THE CIA WORLD FACTBOOK 2016

THE CIA WORLD FACTBOOK 2016

CENTRAL INTELLIGENCE AGENCY

Skyhorse Publishing

Skyhorse Publishing books may be purchased in bulk at special discounts for sales promotion, corporate gifts, fund-raising, or educational purposes. Special editions can also be created to specifications. For details, contact the Special Sales Department, Skyhorse Publishing, 307 West 36th Street, 11th Floor, New York, NY 10018 or info@skyhorsepublishing.com.

Visit our website at www.skyhorsepublishing.com.

10 9 8 7 6 5 4 3 2 1

Library of Congress Cataloging-in-Publication Data is available on file.

Print ISBN: 978-1-63450-328-0
Ebook ISBN: 978-1-5107-0089-5

In general, information available as of September 2015 was used in preparation of this edition.

Printed in Canada

CONTENTS

Introduction viii
A brief history of basic intelligence and *The World Factbook* viii
Notes and Definitions xi
Guide to country profiles xxxiii

A

Afghanistan 1
Akrotiri 4
Albania 5
Algeria 8
American Samoa 12
Andorra 15
Angola 17
Anguilla 21
Antarctica 23
Antigua and Barbuda 25
Arctic Ocean 28
Argentina 28
Armenia 33
Aruba 37
Ashmore and Cartier Islands 39
Atlantic Ocean 40
Australia 41
Austria 45
Azerbaijan 49

B

Bahamas, The 53
Bahrain 56
Bangladesh 59
Barbados 63
Belarus 66
Belgium 70
Belize 74
Benin 77
Bermuda 81
Bhutan 83
Bolivia 87
Bosnia and Herzegovina 91
Botswana 95
Bouvet Island 98
Brazil 99
British Indian Ocean Territory 103
British Virgin Islands 104
Brunei 106
Bulgaria 109
Burkina Faso 113
Burma 116
Burundi 121

C

Cabo Verde 125
Cambodia 128
Cameroon 131
Canada 135
Cayman Islands 139
Central African Republic 141
Chad 144
Chile 148
China 152
Christmas Island 157
Clipperton Island 158
Cocos (Keeling) Islands 158
Colombia 160
Comoros 164
Congo, Democratic Republic of the 167
Congo, Republic of the 172
Cook Islands 175
Coral Sea Islands 178
Costa Rica 178
Cote d'ivoire 182
Croatia 186
Cuba 190
Curacao 194
Cyprus 196
Czech Republic 200

D

Denmark 205
Dhekelia 208
Djibouti 209
Dominica 212
Dominican Republic 215

E

Ecuador 219
Egypt 223
El Salvador 227
Equatorial Guinea 230
Eritrea 234
Estonia 237
Ethiopia 241
European Union 245

F

Falkland Islands (Islas Malvinas) 250
Faroe Islands 252
Fiji 254
Finland 257
France 261
French Polynesia 266
French Southern and Antarctic Lands 268

G

Gabon 271
Gambia, The 274
Gaza Strip 277
Georgia 279
Germany 283
Ghana 287
Gibraltar 291
Greece 293
Greenland 297
Grenada 300
Guam 303
Guatemala 305
Guernsey 309
Guinea 311
Guinea-Bissau 314
Guyana 318

H

Haiti 322
Heard Island and McDonald Islands 325
Holy See (Vatican City) 326
Honduras 327
Hong Kong 331
Howland Island 334
Hungary 335

I

Iceland 339
India 342
Indian Ocean 347
Indonesia 348
Iran 352
Iraq 357
Ireland 361
Isle of Man 365
Israel 367
Italy 371

J

Jamaica 375
Jan Mayen 378
Japan 378
Jarvis Island 382

Jersey 383
Johnston Atoll 385
Jordan 385

K

Kazakhstan 389
Kenya 393
Kingman Reef 397
Kiribati 397
Korea, North 400
Korea, South 403
Kosovo 407
Kuwait 410
Kyrgyzstan 413

L

Laos 417
Latvia 420
Lebanon 423
Lesotho 427
Liberia 430
Libya 434
Liechtenstein 437
Lithuania 439
Luxembourg 443

M

Macau 447
Macedonia 450
Madagascar 453
Malawi 457
Malaysia 460
Maldives 465
Mali 468
Malta 472
Marshall Islands 475
Mauritania 478
Mauritius 481
Mexico 484
Micronesia, Federated States of 489
Midway Islands 491
Moldova 491
Monaco 495
Mongolia 497
Montenegro 501
Montserrat 504
Morocco 506
Mozambique 510

N

Namibia 514
Nauru 517
Navassa Island 520
Nepal 520
Netherlands 524
New Caledonia 528
New Zealand 530
Nicaragua 534
Niger 538
Nigeria 541
Niue 545
Norfolk Island 547
Northern Mariana Islands 549
Norway 551

O

Oman 555

P

Pacific Ocean 559
Pakistan 559
Palau 564
Palmyra Atoll 566
Panama 566
Papua New Guinea 570
Paracel Islands 573
Paraguay 574
Peru 577
Philippines 582
Pitcairn Islands 586
Poland 587
Portugal 591
Puerto Rico 595

Q

Qatar 598

R

Romania 602
Russia 605
Rwanda 611

S

Saint Barthelemy 615
Saint Helena, Ascension, and Tristan da Cunha 616
Saint Kitts and Nevis 618
Saint Lucia 621
Saint Martin 624
Saint Pierre and Miquelon 626
Saint Vincent and the Grenadines 628
Samoa 631
San Marino 634
Sao Tome and Principe 636
Saudi Arabia 639
Senegal 643
Serbia 647
Seychelles 651
Sierra Leone 654
Singapore 657
Sint Maarten 661
Slovakia 662
Slovenia 666
Solomon Islands 670
Somalia 673
South Africa 676
South Georgia and South Sandwich Islands 680
Southern Ocean 681
South Sudan 683
Spain 686
Spratly Islands 690
Sri Lanka 691
Sudan 694
Suriname 698
Svalbard 702
Swaziland 703
Sweden 707
Switzerland 711
Syria 715

T

Taiwan 719
Tajikistan 722
Tanzania 726
Thailand 730
Timor-Leste 734
Togo 737
Tokelau 741
Tonga 742
Trinidad and Tobago 745
Tunisia 749
Turkey 752
Turkmenistan 757
Turks and Caicos Islands 760
Tuvalu 762

U

Uganda 765
Ukraine 768
United Arab Emirates 773
United Kingdom 776
United States 781
United States Pacific Island Wildlife Refuges 786
Uruguay 787
Uzbekistan 791

V

Vanuatu 796
Venezuela 799
Vietnam 803
Virgin Islands 807

W

Wake Island 810
Wallis and Futuna 810
West Bank 812
Western Sahara 815
World 816

Y

Yemen 822

Z

Zambia 826
Zimbabwe 829

APPENDICES

A: Abbreviations 834
B: International Organizations and Groups 840
C: Selected Environmental Agreements 868
D: Cross-Reference List of Country Data Codes 875
E: Cross-Reference List of Hydrographic Data Codes 883
F: Cross-Reference List of Geographic Names 884
G: Weights and Measures 915

REFERENCE MAPS

Africa 926
Antarctic Region 927
Arctic Region 928
Asia 929
Central America and the Caribbean 930
Europe 931
Middle East 932
North America 933
Oceania 934
Physical Map of the World 935
Political Map of the World 935
South America 936
Southeast Asia 937
Standard Time Zone of the World 938
United States 939
Central Balkan Region 940

INTRODUCTION

The *World Factbook* is prepared by the Central Intelligence Agency for the use of US Government officials, and the style, format, coverage, and content are designed to meet their specific requirements. Information is provided by Antarctic Information Program (National Science Foundation), Armed Forces Medical Intelligence Center (Department of Defense), Bureau of the Census (Department of Commerce), Bureau of Labor Statistics (Department of Labor), Central Intelligence Agency, Council of Managers of National Antarctic Programs, Defense Intelligence Agency (Department of Defense), Department of Energy, Department of State, Fish and Wildlife Service (Department of the Interior), Maritime Administration (Department of Transportation), National Geospatial-Intelligence Agency (Department of Defense), Naval Facilities Engineering Command (Department of Defense), Office of Insular Affairs (Department of the Interior), Office of Naval Intelligence (Department of Defense), US Board on Geographic Names (Department of the Interior), US Transportation Command (Department of Defense), Oil & Gas Journal, and other public and private sources.

Comments and queries are welcome and may be addressed to:

Central Intelligence Agency
Attn.: Office of Public Affairs
Washington, DC 20505
Hours: Monday-Friday 8:00 AM-4:30 PM Eastern Standard Time
Telephone: [1] (703) 482-0623
FAX: [1](703) 482-17

A BRIEF HISTORY OF BASIC INTELLIGENCE AND *THE WORLD FACTBOOK*

The Intelligence Cycle is the process by which information is acquired, converted into intelligence, and made available to policymakers. ***Information*** *is raw data from any source, data that may be fragmentary, contradictory, unreliable, ambiguous, deceptive, or wrong.* ***Intelligence*** *is information that has been collected, integrated, evaluated, analyzed, and interpreted.* ***Finished intelligence*** *is the final product of the Intelligence Cycle ready to be delivered to the policymaker.*

The three types of finished intelligence are: basic, current, and estimative. Basic intelligence provides the fundamental and factual reference material on a country or issue. Current intelligence reports on new developments. Estimative intelligence judges probable outcomes. The three are mutually supportive: basic intelligence is the foundation on which the other two are constructed; current intelligence continually updates the inventory of knowledge; and estimative intelligence revises overall interpretations of country and issue prospects for guidance of basic and current intelligence. *The World Factbook, The President's Daily Brief*, and the *National Intelligence Estimates* are examples of the three types of finished intelligence.

The United States has carried on foreign intelligence activities since the days of George Washington but only since World War II have they been coordinated on a government-wide basis. Three programs have highlighted the development of coordinated basic intelligence since that time: (1) *the Joint Army Navy Intelligence Studies* (JANIS), (2) *the National Intelligence Survey* (NIS), and (3) *The World Factbook.*

During World War II, intelligence consumers realized that the production of basic intelligence by different components of the US Government resulted in a great duplication of effort and conflicting information. The Japanese attack on Pearl Harbor in 1941 brought home to leaders in Congress and the executive branch the need for integrating departmental reports to national policymakers. Detailed and coordinated information was needed not only on such major powers as Germany and Japan, but also on places of little previous interest. In the Pacific Theater, for example, the Navy and Marines had to launch amphibious operations against many islands about which information was unconfirmed or nonexistent. Intelligence authorities resolved that the United States should never again be caught unprepared.

In 1943, Gen. George B. Strong (G-2), Adm. H. C. Train (Office of Naval Intelligence—ONI), and Gen. William J. Donovan (Director of the Office of Strategic Services—OSS) decided that a joint effort should be initiated. A steering committee was appointed on 27 April 1943 that recommended the formation of a Joint Intelligence Study Publishing Board to assemble, edit, coordinate, and publish the *Joint Army Navy Intelligence Studies* (JANIS). JANIS was the first interdepartmental basic intelligence program to fulfill the needs of the US Government for an authoritative and coordinated appraisal of strategic basic intelligence. Between April 1943 and July 1947, the board published 34 JANIS studies. JANIS performed well in the war effort, and numerous letters of commendation were received, including a statement from Adm. Forrest Sherman, Chief of Staff, Pacific Ocean Areas, which said, "JANIS has become the indispensable reference work for the shore-based planners."

The need for more comprehensive basic intelligence in the post-war world was well expressed in 1946 by George S. Pettee, a noted author on national security. He wrote in *The Future of American Secret Intelligence* (Infantry Journal Press, 1946, page 46) that world leadership in peace requires even more elaborate intelligence than in war. "The conduct of peace involves all countries, all human activities—not just the enemy and his war production."

The Central Intelligence Agency was established on 26 July 1947 and officially began operating on 18 September 1947. Effective 1 October 1947, the Director of Central Intelligence assumed operational responsibility for JANIS. On 13 January 1948, the National Security Council issued Intelligence Directive (NSCID) No. 3, which authorized the *National Intelligence Survey* (NIS) program as a peacetime replacement for the wartime JANIS program. Before adequate NIS country sections could be produced, government agencies had to develop more comprehensive gazetteers and better maps. The US Board on Geographic Names (BGN) compiled the names; the Department of the Interior produced the gazetteers; and CIA produced the maps.

The Hoover Commission's Clark Committee, set up in 1954 to study the structure and administration of the CIA, reported to Congress in 1955 that: "The National Intelligence Survey is an invaluable publication which provides the essential elements of basic intelligence on all areas of the world. There will always be a continuing requirement for keeping the Survey up-to-date." The *Factbook* was created as an annual summary and update to the encyclopedic NIS studies. The first classified *Factbook* was published in August 1962, and the first unclassified version was published in June 1971. The NIS program was terminated in 1973 except for the *Factbook*, map, and gazetteer components. The 1975 *Factbook* was the first to be made available to the public with sales through the US Government Printing Office (GPO). The *Factbook* was first made available on the Internet in June 1997. The year 2013 marks the 66th anniversary of the establishment of the Central Intelligence Agency and the 70th year of continuous basic intelligence support to the US Government by *The World Factbook* and its two predecessor programs.

The Evolution of The World Factbook

National Basic Intelligence Factbook produced semiannually until 1980. Country entries include sections on Land, Water, People, Government, Economy, Communications, and Defense Forces.

1981—Publication becomes an annual product and is renamed *The World Factbook*. A total of 165 nations are covered on 225 pages.

1983—Appendices (Conversion Factors, International Organizations) first introduced.

1984—Appendices expanded; now include: A. The United Nations, B. Selected United Nations Organizations, C. Selected International Organizations, D. Country Membership in Selected Organizations, E. Conversion Factors.

1987—A new Geography section replaces the former separate Land and Water sections. UN Organizations and Selected International Organizations appendices merged into a new International Organizations appendix. First multi-color-cover *Factbook*.

1988—More than 40 new geographic entities added to provide complete world coverage without overlap or omission. Among the new entities are Antarctica, oceans (Arctic, Atlantic, Indian, Pacific), and the World. The front-of-the-book explanatory introduction expanded and retitled to Notes, Definitions, and Abbreviations. Two new Appendices added: Weights and Measures (in place of Conversion Factors) and a Cross-Reference List of Geographic Names. *Factbook* size reaches 300 pages.

1989—Economy section completely revised and now includes an Overview briefly describing a country's economy. New entries added under People, Government, and Communications.

1990—The Government section revised and considerably expanded with new entries.

1991—A new International Organizations and Groups appendix added. *Factbook* size reaches 405 pages.

1992—Twenty new successor state entries replace those of the Soviet Union and Yugoslavia. New countries are respectively: Armenia, Azerbaijan, Belarus, Estonia, Georgia, Kazakhstan, Kyrgyzstan, Latvia, Lithuania, Moldova, Russia, Tajikistan, Turkmenistan, Ukraine, Uzbekistan; and Bosnia and Hercegovina, Croatia, Macedonia, Serbia and Montenegro, Slovenia. Number of nations in the *Factbook* rises to 188.

1993—Czechoslovakia's split necessitates new Czech Republic and Slovakia entries. New Eritrea entry added after it secedes from Ethiopia. Substantial enhancements made to Geography section.

1994—Two new appendices address Selected International Environmental Agreements. The gross domestic product (GDP) of most developing countries changed to a purchasing power parity (PPP) basis rather than an exchange rate basis. *Factbook* size up to 512 pages.

1995—The GDP of all countries now presented on a PPP basis. New appendix lists estimates of GDP on an exchange rate basis. Communications category split; Railroads, Highways, Inland waterways, Pipelines, Merchant marine, and Airports entries now make up a new Transportation category. *The World Factbook* is first produced on CD-ROM.

1996—Maps accompanying each entry now present more detail. Flags also introduced for nearly all entities. Various new entries appear under Geography and Communications. *Factbook* abbreviations consolidated into a new Appendix A. Two new appendices present a Cross-Reference List of Country Data Codes and a Cross-Reference List of Hydrogeographic Data Codes. Geographic coordinates added to Appendix H, Cross-Reference List of Geographic Names. *Factbook* size expands by 95 pages in one year to reach 652.

1997—*The World Factbook* introduced onto the Internet. A special printed edition prepared for the CIA's 50th anniversary. A schema or Guide to Country Profiles introduced. New color maps and flags now accompany each country profile. Category headings distinguished by shaded backgrounds. Number of categories expanded to nine with the addition of an Introduction (for only a few countries) and Transnational Issues (which includes Disputes-international and Illicit drugs).

1998—The Introduction category with two entries, Current issues and Historical perspective, expanded to more countries. Last year for the production of CD-ROM versions of the *Factbook*.

1999—Historical perspective and Current issues entries in the Introduction category combined into a new Background statement. Several new Economy entries introduced. A new physical map of the world added to the back-of-the-book reference maps.

2000—A new "country profile" added on the Southern Ocean. The Background statements dramatically expanded to over 200 countries and possessions. A number of new Communications entries added.

2001—Background entries completed for all 267 entities in the *Factbook*. Several new HIV/AIDS entries introduced under the People category. Revision begun on individual country maps to include elevation extremes and a partial geographic grid. Weights and Measures appendix deleted.

2002—New entry on Distribution of Family income—Gini index added. Revision of individual country maps continued (process still ongoing).

2003—In the Economy category, petroleum entries added for oil production, consumption, exports, imports, and proved reserves, as well as natural gas proved reserves.

2004—Bi-weekly updates launched on *The World Factbook* website. Additional petroleum entries included for natural gas production, consumption, exports, and imports. In the Transportation category, under Merchant marine, subfields added for foreign-owned vessels and those registered in other countries. Descriptions of the many forms of government mentioned in the Factbook incorporated into the Definitions and Notes.

2005—In the People category, a Major infectious diseases field added for countries deemed to pose a higher risk for travelers. In the Economy category, entries included for Current account balance, Investment, Public debt, and Reserves of foreign exchange and gold. The Transnational issues category expanded to include Refugees and internally displaced persons. Size of the printed *Factbook* reaches 702 pages.

2006—In the Economy category, national GDP figures now presented at Official Exchange Rates (OER) in addition to GDP at purchasing power parity (PPP). Entries in the Transportation section reordered; Highways changed to Roadways, and Ports and harbors to Ports and terminals.

2007—In the Government category, the Capital entry significantly expanded with up to four subfields, including new information having to do with time. The subfields consist of the name of the capital itself, its geographic coordinates, the time difference at the capital from coordinated universal time (UTC), and, if applicable, information on daylight saving time (DST). Where appropriate, a special note is added to highlight those countries with multiple time zones. A Trafficking in persons entry added to the Transnational issues category. A new appendix, Weights and Measures, (re) introduced to the online version of the *Factbook*.

2008—In the Geography category, two fields focus on the increasingly vital resource of water: Total renewable water resources and Freshwater withdrawal. In the Economy category, three fields added for: Stock of direct foreign investment—at home, Stock of direct foreign investment—abroad, and Market value of publicly traded shares. Concise descriptions of all major religions included in the Definitions and Notes. Responsibility for printing of *The World Factbook* turned over to the Government Printing Office.

2009—The online *Factbook* site completely redesigned with many new features. In the People category, two new fields provide information on education in terms of opportunity and resources: School Life Expectancy and Education expenditures. Additionally, the Urbanization entry expanded to include all countries. In the Economy category, five fields added: Central bank discount rate, Commercial bank prime lending rate, Stock of narrow money, Stock of broad money, and Stock of domestic credit.

2010—Weekly updates inaugurated on the *The World Factbook* website. The dissolution of the Netherlands Antilles results in two new listings: Curacao and Sint Maarten. In the Communications category, a Broadcast media field replaces the former Radio broadcast stations and TV broadcast stations entries. In the Geography section, under Natural hazards, a Volcanism subfield added for countries with historically active volcanoes. In the Government category, a new National anthems field introduced. Concise descriptions of all major Legal systems incorporated into the Definitions and Notes. In order to facilitate comparisons over time, dozens of the entries in the Economy category expanded to include two (and in some cases three) years' worth of data.

2011—The People section expanded to People and Society, incorporating ten new fields. The Economy category added Taxes and other revenues and Budget surplus (+) or deficit (–), while the Government section introduced International law organization participation and National symbols. A new African nation, South Sudan, brings the total number of countries in *The World Factbook* to 195.

2012—A new Energy category introduced with 23 energy-related fields. Several distinctive features added to *The World Factbook* website: 1) playable audio files in the Government section for the National Anthems entry, 2) online graphics in the form of a Population Pyramid feature in the People and Society category's Age Structure field, and 3) a Users Guide enabling visitors to navigate the *Factbook* more easily and efficiently. A new and distinctive Map of the World Oceans highlights an expanded array of regional and country maps. Size of the printed *Factbook*'s 50th anniversary edition reaches 847 pages.

2013—In the People and Society section five fields introduced: Demographic profile, Mother's mean age at first birth, Contraceptive prevalence rate, Dependency ratios, and Child labor-children ages 5–14. In the Transnational Issues category, a new *stateless persons* subfield embedded under the Refugees and internally displaced persons entry. In the Economy section two fields added: GDP-composition by end use and Gross national saving. In the Government category the Judicial branch entry revised and expanded to include three new subfields: *highest court(s), judge selection and term of office*, and *subordinate courts.*

NOTES AND DEFINITIONS

Abbreviations This information is included in **Appendix A: Abbreviations,** which includes all abbreviations and acronyms used in the *Factbook*, with their expansions.

Acronyms An acronym is an abbreviation coined from the initial letter of each successive word in a term or phrase. In general, an acronym made up solely from the first letter of the major words in the expanded form is rendered in all capital letters (NATO from North Atlantic Treaty Organization; an exception would be ASEAN for Association of Southeast Asian Nations). In general, an acronym made up of more than the first letter of the major words in the expanded form is rendered with only an initial capital letter (Comsat from Communications Satellite Corporation; an exception would be NAM from Nonaligned Movement). Hybrid forms are sometimes used to distinguish between initially identical terms (ICC for International Chamber of Commerce and ICCt for International Criminal Court).

Administrative divisions This entry generally gives the numbers, designatory terms, and first-order administrative divisions as approved by the US Board on Geographic Names (BGN). Changes that have been reported but not yet acted on by the BGN are noted.

Age structure This entry provides the distribution of the population according to age. Information is included by sex and age group as follows: *0-14 years (children), 15-24 years (early working age), 25-54 years (prime working age), 55-64 years (mature working age), 65 years and over (elderly).* The age structure of a population affects a nation's key socioeconomic issues. Countries with young populations (high percentage under age 15) need to invest more in schools, while countries with older populations (high percentage ages 65 and over) need to invest more in the health sector. The age structure can also be used to help predict potential political issues. For example, the rapid growth of a young adult population unable to find employment can lead to unrest.

Agriculture—products This entry is an ordered listing of major crops and products starting with the most important.

Airports This entry gives the total number of airports or airfields recognizable from the air. The runway(s) may be paved (concrete or asphalt surfaces) or unpaved (grass, earth, sand, or gravel surfaces) and may include closed or abandoned installations. Airports or airfields that are no longer recognizable (overgrown, no facilities, etc.) are not included. Note that not all airports have accommodations for refueling, maintenance, or air traffic control.

Airports—with paved runways This entry gives the total number of airports with paved runways (concrete or asphalt surfaces) by length. For airports with more than one runway, only the longest runway is included according to the following five groups- (1) *over 3,047 m* (over 10,000 ft), (2) *2,438 to 3,047 m* (8,000 to 10,000 ft), (3) *1,524 to 2,437 m* (5,000 to 8,000 ft), (4) *914 to 1,523 m* (3,000 to 5,000 ft), and (5) *under 914 m* (under 3,000 ft). Only airports with usable runways are included in this listing. Not all airports have facilities for refueling, maintenance, or air traffic control. The type aircraft capable of operating from a runway of a given length is dependent upon a number of factors including elevation of the runway, runway gradient, average maximum daily temperature at the airport, engine types, flap settings, and take-off weight of the aircraft.

Airports—with unpaved runways This entry gives the total number of airports with unpaved runways (grass, dirt, sand, or gravel surfaces) by length. For airports with more than one runway, only the longest runway is included according to the following five groups—(1) *over 3,047 m* (over 10,000 ft), (2) *2,438 to 3,047 m* (8,000 to 10,000 ft), (3) *1,524 to 2,437 m* (5,000 to 8,000 ft), (4) *914 to 1,523 m* (3,000 to 5,000 ft), and (5) *under 914 m* (under 3,000 ft). Only airports with usable runways are included in this listing. Not all airports have facilities for refueling, maintenance, or air traffic control. The type aircraft capable of operating from a runway of a given length is dependent upon a number of factors including elevation of the runway, runway gradient, average maximum daily temperature at the airport,engine types, flap settings, and take-off weight of the aircraft.

Appendixes This section includes *Factbook*-related material by topic.

Area This entry includes three subfields. *Total area* is the sum of all land and water areas delimited by international boundaries and/or coastlines. *Land area* is the aggregate of all surfaces delimited by international boundaries and/or coastlines, excluding inland water bodies (lakes, reservoirs, rivers). *Water area* is the sum of the surfaces of all inland water bodies, such as lakes, reservoirs, or rivers, as delimited by international boundaries and/or coastlines.

Area—comparative This entry provides an area comparison based on total area equivalents. Most entities are compared with the entire US or one of the 50 states based on area measurements (1990 revised) provided by the US Bureau of the Census. The smaller entities are compared with Washington, DC (178 sq km, 69 sq mi) or The Mall in Washington, DC (0.59 sq km, 0.23 sq mi, 146 acres).

Background This entry usually highlights major historic events and current issues and may include a statement about one or two key future trends.

Birth rate This entry gives the average annual number of births during a year per 1,000 persons in the population at midyear; also known as crude birth rate. The birth rate is usually the dominant factor in determining the rate of population growth. It depends on both the level of fertility and the age structure of the population.

Broadcast media This entry provides information on the approximate number of public and private TV and radio stations in a country, as well as basic information on the availability of satellite and cable TV services.

Budget This entry includes *revenues, expenditures,* and capital expenditures. These figures are calculated on an exchange rate basis, i.e., not in purchasing power parity (PPP) terms.

Budget surplus (+) or deficit (-) This entry records the difference between national government revenues and expenditures, expressed as a percent of GDP. A positive (+) number indicates that revenues exceeded expenditures (a budget surplus), while a negative (-) number indicates the reverse (a budget deficit). Normalizing the data, by dividing the budget balance by GDP, enables easy comparisons across countries and indicates whether a national government saves or borrows money. Countries with high budget deficits (relative to their GDPs) generally have more difficulty raising funds to finance expenditures, than those with lower deficits.

Capital This entry gives the *name* of the seat of government, its *geographic coordinates*, the *time difference* relative to **Coordinated Universal Time (UTC)** and the time observed in Washington, DC, and, if applicable, information on *daylight saving time* **(DST)**. Where appropriate, a special note has been added to highlight those countries that have multiple time zones.

Carbon dioxide emissions from consumption of energy This entry is the total amount of carbon dioxide, measured in metric tons, released by burning fossil fuels in the process of producing and consuming energy.

Central bank discount rate This entry provides the annualized interest rate a country's central bank charges commercial, depository banks for loans to meet temporary shortages of funds.

Child labor—children ages 5-14 This entry gives the percent of children aged 5-14 (or the age range specified) engaged in child labor. We define "child labor" as work that deprives children of their childhood, their potential, and their dignity, and that is harmful to physical and mental development. It refers to work that is mentally, physically, socially, or morally dangerous and harmful to children. Such labor may deprive them of the opportunity to attend school, oblige them to leave school prematurely, or require them to combine school attendance with excessively long and heavy work. In its most extreme forms, child labor involves children being enslaved, separated from their families,exposed to serious hazards and illnesses, and/or left to fend for themselves on the streets of large cities—often a very early age.

Children under the age of 5 years underweight This entry gives the percent of children under five considered to be underweight. Underweight means weight-for-age is approximately 2 kg below for standard at age one, 3 kg below standard for ages two and three, and 4 kg below standard for ages four and five. This statistic is an indicator of the nutritional status of a community. Children who suffer from growth retardation as a result of poor diets and/or recurrent infections tend to have a greater risk of suffering illness and death.

Climate This entry includes a brief description of typical weather regimes throughout the year.

Coastline This entry gives the total length of the boundary between the land area (including islands) and the sea.

Commercial bank prime lending rate This entry provides a simple average of annualized interest rates commercial banks charge on new loans, denominated in the national currency, to their most credit-worthy customers.

Communications This category deals with the means of exchanging information and includes the telephone, radio, television, and Internet host entries.

Communications—note This entry includes miscellaneous communications information of significance not included elsewhere.

Constitution This entry provides information on a country's constitution. It includes the dates of previous constitutions, the dates of the main steps in making and implementing the latest constitution, and the dates of amendments. For countries with 1-3 previous constitutions, the years are listed; for those with 4-9 previous, the entry is listed as "several previous," and for those with 10 or more, the entry is "many previous." Amendment entries are treated in the same manner, and include the date(s) of the last amendment(s).

The main steps in creating a constitution and amending it usually include drafting, legislative and/or executive branch review and approval, public referendum, and entry into law. In many countries this process is lengthy. Terms commonly used to describe constitutional changes are "amended," "revised," or "reformed." In countries such as South Korea and Turkmenistan, sources differ as to whether changes are stated as new constitutions or are amendments/ revisions to existing ones.

A few countries including Canada, Israel, and UK have no single constitution document, but have various written and unwritten acts, statutes, common laws, and practices that, when taken together, describe a body of fundamental principles or established precedents as to how their countries are governed. Countries including Hong Kong, Macau, Oman, and Saudi Arabia use the term "basic law" instead of constitution.

A number of self-governing dependencies and territories such as the Cayman Islands, Bermuda, and Gibraltar (UK), Greenland and Faroe Islands (Denmark), Aruba, Curacao, and Sint Maarten (Netherlands), and Puerto Rico and the Virgin Islands (US) have their own country-level constitutions.

Contraceptive prevalence rate This field gives the percent of women of reproductive age (15-49) who are married or in union and are using, or whose sexual partner is using, a method of contraception according to the date of the most recent available data. The contraceptive prevalence rate is an indicator of health services, development, and women's empowerment. It is also useful in understanding, past, present, and future fertility trends, especially in developing countries.

Coordinated Universal Time (UTC) UTC is the international atomic time scale that serves as the basis of timekeeping for most of the world. The hours, minutes, and seconds expressed by UTC represent the time of day at the Prime Meridian (0° longitude) located near Greenwich, England as reckoned from midnight. UTC is calculated by the Bureau International des Poids et Measures (BIPM) in Sevres, France. The BIPM averages data collected from more than 200 atomic time and frequency standards located at about 50 laboratories worldwide. UTC is the basis for all civil time with the Earth divided into time zones expressed as positive or negative differences from UTC. UTC is also referred to as "Zulu time." See the Standard Time Zones of the World map included with the **Reference Maps**.

Country data codes See **Data codes**.

Country map Most versions of the *Factbook* provide a country map in color. The maps were produced from the best information available at the time of preparation. Names and/or boundaries may have changed subsequently.

Country name This entry includes all forms of the country's name approved by the US Board on Geographic Names (Italy is used as an example): *conventional long form* (Italian Republic), *conventional short form* (Italy), *local long form* (Repubblica Italiana), *local short form* (Italia), *former* (Kingdom of Italy), as well as the *abbreviation*. Also see the **Terminology** note.

Crude oil—exports This entry is the total amount of crude oil exported, in barrels per day (bbl/day).

Crude oil—imports This entry is the total amount of crude oil imported, in barrels per day (bbl/day).

Crude oil—production This entry is the total amount of crude oil produced, in barrels per day (bbl/day).

Crude oil—proved reserves This entry is the stock of proved reserves of crude oil, in barrels (bbl). Proved reserves are those quantities of petroleum which, by analysis of geological and engineering data, can be estimated with a high degree of confidence to be commercially recoverable from a given date forward, from known reservoirs and under current economic conditions.

Current account balance This entry records a country's net trade in goods and services, plus net earnings from rents, interest, profits, and dividends, and net transfer payments (such as pension funds and worker remittances) to and from the rest of the world during the period specified. These figures are calculated on an exchange rate basis, i.e., not in purchasing power parity (PPP) terms.

Data codes This information is presented in **Appendix D: Cross-Reference List of Country Data Codes and Appendix E: Cross-Reference List of Hydrographic Data Codes.**

Date of information In general, information available as of January in a given year is used in the preparation of the printed edition.

Daylight Saving Time (DST) This entry is included for those entities that have adopted a policy of adjusting the official local time forward, usually one hour, from Standard Time during summer months. Such policies are most common in mid-latitude regions.

Death rate This entry gives the average annual number of deaths during a year per 1,000 population at midyear; also known as crude death rate. The death rate, while only a rough indicator of the mortality situation in a country, accurately indicates the current mortality impact on population growth. This indicator is significantly affected by age distribution, and most countries will eventually show a rise in the overall death rate, in spite of continued decline in mortality at all ages, as declining fertility results in an aging population.

Debt—external This entry gives the total public and private debt owed to nonresidents repayable in internationally accepted currencies, goods, or services. These figures are calculated on an exchange rate basis, i.e., not in purchasing power parity (PPP) terms.

Demographic profile This entry describes a country's key demographic features and trends and how they vary among regional, ethnic, and socioeconomic sub-populations. Some of the topics addressed are population age structure, fertility, health, mortality, poverty, education, and migration.

Dependency ratios Dependency ratios are a measure of the age structure of a population. They relate the number of individuals that are likely to be economically "dependent" on the support of others. Dependency ratios contrast the ratio of youths (ages 0-14) and the elderly (ages 65+) to the number of those in the working-age group (ages 15-64).Changes in the dependency ratio provide an indication of potential social support requirements resulting from changes in population age structures. As fertility levels decline, the dependency ratio initially falls because the proportion of youths decreases while the proportion of the population of working age increases. As fertility levels continue to decline, dependency ratios eventually increase because the proportion of the population of working age starts to decline and the proportion of elderly persons continues to increase.

total dependency ratio—The total dependency ratio is the ratio of combined youth population (ages 0-14) and elderly population (ages 65+) per 100 people of working age (ages 15-64). A high total dependency ratio indicates that the working-age population and the overall economy face a greater burden to support and provide social services for youth and elderly persons, who are often economically dependent.

youth dependency ratio—The youth dependency ratio is the ratio of the youth population (ages 0-14) per 100 people of working age (ages 15-64). A high youth dependency ratio indicates that a greater investment needs to be made in schooling and other services for children.

elderly dependency ratio—The elderly dependency ratio is the ratio of the elderly population (ages 65+) per 100 people of working age (ages 15-64). Increases in the elderly dependency ratio put added pressure on governments to fund pensions and healthcare.

potential support ratio—The potential support ratio is the number of working-age people (ages 15-64) per one elderly person (ages 65+). As a population ages, the potential support ratio tends to fall, meaning there are fewer potential workers to support the elderly.

Dependency status This entry describes the formal relationship between a particular nonindependent entity and an independent state.

Dependent areas This entry contains an alphabetical listing of all nonindependent entities associated in some way with a particular independent state.

Diplomatic representation The US Government has diplomatic relations with 190 independent states, including 188 of the 193 UN members (excluded UN members are Bhutan, Cuba, Iran, North Korea, and the US itself). In addition, the US has diplomatic relations with 2 independent states that are not in the UN, the Holy See and Kosovo, as well as with the EU.

Diplomatic representation from the US This entry includes the *chief of mission*, *embassy* address, *mailing address*, *telephone* number, FAX number, *branch office* locations, *consulate general* locations, and *consulate* locations.

Diplomatic representation in the US This entry includes the *chief of mission, chancery address, telephone, FAX, consulate general locations,* and *consulate locations.* The use of the annotated title Appointed Ambassador refers to a new ambassador who has presented his/her credentials to the secretary of state but not the US president. Such ambassadors fulfill all diplomatic functions except meeting with or appearing at functions attended by the president until such time as they formally present their credentials at a White House ceremony.

Disputes—international This entry includes a wide variety of situations that range from traditional bilateral boundary disputes to unilateral claims of one sort or another. Information regarding disputes over international terrestrial and maritime boundaries has been reviewed by the US Department of State. References to other situations involving borders or frontiers may also be included, such as resource disputes, geopolitical questions, or irredentist issues; however, inclusion does not necessarily constitute official acceptance or recognition by the US Government.

Distribution of family income—Gini index This index measures the degree of inequality in the distribution of family income in a country. The index is calculated from the Lorenz curve, in which cumulative family income is plotted against the number of families arranged from the poorest to the richest. The index is the ratio of (a) the area between a country's Lorenz curve and the 45 degree helping line to (b) the entire triangular area under the 45 degree line. The more nearly equal a country's income distribution, the closer its Lorenz curve to the 45 degree line and the lower its Gini index, e.g., a Scandinavian country with an index of 25. The more unequal a country's income distribution, the farther its Lorenz curve from the 45 degree line and the higher its Gini index, e.g., a Sub-Saharan country with an index of 50. If income were distributed with perfect equality, the Lorenz curve would coincide with the 45 degree line and the index would be zero; if income were distributed with perfect inequality, the Lorenz curve would coincide with the horizontal axis and the right vertical axis and the index would be 100.

Drinking water source This entry provides information about access to improved or unimproved drinking water sources available to segments of the population of a country. *improved* drinking water—use of any of the following sources: piped water into dwelling, yard, or plot; public tap or standpipe; tubewell or borehole; protected dug well; protected spring; or rainwater collection. *unimproved* drinking water—use of any of the following sources: unprotected dug well; unprotected spring; cart with small tank or drum; tanker truck; surface water, which includes rivers, dams, lakes, ponds, streams, canals or irrigation channels; or bottled water.

Economy This category includes the entries dealing with the size, development, and management of productive resources, i.e., land, labor, and capital.

Economy—overview This entry briefly describes the type of economy, including the degree of market orientation, the level of economic development, the most important natural resources, and the unique areas of specialization. It also characterizes major economic events and policy changes in the most recent 12 months and may include a statement about one or two key future macroeconomic trends.

Education expenditures This entry provides the public expenditure on education as a percent of GDP.

Electricity—consumption This entry consists of total electricity generated annually plus imports and minus exports, expressed in kilowatt-hours. The discrepancy between the amount of electricity generated and/or imported and the amount consumed and/or exported is accounted for as loss in transmission and distribution.

Electricity—exports This entry is the total exported electricity in kilowatt-hours.

Electricity—from fossil fuels This entry measures the capacity of plants that generate electricity by burning fossil fuels (such as coal, petroleum products, and natural gas), expressed as a share of the country's total generating capacity.

Electricity—from hydroelectric plants This entry measures the capacity of plants that generate electricity by water-driven turbines, expressed as a share of the country's total generating capacity.

Electricity—from nuclear fuels This entry measures the capacity of plants that generate electricity through radioactive decay of nuclear fuel, expressed as a share of the country's total generating capacity.

Electricity—from other renewable sources This entry measures the capacity of plants that generate electricity by using renewable energy sources other than hydroelectric (including, for example, wind, waves, solar, and geothermal), expressed as a share of the country's total generating capacity.

Electricity—imports This entry is the total imported electricity in kilowatt-hours.

Electricity—installed generating capacity This entry is the total capacity of currently installed generators, expressed in kilowatts (kW), to produce electricity. A 10-kilowatt (kW) generator will produce 10 kilowatt hours (kWh) of electricity, if it runs continuously for one hour.

Electricity—production This entry is the annual electricity generated expressed in kilowatt-hours. The discrepancy between the amount of electricity generated and/or imported and the amount consumed and/or exported is accounted for as loss in transmission and distribution.

Elevation extremes This entry includes both the highest point and the lowest point.

Energy This category includes entries dealing with the production, consumption, import, and export of various forms of energy including electricity, crude oil, refined petroleum products, and natural gas.

Entities Some of the independent states, dependencies, areas of special sovereignty, and governments included in this publication are not independent, and others are not officially recognized by the US Government. "Independent state" refers to a people politically organized into a sovereign state with a definite territory. "Dependencies" and "areas of special sovereignty" refer to a broad category of political entities that are associated in some way with an independent state. "Country" names used in the table of contents or for page headings are usually the short-form names as approved by the US Board on Geographic Names and may include independent states, dependencies, and areas of special sovereignty, or other geographic entities. There are a total of 267 separate geographic entities in The World Factbook that may be categorized as follows:

INDEPENDENT STATES

195 Afghanistan, Albania, Algeria, Andorra, Angola, Antigua and Barbuda, Argentina, Armenia, Australia, Austria, Azerbaijan, The Bahamas, Bahrain, Bangladesh, Barbados, Belarus, Belgium, Belize, Benin, Bhutan, Bolivia, Bosnia and Herzegovina, Botswana, Brazil, Brunei, Bulgaria, Burkina Faso, Burma, Burundi, Cambodia, Cameroon, Canada, Cape Verde, Central African Republic, Chad, Chile, China, Colombia, Comoros, Democratic Republic of the Congo, Republic of the Congo, Costa Rica, Cote d'Ivoire, Croatia, Cuba, Cyprus, Czech Republic, Denmark, Djibouti, Dominica, Dominican Republic, Ecuador, Egypt, El Salvador, Equatorial Guinea, Eritrea, Estonia, Ethiopia, Fiji, Finland, France, Gabon, The Gambia, Georgia, Germany, Ghana, Greece, Grenada, Guatemala, Guinea, Guinea-Bissau, Guyana, Haiti, Holy See, Honduras, Hungary, Iceland, India, Indonesia, Iran, Iraq, Ireland, Israel, Italy, Jamaica, Japan, Jordan, Kazakhstan, Kenya, Kiribati, North Korea, South Korea, Kosovo, Kuwait, Kyrgyzstan, Laos, Latvia, Lebanon, Lesotho, Liberia, Libya, Liechtenstein, Lithuania, Luxembourg, Macedonia, Madagascar, Malawi, Malaysia, Maldives, Mali, Malta, Marshall Islands, Mauritania, Mauritius, Mexico, Federated States of Micronesia, Moldova, Monaco, Mongolia, Montenegro, Morocco, Mozambique, Namibia, Nauru, Nepal, Netherlands, NZ, Nicaragua, Niger, Nigeria, Norway, Oman, Pakistan, Palau, Panama, Papua New Guinea, Paraguay, Peru, Philippines, Poland, Portugal, Qatar, Romania, Russia, Rwanda, Saint Kitts and Nevis, Saint Lucia, Saint Vincent and the Grenadines, Samoa, San Marino, Sao Tome and Principe, Saudi Arabia, Senegal, Serbia, Seychelles, Sierra Leone, Singapore, Slovakia, Slovenia, Solomon Islands, Somalia, South Africa, South Sudan, Spain, Sri Lanka, Sudan, Suriname, Swaziland, Sweden, Switzerland, Syria, Tajikistan, Tanzania, Thailand, Timor-Leste, Togo, Tonga, Trinidad and Tobago, Tunisia, Turkey, Turkmenistan, Tuvalu, Uganda, Ukraine, UAE, UK, US, Uruguay, Uzbekistan, Vanuatu, Venezuela, Vietnam, Yemen, Zambia, Zimbabwe

OTHER

2 Taiwan, European Union

DEPENDENCIES AND AREAS OF SPECIAL SOVEREIGNTY

6 Australia—Ashmore and Cartier Islands, Christmas Island, Cocos (Keeling) Islands, Coral Sea Islands, Heard Island and McDonald Islands, Norfolk Island
2 China—Hong Kong, Macau
2 Denmark—Faroe Islands, Greenland
8 France—Clipperton Island, French Polynesia, French Southern and Antarctic Lands, New Caledonia, Saint Barthelemy, Saint Martin, Saint Pierre and Miquelon, Wallis and Futuna
3 Netherlands—Aruba, Curacao, Sint Maarten
3 New Zealand—Cook Islands, Niue, Tokelau
3 Norway—Bouvet Island, Jan Mayen, Svalbard
17 UK—Akrotiri, Anguilla, Bermuda, British Indian Ocean Territory, British Virgin Islands, Cayman Islands, Dhekelia, Falkland Islands, Gibraltar, Guernsey, Jersey, Isle of Man, Montserrat, Pitcairn Islands, Saint Helena, South Georgia and the South Sandwich Islands, Turks and Caicos Islands
14 US—American Samoa, Baker Island*, Guam, Howland Island*, Jarvis Island*, Johnston Atoll*, Kingman Reef*, Midway Islands*, Navassa Island, Northern Mariana Islands, Palmyra Atoll*, Puerto Rico, Virgin Islands, Wake Island (* consolidated in United States Pacific Island Wildlife Refuges entry)

MISCELLANEOUS

6 Antarctica, Gaza Strip, Paracel Islands, Spratly Islands, West Bank, Western Sahara

OTHER ENTITIES

5 oceans—Arctic Ocean, Atlantic Ocean, Indian Ocean, Pacific Ocean, Southern Ocean
1 World

267 total

Environment—current issues This entry lists the most pressing and important environmental problems. The following terms and abbreviations are used throughout the entry:

Acidification—the lowering of soil and water pH due to acid precipitation and deposition usually through precipitation; this process disrupts ecosystem nutrient flows and may kill freshwater fish and plants dependent on more neutral or alkaline conditions (see acid rain).

Acid rain—characterized as containing harmful levels of sulfur dioxide or nitrogen oxide; acid rain is damaging and potentially deadly to the earth's fragile ecosystems; acidity is measured using the pH scale where 7 is neutral, values greater than 7 are considered alkaline, and values below 5.6 are considered acid precipitation; note—a pH of 2.4 (the acidity of vinegar) has been measured in rainfall in New England.

Aerosol—a collection of airborne particles dispersed in a gas, smoke, or fog. Afforestation—converting a bare or agricultural space by planting trees and plants; reforestation involves replanting trees on areas that have been cut or destroyed by fire.

Asbestos—a naturally occurring soft fibrous mineral commonly used in fireproofing materials and considered to be highly carcinogenic in particulate form.

Biodiversity—also biological diversity; the relative number of species, diverse in form and function, at the genetic, organism, community, and ecosystem level; loss of biodiversity reduces an ecosystem's ability to recover from natural or man-induced disruption.

Bio-indicators—a plant or animal species whose presence, abundance, and health reveal the general condition of its habitat.

Biomass—the total weight or volume of living matter in a given area or volume.

Carbon cycle—the term used to describe the exchange of carbon (in various forms, e.g., as carbon dioxide) between the atmosphere, ocean, terrestrial biosphere, and geological deposits.

Catchments—assemblages used to capture and retain rainwater and runoff; an important water management technique in areas with limited freshwater resources, such as Gibraltar.

DDT (dichloro-diphenyl-trichloro-ethane)—a colorless, odorless insecticide that has toxic effects on most animals; the use of DDT was banned in the US in 1972.
Defoliants—chemicals which cause plants to lose their leaves artificially; often used in agricultural practices for weed control, and may have detrimental impacts on human and ecosystem health.
Deforestation—the destruction of vast areas of forest (e.g., unsustainable forestry practices, agricultural and range land clearing, and the over exploitation of wood products for use as fuel) without planting new growth.
Desertification—the spread of desert-like conditions in arid or semi-arid areas, due to overgrazing, loss of agriculturally productive soils, or climate change.
Dredging—the practice of deepening an existing waterway; also, a technique used for collecting bottom-dwelling marine organisms (e.g., shellfish) or harvesting coral, often causing significant destruction of reef and ocean-floor ecosystems.
Drift-net fishing—done with a net, miles in extent, that is generally anchored to a boat and left to float with the tide; often results in an over harvesting and waste of large populations of non-commercial marine species (by-catch) by its effect of "sweeping the ocean clean."
Ecosystems—ecological units comprised of complex communities of organisms and their specific environments.
Effluents—waste materials, such as smoke, sewage, or industrial waste which are released into the environment, subsequently polluting it.
Endangered species—a species that is threatened with extinction either by direct hunting or habitat destruction.
Freshwater—water with very low soluble mineral content; sources include lakes, streams, rivers, glaciers, and underground aquifers.
Greenhouse gas—a gas that "traps" infrared radiation in the lower atmosphere causing surface warming; water vapor, carbon dioxide, nitrous oxide, methane, hydrofluorocarbons, and ozone are the primary greenhouse gases in the Earth's atmosphere.
Groundwater—water sources found below the surface of the earth often in naturally occurring reservoirs in permeable rock strata; the source for wells and natural springs.
Highlands Water Project—a series of dams constructed jointly by Lesotho and South Africa to redirect Lesotho's abundant water supply into a rapidly growing area in South Africa; while it is the largest infrastructure project in southern Africa, it is also the most costly and controversial; objections to the project include claims that it forces people from their homes, submerges farmlands, and squanders economic resources.
Inuit Circumpolar Conference (ICC)—represents the roughly 150,000 Inuits of Alaska, Canada, Greenland, and Russia in international environmental issues; a General Assembly convenes every three years to determine the focus of the ICC; the most current concerns are long-range transport of pollutants, sustainable development, and climate change.
Metallurgical plants—industries which specialize in the science, technology, and processing of metals; these plants produce highly concentrated and toxic wastes which can contribute to pollution of ground water and air when not properly disposed.
Noxious substances—injurious, very harmful to living beings.
Overgrazing—the grazing of animals on plant material faster than it can naturally regrow leading to the permanent loss of plant cover, a common effect of too many animals grazing limited range land.
Ozone shield—a layer of the atmosphere composed of ozone gas (03) that resides approximately 25 miles above the Earth's surface and absorbs solar ultraviolet radiation that can be harmful to living organisms.
Poaching—the illegal killing of animals or fish, a great concern with respect to endangered or threatened species.
Pollution—the contamination of a healthy environment by man-made waste.
Potable water—water that is drinkable, safe to be consumed.
Salination—the process through which fresh (drinkable) water becomes salt (undrinkable) water; hence, desalination is the reverse process; also involves the accumulation of salts in topsoil caused by evaporation of excessive irrigation water, a process that can eventually render soil incapable of supporting crops.
Siltation—occurs when water channels and reservoirs become clotted with silt and mud, a side effect of deforestation and soil erosion.
Slash-and-burn agriculture—a rotating cultivation technique in which trees are cut down and burned in order to clear land for temporary agriculture; the land is used until its productivity declines at which point a new plot is selected and the process repeats; this practice is sustainable while population levels are low and time is permitted for regrowth of natural vegetation; conversely, where these conditions do not exist, the practice can have disastrous consequences for the environment.
Soil degradation—damage to the land's productive capacity because of poor agricultural practices such as the excessive use of pesticides or fertilizers, soil compaction from heavy equipment, or erosion of topsoil, eventually resulting in reduced ability to produce agricultural products.
Soil erosion—the removal of soil by the action of water or wind, compounded by poor agricultural practices, deforestation, overgrazing, and desertification. Ultraviolet (UV) radiation—a portion of the electromagnetic energy emitted by the sun and naturally filtered in the upper atmosphere by the ozone layer; UV radiation can be harmful to living organisms and has been linked to increasing rates of skin cancer in humans.
Waterborne diseases—those in which bacteria survive in, and are transmitted through, water; always a serious threat in areas with an untreated water supply.

Environment—international agreements This entry separates country participation in international environmental agreements into two levels—*party to* and *signed, but not ratified.* Agreements are listed in alphabetical order by the abbreviated form of the full name.

Environmental agreements This information is presented in **Appendix C: Selected International Environmental Agreements**, which includes the name, abbreviation, date opened for signature, date entered into force, objective, and parties by category.

Ethnic groups This entry provides an ordered listing of ethnic groups starting with the largest and normally includes the percent of total population.

Exchange rates This entry provides the average annual price of a country's monetary unit for the time period specified, expressed in units of local currency per US dollar, as determined by international market forces or by official fiat. The International Organization for Standardization (ISO) 4217 alphabetic currency code for the national medium of exchange is presented in parenthesis. Closing daily exchange rates are not presented in *The World Factbook*, but are used to convert stock values—e.g., the market value of publicly traded shares—to US dollars as of the specified date.

Executive branch This entry includes several subfields. Chief of state includes the name and title of the titular leader of the country who represents the state at official and ceremonial functions but may not be involved with the day-to-day activities of the government. *Head of government* includes the name and title of the top administrative leader who is designated to manage the day-to-day activities of the government. For example, in the UK, the monarch is the chief of state, and the prime minister is the head of government. In the US, the president is both the chief of state and the head of government. *Cabinet* includes the official name for this body of high-ranking advisers and the method for selection of members. *Elections* includes the nature of election process or accession to power, date of the last election, and date of the next election. *Election results* includes the percent of vote for each candidate in the last election.

Exports This entry provides the total US dollar amount of merchandise exports on an f.o.b. (free on board) basis. These figures are calculated on an exchange rate basis, i.e., not in purchasing power parity (PPP) terms.

Exports—commodities This entry provides a listing of the highest-valued exported products; it sometimes includes the percent of total dollar value.

Exports—partners This entry provides a rank ordering of trading partners starting with the most important; it sometimes includes the percent of total dollar value.

Fiscal year This entry identifies the beginning and ending months for a country's accounting period of 12 months, which often is the calendar year but which may begin in any month. All yearly references are for the calendar year (CY) unless indicated as a noncalendar fiscal year (FY).

Flag description This entry provides a written flag description produced from actual flags or the best information available at the time the entry was written. The flags of independent states are used by their dependencies unless there is an officially recognized local flag. Some disputed and other areas do not have flags.

Flag graphic Most versions of the *Factbook* include a color flag at the beginning of the country profile. The flag graphics were produced from actual flags or the best information available at the time of preparation. The flags of independent states are used by their dependencies unless there is an officially recognized local flag. Some disputed and other areas do not have flags.

Freshwater withdrawal (domestic/industrial/agricultural) This entry provides the annual quantity of water in cubic kilometers removed from available sources for use in any purpose. Water drawn-off is not necessarily entirely consumed and some portion may be returned for further use downstream. Domestic sector use refers to water supplied by public distribution systems. Note that some of this total may be used for small industrial and/or limited agricultural purposes. Industrial sector use is the quantity of water used by self-supplied industries not connected to a public distribution system. Agricultural sector use includes water used for irrigation and livestock watering, and does not account for agriculture directly dependent on rainfall. Included are figures for *total* annual water withdrawal and *per capita* water withdrawal.

GDP (official exchange rate) This entry gives the gross domestic product (GDP) or value of all final goods and services produced within a nation in a given year. A nation's GDP at official exchange rates (OER) is the home-currency-denominated annual GDP figure divided by the bilateral average US exchange rate with that country in that year. The measure is simple to compute and gives a precise measure of the value of output. Many economists prefer this measure when gauging the economic power an economy maintains vis-à-vis its neighbors, judging that an exchange rate captures the purchasing power a nation enjoys in the international marketplace. Official exchange rates, however, can be artificially fixed and/or subject to manipulation—resulting in claims of the country having an under-or over-valued currency—and are not necessarily the equivalent of a market-determined exchange rate. Moreover, even if the official exchange rate is market-determined, market exchange rates are frequently established by a relatively small set of goods and services (the ones the country trades) and may not capture the value of the larger set of goods the country produces. Furthermore, OER-converted GDP is not well suited to comparing domestic GDP over time, since appreciation/depreciation from one year to the next will make the OER GDP value rise/fall regardless of whether home-currency-denominated GDP changed.

GDP (purchasing power parity) This entry gives the gross domestic product (GDP) or value of all final goods and services produced within a nation in a given year. A nation's GDP at purchasing power parity (PPP) exchange rates is the sum value of all goods and services produced in the country valued at prices prevailing in the United States in the year noted. This is the measure most economists prefer when looking at per-capita welfare and when comparing living conditions or use of resources across countries. The measure is difficult to compute, as a US dollar value has to be assigned to all goods and services in the country regardless of whether these goods and services have a direct equivalent in the United States (for example, the value of an ox-cart or non-US military equipment); as a result, PPP estimates for some countries are based on a small and sometimes different set of goods and services. In addition, many countries do not formally participate in the World Bank's PPP project that calculates these measures, so the resulting GDP estimates for these countries may lack precision. For many developing countries, PPP-based GDP measures are multiples of the official exchange rate (OER) measure. The differences between the OER-and PPP-denominated GDP values for most of the wealthy industrialized countries are generally much smaller.

GDP—composition, by end use This entry shows who does the spending in an economy: consumers, businesses, government, and foreigners. The distribution gives the percentage contribution to total GDP of *household consumption, government consumption,investment in fixed capital, investment in inventories, exports of goods and services*, and imports of goods and services, and will total 100 percent of GDP if the data are complete.

household consumption—consists of expenditures by resident households, and by nonprofit institutions that serve households, on goods and services that are consumed by individuals. This includes consumption of both domestically produced and foreign goods and services.

government consumption—consists of government expenditures on goods and services. These figures exclude government transfer payments, such as interest on debt, unemployment, and social security, since such payments are not made in exchange for goods and services supplied.

investment in fixed capital—consists of total business spending on fixed assets, such as factories, machinery,equipment, dwellings, and inventories of raw materials, which provide the basis for future production. It is measured gross of the depreciation of the assets, i.e., it includes investment that merely replaces worn-out or scrapped capital. Earlier editions of *The World Factbook* referred to this concept as Investment (gross fixed) and that data now have been moved to this new field.

investment in inventories—consists of net changes to the stock of outputs that are still held by the units that produce them, awaiting further sale to an end user, such as automobiles sitting on a dealer's lot or groceries on the store shelves. This figure may be positive or negative. If the stock of unsold output increases during the relevant time period, *investment in inventories* is positive, but, if the stock of unsold goods declines, it will benegative. *Investment in inventories* normally is an early indicator of the state of the economy. If the stock of unsold items increases unexpectedly – because people stop buying—the economy may be entering a recession;but if the stock of unsold items falls—and goods "go flying off the shelves"—businesses normally try to replace those stocks, and the economy is likely to accelerate.

exports of goods and services—consist of sales, barter, gifts, or grants of goods and services from residents to nonresidents.

imports of goods and services—consist of purchases, barter, or receipts of gifts, or grants of goods and services by residents from nonresidents. *Exports* are treated as a positive item, while imports are treated as a negative item. In a purely accounting sense, *imports* have no direct impact on GDP, which only measures output of the domestic economy. Imports are entered as a negative item to offset the fact that the expenditure figures for consumption, investment, government, and exports also include expenditures on imports. These imports contribute directly to foreign GDP but only indirectly to domestic GDP. Because of this negative offset for imports of goods and services, the sum of the other five items, excluding imports, will always total more than 100 percent of GDP. A surplus of exports of goods and services over imports indicates an economy is investing abroad, while a deficit indicates an economy is borrowing from abroad.

GDP—composition, by sector of origin This entry shows where production takes place in an economy. The distribution gives the percentage contribution of *agriculture, industry*, and *services* to total GDP, and will total 100 percent of GDP if the data are complete. Agriculture includes farming, fishing, and forestry. Industry includes mining, manufacturing, energy production, and construction. Services cover government activities, communications, transportation, finance, and all other private economic activities that do not produce material goods.

GDP—per capita (PPP) This entry shows GDP on a purchasing power parity basis divided by population as of 1 July for the same year.

GDP—real growth rate This entry gives GDP growth on an annual basis adjusted for inflation and expressed as a percent. The growth rates are year-over-year, and not compounded.

GDP methodology In the **Economy** category, GDP dollar estimates for countries are reported both on an official exchange rate (OER) and a purchasing power parity (PPP) basis. Both measures contain information that is useful to the reader. The PPP method involves the use of standardized international dollar price weights, which are applied to the quantities of final goods and services produced in a given economy. The data derived from the PPP method probably provide the best available starting point for comparisons of economic strength and well-being between countries. In contrast, the currency exchange rate method involves a variety of international and domestic financial forces that may not capture the value of domestic output. Whereas PPP estimates for OECD countries are quite reliable, PPP estimates for developing countries are often rough approximations. In developing countries with weak currencies, the exchange rate estimate of GDP in dollars is typically one-fourth to one-half the PPP estimate. Most of the GDP estimates for developing countries are based on extrapolation of PPP numbers published by the UN International Comparison Program (UNICP) and by Professors Robert Summers and Alan Heston of the University of Pennsylvania and their colleagues. GDP derived using the OER method should be used for the purpose of calculating the share of items such as exports, imports, military expenditures, external debt, or the current account balance, because the dollar values presented in the *Factbook* for these items have been converted at official exchange rates, not at PPP. One should use the OER GDP figure to calculate the proportion of, say, Chinese defense expenditures in GDP, because that share will be the same as one calculated in local currency units. Comparison of OER GDP with PPP GDP may also indicate whether a currency is over-or under-valued. If OER GDP is smaller than PPP GDP, the official exchange rate may be undervalued, and vice versa. However, there is no strong historical evidence that market exchange rates move in the direction implied by the PPP rate, at least not in the short-or medium-term. Note: the numbers for GDP and other economic data should not be chained together from successive volumes of the *Factbook* because of changes in the US dollar measuring rod, revisions of data by statistical agencies, use of new or different sources of information, and changes in national statistical methods and practices.

Geographic coordinates This entry includes rounded latitude and longitude figures for the centroid or center point of a country expressed in degrees and minutes; it is based on the locations provided in the Geographic Names Server (GNS), maintained by the National Geospatial-Intelligence Agency on behalf of the US Board on Geographic Names.

Geographic names This information is presented in **Appendix F: Cross Reference List of Geographic Names**. It includes a listing of various alternate names, former names, local names, and regional names referenced to one or more related *Factbook* entries. Spellings are normally, but not always, those approved by the US Board on Geographic Names (BGN). Alternate names and additional information are included in parentheses.

Geography This category includes the entries dealing with the natural environment and the effects of human activity.

Geography—note This entry includes miscellaneous geographic information of significance not included elsewhere.

Gini index See entry for **Distribution of family income—Gini index**

GNP Gross national product (GNP) is the value of all final goods and services produced within a nation in a given year, plus income earned by its citizens abroad, minus income earned by foreigners from domestic production. The *Factbook*, following current practice, uses GDP rather than GNP to measure national production. However, the user must realize that in certain countries net remittances from citizens working abroad may be important to national well-being.

Government This category includes the entries dealing with the system for the adoption and administration of public policy.

Government—note This entry includes miscellaneous government information of significance not included elsewhere.

Government type This entry gives the basic form of government. Definitions of the major governmental terms are as follows. (Note that for some countries more than one definition applies.):

Absolute monarchy—a form of government where the monarch rules unhindered, i.e., without any laws, constitution, or legally organized opposition. Anarchy—a condition of lawlessness or political disorder brought about by the absence of governmental authority.

Authoritarian—a form of government in which state authority is imposed onto many aspects of citizens' lives.

Commonwealth—a nation, state, or other political entity founded on law and united by a compact of the people for the common good.

Communist—a system of government in which the state plans and controls the economy and a single—often authoritarian—party holds power; state controls are imposed with the elimination of private ownership of property or capital while claiming to make progress toward a higher social order in which all goods are equally shared by the people (i.e., a classless society).

Confederacy (Confederation)—a union by compact or treaty between states, provinces, or territories, that creates a central government with limited powers; the constituent entities retain supreme authority over all matters except those delegated to the central government.

Constitutional—a government by or operating under an authoritative document (constitution) that sets forth the system of fundamental laws and principles that determines the nature, functions, and limits of that government. Constitutional democracy—a form of government in which the sovereign power of the people is spelled out in a governing constitution.

Constitutional monarchy—a system of government in which a monarch is guided by a constitution whereby his/her rights, duties, and responsibilities are spelled out in written law or by custom.

Democracy—a form of government in which the supreme power is retained by the people, but which is usually exercised indirectly through a system of representation and delegated authority periodically renewed.

Democratic republic—a state in which the supreme power rests in the body of citizens entitled to vote for officers and representatives responsible to them. Dictatorship—a form of government in which a ruler or small clique wield absolute power (not restricted by a constitution or laws).

Ecclesiastical—a government administrated by a church.

Emirate—similar to a monarchy or sultanate, but a government in which the supreme power is in the hands of an emir (the ruler of a Muslim state); the emir may be an absolute overlord or a sovereign with constitutionally limited authority.

Federal (Federation)—a form of government in which sovereign power is formally divided—usually by means of a constitution—between a central authority and a number of constituent regions (states, colonies, or provinces) so that each region retains some management of its internal affairs; differs from a confederacy in that the central government exerts influence directly upon both individuals as well as upon the regional units.

Federal republic—a state in which the powers of the central government are restricted and in which the component parts (states, colonies, or provinces) retain a degree of

self-government; ultimate sovereign power rests with the voters who chose their governmental representatives.
Islamic republic—a particular form of government adopted by some Muslim states; although such a state is, in theory, a theocracy, it remains a republic, but its laws are required to be compatible with the laws of Islam.
Maoism—the theory and practice of Marxism-Leninism developed in China by Mao Zedong (Mao Tse-tung), which states that a continuous revolution is necessary if the leaders of a communist state are to keep in touch with the people.
Marxism—the political, economic, and social principles espoused by 19th century economist Karl Marx; he viewed the struggle of workers as a progression of historical forces that would proceed from a class struggle of the proletariat (workers) exploited by capitalists (business owners), to a socialist "dictatorship of the proletariat," to, finally, a classless society—Communism. Marxism-Leninism—an expanded form of communism developed by Lenin from doctrines of Karl Marx; Lenin saw imperialism as the final stage of capitalism and shifted the focus of workers' struggle from developed to underdeveloped countries.
Monarchy—a government in which the supreme power is lodged in the hands of a monarch who reigns over a state or territory, usually for life and by hereditary right; the monarch may be either a sole absolute ruler or a sovereign—such as a king, queen, or prince—with constitutionally limited authority.
Oligarchy—a government in which control is exercised by a small group of individuals whose authority generally is based on wealth or power.
Parliamentary democracy—a political system in which the legislature
(parliament) selects the government—a prime minister, premier, or chancellor along with the cabinet ministers—according to party strength as expressed in elections; by this system, the government acquires a dual responsibility: to the people as well as to the parliament.
Parliamentary government (Cabinet-Parliamentary government)—a government in which members of an executive branch (the cabinet and its leader—a prime minister, premier, or chancellor) are nominated to their positions by a legislature or parliament, and are directly responsible to it; this type of government can be dissolved at will by the parliament (legislature) by means of a no confidence vote or the leader of the cabinet may dissolve the parliament if it can no longer function.
Parliamentary monarchy—a state headed by a monarch who is not actively involved in policy formation or implementation (i.e., the exercise of sovereign powers by a monarch in a ceremonial capacity); true governmental leadership is carried out by a cabinet and its head—a prime minister, premier, or chancellor—who are drawn from a legislature (parliament).
Presidential—a system of government where the executive branch exists separately from a legislature (to which it is generally not accountable).
Republic—a representative democracy in which the people's elected deputies (representatives), not the people themselves, vote on legislation.
Socialism—a government in which the means of planning, producing, and distributing goods is controlled by a central government that theoretically seeks a more just and equitable distribution of property and labor; in actuality, most socialist governments have ended up being no more than dictatorships over workers by a ruling elite.
Sultanate—similar to a monarchy, but a government in which the supreme power is in the hands of a sultan (the head of a Muslim state); the sultan may be an absolute ruler or a sovereign with constitutionally limited authority.
Theocracy—a form of government in which a Deity is recognized as the supreme civil ruler, but the Deity's laws are interpreted by ecclesiastical authorities (bishops, mullahs, etc.); a government subject to religious authority.
Totalitarian—a government that seeks to subordinate the individual to the state by controlling not only all political and economic matters, but also the attitudes, values, and beliefs of its population.

Greenwich Mean Time (GMT) The mean solar time at the Greenwich Meridian, Greenwich, England, with the hours and days, since 1925, reckoned from midnight. GMT is now a historical term having been replaced by UTC on 1 January 1972. See **Coordinated Universal Time.**

Gross domestic product See GDP

Gross national product See GNP

Gross national saving Gross national saving is derived by deducting final consumption expenditure (household plus government) from Gross national disposable income, and consists of personal saving, plus business saving (the sum of the capital consumption allowance and retained business profits), plus government saving (the excess of tax revenues over expenditures), but excludes foreign saving (the excess of imports of goods and services over exports). The figures are presented as a percent of GDP. A negative number indicates that the economy as a whole is spending more income than it produces, thus drawing down national wealth (dissaving).

Gross world product See GWP

GWP This entry gives the gross world product (GWP) or aggregate value of all final goods and services produced worldwide in a given year.

Health expenditures This entry provides the total expenditure on health as a percentage of GDP. Health expenditures are broadly defined as activities performed either by institutions or individuals through the application of medical, paramedical, and/or nursing knowledge and technology, the primary purpose of which is to promote, restore, or maintain health.

Heliports This entry gives the total number of heliports with hard-surface runways, helipads, or landing areas that support routine sustained helicopter operations exclusively and have support facilities including one or more of the following facilities: lighting, fuel, passenger handling, or maintenance. It includes former airports used exclusively for helicopter operations but excludes heliports limited to day operations and natural clearings that could support helicopter landings and takeoffs.

HIV/AIDS—adult prevalence rate This entry gives an estimate of the percentage of adults (aged 15-49) living with HIV/AIDS. The adult prevalence rate is calculated by dividing the estimated number of adults living with HIV/AIDS at yearend by the total adult population at yearend.

HIV/AIDS—deaths This entry gives an estimate of the number of adults and children who died of AIDS during a given calendar year.

HIV/AIDS—people living with HIV/AIDS This entry gives an estimate of all people (adults and children) alive at yearend with HIV infection, whether or not they have developed symptoms of AIDS.

Hospital bed density This entry provides the number of hospital beds per 1,000 people; it serves as a general measure of inpatient service availability. Hospital beds include inpatient beds available in public, private, general, and specialized hospitals and rehabilitation centers. In most cases, beds for both acute and chronic care are included. Because the level of inpatient services required for individual countries depends on several factors - such as demographic issues and the burden of disease - there is no global target for the number of hospital beds per country. So, while 2 beds per 1,000 in one country may be sufficient, 2 beds per 1,000 in another may be woefully inadequate because of the number of people hospitalized by disease.

Household income or consumption by percentage share Data on household income or consumption come from household surveys, the results adjusted for household size. Nations use different standards and procedures in collecting and adjusting the data. Surveys based on income will normally show a more unequal distribution than surveys based on consumption. The quality of surveys is improving with time, yet caution is still necessary in making inter-country comparisons.

Hydrographic data codes See **Data codes**

Illicit drugs This entry gives information on the five categories of illicit drugs—narcotics, stimulants, depressants (sedatives), hallucinogens, and cannabis. These categories include many drugs legally produced and prescribed by doctors as well as those illegally produced and sold outside of medical channels.

Cannabis (*Cannabis sativa*) is the common hemp plant, which provides hallucinogens with some sedative properties, and includes marijuana (pot, Acapulco gold, grass, reefer), tetrahydrocannabinol (THC, Marinol), hashish (hash), and hashish oil (hash oil).

Coca (mostly *Erythroxylum* coca) is a bush with leaves that contain the stimulant used to make cocaine. Coca is not to be confused with cocoa, which comes from cacao seeds and is used in making chocolate, cocoa, and cocoa butter.

Cocaine is a stimulant derived from the leaves of the coca bush.

Depressants (sedatives) are drugs that reduce tension and anxiety and include chloral hydrate, barbiturates (Amytal, Nembutal, Seconal, phenobarbital), benzodiazepines (Librium, Valium), methaqualone (Quaalude), glutethimide (Doriden), and others (Equanil, Placidyl, Valmid).

Drugs are any chemical substances that effect a physical, mental, emotional, or behavioral change in an individual.

Drug abuse is the use of any licit or illicit chemical substance that results in physical, mental, emotional, or behavioral impairment in an individual.

Hallucinogens are drugs that affect sensation, thinking, self-awareness, and emotion. Hallucinogens include LSD (acid, microdot), mescaline and peyote (mexc, buttons, cactus), amphetamine variants (PMA, STP, DOB), phencyclidine (PCP, angel dust, hog), phencyclidine analogues (PCE, PCPy, TCP), and others (psilocybin, psilocyn).

Hashish is the resinous exudate of the cannabis or hemp plant (Cannabis sativa).

Heroin is a semisynthetic derivative of morphine.

Mandrax is a trade name for methaqualone, a pharmaceutical depressant.

Marijuana is the dried leaf of the cannabis or hemp plant (*Cannabis sativa*).

Methaqualone is a pharmaceutical depressant, referred to as mandrax in Southwest Asia and Africa.

Narcotics are drugs that relieve pain, often induce sleep, and refer to opium, opium derivatives, and synthetic substitutes. Natural narcotics include opium (paregoric, parepectolin), morphine (MS-Contin, Roxanol), codeine (Tylenol with codeine, Empirin with codeine, Robitussin AC), and thebaine. Semi-synthetic narcotics include heroin (horse, smack), and hydromorphone (Dilaudid). Synthetic narcotics include meperidine or Pethidine (Demerol, Mepergan), methadone (Dolophine, Methadose), and others (Darvon, Lomotil).

Opium is the brown, gummy exudate of the incised, unripe seedpod of the opium poppy.

Opium poppy (*Papaver somniferum*) is the source for the natural and semisynthetic narcotics.

Poppy straw is the entire cut and dried opium poppy-plant material, other than the seeds. Opium is extracted from poppy straw in commercial operations that produce the drug for medical use.

Qat (kat, khat) is a stimulant from the buds or leaves of Catha edulis that is chewed or drunk as tea.

Quaaludes is the North American slang term for methaqualone, a pharmaceutical depressant.

Stimulants are drugs that relieve mild depression, increase energy and activity, and include cocaine (coke, snow, crack), amphetamines (Desoxyn, Dexedrine), ephedrine, ecstasy (clarity, essence, doctor, Adam), phenmetrazine (Preludin), methylphenidate (Ritalin), and others (Cylert, Sanorex, Tenuate).

Imports This entry provides the total US dollar amount of merchandise imports on a c.i.f. (cost, insurance, and freight) or f.o.b. (free on board) basis. These figures are calculated on an exchange rate basis, i.e., not in purchasing power parity (PPP) terms.

Imports—commodities This entry provides a listing of the highest-valued imported products; it sometimes includes the percent of total dollar value.

Imports—partners This entry provides a rank ordering of trading partners starting with the most important; it sometimes includes the percent of total dollar value.

Independence For most countries, this entry gives the date that sovereignty was achieved and from which nation, empire, or trusteeship. For the other countries, the date given may not represent "independence" in the strict sense, but rather some significant nationhood event such as the traditional founding date or the date of unification, federation, confederation, establishment, fundamental change in the form of government, or state succession. For a number of countries, the establishment of statehood was a lengthy evolutionary process occurring over decades or even centuries. In such cases, several significant dates are cited. Dependent areas include the notation "none" followed by the nature of their dependency status. Also see the **Terminology** note.

Industrial production growth rate This entry gives the annual percentage increase in industrial production (includes manufacturing, mining, and construction).

Industries This entry provides a rank ordering of industries starting with the largest by value of annual output.

Infant mortality rate This entry gives the number of deaths of infants under one year old in a given year per 1,000 live births in the same year. This rate is often used as an indicator of the level of health in a country.

Inflation rate (consumer prices) This entry furnishes the annual percent change in consumer prices compared with the previous year's consumer prices.

International disputes see **Disputes—international**

International law organization participation This entry includes information on a country's acceptance of jurisdiction of the International Court of Justice (ICJ) and of the International Criminal Court (ICCt); 55 countries have accepted ICJ jurisdiction with reservations and 11 have accepted ICJ jurisdiction without reservations; 114 countries have accepted ICCt jurisdiction. **Appendix B: International Organizations and Groups** explains the differing mandates of the ICJ and ICCt.

International organization participation This entry lists in alphabetical order by abbreviation those international organizations in which the subject country is a member or participates in some other way.

International organizations This information is presented in **Appendix B: International Organizations and Groups** which includes the name, abbreviation, date established, aim, and members by category.

Internet country code This entry includes the two-letter codes maintained by the International Organization for Standardization (ISO) in the ISO 3166 Alpha-2 list and used by the Internet Assigned Numbers Authority (IANA) to establish country-coded top-level domains (ccTLDs).

Internet hosts This entry lists the number of Internet hosts available within a country. An Internet host is a computer connected directly to the Internet; normally an Internet Service Provider's (ISP) computer is a host. Internet users may use either a hard-wired terminal, at an institution with a mainframe computer connected directly to the Internet, or may connect remotely by way of a modem via telephone line, cable, or satellite to the Internet Service Provider's host computer. The number of hosts is one indicator of the extent of Internet connectivity.

Internet users This entry gives the number of users within a country that access the Internet. Statistics vary from country to country and may include users who access the Internet at least several times a week to those who access it only once within a period of several months.

Introduction This category includes one entry, **Background**.

Investment (gross fixed) This entry records total business spending on fixed assets, such as factories, machinery, equipment, dwellings, and inventories of raw materials, which provide the basis for future production. It is measured gross of the depreciation of the assets, i.e., it includes investment that merely replaces worn-out or scrapped capital.

Irrigated land This entry gives the number of square kilometers of land area that is artificially supplied with water.

Judicial branch This entry includes three subfields. *The highest court(s)* subfield includes the name(s) of a country's highest level court(s), the number and titles of the judges, and the types of cases heard by the court, which commonly are based on civil, criminal, administrative, and constitutional law. A number of countries have separate constitutional courts. The *judge selection and term of office* subfield includes the organizations and associated officials responsible for nominating and appointing judges, and a brief description of the process. The selection process can be indicative of the independence of a country's court system from other branches of its government. Also included in this subfield are judges' tenures, which can range from a few years, to a specified retirement age, to lifelong appointments. *The subordinate courts* subfield lists the courts lower in the hierarchy of a country's court system. A few countries with federal-style governments, such as Brazil, Canada, and the US, in addition to their federal court, have separate state- or province-level court systems, though generally the two systems interact.

Labor force This entry contains the total labor force figure.

Labor force—by occupation This entry lists the percentage distribution of the labor force by sector of occupation. *Agriculture* includes farming, fishing, and forestry. *Industry* includes mining, manufacturing, energy production, and construction. Services cover government activities, communications, transportation, finance, and all other economic activities that do not produce material goods. The distribution will total less than 100 percent if the data are incomplete and may range from 99-101 percent due to rounding.

Land boundaries This entry contains the *total* length of all land boundaries and the individual lengths for each of the contiguous *border countries*. When available, official lengths published by national statistical agencies are used. Because surveying methods may differ, country border lengths reported by contiguous countries may differ.

Land use This entry contains the percentage shares of total land area for three different types of land use: *arable land*—land cultivated for crops like wheat, maize, and rice that are replanted after each harvest; *permanent crops*—land cultivated for crops like citrus, coffee, and rubber that are not replanted after each harvest; includes land under flowering shrubs, fruit trees, nut trees, and vines, but excludes land under trees grown for wood or timber; *other*—any land not arable or under permanent crops; includes permanent meadows and pastures, forests and woodlands, built-on areas, roads, barren land, etc.

Languages This entry provides a rank ordering of languages starting with the largest and sometimes includes the percent of total population speaking that language.

Legal system This entry provides the description of a country's legal system. A statement on judicial review of legislative acts is also included for a number of countries. The legal systems of nearly all countries are generally modeled upon elements of five main types: civil law (including French law, the Napoleonic Code, Roman law, Roman-Dutch law, and Spanish law); common law (including United State law); customary law; mixed or pluralistic law; and religious law (including Islamic law). An additional type of legal system—international law, which governs the conduct of independent nations in their relationships with one another—is also addressed below. The following list describes these legal systems, the countries or world regions where these systems are enforced, and a brief statement on the origins and major features of each.

Civil Law—The most widespread type of legal system in the world, applied in various forms in approximately 150 countries. Also referred to as European continental law, the civil law system is derived mainly from the Roman *Corpus Juris Civilus*, (Body of Civil Law), a collection of laws and legal interpretations compiled under the East Roman (Byzantine) Emperor Justinian I between A.D. 528 and 565. The major feature of civil law systems is that the laws are organized into systematic written codes. In civil law the sources recognized as authoritative are principally legislation—especially codifications in constitutions or statutes enacted by governments—and secondarily, custom. The civil law systems in some countries are based on more than one code.

Common Law—A type of legal system, often synonymous with "English common law," which is the system of England and Wales in the UK, and is also in force in approximately 80 countries formerly part of or influenced by the former British Empire. English common law reflects Biblical influences as well as remnants of law systems imposed by early conquerors including the Romans, Anglo-Saxons, and Normans. Some legal scholars attribute the formation of the English common law system to King Henry II (r. 1154-1189). Until the time of his reign, laws customary among England's various manorial and ecclesiastical (church) jurisdictions were administered locally. Henry II established the king's court and designated that laws were "common" to the entire English realm. The foundation of English common law is "legal precedent"—referred to as *stare decisis*, meaning "to stand by things decided." In the English common law system, court judges are bound in their decisions in large part by the rules and other doctrines developed—and supplemented over time—by the judges of earlier English courts.

Customary Law—A type of legal system that serves as the basis of, or has influenced, the present-day laws in approximately 40 countries—mostly in Africa, but some in the Pacific islands, Europe, and the Near East. Customary law is also referred to as "primitive law," "unwritten law," "indigenous law," and "folk law." There is no single history of customary law such as that found in Roman civil law, English common law, Islamic law, or the Napoleonic Civil Code. The earliest systems of law in human society were customary, and usually developed in small agrarian and hunter-gatherer communities. As the term implies, customary law is based upon the customs of a community. Common attributes of customary legal systems are that they are seldom written down, they embody an organized set of rules reaulating social relations, and they are agreed upon by members of the community. Although such law systems include sanctions for law infractions, resolution tends to be reconciliatory rather than punitive. A number of African states practiced customary law many centuries prior to colonial influences. Following colonization, such laws were written down and incorporated to varying extents into the legal systems imposed by their colonial powers.

European Union Law—A sub-discipline of international law known as "supranational law" in which the rights of sovereign nations are limited in relation to one another. Also referred to as the Law of the European Union or Community Law, it is the unique and complex legal system that operates in tandem with the laws of the 27 member states of the European Union (EU). Similar to federal states, the EU legal system ensures compliance from the member states because of the Union's decentralized political nature. The European Court of Justice (ECJ), established in 1952 by the Treaty of Paris, has been largely responsible for the development of EU law. Fundamental principles of European Union law include: *subsidiarity*—the notion that issues be handled by the smallest, lowest, or least centralized competent authority; *proportionality*—the EU may only act to the extent needed to achieve its objectives; *conferral*—the EU is a union of member states, and all its authorities are voluntarily granted by its members; *legal certainty*—requires that legal rules be clear and precise; and *precautionary principle*—a moral and political principle stating that if an action or policy might cause severe or irreversible harm to the public or to the environment, in the absence of a scientific consensus that harm would not ensue, the burden of proof falls on those who would advocate taking the action.

French Law—A type of civil law that is the legal system of France. The French system also serves as the basis for, or is mixed with, other legal systems in approximately 50 countries, notably in North Africa, the Near East, and the French territories and dependencies. French law is primarily codified or systematic written civil law. Prior to the French Revolution (1789-1799), France had no single national legal system. Laws in the northern areas of present-day France were mostly local customs based on privileges and exemptions granted by kings and feudal lords, while in the southern areas Roman law predominated. The introduction of the Napoleonic Civil Code during the reign of Napoleon I in the first decade of the 19th century brought major reforms to the French legal system, many of which remain part of France's current legal structure, though all have been extensively amended or redrafted to address a modern nation. French law distinguishes between "public law" and "private law." Public law relates to government, the French Constitution, public administration, and criminal law. Private law covers issues between private citizens or corporations. The most recent changes to the French legal system—introduced in the 1980s—were the decentralization laws, which transferred authority from centrally appointed government representatives to locally elected representatives of the people.

International Law—The law of the international community, or the body of customary rules and treaty rules accepted as legally binding by states in their relations with each other. International law differs from other legal systems in that it primarily concerns sovereign political entities. There are three separate disciplines of international law: public international law, which governs the relationship between provinces and international entities and includes treaty law, law of the sea, international criminal law, and international humanitarian law; private international law, which addresses legal jurisdiction; and supranational law—a legal framework wherein countries are bound by regional agreements in which the laws of the member countries are held inapplicable when in conflict with supranational laws. At present the European Union is the only entity under a supranational legal system. The term "international law" was coined by Jeremy Bentham in 1780 in his *Principles of Morals and Legislation*, though laws governing relations between states have been recognized from very early times (many centuries B.C.). Modern international law developed alongside the emergence and growth of the European nationstates beginning in the early 16th century. Other factors that influenced the development of international law included the revival of legal studies, the growth of international trade, and the practice of exchanging emissaries and establishing legations. The sources of International law are set out in Article 38-1 of the Statute of the International Court of Justice within the UN Charter.

Islamic Law—The most widespread type of religious law, it is the legal system enforced in over 30 countries, particularly in the Near East, but also in Central and South Asia, Africa, and Indonesia. In many countries Islamic law operates in tandem with a civil law system. Islamic law is embodied in the sharia, an Arabic word meaning "the right path." Sharia covers all aspects of public and private life and organizes them into five categories: obligatory, recommended, permitted, disliked, and forbidden. The primary sources of sharia law are the Qur'an, believed by Muslims to be the word of God revealed to the Prophet Muhammad by the angel Gabriel, and the Sunnah, the teachings of the Prophet and his works. In addition to these two primary sources, traditional Sunni Muslims recognize the consensus of Muhammad's companions and Islamic jurists on certain issues, called ijmas, and various forms of reasoning, including analogy by legal scholars, referred to as qiyas. Shia Muslims reject ijmas and qiyas as sources of sharia law.

Mixed Law—Also referred to as pluralistic law, mixed law consists of elements of some or all of the other main types of legal systems—civil, common, customary, and religious. The mixed legal systems of a number of countries came about when colonial powers overlaid their own legal systems upon colonized regions but retained elements of the colonies' existing legal systems.

Napoleonic Civil Code—A type of civil law, referred to as the Civil *Code or Code Civil des Francais,* forms part of the legal system of France, and underpins the legal systems of Bolivia, Egypt, Lebanon, Poland, and the US state of Louisiana. The Civil Code was established under Napoleon I, enacted in 1804, and officially designated the *Code Napoleon* in 1807. This legal system combined the Teutonic civil law tradition of the northern provinces of France with the Roman law tradition of the southern and eastern regions of the country. The Civil Code bears similarities in its arrangement to the Roman *Body of Civil Law* (see Civil Law above). As enacted in 1804, the Code addressed personal status, property, and the acquisition of property. Codes added over the following six years included civil procedures, commercial law, criminal law and procedures, and a penal code.

Religious Law—A legal system which stems from the sacred texts of religious traditions and in most cases professes to cover all aspects of life as a seamless part of devotional obligations to a transcendent, imminent, or deep philosophical reality. Implied as the basis of religious law is the concept of unalterability, because the word of God cannot be amended or legislated against by judges or governments. However, a detailed legal system generally requires human elaboration. The main types of religious law are sharia in Islam, halakha in Judaism, and canon law in some Christian groups. Sharia is the most widespread religious legal system (see Islamic Law), and is the sole system of law for countries including Iran, the Maldives, and Saudi Arabia. No country is fully governed by halakha, but Jewish people may decide to settle disputes through Jewish courts and be bound by their rulings. Canon law is not a divine law as such because it is not found in revelation. It is viewed instead as human law inspired by the word of God and applying the demands of that revelation to the actual situation of the church. Canon law regulates the internal ordering of the Roman Catholic Church, the Eastern Orthodox Church, and the Anglican Communion.

Roman Law—A type of civil law developed in ancient Rome and practiced from the time of the city's founding (traditionally 753 B.C.) until the fall of the Western Empire in the 5th century A.D. Roman law remained the legal system of the Byzantine (Eastern Empire) until the fall of Constantinople in 1453. Preserved fragments of the first legal text, known as the Law of the Twelve Tables, dating from the 5th century B.C., contained specific provisions designed to change the prevailing customary law. Early Roman law was drawn from custom and statutes; later, during the time of the empire, emperors asserted their authority as the ultimate source of law. The basis for Roman laws was the idea that the exact form—not the intention—of words or of actions produced legal consequences. It was only in the late 6th century A.D. that a comprehensive Roman code of laws was published (see Civil Law above).

Roman law served as the basis of law systems developed in a number of continental European countries.

Roman-Dutch Law—A type of civil law based on Roman law as applied in the Netherlands. Roman-Dutch law serves as the basis for legal systems in seven African countries, as well as Guyana, Indonesia, and Sri Lanka. This law system, which originated in the province of Holland and expanded throughout the Netherlands (to be replaced by the French Civil Code in 1809), was instituted in a number of sub-Saharan African countries during the Dutch colonial period. The Dutch jurist/philosopher Hugo Grotius was the first to attempt to reduce Roman-Dutch civil law into a system in his *Jurisprudence of Holland* (written 1619-20, commentary published 1621). The Dutch historian/lawyer Simon van Leeuwen coined the term "Roman-Dutch law" in 1652.

Spanish Law—A type of civil law, often referred to as the Spanish Civil Code, it is the present legal system of Spain and is the basis of legal systems in 12 countries mostly in Central and South America, but also in southwestern Europe, northern and western Africa, and southeastern Asia. The Spanish Civil Code reflects a complex mixture of customary, Roman, Napoleonic, local, and modern codified law. The laws of the Visigoth invaders of Spain in the 5th to 7th centuries had the earliest major influence on Spanish legal system development. The Christian Reconquest of Spain in the 11th through 15th centuries witnessed the development of customary law, which combined canon (religious) and Roman law. During several centuries of Hapsburg and Bourbon rule, systematic recompilations of the existing national legal system were attempted, but these often conflicted with local and regional customary civil laws. Legal system development for most of the 19th century concentrated on formulating a national civil law system, which was finally enacted in 1889 as the Spanish Civil Code. Several sections of the code have been revised, the most recent of which are the penal code in 1989 and the judiciary code in 2001. The Spanish Civil Code separates public and private law. Public law includes constitutional law, administrative law, criminal law, process law, financial and tax law, and international public law. Private law includes civil law, commercial law, labor law, and international private law.

United States Law—A type of common law, which is the basis of the legal system of the United States and that of its island possessions in the Caribbean and the Pacific. This legal system has several layers, more possibly than in most other countries, and is due in part to the division between federal and state law. The United States was founded not as one nation but as a union of 13 colonies, each claiming independence from the British Crown. The US Constitution, implemented in 1789, began shifting power away from the states and toward the federal government, though the states today retain substantial legal authority. US law draws its authority from four sources: *constitutional law, statutory law, administrative regulations*, and *case law*. Constitutional law is based on the US Constitution and serves as the supreme federal law. Taken together with those of the state constitutions, these documents outline the general structure of the federal and state governments and provide the rules and limits of power. US statutory law is legislation enacted by the US Congress and is codified in the United States Code. The 50 state legislatures have similar authority to enact state statutes. Administrative law is the authority delegated to federal and state executive agencies. Case law, also referred to as common law, covers areas where constitutional or statutory law is lacking. Case law is a collection of judicial decisions, customs, and general principles that began in England centuries ago, that were adopted in America at the time of the Revolution, and that continue to develop today.

Legislative branch This entry contains information on the structure (unicameral, bicameral, tricameral), formal name, number of seats, and term of office. *Elections* includes the nature of the election process or accession to power, date of the last election, and date of the next election. *Election results* includes the percent of vote and/or number of seats held by each party in the last election.

Life expectancy at birth This entry contains the average number of years to be lived by a group of people born in the same year, if mortality at each age remains constant in the future. Life expectancy at birth is also a measure of overall quality of life in a country and summarizes the mortality at all ages. It can also be thought of as indicating the potential return on investment in human capital and is necessary for the calculation of various actuarial measures.

Literacy This entry includes a *definition* of literacy and Census Bureau percentages for the *total population, males*, and *females*. There are no universal definitions and standards of literacy. Unless otherwise specified, all rates are based on the most common definition—the ability to read and write at a specified age. Detailing the standards that individual countries use to assess the ability to read and write is beyond the scope of the Factbook. Information on literacy, while not a perfect measure of educational results, is probably the most easily available and valid for international comparisons. Low levels of literacy, and education in general, can impede the economic development of a country in the current rapidly changing, technology-driven world.

Location This entry identifies the country's regional location, neighboring countries, and adjacent bodies of water.

Major infectious diseases This entry lists major infectious diseases likely to be encountered in countries where the risk of such diseases is assessed to be very high as compared to the United States. These infectious diseases represent risks to US government personnel traveling to the specified country for a period of less than three years. The **degree of risk** is assessed by considering the foreign nature of these infectious diseases, their severity, and the probability of being affected by the diseases present. The diseases listed do not necessarily represent the total disease burden experienced by the local population.

The risk to an individual traveler varies considerably by the specific location, visit duration, type of activities, type of accommodations, time of year, and other factors. Consultation with a travel medicine physician is needed to evaluate individual risk and recommend appropriate preventive measures such as vaccines.

Diseases are organized into the following six exposure categories shown in italics *and listed in typical descending order of risk.* Note: The sequence of exposure categories listed in individual country entries may vary according to local conditions.

food or waterborne diseases acquired through eating or drinking on the local economy:

Hepatitis A—viral disease that interferes with the functioning of the liver; spread through consumption of food or water contaminated with fecal matter, principally in areas of poor sanitation; victims exhibit fever, jaundice, and diarrhea; 15% of victims will experience prolonged symptoms over 6-9 months; vaccine available.

Hepatitis E—water-borne viral disease that interferes with the functioning of the liver; most commonly spread through fecal contamination of drinking water; victims exhibit jaundice, fatigue, abdominal pain, and dark colored urine.

Typhoid fever—bacterial disease spread through contact with food or water contaminated by fecal matter or sewage; victims exhibit sustained high fevers; left untreated, mortality rates can reach 20%.

vectorborne diseases acquired through the bite of an infected arthropod:

Malaria—caused by single-cell parasitic protozoa Plasmodium; transmitted to humans via the bite of the female Anopheles mosquito; parasites multiply in the liver attacking red blood cells resulting in cycles of fever, chills, and sweats accompanied by anemia; death due to damage to vital organs and interruption of blood supply to the brain; endemic in 100, mostly tropical, countries with 90% of cases and the majority of 1.5-2.5 million estimated annual deaths occurring in sub-Saharan Africa.

Dengue fever—mosquito-borne (*Aedes aegypti*) viral disease associated with urban environments; manifests as sudden onset of fever and severe headache; occasionally produces shock and hemorrhage leading to death in 5% of cases.

Yellow fever—mosquito-borne viral disease; severity ranges from influenza-like symptoms to severe hepatitis and hemorrhagic fever; occurs only in tropical South America and sub-Saharan Africa, where most cases are reported; fatality rate is less than 20%.
Japanese Encephalitis—mosquito-borne (*Culex tritaeniorhynchus*) viral disease associated with rural areas in Asia; acute encephalitis can progress to paralysis, coma, and death; fatality rates 30%.
African Trypanosomiasis—caused by the parasitic protozoa *Trypanosoma*; transmitted to humans via the bite of bloodsucking Tsetse flies; infection leads to malaise and irregular fevers and, in advanced cases when the parasites invade the central nervous system, coma and death; endemic in 36 countries of sub-Saharan Africa; cattle and wild animals act as reservoir hosts for the parasites.
Cutaneous Leishmaniasis—caused by the parasitic protozoa *leishmania*; transmitted to humans via the bite of sandflies; results in skin lesions that may become chronic; endemic in 88 countries; 90% of cases occur in Iran, Afghanistan, Syria, Saudi Arabia, Brazil, and Peru; wild and domesticated animals as well as humans can act as reservoirs of infection.
Plague—bacterial disease transmitted by fleas normally associated with rats; person-to-person airborne transmission also possible; recent plague epidemics occurred in areas of Asia, Africa, and South America associated with rural areas or small towns and villages; manifests as fever, headache, and painfully swollen lymph nodes; disease progresses rapidly and without antibiotic treatment leads to pneumonic form with a death rate in excess of 50%.
Crimea n-Congo hemorrhagic fever—tick-borne viral disease; infection may also result from exposure to infected animal blood or tissue; geographic distribution includes Africa, Asia, the Middle East, and Eastern Europe; sudden onset of fever, headache, and muscle aches followed by hemorrhaging in the bowels, urine, nose, and gums; mortality rate is approximately 30%.
Rift Valley fever—viral disease affecting domesticated animals and humans; transmission is by mosquito and other biting insects; infection may also occur through handling of infected meat or contact with blood; geographic distribution includes eastern and southern Africa where cattle and sheep are raised; symptoms are generally mild with fever and some liver abnormalities, but the disease may progress to hemorrhagic fever, encephalitis, or ocular disease; fatality rates are low at about 1% of cases.
Chikungunya—mosquito-borne (*Aedes aegypti*) viral disease associated with urban environments, similar to Dengue Fever; characterized by sudden onset of fever, rash, and severe joint pain usually lasting 3-7 days, some cases result in persistent arthritis.
water contact diseases acquired through swimming or wading in freshwater lakes, streams, and rivers:
Leptospirosis—bacterial disease that affects animals and humans; infection occurs through contact with water, food, or soil contaminated by animal urine; symptoms include high fever, severe headache, vomiting, jaundice, and diarrhea; untreated, the disease can result in kidney damage, liver failure, meningitis, or respiratory distress; fatality rates are low but left untreated recovery can take months.
Schistosomiasis—caused by parasitic trematode flatworm *Schistosoma*; fresh water snails act as intermediate host and release larval form of parasite that penetrates the skin of people exposed to contaminated water; worms mature and reproduce in the blood vessels, liver, kidneys, and intestines releasing eggs, which become trapped in tissues triggering an immune response; may manifest as either urinary or intestinal disease resulting in decreased work or learning capacity; mortality, while generally low, may occur in advanced cases usually due to bladder cancer; endemic in 74 developing countries with 80% of infected people living in sub-Saharan Africa; humans act as the reservoir for this parasite.
aerosolized dust or soil contact disease acquired through inhalation of aerosols contaminated with rodent urine:
Lassa fever—viral disease carried by rats of the genus Mastomys; endemic in portions of West Africa; infection occurs through direct contact with or consumption of food contaminated by rodent urine or fecal matter containing virus particles; fatality rate can reach 50% in epidemic outbreaks.
respiratory disease acquired through close contact with an infectious person:
Meningococcal meningitis—bacterial disease causing an inflammation of the lining of the brain and spinal cord; one of the most important bacterial pathogens is Neisseria meningitidis because of its potential to cause epidemics; symptoms include stiff neck, high fever, headaches, and vomiting; bacteria are transmitted from person to person by respiratory droplets and facilitated by close and prolonged contact resulting from crowded living conditions, often with a seasonal distribution; death occurs in 5-15% of cases, typically within 24-48 hours of onset of symptoms; highest burden of meningococcal disease occurs in the hyperendemic region of sub-Saharan Africa known as the "Meningitis Belt" which stretches from Senegal east to Ethiopia.
animal contact disease acquired through direct contact with local animals:
Rabies—viral disease of mammals usually transmitted through the bite of an infected animal, most commonly dogs; virus affects the central nervous system causing brain alteration and death; symptoms initially are non-specific fever and headache progressing to neurological symptoms; death occurs within days of the onset of symptoms.

Major urban areas—population This entry provides the population of the capital and up to five major cities defined as urban agglomerations with populations of at least 750,000 people. An *urban agglomeration* is defined as comprising the city or town proper and also the suburban fringe or thickly settled territory lying outside of, but adjacent to, the boundaries of the city. For smaller countries, lacking urban centers of 750,000 or more, only the population of the capital is presented.

Manpower available for military service This entry gives the number of males and females falling in the military age range for a country (defined as being ages 16-49) and assumes that every individual is fit to serve.

Manpower fit for military service This entry gives the number of males and females falling in the military age range for a country (defined as being ages 16-49) and who are not otherwise disqualified for health reasons; accounts for the health situation in the country and provides a more realistic estimate of the actual number fit to serve.

Manpower reaching militarily significant age annually This entry gives the number of males and females entering the military manpower pool (i.e., reaching age 16) in any given year and is a measure of the availability of military-age young adults.

Map references This entry includes the name of the *Factbook* reference map on which a country may be found. Note that boundary representations on these maps are not necessarily authoritative. The entry on **Geographic coordinates** may be helpful in finding some smaller countries.

Maritime claims This entry includes the following claims, the definitions of which are excerpted from the United Nations Convention on the Law of the Sea (UNCLOS), which alone contains the full and definitive descriptions:

territorial sea—the sovereignty of a coastal state extends beyond its land territory and internal waters to an adjacent belt of sea, described as the territorial sea in the UNCLOS (Part II); this sovereignty extends to the air space over the territorial sea as well as its underlying seabed and subsoil; every state has the right to establish the breadth of its territorial sea up to a limit not exceeding 12 nautical miles; the normal baseline for measuring the breadth of the territorial sea is the mean low-water line along the coast as marked on large-scale charts officially recognized by the coastal state; where the coasts of two states are opposite or adjacent to each other, neither state is entitled to extend its territorial sea beyond the median line, every point of which is equidistant from the nearest points on the baseline from which the territorial seas of both states are measured; the UNCLOS describes specific rules for archipelagic states.

contiguous zone—according to the UNCLOS (Article 33), this is a zone contiguous to a coastal state's territorial sea, over which it may exercise the control necessary to: prevent infringement of its customs, fiscal, immigration, or sanitary laws and regulations within its territory or territorial sea; punish infringement of the above laws and regulations committed within its territory or territorial sea; the contiguous zone may not extend beyond 24 nautical miles from the baselines from which the breadth of the territorial sea is measured (e.g., the US has claimed a 12-nautical mile contiguous zone in addition to its 12-nautical mile territorial sea); where the coasts of two states are opposite or adjacent to each other, neither state is entitled to extend its contiguous zone beyond the median line, every point of which is equidistant from the nearest points on the baseline from which the contiguous zone of both states are measured.

exclusive economic zone (EEZ)—the UNCLOS (Part V) defines the EEZ as a zone beyond and adjacent to the territorial sea in which a coastal state has: sovereign rights for the purpose of exploring and exploiting, conserving and managing the natural resources, whether living or non-living, of the waters superjacent to the seabed and of the seabed and its subsoil, and with regard to other activities for the economic exploitation and exploration of the zone, such as the production of energy from the water, currents, and winds; jurisdiction with regard to the establishment and use of artificial islands, installations, and structures; marine scientific research; the protection and preservation of the marine environment; the outer limit of the exclusive economic zone shall not exceed 200 nautical miles from the baselines from which the breadth of the territorial sea is measured.

continental shelf—the UNCLOS (Article 76) defines the continental shelf of a coastal state as comprising the seabed and subsoil of the submarine areas that extend beyond its territorial sea throughout the natural prolongation of its land territory to the outer edge of the continental margin, or to a distance of 200 nautical miles from the baselines from which the breadth of the territorial sea is measured where the outer edge of the continental margin does not extend up to that distance; the continental margin comprises the submerged prolongation of the landmass of the coastal state, and consists of the seabed and subsoil of the shelf, the slope and the rise; wherever the continental margin extends beyond 200 nautical miles from the baseline, coastal states may extend their claim to a distance not to exceed 350 nautical miles from the baseline or 100 nautical miles from the 2,500-meter isobath, which is a line connecting points of 2,500 meters in depth; it does not include the deep ocean floor with its oceanic ridges or the subsoil thereof.

exclusive fishing zone—while this term is not used in the UNCLOS, some states (e.g., the United Kingdom) have chosen not to claim an EEZ, but rather to claim jurisdiction over the living resources off their coast; in such cases, the term exclusive fishing zone is often used; the breadth of this zone is normally the same as the EEZ or 200 nautical miles.

Market value of publicly traded shares This entry gives the value of shares issued by publicly traded companies at a price determined in the national stock markets on the final day of the period indicated. It is simply the latest price per share multiplied by the total number of outstanding shares, cumulated over all companies listed on the particular exchange.

Maternal mortality rate The maternal mortality rate (MMR) is the annual number of female deaths per 100,000 live births from any cause related to or aggravated by pregnancy or its management (excluding accidental or incidental causes). The MMR includes deaths during pregnancy, childbirth, or within 42 days of termination of pregnancy, irrespective of the duration and site of the pregnancy, for a specified year.

Median age This entry is the age that divides a population into two numerically equal groups; that is, half the people are younger than this age and half are older. It is a single index that summarizes the age distribution of a population. Currently, the median age ranges from a low of about 15 in Uganda and Gaza Strip to 40 or more in several European countries and Japan. See the entry for "Age structure" for the importance of a young versus an older age structure and, by implication, a low versus a higher median age.

Merchant marine Merchant marine may be defined as all ships engaged in the carriage of goods; or all commercial vessels (as opposed to all nonmilitary ships), which excludes tugs, fishing vessels, offshore oil rigs, etc. This entry contains information in four fields—*total, ships by type, foreign-owned, and registered in other countries.*

Total includes the number of ships (1,000 GRT or over), total DWT for those ships, and total GRT for those ships. DWT or dead weight tonnage is the total weight of cargo, plus bunkers, stores, etc., that a ship can carry when immersed to the appropriate load line. GRT or gross register tonnage is a figure obtained by measuring the entire sheltered volume of a ship available for cargo and passengers and converting it to tons on the basis of 100 cubic feet per ton; there is no stable relationship between GRT and DWT.

Ships ***by type*** includes a listing of barge carriers, bulk cargo ships, cargo ships, chemical tankers, combination bulk carriers, combination ore/oil carriers, container ships, liquefied gas tankers, livestock carriers, multifunctional large-load carriers, petroleum tankers, passenger ships, passenger/cargo ships, railcar carriers, refrigerated cargo ships, roll-on/roll-off cargo ships, short-sea passenger ships, specialized tankers, and vehicle carriers.

Foreign-owned are ships that fly the flag of one country but belong to owners in another.

Registered in other countries are ships that belong to owners in one country but fly the flag of another.

Military This category includes the entries dealing with a country's military structure, manpower, and expenditures.

Military—note This entry includes miscellaneous military information of significance not included elsewhere.

Military branches This entry lists the service branches subordinate to defense ministries or the equivalent (typically ground, naval, air, and marine forces).

Military expenditures This entry gives spending on defense programs for the most recent year available as a percent of gross domestic product (GDP); the GDP is calculated on an exchange rate basis, i.e., not in terms of purchasing power parity (PPP). For countries with no military forces, this figure can include expenditures on public security and police.

Military service age and obligation This entry gives the required ages for voluntary or conscript military service and the length of service obligation.

Money figures All money figures are expressed in contemporaneous US dollars unless otherwise indicated.

Mother's mean age at first birth This entry provides the mean (average) age of mothers at the birth of their first child. It is a useful indicator for gauging the success of family planning programs aiming to reduce maternal mortality, increase contraceptive use–particularly among married and unmarried adolescents, delay age at first marriage, and improve the health of newborns.

National anthem A generally patriotic musical composition—usually in the form of a song or hymn of praise—that evokes and eulogizes the history, traditions, or struggles of a nation or its people. National anthems can be officially recognized as a national song by a country's constitution or by an enacted law, or simply by tradition. Although most anthems contain lyrics, some do not.

National holiday This entry gives the primary national day of celebration—usually independence day.

National symbol(s) A national symbol is a faunal, floral, or other abstract representation—or some distinctive object—that over time has come to be closely identified with a country or entity. Not all countries have national symbols; a few countries have more than one.

Nationality This entry provides the identifying terms for citizens—*noun* and *adjective*.

Natural gas—consumption This entry is the total natural gas consumed in cubic meters (cu m). The discrepancy between the amount of natural gas produced and/or imported and the amount consumed and/or exported is due to the omission of stock changes and other complicating factors.

Natural gas—exports This entry is the total natural gas exported in cubic meters (cu m).

Natural gas—imports This entry is the total natural gas imported in cubic meters (cu m).

Natural gas—production This entry is the total natural gas produced in cubic meters (cu m). The discrepancy between the amount of natural gas produced and/or imported and the amount consumed and/or exported is due to the omission of stock changes and other complicating factors.

Natural gas—proved reserves This entry is the stock of proved reserves of natural gas in cubic meters (cu m). Proved reserves are those quantities of natural gas, which, by analysis of geological and engineering data, can be estimated with a high degree of confidence to be commercially recoverable from a given date forward, from known reservoirs and under current economic conditions.

Natural hazards This entry lists potential natural disasters. For countries where volcanic activity is common, a *volcanism* subfield highlights historically active volcanoes.

Natural resources This entry lists a country's mineral, petroleum, hydropower, and other resources of commercial importance, such as rare earth elements (REEs). In general, products appear only if they make a significant contribution to the economy, or are likely to do so in the future.

Net migration rate This entry includes the figure for the difference between the number of persons entering and leaving a country during the year per 1,000 persons (based on midyear population). An excess of persons entering the country is referred to as net immigration (e.g., 3.56 migrants/1,000 population); an excess of persons leaving the country as net emigration (e.g., -9.26 migrants/1,000 population). The net migration rate indicates the contribution of migration to the overall level of population change. The net migration rate does not distinguish between economic migrants, refugees, and other types of migrants nor does it distinguish between lawful migrants and undocumented migrants.

Obesity—adult prevalence rate This entry gives the percent of a country's population considered to be obese. Obesity is defined as an adult having a Body Mass Index (BMI) greater to or equal to 30.0. BMI is calculated by taking a person's weight in kg and dividing it by the person's squared height in meters.

People—note This entry includes miscellaneous demographic information of significance not included elsewhere.

People and Society This category includes entries dealing with national identity (including ethnicities, languages, and religions), demography (a variety of population statistics) and societal characteristics (health and education indicators).

Personal Names—Capitalization The *Factbook* capitalizes the surname or family name of individuals for the convenience of our users who are faced with a world of different cultures and naming conventions. The need for capitalization, bold type, underlining, italics, or some other indicator of the individual's surname is apparent in the following examples: MAO Zedong, Fidel CASTRO Ruz, George W. BUSH, and TUNKU SALAHUDDIN Abdul Aziz Shah ibni Al-Marhum Sultan Hisammuddin Alam Shah. By knowing the surname, a short form without all capital letters can be used with confidence as in President Castro, Chairman Mao, President Bush, or Sultan Tunku Salahuddin. The same system of capitalization is extended to the names of leaders with surnames that are not commonly used such as Queen ELIZABETH II. For Vietnamese names, the given name is capitalized because officials are referred to by their given name rather than by their surname. For example, the president of Vietnam is Tran Duc LUONG. His surname is Tran, but he is referred to by his given name—President LUONG.

Personal Names—Spelling The romanization of personal names in the *Factbook* normally follows the same transliteration system used by the US Board on Geographic Names for spelling place names. At times, however, a foreign leader expressly indicates a preference for, or the media or official documents regularly use, a romanized spelling that differs from the transliteration derived from the US Government standard. In such cases, the Factbook uses the alternative spelling.

Personal Names—Titles The *Factbook* capitalizes any valid title (or short form of it) immediately preceding a person's name. A title standing alone is not capitalized. Examples: President PUTIN and President OBAMA are chiefs of state. In Russia, the president is chief of state and the premier is the head of the government, while in the US, the president is both chief of state and head of government.

Petroleum See entries under **Refined petroleum products.**

Petroleum products See entries under **Refined petroleum products.**

Physicians density This entry gives the number of medical doctors (physicians), including generalist and specialist medical practitioners, per 1,000 of the population. Medical doctors are defined as doctors that study, diagnose, treat, and prevent illness, disease, injury, and other physical and mental impairments in humans through the application of modern medicine. They also plan, supervise, and evaluate care and treatment plans by other health care providers. The World Health Organization estimates that fewer than 2.3 health workers (physicians, nurses, and midwives only) per 1,000 would be insufficient to achieve coverage of primary healthcare needs.

Pipelines This entry gives the lengths and types of pipelines for transporting products like natural gas, crude oil, or petroleum products.

Piracy Piracy is defined by the 1982 United Nations Convention on the Law of the Sea as any illegal act of violence, detention, or depredation directed against a ship, aircraft, persons, or property in a place outside the jurisdiction of any State. Such criminal acts committed in the territorial waters of a littoral state are generally considered to be armed robbery against ships. Information on piracy may be found, where applicable, in the **Transportation—note**.

Political parties and leaders This entry includes a listing of significant political parties, coalitions, and electoral lists as of each country's last legislative election, unless otherwise noted.

Political pressure groups and leaders This entry includes a listing of a country's political, social, labor, or religious organizations that are involved in politics, or that exert political pressure, but whose leaders do not stand for legislative election. International movements or organizations are generally not listed.

Population This entry gives an estimate from the US Bureau of the Census based on statistics from population censuses, vital statistics registration systems, or sample surveys pertaining to the recent past and on assumptions about future trends. The total population presents one overall measure of the potential impact of the country on the world and within its region. Note: Starting with the 1993 *Factbook*, demographic estimates for some countries (mostly African) have explicitly taken into account the effects of the growing impact of the HIV/AIDS epidemic. These countries are currently: The Bahamas, Benin, Botswana, Brazil, Burkina Faso, Burma, Burundi, Cambodia, Cameroon, Central African Republic, Democratic Republic of the Congo, Republic of the Congo, Cote d'Ivoire, Ethiopia, Gabon, Ghana, Guyana, Haiti, Honduras, Kenya, Lesotho, Malawi, Mozambique, Namibia, Nigeria, Rwanda, South Africa, Swaziland, Tanzania, Thailand, Togo, Uganda, Zambia, and Zimbabwe.

Population below poverty line National estimates of the percentage of the population falling below the poverty line are based on surveys of sub-groups, with the results weighted by the number of people in each group. Definitions of poverty vary considerably among nations. For example, rich nations generally employ more generous standards of poverty than poor nations.

Population growth rate The average annual percent change in the population, resulting from a surplus (or deficit) of births over deaths and the balance of migrants entering and leaving a country. The rate may be positive or negative. The growth rate is a factor in determining how great a burden would be imposed on a country by the changing needs of its people for infrastructure (e.g., schools, hospitals, housing, roads), resources (e.g., food, water, electricity), and jobs. Rapid population growth can be seen as threatening by neighboring countries.

Population pyramid A population pyramid illustrates the age and sex structure of a country's population and may provide insights about political and social stability, as well as economic development. The population is distributed along the horizontal axis, with males shown on the left and females on the right. The male and female populations are broken down into 5-year age groups represented as horizontal bars along the vertical axis, with the youngest age groups at the bottom and the oldest at the top. The shape of the population pyramid gradually evolves over time based on fertility, mortality, and international migration trends.
Some distinctive types of population pyramids are:

- A **youthful distribution** has a broad base and narrow peak and is characterized by a high proportion of children and low proportion of the elderly. This population distribution results from high fertility, high mortality, low life expectancy, and high population growth. It is typical of developing countries where female education and contraceptive use are low and health care and sanitation are poor.
- A **transitional distribution** is caused by declining fertility and mortality rates, increasing life expectancy, and slowing population growth. The population has a larger proportion of working-age people relative to children and the elderly and produces a barrel-shaped pyramid, where the mid-section bulges and the base and top are narrower. The large proportion of working-age people can create a "demographic bonus" if it is educated and productively employed.
- A **mature distribution** has fairly balanced proportions of the population in the child, working-age, and elderly age groups and will gradually form an inverted triangle population pyramid as population growth continues to fall or ceases and the proportion of older people increases. Low fertility, low mortality, and high life expectancy—made possible by the availability of advanced healthcare, family planning, sanitation, and education—lead to aging populations in industrialized countries.

Ports and terminals This entry lists major ports and terminals primarily on the basis of the amount of cargo tonnage shipped through the facilities on an annual basis. In some instances, the number of containers handled or ship visits were also considered. Most ports service multiple classes of vessels including bulk carriers (dry and liquid), break bulk cargoes (goods loaded individually in bags, boxes, crates, or drums; sometimes palletized), containers,roll-on/roll-off, and passenger ships. The listing leads off with *major seaports* handling all types of cargo. Inland *river and lake ports* are listed separately along with the river or lake name. Ports configured specifically to handle bulk cargoes are designated as *oil/gas terminals or dry bulk cargo ports*. As break bulk cargoes are largely transported by containers today, the entry also includes a listing of major *container ports* with the corresponding throughput measured in twenty-foot equivalent units (TEUs). Some ports are significant for handling passenger traffic and are listed as *cruise/ferry ports*. In addition to commercial traffic, many seaports also provide important military infrastructure as naval bases or dockyards.

Public debt This entry records the cumulative total of all government borrowings less repayments that are denominated in a country's home currency. Public debt should not be confused with external debt, which reflects the foreign currency liabilities of both the private and public sector and must be financed out of foreign exchange earnings.

Railways TThis entry states the *total* route length of the railway network and of its component parts by gauge, which is the measure of the distance between the inner sides of the load-bearing rails. The four typical types of gauges are: *broad broad, standard, narrow*, and *dual*. Other gauges are listed under *note*. Some 60% of the world's railways use the standard gauge of 1.4 m (4.7 ft). Gauges vary by country and sometimes within countries. The choice of gauge during initial construction was mainly in response to local conditions and the intent of the builder. Narrow-gauge railways were cheaper to build and could negotiate sharper curves, broad-gauge railways gave greater stability and permitted higher speeds. Standard-gauge railways were a compromise between narrow and broad gauges.

Rare earth elements Rare earth elements or REEs are 17 chemical elements that are critical in many of today's high-tech industries. They include lanthanum, cerium, praseodymium, neodymium, promethium, samarium, europium, gadolinium, terbium, dysprosium, holmium, erbium, thulium, ytterbium, lutetium, scandium, and yttrium. Typical applications for REEs include batteries in hybrid cars, fiber optic cables, flat panel displays, and permanent magnets, as well as some defense and medical products.

Reference maps This section includes world and regional maps.

Refined petroleum products—consumption This entry is the country's total consumption of refined petroleum products, in barrels per day (bbl/day). The discrepancy between the amount of refined petroleum products produced and/or imported and the amount consumed and/or exported is due to the omission of stock changes, refinery gains, and other complicating factors.

Refined petroleum products—exports This entry is the country's total exports of refined petroleum products, in barrels per day (bbl/day).

Refined petroleum products—imports This entry is the country's total imports of refined petroleum products, in barrels per day (bbl/day).

Refined petroleum products—production This entry is the country's total output of refined petroleum products, in barrels per day (bbl/day). The discrepancy between the amount of refined petroleum products produced and/or imported and the amount consumed and/or exported is due to the omission of stock changes, refinery gains, and other complicating factors.

Refugees and internally displaced persons This entry includes those persons residing in a country as *refugees* or internally displaced persons (*IDPs*). Each country's refugee entry includes only countries of origin that are the source of refugee populations of 5,000 or more. The definition of a refugee according to a United Nations Convention is "a person who is outside his/her country of nationality or habitual residence; has a well-founded fear of persecution because of his/her race, religion, nationality, membership in a particular social group or political opinion; and is unable or unwilling to avail himself/herself of the protection of that country, or to return there, for fear of persecution." The UN established the Office of the UN High Commissioner for Refugees (UNHCR) in 1950 to handle refugee matters worldwide. The UN Relief and Works Agency for Palestine Refugees in the Near East (UNRWA) has a different operational definition for a Palestinian refugee: "a person whose normal place of residence was Palestine during the period 1 June 1946 to 15 May 1948 and who lost both home and means of livelihood as a result of the 1948 conflict." However, UNHCR also assists some 400,000 Palestinian refugees not covered under the UNRWA definition. The term "internally displaced person" is not specifically covered in the UN Convention; it is used to describe people who have fled their homes for reasons similar to refugees, but who remain within their own national territory and are subject to the laws of that state.

Religions This entry is an ordered listing of religions by adherents starting with the largest group and sometimes includes the percent of total population. The core characteristics and beliefs of the world's major religions are described below.

Baha'i—Founded by Mirza Husayn-Ali (known as Baha'u'llah) in Iran in 1852, Baha'i faith emphasizes monotheism and believes in one eternal transcendent God. Its guiding focus is to encourage the unity of all peoples on the earth so that justice and peace may be achieved on earth. Baha'i revelation contends the prophets of major world religions reflect some truth or element of the divine, believes all were manifestations of God given to specific communities in specific times, and that Baha'u'llah is an additional prophet meant to call all humankind. Bahais are an open community, located worldwide, with the greatest concentration of believers in South Asia.

Buddhism—Religion or philosophy inspired by the 5th century B.C. teachings of Siddhartha Gautama (also known as Gautama Buddha "the enlightened one"). Buddhism focuses on the goal of spiritual enlightenment centered on an understanding of Gautama Buddha's Four Noble Truths on the nature of suffering, and on the Eightfold Path of spiritual and moral practice, to break the cycle of suffering of which we are a part. Buddhism ascribes to a karmic system of rebirth. Several schools and sects of Buddhism exist, differing often on the nature of the Buddha, the extent to which enlightenment can be achieved—for one or for all, and by whom—religious orders or laity.

Basic Groupings

Theravada Buddhism: The oldest Buddhist school, Theravada is practiced mostly in Sri Lanka, Cambodia, Laos, Burma, and Thailand, with minority representation elsewhere in Asia and the West. Theravadans follow the Pali Canon of Buddha's teachings, and believe that one may escape the cycle of rebirth, worldly attachment, and suffering for oneself; this process may take one or several lifetimes.

Mahayana Buddhism, including subsets Zen and Tibetan (Lamaistic) Buddhism: Forms of Mahayana Buddhism are common in East Asia and Tibet, and parts of the West. Mahayanas have additional scriptures beyond the Pali Canon and believe the Buddha is eternal and still teaching. Unlike Theravada Buddhism, Mahayana schools maintain the Buddha-nature is present in all beings and all will ultimately achieve enlightenment.

Hoa Hao: a minority tradition of Buddhism practiced in Vietnam that stresses lay participation, primarily by peasant farmers; it eschews expensive ceremonies and temples and relocates the primary practices into the home.

Christianity—Descending from Judaism, Christianity's central belief maintains Jesus of Nazareth is the promised messiah of the Hebrew Scriptures, and that his life, death, and resurrection are salvific for the world. Christianity is one of the three monotheistic Abrahamic faiths, along with Islam and Judaism, which traces its spiritual lineage to Abraham of the Hebrew Scriptures. Its sacred texts include the Hebrew Bible and the New Testament (or the Christian Gospels).

Basic Groupings

Catholicism (or Roman Catholicism): This is the oldest established western Christian church and the world's largest single religious body. It is supranational, and recognizes a hierarchical structure with the Pope, or Bishop of Rome, as its head, located at the Vatican. Catholics believe the Pope is the divinely ordered head of the Church from a direct spiritual legacy of Jesus' apostle Peter. Catholicism is comprised of 23 particular Churches, or Rites—one Western (Roman or Latin-Rite) and 22 Eastern. The Latin Rite is by far the largest, making up about 98% of Catholic membership. Eastern-Rite Churches, such as the Maronite Church and the Ukrainian Catholic Church, are in communion with Rome although they preserve their own worship traditions and their immediate hierarchy consists of clergy within their own rite. The Catholic Church has a comprehensive theological and moral doctrine specified for believers in its catechism, which makes it unique among most forms of Christianity.

Mormonism (including the Church of Jesus Christ of Latter-Day Saints): Originating in 1830 in the United States under Joseph Smith, Mormonism is not characterized as a form of Protestant Christianity because it claims additional revealed Christian scriptures after the Hebrew Bible and New Testament. The Book of Mormon maintains there was an appearance of Jesus in the New World following the Christian account of his resurrection, and that the Americas are uniquely blessed continents. Mormonism believes earlier Christian traditions, such as the Roman Catholic, Orthodox, and Protestant reform faiths, are apostasies and that Joseph Smith's revelation of the Book of Mormon is a restoration of true Christianity. Mormons have a hierarchical religious leadership structure, and actively proselytize their faith; they are located primarily in the Americas and in a number of other Western countries.

Jehovah's Witnesses structure their faith on the Christian Bible, but their rejection of the Trinity is distinct from mainstream Christianity. They believe that a Kingdom of God, the Theocracy, will emerge following Armageddon and usher in a new earthly society. Adherents are required to evangelize and to follow a strict moral code.

Orthodox Christianity: The oldest established eastern form of Christianity, the Holy Orthodox Church, has a ceremonial head in the Bishop of Constantinople (Istanbul), also known as a Patriarch, but its various regional forms (e.g., Greek Orthodox, Russian Orthodox, Serbian Orthodox, Ukrainian Orthodox) are autocephalous (independent of Constantinople's authority, and have their own Patriarchs). Orthodox churches are highly nationalist and ethnic. The Orthodox Christian faith shares many theological tenets with the Roman Catholic Church, but diverges on some key premises and does not recognize the governing authority of the Pope.

Protestant Christianity: Protestant Christianity originated in the 16th century as an attempt to reform Roman Catholicism's practices, dogma, and theology. It encompasses several forms or denominations which are extremely varied in structure, beliefs, relationship to state, clergy, and governance. Many protestant theologies emphasize the primary role of scripture in their faith, advocating individual interpretation of Christian texts without the mediation of a final religious authority such as the Roman Pope. The oldest Protestant Christianities include Lutheranism, Calvinism (Presbyterians), and Anglican Christianity (Episcopalians), which have established liturgies, governing structure, and formal clergy. Other variants on Protestant Christianity, including Pentecostal movements and independent churches, may lack one or more of these elements, and their leadership and beliefs are individualized and dynamic.

Hinduism—Originating in the Vedic civilization of India (second and first millennium B.C.), Hinduism is an extremely diverse set of beliefs and practices with no single founder or religious authority. Hinduism has many scriptures; the Vedas, the Upanishads, and the Bhagavad-Gita are among some of the most important. Hindus may worship one or many deities, usually with prayer rituals within their own home. The most common figures of devotion are the gods Vishnu, Shiva, and a mother goddess, Devi. Most Hindus believe the soul, or atman, is eternal, and goes through a cycle of birth, death, and rebirth (*samsara*) determined by one's positive or negative karma, or the consequences of one's actions. The goal of religious life is to learn to act so as to finally achieve liberation (*moksha*) of one's soul, escaping the rebirth cycle.

Islam—The third of the monotheistic Abrahamic faiths, Islam originated with the teachings of Muhammad in the 7th century. Muslims believe Muhammad is the final of all religious prophets (beginning with Abraham) and that the Qu'ran, which is the Islamic scripture, was revealed to him by God. Islam derives from the word submission, and obedience to God is a primary theme in this religion. In order to live an Islamic life, believers must follow the five pillars, or tenets, of Islam, which are the testimony of faith (*shahada*), daily prayer (*salah*), giving alms (*zakah*), fasting during Ramadan (*sawm*), and the pilgrimage to Mecca (*hajj*).

Basic Groupings

The two primary branches of Islam are Sunni and Shia, which split from each other over a religio-political leadership dispute about the rightful successor to Muhammad. The Shia believe Muhammad's cousin and son-in-law, Ali, was the only divinely ordained Imam (religious leader), while the Sunni maintain the first three caliphs after Muhammad were also legitimate authorities. In modern Islam, Sunnis and Shia continue to have different views of acceptable schools of Islamic jurisprudence, and who is a proper Islamic religious authority. Islam also has an active mystical branch, Sufism, with various Sunni and Shia subsets.

Sunni Islam accounts for over 75% of the world's Muslim population. It recognizes the Abu Bakr as the first caliph after Muhammad. Sunni has four schools of Islamic doctrine and law—Hanafi, Maliki, Shafi'i, and Hanbali—which uniquely interpret the *Hadith*, or recorded oral traditions of Muhammad. A Sunni Muslim may elect to follow any one of these schools, as all are considered equally valid.

Shia Islam represents 10-20% of Muslims worldwide, and its distinguishing feature is its reverence for Ali as an infallible, divinely inspired leader, and as the first Imam of the Muslim community after Muhammad. A majority of Shia are known as "Twelvers," because they believe that the 11 familial successor imams after Muhammad culminate in a 12th Imam (al-Mahdi) who is hidden in the world and will reappear at its end to redeem the righteous.

Variants

Ismaili faith: A sect of Shia Islam, its adherents are also known as "Seveners," because they believe that the rightful seventh Imam in Islamic leadership was Isma'il, the elder son of Imam Jafar al-Sadiq. Ismaili tradition awaits the return of the seventh Imam as the Mahdi, or Islamic messianic figure. Ismailis are located in various parts of the world, particularly South Asia and the Levant.

Alawi faith: Another Shia sect of Islam, the name reflects followers' devotion to the religious authority of Ali. Alawites are a closed, secretive religious group who assert they are Shia Muslims, although outside scholars speculate their beliefs may have a syncretic mix with other faiths originating in the Middle East. Alawis live mostly in Syria, Lebanon, and Turkey.

Druze faith: A highly secretive tradition and a closed community that derives from the Ismaili sect of Islam; its core beliefs are thought to emphasize a combination of Gnostic principles believing that the Fatimid caliph, al-Hakin, is the one who embodies the key aspects of goodness of the universe, which are, the intellect, the word, the soul, the preceder, and the follower. The Druze have a key presence in Syria, Lebanon, and Israel.

Jainism—Originating in India, Jain spiritual philosophy believes in an eternal human soul, the eternal universe, and a principle of "the own nature of things." It emphasizes compassion for all living things, seeks liberation of the human soul from reincarnation through enlightenment, and values personal responsibility due to the belief in the immediate consequences of one's behavior. Jain philosophy teaches non-violence and prescribes vegetarianism for monks and laity alike; its adherents are a highly influential religious minority in Indian society.

Judaism—One of the first known monotheistic religions, likely dating to between 2000-1500 B.C., Judaism is the native faith of the Jewish people, based upon the belief in a covenant of responsibility between a sole omnipotent creator God and Abraham, the patriarch of Judaism's Hebrew Bible, or *Tanakh*. Divine revelation of principles and prohibitions in the Hebrew Scriptures form the basis of Jewish law, or *halakhah*, which is a key component of the faith. While there are extensive traditions of Jewish halakhic and theological discourse, there is no final dogmatic authority in the tradition. Local communities have their own religious leadership. Modern Judaism has three basic categories of faith: Orthodox, Conservative, and Reform/Liberal. These differ in their views and observance of Jewish law, with the Orthodox representing the most traditional practice, and Reform/Liberal communities the most accommodating of individualized interpretations of Jewish identity and faith.

Shintoism—A native animist tradition of Japan, Shinto practice is based upon the premise that every being and object has its own spirit or *kami*. Shinto practitioners worship several particular *kamis*, including the *kamis* of nature, and families often have shrines to their ancestors' *kamis*. Shintoism has no fixed tradition of prayers or prescribed dogma, but is characterized by individual ritual. Respect for the *kamis* in nature is a key Shinto value. Prior to the end of World War II, Shinto was the state religion of Japan, and bolstered the cult of the Japanese emperor.

Sikhism—Founded by the Guru Nanak (born 1469), Sikhism believes in a non-anthropomorphic, supreme, eternal, creator God; centering one's devotion to God is seen as a means of escaping the cycle of rebirth. Sikhs follow the teachings of Nanak and nine subsequent gurus. Their scripture, the Guru Granth Sahib—also known as the Adi Granth—is considered the living Guru, or final authority of Sikh faith and theology. Sikhism emphasizes equality of humankind and disavows caste, class, or gender discrimination.

Taoism—Chinese philosophy or religion based upon Lao Tzu's Tao Te Ching, which centers on belief in the Tao, or the way, as the flow of the universe and the nature of things. Taoism encourages a principle of non-force, or wu-wei, as the means to live harmoniously with the Tao. Taoists believe the esoteric world is made up of a perfect harmonious balance and nature, while in the manifest world—particularly in the body—balance is distorted. The Three Jewels of the Tao—compassion, simplicity, and humility—serve as the basis for Taoist ethics.

Zoroastrianism—Originating from the teachings of Zoroaster in about the 9th or 10th century B.C., Zoroastrianism may be the oldest continuing creedal religion. Its key beliefs center on a transcendent creator God, Ahura Mazda, and the concept of free will. The key ethical tenets of Zoroastrianism expressed in its scripture, the Avesta, are based on a dualistic worldview where one may prevent chaos if one chooses to serve God and exercises good thoughts, good words, and good deeds. Zoroastrianism is generally a closed religion and members are almost always born to Zoroastrian parents. Prior to the spread of Islam, Zoroastrianism dominated greater Iran. Today, though a minority, Zoroastrians remain primarily in Iran, India (where they are known as Parsi), and Pakistan.

Traditional beliefs

Animism: the belief that non-human entities contain souls or spirits.

Badimo: a form of ancestor worship of the Tswana people of Botswana.

Confucianism: an ideology that humans are perfectible through self-cultivation and self-creation; developed from teachings of the Chinese philosopher Confucius. Confucianism has strongly influenced the culture and beliefs of East Asian countries, including China, Japan, Korea, Singapore, Taiwan, and Vietnam.

Inuit beliefs are a form of shamanism (see below) based on animistic principles of the Inuit or Eskimo peoples.

Kirant: the belief system of the Kirat, a people who live mainly in the Himalayas of Nepal. It is primarily a form of polytheistic shamanism, but includes elements of animism and ancestor worship.

Pagan is a blanket term used to describe many unconnected belief practices throughout history, usually in reference to religions outside of the Abrahamic category (monotheistic faiths like Judaism, Christianity, and Islam).

Shamanism: beliefs and practices promoting communication with the spiritual world. Shamanistic beliefs are organized around a shaman or medicine man who—as an intermediary between the human and spirit world—is believed to be able to heal the sick (by healing their souls), communicate with the spirit world, and help souls into the afterlife through the practice of entering a trance. In shaman-based religions, the shaman is also responsible for leading sacred rites.

Spiritualism: the belief that souls and spirits communicate with the living usually through intermediaries called mediums.

Syncretic (fusion of diverse religious beliefs and practices)

Cao Dai: a nationalistic Vietnamese sect, officially established in 1926, that draws practices and precepts from Confucianism, Taoism, Buddhism, and Catholicism.
Chondogyo: or the religion of the Heavenly Way, is based on Korean shamanism, Buddhism, and Korean folk traditions, with some elements drawn from Christianity. Formulated in the 1860s, it holds that God lives in all of us and strives to convert society into a paradise on earth, populated by believers transformed into intelligent moral beings with a high social conscience.
Kimbanguist: a puritan form of the Baptist denomination founded by Simon Kimbangu in the 1920s in what is now the Democratic Republic of Congo. Adherents believe that salvation comes through Jesus' death and resurrection, like Christianity, but additionally that living a spiritually pure life following strict codes of conduct is required for salvation.
Modekngei: a hybrid of Christianity and ancient Palauan culture and oral traditions founded around 1915 on the island of Babeldaob. Adherents simultaneously worship Jesus Christ and Palauan goddesses.
Rastafarian: an afro-centrist ideology and movement based on Christianity that arose in Jamaica in the 1930s; it believes that Haile Selassie I, Emperor of Ethiopia from 1930-74, was the incarnation of the second coming of Jesus.
Santeria: practiced in Cuba, the merging of the Yoruba religion of Nigeria with Roman Catholicism and native Indian traditions. Its practitioners believe that each person has a destiny and eventually transcends to merge with the divine creator and source of all energy, Olorun.
Voodoo/Vodun: a form of spirit and ancestor worship combined with some Christian faiths, especially Catholicism. Haitian and Louisiana Voodoo, which have included more Catholic practices, are separate from West African Vodun, which has retained a focus on spirit worship.
Non-religious
Agnosticism: the belief that most things are unknowable. In regard to religion it is usually characterized as neither a belief nor non belief in a deity.
Atheism: the belief that there are no deities of any kind.

Reserves of foreign exchange and gold This entry gives the dollar value for the stock of all financial assets that are available to the central monetary authority for use in meeting a country's balance of payments needs as of the end-date of the period specified. This category includes not only foreign currency and gold, but also a country's holdings of Special Drawing Rights in the International Monetary Fund, and its reserve position in the Fund.

Roadways This entry gives the total length of the road network and includes the length of the *paved* and *unpaved* portions.

Sanitation facility access This entry provides information about access to improved or unimproved sanitation facilities available to segments of the population of a country. *improved* sanitation—use of any of the following facilities: flush or pour-flush to a piped sewer system, septic tank or pit latrine; ventilated improved pit (VIP) latrine; pit latrine with slab; or a composting toilet, *unimproved* sanitation—use of any of the following facilities: flush or pour-flush not piped to a sewer system, septic tank or pit latrine; pit latrine without a slab or open pit; bucket; hanging toilet or hanging latrine; shared facilities of any type; no facilities; or bush or field.

School life expectancy (primary to tertiary education) School life expectancy (SLE) is the total number of years of schooling (primary to tertiary) that a child can expect to receive, assuming that the probability of his or her being enrolled in school at any particular future age is equal to the current enrollment ratio at that age. Caution must be maintained when utilizing this indicator in international comparisons. For example, a year or grade completed in one country is not necessarily the same in terms of educational content or quality as a year or grade completed in another country. SLE represents the expected number of years of schooling that will be completed, including years spent repeating one or more grades.

Sex ratio This entry includes the number of males for each female in five age groups—*at birth, under 15 years, 15-64 years, 65 years and over*, and for the *total population*. Sex ratio at birth has recently emerged as an indicator of certain kinds of sex discrimination in some countries. For instance, high sex ratios at birth in some Asian countries are now attributed to sex-selective abortion and infanticide due to a strong preference for sons. This will affect future marriage patterns and fertility patterns. Eventually, it could cause unrest among young adult males who are unable to find partners.

Stateless person Statelessness is the condition whereby an individual is not considered a national by any country. Stateless people are denied basic rights, such as access to employment, housing, education, healthcare, and pensions, and they may be unable to vote, own property, open a bank account, or legally register a marriage or birth. They may also be vulnerable to arbitrary treatment and human trafficking. In at least 30 states, women cannot pass their nationality on to their children. In these countries, if a child's father is foreign, stateless, or absent, the child usually becomes stateless. Estimates of the number of stateless people are inherently imprecise because few countries have procedures to identify them; the UN approximates that there are 12 million stateless people worldwide. Stateless people are counted in a country's overall population figure if they have lived there for a year.

Stock of broad money This entry covers all of "Narrow money," plus the total quantity of time and savings deposits, credit union deposits, institutional money market funds, short-term repurchase agreements between the central bank and commercial deposit banks, and other large liquid assets held by nonbank financial institutions, state and local governments, nonfinancial public enterprises, and the private sector of the economy. National currency units have been converted to US dollars at the closing exchange rate for the date of the information. Because of exchange rate movements, changes in money stocks measured in national currency units may vary significantly from those shown in US dollars, and caution is urged when making comparisons over time in US dollars. In addition to serving as a medium of exchange, broad money includes assets that are slightly less liquid than narrow money and the assets tend to function as a "store of value"—a means of holding wealth.

Stock of direct foreign investment—abroad This entry gives the cumulative US dollar value of all investments in foreign countries made directly by residents—primarily companies—of the home country, as of the end of the time period indicated. Direct investment excludes investment through purchase of shares.

Stock of direct foreign investment—at home This entry gives the cumulative US dollar value of all investments in the home country made directly by residents—primarily companies—of other countries as of the end of the time period indicated. Direct investment excludes investment through purchase of shares.

Stock of domestic credit This entry is the total quantity of credit, denominated in the domestic currency, provided by financial institutions to the central bank, state and local governments, public non-financial corporations, and the private sector. The national currency units have been converted to US dollars at the closing exchange rate on the date of the information.

Stock of narrow money This entry, also known as "Ml," comprises the total quantity of currency in circulation (notes and coins) plus demand deposits denominated in the national currency held by nonbank financial institutions, state and local governments, nonfinancial public enterprises, and the private sector of the economy, measured at a specific point in time. National currency units have been converted to US dollars at the closing exchange rate for the date of the information. Because of exchange rate movements, changes in money stocks measured in national currency units may vary significantly from those shown in US dollars, and caution is urged when making comparisons over time in US dollars. Narrow money consists of more liquid assets than broad money and the assets generally function as a "medium of exchange" for an economy.

Suffrage This entry gives the age at enfranchisement and whether the right to vote is universal or restricted.

Taxes and other revenues This entry records total taxes and other revenues received by the national government during the time period indicated, expressed as a percent of GDP. Taxes include personal and corporate income taxes, value added taxes, excise taxes, and tariffs. Other revenues include social contributions—such as payments for social security and hospital insurance—grants, and net revenues from public enterprises. Normalizing the data, by dividing total revenues by GDP, enables easy comparisons across countries, and provides an average rate at which all income (GDP) is paid to the national level government for the supply of public goods and services.

Telephone numbers All telephone numbers in *The World Factbook* consist of the country code in brackets, the city or area code (where required) in parentheses, and the local number. The one component that is not presented is the international access code, which varies from country to country. For example, an international direct dial telephone call placed from the US to Madrid, Spain, would be as follows: 011 [34] (1) 577-xxxx, where is the international access code for station-to-station calls; 01 is for calls other than station-to-station calls, [34] is the country code for Spain, (1) is the city code for Madrid, 577 is the local exchange, and xxxx is the local telephone number. An international direct dial telephone call placed from another country to the US would be as follows: international access code + [1] (202) 939-xxxx, where [1] is the country code for the US, (202) is the area code for Washington, DC, 939 is the local exchange, and xxxx is the local telephone number.

Telephone system This entry includes a brief general assessment of the system with details on the domestic and international components. The following terms and abbreviations are used throughout the entry:

Arabsat—Arab Satellite Communications Organization (Riyadh, Saudi Arabia).
Autodin—Automatic Digital Network (US Department of Defense).
CB—citizen's band mobile radio communications.
Cellular telephone system—the telephones in this system are radio transceivers, with each instrument having its own private radio frequency and sufficient radiated power to reach the booster station in its area (cell), from which the telephone signal is fed to a telephone exchange.
Central American Microwave System—a trunk microwave radio relay system that links the countries of Central America and Mexico with each other.
Coaxial cable—a multichannel communication cable consisting of a central conducting wire, surrounded by and insulated from a cylindrical conducting shell; a large number of telephone channels can be made available within the insulated space by the use of a large number of carrier frequencies.
Comsat—Communications Satellite Corporation (US).
DSN—Defense Switched Network (formerly Automatic Voice Network or Autovon); basic general-purpose, switched voice network of the Defense Communications System (US Department of Defense).
Eutelsat—European Telecommunications Satellite Organization (Paris).
Fiber-optic cable—a multichannel communications cable using a thread of optical glass fibers as a transmission medium in which the signal (voice, video, etc.) is in the form of a coded pulse of light.
GSM—a global system for mobile (cellular) communications devised by the Groupe Special Mobile of the pan-European standardization organization, Conference Europeanne des Posts et Telecommunications (CEPT) in 1982.
HF—high frequency; any radio frequency in the 3,000-to 30,000-kHz range.
Inmarsat—International Maritime Satellite Organization (London); provider of global mobile satellite communications for commercial, distress, and safety applications at sea, in the air, and on land.
Intelsat—International Telecommunications Satellite Organization (Washington, DC).
Intersputnik—International Organization of Space Communications (Moscow); first established in the former Soviet Union and the East European countries, it is now marketing its services worldwide with earth stations in North America,
Africa, and East Asia.
Landline—communication wire or cable of any sort that is installed on poles or buried in the ground.
Marecs—Maritime European Communications Satellite used in the Inmarsat system on lease from the European Space Agency.
Marisat—satellites of the Comsat Corporation that participate in the Inmarsat system.
Medarabtel—the Middle East Telecommunications Project of the International Telecommunications Union (ITU) providing a modern telecommunications network, primarily by microwave radio relay, linking Algeria, Djibouti, Egypt, Jordan, Libya, Morocco, Saudi Arabia, Somalia, Sudan, Syria, Tunisia, and Yemen; it was initially started in Morocco in 1970 by the Arab Telecommunications Union (ATU) and was known at that time as the Middle East Mediterranean Telecommunications Network.
Microwave radio relay—transmission of long distance telephone calls and television programs by highly directional radio microwaves that are received and sent on from one booster station to another on an optical path.
NMT—Nordic Mobile Telephone; an analog cellular telephone system that was developed jointly by the national telecommunications authorities of the Nordic countries (Denmark, Finland, Iceland, Norway, and Sweden).
Orbita—a Russian television service; also the trade name of a packet-switched digital telephone network.
Radiotelephone communications—the two-way transmission and reception of sounds by broadcast radio on authorized frequencies using telephone handsets.
PanAmSat—PanAmSat Corporation (Greenwich, CT).
SAFE—South African Far East Cable
Satellite communication system—a communication system consisting of two or more earth stations and at least one satellite that provide long distance transmission of voice, data, and television; the system usually serves as a trunk connection between telephone exchanges; if the earth stations are in the same country, it is a domestic system.
Satellite earth station—a communications facility with a microwave radio transmitting and receiving antenna and required receiving and transmitting equipment for communicating with satellites.
Satellite link—a radio connection between a satellite and an earth station permitting communication between them, either one-way (down link from satellite to earth station—television receive-only transmission) or two-way (telephone channels).
SHF—super high frequency; any radio frequency in the 3,000- to 30,000-MHz range.
Shortwave—radio frequencies (from 1.605 to 30 MHz) that fall above the commercial broadcast band and are used for communication over long distances.
Solidaridad—geosynchronous satellites in Mexico's system of international telecommunications in the Western Hemisphere.
Statsionar—Russia's geostationary system for satellite telecommunications. Submarine cable—a cable designed for service under water.
TAT—Trans-Atlantic Telephone; any of a number of high-capacity submarine coaxial telephone cables linking Europe with North America.
Telefax—facsimile service between subscriber stations via the public switched telephone network or the international Datel network.
Telegraph—a telecommunications system designed for unmodulated electric impulse transmission.
Telex—a communication service involving teletypewriters connected by wire through automatic exchanges.
Tropospheric scatter—a form of microwave radio transmission in which the troposphere is used to scatter and reflect a

fraction of the incident radio waves back to earth; powerful, highly directional antennas are used to transmit and receive the microwave signals; reliable over-the-horizon communications are realized for distances up to 600 miles in a single hop; additional hops can extend the range of this system for very long distances.

Trunk network—a network of switching centers, connected by multichannel trunk lines.

UHF—ultra high frequency; any radio frequency in the 300-to 3,000-MHz range.

VHF—very high frequency; any radio frequency in the 30-to 300-MHz range.

Telephones—main lines in use This entry gives the total number of main telephone lines in use.

Telephones—mobile cellular This entry gives the total number of mobile cellular telephone subscribers.

Terminology Due to the highly structured nature of the *Factbook* database, some collective generic terms have to be used. For example, the word **Country** in the **Country name** entry refers to a wide variety of dependencies, areas of special sovereignty, uninhabited islands, and other entities in addition to the traditional countries or independent states. **Military** is also used as an umbrella term for various civil defense, security, and defense activities in many entries. The **Independence** entry includes the usual colonial independence dates and former ruling states as well as other significant nationhood dates such as the traditional founding date or the date of unification, federation, confederation, establishment, or state succession that are not strictly independence dates. Dependent areas have the nature of their dependency status noted in this same entry.

Terrain This entry contains a brief description of the topography.

Time difference This entry is expressed in *The World Factbook* in two ways. First, it is stated as the difference in hours between the capital of an entity and **Coordinated Universal Time (UTC)** during Standard Time. Additionally, the difference in time between the capital of an entity and that observed in Washington, D.C. is also provided. Note that the time difference assumes both locations are simultaneously observing Standard Time or Daylight Saving Time.

Time zones Ten countries (Australia, Brazil, Canada, Indonesia, Kazakhstan, Mexico, New Zealand, Russia, Spain, and the United States) and the island of Greenland observe more than one official time depending on the number of designated time zones within their boundaries. An illustration of time zones throughout the world and within countries can be seen in the Standard Time Zones of the World map included in the **Reference Maps** section of *The World Factbook*.

Total fertility rate This entry gives a figure for the average number of children that would be born per woman if all women lived to the end of their childbearing years and bore children according to a given fertility rate at each age. The total fertility rate (TFR) is a more direct measure of the level of fertility than the crude birth rate, since it refers to births per woman. This indicator shows the potential for population change in the country. A rate of two children per woman is considered the replacement rate for a population, resulting in relative stability in terms of total numbers. Rates above two children indicate populations growing in size and whose median age is declining. Higher rates may also indicate difficulties for families, in some situations, to feed and educate their children and for women to enter the labor force. Rates below two children indicate populations decreasing in size and growing older. Global fertility rates are in general decline and this trend is most pronounced in industrialized countries, especially Western Europe, where populations are projected to decline dramatically over the next 50 years.

Total renewable water resources This entry provides the long-term average water availability for a country in cubic kilometers of precipitation, recharged ground water, and surface inflows from surrounding countries. The values have been adjusted to account for overlap resulting from surface flow recharge of groundwater sources. Total renewable water resources provides the water total available to a country but does not include water resource totals that have been reserved for upstream or downstream countries through international agreements. Note that these values are averages and do not accurately reflect the total available in any given year. Annual available resources can vary greatly due to short-term and long-term climatic and weather variations.

Trafficking in persons Trafficking in persons is modern-day slavery, involving victims who are forced, defrauded, or coerced into labor or sexual exploitation. The International Labor Organization (ILO), the UN agency charged with addressing labor standards, employment, and social protection issues, estimates that 12.3 million people worldwide are enslaved in forced labor, bonded labor, forced child labor, sexual servitude, and involuntary servitude at any given time. Human trafficking is a multi-dimensional threat, depriving people of their human rights and freedoms, risking global health, promoting social breakdown, inhibiting development by depriving countries of their human capital, and helping fuel the growth of organized crime. In 2000, the US Congress passed the Trafficking Victims Protection Act (TVPA), reauthorized in 2003 and 2005, which provides tools for the US to combat trafficking in persons, both domestically and abroad. One of the law's key components is the creation of the US Department of State's annual *Trafficking in Persons Report*, which assesses the government response (i.e., the *current situation*) in some 150 countries with a significant number of victims trafficked across their borders who are recruited, harbored, transported, provided, or obtained for forced labor or sexual exploitation. Countries in the annual report are rated in three tiers, based on government efforts to combat trafficking. The countries identified in this entry are those listed in the *2010 Trafficking in Persons Report as Tier 2 Watch List or Tier 3* based on the following *tier rating* definitions:

Tier 2 Watch List *countries do not fully comply with the minimum standards for the elimination of trafficking but are making significant efforts to do so, and meet one of the following criteria:*
1. they display high or significantly increasing number of victims,
2. they have failed to provide evidence of increasing efforts to combat trafficking in persons, or,
3. they have committed to take action over the next year.

Tier 3 *countries neither satisfy the minimum standards for the elimination of trafficking nor demonstrate a significant effort to do so. Countries in this tier are subject to potential non-humanitarian and non-trade sanctions.*

Transnational issues This category includes four entries—**Disputes—international, Refugees and internally displaced persons, Trafficking in persons,** and **Illicit drugs**—that deal with current issues going beyond national boundaries.

Transportation This category includes the entries dealing with the means for movement of people and goods.

Transportation—note This entry includes miscellaneous transportation information of significance not included elsewhere.

Unemployment rate This entry contains the percent of the labor force that is without jobs. Substantial underemployment might be noted.

Unemployment, youth ages 15-24 This entry gives the percent of the total labor force ages 15-24 unemployed during a specified year.

Urbanization This entry provides two measures of the degree of urbanization of a population. The first, *urban population*, describes the percentage of the total population living in urban areas, as defined by the country. The second, *rate of urbanization*, describes the projected average rate of change of the size of the urban population over the given period of time. Additionally, the World entry includes a list of the *ten largest urban agglomerations*. An *urban agglomeration* is defined as comprising the city or town proper and also the suburban fringe or thickly settled territory lying outside of, but adjacent to, the boundaries of the city.

UTC (Coordinated Universal Time) See entry for Coordinated Universal Time.

Waterways This entry gives the total length of navigable rivers, canals, and other inland bodies of water.

Weights and Measures This information is presented in **Appendix G: Weights and Measures** and includes mathematical notations (mathematical powers and names), metric interrelationships (prefix; symbol; length, weight, or capacity; area; volume), and standard conversion factors.

Years All year references are for the calendar year (CY) unless indicated as fiscal year (FY). The calendar year is an accounting period of 12 months from 1 January to 31 December. The fiscal year is an accounting period of 12 months other than 1 January to 31 December.

GUIDE TO COUNTRY PROFILES

INTRODUCTION

Background

GEOGRAPHY

Location
Geographic coordinates
Map references
Area
total
land
water
Area—comparative
Land boundaries
total
border countries
Coastline
Maritime claims
territorial sea
contiguous zone
exclusive economic zone
continental shelf
exclusive fishing zone
Climate
Terrain
Elevation extremes
lowest point
highest point
Natural resources
Land use
arable land
permanent crops
other
Irrigated land
Total renewable water resources
Freshwater withdrawal (domestic/industrial/agricultural)
total
per capita
Natural hazards
volcanism
Environment—current issues
Environment—international agreements
party to
signed, but not ratified
Geography—note

PEOPLE AND SOCIETY

Nationality
noun
adjective
Ethnic groups
Languages
Religions
Demographic profile
Population
Age structure
0-14 years
15-24 years
25-54 years
55-64 years
65 years and over
Median Age
total
male
female
Population growth rate
Birth rate
Death rate
Net migration rate
Urbanization
urban population
rate of urbanization
Major cities—population
Sex ratio
at birth
under 15 years
15-64 years
65 years and over
total population
Maternal mortality rate
Infant mortality rate
total
male
female
Life expectancy at birth
total population
male
female
Total fertility rate
Health expenditures
Physicians density
Hospital bed density
Drinking water source
improved
unimproved
Sanitation facility access
improved
unimproved
HIV/AIDS—adult prevalence rate
HIV/AIDS—people living with HIV/AIDS
HIV/AIDS—deaths
Major infectious diseases
degree of risk
food or waterborne diseases
vectorborne diseases
water contact diseases
aerosolized dust or soil contact disease
respiratory disease
animal contact disease
Obesity—adult prevalence rate
Children under the age of 5 years underweight
Education expenditures
Literacy
definition
total population
male
female
School life expectancy (primary to tertiary)
Unemployment, youth ages 15-24
People—note

GOVERNMENT

Country name
conventional long form
conventional short form
local long form
local short form
former
abbreviation
Dependency status
Government type
Capital
name
geographic coordinates
time difference
daylight saving time
Administrative divisions
Dependent areas
Independence
National holiday
Constitution
Legal system
International law organization participation
Suffrage
Executive branch
chief of state
head of government
cabinet
elections
election results
Legislative branch
elections
election results
Judicial branch
Political parties and leaders
Political pressure groups and leaders
International organization participation
Diplomatic representation in the US
chief of mission
chancery
telephone
FAX
consulate(s) general
consulate(s)
Diplomatic representation from the US
chief of mission
embassy
mailing address
telephone
FAX
consulate(s) general
consulate(s)
branch office(s)
Flag description
National symbol(s)
National anthem
Government—note

ECONOMY

Economy—overview
GDP (purchasing power parity)

GDP (official exchange rate)
GDP—real growth rate
GDP—per capita (PPP)
GDP—composition by sector
agriculture
industry
services
Labor force
Labor force—by occupation
agriculture
industry
services
Unemployment rate
Population below poverty line
Household income or consumption by percentage share
lowest 10%
highest 10%
Distribution of fam ily income—Gini index
Investment (gross fixed)
Budget
revenues
expenditures
Taxes and other revenues
Budget surplus (+) or deficit (–)
Public debt
Inflation rate (consumer prices)
Central bank discount rate
Commercial bank prime lending rate
Stock of narrow money
Stock of broad money
Stock of domestic credit
Market value of publicly traded shares
Agriculture—products
Industries
Industrial production growth rate
Current account balance
Exports
Exports—commodities
Exports—partners
Imports
Imports—commodities
Imports—partners
Reserves of foreign exchange and gold
Debt—external
Stock of direct foreign investment—at home
Stock of direct foreign investment—abroad
Exchange rates
Fiscal year

ENERGY

Electricity—production
Electricity—consumption
Electricity—exports
Electricity—imports
Electricity—installed generating capacity
Electricity—from fossil fuels
Electricity—from nuclear fuels
Electricity—from hydroelectric plants
Electricity—from other renewable sources
Crude oil—production
Crude oil—exports
Crude oil—im ports
Crude oil—proved reserves
Refined petroleum products—production
Refined petroleum products—consumption
Refined petroleum products—exports
Refined petroleum products—imports
Natural gas—production
Natural gas—consumption
Natural gas—exports
Natural gas—imports
Natural gas—proved reserves
Carbon dioxide emissions from consumption of energy

COMMUNICATIONS

Telephones—main lines in use
Telephones—mobile cellular
Telephone system
general assessment
domestic
international
Broadcast media
Internet country code
Internet hosts
Internet users
Communications—note

TRANSPORTATION

Airports
Airports—with paved runways
total
over 3,047 m
2,438 to 3,047 m
1,524 to 2,437 m
914 to 1,523 m
under 914 m
Airports—with unpaved runways
total
over 3,047 m
2,438 to 3,047 m
1,524 to 2,437 m
914 to 1,523 m
under 914 m
Heliports
Pipelines
Railways
total
broad gauge
standard gauge
narrow gauge
dual gauge
Roadways
total
paved
unpaved
Waterways
Merchant marine
total
ships by type
foreign-owned
registered in other countries
Ports and terminals
Transportation—note

MILITARY

Military branches
Military service age and obligation
Manpower available for military service
males age 16-49
females age 16-49
Manpower fit for military service
males age 16-49
females age 16-49
Manpower reaching militarily significant age annually
males
females
Military expenditures—percent of GDP
Military—note

TRANSNATIONAL ISSUES

Disputes—international
Refugees and internally displaced persons
refugees
IDPs
Trafficking in persons
current situation
tier rating
Illicit drugs

AFGHANISTAN

INTRODUCTION

Background: Ahmad Shah DURRANI unified the Pashtun tribes and founded Afghanistan in 1747. The country served as a buffer between the British and Russian Empires until it won independence from notional British control in 1919. A brief experiment in democracy ended in a 1973 coup and a 1978 communist counter-coup. The Soviet Union invaded in 1979 to support the tottering Afghan communist regime, touching off a long and destructive war. The USSR withdrew in 1989 under relentless pressure by internationally supported anti-communist mujahedin rebels. A series of subsequent civil wars saw Kabul finally fall in 1996 to the Taliban, a hardline Pakistani-sponsored movement that emerged in 1994 to end the country's civil war and anarchy. Following the 11 September 2001 terrorist attacks, a US, Allied, and anti-Taliban Northern Alliance military action toppled the Taliban for sheltering Osama BIN LADIN. The UN-sponsored Bonn Conference in 2001 established a process for political reconstruction that included the adoption of a new constitution, a presidential election in 2004, and National Assembly elections in 2005. In December 2004, Hamid KARZAI became the first democratically elected president of Afghanistan and the National Assembly was inaugurated the following December. KARZAI was re-elected in August 2009 for a second term. Despite gains toward building a stable central government, a resurgent Taliban and continuing provincial instability—particularly in the south and the east—remain serious challenges for the Afghan Government.

GEOGRAPHY

Location: Southern Asia, north and west of Pakistan, east of Iran

Geographic coordinates: 33 00 N, 65 00 E

Map references: Asia

Area: *total:* 652,230 sq km
country comparison to the world: 41
land: 652,230 sq km
water: 0 sq km

Area—comparative: almost six time the size of Virginia; slightly smaller than Texas

Land boundaries: *total:* 5,529 km
border countries: China 76 km, Iran 936 km, Pakistan 2,430 km, Tajikistan 1,206 km, Turkmenistan 744 km, Uzbekistan 137 km

Coastline: 0 km (landlocked)

Maritime claims: none (landlocked)

Climate: arid to semiarid; cold winters and hot summers

Terrain: mostly rugged mountains; plains in north and southwest

Elevation extremes: *lowest point:* Amu Darya 258 m
highest point: Noshak 7,485 m

Natural resources: natural gas, petroleum, coal, copper, chromite, talc, barites, sulfur, lead, zinc, iron ore, salt, precious and semiprecious stones

Land use: *arable land:* 11.95%
permanent crops: 0.18%
other: 87.87% (2011)

Irrigated land: 32,080 sq km (2003)

Total renewable water resources: 65.33 cu km (2011)

Freshwater withdrawal (domestic/industrial/agricultural): *total:* 20.28 cu km/yr (1%/1%/98%)
per capita: 823.1 cu m/yr (2005)

Natural hazards: damaging earthquakes occur in Hindu Kush mountains; flooding; droughts

Environment—current issues: limited natural freshwater resources; inadequate supplies of potable water; soil degradation; overgrazing; deforestation (much of the remaining forests are being cut down for fuel and building materials); desertification; air and water pollution

Environment—international agreements: *party to:* Biodiversity, Climate Change, Desertification, Endangered Species, Environmental Modification, Marine Dumping, Ozone Layer Protection
signed, but not ratified: Hazardous Wastes, Law of the Sea, Marine Life Conservation

Geography—note: landlocked; the Hindu Kush mountains that run northeast to southwest divide the northern provinces from the rest of the country; the highest peaks are in the northern Vakhan (Wakhan Corridor)

PEOPLE AND SOCIETY

Nationality: *noun:* Afghan(s)
adjective: Afghan

Ethnic groups: Pashtun 42%, Tajik 27%, Hazara 9%, Uzbek 9%, Aimak 4%, Turkmen 3%, Baloch 2%, other 4%

Languages: Afghan Persian or Dari (official) 50%, Pashto (official) 35%, Turkic languages (primarily Uzbek and Turkmen) 11%, 30 minor languages (primarily Balochi and Pashai) 4%, much bilingualism, but Dari functions as the lingua franca
note: the Turkic languages Uzbek and Turkmen, as well as Balochi, Pashai, Nuristani, and Pamiri are the third official languages in areas where the majority speaks them

Religions: Sunni Muslim 80%, Shia Muslim 19%, other 1%

Population: 31,822,848 (July 2014 est.)
country comparison to the world: 41

Age structure: *0-14 years:* 42% (male 6,793,832/female 6,579,388)
15-24 years: 22.2% (male 3,600,264/female 3,464,781)
25-54 years: 29.4% (male 4,771,323/female 4,586,963)
55-64 years: 2.5% (male 603,197/female 622,539)
65 years and over: 2.5% (male 371,753/female 428,808) (2014 est.)

Dependency ratios:
total dependency ratio: 96%
youth dependency ratio: 91.4%
elderly dependency ratio: 4.6%
potential support ratio: 21.7 (2013)

Median age:
total: 18.1 years
male: 18.1 years
female: 18.2 years (2014 est.)

Population growth rate: 2.29% (2014 est.)
country comparison to the world: 39

Birth rate: 38.84 births/1,000 population (2014 est.)
country comparison to the world: 10

Death rate: 14.12 deaths/1,000 population (2014 est.)
country comparison to the world: 7

Net migration rate: -1.83 migrant(s)/1,000 population (2014 est.)
country comparison to the world: 163

Urbanization: *urban population:* 23.5% of total population (2011)
rate of urbanization: 4.41% annual rate of change (2010–15 est.)

Major urban areas—population: KABUL (capital) 3.097 million (2011)

Sex ratio: *at birth:* 1.05 male(s)/female
0-14 years: 1.03 male(s)/female
15-24 years: 1.04 male(s)/female
25-54 years: 1.04 male(s)/female
55-64 years: 1.03 male(s)/female
65 years and over: 0.87 male(s)/female
total population: 1.03 male(s)/female (2014 est.)

Mother's mean age at first birth: 20.1
note: median age at first birth among women 25–29 (2010 est.)

Maternal mortality rate:
460 deaths/100,000 live births (2010)
country comparison to the world: 22

Infant mortality rate: *total:* 117.23 deaths/1,000 live births
country comparison to the world: 1
male: 124.89 deaths/1,000 live births
female: 109.18 deaths/1,000 live births (2014 est.)

Life expectancy at birth: *total population:* 50.49 years
country comparison to the world: 220
male: 49.17 years
female: 51.88 years (2014 est.)

Total fertility rate: 5.43 children born/woman (2014 est.)
country comparison to the world: 9

Contraceptive prevalence rate: 21.8% (2010)

Health expenditures: 9.6% of GDP (2011)
country comparison to the world: 30

Physicians density: 0.19 physicians/1,000 population (2010)

Hospital bed density: 0.4 beds/1,000 population (2010)

Drinking water source:
Improved:
urban: 85.4% of population
rural: 53% of population
total: 60.6% of population
Unimproved:
urban: 14.6% of population
rural: 47% of population
total: 39.4% of population (2011 est.)

Sanitation facility access:
Improved:
urban: 45.6% of population
rural: 23.2% of population
total: 28.5% of population
Unimproved:
urban: 54.4% of population
rural: 76.8% of population
total: 71.5% of population (2011 est.)

HIV/AIDS—adult prevalence rate: 0.1% (2012 est.)
country comparison to the world: 123

HIV/AIDS—people living with HIV/AIDS: 4,300 (2012 est.)
country comparison to the world: 125

HIV/AIDS—deaths: 300 (2012 est.)
country comparison to the world: 102

Major infectious diseases: *degree of risk:* intermediate
food or waterborne diseases: bacterial diarrhea, hepatitis A, and typhoid fever
vectorborne disease: malaria
animal contact disease: rabies
note: highly pathogenic H5N1 avian influenza has been identified in this country; it poses a negligible risk with extremely rare cases possible among US citizens who have close contact with birds (2013)

Obesity—adult prevalence rate: 2.2% (2008)
country comparison to the world: 182

Children under the age of 5 years underweight: 32.9% (2004)
country comparison to the world: 9

Education expenditures: NA

Literacy: *definition:* age 15 and over can read and write
total population: 28.1%
male: 43.1%
female: 12.6% (2000 est.)

School life expectancy (primary to tertiary education): *total:* 9 years
male: 11 years
female: 7 years (2011)

Child labor—children ages 5–14: *total number:* 3,252,243
percentage: 25 %
note: data on child labor in Afghanistan is uncertain and may be higher than the estimated 25% of children ages 5–14 derived from 2011 survey results; UNICEF estimated that 30% of children ages 5–14 in 2011 were engaged in child labor (2008 est.)

GOVERNMENT

Country name: *conventional long form:* Islamic Republic of Afghanistan
conventional short form: Afghanistan
local long form: Jamhuri-ye Islami-ye Afghanistan
local short form: Afghanistan
former: Republic of Afghanistan

Government type: Islamic republic

Capital: *name:* Kabul
geographic coordinates: 34 31 N, 69 11 E
time difference: UTC+4.5 (9.5 hours ahead of Washington, DC during Standard Time)

Administrative divisions: 34 provinces (welayat, singular—welayat); Badakhshan, Badghis, Baghlan, Balkh, Bamyan, Daykundi, Farah, Faryab, Ghazni, Ghor, Helmand, Herat, Jowzjan, Kabul, Kandahar, Kapisa, Khost, Kunar, Kunduz, Laghman, Logar, Nangarhar, Nimroz, Nuristan, Paktika, Paktiya, Panjshir, Parwan, Samangan, Sar-e Pul, Takhar, Uruzgan, Wardak, Zabul

Independence: 19 August 1919 (from UK control over Afghan foreign affairs)

National holiday: Independence Day, 19 August (1919)

Constitution: several previous; latest drafted 14 December 2003–4 January 2004, signed 16 January 2004, ratified 26 January 2004 (2012)

Legal system: mixed legal system of civil, customary, and Islamic law

International law organization participation: has not submitted an ICJ jurisdiction declaration; accepts ICCt jurisdiction

Suffrage: 18 years of age; universal

Executive branch: *chief of state:* President of the Islamic Republic of Afghanistan Hamid KARZAI (since 7 December 2004); First Vice President vacant); Second Vice President Abdul Karim KHALILI (since 7 December 2004); note—the president is both the chief of state and head of government
head of government: President of the Islamic Republic of Afghanistan Hamid KARZAI (since 7 December 2004); First Vice President vacant); Second Vice President Abdul Karim KHALILI (since 7 December 2004)
cabinet: 25 ministers; note—ministers are appointed by the president and approved by the National Assembly (For more information visit the World Leaders website)
elections: the president is elected by direct vote for a five-year term (eligible for a second term); if no candidate receives 50% or more of the vote in the first round of voting, the two candidates with the most votes will participate in a second round; election last held on 20 August 2009 (next to be held on 5 April 2014)
election results: Hamid KARZAI reelected president; percent of vote (first round)—Hamid KARZAI 49.67%, Abdullah ABDULLAH 30.59%, Ramazan BASHARDOST 10.46%, Ashraf GHANI 2.94%; other 6.34%; note—ABDULLAH conceded the election to KARZAI following the first round vote

Legislative branch: the bicameral National Assembly consists of the Meshrano Jirga or House of Elders (102 seats, two-thirds of members elected from provincial councils for four-year terms, and one-third nominated by the president for five-year terms) and the Wolesi Jirga or House of People (no more than 250 seats; members directly elected for five-year terms)
note: the constitution allows the government to convene a constitutional Loya Jirga (Grand Council) on issues of independence, national sovereignty, and territorial integrity; it can amend the provisions of the constitution and prosecute the president; it is made up of members of the National Assembly and chairpersons of the provincial and district councils; no Loya Jirga of this type has ever been held, and district councils have never been elected
elections: last held on 18 September 2010 (next election expected in 2015)
election results: results by party—NA; note—ethnicity is the main factor influencing political alliances;approximate percentage of seats by ethnic group—Pashtun 39%, Hazara 24%, Tajik 21%, Uzbek 6%, other 10% (including Aimak, Arab, Baloch, Nuristani, Pahhai, Turkmen, Turkic); women hold 69 seats

Judicial branch: *highest court(s):* Supreme Court or Stera Mahkama (consists of the Supreme Court Chief and 8 justices organized into criminal, public security, civil, and commercial divisions or dewans)
judge selection and term of office: court chief and justices appointed by the president with the approval of the Wolesi Jirga; court chief and justices serve single 10-year terms
subordinate courts: Appeals Courts; Primary Courts; Special Courts for issues including narcotics, security,property, family, and juveniles

Political parties and leaders: note—the Ministry of Justice licensed 84 political parties as of December 2012

Political pressure groups and leaders: *other:* religious groups, tribal leaders, ethnically based groups, Taliban

International organization participation: ADB, CICA, CP, ECO, EITI (candidate country), FAO, G-77, IAEA, IBRD, ICAO, ICC (NGOs), ICRM, IDA, IDB, IFAD, IFC, IFRCS, ILO, IMF, Interpol, IOC, IOM, IPU, ISO (correspondent), ITSO, ITU, MIGA, MINUSMA, NAM, OIC, OPCW, OSCE (partner), SAARC, SACEP, SCO (observer), UN, UNCTAD, UNESCO, UNIDO, UNWTO, UPU, WCO, WFTU (NGOs), WHO, WIPO, WMO, WTO

Diplomatic representation in the US: *chief of mission:* Ambassador Eklil Ahmad HAKIMI (since 16 February 2011)
chancery: 2341 Wyoming Avenue NW, Washington, DC 20008
telephone: [1] (202) 483-6410
FAX: [1] (202) 483-6488
consulate(s) general: Los Angeles, New York

Diplomatic representation from the US: *chief of mission:* Ambassador (vacant); Charge d'Affaires Richard YONEOKA
embassy: The Great Masood Road, Kabul
mailing address: U.S. Embassy Kabul, APO, AE 09806
telephone: [93] 0700 108 001
FAX: [93] 0700 108 564

Flag description: three equal vertical bands of black (hoist side), red, and green, with the national emblem in white centered on the red band and slightly overlapping the other two bands; the center of the emblem features a mosque with pulpit and flags on either side, below the mosque are numerals for the solar year 1298 (1919 in the Gregorian calendar, the year of Afghan independence from the UK); this central image is circled by a border consisting of sheaves of wheat on the left and right, in the upper-center is an Arabic inscription of the Shahada (Muslim creed) below which are rays of the rising sun over the Takbir (Arabic expression meaning "God is great"), and at bottom center is a scroll bearing the name Afghanistan; black signifies the past, red is for the blood shed for independence, and green can represent either hope for the future, agricultural prosperity, or Islam
note: Afghanistan had more changes to its national flag in the 20th century than any other country; the colors black, red, and green appeared on most of them

National symbol(s): lion

National anthem: *name:* "Milli Surood" (National Anthem)
lyrics/music: Abdul Bari JAHANI/Babrak WASA
note: adopted 2006; the 2004 constitution of the post-Taliban government mandated that a new national anthem should be written containing the phrase "Allahu Akbar" (God is Great) and mentioning the names of Afghanistan's ethnic groups

ECONOMY

Economy—overview: Afghanistan's economy is recovering from decades of conflict. The economy has improved significantly since the fall of the Taliban regime in 2001 largely because of the infusion of international assistance, the recovery of the agricultural sector, and service sector growth. Despite the progress of the past few years, Afghanistan is extremely poor, landlocked, and highly dependent on foreign aid. Much of the population continues to suffer from shortages of housing, clean water, electricity, medical care, and jobs. Criminality, insecurity, weak governance, lack of infrastructure, and the Afghan Government's difficulty in extending rule of law to all parts of the country pose challenges to future economic growth. Afghanistan's living standards are among the lowest in the world. The international community remains committed to Afghanistan's development, pledging over $67 billion at nine donors' conferences between 2003–10. In July 2012, the donors at the Tokyo conference pledged an additional $16 billion in civilian aid through 2015. Despite this help, the Government of Afghanistan will need to overcome a number of challenges, including low revenue collection, anemic job creation, high levels of corruption, weak government capacity, and poor public infrastructure. Afghanistan's growth rate slowed markedly in 2013.

GDP (purchasing power parity): $45.3 billion (2013 est.)
country comparison to the world: 101
$34.25 billion (2012 est.)
$30.45 billion (2011 est.)
note: data are in 2013 US dollars

GDP (official exchange rate): $20.65 billion (2013 est.)

GDP—real growth rate: 3.1% (2013 est.)
country comparison to the world: 113
12.5% (2012 est.)
6.1% (2011 est.)

GDP—per capita (PPP): $1,100 (2013 est.)
country comparison to the world: 216
$1,100 (2012 est.)
$1,000 (2011 est.)
note: data are in 2013 US dollars

GDP—composition, by end use: household consumption: 96.5%
government consumption: 23.3%
investment in fixed capital: 25.4% investment in inventories: 0%
exports of goods and services: 18.1%
imports of goods and services: –63.4% (2011 est.)

GDP—composition, by sector of origin:
agriculture: 20%
industry: 25.6%
services: 54.4%
note: data exclude opium production (2011 est.)

Agriculture—products: opium, wheat, fruits, nuts; wool, mutton, sheepskins, lambskins

Industries: small-scale production of bricks, textiles, soap, furniture, shoes, fertilizer, apparel, food-products, non-alcoholic beverages, mineral water, cement; handwoven carpets; natural gas, coal, copper

Industrial production growth rate: NA%

Labor force: 7.512 million (2012 est.)
country comparison to the world: 62

Labor force—by occupation: *agriculture:* 78.6%
industry: 5.7%
services: 15.7% (FY08/09 est.)

Unemployment rate: 35% (2008 est.)
country comparison to the world: 186
40% (2005 est.)

Population below poverty line: 36% (FY08/09)

Household income or consumption by percentage share: *lowest 10%:* 3.8%
highest 10%: 24% (2008)

Budget: *revenues:* $2.333 billion
expenditures: $4.122 billion (2012 est.)

Taxes and other revenues: 11.3% of GDP (2012 est.)
country comparison to the world: 206

Budget surplus (+) or deficit (-): –8.7% of GDP (2012 est.)
country comparison to the world: 200

Fiscal year: 21 December—20 December

Inflation rate (consumer prices): 6.8% (2012 est.)
country comparison to the world: 182
5.7% (2011 est.)

Commercial bank prime lending rate: 15% (31 December 2012 est.)
country comparison to the world: 38
15.15% (31 December 2011 est.)

Stock of narrow money: $6.121 billion (31 December 2012 est.)
country comparison to the world: 95
$5.928 billion (31 December 2011 est.)

Stock of broad money: $6.499 billion (31 December 2012 est.)
country comparison to the world: 118
$6.351 billion (31 December 2011 est.)

Stock of domestic credit: $-819.6 million (31 December 2012 est.)
country comparison to the world: 186
$-520.2 million (31 December 2011 est.)

Market value of publicly traded shares: $NA

Current account balance: -$743.9 million (2011 est.)
country comparison to the world: 114
-$736 million (2010 est.)

Exports: $376 million (2012 est.)
country comparison to the world: 180
$388.5 million (2011 est.)
note: not including illicit exports or reexports

Exports—commodities: opium, fruits and nuts, handwoven carpets, wool, cotton, hides and pelts, precious and semi-precious gems

Exports—partners: Pakistan 32.2%, India 27%, Tajikistan 8.5%, US 6.2% (2012)

Imports: $6.39 billion (2012 est.)
country comparison to the world: 118
$5.154 billion (2011 est.)

Imports—commodities: machinery and other capital goods, food, textiles, petroleum products

Imports—partners: Pakistan 24.3%, US 18%, Russia 8.7%, India 5.8%, China 5.6%, Germany 4.4% (2012)

Reserves of foreign exchange and gold: $5.983 billion (31 December 2012 est.)
country comparison to the world: 88
$5.268 billion (31 December 2011 est.)

Debt—external: $1.28 billion (FY10/11)
country comparison to the world: 154
$2.7 billion (FY08/09)

Exchange rates: afghanis (AFA) per US dollar—
50.92 (2012 est.)
46.75 (2011 est.)
46.45 (2010)

ENERGY

Electricity—production: 986.1 million kWh (2010 est.)
country comparison to the world: 146

Electricity—consumption: 2.489 billion kWh (2010 est.)
country comparison to the world: 135

Electricity—exports: 0 kWh (2012 est.)
country comparison to the world: 95

Electricity—imports: 1.572 billion kWh (2010 est.)
country comparison to the world: 57

Electricity—installed generating capacity: 489,100 kW (2010 est.)
country comparison to the world: 140

Electricity—from fossil fuels: 23.5% of total installed capacity (2010 est.)
country comparison to the world: 188

Electricity—from nuclear fuels: 0% of total installed capacity (2010 est.)
country comparison to the world: 34

Electricity—from hydroelectric plants: 76.5% of total installed capacity (2010 est.)
country comparison to the world: 17

Electricity—from other renewable sources: 0% of total installed capacity (2010 est.)
country comparison to the world: 148

Crude oil—production: 1,950 bbl/day (2012 est.)
country comparison to the world: 106

Crude oil—exports: 0 bbl/day (2010 est.)
country comparison to the world: 76

Crude oil—imports: 0 bbl/day (2010 est.)
country comparison to the world: 149

Crude oil—proved reserves: NA bbl (1 January 2013 es)

Refined petroleum products—production: 0 bbl/day (2010 est.)
country comparison to the world: 117

Refined petroleum products—consumption: 4,229 bbl/day (2011 est.)
country comparison to the world: 174

Refined petroleum products—exports: 0 bbl/day (2010 est.)
country comparison to the world: 148

Refined petroleum products—imports: 36,250 bbl/day (2010 est.)
country comparison to the world: 83

Natural gas—production: 140 million cu m (2011 est.)
country comparison to the world: 81

Natural gas—consumption: 140 million cu m (2010 est.)
country comparison to the world: 104

Natural gas—exports: 0 cu m (2011 est.)
country comparison to the world: 55

Natural gas—imports: 0 cu m (2011 est.)
country comparison to the world: 150

Natural gas—proved reserves: 49.55 billion cu m (1 January 2013 es)
country comparison to the world: 65

Carbon dioxide emissions from consumption of energy: 6.589 million Mt (2011 est.)
country comparison to the world: 120

COMMUNICATIONS

Telephones—main lines in use: 13,500 (2012)
country comparison to the world: 198

Telephones—mobile cellular: 18 million (2012)
country comparison to the world: 55

Telephone system: *general assessment:* limited fixed-line telephone service; an increasing number of Afghans utilize mobile-cellular phone networks
domestic: aided by the presence of multiple providers, mobile-cellular telephone service continues to improve rapidly; the Afghan Ministry of Communications and Information claims that more than 90 percent of the population live in areas with access to mobile-cellular services
international: country code—93; multiple VSAT's provide international and domestic voice and data connectivity (2012)

Broadcast media: state-owned broadcaster, Radio Television Afghanistan (RTA), operates a series of radio and television stations in Kabul and the provinces; an estimated 150 private radio stations, 50 TV stations, and about a dozen international broadcasters are available (2007)

Internet country code: .af

Internet hosts: 223 (2012)
country comparison to the world: 199

Internet users: 1 million (2009)
country comparison to the world: 101

Communications—note: Internet access is growing through Internet cafes as well as public "telekiosks" in Kabul (2005)

TRANSPORTATION

Airports: 52 (2013)
country comparison to the world: 91

Airports—with paved runways: *total:* 23
over 3,047 m: 4
2,438 to 3,047 m: 4
1,524 to 2,437 m: 11
914 to 1,523 m: 2
under 914 m: 2 (2013)

Airports—with unpaved runways: *total:* 29
2,438 to 3,047 m: 4
1,524 to 2,437 m: 13
914 to 1,523 m: 6
under 914 m: 6 (2013)

Heliports: 9 (2013)

Pipelines: gas 466 km (2013)

Roadways: *total:* 42,150 km
country comparison to the world: 85
paved: 12,350 km
unpaved: 29,800 km (2006)

Waterways: 1,200 km; (chiefly Amu Darya, which handles vessels up to 500 DWT) (2011)
country comparison to the world: 59

Ports and terminals: *river port(s):* Kheyrabad, Shir Khan

MILITARY

Military branches: *Afghan Armed Forces:* Afghan National Army (ANA, includes Afghan Air Force (AAF)) (2011)

Military service age and obligation: 18 is the legal minimum age for voluntary military service; no conscription (2012)

Manpower available for military service: *males age 16-49:* 7,056,339
females age 16-49: 6,653,419 (2010 est.)

Manpower fit for military service: *males age 16-49:* 4,050,222
females age 16-49: 3,797,087 (2010 est.)

Manpower reaching militarily significant age annually: *male:* 392,116
female: 370,295 (2010 est.)

Military expenditures: NA% (2012)
4.74% of GDP (2011)
NA% (2010)

TRANSNATIONAL ISSUES

Disputes—international: Afghan, Coalition, and Pakistan military meet periodically to clarify the alignment of the boundary on the ground and on maps; Afghan and Iranian commissioners have discussed boundary monument densification and resurvey; Iran protests Afghanistan's restricting flow of dammed Helmand River tributaries during drought; Pakistan has sent troops across and built fences along some remote tribal areas of its treaty-defined Durand Line border with Afghanistan which serve as bases for foreign terrorists and other illegal activities; Russia remains concerned about the smuggling of poppy derivatives from Afghanistan through Central Asian countries

Refugees and internally displaced persons: *Refugees (country of origin):* 16,147 (Pakistan) (2012)
IDPs: about 647,779 (mostly Pashtuns and Kuchis displaced in the south and west due to drought and instability) (2014)

Trafficking in persons: *current situation:* Afghanistan is a source transit, and destination country for men, women, and children subjected to forced labor and sex trafficking, although domestic trafficking is more prevalent than transnational trafficking; Afghan men are subjected to forced labor and debt bondage in Iran, Pakistan,Greece, Turkey, and the Gulf states; Afghan women and girls are forced into prostitution and domestic servitude in Pakistan, Iran, and India, while women and girls from the Philippines, Pakistan, Iran, Tajikistan,and China are reportedly sexually exploited in Afghanistan; children are increasingly subjected to forced labor in carpet-making factories, domestic servitude, forced begging, and commercial sexual exploitation;some children are sold to settle debts
tier rating: Tier 2 Watch List—Afghanistan does not fully comply with the minimum standards for the elimination of trafficking in persons; anti-trafficking law enforcement efforts have improved, though official complicity in human trafficking remains a problem; the first known convictions were made under the government's 2008 anti-trafficking law; Afghanistan has not developed or employed systematic procedures to identify trafficking victims or refer them to protective services and continues to rely on NGOs to provide the vast majority of victim assistance; the government has not made discernible progress in preventing human trafficking or protecting victims but has adopted an anti-trafficking action plan (2013)

Illicit drugs: world's largest producer of opium; poppy cultivation increased 57 percent, from 115,000 hectares in 2011 to 180,000 hectares in 2012; despite the increase in area under cultivation, the effects of poor weather and crop disease resulted in lower yield so potential opium production remained stable at 4,300 mt in 2012 compared to 4,400 mt in 2011; the Taliban and other antigovernment groups participate in and profit from the opiate trade, which is a key source of revenue for the Taliban inside Afghanistan; widespread corruption and instability impede counterdrug efforts; most of the heroin consumed in Europe and Eurasia is derived from Afghan opium; Afghanistan is also struggling to respond to a burgeoning domestic opiate addiction problem; vulnerable to drug money laundering through informal financial networks; regional source of hashish (2013)

AKROTIRI

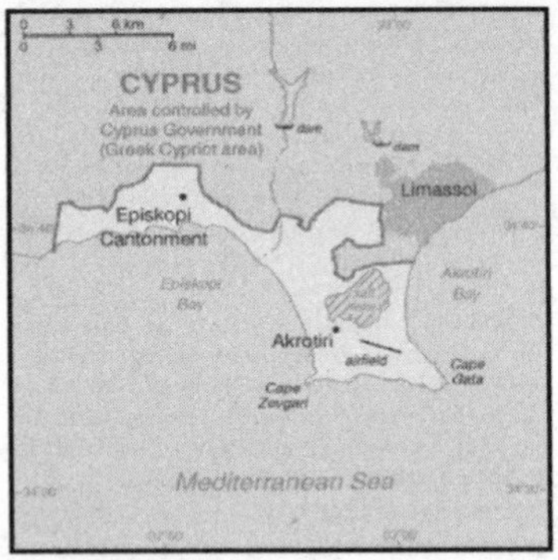

INTRODUCTION

Background: By terms of the 1960 Treaty of Establishment that created the independent Republic of Cyprus, the UK retained full sovereignty and jurisdiction over two areas of almost 254 square kilometers—Akrotiri and Dhekelia. The southernmost and smallest of these is the Akrotiri Sovereign Base Area, which is also referred to as the Western Sovereign Base Area.

GEOGRAPHY

Location: Eastern Mediterranean, peninsula on the southwest coast of Cyprus

Geographic coordinates: 34 37 N, 32 58 E

Map references: Europe

Area: *total:* 123 sq km
country comparison to the world: 224
note: includes a salt lake and wetlands

Area—comparative: about 0.7 times the size of Washington, DC

Land boundaries: *total:* 47.4 km
border countries: Cyprus 47.4 km

Coastline: 56.3 km

Climate: temperate; Mediterranean with hot, dry summers and cool winters

Environment—current issues: hunting around the salt lake; note—breeding place for loggerhead and green turtles; only remaining colony of griffon vultures is on the base

Geography—note: British extraterritorial rights also extended to several small off-post sites scattered across Cyprus; of the Sovereign Base Area (SBA) land, 60% is privately owned and farmed, 20% is owned by the Ministry of Defense, and 20% is SBA Crown land

PEOPLE AND SOCIETY

Languages: English, Greek

Population: approximately 15,700 live on the Sovereign Base Areas of Akrotiri and Dhekelia including 7,700 Cypriots, 3,600 Service and UK-based contract personnel, and 4,400 dependents
country comparison to the world: 223

GOVERNMENT

Country name: *conventional long form:* none
conventional short form: Akrotiri

Dependency status: a special form of UK overseas territory; administered by an administrator who is also the Commander, British Forces Cyprus

Capital: *name:* Episkopi Cantonment (base administrative center for Akrotiri and Dhekelia)
geographic coordinates: 34 40 N, 32 51 E
time difference: UTC+2 (7 hours ahead of Washington, DC during Standard Time)
daylight saving time: +1hr, begins last Sunday in March; ends last Sunday in October

Constitution: presented 3 August 1960, effective 16 August 1960; amended 1966 (The Sovereign Base Areas of Akrotiri and Dhekelia Order in Council 1960, serves as a basic legal document) (2013)

Legal system: the Sovereign Base Area Administration has its own court system to deal with civil and criminal matters; laws applicable to the Cypriot population are, as far as possible, the same as the laws of the Republic of Cyprus

Executive branch: *chief of state:* Queen ELIZABETH II (since 6 February 1952)
head of government: Administrator Major General Richard CRIPWELL (since January 2013) note—reports to the British Ministry of Defense; the Chief Officer is responsible for the day-to-day running of the civil government of the Sovereign Bases
elections: none; the monarchy is hereditary; the administrator appointed by the monarch

Judicial branch: *highest court(s):* Senior Judges' Court (consists of several visiting judges from England and Wales)
judge selection and term of office: judges appointment and tenure NA
subordinate courts: Resident Judges' Court; Courts Martial

Diplomatic representation in the US: none (overseas territory of the UK)

Diplomatic representation from the US: none (overseas territory of the UK)

Flag description: the flag of the UK is used

National anthem: *note:* as a United Kingdom area of special sovereignty, "God Save the Queen" is official (see United Kingdom)

ECONOMY

Economy—overview: Economic activity is limited to providing services to the military and their families located in Akrotiri. All food and manufactured goods must be imported.

Exchange rates: *note:* uses the euro

COMMUNICATIONS

Broadcast media: British Forces Broadcast Service (BFBS) provides multi-channel satellite TV service as well as BFBS radio broadcasts to the Akrotiri Sovereign Base (2009)

MILITARY

Military—note: defense is the responsibility of the UK; Akrotiri has a full RAF base, Headquarters for British Forces Cyprus, and Episkopi Support Unit

ALBANIA

INTRODUCTION

Background: Albania declared its independence from the Ottoman Empire in 1912, but was conquered by Italy in 1939,and occupied by Germany in 1943. Communist partisans took over the country in 1944. Albania allied itself first with the USSR (until 1960), and then with China (to 1978). In the early 1990s, Albania ended 46 years of xenophobic communist rule and established a multiparty democracy. The transition has proven challenging as successive governments have tried to deal with high unemployment, widespread corruption,dilapidated infrastructure, powerful organized crime networks, and combative political opponents. Albania has made progress in its democratic development since first holding multiparty elections in 1991, but deficiencies remain. International observers judged elections to be largely free and fair since the restoration of political stability following the collapse of pyramid schemes in 1997; however, each of Albania's post-communist elections have been marred by claims of electoral fraud. The 2009 general elections resulted in a coalition government, the first such in the country's history. In 2013, general elections achieved a peaceful transition of power and a second successive coalition government. Albania joined NATO in April 2009 and is a potential candidate for EU accession. Although Albania's economy continues to grow, it has slowed, and the country is still one of the poorest in Europe. A large informal economy and an inadequate energy and transportation infrastructure remain obstacles.

GEOGRAPHY

Location: Southeastern Europe, bordering the Adriatic Sea and Ionian Sea, between Greece in the south and Montenegro and Kosovo to the north

Geographic coordinates: 41 00 N, 20 00 E

Map references: Europe

Area: *total:* 28,748 sq km
country comparison to the world: 145
land: 27,398 sq km
water: 1,350 sq km

Area—comparative: slightly smaller than Maryland

Land boundaries: *total:* 717 km
border countries: Greece 282 km, Macedonia 151 km, Montenegro 172 km, Kosovo 112 km

Coastline: 362 km

Maritime claims: *territorial sea:* 12 nm
continental shelf: 200 m depth or to the depth of exploitation

Climate: mild temperate; cool, cloudy, wet winters; hot, clear, dry summers; interior is cooler and wetter

Terrain: mostly mountains and hills; small plains along coast

Elevation extremes: *lowest point:* Adriatic Sea 0 m
highest point: Maja e Korabit (Golem Korab) 2,764 m

Natural resources: petroleum, natural gas, coal, bauxite, chromite, copper, iron ore, nickel, salt, timber, hydropower

Land use: *arable land:* 21.63%
permanent crops: 2.57%
other: 75.79% (2011)

Irrigated land: 1,884 sq km (2006)

Total renewable water resources: 41.7 cu km (2011)

Freshwater withdrawal (domestic/industrial/agricultural): *total:* 1.31 cu km/yr (43%/18%/39%)
per capita: 413.6 cu m/yr (2006)

Natural hazards: destructive earthquakes; tsunamis occur along southwestern coast; floods; drought

Environment—current issues: deforestation; soil erosion; water pollution from industrial and domestic effluents

Environment—international agreements: *party to:* Air Pollution, Biodiversity, Climate Change, Climate Change-Kyoto Protocol, Desertification, Endangered Species, Hazardous Wastes, Law of the Sea, Ozone Layer Protection, Wetlands
signed, but not ratified: none of the selected agreements

Geography—note: strategic location along Strait of Otranto (links Adriatic Sea to Ionian Sea and Mediterranean Sea)

PEOPLE AND SOCIETY

Nationality: *noun:* Albanian(s)
adjective: Albanian

Ethnic groups: Albanian 82.6%, Greek 0.9%, other 1% (including Vlach, Roma (Gypsy), Macedonian, Montenegrin, and Egyptian), unspecified 15.5% (2011 est.)

Languages: Albanian 98.8% (official—derived from Tosk dialect), Greek 0.5%, other 0.6% (including Macedonian, Roma, Vlach, Turkish, Italian, and Serbo-Croatian), unspecified 0.1% (2011 est.)

Religions: Muslim 56.7%, Roman Catholic 10%, Orthodox 6.8%, atheist 2.5%, Bektashi (a Sufi order) 2.1%, other 5.7%,unspecified 16.2%
note: all mosques and churches were closed in 1967 and religious observances prohibited; in November 1990, Albania began allowing private religious practice (2011 est.)

Population: 3,020,209 (July 2014 est.)
country comparison to the world: 138

Age structure: *0-14 years:* 19.3% (male 307,275/female 274,634)
15-24 years: 19.2% (male 297,851/female 282,498)
25-54 years: 40% (male 574,820/female 633,729)
55-64 years: 11.1% (male 157,014/female 158,602)
65 years and over: 10.8% (male 157,143/female 176,643) (2014 est.)

Dependency ratios: *total dependency ratio:* 45.7%
youth dependency ratio: 30.1%
elderly dependency ratio: 15.6%
potential support ratio: 6.4 (2013)

Median age: *total:* 31.6 years
male: 30.3 years
female: 32.9 years (2014 est.)

Population growth rate: 0.3% (2014 est.)
country comparison to the world: 172

Birth rate: 12.73 births/1,000 population (2014 est.)
country comparison to the world: 156

Death rate: 6.47 deaths/1,000 population (2014 est.)
country comparison to the world: 153

Net migration rate: -3.31 migrant(s)/1,000 population (2014 est.)
country comparison to the world: 184

Urbanization: *urban population:* 52% of total population (2010)
rate of urbanization: 2.3% annual rate of change (2010–15 est.)

Major urban areas—population: TIRANA (capital) 419,000 (2011)

Sex ratio: *at birth:* 1.11 male(s)/female
0-14 years: 1.12 male(s)/female
15-24 years: 1.05 male(s)/female
25-54 years: 0.91 male(s)/female
55-64 years: 0.98 male(s)/female
65 years and over: 0.89 male(s)/female
total population: 0.98 male(s)/female (2014 est.)

Mother's mean age at first birth: 23.9
note: median age at first birth among women 25–29 (2009 est.)

Maternal mortality rate: 27 deaths/100,000 live births (2010)
country comparison to the world: 128

Infant mortality rate: *total:* 13.19 deaths/1,000 live births
country comparison to the world: 120
male: 14.68 deaths/1,000 live births
female: 11.54 deaths/1,000 live births (2014 est.)

Life expectancy at birth: *total population:* 77.96 years
country comparison to the world: 60
male: 75.33 years
female: 80.86 years (2014 est.)

Total fertility rate: 1.5 children born/woman (2014 est.)
country comparison to the world: 191

Contraceptive prevalence rate: 69.3% (2008/09)

Health expenditures: 6.3% of GDP (2011)
country comparison to the world: 98

Physicians density: 1.11 physicians/1,000 population (2011)

Hospital bed density: 2.4 beds/1,000 population (2011)

Drinking water source:
Improved:
urban: 95.5% of population
rural: 93.7% of population
total: 94.7% of population
Unimproved:
urban: 4.5% of population
rural: 6.3% of population
total: 5.3% of population (2011 est.)

Sanitation facility access:
Improved:
urban: 94.7% of population
rural: 93% of population
total: 93.9% of population
Unimproved:
urban: 5.3% of population
rural: 7% of population
total: 6.1% of population (2011 est.)

HIV/AIDS—adult prevalence rate: NA

HIV/AIDS—people living with HIV/AIDS: NA

HIV/AIDS—deaths: NA

Obesity—adult prevalence rate: 21.3% (2008)
country comparison to the world: 88

Children under the age of 5 years underweight: 6.3% (2009)
country comparison to the world: 80

Education expenditures: 3.3% of GDP (2007)
country comparison to the world: 130

Literacy: *definition:* age 9 and over can read and write
total population: 96.8%
male: 98%
female: 95.7% (2011 est.)

School life expectancy (primary to tertiary education): *total:* 10 years
male: 10 years
female: 10 years (2001)

Child labor—children ages 5–14: *total number:* 72,818
percentage: 12 % (2005 est.)

Unemployment, youth ages 15–24: *total:* 22.5%
country comparison to the world: 50
male: 23.8%
female: 20.7% (2011)

GOVERNMENT

Country name: *conventional long form:* Republic of Albania
conventional short form: Albania
local long form: Republika e Shqiperise
local short form: Shqiperia
former: People's Socialist Republic of Albania

Government type: parliamentary democracy

Capital: *name:* Tirana (Tirane)
geographic coordinates: 41 19 N, 19 49 E
time difference: UTC+1 (6 hours ahead of Washington, DC during Standard Time)
daylight saving time: +1hr, begins last Sunday in March; ends last Sunday in October

Administrative divisions: 12 counties (qarqe, singular—qark); Berat, Diber, Durres, Elbasan, Fier, Gjirokaster, Korce, Kukes, Lezhe, Shkoder, Tirane, Vlore

Independence: 28 November 1912 (from the Ottoman Empire)

National holiday: Independence Day, 28 November (1912) also known as Flag Day

Constitution: several previous; latest approved by parliament 21 October 1998, adopted by popular referendum 22 November 1998, promulgated 28 November 1998; amended 2007, 2008, 2012 (2014)

Legal system: civil law system except in the northern rural areas where customary law known as the "Code of Leke" prevails

International law organization participation: has not submitted an ICJ jurisdiction declaration; accepts ICCt jurisdiction

Suffrage: 18 years of age; universal

Executive branch: *chief of state:* President of the Republic Bujar NISHANI (since 24 July 2012)
head of government: Prime Minister Edi Rama (since 10 September 2013)
cabinet: Council of Ministers proposed by the prime minister, nominated by the president, and approved by parliament
(For more information visit the World Leaders website)
elections: president is elected by the Assembly for a five-year term and is eligible for a second term (a candidate needs a three-fifths majority of the Assembly's 140 votes (84 votes) in one of the first three rounds of voting or a simple majority in round four or five to become president; up to five rounds of voting are held, if necessary); four election rounds held between 30 May and 11 June 2012 (next election to be held in 2017); prime minister appointed by the president on the proposal of the party or coalition of parties that has the majority of seats in the Assembly
election results: Bujar NISHANI elected president on fourth round of voting; Assembly vote (for first three rounds three-fifths majority, 84 votes, required; fourth round, a simple majority of votes is required): Bujar NISHANI 73 votes

Legislative branch: unicameral Assembly or Kuvendi (140 deputies elected through a regional proportional system from multi-name lists of parties or party coalitions according to their respective order; elected for a four-year term)
elections: last held on 23 June 2013 (next to be held in 2017)
election results: percent of vote by party—PS 41.36%, PD 30.63%, LSI 10.46%, PR 3.02%, PDIU 2.61%, other 11.92%; seats by party—PS 65, PD 50, LSI 16, PDIU 4, PR 3, other 2
note: seats by parliamentary group as of March 2014 - ASHE 85, APMI 55

Judicial branch: *highest court(s):* Constitutional Court (consists of 9 judges, including a chairman); Court of Cassation (consists of 14 judges, including the chief justice)
judge selection and term of office: Constitutional Court judges appointed by the president with the consent of the Assembly to serve single 9-year terms; chairman elected by the People's Assembly for single 3-year term; Court of Cassation judges, including the chairman, appointed by the president with the consent of the Assembly to serve single, 9-year terms)
subordinate courts: Courts of Appeal; Courts of First Instance

Political parties and leaders:
Alliance for Employment, Welfare, and Integration or APMI (coalition of 25 centrist and center-right parties) [Sali BERISHA]: Christian Democratic Party or PDK [Nard NDOKA]
Democratic Party or PD [Lulzim BASHA]
Movement for National Development of LZHK [Dashamir SHEHI]
Party for Justice, Integration and Unity or PDIU [Shpetim IDRIZI]
Republican Party or PR [Fatmir MEDIU]
Alliance for a European Albania or ASHE (coalition of 37 opposition parties from far left to right wing) [Edi RAMA]: Christian Democratic Party of PKD [Mark FRROKU]
Socialist Movement for Integration or LSI [Ilir META]
Socialist Party or PS [Edi RAMA]
Union for Human Rights Party or PBDNJ [Vangjel DULE]
other parties: New Democratic Spirit or FRD [Bamir TOPI]
Red and Black Alliance [Kreshnik SPAHIU]

Political pressure groups and leaders: Confederation of Trade Unions of Albania or KSSH [Kol NIKOLLAJ]
Omonia [Vasil BOLLANO] Union of Independent Trade
Unions of Albania or BSPSH [Gezim KALAJA]

International organization participation: BSEC, CD, CE, CEI, EAPC, EBRD, EITI (candidate country), FAO, IAEA, IBRD, ICAO, ICC (national committees), ICRM, IDA, IDB, IFAD, IFC, IFRCS, ILO, IMF, IMO, Interpol, IOC, IOM, IPU, ISO (correspondent), ITU, ITUC (NGOs), MIGA, NATO, OAS (observer), OIC, OIF, OPCW, OSCE, PCA, SELEC, UN, UNCTAD, UNESCO, UNIDO, UNWTO, UPU, WCO, WFTU (NGOs), WHO, WIPO, WMO, WTO

Diplomatic representation in the US: *chief of mission:* Ambassador Gilbert GALANXHI (since 5 January 2011)
chancery: 1312 18th Street NW, 4th Floor, Washington, DC 20036
telephone: [1] (202) 223-4942
FAX: [1] (202) 628-7342
consulate(s) general: New York

Diplomatic representation from the US: *chief of mission:* Ambassador Alexander ARVIZU (since 10 November 2010)
embassy: Rruga e Elbasanit, 103, Tirana
mailing address: US Department of State, 9510 Tirana Place, Dulles, VA 20189-9510
telephone: [355] (4) 2247-285
FAX: [355] (4) 2232-222

Flag description: red with a black two-headed eagle in the center; the design is claimed to be that of 15th-century hero George Kastrioti SKANDERBEG, who led a successful uprising against the Turks that resulted in a short-lived independence for some Albanian regions (1443-78); an unsubstantiated explanation for the eagle symbol is the tradition that Albanians see themselves as descendants of the eagle; they refer to themselves as "Shqipetare," which translates as "sons of the eagle"

National symbol(s): double-headed eagle

National anthem: *name:* "Hymni i Flamurit" (Hymn to the Flag)
lyrics/music: Aleksander Stavre DRENOVA/Ciprian PORUMBESCU
note: adopted 1912

ECONOMY

Economy—overview: Albania, a formerly closed, centrally-planned state, is making the difficult transition to a more modern open-market economy. Albania managed to weather the first waves of the global financial crisis but, more recently, its negative effects have put some pressure on the Albanian economy. While the government is focused on establishing a favorable business climate through the simplification of licensing requirements and tax codes, it entered into a new arrangement with the IMF for additional financial and technical support. Remittances, a significant catalyst for economic growth declined from 12-15% of GDP before the 2008 financial crisis to 7% of GDP in 2012, mostly from Albanians residing in Greece and Italy. The agricultural sector, which accounts for almost half of employment but only about one-fifth of GDP, is limited primarily to small family operations and subsistence farming, because of a lack of modern equipment, unclear property rights, and the prevalence of small, inefficient plots of land. Complex tax codes and licensing requirements, a weak judicial system, poor enforcement of contracts and property issues, and antiquated infrastructure contribute to Albania's poor business environment and makes attracting foreign investment more difficult. Inward FDI is among the lowest in the region, but the government has embarked on an ambitious program to improve the business climate through fiscal and legislative reforms. Albania's energy supply has improved in recent years mostly due to upgraded transmission capacities that Albania has developed with its neighboring countries. However, technical and non-technical losses—including energy theft and non-payment—continue to be a threat to the financial viability of the entire system. Also, with help from international donors, the government is taking steps to improve the poor national road and rail network, a long-standing barrier to sustained economic growth. The country will continue to face challenges from increasing public debt, having exceeded its former statutory limit of 60% of GDP in 2013. Strong trade, remittance, and banking sector ties with Greece and Italy make Albania vulnerable to spillover effects of debt crises and weak growth in the euro zone.

GDP (purchasing power parity): $26.73 billion (2013 est.)
country comparison to the world: 122
$26.29 billion (2012 est.)
$25.87 billion (2011 est.)
note: data are in 2013 US dollars Albania has an informal, and unreported, sector that may be as large as 50% of official GDP

GDP (official exchange rate): $13.16 billion (2013 est.)

GDP—real growth rate: 1.7% (2013 est.)
country comparison to the world: 148
1.6% (2012 est.)
2.8% (2011 est.)

GDP—per capita (PPP): $8,200 (2013 est.)
country comparison to the world: 131
$8,100 (2012 est.)
$8,000 (2011 est.)
note: data are in 2013 US dollars

Gross national saving: 16.1% of GDP (2013 est.)
country comparison to the world: 105
14.4% of GDP (2012 est.)
12.6% of GDP (2011 est.)

GDP—composition, by end use:
household consumption: 87.6%
government consumption: 8.4%
investment in fixed capital: 25%
investment in inventories: -2.6%
exports of goods and services: 36%
imports of goods and services: -54.4% (2013 est.)

GDP—composition, by sector of origin: *agriculture:* 17.5%
industry: 15.3%
services: 67.2% (2013 est.)

Agriculture—products: wheat, corn, potatoes, vegetables, fruits, sugar beets, grapes; meat, dairy products; sheep

Industries: food and tobacco products; textiles and clothing; lumber, oil, cement, chemicals, mining, basic metals,hydropower

Industrial production growth rate: 0.4% (2013 est.)
country comparison to the world: 163

Labor force:
1.129 million (2013 est.)
country comparison to the world: 140

Labor force—by occupation: *agriculture:* 47.8%
industry: 23%
services: 29.2% (September 2010 es)

Unemployment rate: 12.9% (2013 est.)
country comparison to the world: 128
13% (2012 est.)
note: these are official rates, but actual rates may exceed 30% due to preponderance of near-subsistence farming

Population below poverty line: 12.5% (2008 est.)

Household income or consumption by percentage share: *lowest 10%:* 3.5%
highest 10%: 29% (2008)

Distribution of family income—Gini index: 34.5 (2008)
country comparison to the world: 91
26.7 (2005)

Budget: *revenues:* $3.159 billion
expenditures: $3.709 billion (2013 est.)

Taxes and other revenues: 24% of GDP (2013 est.)
country comparison to the world: 136

Budget surplus (+) or deficit (-): -4.2% of GDP (2013 est.)
country comparison to the world: 153

Public debt: 61.1% of GDP (2013 est.)
country comparison to the world: 47
58.8% of GDP (2012 est.)

Fiscal year: calendar year

Inflation rate (consumer prices): 2% (2013 est.)
country comparison to the world: 65
2% (2012 est.)

Central bank discount rate: 5% (31 December 2010 est.)
country comparison to the world: 66
5.25% (31 December 2009 est.)

Commercial bank prime lending rate: 11.8% (31 December 2013 est.)
country comparison to the world: 80
10.88% (31 December 2012 est.)

Stock of narrow money: $2.576 billion (31 December 2013 est.)
country comparison to the world: 120
$2.657 billion (31 December 2012 est.)

Stock of broad money: $5.882 billion (31 December 2013 est.)
country comparison to the world: 125
$6.326 billion (31 December 2012 est.)

Stock of domestic credit: $8.062 billion (31 December 2013 est.)
country comparison to the world: 103
$8.591 billion (31 December 2012 est.)

Market value of publicly traded shares: $NA

Current account balance: -$1.137 billion (2013 est.)
country comparison to the world: 123
-$1.314 billion (2012 est.)

Exports: $1.226 billion (2013 est.)
country comparison to the world: 153
$1.123 billion (2012 est.)

Exports—commodities: textiles and footwear; asphalt, metals and metallic ores, crude oil; vegetables, fruits, tobacco

Exports—partners: Italy 51.1%, Spain 9.2%, Turkey 6.3%, Greece 4.4% (2012)

Imports: $4.115 billion (2013 est.)
country comparison to the world: 138
$3.984 billion (2012 est.)

Imports—commodities: machinery and equipment, foodstuffs, textiles, chemicals

Imports—partners: Italy 31.9%, Greece 9.5%, China 6.4%, Germany 6%, Turkey 5.7% (2012)

Reserves of foreign exchange and gold: $2.302 billion (31 December 2013 est.)
country comparison to the world: 117
$2.6 billion (31 December 2012 est.)

Debt—external: $6.108 billion (31 December 2013 est.)
country comparison to the world: 117
$5.838 billion (31 December 2012 est.)

Exchange rates: leke (ALL) per US dollar—
109.2 (2013 est.)
108.19 (2012 est.)
103.94 (2010 est.)
94.98 (2009)
79.546 (2008)

ENERGY

Electricity—production: 7.481 billion kWh (2010 est.)
country comparison to the world: 102

Electricity—consumption: 4.669 billion kWh (2010 est.)
country comparison to the world: 116

Electricity—exports: 301 million kWh (2011 est.)
country comparison to the world: 69

Electricity—imports: 3.475 billion kWh (2011 est.)
country comparison to the world: 44

Electricity—installed generating capacity: 1.621 million kW (2010 est.)
country comparison to the world: 112

Electricity—from fossil fuels: 9.9% of total installed capacity (2010 est.)
country comparison to the world: 195

Electricity—from nuclear fuels: 0% of total installed capacity (2010 est.)
country comparison to the world: 37

Electricity—from hydroelectric plants: 90.1% of total installed capacity (2010 est.)
country comparison to the world: 13

Electricity—from other renewable sources: 0% of total installed capacity (2010 est.)
country comparison to the world: 150

Crude oil—production: 16,870 bbl/day (2012 est.)
country comparison to the world: 81

Crude oil—exports: 8,997 bbl/day (2010 est.)
country comparison to the world: 59

Crude oil—imports: 0 bbl/day (2010 est.)
country comparison to the world: 151

Crude oil—proved reserves: 172.4 million bbl (1 January 2013 es)
country comparison to the world: 62

Refined petroleum products—production: 3,121 bbl/day (2010 est.)
country comparison to the world: 108

Refined petroleum products—consumption: 38,390 bbl/day (2011 est.)
country comparison to the world: 109

Refined petroleum products—exports: 67.56 bbl/day (2010 est.)
country comparison to the world: 121

Refined petroleum products—imports: 22,810 bbl/day (2010 est.)
country comparison to the world: 100

Natural gas—production: 10 million cu m (2011 est.)
country comparison to the world: 91

Natural gas—consumption: 10 million cu m (2010 est.)
country comparison to the world: 112

Natural gas—exports: 0 cu m (2011 est.)
country comparison to the world: 56

Natural gas—imports: 0 cu m (2011 est.)
country comparison to the world: 152

Natural gas—proved reserves: 849.5 million cu m (1 January 2013 es)
country comparison to the world: 105

Carbon dioxide emissions from consumption of energy: 4.183 million Mt (2011 est.)
country comparison to the world: 131

COMMUNICATIONS

Telephones—main lines in use: 312,000 (2012)
country comparison to the world: 114

Telephones—mobile cellular: 3.5 million (2012)
country comparison to the world: 125

Telephone system: *general assessment:* despite new investment in fixed lines, teledensity remains low with roughly 10 fixed lines per 100 people; mobile-cellular telephone use is widespread and generally effective
domestic: offsetting the shortage of fixed line capacity, mobile-cellular phone service has been available since 1996; by 2011 multiple companies were providing mobile services and mobile teledensity had reached 100 per 100 persons; Internet broadband services initiated in 2005 but growth has been slow; Internet cafes are popular in Tirana and have started to spread outside the capital
international: country code—355; submarine cable provides connectivity to Italy, Croatia, and Greece; the Trans-Balkan Line, a combination submarine cable and land fiber-optic system, provides additional connectivity to Bulgaria, Macedonia, and Turkey; international traffic carried by fiber-optic cable and, when necessary, by microwave radio relay from the Tirana exchange to Italy and Greece (2011)

Broadcast media: 3 public TV networks, one of which transmits by satellite to Albanian-language communities in neighboring countries; more than 60 private TV stations; many viewers can pick up Italian and Greek TV broadcasts via terrestrial reception; cable TV service is available; 2 public radio networks and roughly 25 private radio stations; several international broadcasters are available (2010)

Internet country code: .al

Internet hosts: 15,528 (2012)
country comparison to the world: 124

Internet users: 1.3 million (2009)
country comparison to the world: 91

TRANSPORTATION

Airports: 4 (2013)
country comparison to the world: 183

Airports—with paved runways: *total:* 4
2,438 to 3,047 m: 3
1,524 to 2,437 m: 1 (2013)

Airports—with unpaved runways: *total:* 1
914 to 1,523 m: 1 (2012)

Heliports: 1 (2013)

Pipelines: gas 331 km; oil 249 km (2013)

Railways: *total:* 339 km
country comparison to the world: 117
standard gauge: 339 km 1.435-m gauge (2009)

Roadways: *total:* 18,000 km
country comparison to the world: 116
paved: 7,020 km
unpaved: 10,980 km (2002)

Waterways: 41 km (on the Bojana River) (2011)
country comparison to the world: 104

Merchant marine: *total:* 17
country comparison to the world: 99
by type: cargo 16, roll on/roll off 1
foreign-owned: 1 (Turkey 1)
registered in other countries: 5 (Antigua and Barbuda 1, Panama 4) (2010)

Ports and terminals: *major seaport(s):* Durres, Sarande, Shengjin, Vlore

MILITARY

Military branches: Land Forces Command, Navy Force Command, Air Forces Command (2013)

Military service age and obligation: 19 is the legal minimum age for voluntary military service; 18 is the legal minimum age in case of general/partial compulsory mobilization (2012)

Manpower available for military service: *males age 16-49:* 731,111
females age 16-49: 780,216 (2010 est.)

Manpower fit for military service: *males age 16-49:* 622,379
females age 16-49: 660,715 (2010 est.)

Manpower reaching militarily significant age annually: *male:* 31,986
female: 29,533 (2010 est.)

Military expenditures: 1.47% of GDP (2012)
country comparison to the world: 66
1.52% of GDP (2011)
1.47% of GDP (2010)

TRANSNATIONAL ISSUES

Disputes—international: none

Refugees and internally displaced persons: *stateless persons:* 7,443 (2012)

Trafficking in persons:
current situation: Albania is a source country for men, women, and children subjected to sex trafficking and forced labor; Albanian victims of sexual exploitation are trafficked within Albania and in Greece, Italy,Macedonia, Kosovo, Belgium, the Netherlands, Germany, Switzerland, Ireland, and the UK; some Albanian women become sex trafficking victims after accepting offers of legitimate jobs; Albanian children are forced to beg or perform other forms of forced labor; Filipino victims of labor trafficking were identified in Albania during 2012

tier rating: Tier 2 Watch List—Albania does not fully comply with the minimum standards for the elimination of trafficking; however, it is making significant efforts to do so; the government decreased its trafficking investigations, prosecutions, and convictions over the last year and, because of inconsistent implementation of operating procedures, continues to punish victims for unlawful acts that are a direct result of being subjected to sex trafficking; the high turnover rate of law enforcement personnel prevents progress at the local level in identifying and protecting trafficking victims; removal of the national anti-trafficking coordinator hinders efforts to implement the 2011 national action plan against trafficking;the government provides limited funding to NGO shelters (2013)

Illicit drugs: increasingly active transshipment point for Southwest Asian opiates, hashish, and cannabis transiting the Balkan route and—to a lesser extent—cocaine from South America destined for Western Europe; limited opium and expanding cannabis production; ethnic Albanian narcotrafficking organizations active and expanding in Europe; vulnerable to money laundering associated with regional trafficking in narcotics, arms, contraband, and illegal aliens

ALGERIA

INTRODUCTION

Background: After more than a century of rule by France, Algerians fought through much of the 1950s to achieve independence in 1962. Algeria's primary political party, the National Liberation Front (FLN), was established in 1954 as part of the struggle for independence and has largely dominated politics since. The Government of Algeria in 1988 instituted a multi-party system in response to public unrest, but the surprising first round success of the Islamic Salvation Front (FIS) in the December 1991 balloting led the Algerian army to intervene and postpone the second round of elections to prevent what the secular elite feared would be an extremist-led government from assuming power. The army began a crackdown on the FIS that spurred FIS supporters to begin attacking government targets. Fighting escalated into an insurgency, which saw intense violence from 1992-98, resulting in over 100,000 deaths—many attributed to indiscriminate massacres of villagers by extremists. The government gained the upper hand by the late-1990s, and FIS's armed wing, the Islamic Salvation Army, disbanded in January 2000. Abdelaziz BOUTEFLIKA, with the backing of the military, won the presidency in 1999 in an election widely viewed as fraudulent. He was reelected to a second term in 2004 and overwhelmingly won a third term in 2009, after the government amended the constitution in 2008 to remove presidential term limits. Longstanding problems continue to face BOUTEFLIKA, including large-scale unemployment, a shortage of housing, unreliable electrical and water supplies, government inefficiencies and corruption, and the continuing activities of extremist militants. The Salafist Group for Preaching and Combat (GSPC) in 2006 merged with al-Qa'ida to form al-Qa'ida in the Lands of the Islamic Maghreb, which has launched an ongoing series of kidnappings and bombings targeting the Algerian Government and Western interests. The government in 2011 introduced some political reforms in response to the Arab Spring, including lifting the 19-year-old state of emergency restrictions and increasing women's quotas for elected assemblies. Parliamentary elections in May 2012 and municipal and provincial elections in November 2012 saw continued dominance by the FLN, with Islamist opposition parties performing poorly. Political protest activity in the country remained low in 2013, but small, sometimes violent socioeconomic demonstrations by disparate groups continued to be a common occurrence. Parliament in 2014 is expected to revise the constitution.

GEOGRAPHY

Location: Northern Africa, bordering the Mediterranean Sea, between Morocco and Tunisia

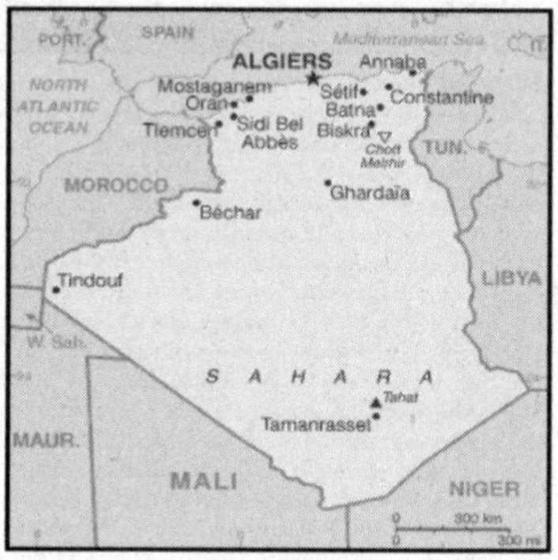

Geographic coordinates: 28 00 N, 3 00 E
Map references: Africa
Area: *total:* 2,381,741 sq km
country comparison to the world: 10
land: 2,381,741 sq km
water: 0 sq km
Area—comparative: slightly less than 3.5 times the size of Texas
Land boundaries: *total:* 6,343 km
border countries: Libya 982 km, Mali 1,376 km, Mauritania 463 km, Morocco 1,559 km, Niger 956 km, Tunisia 965 km, Western Sahara 42 km
Coastline: 998 km
Maritime claims: *territorial sea:* 12 nm
exclusive fishing zone: 32-52 nm
Climate: arid to semiarid; mild, wet winters with hot, dry summers along coast; drier with cold winters and hot summers on high plateau; sirocco is a hot, dust/sand-laden wind especially common in summer
Terrain: mostly high plateau and desert; some mountains; narrow, discontinuous coastal plain
Elevation extremes: *lowest point:* Chott Melrhir -40 m
highest point: Tahat 3,003 m
Natural resources: petroleum, natural gas, iron ore, phosphates, uranium, lead, zinc
Land use: *arable land:* 3.15%
permanent crops: 0.38%
other: 96.46% (2011)
Irrigated land: 5,694 sq km (2003)
Total renewable water resources: 11.67 cu km (2011)
Freshwater withdrawal (domestic/industrial/agricultural): *total:* 5.72 cu km/yr (26%/16%/58%)
per capita: 182 cu m/yr (2005)
Natural hazards: mountainous areas subject to severe earthquakes; mudslides and floods in rainy season
Environment—current issues: soil erosion from overgrazing and other poor farming practices; desertification; dumping of raw sewage, petroleum refining wastes, and other industrial effluents is leading to the pollution of rivers and coastal waters; Mediterranean Sea, in particular, becoming polluted from oil wastes, soil erosion, and fertilizer runoff; inadequate supplies of potable water
Environment—international agreements: *party to:* Biodiversity, Climate Change, Climate Change-Kyoto Protocol, Desertification, Endangered Species, Environmental Modification, Hazardous Wastes, Law of the Sea, Ozone Layer Protection, Ship Pollution, Wetlands
signed, but not ratified: none of the selected agreements
Geography—note: largest country in Africa

PEOPLE AND SOCIETY

Nationality: *noun:* Algerian(s)
adjective: Algerian
Ethnic groups: Arab-Berber 99%, European less than 1%
note: although almost all Algerians are Berber in origin (not Arab), only a minority identify themselves as Berber, about 15% of the total population; these people live mostly in the mountainous region of Kabylie east of Algiers; the Berbers are also Muslim but identify with their Berber rather than Arab cultural heritage; Berbers have long agitated, sometimes violently, for autonomy; the government is unlikely to grant autonomy but has offered to begin sponsoring teaching Berber language in schools
Languages: Arabic (official), French (lingua franca), Berber dialects: Kabylie Berber (Tamazight), Chaouia Berber (Tachawit), Mzab Berber, Tuareg Berber (Tamahaq)
Religions: Muslim (official; predominantly Sunni) 99%, other (includes Christian and Jewish)
Population: 38,813,722 (July 2014 est.)
country comparison to the world: 34
Age structure: *0-14 years:* 28.4% (male 5,641,148/female 5,378,207)
15-24 years: 17.4% (male 3,451,069/female 3,291,166)
25-54 years: 42.8% (male 8,398,770/female 8,209,634)
55-64 years: 5.2% (male 1,230,865/female 1,186,832)
65 years and over: 5.1% (male 931,769/female 1,094,262) (2014 est.)
Dependency ratios: *total dependency ratio:* 47.9 %
youth dependency ratio: 41.1%
elderly dependency ratio: 6.8%
potential support ratio: 14.7 (2013)
Median age: *total:* 27.3 years
male: 27 years
female: 27.5 years (2014 est.)
Population growth rate: 1.88% (2014 est.)
country comparison to the world: 61
Birth rate: 23.99 births/1,000 population (2014 est.)
country comparison to the world: 63
Death rate: 4.31 deaths/1,000 population (2014 est.)
country comparison to the world: 206
Net migration rate: -0.93 migrant(s)/1,000 population (2014 est.)
country comparison to the world: 148
Urbanization: *urban population:* 73% of total population (2011)
rate of urbanization: 2.49% annual rate of change (2010-15 est.)
Major urban areas—population: ALGIERS (capital) 2.916 million; Oran 770,000 (2011)
Sex ratio: *at birth:* 1.05 male(s)/female
0-14 years: 1.05 male(s)/female
15-24 years: 1.05 male(s)/female
25-54 years: 1.02 male(s)/female
55-64 years: 1.03 male(s)/female
65 years and over: 0.84 male(s)/female
total population: 1.03 male(s)/female (2014 est.)
Maternal mortality rate: 97 deaths/100,000 live births (2010)
country comparison to the world: 75
Infant mortality rate: *total:* 21.76 deaths/1,000 live births
country comparison to the world: 82
male: 23.54 deaths/1,000 live births
female: 19.9 deaths/1,000 live births (2014 est.)
Life expectancy at birth: *total population:* 76.39 years
country comparison to the world: 80
male: 75.12 years
female: 77.72 years (2014 est.)
Total fertility rate: 2.78 children born/woman (2014 est.)
country comparison to the world: 69
Contraceptive prevalence rate: 61.4% (2006)
Health expenditures: 3.9% of GDP (2011)
country comparison to the world: 166
Physicians density: 1.21 physicians/1,000 population (2007)
Hospital bed density: 1.7 beds/1,000 population (2004)
Drinking water source:
Improved:
urban: 85.5% of population
rural: 79.5% of population
total: 83.9% of population
Unimproved:
urban: 14.5% of population
rural: 20.5% of population
total: 16.1% of population (2011 est.)
Sanitation facility access:
Improved:
urban: 97.6% of population
rural: 88.4% of population
total: 95.1% of population
Unimproved:
urban: 2.4% of population
rural: 11.6% of population
total: 4.9% of population (2011 est.)
HIV/AIDS—adult prevalence rate: 0.1%; note—no country specific models provided (2009 est.)
country comparison to the world: 124
HIV/AIDS—people living with HIV/AIDS: 18,000 (2009 est.)
country comparison to the world: 84
HIV/AIDS—deaths: fewer than 1,000 (2009 est.)
country comparison to the world: 75
Obesity—adult prevalence rate: 16% (2008)
country comparison to the world: 116
Children under the age of 5 years underweight: 3.7% (2005)
country comparison to the world: 101
Education expenditures: 4.3% of GDP (2008)
country comparison to the world: 97
Literacy: *definition:* age 15 and over can read and write
total population: 72.6%
male: 81.3%
female: 63.9% (2006 est.)
School life expectancy (primary to tertiary education): *total:* 14 years
male: 12 years
female: 14 years (2011)
Child labor—children ages 5-14:
total number: 304,358
percentage: 5 % (2006 est.)
Unemployment, youth ages 15-24: *total:* 28.4%
country comparison to the world: 30
male: 19.1%
female: 38.2% (2011)

GOVERNMENT

Country name: *conventional long form:* People's Democratic Republic of Algeria
conventional short form: Algeria
local long form: Al Jumhuriyah al Jaza'iriyah ad Dimuqratiyah ash Sha'biyah
local short form: Al Jaza'ir
Government type: republic
Capital: *name:* Algiers
geographic coordinates: 36 45 N, 3 03 E
time difference: UTC+1 (6 hours ahead of Washington, DC during Standard Time)
Administrative divisions: 48 provinces (wilayas, singular—wilaya); Adrar, Ain Defla, Ain Temouchent, Alger, Annaba, Batna, Bechar,

Bejaia, Biskra, Blida, Bordj Bou Arreridj, Bouira, Boumerdes, Chlef, Constantine, Djelfa, El Bayadh, El Oued, El Tarf, Ghardaia, Guelma, Illizi, Jijel, Khenchela, Laghouat, Mascara, Medea, Mila, Mostaganem, M'Sila, Naama, Oran, Ouargla, Oum el Bouaghi, Relizane, Saida, Setif, Sidi Bel Abbes, Skikda, Souk Ahras, Tamanrasset, Tebessa, Tiaret, Tindouf, Tipaza, Tissemsilt, Tizi Ouzou, Tlemcen

Independence: 5 July 1962 (from France)

National holiday: Revolution Day, 1 November (1954)

Constitution: adopted 8 September 1963; amended several times, last in 2008 (2013)

Legal system: mixed legal system of French civil law and Islamic law; judicial review of legislative acts in ad hoc Constitutional Council composed of various public officials including several Supreme Court justices

International law organization participation: has not submitted an ICJ jurisdiction declaration; non-party state to the ICCt

Suffrage: 18 years of age; universal

Executive branch: *chief of state:* President Abdelaziz BOUTEFLIKA (since 28 April 1999)
head of government: Prime Minister (Acting) Youcef YOUSFI (since 13 March 2014)
cabinet: Cabinet of Ministers appointed by the president (For more information visit the World Leaders website)
elections: president elected by popular vote for a five-year term (no term limits); election last held on 17 April 2014 (next to be held in April 2019)
election results: Abdelaziz BOUTEFLIKA reelected president for a fourth term; percent of vote—Abdelaziz BOUTEFLIKA 81.5%, Ali BENFLIS 12.2%, Abdelaziz ELAID 3.4%, other 2.9%; voter turnout—51.7%

Legislative branch: bicameral Parliament consists of the Council of the Nation (upper house; 144 seats; one-third of the members appointed by the president, two-thirds elected by indirect vote to serve six-year terms; the constitution requires half the Council to be renewed every three years) and the National People's Assembly (lower house; 462 seats; members elected by popular vote to serve five-year terms)
elections: Council of the Nation—last held on 29 December 2012 (next to be held in December 2017); National People's Assembly—last held on 10 May 2012 (next to be held in 2017)
election results: Council of the Nation election of 29 December 2009—percent of vote by party—NA; seats by party—NA; National People's Assembly election of 10 May 2012—percent of vote by party—NA; seats by party—FLN 221, RND 70, AAV 47, FFS 21, PT 17, FNA 9, El Adala 7, MPA 6, PFJ 5, FC 4, PNSD 4, other 32, independents 19

Judicial branch: *highest court(s):* Supreme Court or Cour Supreme (consists of 150 judges organized into four divisions: civil and commercial; social security and labor; criminal; and administrative; Constitutional Council (consists of 9 members including the court president) note—Algeria's judicial system does not include sharia courts
judge selection and term of office: Supreme Court judges appointed by the High Council of Magistracy, an administrative body presided over by the president of the republic, and includes the republic vice-president and several members; judge tenure NA; Constitutional Council members—3 appointed by the president of the republic, 2 each by the two houses of the Parliament, 1 by the Supreme Court, and 1 by the Council of State; Council president and members appointed for single 6-year terms with half of the membership renewed every 3 years
subordinate courts: appellate or wilaya courts; first instance or daira tribunals

Political parties and leaders: Algerian National Front or FNA [Moussa TOUATI]; Algerian Popular Movement or MPA [Amara BENYOUNES]; Algerian Rally [Ali ZAGHDOUD]; Algeria's Hope Rally or TAJ [Amar GHOUL]; Dignity or El Karama [Mohamed BENHAMOU]; Front for Change or FC [Abdelmadjid MENASRA]; Front for Justice and Development or El Adala [Abdallah DJABALLAH]; Future Front or El Mostakbel [Abdelaziz BELAID]; Green Algeria Alliance or AAV (includes Movement for National Reform, Islamic Renaissance Movement, and Movement of the Society of Peace or Hamas); Islamic Renaissance Movement or EnNahda Movement [Mohamed DHOUIBI]; Movement of the Society of Peace or MSP [Abderrazak MOKRI]; National Democratic Rally (Rassemblement National Democratique) or RND [Bensalah ABDELKADER]; National Liberation Front or FLN [Amar SAIDANI]; National Party for Solidarity and Development or PNSD; National Reform Movement or Islah [Djahid YOUNSI] (see Green Algeria Alliance); New Dawn Party or PFJ; New Generation or Jil Jadid [Soufiane DJILALI]; New Light Party [Bedreddine BELBAZ]; Oath of 1954 or Ahd 54 [Ali Fawzi REBAINE]; Party of Justice and Liberty [Mohammed SAID]; Rally for Culture and Democracy or RCD [Mohcine BELABBAS]; Socialist Forces Front or FFS [Mustafa BOUCHACHI]; Workers Party or PT [Louisa HANOUNE]
note: a law banning political parties based on religion was enacted in March 1997

Political pressure groups and leaders: The Algerian Human Rights League or LADDH [Noureddine BENISSAD]; SOS Disparus [Nacera DUTOUR]; Youth Action Rally or RAJ

International organization participation: ABEDA, AfDB, AFESD, AMF, AMU, AU, BIS, CAEU, CD, FAO, G-15, G-24, G-77, IAEA, IBRD, ICAO, ICC (national committees), ICRM, IDA, IDB, IFAD, IFC, IFRCS, IHO, ILO, IMF, IMO, IMSO, Interpol, IOC, IOM, IPU, ISO, ITSO, ITU, ITUC (NGOs), LAS, MIGA, MONUSCO, NAM, OAPEC, OAS (observer), OIC, OPCW, OPEC, OSCE (partner), UN, UNCTAD, UNESCO, UNHCR, UNIDO, UNITAR, UNWTO, UPU, WCO, WHO, WIPO, WMO, WTO (observer)

Diplomatic representation in the US: *chief of mission:* Ambassador Abdallah BAALI (since 5 November 2008)
chancery: 2118 Kalorama Road NW, Washington, DC 20008
telephone: [1] (202) 265-2800
FAX: [1] (202) 986-5906
consulate(s) general: New York

Diplomatic representation from the US: chief of mission: Ambassador Henry S. ENSHER (since July 2011)
embassy: 05 Chemin Cheikh Bachir, El-Ibrahimi, El-Biar 16030 Algiers
mailing address: B. P. 408, Alger-Gare, 16030 Algiers
telephone: [213] 770-08-2000
FAX: [213] 770-08-2064

Flag description: two equal vertical bands of green (hoist side) and white; a red, five-pointed star within a red crescent centered over the two-color boundary; the colors represent Islam (green), purity and peace (white), and liberty (red); the crescent and star are also Islamic symbols, but the crescent is more closed than those of other Muslim countries because the Algerians believe the long crescent horns bring happiness

National symbol(s): star and crescent; fennec fox

National anthem: name: "Kassaman" (We Pledge)
lyrics/music: Mufdi ZAKARIAH/Mohamed FAWZI
note: adopted 1962; ZAKARIAH wrote "Kassaman" as a poem while imprisoned in Algiers by French colonial forces

ECONOMY

Economy—overview: Algeria's economy remains dominated by the state, a legacy of the country's socialist postindependence development model. In recent years the Algerian Government has halted the privatization of state-owned industries and imposed restrictions on imports and foreign involvement in its economy. Hydrocarbons have long been the backbone of the economy, accounting for roughly 60% of budget revenues, 30% of GDP, and over 95% of export earnings. Algeria has the 10th-largest reserves of natural gas in the world and is the sixth-largest gas exporter. It ranks 16th in oil reserves. Strong revenues from hydrocarbon exports have brought Algeria relative macroeconomic stability, with foreign currency reserves approaching $200 billion and a large budget stabilization fund available for tapping. In addition, Algeria's external debt is extremely low at about 2% of GDP. However, Algeria has struggled to develop non-hydrocarbon industries because of heavy regulation and an emphasis on state-driven growth. The government's efforts have done little to reduce high youth unemployment rates or to address housing shortages. A wave of economic protests in February and March 2011 prompted the Algerian Government to offer more than $23 billion in public grants and retroactive salary and benefit increases, moves which continue to weigh on public finances. Long-term economic challenges include diversifying the economy away from its reliance on hydrocarbon exports, bolstering the private sector, attracting foreign investment, and providing adequate jobs for younger Algerians.

GDP (purchasing power parity): $284.7 billion (2013 est.)
country comparison to the world: 46
$276.2 billion (2012 est.)
$267.4 billion (2011 est.)
note: data are in 2013 US dollars

GDP (official exchange rate): $215.7 billion (2013 est.)

GDP—real growth rate: 3.1% (2013 est.)
country comparison to the world: 110
3.3% (2012 est.)
2.6% (2011 est.)

GDP—per capita (PPP): $7,500 (2013 est.)
country comparison to the world: 137
$7,400 (2012 est.)
$7,300 (2011 est.)
note: data are in 2013 US dollars

Gross national saving: 45.5% of GDP (2013 est.)
country comparison to the world: 7
44.4% of GDP (2012 est.)
47.7% of GDP (2011 est.)

GDP—composition, by end use: *household consumption:* 33.7%
government consumption: 20.6%
investment in fixed capital: 32.9%
investment in inventories: 8.2%
exports of goods and services: 33.3%
imports of goods and services: -28.7% (2013 est.)

GDP—composition, by sector of origin:
agriculture: 9.4%
industry: 62.6%
services: 28% (2013 est.)

Agriculture—products: wheat, barley, oats, grapes, olives, citrus, fruits; sheep, cattle

Industries: petroleum, natural gas, light industries, mining, electrical, petrochemical, food processing

Industrial production growth rate: 2.5% (2013 est.)
country comparison to the world: 120

Labor force: 11.15 million (2013 est.)
country comparison to the world: 48

Labor force—by occupation: *agriculture:* 14%
industry: 13.4%

construction and public works: 10%
trade: 14.6%
government: 32%
other: 16% (2003 est.)

Unemployment rate: 10.3% (2013 est.)
country comparison to the world: 109
10.7% (2012 est.)

Population below poverty line: 23% (2006 est.)

Household income or consumption by percentage share: *lowest 10%:* 2.8%
highest 10%: 26.8% (1995)

Distribution of family income—Gini index: 35.3 (1995)
country comparison to the world: 89

Budget: *revenues:* $80.55 billion
expenditures: $85.58 billion (2013 est.)

Taxes and other revenues: 37.3% of GDP (2013 est.)
country comparison to the world: 53

Budget surplus (+) or deficit (-): -2.3% of GDP (2013 est.)
country comparison to the world: 92

Public debt: 13.2% of GDP (2013 est.)
country comparison to the world: 146
8.3% of GDP (2012 est.)
note: data cover central government debt; the data include debt issued by subnational entities, as well as intra-governmental debt

Fiscal year: calendar year

Inflation rate (consumer prices): 3.9% (2013 est.)
country comparison to the world: 131
8.9% (2012 est.)

Central bank discount rate: 4% (31 December 2010 est.)
country comparison to the world: 93
4% (31 December 2009 est.)

Commercial bank prime lending rate: 8% (31 December 2013 est.)
country comparison to the world: 116
8% (31 December 2012 est.)

Stock of narrow money: $92.91 billion (31 December 2013 est.)
country comparison to the world: 37
$98.36 billion (31 December 2012 est.)

Stock of broad money: $140.2 billion (31 December 2013 est.)
country comparison to the world: 48
$141 billion (31 December 2012 est.)

Stock of domestic credit: $-4.337 billion (31 December 2013 est.)
country comparison to the world: 188
$-4.363 billion (31 December 2012 est.)

Market value of publicly traded shares: $NA

Current account balance: $6.697 billion (2013 est.)
country comparison to the world: 29
$12.3 billion (2012 est.)

Exports: $68.25 billion (2013 est.)
country comparison to the world: 51
$71.74 billion (2012 est.)

Exports—commodities: petroleum, natural gas, and petroleum products 97%

Exports—partners: Italy 16%, US 15%, Spain 10.9%, France 8.5%, Netherlands 7.3%, Canada 7.1%, UK 5.1%, Brazil 4.7% (2012)

Imports: $55.02 billion (2013 est.)
country comparison to the world: 53
$51.57 billion (2012 est.)

Imports—commodities: capital goods, foodstuffs, consumer goods

Imports—partners: France 12.8%, China 11.8%, Italy 10.3%, Spain 8.6%, Germany 5.2% (2012)

Reserves of foreign exchange and gold: $192.5 billion (31 December 2013 est.)
country comparison to the world: 14
$191.6 billion (31 December 2012 est.)

Debt—external: $5.278 billion (31 December 2013 est.)
country comparison to the world: 120
$5.639 billion (31 December 2012 est.)

Stock of direct foreign investment—at home: $25.02 billion (31 December 2013 est.)
country comparison to the world: 67
$23.26 billion (31 December 2012 est.)

Stock of direct foreign investment—abroad: $2.433 billion (31 December 2013 est.)
country comparison to the world: 71
$2.133 billion (31 December 2012 est.)

Exchange rates: Algerian dinars (DZD) per US dollar—
78.77 (2013 est.)
77.536 (2012 est.)
74.386 (2010 est.)
72.65 (2009)
63.25 (2008)

ENERGY

Electricity—production: 46.25 billion kWh (2011 est.)
country comparison to the world: 53

Electricity—consumption: 33.68 billion kWh (2010 est.)
country comparison to the world: 59

Electricity—exports: 803 million kWh (2010 est.)
country comparison to the world: 60

Electricity—imports: 736 million kWh (2010 est.)
country comparison to the world: 66

Electricity—installed generating capacity: 11.33 million kW (2010 est.)
country comparison to the world: 51

Electricity—from fossil fuels: 97.5% of total installed capacity (2010 est.)
country comparison to the world: 61

Electricity—from nuclear fuels: 0% of total installed capacity (2010 est.)
country comparison to the world: 35

Electricity—from hydroelectric plants: 2.5% of total installed capacity (2010 est.)
country comparison to the world: 133

Electricity—from other renewable sources: 0% of total installed capacity (2010 est.)
country comparison to the world: 149

Crude oil—production: 1.875 million bbl/day (2012 est.)
country comparison to the world: 15

Crude oil—exports: 1.097 million bbl/day (2010 est.)
country comparison to the world: 16

Crude oil—imports: 6,400 bbl/day (2010 est.)
country comparison to the world: 79

Crude oil—proved reserves: 12.2 billion bbl (1 January 2013 es)
country comparison to the world: 16

Refined petroleum products—production: 571,400 bbl/day (2010 est.)
country comparison to the world: 29

Refined petroleum products—consumption: 316,400 bbl/day (2011 est.)
country comparison to the world: 40

Refined petroleum products—exports: 471,900 bbl/day (2010 est.)
country comparison to the world: 15

Refined petroleum products—imports: 17,270 bbl/day (2010 est.)
country comparison to the world: 110

Natural gas—production: 82.76 billion cu m (2011 est.)
country comparison to the world: 10

Natural gas—consumption: 28.82 billion cu m (2010 est.)
country comparison to the world: 29

Natural gas—exports: 52.02 billion cu m (2011 est.)
country comparison to the world: 7

Natural gas—imports: 0 cu m (2011 est.)
country comparison to the world: 151

Natural gas—proved reserves: 4.504 trillion cu m (1 January 2013 es)
country comparison to the world: 10

Carbon dioxide emissions from consumption of energy: 117.2 million Mt (2011 est.)
country comparison to the world: 37

COMMUNICATIONS

Telephones—main lines in use: 3.2 million (2012)
country comparison to the world: 49

Telephones—mobile cellular: 37.692 million (2012)
country comparison to the world: 32

Telephone system: *general assessment:* privatization of Algeria's telecommunications sector began in 2000; three mobile cellular licenses have been issued and, in 2005, a consortium led by Egypt's Orascom Telecom won a 15-year license to build and operate a fixed-line network in Algeria; the license will allow Orascom to develop high-speed data and other specialized services and contribute to meeting the large unfulfilled demand for basic residential telephony; Internet broadband services began in 2003
domestic: a limited network of fixed lines with a teledensity of less than 10 telephones per 100 persons has been offset by the rapid increase in mobile-cellular subscribership; in 2011, mobile-cellular teledensity was roughly 100 telephones per 100 persons
international: country code—213; landing point for the SEA-ME-WE-4 fiber-optic submarine cable system that provides links to Europe, the Middle East, and Asia; microwave radio relay to Italy, France, Spain,Morocco, and Tunisia; coaxial cable to Morocco and Tunisia; participant in Medarabtel; satellite earth stations—51 (Intelsat, Intersputnik, and Arabsat) (2011)

Broadcast media: state-run Radio-Television Algerienne operates the broadcast media and carries programming in Arabic, Berber dialects, and French; use of satellite dishes is widespread, providing easy access to European and Arab satellite stations; state-run radio operates several national networks and roughly 40 regional radio stations (2007)

Internet country code: .dz

Internet hosts: 676 (2012)
country comparison to the world: 178

Internet users: 4.7 million (2009)
country comparison to the world: 49

TRANSPORTATION

Airports: 157 (2013)
country comparison to the world: 36

Airports—with paved runways: *total:* 64
over 3,047 m: 12
2,438 to 3,047 m: 29
1,524 to 2,437 m: 17
914 to 1,523 m: 5
under 914 m: 1 (2013)

Airports—with unpaved runways: *total:* 93
2,438 to 3,047 m: 2
1,524 to 2,437 m: 18
914 to 1,523 m: 39
under 914 m: 34 (2013)

Heliports: 3 (2013)

Pipelines: condensate 2,600 km; gas 16,415 km; liquid petroleum gas 3,447 km; oil 7,036 km; refined products 144 km (2013)

Railways: *total:* 3,973 km
country comparison to the world: 45
standard gauge: 2,888 km 1.435-m gauge (283 km electrified)
narrow gauge: 1,085 km 1.055-m gauge (2008)

Roadways: *total:* 113,655 km
country comparison to the world: 42
paved: 87,605 km (includes 645 km of expressways)
unpaved: 26,050 km (2010)

Merchant marine: *total:* 38
country comparison to the world: 77
by type: bulk carrier 6, cargo 8, chemical tanker 3, liquefied gas 11, passenger/cargo 3, petroleum tanker 4,roll on/roll off 3
foreign-owned: 15 (UK, 15) (2010)

Ports and terminals: *major seaport(s):* Algiers, Annaba, Arzew, Bejaia, Djendjene, Jijel, Mostaganem, Oran, Skikda

MILITARY

Military branches: People's National Army (Armee Nationale Populaire, ANP), Land Forces (Forces Terrestres, FT), Navy of the Republic of Algeria (Marine de la Republique Algerienne, MRA), Air Force (Al-Quwwat al-Jawwiya al-Jaza'eriya, QJJ), Territorial Air Defense Force (2009)

Military service age and obligation: 17 is the legal minimum age for voluntary military service; 19-30 years of age for compulsory service; conscript service obligation is 18 months (6 months basic training, 12 months civil projects) (2012)

Manpower available for military service: *males age 16-49:* 10,273,129
females age 16-49: 10,114,552 (2010 est.)

Manpower fit for military service: *males age 16-49:* 8,622,897
females age 16-49: 8,626,222 (2010 est.)

Manpower reaching militarily significant age annually: *male:* 342,895
female: 330,098 (2010 est.)

Military expenditures: 4.48% of GDP (2012)
country comparison to the world: 7
4.36% of GDP (2011)
4.48% of GDP (2010)

TRANSNATIONAL ISSUES

Disputes—international: Algeria and many other states reject Moroccan administration of Western Sahara; the Polisario Front, exiled in Algeria, represents the Sahrawi Arab Democratic Republic; Algeria's border with Morocco remains an irritant to bilateral relations, each nation accusing the other of harboring militants and arms smuggling; dormant disputes include Libyan claims of about 32,000 sq km still reflected on its maps of southeastern Algeria and the National Liberation Front's (FLN) assertions of a claim to Chirac Pastures in southeastern Morocco

Refugees and internally displaced persons: *refugees (country of origin):* 90,000 (Western Saharan Sahrawi, mostly living in Algerian-sponsored camps in the southwestern Algerian town of Tindouf); 1,500 (Mali) (2013)
IDPs: undetermined (civil war during 1990s) (2012)

Trafficking in persons: *current situation:* Algeria is a transit and, to a lesser extent, a destination and source country for women, and, to a lesser extent, men subjected to forced labor and sex trafficking; criminal networks, which sometimes extend to sub-Saharan Africa and to Europe, are involved in both human smuggling and trafficking; sub-Saharan adults enter Algeria voluntarily but illegally, often with the aid of smugglers, for onward travel to Europe, but some of the women are forced into prostitution; some Algerian women are also forced into prostitution; some sub-Saharan men, mostly from Mali, are forced into domestic servitude
tier rating: Tier 3—Algeria does not fully comply with the minimum standards for the elimination of trafficking and is not making significant efforts to do so; the government has not held any perpetrators of sex trafficking or forced labor accountable with jail time; some trafficking victims are treated as illegal migrants and are subject to arrest, detention, and deportation because authorities continue to confuse human trafficking and smuggling; the government has not developed or employed systematic procedures for identifying trafficking victims and referring them for protective services; no public awareness campaigns are conducted and no plan of action was developed to complement Algeria's anti-trafficking law (2013)

AMERICAN SAMOA

INTRODUCTION

Background: Settled as early as 1000 B.C., Samoa was not reached by European explorers until the 18th century. International rivalries in the latter half of the 19th century were settled by an 1899 treaty in which Germany and the US divided the Samoan archipelago. The US formally occupied its portion—a smaller group of eastern islands with the excellent harbor of Pago Pago—the following year.

GEOGRAPHY

Location: Oceania, group of islands in the South Pacific Ocean, about half way between Hawaii and New Zealand

Geographic coordinates: 14 20 S, 170 00 W

Map references: Oceania

Area: *total:* 199 sq km
country comparison to the world: 216
land: 199 sq km
water: 0 sq km
note: includes Rose Island and Swains Island

Area—comparative: slightly larger than Washington, DC

Land boundaries: 0 km

Coastline: 116 km

Maritime claims: *territorial sea:* 12 nm
exclusive economic zone: 200 nm

Climate: tropical marine, moderated by southeast trade winds; annual rainfall averages about 3 m; rainy season (November to April), dry season (May to October); little seasonal temperature variation

Terrain: five volcanic islands with rugged peaks and limited coastal plains, two coral atolls (Rose Island, Swains Island)

Elevation extremes: *lowest point:* Pacific Ocean 0 m
highest point: Lata Mountain 964 m

Natural resources: pumice, pumicite

Land use: *arable land:* 9.5%
permanent crops: 15%
other: 75.5% (2011)

Irrigated land: NA

Natural hazards: typhoons common from December to March
volcanism: limited volcanic activity on the Ofu and Olosega Islands; neither has erupted since the 19th century

Environment—current issues: limited natural freshwater resources; the water division of the government has spent substantial funds in the past few years to improve water catchments and pipelines

Geography—note: Pago Pago has one of the best natural deepwater harbors in the South Pacific Ocean, sheltered by shape from rough seas and protected by peripheral mountains from high winds; strategic location in the South Pacific Ocean

PEOPLE AND SOCIETY

Nationality: *noun:* American Samoan(s) (US nationals)
adjective: American Samoan

Ethnic groups: Native Hawaiian and other Pacific Islander 91.6%, Asian 1%, white 1.1%, mixed 4.2%, other 0.3% (2000 est.)

Languages: Samoan 90.6% (closely related to Hawaiian and other Polynesian languages), English 2.9%, Tongan 2.4%, other Pacific islander 2.1%, other 2%
note: most people are bilingual (2000 census)

Religions: Christian Congregationalist 50%, Roman Catholic 20%, Protestant and other 30%

Population: 54,517 (July 2014 est.)
country comparison to the world: 208

Age structure: *0-14 years:* 24.9% (male 6,671/female 6,917)
15-24 years: 20.2% (male 5,468/female 5,565)
25-54 years: 41.7% (male 11,694/female 11,056)
55-64 years: 4.9% (male 2,211/female 2,260)
65 years and over: 4.7% (male 1,234/female 1,441) (2014 est.)

Median age: *total:* 28.3 years
male: 28.8 years
female: 27.8 years (2014 est.)

Population growth rate: -0.35% (2014 est.)
country comparison to the world: 219

Birth rate: 22.87 births/1,000 population (2014 est.)
country comparison to the world: 72

Death rate: 4.68 deaths/1,000 population (2014 est.)
country comparison to the world: 199

Net migration rate: -21.64 migrant(s)/1,000 population (2014 est.)
country comparison to the world: 221

Urbanization: *urban population:* 93% of total population (2010)
rate of urbanization: 1.8% annual rate of change (2010-15 est.)

Major urban areas—population: PAGO PAGO (capital) 64,000 (2011)

Sex ratio: *at birth:* 1.06 male(s)/female
0-14 years: 0.96 male(s)/female
15-24 years: 0.98 male(s)/female
25-54 years: 1.06 male(s)/female
55-64 years: 1 male(s)/female
65 years and over: 0.86 male(s)/female
total population: 1.01 male(s)/female (2014 est.)

Infant mortality rate: *total:* 8.92 deaths/1,000 live births
country comparison to the world: 150
male: 11.47 deaths/1,000 live births
female: 6.21 deaths/1,000 live births (2014 est.)

Life expectancy at birth: *total population:* 74.91 years
country comparison to the world: 104
male: 71.96 years
female: 78.04 years (2014 est.)

Total fertility rate: 2.98 children born/woman (2014 est.)
country comparison to the world: 57

Drinking water source:
improved:
urban: 100% of population
rural: 100% of population
total: 100% of population
unimproved:
urban: 0% of population
rural: 0% of population
total: 0% of population (2011 est.)

Sanitation facility access:
improved:
urban: 96.9% of population
rural: 96.9% of population
total: 96.9% of population
unimproved:
urban: 3.1% of population
rural: 3.1% of population
total: 3.1% of population (2011 est.)

HIV/AIDS—adult prevalence rate: NA

HIV/AIDS—people living with HIV/AIDS: NA

HIV/AIDS—deaths: NA

Obesity—adult prevalence rate: 74.6% (2007)
country comparison to the world: 1

Literacy: *definition:* age 15 and over can read and write
total population: 97%
male: 98%
female: 97% (1980 est.)

GOVERNMENT

Country name: *conventional long form:* Territory of American Samoa
conventional short form: American Samoa
abbreviation: AS

Dependency status: unincorporated and unorganized territory of the US; administered by the Office of Insular Affairs, US Department of the Interior

Government type: NA

Capital: *name:* Pago Pago
geographic coordinates: 14 16 S, 170 42 W
time difference: UTC-11 (6 hours behind Washington, DC during Standard Time)

Administrative divisions: none (territory of the US); there are no first-order administrative divisions as defined by the US Government, but there are three districts and two islands* at the second order; Eastern, Manu'a, Rose Island*, Swains Island*, Western

Independence: none (territory of the US)

National holiday: Flag Day, 17 April (1900)

Constitution: ratified 2 June 1966, effective 1 July 1967 (2013)

Legal system: mixed legal system of US common law and customary law

Suffrage: 18 years of age; universal

Executive branch: *chief of state:* President Barack H. OBAMA (since 20 January 2009); Vice President Joseph R. BIDEN (since 20 January 2009)
head of government: Governor Lolo Matalasi MOLIGA (since 3 January 2013)
cabinet: Cabinet made up of 12 department directors (For more information visit the World Leaders website)
elections: under the US Constitution, residents of unincorporated territories, such as American Samoa, do not vote in elections for US president and vice president; however, they may vote in Democratic and Republican presidential primary elections; governor and lieutenant governor elected on the same ticket by popular vote for four-year terms (eligible for a second term); election last held on 6 November 2012 with a runoff election held on 20 November 2012 (next to be held in November 2016)
election results: runoff election percent of vote—Lolo Matalasi MOLIGA 52.9%, Faoa Aitofele SUNIA 47.1%

Legislative branch: bicameral Fono or Legislative Assembly consists of the Senate (18 seats; members are elected from local chiefs to serve four-year terms) and the House of Representatives (21 seats; 20 members are elected by popular vote and 1 is an appointed, nonvoting delegate from Swains Island; members serve two-year terms)
elections: House of Representatives—last held on 6 November 2012 (next to be held in November 2014); Senate—last held on 6 November 2012 (next to be held in November 2016)
election results: House of Representatives—percent of vote by party—NA; seats by party—independents 20; Senate—percent of vote by party—NA; seats by party—independents 18
note: American Samoa elects one nonvoting representative to the US House of Representatives; election last held on 6 November 2012 (next to be held in November 2014); results—Eni F. H. FALEOMAVAEGA reelected as delegate

Judicial branch: highest court(s): High Court of American Samoa (consists of the chief justice, associate chief justice, and 6 Samoan associate judges and organized into trial, family, drug, and appellate divisions) note—American Samoa has no US federal courts
judge selection and term of office: chief justice and associate chief justice appointed by the US Secretary of the Interior to serve for life; Samoan associate judges appointed by the governor to serve for life
subordinate courts: district and village courts

Political parties and leaders: Democratic Party [Oreta M. TOGAFAU]; Republican Party [Tautai A. F. FAALEVAO]

Political pressure groups and leaders: Population Pressure LAS (addresses the growing population pressures)

International organization participation: AOSIS, Interpol (subbureau), IOC, PIF (observer), SPC, UPU

Diplomatic representation in the US: none (territory of the US)

Diplomatic representation from the US: none (territory of the US)

Flag description: blue, with a white triangle edged in red that is based on the fly side and extends to the hoist side; a brown and white American bald eagle flying toward the hoist side is carrying two traditional Samoan symbols of authority, a war club known as a "Fa'alaufa'i" (upper; left talon), and a coconut fiber fly whisk known as a "Fue" (lower; right talon); the combination of symbols broadly mimics that seen on the US Great Seal and reflects the relationship between the United States and American Samoa

National anthem: *name:* "Amerika Samoa" (American Samoa)
lyrics/music: Mariota Tiumalu TUIASOSOPO/Napoleon Andrew TUITELELEAPAGA
note: local anthem adopted 1950; as a territory of the United States, "The Star-Spangled Banner" is official (see United States)

ECONOMY

Economy—overview: American Samoa has a traditional Polynesian economy in which more than 90% of the land is communally owned. Economic activity is strongly linked to the US with which American Samoa conducts most of its commerce. Tuna fishing and tuna processing plants are the backbone of the private sector with canned tuna the primary export. The two tuna canneries account for 80% of employment. In late September 2009, an earthquake and the resulting tsunami devastated American Samoa and nearby Samoa, disrupting transportation and power generation, and resulting in about 200 deaths. The US Federal Emergency Management Agency is overseeing a relief program of nearly $25 million. Transfers from the US Government add substantially to American Samoa's economic well being. Attempts by the government to develop a larger and broader economy are restrained by Samoa's remote location, its limited transportation, and its devastating hurricanes. Tourism is a promising developing sector.

GDP (purchasing power parity): $575.3 million (2007 est.)
country comparison to the world: 214
$510.1 million (2003 est.)

GDP (official exchange rate): $462.2 million (2005)

GDP—real growth rate: 3% (2003)
country comparison to the world: 114

GDP—per capita (PPP): $8,000 (2007 est.)
country comparison to the world: 134
$5,800 (2005 est.)

GDP—composition, by sector of origin:
agriculture: NA%
industry: NA%
services: NA%

Agriculture—products: bananas, coconuts, vegetables, taro, breadfruit, yams, copra, pineapples, papayas; dairy products, livestock

Industries: tuna canneries (largely supplied by foreign fishing vessels), handicrafts

Industrial production growth rate: NA%

Labor force: 17,630 (2005)
country comparison to the world: 211

Unemployment rate: 29.8% (2005)
country comparison to the world: 180

Population below poverty line: NA%

Household income or consumption by percentage share: *lowest 10%:* NA%
highest 10%: NA%

Budget: *revenues:* $155.4 million (2007)
expenditures: $183.6 million (2007)

Taxes and other revenues: 33.6% of GDP (2007)
country comparison to the world: 70

Budget surplus (+) or deficit (-): -6.1% of GDP (2007)
country comparison to the world: 180

Fiscal year: 1 October—30 September

Inflation rate (consumer prices): NA%

Exports: $445.6 million (FY04 est.)
country comparison to the world: 177

Exports—commodities: canned tuna 93%

Imports: $308.8 million (FY04 est.)
country comparison to the world: 199

Imports—commodities: raw materials for canneries, food, petroleum products, machinery and parts

Debt—external: $NA

Exchange rates: the US dollar is used

ENERGY

Electricity—production: 155 million kWh (2011 est.)
country comparison to the world: 187

Electricity—consumption: 147.9 million kWh (2010 est.)
country comparison to the world: 191

Electricity—exports: 0 kWh (2012 est.)
country comparison to the world: 98

Electricity—imports: 0 kWh (2012 est.)
country comparison to the world: 114

Electricity—installed generating capacity: 60,000 kW (2010 est.)
country comparison to the world: 183

Electricity—from fossil fuels: 100% of total installed capacity (2010 est.)
country comparison to the world: 3

Electricity—from nuclear fuels: 0% of total installed capacity (2010 est.)
country comparison to the world: 40

Electricity—from hydroelectric plants: 0% of total installed capacity (2010 est.)
country comparison to the world: 154

Electricity—from other renewable sources: 0% of total installed capacity (2010 est.)
country comparison to the world: 152

Crude oil—production: 0 bbl/day (2012 est.)
country comparison to the world: 150

Crude oil—exports: 0 bbl/day (2010 est.)
country comparison to the world: 78

Crude oil—imports: 0 bbl/day (2010 est.)
country comparison to the world: 154

Crude oil—proved reserves: 0 bbl (1 January 2013 es)
country comparison to the world: 104

Refined petroleum products—production: 0 bbl/day (2010 est.)
country comparison to the world: 119

Refined petroleum products—consumption: 5,115 bbl/day (2011 est.)
country comparison to the world: 167

Refined petroleum products—exports: 0 bbl/day (2010 est.)
country comparison to the world: 149

Refined petroleum products—imports: 2,003 bbl/day (2010 est.)
country comparison to the world: 180

Natural gas—production: 0 cu m (2011 est.)
country comparison to the world: 99

Natural gas—consumption: 0 cu m (2010 est.)
country comparison to the world: 117

Natural gas—exports: 0 cu m (2011 est.)
country comparison to the world: 59

Natural gas—imports: 0 cu m (2011 est.)
country comparison to the world: 154

Natural gas—proved reserves: 0 cu m (1 January 2013 es)
country comparison to the world: 110

Carbon dioxide emissions from consumption of energy: 426,200 Mt (2011 est.)
country comparison to the world: 183

COMMUNICATIONS

Telephones—main lines in use: 10,000 (2012)
country comparison to the world: 200

Telephone system: good telex, telegraph, facsimile, and cellular telephone services
domestic: domestic satellite system with 1 Comsat earth station
international: country code—1-684; satellite earth station—1 (Intelsat-Pacific Ocean)

Broadcast media: 3 TV stations; multi-channel pay TV services are available; about a dozen radio stations, some of which are repeater stations (2009)

Internet country code: .as

Internet hosts: 2,387 (2012)
country comparison to the world: 161

Internet users: NA

TRANSPORTATION

Airports: 3 (2013)
country comparison to the world: 193

Airports—with paved runways: *total:* 3
over 3,047 m: 1
914 to 1,523 m: 1
under 914 m: 1 (2013)

Roadways: *total:* 241 km (2008)
country comparison to the world: 206

Ports and terminals: *major seaport(s):* Pago Pago

MILITARY

Manpower fit for military service: *males age 16-49:* 14,562
females age 16-49: 14,129 (2010 est.)

Manpower reaching militarily significant age annually: *male:* 775
female: 762 (2010 est.)

Military—note: defense is the responsibility of the US

TRANSNATIONAL ISSUES

Disputes—international: Tokelau included American Samoa's Swains Island (Olosega) in its 2006 draft independence constitution

ANDORRA

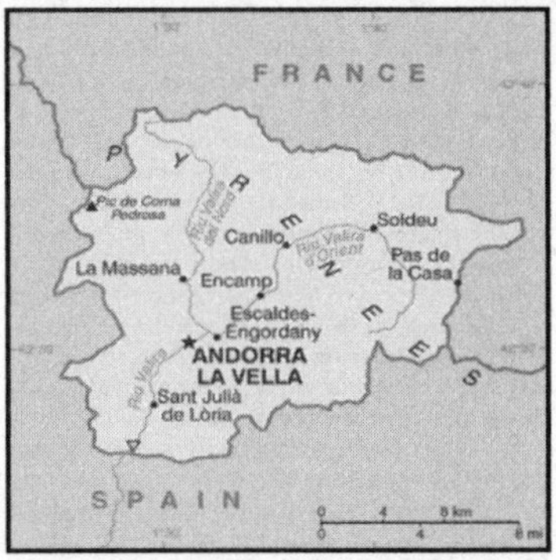

INTRODUCTION

Background: The landlocked Principality of Andorra is one of the smallest states in Europe, nestled high in the Pyrenees between the French and Spanish borders. For 715 years, from 1278 to 1993, Andorrans lived under a unique co-principality, ruled by French and Spanish leaders (from 1607 onward, the French chief of state and the Bishop of Urgell). In 1993, this feudal system was modified with the introduction of a modern,constitution; the co-princes remained as titular heads of state, but the government transformed into a parliamentary democracy. Andorra has become a popular tourist destination visited by approximately ten million people each year drawn by the winter sports, summer climate, and duty-free shopping. Andorra has also become a wealthy international commercial center because of its mature banking sector and low taxes. As part of its effort to modernize its economy, Andorra has opened to foreign investment, and engaged in other reforms, such as advancing tax initiatives aimed at supporting a broader infrastructure. Although not a member of the European Union (EU), Andorra enjoys a special relationship with the EU and uses the euro as its national currency.

GEOGRAPHY

Location: Southwestern Europe, Pyrenees mountains, on the border between France and Spain

Geographic coordinates: 42 30 N, 1 30 E

Map references: Europe

Area: *total:* 468 sq km
country comparison to the world: 196
land: 468 sq km
water: 0 sq km

Area—comparative: 2.5 times the size of Washington, DC

Land boundaries: *total:* 120.3 km
border countries: France 56.6 km, Spain 63.7 km

Coastline: 0 km (landlocked)

Maritime claims: none (landlocked)

Climate: temperate; snowy, cold winters and warm, dry summers

Terrain: rugged mountains dissected by narrow valleys

Elevation extremes: *lowest point:* Riu Runer 840 m
highest point: Pic de Coma Pedrosa 2,946 m

Natural resources: hydropower, mineral water, timber, iron ore, lead

Land use: *arable land:* 5.32%
permanent crops: 0%
other: 94.68% (2011)

Irrigated land: NA

Natural hazards: avalanches

Environment—current issues: deforestation; overgrazing of mountain meadows contributes to soil erosion; air pollution; wastewater treatment and solid waste disposal

Environment—international agreements: *party to:* Biodiversity, Desertification, Hazardous Wastes, Ozone Layer Protection
signed, but not ratified: none of the selected agreements

Geography—note: landlocked; straddles a number of important crossroads in the Pyrenees

PEOPLE AND SOCIETY

Nationality: *noun:* Andorran(s)
adjective: Andorran

Ethnic groups: Spanish 43%, Andorran 33%, Portuguese 11%, French 7%, other 6% (1998)

Languages: Catalan (official), French, Castilian, Portuguese

Religions: Roman Catholic (predominant)

Population: 85,458 (July 2014 est.)
country comparison to the world: 201

Age structure: *0-14 years:* 15.3% (male 6,708/female 6,379)
15-24 years: 9.2% (male 4,078/female 3,766)
25-54 years: 48.7% (male 21,395/female 20,231)
55-64 years: 14.3% (male 5,756/female 4,957)
65 years and over: 13.8% (male 6,145/female 6,043) (2014 est.)

Median age: *total:* 42.4 years
male: 42.6 years
female: 42.2 years (2014 est.)

Population growth rate: 0.17% (2014 est.)
country comparison to the world: 181

Birth rate: 8.48 births/1,000 population (2014 est.)
country comparison to the world: 218

Death rate: 6.82 deaths/1,000 population (2014 est.)
country comparison to the world: 140

Net migration rate: 0 migrant(s)/1,000 population (2014 est.)
country comparison to the world: 94

Urbanization: *urban population:* 88% of total population (2010)
rate of urbanization: 1.1% annual rate of change (2010-15 est.)

Major urban areas—population: ANDORRA LA VELLA (capital) 23,000 (2011)

Sex ratio: *at birth:* 1.07 male(s)/female
0-14 years: 1.05 male(s)/female
15-24 years: 1.08 male(s)/female
25-54 years: 1.06 male(s)/female
55-64 years: 1.07 male(s)/female
65 years and over: 1 male(s)/female
total population: 1.07 male(s)/female (2014 est.)

Infant mortality rate: *total:* 3.69 deaths/1,000 live births
country comparison to the world: 204
male: 3.68 deaths/1,000 live births
female: 3.7 deaths/1,000 live births (2014 est.)

Life expectancy at birth: *total population:* 82.65 years
country comparison to the world: 7
male: 80.51 years
female: 84.92 years (2014 est.)

Total fertility rate: 1.38 children born/woman (2014 est.)
country comparison to the world: 210

Health expenditures: 7.2% of GDP (2011)
country comparison to the world: 82

Physicians density: 3.91 physicians/1,000 population (2009)

Hospital bed density: 2.5 beds/1,000 population (2009)

Drinking water source:
Improved:
urban: 100% of population
rural: 100% of population
total: 100% of population
unimproved:
urban: 0% of population
rural: 0% of population
total: 0% of population (2011 est.)

Sanitation facility access:
improved:
urban: 100% of population
rural: 100% of population
total: 100% of population
unimproved:
urban: 0% of population
rural: 0% of population
total: 0% of population (2011 est.)

HIV/AIDS—adult prevalence rate: NA

HIV/AIDS—people living with HIV/AIDS: NA

HIV/AIDS—deaths: NA

Obesity—adult prevalence rate: 25.2% (2008)
country comparison to the world: 58

Education expenditures: NA

Literacy: *definition:* age 15 and over can read and write
total population: 100%
male: 100%
female: 100%

GOVERNMENT

Country name: *conventional long form:* Principality of Andorra
conventional short form: Andorra
local long form: Principat d'Andorra
local short form: Andorra

Government type: parliamentary democracy (since March 1993) that retains as its chiefs of state a co-principality; the two princes are the President of France and Bishop of Urgell, whose diocese is located in neighboring Spain; both co-princes maintain offices and representatives in Andorra

Capital: *name:* Andorra la Vella
geographic coordinates: 42 30 N, 1 31 E
time difference: UTC+1 (6 hours ahead of Washington, DC during Standard Time)
daylight saving time: +1hr, begins last Sunday in March; ends last Sunday in October

Administrative divisions: 7 parishes (parroquies, singular—parroquia); Andorra la Vella, Canillo, Encamp, Escaldes-Engordany, La Massana, Ordino, Sant Julia de Loria

Independence: 1278 (formed under the joint sovereignty of the French Count of Foix and the Spanish Bishop of Urgell)

National holiday: Our Lady of Meritxell Day, 8 September (1278)

Constitution: drafted 1991, approved by referendum 14 March 1993, effective 28 April 1993 (2013)

Legal system: mixed legal system of civil and customary law with the influence of canon law

International law organization participation: has not submitted an ICJ jurisdiction declaration; accepts ICCt jurisdiction

Suffrage: 18 years of age; universal

Executive branch: *chief of state:* French Co-Prince Francois HOLLANDE (since 15 May 2012); represented by Christian FREMONT (since September 2008) and Spanish Coprince Archbishop Joan-Enric VIVES i Sicilia (since 12 May 2003); represented by Nemesi MARQUES i Oste (since 30 July 2003)
head of government: Head of Government (or Cap de Govern) Antoni MARTI PETIT (since 12 May 2011)
cabinet: Executive Council of nine ministers designated by the Head of Government (For more information visit the World Leaders website)
elections: Head of Government elected by the General Council (Andorran Parliament) and formally appointed by the co-princes for a four-year term; election last held on 3 April 2011 (next to be held in April 2015)
election results: Antoni MARTI PETIT was elected Head of Government; percent of General Council vote—79%; note—the leader of the party which wins a majority of seats in the General Council is usually elected Head of Government

Legislative branch: unicameral General Council of the Valleys or Consell General de las Valls (a minimum of 28 seats; members are elected by direct popular vote, 14 from a single national constituency and 14 to represent each of the seven parishes; to serve four-year terms); note—each voter casts two separate ballots—one for the national list, one for the parish list
elections: last held on 3 April 2011 (next to be held in April 2015)
election results: percent of vote by party—DA 55%, PS 35%, Andorra for Change 7%, VA 3%; seats by party—DA 22, PS 6; note—numbers of votes and percentages are for the respective national list; number of seats include seats won by the parish lists

Judicial branch: *highest court(s):* Supreme Court of Justice of Andorra or Tribunal Superior de la Justicia d'Andorra (consists of the court president and 8 judges organized into civil, criminal, and administrative chambers); Constitutional Court or Tribunal Constitucional (consists of 4 magistrates)
judge selection and term of office: Supreme Court president and judges appointed by the Supreme Council of Justice, a 5-member judicial policy and administrative body appointed 1 each by the co-princes,1 by the General Council, 1 by the executive council president, and 1 by the courts; judges serve 6-year renewable terms; Constitutional magistrates appointed 2 by the co-princes and 2 by the General Council; magistrates' appointments limited to two consecutive 8-year terms
subordinate courts: Tribunal of Judges or Tribunal de Batlles; Tribunal of the Courts or Tribunal de Corts

Political parties and leaders: there are four political parties at the national level: Andorra for Change or ApC [Eusebio NOMEN CALVET]; Democrats for Andorra or DA [Antoni MARTI PETIT], coalition including Liberal Party (PRA) and Reformist Coalition; Greens of Andorra or VA [Isabel LOZANO MUNOZ]; Social Democratic Party or PS [Jaume BARTUMEU CASSANY]; note: there are also several smaller parties at the Parish level (one is Lauredian Union)

International organization participation: CE, FAO, ICAO, ICC (NGOs), ICRM, IFRCS, Interpol, IOC, IPU, ITU, OIF, OPCW, OSCE, UN, UNCTAD, UNESCO, Union Latina, UNWTO, WCO, WHO, WIPO, WTO (observer)

Diplomatic representation in the US: *chief of mission:* Ambassador Narcis CASAL de Fonsdeviela (since 2 November 2009)
chancery: 2 United Nations Plaza, 25th Floor, New York, NY 10017
telephone: [1] (212) 750-8064
FAX: [1] (212) 750-6630

Diplomatic representation from the US: the US does not have an embassy in Andorra; the US Ambassador to Spain is accredited to Andorra; US interests in Andorra are represented by the US Consulate General's office in Barcelona (Spain);
mailing address: Paseo Reina Elisenda de Montcada, 23, 08034 Barcelona, Spain;
telephone: [34] (93) 280-2227;
FAX: [34] (93) 280-6175

Flag description: three vertical bands of blue (hoist side), yellow, and red, with the national coat of arms centered in the yellow band; the latter band is slightly wider than the other two so that the ratio of band widths is 8:9:8; the coat of arms features a quartered shield with the emblems of (starting in the upper left and proceeding clockwise): Urgell, Foix, Bearn, and Catalonia; the motto reads VIRTUS UNITA FORTIOR (Strength United is Stronger); the flag combines the blue and red French colors with the red and yellow of Spain to show Franco-Spanish protection
note: similar to the flags of Chad and Romania, which do not have a national coat of arms in the center, and the flag of Moldova, which does bear a national emblem

National anthem: *name:* "El Gran Carlemany" (The Great Charlemagne)
lyrics/music: Joan BENLLOCH i VIVO/Enric MARFANY BONS
note: adopted 1921; the anthem provides a brief history of Andorra in a first person narrative

ECONOMY

Economy—overview: Tourism, retail sales, and finance are the mainstays of Andorra's tiny, well-to-do economy, accounting for more than three-quarters of GDP. Andorra's duty-free status for some products and its summer and winter resorts attract millions of visitors annually, although the economic downturn in neighboring countries has curtailed the number of tourists. Andorra's comparative advantage as a tax haven eroded when the borders of neighboring France and Spain opened; its bank secrecy laws have been relaxed under pressure from the EU and OECD. Agricultural production is limited—only 5% of the land is arable—and most food has to be imported, making the economy vulnerable to changes in fuel and food prices. The principal livestock is sheep. Manufacturing output and exports consist mainly of perfumes and cosmetic products, products of the printing industry, electrical machinery and equipment, clothing, tobacco products, and furniture. Andorra is a member of the EU Customs Union and is treated as an EU member for trade in manufactured goods (no tariffs) and as a non-EU member for agricultural products. Andorra uses the euro and is effectively subject to the monetary policy of the European Central Bank. Slower growth in Spain and France has dimmed Andorra's economic prospects. Since 2010, a drop in tourism contributed to a contraction in GDP and a sharp deterioration of public finances, prompting the government to begin implementing several austerity measures to reduce the budget deficit, including levying a special corporate tax. To bring in new revenue and diversify future sources of economic growth, the government approved in July 2012 a new foreign investment law opening investment to foreign capital.

GDP (purchasing power parity): $3.163 billion (2012 est.)
country comparison to the world: 180
$3.214 billion (2011 est.)
$3.227 billion (2010 est.)
note: data are in 2013 US dollars

GDP (official exchange rate): $4.8 billion (2012 est.)

GDP—real growth rate: -1.6% (2012 est.)
country comparison to the world: 209
-0.4% (2011 est.)
-1.9% (2010 est.)

GDP—per capita (PPP): $37,200 (2011 est.)
country comparison to the world: 35
$37,700 (2010 est.)
$37,900 (2009 est.)

GDP—composition, by sector of origin:
agriculture: 14%
industry: 79%
services: 6% (2011 est.)

Agriculture—products: small quantities of rye, wheat, barley, oats, vegetables, tobacco; sheep, cattle

Industries: tourism (particularly skiing), banking, timber, furniture

Industrial production growth rate: NA%

Labor force: 36,060 (2012)
country comparison to the world: 201

Labor force—by occupation: *agriculture:* 0.4%
industry: 4.7%
services: 94.9% (2010)

Unemployment rate: 4% (2012 est.)
country comparison to the world: 30
1.9% (2011 est.)

Population below poverty line: NA% (2008)

Household income or consumption by percentage share: *lowest 10%:* NA%
highest 10%: NA%

Budget: *revenues:* $1.029 billion
expenditures: $1.041 billion (2012)

Taxes and other revenues: 21.4% of GDP (2012)
country comparison to the world: 153

Budget surplus (+) or deficit (-): -0.3% of GDP (2012)
country comparison to the world: 51

Public debt: 41.1% of GDP (2012)
country comparison to the world: 86
37.7% of GDP (2011)

Fiscal year: calendar year

Inflation rate (consumer prices): 1.1% (2012 est.)
country comparison to the world: 25
-2.5% (2011 est.)

Exports: $70 million (2012 est.)
country comparison to the world: 193
$72 million (2011 est.)

Exports—commodities: tobacco products, furniture

Imports: $1.43 billion (2012 est.)
country comparison to the world: 173
$1.501 billion (2011 est.)

Imports—commodities: consumer goods, food, fuel, electricity

Debt—external: $NA

Exchange rates: euros (EUR) per US dollar—
0.7778 (2013 est.)
0.7185 (2012 est.)
0.755 (2010 est.)
0.7198 (2009 est.)
0.6827 (2008 est.)

ENERGY

Electricity—production: 91.24 million kWh (2011)
country comparison to the world: 200

Electricity—consumption: 562.4 million kWh (2012)
country comparison to the world: 167

Electricity—exports: 0 kWh (2012 est.)
country comparison to the world: 96

Electricity—imports: 0 kWh (2012 est.)
country comparison to the world: 112

Electricity—installed generating capacity: 520,000 kW
country comparison to the world: 136

Electricity—from fossil fuels: 61.3% of total installed capacity
country comparison to the world: 132

Electricity—from nuclear fuels: 0% of total installed capacity
country comparison to the world: 38

Electricity—from hydroelectric plants: 23.3% of total installed capacity
country comparison to the world: 85

COMMUNICATIONS

Telephones—main lines in use: 39,000 (2012)
country comparison to the world: 170

Telephones—mobile cellular: 65,000 (2012)
country comparison to the world: 198

Telephone system: *general assessment:* modern automatic telephone system
domestic: modern system with microwave radio relay connections between exchanges
international: country code—376; landline circuits to France and Spain (2012)

Broadcast media: 1 public TV station and 2 public radio stations; about 10 commercial radio stations; good reception of radio and TV broadcasts from stations in France and Spain; upgraded to terrestrial digital TV broadcasting in 2007; roughly 25 international TV channels available (2012)

Internet country code: .ad

Internet hosts: 28,383 (2012)
country comparison to the world: 109

Internet users: 67,100 (2009)
country comparison to the world: 171

TRANSPORTATION

Roadways: *total:* 320 km (2008)
country comparison to the world: 203

MILITARY

Military branches: no regular military forces, Police Service of Andorra (2011)

Manpower available for military service: *males age 16-49:* 22,390 (2010 est.)

Manpower fit for military service: *males age 16-49:* 17,977
females age 16-49: 17,069 (2010 est.)

Manpower reaching militarily significant age annually: *male:* 397
female: 347 (2010 est.)

Military—note: defense is the responsibility of France and Spain

TRANSNATIONAL ISSUES

Disputes—international: none

ANGOLA

INTRODUCTION

Background: Angola is still rebuilding its country since the end of a 27-year civil war in 2002. Fighting between the Popular Movement for the Liberation of Angola (MPLA), led by Jose Eduardo DOS SANTOS, and the National Union for the Total Independence of Angola (UNITA), led by Jonas SAVIMBI, followed independence from Portugal in 1975. Peace seemed imminent in 1992 when Angola held national elections, but fighting picked up again in 1993. Up to 1.5 million lives may have been lost—and 4 million people displaced—during the more than a quarter century of fighting. SAVIMBI's death in 2002 ended UNITA's insurgency and cemented the MPLA's hold on power. President DOS SANTOS pushed through a new constitution in 2010; elections held in 2012 saw him installed as president.

GEOGRAPHY

Location: Southern Africa, bordering the South Atlantic Ocean, between Namibia and Democratic Republic of the Congo

Geographic coordinates: 12 30 S, 18 30 E

Map references: Africa

Area: *total:* 1,246,700 sq km
country comparison to the world: 23
land: 1,246,700 sq km
water: 0 sq km

Area—comparative: slightly less than twice the size of Texas

Land boundaries: *total:* 5,198 km
border countries: Democratic Republic of the Congo 2,511 km (of which 225 km is the boundary of discontiguous Cabinda Province), Republic of the Congo 201 km, Namibia 1,376 km, Zambia 1,110 km

Coastline: 1,600 km

Maritime claims: *territorial sea:* 12 nm
contiguous zone: 24 nm
exclusive economic zone: 200 nm

Climate: semiarid in south and along coast to Luanda; north has cool, dry season (May to October) and hot, rainy season (November to April)

Terrain: narrow coastal plain rises abruptly to vast interior plateau

Elevation extremes: *lowest point:* Atlantic Ocean 0 m
highest point: Morro de Moco 2,620 m

Natural resources: petroleum, diamonds, iron ore, phosphates, copper, feldspar, gold, bauxite, uranium

Land use: *arable land:* 3.29%
permanent crops: 0.23%
other: 96.48% (2011)

Irrigated land: 855.3 sq km (2005)

Total renewable water resources: 148 cu km (2011)

Freshwater withdrawal (domestic/industrial/agricultural): *total:* 0.71 cu km/yr (45%/34%/21%)
per capita: 40.27 cu m/yr (2005)

Natural hazards: locally heavy rainfall causes periodic flooding on the plateau

Environment—current issues: overuse of pastures and subsequent soil erosion attributable to population pressures; desertification; deforestation of tropical rain forest, in response to both international demand for tropical timber and to domestic use as fuel, resulting in loss of biodiversity; soil erosion contributing to water pollution and siltation of rivers and dams; inadequate supplies of potable water

Environment—international agreements: *party to:* Biodiversity, Climate Change, Climate Change-Kyoto Protocol, Desertification, Law of the Sea, Marine Dumping, Ozone Layer Protection, Ship Pollution

signed, but not ratified: none of the selected agreements

Geography—note: the province of Cabinda is an exclave, separated from the rest of the country by the Democratic Republic of the Congo

PEOPLE AND SOCIETY

Nationality: *noun:* Angolan(s)
adjective: Angolan

Ethnic groups: Ovimbundu 37%, Kimbundu 25%, Bakongo 13%, mestico (mixed European and native African) 2%, European 1%, other 22%

Languages: Portuguese (official), Bantu and other African languages

Religions: indigenous beliefs 47%, Roman Catholic 38%, Protestant 15% (1998 est.)

Population: 19,088,106 (July 2014 est.)
country comparison to the world: 59

Age structure: *0-14 years:* 43.2% (male 4,206,929/female 4,043,618)
15-24 years: 20.5% (male 1,992,955/female 1,923,932)
25-54 years: 29.3% (male 2,822,164/female 2,777,147)
55-64 years: 2.9% (male 370,181/female 389,885)
65 years and over: 2.9% (male 259,637/female 301,658) (2014 est.)

Dependency ratios: *total dependency ratio:* 99.6 %
youth dependency ratio: 94.8%
elderly dependency ratio: 4.8%
potential support ratio: 20.9 (2013)

Median age: *total:* 17.9 years
male: 17.7 years
female: 18.1 years (2014 est.)

Population growth rate: 2.78% (2014 est.)
country comparison to the world: 19

Birth rate: 38.97 births/1,000 population (2014 est.)
country comparison to the world: 9

Death rate: 11.67 deaths/1,000 population (2014 est.)
country comparison to the world: 29

Net migration rate: 0.47 migrant(s)/1,000 population (2014 est.)
country comparison to the world: 70

Urbanization: *urban population:* 59.2% of total population (2011)
rate of urbanization: 3.97% annual rate of change (2010-15 est.)

Major urban areas—population: LUANDA (capital) 5.068 million; Huambo 979,000 (2011)

Sex ratio: *at birth:* 1.05 male(s)/female
0-14 years: 1.04 male(s)/female
15-24 years: 1.04 male(s)/female
25-54 years: 1.02 male(s)/female
55-64 years: 1.02 male(s)/female
65 years and over: 0.86 male(s)/female
total population: 1.02 male(s)/female (2014 est.)

Maternal mortality rate: 450 deaths/100,000 live births (2010)
country comparison to the world: 25

Infant mortality rate: *total:* 79.99 deaths/1,000 live births
country comparison to the world: 8
male: 83.74 deaths/1,000 live births
female: 76.05 deaths/1,000 live births (2014 est.)

Life expectancy at birth: *total population:* 55.29 years
country comparison to the world: 205
male: 54.16 years
female: 56.47 years (2014 est.)

Total fertility rate: 5.43 children born/woman (2014 est.)
country comparison to the world: 10

Contraceptive prevalence rate: 17.7% (2009)

Health expenditures: 3.5% of GDP (2011)
country comparison to the world: 176

Physicians density: 0.17 physicians/1,000 population (2009)

Hospital bed density: 0.8 beds/1,000 population (2005)

Drinking water source:
Improved:
urban: 66.3% of population
rural: 34.7% of population
total: 53.4% of population
Unimproved:
urban: 33.7% of population
rural: 65.3% of population
total: 46.6% of population (2011 est.)

Sanitation facility access:
Improved:
urban: 85.8% of population
rural: 19.4% of population
total: 58.7% of population
Unimproved:
urban: 14.2% of population
rural: 80.6% of population
total: 41.3% of population (2011 est.)

HIV/AIDS—adult prevalence rate: 2.3% (2012 est.)
country comparison to the world: 26

HIV/AIDS—people living with HIV/AIDS: 248,800 (2012 est.)
country comparison to the world: 24

HIV/AIDS—deaths: 12,600 (2012 est.)
country comparison to the world: 23

Major infectious diseases: *degree of risk:* very high
food or waterborne diseases: bacterial and protozoal diarrhea, hepatitis A, typhoid fever
vectorborne diseases: dengue fever, malaria
water contact disease: schistosomiasis
animal contact disease: rabies (2013)

Obesity—adult prevalence rate: 6.4% (2008)
country comparison to the world: 147

Children under the age of 5 years underweight: 15.6% (2007)
country comparison to the world: 47

Education expenditures: 3.5% of GDP (2010)
country comparison to the world: 127

Literacy: *definition:* age 15 and over can read and write
total population: 70.4%
male: 82.6%
female: 58.6% (2011 est.)

School life expectancy (primary to tertiary education): *total:* 11 years
male: 14 years
female: 9 years (2011)

Child labor—children ages 5-14:
total number: 832,895
percentage: 24 % (2001 est.)

GOVERNMENT

Country name:
conventional long form: Republic of Angola
conventional short form: Angola
local long form: Republica de Angola
local short form: Angola
former: People's Republic of Angola

Government type: republic; multiparty presidential regime

Capital: *name:* Luanda
geographic coordinates: 8 50 S, 13 13 E
time difference: UTC+1 (6 hours ahead of Washington, DC during Standard Time)

Administrative divisions: 18 provinces (provincias, singular—provincia); Bengo, Benguela, Bie, Cabinda, Cunene, Huambo, Huila,Kwando Kubango, Kwanza Norte, Kwanza Sul, Luanda, Lunda Norte, Lunda Sul, Malanje, Moxico, Namibe,Uige, Zaire

Independence: 11 November 1975 (from Portugal)

National holiday: Independence Day, 11 November (1975)

Constitution: previous 1975, 1992; latest adopted 5 February 2010 (2013)

Legal system: civil legal system based on Portuguese civil law; no judicial review of legislation

International law organization participation: has not submitted an ICJ jurisdiction declaration; non-party state to the ICCt

Suffrage: 18 years of age; universal

Executive branch: *chief of state:* President Jose Eduardo DOS SANTOS (since 21 September 1979); Vice President Manuel Domingos VICENTE (since 26 September 2012); note: the president is both chief of state and head of government
head of government: President Jose Eduardo DOS SANTOS (since 21 September 1979); Vice President Manuel Domingos VICENTE (since 26 September 2012)
cabinet: Council of Ministers appointed by the president (For more information visit the World Leaders website)
elections: president indirectly elected by National Assembly for a five-year term (eligible for a second consecutive or discontinuous term) under the 2010 constitution; note—according to the 2010 constitution, ballots are cast for parties rather than candidates, the leader of the party with the most votes becomes president; following the results of the 2012 legislative elections DOS SANTOS became president (eligible for a second term)
election results: NA; as leader of the MPLA, Jose Eduardo DOS SANTOS became pesident following legislative elections on 31 August 2012; DOS SANTOS was inaugurated on 26 September 2012 to serve the first of a possible two terms under the 2010 constitution

Legislative branch: unicameral National Assembly or Assembleia Nacional (220 seats; members elected by proportional vote to serve five-year terms)
elections: last held on 31 August 2012 (next to be held in 2017)
election results: percent of vote by party—MPLA 71.8%, UNITA 18.7%, CASA-CE 6.0%, PRS 1.7%, FNLA 1.1%, other 0.7%; seats by party—MPLA 175, UNITA 32, CASA-CE 8, PRS 3, FNLA 2

Judicial branch: *highest court(s):* Supreme Court or Tribunal da Relacao (consists of the chief justice and NA judges; Constitutional Court or Tribunal Constitucional (consists of 11 members)
judge selection and term of office: Supreme Court judges appointed by the president upon recommendation of the Supreme Judicial Council, an 18-member body presided over by the president; judge tenure NA; Constitutional Court judges—4 nominated by the president, 4 elected by National Assembly, 2 elected by Supreme National Council, 1 elected by competitive submission of curricula; judges serve single 7-year terms

subordinate courts: provincial and municipal courts

Political parties and leaders: Broad Convergence for the Salvation of Angola Electoral Coalition or CASA-CE [Abel CHIVUKUVUKU]; National Front for the Liberation of Angola or FNLA [Lucas NGONDA]; National Union for the Total Independence of Angola or UNITA [Isaias SAMAKUVA] (largest opposition party); Popular Movement for the Liberation of Angola or MPLA [Jose Eduardo DOS SANTOS] (ruling party in power since 1975); Social Renewal Party or PRS [Eduardo KUANGANA]
note: 4 other parties qualified to participate in the national election in August 2012

Political pressure groups and leaders: Front for the Liberation of the Enclave of Cabinda or FLEC [N'zita Henriques TIAGO]
note: FLEC's small-scale armed struggle for the independence of Cabinda Province persists despite the signing of a peace accord with the government in August 2006; Several factions of FLEC have broken off over the past 30 years, including the FLEC-PM [Rodrigues Mingas], which was responsible for a deadly attack on the Togolese soccer team in 2010

International organization participation: ACP, AfDB, AU, CPLP, FAO, G-77, IAEA, IBRD, ICAO, ICRM, IDA, IFAD, IFC, IFRCS, ILO, IMF, IMO, Interpol, IOC, IOM, IPU, ISO (correspondent), ITSO, ITU, ITUC (NGOs), MIGA, NAM, OAS (observer), OPEC, SADC, UN, UNCTAD, UNESCO, UNIDO, Union Latina, UNWTO, UPU, WCO, WFTU (NGOs), WHO, WIPO, WMO, WTO

Diplomatic representation in the US: *chief of mission:* Ambassador Alberto do Carmo BENTO RIBEIRO (since 1 September 2011)
chancery: 2108 16th Street NW, Washington, DC 20009
telephone: [1] (202) 785-1156
FAX: [1] (202) 785-1258
consulate(s) general: Houston, New York

Diplomatic representation from the US: *chief of mission:* Ambassador (vacant); Charge d'Affaires Heather C. Merritt
embassy: number 32 Rua Houari Boumedienne (in the Miramar area of Luanda), Luanda
mailing address: international mail: Caixa Postal 6468, Luanda; pouch: US Embassy Luanda, US Department of State, 2550 Luanda Place, Washington, DC 20521-2550
telephone: [244] (222) 64-1000
FAX: [244] (222) 64-1232

Flag description: two equal horizontal bands of red (top) and black with a centered yellow emblem consisting of a five-pointed star within half a cogwheel crossed by a machete (in the style of a hammer and sickle); red represents liberty, black the African continent, the symbols characterize workers and peasants

National symbol(s): Palanca Negra Gigante (giant black sable antelope)

National anthem: *name:* "Angola Avante" (Forward Angola)
lyrics/music: Manuel Rui Alves MONTEIRO/Rui Alberto Vieira Dias MINGAO
note: adopted 1975

ECONOMY

Economy—overview: Angola's high growth rate in recent years was driven by high international prices for its oil. Angola became a member of OPEC in late 2006 and its current assigned a production quota of 1.65 million barrels a day (bbl/day). Oil production and its supporting activities contribute about 85% of GDP. Diamond exports contribute an additional 5%. Subsistence agriculture provides the main livelihood for most of the people,but half of the country's food is still imported. Increased oil production supported growth averaging more than 17% per year from 2004 to 2008. A postwar reconstruction boom and resettlement of displaced persons has led to high rates of growth in construction and agriculture as well. Much of the country's infrastructure is still damaged or undeveloped from the 27-year-long civil war. Land mines left from the war still mar the countryside, even though peace was established after the death of rebel leader Jonas-SAVIMBI in February 2002. Since 2005, the government has used billions of dollars in credit lines from China, Brazil, Portugal, Germany, Spain, and the EU to rebuild Angola's public infrastructure. The global recession that started in 2008 temporarily stalled economic growth. Lower prices for oil and diamonds during the global recession slowed GDP growth to 2.4% in 2009, and many construction projects stopped because Luanda accrued $9 billion in arrears to foreign construction companies when government revenue fell in 2008 and 2009. Angola abandoned its currency peg in 2009, and in November 2009 signed onto an IMF Stand-By Arrangement loan of $1.4 billion to rebuild international reserves. Consumer inflation declined from 325% in 2000 to about 10% in 2012. Higher oil prices have helped Angola turn a budget deficit of 8.6% of GDP in 2009 into an surplus of 12% of GDP in 2012. Corruption, especially in the extractive sectors, also is a major challenge.

GDP (purchasing power parity): $131.8 billion (2013 est.)
country comparison to the world: 67
$124.8 billion (2012 est.)
$118.7 billion (2011 est.)
note: data are in 2013 US dollars

GDP (official exchange rate): $124 billion (2013 est.)

GDP—real growth rate: 5.6% (2013 est.)
country comparison to the world: 43
5.2% (2012 est.)
3.9% (2011 est.)

GDP—per capita (PPP): $6,300 (2013 est.)
country comparison to the world: 148
$6,200 (2012 est.)
$6,000 (2011 est.)
note: data are in 2013 US dollars

Gross national saving: 19.1% of GDP (2013 est.)
country comparison to the world: 82
23.8% of GDP (2012 est.)
24% of GDP (2011 est.)

GDP—composition, by end use:
household consumption: 49.2%
government consumption: 20%
investment in fixed capital: 11.4%
investment in inventories: -0.1%
exports of goods and services: 59.2%
imports of goods and services: -39.7% (2013 est.)

GDP—composition, by sector of origin:
agriculture: 10.2%
industry: 61.4%
services: 28.4% (2011 est.)

Agriculture—products: bananas, sugarcane, coffee, sisal, corn, cotton, cassava (manioc), tobacco, vegetables, plantains; livestock; forest products; fish

Industries: petroleum; diamonds, iron ore, phosphates, feldspar, bauxite, uranium, and gold; cement; basic metal products; fish processing; food processing, brewing, tobacco products, sugar; textiles; ship repair

Industrial production growth rate: 5.5% (2013 est.)
country comparison to the world: 49

Labor force: 9.018 million (2013 est.)
country comparison to the world: 53

Labor force—by occupation: *agriculture:* 85%
industry and services: 15% (2003 est.)

Unemployment rate: NA%

Population below poverty line: 40.5% (2006 est.)

Household income or consumption by percentage share: *lowest 10%:* 0.6%
highest 10%: 44.7% (2000)

Budget: *revenues:* $52.75 billion
expenditures: $48.48 billion (2013 est.)

Taxes and other revenues: 42.5% of GDP (2013 est.)
country comparison to the world: 27

Budget surplus (+) or deficit (-): 3.4% of GDP (2013 est.)
country comparison to the world: 13

Public debt: 14.7% of GDP (2013 est.)
country comparison to the world: 144
17.2% of GDP (2012 est.)

Fiscal year: calendar year

Inflation rate (consumer prices): 8.9% (2013 est.)
country comparison to the world: 202
10.3% (2012 est.)

Central bank discount rate: 25% (31 December 2010 est.)
country comparison to the world: 2
30% (31 December 2009 est.)

Commercial bank prime lending rate: 15% (31 December 2013 est.)
country comparison to the world: 31
16.81% (31 December 2012 est.)

Stock of narrow money: $16.95 billion (31 December 2013 est.)
country comparison to the world: 69
$13.31 billion (31 December 2012 est.)

Stock of broad money: $50.71 billion (31 December 2013 est.)
country comparison to the world: 69
$40.34 billion (31 December 2012 est.)

Stock of domestic credit: $22.47 billion (31 December 2013 est.)
country comparison to the world: 80
$20.45 billion (31 December 2012 est.)

Current account balance: $10.69 billion (2013 est.)
country comparison to the world: 22
$13.85 billion (2012 est.)

Exports: $70.84 billion (2013 est.)
country comparison to the world: 49
$71.09 billion (2012 est.)

Exports—commodities: crude oil, diamonds, refined petroleum products, coffee, sisal, fish and fish products, timber, cotton

Exports—partners: China 46.3%, US 13.9%, India 10.1%, South Africa 4.2% (2012)

Imports: $26.09 billion (2013 est.)
country comparison to the world: 72
$23.72 billion (2012 est.)

Imports—commodities: machinery and electrical equipment, vehicles and spare parts; medicines, food, textiles, military goods

Imports—partners: China 20.9%, Portugal 19.5%, US 7.7%, South Africa 7.1%, Brazil 5.9% (2012)

Reserves of foreign exchange and gold: $37.94 billion (31 December 2013 est.)
country comparison to the world: 48
$33.41 billion (31 December 2012 est.)

Debt—external: $22.71 billion (31 December 2013 est.)
country comparison to the world: 79
$21.85 billion (31 December 2012 est.)

Stock of direct foreign investment—at home: $17.15 billion (31 December 2012 est.)
country comparison to the world: 78
$12.15 billion (31 December 2011 est.)

Stock of direct foreign investment—abroad: $12.87 billion (31 December 2013 est.)
country comparison to the world: 50
$9.877 billion (31 December 2012 est.)

Exchange rates: kwanza (AOA) per US dollar—
95.97 (2013 est.)
95.468 (2012 est.)
91.906 (2010 est.)
79.33 (2009)
75.023 (2008)

ENERGY

Electricity—production: 5.118 billion kWh (2010 est.)
country comparison to the world: 118

Electricity—consumption: 4.592 billion kWh (2010 est.)
country comparison to the world: 117

Electricity—exports: 0 kWh (2012 est.)
country comparison to the world: 97

Electricity—imports: 0 kWh (2012 est.)
country comparison to the world: 113

Electricity—installed generating capacity: 1.155 million kW (2010 est.)
country comparison to the world: 121

Electricity—from fossil fuels: 56.9% of total installed capacity (2010 est.)
country comparison to the world: 140

Electricity—from nuclear fuels: 0% of total installed capacity (2010 est.)
country comparison to the world: 39

Electricity—from hydroelectric plants: 43.1% of total installed capacity (2010 est.)
country comparison to the world: 55

Electricity—from other renewable sources: 0% of total installed capacity (2010 est.)
country comparison to the world: 151

Crude oil—production: 1.872 million bbl/day (2012 est.)
country comparison to the world: 16

Crude oil—exports: 1.928 million bbl/day (2010 est.)
country comparison to the world: 7

Crude oil—imports: 0 bbl/day (2010 est.)
country comparison to the world: 153

Crude oil—proved reserves: 10.47 billion bbl (1 January 2013 es)
country comparison to the world: 17

Refined petroleum products—production: 38,760 bbl/day (2010 est.)
country comparison to the world: 85

Refined petroleum products—consumption: 79,430 bbl/day (2011 est.)
country comparison to the world: 85

Refined petroleum products—exports: 17,750 bbl/day (2010 est.)
country comparison to the world: 75

Refined petroleum products—imports: 55,740 bbl/day (2010 est.)
country comparison to the world: 66

Natural gas—production: 752 million cu m (2011 est.)
country comparison to the world: 68

Natural gas—consumption: 733 million cu m (2010 est.)
country comparison to the world: 95

Natural gas—exports: 0 cu m (2011 est.)
country comparison to the world: 58

Natural gas—imports: 0 cu m (2011 est.)
country comparison to the world: 153

Natural gas—proved reserves: 366 billion cu m (1 January 2013 es)
country comparison to the world: 37

Carbon dioxide emissions from consumption of energy: 26.97 million Mt (2011 est.)
country comparison to the world: 79

COMMUNICATIONS

Telephones—main lines in use: 303,000 (2012)
country comparison to the world: 116

Telephones—mobile cellular: 9.8 million (2012)
country comparison to the world: 80

Telephone system: *general assessment:* limited system; state-owned telecom had monopoly for fixed-lines until 2005;demand outstripped capacity, prices were high, and services poor; Telecom Namibia, through an Angolan company, became the first private licensed operator in Angola's fixed-line telephone network; by 2010, the number of fixed-line providers had expanded to 5; Angola Telecom established mobile-cellular service in Luanda in 1993 and the network has been extended to larger towns; a privately owned, mobile-cellular service provider began operations in 2001
domestic: only about two fixed-lines per 100 persons; mobile-cellular teledensity about 50 telephones per 100 persons in 2011
international: country code—244; landing point for the SAT-3/WASC fiber-optic submarine cable that provides connectivity to Europe and Asia; satellite earth stations—29 (2009)

Broadcast media: state controls all broadcast media with nationwide reach; state-owned Televisao Popular de Angola (TPA) provides terrestrial TV service on 2 channels; a third TPA channel is available via cable and satellite; TV subscription services are available; state-owned Radio Nacional de Angola (RNA) broadcasts on 5 stations; about a half dozen private radio stations broadcast locally (2008)

Internet country code: .ao

Internet hosts: 20,703 (2012)
country comparison to the world: 116

Internet users: 606,700 (2009)
country comparison to the world: 114

TRANSPORTATION

Airports: 176 (2013)
country comparison to the world: 32

Airports—with paved runways: *total:* 31
over 3,047 m: 7
2,438 to 3,047 m: 8
1,524 to 2,437 m: 12
914 to 1,523 m: 4 (2013)

Airports—with unpaved runways: *total:* 145
over 3,047 m: 2
2,438 to 3,047 m: 3
1,524 to 2,437 m: 31
914 to 1,523 m: 66
under 914 m: 43 (2013)

Heliports: 1 (2013)

Pipelines: gas 352 km; liquid petroleum gas 85 km; oil 1,065 km; oil/gas/water 5 km (2013)

Railways: *total:* 2,764 km
country comparison to the world: 60
narrow gauge: 2,641 km 1.067-m gauge; 123 km 0.600-m gauge (2008)

Roadways: *total:* 51,429 km
country comparison to the world: 76
paved: 5,349 km
unpaved: 46,080 km (2001)

Waterways: 1,300 km (2011)
country comparison to the world: 54

Merchant marine: *total:* 7
country comparison to the world: 123
by type: cargo 1, chemical tanker 1, passenger/cargo 2, petroleum tanker 2, roll on/roll off 1
foreign-owned: 1 (Spain 1)
registered in other countries: 17 (Bahamas 6, Curacao 2, Cyprus 1, Liberia 1, Malta 7) (2010)

Ports and terminals: *major seaport(s):* Cabinda, Lobito, Luanda, Namibe

MILITARY

Military branches: Angolan Armed Forces (Forcas Armadas Angolanas, FAA): Army, Navy (Marinha de Guerra Angola, MGA), Angolan National Air Force (Forca Aerea Nacional Angolana, FANA; under operational control of the Army) (2012)

Military service age and obligation: 20-45 years of age for compulsory male and 18-45 years for voluntary male military service (registration at age 18 is mandatory); 20-45 years of age for voluntary female service; conscript service obligation—2 years; Angolan citizenship required; the Navy (MGA) is entirely staffed with volunteers (2013)

Manpower available for military service:
males age 16-49: 3,062,438
females age 16-49: 2,964,262 (2010 est.)

Manpower fit for military service:
males age 16-49: 1,546,781
females age 16-49: 1,492,308 (2010 est.)

Manpower reaching militarily significant age annually: *male:* 155,476
female: 152,054 (2010 est.)

Military expenditures: 3.63% of GDP (2012)
country comparison to the world: 13
3.5% of GDP (2011)
3.63% of GDP (2010)

TRANSNATIONAL ISSUES

Disputes—international: Democratic Republic of Congo accuses Angola of shifting monuments

Refugees and internally displaced persons: refugees (country of origin): 20,740 (Democratic Republic of Congo) (2012)
IDPs: 19,500 (27-year civil war ending in 2002) (2005)

Trafficking in persons: *current situation:* Angola is a source and destination country for men, women, and children subjected to sex trafficking and forced labor in agriculture, construction, domestic service, and diamond mines; some Angolan girls are forced into domestic prostitution, while some Angolan boys are taken to Namibia as forced laborers or are forced to be cross-border couriers; women and children are also forced into domestic service in South Africa, the Democratic Republic of the Congo, Namibia, and European countries; Vietnamese,Brazilian, and Chinese women are trafficked to Angola for prostitution, while Chinese, Southeast Asian,Namibian, and possibly Congolese migrants are subjected to forced labor in Angola's construction industry

tier rating: Tier 2 Watch List—Angola does not fully comply with the minimum standards for the elimination of trafficking; however, it is making significant efforts to do so; authorities opened one internal labor trafficking investigation but have not initiated the prosecution of any trafficking offenders, has never convicted a trafficking offender, and does not have a law specifically prohibiting all forms of trafficking; the government has not adopted amendments to the penal code reflecting the 2010 constitutional provision prohibiting human trafficking and has not finalized draft anti-trafficking legislation; the government has made minimal efforts to protect trafficking victims but continues to lack a systematic process for identifying trafficking victims and providing legal remedies to victims (2013)

Illicit drugs: used as a transshipment point for cocaine destined for Western Europe and other African states, particularly South Africa

ANGUILLA

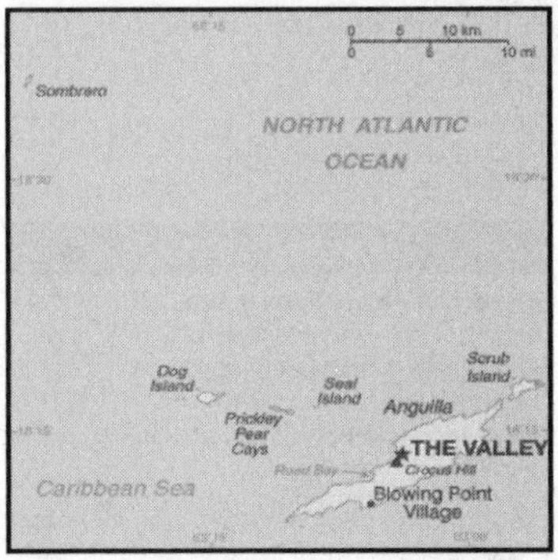

INTRODUCTION

Background: Colonized by English settlers from Saint Kitts in 1650, Anguilla was administered by Great Britain until the early 19th century, when the island—against the wishes of the inhabitants—was incorporated into a single British dependency along with Saint Kitts and Nevis. Several attempts at separation failed. In 1971, two years after a revolt, Anguilla was finally allowed to secede; this arrangement was formally recognized in 1980, with Anguilla becoming a separate British dependency.

GEOGRAPHY

Location: Caribbean, islands between the Caribbean Sea and North Atlantic Ocean, east of Puerto Rico

Geographic coordinates: 18 15 N, 63 10 W

Map references: Central America and the Caribbean

Area: *total:* 91 sq km
country comparison to the world: 227
land: 91 sq km
water: 0 sq km

Area—comparative: about one-half the size of Washington, DC

Land boundaries: 0 km

Coastline: 61 km

Maritime claims: *territorial sea:* 3 nm
exclusive fishing zone: 200 nm

Climate: tropical; moderated by northeast trade winds

Terrain: flat and low-lying island of coral and limestone

Elevation extremes: *lowest point:* Caribbean Sea 0 m
highest point: Crocus Hill 65 m

Natural resources: salt, fish, lobster

Land use: *arable land:* 0%
permanent crops: 0%
other: 100% (mostly rock with sparse scrub oak, few trees, some commercial salt ponds) (2011)

Irrigated land: NA

Natural hazards: frequent hurricanes and other tropical storms (July to October)

Environment—current issues: supplies of potable water sometimes cannot meet increasing demand largely because of poor distribution system

Geography—note: the most northerly of the Leeward Islands in the Lesser Antilles

PEOPLE AND SOCIETY

Nationality: *noun:* Anguillan(s)
adjective: Anguillan

Ethnic groups: black (predominant) 90.1%, mixed, mulatto 4.6%, white 3.7%, other 1.5% (2001 census)

Languages: English (official)

Religions: Protestant 83.1% (Anglican 29%, Methodist 23.9%, other Protestant 30.2%), Roman Catholic 5.7%, other Christian 1.7%, other 5.2%, none or unspecified 4.3% (2001 census)

Population: 16,086 (July 2014 est.)
country comparison to the world: 221

Age structure: *0-14 years:* 23.3% (male 1,918/female 1,826)
15-24 years: 14.1% (male 1,123/female 1,144)
25-54 years: 45% (male 3,269/female 3,965)
55-64 years: 8.3% (male 744/female 763)
65 years and over: 8.1% (male 658/female 676) (2014 est.)

Median age: *total:* 34.1 years
male: 32.4 years
female: 35.7 years (2014 est.)

Population growth rate: 2.06% (2014 est.)
country comparison to the world: 50

Birth rate: 12.68 births/1,000 population (2014 est.)
country comparison to the world: 157

Death rate: 4.54 deaths/1,000 population (2014 est.)
country comparison to the world: 202

Net migration rate: 12.43 migrant(s)/1,000 population (2014 est.)
country comparison to the world: 11

Urbanization: *urban population:* 100% of total population (2010) rate of urbanization: 1.7% annual rate of change (2010-15 est.)

Major cities—population: THE VALLEY (capital) 2,000 (2011)

Sex ratio: *at birth:* 1.03 male(s)/female
0-14 years: 1.05 male(s)/female
15-24 years: 0.98 male(s)/female
25-54 years: 0.82 male(s)/female
55-64 years: 0.92 male(s)/female
65 years and over: 0.96 male(s)/female
total population: 0.93 male(s)/female (2014 est.)

Infant mortality rate: *total:* 3.4 deaths/1,000 live births
country comparison to the world: 210
male: 3.81 deaths/1,000 live births
female: 2.97 deaths/1,000 live births (2014 est.)

Life expectancy at birth: *total population:* 81.2 years
country comparison to the world: 21
male: 78.61 years
female: 83.86 years (2014 est.)

Total fertility rate: 1.75 children born/woman (2014 est.)
country comparison to the world: 166

Contraceptive prevalence rate: 43%
note: percent of women aged 15-45 (2003)

Drinking water source:
Improved:
urban: 94.5% of population
total: 94.5% of population
Unimproved:
urban: 5.5% of population
total: 5.5% of population (2011 est.)

Sanitation facility access:
Improved:
urban: 97.9% of population
total: 97.9% of population
Unimproved:
urban: 2.1% of population
total: 2.1% of population (2011 est.)

HIV/AIDS—adult prevalence rate: NA

HIV/AIDS—people living with HIV/AIDS: NA

HIV/AIDS—deaths: NA

Education expenditures: 2.8% of GDP (2008)
country comparison to the world: 146

Literacy: *definition:* age 12 and over can read and write
total population: 95%
male: 95%
female: 95% (1984 est.)

School life expectancy (primary to tertiary education): *total:* 11 years
male: 11 years
female: 11 years (2008)

GOVERNMENT

Country name: *conventional long form:* none
conventional short form: Anguilla

Dependency status: overseas territory of the UK

Government type: NA

Capital: *name:* The Valley
geographic coordinates: 18 13 N, 63 03 W
time difference: UTC-4 (1 hour ahead of Washington, DC during Standard Time)

Administrative divisions: none (overseas territory of the UK)

Independence: none (overseas territory of the UK)

National holiday: Anguilla Day, 30 May (1967)

Constitution: several previous; latest 1 April 1982; amended 1990 (2013)

Legal system: common law based on the English model

Suffrage: 18 years of age; universal

Executive branch: *chief of state:* Queen ELIZABETH II (since 6 February 1952); represented by Governor Christina SCOTT (since 23 July 2013)
head of government: Chief Minister Hubert HUGHES (since 16 February 2010)
cabinet: Executive Council appointed by the governor from among the elected members of the House of Assembly
(For more information visit the World Leaders website)
elections: the monarchy is hereditary; governor appointed by the monarch; following legislative elections, the leader of the majority party or the leader of the majority coalition usually appointed chief minister by the governor

Legislative branch: unicameral House of Assembly (11 seats; 7 members elected by direct popular vote, 2 ex officio members, and 2 appointed; members serve five-year terms)
elections: last held on 15 February 2010 (next to be held in 2015)
election results: percent of vote by party—NA; seats by party—AUM 4, AUF 2, APP 1

Judicial branch: *highest court(s):* the Eastern Caribbean Supreme Court (ECSC) is the itinerant superior court of record for the 9-member

Organization of Eastern Caribbean States to include Anguilla; the ECSC—headquartered on St. Lucia—is headed by the chief justice and is comprised of the Court of Appeal with 3 justices and the High Court with 16 judges; sittings of the Court of Appeal and High Court rotate among the 9 member states; High Court judges reside in 7 member states, though none resides on Anguilla
judge selection and term of office: Eastern Caribbean Supreme Court chief justice appointed by Her Majesty, Queen ELIZABETH II; other justices and judges appointed by the Judicial and Legal Services Commission; Court of Appeal justices appointed for life with mandatory retirement at age 65; High Court judges appointed for life with mandatory retirement at age 62
subordinate courts: Magistrate's Court; Juvenile Court

Political parties and leaders: Anguilla Progressive Party or APP [Brent DAVIS]; Anguilla Strategic Alternative or ANSA [Edison BAIRD]; Anguilla United Front or AUF [Osbourne FLEMING, Victor BANKS] (a coalition of the Anguilla Democratic Party or ADP and the Anguilla National Alliance or ANA); Anguilla United Movement or AUM [Hubert HUGHES]

International organization participation: Caricom (associate), CDB, Interpol (subbureau), OECS, UPU

Diplomatic representation in the US: none (overseas territory of the UK)

Diplomatic representation from the US: none (overseas territory of the UK)

Flag description: blue, with the flag of the UK in the upper hoist-side quadrant and the Anguillan coat of arms centered in the outer half of the flag; the coat of arms depicts three orange dolphins in an interlocking circular design on a white background with a turquoise-blue field below; the white in the background represents peace; the blue base symbolizes the surrounding sea, as well as faith, youth, and hope; the three dolphins stand for endurance, unity, and strength

National symbol(s): dolphin

National anthem: *name:* "God Bless Anguilla"
lyrics/music: Alex RICHARDSON
note: local anthem adopted 1981; as a territory of the United Kingdom, "God Save the Queen" is official (see United Kingdom)

ECONOMY

Economy—overview: Anguilla has few natural resources, and the economy depends heavily on luxury tourism, offshore banking, lobster fishing, and remittances from emigrants. Increased activity in the tourism industry has spurred the growth of the construction sector contributing to economic growth. Anguillan officials have put substantial effort into developing the offshore financial sector, which is small but growing. In the medium term, prospects for the economy will depend largely on the tourism sector and, therefore, on revived income growth in the industrialized nations as well as on favorable weather conditions.

GDP (purchasing power parity): $175.4 million (2009 est.)
country comparison to the world: 221
$191.7 million (2008 est.)
$108.9 million (2004 est.)

GDP (official exchange rate): $175.4 million (2009 est.)

GDP—real growth rate: -8.5% (2009 est.)
country comparison to the world: 218

GDP—per capita (PPP): $12,200 (2008 est.)
country comparison to the world: 104

GDP—composition, by end use:
household consumption: 74.5%
government consumption: 20.1%
investment in fixed capital: 22.1%
exports of goods and services: 43.7%
imports of goods and services: -60.4% (2013 est.)

GDP—composition, by sector of origin:
agriculture: 2.5%
industry: 23.6%
services: 73.8% (2013 est.)

Agriculture—products: small quantities of tobacco, vegetables; cattle raising

Industries: tourism, boat building, offshore financial services

Industrial production growth rate: 2% (2013 est.)

Labor force: 6,049 (2001)
country comparison to the world: 220

Labor force—by occupation: *agriculture/fishing/forestry/mining:* 4%
manufacturing: 3%
construction: 18%
transportation and utilities: 10%
commerce: 36%
services: 29% (2000 est.)

Unemployment rate: 8% (2002)
country comparison to the world: 88

Population below poverty line: 23% (2002)

Household income or consumption by percentage share: *lowest 10%:* NA%
highest 10%: NA%

Budget: *revenues:* $69.52 million
expenditures: $78.37 million (2012 est.)

Taxes and other revenues: 39.6% of GDP (2012 est.)
country comparison to the world: 45

Budget surplus (+) or deficit (-): -5% of GDP (2012 est.)
country comparison to the world: 165

Public debt: 20% of GDP (2013 est.)
country comparison to the world: 134 21.7% of GDP (2012 est.)

Fiscal year: 1 April–31 March

Inflation rate (consumer prices): 3.1% (2013 est.)
country comparison to the world: 117
4.4% (2012 est.)

Central bank discount rate: 6.5% (31 December 2010 est.)
country comparison to the world: 50
6.5% (31 December 2009 est.)

Commercial bank prime lending rate: 9.4% (31 December 2013 est.)
country comparison to the world: 97
9.38% (31 December 2012 est.)

Stock of narrow money: $16.89 million (31 December 2013 est.)
country comparison to the world: 190
$15.79 million (31 December 2012 est.)

Stock of broad money: $384.4 million (31 December 2013 est.)
country comparison to the world: 182
$373.2 million (31 December 2012 est.)

Stock of domestic credit: $498.1 million (31 December 2013 est.)
country comparison to the world: 169
$483.3 million (31 December 2012 est.)

Current account balance: -$54.3 million (2013 est.)
country comparison to the world: 70
-$44.8 million (2012 est.)

Exports: $12.2 million (2013 est.)
country comparison to the world: 211
$7.3 million (2012 est.)

Exports—commodities: lobster, fish, livestock, salt, concrete blocks, rum

Imports: $140.1 million (2013 est.)
country comparison to the world: 207
$129.3 million (2012 est.)

Imports—commodities: fuels, foodstuffs, manufactures, chemicals, trucks, textiles

Debt—external: $8.8 million (1998)
country comparison to the world: 199

Exchange rates: East Caribbean dollars (XCD) per US dollar—
2.7 (2013 est.)
2.7 (2012 est.)
2.7 (2010 est.), 2.7 (2009)

COMMUNICATIONS

Telephones—main lines in use: 6,000 (2012)
country comparison to the world: 207

Telephones—mobile cellular: 26,000 (2012)
country comparison to the world: 209

Telephone system: *general assessment:* modern internal telephone system
domestic: fixed-line teledensity is roughly 40 per 100 persons; mobile-cellular teledensity is roughly 170 per 100 persons
international: country code—1-264; landing point for the East Caribbean Fiber System submarine cable with links to 13 other islands in the eastern Caribbean extending from the British Virgin Islands to Trinidad; microwave radio relay to island of Saint Martin/Sint Maarten (2011)

Broadcast media: 1 private TV station; multichannel cable TV subscription services are available; about 10 radio stations, one of which is government-owned (2007)

Internet country code: .ai

Internet hosts: 269 (2012)
country comparison to the world: 192

Internet users: 3,700 (2009)
country comparison to the world: 208

TRANSPORTATION

Airports: 2 (2013)
country comparison to the world: 197

Airports—with paved runways: *total:* 1
1,524 to 2,437 m: 1 (2013)

Airports—with unpaved runways: *total:* 1
under 914 m: 1 (2013)

Roadways: *total:* 175 km
country comparison to the world: 210
paved: 82 km
unpaved: 93 km (2004)

Ports and terminals: *major seaport(s):* Blowing Point, Road Bay

MILITARY

Manpower available for military service: *males age 16-49:* 3,641 (2010 est.)

Manpower fit for military service: *males age 16-49:* 3,009
females age 16-49: 3,397 (2010 est.)

Manpower reaching militarily significant age annually: *male:* 111
female: 113 (2010 est.)

Military—note: defense is the responsibility of the UK

TRANSNATIONAL ISSUES

Disputes—international: none

Illicit drugs: transshipment point for South American narcotics destined for the US and Europe

ANTARCTICA

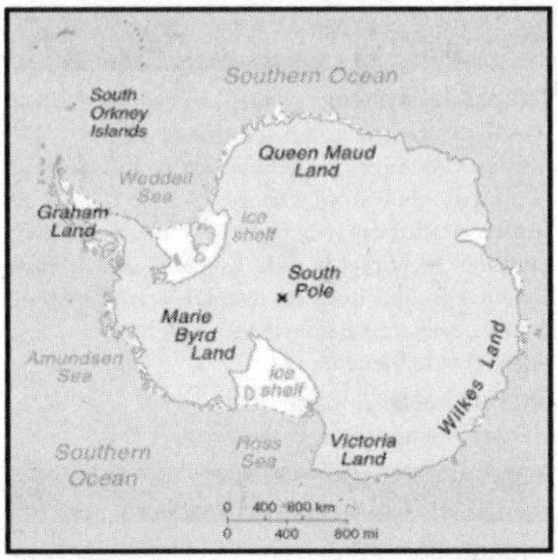

INTRODUCTION

Background: Speculation over the existence of a "southern land" was not confirmed until the early 1820s when British and American commercial operators and British and Russian national expeditions began exploring the Antarctic Peninsula region and other areas south of the Antarctic Circle. Not until 1840 was it established that Antarctica was indeed a continent and not just a group of islands or an area of ocean. Several exploration "firsts" were achieved in the early 20th century, but generally the area saw little human activity. Following World War II, however, the continent experienced an upsurge in scientific research. A number of countries have set up a range of year-round and seasonal stations, camps, and refuges to support scientific research in Antarctica. Seven have made territorial claims, but not all countries recognize these claims. In order to form a legal framework for the activities of nations on the continent, an Antarctic Treaty was negotiated that neither denies nor gives recognition to existing territorial claims; signed in 1959, it entered into force in 1961.

GEOGRAPHY

Location: continent mostly south of the Antarctic Circle

Geographic coordinates: 90 00 S, 0 00 E

Map references: Antarctic Region

Area: *total:* 14 million sq km
land: 14 million sq km (280,000 sq km ice-free, 13.72 million sq km ice-covered) (est.)
note: fifth-largest continent, following Asia, Africa, North America, and South America, but larger than Australia and the subcontinent of Europe

Area—comparative: slightly less than 1.5 times the size of the US

Land boundaries: 0 km
note: see entry on Disputes—international

Coastline: 17,968 km

Maritime claims: Australia, Chile, and Argentina claim Exclusive Economic Zone (EEZ) rights or similar over 200 nm extensions seaward from their continental claims, but like the claims themselves, these zones are not accepted by other countries; 21 of 28 Antarctic consultative nations have made no claims to Antarctic territory (although Russia and the US have reserved the right to do so) and do not recognize the claims of the other nations; also see the Disputes—international entry

Climate: severe low temperatures vary with latitude, elevation, and distance from the ocean; East Antarctica is colder than West Antarctica because of its higher elevation; Antarctic Peninsula has the most moderate climate; higher temperatures occur in January along the coast and average slightly below freezing

Terrain: about 98% thick continental ice sheet and 2% barren rock, with average elevations between 2,000 and 4,000 meters; mountain ranges up to nearly 5,000 meters; ice-free coastal areas include parts of southern Victoria Land, Wilkes Land, the Antarctic Peninsula area, and parts of Ross Island on McMurdo Sound; glaciers form ice shelves along about half of the coastline, and floating ice shelves constitute 11% of the area of the continent

Elevation extremes: *lowest point:* Bentley Subglacial Trench -2,540 m
highest point: Vinson Massif 4,897 m
note: the lowest known land point in Antarctica is hidden in the Bentley Subglacial Trench; at its surface is the deepest ice yet discovered and the world's lowest elevation not under seawater

Natural resources: iron ore, chromium, copper, gold, nickel, platinum and other minerals, and coal and hydrocarbons have been found in small noncommercial quantities; none presently exploited; krill, finfish, and crab have been taken by commercial fisheries

Land use: *arable land:* 0% permanent crops: 0%
other: 100% (ice 98%, barren rock 2%) (2011)

Natural hazards: katabatic (gravity-driven) winds blow coastward from the high interior; frequent blizzards form near the foot of the plateau; cyclonic storms form over the ocean and move clockwise along the coast; volcanism on Deception Island and isolated areas of West Antarctica; other seismic activity rare and weak; large icebergs may calve from ice shelf

Environment—current issues: in 1998, NASA satellite data showed that the Antarctic ozone hole was the largest on record, covering 27 million square kilometers; researchers in 1997 found that increased ultraviolet light passing through the hole damages the DNA of icefish, an Antarctic fish lacking hemoglobin; ozone depletion earlier was shown to harm one-celled Antarctic marine plants; in 2002, significant areas of ice shelves disintegrated in response to regional warming

Geography—note: the coldest, windiest, highest (on average), and driest continent; during summer, more solar radiation reaches the surface at the South Pole than is received at the Equator in an equivalent period; mostly uninhabitable

PEOPLE AND SOCIETY

Population: no indigenous inhabitants, but there are both permanent and summer-only staffed research stations
note: 29 nations, all signatory to the Antarctic Treaty, operate through their National Antarctic Program a number of seasonal-only (summer) and year-round research stations on the continent and its nearby islands south of 60 degrees south latitude (the region covered by the Antarctic Treaty); the population engaging in and supporting science or managing and protecting the Antarctic region varies from approximately 4,400 in summer to 1,100 in winter; in addition, approximately 1,000 personnel, including ship's crew and scientists doing onboard research, are present in the waters of the treaty region; peak summer (December-February) population—4,490 total; Argentina 667, Australia 200, Australia and Romania jointly 13, Belgium 20, Brazil 40, Bulgaria 18, Chile 359, China 90, Czech Republic 20, Ecuador 26, Finland 20, France 125, France and Italy jointly 60, Germany 90, India 65, Italy 102, Japan 125, South Korea 70, NZ 85, Norway 44, Peru 28, Poland 40, Russia 429, South Africa 80, Spain 50, Sweden 20, Ukraine 24, UK 217, US 1,293, Uruguay 70 (2008-2009); winter (June-August) station population—1,106 total; Argentina 176, Australia 62, Brazil 12, Chile 114, China 29, France 26, France and Italy jointly 13, Germany 9, India 25, Japan 40, South Korea 18, NZ 10, Norway 7, Poland 12, Russia 148, South Africa 10, Ukraine 12, UK 37, US 337, Uruguay 9 (2009); research stations operated within the Antarctic Treaty area (south of 60 degrees south latitude) by National Antarctic Programs:; year-round stations—40 total; Argentina 6, Australia 3, Brazil 1, Chile 6, China 2, France 1, France and Italy jointly 1, Germany 1, India 1, Japan 1, South Korea 1, NZ 1, Norway 1, Poland 1, Russia 5, South Africa 1, Ukraine 1, UK 2, US 3, Uruguay 1 (2009); a range of seasonal-only (summer) stations, camps, and refuges—Argentina, Australia, Belgium, Bulgaria, Brazil, Chile, China, Czech Republic, Ecuador, Finland, France, Germany, India, Italy, Japan, South Korea, New Zealand, Norway, Peru, Poland, Romania (with Australia), Russia, South Africa, Spain, Sweden, Ukraine, UK, US, and Uruguay (2008-2009); in addition, during the austral summer some nations have numerous occupied locations such as tent camps, summer-long temporary facilities, and mobile traverses in support of research (May 2009 est.)

GOVERNMENT

Country name: *conventional long form:* none
conventional short form: Antarctica

Government type: Antarctic Treaty Summary—the Antarctic region is governed by a system known as the Antarctic Treaty System; the system includes: 1. the Antarctic Treaty, signed on 1 December 1959 and entered into force on 23 June 1961, which establishes the legal framework for the management of Antarctica, 2. Recommendations and Measures adopted at meetings of Antarctic Treaty countries, 3. The Convention for the Conservation of Antarctic Seals (1972), 4. The Convention for the Conservation of Antarctic Marine Living Resources (1980), and 5. The Protocol on Environmental Protection to the Antarctic Treaty (1991); the 33rd Antarctic Treaty Consultative Meeting was held in Punta del Este, Uruguay in May 2010; at these periodic meetings, decisions are made by consensus (not by vote) of all consultative member nations; by April 2010, there were 48 treaty member nations:

28 consultative and 20 non-consultative; consultative (decision making) members include the seven nations that claim portions of Antarctica as national territory (some claims overlap) and 21 non-claimant nations; the US and Russia have reserved the right to make claims; the US does not recognize the claims of others; Antarctica is administered through meetings of the consultative member nations; decisions from these meetings are carried out by these member nations (with respect to their own nationals and operations) in accordance with their own national laws; the years in parentheses indicate when a consultative member-nation acceded to the Treaty and when it was accepted as a consultative member, while no date indicates the country was an original 1959 treaty signatory; claimant nations are—Argentina, Australia, Chile, France, NZ, Norway, and the UK; nonclaimant consultative nations are—Belgium, Brazil (1975/1983), Bulgaria (1978/1998), China (1983/1985), Ecuador (1987/1990), Finland (1984/1989), Germany (1979/1981), India (1983/1983), Italy (1981/1987), Japan, South Korea (1986/1989), Netherlands (1967/1990), Peru (1981/1989), Poland Article 1—area to be used for peaceful purposes only; military activity, such as weapons testing, is prohibited, but military personnel and equipment may be used for scientific research or any other peaceful purpose; Article 2—freedom of scientific investigation and cooperation shall continue; Article 3—free exchange of information and personnel, cooperation with the UN and other international agencies; Article 4—does not recognize, dispute, or establish territorial claims and no new claims shall be asserted while the treaty is in force; Article 5—prohibits nuclear explosions or disposal of radioactive wastes; Article 6—includes under the treaty all land and ice shelves south of 60 degrees 00 minutes south and reserves high seas rights; Article 7—treaty-state observers have free access, including aerial observation, to any area and may inspect all stations, installations, and equipment; advance notice of all expeditions and of the introduction of military personnel must be given; Article 8—allow s for jurisdiction over observers and scientists by their own states; Article 9—frequent consultative meetings take place among member nations; Article 10—treaty states will discourage activities by any country in Antarctica that are contrary to the treaty; Article 11—disputes to be settled peacefully by the parties concerned or, ultimately, by the ICJ; Articles 12, 13, 14—deal with upholding, interpreting, and amending the treaty among involved nations; other agreements—some 200 recommendations adopted at treaty consultative meetings and ratified by governments; a mineral resources agreement was signed in 1988 but remains unratified; the Protocol on Environmental Protection to the Antarctic Treaty was signed 4 October 1991 and entered into force 14 January 1998; this agreement provides for the protection of the Antarctic environment through six specific annexes: 1) environmental impact assessment, 2) conservation of Antarctic fauna and flora, 3) waste disposal and waste management, 4) prevention of marine pollution, 5) area protection and management and 6) liability arising from environmental emergencies; it prohibits all activities relating to mineral resources except scientific research; a permanent Antarctic Treaty Secretariat was established in 2004 in Buenos Aires, Argentina

Legal system: Antarctica is administered through annual meetings—known as Antarctic Treaty Consultative Meetings—which include consultative member nations, non-consultative member nations, observer organizations, and expert organizations; decisions from these meetings are carried out by these member nations (with respect to their own nationals and operations) in accordance with their own national laws; more generally, access to the Antarctic Treaty area, that is to all areas between 60 and 90 degrees south latitude, is subject to a number of relevant legal instruments and authorization procedures adopted by the states party to the Antarctic Treaty; note—US law, including certain criminal offenses by or against US nationals, such as murder, may apply extraterritorially; some US laws directly apply to Antarctica; for example, the Antarctic Conservation Act, 16 U.S.C. section 2401 et seq., provides civil and criminal penalties for the following activities unless authorized by regulation of statute: the taking of native mammals or birds; the introduction of nonindigenous plants and animals; entry into specially protected areas; the discharge or disposal of pollutants; and the importation into the US of certain items from Antarctica; violation of the Antarctic Conservation Act carries penalties of up to $10,000 in fines and one year in prison; the National Science Foundation and Department of Justice share enforcement responsibilities; Public Law 95-541, the US Antarctic Conservation Act of 1978, as amended in 1996, requires expeditions from the US to Antarctica to notify, in advance, the Office of Oceans, Room 5805, Department of State, Washington, DC 20520, which reports such plans to other nations as required by the Antarctic Treaty; for more information, contact Permit Office, Office of Polar Programs, National Science Foundation, Arlington, Virginia 22230; telephone: (703) 292-8030, or visit its website at www.nsf.gov

ECONOMY

Economy—overview: Scientific undertakings rather than commercial pursuits are the predominate human activity in Antarctica. Fishing off the coast and tourism, both based abroad, account for Antarctica's limited economic activity. Antarctic fisheries, targeting three main species—Patagonian and Antarctic toothfish (Dissostichus eleginoides and D. mawsoni), mackerel icefish (Champsocephalus gunnari), and krill (Euphausia superba)—reported landing 141,147 metric tons in 2008-09 (1 July—30 June). (Estimated fishing is from the area covered by the Convention on the Conservation of Antarctic Marine Living Resources (CCAMLR), which extends slightly beyond the Antarctic Treaty area.) Unregulated fishing, particularly of Patagonian toothfish (also known as Chilean sea bass), is a serious problem. The CCAMLR determines the recommended catch limits for marine species. A total of 37,858 tourists visited the Antarctic Treaty area in the 2008-09 Antarctic summer, down from the 46,265 visitors in 2007-08 (estimates provided to the Antarctic Treaty by the International Association of Antarctica Tour Operators (IAATO); this does not include passengers on overflights). Nearly all of them were passengers on commercial (nongovernmental) ships and several yachts that make trips during the summer.

COMMUNICATIONS

Telephone system: *general assessment:* local systems at some research stations
domestic: commercial cellular networks operating in a small number of locations
international: country code—none allocated; via satellite (including mobile Inmarsat and Iridium systems) to and from all research stations, ships, aircraft, and most field parties (2007)
Internet country code: .aq
Internet hosts: 7,764 (2012)
country comparison to the world: 139

TRANSPORTATION

Airports: 23 (2013)
country comparison to the world: 134
Airports—with unpaved runways: *total: 23*
over 3,047 m: 3
2,438 to 3,047 m: 5
1,524 to 2,437 m: 1
914 to 1,523 m: 8 under 914 m: 6 (2013)
Heliports: 53
note: all year-round and seasonal stations operated by National Antarctic Programs stations have some kind of helicopter landing facilities, prepared (helipads) or unprepared (2012)
Ports and terminals: McMurdo Station; most coastal stations have sparse and intermittent offshore anchorages; a few stations have basic wharf facilities
Transportation—note: US coastal stations include McMurdo (77 51 S, 166 40 E) and Palmer (64 43 S, 64 03 W); government use only except by permit (see Permit Office under "Legal System"); all ships at port are subject to inspection in accordance with Article 7, Antarctic Treaty; relevant legal instruments and authorization procedures adopted by the states parties to the Antarctic Treaty regulating access to the Antarctic Treaty area to all areas between 60 and 90 degrees of latitude south have to be complied with (see "Legal System"); The Hydrographic Commission on Antarctica (HCA), a commission of the International Hydrographic Organization (IHO), is responsible for hydrographic surveying and nautical charting matters in Antarctic Treaty area; it coordinates and facilitates provision of accurate and appropriate charts and other aids to navigation in support of safety of navigation in region; membership of HCA is open to any IHO Member State whose government has acceded to the Antarctic Treaty and which contributes resources or data to IHO Chart coverage of the area

MILITARY

Military—note: the Antarctic Treaty prohibits any measures of a military nature, such as the establishment of military bases and fortifications, the carrying out of military maneuvers, or the testing of any type of weapon; it permits the use of military personnel or equipment for scientific research or for any other peaceful purposes

TRANSNATIONAL ISSUES

Disputes—international: the Antarctic Treaty freezes, and most states do not recognize, the land and maritime territorial claims made by Argentina, Australia, Chile, France, New Zealand, Norway, and the United Kingdom (some overlapping) for three-fourths of the continent; the US and Russia reserve the right to make claims; no formal claims have been made in the sector between 90 degrees west and 150 degrees west; the International Whaling Commission created a sanctuary around the entire continent to deter catches by countries claiming to conduct scientific whaling; Australia has established a similar preserve in the waters around its territorial claim

ANTIGUA AND BARBUDA

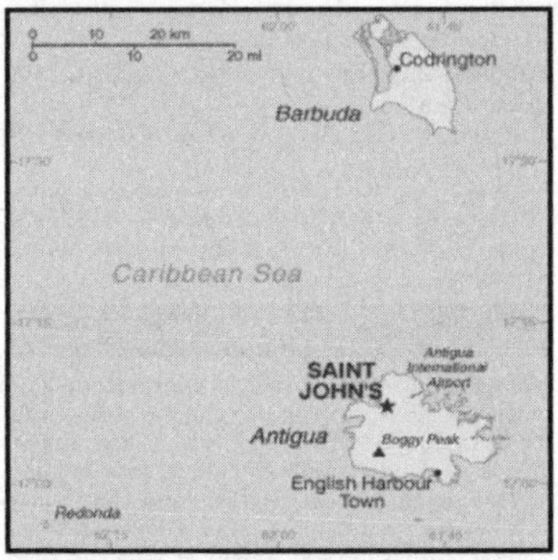

INTRODUCTION

Background: The Siboney were the first people to inhabit the islands of Antigua and Barbuda in 2400 B.C., but Arawak Indians populated the islands when COLUMBUS landed on his second voyage in 1493. Early Spanish and French settlements were succeeded by an English colony in 1667. Slavery, established to run the sugar plantations on Antigua, was abolished in 1834. The islands became an independent state within the British Commonwealth of Nations in 1981.

GEOGRAPHY

Location: Caribbean, islands between the Caribbean Sea and the North Atlantic Ocean, east-southeast of Puerto Rico

Geographic coordinates: 17 03 N, 61 48 W

Map references: Central America and the Caribbean

Area: *total:* 442.6 sq km (Antigua 280 sq km; Barbuda 161 sq km)
country comparison to the world: 201
land: 442.6 sq km
water: 0 sq km
note: includes Redonda, 1.6 sq km

Area—comparative: 2.5 times the size of Washington, DC

Land boundaries: 0 km

Coastline: 153 km

Maritime claims: *territorial sea:* 12 nm
contiguous zone: 24 nm
exclusive economic zone: 200 nm
continental shelf: 200 nm or to the edge of the continental margin

Climate: tropical maritime; little seasonal temperature variation

Terrain: mostly low-lying limestone and coral islands, with some higher volcanic areas

Elevation extremes: *lowest point:* Caribbean Sea 0 m
highest point: Boggy Peak 402 m

Natural resources: NEGL; pleasant climate fosters tourism

Land use: *arable land:* 9.09%
permanent crops: 2.27%
other: 88.64% (2011)

Irrigated land: 1.3 sq km (2003)

Total renewable water resources: 0.05 cu km (2011)

Freshwater withdrawal (domestic/industrial/agricultural): *total:* 0.01 cu km/yr (63%/21%/15%)
per capita: 97.67 cu m/yr (2005)

Natural hazards: hurricanes and tropical storms (July to October); periodic droughts

Environment—current issues: water management—a major concern because of limited natural freshwater resources—is further hampered by the clearing of trees to increase crop production, causing rainfall to run off quickly

Environment—international agreements: *party to:* Biodiversity, Climate Change, Climate Change-Kyoto Protocol, Desertification, Endangered Species, Environmental Modification, Hazardous Wastes, Law of the Sea, Marine Dumping, Ozone Layer Protection, Ship Pollution, Wetlands, Whaling
signed, but not ratified: none of the selected agreements

Geography—note: Antigua has a deeply indented shoreline with many natural harbors and beaches; Barbuda has a large western harbor

PEOPLE AND SOCIETY

Nationality: *noun:* Antiguan(s), Barbudan(s)
adjective: Antiguan, Barbudan

Ethnic groups: black 91%, mixed 4.4%, white 1.7%, other 2.9% (2001 census)

Languages: English (official), local dialects

Religions: Protestant 76.4% (Anglican 25.7%, Seventh-Day Adventist 12.3%, Pentecostal 10.6%, Moravian 10.5%, Methodist 7.9%, Baptist 4.9%, Church of God 4.5%), Roman Catholic 10.4%, other Christian 5.4%, other 2%, none or unspecified 5.8% (2001 census)

Population: 91,295 (July 2014 est.)
country comparison to the world: 199

Age structure: *0-14 years:* 24.3% (male 11,289/female 10,932)
15-24 years: 16.8% (male 7,588/female 7,723)
25-54 years: 42.6% (male 17,789/female 21,137)
55-64 years: 7.3% (male 3,694/female 4,441)
65 years and over: 7.1% (male 2,886/female 3,816) (2014 est.)

Dependency ratios:
total dependency ratio: 47.2%
youth dependency ratio: 36.7%
elderly dependency ratio: 10.5% potential support ratio: 9.5 (2013)

Median age: *total:* 31.1 years
male: 29.4 years
female: 32.6 years (2014 est.)

Population growth rate: 1.25% (2014 est.)
country comparison to the world: 95

Birth rate: 15.94 births/1,000 population (2014 est.)
country comparison to the world: 124

Death rate: 5.7 deaths/1,000 population (2014 est.)
country comparison to the world: 173

Net migration rate: 2.23 migrant(s)/1,000 population (2014 est.)
country comparison to the world: 44

Urbanization: *urban population:* 30% of total population (2010)
rate of urbanization: 1.4% annual rate of change (2010-15 est.)

Major urban areas—population: SAINT JOHN'S (capital) 27,000 (2011)

Sex ratio: *at birth:* 1.05 male(s)/female
0-14 years: 1.03 male(s)/female
15-24 years: 0.98 male(s)/female
25-54 years: 0.84 male(s)/female
55-64 years: 0.9 male(s)/female
65 years and over: 0.76 male(s)/female
total population: 0.9 male(s)/female (2014 est.)

Infant mortality rate: *total:* 13.29 deaths/1,000 live births
country comparison to the world: 119
male: 15.3 deaths/1,000 live births
female: 11.17 deaths/1,000 live births (2014 est.)

Life expectancy at birth: *total population:* 76.12 years
country comparison to the world: 85
male: 74.04 years
female: 78.3 years (2014 est.)

Total fertility rate: 2.03 children born/woman (2014 est.)
country comparison to the world: 120

Health expenditures: 5.9% of GDP (2011)
country comparison to the world: 112

Physicians density: 0.17 physicians/1,000 population (1999)

Hospital bed density: 2.1 beds/1,000 population (2011)

Drinking water source:
Improved:
urban: 97.9% of population
rural: 97.9% of population
total: 97.9% of population
Unimproved:
urban: 2.1% of population
rural: 2.1% of population

total: 2.1% of population (2011 est.)

Sanitation facility access:
Improved:
urban: 91.4% of population
rural: 91.4% of population
total: 91.4% of population
Unimproved:
urban: 8.6% of population
rural: 8.66% of population
total: 8.6% of population (2011 est.)

HIV/AIDS—adult prevalence rate: NA

HIV/AIDS—people living with HIV/AIDS: NA

HIV/AIDS—deaths: NA

Obesity—adult prevalence rate: 25.6% (2008)
country comparison to the world: 52

Education expenditures: 2.4% of GDP (2009)
country comparison to the world: 159

Literacy: *definition:* age 15 and over has completed five or more years of schooling
total population: 99%
male: 98.4%
female: 99.4% (2011 est.)

School life expectancy (primary to tertiary education): *total:* 14 years
male: 13 years
female: 15 years (2012)

Unemployment, youth ages 15-24: *total:* 19.9%
country comparison to the world: 59
male: 18.4%
female: 21.6% (2001)

GOVERNMENT

Country name: *conventional long form:* none
conventional short form: Antigua and Barbuda

Government type: constitutional monarchy with a parliamentary system of government and a Commonwealth realm

Capital: *name:* Saint John's
geographic coordinates: 17 07 N, 61 51 W
time difference: UTC-4 (1 hour ahead of Washington, DC during Standard Time)

Administrative divisions: 6 parishes and 2 dependencies*; Barbuda*, Redonda*, Saint George, Saint John, Saint Mary, Saint Paul, Saint Peter, Saint Philip

Independence: 1 November 1981 (from the UK)

National holiday: Independence Day (National Day), 1 November (1981)

Constitution: several previous; latest presented 31 July 1981; effective 31 October 1981 (Antigua and Barbuda Constitutional Order 1981) (2011)

Legal system: common law based on the English model

International law organization participation: has not submitted an ICJ jurisdiction declaration; accepts ICCt jurisdiction

Suffrage: 18 years of age; universal

Executive branch: *chief of state:* Queen ELIZABETH II (since 6 February 1952); represented by Governor General Louisse LAKE-TACK (since 17 July 2007)
head of government: Prime Minister Winston Baldwin SPENCER (since 24 March 2004)
cabinet: Council of Ministers appointed by the governor general on the advice of the prime minister (For more information visit the World Leaders website)
elections: the monarchy is hereditary; governor general chosen by the monarch on the advice of the prime minister; following legislative elections, the leader of the majority party or the leader of the majority coalition usually appointed prime minister by the governor general

Legislative branch: bicameral Parliament consists of the Senate (17 seats; members appointed by the governor general) and the House of Representatives (17 seats; members are elected by proportional representation to serve five-year terms)
elections: House of Representatives—last held on 12 March 2009 (next to be held in 2014)
election results: percent of vote by party—UPP 50.9%, ALP 47.2%, BPM 1.1%, other 0.8%; seats by party—UPP 9, ALP 7, BPM 1

Judicial branch: *highest court(s):* the Eastern Caribbean Supreme Court (ECSC) is the itinerant superior court of record for the 9-member Organization of Eastern Caribbean States to include Antigua and Barbuda; the ECSC—headquartered on St. Lucia—is headed by the chief justice and is comprised of the Court of Appeal with 3 justices and the High Court with 16 judges; sittings of the Court of Appeal and High Court rotate among the 9 member states; 2 High Court judges reside on Antigua and Barbuda note—Antigua and Barbuda replaced the Judicial Committee of the Privy Council in London as the final appellate court; also a member of the Caribbean Court of Justice
judge selection and term of office: Eastern Caribbean Supreme Court Chief Justice appointed by the Her Majesty, Queen ELIZABETH II; other justices and judges appointed by the Judicial and Legal Services Commission; Court of Appeal justices appointed for life with mandatory retirement at age 65; High Court judges appointed for life with mandatory retirement at age 62
subordinate courts: Industrial Court; Magistrates' Courts

Political parties and leaders: Antigua Labor Party or ALP [Gaston BROWNE]; Barbuda People's Movement or BPM [Trevor WALKER]; Barbuda People's Movement for Change [Arthur NIBBS]; Barbudans for a Better Barbuda [Ordrick SAMUEL]; United Progressive Party or UPP [W. Baldwin SPENCER] (a coalition of three parties—Antigua Caribbean Liberation Movement or ACLM, Progressive Labor Movement or PLM, United National Democratic Party or UNDP)

Political pressure groups and leaders: Antigua Trades and Labor Union or ATLU [Wigley GEORGE]; People's Democratic Movement or PDM [Hugh MARSHALL]

International organization participation: ACP, AOSIS, C, Caricom, CDB, CELAC, FAO, G-77, IBRD, ICAO, ICC (NGOs), ICRM, IDA, IFAD, IFC, IFRCS, ILO, IMF, IMO, IMSO, Interpol, IOC, IOM, ISO (subscriber), ITU, ITUC (NGOs), MIGA, NAM, OAS, OECS, OPANAL, OPCW, Petrocaribe, UN, UNCTAD, UNESCO, UPU, WFTU (NGOs), WHO, WIPO, WMO, WTO

Diplomatic representation in the US: *chief of mission:* Ambassador Deborah Mae LOVELL (since 8 March 2005)
chancery: 3216 New Mexico Avenue NW, Washington, DC 20016
telephone: [1] (202) 362-5122
FAX: [1] (202) 362-5525
consulate(s) general: Miami, New York

Diplomatic representation from the US: the US does not have an embassy in Antigua and Barbuda; the US Ambassador to Barbados is accredited to Antigua and Barbuda

Flag description: red, with an inverted isosceles triangle based on the top edge of the flag; the triangle contains three horizontal bands of black (top), light blue, and white, with a yellow rising sun in the black band; the sun symbolizes the dawn of a new era, black represents the African heritage of most of the population, blue is for hope, and red is for the dynamism of the people; the "V" stands for victory; the successive yellow, blue, and white coloring is also meant to evoke the country's tourist attractions of sun, sea, and sand

National anthem: *name:* "Fair Antigua, We Salute Thee"
lyrics/music: Novelle Hamilton RICHARDS/ Walter Garnet Picart CHAMBERS
note: adopted 1967; as a Commonwealth country, in addition to the national anthem, "God Save the Queen" serves as the royal anthem (see United Kingdom)

ECONOMY

Economy—overview: Tourism continues to dominate Antigua and Barbuda's economy, accounting for nearly 60% of GDP and 40% of investment. The dual-island nation's agricultural production is focused on the domestic market and constrained by a limited water supply and a labor shortage stemming from the lure of higher wages in tourism and construction. Manufacturing comprises enclave-type assembly for export with major products being bedding, handicrafts, and electronic components. Prospects for economic growth in the medium term will continue to depend on tourist arrivals from the US, Canada, and Europe and potential damages from natural disasters. After taking office in 2004, the SPENCER government adopted an ambitious fiscal reform program and was successful in reducing its public debt-to-GDP ratio from approximately 130% in 2010 to 89% in 2012. In 2009, Antigua's economy was severely hit by the global economic crisis and suffered from the collapse of its largest private sector employer, a steep decline in tourism, a rise in debt, and a sharp economic contraction between 2009-11. Antigua has not yet returned to its pre-crisis growth levels.

GDP (purchasing power parity): $1.61 billion (2013 est.)
country comparison to the world: 195
$1.583 billion (2012 est.)
$1.558 billion (2011 est.)
note: data are in 2013 US dollars

GDP (official exchange rate): $1.22 billion (2013 est.)

GDP—real growth rate: 1.7% (2013 est.)
country comparison to the world: 150
1.6% (2012 est.)
-3% (2011 est.)

GDP—per capita (PPP): $18,400 (2013 est.)
country comparison to the world: 76
$18,100 (2012 est.)
$17,800 (2011 est.)
note: data are in 2013 US dollars

Gross national saving: 18% of GDP (2013 est.)
country comparison to the world: 89
18% of GDP (2012 est.)
18.4% of GDP (2011 est.)

GDP—composition, by end use:
household consumption: 55.8%
government consumption: 14.9%
investment in fixed capital: 28%
investment in inventories: 0.1%
exports of goods and services: 46.2%
imports of goods and services: -45% (2013 est.)

GDP—composition, by sector of origin:
agriculture: 2.2%

industry: 16.4%
services: 81.4% (2013 est.)

Agriculture—products: cotton, fruits, vegetables, bananas, coconuts, cucumbers, mangoes, sugarcane; livestock

Industries: tourism, construction, light manufacturing (clothing, alcohol, household appliances)

Industrial production growth rate: 1%
country comparison to the world: 145

Labor force: 30,000 (1991)
country comparison to the world: 205

Labor force—by occupation: *agriculture:* 7%
industry: 11%
services: 82% (1983)

Unemployment rate: 11% (2001 est.)
country comparison to the world: 115

Population below poverty line: NA%

Household income or consumption by percentage share: *lowest 10%:* NA%
highest 10%: NA%

Budget: *revenues:* $239.5 million
expenditures: $248.7 million (2012 est.)

Taxes and other revenues: 19.6% of GDP (2012 est.)
country comparison to the world: 168

Budget surplus (+) or deficit (-): -0.8% of GDP (2012 est.)
country comparison to the world: 60

Public debt: 89% of GDP (2012 est.)
country comparison to the world: 22
130% of GDP (2010 est.)

Fiscal year: 1 April–31 March

Inflation rate (consumer prices): 3% (2013 est.)
country comparison to the world: 113
3.4% (2012 est.)

Central bank discount rate: 6.5% (31 December 2010 est.)
country comparison to the world: 51
6.5% (31 December 2009 est.)

Commercial bank prime lending rate: 10.3% (31 December 2013 est.)
country comparison to the world: 86
10.13% (31 December 2012 est.)

Stock of narrow money: $213 million (31 December 2013 est.)
country comparison to the world: 177
$205.2 million (31 December 2012 est.)

Stock of broad money: $1.044 billion (31 December 2013 est.)
country comparison to the world: 168
$1.033 billion (31 December 2012 est.)

Stock of domestic credit: $1.111 billion (31 December 2013 est.)
country comparison to the world: 152
$1.111 billion (31 December 2012 est.)

Current account balance: -$164.8 million (2013 est.)
country comparison to the world: 82
-$78.5 million (2012 est.)

Exports: $55 million (2013 est.)
country comparison to the world: 195
$56.7 million (2012 est.)

Exports—commodities: petroleum products, bedding, handicrafts, electronic components, transport equipment, food and live animals

Imports: $340.8 million (2013 est.)
country comparison to the world: 195
$402.7 million (2012 est.)

Imports—commodities: food and live animals, machinery and transport equipment, manufactures, chemicals, oil

Debt—external: $441.2 million (31 December 2012)
country comparison to the world: 178
$458 million (June 2010)

Exchange rates: East Caribbean dollars (XCD) per US dollar—
2.7 (2013 est.)
2.7 (2012 est.)
2.7 (2010 est.)
2.7 (2009)

ENERGY

Electricity—production: 115 million kWh (2010 est.)
country comparison to the world: 196

Electricity—consumption: 107 million kWh (2010 est.)
country comparison to the world: 196

Electricity—exports: 0 kWh (2012 est.)
country comparison to the world: 93

Electricity—imports: 0 kWh (2012 est.)
country comparison to the world: 110

Electricity—installed generating capacity: 27,000 kW (2010 est.)
country comparison to the world: 199

Electricity—from fossil fuels: 100% of total installed capacity (2010 est.)
country comparison to the world: 1

Electricity—from nuclear fuels: 0% of total installed capacity (2010 est.)
country comparison to the world: 32

Electricity—from hydroelectric plants: 0% of total installed capacity (2010 est.)
country comparison to the world: 152

Electricity—from other renewable sources: 0% of total installed capacity (2010 est.)
country comparison to the world: 146

Crude oil—production: 0 bbl/day (2012 est.)
country comparison to the world: 148

Crude oil—exports: 0 bbl/day (2010 est.)
country comparison to the world: 75

Crude oil—imports: 0 bbl/day (2010 est.)
country comparison to the world: 147

Crude oil—proved reserves: 0 bbl (1 January 2013 es)
country comparison to the world: 102

Refined petroleum products—production: 0 bbl/day (2010 est.)
country comparison to the world: 116

Refined petroleum products—consumption: 5,000 bbl/day (2011 est.)
country comparison to the world: 168

Refined petroleum products—exports: 239.5 bbl/day (2010 est.)
country comparison to the world: 119

Refined petroleum products—imports: 4,790 bbl/day (2010 est.)
country comparison to the world: 154

Natural gas—production: 0 cu m (2011 est.)
country comparison to the world: 97

Natural gas—consumption: 0 cu m (2010 est.)
country comparison to the world: 116

Natural gas—exports: 0 cu m (2011 est.)
country comparison to the world: 54

Natural gas—imports: 0 cu m (2011 est.)
country comparison to the world: 149

Natural gas—proved reserves: 0 cu m (1 January 2013 es)
country comparison to the world: 108

Carbon dioxide emissions from consumption of energy: 731,600 Mt (2011 est.)
country comparison to the world: 174

COMMUNICATIONS

Telephones—main lines in use: 35,000 (2012)
country comparison to the world: 174

Telephones—mobile cellular: 179,800 (2012)
country comparison to the world: 182

Telephone system: *general assessment:* good automatic telephone system
domestic: fixed-line teledensity roughly 40 per 100 persons; mobile-cellular teledensity is some 200 per 100 persons
international: country code—1-268; landing points for the East Caribbean Fiber System (ECFS) and the Global Caribbean Network (GCN) submarine cable systems with links to other islands in the eastern Caribbean extending from the British Virgin Islands to Trinidad; satellite earth stations—2; tropospheric scatter to Saba (Netherlands) and Guadeloupe (France) (2011)

Broadcast media: state-controlled Antigua and Barbuda Broadcasting Service (ABS) operates 1 TV station; multi-channel cable TV subscription services are available; ABS operates 1 radio station; roughly 15 radio stations, some broadcasting on multiple frequencies (2007)

Internet country code: .ag

Internet hosts: 11,532 (2012)
country comparison to the world: 130

Internet users: 65,000 (2009)
country comparison to the world: 172

TRANSPORTATION

Airports: 3 (2013)
country comparison to the world: 192

Airports—with paved runways: *total:* 2
2,438 to 3,047 m: 1
under 914 m: 1 (2013)

Airports—with unpaved runways: *total:* 1
under 914 m: 1 (2013)

Roadways: *total:* 1,170 km
country comparison to the world: 182
paved: 386 km
unpaved: 784 km (2011)

Merchant marine: *total:* 1,257
country comparison to the world: 9
by type: bulk carrier 49, cargo 753, carrier 6, chemical tanker 4, container 407, liquefied gas 12, refrigerated cargo 7, roll on/roll off 17, vehicle carrier 2
foreign-owned: 1,215 (Albania 1, Colombia 1, Denmark 20, Estonia 10, Germany 1094, Greece 4, Iceland 10, Latvia 16, Lithuania 3, Mexico 1, Netherlands 17, Norway 9, NZ 2, Poland 2, Russia 3, Switzerland 7, Turkey 7, UK 1, US 7) (2010)

Ports and terminals: *major seaport(s):* Saint John's

MILITARY

Military branches: Ministry of National Security, Royal Antigua and Barbuda Defense Force (includes Antigua and Barbuda Coast Guard) (2012)

Military service age and obligation: 18 years of age for voluntary military service; no conscription; Governor-General has powers to call up men for national service and set the age at which they could be called up (2012)

Manpower available for military service: *males age 16-49:* 21,141
females age 16-49: 24,056 (2010 est.)

Manpower fit for military service: *males age 16-49:* 17,676
females age 16-49: 19,960 (2010 est.)

Manpower reaching militarily significant age annually: *male:* 806
female: 799 (2010 est.)

TRANSNATIONAL ISSUES

Disputes—international: none

Illicit drugs: considered a minor transshipment point for narcotics bound for the US and Europe; more significant as an offshore financial center

ARCTIC OCEAN

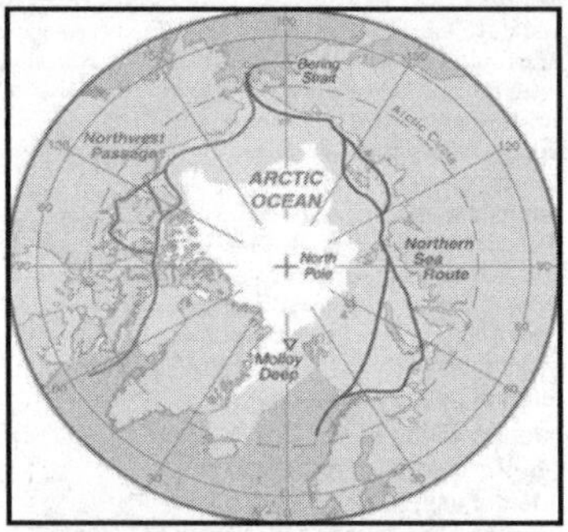

INTRODUCTION

Background: The Arctic Ocean is the smallest of the world's five oceans (after the Pacific Ocean, Atlantic Ocean, Indian Ocean, and the recently delimited Southern Ocean). The Northwest Passage (US and Canada) and Northern Sea Route (Norway and Russia) are two important seasonal waterways. In recent years the polar ice pack has thinned allowing for increased navigation and raising the possibility of future sovereignty and shipping disputes among countries bordering the Arctic Ocean.

GEOGRAPHY

Location: body of water between Europe, Asia, and North America, mostly north of the Arctic Circle

Geographic coordinates: 90 00 N, 0 00 E

Map references: Arctic

Area: *total:* 14.056 million sq km
note: includes Baffin Bay, Barents Sea, Beaufort Sea, Chukchi Sea, East Siberian Sea, Greenland Sea, Hudson Bay, Hudson Strait, Kara Sea, Laptev Sea, Northwest Passage, and other tributary water bodies

Area—comparative: slightly less than 1.5 times the size of the US

Coastline: 45,389 km

Climate: polar climate characterized by persistent cold and relatively narrow annual temperature ranges; winters characterized by continuous darkness, cold and stable weather conditions, and clear skies; summers characterized by continuous daylight, damp and foggy weather, and weak cyclones with rain or snow

Terrain: central surface covered by a perennial drifting polar icepack that, on average, is about 3 meters thick, although pressure ridges may be three times that thickness; clockwise drift pattern in the Beaufort Gyral Stream, but nearly straight-line movement from the New Siberian Islands (Russia) to Denmark Strait (between Greenland and Iceland); the icepack is surrounded by open seas during the summer, but more than doubles in size during the winter and extends to the encircling landmasses; the ocean floor is about 50% continental shelf (highest percentage of any ocean) with the remainder a central basin interrupted by three submarine ridges (Alpha Cordillera, Nansen Cordillera, and Lomonosov Ridge)

Elevation extremes: *lowest point:* Fram Basin -4,665 m
highest point: sea level 0 m

Natural resources: sand and gravel aggregates, placer deposits, polymetallic nodules, oil and gas fields, fish, marine mammals (seals and whales)

Natural hazards: ice islands occasionally break away from northern Ellesmere Island; icebergs calved from glaciers in western Greenland and extreme northeastern Canada; permafrost in islands; virtually ice locked from October to June; ships subject to superstructure icing from October to May

Environment—current issues: endangered marine species include walruses and whales; fragile ecosystem slow to change and slow to recover from disruptions or damage; thinning polar icepack

Geography—note: major chokepoint is the southern Chukchi Sea (northern access to the Pacific Ocean via the Bering Strait); strategic location between North America and Russia; shortest marine link between the extremes of eastern and western Russia; floating research stations operated by the US and Russia; maximum snow cover in March or April about 20 to 50 centimeters over the frozen ocean; snow cover lasts about 10 months

ECONOMY

Economy—overview: Economic activity is limited to the exploitation of natural resources, including petroleum, natural gas, fish, and seals.

TRANSPORTATION

Ports and terminals: *major seaport(s):* Churchill (Canada), Murmansk (Russia), Prudhoe Bay (US)

Transportation—note: sparse network of air, ocean, river, and land routes; the Northwest Passage (North America) and Northern Sea Route (Eurasia) are important seasonal waterways

TRANSNATIONAL ISSUES

Disputes—international: Canada and the United States dispute how to divide the Beaufort Sea and the status of the Northwest Passage but continue to work cooperatively to survey the Arctic continental shelf; Denmark (Greenland) and Norway have made submissions to the Commission on the Limits of the Continental shelf (CLCS) and Russia is collecting additional data to augment its 2001 CLCS submission; record summer melting of sea ice in the Arctic has renewed interest in maritime shipping lanes and sea floor exploration; Norway and Russia signed a comprehensive maritime boundary agreement in 2010

ARGENTINA

INTRODUCTION

Background: In 1816, the United Provinces of the Rio Plata declared their independence from Spain. After Bolivia, Paraguay, and Uruguay went their separate ways, the area that remained became Argentina. The country's population and culture were heavily shaped by immigrants from throughout Europe, with Italy and Spain providing the largest percentage of new comers from 1860 to 1930. Up until about the mid-20th century, much of Argentina's history was dominated by periods of internal political conflict between Federalists and Unitarians and between civilian and military factions. After World War II, an era of Peronist populism and direct and indirect military interference in subsequent governments was follow ed by a military junta that took pow er in 1976. Democracy returned in 1983 after a failed bid to seize the Falkland Islands (Islas Malvinas) by force, and has persisted despite numerous challenges, the most formidable of which was a severe economic crisis in 2001-02 that led to violent public protests and the successive resignations of several presidents. In January 2013, Argentina assumed a nonpermanent seat on the UN Security Council for the 2013-14 term.

GEOGRAPHY

Location: Southern South America, bordering the South Atlantic Ocean, between Chile and Uruguay

Geographic coordinates: 34 00 S, 64 00 W

Map references: South America

Area: *total:* 2,780,400 sq km
country comparison to the world: 8
land: 2,736,690 sq km
water: 43,710 sq km

Area—comparative: slightly less than three-tenths the size of the US

Land boundaries: *total:* 9,861 km

border countries: Bolivia 832 km, Brazil 1,261 km, Chile 5,308 km, Paraguay 1,880 km, Uruguay 580 km

Coastline: 4,989 km

Maritime claims: *territorial sea:* 12 nm
contiguous zone: 24 nm
exclusive economic zone: 200 nm
continental shelf: 200 nm or to the edge of the continental margin

Climate: mostly temperate; arid in southeast; subantarctic in southwest

Terrain: rich plains of the Pampas in northern half, flat to rolling plateau of Patagonia in south, rugged Andes along western border

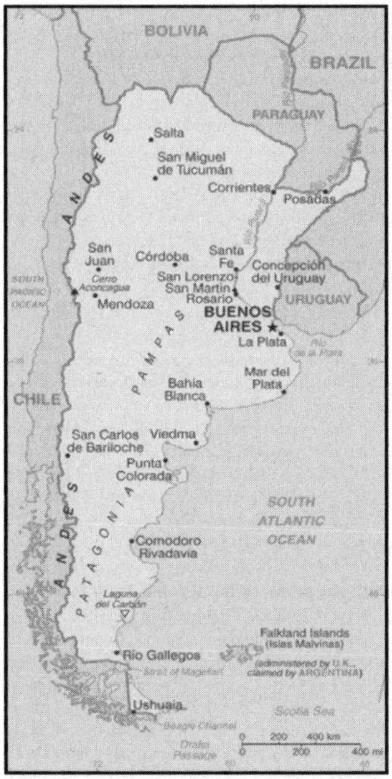

Elevation extremes: *lowest point:* Laguna del Carbon-105 m (located between Puerto San Julian and Comandante Luis Piedra Buena in the province of Santa Cruz)
highest point: Cerro Aconcagua 6,960 m (located in the northwestern corner of the province of Mendoza; highest point in South America)

Natural resources: fertile plains of the pampas, lead, zinc, tin, copper, iron ore, manganese, petroleum, uranium

Land use: *arable land:* 13.68%
permanent crops: 0.36%
other: 85.96% (2011)

Irrigated land: 15,500 sq km (2003)

Total renewable water resources: 814 cu km (2011)

Freshwater withdrawal (domestic/industrial/agricultural): *total:* 32.57 cu km/yr (23%/13%/64%)
per capita: 864.9 cu m/yr (2005)

Natural hazards: San Miguel de Tucuman and Mendoza areas in the Andes subject to earthquakes; pamperos are violent windstorms that can strike the pampas and northeast; heavy flooding in some areas

volcanism: volcanic activity in the Andes Mountains along the Chilean border; Copahue (elev. 2,997 m) last erupted in 2000; other historically active volcanoes include Llullaillaco, Maipo, Planchon-Peteroa, San Jose, Tromen, Tupungatito, and Viedma

Environment—current issues: environmental problems (urban and rural) typical of an industrializing economy such as deforestation, soil degradation, desertification, air pollution, and water pollution
note: Argentina is a world leader in setting voluntary greenhouse gas targets

Environment—international agreements: *party to:* Antarctic-Environmental Protocol, Antarctic-Marine Living Resources, Antarctic Seals, Antarctic Treaty, Biodiversity, Climate Change, Climate Change-Kyoto Protocol, Desertification, Endangered Species, Environmental Modification, Hazardous Wastes, Law of the Sea, Marine Dumping, Ozone Layer Protection, Ship Pollution, Wetlands, Whaling
signed, but not ratified: Marine Life Conservation

Geography—note: second-largest country in South America (after Brazil); strategic location relative to sea lanes between the South Atlantic and the South Pacific Oceans (Strait of Magellan, Beagle Channel, Drake Passage); diverse geophysical landscapes range from tropical climates in the north to tundra in the far south; Cerro Aconcagua is the Western Hemisphere's tallest mountain, while Laguna del Carbon is the lowest point in the Western Hemisphere

PEOPLE AND SOCIETY

Nationality: *noun:* Argentine(s)
adjective: Argentine

Ethnic groups: white (mostly Spanish and Italian) 97%, mestizo (mixed white and Amerindian ancestry), Amerindian, or other non-white groups 3%

Languages: Spanish (official), Italian, English, German, French, indigenous (Mapudungun, Quechua)

Religions: nominally Roman Catholic 92% (less than 20% practicing), Protestant 2%, Jewish 2%, other 4%

Demographic profile: Argentina's population continues to grow but at a slower rate because of its steadily declining birth rate. Argentina's fertility decline began earlier than in the rest of Latin America, occurring most rapidly between the early 20th century and the 1950s and then becoming more gradual. Life expectancy has been improving, most notably among the young and the poor. While the population under age 15 is shrinking, the youth cohort—ages 15-24—is the largest in Argentina's history and will continue to bolster the working-age population. If this large working-age population is well-educated and gainfully employed, Argentina is likely to experience an economic boost and possibly higher per capita savings and investment. Although literacy and primary school enrollment are nearly universal, grade repetition is problematic and secondary school completion is low. Both of these issues vary widely by region and socioeconomic group.

Argentina has been primarily a country of immigration for most of its history, welcoming European immigrants after its independence in the 19th century and attracting especially large numbers from Spain and Italy. European immigration diminished in the 1950s, when Argentina's military dictatorships tightened immigration rules and European economies rebounded. Regional migration, however, continued to supply low-skilled workers and today it accounts for three-quarters of Argentina's immigrant population. The first waves of highly skilled Argentine emigrant workers headed mainly to the United States and Spain in the 1960s and 1970s. The ongoing European economic crisis is driving the return migration of some Argentinean and other Latin American nationals, as well as the immigration of Europeans to South America, where Argentina is a key recipient.

Population: 43,024,374 (July 2014 est.)
country comparison to the world: 33

Age structure: *0-14 years:* 24.9% (male 5,486,989/female 5,233,968)
15-24 years: 15.7% (male 3,445,086/female 3,301,168)
25-54 years: 38.9% (male 8,345,893/female 8,391,445)
55-64 years: 11.4% (male 1,895,965/female 2,017,330)
65 years and over: 11.3% (male 2,036,545/female 2,869,985) (2014 est.)

Dependency ratios: *total dependency ratio:* 54.3%
youth dependency ratio: 37.4%
elderly dependency ratio: 16.9%
potential support ratio: 5.9 (2013)

Median age: *total:* 31.2 years
male: 30.1 years
female: 32.3 years (2014 est.)

Population growth rate: 0.95% (2014 est.)
country comparison to the world: 123

Birth rate: 16.88 births/1,000 population (2014 est.)
country comparison to the world: 113

Death rate: 7.34 deaths/1,000 population (2014 est.)
country comparison to the world: 120

Net migration rate: 0 migrant(s)/1,000 population (2014 est.)
country comparison to the world: 95

Urbanization: *urban population:* 92% of total population (2010)
rate of urbanization: 1.1% annual rate of change (2010-15 est.)

Major urban areas—population: BUENOS AIRES (capital) 13.528 million; Cordoba 1.493 million; Rosario 1.231 million; Mendoza 917,000; San Miguel de Tucuman 831,000 (2011)

Sex ratio: *at birth:* 1.05 male(s)/female
0-14 years: 1.05 male(s)/female
15-24 years: 1.04 male(s)/female
25-54 years: 1 male(s)/female
55-64 years: 0.97 male(s)/female
65 years and over: 0.7 male(s)/female
total population: 0.97 male(s)/female (2014 est.)

Maternal mortality rate: 77 deaths/100,000 live births (2010)
country comparison to the world: 84

Infant mortality rate: *total:* 9.96 deaths/1,000 live births
country comparison to the world: 141
male: 11.15 deaths/1,000 live births
female: 8.71 deaths/1,000 live births (2014 est.)

Life expectancy at birth: *total population:* 77.51 years
country comparison to the world: 66
male: 74.28 years
female: 80.91 years (2014 est.)

Total fertility rate: 2.25 children born/woman (2014 est.)
country comparison to the world: 97

Contraceptive prevalence rate: 78.9% (2004/05)

Health expenditures: 8.1% of GDP (2011)
country comparison to the world: 60

Physicians density: 3.16 physicians/1,000 population (2004)

Hospital bed density: 4.5 beds/1,000 population (2011)

Drinking water source:
Improved:
urban: 99.5% of population
rural: 95.4% of population
total: 99.2% of population
Unimproved:
urban: 0.5% of population
rural: 4.6% of population
total: 0.8% of population (2011 est.)

Sanitation facility access:
Improved:
urban: 96.1% of population
rural: 98.1% of population
total: 96.3% of population
unimproved:
urban: 3.9% of population
rural: 1.9% of population
total: 3.7% of population (2011 est.)

HIV/AIDS—adult prevalence rate: 0.4% (2012 est.)
country comparison to the world: 75

HIV/AIDS—people living with HIV/AIDS: 97,900 (2012 est.)
country comparison to the world: 45

HIV/AIDS—deaths: 3,700 (2012 est.)
country comparison to the world: 47

Obesity—adult prevalence rate: 29.7% (2008)
country comparison to the world: 29

Children under the age of 5 years underweight: 2.3% (2005)
country comparison to the world: 117

Education expenditures: 6.3% of GDP (2011)
country comparison to the world: 32

Literacy: *definition:* age 10 and over can read and write
total population: 97.9%
male: 97.8%
female: 97.9% (2011 est.)

School life expectancy (primary to tertiary education): *total:* 17 years
male: 16 years
female: 18 years (2011)

Child labor—children ages 5-14:
total number: 435,252
percentage: 7%
note: data represents children ages 5-13 (2003 est.)

Unemployment, youth ages 15-24: *total:* 18.3%
country comparison to the world: 68
male: 15.3%
female: 23.1% (2011)

GOVERNMENT

Country name: *conventional long form:* Argentine Republic
conventional short form: Argentina
local long form: Republica Argentina
local short form: Argentina

Government type: republic

Capital: *name:* Buenos Aires
geographic coordinates: 34 35 S, 58 40 W
time difference: UTC-3 (2 hours ahead of Washington, DC during Standard Time)
daylight saving time: none scheduled for 2013

Administrative divisions: 23 provinces (provincias, singular—provincia) and 1 autonomous city*; Buenos Aires, Catamarca, Chaco, Chubut, Ciudad Autonoma de Buenos Aires*, Cordoba, Corrientes, Entre Rios, Formosa, Jujuy, La Pampa, La Rioja, Mendoza, Misiones, Neuquen, Rio Negro, Salta, San Juan, San Luis, Santa Cruz, Santa Fe, Santiago del Estero, Tierra del Fuego—Antartida e Islas del Atlantico Sur (Tierra del Fuego), Tucuman
note: the US does not recognize any claims to Antarctica

Independence: 9 July 1816 (from Spain)

National holiday: Revolution Day, 25 May (1810)

Constitution: several previous; latest effective 11 May 1853; amended many times, last in 1994 (2013)

Legal system: civil law system based on West European legal systems; note—as of January 2013, Congress was deliberating a government-backed reform to the civil code

International law organization participation: has not submitted an ICJ jurisdiction declaration; accepts ICCt jurisdiction

Suffrage: 18-70 years of age; universal and compulsory; 16-17 years of age—optional

Executive branch: *chief of state:* President Cristina FERNANDEZ DE KIRCHNER (since 10 December 2007); Vice President Amado BOUDOU (since 10 December 2011); note—the president is both the chief of state and head of government
head of government: President Cristina FERNANDEZ DE KIRCHNER (since 10 December 2007); Vice President Amado BOUDOU (since 10 December 2011)
cabinet: Cabinet appointed by the president (For more information visit the World Leaders website)
elections: president and vice president elected on the same ticket by popular vote for four-year terms (eligible for a second consecutive term); election last held on 23 October 2011 (next election to be held in October 2015)
election results: Cristina FERNANDEZ DE KIRCHNER reelected president; percent of vote—Cristina FERNANDEZ DE KIRCHNER 54%, Hermes BINNER 16.9%, Ricardo ALFONSIN 11.1%, Alberto Rodriguez SAA 8%, Eduardo DUHALDE 5.9%, other 4.1%

Legislative branch: bicameral National Congress or Congreso Nacional consists of the Senate (72 seats; members are elected by direct vote; presently one-third of the members elected every two years to serve six-year terms) and the Chamber of Deputies (257 seats; members are elected by direct vote; one-half of the members elected every two years to serve four-year terms)
elections: Senate—Senate—last held on 27 October 2013 (next to be held October 2015); Chamber of Deputies—last held on 27 October 2013 (next to be held October 2015)
election results: Senate—percent of vote by bloc or party—NA; seats by bloc or party—FpV 32, FpV allies 6, UCR 17, dissident Peronists 7, FAP and UNEN 7, PRO and allies 3, other 6; Chamber of Deputies—percent of vote by bloc or party—NA; seats by bloc or party—FpV 18, FpV allies 14, UCR 10, dissident Peronists 34, FAP and UNEN 21, PRO 16, CC 3, other 14

Judicial branch: *highest court(s):* Supreme Court or Corte Suprema (consists of the court president,vice-president, and 5 judges)
note—Argentina has a system of federal and provincial courts
judge selection and term of office: judges nominated by the president and approved by the Senate; judges serve for life
subordinate courts: federal level appellate, district, and territorial courts; provincial level supreme, appellate, and first instance courts

Political parties and leaders: Broad Progressive Front or FAP [Hermes BINNER]; Civic Coalition or CC (a broad coalition loosely affiliated with Elisa CARRIO); Dissident Peronists (PJ Disidente) or Federal Peronism (a sector of the Justicialist Party opposed to the Kirchners); Front for Victory or FpV (a broad coalition, including elements of the PJ, UCR, and numerous provincial parties) [Cristina FERNANDEZ DE KIRCHNER]; Peronist (or Justicialist) Party or PJ [vacant]; Radical Civic Union or UCR [Mario BARLETTA]; Republican Proposal or PRO [Mauricio MACRI]; Socialist Party or PS [Ruben GIUSTINIANI]; numerous provincial parties

Political pressure groups and leaders: Argentine Association of Pharmaceutical Labs (CILFA); Argentine Industrial Union (manufacturers' association); Argentine Rural Confederation or CRA (small to medium landowners' association); Argentine Rural Society (large landowners' association); Central of Argentine Workers or CTA (a union for employed and unemployed workers); General Confederation of Labor or CGT (Peronist-leaning umbrella labor organization); Roman Catholic Church; White and Blue CGT (dissident CGT labor confederation);
other: business organizations, Peronist-dominated labor movement, Piquetero groups (popular protest organizations that can be either pro or anti-government), students

International organization participation: AfDB (nonregional member), Australia Group, BCIE, BIS, CAN (associate), CD, CELAC, FAO, FATF, G-15, G-20, G-24, G-77, IADB, IAEA, IBRD, ICAO, ICC (national committees), ICRM, IDA, IFAD, IFC, IFRCS, IHO, ILO, IMF, IMO, IMSO, Interpol, IOC, IOM, IPU, ISO, ITSO, ITU, ITUC (NGOs), LAES, LAIA, Mercosur, MIGA, MINURSO, MINUSTAH, NAM (observer), NSG, OAS, OPANAL, OPCW, Paris Club (associate), PCA, SICA (observer), UN, UN Security Council (temporary), UNASUR, UNCTAD, UNESCO, UNFICYP, UNHCR, UNIDO, Union Latina (observer), UNTSO, UNWTO, UPU, WCO, WFTU (NGOs), WHO, WIPO, WMO, WTO, ZC

Diplomatic representation in the US: *chief of mission:* Ambassador Maria Cecilia NAHON (since 19 February 2013)
chancery: 1600 New Hampshire Avenue NW, Washington, DC 20009
telephone: [1] (202) 238-6400
FAX: [1] (202) 332-3171
consulate(s) general: Atlanta, Chicago, Houston, Los Angeles, Miami, New York

Diplomatic representation from the US: *chief of mission:* Ambassador (vacant); Charge d'Affaires Kevin K. SULLIVAN (since June 2013)
embassy: Avenida Colombia 4300, C1425GMN Buenos Aires

mailing address: international mail: use embassy street address; APO address: US Embassy Buenos Aires, Unit 4334, APO AA 34034
telephone: [54] (11) 5777-4533
FAX: [54] (11) 5777-4240

Flag description: three equal horizontal bands of light blue (top), white, and light blue; centered in the white band is a radiant yellow sun with a human face known as the Sun of May; the colors represent the clear skies and snow of the Andes; the sun symbol commemorates the appearance of the sun through cloudy skies on 25 May 1810 during the first mass demonstration in favor of independence; the sun features are those of Inti, the Inca god of the sun

National symbol(s): Sun of May (a sun-with-face symbol)

National anthem: *name:* "Himno Nacional Argentino" (Argentine National Anthem)
lyrics/music: Vicente LOPEZ y PLANES/Jose Blas PARERA
note: adopted 1813; Vicente LOPEZ was inspired to write the anthem after watching a play about the 1810 May Revolution against Spain

ECONOMY

Economy—overview: Argentina benefits from rich natural resources, a highly literate population, an export-oriented agricultural sector, and a diversified industrial base. Although one of the world's wealthiest countries 100 years ago, Argentina suffered during most of the 20th century from recurring economic crises, persistent fiscal and current account deficits, high inflation, mounting external debt, and capital flight. A severe depression, growing public and external indebtedness, and an unprecedented bank run culminated in 2001 in the most serious economic, social, and political crisis in the country's turbulent history. Interim President Adolfo RODRIGUEZ SAA declared a default—at the time the largest ever—on the government's foreign debt in December of that year, and abruptly resigned only a few days after taking office. His successor, Eduardo DUHALDE, announced an end to the peso's decade-long 1-to-1 peg to the US dollar in early 2002. The economy bottomed out that year, with real GDP 18% smaller than in 1998 and almost 60% of Argentines under the poverty line. Real GDP rebounded to grow by an average 8.5% annually over the subsequent six years, taking advantage of previously idled industrial capacity and labor, an audacious debt restructuring and reduced debt burden, excellent international financial conditions, and expansionary monetary and fiscal policies. Inflation also increased, however, during the administration of President Nestor KIRCHNER, which responded with price restraints on businesses, as well as export taxes and restraints, and beginning in 2007, with understating inflation data. Cristina FERNANDEZ DE KIRCHNER succeeded her husband as President in late 2007, and the rapid economic growth of previous years began to slow sharply the following year as government policies held back exports and the world economy fell into recession. The economy in 2010 rebounded strongly from the 2009 recession, but has slowed since late 2011 even as the government continued to rely on expansionary fiscal and monetary policies, which have kept inflation in the double digits. The government expanded state intervention in the economy throughout 2012. In May the Congress approved the nationalization of the oil company YPF from Spain's Repsol. The government expanded formal and informal measures to restrict imports during the year, including a requirement for pre-registration and pre-approval of all imports. In July the government also further tightened currency controls in an effort to bolster foreign reserves and stem capital flight.

GDP (purchasing power parity): $771 billion (2013 est.)
country comparison to the world: 23
$745.2 billion (2012 est.)
$731.3 billion (2011 est.)
note: data are in 2013 US dollars

GDP (official exchange rate): $484.6 billion (2013 est.)

GDP—real growth rate: 3.5% (2013 est.)
country comparison to the world: 94
1.9% (2012 est.)
8.9% (2011 est.)

GDP—per capita (PPP): $18,600 (2013 est.)
country comparison to the world: 75
$18,200 (2012 est.)
$18,000 (2011 est.)
note: data are in 2013 US dollars

Gross national saving: 24.6% of GDP (2013 est.)
country comparison to the world: 52
24% of GDP (2012 est.)
25.6% of GDP (2011 est.)

GDP—composition, by end use:
household consumption: 55.5%
government consumption: 18%
investment in fixed capital: 22%
investment in inventories: 3.1%
exports of goods and services: 20.3%
imports of goods and services: -18.9% (2013 est.)

GDP—composition, by sector of origin:
agriculture: 9.3%
industry: 29.7%
services: 61% (2013 est.)

Agriculture—products: sunflower seeds, lemons, soybeans, grapes, corn, tobacco, peanuts, tea, wheat; livestock

Industries: food processing, motor vehicles, consumer durables, textiles, chemicals and petrochemicals, printing, metallurgy, steel

Industrial production growth rate: 2.7%
country comparison to the world: 111
note: based on private estimates (2013 est.)

Labor force: 17.32 million
country comparison to the world: 36
note: urban areas only (2013 est.)

Labor force—by occupation: *agriculture:* 5%
industry: 23%
services: 72% (2009 est.)

Unemployment rate: 7.5% (2013 est.)
country comparison to the world: 82
7.2% (2012 est.)

Population below poverty line: 30%
note: data are based on private estimates (2010)

Household income or consumption by percentage share: *lowest 10%:* 1.5%
highest 10%: 32.3% (2010 est.)

Distribution of family income—Gini index: 45.8 (2009)
country comparison to the world: 36

Budget: *revenues:* $129.6 billion
expenditures: $145.3 billion (2013 est.)

Taxes and other revenues: 26.8% of GDP (2013 est.)
country comparison to the world: 111

Budget surplus (+) or deficit (-): -3.2% of GDP (2013 est.)
country comparison to the world: 127

Public debt: 45.8% of GDP (2013 est.)
country comparison to the world: 80
44.8% of GDP (2012 est.)

Fiscal year: calendar year

Inflation rate (consumer prices): 20.8% (2013 est.)
country comparison to the world: 218
25.3% (2012 est.)
note: data are derived from private estimates

Central bank discount rate: NA%

Commercial bank prime lending rate: 16.4% (31 December 2013 est.)
country comparison to the world: 50
14.06% (31 December 2012 est.)

Stock of narrow money: $70.25 billion (31 December 2013 est.)
country comparison to the world: 44
$65.63 billion (31 December 2012 est.)

Stock of broad money: $145 billion (31 December 2013 est.)
country comparison to the world: 47
$145.9 billion (31 December 2012 est.)

Stock of domestic credit: $157.7 billion (31 December 2013 est.)
country comparison to the world: 46
$161.9 billion (31 December 2012 est.)

Market value of publicly traded shares: $34.24 billion (31 December 2012 est.)
country comparison to the world: 52
$43.58 billion (31 December 2011)
$63.91 billion (31 December 2010 est.)

Current account balance: -$2.371 billion (2013 est.)
country comparison to the world: 149
$106.9 million (2012 est.)

Exports: $85.08 billion (2013 est.)
country comparison to the world: 44
$80.91 billion (2012 est.)

Exports—commodities: soybeans and derivatives, petroleum and gas, vehicles, corn, wheat

Exports—partners: Brazil 20.4%, China 7.4%, Chile 6%, US 5.2% (2012)

Imports: $71.3 billion (2013 est.)
country comparison to the world: 41
$65.55 billion (2012 est.)

Imports—commodities: machinery, motor vehicles, petroleum and natural gas, organic chemicals, plastics

Imports—partners: Brazil 27.2%, US 15.6%, China 11.9%, Germany 4.5% (2012)

Reserves of foreign exchange and gold: $33.65 billion (31 December 2013 est.)
country comparison to the world: 50
$43.25 billion (31 December 2012 est.)

Debt—external: $111.5 billion (31 December 2013 est.)
country comparison to the world: 44
$113.7 billion (31 December 2012 est.)

Stock of direct foreign investment—at home: $115.9 billion (31 December 2013 est.)
country comparison to the world: 39
$107.1 billion (31 December 2012 est.)

Stock of direct foreign investment—abroad: $34.21 billion (31 December 2013 est.)
country comparison to the world: 40
$32.91 billion (31 December 2012 est.)

Exchange rates: Argentine pesos (ARS) per US dollar—

5.447 (2013 est.)
4.5369 (2012 est.)
3.8963 (2010 est.)
3.7101 (2009)
3.1636 (2008)

ENERGY

Electricity—production: 119.3 billion kWh (2010 est.)
country comparison to the world: 30

Electricity—consumption: 111.1 billion kWh (2010 est.)
country comparison to the world: 30

Electricity—exports: 1.701 billion kWh (2010 est.)
country comparison to the world: 45

Electricity—imports: 10.3 billion kWh (2010 est.)
country comparison to the world: 23

Electricity—installed generating capacity: 32.87 million kW (2010 est.)
country comparison to the world: 26

Electricity—from fossil fuels: 66.2% of total installed capacity (2010 est.)
country comparison to the world: 118

Electricity—from nuclear fuels: 3.1% of total installed capacity (2010 est.)
country comparison to the world: 24

Electricity—from hydroelectric plants: 27.6% of total installed capacity (2010 est.)
country comparison to the world: 82

Electricity—from other renewable sources: 0.2% of total installed capacity (2010 est.)
country comparison to the world: 92

Crude oil—production: 723,200 bbl/day (2012 est.)
country comparison to the world: 27

Crude oil—exports: 90,920 bbl/day (2010 est.)
country comparison to the world: 38

Crude oil—imports: 0 bbl/day (2010 est.)
country comparison to the world: 155

Crude oil—proved reserves: 2.805 billion bbl (1 January 2013 es)
country comparison to the world: 32

Refined petroleum products—production: 622,200 bbl/day (2010 est.)
country comparison to the world: 27

Refined petroleum products—consumption: 678,100 bbl/day (2011 est.)
country comparison to the world: 27

Refined petroleum products—exports: 94,500 bbl/day (2010 est.)
country comparison to the world: 45

Refined petroleum products—imports: 76,550 bbl/day (2010 est.)
country comparison to the world: 58

Natural gas—production: 38.77 billion cu m (2011 est.)
country comparison to the world: 25

Natural gas—consumption: 43.29 billion cu m (2010 est.)
country comparison to the world: 22

Natural gas—exports: 200 million cu m (2011 est.)
country comparison to the world: 49

Natural gas—imports: 7.57 billion cu m (2011 est.)
country comparison to the world: 33

Natural gas—proved reserves: 332.5 billion cu m (1 January 2013 es)
country comparison to the world: 39

Carbon dioxide emissions from consumption of energy: 190.6 million Mt (2011 est.)
country comparison to the world: 32

COMMUNICATIONS

Telephones—main lines in use: 10 million (2012)
country comparison to the world: 22

Telephones—mobile cellular: 58.6 million (2012)
country comparison to the world: 23

Telephone system: *general assessment:* in 1998 Argentina opened its telecommunications market to competition and foreign investment encouraging the growth of modern telecommunications technology; fiber-optic cable trunk lines are being installed between all major cities; major networks are entirely digital and the availability of telephone service is improving
domestic: microwave radio relay, fiber-optic cable, and a domestic satellite system with 40 earth stations serve the trunk network; fixed-line teledensity is increasing gradually and mobile-cellular subscribership is increasing rapidly; broadband Internet services are gaining ground
international: country code—54; landing point for the Atlantis-2, UNISUR, South America-1, and South American Crossing/Latin American Nautilus submarine cable systems that provide links to Europe, Africa, South and Central America, and US; satellite earth stations—112; 2 international gateways near Buenos Aires (2011)

Broadcast media: government owns a TV station and a radio network; more than 2 dozen TV stations and hundreds of privately-owned radio stations; high rate of cable TV subscription usage (2007)

Internet country code: .ar

Internet hosts: 11.232 million (2012)
country comparison to the world: 13

Internet users: 13.694 million (2009)
country comparison to the world: 28

TRANSPORTATION

Airports: 1,138 (2013)
country comparison to the world: 6

Airports—with paved runways: *total:* 161
over 3,047 m: 4
2,438 to 3,047 m: 29
1,524 to 2,437 m: 65
914 to 1,523 m: 53
under 914 m: 10 (2013)

Airports—with unpaved runways: *total:* 977
over 3,047 m: 1
2,438 to 3,047 m: 1
1,524 to 2,437 m: 43
914 to 1,523 m: 484
under 914 m: 448 (2013)

Heliports: 2 (2013)

Pipelines: gas 29,930 km; liquid petroleum gas 41 km; oil 6,248 km; refined products 3,631 km (2013)

Railways: *total:* 36,966 km
country comparison to the world: 8
broad gauge: 26,475 km 1.676-m gauge (94 km electrified)
standard gauge: 2,780 km 1.435-m gauge (42 km electrified)
narrow gauge: 7,711 km 1.000-m gauge (2008)

Roadways: *total:* 231,374 km
country comparison to the world: 21
paved: 69,412 km (includes 734 km of expressways)
unpaved: 161,962 km (2004)

Waterways: 11,000 km (2012)
country comparison to the world: 11

Merchant marine: *total:* 36
country comparison to the world: 80
by type: bulk carrier 1, cargo 5, chemical tanker 6, container 1, passenger/cargo 1, petroleum tanker 18, refrigerated cargo 4
foreign-owned: 14 (Brazil 1, Chile 6, Spain 3, Taiwan 2, UK 2)
registered in other countries: 15 (Liberia 1, Panama 5, Paraguay 5, Uruguay 1, unknown 3) (2010)

Ports and terminals: *major seaport(s):* Bahia Blanca, Buenos Aires, La Plata, Punta Colorada, Ushuaia
river port(s): Arroyo Seco, Rosario, San Lorenzo-San Martin (Parana)
container port(s) (TEUs): Buenos Aires (1,851,701)

MILITARY

Military branches: Argentine Army (Ejercito Argentino), Navy of the Argentine Republic (Armada Republica; includes naval aviation and naval infantry), Argentine Air Force (Fuerza Aerea Argentina, FAA) (2013)

Military service age and obligation: 18-24 years of age for voluntary military service (18-21 requires parental consent); no conscription; if the number of volunteers fails to meet the quota of recruits for a particular year, Congress can authorize the conscription of citizens turning 18 that year for a period not exceeding one year (2012)

Manpower available for military service: *males age 16-49:* 10,038,967
females age 16-49: 9,959,134 (2010 est.)

Manpower fit for military service: *males age 16-49:* 8,458,362
females age 16-49: 8,414,460 (2010 est.)

Manpower reaching militarily significant age annually: *male:* 339,503
female: 323,170 (2010 est.)

Military expenditures: 0.91% of GDP (2012)
country comparison to the world: 108
0.9% of GDP (2011)
0.91% of GDP (2010)

Military—note: the Argentine military is a well-organized force constrained by the country's prolonged economic hardship; the country has recently experienced a strong recovery, and the military is implementing a modernization plan aimed at making the ground forces lighter and more responsive (2008)

TRANSNATIONAL ISSUES

Disputes—international: Argentina continues to assert its claims to the UK-administered Falkland Islands (Islas Malvinas), South Georgia, and the South Sandwich Islands in its constitution, forcibly occupying the Falklands in 1982, but in 1995 agreed to no longer seek settlement by force; UK continues to reject Argentine requests for sovereignty talks; territorial claim in Antarctica partially overlaps UK and Chilean claims; uncontested dispute between Brazil and Uruguay over Braziliera/Brasiliera Island in the Quarai/Cuareim River leaves the tripoint with Argentina in question; in 2010, the ICJ ruled in favor of Uruguay's operation of two paper mills on the Uruguay River, which forms the border with Argentina; the two countries formed a joint pollution monitoring regime; the joint boundary commission, established by Chile and Argentina in 2001 has yet to map and demarcate the delimited boundary in the inhospitable Andean Southern Ice Field (Campo de Hielo Sur); contraband smuggling, human trafficking, and illegal narcotic trafficking are problems in the porous areas of the border with Bolivia

Illicit drugs: a transshipment country for cocaine headed for Europe, heroin headed for the US, and ephedrine and pseudoephedrine headed for Mexico; some money-laundering activity, especially in the TriBorder Area; law enforcement corruption; a source for precursor chemicals; increasing domestic consumption of drugs in urban centers, especially cocaine base and synthetic drugs (2008)

ARMENIA

INTRODUCTION

Background: Armenia prides itself on being the first nation to formally adopt Christianity (early 4th century). Despite periods of autonomy, over the centuries Armenia came under the sway of various empires including the Roman, Byzantine, Arab,Persian, and Ottoman. During World War I in the western portion of Armenia, Ottoman Turkey instituted a policy of forced resettlement coupled with other harsh practices that resulted in at least 1 million Armenian deaths. The eastern area of Armenia was ceded by the Ottomans to Russia in 1828; this portion declared its independence in 1918, but was conquered by the Soviet Red Army in 1920. Armenian leaders remain preoccupied by the long conflict with Azerbaijan over Nagorno-Karabakh, a primarily Armenian-populated region, assigned to Soviet Azerbaijan in the 1920s by Moscow. Armenia and Azerbaijan began fighting over the area in 1988; the struggle escalated after both countries attained independence from the Soviet Union in 1991. By May 1994, when a cease-fire took hold, ethnic Armenian forces held not only Nagorno-Karabakh but also a significant portion of Azerbaijan proper. The economies of both sides have been hurt by their inability to make substantial progress toward a peaceful resolution. Turkey closed the common border with Armenia in 1993 in support of Azerbaijan in its conflict with Armenia over control of Nagorno-Karabakh and surrounding areas, further hampering Armenian economic growth. In 2009, senior Armenian leaders began pursuing rapprochement with Turkey, aiming to secure an opening of the border, but Turkey has not yet ratified the Protocols normalizing relations between the two countries. In September 2013, President SARGSIAN announced Armenia will join Russia, Belarus, and Kazakhstan as a member of the Customs Union.

GEOGRAPHY

Location: Southwestern Asia, between Turkey (to the west) and Azerbaijan

Geographic coordinates: 40 00 N, 45 00 E

Map references: Middle East

Area: *total:* 29,743 sq km
country comparison to the world: 143 land: 28,203 sq km
water: 1,540 sq km

Area—comparative: slightly smaller than Maryland

Land boundaries: *total:* 1,254 km
border countries: Azerbaijan-proper 566 km, Azerbaijan-Naxcivan exclave 221 km, Georgia 164 km, Iran 35 km, Turkey 268 km

Coastline: 0 km (landlocked)

Maritime claims: none (landlocked)

Climate: highland continental, hot summers, cold winters

Terrain: Armenian Highland with mountains; little forest land; fast flowing rivers; good soil in Aras River valley

Elevation extremes: *lowest point:* Debed River 400 m
highest point: Aragats Lerrnagagat' 4,090 m

Natural resources: small deposits of gold, copper, molybdenum, zinc, bauxite

Land use: *arable land:* 14.47%
permanent crops: 1.8%
other: 83.74% (2011)

Irrigated land: 2,735 sq km (2006)

Total renewable water resources: 7.77 cu km (2011)

Freshwater withdrawal (domestic/industrial/agricultural): *total:* 2.86 cu km/yr (40%/6%/54%)
per capita: 929.7 cu m/yr (2010)

Natural hazards: occasionally severe earthquakes; droughts

Environment—current issues: soil pollution from toxic chemicals such as DDT; the energy crisis of the 1990s led to deforestation when citizens scavenged for firewood; pollution of Hrazdan (Razdan) and Aras Rivers; the draining of Sevana Lich (Lake Sevan), a result of its use as a source for hydropower, threatens drinking water supplies; restart of Metsamor nuclear power plant in spite of its location in a seismically active zone

Environment—international agreements: *party to:* Air Pollution, Biodiversity, Climate Change, Climate Change-Kyoto Protocol, Desertification, Environmental Modification, Hazardous Wastes, Law of the Sea, Ozone Layer Protection, Wetlands
signed, but not ratified: Air Pollution-Persistent Organic Pollutants

Geography—note: landlocked in the Lesser Caucasus Mountains; Sevana Lich (Lake Sevan) is the largest lake in this mountain range

PEOPLE AND SOCIETY

Nationality: *noun:* Armenian(s)
adjective: Armenian

Ethnic groups: Armenian 98.1%, Yezidi (Kurd) 1.1%, other 0.7% (2011 est.)

Languages: Armenian (official) 97.9%, Kurdish (spoken by Yezidi minority) 1%, other 1% (2011 est.)

Religions: Armenian Apostolic 92.6%, Evangelical 1%, other 2.4%, none 1.1%, unspecified 2.9% (2011 est.)

Population: 3,060,631 (July 2014 est.)
country comparison to the world: 137

Age structure: *0-14 years:* 19.1% (male 312,955/female 272,065)
15-24 years: 15.2% (male 236,317/female 228,943)
25-54 years: 43.5% (male 638,141/female 693,397)
55-64 years: 10.5% (male 161,102/female 195,714)
65 years and over: 9.8% (male 128,568/female 193,429) (2014 est.)

Dependency ratios: *total dependency ratio:* 44.1%
youth dependency ratio: 29.2%
elderly dependency ratio: 14.9%
potential support ratio: 6.7 (2013)

Median age: *total:* 33.7 years
male: 31.8 years
female: 35.8 years (2014 est.)

Population growth rate: -0.13% (2014 est.)
country comparison to the world: 209

Birth rate: 13.92 births/1,000 population (2014 est.)
country comparison to the world: 143

Death rate: 9.3 deaths/1,000 population (2014 est.)
country comparison to the world: 62

Net migration rate: -5.88 migrant(s)/1,000 population (2014 est.)
country comparison to the world: 197

Urbanization: *urban population:* 64.1% of total population (2011)
rate of urbanization: 0.34% annual rate of change (2010-15 est.)

Major urban areas—population: YEREVAN (capital) 1.116 million (2011)

Sex ratio: *at birth:* 1.14 male(s)/female
0-14 years: 1.15 male(s)/female
15-24 years: 1.03 male(s)/female
25-54 years: 0.92 male(s)/female
55-64 years: 0.93 male(s)/female
65 years and over: 0.59 male(s)/female
total population: 0.89 male(s)/female (2014 est.)

Mother's mean age at first birth: 24.1
note: median age at first birth among women 25-29 (2010 est.)

Maternal mortality rate: 30 deaths/100,000 live births (2010)
country comparison to the world: 123

Infant mortality rate: *total:* 13.97 deaths/1,000 live births
country comparison to the world: 113
male: 15.39 deaths/1,000 live births
female: 12.36 deaths/1,000 live births (2014 est.)

Life expectancy at birth: *total population:* 74.12 years
country comparison to the world: 116
male: 70.9 years
female: 77.78 years (2014 est.)

Total fertility rate: 1.64 children born/woman (2014 est.)
country comparison to the world: 177

Contraceptive prevalence rate: 54.9% (2010)

Health expenditures: 4.3% of GDP (2011)
country comparison to the world: 156

Physicians density: 2.85 physicians/1,000 population (2011)

Hospital bed density: 4 beds/1,000 population (2011)

Drinking water source:
Improved:
urban: 99.6% of population
rural: 98.4% of population
total: 99.2% of population
Unimproved:
urban: 0.4% of population
rural: 1.6% of population
total: 0.8% of population (2011 est.)

Sanitation facility access:
Improved:
urban: 95.9% of population
rural: 80.5% of population
total: 90.4% of population
Unimproved:
urban: 4.1% of population
rural: 19.5% of population
total: 9.6% of population (2011 est.)

HIV/AIDS—adult prevalence rate: 0.2% (2012 est.)
country comparison to the world: 105

HIV/AIDS—people living with HIV/AIDS: 3,500 (2012 est.)
country comparison to the world: 130

HIV/AIDS—deaths: 200 (2012 est.)
country comparison to the world: 109

Obesity—adult prevalence rate: 24% (2008)
country comparison to the world: 68

Children under the age of 5 years underweight: 5.3% (2010)
country comparison to the world: 89

Education expenditures: 3.3% of GDP (2012)
country comparison to the world: 132

Literacy: *definition:* age 15 and over can read and write
total population: 99.6%
male: 99.7%
female: 99.5% (2011 est.)

School life expectancy (primary to tertiary education): *total:* 12 years
male: 11 years
female: 14 years (2009)

Child labor—children ages 5-14:
total number: 19,596
percentage: 4%
note: data represents children ages 7-17 (2007 est.)

Unemployment, youth ages 15-24: *total:* 39.2%
country comparison to the world: 14
male: 35%
female: 45% (2011)

GOVERNMENT

Country name: *conventional long form:* Republic of Armenia
conventional short form: Armenia
local long form: Hayastani Hanrapetut'yun
local short form: Hayastan
former: Armenian Soviet Socialist Republic, Armenian Republic

Government type: republic

Capital: *name:* Yerevan
geographic coordinates: 40 1 0 N, 44 30 E
time difference: UTC+4 (9 hours ahead of Washington, DC during Standard Time)

Administrative divisions: 11 provinces (marzer, singular—marz); Aragatsotn, Ararat, Armavir, Geghark'unik', Kotayk', Lorri, Shirak, Syunik', Tavush, Vayots' Dzor, Yerevan

Independence: 21 September 1991 (from the Soviet Union)

National holiday: Independence Day, 21 September (1991)

Constitution: previous 1915, 1978; latest adopted 5 July 1995; amended 2005 (2013)

Legal system: civil law system

International law organization participation: has not submitted an ICJ jurisdiction declaration; non-party state to the ICCt

Suffrage: 18 years of age; universal

Executive branch: *chief of state:* President Serzh SARGSIAN (since 9 April 2008)
head of government: Prime Minister Hovik ABRAHAMIAN (since 13 April 2014)
cabinet: Council of Ministers appointed by the prime minister (For more information visit the World Leaders website)
elections: president elected by popular vote for a five-year term (eligible for a second term); election last held on 18 February 2013 (next to be held February 2018); prime minister appointed by the president based on majority or plurality support in parliament; the prime minister and Council of Ministers must resign if the National Assembly refuses to accept their program
election results: Serzh SARGSIAN reelected president; percent of vote—Serzh SARGSIAN 58.6%, Raffi HOVHANNISIAN 36.7%, Hrant BAGRATIAN 2.2%, other 2.5%

Legislative branch: unicameral National Assembly (Parliament) or Azgayin Zhoghov (131 seats; members elected by popular vote, 90 members elected by party list and 41 by direct vote; to serve five-year terms)
elections: last held on 6 May 2012 (next to be held in the spring of 2017)
election results: percent of vote by party—RPA 44%, Prosperous Armenia 30.1%, ANC 7.1%, Heritage Party 5.8%, ARF (Dashnak) 5.7%, Rule of Law 5.5%, other 1.8%; seats by party—RPA 69, Prosperous Armenia 37, ANC 7, Heritage Party 5, ARF (Dashnak) 5, Rule of Law 6, independent 2

Judicial branch: *highest court(s):* Court of Cassation (consists of the court chairman and organized into a criminal chamber and a civil and administrative chamber, each with a court chairman and 2 judges); Constitutional Court (consists of 9 judges)
judge selection and term of office: Court of Cassation judges nominated by the Judicial Council, a 9-member body of selected judges and legal scholars; judges appointed by the president; Constitutional Court judges—4 appointed by the president, and 5 elected by National Assembly; judges of both courts can serve until retirement at age 65
subordinate courts: 2 Courts of Appeal (for civil cases and for criminal and military cases); district courts; Administrative Court

Political parties and leaders: Armenian National Congress or ANC (bloc of independent and opposition parties) [Levon TER-PETROSSIAN]; Armenian National Movement or ANM [Ararat ZURABIAN]; Armenian Revolutionary Federation ("Dashnak" Party) or ARF [Hrant MARKARIAN]; Heritage Party [Raffi HOVHANNISIAN]; People's Party of Armenia [Stepan DEMIRCHIAN]; Prosperous Armenia [Gagik TSARUKIAN]; Republican Party of Armenia or RPA [Serzh SARGSIAN]; Rule of Law Party (Orinats Yerkir) [Artur BAGHDASARIAN]

Political pressure groups and leaders: Aylentrank (Impeachment Alliance) [Nikol PASHINIAN]; Yerkrapah Union [Manvel GRIGORIAN]

International organization participation: ADB, BSEC, CD, CE, CIS, CSTO, EAEC (observer), EAPC, EBRD, FAO, GCTU, IAEA, IBRD, ICAO, ICC (NGOs), ICRM, IDA, IFAD, IFC, IFRCS, ILO, IMF, Interpol, IOC, IOM, IPU, ISO, ITSO, ITU, MIGA, NAM (observer), OAS (observer), OIF, OPCW, OSCE, PFP, UN, UNCTAD, UNESCO, UNIDO, UNIFIL, UNWTO, UPU, WCO, WFTU (NGOs), WHO, WIPO, WMO, WTO

Diplomatic representation in the US: *chief of mission:* Ambassador Tatoul MARKARIAN (since 26 May 2005)
chancery: 2225 R Street NW, Washington, DC 20008
telephone: [1] (202) 319-1976
FAX: [1] (202) 319-2982
consulate(s) general: Glendale (CA), Los Angeles

Diplomatic representation from the US: *chief of mission:* Ambassador John HEFFERN (since 6 October 2011)
embassy: 1 American Ave., Yerevan 0082
mailing address: American Embassy Yerevan, US Department of State, 7020 Yerevan Place, Washington, DC 20521-7020
telephone: [374](10) 464-700
FAX: [374](10) 464-742

Flag description: three equal horizontal bands of red (top), blue, and orange; the color red recalls the blood shed for liberty, blue the Armenian skies as well as hope, and orange the land and the courage of the workers who farm it

National symbol(s): Mount Ararat; eagle; lion

National anthem: *name:* "Mer Hayrenik"(Our Fatherland)
lyrics/music: Mikael NALBANDIAN/Barsegh KANACHYAN
note: adopted 1991; based on the anthem of the Democratic Republic of Armenia (1918-1922) but with different lyrics

ECONOMY

Economy—overview: After several years of double-digit economic growth, Armenia faced a severe economic recession with GDP declining more than 14% in 2009, despite large loans from multilateral institutions. Sharp declines in the construction sector and workers' remittances, particularly from Russia, led the downturn. The economy began to recover in 2010 with 2.1% growth, has grown even faster in the three years since then. Under the old Soviet central planning system, Armenia developed a modern industrial sector, supplying machine tools, textiles, and other manufactured goods to sister republics, in exchange for raw materials and energy. Armenia has since switched to small-scale agriculture and away from the large agroindustrial complexes of the Soviet era. Armenia's geographic isolation, a narrow export base, and pervasive monopolies in important business sectors have made it particularly vulnerable to the sharp deterioration in the global economy and the economic downturn in Russia. Armenia has experienced a sharp currency depreciation. Armenia has only two open trade borders—Iran and Georgia—because its borders with Azerbaijan and Turkey have been closed since 1991 and 1993, respectively, as a result of Armenia's ongoing conflict with Azerbaijan over the separatist Nagorno-Karabakh region. Armenia is particularly dependent on Russian commercial and governmental support and most key Armenian infrastructure is Russian-owned and/or managed, especially in the energy sector. The electricity distribution system was privatized in 2002 and bought by Russia's RAO-UES in 2005. Natural gas is primarily imported from Russia but construction of a pipeline to deliver natural gas from Iran to Armenia was completed in December 2008, and gas deliveries expanded after the April 2010 completion of the Yerevan Thermal Power Plant. Armenia's severe trade imbalance has been offset somewhat by international aid, remittances from Armenians working abroad, and foreign direct investment. Armenia joined the WTO in January 2003. The government made some improvements in tax and customs administration in recent years, but anti-corruption measures have been ineffective and the economic downturn has led to a sharp drop in tax revenue and forced the government to accept large loan packages from Russia, the IMF, and other international financial institutions. Amendments to tax legislation, including the introduction of the first ever "luxury tax" in 2011, aim to increase the ratio of budget revenues to GDP, which still remains at low levels. Armenia will need to pursue additional economic reforms and to strengthen the rule of law in order to regain economic growth and improve economic competitiveness and employment opportunities, especially given its economic isolation from two of its nearest neighbors, Turkey and Azerbaijan.

GDP (purchasing power parity): $20.61 billion (2013 est.)
country comparison to the world: 133
$19.7 billion (2012 est.)
$18.38 billion (2011 est.)
note: data are in 2013 US dollars

GDP (official exchange rate): $10.44 billion (2013 est.)

GDP—real growth rate: 4.6% (2013 est.)
country comparison to the world: 65
7.2% (2012 est.)
4.7% (2011 est.)

GDP—per capita (PPP): $6,300 (2013 est.)
country comparison to the world: 147
$6,000 (2012 est.)
$5,600 (2011 est.)
note: data are in 2013 US dollars

Gross national saving: 16.2% of GDP (2013 est.)
country comparison to the world: 104
13.2% of GDP (2012 est.)
16.1% of GDP (2011 est.)

GDP—composition, by end use:
household consumption: 84.7%
government consumption: 13%
investment in fixed capital: 22.7%
investment in inventories: -0.9%
exports of goods and services: 23.6%
imports of goods and services: -43.1% (2013 est.)

GDP—composition, by sector of origin:
agriculture: 20.6%
industry: 37.3%
services: 42.1% (2013 est.)

Agriculture—products: fruit (especially grapes), vegetables; livestock

Industries: diamond-processing, metal-cutting machine tools, forging-pressing machines, electric motors, tires, knitted wear, hosiery, shoes, silk fabric, chemicals, trucks, instruments, microelectronics, jewelry manufacturing, software development, food processing, brandy, mining

Industrial production growth rate: 3.9% (2013 est.)
country comparison to the world: 77

Labor force: 1.394 million (2013 est.)
country comparison to the world: 133

Labor force—by occupation: *agriculture:* 44.2%
industry: 16.8%
services: 39% (2008 est.)

Unemployment rate: 17.3% (2012 est.)
country comparison to the world: 153
18.4% (2011 est.)

Population below poverty line: 35.8% (2010 est.)

Household income or consumption by percentage share: *lowest 10%:* 3.7%
highest 10%: 25.4% (2008)

Distribution of family income—Gini index: 30.9 (2008)
country comparison to the world: 115
44.4 (1996)

Budget: *revenues:* $2.677 billion
expenditures: $2.707 billion (2013 est.)

Taxes and other revenues: 25.6% of GDP (2013 est.)
country comparison to the world: 119

Budget surplus (+) or deficit (-): -0.3% of GDP (2013 est.)
country comparison to the world: 50

Public debt: 37.7% of GDP (2013 est.)
country comparison to the world: 98
41.4% of GDP (2012 est.)

Fiscal year: calendar year

Inflation rate (consumer prices): 6.2% (2013 est.)
country comparison to the world: 178
2.6% (2012 est.)

Central bank discount rate: 8% (11 January 2012)
country comparison to the world: 37
7.25% (2 December 2008)
note: this is the Refinancing Rate, the key monetary policy instrument of the Armenian National Bank

Commercial bank prime lending rate: 16.5% (31 December 2013 est.)
country comparison to the world: 28
17.23% (31 December 2012 est.)
note: average lending rate on loans up to one year

Stock of narrow money: $1.418 billion (31 December 2013 est.)
country comparison to the world: 141
$1.352 billion (31 December 2012 est.)

Stock of broad money: $2.051 billion (31 December 2013 est.)
country comparison to the world: 148
$1.829 billion (31 December 2012 est.)

Stock of domestic credit: $4.355 billion (31 December 2012 est.)
country comparison to the world: 119
$3.548 billion (31 December 2011 est.)

Market value of publicly traded shares: $132.1 million (31 December 2012 est.)
country comparison to the world: 118
$139.6 million (31 December 2011)
$144.8 million (31 December 2010 est.)

Current account balance: -$720.6 million (2013 est.)
country comparison to the world: 112
-$1.052 billion (2012 est.)

Exports: $1.653 billion (2013 est.)
country comparison to the world: 144
$1.588 billion (2012 est.)

Exports—commodities: pig iron, unwrought copper, nonferrous metals, diamonds, mineral products, foodstuffs, energy

Exports—partners: Russia 19.6%, Germany 10.7%, Bulgaria 9.1%, Belgium 8.9%, Iran 6.9%, US 6.1%, Canada 6%, Georgia 5.7%, Netherlands 5.6%, Switzerland 5% (2012)

Imports: $3.459 billion (2013 est.)
country comparison to the world: 140
$3.656 billion (2012 est.)

Imports—commodities: natural gas, petroleum, tobacco products, foodstuffs, diamonds

Imports—partners: Russia 20%, Germany 11%, Bulgaria 9%, Belgium 9%, Iran 6.5%, US 6.1%, Canada 5.9%, Netherlands 5.6%, Georgia 5.6%, Switzerland 5.2% (2012 est.)

Reserves of foreign exchange and gold: $1.863 billion (31 December 2013 est.)
country comparison to the world: 125
$1.799 billion (31 December 2012 est.)

Debt—external: $7.839 billion (31 December 2013 est.)
country comparison to the world: 106
$7.633 billion (31 December 2012 est.)

Exchange rates: drams (AMD) per US dollar—
410.5 (2013 est.)
401.76 (2012 est.)
373.66 (2010 est.)
363.28 (2009)
303.93 (2008)

ENERGY

Electricity—production: 7.432 billion kWh (2011 est.)
country comparison to the world: 103

Electricity—consumption: 5.8 billion kWh (2011 est.)
country comparison to the world: 108

Electricity—exports: 1.36 billion kWh (2011 est.)
country comparison to the world: 52

Electricity—imports: 246 million kWh (2010 est.)
country comparison to the world: 85

Electricity—installed generating capacity: 3.472 million kW (2010 est.)
country comparison to the world: 84

Electricity—from fossil fuels: 55.6% of total installed capacity (2010 est.)
country comparison to the world: 142

Electricity—from nuclear fuels: 10.8% of total installed capacity (2010 est.)
country comparison to the world: 16

Electricity—from hydroelectric plants: 33.5% of total installed capacity (2010 est.)
country comparison to the world: 67

Electricity—from other renewable sources: 0.1% of total installed capacity (2010 est.)
country comparison to the world: 106

Crude oil—production: 0 bbl/day (2013 est.)
country comparison to the world: 149

Crude oil—exports: 0 bbl/day (2013 est.)
country comparison to the world: 77

Crude oil—imports: 0 bbl/day (2013 est.)
country comparison to the world: 152

Crude oil—proved reserves: 0 bbl (1 January 2013 es)
country comparison to the world: 103

Refined petroleum products—production: 0 bbl/day (2013 est.)
country comparison to the world: 118

Refined petroleum products—consumption: 45,300 bbl/day (2011 est.)
country comparison to the world: 102

Refined petroleum products—exports: 31.78 bbl/day (2010 est.)
country comparison to the world: 124

Refined petroleum products—imports: 46,550 bbl/day (2010 est.)
country comparison to the world: 72

Natural gas—production: 0 cu m (2013 est.)
country comparison to the world: 98

Natural gas—consumption: 2.1 billion cu m (2013 est.)
country comparison to the world: 78

Natural gas—exports: 0 cu m (2013 est.)
country comparison to the world: 57

Natural gas—imports: 2.1 billion cu m (2013 est.)
country comparison to the world: 47

Natural gas—proved reserves: 0 cu m (1 January 2013 es)
country comparison to the world: 109

Carbon dioxide emissions from consumption of energy: 11.74 million Mt (2011 est.)
country comparison to the world: 98

COMMUNICATIONS

Telephones—main lines in use: 584,000 (2012)
country comparison to the world: 92

Telephones—mobile cellular: 3.223 million (2012)
country comparison to the world: 128

Telephone system: *general assessment:* telecommunications investments have made major inroads in modernizing and upgrading the outdated telecommunications network inherited from the Soviet era; now 100% privately owned and undergoing modernization and expansion; mobile-cellular services monopoly terminated in late 2004 and a second provider began operations in mid-2005
domestic: reliable modern fixed-line and mobile-cellular services are available across Yerevan in major cities and towns; significant but ever-shrinking gaps remain in mobile-cellular coverage in rural areas
international: country code—374; Yerevan is connected to the Trans-Asia-Europe fiber-optic cable through Iran; additional international service is available by microwave radio relay and landline connections to the other countries of the Commonwealth of Independent States, through the Moscow international switch, and by satellite to the rest of the world; satellite earth stations—3 (2008)

Broadcast media: 2 public TV networks operating alongside more than 40 privately-owned TV stations that provide local to near nationwide coverage; major Russian broadcast stations are widely available; subscription cable TV services are available in most regions; Public Radio of Armenia is a national, state-run broadcast network that operates alongside about 20 privately owned radio stations; several major international broadcasters are available (2008)

Internet country code: .am

Internet hosts: 194,142 (2012)
country comparison to the world: 73

Internet users: 208,200 (2009)
country comparison to the world: 138

TRANSPORTATION

Airports: 11 (2013)
country comparison to the world: 154

Airports—with paved runways: *total:* 10
over 3,047 m: 2
2,438 to 3,047 m: 2
1,524 to 2,437 m: 4
914 to 1,523 m: 2 (2013)

Airports—with unpaved runways: *total:* 1
914 to 1,523 m: 1 (2013)

Pipelines: gas 2,233 km (2013)

Railways: *total:* 869 km
country comparison to the world: 96
broad gauge: 869 km 1.520-m gauge (818 km electrified)
note: some lines are out of service (2009)

Roadways: *total:* 7,705 km (2012)
country comparison to the world: 143

MILITARY

Military branches: Armenian Armed Forces: Ground Forces, Air Force and Air Defense; "Nagorno-Karabakh Republic": Nagorno-Karabakh Self-Defense Force (NKSDF) (2011)

Military service age and obligation: 18-27 years of age for voluntary or compulsory military service; 2-year conscript service obligation; 17 year olds are eligible to become cadets at military higher education institutes, where they are classified as military personnel (2012)

Manpower available for military service: *males age 16-49:* 805,847
females age 16-49: 854,296 (2010 est.)

Manpower fit for military service: *males age 16-49:* 644,372
females age 16-49: 717,272 (2010 est.)

Manpower reaching militarily significant age annually: *male:* 23,470
female: 21,417 (2010 est.)

Military expenditures: 3.92% of GDP (2012)
country comparison to the world: 12
3.87% of GDP (2011)
3.92% of GDP (2010)

TRANSNATIONAL ISSUES

Disputes—international: the dispute over the break-away Nagorno-Karabakh region and the Armenian military occupation of surrounding lands in Azerbaijan remains the primary focus of regional instability; residents have evacuated the former Soviet-era small ethnic enclaves in Armenia and Azerbaijan; Turkish authorities have complained that blasting from quarries in Armenia might be damaging the medieval ruins of Ani, on the other side of the Arpacay valley; in 2009, Swiss mediators facilitated an accord reestablishing diplomatic ties between Armenia and Turkey, but neither side has ratified the agreement and the rapprochement effort has faltered; local border forces struggle to control the illegal transit of goods and people across the porous, undemarcated Armenian, Azerbaijani, and Georgian borders; ethnic Armenian groups in the Javakheti region of Georgia seek greater autonomy from the Georgian Government

Refugees and internally displaced persons: *refugees (country of origin):* 6,000 Syria (ethnic Armenians) (2013)
IDPs: 8,400 (conflict with Azerbaijan over Nagorno-Karabakh) (2009)
stateless persons: 35 (2012)

Illicit drugs: illicit cultivation of small amount of cannabis for domestic consumption; minor transit point for illicit drugs—mostly opium and hashish—moving from Southwest Asia to Russia and to a lesser extent the rest of Europe

ARUBA

INTRODUCTION

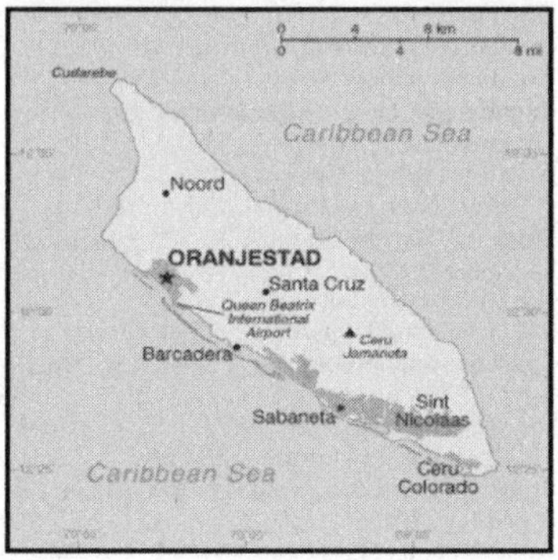

Background: Discovered and claimed for Spain in 1499, Aruba was acquired by the Dutch in 1636. The island's economy has been dominated by three main industries. A 19th century gold rush was followed by prosperity brought on by the opening in 1924 of an oil refinery. The last decades of the 20th century saw a boom in the tourism industry. Aruba seceded from the Netherlands Antilles in 1986 and became a separate, autonomous member of the Kingdom of the Netherlands. Movement toward full independence was halted at Aruba's request in 1990.

GEOGRAPHY

Location: Caribbean, island in the Caribbean Sea, north of Venezuela

Geographic coordinates: 12 30 N, 69 58 W

Map references: Central America and the Caribbean

Area: *total:* 180 sq km
country comparison to the world: 218
land: 180 sq km
water: 0 sq km

Area—comparative: slightly larger than Washington, DC

Land boundaries: 0 km

Coastline: 68.5 km

Maritime claims: *territorial sea:* 12 nm

Climate: tropical marine; little seasonal temperature variation

Terrain: flat with a few hills; scant vegetation

Elevation extremes: *lowest point:* Caribbean Sea 0 m
highest point: Ceru Jamanota 188 m

Natural resources: NEGL; white sandy beaches

Land use: *arable land:* 11.11%
permanent crops: 0%
other: 88.89% (2005)

Irrigated land: NA

Natural hazards: hurricanes; lies outside the Caribbean hurricane belt and is rarely threatened

Environment—current issues: NA

Geography—note: a flat, riverless island renowned for its white sand beaches; its tropical climate is moderated by constant trade winds from the Atlantic Ocean; the temperature is almost constant at about 27 degrees Celsius (81 degrees Fahrenheit)

PEOPLE AND SOCIETY

Nationality: *noun:* Aruban(s)
adjective: Aruban; Dutch

Ethnic groups: Dutch 82.1%, Colombian 6.6%, Venezuelan 2.2%, Dominican 2.2%, Haitian 1.2%, other 5.5%, unspecified 0.1% (2010 est.)

Languages: Papiamento (a Spanish-Portuguese-Dutch-English dialect) 69.4%, Spanish 13.7%, English (widely spoken) 7.1%, Dutch (official) 6.1%, Chinese 1.5%, other 1.7%, unspecified 0.4% (2010 est.)

Religions: Roman Catholic 75.3%, Protestant 4.9% (includes Methodist .9%, Adventist .9%, Anglican .4%, other Protestant 2.7%), Jehovah's Witness 1.7%, other 12%, none 5.5%, unspecified 0.5% (2010 est.)

Population: 110,663 (July 2014 est.)
country comparison to the world: 190
note: estimate based on a revision of the base population, fertility, and mortality numbers, as well as a revision of 1985-99 migration estimates from outmigration to inmigration, which is assumed to continue into the future; the new results are consistent with the 2000 census

Age structure: *0-14 years:* 17.8% (male 9,852/female 9,797)
15-24 years: 13.5% (male 7,469/female 7,427)
25-54 years: 43% (male 22,981/female 24,615)
55-64 years: 12.3% (male 6,804/female 8,093)
65 years and over: 11.9% (male 5,346/female 8,279) (2014 est.)

Dependency ratios: *total dependency ratio:* 44.3%
youth dependency ratio: 28%
elderly dependency ratio: 16.4%
potential support ratio: 6.1 (2013)

Median age: *total:* 38.8 years
male: 36.9 years
female: 40.6 years (2014 est.)

Population growth rate: 1.36% (2014 est.)
country comparison to the world: 90

Birth rate: 12.65 births/1,000 population (2014 est.)
country comparison to the world: 158

Death rate: 8.09 deaths/1,000 population (2014 est.)
country comparison to the world: 97

Net migration rate: 9.04 migrant(s)/1,000 population (2014 est.)
country comparison to the world: 15

Urbanization: *urban population:* 47% of total population (2010)
rate of urbanization: 0.6% annual rate of change (2010-15 est.)

Major urban areas—population: ORANJESTAD (capital) 37,000 (2011)

Sex ratio: *at birth:* 1.02 male(s)/female
0-14 years: 1.01 male(s)/female
15-24 years: 1.01 male(s)/female
25-54 years: 0.93 male(s)/female
55-64 years: 0.9 male(s)/female
65 years and over: 0.65 male(s)/female
total population: 0.9 male(s)/female (2014 est.)

Infant mortality rate: *total:* 11.74 deaths/1,000 live births
country comparison to the world: 128
male: 15.44 deaths/1,000 live births
female: 7.97 deaths/1,000 live births (2014 est.)

Life expectancy at birth: *total population:* 76.35 years
country comparison to the world: 82
male: 73.3 years
female: 79.47 years (2014 est.)

Total fertility rate: 1.84 children born/woman (2014 est.)
country comparison to the world: 150

Drinking water source:
Improved:
urban: 97.8% of population
rural: 97.8% of population
total: 97.8% of population
unimproved:
urban: 2.2% of population
rural: 2.2% of population
total: 2.2% of population (2011 est.)

Sanitation facility access:
improved:
urban: 97.7% of population
rural: 97.7% of population
total: 97.7% of population
unimproved:
urban: 2.3% of population
rural: 2.3% of population
total: 2.3% of population (2011 est.)

HIV/AIDS—adult prevalence rate: NA

HIV/AIDS—people living with HIV/AIDS: NA

HIV/AIDS—deaths: NA

Education expenditures: 6% of GDP (2011)
country comparison to the world: 41

Literacy: *definition:* age 15 and over can read and write total population: 96.8%
male: 96.9%
female: 96.7% (2010 est.)

School life expectancy (primary to tertiary education): *total:* 13 years
male: 13 years
female: 14 years (2011)

Unemployment, youth ages 15-24: *total:* 23.2%
country comparison to the world: 47
male: 24.1%
female: 22.9% (2007)

GOVERNMENT

Country name: *conventional long form:* none
conventional short form: Aruba

Dependency status: constituent country of the Kingdom of the Netherlands; full autonomy in internal affairs obtained in 1986 upon separation from the Netherlands Antilles; Dutch Government responsible for defense and foreign affairs

Government type: parliamentary democracy

Capital: *name:* Oranjestad
geographic coordinates: 12 31 N, 70 02 W
time difference: UTC-4 (1 hour ahead of Washington, DC during Standard Time)

Administrative divisions: none (part of the Kingdom of the Netherlands)

Independence: none (part of the Kingdom of the Netherlands)

National holiday: Flag Day, 18 March (1976)

Constitution: previous 1947, 1955; latest drafted and approved August 1985, enacted 1 January 1986 (regulates governance of Aruba, but is subordinate to the Charter for the Kingdom of the Netherlands); note—in October 2010, following dissolution of the Netherlands Antilles, Aruba became a constituent country within the Kingdom of the Netherlands (2013)

Legal system: civil law system based on the Dutch civil code

Suffrage: 18 years of age; universal

Executive branch: *chief of state:* King WILLEM-ALEXANDER of the Netherlands (since 30 April 2013); represented by Governor General Fredis REFUNJOL (since 11 May 2004)
head of government: Prime Minister Michiel "Mike" Godfried EMAN (since 30 October 2009)
cabinet: Council of Ministers elected by the Staten (For more information visit the World Leaders website)
elections: the monarchy is hereditary; governor general appointed for a six-year term by the monarch; prime minister and deputy prime minister elected by the Staten for four-year terms; election last held on 25 September 2009 (next to be held by September 2013)
election results: Michiel "Mike" Godfried EMAN elected prime minister; percent of legislative vote—NA

Legislative branch: unicameral Legislature or Staten (21 seats; members elected by direct popular vote to serve four-year terms)
elections: last held on 27 September 2013 (next to be held in 2017)
election results: percent of vote by party—NA; seats by party—AVP 13, MEP 8

Judicial branch: *highest court(s):* Joint Court of Justice of Aruba, Curacao, Sint Maarten, and of Bonaire, Sint Eustatius and Saba or "Joint Court of Justice" (consists of the presiding judge, NA members, and NA substitutes); final appeals heard by the Supreme Court, in The Hague, Netherlands
note—prior to 2010, the Joint Court of Justice was the Common Court of Justice of the Netherlands Antilles and Aruba
judge selection and term of office: Joint Court judges appointed by the monarch for life
subordinate courts: Courts in First Instance

Political parties and leaders: Aliansa/Aruban Social Movement or MSA [Robert WEVER]; Aruban Liberal Organization or OLA [Glenbert CROES]; Aruban Patriotic Movement or MPA [Monica ARENDS-KOCK]; Aruban Patriotic Party or PPA [Benny NISBET]; Aruban People's Party or AVP [Michiel "Mike" EMAN]; People's Electoral Movement Party or MEP [Nelson O. ODUBER]; Real Democracy or PDR [Andin BIKKER]; RED [Rudy LAMPE]; Workers Political Platform or PTT [Gregorio WOLFF]

Political pressure groups and leaders: *other:* environmental groups

International organization participation: Caricom (observer), FATF, ILO, IMF, Interpol, IOC, ITUC (NGOs), UNESCO (associate), UNWTO (associate), UPU

Diplomatic representation in the US: none (represented by the Kingdom of the Netherlands); note—Mr. Henry BAARH, Minister Plenipotentiary for Aruba at the Embassy of the Kingdom of the Netherlands

Diplomatic representation from the US: the US does not have an embassy in Aruba; the Consul General to Curacao, currently Consul General Valerie BELON, is accredited to Aruba

Flag description: blue, with two narrow, horizontal, yellow stripes across the lower portion and a red, four-pointed star outlined in white in the upper hoist-side corner; the star represents Aruba and its red soil and white beaches, its four points the four major languages (Papiamento, Dutch, Spanish, English) as well as the four points of a compass, to indicate that its inhabitants come from all over the world; the blue symbolizes Caribbean waters and skies; the stripes represent the island's two main "industries": the flow of tourists to the sun-drenched beaches and the flow of minerals from the earth

National anthem: *name:* "Aruba Deshi Tera" (Aruba Precious Country)
lyrics/music: Juan Chabaya 'Padu' LAMPE/Rufo Inocencio WEVER
note: local anthem adopted 1986; as part of the Kingdom of the Netherlands, "Het Wilhelmus" is official (see Netherlands)

ECONOMY

Economy—overview: Tourism and offshore banking are the mainstays of the small open Aruban economy. Tourist arrivals have rebounded strongly following a dip after the 11 September 2001 attacks. Tourism now accounts for over 80 % of economic activity. Over 1.5 million tourists per year visit Aruba, with 75% of those from the US. The rapid growth of the tourism sector has resulted in a substantial expansion of other activities. Construction continues to boom with hotel capacity five times the 1985 level. Aruba is heavily dependent on imports and is making efforts to expand exports to achieve a more desirable trade balance. Aruba weathered two major shocks in recent years: fallout from the global financial crisis, which had its largest impact on tourism, and the closure of its oil refinery in 2009. Economic recovery is progressing gradually, but output is still 12% below its pre-crisis level. Aruba's banking sector withstood the recession well, and unemployment has significantly decreased.

GDP (purchasing power parity): $2.516 billion (2009 est.)
country comparison to the world: 186
$2.258 billion (2005 est.)
$2.205 billion (2004 est.)

GDP (official exchange rate): $2.516 billion (2009 est.)

GDP—real growth rate: 2.4% (2005 est.)
country comparison to the world: 133

GDP—per capita (PPP): $25,300 (2011 est.)
country comparison to the world: 59

GDP—composition, by sector of origin:
agriculture: 0.4%
industry: 33.3%
services: 66.3% (2002 est.)

Agriculture—products: aloes; livestock; fish

Industries: tourism, transshipment facilities, banking

Industrial production growth rate: NA%

Labor force: 51,610
country comparison to the world: 190
note: of the 51,610 workers aged 15 and over in the labor force, 32,252 were born in Aruba and 19,353 came from abroad; foreign workers are 38% of the employed population (2007 est.)

Labor force—by occupation: *agriculture:* NA%
industry: NA%
services: NA%
note: most employment is in wholesale and retail trade and repair, followed by hotels and restaurants

Unemployment rate: 6.9% (2005 est.)
country comparison to the world: 74

Population below poverty line: NA%

Household income or consumption by percentage share: *lowest* 10%: NA%
highest 10%: NA%

Budget: *revenues:* $625.1 million
expenditures: $813.9 million (2013 est.)

Taxes and other revenues: 24.8% of GDP (2013 est.)
country comparison to the world: 132

Budget surplus (+) or deficit (-): -7.5% of GDP (2013 est.)
country comparison to the world: 192

Public debt: 67% of GDP (2013)
country comparison to the world: 40
55% of GDP (2012)

Fiscal year: calendar year

Inflation rate (consumer prices): -2% (2013 est.)
country comparison to the world: 2
0.6% (2012 est.)

Central bank discount rate: 1% (31 December 2010 est.)
country comparison to the world: 105
3% (31 December 2009 est.)

Commercial bank prime lending rate: 10.5% (31 December 2013 est.)
country comparison to the world: 111
8.4% (31 December 2012 est.)

Stock of narrow money: $1.022 billion (31 December 2012 est.)
country comparison to the world: 151
$868.5 million (31 December 2011 est.)

Stock of broad money: $1.91 billion (31 December 2012 est.)
country comparison to the world: 152
$1.765 billion (31 December 2011 est.)

Stock of domestic credit: $1.594 billion (31 December 2012 est.)
country comparison to the world: 142
$1.448 billion (31 December 2011 est.)

Exports: $2.222 billion (2013 est.)
country comparison to the world: 141
$1.389 billion (2012 est.)

Exports—commodities: live animals and animal products, art and collectibles, machinery and electrical equipment, transport equipment

Exports—partners: Colombia 39.4%, Venezuela 29.3%, US 13%, Netherlands Antilles 4.1% (2012)

Imports: $3.162 billion (2013 est.)
country comparison to the world: 146
$2.039 billion (2012 est.)

Imports—commodities: machinery and electrical equipment, crude oil for refining and reexport, chemicals; foodstuffs

Imports—partners: US 46.4%, Netherlands 11.5%, UK 5.4% (2012)

Debt—external: $533.4 million (2005 est.)
country comparison to the world: 174

Exchange rates: Aruban guilders/florins (AWG) per US dollar—
1.79 (2013 est.)
1.79 (2012 est.)

ENERGY

Electricity—production: 980 million kWh (2010 est.)
country comparison to the world: 147

Electricity—consumption: 911.4 million kWh (2010 est.)
country comparison to the world: 152

Electricity—exports: 0 kWh (2012 est.)
country comparison to the world: 92

Electricity—imports: 0 kWh (2012 est.)
country comparison to the world: 109

Electricity—installed generating capacity: 266,000 kW (2010 est.)
country comparison to the world: 152

Electricity—from fossil fuels: 88.7% of total installed capacity (2010 est.)
country comparison to the world: 80

Electricity—from nuclear fuels: 0% of total installed capacity (2010 est.)
country comparison to the world: 31

Electricity—from hydroelectric plants: 0% of total installed capacity (2010 est.)
country comparison to the world: 151

Electricity—from other renewable sources: 11.3% of total installed capacity (2010 est.)

country comparison to the world: 24
Crude oil—production: 2,811 bbl/day (2012 est.)
country comparison to the world: 103
Crude oil—exports: 0 bbl/day (2010 est.)
country comparison to the world: 74
Crude oil—imports: 228,800 bbl/day (2010 est.)
country comparison to the world: 31
Crude oil—proved reserves: 0 bbl (1 January 2013 es)
country comparison to the world: 101
Refined petroleum products—production: 234,200 bbl/day (2010 est.)
country comparison to the world: 51
Refined petroleum products—consumption: 5,661 bbl/day (2011 est.)
country comparison to the world: 163
Refined petroleum products—exports: 234,200 bbl/day (2010 est.)
country comparison to the world: 27
Refined petroleum products—imports: 6,725 bbl/day (2010 est.)
country comparison to the world: 137
Natural gas—production: 1 cu m (2011 est.)
country comparison to the world: 96
Natural gas—consumption: 1 cu m (2010 est.)
country comparison to the world: 115
Natural gas—exports: 1 cu m (2011 est.)
country comparison to the world: 53
Natural gas—imports: 1 cu m (2011 est.)
country comparison to the world: 77
Natural gas—proved reserves: 0 cu m (1 January 2013 es)
country comparison to the world: 107
Carbon dioxide emissions from consumption of energy: 1.237 million Mt (2011 est.)
country comparison to the world: 161

COMMUNICATIONS

Telephones—main lines in use: 43,000 (2012)
country comparison to the world: 169
Telephones—mobile cellular: 135,000 (2012)
country comparison to the world: 188
Telephone system: *general assessment:* modern fully automatic telecommunications system
domestic: increased competition through privatization; 3 mobile-cellular service providers are now licensed
international: country code—297; landing site for the PAN-AM submarine telecommunications cable system that extends from the US Virgin Islands through Aruba to Venezuela, Colombia, Panama, and the west coast of South America; extensive interisland microwave radio relay links (2007)
Broadcast media: 2 commercial TV stations; cable TV subscription service provides access to foreign channels; about 20 commercial radio stations broadcast (2007)
Internet country code: .aw
Internet hosts: 40,560 (2012)
country comparison to the world: 101
Internet users: 24,000 (2009)
country comparison to the world: 188

TRANSPORTATION

Airports: 1 (2013)
country comparison to the world: 210
Airports—with paved runways: *total:* 1
2,438 to 3,047 m: 1 (2013)
Ports and terminals: *major seaport(s):* Barcadera, Oranjestad
oil terminal(s): Sint Nicolaas
cruise port(s): Oranjestad

MILITARY

Military branches: no regular military forces (2011)
Manpower available for military service: *males age 16-49:* 24,891
females age 16-49: 26,202 (2010 est.)
Manpower fit for military service: *males age 16-49:* 20,527
females age 16-49: 21,493 (2010 est.)
Manpower reaching militarily significant age annually: *male:* 767
female: 743 (2010 est.)
Military—note: defense is the responsibility of the Netherlands; the Aruba security services focus on organized crime and terrorism (2011)

TRANSNATIONAL ISSUES

Disputes—international: none
Illicit drugs: transit point for US-and Europe-bound narcotics with some accompanying money-laundering activity; relatively high percentage of population consumes cocaine

ASHMORE AND CARTIER ISLANDS

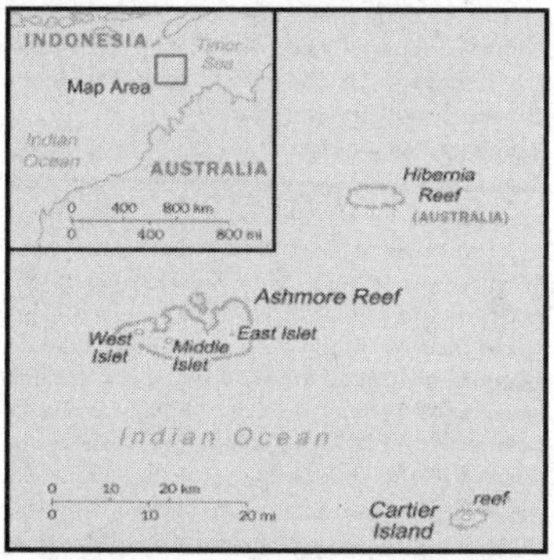

INTRODUCTION

Background: These uninhabited islands came under Australian authority in 1931; formal administration began two years later. Ashmore Reef supports a rich and diverse avian and marine habitat; in 1983, it became a National Nature Reserve. Cartier Island, a former bombing range, became a marine reserve in 2000.

GEOGRAPHY

Location: Southeastern Asia, islands in the Indian Ocean, midway between northwestern Australia and Timor island
Geographic coordinates: 12 14 S, 123 05 E
Map references: Oceania
Area: *total:* 5 sq km
country comparison to the world: 247
land: 5 sq km water: 0 sq km
note: includes Ashmore Reef (West, Middle, and East Islets) and Cartier Island
Area—comparative: about eight times the size of The Mall in Washington, DC
Land boundaries: 0 km
Coastline: 74.1 km
Maritime claims: *territorial sea:* 12 nm
contiguous zone: 12 nm
exclusive fishing zone: 200 nm
continental shelf: 200 m depth or to the depth of exploitation
Climate: tropical
Terrain: low with sand and coral
Elevation extremes: *lowest point:* Indian Ocean 0 m
highest point: unnamed location 3 m
Natural resources: fish
Land use: *arable land:* 0%
permanent crops: 0%
other: 100% (all grass and sand) (2011)
Natural hazards: surrounded by shoals and reefs that can pose maritime hazards
Environment—current issues: illegal killing of protected wildlife by traditional Indonesian fisherman, as well as fishing by non-traditional Indonesian vessels, are ongoing problems
Geography—note: Ashmore Reef National Nature Reserve established in August 1983; Cartier Island Marine Reserve established in 2000

PEOPLE AND SOCIETY

Population: no indigenous inhabitants
note: Indonesian fishermen are allowed access to the lagoon and fresh water at Ashmore Reef's West Island; access to East and Middle Islands is by permit only

GOVERNMENT

Country name: *conventional long form:* Territory of Ashmore and Cartier Islands
conventional short form: Ashmore and Cartier Islands
Dependency status: territory of Australia; administered from Canberra by the Department of Regional Australia, Local Government, Arts and Sport
Legal system: the laws of the Commonwealth of Australia and the laws of the Northern Territory of Australia, where applicable, apply
Diplomatic representation in the US: none (territory of Australia)
Diplomatic representation from the US: none (territory of Australia)
Flag description: the flag of Australia is used

ECONOMY

Economy—overview: no economic activity

TRANSPORTATION

Ports and terminals: none; offshore anchorage only

MILITARY

Military—note: defense is the responsibility of Australia; periodic visits by the Royal Australian Navy and Royal Australian Air Force

TRANSNATIONAL ISSUES

Disputes—international: Australia has closed parts of the Ashmore and Cartier reserve to Indonesian traditional fishing; Indonesian groups challenge Australia's claim to Ashmore Reef

ATLANTIC OCEAN

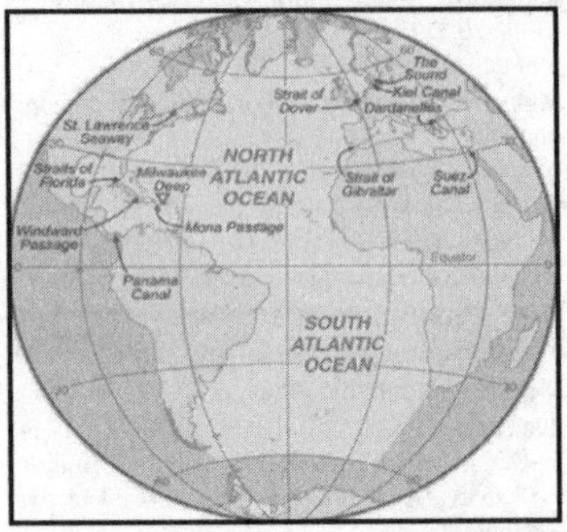

INTRODUCTION

Background: The Atlantic Ocean is the second largest of the world's five oceans (after the Pacific Ocean, but larger than the Indian Ocean, Southern Ocean, and Arctic Ocean). The Kiel Canal (Germany), Oresund (Denmark-Sweden), Bosporus (Turkey), Strait of Gibraltar (Morocco-Spain), and the Saint Lawrence Seaway (Canada-US) are important strategic access waterways. The decision by the International Hydrographic Organization in the spring of 2000 to delimit a fifth world ocean, the Southern Ocean, removed the portion of the Atlantic Ocean south of 60 degrees south latitude.

GEOGRAPHY

Location: body of water between Africa, Europe, the Arctic Ocean, the Americas, and the Southern Ocean

Geographic coordinates: 0 00 N, 25 00 W

Map references: Political Map of the World

Area: *total:* 76.762 million sq km
note: includes Baltic Sea, Black Sea, Caribbean Sea, Davis Strait, Denmark Strait, part of the Drake Passage, Gulf of Mexico, Labrador Sea, Mediterranean Sea, North Sea, Norwegian Sea, almost all of the Scotia Sea, and other tributary water bodies

Area—comparative: slightly less than 6.5 times the size of the US

Coastline: 111,866 km

Climate: tropical cyclones (hurricanes) develop off the coast of Africa near Cabo Verde and move westward into the Caribbean Sea; hurricanes can occur from May to December but are most frequent from August to November

Terrain: surface usually covered with sea ice in Labrador Sea, Denmark Strait, and coastal portions of the Baltic Sea from October to June; clockwise warm-water gyre (broad, circular system of currents) in the northern Atlantic, counterclockwise warm-water gyre in the southern Atlantic; the ocean floor is dominated by the Mid-Atlantic Ridge, a rugged north-south centerline for the entire Atlantic basin

Elevation extremes: *lowest point:* Milwaukee Deep in the Puerto Rico Trench-8,605 m
highest point: sea level 0 m

Natural resources: oil and gas fields, fish, marine mammals (seals and whales), sand and gravel aggregates, placer deposits, polymetallic nodules, precious stones

Natural hazards: icebergs common in Davis Strait, Denmark Strait, and the northwestern Atlantic Ocean from February to August and have been spotted as far south as Bermuda and the Madeira Islands; ships subject to superstructure icing in extreme northern Atlantic from October to May; persistent fog can be a maritime hazard from May to September; hurricanes (May to December)

Environment—current issues: endangered marine species include the manatee, seals, sea lions, turtles, and whales; drift net fishing is hastening the decline of fish stocks and contributing to international disputes; municipal sludge pollution off eastern US, southern Brazil, and eastern Argentina; oil pollution in Caribbean Sea, Gulf of Mexico, Lake Maracaibo, Mediterranean Sea, and North Sea; industrial waste and municipal sewage pollution in Baltic Sea, North Sea, and Mediterranean Sea

Geography—note: major chokepoints include the Dardanelles, Strait of Gibraltar, access to the Panama and Suez Canals; strategic straits include the Strait of Dover, Straits of Florida, Mona Passage, The Sound (Oresund), and Windward Passage; the Equator divides the Atlantic Ocean into the North Atlantic Ocean and South Atlantic Ocean

ECONOMY

Economy—overview: The Atlantic Ocean provides some of the world's most heavily trafficked sea routes, between and within the Eastern and Western Hemispheres. Other economic activity includes the exploitation of natural resources, e.g., fishing, dredging of aragonite sands (The Bahamas), and production of crude oil and natural gas (Caribbean Sea, Gulf of Mexico, and North Sea).

TRANSPORTATION

Ports and terminals: *major seaport(s):* Alexandria (Egypt), Algiers (Algeria), Antwerp (Belgium), Barcelona (Spain), Buenos Aires (Argentina), Casablanca (Morocco), Colon (Panama), Copenhagen (Denmark), Dakar (Senegal), Gdansk (Poland), Hamburg (Germany), Helsinki (Finland), Las Palmas (Canary Islands, Spain), Le Havre (France), Lisbon (Portugal), London (UK), Marseille (France), Montevideo (Uruguay), Montreal (Canada), Naples (Italy), New Orleans (US), New York (US), Oran (Algeria), Oslo (Norway), Peiraiefs or Piraeus (Greece), Rio de Janeiro (Brazil), Rotterdam (Netherlands), Saint Petersburg (Russia), Stockholm (Sweden)

Transportation—note: Kiel Canal and Saint Lawrence Seaway are two important waterways; significant domestic commercial and recreational use of Intracoastal Waterway on central and south Atlantic seaboard and Gulf of Mexico coast of US; the International Maritime Bureau reports the territorial waters of littoral states and offshore Atlantic waters as high risk for piracy and armed robbery against ships, particularly in the Gulf of Guinea off West Africa; in 2012, 58 commercial vessels were attacked in the Gulf of Guinea with 10 hijacked and 207 crew members taken hostage; hijacked vessels are often disguised and cargoes stolen; crews have been robbed and stores or cargoes stolen

TRANSNATIONAL ISSUES

Disputes—international: some maritime disputes (see littoral states)

AUSTRALIA

INTRODUCTION

Background: Prehistoric settlers arrived on the continent from Southeast Asia at least 40,000 years before the first Europeans began exploration in the 17th century. No formal territorial claims were made until 1770, when Capt. James COOK took possession of the east coast in the name of Great Britain (all of Australia was claimed as British territory in 1829 with the creation of the colony of Western Australia). Six colonies were created in the late 18th and 19th centuries; they federated and became the Commonwealth of Australia in 1901. The new country took advantage of its natural resources to rapidly develop agricultural and manufacturing industries and to make a major contribution to the Allied effort in World Wars I and II. In recent decades, Australia has become an internationally competitive, advanced market economy due in large part to economic reforms adopted in the 1980s and its location in one of the fastest growing regions of the world economy. Long-term concerns include aging of the population, pressure on infrastructure, and environmental issues such as floods, droughts, and bushfires. Australia is the driest inhabited continent on earth, making it particularly vulnerable to the challenges of climate change. Australia is home to 10 per cent of the world's biodiversity, and a great number of its flora and fauna exist nowhere else in the world. In January 2013, Australia assumed a nonpermanent seat on the UN Security Council for the 2013-14 term.

GEOGRAPHY

Location: Oceania, continent between the Indian Ocean and the South Pacific Ocean

Geographic coordinates: 27 00 S, 133 00 E

Map references: Oceania

Area: *total:* 7,741,220 sq km
country comparison to the world: 6
land: 7,682,300 sq km
water: 58,920 sq km
note: includes Lord Howe Island and Macquarie Island

Area—comparative: slightly smaller than the US contiguous 48 states

Land boundaries: 0 km

Coastline: 25,760 km

Maritime claims: *territorial sea:* 12 nm
contiguous zone: 24 nm
exclusive economic zone: 200 nm
continental shelf: 200 nm or to the edge of the continental margin

Climate: generally arid to semiarid; temperate in south and east; tropical in north

Terrain: mostly low plateau with deserts; fertile plain in southeast

Elevation extremes: *lowest point:* Lake Eyre-15 m
highest point: Mount Kosciuszko 2,229 m

Natural resources: bauxite, coal, iron ore, copper, tin, gold, silver, uranium, nickel, tungsten, rare earth elements, mineral sands, lead, zinc, diamonds, natural gas, petroleum
note: Australia is the world's largest net exporter of coal accounting for 29% of global coal exports

Land use: *arable land:* 6.16% (includes about 27 million hectares of cultivated grassland)
permanent crops: 0.05%
other: 93.79% (2011)

Irrigated land: 25,460 sq km (2006)

Total renewable water resources: 492 cu km (2011)

Freshwater withdrawal (domestic/industrial/agricultural): *total:* 22.58 cu km/yr (27%/18%/55%)
per capita: 1,152 cu m/yr (2010)

Natural hazards: cyclones along the coast; severe droughts; forest fires
volcanism: volcanic activity on Heard and McDonald Islands

Environment—current issues: soil erosion from overgrazing, industrial development, urbanization, and poor farming practices; soil salinity rising due to the use of poor quality water; desertification; clearing for agricultural purposes threatens the natural habitat of many unique animal and plant species; the Great Barrier Reef off the northeast coast, the largest coral reef in the world, is threatened by increased shipping and its popularity as a tourist site; limited natural freshwater resources

Environment—international agreements: *party to:* Antarctic-Environmental Protocol, Antarctic-Marine Living Resources, Antarctic Seals, Antarctic Treaty, Biodiversity, Climate Change, Climate Change-Kyoto Protocol, Desertification, Endangered Species, Environmental Modification, Hazardous Wastes, Law of the Sea, Marine Dumping, Marine Life Conservation, Ozone Layer Protection, Ship Pollution, Tropical Timber 83, Tropical Timber 94, Wetlands, Whaling
signed, but not ratified: none of the selected agreements

Geography—note: world's smallest continent but sixth-largest country; the only continent without glaciers; population concentrated along the eastern and southeastern coasts; the invigorating sea breeze known as the "Fremantle Doctor" affects the city of Perth on the west coast and is one of the most consistent winds in the world

PEOPLE AND SOCIETY

Nationality: *noun:* Australian(s)
adjective: Australian

Ethnic groups: white 92%, Asian 7%, aboriginal and other 1%

Languages: English 76.8%, Mandarin 1.6%, Italian 1.4%, Arabic 1.3%, Greek 1.2%, Cantonese 1.2%, Vietnamese 1.1%, other 10.4%, unspecified 5% (2011 est.)

Religions: Protestant 28.8% (Anglican 17.1%, Uniting Church 5.0%, Presbyterian and Reformed 2.8%, Baptist, 1.6%, Lutheran 1.2%, Pentecostal 1.1%), Catholic 25.3%, Eastern Orthodox 2.6%, other Christian 4.5%, Buddhist 2.5%, Muslim 2.2%, Hindu 1.3%, other 8.5%, unspecified 2.2%, none 22.3%
note: percentages add up to more than 100% due to rounding (2006 Census)

Population: 22,507,617 (July 2014 est.)
country comparison to the world: 56

Age structure: *0-14 years:* 18% (male 2,075,316/female 1,969,645)
15-24 years: 13.3% (male 1,534,947/female 1,457,250)
25-54 years: 41.8% (male 4,783,473/female 4,626,603)
55-64 years: 15.1% (male 1,321,246/female 1,341,329)
65 years and over: 14.7% (male 1,569,197/female 1,828,611) (2014 est.)

Dependency ratios: *total dependency ratio:* 50.2%
youth dependency ratio: 28.6%
elderly dependency ratio: 21.5%
potential support ratio: 4.6 (2013)

Median age: *total:* 38.3 years
male: 37.5 years
female: 39 years (2014 est.)

Population growth rate: 1.09% (2014 est.)
country comparison to the world: 112

Birth rate: 12.19 births/1,000 population (2014 est.)
country comparison to the world: 162

Death rate: 7.07 deaths/1,000 population (2014 est.)
country comparison to the world: 131

Net migration rate: 5.74 migrant(s)/1,000 population (2014 est.)
country comparison to the world: 23

Urbanization: *urban population:* 89% of total population (2010)
rate of urbanization: 1.2% annual rate of change (2010-15 est.)

Major urban areas—population: Sydney 4.429 million; Melbourne 3.853 million; Brisbane 1.97 million; Perth 1.599 million; CANBERRA (capital) 399,000 (2011)

Sex ratio: *at birth:* 1.06 male(s)/female
0-14 years: 1.05 male(s)/female
15-24 years: 1.05 male(s)/female
25-54 years: 1.03 male(s)/female
55-64 years: 1.01 male(s)/female
65 years and over: 0.85 male(s)/female
total population: 1.01 male(s)/female (2014 est.)

Mother's mean age at first birth: 30.5 (2006 est.)

Maternal mortality rate: 7 deaths/100,000 live births (2010)
country comparison to the world: 164

Infant mortality rate: *total:* 4.43 deaths/1,000 live births
country comparison to the world: 190
male: 4.74 deaths/1,000 live births
female: 4.1 deaths/1,000 live births (2014 est.)

Life expectancy at birth: *total population:* 82.07 years
country comparison to the world: 10
male: 79.63 years
female: 84.64 years (2014 est.)

Total fertility rate: 1.77 children born/woman (2014 est.)
country comparison to the world: 162

Contraceptive prevalence rate: 72.3%
note: percent of women aged 18-44 (2005)

Health expenditures: 9% of GDP (2011)
country comparison to the world: 46

Physicians density: 3.85 physicians/1,000 population (2010)

Hospital bed density: 3.9 beds/1,000 population (2010)

Drinking water source:
Improved:
urban: 100% of population
rural: 100% of population
total: 100% of population
unimproved:
urban: 0% of population
rural: 0% of population
total: 0% of population (2011 est.)

Sanitation facility access:
Improved:
urban: 100% of population
rural: 100% of population
total: 100% of population
unimproved:
urban: 0% of population
rural: 0% of population
total: 0% of population (2011 est.)

HIV/AIDS—adult prevalence rate: 0.1% (2009 est.)
country comparison to the world: 125

HIV/AIDS—people living with HIV/AIDS: 20,000 (2009 est.)
country comparison to the world: 81

HIV/AIDS—deaths: fewer than 100 (2009 est.)
country comparison to the world: 123

Obesity—adult prevalence rate: 26.8% (2008)
country comparison to the world: 44

Children under the age of 5 years underweight: 0.2% (2007)
country comparison to the world: 136

Education expenditures: 5.6% of GDP (2010)
country comparison to the world: 56

Literacy: *definition:* age 15 and over can read and write
total population: 99%
male: 99%
female: 99% (2003 est.)

School life expectancy (primary to tertiary education): *total:* 20 years
male: 19 years
female: 20 years (2011)

Unemployment, youth ages 15-24: *total:* 11.7%
country comparison to the world: 102
male: 12.4%
female: 11% (2012)

GOVERNMENT

Country name: *conventional long form:* Commonwealth of Australia
conventional short form: Australia

Government type: federal parliamentary democracy and a Commonwealth realm

Capital: *name:* Canberra
geographic coordinates: 35 16 S, 149 08 E
time difference: UTC+10 (15 hours ahead of Washington, DC during Standard Time)
daylight saving time: +1hr, begins first Sunday in October; ends first Sunday in April
note: Australia is divided into three time zones

Administrative divisions: 6 states and 2 territories*; Australian Capital Territory*, New South Wales, Northern Territory*, Queensland, South Australia, Tasmania, Victoria, Western Australia

Dependent areas: Ashmore and Cartier Islands, Christmas Island, Cocos (Keeling) Islands, Coral Sea Islands, Heard Island and McDonald Islands, Macquarie Island, Norfolk Island

Independence: 1 January 1901 (from the federation of UK colonies)

National holiday: Australia Day (commemorates the arrival of the First Fleet of Australian settlers), 26 January (1788); ANZAC Day (commemorates the anniversary of the landing of troops of the Australian and New Zealand Army Corps during World War I at Gallipoli, Turkey), 25 April (1915)

Constitution: 9 July 1900; effective 1 January 1901; amended several times, last in 1977; note—a referendum to amend the constitution to reflect the Aboriginal and Torres Strait Islander Peoples Recognition Act 2013 is to be completed by the end of 2014 (2013)

Legal system: common law system based on the English model

International law organization participation: accepts compulsory ICJ jurisdiction with reservations; accepts ICCt jurisdiction

Suffrage: 18 years of age; universal and compulsory

Executive branch: *chief of state:* Queen of Australia ELIZABETH II (since 6 February 1952); represented by Governor General Sir Peter COSGROVE (since 28 March 2014)
head of government: Prime Minister Anthony John "Tony" ABBOTT (since 18 September 2013); Deputy Prime Minister Warren TRUSS (since 18 September 2013)
cabinet: prime minister nominates, from among members of Parliament, candidates who are subsequently sworn in by the governor general to serve as government ministers
(For more information visit the World Leaders website)
elections: the monarchy is hereditary; governor general appointed by the monarch on the recommendation of the prime minister; following legislative elections, the leader of the majority party or leader of a majority coalition is sworn in as prime minister by the governor general

Legislative branch: bicameral Federal Parliament consists of the Senate (76 seats; 12 members from each of the six states and 2 from each of the two mainland territories; one-half of state members are elected every three years by popular vote to serve six-year terms while all territory members are elected every three years) and the House of Representatives (150 seats; members elected by popular vote to serve terms of up to three-years; no state can have fewer than 5 representatives)
elections: Senate—last held on 7 September 2013; House of Representatives—last held on 7 September 2013 (the latest a simultaneous half-Senate and House of Representative elections can be held is 30 November 2016)
election results: Senate NA; House of Representatives—percent of vote by party—Liberal/National Coalition 53.45%, Australian Labor Party 46.55%; seats by party—Liberal/National Coalition 90 (Liberal 58, Liberal National 22, Nationals 9, Country Liberals 1), Australian Labor Party 55, Australian Greens Party 1, Katter's Australian Party 1, Palmer United Party 1, independents 2

Judicial branch: *highest court(s):* High Court of Australia (consists of 7 justices, including the chief justice); note—each of the 6 states, 2 territories,and Norfolk Island has a Supreme Court; the High Court is the final appellate court beyond the state and territory supreme courts
judge selection and term of office: justices appointed by the governor-general in council for life with mandatory retirement at age 70
subordinate courts: subordinate courts at the federal level: Federal Court; Federal Magistrates' Courts of Australia; Family Court;subordinate courts at the state and territory level: Local Court—New South Wales; Magistrates' Courts—Victoria, Queensland, South Australia, Western Australia, Tasmania, Northern Territory, Australian Capital Territory; District Courts—New South Wales, Queensland,South Australia, Western Australia; County Court—Victoria; Family Court—Western Australia; Court of Petty Sessions—Norfolk Island

Political parties and leaders: Australian Greens Party [Christine MILNE]; Australian Labor Party [Bill SHORTEN]; Country Liberal Party [Terry MILLS] Family First Party [Steve FIELDING]; Katter's Australian Party [Bob KATTER]; Liberal National Party of Queensland [Campbell NEWMAN]; Liberal Party [Tony ABBOTT]; National Party of Australia [Warren TRUSS]; Palmer United Party [Clive PALMER]

Political pressure groups and leaders: *other:* business groups, environmental groups, social groups, trade unions

International organization participation: ADB, ANZUS, APEC, ARF, ASEAN (dialogue partner), Australia Group, BIS, C, CD, CP, EAS, EBRD, EITI (implementing country), FAO, FATF, G-20, IAEA, IBRD, ICAO, ICC (national committees), ICRM, IDA, IEA, IFC, IFRCS, IHO, ILO, IMF, IMO, IMSO, Interpol, IOC, IOM, IPU, ISO, ITSO, ITU, ITUC (NGOs), MIGA, NEA, NSG, OECD, OPCW, OSCE (partner), Paris Club, PCA, PIF, SAARC (observer), SICA (observer), Sparteca, SPC, UN, UN Security Council (temporary), UNCTAD, UNESCO, UNHCR, UNMISS, UNMIT, UNRWA, UNTSO, UNWTO, UPU, WCO, WFTU (NGOs), WHO, WIPO, WMO, WTO, ZC

Diplomatic representation in the US: *chief of mission:* Ambassador Kim Christian BEAZLEY (since 7 February 2010)
chancery: 1601 Massachusetts Avenue NW, Washington, DC 20036
telephone: [1] (202) 797-3000
FAX: [1] (202) 797-3168
consulate(s) general: Atlanta, Chicago, Honolulu, Los Angeles, New York, San Francisco

Diplomatic representation from the US: *chief of mission:* Ambassador John BERRY (since 25 September 2013)
embassy: Moonah Place, Yarralumla, Canberra, Australian Capital Territory 2600
mailing address: APO AP 96549
telephone: [61] (02) 6214-5600
FAX: [61] (02) 6214-5970
consulate(s) general: Melbourne, Perth, Sydney

Flag description: blue with the flag of the UK in the upper hoist-side quadrant and a large seven-pointed star in the lower hoist-side quadrant known as the Commonwealth or Federation Star, representing the federation of the colonies of Australia in 1901; the star depicts one point for each of the six original states and one representing all of Australia's internal and external territories; on the fly half is a representation of the Southern Cross constellation in white with one small, five-pointed star and four larger, seven-pointed stars

National symbol(s): Southern Cross constellation (five, seven-pointed stars); kangaroo; emu

National anthem: *name:* "Advance Australia Fair"
lyrics/music: Peter Dodds McCORMICK
note: adopted 1984; although originally written in the late 19th century, the anthem did not become used for all official occasions until 1984; as a Commonwealth country, in addition to the national anthem, "God Save the Queen" is also played at Royal functions (see United Kingdom)

ECONOMY

Economy—overview: The Australian economy has experienced continuous growth and features low unemployment, contained inflation, very low public debt, and a strong and stable financial system. By 2012, Australia had experienced more than 20 years of continued economic growth, averaging 3.5% a year. Demand for resources and energy from Asia and especially China has grown rapidly, creating a channel for resources investments and growth in commodity exports. The high Australian dollar has hurt the manufacturing sector, while the services sector is the largest part of the Australian economy, accounting for about 70% of GDP and 75% of jobs. Australia was comparatively unaffected by the global financial crisis as the banking system has remained strong and inflation is under control. Australia has benefited from a dramatic surge in its terms of trade in recent years, stemming from rising global commodity prices. Australia is a significant exporter of natural resources, energy, and food. Australia's abundant and diverse natural resources attract high levels of foreign investment and include extensive reserves of coal, iron, copper, gold, natural gas, uranium, and renewable energy sources. A series of major investments, such as the US$40 billion Gorgon Liquid Natural Gas project, will significantly expand the resources sector. Australia is an open market with minimal restrictions on imports of goods and services. The process of opening up has increased productivity, stimulated growth, and made the economy more flexible and dynamic. Australia plays an active role in the World Trade Organization, APEC, the G20, and other trade forums. Australia has bilateral free trade agreements (FTAs) with Chile, Malaysia, New Zealand, Singapore, Thailand, and the US, has a regional FTA with ASEAN and New Zealand, is negotiating agreements with China, India, Indonesia, Japan, and the Republic of Korea, as well as with its Pacific neighbors and the Gulf Cooperation Council countries, and is also working on the Trans-Pacific Partnership Agreement with Brunei Darussalam, Canada, Chile, Malaysia, Mexico, New Zealand, Peru, Singapore, the US, and Vietnam.

GDP (purchasing power parity): $998.3 billion (2013 est.)
country comparison to the world: 18
$974.2 billion (2012 est.)
$939.7 billion (2011 est.)
note: data are in 2013 US dollars

GDP (official exchange rate): $1.488 trillion (2013 est.)

GDP—real growth rate: 2.5% (2013 est.)
country comparison to the world: 128
3.7% (2012 est.)
2.4% (2011 est.)

GDP—per capita (PPP): $43,000 (2013 est.)
country comparison to the world: 19
$42,500 (2012 est.)
$41,700 (2011 est.)
note: data are in 2013 US dollars

Gross national saving: 24.4% of GDP (2013 est.)
country comparison to the world: 54
25.2% of GDP (2012 est.)
25.1% of GDP (2011 est.)

GDP—composition, by end use:
household consumption: 54.6%
government consumption: 17.8%
investment in fixed capital: 27.4%
investment in inventories: 0.1%
exports of goods and services: 20.9%
imports of goods and services: -20.8% (2013 est.)

GDP—composition, by sector of origin:
agriculture: 3.8%
industry: 27.4%
services: 68.7% (2013 est.)

Agriculture—products: wheat, barley, sugarcane, fruits; cattle, sheep, poultry

Industries: mining, industrial and transportation equipment, food processing, chemicals, steel

Industrial production growth rate: 3.2% (2013 est.)
country comparison to the world: 91

Labor force: 12.44 million (2013 est.)
country comparison to the world: 43

Labor force—by occupation: *agriculture:* 3.6%
industry: 21.1%
services: 75% (2009 est.)

Unemployment rate: 5.7% (2013 est.)
country comparison to the world: 54
5.2% (2012 est.)

Population below poverty line: NA%

Household income or consumption by percentage share: *lowest 10%:* 2%
highest 10%: 25.4% (1994)

Distribution of family income—Gini index: 30.3 (2008)
country comparison to the world: 119
35.2 (1994)

Budget: *revenues:* $494.3 billion
expenditures: $514.4 billion (2013 est.)

Taxes and other revenues: 33.2% of GDP (2013 est.)
country comparison to the world: 73

Budget surplus (+) or deficit (-): -1.3% of GDP (2013 est.)
country comparison to the world: 67

Public debt: 32.6% of GDP (2013 est.)
country comparison to the world: 111
32.4% of GDP (2012 est.)

Fiscal year: 1 July–30 June

Inflation rate (consumer prices): 2.4% (2013 est.)
country comparison to the world: 89
1.8% (2012 est.)

Central bank discount rate: 3% (February 2013 est.)
country comparison to the world: 83
4.35% (31 December 2010 est.)
note: this is the Reserve Bank of Australia's "cash rate target," or policy rate

Commercial bank prime lending rate: 6.2% (31 December 2013 est.)
country comparison to the world: 125
6.98% (31 December 2012 est.)

Stock of narrow money: $526.5 billion (31 December 2013 est.)
country comparison to the world: 10
$534.8 billion (31 December 2012 est.)

Stock of broad money: $1.661 trillion (31 December 2013 est.)
country comparison to the world: 11
$1.648 trillion (31 December 2012 est.)

Stock of domestic credit: $2.222 trillion (31 December 2013 est.)
country comparison to the world: 12
$2.255 trillion (31 December 2012 est.)

Market value of publicly traded shares: $1.286 trillion (31 December 2012 est.)
country comparison to the world: 9
$1.198 trillion (31 December 2011)
$1.455 trillion (31 December 2010 est.)

Current account balance: -$44.9 billion (2013 est.)
country comparison to the world: 186
-$57.14 billion (2012 est.)

Exports: $251.7 billion (2013 est.)
country comparison to the world: 23
$257.9 billion (2012 est.)

Exports—commodities: coal, iron ore, gold, meat, wool, alumina, wheat, machinery and transport equipment

Exports—partners: China 29.5%, Japan 19.3%, South Korea 8%, India 4.9% (2012)

Imports: $245.8 billion (2013 est.)
country comparison to the world: 22
$263 billion (2012 est.)

Imports—commodities: machinery and transport equipment, computers and office machines, telecommunication equipment and parts; crude oil and petroleum products

Imports—partners: China 18.4%, US 11.7%, Japan 7.9%, Singapore 6%, Germany 4.6%, Thailand 4.2%, South Korea 4.1% (2012)

Reserves of foreign exchange and gold: $48.8 billion (31 December 2013 est.)
country comparison to the world: 41
$49.15 billion (31 December 2012 est.)

Debt—external: $1.506 trillion (31 December 2013 est.)
country comparison to the world: 13
$1.497 trillion (31 December 2012 est.)

Stock of direct foreign investment—at home: $661.6 billion (31 December 2013 est.)
country comparison to the world: 14
$610.8 billion (31 December 2012 est.)

Stock of direct foreign investment—abroad: $440.1 billion (31 December 2013 est.)
country comparison to the world: 17
$426 billion (31 December 2012 est.)

Exchange rates: Australian dollars (AUD) per US dollar—

1.031 (2013 est.)
0.9658 (2012 est.)
1.0902 (2010)
1.2822 (2009) 1.2059 (2008)

ENERGY

Electricity—production: 225.5 billion kWh (2011 est.)
country comparison to the world: 20

Electricity—consumption: 213.5 billion kWh (2010 est.)
country comparison to the world: 17

Electricity—exports: 0 kWh (2012 est.)
country comparison to the world: 99

Electricity—imports: 0 kWh (2012 est.)
country comparison to the world: 115

Electricity—installed generating capacity: 59.13 million kW (2010 est.)
country comparison to the world: 17

Electricity—from fossil fuels: 78.7% of total installed capacity (2010 est.)
country comparison to the world: 93

Electricity—from nuclear fuels: 0% of total installed capacity (2010 est.)
country comparison to the world: 41

Electricity—from hydroelectric plants: 13.6% of total installed capacity (2010 est.)
country comparison to the world: 106

Electricity—from other renewable sources: 5.1% of total installed capacity (2010 est.)
country comparison to the world: 43

Crude oil—production: 519,100 bbl/day (2012 est.)
country comparison to the world: 30

Crude oil—exports: 314,100 bbl/day (2010 est.)
country comparison to the world: 25

Crude oil—imports: 475,900 bbl/day (2010 est.)
country comparison to the world: 19

Crude oil—proved reserves: 1.433 billion bbl (1 January 2013 es)
country comparison to the world: 39

Refined petroleum products—production: 675,200 bbl/day (2010 est.)
country comparison to the world: 25

Refined petroleum products—consumption: 1.023 million bbl/day (2011 est.)
country comparison to the world: 20

Refined petroleum products—exports: 70,810 bbl/day (2010 est.)
country comparison to the world: 54

Refined petroleum products—imports: 304,100 bbl/day (2010 est.)
country comparison to the world: 21

Natural gas—production: 48.24 billion cu m (2012 est.)
country comparison to the world: 20

Natural gas—consumption: 33.39 billion cu m (2010 est.)
country comparison to the world: 27

Natural gas—exports: 30.27 billion cu m (2012 est.)
country comparison to the world: 15

Natural gas—imports: 10.92 billion cu m (2012 est.)
country comparison to the world: 27

Natural gas—proved reserves: 1.219 trillion cu m (1 January 2013 es)
country comparison to the world: 25

Carbon dioxide emissions from consumption of energy: 392.3 million Mt (2011 est.)
country comparison to the world: 18

COMMUNICATIONS

Telephones—main lines in use: 10.47 million (2012)
country comparison to the world: 20

Telephones—mobile cellular: 24.4 million (2012)
country comparison to the world: 43

Telephone system: *general assessment:* excellent domestic and international service
domestic: domestic satellite system; significant use of radiotelephone in areas of low population density; rapid growth of mobile telephones
international: country code—61; landing point for the SEA-ME-WE-3 optical telecommunications submarine cable with links to Asia, the Middle East, and Europe; the Southern Cross fiber optic submarine cable provides links to New Zealand and the United States; satellite earth stations—10 Intelsat (4 Indian Ocean and 6 Pacific Ocean), 2 Inmarsat, 2 Globalstar, 5 other) (2007)

Broadcast media: the Australian Broadcasting Corporation (ABC) runs multiple national and local radio networks and TV stations, as well as Australia Network, a TV service that broadcasts throughout the Asia-Pacific region and is the main public broadcaster; Special Broadcasting Service (SBS), a second large public broadcaster, operates radio and TV networks broadcasting in multiple languages; several large national commercial TV networks, a large number of local commercial TV stations, and hundreds of commercial radio stations are accessible; cable and satellite systems are available (2008)

Internet country code: .au

Internet hosts: 17.081 million (2012)
country comparison to the world: 8

Internet users: 15.81 million (2009)
country comparison to the world: 25

TRANSPORTATION

Airports: 480 (2013)
country comparison to the world: 16

Airports—with paved runways: *total:* 349
over 3,047 m: 11
2,438 to 3,047 m: 14
1,524 to 2,437 m: 155
914 to 1,523 m: 155
under 914 m: 14 (2013)

Airports—with unpaved runways: *total:* 131
1,524 to 2,437 m: 16
914 to 1,523 m: 101
under 914 m: 14 (2013)

Heliports: 1 (2013)

Pipelines: condensate/gas 637 km; gas 30,054 km; liquid petroleum gas 240 km; oil 3,609 km; oil/gas/water 110 km; refined products 72 km (2013)

Railways: *total:* 38,445 km
country comparison to the world: 7
broad gauge: 3,355 km 1.600-m gauge
standard gauge: 21,674 km 1.435-m gauge (650 km electrified)
narrow gauge: 9,539 km 1.067-m gauge (2,067 km electrified); 3,877 km 1.000-m gauge (2008)

Roadways: *total:* 823,217 km
country comparison to the world: 9
paved: 356,343 km
unpaved: 466,874 km (2011)

Waterways: 2,000 km (mainly used for recreation on Murray and Murray-Darling river systems) (2011)
country comparison to the world: 43

Merchant marine: *total:* 41
country comparison to the world: 75
by type: bulk carrier 8, cargo 7, liquefied gas 4, passenger 6, passenger/cargo 6, petroleum tanker 5, roll on/roll off 5
foreign-owned: 17 (Canada 5, Germany 2, Singapore 2, South Africa 1, UK 5, US 2)
registered in other countries: 25 (Bahamas 1, Dominica 1, Fiji 2, Liberia 1, Netherlands 1, Panama 4, Singapore 12, Tonga 1, UK 1, US 1) (2010)

Ports and terminals: *major seaport(s):* Brisbane, Cairns, Darwin, Fremantle, Geelong, Gladstone, Hobart, Melbourne, Newcastle, Port dry Adelaide, Port Kembla, Sydney
bulk cargo port(s): Dampier (iron ore), Dalrymple Bay (coal), Hay Point (coal), Port Hedland (iron ore), Port Walcott (iron ore)
container port(s) (TEUs): Brisbane (1,004,983), Melbourne (2,467,967), Sydney (2,028,074) (2011)

MILITARY

Military branches: Australian Defense Force (ADF): Australian Army; Royal Australian Navy (includes Naval Aviation Force); Royal Australian Air Force; Joint Operations Command (JOC) (2013)

Military service age and obligation: 17 years of age for voluntary military service (with parental consent); no conscription; women allowed to serve in most combat roles, except the Army special forces (2013)

Manpower available for military service: *males age 16-49:* 5,316,464
females age 16-49: 5,116,722 (2010 est.)

Manpower fit for military service: *males age 16-49:* 4,411,958
females age 16-49: 4,239,985 (2010 est.)

Manpower reaching militarily significant age annually: *male:* 143,565
female: 135,800 (2010 est.)

Military expenditures: 1.71% of GDP (2012)
country comparison to the world: 51
1.84% of GDP (2011)
1.71% of GDP (2010)

TRANSNATIONAL ISSUES

Disputes—international: In 2007, Australia and Timor-Leste agreed to a 50-year development zone and revenue sharing arrangement and deferred a maritime boundary; Australia asserts land and maritime claims to Antarctica; Australia's 2004 submission to the Commission on the Limits of the Continental Shelf (CLCS) extends its continental margins over 3.37 million square kilometers, expanding its seabed roughly 30 percent beyond its claimed exclusive economic zone; all borders between Indonesia and Australia have been agreed upon bilaterally, but a 1997 treaty that would settle the last of their maritime and Exclusive Economic Zone (EEZ) boundary has yet to be ratified by Indonesia's legislature; Indonesian groups challenge Australia's claim to Ashmore Reef; Australia closed parts of the Ashmore and Cartier reserve to Indonesian traditional fishing

Refugees and internally displaced persons: *refugees (country of origin):* 7,192 (Afghanistan) (2012)

Illicit drugs: Tasmania is one of the world's major suppliers of licit opiate products; government maintains strict controls over areas of opium poppy cultivation and output of poppy straw concentrate; major consumer of cocaine and amphetamines

AUSTRIA

INTRODUCTION

Background: Once the center of power for the large Austro-Hungarian Empire, Austria was reduced to a small republic after its defeat in World War I. Following annexation by Nazi Germany in 1938 and subsequent occupation by the victorious Allies in 1945, Austria's status remained unclear for a decade. A State Treaty signed in 1955 ended the occupation, recognized Austria's independence, and forbade unification with Germany. A constitutional law that same year declared the country's "perpetual neutrality" as a condition for Soviet military withdraw al. The Soviet Union's collapse in 1991 and Austria's entry into the European Union in 1995 have altered the meaning of this neutrality. A prosperous, democratic country, Austria entered the EU Economic and Monetary Union in 1999.

GEOGRAPHY

Location: Central Europe, north of Italy and Slovenia

Geographic coordinates: 47 20 N, 13 20 E

Map references: Europe

Area: *total:* 83,871 sq km
country comparison to the world: 114
land: 82,445 sq km
water: 1,426 sq km

Area—comparative: slightly smaller than Maine

Land boundaries: *total:* 2,562 km
border countries: Czech Republic 362 km, Germany 784 km, Hungary 366 km, Italy 430 km, Liechtenstein 35 km, Slovakia 91 km, Slovenia 330 km, Switzerland 164 km

Coastline: 0 km (landlocked)

Maritime claims: none (landlocked)

Climate: temperate; continental, cloudy; cold winters with frequent rain and some snow in lowlands and snow in mountains; moderate summers with occasional showers

Terrain: in the west and south mostly mountains (Alps); along the eastern and northern margins mostly flat or gently sloping

Elevation extremes: *lowest point:* Neusiedler See 115 m
highest point: Grossglockner 3,798 m

Natural resources: oil, coal, lignite, timber, iron ore, copper, zinc, antimony, magnesite, tungsten, graphite, salt, hydropower

Land use: *arable land:* 16.25%
permanent crops: 0.77%
other: 82.98% (2011)

Irrigated land: 1,170 sq km (2007)

Total renewable water resources: 77.7 cu km (2011)

Freshwater withdrawal (domestic/industrial/agricultural): *total:* 3.66 cu km/yr (18%/79%/3%)
per capita: 452.4 cu m/yr (2008)

Natural hazards: landslides; avalanches; earthquakes

Environment—current issues: some forest degradation caused by air and soil pollution; soil pollution results from the use of agricultural chemicals; air pollution results from emissions by coal-and oil-fired power stations and industrial plants and from trucks transiting Austria between northern and southern Europe

Environment—international agreements: *party to:* Air Pollution, Air Pollution-Nitrogen Oxides, Air Pollution-Persistent Organic Pollutants, Air Pollution-Sulfur 85, Air Pollution-Sulphur 94, Air Pollution-Volatile Organic Compounds, Antarctic Treaty, Biodiversity, Climate Change, Climate Change-Kyoto Protocol, Desertification, Endangered Species, Environmental Modification, Hazardous Wastes, Law of the Sea, Ozone Layer Protection, Ship Pollution, Tropical Timber 83, Tropical Timber 94, Wetlands, Whaling
signed, but not ratified: none of the selected agreements

Geography—note: landlocked; strategic location at the crossroads of central Europe with many easily traversable Alpine passes and valleys; major river is the Danube; population is concentrated on eastern lowlands because of steep slopes, poor soils, and low temperatures elsewhere

PEOPLE AND SOCIETY

Nationality: *noun:* Austrian(s)
adjective: Austrian

Ethnic groups: Austrians 91.1%, former Yugoslavs 4% (includes Croatians, Slovenes, Serbs, and Bosniaks), Turks 1.6%, German 0.9%, other or unspecified 2.4% (2001 census)

Languages: German (official nationwide) 88.6%, Turkish 2.3%, Serbian 2.2%, Croatian (official in Burgenland) 1.6%, other (includes Slovene, official in Carinthia, and Hungarian, official in Burgenland) 5.3% (2001 census)

Religions: Roman Catholic 73.6%, Protestant 4.7%, Muslim 4.2%, other 3.5%, unspecified 2%, none 12% (2001 census)

Population: 8,223,062 (July 2014 est.)
country comparison to the world: 95

Age structure: *0-14 years:* 13.6% (male 573,146/female 546,596)
15-24 years: 11.6% (male 488,564/female 468,891)
25-54 years: 42.9% (male 1,766,729/female 1,756,880)
55-64 years: 19.2% (male 515,913/female 528,988)
65 years and over: 18.9% (male 670,750/female 906,605) (2014 est.)

Dependency ratios: *total dependency ratio:* 48.9%
youth dependency ratio: 21.6%
elderly dependency ratio: 27.3%
potential support ratio: 3.7 (2013)

Median age: *total:* 44.3 years
male: 43.2 years
female: 45.3 years (2014 est.)

Population growth rate: 0.01% (2014 est.)
country comparison to the world: 191

Birth rate: 8.76 births/1,000 population (2014 est.)
country comparison to the world: 214

Death rate: 10.38 deaths/1,000 population (2014 est.)
country comparison to the world: 42

Net migration rate: 1.76 migrant(s)/1,000 population (2014 est.)
country comparison to the world: 50

Urbanization: *urban population:* 68% of total population (2010)
rate of urbanization: 0.6% annual rate of change (2010-15 est.)

Major urban areas—population: VIENNA (capital) 1.72 million (2011)

Sex ratio: at birth: 1.05 male(s)/female
0-14 years: 1.05 male(s)/female
15-24 years: 1.04 male(s)/female
25-54 years: 1.01 male(s)/female
55-64 years: 0.95 male(s)/female
65 years and over: 0.73 male(s)/female
total population: 0.95 male(s)/female (2014 est.)

Mother's mean age at first birth: 28.5 (2011 est.)

Maternal mortality rate: 4 deaths/100,000 live births (2010)
country comparison to the world: 178

Infant mortality rate: *total:* 4.16 deaths/1,000 live births
country comparison to the world: 196
male: 5.01 deaths/1,000 live births
female: 3.27 deaths/1,000 live births (2014 est.)

Life expectancy at birth: total population: 80.17 years
country comparison to the world: 32
male: 77.25 years
female: 83.24 years (2014 est.)

Total fertility rate: 1.43 children born/woman (2014 est.)
country comparison to the world: 202

Contraceptive prevalence rate: 69.6%
note: percent of women aged 18-46 (2009)

Health expenditures: 10.6% of GDP (2011)
country comparison to the world: 19

Physicians density: 4.86 physicians/1,000 population (2010)

Hospital bed density: 7.6 beds/1,000 population (2010)

Drinking water source:
Improved:
urban: 100% of population
rural: 100% of population
total: 100% of population

unimproved:
urban: 0% of population
rural: 0% of population
total: 0% of population (2011 est.)

Sanitation facility access:
Improved:
urban: 100% of population
rural: 100% of population
total: 100% of population
unimproved:
urban: 0% of population
rural: 0% of population
total: 0% of population (2011 est.)

HIV/AIDS—adult prevalence rate: 0.3% (2009 est.)
country comparison to the world: 88

HIV/AIDS—people living with HIV/AIDS: 15,000 (2009 est.)
country comparison to the world: 90

HIV/AIDS—deaths: fewer than 100 (2009 est.)
country comparison to the world: 124

Obesity—adult prevalence rate: 20.9% (2008)
country comparison to the world: 93

Education expenditures: 5.9% of GDP (2010)
country comparison to the world: 44

Literacy: *definition:* age 15 and over can read and write
total population: 98%
male: NA
female: NA

School life expectancy (primary to tertiary education): *total:* 16 years
male: 15 years
female: 16 years (2011)

Unemployment, youth ages 15-24: *total:* 8.3%
country comparison to the world: 120
male: 8.8%
female: 8.7% (2012)

GOVERNMENT

Country name: *conventional long form:* Republic of Austria
conventional short form: Austria
local long form: Republik Oesterreich
local short form: Oesterreich

Government type: federal republic

Capital: *name:* Vienna
geographic coordinates: 48 12 N, 16 22 E
time difference: UTC+1 (6 hours ahead of Washington, DC during Standard Time)
daylight saving time: +1hr, begins last Sunday in March; ends last Sunday in October

Administrative divisions: 9 states (Bundeslaender, singular—Bundesland); Burgenland, Karnten (Carinthia), Niederoesterreich (Lower Austria), Oberoesterreich (Upper Austria), Salzburg, Steiermark (Styria), Tirol (Tyrol), Vorarlberg, Wien (Vienna)

Independence: 12 November 1918 (republic proclaimed); notable earlier dates: 976 (Margravate of Austria established); 17 September 1156 (Duchy of Austria founded); 11 August 1804 (Austrian Empire proclaimed)

National holiday: National Day, 26 October (1955); note—commemorates the passage of the law on permanent neutrality

Constitution: several previous; latest adopted 1 October 1920, revised 1929, replaced May 1934 (authoritarian-corporate constitution), replaced by German Weimar constitution in 1938 following German annexation; latest reinstated 1 May 1945 (1920 constitution with 1929 revisions); amended many times, last in 2008 (2013)

Legal system: civil law system; judicial review of legislative acts by the Constitutional Court

International law organization participation: accepts compulsory ICJ jurisdiction; accepts ICCt jurisdiction

Suffrage: 16 years of age; universal; note—reduced from 18 years of age in 2007

Executive branch: *chief of state:* President Heinz FISCHER (SPOe) (since 8 July 2004)
head of government: Chancellor Werner FAYMANN (SPOe) (since 2 December 2008); Vice Chancellor Michael SPINDELEGGER (OeVP) (since 21 April 2011)
cabinet: Council of Ministers chosen by the president on the advice of the chancellor (For more information visit the World Leaders website)
elections: president elected for a six-year term (eligible for a second term) by direct popular vote and formally sworn into office before the Federal Assembly or Bundesversammlung; presidential election last held on 25 April 2010 (next to be held on 25 April 2016); chancellor formally chosen by the president but determined by the coalition parties forming a parliamentary majority; vice chancellor chosen by the president on the advice of the chancellor
election results: Heinz FISCHER reelected president; percent of vote—Heinz FISCHER 79.33%, Barbara ROSENKRANZ 15.24%, Rudolf GEHRING 5.43%
note: government coalition—SPOe and OeVP

Legislative branch: bicameral Federal Assembly or Bundesversammlung consists of Federal Council or Bundesrat (62 seats; delegates appointed by state parliaments with each state receiving 3 to 12 seats in proportion to its population; members serve five-or six-year terms) and the National Council or Nationalrat (183 seats; members elected by popular vote for a five-year term under a system of proportional representation with partially-open party lists)
elections: National Council—last held on 29 September 2013 (next to be held by September 2018)
election results: National Council—percent of vote by party—SPOe 27.1%, OeVP 23.8%, FPOe 21.4%, Greens 11.5%, Team Stronach for Austria 5.8%, NEOS—The New Austria 4.8%, other 5.6%; seats by party—SPOe 53, OeVP 46, FPOe 42, Greens 22; Team Stronach for Austria 11, NEOS—The New Austria 9

Judicial branch: *highest court(s):* Supreme Court of Justice or Oberster Gerichtshof (consists of 85 judges organized into 17 senates or panels of five judges each); Constitutional Court or Verfassungsgerichtshof (consists of 20 judges including 6 substitutes; Administrative Court or Verwaltungsgerichtshof—2 judges plus other members depending on the importance of the case)
judge selection and term of office: Supreme Court judges nominated by executive branch departments and appointed by the president; judges serve for life; Constitutional Court judges nominated by several executive branch departments and approved by the president; judges serve for life; Administrative Court judges recommended by executive branch departments and appointed by the president; terms of judges and members determined by the president
subordinate courts: Courts of Appeal (4); Regional Courts (20); district courts (120); county courts

Political parties and leaders: Alliance for the Future of Austria or BZOe [Josef BUCHER]; Austrian People's Party or OeVP [Michael SPINDELEGGER]; Freedom Party of Austria or FPOe [Heinz Christian STRACHE]; Social Democratic Party of Austria or SPOe [Werner FAYMANN]; The Greens [Eva GLAWISCHNIG]; Communist Party of Austria or KPOe [Mirko MESSNER]; "Team Stronach for Austria" [Frank STRONACH]

Political pressure groups and leaders: Austrian Trade Union Federation or OeGB (nominally independent but primarily Social Democratic); Federal Economic Chamber; Labor Chamber or AK (Social Democratic-leaning think tank); OeVP-oriented Association of Austrian Industrialists or IV; Roman Catholic Church, including its chief lay organization, Catholic Action
other: three composite leagues of the Austrian People's Party or OeVP representing business, labor, farmers, and other nongovernment organizations in the areas of environment and human rights

International organization participation: ADB (nonregional member), AfDB (nonregional member), Australia Group, BIS, BSEC (observer), CD, CE, CEI, CERN, EAPC, EBRD, ECB, EIB, EMU, ESA, EU, FAO, FATF, G-9, IADB, IAEA, IBRD, ICAO, ICC (national committees), ICRM, IDA, IEA, IFAD, IFC, IFRCS, IGAD (partners), ILO, IMF, IMO, Interpol, IOC, IOM, IPU, ISO, ITSO, ITU, ITUC (NGOs), MIGA, MINURSO, NEA, NSG, OAS (observer), OECD, OIF (observer), OPCW, OSCE, Paris Club, PCA, PFP, Schengen Convention, SELEC (observer), UN, UNCTAD, UNDOF, UNESCO, UNFICYP, UNHCR, UNIFIL, UNTSO, UNWTO, UPU, WCO, WFTU (NGOs), WHO, WIPO, WMO, WTO, ZC

Diplomatic representation in the US: *chief of mission:* Ambassador Hans Peter MANZ (since 2 December 2011)
chancery: 3524 International Court NW, Washington, DC 20008-3035
telephone: [1] (202) 895-6700
FAX: [1] (202) 895-6750
consulate(s) general: Chicago, Los Angeles, New York

Diplomatic representation from the US: *chief of mission:* Ambassador Alexa L. WESNER (since 6 September 2013)
embassy: Boltzmanngasse 16, A-1090, Vienna
mailing address: use embassy street address
telephone: [43] (1) 31339-0
FAX: [43] (1) 3100682

Flag description: three equal horizontal bands of red (top), white, and red; the flag design is certainly one of the oldest—if not the oldest—national banners in the world; according to tradition, in 1191, following a fierce battle in the Third Crusade, Duke Leopold V of Austria's white tunic became completely blood-spattered; upon removal of his wide belt or sash, a white band was revealed; the red-white-red color combination was subsequently adopted as his banner

National symbol(s): golden eagle, Alpine gentian, edelweiss

National anthem: *name:* "Bundeshymne" (Federal Hymn)
lyrics/music: Paula von PRERADOVIC/Wolfgang Amadeus MOZART or Johann HOLZER (disputed)
note: adopted 1947; the anthem is also known as "Land der Berge, Land am Strome" (Land of the Mountains, Land on the River); Austria adopted a new national anthem after World War II to replace the former imperial anthem composed by Franz Josef HAYDN, which had been appropriated by Germany in 1922 and was now associated with the Nazi regime

ECONOMY

Economy—overview: Austria, with its well-developed market economy, skilled labor force, and high standard of living, is closely tied to other EU economies, especially Germany's. Its economy features a large service sector, a sound industrial sector, and a small, but highly developed agricultural sector. Following several years of solid foreign demand for Austrian exports and record employment growth, the international financial crisis of 2008 and subsequent global economic downturn led to a sharp but brief recession. Austrian GDP contracted 3.8% in 2009 but saw positive growth of about 2% in 2010 and 2.7% in 2011. Growth fell to 0.6% in 2012. Unemployment did not rise as steeply in Austria as elsew here in Europe, partly because the government subsidized reduced working hour schemes to allow companies to retain employees. The 2012 unemployment rate of 4.3% was the lowest within the EU. Stabilization measures, stimulus spending, and an income tax reform pushed the budget deficit to 4.5% in 2010 and 2.6% in 2011, from only about 0.9% in 2008. The international financial crisis of 2008 caused difficulties for Austria's largest banks whose extensive operations in central, eastern, and southeastern Europe faced large losses. The government provided bank support—including in some instances, nationalization—to support aggregate demand and stabilize the banking system. Austria's fiscal position compares favorably with other euro-zone countries, but it faces external risks, such as Austrian banks' continued exposure to Central and Eastern Europe as well as political and economic uncertainties caused by the European sovereign debt crisis. In 2011 the government attempted to pass a constitutional amendment limiting public debt to 60% of GDP by 2020, but it was unable to obtain sufficient support in parliament and instead passed the measure as a simple law. In March 2012, the Austrian parliament approved an austerity package consisting of a mix of expenditure cuts and new revenues that will bring public finances into balance by 2016. In 2012, the budget deficit rose to 3.1% of GDP.

GDP (purchasing power parity): $361 billion (2013 est.)
country comparison to the world: 38
$359.6 billion (2012 est.)
$356.5 billion (2011 est.)
note: data are in 2013 US dollars

GDP (official exchange rate): $417.9 billion (2013 est.)

GDP—real growth rate: 0.4% (2013 est.)
country comparison to the world: 186
0.9% (2012 est.)
2.8% (2011 est.)

GDP—per capita (PPP): $42,600 (2013 est.)
country comparison to the world: 21
$42,500 (2012 est.)
$42,300 (2011 est.)
note: data are in 2013 US dollars

Gross national saving: 23.9% of GDP (2013 est.)
country comparison to the world: 57
24.4% of GDP (2012 est.)
24.5% of GDP (2011 est.)

GDP—composition, by end use:
household consumption: 54.6%
government consumption: 19.2%
investment in fixed capital: 20.8%
investment in inventories: 0.5%
exports of goods and services: 56.9%
imports of goods and services: -52% (2013 est.)

GDP—composition, by sector of origin:
agriculture: 1.6%
industry: 28.6%
services: 69.8% (2013 est.)

Agriculture—products: grains, potatoes, wine, fruit; dairy products, cattle, pigs, poultry; lumber

Industries: construction, machinery, vehicles and parts, food, metals, chemicals, lumber and wood processing, paper and paperboard, communications equipment, tourism

Industrial production growth rate: 0.5% (2013 est.)
country comparison to the world: 161

Labor force: 3.737 million (2013 est.)
country comparison to the world: 94

Labor force—by occupation: *agriculture:* 5.5%
industry: 26%
services: 68.5% (2012 est.)

Unemployment rate: 4.9% (2013 est.)
country comparison to the world: 45
4.4% (2012 est.)

Population below poverty line: 6.2% (2012)

Household income or consumption by percentage share: *lowest 10%:* 4%
highest 10%: 22% (2011)

Distribution of family income—Gini index: 26.3 (2007)
country comparison to the world: 130
31 (1995)

Budget: *revenues:* $200 billion
expenditures: $212.1 billion (2013 est.)

Taxes and other revenues: 47.9% of GDP (2013 est.)
country comparison to the world: 14

Budget surplus (+) or deficit (-): -2.9% of GDP (2013 est.)
country comparison to the world: 119

Public debt: 75.7% of GDP (2013 est.)
country comparison to the world: 32
74.1% of GDP (2012 est.)
note: this is general government gross debt, defined in the Maastricht Treaty as consolidated general government gross debt at nominal value, outstanding at the end of the year; it covers the following categories of government liabilities (as defined in ESA95): currency and deposits (AF.2), securities other than shares excluding financial derivatives (AF.3, excluding AF.34), and loans (AF.4); the general government sector comprises the sub-sectors of central government, state government, local government and social security funds; as a percentage of GDP, the GDP used as a denominator is the gross domestic product in current year prices

Fiscal year: calendar year

Inflation rate (consumer prices): 2.1% (2013 est.)
country comparison to the world: 71
2.6% (2012 est.)

Commercial bank prime lending rate: 2.2% (31 December 2013 est.)
country comparison to the world: 179
2.5% (31 December 2012 est.)

Stock of narrow money: $204.5 billion (31 December 2013 est.)
country comparison to the world: 19
$201.1 billion (31 December 2012 est.)
note: see entry for the European Union for money supply for the entire euro area; the European Central Bank (ECB) controls monetary policy for the 17 members of the Economic and Monetary Union (EMU); individual members of the EMU do not control the quantity of money circulating within their own borders

Stock of broad money: $419 billion (31 December 2013 est.)
country comparison to the world: 24
$414 billion (31 December 2012 est.)

Stock of domestic credit: $544.2 billion (31 December 2013 est.)
country comparison to the world: 25
$543 billion (31 December 2012 est.)

Market value of publicly traded shares: $106 billion (31 December 2012 est.)
country comparison to the world: 43
$82.37 billion (31 December 2011)
$67.68 billion (31 December 2010 est.)

Current account balance: $10.6 billion (2013 est.)
country comparison to the world: 23
$7.085 billion (2012 est.)

Exports: $165.6 billion (2013 est.)
country comparison to the world: 31
$160.1 billion (2012 est.)

Exports—commodities: machinery and equipment, motor vehicles and parts, paper and paperboard, metal goods, chemicals, iron and steel, textiles, foodstuffs

Exports—partners: Germany 29.31%, Italy 6.25%, Switzerland 5.08%, United States 5%, France 4.27% (2013 est.)

Imports: $167.9 billion (2013 est.)
country comparison to the world: 29
$163.2 billion (2012 est.)

Imports—commodities: machinery and equipment, motor vehicles, chemicals, metal goods, oil and oil products; foodstuffs

Imports—partners: Germany 40.39%, Italy 6.13%, Switzerland 5.36% (2013 est.)

Reserves of foreign exchange and gold: $27.21 billion (31 December 2012 est.)
country comparison to the world: 54
$25.16 billion (31 December 2011 est.)

Debt—external: $812 billion (31 December 2012 est.)
country comparison to the world: 19
$786.1 billion (31 December 2011)

Stock of direct foreign investment—at home: $269.5 billion (31 December 2013 est.)
country comparison to the world: 22
$265.3 billion (31 December 2012 est.)

Stock of direct foreign investment—abroad: $345.2 billion (31 December 2013 est.)
country comparison to the world: 19
$331.4 billion (31 December 2012 est.)

Exchange rates: euros (EUR) per US dollar—
0.7634 (2013 est.)
0.7752 (2012 est.)
0.755 (2010 est.)
0.7198 (2009 est.)
0.6827 (2008 est.)

ENERGY

Electricity—production: 69 billion kWh (2012 est.)
country comparison to the world: 40

Electricity—consumption: 63.8 billion kWh (2011 est.)
country comparison to the world: 40

Electricity—exports: 20.46 billion kWh (2012 est.)
country comparison to the world: 9

Electricity—imports: 23.26 billion kWh (2012 est.)
country comparison to the world: 7

Electricity—installed generating capacity: 21.11 million kW (2010 est.)
country comparison to the world: 37

Electricity—from fossil fuels: 27.5% of total installed capacity (2012 est.)
country comparison to the world: 185

Electricity—from nuclear fuels: 0% of total installed capacity (2012 est.)
country comparison to the world: 42

Electricity—from hydroelectric plants: 59.6% of total installed capacity (2012 est.)
country comparison to the world: 32

Electricity—from other renewable sources: 12.8% of total installed capacity (2012 est.)
country comparison to the world: 18

Crude oil—production: 29,480 bbl/day (2012 est.)
country comparison to the world: 67

Crude oil—exports: 0 bbl/day (2011 est.)
country comparison to the world: 79

Crude oil—imports: 139,000 bbl/day (2011 est.)
country comparison to the world: 43

Crude oil—proved reserves: 85 million bbl (1 January 2012 es)
country comparison to the world: 72

Refined petroleum products—production: 159,200 bbl/day (2011 est.)
country comparison to the world: 62

Refined petroleum products—consumption: 210,700 bbl/day (2011 est.)
country comparison to the world: 55

Refined petroleum products—exports: 43,010 bbl/day (2011 est.)
country comparison to the world: 62

Refined petroleum products—imports: 117,100 bbl/day (2011 est.)
country comparison to the world: 46

Natural gas—production: 1.906 billion cu m (2012 est.)
country comparison to the world: 59

Natural gas—consumption: 9 billion cu m (2012 est.)
country comparison to the world: 50

Natural gas—exports: 34.75 billion cu m (2012 est.)
country comparison to the world: 13

Natural gas—imports: 42.56 billion cu m (2012 est.)
country comparison to the world: 12

Natural gas—proved reserves: 10.82 billion cu m (1 January 2013 es)
country comparison to the world: 81

Carbon dioxide emissions from consumption of energy: 67.18 million Mt (2011 est.)
country comparison to the world: 50

COMMUNICATIONS

Telephones—main lines in use: 3.342 million (2012)
country comparison to the world: 46

Telephones—mobile cellular: 13.59 million (2012)
country comparison to the world: 62

Telephone system: *general assessment:* highly developed and efficient
domestic: fixed-line subscribership has been in decline since the mid-1990s with mobile-cellular subscribership eclipsing it by the late 1990s; the fiber-optic net is very extensive; all telephone applications and Internet services are available
international: country code—43; satellite earth stations—15; in addition, there are about 600 VSATs (very small aperture terminals) (2007)

Broadcast media: Austria's public broadcaster, Osterreichischer Rundfunk (ORF), was the main broadcast source until commercial radio and TV service was introduced in the 1990s; cable and satellite TV are available, including German TV stations (2008)

Internet country code: .at

Internet hosts: 3.512 million (2012)
country comparison to the world: 30

Internet users: 6.143 million (2009)
country comparison to the world: 43

TRANSPORTATION

Airports: 52 (2013)
country comparison to the world: 90

Airports—with paved runways: *total:* 24
over 3,047 m: 1
2,438 to 3,047 m: 5
1,524 to 2,437 m: 1
914 to 1,523 m: 4
under 914 m: 13 (2013)

Airports—with unpaved runways: *total:* 28
1,524 to 2,437 m: 1
914 to 1,523 m: 3
under 914 m: 24 (2013)

Heliports: 1 (2013)

Pipelines: gas 4,736 km; oil 663 km; refined products 157 km (2013)

Railways: *total:* 6,399 km
country comparison to the world: 29
standard gauge: 5,927 km 1.435-m gauge (3,853 km electrified)
narrow gauge: 384 km 1.000-m gauge (15 km electrified); 88 km 0.760-m gauge (10 km electrified) (2008)

Roadways: *total:* 124,508 km
country comparison to the world: 39
paved: 124,508 km (includes 1,719 km of expressways) (2012)

Waterways: 358 km (2011)
country comparison to the world: 90

Merchant marine: *registered in other countries:* 3 (Cyprus 1, Kazakhstan 1, Saint Vincent and the Grenadines 1) (2010)
country comparison to the world: 137

Ports and terminals: *river port(s):* Enns, Krems, Linz, Vienna (Danube)

MILITARY

Military branches: Land Forces (KdoLdSK), Air Forces (KdoLuSK)

Military service age and obligation: registration requirement at age 17, the legal minimum age for voluntary military service; 18 is the legal minimum age for compulsory service; males under the age of 35 must complete basic military training (6 month duration); males 18 to 50 years old in the militia or inactive reserve are subject to compulsory service (2012)

Manpower available for military service:
males age 16-49: 1,941,110
females age 16-49: 1,910,434 (2010 est.)

Manpower fit for military service: *males age 16-49:* 1,579,862
females age 16-49: 1,554,130 (2010 est.)

Manpower reaching militarily significant age annually: *male:* 48,108
female: 45,752 (2010 est.)

Military expenditures: 0.81% of GDP (2012)
country comparison to the world: 115
0.82% of GDP (2011)
0.81% of GDP (2010)

TRANSNATIONAL ISSUES

Disputes—international: none

Refugees and internally displaced persons:
refugees (country of origin): 19,517 (Russia); 10,158 (Afghanistan) (2012)
stateless persons: 542 (2012)

Illicit drugs: transshipment point for Southwest Asian heroin and South American cocaine destined for Western Europe; increasing consumption of European-produced synthetic drugs

AZERBAIJAN

INTRODUCTION

Background: Azerbaijan—a nation with a majority-Turkic and majority-Shia Muslim population—was briefly independent (from 1918 to 1920) following the collapse of the Russian Empire; it was subsequently incorporated into the Soviet Union for seven decades. Azerbaijan has yet to resolve its conflict with Armenia over Nagorno-Karabakh, a primarily Armenian-populated region that Moscow recognized in 1923 as an autonomous republic within Soviet Azerbaijan after Armenia and Azerbaijan disputed the territory's status. Armenia and Azerbaijan began fighting over the area in 1988; the struggle escalated after both countries attained independence from the Soviet Union in 1991. By May 1994, when a cease-fire took hold,ethnic Armenian forces held not only Nagorno-Karabakh but also seven surrounding provinces in the territory of Azerbaijan. The OSCE Minsk Group, co-chaired by the United States, France, and Russia, is the framework established to mediate a peaceful resolution of the conflict. Corruption in the country is widespread, and the government, which eliminated presidential term limits in a 2009 referendum, has been accused of authoritarianism. Although the poverty rate has been reduced and infrastructure investment has increased substantially in recent years due to revenue from oil and gas production, reforms have not adequately addressed weaknesses in most government institutions, particularly in the education and health sectors.

GEOGRAPHY

Location: Southwestern Asia, bordering the Caspian Sea, between Iran and Russia, with a small European portion north of the Caucasus range

Geographic coordinates: 40 30 N, 47 30 E

Map references: Middle East

Area: *total:* 86,600 sq km
country comparison to the world: 113
land: 82,629 sq km
water: 3,971 sq km
note: includes the exclave of Naxcivan Autonomous Republic and the Nagorno-Karabakh region; the region's autonomy was abolished by Azerbaijani Supreme Soviet on 26 November 1991

Area—comparative: slightly smaller than Maine

Land boundaries: *total:* 2,013 km
border countries: Armenia (with Azerbaijan-proper) 566 km, Armenia (with Azerbaijan-Naxcivan exclave) 221 km, Georgia 322 km, Iran (with Azerbaijan-proper) 432 km, Iran (with Azerbaijan-Naxcivan exclave) 179 km, Russia 284 km, Turkey 9 km

Coastline: 0 km (landlocked); note—Azerbaijan borders the Caspian Sea (713 km)

Maritime claims: none (landlocked)

Climate: dry, semiarid steppe

Terrain: large, flat Kur-Araz Ovaligi (Kura-Araks Lowland, much of it below sea level) with Great Caucasus Mountains to the north, Qarabag Yaylasi (Karabakh Upland) in west; Baku lies on Abseron Yasaqligi (Apsheron Peninsula) that juts into Caspian Sea

Elevation extremes: *lowest point:* Caspian Sea -28 m
highest point: Bazarduzu Dagi 4,485 m

Natural resources: petroleum, natural gas, iron ore, nonferrous metals, bauxite

Land use: *arable land:* 21.78%
permanent crops: 2.62%
other: 75.6% (2011)

Irrigated land: 14,250 sq km (2010)

Total renewable water resources: 34.68 cu km (2011)

Freshwater withdrawal (domestic/industrial/agricultural): *total:* 12.21 cu km/yr (4%/18%/78%)
per capita: 1,384 cu m/yr (2010)

Natural hazards: droughts

Environment—current issues: local scientists consider the Abseron Yasaqligi (Apsheron Peninsula) (including Baku and Sumqayit) and the Caspian Sea to be the ecologically most devastated area in the world because of severe air, soil, and water pollution; soil pollution results from oil spills, from the use of DDT pesticide, and from toxic defoliants used in the production of cotton

Environment—international agreements: *party to:* Air Pollution, Biodiversity, Climate Change, Climate Change-Kyoto Protocol, Desertification, Endangered Species, Hazardous Wastes, Marine Dumping, Ozone Layer Protection, Ship Pollution, Wetlands
signed, but not ratified: none of the selected agreements

Geography—note: both the main area of the country and the Naxcivan exclave are landlocked

PEOPLE AND SOCIETY

Nationality: *noun:* Azerbaijani(s) adjective: Azerbaijani

Ethnic groups: Azerbaijani 91.6%, Lezgian 2%, Russian 1.3%, Armenian 1.3%, Talysh 1.3%, other 2.4%
note: almost all Armenians live in the separatist Nagorno-Karabakh region (2009 est.)

Languages: Azerbaijani (Azeri) (official) 92.5%, Russian 1.4%, Armenian 1.4%, other 4.7% (2009 est.)

Religions: Muslim 93.4%, Russian Orthodox 2.5%, Armenian Orthodox 2.3%, other 1.8% (1995 est.)
note: religious affiliation is still nominal in Azerbaijan; percentages for actual practicing adherents are much lower

Population: 9,686,210 (July 2014 est.)
country comparison to the world: 92

Age structure: *0-14 years:* 22.7% (male 1,176,438/female 1,017,926)
15-24 years: 17.5% (male 877,773/female 818,380)
25-54 years: 45.1% (male 2,127,239/female 2,236,520)
55-64 years: 6.3% (male 379,081/female 442,970)
65 years and over: 6.3% (male 232,297/female 377,586) (2014 est.)

Dependency ratios: *total dependency ratio:* 38.5 %
youth dependency ratio: 30.8%
elderly dependency ratio: 7.8%
potential support ratio: 12.9 (2013)

Median age: *total:* 30.1 years
male: 28.5 years
female: 31.9 years (2014 est.)

Population growth rate: 0.99% (2014 est.)
country comparison to the world: 121

Birth rate: 16.96 births/1,000 population (2014 est.)
country comparison to the world: 111

Death rate: 7.09 deaths/1,000 population (2014 est.)
country comparison to the world: 129

Net migration rate: 0 migrant(s)/1,000 population (2014 est.)
country comparison to the world: 96

Urbanization: *urban population:* 53.6% of total population (2011)
rate of urbanization: 1.64% annual rate of change (2010-15 est.)

Major urban areas—population: BAKU (capital) 2.123 million (2011)

Sex ratio: *at birth:* 1.12 male(s)/female
0-14 years: 1.16 male(s)/female
15-24 years: 1.07 male(s)/female
25-54 years: 0.95 male(s)/female
55-64 years: 0.98 male(s)/female
65 years and over: 0.62 male(s)/female
total population: 0.98 male(s)/female (2014 est.)

Mother's mean age at first birth: 24.4 (2010 est.)

Maternal mortality rate: 43 deaths/100,000 live births (2010)
country comparison to the world: 113

Infant mortality rate: *total:* 26.67 deaths/1,000 live births
country comparison to the world: 69
male: 27.47 deaths/1,000 live births
female: 25.76 deaths/1,000 live births (2014 est.)

Life expectancy at birth: *total population:* 71.91 years
country comparison to the world: 141
male: 68.92 years
female: 75.26 years (2014 est.)

Total fertility rate: 1.91 children born/woman (2014 est.)
country comparison to the world: 138

Contraceptive prevalence rate: 51.1% (2006)

Health expenditures: 5.2% of GDP (2011)
country comparison to the world: 136

Physicians density: 3.38 physicians/1,000 population (2011)

Hospital bed density: 4.6 beds/1,000 population (2011)

Drinking water source:
Improved:
urban: 88.4% of population
rural: 70.7% of population
total: 80.2% of population
Unimproved:
urban: 11.6% of population
rural: 29.3% of population
total: 19.8% of population (2011 est.)

Sanitation facility access:
Improved:
urban: 85.9% of population
rural: 77.5% of population
total: 82% of population
Unimproved:
urban: 14.1% of population
rural: 22.5% of population
total: 18% of population (2011 est.)

HIV/AIDS—adult prevalence rate: 0.2% (2012 est.)
country comparison to the world: 106

HIV/AIDS—people living with HIV/AIDS: 10,400 (2012 est.)
country comparison to the world: 102

HIV/AIDS—deaths: 600 (2012 est.)
country comparison to the world: 85

Obesity—adult prevalence rate: 23.8% (2008)
country comparison to the world: 71

Children under the age of 5 years underweight: 8.4% (2006)
country comparison to the world: 74

Education expenditures: 2.4% of GDP (2011)
country comparison to the world: 158

Literacy: *definition:* age 15 and over can read and write
total population: 99.8%
male: 99.9%
female: 99.7% (2010 census)

School life expectancy (primary to tertiary education): *total:* 12 years
male: 12 years
female: 12 years (2012)

Child labor—children ages 5-14:
total number: 106,626
percentage: 7 % (2005 est.)

Unemployment, youth ages 15-24: *total:* 14.2%
country comparison to the world: 90
male: 12.2%
female: 16.3% (2012)

GOVERNMENT

Country name: *conventional long form:* Republic of Azerbaijan
conventional short form: Azerbaijan
local long form: Azarbaycan Respublikasi
local short form: Azarbaycan
former: Azerbaijan Soviet Socialist Republic

Government type: republic

Capital: *name:* Baku (Baki, Baky)
geographic coordinates: 40 23 N, 49 52 E
time difference: UTC+4 (9 hours ahead of Washington, DC during Standard Time)
daylight saving time: +1 hr, begins last Sunday in March; ends last Sunday in October

Administrative divisions: 66 rayons (rayonlar; rayon—singular), 11 cities (saharlar; sahar—singular);
rayons: Abseron, Agcabadi, Agdam, Agdas, Agstafa, Agsu, Astara, Babak, Balakan, Barda, Beylaqan, Bilasuvar, Cabrayil, Calilabad, Culfa, Daskasan, Fuzuli, Gadabay, Goranboy, Goycay, Goygol, Haciqabul, Imisli, Ismayilli, Kalbacar, Kangarli, Kurdamir, Lacin, Lankaran, Lerik, Masalli, Neftcala, Oguz, Ordubad, Qabala, Qax, Qazax, Qobustan, Quba, Qubadli, Qusar, Saatli, Sabirabad, Sabran, Sadarak, Sahbuz, Saki, Salyan, Samaxi, Samkir, Samux, Sarur, Siyazan, Susa, Tartar, Tovuz, Ucar, Xacmaz, Xizi, Xocali, Xocavand, Yardimli, Yevlax, Zangilan, Zaqatala, Zardab
cities: Baku, Ganca, Lankaran, Mingacevir, Naftalan, Naxcivan (Nakhichevan), Saki, Sirvan, Sumqayit, Xankandi, Yevlax

Independence: 30 August 1991 (declared from the Soviet Union); 18 October 1991 (adopted by the Supreme Council of Azerbaijan)

National holiday: Founding of the Democratic Republic of Azerbaijan, 28 May (1918)

Constitution: several previous; latest adopted 12 November 1995; amended 1996, 2002, 2009 (2009)

Legal system: civil law system

International law organization participation: has not submitted an ICJ jurisdiction declaration; non-party state to the ICCt

Suffrage: 18 years of age; universal

Executive branch: *chief of state:* President Ilham ALIYEV (since 31 October 2003)
head of government: Prime Minister Artur RASIZADE (since 4 November 2003); First Deputy Prime Minister Yaqub EYYUBOV (since June 2006)
cabinet: Council of Ministers appointed by the president and confirmed by the National Assembly (For more information visit the World Leaders website)
elections: president elected by popular vote for a five-year term (eligible for unlimited terms); election last held on 9 October 2013 (next to be held in October 2018); prime minister and first deputy prime minister appointed by the president and confirmed by the National Assembly
election results: Ilham ALIYEV reelected president; percent of vote—Ilham ALIYEV 84.5%, Jamil HASANLI 5.5%, other 10%
note: OSCE observers concluded that the election did not meet international standards

Legislative branch: unicameral National Assembly or Milli Mejlis (125 seats; members elected by popular vote to serve five-year terms)
elections: last held on 7 November 2010 (next to be held in November 2015)
election results: percent of vote by party—YAP 45.8%, CSP 1.6%, Motherland 1.4%, independents 48.2%, other 3.1%; seats by party—YAP 71, CSP 3, Motherland 2, Democratic Reforms 1, Great Creation 1, Hope Party 1, Social Welfare 1, Civil Unity 1, Whole Azerbaijan Popular Front 1, Justice 1, independents 42

Judicial branch: *highest court(s):* Supreme Court (consists of the chairman, deputy chairman, and at least 24 judges in plenum sessions); Constitutional Court (consists of 9 judges)
judge selection and term of office: Supreme Court judges nominated by the president and appointed by the Milli Majlis; judge tenure NA; Constitutional Court chairman and deputy chairman appointed by the president; other court judges nominated by the president and appointed by the Milli Majlis to serve single 15-year terms
subordinate courts: Courts of Appeal (replaced the Economic Court in 2002); district and municipal courts;

Political parties and leaders: Azerbaijan Democratic Party or ADP [Sardar JALALOGLU]; Azerbaijan Popular Front or AXCP [Ali KARIMLI]; Civil Solidarity Party or CSP [Sabir RUSTAMKHANLI]; Civil Unity Party [Sabir HACIYEV]; Classical Popular Front Party of Azerbaijan [Mirmahmud MIRALI-OGLU]; Democratic Reforms Party [Asim MOLLAZADE]; Great Creation Party [Fazil Gazanfaroglu MUSTAFAYEV]; Hope (Umid) Party [Igbal AGAZADE]; Justice Party [Ilyas ISMAILOV]; Liberal Party of Azerbaijan [Lala Shovkat HACIYEVA, Avaz TEMIRKHAN]; Motherland Party [Fazail AGAMALI]; Musavat (Equality) [Isa GAMBAR]; Open Society Party [Sulhaddin AKBAR]; Social Democratic Party of Azerbaijan or SDP [Araz ALIZADE]; Social Welfare Party [Khanhusein KAZIMLI]; Whole Azerbaijan Popular Front Party [Gudrat HASANGULIYEV]; Yeni (New) Azerbaijan Party or YAP [President Ilham ALIYEV]

Political pressure groups and leaders: EL Movement [Eldar NAMAZOV]; Karabakh Liberation Organization; Forum of Intelligentsia [Rustam IBRAHIMBEYOV]; Republican Alternative (REAL) [Ilgar MAMMADOV]; National Council of Democratic Forces [Jamil HASANLI]; NIDA Youth Movement [Turgut GAMBAR, Zaur GURBANLI (in jail)]; Positive Change Youth Movement [Bakhtiyar HAJIYEV]; Ireli Youth Movement [Rauf MERDIYEV]; Ol! Youth Movement [Vugar SALAMLI]

International organization participation: ADB, BSEC, CD, CE, CICA, CIS, EAPC, EBRD, ECO, EITI (compliant country), FAO, GCTU, GUAM, IAEA, IBRD, ICAO, ICC (NGOs), ICRM, IDA, IDB, IFAD, IFC, IFRCS, ILO, IMF, IMO, Interpol, IOC, IOM, IPU, ISO, ITSO, ITU, ITUC (NGOs), MIGA, NAM, OAS (observer), OIC, OPCW, OSCE, PFP, SELEC (observer), UN, UNCTAD, UNESCO, UNHCR, UNIDO, UNWTO, UPU, WCO, WFTU (NGOs), WHO, WIPO, WMO, WTO (observer)

Diplomatic representation in the US: *chief of mission:* Ambassador Elin SULEYMANOV (since 5 December 2011)
chancery: 2741 34th Street NW, Washington, DC 20008
telephone: [1] (202) 337-3500
FAX: [1] (202) 337-5911
Consulate(s) general: Los Angeles

Diplomatic representation from the US: *chief of mission:* Ambassador Richard L. MORNINGSTAR (since 20 July 2012)
embassy: 111 Azadlig Prospecti, Baku AZ1007
mailing address: American Embassy Baku, US Department of State, 7050 Baku Place, Washington, DC 20521-7050

telephone: [994] (12) 488-3300
FAX: [994] (12) 488-3310

Flag description: three equal horizontal bands of blue (top), red, and green; a crescent and eight-pointed star in white are centered in the red band; the blue band recalls Azerbaijan's Turkic heritage, red stands for modernization and progress, and green refers to Islam; the crescent moon is an Islamic symbol, while the eight-pointed star represents the eight Turkic peoples of the world

National symbol(s): flames of fire

National anthem: *name:* "Azerbaijan Marsi" (March of Azerbaijan)
lyrics/music: Ahmed JAVAD/Uzeyir HAJIBEYOV
note: adopted 1992; although originally written in 1919 during a brief period of independence, "Azerbaijan Marsi" did not become the official anthem until after the dissolution of the Soviet Union

ECONOMY

Economy—overview: Azerbaijan's high economic growth has been attributable to large and growing oil and gas exports, but some non-export sectors also featured double-digit growth, including construction, banking, and real estate. Oil exports through the Baku-Tbilisi-Ceyhan Pipeline, the Baku-Novorossiysk, and the Baku-Supsa pipelines remain the main economic driver, but efforts to boost Azerbaijan's gas production are underway. The eventual completion of the geopolitically important Southern Gas Corridor between Azerbaijan and Europe will open up another, albeit, smaller source of revenue from gas exports. Azerbaijan has made only limited progress on instituting market-based economic reforms. Pervasive public and private sector corruption and structural economic inefficiencies remain a drag on long-term growth, particularly in non-energy sectors. Several other obstacles impede Azerbaijan's economic progress, including the need for stepped up foreign investment in the non-energy sector and the continuing conflict with Armenia over the Nagorno-Karabakh region. Trade with Russia and the other former Soviet republics is declining in importance, while trade is building with Turkey and the nations of Europe. Long-term prospects depend on world oil prices, Azerbaijan's ability to negotiate export routes for its growing gas production, and its ability to use its energy wealth to promote growth and spur employment in non-energy sectors of the economy.

GDP (purchasing power parity): $100.4 billion (2013 est.)
country comparison to the world: 76
$97.04 billion (2012 est.)
$94.98 billion (2011 est.)
note: data are in 2013 US dollars

GDP (official exchange rate): $76.01 billion (2013 est.)

GDP—real growth rate: 3.5% (2013 est.)
country comparison to the world: 96
2.2% (2012 est.)
0.1% (2011 est.)

GDP—per capita (PPP): $10,800 (2013 est.)
country comparison to the world: 114
$10,500 (2012 est.)
$10,400 (2011 est.)
note: data are in 2013 US dollars

Gross national saving: 41% of GDP (2013 est.)
country comparison to the world: 10
44.4% of GDP (2012 est.)
45.1% of GDP (2011 est.)

GDP—composition, by end use:
household consumption: 41.4%
government consumption: 10.5%
investment in fixed capital: 23.3%
investment in inventories: 0.1%
exports of goods and services: 49.9%
imports of goods and services: -25.2% (2013 est.)

GDP—composition, by sector of origin:
agriculture: 6.2%
industry: 63%
services: 30.8% (2013 est.)

Agriculture—products: cotton, grain, rice, grapes, fruit, vegetables, tea, tobacco; cattle, pigs, sheep, goats

Industries: petroleum and natural gas, petroleum products, oilfield equipment; steel, iron ore; cement; chemicals and petrochemicals; textiles

Industrial production growth rate: 3% (2013 est.)
country comparison to the world: 107

Labor force: 6.206 million (2012 est.)
country comparison to the world: 66

Labor force—by occupation: *agriculture:* 38.3%
industry: 12.1%
services: 49.6% (2008)

Unemployment rate: 6% (2013 est.)
country comparison to the world: 58
5.7% (2012 est.)

Population below poverty line: 6% (2012 est.)

Household income or consumption by percentage share: *lowest 10%:* 3.4%
highest 10%: 27.4% (2008)

Distribution of family income—Gini index: 33.7 (2008)
country comparison to the world: 97
36.5 (2001)

Budget: *revenues:* $27.61 billion
expenditures: $27.24 billion (2013 est.)

Taxes and other revenues: 36.3% of GDP (2013 est.)
country comparison to the world: 59

Budget surplus (+) or deficit (-): 0.5% of GDP (2013 est.)
country comparison to the world: 33

Public debt: 7.5% of GDP (2013 est.)
country comparison to the world: 152
7.8% of GDP (2012 est.)

Fiscal year: calendar year

Inflation rate (consumer prices): 2.4% (2013 est.)
country comparison to the world: 87
1.1% (2012 est.)

Central bank discount rate: 5% (31 December 2012 est.)
country comparison to the world: 67
5.25% (31 December 2011 est.)
note: this is the Refinancing Rate, the key policy rate for the National Bank of Azerbaijan

Commercial bank prime lending rate: 17% (31 December 2013 est.)
country comparison to the world: 21
18.5% (31 December 2012 est.)

Stock of narrow money: $17.17 billion (31 December 2013 est.)
country comparison to the world: 67
$14.15 billion (31 December 2012 est.)

Stock of broad money: $21.88 billion (31 December 2013 est.)
country comparison to the world: 83
$17.59 billion (31 December 2012 est.)

Stock of domestic credit: $21.76 billion (31 December 2013 est.)
country comparison to the world: 82
$17.01 billion (31 December 2012 est.)

Market value of publicly traded shares: $NA

Current account balance: $13.28 billion (2013 est.)
country comparison to the world: 20
$14.98 billion (2012 est.)

Exports: $34.46 billion (2013 est.)
country comparison to the world: 63
$32.63 billion (2012 est.)

Exports—commodities: oil and gas 90%, machinery, cotton, foodstuffs

Exports—partners: Italy 27.1%, France 8.1%, Indonesia 6.9%, Germany 5.9%, Israel 5.4%, India 4.2%, US 4.2% (2012)

Imports: $11.98 billion (2013 est.)
country comparison to the world: 94
$10.42 billion (2012 est.)

Imports—commodities: machinery and equipment, oil products, foodstuffs, metals, chemicals

Imports—partners: Turkey 17.8%, Russia 13.7%, China 7.5%, Germany 6.9%, UK 6.8%, Ukraine 5.5%, US 4.9% (2012)

Reserves of foreign exchange and gold: $13.08 billion (31 December 2013 est.)
country comparison to the world: 70
$11.28 billion (31 December 2012 est.)

Debt—external: $9.552 billion (31 December 2013 est.)
country comparison to the world: 101
$9.11 billion (31 December 2012 est.)

Stock of direct foreign investment—at home: $14.35 billion (31 December 2013 est.)
country comparison to the world: 82
$12.35 billion (31 December 2012 est.)

Stock of direct foreign investment—abroad: $8.616 billion (31 December 2013 est.)
country comparison to the world: 57
$7.516 billion (31 December 2012 est.)

Exchange rates: Azerbaijani manats (AZN) per US dollar—
0.785 (2013 est.)
0.7857 (2012 est.)
0.8027 (2010 est.)
0.8038 (2009)
0.8219 (2008)

ENERGY

Electricity—production: 19.44 billion kWh (2011 est.)
country comparison to the world: 75

Electricity—consumption: 13.57 billion kWh (2010 est.)
country comparison to the world: 80

Electricity—exports: 462 million kWh (2010 est.)
country comparison to the world: 66

Electricity—imports: 100 million kWh (2010 est.)
country comparison to the world: 93

Electricity—installed generating capacity: 6.392 million kW (2010 est.)
country comparison to the world: 70

Electricity—from fossil fuels: 84.5% of total installed capacity (2010 est.)
country comparison to the world: 89

Electricity—from nuclear fuels: 0% of total installed capacity (2010 est.)
country comparison to the world: 36

Electricity—from hydroelectric plants: 15.4% of total installed capacity (2010 est.)
country comparison to the world: 100

Electricity—from other renewable sources: 0.1% of total installed capacity (2010 est.)
country comparison to the world: 105

Crude oil—production: 931,900 bbl/day (2012 est.)
country comparison to the world: 25

Crude oil—exports: 821,000 bbl/day (2011 est.)
country comparison to the world: 17

Crude oil—imports: 0 bbl/day (2010 est.)
country comparison to the world: 150

Crude oil—proved reserves: 7 billion bbl (1 January 2013 es)
country comparison to the world: 20

Refined petroleum products—production: 133,500 bbl/day (2010 est.)
country comparison to the world: 65

Refined petroleum products—consumption: 168,000 bbl/day (2011 est.)
country comparison to the world: 63

Refined petroleum products—exports: 53,440 bbl/day (2010 est.)
country comparison to the world: 60

Refined petroleum products—imports: 498.6 bbl/day (2010 est.)
country comparison to the world: 204

Natural gas—production: 17.86 billion cu m (2011 est.)
country comparison to the world: 34

Natural gas—consumption: 9.921 billion cu m (2010 est.)
country comparison to the world: 47

Natural gas—exports: 5.55 billion cu m (2011 est.)
country comparison to the world: 33

Natural gas—imports: 250 million cu m (2011 est.)
country comparison to the world: 70

Natural gas—proved reserves: 991.1 billion cu m (1 January 2013 es)
country comparison to the world: 28

Carbon dioxide emissions from consumption of energy: 36.52 million Mt (2011 est.)
country comparison to the world: 73

COMMUNICATIONS

Telephones—main lines in use: 1.734 million (2012)
country comparison to the world: 64

Telephones—mobile cellular: 10.125 million (2012)
country comparison to the world: 78

Telephone system: *general assessment:* requires considerable expansion and modernization; fixed-line telephone and a broad range of other telecom services are controlled by a state-owned telecommunications monopoly and growth has been stagnant; more competition exists in the mobile-cellular market with four providers in 2009
domestic: teledensity of 17 fixed lines per 100 persons; mobile-cellular teledensity has increased and now exceeds 100 telephones per 100 persons; satellite service connects Baku to a modern switch in its exclave of Naxcivan (Nakhichevan)
international: country code—994; the Trans-Asia-Europe (TAE) fiber-optic link transits Azerbaijan providing international connectivity to neighboring countries; the old Soviet system of cable and microwave is still serviceable; satellite earth stations—2 (2011)

Broadcast media: 3 state-run and 1 public TV channels; 4 domestic commercial TV stations and about 15 regional TV stations; cable TV services are available in Baku; 1 state-run and 1 public radio network operating; a small number of private commercial radio stations broadcasting; local FM relays of Baku commercial stations are available in many localities; local relays of several international broadcasters had been available until late 2008 when their broadcasts were banned from FM frequencies (2010)

Internet country code: .az

Internet hosts: 46,856 (2012)
country comparison to the world: 98

Internet users: 2.42 million (2009)
country comparison to the world: 70

TRANSPORTATION

Airports: 37 (2013)
country comparison to the world: 108

Airports—with paved runways: *total:* 30
over 3,047 m: 5
2,438 to 3,047 m: 5
1,524 to 2,437 m: 13
914 to 1,523 m: 4
under 914 m: 3 (2013)

Airports—with unpaved runways: *total:* 7
under 914 m: 7 (2013)

Heliports: 1 (2012)

Pipelines: condensate 89 km; gas 3,890 km; oil 2,446 km (2013)

Railways: *total:* 2,918 km
country comparison to the world: 59
broad gauge: 2,918 km 1.520-m gauge (1,278 km electrified) (2009)

Roadways: *total:* 52,942 km
country comparison to the world: 75
paved: 26,789 km
unpaved: 26,153 km (2006)

Merchant marine: *total:* 90
country comparison to the world: 53
by type: cargo 27, chemical tanker 1, passenger 2, passenger/cargo 8, petroleum tanker 47, roll on/roll off 3, specialized tanker 2
foreign-owned: 1 (Turkey 1)
registered in other countries: 2 (Malta 1, Saint Vincent and the Grenadines 1) (2010)

Ports and terminals:
major seaport(s): Baku (Baki) located on the Caspian Sea

MILITARY

Military branches: Army, Navy, Air, and Air Defense Forces (2010)

Military service age and obligation: men between 18 and 35 are liable for military service; length of service is 18 months and 12 months for university graduates; 17 years of age for voluntary service; 17 year olds are considered to be on active service at cadet military schools (2012)

Manpower available for military service:
males age 16-49: 2,354,249
females age 16-49: 2,334,632 (2010 est.)

Manpower fit for military service: *males age 16-49:* 1,773,993
females age 16-49: 1,964,012 (2010 est.)

Manpower reaching militarily significant age annually: *male:* 76,923
female: 71,024 (2010 est.)

Military expenditures: 5.2% of GDP (2013)
country comparison to the world: 5
4.64% of GDP (2012)
4.67% of GDP (2011)
4.64% of GDP (2010)

TRANSNATIONAL ISSUES

Disputes—international: Azerbaijan, Kazakhstan, and Russia ratified the Caspian seabed delimitation treaties based on equidistance, while Iran continues to insist on a one-fifth slice of the sea; the dispute over the break-away Nagorno-Karabakh region and the Armenian military occupation of surrounding lands in Azerbaijan remains the primary focus of regional instability; residents have evacuated the former Soviet-era small ethnic enclaves in Armenia and Azerbaijan; local border forces struggle to control the illegal transit of goods and people across the porous, undemarcated Armenian, Azerbaijani, and Georgian borders; bilateral talks continue with Turkmenistan on dividing the seabed and contested oilfields in the middle of the Caspian

Refugees and internally displaced persons:
IDPs: 597,429 (conflict with Armenia over Nagorno-Karabakh; IDPs are mainly ethnic Azerbaijanis but also include ethnic Kurds, Russians, and Turks predominantly from occupied territories around Nagorno-Karabakh; number includes IDPs' descendants, returned IDPs, and people living in insecure areas and excludes people displaced by natural disasters; around half the IDPs live in the capital Baku) (2014)
stateless persons: 3,585 (2012)

Illicit drugs: limited illicit cultivation of cannabis and opium poppy, mostly for CIS consumption; small government eradication program; transit point for Southwest Asian opiates bound for Russia and to a lesser extent the rest of Europe

BAHAMAS, THE

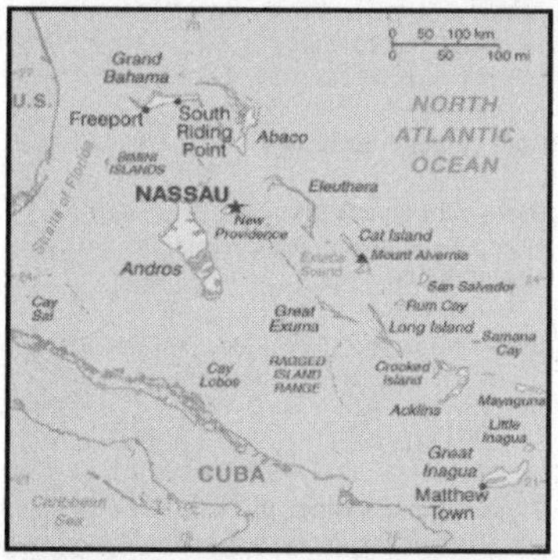

INTRODUCTION

Background: Lucayan Indians inhabited the islands when Christopher COLUMBUS first set foot in the New World on San Salvador in 1492. British settlement of the islands began in 1647; the islands became a colony in 1783. Since attaining independence from the UK in 1973, The Bahamas has prospered through tourism, international banking, and investment management. Because of its geography, the country is a major transshipment point for illegal drugs, particularly shipments to the US and Europe, and its territory is used for smuggling illegal migrants into the US.

GEOGRAPHY

Location: chain of islands in the North Atlantic Ocean, southeast of Florida, northeast of Cuba

Geographic coordinates: 24 15 N, 76 00 W

Map references: Central America and the Caribbean

Area: *total:* 13,880 sq km
country comparison to the world: 161
land: 10,010 sq km
water: 3,870 sq km

Area—comparative: slightly smaller than Connecticut

Land boundaries: 0 km

Coastline: 3,542 km

Maritime claims: territorial sea: 12 nm
exclusive economic zone: 200 nm

Climate: tropical marine; moderated by warm waters of Gulf Stream

Terrain: long, flat coral formations with some low rounded hills

Elevation extremes: *lowest point:* Atlantic Ocean 0 m
highest point: Mount Alvernia on Cat Island 63 m

Natural resources: salt, aragonite, timber, arable land

Land use: *arable land:* 0.65%
permanent crops: 0.29%
other: 99.06% (2011)

Irrigated land: 10 sq km (2003)

Total renewable water resources: 0.02 cu km (2011)

Natural hazards: hurricanes and other tropical storms cause extensive flood and wind damage

Environment—current issues: coral reef decay; solid waste disposal

Environment—international agreements: *party to:* Biodiversity, Climate Change, Climate Change-Kyoto Protocol, Desertification, Endangered Species, Hazardous Wastes, Law of the Sea, Ozone Layer Protection, Ship Pollution, Wetlands
signed, but not ratified: none of the selected agreements

Geography—note: strategic location adjacent to US and Cuba; extensive island chain of which 30 are inhabited

PEOPLE AND SOCIETY

Nationality: *noun:* Bahamian(s)
adjective: Bahamian

Ethnic groups: black 90.6%, white 4.7%, black and white 2.1%, other 1.9%, unspecified 0.7% (2010 est.)

Languages: English (official), Creole (among Haitian immigrants)

Religions: Protestant 69.9% (includes Baptist 34.9%, Anglican 13.7%, Pentecostal 8.9% Seventh Day Adventist 4.4%, Methodist 3.6%, Church of God 1.9%, Brethren 1.6%), Roman Catholic 12%, other Christian 13% (includes Jehovah's Witness 1.1%), other 0.6%, none 1.9%, unspecified 2.6% (2010 est.)

Population: 321,834 (July 2014 est.)
country comparison to the world: 179
note: estimates for this country explicitly take into account the effects of excess mortality due to AIDS; this can result in lower life expectancy, higher infant mortality, higher death rates, lower population growth rates, and changes in the distribution of population by age and sex than would otherwise be expected

Age structure: *0-14 years:* 23.2% (male 37,962/female 36,857)
15-24 years: 17.4% (male 28,387/female 27,639)
25-54 years: 44.1% (male 70,765/female 71,038)
55-64 years: 7% (male 11,882/female 14,885)
65 years and over: 6.7% (male 8,591/female 13,828) (2014 est.)

Dependency ratios: *total dependency ratio:* 40.9%
youth dependency ratio: 30%
elderly dependency ratio: 10.8%
potential support ratio: 9.2% (2013)

Median age: *total:* 31.2 years
male: 30.1 years
female: 32.3 years (2014 est.)

Population growth rate: 0.87% (2014 est.)
country comparison to the world: 128

Birth rate: 15.65 births/1,000 population (2014 est.)
country comparison to the world: 126

Death rate: 7 deaths/1,000 population (2014 est.)
country comparison to the world: 134

Net migration rate: 0 migrant(s)/1,000 population (2014 est.)
country comparison to the world: 97

Urbanization: *urban population:* 84% of total population (2010)
rate of urbanization: 1.3% annual rate of change (2010-15 est.)

Major urban areas: NASSAU (capital) 254,000 (2011)

Sex ratio: *at birth:* 1.03 male(s)/female
0-14 years: 1.03 male(s)/female
15-24 years: 1.03 male(s)/female
25-54 years: 1 male(s)/female
55-64 years: 0.96 male(s)/female
65 years and over: 0.62 male(s)/female
total population: 0.96 male(s)/female (2014 est.)

Maternal mortality rate: 47 deaths/100,000 live births (2010)
country comparison to the world: 111

Infant mortality rate: *total:* 12.5 deaths/1,000 live births
country comparison to the world: 124
male: 12.51 deaths/1,000 live births
female: 12.49 deaths/1,000 live births (2014 est.)

Life expectancy at birth: *total population:* 71.93 years
country comparison to the world: 140
male: 69.48 years
female: 74.46 years (2014 est.)

Total fertility rate: 1.97 children born/woman (2014 est.)
country comparison to the world: 130

Health expenditures: 7.7% of GDP (2011)
country comparison to the world: 67

Physicians density: 2.82 physicians/1,000 population (2008)

Hospital bed density: 3.1 beds/1,000 population (2010)

Drinking water source:
Improved:
urban: 96% of population
rural: 96% of population
total: 96% of population
Unimproved:
urban: 4% of population
rural: 4% of population
total: 4% of population (2011 est.)

Sanitation facility access:
Improved:
urban: 100% of population
rural: 100% of population
total: 100% of population (2010 est.)

HIV/AIDS—adult prevalence rate: 3.3% (2012 est.)
country comparison to the world: 18

HIV/AIDS—people living with HIV/AIDS: 7,000 (2012 est.)
country comparison to the world: 117

HIV/AIDS—deaths: 300 (2012 est.)
country comparison to the world: 105

Obesity—adult prevalence rate: 34.7% (2008)
country comparison to the world: 13

Education expenditures: NA

Literacy: *definition:* age 15 and over can read and write
total population: 95.6%
male: 94.7%
female: 96.5% (2003 est.)

Unemployment, youth ages 15-24: *total:* 30.8%
country comparison to the world: 25
male: 29.6
female: 32.2 (2012)

GOVERNMENT

Country name: *conventional long form:* Commonwealth of The Bahamas
conventional short form: The Bahamas

Government type: constitutional parliamentary democracy and a Commonwealth realm

Capital: *name:* Nassau
geographic coordinates: 25 05 N, 77 21 W
time difference: UTC-5 (same time as Washington, DC during Standard Time)

daylight saving time: +1hr, begins second Sunday in March; ends first Sunday in November

Administrative divisions: 31 districts; Acklins Islands, Berry Islands, Bimini, Black Point, Cat Island, Central Abaco, Central Andros, Central Eleuthera, City of Freeport, Crooked Island and Long Cay, East Grand Bahama, Exuma, Grand Cay, Harbour Island, Hope Town, Inagua, Long Island, Mangrove Cay, Mayaguana, Moore's Island, North Abaco, North Andros, North Eleuthera, Ragged Island, Rum Cay, San Salvador, South Abaco, South Andros, South Eleuthera, Spanish Wells, West Grand Bahama

Independence: 10 July 1973 (from the UK)

National holiday: Independence Day, 10 July (1973)

Constitution: previous 1964 (preindependence); latest adopted 20 June 1973, effective 10 July 1973; amended many times, last in 2002; note - in 2012, a constitutional commission was appointed to review and recommend constitutional changes (2013)

Legal system: common law system based on the English model

International law organization participation: has not submitted an ICJ jurisdiction declaration; non-party state to the ICCt

Suffrage: 18 years of age; universal

Executive branch: *chief of state:* Queen ELIZABETH II (since 6 February 1952); represented by Governor General Sir Arthur A. FOULKES (since 14 April 2010)
head of government: Prime Minister Perry CHRISTIE (since 8 May 2012)
cabinet: Cabinet appointed by the governor general on the prime minister's recommendation (For more information visit the World Leaders website)
elections: the monarchy is hereditary; governor general appointed by the monarch; following legislative elections, the leader of the majority party or the leader of the majority coalition is usually appointed prime minister by the governor general; the prime minister recommends the deputy prime minister

Legislative branch: bicameral Parliament consists of the Senate (16 seats; members appointed by the governor general upon the advice of the prime minister and the opposition leader to serve five-year terms) and the House of Assembly (38 seats; members elected by direct popular vote to serve five-year terms); the government may dissolve the parliament and call elections at any time
elections: last held on 7 May 2012 (next to be held by May 2017)
election results: percent of vote by party—NA; seats by party—PLP 30, FNM 8

Judicial branch: *highest court(s):* The Bahamas Court of Appeal (consists of the court president and 4 justices, sitting in panels of 3 justices) note - as of 2008, the Bahamas was not a party to the agreement establishing the Caribbean Court of Justice as the highest appellate court for the 15-member Caribbean Community (CARICOM); the Judicial Committee of the Privy Council (in London) serves as the final court of appeal for the Bahamas
judge selection and term of office: Court of Appeal justices appointed by the governor-general on the advice of the prime minister and in consultation with the Judicial and Legal Services Commission; justices appointed for life with mandatory retirement at age 68-70
subordinate courts: Supreme Court; Industrial Tribunal; Stipendiary and Magistrates Courts; Family Island Administrators

Political parties and leaders: Free National Movement or FNM [Hubert MINNIS]
Progressive Liberal Party or PLP [Perry CHRISTIE]

Political pressure groups and leaders: Friends of the Environment
other: trade unions

International organization participation: ACP, AOSIS, C, Caricom, CDB, CELAC, FAO, G-77, IADB, IBRD, ICAO, ICRM, IDA, IFAD, IFC, IFRCS, ILO, IMF, IMO, IMSO, Interpol, IOC, IOM, ITSO, ITU, LAES, MIGA, NAM, OAS, OPANAL, OPCW, Petrocaribe, UN, UNCTAD, UNESCO, UNIDO, UNWTO, UPU, WCO, WHO, WIPO, WMO, WTO (observer)

Diplomatic representation in the US: *chief of mission:* Ambassador Dr. Eugene Glenwood NEWRY (since 3 December 2013)
chancery: 2220 Massachusetts Avenue NW, Washington, DC 20008
telephone: [1] (202) 319-2660
FAX: [1] (202) 319-2668
consulate(s) general: Atlanta, Miami, New York

Diplomatic representation from the US: *chief of mission:* Ambassador (vacant); Charge d' Affaires John DINKELMAN (since November 2011)
embassy: 42 Queen Street, Nassau, New Providence
mailing address: local or express mail address: P. O. Box N-8197, Nassau; US Department of State, 3370 Nassau Place, Washington, DC 20521-3370
telephone: [1] (242) 322-1181, 328-2206 (after hours)
FAX: [1] (242) 328-2206

Flag description: three equal horizontal bands of aquamarine (top), gold, and aquamarine, with a black equilateral triangle based on the hoist side; the band colors represent the golden beaches of the islands surrounded by the aquamarine sea; black represents the vigor and force of a united people, while the pointing triangle indicates the enterprise and determination of the Bahamian people to develop the rich resources of land and sea

National symbol(s): blue marlin; flamingo

National anthem: *name:* "March On, Bahamaland!"
lyrics/music: Timothy GIBSON
note: adopted 1973; as a Commonwealth country, in addition to the national anthem, "God Save the Queen" serves as the royal anthem (see United Kingdom)

ECONOMY

Economy—overview: The Bahamas is one of the wealthiest Caribbean countries with an economy heavily dependent on tourism and offshore banking. Tourism together with tourism-driven construction and manufacturing accounts for approximately 60% of GDP and directly or indirectly employs half of the archipelago's labor force. Financial services constitute the second-most important sector of the Bahamian economy and, when combined with business services, account for about 36% of GDP. Manufacturing and agriculture combined contribute less than a 10th of GDP and show little growth, despite government incentives aimed at those sectors. The economy of The Bahamas shrank at an average pace of 0.8% annually between 2007-2011, and tourism, financial services, and construction—pillars of the national economy—remained weak. These challenges, coupled with a growing public debt, high in government expenditures and unemployment, a narrow revenue base, and heavy dependence on customs and property taxes have led to prospects of limited growth for The Bahamas.

GDP (purchasing power parity): $11.4 billion (2013 est.)
country comparison to the world: 153
$11.19 billion (2012 est.)
$10.98 billion (2011 est.)
note: data are in 2013 US dollars

GDP (official exchange rate): $8.373 billion (2013 est.)

GDP—real growth rate: 1.9% (2013 est.)
country comparison to the world: 145
1.8% (2012 est.)
1.7% (2011 est.)

GDP—per capita (PPP): $32,000 (2013 est.)
country comparison to the world: 43
$31,800 (2012 est.)
$31,500 (2011 est.)
note: data are in 2013 US dollars

Gross national saving: 14.3% of GDP (2013 est.)
country comparison to the world: 114
19.3% of GDP (2012 est.)
17.8% of GDP (2011 est.)

GDP—composition, by end use: *household consumption:* 68.7%
government consumption: 15.5%
investment in fixed capital: 34.4%
investment in inventories: 0%
exports of goods and services: 45.8%
imports of goods and services: -64.4% (2013 est.)

GDP—composition by sector of origin: *agriculture:* 2.1%
industry: 7.1%
services: 90.8% (2013 est.)

Agriculture—products: citrus, vegetables; poultry

Industries: tourism, banking, cement, oil transshipment, salt, rum, aragonite, pharmaceuticals

Industrial production growth rate: 1.5% *country comparison to the world:* 134

Labor force: 192,200 (2012)
country comparison to the world: 173

Labor force—by occupation: *agriculture:* 5%
industry: 5%
tourism: 50%
other services: 40% (2005 est.)

Unemployment rate: 14% (2012 est.)
country comparison to the world: 134
14.2% (2009 est.)

Population below poverty line: 9.3% (2004)

Household income or consumption by percentage share: *lowest 10%:* 1%
highest 10%: 22% (2007)

Budget: *revenues:* $1.6 billion
expenditures: $2.1 billion (2013 est.)

Taxes and other: *revenues:* 19.1% of GDP (2013 est.)
country comparison to the world: 172

Budget surplus (+) or deficit (-): -6% of GDP (2013 est.)
country comparison to the world: 179

Fiscal year: 1 July - 30 June

Inflation rate (consumer prices): 1.8% (2013 est.)
country comparison to the world: 53
2% (2012 est.)

Central bank discount rate: 4.5% (31 December 2012 est.)
country comparison to the world: 94
4% (31 December 2011 est.)

Commercial bank prime lending rate: 4.8% (31 December 2013 est.)
country comparison to the world: 159
4.75% (31 December 2012 est.)

Stock of narrow money: $1.577 billion (31 December 2013 est.)
country comparison to the world: 135
$1.575 billion (31 December 2012 est.)

Stock of broad money: $6.465 billion (31 December 2013 est.)
country comparison to the world: 119
$6.088 billion (31 December 2012 est.)

Stock of domestic credit: $9.2 billion (31 December 2013 est.)
country comparison to the world: 101
$8.653 billion (31 December 2012 est.)

Market value of publicly traded shares: $2.78 billion (31 December 2012 est.)

Current account balance: -$1.372 billion (2013 est.)
country comparison to the world: 130
-$1.424 billion (2012 est.)

Exports: $960 million (2013 est.)
country comparison to the world: 161
$984 million (2012 est.)

Exports—commodities: crawfish, aragonite, crude salt, polystyrene products

Exports—partners: Singapore 25.1%, US 20.6%, Dominican Republic 12.9%, Ecuador 9.4%, Canada 5.8%, Switzerland 4.1%, China 4.1% (2012)

Imports: $3.245 billion (2013 est.)
country comparison to the world: 144
$3.386 billion (2012 est.)

Imports—commodities: machinery and transport equipment, manufactures, chemicals, mineral fuels; food and live animals

Imports—partners: US 30.1%, India 20.3%, Singapore 8.7%, South Korea 6.8%, China 5%, Colombia 4.5%, Canada 4.2% (2012)

Reserves of foreign exchange and gold: $830 million (31 December 2013 est.)
country comparison to the world: 142
$846.9 million (31 December 2012 est.)

Debt—external: $17.56 billion (31 December 2013 est.)
country comparison to the world: 85
$16.35 billion (31 December 2012 est.)

Exchange rates: Bahamian dollars (BSD) per US dollar—
1 (2013 est.)
1 (2012 est.)
1 (2010 est.)
1 (2008 est.)
1 (2007 est.)

ENERGY

Electricity—production: 1.93 billion kWh (2010 est.)
country comparison to the world: 137

Electricity—consumption: 1.795 billion kWh (2010 est.)
country comparison to the world: 142

Electricity—exports: 0 kWh (2012 est.)
country comparison to the world: 104

Electricity—imports: 0 kWh (2012 est.)
country comparison to the world: 118

Electricity—installed generating capacity: 493,000 kW (2010 est.)
country comparison to the world: 139

Electricity—from fossil fuels: 100% of total installed capacity (2012 est.)
country comparison to the world: 7

Electricity—from nuclear fuels: 0% of total installed capacity (2012 est.)
country comparison to the world: 47

Electricity—from hydroelectric plants: 0% of total installed capacity (2012 est.)
country comparison to the world: 159

Electricity—from other renewable sources: 0% of total installed capacity (2012 est.)
country comparison to the world: 156

Crude oil—production: 0 bbl/day (2012 est.)
country comparison to the world: 153

Crude oil—exports: 0 bbl/day (2010 est.)
country comparison to the world: 83

Crude oil—imports: 0 bbl/day (2010 est.)
country comparison to the world: 159

Crude oil—proved reserves: 0 bbl (1 January 2013 es)
country comparison to the world: 108

Refined petroleum products—production: 0 bbl/day (2010 est.)
country comparison to the world: 122

Refined petroleum products—consumption: 36,300 bbl/day (2011 est.)
country comparison to the world: 111

Refined petroleum products—exports: 41,770 bbl/day (2010 est.)
country comparison to the world: 63

Refined petroleum products—imports: 64,600 bbl/day (2010 est.)
country comparison to the world: 61

Natural gas—production: 0 cu m (2011 est.)
country comparison to the world: 103

Natural gas—consumption: 0 cu m (2010 est.)
country comparison to the world: 120

Natural gas—exports: 0 cu m (2011 est.)
country comparison to the world: 64

Natural gas—imports: 0 cu m (2011 est.)
country comparison to the world: 159

Natural gas—proved reserves: 0 cu m (1 January 2009 es)
country comparison to the world: 114

Carbon dioxide emissions from consumption of energy: 4.734 million Mt (2011 est.)
country comparison to the world: 128

COMMUNICATIONS

Telephones—main lines in use: 137,000 (2012)
country comparison to the world: 141

Telephones—mobile cellular: 254,000 (2012)
country comparison to the world: 176

Telephone system: *general assessment:* modern facilities
domestic: totally automatic system; highly developed; the Bahamas Domestic Submarine Network links 14 of the islands and is designed to satisfy increasing demand for voice and broadband Internet services
international: country code—1-242; landing point for the Americas Region Caribbean Ring System (ARCOS-1) fiber-optic submarine cable that provides links to South and Central America, parts of the Caribbean, and the US; satellite earth stations—2 (2007)

Broadcast media: 2 TV stations operated by government-owned, commercially run Broadcasting Corporation of the Bahamas (BCB); multi-channel cable TV subscription service is available; about 15 radio stations operating with BCB operating a multi-channel radio broadcasting network alongside privately owned radio stations (2007)

Internet country code: .bs

Internet hosts: 20,661 (2012)
country comparison to the world: 117

Internet users: 115,800 (2009)
country comparison to the world: 156

TRANSPORTATION

Airports: 61 (2013)
country comparison to the world: 79

Airports—with paved runways: *total:* 24
over 3,047 m: 2
2,438 to 3,047 m: 2
1,524 to 2,437 m: 13
914 to 1,523 m: 7 (2013)

Airports—with unpaved runways: *total:* 37
1,524 to 2,437 m: 4
914 to 1,523 m: 16
under 914 m: 17 (2013)

Heliports: 1 (2013)

Roadways: *total:* 2,700 km
country comparison to the world: 170
paved: 1,620 km
unpaved: 1,080 km (2011)

Merchant marine: *total:* 1,160
country comparison to the world: 10
by type: barge carrier 1, bulk carrier 238, cargo 170, carrier 2, chemical tanker 87, combination ore/oil 8, container 57, liquefied gas 71, passenger 102, passenger/cargo 26, petroleum tanker 225, refrigerated cargo 97, roll on/roll off 13, specialized tanker 2, vehicle carrier 61
foreign-owned: 1,063 (Angola 6, Australia 1, Belgium 6, Bermuda 15, Brazil 1, Canada 96, Croatia 1, Cyprus 23, Denmark 69, Finland 8, France 15, Germany 30, Greece 225, Guernsey 6, Hong Kong 3, Indonesia 2, Ireland 3, Italy 1, Japan 88, Jordan 2, Kuwait 1, Malaysia 13, Monaco 8, Montenegro 2, Netherlands 23, Nigeria 2, Norway 186, Poland 34, Saudi Arabia 16, Singapore 7, South Korea 1, Spain 6, Sweden 11, Switzerland 1, Thailand 4, Turkey 3, UAE 23, UK 18, US 109)
registered in other countries: 6 (Panama 6) (2010)

Ports and terminals: *major seaport(s):* Freeport, Nassau, South Riding Point
container port(s) (TEUs): Freeport (1,116,272) (2011)
cruise port(s): Nassau

MILITARY

Military branches: *Royal Bahamas Defense Force:* Land Force, Navy, Air Wing (2011)

Military service age and obligation: 18 years of age for voluntary male and female service; no conscription (2012)

Manpower available for military service: *males age 16-49:* 85,568 (2010 est.)

Manpower fit for military service: *males age 16-49:* 63,429
females age 16-49: 64,645 (2010 est.)

Manpower reaching militarily significant age annually: *male:* 2,829
female: 2,750 (2010 est.)

TRANSNATIONAL ISSUES

Disputes—international: disagrees with the US on the alignment of the northern axis of a potential maritime boundary

Illicit drugs: transshipment point for cocaine and marijuana bound for US and Europe; offshore financial center

BAHRAIN

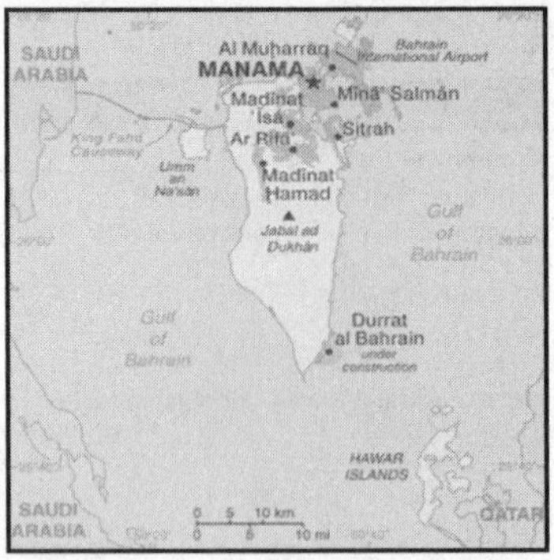

INTRODUCTION

Background: In 1783, the Sunni Al-Khalifa family took power in Bahrain. In order to secure these holdings, it entered into a series of treaties with the UK during the 19th century that made Bahrain a British protectorate. The archipelago attained its independence in 1971. Facing declining oil reserves, Bahrain has turned to petroleum processing and refining and has become an international banking center. Bahrain's small size and central location among Gulf countries require it to play a delicate balancing act in foreign affairs among its larger neighbors. The Sunni-led government has struggled to manage relations with its large Shia-majority population. In early 2011, amid Arab uprisings elsewhere in the region, the Bahraini Government confronted similar protests at home with police and military action. Continued dissatisfaction by Bahraini oppositionists with the political status quo has led to a broader dialogue between government officials, political societies, and legislators.

GEOGRAPHY

Location: Middle East, archipelago in the Persian Gulf, east of Saudi Arabia

Geographic coordinates: 26 00 N, 50 33 E

Map references: Middle East

Area: *total:* 760 sq km
country comparison to the world: 188
land: 760 sq km
water: 0 sq km

Area—comparative: 3.5 times the size of Washington, DC

Land boundaries: 0 km

Coastline: 161 km

Maritime claims: territorial sea: 12 nm
contiguous zone: 24 nm
continental shelf: extending to boundaries to be determined
Climate: arid; mild, pleasant winters; very hot, humid summers

Terrain: mostly low desert plain rising gently to low central escarpment

Elevation extremes: *lowest point:* Persian Gulf 0 m
highest point: Jabal ad Dukhan 122 m

Natural resources: oil, associated and nonassociated natural gas, fish, pearls

Land use: *arable land:* 1.79%
permanent crops: 3.95%
other: 94.26% (2011)

Irrigated land: 40.15 sq km (2003)

Total renewable water resources: 0.12 cu km (2011)

Freshwater withdrawal (domestic/industrial/agricultural): *total:* 0.36 cu km/yr (50%/6%/45%)
per capita: 386 cu m/yr (2003)

Natural hazards: periodic droughts; dust storms

Environment—current issues: desertification resulting from the degradation of limited arable land, periods of drought, and dust storms; coastal degradation (damage to coastlines, coral reefs, and sea vegetation) resulting from oil spills and other discharges from large tankers, oil refineries, and distribution stations; lack of freshwater resources (groundwater and seawater are the only sources for all water needs)

Environment—international agreements: *party to:* Biodiversity, Climate Change, Climate Change-Kyoto Protocol, Desertification, Hazardous Wastes, Law of the Sea, Ozone Layer Protection, Wetlands
signed, but not ratified: none of the selected agreements

Geography—note: close to primary Middle Eastern petroleum sources; strategic location in Persian Gulf, through which much of the Western world's petroleum must transit to reach open ocean

PEOPLE AND SOCIETY

Nationality: *noun:* Bahraini(s)
adjective: Bahraini

Ethnic groups: Bahraini 46%, Asian 45.5%, other Arabs 4.7%, African 1.6%, European 1%, other 1.2% (includes Gulf Co-operative country nationals, North and South Americans, and Oceanians) (2010 est.)

Languages: Arabic (official), English, Farsi, Urdu

Religions: Muslim 70.3%, Christian 14.5%, Hindu 9.8%, Buddhist 2.5%, Jewish 0.6%, folk religion

Population: 1,314,089 (July 2014 est.)
country comparison to the world: 157
note: immigrants make up almost 55% of the total population, according to UN data (2013)

Age structure: *0-14 years:* 19.7% (male 131,698/female 127,663)
15-24 years: 15.9% (male 117,156/female 91,477)
25-54 years: 56.2% (male 483,449/female 254,627)
55-64 years: 2.7% (male 47,172/female 25,354)
65 years and over: 2.6% (male 17,106/female 18,387) (2014 est.)

Dependency ratios: *total dependency ratio:* 30.3%
youth dependency ratio: 27.3%
elderly dependency ratio: 2.9%
potential support ratio: 34.3 (2013)

Median age: *total:* 31.6 years
male: 33 years
female: 28.8 years (2014 est.)

Population growth rate: 2.49% (2014 est.)
country comparison to the world: 31

Birth rate: 13.92 births/1,000 population (2014 est.)
country comparison to the world: 142

Death rate: 2.67 deaths/1,000 population (2014 est.)
country comparison to the world: 223

Net migration rate: 13.6 migrant(s)/1,000 population (2014 est.)
country comparison to the world: 9

Urbanization: *urban population:* 88.7% of total population (2011)
rate of urbanization: 2.21% annual rate of change (2010-15 est.)

Major urban areas—population: MANAMA (capital) 262,000 (2011)

Sex ratio: *at birth:* 1.03 male(s)/female
0-14 years: 1.03 male(s)/female
15-24 years: 1.28 male(s)/female
25-54 years: 1.9 male(s)/female
55-64 years: 1.54 male(s)/female
65 years and over: 0.91 male(s)/female
total population: 1.54 male(s)/female (2014 est.)

Maternal mortality rate: 20 deaths/100,000 live births (2010)
country comparison to the world: 138

Infant mortality rate: *total:* 9.68 deaths/1,000 live births
country comparison to the world: 143
male: 10.69 deaths/1,000 live births
female: 8.65 deaths/1,000 live births (2014 est.)

Life expectancy at birth: *total population:* 78.58 years
country comparison to the world: 51
male: 76.4 years
female: 80.81 years (2014 est.)

Total fertility rate: 1.81 children born/woman (2014 est.)
country comparison to the world: 153

Contraceptive prevalence rate: 61.8% (1995)

Health expenditures: 3.8% of GDP (2011)
country comparison to the world: 168

Physicians density: 1.49 physicians/1,000 population (2010)

Hospital bed density: 1.8 beds/1,000 population (2009)

Drinking water source:
improved:
urban: 100% of population
rural: 100% of population
total: 100% of population
unimproved:
urban: 0% of population
rural: 0% of population
total: 0% of population (2011 est.)

Sanitation facility access:
improved:
urban: 99.2% of population
rural: 99.2% of population
total: 99.2% of population
unimproved:
urban: 0.8% of population
rural: 0.8% of population
total: 0.8% of population (2011 est.)

HIV/AIDS—adult prevalence rate: 0.2% (2001 est.)
country comparison to the world: 107

HIV/AIDS—people living with HIV/AIDS: fewer than 600 (2007 est.)
country comparison to the world: 153

HIV/AIDS—deaths: fewer than 200 (2003 est.)
country comparison to the world: 111

Obesity—adult prevalence rate: 32.9% (2008)
country comparison to the world: 20

Education expenditures: 2.6% of GDP (2012)
country comparison to the world: 153

Literacy: *definition:* age 15 and over can read and write
total population: 94.6%
male: 96.1%

female: 91.6% (2010 est.)

Child labor—children ages 5-14: *total number:* 5,530
percentage: 5 % (2000 est.)

Unemployment, youth ages 15-24: *total:* 5%
country comparison to the world: 138
male: 2.5%
female: 11.6% (2010)

GOVERNMENT

Country name: *conventional long form:* Kingdom of Bahrain
conventional short form: Bahrain
local long form: Mamlakat al Bahrayn
local short form: Al Bahrayn former: Dilmun, State of Bahrain

Government type: constitutional monarchy

Capital: *name:* Manama
geographic coordinates: 26 14 N, 50 34 E
time difference: UTC+3 (8 hours ahead of Washington, DC during Standard Time)

Administrative divisions: 5 governorates (muhafazat, singular - muhafazah); Asamah (Capital), Janubiyah (Southern), Muharraq, Shamaliyah (Northern), Wasat (Central)
note: each governorate administered by an appointed governor

Independence: 15 August 1971 (from the UK)

National holiday: National Day, 16 December (1971); note—15 August 1971 was the date of independence from the UK, 16 December 1971 was the date of independence from British protection

Constitution: adopted 14 February 2002; amended 2012 (2012)

Legal system: mixed legal system of Islamic law, English common law, Egyptian civil, criminal, and commercial codes; customary law

International law organization participation: has not submitted an ICJ jurisdiction declaration; non-party state to the ICCt

Suffrage: 20 years of age; universal; note—Bahraini Cabinet in May 2011 endorsed a draft law lowering eligibility to 18 years

Executive branch: *chief of state:* King HAMAD bin Isa Al-Khalifa (since 6 March 1999); Crown Prince SALMAN bin Hamad Al-Khalifa (son of the monarch, born 21 October 1969)
head of government: Prime Minister KHALIFA bin Salman Al-Khalifa (since 1971); First Deputy Prime Minister SALMAN bin Hamad Al Khalifa (since 11 March 2013); Deputy Prime Ministers ALI bin Khalifa bin Salman Al-Khalifa, Jawad bin Salimal-ARAIDH, KHALID bin Abdallah Al Khalifa, MUHAMMAD bin Mubarak Al-Khalifa
cabinet: Cabinet appointed by the monarch (For more information visit the World Leaders website)
elections: the monarchy is hereditary; prime minister appointed by the monarch

Legislative branch: bicameral National Assembly consists of the Shura Council or Consultative Council (40 members appointed by the King) and the Council of Representatives or Chamber of Deputies (40 seats; members directly elected to serve four-year terms)
elections: Council of Representatives—last held in two rounds on 23 and 30 October 2010 (next election to be held in 2014); byelections to fill 18 vacated seats held in two rounds on 24 September and 1 October 2011
election results: Council of Representatives (2010)—percent of vote by society—NA; seats by society—Wifaq (Shia) 18, Asalah (Sunni Salafi) 3, Minbar (Sunni Muslim Brotherhood) 2, independents 17; Council of Representatives byelection for 18 seats vacated by Wifaq (2011)—seats by society—independent Sunni 8, independent Shia 8, other 2; note—Bahrain has societies rather than parties

Judicial branch: *highest court(s):* Court of Cassation (consists of a chairman and 3 judges); Constitutional Court (consists of a president and 6 members)
note - the judiciary of Bahrain is divided into the civil law and sharia law courts
judge selection and term of office: Court of Cassation and Constitutional Court judges appointed by royal decree and serve for a specified tenure
subordinate courts: High Court of Appeal; middle and lower civil courts; higher and lower shariah courts, and the High Shariah Court of Appeal

Political parties and leaders: *note:* political parties are prohibited but political societies were legalized per a July 2005 law
progovernment: Arab Islamic Center Society [Ahmad Sanad AL-BENALI]; Constitutional Gathering Society; Islamic Asalah [Abd al-Halim MURAD]; Islamic Saff Society [Abdullah Khalil BU GHAMAR]; Islamic Shura Society; Movement of National Justice Society [Muhi al-Din KHAN]; National Action Charter Society [Muhammad AL-BUAYNAYN]; National Dialogue Society; National Islamic Minbar [Ali AHMAD]; National Unity Gathering [Abdullah AL-HUWAYHI]
oppositon: National Democratic Action Society [Ibrahim SHARIF]; National Democratic Assembly [Hasan AL-ALI]; National Fraternity Society [Musa AL-ANSARI]; National Progressive Tribune [Abd al-Nabi SALMAN]; Unitary National Democratic Assemblage [Fadhil ABBAS]; Wifaq National Islamic Society [Ali SALMAN]

Political pressure groups and leaders: *Sunni:* Al-Fatih Awakening
Shia: 14 February Revolution Youth Coalition; Bahrain Islamic Freedom Movement [Said SHIHABI]; Haqq Movement [Hasan MUSHAYMA]; Islamic Amal [Muhammad Ali AL-MAHFUDH]; Khalas [Abd al-Rauf AL-SHAYIB]; Wafa Islamic Society [Abd al-Wahab HUSAYN]

International organization participation: ABEDA, AFESD, AMF, CAEU, CICA, FAO, G-77, GCC, IAEA, IBRD, ICAO, ICC (national committees), ICRM, IDA, IDB, IFC, IFRCS, IHO, ILO, IMF, IMO, IMSO, Interpol, IOC, IOM (observer), IPU, ISO, ITSO, ITU, ITUC (NGOs), LAS, MIGA, NAM, OAPEC, OIC, OPCW, PCA, UN, UNCTAD, UNESCO, UNIDO, UNWTO, UPU, WCO, WFTU (NGOs), WHO, WIPO, WMO, WTO

Diplomatic representation in the US: *chief of mission:* Ambassador Shaikh ABDULLA Mohamed Rashed Al Khalifa (since 26 November 2013)
chancery: 3502 International Drive NW, Washington, DC 20008
telephone: [1] (202) 342-1111
FAX: [1] (202) 362-2192
consulate(s) general: New York

Diplomatic representation from the US: *chief of mission:* Ambassador Thomas C. KRAJESKI (since 26 October 2011)
embassy: Building #979, Road 3119 (next to Al-Ahli Sports Club), Block 331, Zinj District, Manama
mailing address: PSC 451, Box 660, FPO AE 09834-5100; international
mail: American Embassy, Box 26431, Manama
telephone: [973] 1724-2700
FAX: [973] 1727-0547

Flag description: red, the traditional color for flags of Persian Gulf states, with a white serrated band (five white points) on the hoist side; the five points represent the five pillars of Islam
note: until 2002 the flag had eight white points, but this was reduced to five to avoid confusion with the Qatari flag

National anthem: *name:* "Bahrainona" (Our Bahrain)
lyrics/music: unknown
note: adopted 1971; although Mohamed Sudqi AYYASH wrote the original lyrics, they were changed in 2002 following the transformation of Bahrain from an emirate to a kingdom

ECONOMY

Economy—overview: Bahrain has taken great strides in diversifying its economy and its highly developed communication and transport facilities make Bahrain home to numerous multinational firms with business in the Gulf. As part of its diversification plans, Bahrain implemented a Free Trade Agreement (FTA) with the US in August 2006, the first FTA between the US and a Gulf state. Bahrain's economy, however, continues to depend heavily on oil. Petroleum production and refining account for more than 60% of Bahrain's export receipts, 70% of government revenues, and 11% of GDP. Other major economic activities are production of aluminum—Bahrain's second biggest export after oil—finance, and construction. Bahrain competes with Malaysia as a worldwide center for Islamic banking and continues to seek new natural gas supplies as feedstock to support its expanding petrochemical and aluminum industries. In 2011 Bahrain experienced economic setbacks as a result of domestic unrest, however, the economy is recovered in 2012-13, partly as a result of improved tourism. Economic policies aimed at restoring confidence in Bahrain's economy, such as the suspension of an expatriate labor tax and frequent bailouts of Gulf Air, will make Bahrain's long-term economic challenges - youth unemployment and the growth of government debt - more difficult to address.

GDP (purchasing power parity): $34.96 billion (2013 est.)
country comparison to the world: 110
$33.48 billion (2012 est.)
$31.95 billion (2011 est.)
note: data are in 2013 US dollars

GDP (official exchange rate): $28.36 billion (2013 est.)

GDP—real growth rate: 4.4% (2013 est.)
country comparison to the world: 69
4.8% (2012 est.)
2.1% (2011 est.)

GDP—per capita (PPP): $29,800 (2013 est.)
country comparison to the world: 49
$29,100 (2012 est.)
$28,300 (2011 est.)
note: data are in 2013 US dollars

Gross national saving: 27.6% of GDP (2013 est.)
country comparison to the world: 36 27.6% of GDP (2012 est.)
27.5% of GDP (2011 est.)

GDP—composition, by end use: *household consumption:* 39.8%
government consumption: 15.6%
investment in fixed capital: 20.7%
investment in inventories: 0.8%

exports of goods and services: 74.8%
imports of goods and services: -51.7% (2013 est.)

GDP—composition, by sector of origin:
agriculture: 0.3%
industry: 46.7%
services: 53% (2013 est.)

Agriculture—products: fruit, vegetables; poultry, dairy products; shrimp, fish

Industries: petroleum processing and refining, aluminum smelting, iron pelletization, fertilizers, Islamic and offshore banking, insurance, ship repairing, tourism

Industrial production growth rate: 4.7% (2013 est.)
country comparison to the world: 60

Labor force: 716,500
country comparison to the world: 151
note: 44% of the population in the 15-64 age group is non-national (2013 est.)

Labor force—by occupation: *agriculture:* 1%
industry: 79%
services: 20% (1997 est.)

Unemployment rate: 15% (2005 est.)
country comparison to the world: 139

Population below poverty line: NA%

Household income or consumption by percentage share: *lowest 10%:* NA%
highest 10%: NA%

Budget: *revenues:* $8.143 billion
expenditures: $9.232 billion (2013 est.)

Taxes and other revenues: 28.7% of GDP (2013 est.)
country comparison to the world: 99

Budget surplus (+) or deficit (-): -3.8% of GDP (2013 est.)
country comparison to the world: 141

Public debt: 61.2% of GDP (2013 est.)
country comparison to the world: 45
54.2% of GDP (2012 est.)

Fiscal year: calendar year

Inflation rate (consumer prices): 3.1% (2013 est.)
country comparison to the world: 115
2.8% (2012 est.)

Commercial bank prime lending rate: 6.8% (31 December 2013 est.)
country comparison to the world: 135
6.05% (31 December 2012 est.)

Stock of narrow money: $7.431 billion (31 December 2013 est.)
country comparison to the world: 91
$6.944 billion (31 December 2012 est.)

Stock of broad money: $23.93 billion (31 December 2013 est.)
country comparison to the world: 79
$22.51 billion (31 December 2012 est.)

Stock of domestic credit: $25.96 billion (31 December 2013 est.)
country comparison to the world: 72
$22.19 billion (31 December 2012 est.)

Market value of publicly traded shares: $16.06 billion (31 December 2012 est.)
country comparison to the world: 65
$17.15 billion (31 December 2011)
$20.43 billion (31 December 2010 est.)

Current account balance: $1.907 billion (2013 est.)
country comparison to the world: 43
$2.221 billion (2012 est.)

Exports: $20.69 billion (2013 est.)
country comparison to the world: 72
$20.39 billion (2012 est.)

Exports—commodities: petroleum and petroleum products, aluminum, textiles

Exports—partners: Saudi Arabia 3.3%, India 2.2%, UAE 2.2%, South Korea 2% (2012)

Imports: $14.41 billion (2013 est.)
country comparison to the world: 88
$13.24 billion (2012 est.)

Imports—commodities: crude oil, machinery, chemicals

Imports—partners: Saudi Arabia 27.4%, US 9.6%, China 9.5%, Japan 6.4%, India 4.9%, France 4.7% (2012)

Reserves of foreign exchange and gold: $5.933 billion (31 December 2013 est.)
country comparison to the world: 89
$5.211 billion (31 December 2012 est.)

Debt—external: $28.82 billion (31 December 2013 est.)
country comparison to the world: 74
$27.54 billion (31 December 2012 est.)

Stock of direct foreign investment—at home: $17.81 billion (31 December 2013 est.)
country comparison to the world: 76
$16.83 billion (31 December 2012 est.)

Stock of direct foreign investment—abroad: $10.86 billion (31 December 2013 est.)
country comparison to the world: 53
$9.699 billion (31 December 2012 est.)

Exchange rates: Bahraini dinars (BHD) per US dollar—
0.376 (2013 est.)
0.376 (2012 est.)
0.376 (2010 est.)
0.376 (2009)
0.376 (2008)

ENERGY

Electricity—production: 13.16 billion kWh (2011 est.)
country comparison to the world: 87

Electricity—consumption: 12.97 billion kWh (2011 est.)
country comparison to the world: 84

Electricity—exports: 0 kWh (2012 est.)
country comparison to the world: 100

Electricity—imports: 214 million kWh (2011 est.)
country comparison to the world: 86

Electricity—installed generating capacity: 3.169 million kW (2010 est.)
country comparison to the world: 86

Electricity—from fossil fuels: 100% of total installed capacity (2011 est.)
country comparison to the world: 4

Electricity—from nuclear fuels: 0% of total installed capacity (2011 est.)
country comparison to the world: 43

Electricity—from hydroelectric plants: 0% of total installed capacity (2011 est.)
country comparison to the world: 155

Electricity—from other renewable sources: 0% of total installed capacity (2011 est.)
country comparison to the world: 153

Crude oil—production: 49,160 bbl/day (2012 est.)
country comparison to the world: 63

Crude oil—exports: 152,600 bbl/day (2012 est.)
country comparison to the world: 33

Crude oil—imports: 256,000 bbl/day (2011 est.)
country comparison to the world: 30

Crude oil—proved reserves: 124.6 million bbl (1 January 2013 es)
country comparison to the world: 68

Refined petroleum products—production: 270,800 bbl/day (2012 est.)
country comparison to the world: 47

Refined petroleum products—consumption: 51,450 bbl/day (2012 est.)
country comparison to the world: 97

Refined petroleum products—exports: 226,000 bbl/day (2012 est.)
country comparison to the world: 28

Refined petroleum products—imports: 0 bbl/day (2012 est.)
country comparison to the world: 210

Natural gas—production: 12.62 billion cu m (2011 est.)
country comparison to the world: 37

Natural gas—consumption: 12.77 billion cu m (2010 est.)
country comparison to the world: 43

Natural gas—exports: 0 cu m (2011 est.)
country comparison to the world: 60

Natural gas—imports: 0 cu m (2011 est.)
country comparison to the world: 155

Natural gas—proved reserves: 92.03 billion cu m (1 January 2013 es)
country comparison to the world: 56

Carbon dioxide emissions from consumption of energy: 29.7 million Mt (2011 est.)
country comparison to the world: 75

COMMUNICATIONS

Telephones—main lines in use: 290,000 (2012)
country comparison to the world: 118

Telephones—mobile cellular: 2.125 million (2012)
country comparison to the world: 144

Telephone system: *general assessment:* modern system
domestic: modern fiber-optic integrated services; digital network with rapidly growing use of mobile-cellular telephones
international: country code—973; landing point for the Fiber-Optic Link Around the Globe (FLAG) submarine cable network that provides links to Asia, Middle East, Europe, and US; tropospheric scatter to Qatar and UAE; microwave radio relay to Saudi Arabia; satellite earth station—1 (2007)

Broadcast media: state-run Bahrain Radio and Television Corporation (BRTC) operates 5 terrestrial TV networks and several radio stations; satellite TV systems provide access to international broadcasts; 1 private FM station directs broadcasts to Indian listeners; radio and TV broadcasts from countries in the region are available (2007)

Internet country code: .bh

Internet hosts: 47,727 (2012)
country comparison to the world: 97

Internet users: 419,500 (2009)
country comparison to the world: 122

TRANSPORTATION

Airport: 4 (2013)
country comparison to the world: 184

Airports—with paved runways: *total:* 4
over 3,047 m: 3
914 to 1,523 m: 1 (2013)

Heliports: 1 (2013)

Pipelines: gas 20 km; oil 54 km (2013)

Roadways: *total:* 4,122 km
country comparison to the world: 156
paved: 3,392 km

unpaved: 730 km (2010)

Merchant marine: *total:* 8
country comparison to the world: 119
by type: bulk carrier 2, container 4, petroleum tanker 2
foreign-owned: 5 (Kuwait 5)
registered in other countries: 5 (Honduras 5) (2010)

Ports and terminals: Mina' Salman, Sitrah

MILITARY

Military branches: *Bahrain Defense Force (BDF):* Royal Bahraini Army (RBA), Royal Bahraini Navy (RBN), Royal Bahraini Air Force (RBAF), Royal Bahraini Air Defense Force (RBADF) (2013)

Military service age and obligation: 18 years of age for voluntary military service; 15 years of age for NCOs, technicians, and cadets; no conscription (2012)

Manpower available for military service: *males age 16-49:* 508,863
females age 16-49: 290,801 (2010 est.)

Manpower fit for military service: *males age 16-49:* 423,757
females age 16-49: 245,302 (2010 est.)

Manpower reaching militarily significant age annually: *male:* 8,988
female: 8,117 (2010 est.)

Military expenditures: 3.14% of GDP (2012)
country comparison to the world: 18
3.02% of GDP (2011)
3.14% of GDP (2010)

TRANSNATIONAL ISSUES

Disputes—international: none

Trafficking in persons: *current situation:* Bahrain is a destination country for men and women subjected to forced labor and sex trafficking; unskilled and domestic workers from India, Pakistan, Nepal, Sri Lanka, Bangladesh, Indonesia, Thailand, the Philippines, Ethiopia, Ghana, and Eritrea migrate willingly to Bahrain, but some face conditions of forced labor through the withholding of passports, restrictions on movement, nonpayment, threats, and abuse; many Bahraini labor recruitment agencies and some employers charge foreign workers exorbitant fees that make them vulnerable to forced labor and debt bondage; domestic workers are particularly vulnerable to forced labor and sexual exploitation because they are not protected under labor laws; women from Thailand, the Philippines, Morocco, Jordan, Syria, Lebanon, China, Vietnam, Russia, Ukraine, and Eastern European countries are forced into prostitution in Bahrain
tier rating: Tier 2 Watch List - Bahrain does not fully comply with the minimum standards for the elimination of trafficking; however, it is making significant efforts to do so; the government has made few discernible efforts to investigate, prosecute, and convict trafficking offenses; cases of unpaid or withheld wages, passport retention, and other abuses - common indicators of trafficking - are treated as labor disputes and taken to civil court rather than criminal court; the government has made no indication of taking steps to institute a formal trafficking victim identification procedure and referral mechanism, resulting in the majority of victims seeking shelter at their embassies or the NGO-operated trafficking shelter; most victims have not filed lawsuits against employers because of a distrust of the legal system or a fear of reprisals (2013)

BANGLADESH

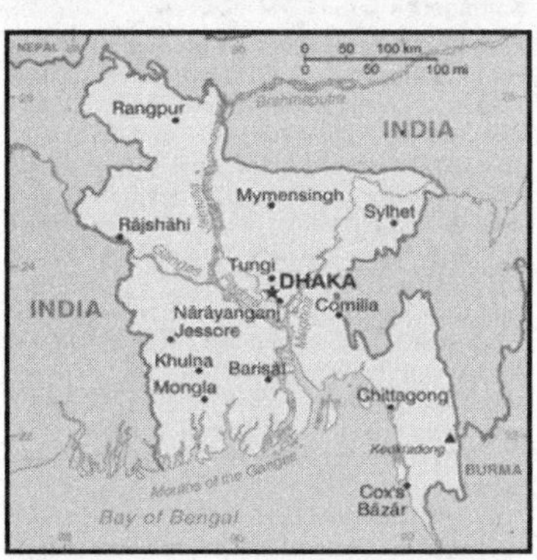

INTRODUCTION

Background: Muslim conversions and settlement in the region now referred to as Bangladesh began in the 10th century, primarily from Arab and Persian traders and preachers. Europeans began to set up trading posts in the area in the 16th century. Eventually the area known as Bengal, primarily Hindu in the western section and mostly Muslim in the eastern half, became part of British India. Partition in 1947 resulted in an eastern wing of Pakistan in the Muslim-majority area, which became East Pakistan. Calls for greater autonomy and animosity between the eastern and western wings of Pakistan led to a Bengali independence movement. That movement, led by the Awami League (AL) and supported by India, won independence for Bangladesh in 1971, although at least 300,000 civilians died in the process. The post-independence, AL government faced daunting challenges and in 1975 was overthrown by the military, triggering a series of military coups that resulted in a military-backed government and subsequent creation of the Bangladesh Nationalist Party (BNP). That government also ended in a coup in 1981, followed by military-backed rule until democratic elections in 1991. The BNP and AL have alternately held power since then, with the exception of a military-backed, emergency caretaker regime that suspended parliamentary elections planned for January 2007 in an effort to reform the political system and root out corruption. That government returned the country to fully democratic rule in December 2008 with the election of the AL and Prime Minister Sheikh HASINA. In January 2014, the AL won the national election by an overwhelming majority after the BNP boycotted, extending HASINA's term as prime minister. With the help of international development assistance, Bangladesh has made great progress in food security since independence, and the economy has grown at an average of about 6 percent over the last two decades.

GEOGRAPHY

Location: Southern Asia, bordering the Bay of Bengal, between Burma and India

Geographic coordinates: 24 00 N, 90 00 E

Map references: Asia

Area: *total:* 143,998 sq km
country comparison to the world: 95
land: 130,168 sq km
water: 13,830 sq km

Area—comparative: slightly smaller than Iowa

Land boundaries: *total:* 4,246 km
border countries: Burma 193 km, India 4,053 km
Coastline: 580 km

Maritime claims: *territorial sea:* 12 nm
contiguous zone: 18 nm
exclusive economic zone: 200 nm
continental shelf: up to the outer limits of the continental margin

Climate: tropical; mild winter (October to March); hot, humid summer (March to June); humid, warm rainy monsoon (June to October)

Terrain: mostly flat alluvial plain; hilly in southeast

Elevation extremes: *lowest point:* Indian Ocean 0 m
highest point: Keokradong 1,230 m

Natural resources: natural gas, arable land, timber, coal

Land use: *arable land:* 52.97%
permanent crops: 6.25%
other: 40.78% (2011)

Irrigated land: 50,500 sq km (2008)

Total renewable water resources: 1,227 cu km (2011)

Freshwater withdrawal (domestic/industrial/agricultural): *total:* 35.87 cu km/yr (10%/2%/88%)
per capita: 238.3 cu m/yr (2008)

Natural hazards: droughts; cyclones; much of the country routinely inundated during the summer monsoon season

Environment—current issues: many people are landless and forced to live on and cultivate flood-prone land; waterborne diseases prevalent in surface water; water pollution, especially of fishing areas, results from the use of commercial pesticides; ground water contaminated by naturally occurring arsenic; intermittent water shortages because of falling water tables in the northern and central parts of the country; soil degradation and erosion; deforestation; severe overpopulation

Environment—international agreements: *party to:* Biodiversity, Climate Change, Climate Change-Kyoto Protocol, Desertification, Endangered Species, Environmental Modification, Hazardous Wastes, Law of the Sea, Ozone Layer Protection, Ship Pollution, Wetlands
signed, but not ratified: none of the selected agreements

Geography—note: *most of the country is situated on deltas of large rivers flowing from the Himalayas:* the Ganges unites with the Jamuna (main channel of the Brahmaputra) and later joins the Meghna to eventually empty into the Bay of Bengal

PEOPLE AND SOCIETY

Nationality: *noun:* Bangladeshi(s)
adjective: Bangladeshi

Ethnic groups: Bengali 98%, other 2% (includes tribal groups, non-Bengali Muslims) (1998)

Languages: Bangla (official, also known as Bengali), English

Religions: Muslim 89.5%, Hindu 9.6%, other 0.9% (2004)

Population: 166,280,712 (July 2014 est.)
country comparison to the world: 9

Age structure: *0-14 years: 32.3% (male 27,268,560/female 26,468,883)*
15-24 years: 18.8% (male 14,637,526/female 16,630,766)
25-54 years: 38% (male 29,853,531/female 33,266,733)
55-64 years: 5% (male 4,964,130/female 4,870,447)
65 years and over: 4.9% (male 4,082,544/female 4,237,592) (2014 est.)

Dependency ratios: *total dependency ratio:* 53.3 %
youth dependency ratio: 46 %
elderly dependency ratio: 7.3 %
potential support ratio: 13.6 (2013)

Median age: *total:* 24.3 years
male: 23.8 years
female: 24.8 years (2014 est.)

Population growth rate: 1.6% (2014 est.)
country comparison to the world: 77

Birth rate: 21.61 births/1,000 population (2014 est.)
country comparison to the world: 76

Death rate: 5.64 deaths/1,000 population (2014 est.)
country comparison to the world: 175

Net migration rate: -0.02 migrant(s)/1,000 population (2014 est.)
country comparison to the world: 110

Urbanization: *urban population:* 28.4% of total population (2011)
rate of urbanization: 2.96% annual rate of change (2010-15 est.)

Major urban areas—population: DHAKA (capital) 15.391 million; Chittagong 4.816 million; Khulna 1.636 million; Rajshahi 853,000 (2011)

Sex ratio: *at birth:* 1.04 male(s)/female
0-14 years: 1.03 male(s)/female
15-24 years: 0.88 male(s)/female
25-54 years: 0.9 male(s)/female
55-64 years: 0.95 male(s)/female
65 years and over: 0.96 male(s)/female
total population: 0.95 male(s)/female (2014 est.)

Mother's mean age at first birth: 18.1 *note:* median age at first birth among women 25-29 (2011 est.)

Maternal mortality rate: 240 deaths/100,000 live births (2010)
country comparison to the world: 49

Infant mortality rate: *total:* 45.67 deaths/1,000 live births
country comparison to the world: 45
male: 48.15 deaths/1,000 live births
female: 43.09 deaths/1,000 live births (2014 est.)

Life expectancy at birth: *total population:* 70.65 years
country comparison to the world: 149
male: 68.75 years
female: 72.63 years (2014 est.)

Total fertility rate: 2.45 children born/woman (2014 est.)
country comparison to the world: 83

Contraceptive prevalence rate: 61.2% (2011/12)

Health expenditures: 3.7% of GDP (2011)
country comparison to the world: 174

Physicians density: 0.36 physicians/1,000 population (2011)

Hospital bed density: 0.6 beds/1,000 population (2011)

Drinking water source:
Improved:
urban: 85.3% of population
rural: 82.4% of population
total: 83.2% of population
Unimproved:
urban: 14.7% of population
rural: 17.6% of population
total: 16.8% of population (2011 est.)

Sanitation facility access:
Improved:
urban: 55.3% of population
rural: 54.5% of population
total: 54.7% of population
Unimproved:
urban: 44.7% of population
rural: 45.5% of population
total: 45.3% of population (2011 est.)

HIV/AIDS—adult prevalence rate: 0.1% (2012 est.)
country comparison to the world: 126

HIV/AIDS—people living with HIV/AIDS: 8,000 (2012 est.)
country comparison to the world: 113

HIV/AIDS—deaths: 400 (2012 est.)
country comparison to the world: 97

Major infectious diseases: *degree of risk:* high
food or waterborne diseases: bacterial and protozoal diarrhea, hepatitis A and E, and typhoid fever
vectorborne diseases: dengue fever and malaria are high risks in some locations
water contact disease: leptospirosis
animal contact disease: rabies
note: highly pathogenic H5N1 avian influenza has been identified in this country; it poses a negligible risk with extremely rare cases possible among US citizens who have close contact with birds (2013)

Obesity—adult prevalence rate: 1.1% (2008)
country comparison to the world: 190

Children under the age of 5 years underweight: 36.8% (2011)
country comparison to the world: 5

Education expenditures: 2.2% of GDP (2009)
country comparison to the world: 161

Literacy: *definition:* age 15 and over can read and write
total population: 57.7%
male: 62%
female: 53.4% (2011 est.)

School life expectancy (primary to tertiary education): *total:* 10 years
male: 10 years
female: 10 years (2011)

Child labor—children ages 5-14: *total number:* 4,485,497
percentage: 13 % (2006 est.)

Unemployment, youth ages 15-24: *total:* 9.3%
country comparison to the world: 114
male: 8%
female: 13.6% (2005)

GOVERNMENT

Country name: *conventional long form:* People's Republic of Bangladesh
conventional short form: Bangladesh
local long form: Gana Prajatantri Bangladesh
local short form: Bangladesh
former: East Bengal, East Pakistan

Government type: parliamentary democracy

Capital: *name:* Dhaka
geographic coordinates: 23 43 N, 90 24 E
time difference: UTC+6 (11 hours ahead of Washington, DC during Standard Time)

Administrative divisions: 7 divisions; Barisal, Chittagong, Dhaka, Khulna, Rajshahi, Rangpur, Sylhet

Independence: 16 December 1971 (from West Pakistan)

National holiday: Independence Day, 26 March (1971); Victory Day; note—March 1971 is the date of the Awami League's declaration of an independent Bangladesh, and 16 December, known as Victory Day, memorializes the military victory over Pakistan and the official creation of the state of Bangladesh

Constitution: previous 1935, 1956, 1962 (preindependence); latest enacted 4 November 1972, effective 16 December 1972, suspended March 1982, restored November 1986; amended many times, last in 2011 (2011)

Legal system: mixed legal system of mostly English common law and Islamic law

International law organization participation: has not submitted an ICJ jurisdiction declaration; accepts ICCt jurisdiction

Suffrage: 18 years of age; universal

Executive branch: *chief of state:* President Abdul HAMID (since 24 April 2013); note - Abdul HAMID served as acting president following the death of Zillur RAHMAN in March 2013; HAMID was subsequently elected by the National Parliament and was sworn in 24 April 2013
head of government: Prime Minister Sheikh HASINA (since 6 January 2009; reelected 5 January 2014)
cabinet: Cabinet selected by the prime minister and appointed by the president (For more information visit the World Leaders website)
elections: president elected by National Parliament for a five-year term (eligible for a second term); last election held on 29 April 2013 (next must be held by 2018)
election results: President Abdul HAMID was elected by the National Parliament unopposed

Legislative branch: unicameral National Parliament or Jatiya Sangsad; 300 seats (45 reserved for women) elected by popular vote from single territorial constituencies; members serve five-year terms
elections: last held on 5 January 2014 (next to be held by January 2019); note - the 5 January 2014 poll was marred by widespread violence, boycotts, general strikes, and low voter turnout
election results: percent of vote by party - AL-led Alliance 77%, JP 33%; seats by party - AL 235, JP 34, other 28

Judicial branch: *highest court(s):* Supreme Court of Bangladesh (organized into the Appellate Division with 7 justices and the High Court Division with 99 justices) *judge selection and term of office:* chief justice and justices appointed by the president; justices serve until retirement at age 67
subordinate courts: civil courts include: Assistant Judge's Court; Joint District Judge's Court; Additional District Judge's Court; District Judge's Court; criminal courts include: Court of Sessions; Court of Metropolitan Sessions; special courts/tribunals; Metropolitan Magistrate Courts; Magistrate Court

Political parties and leaders: Awami League or AL [Sheikh HASINA]; Communist Party of

Bangladesh or CPB [Manjurul A. KHAN]; Bangladesh Nationalist Front or BNF; [Abdul Kalam AZADI]; Bangladesh Nationalist Party or BNP [Khaleda ZIA]; Bikalpa Dhara Bangladesh or BDB [Badrudozza CHOWDHURY]; Islami Oikya Jote or IOJ [multiple leaders] Jatiya Party or JP (Ershad faction) [Hussain Mohammad ERSHAD]; Liberal Democratic Party or LDP [Oli AHMED]; National Socialist Party or JSD [KHALEQUZZAMAN]; Tarikat Foundation [Syed Nozibul Bashar MAIZBHANDARI]; Workers Party or WP [Rashed Khan MENON]

Political pressure groups and leaders: Advocacy to End Gender-based Violence through the MoWCA (Ministry of Women's and Children's Affairs); Ain o Salish Kendro (Law and Order Center); Bangladesh Rural Advancement Committee or BRAC; Bangladesh Center for Worker Solidarity; Federation of Bangladesh Chambers of Commerce and Industry; Odikhar (Human Rights)
other: associations of madrassa teachers; business associations, including those intended to promote international trade; development and advocacy NGOs associated with the Grameen Bank; environmentalists; Islamist groups; labor rights advocacy groups; nongovernmental organizations focused on poverty, alleviation, and socioeconomic international trade; religious leaders; tribal groups and advocacy organizations; union leaders

International organization participation: ADB, ARF, BIMSTEC, C, CD, CICA (observer), CP, D-8, FAO, G-77, IAEA, IBRD, ICAO, ICC (national committees), ICRM, IDA, IDB, IFAD, IFC, IFRCS, IHO, ILO, IMF, IMO, IMSO, Interpol, IOC, IOM, IPU, ISO, ITSO, ITU, ITUC (NGOs), MIGA, MINURSO, MONUSCO, NAM, OIC, OPCW, PCA, SAARC, SACEP, UN, UNAMID, UNCTAD, UNESCO, UNHCR, UNIDO, UNIFIL, UNISFA, UNMIL, UNMISS, UNMIT, UNOCI, UNWTO, UPU, WCO, WFTU (NGOs), WHO, WIPO, WMO, WTO

Diplomatic representation in the US: *chief of mission:* Ambassador Akramul QADER (since 1 September 2009)
chancery: 3510 International Drive NW, Washington, DC 20008
telephone: [1] (202) 244-0183
FAX: [1] (202) 244-7830/2771
consulate(s) general: Los Angeles, New York

Diplomatic representation from the US: *chief of mission:* Ambassador Dan W. MOZENA (since 11 November 2011)
embassy: Madani Avenue, Baridhara, Dhaka 1212
mailing address: G. P. O. Box 323, Dhaka 1000
telephone: [880] (2) 885-5500
FAX: [880] (2) 882-3744

Flag description: green field with a large red disk shifted slightly to the hoist side of center; the red disk represents the rising sun and the sacrifice to achieve independence; the green field symbolizes the lush vegetation of Bangladesh

National symbol(s): Bengal tiger, water lily

National anthem: *name:* "Amar Shonar Bangla" (My Golden Bengal)
lyrics/music: Rabindranath TAGORE
note: adopted 1971; Rabindranath TAGORE, a Nobel laureate, also wrote India's national anthem

ECONOMY

Economy—overview: Bangladesh's economy has grown 6% per year since 1996 despite political instability, poor infrastructure, corruption, insufficient power supplies, slow implementation of economic reforms, and the 2008-09 global financial crisis and recession. Although more than half of GDP is generated through the service sector, almost half of Bangladeshis are employed in the agriculture sector with rice as the single-most-important product. Garment exports, the backbone of Bangladesh's industrial sector and 80% of total exports, surpassed $21 billion last year, 18% of GDP. The sector has remained resilient in recent years amidst a series of factory accidents that have killed over 1,000 workers and crippling strikes that shut down virtually all economic activity. Steady garment export growth combined with remittances from overseas Bangladeshis, which totaled almost $15 billion and 13% of GDP IN 2013, are the largest contributors to Bangladesh's current account surplus and record foreign exchange holdings.

GDP (purchasing power parity): $324.6 billion (2013 est.)
country comparison to the world: 44
$307 billion (2012 est.)
$289.2 billion (2011 est.)
note: data are in 2013 US dollars

GDP (official exchange rate): $140.2 billion (2013 est.)

GDP—real growth rate: 5.8% (2013 est.)
country comparison to the world: 40
6.1% (2012 est.)
6.5% (2011 est.)

GDP—per capita (PPP): $2,100 (2013 est.)
country comparison to the world: 194
$2,000 (2012 est.)
$1,900 (2011 est.)
note: data are in 2013 US dollars

Gross national saving: 28.3% of GDP (2013 est.)
country comparison to the world: 34
27% of GDP (2012 est.)
25% of GDP (2011 est.)

GDP—composition, by end use: *household consumption:* 75.3%
government consumption: 5.7%
investment in fixed capital: 25.6%
investment in inventories: 3.6%
exports of goods and services: 24.5%
imports of goods and services: -34.7% (2013 est.)

GDP—composition, by sector of origin: *agriculture:* 17.2% *industry:* 28.9% *services:* 53.9% (2013 est.)

Agriculture—products: rice, jute, tea, wheat, sugarcane, potatoes, tobacco, pulses, oilseeds, spices, fruit; beef, milk, poultry

Industries: jute, cotton, garments, paper, leather, fertilizer, iron and steel, cement, petroleum products, tobacco, drugs and pharmaceuticals, ceramics, tea, salt, sugar, edible oils, soap and detergent, fabricated metal products, electricity and natural gas

Industrial production growth rate: 9% (2013 est.)
country comparison to the world: 20

Labor force: 78.62 million
country comparison to the world: 7
note: extensive export of labor to Saudi Arabia, Kuwait, UAE, Oman, Qatar, and Malaysia; workers' remittances were $10.9 billion in FY09/10 (2013 est.)

Labor force—by occupation: *agriculture:* 47%
industry: 13%
services: 40% (2010 est.)

Unemployment rate: 5% (2013 est.)
country comparison to the world: 48
5% (2012 est.)
note: about 40% of the population is underemployed; many participants in the labor force work only a few hours a week, at low wages

Population below poverty line: 31.5% (2010 est.)

Household income or consumption by percentage share: lowest 10%: 4%
highest 10%: 27% (2010 est.)

Distribution of family income—Gini index: 32.1 (2010)
country comparison to the world: 105
33.6 (1996)

Budget: *revenues:* $17.19 billion
expenditures: $24.02 billion (2013 est.)

Taxes and other revenues: 12.3% of GDP (2013 est.)
country comparison to the world: 202

Budget surplus (+) or deficit (-): -4.9% of GDP (2013 est.)
country comparison to the world: 163

Public debt: 30.9% of GDP (2013 est.)
country comparison to the world: 118
32.2% of GDP (2012 est.)

Fiscal year: 1 July—30 June

Inflation rate (consumer prices): 7.6% (2013 est.)
country comparison to the world: 190
6.6% (2012 est.)

Central bank discount rate: 5% (31 December 2010 est.)
country comparison to the world: 70
5% (31 December 2009 est.)

Commercial bank prime lending rate: 13% (31 December 2013 est.)
country comparison to the world: 60
13% (31 December 2012 est.)

Stock of narrow money: $17.11 billion (31 December 2013 est.)
country comparison to the world: 68
$14.85 billion (31 December 2012 est.)

Stock of broad money: $85.61 billion (31 December 2013 est.)
country comparison to the world: 58
$70.87 billion (31 December 2012 est.)

Stock of domestic credit: $93.38 billion (31 December 2013 est.)
country comparison to the world: 54
$79.32 billion (31 December 2012 est.)

Market value of publicly traded shares: $37.34 billion (February 2014 est.)
country comparison to the world: 64
$17.48 billion (31 December 2012)
$23.55 billion (31 December 2011 est.)

Current account balance: $3.541 billion (2013 est.)
country comparison to the world: 32
$1.754 billion (2012 est.)

Exports: $26.91 billion (2013 est.)
country comparison to the world: 68
$24.92 billion (2012 est.)

Exports—commodities: garments, knitwear, agricultural products, frozen food (fish and seafood), jute and jute goods, leather

Exports—partners: US 18.7%, Germany 15.8%, UK 10.2%, France 6.2%, Spain 4.6%, Canada 4.3%, Italy 4% (2013 est.)

Imports: $32.94 billion (2013 est.)
country comparison to the world: 64
$32.29 billion (2012 est.)

Imports—commodities: machinery and equipment, chemicals, iron and steel, textiles, foodstuffs, petroleum products, cement

Imports—partners: China 21.7%, India 16.3%, Malaysia 5.2%, Republic of Korea 4.5%, Japan 4.1% (2013 est.)

Reserves of foreign exchange and gold: $15.74 billion (31 December 2013 est.)
country comparison to the world: 68
$12.75 billion (31 December 2012 est.)

Debt—external: $30.69 billion (31 December 2013 est.)
country comparison to the world: 72
$29.53 billion (31 December 2012 est.)

Stock of direct foreign investment—at home: $7.04 billion (31 December 2013 est.)
country comparison to the world: 87
$6.64 billion (31 December 2012 est.)

Stock of direct foreign investment—abroad: $110.1 million (31 December 2013 est.)
country comparison to the world: 86
$108.1 million (31 December 2012 est.)

Exchange rates: taka (BDT) per US dollar—
78.19 (2013 est.)
81.863 (2012 est.)
69.649 (2010 est.)
69.04 (2009)
68.554 (2008)

ENERGY

Electricity—production: 40.08 billion kWh (2011 est.)
country comparison to the world: 59

Electricity—consumption: 38.89 billion kWh (2010 est.)
country comparison to the world: 54

Electricity—exports: 0 kWh (2012 est.)
country comparison to the world: 105

Electricity—imports: 500,000 kWh (2013 est.)
country comparison to the world: 107

Electricity—installed generating capacity: 10.26 million kW (2013 est.)
country comparison to the world: 53

Electricity—from fossil fuels: 97.7% of total installed capacity (2013 est.)
country comparison to the world: 60

Electricity—from nuclear fuels: 0% of total installed capacity (2013 est.)
country comparison to the world: 48

Electricity—from hydroelectric plants: 2.3% of total installed capacity (2013 est.)
country comparison to the world: 134

Electricity—from other renewable sources: 0% of total installed capacity (2013 est.)
country comparison to the world: 157

Crude oil—production: 5,452 bbl/day (2012 est.)
country comparison to the world: 97

Crude oil—exports: 0 bbl/day (2010 est.)
country comparison to the world: 84

Crude oil—imports: 23,620 bbl/day (2010 est.)
country comparison to the world: 66

Crude oil—proved reserves: 28 million bbl (1 January 2013 es)
country comparison to the world: 82

Refined petroleum products—production: 22,710 bbl/day (2010 est.)
country comparison to the world: 90

Refined petroleum products—consumption: 108,900 bbl/day (2011 est.)
country comparison to the world: 74

Refined petroleum products—exports: 3,288 bbl/day (2010 est.)
country comparison to the world: 97

Refined petroleum products—imports: 84,490 bbl/day (2010 est.)
country comparison to the world: 54

Natural gas—production: 20.11 billion cu m (2011 est.)
country comparison to the world: 32

Natural gas—consumption: 19.91 billion cu m (2010 est.)
country comparison to the world: 35

Natural gas—exports: 0 cu m (2011 est.)
country comparison to the world: 65

Natural gas—imports: 0 cu m (2011 est.)
country comparison to the world: 160

Natural gas—proved reserves: 183.7 billion cu m (1 January 2013 es)
country comparison to the world: 47

Carbon dioxide emissions from consumption of energy: 58.81 million Mt (2011 est.)
country comparison to the world: 56

COMMUNICATIONS

Telephones—main lines in use: 962,000 (2012)
country comparison to the world: 78

Telephones—mobile cellular: 97.18 million (2011)
country comparison to the world: 15

Telephone system: *general assessment:* inadequate for a modern country; introducing digital systems; trunk systems include VHF and UHF microwave radio relay links, and some fiber-optic cable in cities
domestic: fixed-line teledensity remains only about 1 per 100 persons; mobile-cellular telephone subscribership has been increasing rapidly and now exceeds 50 telephones per 100 persons international: country code - 880; landing point for the SEA-ME-WE-4 fiber-optic submarine cable system that provides links to Europe, the Middle East, and Asia; satellite earth stations - 6; international radiotelephone communications and landline service to neighboring countries (2011)

Broadcast media: state-owned Bangladesh Television (BTV) operates 1 terrestrial TV station, 3 radio networks, and about 10 local stations; 8 private satellite TV stations and 3 private radio stations also broadcasting; foreign satellite TV stations are gaining audience share in the large cities; several international radio broadcasters are available (2007)

Internet country code: .bd

Internet hosts: 71,164 (2012)
country comparison to the world: 87

Internet users: 617,300 (2009)
country comparison to the world: 112

TRANSPORTATION

Airports: 18 (2013)
country comparison to the world: 139

Airports—with paved runways: *total:* 16
over 3,047 m: 2
2,438 to 3,047 m: 2
1,524 to 2,437 m: 6
914 to 1,523 m: 1
under 914 m: 5 (2013)

Airports—with unpaved runways: *total:* 2
1,524 to 2,437 m: 1
under 914 m: 1 (2013)

Heliports: 3 (2013)

Pipelines: gas 2,950 km (2013)

Railways: *total:* 2,622 km
country comparison to the world: 65
broad gauge: 946 km 1.676-m gauge
narrow gauge: 1,676 km 1.000-m gauge (2008)

Roadways: *total:* 21,269 km
country comparison to the world: 106
paved: 1,063 km
unpaved: 20,206 km (2010)

Waterways: 8,370 km (includes up to 3,060 km of main cargo routes; the network is reduced to 5,200 km in the dry season) (2011)
country comparison to the world: 17

Merchant marine: *total:* 62
country comparison to the world: 64
by type: bulk carrier 25, cargo 28, chemical tanker 1, container 5, petroleum tanker 3
foreign-owned: 8 (China 1, Singapore 7)
registered in other countries: 10 (Comoros 1, Hong Kong 1, Panama 5, Saint Vincent and the Grenadines 1, Sierra Leone 1, Singapore 1) (2010)

Ports and terminals: *major seaport(s):* Chittagong
river port(s): Mongla Port (Sela River)
container port(s): Chittagong (1,392,104) (2011)

Transportation—note: the International Maritime Bureau reports the territorial waters of Bangladesh remain a risk for armed robbery against ships; attacks against vessels have decreased over the last few years in response to improved local security

MILITARY

Military branches: *Bangladesh Defense Force:* Bangladesh Army (Sena Bahini), Bangladesh Navy (Noh Bahini, BN), Bangladesh Air Force (Biman Bahini, BAF) (2013)

Military service age and obligation: 16-19 years of age for voluntary military service; Bangladeshi birth and 10th grade education required; initial obligation 15 years (2012)

Manpower available for military service: *males age 16-49:* 36,520,491 (2010 est.)

Manpower fit for military service: *males age 16-49:* 30,486,086
females age 16-49: 35,616,093 (2010 est.)

Manpower reaching militarily significant age annually: *male:* 1,606,963
female: 1,689,442 (2010 est.)

Military expenditures: 1.35% of GDP (2012)
country comparison to the world: 76
1.44% of GDP (2011)
1.35% of GDP (2010)

TRANSNATIONAL ISSUES

Disputes—international: Bangladesh referred its maritime boundary claims with Burma and India to the International Tribunal on the Law of the Sea; Indian Prime Minister Singh's September 2011 visit to Bangladesh resulted in the signing of a Protocol to the 1974 Land Boundary Agreement between India and Bangladesh, which had called for the settlement of longstanding boundary disputes over undemarcated areas and the exchange of territorial enclaves, but which had never been implemented; Bangladesh struggles to accommodate 29,000 Rohingya, Burmese Muslim minority from Arakan State, living as refugees in Cox's Bazar; Burmese border authorities are constructing a 200 km (124 mi) wire fence designed to deter illegal cross-border transit and tensions from the military build-up along border

Refugees and internally displaced persons: *refugees (country of origin):* 230,674 (Burma) (2012)
IDPs: undetermined (land conflicts, religious persecution) (2012)

Illicit drugs: transit country for illegal drugs produced in neighboring countries

BARBADOS

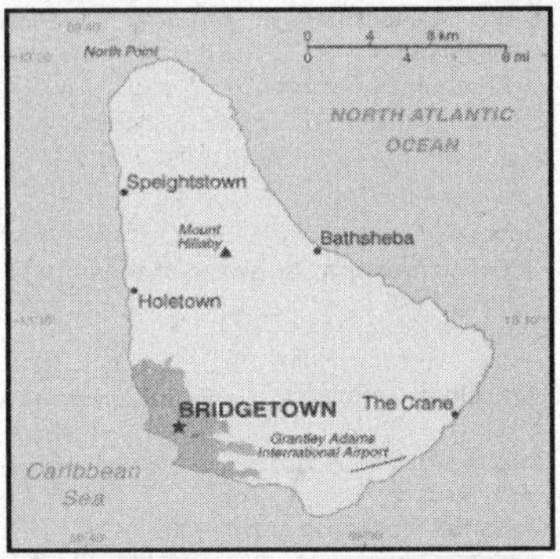

INTRODUCTION

Background: The island was uninhabited when first settled by the British in 1627. African slaves worked the sugar plantations established on the island until 1834 when slavery was abolished. The economy remained heavily dependent on sugar, rum, and molasses production through most of the 20th century. The gradual introduction of social and political reforms in the 1940s and 1950s led to complete independence from the UK in 1966. In the 1990s, tourism and manufacturing surpassed the sugar industry in economic importance.

GEOGRAPHY

Location: Caribbean, island in the North Atlantic Ocean, northeast of Venezuela

Geographic coordinates: 13 10 N, 59 32 W

Map references: Central America and the Caribbean

Area: *total:* 430 sq km
country comparison to the world: 202
land: 430 sq km
water: 0 sq km

Area—comparative: 2.5 times the size of Washington, DC

Land boundaries: 0 km

Coastline: 97 km

Maritime claims: *territorial sea:* 12 nm
exclusive economic zone: 200 nm

Climate: tropical; rainy season (June to October)

Terrain: relatively flat; rises gently to central highland region

Elevation extremes: *lowest point:* Atlantic Ocean 0 m
highest point: Mount Hillaby 336 m

Natural resources: petroleum, fish, natural gas

Land use: *arable land:* 27.91%
permanent crops: 2.33%
other: 69.77% (2011)

Irrigated land: 54.35 sq km (2003)

Total renewable water resources: 0.08 cu km (2011)

Freshwater withdrawal (domestic/industrial/agricultural): *total:* 0.1 cu km/yr (20%/26%/54%)
per capita: 371.3 cu m/yr (2009)

Natural hazards: infrequent hurricanes; periodic landslides

Environment—current issues: pollution of coastal waters from waste disposal by ships; soil erosion; illegal solid waste disposal threatens contamination of aquifers

Environment—international agreements: *party to:* Biodiversity, Climate Change, Climate Change-Kyoto Protocol, Desertification, Endangered Species, Hazardous Wastes, Law of the Sea, Marine Dumping, Ozone Layer Protection, Ship Pollution, Wetlands
signed, but not ratified: none of the selected agreements

Geography—note: easternmost Caribbean island

PEOPLE AND SOCIETY

Nationality: *noun:* Barbadian(s) or Bajan (colloquial)
adjective: Barbadian or Bajan (colloquial)

Ethnic groups: black 92.4%, white 2.7%, mixed 3.1%, East Indian 1.3%, other 0.2%, unspecified 0.2% (2010 est.)

Languages: English (official), Bajan (English-based creole language, widely spoken in informal settings)

Religions: Protestant 66.3% (includes Anglican 23.9%, other Pentecostal 19.5%, Adventist 5.9%, Methodist 4.2%, Wesleyan 3.4%, Nazarene 3.2%, Church of God 2.4%, Baptist 1.8%, Moravian 1.2%, other Protestant .8%), Roman Catholic 3.8%, other Christian 5.4% (includes Jehovah's Witness 2.0%, other 3.4%), Rastafarian 1%, other 1.5%, none 20.6%, unspecified 1.2% (2010 est.)

Population: 289,680 (July 2014 est.)
country comparison to the world: 181

Age structure: *0-14 years:* 18.4% (male 26,709/female 26,716)
15-24 years: 13.6% (male 19,705/female 19,754)
25-54 years: 45% (male 64,821/female 65,394)
55-64 years: 10.5% (male 16,837/female 19,286)
65 years and over: 10.2% (male 12,068/female 18,390) (2014 est.)

Dependency ratios: *total dependency ratio:* 42.3%
youth dependency ratio: 26.9%
elderly dependency ratio: 15.5%
potential support ratio: 6.5% (2013)

Median age: *total:* 37.6 years
male: 36.5 years
female: 38.7 years (2014 est.)

Population growth rate: 0.33% (2014 est.)
country comparison to the world: 169

Birth rate: 11.97 births/1,000 population (2014 est.)
country comparison to the world: 166

Death rate: 8.41 deaths/1,000 population (2014 est.)
country comparison to the world: 83

Net migration rate: -0.3 migrant(s)/1,000 population (2014 est.)
country comparison to the world: 125

Urbanization: *urban population:* 44% of total population (2010)
rate of urbanization: 1.7% annual rate of change (2010-15 est.)

Major urban areas—population: BRIDGETOWN (capital) 122,000 (2011)

Sex ratio: *at birth:* 1.01 male(s)/female
0-14 years: 1 male(s)/female
15-24 years: 1 male(s)/female
25-54 years: 0.99 male(s)/female
55-64 years: 0.94 male(s)/female
65 years and over: 0.65 male(s)/female
total population: 0.94 male(s)/female (2014 est.)

Maternal mortality rate: 51 deaths/100,000 live births (2010)
country comparison to the world: 106

Infant mortality rate: *total:* 10.93 deaths/1,000 live births
country comparison to the world: 132
male: 12.58 deaths/1,000 live births
female: 9.26 deaths/1,000 live births (2014 est.)

Life expectancy at birth: *total population:* 74.99 years
country comparison to the world: 102
male: 72.64 years
female: 77.37 years (2014 est.)

Total fertility rate: 1.68 children born/woman (2014 est.)
country comparison to the world: 174

Health expenditures: 7.7% of GDP (2011)
country comparison to the world: 68

Physicians density: 1.81 physicians/1,000 population (2005)

Hospital bed density: 6.6 beds/1,000 population (2010)

Drinking water source:
Improved:
urban: 99.8% of population
rural: 99.8% of population
total: 99.8% of population
unimproved:
urban: 0.2% of population
rural: 0.2% of population
total: 0.2% of population (2011 est.)

Sanitation facility access:
Improved:
urban: 100% of population
rural: 100% of population
total: 100% of population (2010 est.)

HIV/AIDS—adult prevalence rate: 0.9% (2012 est.)
country comparison to the world: 49

HIV/AIDS—people living with HIV/AIDS: 1,500 (2012 est.)
country comparison to the world: 140

HIV/AIDS—deaths: NA (2009 est.)

Obesity—adult prevalence rate: 34.7% (2008)
country comparison to the world: 14

Education expenditures: 5.6% of GDP (2012)
country comparison to the world: 54

Literacy: *definition:* age 15 and over has ever attended school
total population: 99.7%
male: 99.7%
female: 99.7% (2002 est.)

School life expectancy (primary to tertiary education): *total:* 15 years
male: 14 years
female: 17 years (2011)

Unemployment, youth ages 15-24: *total:* 26.2%
country comparison to the world: 38
male: 24.1%
female: 28.7% (2003)

GOVERNMENT

Country name: *conventional long form:* none
conventional short form: Barbados

Government type: parliamentary democracy and a Commonwealth realm

Capital: *name:* Bridgetown
geographic coordinates: 13 06 N, 59 37 W
time difference: UTC-4 (1 hour ahead of Washington, DC during Standard Time)

Administrative divisions: 11 parishes and 1 city*; Bridgetown*, Christ Church, Saint Andrew, Saint George, Saint James, Saint John, Saint Joseph, Saint Lucy, Saint Michael, Saint Peter, Saint Philip, Saint Thomas

Independence: 30 November 1966 (from the UK)

National holiday: Independence Day, 30 November (1966)

Constitution: adopted 22 November 1966, effective 30 November 1966; amended several times, last in 2003 (2011)

Legal system: English common law; no judicial review of legislative acts

International law organization participation: accepts compulsory ICJ jurisdiction with reservations; accepts ICCt jurisdiction

Suffrage: 18 years of age; universal

Executive branch: *chief of state:* Queen ELIZABETH II (since 6 February 1952); represented by Governor General Elliot BELGRAVE (since 1 June 2012)
head of government: Prime Minister Freundel STUART (since 23 October 2010)
cabinet: Cabinet appointed by the governor general on the advice of the prime minister (For more information visit the World Leaders website)
elections: the monarchy is hereditary; governor general appointed by the monarch; following legislative elections, the leader of the majority party or the leader of the majority coalition is usually appointed prime minister by the governor general; the prime minister recommends the deputy prime minister

Legislative branch: bicameral Parliament consists of the Senate (21 seats; members appointed by the governor general—12 on the advice of the Prime Minister, 2 on the advice of the opposition leader, and 7 at his discretion) and the House of Assembly (30 seats; members are elected by direct popular vote to serve five-year terms)
elections: House of Assembly—last held on 21 February 2013 (next to be called in 2018)
election results: House of Assembly—percent of vote by party—DLP 51.3%, BLP 48.3%, other .4%; seats by party—DLP 16, BLP 14

Judicial branch: *highest court(s):* Supreme Court (consists of the High Court with 8 justices) and the Court of Appeal (consists of the chief Justice and president of the court and 4 justices

note - Barbados, a member of the Caribbean Court of Justice, replaced the Judicial Committee of the Privy Council (in London) as the final court of appeal *judge selection and term of office:* Supreme Court chief justice appointed by the governor-general on the recommendation of the prime minister and opposition leader of Parliament; other justices appointed by the governor-general on the recommendation of the Judicial and Legal Service Commission, a 5-member independent body consisting of the Supreme Court chief justice, the commission head, and governor-general appointees recommended by the prime minister; justices serve until mandatory retirement at age 65

subordinate courts: Magistrates' Courts

Political parties and leaders: Barbados Labor Party or BLP [Owen ARTHUR]; Democratic Labor Party or DLP [Freundel STUART]; People's Empowerment Party or PEP [David COMISSIONG]

Political pressure groups and leaders: Barbados Secondary Teachers' Union or BSTU [Mary REDMAN]; Barbados Union of Teachers or BUT [Karen BEST]; Congress of Trade Unions and Staff Associations of Barbados or CTUSAB, (includes the BWU, NUPW, BUT, and BSTU) [Leroy TROTMAN]; Barbados Workers Union or BWU [Linda BROOKS]; Clement Payne Labor Union [David COMISSIONG]; National Union of Public Workers [Walter MALONEY]

International organization participation: ACP, AOSIS, C, Caricom, CDB, CELAC, FAO, G-77, IADB, IBRD, ICAO, ICRM, IDA, IFAD, IFC, IFRCS, ILO, IMF, IMO, Interpol, IOC, ISO, ITSO, ITU, ITUC (NGOs), LAES, MIGA, NAM, OAS, OPANAL, OPCW, UN, UNCTAD, UNESCO, UNIDO, UPU, WCO, WFTU (NGOs), WHO, WIPO, WMO, WTO

Diplomatic representation in the US: *chief of mission:* Ambassador John E. BEALE (since 29 January 2009)
chancery: 2144 Wyoming Avenue NW, Washington, DC 20008
telephone: [1] (202) 939-9200
FAX: [1] (202) 332-7467
consulate(s) general: Miami, New York
consulate(s): Los Angeles

Diplomatic representation from the US: *chief of mission:* Ambassador Larry L. PALMER (since 9 May 2012); note - also accredited to Antigua and Barbuda, Dominica, Grenada, Saint Kitts and Nevis, Saint Lucia, and Saint Vincent and the Grenadines
embassy: U.S. Embassy, Wildey Business Park, Wildey, St. Michael BB 14006
mailing address: P. O. Box 302, Bridgetown BB 11000; (Department Name) Unit 3120, DPO AA 34055
telephone: [1] (246) 227-4000
FAX: [1] (246) 431-0179

Flag description: three equal vertical bands of blue (hoist side), gold, and blue with the head of a black trident centered on the gold band; the band colors represent the blue of the sea and sky and the gold of the beaches; the trident head represents independence and a break with the past (the colonial coat of arms contained a complete trident)

National symbol(s): Neptune's trident

National anthem: *name:* "The National Anthem of Barbados"
lyrics/music: Irving BURGIE/C. Van Roland EDWARDS
note: adopted 1966; the anthem is also known as "In Plenty and In Time of Need"

ECONOMY

Economy—overview: Barbados is the wealthiest and most developed country in the Eastern Caribbean and enjoys one of the highest per capita incomes in Latin America. Historically, the Barbadian economy was dependent on sugarcane cultivation and related activities. However, in recent years the economy has diversified into light industry and tourism with about four-fifths of GDP and of exports being attributed to services. Offshore finance and information services are important foreign exchange earners and thrive from having the same time zone as eastern US financial centers and a relatively highly educated workforce. Barbados' tourism, financial services, and construction industries have been hard hit since the onset of the global economic crisis in 2008. Barbados' public debt-to-GDP ratio rose from 56% in 2008 to 90.5% in 2013. Growth prospects are limited because of a weak tourism outlook and planned austerity measures.

GDP (purchasing power parity): $7.004 billion (2013 est.)
country comparison to the world: 162
$7.056 billion (2012 est.)
$7.056 billion (2011 est.)
note: data are in 2013 US dollars

GDP (official exchange rate): $4.262 billion (2013 est.)

GDP—real growth rate: -0.8% (2013 est.)
country comparison to the world: 202
0% (2012 est.)
0.8% (2011 est.)

GDP—per capita (PPP): $25,100 (2013 est.)
country comparison to the world: 60
$25,400 (2012 est.)
$25,400 (2011 est.)
note: data are in 2013 US dollars

Gross national saving: 9% of GDP (2013 est.)
country comparison to the world: 142
9.4% of GDP (2012 est.)
3.4% of GDP (2011 est.)

GDP— composition, by end use: household *consumption:* 81.7%
government consumption: 15.4%
investment in fixed capital: 14.3%
investment in inventories: 1.9%
exports of goods and services: 40.5%
imports of goods and services: -53.8% (2013 est.)

GDP—composition, by sector of origin: *agriculture:* 3.1%
industry: 13.9%
services: 83% (2013 est.)

Agriculture—products: sugarcane, vegetables, cotton

Industries: tourism, sugar, light manufacturing, component assembly for export

Industrial production growth rate: -0.7%
country comparison to the world: 173

Labor force: 141,800 (2013 est.)
country comparison to the world: 179

Labor force—by occupation: *agriculture:* 10%
industry: 15%
services: 75% (1996 est.)

Unemployment rate: 11.4% (2013 est.)
country comparison to the world: 119
11.6% (2012 est.)

Population below poverty line: NA%

Household income or consumption by percentage share: *lowest 10%:* NA% *highest 10%:* NA%

Budget: *revenues:* $1.15 billion (2013 est.)
expenditures: $1.45 billion (2013 est.)

Taxes and other revenues: 27% of GDP (2013 est.)
country comparison to the world: 109

Budget surplus (+) or deficit (-): -7% of GDP (2013 est.)
country comparison to the world: 187

Public debt: 90.5% of GDP (2013 est.)
country comparison to the world: 21
85.6% of GDP (2012 est.)

Fiscal year: 1 April—31 March

Inflation rate (consumer prices): 2.1% (2013 est.)
country comparison to the world: 70
4.8% (2012 est.)

Central bank discount rate: 7% (31 December 2010 est.)
country comparison to the world: 43
7% (31 December 2009 est.)

Commercial bank prime lending rate: 8.5% (31 December 2013 est.)
country comparison to the world: 109
8.7% (31 December 2012 est.)

Stock of narrow money: $1.749 billion (31 December 2013 est.)
country comparison to the world: 132
$1.711 billion (31 December 2012 est.)

Stock of broad money: $4.229 billion (31 December 2013 est.)
country comparison to the world: 132
$4.198 billion (31 December 2012 est.)

Stock of domestic credit: $5.035 billion (31 December 2013 est.)
country comparison to the world: 115
$4.874 billion (31 December 2012 est.)

Market value of publicly traded shares: $4.495 billion (31 December 2012 est.)
country comparison to the world: 86
$4.571 billion (31 December 2011)
$4.366 billion (31 December 2010 est.)

Current account balance: -$276.6 million (2013 est.)

country comparison to the world: 90
-$204.4 million (2012 est.)

Exports: $1.051 billion (2013 est.)
country comparison to the world: 157
$1.039 billion (2012 est.)

Exports—commodities: manufactures, sugar and molasses, rum, other foods and beverages, chemicals, electrical components

Exports—partners: Trinidad and Tobago 20.8%, US 11.9%, St. Lucia 9.7%, St. Vincent and the Grenadines 6%, Jamaica 5.6%, Antigua and Barbuda 4.9%, St.Kitts and Nevis 4.6%, UK 4.4% (2012)

Imports: $1.674 billion (2013 est.)
country comparison to the world: 170
$1.584 billion (2012 est.)

Imports—commodities: consumer goods, machinery, foodstuffs, construction materials, chemicals, fuel, electrical components

Imports—partners: Trinidad and Tobago 35.9%, US 26.9%, China 5.6% (2012)

Reserves of foreign exchange and gold: $712.6 million (31 December 2013 est.)
country comparison to the world: 145
$839.7 million (31 December 2012 est.)

Debt—external: $4.49 billion (2010 est.)
country comparison to the world: 125
$668 million (2003 est.)

Exchange rates: Barbadian dollars (BBD) per US dollar—
2 (2013 est.)
2 (2012 est.)
2 (2010 est.)
note: the Barbadian dollar is pegged to the US dollar

ENERGY

Electricity—production: 1.002 billion kWh (2011 est.)
country comparison to the world: 145

Electricity—consumption: 986 million kWh (2010 est.)
country comparison to the world: 150

Electricity—exports: 0 kWh (2012 est.)
country comparison to the world: 101

Electricity—imports: 0 kWh (2012 est.)
country comparison to the world: 116

Electricity—installed generating capacity: 239,000 kW (2010 est.)
country comparison to the world: 157

Electricity—from fossil fuels: 100% of total installed capacity (2010 est.)
country comparison to the world: 5

Electricity—from nuclear fuels: 0% of total installed capacity (2010 est.)
country comparison to the world: 44

Electricity—from hydroelectric plants: 0% of total installed capacity (2010 est.)
country comparison to the world: 156

Electricity—from other renewable sources: 0% of total installed capacity (2010 est.)
country comparison to the world: 154

Crude oil—production: 1,001 bbl/day (2012 est.)
country comparison to the world: 108

Crude oil—exports: 764.5 bbl/day (2010 est.)
country comparison to the world: 70

Crude oil—imports: 0 bbl/day (2010 est.)
country comparison to the world: 156

Crude oil—proved reserves: 2.26 million bbl (1 January 2013 es)
country comparison to the world: 96

Refined petroleum products—production: 31.2 bbl/day (2010 est.)
country comparison to the world: 115

Refined petroleum products—consumption: 8,339 bbl/day (2011 est.)
country comparison to the world: 157

Refined petroleum products—exports: 0 bbl/day (2010 est.)
country comparison to the world: 150

Refined petroleum products—imports: 8,736 bbl/day (2010 est.)
country comparison to the world: 134

Natural gas—production: 20 million cu m (2010 est.)
country comparison to the world: 89

Natural gas—consumption: 20 million cu m (2010 est.)
country comparison to the world: 111

Natural gas—exports: 0 cu m (2011 est.)
country comparison to the world: 61

Natural gas—imports: 0 cu m (2011 est.)
country comparison to the world: 156

Natural gas—proved reserves: 113.3 million cu m (1 January 2013 es)
country comparison to the world: 106

Carbon dioxide emissions from consumption of energy: 1.442 million Mt (2011 est.)
country comparison to the world: 157

COMMUNICATIONS

Telephones—main lines in use: 144,000 (2012)
country comparison to the world: 137

Telephones—mobile cellular: 347,000 (2012)
country comparison to the world: 172

Telephone system: *general assessment:* island-wide automatic telephone system
domestic: fixed-line teledensity of roughly 50 per 100 persons; mobile-cellular telephone density approaching 125 per 100 persons
international: country code—1-246; landing point for the East Caribbean Fiber System (ECFS) submarine cable with links to 13 other islands in the eastern Caribbean extending from the British Virgin Islands to Trinidad; satellite earth stations—1 (Intelsat-Atlantic Ocean); tropospheric scatter to Trinidad and Saint Lucia (2009)

Broadcast media: government-owned Caribbean Broadcasting Corporation (CBC) operates the lone terrestrial TV station; CBC also operates a multi-channel cable TV subscription service; roughly a dozen radio stations, consisting of a CBC-operated network operating alongside privately owned radio stations (2007)

Internet country code: .bb

Internet hosts: 1,524 (2012)
country comparison to the world: 167

Internet users: 188,000 (2008)
country comparison to the world: 143

TRANSPORTATION

Airports: 1 (2013)
country comparison to the world: 236

Airports—with paved runways: *total:* 1
over 3,047 m: 1 (2013)

Pipelines: gas 33 km; oil 64 km; refined products 6 km (2013)

Roadways: *total:* 1,600 km
country comparison to the world: 176
paved: 1,600 km (2011)

Merchant marine: *total:* 109
country comparison to the world: 49
by type: bulk carrier 23, cargo 52, chemical tanker 13, container 6, passenger 1, passenger/cargo 1, petroleum tanker 8, refrigerated cargo 4, roll on/roll off 1
foreign-owned: 83 (Canada 11, Greece 14, Iran 5, Lebanon 2, Norway 38, Sweden 4, Syria 1, Turkey 1, UAE 1, UK 6) (2010)

Ports and terminals: *major seaport(s):* Bridgetown

MILITARY

Military branches: *Royal Barbados Defense Force:* Troops Command, Barbados Coast Guard (2011)

Military service age and obligation: 18 years of age for voluntary military service, or earlier with parental consent; no conscription (2013)

Manpower available for military service: *males age 16-49:* 73,820
females age 16-49: 73,835 (2010 est.)

Manpower fit for military service: *males age 16-49:* 58,125
females age 16-49: 58,016 (2010 est.)

Manpower reaching militarily significant age annually: *male:* 1,842
female: 1,849 (2010 est.)

Military—note: the Royal Barbados Defense Force includes a land-based Troop Command and a small Coast Guard; the primary role of the land element is island defense against external aggression; the Command consists of a single, part-time battalion with a small regular cadre deployed throughout the island; the cadre increasingly supports the police in patrolling the coastline for smuggling and other illicit activities (2007)

TRANSNATIONAL ISSUES

Disputes—international: Barbados and Trinidad and Tobago abide by the April 2006 Permanent Court of Arbitration decision delimiting a maritime boundary and limiting catches of flying fish in Trinidad and Tobago's exclusive economic zone; joins other Caribbean states to counter Venezuela's claim that Aves Island sustains human habitation, a criterion under the UN Convention on the Law of the Sea, which permits Venezuela to extend its Economic Exclusion Zone/continental shelf over a large portion of the eastern Caribbean Sea

Trafficking in persons: *current situation:* Barbados is a source and destination country for men, women, and children subjected to sex trafficking and forced labor; legal and illegal female migrants from Jamaica, the Dominican Republic, and Guyana seem most vulnerable to forced prostitution; Barbadian and immigrant children are prostituted in exchange for material goods; in the past, foreigners are reported to have been forced to work in the domestic service, agriculture, and construction industries
tier rating: Tier 2 Watch List - Barbados does not fully comply with the minimum standards for the elimination of trafficking; however, it is making significant efforts to do so; the country was granted a waiver of an otherwise required downgrade to Tier 3 because the government adopted a national action plan on human trafficking that specifies implementing agencies and addresses prosecution, protection, and prevention measures; the government conducted at least two sex trafficking investigations in 2012, as opposed to none in the previous year but did not report any prosecutions or convictions of trafficking offenses; Barbadian law does not appear to prohibit all forms of human trafficking and does not prescribe sufficiently stringent penalties; government efforts to prevent human trafficking included broadcasting short public awareness messages, holding town hall meetings, and funding a hotline (2013)

Illicit drugs: one of many Caribbean transshipment points for narcotics bound for Europe and the US; offshore financial center

BELARUS

INTRODUCTION

Background: After seven decades as a constituent republic of the USSR, Belarus attained its independence in 1991. It has retained closer political and economic ties to Russia than have any of the other former Soviet republics. Belarus and Russia signed a treaty on a two-state union on 8 December 1999 envisioning greater political and economic integration. Although Belarus agreed to a framework to carry out the accord, serious implementation has yet to take place. Since his election in July 1994 as the country's first directly elected president, Aleksandr LUKASHENKO has steadily consolidated his power through authoritarian means and a centralized economic system. Government restrictions on freedom of speech and the press, peaceful assembly, and religion remain in place.

GEOGRAPHY

Location: Eastern Europe, east of Poland

Geographic coordinates: 53 00 N, 28 00 E

Map references: Europe

Area: *total:* 207,600 sq km
country comparison to the world: 86
land: 202,900 sq km
water: 4,700 sq km

Area—comparative: slightly smaller than Kansas

Land boundaries: *total:* 3,306 km
border countries: Latvia 171 km, Lithuania 680 km, Poland 605 km, Russia 959 km, Ukraine 891 km

Coastline: 0 km (landlocked)

Maritime claims: none (landlocked)

Climate: cold winters, cool and moist summers; transitional between continental and maritime

Terrain: generally flat and contains much marshland

Elevation extremes: *lowest point:* Nyoman River 90 m
highest point: Dzyarzhynskaya Hara 346 m

Natural resources: timber, peat deposits, small quantities of oil and natural gas, granite, dolomitic limestone, marl, chalk, sand, gravel, clay

Land use: *arable land:* 26.63%
permanent crops: 0.59%
other: 72.78% (2011)

Irrigated land: 1,150 sq km (2003)

Total renewable water resources: 58 cu km (2011)

Freshwater withdrawal (domestic/industrial/agricultural): *total:* 4.34 cu km/yr (32%/65%/3%)
per capita: 435.4 cu m/yr (2009)

Natural hazards: NA

Environment—current issues: soil pollution from pesticide use; southern part of the country contaminated with fallout from 1986 nuclear reactor accident at Chornobyl' in northern Ukraine

Environment—international agreements: *party to:* Air Pollution, Air Pollution-Nitrogen Oxides, Air Pollution-Sulfur 85, Biodiversity, Climate Change, Climate Change-Kyoto Protocol, Desertification, Endangered Species, Environmental Modification, Hazardous Wastes, Law of the Sea, Marine Dumping, Ozone Layer Protection, Ship Pollution, Wetlands
signed, but not ratified: none of the selected agreements

Geography—note: landlocked; glacial scouring accounts for the flatness of Belarusian terrain and for its 11,000 lakes

PEOPLE AND SOCIETY

Nationality: *noun:* Belarusian(s)
adjective: Belarusian

Ethnic groups: Belarusian 83.7%, Russian 8.3%, Polish 3.1%, Ukrainian 1.7%, other 2.4%, unspecified 0.9% (2009 est.)

Languages: Belarusian (official) 23.4%, Russian (official) 70.2%, other 3.1% (includes small Polish- and Ukrainian-speaking minorities), unspecified 3.3% (2009 est.)

Religions: Eastern Orthodox 80%, other (including Roman Catholic, Protestant, Jewish, and Muslim) 20% (1997 est.)

Population: 9,608,058 (July 2014 est.)
country comparison to the world: 93

Age structure: *0-14 years:* 15.4% (male 759,285/female 717,118)
15-24 years: 11.7% (male 575,907/female 544,170)
25-54 years: 45.5% (male 2,141,419/female 2,227,433)
55-64 years: 14.2% (male 562,639/female 716,216)
65 years and over: 14% (male 430,225/female 933,646) (2014 est.)

Dependency ratios: *total dependency ratio:* 41.1% *youth dependency ratio:* 21.6% *elderly dependency ratio:* 19.5% *potential support ratio:* 5.1 (2013)

Median age: *total:* 39.4 years
male: 36.3 years
female: 42.4 years (2014 est.)

Population growth rate: -0.19% (2014 est.)
country comparison to the world: 213

Birth rate: 10.86 births/1,000 population (2014 est.)
country comparison to the world: 179

Death rate: 13.51 deaths/1,000 population (2014 est.)
country comparison to the world: 16

Net migration rate: 0.78 migrant(s)/1,000 population (2014 est.)
country comparison to the world: 65

Urbanization: *urban population:* 75% of total population (2011)
rate of urbanization: 0.21% annual rate of change (2010-15 est.)

Major cities—population: MINSK (capital) 1.861 million (2011)

Sex ratio: *at birth:* 1.06 male(s)/female
0-14 years: 1.06 male(s)/female
15-24 years: 1.06 male(s)/female
25-54 years: 0.96 male(s)/female
55-64 years: 0.87 male(s)/female
65 years and over: 0.46 male(s)/female
total population: 0.87 male(s)/female (2014 est.)

Mother's mean age at first birth: 24.9 (2010 est.)

Maternal mortality rate: 4 deaths/100,000 live births (2010)
country comparison to the world: 181

Infant mortality rate: *total:* 3.64 deaths/1,000 live births
country comparison to the world: 206
male: 4.07 deaths/1,000 live births
female: 3.19 deaths/1,000 live births (2014 est.)

Life expectancy at birth: *total population:* 72.15 years
country comparison to the world: 138
male: 66.53 years
female: 78.1 years (2014 est.)

Total fertility rate: 1.47 children born/woman (2014 est.)
country comparison to the world: 195

Contraceptive prevalence rate: 72.6% (2005)

Health expenditures: 5.3% of GDP (2011)
country comparison to the world: 131

Physicians density: 3.76 physicians/1,000 population (2011)

Hospital bed density: 11.1 beds/1,000 population (2011)

Drinking water source:
Improved:
urban: 99.8% of population
rural: 99.4% of population
total: 99.7% of population
Unimproved:
urban: 0.2% of population
rural: 0.6% of population
total: 0.3% of population (2011 est.)

Sanitation facility access:
Improved:
urban: 91.6% of population
rural: 97.2% of population
total: 93% of population
Unimproved:
urban: 8.4% of population
rural: 2.8% of population
total: 7% of population (2011 est.)

HIV/AIDS—adult prevalence rate: 0.4% (2012 est.)
country comparison to the world: 76

HIV/AIDS—people living with HIV/AIDS: 23,200 (2012 est.)
country comparison to the world: 78

HIV/AIDS—deaths: 1,200 (2012 est.)
country comparison to the world: 69

Obesity—adult prevalence rate: 24.3% (2008)
country comparison to the world: 65

Children under the age of 5 years underweight: 1.3% (2005)
country comparison to the world: 130

Education expenditures: 5.1% of GDP (2012)
country comparison to the world: 71

Literacy: *definition:* age 15 and over can read and write
total population: 99.6%

male: 99.8%
female: 99.5% (2009 est.)

School life expectancy (primary to tertiary education): *total:* 16 years
male: 15 years
female: 16 years (2012)

Child labor—children ages 5-14: *total number:* 54,218 *percentage:* 5 % (2005 est.)

Unemployment, youth ages 15-24: *total:* 12.6%
country comparison to the world: 96
male: 12.4%
female: 12.6% (2009)

GOVERNMENT

Country name: *conventional long form:* Republic of Belarus
conventional short form: Belarus
local long form: Respublika Byelarus'/Respublika Belarus'
local short form: Byelarus'
former: Belorussian (Byelorussian) Soviet Socialist Republic

Government type: republic in name, although in fact a dictatorship

Capital: *name:* Minsk
geographic coordinates: 53 54 N, 27 34 E
time difference: UTC+2 (7 hours ahead of Washington, DC during Standard Time) daylight saving time: none scheduled for 2013

Administrative divisions: 6 provinces (voblastsi, singular—voblasts') and 1 municipality* (horad); Brest, Homyel' (Gomel), Horad Minsk* (Minsk City), Hrodna (Grodno), Mahilyow (Mogilev), Minsk, Vitsyebsk (Vitebsk)
note: administrative divisions have the same names as their administrative centers; Russian spelling provided for reference when different from Belarusian

Independence: 25 August 1991 (from the Soviet Union)

National holiday: Independence Day, 3 July (1944); note—3 July 1944 was the date Minsk was liberated from German troops, 25 August 1991 was the date of independence from the Soviet Union

Constitution: several previous; latest drafted between late 1991 and early 1994, signed 15 March 1994; amended 1996, 2004 (2013)

Legal system: civil law system; note—nearly all major codes (civil, civil procedure, criminal, criminal procedure, family and labor) have been revised and came into force in 1999 or 2000

International law organization participation: has not submitted an ICJ jurisdiction declaration; non-party state to the ICCt

Suffrage: 18 years of age; universal

Executive branch: *chief of state:* president Aleksandr LUKASHENKO (since 20 July 1994); note—the US does not recognize the results of the 19 December 2010 elections under which the Central Election Commission of Belarus declared LUKASHENKO president
head of government: prime minister Mikhail MYASNIKOVICH (since 28 December 2010); first deputy prime minister Vladimir SEMASHKO (since December 2003)
cabinet: Council of Ministers (For more information visit the World Leaders website)
elections: president elected by popular vote for a five-year term; first election took place on 23 June and 10 July 1994; according to the 1994 constitution, the next election should have been held in 1999, however, Aleksandr LUKASHENKO extended his term to 2001 via a November 1996 referendum; subsequent election held on 9 September 2001; an October 2004 referendum ended presidential term limits and allowed the president to run in a third (19 March 2006) and fourth election (19 December 2010); prime minister and deputy prime ministers appointed by the president
election results: Aleksandr LUKASHENKO reelected president; percent of vote—Aleksandr LUKASHENKO 79.7%, Andrey SANNIKOV 2.6%, other candidates 17.7%; note—election marred by electoral fraud

Legislative branch: bicameral national assembly or natsionalnoye sobraniye consists of the Council of the Republic or Sovet Respubliki (64 seats; 56 members elected by regional and Minsk city councils and 8 members appointed by the president, to serve four-year terms) and the Chamber of Representatives or Palata Predstaviteley (110 seats; members elected by popular vote to serve four-year terms); note—the US does not recognize the legitimacy of the national assembly
elections: Palata Predstaviteley—last held on 23 September 2012 (next to be held September 2016); OSCE observers determined that the election was neither free nor impartial and that vote counting was problematic in a number of polling stations; pro-LUKASHENKO candidates won every seat with no opposition representation in the chamber; international observers determined that the previous election, on 28 September 2008, despite minor improvements also fell short of democratic standards, with pro-LUKASHENKO candidates winning every seat
election results: Sovet Respubliki—percent of vote by party—NA; seats by party—NA; Palata Predstaviteley [2008]—percent of vote by party—NA; seats by party—KPB 6, AP 1, no affiliation 103; Palata Predstaviteley [2012]—percent of vote by party—NA; seats by party—KPB 3, AP 1, no affiliation 106

Judicial branch: *highest court(s):* Supreme Court (consists of the chairman, deputy chairman, and NA judges);Constitutional Court (consists of 12 judges including a chairman and deputy chairman)
judge selection and term of office: Supreme Court judges appointed by the president with the consent of the Council of the Republic; judges initially appointed for 5 years and evaluated for life appointment;Constitutional Court judges - 6 appointed by the president and 6 elected by the Chamber of Representatives; term of judges is 11 years with an age limit of 70 subordinate courts: regional, district, city, town, and military courts

Political parties and leaders: *pro-government parties:* Belarusian Agrarian Party or AP [Mikhail SHIMANSKY]; Belarusian Patriotic Movement (Belarusian Patriotic Party) or BPR [Nikolay ULAKHOVICH, chairman]; Communist Party of Belarus or KPB [Igor KARPENKO]; Liberal Democratic Party or LDP [Sergey GAYDUKEVICH]; Republican Party of Labor and Justice [Vasiliy ZADNEPRYANYY]
opposition parties: Belarusian Christian Democracy Party [Pavel SEVERINETS] (unregistered): Belarusian Party of the Left "Fair World" [Sergey KALYAKIN]; Belarusian Popular Front or BPF [Aleksey YANUKEVICH]; Belarusian Social-Democratic Hramada [Stanislav SHUSHKEVICH]; Belarusian Social Democratic Party Hramada ("Assembly") or BSDPH [Alrina VESHTARD]; Belarusian Social Democratic Party People's Assembly ("Narodnaya Hramada") [Nikolay STATKEVICH] (unregistered); Christian Conservative Party or BPF [Zyanon PAZNIAK]; European Belarus Campaign [Andrey SANNIKOV]; Party of Freedom and Progress [Vladimir NOVOSYAD] (unregistered); "Tell the Truth" Campaign [Vladimir NEKLYAYEV]; United Civic Party or UCP [Anatoliy LEBEDKO]

Political pressure groups and leaders: Assembly of Pro-Democratic NGOs [Sergey MATSKEVICH] (unregistered)Belarusian Congress of Democratic Trade Unions [Aleksandr YAROSHUK] Belarusian Association of Journalists [Zhana LITVINA] Belarusian Helsinki Committee [Aleh HULAK] Belarusian Independence Bloc (unregistered) and For Freedom movement [Aleksandr MILINKEVICH] Belarusian Organization of Working Women [Irina ZHIKHAR] BPF-Youth [Andrus KRECHKA] (unregistered) Charter 97 [Andrey SANNIKOV] (unregistered) Perspektiva small business association [Anatol SHUMCHENKO] Nasha Vyasna ("Our Spring") human rights center [Ales BYALYATSKI] (unregistered) "Tell the Truth" Movement [Vladimir NEKLYAYEV] (unregistered) Women's Independent Democratic Movement [Ludmila PETINA] Young Belarus (Malady Belarus) [Zmitser KASPYAROVICH] (unregistered) Youth Front (Malady Front) [Zmitser DASHKEVICH] (unregistered)

International organization participation: BSEC (observer), CBSS (observer), CEI, CIS, CSTO, EAEC, EAPC, EBRD, FAO, GCTU, IAEA, IBRD, ICAO, ICC (NGOs), ICRM, IDA, IFC, IFRCS, ILO, IMF, IMSO, Interpol, IOC, IOM, IPU, ISO, ITU, ITUC (NGOs), MIGA, NAM, NSG, OPCW, OSCE, PCA, PFP, SCO (dialogue member), UN, UNCTAD, UNESCO, UNIDO, UNIFIL, UNWTO, UPU, WCO, WFTU (NGOs), WHO, WIPO, WMO, WTO (observer), ZC

Diplomatic representation in the US: *chief of mission:* Ambassador (vacant); Charge d'Affaires Oleg KRAVCHENKO
chancery: 1619 New Hampshire Avenue NW, Washington, DC 20009
telephone: [1] (202) 986-1604
FAX: [1] (202) 986-1805
consulate(s) general: New York

Diplomatic representation from the US: *chief of mission:* Ambassador (vacant); Charge d'Affaires Ethan GOLDRICH (since July 2012)
embassy: 46 Starovilenskaya Street, Minsk 220002
mailing address: PSC 78, Box B Minsk, APO 09723
telephone: [375] (17) 210-12-83
FAX: [375] (17) 234-7853

Flag description: red horizontal band (top) and green horizontal band one-half the width of the red band; a white vertical stripe on the hoist side bears Belarusian national ornamentation in red; the red band color recalls past struggles from oppression, the green band represents hope and the many forests of the country

National symbol(s): mounted knight known as Pahonia (the Chaser)

National anthem: *name:* "My, Bielarusy" (We Belarusians)
lyrics/music: Mikhas KLIMKOVICH and Uladzimir KARYZNA/Nester SAKALOUSKI
note: music adopted 1955, lyrics adopted 2002; after the fall of the Soviet Union, Belarus kept the music of its Soviet-era anthem but adopted new lyrics; also known as "Dziarzauny himn Respubliki Bielarus" (State Anthem of the Republic of Belarus)

ECONOMY

Economy—overview: As part of the former Soviet Union, Belarus had a relatively well-developed industrial base; it retained this industrial base - which is now outdated, energy inefficient, and dependent on subsidized Russian energy and preferential access to Russian markets - following the breakup of the USSR. The country also has a broad agricultural base which is inefficient and dependent on government subsidies. After an initial burst of capitalist reform from 1991-94, including privatization of state enterprises, creation of institutions of private property, and development of entrepreneurship, Belarus' economic development greatly slowed. About 80% of all industry remains in state hands, and foreign investment has been hindered by a climate hostile to business. A few banks, which had been privatized after independence, were renationalized. State banks account for 75% of the banking sector. Economic output, which had declined for several years following the collapse of the Soviet Union, revived in the mid-2000s thanks to the boom in oil prices. Belarus has only small reserves of crude oil, though it imports most of its crude oil and natural gas from Russia at prices substantially below the world market. Belarus exported refined oil products at market prices produced from Russian crude oil purchased at a steep discount. In late 2006, Russia began a process of rolling back its subsidies on oil and gas to Belarus. Tensions over Russian energy reached a peak in 2010, when Russia stopped the export of all subsidized oil to Belarus save for domestic needs. In December 2010, Russia and Belarus reached a deal to restart the export of discounted oil to Belarus. Little new foreign investment has occurred in recent years. In 2011, a financial crisis began, triggered by government directed salary hikes unsupported by commensurate productivity increases. The crisis was compounded by an increased cost in Russian energy inputs and an overvalued Belarusian ruble, and eventually led to a near three-fold devaluation of the Belarusian ruble in 2011. In November 2011, Belarus agreed to sell to Russia its remaining shares in Beltransgaz, the Belarusian natural gas pipeline operator, in exchange for reduced prices for Russian natural gas. Receiving more than half of a $3 billion loan from the Russian-dominated Eurasian Economic Community (EurAsEC) Bailout Fund, a $1 billion loan from the Russian state-owned bank Sberbank, and the $2.5 billion sale of Beltranzgas to Russian state-owned Gazprom helped stabilize the situation in 2012; nevertheless, the Belarusian currency lost more than 60% of its value, as the rate of inflation reached new highs in 2011 and 2012, before calming in 2013. As of January 2014, the final tranche of the EurAsEC loan has been delayed, but in December 2013 Russia announced a new loan for Belarus of up to $2 billion for 2014. Notwithstanding foreign assistance, the Belarusian economy continues to struggle under the weight of high external debt servicing payments, a growing trade deficit, stagnant economic growth, and low foreign reserves.

GDP (purchasing power parity): $150.4 billion (2013 est.)
country comparison to the world: 63
$147.3 billion (2012 est.)
$145 billion (2011 est.)
note: data are in 2013 US dollars

GDP (official exchange rate): $69.24 billion (2013 est.)

GDP—real growth rate: 2.1% (2013 est.)
country comparison to the world: 137
1.5% (2012 est.)
5.5% (2011 est.)

GDP—per capita (PPP): $16,100 (2013 est.)
country comparison to the world: 85
$15,700 (2012 est.)
$15,400 (2011 est.)
note: data are in 2013 US dollars

Gross national saving: 24.8% of GDP (2013 est.)
country comparison to the world: 49
31.8% of GDP (2012 est.)
29.2% of GDP (2011 est.)

GDP—composition, by end use: *household consumption:* 46.3%
government consumption: 15.3%
investment in fixed capital: 30%
investment in inventories: 0.7%
exports of goods and services: 80.2%
imports of goods and services: -72.5% (2013 est.)

GDP—composition, by sector of origin: *agriculture:* 9.2%
industry: 46.2%
services: 44.7% (2013 est.)

Agriculture—products: grain, potatoes, vegetables, sugar beets, flax; beef, milk

Industries: metal-cutting machine tools, tractors, trucks, earthmovers, motorcycles, televisions, synthetic fibers, fertilizer, textiles, radios, refrigerators

Industrial production growth rate: 1% (2013 est.)
country comparison to the world: 149

Labor force: 5 million (2009)
country comparison to the world: 76

Labor force—by occupation: *agriculture:* 9.4%
industry: 45.9%
services: 44.7% (2005 est.)

Unemployment rate: 1% (2009 est.)
country comparison to the world: 6
1.6% (2005)
note: official registered unemployed; large number of underemployed workers

Population below poverty line: 27.1% (2003 est.)

Household income or consumption by percentage share: *lowest 10%:* 3.8%
highest 10%: 21.9% (2008)

Distribution of family income—Gini index: 27.2 (2008)
country comparison to the world: 127
21.7 (1998)

Budget: *revenues:* $26.68 billion
expenditures: $26.79 billion (2013 est.)

Taxes and other revenues: 38.5% of GDP (2013 est.)
country comparison to the world: 50

Budget surplus (+) or deficit (-): -0.2% of GDP (2013 est.)
country comparison to the world: 47

Public debt: 31.5% of GDP (2013 est.)
country comparison to the world: 115
31.5% of GDP (2012 est.)

Fiscal year: calendar year

Inflation rate (consumer prices): 19% (2013 est.)
country comparison to the world: 217
59.1% (2012 est.)

Central bank discount rate: 10.5% (31 December 2010 est.)
country comparison to the world: 14
13.5% (31 December 2009 est.)

Commercial bank prime lending rate: 10% (31 December 2013 est.)
country comparison to the world: 18
19.49% (31 December 2012 est.)

Stock of narrow money: $4.362 billion (31 December 2013 est.)
country comparison to the world: 109
$4.018 billion (31 December 2012 est.)

Stock of broad money: $9.073 billion (31 December 2013 est.)
country comparison to the world: 107
$7.655 billion (31 December 2012 est.)

Stock of domestic credit: $22.68 billion (31 December 2013 est.)
country comparison to the world: 78
$19.82 billion (31 December 2012 est.)

Market value of publicly traded shares: $NA

Current account balance: -$4.245 billion (2013 est.)
country comparison to the world: 163
-$1.688 billion (2012 est.)

Exports: $42.06 billion (2013 est.)
country comparison to the world: 59
$45.57 billion (2012 est.)

Exports—commodities: machinery and equipment, mineral products, chemicals, metals, textiles, foodstuffs

Exports—partners: Russia 35.4%, Netherlands 16.4%, Ukraine 12.1%, Latvia 7.1% (2012)

Imports: $45.17 billion (2013 est.)
country comparison to the world: 58
$45.01 billion (2012 est.)

Imports—commodities: mineral products, machinery and equipment, chemicals, foodstuffs, metals

Imports—partners: Russia 59.4%, Germany 5.9%, China 5.1%, Ukraine 5% (2012)

Reserves of foreign exchange and gold: $4.513 billion (31 December 2013 est.)
country comparison to the world: 97
$5.809 billion (31 December 2012 est.)

Debt—external: $1.204 billion (31 December 2013 est.)
country comparison to the world: 157
$1.225 billion (31 December 2012 est.)

Exchange rates: Belarusian rubles (BYB/BYR) per US dollar—
8,950.7 (2013 est.)
8,336.9 (2012 est.)
2,978.5 (2010 est.)
2,789.49 (2009)
2,130 (2008)

ENERGY

Electricity—production: 32.82 billion kWh (2010 est.)
country comparison to the world: 64

Electricity—consumption: 31.74 billion kWh (2010 est.)
country comparison to the world: 61

Electricity—exports: 5.067 billion kWh (2010 est.)
country comparison to the world: 28

Electricity—imports: 7.767 billion kWh (2010 est.)

country comparison to the world: 29

Electricity—installed generating capacity: 8.032 million kW (2010 est.)
country comparison to the world: 64

Electricity—from fossil fuels: 99.7% of total installed capacity (2010 est.)
country comparison to the world: 48

Electricity—from nuclear fuels: 0% of total installed capacity (2010 est.)
country comparison to the world: 54

Electricity—from hydroelectric plants: 0.2% of total installed capacity (2010 est.)
country comparison to the world: 147

Electricity—from other renewable sources: 0.1% of total installed capacity (2010 est.)
country comparison to the world: 104

Crude oil—production: 32,070 bbl/day (2012 est.)
country comparison to the world: 66

Crude oil—exports: 0 bbl/day (2010 est.)
country comparison to the world: 89

Crude oil—imports: 294,800 bbl/day (2010 est.)
country comparison to the world: 27

Crude oil—proved reserves: 198 million bbl (1 January 2013 es)
country comparison to the world: 40

Refined petroleum products—production: 346,000 bbl/day (2010 est.)
country comparison to the world: 39

Refined petroleum products—consumption: 188,800 bbl/day (2011 est.)
country comparison to the world: 61

Refined petroleum products—exports: 224,200 bbl/day (2010 est.)
country comparison to the world: 29

Refined petroleum products—imports: 43,240 bbl/day (2010 est.)
country comparison to the world: 77

Natural gas—production: 220 million cu m (2011 est.)
country comparison to the world: 78

Natural gas—consumption: 21.82 billion cu m (2010 est.)
country comparison to the world: 34

Natural gas—exports: 0 cu m (2011 est.)
country comparison to the world: 69

Natural gas—imports: 21.02 billion cu m (2011 est.)
country comparison to the world: 20

Natural gas—proved reserves: 2.832 billion cu m (1 January 2013 es)
country comparison to the world: 97

Carbon dioxide emissions from consumption of energy: 67.16 million Mt (2011 est.)
country comparison to the world: 51

COMMUNICATIONS

Telephones—main lines in use: 4.407 million (2012)
country comparison to the world: 37

Telephones—mobile cellular: 10.675 million (2012)
country comparison to the world: 75

Telephone system: *general assessment:* Belarus lags behind its neighbors in upgrading telecommunications infrastructure; modernization of the network progressing with roughly two-thirds of switching equipment now digital
domestic: state-owned Beltelcom is the sole provider of fixed-line local and long distance service; fixed-line teledensity is improving although rural areas continue to be underserved; multiple GSM mobile-cellular networks are experiencing rapid growth; mobile-cellular teledensity now exceeds 100 telephones per 100 persons
international: country code - 375; Belarus is a member of the Trans-European Line (TEL),Trans-Asia-Europe (TAE) fiber-optic line, and has access to the Trans-Siberia Line (TSL); 3 fiber-optic segments provide connectivity to Latvia, Poland, Russia, and Ukraine; worldwide service is available to Belarus through this infrastructure; additional analog lines to Russia; Intelsat, Eutelsat, and Intersputnik earth stations (2008)

Broadcast media: 4 state-controlled national TV channels; Polish and Russian TV broadcasts are available in some areas; state-run Belarusian Radio operates 3 national networks and an external service; Russian and Polish radio broadcasts are available (2007)

Internet country code: .by

Internet hosts: 295,217 (2012)
country comparison to the world: 64

Internet users: 2.643 million (2009)
country comparison to the world: 69

TRANSPORTATION

Airports: 65 (2013)
country comparison to the world: 75

Airports—with paved runways: *total:* 33
over 3,047 m: 1
2,438 to 3,047 m: 20
1,524 to 2,437 m: 4
914 to 1,523 m: 1
under 914 m: 7 (2013)

Airports—with unpaved runways: *total:* 32
over 3,047 m: 1
1,524 to 2,437 m: 1
914 to 1,523 m: 2
under 914 m: 28 (2013)

Heliports: 1 (2013)

Pipelines: gas 5,386 km; oil 1,589 km; refined products 1,730 km (2013)

Railways: *total:* 5,537 km
country comparison to the world: 32
broad gauge: 5,512 km 1.520-m gauge (874 km electrified)
standard gauge: 25 km 1.435-m gauge (2008)

Roadways: *total:* 86,392 km
country comparison to the world: 54
paved: 74,651 km
unpaved: 11,741 km (2010)

Waterways: 2,500 km (use limited by its location on the perimeter of the country and by its shallowness) (2011)
country comparison to the world: 36

Ports and terminals: *river port (s):* Mazyr (Prypyats')

MILITARY

Military branches: *Belarus Armed Forces:* Land Force, Air and Air Defense Force, Special Operations Force (2013)

Military service age and obligation: 18-27 years of age for compulsory military service; conscript service obligation is 12-18 months, depending on academic qualifications; 17 year olds are eligible to become cadets at military higher education institutes, where they are classified as military personnel (2012)

Manpower available for military service: *males age 16-49:* 2,401,785
females age 16-49: 2,429,653 (2010 est.)

Manpower fit for military service: *males age 16-49:* 1,693,626
females age 16-49: 2,012,401 (2010 est.)

Manpower reaching militarily significant age annually: *male:* 51,855
female: 48,760 (2010 est.)

Military expenditures: 1.2% of GDP (2012)
country comparison to the world: 85
1.27% of GDP (2011)
1.2% of GDP (2010)

TRANSNATIONAL ISSUES

Disputes—international: boundary demarcated with Latvia and Lithuania; Poland seeks enhanced demarcation and security along this Schengen hard border with financial assistance from the EU

Refugees and internally displaced persons: **stateless persons:** 6,969 (2012)

Trafficking in persons: *current situation:* Belarus is a source, transit, and destination country for women, men, and children subjected to sex trafficking and forced labor; women and children are trafficked to European and Middle Eastern countries and within Belarus for sexual exploitation; Belarusian men, women, and children are found in forced labor in the construction industry and other sectors in Russia and Belarus; Belarusian men seeking work abroad are increasingly subjected to forced labor
tier rating: Tier 2 Watch List - Belarus does not fully comply with the minimum standards for the elimination of trafficking; however, it is making significant efforts to do so; the government demonstrates decreased law enforcement efforts, conducting fewer trafficking investigations and convicting only one trafficking offender; while two new anti-trafficking laws were passed, they have not been fully implemented and government services to victims remain very limited; the government continues its efforts to prevent trafficking through public awareness campaigns and NGO-operated anti-trafficking hotlines (2013)

Illicit drugs: limited cultivation of opium poppy and cannabis, mostly for the domestic market; transshipment point for illicit drugs to and via Russia, and to the Baltics and Western Europe; a small and lightly regulated financial center; anti-money-laundering legislation does not meet international standards and was weakened further when know-your-customer requirements were curtailed in 2008; few investigations or prosecutions of money-laundering activities (2008)

BELGIUM

INTRODUCTION

Background: Belgium became independent from the Netherlands in 1830; it was occupied by Germany during World Wars I and II. The country prospered in the past half century as a modern, technologically advanced European state and member of NATO and the EU. Political divisions between the Dutch-speaking Flemings of the north and the French-speaking Walloons of the south have led in recent years to constitutional amendments granting these regions formal recognition and autonomy. Its capital, Brussels, is home to numerous international organizations including the EU and NATO.

GEOGRAPHY

Location: Western Europe, bordering the North Sea, between France and the Netherlands

Geographic coordinates: 50 50 N, 4 00 E

Map references: Europe

Area: *total:* 30,528 sq km
country comparison to the world: 141
land: 30,278 sq km
water: 250 sq km

Area—comparative: about the size of Maryland

Land boundaries: *total:* 1,385 km

border countries: France 620 km, Germany 167 km, Luxembourg 148 km, Netherlands 450 km

Coastline: 66.5 km

Maritime claims: *territorial sea:* 12 nm
contiguous zone: 24 nm
exclusive economic zone: geographic coordinates define outer limit continental shelf: median line with neighbors

Climate: temperate; mild winters, cool summers; rainy, humid, cloudy

Terrain: flat coastal plains in northwest, central rolling hills, rugged mountains of Ardennes Forest in southeast

Elevation extremes: *lowest point:* North Sea 0 m
highest point: Botrange 694 m

Natural resources: construction materials, silica sand, carbonates

Land use: *arable land:* 27.06%
permanent crops: 0.72% other: 72.22%
note: includes Luxembourg (2011)

Irrigated land: 233.5 sq km (2007)

Total renewable water resources: 18.3 cu km (2011)

Freshwater withdrawal (domestic/industrial/agricultural): *total:* 6.22 cu km/yr (12%/88%/1%)
per capita: 589.8 cu m/yr (2007)

Natural hazards: flooding is a threat along rivers and in areas of reclaimed coastal land, protected from the sea by concrete dikes

Environment—current issues: the environment is exposed to intense pressures from human activities: urbanization, dense transportation network, industry, extensive animal breeding and crop cultivation; air and water pollution also have repercussions for neighboring countries; uncertainties regarding federal and regional responsibilities (now resolved) had slowed progress in tackling environmental challenges

Environment—international agreements: *party to:* Air Pollution, Air Pollution-Nitrogen Oxides, Air Pollution-Persistent Organic Pollutants, Air Pollution-Sulfur 85, Air Pollution-Sulfur 94, Air Pollution-Volatile Organic Compounds, Antarctic-Environmental Protocol, Antarctic-Marine Living Resources, Antarctic Seals, Antarctic Treaty, Biodiversity, Climate Change, Climate Change-Kyoto Protocol, Desertification, Endangered Species, Environmental Modification, Hazardous Wastes, Law of the Sea, Marine Dumping, Marine Life Conservation, Ozone Layer Protection, Ship Pollution, Tropical Timber 83, Tropical Timber 94, Wetlands, Whaling
signed, but not ratified: none of the selected agreements

Geography—note: crossroads of Western Europe; most West European capitals within 1,000 km of Brussels, the seat of both the European Union and NATO

PEOPLE AND SOCIETY

Nationality: *noun:* Belgian(s)
adjective: Belgian

Ethnic groups: Fleming 58%, Walloon 31%, mixed or other 11%

Languages: Dutch (official) 60%, French (official) 40%, German (official) less than 1%, legally bilingual (Dutch and French)

Religions: Roman Catholic 75%, other (includes Protestant) 25%

Population: 10,449,361 (July 2014 est.)
country comparison to the world: 84

Age structure: *0-14 years:* 15.6% (male 830,980/female 797,624)
15-24 years: 11.7% (male 624,486/female 598,904)
25-54 years: 40.4% (male 2,131,869/female 2,086,212)
55-64 years: 19% (male 690,395/female 704,284)
65 years and over: 18.7% (male 836,685/female 1,147,922) (2014 est.)

Dependency ratios: *total dependency ratio:* 53.8%
youth dependency ratio: 26.1 %
elderly dependency ratio: 27.7 %
potential support ratio: 3.6 (2013)

Median age: *total:* 43.1 years
male: 41.7 years
female: 44.4 years (2014 est.)

Population growth rate: 0.05% (2014 est.)
country comparison to the world: 188

Birth rate: 9.99 births/1,000 population (2014 est.)
country comparison to the world: 193

Death rate: 10.76 deaths/1,000 population (2014 est.)
country comparison to the world: 38

Net migration rate: 1.22 migrant(s)/1,000 population (2014 est.)
country comparison to the world: 57

Urbanization: *urban population:* 97% of total population (2010)

rate of urbanization: 0.4% annual rate of change (2010-15 est.)

Major urban areas—population: BRUSSELS (capital) 1.892 million; Antwerp 961,000 (2009)

Sex ratio: *at birth:* 1.05 male(s)/female
0-14 years: 1.04 male(s)/female
15-24 years: 1.04 male(s)/female
25-54 years: 1.02 male(s)/female
55-64 years: 0.96 male(s)/female
65 years and over: 0.72 male(s)/female
total population: 0.96 male(s)/female (2014 est.)

Mother's mean age at first birth: 28
note: data refer to first birth within current marriage (2008 est.)

Maternal mortality rate: 8 deaths/100,000 live births (2010)
country comparison to the world: 156

Infant mortality rate: *total:* 4.18 deaths/1,000 live births
country comparison to the world: 194
male: 4.67 deaths/1,000 live births
female: 3.66 deaths/1,000 live births (2014 est.)

Life expectancy at birth: *total population:* 79.92 years
country comparison to the world: 36
male: 76.76 years
female: 83.22 years (2014 est.)

Total fertility rate: 1.65 children born/woman (2014 est.)
country comparison to the world: 176

Contraceptive prevalence rate: 70.4%
note: percent of women aged 18-49 (2010)

Health expenditures: 10.6% of GDP (2011)
country comparison to the world: 20

Physicians density: 3.78 physicians/1,000 population (2010)

Hospital bed density: 6.5 beds/1,000 population (2011)

Drinking water source:
Improved:
urban: 100% of population
rural: 100% of population
total: 100% of population
unimproved:
urban: 0% of population
rural: 0% of population
total: 0% of population (2011 est.)

Sanitation facility access:
Improved:
urban: 100% of population

rural: 100% of population
total: 100% of population
unimproved:
urban: 0% of population
rural: 0% of population
total: 0% of population (2011 est.)

HIV/AI DC—adult prevalence rate: 0.2% (2009 est.)
country comparison to the world: 108

HIV/AIDS—people living with HIV/AIDS: 14,000 (2009 est.)
country comparison to the world: 94

HIV/AIDS—deaths: fewer than 100 (2009 est.)
country comparison to the world: 125

Obesity—adult prevalence rate: 22.1% (2008)
country comparison to the world: 83

Education expenditures: 6.6% of GDP (2010)
country comparison to the world: 30

Literacy: *definition:* age 15 and over can read and write
total population: 99%
male: 99%
female: 99% (2003 est.)

School life expectancy (primary to tertiary education): *total:* 16 years
male: 16 years
female: 17 years (2011)

Unemployment, youth ages 15-24: *total:* 19.8%
country comparison to the world: 60
male: 20.4%
female: 19.8% (2012)

GOVERNMENT

Country name: *conventional long form:* Kingdom of Belgium
conventional short form: Belgium local long form: Royaume de Belgique/Koninkrijk Belgie/ Koenigreich Belgien
local short form: Belgique/Belgie/ Belgien

Government type: federal parliamentary democracy under a constitutional monarchy

Capital: *name:* Brussels
geographic coordinates: 50 50 N, 4 20 E
time difference: UTC+1 (6 hours ahead of Washington, DC during Standard Time)
daylight saving time: +1hr, begins last Sunday in March; ends last Sunday in October

Administrative divisions: 3 regions (French: regions, singular - region; Dutch: gewesten, singular - gewest); Brussels-Capital Region, also known as Brussels Hoofdstedelijk Gewest (Dutch), Region de Bruxelles-Capitale (French long form), Bruxelles-Capitale (French short form); Flemish Region (Flanders), also known as Vlaams Gewest (Dutch long form), Vlaanderen (Dutch short form), Region Flamande (French long form), Flandre (French short form); Walloon Region (Wallonia), also known as Region Wallone (French long form), Wallonie (French short form), Waals Gewest (Dutch long form), Wallonie (Dutch short form)
note: as a result of the 1993 constitutional revision that furthered devolution into a federal state, there are now three levels of government (federal, regional, and linguistic community) with a complex division of responsibilities

Independence: 4 October 1830 (a provisional government declared independence from the Netherlands); 21 July 1831 (King LEOPOLD I ascended to the throne)

National holiday: 21 July (1831) ascension to the Throne of King LEOPOLD I

Constitution: drafted 25 November 1830, approved 7 February 1831, entered into force 26 July 1831, revised 14 July 1993 (creating a federal state); amended many times, last in 2012 (2012)

Legal system: civil law system based on the French Civil Code; note—Belgian law continues to be modified in conformance with the legislative norms mandated by the European Union; judicial review of legislative acts

International law organization participation: accepts compulsory ICJ jurisdiction with reservations; accepts ICCt jurisdiction

Suffrage: 18 years of age; universal and compulsory

Executive branch: *chief of state:* King PHILIPPE (since 21 July 2013); Heir Apparent Princess ELISABETH, daughter of the monarch
head of government: Prime Minister Elio DI RUPO (since 6 December 2011); Deputy Prime Minister Alexander DE CROO (since 22 October 2012); Deputy Prime Minister Joelle MILQUET (since 20 March 2008); Deputy Prime Minister Laurette ONKELINX (since 30 December 2008); Deputy Prime Minister Didier REYNDERS (since 30 December 2008); Depurty Prime Minister Johan VANDE LANOTTE (since 16 December 2011); Deputy Prime Minister Pieter DE CREM (since 5 March 2013)
cabinet: Council of Ministers are formally appointed by the monarch (For more information visit the World Leaders website)
elections: the monarchy is hereditary and constitutional; following legislative elections, the leader of the majority party or the leader of the majority coalition usually appointed prime minister by the monarch and then approved by parliament

Legislative branch: bicameral Parliament consists of a Senate or Senaat in Dutch, Senat in French (71 seats; 40 members directly elected by popular vote, 31 indirectly elected; members serve four-year terms) and a Chamber of Deputies or Kamer van Volksvertegenwoordigers in Dutch, Chambre des Representants in French (150 seats; members directly elected by popular vote on the basis of proportional representation to serve four-year terms)
elections: Senate and Chamber of Deputies—last held on 13 June 2010 (next to be held 25 May 2014)
election results: Senate—percent of vote by party—N-VA 19.6%, PS 13.6%, CD&V 10%, SP.A 9.5%, MR 9.3%, Open VLD 8.2%, VB 7.6%, Ecolo 5.5%, CDH 5.1% Groen! 3.9%, other 7.7%; seats by party—N-VA 9, PS 7, CD&V 4, SP.A 4, MR 4, Open VLD 4, VB 3, Ecolo 2, CDH 2, Groen! 1; Chamber of Deputies—percent of vote by party—N-VA 17.4%, PS 13.7%, CD&V 10.9%, MR 9.3%, SP.A 9.2%, Open VLD 8.6%, VB 7.8%, CDH 5.5%, Ecolo 4.8%, Groen! 4.4%, List Dedecker 2.3%, the Popular Party 1.3%, other 4.8%; seats by party—N-VA 27, PS 26, CD&V 17, MR 18, sp.a 13, Open VLD 13, VB 12, CDH 9, Ecolo 8, Groen! 5, List Dedecker 1, the People's Party 1
note: as a result of the 1993 constitutional revision that furthered devolution into a federal state, there are now three levels of government (federal, regional, and linguistic community) with a complex division of responsibilities; this reality leaves six governments, each with its own legislative assembly

Judicial branch: *highest court(s):* Constitutional Court or Grondwettelijk Hof in Dutch and Cour constitutionelle in French (consists of 12 judges - 6 Dutch-speaking and 6 French-speaking); Supreme Court of Justice or Hof van Cassatie in Dutch and Cour de Cassation in French (court organized into 3 chambers: civil and commercial; criminal; social, fiscal, and armed forces; each chamber includes a Dutch division and a French division, each with a chairperson and 5-6 judges)
judge selection and term of office: Constitutional Court judges appointed by the monarch from candidates submitted by Parliament; judges appointed for life with mandatory retirement at age 70; Supreme Court judges appointed by the monarch from candidates submitted by the High Council of Justice, a 44-member independent body of judicial and non-judicial members; judges appointed for life
subordinate courts: Courts of Appeal; regional courts; specialized courts for administrative, commercial, labor, and audit issues; magistrate's courts; justices of the peace

Political parties and leaders: *Flemish parties:* Christian Democratic and Flemish or CD&V [Wouter BEKE]; Flemish Liberals and Democrats or Open VLD [Gwendolyn RUTTEN]; Groen! [Wouter VAN BESIEN] (formerly AGALEV, Flemish Greens); Libertarian, Direct, Democratic or LDD (formerly Dedecker's List) [Jean-Marie DEDECKER]; New Flemish Alliance or N-VA [Bart DE WEVER]; Social Progressive Alternative or SP.A [Bruno TOBBACK]; Vlaams Belang (Flemish Interest) or VB [Gerolf ANNEMANS]
Francophone parties: Ecolo (Francophone Greens) [Olivier DELEUZE, Emily HOYOS] Francophone Federalist Democrats [Olivier MAINGAIN] Humanist and Democratic Center or CDH [Benoit LUTGEN] Reform Movement or MR [Charles MICHEL] Socialist Party or PS [Paul MAGNETTE] other minor parties

Political pressure groups and leaders: Federation of Enterprises in Belgium [Pieter TIMMERMANS/Pierre Alain DE SMEDT]; Confederation of Christan Trade Unions [Luc CORTEBEECK/ Claude ROLIN]; Belgian General Federation of Labor [Rudy DE LEEUW/Anne DEMELENNE]
other: trade unions; numerous other associations representing bankers, manufacturers, middle-class artisans, and the legal and medical professions; various organizations representing the cultural interests of Flanders and Wallonia; various peace groups such as Pax Christi and groups representing immigrants

International organization participation: ADB (nonregional members), AfDB (nonregional members), Australia Group, Benelux, BIS, CD, CE, CERN, EAPC, EBRD, ECB, EIB, EITI (implementing country), EMU, ESA, EU, FAO, FATF, G-9, G-10, IADB, IAEA, IBRD, ICAO, ICC (national committees), ICRM, IDA, IEA, IFAD, IFC, IFRCS, IGAD (partners), IHO, ILO, IMF, IMO, IMSO, Interpol, IOC, IOM, IPU, ISO, ITSO, ITU, ITUC (NGOs), MIGA, MONUSCO, NATO, NEA, NSG, OAS (observer), OECD, OIF, OPCW, OSCE, Paris Club, PCA, Schengen Convention, SELEC (observer), UN, UNCTAD, UNESCO, UNHCR, UNIDO, UNIFIL, UNRWA, UNTSO, UPU, WCO, WHO, WIPO, WMO, WTO, ZC

Diplomatic representation in the US: *chief of mission:* Ambassador Johan VERBEKE (since 10 March 2014); chancery: 3330 Garfield Street NW, Washington, DC 20008
telephone: [1] (202) 333-6900
FAX: [1] (202) 338-4960
consulate(s) general: Atlanta, Los Angeles, New York

Diplomatic representation from the US: *chief of mission:* Ambassador Denise BAUER (since 7 August 2013); embassy: 27 Boulevard du Regent [Regentlaan], B-1000 Brussels
mailing address: PSC 82, Box 002, APO AE 09710
telephone: [32] (2) 811-4000
FAX: [32] (2) 811-4500

Flag description: three equal vertical bands of black (hoist side), yellow, and red; the vertical design was based on the flag of France; the colors are those of the arms of the duchy of Brabant (yellow lion with red claws and tongue on a black field)

National symbol(s): lion

National anthem: name: "La Brabanconne" (The Song of Brabant)
lyrics/music: Louis-Alexandre DECHET [French] Victor CEULEMANS [Dutch]/Francois VAN CAMPENHOUT
note: adopted 1830; Louis-Alexandre DECHET was an actor at the theater in which the revolution against the Netherlands began; according to legend, he wrote the lyrics with a group of young people in a Brussels cafe

ECONOMY

Economy—overview: This modern, open, and private-enterprise-based economy has capitalized on its central geographic location, highly developed transport network, and diversified industrial and commercial base. Industry is concentrated mainly in the more heavily-populated region of Flanders in the north. With few natural resources, Belgium imports substantial quantities of raw materials and exports a large volume of manufactures, making its economy vulnerable to volatility in world markets. Roughly three-quarters of Belgium's trade is with other EU countries, and Belgium has benefited most from its proximity to Germany. In 2013 Belgian GDP grew by 0.1%, the unemployment rate increased to 8.8% from 7.6% the previous year, and the government reduced the budget deficit from a peak of 6% of GDP in 2009 to 3.2%. Despite the relative improvement in Belgium's budget deficit, public debt hovers around 100% of GDP, a factor that has contributed to investor perceptions that the country is increasingly vulnerable to spillover from the euro-zone crisis. Belgian banks were severely affected by the international financial crisis in 2008 with three major banks receiving capital injections from the government, and the nationalization of the Belgian retail arm of a Franco-Belgian bank.

GDP (purchasing power parity): $421.7 billion (2013 est.)
country comparison to the world: 33
$421.3 billion (2012 est.)
$422.5 billion (2011 est.)
note: data are in 2013 US dollars

GDP (official exchange rate): $507.4 billion (2013 est.)

GDP—real growth rate: 0.1% (2013 est.)
country comparison to the world: 194
-0.3% (2012 est.)
1.8% (2011 est.)

GDP—per capita (PPP): $37,800 (2013 est.)
country comparison to the world: 32
$38,000 (2012 est.)
$38,400 (2011 est.)
note: data are in 2013 US dollars

Gross national saving: 19.2% of GDP (2013 est.)
country comparison to the world: 80
19.6% of GDP (2012 est.)
20.8% of GDP (2011 est.)

GDP—composition, by end use: *household consumption:* 53.7%
government consumption: 25%
investment in fixed capital: 20.2%
investment in inventories: 0.8%
exports of goods and services: 81.8%
imports of goods and services: -81.5% (2013 est.)

GDP—composition by sector of origin: *agriculture:* 0.8%
industry: 22.6%
services: 76.6% (2013 est.)

Agriculture—products: sugar beets, fresh vegetables, fruits, grain, tobacco; beef, veal, pork, milk

Industries: engineering and metal products, motor vehicle assembly, transportation equipment, scientific instruments, processed food and beverages, chemicals, basic metals, textiles, glass, petroleum

Industrial production growth rate: 0.2% (2013 est.)
country comparison to the world: 166

Labor force: 5.15 million (2013 est.)
country comparison to the world: 73

Labor force—by occupation: agriculture: 2% industry: 25% services: 73% (2007 est.)

Unemployment rate: 8.8% (2013 est.)
country comparison to the world: 97
7.6% (2012 est.)

Population below poverty line: 15.2% (2007 est.)

Household income or consumption by percentage share: *lowest 10%:* 3.4%
highest 10%: 28.4% (2006)

Distribution of family income—Gini index: 28 (2005)
country comparison to the world: 124 28.7 (1996)

Budget: *revenues:* $241.9 billion
expenditures: $258.2 billion (2013 est.)

Taxes and other revenues: 47.7% of GDP (2013 est.)
country comparison to the world: 15

Budget surplus (+) or deficit (-): -3.2% of GDP (2013 est.)
country comparison to the world: 129

Public debt: 102.4% of GDP (2013 est.)
country comparison to the world: 15
99.6% of GDP (2012 est.)
note: data cover general government debt, and includes debt instruments issued (or owned) by government entities other than the treasury; the data include treasury debt held by foreign entities; the data include debt issued by subnational entities, as well as intra-governmental debt; intra-governmental debt consists of treasury borrowings from surpluses in the social funds, such as for retirement, medical care, and unemployment; debt instruments for the social funds are not sold at public auctions; general government debt is defined by the Maastricht definition and calculated by the National Bank of Belgium as consolidated gross debt; the debt is defined in European Regulation EC479/2009 concerning the implementation of the protocol on the excessive deficit procedure annexed to the Treaty on European Union (Treaty of Maastricht) of 7 February 1992; the sub-sectors of consolidated gross debt are: federal government, communities and regions, local government, and social security funds

Fiscal year: calendar year

Inflation rate (consumer prices): 1.3% (2013 est.)
country comparison to the world: 34
2.6% (2012 est.)

Central bank discount rate: 0.75% (31 December 2013)
country comparison to the world: 126
1.5% (31 December 2010)
note: this is the European Central Bank's rate on the marginal lending facility, which offers overnight credit to banks in the euro area

Commercial bank prime lending rate: 3.5% (31 December 2013 est.)
country comparison to the world: 167
3.62% (31 December 2012 est.)

Stock of narrow money: $185.1 billion (31 December 2013 est.)
country comparison to the world: 21
$185.7 billion (31 December 2012 est.)
note: see entry for the European Union for money supply in the euro area; the European Central Bank (ECB) controls monetary policy for the 17 members of the Economic and Monetary Union (EMU); individual members of the EMU do not control the quantity of money circulating within their own borders

Stock of broad money: $591.7 billion (31 December 2013 est.)
country comparison to the world: 21
$585 billion (31 December 2012 est.)

Stock of domestic credit: $581.4 billion (31 December 2013 est.)
country comparison to the world: 23
$574.8 billion (31 December 2012 est.)

Market value of publicly traded shares: $300.1 billion (31 December 2012 est.)
country comparison to the world: 29
$229.9 billion (31 December 2011)
$269.3 billion (31 December 2010 est.)

Current account balance: -$9.1 billion (2013 est.)
country comparison to the world: 175
-$6.65 billion (2012 est.)

Exports: $295.3 billion (2013 est.)
country comparison to the world: 22
$302.4 billion (2012 est.)

Exports—commodities: machinery and equipment, chemicals, finished diamonds, metals and metal products, foodstuffs

Exports—partners: Germany 18%, France 16.1%, Netherlands 13%, UK 7.3%, US 5.3%, Italy 4.4% (2012)

Imports: $310.2 billion (2013 est.)
country comparison to the world: 18
$311.1 billion (2012 est.)

Imports—commodities: raw materials, machinery and equipment, chemicals, raw diamonds, pharmaceuticals, foodstuffs, transportation equipment, oil products

Imports—partners: Netherlands 20.9%, Germany 14.2%, France 10.6%, US 6.1%, UK 5.5%, Ireland 4.4% (2012)

Reserves of foreign exchange and gold: $30.77 billion (31 December 2012 est.)
country comparison to the world: 52
$29.43 billion (31 December 2011 est.)

Debt—external: $1.424 trillion (31 December 2012 est.)
country comparison to the world: 14
$1.417 trillion (31 December 2011)

Stock of direct foreign investment—at home: $1.195 trillion (31 December 2013 est.)
country comparison to the world: 6
$1.159 trillion (31 December 2012 est.)

Stock of direct foreign investment—abroad: $1.215 trillion (31 December 2013 est.)
country comparison to the world: 7
$1.185 trillion (31 December 2012 est.)

Exchange rates: euros (EUR) per US dollar—
0.7634 (2013 est.)
0.7752 (2012 est.)
0.755 (2010 est.)
0.7198 (2009 est.)
0.6827 (2008 est.)

ENERGY

Electricity—production: 83.37 billion kWh (2011 est.)
country comparison to the world: 38

Electricity—consumption: 84.68 billion kWh (2010 est.)
country comparison to the world: 37

Electricity—exports: 6.911 billion kWh (2012 est.)
country comparison to the world: 23

Electricity—imports: 16.85 billion kWh (2012 est.)
country comparison to the world: 10

Electricity—installed generating capacity: 18.32 million kW (2010 est.)
country comparison to the world: 40

Electricity—from fossil fuels: 43.6% of total installed capacity (2010 est.)
country comparison to the world: 164

Electricity—from nuclear fuels: 32.3% of total installed capacity (2010 est.)
country comparison to the world: 2

Electricity—from hydroelectric plants: 0.6% of total installed capacity (2010 est.)
country comparison to the world: 144

Electricity—from other renewable sources: 16.3% of total installed capacity (2010 est.)
country comparison to the world: 12

Crude oil—production: 10.530 bbl/day (2012 est.)
country comparison to the world: 89

Crude oil—exports: 0 bbl/day (2010 est.)
country comparison to the world: 82

Crude oil—imports: 667,700 bbl/day (2010 est.)
country comparison to the world: 17

Crude oil—proved reserves: 0 bbl (1 January 2013 es)
country comparison to the world: 107

Refined petroleum products—production: 720,000 bbl/day (2010 est.)
country comparison to the world: 24

Refined petroleum products—consumption: 644,400 bbl/day (2011 est.)
country comparison to the world: 28

Refined petroleum products—exports: 442,800 bbl/day (2010 est.)
country comparison to the world: 17

Refined petroleum products—imports: 355,100 bbl/day (2010 est.)
country comparison to the world: 17

Natural gas—production: 0 cu m (2011 est.)
country comparison to the world: 102

Natural gas—consumption: 13.46 billion cu m (2011 est.)
country comparison to the world: 42

Natural gas—exports: 21.18 billion cu m (2012 est.)
country comparison to the world: 18

Natural gas—imports: 38.9 billion cu m (2012 est.)
country comparison to the world: 14

Natural gas—proved reserves: 0 cu m (1 January 2013 es)
country comparison to the world: 113

Carbon dioxide emissions from consumption of energy: 131.1 million Mt (2011 est.)
country comparison to the world: 36

COMMUNICATIONS

Telephones—main lines in use: 4.631 million (2012)
country comparison to the world: 33

Telephones—mobile cellular: 12.88 million (2012)
country comparison to the world: 67

Telephone system: *general assessment:* highly developed, technologically advanced, and completely automated domestic and international telephone and telegraph facilities

domestic: nationwide mobile-cellular telephone system; extensive cable network; limited microwave radio relay network

international: country code—32; landing point for a number of submarine cables that provide links to Europe, the Middle East, and Asia; satellite earth stations—7 (Intelsat—3) (2007)

Broadcast media: a segmented market with the three major communities (Flemish, French, and German-speaking) each having responsibility for their own broadcast media; multiple TV channels exist for each community; additionally, in excess of 90% of households are connected to cable and can access broadcasts of TV stations from neighboring countries; each community has a public radio network co-existing with private broadcasters (2007)

Internet country code: .be

Internet hosts: 5.192 million (2012)
country comparison to the world: 21

Internet users: 8.113 million (2009)
country comparison to the world: 36

TRANSPORTATION

Airports: 41 (2013)
country comparison to the world: 102

Airports—with paved runways: *total:* 26
over 3,047 m: 6
2,438 to 3,047 m: 9
1,524 to 2,437 m: 2
914 to 1,523 m: 1
under 914 m: 8 (2013)

Airports—with unpaved runways: *total:* 15
under 914 m: 15 (2013)

Heliports: 1 (2013)

Pipelines: gas 3,139 km; oil 154 km; refined products 535 km (2013)

Railways: *total:* 3,233 km
country comparison to the world: 55
standard gauge: 3,233 km 1.435-m gauge (2,950 km electrified) (2008)

Roadways: *total:* 154,012 km
country comparison to the world: 31
paved: 120,514 km (includes 1,756 km of expressways)
unpaved: 33,498 km (2010)

Waterways: 2,043 km (1,528 km in regular commercial use) (2012)
country comparison to the world: 42

Merchant marine: *total:* 87
country comparison to the world: 56
by type: bulk carrier 23, cargo 15, chemical tanker 5, container 4, liquefied gas 23, passenger 2, petroleum tanker 8, roll on/roll off 7
foreign-owned: 15 (Denmark 4, France 7, Russia 1, UK 2, US 1)
registered in other countries: 107 (Bahamas 6, Cambodia 1, Cyprus 3, France 7, Gibraltar 1, Greece 17, Hong Kong 26, Liberia 1, Luxembourg 11, Malta 7, Marshall Islands 1, Mozambique 2, North Korea 1, Panama 1, Portugal 8, Russia 4, Saint Kitts and Nevis 1, Saint Vincent and the Grenadines 7, Singapore 1, Vanuatu 1) (2010)

Ports and terminals: *major seaport(s):* Oostende, Zeebrugge
river port(s): Antwerp, Gent (Schelde River); Brussels (Senne River); Liege (Meuse River)
container port(s) (TEUs): Antwerp (8,664,243), Zeebrugge (2,207,257) (2011)

MILITARY

Military branches: Belgian Armed Forces: Land Operations Command, Naval Operations Command, Air Operations Command (2012)

Military service age and obligation: 18 years of age for male and female voluntary military service; conscription abolished in 1994 (2012)

Manpower available for military service: *males age 16-49:* 2,359,232
females age 16-49: 2,291,689 (2010 est.)

Manpower fit for military service: *males age 16-49:* 1,934,957
females age 16-49: 1,877,268 (2010 est.)

Manpower reaching militarily significant age annually: *male:* 59,665
female: 57,142 (2010 est.)

Military expenditures: 1.05% of GDP (2012)
country comparison to the world: 99
1.08% of GDP (2011)
1.05% of GDP (2010)

TRANSNATIONAL ISSUES

Disputes—international: none

Refugees and internally displaced persons: *stateless persons:* 3,898 (2012)

Illicit drugs: growing producer of synthetic drugs and cannabis; transit point for US-bound ecstasy; source of precursor chemicals for South American cocaine processors; transshipment point for cocaine, heroin, hashish, and marijuana entering Western Europe; despite a strengthening of legislation, the country remains vulnerable to money laundering related to narcotics, automobiles, alcohol, and tobacco; significant domestic consumption of ecstasy

BELIZE

INTRODUCTION

Background: Belize was the site of several Mayan city states until their decline at the end of the first millennium A.D. The British and Spanish disputed the region in the 17th and 18th centuries; it formally became the colony of British Honduras in 1854. Territorial disputes between the UK and Guatemala delayed the independence of Belize until 1981. Guatemala refused to recognize the new nation until 1992 and the two countries are involved in an ongoing border dispute. Guatemala and Belize plan to hold a simultaneous referendum, set for 6 October 2013, to determine if this dispute will go before the International Court of Justice at The Hague. Tourism has become the mainstay of the economy. Current concerns include the country's heavy foreign debt burden, high unemployment, growing involvement in the Mexican and South American drug trade, high crime rates, and one of the highest HIV/AIDS prevalence rates in Central America.

GEOGRAPHY

Location: Central America, bordering the Caribbean Sea, between Guatemala and Mexico

Geographic coordinates: 17 15 N, 88 45 W

Map references: Central America and the Caribbean

Area: *total:* 22,966 sq km
country comparison to the world: 152
land: 22,806 sq km
water: 160 sq km

Area—comparative: slightly smaller than Massachusetts

Land boundaries: *total:* 516 km

border countries: Guatemala 266 km, Mexico 250 km

Coastline: 386 km

Maritime claims: *territorial sea:* 12 nm in the north, 3 nm in the south; note—from the mouth of the Sarstoon River to Ranguana Cay, Belize's territorial sea is 3 nm; according to Belize's Maritime Areas Act, 1992, the purpose of this limitation is to provide a framework for negotiating a definitive agreement on territorial differences with Guatemala *exclusive economic zone:* 200 nm

Climate: tropical; very hot and humid; rainy season (May to November); dry season (February to May)

Terrain: flat, swampy coastal plain; low mountains in south

Elevation extremes: *lowest point:* Caribbean Sea 0 m
highest point: Doyle's Delight 1,160 m

Natural resources: arable land potential, timber, fish, hydropower

Land use: *arable land:* 3.27%
permanent crops: 1.39%
other: 95.34% (2011)

Irrigated land: 30 sq km (2003)

Total renewable water resources: 18.55 cu km (2011)

Freshwater withdrawal (domestic/industrial/agricultural): *total:* 0.22 cu km/yr (4%/49%/46%)
per capita: 845.2 cu m/yr (2000)

Natural hazards: frequent, devastating hurricanes (June to November) and coastal flooding (especially in south)

Environment—current issues: deforestation; water pollution from sewage, industrial effluents, agricultural runoff; solid and sewage waste disposal

Environment—international agreements: *party to:* Biodiversity, Climate Change, Climate Change-Kyoto Protocol, Desertification, Endangered Species, Hazardous Wastes, Law of the Sea, Ozone Layer Protection, Ship Pollution, Wetlands, Whaling
signed, but not ratified: none of the selected agreements

Geography—note: only country in Central America without a coastline on the North Pacific Ocean

PEOPLE AND SOCIETY

Nationality: *noun:* Belizean(s)

adjective: Belizean

Ethnic groups: mestizo 48.7%, Creole 24.9%, Maya 10.6%, Garifuna 6.1%, other 9.7% (2000 census)

Languages: Spanish 46%, Creole 32.9%, Mayan dialects 8.9%, English 3.9% (official), Garifuna 3.4% (Carib), German 3.3%, other 1.4%, unknown 0.2% (2000 census)

Religions: Roman Catholic 39.3%, Pentacostal 8.3%, Seventh Day Adventist 5.3%, Anglican 4.5%, Mennonite 3.7%, Baptist 3.5%, Methodist 2.8%, Nazarene 2.8%, Jehovah's Witnesses 1.6%, other 9.9% (includes Bahai Faith, Buddhism, Hinduism, Islam, and Mormon), other (unknown) 3.1%, none 15.2% (2010 census)

Demographic profile: Migration continues to transform Belize's population. About 16% of Belizeans live abroad, while immigrants constitute approximately 15% of Belize's population. Belizeans seeking job and educational opportunities have preferred to emigrate to the United States rather than former colonizer Great Britain because of the United States' closer proximity and stronger trade ties with Belize. Belizeans also emigrate to Canada, Mexico, and English-speaking Caribbean countries. The emigration of a large share of Creoles (Afro-Belizeans) and the influx of Central American immigrants, mainly Guatemalans, Salvadorans, and Hondurans, has changed Belize's ethnic composition. Mestizos have become the largest ethnic group, and Belize now has more native Spanish speakers than English or Creole speakers, despite English being the official language. In addition, Central American immigrants are establishing new communities in rural areas, which contrasts with the urbanization trend seen in neighboring countries. Recently, Chinese, European, and North American immigrants have become more frequent. Immigration accounts for an increasing share of Belize's population growth rate, which is steadily falling due to fertility decline. Belize's declining birth rate and its increased life expectancy are creating an aging population. As the elderly population grows and nuclear families replace extended households, Belize's government will be challenged to balance a rising demand for pensions, social services, and healthcare for its senior citizens with the need to reduce poverty and social inequality and to improve sanitation.

Population: 340,844 (July 2014 est.)
country comparison to the world: 178

Age structure: *0-14 years:* 35.3% (male 61,480/female 59,000)
15-24 years: 21% (male 36,432/female 35,093)
25-54 years: 35.5% (male 61,112/female 59,809)
55-64 years: 3.6% (male 7,719/female 7,807)
65 years and over: 3.6% (male 5,848/female 6,544) (2014 est.)

Dependency ratios: *total dependency ratio:* 60.9%
youth dependency ratio: 54.5%
elderly dependency ratio: 6.4%
potential support ratio: 15.6 (2013)

Median age: *total:* 21.8 years
male: 21.6 years
female: 22 years (2014 est.)

Population growth rate: 1.92% (2014 est.)
country comparison to the world: 58

Birth rate: 25.14 births/1,000 population (2014 est.)
country comparison to the world: 55

Death rate: 5.95 deaths/1,000 population (2014 est.)
country comparison to the world: 167

Net migration rate: 0 migrant(s)/1,000 population (2014 est.)
country comparison to the world: 98

Urbanization: *urban population:* 52% of total population (2010)

Major urban areas—population: BELMOPAN (capital) 14,000 (2011)

Sex ratio: *at birth:* 1.05 male(s)/female
0-14 years: 1.04 male(s)/female
15-24 years: 1.04 male(s)/female
25-54 years: 1.02 male(s)/female
55-64 years: 1.03 male(s)/female
65 years and over: 0.9 male(s)/female
total population: 1.03 male(s)/female (2014 est.)

Maternal mortality rate: 53 deaths/100,000 live births (2010)
country comparison to the world: 105

Infant mortality rate: *total:* 20.31 deaths/1,000 live births
country comparison to the world: 89
male: 22.78 deaths/1,000 live births
female: 17.7 deaths/1,000 live births (2014 est.)

Life expectancy at birth: *total population:* 68.49 years
country comparison to the world: 160
male: 66.88 years

female: 70.17 years (2014 est.)
Total fertility rate: 3.02 children born/woman (2014 est.)
country comparison to the world: 55
Contraceptive prevalence rate: 55.2% (2011)
Health expenditures: 5.7% of GDP (2011)
country comparison to the world: 120
Physicians density: 0.83 physicians/1,000 population (2009)
Hospital bed density: 1.1 beds/1,000 population (2011)
Drinking water source:
Improved:
urban: 96.9% of population
rural: 100% of population
total: 98.6% of population
Unimproved:
urban: 3.1% of population
rural: 0% of population
total: 1.4% of population (2011 est.)
Sanitation facility access:
Improved:
urban: 93.1% of population
rural: 87.2% of population
total: 89.9% of population
Unimproved:
urban: 6.9% of population
rural: 12.8% of population
total: 10.1% of population (2011 est.)
HIV/AIDS—adult prevalence rate: 1.4% (2012 est.)
country comparison to the world: 32
HIV/AIDS—people living with HIV/AIDS: 3,100 (2012 est.)
country comparison to the world: 132
HIV/AIDS—deaths: 100 (2012 est.)
country comparison to the world: 126
Major infectious diseases: *degree of risk:* high
food or waterborne diseases: bacterial diarrhea, hepatitis A, and typhoid fever
vectorborne diseases: dengue fever and malaria (2013)
Obesity—adult prevalence rate: 33.7% (2008)
country comparison to the world: 15
Children under the age of 5 years underweight: 6.2% (2011)
country comparison to the world: 81
Education expenditures: 6.6% of GDP (2010)
country comparison to the world: 29
Literacy: *definition:* age 15 and over can read and write
total population: 76.9%
male: 76.7%
female: 77.1% (2000 census)
School life expectancy (primary to tertiary education): *total:* 14 years
male: 13 years
female: 14 years (2012)
Child labor—children ages 5-14: *total number:* 27,751
percentage: 40 % (2001 est.)
Unemployment, youth ages 15-24: *total:* 19.5%
country comparison to the world: 61
male: 13.8%
female: 28.8% (2005)

GOVERNMENT

Country name: *conventional long form:* none
conventional short form: Belize
former: British Honduras
Government type: parliamentary democracy and a Commonwealth realm
Capital: *name:* Belmopan
geographic coordinates: 17 15 N, 88 46 W
time difference: UTC-6 (1 hour behind Washington, DC during Standard Time)
Administrative divisions: 6 districts; Belize, Cayo, Corozal, Orange Walk, Stann Creek, Toledo
Independence: 21 September 1981 (from the UK)
National holiday: Independence Day, 21 September (1981)
Constitution: previous 1954, 1963 (preindependence); latest signed and entered into force 21 September 1981; amended several times, last in 2012 (2013)
Legal system: English common law
International law organization participation: has not submitted an ICJ jurisdiction declaration; accepts ICCt jurisdiction
Suffrage: 18 years of age; universal
Executive branch: *chief of state:* Queen ELIZABETH II (since 6 February 1952); represented by Governor General Sir Colville YOUNG, Sr. (since 17 November 1993)
head of government: Prime Minister Dean Oliver BARROW (since 8 February 2008); Deputy Prime Minister Gaspar VEGA (since 12 February 2008)
cabinet: Cabinet appointed by the governor general on the advice of the prime minister from the General Assembly (For more information visit the World Leaders website)
elections: the monarchy is hereditary; governor general appointed by the monarch; following legislative elections, the leader of the majority party or the leader of the majority coalition usually appointed prime minister by the governor general; prime minister recommends the deputy prime minister
Legislative branch: bicameral National Assembly consists of the Senate (12 seats; members appointed by the governor general—6 on the advice of the prime minister, 3 on the advice of the leader of the opposition, and 1 each on the advice of the Belize Council of Churches and Evangelical Association of Churches, the Belize Chamber of Commerce and Industry and the Belize Better Business Bureau, and the National Trade Union Congress and the Civil Society Steering Committee; to serve five-year terms) and the House of Representatives (31 seats; members are elected by direct popular vote to serve five-year terms)
elections: House of Representatives—last held on 8 March 2012 (next to be held in 2017)
election results: percent of vote by party—UDP 50.4%, PUP 47.5%, other 2.1%; seats by party—UDP 17, PUP 14
Judicial branch: *highest court(s):* Supreme Court of Judicature (consists of the Court of Appeal with the court president and 3 justices, and the Supreme Court with the chief justice and 2 judges)note - in 2005, Belize ceased final appeals in civil and criminal cases to the Judicial Committee of the Privy Council (in London),replacing it with the Caribbean Court of Justice, the judicial organ of the Caribbean Community *judge selection and term of office:* Court of Appeal president and justices appointed by the governor general upon advice of the prime minister after consultation with the National Assembly opposition leader; justices' tenures vary by terms of appointment; Supreme Court chief justice appointed by the governor-general upon the advice of the prime minister and the National Assembly opposition leader; other judges appointed by the governor-general upon the advice of the Judicial and Legal Services Section of the Public Services Commission and with the concurrence of the prime minister after consultation with the National Assembly opposition leader; judges can be appointed beyond age 65 but must retire by age 75 subordinate courts: Summary Jurisdiction Courts (criminal) and District Courts (civil)
Political parties and leaders: National Alliance for Belizean Rights or NABR; National Reform Party or NRP [Cornelius DUECK]; People's National Party or PNP [Wil MAHEIA]; People's United Party or PUP [John BRICENO]; United Democratic Party or UDP [Dean Oliver BARROW]; Vision Inspired by the People or VIP [Paul MORGAN]; We the People Reform Movement or WTP [Hipolito BAUTISTA]
Political pressure groups and leaders: Society for the Promotion of Education and Research or SPEAR [Nicole HAYLOCK]; Association of Concerned Belizeans or ACB [David VASQUEZ]; National Trade Union Congress of Belize or NTUC/B [Rene GOMEZ]
International organization participation: ACP, AOSIS, C, Caricom, CD, CDB, CELAC, FAO, G-77, IADB, IAEA, IBRD, ICAO, ICC (NGOs), ICRM, IDA, IFAD, IFC, IFRCS, ILO, IMF, IMO, Interpol, IOC, IOM, ITU, LAES, MIGA, NAM, OAS, OPANAL, OPCW, PCA, Petrocaribe, SICA, UN, UNCTAD, UNESCO, UNIDO, UPU, WCO, WHO, WIPO, WMO, WTO
Diplomatic representation in the US: *chief of mission:* Ambassador Nestor MENDEZ (since 10 July 2008)
chancery: 2535 Massachusetts Avenue NW, Washington, DC 20008
telephone: [1] (202) 332-9636
FAX: [1] (202) 332-6888
consulate(s) general: Los Angeles
Diplomatic representation from the US: *chief of mission:* Ambassador (vacant); Charge d'Affaires Margaret HAWTHORNE
embassy: Floral Park Road, Belmopan City, Cayo District
mailing address: P.O. Box 497, Belmopan City, Cayo District, Belize
telephone: [501] 822-4011
FAX: [501] 822-4012
Flag description: blue with a narrow red stripe along the top and the bottom edges; centered is a large white disk bearing the coat of arms; the coat of arms features a shield flanked by two workers in front of a mahogany tree with the related motto SUB UMBRA FLOREO (I Flourish in the Shade) on a scroll at the bottom, all encircled by a green garland of 50 mahogany leaves; the colors are those of the two main political parties: blue for the PUP and red for the UDP; various elements of the coat of arms—the figures, the tools, the mahogany tree, and the garland of leaves—recall the logging industry that led to British settlement of Belize
note: Belize's flag is the only national flag that depicts human beings; two British overseas territories, Montserrat and the British Virgin Islands, also depict humans
National symbol(s): Baird's tapir (a large, browsing, forest-dwelling mammal); keel-billed toucan
National anthem: *name:* "Land of the Free"
lyrics/music: Samuel Alfred HAYNES/Selwyn Walford YOUNG
note: adopted 1981; as a Commonwealth country, in addition to the national anthem, "God Save the Queen" serves as the royal anthem (see United Kingdom)

ECONOMY

Economy—overview: Tourism is the number one foreign exchange earner in this small economy, followed by exports of marine products, citrus, cane sugar, bananas, and garments. The government's expansionary monetary and fiscal policies, initiated in September 1998, led to GDP growth averaging nearly 4% in 1999-2007. Oil discoveries in 2006 bolstered this growth. Exploration efforts have continued and production has increased a small amount. Growth slipped to 0% in 2009, resulting from the global economic slowdown, natural disasters, and a temporary drop in the price of oil, but grew to 2.5% in 2013. With weak economic growth and a large public debt burden, fiscal spending is likely to be tight. In January 2013, the government announced that it had reached a deal with creditors to restructure its $544 million commercial external debt, commonly referred to as the "superbond." The superbond represents one half of the country's public debt. A key government objective remains the reduction of poverty and inequality with the help of international donors. Although Belize has the second highest per capita income in Central America, the average income figure masks a huge income disparity between rich and poor. The sizable trade deficit and heavy foreign debt burden continue to be major concerns.

GDP (purchasing power parity): $3.083 billion (2013 est.)
country comparison to the world: 181
$3.008 billion (2012 est.)
$2.857 billion (2011 est.)
note: data are in 2013 US dollars

GDP (official exchange rate): $1.637 billion (2013 est.)

GDP—real growth rate: 2.5% (2013 est.)
country comparison to the world: 130
5.3% (2012 est.)
1.9% (2011 est.)

GDP—per capita (PPP): $8,800 (2013 est.)
country comparison to the world: 126
$8,800 (2012 est.)
$8,500 (2011 est.)
note: data are in 2013 US dollars

Gross national saving: 31.2% of GDP (2013 est.)
country comparison to the world: 25
29.2% of GDP (2012 est.)
28.2% of GDP (2011 est.)

GDP—composition, by end use: *household consumption:* 79.3%
government consumption: 16.8%
investment in fixed capital: 31.2%
investment in inventories: 1.2%
exports of goods and services: 62.1%
imports of goods and services: -90.6% (2013 est.)

GDP—composition, by sector of origin: *agriculture:* 13%
industry: 23%
services: 64% (2012 est.)

Agriculture—products: bananas, cacao, citrus, sugar; fish, cultured shrimp; lumber

Industries: garment production, food processing, tourism, construction, oil

Industrial production growth rate: -1% (2013 est.)
country comparison to the world: 175

Labor force: 120,500
country comparison to the world: 180
note: shortage of skilled labor and all types of technical personnel (2008 est.)

Labor force - by occupation: *agriculture:* 10.2%
industry: 18.1%
services: 71.7% (2007)

Unemployment rate: 15.5% (2013)
country comparison to the world: 144
11.3% (2012)

Population below poverty line: 41% (2013 est.)

Household income or consumption by percentage share: *lowest 10%:* NA%
highest 10%: NA%

Budget: *revenues:* $410.1 million *expenditures:* $352.4 million (2013 est.)

Taxes and other revenues: 25.1% of GDP (2013 est.)
country comparison to the world: 127

Budget surplus (+) or deficit (-): 3.5% of GDP (2013 est.)
country comparison to the world: 12

Public debt: 75.1% of GDP (2013 est.)
country comparison to the world: 33
84.6% of GDP (2012 est.)

Fiscal year: 1 April—31 March

Inflation rate (consumer prices): 1.3% (2013 est.)
country comparison to the world: 33
1.3% (2012 est.)

Central bank discount rate: 18% (31 December 2010 est.)
country comparison to the world: 18
12% (31 December 2009 est.)

Commercial bank prime lending rate: 11.8% (31 December 2013 est.)
country comparison to the world: 64
12.4% (31 December 2012 est.)

Stock of narrow money: $573 million (31 December 2013 est.)
country comparison to the world: 159
$551.5 million (31 December 2012 est.)

Stock of broad money: $1.3 billion (31 December 2013 est.)
country comparison to the world: 161
$1.222 billion (31 December 2012 est.)

Stock of domestic credit: $1.05 billion (31 December 2013 est.)
country comparison to the world: 153
$1 billion (31 December 2012 est.)

Market value of publicly traded shares: $NA

Current account balance: -$32 million (2013 est.)
country comparison to the world: 64
-$28 million (2012 est.)

Exports: $633 million (2013 est.)
country comparison to the world: 170
$628.3 million (2012 est.)

Exports—commodities: sugar, bananas, citrus, clothing, fish products, molasses, wood, crude oil

Exports—partners: US 31.8%, UK 21.9%, Nigeria 4.8%, Japan 4.1%, Netherlands 4.1% (2012)

Imports: $864 million (2013 est.)
country comparison to the world: 181
$837.1 million (2012 est.)

Imports—commodities: machinery and transport equipment, manufactured goods; fuels, chemicals, pharmaceuticals; food, beverages, tobacco

Imports—partners: US 23.6%, Germany 15%, Mexico 11.5%, Cuba 8.4%, Guatemala 4.8%, China 4.7%, Singapore 4% (2012)

Reserves of foreign exchange and gold: $273 million (31 December 2013 est.)
country comparison to the world: 157
$288.9 million (31 December 2012 est.)

Debt—external: $1.048 billion (31 December 2013 est.)
country comparison to the world: 161
$1.033 billion (31 December 2012 est.)

Exchange rates: Belizean dollars (BZD) per US dollar—
2 (2013 est.)
2 (2012 est.)
2 (2010 est.)
2 (2009)
2 (2008)

ENERGY

Electricity—production: 524.2 million kWh (2010 est.)
country comparison to the world: 162

Electricity—consumption: 630 million kWh (2011 est.)
country comparison to the world: 164

Electricity—exports: 0 kWh (2012 est.)
country comparison to the world: 106

Electricity—imports: 171 million kWh (2011 est.)
country comparison to the world: 87

Electricity—installed generating capacity: 178,100 kW (2010 est.)
country comparison to the world: 160

Electricity—from fossil fuels: 51.1% of total installed capacity (2010 est.)
country comparison to the world: 153

Electricity—from nuclear fuels: 0% of total installed capacity (2010 est.)
country comparison to the world: 49

Electricity—from hydroelectric plants: 32% of total installed capacity (2010 est.)
country comparison to the world: 71

Electricity—from other renewable sources: 16.9% of total installed capacity (2010 est.)
country comparison to the world: 10

Crude oil—production: 3,239 bbl/day (2012 est.)
country comparison to the world: 102

Crude oil—exports: 4,345 bbl/day (2010 est.)
country comparison to the world: 65

Crude oil—imports: 0 bbl/day (2010 est.)
country comparison to the world: 160

Crude oil—proved reserves: 6.7 million bbl (1 January 2013 es)
country comparison to the world: 94

Refined petroleum products—production: 0 bbl/day (2010 est.)
country comparison to the world: 123

Refined petroleum products—consumption: 7,044 bbl/day (2011 est.)
country comparison to the world: 161

Refined petroleum products—exports: 0 bbl/day (2010 est.)
country comparison to the world: 153

Refined petroleum products—imports: 3,493 bbl/day (2010 est.)
country comparison to the world: 166

Natural gas—production: 0 cu m (2011 est.)
country comparison to the world: 104

Natural gas—consumption: 0 cu m (2010 est.)
country comparison to the world: 121

Natural gas—exports: 0 cu m (2011 est.)
country comparison to the world: 66

Natural gas—imports: 0 cu m (2011 est.)

country comparison to the world: 161

Natural gas—proved reserves: 0 cu m (1 January 2013 es)
country comparison to the world: 115

Carbon dioxide emissions from consumption of energy: 536,300 Mt (2011 est.)
country comparison to the world: 179

COMMUNICATIONS

Telephones—main lines in use: 25,400 (2012)
country comparison to the world: 180

Telephones—mobile cellular: 164,200 (2012)
country comparison to the world: 184

Telephone system: *general assessment:* above-average system; trunk network depends primarily on microwave radio relay
domestic: fixed-line teledensity of slightly less than 10 per 100 persons; mobile-cellular teledensity approaching 70 per 100 persons
international: country code—501; landing point for the Americas Region Caribbean Ring System (ARCOS-1) fiber-optic telecommunications submarine cable that provides links to South and Central America, parts of the Caribbean, and the US; satellite earth station—8 (Intelsat—2, unknown—6) (2011)

Broadcast media: 8 privately owned TV stations; multi-channel cable TV provides access to foreign stations; about 25 radio stations broadcasting on roughly 50 different frequencies; state-run radio was privatized in 1998 (2007)

Internet country code: .bz

Internet hosts: 3,392 (2012)
country comparison to the world: 152

Internet users: 36,000 (2009)
country comparison to the world: 178

TRANSPORTATION

Airports: 47 (2013)
country comparison to the world: 92

Airports—with paved runways: *total:* 6
2,438 to 3,047 m: 1
914 to 1,523 m: 2
under 914 m: 3 (2013)

Airports—with unpaved runways: *total:* 41
2,438 to 3,047 m: 1
914 to 1,523 m: 11
under 914 m: 29 (2013)

Roadways: *total:* 2,870 km
country comparison to the world: 169
paved: 488 km
unpaved: 2,382 km (2011)

Waterways: 825 km (navigable only by small craft) (2011)
country comparison to the world: 71

Merchant marine: *total:* 247
country comparison to the world: 33
by type: barge carrier 1, bulk carrier 33, cargo 156, chemical tanker 2, liquefied gas 1, passenger/cargo 4, petroleum tanker 9, refrigerated cargo 30, roll on/roll off 10, specialized tanker 1
foreign-owned: 152 (Bulgaria 1, China 61, Croatia 1, Estonia 1, Greece 2, Iceland 1, Italy 3, Latvia 9, Lithuania 1, Netherlands 1, Norway 2, Russia 30, Singapore 4, Switzerland 1, Syria 4, Thailand 1, Turkey 16, UAE 3, UK 4, Ukraine 6) (2010)

Ports and terminals: *major seaport (s):* Belize City, Big Creek

MILITARY

Military branches: *Belize Defense Force (BDF):* Army, BDF Air Wing (includes Special Boat Unit), BDF Volunteer Guard (2011)

Military service age and obligation: 18 years of age for voluntary military service; laws allow for conscription only if volunteers are insufficient; conscription has never been implemented; volunteers typically outnumber available positions by 3:1; initial service obligation 12 years (2012)

Manpower available for military service:
males age 16-49: 81,284
females age 16-49: 79,185 (2010 est.)

Manpower fit for military service:
males age 16-49: 59,431
females age 16-49: 57,221 (2010 est.)

Manpower reaching militarily significant age annually: *male:* 3,723
female: 3,584 (2010 est.)

Military expenditures: NA% (2012)
1.08% of GDP (2011)
NA% (2010)

TRANSNATIONAL ISSUES

Disputes—international: Guatemala persists in its territorial claim to half of Belize, but agrees to the Line of Adjacency to keep Guatemalan squatters out of Belize's forested interior; both countries agreed in April 2012 to hold simultaneous referenda, scheduled for 6 October 2013, to decide whether to refer the dispute to the ICJ for binding resolution; Belize and Mexico are working to solve minor border demarcation discrepancies arising from inaccuracies in the 1898 border treaty

Illicit drugs: transshipment point for cocaine; small-scale illicit producer of cannabis, primarily for local consumption; offshore sector money-laundering activity related to narcotics trafficking and other crimes (2008)

BENIN

INTRODUCTION

Background: Present day Benin was the site of Dahomey, a West African kingdom that rose to prominence in about 1600 and over the next two and half centuries became a regional power, largely based on its slave trade. Coastal areas of Dahomey began to be controlled by the French in the second half of the 19th century; the entire kingdom was conquered by 1894. French Dahomey achieved independence in 1960; it changed its name to the Republic of Benin in 1975. A succession of military governments ended in 1972 with the rise to power of Mathieu KEREKOU and the establishment of a government based on Marxist-Leninist principles. A move to representative government began in 1989. Two years later, free elections ushered in former Prime Minister Nicephore SOGLO as president, marking the first successful transfer of power in Africa from a dictatorship to a democracy. KEREKOU was returned to power by elections held in 1996 and 2001, though some irregularities were alleged. KEREKOU stepped down at the end of his second term in 2006 and was succeeded by Thomas YAYI Boni, a political outsider and independent. YAYI, who won a second five-year term in March 2011, has attempted to stem corruption and has strongly promoted accelerating Benin's economic growth.

GEOGRAPHY

Location: Western Africa, bordering the Bight of Benin, between Nigeria and Togo

Geographic coordinates: 9 30 N, 2 15 E

Map references: Africa

Area: *total:* 112,622 sq km
country comparison to the world: 102
land: 110,622 sq km
water: 2,000 sq km

Area—comparative: slightly smaller than Pennsylvania

Land boundaries: *total:* 1,989 km
border countries: Burkina Faso 306 km, Niger 266 km, Nigeria 773 km, Togo 644 km

Coastline: 121 km

Maritime claims: *territorial sea:* 200 nm

Climate: tropical; hot, humid in south; semiarid in north Terrain: mostly flat to undulating plain; some hills and low mountains

Elevation extremes: *lowest point:* Atlantic Ocean 0 m
highest point: Mont Sokbaro 658 m

Natural resources: small offshore oil deposits, limestone, marble, timber

Land use: *arable land:* 22.48%
permanent crops: 2.61%
other: 74.9% (2011)

Irrigated land: 230.4 sq km (2008)

Total renewable water resources: 26.39 cu km (2011)

Freshwater withdrawal (domestic/industrial/agricultural): *total:* 0.13 cu km/yr (32%/23%/45%)
per capita: 18.74 cu m/yr (2001)

Natural hazards: hot, dry, dusty harmattan wind may affect north from December to March

Environment—current issues: inadequate supplies of potable water; poaching threatens wildlife populations; deforestation; desertification

Environment—international agreements: *party to:* Biodiversity, Climate Change, Climate Change-Kyoto Protocol, Desertification, Endangered Species, Environmental Modification, Hazardous Wastes, Law of the Sea, Ozone Layer Protection, Ship Pollution, Wetlands, Whaling
signed, but not ratified: none of the selected agreements

Geography—note: sandbanks create difficult access to a coast with no natural harbors, river mouths, or islands

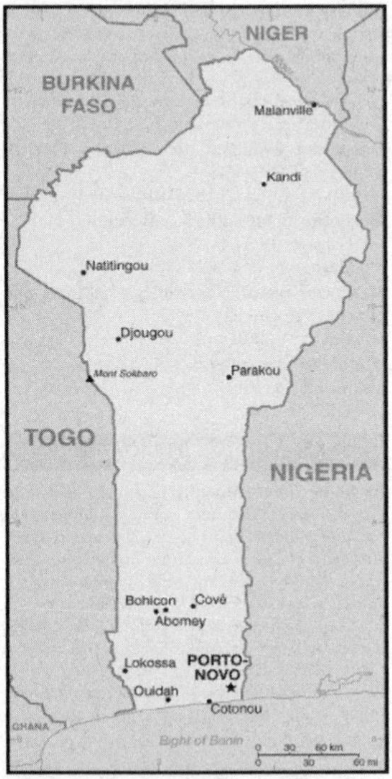

PEOPLE AND SOCIETY

Nationality: *noun:* Beninese (singular and plural)
adjective: Beninese

Ethnic groups: Fon and related 39.2%, Adja and related 15.2%, Yoruba and related 12.3%, Bariba and related 9.2%, Peulh and related 7%, Ottamari and related 6.1%, Yoa-Lokpa and related 4%, Dendi and related 2.5%, other 1.6% (includes Europeans), unspecified 2.9% (2002 census)

Languages: French (official), Fon and Yoruba (most common vernaculars in south), tribal languages (at least six major ones in north)

Religions: Catholic 27.1%, Muslim 24.4%, Vodoun 17.3%, Protestant 10.4% (Celestial 5%, Methodist 3.2%, other Protestant 2.2%), other Christian 5.3%, other 15.5% (2002 census)

Population: 10,160,556 (July 2014 est.)
country comparison to the world: 88
note: estimates for this country explicitly take into account the effects of excess mortality due to AIDS; this can result in lower life expectancy, higher infant mortality, higher death rates, lower population growth rates, and changes in the distribution of population by age and sex than would otherwise be expected

Age structure: *0-14 years:* 43.8% (male 2,269,896/female 2,179,026)
15-24 years: 20.1% (male 1,036,963/female 1,001,400)
25-54 years: 29.9% (male 1,530,283/female 1,504,201)
55-64 years: 2.8% (male 149,883/female 205,701)
65 years and over: 2.8% (male 112,830/female 170,373) (2014 est.)

Dependency ratios: *total dependency ratio:* 84%
youth dependency ratio: 78.7%
elderly dependency ratio: 5.3 %
potential support ratio: 18.8 (2013)

Median age: *total:* 17.7 years
male: 17.4 years
female: 18.1 years (2014 est.)

Population growth rate: 2.81% (2014 est.)
country comparison to the world: 17

Birth rate: 36.51 births/1,000 population (2014 est.)
country comparison to the world: 20

Death rate: 8.39 deaths/1,000 population (2014 est.)
country comparison to the world: 84

Net migration rate: 0 migrant(s)/1,000 population (2014 est.)
country comparison to the world: 99

Urbanization: *urban population:* 44.9% of total population (2011)
rate of urbanization: 4.12% annual rate of change (2010-15 est.)

Major urban areas—population: COTONOU (seat of government) 924,000; PORTO-NOVO (capital) 314,000 (2011)

Sex ratio: *at birth:* 1.05 male(s)/female
0-14 years: 1.04 male(s)/female
15-24 years: 1.04 male(s)/female
25-54 years: 1.02 male(s)/female
55-64 years: 1.01 male(s)/female
65 years and over: 0.67 male(s)/female
total population: 1.01 male(s)/female (2014 est.)

Mother's mean age at first birth: 20 (2006 est.)

Maternal mortality rate: 350 deaths/100,000 live births (2010)
country comparison to the world: 34

Infant mortality rate: *total:* 57.09 deaths/1,000 live births
country comparison to the world: 26
male: 60.26 deaths/1,000 live births
female: 53.76 deaths/1,000 live births (2014 est.)

Life expectancy at birth: *total population:* 61.07 years
country comparison to the world: 191
male: 59.75 years
female: 62.47 years (2014 est.)

Total fertility rate: 5.04 children born/woman (2014 est.)
country comparison to the world: 16

Contraceptive prevalence rate: 12.9% (2012)

Health expenditures: 4.6% of GDP (2011)
country comparison to the world: 149

Physicians density: 0.06 physicians/1,000 population (2008)

Hospital bed density: 0.5 beds/1,000 population (2010)

Drinking water source:
Improved:
urban: 84.5% of population
rural: 69.1% of population
total: 76% of population
Unimproved:
urban: 15.5% of population
rural: 30.9% of population
total: 24% of population (2011 est.)

Sanitation facility access:
Improved:
urban: 25.3% of population
rural: 5.1% of population
total: 14.2% of population
Unimproved:
urban: 74.7% of population
rural: 94.9% of population
total: 85.8% of population (2011 est.)

HIV/AIDS—adult prevalence rate: 1.1% (2012 est.)
country comparison to the world: 45

HIV/AIDS—people living with HIV/AIDS: 71,500 (2012 est.)
country comparison to the world: 53

HIV/AIDS—deaths: 3,100 (2012 est.)
country comparison to the world: 52

Major infectious diseases: *degree of risk:* very high
food or waterborne diseases: bacterial and protozoal diarrhea, hepatitis A, and typhoid fever
vectorborne diseases: dengue fever, malaria, and yellow fever
respiratory disease: meningococcal meningitis
animal contact disease: rabies (2013)

Obesity—adult prevalence rate: 6% (2008)
country comparison to the world: 151

Children under the age of 5 years underweight: 20.2% (2006)
country comparison to the world: 30

Education expenditures: 5.3% of GDP (2010)
country comparison to the world: 64

Literacy: *definition:* age 15 and over can read and write
total population: 42.4%
male: 55.2%
female: 30.3% (2010 census)

School life expectancy (primary to tertiary education): *total:* 11 years
male: 13 years
female: 9 years (2011)

Child labor—children ages 5-14: *total number:* 1,020,981 *percentage:* 46 % (2006 est.)

Unemployment, youth ages 15-24: *total:* 0.8%
country comparison to the world: 147
male: 1.1%
female: 0.6% (2002)

GOVERNMENT

Country name: *conventional long form:* Republic of Benin
conventional short form: Benin
local long form: Republique du Benin
local short form: Benin
former: Dahomey

Government type: republic

Capital: *name:* Porto-Novo (official capital)
geographic coordinates: 6 29 N, 2 37 E
time difference: UTC+1 (6 hours ahead of Washington, DC during Standard Time)
note: Cotonou (seat of government)

Administrative divisions: 12 departments; Alibori, Atakora, Atlantique, Borgou, Collines, Kouffo, Donga, Littoral, Mono, Oueme, Plateau, Zou

Independence: 1 August 1960 (from France)

National holiday: National Day, 1 August (1960)

Constitution: previous 1946, 1958 (preindependence); latest adopted by referendum 2 December 1990, promulgated 11 December 1990 (2012)

Legal system: civil law system modeled largely on the French system and some customary law

International law organization participation: has not submitted an ICJ jurisdiction declaration; accepts ICCt jurisdiction

Suffrage: 18 years of age; universal

Executive branch: *chief of state:* President Thomas YAYI Boni (since 6 April 2006); note—the president is both the chief of state and head of government
head of government: President Thomas YAYI Boni (since 6 April 2006); Prime Minister Pascal KOUPAKI (since 28 May 2011)
cabinet: Council of Ministers appointed by the president (For more information visit the World Leaders website)
elections: president elected by popular vote for a five-year term (eligible for a second term); last held on 13 March 2011 (next to be held in March 2016)
election results: Thomas YAYI Boni re-elected president; percent of vote—Thomas YAYI Boni 53.1%, Adrien HOUNGBEDJI 35.6%, Abdoulaye Bio TCHANE 6.1%, other 5.2%

Legislative branch: unicameral National Assembly or Assemblee Nationale (83 seats; members are elected by direct popular vote to serve four-year terms)
elections: last held on 30 April 2011 (next to be held in 2015)
election results: percent of vote by party—NA; seats by party—FCBE 41, UN 30, other 12

Judicial branch: *highest court(s):* Supreme Court or Cour Supreme (consists of the court president and 3 chamber presidents organized into an administrative division, judicial chamber, and chamber of accounts) Constitutional Court or Cour Constitutionnelle (consists of 7 members including the court president); High Court of Justice (consists of the Constitutional Court members, 6 members appointed by the National Assembly, and the Supreme Court president)note - jurisdiction of the High Court of Justice is to limited cases of high treason by the national president or members of the government
judge selection and term of office: Supreme Court president and judges appointed by the national president upon the advice of the National Assembly; judges appointed for single renewable 5-year terms; Constitutional Court members - 4 appointed by the National Assembly and 3 by the national president; members appointed for single renewable 5-year terms; High Court of Justice "other" members elected by the National Assembly; member tenure NA
subordinate courts: Court of Appeal or Cour d'Appel; district courts; village courts; Assize courts

Political parties and leaders: Be African Movement for Democracy and Progress or MADEP [Sefou FAGBOHOUN]; Alliance of Progress Forces or AFP; Benin Renaissance or RB [Rosine SOGLO]; Democratic Renewal Party or PRD [Adrien HOUNGBEDJI]; Force Cowrie for an Emerging Benin or FCBE [Yayi BONI]; Impulse for Progress and Democracy or IPD [Theophile NATA]; Key Force or FC [Lazare SÈHOUÉTO]; Movement for the People's Alternative or MAP [Olivier CAPO-CHICHI]; Rally for Democracy and Progress or RDP [Dominique HOUNGNINOU]; Social Democrat Party or PSD [Emmanuel GOLOU]; Union for Democracy and National Solidarity or UDS [Sacca LAFIA]; Union for the Relief or UPR [Issa SALIFOU]; Union Makes the Nation or UN [Adrien HOUNGBEDJI] (superceded Alliance for Dynamic Democracy or ADD)
note: approximately 20 additional minor parties

Political pressure groups and leaders: *other:* economic groups; environmentalists; political groups; teachers' unions and other educational groups

International organization participation: ACP, AfDB, AU, CD, ECOWAS, Entente, FAO, FZ, G-77, IAEA, IBRD, ICAO, ICRM, IDA, IDB, IFAD, IFC, IFRCS, ILO, IMF, IMO, Interpol, IOC, IOM, IPU, ISO (correspondent), ITSO, ITU, ITUC (NGOs), MIGA, MINUSMA, MONUSCO, NAM, OAS (observer), OIC, OIF, OPCW, PCA, UN, UNCTAD, UNESCO, UNHCR, UNIDO, UNISFA, UNMIL, UNMISS, UNOCI, UNWTO, UPU, WAEMU, WCO, WFTU (NGOs), WHO, WIPO, WMO, WTO

Diplomatic representation in the US: *chief of mission:* Ambassador Cyrille Segbe OGUIN (since 13 March 2001)
chancery: 2124 Kalorama Road NW, Washington, DC 20008
telephone: [1] (202) 232-6656
FAX: [1] (202) 265-1996

Diplomatic representation from the US: *chief of mission:* Ambassador (Michael RAYNOR since 24 May 2012)
embassy: Rue Caporal Bernard Anani, Cotonou
mailing address: 01 B. P. 2012, Cotonou
telephone: [229] 21-30-06-50
FAX: [229] 21-30-66-82

Flag description: two equal horizontal bands of yellow (top) and red (bottom) with a vertical green band on the hoist side; green symbolizes hope and revival, yellow wealth, and red courage
note: uses the popular Pan-African colors of Ethiopia

National symbol(s): leopard

National anthem: *name:* "L'Aube Nouvelle" (The Dawn of a New Day)
lyrics/music: Gilbert Jean DAGNON
note: adopted 1960

ECONOMY

Economy—overview: The economy of Benin remains underdeveloped and dependent on subsistence agriculture, cotton production, and regional trade. Growth in real output had averaged almost 4% before the global recession and it has returned to roughly that level in 2011-12. Inflation has subsided over the past several years. In order to raise growth, Benin plans to attract more foreign investment, place more emphasis on tourism, facilitate the development of new food processing systems and agricultural products, and encourage new information and communication technology. Specific projects to improve the business climate by reforms to the land tenure system, the commercial justice system, and the financial sector were included in Benin's $307 million Millennium Challenge Account grant signed in February 2006. The 2001 privatization policy continues in telecommunications, water, electricity, and agriculture. The Paris Club and bilateral creditors have eased the external debt situation with Benin benefiting from a G-8 debt reduction announced in July 2005, while pressing for more rapid structural reforms. An insufficient electrical supply continues to adversely affect Benin's economic growth though the government recently has taken steps to increase domestic power production. Private foreign direct investment is small, and foreign aid accounts for the majority of investment in infrastructure projects. Cotton, a key export, suffered from flooding in 2010-11, but high prices supported export earnings. The government agreed to a 25% increase in civil servant salaries in 2011, following a series of strikes, increasing pressure on the national budget. Benin has appealed for international assistance to mitigate piracy against commercial shipping in its territory.

GDP (purchasing power parity): $16.65 billion (2013 est.)
country comparison to the world: 141
$15.86 billion (2012 est.)
$15.04 billion (2011 est.)
note: data are in 2013 US dollars

GDP (official exchange rate): $8.359 billion (2013 est.)

GDP—real growth rate: 5% (2013 est.)
country comparison to the world: 57
5.4% (2012 est.)
3.5% (2011 est.)

GDP—per capita (PPP): $1,600 (2013 est.)
country comparison to the world: 202
$1,600 (2012 est.)
$1,500 (2011 est.)
note: data are in 2013 US dollars

Gross national saving: 9.9% of GDP (2013 est.)
country comparison to the world: 136
9% of GDP (2012 est.)
7.9% of GDP (2011 est.)

GDP—composition, by end use: *household consumption:* 81.3%
government consumption: 12.7%
investment in fixed capital: 18.6%
investment in inventories: 0.2%
exports of goods and services: 13.2%
imports of goods and services: -26% (2013 est.)

GDP—composition, by sector of origin: *agriculture:* 31.6%
industry: 12.9%
services: 55.6% (2013 est.)

Agriculture—products: cotton, corn, cassava (manioc), yams, beans, palm oil, peanuts, cashews; livestock

Industries: textiles, food processing, construction materials, cement

Industrial production growth rate: 3.7% (2013 est.)
country comparison to the world: 80

Labor force: 3.662 million (2007 est.)
country comparison to the world: 96

Unemployment rate: NA%

Population below poverty line: 37.4% (2007 est.)

Household income or consumption by percentage share: *lowest 10%:* 3.1%
highest 10%: 29% (2003)

Distribution of family income—Gini index: 36.5 (2003)
country comparison to the world: 85

Budget: *revenues:* $1.712 billion
expenditures: $1.825 billion (2013 est.)

Taxes and other revenues: 20.5% of GDP (2013 est.)
country comparison to the world: 161

Budget surplus (+) or deficit (-): -1.3% of GDP (2013 est.)
country comparison to the world: 65

Public debt: 29.7% of GDP (2013 est.)
country comparison to the world: 124
31.9% of GDP (2012 est.)

Fiscal year: *calendar year*

Inflation rate (consumer prices): 2.4% (2013 est.)
country comparison to the world: 86
6.8% (2012 est.)

Central bank discount rate: 4.25% (31 December 2010 est.)

country comparison to the world: 90
4.25% (31 December 2009 est.)

Commercial bank prime lending rate: NA%

Stock of narrow money: $1.889 billion (31 December 2013 est.)
country comparison to the world: 128
$1.755 billion (31 December 2012 est.)

Stock of broad money: $3.06 billion (31 December 2013 est.)
country comparison to the world: 144
$2.943 billion (31 December 2012 est.)

Stock of domestic credit: $1.511 billion (31 December 2013 est.)
country comparison to the world: 146
$1.529 billion (31 December 2012 est.)

Market value of publicly traded shares: $NA

Current account balance: -$699.3 million (2013 est.)
country comparison to the world: 111
-$684.9 million (2012 est.)

Exports: $1.108 billion (2013 est.)
country comparison to the world: 155
$1.071 billion (2012 est.)

Exports—commodities: cotton, cashews, shea butter, textiles, palm products, seafood

Exports—partners: China 25%, India 23.5%, Lebanon 18.7%, Niger 4.3%, Nigeria 4% (2012)

Imports: $1.835 billion (2013 est.)
country comparison to the world: 167
$1.755 billion (2012 est.)

Imports—commodities: foodstuffs, capital goods, petroleum products

Imports—partners: China 37.2%, US 8.9%, India 6.7%, France 5.6%, Malaysia 5.3% (2012)

Reserves of foreign exchange and gold: $720.3 million (31 December 2013 est.)
country comparison to the world: 144
$712.8 million (31 December 2012 est.)

Debt—external: $1.236 billion (31 December 2013 est.)
country comparison to the world: 156
$1.123 billion (31 December 2012 est.)

Exchange rates: Communaute Financiere Africaine francs (XOF) per US dollar—
500.7 (2013 est.)
510.53 (2012 est.)
495.28 (2010 est.)
472.19 (2009)
447.81 (2008)

ENERGY

Electricity—production: 142.1 million kWh (2010 est.)
country comparison to the world: 190

Electricity—consumption: 870.1 million kWh (2010 est.)
country comparison to the world: 154

Electricity—exports: 0 kWh (2012 est.)
country comparison to the world: 109

Electricity—imports: 935 million kWh (2010 est.)
country comparison to the world: 65

Electricity—installed generating capacity: 61,000 kW (2010 est.)
country comparison to the world: 182

Electricity—from fossil fuels: 98.4% of total installed capacity (2010 est.)
country comparison to the world: 56

Electricity—from nuclear fuels: 0% of total installed capacity (2010 est.)
country comparison to the world: 53

Electricity—from hydroelectric plants: 1.6% of total installed capacity (2010 est.)
country comparison to the world: 140

Electricity—from other renewable sources: 0% of total installed capacity (2010 est.)
country comparison to the world: 159

Crude oil—production: 0 bbl/day (2012 est.)
country comparison to the world: 155

Crude oil—exports: 0 bbl/day (2010 est.)
country comparison to the world: 88

Crude oil—imports: 0 bbl/day (2010 est.)
country comparison to the world: 163

Crude oil—proved reserves: 8 million bbl (1 January 2013 es)
country comparison to the world: 93

Refined petroleum products—production: 0 bbl/day (2010 est.)
country comparison to the world: 124

Refined petroleum products—consumption: 29,170 bbl/day (2011 est.)
country comparison to the world: 116

Refined petroleum products—exports: 0 bbl/day (2010 est.)
country comparison to the world: 155

Refined petroleum products—imports: 34,840 bbl/day (2010 est.)
country comparison to the world: 87

Natural gas—production: 0 cu m (2011 est.)
country comparison to the world: 106

Natural gas—consumption: 0 cu m (2010 est.)
country comparison to the world: 122

Natural gas—exports: 0 cu m (2011 est.)
country comparison to the world: 68

Natural gas—imports: 0 cu m (2011 est.)
country comparison to the world: 164

Natural gas—proved reserves: 1.133 billion cu m (1 January 2013 es)
country comparison to the world: 102

Carbon dioxide emissions from consumption of energy: 4.655 million Mt (2011 est.)
country comparison to the world: 129

COMMUNICATIONS

Telephones—main lines in use: 156,700 (2012)
country comparison to the world: 135

Telephones—mobile cellular: 8.408 million (2012)
country comparison to the world: 90

Telephone system: *general assessment:* inadequate system of open-wire, microwave radio relay, and cellular connections; fixed-line network characterized by aging, deteriorating equipment
domestic: fixed-line teledensity only about 2 per 100 persons; spurred by the presence of multiple mobile-cellular providers, cellular telephone subscribership has been increasing rapidly
international: country code—229; landing point for the SAT-3/WASC fiber-optic submarine cable that provides connectivity to Europe and Asia; long distance fiber-optic links with Togo, Burkina Faso, Niger, and Nigeria; satellite earth stations—7 (Intelsat-Atlantic Ocean) (2008)

Broadcast media: state-run Office de Radiodiffusion et de Television du Benin (ORTB) operates a TV station with multiple channels giving it a wide broadcast reach; several privately owned TV stations broadcast from Cotonou; satellite TV subscription service is available; state-owned radio, under ORTB control, includes a national station supplemented by a number of regional stations; substantial number of privately owned radio broadcast stations; transmissions of a few international broadcasters are available on FM in Cotonou (2007)

Internet country code: .bj

Internet hosts: 491 (2012)
country comparison to the world: 183

Internet users: 200,100 (2009)
country comparison to the world: 139

TRANSPORTATION

Airports: 6 (2013)
country comparison to the world: 171

Airports—with paved runways: *total:* 1
1,524 to 2,437 m: 1 (2013)

Airports—with unpaved runways: *total:* 5
2,438 to 3,047 m: 2
1,524 to 2,437 m: 1
914 to 1,523 m: 2 (2013)

Railways: *total:* 438 km
country comparison to the world: 113
narrow gauge: 438 km 1.000-m gauge (2008)

Roadways: *total:* 16,000 km
country comparison to the world: 119
paved: 1,400 km
unpaved: 14,600 km (2006)

Waterways: 150 km (seasonal navigation on River Niger along northern border) (2011)
country comparison to the world: 102

Ports and terminals: *major seaport (s):* Cotonou

MILITARY

Military branches: Benin Armed Forces (Forces Armees Beninoises, FAB): Army (l'Arme de Terre), Benin Navy (Forces Navales Beninois, FNB), Benin Air Force (Force Aerienne du Benin, FAB) (2013)

Military service age and obligation: 18-35 years of age for selective compulsory and voluntary military service; a higher education diploma is required; both sexes are eligible for military service; conscript tour of duty—18 months (2013)

Manpower available for military service:
males age 16-49: 2,095,373
females age 16-49: 2,038,351 (2010 est.)

Manpower fit for military service: *males age 16-49:* 1,385,065
females age 16-49: 1,400,045 (2010 est.)

Manpower reaching militarily significant age annually: *male:* 108,496
female: 104,526 (2010 est.)

Military expenditures: 1.03% of GDP (2012)
country comparison to the world: 100
NA% (2011)
1.03% of GDP (2010)

TRANSNATIONAL ISSUES

Disputes—international: talks continue between Benin and Togo on funding the Adjrala hydroelectric dam on the Mona River; Benin retains a border dispute with Burkina Faso around the town of Koualou; location of Benin-Niger-Nigeria tripoint is unresolved

Illicit drugs: transshipment point used by traffickers for cocaine destined for Western Europe; vulnerable to money laundering due to poorly enforced financial regulations (2008)

BERMUDA

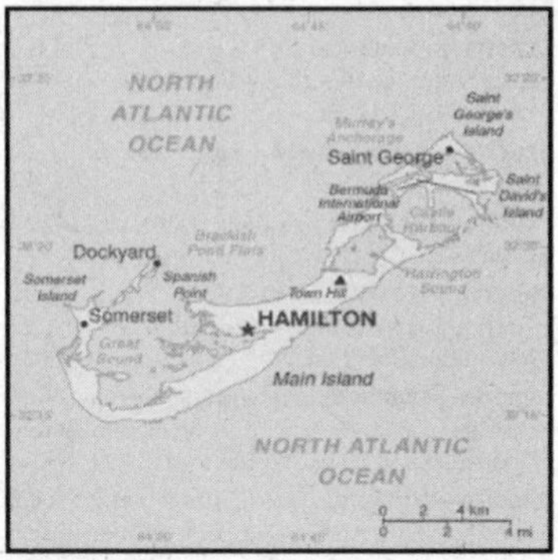

INTRODUCTION

Background: Bermuda was first settled in 1609 by shipwrecked English colonists headed for Virginia. Vacationing to the island to escape North American winters first developed in Victorian times. Tourism continues to be important to the island's economy, although international business has overtaken it in recent years. Bermuda has also developed into a highly successful offshore financial center. A referendum on independence from the UK was soundly defeated in 1995.

GEOGRAPHY

Location: North America, group of islands in the North Atlantic Ocean, east of South Carolina (US)

Geographic coordinates: 32 20 N, 64 45 W

Map references: North America

Area: *total:* 54 sq km
country comparison to the world: 232
land: 54 sq km
water: 0 sq km

Area—comparative: about one-third the size of Washington, DC

Land boundaries: 0 km

Coastline: 103 km

Maritime claims: *territorial sea:* 12 nm
exclusive fishing zone: 200 nm

Climate: subtropical; mild, humid; gales, strong winds common in winter Terrain: low hills separated by fertile depressions Elevation extremes: lowest point: Atlantic Ocean 0 m highest point: Town Hill 76 m

Natural resources: limestone, pleasant climate fostering tourism

Land use: *arable land:* 14.8%
permanent crops: 0%
other: 85.2% (55% developed, 45% rural/open space) (2011)

Irrigated land: NA

Natural hazards: hurricanes (June to November)

Environment—current issues: sustainable development

Geography—note: consists of about 138 coral islands and islets with ample rainfall, but no rivers or freshwater lakes; some land was leased by the US Government from 1941 to 1995

PEOPLE AND SOCIETY

Nationality: *noun:* Bermudian(s)
adjective: Bermudian

Ethnic groups: black 53.8%, white 31%, mixed 7.5%, other 7.1%, unspecified 0.6% (2010 est.)

Languages: English (official), Portuguese

Religions: Protestant 46.1% (Anglican 15.8%, African Methodist Episcopal 8.6%, Seventh Day Adventist 6.7, Pentecostal 3.5%, Methodist 2.7%, Presbyterian 2.0 %, Church of God 1.6%, Baptist 1.2%, Salvation Army 1.1%, Bretheren 1.0%, other Protestant 2.0%), Roman Catholic 14.5%, Jehovah's Witness 1.3%, other Christian 9.1%, Muslim 1%, other 3.9%, none 17.8%, unspecified 6.2% (2010 est.)

Population: 69,839 (July 2014 est.)
country comparison to the world: 204

Age structure: *0-14 years:* 17.5% (male 6,165/female 6,031)
15-24 years: 12.2% (male 4,275/female 4,267)
25-54 years: 39.3% (male 13,706/female 13,741)
55-64 years: 16.4% (male 4,813/female 5,368)
65 years and over: 16% (male 4,821/female 6,652) (2014 est.)

Median age: *total:* 42.9 years
male: 41.1 years
female: 44.6 years (2014 est.)

Population growth rate: 0.52% (2014 est.)
country comparison to the world: 154

Birth rate: 11.35 births/1,000 population (2014 est.)
country comparison to the world: 173

Death rate: 8.06 deaths/1,000 population (2014 est.)
country comparison to the world: 98

Net migration rate: 1.92 migrant(s)/1,000 population (2014 est.)
country comparison to the world: 49

Urbanization: 100% of total population (2010)

rate of urbanization: 0.2% annual rate of change (2010-15 est.)

Major urban areas —population: HAMILTON (capital) 11,000 (2011)

Sex ratio: *at birth:* 1.02 male(s)/female
0-14 years: 1.02 male(s)/female
15-24 years: 1 male(s)/female
25-54 years: 1 male(s)/female
55-64 years: 0.94 male(s)/female
65 years and over: 0.72 male(s)/female
total population: 0.94 male(s)/female (2014 est.)

Infant mortality rate: *total:* 2.48 deaths/1,000 live births
country comparison to the world: 222
male: 2.58 deaths/1,000 live births
female: 2.37 deaths/1,000 live births (2014 est.)

Life expectancy at birth: *total population:* 81.04 years
country comparison to the world: 23
male: 77.83 years
female: 84.31 years (2014 est.)

Total fertility rate: 1.95 children born/woman (2014 est.)
country comparison to the world: 133

HIV/AIDS—adult prevalence rate: 0.3% (2005)
country comparison to the world: 89

HIV/AIDS—people living with HIV/AIDS: 163 (2005)
country comparison to the world: 165

HIV/AIDS—deaths: 392 (2005 est.)
country comparison to the world: 99

Education expenditures: 2.6% of GDP (2010)
country comparison to the world: 151

Literacy: *definition:* age 15 and over can read and write
total population: 98%
male: 98%
female: 99% (2005 est.)

School life expectancy (primary to tertiary education): *total:* 12 years
male: 11 years
female: 13 years (2011)

Unemployment, youth ages 15-24: *total:* 10.8%
country comparison to the world: 106
male: 14.3%
female: 7.6% (2000)

GOVERNMENT

Country name: *conventional long form:* none
conventional short form: Bermuda
former: Somers Islands

Dependency status: overseas territory of the UK

Government type: parliamentary; self-governing territory

Capital: *name:* Hamilton
geographic coordinates: 32 17 N, 64 47 W
time difference: UTC-4 (1 hour ahead of Washington, DC during Standard Time)
daylight saving time: +1hr, begins second Sunday in March; ends first Sunday in November

Administrative divisions: 9 parishes and 2 municipalities*; Devonshire, Hamilton, Hamilton*, Paget, Pembroke, Saint George*, Saint George's, Sandys, Smith's, Southampton, Warwick

Independence: none (overseas territory of the UK)

National holiday: Bermuda Day, 24 May

Constitution: several previous (dating to 1684); latest entered into force 8 June 1968; amended 1989 and 2003 (2013)

Legal system: English common law

International law organization participation: has not submitted an ICJ jurisdiction declaration; non-party state to the ICCt

Suffrage: 18 years of age; universal

Executive branch: *chief of state:* Queen ELIZABETH II (since 6 February 1952); represented by Governor George FERGUSSON (since 23 May 2012)
head of government: Premier Craig CANNONIER (since 18 December 2012)
cabinet: Cabinet nominated by the premier, appointed by the governor (For more information visit the World Leaders website)
elections: the monarchy is hereditary; governor appointed by the monarch; following legislative elections, the leader of the majority party or the leader of the majority coalition usually appointed premier by the governor

Legislative branch: bicameral Parliament consists of the Senate (11 seats; members appointed by the governor, the premier, and the opposition to serve a five-year term) and the House of Assembly (36 seats; members are elected by popular vote to serve up to five-year terms)

elections: last general election held on 17 December 2012 (next to be held not later than 2017) election results: percent of vote by party—OBA 51.7%, PLP 46.1%, other 2.2%; seats by party—OBA 19, PLP 17

Judicial branch: *highest court(s):* Court of Appeal (consists of the court president and 4 justices); Supreme Court (consists of the chief justice, 4 puisne judges, and 1 associate justice)
note - the Judicial Committee of the Privy Council, in London, is the court of last resort
judge selection and term of office: Court of Appeal justice appointed by the governor; justice tenure by individual appointment; Supreme Court judges nominated by the Judicial and Legal Services Commission and appointed by the governor; judge tenure NA subordinate courts: commercial court (began in 2006); magistrates' courts

Political parties and leaders: Progressive Labor Party or PLP [Marc BEAN]; One Bermuda Alliance or OBA [Thad HOLLIS]

Political pressure groups and leaders: Association of Bermuda Insurers and Reinsurers or ABIR [Bradley KADING]; Association of Bermuda International Companies or ABIC [George HUTCHINGS]; Bermuda Employer's Council [Keith JENSEN]; Bermuda Industrial Union or BIU [Chris Furbert]; Bermuda Public Services Union or BPSU [Kevin GRANT and Ed BALL]; Bermuda Union of Teachers [Michael CHARLES]

International organization participation: Caricom (associate), ICC (NGOs), Interpol (subbureau), IOC, ITUC (NGOs), UPU, WCO

Diplomatic representation in the US: none (overseas territory of the UK)

Diplomatic representation from the US: *chief of mission:* Consul General Robert SETTJE (since August 2012)
consulate(s) general: Crown Hill, 16 Middle Road, Devonshire DVO3
mailing address: P. O. Box HM325, Hamilton HMBX; American Consulate General Hamilton, US Department of State, 5300 Hamilton Place, Washington, DC 20520-5300
telephone: [1] (441) 295-1342
FAX: [1] (441) 295-1592, 296-9233

Flag description: red, with the flag of the UK in the upper hoist-side quadrant and the Bermudian coat of arms (a white shield with a red lion standing on a green grassy field holding a scrolled shield showing the sinking of the ship Sea Venture off Bermuda in 1609) centered on the outer half of the flag; it was the shipwreck of the vessel, filled with English colonists originally bound for Virginia, that led to settling of Bermuda
note: the flag is unusual in that it is only British overseas territory that uses a red ensign, all others use blue

National symbol(s): red lion

National anthem: *name:* "Hail to Bermuda"
lyrics/music: Bette JOHNS
note: serves as a local anthem; as a territory of the United Kingdom, "God Save the Queen" is official (see United Kingdom)

ECONOMY

Economy—overview: Despite four years of recession and a public debt of $1.4 billion, Bermuda enjoys the fourth highest per capita income in the world, about 70% higher than that of the US. The average cost of a single-family home in 2012 was $1.1 million. Its economy is primarily based on international business and the provision of financial services to that sector, and to a lesser extent tourism. A number of reinsurance companies relocated to the island following the 11 September 2001 attacks on the US and again after Hurricanes Katrina, Rita, and Wilma in 2005, contributing to the expansion of an already robust international business sector. Bermuda's tourism industry—which derives over 80% of its visitors from the US—continues to struggle and has dropped in its relevant importance to the economy, although it is still important as a job creator. Bermuda must import almost everything. Agriculture is limited due to the small size of the island and Bermuda's industrial sector is small.

GDP (purchasing power parity): $5.6 billion (2011 est.)
country comparison to the world: 169
$5.803 billion (2010 est.)

GDP (official exchange rate): $5.6 billion (2011)

GDP—real growth rate: -3.5% (2011)
country comparison to the world: 213

GDP—per capita (PPP): $86,000 (2011 est.)
country comparison to the world: 3

GDP—composition, by end use: household consumption: 29.4%
government consumption: 15%
investment in fixed capital: 23.3%
investment in inventories: 0%
exports of goods and services: 64.8%
imports of goods and services: 32.5% (2013 est.)

GDP—composition by sector of origin: *agriculture:* 0.7% industry: 5.7%
services: 93.5% (2013 est.)

Agriculture—products: bananas, vegetables, citrus, flowers; dairy products, honey

Industries: international business, tourism, light manufacturing

Industrial production growth rate: 1% country *comparison to the world:* 151

Labor force: 37,400 (2011)
country comparison to the world: 200

Labor force—by occupation: *agriculture and fishing:* 3%
laborers: 17%
clerical: 19%
professional and technical: 21%
administrative and managerial: 15%
sales: 7%
services: 19% (2004 est.)

Unemployment rate: 8% (2012 est.)
country comparison to the world: 87

Population below poverty line: 11% (2008 est.)

Household income or consumption by percentage share: *lowest 10%:* NA%
highest 10%: NA%

Budget: *revenues:* $973.2 million
expenditures: $1.115 billion (FY11/12)

Taxes and other revenues: 17.4% of GDP (FY11/ 12 est.)
country comparison to the world: 178

Budget surplus (+) or deficit (-): -2.5% of GDP (FY11/12 est.)
country comparison to the world: 101

Fiscal year: 1 April—31 March

Inflation rate (consumer prices): 1.8% (2013 est.)
country comparison to the world: 60
2.4% (2012 est.)

Market value of publicly traded shares: $1.487 billion (31 December 2012 est.)
country comparison to the world: 103
$1.436 billion (31 December 2011)
$1.535 billion (31 December 2010 est.)

Exports: $13 million (2013 est.)
country comparison to the world: 209
$12 million (2012 est.)

Exports—commodities: reexports of pharmaceuticals

Exports—partners: Australia 17%, US 14.8%, Indonesia 12.6% (2012)

Imports: $925 million (2013 est.)
country comparison to the world: 178
$900 million (2012 est.)

Imports—commodities: clothing, fuels, machinery and transport equipment, construction materials, chemicals, food and live animals

Imports—partners: South Korea 46.2%, US 21%, Singapore 9.9%, China 7%, Turkmenistan 4.8% (2012)

Debt—external: $1.4 billion (2012 est.)
country comparison to the world: 151

Stock of direct foreign investment—at home: $NA

Stock of direct foreign investment—abroad: $NA

Exchange rates: Bermudian dollars (BMD) per US dollar—
1 (2013 est.)
1 (2012 est.)

ENERGY

Electricity—production: 675 million kWh (2011 est.)
country comparison to the world: 156

Electricity—consumption: 638.4 million kWh (2010 est.)
country comparison to the world: 162

Electricity—exports: 0 kWh (2012 est.)
country comparison to the world: 103

Electricity—imports: 0 kWh (2012 est.)
country comparison to the world: 117

Electricity—installed generating capacity: 165,000 kW (2011 est.)
country comparison to the world: 161

Electricity—from fossil fuels: 98.2% of total installed capacity (2012 est.)
country comparison to the world: 57

Electricity—from nuclear fuels: 0% of total installed capacity (2012 est.)
country comparison to the world: 46

Electricity—from hydroelectric plants: 0% of total installed capacity (2012 est.)
country comparison to the world: 158

Electricity—from other renewable sources: 1.8% of total installed capacity
country comparison to the world: 74
note: the Tynes Bay Waste Treatment Facility turns waste to electric energy (2012 est.)

Crude oil—production: 0 bbl/day (2012 est.)
country comparison to the world: 152

Crude oil—exports: 0 bbl/day (2010 est.)
country comparison to the world: 81

Crude oil—imports: 0 bbl/day (2010 est.)
country comparison to the world: 158

Crude oil—proved reserves: 0 bbl (1 January 2013 es)
country comparison to the world: 106

Refined petroleum products—production: 0 bbl/day (2012 est.)
country comparison to the world: 121

Refined petroleum products—consumption: 2,747 bbl/day (2012 est.)
country comparison to the world: 185

Refined petroleum products—exports: 0 bbl/day (2012 est.)
country comparison to the world: 152

Refined petroleum products—imports: 2,747 bbl/day (2012 est.)
country comparison to the world: 173

Natural gas—production: 0 cu m (2012 est.)
country comparison to the world: 101

Natural gas—consumption: 0 cu m (2012 est.)
country comparison to the world: 119

Natural gas—exports: 0 cu m (2012 est.)
country comparison to the world: 63

Natural gas—imports: 0 cu m (2012 est.)
country comparison to the world: 158

Natural gas—proved reserves: 0 cu m (1 January 2013 es)
country comparison to the world: 112

Carbon dioxide emissions from consumption of energy: 776,900 Mt (2011 est.)
country comparison to the world: 171

COMMUNICATIONS

Telephones—main lines in use: 69,000 (2012)
country comparison to the world: 156

Telephones—mobile cellular: 91,000 (2012)
country comparison to the world: 195

Telephone system: *general assessment:* a good, fully automatic digital telephone system with fiber-optic trunk lines
domestic: the system has a high fixed-line teledensity coupled with a mobile-cellular teledensity of roughly 125 per 100 persons
international: country code—1-441; landing points for the GlobeNet, Gemini Bermuda, CBUS, and the Challenger Bermuda-1 (CB-1)submarine cables; satellite earth stations—3 (2010)

Broadcast media: 3 TV stations; cable and satellite TV subscription services are available; roughly 13 radio stations operating (2012)

Internet country code: .bm

Internet hosts: 20,040 (2012)
country comparison to the world: 119

Internet users: 54,000 (2009)
country comparison to the world: 173

TRANSPORTATION

Airports: 1 (2013)
country comparison to the world: 212

Airports—with paved runways: *total:* 1
2,438 to 3,047 m: 1 (2013)

Roadways: *total:* 447 km
country comparison to the world: 197
paved: 447 km
note: 225 km public roads; 222 km private roads (2010)

Merchant marine: *total:* 139
country comparison to the world: 41
by type: bulk carrier 22, chemical tanker 3, container 14, liquefied gas 43, passenger 27, passenger/cargo 2, petroleum tanker 19, refrigerated cargo 9
foreign-owned: 105 (France 1, Germany 14, Greece 8, Hong Kong 4, Ireland 1, Israel 3, Japan 2, Monaco 2, Nigeria 11, Norway 5, Sweden 14, UK 14, US 26)
registered in other countries: 241 (Bahamas 15, Cyprus 1, France 5, Greece 3, Hong Kong 20, Isle of Man 7, Liberia 4, Malta 15, Marshall Islands 35, Netherlands 1, Norway 24, Panama 27, Philippines 47, Saint Vincent and the Grenadines 1, Singapore 25, UK 6, US 5) (2010)

Ports and terminals: *major seaport(s):* Hamilton, Ireland Island, Saint George

MILITARY

Military branches: Bermuda Regiment (2012)

Military service age and obligation: 18-45 years of age for voluntary male or female enlistment in the Bermuda Regiment; males must register at age 18 and may be subject to conscription; term of service is 38 months for volunteers or conscripts (2012)

Manpower available for military service: *males age 16-49:* 15,081 (2010 est.)

Manpower fit for military service: *males age 16-49:* 12,323
females age 16-49: 12,174 (2010 est.)

Manpower reaching militarily significant age annually: *male:* 433
female: 410 (2010 est.)

Military—note: defense is the responsibility of the UK

TRANSNATIONAL ISSUES

Disputes—international: none

BHUTAN

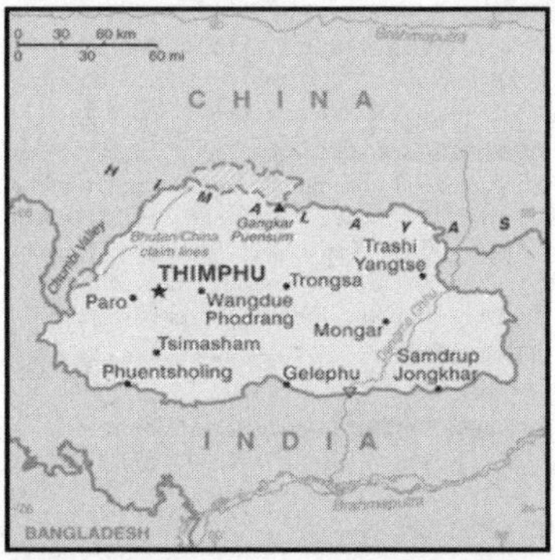

INTRODUCTION

Background: In 1865, Britain and Bhutan signed the Treaty of Sinchulu, under which Bhutan would receive an annual subsidy in exchange for ceding some border land to British India. Under British influence, a monarchy was set up in 1907; three years later, a treaty was signed whereby the British agreed not to interfere in Bhutanese internal affairs, and Bhutan allowed Britain to direct its foreign affairs. This role was assumed by independent India after 1947. Two years later, a formal Indo-Bhutanese accord returned to Bhutan the areas annexed by the British, formalized the annual subsidies the country received, and defined India's responsibilities in defense and foreign relations. In March 2005, King Jigme Singye WANGCHUCK unveiled the government's draft constitution - which introduced major democratic reforms - and pledged to hold a national referendum for its approval. In December 2006, the King abdicated the throne in favor of his son, Jigme Khesar Namgyel WANGCHUCK, in order to give him experience as head of state before the democratic transition. In early 2007, India and Bhutan renegotiated their treaty, eliminating the clause that stated that Bhutan would be "guided by" India in conducting its foreign policy, although Thimphu continues to coordinate closely with New Delhi. Elections for seating the country's first parliament were completed in March 2008; the king ratified the country's first constitution in July 2008. Bhutan experienced a peaceful turnover of power following parliamentary elections in 2013, which routed the incumbent party. The disposition of some 30,000 Bhutanese refugees - housed in two UN refugee camps in Nepal - remains unresolved.

GEOGRAPHY

Location: Southern Asia, between China and India

Geographic coordinates: 27 30 N, 90 30 E

Map references: Asia

Area: *total:* 38,394 sq km
country comparison to the world: 137
land: 38,394 sq km
water: 0 sq km

Area—comparative: about one-half the size of Indiana

Land boundaries: *total:* 1,075 km
border countries: China 470 km, India 605 km

Coastline: 0 km (landlocked)

Maritime claims: none (landlocked)

Climate: varies; tropical in southern plains; cool winters and hot summers in central valleys; severe winters and cool summers in Himalayas

Terrain: mostly mountainous with some fertile valleys and savanna

Elevation extremes: *lowest point:* Drangeme Chhu 97 m
highest point: Gangkar Puensum 7,570 m

Natural resources: timber, hydropower, gypsum, calcium carbonate

Land use: *arable land:* 2.49%
permanent crops: 0.46%
other: 97.06% (2011)

Irrigated land: 319.1 sq km (2010)

Total renewable water resources: 78 cu km (2011)

Freshwater withdrawal (domestic/industrial/agricultural): *total:* 0.34 cu km/yr (5%/1%/94%)
per capita: 458 cu m/yr (2008)

Natural hazards: violent storms from the Himalayas are the source of the country's name, which translates as Land of the Thunder Dragon; frequent landslides during the rainy season

Environment—current issues: soil erosion; limited access to potable water

Environment—international agreements: *party to:* Biodiversity, Climate Change, Climate Change-Kyoto Protocol, Desertification, Endangered Species, Hazardous Wastes, Ozone Layer Protection signed, but not ratified: Law of the Sea

Geography—note: landlocked; strategic location between China and India; controls several key Himalayan mountain passes

PEOPLE AND SOCIETY

Nationality: *noun:* Bhutanese (singular and plural)
adjective: Bhutanese

Ethnic groups: Ngalop (also known as Bhote) 50%, ethnic Nepalese 35% (includes Lhotsampas—one of several Nepalese ethnic groups), indigenous or migrant tribes 15%

Languages: Sharchhopka 28%, Dzongkha (official) 24%, Lhotshamkha 22%, other 26% (includes foreign languages) (2005 est.)

Religions: Lamaistic Buddhist 75.3%, Indian- and Nepalese-influenced Hinduism 22.1%, other 2.6% (2005 est.)

Population: 733,643 (July 2014 est.)
country comparison to the world: 166
note: the Factbook population estimate is consistent with the first modern census of Bhutan, conducted in 2005; previous Factbook population estimates for this country, which were on the order of three times the total population reported here, were based on Bhutanese government publications that did not include the census

Age structure: *0-14 years:* 27.3% (male 102,196/female 97,923)
15-24 years: 20.1% (male 75,327/female 72,472)
25-54 years: 40.8% (male 159,868/female 139,236)
55-64 years: 6% (male 22,769/female 19,699)
65 years and over: 5.9% (male 23,153/female 21,000) (2014 est.)

Dependency ratios: *total dependency ratio:* 48.9%
youth dependency ratio: 41.8%
elderly dependency ratio: 7.1%
potential support ratio: 14 (2013)

Median age: *total:* 26.2 years
male: 26.8 years
female: 25.6 years (2014 est.)

Population growth rate: 1.13% (2014 est.)
country comparison to the world: 106

Birth rate: 18.12 births/1,000 population (2014 est.)
country comparison to the world: 106

Death rate: 6.78 deaths/1,000 population (2014 est.)
country comparison to the world: 141

Net migration rate: 0 migrant(s)/1,000 population (2014 est.)
country comparison to the world: 100

Urbanization: *urban population:* 35.6% of total population (2011)
rate of urbanization: 3.65% annual rate of change (2010-15 est.)

Major urban areas—population: THIMPHU (capital) 99,000 (2011)

Sex ratio: *at birth:* 1.05 male(s)/female
0-14 years: 1.04 male(s)/female
15-24 years: 1.04 male(s)/female
25-54 years: 1.15 male(s)/female
55-64 years: 1.09 male(s)/female
65 years and over: 1.11 male(s)/female
total population: 1.1 male(s)/female (2014 est.)

Maternal mortality rate: 180 deaths/100,000 live births (2010)
country comparison to the world: 59

Infant mortality rate: *total:* 37.89 deaths/1,000 live births
country comparison to the world: 61
male: 38.34 deaths/1,000 live births
female: 37.42 deaths/1,000 live births (2014 est.)

Life expectancy at birth: *total population:* 68.98 years
country comparison to the world: 157
male: 68.06 years female: 69.95 years (2014 est.)

Total fertility rate: 2.02 children born/woman (2014 est.)
country comparison to the world: 121

Contraceptive prevalence rate: 65.6% (2010)

Health expenditures: 4.1% of GDP (2011)
country comparison to the world: 162

Physicians density: 0.07 physicians/1,000 population (2008)

Hospital bed density: 1.8 beds/1,000 population (2011)

Drinking water source:
Improved:
urban: 99.7% of population
rural: 95.8% of population
total: 97.2% of population
Unimproved:
urban: 0.3% of population
rural: 4.2% of population
total: 2.8% of population (2011 est.)

Sanitation facility access:
Improved:
urban: 73.9% of population
rural: 29.3% of population
total: 45.2% of population
Unimproved:
urban: 26.1% of population
rural: 70.7% of population
total: 54.8% of population (2011 est.)

HIV/AIDS—adult prevalence rate: 0.2% (2012 est.)
country comparison to the world: 109

HIV/AIDS—people living with HIV/AIDS: 1,100 (2012 est.)
country comparison to the world: 143

HIV/AIDS—deaths: 100 (2012 est.)
country comparison to the world: 127

Major infectious diseases: *degree of risk:* high
food or waterborne diseases: bacterial and protozoal diarrhea, hepatitis A, and typhoid fever
vectorborne diseases: dengue fever and malaria (2013)

Obesity—adult prevalence rate: 5.3% (2008)
country comparison to the world: 154

Children under the age of 5 years underweight: 12.8% (2010)
country comparison to the world: 59

Education expenditures: 4.7% of GDP (2011)
country comparison to the world: 86

Literacy: *definition:* age 15 and over can read and write
total population: 52.8%
male: 65%
female: 38.7% (2005 est.)

School life expectancy (primary to tertiary education): *total:* 13 years
male: 13 years
female: 13 years (2012)

Child labor—children ages 5-14: *total number:* 25,801
percentage: 18 % (2010 est.)

Unemployment, youth ages 15-24: *total:* 7.2%
country comparison to the world: 127
male: 7.3%
female: 7.2% (2012)

GOVERNMENT

Country name: *conventional long form:* Kingdom of Bhutan
conventional short form: Bhutan
local long form: Druk Gyalkhap
local short form: Druk Yul

Government type: constitutional monarchy

Capital: *name:* Thimphu
geographic coordinates: 27 28 N, 89 38 E
time difference: UTC+6 (11 hours ahead of Washington, DC during Standard Time)

Administrative divisions: 20 districts (dzongkhag, singular and plural); Bumthang, Chhukha, Chirang, Daga, Gasa, Geylegphug, Ha, Lhuntshi, Mongar, Paro, Pemagatsel, Punakha, Samchi, Samdrup Jongkhar, Shemgang, Tashigang, Tashi Yangtse, Thimphu, Tongsa, Wangdi Phodrang

Independence: 1907 (became a unified kingdom under its first hereditary king)

National holiday: National Day (Ugyen WANGCHUCK became first hereditary king), 17 December (1907)

Constitution: previous (various royal decrees); first constitution drafted November 2001 - March 2005, ratified 18 July 2008 (2011)

Legal system: civil law based on Buddhist religious law

International law organization participation: has not submitted an ICJ jurisdiction declaration; non-party state to the ICCt

Suffrage: 18 years of age; universal

Executive branch: *chief of state:* King Jigme Khesar Namgyel WANGCHUCK (since 14 December

2006); note - King Jigme Singye WANGCHUCK abdicated the throne on 14 December 2006 and his son immediately succeeded him; the nearly two-year delay between the former King's abdication and his son's coronation on 6 November 2008 was to ensure an astrologically auspicious coronation date and to give the new king, who had limited experience, deeper administrative expertise under the guidance of his father

head of government: Prime Minister Tshering TOBGAY (since July 2013)

cabinet: Council of Ministers (Lhengye Zhungtshog) nominated by the monarch in consultation with the prime minister and approved by the National Assembly; members serve fixed, five-year terms; the leader of the majority party is nominated as the prime minister (For more information visit the World Leaders website) elections: the monarchy is hereditary, but the 2008 constitution grants the Parliament authority to remove the monarch with two-thirds vote; election of a National Assembly last occurred in July 2013, resulting in the transfer of power to the former opposition party

Legislative branch: bicameral Parliament or Chi Tshog consists of the non-partisan National Council or Gyelyong Tshogde (25 seats; 20 members elected by each of the 20 administrative districts (dzongkhags) for four-year terms and 5 members appointed by the king); and the National Assembly or Tshogdu (47 seats; members nominated by the two parties and elected by direct, popular vote for five-year terms)

elections: National Council elections last held on 23 April 2013 (next to be held in 2017); National Assembly elections (first round) last held on 31 May 2013; second round held on 13 July 2013

election results: National Council - independents 20; note - all candidates required to run as independents; National Assembly - first round poll held on 31 May 2013 - percent of vote by party - DPT 44.52%; PDP 32.53%; DNT 17.04%; DCT 5.9%; second round poll held on 13 July 2013 - percent of vote by party - PDP 54.88%, DPT 45.12%; seats by party - PDP 32, DPT 15

Judicial branch: *highest court(s):* Supreme Court (consists of 5 justices including the chief justice) note - the Supreme Court has sole jurisdiction in constitutional matters

judge selection and term of office: Supreme Court chief justice appointed by the monarch upon the advice of the National Judicial Commission, a 4-member body to include the Legislative Committee of the National Assembly, the attorney general, the Chief Justice of Bhutan and the senior Associate Justice of the Supreme Court; other judges (drangpons) appointed by the monarch from among the High Court judges selected by the National Judicial Commission; chief justice serves a 5-year term or until reaching age 65 years, whichever is earlier; the four other judges serve 10-year terms or until age 65, whichever is earlier subordinate courts: High Court (first appellate court); District or Dzongkhag Courts; sub-district or Dungkhag Courts

Political parties and leaders: Bhutan Peace and Prosperity Party (Druk Phuensum Tshogpa) or DPT [Jigme THINLEY]; Bhutan Kuen-Nyam Party or BNK [Sonam TOBGAY]; People's Democratic Party or PDP [Tshering TOBGAY]; Druk Nymrub Tshogpa or DNT; Druck Chirwang Tshogpa or DCT

Political pressure groups and leaders: United Front for Democracy (exiled); Druk National Congress (exiled)

other: Buddhist clergy; ethnic Nepalese organizations leading militant antigovernment campaign; Indian merchant community

International organization participation: ADB, BIMSTEC, CP, FAO, G-77, IBRD, ICAO, IDA, IFAD, IFC, IMF, Interpol, IOC, IOM (observer), ISO (correspondent), ITSO, ITU, NAM, OPCW, SAARC, SACEP, UN, UNCTAD, UNESCO, UNIDO, UNWTO, UPU, WCO, WHO, WIPO, WMO, WTO (observer)

Diplomatic representation in the US: none; note—the Permanent Mission to the UN for Bhutan has consular jurisdiction in the US; the permanent representative to the UN is Kunzang C. NAMGYEL (since February 2014); address: 343 East 43rd Street, New York, NY 10017; telephone [1] (212) 682-2268; FAX [1] (212) 661-0551

consulate(s) general: New York

Diplomatic representation from the US: the US and Bhutan have no formal diplomatic relations, although frequent informal contact is maintained via the US embasssy in New Delhi (India) and Bhutan's Permanent Mission to the UN

Flag description: divided diagonally from the lower hoist-side corner; the upper triangle is yellow and the lower triangle is orange; centered along the dividing line is a large black and white dragon facing away from the hoist side; the dragon, called the Druk (Thunder Dragon), is the emblem of the nation; its white color stands for purity and the jewels in its claws symbolize wealth; the background colors represent spiritual and secular powers within Bhutan: the orange is associated with Buddhism, while the yellow denotes the ruling dynasty

National symbol(s): thunder dragon known as Druk

National anthem: name: "Druk tsendhen" (The Thunder Dragon Kingdom)

lyrics/music: Gyaldun Dasho Thinley DORJI/Aku TONGMI

note: adopted 1953

ECONOMY

Economy—overview: Bhutan's economy, small and less developed, is based largely on agriculture and forestry, which provide the main livelihood for more than half of the population. Because rugged mountains dominate the terrain and make the building of roads and other infrastructure difficult and expensive, industrial production is primarily of the cottage industry type. The economy is closely aligned with India's through strong trade and monetary links and is dependent on India for financial assistance and migrant laborers for development projects, especially for road construction. Multilateral development organizations administer most educational, social, and environment programs, and take into account the government's desire to protect the country's environment and cultural traditions. For example, the government, in its cautious expansion of the tourist sector, encourages visits by upscale, environmentally conscientious tourists. Complicated controls and uncertain policies in areas such as industrial licensing, trade, labor, and finance continue to hamper foreign investment. Bhutan's largest export - hydropower to India - is creating employment and will probably sustain growth in the coming years. Only 5% of Bhutan's 30,000 megawatt hydropower potential is currently tapped. The large amount of equipment needed to import materials to build hydropower plants has expanded Bhutan's trade and current account deficits. Bhutan's GDP has rebounded strongly since the global recession began in 2008. Bhutan hopes to play a larger role in regional economic integration as a member of the South Asia Association for Regional Cooperation and the Bay of Bengal Initiative for Multi-Sectoral Technical and Economic Cooperation.

GDP (purchasing power parity): $5.235 billion (2013 est.)

country comparison to the world: 170

$4.947 billion (2012 est.)

$4.529 billion (2011 est.)

note: data are in 2013 US dollars

GDP (official exchange rate): $2.133 billion (2013 est.)

GDP—real growth rate: 5.8% (2013 est.)

country comparison to the world: 41

9.2% (2012 est.)

8.5% (2011 est.)

GDP—per capita (PPP): $7,000 (2013 est.)

country comparison to the world: 142

$6,700 (2012 est.)

$6,100 (2011 est.)

note: data are in 2013 US dollars

Gross national saving: 29.6% of GDP

country comparison to the world: 27

29.1% of GDP

29.2% of GDP

GDP—composition, by end use: *household consumption:* 37.9%

government consumption: 21.3%

investment in fixed capital: 64%

investment in inventories: -0.1%

exports of goods and services: 28.6%

imports of goods and services: -51.7% (2013 est.)

GDP—composition, by sector of origin: *agriculture:* 13.8%

industry: 41.2%

services: 45% (2013 est.)

Agriculture—products: rice, corn, root crops, citrus; dairy products, eggs

Industries: cement, wood products, processed fruits, alcoholic beverages, calcium carbide, tourism

Industrial production growth rate: 7%

country comparison to the world: 34

Labor force: 336,400

country comparison to the world: 162

note: major shortage of skilled labor (2012)

Labor force—by occupation: *agriculture:* 62%

industry: 19%

services: 19% (2012 est.)

Unemployment rate: 2.1% (2013)

country comparison to the world: 16

4% (2009)

Population below poverty line: 12% (2012)

Household income or consumption by percentage share: *lowest 10%:* 2.3%

highest 10%: 37.6% (2003)

Distribution of family income—Gini index: 38.7

country comparison to the world: 70

38.1

Budget: *revenues:* $588.2 million
expenditures: $639.5 million
note: the government of India finances nearly one-quarter of Bhutan's budget expenditures (2013 est.)

Taxes and other revenues: 27.6% of GDP (2013 est.)
country comparison to the world: 106

Budget surplus (+) or deficit (-): -2.4% of GDP (2013 est.)
country comparison to the world: 98

Public debt: 38.9% of GDP (2013 est.)
country comparison to the world: 93
44.1% of GDP (2012 est.)

Fiscal year: 1 July—30 June

Inflation rate (consumer prices): 11% (2013 est.)
country comparison to the world: 210
10.9% (2012 est.)

Central bank discount rate: NA%

Commercial bank prime lending rate: 14% (31 December 2013 est.)
country comparison to the world: 52
14% (31 December 2012 est.)

Stock of narrow money: $224.9 million (31 December 2013 est.)
country comparison to the world: 175
$191.9 million (31 December 2012 est.)

Stock of broad money: $1.099 billion (31 December 2013 est.)
country comparison to the world: 166
$1.062 billion (31 December 2012 est.)

Stock of domestic credit: $915 million (31 December 2013 est.)
country comparison to the world: 157
$874.4 million (31 December 2012 est.)

Market value of publicly traded shares: $320 million
country comparison to the world: 113
$283.4 million

Current account balance: $401.5 million (2013 est.)
country comparison to the world: 53
-$311.6 million (2012 est.)

Exports: $721.8 million (2012 est.)
country comparison to the world: 167
$662.2 million (2011 est.)

Exports—commodities: electricity (to India), ferrosilicon, cement, calcium carbide, copper wire, manganese, vegetable oil

Exports—partners: India 83.8% (2013 est.)

Imports: $1.28 billion (2012 est.)
country comparison to the world: 175
$1.185 billion (2011 est.)

Imports—commodities: fuel and lubricants, passenger cars, machinery and parts, fabrics, rice

Imports—partners: South Korea 6% (2013 est.)

Debt—external: $1.275 billion (2011)
country comparison to the world: 155
$836 million (2009)

Stock of direct foreign investment—at home: $63.5 million
country comparison to the world: 106

Exchange rates: ngultrum (BTN) per US dollar—
56.61 (2013 est.)
53.44 (2012 est.)
45.73 (2010 est.)
46.68 (2009 est.)
43.51 (2008 est.)

ENERGY

Electricity—production: 7.23 billion kWh (2010 est.)
country comparison to the world: 108

Electricity—consumption: 1.68 billion kWh (2010 est.)
country comparison to the world: 143

Electricity—exports: 5.4 billion kWh (2010 est.)
country comparison to the world: 27

Electricity—imports: 20 million kWh (2010 est.)
country comparison to the world: 104

Electricity—installed generating capacity: 1.505 million kW (2010 est.)
country comparison to the world: 116

Electricity—from fossil fuels: 1.1% of total installed capacity (2010 est.)
country comparison to the world: 205

Electricity—from nuclear fuels: 0% of total installed capacity (2010 est.)
country comparison to the world: 56

Electricity—from hydroelectric plants: 98.9% of total installed capacity (2010 est.)
country comparison to the world: 6

Electricity—from other renewable sources: 0% of total installed capacity (2010 est.)
country comparison to the world: 161

Crude oil—production: 0 bbl/day (2012 est.)
country comparison to the world: 157

Crude oil—exports: 0 bbl/day (2010 est.)
country comparison to the world: 91

Crude oil—imports: 0 bbl/day (2010 est.)
country comparison to the world: 165

Crude oil—proved reserves: 0 bbl (1 January 2013 es)
country comparison to the world: 111

Refined petroleum products—production: 0 bbl/day (2010 est.)
country comparison to the world: 126

Refined petroleum products—consumption: 1,719 bbl/day (2011 est.)
country comparison to the world: 193

Refined petroleum products—exports: 0 bbl/day (2010 est.)
country comparison to the world: 157

Refined petroleum products—imports: 1,998 bbl/day (2010 est.)
country comparison to the world: 181

Natural gas—production: 0 cu m (2011 est.)
country comparison to the world: 108

Natural gas—consumption: 0 cu m (2010 est.)
country comparison to the world: 124

Natural gas—exports: 0 cu m (2011 est.)
country comparison to the world: 71

Natural gas—imports: 0 cu m (2011 est.)
country comparison to the world: 166

Natural gas—proved reserves: 0 cu m (1 January 2013 es)
country comparison to the world: 118

Carbon dioxide emissions from consumption of energy: 335,700 Mt (2011 est.)
country comparison to the world: 186

COMMUNICATIONS

BHUTAN Telephones—main lines in use: 27,000 (2012)
country comparison to the world: 179

Telephones—mobile cellular: 560,000 (2012)
country comparison to the world: 165

Telephone system: *general assessment:* urban towns and district headquarters have telecommunications services
domestic: low teledensity; domestic service is poor especially in rural areas; mobile-cellular service, started in 2003, is now widely available
international: country code—975; international telephone and telegraph service via landline and microwave relay through India; satellite earth station—1 Intelsat (2012)

Broadcast media: state-owned TV station established in 1999; cable TV service offers dozens of Indian and other international channels; first radio station, privately launched in 1973, is now state-owned; 5 private radio stations are currently broadcasting (2012)

Internet country code: .bt

Internet hosts: 14,590 (2012)
country comparison to the world: 126

Internet users: 50,000 (2009)
country comparison to the world: 174

TRANSPORTATION

Airports: 2 (2013)
country comparison to the world: 198

Airports—with paved runways: *total:* 2
1,524 to 2,437 m: 1
914 to 1,523 m: 1 (2013)

Airports—with unpaved runways: *total:* 1
914 to 1,523 m: 1 (2012)

Roadways: *total:* 8,050 km
country comparison to the world: 140
paved: 4,991 km (includes 622 km of expressways)
unpaved: 3,059 km (2003)

MILITARY

Military branches: Royal Bhutan Army (includes Royal Bodyguard and Royal Bhutan Police) (2009)

Military service age and obligation: 18 years of age for voluntary military service; no conscription; militia training is compulsory for males aged 20-25, over a 3-year period (2012)

Manpower available for military service: *males age 16-49:* 202,407
females age 16-49: 180,349 (2010 est.)

Manpower fit for military service: *males age 16-49:* 157,664
females age 16-49: 144,861 (2010 est.)

Manpower reaching militarily significant age annually: *male:* 7,363
female: 7,095 (2010 est.)

TRANSNATIONAL ISSUES

Disputes—international: lacking any treaty describing the boundary, Bhutan and China continue negotiations to establish a common boundary alignment to resolve territorial disputes arising from substantial cartographic discrepancies, the largest of which lie in Bhutan's northwest and along the Chumbi salient

BOLIVIA

INTRODUCTION

Background: Bolivia, named after independence fighter Simon BOLIVAR, broke away from Spanish rule in 1825; much of its subsequent history has consisted of a series of nearly 200 coups and countercoups. Democratic civilian rule was established in 1982, but leaders have faced difficult problems of deep-seated poverty, social unrest, and illegal drug production. In December 2005, Bolivians elected Movement Toward Socialism leader Evo MORALES president—by the widest margin of any leader since the restoration of civilian rule in 1982—after he ran on a promise to change the country's traditional political class and empower the nation's poor, indigenous majority. However, since taking office, his controversial strategies have exacerbated racial and economic tensions between the Amerindian populations of the Andean west and the non-indigenous communities of the eastern lowlands. In December 2009, President MORALES easily won reelection, and his party took control of the legislative branch of the government, which will allow him to continue his process of change. In October 2011, the country held its first judicial elections to appoint judges to the four highest courts.

GEOGRAPHY

Location: Central South America, southwest of Brazil

Geographic coordinates: 17 00 S, 65 00 W

Map references: South America

Area: *total:* 1,098,581 sq km
country comparison to the world: 28
land: 1,083,301 sq km
water: 15,280 sq km

Area—comparative: slightly less than three times the size of Montana

Land boundaries: *total:* 6,940 km
border countries: Argentina 832 km, Brazil 3,423 km, Chile 860 km, Paraguay 750 km, Peru 1,075 km

Coastline: 0 km (landlocked)

Maritime claims: none (landlocked)

Climate: varies with altitude; humid and tropical to cold and semiarid

Terrain: rugged Andes Mountains with a highland plateau (Altiplano), hills, lowland plains of the Amazon Basin

Elevation extremes: *lowest point:* Rio Paraguay 90 m
highest point: Nevado Sajama 6,542 m

Natural resources: tin, natural gas, petroleum, zinc, tungsten, antimony, silver, iron, lead, gold, timber, hydropower

Land use: *arable land:* 3.49%
permanent crops: 0.2%
other: 96.31% (2011)

Irrigated land: 1,282 sq km (2003)

Total renewable water resources: 622.5 cu km (2011)

Freshwater withdrawal (domestic/industrial/agricultural): *total:* 2.64 cu km/yr (25%/14%/61%)
per capita: 305.8 cu m/yr (2005)

Natural hazards: flooding in the northeast (March to April)
volcanism: volcanic activity in Andes Mountains on the border with Chile; historically active volcanoes in this region are Irruputuncu (elev. 5,163 m), which last erupted in 1995, and Olca-Paruma

Environment—current issues: the clearing of land for agricultural purposes and the international demand for tropical timber are contributing to deforestation; soil erosion from overgrazing and poor cultivation methods (including slash-and-burn agriculture); desertification; loss of biodiversity; industrial pollution of water supplies used for drinking and irrigation

Environment—international agreements: *party to:* Biodiversity, Climate Change, Climate Change-Kyoto Protocol, Desertification, Endangered Species, Hazardous Wastes, Law of the Sea, Marine Dumping, Ozone Layer Protection, Ship Pollution, Tropical Timber 83, Tropical Timber 94, Wetlands
signed, but not ratified: Environmental Modification, Marine Life Conservation

Geography—note: landlocked; shares control of Lago Titicaca, world's highest navigable lake (elevation 3,805 m), with Peru

PEOPLE AND SOCIETY

Nationality: *noun:* Bolivian(s)
adjective: Bolivian

Ethnic groups: Quechua 30%, mestizo (mixed white and Amerindian ancestry) 30%, Aymara 25%, white 15%

Languages: Spanish (official) 60.7%, Quechua (official) 21.2%, Aymara (official) 14.6%, Guarani (official), foreign languages 2.4%, other 1.2%
note: Bolivia's 2009 constitution designates Spanish and all indigenous languages as official; 36 indigenous languages are specified, including some that are extinct (2001 census)

Religions: Roman Catholic 95%, Protestant (Evangelical Methodist) 5%

Demographic profile: Bolivia ranks at or near the bottom among Latin American countries in several areas of health and development, including poverty, education, fertility, malnutrition, mortality, and life expectancy. On the positive side, more children are being vaccinated and more pregnant women are getting prenatal care and having skilled health practitioners attend their births. Bolivia's income inequality is the highest in Latin America and one of the highest in the world. Public education is of poor quality, and educational opportunities are among the most unevenly distributed in Latin America, with girls and indigenous and rural children less likely to be literate or to complete primary school. The lack of access to education and family planning services helps to sustain Bolivia's high fertility rate—approximately three children per woman. Bolivia's lack of clean water and basic sanitation, especially in rural areas, contributes to health problems. Almost 7% of Bolivia's population lives abroad, primarily to work in Argentina, Brazil, Spain, and the United States. In recent years, more restrictive immigration policies in Europe and the United States have increased the flow of Bolivian emigrants to neighboring Argentina and Brazil.

Population: 10,631,486 (July 2014 est.)
country comparison to the world: 82

Age structure: *0-14 years:* 33.3% (male 1,805,121/female 1,737,794)
15-24 years: 19.8% (male 1,063,823/female 1,037,320)
25-54 years: 36.3% (male 1,878,736/female 1,979,819)
55-64 years: 4.9% (male 280,809/female 322,057)
65 years and over: 4.8% (male 232,514/female 293,493) (2014 est.)

Dependency ratios: *total dependency ratio:* 66%
youth dependency ratio: 57.9%
elderly dependency ratio: 8.1%
potential support ratio: 12.3 (2013)

Median age: *total:* 23.4 years
male: 22.6 years
female: 24.1 years (2014 est.)

Population growth rate: 1.6% (2014 est.)
country comparison to the world: 76

Birth rate: 23.28 births/1,000 population (2014 est.)
country comparison to the world: 70

Death rate: 6.59 deaths/1,000 population (2014 est.)
country comparison to the world: 146

Net migration rate: -0.69 migrant(s)/1,000 population (2014 est.)
country comparison to the world: 141

Urbanization: *urban population:* 67% of total population (2010)
rate of urbanization: 2.2% annual rate of change (2010-15 est.)

Major cities—population: LA PAZ (capital) 1.715 million; Santa Cruz 1.584 million; Sucre 307,000 (2011)

Sex ratio: *at birth:* 1.05 male(s)/female
0-14 years: 1.04 male(s)/female
15-24 years: 1.03 male(s)/female
25-54 years: 0.95 male(s)/female
55-64 years: 0.98 male(s)/female
65 years and over: 0.79 male(s)/female
total population: 0.98 male(s)/female (2014 est.)

Mother's mean age at first birth: 21.2
note: median age at first birth among women 25-29 (2008 est.)

Maternal mortality rate: 190 deaths/100,000 live births (2008)
country comparison to the world: 58

Infant mortality rate: *total:* 38.61 deaths/1,000 live births
country comparison to the world: 57
male: 42.23 deaths/1,000 live births
female: 34.81 deaths/1,000 live births (2014 est.)

Life expectancy at birth: *total population:* 68.55 years
country comparison to the world: 159
male: 65.78 years
female: 71.45 years (2014 est.)

Total fertility rate: 2.8 children born/woman (2014 est.)
country comparison to the world: 67

Contraceptive prevalence rate: 60.5% (2008)

Health expenditures: 4.9% of GDP (2011)
country comparison to the world: 144

Physicians density: 1.22 physicians/1,000 population (2001)

Hospital bed density: 1.1 beds/1,000 population (2011)

Drinking water source:
Improved:
urban: 96% of population
rural: 71.9% of population
total: 88% of population
Unimproved:
urban: 4% of population
rural: 28.1% of population
total: 12% of population (2011 est.)

Sanitation facility access:
Improved:
urban: 57.5% of population
rural: 23.7% of population
total: 46.3% of population
Unimproved:
urban: 42.5% of population
rural: 76.3% of population
total: 53.7% of population (2011 est.)

HIV/AIDS—adult prevalence rate: 0.3% (2012 est.)
country comparison to the world: 90

HIV/AIDS—people living with HIV/AIDS: 15,900 (2012 est.)
country comparison to the world: 89

HIV/AIDS—deaths: 1,300 (2012 est.)
country comparison to the world: 67

Major infectious diseases: *degree of risk:* very high
food or waterborne diseases: bacterial diarrhea and, hepatitis A
vectorborne diseases: dengue fever, malaria, and yellow fever (2013)

Obesity—adult prevalence rate: 17.9% (2008)
country comparison to the world: 109

Children under the age of 5 years underweight: 4.5% (2008)
country comparison to the world: 95

Education expenditures: 6.9% of GDP (2011)
country comparison to the world: 24

Literacy: *definition:* age 15 and over can read and write
total population: 91.2%
male: 95.8%
female: 86.8% (2009 est.)

School life expectancy (primary to tertiary education): *total:* 13 years
male: 13 years
female: 13 years (2007)

Child labor—children ages 5-14: *total number:* 553,323
percentage: 26%
note: data represents children ages 5-13 (2008 est.)

Unemployment, youth ages 15-24: *total:* 6.2%
country comparison to the world: 132
male: 4.8%
female: 7.8% (2009)

GOVERNMENT

Country name: *conventional long form:* Plurinational State of Bolivia
conventional short form: Bolivia
local long form: Estado Plurinacional de Bolivia
local short form: Bolivia

Government type: republic; note—the new constitution defines Bolivia as a "Social Unitarian State"

Capital: *name:* La Paz (administrative capital)
geographic coordinates: 16 30 S, 68 09 W
time difference: UTC-4 (1 hour ahead of Washington, DC during Standard Time)
note: Sucre (constitutional capital)

Administrative divisions: 9 departments (departamentos, singular—departamento); Beni, Chuquisaca, Cochabamba, La Paz, Oruro, Pando, Potosi, Santa Cruz, Tarija

Independence: 6 August 1825 (from Spain)

National holiday: Independence Day, 6 August (1825)

Constitution: many previous; latest drafted 6 August 2006 - 9 December 2008, approved by referendum 25 January 2009, effective 7 February 2009; amended 2013 (2013)

Legal system: civil law system with influences from Roman, Spanish, canon (religious), French, and indigenous law

International law organization participation: has not submitted an ICJ jurisdiction declaration; accepts ICCt jurisdiction

Suffrage: 18 years of age, universal and compulsory

Executive branch: *chief of state:* President Juan Evo MORALES Ayma (since 22 January 2006); Vice President Alvaro GARCIA Linera (since 22 January 2006); note—the president is both chief of state and head of government
head of government: President Juan Evo MORALES Ayma (since 22 January 2006); Vice President Alvaro GARCIA Linera (since 22 January 2006)
cabinet: Cabinet appointed by the president (For more information visit the World Leaders website)
elections: president and vice president elected on the same ticket by popular vote for a five-year term and are eligible for re-election once; election last held on 6 December 2009 (next to be held in 2014)
election results: Juan Evo MORALES Ayma reelected president; percent of vote—Juan Evo MORALES Ayma 64%; Manfred REYES VILLA 26%; Samuel DORIA MEDINA Arana 6%; Rene JOAQUINO 2%; other 2%

Legislative branch: bicameral Plurinational Legislative Assembly or Asamblea Legislativa Plurinacional consists of Chamber of Senators or Camara de Senadores (36 seats; members are elected by proportional representation from party lists to serve five-year terms) and Chamber of Deputies or Camara de Diputados (130 seats total; 70 uninominal deputies directly elected from a single district, 7 "special" indigenous deputies directly elected from non-contiguous indigenous districts, and 53 plurinominal deputies elected by proportional representation from party lists; all deputies serve five-year terms)
elections: Chamber of Senators and Chamber of Deputies—last held on 6 December 2009 (next to be held in 2014)
election results: Chamber of Senators—percent of vote by party—NA; seats by party—MAS 26, PPB-CN 10; Chamber of Deputies—percent of vote by party—NA; seats by party—MAS 89, PPB-CN 36, UN 3, AS 2; note—as of 15 February 2013, the current composition of the Chamber of Deputies is: MAS 88, PPB-CN 37, UN 3, AS 2

Judicial branch: *highest court(s):* Supreme Court or Tribunal Supremo de Justicia (consists of 12 judges); Plurinational Constitutional Tribunal (consists of 7 primary and 7 alternate magistrates); Plurinational Electoral Organ (consists of 7 members)
note - the 2009 constitution reformed the procedure for selecting judicial officials for the Supreme Court, Constitutional Tribunal, and the Plurinational Electoral Organ by direct national vote, which occurred in October 2011
judge selection and term of office: Supreme Court and Plurinational Constitutional Tribunal judges elected by popular vote from list of candidates pre-selected by Plurinational Legislative Assembly for 6-year terms);Plurinational Electoral Organ members - 6 judges elected by the Assembly and 1 appointed by the president; judges and members serve 6-year terms
subordinate courts: Agro-Environmental Court; Council of the Judiciary; District Courts (in each of the 9 administrative departments)

Political parties and leaders: Bacada Indigena or BI Bolivia-National Convergence or PPB-CN [Adrian OLIVA] Fearless Movement or MSM [Juan DE GRANADO Cosio] Movement Toward Socialism or MAS [Juan Evo MORALES Ayma] National Unity or UN [Samuel DORIA MEDINA Arana] People or Gente [Roman LOAYZA] Social Alliance or AS [Rene JOAQUINO] Social Democratic Movement or MDS [Ruben COSTAS]

Political pressure groups and leaders: Bolivian Workers Central or COB; Federation of Neighborhood Councils of El Alto or FEJUVE; Landless Movement or MST; National Coordinator for Change or CONALCAM; Sole Confederation of Campesino Workers of Bolivia or CSUTCB
other: Cocalero groups; indigenous organizations (including Confederation of Indigenous Peoples of Eastern Bolivia or CIDOB and National Council of Ayullus and Markas of Quollasuyu or CONAMAQ); Interculturales union or CSCIB; labor unions (including the Central Bolivian Workers' Union or COB and Cooperative Miners Federation or FENCOMIN)

International organization participation: CAN, CD, CELAC, FAO, G-77, IADB, IAEA, IBRD, ICAO, ICC (national committees), ICRM, IDA, IFAD, IFC, IFRCS, ILO, IMF, IMO, Interpol, IOC, IOM, IPU, ISO (correspondent), ITSO, ITU, LAES, LAIA, Mercosur (associate), MIGA, MINUSTAH, MONUSCO, NAM, OAS,

OPANAL, OPCW, PCA, UN, UNASUR, UNCTAD, UNESCO, UNFICYP, UNIDO, Union Latina, UNISFA, UNMIL, UNMISS, UNOCI, UNWTO, UPU, WCO, WFTU (NGOs), WHO, WIPO, WMO, WTO

Diplomatic representation in the US: *chief of mission:* Ambassador (vacant); Charge d'Affaires Freddy BERSATTI Tudela
chancery: 3014 Massachusetts Avenue NW, Washington, DC 20008
telephone: [1] (202) 483-4410
FAX: [1] (202) 328-3712
consulate(s) general: Los Angeles, Miami, New York
note: as of September 2008, the US has expelled the Bolivian ambassador to the US

Diplomatic representation from the US: *chief of mission:* Ambassador (vacant); Charge d'Affaires Aruna AMIRTHANAYAGAM (since 28 February 2014)
embassy: Avenida Arce 2780, Casilla 425, La Paz
mailing address: P. O. Box 425, La Paz; APO AA 34032
telephone: [591] (2) 216-8000
FAX: [591] (2) 216-8111
note: in September 2008, the Bolivian Government expelled the US Ambassador to Bolivia, and the countries have yet to reinstate ambassadors

Flag description: three equal horizontal bands of red (top), yellow, and green with the coat of arms centered on the yellow band; red stands for bravery and the blood of national heroes, yellow for the nation's mineral resources, and green for the fertility of the land
note: similar to the flag of Ghana, which has a large black five-pointed star centered in the yellow band; in 2009, a presidential decree made it mandatory for a so-called wiphala—a square, multicolored flag representing the country's indigenous peoples—to be used alongside the traditional flag

National symbol(s): llama; Andean condor

National anthem: *name:* "Cancion Patriotica" (Patriotic Song)
lyrics/music: Jose Ignacio de SANJINES/Leopoldo Benedetto VINCENTI
note: adopted 1852

ECONOMY

Economy—overview: Bolivia is a resource rich country with strong growth attributed to captive markets for natural gas exports. However, the country remains one of the least developed countries in Latin because of state-oriented policies that deter investment and growth. Following a disastrous economic crisis during the early 1980s, reforms spurred private investment, stimulated economic growth, and cut poverty rates in the 1990s. The period 2003-05 was characterized by political instability, racial tensions, and violent protests against plans - subsequently abandoned - to export Bolivia's newly discovered natural gas reserves to large Northern Hemisphere markets. In 2005, the government passed a controversial hydrocarbons law that imposed significantly higher royalties and required foreign firms then operating under risk-sharing contracts to surrender all production to the state energy company in exchange for a predetermined service fee. The global recession slowed growth, but Bolivia recorded the highest growth rate in South America during 2009. High commodity prices since 2010 sustained rapid growth and large trade surpluses. However, a lack of foreign investment in the key sectors of mining and hydrocarbons, along with growing conflict among social groups pose challenges for the Bolivian economy.

GDP (purchasing power parity): $58.34 billion (2013 est.)
country comparison to the world: 92
$55.35 billion (2012 est.)
$52.63 billion (2011 est.)
note: data are in 2013 US dollars

GDP (official exchange rate): $29.81 billion (2013 est.)

GDP—real growth rate: 6.5% (2013 est.)
country comparison to the world: 29
5.2% (2012 est.)
5.2% (2011 est.)

GDP—per capita (PPP): $5,500 (2013 est.)
country comparison to the world: 156
$5,200 (2012 est.)
$4,900 (2011 est.)
note: data are in 2013 US dollars

Gross national saving: 25.7% of GDP (2013 est.)
country comparison to the world: 46
27.1% of GDP (2012 est.)
25.2% of GDP (2011 est.)

GDP—composition, by end use: *household consumption:* 58.9%
government consumption: 13.4%
investment in fixed capital: 18%
investment in inventories: 0.3%
exports of goods and services: 47.8%
imports of goods and services: -38.4% (2013 est.)

GDP—composition, by sector of origin: *agriculture:* 9.2%
industry: 38.5%
services: 52.3% (2013 est.)

Agriculture—products: soybeans, coffee, coca, cotton, corn, sugarcane, rice, potatoes; Brazil nuts; timber

Industries: mining, smelting, petroleum, food and beverages, tobacco, handicrafts, clothing, jewelry

Industrial production growth rate: 5.6% (2013 est.)
country comparison to the world: 45

Labor force: 4.922 million (2012 est.)
country comparison to the world: 78

Labor force—by occupation: *agriculture:* 32%
industry: 20%
services: 48% (2010 est.)

Unemployment rate: 7.4% (2013 est.)
country comparison to the world: 81
7.5% (2012 est.)
note: data are for urban areas; widespread underemployment

Population below poverty line: 49.6%
note: based on percent of population living on less than the international standard of $2/day (2010 est.)

Household income or consumption by percentage share: *lowest 10%:* 0.5%
highest 10%: 43.3% (2008)

Distribution of family income—Gini index: 53 (2010)
country comparison to the world: 14
57.9 (1999)

Budget: *revenues:* $14.55 billion
expenditures: $13.95 billion (2013 est.)

Taxes and other revenues: 48.8% of GDP (2013 est.)
country comparison to the world: 13

Budget surplus (+) or deficit (-): 2% of GDP (2013 est.)
country comparison to the world: 17

Public debt: 33.3% of GDP (2013 est.)
country comparison to the world: 110
34% of GDP (2012 est.)
note: data cover general government debt, and includes debt instruments issued by government entities other than the treasury; the data include treasury debt held by foreign entities; the data include debt issued by subnational entities

Fiscal year: calendar year

Inflation rate (consumer prices): 5.9% (2013 est.)
country comparison to the world: 170
6.9% (2011 est.)

Central bank discount rate: 4% (31 December 2011 est.)
country comparison to the world: 107
3% (31 December 2010 est.)

Commercial bank prime lending rate: 10.8% (31 December 2013 est.)
country comparison to the world: 77
11.14% (31 December 2012 est.)

Stock of narrow money: $7.446 billion (31 December 2013 est.)
country comparison to the world: 90
$7.32 billion (31 December 2012 est.)

Stock of broad money: $11.28 billion (31 December 2013 est.)
country comparison to the world: 102
$9.562 billion (31 December 2012 est.)

Stock of domestic credit: $10.4 billion (31 December 2013 est.)
country comparison to the world: 99
$9.044 billion (31 December 2012 est.)

Market value of publicly traded shares: $7.69 billion (31 December 2012)
country comparison to the world: 81
$6.089 billion (31 December 2011)
$3.915 billion (31 December 2010)

Current account balance: $2.138 billion (2012 est.)
country comparison to the world: 38
$2.127 billion (2012 est.)

Exports: $12.56 billion (2013 est.)
country comparison to the world: 89
$11.11 billion (2012 est.)

Exports—commodities: natural gas, soybeans and soy products, crude petroleum, zinc ore, tin

Exports—partners: Brazil 41.8%, US 18.4%, Argentina 7.3%, Peru 4.9% (2012)

Imports: $8.224 billion (2013 est.)
country comparison to the world: 108
$7.694 billion (2012 est.)

Imports—commodities: petroleum products, plastics, paper, aircraft and aircraft parts, prepared foods, automobiles, insecticides

Imports—partners: Chile 21.3%, Brazil 20.3%, Argentina 10.9%, US 10.1%, Peru 6.5%, Venezuela 6.2%, China 4.9% (2012)

Reserves of foreign exchange and gold: $14.46 billion (31 December 2013 est.)
country comparison to the world: 69
$13.93 billion (31 December 2012 est.)

Debt—external: $7.429 billion (31 December 2013 est.)
country comparison to the world: 109
$6.89 billion (31 December 2012 est.)

Stock of direct foreign investment—at home: $8.81 billion (31 December 2012)
country comparison to the world: 85

$7.75 billion (31 December 2011)

Stock of direct foreign investment—abroad: $8 million (31 December 2011)
country comparison to the world: 93
$21 million (31 December 2010)

Exchange rates: bolivianos (BOB) per US dollar—
6.91 (2013 est.)
6.94 (2012 est.)
7.0167 (2010 est.)
7.07 (2009)
7.253 (2008)

ENERGY

Electricity—production: 6.94 billion kWh (2012 est.)
country comparison to the world: 110

Electricity—consumption: 7.222 billion kWh (2011 est.)
country comparison to the world: 99

Electricity—exports: 0 kWh (2012 est.)
country comparison to the world: 107

Electricity—imports: 0 kWh (2012 est.)
country comparison to the world: 119

Electricity—installed generating capacity: 1.655 million kW (2010 est.)
country comparison to the world: 111

Electricity—from fossil fuels: 58.9% of total installed capacity (2012 est.)
country comparison to the world: 137

Electricity—from nuclear fuels: 0% of total installed capacity (2012 est.)
country comparison to the world: 51

Electricity—from hydroelectric plants: 39.3% of total installed capacity (2012 est.)
country comparison to the world: 61

Electricity—from other renewable sources: 1.7% of total installed capacity (2012 est.)
country comparison to the world: 75

Crude oil—production: 56,570 bbl/day (2012 est.)
country comparison to the world: 61

Crude oil—exports: 0 bbl/day (2010 est.)
country comparison to the world: 86

Crude oil—imports: 0 bbl/day (2010 est.)
country comparison to the world: 161

Crude oil—proved reserves: 209.8 million bbl (1 January 2013 es)
country comparison to the world: 58

Refined petroleum products—production: 314,700 bbl/day (2012 est.)
country comparison to the world: 40

Refined petroleum products—consumption: 45,840 bbl/day (2012 est.)
country comparison to the world: 101

Refined petroleum products—exports: 864.7 bbl/day (2012 est.)
country comparison to the world: 109

Refined petroleum products—imports: 14,150 bbl/day (2008 est.)
country comparison to the world: 123

Natural gas—production: 48.97 billion cu m (2012 est.)
country comparison to the world: 19

Natural gas—consumption: 8.59 billion cu m (2012 est.)
country comparison to the world: 52

Natural gas—exports: 40.28 billion cu m (2012 est.)
country comparison to the world: 11

Natural gas—imports: 0 cu m (2012 est.)
country comparison to the world: 162

Natural gas—proved reserves: 281.5 billion cu m (1 January 2013 es)
country comparison to the world: 42

Carbon dioxide emissions from consumption of energy: 13.98 million Mt (2011 est.)
country comparison to the world: 93

COMMUNICATIONS

Telephones—main lines in use: 880,600 (2012)
country comparison to the world: 80

Telephones—mobile cellular: 9.494 million (2012)
country comparison to the world: 82

Telephone system: *general assessment:* Bolivian National Telecommunications Company was privatized in 1995 but re-nationalized in 2007; the primary trunk system is being expanded and employs digital microwave radio relay; some areas are served by fiber-optic cable; system operations, reliability, and coverage have steadily improved.
domestic: most telephones are concentrated in La Paz, Santa Cruz, and other capital cities; mobile-cellular telephone use expanding rapidly and, in 2011, teledensity reached about 80 per 100 persons
international: country code - 591; satellite earth station - 1 Intelsat (Atlantic Ocean) (2011)

Broadcast media: large number of radio and TV stations broadcasting with private media outlets dominating; state-owned and private radio and TV stations generally operating freely, although both pro-government and anti-government groups have attacked media outlets in response to their reporting (2010)

Internet country code: .bo

Internet hosts: 180,988 (2012)
country comparison to the world: 75

Internet users: 1.103 million (2009)
country comparison to the world: 95

TRANSPORTATION

Airports: 855 (2013)
country comparison to the world: 7

Airports—with paved runways: *total:* 21
over 3,047 m: 5
2,438 to 3,047 m: 4
1,524 to 2,437 m: 6
914 to 1,523 m: 6 (2013)

Airports—with unpaved runways: total: 834
over 3,047 m: 1
2,438 to 3,047 m: 4
1,524 to 2,437 m: 47
914 to 1,523 m: 151
under 914 m: 631 (2013)

Pipelines: gas 5,457 km; liquid petroleum gas 51 km; oil 2,511 km; refined products 1,627 km (2013)

Railways: *total:* 3,652 km
country comparison to the world: 48
narrow gauge: 3,652 km 1.000-m gauge (2010)

Roadways: *total:* 80,488 km
country comparison to the world: 59
paved: 11,993 km
unpaved: 68,495 km (2010)

Waterways: 10,000 km (commercially navigable almost exclusively in the northern and eastern parts of the country) (2012)
country comparison to the world: 13

Merchant marine: *total:* 18
country comparison to the world: 98
by type: bulk carrier 1, cargo 14, petroleum tanker 1, roll on/roll off 2
foreign-owned: 5 (Syria 4, UK 1, (2010)

Ports and terminals: *river port(s):* Puerto Aguirre (Paraguay/Parana)
note: Bolivia has free port privileges in maritime ports in Argentina, Brazil, Chile, and Paraguay

MILITARY

Military branches: *Bolivian Armed Forces:* Bolivian Army (Ejercito Boliviano, EB), Bolivian Naval Force (Fuerza Naval Boliviana, FNB; includes Marines), Bolivian Air Force (Fuerza Aerea Boliviana, FAB) (2013)

Military service age and obligation: 18-49 years of age for 12-month compulsory male and female military service; Bolivian citizenship required; 17 years of age for voluntary service; when annual number of volunteers falls short of goal, compulsory recruitment is effected, including conscription of boys as young as 14; 15-19 years of age for voluntary premilitary service, provides exemption from further military service (2013)

Manpower available for military service: males age 16-49: 2,472,490
females age 16-49: 2,535,768 (2010 est.)

Manpower fit for military service: *males age 16-49:* 1,762,260
females age 16-49: 2,013,281 (2010 est.)

Manpower reaching militarily significant age annually: *male:* 108,334
female: 104,945 (2010 est.)

Military expenditures: 1.47% of GDP (2012)
country comparison to the world: 62
1.47% of GDP (2011)
1.47% of GDP (2010)

TRANSNATIONAL ISSUES

Disputes—international: Chile and Peru rebuff Bolivia's reactivated claim to restore the Atacama corridor, ceded to Chile in 1884, but Chile offers instead unrestricted but not sovereign maritime access through Chile for Bolivian natural gas; contraband smuggling, human trafficking, and illegal narcotic trafficking are problems in the porous areas of the border with Argentina

Illicit drugs: world's third-largest cultivator of coca (after Colombia and Peru) with an estimated 30,000 hectares under cultivation in 2011, a decrease of 13 percent over 2010; third largest producer of cocaine, estimated at 265 metric tons potential pure cocaine in 2011, a 29 percent increase over 2010; transit country for Peruvian and Colombian cocaine destined for Brazil, Argentina, Chile, Paraguay, and Europe; weak border controls; some money-laundering activity related to narcotics trade; major cocaine consumption (2013)

BOSNIA AND HERZEGOVINA

INTRODUCTION

Background: Bosnia and Herzegovina declared of sovereignty in October 1991 and independence from the former Yugoslavia on 3 March 1992 after a referendum boycotted by ethnic Serbs. The Bosnian Serbs—supported by neighboring Serbia and Montenegro responded with armed resistance aimed at partitioning the republic along ethnic lines and joining Serb-held areas to form a "Greater Serbia." In March 1994, Bosniaks and Croats reduced the number of warring factions from three to two by signing an agreement creating a joint Bosniak/Croat Federation of Bosnia and Herzegovina. On 21 November 1995, in Dayton, Ohio, the warring parties initialed a peace agreement that ended three years of interethnic civil strife (the final agreement was signed in Paris on 14 December 1995). The Dayton Peace Accords retained Bosnia and Herzegovina's international boundaries and created a multi-ethnic and democratic government charged with conducting foreign, diplomatic, and fiscal policy. Also recognized was a second tier of government composed of two entities roughly equal in size: the Bosniak/Bosnian Croat Federation of Bosnia and Herzegovina and the Bosnian Serb-led Republika Srpska (RS). The Federation and RS governments are responsible for overseeing most government functions. Additionally, the Dayton Accords established the Office of the High Representative (OHR) to oversee the implementation of the civilian aspects of the agreement. The Peace Implementation Council (PIC) at its conference in Bonn in 1997 also gave the High Representative the authority to impose legislation and remove officials, the so-called "Bonn Powers." An original NATO-led international peacekeeping force (IFOR) of 60,000 troops assembled in 1995 was succeeded over time by a smaller, NATO-led Stabilization Force (SFOR).

In 2004, European Union peacekeeping troops (EUFOR) replaced SFOR. Currently EUFOR deploys around 600 troops in theater in a policing capacity.

GEOGRAPHY

Location: Southeastern Europe, bordering the Adriatic Sea and Croatia

Geographic coordinates: 44 00 N, 18 00 E

Map references: Europe

Area: *total:* 51,197 sq km
country comparison to the world: 129
land: 51,187 sq km
water: 10 sq km

Area—comparative: slightly smaller than West Virginia

Land boundaries: *total:* 1,538 km

border countries: Croatia 932 km, Montenegro 249 km, Serbia 357 km

Coastline: 20 km

Maritime claims: no data available

Climate: hot summers and cold winters; areas of high elevation have short, cool summers and long, severe winters; mild, rainy winters along coast

Terrain: mountains and valleys

Elevation extremes: lowest point: Adriatic Sea 0 m highest point: Maglic 2,386 m

Natural resources: coal, iron ore, bauxite, copper, lead, zinc, chromite, cobalt, manganese, nickel, clay, gypsum, salt, sand, timber, hydropower

Land use: *arable land:* 19.63%
permanent crops: 1.99%
other: 78.38% (2011)

Irrigated land: 30 sq km (2003)

Total renewable water resources: 37.5 cu km (2011)

Natural hazards: destructive earthquakes

Environment—current issues: air pollution from metallurgical plants; sites for disposing of urban waste are limited; water shortages and destruction of infrastructure because of the 1992-95 civil strife; deforestation

Environment—international agreements: party to: Air Pollution, Biodiversity, Climate Change, Climate Change-Kyoto Protocol, Desertification, Hazardous Wastes, Law of the Sea, Marine Life Conservation, Ozone Layer Protection, Wetlands
signed, but not ratified: none of the selected agreements

Geography—note: within Bosnia and Herzegovina's recognized borders, the country is divided into a joint Bosniak/Croat Federation (about 51% of the territory) and the Bosnian Serb-led Republika Srpska or RS (about 49% of the territory); the region called Herzegovina is contiguous to Croatia and Montenegro, and traditionally has been settled by an ethnic Croat majority in the west and an ethnic Serb majority in the east

PEOPLE AND SOCIETY

Nationality: *noun:* Bosnian(s), Herzegovinian(s)
adjective: Bosnian, Herzegovinian

Ethnic groups: Bosniak 48%, Serb 37.1%, Croat 14.3%, other 0.6% (2000)
note: Bosniak has replaced Muslim as an ethnic term in part to avoid confusion with the religious term Muslim—an adherent of Islam

Languages: Bosnian (official), Croatian (official), Serbian (official)

Religions: Muslim 40%, Orthodox 31%, Roman Catholic 15%, other 14%

Population: 3,871,643 (July 2014 est.)
country comparison to the world: 129

Age structure: *0-14 years:* 13.7% (male 272,812/female 256,152)
15-24 years: 12.7% (male 255,074/female 238,428)
25-54 years: 46.7% (male 906,265/female 899,870)
55-64 years: 13.3% (male 253,045/female 276,769)
65 years and over: 12.9% (male 199,515/female 313,713) (2014 est.)

Dependency ratios: *total dependency ratio:* 45.5%
youth dependency ratio: 22.9%
elderly dependency ratio: 22.7%
potential support ratio: 4.4 (2013)

Median age: *total:* 40.8 years
male: 39.4 years
female: 42.2 years (2014 est.)

Population growth rate: -0.11% (2014 est.)
country comparison to the world: 207

Birth rate: 8.89 births/1,000 population (2014 est.)
country comparison to the world: 211

Death rate: 9.64 deaths/1,000 population (2014 est.)
country comparison to the world: 55

Net migration rate: -0.38 migrant(s)/1,000 population (2014 est.)
country comparison to the world: 132

Urbanization: *urban population:* 49% of total population (2010)
rate of urbanization: 1.1% annual rate of change (2010-15 est.)

Major urban areas—population: SARAJEVO (capital) 389,000 (2011)

Sex ratio: *at birth:* 1.07 male(s)/female
0-14 years: 1.07 male(s)/female
15-24 years: 1.07 male(s)/female
25-54 years: 1.01 male(s)/female
55-64 years: 0.95 male(s)/female
65 years and over: 0.63 male(s)/female
total population: 0.95 male(s)/female (2014 est.)

Mother's mean age at first birth: 25.9 (2010 est.)

Maternal mortality rate: 8 deaths/100,000 live births (2010)
country comparison to the world: 157

Infant mortality rate: *total:* 5.84 deaths/1,000 live births
country comparison to the world: 173
male: 5.91 deaths/1,000 live births
female: 5.78 deaths/1,000 live births (2014 est.)

Life expectancy at birth: *total population:* 76.33 years
country comparison to the world: 84
male: 73.33 years
female: 79.55 years (2014 est.)

Total fertility rate: 1.26 children born/woman (2014 est.)
country comparison to the world: 218

Contraceptive prevalence rate: 45.8% (2012)

Health expenditures: 10.2%of GDP (2011)
country comparison to the world: 23

Physicians density: 1.69 physicians/1,000 population (2010)

Hospital bed density: 3.5 beds/1,000 population (2010)

Drinking water source:
Improved:
urban: 99.7% of population
rural: 98% of population
total: 98.8% of population
Unimproved:
urban: 0.3% of population
rural: 2% of population
total: 1.2% of population (2011 est.)

Sanitation facility access:
Improved:
urban: 99.7% of population
rural: 92.1% of population

total: 95.8% of population
Unimproved:
urban: 0.3% of population
rural: 7.9% of population
total: 4.2% of population (2011 est.)

HIV/AIDS—adult prevalence rate: less than 0.1% (2007 est.)
country comparison to the world: 127

HIV/AIDS—people living with HIV/AIDS: 900 (2007 est.)
country comparison to the world: 151

HIV/AIDS—deaths: 100 (2001 est.)
country comparison to the world: 128

Obesity—adult prevalence rate: 26.5% (2008)
country comparison to the world: 47

Children under the age of 5 years underweight: 1.5% (2012)
country comparison to the world: 128

Education expenditures: NA

Literacy: *definition:* age 15 and over can read and write
total population: 98%
male: 99.5%
female: 96.7% (2011 est.)

Child labor—children ages 5-14: *total number:* 24,722
percentage: 5 % (2006 est.)

Unemployment, youth ages 15-24: *total:* 62.8%
country comparison to the world: 1
male: 62.8%
female: 62.8% (2012)

GOVERNMENT

Country name: *conventional long form:* none
conventional short form: Bosnia and Herzegovina
local long form: none
local short form: Bosnai Hercegovina
former: People's Republic of Bosnia and Herzegovina, Socialist Republic of Bosnia and Herzegovina

Government type: emerging federal democratic republic

Capital: *name:* Sarajevo
geographic coordinates: 43 52 N, 18 25 E
time difference: UTC+1 (6 hours ahead of Washington, DC during Standard Time)
daylight saving time: +1hr, begins last Sunday in March; ends last Sunday in October

Administrative divisions: 2 first-order administrative divisions and 1 internationally supervised district* - the Bosniak/Croat Federation of Bosnia and Herzegovina (Federacija Bosne i Hercegovine), the Bosnian Serb-led Republika Srpska, Brcko District (Brcko Distrikt)*; note - Brcko District is in northeastern Bosnia and is a self-governing administrative unit under the sovereignty of Bosnia and Herzegovina and formally held in condominium between the two entities

Independence: 1 March 1992 (from Yugoslavia; referendum for independence completed on 1 March 1992; independence declared on 3 March 1992)

National holiday: National Day (Statehood Day), 25 November (1943); note—observed only in the Federation of Bosnia and Herzegovina entity

Constitution: 14 December 1995 (constitution included as part of the Dayton Peace Accords); amended several times, last in 2003; note - each of the entities has its own constitution (2011)

Legal system: civil law system; Constitutional Court review of legislative acts

International law organization participation: has not submitted an ICJ jurisdiction declaration; accepts ICCt jurisdiction

Suffrage: 18 years of age, 16 if employed; universal

Executive branch: *chief of state:* Chairman of the Presidency Bakir IZETBEGOVIC (chairman since 10 March 2014; presidency member since 10 November 2010 - Bosniak) ; other members of the three-member presidency rotate every eight months: Zeljko KOMSIC (presidency member since 6 November 2006 - Croat); Nebojsa RADMANOVIC (presidency member since 6 November 2006 - Serb)
head of government: Chairman of the Council of Ministers Vjekoslav BEVANDA (since 12 January 2012)
cabinet: Council of Ministers nominated by the council chairman; approved by the state-level House of Representatives (For more information visit the World Leaders website)
elections: the three members of the presidency (one Bosniak, one Croat, one Serb) elected by popular vote for a four-year term (eligible for a second term, but then ineligible for four years) by constituencies referring to the three ethnic groups; the candidate with the most votes in a constituency is elected; the chairmanship rotates every eight months and resumes where it left off following each general election; election last held on 3 October 2010 (next to be held in October 2014); the chairman of the Council of Ministers appointed by the presidency and confirmed by the state-level House of Representatives
election results: percent of vote—Nebojsa RADMANOVIC with 48.9% of the votes for the Serb seat; Zeljko KOMSIC with 60.6% of the votes for the Croat seat; Bakir IZETBEGOVIC with 34.9% of the votes for the Bosniak seat
note: President of the Federation of Bosnia and Herzegovina: Zivko BUDIMIR (since 17 March 2011); Vice Presidents Svetozar PUDARIC (since 17 March 2011) and Mirsad KEBO (since 17 March 2007); President of the Republika Srpska: Milorad DODIK (since 15 November 2010); Vice Presidents Enes SULJKANOVIC (since 15 November 2010) and Emil VLAJKI (since 15 November 2010)

Legislative branch: bicameral Parliamentary Assembly or Skupstina consists of the House of Peoples or Dom Naroda (15 seats, 5 Bosniak, 5 Croat, 5 Serb; members designated by the Bosniak/Croat Federation's House of Peoples and the Republika Srpska's National Assembly to serve four-year terms); and the state-level House of Representatives or Predstavnicki Dom (42 seats, 28 seats allocated for the Federation of Bosnia and Herzegovina and 14 seats for the Republika Srpska; members elected by popular vote on the basis of proportional representation to serve four-year terms); note—Bosnia's election law specifies four-year terms for the state and first-order administrative division entity legislatures
elections: House of Peoples—last constituted in 9 June 2011 (next likely to be constituted in 2015); state-level House of Representatives—elections last held on 3 October 2010 (next to be held in October 2014)
election results: House of Peoples - percent of vote by party/coalition - NA; seats by party/coalition - NA;state-level House of Representatives - percent of vote by party/coalition - Federation votes: SDP BiH 26.1%,SDA 19.4%, SBB BiH 12.2%, HDZ BiH 11%, SBIH 7.3%, HDZ-1990/HSP BiH 4.9%, NSRzB 4.8%, DNZ 1.5%;Republika Srpska votes: SNSD 43.3%, SDS 22.2%, PDP 6.5%, DNS 4.6%; seats by party/coalition - SDP BiH 8,SNSD 8, SDA 7, SDS 4, SBB BiH 4, HDZ-BiH 3, SBiH 2, HDZ-1990/HSP BiH 2, NSRzB 1, DNZ 1, PDP 1, DNS 1
note: the Bosniak/Croat Federation has a bicameral legislature that consists of a House of Peoples (58 seats- 17 Bosniak, 17 Croat, 17 Serb, 7 other); last constituted May 2011 (next likely to be constituted in 2015); and a House of Representatives (98 seats; members elected by popular vote to serve four-year terms); elections last held on 3 October 2010 (next to be held in October 2014); percent of vote by party - SDP BiH 24.5%, SDA 20.2%, SBB BiH 11.9%, HDZ BiH 10.6%, SBiH 7.6%, NSRzB 4.7%, HDZ 1990/HSP BiH 4.7%, A-SDA 1.9%, DNZ 1.5%, SNSD .9%; seats by party/coalition - SDP BiH 28, SDA 23, SBB BiH 13, HDZ-BiH 12, SBiH 9, NSRzB 5, HDZ-1990/HSP BiH 5, DNZ 1, A-SDA 1, SNSD 1; the Republika Srpska has a National Assembly (83 seats; members elected by popular vote to serve four-year terms); elections last held on 3 October 2010 (next to be held in October 2014); percent of vote by party - SNSD 38%, SDS 19%, PDP 7.6%, DNS 6%, SPRS 4.2%, DP 3.4%, SDP BiH 3%, SDA 2.7%, SRS RS 2.4%, NDS 2.1%; seats by party/coalition - SNSD 37, SDS 18, PDP 7, DNS 6, SPRS 4, DP 3, SDP BiH 3, SDA 2, NDS 2, SRS-RS 1; as a result of the 2002 constitutional reform process, a 28-member Republika Srpska Council of Peoples (COP) was established in the Republika Srpska National Assembly including 8 Croats, 8 Bosniaks, 8 Serbs, and 4 members of the smaller communities

Judicial branch: *highest court(s):* BiH Constitutional Court (consists of 9 members); Court of BiH (consists of 44 national judges and 7 international judges organized into three divisions - Administrative, Appellate, and Criminal, which includes a War Crimes Chamber)
judge selection and term of office: BiH Constitutional Court judges - 4 selected by the Bosniak/Croat Federation's House of Representatives, 2 selected by the Republika Srpska's National Assembly, and 3 non-Bosnian judges selected by the president of the European Court of Human Rights; Court of BiH president and national judges appointed by the High Judicial and Prosecutorial Council; Court of BiH president appointed for renewable 6-year term; other national judges appointed to serve until age 70; international judges recommended by the president of the Court of BiH and appointed by the High Representative for Bosnia and Herzegovina; international judges appointed to serve until age 70 subordinate courts: the Federation has 10 cantonal courts plus a number of municipal courts; the Republika Srpska has a supreme court, 5 district courts, and a number of municipal courts

Political parties and leaders: Activist Democratic Party or A-SDA Alliance for a Better Future of BiH or SBB BiH [Fahrudin RADONCIC] Alliance of Independent Social Democrats or SNSD [Milorad DODIK] Bosnian Party or BOSS [Mirnes AJANOVIC] Bosnian Patriotic Party or BPS [Sefer HALILOVIC] Civic Democratic Party or GDS [Ibrahim SPAHIC] Croat Peasants' Party-New Croat Initiative or HSS-NHI [Ante COLAK] Croatian Christian Democratic Union of Bosnia and Herzegovina or HKDU [Ivan MUSA] Croatian Democratic Union of Bosnia and Herzegovina or HDZ-BiH [Dragan COVIC] Croatian Democratic Union 1990 or HDZ-1990 [Martin RAGUZ] Croatian Party of Rights of Bosnia and Herzegovina or HSP BiH [Zvonko JURISIC] Democratic National Union or DNZ [Rifat DOLIC] Democratic Peoples' Alliance or DNS [Marko PAVIC] Liberal Democratic Party or LDS [Amir HUSARIC] Nasa Stranka or NS [Denis GRATZ] National Democratic Party or NDS New Socialist Party or NSP

[Zdravko KRSMANOVIC] Party for Bosnia and Herzegovina or SBiH [Amer JERLAGIC] Party of Democratic Action or SDA [Sulejman TIHIC] Party of Democratic Progress or PDP [Mladen IVANIC] Party of Justice and Trust or SPP [Zivko BUDIMIR] People's Democratic Movement or NDP [Dragan CAVIC and Krsto JANDRIC] (unification of the Democratic Party or DP and the People's Democratic Party or NDS) 'People's' Party of Work for Progress or NSRzB [Mladen IVANKOVIC-LIJANOVIC] Serb Democratic Party or SDS [Mladen BOSIC] Serb Radical Party of the Republika Srpska or SRS-RS [Milanko MIHAJLICA] Serb Radical Party-Dr. Vojislav Seselj or SRS-VS [Dejan SANTIC] Social Democratic Party of BiH or SDP BiH [Zlatko LAGUMDZIJA] Social Democratic Union or SDU [Miro LAZOVIC] Socialist Party of Republika Srpska or SPRS [Petar DJOKIC]

Political pressure groups and leaders: *other:* war veterans; displaced persons associations; family associations of missing persons; private media

International organization participation: BIS, CD, CE, CEI, EAPC, EBRD, FAO, G-77, IAEA, IBRD, ICAO, ICC (NGOs), ICRM, IDA, IFAD, IFC, IFRCS, ILO, IMF, IMO, IMSO, Interpol, IOC, IOM, IPU, ISO, ITSO, ITU, ITUC (NGOs), MIGA, MONUSCO, NAM (observer), OAS (observer), OIC (observer), OIF (observer), OPCW, OSCE, PFP, SELEC, UN, UNCTAD, UNESCO, UNIDO, UNWTO, UPU, WCO, WHO, WIPO, WMO, WTO (observer)

Diplomatic representation in the US: *chief of mission:* Ambassador Jadranka NEGODIC (since 19 July 2012)
chancery: 2109 E Street NW, Washington, DC 20037
telephone: [1] (202) 337-1500
FAX: [1] (202) 337-1502
consulate(s) general: Chicago, New York

Diplomatic representation from the US: *chief of mission:* Ambassador (vacant); Charge d'Affaires ad interim Nicholas M. HILL (since 24 August 2013)
embassy: 1 Robert C. Frasure Street, 71000 Sarajevo
mailing address: use embassy street address
telephone: [387] (33) 704-000
FAX: [387] (33) 659-722
branch office(s): Banja Luka, Mostar

Flag description: a wide medium blue vertical band on the fly side with a yellow isosceles triangle abutting the band and the top of the flag; the remainder of the flag is medium blue with seven full five-pointed white stars and two half stars top and bottom along the hypotenuse of the triangle; the triangle approximates the shape of the country and its three points stand for the constituent peoples—Bosniaks, Croats, and Serbs; the stars represent Europe and are meant to be continuous (thus the half stars at top and bottom); the colors (white, blue, and yellow) are often associated with neutrality and peace, and traditionally are linked with Bosnia

National symbol(s): golden lily

National anthem: *name:* "Drzavna himna Bosne i Hercegovine" (The National Anthem of Bosnia and Herzegovina)
lyrics/music: Dusan SESTIC and Benjamin ISOVIC/Dusan SESTIC
note: music adopted 1999; lyrics adopted 2009

ECONOMY

Economy—overview: Bosnia has a transitional economy with limited market reforms. The economy relies heavily on the export of metals, energy, textiles and furniture as well as on remittances and foreign aid. A highly decentralized government hampers economic policy coordination and reform, while excessive bureaucracy and a segmented market discourage foreign investment. The interethnic warfare in Bosnia and Herzegovina caused production to plummet by 80% from 1992 to 1995 and unemployment to soar. With an uneasy peace in place, output recovered in 1996-99 but slowed in 2000-02 and picked up again during 2003-08, when GDP growth exceeded 5% per year. However, the country declined in 2009 reflecting local effects of the global economic crisis. GDP growth contracted again in 2012, but posted a small gain in 2013. Foreign banks, primarily from Austria and Italy, now control most of the banking sector. The konvertibilna marka (convertible mark or BAM) - the national currency introduced in 1998 - is pegged to the euro, and confidence in the currency and the banking sector has remained stable. Bosnia's private sector is growing slowly, but foreign investment has dropped sharply since 2007. Government spending - including transfer payments - remains high, at roughly 40% of GDP, because of redundant government offices at the state, entity and municipal level. Privatization of state enterprises has been slow, particularly in the Federation, where political division between ethnically-based political parties makes agreement on economic policy more difficult. High unemployment remains the most serious macroeconomic problem. Successful implementation of a value-added tax in 2006 provided a steady source of revenue for the government and helped rein in gray-market activity. National-level statistics have also improved over time but a large share of economic activity remains unofficial and unrecorded. Bosnia and Herzegovina became a full member of the Central European Free Trade Agreement in September 2007. Bosnia and Herzegovina's top economic priorities are: acceleration of integration into the EU; strengthening the fiscal system; public administration reform; World Trade Organization (WTO) membership; and securing economic growth by fostering a dynamic, competitive private sector. In 2009, Bosnia and Herzegovina was granted an International Monetary Fund (IMF) stand-by arrangement, necessitated by sharply increased social spending and a fiscal crisis exacerbated by the global economic downturn. Disbursement of IMF aid was suspended in 2011 after a parliamentary deadlock left Bosnia without a state-level government for over a year. The IMF concluded a new stand-by arrangement with Bosnia in October 2012 which aims to improve national policy coordination, continue fiscal contraction, improve crisis preparedness, and create an environment conducive to private sector development.

GDP (purchasing power parity): $32.16 billion (2013 est.)
country comparison to the world: 112
$31.9 billion (2012 est.)
$32.26 billion (2011 est.)
note: data are in 2013 US dollars

GDP (official exchange rate): $18.87 billion (2013 est.)

GDP—real growth rate: 0.8% (2013 est.)
country comparison to the world: 178
-1.1% (2012 est.)
1% (2011 est.)

GDP—per capita (PPP): $8,300 (2013 est.)
country comparison to the world: 130
$8,200 (2012 est.)
$8,300 (2011 est.)

note: data are in 2013 US dollars

Gross national saving: 8.6% of GDP
country comparison to the world: 143
6.3% of GDP
6.4% of GDP

GDP—composition, by end use: *household consumption:* 82.1%
government consumption: 22.1%
investment in fixed capital: 17.7%
investment in inventories: 1.5%
exports of goods and services: 29%
imports of goods and services: -52.4% (2012 est.)

GDP—composition, by sector of origin: *agriculture:* 8.1%
industry: 26.4%
services: 65.5% (2013 est.)

Agriculture—products: wheat, corn, fruits, vegetables; livestock

Industries: steel, coal, iron ore, lead, zinc, manganese, bauxite, aluminum, vehicle assembly, textiles, tobacco products, wooden furniture, ammunition, domestic appliances, oil refining

Industrial production growth rate: 11.7% (2013 est.)
country comparison to the world: 8

Labor force: 1.49 million (2012 est.)
country comparison to the world: 129

Labor force—by occupation: *agriculture:* 18.9%
industry: 29.8%
services: 51.3% (2013)

Unemployment rate: 44.3% (2013 est.)
country comparison to the world: 192
44.1% (2012 est.)
note: official rate; actual rate is lower as many technically unemployed persons work in the gray economy

Population below poverty line: 18.6% (2007 est.)

Household income or consumption by percentage share: *lowest 10%:* 2.7%
highest 10%: 27.3% (2007)

Distribution of family income—Gini index: 36.2 (2007)
country comparison to the world: 87

Budget: *revenues:* $7.691 billion
expenditures: $7.497 billion (2013 est.)

Taxes and other revenues: 40.8% of GDP (2013 est.)
country comparison to the world: 32

Budget surplus (+) or deficit (-): 1% of GDP (2013 est.)
country comparison to the world: 25

Public debt: 45.9% of GDP (2013 est.)
country comparison to the world: 79
42.9% of GDP (2012 est.)
note: data cover general government debt, and includes debt instruments issued (or owned) by government entities other than the treasury; the data include treasury debt held by foreign entities; the data include debt issued by subnational entities, as well as intra-governmental debt; intra-governmental debt consists of treasury borrowings from surpluses in the social funds, such as for retirement, medical care, and unemployment; debt instruments for the social funds are not sold at public auctions.

Fiscal year: calendar year

Inflation rate (consumer prices): 0.2% (2013 est.)
country comparison to the world: 9
1.8% (2012 est.)

Commercial bank prime lending rate: 6.73% (31 December 2013 est.)
country comparison to the world: 128
6.8% (31 December 2012 est.)

Stock of narrow money: $4.493 billion (31 December 2013 est.)

country comparison to the world: 107
$4.122 billion (31 December 2012 est.)

Stock of broad money: $10.8 billion (31 December 2013 est.)
country comparison to the world: 104
$10.21 billion (31 December 2012 est.)

Stock of domestic credit: $11 billion (31 December 2013 est.)
country comparison to the world: 96
$10.82 billion (31 December 2012 est.)

Market value of publicly traded shares: $NA

Current account balance: -$939.5 million (2013 est.)
country comparison to the world: 119
$1.639 billion (2012 est.)

Exports: $5.687 billion (2013 est.)
country comparison to the world: 111
$5.161 billion (2012 est.)

Exports—commodities: metals, clothing, wood products

Exports—partners: Germany 15.6%, Croatia 14.2%, Italy 12.1%, Serbia 9.1%, Austria 8.2%, Slovenia 8.1% (2012 est.)

Imports: $10.3 billion (2013 est.)
country comparison to the world: 99
$10.02 billion (2012 est.)

Imports—commodities: machinery and equipment, chemicals, fuels, foodstuffs

Imports—partners: Germany 11.4%, Russian Federation 9.9%, Serbia 9.8%, Italy 9.7%, China 6%, Slovenia 5%, Croatia 12.8% (2012 est.)

Reserves of foreign exchange and gold: $5.002 billion (31 January 2014 est.)
country comparison to the world: 95
$4.852 billion (31 January 2013 est.)

Debt—external: $11.14 billion (31 December 2013 est.)
country comparison to the world: 98
$10.81 billion (31 December 2012 est.)

Stock of direct foreign investment—at home: $7.721 billion
country comparison to the world: 86
$7.58 billion

Exchange rates: konvertibilna markas (BAM) per US dollar—
1.42 (2013 est.)
1.52 (2012 est.)
1.4767 (2010 est.)
1.4079 (2009)
1.3083 (2008)

ENERGY

Electricity—production: 12.93 billion kWh (2012 est.)
country comparison to the world: 89

Electricity—consumption: 12.62 billion kWh (2012 est.)
country comparison to the world: 85

Electricity—exports: 1.569 billion kWh (2012 est.)
country comparison to the world: 48

Electricity—imports: 1.245 billion kWh (2012 est.)
country comparison to the world: 61

Electricity—installed generating capacity: 3.963 million kW (2012 est.)
country comparison to the world: 80

Electricity—from fossil fuels: 43.3% of total installed capacity (2012 est.)
country comparison to the world: 165

Electricity—from nuclear fuels: 0% of total installed capacity (2012 est.)
country comparison to the world: 50

Electricity—from hydroelectric plants: 53.2% of total installed capacity (2012 est.)
country comparison to the world: 39

Electricity—from other renewable sources: 3.5% of total installed capacity (2012 est.)
country comparison to the world: 52

Crude oil—production: 0 bbl/day (2012 est.)
country comparison to the world: 154

Crude oil—exports: 0 bbl/day (2012 est.)
country comparison to the world: 85

Crude oil—imports: 22,140 bbl/day (2010 est.)
country comparison to the world: 68

Crude oil—proved reserves: 0 bbl (1 January 2013 es)
country comparison to the world: 109

Refined petroleum products—production: 22,430 bbl/day (2010 est.)
country comparison to the world: 91

Refined petroleum products—consumption: 27,540 bbl/day (2011 est.)
country comparison to the world: 118

Refined petroleum products—exports: 10,460 bbl/day (2010 est.)
country comparison to the world: 84

Refined petroleum products—imports: 16,330 bbl/day (2010 est.)
country comparison to the world: 113

Natural gas—production: 0 cu m (2013 est.)
country comparison to the world: 105

Natural gas—consumption: 256.9 million cu m (2013 est.)
country comparison to the world: 100

Natural gas—exports: 0 cu m (2013 est.)
country comparison to the world: 67

Natural gas—imports: 256.9 million cu m (2013 est.)
country comparison to the world: 67

Natural gas—proved reserves: 0 cu m (1 January 2013 es)
country comparison to the world: 116

Carbon dioxide emissions from consumption of energy: 22.2 million Mt (2011 est.)
country comparison to the world: 82

COMMUNICATIONS

Telephones—main lines in use: 878,000 (2012)
country comparison to the world: 82

Telephones—mobile cellular: 3.35 million (2012)
country comparison to the world: 127

Telephone system: *general assessment:* post-war reconstruction of the telecommunications network, aided by an internationally sponsored program, resulting in sharp increases in the number of fixed telephone lines available
domestic: fixed-line teledensity roughly 25 per 100 persons; mobile-cellular subscribership has been increasing rapidly and, stands at roughly 80 telephones per 100 persons
international: country code—387; no satellite earth stations (2011)

Broadcast media: 3 public TV broadcasters: Radio and TV of Bosnia and Herzegovina, Federation TV (operating 2 networks), and Republika Srpska Radio-TV; a local commercial network of 5 TV stations; 3 private, near-national TV stations and dozens of small independent TV stations broadcasting; 3 large public radio broadcasters and many private radio stations (2010)

Internet country code: .ba

Internet hosts: 155,252 (2012)
country comparison to the world: 77

Internet users: 1.422 million (2009)
country comparison to the world: 85

TRANSPORTATION

Airports: 24 (2013)
country comparison to the world: 130

Airports—with paved runways: *total:* 7
2,438 to 3,047 m: 4
1,524 to 2,437 m: 1
under 914 m: 2 (2013)

Airports—with unpaved runways: *total:* 17
1,524 to 2,437 m: 1
914 to 1,523 m: 5
under 914 m: 11 (2013)

Heliports: 6 (2013)

Pipelines: gas 147 km; oil 9 km (2013)

Railways: *total:* 601 km
country comparison to the world: 107
standard gauge: 601 km 1.435-m gauge (392 km electrified) (2009)

Roadways: *total:* 22,926 km
country comparison to the world: 101
paved: 19,426 km (4,652 km of interurban roads)
unpaved: 3,500 km (2010)

Waterways: (Sava River on northern border; open to shipping but use limited) (2011)

Ports and terminals: *river port(s):* Bosanska Gradiska, Bosanski Brod, Bosanski Samac, Brcko, Orasje (Sava River)

MILITARY

Military branches: Armed Forces of Bosnia and Herzegovina (AFBiH): Army of Bosnia and Herzegovina, Air and Air Defense Forces of Bosnia and Herzegovina (Zrakoplovstvo i Protuzracna Obrana, ZPO) (2013)

Military service age and obligation: 18 years of age for voluntary military service; mandatory retirement at age 35 or after 15 years of service (2013)

Manpower available for military service: *males age 16-49:* 1,180,829
females age 16-49: 1,143,919 (2010 est.)

Manpower fit for military service: *males age 16-49:* 968,242
females age 16-49: 937,327 (2010 est.)

Manpower reaching militarily significant age annually: *male:* 26,601
female: 24,879 (2010 est.)

Military expenditures: 1.35% of GDP (2012)
country comparison to the world: 75
1.15% of GDP (2011)
1.35% of GDP (2010)

TRANSNATIONAL ISSUES

Disputes—international: Serbia delimited about half of the boundary with Bosnia and Herzegovina, but sections along the Drina River remain in dispute

Refugees and internally displaced persons: *refugees (country of origin):* 6,733 (Croatia) (2012)
IDPs: 113,000 (Bosnian Croats, Serbs, and Bosniaks displaced in 1992-95 war) (2011)
stateless persons: 4,500 (2012)

Illicit drugs: increasingly a transit point for heroin being trafficked to Western Europe; minor transit point for marijuana; remains highly vulnerable to money-laundering activity given a primarily cash-based and unregulated economy, weak law enforcement, and instances of corruption

BOTSWANA

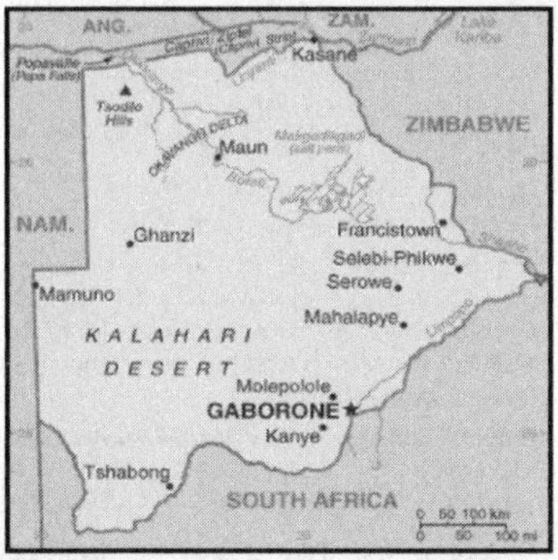

INTRODUCTION

Background: Formerly the British protectorate of Bechuanaland, Botswana adopted its new name upon independence in 1966. More than four decades of uninterrupted civilian leadership, progressive social policies, and significant capital investment have created one of the most stable economies in Africa. Mineral extraction, principally diamond mining, dominates economic activity, though tourism is a growing sector due to the country's conservation practices and extensive nature preserves. Botswana has one of the world's highest known rates of HIV/AIDS infection, but also one of Africa's most progressive and comprehensive programs for dealing with the disease.

GEOGRAPHY

Location: Southern Africa, north of South Africa

Geographic coordinates: 22 00 S, 24 00 E

Map references: Africa

Area: *total:* 581,730 sq km
country comparison to the world: 48
land: 566,730 sq km
water: 15,000 sq km

Area—comparative: slightly smaller than Texas

Land boundaries: *total:* 4,013 km

border countries: Namibia 1,360 km, South Africa 1,840 km, Zimbabwe 813 km

Coastline: 0 km (landlocked)

Maritime claims: none (landlocked)

Climate: semiarid; warm winters and hot summers

Terrain: predominantly flat to gently rolling tableland; Kalahari Desert in southwest

Elevation extremes: *lowest point:* junction of the Limpopo and Shashe Rivers 513 m
highest point: Tsodilo Hills 1,489 m

Natural resources: diamonds, copper, nickel, salt, soda ash, potash, coal, iron ore, silver

Land use: *arable land:* 0.45%
permanent crops: 0%
other: 99.55% (2011)

Irrigated land: 14.39 sq km (2003)

Total renewable water resources: 12.24 cu km (2011)

Freshwater withdrawal (domestic/industrial/agricultural): *total:* 0.19 cu km/yr (42%/19%/39%)
per capita: 107.3 cu m/yr (2005)

Natural hazards: periodic droughts; seasonal August winds blow from the west, carrying sand and dust across the country, which can obscure visibility

Environment—current issues: overgrazing; desertification; limited freshwater resources

Environment—international agreements: *party to:* Biodiversity, Climate Change, Climate Change-Kyoto Protocol, Desertification, Endangered Species, Hazardous Wastes, Law of the Sea, Ozone Layer Protection, Wetlands
signed, but not ratified: none of the selected agreements

Geography—note: landlocked; population concentrated in eastern part of the country

PEOPLE AND SOCIETY

Nationality: *noun:* Motswana (singular), Batswana (plural)
adjective: Motswana (singular), Batswana (plural)

Ethnic groups: Tswana (or Setswana) 79%, Kalanga 11%, Basarwa 3%, other, including Kgalagadi and white 7%

Languages: Setswana 78.2%, Kalanga 7.9%, Sekgalagadi 2.8%, English (official) 2.1%, other 8.6%, unspecified 0.4% (2001 census)

Religions: Christian 71.6%, Badimo 6%, other 1.4%, unspecified 0.4%, none 20.6% (2001 census)

Population: 2,155,784 (July 2014 est.)
country comparison to the world: 145
note: estimates for this country explicitly take into account the effects of excess mortality due to AIDS; this can result in lower life expectancy, higher infant mortality, higher death rates, lower population growth rates, and changes in the distribution of population by age and sex than would otherwise be expected

Age structure: *0-14 years:* 32.9% (male 361,717/female 348,150)
15-24 years: 21.6% (male 231,576/female 234,852)
25-54 years: 37% (male 422,182/female 375,836)
55-64 years: 4% (male 42,099/female 52,917)
65 years and over: 4% (male 34,567/female 51,888) (2014 est.)

Dependency ratios: *total dependency ratio:* 59.1%
youth dependency ratio: 53.3%
elderly dependency ratio: 5.8%
potential support ratio: 17.3 (2013)

Median age: *total:* 22.9 years
male: 22.9 years
female: 22.8 years (2014 est.)

Population growth rate: 1.26% (2014 est.)
country comparison to the world: 92

Birth rate: 21.34 births/1,000 population (2014 est.)
country comparison to the world: 77

Death rate: 13.32 deaths/1,000 population (2014 est.)
country comparison to the world: 17

Net migration rate: 4.62 migrant(s)/1,000 population
country comparison to the world: 28
note: there is an increasing flow of Zimbabweans into South Africa and Botswana in search of better economic opportunities (2014 est.)

Urbanization: *urban population:* 61.7% of total population (2011)
rate of urbanization: 2.07% annual rate of change (2010-15 est.)

Major urban areas—population: GABORONE (capital) 202,000 (2011)

Sex ratio: *at birth:* 1.03 male(s)/female
0-14 years: 1.04 male(s)/female
15-24 years: 0.99 male(s)/female
25-54 years: 1.12 male(s)/female
55-64 years: 1.03 male(s)/female
65 years and over: 0.67 male(s)/female
total population: 1.02 male(s)/female (2014 est.)

Maternal mortality rate: 160 deaths/100,000 live births (2010)
country comparison to the world: 61

Infant mortality rate: *total:* 9.38 deaths/1,000 live births
country comparison to the world: 145
male: 9.77 deaths/1,000 live births
female: 8.99 deaths/1,000 live births (2014 est.)

Life expectancy at birth: *total population:* 54.06 years
country comparison to the world: 210
male: 55.75 years
female: 52.32 years (2014 est.)

Total fertility rate: 2.37 children born/woman (2014 est.)
country comparison to the world: 87

Contraceptive prevalence rate: 52.8%
note: percent of women aged 12-49 (2007/08)

Health expenditures: 5.1% of GDP (2011)
country comparison to the world: 141

Physicians density: 0.34 physicians/1,000 population (2006)

Hospital bed density: 1.8 beds/1,000 population (2010)

Drinking water source:
Improved:
urban: 99.3% of population
rural: 92.8% of population
total: 96.8% of population
Unimproved:
urban: 0.7% of population
rural: 7.2% of population
total: 3.2% of population (2011 est.)

Sanitation facility access:
Improved:
urban: 77.9% of population
rural: 41.8% of population
total: 64% of population
Unimproved:
urban: 22.1% of population
rural: 58.2% of population
total: 36% of population (2011 est.)

HIV/AIDS—adult prevalence rate: 23% (2012 est.)
country comparison to the world: 3

HIV/AIDS—people living with HIV/AIDS: 337,700 (2012 est.)
country comparison to the world: 21

HIV/AIDS—deaths: 5,700 (2012 est.)
country comparison to the world: 33

Major infectious diseases: *degree of risk:* high
food or waterborne diseases: bacterial diarrhea, hepatitis A, and typhoid fever
vectorborne disease: malaria (2013)

Obesity—adult prevalence rate: 11.2% (2008)
country comparison to the world: 128

Children under the age of 5 years underweight: 11.2% (2008)
country comparison to the world: 65

Education expenditures: 9.5% of GDP (2009)
country comparison to the world: 5

Literacy: *definition:* age 15 and over can read and write
total population: 85.1%
male: 84.6%
female: 85.6% (2011 est.)

School life expectancy (primary to tertiary education): *total:* 12 years
male: 12 years
female: 12 years (2006)

Child labor—children ages 5-14: *total number:* 45,036
percentage: 9%
note: data represents children ages 7-17 (2006 est.)

Unemployment, youth ages 15-24: *total:* 13.6%
country comparison to the world: 92
male: 13.2%
female: 14% (2000)

GOVERNMENT

Country name: *conventional long form:* Republic of Botswana
conventional short form: Botswana
local long form: Republic of Botswana
local short form: Botswana
former: Bechuanaland

Government type: parliamentary republic

Capital: *name:* Gaborone
geographic coordinates: 24 38 S, 25 54 E
time difference: UTC+2 (7 hours ahead of Washington, DC during Standard Time)

Administrative divisions: 10 districts and 6 town councils*; Central, Chobe, Francistown*, Gaborone*, Ghanzi, Jwaneng*, Kgalagadi, Kgatleng, Kweneng, Lobatse*, North East, North West, Selebi-Pikwe*, South East, Southern, Sowa Town

Independence: 30 September 1966 (from the UK)

National holiday: Independence Day (Botswana Day), 30 September (1966)

Constitution: previous 1960 (preindependence); latest adopted March 1965, effective 30 September 1966; amended several times, last in 2006 (2006)

Legal system: mixed legal system of civil law influenced by the Roman-Dutch model and also customary and common law

International law organization participation: accepts compulsory ICJ jurisdiction with reservations; accepts ICCt jurisdiction

Suffrage: 18 years of age; universal

Executive branch: *chief of state:* President Seretse Khama Ian KHAMA (since 1 April 2008); Vice President Ponatshego KEDIKILWE (since 2 August 2012); note—the president is both the chief of state and head of government
head of government: President Seretse Khama Ian KHAMA (since 1 April 2008); Vice President Ponatshego KEDIKILWE (since 2 August 2012)
cabinet: Cabinet appointed by the president (For more information visit the World Leaders website)
elections: president indirectly elected for a five-year term (eligible for a second term); election last held on 20 October 2009 (next to be held in October 2014); vice president appointed by the president
election results: Seretse Khama Ian KHAMA elected president; percent of National Assembly vote—NA

Legislative branch: bicameral Parliament consists of the House of Chiefs (a largely advisory 35-member body with 8 ex-officio members consisting of the chiefs of the principal tribes, and 27 non-permanent members serving five-year terms, of which 22 are indirectly elected with the remaining 5 appointed by the President) and the National Assembly (63 seats; 57 members directly elected by popular vote, 4 appointed by the majority party, and 2, the President and Attorney General, serve as ex-officio members; members serve five-year terms)
elections: National Assembly elections last held on 16 October 2009 (next to be held in 2014)
election results: percent of vote by party—BDP 53.3%, BNF 21.9%, BCP 19.2%, BAM 2.3%, other 3.3%; seats by party—BDP 45, BNF 6, BCP 4, BAM 1, other 1

Judicial branch: *highest court(s):* Court of Appeal, High Court (each consists of a chief justice and number of other judges as prescribed by the Parliament)
judge selection and term of office: Court of Appeal and High Court chief justices appointed by the president and other judges appointed by the president upon the advice of the Judicial Service Commission; all judges appointed to serve until age 70
subordinate courts: Industrial Court (with circuits scheduled monthly in the capital city and in three districts); Magistrates Courts (one in each district); Customary Court of Appeal; Paramount Chief's Court/Urban Customary Court; Senior Chief's Representative Court; Chief's Representative's Court; Headman's Court

Political parties and leaders: Botswana Alliance Movement or BAM [Ephraim Lepetu SETSHWAELO]; Botswana Congress Party or BCP [Dumelang SALESHANDO]; Botswana Democratic Party or BDP [Ian KHAMA]; Botswana Movement for Democracy or BMD [Gomolemo MOTSWALEDI]; Botswana National Front or BNF [Duma BOKO]; Botswana Peoples Party or BPP [Bernard BALIKANI]; MELS Movement of Botswana or MELS [Themba JOINA]; New Democratic Front or NDF [Dick BAYFORD]
note: a number of minor parties joined forces in 1999 to form the BAM but did not capture any parliamentary seats—includes the United Action Party [Ephraim Lepetu SETSHWAELO]; the Independence Freedom Party or IFP [Motsamai MPHO]; the Botswana Progressive Union [D. K. KWELE]

Political pressure groups and leaders: First People of the Kalahari (Bushman organization); Pitso Ya Ba Tswana; Society for the Promotion of Ikalanga Language (Kalanga elites)
other: diamond mining companies

International organization participation: ACP, AfDB, AU, C, CD, FAO, G-77, IAEA, IBRD, ICAO, ICRM, IDA, IFAD, IFC, IFRCS, ILO, IMF, Interpol, IOC, IOM, IPU, ISO, ITSO, ITU, ITUC (NGOs), MIGA, NAM, OPCW, SACU, SADC, UN, UNCTAD, UNESCO, UNIDO, UNWTO, UPU, WCO, WFTU (NGOs), WHO, WIPO, WMO, WTO

Diplomatic representation in the US: *chief of mission:* Ambassador Tebelelo Mazile SERETSE (since 16 February 2011)
chancery: 1531-1533 New Hampshire Avenue NW, Washington, DC 20036
telephone: [1] (202) 244-4990
FAX: [1] (202) 244-4164

Diplomatic representation from the US: *chief of mission:* Ambassador Michelle D. GAVIN (since 15 June 2011)
embassy: Embassy Drive, Government Enclave (off Khama Crescent), Gaborone
mailing address: Embassy Enclave, P. O. Box 90, Gaborone
telephone: [267] 395-3982
FAX: [267] 318-0232

Flag description: light blue with a horizontal white-edged black stripe in the center; the blue symbolizes water in the form of rain, while the black and white bands represent racial harmony

National symbol(s): zebra

National anthem: *name:* "Fatshe leno la rona" (Our Land)
lyrics/music: Kgalemang Tumedisco MOTSETE
note: adopted 1966

ECONOMY

Economy—overview: Botswana has maintained one of the world's highest economic growth rates since independence in 1966. However, economic growth was negative in 2009, with the industrial sector shrinking by 30%, after the global crisis reduced demand for Botswana's diamonds. Although the economy recovered in 2010, GDP growth has again slowed. Through fiscal discipline and sound management, Botswana transformed itself from one of the poorest countries in the world to a middle-income country with a per capita GDP of $16,400 in 2013. Two major investment services rank Botswana as the best credit risk in Africa. Diamond mining has fueled much of the expansion and currently accounts for more than one-third of GDP, 70-80% of export earnings, and about one-third of the government's revenues. Botswana's heavy reliance on a single luxury export was a critical factor in the sharp economic contraction of 2009. Tourism, financial services, subsistence farming, and cattle raising are other key sectors. According to official government statistics, unemployment reached 17.8% in 2009, but unofficial estimates run much higher. The prevalence of HIV/AIDS is second highest in the world and threatens Botswana's impressive economic gains. An expected leveling off in diamond production within the next two decades overshadows long-term prospects. A major international diamond company signed a 10-year deal with Botswana in 2012 to move its rough stone sorting and trading division from London to Gaborone by the end of 2013. The move may support Botswana's downstream diamond industry.

GDP (purchasing power parity): $34 billion (2013 est.)
country comparison to the world: 111
$32.71 billion (2012 est.)
$31.4 billion (2011 est.)
note: data are in 2013 US dollars

GDP (official exchange rate): $15.53 billion (2013 est.)

GDP—real growth rate: 3.9% (2013 est.)
country comparison to the world: 82
4.2% (2012 est.)
6.1% (2011 est.)

GDP—per capita (PPP): $16,400 (2013 est.)
country comparison to the world: 82
$15,900 (2012 est.)
$15,500 (2011 est.)
note: data are in 2013 US dollars

Gross national saving: 33.7% of GDP (2013 est.)
country comparison to the world: 16
28.9% of GDP (2012 est.)
41.1% of GDP (2011 est.)

GDP—composition, by end use: *household consumption:* 51.6%
government consumption: 18.3%
investment in fixed capital: 34.1%
investment in inventories: -1.2%
exports of goods and services: 47%
imports of goods and services: -49.8% (2013 est.)

GDP—composition, by sector of origin: *agriculture:* 1.9%
industry: 35.7%
services: 62.4% (2013 est.)

Agriculture—products: livestock, sorghum, maize, millet, beans, sunflowers, groundnuts

Industries: diamonds, copper, nickel, salt, soda ash, potash, coal, iron ore, silver; livestock processing; textiles

Industrial production growth rate: 7.2% (2013 est.)
country comparison to the world: 30

Labor force: 1.308 million (2013 est.)
country comparison to the world: 136

Labor force—by occupation: *agriculture:* NA%
industry: NA%
services: NA%

Unemployment rate: 17.8% (2009 est.)
country comparison to the world: 157
7.5% (2007 est.)

Population below poverty line: 30.3% (2003)

Household income or consumption by percentage share: *lowest 10%:* NA% highest 10%: NA%

Distribution of family income—Gini index: 63 (1993)
country comparison to the world: 3

Budget: *revenues:* $5.04 billion *expenditures:* $4.952 billion (2013 est.)

Taxes and other revenues: 32.4% of GDP (2013 est.)
country comparison to the world: 79

Budget surplus (+) or deficit (-): 0.6% of GDP (2013 est.)
country comparison to the world: 32

Public debt: 17.9% of GDP (2013 est.)
country comparison to the world: 138
17.4% of GDP (2012 est.)

Fiscal year: 1 April—31 March

Inflation rate (consumer prices): 6.1% (2013 est.)
country comparison to the world: 176
7.5% (2012 est.)

Central bank discount rate: 9.5% (31 December 2010 est.)
country comparison to the world: 25
10% (31 December 2009 est.)

Commercial bank prime lending rate: 10% (31 December 2013 est.)
country comparison to the world: 78
11% (31 December 2012 est.)

Stock of narrow money: $1.517 billion (31 December 2013 est.)
country comparison to the world: 139
$1.358 billion (31 December 2012 est.)

Stock of broad money: $8.293 billion (31 December 2013 est.)
country comparison to the world: 110
$7.635 billion (31 December 2012 est.)

Stock of domestic credit: $1.38 billion (31 December 2013 est.)
country comparison to the world: 147
$2.111 billion (31 December 2012 est.)

Market value of publicly traded shares: $4.588 billion (31 December 2012 est.)
country comparison to the world: 87
$4.107 billion (31 December 2011)
$4.076 billion (31 December 2010 est.)

Current account balance: $1.375 billion (2013 est.)
country comparison to the world: 48
-$795.2 million (2012 est.)

Exports: $7.569 billion (2013 est.)
country comparison to the world: 103
$6.011 billion (2012 est.)

Exports—commodities: diamonds, copper, nickel, soda ash, meat, textiles

Imports: $7.389 billion (2013 est.)
country comparison to the world: 111
$7.918 billion (2012 est.)

Imports—commodities: foodstuffs, machinery, electrical goods, transport equipment, textiles, fuel and petroleum products, wood and paper products, metal and metal products

Reserves of foreign exchange and gold: $7.933 billion (31 December 2013 est.)
country comparison to the world: 79
$7.628 billion (31 December 2012 est.)

Debt—external: $2.416 billion (31 December 2013 est.)
country comparison to the world: 141
$2.443 billion (31 December 2012 est.)

Exchange rates: pulas (BWP) per US dollar—
8.732 (2013 est.)
7.6181 (2012 est.)
6.7936 (2010 est.)
7.1551 (2009)
6.7907 (2008)

ENERGY

Electricity—production: 429.6 million kWh (2010 est.)
country comparison to the world: 166

Electricity—consumption: 3.118 billion kWh (2011 est.)
country comparison to the world: 129

Electricity—exports: 0 kWh (2012 est.)
country comparison to the world: 102

Electricity—imports: 2.985 billion kWh (2010 est.)
country comparison to the world: 47

Electricity—installed generating capacity: 132,000 kW (2011 est.)
country comparison to the world: 168

Electricity—from fossil fuels: 100% of total installed capacity (2010 est.)
country comparison to the world: 6

Electricity—from nuclear fuels: 0% of total installed capacity (2010 est.)
country comparison to the world: 45

Electricity—from hydroelectric plants: 0% of total installed capacity (2010 est.)
country comparison to the world: 157

Electricity—from other renewable sources: 0% of total installed capacity (2010 est.)
country comparison to the world: 155

Crude oil—production: 0 bbl/day (2012 est.)
country comparison to the world: 151

Crude oil—exports: 0 bbl/day (2010 est.)
country comparison to the world: 80

Crude oil—imports: 0 bbl/day (2010 est.)
country comparison to the world: 157

Crude oil—proved reserves: 0 bbl (1 January 2013 es)
country comparison to the world: 105

Refined petroleum products—production: 0 bbl/day (2010 est.)
country comparison to the world: 120

Refined petroleum products—consumption: 15,420 bbl/day (2011 est.)
country comparison to the world: 141

Refined petroleum products—exports: 0 bbl/day (2010 est.)
country comparison to the world: 151

Refined petroleum products—imports: 19,360 bbl/day (2010 est.)
country comparison to the world: 107

Natural gas—production: 0 cu m (2011 est.)
country comparison to the world: 100

Natural gas—consumption: 0 cu m (2010 est.)
country comparison to the world: 118

Natural gas—exports: 0 cu m (2011 est.)
country comparison to the world: 62

Natural gas—imports: 0 cu m (2011 est.)
country comparison to the world: 157

Natural gas—proved reserves: 0 cu m (1 January 2013 es)
country comparison to the world: 111

Carbon dioxide emissions from consumption of energy: 3.843 million Mt (2011 est.)
country comparison to the world: 133

COMMUNICATIONS

Telephones—main lines in use: 160,500 (2012)
country comparison to the world: 134

Telephones—mobile cellular: 3.082 million (2012)
country comparison to the world: 129

Telephone system: *general assessment:* Botswana is participating in regional development efforts; expanding fully digital system with fiber-optic cables linking the major population centers in the east as well as a system of open-wire lines, microwave radio relays links, and radiotelephone communication stations
domestic: fixed-line teledensity has declined in recent years and now stands at roughly 7 telephones per 100 persons; mobile-cellular teledensity now pushing 140 telephones per 100 persons
international: country code—267; international calls are made via satellite, using international direct dialing; 2 international exchanges; digital microwave radio relay links to Namibia, Zambia, Zimbabwe, and South Africa; satellite earth station—1 Intelsat (Indian Ocean) (2011)

Broadcast media: 2 TV stations—1 state-owned and 1 privately owned; privately owned satellite TV subscription service is available; 2 state-owned national radio stations; 3 privately owned radio stations broadcast locally (2007)

Internet country code: .bw

Internet hosts: 1,806 (2012)
country comparison to the world: 163

Internet users: 120,000 (2009)
country comparison to the world: 154

TRANSPORTATION

Airports: 74 (2013)
country comparison to the world: 71

Airports—with paved runways: *total:* 10 over 3,047 m: 2

2,438 to 3,047 m: 1
1,524 to 2,437 m: 6
914 to 1,523 m: 1 (2013)

Airports—with unpaved runways: *total:* 64
1,524 to 2,437 m: 5
914 to 1,523 m: 46
under 914 m: 13 (2013)

Railways: *total:* 888 km
country comparison to the world: 93
narrow gauge: 888 km 1.067-m gauge (2008)

Roadways: *total:* 17,916 km
country comparison to the world: 117
note: includes 8,916 km of Public Highway Network roads (6,116 km paved and 2,800 km unpaved) and other 9,000 km of District Council roads (2011)

MILITARY

Military branches: *Botswana Defense Force (BDF):* Ground Forces Command, Air Wing Command, Defense Logistics Command, Special Forces Group (2013)

Military service age and obligation: 18 is the apparent age of voluntary military service; official minimum age is unknown (2001)

Manpower available for military service: *males age 16-49:* 557,647
females age 16-49: 531,095 (2010 est.)

Manpower fit for military service: *males age 16-49:* 340,949
females age 16-49: 302,332 (2010 est.)

Manpower reaching militarily significant age annually: *male:* 23,649
female: 23,063 (2010 est.)

Military expenditures: 2.31% of GDP (2012)
country comparison to the world: 34
2.43% of GDP (2011)
2.31% of GDP (2010)

TRANSNATIONAL ISSUES

Disputes—international: none

BOUVET ISLAND

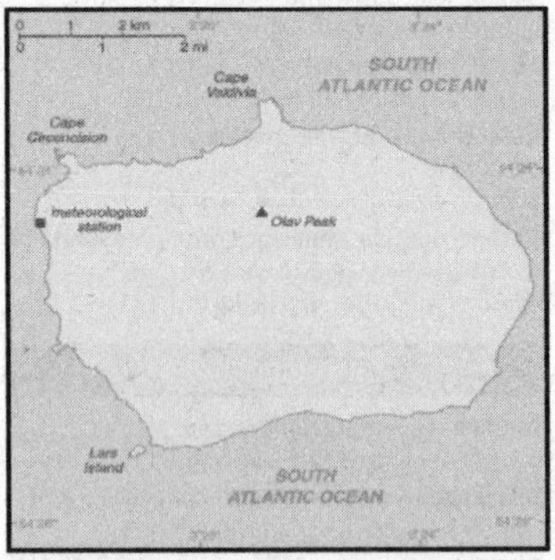

INTRODUCTION

Background: This uninhabited, volcanic, Antarctic island is almost entirely covered by glaciers making it difficult to approach; it is recognized as the most remote island on Earth. Bouvet Island was discovered in 1739 by a French naval officer after whom it is named. No claim was made until 1825, when the British flag was raised. In 1928, the UK waived its claim in favor of Norway, which had occupied the island the previous year. In 1971, Norway designated Bouvet Island and the adjacent territorial waters a nature reserve. Since 1977, Norway has run an automated meteorological station and studied foraging strategies and distribution of fur seals and penguins on the island.

GEOGRAPHY

Location: island in the South Atlantic Ocean, southwest of the Cape of Good Hope (South Africa)

Geographic coordinates: 54 26 S, 3 24 E

Map references: Antarctic Region

Area: *total:* 49 sq km
country comparison to the world: 233
land: 49 sq km
water: 0 sq km

Area—comparative: about 0.3 times the size of Washington, DC

Land boundaries: 0 km

Coastline: 29.6 km

Maritime claims: *territorial sea:* 4 nm

Climate: antarctic

Terrain: volcanic; coast is mostly inaccessible

Elevation extremes: *lowest point:* South Atlantic Ocean 0 m
highest point: Olav Peak 935 m

Natural resources: none

Land use: *arable land:* 0%
permanent crops: 0%
other: 100% (93% ice) (2011)

Natural hazards: NA

Environment—current issues: NA

Geography—note: covered by glacial ice; declared a nature reserve by Norway

PEOPLE AND SOCIETY

Population: uninhabited

GOVERNMENT

Country name: *conventional long form:* none
conventional short form: Bouvet Island

Dependency status: territory of Norway; administered by the Polar Department of the Ministry of Justice and Oslo Police

Legal system: the laws of Norway, where applicable, apply

Flag description: the flag of Norway is used

ECONOMY

Economy—overview: no economic activity; declared a nature reserve

COMMUNICATIONS

Internet country code: .bv

Internet hosts: 6 (2012)
country comparison to the world: 230

Communications—note: has an automatic meteorological station

TRANSPORTATION

Ports and terminals: none; offshore anchorage only

MILITARY

Military—note: defense is the responsibility of Norway

TRANSNATIONAL ISSUES

Disputes—international: none

BRAZIL

INTRODUCTION

Background: Following more than three centuries under Portuguese rule, Brazil gained its independence in 1822, maintaining a monarchical system of government until the abolition of slavery in 1888 and the subsequent proclamation of a republic by the military in 1889. Brazilian coffee exporters politically dominated the country until populist leader Getulio VARGAS rose to power in 1930. By far the largest and most populous country in South America, Brazil underwent more than a half century of populist and military government until 1985, when the military regime peacefully ceded power to civilian rulers. Brazil continues to pursue industrial and agricultural growth and development of its interior. Exploiting vast natural resources and a large labor pool, it is today South America's leading economic power and a regional leader, one of the first in the area to begin an economic recovery. Highly unequal income distribution and crime remain pressing problems.

GEOGRAPHY

Location: Eastern South America, bordering the Atlantic Ocean

Geographic coordinates: 10 00 S, 55 00 W

Map references: South America

Area: *total:* 8,514,877 sq km
country comparison to the world: 5
land: 8,459,417 sq km
water: 55,460 sq km
note: includes Arquipelago de Fernando de Noronha, Atol das Rocas, Ilha da Trindade, Ilhas Martin Vaz, and Penedos de Sao Pedro e Sao Paulo

Area—comparative: slightly smaller than the US

Land boundaries: *total:* 16,885 km
border countries: Argentina 1,261 km, Bolivia 3,423 km, Colombia 1,644 km, French Guiana 730 km, Guyana 1,606 km, Paraguay 1,365 km, Peru 2,995 km, Suriname 593 km, Uruguay 1,068 km, Venezuela 2,200 km

Coastline: 7,491 km

Maritime claims: *territorial sea:* 12 nm
contiguous zone: 24 nm
exclusive economic zone: 200 nm
continental shelf: 200 nm or to edge of the continental margin

Climate: mostly tropical, but temperate in south

Terrain: mostly flat to rolling lowlands in north; some plains, hills, mountains, and narrow coastal belt

Elevation extremes: *lowest point:* Atlantic Ocean 0 m
highest point: Pico da Neblina 2,994 m

Natural resources: bauxite, gold, iron ore, manganese, nickel, phosphates, platinum, tin, rare earth elements, uranium, petroleum, hydropower, timber

Land use: *arable land:* 8.45%
permanent crops: 0.83%
other: 90.72% (2011)

Irrigated land: 54,000 sq km (2011)

Total renewable water resources: 8,233 cu km (2011)

Freshwater withdrawal (domestic/industrial/agricultural): *total:* 58.07 cu km/yr (28%/17%/55%)
per capita: 306 cu m/yr (2006)

Natural hazards: recurring droughts in northeast; floods and occasional frost in south

Environment—current issues: deforestation in Amazon Basin destroys the habitat and endangers a multitude of plant and animal species indigenous to the area; there is a lucrative illegal wildlife trade; air and water pollution in Rio de Janeiro, Sao Paulo, and several other large cities; land degradation and water pollution caused by improper mining activities; wetland degradation; severe oil spills

Environment—international agreements: *party to:* Antarctic-Environmental Protocol, Antarctic-Marine Living Resources, Antarctic Seals, Antarctic Treaty, Biodiversity, Climate Change, Climate Change-Kyoto Protocol, Desertification, Endangered Species, Environmental Modification, Hazardous Wastes, Law of the Sea, Marine Dumping, Ozone Layer Protection, Ship Pollution, Tropical Timber 83, Tropical Timber 94, Wetlands, Whaling
signed, but not ratified: none of the selected agreements

Geography—note: largest country in South America; shares common boundaries with every South American country except Chile and Ecuador

PEOPLE AND SOCIETY

Nationality: *noun:* Brazilian(s)
adjective: Brazilian

Ethnic groups: white 47.7%, mulatto (mixed white and black) 43.1%, black 7.6%, Asian 1.1%, indigenous 0.4% (2010 est.)

Languages: Portuguese (official and most widely spoken language)
note: less common languages include Spanish (border areas and schools), German, Italian, Japanese, English, and a large number of minor Amerindian languages

Religions: Roman Catholic 64.6%, other Catholic 0.4%, Protestant 22.2% (includes Adventist 6.5%, Assembly of God 2.0%, Christian Congregation of Brazil 1.2%, Universal Kingdom of God 1.0%, other Protestant 11.5%), other Christian 0.7%, Spiritist 2.2%, other 1.4%, none 8%, unspecified 0.4% (2010 est.)

Demographic profile: Brazil's rapid fertility decline since the 1960s is the main factor behind the country's slowing population growth rate, aging population, and fast-paced demographic transition. Brasilia has not taken full advantage of its large working-age population to develop its human capital and strengthen its social and economic institutions. The current favorable age structure will begin to shift around 2025, with the labor force shrinking and the elderly starting to compose an increasing share of the total population. Well-funded public pensions have nearly wiped out poverty among the elderly, but limited social spending on children has restricted investment in education—a primary means of escaping poverty. Brazil's poverty and income inequality levels remain high despite improvements in the 2000s and continue to disproportionately affect the Northeast, North, and Center-West, women, and black, mixed race, and indigenous populations. Disparities in opportunities foster social exclusion and contribute to Brazil's high crime rate, particularly violent crime in cities and favelas.

Brazil has traditionally been a net recipient of immigrants, with its southeast being the prime destination. After the importation of African slaves was outlawed in the mid-19th century, Brazil sought Europeans (Italians, Portuguese, Spaniards, and Germans) and later Asians (Japanese) to work in agriculture, especially coffee cultivation. Recent immigrants come mainly from Argentina, Chile, and Andean countries (many are unskilled illegal migrants) or are returning Brazilian nationals. Since Brazil's economic downturn in the 1980s, emigration to the United States, Europe, and Japan has been rising but is negligible relative to Brazil's total population. The majority of these emigrants are well-educated and middle-class. Fewer Brazilian peasants are emigrating to neighboring countries to take up agricultural work.

Population: 202,656,788 (July 2014 est.)
country comparison to the world: 6

Age structure: *0-14 years:* 23.8% (male 24,534,129/female 23,606,332)
15-24 years: 16.5% (male 16,993,708/female 16,521,057)
25-54 years: 43.7% (male 43,910,790/female 44,674,915)
55-64 years: 7.6% (male 8,067,022/female 9,036,519)
65 years and over: 7.3% (male 6,507,069/female 8,805,247) (2014 est.)

Dependency ratios: *total dependency ratio:* 46.2%
youth dependency ratio: 35.2%
elderly dependency ratio: 11%
potential support ratio: 9.1 (2013)

Median age: *total:* 30.7 years
male: 29.9 years
female: 31.5 years (2014 est.)

Population growth rate: 0.8% (2014 est.)
country comparison to the world: 137

Birth rate: 14.72 births/1,000 population (2014 est.)
country comparison to the world: 134

Death rate: 6.54 deaths/1,000 population (2014 est.)
country comparison to the world: 149

Net migration rate: -0.15 migrant(s)/1,000 population (2014 est.)
country comparison to the world: 117

Urbanization: *urban population:* 87% of total population (2010)
rate of urbanization: 1.1% annual rate of change (2010-15 est.)

Major urban areas—population: Sao Paulo 19.96 million; Rio de Janeiro 11.836 million; Belo Horizonte 5.736 million; Porto Alegre 4.034 million; BRASILIA (capital) 3.813 million (2011)

Sex ratio: *at birth:* 1.05 male(s)/female
0-14 years: 1.04 male(s)/female
15-24 years: 1.03 male(s)/female
25-54 years: 0.98 male(s)/female
55-64 years: 0.97 male(s)/female
65 years and over: 0.74 male(s)/female
total population: 0.98 male(s)/female (2014 est.)

Maternal mortality rate: 56 deaths/100,000 live births (2010)
country comparison to the world: 103

Infant mortality rate: *total:* 19.21 deaths/1,000 live births
country comparison to the world: 94
male: 22.47 deaths/1,000 live births
female: 15.78 deaths/1,000 live births (2014 est.)

Life expectancy at birth: *total population:* 73.28 years
country comparison to the world: 126
male: 69.73 years
female: 77 years (2014 est.)

Total fertility rate: 1.79 children born/woman (2014 est.)
country comparison to the world: 155

Contraceptive prevalence rate: 80.3% (2006)

Health expenditures: 8.9% of GDP (2011)
country comparison to the world: 47

Physicians density: 1.76 physicians/1,000 population (2008)

Hospital bed density: 2.3 beds/1,000 population (2011)

Drinking water source:
Improved:
urban: 99.5% of population
rural: 84.5% of population
total: 97.2% of population
Unimproved:
urban: 0.5% of population
rural: 15.5% of population
total: 2.8% of population (2011 est.)

Sanitation facility access:
Improved:
urban: 86.7% of population
rural: 48.4% of population
total: 80.8% of population
Unimproved:
urban: 13.3% of population
rural: 51.6% of population
total: 19.2% of population (2011 est.)

HIV/AIDS—adult prevalence rate: NA

HIV/AIDS—people living with HIV/AIDS: NA

HIV/AIDS—deaths: NA

Obesity—adult prevalence rate: 18.8% (2008)
country comparison to the world: 102

Children under the age of 5 years underweight: 2.2% (2007)
country comparison to the world: 119

Education expenditures: 5.8% of GDP (2010)
country comparison to the world: 49

Literacy: *definition:* age 15 and over can read and write
total population: 90.4%
male: 90.1%
female: 90.7% (2010 est.)

Child labor—children ages 5-14: *total number:* 959,942
percentage: 3%
note: data represents children ages 5-13 (2009 est.)

Unemployment, youth ages 15-24: *total:* 15.4%
country comparison to the world: 82
male: 12.2%
female: 19.8% (2011)

GOVERNMENT

Country name: *conventional long form:* Federative Republic of Brazil
conventional short form: Brazil
local long form: Republica Federativa do Brasil
local short form: Brasil

Government type: federal republic

Capital: name: Brasilia
geographic coordinates: 15 47 S, 47 55 W
time difference: UTC-3 (2 hours ahead of Washington, DC during Standard Time)
daylight saving time: +1hr, begins third Sunday in October; ends third Sunday in February
note: Brazil is divided into three time zones, including one for the Fernando de Noronha Islands

Administrative divisions: 26 states (estados, singular—estado) and 1 federal district* (distrito federal); Acre, Alagoas, Amapa, Amazonas, Bahia, Ceara, Distrito Federal*, Espirito Santo, Goias, Maranhao, Mato Grosso, Mato Grosso do Sul, Minas Gerais, Para, Paraiba, Parana, Pernambuco, Piaui, Rio de Janeiro, Rio Grande do Norte, Rio Grande do Sul, Rondonia, Roraima, Santa Catarina, Sao Paulo, Sergipe, Tocantins

Independence: 7 September 1822 (from Portugal)

National holiday: Independence Day, 7 September (1822)

Constitution: several previous; latest ratified 5 October 1988; amended many times, last in 2012 (2012)

Legal system: civil law; note—a new civil law code was enacted in 2002 replacing the 1916 code

International law organization participation: has not submitted an ICJ jurisdiction declaration; accepts ICCt jurisdiction

Suffrage: voluntary between 16 to under 18 years of age and over 70; compulsory 18 to 70 years of age; note—military conscripts do not vote by law

Executive branch: *chief of state:* President Dilma ROUSSEFF (since 1 January 2011); Vice President Michel Miguel Elias TEMER Lulia (since 1 January 2011); note—the president is both the chief of state and head of government
head of government: President Dilma ROUSSEFF (since 1 January 2011); Vice President Michel Miguel Elias TEMER Lulia (since 1 January 2011)
cabinet: Cabinet appointed by the president (For more information visit the World Leaders website)
elections: president and vice president elected on the same ticket by popular vote for a single four-year term; election last held on 3 October 2010 with runoff on 31 October 2010 (next to be held on 5 October 2014 and, if necessary, a runoff election on 26 October 2014)
election results: Dilma ROUSSEFF (PT) elected president in a runoff election; percent of vote—Dilma ROUSSEFF 56.01%, Jose SERRA (PSDB) 43.99%

Legislative branch: bicameral National Congress or Congresso Nacional consists of the Federal Senate or Senado Federal (81 seats; 3 members from each state and federal district elected according to the principle of majority to serve eight-year terms; one-third and two-thirds of members elected every four years, alternately) and the Chamber of Deputies or Camara dos Deputados (513 seats; members are elected by proportional representation to serve four-year terms)
elections: Federal Senate—last held on 3 October 2010 for two-thirds of the Senate (next to be held in October 2014 for one-third of the Senate); Chamber of Deputies—last held on 3 October 2010 (next to be held in October 2014)
election results: Federal Senate—percent of vote by party—NA; seats by party—PMDB 20, PT 13, PSDB 10, DEM (formerly PFL) 7, PTdoB 6, PP 5, PDT 4, PR 4, PSB 4, PPS 1, PRB 1, other 3; Chamber of Deputies—percent of vote by party—NA; seats by party—PT 87, PMDB 80, PSDB 53, DEM (formerly PFL) 43, PP 41, PR 41, PSB 34, PDT 28, PTdoB 21, PSC 17, PCdoB 15, PV 15, PPS 12, other 26

Judicial branch: *highest court(s):* Supreme Federal Court (consists of 11 justices)
judge selection and term of office: justices appointed by the president and approved by the Federal Senate; justices appointed to serve until mandatory retirement at age 70
subordinate courts: Federal Appeals Court, Superior Court of Justice, Superior Electoral Court,regional federal courts; state court system

Political parties and leaders: Brazilian Communist Party or PCB [Ivan Martins PINHEIRO] Brazilian Democratic Movement Party or PMDB [Michel TEMER] Brazilian Labor Party or PTB [Benito GAMA] Brazilian Renewal Labor Party or PRTB [Jose Levy FIDELIX da Cruz] Brazilian Republican Party or PRB [Marcos Antonio PEREIRA] Brazilian Social Democracy Party or PSDB [Aecio NEVES] Brazilian Socialist Party or PSB [Eduardo CAMPOS] Christian Labor Party or PTC [Daniel TOURINHO] Christian Social Democratic Party or PSDC [Jose Maria EYMAEL] Communist Party of Brazil or PCdoB [Jose Renato RABELO] Democratic Labor Party or PDT [Carlos Roberto LUPI] the Democrats or DEM [Jose AGRIPINO] (formerly Liberal Front Party or PFL) Free Homeland Party or PPL [Sergio RUBENS] Green Party or PV [Jose Luiz PENNA] Humanist Party of Solidarity or PHS [Eduardo MACHADO] Labor Party of Brazil or PTdoB [Luis Henrique de Oliveira RESENDE] National Ecologic Party or PEN [Adilson Barroso OLIVEIRA] National Labor Party or PTN [Jose Masci de ABREU] National Mobilization Party or PMN [Oscar Noronha FILHO] Party of the Republic or PR [Alfredo NASCIMENTO] Popular Socialist Party or PPS [Roberto Joao Pereira FREIRE] Progressive Party or PP [Ciro NOGUEIRA] Progressive Republican Party or PRP [Ovasco Roma Altimari RESENDE] Social Christian Party or PSC [Vitor Jorge Abdala NOSSEIS] Social Democratic Party or PSD [Gilberto KASSAB] Social Liberal Party or PSL [Luciano Caldas BIVAR] Socialism and Freedom Party or PSOL [Luiz ARAUJO] United Socialist Workers' Party or PSTU [Jose Maria DE ALMEIDA] Workers' Cause Party or PCO [Rui Costa PIMENTA] Workers' Party or PT [Rui FALCAO]

Political pressure groups and leaders: Landless Workers' Movement or MST *other:* industrial federations; labor unions and federations; large farmers' associations; religious groups including evangelical Christian churches and the Catholic Church

International organization participation: AfDB (nonregional member), BIS, BRICS, CAN (associate), CD, CELAC, CPLP, FAO, FATF, G-15, G-20, G-24, G-77, IADB, IAEA, IBRD, ICAO, ICC (national committees), ICRM, IDA, IFAD, IFC, IFRCS, IHO, ILO, IMF, IMO, IMSO, Interpol, IOC, IOM, IPU, ISO, ITSO, ITU, ITUC (NGOs), LAES, LAIA, LAS (observer), Mercosur, MIGA, MINURSO, MINUSTAH, NAM (observer), NSG, OAS, OECD (Enhanced Engagement, OPANAL, OPCW, Paris Club (associate), PCA, SICA (observer), UN, UNASUR, UNCTAD, UNESCO, UNFICYP, UNHCR, UNIDO, UNIFIL, Union Latina, UNISFA, UNITAR, UNMIL, UNMISS, UNMIT, UNOCI, UNWTO, UPU, WCO, WFTU (NGOs), WHO, WIPO, WMO, WTO

Diplomatic representation in the US: *chief of mission:* Ambassador Mauro Luiz Iecker VIEIRA (since 11 January 2010)
chancery: 3006 Massachusetts Avenue NW, Washington, DC 20008
telephone: [1] (202) 238-2805
FAX: [1] (202) 238-2827
consulate(s) general: Atlanta, Boston, Chicago, Hartford (CT), Houston, Los Angeles, Miami, New York, San Francisco

Diplomatic representation from the US: *chief of mission:* Ambassador Liliana AYALDE (since 1 August 2013)
embassy: Avenida das Nacoes, Quadra 801, Lote 3, Distrito Federal Cep 70403-900, Brasilia
mailing address: Unit 7500, DPO, AA 34030
telephone: [55] (61) 3312-7000
FAX: [55] (61) 3225-9136
consulate(s) general: Rio de Janeiro, Sao Paulo
consulate(s): Recife

Flag description: green with a large yellow diamond in the center bearing a blue celestial globe with 27 white five-pointed stars; the globe has a white equatorial band with the motto ORDEM E PROGRESSO (Order and Progress); the current flag was inspired by the banner of the former Empire of Brazil (1822–1889); on the imperial flag, the green represented the House of Braganza of Pedro I, the first Emperor of Brazil, while the yellow stood for the Habsburg Family of his wife; on the modern flag the green represents the forests of the country and the yellow rhombus its mineral wealth; the blue circle and stars, which replaced the coat of arms of the original flag, depict the sky over Rio de Janeiro on the morning of 15 November 1889—the day the Republic of Brazil was declared; the number of stars has changed with the creation of new states and has risen from an original 21 to the current 27 (one for each state and the Federal District)

National symbol(s): Southern Cross constellation

National anthem: *name:* "Hino Nacional Brasileiro" (Brazilian National Anthem)
lyrics/music: Joaquim Osorio Duque ESTRADA/ Francisco Manoel DA SILVA
note: music adopted 1890, lyrics adopted 1922; the anthem's music, composed in 1822, was used unofficially for many years before it was adopted

ECONOMY

Economy—overview: Characterized by large and well-developed agricultural, mining, manufacturing, and service sectors, Brazil's economy outweighs that of all other South American countries, and Brazil is expanding its presence in world markets. Since 2003, Brazil has steadily improved its macroeconomic stability, building up foreign reserves, and reducing its debt profile by shifting its debt burden toward real denominated and domestically held instruments. In 2008, Brazil became a net external creditor and two ratings agencies awarded investment grade status to its debt. After strong growth in 2007 and 2008, the onset of the global financial crisis hit Brazil in 2008. Brazil experienced two quarters of recession, as global demand for Brazil's commodity-based exports dwindled and external credit dried up. However, Brazil was one of the first emerging markets to begin a recovery. In 2010, consumer and investor confidence revived and GDP growth reached 7.5%, the highest growth rate in the past 25 years. Rising inflation led the authorities to take measures to cool the economy; these actions and the deteriorating international economic situation slowed growth in 2011-13. Unemployment is at historic lows and Brazil's traditionally high level of income inequality has declined for each of the last 14 years. Brazil's historically high interest rates have made it an attractive destination for foreign investors. Large capital inflows over the past several years have contributed to the appreciation of the currency, hurting the competitiveness of Brazilian manufacturing and leading the government to intervene in foreign exchange markets and raise taxes on some foreign capital inflows. President Dilma ROUSSEFF has retained the previous administration's commitment to inflation targeting by the central bank, a floating exchange rate, and fiscal restraint.

GDP (purchasing power parity): $2.422 trillion (2013 est.)
country comparison to the world: 8
$2.362 trillion (2012 est.)
$2.342 trillion (2011 est.)
note: data are in 2013 US dollars

GDP (official exchange rate): $2.19 trillion (2013 est.)

GDP—real growth rate: 2.5% (2013 est.)
country comparison to the world: 132
0.9% (2012 est.)
2.7% (2011 est.)

GDP—per capita (PPP): $12,100 (2013 est.)
country comparison to the world: 105
$11,900 (2012 est.)
$11,900 (2011 est.)
note: data are in 2013 US dollars

Gross national saving: 14.8% of GDP (2013 est.)
country comparison to the world: 112
15.2% of GDP (2012 est.)
17.6% of GDP (2011 est.)

GDP—composition, by end use: *household consumption:* 62.5%
government consumption: 21.7%
investment in fixed capital: 18.3%
investment in inventories: 0%
exports of goods and services: 12.4%
imports of goods and services: -14.9% (2013 est.)

GDP—composition, by sector of origin: *agriculture:* 5.5%
industry: 26.4%
services: 68.1% (2013 est.)

Agriculture—products: coffee, soybeans, wheat, rice, corn, sugarcane, cocoa, citrus; beef

Industries: textiles, shoes, chemicals, cement, lumber, iron ore, tin, steel, aircraft, motor vehicles and parts, other machinery and equipment

Industrial production growth rate: 3% (2013 est.)
country comparison to the world: 106

Labor force: 107.3 million (2013 est.)
country comparison to the world: 6

Labor force—by occupation: *agriculture:* 15.7%
industry: 13.3%
services: 71% (2011 est.)

Unemployment rate: 5.7% (2013 est.)
country comparison to the world: 53
5.5% (2012 est.)

Population below poverty line: 21.4%
note: official Brazilian data show 4.2% of the population being below the "extreme" poverty line in 2011 (2009 est.)

Household income or consumption by percentage share: *lowest 10%:* 0.8%
highest 10%: 42.9% (2009 est.)

Distribution of family income—Gini index: 51.9 (2012)
country comparison to the world: 17
55.3 (2001)

Budget: *revenues:* $851.1 billion
expenditures: $815.6 billion (2013 est.)

Taxes and other revenues: 38.9% of GDP (2013 est.)
country comparison to the world: 47

Budget surplus (+) or deficit (-): 1.6% of GDP (2013 est.)
country comparison to the world: 21

Public debt: 59.2% of GDP (2013 est.)
country comparison to the world: 49
58.8% of GDP (2012 est.)

Fiscal year: calendar year

Inflation rate (consumer prices): 6.2% (2013 est.)
country comparison to the world: 179
5.4% (2012 est.)

Central bank discount rate: 7.25% (31 December 2012 est.)
country comparison to the world: 23
11% (31 December 2011 est.)

Commercial bank prime lending rate: 26.9% (31 December 2013 est.)
country comparison to the world: 2
36.64% (31 December 2012 est.)

Stock of narrow money: $157.6 billion (31 December 2013 est.)
country comparison to the world: 25
$159.1 billion (31 December 2012 est.)

Stock of broad money: $870.8 billion (31 December 2013 est.)
country comparison to the world: 19
$863.5 billion (31 December 2012 est.)

Stock of domestic credit: $2.435 trillion (31 December 2013 est.)
country comparison to the world: 11
$2.381 trillion (31 December 2012 est.)

Market value of publicly traded shares: $1.23 trillion (31 December 2012 est.)
country comparison to the world: 8
$1.229 trillion (31 December 2011)
$1.546 trillion (31 December 2010 est.)

Current account balance: -$77.63 billion (2013 est.)
country comparison to the world: 191
-$54.23 billion (2012 est.)

Exports: $244.8 billion (2013 est.)
country comparison to the world: 24
$242.6 billion (2012 est.)

Exports—commodities: transport equipment, iron ore, soybeans, footwear, coffee, autos

Exports—partners: China 17%, US 11.1%, Argentina 7.4%, Netherlands 6.2% (2012)

Imports: $241.4 billion (2013 est.)
country comparison to the world: 24
$223.2 billion (2012 est.)

Imports—commodities: machinery, electrical and transport equipment, chemical products, oil, automotive parts, electronics

Imports—partners: China 15.3%, US 14.6%, Argentina 7.4%, Germany 6.4%, South Korea 4.1% (2012)

Reserves of foreign exchange and gold: $378.3 billion (31 December 2013 est.)
country comparison to the world: 8
$373.1 billion (31 December 2012 est.)

Debt—external: $475.9 billion (31 December 2013 est.)
country comparison to the world: 27
$438.9 billion (31 December 2012 est.)

Stock of direct foreign investment—at home: $663.3 billion (31 December 2013 est.)
country comparison to the world: 13
$604.5 billion (31 December 2012 est.)

Stock of direct foreign investment—abroad: $179.6 billion (31 December 2013 est.)
country comparison to the world: 25
$177.1 billion (31 December 2012 est.)

Exchange rates: reals (BRL) per US dollar—
2.153 (2013 est.)
1.9546 (2012 est.)
1.7592 (2010 est.)
2 (2009)
1.8644 (2008)

ENERGY

Electricity—production: 530.7 billion kWh (2011 est.)
country comparison to the world: 8

Electricity—consumption: 455.8 billion kWh (2010 est.)
country comparison to the world: 10

Electricity—exports: 2.544 billion kWh (2011 est.)
country comparison to the world: 39

Electricity—imports: 38.43 billion kWh (2011 est.)
country comparison to the world: 4

Electricity—installed generating capacity: 113.7 million kW (2010 est.)
country comparison to the world: 11

Electricity—from fossil fuels: 19.6% of total installed capacity (2010 est.)
country comparison to the world: 193

Electricity—from nuclear fuels: 1.8% of total installed capacity (2010 est.)
country comparison to the world: 29

Electricity—from hydroelectric plants: 71% of total installed capacity (2010 est.)
country comparison to the world: 21

Electricity—from other renewable sources: 7.7% of total installed capacity (2010 est.)
country comparison to the world: 30

Crude oil—production: 2.652 million bbl/day (2012 est.)
country comparison to the world: 11

Crude oil—exports: 619,100 bbl/day (2010 est.)
country comparison to the world: 21

Crude oil—imports: 343,600 bbl/day (2010 est.)
country comparison to the world: 25

Crude oil—proved reserves: 13.15 billion bbl (1 January 2013 es)
country comparison to the world: 15

Refined petroleum products—production: 2.108 million bbl/day (2010 est.)
country comparison to the world: 9

Refined petroleum products—consumption: 2.594 million bbl/day (2011 est.)
country comparison to the world: 8

Refined petroleum products—exports: 158,400 bbl/day (2010 est.)
country comparison to the world: 36

Refined petroleum products—imports: 457,400 bbl/day (2010 est.)
country comparison to the world: 14

Natural gas—production: 17.03 billion cu m (2012 est.)
country comparison to the world: 35

Natural gas—consumption: 25.2 billion cu m (2010 est.)
country comparison to the world: 31

Natural gas—exports: 400 million cu m (2012 est.)
country comparison to the world: 46

Natural gas—imports: 13.3 billion cu m (2012 est.)
country comparison to the world: 25

Natural gas—proved reserves: 395.5 billion cu m (1 January 2013 es)
country comparison to the world: 34

Carbon dioxide emissions from consumption of energy: 475.4 million Mt (2011 est.)
country comparison to the world: 13

COMMUNICATIONS

Telephones—main lines in use: 44.3 million (2012)
country comparison to the world: 5

Telephones—mobile cellular: 248.324 million (2012)
country comparison to the world: 6

Telephone system: *general assessment:* good working system including an extensive microwave radio relay system and a domestic satellite system with 64 earth stations
domestic: fixed-line connections have remained relatively stable in recent years and stand at about 20 per 100 persons; less expensive mobile-cellular technology has been a major driver in expanding telephone service to the lower-income segments of the population with mobile-cellular teledensity roughly 120 per 100 persons
international: country code—55; landing point for a number of submarine cables, including Americas-1, Americas-2, Atlantis-2, GlobeNet, South America-1, South American Crossing/Latin American Nautilus, and UNISUR that provide direct connectivity to South and Central America, the Caribbean, the US, Africa, and Europe; satellite earth stations—3 Intelsat (Atlantic Ocean), 1 Inmarsat (Atlantic Ocean region east), connected by microwave relay system to Mercosur Brazilsat B3 satellite earth station (2011)

Broadcast media: state-run Radiobras operates a radio and a TV network; more than 1,000 radio stations and more than 100 TV channels operating—mostly privately owned; private media ownership highly concentrated (2007)

Internet country code: .br

Internet hosts: 26.577 million (2012)
country comparison to the world: 3

Internet users: 75.982 million (2009)
country comparison to the world: 4

TRANSPORTATION

Airports: 4,093 (2013)
country comparison to the world: 2

Airports—with paved runways: *total:* 698
over 3,047 m: 7
2,438 to 3,047 m: 27
1,524 to 2,437 m: 179
914 to 1,523 m: 436
under 914 m: 49 (2013)

Airports—with unpaved runways: *total:* 3,395
1,524 to 2,437 m: 92
914 to 1,523 m: 1,619
under 914 m: 1,684 (2013)

Heliports: 13 (2013)

Pipelines: condensate/gas 251 km; gas 17,312 km; liquid petroleum gas 352 km; oil 4,831 km; refined products 4,722 km (2013)

Railways: *total:* 28,538 km
country comparison to the world: 10
broad gauge: 5,627 km 1.600-m gauge (467 km electrified)
standard gauge: 194 km 1.440-m gauge
narrow gauge: 22,717 km 1.000-m gauge (2008)

Roadways: *total:* 1,580,964 km
country comparison to the world: 4
paved: 212,798 km
unpaved: 1,368,166 km
note: does not include urban roads (2010)

Waterways: 50,000 km (most in areas remote from industry and population) (2012)
country comparison to the world: 3

Merchant marine: *total:* 109
country comparison to the world: 48
by type: bulk carrier 18, cargo 16, chemical tanker 7, container 13, liquefied gas 11, petroleum tanker 39, roll on/roll off 5
foreign-owned: 27 (Chile 1, Denmark 3, Germany 6, Greece 1, Norway 3, Spain 12, Turkey 1)
registered in other countries: 36 (Argentina 1, Bahamas 1, Ghana 1, Liberia 20, Marshall Islands 1, Panama 3, Singapore 9) (2010)

Ports and terminals: *major seaport(s):* Belem, Paranagua, Rio Grande, Rio de Janeiro, Santos, Sao Sebastiao, Tubarao
river port(s): Manaus (Amazon)
dry bulk cargo port(s): Sepetiba ore terminal
container ports (TEUs): Santos (2,985,922), Itajai (983,985)(2011)
oil/gas terminal(s): DTSE/Gegua oil terminal, Ilha Grande (Gebig), Guaiba Island terminal, Guamare oil terminal

MILITARY

Military branches: Brazilian Army (Exercito Brasileiro, EB), Brazilian Navy (Marinha do Brasil (MB), includes Naval Air and Marine Corps (Corpo de Fuzileiros Navais)), Brazilian Air Force (Forca Aerea Brasileira, FAB) (2011)

Military service age and obligation: 18-45 years of age for compulsory military service; conscript service obligation is 9-12 months; 17-45 years of age for voluntary service; an increasing percentage of the ranks are "long-service" volunteer professionals; women were allowed to serve in the armed forces beginning in early 1980s when the Brazilian

Army became the first army in South America to accept women into career ranks; women serve in Navy and Air Force only in Women's Reserve Corps (2012)

Manpower available for military service: *males age 16-49:* 53,350,703
females age 16-49: 53,433,918 (2010 est.)

Manpower fit for military service: *males age 16-49:* 38,993,989
females age 16-49: 44,841,661 (2010 est.)

Manpower reaching militarily significant age annually: *male:* 1,733,168
female: 1,672,477 (2010 est.)

Military expenditures: 1.47% of GDP (2012)
country comparison to the world: 63
1.49% of GDP (2011)
1.47% of GDP (2010)

TRANSNATIONAL ISSUES

Disputes—international: uncontested boundary dispute between Brazil and Uruguay over Brazilieira/Brasiliera Island in the Quarai/Cuareim River leaves the tripoint with Argentina in question; smuggling of firearms and narcotics continues to be an issue along the Uruguay-Brazil border; Colombian-organized illegal narcotics and paramilitary activities penetrate Brazil's border region with Venezuela

Illicit drugs: second-largest consumer of cocaine in the world; illicit producer of cannabis; trace amounts of coca cultivation in the Amazon region, used for domestic consumption; government has a large-scale eradication program to control cannabis; important transshipment country for Bolivian, Colombian, and Peruvian cocaine headed for Europe; also used by traffickers as a way station for narcotics air transshipments between Peru and Colombia; upsurge in drug-related violence and weapons smuggling; important market for Colombian, Bolivian, and Peruvian cocaine; illicit narcotics proceeds are often laundered through the financial system; significant illicit financial activity in the Tri-Border Area (2008)

BRITISH INDIAN OCEAN TERRITORY

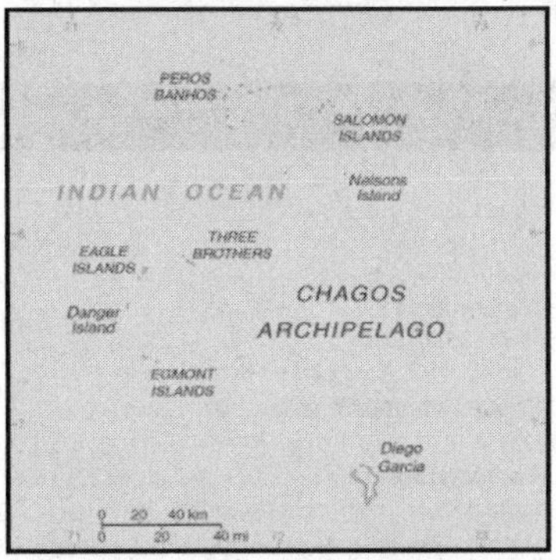

INTRODUCTION

Background: Formerly administered as part of the British Crown Colony of Mauritius, the British Indian Ocean Territory (BIOT) was established as an overseas territory of the UK in 1965. A number of the islands of the territory were later transferred to the Seychelles when it attained independence in 1976. Subsequently, BIOT has consisted only of the six main island groups comprising the Chagos Archipelago. The largest and most southerly of the islands, Diego Garcia, contains a joint UK-US naval support facility. All of the remaining islands are uninhabited. Between 1967 and 1973, former agricultural workers, earlier residents in the islands, were relocated primarily to Mauritius, but also to the Seychelles. Negotiations between 1971 and 1982 resulted in the establishment of a trust fund by the British Government as compensation for the displaced islanders, known as Chagossians. Beginning in 1998, the islanders pursued a series of lawsuits against the British Government seeking further compensation and the right to return to the territory. In 2006 and 2007, British court rulings invalidated the immigration policies contained in the 2004 BIOT Constitution Order that had excluded the islanders from the archipelago, but upheld the special military status of Diego Garcia. In 2008, the House of Lords, as the final court of appeal in the UK, ruled in favor of the British Government by overturning the lower court rulings and finding no right of return for the Chagossians.

GEOGRAPHY

Location: archipelago in the Indian Ocean, south of India, about halfway between Africa and Indonesia

Geographic coordinates: 6 00 S, 71 30 E; note—Diego Garcia 7 20 S, 72 25 E

Map references: Political Map of the World

Area: *total:* 54,400 sq km
country comparison to the world: 128
land: 60 sq km; Diego Garcia 44 sq km
water: 54,340 sq km
note: includes the entire Chagos Archipelago of 55 islands

Area—comparative: land area is about 0.3 times the size of Washington, DC

Land boundaries: 0 km

Coastline: 698 km

Maritime claims: *territorial sea:* 3 nm
exclusive fishing zone: 200 nm

Climate: tropical marine; hot, humid, moderated by trade winds

Terrain: flat and low (most areas do not exceed two meters in elevation)

Elevation extremes: *lowest point:* Indian Ocean 0 m
highest point: unnamed location on Diego Garcia 15 m

Natural resources: coconuts, fish, sugarcane

Land use: *arable land:* 0%
permanent crops: 0%
other: 100% (2011)

Natural hazards: NA

Environment—current issues: NA

Geography—note: archipelago of 55 islands; Diego Garcia, largest and southernmost island, occupies strategic location in central Indian Ocean; island is site of joint US-UK military facility

PEOPLE AND SOCIETY

Population: no indigenous inhabitants
note: approximately 1,200 former agricultural workers resident in the Chagos Archipelago, often referred to as Chagossians or Ilois, were relocated to Mauritius and the Seychelles in the 1960s and 1970s; in November 2004, approximately 4,000 UK and US military personnel and civilian contractors were living on the island of Diego Garcia

GOVERNMENT

Country name: *conventional long form:* British Indian Ocean Territory
conventional short form: none
abbreviation: BIOT

Dependency status: overseas territory of the UK; administered by a commissioner, resident in the Foreign and Commonwealth Office in London

Legal system: the laws of the UK, where applicable, apply

Executive branch: *chief of state:* Queen ELIZABETH II (since 6 February 1952)
head of government: Commissioner Colin ROBERTS (since July 2008); Administrator John MCMANUS (since April 2011); note—both reside in the UK and are represented by the officer commanding British Forces on Diego Garcia
cabinet: NA (For more information visit the World Leaders website)
elections: none; the monarchy is hereditary; commissioner and administrator appointed by the monarch

Diplomatic representation in the US: none (overseas territory of the UK)

Diplomatic representation from the US: none (overseas territory of the UK)

Flag description: white with six blue wavy horizontal stripes; the flag of the UK is in the upper hoist-side quadrant; the striped section bears a palm tree and yellow crown (the symbols of the territory) centered on the outer half of the flag; the wavy stripes represent the Indian Ocean; although not officially described, the six blue stripes may stand for the six main atolls of the archipelago

ECONOMY

Economy—overview: All economic activity is concentrated on the largest island of Diego Garcia, where a joint UK-US military facility is located. Construction projects and various services needed to support the military installation are performed by military and contract employees from the UK, Mauritius, the Philippines, and the US. Some of the natural resources found in this territory include coconuts, fish, and sugarcane. Sugarcane is still a major export for this territory. There are no industrial or agricultural activities on the islands. The territory earns foreign exchange by selling fishing licenses and postage stamps.

Exchange rates: the US dollar is used

COMMUNICATIONS

Telephone system: *general assessment:* separate facilities for military and public needs are available domestic: all commercial telephone services are available, including connection to the Internet international: country code (Diego Garcia)—246; international telephone service is carried by satellite (2000)

Broadcast media: Armed Forces Radio and Television Service (AFRTS) broadcasts over 3 separate frequencies for US and UK military personnel stationed on the islands (2009)

Internet country code: .io

Internet hosts: 75,006 (2012)
country comparison to the world: 85

TRANSPORTATION

Airports: 1 (2013)
country comparison to the world: 220

Airports—with paved runways: *total:* 1
over 3,047 m: 1 (2013)

Roadways: *note:* short section of paved road between port and airfield on Diego Garcia

Ports and terminals: *major seaport(s):* Diego Garcia

MILITARY

Military branches: no regular military forces (2014)

Military—note: defense is the responsibility of the UK; the US lease on Diego Garcia expires in 2016

TRANSNATIONAL ISSUES

Disputes—international: Mauritius and Seychelles claim the Chagos Islands; Negotiations between 1971 and 1982 resulted in the establishment of a trust fund by the British Government as compensation for the displaced islanders, known as Chagossians, who were evicted between 1967-73; in 2001, the former inhabitants of the archipelago were granted UK citizenship and the right of return; in 2006 and 2007, British court rulings invalidated the immigration policies contained in the 2004 BIOT Constitution Order that had excluded the islanders from the archipelago; in 2008 a House of Lords' decision overturned lower court rulings, once again denying the right of return to Chagossians; in addition, the United Kingdom created the world's largest marine protection area around the Chagos islands prohibiting the extraction of any natural resources therein

BRITISH VIRGIN ISLANDS

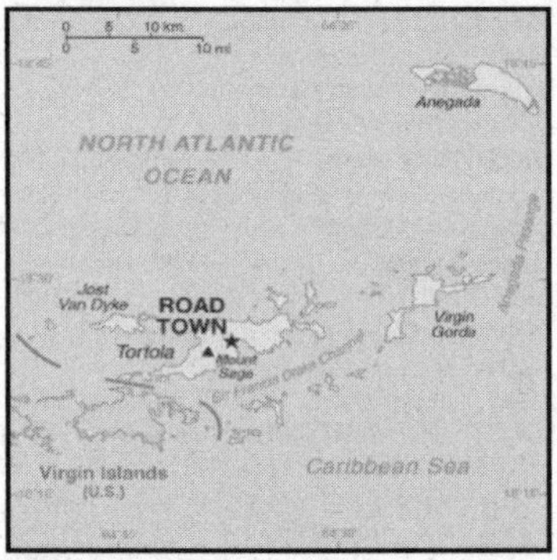

INTRODUCTION

Background: First inhabited by Arawak and later by Carib Indians, the Virgin Islands were settled by the Dutch in 1648 and then annexed by the English in 1672. The islands were part of the British colony of the Leeward Islands from 1872-1960; they were granted autonomy in 1967. The economy is closely tied to the larger and more populous US Virgin Islands to the west; the US dollar is the legal currency.

GEOGRAPHY

Location: Caribbean, between the Caribbean Sea and the North Atlantic Ocean, east of Puerto Rico

Geographic coordinates: 18 30 N, 64 30 W

Map references: Central America and the Caribbean

Area: *total:* 151 sq km
country comparison to the world: 220
land: 151 sq km
water: 0 sq km
note: comprised of 16 inhabited and more than 20 uninhabited islands; includes the islands of Tortola, Anegada, Virgin Gorda, Jost van Dyke

Area—comparative: about 0.9 times the size of Washington, DC

Land boundaries: 0 km

Coastline: 80 km

Maritime claims: *territorial sea:* 3 nm
exclusive fishing zone: 200 nm

Climate: subtropical; humid; temperatures moderated by trade winds

Terrain: coral islands relatively flat; volcanic islands steep, hilly

Elevation extremes: *lowest point:* Caribbean Sea 0 m
highest point: Mount Sage 521 m

Natural resources: NEGL

Land use: *arable land:* 6.67%
permanent crops: 6.67%
other: 86.67% (2011)

Irrigated land: NA

Natural hazards: hurricanes and tropical storms (July to October)

Environment—current issues: limited natural freshwater resources except for a few seasonal streams and springs on Tortola; most of the islands' water supply comes from wells and rainwater catchments

Geography—note: strong ties to nearby US Virgin Islands and Puerto Rico

PEOPLE AND SOCIETY:

Nationality: *noun:* British Virgin Islander(s)
adjective: British Virgin Islander

Ethnic groups: black 82%, white 6.8%, other 11.2% (includes Indian and mixed) (2008)

Languages: English (official)

Religions: Protestant 84% (Methodist 33%, Anglican 17%, Church of God 9%, Seventh-Day Adventist 6%, Baptist 4%, other 15%), Roman Catholic 10%, Jehovah's Witnesses 2%, other 2%, none 2% (1991)

Population: 32,680 (July 2014 est.)
country comparison to the world: 216

Age structure: *0-14 years:* 17.2% (male 2,770/female 2,861)
15-24 years: 14.5% (male 2,252/female 2,472)
25-54 years: 49.8% (male 7,697/female 8,574)
55-64 years: 7.9% (male 1,709/female 1,763)
65 years and over: 7.6% (male 1,258/female 1,324) (2014 est.)

Median age: *total:* 35.6 years
male: 35.5 years
female: 35.7 years (2014 est.)

Population growth rate: 2.36% (2014 est.)
country comparison to the world: 36

Birth rate: 10.83 births/1,000 population (2014 est.)
country comparison to the world: 180

Death rate: 4.93 deaths/1,000 population (2014 est.)
country comparison to the world: 192

Net migration rate: 17.69 migrant(s)/1,000 population (2014 est.)
country comparison to the world: 4

Urbanization: *urban population:* 41% of total population (2010)
rate of urbanization: 1.7% annual rate of change (2010-15 est.)

Major urban areas—population: ROAD TOWN (capital) 10,000 (2011)

Sex ratio: *at birth:* 1.05 male(s)/female
0-14 years: 0.97 male(s)/female
15-24 years: 0.91 male(s)/female
25-54 years: 0.9 male(s)/female
55-64 years: 0.92 male(s)/female
65 years and over: 0.95 male(s)/female
total population: 0.93 male(s)/female (2014 est.)

Infant mortality rate: *total:* 13.45 deaths/1,000 live births
country comparison to the world: 118
male: 15.31 deaths/1,000 live births
female: 11.49 deaths/1,000 live births (2014 est.)

Life expectancy at birth: *total population:* 78.29 years
country comparison to the world: 57
male: 76.99 years
female: 79.66 years (2014 est.)

Total fertility rate: 1.25 children born/woman (2014 est.)
country comparison to the world: 219

Drinking water source:
Improved:
urban: 98% of population

rural: 98% of population
total: 98% of population
Unimproved:
urban: 2% of population
rural: 2% of population
total: 2% of population (2010 est.)

Sanitation facility access:
Improved:
urban: 97.5% of population
rural: 97.5% of population
total: 97.5% of population
Unimproved
urban: 2.5% of population
rural: 2.5% of population
total: 2.5% of population (2011 est.)

HIV/AIDS—adult prevalence rate: NA

HIV/AIDS—people living with HIV/AIDS: NA

HIV/AIDS—deaths: NA

Education expenditures: 4.4% of GDP (2010)
country comparison to the world: 96

Literacy: *definition:* age 15 and over can read and write
total population: 97.8%
male: NA
female: NA (1991 est.)

School life expectancy (primary to tertiary education): *total:* 15 years
male: 15 years
female: 16 years (2009)

GOVERNMENT

Country name: *conventional long form:* none
conventional short form: British Virgin Islands
abbreviation: BVI

Dependency status: overseas territory of the UK; internal self-governing

Government type: NA

Capital: *name:* Road Town
geographic coordinates: 18 25 N, 64 37 W
time difference: UTC-4 (1 hour ahead of Washington, DC during Standard Time)

Administrative divisions: none (overseas territory of the UK)

Independence: none (overseas territory of the UK)

National holiday: Territory Day, 1 July (1956)

Constitution: several previous; latest effective 15 June 2007 (2007)

Legal system: English common law

Suffrage: 18 years of age; universal

Executive branch: *chief of state:* Queen ELIZABETH II (since 6 February 1952); represented by Governor Boyd MCCLEARY (since 20 August 2010)
head of government: Premier Orlando SMITH (since 9 November 2011)
cabinet: Executive Council appointed by the governor from members of the House of Assembly (For more information visit the World Leaders website)
elections: the monarchy is hereditary; governor appointed by the monarch; following legislative elections, the leader of the majority party or the leader of the majority coalition usually appointed premier by the governor

Legislative branch: unicameral House of Assembly (13 elected seats, a speaker elected by the 13 members of the House of Assembly, and 1 non-voting ex officio member in the attorney general; members are elected by direct popular vote, 1 member from each of nine electoral districts, 4 at-large members; members serve four-year terms)
elections: last held on 7 November 2011 (next to be held in 2015)
election results: percent of vote by party—NDP 49.4%, VIP 42%, other 8.6%; seats by party—NDP 9, VIP 4

Judicial branch: *highest court(s):* the Eastern Caribbean Supreme Court (ECSC) is the itinerant superior court of record for the 9-member Organization of Eastern Caribbean States to include the British Virgin Islands; the ECSC - with its headquarters on St. Lucia - is headed by the chief justice and is comprised of the Court of Appeal with 3 justices and the High Court with 16 judges; sittings of the Court of Appeal and High Court rotate among the 9 member states; 3 High Court judges reside in member states; 3 High Court judges reside on the British Virgin Islands
judge selection and term of office: Eastern Caribbean Supreme Court chief justice appointed by Her Majesty, Queen ELIZABETH II; other justices and judges appointed by the Judicial and Legal Services Commission; Court of Appeal justices appointed for life with mandatory retirement at age 65; High Court judges appointed for life with mandatory retirement at age 62
subordinate courts: Magistrates' Courts

Political parties and leaders: Concerned Citizens Movement or CCM [Ethlyn SMITH]; National Democratic Party or NDP [Orlando SMITH]; United Party or UP [Gregory MADURO]; Virgin Islands Party or VIP [Ralph T. O'NEAL]

Political pressure groups and leaders: The Family Support Network; The Women's Desk
other: environmentalists

International organization participation: Caricom (associate), CDB, Interpol (subbureau), IOC, OECS, UNESCO (associate), UPU

Diplomatic representation in the US: none (overseas territory of the UK)

Diplomatic representation from the US: none (overseas territory of the UK)

Flag description: blue, with the flag of the UK in the upper hoist-side quadrant and the Virgin Islander coat of arms centered in the outer half of the flag; the coat of arms depicts a woman flanked on either side by a vertical column of six oil lamps above a scroll bearing the Latin word VIGILATE (Be Watchful); the islands were named by COLUMBUS in 1493 in honor of Saint Ursula and her 11 virgin followers (some sources say 11,000) who reputedly were martyred by the Huns in the 4th or 5th century; the figure on the banner holding a lamp represents the saint, the other lamps symbolize her followers

National anthem: *note:* as a territory of the United Kingdom, "God Save the Queen" is official (see United Kingdom)

ECONOMY

Economy—overview: The economy, one of the most stable and prosperous in the Caribbean, is highly dependent on tourism generating an estimated 45% of the national income. More than 934,000 tourists, mainly from the US, visited the islands in 2008. In the mid-1980s, the government began offering offshore registration to companies wishing to incorporate in the islands, and incorporation fees now generate substantial revenues. Roughly 400,000 companies were on the offshore registry by yearend 2000. The adoption of a comprehensive insurance law in late 1994, which provides a blanket of confidentiality with regulated statutory gateways for investigation of criminal offenses, made the British Virgin Islands even more attractive to international business. Livestock raising is the most important agricultural activity; poor soils limit the islands' ability to meet domestic food requirements. Because of traditionally close links with the US Virgin Islands, the British Virgin Islands has used the US dollar as its currency since 1959.

GDP (purchasing power parity): $500 million (2010 est.)
country comparison to the world: 215

GDP (official exchange rate): $1.095 billion (2008)

GDP—real growth rate: 1.3% (2010 est.)
country comparison to the world: 167
-0.6% (2008 est.)

GDP—per capita (PPP): $42,300 (2010 est.)
country comparison to the world: 22

GDP—composition, by end use: *household consumption:* 34.1%
government consumption: 8.3%
investment in fixed capital: 23.7%
investment in inventories: 0%
exports of goods and services: 107.8%
imports of goods and services: -73.9% (2013 est.)

GDP—composition, by sector of origin: *agriculture:* 1.1%
industry: 11.7%
services: 87.2% (2013 est.)

Agriculture—products: fruits, vegetables; livestock, poultry; fish

Industries: tourism, light industry, construction, rum, concrete block, offshore financial center

Industrial production growth rate: 3%
country comparison to the world: 96

Labor force: 12,770 (2004)
country comparison to the world: 214

Labor force—by occupation: *agriculture:* 0.6%
industry: 40%
services: 59.4% (2005)

Unemployment rate: 8.7% (2010 est.)
country comparison to the world: 96

Population below poverty line: NA%

Household income or consumption by percentage share: *lowest 10%:* NA%
highest 10%: NA%

Budget: *revenues:* $300 million
expenditures: $300 million (2013 est.)

Taxes and other revenues: 27.4% of GDP (2013 est.)
country comparison to the world: 107

Budget surplus (+) or deficit (-): 0% of GDP (2013 est.)
country comparison to the world: 44

Fiscal year: 1 April—31 March

Inflation rate (consumer prices): 1.6% (2013 est.)
country comparison to the world: 44
2.2% (2012 est.)

Current account balance: $362.6 million (2010 est.)
country comparison to the world: 54
$279.8 million (2010 est.)

Exports: $26 million (2012 est.)
country comparison to the world: 203
$25 million (2011 est.)

Exports—commodities: rum, fresh fish, fruits, animals; gravel, sand

Imports: $310 million (2012 est.)
country comparison to the world: 198
$320 million (2011 est.)

Imports—commodities: building materials, automobiles, foodstuffs, machinery

Debt—external: $36.1 million (1997)
country comparison to the world: 195

Exchange rates: the US dollar is used

ENERGY

Electricity—production: 50 million kWh (2010 est.)
country comparison to the world: 206

Electricity—consumption: 46.5 million kWh (2010 est.)
country comparison to the world: 206

Electricity—exports: 0 kWh (2012 est.)
country comparison to the world: 210

Electricity—imports: 0 kWh (2012 est.)
country comparison to the world: 212

Electricity—installed generating capacity: 44,000 kW (2010 est.)
country comparison to the world: 191

Electricity—from fossil fuels: 100% of total installed capacity (2010 est.)
country comparison to the world: 39

Electricity—from nuclear fuels: 0% of total installed capacity (2010 est.)
country comparison to the world: 200

Electricity—from hydroelectric plants: 0% of total installed capacity (2010 est.)
country comparison to the world: 206

Electricity—from other renewable sources: 0% of total installed capacity (2010 est.)
country comparison to the world: 137

Crude oil—production: 0 bbl/day (2012 est.)
country comparison to the world: 142

Crude oil—exports: 0 bbl/day (2010 est.)
country comparison to the world: 202

Crude oil—imports: 0 bbl/day (2010 est.)
country comparison to the world: 138

Crude oil—proved reserves: 0 bbl (1 January 2013 es)
country comparison to the world: 203

Refined petroleum products—production: 0 bbl/day (2010 est.)
country comparison to the world: 206

Refined petroleum products—consumption: 1,000 bbl/day (2011 est.)
country comparison to the world: 202

Refined petroleum products—exports: 0 bbl/day (2010 est.)
country comparison to the world: 142

Refined petroleum products—imports: 772.6 bbl/day (2010 est.)
country comparison to the world: 199

Natural gas—production: 0 cu m (2011 est.)
country comparison to the world: 205

Natural gas—consumption: 0 cu m (2010 est.)
country comparison to the world: 205

Natural gas—exports: 0 cu m (2011 est.)
country comparison to the world: 203

Natural gas—imports: 0 cu m (2011 est.)
country comparison to the world: 146

Natural gas—proved reserves: 0 cu m (1 January 2013 es)
country comparison to the world: 204

Carbon dioxide emissions from consumption of energy: 147,200 Mt (2011 est.)
country comparison to the world: 202

COMMUNICATIONS

Telephones—main lines in use: 12,268 (2012)
country comparison to the world: 199

Telephones—mobile cellular: 48,700 (2012)
country comparison to the world: 202

Telephone system: *general assessment:* good overall telephone service
domestic: fixed line connections exceed 80 per 100 persons and mobile cellular subscribership is roughly 150 per 100 persons
international: country code—1-284; connected via submarine cable to Bermuda; the East Caribbean Fiber System (ECFS) submarine cable provides connectivity to 13 other islands in the eastern Caribbean (2011)

Broadcast media: 1 private TV station; multichannel TV is available from cable and satellite subscription services; about a half dozen private radio stations (2007)

Internet country code: .vg

Internet hosts: 505 (2012)
country comparison to the world: 182

Internet users: 4,000 (2002)
country comparison to the world: 207

TRANSPORTATION

Airports: 4 (2013)
country comparison to the world: 190

Airports—with paved runways: *total:* 2
914 to 1,523 m: 1
under 914 m: 1 (2013)

Airports—with unpaved runways: *total:* 2
914 to 1,523 m: 2 (2013)

Roadways: *total:* 200 km
country comparison to the world: 208
paved: 200 km (2007)

Ports and terminals: Road Harbor

MILITARY

Manpower available for military service: *males age 16-49:* 7,266 (2010 est.)

Manpower fit for military service: *males age 16-49:* 6,057
females age 16-49: 5,805 (2010 est.)

Manpower reaching militarily significant age annually: *male:* 168
female: 162 (2010 est.)

Military—note: defense is the responsibility of the UK

TRANSNATIONAL ISSUES

Disputes—international: none

Illicit drugs: transshipment point for South American narcotics destined for the US and Europe; large offshore financial center makes it vulnerable to money laundering

BRUNEI

INTRODUCTION

Background: The Sultanate of Brunei's influence peaked between the 15th and 17th centuries when its control extended over coastal areas of northwest Borneo and the southern Philippines. Brunei subsequently entered a period of decline brought on by internal strife over royal succession, colonial expansion of European powers, and piracy. In 1888, Brunei became a British protectorate; independence was achieved in 1984. The same family has ruled Brunei for over six centuries. Brunei benefits from extensive petroleum and natural gas fields, the source of one of the highest per capita GDPs in Asia.

GEOGRAPHY

Location: Southeastern Asia, bordering the South China Sea and Malaysia

Geographic coordinates: 4 30 N, 114 40 E

Map references: Southeast Asia

Area: *total:* 5,765 sq km
country comparison to the world: 173
land: 5,265 sq km
water: 500 sq km

Area—comparative: slightly smaller than Delaware

Land boundaries: *total:* 381 km

border countries: Malaysia 381 km

Coastline: 161 km

Maritime claims: territorial sea: 12 nm

exclusive economic zone: 200 nm or to median line

Climate: tropical; hot, humid, rainy

Terrain: flat coastal plain rises to mountains in east; hilly lowland in west

Elevation extremes: *lowest point:* South China Sea 0 m
highest point: Bukit Pagon 1,850 m

Natural resources: petroleum, natural gas, timber

Land use: *arable land:* 0.52%
permanent crops: 0.87%
other: 98.61% (2011)

Irrigated land: 10 sq km (2003)

Total renewable water resources: 8.5 cu km (2011)

Freshwater withdrawal (domestic/industrial/agricultural): *total:* 0.09 cu km/yr (97%/0%/3%)
per capita: 301.6 cu m/yr (2009)

Natural hazards: typhoons, earthquakes, and severe flooding are rare

Environment—current issues: seasonal smoke/haze resulting from forest fires in Indonesia

Environment—international agreements: *party to:* Biodiversity, Climate Change, Desertification, Endangered Species, Hazardous Wastes, Law of the Sea, Ozone Layer Protection, Ship Pollution *signed, but not ratified:* none of the selected agreements

Geography—note: close to vital sea lanes through South China Sea linking Indian and Pacific Oceans; two parts physically separated by Malaysia; almost an enclave within Malaysia

PEOPLE AND SOCIETY

Nationality: *noun:* Bruneian(s)
adjective: Bruneian

Ethnic groups: Malay 65.7%, Chinese 10.3%, other indigenous 3.4%, other 20.6% (2011 est.)

Languages: Malay (official), English, Chinese

Religions: Muslim (official) 78.8%, Christian 8.7%, Buddhist 7.8%, other (includes indigenous beliefs) 4.7% (2011 est.)

Population: 422,675 (July 2014 est.)
country comparison to the world: 175

Age structure: *0-14 years:* 24.2% (male 52,753/female 49,548)
15-24 years: 17.3% (male 36,187/female 36,965)
25-54 years: 46.9% (male 96,006/female 102,028)
55-64 years: 4% (male 16,542/female 15,589)
65 years and over: 3.8% (male 8,301/female 8,756) (2014 est.)

Dependency ratios: *total dependency ratio:* 42%
youth dependency ratio: 36%
elderly dependency ratio: 6.1%
potential support ratio: 16.4 (2013)

Median age: *total:* 29.3 years
male: 28.9 years
female: 29.6 years (2014 est.)

Population growth rate: 1.65% (2014 est.)
country comparison to the world: 74

Birth rate: 17.49 births/1,000 population (2014 est.)
country comparison to the world: 107

Death rate: 3.47 deaths/1,000 population (2014 est.)
country comparison to the world: 217

Net migration rate: 2.47 migrant(s)/1,000 population (2014 est.)
country comparison to the world: 39

Urbanization: *urban population:* 76% of total population (2011)
rate of urbanization: 2.13% annual rate of change (2010-15 est.)

Major cities—population: BANDAR SERI BEGAWAN (capital) 241,000
note: the boundaries of the capital city were expanded in 2007, greatly increasing the city area; the population of the capital increased tenfold (2011)

Sex ratio: *at birth:* 1.05 male(s)/female
0-14 years: 1.07 male(s)/female
15-24 years: 0.98 male(s)/female
25-54 years: 0.94 male(s)/female
55-64 years: 0.99 male(s)/female
65 years and over: 0.95 male(s)/female
total population: 1 male(s)/female (2014 est.)

Maternal mortality rate: 24 deaths/100,000 live births (2010)
country comparison to the world: 132

Infant mortality rate: *total:* 10.48 deaths/1,000 live births
country comparison to the world: 138
male: 12.48 deaths/1,000 live births
female: 8.39 deaths/1,000 live births (2014 est.)

Life expectancy at birth: *total population:* 76.77 years
country comparison to the world: 74
male: 74.46 years
female: 79.19 years (2014 est.)

Total fertility rate: 1.82 children born/woman (2014 est.)
country comparison to the world: 152

Health expenditures: 2.5% of GDP (2011)
country comparison to the world: 187

Physicians density: 1.36 physicians/1,000 population (2010)

Hospital bed density: 2.8 beds/1,000 population (2011)

HIV/AIDS—adult prevalence rate: less than 0.1% (2003 est.)
country comparison to the world: 128

HIV/AIDS—people living with HIV/AIDS: fewer than 200 (2003 est.)
country comparison to the world: 164

HIV/AIDS—deaths: fewer than 200 (2003 est.)
country comparison to the world: 115

Obesity—adult prevalence rate: 7.5% (2008)
country comparison to the world: 141

Education expenditures: 3.5% of GDP (2013)
country comparison to the world: 126

Literacy: *definition:* age 15 and over can read and write
total population: 95.4%
male: 97%
female: 93.9% (2011 est.)

School life expectancy (primary to tertiary education): *total:* 15 years
male: 14 years
female: 15 years (2012)

GOVERNMENT

Country name: *conventional long form:* Brunei Darussalam
conventional short form: Brunei
local long form: Negara Brunei Darussalam local short form: Brunei

Government type: constitutional sultanate (locally known as Malay Islamic Monarchy)

Capital: *name:* Bandar Seri Begawan
geographic coordinates: 4 53 N, 114 56 E
time difference: UTC+8 (13 hours ahead of Washington, DC during Standard Time)

Administrative divisions: 4 districts (daerah-daerah, singular—daerah); Belait, Brunei-Muara, Temburong, Tutong

Independence: 1 January 1984 (from the UK)

National holiday: National Day, 23 February (1984); note—1 January 1984 was the date of independence from the UK, 23 February 1984 was the date of independence from British protection

Constitution: drafted 1954 to 1959, signed 29 September 1959; amended 1984, 2004, 2011; note - some constitutional provisions suspended since 1962 under a State of Emergency, others since independence in 1984 (2011)

Legal system: mixed legal system based on English common law and Islamic law

International law organization participation: has not submitted an ICJ jurisdiction declaration; non-party state to the ICCt

Suffrage: 18 years of age for village elections; universal

Executive branch: *chief of state:* Sultan and Prime Minister Sir HASSANAL Bolkiah (since 5 October 1967); note—the monarch is both the chief of state (Yang Di-Pertuan Agong) and head of government
head of government: Sultan and Prime Minister Sir HASSANAL Bolkiah (since 5 October 1967)
cabinet: Council of Cabinet Ministers appointed and presided over by the monarch; deals with executive matters; note—there is also a Religious Council (members appointed by the monarch) that advises on religious matters, a Privy Council (members appointed by the monarch) that deals with constitutional matters, and the Council of Succession (members appointed by the monarch) that determines the succession to the throne if the need arises (For more information visit the World Leaders website)
elections: none; the monarchy is hereditary

Legislative branch: the Sultan appointed a Legislative Council with 29 members in September 2005; he increased the size of the council to 33 members in June 2011; the council meets annually in March
elections: last held in March 1962 (date of next election NA)
note: the Legislative Council met on 25 September 2004 for first time in 20 years with 21 members appointed by the Sultan; it passed constitutional amendments calling for a 45-seat council with 15 elected members; no timeframe for an election was announced

Judicial branch: *highest court(s):* Supreme Court (consists of Court of Appeal and High Court, each with a chief justice and 2 judges); Sharia Court of Appeal (consists of judges appointed by the monarch)note - Brunei has a dual judicial system of secular and sharia (religious) courts; the Judicial Committee of Privy Council in London serves as the final appellate court for civil cases only
judge selection and term of office: Supreme Court judges appointed by the monarch to serve until age 65, and older if approved by the monarch; Sharia Court of Appeal judges appointed by the monarch; judge tenure NA
subordinate courts: Intermediate Court; Magistrate's Courts; Juvenile Court; small claims courts; lower sharia courts (2006)

Political parties and leaders: National Development Party or NDP [YASSIN Affendi]
note: Brunei National Solidarity Party or PPKB [Abdul LATIF bin Chuchu] and People's Awareness Party or PAKAR [Awang Haji MAIDIN bin Haji Ahmad] were deregistered in 2007; parties are small and have limited activity

Political pressure groups and leaders: NA

International organization participation: ADB, APEC, ARF, ASEAN, C, CP, EAS, G-77, IBRD, ICAO, ICC (NGOs), ICRM, IDA, IDB, IFRCS, ILO, IMF, IMO, IMSO, Interpol, IOC, ISO (correspondent), ITSO, ITU, NAM, OIC, OPCW, UN, UNCTAD, UNESCO, UNIFIL, UNWTO, UPU, WCO, WHO, WIPO, WMO, WTO

Diplomatic representation in the US: *chief of mission:* Ambassador Dato Yusoff Abd HAMID (since 2 October 2009)
chancery: 3520 International Court NW #300, Washington, DC 20008
telephone: [1] (202) 237-1838
FAX: [1] (202) 885-0560

Diplomatic representation from the US: *chief of mission:* Ambassador Daniel L. SHIELDS III (since 28 March 2011)

embassy: Simpang 336-52-16-9, Jalan Datu, Bandar Seri Begawan, BC4115
mailing address: Unit 4280, Box 40, FPO AP 96507; P.O. Box 2991, Bandar Seri Begawan BS8675, Negara Brunei Darussalam
telephone: [673] 238-4616
FAX: [673] 238-4604

Flag description: yellow with two diagonal bands of white (top, almost double width) and black starting from the upper hoist side; the national emblem in red is superimposed at the center; yellow is the color of royalty and symbolizes the sultanate; the white and black bands denote Brunei's chief ministers; the emblem includes five main components: a swallow-tailed flag, the royal umbrella representing the monarchy, the wings of four feathers symbolizing justice, tranquility, prosperity, and peace, the two upraised hands signifying the government's pledge to preserve and promote the welfare of the people, and the crescent moon denoting Islam, the state religion; the state motto "Always render service with God's guidance" appears in yellow Arabic script on the crescent; a ribbon below the crescent reads "Brunei, the Abode of Peace"

National anthem: *name:* "Allah Peliharakan Sultan" (God Bless His Majesty)
lyrics/music: Pengiran Haji Mohamed YUSUF bin Pengiran Abdul Rahim/Awang Haji BESAR bin Sagap
note: adopted 1951

ECONOMY

Economy—overview: Brunei has a small well-to-do economy that depends on revenue from natural resource extraction but encompasses a mixture of foreign and domestic entrepreneurship, government regulation, welfare measures, and village tradition. Crude oil and natural gas production account for 60% of GDP and more than 90% of exports. Per capita GDP is among the highest in Asia, and substantial income from overseas investment supplements income from domestic production. For Bruneian citizens the government provides for all medical services and free education through the university level. The government of Brunei has been emphasizing through policy and resource investments it strong desire to diversity its economy both within the oil and gas sector and to new sectors.

GDP (purchasing power parity): $22.25 billion (2013 est.)
country comparison to the world: 128
$21.93 billion (2012 est.)
$21.73 billion (2011 est.)
note: data are in 2013 US dollars

GDP (official exchange rate): $16.56 billion (2013 est.)

GDP—real growth rate: 1.4% (2013 est.)
country comparison to the world: 162
0.9% (2012 est.)
3.4% (2011 est.)

GDP—per capita (PPP): $54,800 (2013 est.)
country comparison to the world: 11
$54,900 (2012 est.)
$55,200 (2011 est.)
note: data are in 2013 US dollars

GDP—composition, by end use: *household consumption:* 22.1%
government consumption: 18.2%
investment in fixed capital: 14.6%
investment in inventories: 0%
exports of goods and services: 78.4%
imports of goods and services: -33.3% (2013 est.)

GDP—composition by sector of origin: *agriculture:* 0.7%
industry: 70.9%
services: 28.4% (2013 est.)

Agriculture—products: rice, vegetables, fruits; chickens, water buffalo, cattle, goats, eggs

Industries: petroleum, petroleum refining, liquefied natural gas, construction, agriculture, transportation

Industrial production growth rate: 1.5% (2013 est.)
country comparison to the world: 135

Labor force: 205,800 (2011 est.)
country comparison to the world: 169

Labor force—by occupation: *agriculture:* 4.2%
industry: 62.8%
services: 33% (2008 est.)

Unemployment rate: 2.6% (2011)
country comparison to the world: 21
2.7% (2010)

Population below poverty line: NA%

Household income or consumption by percentage share: *lowest 10%:* NA%
highest 10%: NA%

Budget: *revenues:* $6.992 billion
expenditures: $5.366 billion (2013 est.)

Taxes and other revenues: 42.2% of GDP (2013 est.)
country comparison to the world: 28

Budget surplus (+) or deficit (-): 9.8% of GDP (2013 est.)
country comparison to the world: 5

Fiscal year: 1 April—31 March

Inflation rate (consumer prices): 1% (2013 est.)
country comparison to the world: 21
0.5% (2012 est.)

Commercial bank prime lending rate: 5.5% (31 December 2013 est.)
country comparison to the world: 115
5.5% (31 December 2012 est.)

Stock of narrow money: $3.472 billion (31 December 2013 est.)
country comparison to the world: 115
$3.509 billion (31 December 2012 est.)

Stock of broad money: $11.92 billion (31 December 2013 est.)
country comparison to the world: 98
$11.41 billion (31 December 2012 est.)

Stock of domestic credit: $2.846 billion (31 December 2013 est.)
country comparison to the world: 129
$2.351 billion (31 December 2012 est.)

Market value of publicly traded shares: $NA

Current account balance: $3.977 billion (2009 est.)
country comparison to the world: 31

Exports: $12.75 billion (2011)
country comparison to the world: 86
$9.88 billion (2010)

Exports—commodities: crude oil, natural gas, garments

Exports—partners: Japan 45.7%, South Korea 15.1%, Australia 9.1%, NZ 6.6%, India 5.8%, Vietnam 4.7% (2012)

Imports: $3.02 billion (2011 est.)
country comparison to the world: 147
$2.73 billion (2010 est.)

Imports—commodities: iron and steel, motor vehicles, machinery and transport equipment, manufactured goods, food, chemicals

Imports—partners: Singapore 26.3%, China 21.3%, UK 21.3%, Malaysia 11.8% (2012)

Debt—external: $0 (2005)
country comparison to the world: 203

Exchange rates: Bruneian dollars (BND) per US dollar—
1.23 (2013 est.)
1.2496 (2012 est.)
1.3635 (2010 est.)
1.45 (2009)

ENERGY

Electricity—production: 3.723 billion kWh (2011 est.)
country comparison to the world: 126

Electricity—consumption: 3.391 billion kWh (2011 est.)
country comparison to the world: 127

Electricity—exports: 0 kWh (2012 est.)
country comparison to the world: 111

Electricity—imports: 0 kWh (2012 est.)
country comparison to the world: 122

Electricity—installed generating capacity: 759,000 kW (2010 est.)
country comparison to the world: 128

Electricity—from fossil fuels: 100% of total installed capacity (2010 est.)
country comparison to the world: 9

Electricity—from nuclear fuels: 0% of total installed capacity (2010 est.)
country comparison to the world: 57

Electricity—from hydroelectric plants: 0% of total installed capacity (2010 est.)
country comparison to the world: 161

Electricity—from other renewable sources: 0% of total installed capacity (2010 est.)
country comparison to the world: 162

Crude oil—production: 141,000 bbl/day (2012 est.)
country comparison to the world: 44

Crude oil—exports: 147,900 bbl/day (2010 est.)
country comparison to the world: 35

Crude oil—imports: 0 bbl/day (2011 est.)
country comparison to the world: 166

Crude oil—proved reserves: 1.1 billion bbl (1 January 2013 es)
country comparison to the world: 41

Refined petroleum products—production: 13,500 bbl/day (2010 est.)
country comparison to the world: 101

Refined petroleum products—consumption: 14,640 bbl/day (2011 est.)
country comparison to the world: 144

Refined petroleum products—exports: 0 bbl/day (2010 est.)
country comparison to the world: 158

Refined petroleum products—imports: 3,198 bbl/day (2010 est.)
country comparison to the world: 169

Natural gas—production: 12.44 billion cu m (2011 est.)
country comparison to the world: 38

Natural gas—consumption: 2.97 billion cu m (2010 est.)
country comparison to the world: 72

Natural gas—exports: 9.42 billion cu m (2011 est.)
country comparison to the world: 26

Natural gas—imports: 0 cu m (2011 est.)
country comparison to the world: 167

Natural gas—proved reserves: 390.8 billion cu m (1 January 2013 es)
country comparison to the world: 35

Carbon dioxide emissions from consumption of energy: 8.656 million Mt (2011 est.)
country comparison to the world: 105

COMMUNICATIONS

Telephones—main lines in use: 70,933 (2012)
country comparison to the world: 154

Telephones—mobile cellular: 469,700 (2012)
country comparison to the world: 170

Telephone system: *general assessment:* service throughout the country is good; international service is good to Southeast Asia, Middle East, Western Europe, and the US
domestic: every service available
international: country code—673; landing point for the SEA-ME-WE-3 optical telecommunications submarine cable that provides links to Asia, the Middle East, and Europe; the Asia-America Gateway submarine cable network provides new links to Asia and the US; satellite earth stations—2 Intelsat (1 Indian Ocean and 1 Pacific Ocean) (2011)

Broadcast media: state-controlled Radio Television Brunei (RTB) operates 5 channels; 3 Malaysian TV stations are available; foreign TV broadcasts are available via satellite and cable systems; RTB operates 5 radio networks and broadcasts on multiple frequencies; British Forces Broadcast Service (BFBS) provides radio broadcasts on 2 FM stations; some radio broadcast stations from Malaysia are available via repeaters (2009)

Internet country code: .bn

Internet hosts: 49,457 (2012)
country comparison to the world: 96

Internet users: 314,900 (2009)
country comparison to the world: 128

TRANSPORTATION

Airports: 1 (2013)
country comparison to the world: 213

Airports—with paved runways: *total:* 1
over 3,047 m: 1 (2013)

Heliports: 3 (2013)

Pipelines: condensate 33 km; condensate/gas 86 km; gas 628 km; oil 492 km (2013)

Roadways: *total:* 3,029 km
country comparison to the world: 166
paved: 2,425 km
unpaved: 604 km (2010)

Waterways: 209 km (navigable by craft drawing less than 1.2 m; the Belait, Brunei, and Tutong rivers are major transport links) (2012)
country comparison to the world: 97

Merchant marine: *total:* 9
country comparison to the world: 115
by type: chemical tanker 1, liquefied gas 8
foreign-owned: 2 (UK 2) (2010)

Ports and terminals: *major seaport(s):* Muara
oil/gas terminal(s): Lumut, Seria

MILITARY

Military branches: Royal Brunei Armed Forces: Royal Brunei Land Forces, Royal Brunei Navy, Royal Brunei Air Force (Tentera Udara Diraja Brunei) (2013)

Military service age and obligation: 17 years of age for voluntary military service; non-Malays are ineligible to serve; recruits from the army, navy, and air force all undergo 43-week initial training (2013)

Manpower available for military service: *males age 16-49:* 112,688
females age 16-49: 117,536 (2010 est.)

Manpower fit for military service: *males age 16-49:* 95,141
females age 16-49: 99,386 (2010 est.)

Manpower reaching militarily significant age annually: *male:* 3,572
female: 3,465 (2010 est.)

Military expenditures: 2.43% of GDP (2012)
country comparison to the world: 29
2.54% of GDP (2011)
2.43% of GDP (2010)

TRANSNATIONAL ISSUES

Disputes—international: per Letters of Exchange signed in 2009, Malaysia in 2010 ceded two hydrocarbon concession blocks to Brunei in exchange for Brunei's sultan dropping claims to the Limbang corridor, which divides Brunei; nonetheless, Brunei claims a maritime boundary extending as far as a median with Vietnam, thus asserting an implicit claim to Louisa Reef

Refugees and internally displaced persons: stateless persons: 21,009 (2012); note - thousands of stateless persons, often ethnic Chinese, are permanent residents and their families have lived in Brunei for generations; obtaining citizenship is difficult and requires individuals to pass rigorous tests on Malay culture, customs, and language; stateless residents receive an International Certificate of Identity, which enables them to travel overseas; the government is considering changing the law prohibiting non- Bruneians, including stateless permanent residents, from owning land

Illicit drugs: drug trafficking and illegally importing controlled substances are serious offenses in Brunei and carry a mandatory death penalty

BULGARIA

INTRODUCTION

Background: The Bulgars, a Central Asian Turkic tribe, merged with the local Slavic inhabitants in the late 7th century to form the first Bulgarian state. In succeeding centuries, Bulgaria struggled with the Byzantine Empire to assert its place in the Balkans, but by the end of the 14th century the country was overrun by the Ottoman Turks. Northern Bulgaria attained autonomy in 1878 and all of Bulgaria became independent from the Ottoman Empire in 1908. Having fought on the losing side in both World Wars, Bulgaria fell within the Soviet sphere of influence and became a People's Republic in 1946. Communist domination ended in 1990, when Bulgaria held its first multiparty election since World War II and began the contentious process of moving toward political democracy and a market economy while combating inflation, unemployment, corruption, and crime. The country joined NATO in 2004 and the EU in 2007.

GEOGRAPHY

Location: Southeastern Europe, bordering the Black Sea, between Romania and Turkey

Geographic coordinates: 43 00 N, 25 00 E

Map references: Europe

Area: *total:* 110,879 sq km
country comparison to the world: 105
land: 108,489 sq km
water: 2,390 sq km

Area—comparative: slightly larger than Tennessee

Land boundaries: *total:* 1,808 km
border countries: Greece 494 km, Macedonia 148 km, Romania 608 km, Serbia 318 km, Turkey 240 km

Coastline: 354 km

Maritime claims: *territorial sea:* 12 nm
contiguous zone: 24 nm
exclusive economic zone: 200 nm

Climate: temperate; cold, damp winters; hot, dry summers

Terrain: mostly mountains with lowlands in north and southeast

Elevation extremes: *lowest point:* Black Sea 0 m
highest point: Musala 2,925 m

Natural resources: bauxite, copper, lead, zinc, coal, timber, arable land

Land use: *arable land:* 29.28%
permanent crops: 1.44%
other: 69.28% (2011)

Irrigated land: 1,046 sq km (2007)

Total renewable water resources: 21.3 cu km (2011)

Freshwater withdrawal (domestic/industrial/agricultural): *total:* 6.12 cu km/yr (16%/68%/16%)
per capita: 821.8 cu m/yr (2009)

Natural hazards: earthquakes; landslides

Environment—current issues: air pollution from industrial emissions; rivers polluted from raw sewage, heavy metals, detergents; deforestation; forest damage from air pollution and resulting acid rain; soil contamination from heavy metals from metallurgical plants and industrial wastes

Environment—international agreements: *party to:* Air Pollution, Air Pollution-Nitrogen Oxides, Air Pollution-Persistent Organic Pollutants, Air Pollution-Sulfur 85, Air Pollution-Sulfur 94, Air Pollution-Volatile Organic Compounds, Antarctic-Environmental Protocol, Antarctic-Marine Living Resources, Antarctic Treaty, Biodiversity, Climate Change, Climate Change-Kyoto Protocol, Desertification, Endangered Species, Environmental Modification, Hazardous Wastes, Law of the Sea, Marine Dumping, Ozone Layer Protection, Ship Pollution, Wetlands
signed, but not ratified: none of the selected agreements

Geography—note: strategic location near Turkish Straits; controls key land routes from Europe to Middle East and Asia

PEOPLE AND SOCIETY

Nationality: *noun:* Bulgarian(s)
adjective: Bulgarian

Ethnic groups: Bulgarian 76.9%, Turkish 8%, Roma 4.4%, other 0.7% (including Russian, Armenian, and Vlach), other (unknown) 10% (2011 est.)

Languages: Bulgarian (official) 76.8%, Turkish 8.2%, Roma 3.8%, other 0.7%, unspecified 10.5% (2011 est.)

Religions: Eastern Orthodox 59.4%, Muslim 7.8%, other (including Catholic, Protestant, Armenian Apostolic Orthodox, and Jewish) 1.7%, none 3.7%, unspecified 27.4% (2011 est.)

Population: 6,924,716 (July 2014 est.)
country comparison to the world: 103

Age structure: *0-14 years:* 14.2% (male 505,025/female 479,899)
15-24 years: 10.1% (male 359,730/female 340,203)
25-54 years: 42.4% (male 1,459,753/female 1,475,240)
55-64 years: 19.3% (male 446,784/female 519,513)
65 years and over: 18.9% (male 538,720/female 799,849) (2014 est.)

Dependency ratios: *total dependency ratio:* 49.2%
youth dependency ratio: 20.4%
elderly dependency ratio: 28.8%
potential support ratio: 3.5 (2013)

Median age: *total:* 42.6 years
male: 40.3 years
female: 44.8 years (2014 est.)

Population growth rate: -0.83% (2014 est.)
country comparison to the world: 229

Birth rate: 8.92 births/1,000 population (2014 est.)
country comparison to the world: 210

Death rate: 14.3 deaths/1,000 population (2014 est.)
country comparison to the world: 6

Net migration rate: -2.89 migrant(s)/1,000 population (2014 est.)
country comparison to the world: 177

Urbanization: *urban population:* 73.1% of total population (2011)
rate of urbanization: 0.1% annual rate of change (2010-15 est.)

Major urban areas—population: SOFIA (capital) 1.174 million (2011)

Sex ratio: *at birth:* 1.06 male(s)/female
0-14 years: 1.05 male(s)/female
15-24 years: 1.06 male(s)/female
25-54 years: 0.99 male(s)/female
55-64 years: 0.92 male(s)/female
65 years and over: 0.68 male(s)/female
total population: 0.92 male(s)/female (2014 est.)

Mother's mean age at first birth: 26.2 (2010 est.)

Maternal mortality rate: 11 deaths/100,000 live births (2010)
country comparison to the world: 152

Infant mortality rate: *total:* 15.08 deaths/1,000 live births
country comparison to the world: 106
male: 18.07 deaths/1,000 live births
female: 11.91 deaths/1,000 live births (2014 est.)

Life expectancy at birth: *total population:* 74.33 years
country comparison to the world: 112
male: 70.74 years
female: 78.13 years (2014 est.)

Total fertility rate: 1.44 children born/woman (2014 est.)
country comparison to the world: 200

Contraceptive prevalence rate: 69.2%
note: percent of women age 20-49 (2007)

Health expenditures: 7.6% of GDP (2010)
country comparison to the world: 73

Physicians density: 3.76 physicians/1,000 population (2010)

Hospital bed density: 6.5 beds/1,000 population (2010)

Drinking water source:
Improved:
urban: 99.7% of population
rural: 99% of population
total: 99.5% of population
Unimproved:
urban: 0.3% of population
rural: 1% of population
total: 0.5% of population (2011 est.)

Sanitation facility access:
Improved:
urban: 100% of population
rural: 100% of population
total: 100% of population
unimproved:
urban: 0% of population
rural: 0% of population
total: 0% of population (2011 est.)

HIV/AIDS—adult prevalence rate: 0.1% (2009 est.)
country comparison to the world: 129

HIV/AIDS—people living with HIV/AIDS: 3,800 (2009 est.)
country comparison to the world: 128

HIV/AIDS—deaths: fewer than 200 (2009 est.)
country comparison to the world: 116

Obesity—adult prevalence rate: 23.7% (2008)
country comparison to the world: 72

Children under the age of 5 years underweight: 1.6% (2004)
country comparison to the world: 127

Education expenditures: 4.1% of GDP (2010)
country comparison to the world: 108

Literacy: *definition:* age 15 and over can read and write
total population: 98.4%
male: 98.7% female: 98% (2011 est.)

School life expectancy (primary to tertiary education): *total:* 14 years
male: 14 years
female: 15 years (2011)

Unemployment, youth ages 15-24: *total:* 28.1%
country comparison to the world: 32
male: 29.5%
female: 26% (2012)

GOVERNMENT

Country name: *conventional long form:* Republic of Bulgaria
conventional short form: Bulgaria
local long form: Republika Balgariya
local short form: Balgariya

Government type: parliamentary democracy

Capital: *name:* Sofia
geographic coordinates: 42 41 N, 23 19 E
time difference: UTC+2 (7 hours ahead of Washington, DC during Standard Time)
daylight saving time: +1hr, begins last Sunday in March; ends last Sunday in October

Administrative divisions: 28 provinces (oblasti, singular—oblast); Blagoevgrad, Burgas, Dobrich, Gabrovo, Khaskovo, Kurdzhali, Kyustendil, Lovech, Montana, Pazardzhik, Pernik, Pleven, Plovdiv, Razgrad, Ruse, Shumen, Silistra, Sliven, Smolyan, Sofiya (Sofia), Sofiya-Grad (Sofia City), Stara Zagora, Turgovishte, Varna, Veliko Turnovo, Vidin, Vratsa, Yambol

Independence: 3 March 1878 (as an autonomous principality within the Ottoman Empire); 22 September 1908 (complete independence from the Ottoman Empire)

National holiday: Liberation Day, 3 March (1878)

Constitution: several previous; latest drafted between late 1990 and early 1991, adopted 12 July 1991; amended several times, last in 2007 (2007)

Legal system: civil law

International law organization participation: accepts compulsory ICJ jurisdiction with reservations; accepts ICCt jurisdiction

Suffrage: 18 years of age; universal

Executive branch: *chief of state:* President Rosen PLEVNELIEV (since 22 January 2012); Vice President Margarita POPOVA (since 22 January 2012)
head of government: Prime Minister Plamen ORESHARSKI (since 29 May 2013) Deputy Prime Ministers Zinaida ZLATANOVA (since 29 May 2013), Tsvetlin YOVCHEV (since June 2013), and Daniela BOBEVA (since June 2013)
cabinet: Council of Ministers nominated by the prime minister and elected by the National Assembly (For more information visit the World Leaders website)
elections: president and vice president elected on the same ticket by popular vote for a five-year term (eligible for a second term); election last held on 23 and 30 October 2011 (next to be held in 2016); chairman of the Council of Ministers (prime minister) elected by the National Assembly; deputy prime ministers nominated by the prime minister and elected by the National Assembly
election results: Rosen PLEVNELIEV elected president in a runoff election; percent of vote - Rosen PLEVNELIEV 52.6%, Ivailo KALFIN 47.4%; Plamen ORESHARSKI elected prime minister; result of legislative vote - 120 to 97

Legislative branch: unicameral National Assembly or Narodno Sabranie (240 seats; members elected by popular vote to serve four-year terms)
elections: last held on 12 May 2013 (next to be held spring 2017)
election results: percent of vote by party - GERB 30.5%, BSP 26.6%, MRF 11.3%, Ataka 7.3%; seats by party-GERB 97, BSP 84, MRF 36, Ataka 23

Judicial branch: *highest court(s):* Supreme Court of Cassation (consists of a chairman and approximately 72 judges organized into penal, civil, and commercial colleges); Supreme Administrative Court (organized in 2 colleges with various panels of 5 judges each); Constitutional Court (consists of 12 justices); note – Constitutional Court resides outside the Judiciary
judge selection and term of office: Supreme Court of Cassation and Supreme Administrative judges elected by the Supreme Judicial Council or SJC (consists of 25 members with extensive legal

experience) and appointed by the president; judge tenure NA; Constitutional Court justices elected by the National Assembly and appointed by the president and the SJC; justices appointed for 9-year terms with renewal of four justices every 3 years
subordinate courts: appeals courts; regional and district courts; administrative courts; courts martial

Political parties and leaders: Attack (Ataka) [Volen Nikolov SIDEROV]; Bulgarian Socialist Party or BSP [Sergei STANISHEV]; Bulgaria of the Citizens [Meglena KUNEVA]; Citizens for the European Development of Bulgaria or GERB [Boyko BORISOV]; Coalition for Bulgaria or CfB [Sergei STANISHEV] (coalition of parties dominated by BSP); Democrats for a Strong Bulgaria or DSB [Radan KANEV]; Internal Macedonian Revolutionary Organization or IMRO [Krasimir KARAKACHANOV]; Movement for Rights and Freedoms or MRF [Lyutvi MESTAN]; National Front for the Salvation of Bulgaria or NFSB [Valeri SIMEONOV]; National Movement for Stability and Progress or NDSV [Hristina HRISTOVA] (formerly National Movement Simeon II or NMS2); Order, Law, and Justice or RZS [Yane YANEV]; Union of Democratic Forces or UDF [Bozhidar LUKARSKI]

Political pressure groups and leaders: Confederation of Independent Trade Unions of Bulgaria or CITUB Podkrepa Labor Confederation
other: numerous regional, ethnic, and national interest groups with various agendas

International organization participation: Australia Group, BIS, BSEC, CD, CE, CEI, CERN, EAPC, EBRD, EIB, EU, FAO, G-9, IAEA, IBRD, ICAO, ICC (national committees), ICRM, IDA, IFC, IFRCS, IHO (pending member), ILO, IMF, IMO, IMSO, Interpol, IOC, IOM, IPU, ISO, ITSO, ITU, ITUC (NGOs), MIGA, NATO, NSG, OAS (observer), OIF, OPCW, OSCE, PCA, SELEC, UN, UNCTAD, UNESCO, UNHCR, UNIDO, UNMIL, UNWTO, UPU, WCO, WFTU (NGOs), WHO, WIPO, WMO, WTO, ZC

Diplomatic representation in the US: *chief of mission:* Ambassador Elena POPTODOROVA (since 4 August 2010)
chancery: 1621 22nd Street NW, Washington, DC 20008
telephone: [1] (202) 387-0174
FAX: [1] (202) 234-7973
consulate(s) general: Chicago, Los Angeles, New York

Diplomatic representation from the US: *chief of mission:* Ambassador Marcie B. RIES (since 5 September 2012) embassy:
em bassy: 16 Kozyak Street, Sofia 1408
mailing address: American Embassy Sofia, US Department of State, 5740 Sofia Place, Washington, DC 20521-5740
telephone: [359] (2) 937-5100
FAX: [359] (2) 937-5320

Flag description: three equal horizontal bands of white (top), green, and red; the pan-Slavic white-blue-red colors were modified by substituting a green band (representing freedom) for the blue
note: the national emblem, formerly on the hoist side of the white stripe, has been removed

National symbol(s): lion

National anthem: *name:* "Mila Rodino" (Dear Homeland)
lyrics/music: Tsvetan Tsvetkov RADOSLAVOV
note: adopted 1964; the anthem was composed in 1885 by a student en route to fight in the Serbo-Bulgarian War

ECONOMY

Economy—overview: Bulgaria, a former Communist country that entered the EU on 1 January 2007, averaged more than 6% annual growth from 2004 to 2008, driven by significant amounts of bank lending, consumption, and foreign direct investment. Successive governments have demonstrated a commitment to economic reforms and responsible fiscal planning, but the global downturn sharply reduced domestic demand, exports, capital inflows, and industrial production. GDP contracted by 5.5% in 2009, and has been slow to recover in the years since. Despite having a favorable investment regime, including low, flat corporate income taxes, significant challenges remain. Corruption in public administration, a weak judiciary, and the presence of organized crime continue to hamper the country's investment climate and economic prospects.

GDP (purchasing power parity): $104.6 billion (2013 est.)
country comparison to the world: 74
$104.1 billion (2012 est.)
$103.3 billion (2011 est.)
note: data are in 2013 US dollars

GDP (official exchange rate): $53.7 billion (2013 est.)

GDP—real growth rate: 0.5% (2013 est.)
country comparison to the world: 185
0.8% (2012 est.)
1.8% (2011 est.)

GDP—per capita (PPP): $14,400 (2013 est.)
country comparison to the world: 93
$14,300 (2012 est.)
$14,100 (2011 est.)
note: data are in 2013 US dollars

Gross national saving: 23.5% of GDP (2013 est.)
country comparison to the world: 60
22.5% of GDP (2012 est.)
22% of GDP (2011 est.)

GDP—composition, by end use: *household consumption:* 70.4%
government consumption: 7.9%
investment in fixed capital: 21.3%
investment in inventories: 2.5%
exports of goods and services: 69.7%
imports of goods and services: -71.8% (2013 est.)

GDP—composition, by sector of origin: *agriculture:* 6.7%
industry: 30.3%
services: 63% (2013 est.)

Agriculture—products: vegetables, fruits, tobacco, wine, wheat, barley, sunflowers, sugar beets; livestock

Industries: electricity, gas, water; food, beverages, tobacco; machinery and equipment, base metals, chemical products, coke, refined petroleum, nuclear fuel

Industrial production growth rate: 1% (2013 est.)
country comparison to the world: 148

Labor force: 2.551 million (2013 est.)
country comparison to the world: 112

Labor force—by occupation: *agriculture:* 7.1%
industry: 35.2%
services: 57.7% (2009)

Unemployment rate: 11.6% (2013 est.)
country comparison to the world: 120
11.1% (2012 est.)

Population below poverty line: 21.8% (2008)

Household income or consumption by percentage share: *lowest 10%:* 2%
highest 10%: 35.2% (2007)

Distribution of family income—Gini index: 45.3 (2007)
country comparison to the world: 39
26 (2001)

Budget: *revenues:* $18.81 billion
expenditures: $20.12 billion (2013 est.)

Taxes and other revenues: 35% of GDP (2013 est.)
country comparison to the world: 66

Budget surplus (+) or deficit (-): -2.4% of GDP (2013 est.)
country comparison to the world: 97

Public debt: 18.4% of GDP (2013 est.)
country comparison to the world: 137
16.3% of GDP (2012 est.)
defined by the EU's Maastricht Treaty as consolidated general government gross debt at nominal value, outstanding at the end of the year in the following categories of government liabilities: currency and deposits, securities other than shares excluding financial derivatives, and loans; general government sector comprises the subsectors: central government, state government, local government, and social security funds

Fiscal year: calendar year

Inflation rate (consumer prices): 1.5% (2013 est.)
country comparison to the world: 38
3% (2012 est.)

Central bank discount rate: 0.03% (31 December 2012 est.)
country comparison to the world: 142
0.22% (31 December 2011 est.)
note: Bulgarian National Bank (BNB) has had no independent monetary policy since the introduction of the Currency Board regime in 1997; this is BNB's base interest rate

Commercial bank prime lending rate: 9.1% (31 December 2013 est.)
country comparison to the world: 92
9.72% (31 December 2012 est.)

Stock of narrow money: $17.55 billion (31 December 2013 est.)
country comparison to the world: 66
$15.51 billion (31 December 2012 est.)

Stock of broad money: $45.84 billion (31 December 2013 est.)
country comparison to the world: 72
$41.53 billion (31 December 2012 est.)

Stock of domestic credit: $37.6 billion (31 December 2013 est.)
country comparison to the world: 67
$37.12 billion (31 December 2012 est.)

Market value of publicly traded shares: $6.666 billion (31 December 2012 est.)
country comparison to the world: 74
$8.253 billion (31 December 2011)
$7.276 billion (31 December 2010 est.)

Current account balance: -$182.3 million (2013 est.)
country comparison to the world: 83
-$669.5 million (2012 est.)

Exports: $27.9 billion (2013 est.)
country comparison to the world: 67
$26.7 billion (2012 est.)

Exports—commodities: clothing, footwear, iron and steel, machinery and equipment, fuels

Exports—partners: Germany 10.4%, Turkey 9.1%, Italy 8.7%, Romania 8.2%, Greece 7.3%, France 4% (2012)

Imports: $32.88 billion (2013 est.)
country comparison to the world: 65
$31.15 billion (2012 est.)

Imports—commodities: machinery and equipment; metals and ores; chemicals and plastics; fuels, minerals, and raw materials

Imports—partners: Russia 20.9%, Germany 11.3%, Italy 6.7%, Romania 6.6%, Greece 6.1%, Turkey 4.6%, Spain 4.5% (2012)

Reserves of foreign exchange and gold: $20.69 billion (31 December 2013 est.)
country comparison to the world: 59
$20.5 billion (31 December 2012 est.)

Debt—external: $37.85 billion (31 December 2013 est.)
country comparison to the world: 67
$36.52 billion (31 December 2012 est.)

Stock of direct foreign investment—at home: $54.21 billion (31 December 2013 est.)
country comparison to the world: 53
$52.21 billion (31 December 2012 est.)

Stock of direct foreign investment—abroad: $1.939 billion (31 December 2013 est.)
country comparison to the world: 74
$1.82 billion (31 December 2012 est.)

Exchange rates: leva (BGN) per US dollar—
1.478 (2013 est.)
1.5221 (2012 est.)
1.4774 (2010 est.)
1.404 (2009)
1.3171 (2008)

ENERGY

Electricity—production: 43.39 billion kWh (2010 est.)
country comparison to the world: 57

Electricity—consumption: 30.46 billion kWh (2010 est.)
country comparison to the world: 62

Electricity—exports: 12.11 billion kWh (2011 est.)
country comparison to the world: 17

Electricity—imports: 1.45 billion kWh (2011 est.)
country comparison to the world: 58

Electricity—installed generating capacity: 10.01 million kW (2010 est.)
country comparison to the world: 56

Electricity—from fossil fuels: 45.7% of total installed capacity (2010 est.)
country comparison to the world: 163

Electricity—from nuclear fuels: 19% of total installed capacity (2010 est.)
country comparison to the world: 10

Electricity—from hydroelectric plants: 21.8% of total installed capacity (2010 est.)
country comparison to the world: 86

Electricity—from other renewable sources: 4.8% of total installed capacity (2010 est.)
country comparison to the world: 45

Crude oil—production: 3,384 bbl/day (2012 est.)
country comparison to the world: 101

Crude oil—exports: 0 bbl/day (2012 est.)
country comparison to the world: 92

Crude oil—imports: 124,700 bbl/day (2010 est.)
country comparison to the world: 44

Crude oil—proved reserves: 15 million bbl (1 January 2013 es)
country comparison to the world: 85

Refined petroleum products—production: 128,500 bbl/day (2010 est.)
country comparison to the world: 69

Refined petroleum products—consumption: 112,700 bbl/day (2011 est.)
country comparison to the world: 73

Refined petroleum products—exports: 73,740 bbl/day (2010 est.)
country comparison to the world: 53

Refined petroleum products—imports: 50,130 bbl/day (2010 est.)
country comparison to the world: 69

Natural gas—production: 410 million cu m (2011 est.)
country comparison to the world: 73

Natural gas—consumption: 2.54 billion cu m (2010 est.)
country comparison to the world: 77

Natural gas—exports: 0 cu m (2011 est.)
country comparison to the world: 72

Natural gas—imports: 2.64 billion cu m (2011 est.)
country comparison to the world: 44

Natural gas—proved reserves: 5.663 billion cu m (1 January 2013 es)
country comparison to the world: 93

Carbon dioxide emissions from consumption of energy: 52.44 million Mt (2011 est.)
country comparison to the world: 61

COMMUNICATIONS

Telephones—main lines in use: 2.253 million (2012)
country comparison to the world: 55

Telephones—mobile cellular: 10.78 million (2012)
country comparison to the world: 74

Telephone system: *general assessment:* inherited an extensive but antiquated telecommunications network from the Soviet era; quality has improved with a modern digital trunk line now connecting switching centers in most of the regions; remaining areas are connected by digital microwave radio relay
domestic: the Bulgaria Telecommunications Company's fixed-line monopoly terminated in 2005 in an effort to upgrade fixed-line services; mobile-cellular teledensity, fostered by multiple service providers, has reached 150 telephones per 100 persons
international: country code - 359; submarine cable provides connectivity to Ukraine and Russia; a combination submarine cable and land fiber-optic system provides connectivity to Italy, Albania, and Macedonia; satellite earth stations - 3 (1 Intersputnik in the Atlantic Ocean region, 2 Intelsat in the Atlantic and Indian Ocean regions) (2011)

Broadcast media: 4 national terrestrial TV stations with 1 state-owned and 3 privately owned; a vast array of TV stations are available from cable and satellite TV providers; state-owned national radio broadcasts over 3 networks; large number of private radio stations broadcasting, especially in urban areas (2010)

Internet country code: .bg

Internet hosts: 976,277 (2012)
country comparison to the world: 47

Internet users: 3.395 million (2009)
country comparison to the world: 63

TRANSPORTATION

Airports: 68 (2013)
country comparison to the world: 74

Airports—with paved runways: *total:* 57
over 3,047 m: 2
2,438 to 3,047 m: 17
1,524 to 2,437 m: 12
under 914 m: 26 (2013)

Airports—with unpaved runways: *total:* 11
914 to 1,523 m: 2
under 914 m: 9 (2013)

Heliports: 1 (2013)

Pipelines: gas 2,887 km; oil 346 km; refined products 378 km (2013)

Railways: *total:* 4,152 km
country comparison to the world: 41
standard gauge: 4,072 km 1.435-m gauge (2,863 km electrified)
narrow gauge: 80 km 0.760-m gauge (2011)

Roadways: *total:* 19,512 km
country comparison to the world: 111
paved: 19,235 km (includes 458 km of expressways)
unpaved: 277 km
note: does not include Category IV local roads (2011)

Waterways: 470 km (2009)
country comparison to the world: 84

Merchant marine: *total:* 22
country comparison to the world: 93
by type: bulk carrier 9, cargo 8, liquefied gas 2, petroleum tanker 1, roll on/roll off 2
foreign-owned: 14 (Germany 12, Russia 2)
registered in other countries: 30 (Belize 1, Comoros 4, Georgia 1, Malta 8, Moldova 1, Panama 6, Saint Vincent and the Grenadines 9) (2010)

Ports and terminals: *major seaport(s):* Burgas, Varna (Black Sea)

MILITARY

Military branches: Bulgarian Armed Forces: Ground Forces, Naval Forces, Bulgarian Air Forces (Bulgarski Voennovazdyshni Sily, BVVS) (2011)

Military service age and obligation: 18-27 years of age for voluntary military service; conscription ended in January 2008; service obligation 6-9 months (2012)

Manpower available for military service:
males age 16-49: 1,637,470
females age 16-49: 1,621,352 (2010 est.)

Manpower fit for military service: *males age 16-49:* 1,320,955
females age 16-49: 1,337,616 (2010 est.)

Manpower reaching militarily significant age annually: *male:* 33,444
female: 32,075 (2010 est.)

Military expenditures: 1.46% of GDP (2012)
country comparison to the world: 67
1.55% of GDP (2011)
1.46% of GDP (2010)

TRANSNATIONAL ISSUES

Disputes—international: none

Illicit drugs: major European transshipment point for Southwest Asian heroin and, to a lesser degree, South American cocaine for the European market; limited producer of precursor chemicals; vulnerable to money laundering because of corruption, organized crime; some money laundering of drug-related proceeds through financial institutions (2008)

BURKINA FASO

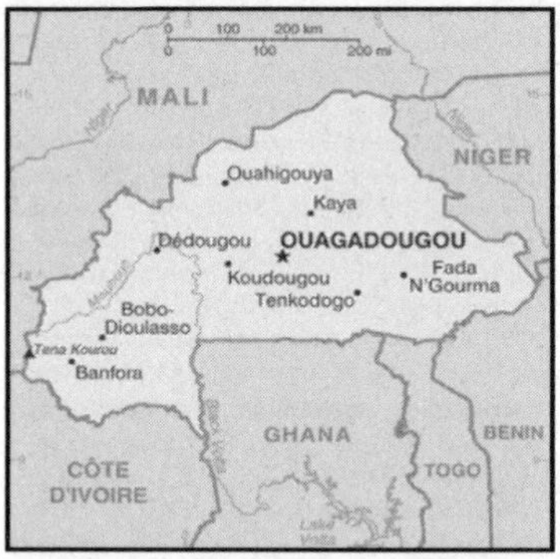

INTRODUCTION

Background: Burkina Faso (formerly Upper Volta) achieved independence from France in 1960. Repeated military coups during the 1970s and 1980s were followed by multiparty elections in the early 1990s. Current President Blaise COMPAORE came to power in a 1987 military coup and has won every election since then. There have been increasing protests over the belief that the president may try to run for a currently unconstitutional third term in the 2015 presidential elections. Burkina Faso's high population growth and limited natural resources result in poor economic prospects for the majority of its citizens.

GEOGRAPHY

Location: Western Africa, north of Ghana

Geographic coordinates: 13 00 N, 2 00 W

Map references: Africa

Area: *total:* 274,200 sq km
country comparison to the world: 75
land: 273,800 sq km
water: 400 sq km

Area—comparative: slightly larger than Colorado

Land boundaries: *total:* 3,193 km
border countries: Benin 306 km, Cote d'Ivoire 584 km, Ghana 549 km, Mali 1,000 km, Niger 628 km, Togo 126 km

Coastline: 0 km (landlocked)

Maritime claims: none (landlocked)

Climate: tropical; warm, dry winters; hot, wet summers

Terrain: mostly flat to dissected, undulating plains; hills in west and southeast

Elevation extremes: *lowest point:* Mouhoun (Black Volta) River 200 m

highest point: Tena Kourou 749 m

Natural resources: manganese, limestone, marble; small deposits of gold, phosphates, pumice, salt

Land use: *arable land:* 20.79%
permanent crops: 0.24%
other: 78.98% (2011)

Irrigated land: 250 sq km (2003)

Total renewable water resources: 12.5 cu km (2011)

Freshwater withdrawal (domestic/industrial/agricultural): *total:* 0.72 cu km/yr (46%/3%/51%)
per capita: 54.99 cu m/yr (2005)

Natural hazards: recurring droughts

Environment—current issues: recent droughts and desertification severely affecting agricultural activities, population distribution, and the economy; overgrazing; soil degradation; deforestation

Environment—international agreements: *party to:* Biodiversity, Climate Change, Climate Change-Kyoto Protocol, Desertification, Endangered Species, Hazardous Wastes, Law of the Sea, Marine Life Conservation, Ozone Layer Protection, Wetlands
signed, but not ratified: none of the selected agreements

Geography—note: landlocked savanna cut by the three principal rivers of the Black, Red, and White Voltas

PEOPLE AND SOCIETY

Nationality: noun: Burkinabe (singular and plural) adjective: Burkinabe

Ethnic groups: Mossi over 40%, other approximately 60% (includes Gurunsi, Senufo, Lobi, Bobo, Mande, and Fulani)

Languages: French (official), native African languages belonging to Sudanic family spoken by 90% of the population

Religions: Muslim 60.5%, Catholic 19%, animist 15.3%, Protestant 4.2%, other 0.6%, none 0.4% (2006 est.)

Population: 18,365,123 (July 2014 est.)
country comparison to the world: 60
note: estimates for this country explicitly take into account the effects of excess mortality due to AIDS; this can result in lower life expectancy, higher infant mortality, higher death rates, lower population growth rates, and changes in the distribution of population by age and sex than would otherwise be expected

Age structure: 0- 14 years: 45.4% (male 4,173,236/female 4,156,245)
15-24 years: 20.1% (male 1,851,801/female 1,833,496)
25-54 years: 29% (male 2,702,573/female 2,622,603)
55-64 years: 2.5% (male 240,520/female 332,421)
65 years and over: 2.5% (male 171,284/female 280,944) (2014 est.)

Dependency ratios: *total dependency ratio:* 92.3%
youth dependency ratio: 87.6%
elderly dependency ratio: 4.7%
potential support ratio: 21.3 (2013)

Median age: *total:* 17 years
male: 16.9 years
female: 17.2 years (2014 est.)

Population growth rate: 3.05% (2014 est.)
country comparison to the world: 11

Birth rate: 42.42 births/1,000 population (2014 est.)
country comparison to the world: 5

Death rate: 11.96 deaths/1,000 population (2014 est.)
country comparison to the world: 27

Net migration rate: 0 migrant(s)/1,000 population (2014 est.)
country comparison to the world: 101

Urbanization: *urban population:* 26.5% of total population (2011)
rate of urbanization: 6.02% annual rate of change (2010-15 est.)

Major urban areas—population: OUAGADOUGOU (capital) 2.053 million (2011)

Sex ratio: *at birth:* 1.03 male(s)/female
0-14 years: 1 male(s)/female
15-24 years: 1.01 male(s)/female
25-54 years: 1.03 male(s)/female
55-64 years: 0.99 male(s)/female
65 years and over: 0.62 male(s)/female
total population: 0.99 male(s)/female (2014 est.)

Mother's mean age at first birth: 19.4
note: median age at first birth among women 25-29 (2010 est.)

Maternal mortality rate: 300 deaths/100,000 live births (2010)
country comparison to the world: 39

Infant mortality rate: *total:* 76.8 deaths/1,000 live births
country comparison to the world: 9
male: 84.1 deaths/1,000 live births
female: 69.28 deaths/1,000 live births (2014 est.)

Life expectancy at birth: *total population:* 54.78 years
country comparison to the world: 207
male: 52.77 years
female: 56.85 years (2014 est.)

Total fertility rate: 5.93 children born/woman (2014 est.)
country comparison to the world: 6

Contraceptive prevalence rate: 16.2% (2010/11)

Health expenditures: 6.5% of GDP (2011)
country comparison to the world: 96

Physicians density: 0.05 physicians/1,000 population (2010)

Hospital bed density: 0.4 beds/1,000 population (2010)

Drinking water source:
Improved:
urban: 96.4% of population
rural: 74.1% of population
total: 80% of population
Unimproved:
urban: 3.6% of population
rural: 25.9% of population
total: 20% of population (2011 est.)

Sanitation facility access:
Improved:
urban: 50.1% of population
rural: 6.5% of population
total: 18% of population
Unimproved:
urban: 49.9% of population
rural: 93.5% of population
total: 82% of population (2011 est.)

HIV/AIDS—adult prevalence rate: 1% (2012 est.)
country comparison to the world: 48

HIV/AIDS—people living with HIV/AIDS: 114,500 (2012 est.)
country comparison to the world: 42

HIV/AIDS—deaths: 5,500 (2012 est.)
country comparison to the world: 36

Major infectious diseases: *degree of risk:* very high
food or waterborne diseases: bacterial and protozoal diarrhea, hepatitis A, and typhoid fever
vectorborne disease: dengue fever, malaria, and yellow fever
water contact disease: schistosomiasis
respiratory disease: meningococcal meningitis
animal contact disease: rabies
note: highly pathogenic H5N1 avian influenza has been identified in this country; it poses a negligible risk with extremely rare cases possible among US citizens who have close contact with birds (2013)

Obesity—adult prevalence rate: 2.3% (2008)
country comparison to the world: 181

Children under the age of 5 years underweight: 26.2% (2010)
country comparison to the world: 24

Education expenditures: 3.4% of GDP (2011)
country comparison to the world: 128

Literacy: *definition:* age 15 and over can read and write
total population: 28.7%
male: 36.7%
female: 21.6% (2007 est.)

School life expectancy (primary to tertiary education): *total:* 8 years
male: 8 years
female: 7 years (2012)

Child labor—children ages 5-14: *total number:* 1,521,006
percentage: 38 % (2006 est.)

Unemployment, youth ages 15-24: *total:* 3.8%
country comparison to the world: 140
male: 4.6%
female: 2.9% (2006)

GOVERNMENT

Country name: *conventional long form:* none
conventional short form: Burkina Faso local long form: none
local short form: Burkina Faso
former: Upper Volta, Republic of Upper Volta

Government type: parliamentary republic

Capital: *name:* Ouagadougou
geographic coordinates: 12 22 N, 1 31 W
time difference: UTC 0 (5 hours ahead of Washington, DC during Standard Time)

Administrative divisions: 13 regions; Boucle du Mouhoun, Cascades, Centre, Centre-Est, Centre-Nord, Centre-Ouest, Centre-Sud, Est, Hauts-Bassins, Nord, Plateau-Central, Sahel, Sud-Ouest

Independence: 5 August 1960 (from France)

National holiday: Republic Day, 11 December (1958); note—commemorates the day that Upper Volta became an autonomous republic in the French Community

Constitution: several previous; latest approved by referendum 2 June 1991, adopted 11 June 1991; amended several times, last in 2012 (2012)

Legal system: civil law based on the French model and customary law

International law organization participation: has not submitted an ICJ jurisdiction declaration; accepts ICCt jurisdiction

Suffrage: 18 years of age; universal

Executive branch: *chief of state:* President Blaise COMPAORE (since 15 October 1987)
head of government: Prime Minister Luc-Adolphe TIAO (since 18 April 2011)
cabinet: Council of Ministers appointed by the president on the recommendation of the prime minister (For more information visit the World Leaders website)
elections: president elected by popular vote for a five-year term (eligible for a second term); election last held on 21 November 2010 (next to be held in 2015); prime minister appointed by the president with the consent of the National Assembly
election results: Blaise COMPAORE reelected president; percent of popular vote—Blaise COMPAORE 80.2%, Hama Arba DIALLO 8.2%, Benewende Stanislas SANKARA 6.3%, other 5.3%

Legislative branch: unicameral National Assembly or Assemblee Nationale (127 seats; members are elected by proportional representation in one national constituency of 16 seats, and 45 multi-member constituencies having between 2 and 9 seats with members serving five-year terms)
elections: National Assembly election last held on 2 December 2012 (next to be held in 2017)
election results: percent of vote by party - NA; seats by party - CDP 70, ADF-RDA 19, Union for Progress and Reform 19, UPR 4, UNIR-MS 4, CFD-B 3, PDS/Metba 2, other 6

Judicial branch: *highest court(s):* Supreme Court of Appeals or Cour de Cassation (consists of NA judges); Constitutional Council or Conseil Constitutionnel (consists of the council president and 3 judges)
judge selection and term of office: Supreme Court judge appointments mostly controlled by the president of Burkina Faso; judge tenure NA; Constitutional Council judges appointed by the president of Burkina Faso upon the proposal of the minister of justice and the president of the National Assembly; judges appointed for 9-year terms with one-third of judges renewed every 3 years
subordinate courts: Appeals Court; High Court; first instance tribunals; district courts; specialized courts relating to issues of labor, children, and juveniles; village (customary) courts

Political parties and leaders: African Democratic Rally-Alliance for Democracy and Federation or ADF-RDA [Gilbert OUEDRAOGO]; Citizen's Popular Rally or RPC [Antoine QUARE]; Coalition of Democratic Forces of Burkina or CFD-B [Zio Eric FRANCOIS]; Congress for Democracy and Progress or CDP [Assimi KOUANDA]; Democratic and Popular Rally or RDP [Nana THIBAUT]; Movement for Tolerance and Progress or MTP [Nayabtigungou Congo KABORE]; Party for African Independence or PAI [Soumane TOURE]; Party for Democracy and Progress-Socialist Party or PDP-PS [Francois O. KABORE]; Party for Democracy and Socialism/Metba or PDS/Metba [Hama Arba DIALLO]; Party for National Rebirth or PAREN [Barry TAHIROU]; People's Movement for Progress or MPP [Roch March KABORE]; Rally for the Development of Burkina or RDB [Celestin Saidou COMPAORE]; Rally of Ecologists of Burkina Faso or RDEB [Ram OUEDRAGO]; Republican Party for Integration and Solidarity or PARIS Union for Democracy and Social Progress or UDPS [Fidele HIEN]; Union for Progress and Change or UPC [Zephirin DIABRE]; Union for Rebirth - Sankarist Movement or UNIR-MS [Benewende Stanislas SANKARA]; Union for the Republic or UPR [Toussaint Abel COULIBALY]; Union of Sankarist Parties or UPS [Ernest Nongma OUEDRAOGO]

Political pressure groups and leaders: Burkinabe General Confederation of Labor or CGTB [Tole SAGNON]; Burkinabe Movement for Human Rights or MBDHP [Chrysigone ZOUGMORE]; Citizen's Resistance Front [Luc Marius IBRIGA] Group of 14 February [Benewende Stanislas SANKARA]; National Confederation of Burkinabe Workers or CNTB [Laurent OUEDRAOGO]; National Organization of Free Unions or ONSL [Paul KABORE]
other: watchdog/political action groups throughout the country in both organizations and communities

International organization participation: ACP, AfDB, AU, CD, ECOWAS, EITI (candidate country), Entente, FAO, FZ, G-77, IAEA, IBRD, ICAO, ICC (NGOs), ICRM, IDA, IDB, IFAD, IFC, IFRCS, ILO, IMF, Interpol, IOC, IOM, IPU, ISO (correspondent), ITSO, ITU, ITUC (NGOs), MIGA, MINUSMA, MONUSCO, NAM, OIC, OIF, OPCW, PCA, UN, UNAMID, UNCTAD, UNESCO, UNIDO, UNISFA, UNITAR, UNWTO, UPU, WADB (regional), WAEMU, WCO, WFTU (NGOs), WHO, WIPO, WMO, WTO

Diplomatic representation in the US: *chief of mission:* Ambassador Seydou BOUDA (since 2 September 2011)
chancery: 2340 Massachusetts Avenue NW, Washington, DC 20008
telephone: [1] (202) 332-5577
FAX: [1] (202) 667-1882

Diplomatic representation from the US: *chief of mission:* Ambassador Tulinabo S. MUSHINGI (since 25 July 2013) *embassy:* 602 Avenue Raoul Follereau, Koulouba, Secteur 4
mailing address: 01 B. P. 35, Ouagadougou 01; pouch mail—US Department of State, 2440 Ouagadougou Place, Washington, DC 20521-2440
telephone: [226] 50-49-53-00
FAX: [226] 50-49-56-28

Flag description: two equal horizontal bands of red (top) and green with a yellow five-pointed star in the center; red recalls the country's struggle for independence, green is for hope and abundance, and yellow represents the country's mineral wealth
note: uses the popular Pan-African colors of Ethiopia

National symbol(s): white stallion

National anthem: *name:* "Le Ditanye" (Anthem of Victory)
lyrics/music: Thomas SANKARA
note: adopted 1974; also known as "Une Seule Nuit" (One Single Night), Burkina Faso's anthem was written by the country's president, an avid guitar player

ECONOMY

Economy—overview: Burkina Faso is a poor, landlocked country that depends on adequate rainfall. About 90% of the population is engaged in subsistence agriculture and cotton is the main cash crop. The country has few natural resources and a weak industrial base. Cotton and gold are key exports. Since 1998, Burkina Faso has begun to privatize state-owned enterprises and in 2004 revised its investment code to attract foreign investment. As a result, the country has seen an upswing in gold exploration, production, and export. The Burkinabe economy experienced high levels of growth over the last few years but growth is highly dependent on swings in gold and cotton prices. In 2013 Burkina Faso experienced a number of public protests over the cost of living, corruption, and other socio-economic issues. To defuse tensions the government has offered higher housing bonuses, reduced income taxes, and price controls. Turmoil in neighboring Mali, unreliable energy supplies, and poor transportation links pose longer-term challenges.

GDP (purchasing power parity): $26.51 billion (2013 est.)
country comparison to the world: 123
$24.9 billion (2012 est.)
$22.85 billion (2011 est.)
note: data are in 2013 US dollars

GDP (official exchange rate): $12.13 billion (2013 est.)

GDP—real growth rate: 6.5% (2013 est.)
country comparison to the world: 28
9% (2012 est.)
5% (2011 est.)

GDP—per capita (PPP): $1,500 (2013 est.)
country comparison to the world: 203
$1,400 (2012 est.)
$1,300 (2011 est.)
note: data are in 2013 US dollars

Gross national saving: 12.2% of GDP (2013 est.)
country comparison to the world: 127
14.1% of GDP (2012 est.)
16.6% of GDP (2011 est.)

GDP—composition, by end use: *household consumption:* 55.2%
government consumption: 16.9%
investment in fixed capital: 18.3%
investment in inventories: 0.2%
exports of goods and services: 34.4%
imports of goods and services: -25% (2013 est.)

GDP—composition, by sector of origin: *agriculture:* 33.6%
industry: 23.6%
services: 42.8% (2013 est.)

Agriculture—products: cotton, peanuts, shea nuts, sesame, sorghum, millet, corn, rice; livestock

Industries: cotton lint, beverages, agricultural processing, soap, cigarettes, textiles, gold

Industrial production growth rate: 6.5% (2013 est.)
country comparison to the world: 40

Labor force: 6.668 million
country comparison to the world: 64
note: a large part of the male labor force migrates annually to neighboring countries for seasonal employment (2007)

Labor force—by occupation: *agriculture:* 90%
industry and services: 10% (2000 est.)

Unemployment rate: 77% (2004)
country comparison to the world: 200

Population below poverty line: 46.7% (2009 est.)

Household income oil consumption by percentage share: *lowest 10%:* 2.9%
highest 10%: 32.2% (2009 est.)

Distribution of family income—Gini index: 39.5 (2007)
country comparison to the world: 62
48.2 (1994)

Budget: *revenues:* $2.838 billion
expenditures: $3.228 billion (2013 est.)

Taxes and other revenues: 23.4% of GDP (2013 est.)
country comparison to the world: 142

Budget surplus (+) or deficit (-): -3.2% of GDP (2013 est.)
country comparison to the world: 128

Fiscal year: calendar year

Inflation rate (consumer prices): 2.1% (2013 est.)
country comparison to the world: 69
3.8% (2012 est.)

Central bank discount rate: 4.25% (31 December 2010 est.)
country comparison to the world: 92
4.25% (31 December 2009 est.)

Commercial bank prime lending rate: NA%

Stock of narrow money: $2.22 billion (31 December 2013 est.)
country comparison to the world: 125
$1.845 billion (31 December 2012 est.)

Stock of broad money: $4.211 billion (31 December 2013 est.)
country comparison to the world: 133
$3.343 billion (31 December 2012 est.)

Stock of domestic credit: $2.711 billion (31 December 2013 est.)
country comparison to the world: 130
$2.123 billion (31 December 2012 est.)

Market value of publicly traded shares: $NA

Current account balance: -$364.9 million (2013 est.)
country comparison to the world: 96
-$247.6 million (2012 est.)

Exports: $2.844 billion (2013 est.)
country comparison to the world: 130
$2.746 billion (2012 est.)

Exports—commodities: gold, cotton, livestock

Exports—partners: China 25.9%, Turkey 24.8%, Belgium 5.2% (2012)

Imports: $2.941 billion (2013 est.)
country comparison to the world: 149
$2.675 billion (2012 est.)

Imports—commodities: capital goods, foodstuffs, petroleum

Imports—partners: Cote dIvoire 17.6%, France 15.2%, Ghana 4.8%, Togo 4.4% (2012)

Reserves of foreign exchange and gold: $1.115 billion (31 December 2013 est.)
country comparison to the world: 132
$1.025 billion (31 December 2012 est.)

Debt—external: $2.863 billion (31 December 2013 est.)
country comparison to the world: 139
$2.607 billion (31 December 2012 est.)

Exchange rates: Communaute Financiere Africaine francs (XOF) per US dollar—
500.7 (2013 est.)
510.53 (2012 est.)
495.28 (2010 est.)
472.19 (2009)
447.81 (2008)

ENERGY

Electricity—production: 670 million kWh (2010 est.)
country comparison to the world: 158

Electricity—consumption: 773.1 million kWh (2010 est.)
country comparison to the world: 157

Electricity—exports: 0 kWh (2012 est.)
country comparison to the world: 208

Electricity—imports: 150 million kWh (2010 est.)
country comparison to the world: 91

Electricity—installed generating capacity: 252,000 kW (2010 est.)
country comparison to the world: 155

Electricity—from fossil fuels: 87.3% of total installed capacity (2010 est.)
country comparison to the world: 84

Electricity—from nuclear fuels: 0% of total installed capacity (2010 est.)
country comparison to the world: 195

Electricity—from hydroelectric plants: 12.7% of total installed capacity (2010 est.)
country comparison to the world: 108

Electricity—from other renewable sources: 0% of total installed capacity (2010 est.)
country comparison to the world: 133

Crude oil—production: 0 bbl/day (2012 est.)
country comparison to the world: 140

Crude oil—exports: 0 bbl/day (2010 est.)
country comparison to the world: 198

Crude oil—imports: 0 bbl/day (2010 est.)
country comparison to the world: 134

Crude oil—proved reserves: 0 bbl (1 January 2013 es)
country comparison to the world: 200

Refined petroleum products—production: 0 bbl/day (2010 est.)
country comparison to the world: 204

Refined petroleum products—consumption: 9,960 bbl/day (2011 est.)
country comparison to the world: 154

Refined petroleum products—exports: 0 bbl/day (2010 est.)
country comparison to the world: 140

Refined petroleum products—imports: 11,660 bbl/day (2010 est.)
country comparison to the world: 128

Natural gas—production: 0 cu m (2011 est.)
country comparison to the world: 202

Natural gas—consumption: 0 cu m (2010 est.)
country comparison to the world: 203

Natural gas—exports: 0 cu m (2011 est.)
country comparison to the world: 199

Natural gas—imports: 0 cu m (2011 est.)
country comparison to the world: 143

Natural gas—proved reserves: 0 cu m (1 January 2013 es)
country comparison to the world: 201

Carbon dioxide emissions from consumption of energy: 1.454 million Mt (2011 est.)
country comparison to the world: 154

COMMUNICATIONS

Telephones—main lines in use: 141,400 (2012)
country comparison to the world: 139

Telephones—mobile cellular: 9.98 million (2012)
country comparison to the world: 79

Telephone system: *general assessment:* system includes microwave radio relay, open-wire, and radiotelephone communication stations; in 2006 the

government sold a 51 percent stake in the national telephone company and ultimately plans to retain only a 23 percent stake in the company *domestic:* fixed-line connections stand at less than 1 per 100 persons; mobile-cellular usage, fostered by multiple providers, is increasing rapidly from a low base
international: country code—226; satellite earth station—1 Intelsat (Atlantic Ocean) (2011)

Broadcast media: 2 TV stations—1 state-owned and 1 privately owned; state-owned radio runs a national and regional network; substantial number of privately owned radio stations; transmissions of several international broadcasters available in Ouagadougou (2007)

Internet country code: .bf

Internet hosts: 1,795 (2012)
country comparison to the world: 164

Internet users: 178,100 (2009)
country comparison to the world: 144

TRANSPORTATION

Airports: 23 (2013)
country comparison to the world: 133

Airports—with paved runways: *total:* 2
over 3,047 m: 1
2,438 to 3,047 m: 1 (2013)

Airports—with unpaved runways: *total:* 21
1,524 to 2,437 m: 3
914 to 1,523 m: 13
under 914 m: 5 (2013)

Railways: *total:* 622 km
country comparison to the world: 106
narrow gauge: 622 km 1.000-m gauge
note: another 660 km of this railway extends into Cote d'Ivoire (2008)

Roadways: *total:* 15,272 km
country comparison to the world: 121
note: does not include urban roads (2010)

MILITARY

Military branches: Army, Air Force of Burkina Faso (Force Aerienne de Burkina Faso, FABF), National Gendarmerie (2011)

Military service age and obligation: 18 years of age for voluntary military service; no conscription; women may serve in supporting roles (2013)

Manpower available for military service: *males age 16-49:* 3,735,735 (2010 est.)

Manpower fit for military service: *males age 16-49:* 2,366,168
females age 16-49: 2,367,673 (2010 est.)

Manpower reaching militarily significant age annually: *male:* 193,905
female: 191,662 (2010 est.)

Military expenditures: 1.39% of GDP (2012)
country comparison to the world: 73
1.34% of GDP (2011)
1.39% of GDP (2010)

TRANSNATIONAL ISSUES

Disputes—international: adding to illicit cross-border activities, Burkina Faso has issues concerning unresolved boundary alignments with its neighbors; demarcation is currently underway with Mali, the dispute with Niger was referred to the ICJ in 2010, and a dispute over several villages with Benin persists; Benin retains a border dispute with Burkina Faso around the town of Koualou

Refugees and internally displaced persons: refugees (country of origin): 32,170 (Mali) (2014)

BURMA

INTRODUCTION

Background: Various ethnic Burmese and ethnic minority city-states or kingdoms occupied the present borders through the 19th century. Over a period of 62 years (1824-1886), Britain conquered Burma and incorporated the country into its Indian Empire. Burma was administered as a province of India until 1937 when it became a separate, self-governing colony; in 1948, Burma attained independence from the Commonwealth. Gen. NE WIN dominated the government from 1962 to 1988, first as military ruler, then as self-appointed president, and later as political kingpin. In response to widespread civil unrest, NE WIN resigned in 1988, but within months the military crushed student-led protests and took power. Multiparty legislative elections in 1990 resulted in the main opposition party—the National League for Democracy (NLD)—winning a landslide victory. Instead of handing over power, the junta placed NLD leader (and Nobel Peace Prize recipient) AUNG SAN SUU KYI (ASSK) under house arrest from 1989 to 1995, 2000 to 2002, and from May 2003 to November 2010. In late September 2007, the ruling junta brutally suppressed protests over increased fuel prices led by prodemocracy activists and Buddhist monks, killing at least 13 people and arresting thousands for participating in the demonstrations. In early May 2008, Burma was struck by Cyclone Nargis, which left over 138,000 dead and tens of thousands injured and homeless. Despite this tragedy, the junta proceeded with its May constitutional referendum, the first vote in Burma since 1990. Parliamentary elections held in November 2010, considered flawed by many in the international community, saw the ruling Union Solidarity and Development Party garner over 75% of the seats. Parliament convened in January 2011 and selected former Prime Minister THEIN SEIN as president. Although the vast majority of national-level appointees named by THEIN SEIN are former or current military officers, the government has initiated a series of political and economic reforms leading to a substantial opening of the long-isolated country. These reforms have included allowing ASSK to contest parliamentary by-elections on 1 April 2012, releasing hundreds of political prisoners, reaching preliminary peace agreements with 10 of the 11 major armed ethnic groups, enacting laws that provide better protections for basic human rights, and gradually reducing restrictions on freedom of the press, association, and civil society. At least due in part to these reforms, ASSK now serves as an elected Member of Parliament and chair of the Committee for Rule of Law and Tranquility. Most political parties have begun building their institutions in preparation for the next round of general elections in 2015. The country is the chair of the Association of Southeast Asian Nations (ASEAN) for 2014.

GEOGRAPHY

Location: Southeastern Asia, bordering the Andaman Sea and the Bay of Bengal, between Bangladesh and Thailand

Geographic coordinates: 22 00 N, 98 00 E

Map references: Southeast Asia

Area: *total:* 676,578 sq km
country comparison to the world: 40
land: 653,508 sq km
water: 23,070 sq km

Area—comparative: slightly smaller than Texas

Land boundaries: *total:* 5,876 km
border countries: Bangladesh 193 km, China 2,185 km, India 1,463 km, Laos 235 km, Thailand 1,800 km

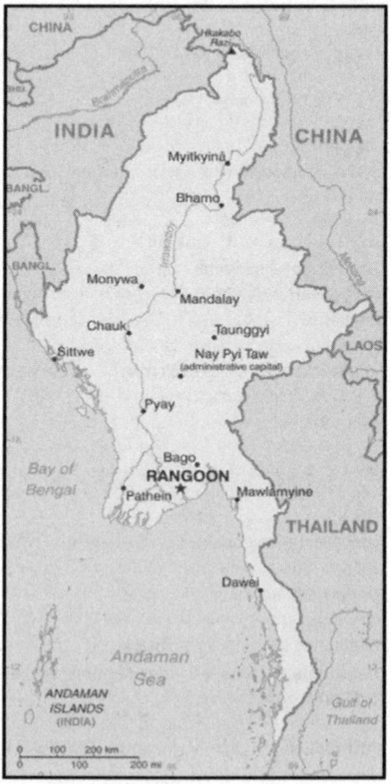

Coastline: 1,930 km

Maritime claims: *territorial sea:* 12 nm
contiguous zone: 24 nm

exclusive economic zone: 200 nm
continental shelf: 200 nm or to the edge of the continental margin
Climate: tropical monsoon; cloudy, rainy, hot, humid summers (southwest monsoon, June to September); less cloudy, scant rainfall, mild temperatures, lower humidity during winter (northeast monsoon, December to April)
Terrain: central lowlands ringed by steep, rugged highlands
Elevation extremes: *lowest point:* Andaman Sea 0 m
highest point: Hkakabo Razi 5,881 m
Natural resources: petroleum, timber, tin, antimony, zinc, copper, tungsten, lead, coal, marble, limestone, precious stones, natural gas, hydropower
Land use: *arable land:* 15.94%
permanent crops: 2.16%
other: 81.89% (2011)
Irrigated land: 21,100 sq km (2004)
Total renewable water resources: 1,168 cu km (2011)
Freshwater withdrawal (domestic/industrial/agricultural): *total:* 33.23 cu km/yr (10%/1%/89%)
per capita: 728.6 cu m/yr (2005)
Natural hazards: destructive earthquakes and cyclones; flooding and landslides common during rainy season (June to September); periodic droughts
Environment—current issues: deforestation; industrial pollution of air, soil, and water; inadequate sanitation and water treatment contribute to disease
Environment—international agreements: *party to:* Biodiversity, Climate Change, Climate Change-Kyoto Protocol, Desertification, Endangered Species, Law of the Sea, Ozone Layer Protection, Ship Pollution, Tropical Timber 83, Tropical Timber 94
signed, but not ratified: none of the selected agreements
Geography—note: strategic location near major Indian Ocean shipping lanes

PEOPLE AND SOCIETY

Nationality: *noun:* Burmese (singular and plural)
adjective: Burmese
Ethnic groups: Burman 68%, Shan 9%, Karen 7%, Rakhine 4%, Chinese 3%, Indian 2%, Mon 2%, other 5%
Languages: Burmese (official)
note: minority ethnic groups have their own languages
Religions: Buddhist 89%, Christian 4% (Baptist 3%, Roman Catholic 1%), Muslim 4%, Animist 1%, other 2%
Population: 55,746,253 (July 2014 est.)
country comparison to the world: 25
note: estimates for this country take into account the effects of excess mortality due to AIDS; this can result in lower life expectancy, higher infant mortality, higher death rates, lower population growth rates, and changes in the distribution of population by age and sex than would otherwise be expected
Age structure: *0-14 years:* 26.4% (male 7,498,179/female 7,209,588)
15-24 years: 18.3% (male 5,163,399/female 5,037,117)
25-54 years: 43.1% (male 11,930,777/female 12,073,741)
55-64 years: 5.3% (male 1,836,463/female 2,059,482)
65 years and over: 5.2% (male 1,277,919/female 1,659,588) (2014 est.)
Dependency ratios: *total dependency ratio:* 43.1%
youth dependency ratio: 35.7%
elderly dependency ratio: 7.5%
potential support ratio: 13.4 (2013)
Median age: *total:* 27.9 years
male: 27.3 years
female: 28.5 years (2014 est.)
Population growth rate: 1.03% (2014 est.)
country comparison to the world: 116
Birth rate: 18.65 births/1,000 population (2014 est.)
country comparison to the world: 97
Death rate: 8.01 deaths/1,000 population (2014 est.)
country comparison to the world: 100
Net migration rate: -0.3 migrant(s)/1,000 population (2014 est.)
country comparison to the world: 124
Urbanization: *urban population:* 32.6% of total population (2011)
rate of urbanization: 2.49% annual rate of change (2010-15 est.)
Major cities—population: RANGOON (capital) 4.259 million; Mandalay 1.009 million; Nay Pyi Taw 992,000 (2009)
Sex ratio: *at birth:* 1.06 male(s)/female
0-14 years: 1.04 male(s)/female
15-24 years: 1.03 male(s)/female
25-54 years: 0.99 male(s)/female
55-64 years: 0.99 male(s)/female
65 years and over: 0.77 male(s)/female
total population: 0.99 male(s)/female (2014 est.)
Maternal mortality rate: 200 deaths/100,000 live births (2010)
country comparison to the world: 54
Infant mortality rate: *total:* 44.91 deaths/1,000 live births
country comparison to the world: 47
male: 51.35 deaths/1,000 live births
female: 38.07 deaths/1,000 live births (2014 est.)
Life expectancy at birth: *total population:* 65.94 years
country comparison to the world: 170
male: 63.57 years
female: 68.46 years (2014 est.)
Total fertility rate: 2.18 children born/woman (2014 est.)
country comparison to the world: 103
Contraceptive prevalence rate: 46% (2009/10)
Health expenditures: 2% of GDP (2011)
country comparison to the world: 189
Physicians density: 0.5 physicians/1,000 population (2010)
Hospital bed density: 0.6 beds/1,000 population (2006)
Drinking water source:
Improved:
urban: 94% of population
rural: 79.3% of population
total: 84.1% of population
Unimproved:
urban: 6% of population
rural: 20.7% of population
total: 15.9% of population (2011 est.)
Sanitation facility access:
Improved:
urban: 83.9% of population
rural: 74.1% of population
total: 77.3% of population
Unimproved:
urban: 16.1% of population
rural: 25.9% of population
total: 22.7% of population (2011 est.)
HIV/AIDS—adult prevalence rate: 0.6% (2012 est.)
country comparison to the world: 61
HIV/AIDS—people living with HIV/AIDS: 195,700 (2012 est.)
country comparison to the world: 31
HIV/AIDS—deaths: 11,600 (2012 est.)
country comparison to the world: 26
Major infectious diseases: *degree of risk:* very high
food or waterborne diseases: bacterial and protozoal diarrhea, hepatitis A, and typhoid fever
vectorborne diseases: dengue fever, malaria, and Japanese encephalitis
water contact disease: leptospirosis
animal contact disease: rabies
note: highly pathogenic H5N1 avian influenza has been identified in this country; it poses a negligible risk with extremely rare cases possible among US citizens who have close contact with birds (2013)
Obesity—adult prevalence rate: 4% (2008)
country comparison to the world: 172
Children under the age of 5 years underweight: 22.6% (2010)
country comparison to the world: 27
Education expenditures: 0.8% of GDP (2011)
country comparison to the world: 172
Literacy: *definition:* age 15 and over can read and write
total population: 92.7%
male: 95.1%
female: 90.4% (2011 est.)
School life expectancy (primary to tertiary education): *total:* 9 years (2007)

GOVERNMENT

Country name: *conventional long form:* Union of Burma
conventional short form: Burma
local long form: Pyidaungzu Thammada Myanma Naingngandaw (translated as the Republic of the Union of Myanmar)
local short form: Myanma/Myanmar
former: Socialist Republic of the Union of Burma, Union of Myanmar
note: since 1989 the military authorities in Burma, and the current parliamentary government, have promoted the name Myanmar as a conventional name for their state; the US Government has not adopted the name
Government type: parliamentary government took power in March 2011
Capital: *name:* Rangoon (Yangon)
geographic coordinates: 16 48 N, 96 09 E

time difference: UTC+6.5 (11.5 hours ahead of Washington, DC during Standard Time)
note: Nay Pyi Taw is the administrative capital

Administrative divisions: 7 regions (taing-myar, singular—taing) and 7 states (pyi ne-myar, singular—pyi ne) regions: Ayeyawady (Irrawaddy), Bago, Magway, Mandalay, Sagaing, Taninthayi, Yangon states: Chin, Kachin, Kayah, Kayin, Mon, Rakhine (Arakan), Shan
union territory: Nay Pyi Taw

Independence: 4 January 1948 (from the UK)

National holiday: Independence Day, 4 January (1948); Union Day, 12 February (1947)

Constitution: previous 1947, 1974 (suspended until 2008); latest approved by referendum 29 May 2008; approved 15 May 2008; reformed 2011 (2011)

Legal system: mixed legal system of English common law (as introduced in codifications designed for colonial India) and customary law

International law organization participation: has not submitted an ICJ jurisdiction declaration; non-party state to the ICCt

Suffrage: 18 years of age; universal

Executive branch: *chief of state:* President THEIN SEIN (since 4 February 2011); Vice President SAI MAUK KHAM (since 3 February 2011); Vice President NYAN TUN (since 15 August 2012)
head of government: President THEIN SEIN (since 4 February 2011)
cabinet: cabinet is appointed by the president and confirmed by the parliament (For more information visit the World Leaders website)
elections: THEIN SEIN elected president by the parliament from among three vice presidents; the upper house, the lower house, and military members of the parliament each nominate one vice president (president serves a five-year term)

Legislative branch: bicameral, consists of the House of Nationalities [Amyotha Hluttaw] (224 seats, 168 directly elected and 56 appointed by the military; members serve five-year terms) and the House of Representatives [Pythu Hluttaw] (440 seats, 330 directly elected and 110 appointed by the military; members serve five-year terms)
elections: last held on 7 November 2010 (next to be held in December 2015)
election results: House of Nationalities—percent of vote by party—USDP 74.8%, others (NUP, SNDP, RNDP, NDF, AMRDP) 25.2%; seats by party—USDP 129, others 39; House of Representatives—percent of vote by party—USDP 79.6%, others (NUP, SNDP, RNDP, NDF, AMRDP) 20.4%; seats by party—USDP 259, others 71

Judicial branch: *highest court(s):* Supreme Court of the Union (consists of the chief justice and 7-11 judges)
judge selection and term of office: chief justice and judges nominated by the president, with approval of the Pythu Hlattaw, and appointed by the president; judges normally serve until mandatory retirement at age 70
subordinate courts: High Courts of the Region; High Courts of the State; Court of the Self-Administered Division;Court of the Self-Administered Zone; district and township courts; special courts (for juvenile, municipal, and traffic offenses); courts martial

Political parties and leaders: All Mon Region Democracy Party or AMRDP [NAING NGWE THEIN]; National Democratic Force or NDF [KHIN MAUNG SWE, Dr.THAN NYEIN]; National League for Democracy or NLD [AUNG SAN S00 KYI]; National Unity Party or NUP [TUN YE]; Rakhine Nationalities Development Party or RNDP [Dr. AYE MG]; Shan Nationalities Democratic Party or SNDP [SAI AIKE PAUNG]; Shan Nationalities League for Democracy or SNLD [HKUN HTUN OO]; Union Solidarity and Development Party or USDP [SHWE MANN, HTAY OO]; numerous smaller parties

Political pressure groups and leaders: *Thai border:* Ethnic Nationalities Council or ENC; Federation of Trade Unions-Burma or FTUB (exile trade union and labor advocates); National Coalition Government of the Union of Burma or NCGUB (self-proclaimed government in exile) ["Prime Minister" Dr. SEIN WIN] consists of individuals, some legitimately elected to the People's Assembly in 1990 (the group fled to a border area and joined insurgents in December 1990 to form a parallel government in exile); National Council-Union of Burma or NCUB (exile coalition of opposition groups); United Nationalities Federal Council (UNFC)
Inside Burma: Karen National Union or KNU; Karenni National People's Party or KNPP; United Wa State Army or UWSA; 88 Generation Students (pro-democracy movement); several other Chin, Karen, Mon, and Shan factions
note: freedom of expression has been highly restricted in Burma; the restrictions are being relaxed by the government; political groups, other than parties approved by the government, are limited in number

International organization participation: ADB, ARF, ASEAN, BIMSTEC, CP, EAS, FAO, G-77, IAEA, IBRD, ICAO, ICRM, IDA, IFAD, IFC, IFRCS, IHO, ILO, IMF, IMO, Interpol, IOC, IOM, IPU, ISO (correspondent), ITU, ITUC (NGOs), NAM, OPCW (signatory), SAARC (observer), UN, UNCTAD, UNESCO, UNIDO, UNWTO, UPU, WCO, WHO, WIPO, WMO, WTO

Diplomatic representation in the US: *chief of mission:* Ambassador KYAW MYO HTUT (since 3 December 2013)
chancery: 2300 S Street NW, Washington, DC 20008
telephone: [1] (202) 332-3344
FAX: [1] (202) 332-4351
consulate(s) general: none; Burma has a Mission to the UN in New York

Diplomatic representation from the US: *chief of mission:* Ambassador Derek J. MITCHELL (since 11 July 2012)
embassy: 110 University Avenue, Kamayut Township, Rangoon
mailing address: Box B, APO AP 96546
telephone: [95] (1) 536-509, 535-756, 538-038
FAX: [95] (1) 511-069

Flag description: design consists of three equal horizontal stripes of yellow (top), green, and red; centered on the green band is a large white five-pointed star that partially overlaps onto the adjacent colored stripes; the design revives the triband colors used by Burma from 1943-45, during the Japanese occupation

National symbol(s): chinthe (mythical lion)

National anthem: *name:* "Kaba Ma Kyei" (Till the End of the World, Myanmar)
lyrics/music: SAYA TIN
note: adopted 1948; Burma is among a handful of non-European nations that have anthems rooted in indigenous traditions; the beginning portion of the anthem is a traditional Burmese anthem before transitioning into a Western-style orchestrated work

ECONOMY

Economy—overview: Since the transition to a civilian government in 2011, Burma has begun an economic overhaul aimed at attracting foreign investment and reintegrating into the global economy. Economic reforms have included establishing a managed float of the Burmese kyat in 2012, granting the Central Bank operational independence in July 2013, and enacting a new Anti-corruption Law in September 2013. The government's commitment to reform, and the subsequent easing of most Western sanctions, has begun to pay dividends. The economy accelerated in 2012 and 2013. And Burma's abundant natural resources, young labor force, and proximity to Asia's dynamic economies have attracted foreign investment in the energy sector, garment industry, information technology, and food and beverages. Foreign direct investment grew from US$1.9 billion in FY 2011 to US$2.7 billion in FY 2012. Despite these improvements, living standards have not improved for the majority of the people residing in rural areas. Burma remains one of the poorest countries in Asia - more than one-fourth of the country's 60 million people live in poverty. The previous government's isolationist policies and economic mismanagement have left Burma with poor infrastructure, endemic corruption, underdeveloped human resources, and inadequate access to capital, which will require a major commitment to reverse. The Burmese government has been slow to address impediments to economic development such as an opaque revenue collection system and antiquated banking system. Key benchmarks of sustained economic progress would include modernizing and opening the financial sector, increasing budget allocations for social services, and accelerating agricultural and land reforms.

GDP (purchasing power parity): $111.1 billion (2013 est.)
country comparison to the world: 71
$104 billion (2012 est.)
$97.81 billion (2011 est.)
note: data are in 2013 US dollars

GDP (official exchange rate): $59.43 billion (2013 est.)

GDP—real growth rate: 6.8% (2013 est.)
country comparison to the world: 26
6.4% (2012 est.)
5.9% (2011 est.)

GDP—per capita (PPP): $1,700 (2013 est.)
country comparison to the world: 201
$1,600 (2012 est.)
$1,600 (2011 est.)
note: data are in 2013 US dollars

Gross national saving: 11.9% of GDP (2013 est.)
country comparison to the world: 129
12.9% of GDP (2012 est.)

13.7% of GDP (2011 est.)

GDP—composition, by end use: *household consumption:* 80.6%
government consumption: 3.8%
investment in fixed capital: 17.5%
investment in inventories: 0.3%
exports of goods and services: 20.1%
imports of goods and services: -22.3% (2013 est.)

GDP—composition, by sector of origin:: *agriculture:* 38%
industry: 20.3%
services: 41.7% (2013 est.)

Agriculture—products: rice, pulses, beans, sesame, groundnuts, sugarcane; fish and fish products; hardwood

Industries: agricultural processing; wood and wood products; copper, tin, tungsten, iron; cement, construction materials; pharmaceuticals; fertilizer; oil and natural gas; garments, jade and gems

Industrial production growth rate: 11.4% (2013 est.)
country comparison to the world: 9

Labor force: 34.31 million (2013 est.)
country comparison to the world: 19

Labor force—by occupation: *agriculture:* 70%
industry: 7%
services: 23% (2001)

Unemployment rate: 5.2% (2013 est.)
country comparison to the world: 50
5.4% (2012 est.)

Population below poverty line: 32.7% (2007 est.)

Household income or consumption by percentage share: *lowest 10%:* 2.8%
highest 10%: 32.4% (1998)

Budget: *revenues:* $2.413 billion
expenditures: $4.443 billion (2013 est.)

Taxes and other revenues: 4.1% of GDP (2013 est.)
country comparison to the world: 213

Budget surplus (+) or deficit (-): -3.4% of GDP (2013 est.)
country comparison to the world: 134

Fiscal year: 1 April—31 March

Inflation rate (consumer prices): 5.7% (2013 est.)
country comparison to the world: 164
1.5% (2012 est.)

Central bank discount rate: 9.95% (31 December 2010 est.)
country comparison to the world: 16
12% (31 December 2009 est.)

Commercial bank prime lending rate: 13% (31 December 2013 est.)
country comparison to the world: 59
13% (31 December 2012 est.)

Stock of narrow money: $12.23 billion (31 December 2013 est.)
country comparison to the world: 73
$11.54 billion (31 December 2012 est.)

Stock of domestic credit: $14.43 billion (31 December 2013 est.)
country comparison to the world: 88
$13.51 billion (31 December 2012 est.)

Market value of publicly traded shares: $NA

Current account balance: -$2.596 billion (2013 est.)
country comparison to the world: 154
-$1.791 billion (2012 est.)

Exports: $9.043 billion (2013 est.)
country comparison to the world: 99
$7.82 billion (2012 est.)
note: official export figures are grossly underestimated due to the value of timber, gems, narcotics, rice, and other products smuggled to Thailand, China, and Bangladesh

Exports—commodities: natural gas, wood products, pulses, beans, fish, rice, clothing, jade and gems

Exports—partners: Thailand 40.7%, India 14.8%, China 14.3%, Japan 7.4% (2012)

Imports: $10.11 billion (2013 est.)
country comparison to the world: 100
$7.998 billion (2012 est.)
note: import figures are grossly underestimated due to the value of consumer goods, diesel fuel, and other products smuggled in from Thailand, China, Malaysia, and India

Imports—commodities: fabric, petroleum products, fertilizer, plastics, machinery, transport equipment; cement, construction materials, crude oil; food products, edible oil

Imports—partners: China 36.9%, Thailand 20.2%, Singapore 8.7%, South Korea 8.7%, Japan 8.2%, Malaysia 4.6% (2012)

Reserves of foreign exchange and gold: $8.278 billion (31 December 2013 est.)
country comparison to the world: 77
$6.977 billion (31 December 2012 est.)

Debt—external: $5.379 billion (31 December 2013 est.)
country comparison to the world: 119
$5.591 billion (31 December 2012 est.)

Exchange rates: kyats (MMK) per US dollar—
947.9 (2013 est.)
853.48 (2012 est.)
5.58 (2010 est.)
1,055 (2009)
1,205 (2008)

ENERGY

Electricity—production: 7.346 billion kWh (2010 est.)
country comparison to the world: 104

Electricity—consumption: 6.093 billion kWh (2010 est.)
country comparison to the world: 107

Electricity—exports: 0 kWh (2012 est.)
country comparison to the world: 108

Electricity—imports: 0 kWh (2012 est.)
country comparison to the world: 120

Electricity—installed generating capacity: 1.713 million kW (2010 est.)
country comparison to the world: 107

Electricity—from fossil fuels: 53.3% of total installed capacity (2010 est.)
country comparison to the world: 147

Electricity—from nuclear fuels: 0% of total installed capacity (2010 est.)
country comparison to the world: 52

Electricity—from hydroelectric plants: 46.7% of total installed capacity (2010 est.)
country comparison to the world: 47

Electricity—from other renewable sources: 0% of total installed capacity (2010 est.)
country comparison to the world: 158

Crude oil—production: 20,830 bbl/day (2012 est.)
country comparison to the world: 76

Crude oil—exports: 0 bbl/day (2010 est.)
country comparison to the world: 87

Crude oil—imports: 0 bbl/day (2010 est.)
country comparison to the world: 162

Crude oil—proved reserves: 50 million bbl (1 January 2013 es)
country comparison to the world: 78

Refined petroleum products—production: 18,920 bbl/day (2010 est.)
country comparison to the world: 94

Refined petroleum products—consumption: 40,620 bbl/day (2011 est.)
country comparison to the world: 106

Refined petroleum products—exports: 0 bbl/day (2010 est.)
country comparison to the world: 154

Refined petroleum products—imports: 4,855 bbl/day (2010 est.)
country comparison to the world: 152

Natural gas—production: 11.91 billion cu m (2011 est.)
country comparison to the world: 39

Natural gas—consumption: 3.24 billion cu m (2010 est.)
country comparison to the world: 70

Natural gas—exports: 8.57 billion cu m (2011 est.)
country comparison to the world: 30

Natural gas—imports: 0 cu m (2011 est.)
country comparison to the world: 163

Natural gas—proved reserves: 283.2 billion cu m (1 January 2013 es)
country comparison to the world: 41

Carbon dioxide emissions from consumption of energy: 13.67 million Mt (2011 est.)
country comparison to the world: 94

COMMUNICATIONS

Telephones—main lines in use: 556,000 (2012)
country comparison to the world: 95

Telephones—mobile cellular: 5.44 million (2012)
country comparison to the world: 106

Telephone system: *general assessment:* meets minimum requirements for local and intercity service for business and government
domestic: system barely capable of providing basic service; mobile-cellular phone system is grossly underdeveloped
international: country code—95; landing point for the SEA-ME-WE-3 optical telecommunications submarine cable that provides links to Asia, the Middle East, and Europe; satellite earth stations—2, Intelsat (Indian Ocean) and ShinSat (2011)

Broadcast media: government controls all domestic broadcast media; 2 state-controlled TV stations with 1 of the stations controlled by the armed forces; 2 pay-TV stations are joint state-private ventures; access to satellite TV is limited; 1 state-controlled domestic radio station and 9 FM stations that are joint state-private ventures; transmissions of several international broadcasters are available in parts of Burma; the Voice of America (VOA), Radio Free Asia (RFA), BBC Burmese service, the Democratic Voice of Burma (DVB), and Radio Australia use shortwave to broadcast in Burma; VOA, RFA, and DVB produce daily TV news programs that are transmitted by satellite to audiences in Burma

Internet country code: .mm

Internet hosts: 1,055 (2012)
country comparison to the world: 172

Internet users: 110,000 (2009)
country comparison to the world: 158

TRANSPORTATION

Airports: 64 (2013)
country comparison to the world: 77

Airports—with paved runways: *total:* 36
over 3,047 m: 12
2,438 to 3,047 m: 11
1,524 to 2,437 m: 12
under 914 m: 1 (2013)

Airports—with unpaved runways: *total:* 28
over 3,047 m: 1
1,524 to 2,437 m: 4
914 to 1,523 m: 10
under 914 m: 13 (2013)

Heliports: 11 (2013)

Pipelines: gas 3,739 km; oil 551 km (2013)

Railways: *total:* 5,031 km
country comparison to the world: 36
narrow gauge: 5,031 km 1.000-m gauge (2008)

Roadways: *total:* 34,377 km (includes 358 km of expressways) (2010)
country comparison to the world: 93

Waterways: 12,800 km (2011)
country comparison to the world: 10

Merchant marine: total: 29
country comparison to the world: 86
by type: cargo 22, passenger 2, passenger/cargo 3, specialized tanker 1, vehicle carrier 1
foreign-owned: 2 (Germany 1, Japan 1)
registered in other countries: 3 (Panama 3) (2010)

Ports and terminals: *major seaport(s):* Moulmein, Sittwe
river port(s): Rangoon (Rangoon River)

MILITARY

Military branches: *Myanmar Armed Forces (Tatmadaw):* Army (Tatmadaw Kyi), Navy (Tatmadaw Yay), Air Force (Tatmadaw Lay) (2013)

Military service age and obligation: 18-35 years of age (men) and 18-27 years of age (women) for voluntary military service; no conscription (a 2010 law reintroducing conscription has not yet entered into force); service obligation 2 years; male (ages 18-45) and female (ages 18-35) professionals (including doctors, engineers, mechanics) serve up to 3 years; service terms may be stretched to 5 years in an officially declared emergency; Burma signed the Convention on the Rights of the Child (CRC) on 15 August 1991; on 27 June 2012, the regime signed a Joint Action Plan on prevention of child recruitment; in February 2013, the military formed a new task force to address forced child conscription, which reportedly continues (2013)

Manpower available for military service: *males age 16-49:* 14,747,845
females age 16-49: 14,710,871 (2010 est.)

Manpower fit for military service: *males age 16-49:* 10,451,515
females age 16-49: 11,181,537 (2010 est.)

Manpower reaching militarily significant age annually: *male:* 522,478
female: 506,388 (2010 est.)

TRANSNATIONAL ISSUES

Disputes—international: over half of Burma's population consists of diverse ethnic groups who have substantial numbers of kin in neighboring countries; the Naf River on the border with Bangladesh serves as a smuggling and illegal transit route; Bangladesh struggles to accommodate 29,000 Rohingya, Burmese Muslim minority from Arakan State, living as refugees in Cox's Bazar; Burmese border authorities are constructing a 200 km (124 mi) wire fence designed to deter illegal cross-border transit and tensions from the military build-up along border with Bangladesh in 2010; Bangladesh referred its maritime boundary claims with Burma and India to the International Tribunal on the Law of the Sea; Burmese forces attempting to dig in to the largely autonomous Shan State to rout local militias tied to the drug trade, prompts local residents to periodically flee into neighboring Yunnan Province in China; fencing along the India-Burma international border at Manipur's Moreh town is in progress to check illegal drug trafficking and movement of militants; 140,000 mostly Karen refugees fleeing civil strife, political upheaval and economic stagnation in Burma live in remote camps in Thailand near the border

Refugees and internally displaced persons: *IDPs:* 649,000 (government offensives against armed ethnic minority groups near its borders with China and Thailand) (2013)
stateless persons: 808,075 (2014); note - Burma's main group of stateless people is the Rohingya, Muslims living in northern Rakhine State; the Burmese Government does not recognize the Rohingya as a "national race" and stripped them of their citizenship under the 1982 Citizenship law, categorizing them as "non-national" or "foreign residents";native-born but non-indigenous people, such as Indians, and children born in Thailand to Burmese parents are also stateless; the Burmese Government does not grant citizenship to children born outside of the country to Burme separents who left the country illegally or fled persecution

Trafficking in persons: *current situation:* Burma is a source country for women, children, and men trafficked for the purpose of forced labor, and for women and children subjected to sex trafficking in other countries; poor economic conditions have led to increased legal and illegal migration of Burmese adults and children throughout East Asia and parts of the Middle East, where they are subject to forced labor and sex trafficking; men are forced to work in the fishing and construction industries, while women and girls are forced into prostitution or domestic servitude; some Burmese economic migrants seeking work in Thailand are subsequently subjected to forced labor or sexual exploitation; military personnel and insurgent militias unlawfully conscript child soldiers and continue to be the leading perpetrators of forced labor inside the country; Burmese children are also forced to work in tea shops, home industries, on plantations, and as beggars
tier rating: Tier 2 Watch List - Burma does not fully comply with the minimum standards for the elimination of trafficking, but it is making significant efforts to do so; anti-trafficking law enforcement efforts focus on the recruitment and transport of Burmese women and girls across international boundaries for forced marriages and sex trafficking; efforts to combat trafficking within Burma remain weak; forced labor of civilians and the recruitment of child soldiers by both military and private entities remain serious problems; the government continues modest efforts to provide temporary shelter and facilitate safe passage to Burmese victims repatriated from abroad, but its overall victim protection efforts are inadequate; in 2012, the government signed a UN-backed action plan for the identification, release, and rehabilitation of children in the Burmese military; as a result, some child soldiers have been released, but the government has not taken steps to prevent recruitment (2013)

Illicit drugs: world's third largest producer of illicit opium with an estimated production in 2012 of 690 metric tons, an increase of 13% over 2011, and poppy cultivation in 2012 totaled 51,000 hectares, a 17% increase over 2011; production in the United Wa State Army's areas of greatest control remains low; Shan state is the source of 94.5% of Burma's poppy cultivation; lack of government will to take on major narcotrafficking groups and lack of serious commitment against money laundering continues to hinder the overall antidrug effort; major source of methamphetamine and heroin for regional consumption (2013)

BURUNDI

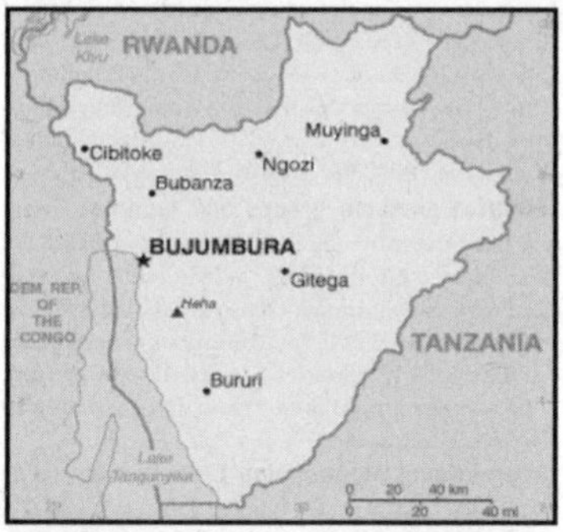

INTRODUCTION

Background: Burundi's first democratically elected president was assassinated in October 1993 after only 100 days in office, triggering widespread ethnic violence between Hutu and Tutsi factions. More than 200,000 Burundians perished during the conflict that spanned almost a dozen years. Hundreds of thousands of Burundians were internally displaced or became refugees in neighboring countries.

An internationally brokered power-sharing agreement between the Tutsi-dominated government and the Hutu rebels in 2003 paved the way for a transition process that led to an integrated defense force, established a new constitution in 2005, and elected a majority Hutu government in 2005. The government of President Pierre NKURUNZIZA, who was reelected in 2010, continues to face many political and economic challenges.

GEOGRAPHY

Location: Central Africa, east of Democratic Republic of the Congo

Geographic coordinates: 3 30 S, 30 00 E

Map references: Africa

Area: *total:* 27,830 sq km
country comparison to the world: 147
land: 25,680 sq km
water: 2,150 sq km

Area—comparative: slightly smaller than Maryland

Land boundaries: *total:* 974 km
border countries: Democratic Republic of the Congo 233 km, Rwanda 290 km, Tanzania 451 km

Coastline: 0 km (landlocked)

Maritime claims: none (landlocked)

Climate: equatorial; high plateau with considerable altitude variation (772 m to 2,670 m above sea level); average annual temperature varies with altitude from 23 to 17 degrees centigrade but is generally moderate as the average altitude is about 1,700 m; average annual rainfall is about 150 cm; two wet seasons (February to May and September to November), and two dry seasons (June to August and December to January)

Terrain: hilly and mountainous, dropping to a plateau in east, some plains

Elevation extremes: *lowest point:* Lake Tanganyika 772 m
highest point: Heha 2,670 m

Natural resources: nickel, uranium, rare earth oxides, peat, cobalt, copper, platinum, vanadium, arable land, hydropower, niobium, tantalum, gold, tin, tungsten, kaolin, limestone

Land use: *arable land:* 33.06%
permanent crops: 14.37%
other: 52.57% (2011)

Irrigated land: 214.3 sq km (2003)

Total renewable water resources: 12.54 cu km (2011)

Freshwater withdrawal (domestic/industrial/agricultural): *total:* 0.29 cu km/yr (15%/5%/79%)
per capita: 43.27 cu m/yr (2005)

Natural hazards: flooding; landslides; drought

Environment—current issues: soil erosion as a result of overgrazing and the expansion of agriculture into marginal lands; deforestation (little forested land remains because of uncontrolled cutting of trees for fuel); habitat loss threatens wildlife populations

Environment—international agreements: *party to:* Biodiversity, Climate Change, Climate Change-Kyoto Protocol, Desertification, Endangered Species, Hazardous Wastes, Ozone Layer Protection, Wetlands
signed, but not ratified: Law of the Sea

Geography—note: landlocked; straddles crest of the Nile-Congo watershed; the Kagera, which drains into Lake Victoria, is the most remote headstream of the White Nile

PEOPLE AND SOCIETY

Nationality: *noun:* Burundian(s)
adjective: Burundian

Ethnic groups: Hutu (Bantu) 85%, Tutsi (Hamitic) 14%, Twa (Pygmy) 1%, Europeans 3,000, South Asians 2,000

Languages: Kirundi 29.7% (official), Kirundi and other language 9.1%, French (official) and French and other language 0.3%, Swahili and Swahili and other language 0.2% (along Lake Tanganyika and in the Bujumbura area), English and English and other language 0.06%, more than 2 languages 3.7%, unspecified 56.9% (2008 est.)

Religions: Catholic 62.1%, Protestant 23.9% (includes Adventist 2.3% and other Protestant 21.6%), Muslim 2.5%, other 3.6%, unspecified 7.9% (2008 est.)

Population: 10,395,931 (July 2014 est.)
country comparison to the world: 86
note: estimates for this country explicitly take into account the effects of excess mortality due to AIDS; this can result in lower life expectancy, higher infant mortality, higher death rates, lower population growth rates, and changes in the distribution of population by age and sex than would otherwise be expected

Age structure: *0-14 years:* 45.7% (male 2,385,571/female 2,361,367)
15-24 years: 19.3% (male 1,001,486/female 1,005,617)
25-54 years: 28.6% (male 1,483,936/female 1,491,401)
55-64 years: 2.5% (male 190,707/female 216,983)
65 years and over: 2.5% (male 109,434/female 149,429) (2014 est.)

Dependency ratios: *total dependency ratio:* 88.6%
youth dependency ratio: 84%
elderly dependency ratio: 4.5%
potential support ratio: 22 (2013)

Median age: *total:* 17 years
male: 16.7 years
female: 17.2 years (2014 est.)

Population growth rate: 3.28% (2014 est.)
country comparison to the world: 8

Birth rate: 42.33 births/1,000 population (2014 est.)
country comparison to the world: 6

Death rate: 9.54 deaths/1,000 population (2014 est.)
country comparison to the world: 56

Net migration rate: 0 migrant(s)/1,000 population (2014 est.)
country comparison to the world: 102

Urbanization: *urban population:* 10.9% of total population (2011)
rate of urbanization: 4.45% annual rate of change (2010-15 est.)

Major urban areas—population: BUJUMBURA (capital) 605,000 (2011)

Sex ratio: *at birth:* 1.03 male(s)/female
0-14 years: 1.01 male(s)/female
15-24 years: 1 male(s)/female
25-54 years: 1 male(s)/female
55-64 years: 0.99 male(s)/female
65 years and over: 0.67 male(s)/female
total population: 0.98 male(s)/female (2014 est.)

Mother's mean age at first birth: 21.3
note: median age at first birth among women 25-29 (2010 est.)

Maternal mortality rate: 800 deaths/100,000 live births (2010)
country comparison to the world: 6

Infant mortality rate: *total:* 63.44 deaths/1,000 live births
country comparison to the world: 20
male: 70.22 deaths/1,000 live births
female: 56.46 deaths/1,000 live births (2014 est.)

Life expectancy at birth: *total population:* 59.55 years
country comparison to the world: 196
male: 57.94 years
female: 61.22 years (2014 est.)

Total fertility rate: 6.14 children born/woman (2014 est.)
country comparison to the world: 3

Contraceptive prevalence rate: 21.9% (2010/11)

Health expenditures: 8.7% of GDP (2011)
country comparison to the world: 50

Physicians density: 0.03 physicians/1,000 population (2004)

Hospital bed density: 1.9 beds/1,000 population (2011)

Drinking water source:
Improved:
urban: 82% of population
rural: 73.4% of population

total: 74.4% of population
Unimproved:
urban: 18% of population
rural: 26.6% of population
total: 25.6% of population (2011 est.)

Sanitation facility access:
Improved:
urban: 44.9% of population
rural: 50.7% of population
total: 50.1% of population
Unimproved:
urban: 55.1% of population
rural: 49.3% of population
total: 49.9% of population (2011 est.)

HIV/AIDS—adult prevalence rate: 1.3% (2012 est.)
country comparison to the world: 36

HIV/AIDS—people living with HIV/AIDS: 89,500 (2012 est.)
country comparison to the world: 46

HIV/AIDS—deaths: 4,800 (2012 est.)
country comparison to the world: 42

Major infectious diseases: *degree of risk:* very high
food or waterborne diseases: bacterial and protozoal diarrhea, hepatitis A, and typhoid fever
vectorborne diseases: malaria and dengue fever
water contact disease: schistosomiasis
animal contact disease: rabies (2013)

Obesity—adult prevalence rate: 2.9% (2008)
country comparison to the world: 176

Children under the age of 5 years underweight: 29.1% (2011)
country comparison to the world: 19

Education expenditures: 5.8% of GDP (2012)
country comparison to the world: 50

Literacy: *definition:* age 15 and over can read and write
total population: 67.2%
male: 72.9%
female: 61.8% (2010 est.)

School life expectancy (primary to tertiary education): *total:* 10 years
male: 11 years
female: 10 years (2010)

Child labor—children ages 5-14: *total number:* 433,187
percentage: 19 % (2005 est.)

GOVERNMENT

Country name: *conventional long form:* Republic of Burundi
conventional short form: Burundi
local long form: Republique du Burundi/Republika y'u Burundi
local short form: Burundi former: Urundi

Government type: republic

Capital: *name:* Bujumbura
geographic coordinates: 3 22 S, 29 21 E
time difference: UTC+2 (7 hours ahead of Washington, DC during Standard Time)

Administrative divisions: 17 provinces; Bubanza, Bujumbura Mairie, Bujumbura Rural, Bururi, Cankuzo, Cibitoke, Gitega, Karuzi, Kayanza, Kirundo, Makamba, Muramvya, Muyinga, Mwaro, Ngozi, Rutana, Ruyigi

Independence: 1 July 1962 (from UN trusteeship under Belgian administration)

National holiday: Independence Day, 1 July (1962)

Constitution: several previous; latest ratified by popular referendum 28 February 2005 (2012)

Legal system: mixed legal system of Belgian civil law and customary law

International law organization participation: has not submitted an ICJ jurisdiction declaration; accepts ICCt jurisdiction

Suffrage: 18 years of age; universal

Executive branch: *chief of state:* President Pierre NKURUNZIZA - Hutu (since 26 August 2005); First Vice President Prosper BAZOMBAZA (since 13 February 2014); Second Vice President Gervais RUFYIKIRI - Hutu (since 29 August 2010); note - the president is both the chief of state and head of government
head of government: President Pierre NKURUNZIZA - Hutu (since 26 August 2005); First Vice President Prosper BAZOMBAZA (since 13 February 2014); Second Vice President Gervais RUFYIKIRI - Hutu (since 29 August 2010)
cabinet: Council of Ministers appointed by president (For more information visit the World Leaders website)
elections: the president elected by popular vote for a five-year term (eligible for a second term); elections last held on 28 June 2010 (next to be held in 2015); vice presidents nominated by the president, endorsed by parliament
election results: Pierre NKURUNZIZA elected president by popular vote; Pierre NKURUNZIZA 91.6%, other 8.4%; note - opposition parties withdrew from the election due to alleged government interference in the electoral process

Legislative branch: bicameral Parliament or Parlement, consists of a Senate (54 seats; 34 members elected by indirect vote to serve five-year terms, with remaining seats assigned to ethnic groups and former chiefs of state) and a National Assembly or Assemblee Nationale (minimum 100 seats, 60% Hutu and 40% Tutsi with at least 30% being women; additional seats appointed by a National Independent Electoral Commission to ensure ethnic representation; members are elected by popular vote to serve five-year terms)
elections: last held on 23 July 2010 (next to be held in 2015)
election results: Senate—percent of vote by party—NA%; seats by party—TBD; National Assembly—percent of vote by party—CNDD-FDD 81.2%, UPRONA 11.6%, FRODEBU 5.9%, others 1.3%; seats by party—CNDD-FDD 81, UPRONA 17, FRODEBU 5, other 3

Judicial branch: *highest court(s):* Supreme Court (consists of 9 judges and organized into Judicial, administrative, and cassation chambers)
judge selection and term of office: judges nominated by the Judicial Service Commission, a 15-member independent body of judicial and legal profession officials); judges appointed by the president with the approval of the Senate; judge tenure NA
subordinate courts: Courts of Appeal; County Courts; Courts of Residence

Political parties and leaders: *governing parties:* Burundi Democratic Front or FRODEBU [Leonce NGENDAKUMANA]; National Council for the Defense of Democracy—Front for the Defense of Democracy or CNDD-FDD [Jeremie NGENDAKUMANA]; Union for National Progress (Union pour le Progress Nationale) or UPRONA [Bonaventure NIYOYANKANA]
note: a multiparty system introduced in 1998 includes: National Council for the Defense of Democracy or CNDD [Leonard NYANGOMA]; National Resistance Movement for the Rehabilitation of the Citizen or MRC-Rurenzangemero [Epitace BANYAGANAKANDI]; Party for National Redress or PARENA [Jean-Baptiste BAGAZA]

Political pressure groups and leaders: Forum for the Strengthening of Civil Society or FORSC [Pacifique NININAHAZWE] (civil society umbrella organization); Observatoire de lutte contre la corruption et les malversations economiques or OLUCOME [Gabriel RUFYIRI] (anti-corruption pressure group) other: Hutu and Tutsi militias (loosely organized)

International organization participation: ACP, AfDB, AU, CEPGL, COMESA, EAC, FAO, G-77, IAEA, IBRD, ICAO, ICRM, IDA, IFAD, IFC, IFRCS, ILO, IMF, Interpol, IOC, IOM, IPU, ISO (correspondent), ITU, ITUC (NGOs), MIGA, NAM, OIF, OPCW, UN, UNAMID, UNCTAD, UNESCO, UNIDO, UNISFA, UNWTO, UPU, WCO, WHO, WIPO, WMO, WTO

Diplomatic representation in the US: *chief of mission:* Ambassador Angele NIYUHIRE (since 18 September 2009)
chancery: Suite 408, 2233 Wisconsin Avenue NW, Washington, DC 20007
telephone: [1] (202) 342-2574
FAX: [1] (202) 342-2578

Diplomatic representation from the US: *chief of mission:* Ambassador Dawn M. LIBERI (since 10 July 2012)
embassy: Avenue des Etats-Unis, Bujumbura
mailing address: B. P. 1720, Bujumbura
telephone: [257] 22-207-000
FAX: [257] 22-222-926

Flag description: divided by a white diagonal cross into red panels (top and bottom) and green panels (hoist side and fly side) with a white disk superimposed at the center bearing three red six-pointed stars outlined in green arranged in a triangular design (one star above, two stars below); green symbolizes hope and optimism, white purity and peace, and red the blood shed in the struggle for independence; the three stars in the disk represent the three major ethnic groups: Hutu, Twa, Tutsi, as well as the three elements in the national motto: unity, work, progress

National symbol(s): lion

National anthem: *name:* "Burundi Bwacu" (Our Beloved Burundi)
lyrics/music: Jean-Baptiste NTAHOKAJA/Marc BARENGAYABO
note: adopted 1962

ECONOMY

Economy—overview: Burundi is a landlocked, resource-poor country with an underdeveloped manufacturing sector. The economy is predominantly agricultural; agriculture accounts for just over 30% of GDP and employs more than 90% of the population. Burundi's primary exports are coffee and tea, which account for 90% of foreign exchange earnings, though exports are a relatively small share of GDP. Burundi's export earnings - and its ability to pay for imports - rests primarily on weather conditions and international coffee and tea prices. An ethnic-based war that lasted for over a decade resulted in more than 200,000 deaths, forced more than 48,000 refugees into Tanzania, and displaced 140,000 others internally. Only one in two children go to school, and approximately one in 15 adults has HIV/AIDS. Food, medicine, and electricity remain in short supply. Less than 2% of the population has electricity in its homes. Burundi's GDP grew around 4% annually in 2006-13. Political stability and the end of the civil war have improved aid flows and economic activity has increased, but underlying weaknesses - a high poverty rate, poor education rates, a weak legal system, a poor transportation network, overburdened utilities, and low administrative capacity - risk undermining planned economic reforms. The purchasing power of most Burundians has decreased as wage increases have not kept up with inflation. Burundi will remain heavily dependent on aid from bilateral and multilateral donors - foreign aid represents 42% of Burundi's national income, the second highest rate in Sub-Saharan Africa. Burundi joined the East African Community in 2009. Government corruption is hindering the development of a healthy private sector as companies seek to navigate an environment with ever changing rules.

GDP (purchasing power parity): $5.75 billion (2013 est.)
country comparison to the world: 166
$5.504 billion (2012 est.)
$5.291 billion (2011 est.)
note: data are in 2013 US dollars

GDP (official exchange rate): $2.676 billion (2013 est.)

GDP—real growth rate: 4.5% (2013 est.)
country comparison to the world: 68
4% (2012 est.)
4.2% (2011 est.)

GDP—per capita (PPP): $600 (2013 est.)
country comparison to the world: 225
$600 (2012 est.)
$600 (2011 est.)
note: data are in 2013 US dollars

Gross national saving: -0.9% of GDP (2013 est.)
country comparison to the world: 151
-0.8% of GDP (2012 est.)
6.3% of GDP (2011 est.)

GDP—composition, by end use: *household consumption:* 88.8%
government consumption: 22.4%
investment in fixed capital: 22.1%
investment in inventories: -4.6%
exports of goods and services: 7.2%
imports of goods and services: -35.9% (2013 est.)

GDP—composition, by sector of origin: *agriculture:* 34.4%
industry: 18.4%
services: 47.2% (2013 est.)

Agriculture—products: coffee, cotton, tea, corn, sorghum, sweet potatoes, bananas, cassava (manioc); beef, milk, hides

Industries: light consumer goods such as blankets, shoes, soap, and beer; assembly of imported components; public works construction; food processing

Industrial production growth rate: 4.5% (2013 est.)
country comparison to the world: 63

Labor force: 4.245 million (2007)
country comparison to the world: 89

Labor force—by occupation: *agriculture:* 93.6%
industry: 2.3%
services: 4.1% (2002 est.)

Unemployment rate: NA%

Population below poverty line: 68% (2002 est.)

Household income or consumption by percentage share: *lowest 10%:* 4.1%
highest 10%: 28% (2006)

Distribution of family income—Gini index: 42.4 (1998)
country comparison to the world: 49

Budget: *revenues:* $766.9 million
expenditures: $855.8 million (2013 est.)

Taxes and other revenues: 28.7% of GDP (2013 est.)
country comparison to the world: 100

Budget surplus (+) or deficit (-): -3.3% of GDP (2013 est.)
country comparison to the world: 131

Public debt: 47.6% of GDP (2013 est.)
country comparison to the world: 72
50.3% of GDP (2012 est.)

Fiscal year: calendar year

Inflation rate (consumer prices): 9.3% (2013 est.)
country comparison to the world: 205
18% (2012 est.)

Central bank discount rate: 11.25% (31 December 2010 est.)
country comparison to the world: 24
10% (31 December 2009 est.)

Commercial bank prime lending rate: 13.7% (31 December 2013 est.)
country comparison to the world: 48
14.32% (31 December 2012 est.)

Stock of narrow money: $339.4 million (31 December 2013 est.)
country comparison to the world: 167
$332.5 million (31 December 2012 est.)

Stock of broad money: $471.1 million (31 December 2013 est.)
country comparison to the world: 177
$458.3 million (31 December 2012 est.)

Stock of domestic credit: $597.2 million (31 December 2013 est.)
country comparison to the world: 165
$572.2 million (31 December 2012 est.)

Market value of publicly traded shares: $NA

Current account balance: -$492.5 million (2013 est.)
country comparison to the world: 100
-$432.1 million (2012 est.)

Exports: $122.8 million (2013 est.)
country comparison to the world: 189
$134.7 million (2012 est.)

Exports—commodities: coffee, tea, sugar, cotton, hides

Exports—partners: Switzerland 23.9%, UK 12.9%, Belgium 7.4%, Pakistan 7.4%, Democratic Republic of the Congo 7.4%, Uganda 5.6%, Germany 5.2%, China 4.9%, Egypt 4.7% (2012)

Imports: $867.2 million (2013 est.)
country comparison to the world: 180
$886.2 million (2012 est.)

Imports—commodities: capital goods, petroleum products, foodstuffs

Imports—partners: Saudi Arabia 11.3%, Belgium 10.1%, China 9.1%, India 7.9%, Tanzania 6.5%, Kenya 6%, Uganda 5.7%, Zambia 4.6%, US 4.1% (2012)

Reserves of foreign exchange and gold: $314.6 million (31 December 2013 est.)
country comparison to the world: 155
$308.8 million (31 December 2012 est.)

Debt—external: $677.2 million (31 December 2013 est.)
country comparison to the world: 170
$641.9 million (31 December 2012 est.)

Exchange rates: Burundi francs (BIF) per US dollar—
1,556.5 (2013 est.)
1,442.51 (2012 est.)
1,230.8 (2010 est.)
1,230.18 (2009)
1,198 (2008)

ENERGY

Electricity—production: 152 million kWh (2010 est.)
country comparison to the world: 188

Electricity—consumption: 221.4 million kWh (2010 est.)
country comparison to the world: 183

Electricity—exports: 0 kWh (2012 est.)
country comparison to the world: 112

Electricity—imports: 80 million kWh (2010 est.)
country comparison to the world: 94

Electricity—installed generating capacity: 52,000 kW (2010 est.)
country comparison to the world: 187

Electricity—from fossil fuels: 1.9% of total installed capacity (2010 est.)
country comparison to the world: 203

Electricity—from nuclear fuels: 0% of total installed capacity (2010 est.)
country comparison to the world: 58

Electricity—from hydroelectric plants: 98.1% of total installed capacity (2010 est.)
country comparison to the world: 8

Electricity—from other renewable sources: 0% of total installed capacity (2010 est.)
country comparison to the world: 163

Crude oil—production: 0 bbl/day (2012 est.)
country comparison to the world: 158

Crude oil—exports: 0 bbl/day (2010 est.)
country comparison to the world: 93

Crude oil—imports: 0 bbl/day (2010 est.)
country comparison to the world: 167

Crude oil—proved reserves: 0 bbl (1 January 2013 es)
country comparison to the world: 112

Refined petroleum products—production: 0 bbl/day (2010 est.)
country comparison to the world: 127

Refined petroleum products—consumption: 2,290 bbl/day (2011 est.)
country comparison to the world: 187

Refined petroleum products—exports: 0 bbl/day (2010 est.)
country comparison to the world: 159

Refined petroleum products—imports: 1,429 bbl/day (2010 est.)
country comparison to the world: 188

Natural gas—production: 0 cu m (2011 est.)
country comparison to the world: 109

Natural gas—consumption: 0 cu m (2010 est.)
country comparison to the world: 125

Natural gas—exports: 0 cu m (2011 est.)
country comparison to the world: 73

Natural gas—imports: 0 cu m (2011 est.)
country comparison to the world: 168

Natural gas—proved reserves: 0 cu m (1 January 2013 es)
country comparison to the world: 119

Carbon dioxide emissions from consumption of energy: 204,700 Mt (2011 est.)
country comparison to the world: 193

COMMUNICATIONS

Telephones—main lines in use: 17,400 (2012)
country comparison to the world: 193

Telephones—mobile cellular: 2.247 million (2012)
country comparison to the world: 140

Telephone system: *general assessment:* sparse system of open-wire, radiotelephone communications, and low—capacity microwave radio relays
domestic: telephone density one of the lowest in the world; fixed-line connections stand at well less than 1 per 100 persons; mobile-cellular usage is increasing but remains at roughly 20 per 100 persons
international: country code—257; satellite earth station—1 Intelsat (Indian Ocean) (2011)

Broadcast media: state-controlled La Radiodiffusion et Television Nationale de Burundi (RTNB) operates the lone TV station and the only national radio network; about 10 privately owned radio stations; transmissions of several international broadcasters are available in Bujumbura (2007)

Internet country code: .bi

Internet hosts: 229 (2012)
country comparison to the world: 198

Internet users: 157,800 (2009)
country comparison to the world: 147

TRANSPORTATION

Airports: 7 (2013)
country comparison to the world: 165

Airports—with paved runways: *total:* 1
over 3,047 m: 1 (2013)

Airports—with unpaved runways: *total:* 6
914 to 1,523 m: 4
under 914 m: 2 (2013)

Heliports: 1 (2012)

Roadways: *total:* 12,322 km
country comparison to the world: 127
paved: 1,286 km
unpaved: 11,036 km (2004)

Waterways: (mainly on Lake Tanganyika between Bujumbura, Burundi's principal port, and lake ports in Tanzania, Zambia, and the Democratic Republic of Congo) (2011)

Ports and terminals: *lake port(s):* Bujumbura (Lake Tanganyika)

MILITARY

Military branches: National Defense Forces (Forces de Defense Nationale, FDN): Army (includes maritime wing, Air Wing), National Gendarmerie (2013)

Military service age and obligation: 18 years of age for voluntary military service; the armed forces law of 31 December 2004 did not specify a minimum age for enlistment, but the government claimed that no one younger than 18 was being recruited; mandatory retirement age 45 (enlisted), 50 (NCOs), and 55 (officers) (2012)

Manpower available for military service: *males age 16-49:* 2,182,327
females age 16-49: 2,202,125 (2010 est.)

Manpower fit for military service: *males age 16-49:* 1,398,769
females age 16-49: 1,481,417 (2010 est.)

Manpower reaching militarily significant age annually: *male:* 117,956
female: 116,956 (2010 est.)

Military expenditures: 2.39% of GDP (2012)
country comparison to the world: 32
NA% (2011)
2.39% of GDP (2010)

TRANSNATIONAL ISSUES

Disputes—international: Burundi and Rwanda dispute two sq km (0.8 sq mi) of Sabanerwa, a farmed area in the Rukurazi Valley where the Akanyaru/Kanyaru River shifted its course southward after heavy rains in 1965; cross-border conflicts persist among Tutsi, Hutu, other ethnic groups, associated political rebels, armed gangs, and various government forces in the Great Lakes region

Refugees and internally displaced persons: *refugees (country of origin):* 41,349 (Democratic Republic of the Congo) (2012)
IDPs: 78,800 (the majority are ethnic Tutsi displaced by inter-communal violence that broke out after the 1993 coup and fighting between government forces and rebel groups; no new displacements since 2008 when the last rebel group laid down its arms) (2012)
stateless persons: 1,302 (2012)

Trafficking in persons: *current situation:* Burundi is a source country for children and possibly women subjected to forced labor and sex trafficking; business people recruit Burundian girls for prostitution domestically, as well as in Rwanda, Kenya, Uganda, and the Middle East, and recruit boys and girls for forced labor in Burundi and Tanzania; children and young adults are coerced into forced labor in farming, mining, construction, or informal commerce; some family members, friends, and neighbors are complicit in exploiting children, luring them in with offers of educational or job opportunities
tier rating: Tier 2 Watch List - Burundi does not comply fully with the minimum standards for the elimination of human trafficking; however, it is making significant efforts to do so; the government fails to prosecute trafficking offenses vigorously or increase its capacity to protect victims; most victim assistance continues to be provided by NGOs without government support; the government also fails to complete its draft anti-trafficking legislation, which is intended to rectify gaps in existing laws; a nationwide awareness-raising campaign continues (2013)

CABO VERDE

INTRODUCTION

Background: The uninhabited islands were discovered and colonized by the Portuguese in the 15th century; Cabo Verde subsequently became a trading center for African slaves and later an important coaling and resupply stop for whaling and transatlantic shipping. Following independence in 1975, and a tentative interest in unification with Guinea-Bissau, a one-party system was established and maintained until multi-party elections were held in 1990. Cabo Verde continues to exhibit one of Africa's most stable democratic governments. Repeated droughts during the second half of the 20th century caused significant hardship and prompted heavy emigration. As a result, Cabo Verde's expatriate population is greater than its domestic one. Most Cabo Verdeans have both African and Portuguese antecedents.

GEOGRAPHY

Location: Western Africa, group of islands in the North Atlantic Ocean, west of Senegal

Geographic coordinates: 16 00 N, 24 00 W

Map references: Africa

Area: *total:* 4,033 sq km
country comparison to the world: 176
land: 4,033 sq km
water: 0 sq km

Area—comparative: slightly larger than Rhode Island

Land boundaries: 0 km

Coastline: 965 km

Maritime claims: measured from claimed archipelagic baselines
territorial sea: 12 nm
contiguous zone: 24 nm
exclusive economic zone: 200 nm

Climate: temperate; warm, dry summer; precipitation meager and erratic

Terrain: steep, rugged, rocky, volcanic

Elevation extremes: *lowest point:* Atlantic Ocean 0 m
highest point: Mt. Fogo 2,829 m (a volcano on Fogo Island)

Natural resources: salt, basalt rock, limestone, kaolin, fish, clay, gypsum

Land use: *arable land:* 11.66%
permanent crops: 0.74%
other: 87.59% (2011)

Irrigated land: 34.76 sq km (2004)

Total renewable water resources: 0.3 cu km (2011)

Freshwater withdrawal (domestic/industrial/agricultural): *total:* 0.02 cu km/yr (6%/1%/93%)
per capita: 48.57 cu m/yr (2004)

Natural hazards: prolonged droughts; seasonal harmattan wind produces obscuring dust; volcanically and seismically active
volcanism: Fogo (elev. 2,829 m), which last erupted in 1995, is Cabo Verde's only active volcano

Environment—current issues: soil erosion; deforestation due to demand for wood used as fuel; water shortages; desertification; environmental damage has threatened several species of birds and reptiles; illegal beach sand extraction; overfishing

Environment—international agreements: *party to:* Biodiversity, Climate Change, Climate Change-Kyoto Protocol, Desertification, Endangered Species, Environmental Modification, Hazardous Wastes, Law of the Sea, Marine Dumping, Ozone Layer Protection, Ship Pollution, Wetlands
signed, but not ratified: none of the selected agreements

Geography—note: strategic location 500 km from west coast of Africa near major north-south sea routes; important communications station; important sea and air refueling site

PEOPLE AND SOCIETY

Nationality: *noun:* Cabo Verdean(s)
adjective: Cabo Verdean

Ethnic groups: Creole (mulatto) 71%, African 28%, European 1%

Languages: Portuguese (official), Crioulo (a blend of Portuguese and West African words)

Religions: Roman Catholic 77.3%, Protestant 3.7% (includes Church of the Nazarene 1.7%, Adventist 1.5%, Universal Kingdom of God .4%, and God and Love .1%), other Christian 4.3% (includes Christian Rationalism 1.9%, Jehovah's Witness 1%, Assembly of God .9%, and New Apostolic .5%), Muslim 1.8%, other 1.3%, none 10.8%, unspecified 0.7% (2010 est.)

Population: 538,535 (July 2014 est.)
country comparison to the world: 173

Age structure: *0-14 years:* 30.6% (male 82,942/female 82,069)
15-24 years: 21.4% (male 57,633/female 57,637)
25-54 years: 38% (male 99,248/female 105,381)
55-64 years: 5.1% (male 10,917/female 15,352)
65 years and over: 5.2% (male 10,322/female 17,034) (2014 est.)

Dependency ratios: *total dependency ratio:* 53.5%
youth dependency ratio: 45.3%
elderly dependency ratio: 8.2%
potential support ratio: 12.2 (2013)

Median age: *total:* 24 years
male: 23.2 years
female: 24.8 years (2014 est.)

Population growth rate: 1.39% (2014 est.)
country comparison to the world: 87

Birth rate: 20.72 births/1,000 population (2014 est.)
country comparison to the world: 82

Death rate: 6.17 deaths/1,000 population (2014 est.)
country comparison to the world: 160

Net migration rate: -0.64 migrant(s)/1,000 population (2014 est.)
country comparison to the world: 139

Urbanization: *urban population:* 62.6% of total population (2011)
rate of urbanization: 2.12% annual rate of change (2010-15 est.)

Major urban areas—population: PRAIA (capital) 132,000 (2011)

Sex ratio: *at birth:* 1.03 male(s)/female
0-14 years: 1.01 male(s)/female
15-24 years: 1 male(s)/female
25-54 years: 0.94 male(s)/female
55-64 years: 0.94 male(s)/female
65 years and over: 0.6 male(s)/female
total population: 0.94 male(s)/female (2014 est.)

Mother's mean age at first birth: 19.5
note: median age at first birth among women 25-29 (2005 est.)

Maternal mortality rate: 79 deaths/100,000 live births (2010)
country comparison to the world: 83

Infant mortality rate: *total:* 24.28 deaths/1,000 live births
country comparison to the world: 76
male: 27.82 deaths/1,000 live births
female: 20.63 deaths/1,000 live births (2014 est.)

Life expectancy at birth: *total population:* 71.57 years
country comparison to the world: 145
male: 69.32 years
female: 73.89 years (2014 est.)

Total fertility rate: 2.34 children born/woman (2014 est.)
country comparison to the world: 92

Contraceptive prevalence rate: 61.3% (2005)

Health expenditures: 4.8% of GDP (2011)
country comparison to the world: 146

Physicians density: 0.3 physicians/1,000 population (2010)

Hospital bed density: 2.1 beds/1,000 population (2010)

Drinking water source:
Improved:
urban: 90.6% of population
rural: 85.6% of population
total: 88.7% of population
unimproved:
urban: 9.4% of population
rural: 14.4% of population
total: 11.3% of population (2011 est.)

Sanitation facility access:
Improved:
urban: 74% of population
rural: 45.3% of population
total: 63.3% of population
unimproved:
urban: 26% of population
rural: 54.7% of population
total: 36.7% of population (2011 est.)

HIV/AIDS—adult prevalence rate: 0.2% (2012 est.)
country comparison to the world: 110

HIV/AIDS—people living with HIV/AIDS: 800 (2001) (2012 est.)
country comparison to the world: 152

HIV/AIDS—deaths: NA

Obesity—adult prevalence rate: 10% (2008)
country comparison to the world: 131

Education expenditures: 5% of GDP (2011)
country comparison to the world: 76

Literacy: *definition:* age 15 and over can read and write
total population: 84.9%
male: 89.7%
female: 80.3% (2011 est.)

School life expectancy (primary to tertiary education): *total:* 13 years
male: 13 years
female: 14 years (2012)

Child labor—children ages 5-14:
total number: 1,948
percentage: 3 %
note: data represents children ages 10-14 (2001 est.)

GOVERNMENT

Country name: *conventional long form:* Republic of Cabo Verde
conventional short form: Cabo Verde
local long form: Republica de Cabo Verde
local short form: Cabo Verde

Government type: republic

Capital: *name:* Praia
geographic coordinates: 14 55 N, 23 31 W
time difference: UTC-1 (4 hours ahead of Washington, DC during Standard Time)

Administrative divisions: 22 municipalities (concelhos, singular—concelho); Boa Vista, Brava, Maio, Mosteiros, Paul, Porto Novo, Praia, Ribeira Brava, Ribeira Grande, Ribeira Grande de Santiago, Sal, Santa Catarina, Santa Catarina do Fogo, Santa Cruz, Sao Domingos, Sao Filipe, Sao Lourenco dos Orgaos, Sao Miguel, Sao Salvador do Mundo, Sao Vicente, Tarrafal, Tarrafal de Sao Nicolau

Independence: 5 July 1975 (from Portugal)

National holiday: Independence Day, 5 July (1975)

Constitution: previous 1981; latest effective 25 September 1992; revised 1995, 1999, 2010 (2010)

Legal system: civil law system of Portugal

International law organization participation: has not submitted an ICJ jurisdiction declaration; non-party state to the ICCt

Suffrage: 18 years of age; universal

Executive branch: *chief of state:* President Jorge Carlos FONSECA (since 9 September 2011)
head of government: Prime Minister Jose Maria Pereira NEVES (since 1 February 2001)
cabinet: Council of Ministers appointed by the president on the recommendation of the prime minister
elections: president elected by popular vote for a five-year term (eligible for a second term); election last held on 7 August 2011 with a second round runoff on 21 August 2011; prime minister nominated by the National Assembly and appointed by the president
election results: percent of vote (second round)—Jorge Carlos FONSECA 53.4%, Manuel Inocencio SOUSA 46.6%

Legislative branch: unicameral National Assembly or Assembleia Nacional (72 seats; members elected by popular vote to serve five-year terms)
elections: last held on 6 February 2011 (next to be held by 2016)
election results: percent of vote by party—NA; seats by party—PAICV 38, MPD 32, UCID 2

Judicial branch: *highest court(s):* Supreme Court of Justice (consists of the chief justice and at least 5 judges)
judge selection and term of office: judges appointments—1 by the president of the republic, 1 elected by the National Assembly, and the remainder by the Supreme Council of Magistrates, a 9-member independent body presided over by the chief justice and includes the high judicial inspector, 2 presidential appointees, 3 elected by the National Assembly, and 2 by their court peers; chief justice appointed by the president of there public from among peers of the Supreme Court and in consultation with the Supreme Council of the Magistrates; judge tenure NA
subordinate courts: first instance (municipal) courts; audit, military, and fiscal and customs courts

Political parties and leaders: African Party for Independence of Cabo Verde or PAICV [Jose Maria Pereira NEVES, chairman]; Democratic and Independent Cabo Verdean Union or UCID [Antonio MONTEIRO]; Democratic Christian Party or PDC [Manuel RODRIGUES]; Democratic Renovation Party or PRD [Victor FIDALGO]; Movement for Democracy or MPD [Jorge SANTOS]; Party for Democratic Convergence or PCD [Dr. Eurico MONTEIRO]; Party of Work and Solidarity or PTS [Isaias RODRIGUES]; Social Democratic Party or PSD [Joao ALEM]

Political pressure groups and leaders: *other:* environmentalists; political pressure groups

International organization participation: ACP, AfDB, AOSIS, AU, CD, CPLP, ECOWAS, FAO, G-77, IAEA, IBRD, ICAO, ICRM, IDA, IFAD, IFC, IFRCS, ILO, IMF, IMO, Interpol, IOC, IOM, IPU, ITSO, ITU, ITUC (NGOs), MIGA, NAM, OIF, OPCW, UN, UNCTAD, UNESCO, UNIDO, Union Latina, UNWTO, UPU, WCO, WHO, WIPO, WMO, WTO

Diplomatic representation in the US: *chief of mission:* Ambassador Maria De Fatima Lima Da VEIGA (since 22 November 2013)
chancery: 3415 Massachusetts Avenue NW, Washington, DC 20007
telephone: [1] (202) 965-6820
FAX: [1] (202) 965-1207
consulate(s) general: Boston

Diplomatic representation from the US: *chief of mission:* Ambassador Adrienne O'NEAL (since 9 December 2011)
embassy: Rua Abilio Macedo 6, Praia
mailing address: C. P. 201, Praia
telephone: [238] 2-60-89-00
FAX: [238] 2-61-13-55

Flag description: five unequal horizontal bands; the top-most band of blue—equal to one half the width of the flag—is follow ed by three bands of white, red, and white, each equal to 1/12 of the width, and a bottom stripe of blue equal to one quarter of the flag width; a circle of 10, yellow, five-pointed stars is centered on the red stripe and positioned 3/8 of the length of the flag from the hoist side; blue stands for the sea and the sky, the circle of stars represents the 10 major islands united into a nation, the stripes symbolize the road to formation of the country through peace (white) and effort (red)

National anthem: *name:* "Cantico da Liberdade" (Song of Freedom)
lyrics/music: Amilcar Spencer LOPES/Adalberto Higino Tavares SILVA
note: adopted 1996

ECONOMY

Economy—overview: The economy is service-oriented with commerce, transport, tourism, and public services accounting for about three-fourths of GDP. Tourism is the mainstay of the economy and it is heavily dependent on conditions in the euro zone countries. This island economy suffers from a poor natural resource base, including serious water shortages exacerbated by cycles of long-term drought and poor soil for agriculture on several of the islands. Although about 40% of the population lives in rural areas, the share of food production in GDP is low. About 82% of food must be imported. The fishing potential, mostly lobster and tuna, is not fully exploited. Cabo Verde annually runs a high trade deficit financed by foreign aid and remittances from its large pool of emigrants; remittances supplement GDP by more than 20%. Despite the lack of resources, sound economic management has produced steadily improving incomes. Continued economic reforms are aimed at developing the private sector and attracting foreign investment to diversify the economy and mitigate high unemployment. Future prospects depend heavily on the maintenance of aid flows, the encouragement of tourism, remittances, and the momentum of the government's development program. Cabo Verde became a member of the WTO in July 2008.

GDP (purchasing power parity): $2.222 billion (2013 est.)
country comparison to the world: 190
$2.19 billion (2012 est.)
$2.135 billion (2011 est.)
note: data are in 2013 US dollars

GDP (official exchange rate): $1.955 billion (2013 est.)

GDP—real growth rate: 1.5% (2013 est.)
country comparison to the world: 159
2.5% (2012 est.)
4% (2011 est.)

GDP—per capita (PPP): $4,400 (2013 est.)
country comparison to the world: 167
$4,400 (2012 est.)
$4,400 (2011 est.)
note: data are in 2013 US dollars

Gross national saving: 38.5% of GDP (2013 est.)
country comparison to the world: 11
34.2% of GDP (2012 est.)
31.2% of GDP (2011 est.)

GDP—composition, by end use:
household consumption: 52.9%
government consumption: 16.6%
investment in fixed capital: 41.9%
investment in inventories: 1.7%
exports of goods and services: 34.3%
imports of goods and services: -47.3% (2013 est.)

GDP—composition, by sector of origin:
agriculture: 9.3%
industry: 18.8%
services: 71.9% (2013 est.)

Agriculture—products: bananas, corn, beans, sweet potatoes, sugarcane, coffee, peanuts; fish

Industries: food and beverages, fish processing, shoes and garments, salt mining, ship repair

Industrial production growth rate: 1.8% (2013 est.)
country comparison to the world: 131

Labor force: 196,100 (2007)
country comparison to the world: 171

Unemployment rate: 21% (2000 est.)
country comparison to the world: 164

Population below poverty line: 30% (2000)

Household income or consumption by percentage share: *lowest 10%:* 1.9%
highest 10%: 40.6% (2001)

Budget: *revenues:* $414.6 million
expenditures: $607 million (2013 est.)

Taxes and other revenues: 21.2% of GDP (2013 est.)
country comparison to the world: 155

Budget surplus (+) or deficit (-): -9.8% of GDP (2013 est.)
country comparison to the world: 205

Public debt: 86.2% of GDP (2012 est.)
country comparison to the world: 24
78.1% of GDP (2011 est.)

Fiscal year: calendar year

Inflation rate (consumer prices): 1.9% (2013 est.)
country comparison to the world: 59
2.5% (2012 est.)

Central bank discount rate: 7.5% (31 December 2010 est.)
country comparison to the world: 35
7.5% (31 December 2009 est.)

Commercial bank prime lending rate: 10.1% (31 December 2013 est.)
country comparison to the world: 89
9.92% (31 December 2012 est.)

Stock of narrow money: $517.4 million (31 December 2013 est.)
country comparison to the world: 161
$490.5 million (31 December 2012 est.)

Stock of broad money: $1.488 billion (31 December 2013 est.)
country comparison to the world: 159
$1.461 billion (31 December 2012 est.)

Stock of domestic credit: $1.523 billion (31 December 2013 est.)
country comparison to the world: 144
$1.496 billion (31 December 2012 est.)

Current account balance: -$100 million (2013 est.)
country comparison to the world: 74
-$209.3 million (2012 est.)

Exports: $159.9 million (2013 est.)
country comparison to the world: 185
$173.1 million (2012 est.)

Exports—commodities: fuel, shoes, garments, fish, hides

Exports—partners: Spain 66.9%, Portugal 13.9%, US 5% (2012)

Imports: $796.3 million (2013 est.)
country comparison to the world: 184
$878.7 million (2012 est.)

Imports—commodities: foodstuffs, industrial products, transport equipment, fuels

Imports—partners: Portugal 38.1%, Netherlands 21.5%, China 7.9%, Spain 7% (2012)

Reserves of foreign exchange and gold: $426.2 million (31 December 2013 est.)
country comparison to the world: 149
$376 million (31 December 2012 est.)

Debt—external: $1.328 billion (31 December 2013 est.)
country comparison to the world: 153
$1.18 billion (31 December 2012 est.)

Exchange rates: Cabo Verdean escudos (CVE) per US dollar—
84.18 (2013 est.)
85.822 (2012 est.)
83.259 (2010 est.)
79.38 (2009)
73.84 (2008)

ENERGY

Electricity—production: 287 million kWh (2010 est.)
country comparison to the world: 174

Electricity—consumption: 266.9 million kWh (2010 est.)
country comparison to the world: 179

Electricity—exports: 0 kWh (2012 est.)
country comparison to the world: 125

Electricity—imports: 0 kWh (2012 est.)
country comparison to the world: 132

Electricity—installed generating capacity: 89,800 kW (2010 est.)
country comparison to the world: 174

Electricity—from fossil fuels: 96.9% of total installed capacity (2010 est.)
country comparison to the world: 64

Electricity—from nuclear fuels: 0% of total installed capacity (2010 est.)
country comparison to the world: 72

Electricity—from hydroelectric plants: 0% of total installed capacity (2010 est.)
country comparison to the world: 164

Electricity—from other renewable sources: 3.1% of total installed capacity (2010 est.)
country comparison to the world: 56

Crude oil—production: 0 bbl/day (2012 est.)
country comparison to the world: 163

Crude oil—exports: 0 bbl/day (2010 est.)
country comparison to the world: 101

Crude oil—imports: 0 bbl/day (2010 est.)
country comparison to the world: 175

Crude oil—proved reserves: 0 bbl (1 January 2013 est.)
country comparison to the world: 120

Refined petroleum products—production: 0 bbl/day (2010 est.)
country comparison to the world: 134

Refined petroleum products—consumption: 2,608 bbl/day (2011 est.)
country comparison to the world: 186

Refined petroleum products—exports: 0 bbl/day (2010 est.)
country comparison to the world: 167

Refined petroleum products—imports: 2,646 bbl/day (2010 est.)
country comparison to the world: 175

Natural gas—production: 0 cu m (2011 est.)
country comparison to the world: 119

Natural gas—consumption: 0 cu m (2010 est.)
country comparison to the world: 135

Natural gas—exports: 0 cu m (2011 est.)
country comparison to the world: 86

Natural gas—imports: 0 cu m (2011 est.)
country comparison to the world: 181

Natural gas—proved reserves: 0 cu m (1 January 2013 es.)
country comparison to the world: 127

Carbon dioxide emissions from consumption of energy: 430,000 Mt (2011 est.)
country comparison to the world: 182

COMMUNICATIONS

Telephones—main lines in use: 70,200 (2012)
country comparison to the world: 155

Telephones—mobile cellular: 425,300 (2012)
country comparison to the world: 171

Telephone system: *general assessment:* effective system, extensive modernization from 1996-2000 following partial privatization in 1995
domestic: major service provider is Cabo Verde Telecom (CVT); fiber-optic ring, completed in 2001, links all islands providing Internet access and ISDN services; cellular service introduced in 1998; broadband services launched in 2004
international: country code—238; landing point for the Atlantis-2 fiber-optic transatlantic telephone cable that provides links to South America, Senegal, and Europe; HF radiotelephone to Senegal and Guinea-Bissau; satellite earth station—1 Intelsat (Atlantic Ocean) (2011)

Broadcast media: state-run TV and radio broadcast network plus a growing number of private broadcasters; Portuguese public TV and radio services for Africa are available; transmissions of a few international broadcasters are available (2007)

Internet country code: .cv

Internet hosts: 38 (2012)
country comparison to the world: 216

Internet users: 150,000 (2009)
country comparison to the world: 148

TRANSPORTATION

Airports: 9 (2013)
country comparison to the world: 157

Airports—with paved runways: *total:* 9
over 3,047 m: 1
1,524 to 2,437 m: 3
914 to 1,523 m: 3
under 914 m: 2 (2013)

Roadways: *total:* 1,350 km
country comparison to the world: 179
paved: 932 km
unpaved: 418 km (2013)

Merchant marine: *total:* 13
country comparison to the world: 104
by type: cargo 3, chemical tanker 2, passenger/cargo 7, petroleum tanker 1
foreign-owned: 3 (Greece 1, Spain 1, UK 1)
registered in other countries: 1 (unknown 1) (2010)

Ports and terminals: *major seaport(s):* Porto Grande

MILITARY

Military branches: *Armed Forces:* Army (also called the National Guard, GN), Cabo Verde Coast Guard (Guardia Costeira de Cabo Verde, GCCV; includes naval infantry) (2013)

Military service age and obligation: 18-35 years of age for male and female selective compulsory military service; conscript service obligation—2 years; 17 years of age for voluntary service (with parental consent) (2013)

Manpower available for military service: *males age 16-49:* 132,087
females age 16-49: 136,956 (2010 est.)

Manpower fit for military service: *males age 16-49:* 106,864
females age 16-49: 117,518 (2010 est.)

Manpower reaching militarily significant age annually: *male:* 6,029
female: 6,026 (2010 est.)

Military expenditures: NA% (2012)
0.51% of GDP (2011)
NA% (2010)

TRANSNATIONAL ISSUES

Disputes—international: none

Illicit drugs: used as a transshipment point for Latin American cocaine destined for Western Europe, particularly because of Lusophone links to Brazil, Portugal, and Guinea-Bissau; has taken steps to deter drug money laundering, including a 2002 anti-money laundering reform that criminalizes laundering the proceeds of narcotics trafficking and other crimes and the establishment in 2008 of a Financial Intelligence Unit (2008)

CAMBODIA

Background: Most Cambodians consider themselves to be Khmers, descendants of the Angkor Empire that extended over much of Southeast Asia and reached its zenith between the 10th and 13th centuries. Attacks by the Thai and Cham (from present-day Vietnam) weakened the empire, ushering in a long period of decline. The king placed the country under French protection in 1863, and it became part of French Indochina in 1887. Following Japanese occupation in World War II, Cambodia gained full independence from France in 1953. In April 1975, after a five-year struggle, communist Khmer Rouge forces captured Phnom Penh and evacuated all cities and towns. At least 1.5 million Cambodians died from execution, forced hardships, or starvation during the Khmer Rouge regime under POL POT. A December 1978 Vietnamese invasion drove the Khmer Rouge into the countryside, began a 10-year Vietnamese occupation, and touched off almost 13 years of civil war. The 1991 Paris Peace Accords mandated democratic elections and a ceasefire, which was not fully respected by the Khmer Rouge. UN-sponsored elections in 1993 helped restore some semblance of normalcy under a coalition government. Factional fighting in 1997 ended the first coalition government, but a second round of national elections in 1998 led to the formation of another coalition government and renewed political stability. The remaining elements of the Khmer Rouge surrendered in early 1999. Some of the surviving Khmer Rouge leaders have been tried or are awaiting trial for crimes against humanity by a hybrid UN-Cambodian tribunal supported by international assistance. Elections in July 2003 were relatively peaceful, but it took one year of negotiations between contending political parties before a coalition government was formed. In October 2004, King Norodom SIHANOUK abdicated the throne and his son, Prince Norodom SIHAMONI, was selected to succeed him. Local elections were held in Cambodia in April 2007, with little of the pre-election violence that preceded prior elections. National elections in July 2008 were relatively peaceful, as were commune council elections in June 2012.

GEOGRAPHY

Location: Southeastern Asia, bordering the Gulf of Thailand, between Thailand, Vietnam, and Laos

Geographic coordinates: 13 00 N, 105 00 E

Map references: Southeast Asia

Area: total: 181,035 sq km
country comparison to the world: 90
land: 176,515 sq km
water: 4,520 sq km

Area—comparative: slightly smaller than Oklahoma

Land boundaries: total: 2,572 km
border countries: Laos 541 km, Thailand 803 km, Vietnam 1,228 km

Coastline: 443 km

Maritime claims: *territorial sea:* 12 nm
contiguous zone: 24 nm
exclusive economic zone: 200 nm
continental shelf: 200 nm

Climate: tropical; rainy, monsoon season (May to November); dry season (December to April); little seasonal temperature variation

Terrain: mostly low, flat plains; mountains in southwest and north

Elevation extremes: *lowest point:* Gulf of Thailand 0 m
highest point: Phnum Aoral 1,810 m

Natural resources: oil and gas, timber, gemstones, iron ore, manganese, phosphates, hydropower potential

Land use: arable land: 22.09%
permanent crops: 0.86%
other: 77.05% (2011)

Irrigated land: 3,536 sq km (2006)

Total renewable water resources: 476.1 cu km (2011)

Freshwater withdrawal (domestic/industrial/agricultural): total: 2.18 cu km/yr (4%/2%/94%)
per capita: 159.8 cu m/yr (2006)

Natural hazards: monsoonal rains (June to November); flooding; occasional droughts

Environment—current issues: illegal logging activities throughout the country and strip mining for gems in the western region along the border with Thailand have resulted in habitat loss and declining biodiversity (in particular, destruction of mangrove swamps threatens natural fisheries); soil erosion; in rural areas, most of the population does not have access to potable water; declining fish stocks because of illegal fishing and overfishing

Environment—international agreements: *party to:* Biodiversity, Climate Change, Climate Change-Kyoto Protocol, Desertification, Endangered Species, Hazardous Wastes, Marine Life Conservation, Ozone Layer Protection, Ship Pollution, Tropical Timber 94, Wetlands, Whaling
signed, but not ratified: Law of the Sea

Geography—note: a land of paddies and forests dominated by the Mekong River and Tonle Sap (Southeast Asia's largest freshwater lake)

PEOPLE AND SOCIETY

Nationality: noun: Cambodian(s)
adjective: Cambodian

Ethnic groups: Khmer 90%, Vietnamese 5%, Chinese 1%, other 4%

Languages: Khmer (official) 96.3%, other 3.7% (2008 est.)

Religions: Buddhist (official) 96.9%, Muslim 1.9%, Christian 0.4%, other 0.8% (2008 est.)

Population: 15,458,332 (July 2014 est.)
country comparison to the world: 69
note: estimates for this country take into account the effects of excess mortality due to AIDS; this can result in lower life expectancy, higher infant mortality, higher death rates, lower population growth rates, and changes in the distribution of population by age and sex than would otherwise be expected

Age structure: 0-14 years: 31.6% (male 2,460,659/female 2,423,619)
15-24 years: 20.5% (male 1,565,135/female 1,596,099)
25-54 years: 38.9% (male 2,938,366/female 3,082,496)
55-64 years: 4% (male 298,733/female 482,588)
65 years and over: 3.9% (male 229,684/female 380,953) (2014 est.)

Dependency ratios: *total dependency ratio:* 57.3%
youth dependency ratio: 48.9%
elderly dependency ratio: 8.4%
potential support ratio: 11.9 (2013)

Median age: *total:* 24.1 years
male: 23.4 years
female: 24.8 years (2014 est.)

Population growth rate: 1.63% (2014 est.)
country comparison to the world: 75

Birth rate: 24.4 births/1,000 population (2014 est.)
country comparison to the world: 60

Death rate: 7.78 deaths/1,000 population (2014 est.)
country comparison to the world: 108

Net migration rate: -0.32 migrant(s)/1,000 population (2014 est.)
country comparison to the world: 127

Urbanization: urban population: 20% of total population (2011)
rate of urbanization: 2.13% annual rate of change (2010-15 est.)

Major urban areas—population: PHNOM PENH (capital) 1.55 million (2011)

Sex ratio: at birth: 1.05 male(s)/female
0-14 years: 1.02 male(s)/female
15-24 years: 0.98 male(s)/female
25-54 years: 0.95 male(s)/female
55-64 years: 0.94 male(s)/female
65 years and over: 0.6 male(s)/female
total population: 0.94 male(s)/female (2014 est.)

Mother's mean age at first birth: 22.8
note: median age at first birth among women 25-29 (2010 est.)

Maternal mortality rate: 250 deaths/100,000 live births (2010)
country comparison to the world: 45

Infant mortality rate: *total:* 51.36 deaths/1,000 live births
country comparison to the world: 36
male: 58.1 deaths/1,000 live births
female: 44.31 deaths/1,000 live births (2014 est.)

Life expectancy at birth: *total population:* 63.78 years
country comparison to the world: 179
male: 61.35 years
female: 66.32 years (2014 est.)

Total fertility rate: 2.66 children born/woman (2014 est.)
country comparison to the world: 74

Contraceptive prevalence rate: 50.5% (2010/11)

Health expenditures: 5.7% of GDP (2011)
country comparison to the world: 118

Physicians density: 0.23 physicians/1,000 population (2008)

Hospital bed density: 0.7 beds/1,000 population (2011)

Drinking water source:
Improved:
urban: 89.6% of population
rural: 61.5% of population
total: 67.1% of population
Unimproved:
urban: 10.4% of population
rural: 38.5% of population
total: 32.9% of population (2011 est.)

Sanitation facility access:
Improved:
urban: 76.4% of population
rural: 22.3% of population
total: 33.1% of population

unimproved:
urban: 23.6% of population
rural: 77.7% of population
total: 66.9% of population (2011 est.)

HIV/AIDS—adult prevalence rate: 0.8% (2012 est.)
country comparison to the world: 53

HIV/AIDS—people living with HIV/AIDS: 76,400 (2012 est.)
country comparison to the world: 50

HIV/AIDS—deaths: 2,700 (2012 est.)
country comparison to the world: 54

Major infectious diseases: *degree of risk:* very high
food or waterborne diseases: bacterial diarrhea, hepatitis A, and typhoid fever
vectorborne diseases: dengue fever, Japanese encephalitis, and malaria
note: highly pathogenic H5N1 avian influenza has been identified in this country; it poses a negligible risk with extremely rare cases possible among US citizens who have close contact with birds (2013)

Obesity—adult prevalence rate: 2.1% (2008)
country comparison to the world: 183

Children under the age of 5 years underweight: 29% (2011)
country comparison to the world: 20

Education expenditures: 2.6% of GDP (2010)
country comparison to the world: 152

Literacy: *definition:* age 15 and over can read and write
total population: 73.9%
male: 82.8%
female: 65.9% (2009 est.)

School life expectancy (primary to tertiary education): *total:* 11 years
male: 12 years
female: 10 years (2008)

Child labor—children ages 5-14:
total number: 1,345,269
percentage: 39 % (2001 est.)

Unemployment, youth ages 15-24: *total:* 3.4%
country comparison to the world: 141
male: 3.5%
female: 3.3% (2008)

GOVERNMENT

Country name: *conventional long form:* Kingdom of Cambodia
conventional short form: Cambodia
local long form: Preahreacheanachakr Kampuchea (phonetic pronunciation)
local short form: Kampuchea
former: Khmer Republic, Democratic Kampuchea, People's Republic of Kampuchea, State of Cambodia

Government type: multiparty democracy under a constitutional monarchy

Capital: *name:* Phnom Penh
geographic coordinates: 11 33 N, 104 55 E
time difference: UTC+7 (12 hours ahead of Washington, DC during Standard Time)

Administrative divisions: 23 provinces (khett, singular and plural) and 1 municipality (krong, singular and plural)
provinces: Banteay Meanchey, Battambang, Kampong Cham, Kampong Chhnang, Kampong Speu, Kampong Thom, Kampot, Kandal, Kep, Koh Kong, Kratie, Mondolkiri, Oddar Meanchey, Pailin, Preah Vihear, Prey Veng, Pursat, Ratanakiri, Siem Reap, Sihanoukville, Stung Treng, Svay Rieng, Takeo
municipalities: Phnom Penh (Phnum Penh)

Independence: 9 November 1953 (from France)

National holiday: Independence Day, 9 November (1953)

Constitution: previous 1947; latest promulgated 21 September 1993; amended 1999, 2008 (2008)

Legal system: civil law system (influenced by the UN Transitional Authority in Cambodia) customary law, Communist legal theory, and common law

International law organization participation: accepts compulsory ICJ jurisdiction with reservations; accepts ICCt jurisdiction

Suffrage: 18 years of age; universal

Executive branch: *chief of state:* King Norodom SIHAMONI (since 29 October 2004)
head of government: Prime Minister HUN SEN (since 14 January 1985) [co-prime minister from 1993 to 1997]; Permanent Deputy Prime Minister MEN SAM AN (since 25 September 2008); Deputy Prime Ministers SAR KHENG (since 3 February 1992); SOK AN, TEA BANH, HOR NAMHONG, NHEK BUNCHHAY (since 16 July 2004); BIN CHHIN (since 5 September 2007); KEAT CHHON, YIM CHHAI LY (since 24 September 2008); KE KIMYAN (since 12 March 2009)
cabinet: Council of Ministers named by the prime minister and appointed by the monarch (For more information visit the World Leaders website)
elections: the king chosen by a Royal Throne Council from among all eligible males of royal descent; following legislative elections, a member of the majority party or majority coalition named prime minister by the Chairman of the National Assembly and appointed by the king

Legislative branch: bicameral, consists of the Senate (61 seats; 2 members appointed by the monarch, 2 elected by the National Assembly, and 57 elected by parliamentarians and commune councils; members serve five-year terms) and the National Assembly (123 seats; members elected by popular vote to serve five-year terms)
elections: Senate—last held on 4 February 2012 (next to be held in February 2018); National Assembly—last held on 28 July 2013 (next to be held in July 2018)
election results: Senate—percent of vote by party—CPP 77.8%, CNRP (SRP) 22.2%; seats by party—CPP 46, CNRP (SRP) 11; National Assembly—percent of vote by party—CPP 48.8%, NRP 44.5%, FUNCINPEC 3.9%, others 2.8%; seats by party—CPP 68, CNRP 55

Judicial branch: *highest court(s):* Supreme Court (organized into 5—and 9-judge panels and includes a court chief and deputy chief); Constitutional Court (consists of 9 members)note—in 1997, the Cambodian Government requested UN assistance in establishing trials to prosecute former Khmer Rouge senior leaders for crimes against humanity committed during the 1975-1979 Khmer Rouge regime; the Extraordinary Chambers of the Courts in Cambodia were established and began hearings for the first case in 2009
judge selection and term of office: Supreme Court and Constitutional Court judge candidates recommended by the Supreme Council of Magistracy, a 9-member body chaired by the monarch and includes other high-level judicial officers; judges of both courts appointed by the monarch; Supreme Court judge tenure NA; Constitutional Court judges appointed for 9-year terms with one-third of the court renewed every 3 years
subordinate courts: municipal and provincial courts; appellate courts; military court

Political parties and leaders: Cambodian People's Party or CPP [CHEA SIM]; Cambodian National Rescue Party or SRP [SAM RANGSI also spelled SAM RAINSY]; National United Front for an Independent, Neutral, Peaceful, and Cooperative Cambodia or FUNCINPEC [KEV PUT REAKSMEI]; Nationalist Party or NP former Norodom Ranariddh Party or NRP [SAO RANY]
note: the CNRP is a merger between the former Human Rights Party or HRP [KHEM SOKHA, also spelled KEM SOKHA] and the Sam Rangsi Party or SRP

Political pressure groups and leaders: Cambodian Freedom Fighters or CFF; Partnership for Transparency Fund or PTF (anti-corruption organization); Students Movement for Democracy; The Committee for Free and Fair Elections or Comfrel
other: human rights organizations; vendors

International organization participation: ADB, ARF, ASEAN, CICA, CICA (observer), EAS, FAO, G-77, IAEA, IBRD, ICAO, ICRM, IDA, IFAD, IFC, IFRCS, ILO, IMF, IMO, Interpol, IOC, IOM, IPU, ISO (correspondent), ITU, MIGA, MINUSMA, NAM, OIF, OPCW, PCA, UN, UNCTAD, UNESCO, UNIDO, UNIFIL, UNMISS, UNWTO, UPU, WCO, WFTU (NGOs), WHO, WIPO, WMO, WTO

Diplomatic representation in the US: *chief of mission:* Ambassador HENG HEM (since 29 January 2009)
chancery: 4530 16th Street NW, Washington, DC 20011
telephone: [1] (202) 726-7742
FAX: [1] (202) 726-8381

Diplomatic representation from the US: *chief of mission:* Ambassador William E. TODD (since 17 April 2012)
embassy: #1, Street 96, Sangkat Wat Phnom, Khan Daun Penh, Phnom Penh
mailing address: Box P, APO AP 96546
telephone: [855] (23) 728-000
FAX: [855] (23) 728-600

Flag description: three horizontal bands of blue (top), red (double width), and blue with a white three-towered temple representing Angkor Wat outlined in black in the center of the red band; red and blue are traditional Cambodian colors
note: only national flag to incorporate an actual building in its design

National symbol(s): Angkor Wat temple; kouprey (wild ox)

National anthem: *name:* "Nokoreach" (Royal Kingdom)
lyrics/music: CHUON NAT/F. PERRUCHOT and J. JEKYLL
note: adopted 1941, restored 1993; the anthem, based on a Cambodian folk tune, was restored after the defeat of the Communist regime

ECONOMY

Economy—overview: Since 2004, garments, construction, agriculture, and tourism have driven Cambodia's growth. GDP climbed more than 7% per year between 2010 and 2013. The garment industry currently employs more about 400,000 people and accounts for about 70% of Cambodia's total exports. In 2005, exploitable oil deposits were found beneath Cambodia's territorial waters, representing a potential revenue stream for the government, if commercial extraction becomes feasible. Mining also is attracting some investor interest and the government has touted opportunities for mining bauxite, gold, iron and gems. The tourism industry has continued to grow rapidly with foreign arrivals exceeding 2 million per year since 2007 and reaching over 3 million visitors in 2012. Cambodia, nevertheless, remains one of the poorest countries in Asia and long-term economic development remains a daunting challenge, inhibited by endemic corruption, limited educational opportunities, high income inequality, and poor job prospects. Approximately 4 million people live on less than $1.25 per day, and 37% of Cambodian children under the age of 5 suffer from chronic malnutrition. More than 50% of the population is less than 25 years old. The population lacks education and productive skills, particularly in the impoverished countryside, which also lacks basic infrastructure. The Cambodian government is working with bilateral and multilateral donors, including the Asian Development Bank, the World Bank and IMF, to address the country's many pressing needs; more than 50% of the government budget comes from donor assistance. The major economic challenge for Cambodia over the next decade will be fashioning an economic environment in which the private sector can create enough jobs to handle Cambodia's demographic imbalance.

GDP (purchasing power parity): $39.64 billion (2013 est.)
country comparison to the world: 107
$37.04 billion (2012 est.)
$34.52 billion (2011 est.)
note: data are in 2013 US dollars

GDP (official exchange rate): $15.64 billion (2013 est.)

GDP—real growth rate: 7% (2013 est.)
country comparison to the world: 21
7.3% (2012 est.)
7.1% (2011 est.)

GDP—per capita (PPP): $2,600 (2013 est.)
country comparison to the world: 183
$2,400 (2012 est.)
$2,300 (2011 est.)
note: data are in 2013 US dollars

Gross national saving: 9.6% of GDP (2013 est.)
country comparison to the world: 138
9.1% of GDP (2012 est.)
12% of GDP (2011 est.)

GDP— composition, by end use:
household consumption: 74.7%
government consumption: 7.7%
investment in fixed capital: 16.4% investment in inventories: 2.1%
exports of goods and services: 65.3%
imports of goods and services: -66.2% (2013 est.)

GDP—composition, by sector of origin:
agriculture: 34.8%
industry: 24.5%
services: 40.7% (2013 est.)

Agriculture—products: rice, rubber, corn, vegetables, cashews, cassava (manioc), silk

Industries: tourism, garments, construction, rice milling, fishing, wood and wood products, rubber, cement, gem mining, textiles

Industrial production growth rate: 9.5% (2013 est.)
country comparison to the world: 17

Labor force: 7.9 million (2011 est.)
country comparison to the world: 60

Labor force—by occupation: *agriculture:* 55.8%
industry: 16.9%
services: 27.3% (2010 est.)

Unemployment rate: 0% (2011 est.)
country comparison to the world: 1
0.3% (2010 est.)

Population below poverty line: 20% (2012 est.)

Household income or consumption by percentage share: lowest 10%: 3%
highest 10%: 37.3% (2007)

Distribution of family income—Gini index: 37.9 (2008 est.)
country comparison to the world: 73
41.9 (2004 est.)

Budget: *revenues:* $2.685 billion
expenditures: $3.1 billion (2013 est.)

Taxes and other revenues: 17.2% of GDP (2013 est.)
country comparison to the world: 181

Budget surplus (+) or deficit (-): -2.7% of GDP (2013 est.)
country comparison to the world: 111

Public debt: NA% of GDP

Fiscal year: calendar year

Inflation rate (consumer prices): 3.2% (2013 est.)
country comparison to the world: 118
2.9% (2012 est.)

Central bank discount rate: NA% (31 December 2012)
country comparison to the world: 68
5.25% (31 December 2007)

Commercial bank prime lending rate: 13% (31 December 2013 est.)
country comparison to the world: 61
12.98% (31 December 2012 est.)

Stock of narrow money: $1.206 billion (31 December 2013 est.)
country comparison to the world: 145
$995.1 million (31 December 2012 est.)

Stock of broad money: $8.373 billion (31 December 2013 est.)
country comparison to the world: 109
$7.1 billion (31 December 2012 est.)

Stock of domestic credit: $5.705 billion (31 December 2013 est.)
country comparison to the world: 112
$4.801 billion (31 December 2012 est.)

Market value of publicly traded shares: $NA

Current account balance: -$1.262 billion (2013 est.)
country comparison to the world: 126
-$1.208 billion (2012 est.)

Exports: $6.781 billion (2013 est.)
country comparison to the world: 104
$6.016 billion (2012 est.)

Exports—commodities: clothing, timber, rubber, rice, fish, tobacco, footwear

Exports—partners: US 32.6%, UK 8.3%, Germany 7.7%, Canada 7.7%, Singapore 6.6%, Vietnam 5.7%, Japan 4.7% (2012)

Imports: $8.895 billion (2013 est.)
country comparison to the world: 106
$7.965 billion (2012 est.)

Imports—commodities: petroleum products, cigarettes, gold, construction materials, machinery, motor vehicles, pharmaceutical products

Imports—partners: Thailand 27.1%, Vietnam 20.3%, China 19.5%, Singapore 7.1%, Hong Kong 5.8%, South Korea 4.3% (2012)

Reserves of foreign exchange and gold: $5.415 billion (31 December 2013 est.)
country comparison to the world: 93
$4.938 billion (31 December 2012 est.)

Debt—external: $4.912 billion (31 December 2013 est.)
country comparison to the world: 123
$4.567 billion (31 December 2012 est.)

Exchange rates: riels (KHR) per US dollar—
4,037.6 (2013 est.)
4,033 (2012 est.)
4,184.9 (2010 est.)
4,139 (2009)
4,070.94 (2008)

ENERGY

Electricity—production: 1.019 billion kWh (2011 est.)
country comparison to the world: 144

Electricity—consumption: 2.573 billion kWh (2011 est.)
country comparison to the world: 134

Electricity—exports: 0 kWh (2012 est.)
country comparison to the world: 113

Electricity—imports: 1.83 billion kWh (2011 est.)
country comparison to the world: 55

Electricity—installed generating capacity: 359,900 kW (2010 est.)
country comparison to the world: 148

Electricity—from fossil fuels: 94.8% of total installed capacity (2010 est.)
country comparison to the world: 69

Electricity—from nuclear fuels: 0% of total installed capacity (2010 est.)
country comparison to the world: 59

Electricity—from hydroelectric plants: 3.6% of total installed capacity (2010 est.)
country comparison to the world: 126

Electricity—from other renewable sources: 1.6% of total installed capacity (2010 est.)
country comparison to the world: 76

Crude oil—production: 0.5 bbl/day (2012 est.)
country comparison to the world: 132

Crude oil—exports: 0 bbl/day (2010 est.)
country comparison to the world: 94

Crude oil—imports: 0 bbl/day (2010 est.)
country comparison to the world: 168

Crude oil—proved reserves: 0 bbl (1 January 2013 es.)
country comparison to the world: 113

Refined petroleum products—production: 0 bbl/day (2010 est.)
country comparison to the world: 128

Refined petroleum products—consumption: 39,350 bbl/day (2011 est.)
country comparison to the world: 108

Refined petroleum products—exports: 0 bbl/day (2010 est.)
country comparison to the world: 160

Refined petroleum products—imports: 26,250 bbl/day (2010 est.)
country comparison to the world: 96

Natural gas—production: 0 cu m (2011 est.)
country comparison to the world: 110

Natural gas—consumption: 0 cu m (2010 est.)
country comparison to the world: 126

Natural gas—exports: 0 cu m (2011 est.)
country comparison to the world: 74

Natural gas—imports: 0 cu m (2011 est.)
country comparison to the world: 169

Natural gas—proved reserves: 0 cu m (1 January 2013 es.)
country comparison to the world: 120

Carbon dioxide emissions from consumption of energy: 4.39 million Mt (2011 est.)
country comparison to the world: 130

COMMUNICATIONS

Telephones—main lines in use: 584,000 (2012)
country comparison to the world: 93

Telephones—mobile cellular: 19.1 million (2012)
country comparison to the world: 53

Telephone system: *general assessment:* adequate fixed-line and/or cellular service in Phnom Penh and other provincial cities; mobile-cellular phone systems are widely used in urban areas to bypass deficiencies in the fixed-line network; mobile-phone coverage is rapidly expanding in rural areas
domestic: fixed-line connections stand at about 4 per 100 persons; mobile-cellular usage, aided by competition among service providers, is increasing rapidly and stands at 92 per 100 persons
international: country code—855; adequate but expensive landline and cellular service available to all countries from Phnom Penh and major provincial cities; satellite earth station—1 Intersputnik (Indian Ocean region) (2011)

Broadcast media: mixture of state-owned, joint public-private, and privately owned broadcast media; 9 TV broadcast stations with most operating on multiple channels, including 1 state-operated station broadcasting from multiple locations, 6 stations either jointly operated or privately owned with some broadcasting from several locations, and 2 TV relay stations—one relaying a French TV station and the other relaying a Vietnamese TV station; multi-channel cable and satellite systems are available; roughly 50 radio broadcast stations—1 state-owned broadcaster with multiple stations and a large mixture of public and private broadcasters; several international broadcasters are available (2009)

Internet country code: .kh

Internet hosts: 13,784 (2012)
country comparison to the world: 129

Internet users: 78,500 (2009)
country comparison to the world: 167

TRANSPORTATION

Airports: 16 (2013)
country comparison to the world: 142

Airports—with paved runways: *total:* 6
2,438 to 3,047 m: 3
1,524 to 2,437 m: 2
914 to 1,523 m: 1 (2013)

Airports—with unpaved runways: *total:* 10
1,524 to 2,437 m: 2
914 to 1,523 m: 7
under 914 m: 1 (2013)

Heliports: 1 (2013)

Railways: *total:* 690 km
country comparison to the world: 101
narrow gauge: 690 km 1.000-m gauge
note: under restoration (2010)

Roadways: *total:* 39,618 km
country comparison to the world: 88
paved: 2,492 km
unpaved: 37,126 km (2009)

Waterways: 3,700 km (mainly on Mekong River) (2012)
country comparison to the world: 29

Merchant marine: *total:* 544
country comparison to the world: 21
by type: bulk carrier 38, cargo 459, carrier 7, chemical tanker 4, container 4, liquefied gas 1, passenger 1, passenger/cargo 6, petroleum tanker 8, refrigerated cargo 11, roll on/roll off 4, vehicle carrier 1
foreign-owned: 352 (Belgium 1, Canada 2, China 177, Cyprus 4, Egypt 4, Estonia 1, French Polynesia 1, Gabon 1, Greece 2, Hong Kong 10, Indonesia 2, Ireland 1, Japan 1, Lebanon 5, Russia 50, Singapore 3, South Korea 10, Syria 22, Taiwan 1, Turkey 15, UAE 2, UK 1, Ukraine 35, Vietnam 1) (2010)

Ports and terminals: *major seaport(s):* Sihanoukville (Kampong Saom)
river port(s): Phnom Penh (Mekong)

MILITARY

Military branches: *Royal Cambodian Armed Forces:* Royal Cambodian Army, Royal Khmer Navy, Royal Cambodian Air Force (2013)

Military service age and obligation: 18 is the legal minimum age for compulsory and voluntary military service (2012)

Manpower available for military service:
males age 16-49: 3,883,724
females age 16-49: 4,003,585 (2010 est.)

Manpower fit for military service: *males age 16-49:* 2,638,167
females age 16-49: 2,965,328 (2010 est.)

Manpower reaching militarily significant age annually:
male: 151,143
female: 154,542 (2010 est.)

Military expenditures: 1.54% of GDP (2012)
country comparison to the world: 60
1.5% of GDP (2011)
1.54% of GDP (2010)

TRANSNATIONAL ISSUES

Disputes—international: Cambodia is concerned about Laos' extensive upstream dam construction; Cambodia and Thailand dispute sections of boundary; in 2011 Thailand and Cambodia resorted to arms in the dispute over the location of the boundary on the precipice surmounted by Preah Vihear Temple ruins, awarded to Cambodia by ICJ decision in 1962 and part of a UN World Heritage site; Cambodia accuses Vietnam of a wide variety of illicit cross-border activities; progress on a joint development area with Vietnam is hampered by an unresolved dispute over sovereignty of offshore islands

Trafficking in persons: *current situation:* Cambodia is a source, transit, and destination country for men, women, and children subjected to forced labor and sex trafficking; Cambodian men, women, and children migrate to countries within the region for legitimate work but are subsequently subjected to sex trafficking, domestic servitude,debt bondage, or forced labor; the inability to understand formal obligations, read contracts, or pay processing fees, and inadequate government regulatory oversight renders some Cambodian migrant workers vulnerable to such exploitation; poor Cambodian children are subject to forced labor, including forced begging in Thailand and Vietnam; Cambodian and ethnic Vietnamese women and girls are trafficked from rural areas to urban centers for sexual exploitation; Cambodian men are the main exploiters of child prostitutes, but men from other Asian countries, the US, and Europe travel to Cambodia for child sex tourism

tier rating: Tier 2 Watch List—Cambodia does not fully comply with the minimum standards for the elimination of trafficking; however, it is making significant efforts to do so; the government has prosecuted and convicted fewer trafficking offenders and identified fewer victims than in the previous year; corruption continues to impede anti-trafficking endeavors; authorities systematically refer identified victims to NGO shelters, which provide the majority of services but lack long-term care services, making victims, particularly children, vulnerable to re-trafficking; the government has established a migration working group within its anti-trafficking committee to better address the exploitation of Cambodian workers abroad, but laws governing migrant workers abroad remain weak (2013)

Illicit drugs: narcotics-related corruption reportedly involving some in the government, military, and police; limited methamphetamine production; vulnerable to money laundering due to its cash-based economy and porous borders

CAMEROON

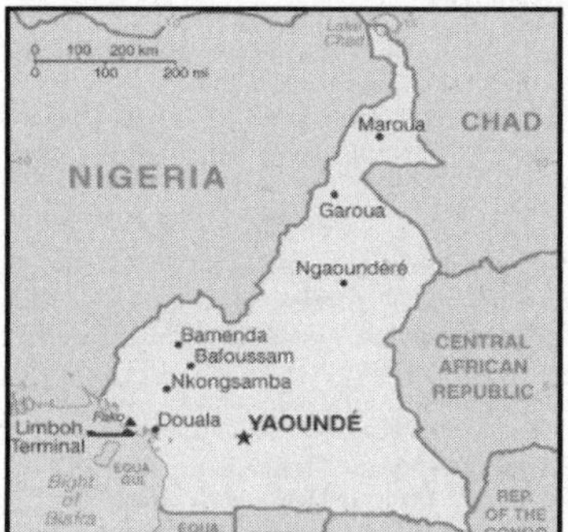

INTRODUCTION

Background: French Cameroon became independent in 1960 as the Republic of Cameroon. The following year the southern portion of neighboring British Cameroon voted to merge with the new country to form the Federal Republic of Cameroon. In 1972, a new constitution replaced the federation with a unitary state, the United Republic of Cameroon. The country has generally enjoyed stability, which has permitted the development of agriculture, roads, and railways, as well as a petroleum industry. Despite slow movement toward democratic reform, political power remains firmly in the hands of President Paul BIYA.

GEOGRAPHY

Location: Central Africa, bordering the Bight of Biafra, between Equatorial Guinea and Nigeria

Geographic coordinates: 6 00 N, 12 00 E

Map references: Africa

Area: *total:* 475,440 sq km
country comparison to the world: 54
land: 472,710 sq km
water: 2,730 sq km

Area—comparative: slightly larger than California

Land boundaries: *total:* 4,591 km
border countries: Central African Republic 797 km, Chad 1,094 km, Republic of the Congo 523 km,

Equatorial Guinea 189 km, Gabon 298 km, Nigeria 1,690 km

Coastline: 402 km

Maritime claims: *territorial sea:* 12 nm
contiguous zone: 24 nm

Climate: varies with terrain, from tropical along coast to semiarid and hot in north

Terrain: diverse, with coastal plain in southwest, dissected plateau in center, mountains in west, plains in north

Elevation extremes: *lowest point:* Atlantic Ocean 0 m
highest point: Fako 4,095 m (on Mt. Cameroon)

Natural resources: petroleum, bauxite, iron ore, timber, hydropower

Land use: *arable land:* 13.04%
permanent crops: 2.94%
other: 84.01% (2011)

Irrigated land: 256.5 sq km (2003)

Total renewable water resources: 285.5 cu km (2011)

Freshwater withdrawal (domestic/industrial/agricultural): *total:* 0.97 cu km/yr (23%/10%/68%)
per capita: 58.9 cu m/yr (2005)

Natural hazards: volcanic activity with periodic releases of poisonous gases from Lake Nyos and Lake Monoun volcanoes
volcanism: Mt. Cameroon (elev. 4,095 m), which last erupted in 2000, is the most frequently active volcano in West Africa; lakes in Oku volcanic field have released fatal levels of gas on occasion, killing some 1,700 people in 1986

Environment—current issues: waterborne diseases are prevalent; deforestation; overgrazing; desertification; poaching; overfishing

Environment—international agreements: *party to:* Biodiversity, Climate Change, Climate Change-Kyoto Protocol, Desertification, Endangered Species, Hazardous Wastes, Law of the Sea, Ozone Layer Protection, Tropical Timber 83, Tropical Timber 94, Wetlands, Whaling
signed, but not ratified: none of the selected agreements

Geography—note: sometimes referred to as the hinge of Africa; throughout the country there are areas of thermal springs and indications of current or prior volcanic activity; Mount Cameroon, the highest mountain in Sub-Saharan west Africa, is an active volcano

PEOPLE AND SOCIETY

Nationality: *noun:* Cameroonian(s)
adjective: Cameroonian

Ethnic groups: Cameroon Highlanders 31%, Equatorial Bantu 19%, Kirdi 11%, Fulani 10%, Northwestern Bantu 8%, Eastern Nigritic 7%, other African 13%, non-African less than 1%

Languages: 24 major African language groups, English (official), French (official)

Religions: indigenous beliefs 40%, Christian 40%, Muslim 20%

Population: 23,130,708 (July 2014 est.)
country comparison to the world: 54
note: estimates for this country explicitly take into account the effects of excess mortality due to AIDS; this can result in lower life expectancy, higher infant mortality, higher death rates, lower population growth rates, and changes in the distribution of population by age and sex than would otherwise be expected

Age structure: *0-14 years:* 42.9% (male 5,001,984/female 4,927,122)
15-24 years: 19.6% (male 2,286,244/female 2,257,231)
25-54 years: 30.4% (male 3,529,203/female 3,491,125)
55-64 years: 3.1% (male 445,181/female 468,388)
65 years and over: 3.4% (male 337,490/female 386,740) (2014 est.)

Dependency ratios: *total dependency ratio:* 85.8 %
youth dependency ratio: 79.8%
elderly dependency ratio: 6%
potential support ratio: 16.7 (2013)

Median age: *total:* 18.3 years
male: 18.2 years
female: 18.4 years (2014 est.)

Population growth rate: 2.6% (2014 est.)
country comparison to the world: 26

Birth rate: 36.58 births/1,000 population (2014 est.)
country comparison to the world: 19

Death rate: 10.4 deaths/1,000 population (2014 est.)
country comparison to the world: 41

Net migration rate: -0.15 migrant(s)/1,000 population (2014 est.)
country comparison to the world: 118

Urbanization: *urban population:* 52.1% of total population (2011)
rate of urbanization: 3.23% annual rate of change (2010-15 est.)

Major urban areas—population: YAOUNDE (capital) 2.432 million; Douala 2.053 million (2011)

Sex ratio: *at birth:* 1.03 male(s)/female
0-14 years: 1.02 male(s)/female
15-24 years: 1.01 male(s)/female
25-54 years: 1.01 male(s)/female
55-64 years: 1.01 male(s)/female
65 years and over: 0.84 male(s)/female
total population: 1.01 male(s)/female (2014 est.)

Mother's mean age at first birth: 19.7
note: median age at first birth among women 25-29 (2011 est.)

Maternal mortality rate: 690 deaths/100,000 live births (2010)
country comparison to the world: 10

Infant mortality rate: *total:* 55.1 deaths/1,000 live births
country comparison to the world: 31
male: 58.78 deaths/1,000 live births
female: 51.31 deaths/1,000 live births (2014 est.)

Life expectancy at birth: *total population:* 57.35 years
country comparison to the world: 202
male: 56.09 years
female: 58.65 years (2014 est.)

Total fertility rate: 4.82 children born/woman (2014 est.)
country comparison to the world: 20

Contraceptive prevalence rate: 23.4% (2011)

Health expenditures: 5.2% of GDP (2011)
country comparison to the world: 137

Physicians density: 0.08 physicians/1,000 population (2009)

Hospital bed density: 1.3 beds/1,000 population (2010)

Drinking water source:
Improved:
urban: 94.9% of population
rural: 52.1% of population
total: 74.4% of population
unimproved:
urban: 5.1% of population
rural: 47.9% of population
total: 25.6% of population (2011 est.)

Sanitation facility access:
Improved:
urban: 58.3% of population
rural: 36.4% of population
total: 47.8% of population
unimproved:
urban: 41.7% of population
rural: 63.6% of population
total: 52.2% of population (2011 est.)

HIV/AIDS—adult prevalence rate: 4.5% (2012 est.)
country comparison to the world: 15

HIV/AIDS—people living with HIV/AIDS: 600,500 (2012 est.)
country comparison to the world: 16

HIV/AIDS—deaths: 34,600 (2012 est.)
country comparison to the world: 11

Major infectious diseases: *degree of risk:* very high
food or waterborne diseases: bacterial and protozoal diarrhea, hepatitis A, and typhoid fever
vectorborne diseases: malaria, dengue fever, and yellow fever
water contact disease: schistosomiasis
respiratory disease: meningococcal meningitis
animal contact disease: rabies (2013)

Obesity—adult prevalence rate: 10.3% (2008)
country comparison to the world: 130

Children under the age of 5 years underweight: 15.1% (2011)
country comparison to the world: 48

Education expenditures: 3.2% of GDP (2011)
country comparison to the world: 133

Literacy: *definition:* age 15 and over can read and write
total population: 71.3%
male: 78.3%
female: 64.8% (2010 est.)

School life expectancy (primary to tertiary education): *total:* 10 years
male: 11 years
female: 10 years (2011)

Child labor - children ages 5-14:
total number: 1,396,281
percentage: 31 % (2006 est.)

GOVERNMENT

Country name: *conventional long form:* Republic of Cameroon
conventional short form: Cameroon
local long form: Republique du Cameroun/Republic of Cameroon
local short form: Cameroun/Cameroon
former: French Cameroon, British Cameroon, Federal Republic of Cameroon, United Republic of Cameroon

Government type: republic; multiparty presidential regime

Capital: *name:* Yaounde
geographic coordinates: 3 52 N, 11 31 E
time difference: UTC+1 (6 hours ahead of Washington, DC during Standard Time)

Administrative divisions: 10 regions (regions, singular—region); Adamaoua, Centre, East (Est), Far North (Extreme-Nord), Littoral, North (Nord), North-West (Nord-Ouest), West (Ouest), South (Sud), South-West (Sud-Ouest)

Independence: 1 January 1960 (from French-administered UN trusteeship)

National holiday: Republic Day (National Day), 20 May (1972)

Constitution: several previous; latest effective 18 January 1996; amended 2008 (2008)

Legal system: mixed legal system of English common law, French civil law, and customary law

International law organization participation: accepts compulsory ICJ jurisdiction; non-party state to the ICCt

Suffrage: 20 years of age; universal

Executive branch: *chief of state:* President Paul BIYA (since 6 November 1982)
head of government: Prime Minister Philemon YANG (since 30 June 2009)
cabinet: Cabinet appointed by the president from proposals submitted by the prime minister (For more information visit the World Leaders website)
elections: president elected by popular vote for a seven-year term (with no term limits per 2008 constitutional amendment); election last held on 9 October 2011 (next to be held in October 2018); prime minister appointed by the president
election results: President Paul BIYA reelected; percent of vote—Paul BIYA 78.0%, John FRU NDI 10.7%, Garga Haman ADJI 3.2%, Adamou Ndam NJOYA 1.7%, Paul Abine AYAH 1.3%, other 5.1%

Legislative branch: bicameral legislature consisting of an upper house or Senate (100 seats; 70 indirectly elected by municipal councils, 30 appointed by the President) and a National Assembly or Assemblee Nationale (180 seats; members are elected by direct popular vote to serve five-year terms); note—the president can either lengthen or shorten the term of the legislature; a senate was initially designated in 1996 by constitutional amendment but was only convened following a presidential decree in 2013
elections: Senate last held on 14 April 2013 (next to be held NA); National Assembly last held on 30 September 2013 (next to be held in 2018)
election results: Senate percent of vote by party—NA; seats by party—CPDM 56, SDF 14; National Assembley percent of vote by party—NA; seats by party—CPDM 148, SDF 18, UNDP 5, UDC 4, UPC 3, other 2

Judicial branch: *highest court(s):* Supreme Court of Cameroon (consists of 9 titular and 6 surrogate judges and organized into judicial, administrative, and audit chambers); Constitutional Council (consists of 11 members)
judge selection and term of office: Supreme Court judges appointed by the president with the advice of the Higher Judicial Council of Cameroon (a body chaired by the president and includes the minister of justice, selected magistrates, and representatives of the National Assembly); judge term NA; Constitutional Council members appointed by the president for single 9-year terms
subordinate courts: Parliamentary Court of Justice (jurisdiction limited to cases involving the president and prime minister); appellate and first instance courts; circuit and magistrate's courts

Political parties and leaders: Cameroon People's Democratic Movement or CPDM [Paul BIYA]; Cameroon People's Party [Edith Kah WALLA]; Cameroonian Democratic Union or UDC [Adamou Ndam NJOYA]; Movement for the Defense of the Republic or MDR [Dakole DAISSALA]; Movement for the Liberation and Development of Cameroon or MLDC [Marcel YONDO]; National Union for Democracy and Progress or UNDP [Maigari BELLO BOUBA]; Progressive Movement or MP; Social Democratic Front or SDF [John FRU NDI]; Union of Peoples of Cameroon or UPC [Augustin Frederic KODOCK]

Political pressure groups and leaders: Human Rights Defense Group [Albert MUKONG, president]; Southern Cameroon National Council [Ayamba Ette OTUN]

International organization participation: ACP, AfDB, AU, BDEAC, C, CEMAC, EITI (candidate country), FAO, FZ, G-77, IAEA, IBRD, ICAO, ICC (national committees), ICRM, IDA, IDB, IFAD, IFC, IFRCS, IHO, ILO, IMF, IMO, IMSO, Interpol, IOC, IOM, IPU, ISO, ITSO, ITU, ITUC (NGOs), MIGA, MONUSCO, NAM, OIC, OIF, OPCW, PCA, UN, UNAMID, UNCTAD, UNESCO, UNHCR, UNIDO, UNWTO, UPU, WCO, WFTU (NGOs), WHO, WIPO, WMO, WTO

Diplomatic representation in the US: *chief of mission:* Ambassador Joseph FOE-ATANGANA (since 12 September 2008)
chancery: 2349 Massachusetts Avenue NW, Washington, DC 20008; current temporary address—3400 International Drive NW, Washington, DC 20008
telephone: [1] (202) 265-8790
FAX: [1] (202) 387-3826

Diplomatic representation from the US: *chief of mission:* Ambassador (vacant); Charge d'Affaires Gregory THOME
embassy: Avenue Rosa Parks, Yaounde
mailing address: P. O. Box 817, Yaounde; pouch: American Embassy, US Department of State, Washington, DC 20521-2520
telephone: [237] 2220 15 00; Consular: [237] 2220 16 03
FAX: [237] 2220 15 00 Ext. 4531; Consular FAX: [237] 2220 17 52
branch office(s): Douala

Flag description: three equal vertical bands of green (hoist side), red, and yellow, with a yellow five-pointed star centered in the red band; the vertical tricolor recalls the flag of France; red symbolizes unity, yellow the sun, happiness, and the savannahs in the north, and green hope and the forests in the south; the star is referred to as the "star of unity"
note: uses the popular Pan-African colors of Ethiopia

National symbol(s): lion

National anthem: *name:* "O Cameroun, Berceau de nos Ancetres" (O Cameroon, Cradle of Our Forefathers)
lyrics/music: Rene Djam AFAME, Samuel Minkio BAMBA, Moise Nyatte NKO'O [French], Benard Nsokika FONLON [English]/Rene Djam AFAME
note: adopted 1957; Cameroon's anthem, also known as "Chant de Ralliement" (The Rallying Song), has been used unofficially since 1948 and officially adopted in 1957; the anthem has French and English versions whose lyrics differ

ECONOMY

Economy—overview: Because of its modest oil resources and favorable agricultural conditions, Cameroon has one of the best-endowed primary commodity economies in sub-Saharan Africa. Still, it faces many of the serious problems confronting other underdeveloped countries, such as stagnant per capita income, a relatively inequitable distribution of income, a top-heavy civil service, endemic corruption, and a generally unfavorable climate for business enterprise. Since 1990, the government has embarked on various IMF and World Bank programs designed to spur business investment, increase efficiency in agriculture, improve trade, and recapitalize the nation's banks. The IMF is pressing for more reforms, including increased budget transparency, privatization, and poverty reduction programs. Subsidies for electricity, food, and fuel have strained the budget. Cameroon has several large infrastructure projects under construction, including a deep sea port in Kribi and the Lom Pangar Hydropower Project. It also recently opened a natural gas powered electricity generating plant. Cameroon must attract more investment to improve its inadequate infrastructure, but its business environment is a deterrent to foreign investment.

GDP (purchasing power parity): $53.16 billion (2013 est.)
country comparison to the world: 97
$50.85 billion (2012 est.)
$48.62 billion (2011 est.)
note: data are in 2013 US dollars

GDP (official exchange rate): $27.88 billion (2013 est.)

GDP—real growth rate: 4.6% (2013 est.)
country comparison to the world: 66
4.6% (2012 est.)
4.1% (2011 est.)

GDP—per capita (PPP): $2,400 (2013 est.)
country comparison to the world: 188
$2,400 (2012 est.)
$2,300 (2011 est.)
note: data are in 2013 US dollars

Gross national saving: 21.6% of GDP (2013 est.)
country comparison to the world: 70
21% of GDP (2012 est.)
19.8% of GDP (2011 est.)

GDP—composition, by end use:
household consumption: 65.6%
government consumption: 16%
investment in fixed capital: 21.7%
investment in inventories: 0%
exports of goods and services: 31.7%
imports of goods and services: -35% (2013 est.)

GDP—composition, by sector of origin:
agriculture: 20.6%
industry: 27.3%
services: 52.1% (2013 est.)

Agriculture—products: coffee, cocoa, cotton, rubber, bananas, oilseed, grains, cassava (manioc); livestock; timber

Industries: petroleum production and refining, aluminum production, food processing, light consumer goods, textiles, lumber, ship repair

Industrial production growth rate: 4.1% (2013 est.)
country comparison to the world: 69

Labor force: 8.426 million (2013 est.)
country comparison to the world: 56

Labor force—by occupation: *agriculture:* 70%
industry: 13%
services: 17% (2001 est.)

Unemployment rate: 30% (2001 est.)
country comparison to the world: 181

Population below poverty line: 48% (2000 est.)

Household income or consumption by percentage share: *lowest 10%:* 2.3%
highest 10%: 35.4% (2001)

Distribution of family income—Gini index: 44.6 (2001)
country comparison to the world: 43
47.7 (1996)

Budget: *revenues:* $5.089 billion
expenditures: $6.28 billion (2013 est.)

Taxes and other revenues: 18.3% of GDP (2013 est.)
country comparison to the world: 175

Budget surplus (+) or deficit (-): -4.3% of GDP (2013 est.)
country comparison to the world: 155

Public debt: 16.7% of GDP (2013 est.)
country comparison to the world: 139
16.1% of GDP (2012 est.)

Fiscal year: 1 July—30 June

Inflation rate (consumer prices): 2.6% (2013 est.)
country comparison to the world: 95
2.9% (2012 est.)

Central bank discount rate: 4.25% (31 December 2009 est.)

Commercial bank prime lending rate: 14% (31 December 2013 est.)

country comparison to the world: 51
14% (31 December 2012 est.)

Stock of narrow money: $3.764 billion (31 December 2013 est.)
country comparison to the world: 112
$3.482 billion (31 December 2012 est.)

Stock of broad money: $6.195 billion (31 December 2013 est.)
country comparison to the world: 122
$5.731 billion (31 December 2012 est.)

Stock of domestic credit: $2.898 billion (31 December 2013 est.)
country comparison to the world: 128
$2.772 billion (31 December 2012 est.)

Market value of publicly traded shares: $230 million (31 December 2012 est.)

Current account balance: -$1.461 billion (2013 est.)
country comparison to the world: 133
-$956.2 million (2012 est.)

Exports: $6.002 billion (2013 est.)
country comparison to the world: 108
$6.015 billion (2012 est.)

Exports—commodities: crude oil and petroleum products, lumber, cocoa beans, aluminum, coffee, cotton

Exports—partners: China 15.2%, Netherlands 9.7%, Spain 9.1%, India 8.6%, Portugal 8.1%, Italy 6%, US 5.5%, France 4% (2012)

Imports: $6.795 billion (2013 est.)
country comparison to the world: 115
$6.321 billion (2012 est.)

Imports—commodities: machinery, electrical equipment, transport equipment, fuel, food

Imports—partners: China 18.7%, France 14.9%, Nigeria 12.3%, Belgium 5.2%, US 4.4%, India 4.2% (2012)

Reserves of foreign exchange and gold: $3.353 billion (31 December 2013 est.)
country comparison to the world: 104
$3.431 billion (31 December 2012 est.)

Debt—external: $3.455 billion (31 December 2013 est.)
country comparison to the world: 130
$3.207 billion (31 December 2012 est.)

Exchange rates: Cooperation Financiere en Afrique Centrale francs (XAF) per dollar—
500.7 (2013 est.)
510.53 (2012 est.)
495.28 (2010 est.)
472.19 (2009)
447.81 (2008)

ENERGY

Electricity—production: 5.761 billion kWh (2010 est.)
country comparison to the world: 114

Electricity—consumption: 5.181 billion kWh (2010 est.)
country comparison to the world: 114

Electricity—exports: 0 kWh (2012 est.)
country comparison to the world: 120

Electricity—imports: 0 kWh (2012 est.)
country comparison to the world: 127

Electricity—installed generating capacity: 1.115 million kW (2010 est.)
country comparison to the world: 122

Electricity—from fossil fuels: 27.8% of total installed capacity (2010 est.)
country comparison to the world: 184

Electricity—from nuclear fuels: 0% of total installed capacity (2010 est.)
country comparison to the world: 66

Electricity—from hydroelectric plants: 72.2% of total installed capacity (2010 est.)
country comparison to the world: 20

Electricity—from other renewable sources: 0% of total installed capacity (2010 est.)
country comparison to the world: 168

Crude oil—production: 63,520 bbl/day (2012 est.)
country comparison to the world: 58

Crude oil—exports: 55,680 bbl/day (2010 est.)
country comparison to the world: 45

Crude oil—imports: 34,220 bbl/day (2010 est.)
country comparison to the world: 61

Crude oil—proved reserves: 200 million bbl (1 January 2013 es)
country comparison to the world: 59

Refined petroleum products—production: 43,500 bbl/day (2010 est.)
country comparison to the world: 83

Refined petroleum products—consumption: 29,410 bbl/day (2011 est.)
country comparison to the world: 114

Refined petroleum products—exports: 13,370 bbl/day (2010 est.)
country comparison to the world: 81

Refined petroleum products—imports: 6,018 bbl/day (2010 est.)
country comparison to the world: 143

Natural gas—production: 150 million cu m (2011 est.)
country comparison to the world: 80

Natural gas—consumption: 210 million cu m (2010 est.)
country comparison to the world: 101

Natural gas—exports: 0 cu m (2011 est.)
country comparison to the world: 81

Natural gas—imports: 0 cu m (2011 est.)
country comparison to the world: 176

Natural gas—proved reserves: 135.1 billion cu m (1 January 2013 es)
country comparison to the world: 50

Carbon dioxide emissions from consumption of energy: 8.126 million Mt (2011 est.)
country comparison to the world: 108

COMMUNICATIONS

Telephones—main lines in use: 737,400 (2012)
country comparison to the world: 88

Telephones—mobile cellular: 13.1 million (2012)
country comparison to the world: 64

Telephone system: *general assessment:* system includes cable, microwave radio relay, and tropospheric scatter; Camtel, the monopoly provider of fixed-line service, provides connections for only about 3 per 100 persons; equipment is old and outdated, and connections with many parts of the country are unreliable
domestic: mobile-cellular usage, in part a reflection of the poor condition and general inadequacy of the fixed-line network, has increased sharply, reaching a subscribership base of 50 per 100 persons
international: country code—237; landing point for the SAT-3/WASC fiber-optic submarine cable that provides connectivity to Europe and Asia; satellite earth stations—2 Intelsat (Atlantic Ocean) (2011)

Broadcast media: government maintains tight control over broadcast media; state-owned Cameroon Radio Television (CRTV), broadcasting on both a TV and radio network, was the only officially recognized and fully licensed broadcaster until August 2007 when the government finally issued licenses to 2 private TV broadcasters and 1 private radio broadcaster; about 70 privately owned, unlicensed radio stations operating but are subject to closure at any time; foreign news services required to partner with state-owned national station (2007)

Internet country code: .cm

Internet hosts: 10,207 (2012)
country comparison to the world: 134

Internet users: 749,600 (2009)
country comparison to the world: 106

TRANSPORTATION

Airports: 33 (2013)
country comparison to the world: 112

Airports—with paved runways: *total:* 11
over 3,047 m: 2
2,438 to 3,047 m: 5
1,524 to 2,437 m: 3
914 to 1,523 m: 1 (2013)

Airports—with unpaved runways: *total:* 22
1,524 to 2,437 m: 4
914 to 1,523 m: 10
under 914 m: 8 (2013)

Pipelines: gas 53 km; liquid petroleum gas 5 km; oil 1,107 km; water 35 km (2013)

Railways: *total:* 1,245 km
country comparison to the world: 82
narrow gauge: 1,245 km 1.000-m gauge (2008)

Roadways: *total:* 51,350 km
country comparison to the world: 77
paved: 4,108 km
unpaved: 47,242 km
note: there are 28,857 km of national roads (2011)

Waterways: (major rivers in the south, such as the Wouri and the Sanaga, are largely non-navigable; in the north, the Benue, which connects through Nigeria to the Niger River, is navigable in the rainy season only to the port of Garoua) (2010)

Ports and terminals: *river port(s):* Douala (Wouri); Garoua (Benoue)
oil/gas terminal(s): Limboh Terminal

MILITARY

Military branches: Cameroon Armed Forces (Forces Armees Camerounaises, FAC), Army (L'Armee de Terre), Navy (Marine Nationale Republique (MNR), includes naval infantry), Air Force (Armee de l'Air du Cameroun, AAC), Fire Fighter Corps, Gendarmerie (2013)

Military service age and obligation: 18-23 years of age for male and female voluntary military service; no conscription; high school graduation required; service obligation 4 years; the government makes periodic calls for volunteers (2012)

Manpower available for military service: *males age 16-49:* 4,667,251
females age 16-49: 4,548,909 (2010 est.)

Manpower fit for military service: *males age 16-49:* 2,794,998
females age 16-49: 2,718,110 (2010 est.)

Manpower reaching militarily significant age annually: *male:* 215,248
female: 211,636 (2010 est.)

Military expenditures: 1.42% of GDP (2012)
country comparison to the world: 70
1.37% of GDP (2011)
1.42% of GDP (2010)

TRANSNATIONAL ISSUES

Disputes—international: Joint Border Commission with Nigeria reviewed 2002 ICJ ruling on the entire boundary and bilaterally resolved differences, including June 2006 Greentree Agreement that immediately ceded sovereignty of the Bakassi Peninsula to Cameroon with a full phase-out of Nigerian control and patriation of residents in 2008; Cameroon and Nigeria agreed on maritime delimitation in March 2008; sovereignty dispute between Equatorial Guinea and Cameroon over an island at the mouth of the Ntem River; only Nigeria and Cameroon have heeded the Lake Chad Commission's admonition to ratify the delimitation treaty, which also includes the Chad-Niger and Niger-Nigeria boundaries

Refugees and internally displaced persons: *refugees (country of origin):* 166,000 (Central African Republic); 12,400 (Nigeria) (2014)

CANADA

INTRODUCTION

Background: A land of vast distances and rich natural resources, Canada became a self-governing dominion in 1867 while retaining ties to the British crown. Economically and technologically, the nation has developed in parallel with the US, its neighbor to the south across the world's longest unfortified border. Canada faces the political challenges of meeting public demands for quality improvements in health care, education, social services, and economic competitiveness, as well as responding to the particular concerns of predominantly francophone Quebec. Canada also aims to develop its diverse energy resources while maintaining its commitment to the environment.

GEOGRAPHY

Location: Northern North America, bordering the North Atlantic Ocean on the east, North Pacific Ocean on the west, and the Arctic Ocean on the north, north of the conterminous US

Geographic coordinates: 60 00 N, 95 00 W

Map references: North America

Area: *total:* 9,984,670 sq km
country comparison to the world: 2
land: 9,093,507 sq km
water: 891,163 sq km

Area—comparative: slightly larger than the US

Land boundaries: *total:* 8,893 km
border countries: US 8,893 km (includes 2,477 km with Alaska)
note: Canada is the World's largest country that borders only one country

Coastline: 202,080 km

Maritime claims: *territorial sea:* 12 nm
contiguous zone: 24 nm
exclusive economic zone: 200 nm
continental shelf: 200 nm or to the edge of the continental margin

Climate: varies from temperate in south to subarctic and arctic in north

Terrain: mostly plains with mountains in west and lowlands in southeast

Elevation extremes: *lowest point:* Atlantic Ocean 0 m
highest point: Mount Logan 5,959 m

Natural resources: iron ore, nickel, zinc, copper, gold, lead, rare earth elements, molybdenum, potash, diamonds, silver, fish, timber, wildlife, coal, petroleum, natural gas, hydropower

Land use: *arable land:* 4.3%
permanent crops: 0.49%
other: 95.2% (2011)

Irrigated land: 8,699 sq km (2004)

Total renewable water resources: 2,902 cu km (2011)

Freshwater withdrawal (domestic/industrial/agricultural): *total:* 42.2 cu km/yr (20%/70%/10%)
per capita: 1,589 cu m/yr (2010)

Natural hazards: continuous permafrost in north is a serious obstacle to development; cyclonic storms form east of the Rocky Mountains, a result of the mixing of air masses from the Arctic, Pacific, and North American interior, and produce most of the country's rain and snow east of the mountains
volcanism: the vast majority of volcanoes in Western Canada's Coast Mountains remain dormant

Environment—current issues: air pollution and resulting acid rain severely affecting lakes and damaging forests; metal smelting, coal-burning utilities, and vehicle emissions impacting on agricultural and forest productivity; ocean waters becoming contaminated due to agricultural, industrial, mining, and forestry activities

Environment—international agreements: *party to:* Air Pollution, Air Pollution-Nitrogen Oxides, Air Pollution-Persistent Organic Pollutants, Air Pollution-Sulfur 85, Air Pollution-Sulfur 94, Antarctic-Environmental Protocol, Antarctic-Marine Living Resources, Antarctic Seals, Antarctic Treaty, Biodiversity, Climate Change, Desertification, Endangered Species, Environmental Modification, Hazardous Wastes, Law of the Sea, Marine Dumping, Ozone Layer Protection, Ship Pollution, Tropical Timber 83, Tropical Timber 94, Wetlands
signed, but not ratified: Air Pollution-Volatile Organic Compounds, Marine Life Conservation

Geography—note: second-largest country in world (after Russia); strategic location between Russia and US via north polar route; approximately 90% of the population is concentrated within 160 km (100 mi) of the US border; Canada has more fresh water than any other country and almost 9% of Canadian territory is water; Canada has at least 2 million and possibly over 3 million lakes—that is more than all other countries combined

PEOPLE AND SOCIETY

Nationality: *noun:* Canadian(s)
adjective: Canadian

Ethnic groups: Canadian 32.2%, English 19.8%, French 15.5%, Scottish 14.4%, Irish 13.8%, German 9.8%, Italian 4.5%, Chinese 4.5%, North American Indian 4.2%, other 50.9% (2011 est.)

Languages: English (official) 58.7%, French (official) 22%, Punjabi 1.4%, Italian 1.3%, Spanish 1.3%, German 1.3%, Cantonese 1.2%, Tagalog 1.2%, Arabic 1.1%, other 10.5%
note: shares sum to more than 100% because some respondents gave more than one answer on the census (2011 est.)

Religions: Catholic 40.5% (includes Roman Catholic 38.7%, Orthodox 1.6%, other Catholic .2%), Protestant 20.3% (includes United Church 6.1%, Anglican 5%, Baptist 1.9%, Lutheran 1.5%, Pentecostal 1.5%, Presbyterian 1.4%, other Protestant 2.9%), other Christian 6.3%, Muslim 3.2%, Hindu 1.5%, Sikh 1.4%, Buddhist 1.1%, Jewish 1%, other 0.6%, none 23.9% (2011 est.)

Population: 34,834,841 (July 2014 est.)
country comparison to the world: 38

Age structure: *0-14 years:* 15.5% (male 2,764,691/female 2,628,413)
15-24 years: 12.7% (male 2,267,210/female 2,142,085)
25-54 years: 41% (male 7,244,109/female 7,052,512)
55-64 years: 17.3% (male 2,336,202/female 2,380,703)
65 years and over: 16.8% (male 2,670,482/female 3,348,434) (2014 est.)

Dependency ratios: *total dependency ratio:* 46.3%
youth dependency ratio: 24%
elderly dependency ratio: 22.2%
potential support ratio: 4.5 (2013)

Median age: *total:* 41.7 years
male: 40.4 years
female: 42.9 years (2014 est.)

Population growth rate: 0.76% (2014 est.)
country comparison to the world: 144

Birth rate: 10.29 births/1,000 population (2014 est.)
country comparison to the world: 188

Death rate: 8.31 deaths/1,000 population (2014 est.)
country comparison to the world: 90

Net migration rate: 5.66 migrant(s)/1,000 population (2014 est.)
country comparison to the world: 24

Urbanization: *urban population:* 81% of total population (2010)
rate of urbanization: 1.1% annual rate of change (2010-15 est.)

Major urban areas—population: Toronto 5.377 million; Montreal 3.75 million; Vancouver 2.197 million; OTTAWA (capital) 1.208 million; Calgary 1.16 million (2011)

Sex ratio: *at birth:* 1.06 male(s)/female
0-14 years: 1.05 male(s)/female
15-24 years: 1.06 male(s)/female
25-54 years: 1.03 male(s)/female
55-64 years: 0.99 male(s)/female
65 years and over: 0.79 male(s)/female
total population: 0.99 male(s)/female (2014 est.)

Mother's mean age at first birth: 27.6 (2007 est.)

Maternal mortality rate: 12 deaths/100,000 live births (2010)
country comparison to the world: 147

Infant mortality rate: *total:* 4.71 deaths/1,000 live births
country comparison to the world: 182
male: 5.04 deaths/1,000 live births
female: 4.37 deaths/1,000 live births (2014 est.)

Life expectancy at birth: *total population:* 81.67 years
country comparison to the world: 14
male: 79.07 years
female: 84.42 years (2014 est.)

Total fertility rate: 1.59 children born/woman (2014 est.)
country comparison to the world: 181

Contraceptive prevalence rate: 74%
note: percent of women aged 18-44 (2002)

Health expenditures: 11.2% of GDP (2011)
country comparison to the world: 13

Physicians density: 2.07 physicians/1,000 population (2010)

Hospital bed density: 3.2 beds/1,000 population (2010)

Drinking water source:
Improved:
urban: 100% of population
rural: 99% of population
total: 99.8% of population
unimproved:
urban: 0% of population
rural: 1% of population
total: 0.2% of population (2011 est.)

Sanitation facility access:
Improved:
urban: 100% of population
rural: 99% of population
total: 99.8% of population
unimproved:
urban: 0% of population
rural: 1% of population
total: 0.2% of population (2010 est.)

HIV/AIDS—adult prevalence rate: 0.3% (2009 est.)
country comparison to the world: 91

HIV/AIDS—people living with HIV/AIDS: 68,000 (2009 est.)
country comparison to the world: 55

HIV/AIDS—deaths: fewer than 1,000 (2009 est.)
country comparison to the world: 72

Obesity—adult prevalence rate: 26.2% (2008)
country comparison to the world: 48

Education expenditures: 5.4% of GDP (2011)
country comparison to the world: 62

Literacy: *definition:* age 15 and over can read and write
total population: 99%
male: 99%
female: 99% (2003 est.)

School life expectancy (primary to tertiary education): *total:* 16 years
male: 15 years
female: 16 years (2000)

Unemployment, youth ages 15-24: *total:* 14.3%
country comparison to the world: 88
male: 15.9%
female: 12.6% (2012)

GOVERNMENT

Country name: *conventional long form:* none
conventional short form: Canada

Government type: a parliamentary democracy, a federation, and a constitutional monarchy

Capital: *name:* Ottawa
geographic coordinates: 45 25 N, 75 42 W
time difference: UTC-5 (same time as Washington, DC during Standard Time)
daylight saving time: +1hr, begins second Sunday in March; ends first Sunday in November
note: Canada is divided into six time zones

Administrative divisions: 10 provinces and 3 territories*; Alberta, British Columbia, Manitoba, New Brunswick, Newfoundland and Labrador, Northwest Territories*, Nova Scotia, Nunavut*, Ontario, Prince Edward Island, Quebec, Saskatchewan, Yukon*

Independence: 1 July 1867 (union of British North American colonies); 11 December 1931 (recognized by UK per Statute of Westminster)

National holiday: Canada Day, 1 July (1867)

Constitution: made up of unwritten and written acts, customs, judicial decisions, and traditions dating from 1763; the written part of the constitution consists of the Constitution Act of 29 March 1867, which created a federation of four provinces, and the Constitution Act of 17 April 1982; several amendments to Constitution Act, 1982, last in 2011 (2011)

Legal system: common law system except in Quebec where civil law based on the French civil code prevails

International law organization participation: accepts compulsory ICJ jurisdiction with reservations; accepts ICCt jurisdiction

Suffrage: 18 years of age; universal

Executive branch: *head of state:* Queen ELIZABETH II (since 6 February 1952); represented by Governor General David JOHNSTON (since 1 October 2010)
head of government: Prime Minister Stephen Joseph HARPER (since 6 February 2006)
cabinet: Federal Ministry chosen by the prime minister usually from among the members of his own party sitting in Parliament (For more information visit the World Leaders website)
elections: the monarchy is hereditary; governor general appointed by the monarch on the advice of the prime minister for a five-year term; following legislative elections, the leader of the majority party or the leader of the majority coalition in the House of Commons generally designated prime minister by the governor general

Legislative branch: bicameral Parliament or Parlement consists of the Senate or Senat (105 seats; members appointed by the governor general on the advice of the prime minister and serve until 75 years of age) and the House of Commons or Chambre des Communes (308 seats; members elected by direct, popular vote to serve a maximum of four-year terms)
elections: House of Commons—last held on 2 May 2011 (next to be held no later than 19 October 2015)
election results: House of Commons—percent of vote by party—Conservative Party 39.6%, NDP 30.6%, Liberal Party 18.9%, Bloc Quebecois 6%, Greens 3.9%; seats by party—Conservative Party 166, NDP 103, Liberal Party 34, Bloc Quebecois 4, Greens 1

Judicial branch: *highest court(s):* Supreme Court of Canada (consists of the chief justice and 8 judges)note—in 1949, Canada finally abolished all appeals beyond its Supreme Court to the Judicial Committee of the Privy Council (in London)
judge selection and term of office: chief justice and judges appointed by the prime minister in council; all judges appointed for life with mandatory retirement at age 75
subordinate courts: federal level: Federal Court of Appeal; Federal Court; Tax Court; federal administrative tribunals; courts martial;provincial/territorial: provincial superior, appeals, first instance, and specialized courts; in 1999, the Nunavut Court—a circuit court with the power of a superior court and the territorial courts—was established to serve isolated settlements

Political parties and leaders: Bloc Quebecois [Daniel PAILLE]; Conservative Party of Canada [Stephen HARPER]; Green Party [Elizabeth MAY]; Liberal Party [Justin TRUDEAU]; New Democratic Party or NDP [Thomas MULCAIR]

Political pressure groups and leaders: *other:* agricultural sector; automobile industry; business groups; chemical industry; commercial banks; communications sector; energy industry; environmentalists; public administration groups; steel industry; trade unions

International organization participation: ADB (nonregional member), AfDB (nonregional member), APEC, Arctic Council, ARF, ASEAN (dialogue partner), Australia Group, BIS, C, CD, CDB, CE (observer), EAPC, EBRD, EITI (implementing country), FAO, FATF, G-20, G-7, G-8, G-10, IADB, IAEA, IBRD, ICAO, ICC (national committees), ICRM, IDA, IEA, IFAD, IFC, IFRCS, IGAD (partners), IHO, ILO, IMF, IMO, IMSO, Interpol, IOC, IOM, IPU, ISO, ITSO, ITU, ITUC (NGOs), MIGA, MINUSTAH, MONUSCO, NAFTA, NATO, NEA, NSG, OAS, OECD, OIF, OPCW, OSCE, Paris Club, PCA, PIF (partner), UN, UNAMID, UNCTAD, UNESCO, UNFICYP, UNHCR, UNMISS, UNRWA, UNTSO, UPU, WCO, WFTU (NGOs), WHO, WIPO, WMO, WTO, ZC

Diplomatic representation in the US: *chief of mission:* Ambassador Gary DOER (since 23 October 2009)
chancery: 501 Pennsylvania Avenue NW, Washington, DC 20001
telephone: [1] (202) 682-1740
FAX: [1] (202) 682-7726

consulate(s) general: Atlanta, Boston, Buffalo, Chicago, Dallas, Denver, Detroit, Los Angeles, Miami, Minneapolis, New York, San Francisco/Silicon Valley, Seattle
consulate(s): Anchorage (AK), Houston, Palo Alto (CA), Philadelphia, Phoenix, Raleigh (NC), Salt Lake City, San Diego, Tucson

Diplomatic representation from the US: *chief of mission:* Ambassador (Bruce A. Heyman has been nominated; The ambassador is scheduled to present his credentials on 8 April 2014); Charge d'Affaires Richard M. Sanders (since 25 July 2013)
embassy: 490 Sussex Drive, Ottawa, Ontario K1N 1G8
mailing address: P. O. Box 5000, Ogdensburg, NY 13669-0430; P.O. Box 866, Station B, Ottawa, Ontario K1P 5T1
telephone: [1] (613) 688-5335
FAX: [1] (613) 688-3082
consulate(s) general: Calgary, Halifax, Montreal, Quebec City, Toronto, Vancouver, Winnipeg

Flag description: two vertical bands of red (hoist and fly side, half width) with white square between them; an 11-pointed red maple leaf is centered in the white square; the maple leaf has long been a Canadian symbol; the official colors of Canada are red and white

National symbol(s): maple leaf

National anthem: *name:* "O Canada"
lyrics/music: Adolphe-Basile ROUTHIER [French], Robert Stanley WEIR [English]/Calixa LAVALLEE
note: adopted 1980; originally written in 1880, "O Canada" served as an unofficial anthem many years before its official adoption; the anthem has French and English versions whose lyrics differ; as a Commonwealth realm, in addition to the national anthem, "God Save the Queen" serves as the royal anthem (see United Kingdom)

ECONOMY

Economy—overview: As a, high-tech industrial society in the trillion-dollar class, Canada resembles the US in its market-oriented economic system, pattern of production, and high living standards. Since World War II, the impressive growth of the manufacturing, mining, and service sectors has transformed the nation from a largely rural economy into one primarily industrial and urban. The 1989 US-Canada Free Trade Agreement (FTA) and the 1994 North American Free Trade Agreement (NAFTA) (which includes Mexico) touched off a dramatic increase in trade and economic integration with the US, its principal trading partner. Canada enjoys a substantial trade surplus with the US, which absorbs about three-fourths of Canadian merchandise exports each year. Canada is the US's largest foreign supplier of energy, including oil, gas, uranium, and electric power. Given its abundant natural resources, highly skilled labor force, and modern capital plant, Canada enjoyed solid economic growth from 1993 through 2007. Buffeted by the global economic crisis, the economy dropped into a sharp recession in the final months of 2008, and Ottawa posted its first fiscal deficit in 2009 after 12 years of surplus. Canada's major banks, however, emerged from the financial crisis of 2008-09 among the strongest in the world, owing to the financial sector's tradition of conservative lending practices and strong capitalization. Canada achieved marginal growth in 2010-13 and plans to balance the budget by 2015. In addition, the country's petroleum sector is rapidly expanding, because Alberta's oil sands significantly boosted Canada's proven oil reserves. Canada now ranks third in the world in proved oil reserves behind Saudi Arabia and Venezuela.

GDP (purchasing power parity): $1.518 trillion (2013 est.)
country comparison to the world: 14
$1.494 trillion (2012 est.)
$1.469 trillion (2011 est.)
note: data are in 2013 US dollars

GDP (official exchange rate): $1.825 trillion (2013 est.)

GDP—real growth rate: 1.6% (2013 est.)
country comparison to the world: 152
1.7% (2012 est.)
2.5% (2011 est.)

GDP—per capita (PPP): $43,100 (2013 est.)
country comparison to the world: 18
$42,900 (2012 est.)
$42,700 (2011 est.)
note: data are in 2013 US dollars

Gross national saving: 21.5% of GDP (2013 est.)
country comparison to the world: 71
21.2% of GDP (2012 est.)
21.1% of GDP (2011 est.)

GDP—composition, by end use:
household consumption: 55.8%
government consumption: 21.6%
investment in fixed capital: 24.6%
investment in inventories: 0.2%
exports of goods and services: 30.1%
imports of goods and services: -32.3% (2013 est.)

GDP—composition, by sector of origin:
agriculture: 1.7%
industry: 28.4%
services: 69.9% (2013 est.)

Agriculture—products: wheat, barley, oilseed, tobacco, fruits, vegetables; dairy products; fish; forest products

Industries: transportation equipment, chemicals, processed and unprocessed minerals, food products, wood and paper products, fish products, petroleum and natural gas

Industrial production growth rate: 1.4% (2013 est.)
country comparison to the world: 139

Labor force: 19.08 million (2013 est.)
country comparison to the world: 32

Labor force—by occupation: *agriculture:* 2%
manufacturing: 13%
construction: 6%
services: 76%
other: 3% (2006 est.)

Unemployment rate: 7.1% (2013 est.)
country comparison to the world: 77
7.3% (2012 est.)

Population below poverty line: 9.4%
note: this figure is the Low Income Cut-Off (LICO), a calculation that results in higher figures than found in many comparable economies; Canada does not have an official poverty line (2008)

Household income or consumption by percentage share: *lowest 10%:* 2.6%
highest 10%: 24.8% (2000)

Distribution of family income—Gini index: 32.1 (2005)
country comparison to the world: 106
31.5 (1994)

Budget: *revenues:* $687.8 billion
expenditures: $740.8 billion (2013 est.)

Taxes and other revenues: 37.7% of GDP (2013 est.)
country comparison to the world: 52

Budget surplus (+) or deficit (-): -2.9% of GDP (2013 est.)
country comparison to the world: 117

Public debt: 86.3% of GDP (2013 est.)
country comparison to the world: 23
85.4% of GDP (2012 est.)
note: figures are for gross general government debt, as opposed to net federal debt; gross general government debt includes both intragovernmental debt and the debt of public entities at the subnational level

Fiscal year: 1 April–31 March

Inflation rate (consumer prices): 1% (2013 est.)
country comparison to the world: 22
1.5% (2012 est.)

Central bank discount rate: 1% (31 December 2010 est.)
country comparison to the world: 141
0.25% (31 December 2009 est.)

Commercial bank prime lending rate: 3% (31 December 2013 est.)
country comparison to the world: 175
3% (31 December 2012 est.)

Stock of narrow money: $699.1 billion (31 December 2013 est.)
country comparison to the world: 9
$648.8 billion (31 December 2012 est.)

Stock of broad money: $1.539 trillion (31 December 2013 est.)
country comparison to the world: 12
$1.488 trillion (31 December 2012 est.)

Stock of domestic credit: $3.126 trillion (31 December 2013 est.)
country comparison to the world: 9
$3.091 trillion (31 December 2012 est.)

Market value of publicly traded shares: $2.016 trillion (31 December 2012 est.)
country comparison to the world: 6
$1.907 trillion (31 December 2011)
$2.16 trillion (31 December 2010 est.)

Current account balance: -$59.5 billion (2013 est.)
country comparison to the world: 189
-$62.27 billion (2012 est.)

Exports: $458.7 billion (2013 est.)
country comparison to the world: 13
$462.9 billion (2012 est.)

Exports—commodities: motor vehicles and parts, industrial machinery, aircraft, telecommunications equipment; chemicals, plastics, fertilizers; wood pulp, timber, crude petroleum, natural gas, electricity, aluminum

Exports—partners: US 74.5%, China 4.3%, UK 4.1% (2012)

Imports: $471 billion (2013 est.)
country comparison to the world: 11
$474.9 billion (2012 est.)

Imports—commodities: machinery and equipment, motor vehicles and parts, crude oil, chemicals, electricity, durable consumer goods

Imports—partners: US 50.6%, China 11%, Mexico 5.5% (2012)

Reserves of foreign exchange and gold: $68.55 billion (31 December 2012 est.)
country comparison to the world: 30
$65.82 billion (31 December 2011 est.)

Debt—external: $1.331 trillion (31 December 2012 est.)
country comparison to the world: 15
$1.191 trillion (31 December 2011)

Stock of direct foreign investment—at home: $1.038 trillion (31 December 2013 est.)
country comparison to the world: 8
$992.2 billion (31 December 2012 est.)

Stock of direct foreign investment—abroad: $1.047 trillion (31 December 2013 est.)

country comparison to the world: 9
$991.6 billion (31 December 2012 est.)

Exchange rates: Canadian dollars (CAD) per US dollar—
1.03 (2013 est.)
0.9992 (2012 est.)
1.0302 (2010 est.)
1.1431 (2009)
1.0364 (2008)

ENERGY

Electricity—production: 618.9 billion kWh (2011 est.)
country comparison to the world: 7

Electricity—consumption: 499.9 billion kWh (2010 est.)
country comparison to the world: 8

Electricity—exports: 57.97 billion kWh (2012 est.)
country comparison to the world: 2

Electricity—imports: 11.39 billion kWh (2012 est.)
country comparison to the world: 19

Electricity—installed generating capacity: 136.9 million kW (2010 est.)
country comparison to the world: 8

Electricity—from fossil fuels: 31.7% of total installed capacity (2010 est.)
country comparison to the world: 179

Electricity—from nuclear fuels: 9.2% of total installed capacity (2010 est.)
country comparison to the world: 20

Electricity—from hydroelectric plants: 54.7% of total installed capacity (2010 est.)
country comparison to the world: 37

Electricity—from other renewable sources: 4.2% of total installed capacity (2010 est.)
country comparison to the world: 48

Crude oil—production: 3.856 million bbl/day (2012 est.)
country comparison to the world: 5

Crude oil—exports: 1.44 million bbl/day (2010 est.)
country comparison to the world: 11

Crude oil—imports: 770,300 bbl/day (2010 est.)
country comparison to the world: 16

Crude oil—proved reserves: 173.1 billion bbl (1 January 2013 es)
country comparison to the world: 3

Refined petroleum products—production: 2.016 million bbl/day (2010 est.)
country comparison to the world: 10

Refined petroleum products—consumption: 2.259 million bbl/day (2011 est.)
country comparison to the world: 11

Refined petroleum products—exports: 1.073 million bbl/day (2010 est.)
country comparison to the world: 8

Refined petroleum products—imports: 249,500 bbl/day (2010 est.)
country comparison to the world: 24

Natural gas—production: 143.1 billion cu m (2012 est.)
country comparison to the world: 5

Natural gas—consumption: 82.48 billion cu m (2010 est.)
country comparison to the world: 8

Natural gas—exports: 88.29 billion cu m (2012 est.)
country comparison to the world: 5

Natural gas—imports: 31.31 billion cu m (2012 est.)
country comparison to the world: 19

Natural gas—proved reserves: 1.93 trillion cu m (1 January 2013 es)
country comparison to the world: 19

Carbon dioxide emissions from consumption of energy: 552.6 million Mt (2011 est.)
country comparison to the world: 10

COMMUNICATIONS

Telephones—main lines in use: 18.01 million (2012)
country comparison to the world: 16

Telephones—mobile cellular: 26.263 million (2012)
country comparison to the world: 41

Telephone system: *general assessment:* excellent service provided by modern technology
domestic: domestic satellite system with about 300 earth stations
international: country code—1; submarine cables provide links to the US and Europe; satellite earth stations—7 (5 Intelsat—4 Atlantic Ocean and 1 Pacific Ocean, and 2 Intersputnik—Atlantic Ocean region) (2011)

Broadcast media: 2 public TV broadcasting networks each with a large number of network affiliates; several private-commercial networks also with multiple network affiliates; overall, about 150 TV stations; multi-channel satellite and cable systems provide access to a wide range of stations including US stations; mix of public and commercial radio broadcasters with the Canadian Broadcasting Corporation (CBC), the public radio broadcaster, operating 4 radio networks, Radio Canada International, and radio services to indigenous populations in the north; roughly 2,000 licensed radio stations in Canada (2008)

Internet country code: .ca

Internet hosts: 8.743 million (2012)
country comparison to the world: 14

Internet users: 26.96 million (2009)
country comparison to the world: 16

TRANSPORTATION

Airports: 1,467 (2013)
country comparison to the world: 4

Airports—with paved runways: *total:* 523
over 3,047 m: 21
2,438 to 3,047 m: 19
1,524 to 2,437 m: 147
914 to 1,523 m: 257
under 914 m: 79 (2013)

Airports—with unpaved runways: *total:* 944
1,524 to 2,437 m: 75
914 to 1,523 m: 385
under 914 m: 484 (2013)

Heliports: 26 (2013)

Pipelines: gas and liguid petroleum 100,000 km (2013)

Railways: *total:* 46,552 km
country comparison to the world: 5
standard gauge: 46,552 km 1.435-m gauge (2008)

Roadways: *total:* 1,042,300 km
country comparison to the world: 7
paved: 415,600 km (includes 17,000 km of expressways)
unpaved: 626,700 km (2008)

Waterways: 636 km (Saint Lawrence Seaway of 3,769 km, including the Saint Lawrence River of 3,058 km, shared with United States) (2011)
country comparison to the world: 78

Merchant marine: *total:* 181
country comparison to the world: 35
by type: bulk carrier 62, cargo 15, carrier 1, chemical tanker 15, combination ore/oil 1, container 2, passenger 5, passenger/cargo 63, petroleum tanker 11, roll on/roll off 6
foreign-owned: 19 (Estonia 1, France 1, Netherlands 1, Norway 4, Sweden 2, US 10)
registered in other countries: 225 (Australia 5, Bahamas 96, Barbados 11, Cambodia 2, Cyprus 2, Honduras 1, Hong Kong 77, Liberia 2, Malta 5, Marshall Islands 8, Norway 1, Panama 6, Spain 4, Vanuatu 5) (2010)

Ports and terminals: *major seaport(s):* Halifax, Saint John (New Brunswick), Vancouver
river and lake port(s): Montreal, Quebec City, Sept-Isles (St. Lawrence); Fraser River Port (Fraser); Hamilton (Lake Ontario)
oil/gas terminal(s): Lower Lakes terminal
dry bulk cargo port(s): Port-Cartier (iron ore and grain),
container port(s): Montreal (1,362,975), Vancouver (2,507,032)(2011)

MILITARY

Military branches: Canadian Forces: Canadian Army, Royal Canadian Navy, Royal Canadian Air Force, Canada Command (homeland security) (2011)

Military service age and obligation: 17 years of age for voluntary male and female military service (with parental consent); 16 years of age for Reserve and Military College applicants; Canadian citizenship or permanent residence status required; maximum 34 years of age; service obligation 3-9 years (2012)

Manpower available for military service: males age 16-49: 8,031,266
females age 16-49: 7,755,550 (2010 est.)

Manpower fit for military service: *males age 16-49:* 6,633,472
females age 16-49: 6,389,669 (2010 est.)

Manpower reaching militarily significant age annually: *male:* 218,069
female: 206,195 (2010 est.)

Military expenditures: 1.24% of GDP (2012)
country comparison to the world: 83
1.31% of GDP (2011)
1.24% of GDP (2010)

TRANSNATIONAL ISSUES

Disputes—international: managed maritime boundary disputes with the US at Dixon Entrance, Beaufort Sea, Strait of Juan de Fuca, and the Gulf of Maine including the disputed Machias Seal Island and North Rock; Canada and the United States dispute how to divide the Beaufort Sea and the status of the Northwest Passage but continue to work cooperatively to survey the Arctic continental shelf; US works closely with Canada to intensify security measures for monitoring and controlling legal and illegal movement of people, transport, and commodities across the international border; sovereignty dispute with Denmark over Hans Island in the Kennedy Channel between Ellesmere Island and Greenland; commencing the collection of technical evidence for submission to the Commission on the Limits of the Continental Shelf in support of claims for continental shelf beyond 200 nautical miles from its declared baselines in the Arctic, as stipulated in Article 76, paragraph 8, of the United Nations Convention on the Law of the Sea

Refugees and internally displaced persons: *refugees (country of origin):* 17,563 (Colombia); 16,813 (China); 13,705 (Sri Lanka); 11,605 (Pakistan); 6,798 (Haiti); 5,995 (Mexico); 5,287 (India) (2012)

Illicit drugs: illicit producer of cannabis for the domestic drug market and export to US; use of hydroponics technology permits growers to plant large quantities of high-quality marijuana indoors; increasing ecstasy production, some of which is destined for the US; vulnerable to narcotics money laundering because of its mature financial services sector

CAYMAN ISLANDS

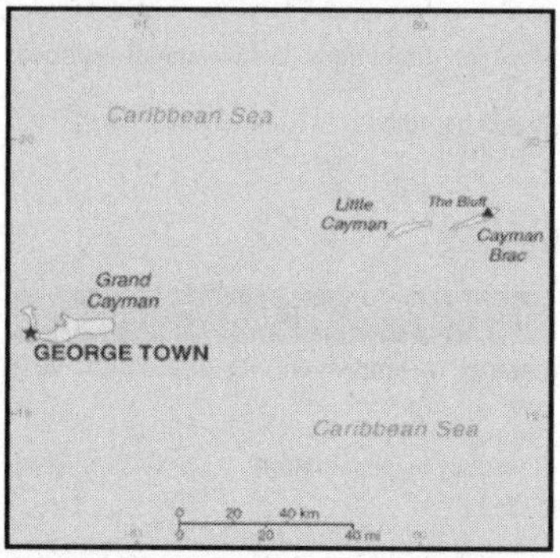

INTRODUCTION

Background: The Cayman Islands were colonized from Jamaica by the British during the 18th and 19th centuries and were administered by Jamaica after 1863. In 1959, the islands became a territory within the Federation of the West Indies. When the Federation dissolved in 1962, the Cayman Islands chose to remain a British dependency.

GEOGRAPHY

Location: Caribbean, three-island group (Grand Cayman, Cayman Brac, Little Cayman) in Caribbean Sea, 240 km south of Cuba and 268 km northwest of Jamaica

Geographic coordinates: 19 30 N, 80 30 W

Map references: Central America and the Caribbean

Area: *total:* 264 sq km
country comparison to the world: 211
land: 264 sq km
water: 0 sq km

Area—comparative: 1.5 times the size of Washington, DC

Land boundaries: 0 km

Coastline: 160 km

Maritime claims: *territorial sea:* 12 nm
exclusive fishing zone: 200 nm

Climate: tropical marine; warm, rainy summers (May to October) and cool, relatively dry winters (November to April)

Terrain: low-lying limestone base surrounded by coral reefs

Elevation extremes: *lowest point:* Caribbean Sea 0 m
highest point: The Bluff on Cayman Brac 43 m

Natural resources: fish, climate and beaches that foster tourism

Land use: *arable land:* 0.83%
permanent crops: 2.08%
other: 97.08% (2011)

Irrigated land: NA

Natural hazards: hurricanes (July to November)

Environment—current issues: no natural freshwater resources; drinking water supplies must be met by rainwater catchments

Geography—note: important location between Cuba and Central America

PEOPLE AND SOCIETY

Nationality: *noun:* Caymanian(s)
adjective: Caymanian

Ethnic groups: mixed 40%, white 20%, black 20%, expatriates of various ethnic groups 20%

Languages: English (official) 90.9%, Spanish 4%, Filipino 3.3%, other 1.7%, unspecified 0.1% (2010 est.)

Religions: Protestant 67.8% (includes Church of God 22.6%, Seventh Day Adventist 9.4%, Presbyterian/United Church 8.6%, Baptist 8.3%,Pentecostal 7.1%, non-denominational 5.3%, Anglican 4.1%, Wesleyan Holiness 2.4%), Roman Catholic 14.1%, Jehovah's Witness 1.1%, other 7%, none 9.3%, unspecified 0.7% (2010 est.)

Population: 54,914 (July 2013 est.)
country comparison to the world: 207
note: most of the population lives on Grand Cayman (July 2014 est.)

Age structure: *0-14 years:* 18.4% (male 5,093/female 5,022)
15-24 years: 12.9% (male 3,505/female 3,579)
25-54 years: 44% (male 11,771/female 12,384)
55-64 years: 11.1% (male 3,549/female 3,922)
65 years and over: 10.7% (male 2,870/female 3,219) (2014 est.)

Median age: *total:* 39.5 years
male: 38.8 years
female: 40.1 years (2014 est.)

Population growth rate: 2.14% (2014 est.)
country comparison to the world: 45

Birth rate: 12.13 births/1,000 population (2014 est.)
country comparison to the world: 164

Death rate: 5.41 deaths/1,000 population (2014 est.)
country comparison to the world: 178

Net migration rate: 14.71 migrant(s)/1,000 population
country comparison to the world: 7
note: major destination for Cubans trying to migrate to the US (2014 est.)

Urbanization: *urban population:* 100% of total population (2010)
rate of urbanization: 0.9% annual rate of change (2010-15 est.)

Major urban areas—population: GEORGE TOWN (capital) 28,000 (2011)

Sex ratio: *at birth:* 1.02 male(s)/female
0-14 years: 1.01 male(s)/female
15-24 years: 0.98 male(s)/female
25-54 years: 0.95 male(s)/female
55-64 years: 0.95 male(s)/female
65 years and over: 0.9 male(s)/female
total population: 0.95 male(s)/female (2014 est.)

Infant mortality rate: *total:* 6.21 deaths/1,000 live births
country comparison to the world: 167
male: 7.1 deaths/1,000 live births
female: 5.31 deaths/1,000 live births (2014 est.)

Life expectancy at birth: *total population:* 81.02 years
country comparison to the world: 24
male: 78.33 years
female: 83.76 years (2014 est.)

Total fertility rate: 1.86 children born/woman (2014 est.)
country comparison to the world: 144

Drinking water source:
Improved:
urban: 95.6% of population
total: 95.6% of population
unimproved:
urban: 4.4% of population
total: 4.4% of population (2011 est.)

Sanitation facility access:
Improved:
urban: 96.3% of population
total: 96.3% of population
unimproved:
urban: 3.7% of population
total: 3.7% of population (2011 est.)

HIV/AIDS—adult prevalence rate: NA

HIV/AIDS—people living with HIV/AIDS: NA

HIV/AIDS—deaths: NA

Education expenditures: NA

Literacy: *definition:* age 15 and over has ever attended school
total population: 98.9%
male: 98.7%
female: 99% (2007 est.)

Unemployment, youth ages 15-24:
total: 13.5%
country comparison to the world: 94
male: 13.6%
female: 13.3% (2008)

GOVERNMENT

Country name: *conventional long form:* none
conventional short form: Cayman Islands

Dependency status: overseas territory of the UK

Government type: parliamentary democracy

Capital: *name:* George Town (on Grand Cayman)
geographic coordinates: 19 18 N, 81 23 W
time difference: UTC-5 (same time as Washington, DC during Standard Time)

Administrative divisions: 6 districts; Bodden Town, Cayman Brac and Little Cayman, East End, George Town, North Side, West Bay

Independence: none (overseas territory of the UK)

National holiday: Constitution Day, first Monday in July

Constitution: several previous; latest approved 10 June 2009, entered into force 6 November 2009 (The Cayman Islands Constitution Order 2009) (2013)

Legal system: English common law and local statutes

Suffrage: 18 years of age; universal

Executive branch: *chief of state:* Queen ELIZABETH II (since 6 February 1952); represented by Governor Helen KILPATRICK (since 6 September 2013)
head of government: Premier Alden MCLAUGHLIN (since 29 May 2013)
cabinet: The Cabinet (six members are appointed by the governor on the advice of the premier, selected from among the elected members of the Legislative Assembly)
(For more information visit the World Leaders website)
elections: the monarchy is hereditary; the governor appointed by the monarch; following legislative elections, the leader of the majority party or coalition appointed by the governor as premier

Legislative branch: unicameral Legislative Assembly (21 seats; 18 members elected by popular vote, Speaker, and 2 ex officio members - Deputy Governor and Attorney General; to serve four-year terms)
elections: last held on 22 May 2013 (next to be held in 2017)
election results: percent of vote by party—PPM 36.1%, UDP 27.8%, C4C 18.6%, independents 11.9%, PNA 5.7%; seats by party—PPM 9 , UDP 3, C4C 3, independent 2, PNA 1

Judicial branch: *highest court(s):* Court of Appeal (consists of the court president and at least 2 judges); Grand Court (consists of the court president and at least 2 judges)
note—appeals beyond the Court of Appeal are heard by the Judicial Committee of the Privy Council (in London)
judge selection and term of office: Court of Appeal and Grand Court judges appointed by the governor on the advice of the Judicial and Legal Services Commission, an 8-member independent body consisting of governor appointees, Court of Appeal president, and attorneys; Court of Appeal judges' tenure based on their individual instruments of appointment; Grand Court judges normally appointed until retirement at age 65 but can be extended until age 70
subordinate courts: Summary Court

Political parties and leaders: People's Progressive Movement or PPM [Kurt TIBBETTS]; United Democratic Party or UDP [McKeeva BUSH]

Political pressure groups and leaders: Coalition for Cayman or C4C; National People's Alliance or PNA; National Trust
other: environmentalists

International organization participation: Caricom (associate), CDB, Interpol (subbureau), IOC, UNESCO (associate), UPU

Diplomatic representation in the US: none (overseas territory of the UK)

Diplomatic representation from the US: none (overseas territory of the UK); consular services provided through the US Embassy in Jamaica

Flag description: a blue field, with the flag of the UK in the upper hoist-side quadrant and the Caymanian coat of arms centered on the outer half of the flag; the coat of arms includes a crest with a pineapple, representing the connection with Jamaica, and a turtle, representing Cayman's seafaring tradition, above a shield bearing a golden lion, symbolizing Great Britain, below which are three green stars (representing the three islands) surmounting white and blue wavy lines representing the sea and a scroll at the bottom bearing the motto HE HATH FOUNDED IT UPON THE SEAS

National anthem: *name:* "Beloved Isle Cayman"
lyrics/music: Leila E. ROSS
note: adopted 1993; served as an unofficial anthem since 1930; as a territory of the United Kingdom, in addition to the local anthem, "God Save the Queen" is official (see United Kingdom)

ECONOMY

Economy—overview: With no direct taxation, the islands are a thriving offshore financial center. More than 93,000 companies were registered in the Cayman Islands as of 2008, including almost 300 banks, 800 insurers, and 10,000 mutual funds. A stock exchange was opened in 1997. Tourism is also a mainstay, accounting for about 70% of GDP and 75% of foreign currency earnings. The tourist industry is aimed at the luxury market and caters mainly to visitors from North America. Total tourist arrivals exceeded 1.9 million in 2008, with about half from the US. Nearly 90% of the islands' food and consumer goods must be imported. The Caymanians enjoy a standard of living comparable to that of Switzerland.

GDP (purchasing power parity): $2.25 billion (2008 est.)
country comparison to the world: 189
$2.23 billion (2003 est.)

GDP (official exchange rate): $2.25 billion (2008 est.)

GDP—real growth rate: 1.1% (2008 est.)
country comparison to the world: 171
0.9% (2004 est.)

GDP—per capita (PPP): $43,800 (2004 est.)
country comparison to the world: 17

GDP—composition, by end use:
household consumption: 62.7%
government consumption: 14.8%
investment in fixed capital: 22.3%
exports of goods and services: 57.4%
imports of goods and services: -57.1% (2013 est.)

GDP—composition, by sector of origin:
agriculture: 0.3%
industry: 27.4%
services: 72.3% (2013 est.)

Agriculture—products: vegetables, fruit; livestock; turtle farming

Industries: tourism, banking, insurance and finance, construction, construction materials, furniture

Industrial production growth rate: 1.5%
country comparison to the world: 133

Labor force: 39,000
country comparison to the world: 198
note: nearly 55% are non-nationals (2007)

Labor force—by occupation: *agriculture:* 1.9%
industry: 19.1%
services: 79% (2008 est.)

Unemployment rate: 4% (2008)
country comparison to the world: 31
4.4% (2004)

Population below poverty line: NA%

Household income or consumption by percentage share: *lowest 10%:* NA%
highest 10%: NA%

Budget: *revenues:* $700.5 million
expenditures: $757.5 million (2013 est.)

Taxes and other revenues: 31.1% of GDP (2013 est.)
country comparison to the world: 87

Budget surplus (+) or deficit (-): -2.5% of GDP (2013 est.)
country comparison to the world: 104

Fiscal year: 1 April–31 March

Inflation rate (consumer prices): 1.8% (2013 est.)
country comparison to the world: 57
1.2% (2012 est.)

Stock of narrow money: $334.3 million (31 December 2008)
country comparison to the world: 169

Stock of broad money: $5.564 billion (31 December 2008 est.)
country comparison to the world: 126

Market value of publicly traded shares: $NA (31 December 2008)
country comparison to the world: 115
$183.5 million (31 December 2007)
$188.4 million (31 December 2006)

Exports: $13.9 million (2013 est.)
country comparison to the world: 208
$15 million (2012 est.)

Exports—commodities: turtle products, manufactured consumer goods

Imports: $719 million (2013 est.)
country comparison to the world: 187
$698.1 million (2012 est.)

Imports—commodities: foodstuffs, manufactured goods, fuels

Stock of direct foreign investment—at home: $NA

Stock of direct foreign investment—abroad: $NA

Exchange rates: Caymanian dollars (KYD) per US dollar—
0.83 (2013 est.)
0.83 (2012 est.)
0.83 (2010 est.)

ENERGY

Electricity—production: 594 million kWh (2011 est.)
country comparison to the world: 159

Electricity—consumption: 552 million kWh (2010 est.)
country comparison to the world: 168

Electricity—exports: 0 kWh (2012 est.)
country comparison to the world: 119

Electricity—imports: 0 kWh (2012 est.)
country comparison to the world: 126

Electricity—installed generating capacity: 151,000 kW (2010 est.)
country comparison to the world: 162

Electricity—from fossil fuels: 100% of total installed capacity (2010 est.)
country comparison to the world: 11

Electricity—from nuclear fuels: 0% of total installed capacity (2010 est.)
country comparison to the world: 65

Electricity—from hydroelectric plants: 0% of total installed capacity (2010 est.)
country comparison to the world: 163

Electricity—from other renewable sources: 0% of total installed capacity (2010 est.)
country comparison to the world: 167

Crude oil—production: 0 bbl/day (2012 est.)
country comparison to the world: 160

Crude oil—exports: 0 bbl/day (2010 est.)
country comparison to the world: 97

Crude oil—imports: 0 bbl/day (2010 est.)
country comparison to the world: 172

Crude oil—proved reserves: 0 bbl (1 January 2013 es)
country comparison to the world: 116

Refined petroleum products—production: 0 bbl/day (2010 est.)
country comparison to the world: 131

Refined petroleum products—consumption: 3,141 bbl/day (2011 est.)
country comparison to the world: 180

Refined petroleum products—exports: 0 bbl/day (2010 est.)
country comparison to the world: 164

Refined petroleum products—imports: 3,754 bbl/day (2010 est.)
country comparison to the world: 163

Natural gas—production: 0 cu m (2011 est.)
country comparison to the world: 115

Natural gas—consumption: 0 cu m (2010 est.)
country comparison to the world: 131

Natural gas—exports: 0 cu m (2011 est.)
country comparison to the world: 80

Natural gas—imports: 0 cu m (2011 est.)
country comparison to the world: 175

Natural gas—proved reserves: 0 cu m (1 January 2013 es.)
country comparison to the world: 123

Carbon dioxide emissions from consumption of energy: 592,800 Mt (2011 est.)
country comparison to the world: 177

COMMUNICATIONS

Telephones—main lines in use: 37,400 (2012)
country comparison to the world: 171

Telephones—mobile cellular: 96,300 (2012)
country comparison to the world: 194

Telephone system: *general assessment:* reasonably good overall telephone system with a high fixed-line teledensity
domestic: liberalization of telecom market in 2003; introduction of competition in the mobile-cellular market in 2004
international: country code—1-345; landing points for the Maya-1, Eastern Caribbean Fiber System (ECFS), and the Cayman-Jamaica Fiber System submarine cables that provide links to the US and parts of Central and South America; satellite earth station—1 Intelsat (Atlantic Ocean) (2011)

Broadcast media: 4 TV stations; cable and satellite subscription services offer a variety of international programming; government-owned Radio Cayman operates 2 networks broadcasting on 5 stations; 10 privately owned radio stations operate alongside Radio Cayman (2007)

Internet country code: .ky

Internet hosts: 23,472 (2012)
country comparison to the world: 114

Internet users: 23,000 (2008)
country comparison to the world: 189

TRANSPORTATION

Airports: 3 (2013)
country comparison to the world: 196

Airports—with paved runways: *total:* 3
1,524 to 2,437 m: 2
914 to 1,523 m: 1 (2013)

Airports—with unpaved runways: *total:* 1
914 to 1,523 m: 1 (2012)

Roadways: *total:* 785 km
country comparison to the world: 188
paved: 785 km (2007)

Merchant marine: *total:* 116
country comparison to the world: 46
by type: bulk carrier 19, cargo 3, chemical tanker 61, liquefied gas 1, passenger 1, petroleum tanker 5, refrigerated cargo 10, vehicle carrier 16
foreign-owned: 102 (Germany 3, Greece 9, Italy 7, Japan 23, Switzerland 1, UK 2, US 57) (2010)

Ports and terminals: *major seaport(s):* Cayman Brac, George Town

MILITARY

Military branches: no regular military forces; Royal Cayman Islands Police Force (2012)

Manpower available for military service:
males age: 16-49: 12,238 (2010 est.)

Manpower fit for military service:
males age: 16-49: 9,981
females age 16-49: 10,417 (2010 est.)

Manpower reaching militarily significant age annually: *male:* 333
female: 342 (2010 est.)

Military—note: defense is the responsibility of the UK

TRANSNATIONAL ISSUES

Disputes—international: none

Illicit drugs: major offshore financial center; vulnerable to drug transshipment to the US and Europe (2008)

CENTRAL AFRICAN REPUBLIC

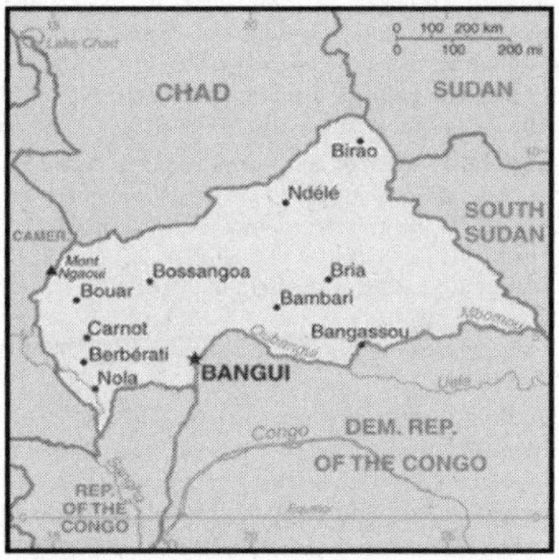

INTRODUCTION

Background: The former French colony of Ubangi-Shari became the Central African Republic upon independence in 1960. After three tumultuous decades of misrule—mostly by military governments—civilian rule was established in 1993 and lasted for one decade. In March, 2003 President Ange-Felix PATASSE was deposed in a military coup led by General Francois BOZIZE, who established a transitional government. Elections held in 2005 affirmed General BOZIZE as president; he was reelected in 2011 in voting widely viewed as flawed. The government still does not fully control the countryside, where pockets of law lessness persist. The militant group the Lord's Resistance Army continues to destabilize southeastern Central African Republic, and several rebel groups joined together in early December 2012 to launch a series of attacks that left them in control of numerous towns in the northern and central parts of the country. The rebels—who are unhappy with BOZIZE's government—participated in peace talks in early January 2013 which resulted in a coalition government including the rebellion's leadership. In March 2013, the coalition government dissolved, rebels seized the capital, and President BOZIZE fled the country. Rebel leader Michel DJOTODIA assumed the presidency, reappointed Nicolas TIANGAYE as Prime Minister, and established a transitional government on 31 March. On 13 April 2013, the National Transitional Council affirmed DJOTODIA as President.

GEOGRAPHY

Location: Central Africa, north of Democratic Republic of the Congo

Geographic coordinates: 7 00 N, 21 00 E

Map references: Africa

Area: *total:* 622,984 sq km
country comparison to the world: 45
land: 622,984 sq km
water: 0 sq km

Area—comparative: slightly smaller than Texas

Land boundaries: *total:* 5,203 km
border countries: Cameroon 797 km, Chad 1,197 km, Democratic Republic of the Congo 1,577 km, Republic of the Congo 467 km, South Sudan 990 km, Sudan 175 km

Coastline: 0 km (landlocked)

Maritime claims: none (landlocked)

Climate: tropical; hot, dry winters; mild to hot, wet summers

Terrain: vast, flat to rolling, monotonous plateau; scattered hills in northeast and southwest

Elevation extremes: *lowest point:* Oubangui River 335 m
highest point: Mont Ngaoui 1,420 m

Natural resources: diamonds, uranium, timber, gold, oil, hydropower

Land use: *arable land:* 2.89%
permanent crops: 0.13%
other: 96.98% (2011)

Irrigated land: 1.35 sq km (2003)

Total renewable water resources: 144.4 cu km (2011)

Freshwater withdrawal (domestic/industrial/agricultural): *total:* 0.07 cu km/yr (83%/17%/1%)
per capita: 17.42 cu m/yr (2005)

Natural hazards: hot, dry, dusty harmattan winds affect northern areas; floods are common

Environment—current issues: tap water is not potable; poaching has diminished the country's reputation as one of the last great wildlife refuges; desertification; deforestation

Environment—international agreements: *party to:* Biodiversity, Climate Change, Climate Change-Kyoto Protocol, Desertification, Endangered Species, Hazardous Wastes, Ozone Layer Protection, Tropical Timber 94, Wetlands
signed, but not ratified: Law of the Sea

Geography—note: landlocked; almost the precise center of Africa

PEOPLE AND SOCIETY

Nationality: *noun:* Central African(s)
adjective: Central African

Ethnic groups: Baya 33%, Banda 27%, Mandjia 13%, Sara 10%, Mboum 7%, M'Baka 4%, Yakoma 4%, other 2%

Languages: French (official), Sangho (lingua franca and national language), tribal languages

Religions: indigenous beliefs 35%, Protestant 25%, Roman Catholic 25%, Muslim 15%
note: animistic beliefs and practices strongly influence the Christian majority

Population: 5,277,959 (July 2014 est.)
country comparison to the world: 118

note: estimates for this country explicitly take into account the effects of excess mortality due to AIDS; this can result in lower life expectancy, higher infant mortality, higher death rates, lower population growth rates, and changes in the distribution of population by age and sex than would otherwise be expected

Age structure: *0-14 years:* 40.6% (male 1,077,247/female 1,064,660)
15-24 years: 20.1% (male 534,257/female 528,822)
25-54 years: 31.8% (male 838,484/female 838,858)
55-64 years: 3.6% (male 91,696/female 115,600)
65 years and over: 3.6% (male 73,914/female 114,421) (2014 est.)

Dependency ratios: *total dependency ratio:* 77.5%
youth dependency ratio: 70.7%
elderly dependency ratio: 6.8%
potential support ratio: 14.7 (2013)

Median age: *total:* 19.4 years
male: 19.1 years
female: 19.8 years (2014 est.)

Population growth rate: 2.13% (2014 est.)
country comparison to the world: 46

Birth rate: 35.45 births/1,000 population (2014 est.)
country comparison to the world: 23

Death rate: 14.11 deaths/1,000 population (2014 est.)
country comparison to the world: 8

Net migration rate: 0 migrant(s)/1,000 population (2014 est.)
country comparison to the world: 103

Urbanization: *urban population:* 39.1% of total population (2011)
rate of urbanization: 2.6% annual rate of change (2010-15 est.)

Major urban areas—population: BANGUI (capital) 740,000 (2011)

Sex ratio: *at birth:* 1.03 male(s)/female
0-14 years: 1.01 male(s)/female
15-24 years: 1.01 male(s)/female
25-54 years: 1 male(s)/female
55-64 years: 0.98 male(s)/female
65 years and over: 0.66 male(s)/female
total population: 0.98 male(s)/female (2014 est.)

Maternal mortality rate: 890 deaths/100,000 live births (2010)
country comparison to the world: 4

Infant mortality rate: *total:* 92.86 deaths/1,000 live births
country comparison to the world: 4
male: 100.55 deaths/1,000 live births
female: 84.93 deaths/1,000 live births (2014 est.)

Life expectancy at birth: *total population:* 51.35 years
country comparison to the world: 218
male: 50.06 years
female: 52.67 years (2014 est.)

Total fertility rate: 4.46 children born/woman (2014 est.)
country comparison to the world: 31

Contraceptive prevalence rate: 19% (2006)

Health expenditures: 3.8% of GDP (2011)
country comparison to the world: 171

Physicians density: 0.05 physicians/1,000 population (2009)

Hospital bed density: 1 beds/1,000 population (2011)

Drinking water source:
Improved:
urban: 92.1% of population
rural: 51.1% of population
total: 67.1% of population
unimproved:
urban: 7.9% of population
rural: 48.9% of population
total: 32.9% of population (2011 est.)

Sanitation facility access:
Improved:
urban: 43.1% of population
rural: 27.8% of population
total: 33.8% of population
unimproved:
urban: 56.9% of population
rural: 72.2% of population
total: 66.2% of population (2011 est.)

HIV/AIDS—adult prevalence rate: 4.7% (2009 est.)
country comparison to the world: 14

HIV/AIDS—people living with HIV/AIDS: 130,000 (2009 est.)
country comparison to the world: 39

HIV/AIDS—deaths: 11,000 (2009 est.)
country comparison to the world: 28

Major infectious diseases: *degree of risk:* very high
food or waterborne diseases: bacterial and protozoal diarrhea, hepatitis A and E, and typhoid fever
vectorborne disease: malaria and dengue fever
respiratory disease: meningococcal meningitis
water contact disease: schistosomiasis
animal contact disease: rabies (2013)

Obesity—adult prevalence rate: 3.5% (2008)
country comparison to the world: 175

Children under the age of 5 years underweight: 28% (2006)
country comparison to the world: 22

Education expenditures: 1.2% of GDP (2011)
country comparison to the world: 171

Literacy: *definition:* age 15 and over can read and write
total population: 56.6%
male: 69.6%
female: 44.2% (2011 est.)

School life expectancy (primary to tertiary education): *total:* 7 years
male: 9 years
female: 6 years (2012)

Child labor—children ages 5-14:
total number: 532,518
percentage: 47 % (2006 est.)

GOVERNMENT

Country name: *conventional long form:* Central African Republic
conventional short form: none
local long form: Republique Centrafricaine
local short form: none
former: Ubangi-Shari, Central African Empire
abbreviation: CAR

Government type: republic

Capital: *name:* Bangui
geographic coordinates: 4 22 N, 18 35 E
time difference: UTC+1 (6 hours ahead of Washington, DC during Standard Time)

Administrative divisions: 14 prefectures (prefectures, singular—prefecture), 2 economic prefectures* (prefectures economiques, singular—prefecture economique), and 1 commune**; Bamingui-Bangoran, Bangui**, Basse-Kotto, Haute-Kotto, Haut-Mbomou, Kemo, Lobaye, Mambere-Kadei, Mbomou, Nana-Grebizi*, Nana-Mambere, Ombella-Mpoko, Ouaka, Ouham, Ouham-Pende, Sangha-Mbaere*, Vakaga

Independence: 13 August 1960 (from France)

National holiday: Republic Day, 1 December (1958)

Constitution: several previous; latest ratified by referendum 5 December 2004, effective 27 December 2004; amended 2010 (2010)

Legal system: civil law system based on the French model

International law organization participation: has not submitted an ICJ jurisdiction declaration; accepts ICCt jurisdiction

Suffrage: 18 years of age; universal

Executive branch: *chief of state:* Interim President Catherine SAMBA-PANZA (since 20 January 2014); elected by the National Transitional Council to replace Interim President Alexandre-Ferdinand NGUENDET, who took over after the resignation of Interim President DJOTODIA
head of government: Prime Minister Andre NZAPAYEKE (since 25 January 2014); note—Prime Minister Nicolas TIANGAYE resigned 10 January 2014
cabinet: Council of Ministers (For more information visit the World Leaders website)
elections: president elected for a five-year term (eligible for a second term); elections last held on 23 January 2011 (next to be held in 2014—as specified in the January 2013 Libreville agreement); prime minister appointed by the president
election results: Francois BOZIZE elected to a second term as president; percent of vote—Francois BOZIZE (KNK) 64.4%, Ange-Felix PATASSE 21.4%, Martin ZIGUELE (MLPC) 6.8%, Emile Gros Raymond NAKOMBO (RDC) 4.6%, Jean-Jacques DEMAFOUTH (NAP) 2.8%; note—rebel forces seized the capital in March 2013, forcing former president BOZIZE to flee the country; Interim President Michel DJOTODIA assumed the presidency, reinstated the Prime Minister, established a transitional government, and was subsequently affirmed as President by the National Transitional Council on 13 April 2013

Legislative branch: unicameral National Assembly or Assemblee Nationale (105 seats; members are elected by popular vote to serve five-year terms)
elections: last held on 23 January 2011 and 27 March 2011 (next to be held in 2016)
election results: percent of vote by party—NA; seats by party—KNK 62, independents 26, MLPC 2, other 15

Judicial branch: *highest court(s):* Supreme Court (consists of NA judges); Constitutional Court (consists of 9 judges, at least 3 of which are women)
judge selection and term of office: Supreme Court judges appointed by the president; Constitutional Court judge appointments—2 by the president, 1 by the speaker of the National Assembly, 2 elected by their peers, 2 are advocates elected by their peers, and 2 are law professors elected by their peers; judges serve 7-year non-renewable terms
subordinate courts: high courts; magistrates' courts

Political parties and leaders: Alliance for Democracy and Progress or ADP [Jacques MBOLIEDAS]; Central African Democratic Rally or RDC [Louis-Pierre GAMBA]; Civic Forum or FC [Gen. Timothee MALENDOMA]; Democratic Forum for Modernity or FODEM [Saturnin NDOMBY]; Liberal Democratic Party or PLD [Nestor KOMBO-NAGUEMON]; Londo Association or LONDO; Movement for Democracy and Development or MDD; Movement for the Liberation of the Central African People or MLPC [Martin ZIGUELE]; National Convergence or KNK [Francois BOZIZE]; National Unity Party or PUN [Jean-Paul NGOUPANDE]; New Alliance for Progress or NAP [Jean-Jacques DEMAFOUTH]; Patriotic Front for Progress or FPP [Alexandre Philippe GOUMBA]; People's Union for the Republic or UPR [Pierre Sammy MAKFOY]; Social Democratic Party or PSD [Enoch LAKOUE]

Political pressure groups and leaders: NA

International organization participation: ACP, AfDB, AU, BDEAC, CEMAC, EITI (compliant country), FAO, FZ, G-77, IAEA, IBRD, ICAO, ICRM, IDA, IFAD, IFC, IFRCS, ILO, IMF, Interpol, IOC, IOM, ITSO, ITU, ITUC (NGOs), MIGA, NAM, OIC, OIF, OPCW, UN, UNCTAD, UNESCO, UNIDO, UNWTO, UPU, WCO, WHO, WIPO, WMO, WTO

Diplomatic representation in the US: *chief of mission:* Ambassador Stanislas MOUSSA-KEMBE (since 24 August 2009)
chancery: 1618 22nd Street NW, Washington, DC 20008
telephone: [1] (202) 483-7800
FAX: [1] (202) 332-9893

Diplomatic representation from the US: *chief of mission:* Ambassador Laurence D. WOHLERS (since September 2010)
embassy: Avenue David Dacko, Bangui
mailing address: B. P. 924, Bangui
telephone: [236] 21 61 02 00
FAX: [236] 21 61 44 94
note: the embassy temporarily suspended operations in December, 2012

Flag description: four equal horizontal bands of blue (top), white, green, and yellow with a vertical red band in center; a yellow five-pointed star to the hoist side of the blue band; banner combines the Pan-African and French flag colors; red symbolizes the blood spilled in the struggle for independence, blue represents the sky and freedom, white peace and dignity, green hope and faith, and yellow tolerance; the star represents aspiration towards a vibrant future

National symbol(s): elephant

National anthem: *name:* "Le Renaissance" (The Renaissance)
lyrics/music: Barthelemy BOGANDA/Herbert PEPPER
note: adopted 1960; Barthelemy BOGANDA, who wrote the anthem's lyrics, was the first prime minister of the autonomous French territory

ECONOMY

Economy—overview: Subsistence agriculture, together with forestry and mining, remains the backbone of the economy of the Central African Republic (CAR), with about 60% of the population living in outlying areas. The agricultural sector generates more than half of GDP. Timber and diamonds account for most export earnings, followed by cotton. Important constraints to economic development include the CAR's landlocked position, a poor transportation system, a largely unskilled work force, and a legacy of misdirected macroeconomic policies. Factional fighting between the government and its opponents remains a drag on economic revitalization. Since 2009 the IMF has worked closely with the government to institute reforms that have resulted in some improvement in budget transparency, but other problems remain. The government's additional spending in the run-up to the election in 2011 worsened CAR's fiscal situation. Distribution of income is extraordinarily unequal. Grants from France and the international community can only partially meet humanitarian needs. In 2012 the World Bank approved $125 million in funding for transport infrastructure and regional trade, focused on the route between CAR's capital and the port of Douala in Cameroon. After a two year lag in donor support, the IMF's first review of CAR's extended credit facility for 2012-2015 praised improvements in revenue collection but warned of weak management of spending.

GDP (purchasing power parity): $3.336 billion (2013 est.)
country comparison to the world: 178
$3.902 billion (2012 est.)
$3.748 billion (2011 est.)
note: data are in 2013 US dollars

GDP (official exchange rate): $2.05 billion (2013 est.)

GDP—real growth rate: -14.5% (2013 est.)
country comparison to the world: 220
4.1% (2012 est.)
3.3% (2011 est.)

GDP—per capita (PPP): $700 (2013 est.)
country comparison to the world: 224
$900 (2012 est.)
$800 (2011 est.)
note: data are in 2013 US dollars

Gross national saving: 2.4% of GDP (2013 est.)
country comparison to the world: 150
3.8% of GDP (2012 est.)
3.7% of GDP (2011 est.)

GDP—composition, by end use:
household consumption: 91.5%
government consumption: 6.1%
investment in fixed capital: 8.3%
investment in inventories: 0%
exports of goods and services: 9.7%
imports of goods and services: -15.6% (2013 est.)

GDP—composition, by sector of origin:
agriculture: 56.6%
industry: 14.5%
services: 28.9% (2013 est.)

Agriculture—products: cotton, coffee, tobacco, manioc (tapioca), yams, millet, corn, bananas; timber

Industries: gold and diamond mining, logging, brewing, sugar refining

Industrial production growth rate: -11% (2013 est.)
country comparison to the world: 192

Labor force: 2.082 million (2011 est.)
country comparison to the world: 121

Unemployment rate: 8% (2001 est.)
country comparison to the world: 90
note: 23% unemployment in Bangui

Population below poverty line: NA%

Household income or consumption by percentage share: *lowest 10%:* 2.1%
highest 10%: 33% (2003)

Distribution of family income—Gini index: 61.3 (1993)
country comparison to the world: 5

Budget: *revenues:* $186.2 million
expenditures: $270.7 million (2013 est.)

Taxes and other revenues: 9.1% of GDP (2013 est.)
country comparison to the world: 209

Budget surplus (+) or deficit (-): -4.1% of GDP (2013 est.)
country comparison to the world: 149

Fiscal year: calendar year

Inflation rate (consumer prices): 7% (2013 est.)
country comparison to the world: 186
5.8% (2012 est.)

Central bank discount rate: 4.25% (31 December 2009)
country comparison to the world: 77
4.75% (31 December 2008)

Commercial bank prime lending rate: 15% (31 December 2013 est.)
country comparison to the world: 39
15% (31 December 2012 est.)

Stock of narrow money: $308.3 million (31 December 2013 est.)
country comparison to the world: 170
$337.7 million (31 December 2012 est.)

Stock of broad money: $376.4 million (31 December 2013 est.)
country comparison to the world: 183
$421.6 million (31 December 2012 est.)

Stock of domestic credit: $478.7 million (31 December 2013 est.)
country comparison to the world: 170
$507.7 million (31 December 2012 est.)

Market value of publicly traded shares: $NA

Current account balance: -$133.8 million (2013 est.)
country comparison to the world: 79
-$197.6 million (2012 est.)

Exports: $138.9 million (2013 est.)
country comparison to the world: 187
$207.7 million (2012 est.)

Exports—commodities: diamonds, timber, cotton, coffee

Exports—partners: Belgium 31.7%, China 27.9%, Democratic Republic of the Congo 7.8%, Indonesia 5.2%, France 4.5% (2012)

Imports: $218.6 million (2013 est.)
country comparison to the world: 203
$333.7 million (2012 est.)

Imports—commodities: food, textiles, petroleum products, machinery, electrical equipment, motor vehicles, chemicals, pharmaceuticals

Imports—partners: Netherlands 20.3%, France 9.7%, Cameroon 9.1%, South Korea 9.1% (2012)

Debt—external: $634.2 million (31 December 2013 est.)
country comparison to the world: 171
$632.7 million (31 December 2012 est.)

Exchange rates: Cooperation Financiere en Afrique Centrale francs (XAF) per US dollar—
500.7 (2013 est.)
510.53 (2012 est.)
495.28 (2010)
472.19 (2009)
447.81 (2008)

ENERGY

Electricity—production: 160 million kWh (2010 est.)
country comparison to the world: 186

Electricity—consumption: 148.8 million kWh (2010 est.)
country comparison to the world: 190

Electricity—exports: 0 kWh (2012 est.)
country comparison to the world: 123

Electricity—imports: 0 kWh (2012 est.)
country comparison to the world: 130

Electricity—installed generating capacity: 44,000 kW (2010 est.)
country comparison to the world: 192

Electricity—from fossil fuels: 43.2% of total installed capacity (2010 est.)
country comparison to the world: 166

Electricity—from nuclear fuels:0% of total installed capacity (2010 est.)
country comparison to the world: 70

Electricity—from hydroelectric plants: 56.8% of total installed capacity (2010 est.)
country comparison to the world: 35

Electricity—from other renewable sources: 0% of total installed capacity (2010 est.)
country comparison to the world: 170

Crude oil—production: 0 bbl/day (2012 est.)
country comparison to the world: 162

Crude oil—exports: 0 bbl/day (2010 est.)
country comparison to the world: 100

Crude oil—imports: 0 bbl/day (2010 est.)
country comparison to the world: 174

Crude oil—proved reserves: 0 bbl (1 January 2013 es.)
country comparison to the world: 119

Refined petroleum products—production: 0 bbl/day (2010 est.)
country comparison to the world: 133

Refined petroleum products—consumption: 3,175 bbl/day (2011 est.)
country comparison to the world: 179

Refined petroleum products—exports: 0 bbl/day (2010 est.)
country comparison to the world: 166

Refined petroleum products—imports: 2,318 bbl/day (2010 est.)
country comparison to the world: 178

Natural gas—production: 0 cu m (2011 est.)
country comparison to the world: 118

Natural gas—consumption: 0 cu m (2010 est.)
country comparison to the world: 134

Natural gas—exports: 0 cu m (2011 est.)
country comparison to the world: 84

Natural gas—imports: 0 cu m (2011 est.)
country comparison to the world: 179

Natural gas—proved reserves: 0 cu m (1 January 2013 es)
country comparison to the world: 126

Carbon dioxide emissions from consumption of energy: 293,900 Mt (2011 est.)
country comparison to the world: 189

COMMUNICATIONS

Telephones—main lines in use: 5,600 (2012)
country comparison to the world: 209

Telephones—mobile cellular: 1.07 million (2012)
country comparison to the world: 157

Telephone system: *general assessment:* network consists principally of microwave radio relay and low-capacity, low-powered radiotelephone communication
domestic: limited telephone service with less than 1 fixed-line connection per 100 persons; spurred by the presence of multiple mobile-cellular service providers, cellular usage is increasing from a low base; most fixed-line and mobile-cellular telephone services are concentrated in Bangui
international: country code—236; satellite earth station—1 Intelsat (Atlantic Ocean) (2011)

Broadcast media: government-owned network, Radiodiffusion Television Centrafricaine, provides domestic TV broadcasting; licenses for 2 private TV stations are pending; state-owned radio network is supplemented by a small number of privately owned broadcast stations as well as a few community radio stations; transmissions of at least 2 international broadcasters are available (2007)

Internet country code: .cf

Internet hosts: 20 (2012)
country comparison to the world: 221

Internet users: 22,600 (2009)
country comparison to the world: 192

TRANSPORTATION

Airports: 39 (2013)
country comparison to the world: 106

Airports—with paved runways: *total:* 2
2,438 to 3,047 m: 1
1,524 to 2,437 m: 1 (2013)

Airports—with unpaved runways: *total:* 37
2,438 to 3,047 m: 1
1,524 to 2,437 m: 11
914 to 1,523 m: 19
under 914 m: 6 (2013)

Roadways: *total:* 20,278 km (2010)
country comparison to the world: 107

Waterways: 2,800 km (the primary navigable river is the Ubangi, which joins the River Congo; it was the traditional route for the export of products because it connected with the Congo-Ocean railway at Brazzaville; because of the warfare on both sides of the River Congo from 1997, however, routes through Cameroon became preferred by importers and exporters) (2011)
country comparison to the world: 35

Ports and terminals: *river port(s):* Bangui (Oubangui); Nola (Sangha)

MILITARY

Military branches: Central African Armed Forces (Forces Armees Centrafricaines, FACA): Ground Forces (includes Military Air Service), General Directorate of Gendarmerie Inspection (DGIG), National Police (2011)

Military service age and obligation: 18 years of age for selective military service; 2-year conscript service obligation (2012)

Manpower available for military service: *males age 16-49:* 1,149,856
females age 16-49: 1,145,897 (2010 est.)

Manpower fit for military service: *males age 16-49:* 655,875
females age 16-49: 661,308 (2010 est.)

Manpower reaching militarily significant age annually: *male:* 54,843
female: 53,999 (2010 est.)

TRANSNATIONAL ISSUES

Disputes—international: periodic skirmishes over water and grazing rights among related pastoral populations along the border with southern Sudan persist

Refugees and internally displaced persons: *refugees (country of origin):* 10,662 (Democratic Republic of the Congo) (2012)
IDPs: 644,000 (clashes between army and rebel groups since 2005; tensions between ethnic groups) (2014)

Trafficking in persons: *current situation:* Central African Republic (CAR) is a source and destination country for children subjected to forced labor and sex trafficking and possibly women subjected to forced prostitution; most victims appear to be CAR citizens exploited within the country, and that a smaller number are transported back and forth between the CAR and Cameroon, Chad, Nigeria, Republic of the Congo, Democratic Republic of the Congo, Sudan, and South Sudan; children are forced into domestic servitude, commercial sexual exploitation, agricultural labor, mining, and street vending; armed groups operating in the CAR, including the Lord's Resistance Army, continue to recruit and use children for military activities, while village self-defense units use children as combatants, lookouts, and porters tier

rating: Tier 3—Central African Republic does not fully comply with the minimum standards for the elimination of trafficking and is not making significant efforts to do so; the government does not investigate or prosecute any suspected cases of human trafficking, including the use of child soldiers; the government also fails to identify, provide protection to, or refer to service providers any trafficking victims; in collaboration with an NGO, the government has convened a working group to develop a national action plan to combat human trafficking (2013)

CHAD

INTRODUCTION

Background: Chad, part of France's African holdings until 1960, endured three decades of civil warfare, as well as invasions by Libya, before a semblance of peace was finally restored in 1990. The government eventually drafted a democratic constitution and held flawed presidential elections in 1996 and 2001. In 1998, a rebillion broke out in northern Chad, which has sporadically flared up despite several peace agreements between the government and the insurgents. In 2005, new rebel groups emerged in western Sudan and made probing attacks into eastern Chad despite signing peace agreements in December 2006 and October 2007. In June 2005, President Idriss DEBY held a referendum successfully removing constitutional term limits and won another controversial election in 2006. Sporadic rebel campaigns continued throughout 2006 and 2007. The capital experienced a significant insurrection in early 2008, but has had no significant rebel threats since then, in part due to Chad's 2010 rapprochement with Sudan, which previously used Chadian rebels as proxies. DEBY in 2011 was reelected to his fourth term in an election that international observers described as proceeding without incident. Power remains in the hands of an ethnic minority. In January 2014, Chad began a two year rotation on the UN Security Council.

GEOGRAPHY

Location: Central Africa, south of Libya

Geographic coordinates: 15 00 N, 19 00 E

Map references: Africa

Area: *total:* 1.284 million sq km
country comparison to the world: 21
land: 1,259,200 sq km
water: 24,800 sq km

Area—comparative: slightly more than three times the size of California

Land boundaries: *total:* 5,968 km

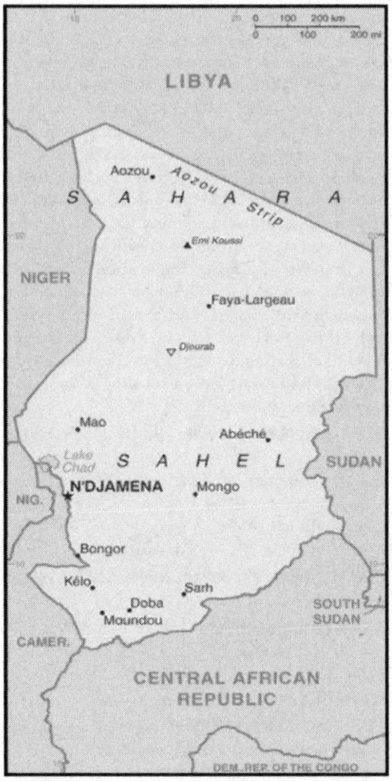

border countries: Cameroon 1,094 km, Central African Republic 1,197 km, Libya 1,055 km, Niger 1,175 km, Nigeria 87 km, Sudan 1,360 km

Coastline: 0 km (landlocked)

Maritime claims: none (landlocked)

Climate: tropical in south, desert in north

Terrain: broad, arid plains in center, desert in north, mountains in northwest, lowlands in south

Elevation extremes: *lowest point:* Djourab 160 m
highest point: Emi Koussi 3,415 m

Natural resources: petroleum, uranium, natron, kaolin, fish (Lake Chad), gold, limestone, sand and gravel, salt

Land use: *arable land:* 3.82%
permanent crops: 0.02%
other: 96.16% (2011)

Irrigated land: 302.7 sq km (2003)

Total renewable water resources: 43 cu km (2011)

Freshwater withdrawal (domestic/industrial/agricultural): *total:* 0.88 cu km/yr (12%/12%/76%)
per capita: 84.81 cu m/yr (2005)

Natural hazards: hot, dry, dusty harmattan winds occur in north; periodic droughts; locust plagues

Environment—current issues: inadequate supplies of potable water; improper waste disposal in rural areas contributes to soil and water pollution; desertification

Environment—international agreements: *party to:* Biodiversity, Climate Change, Desertification, Endangered Species, Hazardous Wastes, Ozone Layer Protection, Wetlands
signed, but not ratified: Law of the Sea, Marine Dumping

Geography—note: landlocked; Lake Chad is the most significant water body in the Sahel

PEOPLE AND SOCIETY

Nationality: *noun:* Chadian(s)
adjective: Chadian

Ethnic groups: Sara 27.7%, Arab 12.3%, Mayo-Kebbi 11.5%, Kanem-Bornou 9%, Ouaddai 8.7%, Hadjarai 6.7%, Tandjile 6.5%, Gorane 6.3%, Fitri-Batha 4.7%, other 6.4%, unknown 0.3% (1993 census)

Languages: French (official), Arabic (official), Sara (in south), more than 120 different languages and dialects

Religions: Muslim 53.1%, Catholic 20.1%, Protestant 14.2%, animist 7.3%, other 0.5%, unknown 1.7%, atheist 3.1% (1993 census)

Population: 11,412,107 (July 2014 est.)
country comparison to the world: 77

Age structure: *0-14 years:* 44.7% (male 2,588,424/female 2,515,935)
15-24 years: 20.6% (male 1,143,812/female 1,211,136)
25-54 years: 27.8% (male 1,436,018/female 1,737,901)
55-64 years: 3% (male 193,173/female 247,584)
65 years and over: 2.9% (male 140,592/female 197,532) (2014 est.)

Dependency ratios: *total dependency ratio:* 103.3%
youth dependency ratio: 98.4%
elderly dependency ratio: 4.9%
potential support ratio: 20.4 (2013)

Median age: *total:* 17.2 years
male: 16.1 years
female: 18.2 years (2014 est.)

Population growth rate: 1.92% (2014 est.)
country comparison to the world: 59

Birth rate: 37.29 births/1,000 population (2014 est.)
country comparison to the world: 16

Death rate: 14.56 deaths/1,000 population (2014 est.)
country comparison to the world: 4

Net migration rate: -3.54 migrant(s)/1,000 population (2014 est.)
country comparison to the world: 187

Urbanization: *urban population:* 21.8% of total population (2011)
rate of urbanization: 3% annual rate of change (2010-15 est.)

Major urban areas—population: N'DJAMENA (capital) 1.079 million (2011)

Sex ratio: *at birth:* 1.04 male(s)/female
0-14 years: 1.03 male(s)/female
15-24 years: 0.94 male(s)/female
25-54 years: 0.83 male(s)/female
55-64 years: 0.93 male(s)/female
65 years and over: 0.72 male(s)/female
total population: 0.93 male(s)/female (2014 est.)

Mother's mean age at first birth: 18.2 (2004 est.)

Maternal mortality rate: 1,100 deaths/100,000 live births (2010)
country comparison to the world: 2

Infant mortality rate: *total:* 90.3 deaths/1,000 live births
country comparison to the world: 6
male: 95.92 deaths/1,000 live births
female: 84.46 deaths/1,000 live births (2014 est.)

Life expectancy at birth: *total population:* 49.44 years
country comparison to the world: 223
male: 48.3 years
female: 50.63 years (2014 est.)

Total fertility rate: 4.68 children born/woman (2014 est.)
country comparison to the world: 24

Contraceptive prevalence rate: 4.8% (2010)

Health expenditures: 4.3% of GDP (2011)
country comparison to the world: 158

Physicians density: 0.04 physicians/1,000 population (2006)

Hospital bed density: 0.43 beds/1,000 population (2005)

Drinking water source:
Improved:
urban: 70.8% of population
rural: 44.4% of population
total: 55.6% of population
unimproved:
urban: 29.2% of population
rural: 55.6% of population
total: 49.8% of population (2011 est.)

Sanitation facility access:
Improved:
urban: 30.9% of population
rural: 6.4% of population
total: 11.7% of population
unimproved:
urban: 69.1% of population
rural: 93.6% of population
total: 88.3% of population (2011 est.)

HIV/AIDS—adult prevalence rate: 2.7% (2012 est.)
country comparison to the world: 25

HIV/AIDS—people living with HIV/AIDS: 213,100 (2012 est.)
country comparison to the world: 28

HIV/AIDS—deaths: 14,400 (2012 est.)
country comparison to the world: 21

Major infectious diseases: *degree of risk:* very high
food or waterborne diseases: bacterial and protozoal diarrhea, hepatitis A and E, and typhoid fever
vectorborne disease: malaria and dengue fever
water contact disease: schistosomiasis
respiratory disease: meningococcal meningitis
animal contact disease: rabies (2013)

Obesity—adult prevalence rate: 2.7% (2008)
country comparison to the world: 177

Children under the age of 5 years underweight: 33.9% (2004)
country comparison to the world: 8

Education expenditures: 2.3% of GDP (2011)
country comparison to the world: 160

Literacy: *definition:* age 15 and over can read and write French or Arabic
total population: 35.4%
male: 45.6%
female: 25,4% (2011 est.)

School life expectancy (primary to tertiary education): *total:* 7 years
male: 9 years
female: 6 years (2011)

Child labor—children ages 5-14:
total number: 1,475,960
percentage: 48 % (2010 est.)

GOVERNMENT

Country name: *conventional long form:* Republic of Chad
conventional short form: Chad

local long form: Republique du Tchad/Jumhuriyat Tshad
local short form: Tchad/Tshad

Government type: republic

Capital: *name:* N'Djamena
geographic coordinates: 12 06 N, 15 02 E
time difference: UTC+1 (6 hours ahead of Washington, DC during Standard Time)

Administrative divisions: 23 regions (regions, singular—region); Barh el Gazel, Batha, Borkou, Chari-Baguirmi, Ennedi-Est, Ennedi-Ouest, Guera, Hadjer-Lamis, Kanem, Lac, Logone Occidental, Logone Oriental, Mandoul, Mayo-Kebbi Est, Mayo-Kebbi Ouest, Moyen-Chari, Ouaddai, Salamat, Sila, Tandjile, Tibesti, Ville de N'Djamena, Wadi Fira

Independence: 11 August 1960 (from France)

National holiday: Independence Day, 11 August (1960)

Constitution: several previous; latest passed by referendum 31 March 1996, entered into force 8 April 1996; amended 2005 (2010)

Legal system: mixed legal system of civil and customary law

International law organization participation: has not submitted an ICJ jurisdiction declaration; accepts ICCt jurisdiction

Suffrage: 18 years of age; universal

Executive branch: *chief of state:* President Lt. Gen. Idriss DEBY Itno (since 4 December 1990)
head of government: Prime Minister Kalzeube Pahimi DEUBET (since 21 November 2013)
cabinet: Council of State; members are appointed by the president on the recommendation of the prime minister (For more information visit the World Leaders website)
elections: president elected by popular vote for a five-year term; if no candidate receives at least 50% of the total vote, the two candidates receiving the most votes must stand for a second round of voting; last election held on 25 April 2011 (next to be held by 2016); prime minister appointed by the president
election results: Lt. Gen. Idriss DEBY Itno reelected president; percent of vote—Lt. Gen. Idriss DEBY 83.6%, Albert Pahimi PADACKE 8.6%, Nadji MADOU 7.8%

Legislative branch: unicameral National Assembly (188 seats; members elected by popular vote to serve four-year terms)
elections: National Assembly—last held on 13 February 2011 (next to be held by 2015); note—legislative elections, originally scheduled for 2006, were first delayed by National Assembly action and subsequently by an accord, signed in August 2007, between government and opposition parties
election results: percent of vote by party—NA; seats by party—ART 133, UNDR 11, others 44

Judicial branch: *highest court(s):* Supreme Court (consists of a chief justice and 15 judges or councilors and divided into 3 chambers); Constitutional Council (consists of 3 judges and 6 jurists)
judge selection and term of office: Supreme Court chief justice selected by the president; councilors—8 designated by the president and 7 by the speaker of the National Assembly; chief justice and councilors appointed for life; Constitutional Council judges—2 appointed by the president and 1 by the speaker of the National Assembly; jurists—3 each by the president and by the speaker of the National Assembly; judges term NA
subordinate courts: High Court of Justice; Courts of Appeal; tribunals; justices of the peace

Political parties and leaders: Alliance for the Renaissance of Chad or ART, an alliance among the ruling MPS, RDP, and Viva-RNDP; Federation Action for the Republic or FAR [Ngarledjy YORONGAR]; National Rally for Development and Progress or Viva-RNDP [Albert Pahimi PADACKE]; National Union for Democracy and Renewal or UNDR [Saleh KEBZABO]; Party for Liberty and Development or PLD [Jean-Baptiste LAOKOLE]; Patriotic Salvation Movement or MPS [Mahamat Saleh AHMAT, chairman]; Rally for Democracy and Progress or RDP [Lol Mahamat CHOUA]; Union for Renewal and Democracy or URD [Sande NGARYIMBE]

Political pressure groups and leaders: rebel groups

International organization participation: ACP, AfDB, AU, BDEAC, CEMAC, EITI (candidate country), FAO, FZ, G-77, IAEA, IBRD, ICAO, ICRM, IDA, IDB, IFAD, IFC, IFRCS, ILO, IMF, Interpol, IOC, IOM, IPU, ITSO, ITU, ITUC (NGOs), MIGA, MINUSMA, NAM, OIC, OIF, OPCW, UN, UN Security Council (temporary), UNCTAD, UNESCO, UNIDO, UNOCI, UNWTO, UPU, WCO, WHO, WIPO, WMO, WTO

Diplomatic representation in the US: *chief of mission:* Ambassador Maitine DJOUMBE (since 12 July 2012)
chancery: 2401 Massachusetts Avenue NW, Washington, DC 20008
telephone: [1] (202) 462-4009
FAX: [1] (202) 265-1937

Diplomatic representation from the US: *chief of mission:* Ambassador James KNIGHT (since 13 March 2013)
embassy: Avenue Felix Eboue, N'Djamena
mailing address: B. P. 413, N'Djamena
telephone: [235] 2251-70-09
FAX: [235] 2251-56-54

Flag description: three equal vertical bands of blue (hoist side), yellow, and red; the flag combines the blue and red French (former colonial) colors with the red and yellow of the Pan-African colors; blue symbolizes the sky, hope, and the south of the country, which is relatively well-watered; yellow represents the sun, as well as the desert in the north of the country; red stands for progress, unity, and sacrifice
note: similar to the flag of Romania; also similar to the flags of Andorra and Moldova, both of which have a national coat of arms centered in the yellow band; design was based on the flag of France

National symbol(s): goat (north); lion (south)

National anthem: *name:* "La Tchadienne" (The Chadian)
lyrics/music: Louis GIDROL and his students/ Paul VILLARD
note: adopted 1960

ECONOMY

Economy—overview: Oil and agriculture drive Chad's economy. At least 80% of Chad's population relies for its livelihood on subsistence farming and livestock raising and oil provides the bulk of export revenues. Cotton, cattle, and gum arabic provide the bulk of Chad's non-oil export earnings. Remittances have also been an important source of income and Chad relies on foreign assistance and foreign capital for most public and private sector investment. Oil production came on stream in late 2003 and Chad began to export oil in 2004. Economic growth has been positive in recent years due to high oil prices and strong local harvests, but Chad's fiscal situation is repeatedly exposed to declining oil prices and drought . Recently, the economy has been strained by the costs of repatriating Chadians fleeing the violence in South Sudan and the Central African Republic. Chad's investment climate remains challenging due to limited infrastructure, a lack of trained workers, extensive government bureaucracy, and corruption.

GDP (purchasing power parity): $28 billion (2013 est.)
country comparison to the world: 117
$26.94 billion (2012 est.)
$24.74 billion (2011 est.)
note: data are in 2013 US dollars

GDP (official exchange rate): $13.59 billion (2013 est.)

GDP—real growth rate: 3.9% (2013 est.)
country comparison to the world: 83
8.9% (2012 est.)
0.1% (2011 est.)

GDP—per capita (PPP): $2,500 (2013 est.)
country comparison to the world: 184
$2,500 (2012 est.)
$2,400 (2011 est.)
note: data are in 2013 US dollars

Gross national saving: 46.4% of GDP (2013 est.)
country comparison to the world: 6
45.6% of GDP (2012 est.)
45.4% of GDP (2011 est.)

GDP - composition, by end use:
household consumption: 25.9%
government consumption: 12.2%
investment in fixed capital: 53%
investment in inventories: 0.3%
exports of goods and services:
32% *imports of goods and services:* -23.4% (2013 est.)

GDP—composition, by sector of origin:
agriculture: 46.3%
industry: 9.9%
services: 43.8% (2013 est.)

Agriculture—products: cotton, sorghum, millet, peanuts, rice, potatoes, manioc (tapioca); cattle, sheep, goats, camels

Industries: oil, cotton textiles, meatpacking, brewing, natron (sodium carbonate), soap, cigarettes, construction materials

Industrial production growth rate: 10% (2013 est.)
country comparison to the world: 14

Labor force: 4.293 million (2007)
country comparison to the world: 87

Labor force—by occupation: *agriculture:* 80% (2006 est.)
industry and services: 20% (2006 est.)

Unemployment rate: NA%

Population below poverty line: 80% (2001 est.)

Household income or consumption by percentage share: *lowest 10%:* 2.6%
highest 10%: 30.8% (2003)

Budget: *revenues:* $2.753 billion
expenditures: $3.557 billion (2013 est.)

Taxes and other revenues: 20.3% of GDP (2013 est.)
country comparison to the world: 163

Budget surplus (+) or deficit (-): -5.9% of GDP (2013 est.)
country comparison to the world: 178

Public debt: 30.5% of GDP (2013 est.)
country comparison to the world: 121
31.3% of GDP (2012 est.)

Fiscal year: calendar year

Inflation rate (consumer prices): 4.5% (2013 est.)
country comparison to the world: 147
10.2% (2012 est.)

Central bank discount rate: 4.25% (31 December 2009)
country comparison to the world: 80
4.75% (31 December 2008)

Commercial bank prime lending rate: 15.5% (31 December 2013 est.)
country comparison to the world: 35
15.5% (31 December 2012 est.)

Stock of narrow money: $1.598 billion (31 December 2013 est.)
country comparison to the world: 134
$1.442 billion (31 December 2012 est.)

Stock of broad money: $1.804 billion (31 December 2013 est.)
country comparison to the world: 154
$1.559 billion (31 December 2012 est.)

Stock of domestic credit: $832.4 million (31 December 2013 est.)
country comparison to the world: 158
$550.7 million (31 December 2012 est.)

Market value of publicly traded shares: $NA

Current account balance: -$827.1 million (2013 est.)
country comparison to the world: 115
-$378.9 million (2012 est.)

Exports: $3.865 billion (2013 est.)
country comparison to the world: 124
$4.126 billion (2012 est.)

Exports—commodities: oil, cattle, cotton, gum arabic

Exports—partners: US 81.9%, China 6.7% (2012)

Imports: $2.701 billion (2013 est.)
country comparison to the world: 152
$2.672 billion (2012 est.)

Imports—commodities: machinery and transportation equipment, industrial goods, foodstuffs, textiles

Imports—partners: China 20.2%, Cameroon 18.2%, France 16.1%, Saudi Arabia 5.6%, US 4.2% (2012)

Reserves of foreign exchange and gold: $1.304 billion (31 December 2013 est.)
country comparison to the world: 130
$1.174 billion (31 December 2012 est.)

Debt—external: $1.828 billion (31 December 2013 est.)
country comparison to the world: 145
$1.794 billion (31 December 2012 est.)

Stock of direct foreign investment—at home: $NA
$4.5 billion (2006 est.)

Stock of direct foreign investment—abroad: $NA

Exchange rates: Cooperation Financiere en Afrique Centrale francs (XAF) per US dollar—
500.7 (2013 est.)
510.53 (2012 est.)
495.28 (2010 est.)
472.19 (2009)
447.81 (2008)

ENERGY

Electricity—production: 98 million kWh (2010 est.)
country comparison to the world: 198

Electricity—consumption: 91.14 million kWh (2010 est.)
country comparison to the world: 198

Electricity—exports: 0 kWh (2012 est.)
country comparison to the world: 115

Electricity—imports: 0 kWh (2012 est.)
country comparison to the world: 124

Electricity—installed generating capacity: 31,000 kW (2010 est.)
country comparison to the world: 197

Electricity—from fossil fuels: 100% of total installed capacity (2010 est.)
country comparison to the world: 10

Electricity—from nuclear fuels: 0% of total installed capacity (2010 est.)
country comparison to the world: 60

Electricity—from hydroelectric plants: 0% of total installed capacity (2010 est.)
country comparison to the world: 162

Electricity—from other renewable sources: 0% of total installed capacity (2010 est.)
country comparison to the world: 164

Crude oil—production: 104,500 bbl/day (2012 est.)
country comparison to the world: 48

Crude oil—exports: 125,700 bbl/day (2010 est.)
country comparison to the world: 36

Crude oil—imports: 0 bbl/day (2010 est.)
country comparison to the world: 169

Crude oil—proved reserves: 1.5 billion bbl (1 January 2013 es)
country comparison to the world: 38

Refined petroleum products—production: 0 bbl/day (2010 est.)
country comparison to the world: 129

Refined petroleum products—consumption: 1,817 bbl/day (2011 est.)
country comparison to the world: 190

Refined petroleum products—exports: 0 bbl/day (2010 est.)
country comparison to the world: 161

Refined petroleum products—imports: 1,754 bbl/day (2010 est.)
country comparison to the world: 183

Natural gas—production: 0 cu m (2011 est.)
country comparison to the world: 112

Natural gas—consumption: 0 cu m (2010 est.)
country comparison to the world: 128

Natural gas—exports: 0 cu m (2011 est.)
country comparison to the world: 76

Natural gas—imports: 0 cu m (2011 est.)
country comparison to the world: 171

Natural gas—proved reserves: 999.5 billion cu m (1 January 2012 es)
country comparison to the world: 27

Carbon dioxide emissions from consumption of energy: 289,800 Mt (2011 est.)
country comparison to the world: 190

COMMUNICATIONS

Telephones—main lines in use: 29,900 (2012)
country comparison to the world: 176

Telephones—mobile cellular: 4.2 million (2012)
country comparison to the world: 119

Telephone system: *general assessment:* inadequate system of radiotelephone communication stations with high costs and low telephone density
domestic: fixed-line connections for less than 1 per 100 persons coupled with mobile-cellular subscribership base of only about 35 per 100 persons
international: country code—235; satellite earth station—1 Intelsat (Atlantic Ocean) (2011)

Broadcast media: 1 state-owned TV station; state-owned radio network, Radiodiffusion Nationale Tchadienne (RNT), operates national and regional stations; about 10 private radio stations; some stations rebroadcast programs from international broadcasters (2007)

Internet country code: .td

Internet hosts: 6 (2012)
country comparison to the world: 229

Internet users: 168,100 (2009)
country comparison to the world: 145

TRANSPORTATION

Airports: 59 (2013)
country comparison to the world: 82

Airports—with paved runways: *total:* 9
over 3,047 m: 2
2,438 to 3,047 m: 4
1,524 to 2,437 m: 2
under 914 m: 1 (2013)

Airports—with unpaved runways: *total:* 50
over 3,047 m: 1
2,438 to 3,047 m: 2
1,524 to 2,437 m: 14
914 to 1,523 m: 22
under 914 m: 11 (2013)

Pipelines: oil 582 km (2013)

Roadways: *total:* 40,000 km
country comparison to the world: 87
note: consists of 25,000 km of national and regional roads and 15,000 km of local roads; 206 km of urban roads are paved (2011)

Waterways: (Chari and Legone rivers are navigable only in wet season) (2012)

MILITARY

Military branches: Chadian National Army (Armee Nationale du Tchad, ANT): Ground Forces (l'Armee de Terre, AdT), Chadian Air Force (l'Armee de l'Air Tchadienne, AAT), National Gendarmerie, National and Nomadic Guard of Chad (GNNT) (2013)

Military service age and obligation: 20 is the legal minimum age for compulsory military service, with a 3-year service obligation; 18 is the legal minimum age for voluntary service; no minimum age restriction for volunteers with consent from a parent or guardian; women are subject to 1 year of compulsory military or civic service at age of 21 (2012)

Manpower available for military service:
males age 16-49: 2,090,244
females age 16-49: 2,441,321 (2010 est.)

Manpower fit for military service: *males age 16-49:* 1,183,242
females age 16-49: 1,395,811 (2010 est.)

Manpower reaching militarily significant age annually: *male:* 128,723
female: 128,244 (2010 est.)

Military expenditures:
NA% (2012)
2.28% of GDP (2011)
NA% (2010)

TRANSNATIONAL ISSUES

Disputes—international: since 2003, ad hoc armed militia groups and the Sudanese military have driven hundreds of thousands of Darfur residents into Chad; Chad wishes to be a helpful mediator in resolving the Darfur conflict, and in 2010 established a joint border monitoring force with Sudan, which has helped to reduce cross-border banditry and violence; only Nigeria and Cameroon have heeded the Lake Chad Commission's admonition to ratify the delimitation treaty, which also includes the Chad-Niger and Niger-Nigeria boundaries

Refugees and internally displaced persons: *refugees (country of origin):* 352,948 (Sudan); 90,000 (Central African Republic) (2014)
IDPs: 90,000 (majority are in the east) (2012)

Trafficking in persons: *current situation:* Chad is a source, transit, and destination country for children subjected to forced labor and sex trafficking; the trafficking problem is mainly internal and frequently involves family members entrusting children to relatives or intermediaries in return for promises of education, apprenticeships,goods, or money; child trafficking victims are subjected to involuntary domestic servitude, forced cattle herding, forced begging, involuntary agricultural labor, or commercial sexual exploitation; some Chadian girls who travel to larger towns in search of work are forced into prostitution; in 2012, Chadian children were identified in some government military training centers and among rebel groups
tier rating: Tier 2 Watch List - Chad does not fully comply with the minimum standards for the elimination of trafficking; however, it is making significant efforts to do so; the government has made a limited commitment to increased anti-trafficking law enforcement but continues to lack formal victim identification procedures; draft revisions to Chad's penal code that would prohibit child trafficking and provide protection for victims were not enacted for the third consecutive year; the government continues its nationwide campaign on human rights issues, including human trafficking, and high-ranking officials, such as the president and prime minister, are speaking out publicly against human trafficking (2013)

CHILE

INTRODUCTION

Background: Prior to the arrival of the Spanish in the 16th century, the Inca ruled northern Chile while the Mapuche inhabited central and southern Chile. Although Chile declared its independence in 1810, decisive victory over the Spanish was not achieved until 1818. In the War of the Pacific (1879-83), Chile defeated Peru and Bolivia and won its present northern regions. It was not until the 1880s that the Mapuche were brought under central government control. After a series of elected governments, the three-year-old Marxist government of Salvador ALLENDE was overthrown in 1973 by a military coup led by Augusto PINOCHET, who ruled until a freely elected president was inaugurated in 1990. Sound economic policies, maintained consistently since the 1980s, contributed to steady growth, reduced poverty rates by over half, and helped secure the country's commitment to democratic and representative government. Chile has increasingly assumed regional and international leadership roles befitting its status as a stable, democratic nation. In January 2014, Chile assumed a nonpermanent seat on the UN Security Council for the 2014-15 term.

GEOGRAPHY

Location: Southern South America, bordering the South Pacific Ocean, between Argentina and Peru

Geographic coordinates: 30 00 S, 71 00 W

Map references: South America

Area: *total:* 756,102 sq km
country comparison to the world: 38
land: 743,812 sq km
water: 12,290 sq km
note: includes Easter Island (Isla de Pascua) and Isla Sala y Gomez

Area—comparative: slightly smaller than twice the size of Montana

Land boundaries: *total:* 6,339 km
border countries: Argentina 5,308 km, Bolivia 860 km, Peru 171 km

Coastline: 6,435 km

Maritime claims: *territorial sea:* 12 nm
contiguous zone: 24 nm
exclusive economic zone: 200 nm
continental shelf: 200/350 nm

Climate: temperate; desert in north; Mediterranean in central region; cool and damp in south

Terrain: low coastal mountains; fertile central valley; rugged Andes in east

Elevation extremes: *lowest point:* Pacific Ocean 0 m
highest point: Nevado Ojos del Salado 6,880 m

Natural resources: copper, timber, iron ore, nitrates, precious metals, molybdenum, hydropower

Land use: *arable land:* 1.74%
permanent crops: 0.6%
other: 97.65% (2011)

Irrigated land: 11,990 sq km (2003)

Total renewable water resources: 922 cu km (2011)

Freshwater withdrawal (domestic/industrial/agricultural): *total:* 26.67 cu km/yr (4%/10%/86%)
per capita: 1,603 cu m/yr (2007)

Natural hazards: severe earthquakes; active volcanism; tsunamis
volcanism: significant volcanic activity due to more than three-dozen active volcanoes along the Andes Mountains; Lascar (elev. 5,592 m), which last erupted in 2007, is the most active volcano in the northern Chilean Andes; Llaima (elev. 3,125 m) in central Chile, which last erupted in 2009, is another of the country's most active; Chaiten's 2008 eruption forced major evacuations; other notable historically active volcanoes include Cerro Hudson, Copahue, Guallatiri, Llullaillaco, Nevados de Chillan, Puyehue, San Pedro, and Villarrica

Environment—current issues: widespread deforestation and mining threaten natural resources; air pollution from industrial and vehicle emissions; water pollution from raw sewage

Environment—international agreements: *party to:* Antarctic-Environmental Protocol, Antarctic-Marine Living Resources, Antarctic Seals, Antarctic Treaty, Biodiversity, Climate Change, Climate Change-Kyoto Protocol, Desertification, Endangered Species, Environmental Modification, Hazardous Wastes, Law of the Sea, Marine Dumping, Ozone Layer Protection, Ship Pollution, Wetlands, Whaling
signed, but not ratified: none of the selected agreements

Geography—note: the longest north-south trending country in the world, extending across 38 degrees of latitude; strategic location relative to sea lanes between the Atlantic and Pacific Oceans (Strait of Magellan, Beagle Channel, Drake Passage); Atacama Desert—the driest desert in the world—spreads across the northern part of the country; the crater lake of Ojos del Salado is the world's *highest lake (at 6,390 m)*

PEOPLE AND SOCIETY

Nationality: *noun:* Chilean(s)
adjective: Chilean

Ethnic groups: white and non-indigenous 88.9%, Mapuche 9.1%, Aymara 0.7%, other indigenous groups 1% (includes Rapa Nui, Likan Antai, Quechua, Colla, Diaguita, Kawesqar, Yagan or Yamana), unspecified 0.3% (2012 est.)

Languages: Spanish 99.5% (official), English 10.2%, indigenous 1% (includes Mapudungun, Aymara, Quechua, Rapa Nui), other 2.3%, unspecified 0.2%
note: shares sum to more than 100% because some respondents gave more than one answer on the census (2012 est.)

Religions: Roman Catholic 66.7%, Evangelical or Protestant 16.4%, Jehovah's Witnesses 1%, other 3.4%, none 11.5%, unspecified 1.1% (2012 est.)

Demographic profile: Chile is in the advanced stages of demographic transition and is becoming an aging society—with fertility below replacement level, low mortality rates, and life expectancy on par with developed countries. Nevertheless, with its dependency ratio nearing its low point, Chile could benefit from its favorable age structure. It will need to keep its large working-age population productively employed, while preparing to provide for the needs of its growing proportion of elderly people, especially as women—the traditional caregivers—increasingly enter the workforce. Over the last two decades, Chile has made great strides in reducing its poverty rate, which is now lower than most Latin American countries. However, its severe income inequality ranks as the worst among members of the Organization for Economic Cooperation and Development. Unequal access to quality education perpetuates this uneven income distribution.

Chile has historically been a country of emigration but has slowly become more attractive to immigrants since transitioning to democracy in 1990 and improving its economic stability (other regional destinations have concurrently experienced deteriorating economic and political conditions). Most of Chile's small but growing foreign-born population consists of transplants from other Latin American countries, especially Peru.

Population: 17,363,894 (July 2014 est.)
country comparison to the world: 65

Age structure: *0-14 years:* 20.7% (male 1,834,247/female 1,760,315)
15-24 years: 16.3% (male 1,442,610/female 1,383,738)
25-54 years: 43.2% (male 3,733,261/female 3,766,912)
55-64 years: 9.9% (male 806,044/female 910,818)
65 years and over: 9.7% (male 720,681/female 1,005,268) (2014 est.)

Dependency ratios:
total dependency ratio: 45%
youth dependency ratio: 30.6%
elderly dependency ratio: 14.5%
potential support ratio: 6.9 (2013)

Median age: *total:* 33.3 years
male: 32.2 years
female: 34.6 years (2014 est.)

Population growth rate: 0.84% (2014 est.)
country comparison to the world: 131

Birth rate: 13.97 births/1,000 population (2014 est.)
country comparison to the world: 140

Death rate: 5.93 deaths/1,000 population (2014 est.)
country comparison to the world: 170

Net migration rate: 0.35 migrant(s)/1,000 population (2014 est.)
country comparison to the world: 74

Urbanization: *urban population:* 89% of total population (2010)
rate of urbanization: 1.1% annual rate of change (2010-15 est.)

Major urban areas—population: SANTIAGO (capital) 6.034 million; Valparaiso 865,000 (2011)

Sex ratio: *at birth:* 1.04 male(s)/female
0-14 years: 1.04 male(s)/female
15-24 years: 1.04 male(s)/female
25-54 years: 0.99 male(s)/female
55-64 years: 0.97 male(s)/female
65 years and over: 0.71 male(s)/female
total population: 0.97 male(s)/female (2014 est.)

Mother's mean age at first birth: 23.7 (2004 est.)

Maternal mortality rate: 25 deaths/100,000 live births (2010)
country comparison to the world: 131

Infant mortality rate: *total:* 7.02 deaths/1,000 live births
country comparison to the world: 161
male: 7.51 deaths/1,000 live births
female: 6.52 deaths/1,000 live births (2014 est.)

Life expectancy at birth: *total population:* 78.44 years
country comparison to the world: 52
male: 75.42 years
female: 81.59 years (2014 est.)

Total fertility rate: 1.84 children born/woman (2014 est.)
country comparison to the world: 148

Contraceptive prevalence rate: 64.2%
note: percent of women aged 15-44 (2006)

Health expenditures: 7.5% of GDP (2011)
country comparison to the world: 74

Physicians density: 1.03 physicians/1,000 population (2009)

Hospital bed density: 2 beds/1,000 population (2010)

Drinking water source:
Improved:
urban: 99.5% of population
rural: 90.1% of population
total: 98.5% of population
unimproved:
urban: 0.5% of population
rural: 9.9% of population
total: 1.5% of population (2011 est.)

Sanitation facility access:
Improved:
urban: 99.8% of population
rural: 89.4% of population
total: 98.7% of population
unimproved:
urban: 0.2% of population
rural: 10.6% of population
total: 1.3% of population (2011 est.)

HIV/AIDS—adult prevalence rate: 0.4% (2012 est.)
country comparison to the world: 77

HIV/AIDS—people living with HIV/AIDS: 38,700 (2012 est.)
country comparison to the world: 68

HIV/AIDS—deaths: NA

Obesity—adult prevalence rate: 29.4% (2008)
country comparison to the world: 30

Children under the age of 5 years underweight: 0.5% (2008)
country comparison to the world: 135

Education expenditures: 4.5% of GDP (2012)
country comparison to the world: 90

Literacy: *definition:* age 15 and over can read and write
total population: 98.6%
male: 98.6%
female: 98.5% (2009 est.)

School life expectancy (primary to tertiary education): *total:* 15 years
male: 15 years
female: 16 years (2012)

Child labor—children ages 5-14:
total number: 82,882
percentage: 3 % (2003 est.)

unemployment, youth ages 15-24: *total:* 16.3%
country comparison to the world: 80
male: 14.3%
female: 19.1% (2012)

GOVERNMENT

Country name: *conventional long form:* Republic of Chile
conventional short form: Chile
local long form: Republica de Chile
local short form: Chile

Government type: republic

Capital: *name:* Santiago
geographic coordinates: 33 27 S, 70 40 W
time difference: UTC-4 (1 hour ahead of Washington, DC during Standard Time)
daylight saving time: +1hr, under a new pilot program begins second Sunday in September; ends fourth Sunday in April
note: Valparaiso is the seat of the national legislature

Administrative divisions: 15 regions (regiones, singular—region); Aysen, Antofagasta, Araucania, Arica y Parinacota, Atacama, Biobio, Coquimbo, Libertador General Bernardo O'Higgins, Los Lagos, Los Rios, Magallanes y de la Antartica Chilena, Maule, Region Metropolitana (Santiago), Tarapaca, Valparaiso
note: the US does not recognize claims to Antarctica

Independence: 18 September 1810 (from Spain)

National holiday: Independence Day, 18 September (1810)

Constitution: many previous; latest adopted 11 September 1980, effective 11 March 1981; amended many times, last in 2011 (2011)

Legal system: civil law system influenced by several West European civil legal systems; judicial review of legislative acts by the Constitutional Tribunal

International law organization participation: has not submitted an ICJ jurisdiction declaration; accepts ICCt jurisdiction

Suffrage: 18 years of age; universal and voluntary

Executive branch: *chief of state:* President Michelle BACHELET Jeria (since 11 March 2014); note—the president is both the chief of state and head of government
head of government: President Michelle BACHELET Jeria (since 11 March 2014)
cabinet: Cabinet appointed by the president (For more information visit the World Leaders website)
elections: president elected by popular vote for a single four-year term; election last held on 17 November 2013 with a runoff election held on 15 December 2013 (next to be held 19 November 2017)
election results: Michelle BACHELET Jeria elected president; percent of vote - Michelle BACHELET Jeria 62.2%; Evelyn Rose MATTHEI Fornet 37.8%

Legislative branch: bicameral National Congress or Congreso Nacional consists of the Senate or Senado (38 seats; members elected by popular vote to serve eight-year terms; one-half elected every four years) and the Chamber of Deputies or Camara de Diputados (120 seats; members are elected by popular vote to serve four-year terms)
elections: Senate—last held on 13 December 2009 (next to be held in November 2013); Chamber of Deputies—last held on 13 December 2009 (next to be held in November 2013)
election results: Senate—percent of vote by party—NA; seats by party—CPD 9 (PDC 4, PPD 3, PS 2), APC 9 (RN 6, UDI 3); Chamber of Deputies—percent of vote by party—NA; seats by party—APC 58 (UDI 37, RN 18, other 3), CPD

57 (PDC 19, PPD 18, PS 11, PRSD 5, PC 3, other 1), PRI 3, independent 2; note—as of 19 February 2013, the composition of the entire legislature is as follows: Senate—seats by party—CPD 19 (PDC 9, PPD 4, PS 5, PRSD 1), Coalition for Change (former APC) 16 (RN 8, UDI 8), independent 2, MAS 1; Chamber of Deputies—seats by party—Coalition for Change (former APC) 56 (UDI 39, RN 17), CPD 53 (PDC 19, PPD 18, PS 11, PRSD 5), independent 5, PC 3, PRI 2, IC 1

Judicial branch: *highest court(s):* Supreme Court or Corte Suprema (consists of a court president and 20 members or ministros); Constitutional Court (consists of 7 members); Electoral Court (consists of 5 members)
judge selection and term of office: Supreme Court judges appointed by the president and ratified by the Senate from lists of candidates provided by the court itself; judges appointed for life with mandatory retirement at age 70; Constitutional Court members appointed—3 by the Supreme Court, 1 by the president of the republic, 2 by the National Security Council, and 1 by the Senate; members serve 8-year terms with partial court replacement every 4 years (the court reviews constitutionality of legislation); Electoral Court member appointments—4 by the Supreme Court and 1 a former president or vice-president of the Senate or Chamber of Deputies selected by the Supreme Court; member term NA
subordinate courts: Courts of Appeal; oral criminal tribunals; military tribunals; local police courts; specialized tribunals and courts in matters such as family, labor, customs, taxes, and electoral affairs

Political parties and leaders: Broad Social Movement or MAS [Alejandro NAVARRO Brain]; Citizen Left or IC; Equality Party [Lautaro GUANCA Vallejos]; Coalition for Change or CC (also known as the Alliance for Chile (Alianza) or APC) (including National Renewal or RN [Carlos LARRAIN Pena], and Independent Democratic Union or UDI [Patricio MELERO]; Coalition of Parties for Democracy (Concertacion) or CPD (including Christian Democratic Party or PDC [Ignacio WALKER Prieto], Party for Democracy or PPD [Jaime Daniel QUINTANA Leal], Radical Social Democratic Party or PRSD [Jose Antonio GOMEZ Urrutia], and Socialist Party or PS [Osvaldo ANDRADE Lara]); Communist Party of Chile (Partido Comunista de Chile) or PC [Guillermo TEILLIER del Valle]; Ecological Green Party [Cristian VILLAROEL Novoa]; Humanist Party or PH [Danilo MONTEVERDE Reyes]; Independent Regionalist Party or PRI [Carlos OLIVARES Zepeda]; Progressive Party or PRO [Marco ENRIQUEZ-OMINAMI Gumucio]

Political pressure groups and leaders: Roman Catholic Church, particularly conservative groups such as Opus Dei; United Labor Central or CUT includes trade unionists from the country's five largest labor confederations
other: university student federations at all major universities

International organization participation: APEC, BIS, BRICS, CAN (associate), CD, CELAC, FAO, G-15, G-77, IADB, IAEA, IBRD, ICAO, ICC (national committees), ICRM, IDA, IFAD, IFC, IFRCS, IHO, ILO, IMF, IMO, IMSO, Interpol, IOC, IOM, IPU, ISO, ITSO, ITU, ITUC (NGOs), LAES, LAIA, Mercosur (associate), MIGA, MINUSTAH, NAM, OAS, OECD (Enhanced Engagement, OPANAL, OPCW, PCA, SICA (observer), UN, UNASUR, UNCTAD, UNESCO, UNFICYP, UNHCR, UNIDO, Union Latina, UNMOGIP, UNTSO, UNWTO, UPU, WCO, WFTU (NGOs), WHO, WIPO, WMO, WTO

Diplomatic representation in the US: *chief of mission:* Ambassador Felipe BULNES Serrano (since 5 April 2012)
chancery: 1732 Massachusetts Avenue NW, Washington, DC 20036
telephone: [1] (202) 785-1746
FAX: [1] (202) 887-5579
consulate(s) general: Chicago, Los Angeles, Miami, New York, Philadelphia, San Francisco

Diplomatic representation from the US: *chief of mission:* Ambassador (vacant); Charge d'Affaires Stephen M. LISTON
embassy: Avenida Andres Bello 2800, Las Condes, Santiago
mailing address: APO AA 34033
telephone: [56] (2) 330-3000
FAX: [56] (2) 330-3710, 330-3160

Flag description: two equal horizontal bands of white (top) and red; a blue square the same height as the white band at the hoist-side end of the white band; the square bears a white five-pointed star in the center representing a guide to progress and honor; blue symbolizes the sky, white is for the snow-covered Andes, and red represents the blood spilled to achieve independence
note: design was influenced by the US flag

National symbol(s): huemul (mountain deer); Andean condor

National anthem: *name:* "Himno Nacional de Chile" (National Anthem of Chile)
lyrics/music: Eusebio LILLO Robles and Bernardo DE VERA y Pintado/Ramon CARNICER y Battle
note: music adopted 1828, original lyrics adopted 1818, adapted lyrics adopted 1847; under Augusto PINOCHET's military rule, a verse glorifying the army was added; however, as a protest, some citizen refused to sing this verse; it was removed when democracy was restored in 1990

ECONOMY

Economy—overview: Chile has a market-oriented economy characterized by a high level of foreign trade and a reputation for strong financial institutions and sound policy that have given it the strongest sovereign bond rating in South America. Exports of goods and services account for approximately one-third of GDP, with commodities making up some three-quarters of total exports. Copper alone provides 19% of government revenue. From 2003 through 2013, real growth averaged almost 5% per year, despite the slight contraction in 2009 that resulted from the global financial crisis. Chile deepened its longstanding commitment to trade liberalization with the signing of a free trade agreement with the US, which took effect on 1 January 2004. Chile has 22 trade agreements covering 60 countries including agreements with the European Union, Mercosur, China, India, South Korea, and Mexico. Chile has joined the United States and nine other countries in negotiating the Trans-Pacific-Partnership trade agreement. The Chilean Government has generally followed a countercyclical fiscal policy, accumulating surpluses in sovereign wealth funds during periods of high copper prices and economic growth, and generally allowing deficit spending only during periods of low copper prices and growth. As of 31 December 2012, those sovereign wealth funds—kept mostly outside the country and separate from Central Bank reserves—amounted to more than $20.9 billion. Chile used these funds to finance fiscal stimulus packages during the 2009 economic downturn. In May 2010 Chile signed the OECD Convention, becoming the first South American country to join the OECD.

GDP (purchasing power parity): $335.4 billion (2013 est.)
country comparison to the world: 43
$321.3 billion (2012 est.)
$304.2 billion (2011 est.)
note: data are in 2013 US dollars

GDP (official exchange rate): $281.7 billion (2013 est.)

GDP—real growth rate: 4.4% (2013 est.)
country comparison to the world: 70
5.6% (2012 est.)
5.8% (2011 est.)

GDP—per capita (PPP): $19,100 (2013 est.)
country comparison to the world: 74
$18,500 (2012 est.)
$17,600 (2011 est.)
note: data are in 2013 US dollars

Gross national saving:
20.8% of GDP (2013 est.)
country comparison to the world: 77
21.4% of GDP (2012 est.)
22.2% of GDP (2011 est.)

GDP—composition, by end use:
household consumption: 63.2%
government consumption: 12%
investment in fixed capital: 25%
investment in inventories: 0.6%
exports of goods and services: 32.7%
imports of goods and services: -33.5% (2013 est.)

GDP—composition, by sector of origin:
agriculture: 3.6%
industry: 35.4%
services: 61% (2013 est.)

Agriculture—products: grapes, apples, pears, onions, wheat, corn, oats, peaches, garlic, asparagus, beans; beef, poultry, wool; fish; timber

Industries: copper, lithium, other minerals, foodstuffs, fish processing, iron and steel, wood and wood products, transport equipment, cement, textiles

Industrial production growth rate: 3% (2013 est.)
country comparison to the world: 105

Labor force: 8.367 million (2013 est.)
country comparison to the world: 58

Labor force—by occupation: *agriculture:* 13.2%
industry: 23%
services: 63.9% (2005)

Unemployment rate: 6% (2013 est.)
country comparison to the world: 59
6.3% (2012 est.)

Population below poverty line: 15.1% (2009 est.)

Household income or consumption by percentage share: *lowest 10%:* 1.5%
highest 10%: 42.8% (2009 est.)

Distribution of family income—Gini index: 52.1 (2009)
country comparison to the world: 15
57.1 (2000)

Budget: *revenues:* $58.49 billion
expenditures: $61.26 billion (2013 est.)

Taxes and other revenues: 20.8% of GDP (2013 est.)
country comparison to the world: 158

Budget surplus (+) or deficit (-): -1% of GDP (2013 est.)
country comparison to the world: 63

Public debt: 13.9% of GDP (2013 est.)
country comparison to the world: 145
11.9% of GDP (2012 est.)

Fiscal year: calendar year

Inflation rate (consumer prices): 1.7% (2013 est.)
country comparison to the world: 52
3% (2012 est.)

Central bank discount rate: 3.12% (31 December 2010 est.)
country comparison to the world: 136
0.5% (31 December 2009 est.)

Commercial bank prime lending rate: 9.5% (31 December 2013 est.)
country comparison to the world: 88
10.06% (31 December 2012 est.)

Stock of narrow money: $41.61 billion (31 December 2013 est.)
country comparison to the world: 53
$40.95 billion (31 December 2012 est.)

Stock of broad money: $159 billion (31 December 2013 est.)
country comparison to the world: 44
$150.5 billion (31 December 2012 est.)

Stock of domestic credit: $214 billion (31 December 2013 est.)
country comparison to the world: 39
$202.5 billion (31 December 2012 est.)

Market value of publicly traded shares: $313.3 billion (31 December 2012 est.)
country comparison to the world: 27
$270.3 billion (31 December 2011)
$341.6 billion (31 December 2010 est.)

Current account balance: -$10.97 billion (2013 est.)
country comparison to the world: 178
-$9.499 billion (2012 est.)

Exports: $77.94 billion (2013 est.)
country comparison to the world: 46
$78.28 billion (2012 est.)

Exports—commodities: copper, fruit, fish products, paper and pulp, chemicals, wine

Exports—partners: China 23.3%, US 12.3%, Japan 10.7%, South Korea 5.8%, Brazil 5.5% (2012)

Imports: $75.7 billion (2013 est.)
country comparison to the world: 40
$74.86 billion (2012 est.)

Imports—commodities: petroleum and petroleum products, chemicals, electrical and telecommunications equipment, industrial machinery, vehicles, natural gas

Imports—partners: US 22.9%, China 18.2%, Argentina 6.6%, Brazil 6.5% (2012)

Reserves of foreign exchange and gold: $39.89 billion (31 December 2013 est.)
country comparison to the world: 46
$41.65 billion (31 December 2012 est.)

Debt—external: $119 billion (31 December 2013 est.)
country comparison to the world: 43
$112.7 billion (31 December 2012 est.)

Stock of direct foreign investment—at home: $214.8 billion (31 December 2013 est.)
country comparison to the world: 26
$192.8 billion (31 December 2012 est.)

Stock of direct foreign investment—abroad: $109.2 billion (31 December 2013 est.)
country comparison to the world: 29
$91.3 billion (31 December 2012 est.)

Exchange rates: Chilean pesos (CLP) per US dollar—
491.7 (2013 est.)
486.49 (2012 est.)
510.25 (2010 est.)
560.86 (2009)
509.02 (2008)

ENERGY

Electricity—production: 62.86 billion kWh (2011 est.)
country comparison to the world: 4 2

Electricity—consumption: 53.93 billion kWh (2010 est.)
country comparison to the world: 44

Electricity—exports: 0 kWh (2012 est.)
country comparison to the world: 118

Electricity—imports: 734 million kWh (2011 est.)
country comparison to the world: 67

Electricity—installed generating capacity: 16.21 million kW (2010 est.)
country comparison to the world: 44

Electricity—from fossil fuels: 62% of total installed capacity (2010 est.)
country comparison to the world: 130

Electricity—from nuclear fuels: 0% of total installed capacity (2010 est.)
country comparison to the world: 64

Electricity—from hydroelectric plants: 33.7% of total installed capacity (2010 est.)
country comparison to the world: 65

Electricity—from other renewable sources: 4.3% of total installed capacity (2010 est.)
country comparison to the world: 46

Crude oil—production: 17,340 bbl/day (2012 est.)
country comparison to the world: 80

Crude oil—exports: 0 bbl/day (2010 est.)
country comparison to the world: 96

Crude oil—imports: 169,700 bbl/day (2010 est.)
country comparison to the world: 36

Crude oil—proved reserves: 150 million bbl (1 January 2013 es)
country comparison to the world: 66

Refined petroleum products—production: 187,200 bbl/day (2010 est.)
country comparison to the world: 56

Refined petroleum products—consumption: 321,700 bbl/day (2011 est.)
country comparison to the world: 38

Refined petroleum products—exports: 13,040 bbl/day (2010 est.)
country comparison to the world: 82

Refined petroleum products—imports: 154,100 bbl/day (2010 est.)
country comparison to the world: 37

Natural gas—production: 1.144 billion cu m (2012 est.)
country comparison to the world: 63

Natural gas—consumption: 5.296 billion cu m (2010 est.)
country comparison to the world: 60

Natural gas—exports: 0 cu m (2011 est.)
country comparison to the world: 79

Natural gas—imports: 3.83 billion cu m (2012 est.)
country comparison to the world: 38

Natural gas—proved reserves: 97.97 billion cu m (1 January 2013 es)
country comparison to the world: 55

Carbon dioxide emissions from consumption of energy: 80.1 million Mt (2011 est.)
country comparison to the world: 46

COMMUNICATIONS

Telephones—main lines in use: 3.276 million (2012)
country comparison to the world: 48

Telephones—mobile cellular: 24.13 million (2012)
country comparison to the world: 44

Telephone system: *general assessment:* privatization began in 1988; most advanced telecommunications infrastructure in South America; modern system based on extensive microwave radio relay facilities; domestic satellite system with 3 earth stations
domestic: number of fixed-line connections have stagnated in recent years as mobile-cellular usage continues to increase, reaching 130 telephones per 100 persons
international: country code—56; landing points for the Pan American, South America-1, and South American Crossing/Latin America Nautilus submarine cables providing links to the US and to Central and South America; satellite earth stations—2 Intelsat (Atlantic Ocean) (2011)

Broadcast media: national and local terrestrial TV channels, coupled with extensive cable TV networks; the state-owned Television Nacional de Chile (TVN) network is self-financed through commercial advertising revenues and is not under direct government control; large number of privately-owned TV stations; about 250 radio stations (2007)

Internet country code: .cl

Internet hosts: 2.152 million (2012)
country comparison to the world: 38

Internet users: 7.009 million (2009)
country comparison to the world: 39

TRANSPORTATION

Airports: 481 (2013)
country comparison to the world: 15

Airports—with paved runways: *total:* 90
over 3,047 m: 5
2,438 to 3,047 m: 7
1,524 to 2,437 m: 23
914 to 1,523 m: 31
under 914 m: 24 (2013)

Airports—with unpaved runways: *total:* 391
2,438 to 3,047 m: 5
1,524 to 2,437 m: 11
914 to 1,523 m: 56
under 914 m: 319 (2013)

Heliports: 1 (2013)

Pipelines: gas 3,160 km; liquid petroleum gas 781 km; oil 985 km; refined products 722 km (2013)

Railways: *total:* 7,082 km
country comparison to the world: 28
broad gauge: 3,435 km 1.676-m gauge (850 km electrified)
narrow gauge: 3,647 km 1.000-m gauge (2008)

Roadways: *total:* 77,764 km
country comparison to the world: 61
paved: 18,119 km (includes 2,387 km of expressways)
unpaved: 59,645 km (2010)

Merchant marine: *total:* 42
country comparison to the world: 74
by type: bulk carrier 13, cargo 5, chemical tanker 7, container 2, liquefied gas 1, passenger 3, passenger/cargo 2, petroleum tanker 8, roll on/roll off 1
foreign-owned: 1 (Norway 1)

registered in other countries: 52 (Argentina 6, Brazil 1, Honduras 1, Isle of Man 9, Liberia 9, Panama 14, Peru 6, Singapore 6) (2010)

Ports and terminals: *major seaport(s):* Coronel, Huasco, Lirquen, Puerto Ventanas, San Antonio, San Vicente, Valparaiso

MILITARY

Military branches: Army of the Nation, Chilean Navy (Armada de Chile, includes Naval Aviation, Marine Corps, and Maritime Territory and Merchant Marine Directorate (Directemar)), Chilean Air Force (Fuerza Aerea de Chile, FACh), Carabineros Corps (Cuerpo de Carabineros) (2011)

Military service age and obligation: 18-45 years of age for voluntary male and female military service, although the right to compulsory recruitment of males 18-45 is retained; service obligation is 12 months for Army and 22 months for Navy and Air Force (2012)

Manpower available for military service: *males age 16-49:* 4,324,732
females age 16-49: 4,251,954 (2010 est.)

Manpower fit for military service: *males age 16-49:* 3,621,475
females age 16-49: 3,561,099 (2010 est.)

Manpower reaching militarily significant age annually: *male:* 141,500
female: 135,709 (2010 est.)

Military expenditures: 2.04% of GDP (2012)
country comparison to the world: 39
2.17% of GDP (2011)
2.04% of GDP (2010)

TRANSNATIONAL ISSUES

Disputes—international: Chile and Peru rebuff Bolivia's reactivated claim to restore the Atacama corridor, ceded to Chile in 1884, but Chile has offered instead unrestricted but not sovereign maritime access through Chile to Bolivian natural gas; Chile rejects Peru's unilateral legislation to change its latitudinal maritime boundary with Chile to an equidistance line with a southwestern axis favoring Peru; in October 2007, Peru took its maritime complaint with Chile to the ICJ; territorial claim in Antarctica (Chilean Antarctic Territory) partially overlaps Argentine and British claims; the joint boundary commission, established by Chile and Argentina in 2001, has yet to map and demarcate the delimited boundary in the inhospitable Andean Southern Ice Field (Campo de Hielo Sur)

Illicit drugs: transshipment country for cocaine destined for Europe and the region; some money laundering activity, especially through the Iquique Free Trade Zone; imported precursors passed on to Bolivia; domestic cocaine consumption is rising, making Chile a significant consumer of cocaine (2008)

CHINA

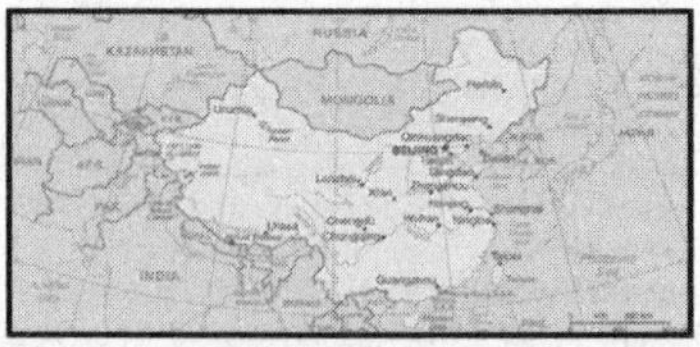

INTRODUCTION

Background: For centuries China stood as a leading civilization, outpacing the rest of the world in the arts and sciences, but in the 19th and early 20th centuries, the country was beset by civil unrest, major famines, military defeats, and foreign occupation. After World War II, the communists under MAO Zedong established an autocratic socialist system that, while ensuring China's sovereignty, imposed strict controls over everyday life and cost the lives of tens of millions of people. After 1978, MAO's successor DENG Xiaoping and other leaders focused on market-oriented economic development and by 2000 output had quadrupled. For much of the population, living standards have improved dramatically and the room for personal choice has expanded, yet political controls remain tight. Since the early 1990s, China has increased its global outreach and participation in international organizations.

GEOGRAPHY

Location: Eastern Asia, bordering the East China Sea, Korea Bay, Yellow Sea, and South China Sea, between North Korea and Vietnam

Geographic coordinates: 35 00 N, 105 00 E

Map references: Asia

Area: *total:* 9,596,961 sq km
country comparison to the world: 4
land: 9,569,901 sq km
water: 27,060 sq km

Area—comparative: slightly smaller than the US

Land boundaries: *total:* 22,117 km
border countries: Afghanistan 76 km, Bhutan 470 km, Burma 2,185 km, India 3,380 km, Kazakhstan 1,533 km, North Korea 1,416 km, Kyrgyzstan 858 km, Laos 423 km, Mongolia 4,677 km, Nepal 1,236 km, Pakistan 523 km, Russia (northeast) 3,605 km, Russia (northwest) 40 km, Tajikistan 414 km, Vietnam 1,281 km regional borders: Hong Kong 30 km, Macau 0.34 km

Coastline: 14,500 km

Maritime claims: *territorial sea:* 12 nm
contiguous zone: 24 nm
exclusive economic zone: 200 nm
continental shelf: 200 nm or to the edge of the continental margin

Climate: extremely diverse; tropical in south to subarctic in north

Terrain: mostly mountains, high plateaus, deserts in west; plains, deltas, and hills in east

Elevation extremes: *lowest point:* Turpan Pendi -154 m
highest point: Mount Everest 8,850 m (highest point in Asia)

Natural resources: coal, iron ore, petroleum, natural gas, mercury, tin, tungsten, antimony, manganese, molybdenum, vanadium, magnetite, aluminum, lead, zinc, rare earth elements, uranium, hydropower potential (world's largest)

Land use: *arable land:* 11.62%
permanent crops: 1.53%
other: 86.84% (2011)

Irrigated land: 629,380 sq km (2006)

Total renewable water resources: 2,840 cu km (2011)

Freshwater withdrawal (domestic/industrial/agricultural): *total:* 554.1 cu km/yr (12%/23%/65%)
per capita: 409.9 cu m/yr (2005)

Natural hazards: frequent typhoons (about five per year along southern and eastern coasts); damaging floods; tsunamis; earthquakes; droughts; land subsidence
volcanism: China contains some historically active volcanoes including Changbaishan (also known as Baitoushan, Baegdu, or P'aektu-san), Hainan Dao, and Kunlun although most have been relatively inactive in recent centuries

Environment—current issues: air pollution (greenhouse gases, sulfur dioxide particulates) from reliance on coal produces acid rain; China is the world's largest single emitter of carbon dioxide from the burning of fossil fuels; water shortages, particularly in the north; water pollution from untreated wastes; deforestation; estimated loss of one-fifth of agricultural land since 1949 to soil erosion and economic development; desertification; trade in endangered species

Environment—international agreements: *party to:* Antarctic-Environmental Protocol, Antarctic Treaty, Biodiversity, Climate Change, Climate Change-Kyoto Protocol, Desertification, Endangered Species, Environmental Modification, Hazardous Wastes, Law of the Sea, Marine Dumping, Ozone Layer Protection, Ship Pollution, Tropical Timber 83, Tropical Timber 94, Wetlands, Whaling
signed, but not ratified: none of the selected agreements

Geography—note: world's fourth largest country (after Russia, Canada, and US); Mount Everest on the border with Nepal is the world's tallest peak

PEOPLE AND SOCIETY

Nationality: *noun:* Chinese (singular and plural)
adjective: Chinese

Ethnic groups: Han Chinese 91.6%, Zhuang 1.3%, other (includes Hui, Manchu, Uighur, Miao, Yi, Tujia, Tibetan, Mongol, Dong, Buyei, Yao, Bai, Korean, Hani, Li, Kazakh, Dai and other nationalities) 7.1%
note: the Chinese government officially recognizes 56 ethnic groups (2010 est.)

Languages: Standard Chinese or Mandarin (official; Putonghua, based on the Beijing dialect), Yue (Cantonese), Wu (Shanghainese), Minbei (Fuzhou), Minnan (Hokkien-Taiwanese), Xiang, Gan, Hakka dialects, minority languages (see Ethnic groups entry)
note: Zhuang is official in Guangxi Zhuang, Yue is official in Guangdong, Mongolian is official in Nei Mongol, Uighur is official in Xinjiang Uygur, Kyrgyz is official in Xinjiang Uyghur, and Tibetan is official in Xizang (Tibet)

Religions: Buddhist 18.2%, Christian 5.1%, Muslim 1.8%, folk religion < .1%, Hindu < .1%, Jewish < .1%, other 0.7% (includes Daoist (Taoist)), unaffiliated 52.2%
note: officially atheist (2010 est.)

Population: 1,355,692,576 (July 2014 est.)
country comparison to the world: 1

Age structure: *0-14 years:* 17.1% (male 124,340,516/female 107,287,324)
15-24 years: 14.7% (male 105,763,058/female 93,903,845)
25-54 years: 47.2% (male 327,130,324/female 313,029,536)
55-64 years: 9.6% (male 77,751,100/female 75,737,968)
65 years and over: 9.4% (male 62,646,075/female 68,102,830) (2014 est.)

Dependency ratios:
total dependency ratio: 36.8 %
youth dependency ratio: 24.7 %
elderly dependency ratio: 12.1 %
potential support ratio: 8.2 (2013)

Median age:
total: 36.7 years
male: 35.8 years
female: 37.5 years (2014 est.)

Population growth rate: 0.44% (2014 est.)
country comparison to the world: 159

Birth rate: 12.17 births/1,000 population (2014 est.)
country comparison to the world: 163

Death rate: 7.44 deaths/1,000 population (2014 est.)
country comparison to the world: 116

Net migration rate:-0.32 migrant(s)/1,000 population (2014 est.)
country comparison to the world: 128

Urbanization: *urban population:* 50.6% of total population (2011)
rate of urbanization: 2.85% annual rate of change (2010-15 est.)

Major urban areas—population: Shanghai 16.575 million; BEIJING (capital) 15.594 million; Chongqing 9.401 million; Shenzhen 9.005 million; Guangzhou 8.884 million (2011)

Sex ratio: *at birth:* 1.11 male(s)/female
0-14 years: 1.16 male(s)/female
15-24 years: 1.13 male(s)/female
25-54 years: 1.05 male(s)/female
55-64 years: 1.06 male(s)/female
65 years and over: 0.92 male(s)/female
total population: 1.06 male(s)/female (2014 est.)

Maternal mortality rate: 37 deaths/100,000 live births (2010)
country comparison to the world: 116

Infant mortality rate: *total:* 14.79 deaths/1,000 live births
country comparison to the world: 108
male: 14.93 deaths/1,000 live births
female: 14.63 deaths/1,000 live births (2014 est.)

Life expectancy at birth: total population: 75.15 years
country comparison to the world: 100
male: 73.09 years
female: 77.43 years (2014 est.)

Total fertility rate: 1.55 children born/woman (2014 est.)
country comparison to the world: 185

Contraceptive prevalence rate: 84.6% (2006)

Health expenditures: 5.2% of GDP (2011)
country comparison to the world: 135

Physicians density: 1.46 physicians/1,000 population (2010)

Hospital bed density: 3.8 beds/1,000 population (2011)

Drinking water source:
Improved:
urban: 98.4% of population
rural: 84.9% of population
total: 91.7% of population
unimproved:
urban: 1.6% of population
rural: 15.1% of population
total: 8.3% of population (2011 est.)

Sanitation facility access:
Improved:
urban: 74.1% of population
rural: 55.8% of population
total: 65.1% of population
unimproved:
urban: 25.9% of population
rural: 44.2% of population
total: 34.9% of population (2011 est.)

HIV/AIDS—adult prevalence rate: 0.1% (2012 est.)
country comparison to the world: 130

HIV/AIDS—people living with HIV/AIDS: 780,000 (2012 est.)
country comparison to the world: 13

HIV/AIDS—deaths: 26,000 (2009 est.)
country comparison to the world: 16

Major infectious diseases: *degree of risk:* intermediate
food or waterborne: bacterial diarrhea, hepatitis A, and typhoid fever
vectorborne diseases: disease: Japanese encephalitis
soil contact disease: hantaviral hemorrhagic fever with renal syndrome (HFRS)
note: highly pathogenic H5N1 avian influenza has been identified in this country; it poses a negligible risk with extremely rare cases possible among US citizens who have close contact with birds (2013)

Obesity—adult prevalence rate: 5.7% (2008)
country comparison to the world: 152

Children under the age of 5 years underweight: 3.4% (2010)
country comparison to the world: 105

Education expenditures: NA

Literacy: *definition:* age 15 and over can read and write
total population: 95.1%
male: 97.5%
female: 92.7% (2010 est.)

School life expectancy (primary to tertiary education): *total:* 13 years
male: 13 years
female: 13 years (2012)

GOVERNMENT

Country name: *conventional long form:* People's Republic of China
conventional short form: China
local long form: Zhonghua Renmin Gongheguo
local short form: Zhongguo
abbreviation: PRC

Government type: Communist state

Capital: *name:* Beijing
geographic coordinates: 39 55 N, 116 23 E
time difference: UTC+8 (13 hours ahead of Washington, DC during Standard Time)
note: despite its size, all of China falls within one time zone; many people in Xinjiang Province observe an unofficial "Xinjiang time zone" of UTC+6, two hours behind Beijing

Administrative divisions: 23 provinces (sheng, singular and plural), 5 autonomous regions (zizhiqu, singular and plural), and 4 municipalities (shi, singular and plural)
provinces: Anhui, Fujian, Gansu, Guangdong, Guizhou, Hainan, Hebei, Heilongjiang, Henan, Hubei, Hunan, Jiangsu, Jiangxi, Jilin, Liaoning, Qinghai, Shaanxi, Shandong, Shanxi, Sichuan, Yunnan, Zhejiang; (see note on Taiwan)
autonomous regions: Guangxi, Nei Mongol (Inner Mongolia), Ningxia, Xinjiang Uygur, Xizang (Tibet)
municipalities: Beijing, Chongqing, Shanghai, Tianjin
note: China considers Taiwan its 23rd province; see separate entries for the special administrative regions of Hong Kong and Macau

Independence: 1 October 1949 (People's Republic of China established); notable earlier dates: 221 B.C. (unification under the Qin Dynasty); 1 January 1912 (Qing Dynasty replaced by the Republic of China)

National holiday: Anniversary of the founding of the People's Republic of China, 1 October (1949)

Constitution: several previous; latest promulgated 4 December 1982; amended several times, last in 2005 (2005)

Legal system: civil law influenced by Soviet and continental European civil law systems; legislature retains power to interpret statutes; note—criminal procedure law revised in early 2012

International law organization participation: has not submitted an ICJ jurisdiction declaration; non-party state to the ICCt

Suffrage: 18 years of age; universal

Executive branch: *chief of state:* President XI Jinping (since 14 March 2013); Vice President LI Yuanchao (since 14 March 2013)
head of government: Premier LI Keqiang (since 16 March 2013); Executive Vice Premier ZHANG Gaoli (since 16 March 2013), Vice Premier LIU Yandong (since 16 March 2013), Vice Premier MA Kai (since 16 March 2013), and Vice Premier WANG Yang (since 16 March 2013)
cabinet: State Council appointed by National People's Congress (For more information visit the World Leaders website)
elections: president and vice president elected by National People's Congress for a five-year term (eligible for a second term); elections last held on 5-17 March 2013 (next to be held in March 2018); premier nominated by president, confirmed by National People's Congress
election results: XI Jinping elected president by National People's Congress with a total of 2,952 votes; LI Yuanchao elected vice president with a total of 2,940 votes

Legislative branch: unicameral National People's Congress or Quanguo Renmin Daibiao Dahui (2,987 seats; members elected by municipal, regional, and provincial people's congresses, and People's Liberation Army to serve five-year terms)
elections: last held in December 2012-February 2013 (next to be held in late 2017 to early 2018)
election results: percent of vote—NA; seats—2,987
note: in practice, only members of the CCP, its eight allied parties, and CCP-approved independent candidates are elected

Judicial branch: *highest court(s):* Supreme People's Court (consists of over 340 judges including the chief justice, 13 grand justices organized into a civil committee and tribunals for civil, economic, administrative, complaint and appeal, and communication and transportation cases) note—in October 2012, China issued a white paper on planned judicial reform
judge selection and term of office: chief justice appointed by the People's National Congress; term limited to two consecutive 5-year terms; other justices and judges nominated by the chief justice and appointed by the Standing Committee of the People's National Congress; term of other justices and judges NA

subordinate courts: Higher People's Courts; Intermediate People's Courts; District and County People's Courts; Autonomous Region People's Courts; Special People's Courts for military, maritime, transportation, and forestry issues

Political parties and leaders: Chinese Communist Party or CCP [XI Jinping]; eight nominally independent small parties ultimately controlled by the CCP

Political pressure groups and leaders: no substantial political opposition groups exist

International organization participation: ADB, AfDB (nonregional member), APEC, ARF, ASEAN (dialogue partner), BIS, CDB, CICA, EAS, FAO, FATF, G-20, G-24 (observer), G-77, IADB, IAEA, IBRD, ICAO, ICC (national committees), ICRM, IDA, IFAD, IFC, IFRCS, IHO, ILO, IMF, IMO, IMSO, Interpol, IOC, IOM (observer), IPU, ISO, ITSO, ITU, LAIA (observer), MIGA, MINURSO, MINUSMA, MONUSCO, NAM (observer), NSG, OAS (observer), OPCW, PCA, PIF (partner), SAARC (observer), SCO, SICA (observer), UN, UNAMID, UNCTAD, UNESCO, UNFICYP, UNHCR, UNIDO, UNIFIL, UNISFA, UNMIL, UNMISS, UNMIT, UNOCI, UNSC (permanent), UNTSO, UNWTO, UPU, WCO, WHO, WIPO, WMO, WTO, ZC

Diplomatic representation in the US: *chief of mission:* Ambassador CUI Tiankai (since 3 April 2013)
chancery: 3505 International Place NW, Washington, DC 20008
telephone: [1] (202) 495-2266
FAX: [1] (202) 495-2138
consulate(s) general: Chicago, Houston, Los Angeles, New York, San Francisco

Diplomatic representation from the US:
chief of mission: Ambassador Max Sieben BAUCUS (since 21 February 2014)
embassy: 55 An Jia Lou Lu, 100600 Beijing
mailing address: PSC 461, Box 50, FPO AP 96521-0002
telephone: [86] (10) 8531-3000
FAX: [86] (10) 8531-3300
consulate(s) general: Chengdu, Guangzhou, Shanghai, Shenyang, Wuhan

Flag description: red with a large yellow five-pointed star and four smaller yellow five-pointed stars (arranged in a vertical arc toward the middle of the flag) in the upper hoist-side corner; the color red represents revolution, while the stars symbolize the four social classes—the working class, the peasantry, the urban petty bourgeoisie, and the national bourgeoisie (capitalists)—united under the Communist Party of China

National symbol(s): dragon

National anthem: *name:* "Yiyongjun Jinxingqu" (The March of the Volunteers)
lyrics/music: TIAN Han/NIE Er
note: adopted 1949; the anthem, though banned during the Cultural Revolution, is more commonly known as "Zhongguo Guoge" (Chinese National Song); it was originally the theme song to the 1935 Chinese movie, "Sons and Daughters in a Time of Storm"

ECONOMY

Economy—overview: Since the late 1970s China has moved from a closed, centrally planned system to a more market-oriented one that plays a major global role—in 2010 China became the world's largest exporter. Reforms began with the phasing out of collectivized agriculture, and expanded to include the gradual liberalization of prices, fiscal decentralization, increased autonomy for state enterprises, growth of the private sector, development of stock markets and a modern banking system, and opening to foreign trade and investment. China has implemented reforms in a gradualist fashion. In recent years, China has renewed its support for state-owned enterprises in sectors considered important to "economic security," explicitly looking to foster globally competitive industries. After keeping its currency tightly linked to the US dollar for years, in July 2005 China moved to an exchange rate system that references a basket of currencies. From mid 2005 to late 2008 cumulative appreciation of the renminbi against the US dollar was more than 20%, but the exchange rate remained virtually pegged to the dollar from the onset of the global financial crisis until June 2010, when Beijing allowed resumption of a gradual appreciation and expanded the daily trading band within which the RMB is permitted to fluctuate. The restructuring of the economy and resulting efficiency gains have contributed to a more than tenfold increase in GDP since 1978. Measured on a purchasing power parity (PPP) basis that adjusts for price differences, China in 2013 stood as the second-largest economy in the world after the US, having surpassed Japan in 2001. The dollar values of China's agricultural and industrial output each exceed those of the US; China is second to the US in the value of services it produces. Still, per capita income is below the world average. The Chinese government faces numerous economic challenges, including: (a) reducing its high domestic savings rate and correspondingly low domestic consumption; (b) facilitating higher-wage job opportunities for the aspiring middle class, including rural migrants and increasing numbers of college graduates; (c) reducing corruption and other economic crimes; and (d) containing environmental damage and social strife related to the economy's rapid transformation. Economic development has progressed further in coastal provinces than in the interior, and by 2011 more than 250 million migrant workers and their dependents had relocated to urban areas to find work. One consequence of population control policy is that China is now one of the most rapidly aging countries in the world. Deterioration in the environment—notably air pollution, soil erosion, and the steady fall of the water table, especially in the North—is another long-term problem. China continues to lose arable land because of erosion and economic development. The Chinese government is seeking to add energy production capacity from sources other than coal and oil, focusing on nuclear and alternative energy development. Several factors are converging to slow China's growth, including debt overhang from its credit-fueled stimulus program, industrial overcapacity, inefficient allocation of capital by state-owned banks, and the slow recovery of China's trading partners. The government's 12th Five-Year Plan, adopted in March 2011 and reiterated at the Communist Party's "Third Plenum" meeting in November 2013, emphasizes continued economic reforms and the need to increase domestic consumption in order to make the economy less dependent in the future on fixed investments, exports, and heavy industry. However, China has made only marginal progress toward these rebalancing goals. The new government of President XI Jinping has signaled a greater willingness to undertake reforms that focus on China's long-term economic health, including giving the market a more decisive role in allocating resources.

GDP (purchasing power parity):
$13.37 trillion (2013 est.)
country comparison to the world: 3
$12.43 trillion (2012 est.)
$11.54 trillion (2011 est.)
note: data are in 2013 US dollars

GDP (official exchange rate): $8.939 trillion
note: because China's exchange rate is determine by fiat, rather than by market forces, the official exchange rate measure of GDP is not an accurate measure of China's output; GDP at the official exchange rate substantially understates the actual level of China's output vis-a-vis the rest of the world; in China's situation, GDP at purchasing power parity provides the best measure for comparing output across countries (2013 est.)

GDP—real growth rate: 7.6% (2013 est.)
country comparison to the world: 14
7.7% (2012 est.)
9.3% (2011 est.)

GDP—per capita (PPP): $9,800 (2013 est.)
country comparison to the world: 120
$9,200 (2012 est.)
$8,600 (2011 est.)
note: data are in 2013 US dollars

Gross national saving:
49% of GDP (2013 est.)
country comparison to the world: 4
50.1% of GDP (2012 est.)
50.2% of GDP (2011 est.)

GDP—composition, by end use:
household consumption: 36.3%
government consumption: 13.7%
investment in fixed capital: 46%
investment in inventories: 1.2%
exports of goods and services: 25.1%
imports of goods and services: -22.2% (2013 est.)

GDP—composition, by sector of origin:
agriculture: 9.7%
industry: 45.3%
services: 45% (2013 est.)

Agriculture—products: world leader in gross value of agricultural output; rice, wheat, potatoes, corn, peanuts, tea, millet, barley, apples, cotton, oilseed; pork; fish

Industries: world leader in gross value of industrial output; mining and ore processing, iron, steel, aluminum, and other metals, coal; machine building; armaments; textiles and apparel; petroleum; cement; chemicals; fertilizers; consumer products, including footwear, toys, and electronics; food processing; transportation equipment, including automobiles, rail cars and locomotives, ships, and aircraft; telecommunications equipment, commercial space launch vehicles, satellites

Industrial production growth rate: 7.7% (2013 est.)
country comparison to the world: 28

Labor force: 797.6 million
country comparison to the world: 1
note: by the end of 2012, China's population at working age (15-64 years) was 1.0040 billion (2013 est.)

Labor force—by occupation: *agriculture:* 34.8%
industry: 29.5%
services: 35.7% (2011 est.)

Unemployment rate: 6.4% (2013 est.)
country comparison to the world: 64
6.5% (2012 est.)
note: registered urban unemployment, which excludes private enterprises and migrants, was 4.1% in 2012

Population below poverty line: 13.4%
note: in 2011, China set a new poverty line at RMB 2300 (approximately US $3,630) (2011)

Household income or consumption by percentage share: *lowest 10%:* 3.5%
highest 10%: 15%
note: data are for urban households only (2008)

Distribution of family income—Gini index: 47.4 (2012)
country comparison to the world: 30
48.4 (2007)

Budget: *revenues:* $2.064 trillion
expenditures: $2.251 trillion (2013 est.)

Taxes and other revenues: 23.1% of GDP (2013 est.)
country comparison to the world: 146

Budget surplus (+) or deficit (-): -2.1% of GDP (2013 est.)
country comparison to the world: 89

Public debt: 31.7% of GDP (2012 est.)
country comparison to the world: 114
38.5% of GDP (2011)
note: official data; data cover both central government debt and local government debt, which China's National Audit Office estimated at RMB 10.72 trillion (approximately US$1.66 trillion) in 2011; data exclude policy bank bonds, Ministry of Railway debt, China Asset Management Company debt, and non-performing loans

Fiscal year: calendar year

Inflation rate (consumer prices): 2.6% (2013 est.)
country comparison to the world: 97
2.6% (2012 est.)

Central bank discount rate: 2.25% (31 December 2013 est.)
country comparison to the world: 111
2.25% (31 December 2012 est.)

Commercial bank prime lending rate: 5.73% (31 December 2013 est.)
country comparison to the world: 138
6% (31 December 2012 est.)

Stock of narrow money: $5.515 trillion (31 December 2013 est.)
country comparison to the world: 3
$4.907 trillion (31 December 2012 est.)

Stock of broad money: $18.05 trillion (31 December 2013 est.)
country comparison to the world: 1
$15.49 trillion (31 December 2012 est.)

Stock of domestic credit: $11.76 trillion (31 December 2013 est.)
country comparison to the world: 4
$10.01 trillion (31 December 2012 est.)

Market value of publicly traded shares: $6.499 trillion (31 December 2013 est.)
country comparison to the world: 3
$5.753 trillion (31 December 2012)
$3.389 trillion (31 December 2011 est.)

Current account balance: $176.6 billion (2013 est.)
country comparison to the world: 2
$193.1 billion (2012 est.)

Exports: $2.21 trillion (2013 est.)
country comparison to the world: 1
$1.818 trillion (2012 est.)

Exports—commodities: electrical and other machinery, including data processing equipment, apparel, radio telephone handsets, textiles, integrated circuits

Exports—partners: Hong Kong 17.4%, US 16.7%, Japan 6.8%, South Korea 4.1% (2013 est.)

Imports: $1.772 trillion (2013 est.)
country comparison to the world: 3
$1.653 trillion (2012 est.)

Imports—commodities: electrical and other machinery, oil and mineral fuels; nuclear reactor, boiler, and machinery components; optical and medical equipment, metal ores, motor vehicles; soybeans

Imports—partners: South Korea 9.4%, Japan 8.3%, Taiwan 8%, United States 7.8%, Australia 5%, Germany 4.8% (2013 est.)

Reserves of foreign exchange and gold: $3.82 trillion (31 December 2013 est.)
country comparison to the world: 1
$3.312 trillion (31 December 2012 est.)

Debt—external: $784.8 billion (31 December 2013 est.)
country comparison to the world: 20
$737 billion (31 December 2012 est.)

Stock of direct foreign investment—at home: $1.344 trillion (31 December 2012 est.)
country comparison to the world: 4
$1.232 trillion (31 December 2011 est.)

Stock of direct foreign investment—abroad: $644.2 billion (31 December 2013 est.)
country comparison to the world: 14
$532 billion (31 December 2012 est.)

Exchange rates: Renminbi yuan (RMB) per US dollar—
6.2 (2013 est.)
6.3123 (2012 est.)
6.7703 (2010 est.)
6.8314 (2009)
6.9385 (2008)

ENERGY

Electricity—production: 4.977 trillion kWh (2012)
country comparison to the world: 1

Electricity—consumption: 4.951 trillion kWh (2012)
country comparison to the world: 1

Electricity—exports: 17.65 billion kWh (2012)
country comparison to the world: 12

Electricity—imports: 6.874 billion kWh (2012)
country comparison to the world: 30

Electricity—installed generating capacity: *1.146 billion kW (2012 est.)*
country comparison to the world: 1

Electricity—from fossil fuels: 69.5% of total installed capacity (2012 est.)
country comparison to the world: 107

Electricity—from nuclear fuels: 1.1% of total installed capacity (2012 est.)
country comparison to the world: 30

Electricity—from hydroelectric plants: 21.8% of total installed capacity (2012 est.)
country comparison to the world: 87

Electricity—from other renewable sources: 7.6% of total installed capacity (2012 est.)
country comparison to the world: 32

Crude oil—production: 4.155 million bbl/day (2012 est.)
country comparison to the world: 4

Crude oil—exports: 26,000 bbl/day (2012 est.)
country comparison to the world: 51

Crude oil—imports: 5.433 million bbl/day (2012 est.)
country comparison to the world: 3

Crude oil—proved reserves: 17.3 billion bbl (1 January 2013 es)
country comparison to the world: 14

Refined petroleum products—production: 9.371 million bbl/day (2012 est.)
country comparison to the world: 3

Refined petroleum products—consumption: 9.79 million bbl/day (2011 est.)
country comparison to the world: 3

Refined petroleum products—exports: 538,000 bbl/day (2012 est.)
country comparison to the world: 14

Refined petroleum products—imports: 1.729 million bbl/day (2012 est.)
country comparison to the world: 4

Natural gas—production: 107.2 billion cu m (2012 est.)
country comparison to the world: 8

Natural gas—consumption 143 billion cu m (2012 est.)
country comparison to the world: 5

Natural gas—exports: 3.195 billion cu m (2011 est.)
country comparison to the world: 39

Natural gas—imports: 41.4 billion cu m (2012 est.)
country comparison to the world: 13

Natural gas—proved reserves: 3.1 trillion cu m (1 January 2013 es)
country comparison to the world: 12

Carbon dioxide emissions from consumption of energy: 8.715 billion Mt (2011 est.)
country comparison to the world: 1

COMMUNICATIONS

Telephones—main lines in use: 278.86 million (2012)
country comparison to the world: 1

Telephones—mobile cellular: 1.1 billion (2012)
country comparison to the world: 1

Telephone system: *general assessment:* domestic and international services are increasingly available for private use; unevenly distributed domestic system serves principal cities, industrial centers, and many towns; China continues to develop its telecommunications infrastructure; China in the summer of 2008 began a major restructuring of its telecommunications industry, resulting in the consolidation of its six telecom service operators to three, China Telecom, China Mobile and China Unicom, each providing both fixed-line and mobile services
domestic: interprovincial fiber-optic trunk lines and cellular telephone systems have been installed; mobile-cellular subscribership is increasing rapidly; the number of Internet users exceeded 564 million by the end of 2012; a domestic satellite system with several earth stations is in place
international: country code—86; a number of submarine cables provide connectivity to Asia, the Middle East, Europe, and the US; satellite earth stations—7 (5 Intelsat—4 Pacific Ocean and 1 Indian Ocean; 1 Intersputnik—Indian Ocean region; and 1 Inmarsat—Pacific and Indian Ocean regions) (2012)

Broadcast media: all broadcast media are owned by, or affiliated with, the Communist Party of China or a government agency; no privately owned TV or radio stations; state-run Chinese Central TV, provincial, and municipal stations offer more than 2,000 channels; the Central Propaganda Department lists subjects that are off limits to domestic broadcast media with the government maintaining authority to approve all programming; foreign-made TV programs must be approved prior to broadcast

Internet country code: .cn

Internet hosts: 20.602 million (2012)

country comparison to the world: 5

Internet users: 389 million (2009)
country comparison to the world: 1

TRANSPORTATION

Airports: 507 (2013)
country comparison to the world: 14

Airports—with paved runways: total: 463
over 3,047 m: 71
2,438 to 3,047 m: 158
1,524 to 2,437 m: 123
914 to 1,523 m: 25
under 914 m: 86 (2013)

Airports—with unpaved runways: total: 44
over 3,047 m: 4
2,438 to 3,047 m: 7
1,524 to 2,437 m: 6
914 to 1,523 m: 9
under 914 m: 18 (2013)

Heliports: 47 (2013)

Pipelines: condensate 9 km; gas 48,502 km; oil 23,072 km; oil/gas/water 31 km; refined products 15,298 km; water 9 km (2013)

Railways: *total:* 86,000 km
country comparison to the world: 3
standard gauge: 86,000 km 1.435-m gauge (36,000 km electrified) (2008)

Roadways: total: 4,106,387 km
country comparison to the world: 3
paved: 3,453,890 km (includes 84,946 km of expressways)
unpaved: 652,497 km (2011)

Waterways: 110,000 km (navigable waterways) (2011)
country comparison to the world: 1

Merchant marine: *total:* 2,030
country comparison to the world: 3
by type: barge carrier 7, bulk carrier 621, cargo 566, carrier 10, chemical tanker 140, container 206, liquefied gas 60, passenger 9, passenger/cargo 81, petroleum tanker 264, refrigerated cargo 33, roll on/roll off 8, specialized tanker 2, vehicle carrier 23
foreign-owned: 22 (Hong Kong 18, Indonesia 2, Japan 2)
registered in other countries: 1,559 (Bangladesh 1, Belize 61, Cambodia 177, Comoros 1, Cyprus 6, Georgia 10, Honduras 2, Hong Kong 500, India 1, Indonesia 1, Kiribati 26, Liberia 4, Malta 6, Marshall Islands 14, North Korea 3, Panama 534, Philippines 4, Saint Kitts and Nevis 1, Saint Vincent and the Grenadines 65, Sao Tome and Principe 1, Sierra Leone 19, Singapore 29, South Korea 6, Thailand 1, Togo 1, Tuvalu 4, UK 7, Vanuatu 1, unknown 73) (2010)

Ports and terminals: *major seaport(s):* Dalian, Ningbo, Qingdao, Qinhuangdao, Shanghai, Shenzhen, Tianjin
river port(s): Guangzhou (Pearl)
container port(s) (TEUs): Dalian (6,400,300), Guangzhou (14,260,400), Ningbo (14,719,200), Qingdao (13,020,100), Shanghai (31,739,000), Shenzhen (22,570,800), Tianjin (11,587,600) (2011)

MILITARY

Military branches: People's Liberation Army (PLA): Ground Forces, Navy (PLAN; includes marines and naval aviation), Air Force (Zhongguo Renmin Jiefangjun Kongjun, PLAAF; includes Airborne Forces), and Second Artillery Corps (strategic missile force); People's Armed Police (Renmin Wuzhuang Jingcha Budui, PAP); PLA Reserve Force (2012)
Military service age and obligation: 18-24 years of age for selective compulsory military service, with a 2-year service obligation; no minimum age for voluntary service (all officers are volunteers); 18-19 years of age for women high school graduates who meet requirements for specific military jobs; a recent military decision allows women in combat roles; the first class of women warship commanders was in 2011 (2012)

Manpower available for military service:
males age 16-49: 385,821,101
females age 16-49: 363,789,674 (2010 est.)

Manpower fit for military service:
males age 16-49: 318,265,016
females age 16-49: 300,323,611 (2010 est.)

Manpower reaching militarily significant age annually: *male:* 10,406,544
female: 9,131,990 (2010 est.)

Military expenditures: 1.99% of GDP (2012)
country comparison to the world: 41
2% of GDP (2011)
1.99% of GDP (2010)

TRANSNATIONAL ISSUES

Disputes—international: continuing talks and confidence-building measures work toward reducing tensions over Kashmir that nonetheless remains militarized with portions under the de facto administration of China (Aksai Chin), India (Jammu and Kashmir), and Pakistan (Azad Kashmir and Northern Areas); India does not recognize Pakistan's ceding historic Kashmir lands to China in 1964; China and India continue their security and foreign policy dialogue started in 2005 related to the dispute over most of their rugged, militarized boundary, regional nuclear proliferation, and other matters; China claims most of India's Arunachal Pradesh to the base of the Himalayas; lacking any treaty describing the boundary, Bhutan and China continue negotiations to establish a common boundary alignment to resolve territorial disputes arising from substantial cartographic discrepancies, the largest of which lie in Bhutan's northwest and along the Chumbi salient; Burmese forces attempting to dig in to the largely autonomous Shan State to rout local militias tied to the drug trade, prompts local residents to periodically flee into neighboring Yunnan Province in China; Chinese maps show an international boundary symbol off the coasts of the littoral states of the South China Seas, where China has interrupted Vietnamese hydrocarbon exploration; China asserts sovereignty over Scarborough Reef along with the Philippines and Taiwan, and over the Spratly Islands together with Malaysia, the Philippines, Taiwan, Vietnam, and Brunei; the 2002 Declaration on the Conduct of Parties in the South China Sea eased tensions in the Spratlys but is not the legally binding code of conduct sought by some parties; Vietnam and China continue to expand construction of facilities in the Spratlys and in March 2005, the national oil companies of China, the Philippines, and Vietnam signed a joint accord on marine seismic activities in the Spratly Islands; China occupies some of the Paracel Islands also claimed by Vietnam and Taiwan; China and Taiwan continue to reject both Japan's claims to the uninhabited islands of Senkaku-shoto (Diaoyu Tai) and Japan's unilaterally declared equidistance line in the East China Sea, the site of intensive hydrocarbon exploration and exploitation; certain islands in the Yalu and Tumen rivers are in dispute with North Korea; North Korea and China seek to stem illegal migration to China by North Koreans, fleeing privations and oppression, by building a fence along portions of the border and imprisoning North Koreans deported by China; China and Russia have demarcated the once disputed islands at the Amur and Ussuri confluence and in the Argun River in accordance with their 2004 Agreement; China and Tajikistan have begun demarcating the revised boundary agreed to in the delimitation of 2002; the decade-long demarcation of the China-Vietnam land boundary was completed in 2009; citing environmental, cultural, and social concerns, China has reconsidered construction of 13 dams on the Salween River, but energy-starved Burma, with backing from Thailand, remains intent on building five hydro-electric dams downstream despite regional and international protests; Chinese and Hong Kong authorities met in March 2008 to resolve ownership and use of lands recovered in Shenzhen River channelization, including 96-hectare Lok Ma Chau Loop; Hong Kong developing plans to reduce 2,000 out of 2,800 hectares of its restricted Closed Area by 2010

Refugees and internally displaced persons: *refugees (country of origin):* 300,897 Vietnam); (2012); estimated 30,000-50,000 (North Korea)
IDPs: 90,000 (2010)

Trafficking in persons: *current situation:* China is a source, transit, and destination country for men, women, and children trafficked for the purposes of sexual exploitation and forced labor; the majority of trafficking in China occurs within the country's borders, there are many reports that Chinese men, women, and children may be subjected to conditions of sex trafficking and forced labor in numerous countries and territories worldwide; women and children are trafficked to China from Burma, Vietnam, Laos, Mongolia, Russia, North Korea, and even as far away as Europe and Africa for forced labor and prostitution; some Chinese adults and children are forced into prostitution and various forms of forced labor, including begging, stealing, and working in brick kilns, coal mines, and factories

tier rating: Tier 3—China does not fully comply with the minimum standards for the elimination of trafficking and was downgraded to Tier 3 after the maximum of two consecutive annual waivers; the government has not demonstrated significant efforts to comprehensively prohibit and punish all forms of trafficking and to prosecute traffickers; the government also has not reported providing comprehensive victim protection services to domestic or foreign, male or female victims of trafficking; in 2013, the government released an eight-year national action plan, which includes measures to improve interagency and other internal coordination among anti-trafficking stakeholders and victim protection (2013)

Illicit drugs: major transshipment point for heroin produced in the Golden Triangle region of Southeast Asia; growing domestic consumption of synthetic drugs, and heroin from Southeast and Southwest Asia; source country for methamphetamine and heroin chemical precursors, despite new regulations on its large chemical industry (2008)

CHRISTMAS ISLAND

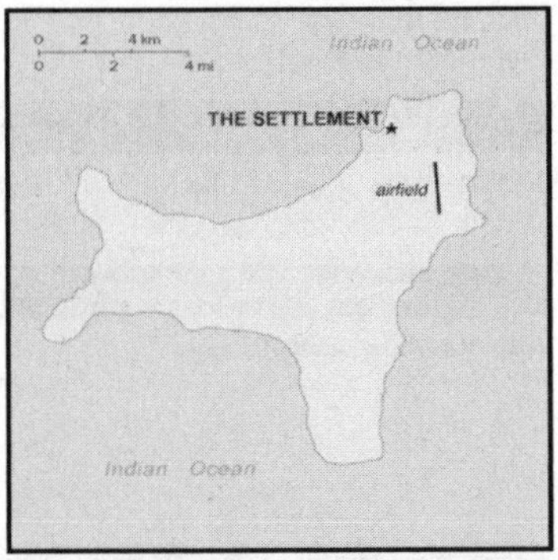

INTRODUCTION

Background: Named in 1643 for the day of its discovery, the island was annexed and settlement began by the UK in 1888 with the discovery of the island's phosphate deposits. Following the Second World War, Christmas Island came under the jurisdiction of the new British Colony of Singapore. The island existed as a separate Crown colony from 1 January 1958 to 1 October 1958 when its transfer to Australian jurisdiction was finalized. That date is still celebrated on the first Monday in October as Territory Day. Almost two-thirds of the island has been declared a national park.

GEOGRAPHY

Location: Southeastern Asia, island in the Indian Ocean, south of Indonesia

Geographic coordinates: 10 30 S, 105 40 E

Map references: Oceania

Area: *total:* 135 sq km
country comparison to the world: 222
land: 135 sq km
water: 0 sq km

Area—comparative: about three-quarters the size of Washington, DC

Land boundaries: 0 km

Coastline: 138.9 km

Maritime claims: *territorial sea:* 12 nm
contiguous zone: 12 nm
exclusive fishing zone: 200 nm

Climate: tropical with a wet season (December to April) and dry season; heat and humidity moderated by trade winds

Terrain: steep cliffs along coast rise abruptly to central plateau

Elevation extremes: *lowest point:* Indian Ocean 0 m
highest point: Murray Hill 361 m

Natural resources: phosphate, beaches

Land use: *arable land:* 0%
permanent crops: 0%
other: 100% (mainly tropical rainforest; 63% of the island is a national park) (2011)

Irrigated land: NA

Natural hazards: the narrow fringing reef surrounding the island can be a maritime hazard

Environment—current issues: loss of rainforest; impact of phosphate mining

Geography—note: located along major sea lanes of Indian Ocean

PEOPLE AND SOCIETY

Nationality: *noun:* Christmas Islander(s)
adjective: Christmas Island

Ethnic groups: Chinese 70%, European 20%, Malay 10%
note: no indigenous population (2001)

Languages: English (official), Chinese, Malay

Religions: Buddhist 36%, Muslim 25%, Christian 18%, other 21% (1997)

Population: 1,530 (July 2014 est.)
country comparison to the world: 235

Population growth rate: 1.11% (2014 est.)
country comparison to the world: 111

Sex ratio: NA (2009 est.)

Infant mortality rate: total: NA
male: NA
female: NA

Life expectancy at birth: total population: NA
male: NA
female: NA

Total fertility rate: NA (2014 est.)

HIV/AIDS—adult prevalence rate: NA

HIV/AIDS—people living with HIV/AIDS: NA

HIV/AIDS—deaths: NA

Literacy: NA

GOVERNMENT

Country name: *conventional long form:* Territory of Christmas Island
conventional short form: Christmas Island

Dependency status: non-self governing territory of Australia; administered from Canberra by the Department of Regional Australia, Local Government, Arts and Sport

Government type: NA

Capital: *name:* The Settlement
geographic coordinates: 10 25 S, 105 43 E
time difference: UTC+7 (12 hours ahead of Washington, DC during Standard Time)

Administrative divisions: none (territory of Australia)

Independence: none (territory of Australia)

National holiday: Australia Day, 26 January (1788)

Constitution: 1 October 1958 (Christmas Island Act 1958); amended many times, last in 2010 (Territories Law Reform Act 2010) (2010)

Legal system: legal system is under the authority of the governor general of Australia and Australian law

Suffrage: 18 years of age

Executive branch: *chief of state:* Queen ELIZABETH II (since 6 February 1952) represented by the Australian governor general
head of government: Administrator Jon STANHOPE (since 5 October 2012)
elections: the monarchy is hereditary; governor general appointed by the monarch on the recommendation of the Australian prime minister; administrator appointed by the governor general of Australia for a two-year term and represents the monarch and Australia

Legislative branch: unicameral Christmas Island Shire Council (9 seats; members elected by popular vote to serve four-year terms)
elections: held every two years with half the members standing for election; last held In 2011 (next to be held in 2013)
election results: percent of vote—NA; seats—independents 9

Judicial branch: *highest court(s):* under the terms of the Territorial Law Reform Act 1992, Western Australia provides court services as needed for the island including the Supreme Court and subordinate courts (District Court, Magistrate Court, Family Court, Children's Court, and Coroners' Court)
judge selection and term of office:
subordinate courts:

Political parties and leaders: none

Political pressure groups and leaders: none

International organization participation: none

Diplomatic representation in the US: none (territory of Australia)

Diplomatic representation from the US: none (territory of Australia)

Flag description: territorial flag; divided diagonally from upper hoist to lower fly; the upper triangle is green with a yellow image of the Golden Bosun Bird superimposed; the lower triangle is blue with the Southern Cross constellation, representing Australia, superimposed; a centered yellow disk displays a green map of the island
note: the flag of Australia is used for official purposes

National symbol(s): golden bosun bird

National anthem: *note:* as a territory of Australia, "Advance Australia Fair" remains official as the national anthem, while "God Save the Queen" serves as the royal anthem (see Australia)

ECONOMY

Economy—overview: The main economic activities on Christmas Island are the mining of low grade phosphate, limited tourism, the provision of government services and more recently the construction and operation of the Immigration Detention Center. The government sector includes administration, health, education, policing, customs, quarantine and defense.

GDP (purchasing power parity): $NA

Agriculture—products: NA

Industries: tourism, phosphate extraction (near depletion)

Labor force: NA

Budget: *revenues:* $NA
expenditures: $NA

Fiscal year: 1 July–30 June

Exports: $NA

Exports—commodities: phosphate

Imports: $NA

Imports—commodities: consumer goods

Exchange rates: Australian dollars (AUD) per US dollar—
1.031 (2013)
0.9658 (2012)
1.0902 (2010)
1.2822 (2009)
1.2059 (2008)

COMMUNICATIONS

Telephone system: *general assessment:* service provided by the Australian network
domestic: GSM mobile-cellular telephone service replaced older analog system in February 2005
international: country code—61-8; satellite earth station—1 (Intelsat provides telephone and telex service) (2005)

Broadcast media: 1 community radio station; satellite broadcasts of several Australian radio and TV stations (2009)

Internet country code: .cx

Internet hosts: 3,028 (2012)
country comparison to the world: 155

Internet users: 464 (2001)
country comparison to the world: 217

TRANSPORTATION

Airports: 1 (2013)
country comparison to the world: 223

Airports—with paved runways: *total:* 1
1,524 to 2,437 m: 1 (2013)

Railways: *total:* 18 km
country comparison to the world: 133
standard gauge: 18 km 1.435-m (not in operation) (2010)

Roadways: *total:* 140 km
country comparison to the world: 211
paved: 30 km
unpaved: 110 km (2011)

Ports and terminals:
major seaport(s): Flying Fish Cove

MILITARY

Military—note: defense is the responsibility of Australia

TRANSNATIONAL ISSUES

Disputes—international: none

CLIPPERTON ISLAND

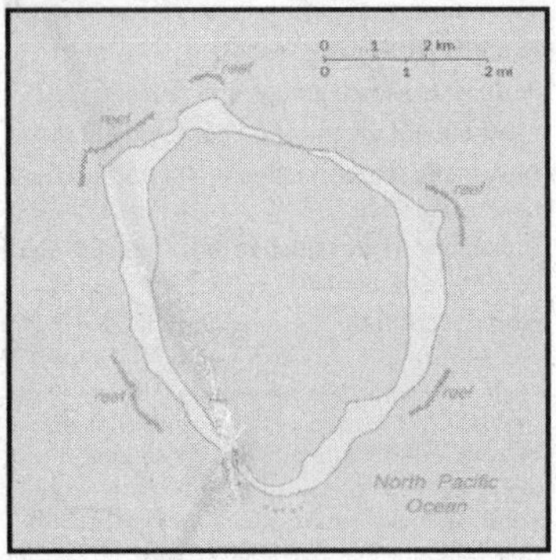

INTRODUCTION

Background: This isolated atoll was named for John CLIPPERTON, a pirate who was rumored to have made it his hideout early in the 18th century. Annexed by France in 1855 and claimed by the United States, it was seized by Mexico in 1897. Arbitration eventually awarded the island to France in 1931, which took possession in 1935.

GEOGRAPHY

Location: Middle America, atoll in the North Pacific Ocean, 1,120 km southwest of Mexico

Geographic coordinates: 10 17 N, 109 13 W

Map references: Political Map of the World

Area: *total:* 6 sq km
country comparison to the world: 245
land: 6 sq km
water: 0 sq km

Area—comparative: about 12 times the size of The Mall in Washington, DC

Land boundaries: 0 km

Coastline: 11.1 km

Maritime claims: *territorial sea:* 12 nm
exclusive economic zone: 200 nm

Climate: tropical; humid, average temperature 20-32 degrees C, wet season (May to October)

Terrain: coral atoll

Elevation extremes: *lowest point:* Pacific Ocean 0 m
highest point: Rocher Clipperton 29 m

Natural resources: fish

Land use: *arable land:* 0%
permanent crops: 0%
other: 100% (all coral) (2011)

Natural hazards: NA

Environment—current issues: NA

Geography—note: the atoll reef is approximately 12 km (7.5 mi) in circumference; an effort to colonize the atoll in the early 20th century ended in disaster and was abandoned in 1917

PEOPLE AND SOCIETY

Population: uninhabited

GOVERNMENT

Country name: *conventional long form:* none
conventional short form: Clipperton Island
local long form: none
local short form: Ile Clipperton
former: sometimes called Ile de la Passion

Dependency status: possession of France; administered directly by the Minister of Overseas France

Legal system: the laws of France apply

Flag description: the flag of France is used

ECONOMY

Economy—overview: Although 115 species of fish have been identified in the territorial waters of Clipperton Island, the only economic activity is tuna fishing.

TRANSPORTATION

Ports and terminals: none; offshore anchorage only

MILITARY

Military—note: defense is the responsibility of France

TRANSNATIONAL ISSUES

Disputes—international: none

COCOS (KEELING) ISLANDS

INTRODUCTION

Background: There are 27 coral islands in the group. Captain William KEELING discovered the islands in 1609, but they remained uninhabited until the 19th century. From the 1820s to 1978, members of the CLUNIE-ROSS family controlled the islands and the copra produced from local coconuts. Annexed by the UK in 1857, the Cocos Islands were transferred to the Australian Government in 1955. Apart from North Keeling Island, which lies 30 kilometers north of the main group, the islands form a horseshoe-shaped atoll surrounding a lagoon. North Keeling Island was declared a national park in 1995 and is administered by Parks Australia. The population on the two inhabited islands generally is split between the ethnic Europeans on West Island and the ethnic Malays on Home Island.

GEOGRAPHY

Location: Southeastern Asia, group of islands in the Indian Ocean, southwest of Indonesia, about halfway between Australia and Sri Lanka

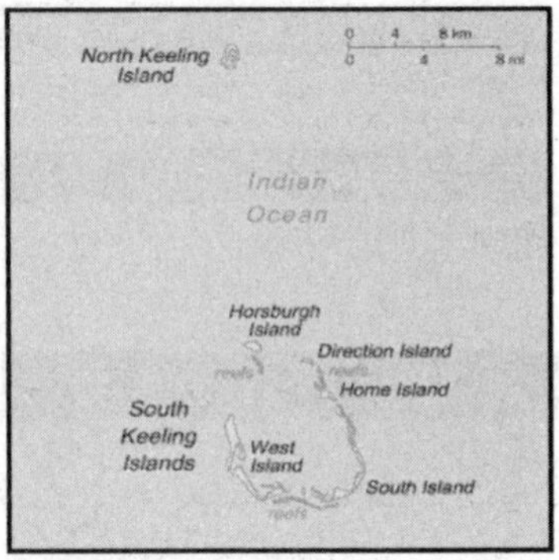

Geographic coordinates: 12 30 S, 96 50 E

Map references: Oceania

Area: *total:* 14 sq km
country comparison to the world: 241
land: 14 sq km
water: 0 sq km
note: includes the two main islands of West Island and Home Island

Area—comparative: about 24 times the size of The Mall in Washington, DC

Land boundaries: 0 km

Coastline: 26 km

Maritime claims: *territorial sea:* 12 nm
exclusive fishing zone: 200 nm

Climate: tropical with high humidity, moderated by the southeast trade winds for about nine months of the year

Terrain: flat, low-lying coral atolls

Elevation extremes:
lowest point: Indian Ocean 0 m
highest point: unnamed location 5 m

Natural resources: fish

Land use: *arable land:* 0%
permanent crops: 0%
other: 100% (2011)

Irrigated land: NA

Natural hazards: cyclone season is October to April

Environment—current issues: freshwater resources are limited to rainwater accumulations in natural underground reservoirs

Geography—note: islands are thickly covered with coconut palms and other vegetation; site of a World War I naval battle in November 1914 between the Australian light cruiser HMAS Sydney and the German raider SMS Emden; after being heavily damaged in the engagement, the Emden was beached by her captain on North Keeling Island

PEOPLE AND SOCIETY

Nationality: *noun:* Cocos Islander(s)
adjective: Cocos Islander

Ethnic groups: Europeans, Cocos Malays

Languages: Malay (Cocos dialect), English

Religions: Sunni Muslim 80%, other 20% (2002 est.)

Population: 596 (July 2014 est.)
country comparison to the world: 239

Population growth rate: 0% (2014 est.)
country comparison to the world: 196

Infant mortality rate: *total:* NA
male: NA
female: NA

Life expectancy at birth: *total population:* NA
male: NA
female: NA

Total fertility rate: NA (2014 est.)

HIV/AIDS—adult prevalence rate: NA

HIV/AIDS—people living with HIV/AIDS: NA

HIV/AIDS—deaths: NA

Literacy: NA

GOVERNMENT

Country name: *conventional long form:* Territory of Cocos (Keeling) Islands
conventional short form: Cocos (Keeling) Islands

Dependency status: non-self governing territory of Australia; administered from Canberra by the Department of Regional Australia, Local Government, Arts and Sport

Government type: NA

Capital: *name:* West Island
geographic coordinates: 12 10 S, 96 50 E
time difference: UTC+6.5 (11.5 hours ahead of Washington, DC during Standard Time)

Administrative divisions: none (territory of Australia)

Independence: none (territory of Australia)

National holiday: Australia Day, 26 January (1788)

Constitution: 23 November 1955 (Cocos (Keeling) Islands Act 1955); amended many times, last in 2010 (2010)

Legal system: common law based on the Australian model

Suffrage: 18 years of age

Executive branch: *chief of state:* Queen ELIZABETH II (since 6 February 1952); represented by the Australian governor general
head of government: Administrator (nonresident) Jon STANHOPE (since 5 October 2012)
cabinet: NA
(For more information visit the World Leaders website)
elections: the monarchy is hereditary; governor general appointed by the monarch on the recommendation of the Australian prime minister; administrator appointed by the governor general of Australia for a two-year term and represents the monarch and Australia

Legislative branch: unicameral Cocos (Keeling) Islands Shire Council (7 seats)
elections: held every two years with half the members standing for election; last held in October 2011 (next to be held in October 2013)

Judicial branch: *highest court(s):* under the terms of the Territorial Law Reform Act 1992, Western Australia provides court services as needed for the island including the Supreme Court and subordinate courts (District Court, Magistrate Court, Family Court, Children's Court, and Coroners' Court)
judge selection and term of office: NA
subordinate courts: NA

Political parties and leaders: none

Political pressure groups and leaders: The Cocos Islands Youth Support Centre

International organization participation: none

Diplomatic representation in the US: none (territory of Australia)

Diplomatic representation from the US: none (territory of Australia)

Flag description: the flag of Australia is used

National anthem: *note:* as a territory of Australia, "Advance Australia Fair" remains official as the national anthem, while "God Save the Queen" serves as the royal anthem (see Australia)

ECONOMY

Economy—overview: Coconuts, grown throughout the islands, are the sole cash crop. Small local gardens and fishing contribute to the food supply, but additional food and most other necessities must be imported from Australia. There is a small tourist industry.

GDP (purchasing power parity): $NA

GDP—real growth rate: 1% (2003)
country comparison to the world: 174

Agriculture—products: vegetables, bananas, pawpaws, coconuts

Industries: copra products, tourism

Labor force: NA

Labor force—by occupation: *note:* the Cocos Islands Cooperative Society Ltd. employs construction workers, stevedores, and lighterage workers; tourism is the other main source of employment

Unemployment rate: 60% (2000 est.)
country comparison to the world: 198

Budget: *revenues:* $NA
expenditures: $NA

Fiscal year: 1 July—30 June

Exports: $NA

Exports—commodities: copra

Imports: $NA

Imports—commodities: foodstuffs

Exchange rates: Australian dollars (AUD) per US dollar—
1.031 (2013)
0.9658 (2012)
1.0902 (2010)
1.2822 (2009)
1.2059 (2008)

COMMUNICATIONS

Telephone system: *general assessment:* telephone service is part of the Australian network; an operational local mobile-cellular network available; wireless Internet connectivity available
domestic: NA
international: country code—61; telephone, telex, and facsimile communications with Australia and elsewhere via satellite; satellite earth station—1 (Intelsat) (2001)

Broadcast media: 1 local radio station staffed by community volunteers; satellite broadcasts of several Australian radio and TV stations available (2009)

Internet country code: .cc

Internet hosts: 42,820 (2012)
country comparison to the world: 99

TRANSPORTATION

Airports: 1 (2013)
country comparison to the world: 214

Airports—with paved runways: *total:* 1
2,438 to 3,047 m: 1 (2013)

Roadways: *total:* 22 km
country comparison to the world: 221
paved: 10 km
unpaved: 12 km (2007)

Ports and terminals:
major seaport(s): Port Refuge

MILITARY

Military—note: defense is the responsibility of Australia; the territory has a five-person police force

TRANSNATIONAL ISSUES

Disputes—international: none

COLOMBIA

INTRODUCTION

Background: Colombia was one of the three countries that emerged from the collapse of Gran Colombia in 1830 (the others are Ecuador and Venezuela). A nearly five-decade long conflict between government forces and anti-government insurgent groups, principally the Revolutionary Armed Forces of Colombia (FARC) heavily funded by the drug trade, escalated during the 1990s. More than 31,000 former paramilitaries had demobilized by the end of 2006 and the United Self Defense Forces of Colombia as a formal organization had ceased to function. In the wake of the paramilitary demobilization, emerging criminal groups arose, whose members include some former paramilitaries. The insurgents lack the military or popular support necessary to overthrow the government, but continue attacks against civilians. Large areas of the countryside are under guerrilla influence or are contested by security forces. In November 2012, the Colombian Government started formal peace negotiations with the FARC aimed at reaching a definitive bilateral ceasefire and incorporating demobilized FARC members into mainstream society and politics. The Colombian Government has stepped up efforts to reassert government control throughout the country, and now has a presence in every one of its administrative departments. Despite decades of internal conflict and drug related security challenges, Colombia maintains relatively strong democratic institutions characterized by peaceful, transparent elections and the protection of civil liberties.

GEOGRAPHY

Location: Northern South America, bordering the Caribbean Sea, between Panama and Venezuela, and bordering the North Pacific Ocean, between Ecuador and Panama

Geographic coordinates: 4 00 N, 72 00 W

Map references: South America

Area: *total:* 1,138,910 sq km
country comparison to the world: 26
land: 1,038,700 sq km
water: 100,210 sq km
note: includes Isla de Malpelo, Roncador Cay, and Serrana Bank

Area—comparative: slightly less than twice the size of Texas

Land boundaries: *total:* 6,309 km
border countries: Brazil 1,644 km, Ecuador 590 km, Panama 225 km, Peru 1,800 km, Venezuela 2,050 km

Coastline:
3,208 km (Caribbean Sea 1,760 km, North Pacific Ocean 1,448 km)

Maritime claims: *territorial sea:* 12 nm
exclusive economic zone: 200 nm
continental shelf: 200 m depth or to the depth of exploitation

Climate: tropical along coast and eastern plains; cooler in highlands

Terrain: flat coastal lowlands, central highlands, high Andes Mountains, eastern lowland plains (Llanos)

Elevation extremes: *lowest point:* Pacific Ocean 0 m
highest point: Pico Cristobal Colon 5,775 m
note: nearby Pico Simon Bolivar also has the same elevation

Natural resources: petroleum, natural gas, coal, iron ore, nickel, gold, copper, emeralds, hydropower

Land use: *arable land:* 1.84%
permanent crops: 1.66%
other: 96.5% (2011)

Irrigated land: 10,870 sq km (2011)

Total renewable water resources: 2,132 cu km (2011)

Freshwater withdrawal (domestic/industrial/agricultural): *total:* 12.65 cu km/yr (55%/4%/41%)
per capita: 308 cu m/yr (2010)

Natural hazards: highlands subject to volcanic eruptions; occasional earthquakes; periodic droughts

volcanism: Galeras (elev. 4,276 m) is one of Colombia's most active volcanoes, having erupted in 2009 and 2010 causing major evacuations; it has been deemed a "Decade Volcano" by the International Association of Volcanology and Chemistry of the Earth's Interior, worthy of study due to its explosive history and close proximity to human populations; Nevado del Ruiz (elev. 5,321 m), 129 km (80 mi) west of Bogota, erupted in 1985 producing lahars that killed 23,000 people; the volcano last erupted in 1991; additionally, after 500 years of dormancy, Nevado del Huila reawakened in 2007 and has experienced frequent eruptions since then; other historically active volcanoes include Cumbal, Dona Juana, Nevado del Tolima, and Purace

Environment—current issues: deforestation; soil and water quality damage from overuse of pesticides; air pollution, especially in Bogota, from vehicle emissions

Environment—international agreements: *party to:* Antarctic Treaty, Biodiversity, Climate Change, Climate Change-Kyoto Protocol, Desertification, Endangered Species, Hazardous Wastes, Marine Life Conservation, Ozone Layer Protection, Ship Pollution, Tropical Timber 83, Tropical Timber 94, Wetlands
signed, but not ratified: Law of the Sea

Geography—note: only South American country with coastlines on both the North Pacific Ocean and Caribbean Sea

PEOPLE AND SOCIETY

Nationality: *noun:* Colombian(s)
adjective: Colombian

Ethnic groups: mestizo 58%, white 20%, mulatto 14%, black 4%, mixed black-Amerindian 3%, Amerindian 1%

Languages: Spanish (official)

Religions: Roman Catholic 90%, other 10%

Demographic profile: Colombia is in the midst of a demographic transition resulting from steady declines in its fertility, mortality, and population growth rates. The birth rate has fallen from more than 6 children per woman in the 1960s to just above replacement level today as a result of increased literacy, family planning services, and urbanization. However, income inequality is among the worst in the world, and more than a third of the population lives below the poverty line.

Colombia experiences significant legal and illegal economic emigration and refugee flows. Large-scale labor emigration dates to the 1960s; Venezuela and the United States continue to be the main host countries. Colombia is the largest source of Latin American refugees in Latin America, nearly 400,000 of whom live primarily in Venezuela and Ecuador. Forced displacement remains prevalent because of violence among guerrillas, paramilitary groups, and Colombian security forces. Afro-Colombian and indigenous populations are disproportionately affected. A leading

NGO estimates that 5.2 million people have been displaced since 1985, while the Colombian Government estimates 3.6 million since 2000. These estimates may undercount actual numbers because not all internally displaced persons are registered. Historically, Colombia also has one of the world's highest levels of forced disappearances. About 30,000 cases have been recorded over the last four decades—although the number is likely to be much higher—including human rights activists, trade unionists, Afro-Colombians, indigenous people, and farmers in rural conflict zones.

Population: 46,245,297 (July 2014 est.)
country comparison to the world: 30

Age structure: *0-14 years:* 25.3% (male 5,998,645/female 5,720,229)
15-24 years: 18% (male 4,243,251/female 4,099,299)
25-54 years: 41.6% (male 9,515,723/female 9,720,894)
55-64 years: 6.7% (male 1,796,050/female 2,051,948)
65 years and over: 6.5% (male 1,293,258/female 1,806,000) (2014 est.)

Dependency ratios:
total dependency ratio: 51.2 %
youth dependency ratio: 41.9 %
elderly dependency ratio: 9.3 %
potential support ratio: 10.7 (2013)

Median age: *total:* 28.9 years
male: 27.9 years
female: 29.9 years (2014 est.)

Population growth rate: 1.07% (2014 est.)
country comparison to the world: 114

Birth rate: 16.73 births/1,000 population (2014 est.)
country comparison to the world: 117

Death rate: 5.36 deaths/1,000 population (2014 est.)
country comparison to the world: 179

Net migration rate: -0.65 migrant(s)/1,000 population (2014 est.)
country comparison to the world: 140

Urbanization: *urban population:* 75% of total population (2010)
rate of urbanization: 1.7% annual rate of change (2010-15 est.)

Major urban areas—population: BOGOTA (capital) 8.744 million; Medellin 3.497 million; Cali 2.352 million; Barranquilla 1.836 million; Bucaramanga 1.065 million (2011)

Sex ratio: *at birth:* 1.06 male(s)/female
0-14 years: 1.05 male(s)/female
15-24 years: 1.04 male(s)/female
25-54 years: 0.98 male(s)/female
55-64 years: 0.98 male(s)/female
65 years and over: 0.72 male(s)/female
total population: 0.98 male(s)/female (2014 est.)

Mother's mean age at first birth: 21.4
note: median age at first birth among women 25-29 (2010 est.)

Maternal mortality rate: 92 deaths/100,000 live births (2010)
country comparison to the world: 80

Infant mortality rate: total: 15.02 deaths/1,000 live births
country comparison to the world: 107
male: 18.22 deaths/1,000 live births
female: 11.62 deaths/1,000 live births (2014 est.)

Life expectancy at birth: total population: 75.25 years
country comparison to the world: 97
male: 72.08 years
female: 78.61 years (2014 est.)

Total fertility rate: 2.07 children born/woman (2014 est.)
country comparison to the world: 115

Contraceptive prevalence rate: 79.1% (2010)

Health expenditures: 6.1% of GDP (2011)
country comparison to the world: 106

Physicians density: 1.47 physicians/1,000 population (2010)

Hospital bed density: 1.4 beds/1,000 population (2011)

Drinking water source:
Improved:
urban: 99.6% of population
rural: 72.5% of population
total: 92.9% of population
unimproved:
urban: 0.4% of population
rural: 27.5% of population
total: 7.1% of population (2011 est.)

Sanitation facility access:
Improved:
urban: 82.3% of population
rural: 65.4% of population
total: 78.1% of population
unimproved:
urban: 17.7% of population
rural: 34.6% of population
total: 21.9% of population (2011 est.)

HIV/AIDS—adult prevalence rate: 0.5% (2012 est.)
country comparison to the world: 67

HIV/AIDS—people living with HIV/AIDS: 146,500 (2012 est.)
country comparison to the world: 35

HIV/AIDS—deaths: 6,500 (2012 est.)
country comparison to the world: 31

Major infectious diseases: *degree of risk:* high
food or waterborne diseases: bacterial diarrhea
vectorborne diseases: dengue fever, malaria, and yellow fever (2013)

Obesity—adult prevalence rate: 17.3% (2008)
country comparison to the world: 112

Children under the age of 5 years underweight: 3.4% (2010)
country comparison to the world: 108

Education expenditures: 4.4% of GDP (2012)
country comparison to the world: 95

Literacy: *definition:* age 15 and over can read and write
total population: 93.6%
male: 93.5%
female: 93.7% (2011 est.)

School life expectancy (primary to tertiary education):
total: 13 years
male: 13 years
female: 14 years (2012)

Child labor—children ages 5-14: total number: 988,362
percentage: 9 %
note: data represents children ages 5-17 (2009 est.)

Unemployment, youth ages 15-24: *total:* 21.9%
country comparison to the world: 53
male: 17%
female: 28.9% (2011)

GOVERNMENT

Country name: *conventional long form:* Republic of Colombia
conventional short form: Colombia
local long form: Republica de Colombia
local short form: Colombia

Government type: republic; executive branch dominates government structure

Capital: *name:* Bogota
geographic coordinates: 4 36 N, 74 05 W
time difference: UTC-5 (same time as Washington, DC during Standard Time)

Administrative divisions: 32 departments (departamentos, singular—departamento) and 1 capital district* (distrito capital); Amazonas, Antioquia, Arauca, Atlantico, Bogota*, Bolivar, Boyaca, Caldas, Caqueta, Casanare, Cauca, Cesar, Choco, Cordoba, Cundinamarca, Guainia, Guaviare, Huila, La Guajira, Magdalena, Meta, Narino, Norte de Santander, Putumayo, Quindio, Risaralda, Archipielago de San Andres, Providencia y Santa Catalina (colloquially San Andres y Providencia), Santander, Sucre, Tolima, Valle del Cauca, Vaupes, Vichada

Independence: 20 July 1810 (from Spain)

National holiday: Independence Day, 20 July (1810)

Constitution: several previous; latest promulgated 5 July 1991; amended many times, last in 2011 (2013)

Legal system: civil law system influenced by the Spanish and French civil codes

International law organization participation: has not submitted an ICJ jurisdiction declaration; accepts ICCt jurisdiction

Suffrage: 18 years of age; universal

Executive branch: *chief of state:* President Juan Manuel SANTOS Calderon (since 7 August 2010); Vice President Angelino GARZON (since 7 August 2010); note—the president is both the chief of state and head of government
head of government: President Juan Manuel SANTOS Calderon (since 7 August 2010); Vice President Angelino GARZON (since 7 August 2010)
cabinet: Cabinet appointed by the president (For more information visit the World Leaders website)
elections: president and vice president elected by popular vote for a four-year term (eligible for a second term); election last held on 30 May 2010 with a runoff election 20 June 2010 (next to be held on 25 May 2014)
election results: Juan Manuel SANTOS Calderon elected president in runoff election; percent of vote—Juan Manuel SANTOS Calderon 69.06%, Antanas MOCKUS 27.52%

Legislative branch: bicameral Congress or Congreso consists of the Senate or Senado (102 seats; members elected by popular vote to serve four-year terms) and the Chamber of Representatives or Camara de Representantes (166 seats; members elected by popular vote to serve four-year terms)
elections: Senate—last held on 14 March 2010 (next to be held in March 2014); Chamber of

Representatives—last held on 14 March 2010 (next to be held in March 2014)
election results: Senate—percent of vote by party—NA; seats by party—U Party 28, PC 22, PL 17, PIN 9, CR 8, PDA 8, Green Party 5, other parties 5; Chamber of Representatives—percent of vote by party—NA; seats by party—U Party 47, PC 38, PL 37, CR 15, PIN 12, PDA 4, Green Party 3, other parties 10; note—as of 1 January 2011, the Senate currently has 101 seats after one seat became vacant due to a PL senator losing his seat for illegal collusion with the FARC; the Chamber of Representatives also has one seat vacant after only 165 of the 166 candidates were credentialed

Judicial branch: *highest court(s):* Supreme Court of Justice or Corte Suprema de Justicia (consists of the Civil-Agrarian and Labor Chambers each with 7 judges, and the Penal Chamber with 9 judges); Constitutional Court (consists of 9 magistrates); Council of State (consists of 27 magistrates)
judge selection and term of office: Supreme Court judges appointed by the Congress from candidates submitted by the president; judges appointed for life; Constitutional Court magistrates—3 nominated by the president, 3 by the Supreme Court, and 3 elected by the Senate; judges elected for individual 2-8 year terms
subordinate courts: Superior Tribunals (appellate courts for each of the judicial districts); regional courts; civil municipal courts; Superior Military Tribunal; first instance administrative courts

Political parties and leaders: Alternative Democratic Pole or PDA [Clara LOPEZ]; Conservative Party or PC [Omar YEPES Alzate]; Democratic Center Party or CD [Alvaro URIBE Velez]; Green Party [Alfonso PRADA]; Liberal Party or PL [Simon GAVIRIA Munoz]; National Integration Party or PIN [Angel ALIRIO Moreno]; Radical Change or CR [Carlos Fernando GALAN]; Social National Unity Party or U Party [Sergio Diaz GANADOS]
note: Colombia has seven major political parties, and numerous smaller movements

Political pressure groups and leaders: Central Union of Workers or CUT; Colombian Confederation of Workers or CTC; General Confederation of Workers or CGT; National Liberation Army or ELN; Revolutionary Armed Forces of Colombia or FARC
note: FARC and ELN are the two largest insurgent groups active in Colombia

International organization participation: BCIE, BIS, CAN, Caricom (observer), CD, CDB, CELAC, FAO, G-3, G-24, G-77, IADB, IAEA, IBRD, ICAO, ICC (national committees), ICRM, IDA, IFAD, IFC, IFRCS, IHO, ILO, IMF, IMO, IMSO, Interpol, IOC, IOM, IPU, ISO, ITSO, ITU, ITUC (NGOs), LAES, LAIA, Mercosur (associate), MIGA, NAM, OAS, OPANAL, OPCW, PCA, UN, UNASUR, UNCTAD, UNESCO, UNHCR, UNIDO, Union Latina, UNSC (temporary), UNWTO, UPU, WCO, WFTU (NGOs), WHO, WIPO, WMO, WTO

Diplomatic representation in the US:
chief of mission: Ambassador Luis Carlos VILLEGAS Echeverri (since 3 December 2013)
chancery: 2118 Leroy Place NW, Washington, DC 20008
telephone: [1] (202) 387-8338
FAX: [1] (202) 232-8643
consulate(s) general: Atlanta, Beverly Hills (CA), Boston, Chicago, Houston, Miami, New York, San Francisco, San Juan (Puerto Rico)
consulate(s): Newark (NJ)

Diplomatic representation from the US:
chief of mission: Ambassador (vacant); Charge d'Affaires Benjamin ZIFF
embassy: Calle 24 Bis No. 48-50, Bogota, D.C.
mailing address: Carrera 45 No. 24B-27, Bogota, D.C.
telephone: [57] (1) 275-2000
FAX: [57] (1) 275-4600

Flag description: three horizontal bands of yellow (top, double-width), blue, and red; the flag retains the three main colors of the banner of Gran Colombia, the short-lived South American republic that broke up in 1830; various interpretations of the colors exist and include: yellow for the gold in Colombia's land, blue for the seas on its shores, and red for the blood spilled in attaining freedom; alternatively, the colors have been described as representing more elemental concepts such as sovereignty and justice (yellow), loyalty and vigilance (blue), and valor and generosity (red); or simply the principles of liberty, equality, and fraternity
note: similar to the flag of Ecuador, which is longer and bears the Ecuadorian coat of arms superimposed in the center

National symbol(s): Andean condor

National anthem: *name:* "Himno Nacional de la Republica de Colombia" (National Anthem of the Republic of Colombia)
lyrics/music: Rafael NUNEZ/Oreste SINDICI
note: adopted 1920; the anthem was created from an inspirational poem written by President Rafael NUNEZ

ECONOMY

Economy—overview: Colombia's consistently sound economic policies and aggressive promotion of free trade agreements in recent years have bolstered its ability to face external shocks. Real GDP has grown more than 4% per year for the past three years, continuing almost a decade of strong economic performance. All three major ratings agencies have upgraded Colombia's government debt to investment grade. Nevertheless, Colombia depends heavily on energy and mining exports, making it vulnerable to a drop in commodity prices. Colombia is the world's fourth largest coal exporter and Latin America's fourth largest oil producer. Economic development is stymied by inadequate infrastructure and an uncertain security situation. Moreover, the unemployment rate of 9.7% in 2013 is still one of Latin America's highest. The SANTOS Administration's foreign policy has focused on bolstering Colombia's commercial ties and boosting investment at home. The US-Colombia Free Trade Agreement (FTA) was ratified by the US Congress in October 2011 and implemented in 2012. Colombia has signed or is negotiating FTAs with a number of other countries, including Canada, Chile, Mexico, Switzerland, the EU, Venezuela, South Korea, Turkey, Japan, China, Costa Rica, Panama, and Israel. Colombia is also a founding member of the Pacific Alliance—a group formed in 2012 among Chile, Colombia, Mexico, and Peru to promote regional trade and integration. In 2013, Colombia began its ascension process to the OECD. The annual level of foreign direct investment—notably in the oil and gas sectors—reached $10 billion in 2008 but dropped to $7.2 billion in 2009, before beginning to recover in 2010, and reached a record high of nearly $16 billion in 2012. Inequality, poverty, and narcotrafficking remain significant challenges, and Colombia's infrastructure requires major improvements to sustain economic expansion.

GDP (purchasing power parity):
$526.5 billion (2013 est.)
country comparison to the world: 29
$505.2 billion (2012 est.)
$484.9 billion (2011 est.)
note: data are in 2013 US dollars GDP (official exchange rate):
$369.2 billion (2013 est.)

GDP—real growth rate: 4.2% (2013 est.)
country comparison to the world: 73
4.2% (2012 est.)
6.6% (2011 est.)

GDP—per capita (PPP): $11,100 (2013 est.)
country comparison to the world: 112
$10,800 (2012 est.)
$10,500 (2011 est.)
note: data are in 2013 US dollars Gross national saving:
21.9% of GDP (2013 est.)
country comparison to the world: 69
22.8% of GDP (2012 est.)
20.3% of GDP (2011 est.)

GDP—composition, by end use:
household consumption: 61.7%
government consumption: 16.7%
investment in fixed capital: 23.8%
investment in inventories: -0.3%
exports of goods and services: 17.3%
imports of goods and services: -19.3% (2013 est.)

GDP—composition, by sector of origin:
agriculture: 6.6%
industry: 37.8%
services: 55.6% (2013 est.)

Agriculture—products: coffee, cut flowers, bananas, rice, tobacco, corn, sugarcane, cocoa beans, oilseed, vegetables; shrimp; forest products

Industries: textiles, food processing, oil, clothing and footwear, beverages, chemicals, cement; gold, coal, emeralds

Industrial production growth rate: 2.5% (2013 est.)
country comparison to the world: 119

Labor force: 23.75 million (2013 est.)
country comparison to the world: 28

Labor force—by occupation: *agriculture:* 17%
industry: 21%
services: 62% (2011 est.)

Unemployment rate: 9.7% (2013 est.)
country comparison to the world: 104
10.4% (2012 est.)

Population below poverty line: 32.7% (2012 est.)

Household income or consumption by percentage share: *lowest 10%:* 0.9%
highest 10%: 44.4% (2010 est.)

Distribution of family income—Gini index:
55.9 (2010)
country comparison to the world: 9
56.9 (1996)

Budget: revenues: $107.4 billion
expenditures: $106 billion (2013 est.)

Taxes and other revenues: 29.1% of GDP (2012 est.)
country comparison to the world: 95

Budget surplus (+) or deficit (-):
0.4% of GDP (2012 est.)
country comparison to the world: 36

Public debt: 39.6% of GDP (2013 est.)
country comparison to the world: 91
40.5% of GDP (2012 est.)
note: data cover general government debt, and includes debt instruments issued (or owned) by government entities other than the treasury; the data include treasury debt held by foreign entities; the data include debt issued by subnational entities

Fiscal year: calendar year

Inflation rate (consumer prices): 2.2% (2013 est.)
country comparison to the world: 79
3.4% (2011 est.)

Central bank discount rate: 4.75% (31 December 2011)
country comparison to the world: 72
5% (31 December 2010)

Commercial bank prime lending rate: 11% (31 December 2013 est.)
country comparison to the world: 62
12.6% (31 December 2012 est.)

Stock of narrow money: $42.28 billion (31 December 2013 est.)
country comparison to the world: 52
$41.7 billion (31 December 2012 est.)

Stock of broad money: $163.2 billion (31 December 2013 est.)
country comparison to the world: 43
$153.1 billion (31 December 2012 est.)

Stock of domestic credit: $192.6 billion (31 December 2013 est.)
country comparison to the world: 41
$180.7 billion (31 December 2012 est.)

Market value of publicly traded shares: $262.1 billion (31 December 2012 est.)
country comparison to the world: 32
$201.3 billion (31 December 2011)
$208.5 billion (31 December 2010 est.)

Current account balance: -$11.02 billion (2013 est.)
country comparison to the world: 179
-$12.17 billion (2012 est.)

Exports: $58.7 billion (2013 est.)
country comparison to the world: 56
$59.85 billion (2012 est.)

Exports—commodities: petroleum, coal, emeralds, coffee, nickel, cut flowers, bananas, apparel

Exports—partners: US 36.6%, China 5.5%, Spain 4.8%, Panama 4.7%, Venezuela 4.4%, Netherlands 4.1% (2012)

Imports: $53.5 billion (2013 est.)
country comparison to the world: 54
$54.64 billion (2012 est.)

Imports—commodities: industrial equipment, transportation equipment, consumer goods, chemicals, paper products, fuels, electricity

Imports—partners: US 24.2%, China 16.3%, Mexico 10.9%, Brazil 4.8% (2012)

Reserves of foreign exchange and gold: $43.74 billion (31 December 2013 est.)
country comparison to the world: 44
$37 billion (31 December 2012 est.)

Debt—external: $85.83 billion (31 December 2013 est.)
country comparison to the world: 51
$80.72 billion (31 December 2012 est.)

Stock of direct foreign investment—at home: $128.1 billion (31 December 2013 est.)
country comparison to the world: 36
$111.7 billion (31 December 2012 est.)

Stock of direct foreign investment—abroad: $33.7 billion (31 December 2013 est.)
country comparison to the world: 41
$31.65 billion (31 December 2012 est.)

Exchange rates: Colombian pesos (COP) per US dollar—
1,865.8 (2013 est.)
1,798 (2012 est.)
1,898.6 (2010 est.)
2,157.6 (2009)
2,243.6 (2008)

ENERGY

Electricity—production: 61.82 billion kWh (2011 est.)
country comparison to the world: 43

Electricity—consumption: 45.35 billion kWh (2010 est.)
country comparison to the world: 49

Electricity—exports: 1.294 billion kWh (2011 est.)
country comparison to the world: 53

Electricity—imports: 8.22 billion kWh (2011 est.)
country comparison to the world: 27

Electricity—installed generating capacity: 13.54 million kW (2010 est.)
country comparison to the world: 48

Electricity—from fossil fuels: 32.9% of total installed capacity (2010 est.)
country comparison to the world: 176

Electricity—from nuclear fuels: 0% of total installed capacity (2010 est.)
country comparison to the world: 68

Electricity—from hydroelectric plants: 66.6% of total installed capacity (2010 est.)
country comparison to the world: 25

Electricity—from other renewable sources: 0.4% of total installed capacity (2010 est.)
country comparison to the world: 87

Crude oil—production: 969,100 bbl/day (2012 est.)
country comparison to the world: 24

Crude oil—exports: 777,900 bbl/day (2009)
country comparison to the world: 18

Crude oil—imports: 10 bbl/day (2011 est.)
country comparison to the world: 81

Crude oil—proved reserves: 2.2 billion bbl (1 January 2013 es)
country comparison to the world: 35

Refined petroleum products—production: 313,100 bbl/day (2010 est.)
country comparison to the world: 41

Refined petroleum products—consumption: 287,000 bbl/day (2011 est.)
country comparison to the world: 44

Refined petroleum products—exports: *92,410 bbl/day (2010 est.)*
country comparison to the world: 46

Refined petroleum products—imports: 49,790 bbl/day (2010 est.)
country comparison to the world: 70

Natural gas—production: 10.95 billion cu m (2011 est.)
country comparison to the world: 40

Natural gas—consumption: 9.08 billion cu m (2010 est.)
country comparison to the world: 49

Natural gas—exports: 2.11 billion cu m (2011 est.)
country comparison to the world: 43

Natural gas—imports: 40,290 cu m (2011 est.)
country comparison to the world: 75

Natural gas—proved reserves: 169.9 billion cu m (1 January 2013 es)
country comparison to the world: 48

Carbon dioxide emissions from consumption of energy: 71.15 million Mt (2011 est.)
country comparison to the world: 49

COMMUNICATIONS

Telephones—main lines in use: 6.291 million (2012)
country comparison to the world: 27

Telephones—mobile cellular: 49.066 million (2012)
country comparison to the world: 29

Telephone system: *general assessment:* modern system in many respects with a nationwide microwave radio relay system, a domestic satellite system with 41 earth stations, and a fiber-optic network linking 50 cities; telecommunications sector liberalized during the 1990s; multiple providers of both fixed-line and mobile-cellular services
domestic: fixed-line connections stand at about 15 per 100 persons; mobile cellular telephone subscribership is about 100 per 100 persons; competition among cellular service providers is resulting in falling local and international calling rates and contributing to the steep decline in the market share of fixed line services
international: country code—57; multiple submarine cable systems provide links to the US, parts of the Caribbean, and Central and South America; satellite earth stations—10 (6 Intelsat, 1 Inmarsat, 3 fully digitalized international switching centers) (2011)

Broadcast media: combination of state-owned and privately owned broadcast media provide service; more than 500 radio stations and many national, regional, and local TV stations (2007)

Internet country code: .co

Internet hosts: 4.41 million (2012)
country comparison to the world: 24

Internet users: 22.538 million (2009)
country comparison to the world: 18

TRANSPORTATION

Airports: 836 (2013)
country comparison to the world: 8
Airports—with paved runways: total: 121
over 3,047 m: 2
2,438 to 3,047 m: 9
1,524 to 2,437 m: 39
914 to 1,523 m: 53
under 914 m: 18 (2013)

Airports—with unpaved runways: *total:* 715
over 3,047 m: 1
1,524 to 2,437 m: 25
914 to 1,523 m: 201
under 914 m: 488 (2013)

Heliports: 3 (2013)

Pipelines: gas 4,991 km; oil 6,796 km; refined products 3,429 km (2013)

Railways: *total:* 874 km
country comparison to the world: 95
standard gauge: 150 km 1.435-m gauge
narrow gauge: 498 km 0.950-m gauge; 226 km 0.914-m gauge (2008)

Roadways: *total:* 141,374 km (2010)
country comparison to the world: 34

Waterways: 24,725 km (18,300 km navigable; the most important waterway, the River Magdalena, of which 1,488 km is navigable, is dredged regularly to ensure the safe passage of cargo vessels and container barges) (2012)
country comparison to the world: 6

Merchant marine: *total:* 12
country comparison to the world: 106
by type: cargo 9, chemical tanker 1, petroleum tanker 2

registered in other countries: 4 (Antigua and Barbuda 1, Panama 2, Portugal 1) (2010)

Ports and terminals:
major seaport(s): Atlantic Ocean (Caribbean)—Cartagena, Santa Marta, Turbo; Pacific Ocean—Buenaventura
river port(s): Barranquilla (Rio Magdalena)
oil/gas terminal(s): Covenas offshore terminal
dry bulk cargo port(s): Puerto Bolivar (coal)
container port(s) (TEUs): Cartagena (1,853,342)

MILITARY

Military branches: National Army (Ejercito Nacional), Republic of Colombia Navy (Armada Republica de Colombia, ARC, includes Naval Aviation, Naval Infantry (Infanteria de Marina, IM), and Coast Guard), Colombian Air Force (Fuerza Aerea de Colombia, FAC) (2012)

Military service age and obligation: 18-24 years of age for compulsory and voluntary military service; service obligation is 18 months (2012)

Manpower available for military service:
males age 16-49: 11,692,647
females age 16-49: 11,727,625 (2010 est.)

Manpower fit for military service: *males age 16-49:* 9,150,400
females age 16-49: 9,861,760 (2010 est.)

Manpower reaching militarily significant age annually: *male:* 430,634
female: 413,974 (2010 est.)

Military expenditures: 3.28% of GDP (2012)
country comparison to the world: 16
3.06% of GDP (2011)
3.28% of GDP (2010)

TRANSNATIONAL ISSUES

Disputes—international: in December 2007, ICJ allocated San Andres, Providencia, and Santa Catalina islands to Colombia under 1928 Treaty but did not rule on 82 degrees W meridian as maritime boundary with Nicaragua; managed dispute with Venezuela over maritime boundary and Venezuelan-administered Los Monjes Islands near the Gulf of Venezuela; Colombian-organized illegal narcotics, guerrilla, and paramilitary activities penetrate all neighboring borders and have caused Colombian citizens to flee mostly into neighboring countries; Colombia, Honduras, Nicaragua, Jamaica, and the US assert various claims to Bajo Nuevo and Serranilla Bank

Refugees and internally displaced persons: *IDPs:* 4.9–5.7 million (conflict between government and illegal armed groups and drug traffickers since 1985) (2013)
stateless persons: 12 (2012)

Illicit drugs: illicit producer of coca, opium poppy, and cannabis; world's leading coca cultivator with 83,000 hectares in coca cultivation in 2011, a 17% decrease over 2010, producing a potential of 195 mt of pure cocaine; the world's largest producer of coca derivatives; supplies cocaine to nearly all of the US market and the great majority of other international drug markets; in 2012, aerial eradication dispensed herbicide to treat over 100,549 hectares combined with manual eradication of 30,486 hectares; a significant portion of narcotics proceeds are either laundered or invested in Colombia through the black market peso exchange; important supplier of heroin to the US market; opium poppy cultivation is estimated to have fallen to 1,100 hectares in 2009 while pure heroin production declined to 2.1 mt; most Colombian heroin is destined for the US market (2013)

COMOROS

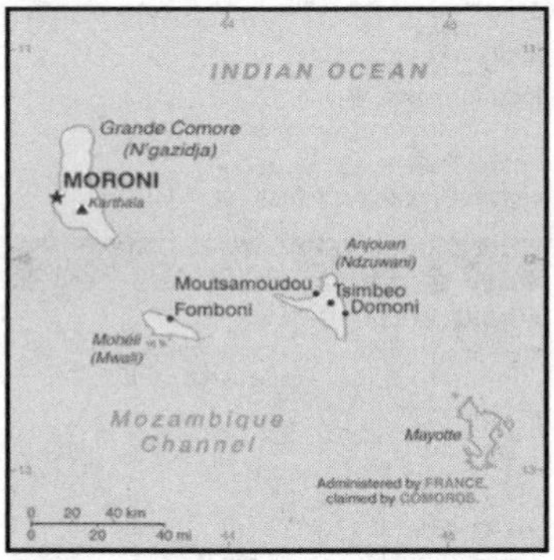

INTRODUCTION

Background: Comoros has endured more than 20 coups or attempted coups since gaining independence from France in 1975. In 1997, the islands of Anjouan and Moheli declared independence from Comoros. In 1999, military chief Col. AZALI seized power of the entire government in a bloodless coup, and helped negotiate the 2000 Fomboni Accords power-sharing agreement in which the federal presidency rotates among the three islands, and each island maintains its local government. AZALI won the 2002 federal presidential election, and each island in the archipelago elected its president. AZALI stepped down in 2006 and President SAMBI was elected to office. In 2007, Mohamed BACAR effected Anjouan's de-facto secession from the Union of Comoros, refusing to step down when Comoros' other islands held legitimate elections in July. The African Union (AU) initially attempted to resolve the political crisis by applying sanctions and a naval blockade to Anjouan, but in March 2008 the AU and Comoran soldiers seized the island. The island's inhabitants generally welcomed the move. In May 2011, Ikililou DHOININE won the presidency in peaceful elections widely deemed to be free and fair.

GEOGRAPHY

Location: Southern Africa, group of islands at the northern mouth of the Mozambique Channel, about two-thirds of the way between northern Madagascar and northern Mozambique

Geographic coordinates: 12 10 S, 44 15 E

Map references: Africa

Area: *total:* 2,235 sq km
country comparison to the world: 180
land: 2,235 sq km water: 0 sq km

Area—comparative: slightly more than 12 times the size of Washington, DC

Land boundaries: 0 km

Coastline: 340 km

Maritime claims: *territorial sea:* 12 nm
exclusive economic zone: 200 nm

Climate: tropical marine; rainy season (November to May)

Terrain: volcanic islands, interiors vary from steep mountains to low hills

Elevation extremes: *lowest point:* Indian Ocean 0 m
highest point: Karthala 2,360 m

Natural resources: NEGL

Land use: *arable land:* 44.06%
permanent crops: 31.17%
other: 24.77% (2011)

Irrigated land: 1.3 sq km NA (2003)

Total renewable water resources: 1.2 cu km (2011)

Freshwater withdrawal (domestic/industrial/agricultural): *total:* 0.01 cu km/yr (48%/5%/47%)
per capita: 16.86 cu m/yr (1999)

Natural hazards: cyclones possible during rainy season (December to April); volcanic activity on Grand Comore
volcanism: Karthala (elev. 2,361 m) on Grand Comore Island last erupted in 2007; a 2005 eruption forced thousands of people to be evacuated and produced a large ash cloud

Environment—current issues: soil degradation and erosion results from crop cultivation on slopes without proper terracing; deforestation

Environment—international agreements: *party to:* Biodiversity, Climate Change, Climate Change-Kyoto Protocol, Desertification, Endangered Species, Hazardous Wastes, Law of the Sea, Ozone Layer Protection, Ship Pollution, Wetlands
signed, but not ratified: none of the selected agreements

Geography—note: important location at northern end of Mozambique Channel

PEOPLE AND SOCIETY

Nationality: *noun:* Comoran(s)
adjective: Comoran

Ethnic groups: Antalote, Cafre, Makoa, Oimatsaha, Sakalava

Languages: Arabic (official), French (official), Shikomoro (a blend of Swahili and Arabic)

Religions: Sunni Muslim 98%, Roman Catholic 2%

Population: 766,865 (July 2014 est.)
country comparison to the world: 164

Age structure: 0-14 years: 41.3% (male 157,996/female 159,088)
15-24 years: 18.8% (male 69,688/female 74,418)
25-54 years: 31.9% (male 116,235/female 128,647)
55-64 years: 3.8% (male 14,074/female 17,700)
65 years and over: 3.7% (male 13,696/female 15,323) (2014 est.)

Dependency ratios: *total dependency ratio:* 81.6 %
youth dependency ratio: 76.4 %
elderly dependency ratio: 5.2 %
potential support ratio: 19.3 (2013)

Median age: *total:* 19.2 years
male: 18.5 years
female: 19.8 years (2014 est.)

Population growth rate: 1.87% (2014 est.)
country comparison to the world: 62

Birth rate: 29.05 births/1,000 population (2014 est.)
country comparison to the world: 44

Death rate: 7.76 deaths/1,000 population (2014 est.)
country comparison to the world: 109

Net migration rate: -2.58 migrant(s)/1,000 population (2014 est.)
country comparison to the world: 174

Urbanization: *urban population:* 28% of total population (2011)
rate of urbanization: 2.84% annual rate of change (2010-15 est.)

Major urban areas—population: MORONI (capital) 54,000 (2011)

Sex ratio: at birth: 1.03 male(s)/female
0-14 years: 0.99 male(s)/female
15-24 years: 0.94 male(s)/female
25-54 years: 0.9 male(s)/female
55-64 years: 0.94 male(s)/female
65 years and over: 0.92 male(s)/female
total population: 0.94 male(s)/female (2014 est.)

Maternal mortality rate: 280 deaths/100,000 live births (2010)
country comparison to the world: 42

Infant mortality rate: total: 65.31 deaths/1,000 live births
country comparison to the world: 19
male: 76.11 deaths/1,000 live births
female: 54.18 deaths/1,000 live births (2014 est.)

Life expectancy at birth: total population: 63.48 years
country comparison to the world: 184
male: 61.23 years
female: 65.8 years (2014 est.)

Total fertility rate: 3.76 children born/woman (2014 est.)
country comparison to the world: 42

Contraceptive prevalence rate: 25.7% (2000)

Health expenditures: 5.3% of GDP (2011)
country comparison to the world: 130

Physicians density: 0.15 physicians/1,000 population (2004)

Hospital bed density: 2.2 beds/1,000 population (2006)

Drinking water source:
Improved:
rural: 96.7% of population
unimproved:
rural: 0.3% of population (2011 est.)

Sanitation facility access:
Improved:
urban: 50% of population
rural: 29.7% of population
total: 35.4% of population
unimproved:
urban: 50% of population
rural: 70.3% of population
total: 64.6% of population (2010 est.)

HIV/AIDS—adult prevalence rate: 0.1% (2009 est.)
country comparison to the world: 131

HIV/AIDS—people living with HIV/AIDS: fewer than 500 (2009 est.)
country comparison to the world: 155

HIV/AIDS—deaths: fewer than 100 (2009 est.)
country comparison to the world: 129

Obesity—adult prevalence rate: 4.4% (2008)
country comparison to the world: 164

Children under the age of 5 years underweight: 25% (2000)
country comparison to the world: 25

Education expenditures: 7.6% of GDP (2008)
country comparison to the world: 15

Literacy: *definition:* age 15 and over can read and write
total population: 75.5%
male: 80.5%
female: 70.6% (2011 est.)

School life expectancy (primary to tertiary education): *total:* 13 years
male: 13 years
female: 12 years (2012)

Child labor—children ages 5-14: total number: 39,550
percentage: 27 % (2000 est.)

GOVERNMENT

Country name: *conventional long form:* Union of the Comoros
conventional short form: Comoros
local long form: Udzima wa Komori (Comorian); Union des Comores (French); Jumhuriyat al Qamar al Muttahidah (Arabic)
local short form: Komori (Comorian); Comores (French); Juzur al Qamar (Arabic)

Government type: republic

Capital: *name:* Moroni
geographic coordinates: 11 42 S, 43 14 E
time difference: UTC+3 (8 hours ahead of Washington, DC during Standard Time)

Administrative divisions: 3 islands and 4 municipalities*; Anjouan (Ndzuwani), Domoni*, Fomboni*, Grande Comore (N'gazidja), Moheli (Mwali), Moroni*, Moutsamoudou*

Independence: 6 July 1975 (from France)

National holiday: Independence Day, 6 July (1975)

Constitution: previous 1996; latest ratified 23 December 2001; amended 2009 and 2014 (2009)

Legal system: mixed legal system of Islamic religious law, the French civil code of 1975, and customary law

International law organization participation: has not submitted an ICJ jurisdiction declaration; accepts ICCt jurisdiction

Suffrage: 18 years of age; universal

Executive branch: chief of state: President Ikililou DHOININE (since 26 May 2011)
head of government: President Ikililou DHOININE (since 26 May 2011)
cabinet: Council of Ministers appointed by the president (For more information visit the World Leaders website)
elections: as defined by the 2001 constitution, the presidency rotates every four years among the elected presidents from the three main islands in the Union; election last held on 7 November and 26 December 2010 (next to be held in 2015)
election results: Ikililou DHOININE elected president; percent of vote—Ikililou DHOININE 61.1%, Mohamed Said FAZUL 32.7%, Abdou DJABIR 6.2%

Legislative branch: unicameral Assembly of the Union (33 seats; 15 deputies are selected by the individual islands' local assemblies and 18 by universal suffrage to serve for five years);
elections: last held on 6 and 20 December 2009 (next to be held in 2014)
election results: percent of vote by party—NA; seats by party—pro-union coalition 19, autonomous coalition 4, independents 1; note—9 additional seats are filled by deputies from local island assemblies

Judicial branch: *highest court(s):* Supreme Court or Cour Supreme (consists of 7 judges); Constitutional Court (consists of 8 members)
judge selection and term of office: Supreme Court judges selected—2 by the president of the Union, 2 by the Assembly of the Union, and 1 each by the 3 island councils; judges appointed for life; Constitutional Court members appointed—1 by the president, 1 each by the 3 vice presidents, 1 by the Assembly, and 1 each by the island executives; all members serve 6-year renewable terms
subordinate courts: Court of Appeals (in Moroni); Tribunal de premiere; island village (community) courts; religious courts

Political parties and leaders: Camp of the Autonomous Islands or CdIA (a coalition of parties organized by the islands' presidents in opposition to the Union President); Convention for the Renewal of the Comoros or CRC [AZALI Assowmani]; Front National pour la Justice or FNJ [Ahmed RACHID] (Islamic party in opposition); Mouvement pour la Democratie et le Progress or MDP-NGDC [Abbas DJOUSSOUF]; Parti Comorien pour la Democratie et le Progress or PCDP [Ali MROUDJAE]; Rassemblement National pour le Development or RND [Omar TAMOU, Abdoulhamid AFFRAITANE]

Political pressure groups and leaders: *other:* environmentalists

International organization participation: ACP, AfDB, AMF, AOSIS, AU, CAEU (candidates), COMESA, FAO, FZ, G-77, IBRD, ICAO, ICRM, IDA, IDB, IFAD, IFC, IFRCS, ILO, IMF, IMO, IMSO, InOC, Interpol, IOC, IOM, ITSO, ITU, ITUC (NGOs), LAS, NAM, OIC, OIF, OPCW, UN, UNCTAD, UNESCO, UNIDO, UPU, WCO, WHO, WIPO, WMO, WTO (observer)

Diplomatic representation in the US: chief of mission: Ambassador Roubani KAAMBI (since 6 September 2012); note—also serves as Permanent Representative to the UN
chancery: Mission to the US, 866 United Nations Plaza, Suite 418, New York, NY 10017
telephone: [1] (212) 750-1637
FAX: [1] (212) 750-1657

Diplomatic representation from the US: the US does not have an embassy in Comoros; the ambassador to Madagascar is accredited to Comoros

Flag description: four equal horizontal bands of yellow (top), white, red, and blue, with a green isosceles triangle based on the hoist; centered within the triangle is a white crescent with the convex side facing the hoist and four white, five-pointed stars placed vertically in a line between the points of the crescent; the horizontal bands and the four stars represent the four main islands of the archipelago—Mwali, N'gazidja, Ndzuwani, and Mahore (Mayotte— department of France, but claimed by Comoros)
note: the crescent, stars, and color green are traditional symbols of Islam

National symbol(s): four stars and crescent

National anthem: *name:* "Udzima wa ya Masiwa" (The Union of the Great Islands)
lyrics/music: Said Hachim SIDI ABDEREMANE/ Said Hachim SIDI ABDEREMANE and Kamildine ABDALLAH
note: adopted 1978

ECONOMY

Economy—overview: One of the world's poorest countries, Comoros is made up of three islands that have inadequate transportation links, a young and rapidly increasing population, and few natural resources. The low educational level of the labor force contributes to a subsistence level of economic activity, high unemployment, and a heavy dependence on foreign grants and technical assistance. Agriculture, including fishing, hunting, and forestry, contributes 50% to GDP, employs 80% of the labor force, and provides most of the exports. Export income is heavily reliant on the three main crops of vanilla, cloves, and ylang-ylang; and Comoros' export earnings are easily disrupted by disasters such as fires. The country is not self-sufficient in food production; rice, the main staple, accounts for the bulk of imports. The government—which is hampered by internal political disputes—lacks a comprehensive strategy to attract foreign investment and is struggling to upgrade education and technical training, privatize commercial and industrial enterprises, improve health services, diversify exports, promote tourism, and reduce the high population growth rate. Political problems have inhibited growth. Remittances from 200,000 Comorans abroad help supplement GDP. In December 2012, IMF and the World Bank's International Development Association supported $176 million in debt relief for Comoros, resulting in a 59% reduction of its future external debt service over a period of 40 years.

GDP (purchasing power parity): $911 million (2013 est.)
country comparison to the world: 206
$879.9 million (2012 est.)
$855.1 million (2011 est.)
note: data are in 2013 US dollars

GDP (official exchange rate): $658 million (2013 est.)

GDP—real growth rate: 3.5% (2013 est.)
country comparison to the world: 98
3% (2012 est.)
2.2% (2011 est.)

GDP—per capita (PPP): $1,300 (2013 est.)
country comparison to the world: 209
$1,300 (2012 est.)
$1,300 (2011 est.)
note: data are in 2013 US dollars

GDP—composition, by end use: household consumption: 97.2%
government consumption: 17.4%
investment in fixed capital: 21.6%
investment in inventories: 5.1%
exports of goods and services: 15%
imports of goods and services: -56.4% (2013 est.)

GDP—composition, by sector of origin:
agriculture: 51%
industry: 10%
services: 39% (2012 est.)

Agriculture—products: vanilla, cloves, ylang-ylang (perfume essence), copra, coconuts, bananas, cassava (manioc)

Industries: fishing, tourism, perfume distillation

Industrial production growth rate: 4%
country comparison to the world: 75

Labor force: 233,500 (2011 est.)
country comparison to the world: 167

Labor force—by occupation: agriculture: 80%
industry and services: 20% (1996 est.)

Unemployment rate: 20% (1996 est.)
country comparison to the world: 160

Population below poverty line: 60% (2002 est.)

Household income or consumption by percentage share: lowest 10%: 0.9%
highest 10%: 55.2% (2004)

Budget: *revenues:* $170.1 million
expenditures: $167.4 million (2013 est.)

Taxes and other revenues: 25.8% of GDP (2013 est.)
country comparison to the world: 116

Budget surplus (+) or deficit (-): 0.4% of GDP (2013 est.)
country comparison to the world: 37

Fiscal year: calendar year

Inflation rate (consumer prices): 2.5% (2013 est.)
country comparison to the world: 92
6.3% (2012 est.)

Central bank discount rate: 1.93% (31 December 2010 est.)
country comparison to the world: 112
2.21% (31 December 2009 est.)

Commercial bank prime lending rate: 9% (31 December 2013 est.)
country comparison to the world: 83
10.5% (31 December 2012 est.)

Stock of narrow money: $162.2 million (31 December 2013 est.)
country comparison to the world: 180
$151.6 million (31 December 2012 est.)

Stock of broad money: $261.6 million (31 December 2013 est.)
country comparison to the world: 186
$234.4 million (31 December 2012 est.)

Stock of domestic credit: $156.8 million (31 December 2013 est.)
country comparison to the world: 176
$132.4 million (31 December 2012 est.)

Current account balance: -$45.2 million (2013 est.)
country comparison to the world: 68
-$40.9 million (2012 est.)

Exports: $19.7 million (2013 est.)
country comparison to the world: 206
$19.6 million (2012 est.)

Exports—commodities: vanilla, ylang-ylang (perfume essence), cloves, copra

Exports—partners: Netherlands 58.6%, Singapore 10.6%, Turkey 9.3%, France 5.6%, India 5% (2012)

Imports: $208.8 million (2013 est.)
country comparison to the world: 205
$208 million (2012 est.)

Imports—commodities: rice and other foodstuffs, consumer goods, petroleum products, cement, transport equipment

Imports—partners: Pakistan 15.7%, France 14.2%, UAE 11.5%, India 8.5%, China 6.7%, Kenya 5.3%, Singapore 5.2% (2012)

Debt—external: $142.9 million (31 December 2013 est.)
country comparison to the world: 189
$136.1 million (31 December 2012 est.)

Exchange rates: Comoran francs (KMF) per US dollar—
378.7 (2013 est.)
382.9 (2012 est.)
371.46 (2010 est.)

ENERGY

Electricity—production: 40 million kWh (2010 est.)
country comparison to the world: 208

Electricity—consumption: 37.2 million kWh (2010 est.)
country comparison to the world: 208

Electricity—exports: 0 kWh (2012 est.)
country comparison to the world: 121

Electricity—imports: 0 kWh (2012 est.)
country comparison to the world: 128

Electricity—installed generating capacity: 6,000 kW (2010 est.)
country comparison to the world: 207

Electricity—from fossil fuels: 83.3% of total installed capacity (2010 est.)
country comparison to the world: 91

Electricity—from nuclear fuels: 0% of total installed capacity (2010 est.)
country comparison to the world: 67

Electricity—from hydroelectric plants: 16.7% of total installed capacity (2010 est.)
country comparison to the world: 97

Electricity—from other renewable sources: 0% of total installed capacity (2010 est.)
country comparison to the world: 169

Crude oil—production: 0 bbl/day (2012 est.)
country comparison to the world: 161

Crude oil—exports: 0 bbl/day (2010 est.)
country comparison to the world: 98

Crude oil—imports: 0 bbl/day (2010 est.)
country comparison to the world: 173

Crude oil—proved reserves: 0 bbl (1 January 2013 es)
country comparison to the world: 117

Refined petroleum products—production: 0 bbl/day (2010 est.)
country comparison to the world: 132

Refined petroleum products —consumption: 1,025 bbl/day (2011 est.)
country comparison to the world: 199

Refined petroleum products—exports: 0 bbl/day (2010 est.)
country comparison to the world: 165

Refined petroleum products—imports: 877.1 bbl/day (2010 est.)
country comparison to the world: 197

Natural gas—production: 0 cu m (2011 est.)
country comparison to the world: 116

Natural gas—consumption: 0 cu m (2010 est.)
country comparison to the world: 132

Natural gas—exports: 0 cu m (2011 est.)
country comparison to the world: 82

Natural gas—imports: 0 cu m (2011 est.)
country comparison to the world: 177

Natural gas—proved reserves: 0 cu m (1 January 2013 es)
country comparison to the world: 124

Carbon dioxide emissions from consumption of energy: 148,400 Mt (2011 est.)
country comparison to the world: 201

COMMUNICATIONS

Telephones—main lines in use: 24,000 (2012)
country comparison to the world: 181

Telephones—mobile cellular: 250,000 (2012)
country comparison to the world: 177

Telephone system: *general assessment:* sparse system of microwave radio relay and HF radiotelephone communication stations
domestic: fixed-line connections only about 3 per 100 persons; mobile cellular usage about 30 per 100 persons
international: country code—269; landing point for the EASSy fiber-optic submarine cable system connecting East Africa with Europe and North America; HF radiotelephone communications to Madagascar and Reunion (2010)

Broadcast media: national state-owned TV station and a TV station run by Anjouan regional government; national state-owned radio; regional governments on the islands of Grande Comore and Anjouan each operate a radio station; a few independent and small community radio stations operate on the islands of Grande Comore and Moheli, and these two islands have access to Mayotte Radio and French TV (2007)

Internet country code: .km

Internet hosts: 14 (2012)
country comparison to the world: 225

Internet users: 24,300 (2009)
country comparison to the world: 187

TRANSPORTATION

Airports: 4 (2013)
country comparison to the world: 185

Airports—with paved runways: total: 4
2,438 to 3,047 m: 1
914 to 1,523 m: 3 (2013)

Roadways: *total:* 880 km
country comparison to the world: 186
paved: 673 km
unpaved: 207 km (2002)

Merchant marine: *total:* 149
country comparison to the world: 39
by type: bulk carrier 16, cargo 83, carrier 5, chemical tanker 5, container 2, passenger 2, passenger/cargo 1, petroleum tanker 17, refrigerated cargo 10, roll on/roll off 8
foreign-owned: 73 (Bangladesh 1, Bulgaria 4, China 1, Cyprus 2, Greece 4, Kenya 2, Kuwait 1, Latvia 2, Lebanon 2, Lithuania 1, Nigeria 1, Norway 1, Pakistan 5, Russia 12, Syria 5, Turkey 8, UAE 8, UK 1, Ukraine 10, US 2) (2010)

Ports and terminals:
major seaport(s): Moroni, Mutsamudu

MILITARY

Military branches: Army of National Development (l'Armee du Developpement Nationale, AND): Comoran Security Force (also called Comoran Defense Force (Force Comorienne de Defense, FCD), includes Gendarmerie), Comoran Coast Guard, Comoran Federal Police (2013)

Military service age and obligation: 18 years of age for 2-year voluntary military service; no conscription; women first inducted into the Army in 2004 (2012)

Manpower available for military service: males age 16-49: 184,236
females age 16-49: 183,363 (2010 est.)

Manpower fit for military service:
males age 16-49: 134,562
females age 16-49: 145,797 (2010 est.)

Manpower reaching militarily significant age annually: *male:* 8,831
female: 8,809 (2010 est.)

TRANSNATIONAL ISSUES

Disputes—international: claims French-administered Mayotte and challenges France's and Madagascar's claims to Banc du Geyser, a drying reef in the Mozambique Channel; in May 2008, African Union forces were called in to assist the Comoros military recapture Anjouan Island from rebels who seized it in 2001

Trafficking in persons:
current situation: Comoros is a source country for children subjected to forced labor and reportedly sex trafficking; Comoran children are forced to labor within the country in domestic service, roadside and street vending, baking, agriculture, and sometimes criminal activities; some Comoran students at Koranic schools are exploited for forced agricultural or domestic labor, sometimes being subjected to physical and sexual abuse; Comoros may be particularly vulnerable to transnational trafficking because of inadequate border controls, government corruption, and the presence of criminal networks

tier rating: Tier 2 Watch List—Comoros does not comply fully with the minimum standards for the elimination of trafficking; however, it is making significant efforts to do so; although the government provided some funding to UNICEF-supported, NGO-run centers, victim protection provisions remained very modest; the government relies on donor funding and international organization partners for the majority of its anti-trafficking efforts; a new law was passed prohibiting child trafficking and the penal code was revised to include prohibitions against and penalties for human trafficking, but these modifications await parliamentary adoption (2013)

CONGO, DEMOCRATIC REPUBLIC OF THE

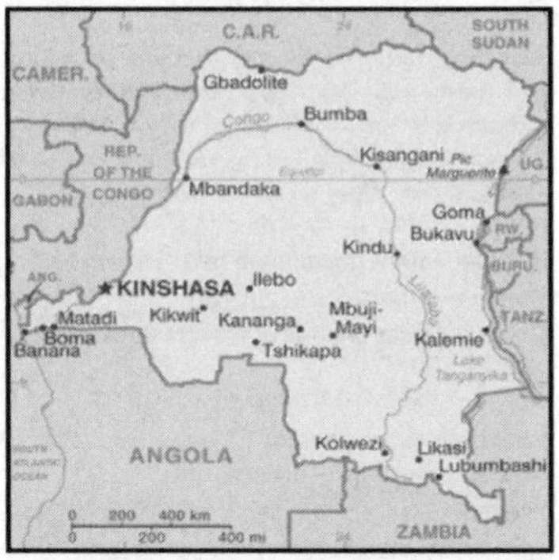

INTRODUCTION

Background: Established as a Belgian colony in 1908, the then-Republic of the Congo gained its independence in 1960, but its early years were marred by political and social instability. Col. Joseph MOBUTU seized power and declared himself president in a November 1965 coup. He subsequently changed his name—to MOBUTU Sese Seko—as well as that of the country—to Zaire. MOBUTU retained his position for 32 years through several sham elections, as well as through brutal force. Ethnic strife and civil war, touched off by a massive inflow of refugees in 1994 from fighting in Rwanda and Burundi, led in May 1997 to the toppling of the MOBUTU regime by a rebellion backed by Rwanda and Uganda and fronted by Laurent KABILA. He renamed the country the Democratic Republic of the Congo (DRC), but in August 1998 his regime was itself challenged by a second insurrection again backed by Rwanda and Uganda. Troops from Angola, Chad, Namibia, Sudan, and Zimbabwe intervened to support KABILA's regime. In January 2001, KABILA was assassinated and his son, Joseph KABILA, was named head of state. In October 2002, the new president was successful in negotiating the withdrawal of Rwandan forces occupying the eastern DRC; two months later, the Pretoria Accord was signed by all remaining warring parties to end the fighting and establish a government of national unity. A transitional government was set up in July 2003; it held a successful constitutional referendum in December 2005 and elections for the presidency, National Assembly, and provincial legislatures took place in 2006. In 2009, following a resurgence of conflict in the eastern DRC, the government signed a peace agreement with the National Congress for the Defense of the People (CNDP), a primarily Tutsi rebel group. An attempt to integrate CNDP members into the Congolese military failed, prompting their defection in 2012 and the formation of the M23 armed group—named after the 23 March 2009 peace agreements. Renewed conflict has lead to the displacement of large numbers of persons and significant human rights abuses. As of February 2013, peace talks between the Congolese government and the M23 were on-going. In addition, the DRC continues to experience violence committed by other armed groups including the Democratic Forces for the Liberation of Rwanda and Mai Mai groups. In the most recent national elections, held in November 2011, disputed results allowed Joseph KABILA to be reelected to the presidency.

GEOGRAPHY

Location: Central Africa, northeast of Angola

Geographic coordinates: 0 00 N, 25 00 E

Map references: Africa

Area: *total:* 2,344,858 sq km
country comparison to the world: 11
land: 2,267,048 sq km
water: 77,810 sq km

Area—comparative: slightly less than one-fourth the size of the US

Land boundaries: *total:* 10,730 km
border countries: Angola 2,511 km (of which 225 km is the boundary of Angola's discontiguous Cabinda Province), Burundi 233 km, Central African Republic 1,577 km, Republic of the Congo 2,410 km, Rwanda 217 km, South Sudan 628 km, Tanzania 459 km, Uganda 765 km, Zambia 1,930 km

Coastline: 37 km

Maritime claims: *territorial sea:* 12 nm
exclusive economic zone: boundaries with neighbors

Climate: tropical; hot and humid in equatorial river basin; cooler and drier in southern highlands; cooler and wetter in eastern highlands; north of Equator—wet season (April to October), dry season (December to February); south of Equator—wet season (November to March), dry season (April to October)

Terrain: vast central basin is a low-lying plateau; mountains in east

Elevation extremes: *lowest point:* Atlantic Ocean 0 m
highest point: Pic Marguerite on Mont Ngaliema (Mount Stanley) 5,110 m

Natural resources: cobalt, copper, niobium, tantalum, petroleum, industrial and gem diamonds, gold, silver, zinc, manganese, tin, uranium, coal, hydropower, timber

Land use: *arable land:* 2.9%
permanent crops: 0.32%
other: 96.78% (2011)

Irrigated land: 105 sq km (2003)

Total renewable water resources: 1,283 cu km (2011)

Freshwater withdrawal (domestic/industrial/agricultural): *total:* 0.68 cu km/yr (68%/21%/11%)
per capita: 11.25 cu m/yr (2005)

Natural hazards: periodic droughts in south; Congo River floods (seasonal); active volcanoes in the east along the Great Rift Valley
volcanism: Nyiragongo (elev. 3,470 m), which erupted in 2002 and is experiencing ongoing activity, poses a major threat to the city of Goma, home to a quarter million people; the volcano produces unusually fast-moving lava, known to travel up to 100 km /hr; Nyiragongo has been deemed a "Decade Volcano" by the International Association of Volcanology and Chemistry of the Earth's Interior, worthy of study due to its explosive history and close proximity to human populations; its neighbor, Nyamuragira, which erupted in 2010, is Africa's most active volcano; Visoke is the only other historically active volcano

Environment—current issues: poaching threatens wildlife populations; water pollution; deforestation; refugees responsible for significant deforestation, soil erosion, and wildlife poaching; mining of minerals (coltan—a mineral used in creating capacitors, diamonds, and gold) causing environmental damage

Environment—international agreements: *party to:* Biodiversity, Climate Change, Climate Change-Kyoto Protocol, Desertification, Endangered Species, Hazardous Wastes, Law of the Sea, Marine Dumping, Ozone Layer Protection, Tropical Timber 83, Tropical Timber 94, Wetlands
signed, but not ratified: Environmental Modification

Geography—note: straddles equator; has narrow strip of land that controls the lower Congo River and is only outlet to South Atlantic Ocean; dense tropical rain forest in central river basin and eastern highlands; second largest country in Africa (after Algeria)

PEOPLE AND SOCIETY

Nationality: *noun:* Congolese (singular and plural)
adjective: Congolese or Congo

Ethnic groups: over 200 African ethnic groups of which the majority are Bantu; the four largest tribes—Mongo, Luba, Kongo (all Bantu), and the Mangbetu-Azande (Hamitic) make up about 45% of the population

Languages: French (official), Lingala (a lingua franca trade language), Kingwana (a dialect of Kiswahili or Swahili), Kikongo, Tshiluba

Religions: Roman Catholic 50%, Protestant 20%, Kimbanguist 10%, Muslim 10%, other (includes syncretic sects and indigenous beliefs) 10%

Population: 77,433,744 (July 2014 est.)
country comparison to the world: 20

note: estimates for this country explicitly take into account the effects of excess mortality due to AIDS; this can result in lower life expectancy, higher infant mortality, higher death rates, lower population growth rates, and changes in the distribution of population by age and sex than would otherwise be expected

Age structure: 0-14 years: 43.1% (male 16,810,549/female 16,552,685)
15-24 years: 21.4% (male 8,292,444/female 8,248,326)
25-54 years: 29.4% (male 11,359,385/female 11,405,442)
55-64 years: 2.6% (male 1,287,895/female 1,457,499)
65 years and over: 2.6% (male 849,840/female 1,169,679) (2014 est.)

Dependency ratios: *total dependency ratio:* 91.9 %
youth dependency ratio: 86.4 %
elderly dependency ratio: 5.5 %
potential support ratio: 18.2 (2013)

Median age: *total:* 17.9 years
male: 17.7 years
female: 18.1 years (2014 est.)

Population growth rate: 2.5% (2014 est.)
country comparison to the world: 30

Birth rate: 35.62 births/1,000 population (2014 est.)
country comparison to the world: 22

Death rate: 10.3 deaths/1,000 population (2014 est.)
country comparison to the world: 44

Net migration rate: -0.33 migrant(s)/1,000 population (2014 est.)
country comparison to the world: 130

Urbanization: *urban population:* 34.3% of total population (2011)
rate of urbanization: 4.19% annual rate of change (2010-15 est.)

Major urban areas—population: KINSHASA (capital) 8.798 million; Lubumbashi 1.543 million; Mbuji-Mayi 1.488 million; Kananga 878,000; Kisangani
812,000 (2011)

Sex ratio: *at birth:* 1.03 male(s)/female
0-14 years: 1.02 male(s)/female
15-24 years: 1.01 male(s)/female
25-54 years: 1 male(s)/female
55-64 years: 0.99 male(s)/female
65 years and over: 0.72 male(s)/female
total population: 0.99 male(s)/female (2014 est.)

Mother's mean age at first birth: 20.2 (2007 est.)

Maternal mortality rate: 540 deaths/100,000 live births (2010)
country comparison to the world: 17

Infant mortality rate: total: 73.15 deaths/1,000 live births
country comparison to the world: 12
male: 76.8 deaths/1,000 live births
female: 69.39 deaths/1,000 live births (2014 est.)

Life expectancy at birth: *total population:* 56.54 years
country comparison to the world: 203
male: 55.03 years
female: 58.09 years (2014 est.)

Total fertility rate: 4.8 children born/woman (2014 est.)
country comparison to the world: 22

Contraceptive prevalence rate: 17.7% (2010)

Health expenditures: 8.5% of GDP (2011)
country comparison to the world: 52

Physicians density: 0.11 physicians/1,000 population (2004)

Hospital bed density: 0.8 beds/1,000 population (2006)

Drinking water source:
improved:
urban: 79.6% of population
rural: 28.9% of population
total: 46.2% of population
unimproved:
urban: 20.4% of population
rural: 71.1% of population
total: 53.8% of population (2011 est.)

Sanitation facility access:
improved:
urban: 29.2% of population
rural: 31.5% of population
total: 30.7% of population
unimproved:
urban: 70.8% of population
rural: 68.5% of population
total: 69.3% of population (2011 est.)

HIV/AIDS—adult prevalence rate: 1.1% (2012 est.)
country comparison to the world: 44

HIV/AIDS—people living with HIV/AIDS: 481,500 (2012 est.)
country comparison to the world: 17

HIV/AIDS—deaths: 31,700 (2012 est.)
country comparison to the world: 12

Major infectious diseases: *degree of risk:* very high
food or waterborne diseases: bacterial and protozoal diarrhea, hepatitis A, and typhoid fever vectorborne diseases: malaria, dengue fever, and trypanosomiasis-gambiense (African sleeping sickness)
water contact disease: schistosomiasis
animal contact disease: rabies (2013)

Obesity—adult prevalence rate: 1.7% (2008)
country comparison to the world: 185

Children under the age of 5 years underweight: 28.2% (2007)
country comparison to the world: 21

Education expenditures: 2.5% of GDP (2010)
country comparison to the world: 157

Literacy:
definition: age 15 and over can read and write French, Lingala, Kingwana, or Tshiluba
total population: 66.8%
male: 76.9%
female: 57% (2010 est.)

School life expectancy (primary to tertiary education):
total: 10 years
male: 11 years
female: 8 years (2012)

Child labor—children ages 5-14:
total number: 8,284,395
percentage: 42 % (2010 est.)

GOVERNMENT

Country name: *conventional long form:* Democratic Republic of the Congo
conventional short form: DRC
local long form: Republique Democratique du Congo

local short form: RDC
former: Congo Free State, Belgian Congo, Congo/Leopoldville, Congo/Kinshasa, Zaire
abbreviation: DRC

Government type: republic

Capital: *name:* Kinshasa
geographic coordinates: 4 19 S, 15 18 E
time difference: UTC+1 (6 hours ahead of Washington, DC during Standard Time)

Administrative divisions: 10 provinces (provinces, singular—province) and 1 city* (ville); Bandundu, Bas-Congo (Lower Congo), Equateur, Kasai-Occidental (West Kasai), Kasai-Oriental (East Kasai), Katanga, Kinshasa*, Maniema, Nord-Kivu (North Kivu), Orientale, Sud-Kivu (South Kivu)
note: according to the Constitution adopted in December 2005, the current administrative divisions were to be subdivided into 26 new provinces by 2009 but this has yet to be implemented

Independence: 30 June 1960 (from Belgium)

National holiday: Independence Day, 30 June (1960)

Constitution: several previous; latest adopted 13 May 2005, approved by referendum 18-19 December 2005, promulgated 18 February 2006; revised 2011 (2011)

Legal system: civil legal system based on Belgian version of French civil law

International law organization participation: accepts compulsory ICJ jurisdiction with reservations; accepts ICCt jurisdiction

Suffrage: 18 years of age; universal and compulsory

Executive branch: *chief of state:* President Joseph KABILA (since 17 January 2001)
head of government: Prime Minister Augustin MATATA PONYO Mapon (since 18 April 2012)
cabinet: Ministers of State appointed by the president (For more information visit the World Leaders website)
elections: under the new constitution the president elected by popular vote for a five-year term (eligible for a second term); elections last held on 28 November 2011 (next to be held in November 2016); prime minister appointed by the president
election results: Joseph KABILA reelected president; percent of vote—Joseph KABILA 49%, Etienne TSHISEKEDI 32.3%, other 18.7%; note—election marred by serious voting irregularities
note: Joseph KABILA succeeded his father, Laurent Desire KABILA, following the latter's assassination in January 2001; negotiations with rebel leaders led to the establishment of a transitional government in July 2003 with free elections held on 30 July 2006 and a run-off on 29 October 2006 confirming Joseph KABILA as president

Legislative branch: bicameral legislature consists of a Senate (108 seats; members elected by provincial assemblies to serve five-year terms) and a National Assembly (500 seats; 61 members elected by majority vote in single-member constituencies, 439 members elected by open list proportional-representation in multi-member constituencies to serve five-year terms)
elections: Senate—last held on 19 January 2007 (next scheduled for 5 June 2013; though likely to be delayed); National Assembly—last held on 28 November 2011 (next to be held in 2016)
election results: Senate—percent of vote by party—NA; seats by party—PPRD 22, MLC 14, FR 7, RCD 7, PDC 6, CDC 3, MSR 3, PALU 2, independents 26, others 18 (political parties that won a single seat); National Assembly—percent of vote by party—NA; seats by party—PPRD 62, UDPS 41, PPPD 29, MSR 27, MLC 22, PALU 19, UNC 17, ARC 16, AFDC 15, ECT 11, RRC 11, independents 16, others 214 (includes numerous political parties that won 10 or fewer seats and 2 constituencies where voting was halted); note—the November 2011 elections were married by violence including the destruction of ballots in two constituencies resulting in the closure of polling sites; election results were delayed three months, stongly contested, and continue to be unresolved

Judicial branch: *highest court(s):* Supreme Court of Justice (organized into legislative and judiciary sections and consists of 26 justices); Constitutional Court (consists of 9 judges)
judge selection and term of office: Supreme Court of Justice judges nominated by the Judicial Service Council, an independent body of public prosecutors and selected judges of the lower courts; judges tenure NA; Constitutional Court judges—3 nominated by the president, 3 by the Judicial Service Council, and 3 by the legislature; judges appointed by the president to serve 9-year non-renewable terms
subordinate courts: State Security Court; Court of Appeals (organized into administrative and judiciary sections); Tribunal de Grande; magistrates' courts; customary courts

Political parties and leaders: Christian Democrat Party or PDC [Jose ENDUNDO]; Congolese Rally for Democracy or RCD [Azarias RUBERWA]; Convention of Christian Democrats or CDC; Forces of Renewal or FR [Mbusa NYAMWISI]; Movement for the Liberation of the Congo or MLC [Jean-Pierre BEMBA]; People's Party for Reconstruction and Democracy or PPRD [Joseph KABILA]; Social Movement for Renewal or MSR [Pierre LUMBI]; Unified Lumumbist Party or PALU [Antoine GIZENGA]; Union for the Congolese Nation or UNC [Vital KAMERHE]; Union for Democracy and Social Progress or UDPS [Etienne TSHISEKEDI]; Union of Mobutuist Democrats or UDEMO [MOBUTU Nzanga]

Political pressure groups and leaders: FARDC (Forces Armées de la République Démocratique du Congo)—Army of the Democratic Republic of the Congo, which commits atrocities on citizens; FDLR (Forces Democratiques de Liberation du Rwanda)—Rwandan militia group made up of some of the perpetrators of Rwanda's Genocide in 1994; CNDP (National Congress for the Defense of the People)—mainly Congolese Tutsis who want refugees returned and more representation in government; M23—rebel group comprised largely from ex-CNDP forces

International organization participation: ACP, AfDB, AU, CEPGL, COMESA, EITI (candidate country), FAO, G-24, G-77, IAEA, IBRD, ICAO, ICRM, IDA, IFAD, IFC, IFRCS, IHO, ILO, IMF, IMO, Interpol, IOC, IOM, IPU, ISO, ITSO, ITU, ITUC (NGOs), MIGA, NAM, OIF, OPCW, PCA, SADC, UN, UNCTAD, UNESCO, UNHCR, UNIDO, UNWTO, UPU, WCO, WFTU (NGOs), WHO, WIPO, WMO, WTO

Diplomatic representation in the US: *chief of mission:* Ambassador Faida Maramuke MITIFU (since 3 February 2000)
chancery: Suite 601, 1726 M Street, NW, Washington, DC, 20036
telephone: [1] (202) 234-7690 through 7691
FAX: [1] (202) 234-2609
consulate(s) general: New York

Diplomatic representation from the US: *chief of mission:* Ambassador James C. SWAN (since 5 September 2013)
embassy: 310 Avenue des Aviateurs, Kinshasa
mailing address: Unit 2220, DPO AE 09828
telephone: [243] (081) 556-0151
FAX: [243] (081) 556-0175

Flag description: sky blue field divided diagonally from the lower hoist corner to upper fly corner by a red stripe bordered by two narrow yellow stripes; a yellow, five-pointed star appears in the upper hoist corner; blue represents peace and hope, red the blood of the country's martyrs, and yellow the country's wealth and prosperity; the star symbolizes unity and the brilliant future for the country

National symbol(s): leopard

National anthem: *name:* "Debout Congolaise" (Arise Congolese)
lyrics/music: Joseph LUTUMBA/Simon-Pierre BOKA di Mpasi Londi
note: adopted 1960; the anthem was replaced during the period in which the country was known as Zaire, but was readopted in 1997

ECONOMY

Economy—overview: The economy of the Democratic Republic of the Congo—a nation endowed with vast natural resource wealth—is slowly recovering after decades of decline. Systemic corruption since independence in 1960, combined with country-wide instability and conflict that began in the mid-90s has dramatically reduced national output and government revenue and increased external debt. With the installation of a transitional government in 2003 after peace accords, economic conditions slowly began to improve as the transitional government reopened relations with international financial institutions and international donors, and President KABILA began implementing reforms. Progress has been slow to reach the interior of the country although clear changes are evident in Kinshasa and Lubumbashi. An uncertain legal framework, corruption, and a lack of transparency in government policy are long-term problems for the mining sector and for the economy as a whole. Much economic activity still occurs in the informal sector and is not reflected in GDP data. Renewed activity in the mining sector, the source of most export income, has boosted Kinshasa's fiscal position and GDP growth in recent years. The global recession cut economic growth in 2009 to less than half its 2008 level, but growth returned to around 7% per year in 2010-12. The DRC signed a Poverty Reduction and Growth Facility with the IMF in 2009 and received $12 billion in multilateral and bilateral debt relief in 2010, but the IMF at the end of 2012 suspended the last three payments under the loan facility—worth $240 million—because of concerns about the lack of transparency in mining contracts. In 2012, the DRC updated its business laws by adhering to OHADA, the Organization for the Harmonization of Business Law in Africa. The country marked its tenth consecutive year of positive economic expansion in 2012.

GDP (purchasing power parity): $29.39 billion (2013 est.)
country comparison to the world: 115
$27.66 billion (2012 est.)
$25.82 billion (2011 est.)
note: data are in 2013 US dollars

GDP (official exchange rate): $18.56 billion (2013 est.)

GDP—real growth rate: 6.2% (2013 est.)
country comparison to the world: 36
7.2% (2012 est.)
6.9% (2011 est.)

GDP—per capita (PPP): $400 (2013 est.)
country comparison to the world: 228
$400 (2012 est.)
$400 (2011 est.)
note: data are in 2013 US dollars

GDP—composition, by end use:
household consumption: 65.9%
government consumption: 12.5%
investment in fixed capital: 27.9%
investment in inventories: 1%
exports of goods and services: 49.9%
imports of goods and services: -56.3% (2013 est.)

GDP—composition, by sector of origin:
agriculture: 44.3%
industry: 21.7%
services: 34% (2013 est.)

Agriculture—products: coffee, sugar, palm oil, rubber, tea, cotton, cocoa, quinine, cassava (manioc), bananas, plantains, peanuts, root crops, *corn, fruits; wood products*

Industries: mining (copper, cobalt, gold, diamonds, coltan, zinc, tin, tungsten), mineral processing, consumer products (textiles, plastics, footwear, cigarettes), metal products, processed foods and beverages, timber, cement, commercial ship repair

Industrial production growth rate: 12%
country comparison to the world: 7

Labor force: 35.18 million (2013 est.)
country comparison to the world: 18

Labor force—by occupation: agriculture: NA%
industry: NA%
services: NA%

Unemployment rate: NA%
Population below poverty line:
71% (2006 est.)

Household income or consumption by percentage share: *lowest 10%:* 2.3%
highest 10%: 34.7% (2006)

Budget: revenues: $5.817 billion
expenditures: $6.472 billion (2013 est.)

Taxes and other revenues: 31.3% of GDP (2013 est.)
country comparison to the world: 85

Budget surplus (+) or deficit (-): -3.5% of GDP (2013 est.)
country comparison to the world: 137

Fiscal year: calendar year

Inflation rate (consumer prices):
7.1% (2013 est.)
country comparison to the world: 187
9.5% (2012 est.)

Central bank discount rate: 4% (31 December 2012 est.)
country comparison to the world: 7
20% (31 December 2011 est.)

Commercial bank prime lending rate: 18.6% (31 December 2013 est.)
country comparison to the world: 6
28.45% (31 December 2012 est.)

Stock of narrow money: $1.06 billion (31 December 2013 est.)
country comparison to the world: 149
$986.6 million (31 December 2012 est.)

Stock of broad money: $3.502 billion (31 December 2013 est.)
country comparison to the world: 140
$3.042 billion (31 December 2012 est.)

Stock of domestic credit: $1.862 billion (31 December 2013 est.)
country comparison to the world: 134
$1.708 billion (31 December 2012 est.)

Market value of publicly traded shares: $NA

Current account balance: -$2.544 billion (2013 est.)
country comparison to the world: 153
-$2.254 billion (2012 est.)

Exports: $9.936 billion (2013 est.)
country comparison to the world: 95
$8.872 billion (2012 est.)

Exports—commodities: diamonds, copper, gold, cobalt, wood products, crude oil, coffee

Exports—partners: China 54.3%, Zambia 22.6%, Belgium 5.7% (2012)

Imports: $8.924 billion (2013 est.)
country comparison to the world: 104
$8.187 billion (2012 est.)

Imports—commodities: foodstuffs, mining and other machinery, transport equipment, fuels

Imports—partners: South Africa 22.3%, China 15.3%, Belgium 8%, Zambia 6.9%, Zimbabwe 5.6%, France 4.9%, Kenya 4.7% (2012)

Reserves of foreign exchange and gold:
$1.582 billion (31 December 2013 est.)
country comparison to the world: 127
$1.633 billion (31 December 2012 est.)

Debt—external: $6.874 billion (31 December 2013 est.)
country comparison to the world: 111
$6.087 billion (31 December 2012 est.)

Exchange rates: Congolese francs (CDF) per US dollar —
918 (2013 est.)
920.25 (2012 est.)
905.91 (2010 est.)
472.19 (2009)
559 (2008)

ENERGY

Electricity—production: 7.804 billion kWh (2010 est.)
country comparison to the world: 101

Electricity—consumption: 6.197 billion kWh (2010 est.)
country comparison to the world: 105

Electricity—exports: 916 million kWh (2010 est.)
country comparison to the world: 59

Electricity—imports: 161 million kWh (2010 est.)
country comparison to the world: 89

Electricity—installed generating capacity:
2.437 million kW (2010 est.)
country comparison to the world: 95

Electricity—from fossil fuels: 1.4% of total installed capacity (2010 est.)
country comparison to the world: 204

Electricity—from nuclear fuels: 0% of total installed capacity (2010 est.)
country comparison to the world: 63

Electricity—from hydroelectric plants:
98.6% of total installed capacity (2010 est.)
country comparison to the world: 7

Electricity—from other renewable sources:
0% of total installed capacity (2010 est.)
country comparison to the world: 166

Crude oil—production: 20,000 bbl/day (2012 est.)
country comparison to the world: 78

Crude oil—exports: 22,240 bbl/day (2010 est.)
country comparison to the world: 52

Crude oil—imports: 0 bbl/day (2010 est.)
country comparison to the world: 171

Crude oil—proved reserves: 180 million bbl (1 January 2013 es)
country comparison to the world: 61

Refined petroleum products—production:
0 bbl/day (2010 est.)
country comparison to the world: 130

Refined petroleum products—consumption:
10,240 bbl/day (2011 est.)
country comparison to the world: 153

Refined petroleum products—exports:
0 bbl/day (2010 est.)
country comparison to the world: 163

Refined petroleum products—imports:
16,200 bbl/day (2010 est.)
country comparison to the world: 115

Natural gas—production: 0 cu m (2011 est.)
country comparison to the world: 114

Natural gas—consumption: 0 cu m (2010 est.)
country comparison to the world: 130

Natural gas—exports: 0 cu m (2011 est.)
country comparison to the world: 78

Natural gas—imports: 0 cu m (2011 est.)
country comparison to the world: 174

Natural gas—proved reserves: 991.1 million cu m (1 January 2013 es)
country comparison to the world: 104

Carbon dioxide emissions from consumption of energy: 2.721 million Mt (2011 est.)
country comparison to the world: 141

COMMUNICATIONS

Telephones—main lines in use: 58,200 (2012)
country comparison to the world: 161

Telephones—mobile cellular: 19.487 million (2012)
country comparison to the world: 52
Telephone system: general assessment: barely adequate wire and microwave radio relay service in and between urban areas; domestic satellite system with 14 earth stations; inadequate fixed line infrastructure
domestic: state-owned operator providing less than 1 fixed-line connection per 1000 persons; given the backdrop of a wholly inadequate fixed-line infrastructure, the use of mobile-cellular services has surged and mobile teledensity is roughly 20 per 100 persons
international: country code—243; satellite earth station—1 Intelsat (Atlantic Ocean) (2011)

Broadcast media: state-owned TV broadcast station with near national coverage; more than a dozen privately owned TV stations with 2 having near national coverage; 2 state-owned radio stations are supplemented by more than 100 private radio stations; transmissions of at least 2 international broadcasters are available (2007)

Internet country code: .cd

Internet hosts: 2,515 (2012)
country comparison to the world: 159

Internet users: 290,000 (2008)
country comparison to the world: 132

TRANSPORTATION

Airports: 198 (2013)
country comparison to the world: 27

Airports—with paved runways:
total: 26
over 3,047 m: 3
2,438 to 3,047 m: 3
1,524 to 2,437 m: 17
914 to 1,523 m: 2
under 914 m: 1 (2013)

Airports—with unpaved runways: *total:* 172
1,524 to 2,437 m: 20
914 to 1,523 m: 87
under 914 m: 65 (2013)

Heliports: 1 (2013)

Pipelines: gas 62 km; oil 77 km; refined products 756 km (2013)

Railways: total: 4,007 km
country comparison to the world: 44
narrow gauge: 3,882 km 1.067-m gauge (858 km electrified); 125 km 1.000-m gauge (2008)

Roadways: total: 153,497 km
country comparison to the world: 32
paved: 2,794 km
unpaved: 150,703 km (2004)

Waterways: 15,000 km (including the Congo, its tributaries, and unconnected lakes) (2011)
country comparison to the world: 8

Merchant marine: *total:* 1
country comparison to the world: 151
by type: petroleum tanker 1
foreign-owned: 1 (Republic of the Congo 1) (2010)

Ports and terminals: *major seaport(s):* Banana
river or lake port(s): Boma, Bumba, Kinshasa, Kisangani, Matadi, Mbandaka (Congo); Kindu (Lualaba); Bukavu, Goma (Lake Kivu); Kalemie (Lake Tanganyika)

MILITARY

Military branches: Armed Forces of the Democratic Republic of the Congo (Forces d'Armees de la Republique Democratique du Congo, FARDC): Army, National Navy (La Marine Nationale), Congolese Air Force (Force Aerienne Congolaise, FAC) (2011)

Military service age and obligation: 18-45 years of age for voluntary and compulsory military service (2012)

Manpower available for military service:
males age 16-49: 15,980,106 (2010 est.)

Manpower fit for military service:
males age 16-49: 10,168,258
females age 16-49: 10,331,693 (2010 est.)

Manpower reaching militarily significant age annually: *male:* 877,684
female: 871,880 (2010 est.)

Military expenditures: 1.72% of GDP (2012)
country comparison to the world: 50
1.53% of GDP (2011)
1.72% of GDP (2010)

TRANSNATIONAL ISSUES

Disputes—international: heads of the Great Lakes states and UN pledged in 2004 to abate tribal, rebel, and militia fighting in the region, including northeast Congo, where the UN Organization Mission in the Democratic Republic of the Congo (MONUC), organized in 1999, maintains over 16,500 uniformed peacekeepers; members of Uganda's Lords Resistance Army forces continue to seek refuge in Congo's Garamba National Park as peace talks with the Uganda government evolve; the location of the boundary in the broad Congo River with the Republic of the Congo is indefinite except in the Pool Malebo/Stanley Pool area; Uganda and DRC dispute Rukwanzi Island in Lake Albert and other areas on the Semliki River with hydrocarbon potential; boundary commission continues discussions over Congolese-administered triangle of land on the right bank of the Lunkinda River claimed by Zambia near the DRC village of Pweto; DRC accuses Angola of shifting monuments

Refugees and internally displaced persons: *refugees (country of origin):* 50,736 (Rwanda); 9,368 (Burundi) (2012); 54,000 (Central African Republic) (2014)IDPs: 2,669,069 (fighting between government forces and rebels since mid-1990s; most IDPs are in eastern provinces) (2012)

Trafficking in persons: *current situation:* Democratic Republic of the Congo is a source, destination, and possibly a transit country for men, women, and children subjected to forced labor and sex trafficking; the majority of this trafficking is internal, and much of it is perpetrated by armed groups and government forces outside government control within the country's unstable eastern provinces; Congolese women and children have been exploited internally as domestic servants, while others migrate to Angola, South Africa, Republic of the Congo, and South Sudan, as well as East African, Middle Eastern, and European nations where they are subjected to forced prostitution, domestic servitude, and forced labor in agriculture and diamond mines; indigenous and foreign armed groups (including the Lord's Resistance Army) abduct and forcibly recruit Congolese adults and children to serve as laborers, porters, domestics, combatants, and sex slaves; some commanders of the Congolese national army also recruit, at times through force, men and children for use as combatants, escorts, and porters
tier rating: Tier 3—The Democratic Republic of the Congo does not fully comply with the minimum standards for the elimination of trafficking and is not making significant efforts to do so; the government signed a UN-backed action plan to end the recruitment and use of child soldiers within its armed forces but has not applied legal sanctions against those who recruit and use child soldiers and has not reported any law enforcement efforts to combat any other forms of trafficking; besides child soldiers, the government has not reported identifying any other victims of forced labor or sex trafficking or providing protective services or referrals to NGO-operated care facilities; NGOs continue to provide the vast majority of the limited shelter, legal, medical, and psychological services available to victims (2013)

Illicit drugs: one of Africa's biggest producers of cannabis, but mostly for domestic consumption; traffickers exploit lax shipping controls to transit pseudoephedrine through the capital; while rampant corruption and inadequate supervision leaves the banking system vulnerable to money laundering, the lack of a well-developed financial system limits the country's utility as a money-laundering center (2008)

CONGO, REPUBLIC OF THE

INTRODUCTION

Background: Upon independence in 1960, the former French region of Middle Congo became the Republic of the Congo. A quarter century of experimentation with Marxism was abandoned in 1990 and a democratically elected government took office in 1992. A brief civil war in 1997 restored former Marxist President Denis SASSOU-Nguesso, and ushered in a period of ethnic and political unrest. Southern-based rebel groups agreed to a final peace accord in March 2003, but the calm is tenuous and refugees continue to present a humanitarian crisis. The Republic of Congo is one of Africa's largest petroleum producers, but with declining production it will need new offshore oil finds to sustain its oil earnings over the long term.

GEOGRAPHY

Location: Central Africa, bordering the South Atlantic Ocean, between Angola and Gabon

Geographic coordinates: 1 00 S, 15 00 E

Map references: Africa

Area: *total:* 342,000 sq km
country comparison to the world: 64
land: 341,500 sq km
water: 500 sq km

Area—comparative: slightly smaller than Montana

Land boundaries: *total:* 5,504 km
border countries: Angola 201 km, Cameroon 523 km, Central African Republic 467 km, Democratic Republic of the Congo 2,410 km, Gabon 1,903 km

Coastline: 169 km

Maritime claims: territorial sea: 200 nm

Climate: tropical; rainy season (March to June); dry season (June to October); persistent high temperatures and humidity; particularly enervating climate astride the Equator

Terrain: coastal plain, southern basin, central plateau, northern basin

Elevation extremes: *lowest point:* Atlantic Ocean 0 m
highest point: Mount Berongou 903 m

Natural resources: petroleum, timber, potash, lead, zinc, uranium, copper, phosphates, gold, magnesium, natural gas, hydropower

Land use: *arable land:* 1.46%
permanent crops: 0.18%
other: 98.36% (2011)

Irrigated land: 20 sq km (2003)

Total renewable water resources: 832 cu km (2011)

Freshwater withdrawal (domestic/industrial/agricultural): *total:* 0.05 cu km/yr (69%/26%/4%)
per capita: 13.99 cu m/yr (2005)

Natural hazards: seasonal flooding

Environment—current issues: air pollution from vehicle emissions; water pollution from the dumping of raw sewage; tap water is not potable; deforestation

Environment—international agreements:
party to: Biodiversity, Climate Change, Climate Change-Kyoto Protocol, Desertification, Endangered Species, Hazardous Wastes, Law of the Sea, Ozone Layer Protection, Ship Pollution, Tropical Timber 83, Tropical Timber 94, Wetlands
signed, but not ratified: none of the selected agreements

Geography—note: about 70% of the population lives in Brazzaville, Pointe-Noire, or along the railroad between them

PEOPLE AND SOCIETY

Nationality: noun: Congolese (singular and plural)
adjective: Congolese or Congo

Ethnic groups: Kongo 48%, Sangha 20%, M'Bochi 12%, Teke 17%, Europeans and other 3%

Languages: French (official), Lingala and Monokutuba (lingua franca trade languages), many local languages and dialects (of which Kikongo is the most widespread)

Religions: Roman Catholic 33.1%, Awakening Churches/Christian Revival 22.3%, Protestant 19.9%, Salutiste 2.2%, Muslim 1.6%, Kimbanguiste 1.5%, other 8.1%, none 11.3% (2010 est.)

Population: 4,662,446 (July 2014 est.)
country comparison to the world: 125
note: estimates for this country explicitly take into account the effects of excess mortality due to AIDS; this can result in lower life expectancy, higher infant mortality, higher death rates, lower population growth rates, and changes in the distribution of population by age and sex than would otherwise be expected

Age structure: *0-14 years:* 41.1% (male 966,852/female 950,411)
15-24 years: 17.7% (male 411,263/female 413,594)
25-54 years: 34.2% (male 808,181/female 787,554)
55-64 years: 3% (male 90,795/female 94,837)
65 years and over: 2.7% (male 60,400/female 78,559) (2014 est.)

Dependency ratios: *total dependency ratio:* 84.9 %
youth dependency ratio: 78.7 %
elderly dependency ratio: 6.3 %
potential support ratio: 15.9 (2013)

Median age: total: 19.8 years
male: 19.7 years
female: 20 years (2014 est.)

Population growth rate: 1.94% (2014 est.)
country comparison to the world: 55

Birth rate: 36.59 births/1,000 population (2014 est.)
country comparison to the world: 18

Death rate: 10.17 deaths/1,000 population (2014 est.)
country comparison to the world: 47

Net migration rate: -7.02 migrant(s)/1,000 population (2014 est.)
country comparison to the world: 204

Urbanization: *urban population:* 63.7% of total population (2011)
rate of urbanization: 2.84% annual rate of change (2010-15 est.)

Major urban areas—population: BRAZZAVILLE (capital) 1.611 million (2011)

Sex ratio: *at birth:* 1.03 male(s)/female
0-14 years: 1.02 male(s)/female
15-24 years: 0.99 male(s)/female
25-54 years: 1.03 male(s)/female
55-64 years: 1.01 male(s)/female
65 years and over: 0.69 male(s)/female
total population: 0.99 male(s)/female (2014 est.)

Mother's mean age at first birth: 19.8 (2011-12 est.)

Maternal mortality rate: 560 deaths/100,000 live births (2010)
country comparison to the world: 16

Infant mortality rate: total: 59.34 deaths/1,000 live births
country comparison to the world: 24
male: 64.49 deaths/1,000 live births
female: 54.04 deaths/1,000 live births (2014 est.)

Life expectancy at birth: total population: 58.52 years
country comparison to the world: 198
male: 57.38 years
female: 59.7 years (2014 est.)

Total fertility rate: 4.73 children born/woman (2014 est.)
country comparison to the world: 23

Contraceptive prevalence rate: 44.7% (2011/12)

Health expenditures: 2.5% of GDP (2011)
country comparison to the world: 186

Physicians density: 0.1 physicians/1,000 population (2007)

Hospital bed density: 1.6 beds/1,000 population (2005)

Drinking water source:
improved:
urban: 95.5% of population
rural: 31.9% of population
total: 72.4% of population
unimproved:
urban: 4.5% of population
rural: 68.1% of population
total: 27.6% of population (2011 est.)

Sanitation facility access:
improved:
urban: 19.5% of population
rural: 14.8% of population
total: 17.8% of population
unimproved:
urban: 80.5% of population
rural: 85.2% of population
total: 82.2% of population (2011 est.)

HIV/AIDS—adult prevalence rate: 2.8% (2012 est.)
country comparison to the world: 23

HIV/AIDS—people living with HIV/AIDS: 74,500 (2012 est.)
country comparison to the world: 52

HIV/AIDS—deaths: 5,200 (2012 est.)
country comparison to the world: 37

Major infectious diseases: *degree of risk:* very high
food or waterborne diseases: bacterial and protozoal diarrhea, hepatitis A, and typhoid fever vectorborne disease: malaria and dengue fever
animal contact disease: rabies
water contact disease: schistosomiasis (2013)

Obesity—adult prevalence rate: 4.7% (2008)
country comparison to the world: 163

Children under the age of 5 years underweight: 11.8% (2005)
country comparison to the world: 61

Education expenditures: 6.2% of GDP (2010)
country comparison to the world: 39

Literacy: *definition:* age 15 and over can read and write
total population: 83.8%
male: 89.6%
female: 78.4% (2003 est.)

School life expectancy (primary to tertiary education): *total:* 11 years
male: 11 years
female: 11 years (2012)

Child labor—children ages 5-14: total number: 252,171
percentage: 25 % (2005 est.)

GOVERNMENT

Country name: conventional long form: Republic of the Congo
conventional short form: Congo (Brazzaville)
local long form: Republique du Congo
local short form: none
former: Middle Congo, Congo/Brazzaville, Congo

Government type: republic
Capital: name: Brazzaville
geographic coordinates: 4 15 S, 15 17 E
time difference: UTC+1 (6 hours ahead of Washington, DC during Standard Time)

Administrative divisions: 12 departments (departments, singular—department); Bouenza, Brazzaville, Cuvette, Cuvette-Ouest, Kouilou, Lekoumou, Likouala, Niari, Plateaux, Pointe-Noire, Pool, Sangha

Independence: 15 August 1960 (from France)

National holiday: Independence Day, 15 August (1960)

Constitution: previous 1992; latest approved by referendum 20 January 2002 (2002)

Legal system: mixed legal system of French civil law and customary law

International law organization participation: has not submitted an ICJ jurisdiction declaration; accepts ICCt jurisdiction

Suffrage: 18 years of age; universal

Executive branch: *chief of state:* President Denis SASSOU-Nguesso (since 25 October 1997, following the civil war in which he toppled elected president Pascal LISSOUBA); note—the president is both the chief of state and head of government
head of government: President Denis SASSOU-Nguesso (since 25 October 1997); note—the position of prime minister was abolished in September 2009
cabinet: Council of Ministers appointed by the president (For more information visit the World Leaders website)
elections: president elected by popular vote for a seven-year term (eligible for a second term); election last held on 12 July 2009 (next to be held in 2016)
election results: Denis SASSOU-Nguesso reelected president; percent of vote—Denis SASSOU-Nguesso 78.6%, Joseph Kignoumbi Kia MBOUNGOU 7.5%, Nicephore Fylla de SAINT-EUDES 7%, other 6.9%

Legislative branch: bicameral Parliament consists of the Senate (72 seats; members elected by indirect vote to serve five-year terms) and the National Assembly (139 seats; members elected by popular vote to serve six-year terms)
elections: Senate—last held on 5 August 2008 (next to be held in July 2014); National Assembly—last held on 15 July and 5 August 2012 (next to be held in 2018)
election results: Senate—percent of vote by party—NA; seats by party—RMP 33, FDU 23, UPADS 2, independents 7, other 7; National Assembly—percent of vote by party—NA; seats by party—PCT (and allies) 117, UPADS 7, independents 12, vacant 3

Judicial branch:
highest court(s): Supreme Court or Cour Supreme (consists of NA judges) note—the High Court of Justice, outside the judicial authority, tries cases involving treason by the president of the republic
judge selection and term of office: judges elected by parliament and serve until retirement age
subordinate courts: courts of appeal; regional and district courts; employment tribunals; juvenile courts

Political parties and leaders: Action Movement for Renewal or MAR; Congolese Labour Party or PCT; Congolese Movement for Democracy and Integral Development or MCDDI [Michel MAMPOUYA]; Movement for Solidarity and Development or MSD; Pan-African Union for Social Development or UPADS [Martin MBERI]; Rally for Democracy and the Republic or RDR [Raymond Damasge NGOLLO]; Rally for Democracy and Social Progress or RDPS [Jean-Pierre Thystere TCHICAYA, president]; Rally of the Presidential Majority or RMP; Union for Democracy and Republic or UDR; United Democratic Forces or FDU [Sebastian EBAO]; many smaller parties

Political pressure groups and leaders: Congolese Trade Union Congress or CSC; General Union of Congolese Pupils and Students or UGEEC; Revolutionary Union of Congolese Women or URFC; Union of Congolese Socialist Youth or UJSC

International organization participation: ACP, AfDB, AU, BDEAC, CEMAC, EITI (candidate country), FAO, FZ, G-77, IAEA, IBRD, ICAO, ICRM, IDA, IFAD, IFC, IFRCS, ILO, IMF, IMO, Interpol, IOC, IOM, IPU, ISO (correspondent), ITSO, ITU, ITUC (NGOs), MIGA, NAM, OIF, OPCW, UN, UNCTAD, UNESCO, UNHCR, UNIDO, UNITAR, UNWTO, UPU, WCO, WFTU (NGOs), WHO, WIPO, WMO, WTO

Diplomatic representation in the US:
chief of mission: Ambassador Serge MOMBOULI (since 31 July 2001)
chancery: 1720 16th Street NW, Washington, DC 20009
telephone: [1] (202) 726-5500
FAX: [1] (202) 726-1860

Diplomatic representation from the US:
chief of mission: Ambassador Stephanie S. Sullivan (since 12 August 2013)
embassy: 70-83 Section D, Maya-Maya Boulevard, Brazzaville;
mailing address: B.P. 1015, Brazzaville
telephone: [242] 06 612-200

Flag description: divided diagonally from the lower hoist side by a yellow band; the upper triangle (hoist side) is green and the lower triangle is red; green symbolizes agriculture and forests, yellow the friendship and nobility of the people, red is *unexplained but has been associated with the struggle for independence note:* uses the popular Pan-African colors of Ethiopia

National symbol(s): lion; elephant

National anthem:
name: "La Congolaise" (The Congolese)
lyrics/music: Jacques TONDRA and Georges KIBANGHI/Jean ROYER and Joseph SPADILIERE
note: originally adopted 1959, restored 1991

ECONOMY

Economy—overview: The economy is a mixture of subsistence hunting and agriculture, an industrial sector based largely on oil and support services, and government spending. Oil has supplanted forestry as the mainstay of the economy, providing a major share of government revenues and exports. Natural gas is increasingly being converted to electricity rather than being flared, greatly improving energy prospects. New mining projects, particularly iron ore, that entered production in late 2013 may add as much as $1 billion to annual government revenue. Economic reform efforts have been undertaken with the support of international organizations, notably the World Bank and the IMF, including recently concluded Article IV consultations. The current administration faces difficult economic challenges of stimulating recovery and reducing poverty. The drop in oil prices during the global crisis reduced oil revenue by about 30%, but the subsequent recovery of oil prices boosted the economy's GDP from 2009-13. Officially the country became a net external creditor as of 2011, with external debt representing only about 16% of GDP and debt servicing less than 3% of government revenue.

GDP (purchasing power parity): $20.26 billion (2013 est.)
country comparison to the world: 134
$19.15 billion (2012 est.)
$18.44 billion (2011 est.)
note: data are in 2013 US dollars

GDP (official exchange rate): $14.25 billion (2013 est.)

GDP—real growth rate: 5.8% (2013 est.)
country comparison to the world: 39
3.8% (2012 est.)
3.4% (2011 est.)

GDP—per capita (PPP): $4,800 (2013 est.)
country comparison to the world: 162
$4,700 (2012 est.)
$4,600 (2011 est.)
note: data are in 2013 US dollars

Gross national saving: 61.4% of GDP (2013 est.)
country comparison to the world: 1
56.2% of GDP (2012 est.)
61.3% of GDP (2011 est.)

GDP—composition, by end use:
household consumption: 24.8%
government consumption: 11.1%
investment in fixed capital: 55.4%
investment in inventories: 0.9%
exports of goods and services: 91.8%
imports of goods and services: -84.1% (2013 est.)

GDP—composition, by sector of origin:
agriculture: 3.3%
industry: 73.9%
services: 22.9% (2013 est.)

Agriculture—products: cassava (tapioca), sugar, rice, corn, peanuts, vegetables, coffee, cocoa; forest products

Industries: petroleum extraction, cement, lumber, brewing, sugar, palm oil, soap, flour, cigarettes

Industrial production growth rate: 2% (2013 est.)
country comparison to the world: 126

Labor force: 2.89 million (2011 est.)
country comparison to the world: 105

Unemployment rate: 53% (2012 est.)
country comparison to the world: 196

Population below poverty line: 46.5% (2011 est.)

Household income or consumption by percentage share: *lowest 10%:* 2.1%
highest 10%: 37.1% (2005)

Budget: *revenues:* $6.608 billion
expenditures: $4.618 billion (2013 est.)

Taxes and other revenues:
46.4% of GDP (2013 est.)
country comparison to the world: 18

Budget surplus (+) or deficit (-):
14% of GDP (2013 est.)
country comparison to the world: 3

Public debt: 32.1% of GDP (2013 est.)
country comparison to the world: 112
31.8% of GDP (2012 est.)

Fiscal year: calendar year
Inflation rate (consumer prices):
1.7% (2013 est.)
country comparison to the world: 46
3.9% (2012 est.)

Central bank discount rate: 4.25% (31 December 2009)
country comparison to the world: 78
4.75% (31 December 2008)

Commercial bank prime lending rate:
14.8% (31 December 2013 est.)
country comparison to the world: 44
14.8% (31 December 2012 est.)

Stock of narrow money: $4.678 billion (31 December 2013 est.)
country comparison to the world: 102
$4.403 billion (31 December 2012 est.)

Stock of broad money: $5.119 billion (31 December 2013 est.)
country comparison to the world: 127
$4.795 billion (31 December 2012 est.)

Stock of domestic credit: $-1.053 billion (31 December 2013 est.)
country comparison to the world: 187
$-1.448 billion (31 December 2012 est.)

Market value of publicly traded shares: $NA

Current account balance: $638.2 million (2013 est.)
country comparison to the world: 51
$187.9 million (2012 est.)

Exports: $9.912 billion (2013 est.)
country comparison to the world: 96
$10.53 billion (2012 est.)

Exports—commodities: petroleum, lumber, plywood, sugar, cocoa, coffee, diamonds

Exports—partners: China 39%, US 13%, France 9.5%, Australia 8.8%, Netherlands 6.8%, Spain 5.3%, India 5.2% (2012)

Imports: $4.297 billion (2013 est.)
country comparison to the world: 136
$4.45 billion (2012 est.)

Imports—commodities: capital equipment, construction materials, foodstuffs

Imports—partners: France 19.5%, China 13.5%, Brazil 9.1%, US 6.1%, India 5.8%, Italy 4.8%, Belgium 4.4% (2012)

Reserves of foreign exchange and gold: $5.239 billion (31 December 2013 est.)
country comparison to the world: 94
$5.568 billion (31 December 2012 est.)

Debt—external: $3.274 billion (31 December 2013 est.)
country comparison to the world: 134
$2.999 billion (31 December 2012 est.)

Exchange rates: Cooperation Financiere en Afrique Centrale francs (XAF) per US dollar -
500.7 (2013 est.)
510.53 (2012 est.)
495.28 (2010 est.)
472.19 (2009)
447.81 (2008)

ENERGY

Electricity—production: 559 million kWh (2012 est.)
country comparison to the world: 161

Electricity—consumption: 588 million kWh (2012 est.)
country comparison to the world: 166

Electricity—exports: 0 kWh (2012 est.)
country comparison to the world: 117

Electricity—imports: 495 million kWh (2010 est.)
country comparison to the world: 79

Electricity—installed generating capacity:
559,000 kW (2012 est.)
country comparison to the world: 133

Electricity—from fossil fuels: 51.2% of total installed capacity (2012 est.)
country comparison to the world: 152

Electricity—from nuclear fuels: 0% of total installed capacity (2012 est.)
country comparison to the world: 62

Electricity—from hydroelectric plants: 48.8% of total installed capacity (2012 est.)
country comparison to the world: 44

Electricity—from other renewable sources:
0% of total installed capacity (2012 est.)
country comparison to the world: 165

Crude oil—production: 291,900 bbl/day (2012 est.)
country comparison to the world: 35

Crude oil—exports: 290,000 bbl/day (2011 est.)
country comparison to the world: 27

Crude oil—imports: 0 bbl/day (2011 est.)
country comparison to the world: 170

Crude oil—proved reserves: 1.6 billion bbl (1 January 2013 es)
country comparison to the world: 37

Refined petroleum products—production:
13,820 bbl/day (2010 est.)
country comparison to the world: 100

Refined petroleum products—consumption:
10,710 bbl/day (2011 est.)
country comparison to the world: 152

Refined petroleum products—exports:
4,288 bbl/day (2010 est.)
country comparison to the world: 93

Refined petroleum products—imports:
4,156 bbl/day (2010 est.)
country comparison to the world: 161

Natural gas—production: 946 million cu m (2012 est.)
country comparison to the world: 65

Natural gas—consumption: 930 million cu m (2010 est.)
country comparison to the world: 90

Natural gas—exports: 39 million cu m (2012 est.)
country comparison to the world: 50

Natural gas—imports: 0 cu m (2012 est.)
country comparison to the world: 173

Natural gas—proved reserves: 90.61 billion cu m (1 January 2013 es)
country comparison to the world: 58

Carbon dioxide emissions from consumption of energy: 6.858 million Mt (2011 est.)
country comparison to the world: 114

COMMUNICATIONS

Telephones—main lines in use: 14,900 (2012)
country comparison to the world: 196

Telephones—mobile cellular: 4.283 million (2012)
country comparison to the world: 118

Telephone system: *general assessment:* primary network consists of microwave radio relay and coaxial cable with services barely adequate for government use; key exchanges are in Brazzaville, Pointe-Noire, and Loubomo; intercity lines frequently out of order

domestic: fixed-line infrastructure inadequate providing less than 1 connection per 100 persons; in the absence of an adequate fixed line infrastructure, mobile-cellular subscribership has surged to 90 per 100 persons
international: country code—242; satellite earth station—1 Intelsat (Atlantic Ocean) (2011)

Broadcast media:
1 state-owned TV and 3 state-owned radio stations; several privately owned TV and radio stations; satellite TV service is available; rebroadcasts of several international broadcasters are available (2007)

Internet country code: .cg

Internet hosts: 45 (2012)
country comparison to the world: 215

Internet users: 245,200 (2009)
country comparison to the world: 136

TRANSPORTATION

Airports: 27 (2013)
country comparison to the world: 125

Airports—with paved runways:
total: 8
over 3,047 m: 2
2,438 to 3,047 m: 1
1,524 to 2,437 m: 5 (2013)

Airports—with unpaved runways:
total: 1 9
1,524 to 2,437 m: 8
914 to 1,523 m: 9
under 914 m: 2 (2013)

Pipelines:
gas 232 km; liquid petroleum gas 4 km; oil 982 km (2013)

Railways: total: 886 km
country comparison to the world: 94
narrow gauge: 886 km 1.067-m gauge (2008)

Roadways: total: 17,289 km
country comparison to the world: 118
paved: 864 km
unpaved: 16,425 km (2004)

Waterways: 1,120 km (commercially navigable on Congo and Oubanqui rivers above Brazzaville; there are many ferries across the river to Kinshasa; the Congo south of Brazzaville-Kinshasa to the coast is not navigable because of rapids, thereby necessitating a rail connection to Pointe Noire; other rivers are used for local traffic only) (2011)
country comparison to the world: 62

Merchant marine:
registered in other countries: 1 (Democratic Republic of the Congo 1) (2010)
country comparison to the world: 155

Ports and terminals:
major seaport(s): Pointe-Noire
river port(s): Brazzaville (Congo); Impfondo (Oubangi); Ouesso (Sangha); Oyo (Alima)
oil/gas terminal(s): Djeno

MILITARY

Military branches: Congolese Armed Forces (Forces Armees Congolaises, FAC): Army (Armee de Terre), Navy, Congolese Air Force (Armee de l'Air Congolaise); Gendarmerie; Special Presidential Security Guard (GSSP) (2013)

Military service age and obligation:
18 years of age for voluntary military service; women can serve in the Armed Forces (2012)

Manpower available for military service:
males age 16-49: 928,664
females age 16-49: 914,265 (2010 est.)

Manpower fit for military service:
males age 16-49: 577,944
females age 16-49: 566,587 (2010 est.)

Manpower reaching militarily significant age annually:
male: 50,000
female: 49,641 (2010 est.)

TRANSNATIONAL ISSUES

Disputes—international:
the location of the boundary in the broad Congo River with the Democratic Republic of the Congo is undefined except in the Pool Malebo/Stanley Pool area

Refugees and internally displaced persons:
refugees (country of origin): 89,424 (Democratic Republic of Congo) (2012); 8,404 (Rwanda); 15,000 (Central African Republic) (2014)
IDPs: 7,800 (multiple civil wars since 1992) (2009)

COOK ISLANDS

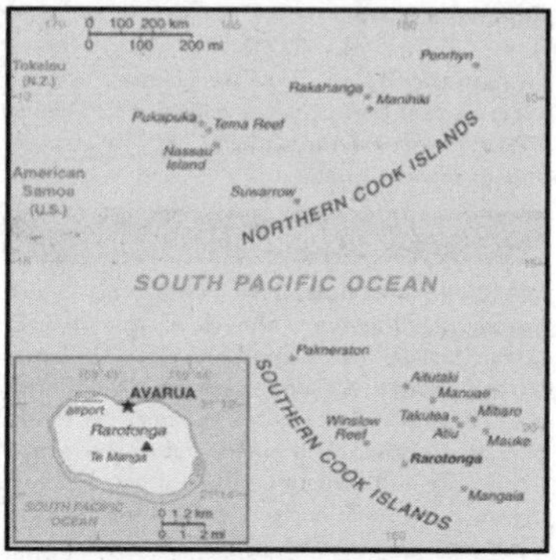

INTRODUCTION

Background: Named after Captain COOK, who sighted them in 1770, the islands became a British protectorate in 1888. By 1900, administrative control was transferred to New Zealand; in 1965, residents chose self-government in free association with New Zealand. The emigration of skilled workers to New Zealand and government deficits are continuing problems.

GEOGRAPHY

Location: Oceania, group of islands in the South Pacific Ocean, about half way between Hawaii and New Zealand

Geographic coordinates: 21 14 S, 159 46 W

Map references: Oceania

Area: *total:* 236 sq km
country comparison to the world: 215
land: 236 sq km
water: 0 sq km

Area—comparative: 1.3 times the size of Washington, DC

Land boundaries: 0 km

Coastline: 120 km

Maritime claims: *territorial sea:* 12 nm
exclusive economic zone: 200 nm
continental shelf: 200 nm or to the edge of the continental margin

Climate: tropical oceanic; moderated by trade winds; a dry season from April to November and a more humid season from December to March

Terrain: low coral atolls in north; volcanic, hilly islands in south

Elevation extremes: *lowest point:* Pacific Ocean 0 m
highest point: Te Manga 652 m

Natural resources: NEGL

Land use: *arable land:* 8.33%
permanent crops: 4.17%
other: 87.5% (2011)

Irrigated land: NA

Natural hazards: typhoons (November to March)

Environment—current issues: NA

Environment—international agreements:
party to: Biodiversity, Climate Change, Climate Change-Kyoto Protocol, Desertification, Hazardous Wastes, Law of the Sea, Ozone Layer Protection

Geography—note: the northern Cook Islands are seven low-lying, sparsely populated, coral atolls; the southern Cook Islands, where most of the population lives, consist of eight elevated, fertile, volcanic isles, including the largest, Rarotonga, at 67 sq km

PEOPLE AND SOCIETY

Nationality: *noun:* Cook Islander(s)
adjective: Cook Islander

Ethnic groups: Cook Island Maori (Polynesian) 81.3%, part Cook Island Maori 6.7%, other 11.9% (2011 est.)

Languages: English (official) 86.4%, Cook Islands Maori (Rarotongan) (official) 76.2%, other 8.3% (2011 est.)

Religions: Protestant 62.8% (Cook Islands Christian Church 49.1%, Seventh-Day Adventist 7.9%, Assemblies of God 3.7%, Apostolic Church 2.1%), Roman Catholic 17%, Mormon 4.4%, other 8%, none 5.6%, no response 2.2% (2011 est.)

Population: 10,134
country comparison to the world: 226
note: the Cook Islands' Ministry of Finance & Economic Management estimated the resident population to have been 13,700 in September 2013 (July 2014 est.)
Age structure: *0-14 years:* 22.8% (male 1,224/female 1,084)
15-24 years: 17.9% (male 971/female 845)
25-54 years: 38% (male 1,937/female 1,917)
55-64 years: 11% (male 555/female 487)

65 years and over: 10.6% (male 548/female 566) (2014 est.)

Median age: *total:* 34.4 years
male: 33.8 years
female: 35 years (2014 est.)

Population growth rate: -3% (2014 est.)
country comparison to the world: 232

Birth rate: 14.7 births/1,000 population (2014 est.)
country comparison to the world: 135

Death rate: 7.8 deaths/1,000 population (2014 est.)
country comparison to the world: 107

Urbanization: *urban population:* 75% of total population (2008)
rate of urbanization: 1.4% annual rate of change (2010-15 est.)

Sex ratio: *at birth:* 1.04 male(s)/female
0-14 years: 1.13 male(s)/female
15-24 years: 1.15 male(s)/female
25-54 years: 1.01 male(s)/female
55-64 years: 1.07 male(s)/female
65 years and over: 0.96 male(s)/female
total population: 1.07 male(s)/female (2014 est.)

Infant mortality rate: *total:* 14.33 deaths/1,000 live births
country comparison to the world: 111
male: 17.43 deaths/1,000 live births
female: 11.08 deaths/1,000 live births (2014 est.)

Life expectancy at birth:
total population: 75.38 years
country comparison to the world: 95
male: 72.56 years
female: 78.33 years (2014 est.)

Total fertility rate:
2.27 children born/woman (2014 est.)
country comparison to the world: 96

Contraceptive prevalence rate: 43.2% (1999)

Health expenditures: 5.5% of GDP (2011)
country comparison to the world: 121

Physicians density:
2.89 physicians/1,000 population (2009)

Drinking water source:
improved:
urban: 99.6% of population
rural: 99.6% of population
total: 99.6% of population
unimproved:
urban: 0.4% of population
rural: 0.4% of population
total: 0.4% of population (2011 est.)

Sanitation facility access:
improved:
urban: 94.6% of population
rural: 94.6% of population
total: 94.6% of population
unimproved:
urban: 5.4% of population
rural: 5.4% of population
total: 5.4% of population (2011 est.)

HIV/AIDS—adult prevalence rate: NA

HIV/AIDS—people living with HIV/AIDS: NA

HIV/AIDS—deaths: NA

Obesity—adult prevalence rate: 63.7% (2008)
country comparison to the world: 3

Education expenditures: 3.1% of GDP (2011)
country comparison to the world: 137

Literacy: *definition:* age 15 and over can read and write
total population: 95%
male: NA
female: NA

School life expectancy (primary to tertiary education): *total:* 13 years
male: 12 years
female: 13 years (2011)

GOVERNMENT

Country name: *conventional long form:* none
conventional short form: Cook Islands
former: Harvey Islands

Dependency status: self-governing in free association with New Zealand; Cook Islands is fully responsible for internal affairs; New Zealand retains responsibility for external affairs and defense in consultation with the Cook Islands

Government type: self-governing parliamentary democracy

Capital: *name:* Avarua
geographic coordinates: 21 12 S, 159 46 W
time difference: UTC-10 (5 hours behind Washington, DC during Standard Time)

Administrative divisions: none

Independence: none (became self-governing in free association with New Zealand on 4 August 1965 and has the right at any time to move to full independence by unilateral action)

National holiday: Constitution Day, first Monday in August (1965)

Constitution: effective 4 August 1965 (Cook islands Constitution Act 1964); amended many times, last in 2004 (2004)

Legal system: common law similar to New Zealand common law

International law organization participation: has not submitted an ICJ jurisdiction declaration (New Zealand normally retains responsibility for external affairs); accepts ICCt jurisdiction

Suffrage: 18 years of age; universal

Executive branch: *chief of state:* Queen ELIZABETH II (since 6 February 1952) represented by Tom J. MARSTERS (since 9 August 2013); New Zealand High Commissioner Joanna KEMPKERS (since 19 July 2013)
head of government: Prime Minister Henry PUNA (since 30 November 2010)
cabinet: Cabinet chosen by the prime minister; collectively responsible to Parliament (For more information visit the World Leaders website)
elections: the monarchy is hereditary; the UK representative appointed by the monarch; the New Zealand high commissioner appointed by the New Zealand Government; following legislative elections, the leader of the majority party or the leader of the majority coalition usually becomes prime minister

Legislative branch: bicameral Parliament consists of a House of Ariki, or upper house, made up of traditional leaders and a Legislative Assembly, or lower house, (24 seats; members elected by popular vote to serve four-year terms)
note: the House of Ariki advises on traditional matters and maintains considerable influence but has no legislative powers
elections: last held on 17 November 2010 (next to be held by 2014)
election results: percent of vote by party—NA; seats by party—CIP 16, Demo 8

Judicial branch: *highest court(s):* Court of Appeal (consists of the chief justice and 3 judges of the High Court); High Court (consists of the chief justice and at least 4 judges and organized into civil, criminal, and land divisions)
note—appeals beyond the Cook Islands Court of Appeal are brought before the Judicial Committee of the Privy Council (in London)
judge selection and term of office: High Court chief justice appointed by the Queen's Representative on the advice of the Executive Council tendered by the prime minister; other judges appointed by the Queen's Representative, on the advice of the Executive Council tendered by the chief justice, High Court chief justice, and the minister of justice; chief justice and judges appointed for 3-year renewable terms
subordinate courts: justices of the peace

Political parties and leaders: Cook Islands Party or CIP [Henry PUNA]; Democratic Party or Demo [Dr. Terepai MAOATE]

Political pressure groups and leaders:
Reform Conference (lobby for political system changes)
other: various groups lobbying for political change

International organization participation:
ACP, ADB, AOSIS, FAO, ICAO, ICRM, IFAD, IFRCS, IMO, IMSO, IOC, ITUC (NGOs), OPCW, PIF, Sparteca, SPC, UNESCO, UPU, WHO, WMO

Diplomatic representation in the US: none (self-governing in free association with New Zealand)

Diplomatic representation from the US: none (self-governing in free association with New Zealand)

Flag description: blue, with the flag of the UK in the upper hoist-side quadrant and a large circle of 15 white five-pointed stars (one for every island) centered in the outer half of the flag

National anthem:
name: "Te Atua Mou E" (To God Almighty)
lyrics/music: Tepaeru Te RITO/Thomas DAVIS
note: adopted 1982; as prime minister, Sir Thomas DAVIS composed the anthem; his wife, a tribal chief, wrote the lyrics

ECONOMY

Economy—overview: Like many other South Pacific island nations, the Cook Islands' economic development is hindered by the isolation of the country from foreign markets, the limited size of domestic markets, lack of natural resources, periodic devastation from natural disasters, and inadequate infrastructure. Agriculture, employing more than one-quarter of the working population, provides the economic base with major exports of copra and citrus fruit. Black pearls are the Cook Islands' leading export. Manufacturing activities are limited to fruit processing, clothing, and handicrafts. Trade deficits are offset by remittances from emigrants and by foreign aid overwhelmingly from New Zealand. In the 1980s and 1990s, the country lived beyond its means, maintaining a bloated public service and accumulating a large foreign debt. Subsequent reforms, including the sale of state assets, the strengthening of economic management, the encouragement of tourism, and a debt restructuring agreement, have rekindled investment and growth.

GDP (purchasing power parity):
$183.2 million (2005 est.)

country comparison to the world: 220

GDP (official exchange rate): $183.2 million (2005 est.)

GDP—real growth rate: 0.1% (2005 est.)
country comparison to the world: 193

GDP—per capita (PPP): $9,100 (2005 est.)
country comparison to the world: 123

GDP—composition, by sector of origin:
agriculture: 5.1%
industry: 12.7%
services: 82.1% (2010 est.)

Agriculture—products: copra, citrus, pineapples, tomatoes, beans, pawpaws, bananas, yams, taro, coffee; pigs, poultry

Industries: fruit processing, tourism, fishing, clothing, handicrafts

Industrial production growth rate: 1% (2002)
country comparison to the world: 147

Labor force: 6,820 (2001)
country comparison to the world: 219

Labor force—by occupation:
agriculture: 29%
industry: 15%
services: 56% (1995)

Unemployment rate: 13.1% (2005)
country comparison to the world: 130

Population below poverty line: NA%

Household income or consumption by percentage share: *lowest 10%:* NA%
highest 10%: NA%

Budget: *revenues:* $70.95 million
expenditures: $69.05 million (FY05/06)

Taxes and other revenues: 38.7% of GDP (FY05/06)
country comparison to the world: 49

Budget surplus (+) or deficit (-):
1% of GDP (FY05/06)
country comparison to the world: 27

Fiscal year: 1 April—31 March

Inflation rate (consumer prices): 2.2% (2011 est.)
country comparison to the world: 75
2.2% (2011 est.)

Stock of narrow money: $38.99 million (31 December 2011 est.)
country comparison to the world: 187
$38.99 million (31 December 2011 est.)

Stock of broad money: $148.2 million (31 December 2011 est.)
country comparison to the world: 188
$170.9 million (31 December 2010 est.)

Current account balance: $26.67 million (2005)
country comparison to the world: 59

Exports: $5.222 million (2005 est.)
country comparison to the world: 217
$3,000

Exports—commodities: copra, papayas, fresh and canned citrus fruit, coffee; fish; pearls and pearl shells; clothing

Imports: $83.49 million (2011 est.)
country comparison to the world: 215
$80.55 million

Imports—commodities: foodstuffs, textiles, fuels, timber, capital goods

Debt—external: $141 million (1996 est.)
country comparison to the world: 190

Exchange rates: NZ dollars (NZD) per US dollar—
1.247 (2013)
1.2659 (2011 est.)
1.3874 (2010)
1.6002 (2009)
1.4151 (2008)

ENERGY

Electricity—production: 31.13 million kWh (2010 est.)
country comparison to the world: 210

Electricity—consumption: 28.95 million kWh (2010 est.)
country comparison to the world: 210

Electricity—exports: 0 kWh (2012 est.)
country comparison to the world: 126

Electricity—imports: 0 kWh (2012 est.)
country comparison to the world: 133

Electricity—installed generating capacity: 8,090 kW (2010 est.)
country comparison to the world: 206

Electricity—from fossil fuels: 98.9% of total installed capacity (2010 est.)
country comparison to the world: 53

Electricity—from nuclear fuels: 0% of total installed capacity (2010 est.)
country comparison to the world: 73

Electricity—from hydroelectric plants: 0% of total installed capacity (2010 est.)
country comparison to the world: 165

Electricity—from other renewable sources: 1.1% of total installed capacity (2010 est.)
country comparison to the world: 82

Crude oil—production: 0 bbl/day (2012 est.)
country comparison to the world: 164

Crude oil—exports:
0 bbl/day (2010 est.)
country comparison to the world: 102

Crude oil—imports: 0 bbl/day (2010 est.)
country comparison to the world: 176

Crude oil—proved reserves: 0 bbl (1 January 2013 es)
country comparison to the world: 121

Refined petroleum products—production:
0 bbl/day (2010 est.)
country comparison to the world: 135

Refined petroleum products—consumption:
974.1 bbl/day (2011 est.)
country comparison to the world: 204

Refined petroleum products—exports:
0 bbl/day (2010 est.)
country comparison to the world: 168

Refined petroleum products—imports:
484.7 bbl/day (2010 est.)
country comparison to the world: 205

Natural gas—production: 0 cu m (2011 est.)
country comparison to the world: 120

Natural gas—consumption: 0 cu m (2010 est.)
country comparison to the world: 136

Natural gas—exports: 0 cu m (2011 est.)
country comparison to the world: 87

Natural gas—imports: 0 cu m (2011 est.)
country comparison to the world: 182

Natural gas—proved reserves: 0 cu m (1 January 2013 es)
country comparison to the world: 128

Carbon dioxide emissions from consumption of energy: 75,400 Mt (2011 est.)
country comparison to the world: 207

COMMUNICATIONS

Telephones—main lines in use: 7,200 (2009)
country comparison to the world: 206

Telephones—mobile cellular: 7,800 (2009)
country comparison to the world: 212

Telephone system: *general assessment:* Telecom Cook Islands offers international direct dialing, Internet, email, fax, and Telex
domestic: individual islands are connected by a combination of satellite earth stations, microwave systems, and VHF and HF radiotelephone; within the islands, service is provided by small exchanges connected to subscribers by open-wire, cable, and fiber-optic cable
international: country code—682; satellite earth station—1 Intelsat (Pacific Ocean)

Broadcast media: 1 privately owned TV station broadcasts from Rarotonga providing a mix of local news and overseas-sourced programs; a satellite program package is available; 6 radio stations broadcast with 1 reportedly reaching all of the islands (2009)

Internet country code: .ck

Internet hosts: 3,562 (2012)
country comparison to the world: 150

Internet users: 6,000 (2009)
country comparison to the world: 205

TRANSPORTATION

Airports: 11 (2013)
country comparison to the world: 153

Airports—with paved runways: *total:* 1
1,524 to 2,437 m: 1 (2013)

Airports—with unpaved runways: *total:* 10
1,524 to 2,437 m: 2
914 to 1,523 m: 7
under 914 m: 1 (2013)

Roadways: *total:* 320 km
country comparison to the world: 204
paved: 33 km
unpaved: 287 km (2003)

Merchant marine: *total:* 35
country comparison to the world: 81
by type: bulk carrier 2, cargo 25, passenger 1, refrigerated cargo 6, roll on/roll off 1
foreign-owned: 23 (Estonia 1, Germany 1, Lithuania 1, Norway 8, NZ 2, Russia 1, Sweden 3, Turkey 4, UK 2) (2010)
Ports and terminals: major seaport(s): Avatiu

MILITARY

Military branches: no regular military forces; National Police Department (2009)

Manpower fit for military service: *males age 16-49:* 2,198
females age 16-49: 2,156 (2010 est.)

Manpower reaching militarily significant age annually: *male:* 127
female: 107 (2010 est.)

Military—note: defense is the responsibility of New Zealand in consultation with the Cook Islands and at its request

TRANSNATIONAL ISSUES

Disputes—international: none

CORAL SEA ISLANDS

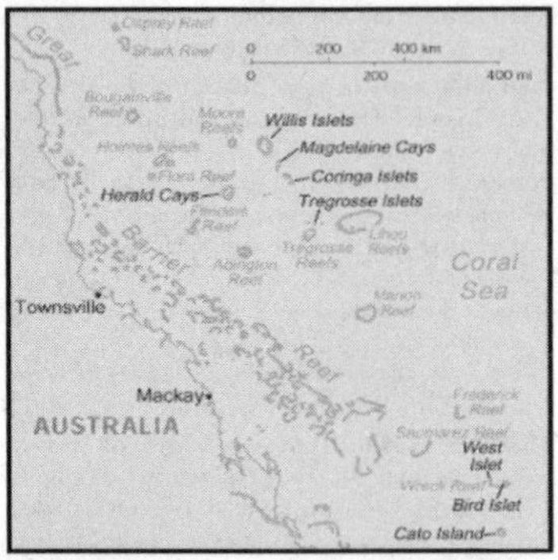

INTRODUCTION

Background: Scattered over more than three-quarters of a million square kilometers of ocean, the Coral Sea Islands were declared a territory of Australia in 1969. They are uninhabited except for a small meteorological staff on the Willis Islets. Automated weather stations, beacons, and a lighthouse occupy many other islands and reefs. The Coral Sea Islands Act 1969 was amended in 1997 to extend the boundaries of the Coral Sea Islands Territory around Elizabeth and Middleton Reefs.

GEOGRAPHY

Location: Oceania, islands in the Coral Sea, northeast of Australia

Geographic coordinates: 18 00 S, 152 00 E

Map references: Oceania

Area: *total:* less than 3 sq km
country comparison to the world: 249
land: less than 3 sq km
water: 0 sq km
note: includes numerous small islands and reefs scattered over a sea area of about 780,000 sq km with the Willis Islets the most important

Area—comparative: NA

Land boundaries: 0 km

Coastline: 3,095 km

Maritime claims: *territorial sea:* 3 nm
exclusive fishing zone: 200 nm

Climate: tropical

Terrain: sand and coral reefs and islands (or cays)

Elevation extremes: *lowest point:* Pacific Ocean 0 m
highest point: unnamed location on Cato Island 6 m

Natural resources: NEGL

Land use: *arable land:* 0%
permanent crops: 0%
other: 100% (mostly grass or scrub cover) (2011)

Irrigated land: 0 sq km (2011)

Natural hazards: occasional tropical cyclones

Environment—current issues: no permanent freshwater resources

Geography—note: important nesting area for birds and turtles

PEOPLE AND SOCIETY

Population: no indigenous inhabitants
note: there is a staff of three to four at the meteorological station on Willis Island (July 2007 est.)

GOVERNMENT

Country name: conventional long form: Coral Sea Islands Territory
conventional short form: Coral Sea Islands

Dependency status: territory of Australia; administered from Canberra by the Department of Regional Australia, Local Government, Arts and Sport

Legal system: the common law legal system of Australia, where applicable, applies

Diplomatic representation in the US: none (territory of Australia)

Diplomatic representation from the US: none (territory of Australia)

Flag description: the flag of Australia is used

ECONOMY

Economy—overview: no economic activity

COMMUNICATIONS

Communications—note: automatic weather stations on many of the isles and reefs relay data to the mainland

TRANSPORTATION

Ports and terminals: none; offshore anchorage only

MILITARY

Military—note: defense is the responsibility of Australia

TRANSNATIONAL ISSUES

Disputes—international: none

COSTA RICA

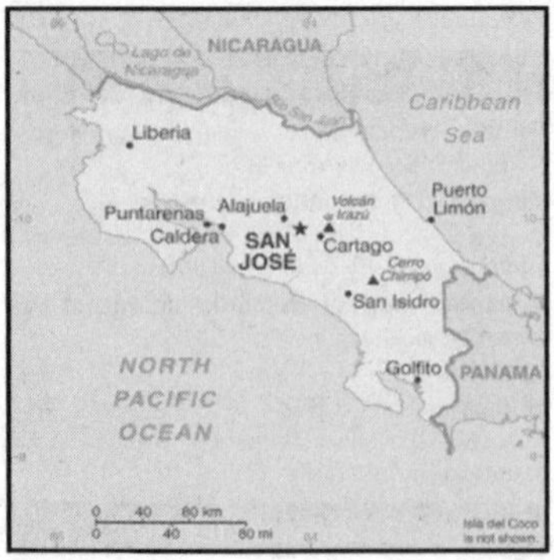

INTRODUCTION

Background: Although explored by the Spanish early in the 16th century, initial attempts at colonizing Costa Rica proved unsuccessful due to a combination of factors, including disease from mosquito-infested swamps, brutal heat, resistance by natives, and pirate raids. It was not until 1563 that a permanent settlement of Cartago was established in the cooler, fertile central highlands. The area remained a colony for some two and a half centuries. In 1821, Costa Rica became one of several Central American provinces that jointly declared their independence from Spain. Two years later it joined the United Provinces of Central America, but this federation disintegrated in 1838, at which time Costa Rica proclaimed its sovereignty and independence. Since the late 19th century, only two brief periods of violence have marred the country's democratic development. In 1949, Costa Rica dissolved its armed forces. Although it still maintains a large agricultural sector, Costa Rica has expanded its economy to include strong technology and tourism industries. The standard of living is relatively high. Land ownership is widespread.

GEOGRAPHY

Location: Central America, bordering both the Caribbean Sea and the North Pacific Ocean, between Nicaragua and Panama

Geographic coordinates: 10 00 N, 84 00 W

Map references: Central America and the Caribbean

Area: *total:* 51,100 sq km
country comparison to the world: 130
land: 51,060 sq km
water: 40 sq km
note: includes Isla del Coco

Area—comparative: slightly smaller than West Virginia

Land boundaries: *total:* 639 km
border countries: Nicaragua 309 km, Panama 330 km

Coastline: 1,290 km

Maritime claims: *territorial sea:* 12 nm
exclusive economic zone: 200 nm
continental shelf: 200 nm

Climate: tropical and subtropical; dry season (December to April); rainy season (May to November); cooler in highlands

Terrain: coastal plains separated by rugged mountains including over 100 volcanic cones, of which several are major volcanoes

Elevation extremes: *lowest point:* Pacific Ocean 0 m
highest point: Cerro Chirripo 3,810 m

Natural resources: hydropower

Land use: *arable land:* 4.89%
permanent crops: 6.46%
other: 88.65% (2011)

Irrigated land: 1,031 sq km (2003)

Total renewable water resources: 112.4 cu km (2011)

Freshwater withdrawal (domestic/industrial/agricultural): *total:* 5.77 cu km/yr (15%/9%/77%)
per capita: 1,582 cu m/yr (2006)

Natural hazards: occasional earthquakes, hurricanes along Atlantic coast; frequent flooding of lowlands at onset of rainy season and landslides; active volcanoes
volcanism: Arenal (elev. 1,670 m), which erupted in 2010, is the most active volcano in Costa Rica; a 1968 eruption destroyed the town of Tabacon; Irazu (elev. 3,432 m), situated just east of San Jose, has the potential to spewash over the capital city as it did between 1963 and 1965; other historically active volcanoes include Miravalles, Poas, Rincon de la Vieja, and Turrialba

Environment—current issues: deforestation and land use change, largely a result of the clearing of land for cattle ranching and agriculture; soil erosion; coastal marine pollution; fisheries protection; solid waste management; air pollution

Environment—international agreements: *party to:* Biodiversity, Climate Change, Climate Change-Kyoto Protocol, Desertification, Endangered Species, Environmental Modification, Hazardous Wastes, Law of the Sea, Marine Dumping, Ozone Layer Protection, Wetlands, Whaling
signed, but not ratified: Marine Life Conservation

Geography—note: four volcanoes, two of them active, rise near the capital of San Jose in the center of the country; one of the volcanoes, Irazu, erupted destructively in 1963-65

PEOPLE AND SOCIETY

Nationality: *noun:* Costa Rican(s)
adjective: Costa Rican

Ethnic groups: white or mestizo 83.6%, mulato 6.7%, indigenous 2.4%, black of African descent 1.1%, other 1.1%, none 2.9%, unspecified 2.2% (2011 est.)

Languages: Spanish (official), English

Religions: Roman Catholic 76.3%, Evangelical 13.7%, Jehovah's Witnesses 1.3%, other Protestant 0.7%, other 4.8%, none 3.2%

Demographic profile: Costa Rica's political stability, high standard of living, and well-developed social benefits system set it apart from its Central American neighbors. Through the government's sustained social spending—almost 20% of GDP annually—Costa Rica has made tremendous progress toward achieving its goal of providing universal access to education, healthcare, clean water, sanitation, and electricity. Since the 1970s, expansion of these services has led to a rapid decline in infant mortality, an increase in life expectancy at birth, and a sharp decrease in the birth rate. The average number of children born per women has fallen from about 7 in the 1960s to 3.5 in the early 1980s to below replacement level today. Costa Rica's poverty rate is lower than in most Latin American countries, but it has stalled at around 20% for almost two decades.
Costa Rica is a popular regional immigration destination because of its job opportunities and social programs. Almost 9% of the population is foreign-born, with Nicaraguans comprising nearly three-quarters of the foreign population. Many Nicaraguans who perform unskilled seasonal labor enter Costa Rica illegally or overstay their visas, which continues to be a source of tension. Less than 3% of Costa Rica's population lives abroad. The overwhelming majority of expatriates have settled in the United States after completing a university degree or in order to work in a highly skilled field.

Population: 4,755,234 (July 2014 est.)
country comparison to the world: 124
Age structure: 0-14 years: 23.5% (male 570,311/female 545,026)
15-24 years: 17.5% (male 423,340/female 407,335)
25-54 years: 43.8% (male 1,045,296/female 1,035,273)
55-64 years: 7% (male 193,205/female 201,377)
65 years and over: 6.8% (male 154,467/female 179,604) (2014 est.)

Dependency ratios: *total dependency ratio:* 44 %
youth dependency ratio: 33.9 %
elderly dependency ratio: 10.1 %
potential support ratio: 9.9 (2013)

Median age: *total:* 30 years
male: 29.5 years
female: 30.5 years (2014 est.)

Population growth rate: 1.24% (2014 est.)
country comparison to the world: 96

Birth rate: 16.08 births/1,000 population (2014 est.)
country comparison to the world: 123

Death rate: 4.49 deaths/1,000 population (2014 est.)
country comparison to the world: 205

Net migration rate: 0.84 migrant(s)/1,000 population (2014 est.)
country comparison to the world: 64

Urbanization: *urban population:* 64% of total population (2010)
rate of urbanization: 2.1% annual rate of change (2010-15 est.)

Major urban areas—population: SAN JOSE (capital) 1.515 million (2011)

Sex ratio: *at birth:* 1.05 male(s)/female
0-14 years: 1.05 male(s)/female
15-24 years: 1.04 male(s)/female
25-54 years: 1.01 male(s)/female
55-64 years: 1.01 male(s)/female
65 years and over: 0.86 male(s)/female
total population: 1.01 male(s)/female (2014 est.)

Maternal mortality rate: 40 deaths/100,000 live births (2010)
country comparison to the world: 115

Infant mortality rate: *total:* 8.7 deaths/1,000 live births
country comparison to the world: 151
male: 9.5 deaths/1,000 live births
female: 7.86 deaths/1,000 live births (2014 est.)

Life expectancy at birth: total population: 78.23 years
country comparison to the world: 58
male: 75.59 years
female: 81.01 years (2014 est.)

Total fertility rate: 1.91 children born/woman (2014 est.)
country comparison to the world: 139

Contraceptive prevalence rate: 82.2% (2010)

Health expenditures: 10.9% of GDP (2011)
country comparison to the world: 16

Physicians density: 1.32 physicians/1,000 population (2000)

Hospital bed density: 1.2 beds/1,000 population (2011)

Drinking water source:
improved:
urban: 99.6% of population
rural: 90.7% of population
total: 96.4% of population
unimproved:
urban: 0.4% of population
rural: 9.3% of population
total: 3.6% of population (2011 est.)

Sanitation facility access:
improved:
urban: 94.8% of population
rural: 91.6% of population
total: 93.7% of population
unimproved:
urban: 5.2% of population
rural: 8.4% of population
total: 6.3% of population (2011 est.)

HIV/AIDS—adult prevalence rate: 0.3% (2012 est.)
country comparison to the world: 92

HIV/AIDS—people living with HIV/AIDS: 9,800 (2012 est.)
country comparison to the world: 105

HIV/AIDS—deaths: 300 (2012 est.)
country comparison to the world: 100

Major infectious diseases: *degree of risk:* intermediate
food or waterborne diseases: bacterial diarrhea
vectorborne diseases: dengue fever (2013)

Obesity—adult prevalence rate: 23.7% (2008)
country comparison to the world: 73

Children under the age of 5 years underweight: 1.1% (2009)
country comparison to the world: 131

Education expenditures: 6.3% of GDP (2009)
country comparison to the world: 34

Literacy: *definition:* age 15 and over can read and write
total population: 96.3%
male: 96%
female: 96.5% (2011 est.)

School life expectancy (primary to tertiary education): *total:* 14 years
male: 13 years
female: 14 years (2012)

Child labor—children ages 5-14:
total number: 39,082
percentage: 5 % (2002 est.)

Unemployment, youth ages 15-24: total: 18.4%
country comparison to the world: 67
male: 15%
female: 24.2% (2012)

GOVERNMENT

Country name: *conventional long form:* Republic of Costa Rica
conventional short form: Costa Rica
local long form: Republica de Costa Rica
local short form: Costa Rica

Government type: democratic republic

Capital: *name:* San Jose
geographic coordinates: 9 56 N, 84 05 W
time difference: UTC-6 (1 hour behind Washington, DC during Standard Time)

Administrative divisions: 7 provinces (provincias, singular—provincia); Alajuela, Cartago, Guanacaste, Heredia, Limon, Puntarenas, San Jose

Independence: 15 September 1821 (from Spain)

National holiday: Independence Day, 15 September (1821)

Constitution: previous 1825; latest adopted 7 November 1949; amended many times, last in 2005 (2005)

Legal system: civil law system based on Spanish civil code; judicial review of legislative acts in the Supreme Court

International law organization participation: *accepts compulsory ICJ jurisdiction; accepts ICCt jurisdiction*

Suffrage: 18 years of age; universal and compulsory

Executive branch: *chief of state:* President Laura CHINCHILLA Miranda (since 8 May 2010); First Vice President Alfio PIVA Mesen (since 8 May 2010); Second Vice President Luis LIBERMAN Ginsburg (since 8 May 2010); note—the president is both the chief of state and head of government
head of government: President Laura CHINCHILLA Miranda (since 8 May 2010); First Vice President Alfio PIVA Mesen (since 8 May 2010); Second Vice President Luis LIBERMAN Ginsburg (since 8 May 2010)
cabinet: Cabinet selected by the president (For more information visit the World Leaders website)
elections: president and vice presidents elected on the same ticket by popular vote for a single four-year term; election last held on 7 February 2010 (next to be held in February 2014)
election results: Laura CHINCHILLA Miranda elected president; percent of vote—Laura CHINCHILLA Miranda (PLN) 46.7%; Otton SOLIS (PAC) 25.1%, Otto GUEVARA Guth (ML) 20.8%, other 7.4%

Legislative branch: unicameral Legislative Assembly or Asamblea Legislativa (57 seats; members elected by direct, popular vote to serve four-year terms)
elections: last held on 2 February 2014 (next to be held in February 2018)
election results: percent of vote by party—NA; seats by party—PLN 18, PAC 13, FA 9, PUSC 9, PML 3, other 5

Judicial branch: *highest court(s):* Supreme Court of Justice (consists of 22 judges organized into 3 cassation chambers each with 5 judges, and the Constitutional Chamber with 7 judges)
judge selection and term of office: Supreme Court of Justice judges elected by the National Assembly for 8-year terms with renewal decided by the National Assembly
subordinate courts: appellate courts; first instance and justice of the peace courts; Superior Electoral Tribunal

Political parties and leaders: Accessibility Without Exclusion or PASE [Oscar Andres LOPEZ Arias]; Citizen Action Party or PAC [Olivier PEREZ Gonzalez]; Costa Rican Renovation Party or PRC [Gerardo Justo OROZCO Alvarez]; Broad Front (Frente Amplio) or PFA [Jose MERINO del Rio]; Libertarian Movement Party or ML [Otto GUEVARA Guth]; National Integration Party or PIN [Walter MUNOZ Cespedes]; National Liberation Party or PLN [Bernal JIMENEZ]; National Restoration Party or PRN; Patriotic Alliance [Mariano FIGUERES Olsen]; Popular Vanguard [Trino BARRANTES Araya]; Social Christian Unity Party or PUSC [Gerardo VARGAS]

Political pressure groups and leaders: Authentic Confederation of Democratic Workers or CATD (Communist Party affiliate); Chamber of Coffee Growers; Confederated Union of Workers or CUT (Communist Party affiliate); Costa Rican Confederation of Democratic Workers or CCTD (Liberation Party affiliate); Costa Rican Exporter's Chamber or CADEXCO; Costa Rican Solidarity Movement; Costa Rican Union of Private Sector Enterprises or UCCAEP; Federation of Public Service Workers or FTSP; National Association for Economic Development or ANFE; National Association of Educators or ANDE; National Association of Public and Private Employees or ANEP; ANEP Confederation of Workers Rerum Novarum or CTRN (PLN affiliate)

International organization participation: BCIE, CACM, CD, CELAC, FAO, G-77, IADB, IAEA, IBRD, ICAO, ICC (national committees), ICRM, IDA, IFAD, IFC, IFRCS, ILO, IMF, IMO, IMSO, Interpol, IOC, IOM, IPU, ISO, ITSO, ITU, ITUC (NGOs), LAES, LAIA (observer), MIGA, NAM (observer), OAS, OPANAL, OPCW, PCA, SICA, UN, UNCTAD, UNESCO, UNHCR, UNIDO, Union Latina, UNWTO, UPU, WCO, WFTU (NGOs), WHO, WIPO, WMO, WTO

Diplomatic representation in the US:
chief of mission: Ambassador Shanon Muni FIGUERES Boggs (since 7 September 2010)
chancery: 2114 S Street NW, Washington, DC 20008
telephone: [1] (202) 480-2200
FAX: [1] (202) 265-4795
consulate(s) general: Atlanta, Chicago, Houston, Los Angeles, Miami, New York, Washington DC; note—Honorary Consulate: Saint Paul (Minnesota), Tucson (Arizona)
consulate(s): Austin

Diplomatic representation from the US:
chief of mission: Ambassador (vacant); Charge d'Affaires Gonzalo GALLEGOS
embassy: Calle 120 Avenida O, Pavas, San Jose
mailing address: APO AA 34020
telephone: [506] 2519-2000
FAX: [506] 2519-2305

Flag description: five horizontal bands of blue (top), white, red (double width), white, and blue, with the coat of arms in a white elliptical disk toward the hoist side of the red band; Costa Rica retained the earlier blue-white-blue flag of Central America until 1848 when, in response to revolutionary activity in Europe, it was decided to incorporate the French colors into the national flag and a central red stripe was added; today the blue color is said to stand for the sky, opportunity, and perseverance, white denotes peace, happiness, and wisdom, while red represents the blood shed for freedom, as well as the generosity and vibrancy of the people
note: somewhat resembles the flag of North Korea; similar to the flag of Thailand but with the blue and red colors reversed

National symbol(s): clay-colored robin known as Yiguirro

National anthem: *name:* "Himno Nacional de Costa Rica" (National Anthem of Costa Rica)
lyrics/music: Jose Maria ZELEDON Brenes/ Manuel Maria GUTIERREZ
note: adopted 1949; the anthem's music was originally written for an 1853 welcome ceremony for diplomatic missions from the United States and United Kingdom; the lyrics were added in 1903

ECONOMY

Economy—overview: Prior to the global economic crisis, Costa Rica enjoyed stable economic growth. The economy contracted 1.3% in 2009 but resumed growth at about 4.5% per year in 2010-12. While the traditional agricultural exports of bananas, coffee, sugar, and beef are still the backbone of commodity export trade, a variety of industrial and specialized agricultural products have broadened export trade in recent years. High value-added goods and services, including microchips, have further bolstered exports. Tourism continues to bring in foreign exchange, as Costa Rica's impressive biodiversity makes it a key destination for ecotourism. Foreign investors remain attracted by the country's political stability and relatively high education levels, as well as the incentives offered in the free-trade zones; and Costa Rica has attracted one of the highest levels of foreign direct investment per capita in Latin America. However, many business impediments remain, such as high levels of bureaucracy, legal uncertainty due to overlapping and at times conflicting responsibilities between agencies, difficulty of enforcing contracts, and weak investor protection. Poverty has remained around 20-25% for nearly 20 years, and the strong social safety net that had been put into place by the government has eroded due to increased financial constraints on government expenditures. Unlike the rest of Central America, Costa Rica is not highly dependent on remittances as they only represent about 2% of

GDP. Immigration from Nicaragua has increasingly become a concern for the government. The estimated 300,000- 500,000 Nicaraguans in Costa Rica legally and illegally are an important source of mostly unskilled labor but also place heavy demands on the social welfare system. The US-Central American-Dominican Republic Free Trade Agreement (CAFTA-DR) entered into force on 1 January 2009 after significant delays within the Costa Rican legislature. CAFTA-DR has increased foreign direct investment in key sectors of the economy, including the insurance and telecommunications sectors recently opened to private investors. President CHINCHILLA was not able to gain legislative approval for fiscal reform, her top priority, though she continued to pursue fiscal reform in 2012. President CHINCHILLA and the PLN were successful in passing a tax on corporations to fund an increase for security services.

GDP (purchasing power parity): $61.43 billion (2013 est.)
country comparison to the world: 91
$59.35 billion (2012 est.)
$56.45 billion (2011 est.)
note: data are in 2013 US dollars

GDP (official exchange rate): $48.51 billion (2013 est.)

GDP—real growth rate: 3.5% (2013 est.)
country comparison to the world: 93
5.1% (2012 est.)
4.4% (2011 est.)

GDP—per capita (PPP): $12,900 (2013 est.)
country comparison to the world: 102
$12,700 (2012 est.)
$12,200 (2011 est.)
note: data are in 2013 US dollars

Gross national saving: 16.3% of GDP (2013 est.)
country comparison to the world: 102
15.9% of GDP (2012 est.)
16.2% of GDP (2011 est.)

GDP—composition, by end use:
household consumption: 64.7%
government consumption: 17.9%
investment in fixed capital: 20.9%
investment in inventories: 0.8%
exports of goods and services: 35.2%
imports of goods and services: -39.5% (2013 est.)

GDP—composition, by sector of origin:
agriculture: 6.2%
industry: 21.3%
services: 72.5% (2013 est.)

Agriculture—products: bananas, pineapples, coffee, melons, ornamental plants, sugar, corn, rice, beans, potatoes; beef, poultry, dairy; timber

Industries: microprocessors, food processing, medical equipment, textiles and clothing, construction materials, fertilizer, plastic products

Industrial production growth rate: 4.3% (2013 est.)
country comparison to the world: 65

Labor force: 2.222 million
country comparison to the world: 117
note: this official estimate excludes Nicaraguans living in Costa Rica (2013 est.)

Labor force—by occupation: *agriculture:* 14%
industry: 22%
services: 64% (2006 est.)

Unemployment rate: 7.9% (2013 est.)
country comparison to the world: 85
7.8% (2012 est.)

Population below poverty line: 24.8% (2011 est.)

Household income or consumption by percentage share: *lowest 10%:* 1.2%
highest 10%: 39.5% (2009 est.)

Distribution of family income—Gini index:
50.3 (2009)
country comparison to the world: 21
45.9 (1997)

Budget: *revenues:* $7.197 billion
expenditures: $9.621 billion (2013 est.)

Taxes and other revenues: 14.8% of GDP (2013 est.)
country comparison to the world: 193

Budget surplus (+) or deficit (-):
-5% of GDP (2013 est.)
country comparison to the world: 168

Public debt: 55% of GDP (2013 est.)
country comparison to the world: 57
51.9% of GDP (2012 est.)

Fiscal year: calendar year

Inflation rate (consumer prices): 5.6% (2013 est.)
country comparison to the world: 163
4.5% (2012 est.)

Central bank discount rate:
21.5% (31 December 2010 est.)
country comparison to the world: 5
23% (31 December 2009 est.)

Commercial bank prime lending rate:
18% (31 December 2013 est.)
country comparison to the world: 24
18.21% (31 December 2012 est.)

Stock of narrow money: $4.633 billion (31 December 2013 est.)
country comparison to the world: 104
$4.197 billion (31 December 2012 est.)

Stock of broad money: $14.57 billion (31 December 2013 est.)
country comparison to the world: 90
$14.95 billion (31 December 2012 est.)

Stock of domestic credit: $22.92 billion (31 December 2013 est.)
country comparison to the world: 77
$21.93 billion (31 December 2012 est.)

Market value of publicly traded shares:
$2.015 billion (31 December 2012 est.)
country comparison to the world: 102
$1.443 billion (31 December 2011)
$1.445 billion (31 December 2010 est.)

Current account balance: -$2.673 billion (2013 est.)
country comparison to the world: 155
-$2.341 billion (2012 est.)

Exports: $11.66 billion (2013 est.)
country comparison to the world: 91
$11.44 billion (2012 est.)

Exports—commodities: bananas, pineapples, coffee, melons, ornamental plants, sugar; beef; seafood; electronic components, medical equipment

Exports—partners: US 38.9%, Netherlands 7.5%, Panama 5.1%, Hong Kong 4.6%, Nicaragua 4.4% (2012)

Imports: $17.56 billion (2013 est.)
country comparison to the world: 82
$16.75 billion (2012 est.)

Imports—commodities: raw materials, consumer goods, capital equipment, petroleum, construction materials

Imports—partners: US 49.8%, China 8.2%, Mexico 6.6% (2012)

Reserves of foreign exchange and gold:
$7.406 billion (31 December 2013 est.)
country comparison to the world: 80
$6.857 billion (31 December 2012 est.)

Debt—external: $15.1 billion (31 December 2013 est.)
country comparison to the world: 89
$13.81 billion (31 December 2012 est.)

Stock of direct foreign investment—at home:
$21.7 billion (31 December 2013 est.)
country comparison to the world: 70
$18.98 billion (31 December 2012 est.)

Stock of direct foreign investment—abroad:
$1.681 billion (31 December 2013 est.)
country comparison to the world: 75
$1.481 billion (31 December 2012 est.)

Exchange rates: Costa Rican colones (CRC) per US dollar—
500.9 (2013 est.)
502.9 (2012 est.)
525.83 (2010 est.)
573.29 (2009)
530.41 (2008)

ENERGY

Electricity—production: 9.473 billion kWh (2010 est.)
country comparison to the world: 9 6

Electricity—consumption: 8.532 billion kWh (2010 est.)
country comparison to the world: 92

Electricity—exports: 135 million kWh (2010 est.)
country comparison to the world: 73

Electricity—imports: 164 million kWh (2010 est.)
country comparison to the world: 88

Electricity—installed generating capacity:
2.8 million kW (2010 est.)
country comparison to the world: 89

Electricity—from fossil fuels: 32.4% of total installed capacity (2010 est.)
country comparison to the world: 177

Electricity—from nuclear fuels: 0% of total installed capacity (2010 est.)
country comparison to the world: 69

Electricity—from hydroelectric plants:
55.5% of total installed capacity (2010 est.)
country comparison to the world: 36

Electricity—from other renewable sources:
12.1% of total installed capacity (2010 est.)
country comparison to the world: 22

Crude oil—production: 290.7 bbl/day (2012 est.)
country comparison to the world: 116

Crude oil—exports: 0 bbl/day (2010 est.)
country comparison to the world: 99

Crude oil—imports: 10,040 bbl/day (2010 est.)
country comparison to the world: 78

Crude oil—proved reserves: 0 bbl (1 January 2013 es)
country comparison to the world: 118

Refined petroleum products—production:
10,630 bbl/day (2010 est.)
country comparison to the world: 104

Refined petroleum products—consumption:
50,200 bbl/day (2011 est.)
country comparison to the world: 99

Refined petroleum products—exports:
1,898 bbl/day (2010 est.)
country comparison to the world: 102

Refined petroleum products—imports:
40,290 bbl/day (2010 est.)
country comparison to the world: 81

Natural gas—production: 0 cu m (2011 est.)
country comparison to the world: 117

Natural gas—consumption: 0 cu m (2010 est.)
country comparison to the world: 133

Natural gas—exports: 0 cu m (2011 est.)

country comparison to the world: 83

Natural gas—imports: 0 cu m (2011 est.)
country comparison to the world: 178

Natural gas—proved reserves: 0 cu m (1 January 2013 es)
country comparison to the world: 125

Carbon dioxide emissions from consumption of energy: 6.806 million Mt (2011 est.)
country comparison to the world: 116

COMMUNICATIONS

Telephones—main lines in use: 1.018 million (2012)
country comparison to the world: 75

Telephones—mobile cellular: 6.151 million (2012)
country comparison to the world: 100

Telephone system: *general assessment:* good domestic telephone service in terms of breadth of coverage; under the terms of CAFTA-DR, the state-run telecommunications monopoly is scheduled to be opened to competition from domestic and international firms, but has been slow to open to competition
domestic: point-to-point and point-to-multi-point microwave, fiber-optic, and coaxial cable link rural areas; Internet service is available
international: country code—506; landing points for the Americas Region Caribbean Ring System (ARCOS-1), MAYA-1, and the Pan American Crossing submarine cables that provide links to South and Central America, parts of the Caribbean, and the US; connected to Central American Microwave System; satellite earth stations—2 Intelsat (Atlantic Ocean) (2011)

Broadcast media: multiple privately owned TV stations and 1 publicly owned TV station; cable network services are widely available; more than 100 privately owned radio stations and a public radio network (2007)

Internet country code: .cr

Internet hosts: 147,258 (2012)
country comparison to the world: 78

Internet users: 1.485 million (2009)
country comparison to the world: 82

TRANSPORTATION

Airports: 161 (2013)
country comparison to the world: 35

Airports—with paved runways: *total:* 47
2,438 to 3,047 m: 2
1,524 to 2,437 m: 2
914 to 1,523 m: 27
under 914 m: 16 (2013)

Airports—with unpaved runways: *total:* 114
914 to 1,523 m: 18
under 914 m: 96 (2013)

Pipelines: refined products 662 km (2013)

Railways: total: 278 km
country comparison to the world: 122
narrow gauge: 278 km 1.067-m gauge
note: none of the railway network is in use (2008)

Roadways: total: 39,018 km
country comparison to the world: 90
paved: 10,133 km
unpaved: 28,885 km (2010)

Waterways: 730 km (seasonally navigable by small craft) (2011)
country comparison to the world: 75

Merchant marine: total: 1
country comparison to the world: 154
by type: passenger/cargo 1 (2010)

Ports and terminals:
major seaport(s): Atlantic Ocean (Caribbean) Puerto Limon; Pacific Ocean—Caldera

MILITARY

Military branches: no regular military forces; Ministry of Public Security, Government, and Police (2011)

Manpower available for military service: *males age 16-49:* 1,255,798
females age 16-49: 1,230,202 (2010 est.)

Manpower fit for military service: *males age 16-49:* 1,058,419
females age 16-49: 1,037,053 (2010 est.)

Manpower reaching militarily significant age annually: *male:* 42,201
female: 40,444 (2010 est.)

TRANSNATIONAL ISSUES

Disputes—international: the ICJ had given Costa Rica until January 2008 to reply and Nicaragua until July 2008 to rejoin before rendering its decision on the navigation, security, and commercial rights of Costa Rican vessels on the Rio San Juan over which Nicaragua retains sovereignty

Refugees and internally displaced persons: *refugees (country of origin):* 10,305 (Colombia) (2012)

Illicit drugs: transshipment country for cocaine and heroin from South America; illicit production of cannabis in remote areas; domestic cocaine consumption, particularly crack cocaine, is rising; significant consumption of amphetamines; seizures of smuggled cash in Costa Rica and at the main border crossing to enter Costa Rica from Nicaragua have risen in recent years (2008)

COTE D'IVOIRE

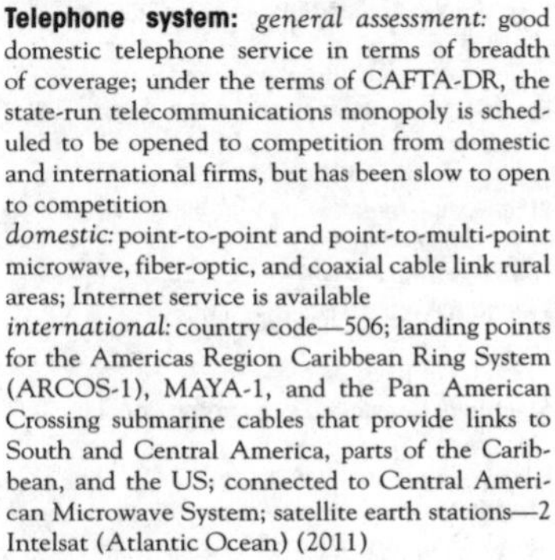

INTRODUCTION

Background: Close ties to France following independence in 1960, the development of cocoa production for export, and foreign investment all made Cote d'Ivoire one of the most prosperous of the West African states but did not protect it from political turmoil. In December 1999, a military coup—the first ever in Cote d'Ivoire's history—overthrew the government. Junta leader Robert GUEI blatantly rigged elections held in late 2000 and declared himself the winner. Popular protest forced him to step aside and brought Laurent GBAGBO into power. Ivorian dissidents and disaffected members of the military launched a failed coup attempt in September 2002 that developed into a rebellion and then a civil war. The war ended in 2003 with a cease fire that left the country divided with the rebels holding the north, the government the south, and peacekeeping forces a buffer zone between the two. In March 2007, President GBAGBO and former New Forces rebel leader Guillaume SORO signed an agreement in which SORO joined GBAGBO's government as prime minister and the two agreed to reunite the country by dismantling the buffer zone, integrating rebel forces into the national armed forces, and holding elections. Difficulties in preparing electoral registers delayed balloting until 2010. In November 2010, Alassane Dramane OUATTARA won the presidential election over GBAGBO, but GBAGBO refused to hand over power, resulting in a five-month stand-off. In April 2011, after widespread fighting, GBAGBO was formally forced from office by armed OUATTARA supporters with the help of UN and French forces. Several thousand UN peacekeepers and several hundred French troops remain in Cote d'Ivoire to support the transition process. OUATTARA is focused on rebuilding the country's infrastructure and military after the five months of post-electoral fighting and faces ongoing threats from GBAGBO supporters, many of whom have sought shelter in Ghana. GBAGBO is in The Hague awaiting trial for crimes against humanity.

GEOGRAPHY

Location: Western Africa, bordering the North Atlantic Ocean, between Ghana and Liberia

Geographic coordinates: 8 00 N, 5 00 W

Map references: Africa

Area: *total:* 322,463 sq km
country comparison to the world: 69
land: 318,003 sq km
water: 4,460 sq km

Area—comparative: slightly larger than New Mexico

Land boundaries: *total:* 3,110 km

border countries: Burkina Faso 584 km, Ghana 668 km, Guinea 610 km, Liberia 716 km, Mali 532 km

Coastline: 515 km

Maritime claims: *territorial sea:* 12 nm
exclusive economic zone: 200 nm
continental shelf: 200 nm

Climate: tropical along coast, semiarid in far north; three seasons—warm and dry (November to March), hot and dry (March to May), hot and wet (June to October)

Terrain: mostly flat to undulating plains; mountains in northwest

Elevation extremes: *lowest point:* Gulf of Guinea 0 m
highest point: Monts Nimba 1,752 m

Natural resources: petroleum, natural gas, diamonds, manganese, iron ore, cobalt, bauxite, copper, gold, nickel, tantalum, silica sand, clay, cocoa beans, coffee, palm oil, hydropower

Land use: *arable land:* 8.99%
permanent crops: 13.65%
other: 77.36% (2011)

Irrigated land: 727.5 sq km (2003)

Total renewable water resources: 81.14 cu km (2011)

Freshwater withdrawal (domestic/industrial/agricultural): *total:* 1.55 cu km/yr (41%/21%/38%)
per capita: 83.07 cu m/yr (2008)

Natural hazards: coast has heavy surf and no natural harbors; during the rainy season torrential flooding is possible

Environment—current issues: deforestation (most of the country's forests—once the largest in West Africa—have been heavily logged); water pollution from sewage and industrial and agricultural effluents

Environment—international agreements: *party to:* Biodiversity, Climate Change, Climate Change-Kyoto Protocol, Desertification, Endangered Species, Hazardous Wastes, Law of the Sea, Marine Dumping, Ozone Layer Protection, Ship Pollution, Tropical Timber 83, Tropical Timber 94, Wetlands, Whaling
signed, but not ratified: none of the selected agreements

Geography—note: most of the inhabitants live along the sandy coastal region; apart from the capital area, the forested interior is sparsely populated

PEOPLE AND SOCIETY

Nationality: *noun:* Ivoirian(s)
adjective: Ivoirian
Ethnic groups: Akan 42.1%, Voltaiques or Gur 17.6%, Northern Mandes 16.5%, Krous 11%, Southern Mandes 10%, other 2.8% (includes 130,000 Lebanese and 14,000 French) (1998)

Languages: French (official), 60 native dialects of which Dioula is the most widely spoken

Religions: Muslim 38.6%, Christian 32.8%, indigenous 11.9%, none 16.7% (2008 est.)
note: the majority of foreigners (migratory workers) are Muslim (70%) and Christian (20%)

Population: 22,848,945 (July 2014 est.)
country comparison to the world: 55
note: estimates for this country explicitly take into account the effects of excess mortality due to AIDS; this can result in lower life expectancy, higher infant mortality, higher death rates, lower population growth rates, and changes in the distribution of population by age and sex than would otherwise be expected

Age structure: *0-14 years:* 38.4% (male 4,427,193/female 4,353,342)
15-24 years: 21% (male 2,415,504/female 2,378,196)
25-54 years: 33% (male 3,864,593/female 3,677,996)
55-64 years: 3.3% (male 494,063/female 493,213)
65 years and over: 3.2% (male 361,135/female 383,710) (2014 est.)

Dependency ratios:
total dependency ratio: 80.2 %
youth dependency ratio: 74.5 %
elderly dependency ratio: 5.7 %
potential support ratio: 17.5 (2013)

Median age: *total:* 20.3 years
male: 20.3 years
female: 20.2 years (2014 est.)

Population growth rate: 1.96% (2014 est.)
country comparison to the world: 53

Birth rate: 29.25 births/1,000 population (2014 est.)
country comparison to the world: 43

Death rate: 9.67 deaths/1,000 population (2014 est.)
country comparison to the world: 54

Net migration rate: 0 migrant(s)/1,000 population (2014 est.)
country comparison to the world: 104

Urbanization: *urban population:* 51.3% of total population (2011)
rate of urbanization: 3.56% annual rate of change (2010-15 est.)

Major urban areas—population:
ABIDJAN (seat of government) 4.288 million; YAMOUSSOUKRO (capital) 966,000 (2011)

Sex ratio: *at birth:* 1.03 male(s)/female
0-14 years: 1.02 male(s)/female
15-24 years: 1.02 male(s)/female
25-54 years: 1.05 male(s)/female
55-64 years: 1.02 male(s)/female
65 years and over: 0.96 male(s)/female
total population: 1.03 male(s)/female (2014 est.)

Mother's mean age at first birth: 19.8
note: median age at first birth among women 25-29 (2011-12 est.)

Maternal mortality rate:
400 deaths/100,000 live births (2010)
country comparison to the world: 27

Infant mortality rate: *total:* 60.16 deaths/1,000 live births
country comparison to the world: 22
male: 66.4 deaths/1,000 live births
female: 53.73 deaths/1,000 live births (2014 est.)

Life expectancy at birth: *total population:* 58.01 years
country comparison to the world: 200
male: 56.9 years
female: 59.16 years (2014 est.)

Total fertility rate: 3.63 children born/woman (2014 est.)
country comparison to the world: 43

Contraceptive prevalence rate: 18.2% (2012)

Health expenditures: 6.8% of GDP (2011)
country comparison to the world: 89

Physicians density: 0.14 physicians/1,000 population (2008)

Hospital bed density: 0.4 beds/1,000 population (2006)

Drinking water source:
improved:
urban: 91.1% of population
rural: 68% of population
total: 79.9% of population
unimproved:
urban: 8.9% of population
rural: 32% of population
total: 20.1% of population (2011 est.)

Sanitation facility access:
improved:
urban: 35.8% of population
rural: 11.4% of population
total: 23.9% of population
unimproved:
urban: 64.2% of population
rural: 88.6% of population
total: 76.1% of population (2011 est.)

HIV/AIDS—adult prevalence rate: 3.2% (2012 est.)
country comparison to the world: 19

HIV/AIDS—people living with HIV/AIDS: 450,000 (2012 est.)
country comparison to the world: 18

HIV/AIDS—deaths: 31,200 (2012 est.)
country comparison to the world: 13

Major infectious diseases: degree of risk: very high
food or waterborne diseases: bacterial diarrhea, hepatitis A, and typhoid fever
vectorborne diseases: malaria, dengue fever, and yellow fever
water contact disease: schistosomiasis
animal contact disease: rabies
respiratory disease: meningococcal meningitis
note: highly pathogenic H5N1 avian influenza has been identified in this country; it poses a negligible risk with extremely rare cases possible among US citizens who have close contact with birds (2013)

Obesity—adult prevalence rate: 6.2% (2008)
country comparison to the world: 149

Children under the age of 5 years underweight: *29.4% (2007)*
country comparison to the world: 16

Education expenditures: 4.6% of GDP (2008)
country comparison to the world: 89

Literacy: *definition:* age 15 and over can read and write
total population: 56.9%
male: 65.6%
female: 47.6% (2011 est.)

Child labor—children ages 5-14:
total number: 1,796,802
percentage: 35 % (2006 est.)

GOVERNMENT

Country name: *conventional long form:* Republic of Cote d'Ivoire
conventional short form: Cote d'Ivoire
local long form: Republique de Cote d'Ivoire
local short form: Cote d'Ivoire
note: pronounced coat-div-whar
former: Ivory Coast

Government type: republic; multiparty presidential regime established 1960

Capital: *name:* Yamoussoukro
geographic coordinates: 6 49 N, 5 16 W
time difference: UTC 0 (5 hours ahead of Washington, DC during Standard Time)
note: although Yamoussoukro has been the official capital since 1983, Abidjan remains the commercial and administrative center; the US, like other countries, maintains its Embassy in Abidjan

Administrative divisions: 12 districts and 2 autonomous districts*; Abidjan*, Bas-Sassandra, Comoe, Denguele, Goh-Djiboua, Lacs, Lagunes, Montagnes, Sassandra-Marahoue, Savanes, Vallee du Bandama, Woroba, Yamoussoukro*, Zanzan

Independence: 7 August 1960 (from France)

National holiday: Independence Day, 7 August (1960)

Constitution: previous 1960; latest approved by referendum 23 July 2000; amended 2012 (2012)

Legal system: civil law system based on the French civil code; judicial review in the Constitutional Chamber of the Supreme Court

International law organization participation: accepts compulsory ICJ jurisdiction with reservations; accepts ICCt jurisdiction under Article 12(3)of the Rome Statute

Suffrage: 18 years of age; universal

Executive branch: *chief of state:* President Alassane Dramane OUATTARA (since 4 December 2010)
head of government: Prime Minister Daniel Kablan DUNCAN (since 21 November 2012)
cabinet: Council of Ministers appointed by the president (For more information visit the World Leaders website)
elections: president elected by popular vote for a five-year term (no term limits); election last held on 31 October and 28 November 2010 (next to be held in 2015); prime minister appointed by the president
election results: Alassane OUATTARA elected president; percent of vote—Alassane OUATTARA 54.1%, Laurent GBAGBO 45.9%; note—President OUATTARA was declared winner by the election commission and took the oath of *office on 4 December, Prime Minister SORO resigned from the incumbent administration and was subsequently appointed to the same position by OUATTARA; former president GBAGBO refused to cede resulting in a 5-month stand-off, he was finally forced to stand down in April 2011*

Legislative branch: unicameral National Assembly or Assemblee Nationale (255 seats; members elected in single- and multi-district elections by direct popular vote to serve five-year terms)
elections: elections last held on 11 December 2011 (next to be held in 2016)
election results: percent of vote by party—RDR 42.1%, PDCI 28.6%, UDPCI 3.1%, RDP 1.7%, other 24.5% ; seats by party—RDR 127, PDCI 76, UDPCI 7, RDP 4, other 2, independents 39

Judicial branch: *highest court(s):* Supreme Court or Cour Supreme (organized into Judicial, Audit, Constitutional, and Administrative Chambers; consists of the court president, 3 vice-presidents for the Judicial, Audit, and Administrative chambers, and 9 associate justices or magistrates) judges nominated by the Superior Council of the Magistrature, a 7-member body consisting of the national president (chairman), 3 "Bench" judges, and 3 public prosecutors; judges appointed for life
subordinate courts: Courts of Appeal (organized into civil, criminal, and social chambers); first instance courts; peace courts

Political parties and leaders: Citizen's Democratic Union or UDCY [Theodore MEL EG]; Democracy and Liberty for the Republic or LIDER [Mamadou KOULIBALY]; Democratic Party of Cote d'Ivoire or PDCI [Henri Konan BEDIE]; Ivorian Popular Front or FPI [Pascal AFFI NGUESSAN]; Ivorian Worker's Party or PIT [Daniel AKA AHIZ]; Movement of the Future Forces or MFA [Innocent Augustin ANAKY KOBENA]; Rally of the Republicans or RDR [Alassane OUATTARA]; Union for Democracy and Peace in Cote d'Ivoire or UDPCI [Toikeuse MABRI]; over 144 smaller registered parties

Political pressure groups and leaders: Federation of University and High School Students of Cote d'Ivoire or FESCI [Augustin MIAN]; National Congress for the Resistance and Democracy or CNRD [Bernard DADIE]; Panafrican Congress for Justice and Peoples Equality or COJEP [Roselin BLY]; Rally of Houphouetists for Democracy and Peace or RHDP

International organization participation: ACP, AfDB, AU, ECOWAS, EITI (candidate country), Entente, FAO, FZ, G-24, G-77, IAEA, IBRD, ICAO, ICC, ICRM, IDA, IDB, IFAD, IFC, IFRCS, ILO, IMF, IMO, Interpol, IOC, IOM, IPU, ISO, ITSO, ITU, ITUC (NGOs), MIGA, MINUSMA, NAM, OIC, OIF, OPCW, UN, UNCTAD, UNESCO, UNHCR, UNIDO, Union Latina, UNWTO, UPU, WADB (regional), WAEMU, WCO, WFTU (NGOs), WHO, WIPO, WMO, WTO

Diplomatic representation in the US: *chief of mission:* Ambassador Daouda DIABATE (since 11 February 2011)
chancery: 2424 Massachusetts Avenue NW, Washington, DC 20008
telephone: [1] (202) 797-0300
FAX: [1] (202) 462-9444

Diplomatic representation from the US: *chief of mission:* Ambassador Terrance MCCULLEY
embassy: Cocody Riviera Golf 01, Abidjan
mailing address: B. P. 1712, Abidjan 01
telephone: [225] 22 49 40 00
FAX: [225] 22 49 43 32

Flag description: three equal vertical bands of orange (hoist side), white, and green; orange symbolizes the land (savannah) of the north and fertility, white stands for peace and unity, green represents the forests of the south and the hope for a bright future
note: similar to the flag of Ireland, which is longer and has the colors reversed—green (hoist side), white, and orange; also similar to the flag of Italy, which is green (hoist side), white, and red; design was based on the flag of France

National symbol(s): elephant

National anthem: *name:* "L'Abidjanaise" (Song of Abidjan)
lyrics/music: Mathieu EKRA, Joachim BONY, and Pierre Marie COTY/Pierre Marie COTY and Pierre Michel PANGO
note: adopted 1960; although the nation's capital city moved from Abidjan to Yamoussoukro in 1983, the anthem still owes its name to the former capital

ECONOMY

Economy—overview: Cote d'Ivoire is heavily dependent on agriculture and related activities, which engage roughly two-thirds of the population. Cote d'Ivoire is the world's largest producer and exporter of cocoa beans and a significant producer and exporter of coffee and palm oil. Consequently, the economy is highly sensitive to fluctuations in international prices for these products and in climatic conditions. Cocoa, oil, and coffee are the country's top export revenue earners, but the country is also producing gold. The country also produces oil and boasted two offshore oil finds in 2012. Since the end of the civil war in 2003, political turmoil has continued to damage the economy, resulting in the loss of foreign investment and slow economic growth. In June 2012, the IMF and the World Bank announced $4.4 billion in debt relief for Cote d'Ivoire under the Highly Indebted Poor Countries Initiative. Cote d'Ivoire's long-term challenges include political instability and degrading infrastructure.

GDP (purchasing power parity): $43.67 billion (2013 est.)
country comparison to the world: 102
$40.43 billion (2012 est.)
$36.84 billion (2011 est.)
note: data are in 2013 US dollars

GDP (official exchange rate): $28.28 billion (2013 est.)

GDP—real growth rate: 8% (2013 est.)
country comparison to the world: 12
9.8% (2012 est.)
-4.7% (2011 est.)

GDP—per capita (PPP): $1,800 (2013 est.)
country comparison to the world: 196
$1,700 (2012 est.)
$1,600 (2011 est.)
note: data are in 2013 US dollars

GDP—composition, by end use:
household consumption: 79.1%
government consumption: 9.1%
investment in fixed capital: 12.7%
investment in inventories: 0%
exports of goods and services: 53.2%
imports of goods and services: -54.1% (2013 est.)

GDP—composition, by sector of origin:
agriculture: 26.3%
industry: 21.3%
services: 52.4% (2013 est.)

Agriculture—products: coffee, cocoa beans, bananas, palm kernels, corn, rice, cassava (manioc), sweet potatoes, sugar, cotton, rubber; timber

Industries: foodstuffs, beverages; wood products, oil refining, gold mining, truck and bus assembly, textiles, fertilizer, building materials, electricity

Industrial production growth rate: 7% (2013 est.)
country comparison to the world: 33

Labor force: 7.928 million (2013 est.)
country comparison to the world: 59

Labor force—by occupation: agriculture: 68%
industry and services: NA% (2007 est.)

Unemployment rate: NA%

Population below poverty line: 42% (2006 est.)

Household income or consumption by percentage share: *lowest 10%:* 2.2%
highest 10%: 31.8% (2008)

Distribution of family income—Gini index: 41.5 (2008)
country comparison to the world: 51
36.7 (1995)

Budget: *revenues:* $5.7 billion
expenditures: $6.665 billion (2013 est.)

Taxes and other revenues: 20.2% of GDP (2013 est.)
country comparison to the world: 166

Budget surplus (+) or deficit (-):
-3.4% of GDP (2013 est.)
country comparison to the world: 135

Public debt: 45.2% of GDP (2013 est.)
country comparison to the world: 82
47.8% of GDP (2012 est.)

Fiscal year: calendar year
Inflation rate (consumer prices):
2.9% (2013 est.)
country comparison to the world: 111
1.3% (2012 est.)

Central bank discount rate: 4.25% (31 December 2010 est.)
country comparison to the world: 89
4.25% (31 December 2009 est.)

Commercial bank prime lending rate: 3.8% (31 December 2013 est.)
country comparison to the world: 165
4% (31 December 2012 est.)

Stock of narrow money: $7.606 billion (31 December 2013 est.)
country comparison to the world: 89
$6.552 billion (31 December 2012 est.)

Stock of broad money: $11.46 billion (31 December 2013 est.)
country comparison to the world: 101
$9.877 billion (31 December 2012 est.)

Stock of domestic credit: $7.953 billion (31 December 2013 est.)
country comparison to the world: 104
$6.918 billion (31 December 2012 est.)

Market value of publicly traded shares:
$7.829 billion (31 December 2012 est.)
country comparison to the world: 80
$6.288 billion (31 December 2011)
$7.099 billion (31 December 2010 est.)

Current account balance: -$623 million (2013 est.)
country comparison to the world: 108
-$266.5 million (2012 est.)

Exports: $12.96 billion (2013 est.)
country comparison to the world: 84
$12.53 billion (2012 est.)

Exports—commodities: cocoa, coffee, timber, petroleum, cotton, bananas, pineapples, palm oil, fish

Exports—partners: Netherlands 8.8%, US 8.1%, Nigeria 8%, Germany 7.5%, France 4.5%, Canada 4.2% (2012)

Imports: $9.859 billion (2013 est.)
country comparison to the world: 102
$8.973 billion (2012 est.)

Imports—commodities: fuel, capital equipment, foodstuffs

Imports—partners: Nigeria 25%, France 11%, China 7.2% (2012)

Reserves of foreign exchange and gold:
$4.085 billion (31 December 2013 est.)
country comparison to the world: 100
$3.928 billion (31 December 2012 est.)

Debt—external: $8.959 billion (31 December 2013 est.)
country comparison to the world: 102
$8.096 billion (31 December 2012 est.)

Stock of direct foreign investment—at home:
$NA

Stock of direct foreign investment—abroad:
$NA

Exchange rates: Communaute Financiere Africaine francs (XOF) per US dollar—
504.6 (2013 est.)
510.29 (2012 est.)
495.28 (2010 est.)
472.19 (2009)
447.81 (2008)

ENERGY

Electricity—production: 5.721 billion kWh (2010 est.)
country comparison to the world: 116

Electricity—consumption: 3.865 billion kWh (2010 est.)
country comparison to the world: 124

Electricity—exports: 471 million kWh (2010 est.)
country comparison to the world: 65

Electricity—imports: 0 kWh (2012 est.)
country comparison to the world: 157

Electricity—installed generating capacity:
1.222 million kW (2010 est.)
country comparison to the world: 119

Electricity—from fossil fuels: 50.6% of total installed capacity (2010 est.)
country comparison to the world: 155

Electricity—from nuclear fuels: 0% of total installed capacity (2010 est.)
country comparison to the world: 112

Electricity—from hydroelectric plants: 49.4% of total installed capacity (2010 est.)
country comparison to the world: 43

Electricity—from other renewable sources:
0% of total installed capacity (2010 est.)
country comparison to the world: 184

Crude oil—production: 38,560 bbl/day (2012 est.)
country comparison to the world: 65

Crude oil—exports: 32,190 bbl/day (2010 est.)
country comparison to the world: 49

Crude oil—imports: 49,780 bbl/day (2010 est.)
country comparison to the world: 57

Crude oil—proved reserves: 100 million bbl (1 January 2013 es)
country comparison to the world: 70

Refined petroleum products—production:
55,890 bbl/day (2010 est.)
country comparison to the world: 82

Refined petroleum products—consumption:
24,630 bbl/day (2011 est.)
country comparison to the world: 123

Refined petroleum products—exports:
38,300 bbl/day (2010 est.)
country comparison to the world: 64

Refined petroleum products—imports:
4,810 bbl/day (2010 est.)
country comparison to the world: 153

Natural gas—production: 1.5 billion cu m (2011 est.)
country comparison to the world: 61

Natural gas—consumption: 1.5 billion cu m (2010 est.)
country comparison to the world: 83

Natural gas—exports: 0 cu m (2011 est.)
country comparison to the world: 121

Natural gas—imports: 0 cu m (2011 est.)
country comparison to the world: 208

Natural gas—proved reserves: 28.32 billion cu m (1 January 2013 es)
country comparison to the world: 72

Carbon dioxide emissions from consumption of energy: 6.68 million Mt (2011 est.)
country comparison to the world: 119

COMMUNICATIONS

Telephones—main lines in use: 268,000 (2012)
country comparison to the world: 121

Telephones—mobile cellular: 19.827 million (2012)
country comparison to the world: 49

Telephone system: *general assessment:* well-developed by African standards; telecommunications sector privatized in late 1990s and operational fixed-lines have increased since that time with two fixed-line providers operating over open-wire lines, microwave radio relay, and fiber-optics; 90% digitalized
domestic: with multiple mobile-cellular service providers competing in the market, usage has increased sharply to roughly 80 per 100 persons
international: country code—225; landing point for the SAT-3/WASC fiber-optic submarine cable that provides connectivity to Europe and Asia; satellite earth stations—2 Intelsat (1 Atlantic Ocean and 1 Indian Ocean) (2011)

Broadcast media: 2 state-owned TV stations; no private terrestrial TV stations, but satellite TV subscription service is available; 2 state-owned radio stations; some private radio stations; transmissions of several international broadcasters are available (2007)

Internet country code: .ci

Internet hosts: 9,115 (2012)
country comparison to the world: 137

Internet users: 967,300 (2009)
country comparison to the world: 103

TRANSPORTATION

Airports: 27 (2013)
country comparison to the world: 124

Airports—with paved runways: *total:* 7
over 3,047 m: 1
2,438 to 3,047 m: 2
1,524 to 2,437 m: 4 (2013)

Airports—with unpaved runways: *total:* 2 0
1,524 to 2,437 m: 6
914 to 1,523 m: 11
under 914 m: 3 (2013)

Heliports: 1 (2013)

Pipelines: condensate 101 km; gas 256 km; oil 118 km; oil/gas/water 5 km; water 7 km (2013)

Railways: total: 660 km
country comparison to the world: 104
narrow gauge: 660 km 1.000-m gauge
note: an additional 622 km of this railroad extends into Burkina Faso (2008)

Roadways: total: 81,996 km
country comparison to the world: 58
paved: 6,502 km
unpaved: 75,494 km
note: includes intercity and urban roads; another 20,000 km of dirt roads are in poor condition and 150,000 km of dirt roads are impassable (2007)

Waterways:
980 km (navigable rivers, canals, and numerous coastal lagoons) (2011)
country comparison to the world: 67

Ports and terminals:
major seaport(s): Abidjan, San-Pedro
oil/gas terminal(s): Espoir Offshore Terminal

MILITARY

Military branches: Republican Forces of Cote d'Ivoire (Force Republiques de Cote d'Ivoire, FRCI): Army, Navy, Cote d'Ivoire Air Force (Force Aerienne de la Cote d'Ivoire)
note: FRCI is the former Armed Forces of the New Forces (FAFN) (2013)

Military service age and obligation: 18-25 years of age for compulsory and voluntary male and female military service; conscription is not enforced; voluntary recruitment of former rebels into the new national army is restricted to ages 22-29 (2012)

Manpower available for military service:
males age 16-49: 5,247,522
females age 16-49: 5,047,901 (2010 est.)

Manpower fit for military service:
males age 16-49: 3,360,087
females age 16-49: 3,196,033 (2010 est.)

Manpower reaching militarily significant age annually: *male:* 247,011
female: 242,958 (2010 est.)

Military expenditures: 1.65% of GDP (2012)
country comparison to the world: 56
1.49% of GDP (2011)
1.65% of GDP (2010)

TRANSNATIONAL ISSUES

Disputes—international: disputed maritime border between Cote d'Ivoire and Ghana

Refugees and internally displaced persons: *refugees (country of origin):* 9,126 (Liberia) (2012)
IDPs: 40,000—80,000 (post-election conflict in 2010-2011, as well as civil war from 2002-2004; most pronounced in western and southwestern regions) (2011)
stateless persons: 700,000 (2012); note - many Ivoirians lack documentation proving their nationality, which prevent them from accessing education and healthcare; birth on Ivorian soil does not automatically result in citizenship; disputes over citizenship and the associated rights of the large population descended from migrants from neighboring countries is an ongoing source of tension and contributed to the country's 2002 civil war; some observers believe the government's mass naturalizations of thousands of people over the last couple of years is intended to boost its electoral support base; the government in October 2013 acceded to international conventions on statelessness and in August 2013 reformed its nationality law, key steps to clarify the nationality of thousands of residents

Illicit drugs: illicit producer of cannabis, mostly for local consumption; utility as a narcotic transshipment point to Europe reduced by ongoing political instability; while rampant corruption and inadequate supervision leave the banking system vulnerable to money laundering, the lack of a developed financial system limits the country's utility as a major money-laundering center (2008)

CROATIA

INTRODUCTION

Background: The lands that today comprise Croatia were part of the Austro-Hungarian Empire until the close of World War I. In 1918, the Croats, Serbs, and Slovenes formed a kingdom known after 1929 as Yugoslavia. Following World War II, Yugoslavia became a federal independent communist state under the strong hand of Marshal TITO. Although Croatia declared its independence from Yugoslavia in 1991, it took four years of sporadic, but often bitter, fighting before occupying Serb armies were mostly cleared from Croatian lands, along with a majority of Croatia's ethnic Serb population. Under UN supervision, the last Serb-held enclave in eastern Slavonia was returned to Croatia in 1998. The country joined NATO in April 2009 and the EU in July 2013.

GEOGRAPHY

Location: Southeastern Europe, bordering the Adriatic Sea, between Bosnia and Herzegovina and Slovenia

Geographic coordinates: 45 10 N, 15 30 E

Map references: Europe

Area: *total:* 56,594 sq km
country comparison to the world: 127
land: 55,974 sq km
water: 620 sq km

Area—comparative: slightly smaller than West Virginia

Land boundaries: *total:* 1,982 km
border countries: Bosnia and Herzegovina 932 km, Hungary 329 km, Serbia 241 km, Montenegro 25 km, Slovenia 455 km

Coastline: 5,835 km (mainland 1,777 km, islands 4,058 km)

Maritime claims: *territorial sea:* 12 nm
continental shelf: 200 m depth or to the depth of exploitation

Climate: Mediterranean and continental; continental climate predominant with hot summers and cold winters; mild winters, dry summers along coast

Terrain: geographically diverse; flat plains along Hungarian border, low mountains and highlands near Adriatic coastline and islands

Elevation extremes: *lowest point:* Adriatic Sea 0 m
highest point: Dinara 1,831 m

Natural resources: oil, some coal, bauxite, low-grade iron ore, calcium, gypsum, natural asphalt, silica, mica, clays, salt, hydropower

Land use: *arable land:* 15.85%
permanent crops: 1.47%
other: 82.69% (2011)

Irrigated land: 36.27 sq km (2010)

Total renewable water resources: 105.5 cu km (2011)

Natural hazards: destructive earthquakes

Environment—current issues: air pollution (from metallurgical plants) and resulting acid rain is damaging the forests; coastal pollution from industrial and domestic waste; landmine removal and reconstruction of infrastructure consequent to 1992-95 civil strife

Environment—international agreements: *party to:* Air Pollution, Air Pollution-Nitrogen Oxides, Air Pollution-Persistent Organic Pollutants, Air Pollution-Sulfur 94, Air Pollution-Volatile Organic Compounds, Biodiversity, Climate Change, Climate Change-Kyoto Protocol, Desertification, Endangered Species, Hazardous Wastes, Law of the Sea, Marine Dumping, Ozone Layer Protection, Ship Pollution, Wetlands, Whaling
signed, but not ratified: none of the selected agreements

Geography—note: controls most land routes from Western Europe to Aegean Sea and Turkish Straits; most Adriatic Sea islands lie off the coast of Croatia—some 1,200 islands, islets, ridges, and rocks

PEOPLE AND SOCIETY

Nationality: *noun:* Croat(s), Croatian(s)
adjective: Croatian

Ethnic groups: Croat 90.4%, Serb 4.4%, other 4.4% (including Bosniak, Hungarian, Slovene, Czech, and Roma), unspecified 0.8% (2011 est.)

Languages: Croatian (official) 95.6%, Serbian 1.2%, other 3% (including Hungarian, Czech, Slovak, and Albanian), unspecified 0.2% (2011 est.)

Religions: Roman Catholic 86.3%, Orthodox 4.4%, Muslim 1.5%, other 1.5%, unspecified 2.5%, not religious or atheist 3.8% (2011 est.)

Population: 4,470,534 (July 2014 est.)
country comparison to the world: 126

Age structure: *0-14 years:* 14.5% (male 332,079/female 314,842)
15-24 years: 12.1% (male 275,957/female 263,796)
25-54 years: 41.1% (male 910,591/female 928,434)
55-64 years: 17.8% (male 315,791/female 334,017)
65 years and over: 17.4% (male 320,898/female 474,129) (2014 est.)

Dependency ratios:
total dependency ratio: 49.6 %
youth dependency ratio: 22.3 %
elderly dependency ratio: 27.4 %
potential support ratio: 3.7 (2013)

Median age: *total:* 42.1 years
male: 40.2 years
female: 43.9 years (2014 est.)

Population growth rate: -0.12% (2014 est.)
country comparison to the world: 208

Birth rate: 9.49 births/1,000 population (2014 est.)
country comparison to the world: 201

Death rate: 12.13 deaths/1,000 population (2014 est.)
country comparison to the world: 26

Net migration rate: 1.43 migrant(s)/1,000 population (2014 est.)
country comparison to the world: 54

Urbanization: *urban population:* 58% of total population (2010)
rate of urbanization: 0.4% annual rate of change (2010-15 est.)

Major urban areas—population:
ZAGREB (capital) 686,000 (2011)

Sex ratio: *at birth:* 1.06 male(s)/female
0-14 years: 1.06 male(s)/female
15-24 years: 1.05 male(s)/female
25-54 years: 0.98 male(s)/female
55-64 years: 0.93 male(s)/female
65 years and over: 0.66 male(s)/female
total population: 0.93 male(s)/female (2014 est.)

Mother's mean age at first birth: 27.7 (2010 est.)

Maternal mortality rate:
17 deaths/100,000 live births (2010)
country comparison to the world: 142

Infant mortality rate: *total:* 5.87 deaths/1,000 live births
country comparison to the world: 172
male: 5.99 deaths/1,000 live births
female: 5.73 deaths/1,000 live births (2014 est.)

Life expectancy at birth: *total population:* 76.41 years
country comparison to the world: 79
male: 72.81 years
female: 80.2 years (2014 est.)

Total fertility rate: 1.45 children born/woman (2014 est.)
country comparison to the world: 199

Health expenditures: 7.8% of GDP (2010)
country comparison to the world: 66

Physicians density: 2.72 physicians/1,000 population (2010)

Hospital bed density: 6 beds/1,000 population (2011)

Drinking water source:
improved:
urban: 99.8% of population
rural: 96.8% of population
total: 98.5% of population
unimproved:
urban: 0.2% of population
rural: 3.2% of population
total: 1.5% of population (2011 est.)

Sanitation facility access:
improved:
urban: 98.6% of population
rural: 97.6% of population
total: 98.2% of population
unimproved:
urban: 1.4% of population
rural: 2.4% of population
total: 1.8% of population (2011 est.)

HIV/AIDS—adult prevalence rate:
less than 0.1% (2009 est.)
country comparison to the world: 132

HIV/AIDS—people living with HIV/AIDS:
fewer than 1,000 (2009 est.)
country comparison to the world: 149

HIV/AIDS—deaths: fewer than 100 (2009 est.)
country comparison to the world: 130

Major infectious diseases: *degree of risk:* intermediate
vectorborne diseases: tickborne encephalitis
note: highly pathogenic H5N1 avian influenza has been identified in this country; it poses a negligible risk with extremely rare cases possible among US citizens who have close contact with birds (2013)

Obesity—adult prevalence rate: 24.2% (2008)
country comparison to the world: 66

Education expenditures: 4.3% of GDP (2010)
country comparison to the world: 99

Literacy: *definition:* age 15 and over can read and write
total population: 98.9%
male: 99.5%
female: 98.3% (2011 est.)

School life expectancy (primary to tertiary education): *total:* 15 years
male: 14 years
female: 15 years (2011)

Unemployment, youth ages 15-24: *total:* 43.1%
country comparison to the world: 9
male: 42.3%
female: 44.3% (2012)

GOVERNMENT

Country name: *conventional long form:* Republic of Croatia
conventional short form: Croatia
local long form: Republika Hrvatska
local short form: Hrvatska
former: People's Republic of Croatia, Socialist Republic of Croatia

Government type: parliamentary democracy

Capital: *name:* Zagreb
geographic coordinates: 45 48 N, 16 00 E
time difference: UTC+1 (6 hours ahead of Washington, DC during Standard Time)
daylight saving time: +1hr, begins last Sunday in March; ends last Sunday in October

Administrative divisions: 20 counties (zupanije, zupanija—singular) and 1 city* (grad—singular) with special county status; Bjelovarsko-Bilogorska, Brodsko-Posavska, Dubrovacko-Neretvanska (Dubrovnik-Neretva), Istarska (Istria), Karlovacka, Koprivnicko-Krizevacka, Krapinsko-Zagorska, Licko-Senjska (Lika-Senj), Medimurska, Osjecko-Baranjska, Pozesko-Slavonska (Pozega-Slavonia), Primorsko-Goranska, Sibensko-Kninska, Sisacko-Moslavacka, Splitsko-Dalmatinska (Split-Dalmatia), Varazdinska, Viroviticko-Podravska, Vukovarsko-Srijemska, Zadarska, Zagreb*, Zagrebacka (Zagreb county)

Independence: 25 June 1991 (from Yugoslavia)

National holiday: Independence Day, 8 October (1991) and Statehood Day, 25 June (1991); note—25 June 1991 was the day the Croatian parliament voted for independence; following a three-month moratorium to allow the European Community to solve the Yugoslav crisis peacefully, Parliament adopted a decision on 8 October 1991 to sever constitutional relations with Yugoslavia

Constitution: several previous; latest adopted 22 December 1990; amended several times, last in December 2013 through public referendum (2012)

Legal system: civil law system influenced by legal heritage of Austria-Hungary; note—Croatian law was fully harmonized with the European Community acquis as of the June 2010 completion of EU accession negotiations

International law organization participation: has not submitted an ICJ jurisdiction declaration; accepts ICCt jurisdiction

Suffrage: 18 years of age, 16 if employed; universal

Executive branch: *chief of state:* President Ivo JOSIPOVIC (since 18 February 2010)
head of government: Prime Minister Zoran MILANOVIC (since 23 December 2011); First Deputy Prime Minister Vesna PUSIC (since 16 November 2012)
cabinet: Council of Ministers named by the prime minister and approved by the parliamentary assembly (For more information visit the World Leaders website)
elections: president elected by popular vote for a five-year term (eligible for a second term); election last held on 10 January 2010 (next to be held in December 2014); the leader of the majority party or the leader of the majority coalition usually appointed prime minister by the president and then approved by the assembly
election results: Ivo JOSIPOVIC elected president; percent of vote in the second round—Ivo JOSIPOVIC 60%, Milan BANDIC 40%

Legislative branch: unicameral Assembly or Sabor (151 seats; members elected from party lists by popular vote to serve four-year terms; each of 10 electoral districts elect 14 members, Croatian citizens abroad vote as an electoral district and elect 3 members, national minorities vote as an electoral district and elect 8 members)
elections: last held on 4 December 2011 (next to be held in late 2015)
election results: percent of vote by party/coalition—Kukuriku 40.0%, HDZ-led Coalitiion 23.8%, Croatian Laborists-Labor Party 5.1%, HSS 3.0%, HDSSB 2.9%, Independent list of Ivan Grubisic 2.8%, HCSP-HSP AS 2.8%, other 19.6%; number of seats by party/coalition—Kukuriku 80 (SDP 61, HNS 13, IDS 3, HSU 3), HDZ-led coalition 47 (HDZ 44, HGS 2, DC 1), Croatian Laborists-Labor Party 6, HDSSB 6, SDSS 3, Independent list of Ivan Grubisic 2, HSS 1, HCSP-HSP AS 1, other 5
note: seats by party as of 25 March 2014—SDP 58, HDZ 42, HNS 13, HDSSB 7, Croatian Laborists—Labor Party 6, HSU 4, SDSS 3, HGS 2, IDS 2, BDSH 1, DC 1, HSS 1, HSP AS 1, ORaH 1, independents 9

Judicial branch: *highest court(s):* Supreme Court (consists of the court president and vice president, 25 civil department justices, and 16 criminal department justices)
judge selection and term of office: president of Supreme Court nominated by president of Croatia and elected by Croatian Sabor for a 4-year term; other Supreme Court justices appointed by National Judicial Council; all judges serve until age 70
subordinate courts: Administrative Court; county, municipal, and specialized courts; note—there is an 11-member Constitutional Court with jurisdiction limited to constitutional issues but is outside Croatia's judicial system

Political parties and leaders: Bosniak Democratic Party of Croatia or BDSH [Medzad HODZIC]; Croatian Civic Party or HGS [Zeljko KERUM]; Croatian Democratic Congress of Slavonia and Baranja or HDSSB [Vladimir SISLJAGIC]; Croatian Democratic Union or HDZ [Tomislav KARAMARKO]; Croatian Laborists—Labor Party [Dragutin LESAR]; Croatian Party of Rights—dr. Ante Starcevic or HSP AS [Ruza TOMASIC]; Croatian Peasant Party or HSS [Branko HRG]; Croatian Pensioner Party or HSU [Silvano HRELJA]; Croatian People's Party—Liberal Democrats or HNS [Vesna

PUSIC]; Croatian Pure Party of Rights or HCSP [Josip MILJIC]; Democratic Centre or DC [Vesna SKARE-OZBOLT]; HDZ-led Coalition [Tomislav KARAMARKO] (includes HDZ, HGS, and DC); Independent Democratic Serb Party or SDSS [Vojislav STANIMIROVIC]; Independent List of Ivan Grubisic [Ivan GRUBISIC]; Istrian Democratic Assembly or IDS [Ivan JAKOVCIC]; Kukuriku Coalition [Zoran MILANOVIC] (includes SDP, HNS, IDS, and HSU); Social Democratic Party of Croatia or SDP [Zoran MILANOVIC]; Sustainable Development for Croatia or ORaH [Mirela HOLY]

Political pressure groups and leaders: *other:* human rights groups

International organization participation: Australia Group, BIS, BSEC (observer), CD, CE, CEI, EAPC, EBRD, EU, FAO, G-11, IADB, IAEA, IBRD, ICAO, ICC (national committees), ICRM, IDA, IFAD, IFC, IFRCS, IHO, ILO, IMF, IMO, IMSO, Interpol, IOC, IOM, IPU, ISO, ITSO, ITU, ITUC (NGOs), MIGA, MINURSO, MINUSTAH, NAM (observer), NATO, NSG, OAS (observer), OIF (observer), OPCW, OSCE, PCA, SELEC, UN, UNCTAD, UNDOF, UNESCO, UNFICYP, UNHCR, UNIDO, UNIFIL, UNMIL, UNMOGIP, UNWTO, UPU, WCO, WHO, WIPO, WMO, WTO, ZC

Diplomatic representation in the US:
chief of mission: Ambassador Josko PARO (since 20 April 2012)
chancery: 2343 Massachusetts Avenue NW, Washington, DC 20008
telephone: [1] (202) 588-5899
FAX: [1] (202) 588-8936
consulate(s) general: Chicago, Los Angeles, New York

Diplomatic representation from the US:
chief of mission: Ambassador Kenneth MERTEN (since 3 October 2012)
embassy: 2 Thomas Jefferson Street, 10010 Zagreb
mailing address: use street address
telephone: [385] (1) 661-2200
FAX: [385] (1) 661-2373

Flag description: three equal horizontal bands of red (top), white, and blue—the Pan-Slav colors—superimposed by the Croatian coat of arms; the coat of arms consists of one main shield (a checkerboard of 13 red and 12 silver (white) fields) surmounted by five smaller shields that form a crown over the main shield; the five small shields represent five historic regions, they are (from left to right): Croatia, Dubrovnik, Dalmatia, Istria, and Slavonia
note: the Pan-Slav colors were inspired by the 19th-century flag of Russia

National symbol(s): red-white checkerboard

National anthem: *name:* "Lijepa nasa domovino" (Our Beautiful Homeland)
lyrics/music: Antun MIHANOVIC/Josip RUNJANIN
note: adopted 1972; "Lijepa nasa domovino," whose lyrics were written in 1835, served as an unofficial anthem beginning in 1891

ECONOMY

Economy—overview: Though still one of the wealthiest of the former Yugoslav republics, Croatia's economy suffered badly during the 1991-95 war. The country's output during that time collapsed and Croatia missed the early waves of investment in Central and Eastern Europe that followed the fall of the Berlin Wall. Between 2000 and 2007, however, Croatia's economic fortunes began to improve with moderate but steady GDP growth between 4% and 6% led by a rebound in tourism and credit-driven consumer spending. Inflation over the same period remained tame and the currency, the kuna, stable. Croatia experienced an abrupt slowdown in the economy in 2008 and has yet to recover; economic growth was stagnant or negative in each year since 2009. Difficult problems still remain, including a stubbornly high unemployment rate, uneven regional development, and a challenging investment climate. Croatia continues to face reduced foreign investment. On 1 July 2013 Croatia joined the EU, following a decade-long application process. Croatia will be a member of the European Exchange Rate Mechanism until it meets the criteria for joining the Economic and Monetary Union and adopts the euro as its currency. EU accession has increased pressure on the government to reduce Croatia's relatively high public debt, which triggered the EU's excessive deficit procedure for fiscal consolidation. Zagreb has cut spending since 2012, and the government also raised additional revenues through more stringent tax collection and by raising the Value Added Tax. The government has also sought to accelerate privatization of non-strategic assets, with mixed success.

GDP (purchasing power parity): $78.9 billion (2013 est.)
country comparison to the world: 84
$79.7 billion (2012 est.)
$81.3 billion (2012 est.)
note: data are in 2013 US dollars

GDP (official exchange rate):
$59.14 billion (2013 est.)

GDP—real growth rate: -1% (2013 est.)
country comparison to the world: 204
-1.9% (2012 est.)
-0.2% (2011 est.)

GDP—per capita (PPP): $17,800 (2013 est.)
country comparison to the world: 78
$17,900 (2012 est.)
$18,200 (2011 est.)
note: data are in 2013 US dollars

Gross national saving: 19.9% of GDP (2013 est.)
country comparison to the world: 78
19.3% of GDP (2012 est.)
19.5% of GDP (2011 est.)

GDP—composition, by end use:
household consumption: 59.2%
government consumption: 20%
investment in fixed capital: 18.5%
investment in inventories: 1.7%
exports of goods and services: 44.4%
imports of goods and services: -43.8% (2013 est.)

GDP—composition, by sector of origin:
agriculture: 5%
industry: 25.8%
services: 69.2% (2013 est.)

Agriculture—products: arable crops (wheat, corn, barley, sugar beet, sunflower, rapeseed, alfalfa, clover); vegetables (potatoes, cabbage, onion, tomato, pepper); fruits (apples, plum, mandarins, olives), grapes for wine; livestock (cattle, cows, pigs); dairy products

Industries: chemicals and plastics, machine tools, fabricated metal, electronics, pig iron and rolled steel products, aluminum, paper, wood products, construction materials, textiles, shipbuilding, petroleum and petroleum refining, food and beverages, tourism

Industrial production growth rate: -1.8% (2013 est.)
country comparison to the world: 182

Labor force: 1.715 million (2013 est.)
country comparison to the world: 124

Labor force—by occupation: *agriculture:* 2.1%
industry: 29%
services: 69% (2012)

Unemployment rate: 21.6% (2013 est.)
country comparison to the world: 166
19.1% (2012 est.)

Population below poverty line: 21.1% (2011)

Household income or consumption by percentage share: *lowest 10%:* 3.3%
highest 10%: 27.5% (2008 est.)

Distribution of family income—Gini index:
32 (2010)
country comparison to the world: 108
29 (1998)

Budget: *revenues:* $17.87 billion
expenditures: $20.43 billion (2013 est.)

Taxes and other revenues:
36.9% of GDP (2013 est.)
country comparison to the world: 57

Budget surplus (+) or deficit (-):
-4.4% of GDP (2013 est.)
country comparison to the world: 157

Public debt: 66.2% of GDP (2013 est.)
country comparison to the world: 41
55.6% of GDP (2012 est.)

Fiscal year: calendar year
Inflation rate (consumer prices):
2.2% (2013 est.)
country comparison to the world: 82
3.4% (2012 est.)

Central bank discount rate: 7% (31 December 2013 est.)
country comparison to the world: 41
7% (31 December 2012 est.)

Commercial bank prime lending rate:
9% (31 December 2013 est.)
country comparison to the world: 95
9.48% (31 December 2012 est.)

Stock of narrow money: $10.38 billion (31 January 2014 est.)
country comparison to the world: 77
$10.64 billion (31 December 2012 est.)

Stock of broad money: $49.3 billion (31 December 2013 est.)
country comparison to the world: 70
$493.7 billion (31 December 2012 est.)

Stock of domestic credit: $46.65 billion (31 December 2013 est.)
country comparison to the world: 62
$46.23 billion (31 December 2012 est.)

Market value of publicly traded shares:
$21.63 billion (31 December 2013 est.)
country comparison to the world: 60
$23.24 billion (31 December 2012)
$23.75 billion (31 December 2011 est.)

Current account balance: -$102.3 million (2013 est.)
country comparison to the world: 76
-$17.59 million (2012 est.)

Exports: $12.36 billion (2013 est.)
country comparison to the world: 90
$13.16 billion (2012 est.)

Exports—commodities: transport equipment, machinery, textiles, chemicals, foodstuffs, fuels

Exports—partners: Italy 14.1%, Bosnia Herzegovina 13.1%, Germany 11.1%, Slovenia 10.1%, Austria 6.3% (2012 est.)

Imports: $21.74 billion (2013 est.)

country comparison to the world: 76
$22.16 billion (2012 est.)

Imports—commodities: machinery, transport and electrical equipment; chemicals, fuels and lubricants; foodstuffs

Imports—partners: Germany 13.7%, Italy 12.5%, Slovenia 11.5%, Austria 9.1%, Hungary 6.2%, Russia 5.4% (2012 est.)

Reserves of foreign exchange and gold: $11.46 billion (31 December 2013 est.)
country comparison to the world: 72
$11.95 billion (31 December 2012 est.)

Debt—external: $60.47 billion (31 December 2013 est.)
country comparison to the world: 57
$61.39 billion (2012 est.)

Stock of direct foreign investment—at home: $37.5 billion (31 December 2013 est.)
country comparison to the world: 58
$36.08 billion (31 December 2012 est.)

Stock of direct foreign investment—abroad: $6.081 billion (31 December 2013 est.)
country comparison to the world: 63
$5.581 billion (31 December 2012 est.)

Exchange rates: kuna (HRK) per US dollar—
5.775 (2013 est.)
5.8503 (2012 est.)
5.498 (2010 est.)
5.2692 (2009)
4.98 (2008)

ENERGY

Electricity—production: 14.24 billion kWh (2013 est.)
country comparison to the world: 86

Electricity—consumption: 16.7 billion kWh (2012 est.)
country comparison to the world: 73

Electricity—exports: 3.294 billion kWh (2013 est.)
country comparison to the world: 33

Electricity—imports: 6.844 billion kWh (2013 est.)
country comparison to the world: 31

Electricity—installed generating capacity: 4.132 million kW (2010 est.)
country comparison to the world: 79

Electricity—from fossil fuels: 45.9% of total installed capacity (2010 est.)
country comparison to the world: 162

Electricity—from nuclear fuels: 0% of total installed capacity (2010 est.)
country comparison to the world: 106

Electricity—from hydroelectric plants: 44.7% of total installed capacity (2010 est.)
country comparison to the world: 53

Electricity—from other renewable sources: 2.3% of total installed capacity (2010 est.)
country comparison to the world: 66

Crude oil—production: 11,930 bbl/day (2013 est.)
country comparison to the world: 86

Crude oil—exports: 0 bbl/day (2013 est.)
country comparison to the world: 127

Crude oil—imports: 51,470 bbl/day (2013 est.)
country comparison to the world: 56

Crude oil—proved reserves: 71 million bbl (1 January 2013 es)
country comparison to the world: 77

Refined petroleum products—production: 65,410 bbl/day (2013 est.)
country comparison to the world: 80

Refined petroleum products—consumption: 74,410 bbl/day (2012 est.)
country comparison to the world: 88

Refined petroleum products—exports: 30,120 bbl/day (2013 est.)
country comparison to the world: 69

Refined petroleum products—imports: 26,670 bbl/day (2013 est.)
country comparison to the world: 95

Natural gas—production: 1.863 billion cu m (2013 est.)
country comparison to the world: 60

Natural gas—consumption: 2.755 billion cu m (2012 est.)
country comparison to the world: 76

Natural gas—exports: 392 million cu m (2013 est.)
country comparison to the world: 47

Natural gas—imports: 1.137 billion cu m (2013 est.)
country comparison to the world: 55

Natural gas—proved reserves: 24.92 billion cu m (1 January 2013 es)
country comparison to the world: 74

Carbon dioxide emissions from consumption of energy: 22.35 million Mt (2011 est.)
country comparison to the world: 81

COMMUNICATIONS

Telephones—main lines in use: 1.64 million (2012)
country comparison to the world: 65

Telephones—mobile cellular: 4.97 million (2012)
country comparison to the world: 112

Telephone system: *general assessment:* the telecommunications network has improved steadily since the mid-1990s, covering much of what were once inaccessible areas; local lines are digital
domestic: fixed-line teledensity holding steady at about 40 per 100 persons; mobile-cellular telephone subscriptions exceed the population
international: country code—385; digital international service is provided through the main switch in Zagreb; Croatia participates in the Trans-Asia-Europe (TEL) fiber-optic project, which consists of 2 fiber-optic trunk connections with Slovenia and a fiber-optic trunk line from Rijeka to Split and Dubrovnik; the ADRIA-1 submarine cable provides connectivity to Albania and Greece (2011)

Broadcast media: the national state-owned public broadcaster, Croatian Radio television (HRT), operates 4 terrestrial TV networks, a satellite channel that rebroadcasts programs for Croatians living abroad, and 6 regional TV centers; 2 private broadcasters operate national terrestrial networks; roughly 25 privately owned regional TV stations; multi-channel cable and satellite TV subscription services are available; state-owned public broadcaster operates 3 national radio networks and 9 regional radio stations; 2 privately owned national radio networks and more than 170 regional, county, city, and community radio stations (2012)

Internet country code: .hr

Internet hosts:729,420 (2012)
country comparison to the world: 50

Internet users: 2.234 million (2009)
country comparison to the world: 73

TRANSPORTATION

Airports: 69 (2013)
country comparison to the world: 7 2

Airports—with paved runways: *total:* 2 4
over 3,047 m: 2
2,438 to 3,047 m: 6
1,524 to 2,437 m: 3
914 to 1,523 m: 3
under 914 m: 10 (2013)

Airports—with unpaved runways: *total:* 4 5
1,524 to 2,437 m: 1
914 to 1,523 m: 6
under 914 m: 38 (2013)

Heliports: 1 (2013)

Pipelines: gas 2,410 km; oil 610 km (2011)

Railways: *total:* 2,722 km
country comparison to the world: 61
standard gauge: 2,722 km 1.435-m gauge (984 km electrified) (2011)

Roadways: total: 29,410 km (includes 1,254 km of expressways) (2011)
country comparison to the world: 97

Waterways: 785 km (2009)
country comparison to the world: 74

Merchant marine: *total:* 7 7
country comparison to the world: 59
by type: bulk carrier 24, cargo 7, chemical tanker 8, passenger/cargo 27, petroleum tanker 10, refrigerated cargo 1
foreign-owned: 2 (Norway 2)
registered in other countries: 31 (Bahamas 1, Belize 1, Liberia 1, Malta 6, Marshall Islands 12, Panama 2, Saint Vincent and the Grenadines 8) (2010)

Ports and terminals:
major seaport(s): Ploce, Rijeka, Sibernik, Split
river port(s): Vukovar (Danube)
oil/gas terminal(s): Omisalj

MILITARY

Military branches: Armed Forces of the Republic of Croatia (Oruzane Snage Republike Hrvatske, OSRH) consists of five major commands directly subordinate to a General Staff: Ground Forces (Hrvatska Kopnena Vojska, HKoV), Naval Forces (Hrvatska Ratna Mornarica, HRM; includes coast guard), Air Force and Air Defense Command (Hrvatsko Ratno Zrakoplovstvo I Protuzracna Obrana), Joint Education and Training Command, Logistics Command; Military Police Force supports each of the three Croatian military forces (2012)

Military service age and obligation: 18-27 years of age for voluntary military service; 6-month service obligation (2012)

Manpower available for military service:
males age 16-49: 1,016,234
females age 16-49: 1,017,355 (2010 est.)

Manpower fit for military service:
males age 16-49: 770,710
females age 16-49: 839,732 (2010 est.)

Manpower reaching militarily significant age annually: *male:* 28,334
female: 27,015 (2010 est.)

Military expenditures: 1.7% of GDP (2012)
country comparison to the world: 52
1.77% of GDP (2011)
1.7% of GDP (2010)

TRANSNATIONAL ISSUES

Disputes—international: dispute remains with Bosnia and Herzegovina over several small sections of the boundary related to maritime access that hinders ratification of the 1999 border agreement; since the breakup of Yugoslavia in the early 1990s, Croatia and Slovenia have each claimed sovereignty over Pirin Bay and four villages, and Slovenia has objected to Croatia's claim of an exclusive economic zone in the Adriatic Sea; in 2009, however Croatia and Slovenia signed a binding international arbitration agreement to define their disputed land and maritime borders, which led to Slovenia lifting its objections to Croatia joining the EU; Slovenia continues to impose a hard border Schengen regime with Croatia, which joined the EU in 2013 but has not yet fulfilled Schengen requirements; as a European Union peripheral state, Slovenia imposed a hard border Schengen regime with non-member Croatia in December 2007

Refugees and internally displaced persons: *stateless persons:* 2,886 (2012)

Illicit drugs: transit point along the Balkan route for Southwest Asian heroin to Western Europe; has been used as a transit point for maritime shipments of South American cocaine bound for Western Europe (2008)

CUBA

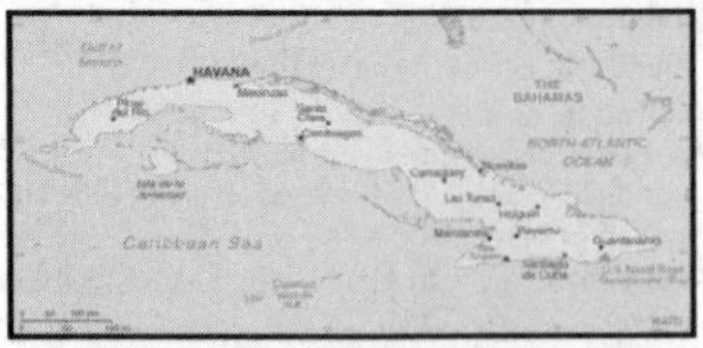

INTRODUCTION

Background: The native Amerindian population of Cuba began to decline after the European discovery of the island by Christopher COLUMBUS in 1492 and following its development as a Spanish colony during the next several centuries. Large numbers of African slaves were imported to work the coffee and sugar plantations, and Havana became the launching point for the annual treasure fleets bound for Spain from Mexico and Peru. Spanish rule eventually provoked an independence movement and occasional rebellions that were harshly suppressed. US intervention during the Spanish-American War in 1898 assisted the Cubans in overthrowing Spanish rule. Subsequently, the 1901 Platt Amendment to the Cuban constitution authorized the US to intevene in Cuba in the event of instability. The Treaty of Paris established Cuban independence from the US in 1902 after which the island experienced a string of governments mostly dominated by the military and corrupt politicians. Fidel CASTRO led a rebel army to victory in 1959; his iron rule held the subsequent regime together for nearly five decades. He stepped down as president in February 2008 in favor of his younger brother Raul CASTRO. Cuba's communist revolution, with Soviet support, was exported throughout Latin America and Africa during the 1960s, 1970s, and 1980s. The country faced a severe economic downturn in 1990 following the withdrawal of former Soviet subsidies worth $4-6 billion annually. Cuba at times portrays the US embargo, in place since 1961, as the source if its difficulties. Illicit migration to the US—using homemade rafts, alien smugglers, air flights, or via the US's southwest border—is a continuing problem. The US Coast Guard interdicted 1,357 Cuban nationals attempting to cross the Straits of Florida in 2013. Also in 2013, 14,251 Cuban migrants presented themselves at various land border ports of entry through out the US.

GEOGRAPHY

Location: Caribbean, island between the Caribbean Sea and the North Atlantic Ocean, 150 km south of Key West, Florida

Geographic coordinates: 21 30 N, 80 00 W

Map references: Central America and the Caribbean

Area: *total:* 110,860 sq km
country comparison to the world: 106
land: 109,820 sq km water: 1,040 sq km

Area—comparative: slightly smaller than Pennsylvania

Land boundaries: *total:* 29 km
border countries: US Naval Base at Guantanamo Bay 29 km
note: Guantanamo Naval Base is leased by the US and remains part of Cuba

Coastline: 3,735 km

Maritime claims: *territorial sea:* 12 nm
contiguous zone: 24 nm
exclusive economic zone: 200 nm

Climate: tropical; moderated by trade winds; dry season (November to April); rainy season (May to October)

Terrain: mostly flat to rolling plains, with rugged hills and mountains in the southeast

Elevation extremes: *lowest point:* Caribbean Sea 0 m
highest point: Pico Turquino 2,005 m

Natural resources: cobalt, nickel, iron ore, chromium, copper, salt, timber, silica, petroleum, arable land

Land use: *arable land:* 32.31%
permanent crops: 3.55%
other: 64.15% (2011)

Irrigated land: 8,703 sq km (2003)

Total renewable water resources: 38.12 cu km (2011)

Freshwater withdrawal (domestic/industrial/agricultural): *total:* 4.42 cu km/yr (22%/14%/65%)
per capita: 392.6 cu m/yr (2010)

Natural hazards: the east coast is subject to hurricanes from August to November (in general, the country averages about one hurricane every other year); droughts are common

Environment—current issues: air and water pollution; biodiversity loss; deforestation

Environment—international agreements: *party to:* Antarctic Treaty, Biodiversity, Climate Change, Climate Change-Kyoto Protocol, Desertification, Endangered Species, Environmental Modification, Hazardous Wastes, Law of the Sea, Marine Dumping, Ozone Layer Protection, Ship Pollution, Wetlands
signed, but not ratified: Marine Life Conservation

Geography—note: largest country in Caribbean and westernmost island of the Greater Antilles

PEOPLE AND SOCIETY

Nationality: *noun:* Cuban(s)
adjective: Cuban

Ethnic groups: white 64.1%, mestizo 26.6%, black 9.3% (2012 est.)

Languages: Spanish (official)

Religions: nominally Roman Catholic 85%, Protestant, Jehovah's Witnesses, Jewish, Santeria
note: prior to CASTRO assuming power

Population: 11,047,251 (July 2014 est.)
country comparison to the world: 78
Age structure: 0-14 years: 16.3% (male 923,602/female 873,156)
15-24 years: 13.6% (male 770,515/female 732,056)
25-54 years: 47.1% (male 2,618,089/female 2,581,895)
55-64 years: 12.6% (male 551,637/female 602,658)
65 years and over: 12.3% (male 625,330/female 768,313) (2014 est.)

Dependency ratios:
total dependency ratio: 41.9 %
youth dependency ratio: 23 %
elderly dependency ratio: 18.9 %
potential support ratio: 5.3 (2013)

Median age: *total:* 39.9 years
male: 39.1 years
female: 40.8 years (2014 est.)

Population growth rate: -0.14% (2014 est.)
country comparison to the world: 211

Birth rate: 9.9 births/1,000 population (2014 est.)
country comparison to the world: 195

Death rate: 7.64 deaths/1,000 population (2014 est.)
country comparison to the world: 113

Net migration rate: -3.64 migrant(s)/1,000 population (2014 est.)
country comparison to the world: 188

Urbanization: *urban population:* 75% of total population (2010)
rate of urbanization: 0% annual rate of change (2010-15 est.)

Major urban areas—population: HAVANA (capital) 2.116 million (2011)

Sex ratio: *at birth:* 1.06 male(s)/female
0-14 years: 1.06 male(s)/female
15-24 years: 1.05 male(s)/female
25-54 years: 1.01 male(s)/female
55-64 years: 0.99 male(s)/female

65 years and over: 0.82 male(s)/female
total population: 0.99 male(s)/female (2014 est.)

Maternal mortality rate: 73 deaths/100,000 live births (2010)
country comparison to the world: 85

Infant mortality rate: *total:* 4.7 deaths/1,000 live births
country comparison to the world: 183
male: 5.04 deaths/1,000 live births
female: 4.33 deaths/1,000 live births (2014 est.)

Life expectancy at birth: total population: 78.22 years
country comparison to the world: 59
male: 75.92 years
female: 80.65 years (2014 est.)

Total fertility rate: 1.46 children born/woman (2014 est.)
country comparison to the world: 197

Contraceptive prevalence rate: 74.3% (2011)

Health expenditures: 10% of GDP (2011)
country comparison to the world: 27

Physicians density: 6.72 physicians/1,000 population (2010)

Hospital bed density: 5.1 beds/1,000 population (2011)

Drinking water source:
improved:
urban: 96.2% of population
rural: 86.4% of population
total: 93.8% of population
unimproved:
urban: 3.8% of population
rural: 13.6% of population
total: 6.2% of population (2011 est.)

Sanitation facility access:
improved:
urban: 93.7% of population
rural: 87.3% of population
total: 92.1% of population
unimproved:
urban: 6.3% of population
rural: 12.7% of population
total: 7.9% of population (2011 est.)

HIV/AIDS—adult prevalence rate: 0.1% (2012 est.)
country comparison to the world: 133

HIV/AIDS—people living with HIV/AIDS: 4,700 (2012 est.)
country comparison to the world: 123

HIV/AIDS—deaths: fewer than 100 (2009 est.)
country comparison to the world: 131

Major infectious diseases: *degree of risk:* intermediate
food or waterborne diseases: bacterial diarrhea and hepatitis A
vectorborne diseases: dengue fever (2013)

Obesity—adult prevalence rate: 21.5% (2008)
country comparison to the world: 85

Children under the age of 5 years underweight: 3.4% (2000)
country comparison to the world: 107

Education expenditures: 12.8% of GDP (2010)
country comparison to the world: 2

Literacy: *definition:* age 15 and over can read and write
total population: 99.8%
male: 99.8%
female: 99.8% (2011 est.)

School life expectancy (primary to tertiary education): *total:* 15 years
male: 14 years
female: 15 years (2012)

Unemployment, youth ages 15-24:
total: 3.1%
country comparison to the world: 143
male: 2.8%
female: 3.5% (2008)

People—note: illicit emigration is a continuing problem; Cubans attempt to depart the island and enter the US using homemade rafts, alien smugglers, direct flights, or falsified visas; Cubans also use non-maritime routes to enter the US including direct flights to Miami and over-land via the southwest border

GOVERNMENT

Country name: *conventional long form:* Republic of Cuba
conventional short form: Cuba local
long form: Republica de Cuba
local short form: Cuba

Government type: Communist state

Capital: *name:* Havana
geographic coordinates: 23 07 N, 82 21 W
time difference: UTC-5 (same time as Washington, DC during Standard Time)
daylight saving time: +1hr, begins second Sunday in March; ends first Sunday in November; note—Cuba has been known to alter the schedule of DST on short notice in an attempt to conserve electricity for lighting

Administrative divisions: 15 provinces (provincias, singular - provincia) and 1 special municipality* (municipio especial); Artemisa, Camaguey, Ciego de Avila, Cienfuegos, Granma, Guantanamo, Holguin, Isla de la Juventud*, La Habana, Las Tunas, Matanzas, Mayabeque, Pinar del Rio, Sancti Spiritus, Santiago de Cuba, Villa Clara

Independence: 20 May 1902 (from Spain 10 December 1898; administered by the US from 1898 to 1902); not acknowledged by the Cuban Government as a day of independence

National holiday: Triumph of the Revolution, 1 January (1959)

Constitution: several previous; latest adopted by referendum 15 February 1976, effective 24 February 1976; amended 1978, 1992, 2002 (2010)

Legal system: civil law system based on Spanish civil code

International law organization participation: has not submitted an ICJ jurisdiction declaration; non-party state to the ICCt

Suffrage: 16 years of age; universal

Executive branch: *chief of state:* President of the Council of State and President of the Council of Ministers Gen. Raul CASTRO Ruz (president since 24 February 2008); First Vice President of the Council of State and First Vice President of the Council of Ministers Miguel DIAZ-CANEL Bermudez (since 24 February 2013); note—the *president is both the chief of state and head of government*
head of government: President of the Council of State and President of the Council of Ministers Gen. Raul CASTRO Ruz (president since 24 February 2008); First Vice President of the Council of State and First Vice President of the Council of Ministers Miguel DIAZ-CANEL Bermudez (since 24 February 2013)
cabinet: Council of Ministers proposed by the president of the Council of State and appointed by the National Assembly or the 28-member Council of State, elected by the assembly to act on its behalf when it is not in session (For more information visit the World Leaders website)
elections: president and vice presidents elected by the National Assembly for a five-year term; election last held on 24 February 2013 (next to be held in 2018)
election results: Gen. Raul CASTRO Ruz reelected president; percent of legislative vote—100%; Miguel DIAZ-CANEL Bermudez elected vice president; percent of legislative vote—100%

Legislative branch: unicameral National Assembly of People's Power or Asemblea Nacional del Poder Popular (number of seats in the National Assembly is based on population; 614 seats; members elected directly from slates approved by special candidacy commissions to serve five-year terms)
elections: last held on 3 February 2013 (next to be held in 2018)
election results: Cuba's Communist Party is the only legal party, and officially sanctioned candidates run unopposed

Judicial branch: *highest court(s):* People's Supreme Court (consists of court president, vice president, 41 professional justices, and NA lay judges; organized into the "Whole," State Council, and criminal, civil, administrative, labor, crimes against the state, and military courts)
judge selection and term of office: professional judges elected by the National Assembly to serve 2.5-year terms; lay judges nominated by workplace collectives and neighborhood associations and elected by municipal or provincial assemblies; lay judges appointed for 5-year terms and serve up to 30 days per year
subordinate courts: People's Provincial Courts; People's Regional Courts; People's Courts

Political parties and leaders:
Cuban Communist Party or PCC [Raul CASTRO Ruz, first secretary]

Political pressure groups and leaders:
Human Rights Watch National Association of Small Farmers

International organization participation: ACP, ALBA, AOSIS, CELAC, FAO, G-77, IAEA, ICAO, ICC (national committees), ICRM, IFAD, IFRCS, IHO, ILO, IMO, IMSO, Interpol, IOC, IOM (observer), IPU, ISO, ITSO, ITU, LAES, LAIA, NAM, OAS (excluded from formal participation since 1962), OPANAL, OPCW, PCA, Petrocaribe, UN, UNCTAD, UNESCO, UNIDO, Union Latina, UNWTO, UPU, WCO, WFTU (NGOs), WHO, WIPO, WMO, WTO

Diplomatic representation in the US: *none; note*—Cuba has an Interests Section in the Swiss Embassy, headed by Principal Officer Jorge BOLANOS Suarez (since November 2007); address: Cuban Interests Section, Swiss Embassy, 2630 16th Street NW, Washington, DC 20009; telephone: [1] (202) 797-8518; FAX: [1] (202) 797-8521

Diplomatic representation from the US: *none; note*—the US has an Interests Section in the Swiss Embassy, headed by Chief of Mission John P. CAULFIELD (since September 2011); address:

USINT, Swiss Embassy, Calzada between L and M Streets, Vedado, Havana; telephone: [53] (7) 839-4100; FAX: [53] (7) 839-4247; protecting power in Cuba is Switzerland

Flag description: five equal horizontal bands of blue (top, center, and bottom) alternating with white; a red equilateral triangle based on the hoist side bears a white, five-pointed star in the center; the blue bands refer to the three old divisions of the island: central, occidental, and oriental; the white bands describe the purity of the independence ideal; the triangle symbolizes liberty, equality, and fraternity, while the red color stands for the blood shed in the independence struggle; the white star, called La Estrella Solitaria (the Lone Star) lights the way to freedom and was taken from the flag of Texas
note: design similar to the Puerto Rican flag, with the colors of the bands and triangle reversed

National anthem: *name:* "La Bayamesa" (The Bayamo Song)
lyrics/music: Pedro FIGUEREDO
note: adopted 1940; Pedro FIGUEREDO first performed "La Bayamesa" in 1868 during the Ten Years War against the Spanish; a leading figure in the uprising, FIGUEREDO was captured in 1870 and executed by a firing squad; just prior to the fusillade he is reputed to have shouted, "Morir por la Patria es vivir" (To die for the country is to live), a line from the anthem

ECONOMY

Economy—overview: The government continues to balance the need for loosening its socialist economic system against a desire for firm political control. The government in April 2011 held the first Cuban Communist Party Congress in almost 13 years, during which leaders approved a plan for wide-ranging economic changes. President Raul CASTRO said such changes were needed to update the economic model to ensure the survival of socialism. The government has expanded opportunities for self-employment and has introduced limited reforms, some initially implemented in the 1990s, to increase enterprise efficiency and alleviate serious shortages of food, consumer goods, services, and housing. The average Cuban's standard of living remains at a lower level than before the downturn of the 1990s, which was caused by the loss of Soviet aid and domestic inefficiencies. Since late 2000, Venezuela has been providing oil on preferential terms, and it currently supplies over 100,000 barrels per day of petroleum products. Cuba has been paying for the oil, in part, with the services of Cuban personnel in Venezuela including some 30,000 medical professionals.

GDP (purchasing power parity): $121 billion (2012 est.)
country comparison to the world: 68
$117.3 billion (2011 est.)
$114.1 billion (2010 est.)
note: data are in 2013 US dollars

GDP (official exchange rate): $72.3 billion (2012 est.)

GDP—real growth rate: 3.1% (2012 est.)
country comparison to the world: 109
2.8% (2011 est.)
2.4% (2010 est.)

GDP—per capita (PPP): $10,200 (2010 est.)
country comparison to the world: 117
$10,000 (2009 est.)
$10,000 (2008 est.)
note: data are in 2010 US dollars

Gross national saving: 13.4% of GDP (2013 est.)
country comparison to the world: 119
11.1% of GDP (2012 est.)
11.7% of GDP (2011 est.)

GDP—composition, by end use:
household consumption: 52.1%
government consumption: 34.4%
investment in fixed capital: 10%
investment in inventories: -3.4%
exports of goods and services: 26%
imports of goods and services: -19.2% (2013 est.)

GDP—composition, by sector of origin:
agriculture: 3.8%
industry: 22.3%
services: 73.9% (2013 est.)

Agriculture—products: sugar, tobacco, citrus, coffee, rice, potatoes, beans; livestock

Industries: petroleum, nickel/cobalt, pharmaceuticals, tobacco, construction, steel, cement, agricultural machinery, sugar

Industrial production growth rate: 2.6% (2013 est.)
country comparison to the world: 113

Labor force: 5.233 million
country comparison to the world: 72
note: state sector 72.3%, non-state sector 27.7% (2013 est.)

Labor force—by occupation: *agriculture:* 19.7%
industry: 17.1%
services: 63.2% (2011)

Unemployment rate: 4.3% (2013 est.)
country comparison to the world: 37
3.8% (2012 est.)
note: these are official rates; unofficial estimates are about double the official figures

Population below poverty line: NA%

Household income or consumption by percentage share:
lowest 10%: NA%
highest 10%: NA%

Budget: *revenues:* $47.62 billion
expenditures: $50.29 billion (2013 est.)

Taxes and other revenues: 65.9% of GDP (2013 est.)
country comparison to the world: 2

Budget surplus (+) or deficit (-):
-3.7% of GDP (2013 est.)
country comparison to the world: 140

Public debt: 35.9% of GDP (2013 est.)
country comparison to the world: 104
35.8% of GDP (2012 est.)

Fiscal year: calendar year

Inflation rate (consumer prices): 6% (2013 est.)
country comparison to the world: 171
5.5% (2012 est.)

Central bank discount rate: NA%

Commercial bank prime lending rate: NA%

Stock of narrow money: $11.21 billion (31 December 2013 est.)
country comparison to the world: 75
$10.97 billion (31 December 2012 est.)

Stock of broad money: $24.63 billion (31 December 2013 est.)
country comparison to the world: 78
$24.08 billion (31 December 2012 est.)

Stock of domestic credit: $NA

Current account balance: $289.8 million (2013 est.)
country comparison to the world: 55
-$134.4 million (2012 est.)

Exports: $6.252 billion (2013 est.)
country comparison to the world: 107
$5.972 billion (2012 est.)

Exports—commodities: petroleum, nickel, medical products, sugar, tobacco, fish, citrus, coffee

Exports—partners: Canada 17.7%, China 16.9%, Venezuela 12.5%, Netherlands 9%, Spain 5.9% (2012)

Imports: $13.6 billion (2013 est.)
country comparison to the world: 89
$13.72 billion (2012 est.)

Imports—commodities: petroleum, food, machinery and equipment, chemicals

Imports—partners: Venezuela 38.3%, China 10.8%, Spain 8.9%, Brazil 5.2%, US 4.3% (2012)

Reserves of foreign exchange and gold:
$4.993 billion (31 December 2013 est.)
country comparison to the world: 96
$4.693 billion (31 December 2012 est.)

Debt—external: $23.44 billion (31 December 2013 est.)
country comparison to the world: 78
$22.51 billion (31 December 2012 est.)

Stock of direct foreign investment—at home: $NA

Stock of direct foreign investment—abroad:
$4.138 billion (2006 est.)
country comparison to the world: 64

Exchange rates: Cuban pesos (CUP) per US dollar—
1 (2013 est.)
1 (2012 est.)
0.9259 (2010 est.)
0.9259 (2009)
0.9259 (2008)

ENERGY

Electricity—production: 17.8 billion kWh (2011 est.)
country comparison to the world: 7 7

Electricity—consumption: 13.64 billion kWh (2010 est.)
country comparison to the world: 79

Electricity—exports: 0 kWh (2012 est.)
country comparison to the world: 124

Electricity—imports: 0 kWh (2012 est.)
country comparison to the world: 131

Electricity—installed generating capacity:
5.914 million kW (2011 est.)
country comparison to the world: 71

Electricity—from fossil fuels: 99.3% of total installed capacity (2011 est.)
country comparison to the world: 52

Electricity—from nuclear fuels: 0% of total installed capacity (2011 est.)
country comparison to the world: 71

Electricity—from hydroelectric plants: 0.6% of total installed capacity (2011 est.)
country comparison to the world: 143

Electricity—from other renewable sources:
0.1% of total installed capacity (2011 est.)
country comparison to the world: 103

Crude oil—production: 50,800 bbl/day (2012 est.)

country comparison to the world: 62

Crude oil—exports: 83,000 bbl/day (2012 est.)
country comparison to the world: 41

Crude oil—imports: 165,000 bbl/day (2012 est.)
country comparison to the world: 37

Crude oil—proved reserves: 124 million bbl (1 January 2013 es)
country comparison to the world: 69

Refined petroleum products—production: 100,600 bbl/day (2010 est.)
country comparison to the world: 74

Refined petroleum products—consumption: 150,200 bbl/day (2011 est.)
country comparison to the world: 66

Refined petroleum products—exports: 11,320 bbl/day (2010 est.)
country comparison to the world: 83

Refined petroleum products—imports: 4,877 bbl/day (2010 est.)
country comparison to the world: 151

Natural gas—production: 1.03 billion cu m (2012 est.)
country comparison to the world: 64

Natural gas—consumption: 1.03 billion cu m (2012 est.)
country comparison to the world: 89

Natural gas—exports: 0 cu m (2012 est.)
country comparison to the world: 85

Natural gas—imports: 0 cu m (2012 est.)
country comparison to the world: 180

Natural gas—proved reserves: 70.79 billion cu m (1 January 2013 es)
country comparison to the world: 59

Carbon dioxide emissions from consumption of energy: 28.41 million Mt (2011 est.)
country comparison to the world: 78

COMMUNICATIONS

Telephones—main lines in use: 1.217 million (2012)
country comparison to the world: 68

Telephones—mobile cellular: 1.682 million (2012)
country comparison to the world: 149

Telephone system: *general assessment:* greater investment beginning in 1994 and the establishment of a new Ministry of Information Technology and Communications in 2000 has resulted in improvements in the system; national fiber-optic system under development; 95% of switches digitized by end of 2006; mobile-cellular telephone service is expensive and must be paid in convertible pesos, which effectively limits subscribership
domestic: fixed-line density remains low at 10 per 100 inhabitants; mobile-cellular service expanding but remains only about 10 per 100 persons
international: country code—53; the ALBA—1 fiber- optic submarine cable links Cuba, Jamaica, and Venezuela; fiber-optic cable laid to but not linked to US network; satellite earth station—1 Intersputnik (Atlantic Ocean region) (2010)

Broadcast media: government owns and controls all broadcast media with private ownership of electronic media prohibited; government operates 4 national TV networks and many local TV stations; government operates 6 national radio networks, an international station, and many local radio stations; Radio-TV Marti is beamed from the US (2007)

Internet country code: .cu

Internet hosts: 3,244 (2012)
country comparison to the world: 154

Internet users: 1.606 million
country comparison to the world: 79
note: private citizens are prohibited from buying computers or accessing the Internet without special authorization; foreigners may access the Internet in large hotels but are subject to firewalls; some Cubans buy illegal passwords on the black market or take advantage of public outlets to access limited email and the government-controlled "intranet" (2009)

TRANSPORTATION

Airports: 133 (2013)
country comparison to the world: 4 2

Airports—with paved runways: *total:* 6 4
over 3,047 m: 7
2,438 to 3,047 m: 10
1,524 to 2,437 m: 16
914 to 1,523 m: 4
under 914 m: 27 (2013)

Airports—with unpaved runways: *total:* 6 9
914 to 1,523 m: 11
under 914 m: 58 (2013)

Pipelines: gas 41 km; oil 230 km (2013)

Railways: *total:* 8,203 km
country comparison to the world: 25
standard gauge: 8,134 km 1.435-m gauge (124 km electrified)
narrow gauge: 69 km 1.000-m gauge
note: 48 km of standard gauge track is not for public use (2011)

Roadways: total: 60,858 km
country comparison to the world: 69
paved: 29,820 km (includes 639 km of expressways)
unpaved: 31,038 km (2001)

Waterways: 240 km (almost all navigable inland waterways are near the mouths of rivers) (2011)
country comparison to the world: 95

Merchant marine: total: 3
country comparison to the world: 136
by type: cargo 1, passenger 1, refrigerated cargo 1
registered in other countries: 5 (Curacao 1, Panama 2, unknown 2) (2010)

Ports and terminals: *major seaport(s):* Antilla, Cienfuegos, Guantanamo, Havana, Matanzas, Mariel, Nuevitas Bay, Santiago de Cuba

MILITARY

Military branches: Revolutionary Armed Forces (Fuerzas Armadas Revolucionarias, FAR): Revolutionary Army (Ejercito Revolucionario, ER, includes Territorial Militia Troops (Milicia de Tropas de Territoriales, MTT)); Revolutionary Navy (Marina de Guerra Revolucionaria, MGR, includes Marine Corps); Revolutionary Air and Air Defense Forces (Defensas Anti-Aereas y Fuerza Aerea Revolucionaria, DAAFAR), Youth Labor Army (Ejercito Juvenil del Trabajo, EJT) (2013)

Military service age and obligation:
17-28 years of age for compulsory military service; 2-year service obligation; both sexes subject to military service (2012)

Manpower available for military service:
males age 16-49: 2,998,201
females age 16-49: 2,919,107 (2010 est.)

Manpower fit for military service:
males age 16-49: 2,446,131
females age 16-49: 2,375,590 (2010 est.)

Manpower reaching militarily significant age annually: *male:* 72,823
female: 69,108 (2010 est.)

Military—note:
the collapse of the Soviet Union deprived the Cuban military of its major economic and logistic support and had a significant impact on the state of Cuban equipment; the army remains well trained and professional in nature; while the lack of replacement parts for its existing equipment has increasingly affected operational capabilities, Cuba remains able to offer considerable resistance to any regional power (2010)

TRANSNATIONAL ISSUES

Disputes—international: US Naval Base at Guantanamo Bay is leased to US and only mutual agreement or US abandonment of the facility can terminate the lease

Trafficking in persons: *current situation:* Cuba is a source country for adults and children subjected to forced labor and sex trafficking; child prostitution and child sex tourism reportedly occurs in Cuba, and laws do not appear to penalize the prostitution of children between the ages of 16 and 18; allegations have been made of Cubans being subjected to forced labor, particularly with Cuban work missions abroad; the scope of trafficking within Cuba is particularly difficult to gauge due to the closed nature of the government and sparse non-governmental or independent reporting

tier rating: Tier 3—Cuba does not fully comply with the minimum standards for the elimination of trafficking and is not making significant efforts to do so; the government has not publicized information about government measures to address human trafficking through prosecution, protection, or prevention efforts but did share information about its general approach to protection for children and youth; the government has a network of shelters for victims of domestic violence and child abuse but has not verified if trafficking victims receive care in those centers (2013)

Illicit drugs: territorial waters and air space serve as transshipment zone for US- and European-bound drugs; established the death penalty for certain drug-related crimes in 1999 (2008)

CURACAO

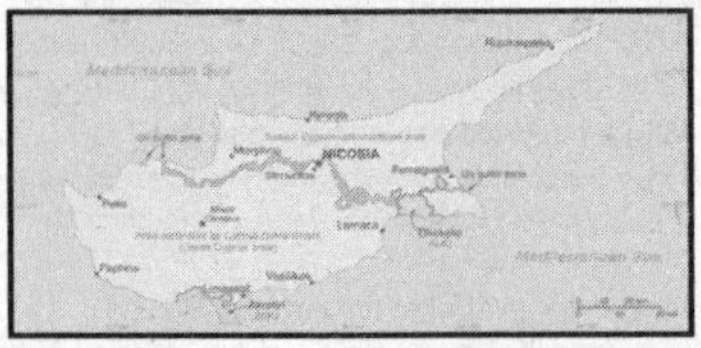

INTRODUCTION

Background: Originally settled by Arawak Indians, Curacao was seized by the Dutch in 1634 along with the neighboring island of Bonaire. Once the center of the Caribbean slave trade, Curacao was hard hit economically by the abolition of slavery in 1863. Its prosperity (and that of neighboring Aruba) was restored in the early 20th century with the construction of the Isla Refineria to service the newly discovered Venezuelan oil fields. In 1954, Curacao and several other Dutch Caribbean possessions were reorganized as the Netherlands Antilles, part of the Kingdom of the Netherlands. In referenda in 2005 and 2009, the citizens of Curacao voted to become a self-governing country within the Kingdom of the Netherlands. The change in status became effective in October 2010 with the dissolution of the Netherlands Antilles.

GEOGRAPHY

Location: Caribbean, an island in the Caribbean Sea—55 km off the coast of Venezuela

Geographic coordinates: 12 10 N, 69 00 W

Map references: Central America and the Caribbean

Area: total: 444 sq km
country comparison to the world: 200
land: 444 sq km
water: 0 sq km

Area—comparative: more than twice the size of Washington, DC

Land boundaries: 0 km

Coastline: 364 km

Maritime claims: territorial sea: 12 nm
exclusive fishing zone: 12 nm

Climate: tropical marine climate, ameliorated by northeast trade winds, results in mild temperatures; semiarid with average rainfall of 600 mm/year

Terrain: generally low, hilly terrain

Elevation extremes: lowest point: Caribbean Sea 0 m
highest point: Mt. Christoffel, 372m

Natural resources: calcium phosphates, aloes, sorghum, peanuts, vegetables, tropical fruit

Land use: *arable land:* 10%
permanent crops: 0%
other: 90% (2011)

Irrigated land: NA

Total renewable water resources: NA

Natural hazards: Curacao is south of the Caribbean hurricane belt and is rarely threatened

Environment—current issues: NA

Geography—note: Curacao is a part of the Windward Islands (southern) group

PEOPLE AND SOCIETY

Nationality: noun: Curacaoan
adjective: Curacaoan; Dutch

Ethnic groups: Afro-Caribbean majority; Dutch, French, Latin American, East Asian, South Asian, Jewish minorities

Languages: Papiamentu (a Spanish-Portuguese-Dutch-English dialect) 81.2%, Dutch (official) 8%, Spanish 4%, English 2.9%, other 3.9% (2001 census)

Religions: Roman Catholic 72.8%, Pentecostal 6.6%, Protestant 3.2%, Adventist 3%, Jehovah's Witness 2%, Evangelical 1.9%, other 3.8%, none 6%, unspecified 0.6% (2011 est.)

Population: 146,836 (July 2013 est.)
country comparison to the world: 189

Age structure: *0-14 years:* 20.6% (male 15,342/female 14,645)
15-24 years: 15.4% (male 11,599/female 10,790)
25-54 years: 38.5% (male 26,869/female 29,348)
55-64 years: 12.6% (male 8,059/female 10,259)
65 years and over: 13% (male 7,833/female 11,090) (2013 est.)

Dependency ratios:
total dependency ratio: 50.1 %
youth dependency ratio: 29 %
elderly dependency ratio: 21 %
potential support ratio: 4.8 (2013)

Median age: *total:* 36.2 years
male: 32.7 years
female: 39.9 years (2013 est.)

Population growth rate: NA

Birth rate: NA

Death rate: 8 deaths/1,000 population (2009)
country comparison to the world: 101

Net migration rate: 1.27 migrant(s)/1,000 population (2008)
country comparison to the world: 56

Sex ratio: *at birth:* 1.15 male(s)/female
0-14 years: 1.05 male(s)/female
15-24 years: 1.08 male(s)/female
25-54 years: 0.92 male(s)/female
55-64 years: 0.79 male(s)/female
65 years and over: 0.71 male(s)/female
total population: 0.92 male(s)/female (2013 est.)

Life expectancy at birth: *total:* NA
males: 72.4 years
females: 80.1 years (2009)

Total fertility rate: 2.09 children born/woman (2013 est.)
country comparison to the world: 111

HIV/AIDS—adult prevalence rate: NA

HIV/AIDS—people living with HIV/AIDS: NA

HIV/AIDS—deaths: NA

GOVERNMENT

Country name: Dutch long form: Land Curacao
Dutch short form: Curacao
Papiamentu long form: Pais Korsou
Papiamentu short form: Korsou
former: Netherlands Antilles; Curacao and Dependencies

Dependency status: constituent country within the Kingdom of the Netherlands; full autonomy in internal affairs granted in 2010; Dutch Government responsible for defense and foreign affairs

Government type: parliamentary

Capital: name: Willemstad
geographic coordinates: 12 06 N, 68 55 W
time difference: UTC-4 (1 hour ahead of Washington, DC during Standard Time)

Administrative divisions: none (part of the Kingdom of the Netherlands)

Independence: none (part of the Kingdom of the Netherlands)

National holiday: Queen's Day (Birthday of Queen-Mother JULIANA and accession to the throne of her oldest daughter BEATRIX), 30 April (1909 and 1980)

Constitution: previous 1947, 1955; latest adopted 5 September 2010, entered into force 10 October 2010 (regulates governance of Curacao but is subordinate to the Charter for the Kingdom of the Netherlands); note—in October 2010, with the dissolution of the Netherlands Antilles, Curacao became a constituent country within the Kingdom of the Netherlands (2013)

Legal system: based on Dutch civil law system with some English common law influence

Suffrage: 18 years of age; universal

Executive branch: *chief of state:* King WILLEM-ALEXANDER of the Netherlands (since 30 April 2013); represented by Governor Lucille A. GEORGE-WOUT (since 4 November 2013)
head of government: Prime Minister Ivar ASJES (since 7 June 2013)
cabinet: Cabinet appointed by the governor
(For more information visit the World Leaders website)
elections: the monarch is hereditary; governor general appointed by the monarch; following legislative elections, the leader of the majority party is usually elected prime minister by the parliament; next election is scheduled for 2016

Legislative branch: unicameral Estates of Curacao (21 seats; members elected by popular vote for four year terms)
elections: last held 19 October 2012 (next to be held in 2016)
election results: percent of vote by party—PS 22.6%, MFK 21.2%, PAR 19.7%, PAIS 17.7%, MAN 9.5%, PNP 5.9%, other 3.4%; seats by party—PS 5, MFK 5, PAR 4, PAIS 4, MAN 2, PNP 1

Judicial branch: *highest court(s):*

Political parties and leaders: Frente Obrero Liberashon (Workers' Liberation Front) or FOL [Anthony GODETT]; Movementu Futuro Korsou or MFK [Gerrit SCHOTTE]; Movishon Antia Nobo or MAN [Eunice EISDEN]; Partido Antia Restruktura or PAR [Emily DE JONGH-ELHAGE] *Partido pa Adelanto I Inovashon Soshal or PAIS [Alex ROSARIA]; Partido Nashonal di Pueblo or PNP [Humphrey DAVELAAR]; Pueblo Soberano or PS [Helmin WIELS]*

Diplomatic representation in the US: none (represented by the Kingdom of the Netherlands)

Diplomatic representation from the US: *chief of mission:* Consul General James R. Moore (since June 2013); note—also accredited to Aruba and Sint Martin
consulate(s) general: J. B. Gorsiraweg #1, Willemstad, Curacao
mailing address: P. O. Box 158, Willemstad, Curacao
telephone: [599] (9) 4613066
FAX: [599] (9) 4616489

Flag description: on a blue field a horizontal yellow band somewhat below the center divides the flag into proportions of 5:1:2; two five-pointed white stars—the smaller above and to the left of the larger—appear in the canton; the blue of the upper and lower sections symbolizes the sky and sea respectively; yellow represents the sun; the stars symbolize Curacao and its uninhabited smaller sister island of Klein Curacao; the five star points signify the five continents from which Curacao's people derive

National anthem: name: Himmo di Korsou (Anthem of Curacao)
lyrics/music: Guillermo ROSARIO, Mae HENRIQUEZ, Enrique MULLER, Betty DORAN/ Frater Candidus NOWENS, Errol "El Toro" COLINA
note: adapted 1978; the lyrics, originally written in 1899, were rewritten in 1978 to make them less colonial in nature

ECONOMY

Economy—overview: Tourism, petroleum refining, offshore finance, and trade and transport are the mainstays of this small economy, which is closely tied to the outside world. Although GDP grew slightly during the past decade, the island enjoys a high per capita income and a well-developed infrastructure compared with other countries in the region. Curacao has an excellent natural harbor that can accommodate large oil tankers. Venezuelan state oil company PdVSA, under a contract in effect until 2019, leases the single refinery on the island from the government, employing some 1,500 people; most of the oil for the refinery is imported from Venezuela; most of the refined products are exported to the US. Almost all consumer and capital goods are imported, with the US, Brazil, Italy, and Mexico being the major suppliers. The government is attempting to diversify its industry and trade and has signed an Association Agreement with the EU to expand business there. Most of Curacao's GDP results from services. Curacao has limited natural resources, poor soils, and inadequate water supplies, and budgetary problems complicate reform of the health and education systems. In 2013 the government implemented changes to the sales tax and reformed the public pension and health care systems, including increasing the sales tax from 5% to as high as 9% on some products, raising the age for public pension withdrawals to 65, and requiring citizens to pay higher premiums.

GDP (purchasing power parity): $2.838 billion (2008 est.)
country comparison to the world: 184
$2.606 billion (2007 est.)
$2.452 billion (2006 est.)
note: data are in 2008 US dollars

GDP (official exchange rate): $5.08 billion (2008 est.)

GDP—real growth rate: 0% (2012 est.)
country comparison to the world: 196
3.5% (2008)
2.2% (2007)

GDP—per capita (PPP): $15,000 (2004 est.)
country comparison to the world: 91

GDP—composition, by sector of origin: agriculture: 0.7%
industry: 15.5%
services: 83.8% (2012 est.)

Agriculture—products: aloe, sorghum, peanuts, vegetables, tropical fruit

Industries: tourism, petroleum refining, petroleum transshipment facilities, light manufacturing

Industrial production growth rate: NA%

Labor force: 62,040 (2011)
country comparison to the world: 186

Labor force—by occupation: *agriculture:* 1.2%
industry: 16.9%
services: 81.8% (2008 est.)

Unemployment rate: 9.8% (2011 est.)
country comparison to the world: 105
10.3% (2008 est.)

Taxes and other revenues: 10.8% of GDP (2011 est.)
country comparison to the world: 207

Budget surplus (+) or deficit (-):
-0.9% of GDP (2011 est.)
country comparison to the world: 61

Inflation rate (consumer prices): 2.3% (2011 est.)
country comparison to the world: 84
1.3% (2010 est.)

Exports: $1.5 billion (2011 est.)
country comparison to the world: 148
$1.4 billion (2010 est.)

Exports—commodities: petroleum products

Imports: $2.5 billion (2011 est.)
country comparison to the world: 155
$2.648 billion (2009 est.)

Imports—commodities: crude petroleum, food, manufactures

Exchange rates: Netherlands Antillean guilders (ANG) per US dollar—
1.79 (2011)
1.79 (2011 est.)
1.79 (2010 est.)
1.79 (2009)
1.79 (2008)
note: the Netherland Antillean guilder was replaced by the newly created Caribbean guilder in 2013

ENERGY

Electricity—production: 1.167 billion kWh (2008 est.)
country comparison to the world: 143

Electricity—consumption: 968 million kWh (2008 est.)
country comparison to the world: 151

Electricity—exports: 0 kWh (2009 est.)
country comparison to the world: 114

Electricity—imports: 0 kWh (2009 est.)
country comparison to the world: 123

Crude oil—proved reserves: 0 bbl (1 January 2011 es)
country comparison to the world: 114

Refined petroleum products—production:
531.1 bbl/day (2010 est.)
country comparison to the world: 112

Refined petroleum products—consumption:
72,000 bbl/day (2010 est.)
country comparison to the world: 90

Refined petroleum products—exports:
211,100 bbl/day (2009 est.)
country comparison to the world: 30

Refined petroleum products—imports:
291,700 bbl/day (2009 est.)
country comparison to the world: 23

Natural gas—production: 0 cu m (2009 est.)
country comparison to the world: 111

Natural gas—consumption: 0 cu m (2009 est.)
country comparison to the world: 127

Natural gas—exports: 0 cu m (2009 est.)
country comparison to the world: 75

Natural gas—imports: 0 cu m (2009 est.)
country comparison to the world: 170

Natural gas—proved reserves: 0 cu m (1 January 2011 es)
country comparison to the world: 121

COMMUNICATIONS

Telephone system: international: country code—599

Broadcast media: government-run Telecuracao operates a TV station and a radio station; several privately-owned radio stations

Internet country code: .cw

Internet hosts: NA

Internet users: NA

TRANSPORTATION

Roadways: total: 550 km
country comparison to the world: 192

Ports and terminals: *major seaport(s):* Willemstad
oil/gas terminal(s): Bullen Baai (Curacao Terminal)
bulk cargo port(s): Fuik Bay (phosphate rock)

MILITARY

Military branches: no regular military forces; the Dutch Government controls foreign and defense policy (2012)

Military service age and obligation:
no conscription (2010)

Military—note: defense is the responsibility of the Kingdom of the Netherlands

CYPRUS

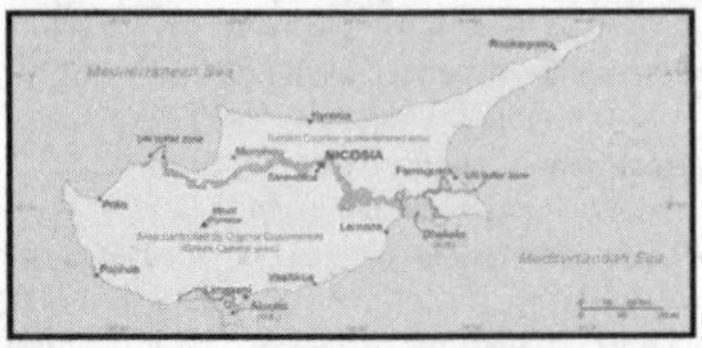

INTRODUCTION

Background: A former British colony, Cyprus became independent in 1960 following years of resistance to British rule. Tensions between the Greek Cypriot majority and Turkish Cypriot minority came to a head in December 1963, when violence broke out in the capital of Nicosia. Despite the deployment of UN peacekeepers in 1964, sporadic intercommunal violence continued forcing most Turkish Cypriots into enclaves throughout the island. In 1974, a Greek Government-sponsored attempt to overthrow the elected president of Cyprus was met by military intervention from Turkey, which soon controlled more than a third of the island. In 1983, the Turkish Cypriot-occupied area declared itself the "Turkish Republic of Northern Cyprus" ("TRNC"), but it is recognized only by Turkey. In February 2014, after a hiatus of nearly two years, the leaders of the two communities resumed formal discussions under UN auspices aimed at reuniting the divided island. The talks are ongoing. The entire island entered the EU on 1 May 2004, although the EU acquis - the body of common rights and obligations - applies only to the areas under the internationally recognized government, and is suspended in the areas administered by Turkish Cypriots. However, individual Turkish Cypriots able to document their eligibility for Republic of Cyprus citizenship legally enjoy the same rights accorded to other citizens of European Union states.

GEOGRAPHY

Location: Middle East, island in the Mediterranean Sea, south of Turkey

Geographic coordinates: 35 00 N, 33 00 E

Map references: Europe

Area: *total:* 9,251 sq km (of which 3,355 sq km are in north Cyprus)
country comparison to the world: 171
land: 9,241 sq km
water: 10 sq km

Area—comparative: about 0.6 times the size of Connecticut

Land boundaries: *total:* 150.4 km (approximately)
border sovereign base areas: Akrotiri 47.4 km, Dhekelia 103 km (approximately)

Coastline: 648 km

Maritime claims: *territorial sea:* 12 nm
contiguous zone: 24 nm
continental shelf: 200 m depth or to the depth of exploitation

Climate: temperate; Mediterranean with hot, dry summers and cool winters

Terrain: central plain with mountains to north and south; scattered but significant plains along southern coast

Elevation extremes: *lowest point:* Mediterranean Sea 0 m
highest point: Mount Olympus 1,951 m

Natural resources: copper, pyrites, asbestos, gypsum, timber, salt, marble, clay earth pigment

Land use: *arable land:* 9.06%
permanent crops: 3.54%
other: 87.41% (2011)

Irrigated land: 457.9 sq km (2007)

Total renewable water resources: 0.78 cu km (2011)

Freshwater withdrawal (domestic/industrial/agricultural): *total:* 0.18 cu km/yr (10%/3%/86%)
per capita: 164.7 cu m/yr (2009)

Natural hazards: moderate earthquake activity; droughts

Environment—current issues: water resource problems (no natural reservoir catchments, seasonal disparity in rainfall, sea water intrusion to island's largest aquifer, increased salination in the north); water pollution from sewage and industrial wastes; coastal degradation; loss of wildlife habitats from urbanization

Environment—international agreements: *party to:* Air Pollution, Air Pollution-Nitrogen Oxides, Air Pollution-Persistent Organic Pollutants, Air Pollution-Sulfur 94, Biodiversity, Climate Change, Climate Change-Kyoto Protocol, Desertification, Endangered Species, Environmental Modification, Hazardous Wastes, Law of the Sea, Marine Dumping, Ozone Layer Protection, Ship Pollution, Wetlands
signed, but not ratified: none of the selected agreements

Geography—note: the third largest island in the Mediterranean Sea (after Sicily and Sardinia)

PEOPLE AND SOCIETY

Nationality: *noun:* Cypriot(s)
adjective: Cypriot

Ethnic groups: Greek 77%, Turkish 18%, other 5% (2001)

Languages: Greek (official) 80.9%, Turkish (official) 0.2%, English 4.1%, Romanian 2.9%, Russian 2.5%, Bulgarian 2.2%, Arabic 1.2%, Filippino 1.1%, other 4.3%, unspecified 0.6% (2011 est.)

Religions: Greek Orthodox 78%, Muslim 18%, other (includes Maronite and Armenian Apostolic) 4%

Population: 1,172,458 (July 2014 est.)
country comparison to the world: 161

Age structure: *0-14 years:* 15.7% (male 94,437/female 89,174)
15-24 years: 15.3% (male 97,773/female 82,053)
25-54 years: 46.9% (male 288,673/female 261,651)
55-64 years: 11.2% (male 60,639/female 66,336)
65 years and over: 11% (male 57,188/female 74,534) (2014 est.)

Dependency ratios:
total dependency ratio: 41.3 %
youth dependency ratio: 24 %
elderly dependency ratio: 17.3 %
potential support ratio: 5.8 (2013)

Median age: *total:* 35.7 years
male: 34.4 years
female: 37.4 years (2014 est.)

Population growth rate: 1.48% (2014 est.)
country comparison to the world: 82

Birth rate: 11.44 births/1,000 population (2014 est.)
country comparison to the world: 172

Death rate: 6.57 deaths/1,000 population (2014 est.)
country comparison to the world: 148

Net migration rate: 9.89 migrant(s)/1,000 population (2014 est.)
country comparison to the world: 14

Urbanization: *urban population:* 70.5% of total population (2011)
rate of urbanization: 1.36% annual rate of change (2010-15 est.)

Major urban areas—population: NICOSIA (capital) 253,000 (2011)

Sex ratio: *at birth:* 1.05 male(s)/female
0-14 years: 1.06 male(s)/female
15-24 years: 1.19 male(s)/female
25-54 years: 1.1 male(s)/female
55-64 years: 1.04 male(s)/female
65 years and over: 0.77 male(s)/female
total population: 1.04 male(s)/female (2014 est.)

Mother's mean age at first birth: 27.5 (2005 est.)

Maternal mortality rate:
10 deaths/100,000 live births (2010)
country comparison to the world: 154

Infant mortality rate: *total:* 8.54 deaths/1,000 live births
country comparison to the world: 152
male: 10.1 deaths/1,000 live births
female: 6.91 deaths/1,000 live births (2014 est.)

Life expectancy at birth: *total population:* 78.34 years
country comparison to the world: 54
male: 75.54 years
female: 81.27 years (2014 est.)

Total fertility rate: 1.46 children born/woman (2014 est.)
country comparison to the world: 198

Health expenditures: 7.4% of GDP (2011)
country comparison to the world: 76

Physicians density: 2.75 physicians/1,000 population (2010)

Hospital bed density: 3.5 beds/1,000 population (2010)

Drinking water source:
improved:
urban: 100% of population
rural: 100% of population
total: 100% of population
unimproved:
urban: 0% of population
rural: 0% of population
total: 0% of population (2011 est.)

Sanitation facility access:
improved:
urban: 100% of population
rural: 100% of population

total: 100% of population
unimproved:
urban: 0% of population
rural: 0% of population
total: 0% of population (2011 est.)

HIV/AIDS—adult prevalence rate: 0.1% (2003 est.)
country comparison to the world: 134

HIV/AIDS—people living with HIV/AIDS: fewer than 1,000 (2007 est.)
country comparison to the world: 146

HIV/AIDS—deaths: NA

Obesity—adult prevalence rate: 25.5% (2008)
country comparison to the world: 53

Education expenditures: 7.3% of GDP (2010)
country comparison to the world: 19

Literacy: *definition:* age 15 and over can read and write
total population: 98.7%
male: 99.3%
female: 98.1% (2011 est.)

School life expectancy (primary to tertiary education): *total:* 14 years
male: 14 years
female: 14 years (2011)

Unemployment, youth ages 15-24: *total:* 27.8%
country comparison to the world: 34
male: 28.8%
female: 26.6% (2012)

GOVERNMENT

Country name: *conventional long form:* Republic of Cyprus
conventional short form: Cyprus
local long form: Kypriaki Dimokratia/Kibris Cumhuriyeti
local short form: Kypros/Kibris
note: the Turkish Cypriot community, which administers the northern part of the island, refers to itself as the "Turkish Republic of Northern Cyprus" or "TRNC" (Kuzey Kibris Turk Cumhuriyeti or KKTC)

Government type: republic
note: a separation of the two ethnic communities inhabiting the island began following the outbreak of communal strife in 1963; this separation was further solidified after the Turkish intervention in July 1974, following a Greek military-junta-supported coup attempt that gave the Turkish Cypriots de facto control in the north; Greek Cypriots control the only internationally recognized government; on 15 November 1983 Turkish Cypriot "President" Rauf DENKTAS declared independence and the formation of a "Turkish Republic of Northern Cyprus" ("TRNC"), which is recognized only by Turkey

Capital: *name:* Nicosia (Lefkosia/Lefkosa)
geographic coordinates: 35 10 N, 33 22 E
time difference: UTC+2 (7 hours ahead of Washington, DC during Standard Time)
daylight saving time: +1hr, begins last Sunday in March; ends last Sunday in October

Administrative divisions: 6 districts; Ammochostos (Famagusta; all but a small part administered by Turkish Cypriots), Keryneia (Kyrenia; the only district completely administered by Turkish Cypriots), Larnaka (Larnaca; a small part administered by Turkish Cypriots), Lemesos (Limassol), Lefkosia (Nicosia; a small part administered by Turkish Cypriots), Pafos (Paphos); note—the five districts of Turkish Cypriot-administered part of Cyprus are Gazimagusa (Famagusta), Girne (Kyrenia), Guzelyurt (Morphou), Lefkosia (Nicosia) and Iskele (Trikomo)

Independence: 16 August 1960 (from the UK); note—Turkish Cypriots proclaimed self-rule on 13 February 1975 and independence in 1983, but these proclamations are only recognized by Turkey

National holiday: Independence Day, 1 October (1960); note—Turkish Cypriots celebrate 15 November (1983) as "Independence Day"

Constitution: ratified 16 August 1960; note - in 1963, the constitution was partly suspended as Turkish Cypriots withdrew from the government; Turkish-held territory in 1983 was declared the "Turkish Republic of Northern Cyprus" ("TRNC"); in 1985, the "TRNC" approved its own constitution (2013)

Legal system: mixed legal system of English common law and civil law with Greek Orthodox religious law influence

International law organization participation: accepts compulsory ICJ jurisdiction with reservations; accepts ICCt jurisdiction

Suffrage: 18 years of age; universal

Executive branch: chief of state: President Nicos ANASTASIADES (since 28 February 2013); note—the president is both the chief of state and head of government; post of vice president is currently vacant; under the 1960 constitution, the post is reserved for a Turkish Cypriot
head of government: President Nicos ANASTASIADES (since 28 February 2013)
cabinet: Council of Ministers appointed by the president; note—under the 1960 Constitution, three of the ministerial posts are reserved for Turkish Cypriots appointed by the Vice President but the positions are currently filled by Greek Cypriots (For more information visit the World Leaders website)
elections: president elected by popular vote for a five-year term; election last held on 17 and 24 February 2013 (next to be held in February 2018)
election results: Nicos ANASTASIADES elected president; percent of vote (first round)—Nicos ANASTASIADES 45.46%, Stavros MALAS 26.91%, Giorgos LILLIKAS 24.93%, other 2.7%; (second round) Nicos ANASTASIADES 57.48%, Savros MALAS 42.52%
note: Dervis EROGLU became "president" of the "TRNC" on 23 April 2010 after "presidential" elections on 18 April 2010; results—Dervis EROGLU 50.4%, Mehmet Ali TALAT 42.9%; Ozkan YORGANCIOGLU is "TRNC prime minister"

Legislative branch: *unicameral—area under government control:* House of Representatives or Vouli Antiprosopon (80 seats; 56 assigned to the Greek Cypriots, 24 to Turkish Cypriots; note—only those assigned to Greek Cypriots are filled; members are elected by popular vote to serve five-year terms); area administered by Turkish Cypriots: "Assembly of the Republic" or Cumhuriyet Meclisi (50 seats; members elected by popular vote to serve five-year terms)
elections: area under government control: last held on 22 May 2011 (next to be held in May 2016); area administered by Turkish Cypriots: last held on 28 July 2013 (next to be held on July 2018)
election results: area under government control: House of Representatives—percent of vote by party—DISY 34.3%, AKEL 32.7%, DIKO 15.8%, KS-EDEK 8.9%, EVROKO 3.9%, other 4.4%; seats by party—DISY 20, AKEL 19, DIKO 9, KS-EDEK 5, EVROKO 2, KOP 1; note—as of 1 January 2014, the composition of the Cypriot House of Representatives was DISY 20, AKEL 19, DIKO 8, KS-EDEK 5, EVROKO 1, SP 1, KOP 1, independent 1; area administered by Turkish Cypriots: "Assembly of the Republic"—percent of vote by party—CTP-BG 38%, UBP 27%, DP-UG 23%, TDP 7%, other 5%; seats by party—CTP-BG 21, UBP 14, DP-UG 12, TDP 3

Judicial branch: highest court(s): Supreme Court of Cyprus (consists of 13 judges including the court president); note—the highest court in the "Turkish Republic of Northern Cyprus (TRNC)" is the "Supreme Court" (consists of 8 "judges" including the "court president")
judge selection and term of office: Republic of Cyprus Supreme Court judges appointed by the president of the republic upon the recommendation of the Supreme Court judges; judges tenure is until the age of 68; "TRNC Supreme Court" judges appointed by the "Supreme Council of Judicature", a 12-member body of "judges", the "attorney general", "appointees"—one each by the "president" of the "TRNC" and by the "Legislative Assembly", and a member elected by the Bar Association; "judge" tenure NA
subordinate courts: Republic of Cyprus district courts; Assize Courts; specialized courts for issues relating to family, industrial disputes, military, and rent control; "TRNC Assize Courts"; "district and family courts"

Political parties and leaders: *area under government control:* Citizens' Alliance or SP [Giorgos LILLIKAS]; Democratic Party or DIKO [Nicolas PAPADOPOULOS]; Democratic Rally or DISY [Averof NEOPHYTOU (Neofytou)]; European Party or EVROKO [Dimitris SYLLOURIS]; Ecological and Environmental Movement of KOP (Green Party) [Giorgos PERDIKIS]; Movement of Social Democrats or KS-EDEK [Yiannakis OMIROU]; National Popular Front or ELAM [Christos CHRISTOU]; Progressive Party of the Working People or AKEL (Communist Party) [Andros KYPRIANOU]; Frontt for the Restoration of the Center or EPALXI [Kypros CHRYSOSTOMIDIS]; United Democrats or EDI [Praxoula ANTONIADOU]
area administered by Turkish Cypriots: Communal Democracy Party or TDP [Cemal OZYIGIT]; Cyprus Socialist Party or KSP [Mehmet BIRINCI]; Democrat Party- National Forces or DP-UG [Serdar DENKTAS]; National Unity Party or UBP [Huseyin OZGURGUN]; New Cyprus Party or YKP [Murat KANATLI]; Republican Turkish Party-United Forces or CTP-BG [Ozkan YORGANCIOGLU]; United Cyprus Party or BKP [Izzet IZCAN]

Political pressure groups and leaders: Confederation of Cypriot Workers or SEK (pro-West) Pan-Cyprian Labor Federation or PEO (Communist controlled)
area administered by Turkish Cypriots: Federation of Turkish Cypriot Labor Unions or Turk-Sen Confederation of Revolutionary Labor Unions or Dev-Is

International organization participation: Australia Group, C, CD, CE, EBRD, ECB, EIB, EMU,

EU, FAO, IAEA, IBRD, ICAO, ICC (national committees), IDA, IFAD, IFC, IFRCS (observer), IHO, ILO, IMF, IMO, IMSO, Interpol, IOC, IOM, IPU, ISO, ITSO, ITU, ITUC (NGOs), MIGA, NAM, NSG, OAS (observer), OIF, OPCW, OSCE, PCA, UN, UNCTAD, UNESCO, UNHCR, UNIDO, UNIFIL, UNWTO, UPU, WCO, WFTU (NGOs), WHO, WIPO, WMO, WTO

Diplomatic representation in the US: *chief of mission:* Ambassador George CHACALLI (since 30 May 2013)

chancery: 2211 R Street NW, Washington, DC 20008
telephone: [1] (202) 462-5772, 462-0873
FAX: [1] (202) 483-6710
consulate(s) general: New York
note: representative of the Turkish Cypriot community in the US is Ahmet ERDENGIZ; office at 1667 K Street NW, Washington, DC; telephone [1] (202) 887-6198

Diplomatic representation from the US:
chief of mission: Ambassador John M. KOENIG (since 17 August 2012)
embassy: corner of Metochiou and Ploutarchou Streets, 2407 Engomi, Nicosia
mailing address: P. O. Box 24536, 1385 Nicosia
telephone: [357] (22) 393939
FAX: [357] (22) 780944

Flag description: white with a copper-colored silhouette of the island (the name Cyprus is derived from the Greek word for copper) above two green crossed olive branches in the center of the flag; the branches symbolize the hope for peace and reconciliation between the Greek and Turkish communities
note: the "Turkish Republic of Northern Cyprus" flag retains the white field of the Cyprus national flag but displays narrow horizontal red stripes positioned a small distance from the top and bottom edges between which are centered a red crescent and a red five-pointed star; the banner is modeled after the Turkish national flag but with the colors reversed

National symbol(s): Cypriot mouflon (wild sheep); white dove

National anthem: *name:* "Ymnos eis tin Eleftherian" (Hymn to Liberty) lyrics/music: Dionysios SOLOMOS/Nikolaos MANTZAROS
note: adopted 1960; Cyprus adopted the Greek national anthem as its own; the Turkish community in Cyprus uses the anthem of Turkey

ECONOMY

Economy—overview: The area of the Republic of Cyprus under government control has a market economy dominated by the service sector, which accounts for four-fifths of GDP. Tourism, financial services, and real estate have traditionally been the most important sectors. Cyprus has been a member of the European Union (EU) since May 2004 and adopted the euro as its national currency in January 2008. During the first five years of EU membership, the Cyprus economy grew at an average rate of about 4%, with unemployment between 2004 and 2008 averaging about 3%. An overextended banking sector with excessive exposure to Greek debt resulted in a contraction in economic growth. Two of Cyprus' biggest banks were among the largest holders of Greek bonds in Europe and had a substantial presence in Greece through bank branches and subsidiaries. Following numerous downgrades of its credit rating, Cyprus lost access to international capital markets in May 2011. The economy contracted by an accumulated 8.2% between 2009 and 2013 and is not expected to return to positive growth before 2015. Unemployment is currently over 17% and expected to reach 19% in 2014. In July 2012, Cyprus became the fifth eurozone government to request an economic bailout program from the European Commission, European Central Bank and the International Monetary Fund—known collectively as the "Troika". Shortly after the election of President Nicos ANASTASIADES in February 2013, Cyprus faced an economic crisis and agreed with the Troika to a $13 billion bailout that included losses on uninsured bank deposits. The bailout triggered a two-week bank closure and the imposition of capital controls, some of which remained in place through 2014. Cyprus' two largest banks merged and the combined entity was recapitalized through conversion of some large bank deposits to shares and imposition of losses on some bank bondholders. The Troika conditioned the bailout on progress in financial and structural reforms and privatization of state-owned enterprises. Cyprus has downsized and restructured its banking sector significantly. Three positive reviews by the Troika since May 2013 indicate that Cyprus' bailout program is on track with a fourth review scheduled in May 2014. In October 2013, Cyprus completed preliminary appraisal of hydrocarbon deposits in its territorial waters, which revealed less than anticipated natural gas reserves. Additional exploration drilling is likely to continue in 2014-2015.

GDP (purchasing power parity): $21.62 billion (2013 est.)
country comparison to the world: 130
$23.68 billion (2012 est.)
$24.27 billion (2011 est.)
note: data are in 2013 US dollars

GDP (official exchange rate): $21.78 billion (2013 est.)

GDP—real growth rate: -8.7% (2013 est.)
country comparison to the world: 219
-2.4% (2012 est.)
0.5% (2011 est.)

GDP—per capita (PPP): $24,500 (2013 est.)
country comparison to the world: 62
$27,200 (2012 est.)
$28,200 (2011 est.)
note: data are in 2013 US dollars

Gross national saving: 8.4% of GDP (2013 est.)
country comparison to the world: 144
6.6% of GDP (2012 est.)
14.2% of GDP (2011 est.)

GDP—composition, by end use:
household consumption: 67.2%
government consumption: 20.1%
investment in fixed capital: 10.5%
investment in inventories: -4.8%
exports of goods and services: 45.5%
imports of goods and services: -38.5% (2013 est.)

GDP—composition, by sector of origin:
agriculture: 2.4%
industry: 15.9%
services: 81.7% (2013 est.)

Agriculture—products: citrus, vegetables, barley, grapes, olives, vegetables; poultry, pork, lamb; dairy, cheese

Industries: tourism, food and beverage processing, cement and gypsum production, ship repair and refurbishment, textiles, light chemicals, metal products, wood, paper, stone and clay products

Industrial production growth rate: -3.5% (2013 est.)
country comparison to the world: 186

Labor force: 443,500 (2013 est.)
country comparison to the world: 157

Labor force—by occupation: *agriculture:* 8.5%
industry: 20.5%
services: 71% (2006 est.)

Unemployment rate: 17.4% (2013 est.)
country comparison to the world: 154
11.9% (2012 est.)

Population below poverty line: NA%

Household income or consumption by percentage share: *lowest 10%:* NA%
highest 10%: NA%

Distribution of family income—Gini index: 31 (2012 est.)
country comparison to the world: 113
29 (2005 est.)

Budget: *revenues:* $8.799 billion
expenditures: $10.04 billion (2013 est.)

Taxes and other revenues: 40.4% of GDP (2013 est.)
country comparison to the world: 39

Budget surplus (+) or deficit (-):
-5.7% of GDP (2013 est.)
country comparison to the world: 176

Public debt: 113.1% of GDP (2013 est.)
country comparison to the world: 11
85.8% of GDP (2012 est.)
note: data cover general government debt, and includes debt instruments issued (or owned) by government entities other than the treasury; the data include treasury debt held by foreign entities; the data exclude debt issued by subnational entities, as well as intra-governmental debt; intra-governmental debt consists of treasury borrowings from surpluses in the social funds, such as for *retirement, medical care, and unemployment*

Fiscal year: calendar year

Inflation rate (consumer prices): 0.2% (2013 est.)
country comparison to the world: 8
2.4% (2012 est.)

Central bank discount rate: 0.75% (31 December 2013)
country comparison to the world: 125
1.5% (31 December 2010)
note: this is the European Central Bank's rate on the marginal lending facility, which offers overnight credit to banks in the euro area

Commercial bank prime lending rate:
7% (31 December 2013 est.)
country comparison to the world: 123
7.05% (31 December 2012 est.)

Stock of narrow money: $14.73 billion (31 December 2011 est.)
country comparison to the world: 70
$14.6 billion (31 December 2010 est.)
note: see entry for the European Union for money supply in the euro area; the European Central Bank (ECB) controls monetary policy for the 17 members of the EMU; individual members of the EMU do not control the quantity of money circulating within their own borders

Stock of broad money: $46.46 billion (31 December 2013 est.)
country comparison to the world: 71
$50.06 billion (31 December 2012 est.)

Stock of domestic credit: $50.39 billion (31 December 2013 est.)
country comparison to the world: 61
$54.29 billion (31 December 2012 est.)

Market value of publicly traded shares: $1.996 billion (31 December 2012 est.)
country comparison to the world: 94

$2.853 billion (31 December 2011)
$6.834 billion (31 December 2010 est.)

Current account balance: -$358.2 million (2013 est.)
country comparison to the world: 95
-$1.506 billion (2012 est.)

Exports: $2.42 billion (2013 est.)
country comparison to the world: 138
$2.602 billion (2012 est.)

Exports—commodities: citrus, potatoes, pharmaceuticals, cement, clothing

Exports—partners: Greece 23%, UK 10.1% (2012)

Imports: $4.747 billion (2013 est.)
country comparison to the world: 131
$6.755 billion (2012 est.)

Imports—commodities: consumer goods, petroleum and lubricants, machinery, transport equipment

Imports—partners: Greece 21.6%, Israel 11.9%, Italy 8.3%, UK 7.3%, Germany 7.1%, Netherlands 6.7%, France 6%, China 4.5% (2012)

Reserves of foreign exchange and gold:
$853 million (31 December 2013 est.)
country comparison to the world: 140
$1.191 billion (31 December 2012 est.)

Debt—external: $95.28 billion (31 December 2013 est.)
country comparison to the world: 49
$103.5 billion (31 December 2012 est.)

Stock of direct foreign investment—at home:
$28.53 billion (31 December 2013 est.)
country comparison to the world: 63
$26.28 billion (31 December 2012 est.)

Stock of direct foreign investment—abroad:
$12.11 billion (31 December 2013 est.)
country comparison to the world: 51
$11.16 billion (31 December 2012 est.)

Exchange rates: euros (EUR) per US dollar—
0.7634 (2013 est.)
0.7752 (2012 est.)
0.755 (2010 est.)
0.7198 (2009 est.)
0.6827 (2008 est.)

Economy of the area administered by Turkish Cypriots: *Economy—overview:* The market-based economy of the area administered by Turkish Cypriots, known locally as the "Turkish Republic of Northern Cyprus" ("TRNC"), is roughly half the size of its southern neighbor and is likewise dominated by the service sector with a large portion of the population employed by the government. Since its creation, the "TRNC" has heavily relied on financial assistance from Turkey which supports the "TRNC" defense, telecommunications, water and postal services, and the "TRNC" remains vulnerable to the Turkish market and monetary policy through its use of the Turkish Lira. The "TRNC" weathered the European financial crisis relatively unscathed-compared to the Republic of Cyprus-because of the lack of financial sector development, health of the Turkish economy, and its separation from the rest of the island.

GDP (purchasing power parity): $1.829 billion (2007 est.)

GDP—real growth rate: -0.6% (2010 est.)

GDP—per capita: $11,700 (2007 est.)

GDP—composition by sector: agriculture: 8.6%, industry: 22.4%, services: 69.1% (2006 est.)

Labor force: 95,030 (2007 est.)

Labor force—by occupation: agriculture: 14.5%, industry: 29%, services: 56.5% (2004)

Unemployment rate: 9.4% (2005 est.)

Population below poverty line: %NA

Inflation rate: 11.4% (2006)

Budget: revenues: $2.5 billion, expenditures: $2.5 billion (2006)

Agriculture—products: citrus fruit, dairy, potatoes, grapes, olives, poultry, lamb

Industries: foodstuffs, textiles, clothing, ship repair, clay, gypsum, copper, furniture

Industrial production growth rate: -0.3% (2007 est.)

Electricity production: 998.9 million kWh (2005)

Electricity consumption: 797.9 million kWh (2005)

Exports: $68.1 million, f.o.b. (2007 est.)

Export—commodities: citrus, dairy, potatoes, textiles

Export—partners: Turkey 40%; direct trade between the area administered by Turkish Cypriots and the area under government control remains limited

Imports: $1.2 billion, f.o.b. (2007 est.)

Import—commodities: vehicles, fuel, cigarettes, food, minerals, chemicals, machinery

Import—partners: Turkey 60%; direct trade between the area administered by Turkish Cypriots and the area under government control remains limited

Reserves of foreign exchange and gold: $NA

Debt—external: $NA

Currency (code): Turkish new lira (YTL)

Exchange rates: Turkish new lira per US dollar: 1.668 (2011) 1.5026 (2010) 1.55 (2009) 1.3179 (2008) 1.319 (2007)

ENERGY

Electricity—production: 4.443 billion kWh (2012 est.)
country comparison to the world: 121

Electricity—consumption: 4.356 billion kWh (2012 est.)
country comparison to the world: 120

Electricity—exports: 0 kWh (2012 est.)
country comparison to the world: 127

Electricity—imports: 0 kWh (2012 est.)
country comparison to the world: 134

Electricity—installed generating capacity:
1.493 million kW (2012 est.)
country comparison to the world: 117

Electricity—from fossil fuels: 94.2% of total installed capacity (2010 est.)
country comparison to the world: 70

Electricity—from nuclear fuels: 0% of total installed capacity (2010 est.)
country comparison to the world: 74

Electricity—from hydroelectric plants:
0% of total installed capacity (2010 est.)
country comparison to the world: 166

Electricity—from other renewable sources:
5.8% of total installed capacity (2010 est.)
country comparison to the world: 39

Crude oil—production: 8.47 bbl/day (2012 est.)
country comparison to the world: 131

Crude oil—exports: 0 bbl/day (2010 est.)
country comparison to the world: 103

Crude oil—imports: 0 bbl/day (2010 est.)
country comparison to the world: 177

Crude oil—proved reserves: 0 bbl (1 January 2013 es)
country comparison to the world: 122

Refined petroleum products—production:
0 bbl/day (2010 est.)
country comparison to the world: 136

Refined petroleum products—consumption:
58,430 bbl/day (2011 est.)
country comparison to the world: 94

Refined petroleum products—exports:
0 bbl/day (2010 est.)
country comparison to the world: 169

Refined petroleum products—imports:
58,310 bbl/day (2010 est.)
country comparison to the world: 63

Natural gas—production: 0 cu m (2011 est.)
country comparison to the world: 121

Natural gas—consumption: 0 cu m (2010 est.)
country comparison to the world: 137

Natural gas—exports: 0 cu m (2011 est.)
country comparison to the world: 88

Natural gas—imports: 0 cu m (2011 est.)
country comparison to the world: 183

Natural gas—proved reserves: 0 cu m (1 January 2013 es)
country comparison to the world: 129

Carbon dioxide emissions from consumption of energy: 9.503 million Mt (2011 est.)
country comparison to the world: 102

COMMUNICATIONS

Telephones—main lines in use: 373,200 (2012)
country comparison to the world: 108

Telephones—mobile cellular: 1.11 million (2012)
country comparison to the world: 155

Telephone system: *general assessment:* excellent in both area under government control and area administered by Turkish Cypriots
domestic: open-wire, fiber-optic cable, and microwave radio relay
international: country code—357 (area administered by Turkish Cypriots uses the country code of Turkey—90); a number of submarine cables, including the SEA-ME-WE-3, combine to provide connectivity to Western Europe, the Middle East, and Asia; tropospheric scatter; satellite earth stations—8 (3 Intelsat—1 Atlantic Ocean and 2 Indian Ocean, 2 Eutelsat, 2 Intersputnik, and 1 Arabsat)

Broadcast media: mixture of state and privately run TV and radio services; the public broadcaster operates 2 TV channels and 4 radio stations; 6 private TV broadcasters, satellite and cable TV services including telecasts from Greece and Turkey, and a number of private radio stations are available; in areas administered by Turkish Cypriots, there are 2 public TV stations, 4 public radio stations, and privately owned TV and radio broadcast stations (2007)

Internet country code: .cy

Internet hosts: 252,013 (2012)
country comparison to the world: 67

Internet users: 433,900 (2009)
country comparison to the world: 120

TRANSPORTATION

Airports: 15 (2013)
country comparison to the world: 145

Airports—with paved runways: *total:* 1 3
2,438 to 3,047 m: 7

1,524 to 2,437 m: 2
914 to 1,523 m: 3
under 914 m: 1 (2013)

Airports—with unpaved runways: total: 2
under 914 m: 2 (2013)

Heliports: 9 (2013)

Roadways: total: 20,006 km
country comparison to the world: 108
government control: 13,006 km (includes 2,277 km of expressways)
paved: 8,564 km
unpaved: 4,442 km
Turkish Cypriot control: 7,000 km (2011)

Merchant marine: total: 838
country comparison to the world: 13
by type: bulk carrier 278, cargo 163, chemical tanker 77, container 201, liquefied gas 11, passenger 3, passenger/cargo 25, petroleum tanker 62, refrigerated cargo 5, roll on/roll off 9, vehicle carrier 4
foreign-owned: 622 (Angola 1, Austria 1, Belgium 3, Bermuda 1, Canada 2, China 6, Denmark 6, Estonia 6, France 16, Germany 192, Greece 201, Hong Kong 2, India 4, Iran 10, Ireland 3, Italy 6, Japan 16, Netherlands 23, Norway 14, Philippines 1, Poland 24, Portugal 2, Russia 46, Singapore 1, Slovenia 5, Spain 6, Sweden 5, Turkey 1, UAE 3, UK 7, Ukraine 3, US 5)
registered in other countries: 152 (Bahamas 23, Cambodia 4, Comoros 2, Finland 1, Gibraltar 1, Greece 3, Hong Kong 3, Liberia 9, Malta 32, Marshall Islands 40, Norway 1, Panama 5, Russia 13, Saint Vincent and the Grenadines 3, Sierra Leone 2, Singapore 6, unknown 4) (2010)

Ports and terminals:
major seaport(s): area under government control: Larnaca, Limassol, Vasilikos; area administered by Turkish Cypriots: Famagusta, Kyrenia

MILITARY

Military branches: Republic of Cyprus: Cypriot National Guard (Ethniki Froura, EF; includes naval and air elements); Northern Cyprus: Turkish Cypriot Security Force (GKK) (2014)

Military service age and obligation: Cypriot National Guard (CNG): 18-50 years of age for compulsory military service for all Greek Cypriot males; 17 years of age for voluntary service; length of service obligation is 24 months (2014)

Manpower available for military service: Cypriot National Guard (GCNG):
males age 16-49: 327,875
females age 16-49: 287,891 (2010 est.)

Manpower fit for military service: Cypriot National Guard (GCNG):
males age 16-49: 275,842
females age 16-49: 239,862 (2010 est.)

Manpower reaching militarily significant age annually: *male:* 8,167
female: 7,398 (2010 est.)

Military expenditures: 2.05% of GDP (2012)
country comparison to the world: 38
2.14% of GDP (2011)
2.05% of GDP (2010) (U)

TRANSNATIONAL ISSUES

Disputes—international: hostilities in 1974 divided the island into two de facto autonomous entities, the internationally recognized Cypriot Government and a Turkish-Cypriot community (north Cyprus); the 1,000-strong UN Peacekeeping Force in Cyprus (UNFICYP) has served in Cyprus since 1964 and maintains the buffer zone between north and south; on 1 May 2004, Cyprus entered the European Union still divided, with the EU's body of legislation and standards (acquis communitaire) suspended in the north; Turkey protests Cypriot Government creating hydrocarbon blocks and maritime boundary with Lebanon in March 2007

Refugees and internally displaced persons: *IDPs:* 208,000 (both Turkish and Greek Cypriots; many displaced since 1974) (2012)

Illicit drugs: minor transit point for heroin and hashish via air routes and container traffic to Europe, especially from Lebanon and Turkey; some cocaine transits as well; despite a strengthening of anti-money-laundering legislation, remains vulnerable to money laundering; reporting of suspicious transactions in offshore sector remains weak (2008)

CZECH REPUBLIC

INTRODUCTION

Background: At the close of World War I, the Czechs and Slovaks of the former Austro-Hungarian Empire merged to form Czechoslovakia. During the interw ar years, having rejected a federal system, the new country's predominantly Czech leaders were frequently preoccupied with meeting the increasingly strident demands of other ethnic minorities within the republic, most notably the Slovaks, the Sudeten Germans, and the Ruthenians (Ukrainians). On the eve of World War II, Nazi Germany occupied the Czech part of the country and Slovakia became an independent state allied with Germany. After the war, a reunited but truncated Czechoslovakia (less Ruthenia) fell within the Soviet sphere of influence. In 1968, an invasion by Warsaw Pact troops ended the efforts of the country's leaders to liberalize Communist rule and create "socialism with a human face," ushering in a period of repression known as "normalization." The peaceful "Velvet Revolution" swept the Communist Party from power at the end of 1989 and inaugurated a return to democratic rule and a market economy. On 1 January 1993, the country underw ent a nonviolent "velvet divorce" into its two national components, the Czech Republic and Slovakia. The Czech Republic joined NATO in 1999 and the European Union in 2004.

GEOGRAPHY

Location: Central Europe, between Germany, Poland, Slovakia, and Austria

Geographic coordinates: 49 45 N, 15 30 E

Map references: Europe

Area: *total:* 78,867 sq km
country comparison to the world: 116
land: 77,247 sq km
water: 1,620 sq km

Area—comparative: slightly smaller than South Carolina

Land boundaries: *total:* 1,989 km
border countries: Austria 362 km, Germany 815 km, Poland 615 km, Slovakia 197 km

Coastline: km (landlocked)

Maritime claims: none (landlocked)

Climate: temperate; cool summers; cold, cloudy, humid winters

Terrain: Bohemia in the west consists of rolling plains, hills, and plateaus surrounded by low mountains; Moravia in the east consists of very hilly country

Elevation extremes: *lowest point:* Labe (Elbe) River 115 m
highest point: Snezka 1,602 m

Natural resources: hard coal, soft coal, kaolin, clay, graphite, timber

Land use: *arable land:* 40.12%
permanent crops: 0.96%
other: 58.92% (2011)

Irrigated land: 385.3 sq km (2007)

Total renewable water resources: 13.15 cu km (2011)

Freshwater withdrawal (domestic/industrial/agricultural): *total:* 1.7 cu km/yr (41%/56%/2%)
per capita: 164.7 cu m/yr (2009)

Natural hazards: flooding

Environment—current issues: air and water pollution in areas of northwest Bohemia and in northern Moravia around Ostrava present health risks; acid rain damaging forests; efforts to bring industry up to EU code should improve domestic pollution

Environment—international agreements: *party to:* Air Pollution, Air Pollution-Nitrogen Oxides, Air Pollution-Persistent Organic Pollutants, Air Pollution-Sulfur 85, Air Pollution-Sulfur 94, Air Pollution-Volatile Organic Compounds, Antarctic-Environmental Protocol, Antarctic

Treaty, Biodiversity, Climate Change, Climate Change-Kyoto Protocol, Desertification, Endangered Species, Environmental Modification, Hazardous Wastes, Law of the Sea, Ozone Layer Protection, Ship Pollution, Wetlands, Whaling
signed, but not ratified: none of the selected agreements

Geography—note: landlocked; strategically located astride some of oldest and most significant land routes in Europe; Moravian Gate is a traditional military corridor between the North European Plain and the Danube in central Europe

PEOPLE AND SOCIETY

Nationality: *noun:* Czech(s)
adjective: Czech

Ethnic groups: Czech 64.3%, Moravian 5%, Slovak 1.4%, other 1.8%, unspecified 27.5% (2011 est.)

Languages: Czech 95.4%, Slovak 1.6%, other 3% (2011 census)

Religions: Roman Catholic 10.4%, Protestant (includes Czech Brethren and Hussite) 1.1%, other and unspecified 54%, none 34.5% (2011 est.)

Population: 10,627,448 (July 2014 est.)
country comparison to the world: 83

Age structure: *0-14 years:* 14.9% (male 812,503/female 769,849)
15-24 years: 10.6% (male 576,304/female 547,765)
25-54 years: 43.6% (male 2,377,962/female 2,256,989)
55-64 years: 17.5% (male 687,155/female 735,277)
65 years and over: 17.6% (male 766,402/female 1,097,242) (2014 est.)

Dependency ratios:
total dependency ratio: 46.1 %
youth dependency ratio: 21.7 %
elderly dependency ratio: 24.4 %
potential support ratio: 4.1 (2013)

Median age: *total:* 40.9 years
male: 39.6 years
female: 42.3 years (2014 est.)

Population growth rate: 0.17% (2014 est.)
country comparison to the world: 182

Birth rate: 9.79 births/1,000 population (2014 est.)
country comparison to the world: 199

Death rate: 10.29 deaths/1,000 population (2014 est.)
country comparison to the world: 45

Net migration rate: 2.15 migrant(s)/1,000 population (2014 est.)
country comparison to the world: 46

Urbanization: *urban population:* 73.4% of total population (2011)
rate of urbanization: 0.24% annual rate of change (2010-15 est.)

Major urban areas—population: PRAGUE (capital) 1.276 million (2011)

Sex ratio: *at birth:* 1.06 male(s)/female
0-14 years: 1.06 male(s)/female
15-24 years: 1.05 male(s)/female
25-54 years: 1.05 male(s)/female
55-64 years: 0.97 male(s)/female
65 years and over: 0.67 male(s)/female
total population: 0.95 male(s)/female (2014 est.)

Mother's mean age at first birth: 27.6 (2010 est.)

Maternal mortality rate: 5 deaths/100,000 live births (2010)
country comparison to the world: 173

Infant mortality rate: *total:* 2.63 deaths/1,000 live births
country comparison to the world: 218
male: 2.76 deaths/1,000 live births
female: 2.49 deaths/1,000 live births (2014 est.)

Life expectancy at birth: *total population:* 78.31 years
country comparison to the world: 55
male: 75.34 years
female: 81.45 years (2014 est.)

Total fertility rate: 1.43 children born/woman (2014 est.)
country comparison to the world: 201

Contraceptive prevalence rate: 86.3%
note: percent of women aged 18-49 (2008)

Health expenditures: 7.4% of GDP (2011)
country comparison to the world: 75

Physicians density: 3.71 physicians/1,000 population (2010)

Hospital bed density: 7 beds/1,000 population (2010)

Drinking water source:
improved:
urban: 99.9% of population
rural: 99.6% of population
total: 99.8% of population
unimproved:
urban: 0.1% of population
rural: 0.4% of population
total: 0.2% of population (2011 est.)

Sanitation facility access:
improved:
urban: 100% of population
rural: 100% of population
total: 100% of population
unimproved:
urban: 0% of population
rural: 0% of population
total: 0% of population (2011 est.)

HIV/AIDS—adult prevalence rate: less than 0.1% (2009 est.)
country comparison to the world: 135

HIV/AIDS—people living with HIV/AIDS: 2,000 (2009 est.)
country comparison to the world: 139

HIV/AIDS—deaths: fewer than 100 (2009 est.)
country comparison to the world: 132

Obesity—adult prevalence rate: 32.7% (2008)
country comparison to the world: 21

Children under the age of 5 years underweight: 2% (2007)
country comparison to the world: 122

Education expenditures: 4.2% of GDP (2010)
country comparison to the world: 106

Literacy: *definition:* NA
total population: 99%
male: 99%
female: 99% (2011 est.)

School life expectancy (primary to tertiary education): *total:* 16 years
male: 16 years
female: 17 years (2011)

Unemployment, youth ages 15-24: *total:* 19.5%
country comparison to the world: 62
male: 19.9%
female: 19% (2012)

GOVERNMENT

Country name: *conventional long form:* Czech Republic
conventional short form: Czech Republic
local long form: Ceska republika
local short form: Cesko

Government type: parliamentary democracy

Capital: *name:* Prague
geographic coordinates: 50 05 N, 14 28 E
time difference: UTC+1 (6 hours ahead of Washington, DC during Standard Time)
daylight saving time: +1hr, begins last Sunday in March; ends last Sunday in October

Administrative divisions: 13 regions (kraje, singular—kraj) and 1 capital city* (hlavni mesto); Jihocesky (South Bohemia), Jihomoravsky (South Moravia), Karlovarsky (Karlovy Vary), Kralovehradecky (Hradec Kralove), Liberecky (Liberec), Moravskoslezsky (Moravia-Silesia), Olomoucky (Olomouc), Pardubicky (Pardubice), Plzensky (Pilsen), Praha (Prague)*, Stredocesky (Central Bohemia), Ustecky (Usti), Vysocina (Highlands), Zlinsky (Zlin)

Independence: 1 January 1993 (Czechoslovakia split into the Czech Republic and Slovakia); note—although 1 January is the day the Czech Republic came into being, the Czechs commemorate 28 October 1918, the day the former Czechoslovakia declared its independence from the Austro-Hungarian Empire, as their independence day

National holiday: Czechoslovak Founding Day, 28 October (1918)

Constitution: previous 1960; latest ratified 16 December 1992, effective 1 January 1993; amended several times, last in 2013 (2013)

Legal system: in 2014, a new civil code will replace the existing civil law system, which is based on former Austro-Hungarian civil codes and socialist theory and has been amended 40 times since the Communist regime fell in 1989

International law organization participation: has not submitted an ICJ jurisdiction declaration; accepts ICCt jurisdiction

Suffrage: 18 years of age; universal

Executive branch: *chief of state:* President Milos ZEMAN (since 8 March 2013)
head of government: Prime Minister Bohuslav SOBOTKA (since 17 January 2014); First Deputy Prime Minister Andrej BABIS and Deputy Prime Minister Pavel BELOBRADEK (both since 29 January 2014)
cabinet: Cabinet appointed by the president on the recommendation of the prime minister (For more information visit the World Leaders website)
elections: constitutional amendment passed in 2012 introduced presidential election by popular vote instead of by Parliament; president elected for a five-year term (may not serve more than two consecutive terms); elections last held on 11-12 January 2013 with a runoff on 25-26 January 2013 (next to be held in January 2018); prime minister appointed by the president
election results: Milos ZEMAN elected president; percent of popular vote—Milos ZEMAN 54.8%, Karel SCHWARZENBERG 45.2%

Legislative branch: bicameral Parliament or Parlament consists of the Senate or Senat (81 seats; members elected by popular vote to serve six-year

terms; one-third elected every two years) and the Chamber of Deputies or Poslanecka Snemovna (200 seats; members elected by popular vote to serve four-year terms)
elections: Senate—last held in two rounds on 12-13 and 19-20 October 2012 (next to be held in October 2014); Chamber of Deputies—last held on 25-26 October 2013 (next to be held in 2017)
election results: Senate—percent of vote by party—NA; seats by party—CSSD 48, ODS 15, KDU-CSL 4, TOP 09 4, North Bohemians 2, KSCM 2, Green 1, Ostravak 1, Pirate 1, independent 3; Chamber of Deputies—percent of vote by party—CSSD 20.5%, ANO 2011 18.7%, KSCM 14.9%, TOP 09 12%, ODS 7.7%, Usvit 6.9%, KDU-CSL 6.8% other 12.5%; seats by party—CSSD 50, ANO 2011 47, KSCM 33, TOP 09 26, ODS 16, Usvit 14, KDU-CSL 14

Judicial branch: *highest court(s):* Supreme Court (organized into Civil Law and Commercial Division, and Criminal Division each with a court chief justice, vice justice, and several judges); Constitutional Court (consists of 15 justices); Supreme Administrative Court (consists of 28 judges)
judge selection and term of office: Supreme Court judges proposed by the Chamber of Deputies and appointed by the president; judges appointed for life; Constitutional Court judges appointed by the president and confirmed by the Senate; judges appointed for 10-year, renewable terms; Supreme Administrative Court judges selected by the president of the Court; judge term NA
subordinate courts: High Court; superior, regional, and district courts

Political parties and leaders:
Association of Independent Candidates-European Democrats or SNK-ED [Zdenka MARKOVA]; Christian Democratic Union-Czechoslovak People's Party or KDU-CSL [Pavel BELOBRADEK]; Civic Democratic Party or ODS [Petr FIALA]; Communist Party of Bohemia and Moravia or KSCM [Vojtech FILIP]; Czech Pirate Party [Ivan BARTOS]; Czech Social Democratic Party or CSSD [Bohuslav SOBOTKA]; Dawn of Direct Democracy or Usvit [Tomio OKAMURA]; Green Party [Ondrej LISKA]; Liberal Democrats or LIDEM [Dagmar NAVRATILOVA]; Liberal Environmental Party or LES [Martin BURSYK]; Movement of Dissatisfied Citizens or ANO [Andrej BABIS]; North Bohemians; Ostravak Movement; Public Affairs or VV [Radek JOHN]; Tradition Responsibility Prosperity 09 or TOP 09 [Karel SCHWARZENBERG]

Political pressure groups and leaders:
Czech-Moravian Confederation of Trade Unions or CMKOS [Jaroslav ZAVADIL];

International organization participation: Australia Group, BIS, BSEC (observer), CD, CE, CEI, CERN, EAPC, EBRD, EIB, ESA, EU, FAO, IAEA, IBRD, ICAO, ICC (national committees), ICRM, IDA, IEA, IFC, IFRCS, ILO, IMF, IMO, IMSO, Interpol, IOC, IOM, IPU, ISO, ITSO, ITU, ITUC (NGOs), MIGA, MONUSCO, NATO, NEA, NSG, OAS (observer), OECD, OIF (observer), OPCW, OSCE, PCA, Schengen Convention, SELEC (observer), UN, UNCTAD, UNESCO, UNIDO, UNWTO, UPU, WCO, WFTU (NGOs), WHO, WIPO, WMO, WTO, ZC

Diplomatic representation in the US:
chief of mission: Ambassador Petr GANDALOVIC (since 23 May 2011)
chancery: 3900 Spring of Freedom Street NW, Washington, DC 20008
telephone: [1] (202) 274-9100
FAX: [1] (202) 966-8540
consulate(s) general: Chicago, Los Angeles, New York

Diplomatic representation from the US:
chief of mission: Ambassador Norman L. EISEN (since 14 January 2011)
embassy: Trziste 15, 118 01 Prague 1—Mala Strana
mailing address: use embassy street address
telephone: [420] 257 022 000
FAX: [420] 257 022 809

Flag description: two equal horizontal bands of white (top) and red with a blue isosceles triangle based on the hoist side
note: is identical to the flag of the former Czechoslovakia

National symbol(s): double-tailed lion

National anthem: *name:* "Kde domov muj?" (Where is My Home?)
lyrics/music: Josef Kajetan TYL/Frantisek Jan SKROUP
note: adopted 1993; the anthem is a verse from the former Czechoslovak anthem originally written as part of the opera "Fidlovacka"

ECONOMY

Economy—overview: The Czech Republic is a stable and prosperous market economy closely integrated with the EU, especially since the country's EU accession in 2004. The auto industry is the largest single industry, and, together with its upstream suppliers, accounts for nearly 24% of Czech manufacturing. The Czech Republic produced more than a million cars for the first time in 2010, over 80% of which were exported. While the conservative, inward-looking Czech financial system has remained relatively healthy, the small, open, export-driven Czech economy remains sensitive to changes in the economic performance of its main export markets, especially Germany. When Western Europe and Germany fell into recession in late 2008, demand for Czech goods plunged, leading to double digit drops in industrial production and exports. As a result, real GDP fell sharply in 2009. The economy slowly recovered in the second half of 2009 and registered weak growth in the next two years. In 2012, however, the economy fell into a recession again, due both to a slump in external demand and to the government's austerity measures. The country pulled out of recession in the second half of 2013, and most analysts expect modest, but steady, growth through 2014. Foreign and domestic businesses alike voice concerns about corruption, especially in public procurement. Other long term challenges include dealing with a rapidly aging population, funding an unsustainable pension and health care system, and diversifying away from manufacturing and toward a unsustainable pension and health care system, and diversifying away from manufacturing and toward a more high-tech, services-based, knowledge economy.

GDP (purchasing power parity): $285.6 billion (2013 est.)
country comparison to the world: 45
$288.2 billion (2012 est.)
$291.1 billion (2011 est.)
note: data are in 2013 US dollars

GDP (official exchange rate): $194.8 billion (2013 est.)

GDP—real growth rate: -0.9% (2013 est.)
country comparison to the world: 203
-1% (2012 est.)
1.8% (2011 est.)

GDP—per capita (PPP): $26,300 (2013 est.)
country comparison to the world: 56
$26,500 (2012 est.)
$28,300 (2011 est.)
note: data are in 2013 US dollars

Gross national saving: 21.1% of GDP (2013 est.)
country comparison to the world: 73
20.7% of GDP (2012 est.)
21.2% of GDP (2011 est.)

GDP—composition, by end use:
household consumption: 45.1%
government consumption: 18.3%
investment in fixed capital: 27%
investment in inventories: 0.1%
exports of goods and services: 81.1%
imports of goods and services: -71.5% (2013 est.)

GDP—composition, by sector of origin:
agriculture: 2.4%
industry: 37.3%
services: 60.3% (2012 est.)

Agriculture—products: wheat, potatoes, sugar beets, hops, fruit; pigs, poultry

Industries: motor vehicles, metallurgy, machinery and equipment, glass, armaments

Industrial production growth rate: 0.5% (2013 est.)
country comparison to the world: 157

Labor force: 5.304 million (2013 est.)
country comparison to the world: 71

Labor force—by occupation: agriculture: 2.6%
industry: 37.4%
services: 60% (2012)

Unemployment rate: 7.1% (2013 est.)
country comparison to the world: 76
7% (2012 est.)

Population below poverty line: 9.8% (2011 est.)

Household income or consumption by percentage share: *lowest 10%:* 1.5%
highest 10%: 29.1% NA% (2012 est.)

Distribution of family income—Gini index:
24.9 (2012)
country comparison to the world: 134
25.4 (1996)

Budget: *revenues:* $55.81 billion
expenditures: $59.96 billion (2013 est.)

Taxes and other revenues: 28.6% of GDP (2013 est.)
country comparison to the world: 101

Budget surplus (+) or deficit (-):
-2.1% of GDP (2013 est.)
country comparison to the world: 88

Public debt: 48.8% of GDP (2013 est.)
country comparison to the world: 69
46.2% of GDP (2012 est.)

Fiscal year: calendar year

Inflation rate (consumer prices): 1.4% (2013 est.)
country comparison to the world: 37
3.3% (2012 est.)

Central bank discount rate: 0.05% (31 December 2013 est.)
country comparison to the world: 144
0.05% (31 December 2012)
note: this is the two-week repo, the main rate CNB uses

Commercial bank prime lending rate:
5.1% (31 December 2013 est.)
country comparison to the world: 148
5.41% (31 December 2012 est.)

Stock of narrow money: $124.1 billion (30 September 2013 est.)
country comparison to the world: 30
$114.2 billion (30 September 2012 est.)

Stock of broad money: $154 billion (30 September 2013 est.)
country comparison to the world: 45
$146.5 billion (30 September 2012 est.)

Stock of domestic credit: $134.3 billion (30 September 2012 est.)
country comparison to the world: 48
$130.2 billion (31 December 2011 est.)

Market value of publicly traded shares: $54.92 billion (30 December 3013 est.)
country comparison to the world: 49
$59.88 billion (28 December 2012)
$53.2 billion (30 December 2011 est.)

Current account balance: -$3.27 billion (2013 est.)
country comparison to the world: 160
-$4.798 billion (2012 est.)

Exports: $161.4 billion (2013 est.)
country comparison to the world: 32
$157 billion (2012 est.)

Exports—commodities: machinery and transport equipment, raw materials and fuel, chemicals

Exports—partners: Germany 31.8%, Slovakia 9.1%, Poland 6.1%, France 5.1%, UK 4.9%, Austria 4.7% (2012)

Imports: $143.4 billion (2013 est.)
country comparison to the world: 32
$141.4 billion (2012 est.)

Imports—commodities: machinery and transport equipment, raw materials and fuels, chemicals

Imports—partners: Germany 29.5%, Poland 7.7%, Slovakia 7.4%, China 6.3%, Netherlands 5.8%, Russia 5.3%, Austria 4.3% (2012)

Reserves of foreign exchange and gold:
$56.22 billion (31 December 2013 est.)
country comparison to the world: 34
$44.88 billion (31 December 2012 est.)

Debt—external: $102.1 billion (30 September 2013 est.)
country comparison to the world: 45
$101.9 billion (31 December 2012 est.)

Stock of direct foreign investment—at home:
$144.2 billion (31 December 2013 est.)
country comparison to the world: 32
$136.5 billion (31 December 2012 est.)

Stock of direct foreign investment—abroad:
$16.63 billion (31 December 2013 est.)
country comparison to the world: 49
$17.37 billion (31 December 2012 est.)

Exchange rates: koruny (CZK) per US dollar—
19.57 (2013 est.)
19.59 (2012 est.)
19.098 (2010 est.)
19.063 (2009)
17.064 (2008)

ENERGY

Electricity—production: 87.57 billion kWh (2012 est.)
country comparison to the world: 37

Electricity—consumption: 70.45 billion kWh (2012 est.)
country comparison to the world: 38

Electricity—exports: 27.45 billion kWh (2012 est.)
country comparison to the world: 7

Electricity—imports: 10.33 billion kWh (2012 est.)
country comparison to the world: 22

Electricity—installed generating capacity:
NA Kw (2012 est.)

Electricity—from fossil fuels: 63.6% of total installed capacity (2012 est.)
country comparison to the world: 126

Electricity—from nuclear fuels: 19.7% of total installed capacity (2012 est.)
country comparison to the world: 9

Electricity—from hydroelectric plants: 5.2% of total installed capacity (2012 est.)
country comparison to the world: 125

Electricity—from other renewable sources:
11.5% of total installed capacity (2012 est.)
country comparison to the world: 23

Crude oil—production: 10,010 bbl/day (2012 est.)
country comparison to the world: 90

Crude oil—exports: 403.8 bbl/day (2010 est.)
country comparison to the world: 72

Crude oil—imports: 154,000 bbl/day (2010 est.)
country comparison to the world: 41

Crude oil—proved reserves: 15 million bbl (1 January 2013 es)
country comparison to the world: 87

Refined petroleum products—production:
178,900 bbl/day (2010 est.)
country comparison to the world: 58

Refined petroleum products—consumption:
199,000 bbl/day (2011 est.)
country comparison to the world: 59

Refined petroleum products—exports:
35,720 bbl/day (2010 est.)
country comparison to the world: 67

Refined petroleum products—imports:
54,240 bbl/day (2010 est.)
country comparison to the world: 67

Natural gas—production:
200 million cu m (2012 est.)
country comparison to the world: 79

Natural gas—consumption: 8.158 billion cu m (2012 est.)
country comparison to the world: 53

Natural gas—exports: 7.4 million cu m (2012 est.)
country comparison to the world: 52

Natural gas—imports: 7.471 billion cu m (2012 est.)
country comparison to the world: 34

Natural gas—proved reserves: 1.922 billion cu m (1 January 2013 es)
country comparison to the world: 100

Carbon dioxide emissions from consumption of energy: 106.3 million Mt (2011 est.)
country comparison to the world: 40

COMMUNICATIONS

Telephones—main lines in use: 2.1 million (2012)
country comparison to the world: 56

Telephones—mobile cellular: 12.973 million (2012)
country comparison to the world: 65

Telephone system: *general assessment:* privatization and modernization of the Czech telecommunication system got a late start but is advancing steadily; virtually all exchanges now digital; existing copper subscriber systems enhanced with Asymmetric Digital Subscriber Line (ADSL) equipment to accommodate Internet and other digital signals; trunk systems include fiber-optic cable and microwave radio relay
domestic: access to the fixed-line telephone network expanded throughout the 1990s but the number of fixed line connections has been dropping since then; mobile telephone usage increased sharply beginning in the mid-1990s and the number of cellular telephone subscriptions now greatly exceeds the population
international: country code—420; satellite earth stations—6 (2 Intersputnik—Atlantic and Indian Ocean regions, 1 Intelsat, 1 Eutelsat, 1 Inmarsat, 1 Globalstar) (2011)

Broadcast media: roughly 130 TV broadcasters operating some 350 channels with 4 publicly operated and the remainder in private hands; 16 TV stations have national coverage with 4 being publicly operated; cable and satellite TV subscription services are available; 63 radio broadcasters are registered operating roughly 80 radio stations with 15 stations publicly operated; 10 radio stations provide national coverage with the remainder local or regional (2008)

Internet country code: .cz

Internet hosts: 4.148 million (2012)
country comparison to the world: 27

Internet users: 6.681 million (2009)
country comparison to the world: 40

TRANSPORTATION

Airports: 128 (2013)
country comparison to the world: 4 6

Airports—with paved runways: *total:* 4 1
over 3,047 m: 2
2,438 to 3,047 m: 9
1,524 to 2,437 m: 12
914 to 1,523 m: 2
under 914 m: 16 (2013)

Airports—with unpaved runways: *total:* 8 7
1,524 to 2,437 m: 1
914 to 1,523 m: 25
under 914 m: 61 (2013)

Heliports: 1 (2013)

Pipelines: gas 7,160 km; oil 536 km; refined products 94 km (2013)

Railways: total: 9,469 km
country comparison to the world: 23

standard gauge: 9,449 km 1.435-m gauge (3,165 km electrified)
narrow gauge: 20 km 0.750-m gauge (2008)

Roadways: total: 130,671 km (includes urban roads)
country comparison to the world: 38
paved: 130,671 km (includes 730 km of expressways) (2010)

Waterways: 664 km (principally on Elbe, Vltava, Oder, and other navigable rivers, lakes, and canals) (2010)
country comparison to the world: 77

Merchant marine: registered in other countries: 1 (Saint Vincent and the Grenadines 1) (2010)
country comparison to the world: 147

Ports and terminals: *river port(s):* Prague (Vltava); Decin, Usti nad Labem (Elbe)

MILITARY

Military branches: Army of the Czech Republic (Armada Ceske Republiky): Joint Forces Command (Spolocene Sily; includes Land Forces (Pozemni Sily) and Air Forces (Vzdusne Sily)) (2013)

Military service age and obligation:
18-28 years of age for male and female voluntary military service; no conscription (2012)

Manpower available for military service:
males age 16-49: 2,506,826
females age 16-49: 2,407,634 (2010 est.)

Manpower fit for military service:
males age 16-49: 2,072,267
females age 16-49: 1,988,839 (2010 est.)

Manpower reaching militarily significant age annually:
male: 49,999
female: 47,501 (2010 est.)

Military expenditures: 1.08% of GDP (2013)
country comparison to the world: 95
1.13% of GDP (2012)
1.15% of GDP (2011)
1.13% of GDP (2010)

TRANSNATIONAL ISSUES

Disputes—international: while threats of international legal action never materialized in 2007, 915,220 Austrians, with the support of the popular Freedom Party, signed a petition in January 2008, demanding that Austria block the Czech Republic's accession to the EU unless Prague closes its controversial Soviet-style nuclear plant in Temelin, bordering Austria

Refugees and internally displaced persons:
stateless persons: 1,502 (2012)

Illicit drugs: transshipment point for Southwest Asian heroin and minor transit point for Latin American cocaine to Western Europe; producer of synthetic drugs for local and regional markets; susceptible to money laundering related to drug trafficking, organized crime; significant consumer of ecstasy (2008)

DENMARK

Background: Once the seat of Viking raiders and later a major north European power, Denmark has evolved into a modern, prosperous nation that is participating in the general political and economic integration of Europe. It joined NATO in 1949 and the EEC (now the EU) in 1973. However, the country has opted out of certain elements of the European Union's Maastricht Treaty, including the European Economic and Monetary Union (EMU), European defense cooperation, and issues concerning certain justice and home affairs.

GEOGRAPHY

Location: Northern Europe, bordering the Baltic Sea and the North Sea, on a peninsula north of Germany (Jutland); also includes several major islands (Sjaelland, Fyn, and Bornholm)

Geographic coordinates: 56 00 N, 10 00 E

Map references: Europe

Area: *total:* 43,094 sq km country *comparison to the world:* 134
land: 42,434 sq km
water: 660 sq km
note: includes the island of Bornholm in the Baltic Sea and the rest of metropolitan Denmark (the Jutland Peninsula, and the major islands of Sjaelland and Fyn), but excludes the Faroe Islands and Greenland

Area—comparative: slightly less than twice the size of Massachusetts

Land boundaries: *total:* 68 km
border countries: Germany 68 km

Coastline: 7,314 km

Maritime claims: *territorial sea:* 12 nm
contiguous zone: 24 nm
exclusive economic zone: 200 nm
continental shelf: 200 m depth or to the depth of exploitation

Climate: temperate; humid and overcast; mild, windy winters and cool summers

Terrain: low and flat to gently rolling plains

Elevation extremes: *lowest point:* Lammefjord -7 m
highest point: Mollehoj/Ejer Bavnehoj 171 m

Natural resources: petroleum, natural gas, fish, salt, limestone, chalk, stone, gravel and sand

Land use: *arable land:* 57.99%
permanent crops: 0.09%
other: 41.91% (2011)

Irrigated land: 4,354 sq km (2007)

Total renewable water resources: 6 cu km (2011)

Freshwater withdrawal (domestic/industrial/agricultural): *total:* 0.66 cu km/yr (58%/5%/36%)
per capita: 118.4 cu m/yr (2009)

Natural hazards: flooding is a threat in some areas of the country (e.g., parts of Jutland, along the southern coast of the island of Lolland) that are protected from the sea by a system of dikes

Environment—current issues: air pollution, principally from vehicle and power plant emissions; nitrogen and phosphorus pollution of the North Sea; drinking and surface water becoming polluted from animal wastes and pesticides

Environment—international agreements: *party to:* Air Pollution, Air Pollution-Nitrogen Oxides, Air Pollution-Persistent Organic Pollutants, Air Pollution-Sulfur 85, Air Pollution-Sulfur 94, Air Pollution-Volatile Organic Compounds, Antarctic Treaty, Biodiversity, Climate Change, Climate Change-Kyoto Protocol, Desertification, Endangered Species, Environmental Modification, Hazardous Wastes, Law of the Sea, Marine Dumping, Marine Life Conservation, Ozone Layer Protection, Ship Pollution, Tropical Timber 83, Tropical Timber 94, Wetlands, Whaling
signed, but not ratified: none of the selected agreements

Geography—note: controls Danish Straits (Skagerrak and Kattegat) linking Baltic and North Seas; about one-quarter of the population lives in greater Copenhagen

PEOPLE AND SOCIETY

Nationality: *noun:* Dane(s)
adjective: Danish

Ethnic groups: Scandinavian, Inuit, Faroese, German, Turkish, Iranian, Somali

Languages: Danish, Faroese, Greenlandic (an Inuit dialect), German (small minority)
note: English is the predominant second language

Religions: Evangelical Lutheran (official) 80%, Muslim 4%, other (denominations of less than 1% each, includes Roman Catholic, Jehovah's Witness, Serbian Orthodox Christian, Jewish, Baptist, and Buddhist) 16% (2012 est.)

Population: 5,569,077 (July 2014 est.)
country comparison to the world: 115

Age structure: *0-14 years:* 17% (male 485,115/female 460,682)
15-24 years: 13.1% (male 371,258/female 355,984)
25-54 years: 39.2% (male 1,087,993/female 1,093,545)
55-64 years: 18.4% (male 343,685/female 347,732)
65 years and over: 18% (male 457,175/female 565,908) (2014 est.)

Dependency ratios:
total dependency ratio: 55 %
youth dependency ratio: 27.2 %
elderly dependency ratio: 27.7 %
potential support ratio: 3.6 (2013)

Median age: *total:* 41.6 years
male: 40.7 years
female: 42.5 years (2014 est.)

Population growth rate: 0.22% (2014 est.)
country comparison to the world: 178

Birth rate: 10.22 births/1,000 population (2014 est.)
country comparison to the world: 190

Death rate: 10.23 deaths/1,000 population (2014 est.)
country comparison to the world: 46

Net migration rate: 2.25 migrant(s)/1,000 population (2014 est.)
country comparison to the world: 43

Urbanization: *urban population:* 86.9% of total population (2011)
rate of urbanization: 0.5% annual rate of change (2010-15 est.)

Major urban areas—population:
COPENHAGEN (capital) 1.206 million (2011)

Sex ratio: *at birth:* 1.06 male(s)/female
0-14 years: 1.05 male(s)/female
15-24 years: 1.04 male(s)/female
25-54 years: 1 male(s)/female
55-64 years: 0.97 male(s)/female
65 years and over: 0.8 male(s)/female
total population: 0.97 male(s)/female (2014 est.)

Mother's mean age at first birth: 29.1 (2010 est.)

Maternal mortality rate:
12 deaths/100,000 live births (2010)
country comparison to the world: 151

Infant mortality rate: total: 4.1 deaths/1,000 live births
country comparison to the world: 197
male: 4.17 deaths/1,000 live births
female: 4.02 deaths/1,000 live births (2014 est.)

Life expectancy at birth: *total population:* 79.09 years
country comparison to the world: 48
male: 76.68 years
female: 81.64 years (2014 est.)

Total fertility rate: 1.73 children born/woman (2014 est.)
country comparison to the world: 168

Health expenditures: 11.2% of GDP (2011)
country comparison to the world: 12

Physicians density: 3.42 physicians/1,000 population (2007)

Hospital bed density: 3.5 beds/1,000 population (2010)

Drinking water source:
improved:
urban: 100% of population
rural: 100% of population
total: 100% of population
unimproved:
urban: 0% of population
rural: 0% of population
total: 0% of population (2011 est.)

Sanitation facility access:
improved:
urban: 100% of population
rural: 100% of population
total: 100% of population
unimproved:
urban: 0% of population
rural: 0% of population
total: 0% of population (2011 est.)

HIV/AIDS—adult prevalence rate: 0.2% (2009 est.)
country comparison to the world: 111

HIV/AIDS—people living with HIV/AIDS:
5,300 (2009 est.)
country comparison to the world: 122

HIV/AIDS—deaths: fewer than 100 (2009 est.)
country comparison to the world: 133

Obesity—adult prevalence rate: 18.2% (2008)
country comparison to the world: 107

Education expenditures: 8.7% of GDP (2009)
country comparison to the world: 8

Literacy: *definition:* age 15 and over can read and write

total population: 99%
male: 99%
female: 99% (2003 est.)

School life expectancy (primary to tertiary education): *total:* 17 years
male: 16 years
female: 18 years (2010)

Unemployment, youth ages 15-24: *total:* 14.2%
country comparison to the world: 89
male: 14.8%
female: 14.1% (2012)

GOVERNMENT

Country name: conventional long form: Kingdom of Denmark
conventional short form: Denmark local
long form: Kongeriget Danmark
local short form: Danmark

Government type: constitutional monarchy

Capital: *name:* Copenhagen
geographic coordinates: 55 40 N, 12 35 E
time difference: UTC+1 (6 hours ahead of Washington, DC during Standard Time)
daylight saving time: +1hr, begins last Sunday in March; ends last Sunday in October
note: applies to continental Denmark only, not to its North Atlantic components

Administrative divisions: metropolitan Denmark—5 regions (regioner, singular—region); Hovedstaden, Midtjylland, Nordjylland, Sjaelland, Syddanmark
note: an extensive local government reform merged 271 municipalities into 98 and 13 counties into five regions, effective 1 January 2007

Independence: ca. 965 (unified and Christianized under HARALD I Gormson); 5 June 1849 (became a constitutional monarchy)

National holiday: none designated; Constitution Day, 5 June (1849) is generally viewed as the National Day

Constitution: previous 1665; latest adopted 5 June 1849; amended several times, last in 2009 (2009)

Legal system: civil law; judicial review of legislative acts

International law organization participation: accepts compulsory ICJ jurisdiction with reservations; accepts ICCt jurisdiction

Suffrage: 18 years of age; universal

Executive branch: *chief of state:* Queen MARGRETHE II (since 14 January 1972); Heir Apparent Crown Prince FREDERIK, elder son of the monarch (born on 26 May 1968)
head of government: Prime Minister Helle THORNING-SCHMIDT (since 3 October 2011)
cabinet: Council of State appointed by the monarch (For more information visit the World Leaders website)
elections: the monarchy is hereditary; following legislative elections, the leader of the majority party or the leader of the majority coalition usually appointed prime minister by the monarch

Legislative branch: unicameral People's Assembly or Folketing (179 seats, including 2 from Greenland and 2 from the Faroe Islands; members elected by popular vote on the basis of proportional representation to serve four-year terms unless the Folketing is dissolved earlier)
elections: last held on 15 September 2011 (next to be held by September 2015)
election results: percent of vote by party—V 26.7%, SDP 24.9%, DF 12.3%, SLP 9.5%, SF 9.2%, O 6.7%, LA 5%, C 4.9%, other 0.8%; seats by party—V 47, SDP 44, DF 22, SLP 17, SF 16, O 12, LA 9, C 8; note—does not include the two seats from Greenland and the two seats from the Faroe Islands

Judicial branch: *highest court(s):* Supreme Court (consists of the court president and 18 judges)
judge selection and term of office: judges appointed by the monarch upon the recommendation of the Minister of Justice with the advice of the Judicial Appointments Council, a 6-member independent body of judges and lawyers; judges appointed for life with retirement at age 70
subordinate courts: Special Court of Indictment and Revision; 2 High Courts; Maritime and Commercial Court; county courts

Political parties and leaders: Conservative People's Party or C [Lars BARFOED]; Danish People's Party or DF [Kristian THULESEN DAHL]; Liberal Alliance or LA [Anders SAMUELSEN]; Liberal Party or V [Lars LOKKE RAMUSSEN]; Red-Green Alliance (Unity List) or O [collective leadership, spokesperson Johanne SCHMIDT-NIELSEN]; Social Democratic Party or SDP [Helle THORNING-SCHMIDT]; Social Liberal Party or SLP [Margrethe VESTAGER]; Socialist People's Party or SF [Annette VILHELMSEN]

Political pressure groups and leaders: Confederation of Danish Employers or DA [President Jorn Neergaard LARSEN]; Confederation of Danish Industries [CEO Karsten DYBVAD]; Confederation of Danish Labor Unions (Landsorganisationen) or LO [President Harald BORSTING]; Danish Shipowners' Association [Chairman Carsten MORTENSEN]; Danish Bankers Association [CEO Joergen HORWITZ]; DaneAge Association [President Bjarne HASTRUP]; Danish Society for Nature Conservation [President Ella Maria BISSCHOP-LARSEN]
other: environmental groups; humanitarian relief; development assistance; human rights NGOs

International organization participation: ADB (nonregional member), AfDB (nonregional member), Arctic Council, Australia Group, BIS, CBSS, CD, CE, CERN, EAPC, EBRD, EIB, EITI (implementing country), ESA, EU, FAO, FATF, G-9, IADB, IAEA, IBRD, ICAO, ICC (national committees), ICRM, IDA, IEA, IFAD, IFC, IFRCS, IGAD (partners), IHO, ILO, IMF, IMO, IMSO, Interpol, IOC, IOM, IPU, ISO, ITSO, ITU, ITUC (NGOs), MIGA, NATO, NC, NEA, NIB, NSG, OAS (observer), OECD, OPCW, OSCE, Paris Club, PCA, Schengen Convention, UN, UNCTAD, UNESCO, UNHCR, UNIDO, UNMIL, UNMISS, UNRWA, UNTSO, UPU, WCO, WHO, WIPO, WMO, WTO, ZC

Diplomatic representation in the US: chief of mission: Ambassador Peter TAKSOE-JENSEN (since 1 September 2010)
chancery: 3200 Whitehaven Street NW, Washington, DC 20008
telephone: [1] (202) 234-4300
FAX: [1] (202) 328-1470
consulate(s) general: Chicago, New York

Diplomatic representation from the US: *chief of mission:* Ambassador Rufus GIFFORD (since 15 August 2013)
embassy: Dag Hammarskjolds Alle 24, 2100 Copenhagen 0
mailing address: Unit 5280, DPO, AE 09716
telephone: [45] 33 41 71 00
FAX: [45] 35 43 02 23

Flag description: red with a white cross that extends to the edges of the flag; the vertical part of the cross is shifted to the hoist side; the banner is referred to as the Dannebrog (Danish flag) and is one of the oldest national flags in the world; traditions as to the origin of the flag design vary, but the best known is a legend that the banner fell from the sky during an early-13th century battle; caught up by the Danish king before it ever touched the earth, this heavenly talisman inspired the royal army to victory; in actuality, the flag may derive from a crusade banner or ensign
note: the shifted design element was subsequently adopted by the other Nordic countries of Finland, Iceland, Norway, and Sweden

National symbol(s): lion; mute swan

National anthem: *name:* "Der er et yndigt land" (There is a Lovely Land); "Kong Christian" (King Christian)
lyrics/music: Adam Gottlob OEHLENSCHLAGER/Hans Ernst KROYER; Johannes EWALD/unknown
note: Denmark has two national anthems with equal status; "Der er et yndigt land," adopted 1844, is a national anthem, while "Kong Christian," adopted 1780, serves as both a national and royal anthem; "Kong Christian" is also known as "Kong Christian stod ved hojen mast" (King Christian Stood by the Lofty Mast) and "Kongesangen" (The King's Anthem); within Denmark, the royal anthem is played only when royalty is present and is usually followed by the national anthem; when royalty is not present, only the national anthem is performed; outside Denmark, the royal anthem is played, unless the national anthem is requested

ECONOMY

Economy—overview: This thoroughly modern market economy features a high-tech agricultural sector, state-of-the-art industry with world-leading firms in pharmaceuticals, maritime shipping and renewable energy, and a high dependence on foreign trade. Denmark is a member of the European Union (EU); Danish legislation and regulations conform to EU standards on almost all issues. Danes enjoy a high standard of living and the Danish economy is characterized by extensive government welfare measures and an equitable distribution of income. Denmark is a net exporter of food and energy and enjoys a comfortable balance of payments surplus, but depends on imports of raw materials for the manufacturing sector. Within the EU, Denmark is among the strongest supporters of trade liberalization. After a long consumption-driven upswing, Denmark's economy began slowing in 2007 with the end of a housing boom. Housing prices dropped markedly in 2008-09 and, following a short respite in 2010, have since continued to decline. Household indebtedness is still relatively high at more than 275% of gross disposable income in the first half of 2013. The global financial crisis has exacerbated this cyclical slowdown through increased borrowing costs and lower export demand, consumer confidence, and investment. Denmark made a modest recovery in 2010, in part because of increased government spending; however, the country experienced a technical recession in late 2010-early 2011. Historically low levels of unemployment rose sharply with the recession and have remained at about 6% in 2010-13, based on the national measure, about two-thirds average EU unemployment. An impending decline in the ratio of workers to retirees will be a major long-term issue. Denmark maintained a healthy budget surplus for many years up to 2008, but the budget balance swung into deficit in 2009, where it remains. In spite of the deficits, the new coalition government delivered a modest stimulus to the economy in 2012. Nonetheless, Denmark's fiscal position remains among the strongest in the EU with public debt at about 46% of GDP in 2013. Despite previously meeting the criteria to join the

European Economic and Monetary Union (EMU), so far Denmark has decided not to join, although the Danish krone remains pegged to the euro.

GDP (purchasing power parity): $211.3 billion (2013 est.)
country comparison to the world: 55
$211.1 billion (2012 est.)
$211.9 billion (2011 est.)
note: data are in 2013 US dollars

GDP (official exchange rate): $324.3 billion (2013 est.)

GDP—real growth rate: 0.1% (2013 est.)
country comparison to the world: 192
-0.4% (2012 est.)
1.1% (2011 est.)

GDP—per capita (PPP): $37,800 (2013 est.)
country comparison to the world: 31
$37,800 (2012 est.)
$38,100 (2011 est.)
note: data are in 2013 US dollars

Gross national saving: 24.1% of GDP (2013 est.)
country comparison to the world: 55
22.6% of GDP (2012 est.)
23.3% of GDP (2011 est.)

GDP—composition, by end use:
household consumption: 49.1%
government consumption: 28.8%
investment in fixed capital: 17.7%
investment in inventories: 0.2%
exports of goods and services: 53.4%
imports of goods and services: -49.2% (2013 est.)

GDP—composition, by sector of origin:
agriculture: 1.5%
industry: 21.7%
services: 76.8% (2013 est.)

Agriculture—products: barley, wheat, potatoes, sugar beets; pork, dairy products; fish

Industries: iron, steel, nonferrous metals, chemicals, food processing, machinery and transportation equipment, textiles and clothing, electronics, construction, furniture and other wood products, shipbuilding and refurbishment, windmills, pharmaceuticals, medical equipment

Industrial production growth rate: 1.1% (2013 est.)
country comparison to the world: 144

Labor force: 2.795 million (2013 est.)
country comparison to the world: 106

Labor force—by occupation: *agriculture:* 2.6%
industry: 20.3%
services: 77.1% (2011 est.)

Unemployment rate: 6% (2013 est.)
country comparison to the world: 60
6% (2012 est.)

Population below poverty line: 13.4% (2011)

Household income or consumption by percentage share:
lowest 10%: 1.9%
highest 10%: 28.7% (2007)

Distribution of family income—Gini index:
24.8 (2011 est.)
country comparison to the world: 135
24.7 (1992)

Budget: *revenues:* $181.4 billion
expenditures: $189.7 billion (2013 est.)

Taxes and other revenues: 55.9% of GDP (2013 est.)
country comparison to the world: 8

Budget surplus (+) or deficit (-):
-2.5% of GDP (2013 est.)
country comparison to the world: 103

Public debt: 47% of GDP (2013 est.)
country comparison to the world: 75
45.6% of GDP (2012 est.)
note: data cover general government debt, and includes debt instruments issued (or owned) by government entities other than the treasury; the data include treasury debt held by foreign entities; the data include debt issued by subnational entities, as well as intra-governmental debt; intra-governmental debt consists of treasury borrowings from surpluses in the social funds, such as for retirement, medical care, and unemployment; debt instruments for the social funds are not sold at public auctions

Fiscal year: calendar year

Inflation rate (consumer prices): 0.8% (2013 est.)
country comparison to the world: 18
2.4% (2012 est.)

Central bank discount rate:
0.75% (31 December 2011 est.)
country comparison to the world: 132
0.75% (31 December 2010 est.)

Commercial bank prime lending rate:
3.6% (31 December 2013 est.)
country comparison to the world: 168
3.6% (31 December 2012 est.)

Stock of narrow money: $147.6 billion (31 December 2013 est.)
country comparison to the world: 26
$150.4 billion (31 December 2012 est.)

Stock of broad money: $180.2 billion (31 December 2013 est.)
country comparison to the world: 42
$174.3 billion (31 December 2012 est.)

Stock of domestic credit: $675 billion (31 December 2013 est.)
country comparison to the world: 22
$664.5 billion (31 December 2012 est.)

Market value of publicly traded shares:
$224.9 billion (31 December 2012 est.)
country comparison to the world: 34
$179.5 billion (31 December 2011)
$231.7 billion (31 December 2010 est.)

Current account balance: $19.6 billion (2013 est.)
country comparison to the world: 16
$17.44 billion (2012 est.)

Exports: $106 billion (2013 est.)
country comparison to the world: 37
$104.9 billion (2012 est.)

Exports—commodities: machinery and instruments, meat and meat products, dairy products, fish, pharmaceuticals, furniture, windmills

Exports—partners: Germany 15.9%, Sweden 13.5%, UK 9.6%, US 6.6%, Norway 6.3%, Netherlands 4.6% (2012)

Imports: $98.45 billion (2013 est.)
country comparison to the world: 35
$96.77 billion (2012 est.)

Imports—commodities: machinery and equipment, raw materials and semimanufactures for industry, chemicals, grain and foodstuffs, consumer goods

Imports—partners: Germany 21.2%, Sweden 13.5%, Netherlands 7.5%, China 6.4%, Norway 6.3%, UK 5.6% (2012)

Reserves of foreign exchange and gold:
$89.5 billion (31 December 2013 est.)
country comparison to the world: 25
$89.7 billion (31 December 2012 est.)

Debt—external: $586.7 billion (31 December 2012 est.)
country comparison to the world: 24
$571.4 billion (31 December 2011)

Stock of direct foreign investment—at home:
$146 billion (31 December 2013 est.)
country comparison to the world: 31
$147.1 billion (31 December 2012 est.)

Stock of direct foreign investment—abroad:
$248.3 billion (31 December 2013 est.)
country comparison to the world: 21
$241.7 billion (31 December 2012 est.)

Exchange rates: Danish kroner (DKK) per US dollar—
5.695 (2013 est.)
5.7925 (2012 est.)
5.6241 (2010 est.)
5.361 (2009)
5.0236 (2008)

ENERGY

Electricity—production: 33.71 billion kWh (2011 est.)
country comparison to the world: 6 3

Electricity—consumption: 33.56 billion kWh (2010 est.)
country comparison to the world: 60

Electricity—exports: 10.71 billion kWh (2012 est.)
country comparison to the world: 20

Electricity—imports: 15.92 billion kWh (2012 est.)
country comparison to the world: 11

Electricity—installed generating capacity:
13.71 million kW (2010 est.)
country comparison to the world: 47

Electricity—from fossil fuels:
63% of total installed capacity (2010 est.)
country comparison to the world: 129

Electricity—from nuclear fuels:
0% of total installed capacity (2010 est.)
country comparison to the world: 75

Electricity—from hydroelectric plants:
0.1% of total installed capacity (2010 est.)
country comparison to the world: 150

Electricity—from other renewable sources:
36.9% of total installed capacity (2010 est.)
country comparison to the world: 2

Crude oil—production: 207,400 bbl/day (2012 est.)
country comparison to the world: 38

Crude oil—exports: 155,200 bbl/day (2010 est.)
country comparison to the world: 32

Crude oil—imports: 55,010 bbl/day (2010 est.)
country comparison to the world: 55

Crude oil—proved reserves: 805 million bbl (1 January 2013 es)
country comparison to the world: 43

Refined petroleum products—production:
145,300 bbl/day (2010 est.)
country comparison to the world: 63

Refined petroleum products—consumption:
160,200 bbl/day (2011 est.)
country comparison to the world: 64

Refined petroleum products—exports:
104,400 bbl/day (2010 est.)
country comparison to the world: 44

Refined petroleum products—imports:
124,100 bbl/day (2010 est.)
country comparison to the world: 44

Natural gas—production: 6.412 billion cu m (2012 est.)
country comparison to the world: 50

Natural gas—consumption:
4.994 billion cu m (2010 est.)
country comparison to the world: 63

Natural gas—exports: 2.983 billion cu m (2012 est.)
country comparison to the world: 40

Natural gas—imports:
254 million cu m (2012 est.)
country comparison to the world: 68

Natural gas—proved reserves:

42.98 billion cu m (1 January 2013 es)
country comparison to the world: 67

Carbon dioxide emissions from consumption of energy: 46.66 million Mt (2011 est.)
country comparison to the world: 66

COMMUNICATIONS

Telephones—main lines in use: 2.431 million (2012)
country comparison to the world: 53

Telephones—mobile cellular: 6.6 million (2012)
country comparison to the world: 97

Telephone system: *general assessment:* excellent telephone and telegraph services
domestic: buried and submarine cables and microwave radio relay form trunk network, multiple cellular mobile communications systems
international: country code—45; a series of fiber-optic submarine cables link Denmark with Canada, Faroe Islands, Germany, Iceland, Netherlands, Norway, Poland, Russia, Sweden, and UK; satellite earth stations—18 (6 Intelsat, 10 Eutelsat, 1 Orion, 1 Inmarsat (Blaavand-Atlantic-East)); note—the Nordic countries (Denmark, Finland, Iceland, Norway, and Sweden) share the Danish earth station and the Eik, Norway, station for worldwide Inmarsat access (2011)

Broadcast media: strong public-sector TV presence with state-owned Danmarks Radio (DR) operating 4 channels and publicly owned TV2 operating roughly a half dozen channels; broadcasts of privately owned stations are available via satellite and cable feed; DR operates 4 nationwide FM radio stations, 15 digital audio broadcasting stations, and about 15 web-based radio stations; approximately 250 commercial and community radio stations (2007)

Internet country code: .dk

Internet hosts: 4.297 million (2012)
country comparison to the world: 25

Internet users: 4.75 million (2009)
country comparison to the world: 48

TRANSPORTATION

Airports: 80 (2013)
country comparison to the world: 6 8

Airports—with paved runways: *total:* 2 8
over 3,047 m: 2
2,438 to 3,047 m: 7
1,524 to 2,437 m: 5
914 to 1,523 m: 12
under 914 m: 2 (2013)

Airports—with unpaved runways: *total:* 5 2
914 to 1,523 m: 5
under 914 m: 47 (2013)

Pipelines: condensate 11 km; gas 4,377 km; oil 647 km; oil/gas/water 2 km (2013)

Railways: *total:* 2,667 km
country comparison to the world: 62
standard gauge: 2,667 km 1.435-m gauge (640 km electrified) (2008)

Roadways: total: 73,929 km
country comparison to the world: 63
paved: 73,929 km (includes 1,143 km of expressways) (2012)

Waterways: 400 km (2010)
country comparison to the world: 88

Merchant marine: *total:* 367
country comparison to the world: 27
by type: bulk carrier 4, cargo 48, carrier 1, chemical tanker 125, container 94, liquefied gas 4, passenger 1, passenger/cargo 40, petroleum tanker 36, refrigerated cargo 3, roll on/roll off 8, specialized tanker 3
foreign-owned: 27 (Germany 9, Greenland 1, Norway 2, Sweden 15) registered in other countries: 582 (Antigua and Barbuda 20, Bahamas 69, Belgium 4, Brazil 3, Curacao 1, Cyprus 6, Egypt 1, France 11, Gibraltar 7, Hong Kong 42, Isle of Man 30, Italy 4, Jamaica 1, Liberia 8, Lithuania 8, Luxembourg 1, Malaysia 1, Malta 34, Marshall Islands 7, Moldova 1, Netherlands 27, Norway 7, Panama 41, Philippines 2, Portugal 4, Saint Vincent and the Grenadines 9, Singapore 149, Sweden 4, UK 43, Uruguay 1, US 31, Venezuela 1, unknown 4) (2010)

Ports and terminals:
major seaport(s): Baltic Sea—Aarhus, Copenhagen, Fredericia, Kalundborg; North Sea—Esbjerg,
river port(s): Aalborg (Langerak)
dry bulk cargo port(s): Ensted (coal)
cruise port(s): Copenhagen

MILITARY

Military branches: Defense Command: Army Operational Command, Admiral Danish Fleet, Arctic Command, Tactical Air Command, Home Guard (2010)

Military service age and obligation: 18 years of age for compulsory and voluntary military service; conscripts serve an initial training period that varies from 4 to 12 months according to specialization; reservists are assigned to mobilization units following completion of their conscript service; women eligible to volunteer for military service (2012)

Manpower available for military service:
males age 16-49: 1,236,337
females age 16-49: 1,224,182 (2010 est.)

Manpower fit for military service:
males age 16-49: 1,014,560
females age 16-49: 1,003,921 (2010 est.)

Manpower reaching militarily significant age annually: *male:* 37,913
female: 35,865 (2010 est.)

Military expenditures:
1.41% of GDP (2012)
country comparison to the world: 71
1.35% of GDP (2011)
1.41% of GDP (2010)

TRANSNATIONAL ISSUES

Disputes—international: Iceland, the UK, and Ireland dispute Denmark's claim that the Faroe Islands' continental shelf extends beyond 200 nm; Faroese continue to study proposals for full independence; sovereignty dispute with Canada over Hans Island in the Kennedy Channel between Ellesmere Island and Greenland; Denmark (Greenland) and Norway have made submissions to the Commission on the Limits of the Continental Shelf (CLCS) and Russia is collecting additional data to augment its 2001 CLCS submission

Refugees and internally displaced persons:
stateless persons: 3,623 (2012)

DHEKELIA

INTRODUCTION

Background: By terms of the 1960 Treaty of Establishment that created the independent Republic of Cyprus, the UK retained full sovereignty and jurisdiction over two areas of almost 254 square kilometers—Akrotiri and Dhekelia. The larger of these is the Dhekelia Sovereign Base Area, which is also referred to as the Eastern Sovereign Base Area.

GEOGRAPHY

Location: Eastern Mediterranean, on the southeast coast of Cyprus near Famagusta

Geographic coordinates: 34 59 N, 33 45 E

Map references: Europe

Area: *total:* 130.8 sq km
country comparison to the world: 223
note: area surrounds three Cypriot enclaves

Area—comparative: about three-quarters the size of Washington, DC

Land boundaries: *total:* 103 km (approximately)
border countries: Cyprus 103 km (approximately)

Coastline: 27.5 km

Climate: temperate; Mediterranean with hot, dry summers and cool winters

Environment—current issues: netting and trapping of small migrant songbirds in the spring and autumn

Geography—note: British extraterritorial rights also extended to several small off-post sites scattered across Cyprus; of the Sovereign Base Area land 60% is privately owned and farmed, 20% is owned by the Ministry of Defense, and 20% is SBA Crown land

PEOPLE AND SOCIETY

Languages: English, Greek

Population: approximately 15,700 live on the Sovereign Base Areas of Akrotiri and Dhekelia including 7,700 Cypriots, 3,600 service and UK based contract personnel, and 4,400 dependents
country comparison to the world: 222

GOVERNMENT

Country name: *conventional long form:* none
conventional short form: Dhekelia

Dependency status: a special form of UK overseas territory; administered by an administrator who is also the Commander, British Forces Cyprus

Capital: *name:* Episkopi Cantonment (base administrative center for Akrotiri and Dhekelia); located in Akrotiri
geographic coordinates: 34 40 N, 32 51 E
time difference: UTC+2 (7 hours ahead of Washington, DC during Standard Time)
daylight saving time: +1hr, begins last Sunday in March; ends last Sunday in October

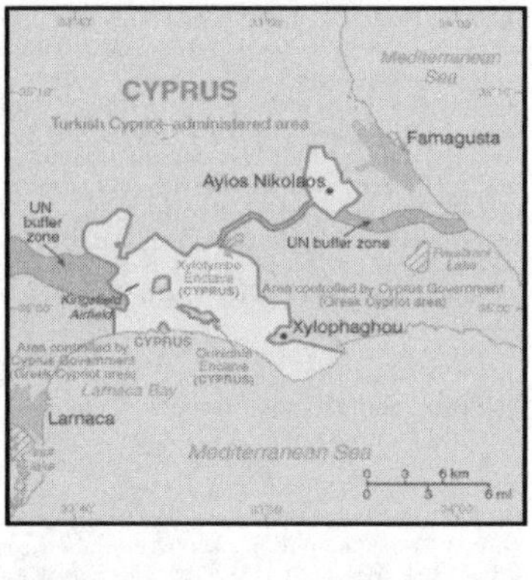

Constitution: presented 3 August 1960, effective 16 August 1960; amended 1966 (The Sovereign Base Areas of Akrotiri and Dhekelia Order in Council 1960, serves as a basic legal document) (2013)

Legal system: the Sovereign Base Area Administration has its own court system to deal with civil and criminal matters; laws applicable to the Cypriot population are, as far as possible, the same as the law s of the Republic of Cyprus

Executive branch: *chief of state:* Queen ELIZABETH II (since 6 February 1952)
head of government: Administrator Air Vice Marshall Graham STACEY (since 4 November 2010); note—reports to the British Ministry of Defense
elections: none; the monarchy is hereditary; the administrator appointed by the monarch

Judicial branch: *highest court(s):* Senior Judges' Court (consists of several visiting judges from England and Wales)
judge selection and term of office: judges appointment and tenure NA
subordinate courts: Resident Judges' Court; Courts Martial

Diplomatic representation in the US: none (overseas territory of the UK)

Diplomatic representation from the US: none (overseas territory of the UK)

Flag description: the flag of the UK is used

National anthem: *note:* as a United Kingdom area of special sovereignty, "God Save the Queen" is official (see United Kingdom)

ECONOMY

Economy—overview: Economic activity is limited to providing services to the military and their families located in Dhekelia. All food and manufactured goods must be imported.

Industries: none

Exchange rates: *note:* uses the euro

COMMUNICATIONS

Broadcast media: British Forces Broadcast Service (BFBS) provides multi-channel satellite TV service as well as BFBS radio broadcasts to the Dhekelia Sovereign Base (2009)

MILITARY

Military—note: defense is the responsibility of the UK; includes Dhekelia Garrison and Ayios Nikolaos Station connected by a roadway

DJIBOUTI

INTRODUCTION

Background: The French Territory of the Afars and the Issas became Djibouti in 1977. Hassan Gouled APTIDON installed an authoritarian one-party state and proceeded to serve as president until 1999. Unrest among the Afar minority during the 1990s led to a civil war that ended in 2001 with a peace accord between Afar rebels and the Somali Issa-dominated government. In 1999, Djibouti's first multiparty presidential elections resulted in the election of Ismail Omar GUELLEH as president; he was reelected to a second term in 2005 and extended his tenure in office via a constitutional amendment, which allowed him to begin a third term in 2011. Djibouti occupies a strategic geographic location at the intersection of the Red Sea and the Gulf of Aden and serves as an important shipping portal for goods entering and leaving the east African highlands and transshipments between Europe, the Middle East, and Asia. The government holds longstanding ties to France, which maintains a significant military presence in the country, and has strong ties with the United States. Djibouti hosts several thousand members of US armed services at US-run Camp Lemonnier.

GEOGRAPHY

Location: Eastern Africa, bordering the Gulf of Aden and the Red Sea, between Eritrea and Somalia

Geographic coordinates: 11 30 N, 43 00 E

Map references: Africa

Area: *total:* 23,200 sq km
country comparison to the world: 151
land: 23,180 sq km
water: 20 sq km

Area—comparative: slightly smaller than New Jersey

Land boundaries: *total:* 516 km
border countries: Eritrea 109 km, Ethiopia 349 km, Somalia 58 km

Coastline: 314 km

Maritime claims: territorial sea: 12 nm
contiguous zone: 24 nm
exclusive economic zone: 200 nm

Climate: desert; torrid, dry

Terrain: coastal plain and plateau separated by central mountains

Elevation extremes: *lowest point:* Lac Assal-155 m
highest point: Moussa Ali 2,028 m

Natural resources: potential geothermal power, gold, clay, granite, limestone, marble, salt, diatomite, gypsum, pumice, petroleum

Land use: *arable land:* 0.09%
permanent crops: 0%
other: 99.91% (2011)

Irrigated land: 10.12 sq km (2003)

Total renewable water resources: 0.3 cu km (2011)

Freshwater withdrawal (domestic/industrial/agricultural): *total:* 0.02 cu km/yr (84%/0%/16%)
per capita: 24.84 cu m/yr (2000)

Natural hazards: earthquakes; droughts; occasional cyclonic disturbances from the Indian Ocean bring heavy rains and flash floods
volcanism: experiences limited volcanic activity; Ardoukoba (elev. 298 m) last erupted in 1978; Manda-Inakir, located along the Ethiopian border, is also historically active

Environment—current issues: inadequate supplies of potable water; limited arable land; desertification; endangered species

Environment—international agreements: *party to:* Biodiversity, Climate Change, Climate Change-Kyoto Protocol, Desertification, Endangered Species, Hazardous Wastes, Law of the Sea, Ozone Layer Protection, Ship Pollution, Wetlands
signed, but not ratified: none of the selected agreements

Geography—note: strategic location near world's busiest shipping lanes and close to Arabian oilfields; terminus of rail traffic into Ethiopia; mostly wasteland; Lac Assal (Lake Assal) is the lowest point in Africa and the saltiest lake in the world

PEOPLE AND SOCIETY

Nationality: *noun:* Djiboutian(s) adjective: Djiboutian

Ethnic groups: Somali 60%, Afar 35%, other 5% (includes French, Arab, Ethiopian, and Italian)

Languages: French (official), Arabic (official), Somali, Afar

Religions: Muslim 94%, Christian 6%

Population: 810,179 (July 2014 est.)
country comparison to the world: 163

Age structure: *0-14 years:* 32.9% (male 133,786/female 133,163)
15-24 years: 22% (male 83,871/female 94,316)
25-54 years: 36.9% (male 124,198/female 174,557)
55-64 years: 3.5% (male 17,694/female 19,931)
65 years and over: 3.5% (male 12,875/female 15,788) (2014 est.)

Dependency ratios:
total dependency ratio: 60.5 %
youth dependency ratio: 54.1 %
elderly dependency ratio: 6.4 %
potential support ratio: 15.7 (2013)

Median age: total: 22.8 years
male: 21.1 years
female: 24.1 years (2014 est.)

Population growth rate: 2.23% (2014 est.)
country comparison to the world: 41

Birth rate: 24.08 births/1,000 population (2014 est.)
country comparison to the world: 62

Death rate: 7.84 deaths/1,000 population (2014 est.)
country comparison to the world: 106
Net migration rate: 6.06 migrant(s)/1,000 population (2014 est.)
country comparison to the world: 22
Urbanization: *urban population:* 77.1% of total population (2011)
rate of urbanization: 1.96% annual rate of change (2010-15 est.)
Major urban areas—population:
DJIBOUTI (capital) 496,000 (2011)
Sex ratio: *at birth:* 1.03 male(s)/female
0-14 years: 1.01 male(s)/female
15-24 years: 0.89 male(s)/female
25-54 years: 0.71 male(s)/female
55-64 years: 0.85 male(s)/female
65 years and over: 0.82 male(s)/female
total population: 0.86 male(s)/female (2014 est.)
Maternal mortality rate:
200 deaths/100,000 live births (2010)
country comparison to the world: 56
Infant mortality rate:
total: 50.2 deaths/1,000 live births
country comparison to the world: 39
male: 57.46 deaths/1,000 live births
female: 42.72 deaths/1,000 live births (2014 est.)
Life expectancy at birth: *total population:* 62.4 years
country comparison to the world: 187
male: 59.93 years
female: 64.94 years (2014 est.)
Total fertility rate: 2.47 children born/woman (2014 est.)
country comparison to the world: 82
Contraceptive prevalence rate: 17.8% (2006)
Health expenditures: 7.9% of GDP (2011)
country comparison to the world: 64
Physicians density: 0.23 physicians/1,000 population (2006)
Hospital bed density:
1.4 beds/1,000 population (2010)
Drinking water source:
improved:
urban: 100% of population
rural: 67.3% of population
total: 92.5% of population
unimproved:
urban: 0% of population
rural: 32.7% of population
total: 7.5% of population (2011 est.)
Sanitation facility access:
improved:
urban: 73.1% of population
rural: 21.6% of population
total: 61.3% of population
unimproved:
urban: 26.9% of population
rural: 78.4% of population
total: 38.7% of population (2011 est.)
HIV/AIDS—adult prevalence rate: 1.2% (2012 est.)
country comparison to the world: 39
HIV/AIDS—people living with HIV/AIDS:
7,700 (2012 est.)
country comparison to the world: 114
HIV/AIDS—deaths: 800 (2012 est.)
country comparison to the world: 83
Major infectious diseases: *degree of risk:* high
food or waterborne diseases: *bacterial and protozoal diarrhea, hepatitis A, and typhoid fever*
vectorborne disease: *dengue fever*
note: highly pathogenic H5N1 avian influenza has been identified in this country; it poses a negligible risk with extremely rare cases possible among US citizens who have close contact with birds (2013)

Obesity—adult prevalence rate: 9.4% (2008)
country comparison to the world: 134
Children under the age of 5 years underweight:
29.8% (2012)
country comparison to the world: 15
Education expenditures: 8.4% of GDP (2007)
country comparison to the world: 11
Literacy: *definition:* age 15 and over can read and write
total population: 67.9%
male: 78%
female: 58.4% (2003 est.)
School life expectancy (primary to tertiary education): *total: 6 years*
male: 7 years
female: 6 years (2011)
Child labor—children ages 5-14:
total number: 13,176
percentage: 8 % (2006 est.)

GOVERNMENT

Country name: *conventional long form:* Republic of Djibouti
conventional short form: Djibouti
local long form: Republique de Djibouti/Jumhuriyat Jibuti
local short form: Djibouti/Jibuti
former: French Territory of the Afars and Issas, French Somaliland
Government type: republic
Capital: *name:* Djibouti
geographic coordinates: 11 35 N, 43 09 E
time difference: UTC+3 (8 hours ahead of Washington, DC during Standard Time)
Administrative divisions: 6 districts (cercles, singular—cercle); Ali Sabieh, Arta, Dikhil, Djibouti, Obock, Tadjourah
Independence: 27 June 1977 (from France)
National holiday: Independence Day, 27 June (1977)
Constitution: approved by referendum 4 September 1992; amended 2006, 2008, 2010 (2010)
Legal system: mixed legal system based primarily on the French civil code (as it existed in 1997), Islamic religious law (in matters of family law and successions), and customary law
International law organization participation:
accepts compulsory ICJ jurisdiction with reservations; accepts ICCt jurisdiction
Suffrage: 18 years of age; universal
Executive branch: *chief of state:* President Ismail Omar GUELLEH (since 8 May 1999)
head of government: Prime Minister Abdoulkader Kamil MOHAMED (since 1 April 2013)
cabinet: Council of Ministers (responsible to the president) (For more information visit the World Leaders website)
elections: president elected by popular vote for a five-year term; president is eligible to hold office until age 75; election last held on 8 April 2011 (next to be held by 2016); prime minister appointed by the president
election results: Ismail Omar GUELLEH reelected president for a third term; percent of vote—Ismail Omar GUELLEH 80.6%, Mohamed Warsama RAGUEH 19.4%
Legislative branch: unicameral Chamber of Deputies or Chambre des Deputes (65 seats; members elected by popular vote to serve five-year terms); note—constitutional amendments in 2010 provided for the establishment of a senate
elections: last held on 22 February 2013 (next to be held in 2018)
election results: percent of vote by party—NA; seats—UMP (coalition of parties associated with President Ismail Omar GUELLEH) 49, USN 16

Judicial branch: *highest court(s):* Supreme Court or Cour Supreme (consists of NA magistrates); Constitutional Council (consists of 6 magistrates)
judge selection and term of office: Supreme Court magistrates appointed by the president with the advice of the Superior Council of the Magistracy; magistrates appointed for life with retirement at age 65; Constitutional magistrates—2 appointed by the president, 2 by the president of the National Assembly, and 2 by High Council of the Judiciary; magistrates appointed for 8-year, non-renewable terms
subordinate courts: High Court of Appeal; 5 Courts of First Instance; customary courts
Political parties and leaders: Democratic National Party or PND [ADEN Robleh Awaleh]; Democratic Renewal Party or PRD [Abdillahi HAMARITEH]; Djibouti Development Party or PDD [Mohamed Daoud CHEHEM]; Front pour la Restauration de l'Unite Democratique or FRUD [Ali Mohamed DAOUD]; Movement for Development and Liberty or MODEL [Sheikh Guirreh MEIDAL]; People's Rally for Progress or RPP [Ismail Omar GUELLEH] (governing party); Peoples Social Democratic Party or PPSD [Moumin Bahdon FARAH]; Republican Alliance for Democracy or ARD [Ahmed YOUSSOUF]; Union for a Presidential Majority or UMP (a coalition of parties including RPP, FRUD, PND, and PPSD); Union for Democracy and Justice or UDJ [Ismail GUEDI Hared]; Union for National Salvation or USN (an umbrella coalition comprising PRD, PDD, MODEL, ARD, and UDJ); [Ahmed Youssouf HOUMER]
Political pressure groups and leaders: NA
International organization participation:
ACP, AfDB, AFESD, AMF, AU, CAEU (candidates), COMESA, FAO, G-77, IBRD, ICAO, ICRM, IDA, IDB, IFAD, IFC, IFRCS, IGAD, ILO, IMF, IMO, Interpol, IOC, IOM, IPU, ITU, ITUC (NGOs), LAS, MIGA, MINURSO, NAM, OIC, OIF, OPCW, UN, UNCTAD, UNESCO, UNHCR, UNIDO, UNWTO, UPU, WCO, WFTU (NGOs), WHO, WIPO, WMO, WTO
Diplomatic representation in the US:
chief of mission: Ambassador Roble OLHAYE Oudine (since 22 March 1988)
chancery: Suite 515, 1156 15th Street NW, Washington, DC 20005
telephone: [1] (202) 331-0270
FAX: [1] (202) 331-0302
Diplomatic representation from the US:
chief of mission: Ambassador Geeta PASI (since 29 August 2011)
embassy: Lot 350-B, Haramouss, Djibouti
mailing address: B. P. 185, Djibouti
telephone: [253] 21 45 30 00
FAX: [253] 21 45 30 20
Flag description: two equal horizontal bands of light blue (top) and light green with a white isosceles triangle based on the hoist side bearing a red five-pointed star in the center; blue stands for sea and sky and the Issa Somali people; green symbolizes earth and the Afar people; white represents peace; the red star recalls the struggle for independence and stands for unity
National anthem: *name:* "Jabuuti" (Djibouti)
lyrics/music: Aden ELMI/Abdi ROBLEH
note: adopted 1977

ECONOMY

Economy—overview: Djibouti's economy is based on service activities connected with the country's strategic location as a deepwater port on the Red Sea. Three-fourths of Djibouti's inhabitants live in the capital city; the remainder are mostly nomadic herders. Scant rainfall limits crop production to small quantities of fruits and vegetables, and most food must be imported.

Djibouti provides services as both a transit port for the region and an international transshipment and refueling center. Imports, exports, and re-exports—primarily of coffee from landlocked neighbor Ethiopia—represent 70% of port activity at Djibouti's container terminal. Djibouti has few natural resources and little industry. The nation is, therefore, heavily dependent on foreign assistance to help support its balance of payments and to finance development projects. An unemployment rate of nearly 60% continues to be a major problem. While inflation is not a concern, due to the fixed tie of the Djiboutian franc to the US dollar, the artificially high value of the Djiboutian franc adversely affects Djibouti's balance of payments. Djibouti holds foreign reserves amounting to less than six months of import coverage. Djibouti has experienced relatively minimal impact from the global economic downturn, but its reliance on diesel-generated electricity and imported food leave average consumers vulnerable to global price shocks. President GUELLEH in 2013 told international investors that Djibouti's development plan is to increase its prominence in financial and communication sectors.

GDP (purchasing power parity): $2.505 billion (2013 est.)
country comparison to the world: 187
$2.386 billion (2012 est.)
$2.275 billion (2011 est.)
note: data are in 2013 US dollars

GDP (official exchange rate): $1.459 billion (2013 est.)

GDP—real growth rate: 5% (2013 est.)
country comparison to the world: 58
4.8% (2012 est.)
4.5% (2011 est.)

GDP—per capita (PPP): $2,700 (2013 est.)
country comparison to the world: 181
$2,700 (2012 est.)
$2,600 (2011 est.)
note: data are in 2013 US dollars

Gross national saving: 21.5% of GDP (2013 est.)
country comparison to the world: 72
17% of GDP (2012 est.)
16.2% of GDP (2011 est.)

GDP—composition, by end use:
household consumption: 56.6%
government consumption: 23.1%
investment in fixed capital: 35.7%
investment in inventories: 0.5%
exports of goods and services: 35.2%
imports of goods and services: -51.1% (2013 est.)

GDP—composition, by sector of origin:
agriculture: 3%
industry: 17.3%
services: 79.7% (2013 est.)

Agriculture—products: fruits, vegetables; goats, sheep, camels, animal hides

Industries: construction, agricultural processing

Industrial production growth rate: 8% (2013 est.)
country comparison to the world: 22

Labor force: 294,600 (2012)
country comparison to the world: 165

Labor force—by occupation:
agriculture: NA%
industry: NA%
services: NA%

Unemployment rate: 59% (2007 est.)
country comparison to the world: 197
note: data are for urban areas, 83% in rural areas

Population below poverty line: 18.8%
note: percent of population below $1.25 per day at purchasing power parity (2012 est.)

Household income or consumption by percentage share:
lowest 10%: 2.4%
highest 10%: 30.9% (2002)

Distribution of family income—Gini index:
40.9 (2002)
country comparison to the world: 53

Budget: revenues: $512.7 million
expenditures: $532.9 million (2013 est.)

Taxes and other revenues:
35.1% of GDP (2013 est.)
country comparison to the world: 65

Budget surplus (+) or deficit (-): -1.4% of GDP (2013 est.)
country comparison to the world: 70

Public debt: 38.6% of GDP (2012 est.)
country comparison to the world: 95

Fiscal year: calendar year
Inflation rate (consumer prices):
2.5% (2013 est.)
country comparison to the world: 91
7.9% (2012 est.)

Commercial bank prime lending rate:
11% (31 December 2013 est.)
country comparison to the world: 68
12% (31 December 2012 est.)

Stock of narrow money:
$850.8 million (31 December 2013 est.)
country comparison to the world: 153
$758.9 million (31 December 2012 est.)

Stock of broad money:
$1.256 billion (31 December 2013 est.)
country comparison to the world: 163
$1.16 billion (31 December 2012 est.)

Stock of domestic credit: $523.4 million (31 December 2013 est.)
country comparison to the world: 168
$483.4 million (31 December 2012 est.)

Current account balance:
-$219.5 million (2013 est.)
country comparison to the world: 89
-$216.2 million (2012 est.)

Exports: $90.8 million (2013 est.)
country comparison to the world: 192
$87.9 million (2012 est.)

Exports—commodities: reexports, hides and skins, coffee (in transit)

Exports—partners: Somalia 80.1%, UAE 4.4%, Yemen 4.1% (2012)

Imports: $593.3 million (2013 est.)
country comparison to the world: 189
$574.2 million (2012 est.)

Imports—commodities: foods, beverages, transport equipment, chemicals, petroleum products

Imports—partners: China 24.4%, Saudi Arabia 16.4%, India 10.6%, Indonesia 7.3% (2012)

Debt—external: $821.6 million (31 December 2013 est.)
country comparison to the world: 166
$773.9 million (31 December 2012 est.)

Stock of direct foreign investment—at home:
$630.6 million (31 December 2013 est.)
country comparison to the world: 103
$510.6 million (31 December 2012 est.)

Exchange rates: Djiboutian francs (DJF) per US dollar—
177.7 (2013 est.)
177.72 (2012 est.)
177.72 (2010 est.)

ENERGY

Electricity—production: 325 million kWh (2010 est.)
country comparison to the world: 169

Electricity—consumption: 302.3 million kWh (2010 est.)
country comparison to the world: 175

Electricity—exports: 0 kWh (2012 est.)
country comparison to the world: 128

Electricity—imports: 0 kWh (2012 est.)
country comparison to the world: 135

Electricity—installed generating capacity:
130,000 kW (2010 est.)
country comparison to the world: 169

Electricity—from fossil fuels: 100% of total installed capacity (2010 est.)
country comparison to the world: 12

Electricity—from nuclear fuels: 0% of total installed capacity (2010 est.)
country comparison to the world: 76

Electricity—from hydroelectric plants:
0% of total installed capacity (2010 est.)
country comparison to the world: 167

Electricity—from other renewable sources:
0% of total installed capacity (2010 est.)
country comparison to the world: 171

Crude oil—production: 0 bbl/day (2012 est.)
country comparison to the world: 165

Crude oil—exports: 0 bbl/day (2010 est.)
country comparison to the world: 104

Crude oil—imports: 0 bbl/day (2010 est.)
country comparison to the world: 178

Crude oil—proved reserves: 0 bbl (1 January 2013 es)
country comparison to the world: 123

Refined petroleum products—production:
0 bbl/day (2010 est.)
country comparison to the world: 137

Refined petroleum products—consumption:
12,460 bbl/day (2011 est.)
country comparison to the world: 149

Refined petroleum products—exports:
19.18 bbl/day (2010 est.)
country comparison to the world: 126

Refined petroleum products—imports:
8,089 bbl/day (2010 est.)
country comparison to the world: 135

Natural gas—production: 0 cu m (2011 est.)
country comparison to the world: 122

Natural gas—consumption: 0 cu m (2010 est.)
country comparison to the world: 138

Natural gas—exports: 0 cu m (2011 est.)
country comparison to the world: 89

Natural gas—imports:
0 cu m (2011 est.)
country comparison to the world: 184

Natural gas—proved reserves: 0 cu m (1 January 2013 es)
country comparison to the world: 130

Carbon dioxide emissions from consumption of energy: 1.15 million Mt (2011 est.)
country comparison to the world: 163

COMMUNICATIONS

Telephones—main lines in use: 18,000 (2012)
country comparison to the world: 191

Telephones—mobile cellular: 209,000 (2012)
country comparison to the world: 181

Telephone system: *general assessment:* telephone facilities in the city of Djibouti are adequate, as are the microwave radio relay connections to outlying areas of the country
domestic: Djibouti Telecom is the sole provider of telecommunications services and utilizes mostly a microwave radio relay network; fiber-optic cable is installed in the capital; rural areas connected via wireless local loop radio systems; mobile cellular coverage is primarily limited to the area in and around Djibouti city

international: country code—253; landing point for the SEA-ME-WE-3 and EASSy fiber-optic submarine cable systems providing links to Asia, the Middle East, Europe and North America; satellite earth stations—2 (1 Intelsat—Indian Ocean and 1 Arabsat); Medarabtel regional microwave radio relay telephone network (2009)

Broadcast media: state-owned Radiodiffusion-Television de Djibouti (RTD) operates the sole terrestrial TV station as well as the only 2 domestic radio networks; no private TV or radio stations; transmissions of several international broadcasters are available (2007)

Internet country code: .dj

Internet hosts: 215 (2012)
country comparison to the world: 200

Internet users: 25,900 (2009) country *comparison to the world:* 185

TRANSPORTATION

Airports: 13 (2013)
country comparison to the world: 152

Airports—with paved runways: total: 3
over 3,047 m: 1
2,438 to 3,047 m: 1
1,524 to 2,437 m: 1 (2013)

Airports—with unpaved runways: total: 1 0
1,524 to 2,437 m: 1
914 to 1,523 m: 7
under 914 m: 2 (2013)

Railways: *total:* 100 km (Djibouti segment of the 781 km Addis Ababa-Djibouti railway)
country comparison to the world: 126
narrow gauge: 100 km 1.000-m gauge
note: railway is under joint control of Djibouti and Ethiopia but is largely inoperable (2008)

Roadways: total: 3,065 km
country comparison to the world: 165
paved: 1,226 km
unpaved: 1,839 km (2000)

Ports and terminals: *major seaport(s):* Djibouti

Transportation—note: while attacks decreased significantly in 2012, the International Maritime Bureau reports offshore waters in the Gulf of Aden remain a high risk for piracy; the presence of several naval task forces in the Gulf of Aden and additional anti-piracy measures on the part of ship operators, including the use of on-board armed security teams, contributed to the drop in incidents

MILITARY

Military branches: Djibouti Armed Forces (Forces Armees Djiboutiennes, FAD): Djibouti National Army (includes Navy, Djiboutian Air Force (Force Aerienne Djiboutienne, FAD), National Gendarmerie (GN)) (2013)

Military service age and obligation: 18 years of age for voluntary military service; 16-25 years of age for voluntary military training; no conscription (2012)

Manpower available for military service:
males age 16-49: 170,386
females age 16-49: 221,411 (2010 est.)

Manpower fit for military service:
males age 16-49: 114,557
females age 16-49: 154,173 (2010 est.)

Manpower reaching militarily significant age annually:
male: 8,360
female: 8,602 (2010 est.)

TRANSNATIONAL ISSUES

Disputes—international: Djibouti maintains economic ties and border accords with "Somaliland" leadership while maintaining some political ties to various factions in Somalia; Kuwait is chief investor in the 2008 restoration and upgrade of the Ethiopian-Djibouti rail link; in 2008, Eritrean troops moved across the border on Ras Doumera peninsula and occupied Doumera Island with undefined sovereignty in the Red Sea

Refugees and internally displaced persons: *refugees (country of origin): 19,168 (Somalia) (2014)*

Trafficking in persons: *current situation:* Djibouti is a transit, source, and destination country for men, women, and children subjected to forced labor and sex trafficking; economic migrants from East Africa en route to Yemen and other Middle East locations are vulnerable to exploitation in Djibouti; some woman and girls may be forced into domestic servitude or prostitution after reaching Djibouti City, the Ethiopian-Djiboutian trucking corridor, or Obock - the main crossing point into Yemen; Djiboutian and foreign children may be forced to beg, to work as domestic servants, or to commit theft and other petty crimes

tier rating: Tier 2 Watch List - Djibouti does not fully comply with the minimum standards for the elimination of trafficking; however, it is making significant efforts to do so; outside of child prostitution, the government fails to investigate or prosecute any other trafficking offenses, including those allegedly committed by complicit officials; it has made no attempt to implement the protection or prevention components of its anti-trafficking law, and its working group on trafficking was inactive in 2012; a draft national action plan against human trafficking remains incomplete (2013)

DOMINICA

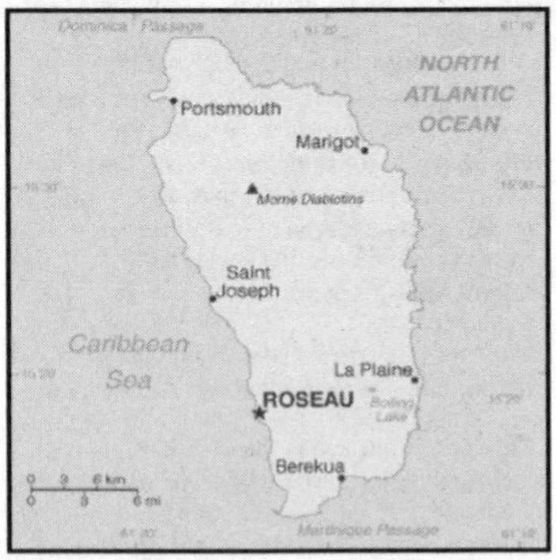

INTRODUCTION

Background: Dominica was the last of the Caribbean islands to be colonized by Europeans due chiefly to the fierce resistance of the native Caribs. France ceded possession to Great Britain in 1763, which made the island a colony in 1805. In 1980, two years after independence, Dominica's fortunes improved when a corrupt and tyrannical administration was replaced by that of Mary Eugenia CHARLES, the first female prime minister in the Caribbean, who remained in office for 15 years. Some 3,000 Carib Indians still living on Dominica are the only pre-Columbian population remaining in the eastern Caribbean.

GEOGRAPHY

Location: Caribbean, island between the Caribbean Sea and the North Atlantic Ocean, about half way between Puerto Rico and Trinidad and Tobago

Geographic coordinates: 15 25 N, 61 20 W

Map references: Central America and the Caribbean

Area: *total:* 751 sq km
country comparison to the world: 189
land: 751 sq km
water: 0 sq km

Area—comparative: slightly more than four times the size of Washington, DC

Land boundaries: 0 km

Coastline: 148 km

Maritime claims: *territorial sea:* 12 nm
contiguous zone: 24 nm
exclusive economic zone: 200 nm

Climate: tropical; moderated by northeast trade winds; heavy rainfall

Terrain: rugged mountains of volcanic origin

Elevation extremes: *lowest point:* Caribbean Sea 0 m
highest point: Morne Diablotins 1,447 m

Natural resources: timber, hydropower, arable land

Land use: *arable land:* 8%
permanent crops: 24%
other: 68% (2011)

Irrigated land: NA

Total renewable water resources: NA

Freshwater withdrawal (domestic/industrial/agricultural): *total:* 0.02 cu km/yr
per capita: 244.1 cu m/yr (2004)

Natural hazards: flash floods are a constant threat; destructive hurricanes can be expected during the late summer months

Environment—current issues: NA

Environment—international agreements: *party to:* Biodiversity, Climate Change, Climate Change-Kyoto Protocol, Desertification, Endangered Species, Environmental Modification, Hazardous Wastes, Law of the Sea, Ozone Layer Protection, Ship Pollution, Whaling
signed, but not ratified: none of the selected agreements

Geography—note: known as "The Nature Island of the Caribbean" due to its spectacular, lush, and varied flora and fauna, which are protected by an extensive natural park system; the most mountainous of the Lesser Antilles, its volcanic peaks are cones of lava craters and include Boiling Lake, the second-largest, thermally active lake in the world

PEOPLE AND SOCIETY

Nationality: *noun:* Dominican(s)
adjective: Dominican

Ethnic groups: black 86.8%, mixed 8.9%, Carib Amerindian 2.9%, white 0.8%, other 0.7% (2001 census)

Languages: English (official), French patois

Religions: Roman Catholic 61.4%, Protestant 20.6% (Seventh-Day Adventist 6%, Pentecostal 5.6%, Baptist 4.1%, Methodist 3.7%, Church of God 1.2%), Jehovah's Witnesses 1.2%, other Christian 7.7%, Rastafarian 1.3%, other or unspecified 1.6%, none 6.1% (2001 census)

Population: 73,449 (July 2014 est.)
country comparison to the world: 202

Age structure: *0-14 years:* 22.1% (male 8,300/female 7,939)
15-24 years: 16.7% (male 6,311/female 5,946)
25-54 years: 41.5% (male 15,470/female 15,004)
55-64 years: 10.5% (male 3,604/female 3,147)
65 years and over: 10.4% (male 3,386/female 4,342) (2014 est.)

Median age: *total:* 32.1 years
male: 31.7 years
female: 32.6 years (2014 est.)

Population growth rate: 0.22% (2014 est.)
country comparison to the world: 179

Birth rate: 15.53 births/1,000 population (2014 est.)
country comparison to the world: 130

Death rate: 7.94 deaths/1,000 population (2014 est.)
country comparison to the world: 102

Net migration rate:
-5.39 migrant(s)/1,000 population (2014 est.)
country comparison to the world: 196

Urbanization: *urban population:* 67% of total population (2010)
rate of urbanization: 0.3% annual rate of change (2010-15 est.)

Major urban areas—population: ROSEAU (capital) 14,000 (2011)

Sex ratio: *at birth:* 1.05 male(s)/female
0-14 years: 1.05 male(s)/female
15-24 years: 1.06 male(s)/female
25-54 years: 1.03 male(s)/female
55-64 years: 1.02 male(s)/female
65 years and over: 0.77 male(s)/female
total population: 1.02 male(s)/female (2014 est.)

Infant mortality rate:
total: 11.61 deaths/1,000 live births
country comparison to the world: 129
male: 15.46 deaths/1,000 live births
female: 7.57 deaths/1,000 live births (2014 est.)

Life expectancy at birth: *total population:* 76.59 years
country comparison to the world: 77
male: 73.63 years
female: 79.7 years (2014 est.)

Total fertility rate: 2.05 children born/woman (2014 est.)
country comparison to the world: 117

Health expenditures: 5.9% of GDP (2011)
country comparison to the world: 113

Physicians density: 1.59 physicians/1,000 population (2001)

Hospital bed density: 3.8 beds/1,000 population (2011)

Drinking water source:
improved:
urban: 95.7% of population
unimproved:
urban: 4.3% of population (2011 est.)

Sanitation facility access:

improved:
urban: 79.6% of population
rural: 84.3% of population
total: 81.1% of population
unimproved:
urban: 20.4% of population
rural: 15.7% of population
total: 18.9% of population (2007 est.)

HIV/AIDS—adult prevalence rate: NA

HIV/AIDS—people living with HIV/AIDS: NA

HIV/AIDS—deaths: NA

Obesity—adult prevalence rate: 24.9% (2008)
country comparison to the world: 61

Education expenditures: 3.5% of GDP (2010)
country comparison to the world: 125

Literacy: *definition:* age 15 and over has ever attended school
total population: 94%
male: 94%
female: 94% (2003 est.)

Unemployment, youth ages 15-24: *total:* 26%
country comparison to the world: 39
male: 26.2%
female: 25.4% (2001)

GOVERNMENT

Country name: *conventional long form:* Commonwealth of Dominica
conventional short form: Dominica

Government type: parliamentary democracy

Capital: *name:* Roseau
geographic coordinates: 15 18 N, 61 24 W
time difference: UTC-4 (1 hour ahead of Washington, DC during Standard Time)

Administrative divisions: 10 parishes; Saint Andrew, Saint David, Saint George, Saint John, Saint Joseph, Saint Luke, Saint Mark, Saint Patrick, Saint Paul, Saint Peter

Independence: 3 November 1978 (from the UK)

National holiday: Independence Day, 3 November (1978)

Constitution: previous 1967 (preindependence); latest presented 25 July 1978, entered into force 3 November 1978; amended several times, last in *1984 (2011)*

Legal system: common law based on the English model

International law organization participation: accepts compulsory ICJ jurisdiction; accepts ICCt jurisdiction

Suffrage: 18 years of age; universal

Executive branch: *chief of state:* President Charles A. SAVARIN (since 2 October 2013)
head of government: Prime Minister Roosevelt SKERRIT (since 8 January 2004)
cabinet: Cabinet appointed by the president on the advice of the prime minister (For more information visit the World Leaders website)
elections: president elected by the House of Assembly for a five-year term; election last held on 30 September 2013 (next to be held in October 2018); prime minister appointed by the president
election results: Charles A. SAVARIN elected president 19-0 on 30 September 2013

Legislative branch: unicameral House of Assembly (32 seats; 9 members appointed, 21 elected by popular vote to serve five-year terms, 1 speaker elected from among persons who are not members of the House, responsible for the management and general administration of the House, and one ex-officio Clerk of the House)
elections: last held on 18 December 2009 (next to be held in 2015); note—tradition dictates that the election will be held within five years of the last election, but technically it is five years from the first seating of parliament (12 May 2005) plus a 90-day grace period
election results: percent of vote by party—DLP 61.2%, UWP 34.9%, other 3.9%; seats by party—DLP 18, UWP 3

Judicial branch: *highest court(s):* The Eastern Caribbean Supreme Court (ECSC) is the itinerant superior court of record for the 9-member Organization of Eastern Caribbean States to include Dominica; the ECSC—based on St. Lucia—is headed by the chief justice and is comprised of the Court of Appeal with 3 justices and the High Court with 16 judges; sittings of the Court of Appeal and High Court rotate among the 9 member states; 2 High Court judges reside in Dominica
note—Dominica is a member of the Caribbean Court of Justice
judge selection and term of office: ECSC chief justice appointed by Her Majesty, Queen ELIZABETH II; other justices and judges appointed by the Judicial and Legal Services Commission; Court of Appeal justices appointed for life with mandatory retirement at age 65; High Court judges appointed for life with mandatory retirement at age 62
subordinate courts: Court of Summary Jurisdiction; magistrates' courts

Political parties and leaders: Dominica Freedom Party or DFP [Judith PESTAINA]; Dominica Labor Party or DLP [Roosevelt SKERRIT]; Dominica United Workers Party or UWP [Hector JOHN]

Political pressure groups and leaders: Dominica Liberation Movement or DLM (a small leftist party)

International organization participation: ACP, AOSIS, C, Caricom, CD, CDB, CELAC, Commonwealth of Nations, ECCU, FAO, G-77, IAEA, IBRD, ICRM, IDA, IFAD, IFC, IFRCS, ILO, IMF, IMO, Interpol, IOC, ISO (subscriber), ITU, ITUC (NGOs), MIGA, NAM, OAS, OECS, OIF, OPANAL, OPCW, Petrocaribe, UN, UNCTAD, UNESCO, UNIDO, UPU, WCL, WFTU, WHO, WIPO, WMO, WTO

Diplomatic representation in the US: chief of mission: Ambassador Hubert J. CHARLES (since 16 July 2010)
chancery: 3216 New Mexico Avenue NW, Washington, DC 20016
telephone: [1] (202) 364-6781
FAX: [1] (202) 364-6791
consulate(s) general: New York

Diplomatic representation from the US:
the US does not have an embassy in Dominica; the US Ambassador to Barbados is accredited to Dominica

Flag description: green, with a centered cross of three equal bands—the vertical part is yellow (hoist side), black, and white and the horizontal part is yellow (top), black, and white; superimposed in the center of the cross is a red disk bearing a Sisserou parrot, unique to Dominica, encircled by 10 green, five-pointed stars edged in yellow; the 10 stars represent the 10 administrative divisions (parishes); green symbolizes the island's lush vegetation; the triple-colored cross represents the Christian Trinity; the yellow color denotes sunshine, the main agricultural products (citrus and bananas), and the native Carib Indians; black is for the rich soil and the African heritage of most citizens; white signifies rivers, waterfalls, and the purity of aspirations; the red disc stands for social justice

National symbol(s): Sisserou parrot

National anthem: name: "Isle of Beauty"
lyrics/music: Wilfred Oscar Morgan POND/Lemuel McPherson CHRISTIAN
note: adopted 1967

ECONOMY

Economy—overview: The Dominican economy has been dependent on agriculture—primarily bananas—in years past, but increasingly has been driven by tourism as the government seeks to promote Dominica as an "ecotourism" destination. Moreover, Dominica has successfully developed an offshore medical education sector. In order to diversify the island's economy, the government is also attempting to develop an offshore financial sector and plans to sign agreements with the private sector to develop geothermal energy resources. In 2003, the government began a comprehensive restructuring of the economy—including elimination of price controls, privatization of the state banana company, and tax increases—to address an economic and financial crisis and to meet IMF requirements. In 2009, the economy contracted as a result of the global recession; growth remains anemic. Although public debt levels continue to exceed pre-recession levels, the debt burden declined from 78% of GDP in 2011 to approximately 70% in 2012, one of the lowest levels in the Eastern Caribbean.

GDP (purchasing power parity): $1.015 billion (2013 est.)
country comparison to the world: 204
$1.004 billion (2012 est.)
$1.021 billion (2011 est.)
note: data are in 2013 US dollars

GDP (official exchange rate): $495 million (2013 est.)

GDP—real growth rate: 1.1% (2013 est.)
country comparison to the world: 173
-1.7% (2012 est.)
1% (2011 est.)

GDP—per capita (PPP): $14,300 (2013 est.)
country comparison to the world: 94
$14,200 (2012 est.)
$14,400 (2011 est.)
note: data are in 2013 US dollars

Gross national saving: 9.2% of GDP (2012 est.)
country comparison to the world: 139
8.5% of GDP (2011 est.)
7.8% of GDP (2010 est.)

GDP—composition, by end use:
household consumption: 65.5%
government consumption: 18.9%
investment in fixed capital: 24.8%
investment in inventories: 0%
exports of goods and services: 46.4%
imports of goods and services: -55.6% (2013 est.)

GDP—composition, by sector of origin:
agriculture: 15.7%
industry: 15.6%
services: 68.7% (2013 est.)

Agriculture—products: bananas, citrus, mangos, root crops, coconuts, cocoa
note: forest and fishery potential not exploited

Industries: soap, coconut oil, tourism, copra, furniture, cement blocks, shoes

Industrial production growth rate: -1%
country comparison to the world: 174

Labor force: 25,000 (2000 est.)
country comparison to the world: 207

Labor force—by occupation: *agriculture:* 40%
industry: 32%
services: 28% (2002 est.)

Unemployment rate: 23% (2000 est.)
country comparison to the world: 171

Population below poverty line: 29% (2009 est.)

Household income or consumption by percentage share:
lowest 10%: NA%
highest 10%: NA%

Budget: *revenues:* $148.1 million
expenditures: $185.2 million (2013 est.)

Taxes and other revenues:
29.9% of GDP (2013 est.)
country comparison to the world: 93

Budget surplus (+) or deficit (-):
-7.5% of GDP (2013 est.)
country comparison to the world: 190

Public debt: 70% of GDP (2012 est.)
country comparison to the world: 37
78% of GDP (2009 est.)

Fiscal year: 1 July–30 June

Inflation rate (consumer prices): 1.8% (2013 est.)
country comparison to the world: 56
1.4% (2012 est.)

Central bank discount rate:
6.5% (31 December 2010 est.)
country comparison to the world: 46
6.5% (31 December 2009 est.)

Commercial bank prime lending rate:
9.1% (31 December 2013 est.)
country comparison to the world: 100
9.03% (31 December 2012 est.)

Stock of narrow money: $94.41 million (31 December 2013 est.)
country comparison to the world: 184
$84.39 million (31 December 2012 est.)

Stock of broad money: $455.2 million (31 December 2013 est.)
country comparison to the world: 179
$421.6 million (31 December 2012 est.)

Stock of domestic credit: $333.3 million (31 December 2013 est.)
country comparison to the world: 173
$304.1 million (31 December 2012 est.)

Current account balance: -$91.5 million (2013 est.)
country comparison to the world: 73
-$54.9 million (2012 est.)

Exports: $40.4 million (2013 est.)
country comparison to the world: 201
$40.6 million (2012 est.)

Exports—commodities: bananas, soap, bay oil, vegetables, grapefruit, oranges

Exports—partners: Japan 38.8%, Jamaica 8.3%, Antigua and Barbuda 7.7%, Guyana 6.5%, Paraguay 5.6%, Trinidad and Tobago 4.2% (2012)

Imports: $219.6 million (2013 est.)
country comparison to the world: 202
$182.7 million (2012 est.)

Imports—commodities: manufactured goods, machinery and equipment, food, chemicals

Imports—partners: Japan 39.3%, US 15.6%, Trinidad and Tobago 13.5%, China 5.1% (2012)

Reserves of foreign exchange and gold:
$90 million (31 December 2013 est.)
country comparison to the world: 166
$94.56 million (31 December 2012 est.)

Debt—external: $274.9 million (31 December 2013 est.)
country comparison to the world: 184
$272.1 million (31 December 2012 est.)

Exchange rates: East Caribbean dollars (XCD) per US dollar—
2.7 (2013 est.)
2.7 (2012 est.)
2.7 (2010 est.)
2.7 (2009)

ENERGY

Electricity—production: 100.5 million kWh (2010 est.)
country comparison to the world: 197

Electricity—consumption: 93.47 million kWh (2010 est.)
country comparison to the world: 197

Electricity—exports: 0 kWh (2012 est.)
country comparison to the world: 129

Electricity—imports: 0 kWh (2012 est.)
country comparison to the world: 136

Electricity—installed generating capacity:
97,000 kW (2010 est.)
country comparison to the world: 173

Electricity—from fossil fuels: 19.6% of total installed capacity (2010 est.)
country comparison to the world: 192

Electricity—from nuclear fuels: 0% of total installed capacity (2010 est.)
country comparison to the world: 77

Electricity—from hydroelectric plants:
6.2% of total installed capacity (2010 est.)
country comparison to the world: 122

Electricity—from other renewable sources:
74.2% of total installed capacity (2010 est.)
country comparison to the world: 1

Crude oil—production: 0 bbl/day (2012 est.)
country comparison to the world: 166

Crude oil—exports: 0 bbl/day (2010 est.)
country comparison to the world: 105

Crude oil—imports: 0 bbl/day (2010 est.)
country comparison to the world: 179

Crude oil—proved reserves: 0 bbl (1 January 2013 es)
country comparison to the world: 124

Refined petroleum products—production:
0 bbl/day (2010 est.)
country comparison to the world: 138

Refined petroleum products—consumption:
917.7 bbl/day (2011 est.)
country comparison to the world: 206

Refined petroleum products—exports:
0 bbl/day (2010 est.)
country comparison to the world: 170

Refined petroleum products—imports:
915.9 bbl/day (2010 est.)
country comparison to the world: 195

Natural gas—production: 0 cu m (2011 est.)
country comparison to the world: 123

Natural gas—consumption: 0 cu m (2010 est.)
country comparison to the world: 139

Natural gas—exports: 0 cu m (2011 est.)
country comparison to the world: 90

Natural gas—imports: 0 cu m (2011 est.)
country comparison to the world: 185

Natural gas—proved reserves: 0 cu m (1 January 2013 es)
country comparison to the world: 131

Carbon dioxide emissions from consumption of energy: 141,600 Mt (2011 est.)
country comparison to the world: 204

COMMUNICATIONS

Telephones—main lines in use: 14,600 (2012)
country comparison to the world: 197

Telephones—mobile cellular: 109,300 (2012)
country comparison to the world: 191

Telephone system: *general assessment:* fully automatic network
domestic: fixed-line connections continued to decline slowly with the two active operators providing about 20 fixed-line connections per 100 persons; subscribership among the three mobile-cellular providers continued to increase with teledensity reaching 150 per 100 persons
international: country code—1-767; landing points for the East Caribbean Fiber Optic System (ECFS) and the Global Caribbean Network (GCN) submarine cables providing connectivity to other islands in the eastern Caribbean extending from the British Virgin Islands to Trinidad; microwave radio relay and SHF radiotelephone links to Martinique and Guadeloupe; VHF and UHF radiotelephone links to Saint Lucia (2010)

Broadcast media: no terrestrial TV service available; subscription cable TV provider offers some locally produced programming plus channels from the US, Latin America, and the Caribbean; state-operated radio broadcasts on 6 stations; privately owned radio broadcasts on about 15 stations (2007)

Internet country code: .dm

Internet hosts: 723 (2012)
country comparison to the world: 175

Internet users: 28,000 (2009)
country comparison to the world: 183

TRANSPORTATION

Airports: 2 (2013)
country comparison to the world: 199

Airports—with paved runways: *total:* 2
1,524 to 2,437 m: 1
914 to 1,523 m: 1 (2013)

Roadways: *total:* 1,512 km
country comparison to the world: 177
paved: 762 km
unpaved: 750 km (2010)

Merchant marine: *total:* 43
country comparison to the world: 73
by type: bulk carrier 11, cargo 22, chemical tanker 2, petroleum tanker 4, refrigerated cargo 3, roll on/roll off 1
foreign-owned: 32 (Australia 1, Estonia 6, Germany 5, Greece 4, India 2, Latvia 2, Norway 1, Russia 3, Saudi Arabia 2, Syria 4, Turkey 1, Ukraine 1)
registered in other countries: 1 (Saint Vincent and the Grenadines 1) (2010)

Ports and terminals: *major seaport(s):* Portsmouth, Roseau

MILITARY

Military branches: no regular military forces; Commonwealth of Dominica Police Force (includes Coast Guard) (2012)

Manpower available for military service: *males age 16-49:* 19,075 (2010 est.)

Manpower fit for military service: *males age 16-49:* 16,035
females age 16-49: 15,499 (2010 est.)

Manpower reaching militarily significant age annually: *male:* 675
female: 636 (2010 est.)

TRANSNATIONAL ISSUES

Disputes—international: Dominica is the only Caribbean state to challenge Venezuela's sovereignty claim over Aves Island and joins the other island nations in challenging whether the feature sustains human habitation, a criterion under the UN Convention on the Law of the Sea (UNCLOS), which permits Venezuela to extend its Exclusive Economic Zone (EEZ) and continental shelf claims over a large portion of the eastern Caribbean Sea

Illicit drugs: transshipment point for narcotics bound for the US and Europe; minor cannabis producer (2008)

DOMINICAN REPUBLIC

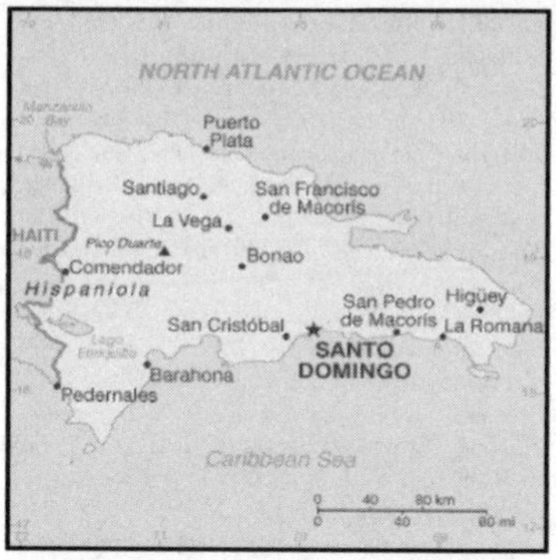

INTRODUCTION

Background: The Taino—indigenous inhabitants of Hispaniola prior to the arrival of the Europeans—divided the island into five chiefdoms and territories. Christopher COLUMBUS explored and claimed the island on his first voyage in 1492; it became a springboard for Spanish conquest of the Caribbean and the American mainland. In 1697, Spain recognized French dominion over the western third of the island, which in 1804 became Haiti. The remainder of the island, by then known as Santo Domingo, sought to gain its own independence in 1821 but was conquered and ruled by the Haitians for 22 years; it finally attained independence as the Dominican Republic in 1844. In 1861, the Dominicans voluntarily returned to the Spanish Empire, but two years later they launched a war that restored independence in 1865. A legacy of unsettled, mostly non-representative rule followed, capped by the dictatorship of Rafael Leonidas TRUJILLO from 1930 to 1961. Juan BOSCH was elected president in 1962 but was deposed in a military coup in 1963. In 1965, the United States led an intervention in the midst of a civil war sparked by an uprising to restore BOSCH. In 1966, Joaquin BALAGUER defeated BOSCH in an election to become president. BALAGUER maintained a tight grip on power for most of the next 30 years when international reaction to flawed elections forced him to curtail his term in 1996. Since then, regular competitive elections have been held in which opposition candidates have won the presidency. Former President Leonel FERNANDEZ Reyna (first term 1996-2000) won election to a new term in 2004 following a constitutional amendment allowing presidents to serve more than one term, and was later reelected to a second consecutive term. In 2012, Danilo MEDINA was elected president.

GEOGRAPHY

Location: Caribbean, eastern two-thirds of the island of Hispaniola, between the Caribbean Sea and the North Atlantic Ocean, east of Haiti

Geographic coordinates: 19 00 N, 70 40 W

Map references: Central America and the Caribbean

Area: *total:* 48,670 sq km
country comparison to the world: 132
land: 48,320 sq km
water: 350 sq km

Area—comparative: slightly more than twice the size of New Hampshire

Land boundaries: *total:* 360 km
border countries: Haiti 360 km

Coastline: 1,288 km

Maritime claims: measured from claimed archipelagic straight baselines
territorial sea: 12 nm
contiguous zone: 24 nm
exclusive economic zone: 200 nm
continental shelf: 200 nm or to the edge of the continental margin

Climate: tropical maritime; little seasonal temperature variation; seasonal variation in rainfall

Terrain: rugged highlands and mountains with fertile valleys interspersed

Elevation extremes: *lowest point:* Lago Enriquillo-46 m
highest point: Pico Duarte 3,175 m

Natural resources: nickel, bauxite, gold, silver

Land use: *arable land:* 16.44%
permanent crops: 9.25%
other: 74.32% (2011)

Irrigated land: 3,065 sq km (2009)

Total renewable water resources: 21 cu km (2011)

Freshwater withdrawal (domestic/industrial/agricultural): *total:* 5.47 cu km/yr (26%/1%/72%)
per capita: 574.2 cu m/yr (2005)

Natural hazards: lies in the middle of the hurricane belt and subject to severe storms from June to October; occasional flooding; periodic droughts

Environment—current issues: water shortages; soil eroding into the sea damages coral reefs; deforestation

Environment—international agreements: *party to:* Biodiversity, Climate Change, Climate Change-Kyoto Protocol, Desertification, Endangered Species, Hazardous Wastes, Marine Dumping, Marine Life Conservation, Ozone Layer Protection, Ship Pollution, Wetlands
signed, but not ratified: Law of the Sea

Geography—note: shares island of Hispaniola with Haiti

PEOPLE AND SOCIETY

Nationality: *noun:* Dominican(s)
adjective: Dominican

Ethnic groups: mixed 73%, white 16%, black 11%

Languages: Spanish (official)

Religions: Roman Catholic 95%, other 5%

Population: 10,349,741 (July 2014 est.)
country comparison to the world: 87

Age structure: *0-14 years:* 28% (male 1,474,170/female 1,423,573)
15-24 years: 18.5% (male 974,688/female 937,103)
25-54 years: 39.3% (male 2,078,915/female 1,984,585)
55-64 years: 7% (male 376,175/female 371,152)
65 years and over: 6.9% (male 336,712/female 392,668) (2014 est.)

Dependency ratios:
total dependency ratio: 57.5 %
youth dependency ratio: 47.6 %
elderly dependency ratio: 9.9 %
potential support ratio: 10.1 (2013)

Median age: *total:* 27.1 years
male: 26.9 years
female: 27.3 years (2014 est.)

Population growth rate: 1.25% (2014 est.)
country comparison to the world: 93

Birth rate: 18.97 births/1,000 population (2014 est.)
country comparison to the world: 92

Death rate: 4.5 deaths/1,000 population (2014 est.)
country comparison to the world: 204

Net migration rate: -1.93 migrant(s)/1,000 population (2014 est.)
country comparison to the world: 165

Urbanization: *urban population:* 69% of total population (2010)
rate of urbanization: 2.1% annual rate of change (2010-15 est.)

Major urban areas—population: SANTO DOMINGO (capital) 2.191 million (2011)
Sex ratio: at birth: 1.04 male(s)/female
0-14 years: 1.04 male(s)/female
15-24 years: 1.04 male(s)/female
25-54 years: 1.05 male(s)/female
55-64 years: 1.03 male(s)/female
65 years and over: 0.86 male(s)/female
total population: 1.03 male(s)/female (2014 est.)

Mother's mean age at first birth: 20.3 (2007 est.)

Maternal mortality rate:
150 deaths/100,000 live births (2010)
country comparison to the world: 62

Infant mortality rate: total: 19.63 deaths/1,000 live births
country comparison to the world: 92
male: 21.56 deaths/1,000 live births
female: 17.62 deaths/1,000 live births (2014 est.)

Life expectancy at birth: *total population:* 77.8 years
country comparison to the world: 62
male: 75.6 years
female: 80.08 years (2014 est.)

Total fertility rate: 2.36 children born/woman (2014 est.)
country comparison to the world: 88

Contraceptive prevalence rate: 72.9% (2007)

Health expenditures: 5.4% of GDP (2011)
country comparison to the world: 124

Physicians density: 1.88 physicians/1,000 population (2000)

Hospital bed density: 1.7 beds/1,000 population (2011)

Drinking water source:
improved:
urban: 82% of population
rural: 80.6% of population
total: 81.6% of population
unimproved:
urban: 18% of population
rural: 19.4% of population
total: 18.4% of population (2011 est.)

Sanitation facility access:
improved:
urban: 85.7% of population
rural: 74.5% of population
total: 82.3% of population
unimproved:
urban: 14.3% of population
rural: 25.5% of population
total: 17.7% of population (2011 est.)

HIV/AIDS—adult prevalence rate: 0.7% (2012 est.)
country comparison to the world: 54

HIV/AIDS—people living with HIV/AIDS: 45,000 (2012 est.)
country comparison to the world: 63

HIV/AIDS—deaths: 1,900 (2012 est.)
country comparison to the world: 59

Major infectious diseases: *degree of risk:* high
food or waterborne diseases: bacterial diarrhea, hepatitis A, and typhoid fever
vectorborne disease: dengue fever (2013)

Obesity—adult prevalence rate: 21.2% (2008)
country comparison to the world: 90

Children under the age of 5 years underweight: *3.4% (2007)*
country comparison to the world: 106

Education expenditures: 2.2% of GDP (2012)
country comparison to the world: 163

Literacy: *definition:* age 15 and over can read and write
total population: 90.1%
male: 90%
female: 90.2% (2011 est.)

Child labor—children ages 5-14:
total number: 180,423
percentage: 10 % (2000 est.)

Unemployment, youth ages 15-24: total: 29.4%
country comparison to the world: 26
male: 22.6%
female: 40.8% (2011)

GOVERNMENT

Country name: *conventional long form:* Dominican Republic
conventional short form: The Dominican
local long form: Republica Dominicana
local short form: La Dominicana

Government type: democratic republic

Capital: *name:* Santo Domingo
geographic coordinates: 18 28 N, 69 54 W
time difference: UTC-4 (1 hour ahead of Washington, DC during Standard Time)

Administrative divisions: 31 provinces (provincias, singular—provincia) and 1 district* (distrito); Azua, Baoruco, Barahona, Dajabon, Distrito Nacional*, Duarte, El Seibo, Elias Pina, Espaillat, Hato Mayor, Hermanas Mirabal, Independencia, La Altagracia, La Romana, La Vega, Maria Trinidad Sanchez, Monsenor Nouel, Monte Cristi, Monte Plata, Pedernales, Peravia, Puerto Plata, Samana, San Cristobal, San Jose de Ocoa, San Juan, San Pedro de Macoris, Sanchez Ramirez, Santiago, Santiago Rodriguez, Santo Domingo, Valverde

Independence: 27 February 1844 (from Haiti)

National holiday: Independence Day, 27 February (1844)

Constitution: many previous (38 total); latest proclaimed 26 January 2010; note—the Dominican Republic Government has a practice of promulgating a "new" constitution whenever an amendment is ratified (2013)

Legal system: civil law system based on the French civil code; Criminal Procedures Code modified in 2004 to include important elements of an accusatory system

International law organization participation: accepts compulsory ICJ jurisdiction; accepts ICCt jurisdiction

Suffrage: 18 years of age, universal and compulsory; married persons regardless of age can vote; note—members of the armed forces and national police cannot vote by law

Executive branch: *chief of state:* President Danilo MEDINA Sanchez (since 16 August 2012); Vice President Margarita CEDENO DE FERNANDEZ (since 16 August 2012); note—the president is both the chief of state and head of government
head of government: President Danilo MEDINA Sanchez (since 16 August 2012); Vice President Margarita CEDENO DE FERNANDEZ (since 16 August 2012)
cabinet: Cabinet nominated by the president (For more information visit the World Leaders website)
elections: president and vice president elected on the same ticket by popular vote for four-year terms; election last held on 20 May 2012 (next to be held in 2016)
election results: Danilo MEDINA Sanchez elected president; percent of vote—Danilo MEDINA Sanchez 51.2%, Hipolito MEJIA 47%, other 1.8%; Margarita CEDENO DE FERNANDEZ elected vice president

Legislative branch: bicameral National Congress or Congreso Nacional consists of the Senate or Senado (32 seats; members elected by popular vote to serve four-year terms) and the House of Representatives or Camara de Diputados (183 seats; members are elected by popular vote to serve four-year terms)
elections: Senate—last held on 16 May 2010 (next to be held in May 2016); House of Representatives—last held on 16 May 2010 (next to be held in May 2016); in order to synchronize presidential, legislative, and local elections for 2016, those members elected in 2010 will actually serve six-year terms
election results: Senate—percent of vote by party—NA; seats by party—PLD 31, PRSC 1; House of Representatives—percent of vote by

party—NA; seats by party—PLD 105, PRD 75, PRSC 3

Judicial branch: *highest court(s):* Supreme Court of Justice or Suprema Corte de Justicia (consists of a minimum of 16 magistrates); Constitutional Court or Tribunal Constitucional (consists of 13 judges) note—the Constitutional Court was established in 2010 by constitutional amendment
judge selection and term of office: Supreme Court and Constitutional Court judges appointed by the National Council of the Judiciary comprised of the president, the leaders of both chambers of congress, the president of the Supreme Court, and a non-governing party congressional representative; Supreme Court judges appointed for 7- year terms; Constitutional Court judges appointed for 9-year terms
subordinate courts: courts of appeal; courts of first instance; justices of the peace; special courts for juvenile, labor, and land cases; Contentious Administrative Court for cases filed against the government

Political parties and leaders: Dominican Liberation Party or PLD [Leonel FERNANDEZ Reyna]; Dominican Revolutionary Party or PRD [Miguel VARGAS Maldonado]; National Progressive Front [Vinicio CASTILLO, Pelegrin CASTILLO]; Social Christian Reformist Party or PRSC [Carlos MORALES Troncoso]

Political pressure groups and leaders: Citizen Participation Group (Participacion Ciudadania); Collective of Popular Organizations or COP; Foundation for Institution-Building and Justice or FINJUS

International organization participation: ACP, AOSIS, BCIE, Caricom (observer), CD, CELAC, FAO, G-77, IADB, IAEA, IBRD, ICAO, ICC (national committees), ICRM, IDA, IFAD, IFC, IFRCS, IHO, ILO, IMF, IMO, Interpol, IOC, IOM, IPU, ISO (correspondent), ITSO, ITU, ITUC (NGOs), LAES, LAIA (observer), MIGA, MINUSMA, NAM, OAS, OIF (observer), OPANAL, OPCW, PCA, Petrocaribe, SICA (associated member), UN, UNCTAD, UNESCO, UNIDO, Union Latina, UNWTO, UPU, WCO, WFTU (NGOs), WHO, WIPO, WMO, WTO

Diplomatic representation in the US:
chief of mission: Ambassador Anibal de Jesus de CASTRO Rodriguez (since 5 July 2011)
chancery: 1715 22nd Street NW, Washington, DC 20008
telephone: [1] (202) 332-6280
FAX: [1] (202) 265-8057
consulate(s) general: Boston, Chicago, Glendale (CA), Mayaguez (Puerto Rico), Miami, New Orleans, New York, San Juan (Puerto Rico)

Diplomatic representation from the US:
chief of mission: Ambassador (vacant); Charge d'Affaires Daniel L. FOOTE
embassy: corner of Calle Cesar Nicolas Penson and Calle Leopoldo Navarro, Santo Domingo
mailing address: Unit 5500, APO AA 34041-5500
telephone: [1] (809) 221-2171
FAX: [1] (809) 686-7437

Flag description: a centered white cross that extends to the edges divides the flag into four rectangles—the top ones are blue (hoist side) and red, and the bottom ones are red (hoist side) and blue; a small coat of arms featuring a shield supported by a laurel branch (left) and a palm branch (right) is at the center of the cross; above the shield a blue ribbon displays the motto, DIOS, PATRIA, LIBERTAD (God, Fatherland, Liberty), and below the shield, REPUBLICA DOMINICANA appears on a red ribbon; in the shield a bible is opened to a verse that reads "Y la verdad nos hara libre" (And the truth shall set you free); blue stands for liberty, white for salvation, and red for the blood of heroes

National symbol(s): palmchat (bird)

National anthem: *name:* "Himno Nacional" (National Anthem)
lyrics/music: Emilio PRUD"HOMME/Jose REYES
note: adopted 1934; also known as "Quisqueyanos valientes" (Valient Sons of Quisqueye); the anthem never refers to the people as Dominican but rather calls them "Quisqueyanos," a reference to the indigenous name of the island

ECONOMY

Economy—overview: The Dominican Republic has long been viewed primarily as an exporter of sugar, coffee, and tobacco, but in recent years the service sector has overtaken agriculture as the economy's largest employer, due to growth in telecommunications, tourism, and free trade zones. The economy is highly dependent upon the US, the destination for more than half of exports. Remittances from the US amount to about one-tenth of GDP, equivalent to almost half of exports and three-quarters of tourism receipts. The country suffers from marked income inequality; the poorest half of the population receives less than one-fifth of GDP, while the richest 10% enjoys nearly 40% of GDP. High unemployment and underemployment remains an important long-term challenge. The Central America-Dominican Republic Free Trade Agreement (CAFTA-DR) came into force in March 2007, boosting investment and exports and reducing losses to the Asian garment industry. The Dominican Republic's economy rebounded from the global recession in 2010-13, and it's fiscal situation is improving. A tax reform package passed in November 2012 and a successful government bond sale in 2013 helped to narrow the budget deficit from 8% of GDP in 2012 to 3% in 2013.

GDP (purchasing power parity): $101 billion (2013 est.)
country comparison to the world: 75
$99.02 billion (2012 est.)
$95.32 billion (2011 est.)
note: data are in 2013 US dollars

GDP (official exchange rate): $59.27 billion (2013 est.)

GDP—real growth rate: 2% (2013 est.)
country comparison to the world: 140
3.9% (2012 est.)
4.5% (2011 est.)

GDP—per capita (PPP): $9,700 (2013 est.)
country comparison to the world: 121
$9,700 (2012 est.)
$9,500 (2011 est.)
note: data are in 2013 US dollars

GDP—composition, by end use:
household consumption: 83.3%
government consumption: 7.7%
investment in fixed capital: 15.6%
investment in inventories: 0.1%
exports of goods and services: 26.4%
imports of goods and services: -33.2% (2013 est.)

GDP—composition, by sector of origin:
agriculture: 6%
industry: 29.1%
services: 64.9% (2013 est.)

Agriculture—products: sugarcane, coffee, cotton, cocoa, tobacco, rice, beans, potatoes, corn, bananas; cattle, pigs, dairy products, beef, eggs

Industries: tourism, sugar processing, ferronickel and gold mining, textiles, cement, tobacco

Industrial production growth rate: 2.5% (2013 est.)
country comparison to the world: 118

Labor force: 4.912 million (2013 est.)
country comparison to the world: 80

Labor force—by occupation: *agriculture:* 14.6%
industry: 22.3%
services: 63.1% (2005)

Unemployment rate: 15% (2013 est.)
country comparison to the world: 140
14.3% (2012 est.)

Population below poverty line: 34.4% (2010 est.)

Household income or consumption by percentage share:
lowest 10%: 1.8%
highest 10%: 36.4% (2010 est.)

Distribution of family income—Gini index:
47.2 (2010 est.)
country comparison to the world: 31
52 (2000 est.)

Budget: *revenues:* $9.012 billion
expenditures: $10.79 billion (2013 est.)

Taxes and other revenues: 15.2% of GDP (2013 est.)
country comparison to the world: 192

Budget surplus (+) or deficit (-):
-3% of GDP (2013 est.)
country comparison to the world: 122

Public debt: 47% of GDP (2013 est.)
country comparison to the world: 76
41.5% of GDP (2012 est.)

Fiscal year: calendar year

Inflation rate (consumer prices): 5% (2013 est.)
country comparison to the world: 155
3.7% (2012 est.)

Commercial bank prime lending rate:
13.6% (31 December 2013 est.)
country comparison to the world: 36
15.48% (31 December 2012 est.)

Stock of narrow money: $4.943 billion (31 December 2013 est.)
country comparison to the world: 100
$4.738 billion (31 December 2012 est.)

Stock of broad money: $15.54 billion (31 December 2013 est.)
country comparison to the world: 88
$14.83 billion (31 December 2012 est.)

Stock of domestic credit: $25.09 billion (31 December 2013 est.)
country comparison to the world: 75
$23.71 billion (31 December 2012 est.)

Market value of publicly traded shares: $NA

Current account balance: -$2.33 billion (2013 est.)
country comparison to the world: 147
-$4.037 billion (2012 est.)

Exports: $9.825 billion (2013 est.)
country comparison to the world: 97
$9.079 billion (2012 est.)

Exports—commodities: ferronickel, sugar, gold, silver, coffee, cocoa, tobacco, meats, consumer goods

Exports—partners: US 47%, Haiti 16.1%, China 4.3% (2012)

Imports: $16.8 billion (2013 est.)
country comparison to the world: 83
$17.76 billion (2012 est.)

Imports—commodities: foodstuffs, petroleum, cotton and fabrics, chemicals and pharmaceuticals

Imports—partners: US 43.3%, Venezuela 7.7%, China 6.3%, Mexico 5.3%, Colombia 4.1% (2012)

Reserves of foreign exchange and gold: $4.379 billion (31 December 2013 est.)
country comparison to the world: 98
$3.579 billion (31 December 2012 est.)

Debt—external: $18.01 billion (31 December 2013 est.)
country comparison to the world: 82
$16.33 billion (31 December 2012 est.)

Stock of direct foreign investment—at home: $26.76 billion (31 December 2013 est.)
country comparison to the world: 64
$24.86 billion (31 December 2012 est.)

Stock of direct foreign investment—abroad: $59 million (31 December 2013 est.)
country comparison to the world: 88
$59 million (31 December 2012 est.)

Exchange rates: Dominican pesos (DOP) per US dollar—
41.8 (2013 est.)
39.336 (2012 est.)
37.307 (2010 est.)
36.03 (2009)
34.775 (2008)

ENERGY

Electricity—production: 13.09 billion kWh (2011 est.)
country comparison to the world: 8 8

Electricity—consumption: 13.11 billion kWh (2010 est.)
country comparison to the world: 83

Electricity—exports: 0 kWh (2012 est.)
country comparison to the world: 130

Electricity—imports: 0 kWh (2012 est.)
country comparison to the world: 137

Electricity—installed generating capacity: 5.701 million kW (2010 est.)
country comparison to the world: 73

Electricity—from fossil fuels: 90.6% of total installed capacity (2010 est.)
country comparison to the world: 74

Electricity—from nuclear fuels: 0% of total installed capacity (2010 est.)
country comparison to the world: 78

Electricity—from hydroelectric plants: 9.2% of total installed capacity (2010 est.)
country comparison to the world: 117

Electricity—from other renewable sources: 0.2% of total installed capacity (2010 est.)
country comparison to the world: 97

Crude oil—production: 61.1 bbl/day (2012 est.)
country comparison to the world: 124

Crude oil—exports: 0 bbl/day (2010 est.)
country comparison to the world: 106

Crude oil—imports: 27,260 bbl/day (2010 est.)
country comparison to the world: 65

Crude oil—proved reserves: 0 bbl (1 January 2013 es)
country comparison to the world: 125

Refined petroleum products—production: 28,050 bbl/day (2010 est.)
country comparison to the world: 88

Refined petroleum products—consumption: 122,300 bbl/day (2011 est.)
country comparison to the world: 72

Refined petroleum products—exports: 0 bbl/day (2010 est.)
country comparison to the world: 171

Refined petroleum products—imports: 85,490 bbl/day (2010 est.)
country comparison to the world: 53

Natural gas—production: 0 cu m (2011 est.)
country comparison to the world: 124

Natural gas—consumption: 820 million cu m (2010 est.)
country comparison to the world: 92

Natural gas—exports: 0 cu m (2011 est.)
country comparison to the world: 91

Natural gas—imports: 930 million cu m (2011 est.)
country comparison to the world: 58

Natural gas—proved reserves: 0 cu m (1 January 2013 es)
country comparison to the world: 132

Carbon dioxide emissions from consumption of energy: 20.64 million Mt (2011 est.)
country comparison to the world: 83

COMMUNICATIONS

Telephones—main lines in use: 1.065 million (2012)
country comparison to the world: 73

Telephones—mobile cellular: 9.038 million (2012)
country comparison to the world: 86

Telephone system: *general assessment:* relatively efficient system based on island-wide microwave radio relay network
domestic: fixed-line teledensity is about 10 per 100 persons; multiple providers of mobile-cellular service with a subscribership of nearly 90 per 100 persons
international: country code—1-809; landing point for the Americas Region Caribbean Ring System (ARCOS-1), Antillas 1, and the Fibralink submarine cables that provide links to South and Central America, parts of the Caribbean, and US; satellite earth station—1 Intelsat (Atlantic Ocean) (2011)

Broadcast media: combination of state-owned and privately owned broadcast media; 1 state-owned TV network and a number of private TV networks; networks operate repeaters to extend signals throughout country; combination of state-owned and privately owned radio stations with more than 300 radio stations operating (2007)

Internet country code: .do

Internet hosts: 404,500 (2012)
country comparison to the world: 55

Internet users: 2.701 million (2009)
country comparison to the world: 68

TRANSPORTATION

Airports: 36 (2013)
country comparison to the world: 109

Airports—with paved runways: total: 1 6
over 3,047 m: 3
2,438 to 3,047 m: 4
1,524 to 2,437 m: 4
914 to 1,523 m: 4
under 914 m: 1 (2013)

Airports—with unpaved runways: *total:* 2 0
1,524 to 2,437 m: 1
914 to 1,523 m: 1
under 914 m: 18 (2013)

Heliports: 1 (2013)

Pipelines: gas 27 km; oil 103 km (2013)

Railways: *total:* 142 km
country comparison to the world: 125
standard gauge: 142 km 1.435-m gauge (2008)

Roadways: total: 19,705 km
country comparison to the world: 110
paved: 9,872 km
unpaved: 9,833 km (2002)

Ports and terminals: *major seaport(s):* Puerto Haina, Puerto Plata, Santo Domingo
oil/gas terminal(s): Andres LNG terminal (Boca Chica), Punta Nizao oil terminal

MILITARY

Military branches: Army (Ejercito Nacional, EN), Navy (Marina de Guerra, MdG; includes naval infantry), Dominican Air Force (Fuerza Aerea Dominicana, FAD) (2013)

Military service age and obligation: 17-21 years of age for voluntary military service; recruits must have completed primary school and be Dominican Republic citizens; women may volunteer (2012)

Manpower available for military service:
males age 16-49: 2,580,083
females age 16-49: 2,464,698 (2010 est.)

Manpower fit for military service:
males age 16-49: 2,188,358
females age 16-49: 2,090,180 (2010 est.)

Manpower reaching militarily significant age annually: male: 100,047
female: 96,302 (2010 est.)

Military expenditures: 0.61% of GDP (2012)
country comparison to the world: 121
0.63% of GDP (2011)
0.61% of GDP (2010)

TRANSNATIONAL ISSUES

Disputes—international: Haitian migrants cross the porous border into the Dominican Republic to find work; illegal migrants from the Dominican Republic cross the Mona Passage each year to Puerto Rico to find better work

Illicit drugs: transshipment point for South American drugs destined for the US and Europe; has become a transshipment point for ecstasy from the Netherlands and Belgium destined for US and Canada; substantial money laundering activity in particular by Colombian narcotics traffickers; significant amphetamine consumption (2008)

ECUADOR

INTRODUCTION

Background: What is now Ecuador formed part of the northern Inca Empire until the Spanish conquest in 1533. Quito became a seat of Spanish colonial government in 1563 and part of the Viceroyalty of New Granada in 1717. The territories of the Viceroyalty—New Granada (Colombia), Venezuela, and Quito—gained their independence between 1819 and 1822 and formed a federation known as Gran Colombia. When Quito withdrew in 1830, the traditional name was changed in favor of the "Republic of the Equator." Between 1904 and 1942, Ecuador lost territories in a series of conflicts with its neighbors. A border war with Peru that flared in 1995 was resolved in 1999. Although Ecuador marked 30 years of civilian governance in 2004, the period was marred by political instability. Protests in Quito contributed to the mid-term ouster of three of Ecuador's last four democratically elected Presidents. In late 2008, voters approved a new constitution, Ecuador's 20th since gaining independence. General elections were held in February 2013, and voters re-elected President Rafael CORREA.

GEOGRAPHY

Location: Western South America, bordering the Pacific Ocean at the Equator, between Colombia and Peru

Geographic coordinates: 2 00 S, 77 30 W

Map references: South America

Area: *total:* 283,561 sq km
country comparison to the world: 74
land: 276,841 sq km
water: 6,720 sq km
note: includes Galapagos Islands

Area—comparative: slightly smaller than Nevada

Land boundaries: *total:* 2,010 km
border countries: Colombia 590 km, Peru 1,420 km

Coastline: 2,237 km

Maritime claims: *territorial sea:* 200 nm
continental shelf: 100 nm from 2,500-m isobath

Climate: tropical along coast, becoming cooler inland at higher elevations; tropical in Amazonian jungle lowlands

Terrain: coastal plain (costa), inter-Andean central highlands (sierra), and flat to rolling eastern jungle (oriente)

Elevation extremes: *lowest point:* Pacific Ocean 0 m
highest point: Chimborazo 6,267 m
note: due to the fact that the earth is not a perfect sphere and has an equatorial bulge, the highest point on the planet furthest from its center is Mount Chimborazo not Mount Everest, which is merely the highest peak above sea-level

Natural resources: petroleum, fish, timber, hydropower

Land use: *arable land:* 4.51%
permanent crops: 5.38%
other: 90.11% (2011)

Irrigated land: 8,534 sq km (2003)

Total renewable water resources: 424.4 cu km (2011)

Freshwater withdrawal (domestic/industrial/agricultural): *total:* 9.92 cu km/yr (13%/6%/81%)
per capita: 716.1 cu m/yr (2005)

Natural hazards: frequent earthquakes; landslides; volcanic activity; floods; periodic droughts
volcanism: volcanic activity concentrated along the Andes Mountains; Sangay (elev. 5,230 m), which erupted in 2010, is mainland Ecuador's most active volcano; other historically active volcanoes in the Andes include Antisana, Cayambe, Chacana, Cotopaxi, Guagua Pichincha, Reventador, Sumaco, and Tungurahua; Fernandina (elev. 1,476 m), a shield volcano that last erupted in 2009, is the most active of the many Galapagos volcanoes; other historically active Galapagos volcanoes include Wolf, Sierra Negra, Cerro Azul, Pinta, Marchena, and Santiago

Environment—current issues: deforestation; soil erosion; desertification; water pollution; pollution from oil production wastes in ecologically sensitive areas of the Amazon Basin and Galapagos Islands

Environment—international agreements: *party to:* Antarctic-Environmental Protocol, Antarctic Treaty, Biodiversity, Climate Change, Climate Change-Kyoto Protocol, Desertification, Endangered Species, Hazardous Wastes, Ozone Layer Protection, Ship Pollution, Tropical Timber 83, Tropical Timber 94, Wetlands
signed, but not ratified: none of the selected agreements

Geography—note: Cotopaxi in Andes is highest active volcano in world

PEOPLE AND SOCIETY

Nationality: *noun: Ecuadorian(s)*
adjective: Ecuadorian

Ethnic groups: mestizo (mixed Amerindian and white) 71.9%, Montubio 7.4%, Afroecuadorian 7.2%, Amerindian 7%, white 6.1%, other 0.4% (2010 census)

Languages: Spanish (Castillian) 93% (official), Quechua 4.1%, other indigenous 0.7%, foreign 2.2%
note: (Quechua and Shuar are official languages of intercultural relations; other indigenous languages are in official use by indigenous peoples in the areas they inhabit) (2010 est.)

Religions: Roman Catholic 95%, other 5%

Demographic profile: Ecuador's high poverty and income inequality most affect indigenous, mixed race, and rural populations. The government has increased its social spending to ameliorate these problems, but critics question the efficiency and implementation of its national development plan. Nevertheless, the conditional cash transfer program, which requires participants' children to attend school and have medical check-ups, has helped improve educational attainment and healthcare among poor children. Ecuador is stalled at above replacement level fertility and the population most likely will keep growing rather than stabilize. An estimated 2 to 3 million Ecuadorians live abroad, but increased unemployment in key receiving countries—Spain, the United States, and Italy—is slowing emigration and increasing the likelihood of returnees to Ecuador. The first large-scale emigration of Ecuadorians occurred between 1980 and 2000, when an economic crisis drove Ecuadorians from southern provinces to New York City, where they had trade contacts. A second, nationwide wave of emigration in the late 1990s was caused by another economic downturn, political instability, and a currency crisis. Spain was the logical destination because of its shared language and the wide availability of low-skilled, informal jobs at a time when increased border surveillance made illegal migration to the US difficult. Ecuador has a small but growing immigrant population and is Latin America's top recipient of refugees; 98% are neighboring Colombians fleeing violence in their country.

Population: 15,654,411 (July 2014 est.)
country comparison to the world: 68
Age structure: *0-14 years:* 28.5% (male 2,275,448/female 2,184,706)
15-24 years: 18.6% (male 1,478,184/female 1,439,288)
25-54 years: 38.9% (male 2,968,757/female 3,124,938)
55-64 years: 6.9% (male 544,097/female 562,326)
65 years and over: 6.7% (male 514,549/female 562,118) (2014 est.)

Dependency ratios:
total dependency ratio: 57.4 %
youth dependency ratio: 47.2 %
elderly dependency ratio: 10.3 %
potential support ratio: 9.8 (2013)

Median age: total: 26.7 years
male: 26 years
female: 27.3 years (2014 est.)

Population growth rate: 1.37% (2014 est.)
country comparison to the world: 88

Birth rate: 18.87 births/1,000 population (2014 est.)
country comparison to the world: 95

Death rate: 5.04 deaths/1,000 population (2014 est.)
country comparison to the world: 186

Net migration rate: -0.13 migrant(s)/1,000 population (2014 est.)
country comparison to the world: 116

Urbanization: *urban population:* 67% of total population (2010)
rate of urbanization: 2% annual rate of change (2010-15 est.)

Major urban areas—population: Guayaquil 2.634 million; QUITO (capital) 1.622 million (2011)

Sex ratio: *at birth:* 1.05 male(s)/female
0-14 years: 1.04 male(s)/female
15-24 years: 1.03 male(s)/female
25-54 years: 0.95 male(s)/female
55-64 years: 0.99 male(s)/female
65 years and over: 0.92 male(s)/female
total population: 0.99 male(s)/female (2014 est.)

Mother's mean age at first birth: 21.8 (2004 est.)

Maternal mortality rate:
110 deaths/100,000 live births (2010)
country comparison to the world: 67

Infant mortality rate: *total:* 17.93 deaths/1,000 live births
country comparison to the world: 98
male: 21.11 deaths/1,000 live births
female: 14.58 deaths/1,000 live births (2014 est.)

Life expectancy at birth: *total population:* 76.36 years
country comparison to the world: 81
male: 73.4 years
female: 79.46 years (2014 est.)

Total fertility rate: 2.29 children born/woman (2014 est.)
country comparison to the world: 94

Contraceptive prevalence rate: 72.7% (2004)

Health expenditures: 7.3% of GDP (2011)
country comparison to the world: 79

Physicians density: 1.69 physicians/1,000 population (2009)

Hospital bed density: 1.6 beds/1,000 population (2010)

Drinking water source:
improved:
urban: 96.5% of population
rural: 82.2% of population
total: 91.8% of population
unimproved:
urban: 3.5% of population
rural: 17.8% of population
total: 8.2% of population (2011 est.)

Sanitation facility access:
improved:
urban: 96.2% of population
rural: 86.1% of population
total: 92.9% of population
unimproved:
urban: 3.8% of population
rural: 13.9% of population
total: 7.1% of population (2011 est.)

HIV/AIDS—adult prevalence rate: 0.6% (2012 est.)
country comparison to the world: 62

HIV/AIDS—people living with HIV/AIDS:
52,300 (2012 est.)
country comparison to the world: 60

HIV/AIDS—deaths: 2,700 (2012 est.)
country comparison to the world: 53

Major infectious diseases: *degree of risk:* high
food or waterborne diseases: bacterial diarrhea, hepatitis A, and typhoid fever
vectorborne diseases: dengue fever and malaria (2013)

Obesity—adult prevalence rate: 21.4% (2008)
country comparison to the world: 86

Children under the age of 5 years underweight:
6.2% (2004)
country comparison to the world: 82

Education expenditures: 4.4% of GDP (2012)
country comparison to the world: 94

Literacy: definition: age 15 and over can read and write
total population: 91.6%
male: 93.1%
female: 90.2% (2011 est.)

Child labor—children ages 5-14:
total number: 227,599
percentage: 8 % (2008 est.)

Unemployment, youth ages 15-24: *total:* 11.1%
country comparison to the world: 105
male: 9%
female: 15% (2011)

GOVERNMENT

Country name: *conventional long form:* Republic of Ecuador
conventional short form: Ecuador
local long form: Republica del Ecuador
local short form: Ecuador

Government type: republic

Capital: *name:* Quito
geographic coordinates: 0 13 S, 78 30 W
time difference: UTC-5 (same time as Washington, DC during Standard Time)

Administrative divisions: 24 provinces (provincias, singular—provincia); Azuay, Bolivar, Canar, Carchi, Chimborazo, Cotopaxi, El Oro, Esmeraldas, Galapagos, Guayas, Imbabura, Loja, Los Rios, Manabi, Morona-Santiago, Napo, Orellana, Pastaza, Pichincha, Santa Elena, Santo Domingo de los Tsachilas, Sucumbios, Tungurahua, Zamora-Chinchipe

Independence: 24 May 1822 (from Spain)

National holiday: Independence Day (independence of Quito), 10 August (1809)

Constitution: many previous; latest approved 20 October 2008; amended 2011 (2011)

Legal system: civil law based on the Chilean civil code with modifications

International law organization participation:
has not submitted an ICJ jurisdiction declaration; accepts ICCt jurisdiction

Suffrage: 18-65 years of age, universal and compulsory; 16-18, over 65, and other eligible voters, optional

Executive branch: *chief of state:* President Rafael CORREA Delgado (since 15 January 2007); Vice President Jorge GLAS Espinel (since 24 May 2013); note—the president is both the chief of state and head of government
head of government: President Rafael CORREA Delgado (since 15 January 2007); Vice President Jorge GLAS Espinel (since 24 May 2013)
cabinet: Cabinet appointed by the president (For more information visit the World Leaders website)
elections: the president and vice president elected on the same ticket by popular vote for a four-year term and can be re-elected for another consecutive term; election last held on 17 February 2013 (next to be held in 2017)
election results: President Rafael CORREA Delgado reelected president; percent of vote—Rafael CORREA Delgado 57.2%, Guillermo LASSO 22.7%, Lucio GUTIERREZ 6.8%, Mauricio RODAS 3.9%, other 9.4%

Legislative branch: unicameral National Assembly or Asamblea Nacional (137 seats; members are elected through a party-list *proportional representation system to serve four-year terms)*
elections: last held on 17 February 2013 (next to be held in 2017)
election results: percent of vote by party—NA; seats by party—PAIS 100, CREO 11, PSC 6, AVANZA 5, MUPP 5, PSP 5, other 5; note—defections by members of National Assembly are commonplace, resulting in frequent changes in the numbers of seats held by the various parties

Judicial branch: *highest court(s):* National Court of Justice or Corte Nacional de Justicia (consists of 21 judges including a chief justice and organized into 5 specialized chambers); Constitutional Court or Corte Constitutional (consists of 11 judges)
judge selection and term of office: justices of National Court of Justice elected by the Judiciary Council, a 9-member independent body of professionals; judges elected for 9-year, non-renewable terms, with one-third of the judges renewed every 3 years; Constitutional Court judges appointed by the National Assembly from candidates selected by the president, Supreme Court, and other government officials; judges appointed for 2-year terms
subordinate courts: Fiscal Tribunal; Superior Court (one for each province); lower provincial and cantonal courts

Political parties and leaders: Alianza PAIS movement [Rafael Vicente CORREA Delgado]; Avanza Party or AVANZA [Ramiro GONZALEZ]; Breakaway Party [Martha ROLDOS]; Creating Opportunities Movement or CREO [Guillermo LASSO]; Institutional Renewal and National Action Party or PRIAN [Alvaro NOBOA]; Pachakutik Plurinational Unity Movement or MUPP [Rafael ANTUNI]; Patriotic Society Party or PSP [Lucio GUTIERREZ Borbua]; Plurinational Union Movement of the Left [Alberto ACOSTA]; Roldosist Party or PRE [Abdala BUCARAM Pulley, director]; Social Christian Party or PSC [Pascual DEL CIOPPO]; Socialist Party; Society United for More Action or SUMA [Mauricio RODAS]; Warrior's Spirit Movement [Jaime NEBOT]

Political pressure groups and leaders: Confederation of Indigenous Nationalities of Ecuador or CONAIE [Humberto CHOLANGO]; Federation of Indigenous Evangelists of Ecuador or FEINE [Manuel CHUGCHILAN, president]; National Federation of Indigenous Afro-Ecuatorianos and Peasants or FENOCIN; National Teacher's Union or UNE [Mariana PALLASCO]

International organization participation: CAN, CD, CELAC, FAO, G-11, G-77, IADB, IAEA, IBRD, ICAO, ICC (national committees), ICRM, IDA, IFAD, IFC, IFRCS, IHO, ILO, IMF, IMO, Interpol, IOC, IOM, IPU, ISO, ITSO, ITU, ITUC (NGOs), LAES, LAIA, Mercosur (associate), MIGA, MINUSTAH, NAM, OAS, OPANAL, OPCW, OPEC, PCA, UN, UNAMID, UNASUR, UNCTAD, UNESCO, UNHCR, UNIDO, Union Latina, UNMIL, UNMISS, UNOCI, UNWTO, UPU, WCO, WFTU (NGOs), WHO, WIPO, WMO, WTO

Diplomatic representation in the US:
chief of mission: Ambassador Saskia Nathalie CELY Suarez (since 2 December 2011)
chancery: 1050 30th Street, NW, Washington, DC 20007
telephone: [1] (202) 465-8140
FAX: [1] (202) 333-2893

consulate(s) general: Atlanta, Boston, Chicago, Houston, Los Angeles, Miami, New Haven (CT), New Orleans, New York, Newark (NJ), Phoenix, San Francisco, San Juan (Puerto Rico)

Diplomatic representation from the US:
chief of mission: Ambassador Adam E. NAMM (since 26 April 2012)
embassy: Avenida Avigiras E12-170 y Avenida Eloy Alfaro, Quito
mailing address: Avenida Guayacanes N52-205 y Avenida Avigiras
telephone: [593] (2) 398-5000
FAX: [593] (2) 398-5100
consulate(s) general: Guayaquil

Flag description: three horizontal bands of yellow (top, double width), blue, and red with the coat of arms superimposed at the center of the flag; the flag retains the three main colors of the banner of Gran Columbia, the South American republic that broke up in 1830; the yellow color represents sunshine, grain, and mineral wealth, blue the sky, sea, and rivers, and red the blood of patriots spilled in the struggle for freedom and justice
note: similar to the flag of Colombia, which is shorter and does not bear a coat of arms

National symbol(s): Andean condor

National anthem: *name:* "Salve, Oh Patria!" (We Salute You Our Homeland)
lyrics/music: Juan Leon MERA/Antonio NEUMANE
note: adopted 1948; Juan Leon MERA wrote the lyrics in 1865; only the chorus and second verse are sung

ECONOMY

Economy—overview: Ecuador is substantially dependent on its petroleum resources, which have accounted for more than half of the country's export earnings and approximately two-fifths of public sector revenues in recent years. In 1999/2000, Ecuador's economy suffered from a banking crisis, with GDP contracting by 5.3% and poverty increasing significantly. In March 2000, the Congress approved a series of structural reforms that also provided for the adoption of the US dollar as legal tender. Dollarization stabilized the economy, and positive growth returned in the years that followed, helped by high oil prices, remittances, and increased non-traditional exports. From 2002-06 the economy grew an average of 4.3% per year, the highest five-year average in 25 years. After moderate growth in 2007, the economy reached a growth rate of 6.4% in 2008, buoyed by high global petroleum prices and increased public sector investment. President Rafael CORREA, who took office in January 2007, defaulted in December 2008 on Ecuador's sovereign debt, which, with a total face value of approximately US$3.2 billion, represented about 30% of Ecuador's public external debt. In May 2009, Ecuador bought back 91% of its "defaulted" bonds via an international reverse auction. Economic policies under the CORREA administration—for example, an announcement in late 2009 of its intention to terminate 13 bilateral investment treaties, including one with the United States—have generated economic uncertainty and discouraged private investment. China has become Ecuador's largest foreign lender since Quito defaulted in 2008, allowing the government to maintain a high rate of social spending; Ecuador contracted with the Chinese government for more than $9 billion in oil for cash and project loans as of December 2012.

GDP (purchasing power parity): $157.6 billion (2013 est.)
country comparison to the world: 62
$151.5 billion (2012 est.)
$144.2 billion (2011 est.)
note: data are in 2013 US dollars

GDP (official exchange rate): $91.41 billion (2013 est.)

GDP—real growth rate: 4% (2013 est.)
country comparison to the world: 77
5.1% (2012 est.)
7.8% (2011 est.)

GDP—per capita (PPP): $10,600 (2013 est.)
country comparison to the world: 115
$9,600 (2012 est.)
$9,200 (2011 est.)
note: data are in 2013 US dollars

Gross national saving: 26% of GDP (2013 est.)
country comparison to the world: 44
21.3% of GDP (2012 est.)
19.7% of GDP (2011 est.)

GDP—composition, by end use:
household consumption: 62.4%
government consumption: 13.4%
investment in fixed capital: 26.6%
investment in inventories: 0.3%
exports of goods and services: 29.4%
imports of goods and services: -32.1% (2013 est.)

GDP—composition, by sector of origin:
agriculture: 5.9%
industry: 35.1%
services: 59% (2013 est.)

Agriculture—products: bananas, coffee, cocoa, rice, potatoes, manioc (tapioca), plantains, sugarcane; cattle, sheep, pigs, beef, pork, dairy products; fish, shrimp; balsa wood

Industries: petroleum, food processing, textiles, wood products, chemicals

Industrial production growth rate: 3.1%
country comparison to the world: 94
note: excludes oil refining (2013 est.)

Labor force: 4.854 million (2013 est.)
country comparison to the world: 81

Labor force—by occupation: *agriculture:* 27.8%
industry: 17.8%
services: 54.4% (2012)

Unemployment rate: 4.9% (2013 est.)
country comparison to the world: 43
4.2% (2011 est.)

Population below poverty line: 27.3% (December 2012 est)

Household income or consumption by percentage share:
lowest 10%: 1.4%
highest 10%: 38.3%
note: data for urban households only (2010 est.)

Distribution of family income—Gini index:
47.7 (December 2012)
country comparison to the world: 28
50.5 (2006)
note: data are for urban households

Budget: *revenues:* $37 billion
expenditures: $39.3 billion (2013 est.)

Taxes and other revenues: 40.5% of GDP (2013 est.)
country comparison to the world: 37

Budget surplus (+) or deficit (-):
-2.5% of GDP (2013 est.)
country comparison to the world: 102

Public debt: 23.2% of GDP (2013 est.)
country comparison to the world: 131
21% of GDP (2012 est.)

Fiscal year: calendar year

Inflation rate (consumer prices): 2.6% (2013 est.)
country comparison to the world: 96
4.5% (2011 est.)

Central bank discount rate: 8.17% (31 December 2011)
country comparison to the world: 30
8.68% (31 December 2010)

Commercial bank prime lending rate:
8.7% (31 December 2013 est.)
country comparison to the world: 114
8.17% (31 December 2012 est.)

Stock of narrow money: $8.59 billion (31 December 2013 est.)
country comparison to the world: 84
$7.801 billion (31 December 2012 est.)

Stock of broad money: $27.75 billion (31 December 2013 est.)
country comparison to the world: 76
$24.68 billion (31 December 2012 est.)

Stock of domestic credit: $25.4 billion (31 December 2013 est.)
country comparison to the world: 74
$22.5 billion (31 December 2012 est.)

Market value of publicly traded shares:
$5.911 billion (31 December 2012 est.)
country comparison to the world: 82
$5.779 billion (31 December 2011)
$5.263 billion (31 December 2010 est.)

Current account balance: -$827.1 million (2013 est.)
country comparison to the world: 116
-$177 million (2012 est.)

Exports: $25.48 billion (2013 est.)
country comparison to the world: 69
$24.65 billion (2012 est.)

Exports—commodities: petroleum, bananas, cut flowers, shrimp, cacao, coffee, wood, fish

Exports—partners: US 37.3%, Chile 8.1%, Peru 6.5%, Japan 4.5%, Russia 4.5%, Colombia 4% (2012)

Imports: $26.22 billion (2013 est.)
country comparison to the world: 71
$24.58 billion (2012 est.)

Imports—commodities: industrial materials, fuels and lubricants, nondurable consumer goods

Imports—partners: US 28.4%, China 11.3%, Colombia 8.8%, Peru 4.5% (2012)

Reserves of foreign exchange and gold:
$2.625 billion (31 December 2013 est.)
country comparison to the world: 114
$2.483 billion (31 December 2012 est.)

Debt—external: $19.91 billion (31 December 2013 est.)
country comparison to the world: 81
$17.68 billion (31 December 2012 est.)

Stock of direct foreign investment—at home:
$17.89 billion (31 December 2013 est.)
country comparison to the world: 75
$17.3 billion (31 December 2012 est.)

Stock of direct foreign investment—abroad:
$6.33 billion (31 December 2012 est.)
country comparison to the world: 62
$6.33 billion (31 December 2011 est.)

Exchange rates: the US dollar became Ecuador's currency in 2001

ENERGY

Electricity—production: 21.84 billion kWh (2011 est.)
country comparison to the world: 7 0

Electricity—consumption: 14.92 billion kWh (2010 est.)
country comparison to the world: 77

Electricity—exports: 14.1 million kWh (2010 est.)
country comparison to the world: 90

Electricity—imports: 1.3 billion kWh (2010 est.)
country comparison to the world: 59

Electricity—installed generating capacity: 5.243 million kW (2010 est.)
country comparison to the world: 75

Electricity—from fossil fuels: *55.3% of total installed capacity (2010 est.)*
country comparison to the world: 143

Electricity—from nuclear fuels: 0% of total installed capacity (2010 est.)
country comparison to the world: 79

Electricity—from hydroelectric plants: 42.8% of total installed capacity (2010 est.)
country comparison to the world: 57

Electricity—from other renewable sources: 2% of total installed capacity (2010 est.)
country comparison to the world: 67

Crude oil—production: 504,500 bbl/day (2012 est.)
country comparison to the world: 31

Crude oil—exports: 366,000 bbl/day (2012 est.)
country comparison to the world: 22

Crude oil—imports: 154,000 bbl/day (2012 est.)
country comparison to the world: 40

Crude oil—proved reserves: 8.24 billion bbl (1 January 2013 es)
country comparison to the world: 19

Refined petroleum products—production: 198,700 bbl/day (2012 est.)
country comparison to the world: 54

Refined petroleum products—consumption: 280,000 bbl/day (2012 est.)
country comparison to the world: 45

Refined petroleum products—exports: 28,000 bbl/day (2012 est.)
country comparison to the world: 70

Refined petroleum products—imports: 111,000 bbl/day (2012 est.)
country comparison to the world: 49

Natural gas—production: 240 million cu m (2011 est.)
country comparison to the world: 76

Natural gas—consumption: 330 million cu m (2010 est.)
country comparison to the world: 99

Natural gas—exports: 0 cu m (2011 est.)
country comparison to the world: 92

Natural gas—imports: 25,000 cu m (2012 est.)
country comparison to the world: 76

Natural gas—proved reserves: 6.994 billion cu m (1 January 2013 es)
country comparison to the world: 86

Carbon dioxide emissions from consumption of energy: 29.13 million Mt (2011 est.)
country comparison to the world: 76

COMMUNICATIONS

Telephones—main lines in use: 2.31 million (2012)
country comparison to the world: 54

Telephones—mobile cellular: 16.457 million (2012)
country comparison to the world: 56

Telephone system: *general assessment:* elementary fixed-line service, but increasingly sophisticated mobile-cellular network
domestic: fixed-line services provided by multiple telecommunications operators; fixed-line teledensity stands at about 15 per 100 persons; mobile-cellular use has surged and subscribership has reached 100 per 100 persons
international: country code—593; landing points for the PAN-AM and South America-1 submarine cables that provide links to the west coast of South America, Panama, Colombia, Venezuela, and extending onward to Aruba and the US Virgin Islands in the Caribbean; satellite earth station—1 Intelsat (Atlantic Ocean) (2011)

Broadcast media: Ecuador has multiple TV networks and many local channels, as well as more than 300 radio stations; many TV and radio stations are privately owned; the government owns or controls 5 national TV stations and multiple radio stations; broadcast media required by law to give the government free air time to broadcast programs produced by the state (2007)

Internet country code: .ec

Internet hosts: 170,538 (2012)
country comparison to the world: 76

Internet users: 3.352 million (2009)
country comparison to the world: 64

TRANSPORTATION

Airports: 432 (2013)
country comparison to the world: 2 0

Airports—with paved runways: *total:* 104
over 3,047 m: 4
2,438 to 3,047 m: 5
1,524 to 2,437 m: 18
914 to 1,523 m: 26
under 914 m: 51 (2013)

Airports—with unpaved runways: *total:* 328
914 to 1,523 m: 37
under 914 m: 291 (2013)

Heliports: 2 (2013)

Pipelines: extra heavy crude 527 km; gas 71 km; oil 2,131 km; refined products 1,526 km (2013)

Railways: *total:* 965 km
country comparison to the world: 90
narrow gauge: 965 km 1.067-m gauge (2008)

Roadways: total: 43,670 km
country comparison to the world: 84
paved: 6,472 km
unpaved: 37,198 km (2007)

Waterways: 1,500 km (most inaccessible) (2012)
country comparison to the world: 53

Merchant marine: *total:* 4 4
country comparison to the world: 72
by type: cargo 1, chemical tanker 4, liquefied gas 1, passenger 9, petroleum tanker 28, refrigerated cargo 1
registered in other countries: 4 (Panama 3, Peru 1) (2010)

Ports and terminals: *major seaport(s):* Esmeraldas, Manta, Puerto Bolivar river port(s): Guayaquil (Guayas)
container port(s) (TEUs): Guayaquil (1,405,762)

MILITARY

Military branches: Ecuadorian Armed Forces: Ecuadorian Land Force (Fuerza Terrestre Ecuatoriana, FTE), Ecuadorian Navy (Fuerza Naval del Ecuador (FNE), includes Naval Infantry, Naval Aviation, Coast Guard), Ecuadorian Air Force (Fuerza Aerea Ecuatoriana, FAE) (2012)

Military service age and obligation: 18 years of age for selective conscript military service; conscription has been suspended; 18 years of age for voluntary military service; Air Force 18-22 years of age, Ecadorian birth requirement; 1-year service *obligation (2012)*

Manpower available for military service:
males age 16-49: 3,728,906
females age 16-49: 3,844,918 (2010 est.)

Manpower fit for military service:
males age 16-49: 2,834,213
females age 16-49: 3,269,535 (2010 est.)

Manpower reaching militarily significant age annually: *male:* 152,593
female: 147,143 (2010 est.)

Military expenditures: 2.83% of GDP (2012)
country comparison to the world: 25
3.2% of GDP (2011)
2.83% of GDP (2010)

TRANSNATIONAL ISSUES

Disputes—international: organized illegal narcotics operations in Colombia penetrate across Ecuador's shared border, which thousands of Colombians also cross to escape the violence in their home country

Refugees and internally displaced persons: *refugees (country of origin):* 122,964 (Colombia) (2012)

Illicit drugs: significant transit country for cocaine originating in Colombia and Peru, with much of the US-bound cocaine passing through Ecuadorian Pacific waters; importer of precursor chemicals used in production of illicit narcotics; attractive location for cash-placement by drug traffickers laundering money because of dollarization and weak anti-money-laundering regime; increased activity on the northern frontier by trafficking groups and Colombian insurgents (2008)

EGYPT

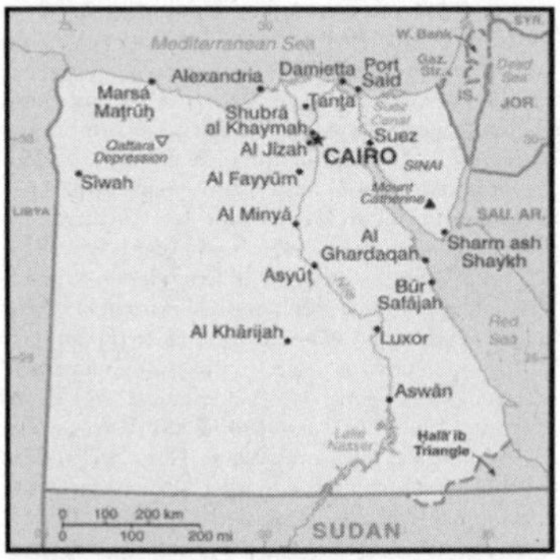

INTRODUCTION

Background: The regularity and richness of the annual Nile River flood, coupled with semi-isolation provided by deserts to the east and west, allowed for the development of one of the world's great civilizations. A unified kingdom arose circa 3200 B.C., and a series of dynasties ruled in Egypt for the next three millennia. The last native dynasty fell to the Persians in 341 B.C., who in turn were replaced by the Greeks, Romans, and Byzantines. It was the Arabs who introduced Islam and the Arabic language in the 7th century and who ruled for the next six centuries. A local military caste, the Mamluks took control about 1250 and continued to govern after the conquest of Egypt by the Ottoman Turks in 1517. Completion of the Suez Canal in 1869 elevated Egypt as an important world transportation hub. Ostensibly to protect its investments, Britain seized control of Egypt's government in 1882, but nominal allegiance to the Ottoman Empire continued until 1914. Partially independent from the UK in 1922, Egypt acquired full sovereignty from Britain in 1952. The completion of the Aswan High Dam in 1971 and the resultant Lake Nasser have altered the time-honored place of the Nile River in the agriculture and ecology of Egypt. A rapidly growing population (the largest in the Arab world), limited arable land, and dependence on the Nile all continue to overtax resources and stress society. The government has struggled to meet the demands of Egypt's population through economic reform and massive investment in communications and physical infrastructure. Inspired by the 2010 Tunisian revolution, Egyptian opposition groups led demonstrations and labor strikes countrywide, culminating in President Hosni MUBARAK's ouster. Egypt's military assumed national leadership until a new parliament was in place in early 2012; later that same year, Mohammed MURSI won the presidential election. Following often violent protests throughout the spring of 2013 against MORSI's government and the Muslim Brotherhood (MB), and massive anti-government demonstrations, the Egyptian Armed Forces (EAF) intervened and removed MORSI from power in mid-July 2013 and replaced him with interim president Adly MANSOUR. In mid-January 2014, voters approved a new constitution by referendum. Presidential elections to replace MANSOUR are scheduled for late May 2014. According to the constitution and the government's transitional road map, preparations for parliamentary elections will begin by mid-July 2014.

GEOGRAPHY

Location: Northern Africa, bordering the Mediterranean Sea, between Libya and the Gaza Strip, and the Red Sea north of Sudan, and includes the Asian Sinai Peninsula

Geographic coordinates: 27 00 N, 30 00 E

Map references: Africa

Area: *total:* 1,001,450 sq km
country comparison to the world: 30
land: 995,450 sq km
water: 6,000 sq km

Area—comparative: more than eight times the size of Ohio; slightly more than three times the size of New Mexico

Land boundaries: *total:* 2,665 km
border countries: Gaza Strip 11 km, Israel 266 km, Libya 1,115 km, Sudan 1,273 km

Coastline: 2,450 km

Maritime claims: *territorial sea:* 12 nm
contiguous zone: 24 nm
exclusive economic zone: 200 nm
continental shelf: 200 m depth or to the depth of exploitation

Climate: desert; hot, dry summers with moderate winters

Terrain: vast desert plateau interrupted by Nile valley and delta

Elevation extremes: *lowest point:* Qattara Depression -133 m
highest point: Mount Catherine 2,629 m

Natural resources: petroleum, natural gas, iron ore, phosphates, manganese, limestone, gypsum, talc, asbestos, lead, rare earth elements, zinc

Land use: *arable land:* 2.87%
permanent crops: 0.79%
other: 96.34% (2011)

Irrigated land: 34,220 sq km (2003)

Total renewable water resources: 57.3 cu km (2011)

Freshwater withdrawal (domestic/industrial/agricultural): *total:* 68.3 cu km/yr (8%/6%/86%)
per capita: 973.3 cu m/yr (2000)

Natural hazards: periodic droughts; frequent earthquakes; flash floods; landslides; hot, driving windstorms called khamsin occur in spring; dust storms; sandstorms

Environment—current issues: agricultural land being lost to urbanization and windblown sands; increasing soil salination below Aswan High Dam; desertification; oil pollution threatening coral reefs, beaches, and marine habitats; other water pollution from agricultural pesticides, raw sewage, and industrial effluents; limited natural freshwater resources away from the Nile, which is the only perennial water source; rapid growth in population overstraining the Nile and natural resources

Environment—international agreements: *party to:* Biodiversity, Climate Change, Climate Change-Kyoto Protocol, Desertification, Endangered Species, Environmental Modification, Hazardous Wastes, Law of the Sea, Marine Dumping, Ozone Layer Protection, Ship Pollution, Tropical Timber 83, Tropical Timber 94, Wetlands
signed, but not ratified: none of the selected agreements

Geography—note: controls Sinai Peninsula, only land bridge between Africa and remainder of Eastern Hemisphere; controls Suez Canal, a sea link between Indian Ocean and Mediterranean Sea; size, and juxtaposition to Israel, establish its major role in Middle Eastern geopolitics; dependence on upstream neighbors; dominance of Nile basin issues; prone to influxes of refugees from Sudan and the Palestinian territories

PEOPLE AND SOCIETY

Nationality: *noun:* Egyptian(s)
adjective: Egyptian

Ethnic groups: Egyptian 99.6%, other 0.4% (2006 census)

Languages: Arabic (official), English and French widely understood by educated classes

Religions: Muslim (predominantly Sunni) 90%, Christian (majority Coptic Orthodox, other Christians include Armenian Apostolic, Catholic, Maronite, Orthodox, and Anglican) 10% (2012 est.)

Population: 86,895,099 (July 2014 est.)
country comparison to the world: 16

Age structure: *0-14 years:* 32.1% (male 14,272,494/female 13,639,550)
15-24 years: 17.8% (male 7,913,351/female 7,536,925)
25-54 years: 38.4% (male 16,942,145/female 16,398,524)
55-64 years: 5% (male 2,888,193/female 2,973,531)
65 years and over: 4.8% (male 1,949,145/female 2,381,241) (2014 est.)

Dependency ratios:
total dependency ratio: 58.5 %
youth dependency ratio: 49.4 %
elderly dependency ratio: 9.1 %
potential support ratio: 10.9 (2013)

Median age: *total:* 25.1 years
male: 24.7 years
female: 25.4 years (2014 est.)

Population growth rate: 1.84% (2014 est.)
country comparison to the world: 64

Birth rate: 23.35 births/1,000 population (2014 est.)
country comparison to the world: 68

Death rate: 4.77 deaths/1,000 population (2014 est.)
country comparison to the world: 197

Net migration rate: -0.19 migrant(s)/1,000 population (2014 est.)
country comparison to the world: 119

Urbanization: *urban population:* 43.5% of total population (2011)
rate of urbanization: 2.04% annual rate of change (2010-15 est.)

Major urban areas—population: CAIRO (capital) 11.169 million; Alexandria 4.387 million (2011)

Sex ratio: *at birth:* 1.05 male(s)/female
0-14 years: 1.05 male(s)/female
15-24 years: 1.05 male(s)/female
25-54 years: 1.03 male(s)/female
55-64 years: 1.02 male(s)/female
65 years and over: 0.82 male(s)/female
total population: 1.03 male(s)/female (2014 est.)

Mother's mean age at first birth: 22.9 (2008 est.)

Maternal mortality rate:
66 deaths/100,000 live births (2010)
country comparison to the world: 92

Infant mortality rate: total: 22.41 deaths/1,000 live births
country comparison to the world: 80
male: 23.9 deaths/1,000 live births
female: 20.84 deaths/1,000 live births (2014 est.)

Life expectancy at birth: *total population:* 73.45 years
country comparison to the world: 122
male: 70.82 years
female: 76.2 years (2014 est.)

Total fertility rate: 2.87 children born/woman (2014 est.)
country comparison to the world: 62

Contraceptive prevalence rate: 60.3% (2008)

Health expenditures: 4.9% of GDP (2011)
country comparison to the world: 143

Physicians density: 2.83 physicians/1,000 population (2009)

Hospital bed density: 1.7 beds/1,000 population (2010)

Drinking water source:
improved:
urban: 100% of population
rural: 98.8% of population
total: 99.3% of population
unimproved:
urban: 0% of population
rural: 1.2% of population
total: 0.7% of population (2011 est.)

Sanitation facility access:
improved:
urban: 96.9% of population
rural: 93.5% of population
total: 95% of population
unimproved:
urban: 3.1% of population
rural: 6.5% of population
total: 5% of population (2011 est.)

HIV/AIDS—adult prevalence rate: 0.1% (2012 est.)
country comparison to the world: 136

HIV/AIDS—people living with HIV/AIDS: 6,500 (2012 est.)
country comparison to the world: 120

HIV/AIDS—deaths: 300 (2012 est.)
country comparison to the world: 103

Major infectious diseases: *degree of risk:* intermediate
food or waterborne diseases: bacterial diarrhea, hepatitis A, and typhoid fever
water contact disease: schistosomiasis
note: highly pathogenic H5N1 avian influenza has been identified in this country; it poses a negligible risk with extremely rare cases possible among US citizens who have close contact with birds (2013)

Obesity—adult prevalence rate: 33.1% (2008)
country comparison to the world: 17

Children under the age of 5 years underweight: 6.8% (2008)
country comparison to the world: 77

Education expenditures: 3.8% of GDP (2008)
country comparison to the world: 117

Literacy: *definition:* age 15 and over can read and write
total population: 73.9%
male: 81.7%
female: 65.8% (2012 est.)

School life expectancy (primary to tertiary education): *total:* 13 years
male: 13 years
female: 13 years (2011)

Child labor—children ages 5-14: *total number:* 1,066,526
percentage: 7 % (2005 est.)

Unemployment, youth ages 15-24: total: 24.8%
country comparison to the world: 41
male: 14.7%
female: 54.1% (2010)

GOVERNMENT

Country name: *conventional long form:* Arab Republic of Egypt
conventional short form: Egypt
local long form: Jumhuriyat Misr al-Arabiyah
local short form: Misr
former: United Arab Republic (with Syria)

Government type: republic

Capital: *name:* Cairo
geographic coordinates: 30 03 N, 31 15 E
time difference: UTC+2 (7 hours ahead of Washington, DC during Standard Time)

Administrative divisions: 27 governorates (muhafazat, singular - muhafazat); Ad Daqahliyah, Al Bahr al Ahmar (Red Sea), Al Buhayrah, Al Fayyum, Al Gharbiyah, Al Iskandariyah (Alexandria), Al Isma'iliyah (Ismailia), Al Jizah (Giza), Al Minufiyah, Al Minya, Al Qahirah (Cairo), Al Qalyubiyah, Al Uqsur (Luxor), Al Wadi al Jadid (New Valley), As Suways (Suez), Ash Sharqiyah, Aswan, Asyut, Bani Suwayf, Bur Sa'id (Port Said), Dumyat (Damietta), Janub Sina' (South Sinai), Kafr ash Shaykh, Matruh, Qina, Shamal Sina' (North Sinai), Suhaj

Independence: 28 February 1922 (from UK protectorate status; the revolution that began on 23 July 1952 led to a republic being declared on 18 June 1953 and all British troops withdrawn on 18 June 1956); note—it was ca. 3200 B.C. that the Two Lands of Upper (southern) and Lower (northern) Egypt were first united politically

National holiday: National Day, 23 July (1952)

Constitution: several previous; latest approved by a constitutional committee in December 2013, approved by referenfum held on 14-15 January 2014, ratified by interim president on 19 January 2014 (2012)

Legal system: mixed legal system based on Napoleonic civil and penal law, Islamic religious law, and vestiges of colonial-era laws; judicial review of the constitutionality of laws by the Supreme Constitutional Court

International law organization participation: accepts compulsory ICJ jurisdiction with reservations; non-party state to the ICCt

Suffrage: 18 years of age; universal and compulsory

Executive branch: *Chief of state:* Interim President Adly MANSOUR (since 1 July 2013)
head of government: Interim Prime Minister Ibrahim MEHLAB (since 1 March 2014)
cabinet: interim cabinet sworn in 1 March 2014 (For more information visit the World Leaders website)
elections: last presidential election (first round held on 23-24 May 2012; runoff held on 16-17 June 2012 (next election expected 26-27 May 2014)
election results: percent of vote (first round)—Mohammed MURSI 24.3%, Ahmed SHAFIQ 23.3%, Hamdeen SABAHI 20.4%, Abdel Moneim Aboul FOTOUH 17.2%, Amre MOUSSA 11.1%, other 3.7%; (runoff)—Mohammed MURSI 51.7%, Ahmed SHAFIQ 48.3%

Legislative branch:
note: the previous bicameral legislature was dissolved in July 2013 and under the 2014 constitution was changed to the unicameral House of Representatives (minimum of 450 seats with up to 5 percent appointed by the president; members to serve 5-year terms); the process for elected members as stated in Article 102 of the 2014 constitution may be majoritarian, proportional list, or a mixed system; the previous bicameral parliament consisted of the Shura Council (at least 150 seats with up to one-tenth of body appointed by the president to serve six-year terms) and the House of Representatives(at least 350 seats); members elected by popular vote to serve five-year terms)
elections (for new House of Representatives): unscheduled but expected in mid- to late-2014
election results (for previous legislature): Advisory Council (held 29 January and 14 February 2012)—percent of vote by party—Democratic Alliance for Egypt 45%, Alliance for Egypt (Islamic Bloc) 28.6%, New Wafd Party 8.5%, Egyptian Bloc 5.4%, other 12.5%; seats by party—Democratic Alliance for Egypt 105, Alliance for Egypt (Islamic Bloc) 45, New Wafd Party 14, Egyptian Bloc 8, other 4, independents 4, presidential appointees 90; People's Assembly (held in three stages 28 November 2011 to 11 January 2012)—percent of vote by party—Democratic Alliance for Egypt 37.5%, Alliance for Egypt (Islamic Bloc) 27.8%, New Wafd Party 9.2%, Egyptian Bloc 8.9%, Al-Wasat Party 3.7%, The Revolution Continues Alliance 2.8%, Reform and Development Party 2.2%, National Party of Egypt 1.6%, Freedom Party 1.9%, Egyptian Citizen Party 0.9%, other 3.5%; seats by party—Democratic Alliance of Egypt 235, Alliance for Egypt (Islamic Bloc) 123, New Wafd Party 38, Egyptian Bloc 35, Al-Wasat 10, Reform and Development Party 9, The Revolution Continues Alliance 8, National Party of Egypt 5, Egyptian Citizen Party 4, Freedom Party 4, independents 21, other 6, SCAF appointees 10

Judicial branch: *highest court(s):* Court of Cassation (consists of the court president and 550 judges organized in circuits with cases heard by panels of 5 judges); Supreme Constitutional Court or SCC (consists of the court president and 10 justices); Supreme Administrative Court—the highest court of the State Council (consists of the court president and organized in circuits with cases heard by panels of 5 judges)
judge selection and term of office: under the 2014 constitution, all judges and justices selected by the Supreme Judiciary Council and appointed by the president of the Republic; tenure NA
subordinate courts: Courts of Appeal; Courts of First Instance; courts of limited jurisdiction; Family Court (established in 2004)

Political parties and leaders: Al-Asala [Ehab SHIHA]; Al-Nour [Yunis MAKHYUN]; Al-Wasat Party [Abou Elela MADY]; Al-Watan [Imad Abd al-GHAFUR]; Building and Development Party or BDP [Nasr Abdul-SALAM]; Dustour (Constitution) Party [Hala SHUKRALLAH]; Egyptian Current Party; Egypt of Freedom Party [Amr HAMZAWY]; El Tagamu'u Party [Sayed Abdel AAL]; Freedom and Justice Party [Muhammad Saad al-KATATNI]; Free Egyptians Party [Ahmad SAID]; New Wafd Party [Sayed al-BADAWI]; Reform and Development Party [Muhammad Anwar al-SADAT]; Strong Egypt Party [Abdel Aboul FOTOUH]; The Conference Party [Ambassador Mohamed ORABI]; The Egyptian Social Democratic Party [Mohamed Aboul GHAR]; The Popular Current Party [Hamdeen SABAHI]; The Popular Socialist Alliance Party [Abdel Ghafar SHOUKR]

Political pressure groups and leaders: NA

International organization participation: ABEDA, AfDB, AFESD, AMF, AU, BSEC (observer), CAEU, CD, CICA, COMESA, D-8, EBRD, FAO, G-15, G-24, G-77, IAEA, IBRD, ICAO, ICC (national committees), ICRM, IDA, IDB, IFAD, IFC, IFRCS, IHO, ILO, IMF, IMO, IMSO, Interpol, IOC, IOM, IPU, ISO, ITSO, ITU, LAS, MIGA, MINURSO, MONUSCO, NAM, OAPEC, OAS (observer), OIC, OIF, OSCE (partner), PCA, UN, UNAMID, UNCTAD, UNESCO, UNHCR, UNIDO,

UNISFA, UNMIL, UNMISS, UNOCI, UNRWA, UNWTO, UPU, WCO, WFTU (NGOs), WHO, WIPO, WMO, WTO

Diplomatic representation in the US:
chief of mission: Ambassador Mohamed M. TAWFIK (since 7 September 2012)
chancery: 3521 International Court NW, Washington, DC 20008
telephone: [1] (202) 895-5400
FAX: [1] (202) 244-5131
consulate(s) general: Chicago, Houston, Los Angeles, New York

Diplomatic representation from the US:
chief of mission: Ambassador (vacant); Charge d'Affaires Marc J. SIEVERS (since 21 January 2014)
embassy: 5 Tawfik Diab St., Garden City, Cairo
mailing address: Unit 64900, Box 15, APO AE 09839-4900; 5 Tawfik Diab Street, Garden City, Cairo
telephone: [20] (2) 2797-3300
FAX: [20] (2) 2797-3200

Flag description: three equal horizontal bands of red (top), white, and black; the national emblem (a gold Eagle of Saladin facing the hoist side with a shield superimposed on its chest above a scroll bearing the name of the country in Arabic) centered in the white band; the band colors derive from the Arab Liberation flag and represent oppression (black), overcome through bloody struggle (red), to be replaced by a bright future (white)
note: similar to the flag of Syria, which has two green stars in the white band, Iraq, which has an Arabic inscription centered in the white band, and Yemen, which has a plain white band

National symbol(s): golden eagle

National anthem: *name:* "Bilady, Bilady, Bilady" (My Homeland, My Homeland, My Homeland)
lyrics/music: Younis-al QADI/Sayed DARWISH
note: adopted 1979; after the signing of the 1979 peace with Israel, Egypt sought to create an anthem less militaristic than its previous one; Sayed DARWISH, commonly considered the father of modern Egyptian music, composed the anthem

ECONOMY

Economy—overview: Occupying the northeast corner of the African continent, Egypt is bisected by the highly fertile Nile valley, where most economic activity takes place. Egypt's economy was highly centralized during the rule of former President Gamal Abdel NASSER but opened up considerably under former Presidents Anwar EL-SADAT and Mohamed Hosni MUBARAK. Cairo from 2004 to 2008 aggressively pursued economic reforms to attract foreign investment and facilitate growth. Poor living conditions combined with limited job opportunities for the average Egyptian contribute to public discontent. After unrest erupted in January 2011, the Egyptian Government backtracked on economic reforms, drastically increasing social spending to address public dissatisfaction, but political uncertainty at the same time caused economic growth to slow significantly, reducing the government's revenues. Tourism, manufacturing, and construction were among the hardest hit sectors of the Egyptian economy, pushing up unemployment levels, and economic growth remains slow amid political uncertainty, government transitions, unrest, and cycles of violence. Cairo since 2011 has drawn down foreign exchange reserves and depended on foreign assistance, particularly from Gulf countries, to finance imports and energy products and prevent further devaluation of the Egyptian pound, fearing higher inflation from a weaker currency.

GDP (purchasing power parity): $551.4 billion (2013 est.)
country comparison to the world: 28
$541.5 billion (2012 est.)
$529.7 billion (2011 est.)
note: data are in 2013 US dollars

GDP (official exchange rate): $262 billion (2013 est.)

GDP—real growth rate: 1.8% (2013 est.)
country comparison to the world: 147
2.2% (2012 est.)
1.8% (2011 est.)

GDP—per capita (PPP): $6,600 (2013 est.)
country comparison to the world: 144
$6,600 (2012 est.)
$6,600 (2011 est.)
note: data are in 2013 US dollars

Gross national saving: 12.3% of GDP (2013 est.)
country comparison to the world: 126
13.1% of GDP (2012 est.)
13.8% of GDP (2011 est.)

GDP—composition, by end use:
household consumption: 78.6%
government consumption: 11.8%
investment in fixed capital: 14.3%
investment in inventories: 0.4%
exports of goods and services: 18%
imports of goods and services: -23.2% (2013 est.)

GDP—composition, by sector of origin:
agriculture: 14.5%
industry: 37.5%
services: 48% (2013 est.)

Agriculture—products: cotton, rice, corn, wheat, beans, fruits, vegetables; cattle, water buffalo, sheep, goats

Industries: textiles, food processing, tourism, chemicals, pharmaceuticals, hydrocarbons, construction, cement, metals, light manufactures

Industrial production growth rate: 1.4% (2013 est.)
country comparison to the world: 140

Labor force: 27.69 million (2013 est.)
country comparison to the world: 24

Labor force—by occupation: agriculture: 29%
industry: 24%
services: 47% (2011 est.)

Unemployment rate: 13.4% (2013 est.)
country comparison to the world: 131
12.7% (2012 est.)

Population below poverty line: 22% (2008 est.)

Household income or consumption by percentage share: *lowest 10%:* 4%
highest 10%: 26.6% (2008)

Distribution of family income—Gini index: 30.8 (2008)
country comparison to the world: 116
32.1 (2005)

Budget: *revenues:* $45.57 billion
expenditures: $80.42 billion (2013 est.)

Taxes and other revenues: 17.4% of GDP (2013 est.)
country comparison to the world: 180

Budget surplus (+) or deficit (-): -13.3% of GDP (2013 est.)
country comparison to the world: 213

Public debt: 92.2% of GDP (2013 est.)
country comparison to the world: 19
88% of GDP (2012 est.)
note: data cover central government debt, and includes debt instruments issued (or owned) by government entities other than the treasury; the data include treasury debt held by foreign entities; the data include debt issued by subnational entities, as well as intra-governmental debt; intra-governmental debt consists of treasury borrowings from surpluses in the social funds, such as for retirement, medical care, and unemployment; debt instruments for the social funds are sold at public auctions

Fiscal year: 1 July—30 June

Inflation rate (consumer prices): 9% (2013 est.)
country comparison to the world: 204
7.1% (2012 est.)

Central bank discount rate:
8.75% (5 December 2013 est.)
country comparison to the world: 31
8.68% (31 December 2010 est.)

Commercial bank prime lending rate:
11% (31 December 2013 est.)
country comparison to the world: 69
12% (31 December 2012 est.)

Stock of narrow money: $47.8 billion (31 December 2013 est.)
country comparison to the world: 47
$45.33 billion (31 December 2012 est.)

Stock of broad money: $191.2 billion (31 December 2013 est.)
country comparison to the world: 38
$183.6 billion (31 December 2012 est.)

Stock of domestic credit:
$163.6 billion (31 December 2013 est.)
country comparison to the world: 45
$192.5 billion (31 December 2012 est.)

Market value of publicly traded shares:
$63.49 billion (23 January 2014 est.)
country comparison to the world: 50
$58.01 billion (31 December 2012)
$48.68 billion (31 December 2011 est.)
Current account balance:

-$6.035 billion (2013 est.) country comparison to the world: 172
-$9.136 billion (2012 est.)

Exports: $24.81 billion (2013 est.)
country comparison to the world: 71
$24.93 billion (2012 est.)

Exports—commodities: crude oil and petroleum products, cotton, textiles, metal products, chemicals, processed food

Exports—partners: Italy 7.9%, India 6.9%, US 6.8%, Saudi Arabia 6.2%, Turkey 5.3%, Libya 4.9% (2012)

Imports: $59.22 billion (2013 est.)
country comparison to the world: 50
$60.26 billion (2012 est.)

Imports—commodities: machinery and equipment, foodstuffs, chemicals, wood products, fuels

Imports—partners: China 9.5%, US 7.6%, Germany 6.7%, Russia 5.3%, Ukraine 5.3%, Turkey 5.1%, Italy 5% (2012)

Reserves of foreign exchange and gold:
$17.03 billion (31 December 2013 est.)
country comparison to the world: 63
$14.93 billion (31 December 2012 est.)

Debt—external: $48.76 billion (31 December 2013 est.)
country comparison to the world: 63
$38.69 billion (31 December 2012 est.)

Stock of direct foreign investment—at home:
$76.76 billion (31 December 2013 est.)
country comparison to the world: 48
$75.41 billion (31 December 2012 est.)

Stock of direct foreign investment—abroad:
$6.475 billion (31 December 2013 est.)
country comparison to the world: 61
$6.285 billion (31 December 2012 est.)

Exchange rates: Egyptian pounds (EGP) per US dollar—
6.91 (2013 est.)
6.0608 (2012 est.)
5.6219 (2010 est.)

5.545 (2009)
5.4 (2008)

ENERGY

Electricity—production: 138.7 billion kWh (2011 est.)
country comparison to the world: 2 7

Electricity—consumption: 122.4 billion kWh (2010 est.)
country comparison to the world: 27

Electricity—exports: 1.595 billion kWh (2010 est.)
country comparison to the world: 47

Electricity—imports: 156 million kWh (2010 est.)
country comparison to the world: 90

Electricity—installed generating capacity:
26.91 million kW (2010 est.)
country comparison to the world: 30

Electricity—from fossil fuels:
87.6% of total installed capacity (2010 est.)
country comparison to the world: 83

Electricity—from nuclear fuels:
0% of total installed capacity (2010 est.)
country comparison to the world: 80

Electricity—from hydroelectric plants:
10.4% of total installed capacity (2010 est.)
country comparison to the world: 113

Electricity—from other renewable sources:
2% of total installed capacity (2010 est.)
country comparison to the world: 68

Crude oil—production: 720,000 bbl/day (2012 est.)
country comparison to the world: 28

Crude oil—exports: 85,000 bbl/day (2010 est.)
country comparison to the world: 40

Crude oil—imports: 48,740 bbl/day (2010 est.)
country comparison to the world: 58

Crude oil—proved reserves: 4.4 billion bbl (1 January 2013 es)
country comparison to the world: 25

Refined petroleum products—production:
602,600 bbl/day (2010 est.)
country comparison to the world: 28

Refined petroleum products—consumption:
816,300 bbl/day (2011 est.)
country comparison to the world: 23

Refined petroleum products—exports:
90,050 bbl/day (2010 est.)
country comparison to the world: 47

Refined petroleum products—imports:
164,200 bbl/day (2010 est.)
country comparison to the world: 35

Natural gas—production: 61.26 billion cu m (2011 est.)
country comparison to the world: 16

Natural gas—consumption: 46.17 billion cu m (2010 est.)
country comparison to the world: 20

Natural gas—exports: 10.51 billion cu m (2011 est.)
country comparison to the world: 24

Natural gas—imports: 0 cu m (2011 est.)
country comparison to the world: 186

Natural gas—proved reserves:
2.186 trillion cu m (1 January 2013 es)
country comparison to the world: 16

Carbon dioxide emissions from consumption of energy: 201.7 million Mt (2011 est.)
country comparison to the world: 29

COMMUNICATIONS

Telephones—main lines in use: 8.557 million (2012)
country comparison to the world: 23

Telephones—mobile cellular: 96.8 million (2012)
country comparison to the world: 16

Telephone system: *general assessment:* underwent extensive upgrading during 1990s; principal centers at Alexandria, Cairo, Al Mansurah, Ismailia, Suez, and Tanta are connected by coaxial cable and microwave radio relay
domestic: largest fixed-line system in the region; as of 2011 there were multiple mobile-cellular networks with a total of roughly 83 million subscribers
international: country code—20; landing point for Aletar, the SEA-ME-WE-3 and SEA-ME-WE-4 submarine cable networks, Link Around the Globe (FLAG) Falcon and FLAG FEA; satellite earth stations—4 (2 Intelsat—Atlantic Ocean and Indian Ocean, 1 Arabsat, and 1 Inmarsat); tropospheric scatter to Sudan; microwave radio relay to Israel; a participant in Medarabtel (2011)

Broadcast media: mix of state-run and private broadcast media; state-run TV operates 2 national and 6 regional terrestrial networks as well as a few satellite channels; about 20 private satellite channels and a large number of Arabic satellite channels are available via subscription; state-run radio operates about 70 stations belonging to 8 networks; 2 privately owned radio stations operational (2008)

Internet country code: .eg

Internet hosts: 200,430 (2012)
country comparison to the world: 71

Internet users: 20.136 million (2009)
country comparison to the world: 21

TRANSPORTATION

Airports: 83 (2013)
country comparison to the world: 6 5

Airports—with paved runways: *total:* 7 2
over 3,047 m: 15
2,438 to 3,047 m: 36
1,524 to 2,437 m: 15
under 914 m: 6 (2013)

Airports—with unpaved runways: *total:* 1 1
2,438 to 3,047 m: 1
1,524 to 2,437 m: 3
914 to 1,523 m: 4
under 914 m: 3 (2013)

Heliports: 7 (2013)

Pipelines: condensate 486 km; condensate/gas 74 km; gas 7,986 km; liquid petroleum gas 957 km; oil 5,225 km;
oil/gas/water 37 km; refined products 895 km; water 65 km (2013)

Railways: *total:* 5,083 km
country comparison to the world: 34
standard gauge: 5,083 km 1.435-m gauge (62 km electrified) (2009)

Roadways: total: 137,430 km
country comparison to the world: 37
paved: 126,742 km (includes 838 km of expressways)
unpaved: 10,688 km (2010)

Waterways: 3,500 km (includes the Nile River, Lake Nasser, Alexandria-Cairo Waterway, and numerous smaller canals in Nile Delta; the Suez Canal (193.5 km including approaches) is navigable by oceangoing vessels drawing up to 17.68 m) (2011)
country comparison to the world: 30

Merchant marine: *total:* 6 7
country comparison to the world: 62
by type: bulk carrier 16, cargo 20, container 3, passenger/cargo 7, petroleum tanker 12, roll on/roll off 9
foreign-owned: 13 (Denmark 1, France 1, Greece 8, Jordan 2, Lebanon 1)
registered in other countries: 42 (Cambodia 4, Georgia 7, Honduras 2, Liberia 3, Malta 1, Marshall Islands
1, Moldova 5, Panama 11, Saint Kitts and Nevis 1, Saint Vincent and the Grenadines 2, Saudi Arabia 1, Sierra Leone 3, unknown 1) (2010)

Ports and terminals: *major seaport(s):* Mediterranean Sea—Alexandria, Damietta, El Dekheila, Port Said; Gulf of Suez—Suez
oil/gas terminal(s): Ain Sukhna terminal, Sidi Kerir terminal
container port(s) (TEUs): Alexandria (1,108,826), Port Said(East) (2,617,043), Port Said(West) (1,138,753)

MILITARY

Military branches: Army, Navy, Egyptian Air Force (Al-Quwwat al-Jawwiya il-Misriya), Egyptian Air Defense Command (2013)

Military service age and obligation: 18-30 years of age for male conscript military service; service obligation—18-36 months, followed by a 9-year reserve obligation; voluntary enlistment possible from age 16 (2012)

Manpower available for military service:
males age 16-49: 21,012,199
females age 16-49: 20,145,021 (2010 est.)

Manpower fit for military service:
males age 16-49: 18,060,543
females age 16-49: 17,244,838 (2010 est.)

Manpower reaching militarily significant age annually: *male:* 783,405
female: 748,647 (2010 est.)

Military expenditures: 1.72% of GDP (2012)
country comparison to the world: 49
1.86% of GDP (2011)
1.72% of GDP (2010)

TRANSNATIONAL ISSUES

Disputes—international: Sudan claims but Egypt de facto administers security and economic development of Halaib region north of the 22nd parallel boundary; Egypt no longer shows its administration of the Bir Tawil trapezoid in Sudan on its maps; Gazan breaches in the security wall with Egypt in January 2008 highlight difficulties in monitoring the Sinai border; Saudi Arabia claims Egyptian-administered islands of Tiran and Sanafir

Refugees and internally displaced persons: *refugees (country of origin): 70,028 (West Bank and Gaza Strip); 12,124 (Sudan); 5,703 (Iraq) (2012); 7,957 (Somalia) (2013); 136,512 (Syria) (2014)*
stateless persons: 60 (2012)

Illicit drugs: transit point for cannabis, heroin, and opium moving to Europe, Israel, and North Africa; transit stop for Nigerian drug couriers; concern as money laundering site due to lax enforcement of financial regulations

EL SALVADOR

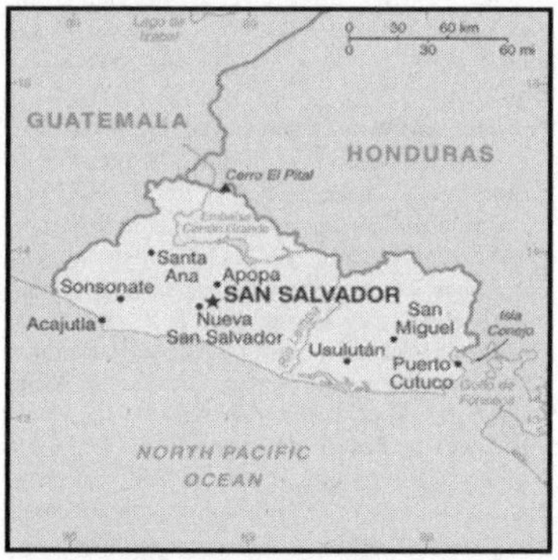

INTRODUCTION

Background: El Salvador achieved independence from Spain in 1821 and from the Central American Federation in 1839. A 12-year civil war, which cost about 75,000 lives, was brought to a close in 1992 when the government and leftist rebels signed a treaty that provided for military and political reforms.

GEOGRAPHY

Location: Central America, bordering the North Pacific Ocean, between Guatemala and Honduras

Geographic coordinates: 13 50 N, 88 55 W

Map references: Central America and the Caribbean

Area: *total:* 21,041 sq km
country comparison to the world: 153
land: 20,721 sq km
water: 320 sq km

Area—comparative: slightly smaller than Massachusetts

Land boundaries: *total:* 545 km
border countries: Guatemala 203 km, Honduras 342 km

Coastline: 307 km

Maritime claims: *territorial sea:* 12 nm
contiguous zone: 24 nm
exclusive economic zone: 200 nm

Climate: tropical; rainy season (May to October); dry season (November to April); tropical on coast; temperate in uplands

Terrain: mostly mountains with narrow coastal belt and central plateau

Elevation extremes: *lowest point:* Pacific Ocean 0 m
highest point: Cerro El Pital 2,730 m

Natural resources: hydropower, geothermal power, petroleum, arable land

Land use: *arable land:* 31.61%
permanent crops: 10.93%
other: 57.46% (2011)

Irrigated land: 449.9 sq km (2003)

Total renewable water resources: 25.23 cu km (2011)

Freshwater withdrawal (domestic/industrial/agricultural): *total:* 1.84 cu km/yr (22%/14%/64%)
per capita: 301.9 cu m/yr (2007)

Natural hazards: known as the Land of Volcanoes; frequent and sometimes destructive earthquakes and volcanic activity; extremely susceptible to hurricanes
volcanism: significant volcanic activity; San Salvador (elev. 1,893 m), which last erupted in 1917, has the potential to cause major harm to the country's capital, which lies just below the volcano's slopes; San Miguel (elev. 2,130 m), which last erupted in 2002, is one of the most active volcanoes in the country; other historically active volcanoes include Conchaguita, Ilopango, Izalco, and Santa Ana

Environment—current issues: deforestation; soil erosion; water pollution; contamination of soils from disposal of toxic wastes

Environment—international agreements: *party to:* Biodiversity, Climate Change, Climate Change-Kyoto Protocol, Desertification, Endangered Species, Hazardous Wastes, Ozone Layer Protection, Wetlands
signed, but not ratified: Law of the Sea

Geography—note: smallest Central American country and only one without a coastline on Caribbean Sea

PEOPLE AND SOCIETY

Nationality: *noun:* Salvadoran(s)
adjective: Salvadoran

Ethnic groups: mestizo 86.3%, white 12.7%, Amerindian 1% (2007 census)

Languages: Spanish (official), Nahua (among some Amerindians)

Religions: Roman Catholic 57.1%, Protestant 21.2%, Jehovah's Witnesses 1.9%, Mormon 0.7%, other religions 2.3%, none 16.8% (2003 est.)

Demographic profile: El Salvador is the smallest and most densely populated country in Central America. It is well into its demographic transition, experiencing slower population growth, a decline in its number of youths, and the gradual aging of its population. The increased use of family planning has substantially lowered El Salvador's fertility rate, from approximately 6 children per woman in the 1970s to replacement level today. A 2008 national family planning survey showed that female sterilization remained the most common contraception method in El Salvador—its sterilization rate is among the highest in Latin America and the Caribbean—but that the use of injectable contraceptives is growing. Fertility differences between rich and poor and urban and rural women are narrowing.
Salvadorans fled during the 1979 to 1992 civil war mainly to the United States but also to Canada and to neighboring Mexico, Guatemala, Honduras, Nicaragua, and Costa Rica. Emigration to the United States increased again in the 1990s and 2000s as a result of deteriorating economic conditions, natural disasters (Hurricane Mitch in 1998 and earthquakes in 2001), and family reunification. At least 20% of El Salvador's population lives abroad. The remittances they send home account for close to 20% of GDP, are the second largest source of external income after exports, and have helped reduce poverty.

Population: 6,125,512 (July 2014 est.)
country comparison to the world: 109

Age structure: *0-14 years:* 28.1% (male 882,185/female 837,646)
15-24 years: 20.8% (male 640,322/female 635,409)
25-54 years: 37.5% (male 1,056,779/female 1,243,220)
55-64 years: 6.9% (male 182,937/female 224,019)
65 years and over: 6.7% (male 187,664/female 235,331) (2014 est.)

Dependency ratios:
total dependency ratio: 59 %
youth dependency ratio: 47.6 %
elderly dependency ratio: 11.3 %
potential support ratio: 8.8 (2013)

Median age: *total:* 25.6 years
male: 24.1 years
female: 27.1 years (2014 est.)

Population growth rate: 0.27% (2014 est.)
country comparison to the world: 174

Birth rate: 16.79 births/1,000 population (2014 est.)
country comparison to the world: 115

Death rate: 5.67 deaths/1,000 population (2014 est.)
country comparison to the world: 174

Net migration rate: -8.44 migrant(s)/1,000 population (2014 est.)
country comparison to the world: 208

Urbanization: *urban population:* 64% of total population (2010)
rate of urbanization: 1.4% annual rate of change (2010-15 est.)

Major urban areas—population:
SAN SALVADOR (capital) 1.605 million (2011)

Sex ratio: *at birth:* 1.05 male(s)/female
0-14 years: 1.05 male(s)/female
15-24 years: 1.01 male(s)/female
25-54 years: 0.85 male(s)/female
55-64 years: 0.93 male(s)/female
65 years and over: 0.8 male(s)/female
total population: 0.93 male(s)/female (2014 est.)

Mother's mean age at first birth: 20.8 (2008 est.)

Maternal mortality rate:
81 deaths/100,000 live births (2010)
country comparison to the world: 81

Infant mortality rate: *total:* 18.44 deaths/1,000 live births
country comparison to the world: 97
male: 20.52 deaths/1,000 live births
female: 16.27 deaths/1,000 live births (2014 est.)

Life expectancy at birth: *total population:* 74.18 years
country comparison to the world: 114
male: 70.9 years
female: 77.62 years (2014 est.)

Total fertility rate: 1.95 children born/woman (2014 est.)
country comparison to the world: 134

Contraceptive prevalence rate: 72.5%
note: percent of women aged 15-44 (2008)

Health expenditures: 6.8% of GDP (2011)
country comparison to the world: 87

Physicians density: 1.6 physicians/1,000 population (2008)

Hospital bed density: 1 beds/1,000 population (2011)

Drinking water source:
improved:
urban: 94.2% of population
rural: 81.4% of population
total: 89.7% of population
unimproved:
urban: 5.8% of population
rural: 18.6% of population
total: 10.3% of population (2011 est.)

Sanitation facility access:
improved:
urban: 79.4% of population
rural: 52.6% of population
total: 70% of population
unimproved:
urban: 20.6% of population
rural: 47.4% of population
total: 30% of population (2011 est.)

HIV/AIDS—adult prevalence rate: 0.6% (2012 est.)
country comparison to the world: 66

HIV/AIDS—people living with HIV/AIDS: 24,900 (2012 est.)
country comparison to the world: 77

HIV/AIDS—deaths: 1,000 (2012 est.)
country comparison to the world: 80

Major infectious diseases: *degree of risk:* high food or waterborne diseases: bacterial and protozoal diarrhea
vectorborne diseases: dengue fever (2013)
Obesity—adult prevalence rate: 25.8% (2008)
country comparison to the world: 51

Children under the age of 5 years underweight: 6.6% (2008)
country comparison to the world: 78

Education expenditures: 3.4% of GDP (2011)
country comparison to the world: 129

Literacy: *definition:* age 15 and over can read and write
total population: 84.5%
male: 87.1%
female: 82.3% (2010 est.)

School life expectancy (primary to tertiary education): *total:* 12 years
male: 12 years
female: 12 years (2012)

Child labor—children ages 5-14:
total number: 179,303
percentage: 4 %
note: data represents children ages 5-17 (2007 est.)

Unemployment, youth ages 15-24: *total:* 12.4%
country comparison to the world: 97
male: 12.8%
female: 11.7% (2012)

GOVERNMENT

Country name: *conventional long form:* Republic of El Salvador
conventional short form: El Salvador
local long form: Republica de El Salvador
local short form: El Salvador

Government type: republic

Capital: *name:* San Salvador
geographic coordinates: 13 42 N, 89 12 W
time difference: UTC-6 (1 hour behind Washington, DC during Standard Time)
daylight saving time: none scheduled for 2013

Administrative divisions: 14 departments (departamentos, singular—departamento); Ahuachapan, Cabanas, Chalatenango, Cuscatlan, La Libertad, La Paz, La Union, Morazan, San Miguel, San Salvador, San Vicente, Santa Ana, Sonsonate, Usulutan

Independence: 15 September 1821 (from Spain)

National holiday: Independence Day, 15 September (1821)

Constitution: many previous; latest drafted 16 December 1983, enacted 23 December 1983; amended many times, last in 2009 (2012)

Legal system: civil law system with minor common law influence; judicial review of legislative acts in the Supreme Court

International law organization participation: has not submitted an ICJ jurisdiction declaration; non-party state to the ICCt

Suffrage: 18 years of age; universal

Executive branch: *chief of state:* President Carlos Mauricio FUNES Cartagena (since 1 June 2009); Vice President Salvador SANCHEZ CEREN (since 1 June 2009); note—the president is both the chief of state and head of government
head of government: President Carlos Mauricio FUNES Cartagena (since 1 June 2009); Vice President Salvador SANCHEZ CEREN (since
1 June 2009)
cabinet: Council of Ministers selected by the president (For more information visit the World Leaders website)
elections: president and vice president elected on the same ticket by popular vote for a single five-year term; election last held on 2 February 2014, with a runoff on 9 March 2014 (next to be held in February 2019)
election results: percent of vote—Salvador SANCHEZ Ceren 48.9%, Norman QUIJANO 39%, Antonio SACA 11.4%; note—a runoff election is scheduled for 9 March 2014

Legislative branch: unicameral Legislative Assembly or Asamblea Legislativa (84 seats; members elected by direct, popular vote to serve three-year terms)
elections: last held on 11 March 2012 (next to be held in 2015)
election results: percent of vote by party—NA; seats by party—ARENA 33, FMLN 31, GANA 11, CN 7, PES 1, PCD 1; note—changes in party affiliation now reflect the following seat distribution: as of 8 May 2013—FMLN 31, ARENA 28, GANA 11, CN 7, Unidos por El Salvador 5, CD 1, PDC 1

Judicial branch: *highest court(s):* Supreme Court or Corte Suprema (consists of 15 judges assigned to constitutional, civil, penal, and administrative *conflict divisions)*
judge selection and term of office: judges elected by the Legislative Assembly on the recommendation of the National Council of the Judicature, an independent body elected by the Legislative Assembly; judges elected for single, 9-year terms with renewal of one-third of judges every 3 years.
subordinate courts: Chambers of Second Instance; Courts of First Instance; Courts of Peace

Political parties and leaders: Democratic Change (Cambio Democratico) or CD [Tomas CHEVEZ] (formerly United Democratic Center or CDU); Farabundo Marti National Liberation Front or FMLN [Medardo GONZALEZ]; Great Alliance for National Unity or GANA (Jose Andres ROVIRA Caneles); National Coalition (Concertation Nacional) or CN [Ciro CRUZ ZEPEDA] (formerly the National Conciliation Party or PCN); Nationalist Republican Alliance or ARENA [Alfredo CRISTIANI]; Party of Hope or PES [Rodolfo Antonio PARKER Soto] (formerly the Christian Democratic Party or PCD); Unidos por El Salvador [Manuel Rigoberto SOTO Lazo]

Political pressure groups and leaders: labor organizations—Electrical Industry Union of El Salvador or SIES; Federation of the Construction Industry, Similar Transport and other activities, or FESINCONTRANS; National Confederation of Salvadoran Workers or CNTS; National Union of Salvadoran Workers or UNTS; Port Industry Union of El Salvador or SIPES; Salvadoran Union of Ex-Petrolleros and Peasant Workers or USEPOC; Salvadoran Workers Central or CTS; Workers Union of Electrical Corporation or STCEL; business organizations—National Association of Small Enterprise or ANEP; Salvadoran Assembly Industry Association or ASIC; Salvadoran Industrial Association or ASI

International organization participation: BCIE, CACM, CD, CELAC, FAO, G-11, G-77, IADB, IAEA, IBRD, ICAO, ICC (national committees), ICRM, IDA, IFAD, IFC, IFRCS, ILO, IMF, IMO, Interpol, IOC, IOM, IPU, ISO (correspondent), ITSO, ITU, ITUC (NGOs), LAES, LAIA (observer), MIGA, MINURSO, NAM (observer), OAS, OPANAL, OPCW, PCA, SICA, UN, UNCTAD, UNESCO, UNIDO, UNIFIL, Union Latina, UNMIL, UNMISS, UNOCI, UNWTO, UPU, WCO, WFTU (NGOs), WHO, WIPO, WMO, WTO

Diplomatic representation in the US:
chief of mission: Ambassador Ruben Ignacio ZAMORA Rivas (since 12 April 2013)
chancery: Suite 100, 1400 16th Street, Washington, DC 20036
telephone: [1] (202) 595-7500
FAX: [1] (202) 232-3763
consulate(s) general: Brentwood (NY), Chicago, Coral Gables (FL), Dallas, Houston, Las Vegas, Los Angeles, New York, San Francisco, Santa Ana (CA), Seattle, Tucson, Woodbridge (VA), Woodstock (GA)
consulate(s): Elizabeth (NJ)

Diplomatic representation from the US:
chief of mission: Ambassador Mari Carmen APONTE (since 22 September 2010)
embassy: Final Boulevard Santa Elena Sur, Antiguo Cuscatlan, La Libertad, San Salvador
mailing address: Unit 3450, APO AA 34023; 3450 San Salvador Place, Washington, DC 20521-3450
telephone: [503] 2501-2999
FAX: [503] 2501-2150

Flag description: three equal horizontal bands of blue (top), white, and blue with the national coat of arms centered in the white band; the coat of arms features a round emblem encircled by the words REPUBLICA DE EL SALVADOR EN LA AMERICA CENTRAL; the banner is based on the former blue-white-blue flag of the Federal Republic of Central America; the blue bands symbolize the Pacific Ocean and the Caribbean Sea, while the white band represents the land between the two bodies of water, as well as peace and prosperity
note: similar to the flag of Nicaragua, which has a different coat of arms centered in the white band—it features a triangle encircled by the

words REPUBLICA DE NICARAGUA on top and AMERICA CENTRAL on the bottom; also similar to the flag of Honduras, which has five blue stars arranged in an X pattern centered in the white band

National symbol(s): turquoise-browed motmot (bird)

National anthem: *name:* "Himno Nacional de El Salvador" (National Anthem of El Salvador)
lyrics/music: Juan Jose CANAS/Juan ABERLE
note: officially adopted 1953, in use since 1879; the anthem of El Salvador is one of the world's longest

ECONOMY

overview: The smallest country in Central America geographically, El Salvador has the third largest economy in the region. With the global recession, real GDP began contracting in 2009 and continued downward during 2010-13. Remittances accounted for 17% of GDP in 2013 and were received by about a third of all households. In 2006, El Salvador was the first country to ratify the Dominican Republic-Central American Free Trade Agreement (CAFTA-DR), which has bolstered the export of processed foods, sugar, and ethanol, and supported investment in the apparel sector amid increased Asian competition. The Salvadoran Government maintained fiscal discipline during post-war reconstruction and reconstruction following earthquakes in 2001 and hurricanes in 1998 and 2005, but El Salvador's external debt has been mounting over the last several years, amounting to some 57% of GDP in 2013. In September 2013, El Salvador was awarded a $277 million compact with with the Millennium Challenge Corporation (MCC)—a United States Government agency aimed at stimulating economic growth and reducing poverty—in the country's northern region, the primary conflict zone during the civil war, through investments in education, public services, enterprise development, and transportation infrastructure. However, the signing of the compact has been delayed until after the February 2014 presidential elections.

GDP (purchasing power parity): $47.47 billion (2013 est.)
country comparison to the world: 98
$46.72 billion (2012 est.)
$45.84 billion (2011 est.)
note: data are in 2013 US dollars

GDP (official exchange rate): $24.67 billion (2013 est.)

GDP—real growth rate: 1.6% (2013 est.)
country comparison to the world: 155
1.9% (2012 est.)
2.2% (2011 est.)

GDP—per capita (PPP): $7,500 (2013 est.)
country comparison to the world: 138
$7,400 (2012 est.)
$7,300 (2011 est.)
note: data are in 2013 US dollars

Gross national saving: 9% of GDP (2013 est.)
country comparison to the world: 141
8.9% of GDP (2012 est.)
9.3% of GDP (2011 est.)

GDP—composition, by end use:
household consumption: 93.9%
government consumption: 11.1%
investment in fixed capital: 14.5%
investment in inventories: 0%
exports of goods and services: 29%
imports of goods and services: -48.5% (2013 est.)

GDP—composition, by sector of origin:
agriculture: 10.3%
industry: 29.5%
services: 60.1% (2013 est.)

Agriculture—products: coffee, sugar, corn, rice, beans, oilseed, cotton, sorghum; beef, dairy products

Industries: food processing, beverages, petroleum, chemicals, fertilizer, textiles, furniture, light metals

Industrial production growth rate: 2.1% (2013 est.)
country comparison to the world: 124

Labor force: 2.738 million (2013 est.)
country comparison to the world: 107

Labor force—by occupation: agriculture: 21%
industry: 20%
services: 58% (2011 est.)

Unemployment rate: 6.3% (2013 est.)
country comparison to the world: 63
6.1% (2012 est.)
note: data are official rates; but the economy has much underemployment

Population below poverty line: 36.5% (2010 est.)

Household income or consumption by percentage share: *lowest* 10%: 1%
highest 10%: 37% (2009 est.)

Distribution of family income—Gini index:
46.9 (2007)
country comparison to the world: 32
52.5 (2001)

Budget: *revenues:* $4.683 billion
expenditures: $5.666 billion (2013 est.)

Taxes and other revenues: 19% of GDP (2013 est.)
country comparison to the world: 173

Budget surplus (+) or deficit (-):
-4% of GDP (2013 est.)
country comparison to the world: 145

Public debt: 62% of GDP (2013 est.)
country comparison to the world: 44
59.2% of GDP (2012 est.)
note: El Salvador's total public debt includes nonfinancial public sector debt, financial public sector debt, and central bank debt

Fiscal year: calendar year
Inflation rate (consumer prices):
0.9% (2013 est.)
country comparison to the world: 19
1.8% (2012 est.)

Commercial bank prime lending rate:
5.8% (31 December 2013 est.)
country comparison to the world: 145
5.6% (31 December 2012 est.)

Stock of narrow money: $2.914 billion (31 December 2013 est.)
country comparison to the world: 117
$2.796 billion (31 December 2012 est.)

Stock of broad money: $10.12 billion (31 December 2013 est.)
country comparison to the world: 105
$9.847 billion (31 December 2012 est.)

Stock of domestic credit: $11.16 billion (31 December 2013 est.)
country comparison to the world: 95
$10.51 billion (31 December 2012 est.)

Market value of publicly traded shares:
$10.74 billion (31 December 2012 est.)
country comparison to the world: 83
$5.474 billion (31 December 2011)
$4.227 billion (31 December 2010 est.)

Current account balance: -$1.331 billion (2013 est.)
country comparison to the world: 129
-$1.257 billion (2012 est.)

Exports: $5.112 billion (2013 est.)
country comparison to the world: 115
$5.447 billion (2012 est.)

Exports—commodities: offshore assembly exports, coffee, sugar, textiles and apparel, gold, ethanol, chemicals, electricity, iron and steel manufactures

Exports—partners: US 47.3%, Guatemala 13.8%, Honduras 9.6%, Nicaragua 5.4% (2012)

Imports: $10.03 billion (2013 est.)
country comparison to the world: 101
$9.912 billion (2012 est.)

Imports—commodities: raw materials, consumer goods, capital goods, fuels, foodstuffs, petroleum, electricity

Imports—partners: US 35.4%, Guatemala 12.7%, Mexico 7%, China 5.6%, Germany 4.2% (2012)

Reserves of foreign exchange and gold:
$2.855 billion (31 December 2013 est.)
country comparison to the world: 109
$3.176 billion (31 December 2012 est.)

Debt—external: $14.44 billion (31 December 2013 est.)
country comparison to the world: 91
$13.56 billion (31 December 2012 est.)

Stock of direct foreign investment—at home:
$8.879 billion (31 December 2013 est.)
country comparison to the world: 84
$8.635 billion (31 December 2012 est.)

Stock of direct foreign investment—abroad:
$5.7 million (31 December 2013 est.)
country comparison to the world: 94
$5.7 million (31 December 2012 est.)

Exchange rates: note: the US dollar is used as a medium of exchange and circulates freely in the economy, 1 (2013 est.)
1 (2012 est.)

ENERGY

Electricity—production: 5.728 billion kWh (2011 est.)
country comparison to the world: 115

Electricity—consumption: 5.756 billion kWh (2011 est.)
country comparison to the world: 109

Electricity—exports: 101.6 million kWh (2011 est.)
country comparison to the world: 76

Electricity—imports: 251 million kWh (2011 est.)
country comparison to the world: 83

Electricity—installed generating capacity:
1.491 million kW (2010 est.)
country comparison to the world: 118

Electricity—from fossil fuels: 52.6% of total installed capacity (2010 est.)
country comparison to the world: 149

Electricity—from nuclear fuels:
0% of total installed capacity (2010 est.)
country comparison to the world: 85

Electricity—from hydroelectric plants:
31.6% of total installed capacity (2010 est.)
country comparison to the world: 73

Electricity—from other renewable sources:
15.7% of total installed capacity (2010 est.)
country comparison to the world: 14

Crude oil—production: 0 bbl/day (2011 est.)

country comparison to the world: 168

Crude oil—exports: 0 bbl/day (2010 est.)
country comparison to the world: 108

Crude oil—imports: 16,160 bbl/day (2010 est.)
country comparison to the world: 70

Crude oil—proved reserves: 0 bbl (1 January 2013 es)
country comparison to the world: 129

Refined petroleum products—production: 16,620 bbl/day (2010 est.)
country comparison to the world: 97

Refined petroleum products—consumption: 44,040 bbl/day (2011 est.)
country comparison to the world: 103

Refined petroleum products—exports: 2,425 bbl/day (2010 est.)
country comparison to the world: 100

Refined petroleum products—imports: 29,020 bbl/day (2010 est.)
country comparison to the world: 92

Natural gas—production: 0 cu m (2011 est.)
country comparison to the world: 127

Natural gas—consumption: 0 cu m (2010 est.)
country comparison to the world: 141

Natural gas—exports: 0 cu m (2011 est.)
country comparison to the world: 96

Natural gas—imports: 0 cu m (2011 est.)
country comparison to the world: 189

Natural gas—proved reserves: 0 cu m (1 January 2013 es)
country comparison to the world: 135

Carbon dioxide emissions from consumption of energy: 6.713 million Mt (2011 est.)
country comparison to the world: 117

COMMUNICATIONS

Telephones—main lines in use: 1.06 million (2012)
country comparison to the world: 74

Telephones—mobile cellular: 8.65 million (2012)
country comparison to the world: 88

Telephone system: *general assessment:* multiple mobile-cellular providers are expanding services rapidly and in 2011 teledensity exceeded 135 per 100 persons; growth in fixed-line services has slowed in the face of mobile-cellular competition
domestic: nationwide microwave radio relay system
international: country code—503; satellite earth station—1 Intelsat (Atlantic Ocean); connected to Central American Microwave System (2011)

Broadcast media: multiple privately owned national terrestrial TV networks, supplemented by cable TV networks that carry international channels; hundreds of commercial radio broadcast stations and 1 government-owned radio broadcast station (2007)

Internet country code: .sv

Internet hosts: 24,070 (2012)
country comparison to the world: 113

Internet users: 746,000 (2009)
country comparison to the world: 107

TRANSPORTATION

Airports: 68 (2013)
country comparison to the world: 7 3

Airports—with paved runways: *total:* 5
over 3,047 m: 1
1,524 to 2,437 m: 1
914 to 1,523 m: 2
under 914 m: 1 (2013)

Airports—with unpaved runways: *total:* 6 3
1,524 to 2,437 m: 1
914 to 1,523 m: 11
under 914 m: 51 (2013)

Heliports: 2 (2013)

Railways: total: 283 km
country comparison to the world: 121
narrow gauge: 283 km 0.600-m gauge
note: railways have been inoperable since 2005 because of disuse and high costs that led to a lack of maintenance (2008)

Roadways: *total:* 6,918 km
country comparison to the world: 147
paved: 3,247 km (includes 341 km of expressways)
unpaved: 3,671 km (2010)

Waterways: (Rio Lempa is partially navigable for small craft) (2011)

Ports and terminals: *major seaport(s):* Puerto Cutuco
oil/gas terminal(s): Acajutla offshore terminal

MILITARY

Military branches: Salvadoran Armed Forces (Fuerza Armada de El Salvador, FAES): Salvadoran Army (Ejercito de El Salvador, ES), Salvadoran Navy (Fuerza Naval de El Slavador, FNES), Salvadoran Air Force (Fuerza Aerea Salvadorena, FAS) (2013)

Military service age and obligation: 18 years of age for selective compulsory military service; 16-22 years of age for voluntary male or female service; service obligation is 12 months, with 11 months for officers and NCOs (2012)

Manpower available for military service:
males age 16-49: 1,449,214
females age 16-49: 1,611,248 (2010 est.)

Manpower fit for military service:
males age 16-49: 1,079,038
females age 16-49: 1,373,368 (2010 est.)

Manpower reaching militarily significant age annually: *male:* 71,530
female: 68,971 (2010 est.)

Military expenditures:
0.99% of GDP (2012)
country comparison to the world: 102
1.11% of GDP (2011)
0.99% of GDP (2010)

TRANSNATIONAL ISSUES

Disputes—international: International Court of Justice (ICJ) ruled on the delimitation of "bolsones" (disputed areas) along the El Salvador-Honduras boundary, in 1992, with final agreement by the parties in 2006 after an Organization of American States survey and a further ICJ ruling in 2003; the 1992 ICJ ruling advised a tripartite resolution to a maritime boundary in the Gulf of Fonseca advocating Honduran access to the Pacific; El Salvador continues to claim tiny Conejo Island, not identified in the ICJ decision, off Honduras in the Gulf of Fonseca

Illicit drugs: transshipment point for cocaine; small amounts of marijuana produced for local consumption; significant use of cocaine

EQUATORIAL GUINEA

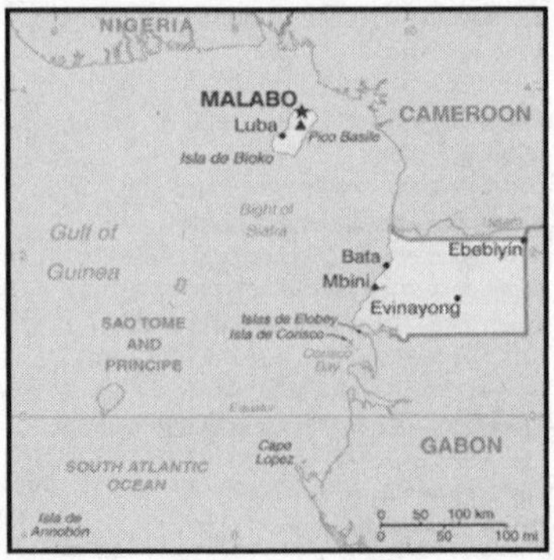

INTRODUCTION

Background: Equatorial Guinea gained independence in 1968 after 190 years of Spanish rule. This tiny country, composed of a mainland portion plus five inhabited islands, is one of the smallest on the African continent. President Teodoro Obiang NGUEMA MBASOGO has ruled the country since 1979 when he seized power in a coup. Although nominally a constitutional democracy since 1991, the 1996, 2002, and 2009 presidential elections—as well as the 1999, 2004, 2008, and 2013 legislative elections—were widely seen as flawed. The president exerts almost total control over the political system and has discouraged political opposition. Equatorial Guinea has experienced rapid economic growth due to the discovery of large offshore oil reserves, and in the last decade has become Sub-Saharan Africa's third largest oil exporter. Despite the country's economic windfall from oil production, resulting in a massive increase in government revenue in recent years, improvements in the population's living standards have been slow to develop.

GEOGRAPHY

Location: Central Africa, bordering the Bight of Biafra, between Cameroon and Gabon

Geographic coordinates: 2 00 N, 10 00 E

Map references: Africa

Area: *total:* 28,051 sq km
country comparison to the world: 146

land: 28,051 sq km
water: 0 sq km

Area—comparative: slightly smaller than Maryland

Land boundaries: *total:* 539 km
border countries: Cameroon 189 km, Gabon 350 km

Coastline: 296 km

Maritime claims: *territorial sea:* 12 nm
exclusive economic zone: 200 nm

Climate: tropical; always hot, humid

Terrain: coastal plains rise to interior hills; islands are volcanic

Elevation extremes: *lowest point:* Atlantic Ocean 0 m
highest point: Pico Basile 3,008 m

Natural resources: petroleum, natural gas, timber, gold, bauxite, diamonds, tantalum, sand and gravel, clay

Land use: *arable land:* 4.63%
permanent crops: 2.5%
other: 92.87% (2011)

Irrigated land: NA

Total renewable water resources: 26 cu km (2011)

Freshwater withdrawal (domestic/industrial/agricultural): *total:* 0.02 cu km/yr (80%/15%/5%)
per capita: 31.41 cu m/yr (2005)

Natural hazards: violent windstorms; flash floods
volcanism: Santa Isabel (elev. 3,007 m), which last erupted in 1923, is the country's only historically active volcano; Santa Isabel, along with two dormant volcanoes, form Bioko Island in the Gulf of Guinea

Environment—current issues: tap water is not potable; deforestation

Environment—international agreements:
party to: Biodiversity, Climate Change, Climate Change-Kyoto Protocol, Desertification, Endangered Species, Hazardous Wastes, Law of the Sea, Marine Dumping, Ozone Layer Protection, Ship Pollution, Wetlands
signed, but not ratified: none of the selected agreements

Geography—note: insular and continental regions widely separated

PEOPLE AND SOCIETY

Nationality: noun: Equatorial Guinean(s) or Equatoguinean(s)
adjective: Equatorial Guinean or Equatoguinean
Ethnic groups: Fang 85.7%, Bubi 6.5%, Mdowe 3.6%, Annobon 1.6%, Bujeba 1.1%, other 1.4% (1994 census)

Languages: Spanish (official) 67.6%, other (includes French (official), Fang, Bubi) 32.4% (1994 census)

Religions: nominally Christian and predominantly Roman Catholic, pagan practices

Population: 722,254 (July 2014 est.)
country comparison to the world: 167

Age structure: *0-14 years:* 40.8% (male 149,597/female 144,788)
15-24 years: 19.5% (male 71,609/female 69,061)
25-54 years: 31.5% (male 112,956/female 114,785)
55-64 years: 4% (male 13,052/female 17,247)
65 years and over: 4.1% (male 12,310/female 16,849) (2014 est.)

Dependency ratios:
total dependency ratio: 71.4 %
youth dependency ratio: 66.6 %
elderly dependency ratio: 4.8 %
potential support ratio: 21 (2013)

Median age: *total:* 19.4 years
male: 18.8 years
female: 19.9 years (2014 est.)

Population growth rate: 2.54% (2014 est.)
country comparison to the world: 28

Birth rate: 33.83 births/1,000 population (2014 est.)
country comparison to the world: 32

Death rate: 8.39 deaths/1,000 population (2014 est.)
country comparison to the world: 85

Net migration rate: 0 migrant(s)/1,000 population (2014 est.)
country comparison to the world: 105

Urbanization: *urban population:* 39.5% of total population (2011)
rate of urbanization: 3.16% annual rate of change (2010-15 est.)

Major urban areas—population: MALABO (capital) 137,000 (2011)

Sex ratio: *at birth:* 1.03 male(s)/female
0-14 years: 1.03 male(s)/female
15-24 years: 1.04 male(s)/female
25-54 years: 0.98 male(s)/female
55-64 years: 0.99 male(s)/female
65 years and over: 0.75 male(s)/female
total population: 0.99 male(s)/female (2014 est.)

Maternal mortality rate:
240 deaths/100,000 live births (2010)
country comparison to the world: 47

Infant mortality rate:
total: 71.12 deaths/1,000 live births
country comparison to the world: 14
male: 72.17 deaths/1,000 live births
female: 70.04 deaths/1,000 live births (2014 est.)

Life expectancy at birth: *total population:* 63.49 years
country comparison to the world: 183
male: 62.43 years
female: 64.58 years (2014 est.)

Total fertility rate: 4.66 children born/woman (2014 est.)
country comparison to the world: 26

Contraceptive prevalence rate: 10.1% (2000)

Health expenditures: 4% of GDP (2011)
country comparison to the world: 164

Physicians density: 0.3 physicians/1,000 population (2004)

Hospital bed density: 2.1 beds/1,000 population (2010)

Drinking water source:
improved:
urban: 65.5% of population
rural: 41.6% of population
total: 50.9% of population
unimproved:
urban: 34.5% of population
rural: 58.4% of population
total: 49.1% of population (2006 est.)

HIV/AIDS—adult prevalence rate: 6.2% (2012 est.)
country comparison to the world: 11

HIV/AIDS—people living with HIV/AIDS: 31,400 (2012 est.)
country comparison to the world: 69

HIV/AIDS—deaths: 1,400 (2012 est.)
country comparison to the world: 65

Major infectious diseases: *degree of risk:* very high
food or waterborne diseases: bacterial and protozoal diarrhea, hepatitis A, and typhoid fever
vectorborne disease: malaria and dengue fever
animal contact disease: rabies (2013)

Obesity—adult prevalence rate: 10.6% (2008)
country comparison to the world: 129

Children under the age of 5 years underweight: 10.6% (2004)
country comparison to the world: 67

Education expenditures: 0.6% of GDP (2002)
country comparison to the world: 173

Literacy: *definition:* age 15 and over can read and write
total population: 94.2%
male: 97.1%
female: 91.1% (2011 est.)

School life expectancy (primary to tertiary education): *total:* 9 years
male: 10 years
female: 7 years (2000)

Child labor—children ages 5-14: *total number:* 35,382
percentage: 28 % (2000 est.)

GOVERNMENT

conventional long form: Republic of Equatorial Guinea
conventional short form: Equatorial Guinea
local long form: Republica de Guinea Ecuatorial/Republique de Guinee equatoriale
local short form: Guinea Ecuatorial/Guinee equatoriale
former: Spanish Guinea

Government type: republic

Capital: name: Malabo
geographic coordinates: 3 45 N, 8 47 E
time difference: UTC+1 (6 hours ahead of Washington, DC during Standard Time)

Administrative divisions: 7 provinces (provincias, singular—provincia); Annobon, Bioko Norte, Bioko Sur, Centro Sur, Kie-Ntem, Litoral, Wele-Nzas

Independence: 12 October 1968 (from Spain)

National holiday: Independence Day, 12 October (1968)

Constitution: approved by referendum 17 November 1991; amended several times, last in 2012 (2012)

Legal system: mixed system of civil and customary law

International law organization participation: has not submitted an ICJ jurisdiction declaration; non-party state to the ICCt

Suffrage: 18 years of age; universal

Executive branch: *chief of state:* President Brig. Gen. (Ret.) Teodoro Obiang NGUEMA MGASOGO (since 3 August 1979 when he seized power in a military coup)
head of government: Prime Minister Vicente Ehate TOMI (since 22 May 2012)

cabinet: Council of Ministers appointed by the president (For more information visit the World Leaders website)
elections: president elected by popular vote for a seven-year term (two term limits); election last held on 29 November 2009 (next to be held in 2016); prime minister and deputy prime ministers appointed by the president; note—according to the constitutional referendum on November 2011, elections are to be held in 2016 and the presidency is limited to two terms
election results: Teodoro Obiang NGUEMA MBASOGO reelected president; percent of vote—Teodoro Obiang NGUEMA MBASOGO 95.8%, Placido MICO Abogo 3.6%, other 0.6%

Legislative branch: bicameral Parliament consists of the Senate (70 seats; 55 seats directly elected and 15 appointed by the president) and the House of People's Representatives or Camara de los Diputdos or Chamber of Deputies (100 seats; members directly elected by popular vote to serve five-year terms)
elections: last held on 26 May 2013 (next to be held in 2018)
election results: Senate—percent of vote by party—NA; seats by party—PDGE 54, CPDS 1; Chamber of Deputies—percent of vote by party—NA; seats by party—PDGE 99, CPDS 1
note: note—Parliament has little power since the constitution vests all executive authority in the president; the constitutional referendum of 2011 established a bicameral legislature formed following the May 2013 elections; the newly formed Senate consists of elected and appointed (by the President) members

Judicial branch: *highest court(s):* Supreme Court of Justice (consists of the chief justice and NA judges); Constitutional Court (consists of the court president and 4 members)
judge selection and term of office: Supreme Court judges appointed by the president for 5-year terms; *Constitutional Court members appointed by the president, two of which are nominated by the Chamber of Deputies*
subordinate courts: Court of Guarantees; military courts; Courts of Appeal; first instance tribunals; district and county tribunals

Political parties and leaders: Convergence Party for Social Democracy or CPDS [Andres Esono ONDO]; Democratic Party for Equatorial Guinea or PDGE [Jeronimo Osa Osa ECORO] (ruling party); Electoral Coalition or EC; Party for Progress of Equatorial Guinea or PPGE [Severo MOTO]; Popular Action of Equatorial Guinea or APGE [Carmelo Mba BACALE]; Popular Union or UP [Daniel MARTINEZ Ayecaba]

Political pressure groups and leaders: ASODEGUE (Madrid-based pressure group for democratic reform); EG Justice (US-based anti-corruption group);

International organization participation: ACP, AfDB, AU, BDEAC, CEMAC, CPLP (associate), FAO, FZ, G-77, IBRD, ICAO, ICRM, IDA, IFAD, IFC, IFRCS, ILO, IMF, IMO, Interpol, IOC, IPU, ITSO, ITU, MIGA, NAM, OAS (observer), OIF, OPCW, UN, UNCTAD, UNESCO, UNIDO, UNWTO, UPU, WHO, WIPO, WTO (observer)

Diplomatic representation in the US:
chief of mission: Ambassador Ruben Maye Nsue MANGUE (since 10 September 2013)
chancery: 2020 16th Street NW, Washington, DC 20009
telephone: [1] (202) 518-5700
FAX: [1] (202) 518-5252
consul general(s): Houston

Diplomatic representation from the US:
chief of mission: Ambassador Mark L. ASQUINO (since 29 June 2012)
embassy: Carretera Malabo II, Malabo, Guinea Ecuatorial
mailing address: US Embassy Malabo, US Department of State, Washington, DC 20521-2520
telephone: [240] 333 09 57 41

Flag description: three equal horizontal bands of green (top), white, and red, with a blue isosceles triangle based on the hoist side and the coat of arms centered in the white band; the coat of arms has six yellow six-pointed stars (representing the mainland and five offshore islands) above a gray shield bearing a silk-cotton tree and below which is a scroll with the motto UNIDAD, PAZ, JUSTICIA (Unity, Peace, Justice); green symbolizes the jungle and natural resources, blue represents the sea that connects the mainland to the islands, white stands for peace, and red recalls the fight for independence

National symbol(s): silk cotton tree

National anthem: name: "Caminemos pisando la senda" (Let Us Tread the Path)
lyrics/music: Atanasio Ndongo MIYONO/Atanasio Ndongo MIYONO or Ramiro Sanchez LOPEZ (disputed)
note: adopted 1968

ECONOMY

Economy—overview: The discovery and exploitation of large oil and gas reserves have contributed to dramatic economic growth, but fluctuating oil prices along with slowing or declining oil production have resulted in much lower GDP growth in recent years. The economy is still dominated by hydrocarbon production. The government has solicited foreign investment, particularly from the United States, to diversify the economy and in February 2014 the government hosted an economic diversification symposium focused on attracting investment in five sectors: agriculture and animal ranching, fishing, mining and petrochemicals, tourism, and financial services. Undeveloped mineral resources include gold, zinc, diamonds, columbite-tantalite, and other base metals. Forestry and farming are also minor components of GDP. Subsistence farming is the dominant form of livelihood. Although pre-independence Equatorial Guinea counted on cocoa production for hard currency earnings, the neglect of the rural economy under successive regimes has diminished potential for agriculture-led growth. The government has stated its intention to reinvest some oil revenue into agriculture. A number of aid programs sponsored by the World Bank and the IMF have been cut off since 1993 because of corruption and mismanagement. The government has been widely criticized for its lack of transparency and misuse of oil revenues and has attempted to address this issue by working towards compliance with the Extractive Industries Transparency Initiative.

GDP (purchasing power parity): $19.68 billion (2013 est.)
country comparison to the world: 136
$19.97 billion (2012 est.)
$18.96 billion (2011 est.)
note: data are in 2013 US dollars

GDP (official exchange rate): $17.08 billion (2013 est.)

GDP—real growth rate: -1.5% (2013 est.)
country comparison to the world: 208
5.3% (2012 est.)
4.6% (2011 est.)

GDP—per capita (PPP): $25,700 (2013 est.)
country comparison to the world: 58
$26,900 (2012 est.)
$26,200 (2011 est.)
note: data are in 2010 US dollars; population figures are uncertain for Equatorial Guinea; these per capita income figures are based on a estimated population of less than 700,000; some estimates put the figure as high as 1.2 million people; if true, the per capita GDP figures would be significantly lower

Gross national saving: 22.6% of GDP (2013 est.)
country comparison to the world: 64
26.4% of GDP (2012 est.)
32% of GDP (2011 est.)

GDP—composition, by end use:
household consumption: 26.7%
government consumption: 3.7%
investment in fixed capital: 37.9%
investment in inventories: 1%
exports of goods and services: 80.8%
imports of goods and services: -50.1% (2013 est.)

GDP—composition, by sector of origin:
agriculture: 4.6%
industry: 87.3%
services: 8.1% (2013 est.)

Agriculture—products: coffee, cocoa, rice, yams, cassava (manioc), bananas, palm oil nuts; livestock; timber

Industries: petroleum, natural gas, sawmilling
Industrial production growth rate:
3.2% (2013 est.)
country comparison to the world: 93

Labor force: 195,200 (2007)
country comparison to the world: 172

Unemployment rate: 22.3% (2009 est.)
country comparison to the world: 168

Population below poverty line: NA%

Household income or consumption by percentage share: *lowest 10%:* NA%
highest 10%: NA%

Budget: *revenues:* $6.837 billion
expenditures: $6.795 billion (2013 est.)

Taxes and other revenues: 40% of GDP (2013 est.)
country comparison to the world: 42

Budget surplus (+) or deficit (-):
0.2% of GDP (2013 est.)
country comparison to the world: 39

Public debt: 11% of GDP (2013 est.)
country comparison to the world: 148
9.3% of GDP (2012 est.)

Fiscal year: calendar year

Inflation rate (consumer prices): 6% (2013 est.)
country comparison to the world: 172
6.1% (2012 est.)

Central bank discount rate: 8.5% (31 December 2010 est.)
country comparison to the world: 88
4.25% (31 December 2009 est.)

Commercial bank prime lending rate: 15% (31 December 2013 est.)
country comparison to the world: 40
15% (31 December 2012 est.)

Stock of narrow money: $3.001 billion (31 December 2013 est.)
country comparison to the world: 116
$3.023 billion (31 December 2012 est.)

Stock of broad money: $3.382 billion (31 December 2013 est.)
country comparison to the world: 141
$3.438 billion (31 December 2012 est.)

Stock of domestic credit: $-424.6 million (31 December 2013 est.)
country comparison to the world: 185
$-631.4 million (31 December 2012 est.)

Current account balance: -$2.916 billion (2013 est.)
country comparison to the world: 158
-$2.945 billion (2012 est.)

Exports: $15.44 billion (2013 est.)
country comparison to the world: 78
$14.86 billion (2012 est.)

Exports—commodities: petroleum products, timber

Exports—partners: Japan 18.8%, France 16.1%, China 11.7%, US 11.3%, Netherlands 7.2%, Spain 7.1%, Italy 5.1% (2012)

Imports: $7.943 billion (2013 est.)
country comparison to the world: 110
$8.045 billion (2012 est.)

Imports—commodities: petroleum sector equipment, other equipment, construction materials, vehicles

Imports—partners: Spain 18.4%, China 17.4%, US 11.1%, France 8%, Italy 5.9%, Cote dIvoire 5.3%, Brazil 4.4% (2012)

Reserves of foreign exchange and gold: $4.027 billion (31 December 2013 est.)
country comparison to the world: 101
$4.397 billion (31 December 2012 est.)

Debt—external: $2.104 billion (31 December 2013 est.)
country comparison to the world: 143
$1.858 billion (31 December 2012 est.)

Exchange rates: Cooperation Financiere en Afrique Centrale francs (XAF) per US dollar—
500.7 (2013 est.)
510.53 (2012 est.)
495.28 (2010 est.)
472.19 (2009)
447.81 (2008)

ENERGY

Electricity—production: 97 million kWh (2010 est.)
country comparison to the world: 199

Electricity—consumption: 90.21 million kWh (2010 est.)
country comparison to the world: 199

Electricity—exports: 0 kWh (2012 est.)
country comparison to the world: 131

Electricity—imports: 0 kWh (2012 est.)
country comparison to the world: 138

Electricity—installed generating capacity: 38,000 kW (2010 est.)
country comparison to the world: 195

Electricity—from fossil fuels: 97.4% of total installed capacity (2010 est.)
country comparison to the world: 62

Electricity—from nuclear fuels: 0% of total installed capacity (2010 est.)
country comparison to the world: 82

Electricity—from hydroelectric plants: 2.6% of total installed capacity (2010 est.)
country comparison to the world: 132

Electricity—from other renewable sources: 0% of total installed capacity (2010 est.)
country comparison to the world: 172

Crude oil—production: 318,000 bbl/day (2012 est.)
country comparison to the world: 34

Crude oil—exports: 319,100 bbl/day (2010 est.)
country comparison to the world: 24

Crude oil—imports: 0 bbl/day (2010 est.)
country comparison to the world: 180

Crude oil—proved reserves: 1.1 billion bbl (1 January 2013 es)
country comparison to the world: 42

Refined petroleum products—production: 3,074 bbl/day (2010 est.)
country comparison to the world: 109

Refined petroleum products—consumption: 1,588 bbl/day (2011 est.)
country comparison to the world: 194

Refined petroleum products—exports: 2,320 bbl/day (2010 est.)
country comparison to the world: 101

Refined petroleum products—imports: 4,561 bbl/day (2010 est.)
country comparison to the world: 159

Natural gas—production: 6.88 billion cu m (2011 est.)
country comparison to the world: 48

Natural gas—consumption: 1.58 billion cu m (2010 est.)
country comparison to the world: 80

Natural gas—exports: 5.26 billion cu m (2011 est.)
country comparison to the world: 34

Natural gas—imports: 0 cu m (2011 est.)
country comparison to the world: 187

Natural gas—proved reserves: 36.81 billion cu m (1 January 2013 es)
country comparison to the world: 68

Carbon dioxide emissions from consumption of energy: 5.232 million Mt (2011 est.)
country comparison to the world: 123

COMMUNICATIONS

Telephones—main lines in use: 14,900 (2012)
country comparison to the world: 195

Telephones—mobile cellular: 501,000 (2012)
country comparison to the world: 169

Telephone system: *general assessment:* digital fixed-line network in most major urban areas and good mobile coverage
domestic: fixed-line density is about 2 per 100 persons; mobile-cellular subscribership has been increasing and in 2011 stood at about 60 percent of the population
international: country code—240; international communications from Bata and Malabo to African and European countries; satellite earth station—1 Intelsat (Indian Ocean) (2011)

Broadcast media: state maintains control of broadcast media with domestic broadcast media limited to 1 state-owned TV station, 1 private TV station owned by the president's eldest son, 1 state-owned radio station, and 1 private radio station owned by the president's eldest son; satellite TV service is available; transmissions of multiple international broadcasters are accessible (2013)

Internet country code: .gq

Internet hosts: 7 (2012)
country comparison to the world: 227

Internet users: 14,400 (2009)
country comparison to the world: 200

TRANSPORTATION

Airports: 7 (2013)
country comparison to the world: 166

Airports—with paved runways: *total:* 6
over 3,047 m: 1
2,438 to 3,047 m: 2
1,524 to 2,437 m: 1
under 914 m: 2 (2013)

Airports—with unpaved runways: total: 1
2,438 to 3,047 m: 1 (2013)

Pipelines: condensate 42 km; condensate/gas 5 km; gas 79 km; oil 71 km (2013)

Roadways: total: 2,880 km (2000)
country comparison to the world: 168

Merchant marine: *total:* 5
country comparison to the world: 128
by type: cargo 1, chemical tanker 1, petroleum tanker 3
foreign-owned: 1 (Norway 1) (2010)

Ports and terminals: *major seaport(s):* Bata, Luba, Malabo

MILITARY

Military branches: Equatorial Guinea Armed Forces (FAGE): Equatorial Guinea National Guard (Guardia Nacional de Guinea Ecuatoria, GNGE (Army), with Navy and Air Force (2013)

Military service age and obligation: 18 years of age for selective compulsory military service, although conscription is rare in practice; 2-year service obligation; women hold only administrative positions in the Coast Guard (2013)

Manpower available for military service:
males age 16-49: 151,147
females age 16-49: 150,345 (2010 est.)

Manpower fit for military service:
males age 16-49: 113,277
females age 16-49: 115,320 (2010 est.)

Manpower reaching militarily significant age annually: *male:* 7,398
female: 7,126 (2010 est.)

TRANSNATIONAL ISSUES

Disputes—international: in 2002, ICJ ruled on an equidistance settlement of Cameroon-Equatorial Guinea-Nigeria maritime boundary in the Gulf of Guinea, but a dispute between Equatorial Guinea and Cameroon over an island at the mouth of the Ntem River and imprecisely defined maritime coordinates in the ICJ decision delayed final delimitation; UN urged Equatorial Guinea and Gabon to resolve the sovereignty dispute over Gabon-occupied Mbane and lesser islands and to create a maritime boundary in the hydrocarbon-rich Corisco Bay

Trafficking in persons: *current situation:* Equatorial Guinea is a source and destination country for women and children subjected to forced labor and sexual exploitation; children have been trafficked from nearby countries for work as domestic servants, market laborers, ambulant vendors, and launderers; women may also be trafficked to Equatorial Guinea from Cameroon, Benin, other neighboring countries, and China for forced labor or prostitution; Equatorial Guinean girls may be encouraged by their parents to engage in the sex trade in urban centers to receive groceries, gifts, housing, and money

tier rating: Tier 3—Equatorial Guinea does not fully comply with the minimum standards on the elimination of trafficking and is not making significant efforts to do so; the government has initiated no investigations or prosecutions of suspected trafficking offenses and demonstrated no efforts to identify victims or to provide them with necessary services, despite being required to do so under its 2004 anti-trafficking law; the government shows a slight increase in its efforts to prevent trafficking with the creation in 2012 of a working-level committee to combat human trafficking, but it has not launched any public anti-trafficking campaigns or implemented any programs to address forced child labor (2013)

ERITREA

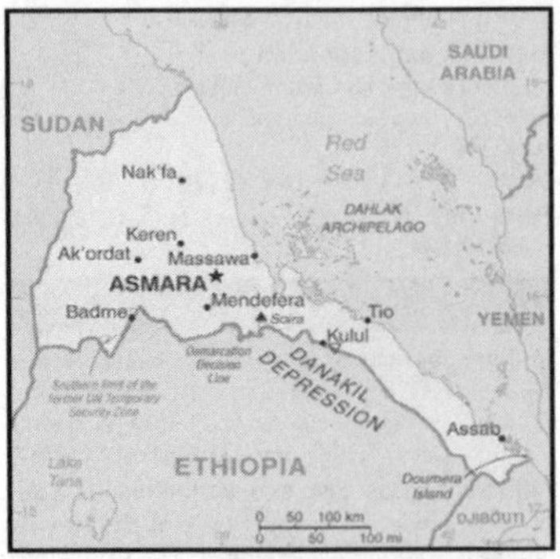

INTRODUCTION

Background: After independence from Italian colonial control in 1941 and 10 years of British administrative control, the UN established Eritrea as an autonomous region within the Ethiopian federation in 1952. Ethiopia's full annexation of Eritrea as a province 10 years later sparked a violent 30-year struggle for independence that ended in 1991 with Eritrean rebels defeating government forces. Eritreans overwhelmingly approved independence in a 1993 referendum. ISAIAS Afworki has been Eritrea's only president since independence; his rule, particularly since 2001, has been highly autocratic and repressive. His government has created a highly militarized society by pursuing an unpopular program of mandatory conscription into national service, sometimes of indefinite length. A two-and-a-half-year border war with Ethiopia that erupted in 1998 ended under UN auspices in December 2000. A UN peacekeeping operation was established that monitored a 25 km-wide Temporary Security Zone. The Eritrea-Ethiopia Boundary Commission (EEBC) created in April 2003 was tasked "to delimit and demarcate the colonial treaty border based on pertinent colonial treaties (1900, 1902, and 1908) and applicable international law." The EEBC on 30 November 2007 remotely demarcated the border, assigning the town of Badme to Eritrea, despite Ethiopia's maintaining forces there from the time of the 1998-2000 war. Eritrea insisted that the UN terminate its peacekeeping mission on 31 July 2008. Eritrea has accepted the EEBC's "virtual demarcation" decision and repeatedly called on Ethiopia to remove its troops. Ethiopia has not accepted the demarcation decision, and neither party has entered into meaningful dialogue to resolve the impasse. Eritrea is subject to several UN Security Council Resolutions (from 2009, 2011, and 2012) imposing various military and economic sanctions, in view of evidence that it has supported armed opposition groups in the region.

GEOGRAPHY

Location: Eastern Africa, bordering the Red Sea, between Djibouti and Sudan

Geographic coordinates: 15 00 N, 39 00 E

Map references: Africa

Area: *total:* 117,600 sq km
country comparison to the world: 101
land: 101,000 sq km
water: 16,600 sq km

Area—comparative: slightly larger than Pennsylvania

Land boundaries: total: 1,626 km
border countries: Djibouti 109 km, Ethiopia 912 km, Sudan 605 km

Coastline: 2,234 km (mainland on Red Sea 1,151 km, islands in Red Sea 1,083 km)

Maritime claims: territorial sea: 12 nm

Climate: hot, dry desert strip along Red Sea coast; cooler and wetter in the central highlands (up to 61 cm of rainfall annually, heaviest June to September); semiarid in western hills and lowlands

Terrain: dominated by extension of Ethiopian north-south trending highlands, descending on the east to a coastal desert plain, on the northwest to hilly terrain and on the southwest to flat-to-rolling plains

Elevation extremes: *lowest point:* near Kulul within the Danakil Depression -75 m
highest point: Soira 3,018 m

Natural resources: gold, potash, zinc, copper, salt, possibly oil and natural gas, fish

Land use: arable land: 5.87%
permanent crops: 0.02%
other: 94.12% (2011)

Irrigated land: 215.9 sq km (2003)

Total renewable water resources: 6.3 cu km (2011)

Freshwater withdrawal (domestic/industrial/agricultural): *total:* 0.58 cu km/yr (5%/0%/95%)
per capita: 121.3 cu m/yr (2004)

Natural hazards: frequent droughts, rare earthquakes and volcanoes; locust swarms
volcanism: Dubbi (elev. 1,625 m), which last erupted in 1861, was the country's only historically active volcano until Nabro (2,218 m) came to life on 12 June 2011

Environment—current issues: deforestation; desertification; soil erosion; overgrazing; loss of infrastructure from civil warfare

Environment—international agreements:
party to: Biodiversity, Climate Change, Climate Change-Kyoto Protocol, Desertification, Endangered Species, Hazardous Wastes, Ozone Layer Protection signed, but not ratified: none of the selected agreements

Geography—note: strategic geopolitical position along world's busiest shipping lanes; Eritrea retained the entire coastline of Ethiopia along the Red Sea upon de jure independence from Ethiopia on 24 May 1993

PEOPLE AND SOCIETY

Nationality: *noun:* Eritrean(s)
adjective: Eritrean

Ethnic groups: nine recognized ethnic groups: Tigrinya 55%, Tigre 30%, Saho 4%, Kunama 2%, Rashaida 2%, Bilen 2%, other (Afar, Beni Amir, Nera) 5% (2010 est.)

Languages: Tigrinya (official), Arabic (official), English (official), Tigre, Kunama, Afar, other Cushitic languages

Religions: Muslim, Coptic Christian, Roman Catholic, Protestant

Population: 6,380,803 (July 2014 est.)
country comparison to the world: 107

Age structure: *0-14 years:* 40.8% (male 1,307,550/female 1,293,867)
15-24 years: 20.2% (male 644,878/female 646,518)
25-54 years: 31.5% (male 996,856/female 1,014,798)
55-64 years: 3.7% (male 101,549/female 138,016)
65 years and over: 3.7% (male 102,525/female 134,246) (2014 est.)

Dependency ratios:
total dependency ratio: 83.2 %
youth dependency ratio: 79.1 %
elderly dependency ratio: 4.1 %
potential support ratio: 24.1 (2013)

Median age: *total:* 19.1 years
male: 18.8 years
female: 19.5 years (2014 est.)

Population growth rate: 2.3% (2014 est.)
country comparison to the world: 38

Birth rate: 30.69 births/1,000 population (2014 est.)
country comparison to the world: 41

Death rate: 7.65 deaths/1,000 population (2014 est.)
country comparison to the world: 112

Net migration rate: 0 migrant(s)/1,000 population (2014 est.)
country comparison to the world: 106

Urbanization: *urban population:* 21.3% of total population (2011)
rate of urbanization: 5.01% annual rate of change (2010-15 est.)

Major urban areas—population: ASMARA (capital) 649,000 (2009)

Sex ratio: *at birth:* 1.03 male(s)/female
0-14 years: 1.01 male(s)/female
15-24 years: 1 male(s)/female
25-54 years: 0.98 male(s)/female
55-64 years: 0.98 male(s)/female
65 years and over: 0.79 male(s)/female
total population: 0.98 male(s)/female (2014 est.)

Mother's mean age at first birth: 20.6 (2002 est.)

Maternal mortality rate: 240 deaths/100,000 live births (2010)
country comparison to the world: 46

Infant mortality rate: *total:* 38.44 deaths/1,000 live births
country comparison to the world: 59
male: 43.61 deaths/1,000 live births
female: 33.12 deaths/1,000 live births (2014 est.)

Life expectancy at birth: *total population:* 63.51 years
country comparison to the world: 181
male: 61.36 years
female: 65.72 years (2014 est.)

Total fertility rate: 4.14 children born/woman (2014 est.)
country comparison to the world: 35

Contraceptive prevalence rate: 8% (2002)

Health expenditures: 2.6% of GDP (2011)
country comparison to the world: 184

Physicians density: 0.05 physicians/1,000 population (2004)

Hospital bed density: 0.7 beds/1,000 population (2011)

Drinking water source:
improved:
urban: 73.7% of population
rural: 56.7% of population
total: 60.2% of population
unimproved:
urban: 26.3% of population
rural: 43.3% of population
total: 39.8% of population (2008 est.)

Sanitation facility access:
improved:
urban: 52% of population

rural: 4% of population
total: 14% of population
unimproved:
urban: 48% of population
rural: 96% of population
total: 86% of population (2008 est.)

HIV/AIDS—adult prevalence rate: 0.7% (2012 est.)
country comparison to the world: 55

HIV/AIDS—people living with HIV/AIDS: 17,800 (2012 est.)
country comparison to the world: 86

HIV/AIDS—deaths: 1,200 (2012 est.)
country comparison to the world: 71

Major infectious diseases: *degree of risk:* high
food or waterborne diseases: bacterial diarrhea, hepatitis A, and typhoid fever
vectorborne diseases: malaria and dengue fever (2013)

Obesity—adult prevalence rate: 1.5% (2008)
country comparison to the world: 188

Children under the age of 5 years underweight: 34.5% (2002)
country comparison to the world: 7

Education expenditures: 2.1% of GDP (2006)
country comparison to the world: 165

Literacy: *definition:* age 15 and over can read and write
total population: 68.9%
male: 79.5%
female: 59% (2011 est.)

School life expectancy (primary to tertiary education): *total:* 4 years
male: 5 years
female: 4 years (2010)

GOVERNMENT

Country name: conventional long form: State of Eritrea
conventional short form: Eritrea
local long form: Hagere Ertra
local short form: Ertra
former: Eritrea Autonomous Region in Ethiopia

Government type: transitional government
note: following a successful referendum on independence for the Autonomous Region of Eritrea on 23-25 April 1993, a National Assembly, composed entirely of the People's Front for Democracy and Justice or PFDJ, was established as a transitional legislature and a Constitutional Commission was established to draft a constitution; ISAIAS Afworki was named president by the transitional legislature; the constitution, ratified in May 1997, did not enter into effect, pending parliamentary and presidential elections; parliamentary elections were scheduled in December 2001 but were postponed indefinitely; currently the PFDJ is the sole legal party and controls all national, regional, and local political offices

Capital: *name:* Asmara (Asmera)
geographic coordinates: 15 20 N, 38 56 E
time difference: UTC+3 (8 hours ahead of Washington, DC during Standard Time)

Administrative divisions: 6 regions (zobatat, singular—zoba); Anseba, Debub (South), Debubawi K'eyih Bahri (Southern Red Sea), Gash Barka, Ma'akel (Central), Semenawi Keyih Bahri (Northern Red Sea)

Independence: 24 May 1993 (from Ethiopia)

National holiday: Independence Day, 24 May (1993)

Constitution: adopted 23 May 1997 (not fully implemented) (2014)

Legal system: mixed legal system of civil, customary, and Islamic religious law

International law organization participation: has not submitted an ICJ jurisdiction declaration; non-party state to the ICCt

Suffrage: 18 years of age; universal

Executive branch: *chief of state:* President ISAIAS Afworki (since 8 June 1993); note—the president is both the chief of state and head of government and is head of the State Council and National Assembly
head of government: President ISAIAS Afworki (since 8 June 1993)
cabinet: State Council the collective exercises executive authority; members appointed by the president (For more information visit the World Leaders website)
elections: president elected by the National Assembly for a five-year term (eligible for a second term); the most recent and only election was held on 8 June 1993 (next election date uncertain as the National Assembly did not hold a presidential election in December 2001 as anticipated)
election results: ISAIAS Afworki elected president by the transitional National Assembly; percent of National Assembly vote—ISAIAS Afworki 95%, other 5%

Legislative branch: unicameral National Assembly (150 seats; members elected by direct popular vote to serve five-year terms)
elections: in May 1997, following the adoption of the new constitution, 75 members of the PFDJ Central Committee (the old Central Committee of the EPLF), 60 members of the 527-member Constituent Assembly, which had been established in 1997 to discuss and ratify the new constitution, and 15 representatives of Eritreans living abroad were formed into a Transitional National Assembly to serve as the country's legislative body until countrywide elections to a National Assembly were held; although only 75 of 150 members of the Transitional National Assembly were elected, the constitution stipulates that once past the transition stage, all members of the National Assembly will be elected by secret ballot of all eligible voters; National Assembly elections scheduled for December 2001 were postponed indefinitely due to the war with Ethiopia

Judicial branch: *highest court(s):* High Court (organized into civil, commercial, criminal, labor, administrative, and customary sections with 20 judges)
judge selection and term of office: High Court judges appointed by the president
subordinate courts: regional/zonal courts; community courts; special courts; sharia courts (for issues dealing with Muslim marriage, inheritance, and family); military courts

Political parties and leaders: People's Front for Democracy and Justice or PFDJ [ISAIAS Afworki] (the only party recognized by the government); note—a National Assembly committee drafted a law on political parties in January 2001, but the full National Assembly never debated or voted on it

Political pressure groups and leaders: Democratic Movement for the Liberation of Eritrean Kunama (DMLEK); Eritrean Democratic Alliance (EDA); Eritrean National Congress for Democratic Change (ENCDC); Eritrean National Salvation Front (ENSF); Eritrean Islamic Party for Justice and Development (EIPJD) (includes the Eritrean Islamic Jihad (EIJ), Eritrean Islamic; Jihad Movement (EIJM), Eritrean Islamic Salvation, and the Eritrean Islamic Foundation); Eritrean People's Democratic Party (EPDP); Red Sea Afar Democratic Organization (RSADO)

International organization participation: ACP, AfDB, AU, COMESA, FAO, G-77, IAEA, IBRD, ICAO, ICC (NGOs), IDA, IFAD, IFC, IFRCS (observer), ILO, IMF, IMO, Interpol, IOC, ISO (subscriber), ITU, ITUC (NGOs), LAS (observer), MIGA, NAM, OPCW, PCA, UN, UNCTAD, UNESCO, UNIDO, UNWTO, UPU, WCO, WFTU (NGOs), WHO, WIPO, WMO

Diplomatic representation in the US: *chief of mission:* Ambassador (vacant); Charge d'Affaires BERHANE Gebrehiwet Solomon (since 15 March 2011)
chancery: 1708 New Hampshire Avenue NW, Washington, DC 20009
telephone: [1] (202) 319-1991
FAX: [1] (202) 319-1304

Diplomatic representation from the US: *chief of mission:* Ambassador (vacant); Charge d'Affaires Sue BREMNER (since July 2012)
embassy: 179 Ala Street, Asmara
mailing address: P. O. Box 211, Asmara
telephone: [291] (1) 120004
FAX: [291] (1) 127584

Flag description: red isosceles triangle (based on the hoist side) dividing the flag into two right triangles; the upper triangle is green, the lower one is blue; a gold wreath encircling a gold olive branch is centered on the hoist side of the red triangle; green stands for the country's agriculture economy, red signifies the blood shed in the fight for freedom, and blue symbolizes the bounty of the sea; the wreath-olive branch symbol is similar to that on the first flag of Eritrea from 1952; the shape of the red triangle broadly mimics the shape of the country

National symbol(s): camel

National anthem: *name:* "Ertra, Ertra, Ertra" (Eritrea, Eritrea, Eritrea)
lyrics/music: SOLOMON Tsehaye Beraki/Isaac Abraham MEHAREZGI and ARON Tekle Tesfatsion
note: adopted 1993; upon independence from Ethiopia

ECONOMY

Economy—overview: Since formal independence from Ethiopia in 1993, Eritrea has faced many economic problems, including lack of resources and chronic drought, which have been exacerbated by restrictive economic policies. Eritrea has a command economy under the control of the sole political party, the People's Front for Democracy and Justice (PFDJ). Like the economies of many African nations, a large share of the population—nearly 80%—is engaged in subsistence agriculture, but the sector only produces a small share of the country's total output. Since the conclusion of the Ethiopian-Eritrea war in 2000, the government has expanded use of military and party-owned businesses to complete President ISAIAS's development agenda. The government has strictly controled the use of foreign currency by limiting access and availability; new regulations in 2013 have slightly relaxed currently controls. Few large private enterprises exist in Eritrea and most operate in conjunction with government partners, including a number of large international mining ventures that have recently begun production. While reliable statistics on food security are difficult to obtain, erratic rainfall and the percentage of the labor force tied up in national service continue to interfere with agricultural production and economic development. Eritrea's harvests generally cannot meet the food needs of the country without supplemental grain purchases. Copper, potash, and gold production is likely to drive economic growth over the next few years, but military spending will continue to compete with development and investment plans. Eritrea's economic future will depend on market reform, international sanctions, global food prices, and success at addressing social problems such as illiteracy and low skills.

GDP (purchasing power parity): $4.717 billion (2013 est.)
country comparison to the world: 172
$4.409 billion (2012 est.)
$4.12 billion (2011 est.)
note: data are in 2013 US dollars

GDP (official exchange rate): $3.438 billion (2013 est.)

GDP—real growth rate: 7% (2013 est.)
country comparison to the world: 20
7% (2012 est.)
8.7% (2011 est.)

GDP—per capita (PPP): $1,200 (2013 est.)
country comparison to the world: 212
$1,100 (2012 est.)
$1,100 (2011 est.)
note: data are in 2013 US dollars

Gross national saving: 13% of GDP (2013 est.)
country comparison to the world: 120
10.9% of GDP (2012 est.)
5.3% of GDP (2011 est.)

GDP—composition, by end use:
household consumption: 75.1%
government consumption: 18.4%
investment in fixed capital: 15.7%
exports of goods and services: 10.2%
imports of goods and services: -19.4% (2013 est.)

GDP—composition, by sector of origin:
agriculture: 11.7%
industry: 26.9%
services: 61.4% (2013 est.)

Agriculture—products: sorghum, lentils, vegetables, corn, cotton, tobacco, sisal; livestock, goats; fish

Industries: food processing, beverages, clothing and textiles, light manufacturing, salt, cement

Industrial production growth rate: 7% (2013 est.)
country comparison to the world: 35

Labor force: 2.955 million (2012 est.)
country comparison to the world: 104

Labor force—by occupation: *agriculture:* 80%
industry and services: 20% (2004 est.)

Unemployment rate: NA%

Population below poverty line: 50% (2004 est.)

Household income or consumption by percentage share: *lowest 10%:* NA%
highest 10%: NA%

Budget: *revenues:* $968.8 million
expenditures: $1.417 billion (2013 est.)

Taxes and other revenues: 28.2% of GDP (2013 est.)
country comparison to the world: 103

Budget surplus (+) or deficit (-):
-13% of GDP (2013 est.)
country comparison to the world: 212

Public debt: 104.7% of GDP (2013 est.)
country comparison to the world: 14
125.8% of GDP (2012 est.)

Fiscal year: calendar year

Inflation rate (consumer prices): 13% (2013 est.)
country comparison to the world: 216
17% (2012 est.)

Commercial bank prime lending rate: NA%

Stock of narrow money: $1.798 billion (31 December 2013 est.)
country comparison to the world: 130
$1.396 billion (31 December 2012 est.)

Stock of broad money: $4.077 billion (31 December 2013 est.)
country comparison to the world: 134
$3.11 billion (31 December 2012 est.)

Stock of domestic credit: $3.602 billion (31 December 2013 est.)
country comparison to the world: 123
$2.777 billion (31 December 2012 est.)

Current account balance: -$210.1 million (2013 est.)
country comparison to the world: 86
$174.5 million (2012 est.)

Exports: $496.2 million (2013 est.)
country comparison to the world: 174
$454.9 million (2012 est.)

Exports—commodities: livestock, sorghum, textiles, food, small manufactures

Imports: $1.027 billion (2013 est.)
country comparison to the world: 177
$972.8 million (2012 est.)

Imports—commodities: machinery, petroleum products, food, manufactured goods

Reserves of foreign exchange and gold:
$192.9 million (31 December 2013 est.)
country comparison to the world: 160
$174.4 million (31 December 2012 est.)

Debt—external: $1.094 billion (31 December 2013 est.)
country comparison to the world: 160
$1.057 billion (31 December 2012 est.)

Exchange rates: nakfa (ERN) per US dollar—
15.38 (2013 est.)
15.375 (2012 est.)
15.375 (2010 est.)
15.375 (2009)
15.38 (2008)

ENERGY

Electricity—production: 292.5 million kWh (2010 est.)
country comparison to the world: 173

Electricity—consumption: 253.5 million kWh (2010 est.)
country comparison to the world: 181

Electricity—exports: 0 kWh (2012 est.)
country comparison to the world: 132

Electricity—imports: 0 kWh (2012 est.)
country comparison to the world: 139

Electricity—installed generating capacity:
140,800 kW (2010 est.)
country comparison to the world: 164

Electricity—from fossil fuels: 98.7% of total installed capacity (2010 est.)
country comparison to the world: 54

Electricity—from nuclear fuels: 0% of total installed capacity (2010 est.)
country comparison to the world: 84

Electricity—from hydroelectric plants:
0% of total installed capacity (2010 est.)
country comparison to the world: 168

Electricity—from other renewable sources:
1.3% of total installed capacity (2010 est.)
country comparison to the world: 81

Crude oil—production: 0 bbl/day (2012 est.)
country comparison to the world: 167

Crude oil—exports: 0 bbl/day (2010 est.)
country comparison to the world: 107

Crude oil—imports: 0 bbl/day (2010 est.)
country comparison to the world: 182

Crude oil—proved reserves: 0 bbl (1 January 2013 es)
country comparison to the world: 128

Refined petroleum products—production:
0 bbl/day (2010 est.)
country comparison to the world: 140

Refined petroleum products—consumption:
4,480 bbl/day (2011 est.)
country comparison to the world: 172

Refined petroleum products—exports:
0 bbl/day (2010 est.)
country comparison to the world: 173

Refined petroleum products—imports:
3,160 bbl/day (2010 est.)
country comparison to the world: 171

Natural gas—production: 0 cu m (2011 est.)
country comparison to the world: 126

Natural gas—consumption: 0 cu m (2010 est.)
country comparison to the world: 140

Natural gas—exports: 0 cu m (2011 est.)
country comparison to the world: 95

Natural gas—imports: 0 cu m (2011 est.)
country comparison to the world: 188

Natural gas—proved reserves: 0 cu m (1 January 2013 es)
country comparison to the world: 134

Carbon dioxide emissions from consumption of energy: 625,600 Mt (2011 est.)
country comparison to the world: 175

COMMUNICATIONS

Telephones—main lines in use: 60,000 (2012)
country comparison to the world: 160

Telephones—mobile cellular: 305,300 (2012)
country comparison to the world: 174

Telephone system: *general assessment:* inadequate; most fixed-line telephones are in Asmara; government is seeking international tenders to improve the system; cell phones in increasing use throughout the country
domestic: combined fixed-line and mobile-cellular subscribership is less than 5 per 100 persons
international: country code—291 (2011)

Broadcast media: government controls broadcast media with private ownership prohibited; 1 state-owned TV station; state-owned radio operates 2 networks; purchases of satellite dishes and subscriptions to international broadcast media are permitted (2007)

Internet country code: .er

Internet hosts: 701 (2012)
country comparison to the world: 177

Internet users: 200,000 (2008)
country comparison to the world: 140

TRANSPORTATION

Airports: 13 (2013)
country comparison to the world: 151

Airports—with paved runways: total: 4
over 3,047 m: 2
2,438 to 3,047 m: 2 (2013)

Airports—with unpaved runways: total: 9
over 3,047 m: 1
2,438 to 3,047 m: 1
1,524 to 2,437 m: 5
914 to 1,523 m: 2 (2013)

Heliports: 1 (2013)

Railways: total: 306 km
country comparison to the world: 119
narrow gauge: 306 km 0.950-m gauge (2008)

Roadways: total: 4,010 km
country comparison to the world: 158
paved: 874 km
unpaved: 3,136 km (2000)

Merchant marine: *total:* 4
country comparison to the world: 133
by type: cargo 2, petroleum tanker 1, roll on/roll off 1 (2010)

Ports and terminals: *major seaport(s):* Assab, Massawa

MILITARY

Military branches: Eritrean Armed Forces: Eritrean Ground Forces, Eritrean Navy, Eritrean Air Force (includes Air Defense Force) (2011)

Military service age and obligation: 18-40 years of age for male and female voluntary and compulsory military service; 16-month conscript service obligation (2012)

Manpower available for military service:
males age 16-49: 1,350,446
females age 16-49: 1,362,575 (2010 est.)

Manpower fit for military service: males age 16-49: 896,096
females age 16-49: 953,757 (2010 est.)

Manpower reaching militarily significant age annually: *male:* 66,829
female: 66,731 (2010 est.)

TRANSNATIONAL ISSUES

Disputes—international: Eritrea and Ethiopia agreed to abide by 2002 Ethiopia-Eritrea Boundary Commission's (EEBC) delimitation decision, but neither party responded to the revised line detailed in the November 2006 EEBC Demarcation Statement; Sudan accuses Eritrea of supporting eastern Sudanese rebel groups; in 2008 Eritrean troops moved across the border on Ras Doumera peninsula and occupied Doumera Island with undefined sovereignty in the Red Sea

Refugees and internally displaced persons: *IDPs:* 10,000 (border war with Ethiopia from 1998-2000; it has not been possible to confirm whether remaining IDPs are still living with hosts or have been returned or resettled) (2009)

Trafficking in persons: current situation: Eritrea is a source country for men, women, and children trafficked for the purposes of forced labor and, to a lesser extent, sex and labor trafficking abroad; the country's national service program is often abused to keep conscripts indefinitely and to force them to perform labor outside the scope of their duties; each year large numbers of migrants, often fleeing national service, depart Eritrea in search of work, particularly in the Gulf States, where some are likely to become victims of forced labor; Eritrean children working in various economic sectors, including domestic service, street vending, small-scale manufacturing, garages, bicycle repair shops, tea and coffee shops, metal workshops, and agriculture may be subjected to conditions of forced labor; some Eritrean refugees from Sudanese camps are extorted and tortured by traffickers as they are transported through the Sinai Peninsula
tier rating: Tier 3—Eritrea does not fully comply with the minimum standards for the elimination of trafficking and is not making significant efforts to do so; the Eritrean Government does not operate with transparency and has published neither data nor statistics regarding its efforts to combat human trafficking; the government did not report prosecuting or convicting any traffickers and did not identify or refer any victims to protective services in 2012; authorities largely lack an understanding of human trafficking, confusing it with all forms of transnational migration from Eritrea; the government made its first-ever efforts to prevent trafficking, warning about the hazards its citizens faced when attempting to migrate abroad (2013)

ESTONIA

INTRODUCTION

Background: After centuries of Danish, Swedish, German, and Russian rule, Estonia attained independence in 1918. Forcibly incorporated into the USSR in 1940—an action never recognized by the US—it regained its freedom in 1991 with the collapse of the Soviet Union. Since the last Russian troops left in 1994, Estonia has been free to promote economic and political ties with the West. It joined both NATO and the EU in the spring of 2004, formally joined the OECD in late 2010, and adopted the euro as its official currency on 1 January 2011.

GEOGRAPHY

Location: Eastern Europe, bordering the Baltic Sea and Gulf of Finland, between Latvia and Russia

Geographic coordinates: 59 00 N, 26 00 E

Map references: Europe

Area: *total:* 45,228 sq km
country comparison to the world: 133
land: 42,388 sq km
water: 2,840 sq km
note: includes 1,520 islands in the Baltic Sea

Area—comparative: slightly smaller than New Hampshire and Vermont combined

Land boundaries: *total:* 633 km
border countries: Latvia 343 km, Russia 290 km

Coastline: 3,794 km

Maritime claims: *territorial sea:* 12 nm
exclusive economic zone: limits fixed in coordination with neighboring states

Climate: maritime; wet, moderate winters, cool summers

Terrain: marshy, lowlands; flat in the north, hilly in the south

Elevation extremes: *lowest point:* Baltic Sea 0 m
highest point: Suur Munamagi 318 m

Natural resources: oil shale, peat, rare earth elements, phosphorite, clay, limestone, sand, dolomite, arable land, sea mud

Land use: *arable land:* 13.97%
permanent crops: 0.13%
other: 85.89% (2011)

Irrigated land: 4.58 sq km (2010)

Total renewable water resources: 12.81 cu km (2011)

Freshwater withdrawal (domestic/industrial/agricultural): *total:* 1.8 cu km/yr (3%/97%/0%)
per capita: 1,337 cu m/yr (2009)

Natural hazards: sometimes flooding occurs in the spring

Environment—current issues: air polluted with sulfur dioxide from oil-shale burning power plants in northeast; however, the amount of pollutants emitted to the air have fallen steadily, the emissions of 2000 were 80% less than in 1980; the amount of unpurified wastewater discharged to water bodies in 2000 was 1/20 the level of 1980; in connection with the start-up of new water purification plants, the pollution load of wastewater decreased; Estonia has more than 1,400 natural and manmade lakes, the smaller of which in agricultural areas need to be monitored; coastal seawater is polluted in certain locations

Environment—international agreements: *party to:* Air Pollution, Air Pollution-Nitrogen Oxides, Air Pollution-Persistent Organic Pollutants, Air *Pollution-Sulfur 85, Air Pollution-Volatile Organic Compounds, Antarctic Treaty, Biodiversity, Climate Change, Climate Change-Kyoto Protocol, Endangered Species, Hazardous Wastes, Law of the Sea, Ozone Layer Protection, Ship Pollution, Wetlands*
signed, but not ratified: none of the selected agreements

Geography—note: the mainland terrain is flat, boggy, and partly wooded; offshore lie more than 1,500 islands

PEOPLE AND SOCIETY

Nationality: *noun:* Estonian(s)
adjective: Estonian

Ethnic groups: Estonian 68.7%, Russian 24.8%, Ukrainian 1.7%, Belarusian 1%, Finn 0.6%, other 1.6%, unspecified 1.6% (2011 est.)

Languages: Estonian (official) 68.5%, Russian 29.6%, Ukrainian 0.6%, other 1.2%, unspecified 0.1% (2011 est.)

Religions: Lutheran 9.9%, Orthodox 16.2%, other Christian (including Methodist, Seventh-Day Adventist, Roman Catholic, Pentecostal) 2.2%, other 0.9%, none 54.1%, unspecified 16.7% (2011 est.)

Population: 1,257,921 (July 2014 est.)
country comparison to the world: 158

Age structure: *0-14 years:* 15.6% (male 101,018/female 95,204)
15-24 years: 11.2% (male 72,318/female 68,373)
25-54 years: 41.5% (male 250,244/female 271,450)
55-64 years: 18.6% (male 71,518/female 94,029)
65 years and over: 18.2% (male 77,492/female 156,275) (2014 est.)

Dependency ratios:
total dependency ratio: 51.2 %
youth dependency ratio: 23.9 %
elderly dependency ratio: 27.3 %
potential support ratio: 3.7 (2013)

Median age: *total:* 41.2 years
male: 37.6 years
female: 44.5 years (2014 est.)

Population growth rate: -0.68% (2014 est.)
country comparison to the world: 228

Birth rate: 10.29 births/1,000 population (2014 est.)
country comparison to the world: 187

Death rate: 13.69 deaths/1,000 population (2014 est.)
country comparison to the world: 13

Net migration rate: -3.37 migrant(s)/1,000 population (2014 est.)
country comparison to the world: 185

Urbanization: *urban population:* 69.5% of total population (2011)
rate of urbanization: 0.02% annual rate of change (2010-15 est.)

Major urban areas—population: TALLINN (capital) 399,000 (2009)

Sex ratio: *at birth:* 1.06 male(s)/female
0-14 years: 1.06 male(s)/female
15-24 years: 1.06 male(s)/female
25-54 years: 0.92 male(s)/female
55-64 years: 0.84 male(s)/female
65 years and over: 0.49 male(s)/female
total population: 0.84 male(s)/female (2014 est.)

Mother's mean age at first birth: 26.3 (2010 est.)

Maternal mortality rate: 2 deaths/100,000 live births (2010)
country comparison to the world: 184

Infant mortality rate: total: 6.7 deaths/1,000 live births
country comparison to the world: 164
male: 7.81 deaths/1,000 live births
female: 5.52 deaths/1,000 live births (2014 est.)

Life expectancy at birth: *total population:* 74.07 years
country comparison to the world: 118
male: 68.85 years
female: 79.61 years (2014 est.)

Total fertility rate: 1.46 children born/woman (2014 est.)
country comparison to the world: 196

Contraceptive prevalence rate: 63.4%
note: percent of women aged 18-49 (2005)

Health expenditures: 6% of GDP (2011)
country comparison to the world: 108

Physicians density: 3.34 physicians/1,000 population (2010)

Hospital bed density: 5.3 beds/1,000 population (2010)

Drinking water source:
improved:
urban: 99.5% of population
rural: 97.1% of population
total: 98.8% of population
unimproved:
urban: 0.5% of population
rural: 2.9% of population
total: 1.2% of population (2011 est.)

Sanitation facility access:
improved:
urban: 99.7% of population
rural: 93.7% of population
total: 97.9% of population
unimproved:
urban: 0.3% of population
rural: 6.3% of population
total: 2.1% of population (2011 est.)

HIV/AIDS—adult prevalence rate: 1.2% (2009 est.)
country comparison to the world: 38

HIV/AIDS—people living with HIV/AIDS: 9,900 (2009 est.)
country comparison to the world: 104

HIV/AIDS—deaths: fewer than 500 (2009 est.)
country comparison to the world: 94

Major infectious diseases:
degree of risk: intermediate
vectorborne disease: tickborne encephalitis (2013)

Obesity—adult prevalence rate: 20.6% (2008)
country comparison to the world: 95

Education expenditures: 5.7% of GDP (2010)
country comparison to the world: 52

Literacy: *definition:* age 15 and over can read and write
total population: 99.8%
male: 99.8%
female: 99.8% (2011 est.)

School life expectancy (primary to tertiary education): *total:* 17 years
male: 16 years
female: 18 years (2010)

Unemployment, youth ages 15-24: total: 20.9%
country comparison to the world: 56
male: 23.4%
female: 17.9% (2012)

GOVERNMENT

Country name:
conventional long form: Republic of Estonia
conventional short form: Estonia
local long form: Eesti Vabariik
local short form: Eesti
former: Estonian Soviet Socialist Republic

Government type: parliamentary republic

Capital: name: Tallinn
geographic coordinates: 59 26 N, 24 43 E
time difference: UTC+2 (7 hours ahead of Washington, DC during Standard Time)
daylight saving time: +1hr, begins last Sunday in March; ends last Sunday in October

Administrative divisions: 15 counties (maakonnad, singular—maakond); Harjumaa (Tallinn), Hiiumaa (Kardla), Ida-Virumaa (Johvi), Jarvamaa (Paide), Jogevamaa (Jogeva), Laanemaa (Haapsalu), Laane-Virumaa (Rakvere), Parnumaa (Parnu), Polvamaa (Polva), Raplamaa (Rapla), Saaremaa (Kuressaare), Tartumaa (Tartu), Valgamaa (Valga), Viljandimaa (Viljandi), Vorumaa (Voru)
note: counties have the administrative center name following in parentheses

Independence: 20 August 1991 (declared); 6 September 1991 (recognized by the Soviet Union)

National holiday: Independence Day, 24 February (1918); note—24 February 1918 was the date Estonia declared its independence from Soviet Russia and established its statehood; 20 August 1991 was the date it declared its independence from the Soviet Union

Constitution: several previous; latest adopted 28 June 1992; amended several times, last in 2012 (2012)

Legal system: civil law system

International law organization participation: accepts compulsory ICJ jurisdiction with reservations; accepts ICCt jurisdiction

Suffrage: 18 years of age; universal for all Estonian citizens

Executive branch: *chief of state:* President Toomas Hendrik ILVES (since 9 October 2006)
head of government: Taavi ROIVAS (since 26 March 2014)
cabinet: Ministers appointed by the prime minister, approved by Parliament (For more information visit the World Leaders website)
elections: president elected by Parliament for a five-year term (eligible for a second term); if a candidate does not secure two-thirds of the votes after three rounds of balloting in the Parliament, then an electoral assembly (made up of Parliament plus members of local councils) elects the president, choosing between the two candidates with the largest number of votes; election last held on 29 August 2011 (next to be held in the fall of 2016); prime minister nominated by the president and approved by Parliament
election results: Toomas Hendrik ILVES reelected president; parliamentary vote—Toomas Hendrik ILVES 73, Indrek TARAND 25

Legislative branch: unicameral Parliament or Riigikogu (101 seats; members elected by popular vote to serve four-year terms)
elections: last held on 6 March 2011 (next to be held in March 2015)
election results: percent of vote by party—Estonian Reform Party 28.6%, Center Party of Estonia 23.3%, IRL 20.5%, SDE 17.1%, Estonian Greens 3.8%, Estonian People's Union 2.1%, other 4.6%; seats by party—Estonian Reform Party 33, Center Party 21, IRL 23, SDE 19, unaffiliated 5

Judicial branch: *highest court(s):* Supreme Court (consists of the chief justice and organized into the Civil Chamber with a chamber chairman and 6 justices, the Criminal Chamber with a chamber chairman and 5 justices, the Administrative Law Chamber with a chamber chairman and 4 justices, and the Constitutional Review Chamber with 9 members—the chief justice and 2 justices from the Civil Chamber, 3 from the Criminal Chamber and 3 from the Administrative chamber)
judge selection and term of office: the chief justice is proposed by the president and appointed by the Riigikogu; other justices proposed by the chief justice and appointed by the Riigikogu; justices appointed for life

subordinate courts: circuit (appellate) courts; administrative, county, city, and specialized courts

Political parties and leaders: Center Party of Estonia (Keskerakond) [Edgar SAVISAAR]; Estonian Greens (Rohelised) [Aleksander LAANE]; Estonian Conservative People's Party (Konservatiivne Rahvaerakond) or EKRE [Mart HELME]; Estonian Reform Party (Reformierakond) [Taavi ROIVAS]; Social Democratic Party or SDE [Sven MIKSER]; Union of Pro Patria and Res Publica (Isamaa je Res Publica Liit) or IRL [Urmas REINSALU]

International organization participation: Australia Group, BA, BIS, CBSS, CD, CE, EAPC, EBRD, ECB, EIB, EMU, ESA (cooperating state), EU, FAO, IAEA, IBRD, ICAO, ICC (national committees), ICRM, IDA, IEA, IFC, IFRCS, IHO, ILO, IMF, IMO, Interpol, IOC, IOM, IPU, ISO, ITSO, ITU, ITUC (NGOs), MIGA, MINUSMA, NATO, NIB, NSG, OAS (observer), OECD, OIF (observer), OPCW, OSCE, PCA, Schengen Convention, UN, UNCTAD, UNESCO, UNHCR, UNTSO, UPU, WCO, WHO, WIPO, WMO, WTO

Diplomatic representation in the US: *chief of mission:* Ambassador Marina KALJURAND (since 6 September 2011)
chancery: 2131 Massachusetts Avenue NW, Washington, DC 20008
telephone: [1] (202) 588-0101
FAX: [1] (202) 588-0108
consulate(s) general: New York

Diplomatic representation from the US: chief of mission: Ambassador Jeffrey D. LEVINE (since 24 July 2012)
embassy: Kentmanni 20, 15099 Tallinn
mailing address: use embassy street address
telephone: [372] 668-8100
FAX: [372] 668-8134

Flag description: three equal horizontal bands of blue (top), black, and white; various interpretations are linked to the flag colors; blue represents faith, loyalty, and devotion, while also reminiscent of the sky, sea, and lakes of the country; black symbolizes the soil of the country and the dark past and suffering endured by the Estonian people; white refers to the striving towards enlightenment and virtue, and is the color of birch bark and snow, as well as summer nights illuminated by the midnight sun

National symbol(s): barn swallow, cornflower

National anthem: *name:* "Mu isamaa, mu onn ja room" (My Native Land, My Pride and Joy)
lyrics/music: Johann Voldemar JANNSEN/Fredrik PACIUS
note: adopted 1920, though banned between 1940 and 1990 under Soviet occupation; the anthem, used in Estonia since 1869, shares the same melody with that of Finland but has different lyrics

ECONOMY

Economy—overview: Estonia, a member of the European Union and the eurozone since 2004, has a modern market-based economy and one of the higher per capita income levels in Central Europe and the Baltic region. Estonia's successive governments have pursued a free market, pro-business economic agenda and have wavered little in their commitment to pro-market reforms. The current government has followed sound fiscal policies that have resulted in balanced budgets and low public debt. The economy benefits from strong electronics and telecommunications sectors and strong trade ties with Finland, Sweden, Russia, and Germany. Estonia's economy fell into recession in mid-2008, as a result of an investment and consumption slump following the bursting of the real estate market bubble and a decrease in export demand as result of economic slowdown in the rest of Europe, but the economy has recovered strongly in the last five years. Growth was expected to top 2% in 2014, before the events in Ukraine. Estonia adopted the euro on 1 January 2011.

GDP (purchasing power parity): $29.94 billion (2013 est.)
country comparison to the world: 114
$29.49 billion (2012 est.)
$28.37 billion (2011 est.)
note: data are in 2013 US dollars

GDP (official exchange rate): $24.28 billion (2013 est.)

GDP—real growth rate: 1.5% (2013 est.)
country comparison to the world: 158
3.9% (2012 est.)
9.6% (2011 est.)

GDP—per capita (PPP): $22,400 (2013 est.)
country comparison to the world: 66
$22,000 (2012 est.)
$21,200 (2011 est.)
note: data are in 2013 US dollars

Gross national saving: 23.9% of GDP (2013 est.)
country comparison to the world: 56
26.4% of GDP (2012 est.)
26.9% of GDP (2011 est.)

GDP—composition, by end use:
household consumption: 50.6%
government consumption: 19%
investment in fixed capital: 24.5%
investment in inventories: 0.9%
exports of goods and services: 90.4%
imports of goods and services: -90.3% (2013 est.)

GDP—composition, by sector of origin:
agriculture: 3.9%
industry: 30%
services: 66.2% (2013 est.)

Agriculture—products: grain, potatoes, vegetables; livestock and dairy products; fish

Industries: engineering, electronics, wood and wood products, textiles; information technology, telecommunications

Industrial production growth rate: 3% (2013 est.)
country comparison to the world: 104

Labor force: 692,900 (2013 est.)
country comparison to the world: 152

Labor force—by occupation:
agriculture: 4.2%
industry: 20.2%
services: 75.6% (2010)

Unemployment rate: 10.9% (2013 est.)
country comparison to the world: 114
10.2% (2012 est.)

Population below poverty line: 17.5% (2010)

Household income or consumption by percentage share: *lowest* 10%: 2.7%
highest 10%: 27.7% (2004)

Distribution of family income—Gini index: 31.3 (2010)
country comparison to the world: 111
37 (1999)

Budget: *revenues:* $8.489 billion
expenditures: $8.615 billion (2013 est.)

Taxes and other revenues: 35% of GDP (2013 est.)
country comparison to the world: 67

Budget surplus (+) or deficit (-):
-0.5% of GDP (2013 est.)
country comparison to the world: 57

Public debt: 6% of GDP (2013 est.)
country comparison to the world: 156
5.8% of GDP (2012 est.)
note: data cover general government debt, and includes debt instruments issued (or owned) by government entities, including sub-sectors of central government, state government, local government, and social security funds

Fiscal year: calendar year

Inflation rate (consumer prices): 3.4% (2013 est.)
country comparison to the world: 120
3.9% (2012 est.)

Commercial bank prime lending rate:
5.5% (31 December 2013 est.)
country comparison to the world: 141
5.75% (31 December 2012 est.)

Stock of narrow money: $9.994 billion (31 December 2013 est.)
country comparison to the world: 78
$8.191 billion (31 December 2012 est.)
note: this figure represents the US dollar value of Estonian kroon in circulation prior to Estonia's joining the Economic and Monetary Union (EMU); see entry for the European Union for money supply in the euro area; the European Central Bank (ECB) controls monetary policy for the 17 members of the EMU; individual members of the EMU do not control the quantity of money circulating within their own borders

Stock of broad money: $13.64 billion (31 December 2013 est.)
country comparison to the world: 92
$12.71 billion (31 December 2012 est.)

Stock of domestic credit: $19.16 billion (31 December 2013 est.)
country comparison to the world: 84
$19.24 billion (31 December 2012 est.)

Market value of publicly traded shares:
$2.332 billion (31 December 2012 est.)
country comparison to the world: 99
$1.611 billion (31 December 2011)
$2.26 billion (31 December 2010 est.)

Current account balance: -$352.3 million (2013 est.)
country comparison to the world: 93
-$267.7 million (2012 est.)

Exports: $15.11 billion (2013 est.)
country comparison to the world: 79
$14.46 billion (2012 est.)

Exports—commodities: machinery and electrical equipment 21%, wood and wood products 9%, metals 9%, furniture 7%, vehicles and parts 5%, food products and beverages 4%, textiles 4%, plastics 3%

Exports—partners: Sweden 16.8%, Finland 15.3%, Russia 12.7%, Latvia 9.2%, Lithuania 5.7%, Germany 4.8% (2012)

Imports: $16.38 billion (2013 est.)
country comparison to the world: 85
$15.6 billion (2012 est.)

Imports—commodities: machinery and electrical equipment, mineral fuels, chemical products, foodstuffs, plastics, textiles

Imports—partners: Finland 15.1%, Germany 10.7%, Sweden 10.7%, Latvia 10%, Lithuania 9%, Poland 6.6%, China 4.4%, Russia 4.1% (2012)

Reserves of foreign exchange and gold:
$372.3 million (31 December 2013 est.)
country comparison to the world: 151
$300.7 million (31 December 2012 est.)

Debt—external: $26.74 billion (31 December 2013 est.)
country comparison to the world: 76
$25.69 billion (31 December 2012 est.)

Stock of direct foreign investment—at home: $21.73 billion (31 December 2013 est.)
country comparison to the world: 69
$20.87 billion (31 December 2012 est.)

Stock of direct foreign investment—abroad: $7.34 billion (31 December 2013 est.)
country comparison to the world: 60
$7.84 billion (31 December 2012 est.)

Exchange rates: kroon (EEK) per US dollar—
0.7697 (2013 est.)
0.7778 (2012 est.)
11.81 (2010 est.)
11.23 (2009)
10.7 (2008)

ENERGY

Electricity—production: 12.19 billion kWh (2011 est.)
country comparison to the world: 9 1

Electricity—consumption: 7.948 billion kWh (2010 est.)
country comparison to the world: 96

Electricity—exports: 4.95 billion kWh (2012 est.)
country comparison to the world: 29

Electricity—imports: 2.71 billion kWh (2012 est.)
country comparison to the world: 48

Electricity—installed generating capacity: 2.751 million kW (2010 est.)
country comparison to the world: 90

Electricity—from fossil fuels: 93.4% of total installed capacity (2010 est.)
country comparison to the world: 71

Electricity—from nuclear fuels: 0% of total installed capacity (2010 est.)
country comparison to the world: 83

Electricity—from hydroelectric plants: 0.2% of total installed capacity (2010 est.)
country comparison to the world: 148

Electricity—from other renewable sources: 6.4% of total installed capacity (2010 est.)
country comparison to the world: 37

Crude oil—production: 11,000 bbl/day (2012 est.)
country comparison to the world: 88

Crude oil—exports: 7,624 bbl/day (2010 est.)
country comparison to the world: 60

Crude oil—imports: 0 bbl/day (2010 est.)
country comparison to the world: 181

Crude oil—proved reserves: 0 bbl (1 January 2013 es)
country comparison to the world: 127

Refined petroleum products—production: 0 bbl/day (2010 est.)
country comparison to the world: 139

Refined petroleum products—consumption: 26,340 bbl/day (2011 est.)
country comparison to the world: 120

Refined petroleum products—exports: 0 bbl/day (2010 est.)
country comparison to the world: 172

Refined petroleum products—imports: 22,670 bbl/day (2010 est.)
country comparison to the world: 101

Natural gas—production: 0 cu m (2012 est.)
country comparison to the world: 125

Natural gas—consumption: 701 million cu m (2010 est.)
country comparison to the world: 96

Natural gas—exports: 0 cu m (2012 est.)
country comparison to the world: 94

Natural gas—imports: 670 million cu m (2012 est.)
country comparison to the world: 65

Natural gas—proved reserves: 0 cu m (1 January 2013 es)
country comparison to the world: 133

Carbon dioxide emissions from consumption of energy: 20.26 million Mt (2011 est.)
country comparison to the world: 85

COMMUNICATIONS

Telephones—main lines in use: 448,200 (2012)
country comparison to the world: 9 9

Telephones—mobile cellular: 2.07 million (2012)
country comparison to the world: 145

Telephone system: *general assessment:* foreign investment in the form of joint business ventures greatly improved telephone service with a wide range of high quality voice, data, and Internet services available
domestic: substantial fiber-optic cable systems carry telephone, TV, and radio traffic in the digital mode; Internet services are widely available; schools and libraries are connected to the Internet, a large percentage of the population files income-tax returns online, and online voting was used for the first time in the 2005 local elections
international: country code—372; fiber-optic cables to Finland, Sweden, Latvia, and Russia provide worldwide packet-switched service; 2 international switches are located in Tallinn (2011)

Broadcast media: the publicly owned broadcaster, Eesti Rahvusringhaaling (ERR), operates 2 TV channels and 5 radio networks; growing number of private commercial radio stations broadcasting nationally, regionally, and locally; fully transitioned to digital television in 2010; national private TV channels expanding service; a range of channels are aimed at Russian-speaking viewers; high penetration rate for cable TV services with *more than half of Estonian households connected (2008)*

Internet country code: .ee

Internet hosts: 865,494 (2012)
country comparison to the world: 49

Internet users: 971,700 (2009)
country comparison to the world: 102

TRANSPORTATION

Airports: 18 (2013)
country comparison to the world: 141

Airports—with paved runways: *total:* 1 3
over 3,047 m: 2
2,438 to 3,047 m: 8
1,524 to 2,437 m: 2
914 to 1,523 m: 1 (2013)

Airports—with unpaved runways: *total:* 5
1,524 to 2,437 m: 1
914 to 1,523 m: 1
under 914 m: 3 (2013)

Heliports: 1 (2012)

Pipelines: gas 868 km (2013)

Railways: *total:* 1,196 km
country comparison to the world: 85
broad gauge: 1,196 km 1.520-m and 1.524-m gauge (133 km electrified) (2011)

Roadways: *total:* 58,412 km (includes urban roads)
country comparison to the world: 73
paved: 10,427 km (includes 115 km of expressways)
unpaved: 47,985 km (2011)

Waterways: 335 km (320 km are navigable year round) (2011)
country comparison to the world: 91

Merchant marine: *total:* 2 5
country comparison to the world: 89
by type: cargo 4, chemical tanker 1, passenger/cargo 18, petroleum tanker 2
foreign-owned: 3 (Germany 1, Norway 2)
registered in other countries: 63 (Antigua and Barbuda 10, Belize 1, Cambodia 1, Canada 1, Cook Islands 1, Cyprus 6, Dominica 6, Finland 2, Latvia 3, Malta 16, Russia 1, Saint Vincent and the Grenadines 8, Sierra Leone 2, Sweden 3, Venezuela 1, unknown 1) (2010)

Ports and terminals: *major seaport(s):* Kuivastu, Kunda, Muuga, Parnu Reid, Sillamae, Tallinn

MILITARY

Military branches: Estonian Defense Forces (Eesti Kaitsevagi): Land Force (Maavagi), Navy (Merevagi), Air Force (Ohuvagi), Defense League (Kaitseliit) (2012)

Military service age and obligation: 18-27 for compulsory military or governmental service, conscript service requirement 8-11 months depending on education; NCOs, reserve officers, and specialists serve 11 months (2013)

Manpower available for military service:
males age 16-49: 291,801
females age 16-49: 302,696 (2010 est.)

Manpower fit for military service:
males age 16-49: 210,854
females age 16-49: 251,185 (2010 est.)

Manpower reaching militarily significant age annually: *male:* 6,668
female: 6,309 (2010 est.)

Military expenditures: 2% of GDP (2013)
country comparison to the world: 40
1.92% of GDP (2012)
1.69% of GDP (2011)
1.92% of GDP (2010)

TRANSNATIONAL ISSUES

Disputes—international: Russia and Estonia in May 2005 signed a technical border agreement, but Russia in June 2005 recalled its signature after the Estonian parliament added to its domestic ratification act a historical preamble referencing the Soviet occupation and Estonia's pre-war borders under the 1920 Treaty of Tartu; Russia contends that the preamble allows Estonia to make territorial claims on Russia in the future, while Estonian officials deny that the preamble has any legal impact on the treaty text; Russia demands better treatment of the Russian-speaking population in Estonia; as a member state that forms part of the EU's external border, Estonia implements strict Schengen border rules with Russia

Refugees and internally displaced persons: *stateless persons:* 94,235 (2012); note—following independence in 1991, automatic citizenship was restricted to those who were Estonian citizens prior to the 1940 Soviet occupation and their descendants; thousands of ethnic Russians remained stateless when forced to choose between passing Estonian language and citizenship tests or applying for Russian citizenship; one reason for demurring on Estonian citizenship was to retain the right of visa-free travel to Russia; stateless residents can vote in local elections but not general elections; stateless parents who have been lawful residents of Estonia for at least five years can apply for citizenship for their children before they turn 15

Illicit drugs: growing producer of synthetic drugs; increasingly important transshipment zone for cannabis, cocaine, opiates, and synthetic drugs since joining the European Union and the Schengen Accord; potential money laundering related to organized crime and drug trafficking is a concern, as is possible use of the gambling sector to launder funds; major use of opiates and ecstasy

ETHIOPIA

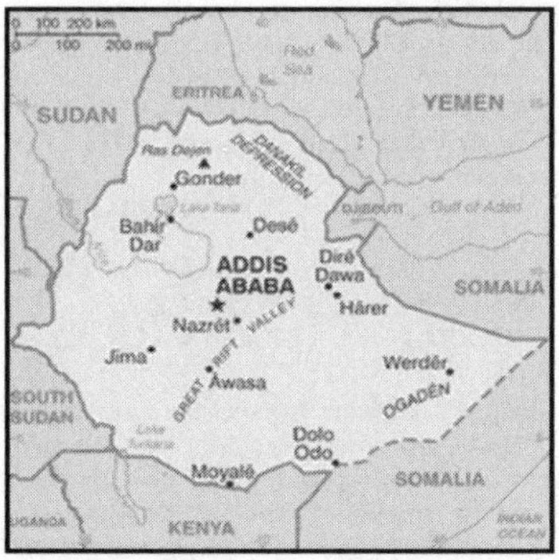

INTRODUCTION

Background: Unique among African countries, the ancient Ethiopian monarchy maintained its freedom from colonial rule with the exception of a short-lived Italian occupation from 1936-41. In 1974, a military junta, the Derg, deposed Emperor Haile SELASSIE (who had ruled since 1930) and established a socialist state. Torn by bloody coups, uprisings, wide-scale drought, and massive refugee problems, the regime was finally toppled in 1991 by a coalition of rebel forces, the Ethiopian People's Revolutionary Democratic Front (EPRDF). A constitution was adopted in 1994, and Ethiopia's first multiparty elections were held in 1995. A border war with Eritrea late in the 1990s ended with a peace treaty in December 2000. In November 2007, the Eritrea-Ethiopia Border Commission (EEBC) issued specific coordinates as virtually demarcating the border and pronounced its work finished. Alleging that the EEBC acted beyond its mandate in issuing the coordinates, Ethiopia has not accepted them and has not withdrawn troops from previously contested areas pronounced by the EEBC as belonging to Eritrea. In August 2012, longtime leader Prime Minister MELES Zenawi died in office and was replaced by his Deputy Prime Minister HAILEMARIAM Desalegn, marking the first peaceful transition of power in decades.

GEOGRAPHY

Location: Eastern Africa, west of Somalia

Geographic coordinates: 8 00 N, 38 00 E

Map references: Africa

Area: *total:* 1,104,300 sq km
country comparison to the world: 27
land: 1 million sq km
water: 104,300 sq km

Area—comparative: slightly less than twice the size of Texas

Land boundaries: *total:* 5,328 km
border countries: Djibouti 349 km, Eritrea 912 km, Kenya 861 km, Somalia 1,600 km, South Sudan 837 km, Sudan 769 km

Coastline: 0 km (landlocked)

Maritime claims: none (landlocked)

Climate: tropical monsoon with wide topographic-induced variation

Terrain: high plateau with central mountain range divided by Great Rift Valley

Elevation extremes:
lowest point: Danakil Depression -125 m
highest point: Ras Dejen 4,533 m

Natural resources: small reserves of gold, platinum, copper, potash, natural gas, hydropower

Land use: *arable land:* 13.19%
permanent crops: 1.01%
other: 85.8% (2011)

Irrigated land: 2,896 sq km (2003)

Total renewable water resources: 122 cu km (2011)

Freshwater withdrawal (domestic/industrial/agricultural):
total: 5.56 cu km/yr (13%/1%/86%)
per capita: 80.5 cu m/yr (2005)

Natural hazards: geologically active Great Rift Valley susceptible to earthquakes, volcanic eruptions; frequent droughts volcanism: volcanic activity in the Great Rift Valley; Erta Ale (elev. 613 m), which has caused frequent lava flows in recent years, is the country's most active volcano; Dabbahu became active in 2005, causing evacuations; other historically active volcanoes include Alayta, Dalaffilla, Dallol, Dama Ali, Fentale, Kone, Manda Hararo, and Manda-Inakir

Environment—current issues: deforestation; overgrazing; soil erosion; desertification; water shortages in some areas from water-intensive farming and poor management

Environment—international agreements:
party to: Biodiversity, Climate Change, Climate Change-Kyoto Protocol, Desertification, Endangered Species, Hazardous Wastes, Ozone Layer Protection signed, but not ratified: Environmental Modification, Law of the Sea

Geography—note: landlocked—entire coastline along the Red Sea was lost with the de jure independence of Eritrea on 24 May 1993; Ethiopia is, therefore, the most populous landlocked country in the world; the Blue Nile, the chief headstream of the Nile by water volume, rises in T'ana Hayk (Lake Tana) in northwest Ethiopia; three major crops are believed to have originated in Ethiopia: coffee, grain sorghum, and castor bean

PEOPLE AND SOCIETY

Nationality: *noun:* Ethiopian(s)
adjective: Ethiopian

Ethnic groups: Oromo 34.5%, Amhara (Amara) 26.9%, Somali (Somalie) 6.2%, Tigray (Tigrigna) 6.1%, Sidama 4%, Gurage 2.5%, Welaita 2.3%, Hadiya 1.7%, Afar (Affar) 1.7%, Gamo 1.5%, Gedeo 1.3%, other 11.3% (2007 Census)

Languages: Oromo (official working language in the State of Oromiya) 33.8%, Amharic (official national language) 29.3%, Somali (official working language of the State of Sumale) 6.2%, Tigrayan (official working language of the State of Tigray) 5.9%, Sidamo 4%, Wolaytta 2.2%, Guragiegna 2%, Afar (official working language of the State of Afar) 1.7%, Hadiyya 1.7%, Gamo 1.5%, other 11.7%, English (major foreign language taught in schools), Arabic (2007 census)

Religions: Ethiopian Orthodox 43.5%, Muslim 33.9%, Protestant 18.6%, traditional 2.6%, Catholic 0.7%, other 0.7% (2007 Census)

Population: 96,633,458 (July 2014 est.)
country comparison to the world: 14
note: estimates for this country explicitly take into account the effects of excess mortality due to AIDS; this can result in lower life expectancy, higher infant mortality, higher death rates, lower population growth rates, and changes in the distribution of population by age and sex than would otherwise be expected
Age structure: 0-14 years: 44.2% (male 21,376,243/female 21,308,454)
15-24 years: 19.9% (male 9,557,462/female 9,692,275)
25-54 years: 29.2% (male 14,023,218/female 14,176,263)
55-64 years: 2.8% (male 1,826,602/female 1,919,212)
65 years and over: 2.8% (male 1,242,171/female 1,511,558) (2014 est.)

Dependency ratios:
total dependency ratio: 85.5 %
youth dependency ratio: 79.2 %
elderly dependency ratio: 6.3 %
potential support ratio: 15.8 (2013)

Median age: total: 17.6 years
male: 17.4 years
female: 17.7 years (2014 est.)

Population growth rate: 2.89% (2014 est.)
country comparison to the world: 14

Birth rate: 37.66 births/1,000 population (2014 est.)
country comparison to the world: 14

Death rate: 8.52 deaths/1,000 population (2014 est.)
country comparison to the world: 78

Net migration rate: -0.23 migrant(s)/1,000 population
country comparison to the world: 122
note: repatriation of Ethiopian refugees residing in Sudan is expected to continue for several years; some Sudanese, Somali, and Eritrean refugees, who fled to Ethiopia from the fighting or famine in their own countries, continue to return to their homes (2014 est.)
Urbanization: urban population: 17% of total population (2011)
rate of urbanization: 3.57% annual rate of change (2010-15 est.)

Major urban areas—population: ADDIS ABABA (capital) 2.863 million (2009)
Sex ratio: at birth: 1.03 male(s)/female
0-14 years: 1 male(s)/female
15-24 years: 0.99 male(s)/female
25-54 years: 0.99 male(s)/female
55-64 years: 0.99 male(s)/female
65 years and over: 0.83 male(s)/female
total population: 0.99 male(s)/female (2014 est.)

Mother's mean age at first birth: 19.6
note: median age at first birth among women 25-29 (2011 est.)

Maternal mortality rate: 350 deaths/100,000 live births (2010)
country comparison to the world: 33

Infant mortality rate: total: 55.77 deaths/1,000 live births
country comparison to the world: 29
male: 63.77 deaths/1,000 live births
female: 47.53 deaths/1,000 live births (2014 est.)

Life expectancy at birth: *total population:* 60.75 years
country comparison to the world: 193
male: 58.43 years
female: 63.15 years (2014 est.)

Total fertility rate: 5.23 children born/woman (2014 est.)
country comparison to the world: 14

Contraceptive prevalence rate: 28.6% (2010/11)

Health expenditures: 4.7% of GDP (2011)
country comparison to the world: 148

Physicians density: 0.03 physicians/1,000 population (2009)

Hospital bed density: 6.3 beds/1,000 population (2011)

Drinking water source:
improved:
urban: 96.6% of population
rural: 39.3% of population
total: 49% of population
unimproved:
urban: 3.4% of population
rural: 60.7% of population
total: 51% of population (2011 est.)

Sanitation facility access:
improved:
urban: 27.3% of population
rural: 19.4% of population
total: 20.7% of population
unimproved:
urban: 72.7% of population
rural: 80.6% of population
total: 79.3% of population (2011 est.)

HIV/AIDS—adult prevalence rate:
1.3% (2012 est.)
country comparison to the world: 34

HIV/AIDS—people living with HIV/AIDS:
758,600 (2012 est.)
country comparison to the world: 14

HIV/AIDS—deaths: 47,200 (2012 est.)
country comparison to the world: 8

Major infectious diseases: *degree of risk:* very high
food or waterborne diseases: bacterial and protozoal diarrhea, hepatitis A, and typhoid fever
vectorborne diseases: malaria and dengue fever
respiratory disease: meningococcal meningitis
animal contact disease: rabies
water contact disease: schistosomiasis (2013)

Obesity—adult prevalence rate: 1.1% (2008)
country comparison to the world: 191

Children under the age of 5 years underweight:
29.2% (2011)
country comparison to the world: 17

Education expenditures: 4.7% of GDP (2010)
country comparison to the world: 85

Literacy: *definition:* age 15 and over can read and write
total population: 39%
male: 49.1%
female: 28.9% (2007 est.)

School life expectancy (primary to tertiary education): *total:* 7 years
male: 8 years
female: 6 years (2005)

Child labor—children ages 5-14:
total number: 10,693,164
percentage: 53 % (2005 est.)

Unemployment, youth ages 15-24: *total:* 24.9%
country comparison to the world: 40
male: 19.5%
female: 29.4% (2006)

GOVERNMENT

Country name: *conventional long form:* Federal Democratic Republic of Ethiopia
conventional short form: Ethiopia
local long form: Ityop'iya Federalawi Demokrasiyawi Ripeblik
local short form: Ityop'iya
former: Abyssinia, Italian East Africa
abbreviation: FDRE

Government type: federal republic

Capital: *name:* Addis Ababa
geographic coordinates: 9 02 N, 38 42 E
time difference: UTC+3 (8 hours ahead of Washington, DC during Standard Time)

Administrative divisions: 9 ethnically based states (kililoch, singular—kilil) and 2 self-governing administrations* (astedaderoch, singular—astedader); Adis Abeba* (Addis Ababa), Afar, Amara (Amhara), Binshangul Gumuz, Dire Dawa*, Gambela Hizboch (Gambela Peoples), Hareri Hizb (Harari People), Oromiya (Oromia), Sumale (Somali), Tigray, Ye Debub Biheroch Bihereseboch na Hizboch (Southern Nations, Nationalities, and Peoples)

Independence: oldest independent country in Africa and one of the oldest in the world—at least 2,000 years (may be traced to the Aksumite Kingdom, which coalesced in the first century B.C.)

National holiday: National Day (defeat of MENGISTU regime), 28 May (1991)

Constitution: several previous; latest drafted June 1994, adopted 8 December 1994, entered into force 21 August 1995 (2013)

Legal system: civil law system

International law organization participation:
has not submitted an ICJ jurisdiction declaration; non-party state to the ICCt

Suffrage: 18 years of age; universal

Executive branch: *chief of state:* President MULATU Teshome Wirtu (since 7 October 2013)
head of government: Prime Minister HAILEMARIAM Desalegn (since 21 September 2012); Deputy Prime Ministers ASTER Mamo, DEBRETSION Gebre-Michael, DEMEKE Mekonnen Hassen; note—prior to his approval as prime minister, HAILEMARIAM had been acting prime minister due to the death of former Prime Minister MELES
cabinet: Council of Ministers—ministers selected by the prime minister and approved by the House of People's Representatives (For more information visit the World Leaders website)
elections: president elected by both chambers of Parliament for a six-year term (eligible for a second term); election last held on 7 October 2013 (next to be held in October 2019); prime minister designated by the party in power following legislative elections
election results: MULATU Teshome Wirtu elected president by acclamation

Legislative branch: bicameral Parliament consists of the House of Federation (or upper chamber responsible for interpreting the constitution and federal-regional issues) (108 seats; members chosen by state assemblies to serve five-year terms) and the House of People's Representatives (or lower chamber responsible for passing legislation) (547 seats; members directly elected by popular vote from single-member districts to serve five-year terms)
elections: last held on 23 May 2010 (next to be held in 2015)
election results: percent of vote—NA; seats by party—EPRDF 499, SPDP 24, BGPDP 9, ANDP 8, GPUDM 3, HNL 1, FORUM 1, APDO 1, independent 1

Judicial branch: *highest court(s):* Federal Supreme Court or Supreme Imperial Court (consists of 11 judges) note—the Federal Supreme Court has jurisdiction for all constitutional issues
judge selection and term of office: president and vice president of Federal Supreme Court nominated by the prime minister and appointed by the House of People's Representatives; other Supreme Court judges nominated by the Federal Judicial Administrative Council and appointed by the House of People's Representatives; judges serve until retirement at age 60
subordinate courts: federal high courts and federal courts of first instance; state court systems (mirror structure of federal system); sharia courts and customary and traditional courts

Political parties and leaders: Afar National Democratic Party or ANDP [Mohammed KEDIR]; All Ethiopian Unity Organization or AEUO [Hailu SHAWEL]; Arena Tigray [GEBRU Asrat]; Argoba People's Democratic Organization or APDO [Abdulkader MOHAMMED]; Benishangul Gumuz People's Democratic Party or BGPDP [Mulualem BESSE]; Coalition for Unity and Democratic Party or CUDP [AYELE Chamiso]; Ethiopian Democratic Party or EDP [MUSHE Semu]; Ethiopian Federal Democratic Forum or FORUM (a UDJ-led 6-party alliance established for the 2010 parliamentary; elections) [Dr. Moga FRISSA]; Ethiopian People's Revolutionary Democratic Front or EPRDF (including the following organizations: Amhara National; Democratic Movement or ANDM; Oromo People's Democratic Organization or OPDO; Southern Ethiopian People's; Democratic Movement or SEPDM; and Tigray People's Liberation Front or TPLF); Gambella Peoples Unity Democratic Movement or GPUDM; Gurage Peoples Democratic Front [GIRMA Bogale]; Harari National League or HNL [YASIN Husein]; Oromo Federalist Democratic Movement or OFDM; Oromo People's Congress or OPC [IMERERA Gudina]; Somali Democratic Alliance Forces or SODAF [BUH Hussien]; Somali People's Democratic Party or SPDP [Abdulfetah Sheck ABDULAHI]; South Ethiopian People's Democratic Union or SEPDU [TILAHUN Endeshaw]; United Ethiopian Democratic Forces or UEDF [BEYENE Petros]; Unity for Democracy and Justice or UDJ [Dr. NEGASSO Gidada]

Political pressure groups and leaders: Ethiopian People's Patriotic Front or EPPF; Ogaden National Liberation Front or ONLF; Oromo Liberation Front or OLF [DAOUD Ibsa]

International organization participation: ACP, AfDB, AU, COMESA, FAO, G-24, G-77, IAEA, IBRD, ICAO, ICRM, IDA, IFAD, IFC, IFRCS, IGAD, ILO, IMF, IMO, Interpol, IOC, IOM, IPU, ISO, ITSO, ITU, ITUC (NGOs), MIGA, NAM, OPCW, PCA, UN, UNAMID, UNCTAD, UNESCO, UNHCR, UNIDO, UNISFA, UNMIL, UNOCI, UNWTO, UPU, WCO, WFTU (NGOs), WHO, WIPO, WMO, WTO (observer)

Diplomatic representation in the US: *chief of mission:* Ambassador GIRMA Birru (since 6 January 2011)
chancery: 3506 International Drive NW, Washington, DC 20008
telephone: [1] (202) 364-1200
FAX: [1] (202) 587-0195
consulate(s) general: Los Angeles
consulate(s): New York

Diplomatic representation from the US:
chief of mission: Ambassador Patricia Marie HASLACH (since 14 August 2013)
embassy: Entoto Street, Addis Ababa
mailing address: P. O. Box 1014, Addis Ababa
telephone: 130-6000
FAX: 124-2401

Flag description: three equal horizontal bands of green (top), yellow, and red, with a yellow pentagram and single yellow rays emanating from the angles between the points on a light blue disk centered on the three bands; green represents hope and the fertility of the land, yellow symbolizes justice and harmony, while red stands for sacrifice and heroism in the defense of the land; the blue of the disk symbolizes peace and the pentagram represents the unity and equality of the nationalities and peoples of Ethiopia
note: Ethiopia is the oldest independent country in Africa, and the three main colors of her flag (adopted ca. 1895) were so often adopted by other African countries upon independence that they became known as the Pan-African colors; the emblem in the center of the current flag was added in 1996

National symbol(s): Abyssinian lion

National anthem: *name:* "Whedefit Gesgeshi Woud Enat Ethiopia" (March Forward, Dear Mother Ethiopia)
lyrics/music: DEREJE Melaku Mengesha/SOLOMON Lulu
note: adopted 1992

ECONOMY

overview: Ethiopia's economy is based on agriculture but the government is pushing to diversify into manufacturing, textiles, and energy generation.. Coffee is a major export crop. The agricultural sector suffers from poor cultivation practices and frequent drought, but recent joint efforts by the Government of Ethiopia and donors have strengthened Ethiopia's agricultural resilience, contributing to a reduction in the number of Ethiopians threatened with starvation. The banking, insurance, telecommunications, and micro-credit industries are restricted to domestic investors, but Ethiopia has attracted significant foreign investment in textiles, leather, commercial agriculture and manufacturing. Under Ethiopia's constitution, the state owns all land and provides long-term leases to the tenants; land use certificates are now being issued in some areas so that tenants have more recognizable rights to continued occupancy and hence make more concerted efforts to improve their leaseholds. While GDP growth has remained high, per capita income is among the lowest in the world. Ethiopia's economy continues on its state-led Growth and Transformation Plan under the new collective leadership that followed Prime Minister MELES's death. The five-year economic plan has achieved high single-digit growth rates through government-led infrastructure expansion and commercial agriculture development. Ethiopia in 2014 will continue construction of its Grand Renaissance Dam on the Nile – a controversial five billion dollar effort to develop electricity for domestic consumption and export.

GDP (purchasing power parity): $118.2 billion (2013 est.)
country comparison to the world: 69
$110.4 billion (2012 est.)
$101.8 billion (2011 est.)
note: data are in 2013 US dollars

GDP (official exchange rate): $47.34 billion (2013 est.)

GDP—real growth rate: 7% (2013 est.)
country comparison to the world: 24
8.5% (2012 est.)
11.4% (2011 est.)

GDP—per capita (PPP): $1,300 (2013 est.)
country comparison to the world: 211
$1,300 (2012 est.)
$1,200 (2011 est.)
note: data are in 2013 US dollars

Gross national saving: 18.8% of GDP (2013 est.)
country comparison to the world: 84
18.2% of GDP (2012 est.)
22.9% of GDP (2011 est.)

GDP—composition, by end use:
household consumption: 83.1%
government consumption: 8.6%
investment in fixed capital: 26.1%
investment in inventories: 0%
exports of goods and services: 11.5%
imports of goods and services: -29.3% (2013 est.)

GDP—composition, by sector of origin:
agriculture: 47%
industry: 10.8%
services: 42.2% (2013 est.)

Agriculture—products: cereals, pulses, coffee, oilseed, cotton, sugarcane, potatoes, khat, cut flowers; hides, cattle, sheep, goats; fish

Industries: food processing, beverages, textiles, leather, chemicals, metals processing, cement

Industrial production growth rate: 9% (2013 est.)
country comparison to the world: 21

Labor force: 45.65 million (2013 est.)
country comparison to the world: 14

Labor force—by occupation: *agriculture:* 85%
industry: 5%
services: 10% (2009 est.)

Unemployment rate: 17.5% (2012 est.)
country comparison to the world: 155
18% (2011 est.)

Population below poverty line: 39% (2012 est.)

Household income or consumption by percentage share: *lowest 10%:* 4.1%
highest 10%: 25.6% (2005)

Distribution of family income—Gini index:
33 (2011)
country comparison to the world: 101
30 (2000)

Budget: *revenues:* $6.702 billion
expenditures: $8.042 billion (2013 est.)

Taxes and other revenues: 14.2% of GDP (2013 est.)
country comparison to the world: 196

Budget surplus (+) or deficit (-):
-2.8% of GDP (2013 est.)
country comparison to the world: 115

Public debt: 50.4% of GDP (2013 est.)
country comparison to the world: 67
39.7% of GDP (2012 est.)
note: official data cover central government debt, including debt instruments issued (or owned) by government entities other than the treasury and treasury debt owned by foreign entities; the data exclude debt issued by subnational entities, as well as intragovernmental debt; debt instruments for the social funds are not sold at public auctions

Fiscal year: 8 July–7 July

Inflation rate (consumer prices): 8.4% (2013 est.)
country comparison to the world: 197
22.9% (2012 est.)

Central bank discount rate: NA%

Commercial bank prime lending rate:
12% (31 December 2013 est.)
country comparison to the world: 45
14.5% (31 December 2012 est.)

Stock of narrow money: $9.006 billion (31 December 2013 est.)
country comparison to the world: 82
$9.107 billion (31 December 2012 est.)

Stock of broad money: $15.43 billion (31 December 2013 est.)
country comparison to the world: 89
$15.45 billion (31 December 2012 est.)

Stock of domestic credit: $16.07 billion (31 December 2013 est.)
country comparison to the world: 87
$16.09 billion (31 December 2012 est.)

Market value of publicly traded shares: $NA

Current account balance: -$2.744 billion (2013 est.)
country comparison to the world: 157
-$2.031 billion (2012 est.)

Exports: $3.214 billion (2013 est.)
country comparison to the world: 127
$3.039 billion (2012 est.)

Exports—commodities: coffee, khat, gold, leather products, live animals, oilseeds

Exports—partners: China 13%, Germany 10.8%, US 8%, Belgium 7.7%, Saudi Arabia 7.6% (2012)

Imports: $10.68 billion (2013 est.)
country comparison to the world: 98
$10.25 billion (2012 est.)

Imports—commodities: food and live animals, petroleum and petroleum products, chemicals, machinery, motor vehicles, cereals, textiles

Imports—partners: China 13.1%, US 11%, Saudi Arabia 8.4%, India 5.4% (2012)

Reserves of foreign exchange and gold:
$3.382 billion (31 December 2013 est.)
country comparison to the world: 103
$3.272 billion (31 December 2012 est.)

Debt—external: $11.99 billion (31 December 2013 est.)
country comparison to the world: 95
$10.03 billion (31 December 2012 est.)

Exchange rates: birr (ETB) per US dollar—

19.92 (2013 est.)
17.705 (2012 est.)
14.41 (2010 est.)
11.78 (2009)
9.57 (2008)

ENERGY

Electricity—production: 4.929 billion kWh (2010 est.)
country comparison to the world: 119

Electricity—consumption: 4.451 billion kWh (2010 est.)
country comparison to the world: 119

Electricity—exports: 0 kWh (2012 est.)
country comparison to the world: 133

Electricity—imports: 0 kWh (2012 est.)
country comparison to the world: 140

Electricity—installed generating capacity: 2.061 million kW (2010 est.)
country comparison to the world: 100

Electricity—from fossil fuels: 9.9% of total installed capacity (2010 est.)
country comparison to the world: 196

Electricity—from nuclear fuels: 0% of total installed capacity (2010 est.)
country comparison to the world: 86

Electricity—from hydroelectric plants: 89.7% of total installed capacity (2010 est.)
country comparison to the world: 14

Electricity—from other renewable sources: 0.4% of total installed capacity (2010 est.)
country comparison to the world: 85

Crude oil—production: 100 bbl/day (2012 est.)
country comparison to the world: 122

Crude oil—exports: 0 bbl/day (2010 est.)
country comparison to the world: 109

Crude oil—imports: 0 bbl/day (2010 est.)
country comparison to the world: 183

Crude oil—proved reserves: 430,000 bbl (1 January 2013 es)
country comparison to the world: 99

Refined petroleum products—production: 0 bbl/day (2010 est.)
country comparison to the world: 141

Refined petroleum products—consumption: 49,080 bbl/day (2011 est.)
country comparison to the world: 100

Refined petroleum products—exports: 0 bbl/day (2010 est.)
country comparison to the world: 174

Refined petroleum products—imports: 42,500 bbl/day (2010 est.)
country comparison to the world: 78

Natural gas—production: 0 cu m (2011 est.)
country comparison to the world: 128

Natural gas—consumption: 0 cu m (2010 est.)
country comparison to the world: 142

Natural gas—exports: 0 cu m (2011 est.)
country comparison to the world: 97

Natural gas—imports: 0 cu m (2011 est.)
country comparison to the world: 190

Natural gas—proved reserves: 24.92 billion cu m (1 January 2013 es)
country comparison to the world: 73

Carbon dioxide emissions from consumption of energy: 6.703 million Mt (2011 est.)
country comparison to the world: 118

COMMUNICATIONS

Telephones—main lines in use: 797,500 (2012)
country comparison to the world: 8 6

Telephones—mobile cellular: 20.524 million (2012)
country comparison to the world: 47

Telephone system: *general assessment:* inadequate telephone system with the Ethio Telecom maintaining a monopoly over telecommunication services; open-wire, microwave radio relay; radio communication in the HF, VHF, and UHF frequencies; 2 domestic satellites provide the national trunk service
domestic: the number of fixed lines and mobile telephones is increasing from a small base; combined fixed and mobile-cellular teledensity is roughly 15 per 100 persons
international: country code—251; open-wire to Sudan and Djibouti; microwave radio relay to Kenya and Djibouti; satellite earth stations—3 Intelsat (1 Atlantic Ocean and 2 Pacific Ocean) (2011)

Broadcast media: 1 public TV station broadcasting nationally and 1 public radio broadcaster with stations in each of the 13 administrative districts; a few commercial radio stations and roughly a dozen community radio stations (2009)

Internet country code: .et

Internet hosts: 179 (2012)
country comparison to the world: 203

Internet users: 447,300 (2009)
country comparison to the world: 119

TRANSPORTATION

Airports: 57 (2013)
country comparison to the world: 8 4

Airports—with paved runways: *total:* 1 7
over 3,047 m: 3
2,438 to 3,047 m: 8
1,524 to 2,437 m: 4
under 914 m: 2 (2013)

Airports—with unpaved runways: *total:* 4 0
2,438 to 3,047 m: 3
1,524 to 2,437 m: 9
914 to 1,523 m: 20
under 914 m: 8 (2013)

Railways: *total:* 681 km (Ethiopian segment of the 781 km Addis Ababa-Djibouti railroad)
country comparison to the world: 102
narrow gauge: 681 km 1.000-m gauge
note: railway is under joint control of Djibouti and Ethiopia but is largely inoperable (2008)

Roadways: *total:* 44,359 km
country comparison to the world: 79
paved: 6,064 km
unpaved: 38,295 km (2007)

Merchant marine: *total:* 8
country comparison to the world: 121
by type: cargo 8 (2010)

Ports and terminals: Ethiopia is landlocked and uses the ports of Djibouti in Djibouti and Berbera in Somalia

MILITARY

Military branches: Ethiopian National Defense Force (ENDF): Ground Forces, Ethiopian Air Force (Ye Ityopya Ayer Hayl, ETAF) (2013)

Military service age and obligation: 18 years of age for voluntary military service; no compulsory military service, but the military can conduct callups when necessary and compliance is compulsory (2012)

Manpower available for military service:
males age 16-49: 19,067,499
females age 16-49: 19,726,816 (2010 est.)

Manpower fit for military service:
males age 16-49: 11,868,084
females age 16-49: 12,889,260 (2010 est.)

Manpower reaching militarily significant age annually:
male: 967,411
female: 981,714 (2010 est.)

Military expenditures: 0.91% of GDP (2012)
country comparison to the world: 107
1.1% of GDP (2011)
0.91% of GDP (2010)

TRANSNATIONAL ISSUES

Disputes—international: Eritrea and Ethiopia agreed to abide by the 2002 Eritrea-Ethiopia Boundary Commission's (EEBC) delimitation decision, but neither party responded to the revised line detailed in the November 2006 EEBC Demarcation Statement; the undemarcated former British administrative line has little meaning as a political separation to rival clans within Ethiopia's Ogaden and southern Somalia's Oromo region; Ethiopian forces invaded southern Somalia and routed Islamist Courts from Mogadishu in January 2007; "Somaliland" secessionists provide port facilities in Berbera and trade ties to landlocked Ethiopia; civil unrest in eastern Sudan has hampered efforts to demarcate the porous boundary with Ethiopia

Refugees and internally displaced persons: *refugees (country of origin):* 243,824 (Somalia); 136,284 (South Sudan); 84,271 (Eritrea); 40,781 (Sudan) (2014)
IDPs: 200,000-300,000 (border war with Eritrea from 1998-2000, ethnic clashes in Gambela, and ongoing Ethiopian military counterinsurgency in Somali region; most IDPs are in Tigray and Gambela Provinces) (2008)

Illicit drugs: transit hub for heroin originating in Southwest and Southeast Asia and destined for Europe, as well as cocaine destined for markets in southern Africa; cultivates qat (khat) for local use and regional export, principally to Djibouti and Somalia (legal in all three countries); the lack of a well-developed financial system limits the country's utility as a money laundering center

EUROPEAN UNION

INTRODUCTION

Background: Following the two devastating World Wars in the first half of the 20th century, a number of European leaders in the late 1940s became convinced that the only way to establish a lasting peace was to reconcile the two chief belligerent nations—France and Germany—both economically and politically. In 1950, the French Foreign Minister Robert SCHUMAN proposed an eventual union of all Europe, the first step of which would be the integration of the coal and steel industries of Western Europe. The following year, the European Coal and Steel Community (ECSC) was set up when six members, Belgium, France, West Germany, Italy, Luxembourg, and the Netherlands, signed the Treaty of Paris.

The ECSC was so successful that within a few years the decision was made to integrate other elements of the countries' economies. In 1957, envisioning an "ever closer union," the Treaties of Rome created the European Economic Community (EEC) and the European Atomic Energy Community (Euratom), and the six member states undertook to eliminate trade barriers among themselves by forming a common market. In 1967, the institutions of all three communities were formally merged into the European Community (EC), creating a single Commission, a single Council of Ministers, and the body known today as the European Parliament. Members of the European Parliament were initially selected by national parliaments, but in 1979 the first direct elections were undertaken and have been held every five years since.

In 1973, the first enlargement of the EC took place with the addition of Denmark, Ireland, and the United Kingdom. The 1980s saw further membership expansion with Greece joining in 1981 and Spain and Portugal in 1986. The 1992 Treaty of Maastricht laid the basis for further forms of cooperation in foreign and defense policy, in judicial and internal affairs, and in the creation of an economic and monetary union—including a common currency. This further integration created the European Union (EU), at the time standing alongside the European Community. In 1995, Austria, Finland, and Sweden joined the EU/EC, raising the membership total to 15.

A new currency, the euro, was launched in world money markets on 1 January 1999; it became the unit of exchange for all EU member states except Denmark, Sweden, and the United Kingdom. In 2002, citizens of those 12 countries began using euro banknotes and coins. Ten new countries joined the EU in 2004—Cyprus, the Czech Republic, Estonia, Hungary, Latvia, Lithuania, Malta, Poland, Slovakia, and Slovenia. Bulgaria and Romania joined in 2007 and Croatia in 2013, bringing the current membership to 28.

In an effort to ensure that the EU could function efficiently with an expanded membership, the Treaty of Nice (signed in 2000) set forth rules aimed at streamlining the size and procedures of EU institutions. An effort to establish a "Constitution for Europe," growing out of a Convention held in 2002-2003, foundered when it was rejected in referenda in France and the Netherlands in 2005. A subsequent effort in 2007 incorporated many of the features of the rejected Constitution while also making a number of substantive and symbolic changes. The new treaty, initially known as the Reform Treaty but subsequently referred to as the Treaty of Lisbon, sought to amend existing treaties rather than replace them. The treaty was approved at the EU intergovernmental conference of the 27 member states held in Lisbon in December 2007, after which the process of national ratifications began. In October 2009, an Irish referendum approved the Lisbon Treaty (overturning a previous rejection) and cleared the way for an ultimate unanimous endorsement. Poland and the Czech Republic signed on soon after. The Lisbon Treaty, again invoking the idea of an "ever closer union," came into force on 1 December 2009 and the European Union officially replaced and succeeded the European Community.

Preliminary statement: The evolution of what is today the European Union (EU) from a regional economic agreement among six neighboring states in 1951 to today's hybrid intergovernmental and supranational organization of 28 countries across the European continent stands as an unprecedented phenomenon in the annals of history. Dynastic unions for territorial consolidation were long the norm in Europe; on a few occasions even country-level unions were arranged—the Polish-Lithuanian Commonwealth and the Austro-Hungarian Empire were examples. But for such a large number of nation-states to cede some of their sovereignty to an overarching entity is unique.

Although the EU is not a federation in the strict sense, it is far more than a free-trade association such as ASEAN, NAFTA, or Mercosur, and it has certain attributes associated with independent nations: its own flag, currency (for some members), and law-making abilities, as well as diplomatic representation and a common foreign and security policy in its dealings with external partners.

Thus, inclusion of basic intelligence on the EU has been deemed appropriate as a new, separate entity in The World Factbook. However, because of the EU's special status, this description is placed after the regular country entries.

GEOGRAPHY

Location: Europe between the North Atlantic Ocean in the west and Russia, Belarus, and Ukraine to the east

Map references: Europe

Area: total: 4,324,782 sq km

Area—comparative: less than one-half the size of the US

Land boundaries: total: 12,440.8 km
border countries: Albania 282 km, Andorra 120.3 km, Belarus 1,050 km, Croatia 999 km, Holy See 3.2 km, Liechtenstein 34.9 km, Macedonia 394 km, Moldova 450 km, Monaco 4.4 km, Norway 2,348 km, Russia 2,257 km, San Marino 39 km, Serbia 945 km, Switzerland 1,811 km, Turkey 446 km, Ukraine 1,257 km
note: data for European Continent only

Coastline: 65,992.9 km

Maritime claims: NA

Climate: cold temperate; potentially subarctic in the north to temperate; mild wet winters; hot dry summers in the south

Terrain: fairly flat along the Baltic and Atlantic coast; mountainous in the central and southern areas

Elevation extremes: *lowest point:* Lammefjord, Denmark -7 m; Zuidplaspolder, Netherlands -7 m
highest point: Mont Blanc 4,807 m; note—situated on the border between France and Italy

Natural resources: iron ore, natural gas, petroleum, coal, copper, lead, zinc, bauxite, uranium, potash, salt, hydropower, arable land, timber, fish

Land use: arable land: 24.91
permanent crops: 2.75
other: 72.34 (2011)

Irrigated land: 154,539.82 sq km (2011 est.)

Total renewable water resources: 2,057.76 cu km (2011)

Natural hazards: flooding along coasts; avalanches in mountainous area; earthquakes in the south; volcanic eruptions in Italy; periodic droughts in Spain; ice floes in the Baltic

Environment—current issues: NA

Environment—international agreements: *party to:* Air Pollution, Air Pollution-Nitrogen Oxides, Air Pollution-Persistent Organic Pollutants, Air Pollution-Sulphur 94, Antarctic-Marine Living Resources, Biodiversity, Climate Change, Climate Change-Kyoto Protocol, Desertification, Hazardous Wastes, Law of the Sea, Ozone Layer Protection, Tropical Timber 83, Tropical Timber 94
signed but not ratified: Air Pollution-Volatile Organic Compounds

PEOPLE AND SOCIETY

Languages: Bulgarian, Croatian, Czech, Danish, Dutch, English, Estonian, Finnish, French, Gaelic, German, Greek, Hungarian, Italian, Latvian, Lithuanian, Maltese, Polish, Portuguese, Romanian, Slovak, Slovene, Spanish, Swedish
note: only the 24 official languages are listed; German, the major language of Germany, Austria, and Switzerland, is the most widely spoken mother tongue—about 18% of the EU population; English is the most widely spoken foreign language—about 38% of the EU population is conversant with it (2013)

Religions: Roman Catholic, Protestant, Orthodox, Muslim, Jewish

Population: 509,365,627 (July 2013 est.)
country comparison to the world: 3

Age structure: *0-14 years:* 15.41% (male 40,260,485/female 38,227,892)
15-24 years: 11.39% (male 29,658,221/female 28,372,384)
25-54 years: 42.31% (male 108,552,954/female 106,950,141)
55-64 years: 12.68% (male 31,342,550/female 33,262,502)
65 years and over: 18.21% (male 39,348,896/female 53,389,602) (2013 est.)

Median age: note—see individual country entries of member states

Population growth rate: 0.21% (2013 est.)

Birth rate: 10.19 births/1,000 population (2013 est.)

Death rate: 10.13 deaths/1,000 population
country comparison to the world: 48

Net migration rate: 2.02 migrant(s)/1,000 population (2013 est.)

Sex ratio: *at birth:* 1.06 male(s)/female
0-14 years: 1.05 male(s)/female
15-24 years: 1.05 male(s)/female
25-54 years: 1.02 male(s)/female
55-64 years: 0.94 male(s)/female
65 years and over: 0.74 male(s)/female
total population: 0.96 male(s)/female (2013 est.)

Infant mortality rate: total: 4.43 deaths/1,000 live births
country comparison to the world: 191
male: 4.89 deaths/1,000 live births
female: 3.95 deaths/1,000 live births (2013 est.)

Life expectancy at birth: *total population:* 79.86 years
country comparison to the world: 37
male: 77.01 years
female: 82.87 years (2013 est.)

Total fertility rate: 1.59 children born/woman (2013 est.)

Hospital bed density: 5.5 beds/1,000 population (2010)

HIV/AIDS—adult prevalence rate: note—see individual country entries of member states

HIV/AIDS—people living with HIV/AIDS: note—see individual country entries of member states

HIV/AIDS—deaths: note—see individual country entries of member states

GOVERNMENT

Union name: conventional long form: European Union
abbreviation: EU
Political structure: a hybrid and unique intergovernmental and supranational organization

Capital: name: Brussels (Belgium), Strasbourg (France), Luxembourg geographic coordinates: (Brussels) 50 50 N, 4 20 E
time difference: UTC+1 (6 hours ahead of Washington, DC during Standard Time)
daylight saving time: +1hr, begins last Sunday in March; ends last Sunday in October
note: the European Council and the Council of the European Union meet in Brussels, Belgium; the European Parliament meets in Brussels and Strasbourg, France, and has administrative offices in Luxembourg; the Court of Justice of the European Union meets in Luxembourg

Member states: 28 countries: Austria, Belgium, Bulgaria, Croatia, Cyprus, Czech Republic, Denmark, Estonia, Finland, France, Germany, Greece, Hungary, Ireland, Italy, Latvia, Lithuania, Luxembourg, Malta, Netherlands, Poland, Portugal, Romania, Slovakia, Slovenia, Spain, Sweden, UK; note—candidate countries: Iceland, Macedonia, Montenegro, Serbia, Turkey

Independence: 7 February 1992 (Maastricht Treaty signed establishing the European Union); 1 November 1993 (Maastricht Treaty entered into force)
note: the Treaties of Rome, signed on 25 March 1957 and subsequently entered into force on 1 January 1958, created the European Economic Community and the European Atomic Energy Community; a series of subsequent treaties have been adopted to increase efficiency and transparency, to prepare for new member states, and to introduce new areas of cooperation—such as single currency; the Treaty of Lisbon, signed on 13 December 2007 and entered into force on 1 December 2009 is the most recent of these treaties and is intended to make the EU more democratic, more efficient, and better able to address global problems with one voice

National holiday: Europe Day 9 May (1950); note—the day in 1950 that Robert SCHUMAN proposed the creation of what became the European Coal and Steel Community, the progenitor of today's European Union, with the aim of achieving a united Europe
Constitution: none
note: the EU legal order, although based on a series of treaties, has often been described as "constitutional" in nature; the Treaty on European Union (TEU), as modified by the Lisbon Treaty, states in Article 1 that "the HIGH CONTRACTING PARTIES establish among themselves a EUROPEAN UNION ... on which the Member States confer competences to attain objectives they have in common"; Article 1 of the TEU states further that the EU is "founded on the present Treaty and on the Treaty on the Functioning of the European Union (hereinafter referred to as 'the Treaties')," both possessing the same legal value; Article 6 of the TEU provides that a separately adopted Charter of Fundamental Rights of the European Union "shall have the same legal value as the Treaties" (2013)

Legal system: unique supranational law system in which, according to an interpretive declaration of member-state governments appended to the Treaty of Lisbon, "the Treaties and the law adopted by the Union on the basis of the Treaties have primacy over the law of Member States" under conditions laid down in the case law of the Court of Justice; key principles of EU law include fundamental rights as guaranteed by the Charter of Fundamental Rights and as resulting from constitutional traditions common to the EU's states; EU law is divided into 'primary' and 'secondary' legislation; the treaties (primary legislation) are the basis for all EU action; secondary legislation—which includes regulations, directives and decisions—are derived from the principles and objectives set out in the treaties

Suffrage: 18 years of age; universal; voting for the European Parliament is permitted in each member state

Executive branch: under the EU treaties there are three distinct institutions, each of which conducts functions that may be regarded as executive in nature:
the European Council: brings together heads of state and government, along with the president of the European Commission, and meets at least four times a year; its aim is to provide the impetus for the development of the Union and to issue general policy guidelines; leaders of the EU member states appointed former Belgian Prime Minister Herman VAN ROMPUY to be the first full-time president of the European Council in November 2009; he took office on 1 December 2009 for a two-and-one-half-year term, renewable once; EU member state leaders confirmed Herman VAN ROMPUY for a second and final two-and-one-half-year term in March 2012; his core responsibilities include chairing the EU summits and providing policy and organizational continuity
the Council of the European Union: consists of ministers of each EU member state and meets regularly in different configurations depending on the subject matter; it carries out policy-making and coordinating functions (as well as legislative functions); ministers of EU member states chair meetings of the Council of the EU based on a six-month rotating presidency
the European Commission: is headed by a College of Commissioners composed of 28 members, one from each member country; each commissioner is responsible for one or more policy areas; the Commission's responsibilities include the sole right to initiate EU legislation (except for foreign and defense policy), promoting the general interest of the EU, acting as "guardian of the Treaties," executing the budget and managing programs, ensuring the Union's external representation, and additional duties; its president is Jose Manuel BARROSO (since 2004); the president of the European Commission is nominated by member state governments taking into account the results of the European Parliament elections and elected by the European Parliament; working from member state recommendations, the Commission president then assembles the "college" of Commission members; the European Parliament confirms the *entire Commission for a five-year term; the next confirmation process will likely be held in the fall of 2014*
note: for external representation and foreign policy making, leaders of the EU member states appointed Catherine ASHTON of the United Kingdom to be the first High Representative of the Union for Foreign Affairs and Security Policy; ASHTON took office on 1 December 2009; her concurrent appointment as Vice President of the European Commission endows her position with the policymaking influence of the Council of the EU and the budgetary influence of the European Commission; the High Representative helps develop and implement the EU's Common Foreign and Security Policy (CFSP) and Common Security and Defense Policy (CSDP), chairs the Foreign Affairs Council, represents and acts for the Union in many international contexts, and oversees the European External Action Service (EEAS), the diplomatic corps of the EU, established on 1 December 2010 External Action Service (EEAS), the diplomatic corps of the EU, established on 1 December 2010

Legislative branch: two legislative bodies consisting of the Council of the European Union (28 member-state ministers having 352 votes; the number of votes is roughly proportional to member-states' population, and 255 votes plus a majority of member states forms a "qualified majority" to pass a measure) and the European Parliament (766

seats; seats allocated among member states in proportion to population; members elected by direct universal suffrage for a five-year term); note—the European Parliament President is elected by a majority of fellow members of the European Parliament (MEP), and represents the Parliament within the EU and internationally; German MEP Martin SCHULZ from the Group of the Progressive Alliance of Socialists and Democrats (S&D) was elected in January 2012; the Council of the EU is the main decision-making body of the EU, although the European Parliament must also approve almost all EU legislation; the Parliament does not have the right to initiate legislation
elections: last held on 4-7 June 2009 (next to be held 22-25 May 2014)
election results: percent of vote—EPP 36%, S&D 25%, ALDE 11.4%, Greens/EFA 7.5%, ECR 7.3%, GUE/NGL 4.8%, EFD 4.3%, independents 3.7%; seats by party—EPP 265, S&D 184, ALDE 84, Greens/EFA 55, ECR 54, GUE/NGL 35, EFD 32, nonaffiliated 27, plus 18 "observers"; note—current seats by party as of July 2013—EPP 275, S&D 195, ALDE 84, Greens/EFA 58, ECR 56, GUE/NGL 36, EFD 33, nonaffiliated 29

Judicial branch: *highest court(s):* Court of Justice of the European Union (organized into Court of Justice, General Court, and Civil Service Tribunal; consists of 27 judges, one from each of the member states) note—the Court of Justice ensures that treaties are interpreted and applied uniformly throughout the EU, resolves disputed issues among the EU institutions, issues opinions on questions of EU law referred by member state courts;
judge selection and term of office: judges appointed for 6-year terms; note—the court can sit in chambers, in a "Grand Chamber" of 13 judges, or as the full court; General Court (a court below the Court of Justice)—27 judges appointed for six-year terms; Civil Service Tribunal—7 judges appointed for 3-year terms
subordinate courts:

Political parties and leaders: Confederal Group of the European United Left-Nordic Green Left or GUE/NGL [Gabriele ZIMMER]; Europe of Freedom and Democracy Group or EFD [Nigel FARAGE and Francesco SPERONI]; European Conservatives and Reformists Group or ECR [Martin CALLANAN]; Group of Greens/European Free Alliance or Greens/EFA [Rebecca HARMS and Daniel COHN-BENDIT]; Group of the Alliance of Liberals and Democrats for Europe or ALDE [Guy VERHOFSTADT]; Group of the European People's Party or EPP [Joseph DAUL]; Group of the Progressive Alliance of Socialists and Democrats or S&D [Hannes SWOBODA]

International organization participation: ARF (dialogue member), ASEAN (dialogue member), Australian Group, BIS, BSEC (observer), CBSS, CERN, EBRD, FAO, FATF, G-8, G-10, G-20, IDA, IEA, IGAD (partners), LAIA (observer), NSG (observer), OAS (observer), OECD, PIF (partner), SAARC (observer), UN (observer), UNRWA (observer), WCO, WTO, ZC (observer)

Diplomatic representation in the US: *chief of mission:* Ambassador Joao VALE DE ALMEIDA (since 16 July 2010)
chancery: 2175 K Street, NW, Washington, DC 20037
telephone: [1] (202) 862-9500
FAX: [1] (202) 429-1766

Diplomatic representation from the US:
chief of mission: Ambassador Anthony L. GARDNER (since 12 February 2014)
embassy: 13 Zinnerstraat/Rue Zinner, B-1000 Brussels
mailing address: same as above
telephone: [32] (2) 811-4100
FAX: [32] (2) 811-5154

Flag description: a blue field with 12 five-pointed gold stars arranged in a circle in the center; blue represents the sky of the Western world, the stars are the peoples of Europe in a circle, a symbol of unity; the number of stars is fixed

National symbol(s): a circle of 12 stars

National anthem: name: "Ode to Joy"
lyrics/music: none/Ludwig VON BEETHOVEN, arranged by Herbert VON KARAJAN
note: adopted 1972, not in use until 1986; according to the European Union, the song is meant to represent all of Europe rather than just the organization; the song also serves as the anthem for the Council of Europe

ECONOMY

Economy—overview: Internally, the EU has adopted the framework of a single market with free movement of goods, services and capital and a common currency amongst 18 member states. Internationally, the EU aims to bolster Europe's trade position and its political and economic weight. Despite great differences in per capita income among member states (from $13,000 to $82,000) and in national attitudes toward issues like inflation, debt, and foreign trade, the EU has achieved a high degree of coordination of economic and fiscal policies. Eleven established EU member states, under the auspices of the European Economic and Monetary Union (EMU), introduced the euro as their common currency on 1 January 1999 (Greece did so two years later). Between 2004 and 2007, 12 states acceded to the EU that are, in general, less advanced economically than the other 15 member states. On 1 July 2013 Croatia became the most recent member of the EU, following a decade long application process. Of the 13 most recent entrants, Slovenia (1 January 2007), Cyprus and Malta (1 January 2008), Slovakia (1 January 2009), Estonia (1 January 2011) and Latvia (2014) have adopted the euro; 11 other member states—other than the UK and Denmark, which have formal opt-outs—are required by EU treaties to adopt the common currency upon meeting fiscal and monetary convergence criteria. Following the 2008-09 global economic crisis, the EU economy saw moderate GDP growth in 2010 and 2011, but a sovereign debt crisis in the eurozone intensified in 2011, making it impossible for several member states to gain market financing for new sovereign debt to sustain fiscal deficits. As a result, the eurozone crisis became the bloc's top economic and political priority. Despite EU/IMF rescue programs in Greece, Ireland, Portugal, Spain and Cyprus, and fiscal consolidation measures in many other EU member states, significant risks to growth remain, including high public and private debt loads, crimped lending as banks raise capital, aging populations, onerous regulations, and high unemployment. In response, eurozone leaders in 2011 boosted funding levels for the temporary European Financial Stability Facility (EFSF) to almost $600 billion and made loan terms more favorable for crisis-hit countries, followed in July 2012 by the permanent European Stabilization Mechanism (ESM). In addition, 26 of 28 EU member states (all except the UK and Czech Republic) enacted a "fiscal compact" treaty to boost long-term budgetary discipline and coordination. In September 2012 the European Central Bank indicated its willingness to purchase bonds from troubled eurozone member states that agree to a formal program of fiscal and structural reforms, aiming to reduce their borrowing costs and restore confidence in the eurozone. The eurozone has since made great strides towards a banking union to increase financial stability and improve lending conditions. In an effort to restore economic growth and create jobs, in 2013 the EU and the United States started negotiations on an ambitious and comprehensive free trade agreement with the goal of expanding already massive trade and investment flows.

GDP (purchasing power parity): $15.83 trillion (2013 est.)
country comparison to the world: 2
$15.84 trillion (2012 est.)
$15.89 trillion (2011 est.)
note: data are in 2013 US dollars

GDP (official exchange rate): $17.03 trillion (2013 est.)

GDP—real growth rate: 0% (2013 est.)
country comparison to the world: 198
-0.3% (2012 est.)
1.7% (2011 est.)

GDP—per capita (PPP): $34,500 (2013 est.)
country comparison to the world: 41
$34,500 (2012 est.)
$34,700 (2011 est.)
note: data are in 2013 US dollars

Gross national saving: 19.2% of GDP (2013)
country comparison to the world: 81
19% of GDP (2012)
19.5% of GDP (2011)

GDP—composition, by end use:
household consumption: 56.9%
government consumption: 21.6%
investment in fixed capital: 17.9%
investment in inventories: 0.1%
exports of goods and services: 44.9%
imports of goods and services: -42.9% (2012 est.)

GDP—composition, by sector of origin:
agriculture: 1.8%
industry: 25.2%
services: 72.8% (2013 est.)

Agriculture—products: wheat, barley, oilseeds, sugar beets, wine, grapes; dairy products, cattle, sheep, pigs, poultry; fish

Industries: among the world's largest and most technologically advanced, the EU industrial base includes: ferrous and non-ferrous metal production and processing, metal products, petroleum, coal, cement, chemicals, pharmaceuticals, aerospace, rail transportation equipment, passenger and commercial vehicles, construction equipment, industrial equipment, shipbuilding, electrical power equipment, machine tools and automated manufacturing systems, electronics and telecommunications equipment, fishing, food and beverage processing, furniture, paper, textiles

Industrial production growth rate: -0.3% (2013 est.)
country comparison to the world: 170

Labor force: 230.7 million (2013 est.)
country comparison to the world: 3

Labor force—by occupation: agriculture: 5.2%
industry: 22.7%
services: 72.2% (2012 est.)

Unemployment rate: 10.8% (2013 est.)
country comparison to the world: 113
10.2% (2012)

Population below poverty line: note—see individual country entries of member states

Household income or consumption by percentage share: *lowest 10%:* 2.9%
highest 10%: 23.9% (2012 est.)

Distribution of family income—Gini index: 30.6 (2012 est.)
country comparison to the world: 118
30.8 (2011 est.)

Fiscal year: NA

Inflation rate (consumer prices): 1.5% (2013 est.)
country comparison to the world: 39
2.6% (2012 est.)

Central bank discount rate: 0.75% (31 December 2013)
country comparison to the world: 124
1.5% (31 December 2012)
note: this is the European Central Bank's rate on the marginal lending facility, which offers overnight credit to banks in the euro area

Commercial bank prime lending rate: 5.9% (31 December 2010 est.)
country comparison to the world: 119
7.52% (31 December 2009 est.)

Stock of narrow money: $6.736 trillion (31 December 2013)
country comparison to the world: 1
$6.219 trillion (31 December 2012)
note: this is the quantity of money, M1, for the euro area, converted into US dollars at the exchange rate for the date indicated; it excludes the stock of money carried by non-euro-area members of the European Union

Stock of broad money: $12.9 trillion (31 December 2012 est.)
country comparison to the world: 4
$12.29 trillion (31 December 2011 est.)
note: this is the quantity of broad money for the euro area, converted into US dollars at the exchange rate for the date indicated; it excludes the stock of broad money carried by non-euro-area members of the European Union

Stock of domestic credit: $21.71 trillion (31 December 2012 est.)
country comparison to the world: 1
$21.29 trillion (31 December 2011 est.)
note: this figure refers to the euro area only; it excludes credit data for non-euro-area members of the EU

Market value of publicly traded shares: $10.4 trillion (31 December 2012 est.)
country comparison to the world: 2
$9.36 trillion (31 December 2011)
$10.56 trillion (31 December 2010 est.)

Current account balance: -$34.49 billion (2011 est.)
country comparison to the world: 185
-$5.73 billion (2010 est.)

Exports: $2.173 trillion (2012 est.)
country comparison to the world: 2
$2.174 trillion (2011 est.)
note: external exports, excluding intra-EU trade

Exports—commodities: machinery, motor vehicles, pharmaceuticals and other chemicals, fuels, aircraft, plastics, iron and steel, wood pulp and paper products, alcoholic beverages, furniture

Imports: $2.312 trillion (2012 est.)
country comparison to the world: 1
$2.404 trillion (2011 est.)
note: external imports, excluding intra-EU trade

Imports—commodities: fuels and crude oil, machinery, vehicles, pharmaceuticals and other chemicals, precious gemstones, textiles, aircraft, plastics, metals, ships

Reserves of foreign exchange and gold: $812.1 billion (31 December 2011)
country comparison to the world: 3
note: $863.8 billion (31 December 2011); this includes reserves held by the European Central Bank and euro-zone national central banks; it excludes reserves for non-euro-area members of the EU

Debt—external: $15.95 trillion (31 December 2012 est.)
country comparison to the world: 1
$14.78 trillion (31 December 2011)

Stock of direct foreign investment—at home: $NA

Exchange rates: euros per US dollar—
0.7634 (2013 est.)
0.7752 (2012 est.)
0.755 (2010 est.)
0.7198 (2009 est.)
0.6827 (2008 est.)

ENERGY

Electricity—production: 3.255 trillion kWh (2011 est.)
country comparison to the world: 3

Electricity—consumption: 3.037 trillion kWh (2009 est.)
country comparison to the world: 3

Electricity—installed generating capacity: 868.4 million kW (2010 est.)
country comparison to the world: 3

Crude oil—production: 1.857 million bbl/day (2012 est.)
country comparison to the world: 17

Crude oil—proved reserves: 5.568 billion bbl (1 January 2013 es)
country comparison to the world: 21

Refined petroleum products—production: 12.05 million bbl/day (2012 est.)
country comparison to the world: 2

Refined petroleum products—consumption: 12.8 million bbl/day (2012 est.)
country comparison to the world: 2

Refined petroleum products—exports: 2.196 million bbl/day (2010 est.)
country comparison to the world: 3

Refined petroleum products—imports: 8.613 million bbl/day (2010 est.)
country comparison to the world: 1

Natural gas—production: 164.6 billion cu m (2012 est.)
country comparison to the world: 3

Natural gas—consumption: 443.9 billion cu m (2012 est.)
country comparison to the world: 3

Natural gas—exports: 93.75 billion cu m (2010 est.)
country comparison to the world: 4

Natural gas—imports: 420.6 billion cu m (2010 est.)
country comparison to the world: 1

Natural gas—proved reserves: 1.953 trillion cu m (1 January 2012 es)
country comparison to the world: 18

Carbon dioxide emissions from consumption of energy: 3.978 billion Mt (2012 est.)
country comparison to the world: 3

COMMUNICATIONS

Telephones—main lines in use: 226 million (2011)

Telephones—mobile cellular: 629 million (2011)

Telephone system: note—see individual country entries of member states

Internet country code: .eu; note—see country entries of member states for individual country codes

Internet hosts: 201,116; note—this sum reflects the number of Internet hosts assigned the .eu Internet country code (2012)

Internet users: 340 million (2009)

TRANSPORTATION

Airports: 3,102 (2013)

Airports—with paved runways: *total:* 1,858
over 3,047 m: 118
2,438 to 3,047 m: 335
1,524 to 2,437 m: 504
914 to 1,523 m: 422
under 914 m: 479 (2013)

Airports—with unpaved runways: total: 1,244
over 3,047 m: 1
2,437 to 3,047 m: 1
1,524 to 2,437 m: 15
914 to 1,523 m: 245
under 914 m: 982 (2013)

Heliports: 90 (2013)

Railways: total: 461,096 km (2013)

Roadways: total: 10,582,653 km (2013)

Waterways: 53,384 km (2013)

Ports and terminals: *major port(s):* Antwerp (Belgium), Barcelona (Spain), Braila (Romania), Bremen (Germany), Burgas (Bulgaria), Constanta (Romania), Copenhagen (Denmark), Galati (Romania), Gdansk (Poland), Hamburg (Germany), Helsinki (Finland), Las Palmas (Canary Islands, Spain), Le Havre (France), Lisbon (Portugal), London (UK), Marseille (France), Naples (Italy), Peiraiefs or Piraeus (Greece), Riga (Latvia), Rotterdam (Netherlands), Stockholm (Sweden), Talinn (Estonia), Tulcea (Romania), Varna (Bulgaria)

MILITARY

Military expenditures: 1.65% of GDP (2012)
country comparison to the world: 5 5
1.66% of GDP (2011)

1.65% of GDP (2010)

Military—note: the five-nation Eurocorps—created in 1992 by France, Germany, Belgium, Spain, and Luxembourg—has deployed troops and police on peacekeeping missions to Bosnia-Herzegovina, Macedonia, and the Democratic Republic of the Congo and assumed command of the ISAF in Afghanistan in August 2004; Eurocorps directly commands the 5,000-man Franco-German Brigade, the Multinational Command Support Brigade, and EUFOR in Bosnia and Herzegovina; in November 2004, the EU Council of Ministers formally committed to creating 13 1,500-man battle groups by the end of 2007, to respond to international crises on a rotating basis; 22 of the EU's 27 nations have agreed to supply troops; France, Italy, and the UK formed the first of three battle groups in 2005; Norway, Sweden, Estonia, and Finland established the Nordic Battle Group effective 1 January 2008; nine other groups are to be formed; a rapid-reaction naval EU Maritime Task Group was stood up in March 2007 (2007)

TRANSNATIONAL ISSUES

Disputes—international: as a political union, the EU has no border disputes with neighboring countries, but Estonia has no land boundary agreements with Russia, Slovenia disputes its land and maritime boundaries with Croatia, and Spain has territorial and maritime disputes with Morocco and with the UK over Gibraltar; the EU has set up a Schengen area—consisting of 22 EU member states that have signed the convention implementing the Schengen agreements or "acquis" (1985 and 1990) on the free movement of persons and the harmonization of border controls in Europe; these agreements became incorporated into EU law with the implementation of the 1997 Treaty of Amsterdam on 1 May 1999; in addition, non-EU states Iceland and Norway (as part of the Nordic Union) have been included in the Schengen area since 1996 (full members in 2001), Switzerland since 2008, and Liechtenstein since 2011 bringing the total current membership to 26; the UK (since 2000) and Ireland (since 2002) take part in only some aspects of the Schengen area, especially with respect to police and criminal matters; nine of the 12 new member states that joined the EU since 2004 joined Schengen on 21 December 2007; of the three remaining EU states, Romania and Bulgaria may join in 2013 or 2014, while Cyprus' entry is held up by the ongoing Cyprus dispute

FALKLAND ISLANDS (ISLAS MALVINAS)

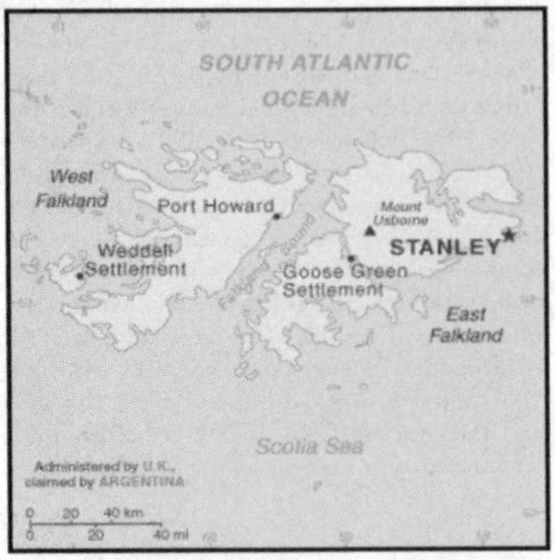

INTRODUCTION

Background: Although first sighted by an English navigator in 1592, the first landing (English) did not occur until almost a century later in 1690, and the first settlement (French) was not established until 1764. The colony was turned over to Spain two years later and the islands have since been the subject of a territorial dispute, first between Britain and Spain, then between Britain and Argentina. The UK asserted its claim to the islands by establishing a naval garrison there in 1833. Argentina invaded the islands on 2 April 1982. The British responded with an expeditionary force that landed seven weeks later and after fierce fighting forced an Argentine surrender on 14 June 1982. With hostilities ended and Argentine forces withdrawn, UK administration resumed. In response to renewed calls from Argentina for Britain to relinquish control of the islands, a referendum was held in March 2013, which resulted in 99.8% of the population voting to remain a part of the UK.

GEOGRAPHY

Location: Southern South America, islands in the South Atlantic Ocean, east of southern Argentina

Geographic coordinates: 51 45 S, 59 00 W

Map references: South America

Area: *total:* 12,173 sq km
country comparison to the world: 165
land: 12,173 sq km
water: 0 sq km
note: includes the two main islands of East and West Falkland and about 200 small islands

Area—comparative: slightly smaller than Connecticut

Land boundaries: 0 km

Coastline: 1,288 km

Maritime claims: *territorial sea:* 12 nm
continental shelf: 200 nm
exclusive fishing zone: 200 nm

Climate: cold marine; strong westerly winds, cloudy, humid; rain occurs on more than half of days in year; average annual rainfall is 24 inches in Stanley; occasional snow all year, except in January and February, but typically does not accumulate

Terrain: rocky, hilly, mountainous with some boggy, undulating plains

Elevation extremes: *lowest point:* Atlantic Ocean 0 m
highest point: Mount Usborne 705 m

Natural resources: fish, squid, wildlife, calcified seaweed, sphagnum moss

Land use: *arable land:* 0%
permanent crops: 0%
other: 100% (99% permanent pastures, 1% other) (2011)

Irrigated land: NA

Natural hazards: strong winds persist throughout the year

Environment—current issues: overfishing by unlicensed vessels is a problem; reindeer were introduced to the islands in 2001 for commercial reasons; this is the only commercial reindeer herd in the world unaffected by the 1986 Chornobyl disaster

Geography—note: deeply indented coast provides good natural harbors; short growing season

PEOPLE AND SOCIETY

Nationality: *noun:* Falkland Islander(s)
adjective: Falkland Island

Ethnic groups: Falkland Islander 57%, British 24.6%, St. Helenian 9.8%, Chilean 5.3%, other 3.4% (2012 est.)

Languages: English 89%, Spanish 7.7%, other 3.3% (2006 est.)

Religions: Christian 66%, none 32%, other 2% (2012 est.)

Population: 3,140 (July 2008 est.)
country comparison to the world: 232

Population growth rate: 0.01% (2009 est.)
country comparison to the world: 193

Birth rate: NA

Net migration rate: NA

Urbanization: *urban population:* 74% of total population (2010)
rate of urbanization: 0.9% annual rate of change (2010-15 est.)

Major urban areas—population: STANLEY (capital) 2,000 (2009)

Infant mortality rate: *total:* NA
male: NA
female: NA

Life expectancy at birth: *total population:* NA
male: NA
female: NA

Total fertility rate: NA

HIV/AIDS—adult prevalence rate: NA

HIV/AIDS—people living with HIV/AIDS: NA

HIV/AIDS—deaths: NA

Literacy: NA

GOVERNMENT

Country name: *conventional long form:* none
conventional short form: Falkland Islands (Islas Malvinas)
Dependency status: overseas territory of the UK; also claimed by Argentina

Government type: NA

Capital: *name:* Stanley
geographic coordinates: 51 42 S, 57 51 W
time difference: UTC-4 (1 hour ahead of Washington, DC during Standard Time)
daylight saving time: +1hr, observed all year in 2013

Administrative divisions: none (overseas territory of the UK; also claimed by Argentina)

Independence: none (overseas territory of the UK; also claimed by Argentina)

National holiday: Liberation Day, 14 June (1982)

Constitution: previous 1985; latest entered into force 1 January 2009 (2011)

Legal system: English common law and local statutes

Suffrage: 18 years of age; universal

Executive branch: *chief of state:* Queen ELIZABETH II (since 6 February 1952)
head of government: Governor Nigel HAYWOOD (since 16 October 2010) is the Queen's representative; Chief Executive Keith PADGETT (since 1 February 2012)
cabinet: Executive Council; three members elected by the Legislative Council, two ex officio members (chief executive and the financial secretary), and the governor; the governor must obey the rulings of the Executive Council on domestic affairs (For more information visit the World Leaders website)
elections: the monarchy is hereditary; governor appointed by the monarch; chief executive appointed by the governor

Legislative branch: unicameral Legislative Assembly (10 seats; 2 members are ex officio and 8 are elected by popular vote; members to serve four-year terms); presided over by the governor
elections: last held on 7 November 2013 (next to be held in November 2017)
election results: percent of vote—NA; seats—independents 8

Judicial branch: *highest court(s):* Court of Appeal (consists of the court president, the chief justice as an ex officio, non-resident member, and 2 justices of appeal); Supreme Court (consists of the chief justice) note—appeals beyond the Court of Appeal are referred to the Judicial Committee of the Privy Council (in London)
judge selection and term of office: all justices appointed by the governor; tenure specified in each justice's instrument of appointment
subordinate courts: Magistrate's Court (senior magistrate presides over civil and criminal divisions); Court of Summary Jurisdiction

Political parties and leaders: none; all independents

Political pressure groups and leaders: Falkland Islands Association (supports freedom of the people from external causes)

International organization participation: UPU

Diplomatic representation in the US: none (overseas territory of the UK)

Diplomatic representation from the US: none (overseas territory of the UK; also claimed by Argentina)

Flag description: blue with the flag of the UK in the upper hoist-side quadrant and the Falkland Island coat of arms centered on the outer half of the flag; the coat of arms contains a white ram (sheep raising was once the major economic activity) above the sailing ship Desire (whose crew discovered the islands) with a scroll at the bottom bearing the motto DESIRE THE RIGHT

National symbol(s): r a m

National anthem: name: "Song of the Falklands"
lyrics/music: Christopher LANHAM
note: adopted 1930s; the song is the local unofficial anthem; as a territory of the United Kingdom, "God Save the Queen" is official (see United Kingdom)

ECONOMY

Economy—overview: The economy was formerly based on agriculture, mainly sheep farming but fishing and tourism currently comprise the bulk of economic activity. In 1987, the government began selling fishing licenses to foreign trawlers operating within the Falkland Islands' exclusive fishing zone. These license fees net more than $40 million per year, which help support the island's health, education, and welfare system. The waters around the Falkland Islands are known for their squid, which account for around 75% of the annual 200,000 ton fish catch. Dairy farming supports domestic consumption; crops furnish winter fodder. Foreign exchange earnings come from shipments of high-grade wool to the UK and from the sale of postage stamps and coins. In 2001, the government purchased 100 reindeer with the intent to increase the number to 10,000 over the following 20 years so that venison could be exported to Scandinavia and Chile. Tourism, especially eco-tourism, is increasing rapidly, with about 69,000 visitors in 2009. The British military presence also provides a sizeable economic boost. The islands are now self-financing except for defense. In 1993 the British Geological Survey announced a 200-mile oil exploration zone around the islands, and early seismic surveys suggest substantial reserves capable of producing 500,000 barrels per day. Political tensions between the UK and Argentina remain high following the start of oil drilling activities in the waters. In September 2011, a British exploration firm announced that it plans to commence oil production in 2016.

GDP (purchasing power parity): $164.5 million (2007 est.)
country comparison to the world: 222
$105.1 million (2002 est.)

GDP (official exchange rate): $164.5 million (2007 est.)

GDP—per capita (PPP): $55,400 (2002 est.)
country comparison to the world: 9

GDP—composition, by sector of origin:
agriculture: 95%
industry: NA%
services: NA% (1996)

Agriculture—products: fodder and vegetable crops; venison, sheep, dairy products; fish, squid

Industries: fish and wool processing; tourism

Industrial production growth rate: NA%

Labor force: 5,246 (2006)
country comparison to the world: 221

Labor force—by occupation: *agriculture:* 95% (mostly sheepherding and fishing)
industry and services: 5% (1996)

Unemployment rate: 4.1% (2010)
country comparison to the world: 34

Population below poverty line: NA%

Household income or consumption by percentage share: *lowest 10%:* NA%
highest 10%: NA%

Budget: *revenues:* $67.1 million
expenditures: $75.3 million (FY09/10)

Taxes and other revenues: 40.8% of GDP (FY09/10)
country comparison to the world: 33

Budget surplus (+) or deficit (-):
-5% of GDP (FY09/10)
country comparison to the world: 167

Fiscal year: 1 April—31 March

Inflation rate (consumer prices): 1.2% (2003)
country comparison to the world: 30
3.6% (1998)

Exports: $125 million (2004 est.)
country comparison to the world: 188

Exports—commodities: wool, hides, meat, venison, fish, squid

Imports: $90 million (2004 est.)
country comparison to the world: 214

Imports—commodities: fuel, food and drink, building materials, clothing

Debt—external: $NA

Exchange rates: Falkland pounds (FKP) per US dollar—
0.6391 (2013)
0.6307 (2012)
0.6472 (2010)
0.6175 (2009)

ENERGY

Electricity—production: 19 million kWh (2010 est.)
country comparison to the world: 214

Electricity—consumption: 17.67 million kWh (2010 est.)
country comparison to the world: 214

Electricity—exports: 0 kWh (2012 est.)
country comparison to the world: 135

Electricity—imports: 0 kWh (2012 est.)
country comparison to the world: 142

Electricity—installed generating capacity:
10,000 kW (2010 est.)
country comparison to the world: 204

Electricity—from fossil fuels: 90% of total installed capacity (2010 est.)
country comparison to the world: 75

Electricity—from nuclear fuels:
0% of total installed capacity (2010 est.)
country comparison to the world: 88

Electricity—from hydroelectric plants: 0% of total installed capacity (2010 est.)
country comparison to the world: 169

Electricity—from other renewable sources:
10% of total installed capacity (2010 est.)
country comparison to the world: 27

Crude oil—production: 0 bbl/day (2012 est.)
country comparison to the world: 169

Crude oil—exports: 0 bbl/day (2010 est.)
country comparison to the world: 112

Crude oil—imports: 0 bbl/day (2010 est.)
country comparison to the world: 185

Crude oil—proved reserves: 0 bbl (1 January 2013 es)
country comparison to the world: 132

Refined petroleum products—production:
0 bbl/day (2010 est.)
country comparison to the world: 143

Refined petroleum products—consumption:
300 bbl/day (2011 est.)
country comparison to the world: 208

Refined petroleum products—exports:
0 bbl/day (2010 est.)
country comparison to the world: 175

Refined petroleum products—imports:
312.5 bbl/day (2010 est.)
country comparison to the world: 207

Natural gas—production:
0 cu m (2011 est.)
country comparison to the world: 131

Natural gas—consumption: 0 cu m (2010 est.)
country comparison to the world: 144

Natural gas—exports: 0 cu m (2011 est.)
country comparison to the world: 100

Natural gas—imports: 0 cu m (2011 est.)
country comparison to the world: 192

Natural gas—proved reserves: 0 cu m (1 January 2013 es)
country comparison to the world: 138

Carbon dioxide emissions from consumption of energy: 45,740 Mt (2011 est.)
country comparison to the world: 209

COMMUNICATIONS

Telephones—main lines in use: 1,980 (2012)
country comparison to the world: 218

Telephones—mobile cellular: 3,450 (2012)
country comparison to the world: 216

Telephone system: *domestic:* government-operated radiotelephone and private VHF/CB radiotelephone networks provide effective service to almost all points on both islands
international: country code—500; satellite earth station—1 Intelsat (Atlantic Ocean) with links through London to other countries (2011)

Broadcast media: TV service provided by a multi-channel service provider; radio services provided by the public broadcaster, Falkland Islands Radio Service, broadcasting on both AM and FM frequencies, and by the British Forces Broadcasting Service (BFBS) (2007)

Internet country code: .fk

Internet hosts: 110 (2012)
country comparison to the world: 206

Internet users: 2,900 (2009)
country comparison to the world: 209

TRANSPORTATION

Airports: 7 (2013)
country comparison to the world: 170

Airports—with paved runways: *total:* 2
2,438 to 3,047 m: 1
914 to 1,523 m: 1 (2013)

Airports—with unpaved runways: *total:* 5
under 914 m:
5 (2013)

Roadways: total: 440 km
country comparison to the world: 198
paved: 50 km
unpaved: 390 km (2008)

Ports and terminals: *major seaport(s):* Stanley

MILITARY

Military branches: no regular military forces

Military—note: defense is the responsibility of the UK

TRANSNATIONAL ISSUES

Disputes—international: Argentina, which claims the islands in its constitution and briefly occupied them by force in 1982, agreed in 1995 to no longer seek settlement by force; UK continues to reject Argentine requests for sovereignty talks

FAROE ISLANDS

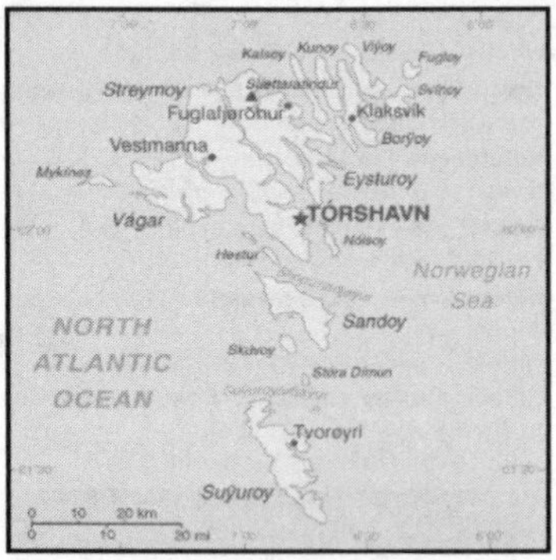

INTRODUCTION

Background: The population of the Faroe Islands is largely descended from Viking settlers who arrived in the 9th century. The islands have been connected politically to Denmark since the 14th century. A high degree of self-government was granted the Faroese in 1948, who have autonomy over most internal affairs while Denmark is responsible for justice, defense, and foreign affairs. The Faroe Islands are not part of the European Union.

GEOGRAPHY

Location: Northern Europe, island group between the Norwegian Sea and the North Atlantic Ocean, about half way between Iceland and Norway

Geographic coordinates: 62 00 N, 7 00 W

Map references: Europe

Area: *total:* 1,393 sq km
country comparison to the world: 183
land: 1,393 sq km
water: 0 sq km (some lakes and streams)

Area—comparative: eight times the size of Washington, DC

Land boundaries: 0 km

Coastline: 1,117 km

Maritime claims: territorial sea: 3 nm
continental shelf: 200 nm or agreed boundaries or median line
exclusive fishing zone: 200 nm or agreed boundaries or median line

Climate: mild winters, cool summers; usually overcast; foggy, windy

Terrain: rugged, rocky, some low peaks; cliffs along most of coast

Elevation extremes: *lowest point:* Atlantic Ocean 0 m
highest point: Slaettaratindur 882 m

Natural resources: fish, whales, hydropower, possible oil and gas

Land use: arable land: 2.15%
permanent crops: 0%
other: 97.85% (2011)

Irrigated land: 0 sq km (2011)

Natural hazards: NA

Environment—current issues: NA

Environment—international agreements: party to: Marine Dumping—associate member to the London Convention and Ship Pollution

Geography—note: archipelago of 17 inhabited islands and one uninhabited island, and a few uninhabited islets; strategically located along important sea lanes in northeastern Atlantic; precipitous terrain limits habitation to small coastal lowlands

PEOPLE AND SOCIETY

Nationality: *noun:* Faroese (singular and plural)
adjective: Faroese

Ethnic groups: Scandinavian

Languages: Faroese (derived from Old Norse), Danish

Religions: Evangelical Lutheran 83.8%, other and unspecified 16.2% (2006 census)

Population: 49,947 (July 2014 est.)
country comparison to the world: 211

Age structure: *0-14 years:* 20.3% (male 5,251/female 4,877)
15-24 years: 15.3% (male 3,942/female 3,701)
25-54 years: 36.8% (male 9,958/female 8,445)
55-64 years: 15.8% (male 3,035/female 2,859)
65 years and over: 15.4% (male 3,819/female 4,060) (2014 est.)

Median age: total: 37.7 years
male: 37.1 years
female: 38.4 years (2014 est.)

Population growth rate: 0.49% (2014 est.)
country comparison to the world: 156

Birth rate: 13.57 births/1,000 population (2014 est.)
country comparison to the world: 147

Death rate: 8.71 deaths/1,000 population (2014 est.)
country comparison to the world: 73

Net migration rate: 0 migrant(s)/1,000 population (2014 est.)
country comparison to the world: 107

Urbanization: *urban population:* 40% of total population (2010)
rate of urbanization: 0.9% annual rate of change (2010-15 est.)

Sex ratio: *at birth:* 1.07 male(s)/female
0-14 years: 1.08 male(s)/female
15-24 years: 1.07 male(s)/female
25-54 years: 1.18 male(s)/female
55-64 years: 1.09 male(s)/female
65 years and over: 0.93 male(s)/female
total population: 1.09 male(s)/female (2014 est.)

Infant mortality rate: *total:* 5.71 deaths/1,000 live births
country comparison to the world: 174
male: 5.97 deaths/1,000 live births
female: 5.43 deaths/1,000 live births (2014 est.)

Life expectancy at birth: *total population:* 80.11 years
country comparison to the world: 34
male: 77.61 years
female: 82.79 years (2014 est.)

Total fertility rate: 2.38 children born/woman (2014 est.)
country comparison to the world: 86

Hospital bed density: 4.7 beds/1,000 population (2012)

HIV/AIDS—adult prevalence rate: NA

HIV/AIDS—people living with HIV/AIDS: NA

HIV/AIDS—deaths: NA

Literacy: NA; note—probably 99%, the same as Denmark proper

Unemployment, youth ages 15-24: *total:* 9.4%
country comparison to the world: 112
male: 6.9%
female: 12.5% (2005)

GOVERNMENT

Country name: *conventional long form:* none
conventional short form: Faroe Islands
local long form: none
local short form: Foroyar

Dependency status: part of the Kingdom of Denmark; self-governing overseas administrative division of Denmark since 1948

Government type: NA

Capital: name: Torshavn
geographic coordinates: 62 00 N, 6 46 W
time difference: UTC 0 (5 hours ahead of Washington, DC during Standard Time)
daylight saving time: +1hr, begins last Sunday in March; ends last Sunday in October

Administrative divisions: none (part of the Kingdom of Denmark; self-governing overseas administrative division of Denmark); there are no first-order administrative divisions as defined by the US Government, but there are 34 municipalities

Independence: none (part of the Kingdom of Denmark; self-governing overseas administrative division of Denmark)

National holiday: Olaifest (Olavsoka), 29 July
Constitution: 5 June 1953 (Danish Constitution), 23 March 1948 (Home Rule Act), and 24 June 2005 (Takeover Act) serve as the Faroe Islands' constitutional position in the Unity of the Realm (2013)

Legal system: the laws of Denmark, where applicable, apply

Suffrage: 18 years of age; universal

Executive branch: *chief of state:* Queen MARGRETHE II of Denmark (since 14 January 1972), represented by High Commissioner Dan Michael KNUDSEN, chief administrative officer (since 2008)
head of government: Prime Minister Kaj Leo JOHANNESSEN (since 26 September 2008)
cabinet: Landsstyri appointed by the prime minister (For more information visit the World Leaders website)
elections: the monarchy is hereditary; high commissioner appointed by the monarch; following legislative elections, the leader of the majority party or the leader of the majority coalition is usually elected prime minister by the Faroese Parliament; election last held on 14 November 2011 (next to be held no later than November 2015)
election results: Kaj Leo JOHANNESSEN reelected prime minister in 2011

Legislative branch: unicameral Faroese Parliament or Logting (33 seats; members elected by popular vote on a proportional basis from the seven constituencies to serve four-year terms)
elections: last held on 29 October 2011 (next to be held no later than October 2015)
election results: percent of vote by party—Union Party 24.7%, People's Party 22.5%, Republican Party 18.3%, Social Democratic Party 17.7%,

Progressive Party 6.3%, Center Party 6.2%, Independence Party 4.2%, other 0.1%; seats by party—Union Party 8, People's Party 8, Republican Party 6, Social Democratic Party 6, Progressive Party 2, Center Party 2, Independence Party 1
note: election of two seats to the Danish Parliament was last held on 15 September 2011 (next to be held no later than September 2015); results—percent of vote by party—NA; seats by party—Social Democratic Party 1, Union Party 1

Judicial branch: the Faroese Court or Raett (Rett—Danish) decides both civil and criminal cases; the Court is part of the Danish legal system

Political parties and leaders: Center Party (Midflokkurin) [Jenis av RANA]; Independence Party (Sjalvstyrisflokkurin) [Kari P. HOJGAARD]; People's Party (Folkaflokkurin) [Jorgen NICLASEN]; Progressive Party (Framsokn) [Poul MICHELSEN]; Republican Party (Tjodveldi) [Hogni HOYDAL]; Social Democratic Party (Javnadarflokkurin) [Aksel JOHANNESEN]; Union Party (Sambandsflokkurin) [Kaj Leo JOHANNESEN]

Political pressure groups and leaders:
conservationists

International organization participation:
Arctic Council, IMO (associate), NC, NIB, UNESCO (associate), UPU

Diplomatic representation in the US: none (self-governing overseas administrative division of Denmark)

Diplomatic representation from the US: none (self-governing overseas administrative division of Denmark)

Flag description: white with a red cross outlined in blue extending to the edges of the flag; the vertical part of the cross is shifted toward the hoist side in the style of the Dannebrog (Danish flag); referred to as Merkid, meaning "the banner" or "the mark," the flag resembles those of neighboring Iceland and Norway, and uses the same three colors—but in a different sequence; white represents the clear Faroese sky as well as the foam of the waves; red and blue are traditional Faroese colors

National symbol(s): ram

National anthem: *name:* "Mitt alfagra land" (My Fairest Land)
lyrics/music: Simun av SKAROI/Peter ALBERG
note: adopted 1948; the anthem is also known as "Tu alfagra land mitt" (Thou Fairest Land of Mine); as an autonomous overseas division of Denmark, the Faroe Islands are permitted their own national anthem

ECONOMY

overview: The Faroese economy is dependent on fishing, which makes the economy vulnerable to price fluctuations. The sector normally accounts for about 95% of exports and nearly half of GDP. In early 2008 the Faroese economy began to slow as a result of smaller catches and historically high oil prices. The slowdown in the Faroese economy followed a strong performance since the mid-1990s with annual growth rates averaging close to 6%, mostly a result of increased fish landings and salmon farming, and high export prices. Unemployment reached its lowest level in June 2008 at 1.1% but gradually increased to about 5.5% in 2012. The Faroese Home Rule Government produced increasing budget surpluses in that period, which helped to reduce the large public debt, most of it to Denmark. However, total dependence on fishing and salmon farming make the Faroese economy vulnerable to fluctuations in world demand. Initial discoveries of oil in the Faroese area give hope for eventual oil production, which may provide a foundation for a more diversified economy and less dependence on Danish economic assistance. Aided by an annual subsidy from Denmark amounting to about 3% of Faroese GDP, the Faroese have a standard of living almost equal to that of Denmark and Greenland. The Faroese Government ran relatively large deficits from 2008 to 2010 and budget deficits are forecast for several years ahead. At year-end 2010 gross external debt had reached approximately US$900 million.

GDP (purchasing power parity): $1.471 billion (2010 est.)
country comparison to the world: 197
$1.389 billion (2008 est.)

GDP (official exchange rate): $2.32 billion (2010 est.)

GDP—real growth rate: 2.9% (2010 est.)
country comparison to the world: 121
0.5% (2008 est.)

GDP—per capita (PPP): $30,500 (2008 est.)
country comparison to the world: 45

GDP—composition, by sector of origin:
agriculture: 16%
industry: 29%
services: 55% (2007 est.)

Agriculture—products: milk, potatoes, vegetables; sheep; salmon, other fish

Industries: fishing, fish processing, small ship repair and refurbishment, handicrafts

Industrial production growth rate: 3.4% (2009 est.)
country comparison to the world: 88

Labor force: 34,710 (November 2010)
country comparison to the world: 203

Labor force—by occupation: agriculture: 10.7%
industry: 18.9%
services: 70.3% (November 2010)

Unemployment rate: 6.8% (2011)
country comparison to the world: 73
5.7% (2010)

Population below poverty line: NA%

Household income or consumption by percentage share: *lowest 10%:* NA%
highest 10%: NA%

Budget: revenues: $1.025 billion
expenditures: $1.301 billion
note: Denmark supplies the Faroe Islands with almost one-third of their public funds (2010 est.)

Taxes and other revenues: 44.2% of GDP (2010 est.)
country comparison to the world: 22

Budget surplus (+) or deficit (-):
-11.9% of GDP (2010 est.)
country comparison to the world: 209

Fiscal year: calendar year

Inflation rate (consumer prices): 2.3% (2011)
country comparison to the world: 83
0.4% (2010)

Exports: $824 million (2010)
country comparison to the world: 165
$767 million (2009)

Exports—commodities: fish and fish products 94%, stamps, ships

Exports—partners: Denmark 23.4%, UK 21%, Nigeria 13.4%, US 8.9%, Netherlands 8.4%, Russia 7%, China 4.4% (2012)

Imports: $776 million (2010)
country comparison to the world: 186
$786 million (2009)

Imports—commodities: goods for household consumption 24%, machinery and transport equipment 23.5%, fuels 21.4%, raw materials and semi-manufactures, salt

Imports—partners: Denmark 42%, Norway 32%, Germany 8.7%, Iceland 5.3% (2012)

Debt—external: $888.8 million (2010)
country comparison to the world: 164
$68.1 million (2006)

Exchange rates: Danish kroner (DKK) per US dollar—
5.695 (2011)
5.6241 (2011 est.)
5.6241 (2010 est.)
5.361 (2009)
5.0236 (2008)

ENERGY

Electricity—production: 261 million kWh (2011 est.)
country comparison to the world: 178

Electricity—consumption: 249 million kWh (2010 est.)
country comparison to the world: 182

Electricity—exports: 0 kWh (2012 est.)
country comparison to the world: 137

Electricity—imports: 0 kWh (2012 est.)
country comparison to the world: 144

Electricity—installed generating capacity:
100,100 kW (2010 est.)
country comparison to the world: 172

Electricity—from fossil fuels: 64.9% of total installed capacity (2010 est.)
country comparison to the world: 123

Electricity—from nuclear fuels: 0% of total installed capacity (2010 est.)
country comparison to the world: 89

Electricity—from hydroelectric plants: 31% of total installed capacity (2010 est.)
country comparison to the world: 76

Electricity—from other renewable sources:
4.1% of total installed capacity (2010 est.)
country comparison to the world: 49

Crude oil—production: 0 bbl/day (2012 est.)
country comparison to the world: 170

Crude oil—exports: 0 bbl/day (2010 est.)
country comparison to the world: 113

Crude oil—imports: 0 bbl/day (2010 est.)
country comparison to the world: 186

Crude oil—proved reserves: 0 bbl (1 January 2013 es)
country comparison to the world: 133

Refined petroleum products—production:
0 bbl/day (2010 est.)
country comparison to the world: 144

Refined petroleum products—consumption:
4,871 bbl/day (2011 est.)
country comparison to the world: 170

Refined petroleum products—exports:
0 bbl/day (2010 est.)
country comparison to the world: 176

Refined petroleum products—imports:
4,661 bbl/day (2010 est.)

country comparison to the world: 157
Natural gas—production: 0 cu m (2011 est.)
country comparison to the world: 132
Natural gas—consumption: 0 cu m (2010 est.)
country comparison to the world: 145
Natural gas—exports: 0 cu m (2011 est.)
country comparison to the world: 101
Natural gas—imports: 0 cu m (2011 est.)
country comparison to the world: 193
Natural gas—proved reserves: 0 cu m (1 January 2013 es)
country comparison to the world: 139
Carbon dioxide emissions from consumption of energy: 785,300 Mt (2011 est.)
country comparison to the world: 170

COMMUNICATIONS

Telephones—main lines in use: 24,000 (2012)
country comparison to the world: 182
Telephones—mobile cellular: 61,000 (2012)
country comparison to the world: 199
Telephone system: *general assessment:* good international communications; good domestic facilities
domestic: conversion to digital system completed in 1998; both NMT (analog) and GSM (digital) mobile telephone systems are installed
international: country code—298; satellite earth stations—1 Orion; 1 fiber-optic submarine cable to the Shetland Islands, linking the Faroe Islands with Denmark and Iceland; fiber-optic submarine cable connection to Canada-Europe cable (2011)
Broadcast media: 1 publicly owned TV station; the Faroese telecommunications company distributes local and international channels through its digital terrestrial network; publicly owned radio station supplemented by 2 privately owned stations broadcasting over multiple frequencies (2008)
Internet country code: .fo
Internet hosts: 7,575 (2012)
country comparison to the world: 140
Internet users: 37,500 (2009)
country comparison to the world: 176

TRANSPORTATION

Airports: 1 (2013)
country comparison to the world: 215
Airports—with paved runways: *total:* 1
1,524 to 2,437 m: 1 (2013)
Roadways: *total:* 463 km (2006)
country comparison to the world: 196
Merchant marine: *total:* 3 7
country comparison to the world: 79
by type: cargo 20, chemical tanker 7, container 2, passenger/cargo 3, refrigerated cargo 3, roll on/roll off 2
foreign-owned: 28 (Iceland 4, Norway 13, Sweden 11) (2010)
Ports and terminals: major seaport(s): Fuglafjordur, Torshavn, Vagur

MILITARY

Military branches: no regular military forces (2012)
Manpower available for military service:
males age 16-49: 11,831 (2010 est.)
Manpower fit for military service: *males age 16-49:* 9,827
females age 16-49: 8,418 (2010 est.)
Manpower reaching militarily significant age annually:
male: 372
female: 373 (2010 est.)
Military—note: defense is the responsibility of Denmark

TRANSNATIONAL ISSUES

Disputes—international: because anticipated offshore hydrocarbon resources have not been realized, earlier Faroese proposals for full independence have been deferred; Iceland, the UK, and Ireland dispute Denmark's claim that the Faroe Islands' continental shelf extends beyond 200 nm

FIJI

INTRODUCTION

Background: Fiji became independent in 1970 after nearly a century as a British colony. Democratic rule was interrupted by two military coups in 1987 caused by concern over a government perceived as dominated by the Indian community (descendants of contract laborers brought to the islands by the British in the 19th century). The coups and a 1990 constitution that cemented native Melanesian control of Fiji led to heavy Indian emigration; the population loss resulted in economic difficulties, but ensured that Melanesians became the majority. A new constitution enacted in 1997 was more equitable. Free and peaceful elections in 1999 resulted in a government led by an Indo-Fijian, but a civilian-led coup in May 2000 ushered in a prolonged period of political turmoil. Parliamentary elections held in August 2001 provided Fiji with a democratically elected government led by Prime Minister Laisenia QARASE. Re-elected in May 2006, QARASE was ousted in a December 2006 military coup led by Commodore Voreqe BAINIMARAMA, who initially appointed himself acting president but in January 2007 became interim prime minister. Since taking power BAINIMARAMA has neutralized his opponents, crippled Fiji's democratic institutions, and initially refused to hold elections. In 2012, he promised to hold elections in 2014.

GEOGRAPHY

Location: Oceania, island group in the South Pacific Ocean, about two-thirds of the way from Hawaii to New Zealand
Geographic coordinates: 18 00 S, 175 00 E
Map references: Oceania
Area: *total:* 18,274 sq km
country comparison to the world: 157
land: 18,274 sq km
water: 0 sq km
Area—comparative: slightly smaller than New Jersey
Land boundaries: 0 km
Coastline: 1,129 km
Maritime claims: measured from claimed archipelagic straight baselines
territorial sea: 12 nm
exclusive economic zone: 200 nm
continental shelf: 200 m depth or to the depth of exploitation; rectilinear shelf claim added
Climate: tropical marine; only slight seasonal temperature variation
Terrain: mostly mountains of volcanic origin
Elevation extremes: *lowest point:* Pacific Ocean 0 m
highest point: Tomanivi 1,324 m
Natural resources: timber, fish, gold, copper, offshore oil potential, hydropower
Land use: arable land: 9.17%
permanent crops: 4.65%
other: 86.17% (2011)
Irrigated land: 30 sq km (2003)
Total renewable water resources: 28.55 cu km (2011)
Freshwater withdrawal (domestic/industrial/agricultural): *total:* 0.08 cu km/yr (30%/11%/59%)
per capita: 100.1 cu m/yr (2005)
Natural hazards: cyclonic storms can occur from November to January
Environment—current issues: deforestation; soil erosion
Environment—international agreements:
party to: Biodiversity, Climate Change, Climate Change-Kyoto Protocol, Desertification, Endangered Species, Law of the Sea, Marine Life *Conservation, Ozone Layer Protection, Tropical Timber 83, Tropical Timber 94, Wetlands*
signed, but not ratified: none of the selected agreements
Geography—note: includes 332 islands; approximately 110 are inhabited

PEOPLE AND SOCIETY

Nationality: *noun:* Fijian(s)
adjective: Fijian
Ethnic groups: iTaukei 56.8% (predominantly Melanesian with a Polynesian admixture), Indian 37.5%, Rotuman 1.2%, other 4.5% (European, part European, other Pacific Islanders, Chinese)

note: a 2010 law replaces 'Fijian' with 'iTuakei' when referring to the original and native settlers of Fiji (2007 est.)

Languages: English (official), Fijian (official), Hindustani

Religions: Protestant 45% (Methodist 34.6%, Assembly of God 5.7%, Seventh Day Adventist 3.9%, and Anglican 0.8%), Hindu 27.9%, other Christian 10.4%, Roman Catholic 9.1%, Muslim 6.3%, Sikh 0.3%, other 0.3%, none 0.8% (2007 est.)

Population: 903,207 (July 2014 est.)
country comparison to the world: 162

Age structure: *0-14 years:* 28.2% (male 130,013/female 124,423)
15-24 years: 17.1% (male 78,751/female 75,358)
25-54 years: 41.1% (male 190,035/female 181,268)
55-64 years: 5.8% (male 35,616/female 34,920)
65 years and over: 5.6% (male 24,282/female 28,541) (2014 est.)

Dependency ratios:
total dependency ratio: 52.2 %
youth dependency ratio: 43.9 %
elderly dependency ratio: 8.3 %
potential support ratio: 12.1 (2013)

Median age: *total:* 27.9 years
male: 27.7 years
female: 28.1 years (2014 est.)

Population growth rate: 0.7% (2014 est.)
country comparison to the world: 145

Birth rate: 19.86 births/1,000 population (2014 est.)
country comparison to the world: 87

Death rate: 6 deaths/1,000 population (2014 est.)
country comparison to the world: 165

Net migration rate: -6.86 migrant(s)/1,000 population (2014 est.)
country comparison to the world: 203

Urbanization: *urban population:* 52% of total population (2010)
rate of urbanization: 1.3% annual rate of change (2010-15 est.)

Major urban areas—population: SUVA (capital) 174,000 (2009)

Sex ratio: *at birth:* 1.05 male(s)/female
0-14 years: 1.05 male(s)/female
15-24 years: 1.05 male(s)/female
25-54 years: 1.05 male(s)/female
55-64 years: 1.03 male(s)/female
65 years and over: 0.85 male(s)/female
total population: 1.03 male(s)/female (2014 est.)

Maternal mortality rate: 26 deaths/100,000 live births (2010)
country comparison to the world: 129

Infant mortality rate: total: 10.2 deaths/1,000 live births
country comparison to the world: 139
male: 11.24 deaths/1,000 live births
female: 9.1 deaths/1,000 live births (2014 est.)

Life expectancy at birth: total population: 72.15 years
country comparison to the world: 139
male: 69.53 years
female: 74.91 years (2014 est.)

Total fertility rate: 2.51 children born/woman (2014 est.)
country comparison to the world: 80

Health expenditures: 3.8% of GDP (2011)
country comparison to the world: 169

Physicians density: 0.43 physicians/1,000 population (2009)

Hospital bed density: 2.1 beds/1,000 population (2009)

Drinking water source:
improved:
urban: 100% of population
rural: 92.2% of population
total: 96.3% of population
unimproved:
urban: 0% of population
rural: 7.8% of population
total: 3.7% of population (2011 est.)

Sanitation facility access:
improved:
urban: 92.1% of population
rural: 81.7% of population
total: 87.1% of population
unimproved:
urban: 7.9% of population
rural: 18.3% of population
total: 12.9% of population (2011 est.)

HIV/AIDS—adult prevalence rate: 0.2% (2012 est.)
country comparison to the world: 112

HIV/AIDS—people living with HIV/AIDS: 900 (2012 est.)
country comparison to the world: 150

HIV/AIDS—deaths: fewer than 100 (2009 est.)
country comparison to the world: 156

Obesity—adult prevalence rate: 30.6% (2008)
country comparison to the world: 25

Children under the age of 5 years underweight: *5.3% (2004)*
country comparison to the world: 90

Education expenditures: 4.2% of GDP (2011)
country comparison to the world: 102

Literacy: *definition:* age 15 and over can read and write
total population: 93.7%
male: 95.5%
female: 91.9% (2003 est.)

School life expectancy (primary to tertiary education): *total:* 16 years (2011)

GOVERNMENT

Country name: conventional long form: Republic of Fiji
conventional short form: Fiji
local long form: Republic of Fiji/Matanitu ko Viti
local short form: Fiji/Viti

Government type: republic

Capital: name: Suva (on Viti Levu)
geographic coordinates: 18 08 S, 178 25 E
time difference: UTC+12 (17 hours ahead of Washington, DC during Standard Time)
daylight saving time: +1hr, begins fourth Sunday in October; ends third Sunday in January

Administrative divisions: 4 divisions and 1 dependency*; Central, Eastern, Northern, Rotuma*, Western

Independence: 10 October 1970 (from the UK)

National holiday: Independence Day, second Monday of October (1970)

Constitution: several previous; latest approved July 1997 (suspended in 2009); note—the prime minister submitted a new draft constitution in March 2013 (2013)

Legal system: common law system based on the English model

International law organization participation: has not submitted an ICJ jurisdiction declaration; accepts ICCt jurisdiction

Suffrage: 21 years of age; universal

Executive branch: *chief of state:* President Ratu Epeli NAILATIKAU (since 30 July 2009) head of government: Prime Minister Laisenia QARASE (since 10 September 2000); note—although QARASE is still the legal prime minister, he has been confined to his home island; former President ILOILOVATU appointed Commodore Voreqe "Frank" BAINIMARAMA interim prime minister under the military regime
cabinet: Cabinet appointed by the prime minister from among the members of Parliament and responsible to Parliament; note—coup leader Commodore Voreqe BAINIMARAMA has appointed an interim cabinet (For more information visit the World Leaders website)
elections: under the constitution, president elected by the Great Council of Chiefs for a five-year term (eligible for a second term); in 2007 the Great Council of Chiefs was suspended from its role in electing the president; prime minister appointed by the president
election results: Ratu Epeli NAILATIKAU was appointed by Chief Justice Anthony GATES

Legislative branch: bicameral Parliament consists of the Senate (32 seats; 14 members appointed by the president on the advice of the Great Council of Chiefs, 9 appointed by the president on the advice of the Prime Minister, 8 on the advice of the opposition leader, and 1 appointed on the advice of the council of Rotuma) and the House of Representatives (71 seats; 23 members reserved for ethnic Fijians, 19 reserved for ethnic Indians, 3 reserved for other ethnic groups, 1 reserved for the council of Rotuma constituency encompassing the whole of Fiji, and 25 open seats; members serve five-year terms)
elections: House of Representatives—last held on 6-13 May 2006 (long delayed, the next elections reportedly will be held in 2014)
election results: House of Representatives—percent of vote by party—SDL 44.6%, FLP 39.2%, UPP 0.8%, independents 4.9%, other 10.5%; seats by party—SDL 36, FLP 31, UPP 2, independents 2

Judicial branch: *highest court(s):* Supreme Court (consists of the chief justice, all justices of the Court of Appeal, and judges appointed specifically as Supreme Court judges); Court of Appeal (consists of the court president, all puisne judges of the High Court, and judges specifically appointed to the Court of Appeal); High Court (chaired by the chief justice and includes a minimum of 10 puisne judges; High Court organized into civil, criminal, family, employment, and tax divisions) note—in 1987, the Supreme Court assumed functions formerly performed by the Judicial Committee of the Privy Council (in London)
judge selection and term of office: chief justice appointed by the president of Fiji on the advice of the prime minister following consultation with the parliamentary leader of the opposition; judges of the Supreme Court, the president of the Court of Appeal, the justices of the Court of Appeal, and puisne judges of the High Court are appointed by the president of Fiji, upon the nomination of the Judicial Service Commission, after consulting with the cabinet minister and the committee of the House of Representatives responsible for the administration of justice; the chief justice, Supreme Court judges, and justices of Appeal generally required to retire at age 70, but may be waived for one or more sessions of the court; puisne judges appointed for not less than 4 years nor more than 7 years with mandatory retirement at age 65
subordinate courts: Magistrates' Court (organized into civil, criminal, juvenile, and small claims divisions)

Political parties and leaders: Dodonu Ni Taukei Party or DNT [Fereti S. DEWA]; Fiji Democratic Party or FDP [Filipe BOLE] (a merger of the Christian Democrat Alliance or VLV [Poesci Waqalevu

BUNE], Fijian; Association Party or FAP, Fijian Political Party or SVT [Sitiveni RABUKA] (primarily Fijian), and New Labor Unity Party or NLUP [Ofa; SWANN]); Fiji Labor Party or FLP [Mahendra CHAUDHRY]; General Voters Party or GVP (became part of United General Party); Girmit Heritage Party or GHP; Justice and Freedom Party or AIM; Lio 'On Famor Rotuma Party or LFR; National Federation Party or NFP [Pramond RAE] (primarily Indian); Nationalist Vanua Takolavo Party or NVTLP [Saula TELAWA]; Party of National Unity or PANU [Ponipate LESAVUA]; Party of the Truth or POTT; United Fiji Party/Sogosogo Duavata ni Lewenivanua or SDL [Laisenia QARASE]; United Peoples Party or UPP [Millis Mick BEDDOES]

Political pressure groups and leaders: Group Against Racial Discrimination or GARD [Dr. Anirudk SINGH] (for restoration of a democratic government)] Viti Landowners Association

International organization participation: ACP, ADB, AOSIS, C (suspended), CP, FAO, G-77, IAEA, IBRD, ICAO, ICRM, IDA, IFAD, IFC, IFRCS, IHO, ILO, IMF, IMO, Interpol, IOC, ISO, *ITSO, ITU, ITUC (NGOs), MIGA, NAM, OPCW, PCA, PIF, Sparteca (suspended), SPC, UN, UNCTAD, UNESCO, UNIDO, UNMISS, UNMIT, UNWTO, UPU, WCO, WFTU (NGOs), WHO, WIPO, WMO, WTO*

Diplomatic representation in the US:
chief of mission: Ambassador Winston THOMPSON (since 20 April 2009)
chancery: 2000 M Street, NW, Suite 710, Washington, DC 20036
telephone: [1] (202) 466-8320
FAX: [1] (202) 466-8325

Diplomatic representation from the US:
chief of mission: Ambassador Frankie A. REED (since 15 October 2011) note—also accredited to Kiribati, Nauru, Tonga, and Tuvalu
embassy: 158 Princes Rd, Tamavua
mailing address: P. O. Box 218, Suva
telephone: [679] 331-4466
FAX: [679] 330-2267

Flag description: light blue with the flag of the UK in the upper hoist-side quadrant and the Fijian shield centered on the outer half of the flag; the blue symbolizes the Pacific ocean and the Union Jack reflects the links with Great Britain; the shield—taken from Fiji's coat of arms—depicts a yellow lion above a white field quartered by the cross of Saint George; the four quarters depict stalks of sugarcane, a palm tree, bananas, and a white dove

National anthem: name: "God Bless Fiji"
lyrics/music: Michael Francis Alexander PRESCOTT/C. Austin MILES (adapted by Michael Francis Alexander PRESCOTT)
note: adopted 1970; the anthem is known in Fijian as "Meda Dau Doka" (Let Us Show Pride); adapted from the hymn, "Dwelling in Beulah Land," the anthem's English lyrics are generally sung, although they differ in meaning from the official Fijian lyrics

ECONOMY

Economy—overview: Fiji, endowed with forest, mineral, and fish resources, is one of the most developed of the Pacific island economies though still with a large subsistence sector. Sugar exports, remittances from Fijians working abroad, and a growing tourist industry—with 400,000 to 500,000 tourists annually—are the major sources of foreign exchange. Fiji's sugar has special access to European Union markets but will be harmed by the EU's decision to cut sugar subsidies. Sugar processing makes up one-third of industrial activity but is not efficient. Fiji's tourism industry was damaged by the December 2006 coup and is facing an uncertain recovery time. In 2007 tourist arrivals were down almost 6%, with substantial job losses in the service sector, and GDP dipped. The coup has created a difficult business climate. The EU has suspended all aid until the interim government takes steps toward new elections. Long-term problems include low investment, uncertain land ownership rights, and the government's inability to manage its budget. Overseas remittances from Fijians working in Kuwait and Iraq have decreased significantly. Fiji's current account deficit peaked at 23% of GDP in 2006, and declined to less than 12% of GDP in 2013.

GDP (purchasing power parity): $4.45 billion (2013 est.)
country comparison to the world: 174
$4.319 billion (2012 est.)
$4.226 billion (2011 est.)
note: data are in 2013 US dollars

GDP (official exchange rate): $4.218 billion (2013 est.)

GDP—real growth rate: 3% (2013 est.)
country comparison to the world: 115
2.2% (2012 est.)
1.9% (2011 est.)

GDP—per capita (PPP): $4,900 (2013 est.)
country comparison to the world: 161
$4,800 (2012 est.)
$4,700 (2011 est.)
note: data are in 2013 US dollars

GDP—composition, by end use:
household consumption: 90.4%
government consumption: 16%
investment in fixed capital: 22.7%
investment in inventories: 0%
exports of goods and services: 39.7%
imports of goods and services: -68.8% (2013 est.)

GDP—composition, by sector of origin:
agriculture: 11.7%
industry: 18.1%
services: 70.2% (2013 est.)

Agriculture—products: sugarcane, coconuts, cassava (manioc), rice, sweet potatoes, bananas; cattle, pigs, horses, goats; fish

Industries: tourism, sugar, clothing, copra, gold, silver, lumber, small cottage industries

Industrial production growth rate: 2.5%
country comparison to the world: 117

Labor force: 335,000 (2007 est.)
country comparison to the world: 163

Labor force—by occupation: agriculture: 70%
industry and services: 30% (2001 est.)

Unemployment rate: 7.6% (1999)
country comparison to the world: 83

Population below poverty line: 31% (2009 est.)

Household income or consumption by percentage share: *lowest 10%:* 2.6%
highest 10%: 34.9% (2009 est.)

Budget: *revenues:* $1.084 billion
expenditures: $1.192 billion (2013 est.)

Taxes and other revenues: 25.7% of GDP (2013 est.)
country comparison to the world: 117

Budget surplus (+) or deficit (-):
-2.6% of GDP (2013 est.)
country comparison to the world: 106

Public debt: 56.2% of GDP (2013 est.)
country comparison to the world: 55
53.5% of GDP (2012 est.)

Fiscal year: calendar year

Inflation rate (consumer prices): 3% (2013 est.)
country comparison to the world: 114
4.4% (2012 est.)

Central bank discount rate: 1.75% (31 December 2010 est.)
country comparison to the world: 106
3% (31 December 2009 est.)

Commercial bank prime lending rate: 6.2% (31 December 2013 est.)
country comparison to the world: 124
7% (31 December 2012 est.)

Stock of narrow money: $1.549 billion (31 December 2013 est.)
country comparison to the world: 137
$1.453 billion (31 December 2012 est.)

Stock of broad money: $2.697 billion (31 December 2013 est.)
country comparison to the world: 146
$2.578 billion (31 December 2012 est.)

Stock of domestic credit: $2.168 billion (31 December 2013 est.)
country comparison to the world: 133
$1.958 billion (31 December 2012 est.)

Market value of publicly traded shares:
$452.5 million (31 December 2012 est.)
country comparison to the world: 112
$392.2 million (31 December 2011)
$418.8 million (31 December 2010 est.)

Current account balance: -$492.3 million (2013 est.)
country comparison to the world: 99
-$425.1 million (2012 est.)

Exports: $1.026 billion (2013 est.)
country comparison to the world: 158
$932.4 million (2012 est.)

Exports—commodities: sugar, garments, gold, timber, fish, molasses, coconut oil

Exports—partners: US 14.6%, Australia 13.2%, Japan 6.9%, Samoa 5.8%, Tonga 5.1% (2012)

Imports: $2.054 billion (2013 est.)
country comparison to the world: 164
$1.867 billion (2012 est.)

Imports—commodities: manufactured goods, machinery and transport equipment, petroleum products, food, chemicals

Imports—partners: Singapore 32.8%, Australia 15.5%, NZ 14.5%, China 10.7% (2012)

Reserves of foreign exchange and gold:
$963.7 million (31 December 2013 est.)
country comparison to the world: 137
$921.4 million (31 December 2012 est.)

Debt—external: $779.9 million (31 December 2013 est.)
country comparison to the world: 168
$685.5 million (31 December 2012 est.)

Stock of direct foreign investment—at home:
$3.17 billion (31 December 2013 est.)
country comparison to the world: 94
$2.903 billion (31 December 2012 est.)

Stock of direct foreign investment—abroad:
$43.03 million (31 December 2013 est.)
country comparison to the world: 89
$44.08 million (31 December 2012 est.)

Exchange rates: Fijian dollars (FJD) per US dollar—
1.845 (2013 est.)
1.7899 (2012 est.)
1.9183 (2010 est.)

ENERGY

Electricity—production: 836.1 million kWh (2011 est.)
country comparison to the world: 151

Electricity—consumption: 808.3 million kWh (2010 est.)
country comparison to the world: 156

Electricity—exports: 0 kWh (2012 est.)

country comparison to the world: 134
Electricity—imports: 0 kWh (2012 est.)
country comparison to the world: 141
Electricity—installed generating capacity: 245,100 kW (2010 est.)
country comparison to the world: 156
Electricity—from fossil fuels: 49% of total installed capacity (2010 est.)
country comparison to the world: 156
Electricity—from nuclear fuels: 0% of total installed capacity (2010 est.)
country comparison to the world: 87
Electricity—from hydroelectric plants: 45.3% of total installed capacity (2010 est.)
country comparison to the world: 50
Electricity—from other renewable sources: 5.7% of total installed capacity (2010 est.)
country comparison to the world: 40
Crude oil—production: 30 bbl/day (2012 est.)
country comparison to the world: 125
Crude oil—exports: 0 bbl/day (2010 est.)
country comparison to the world: 111
Crude oil—imports: 0 bbl/day (2010 est.)
country comparison to the world: 184
Crude oil—proved reserves: 0 bbl (1 January 2013 es)
country comparison to the world: 131
Refined petroleum products—production: 0 bbl/day (2010 est.)
country comparison to the world: 142
Refined petroleum products—consumption: 17,810 bbl/day (2011 est.)
country comparison to the world: 134
Refined petroleum products—exports: 691.6 bbl/day (2010 est.)
country comparison to the world: 110
Refined petroleum products—imports: 10,050 bbl/day (2010 est.)
country comparison to the world: 130
Natural gas—production: 0 cu m (2011 est.)
country comparison to the world: 130
Natural gas—consumption: 0 cu m (2010 est.)
country comparison to the world: 143
Natural gas—exports: 0 cu m (2011 est.)
country comparison to the world: 99
Natural gas—imports: 0 cu m (2011 est.)
country comparison to the world: 191
Natural gas—proved reserves: 0 cu m (1 January 2013 es)
country comparison to the world: 137
Carbon dioxide emissions from consumption of energy: 1.445 million Mt (2011 est.)
country comparison to the world: 155

COMMUNICATIONS

Telephones—main lines in use: 88,400 (2012)
country comparison to the world: 147
Telephones—mobile cellular: 858,800 (2012)
country comparison to the world: 159
Telephone system: *general assessment:* modern local, interisland, and international (wire/radio integrated) public and special-purpose telephone, *telegraph, and teleprinter facilities; regional radio communications center*
domestic: telephone or radio telephone links to almost all inhabited islands; most towns and large villages have automatic telephone exchanges and direct dialing; combined fixed and mobile-cellular teledensity roughly 100 per 100 persons
international: country code—679; access to important cable links between US and Canada as well as between NZ and Australia; satellite earth stations—2 Inmarsat (Pacific Ocean) (2011)
Broadcast media: Fiji TV, a publicly traded company, operates a free-to-air channel as well as Sky Fiji and Sky Pacific multi-channel pay-TV services; state-owned commercial company, Fiji Broadcasting Corporation, Ltd, operates 6 radio stations—2 public broadcasters and 4 commercial broadcasters with multiple repeaters; 5 radio stations with repeaters operated by Communications Fiji, Ltd; transmissions of multiple international broadcasters are available (2009)
Internet country code: .fj
Internet hosts: 21,739 (2012)
country comparison to the world: 115
Internet users: 114,200 (2009)
country comparison to the world: 157

TRANSPORTATION

Airports: 28 (2013)
country comparison to the world: 121
Airports—with paved runways: *total:* 4
over 3,047 m: 1
1,524 to 2,437 m: 1
914 to 1,523 m: 2 (2013)
Airports—with unpaved runways: *total:* 2 4
914 to 1,523 m: 5
under 914 m: 19 (2013)
Railways: total: 597 km
country comparison to the world: 108
narrow gauge: 597 km 0.600-m gauge
note: belongs to the government-owned Fiji Sugar Corporation; used to haul sugarcane during the harvest season, which runs from May to December (2008)
Roadways: *total:* 3,440 km
country comparison to the world: 162
paved: 1,686 km
unpaved: 1,754 km (2011)
Waterways: 203 km (122 km are navigable by motorized craft and 200-metric-ton barges) (2012)
country comparison to the world: 98
Merchant marine: *total:* 1 1
country comparison to the world: 108
by type: passenger 4, passenger/cargo 4, refrigerated cargo 1, roll on/roll off 2
foreign-owned: 2 (Australia 2) (2010)
Ports and terminals: *major seaport(s):* Lautoka, Levuka, Suva

MILITARY

Military branches: Republic of Fiji Military Forces (RFMF): Land Forces, Naval Forces (2011)
Military service age and obligation: 18 years of age for voluntary military service; mandatory retirement at age 55 (2013)
Manpower available for military service: males age 16-49: 233,240
females age 16-49: 222,587 (2010 est.)
Manpower fit for military service:
males age 16-49: 183,730
females age 16-49: 188,325 (2010 est.)
Manpower reaching militarily significant age annually: *male:* 8,403
female: 8,039 (2010 est.)
Military expenditures: 1.47% of GDP (2012)
country comparison to the world: 64
1.44% of GDP (2011)
1.47% of GDP (2010)

TRANSNATIONAL ISSUES

Disputes—international: none

FINLAND

INTRODUCTION

Background: Finland was a province and then a grand duchy under Sweden from the 12th to the 19th centuries, and an autonomous grand duchy of Russia after 1809. It gained complete independence in 1917. During World War II, it successfully defend its independence through cooperation with Germany and resisted subsequent invasions by the Soviet Union—albeit with some loss of territory. In the subsequent half century, Finland transformed from a farm/forest economy to a diversified modern industrial economy; per capita income is among the highest in Western Europe. A member of the European Union since 1995, Finland was the only Nordic state to join the euro single currency at its initiation in January 1999. In the 21st century, the key features of Finland's modern welfare state are high quality education, promotion of equality, and a national social welfare system—currently challenged by an aging population and the fluctuations of an export-driven economy.

GEOGRAPHY

Location: Northern Europe, bordering the Baltic Sea, Gulf of Bothnia, and Gulf of Finland, between Sweden and Russia
Geographic coordinates: 64 00 N, 26 00 E
Map references: Europe
Area: *total:* 338,145 sq km
country comparison to the world: 65
land: 303,815 sq km
water: 34,330 sq km
Area—comparative: slightly smaller than Montana
Land boundaries: total: 2,654 km
border countries: Norway 727 km, Sweden 614 km, Russia 1,313 km
Coastline: 1,250 km
Maritime claims: *territorial sea:* 12 nm (in the Gulf of Finland—3 nm)
contiguous zone: 24 nm
exclusive fishing zone: 12 nm; extends to continental shelf boundary with Sweden
continental shelf: 200 m depth or to the depth of exploitation
Climate: cold temperate; potentially subarctic but comparatively mild because of moderating influence of the North Atlantic Current, Baltic Sea, and more than 60,000 lakes
Terrain: mostly low, flat to rolling plains interspersed with lakes and low hills
Elevation extremes: *lowest point:* Baltic Sea 0 m

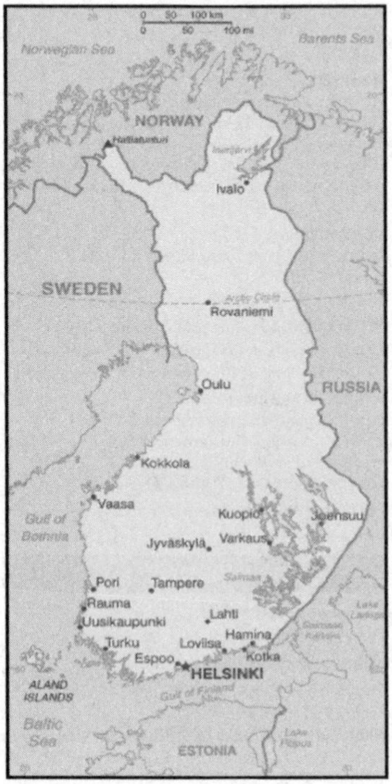

highest point: Halti (alternatively Haltia, Haltitunturi, Haltiatunturi) 1,328 m

Natural resources: timber, iron ore, copper, lead, zinc, chromite, nickel, gold, silver, limestone

Land use: arable land: 6.65%
permanent crops: 0.01%
other: 93.34% (2011)

Irrigated land: 685.8 sq km (2010)

Total renewable water resources: 110 cu km (2011)

Freshwater withdrawal (domestic/industrial/agricultural): *total:* 1.63 cu km/yr (25%/72%/3%)
per capita: 308.9 cu m/yr (2005)

Natural hazards: NA

Environment—current issues: air pollution from manufacturing and power plants contributing to acid rain; water pollution from industrial wastes, agricultural chemicals; habitat loss threatens wildlife populations

Environment—international agreements: *party to:* Air Pollution, Air Pollution-Nitrogen Oxides, Air Pollution-Persistent Organic Pollutants, Air Pollution-Sulfur 85, Air Pollution-Sulfur 94, Air Pollution-Volatile Organic Compounds, Antarctic-Environmental Protocol, Antarctic-Marine Living Resources, Antarctic Treaty, Biodiversity, Climate Change, Climate Change-Kyoto Protocol, Desertification, Endangered Species, Environmental Modification, Hazardous Wastes, Law of the Sea, Marine Dumping, Marine Life Conservation, Ozone Layer Protection, Ship Pollution, Tropical Timber 83, Tropical Timber 94, Wetlands, Whaling signed, but not ratified: none of the selected agreements

Geography—note: long boundary with Russia; Helsinki is northernmost national capital on European continent; population concentrated on small southwestern coastal plain

PEOPLE AND SOCIETY

Nationality: *noun:* Finn(s)
adjective: Finnish

Ethnic groups: Finn 93.4%, Swede 5.6%, Russian 0.5%, Estonian 0.3%, Roma (Gypsy) 0.1%, Sami 0.1% (2006)

Languages: Finnish (official) 94.2%, Swedish (official) 5.5%, other (small Sami- and Russian-speaking minorities) 0.2% (2012 est.)

Religions: Lutheran 78.4%, Orthodox 1.1%, other Christian 1.1%, other 0.2%, none 19.2% (2010 est.)

Population: 5,268,799 (July 2014 est.)
country comparison to the world: 119

Age structure: *0-14 years:* 15.8% (male 423,011/female 408,664)
15-24 years: 12.1% (male 326,140/female 313,621)
25-54 years: 38.1% (male 1,021,798/female 983,423)
55-64 years: 19.8% (male 368,355/female 379,957)
65 years and over: 19.2% (male 439,014/female 604,816) (2014 est.)

Dependency ratios: *total dependency ratio:* 55 %
youth dependency ratio: 25.5 %
elderly dependency ratio: 29.5 %
potential support ratio: 3.4 (2013)

Median age: *total:* 43.2 years
male: 41.2 years
female: 45 years (2014 est.)

Population growth rate: 0.05% (2014 est.)
country comparison to the world: 187

Birth rate: 10.35 births/1,000 population (2014 est.)
country comparison to the world: 186

Death rate: 10.51 deaths/1,000 population (2014 est.)
country comparison to the world: 40

Net migration rate: 0.62 migrant(s)/1,000 population (2014 est.)
country comparison to the world: 67

Urbanization: *urban population:* 85% of total population (2010)
rate of urbanization: 0.6% annual rate of change (2010-15 est.)

Major urban areas—population: HELSINKI (capital) 1.107 million (2009)

Sex ratio: *at birth:* 1.04 male(s)/female
0-14 years: 1.04 male(s)/female
15-24 years: 1.04 male(s)/female
25-54 years: 1.04 male(s)/female
55-64 years: 0.96 male(s)/female
65 years and over: 0.71 male(s)/female
total population: 0.96 male(s)/female (2014 est.)

Mother's mean age at first birth: 27.9 (2005 est.)

Maternal mortality rate: 5 deaths/100,000 live births (2010)
country comparison to the world: 174

Infant mortality rate: *total:* 3.36 deaths/1,000 live births
country comparison to the world: 211
male: 3.65 deaths/1,000 live births
female: 3.06 deaths/1,000 live births (2014 est.)

Life expectancy at birth: total population: 79.69 years
country comparison to the world: 41
male: 76.24 years
female: 83.29 years (2014 est.)

Total fertility rate: 1.73 children born/woman (2014 est.)
country comparison to the world: 169

Health expenditures: 8.9% of GDP (2011)
country comparison to the world: 48

Physicians density: 2.9 physicians/1,000 population (2010)

Hospital bed density: 5.9 beds/1,000 population (2010)

Drinking water source:
improved:
urban: 100% of population
rural: 100% of population
total: 100% of population
unimproved:
urban: 0% of population
rural: 0% of population
total: 0% of population (2011 est.)

Sanitation facility access:
improved:
urban: 100% of population
rural: 100% of population
total: 100% of population
unimproved:
urban: 0% of population
rural: 0% of population
total: 0% of population (2011 est.)

HIV/AIDS—adult prevalence rate: 0.1% (2009 est.)
country comparison to the world: 137

HIV/AIDS—people living with HIV/AIDS:
2,600 (2009 est.)
country comparison to the world: 135

HIV/AIDS—deaths: fewer than 100 (2009 est.)
country comparison to the world: 157

Obesity—adult prevalence rate: 23% (2008)
country comparison to the world: 77

Education expenditures: 6.8% of GDP (2010)
country comparison to the world: 27

Literacy: *definition:* age 15 and over can read and write
total population: 100%
male: 100%
female: 100% (2000 est.)

School life expectancy (primary to tertiary education): *total:* 17 years
male: 16 years
female: 18 years (2011)

Unemployment, youth ages 15-24: total: 17.7%
country comparison to the world: 70
male: 17.6%
female: 17.9% (2012)

GOVERNMENT

Country name: *conventional long form:* Republic of Finland
conventional short form: Finland
local long form: Suomen tasavalta/Republiken Finland
local short form: Suomi/Finland

Government type: republic

Capital: *name:* Helsinki
geographic coordinates: 60 10 N, 24 56 E
time difference: UTC+2 (7 hours ahead of Washington, DC during Standard Time)
daylight saving time: +1hr, begins last Sunday in March; ends last Sunday in October

Administrative divisions: 19 regions (maakunnat, singular—maakunta (Finnish); landskapen, singular—landskapet (Swedish)); Aland (Swedish), Ahvenanmaa (Finnish); Etela-Karjala (Finnish), Sodra Karelen (Swedish) [South Karelia]; Etela-Pohjanmaa (Finnish), Sodra Osterbotten (Swedish) [South Ostrobothnia]; Etela-Savo (Finnish), Sodra Savolax (Swedish) [South Savo]; Kanta-Hame (Finnish), Egentliga Tavastland (Swedish); Kainuu (Finnish), Kajanaland (Swedish); Keski-Pohjanmaa (Finnish), Mellersta Osterbotten (Swedish) [Central Ostrobothnia]; Keski-Suomi (Finnish), Mellersta Finland (Swedish) [Central Finland]; Kymenlaakso (Finnish), Kymmenedalen (Swedish); Lappi (Finnish), Lappland (Swedish); Paijat-Hame (Finnish),

Paijanne-Tavastland (Swedish); Pirkanmaa (Finnish), Birkaland (Swedish) [Tampere]; Pohjanmaa (Finnish), Osterbotten (Swedish) [Ostrobothnia]; Pohjois-Karjala (Finnish), Norra Karelen (Swedish) [North Karelia]; Pohjois-Pohjanmaa (Finnish), Norra Osterbotten (Swedish) [North Ostrobothnia]; Pohjois-Savo (Finnish), Norra Savolax (Swedish) [North Savo]; Satakunta (Finnish and Swedish); Uusimaa (Finnish), Nyland (Swedish) [Newland]; Varsinais-Suomi (Finnish), Egentliga Finland (Swedish) [Southwest Finland]

Independence: 6 December 1917 (from Russia)

National holiday: Independence Day, 6 December (1917)

Constitution: previous 1906, 1919; latest drafted 17 June 1997, approved by Parliament 11 June 1999, entered into force 1 March 2000; amended several times, last in 2011 (2011)

Legal system: civil law system based on the Swedish model

International law organization participation: accepts compulsory ICJ jurisdiction with reservations; accepts ICCt jurisdiction

Suffrage: 18 years of age; universal

Executive branch: *chief of state:* President Sauli NIINISTO (since 1 March 2012)
head of government: Prime Minister Jyrki KATAINEN (since 22 June 2011)
cabinet: Council of State or Valtioneuvosto appointed by the president, responsible to parliament (For more information visit the World Leaders website)
elections: president elected by popular vote for a six-year term (eligible for a second term); election last held on 5 February 2012 (next to be held in February 2018); the parliament elects a prime minister who is then appointed to office by the president
election results: percent of vote—Sauli NIINISTO (Kok) 36.96%, Pekka HAAVISTO (Vihr) 18.76%, Paavo VAYRYNEN (Kesk) 17.53%, Timo SOINI (TF) 9.4%, Paavo LIPPONEN (SDP) 6.7%, Paavo ARHINMÄKI (Vas) 5.48%, Eva BIAUDET (SFP) 2.7%, Sari ESSAYAH (KD) 2.47%; a runoff election between NIINISTO and HAAVISTO was held 5 February 2012—NIINISTO 62.59%, HAAVISTO 37.41%; Jyrki KATAINEN elected prime minister; election results 118-72
note: government coalition—Kok, SDP, Vihr, SFP, Vas, and KD (2013)

Legislative branch: unicameral Parliament or Eduskunta (200 seats; members elected by popular vote on a proportional basis to serve four-year terms)
elections: last held on 17 April 2011 (next to be held in April 2015)
election results: percent of vote by party—Kok 20.4%, SDP 19.1%, PS 19.1%, Kesk 15.8%, Vas 8.1%, Vihr 7.3%, SFP 4.3%, KD 4%, other 1.9%; seats by party—Kok 44, SDP 42, TF 39, Kesk 35, Vas 14, Vihr 10, SFP 9, KD 6, other 1 (the constituency of Aland)

Judicial branch: *highest court(s):* Supreme Court or Korkein Oikeus (consists of the court president and 18 judges); Supreme Administrative Court (consists of 21 judges including the court president and organized into 3 chambers) note—Finland has a dual judicial system—courts with civil and criminal jurisdiction, and administrative courts with jurisdiction for litigation between individuals and administrative organs of the state and communities
judge selection and term of office: Supreme Court and Supreme Administrative Court judges appointed by the president of the republic; judges serve until mandatory retirement at age 65
subordinate courts: 6 Courts of Appeal; 8 regional administrative courts; 27 district courts; special courts for issues relating to markets, labor, insurance, impeachment, land, tenancy, and water rights

Political parties and leaders: Center Party or Kesk [Juha SIPILA]; Christian Democrats or KD [Paivi RASANEN]; Green League or Vihr [Ville NIINISTO]; Left Alliance or Vas [Paavo ARHINMAKI]; National Coalition Party or Kok [Jyrki KATAINEN]; Social Democratic Party or SDP [Jutta URPILAINEN]; Swedish People's Party or SFP [Carl HAGLUND]; The Finns Party or PS [Timo SOINI]

International organization participation: ADB (nonregional member), AfDB (nonregional member), Arctic Council, Australia Group, BIS, CBSS, CD, CE, CERN, EAPC, EBRD, ECB, EIB, EITI (implementing country), EMU, ESA, EU, FAO, FATF, G-9, IADB, IAEA, IBRD, ICAO, ICC (national committees), ICRM, IDA, IEA, IFAD, IFC, IFRCS, IHO, ILO, IMF, IMO, IMSO, Interpol, IOC, IOM, IPU, ISO, ITSO, ITU, ITUC (NGOs), MIGA, MINUSMA, NC, NEA, NIB, NSG, OAS (observer), OECD, OPCW, OSCE, Paris Club, PCA, PFP, Schengen Convention, UN, UNCTAD, UNESCO, UNHCR, UNIDO, UNIFIL, UNMIL, UNMOGIP, UNRWA, UNTSO, UPU, WCO, WFTU (NGOs), WHO, WIPO, WMO, WTO, ZC

Diplomatic representation in the US: *chief of mission:* Ambassador Ritva KOUKKU-RONDE (since 1 September 2011)
chancery: 3301 Massachusetts Avenue NW, Washington, DC 20008
telephone: [1] (202) 298-5800
FAX: [1] (202) 298-6030
consulate(s) general: Los Angeles (Juha Pekka MARKKANEN), New York (Jukka PIETIKAINEN)

Diplomatic representation from the US:
chief of mission: Ambassador Bruce J. ORECK (since 12 August 2009)
embassy: Itainen Puistotie 14B, 00140 Helsinki
mailing address: APO AE 09723
telephone: [358] (9) 616250
FAX: [358] (9) 6162 5800

Flag description: white with a blue cross extending to the edges of the flag; the vertical part of the cross is shifted to the hoist side in the style of the Dannebrog (Danish flag); the blue represents the thousands of lakes scattered across the country, while the white is for the snow that covers the land in winter

National symbol(s): lion

National anthem: *name:* "Maamme" (Our Land)
lyrics/music: Johan Ludvig RUNEBERG/Fredrik PACIUS
note: in use since 1848; although never officially adopted by law, the anthem has been popular since it was first sung by a student group in 1848; Estonia's anthem uses the same melody as that of Finland

Economy

Economy—overview: Finland has a highly industrialized, largely free-market economy with per capita output almost as high as that of Austria, Belgium, the Netherlands, or Sweden. Trade is important, with exports accounting for over one-third of GDP in recent years. Finland is historically competitive in manufacturing—principally the wood, metals, engineering, telecommunications, and electronics industries. Finland excels in export of technology for mobile phones as well as promotion of startups in the ICT, gaming, cleantech, and biotechnology sectors. Except for timber and several minerals, Finland depends on imports of raw materials, energy, and some components for manufactured goods. Because of the climate, agricultural development is limited to maintaining self-sufficiency in basic products. Forestry, an important export earner, provides a secondary occupation for the rural population. Finland had been one of the best performing economies within the EU in recent years and its banks and financial markets avoided the worst of global financial crisis. However, the world slowdown hit exports and domestic demand hard in 2009, with Finland experiencing one of the deepest contractions in the euro zone. A recovery of exports, domestic trade, and household consumption stimulated economic growth in 2010-11, however, continued recession within the EU dampened the economy in 2012-13. The recession affected general government finances and the debt ratio, turning previously strong budget surpluses into deficits, but Finland took action to ensure it that it met the EU deficit targets in 2013 and retained its triple-A credit rating. Finland's main challenge will be to stimulate growth while faced with weak export demand in the EU and its own government austerity measures. Longer-term, Finland must address a rapidly aging population and decreasing productivity in traditional industries that threaten competitiveness, fiscal sustainability, and economic growth.

GDP (purchasing power parity): $195.5 billion (2013 est.)
country comparison to the world: 58
$196.8 billion (2012 est.)
$198.4 billion (2011 est.)
note: data are in 2013 US dollars

GDP (official exchange rate): $259.6 billion (2013 est.)

GDP—real growth rate: -0.6% (2013 est.)
country comparison to the world: 201
-0.8% (2012 est.)
2.7% (2011 est.)

GDP—per capita (PPP): $35,900 (2013 est.)
country comparison to the world: 37
$36,300 (2012 est.)
$36,700 (2011 est.)
note: data are in 2013 US dollars

Gross national saving: 17.9% of GDP (2013 est.)
country comparison to the world: 91
19.6% of GDP (2012 est.)
21.2% of GDP (2011 est.)

GDP—composition, by end use:
household consumption: 56.3%
government consumption: 24.3%
investment in fixed capital: 18.3%
investment in inventories: 0.3%
exports of goods and services: 38%
imports of goods and services: -37.3% (2013 est.)

GDP—composition, by sector of origin:
agriculture: 2.9%
industry: 25.1%
services: 71.9% (2013 est.)

Agriculture—products: barley, wheat, sugar beets, potatoes; dairy cattle; fish

Industries: metals and metal products, electronics, machinery and scientific instruments, shipbuilding, pulp and paper, foodstuffs, chemicals, textiles, clothing

Industrial production growth rate: -4.2% (2013 est.)
country comparison to the world: 188

Labor force: 2.685 million (2013 est.)
country comparison to the world: 110

Labor force—by occupation: *agriculture and forestry:* 4.4%
industry: 15.5%
construction: 7.1%
commerce: 21.3%
finance, insurance, and business services: 13.3%

transport and communications: 9.9%
public services: 28.5% (2011)
Unemployment rate: 8.1% (2013 est.)
country comparison to the world: 91
7.8% (2012 est.)
Population below poverty line: NA%
Household income or consumption by percentage share: *lowest 10%:* 3.6%
highest 10%: 24.7% (2007)
Distribution of family income—Gini index: 26.8 (2008)
country comparison to the world: 129
25.6 (1991)
Budget: *revenues:* $139.4 billion
expenditures: $145.3 billion
note: Central Government Budget (2013 est.)
Taxes and other revenues: 53.7% of GDP (2013 est.)
country comparison to the world: 10
Budget surplus (+) or deficit (-): -2.3% of GDP (2013 est.)
country comparison to the world: 93
Public debt: 56.5% of GDP (2013 est.)
country comparison to the world: 54
53.1% of GDP (2012 est.)
note: data cover general government debt, and includes debt instruments issued (or owned) by government entities other than the treasury; the data include treasury debt held by foreign entities; the data include debt issued by subnational entities, as well as intra-governmental debt; intra-governmental debt consists of treasury borrowings from surpluses in the social funds, such as for retirement, medical care, and unemployment; debt instruments for the social funds are not sold at public auctions
Fiscal year: calendar year
Inflation rate (consumer prices): 2.2% (2013 est.)
country comparison to the world: 77
3.2% (2012 est.)
Central bank discount rate: 0.75% (31 December 2013)
country comparison to the world: 122
1.5% (31 December 2010)
note: this is the European Central Bank's rate on the marginal lending facility, which offers overnight credit to banks in the euro area
Commercial bank prime lending rate: 2% (31 December 2013 est.)
country comparison to the world: 180
2.06% (31 December 2012 est.)
Stock of narrow money: $130.8 billion (31 December 2013 est.)
country comparison to the world: 28
$126.5 billion (31 December 2012 est.)
note: see entry for the European Union for money supply in the euro area; the European Central Bank (ECB) controls monetary policy for the 17 members of the Economic and Monetary Union (EMU); individual members of the EMU do not control the quantity of money circulating within their own borders
Stock of broad money: $183.3 billion (31 December 2013 est.)
country comparison to the world: 41
$182.4 billion (31 December 2012 est.)
Stock of domestic credit: $267.8 billion (31 December 2013 est.)
country comparison to the world: 36
$265.3 billion (31 December 2012 est.)
Market value of publicly traded shares: $158.7 billion (31 December 2012 est.)
country comparison to the world: 36
$143.1 billion (31 December 2011)
$118.2 billion (31 December 2010 est.)
Current account balance: -$2 billion (2013 est.)
country comparison to the world: 144
-$3.679 billion (2012 est.)
Exports: $75.7 billion (2013 est.)
country comparison to the world: 47
$76.46 billion (2012 est.)
Exports—commodities: electrical and optical equipment, machinery, transport equipment, paper and pulp, chemicals, basic metals; timber
Exports—partners: Sweden 11.1%, Russia 9.9%, Germany 9.3%, Netherlands 6.3%, US 6.2%, UK 5.1%, China 4.6% (2012)
Imports: $70.67 billion (2013 est.)
country comparison to the world: 42
$72.13 billion (2012 est.)
Imports—commodities: foodstuffs, petroleum and petroleum products, chemicals, transport equipment, iron and steel, machinery, computers, electronic industry products, textile yarn and fabrics, grains
Imports—partners: Russia 17.7%, Sweden 14.8%, Germany 13.9%, Netherlands 8.1%, China 4.4% (2012)
Reserves of foreign exchange and gold: $10.6 billion (31 December 2013 est.)
country comparison to the world: 74
$11.08 billion (31 December 2012 est.)
Debt—external: $586.9 billion (31 December 2012 est.)
country comparison to the world: 23
$478.5 billion (31 December 2011)
Stock of direct foreign investment—at home: $138.7 billion (31 December 2013 est.)
country comparison to the world: 35
$134.4 billion (31 December 2012 est.)
Stock of direct foreign investment—abroad: $197.2 billion (31 December 2013 est.)
country comparison to the world: 24
$186.7 billion (31 December 2012 est.)
Exchange rates: euros (EUR) per US dollar—
0.7634 (2013 est.)
0.7752 (2012 est.)
0.755 (2010 est.)
0.7198 (2009 est.)
0.6827 (2008 est.)

ENERGY

Electricity—production: 70.34 billion kWh (2011 est.)
country comparison to the world: 3 9
Electricity—consumption: 84.83 billion kWh (2010 est.)
country comparison to the world: 36
Electricity—exports: 1.645 billion kWh (2012 est.)
country comparison to the world: 46
Electricity—imports: 19.09 billion kWh (2012 est.)
country comparison to the world: 8
Electricity—installed generating capacity: 16.68 million kW (2010 est.)
country comparison to the world: 42
Electricity—from fossil fuels: 52.3% of total installed capacity (2010 est.)
country comparison to the world: 151
Electricity—from nuclear fuels: 16.2% of total installed capacity (2010 est.)
country comparison to the world: 14
Electricity—from hydroelectric plants: 18.8% of total installed capacity (2010 est.)
country comparison to the world: 94
Electricity—from other renewable sources: 12.7% of total installed capacity (2010 est.)
country comparison to the world: 19
Crude oil—production: 13,530 bbl/day (2012 est.)
country comparison to the world: 85
Crude oil—exports: 0 bbl/day (2010 est.)
country comparison to the world: 110
Crude oil—imports: 214,700 bbl/day (2010 est.)
country comparison to the world: 33
Crude oil—proved reserves: 0 bbl (1 January 2013 es)
country comparison to the world: 130
Refined petroleum products—production: 282,300 bbl/day (2010 est.)
country comparison to the world: 45
Refined petroleum products—consumption: 204,800 bbl/day (2011 est.)
country comparison to the world: 57
Refined petroleum products—exports: 144,400 bbl/day (2010 est.)
country comparison to the world: 39
Refined petroleum products—imports: 113,800 bbl/day (2010 est.)
country comparison to the world: 47
Natural gas—production: 0 cu m (2011 est.)
country comparison to the world: 129
Natural gas—consumption: 4.7 billion cu m (2010 est.)
country comparison to the world: 64
Natural gas—exports: 0 cu m (2011 est.)
country comparison to the world: 98
Natural gas—imports: 3.661 billion cu m (2012 est.)
country comparison to the world: 39
Natural gas—proved reserves: 0 cu m (1 January 2013 es)
country comparison to the world: 136
Carbon dioxide emissions from consumption of energy: 54.06 million Mt (2011 est.)
country comparison to the world: 58

COMMUNICATIONS

Telephones—main lines in use: 890,000 (2012)
country comparison to the world: 7 9
Telephones—mobile cellular: 9.32 million (2012)
country comparison to the world: 83
Telephone system: *general assessment:* modern system with excellent service
domestic: digital fiber-optic fixed-line network and an extensive mobile-cellular network provide domestic needs
international: country code—358; submarine cables provide links to Estonia and Sweden; satellite earth stations—access to Intelsat transmission service via a Swedish satellite earth station, 1 Inmarsat (Atlantic and Indian Ocean regions); note—Finland shares the Inmarsat earth station with the other Nordic countries (Denmark, Iceland, Norway, and Sweden) (2011)
Broadcast media: a mix of publicly operated TV stations and privately owned TV stations; the 2 publicly owned TV stations recently expanded services and the largest private TV station has introduced several special-interest pay-TV channels; cable and satellite multi-channel subscription services are available; all TV signals have been broadcast digitally since September 2007; analog broadcasts via cable networks were terminated in February 2008; public broadcasting maintains a network of 13 national and 25 regional radio stations; a large number of private radio broadcasters (2008)
Internet country code: .fi; note—Aland Islands assigned .ax
Internet hosts: 4.763 million (2012)
country comparison to the world: 22

Internet users: 4.393 million (2009)
country comparison to the world: 55

TRANSPORTATION

Airports: 148 (2013)
country comparison to the world: 3 9

Airports—with paved runways: *total:* 7 4
over 3,047 m: 3
2,438 to 3,047 m: 26
1,524 to 2,437 m: 10
914 to 1,523 m: 21
under 914 m: 14 (2013)

Airports—with unpaved runways: total: 7 4
914 to 1,523 m: 3
under 914 m: 71 (2013)

Pipelines: gas 1,689 km (2010)

Railways: total: 5,944 km
country comparison to the world: 31
broad gauge: 5,944 km 1.524-m gauge (3,067 km electrified) (2013)

Roadways: total: 78,000 km
country comparison to the world: 60
paved: 50,000 km (includes 700 km of expressways)
unpaved: 28,000 km
note: there 78,000 km of highways, 350,000 km of private and forest roads, and 26,000 km of urban roads giving Finland a total road network of 450,000 km (2012)

Waterways: 8,000 km (includes Saimaa Canal system of 3,577 km; southern part leased from Russia; water transport is used frequently in the summer and is widely replaced with sledges on the ice in winter; there are 187,888 lakes in Finland that cover 31,500 km); Finand also maintains 8,200 km of coastal fairways (2013)
country comparison to the world: 18

Merchant marine: *total:* 9 7
country comparison to the world: 51
by type: bulk carrier 2, cargo 25, carrier 1, chemical tanker 6, container 3, passenger 5, passenger/cargo 16, petroleum tanker 5, roll on/roll off 31, vehicle carrier 3
foreign-owned: 5 (Cyprus 1, Estonia 2, Iceland 1, Sweden 1) registered in other countries: 47 (Bahamas 8, Germany 3, Gibraltar 2, Malta 3, Netherlands 13, Panama 2, Sweden 16) (2010)

Ports and terminals: *major seaport(s):* Helsinki, Kotka, Naantali, Porvoo, Raahe, Rauma

MILITARY

Military branches: Finnish Defense Forces (FDF): Army (Puolustusvoimat), Navy (Merivoimat; includes Coastal Defense Forces), Air Force (Ilmavoimat) (2013)

Military service age and obligation: 18 years of age for male voluntary and compulsory—and female voluntary—national military and nonmilitary service; service obligation 6-12 months; military obligation to age 60 (2012)

Manpower available for military service:
males age 16-49: 1,155,368
females age 16-49: 1,106,193 (2010 est.)

Manpower fit for military service:
males age 16-49: 955,151
females age 16-49: 912,983 (2010 est.)

Manpower reaching militarily significant age annually: *male:* 32,599
female: 31,416 (2010 est.)

Military expenditures: 1.47% of GDP (2012)
country comparison to the world: 65
1.42% of GDP (2011)
1.47% of GDP (2010)

TRANSNATIONAL ISSUES

Disputes—international: various groups in Finland advocate restoration of Karelia and other areas ceded to the Soviet Union, but the Finnish Government asserts no territorial demands

Refugees and internally displaced persons:
stateless persons: 2,017 (2012)

FRANCE

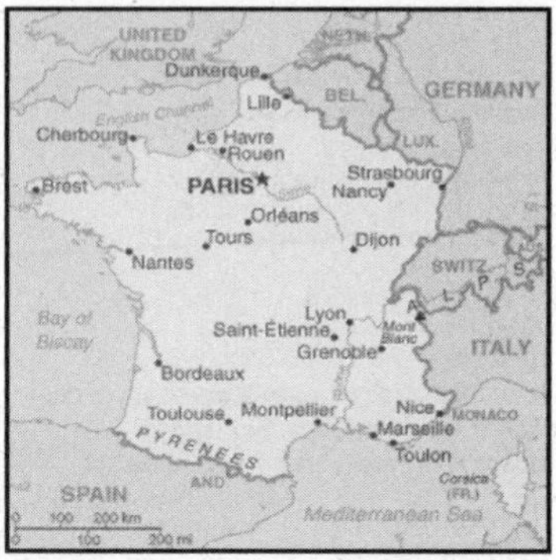

INTRODUCTION

Background: France today is one of the most modern countries in the world and is a leader among European nations. It plays an influential global role as a permanent member of the United Nations Security Council, NATO, the G-8, the G-20, the EU and other multilateral organizations. France rejoined NATO's integrated military command structure in 2009, reversing de Gaulle's 1966 decision to take French forces out of NATO. Since 1958, it has constructed a hybrid presidential-parliamentary governing system resistant to the instabilities experienced in earlier, more purely parliamentary administrations. In recent decades, its reconciliation and cooperation with Germany have proved central to the economic integration of Europe, including the introduction of a common currency, the euro, in January 1999. In the early 21st century, five French overseas entities—French Guiana, Guadeloupe, Martinique, Mayotte, and Reunion—became French regions and were made part of France proper.

GEOGRAPHY

Location: metropolitan France: Western Europe, bordering the Bay of Biscay and English Channel, between Belgium and Spain, southeast of the UK; bordering the Mediterranean Sea, between Italy and Spain
French Guiana: Northern South America, bordering the North Atlantic Ocean, between Brazil and Suriname
Guadeloupe: Caribbean, islands between the Caribbean Sea and the North Atlantic Ocean, southeast of Puerto Rico
Martinique: Caribbean, island between the Caribbean Sea and North Atlantic Ocean, north of Trinidad and Tobago
Mayotte: Southern Indian Ocean, island in the Mozambique Channel, about half way between northern Madagascar and northern Mozambique
Reunion: Southern Africa, island in the Indian Ocean, east of Madagascar

Geographic coordinates:
metropolitan France: 46 00 N, 2 00 E
French Guiana: 4 00 N, 53 00 W
Guadeloupe: 16 15 N, 61 35 W
Martinique: 14 40 N, 61 00 W
Mayotte: 12 50 S, 45 10 E
Reunion: 21 06 S, 55 36 E

Map references: metropolitan France: Europe
French Guiana: South America
Guadeloupe: Central America and the Caribbean
Martinique: Central America and the Caribbean
Mayotte: Africa
Reunion: World

Area: *total:* 643,801 sq km; 551,500 sq km (metropolitan France)
country comparison to the world: 43
land: 640,427 sq km; 549,970 sq km (metropolitan France)
water: 3,374 sq km; 1,530 sq km (metropolitan France)
note: the first numbers include the overseas regions of French Guiana, Guadeloupe, Martinique, Mayotte, and Reunion

Area—comparative: slightly more than four times the size of Georgia; slightly less than the size of Texas

Land boundaries: metropolitan France—total: 2,889 km
border countries: Andorra 56.6 km, Belgium 620 km, Germany 451 km, Italy 488 km, Luxembourg 73 km, Monaco 4.4 km, Spain 623 km, Switzerland 573 km French Guiana—total: 1,183 km
border countries: Brazil 673 km, Suriname 510 km

Coastline: *total:* 4,853 km
metropolitan France: 3,427 km

Maritime claims: territorial sea: 12 nm
contiguous zone: 24 nm
exclusive economic zone: 200 nm (does not apply to the Mediterranean)
continental shelf: 200 m depth or to the depth of exploitation

Climate: metropolitan France: generally cool winters and mild summers, but mild winters and hot summers along the Mediterranean; occasional strong, cold, dry, north-to-northwesterly wind known as mistral
French Guiana: tropical; hot, humid; little seasonal temperature variation
Guadeloupe and Martinique: subtropical tempered by trade winds; moderately high humidity; rainy season (June to October); vulnerable to

devastating cyclones (hurricanes) every eight years on average
Mayotte: tropical; marine; hot, humid, rainy season during northeastern monsoon (November to May); dry season is cooler (May to November)
Reunion: tropical, but temperature moderates with elevation; cool and dry (May to November), hot and rainy (November to April)

Terrain: metropolitan France: mostly flat plains or gently rolling hills in north and west; remainder is mountainous, especially Pyrenees in south, Alps in east
French Guiana: low-lying coastal plains rising to hills and small mountains
Guadeloupe: Basse-Terre is volcanic in origin with interior mountains; Grande-Terre is low limestone
formation; most of the seven other islands are volcanic in origin
Martinique: mountainous with indented coastline; dormant volcano
Mayotte: generally undulating, with deep ravines and ancient volcanic peaks
Reunion: mostly rugged and mountainous; fertile lowlands along coast

Elevation extremes: *lowest point:* Rhone River delta -2 m
highest point: Mont Blanc 4,807 m
note: in order to assess the possible effects of climate change on the ice and snow cap of Mont Blanc, its surface and peak have been extensively measured in recent years; these new peak measurements have exceeded the traditional height of 4,807 m and have varied between 4,808 m and 4,811 m; the actual rock summit is 4,792 m and is 40 m away from the ice-covered summit

Natural resources: metropolitan France: coal, iron ore, bauxite, zinc, uranium, antimony, arsenic, potash, feldspar, fluorspar, gypsum, timber, fish
French Guiana: gold deposits, petroleum, kaolin, niobium, tantalum, clay

Land use: *arable land:* 33.45%
permanent crops: 1.86%
other: 64.69%
note: French Guiana—arable land 0.13%, permanent crops 0.04%, other 99.83% (90% forest, 10% other); Guadeloupe—arable land 11.70%, permanent crops 2.92%, other 85.38%; Martinique—arable land 9.09%, permanent crops 10.0%, other 80.91%; Reunion—arable land 13.94%, permanent crops 1.59%, other 84.47% (2011)

Irrigated land: *total:* 26,420 sq km 26,950 sq km
metropolitan France: 27,230 sq km (2007)

Total renewable water resources: 211 cu km (2011)

Freshwater withdrawal (domestic/industrial/agricultural): *total:* 31.62 cu km/yr (19%/71%/10%)
per capita: 512.1 cu m/yr (2009)

Natural hazards: metropolitan France: flooding; avalanches; midwinter windstorms; drought; forest fires in south near the Mediterranean
overseas departments: hurricanes (cyclones); flooding; volcanic activity (Guadeloupe, Martinique, Reunion)

Environment—current issues: some forest damage from acid rain; air pollution from industrial and vehicle emissions; water pollution from urban wastes, agricultural runoff

Environment—international agreements:
party to: Air Pollution, Air Pollution-Nitrogen Oxides, Air Pollution-Persistent Organic Pollutants, Air Pollution-Sulfur 85, Air Pollution-Sulfur 94, Air Pollution-Volatile Organic Compounds, Antarctic-Environmental Protocol, Antarctic-Marine Living Resources, Antarctic Seals, Antarctic Treaty, Biodiversity, Climate Change, Climate Change-Kyoto Protocol, Desertification, Endangered Species, Hazardous Wastes, Law of the Sea, Marine Dumping, Marine Life Conservation, Ozone Layer Protection, Ship Pollution, Tropical Timber 83, Tropical Timber 94, Wetlands, Whaling
signed, but not ratified: none of the selected agreements

Geography—note: largest West European nation

PEOPLE AND SOCIETY

Nationality: *noun:* Frenchman(men), Frenchwoman (women)
adjective: French

Ethnic groups: Celtic and Latin with Teutonic, Slavic, North African, Indochinese, Basque minorities
overseas departments: black, white, mulatto, East Indian, Chinese, Amerindian

Languages: French (official) 100%, rapidly declining regional dialects and languages (Provencal, Breton, Alsatian, Corsican, Catalan, Basque, Flemish)
overseas departments: French, Creole patois, Mahorian (a Swahili dialect)

Religions: Roman Catholic 83%-88%, Protestant 2%, Jewish 1%, Muslim 5%-10%, unaffiliated 4%
overseas departments: Roman Catholic, Protestant, Hindu, Muslim, Buddhist, pagan

Population: 66,259,012 (July 2014 est.)
country comparison to the world: 22
note: the above figure is for metropolitan France and five overseas regions; the metropolitan France *population is 62,814,233*

Age structure: *0-14 years:* 18.7% (male 6,337,877/female 6,053,185)
15-24 years: 11.9% (male 4,018,044/female 3,837,191)
25-54 years: 38.6% (male 12,851,278/female 12,719,073)
55-64 years: 18.3% (male 4,012,614/female 4,290,624)
65 years and over: 17.9% (male 5,197,519/female 6,941,607) (2014 est.)

Dependency ratios:
total dependency ratio: 56.5 %
youth dependency ratio: 28.5 %
elderly dependency ratio: 27.9 %
potential support ratio: 3.6 (2013)

Median age: *total:* 40.9 years
male: 39.3 years
female: 42.4 years (2014 est.)
Population growth rate:
0.45% (2014 est.)
country comparison to the world: 158

Birth rate: 12.49 births/1,000 population (2014 est.)
country comparison to the world: 159

Death rate: 9.06 deaths/1,000 population (2014 est.)
country comparison to the world: 66

Net migration rate: 1.09 migrant(s)/1,000 population (2014 est.)
country comparison to the world: 59

Urbanization: *urban population:* 85% of total population (2010)
rate of urbanization: 1% annual rate of change (2010-15 est.)

Major urban areas—population: PARIS (capital) 10.41 million; Marseille-Aix-en-Provence 1.457 million; Lyon 1.456 million; Lille 1.028 million; Nice-Cannes 977,000 (2009)

Sex ratio: *at birth:* 1.05 male(s)/female
0-14 years: 1.05 male(s)/female
15-24 years: 1.05 male(s)/female
25-54 years: 1.01 male(s)/female
55-64 years: 0.96 male(s)/female
65 years and over: 0.74 male(s)/female
total population: 0.96 male(s)/female (2014 est.)

Mother's mean age at first birth: 28.6 (2006 est.)

Maternal mortality rate: 8 deaths/100,000 live births (2010)
country comparison to the world: 158

Infant mortality rate: *total:* 3.31 deaths/1,000 live births
country comparison to the world: 214
male: 3.63 deaths/1,000 live births
female: 2.97 deaths/1,000 live births (2014 est.)

Life expectancy at birth:
total population: 81.66 years
country comparison to the world: 15
male: 78.55 years
female: 84.91 years (2014 est.)

Total fertility rate: 2.08 children born/woman (2014 est.)
country comparison to the world: 112

Contraceptive prevalence rate: 76.4%
note: percent of women aged 20-49 (2008)

Health expenditures: 11.6% of GDP (2011)
country comparison to the world: 10

Physicians density: 3.38 physicians/1,000 population (2011)

Hospital bed density: 6.6 beds/1,000 population (2010)

Drinking water source:
improved:
urban: 100% of population
rural: 100% of population
total: 100% of population
unimproved:
urban: 0% of population
rural: 0% of population
total: 0% of population (2011 est.)

Sanitation facility access:
improved:
urban: 100% of population
rural: 100% of population
total: 100% of population
unimproved:
urban: 0% of population
rural: 0% of population
total: 0% of population (2011 est.)

HIV/AIDS—adult prevalence rate: 0.4% (2009 est.)
country comparison to the world: 78

HIV/AIDS—people living with HIV/AIDS: 150,000 (2009 est.)
country comparison to the world: 34

HIV/AIDS—deaths: 1,700 (2009 est.)
country comparison to the world: 62

Obesity—adult prevalence rate: 18.2% (2008)
country comparison to the world: 108

Education expenditures: 5.9% of GDP (2010)
country comparison to the world: 43

Literacy: *definition:* age 15 and over can read and write
total population: 99%
male: 99%
female: 99% (2003 est.)

School life expectancy (primary to tertiary education): *total:* 16 years
male: 16 years
female: 16 years (2011)

Unemployment, youth ages 15-24: *total:* 23.8%
country comparison to the world: 43
male: 23.9%
female: 23.7% (2012)

GOVERNMENT

Country name: conventional long form: French Republic
conventional short form: France
local long form: Republique francaise
local short form: France

Government type: republic

Capital: *name:* Paris
geographic coordinates: 48 52 N, 2 20 E
time difference: UTC+1 (6 hours ahead of Washington, DC during Standard Time)
daylight saving time: +1hr, begins last Sunday in March; ends last Sunday in October
note: applies to metropolitan France only, not to its overseas departments, collectivities, or territories

Administrative divisions: 27 regions (regions, singular—region); Alsace, Aquitaine, Auvergne, Basse-Normandie (Lower Normandy), Bourgogne (Burgundy), Bretagne (Brittany), Centre, Champagne-Ardenne, Corse (Corsica), Franche-Comte, Guadeloupe, Guyane (French Guiana), Haute-Normandie (Upper Normandy), Ile-de-France, Languedoc-Roussillon, Limousin, Lorraine, Martinique, Mayotte, Midi-Pyrenees, Nord-Pas-de-Calais, Pays de la Loire, Picardie, Poitou-Charentes, Provence-Alpes-Cote d'Azur, Reunion, Rhone-Alpes
note: France is divided into 22 metropolitan regions (including the "territorial collectivity" of Corse or Corsica) and 5 overseas regions (French Guiana, Guadeloupe, Martinique, Mayotte, and Reunion) and is subdivided into 96 metropolitan departments and 5 overseas departments (which are the same as the overseas regions)

Dependent areas: Clipperton Island, French Polynesia, French Southern and Antarctic Lands, New Caledonia, Saint Barthelemy, Saint Martin, Saint Pierre and Miquelon, Wallis and Futuna
note: the US does not recognize claims to Antarctica; New Caledonia has been considered a "sui generis" collectivity of France since 1998, a unique status falling between that of an independent country and a French overseas department

Independence: no official date of independence: 486 (Frankish tribes unified under Merovingian kingship); 10 August 843 (Western Francia established from the division of the Carolingian Empire); 14 July 1789 (French monarchy overthrown); 22 September 1792 (First French Republic founded); 4 October 1958 (Fifth French Republic established)

National holiday: Fete de la Federation, 14 July (1790); note—although often incorrectly referred to as Bastille Day, the celebration actually commemorates the holiday held on the first anniversary of the storming of the Bastille (on 14 July 1789) and the establishment of a constitutional monarchy; other names for the holiday are Fete Nationale (National Holiday) and quatorze juillet (14th of July)

Constitution: 4 October 1958 (French Constitution) (2013)

Legal system: civil law; review of administrative but not legislative acts

International law organization participation: has not submitted an ICJ jurisdiction declaration; accepts ICCt jurisdiction

Suffrage: 18 years of age; universal

Executive branch: *chief of state:* President Francois HOLLANDE (since 15 May 2012)
head of government: Prime Minister Manuel VALLS (since 1 April 2014)
cabinet: Council of Ministers appointed by the president at the suggestion of the prime minister (For more information visit the World Leaders website)
elections: president elected by popular vote for a five-year term (eligible for a second term); election last held on 22 April and 6 May 2012 (next to be held in the spring of 2017); prime minister appointed by the president
election results: Francois HOLLANDE elected; first round: percent of vote—Francois HOLLANDE 28.6%, Nicolas SARKOZY 27.2%, Marine LE PEN 17.9%, Jean-Luc MELENCHON 11.1%, Francois BAYROU, 9.1%, others 6.1%; second round: HOLLANDE 51.6%, SARKOZY 48.4%

Legislative branch: bicameral Parliament or Parlement consists of the Senate or Senat (348 seats; 328 for metropolitan France and overseas departments, 2 for New Caledonia, 2 for French Polynesia, 1 for Saint-Pierre and Miquelon, 1 for Saint-Barthelemy, 1 for Saint-Martin, 1 for Wallis and Futuna, and 12 for French nationals abroad; members indirectly elected by an electoral college to serve six-year terms; one third elected every three years); and the National Assembly or Assemblee Nationale (577 seats; 555 for metropolitan France, 15 for overseas departments, 7 for overseas dependencies; members elected by popular vote under a single-member majority system to serve five-year terms)
elections: Senate—last held on 25 September 2011 (next to be held in September 2014); National Assembly—last held on 10 and 17 June 2012 (next to be held in June 2017)
election results: Senate—percent of vote by party—NA; seats by party—PS/Greens 140, UMP 132, UDF 31, PCF/MRC 21, PRG 17, other 7; National Assembly—percent of vote by party—PS 48.5%, UMP 33.6%, miscellaneous left wing parties 3.8%, Greens 3.0%, miscellaneous right wing parties 2.6%, NC 2.1%, PRG 2.1%, FDG 1.7%, other 2.6%; seats by party—PS 280, UMP 194, miscellaneous left wing parties 22, Greens 17, miscellaneous right wing parties 15, NC 12, PRG 12, FDG 10, other 15

Judicial branch: *highest court(s):* Court of Cassation or Cour de Cassation (consists of the court president, 6 divisional presiding judges, 120 trial judges, and 70 deputy judges organized into 6 divisions—3 civil, 1 commercial, 1 labor, and 1 criminal); Constitutional Council (consists of 9 members)
judge selection and term of office: Court of Cassation judges appointed by the president of the republic from nominations from the High Council of the Judiciary, presided by the Court of Cassation and 15 appointed members; judge term of appointment NA; Constitutional Council members appointed—3 by the president of the republic and 3 each by the National Assembly and Senate presidents; members serve 9-year, non-renewable terms with one third of the membership renewed every 3 years
subordinate courts: appellate courts or Cour d'Appel; regional courts or Tribunal de Grande Instance; first instance courts or Tribunal' d'instance

Political parties and leaders: Europe Ecology—The Greens or EELV [Emmanuelle COSSE]; French Communist Party or PCF [Pierre LAURENT]; Left Front Coalition or FDG [Jean-Luc MELENCHON]; Left Party or PG [Jean-Luc MELENCHON and Martine BILLARD]; Left Radical Party or PRG [Jean-Michel BAYLET] (previously Radical Socialist Party or PRS and the Left; Radical Movement or MRG); Movement for France or MPF [Philippe DE VILLIERS]; National Front or FN [Marine LE PEN]; New Anticapitalist Party or NPA [collective leadership; main spokesperson Christine POUPIN]; New Center or NC [Herve MORIN]; Radical Party [Jean-Louis BORLOO]; Rally for France or RPF [Charles PASQUA]; Republican and Citizen Movement or MRC [Jean-Luc LAURENT]; Socialist Party or PS [Haerlem DESIR]; United Republic or RS [Dominique DE VILLEPIN]; Union for a Popular Movement or UMP [Jean-Francois COPE]; Union des Democrates et Independants or UDI [Jean-Louis BORLOO] and Democratic Movement or MoDem; [Francois BAYROU] (previously Union for French Democracy or UDF); together known as UDI-Modem; Worker's Struggle (Lutte Ouvriere) or LO [collective leadership; spokespersons Nathalie ARTHAUD and; Arlette LAQUILLER]

Political pressure groups and leaders: Confederation Francaise Democratique du Travail (French Democratic Confederation of Labor) or CFDT, left-leaning labor union with approximately 875,000 members [Laurent BERGER, Secretary General]
Confederation francaise de l'encadrement—Confederation generale des cadres (French Confederation of Management—General Confederation of Executives) or CFE-CGC, independent white-collar union with 140,000 members [Carole COUVERT, president]
Confederation francaise des travailleurs chretiens (French Confederation of Christian Workers) or CFTC, independent labor union founded by Catholic workers that claims 142,000 members [Philippe LOUIS, president]
Confederation generale du travail (General Confederation of Labor) or CGT, historically communist labor union with approximately 710,000 members [Bernard THIBAULT, secretary general] Confederation generale du travail—Force ouvriere (General Confederation of Labor—Worker's Force) or FO, independent labor union with an estimated 300,000 members [Jean-Claude MAILLY, secretary general]
Mouvement des entreprises de France or MEDEF, employers' union with 750,000 companies as members (claimed) [Pierre GATTAZ, president]

French Guiana:
conservationists
gold mining pressure groups
hunting pressure groups

Guadeloupe:
Christian Movement for the Liberation of Guadeloupe or KLPG; General Federation of Guadeloupe Workers or CGT-G; General Union of Guadeloupe Workers or UGTG; Movement for an Independent Guadeloupe or MPGI; The Socialist Renewal Movement

Martinique:
Caribbean Revolutionary Alliance or ARC; Central Union for Martinique Workers or CSTM; Frantz Fanon Circle; League of Workers and Peasants; Proletarian Action Group or GAP

Reunion: NA

International organization participation: ADB (nonregional member), AfDB (nonregional member), Arctic Council (observer), Australia Group, BDEAC, BIS, BSEC (observer), CBSS (observer), CE, CERN, EAPC, EBRD, ECB, EIB, EITI (implementing country), EMU, ESA, EU, FAO, FATF, FZ, G-20, G-5, G-7, G-8, G-10, IADB, IAEA, IBRD, ICAO, ICC (national committees), ICRM, IDA, IEA, IFAD, IFC, IFRCS, IGAD (partners), IHO, ILO, IMF, IMO, IMSO, InOC, Interpol, IOC, IOM, IPU, ISO, ITSO,

ITU, ITUC (NGOs), MIGA, MINURSO, MINUSMA, MINUSTAH, MONUSCO, NATO, NEA, NSG, OAS; (observer), OECD, OIF, OPCW, OSCE, Paris Club, PCA, PIF (partner), Schengen Convention, SELEC (observer), SPC, UN, UN Security Council, UNCTAD, UNESCO, UNHCR, UNIDO, UNIFIL, Union Latina, UNMIL, UNOCI, UNRWA, UNSC (permanent), UNTSO, UNWTO, UPU, WCO, WFTU (NGOs), WHO, WIPO, WMO, WTO, ZC

Diplomatic representation in the US:
chief of mission: Ambassador Francois M. DELATTRE (since 18 February 2011)
chancery: 4101 Reservoir Road NW, Washington, DC 20007
telephone: [1] (202) 944-6000
FAX: [1] (202) 944-6166
consulate(s) general: Atlanta, Boston, Chicago, Houston, Los Angeles, Miami, New Orleans, New York, San Francisco

Diplomatic representation from the US:
chief of mission: Ambassador (vacant); Charge d'Affaires Mark A. TAPLIN; note—also accredited to Monaco
embassy: 2 Avenue Gabriel, 75382 Paris Cedex 08
mailing address: PSC 116, APO AE 09777
telephone: [33] (1) 43-12-22-22
FAX: [33] (1) 42 66 97 83
consulate(s) general: Marseille, Strasbourg

Flag description: three equal vertical bands of blue (hoist side), white, and red; known as the "Le drapeau tricolore" (French Tricolor), the origin of the flag dates to 1790 and the French Revolution when the "ancient French color" of white was combined with the blue and red colors of the Parisian militia; the official flag for all French dependent areas
note: the design and/or colors are similar to a number of other flags, including those of Belgium, Chad, Cote d'Ivoire, Ireland, Italy, Luxembourg, and Netherlands

National symbol(s): Gallic rooster, fleur-de-lis, Marianne

National anthem: *name:* "La Marseillaise" (The Song of Marseille)
lyrics/music: Claude-Joseph ROUGET de Lisle
note: adopted 1795, restored 1870; originally known as "Chant de Guerre pour l'Armee du Rhin" (War Song for the Army of the Rhine), the National Guard of Marseille made the song famous by singing it while marching into Paris in 1792 during the French Revolutionary Wars

ECONOMY

Economy—overview: The French economy is diversified across all sectors. The government has partially or fully privatized many large companies, including Air France, France Telecom, Renault, and Thales. However, the government maintains a strong presence in some sectors, particularly power, public transport, and defense industries. With at least 82 million foreign tourists per year, France is the most visited country in the world and maintains the third largest income in the world from tourism. France's leaders remain committed to a capitalism in which they maintain social equity by means of laws, tax policies, and social spending that mitigate economic inequality. France's real GDP stagnated in 2012 and 2013. The unemployment rate (including overseas territories) increased from 7.8% in 2008 to 10.2% in 2013. Youth unemployment in metropolitan France decreased from a high of 25.4% in the fourth quarter of 2012 to 22.8% in the fourth quarter of 2013. Lower-than-expected growth and high spending have strained France's public finances. The budget deficit rose sharply from 3.3% of GDP in 2008 to 7.5% of GDP in 2009 before improving to 4.1% of GDP in 2013, while France's public debt rose from 68% of GDP to nearly 94% over the same period. In accordance with its EU obligations, France is targeting a deficit of 3.6% of GDP in 2014 and 2.8% in 2015. The administration of President Francois HOLLANDE has implemented greater state support for employment, the separation of banks' traditional deposit taking and lending activities from more speculative businesses, increasing the top corporate and personal tax rates, including a temporary 75% tax on wages over one million euros, and hiring an additional 60,000 teachers during his five-year term. In January 2014 HOLLANDE proposed a "Responsibility Pact" aimed primarily at lowering labor costs in return for businesses' commitment to create jobs. Despite stagnant growth and fiscal challenges, France's borrowing costs have declined in recent years because investors remain attracted to the liquidity of France's bonds.

GDP (purchasing power parity): $2.273 trillion (2013 est.)
country comparison to the world: 10
$2.269 trillion (2012 est.)
$2.268 trillion (2011 est.)
note: data are in 2013 US dollars

GDP (official exchange rate): $2.739 trillion (2013 est.)

GDP—real growth rate: 0.2% (2013 est.)
country comparison to the world: 189
0% (2012 est.)
2% (2011 est.)

GDP—per capita (PPP): $35,700 (2013 est.)
country comparison to the world: 38
$35,800 (2012 est.)
$36,000 (2011 est.)
note: data are in 2013 US dollars

Gross national saving: 17.1% of GDP (2013 est.)
country comparison to the world: 97
17.6% of GDP (2012 est.)
18.9% of GDP (2011 est.)

GDP—composition, by end use:
household consumption: 57.6%
government consumption: 25.1%
investment in fixed capital: 18.7%
investment in inventories: 0.1%
exports of goods and services: 27.3%
imports of goods and services: -28.8% (2013 est.)

GDP—composition, by sector of origin:
agriculture: 1.9%
industry: 18.7%
services: 79.4% (2013 est.)

Agriculture—products: wheat, cereals, sugar beets, potatoes, wine grapes; beef, dairy products; fish

Industries: machinery, chemicals, automobiles, metallurgy, aircraft, electronics; textiles, food processing; tourism

Industrial production growth rate: -0.4% (2013 est.)
country comparison to the world: 172

Labor force: 29.94 million (2013 est.)
country comparison to the world: 21

Labor force—by occupation: agriculture: 3.8%
industry: 24.3%
services: 71.8% (2005)

Unemployment rate: 10.5% (2013 est.)
country comparison to the world: 111
9.8% (2012 est.)
note: includes overseas territories

Population below poverty line: 7.8% (2010)

Household income or consumption by percentage share: *lowest 10%:* 3%
highest 10%: 24.8% (2004)

Distribution of family income—Gini index:
32.7 (2008)
country comparison to the world: 103
32.7 (1995)

Budget: revenues: $1.41 trillion
expenditures: $1.52 trillion (2013 est.)

Taxes and other revenues: 51.5% of GDP (2013 est.)
country comparison to the world: 11

Budget surplus (+) or deficit (-):
-4% of GDP (2013 est.)
country comparison to the world: 143

Public debt: 93.8% of GDP (2013 est.)
country comparison to the world: 17
90.3% of GDP (2012 est.)
note: data cover general government debt, and includes debt instruments issued (or owned) by government entities other than the treasury; the data include treasury debt held by foreign entities; the data include debt issued by subnational entities, as well as intra-governmental debt; intra-governmental debt consists of treasury borrowings from surpluses in the social funds, such as for retirement, medical care, and unemployment; debt instruments for the social funds are not sold at public auctions

Fiscal year: calendar year

Inflation rate (consumer prices): 1.1% (2013 est.)
country comparison to the world: 28
2.2% (2012 est.)

Central bank discount rate: 0.75% (31 December 2013)
country comparison to the world: 121
1.5% (31 December 2010)
note: this is the European Central Bank's rate on the marginal lending facility, which offers overnight credit to banks in the euro area

Commercial bank prime lending rate:
3.1% (31 December 2013 est.)
country comparison to the world: 172
3.44% (31 December 2012 est.)

Stock of narrow money: $951 billion (31 December 2013 est.)
country comparison to the world: 7
$939.1 billion (31 December 2012 est.)
note: see entry for the European Union for money supply in the euro area; the European Central Bank (ECB) controls monetary policy for the 17 members of the Economic and Monetary Union (EMU); individual members of the EMU do not control the quantity of money circulating within their own borders

Stock of broad money: $2.656 trillion (31 December 2013 est.)
country comparison to the world: 7
$2.611 trillion (31 December 2012 est.)

Stock of domestic credit:
$3.687 trillion (31 December 2013 est.)
country comparison to the world: 6
$3.631 trillion (31 December 2012 est.)

Market value of publicly traded shares:
$1.823 trillion (31 December 2012 est.)
country comparison to the world: 7
$1.569 trillion (31 December 2011)
$1.926 trillion (31 December 2010 est.)

Current account balance: -$47.3 billion (2013 est.)
country comparison to the world: 187
-$57.2 billion (2012 est.)

Exports: $570.1 billion (2013 est.)
country comparison to the world: 6
$567.4 billion (2012 est.)

Exports—commodities: machinery and transportation equipment, aircraft, plastics, chemicals, pharmaceutical products, iron and steel, beverages

Exports—partners: Germany 16.7%, Belgium 7.5%, Italy 7.5%, Spain 6.9%, UK 6.9%, US 5.6%, Netherlands 4.3% (2012)

Imports: $640.1 billion (2013 est.)
country comparison to the world: 7
$643.4 billion (2012 est.)

Imports—commodities: machinery and equipment, vehicles, crude oil, aircraft, plastics, chemicals

Imports—partners: Germany 19.5%, Belgium 11.3%, Italy 7.6%, Netherlands 7.4%, Spain 6.6%, UK 5.1%, China 4.9% (2012)

Reserves of foreign exchange and gold: $184.5 billion (31 December 2012 est.)
country comparison to the world: 15
$171.9 billion (31 December 2011 est.)

Debt—external: $5.371 trillion (31 December 2012 est.)
country comparison to the world: 5
$5.004 trillion (31 December 2011)

Stock of direct foreign investment—at home: $1.103 trillion (31 December 2013 est.)
country comparison to the world: 7
$1.095 trillion (31 December 2012 est.)

Stock of direct foreign investment—abroad: $1.489 trillion (31 December 2013 est.)
country comparison to the world: 4
$1.497 trillion (31 December 2012 est.)

Exchange rates: euros (EUR) per US dollar—
0.7634 (2013 est.)
0.7752 (2012 est.)
0.755 (2010 est.)
0.7198 (2009 est.)
0.6827 (2008 est.)

ENERGY

Electricity—production: 530.6 billion kWh (2011 est.)
country comparison to the world: 9

Electricity—consumption: 471 billion kWh (2010 est.)
country comparison to the world: 9

Electricity—exports: 56.69 billion kWh (2012 est.)
country comparison to the world: 3

Electricity—imports: 12.52 billion kWh (2012 est.)
country comparison to the world: 14

Electricity—installed generating capacity: 124.3 million kW (2010 est.)
country comparison to the world: 9

Electricity—from fossil fuels: 22.1% of total installed capacity (2010 est.)
country comparison to the world: 189

Electricity—from nuclear fuels: 50.8% of total installed capacity (2010 est.)
country comparison to the world: 1

Electricity—from hydroelectric plants: 14.7% of total installed capacity (2010 est.)
country comparison to the world: 104

Electricity—from other renewable sources: 6.9% of total installed capacity (2010 est.)
country comparison to the world: 36

Crude oil—production: 72,300 bbl/day (2012 est.)
country comparison to the world: 55

Crude oil—exports: 0 bbl/day (2010 est.)
country comparison to the world: 115

Crude oil—imports: 1.298 million bbl/day (2010 est.)
country comparison to the world: 9

Crude oil—proved reserves: 85.18 million bbl (1 January 2013 es)
country comparison to the world: 71

Refined petroleum products—production: 1.55 million bbl/day (2010 est.)
country comparison to the world: 13

Refined petroleum products—consumption: 1.792 million bbl/day (2011 est.)
country comparison to the world: 13

Refined petroleum products—exports: 464,300 bbl/day (2010 est.)
country comparison to the world: 16

Refined petroleum products—imports: 834,800 bbl/day (2010 est.)
country comparison to the world: 7

Natural gas—production: 508 million cu m (2012 est.)
country comparison to the world: 70

Natural gas—consumption: 47.99 billion cu m (2010 est.)
country comparison to the world: 18

Natural gas—exports: 5.994 billion cu m (2012 est.)
country comparison to the world: 32

Natural gas—imports: 47.71 billion cu m (2012 est.)
country comparison to the world: 8

Natural gas—proved reserves: 10.7 billion cu m (1 January 2013 es)
country comparison to the world: 82

Carbon dioxide emissions from consumption of energy: 374.3 million Mt (2011 est.)
country comparison to the world: 19

COMMUNICATIONS

Telephones—main lines in use: 39.29 million (2012)
country comparison to the world: 7

Telephones—mobile cellular: 62.28 million (2012)
country comparison to the world: 21

Telephone system: *general assessment:* highly developed
domestic: extensive cable and microwave radio relay; extensive use of fiber-optic cable; domestic satellite system
international: country code—33; numerous submarine cables provide links throughout Europe, Asia, Australia, the Middle East, and US; satellite earth stations—more than 3 (2 Intelsat (with total of 5 antennas - 2 for Indian Ocean and 3 for Atlantic Ocean), NA Eutelsat, 1 Inmarsat—Atlantic Ocean region); HF radiotelephone communications with more than 20 countries
overseas departments: country codes: French Guiana—594; Guadeloupe—590; Martinique—596; Mayotte—262; Reunion—262 (2011)

Broadcast media: a mix of both publicly operated and privately owned TV stations; state-owned France Televisions operates 4 networks, one of which is a network of regional stations, and has part-interest in several thematic cable/satellite channels and international channels; a large number of privately owned regional and local TV stations; multi-channel satellite and cable services provide a large number of channels; public broadcaster Radio France operates 7 national networks, a series of regional networks, and operates services for overseas territories and foreign audiences; Radio France Internationale (RFI), under the Ministry of Foreign Affairs, is a leading international broadcaster; a large number of commercial FM stations, with many of them consolidating into commercial networks (2008)

Internet country code: metropolitan France—.fr; French Guiana—.gf; Guadeloupe—.gp; Martinique—.mq; Mayotte—.yt; Reunion—.re

Internet hosts: 17.266 million (2012)
country comparison to the world: 7

Internet users: 45.262 million; 44.625 million (metropolitan France) (2009)
country comparison to the world: 8

TRANSPORTATION

Airports: 464 (2013)
country comparison to the world: 1 7

Airports—with paved runways: *total:* 294
over 3,047 m: 14
2,438 to 3,047 m: 25
1,524 to 2,437 m: 97
914 to 1,523 m: 83
under 914 m: 75 (2013)

Airports—with unpaved runways: *total:* 170
1,524 to 2,437 m: 1
914 to 1,523 m: 64
under 914 m: 105 (2013)

Heliports: 1 (2013)

Pipelines: gas 15,322 km; oil 2,939 km; refined products 5,084 km (2013)

Railways: total: 29,640 km
country comparison to the world: 9
standard gauge: 29,473 km 1.435-m gauge (15,361 km electrified)
narrow gauge: 167 km 1.000-m gauge (63 km electrified) (2008)

Roadways: total: 1,028,446 km (metropolitan France; includes 11,416 km of expressways)
country comparison to the world: 8
note: there are another 5,100 km of roadways in overseas departments (2010)

Waterways: metropolitan France: 8,501 km (1,621 km accessible to craft of 3,000 metric tons) (2010)
country comparison to the world: 16

Merchant marine: total: 162
country comparison to the world: 36
by type: bulk carrier 3, cargo 7, chemical tanker 34, container 27, liquefied gas 12, passenger 10, passenger/cargo 41, petroleum tanker 16, refrigerated cargo 1, roll on/roll off 11
foreign-owned: 50 (Belgium 7, Bermuda 5, Denmark 11, French Polynesia 11, Germany 1, New Caledonia 3, Singapore 3, Sweden 4, Switzerland 5)
registered in other countries: 151 (Bahamas 15, Belgium 7, Bermuda 1, Canada 1, Cyprus 16, Egypt 1, Hong Kong 4, Indonesia 1, Ireland 2, Italy 2, Luxembourg 15, Malta 8, Marshall Islands 7, Mexico 1, Morocco 3, Netherlands 2, Norway 5, Panama 7, Saint Vincent and the Grenadines 2, Singapore 3, South Korea 2, Taiwan 2, UK 39, US 4, unknown 1) (2010)

Ports and terminals: *major seaport(s):* Brest, Calais, Dunkerque, Le Havre, Marseille, Nantes,
river port(s): Paris, Rouen (Seine); Strasbourg (Rhine); Bordeaux (Garronne)
container port(s): Le Havre (2,215,262)(2011)
cruise/ferry port(s): Calais, Cherbourg, Le Havre

MILITARY

Military branches: Army (Armee de Terre; includes Marines, Foreign Legion, Army Light Aviation), Navy (Marine Nationale), Air Force (Armee de l'Air (AdlA); includes Air Defense) (2011)

Military service age and obligation: 17-40 years of age for male and female voluntary military service (with parental consent); no conscription; 1-year service obligation; women serve in non-combat posts (2013)

Manpower available for military service:
males age 16-49: 14,563,662
females age 16-49: 14,238,434 (2010 est.)

Manpower fit for military service:
males age 16-49: 12,025,341
females age 16-49: 11,721,827 (2010 est.)

Manpower reaching militarily significant age annually: *male:* 396,050
female: 377,839 (2010 est.)

Military expenditures: 2.26% of GDP (2012)
country comparison to the world: 36
2.25% of GDP (2011)
2.26% of GDP (2010)

TRANSNATIONAL ISSUES

Disputes—international: Madagascar claims the French territories of Bassas da India, Europa Island, Glorioso Islands, and Juan de Nova Island; Comoros claims Mayotte; Mauritius claims Tromelin Island; territorial dispute between Suriname and the French overseas department of French Guiana; France asserts a territorial claim in Antarctica (Adelie Land); France and Vanuatu claim Matthew and Hunter Islands, east of New Caledonia

Refugees and internally displaced persons:
refugees (country of origin): 23,225 (Sri Lanka); 12,666 (Cambodia); 12,585 (Democratic Republic of the Congo); 11,767 (Russia); 11,506 (Serbia); 10,887 (Turkey); 8,605 (Vietnam); 7,335 (Laos) (2012)
stateless persons: 1,210 (2012)

Illicit drugs: *metropolitan France:* transshipment point for South American cocaine, Southwest Asian heroin, and European synthetics
French Guiana: small amount of marijuana grown for local consumption; minor transshipment point to Europe
Martinique: transshipment point for cocaine and marijuana bound for the US and Europee

FRENCH POLYNESIA

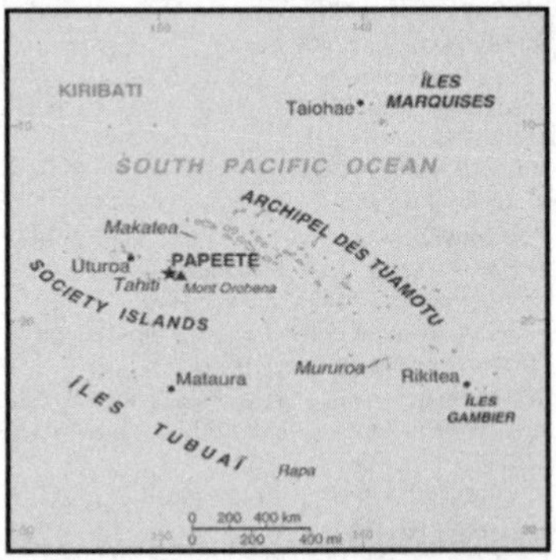

INTRODUCTION

Background: The French annexed various Polynesian island groups during the 19th century. In September 1995, France stirred up widespread protests by resuming nuclear testing on the Mururoa atoll after a three-year moratorium. The tests were halted in January 1996. In recent years, French Polynesia's autonomy has been considerably expanded.

GEOGRAPHY

Location: Oceania, five archipelagoes (Archipel des Tuamotu, Iles Gambier, Iles Marquises, Iles Tubuai, Society Islands) in the South Pacific Ocean about half way between South America and Australia

Geographic coordinates: 15 00 S, 140 00 W

Map references: Oceania

Area: *total:* 4,167 sq km (118 islands and atolls)
country comparison to the world: 175
land: 3,827 sq km
water: 340 sq km

Area—comparative: slightly less than one-third the size of Connecticut

Land boundaries: 0 km

Coastline: 2,525 km

Maritime claims: *territorial sea:* 12 nm
exclusive economic zone: 200 nm

Climate: tropical, but moderate

Terrain: mixture of rugged high islands and low islands with reefs

Elevation extremes: *lowest point:* Pacific Ocean 0 m
highest point: Mont Orohena 2,241 m

Natural resources: timber, fish, cobalt, hydropower

Land use: *arable land:* 0.68%
permanent crops: 6.28%
other: 93.03% (2011)

Irrigated land: 10 sq km (2003)

Natural hazards: occasional cyclonic storms in January

Environment—current issues: NA
Geography—note:
includes five archipelagoes: four volcanic (Iles Gambier, Iles Marquises, Iles Tubuai, Society Islands) and one coral (Archipel des Tuamotu); Makatea in French Polynesia is one of the three great phosphate rock islands in the Pacific Ocean—the others are Banaba (Ocean Island) in Kiribati and Nauru

PEOPLE AND SOCIETY

Nationality: *noun:* French Polynesian(s)
adjective: French Polynesian

Ethnic groups: Polynesian 78%, Chinese 12%, local French 6%, metropolitan French 4%

Languages: French (official) 61.1%, Polynesian (official) 31.4%, Asian languages 1.2%, other 0.3%, unspecified 6% (2002 census)

Religions: Protestant 54%, Roman Catholic 30%, other 10%, no religion 6%

Population: 280,026 (July 2014 est.)
country comparison to the world: 182

Age structure: *0-14 years:* 23.7% (male 34,182/female 32,276)
15-24 years: 16.7% (male 24,219/female 22,559)
25-54 years: 43.9% (male 63,034/female 59,859)
55-64 years: 7.1% (male 12,305/female 11,599)
65 years and over: 6.9% (male 9,713/female 10,280) (2014 est.)

Dependency ratios:
total dependency ratio: 42.4 %
youth dependency ratio: 32.2 %
elderly dependency ratio: 10.2 %
potential support ratio: 9.8 (2013)

Median age: *total:* 30.6 years
male: 30.5 years
female: 30.7 years (2014 est.)

Population growth rate: 0.97% (2014 est.)
country comparison to the world: 122

Birth rate: 15.47 births/1,000 population (2014 est.)
country comparison to the world: 131

Death rate: 4.93 deaths/1,000 population (2014 est.)
country comparison to the world: 191

Net migration rate: -0.87 migrant(s)/1,000 population (2014 est.)
country comparison to the world: 147

Urbanization: *urban population:* 51% of total population (2010)
rate of urbanization: 1.3% annual rate of change (2010-15 est.)

Major urban areas—population: PAPEETE (capital) 133,000 (2009)

Sex ratio: *at birth:* 1.05 male(s)/female
0-14 years: 1.06 male(s)/female
15-24 years: 1.07 male(s)/female
25-54 years: 1.05 male(s)/female
55-64 years: 1.05 male(s)/female
65 years and over: 0.95 male(s)/female
total population: 1.05 male(s)/female (2014 est.)

Infant mortality rate: *total:* 4.78 deaths/1,000 live births
country comparison to the world: 180
male: 5.31 deaths/1,000 live births
female: 4.22 deaths/1,000 live births (2014 est.)

Life expectancy at birth: *total population:* 76.79 years
country comparison to the world: 73
male: 74.54 years
female: 79.15 years (2014 est.)

Total fertility rate: 1.95 children born/woman (2014 est.)
country comparison to the world: 132

Drinking water source:
improved:
urban: 100% of population
rural: 100% of population
total: 100% of population
unimproved:
urban: 0% of population
rural: 0% of population
total: 0% of population (2011 est.)

Sanitation facility access:
improved:
urban: 97.1% of population
rural: 97.1% of population
total: 97.1% of population
unimproved:
urban: 2.9% of population
rural: 2.9% of population

total: 2.9% of population (2011 est.)

HIV/AIDS—adult prevalence rate: NA

HIV/AIDS—people living with HIV/AIDS: NA

HIV/AIDS—deaths: NA

Literacy: *definition:* age 14 and over can read and write
total population: 98%
male: 98%
female: 98% (1977 est.)

Unemployment, youth ages 15-24: total: 33.2%
country comparison to the world: 24
male: 29.3%
female: 39.1% (2002)

GOVERNMENT

Country name: *conventional long form:* Overseas Lands of French Polynesia
conventional short form: French Polynesia
local long form: Pays d'outre-mer de la Polynesie Francaise
local short form: Polynesie Francaise
former: French Colony of Oceania

Dependency status: *overseas lands of France*; overseas territory of France from 1946-2003; overseas collectivity of France since 2003, though it is often referred to as an overseas country due to its degree of autonomy

Government type: parliamentary representative democratic French overseas collectivity

Capital: *name:* Papeete (located on Tahiti)
geographic coordinates: 17 32 S, 149 34 W
time difference: UTC-10 (5 hours behind Washington, DC during Standard Time)

Administrative divisions: none (overseas lands of France); there are no first-order administrative divisions as defined by the US Government, but there are five second order administrative units named Iles Australes, Iles du Vent, Iles Marquises, Iles Sous le Vent, Iles Tuamotu et Gambier

Independence: none (overseas lands of France)

National holiday: Fete de la Federation, 14 July (1789); note—the local holiday is Internal Autonomy Day, 29 June (1880)

Constitution: 4 October 1958 (French Constitution)

Legal system: the laws of France, where applicable, apply

Suffrage: 18 years of age; universal

Executive branch: *chief of state:* President Francois HOLLANDE (since 15 May 2012), represented by High Commissioner of the Republic Lionel BEFFRE (since 16 September 2013)
head of government: President of French Polynesia Gaston FLOSS (since 17 May 2013); President of the Assembly of French Polynesia L. Edouard FRITCH (since 16 May 2013)
cabinet: Council of Ministers; president submits a list of members of the Assembly for approval by them to serve as ministers (For more information visit the World Leaders website)
elections: French president elected by popular vote for a five-year term; high commissioner appointed by the French president on the advice of the French Ministry of Interior; president of the French Polynesia government and the president of the Assembly of French Polynesia elected by the members of the assembly for five-year terms (no term limits)

Legislative branch: unicameral Assembly of French Polynesia or Assemblee de la Polynesia francaise (57 seats; members elected by popular vote to serve five-year terms)
elections: last held on 21 April 2013 (first round) and 5 May 2013 (second round) (next to be held in 2018)
election results: percent of vote by party—Popular Rally 45.1%, Union for Democracy alliance 29.3%, A Tia Porinetia 25.6%, other 15.8%; seats by party—Popular Rally 38, Union for Democracy alliance 11, A Tia Porinetia 8
note: two seats were elected to the French Senate on 21 September 2008 (next to be held in September 2014); results—percent of vote by party—NA; seats by party—UMP 1, independent 1; three seats were elected to the French National Assembly on 17 June 2012 (next to be held by June 2017); results—percent of vote by party—NA; seats by party—UMP 3

Judicial branch: *highest court(s):* Court of Appeal or Cour d'Appel (composition NA) note—appeals beyond the French Polynesia Court of Appeal are heard by the Court of Cassation (in Paris)

judge selection and term of office: NA
subordinate courts: Court of the First Instance or Tribunal de Premiere Instance; Court of Administrative Law or Tribunal Administratif

Political parties and leaders: A Tia Porinetia [Teva ROHFRITSCH]; Alliance for a New Democracy or ADN (includes the parties The New Star and This Country is Yours); New Fatherland Party (Ai'a Api) [Emile Vernaudon]; Our Home alliance; People's Servant Party (Tavini Huiraatira) [Oscar TEMARU]; Popular Rally (Tahoeraa Huiraatira) [Gaston FLOSSE]; Union for Democracy alliance or UPD [Oscar TEMARU]

Political pressure groups and leaders: NA

International organization participation: ITUC (NGOs), PIF (associate member), SPC, UPU

Diplomatic representation in the US: none (overseas lands of France)

Diplomatic representation from the US: none (overseas lands of France)

Flag description: two red horizontal bands encase a wide white band in a 1:2:1 ratio; centered on the white band is a disk with a blue and white wave pattern depicting the sea on the lower half and a gold and white ray pattern depicting the sun on the upper half; a Polynesian canoe rides on the wave pattern; the canoe has a crew of five represented by five stars that symbolize the five island groups; red and white are traditional Polynesian colors
note: similar to the red-white-red flag of Tahiti, the largest of the islands in French Polynesia, which has no emblem in the white band; the flag of France is used for official occasions

National symbol(s): outrigger canoe

National anthem: name: "Ia Ora 'O Tahiti Nui" (Long Live Tahiti Nui)
lyrics/music: Maeva BOUGES, Irmine TEHEI, Angele TEROROTUA, Johanna NOUVEAU, Patrick AMARU, Louis MAMATUI and Jean-Pierre CELESTIN
note: adopted 1993; serves as a local anthem; as a territory of France, "La Marseillaise" is official (see France)

Government—note: under certain acts of France, French Polynesia has acquired autonomy in all areas except those relating to police and justice, monetary policy, tertiary education, immigration, and defense and foreign affairs; the duties of its president are fashioned after those of the French prime minister

ECONOMY

Economy—overview: Since 1962, when France stationed military personnel in the region, French Polynesia has changed from a subsistence agricultural economy to one in which a high proportion of the work force is either employed by the military or supports the tourist industry. With the halt of French nuclear testing in 1996, the military contribution to the economy fell sharply. Tourism accounts for about one-fourth of GDP and is a primary source of hard currency earnings. Other sources of income are handicrafts, public works projects, aquaculture, pearl farming and deep-sea commercial fishing. The small manufacturing sector primarily processes agricultural products. The territory benefits substantially from development agreements with France aimed principally at creating new businesses and strengthening social services.

GDP (purchasing power parity): $5.65 billion (2006 est.)
country comparison to the world: 168
$5.674 billion (2005 est.)
$5.525 billion (2004 est.)

GDP (official exchange rate): $5.65 billion (2006)

GDP—real growth rate: -0.4% (2006)
country comparison to the world: 199
2.7% (2005)

GDP—per capita (PPP): $22,000 (2006 est.)
country comparison to the world: 67
$18,000 (2004 est.)

GDP—composition, by sector of origin:
agriculture: 3.1%
industry: 20%
services: 76.9% (2006)

Agriculture—products: coconuts, vanilla, vegetables, fruits, coffee; poultry, beef, dairy products; fish

Industries: tourism, pearls, agricultural processing, handicrafts, phosphates

Industrial production growth rate: NA%

Labor force: 116,000 (2007)
country comparison to the world: 181

Labor force—by occupation: agriculture: 13%
industry: 19%
services: 68% (2002)

Unemployment rate: 11.7% (2010)
country comparison to the world: 121
11.7% (2005)

Population below poverty line: 19.7% (2009)

Household income or consumption by percentage share: *lowest* 10%: NA%
highest 10%: NA%

Budget: *revenues:* $865 million
expenditures: $644.1 million (1999)

Taxes and other revenues: 15.3% of GDP (1999)
country comparison to the world: 191

Budget surplus (+) or deficit (-):
3.9% of GDP (1999)
country comparison to the world: 11

Fiscal year: calendar year

Inflation rate (consumer prices): 1.1% (2007)
country comparison to the world: 24
1.1% (2006 est.)

Market value of publicly traded shares: $NA

Exports: $200 million (2008 est.)
country comparison to the world: 184
$211 million (2005 est.)

Exports—commodities: cultured pearls, coconut products, mother-of-pearl, vanilla, shark meat
Imports:
$2.2 billion (2008 est.)
country comparison to the world: 162
$1.706 billion (2005 est.)

Imports—commodities: fuels, foodstuffs, machinery and equipment

Debt—external: $NA

Exchange rates: Comptoirs Francais du Pacifique francs (XPF) per US dollar—
90.01 (2010 est.)
87.59 (2007)

ENERGY

Electricity—production: 672 million kWh (2010 est.)
country comparison to the world: 157

Electricity—consumption: 625 million kWh (2010 est.)
country comparison to the world: 165

Electricity—exports: 0 kWh (2012 est.)
country comparison to the world: 138

Electricity—imports: 0 kWh (2012 est.)
country comparison to the world: 145

Electricity—installed generating capacity: 186,000 kW (2010 est.)
country comparison to the world: 159

Electricity—from fossil fuels: 74.7% of total installed capacity (2010 est.)
country comparison to the world: 101

Electricity—from nuclear fuels: 0% of total installed capacity (2010 est.)
country comparison to the world: 90

Electricity—from hydroelectric plants: 25.3% of total installed capacity (2010 est.)
country comparison to the world: 84

Electricity—from other renewable sources: 0% of total installed capacity (2010 est.)
country comparison to the world: 173

Crude oil—production: 0 bbl/day (2012 est.)
country comparison to the world: 171

Crude oil—exports: 0 bbl/day (2010 est.)
country comparison to the world: 114

Crude oil—imports: 0 bbl/day (2010 est.)
country comparison to the world: 187

Crude oil—proved reserves: 0 bbl (1 January 2013 es)
country comparison to the world: 134

Refined petroleum products—production: 0 bbl/day (2010 est.)
country comparison to the world: 145

Refined petroleum products—consumption: 8,000 bbl/day (2011 est.)
country comparison to the world: 158

Refined petroleum products—exports: 0 bbl/day (2010 est.)
country comparison to the world: 177

Refined petroleum products—imports: 7,190 bbl/day (2010 est.)
country comparison to the world: 136

Natural gas—production: 0 cu m (2011 est.)
country comparison to the world: 133

Natural gas—consumption: 0 cu m (2010 est.)
country comparison to the world: 146

Natural gas—exports: 0 cu m (2011 est.)
country comparison to the world: 102

Natural gas—imports: 0 cu m (2011 est.)
country comparison to the world: 194

Natural gas—proved reserves: 0 cu m (1 January 2013 es)
country comparison to the world: 140

Carbon dioxide emissions from consumption of energy: 1.22 million Mt (2011 est.)
country comparison to the world: 162

COMMUNICATIONS

Telephones—main lines in use: 55,000 (2012)
country comparison to the world: 162

Telephones—mobile cellular: 226,000 (2012)
country comparison to the world: 180

Telephone system: *domestic:* combined fixed and mobile-cellular density is roughly 100 per 100 persons
international: country code—689; satellite earth station—1 Intelsat (Pacific Ocean) (2011)

Broadcast media: the publicly owned French Overseas Network (RFO), which operates in France's overseas departments and territories, broadcasts on 2 TV channels and 1 radio station; 1 government-owned TV station; a small number of privately owned radio stations (2008)

Internet country code: .pf

Internet hosts: 37,949 (2012)
country comparison to the world: 103

Internet users: 120,000 (2009)
country comparison to the world: 153

TRANSPORTATION

Airports: 54 (2013)
country comparison to the world: 8 8

Airports—with paved runways: total: 4 5
over 3,047 m: 2
1,524 to 2,437 m: 5
914 to 1,523 m: 33
under 914 m: 5 (2013)

Airports—with unpaved runways: total: 9
914 to 1,523 m: 4
under 914 m: 5 (2013)

Heliports: 1 (2013)

Roadways: total: 2,590 km
country comparison to the world: 171
paved: 1,735 km
unpaved: 855 km (1999)

Merchant marine: registered in other countries: 12 (Cambodia 1, France 11) (2010)
country comparison to the world: 105

Ports and terminals: *major seaport(s):* Papeete

MILITARY

Military branches: no regular military forces (2011)

Manpower available for military service:
males age 16-49: 82,722 (2010 est.)

Manpower fit for military service:
males age 16-49: 67,363
females age 16-49: 66,053 (2010 est.)

Manpower reaching militarily significant age annually: *male:* 2,498
female: 2,390 (2010 est.)

Military—note: defense is the responsibility of France

TRANSNATIONAL ISSUES

Disputes—international: none

FRENCH SOUTHERN AND ANTARCTIC LANDS

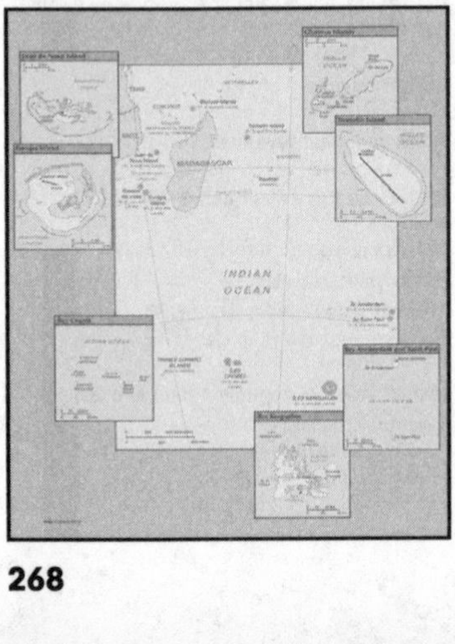

INTRODUCTION

Background: In February 2007, the Iles Eparses became an integral part of the French Southern and Antarctic Lands (TAAF). The Southern Lands are now divided into five administrative districts, two of which are archipelagos, Iles Crozet and Iles Kerguelen; the third is a district composed of two volcanic islands, Ile Saint-Paul and Ile Amsterdam; the fourth, Iles Eparses, consists of five scattered tropical islands around Madagascar. They contain no permanent inhabitants and are visited only by researchers studying the native fauna, scientists at the various scientific stations, fishermen, and military personnel. The fifth district is the Antarctic portion, which consists of "Adelie Land," a thin slice of the Antarctic continent discovered and claimed by the French in 1840.

Ile Amsterdam: Discovered but not named in 1522 by the Spanish, the island subsequently received the appellation of Nieuw Amsterdam from a Dutchman; it was claimed by France in 1843. A short-lived attempt at cattle farming began in 1871. A French meteorological station established on the island in 1949 is still in use. Ile Saint Paul: Claimed by France since 1893, the island was a fishing industry center from 1843 to 1914. In 1928, a spiny lobster cannery was established, but when the company went bankrupt in 1931, seven workers were abandoned. Only two survived until 1934 when rescue finally arrived. Iles Crozet: A large archipelago formed from the Crozet Plateau, Iles Crozet is divided into two main groups: L'Occidental (the West), which includes Ile aux Cochons, Ilots des Apotres, Ile des Pingouins, and the reefs Brisants de l'Heroine; and L'Oriental (the East), which includes Ile d'Est and Ile de la Possession (the largest island of the Crozets). Discovered and claimed by France in 1772, the islands were used for seal hunting and as a base for whaling. Originally administered as a dependency of Madagascar, they became part of the TAAF in 1955.

Iles Kerguelen: This island group, discovered in 1772, is made up of one large island (Ile Kerguelen) and about 300 smaller islands. A permanent group of 50 to 100 scientists resides at the main base at Port-aux-Francais.

Adelie Land: The only non-insular district of the TAAF is the Antarctic claim known as "Adelie Land." The US Government does not recognize it as a French dependency.

Bassas da India: A French possession since 1897, this atoll is a volcanic rock surrounded by reefs and is awash at high tide.

Europa Island: This heavily wooded island has been a French possession since 1897; it is the site of a small military garrison that staffs a weather station.

Glorioso Islands: A French possession since 1892, the Glorioso Islands are composed of two lushly vegetated coral islands (Ile Glorieuse and Ile du Lys) and three rock islets. A military garrison operates a weather and radio station on Ile Glorieuse.

Juan de Nova Island: Named after a famous 15th century Spanish navigator and explorer, the island has been a French possession since 1897. It has been exploited for its guano and phosphate. Presently a small military garrison oversees a meteorological station.

Tromelin Island: First explored by the French in 1776, the island came under the jurisdiction of Reunion in 1814. At present, it serves as a sea turtle sanctuary and is the site of an important meteorological station.

GEOGRAPHY

Location: southeast and east of Africa, islands in the southern Indian Ocean, some near Madagascar and others about equidistant between Africa, Antarctica, and Australia; note—French Southern and Antarctic Lands include Ile Amsterdam, Ile Saint-Paul, Iles Crozet, Iles Kerguelen, Bassas da India, Europa Island, Glorioso Islands, Juan de Nova Island, and Tromelin Island in the southern Indian Ocean, along with the French-claimed sector of Antarctica, "Adelie Land"; the US does not recognize the French claim to "Adelie Land"

Geographic coordinates:
Ile Amsterdam (Ile Amsterdam et Ile Saint-Paul): 37 50 S, 77 32 E
Ile Saint-Paul (Ile Amsterdam et Ile Saint-Paul): 38 72 S, 77 53 E
Iles Crozet: 46 25 S, 51 00 E
Iles Kerguelen: 49 15 S, 69 35 E
Bassas da India (Iles Eparses): 21 30 S, 39 50 E
Europa Island (Iles Eparses): 22 20 S, 40 22 E
Glorioso Islands (Iles Eparses): 11 30 S, 47 20 E
Juan de Nova Island (Iles Eparses): 17 03 S, 42 45 E
Tromelin Island (Iles Eparses): 15 52 S, 54 25 E

Map references: Antarctic Region

Area:
Ile Amsterdam (Ile Amsterdam et Ile Saint-Paul): total—55 sq km; land—55 sq km; water—0 sq km
country comparison to the world: 230
Ile Saint-Paul (Ile Amsterdam et Ile Saint-Paul): total—7 sq km; land—7 sq km; water—0 sq km
Iles Crozet: total—352 sq km; land—352 sq km; water—0 sq km
Iles Kerguelen: total—7,215 sq km; land—7,215 sq km; water—0 sq km
Bassas da India (Iles Eparses): total—80 sq km; land—0.2 sq km; water—79.8 sq km (lagoon)
Europa Island (Iles Eparses): total—28 sq km; land—28 sq km; water—0 sq km
Glorioso Islands (Iles Eparses): total—5 sq km; land—5 sq km; water—0 sq km
Juan de Nova Island (Iles Eparses): total—4.4 sq km; land—4.4 sq km; water—0 sq km
Tromelin Island (Iles Eparses): total—1 sq km; land—1 sq km; water—0 sq km
note: excludes "Adelie Land" claim of about 500,000 sq km in Antarctica that is not recognized by the US

Area—comparative:
Ile Amsterdam (Ile Amsterdam et Ile Saint-Paul): less than one-half the size of Washington, DC
Ile Saint-Paul (Ile Amsterdam et Ile Saint-Paul): more than 10 times the size of The Mall in Washington, DC
Iles Crozet: about twice the size of Washington, DC
Iles Kerguelen: slightly larger than Delaware
Bassas da India (Iles Eparses): land area about one-third the size of The Mall in Washington, DC
Europa Island (Iles Eparses): about one-sixth the size of Washington, DC
Glorioso Islands (Iles Eparses): about eight times the size of The Mall in Washington, DC
Juan de Nova Island (Iles Eparses): about seven times the size of The Mall in Washington, DC
Tromelin Island (Iles Eparses): about 1.7 times the size of The Mall in Washington, DC

Land boundaries: 0 km

Coastline:
Ile Amsterdam (Ile Amsterdam et Ile Saint-Paul): 28 km
Ile Saint-Paul (Ile Amsterdam et Ile Saint-Paul):
Iles Kerguelen: 2,800 km
Bassas da India (Iles Eparses): 35.2 km
Europa Island (Iles Eparses): 22.2 km
Glorioso Islands (Iles Eparses): 35.2 km
Juan de Nova Island (Iles Eparses): 24.1 km
Tromelin Island (Iles Eparses): 3.7 km

Maritime claims: *territorial sea:* 12 nm
exclusive economic zone: 200 nm from Iles Kerguelen and Iles Eparses (does not include the rest of French Southern and Antarctic Lands); Juan de Nova Island and Tromelin Island
claim a continental shelf of 200-m depth or to the depth of exploitation

Climate:
Ile Amsterdam et Ile Saint-Paul: oceanic with persistent westerly winds and high humidity
Iles Crozet: windy, cold, wet, and cloudy
Iles Kerguelen: oceanic, cold, overcast, windy
Iles Eparses: tropical

Terrain:
Ile Amsterdam (Ile Amsterdam et Ile Saint-Paul): a volcanic island with steep coastal cliffs; the center floor of the volcano is a large plateau
Ile Saint-Paul (Ile Amsterdam et Ile Saint-Paul): triangular in shape, the island is the top of a volcano, rocky with steep cliffs on the eastern side; has active thermal springs
Iles Crozet: a large archipelago formed from the Crozet Plateau is divided into two groups of islands
Iles Kerguelen: the interior of the large island of Ile Kerguelen is composed of rugged terrain of high mountains, hills, valleys, and plains with a number of peninsulas stretching off its coasts
Bassas da India (Iles Eparses): atoll, awash at high tide; shallow (15 m) lagoon
Europa Island, Glorioso Islands, Juan de Nova Island: low, flat, and sandy
Tromelin Island (Iles Eparses): low, flat, sandy; likely volcanic seamount

Elevation extremes: *lowest point:* Indian Ocean 0 m
highest point: Mont de la Dives on Ile Amsterdam (Ile Amsterdam et Ile Saint-Paul) 867 m; unnamed location on Ile Saint-Paul (Ile Amsterdam et Ile Saint-Paul) 272 m; Pic Marion-Dufresne in Iles Crozet 1,090 m; Mont Ross in Iles Kerguelen 1,850 m; unnamed location on Bassas de India (Iles Eparses) 2.4 m; unnamed location on Europa Island (Iles Eparses) 24 m; unnamed location on Glorioso Islands (Iles Eparses) 12 m; unnamed location on Juan de Nova Island (Iles Eparses) 10 m; unnamed location on Tromelin Island (Iles Eparses) 7 m

Natural resources: fish, crayfish
note: Glorioso Islands and Tromelin Island (Iles Eparses) have guano, phosphates, and coconuts

Land use: Ile Amsterdam (Ile Amsterdam et Ile Saint-Paul)—100% trees, grasses, ferns, and moss; Ile Saint-Paul (Ile Amsterdam et Ile Saint-Paul)—100% grass, ferns, and moss; Iles Crozet—100% tossock grass, heath, and fern; Iles Kerguelen—100% tossock grass and Kerguelen cabbage; Bassas da India (Iles Eparses)—100% rock, coral reef, and sand; Europa Island (Iles Eparses)—100% mangrove swamp and dry woodlands; Glorioso Islands (Iles Eparses)—100% lush vegetation and coconut palms; Juan de Nova Island (Iles Eparses)—90% forest, 10% other; Tromelin Island (Iles Eparses)—100% grasses and scattered brush (2011)

Irrigated land: 0 sq km (2011)

Natural hazards: Ile Amsterdam and Ile Saint-Paul are inactive volcanoes; Iles Eparses subject to periodic cyclones; Bassas da India is a maritime hazard since it is under water for a period of three hours prior to and following the high tide and surrounded by reefs
volcanism: Reunion Island—Piton de la Fournaise (elev. 2,632 m,), which has erupted many times in recent years including 2010, is one of the world's most active volcanoes; although rare, eruptions outside the volcano's caldera could threaten nearby cities

Environment—current issues: introduction of foreign species on Iles Crozet has caused severe damage to the original ecosystem; overfishing of Patagonian toothfish around Iles Crozet and Iles Kerguelen

Geography—note: islands component is widely scattered across remote locations in the southern Indian Ocean
Bassas da India (Iles Eparses): the atoll is a circular reef that sits atop a long-extinct, submerged volcano

Europa Island and Juan de Nova Island (Iles Eparses): wildlife sanctuary for seabirds and sea turtles
Glorioso Island (Iles Eparses): the islands and rocks are surrounded by an extensive reef system
Tromelin Island (Iles Eparses): climatologically important location for forecasting cyclones in the western Indian Ocean; wildlife sanctuary (seabirds, tortoises)

PEOPLE AND SOCIETY

Population: no indigenous inhabitants
Ile Amsterdam (Ile Amsterdam et Ile Saint-Paul): has no permanent residents but has a meteorological station
Ile Saint-Paul (Ile Amsterdam et Ile Saint-Paul): is uninhabited but is frequently visited by fishermen and has a scientific research cabin for short stays
Iles Crozet: are uninhabited except for 18 to 30 people staffing the Alfred Faure research station on Ile del la Possession
Iles Kerguelen: 50 to 100 scientists are located at the main base at Port-aux-Francais on Ile Kerguelen
Bassas da India (Iles Eparses): uninhabitable
Europa Island, Glorioso Islands, Juan de Nova Island (Iles Eparses): a small French military garrison and a few meteorologists on each possession; visited by scientists
Tromelin Island (Iles Eparses): uninhabited, except for visits by scientists

GOVERNMENT

Country name: *conventional long form:* Territory of the French Southern and Antarctic Lands
conventional short form: French Southern and Antarctic Lands
local long form: Territoire des Terres Australes et Antarctiques Francaises
local short form: Terres Australes et Antarctiques Francaises
abbreviation: TAAF

Dependency status:
overseas territory of France since 1955

Administrative divisions: none (overseas territory of France); there are no first-order administrative divisions as defined by the US Government, but there are five administrative districts named Iles Crozet, Iles Eparses, Iles Kerguelen, Ile Saint-Paul et Ile Amsterdam; the fifth district is the "Adelie Land" claim in Antarctica that is not recognized by the US

Legal system: the laws of France, where applicable, apply

Executive branch: *chief of state:* President Francois HOLLANDE (since 15 May 2012), represented by Senior Administrator Pascal BOLOT (since 29 February 2012)

International organization participation: UPU

Diplomatic representation in the US: none (overseas territory of France)

Diplomatic representation from the US: none (overseas territory of France)

Flag description: the flag of France is used

National symbol(s): sea lion

National anthem: note: as a territory of France, "La Marseillaise" is official (see France)

ECONOMY

overview: Economic activity is limited to servicing meteorological and geophysical research stations, military bases, and French and other fishing fleets. The fish catches landed on Iles *Kerguelen by foreign ships are exported to France and Reunion.*

COMMUNICATIONS

Internet country code: .tf

Internet hosts: 53 (2012)
country comparison to the world: 214

Communications—note: has one or more meteorological stations on each possession

TRANSPORTATION

Airports: 4; note—one each on Europa Island, Glorioso Islands, Juan de Nova Island, and Tromelin Island in the Iles Eparses district (2013)
country comparison to the world: 186

Ports and terminals: none; offshore anchorage only

MILITARY

Military—note: defense is the responsibility of France

TRANSNATIONAL ISSUES

Disputes—international: French claim to "Adelie Land" in Antarctica is not recognized by the US
Bassas da India, Europa Island, Glorioso Islands, Juan de Nova Island (Iles Eparses): claimed by Madagascar; the vegetated drying cays of Banc du Geyser, which were claimed by Madagascar in 1976, also fall within the EEZ claims of the Comoros and France (Glorioso Islands)
Tromelin Island (Iles Eparses): claimed by Mauritius

GABON

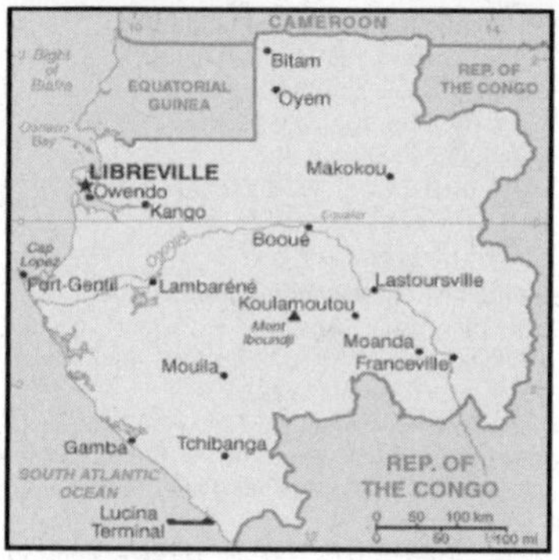

INTRODUCTION

Background: El Hadj Omar BONGO Ondimba—one of the longest-serving heads of state in the world—dominated the country's political scene for four decades (1967-2009) following independence from France in 1960. President BONGO introduced a nominal multiparty system and a new constitution in the early 1990s. However, allegations of electoral fraud during local elections in December 2002 and the presidential elections in 2005 exposed the weaknesses of formal political structures in Gabon. Following President BONGO's death in 2009, new elections brought Ali BONGO Ondimba, son of the former president, to power. Despite constrained political conditions, Gabon's small population, abundant natural resources, and considerable foreign support have helped make it one of the more stable African countries.

GEOGRAPHY

Location: Central Africa, bordering the Atlantic Ocean at the Equator, between Republic of the Congo and Equatorial Guinea

Geographic coordinates: 1 00 S, 11 45 E

Map references: Africa

Area: *total:* 267,667 sq km
country comparison to the world: 77
land: 257,667 sq km
water: 10,000 sq km

Area—comparative: slightly smaller than Colorado

Land boundaries: *total:* 2,551 km
border countries: Cameroon 298 km, Republic of the Congo 1,903 km, Equatorial Guinea 350 km

Coastline: 885 km

Maritime claims: *territorial sea:* 12 nm
contiguous zone: 24 nm
exclusive economic zone: 200 nm

Climate: tropical; always hot, humid

Terrain: narrow coastal plain; hilly interior; savanna in east and south

Elevation extremes: *lowest point:* Atlantic Ocean 0 m
highest point: Mont Iboundji 1,575 m

Natural resources: petroleum, natural gas, diamond, niobium, manganese, uranium, gold, timber, iron ore, hydropower

Land use: *arable land:* 1.21%
permanent crops: 0.64%
other: 98.15% (2011)

Irrigated land: 44.5 sq km (2003)

Total renewable water resources: 164 cu km (2011)

Freshwater withdrawal (domestic/industrial/agricultural): *total:* 0.14 cu km/yr (61%/10%/29%)
per capita: 97.68 cu m/yr (2005)

Natural hazards: NA

Environment—current issues: deforestation; poaching

Environment—international agreements:
party to: Biodiversity, Climate Change, Climate Change-Kyoto Protocol, Desertification, Endangered Species, Hazardous Wastes, Law of the Sea, Marine Dumping, Ozone Layer Protection, Ship Pollution, Tropical Timber 83, Tropical Timber 94, Wetlands, Whaling
signed, but not ratified: none of the selected agreements

Geography—note: a small population and oil and mineral reserves have helped Gabon become one of Africa's wealthier countries; in general, these circumstances have allowed the country to maintain and conserve its pristine rain forest and rich biodiversity

PEOPLE AND SOCIETY

Nationality: *noun:* Gabonese (singular and plural)
adjective: Gabonese

Ethnic groups: Bantu tribes, including four major tribal groupings (Fang, Bapounou, Nzebi, Obamba); other Africans and Europeans, 154,000, including 10,700 French and 11,000 persons of dual nationality

Languages: French (official), Fang, Myene, Nzebi, Bapounou/Eschira, Bandjabi

Religions: Christian 55%-75%, animist, Muslim less than 1%

Population: 1,672,597 (July 2014 est.)
country comparison to the world: 154
note: estimates for this country explicitly take into account the effects of excess mortality due to AIDS; this can result in lower life expectancy, higher infant mortality, higher death rates, lower population growth rates, and changes in the distribution of population by age and sex than would otherwise be expected

Age structure: *0-14 years:* 42.1% (male 353,863/female 350,456)
15-24 years: 20.3% (male 169,681/female 169,082)
25-54 years: 29.7% (male 248,328/female 248,063)
55-64 years: 3.8% (male 33,608/female 35,838)
65 years and over: 3.8% (male 27,117/female 36,561) (2014 est.)

Dependency ratios:
total dependency ratio: 77.4 %
youth dependency ratio: 68.3 %
elderly dependency ratio: 9.2 %
potential support ratio: 10.9 (2013)

Median age: total: 18.6 years
male: 18.4 years
female: 18.8 years (2014 est.)

Population growth rate: 1.94% (2014 est.)
country comparison to the world: 54

Birth rate: 34.64 births/1,000 population (2014 est.)
country comparison to the world: 27

Death rate: 13.13 deaths/1,000 population (2014 est.)
country comparison to the world: 20

Net migration rate: -2.07 migrant(s)/1,000 population (2014 est.)
country comparison to the world: 168

Urbanization: *urban population:* 86.2% of total population (2011)
rate of urbanization: 2.27% annual rate of change (2010-15 est.)

Major urban areas—population: LIBREVILLE (capital) 619,000 (2009)

Sex ratio: *at birth:* 1.03 male(s)/female
0-14 years: 1.01 male(s)/female
15-24 years: 1 male(s)/female
25-54 years: 1 male(s)/female
55-64 years: 0.99 male(s)/female
65 years and over: 0.73 male(s)/female
total population: 0.99 male(s)/female (2014 est.)

Mother's mean age at first birth: 20.3
note: median age at first birth among women 25-29 (2012 est.)

Maternal mortality rate:
230 deaths/100,000 live births (2010)
country comparison to the world: 50

Infant mortality rate: *total:* 47.03 deaths/1,000 live births
country comparison to the world: 43
male: 54.27 deaths/1,000 live births
female: 39.57 deaths/1,000 live births (2014 est.)

Life expectancy at birth: *total population:* 52.06 years
country comparison to the world: 214
male: 51.54 years
female: 52.6 years (2014 est.)

Total fertility rate: 4.49 children born/woman (2014 est.)
country comparison to the world: 30

Contraceptive prevalence rate: 31.1% (2012)

Health expenditures: 3.2% of GDP (2011)
country comparison to the world: 179

Physicians density: 0.29 physicians/1,000 population (2004)

Hospital bed density: 6.3 beds/1,000 population (2010)

Drinking water source:
improved:
urban: 95.3% of population
rural: 41.3% of population
total: 87.9% of population
unimproved:
urban: 4.7% of population
rural: 58.7% of population
total: 12.1% of population (2011 est.)

Sanitation facility access:
improved:
urban: 33.3% of population
rural: 30.4% of population
total: 32.9% of population
unimproved:
urban: 66.7% of population
rural: 69.6% of population
total: 67.1% of population (2011 est.)

HIV/AIDS—adult prevalence rate: 4% (2012 est.)
country comparison to the world: 16

HIV/AIDS—people living with HIV/AIDS: 40,700 (2012 est.)

country comparison to the world: 67

HIV/AIDS—deaths: 2,300 (2012 est.)
country comparison to the world: 58

Major infectious diseases: *degree of risk:* very high
food or waterborne diseases: bacterial diarrhea, hepatitis A, and typhoid fever
vectorborne disease: malaria and dengue fever
water contact disease: schistosomiasis
animal contact disease: rabies (2013)

Obesity—adult prevalence rate: 13.9% (2008)
country comparison to the world: 124

Children under the age of 5 years underweight: 6.5% (2012)
country comparison to the world: 79

Education expenditures: NA

Literacy: *definition:* age 15 and over can read and write
total population: 89%
male: 92.3%
female: 85.6% (2011 est.)

GOVERNMENT

Country name: conventional long form: Gabonese Republic
conventional short form: Gabon
local long form: Republique Gabonaise
local short form: Gabon

Government type: republic; multiparty presidential regime

Capital: name: Libreville

geographic coordinates: 0 23 N, 9 27 E
time difference: UTC+1 (6 hours ahead of Washington, DC during Standard Time)

Administrative divisions: 9 provinces; Estuaire, Haut-Ogooue, Moyen-Ogooue, Ngounie, Nyanga, Ogooue-Ivindo, Ogooue-Lolo, Ogooue-Maritime, Woleu-Ntem

Independence: 17 August 1960 (from France)

National holiday: Independence Day, 17 August (1960)

Constitution: previous 1961; latest drafted May 1990, adopted 15 March 1991, promulgated 26 March 1991; amended several times, including 2003 and 2011 (2013)

Legal system: mixed legal system of French civil law and customary law

International law organization participation: has not submitted an ICJ jurisdiction declaration; accepts ICCt jurisdiction

Suffrage: 18 years of age; universal

Executive branch: *chief of state:* President Ali BONGO ONDIMBA (since 16 October 2009)
head of government: Prime Minister Daniel ONA ONDO (since 27 January 2014)
cabinet: Council of Ministers appointed by the prime minister in consultation with the president (For more information visit the World Leaders website)
elections: president elected by popular vote for a seven-year term (no term limits); election last held on 30 August 2009 (next to be held in 2016); prime minister appointed by the president
election results: President Ali BONGO ONDIMBA elected; percent of vote—Ali BONGO ONDIMBA 41.7%, Andre MBA OBAME 25.9%, Pierre MAMBOUNDOU 25.2%, Zacharie MYBOTO 3.9%, other 3.3%
note: President BONGO died on 8 June 2009 after serving as president for 32 years; in accordance with the constitution he was replaced on an interim basis by the president of the Senate, Rose Francine ROGOMBE on 10 June 2009; new elections were held on 30 August 2009 and the son of the former president, Ali BONGO Ondimba, was elected president

Legislative branch: bicameral legislature consists of the Senate (102 seats; members elected by members of municipal councils and departmental assemblies to serve six-year terms) and the National Assembly or Assemblee Nationale (120 seats; members are elected by direct, popular vote to serve five-year terms)
elections: Senate—last held on 18 January 2009 (next to be held in January 2015); National Assembly—last held on 17 December 2011 (next to be held in December 2016)
election results: Senate—percent of vote by party—NA; seats by party—PDG 75, RPG 6, UGDD 3, CLR 2, PGCI 2, PSD 2, UPG 2, ADERE 1, independents 9; National Assembly—percent of vote by party—NA; seats by party—PDG 114, RPG 3, others 3

Judicial branch: *highest court(s):* Supreme Court (organized into Judicial, Administrative, and Accounts chambers and consists of NA judges); Constitutional Court (consists of 9 judges)
judge selection and term of office: Supreme Court judges appointment and tenure NA; Constitutional Court judges appointed—3 by the national president, 3 by the president of the Senate, and 3 by the president of the National Assembly; judges serve 7-year, single renewable terms
subordinate courts: Courts of Appeal; Court of State Security; county courts; military courts

Political parties and leaders: Alliance for National Rebirth or ARENA [Richard MOULOMBA]; Circle of Liberal Reformers or CLR [General Jean Boniface ASSELE]; Congress for Democracy and Justice or CDJ [Jules Aristide Bourdes OGOULIGUENDE]; Democratic and Republican Alliance or ADERE [Divungui-di-Ndinge DIDJOB]; Gabonese Democratic Party or PDG [Ali BONGO ONDIMBA]; Gabonese Party for Progress or PGP [Benoit Mouity NZAMBA]; Gabonese Union for Democracy and Development or UGDD [Zacharie MYBOTO]; Independent Center Party of Gabon or PGCI [Luccheri GAHILA, interim head of party]; National Rally of Woodcutters-Democratic or RNB [Pierre Andre KOMBILA]; National Rally of Woodcutters-Rally for Gabon-Rally for Gabon or RNB-RPG (Bucherons) [Fr. Paul M'BA-ABESSOLE]; Party of Development and Social Solidarity or PDS [Seraphin Ndoat REMBOGO]; Social Democratic Party or PSD [Pierre Claver MAGANGA-MOUSSAVOU]; Union for Democracy and Social Integration or UDIS; Union for the New Republic or UPRN [Louis Gaston MAYILA]; Union of Gabonese People or UPG [Mathieu Mboumba NZIENGUI (until the next Congress)]

Political pressure groups and leaders: NA

International organization participation: ACP, AfDB, AU, BDEAC, CEMAC, FAO, FZ, G-24, G-77, IAEA, IBRD, ICAO, ICRM, IDA, IDB, IFAD, IFC, IFRCS, ILO, IMF, IMO, IMSO, Interpol, IOC, IOM, IPU, ISO, ITSO, ITU, ITUC (NGOs), MIGA, NAM, OIC, OIF, OPCW, UN, UNCTAD, UNESCO, UNIDO, UNWTO, UPU, WCO, WHO, WIPO, WMO, WTO

Diplomatic representation in the US:
chief of mission: Ambassador Michael MOUSSA-ADAMO (since 2 September 2011)
chancery: Suite 200, 2034 20th Street NW, Washington, DC 20009
telephone: [1] (202) 797-1000
FAX: [1] (202) 332-0668
consulate(s): New York

Diplomatic representation from the US:
chief of mission: Ambassador (vacant); Charge d'Affaires Dante PARADISO; note—also accredited to Sao Tome and Principe
embassy: Boulevard du Bord de Mer, Libreville
mailing address: Centre Ville, B. P. 4000, Libreville; pouch: 2270 Libreville Place, Washington, DC 20521-2270
telephone: [241] 01-45-71-00, after hours—07380171
FAX: [241] 74 55 07

Flag description: three equal horizontal bands of green (top), yellow, and blue; green represents the country's forests and natural resources, gold represents the equator (which transects Gabon) as well as the sun, blue represents the sea

National symbol(s): black panther

National anthem: name: "La Concorde" (The Concorde)
lyrics/music: Georges Aleka DAMAS
note: adopted 1960

ECONOMY

Economy—overview: Gabon enjoys a per capita income four times that of most sub-Saharan African nations, but because of high income inequality, a large proportion of the population remains poor. Gabon depended on timber and manganese until oil was discovered offshore in the early 1970s. The economy was reliant on oil for about 50% of its GDP, about 70% of revenues, and 87% of goods exports for 2010, although some fields have passed their peak production. A rebound of oil prices from 1999 to 2008 helped growth, but declining production has hampered Gabon from fully realizing potential gains. Gabon signed a 14-month Stand-By Arrangement with the IMF in May 2007, and later that year issued a $1 billion sovereign bond to buy back a sizable portion of its Paris Club debt. Gabon continues to face fluctuating prices for its oil, timber, and manganese exports. Despite the abundance of natural wealth, poor fiscal management has stifled the economy. However, President BONGO ONDIMBA has made efforts to increase transparency and is taking steps to make Gabon a more attractive investment destination to diversify the economy. BONGO ONDIMBA has attempted to boost growth by increasing government investment in human resources and infrastructure. GDP grew more than 6% per year over the 2010-13 period.

GDP (purchasing power parity): $30.06 billion (2013 est.)
country comparison to the world: 113
$28.19 billion (2012 est.)
$26.7 billion (2011 est.)
note: data are in 2013 US dollars

GDP (official exchange rate): $19.97 billion (2013 est.)

GDP—real growth rate: 6.6% (2013 est.)

country comparison to the world: 27
5.6% (2012 est.)
7.1% (2011 est.)

GDP—per capita (PPP): $19,200 (2013 est.)
country comparison to the world: 72
$18,300 (2012 est.)
$17,600 (2011 est.)
note: data are in 2013 US dollars

Gross national saving: 44.7% of GDP (2013 est.)
country comparison to the world: 9
47.1% of GDP (2012 est.)
44.9% of GDP (2011 est.)

GDP—composition, by end use:
household consumption: 39.1%
government consumption: 10.5%
investment in fixed capital: 33.7%
investment in inventories: 0%
exports of goods and services: 58.1%
imports of goods and services: -41.4% (2013 est.)

GDP—composition, by sector of origin:
agriculture: 3.6%
industry: 63.9%
services: 32.5% (2013 est.)

Agriculture—products: cocoa, coffee, sugar, palm oil, rubber; cattle; okoume (a tropical softwood); fish

Industries: petroleum extraction and refining; manganese, gold; chemicals, ship repair, food and beverages, textiles, lumbering and plywood, cement

Industrial production growth rate: 4.4% (2013 est.)
country comparison to the world: 64

Labor force: 629,100 (2013 est.)
country comparison to the world: 155

Labor force—by occupation: agriculture: 60%
industry: 15%
services: 25% (2000 est.)

Unemployment rate: 21% (2006 est.)
country comparison to the world: 165

Population below poverty line: NA%

Household income or consumption by percentage share: *lowest* 10%: 2.5%
highest 10%: 32.7% (2005)

Budget: *revenues:* $5.031 billion
expenditures: $4.896 billion (2013 est.)

Taxes and other revenues: 25.2% of GDP (2013 est.)
country comparison to the world: 122

Budget surplus (+) or deficit (-):
0.7% of GDP (2013 est.)
country comparison to the world: 29

Public debt: 23.2% of GDP (2013 est.)
country comparison to the world: 132
22.2% of GDP (2012 est.)

Fiscal year: calendar year
Inflation rate (consumer prices):
1.2% (2013 est.)
country comparison to the world: 32
2.7% (2012 est.)

Central bank discount rate: 3% (31 December 2010 est.)
country comparison to the world: 84
4.25% (31 December 2009 est.)

Commercial bank prime lending rate:
15% (31 December 2013 est.)
country comparison to the world: 41
15% (31 December 2012 est.)

Stock of narrow money: $2.497 billion (31 December 2013 est.)
country comparison to the world: 121
$2.552 billion (31 December 2012 est.)

Stock of broad money: $3.973 billion (31 December 2013 est.)
country comparison to the world: 137
$3.908 billion (31 December 2012 est.)

Stock of domestic credit: $1.7 billion (31 December 2013 est.)
country comparison to the world: 137
$1.672 billion (31 December 2012 est.)

Market value of publicly traded shares: $NA

Current account balance: $1.783 billion (2013 est.)
country comparison to the world: 45
$2.687 billion (2012 est.)

Exports: $9.777 billion (2013 est.)
country comparison to the world: 98
$10.2 billion (2012 est.)

Exports—commodities: crude oil, timber, manganese, uranium

Exports—partners: Japan 24.1%, US 17%, Australia 11.3%, India 7.4%, China 5.4%, Spain 4.1% (2012)

Imports: $3.934 billion (2013 est.)
country comparison to the world: 139
$3.638 billion (2012 est.)

Imports—commodities: machinery and equipment, foodstuffs, chemicals, construction materials

Imports—partners: France 28.2%, China 12.6%, US 9.4%, Belgium 5.8%, Cameroon 4.3% (2012)

Reserves of foreign exchange and gold:
$2.47 billion (31 December 2013 est.)
country comparison to the world: 115
$2.373 billion (31 December 2012 est.)

Debt—external: $3.433 billion (31 December 2013 est.)
country comparison to the world: 131
$3.196 billion (31 December 2012 est.)

Exchange rates: Cooperation Financiere en Afrique Centrale francs (XAF) per US dollar—
504.9 (2013 est.)
510.53 (2012 est.)
495.28 (2010 est.)
472.19 (2009)
447.81 (2008)

ENERGY

Electricity—production: 1.777 billion kWh (2010 est.)
country comparison to the world: 138

Electricity—consumption: 1.442 billion kWh (2010 est.)
country comparison to the world: 146

Electricity—exports: 0 kWh (2012 est.)
country comparison to the world: 140

Electricity—imports: 0 kWh (2012 est.)
country comparison to the world: 147

Electricity—installed generating capacity:
415,000 kW (2010 est.)
country comparison to the world: 144

Electricity—from fossil fuels:
59% of total installed capacity (2010 est.)
country comparison to the world: 136

Electricity—from nuclear fuels: 0% of total installed capacity (2010 est.)
country comparison to the world: 92

Electricity—from hydroelectric plants:
41% of total installed capacity (2010 est.)
country comparison to the world: 58

Electricity—from other renewable sources:
0% of total installed capacity (2010 est.)
country comparison to the world: 175

Crude oil—production: 242,000 bbl/day (2012 est.)
country comparison to the world: 37

Crude oil—exports: 225,300 bbl/day (2010 est.)
country comparison to the world: 29

Crude oil—imports: 0 bbl/day (2010 est.)
country comparison to the world: 189

Crude oil—proved reserves: 2 billion bbl (1 January 2013 es)
country comparison to the world: 36

Refined petroleum products—production:
19,280 bbl/day (2010 est.)
country comparison to the world: 93

Refined petroleum products—consumption:
15,800 bbl/day (2011 est.)
country comparison to the world: 140

Refined petroleum products—exports:
7,670 bbl/day (2010 est.)
country comparison to the world: 86

Refined petroleum products—imports:
4,594 bbl/day (2010 est.)
country comparison to the world: 158

Natural gas—production: 70 million cu m (2011 est.)
country comparison to the world: 84

Natural gas—consumption: 80 million cu m (2010 est.)
country comparison to the world: 109

Natural gas—exports: 0 cu m (2011 est.)
country comparison to the world: 104

Natural gas—imports: 0 cu m (2011 est.)
country comparison to the world: 196

Natural gas—proved reserves: 28.32 billion cu m (1 January 2013 es)
country comparison to the world: 70

Carbon dioxide emissions from consumption of energy: 4.758 million Mt (2011 est.)
country comparison to the world: 127

COMMUNICATIONS

Telephones—main lines in use: 17,000 (2012)
country comparison to the world: 194

Telephones—mobile cellular: 2.93 million (2012)
country comparison to the world: 133

Telephone system: *general assessment:* adequate system of cable, microwave radio relay, tropospheric scatter, radiotelephone communication stations, and a domestic satellite system with 12 earth stations
domestic: a growing mobile-cellular network with multiple providers is making telephone service more widely available with mobile-cellular teledensity exceeding 100 per 100 persons
international: country code—241; landing point for the SAT-3/WASC fiber-optic submarine cable that provides connectivity to Europe and Asia; satellite earth stations—3 Intelsat (Atlantic Ocean) (2011)

Broadcast media: state owns and operates 2 TV stations and 2 radio broadcast stations; a few private radio and TV stations; transmissions of at least 2 international broadcasters are accessible; satellite service subscriptions are available (2007)

Internet country code: .ga

Internet hosts: 127 (2012)
country comparison to the world: 205

Internet users: 98,800 (2009)
country comparison to the world: 160

TRANSPORTATION

Airports: 44 (2013)
country comparison to the world: 99

Airports—with paved runways: *total:* 14
over 3,047 m: 1
2,438 to 3,047 m: 2
1,524 to 2,437 m: 9
914 to 1,523 m: 1
under 914 m: 1 (2013)

Airports—with unpaved runways: *total:* 30
1,524 to 2,437 m: 7
914 to 1,523 m: 9
under 914 m: 14 (2013)

Pipelines: gas 807 km; oil 1,639 km; water 3 km (2013)

Railways: total: 649 km
country comparison to the world: 105
standard gauge: 649 km 1.435-m gauge (2008)

Roadways: total: 9,170 km
country comparison to the world: 138
paved: 1,097 km
unpaved: 8,073 km (2007)

Waterways: 1,600 km (310 km on Ogooue River) (2010)
country comparison to the world: 49

Merchant marine: *registered in other countries:* 2 (Cambodia 1, Panama 1) (2010)
country comparison to the world: 145

Ports and terminals: major seaport(s): Libreville, Owendo, Port-Gentil
oil/gas terminal(s): Gamba, Lucina

MILITARY

Military branches: Gabonese Defense Forces (Forces de Defense Gabonaise): Land Force (Force Terrestre), Gabonese Navy (Marine Gabonaise), Gabonese Air Forces (Forces Aerienne Gabonaises, FAG) (2012)

Military service age and obligation: 20 years of age for voluntary military service; no conscription (2012)

Manpower available for military service:
males age 16-49: 350,640
females age 16-49: 351,718 (2010 est.)

Manpower fit for military service:
males age 16-49: 202,404
females age 16-49: 195,389 (2010 est.)

Manpower reaching militarily significant age annually: *male:* 17,638
female: 17,614 (2010 est.)

Military expenditures: 1.34% of GDP (2012)
country comparison to the world: 78
NA% (2011)
1.34% of GDP (2010)

TRANSNATIONAL ISSUES

Disputes—international: UN urges Equatorial Guinea and Gabon to resolve the sovereignty dispute over Gabon-occupied Mbane Island and lesser islands and to establish a maritime boundary in hydrocarbon-rich Corisco Bay

GAMBIA, THE

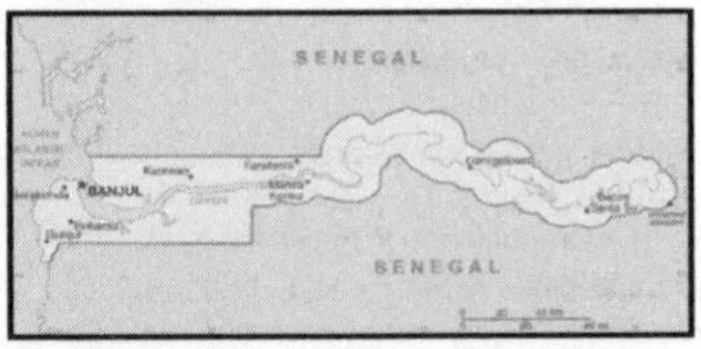

INTRODUCTION

Background: The Gambia gained its independence from the UK in 1965. Geographically surrounded by Senegal, it formed a short-lived federation of Senegambia between 1982 and 1989. In 1991 the two nations signed a friendship and cooperation treaty, but tensions have flared up intermittently since then. Yahya JAMMEH led a military coup in 1994 that overthrew the president and banned political activity. A new constitution and presidential elections in 1996, followed by parliamentary balloting in 1997, completed a nominal return to civilian rule. JAMMEH has been elected president in all subsequent elections including most recently in late 2011.

GEOGRAPHY

Location: Western Africa, bordering the North Atlantic Ocean and Senegal

Geographic coordinates: 13 28 N, 16 34 W

Map references: Africa

Area: *total:* 11,295 sq km
country comparison to the world: 167
land: 10,000 sq km
water: 1,295 sq km

Area—comparative: slightly less than twice the size of Delaware

Land boundaries: *total:* 740 km
border countries: Senegal 740 km

Coastline: 80 km

Maritime claims: *territorial sea:* 12 nm
contiguous zone: 18 nm
exclusive fishing zone: 200 nm
continental shelf: extent not specified

Climate: tropical; hot, rainy season (June to November); cooler, dry season (November to May)

Terrain: flood plain of the Gambia River flanked by some low hills

Elevation extremes: *lowest point:* Atlantic Ocean 0 m
highest point: unnamed elevation 53 m

Natural resources: fish, clay, silica sand, titanium (rutile and ilmenite), tin, zircon

Land use: arable land: 39.82%
permanent crops: 0.44%
other: 59.73% (2011)

Irrigated land: 50 sq km (2011)

Total renewable water resources: 8 cu km (2011)

Freshwater withdrawal (domestic/industrial/agricultural): *total:* 0.09 cu km/yr (41%/21%/39%)
per capita: 65.77 cu m/yr (2005)

Natural hazards: drought (rainfall has dropped by 30% in the last 30 years)

Environment—current issues: deforestation; desertification; water-borne diseases prevalent

Environment—international agreements: *party to:* Biodiversity, Climate Change, Climate Change-Kyoto Protocol, Desertification, Endangered Species, Hazardous Wastes, Law of the Sea, Ozone Layer Protection, Ship Pollution, Wetlands, Whaling
signed, but not ratified: none of the selected agreements

Geography—note: almost an enclave of Senegal; smallest country on the continent of Africa

PEOPLE AND SOCIETY

Nationality: *noun:* Gambian(s)
adjective: Gambian

Ethnic groups: African 99% (Mandinka 42%, Fula 18%, Wolof 16%, Jola 10%, Serahuli 9%, other 4%), non-African 1% (2003 census)

Languages: English (official), Mandinka, Wolof, Fula, other indigenous vernaculars

Religions: Muslim 90%, Christian 8%, indigenous beliefs 2%

Population: 1,925,527 (July 2014 est.)
country comparison to the world: 150

Age structure: *0-14 years:* 38.7% (male 374,353/female 371,488)
15-24 years: 21% (male 199,306/female 204,324)
25-54 years: 33% (male 310,901/female 324,227)
55-64 years: 3.3% (male 37,506/female 39,958)
65 years and over: 3.2% (male 29,793/female 33,671) (2014 est.)

Dependency ratios:
total dependency ratio: 93.5 %
youth dependency ratio: 88.9 %
elderly dependency ratio: 4.6 %
potential support ratio: 21.6 (2013)

Median age: total: 20.2 years
male: 19.9 years
female: 20.5 years (2014 est.)

Population growth rate: 2.23% (2014 est.)
country comparison to the world: 43

Birth rate: 31.75 births/1,000 population (2014 est.)
country comparison to the world: 37

Death rate: 7.26 deaths/1,000 population (2014 est.)
country comparison to the world: 125

Net migration rate: -2.23 migrant(s)/1,000 population (2014 est.)
country comparison to the world: 170

Urbanization: *urban population:* 57.3% of total population (2011)
rate of urbanization: 3.63% annual rate of change (2010-15 est.)

Major urban areas—population: BANJUL (capital) 436,000 (2009)

Sex ratio: *at birth:* 1.03 male(s)/female
0-14 years: 1.01 male(s)/female
15-24 years: 0.98 male(s)/female
25-54 years: 0.96 male(s)/female
55-64 years: 0.98 male(s)/female
65 years and over: 0.9 male(s)/female
total population: 0.98 male(s)/female (2014 est.)

Maternal mortality rate: 360 deaths/100,000 live births (2010)
country comparison to the world: 29

Infant mortality rate: total: 65.74 deaths/1,000 live births
country comparison to the world: 18
male: 71.21 deaths/1,000 live births
female: 60.11 deaths/1,000 live births (2014 est.)

Life expectancy at birth: total population: 64.36 years
country comparison to the world: 176
male: 62.04 years
female: 66.74 years (2014 est.)

Total fertility rate: 3.85 children born/woman (2014 est.)
country comparison to the world: 41

Contraceptive prevalence rate: 13.3% (2010)

Health expenditures: 4.4% of GDP (2011)
country comparison to the world: 154

Physicians density: 0.11 physicians/1,000 population (2008)

Hospital bed density: 1.1 beds/1,000 population (2011)

Drinking water source:
improved:
urban: 92.4% of population
rural: 85.2% of population
total: 89.3% of population
unimproved:
urban: 7.6% of population
rural: 14.8% of population
total: 10.7% of population (2011 est.)

Sanitation facility access:
improved:
urban: 69.8% of population
rural: 64.8% of population
total: 67.7% of population
unimproved:
urban: 30.2% of population
rural: 35.2% of population
total: 32.3% of population (2011 est.)

HIV/AIDS—adult prevalence rate:
1.3% (2012 est.)
country comparison to the world: 35

HIV/AIDS—people living with HIV/AIDS:
14,300 (2012 est.)
country comparison to the world: 92

HIV/AIDS—deaths: 500 (2012 est.)
country comparison to the world: 95

Major infectious diseases: *degree of risk:* very high
food or waterborne diseases: bacterial and protozoal diarrhea, hepatitis A, and typhoid fever
vectorborne diseases: malaria and dengue fever
water contact disease: schistosomiasis
respiratory disease: meningococcal meningitis
animal contact disease: rabies (2013)

Obesity—adult prevalence rate: 7.9% (2008)
country comparison to the world: 138

Children under the age of 5 years underweight:
15.8% (2006)
country comparison to the world: 45

Education expenditures: 4.1% of GDP (2012)
country comparison to the world: 109

Literacy: *definition:* age 15 and over can read and write
total population: 51.1%
male: 60.9%
female: 41.9% (2011 est.)

School life expectancy (primary to tertiary education): *total:* 9 years (2008)
Child labor—children ages 5-14:
total number: 103,389
percentage: 25 % (2006 est.)

GOVERNMENT

Country name: *conventional long form:* Republic of The Gambia
conventional short form: The Gambia

Government type: republic

Capital: *name:* Banjul
geographic coordinates: 13 27 N, 16 34 W
time difference: UTC 0 (5 hours ahead of Washington, DC during Standard Time)

Administrative divisions: 5 divisions and 1 city*; Banjul*, Central River, Lower River, North Bank, Upper River, Western

Independence: 18 February 1965 (from the UK)

National holiday: Independence Day, 18 February (1965)

Constitution: previous 1970; latest adopted 8 April 1996, approved by referendum 8 August 1996, effective 16 January 1997; amended several times, last in 2009 (2009)

Legal system: mixed legal system of English common law, Islamic law, and customary law

International law organization participation: accepts compulsory ICJ jurisdiction with reservations; accepts ICCt jurisdiction

Suffrage: 18 years of age; universal

Executive branch: *chief of state:* President Yahya JAMMEH (since 18 October 1996); note—from 1994 to 1996 he was chairman of the junta; Vice President Isatou NJIE-SAIDY (since 20 March 1997); note—the president is both the chief of state and head of government
head of government: President Yahya JAMMEH (since 18 October 1996); Vice President Isatou NJIE-SAIDY (since 20 March 1997)
cabinet: Cabinet appointed by the president (For more information visit the World Leaders website)
elections: president elected by popular vote for a five-year term (no term limits); election last held on 24 November 2011 (next to be held in 2016)
election results: Yahya JAMMEH reelected president; percent of vote—Yahya JAMMEH 71.5%, Ousainou DARBOE 17.4%, Hamat BAH 11.1%

Legislative branch: unicameral National Assembly (53 seats; 48 members elected by popular vote, 5 appointed by the president; members to serve five-year terms)
elections: last held on 29 March 2012 (next to be held in 2017)
election results: percent of vote by party—APRC 51.8%, independents 38.8%, NRP 9.4%; seats by party—APRC 43, independents 4, NRP 1
note: except for the NRP, all opposition parties boycotted the 29 March 2012 legislative elections

Judicial branch: *highest court(s):* Supreme Court of The Gambia (consists of the chief justice and 6 other justices); note—court sessions held with 5 justices
judge selection and term of office: justices appointed by the president after consultation with the Judicial Service Commission, a 6-member independent body of high-level judicial officials, a presidential appointee, and a National Assembly appointee; justices appointed for life or until mandatory retirement age
subordinate courts: Court of Appeal; High Court; Special Criminal Court; Khadis or Muslim courts; district tribunals; magistrates courts

Political parties and leaders: Alliance for Patriotic Reorientation and Construction or APRC [Yahya JAMMEH] (the ruling party); Gambia People's Democratic Party or GPDP [Henry GOMEZ]; National Alliance for Democracy and Development or NADD [Halifa SALLAH]; National Convention Party or NCP [Sheriff DIBBA]; National Reconciliation Party or NRP [Hamat BAH]; People's Democratic Organization for Independence and Socialism or PDOIS [Halifa SALLAH]; United Democratic Party or UDP [Ousainou DARBOE]

Political pressure groups and leaders: National Environment Agency or NEA; West African Peace Building Network-Gambian Chapter or WANEB-GAMBIA; Youth Employment Network Gambia or YENGambia; other: special needs group advocates; teachers and principals

International organization participation: ACP, AfDB, AU, C, ECOWAS, FAO, G-77, IBRD, ICAO, ICRM, IDA, IDB, IFAD, IFC, IFRCS, ILO, IMF, IMO, Interpol, IOC, IOM, IPU, ISO (correspondent), ITSO, ITU, ITUC (NGOs), MIGA, MINUSMA, NAM, OIC, OPCW, UN, UNAMID, UNCTAD, UNESCO, UNIDO, UNMIL, UNOCI, UNWTO, UPU, WCO, WFTU (NGOs), WHO, WIPO, WMO, WTO

Diplomatic representation in the US: *chief of mission:* Ambassador (vacant); Charge d'Affaires Baboucarr JALLOW (since 25 June 2013)
chancery: Suite 240, Georgetown Plaza, 2233 Wisconsin Avenue NW, Washington, DC 20007
telephone: [1] (202) 785-1379, 1399, 1425
FAX: [1] (202) 342-0240

Diplomatic representation from the US: *chief of mission:* Ambassador (vacant); Charge d'Affaires Michael ARIETTI (since 2014)
embassy: Kairaba Avenue, Fajara, Banjul
mailing address: P. M. B. No. 19, Banjul
telephone: [220] 439-2856, 437-6169, 437-6170
FAX: [220] 439-2475

Flag description: three equal horizontal bands of red (top), blue with white edges, and green; red stands for the sun and the savannah, blue represents the Gambia River, and green symbolizes forests and agriculture; the white stripes denote unity and peace

National symbol(s): lion

National anthem: *name:* "For The Gambia, Our Homeland"
lyrics/music: Virginia Julie HOWE/adapted by Jeremy Frederick HOWE
note: adopted 1965; the music is an adaptation of the traditional Mandinka song "Foday Kaba Dumbuya"

ECONOMY

Economy—overview: The Gambia has sparse natural resource deposits and a limited agricultural base, and relies in part on remittances from workers overseas and tourist receipts. About three-quarters of the population depends on the agricultural sector for its livelihood and the sector provides for about one-fifth of GDP. The agricultural sector has untapped potential—less than half of arable land is cultivated. Small-scale manufacturing activity features the processing of peanuts, fish, and hides. The Gambia's natural beauty and proximity to Europe has made it one of the larger markets for tourism in West Africa, boosted by government and private sector investments in eco-tourism and upscale facilities. In 2012, however, sluggish tourism led to a decline in GDP. Tourism brings in about one-fifth of GDP. Agriculture also took a hit in 2012 due to unfavorable weather patterns. The Gambia's re-export trade accounts for almost 80% of goods exports. Unemployment and underemployment rates remain high. Economic progress depends on sustained bilateral and multilateral aid, on responsible government economic management, and on continued technical assistance from multilateral and bilateral donors. International donors and lenders continue to be concerned about the quality of fiscal management and The Gambia's debt burden.

GDP (purchasing power parity): $3.678 billion (2013 est.)
country comparison to the world: 177
$3.456 billion (2012 est.)
$3.283 billion (2011 est.)
note: data are in 2013 US dollars

GDP (official exchange rate): $896 million (2013 est.)

GDP—real growth rate: 6.4% (2013 est.)
country comparison to the world: 30
5.3% (2012 est.)
-4.3% (2011 est.)

GDP—per capita (PPP): $2,000 (2013 est.)
country comparison to the world: 195
$1,900 (2012 est.)
$1,800 (2011 est.)
note: data are in 2013 US dollars

Gross national saving: 16.3% of GDP (2013 est.)
country comparison to the world: 103
17.5% of GDP (2012 est.)
23.6% of GDP (2011 est.)

GDP—composition, by end use:
household consumption: 89.2%
government consumption: 10.9%
investment in fixed capital: 19.1%
investment in inventories: 0%
exports of goods and services: 28%
imports of goods and services: -47.3% (2013 est.)

GDP—composition, by sector of origin:
agriculture: 19.7%
industry: 12.6%
services: 67.7% (2013 est.)

Agriculture—products: rice, millet, sorghum, peanuts, corn, sesame, cassava (manioc), palm kernels; cattle, sheep, goats

Industries: processing peanuts, fish, and hides; tourism, beverages, agricultural machinery assembly, woodworking, metalworking, clothing

Industrial production growth rate: 3.4% (2013 est.)
country comparison to the world: 89

Labor force: 777,100 (2007)
country comparison to the world: 150

Labor force—by occupation: agriculture: 75%
industry: 19%
services: 6% (1996)

Unemployment rate: NA%

Population below poverty line: 48.4% (2010 est.)

Household income or consumption by percentage share: *lowest 10%:* 2%
highest 10%: 36.9% (2003)

Distribution of family income—Gini index:
50.2 (1998)
country comparison to the world: 22

Budget: *revenues:* $229.6 million
expenditures: $265.1 million (2013 est.)

Taxes and other revenues: 25.6% of GDP (2013 est.)
country comparison to the world: 118

Budget surplus (+) or deficit (-):
-4% of GDP (2013 est.)
country comparison to the world: 147

Fiscal year: calendar year
Inflation rate (consumer prices):
6% (2013 est.)
country comparison to the world: 173
4.6% (2012 est.)

Central bank discount rate: 9% (31 December 2009)
country comparison to the world: 22
11% (31 December 2008)

Commercial bank prime lending rate:
30.5% (31 December 2013 est.)
country comparison to the world: 8
28% (31 December 2012 est.)

Stock of narrow money: $207.1 million (31 December 2013 est.)
country comparison to the world: 178
$217.9 million (31 December 2012 est.)

Stock of broad money: $479.8 million (31 December 2013 est.)
country comparison to the world: 176
$494.1 million (31 December 2012 est.)

Stock of domestic credit: $375 million (31 December 2013 est.)
country comparison to the world: 172
$386.2 million (31 December 2012 est.)

Market value of publicly traded shares: $NA

Current account balance: -$163.7 million (2013 est.)
country comparison to the world: 81
-$152.5 million (2012 est.)

Exports: $113.2 million (2013 est.)
country comparison to the world: 190
$111.8 million (2012 est.)

Exports—commodities: peanut products, fish, cotton lint, palm kernels

Exports—partners: China 57.1%, India 18.6%, France 4.6%, UK 4% (2012)

Imports: $359.7 million (2013 est.)
country comparison to the world: 193
$365.8 million (2012 est.)

Imports—commodities: foodstuffs, manufactures, fuel, machinery and transport equipment

Imports—partners: China 27.6%, Senegal 8.5%, Brazil 8.1%, UK 6.4%, India 6.1%, Indonesia 4.1% (2012)
Reserves of foreign exchange and gold:
$251.2 million (31 December 2013 est.)
country comparison to the world: 158
$236.2 million (31 December 2012 est.)

Debt—external: $517.7 million (31 December 2013 est.)
country comparison to the world: 175
$481.5 million (31 December 2012 est.)

Exchange rates: dalasis (GMD) per US dollar—
36.59 (2013 est.)
32.0771 (2012 est.)
28.012 (2010 est.)
26.6444 (2009)
22.75 (2008)

ENERGY

Electricity—production: 230 million kWh (2010 est.)
country comparison to the world: 180

Electricity—consumption: 213.9 million kWh (2010 est.)
country comparison to the world: 184

Electricity—exports: 0 kWh (2012 est.)
country comparison to the world: 139

Electricity—imports: 0 kWh (2012 est.)
country comparison to the world: 146

Electricity—installed generating capacity:
62,000 kW (2010 est.)
country comparison to the world: 181

Electricity—from fossil fuels: 100% of total installed capacity (2010 est.)
country comparison to the world: 13

Electricity—from nuclear fuels: 0% of total installed capacity (2010 est.)
country comparison to the world: 91

Electricity—from hydroelectric plants: 0% of total installed capacity (2010 est.)
country comparison to the world: 170

Electricity—from other renewable sources:
0% of total installed capacity (2010 est.)
country comparison to the world: 174

Crude oil—production: 0 bbl/day (2012 est.)
country comparison to the world: 172

Crude oil—exports: 0 bbl/day (2010 est.)
country comparison to the world: 116

Crude oil—imports: 0 bbl/day (2010 est.)
country comparison to the world: 188

Crude oil—proved reserves: 0 bbl (1 January 2013 es)
country comparison to the world: 135

Refined petroleum products—production:
0 bbl/day (2010 est.)
country comparison to the world: 146

Refined petroleum products—consumption:
3,181 bbl/day (2011 est.)
country comparison to the world: 178

Refined petroleum products—exports:
41.62 bbl/day (2010 est.)
country comparison to the world: 123

Refined petroleum products—imports:
3,434 bbl/day (2010 est.)
country comparison to the world: 167

Natural gas—production: 0 cu m (2011 est.)
country comparison to the world: 134

Natural gas—consumption: 0 cu m (2010 est.)
country comparison to the world: 147

Natural gas—exports: 0 cu m (2011 est.)
country comparison to the world: 103

Natural gas—imports: 0 cu m (2011 est.)
country comparison to the world: 195

Natural gas—proved reserves: 0 cu m (1 January 2013 es)
country comparison to the world: 141

Carbon dioxide emissions from consumption of energy: 425,600 Mt (2011 est.)
country comparison to the world: 184

COMMUNICATIONS

Telephones—main lines in use: 64,200 (2012)
country comparison to the world: 159

Telephones—mobile cellular: 1.526 million (2012)
country comparison to the world: 151

Telephone system: *general assessment:* adequate microwave radio relay and open-wire network; state-owned Gambia Telecommunications partially privatized in 2007
domestic: combined fixed-line and mobile-cellular teledensity, aided by multiple mobile-cellular providers, is roughly 80 per 100 persons
international: country code—220; microwave radio relay links to Senegal and Guinea-Bissau; a landing station for the Africa Coast to Europe (ACE) undersea fiber-optic cable is scheduled for completion in 2011; satellite earth station—1 Intelsat (Atlantic Ocean) (2011)

Broadcast media: state-owned, single-channel TV service; state-owned radio station and 4 privately owned radio stations; transmissions of multiple international broadcasters are available, some via shortwave radio; cable and satellite TV subscription services are obtainable in some parts of the country (2007)

Internet country code: .gm

Internet hosts: 656 (2012)
country comparison to the world: 179

Internet users: 130,100 (2009)
country comparison to the world: 150

TRANSPORTATION

Airports: 1 (2013)
country comparison to the world: 216

Airports—with paved runways: total: 1
over 3,047 m: 1 (2013)

Roadways: total: 3,740 km
country comparison to the world: 159
paved: 711 km
unpaved: 3,029 km (2011)

Waterways: 390 km (on River Gambia; small ocean-going vessels can reach 190 km) (2010)
country comparison to the world: 89

Merchant marine: *total:* 4
country comparison to the world: 132
by type: passenger/cargo 3, petroleum tanker 1 (2010)

Ports and terminals: *major seaport(s):* Banjul

MILITARY

Military branches: Office of the Chief of Defense Staff: Gambian National Army (GNA), Gambian Navy (GN), Republican National Guard (RNG) (2010)

Military service age and obligation: 18 years of age for male and female voluntary military service; no conscription; service obligation 6 months (2012)

Manpower available for military service:
males age 16-49: 423,306
females age 16-49: 438,641 (2010 est.)

Manpower fit for military service:
males age 16-49: 315,176
females age 16-49: 347,017 (2010 est.)

Manpower reaching militarily significant age annually: *male:* 20,508
female: 20,853 (2010 est.)

TRANSNATIONAL ISSUES

Disputes—international: attempts to stem refugees, cross-border raids, arms smuggling, and other illegal activities by separatists from southern Senegal's Casamance region, as well as from conflicts in other west African states

Refugees and internally displaced persons: *refugees (country of origin):* 9,042 (Senegal) (2012)

Trafficking in persons: *current situation:* The Gambia is a source, transit, and destination country for women and children subjected to forced labor and sex trafficking; Gambian women, children, and, to a lesser extent, boys are exploited for prostitution and domestic servitude; women, girls, and boys from West African countries are trafficked to the Gambia for sexual exploitation, particularly catering to European tourists seeking sex with children; some Gambian trafficking victims have been identified in neighboring West African countries and the UK; boys in some Koranic schools are forced into street vending or begging
tier rating: Tier 2 Watch List—The Gambia does not fully comply with the minimum standards for the elimination of trafficking; however, it is making significant efforts to do so; the government has sustained its modest anti-trafficking law enforcement efforts, opening some investigations but failing to initiate any prosecutions or to formally identify any victims; a government program was launched providing resources and financial support to 12 Koranic schools on the condition that their students are not forced to beg (2013)

GAZA STRIP

INTRODUCTION

Background: Inhabited since at least the 15th century B.C., Gaza has been dominated by many different peoples and empires throughout its history; it was incorporated into the Ottoman Empire in the early 16th century. Gaza fell to British forces during World War I, becoming a part of the British Mandate of Palestine. Following the 1948 Arab-Israeli War, Egypt administered the newly formed Gaza Strip; it was captured by Israel in the Six-Day War in 1967. Under a series of agreements signed between 1994 and 1999, Israel transferred to the Palestinian Authority (PA) security and civilian responsibility for many Palestinian-populated areas of the Gaza Strip as well as the West Bank. Negotiations to determine the permanent status of the West Bank and Gaza Strip stalled after the outbreak of an intifada in mid- 2000. In early 2003, the "Quartet" of the US, EU, UN, and Russia, presented a roadmap to a final peace settlement by 2005, calling for two states—Israel and a democratic Palestine. Following Palestinian leader Yasir ARAFAT's death in late 2004 and the subsequent election of Mahmud ABBAS (head of the Fatah political party) as the PA president, Israel and the PA agreed to move the peace process forward. Israel in late 2005 unilaterally withdrew all of its settlers and soldiers and dismantled its military facilities in the Gaza Strip, but continues to control maritime, airspace, and other access. In early 2006, the Islamic Resistance Movement, HAMAS, won the Palestinian Legislative Council election and took control of the PA government. Attempts to form a unity government between Fatah and HAMAS failed, and violent clashes between Fatah and HAMAS supporters ensued, culminating in HAMAS's violent seizure of all military and governmental institutions in the Gaza Strip in June 2007. Fatah and HAMAS in early 2011 agreed to reunify the Gaza Strip and West Bank, but the factions have struggled to implement details on governance and security. Brief periods of increased violence between Israel and Palestinian militants in the Gaza Strip in 2007-08 and again in 2012, both led to Egyptian-brokered truces. The status quo remains with HAMAS in control of the Gaza Strip and the PA governing the West Bank.

GEOGRAPHY

Location: Middle East, bordering the Mediterranean Sea, between Egypt and Israel

Geographic coordinates: 31 25 N, 34 20 E

Map references: Middle East

Area: *total:* 360 sq km
country comparison to the world: 206
land: 360 sq km
water: 0 sq km

Area—comparative: slightly more than twice the size of Washington, DC

Land boundaries: *total:* 62 km
border countries: Egypt 11 km, Israel 51 km

Coastline: 40 km

Maritime claims: see entry for Israel
note: effective 3 January 2009 the Gaza maritime area is closed to all maritime traffic and is under blockade imposed by Israeli Navy until further notice

Climate: temperate, mild winters, dry and warm to hot summers

Terrain: flat to rolling, sand- and dune-covered coastal plain

Elevation extremes: *lowest point:* Mediterranean Sea 0 m
highest point: Abu 'Awdah (Joz Abu 'Awdah) 105 m

Natural resources: arable land, natural gas

Land use: arable land: 7.39%
permanent crops: 10.96%
other: 81.64% (2011)

Irrigated land: 240 sq km; note—includes West Bank (2003)

Natural hazards: droughts

Environment—current issues: desertification; salination of fresh water; sewage treatment; water-borne disease; soil degradation; depletion and contamination of underground water resources

Geography—note: strategic strip of land along Mideast-North African trade routes has experienced an incredibly turbulent history; the town of Gaza itself has been besieged countless times in its history

PEOPLE AND SOCIETY

Nationality: *noun:* NA
adjective: NA

Ethnic groups: Palestinian Arab

Languages: Arabic, Hebrew (spoken by many Palestinians), English (widely understood)

Religions: Muslim (predominantly Sunni), Jewish, Christian

Population: 1,816,379 (July 2014 est.)
country comparison to the world: 152

Age structure: *0-14 years:* 43.2% (male 402,848/female 381,155)
15-24 years: 20.6% (male 191,710/female 182,405)
25-54 years: 30.1% (male 280,551/female 266,756)
55-64 years: 2.6% (male 31,711/female 31,515)
65 years and over: 2.6% (male 19,617/female 28,111) (2014 est.)

Dependency ratios:
total dependency ratio: 75.6 %
youth dependency ratio: 70.4 %
elderly dependency ratio: 5.2 %
potential support ratio: 19.2
note: data represents the Palestinian Territories (2013)

Median age: total: 18.2 years
male: 18 years
female: 18.4 years (2014 est.)

Population growth rate: 2.91% (2014 est.)
country comparison to the world: 13

Birth rate: 32.2 births/1,000 population (2014 est.)
country comparison to the world: 35

Death rate: 3.09 deaths/1,000 population (2014 est.)
country comparison to the world: 221

Net migration rate: 0 migrant(s)/1,000 population (2014 est.)
country comparison to the world: 108

Urbanization: *urban population:* 74.3% of total population (2011)
rate of urbanization: 3.1% annual rate of change (2005-10 est.)

Sex ratio: *at birth:* 1.06 male(s)/female
0-14 years: 1.06 male(s)/female
15-24 years: 1.05 male(s)/female
25-54 years: 1.05 male(s)/female
55-64 years: 1.04 male(s)/female
65 years and over: 0.68 male(s)/female
total population: 1.04 male(s)/female (2014 est.)

Maternal mortality rate: 64 deaths/100,000 live births (2010)
country comparison to the world: 94

Infant mortality rate: total: 15.46 deaths/1,000 live births
country comparison to the world: 105
male: 16.51 deaths/1,000 live births
female: 14.35 deaths/1,000 live births (2014 est.)

Life expectancy at birth: total population: 74.64 years
country comparison to the world: 109
male: 72.9 years
female: 76.48 years (2014 est.)

Total fertility rate: 4.24 children born/woman (2014 est.)
country comparison to the world: 34

HIV/AIDS—adult prevalence rate: NA

HIV/AIDS—people living with HIV/AIDS: NA

HIV/AIDS—deaths: NA

Literacy: *definition:* age 15 and over can read and write
total population: 95.3%
male: 97.9%
female: 92.6%
note: estimates are for the Palestinian Territories (2011 est.)

Unemployment, youth ages 15-24: total: 38.8%
country comparison to the world: 16
male: 34.5%
female: 62.2%
note: includes West Bank (2012)

GOVERNMENT

Country name: conventional long form: none
conventional short form: Gaza Strip
local long form: none
local short form: Qita' Ghazzah

ECONOMY

Economy—overview: Israeli security controls imposed since the end of the second intifada have degraded economic conditions in the Gaza Strip, the smaller of the two areas comprising the Palestinian territories. Israeli-imposed border closures, which became more restrictive after HAMAS seized control of the territory in June 2007, have resulted in high unemployment, elevated poverty rates, and a sharp contraction of the private sector that had relied primarily on export markets. Gazans increasingly turned to tunnels that ran under the Egyptian border to bring in fuel, construction materials, and consumer goods. In July 2013, Egyptian authorities began a serious crackdown on the tunnels, causing shortages in Gaza. The population depends on government spending—by both the Palestinian Authority and HAMAS's de facto government—and humanitarian assistance. Changes to Israeli restrictions on imports in 2010 resulted in a rebound in some economic activity, but regular exports from Gaza still are not permitted. Standard-of-living measures remain below levels seen in the mid-1990s.

GDP (purchasing power parity): see entry for West Bank

GDP—real growth rate: see entry for West Bank

GDP—per capita (PPP): see entry for West Bank

GDP—composition, by end use:
household consumption: 99.5%
government consumption: 29.5%
investment in fixed capital: 18%
investment in inventories: 0%
exports of goods and services: 14.9%
imports of goods and services: -62% (2013 est.)

GDP—composition, by sector of origin: see entry for West Bank

Agriculture—products: olives, fruit, vegetables, flowers; beef, dairy products

Industries: textiles, food processing, furniture

Industrial production growth rate: (2013 est.)

Labor force: 348,200 (2010 est.)
country comparison to the world: 161

Labor force—by occupation: agriculture: 5.1%
industry: 15.6%
services: 79.3% (2010 est.)

Unemployment rate: 22.5% (2013 est.)
country comparison to the world: 170
23% (2012 est.)

Population below poverty line: 38% (2010 est.)

Budget: see entry for West Bank

Fiscal year: calendar year

Inflation rate (consumer prices): 1.7% (2013 est.)
country comparison to the world: 50
2.8% (2012 est.)
note: includes West Bank

Commercial bank prime lending rate: see entry for West Bank

Stock of broad money: $2.1 billion (31 December 2013 est.)
country comparison to the world: 147
$1.814 billion (31 December 2012 est.)

Stock of domestic credit: $1.248 billion (31 December 2013 est.)
country comparison to the world: 150
$1.042 billion (31 December 2012 est.)

Current account balance: (2011 est.)

Exports: (2011 est.)

Exports—commodities: strawberries, carnations, vegetables (small and irregular shipments, as permitted to transit the Israeli-controlled Kerem Shalom crossing)

Imports: see entry for West Bank

Imports—commodities: food, consumer goods
note: Israel permits basic commercial imports through the Kerem Shalom crossing, but many "dual use" goods, such as construction materials and electronics, are smuggled through tunnels beneath Gaza's border with Egypt

Debt—external: see entry for West Bank

Exchange rates: new Israeli shekels (ILS) per US dollar—
3.621 (2012 est.)
3.5781 (2012 est.)
3.739 (2010 est.)
3.9323 (2009)
3.56 (2008)

ENERGY

Electricity—production: 51,000 kWh (2011 est.)
country comparison to the world: 218

Electricity—consumption: 202,000 kWh (2009)
country comparison to the world: 217

Electricity—exports: 0 kWh (2011 est.)
country comparison to the world: 147

Electricity—imports: 193,000 kWh (2011 est.)
country comparison to the world: 108

Crude oil—proved reserves: 0 bbl (1 January 2010 es)
country comparison to the world: 142

COMMUNICATIONS

Telephones—main lines in use: 406,000 (includes West Bank) (2012)
country comparison to the world: 105

Telephones—mobile cellular: 3.041 million (includes West Bank) (2012)
country comparison to the world: 131

Telephone system: *general assessment:* Gaza continues to repair the damage to its telecommunications infrastructure caused by fighting in 2009
domestic: Israeli company BEZEK and the Palestinian company PALTEL are responsible for fixed-line services; the Palestinian JAWWAL company provides cellular services
international: country code—970 (2009) Broadcast media: 1 TV station and about 10 radio stations (2008)

Internet country code: .ps; note—same as West Bank

Internet users: 1.379 million (includes West Bank) (2009)
country comparison to the world: 87

TRANSPORTATION

Airports: 1 (2013)
country comparison to the world: 218
Airports—with paved runways: total: 1
over 3,047 m: 1 (2013)
Heliports: 1 (2013)
Roadways: *note:* see entry for West Bank
Ports and terminals: *major seaport(s):* Gaza

MILITARY

Military branches: Hamas does not have a conventional military in the Gaza Strip, but maintains security forces in addition to its military wing, the 'Izz al-Din al-Qassam Brigades; the military wing reports to the external Hamas Political Bureau leadership, which has been in exile in Cairo and Doha since closing its Damascus headquarters in late 2011 (2013)
Manpower available for military service:
males age 16-49: 385,961 (2010 est.)
Manpower fit for military service:
males age 16-49: 335,820
females age 16-49: 319,847 (2010 est.)
Manpower reaching militarily significant age annually: *male:* 18,805
female: 17,903 (2010 est.)

TRANSNATIONAL ISSUES

Disputes—international: the status of the Gaza Strip is a final status issue to be resolved through negotiations; Israel removed settlers and military personnel from Gaza Strip in August 2005
Refugees and internally displaced persons: *refugees* (country of origin): 1,221,110 (Palestinian refugees (UNRWA)) (2013)
IDPs: 160,000 (persons displaced within both the Gaza strip and the West Bank since 1967; as estimated by unofficial sources) (2011)

GEORGIA

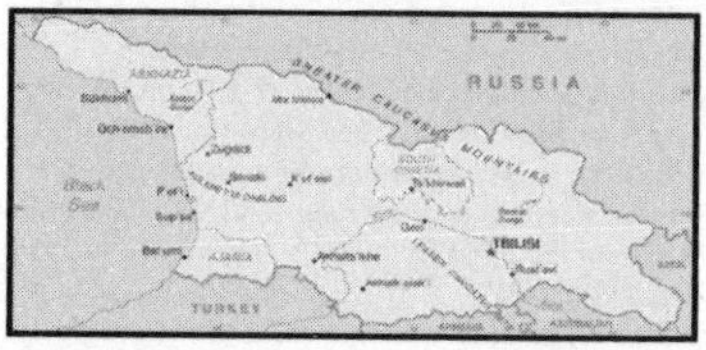

INTRODCTION

Background: The region of present day Georgia contained the ancient kingdoms of Colchis and Kartli-Iberia. The area came under Roman influence in the first centuries A.D., and Christianity became the state religion in the 330s. Domination by Persians, Arabs, and Turks was followed by a Georgian golden age (11th-13th centuries) that was cut short by the Mongol invasion of 1236. Subsequently, the Ottoman and Persian empires competed for influence in the region. Georgia was absorbed into the Russian Empire in the 19th century. Independent for three years (1918-1921) following the Russian revolution, it was forcibly incorporated into the USSR in 1921 and regained its independence when the Soviet Union dissolved in 1991. Mounting public discontent over rampant corruption and ineffective government services, followed by an attempt by the incumbent Georgian Government to manipulate national legislative elections in November 2003 touched off widespread protests that led to the resignation of Eduard SHEVARDNADZE, president since 1995. In the aftermath of that popular movement, which became known as the "Rose Revolution," new elections in early 2004 swept Mikheil SAAKASHVILI into power along with his United National Movement (UNM) party. Progress on market reforms and democratization has been made in the years since independence, but this progress has been complicated by Russian assistance and support to the separatist regions of Abkhazia and South Ossetia. Periodic flare-ups in tension and violence culminated in a five-day conflict in August 2008 between Russia and Georgia, including the invasion of large portions of undisputed Georgian territory. Russian troops pledged to pull back from most occupied Georgian territory, but in late August 2008 Russia unilaterally recognized the independence of Abkhazia and South Ossetia, and Russian military forces remain in those regions. Billionaire philanthropist Bidzina IVANISHVILI's unexpected entry into politics in October 2011 brought the divided opposition together under his Georgian Dream coalition, which won a majority of seats in the October 2012 parliamentary election and removed UNM from power. Conceding defeat, SAAKASHVILI named IVANISHVILI as prime minister and allowed Georgian Dream to create a new government. Georgian Dream's Giorgi MARGVELASHVILI was inaugurated as president on 17 November 2013, ending a tense year of power-sharing between SAAKASHVILI and IVANISHVILI. IVANISHVILI voluntarily resigned from office after the presidential succession, and Georgia's legislature on 20 November 2013 confirmed Irakli GARIBASHVILI as his replacement. Georgia's recent elections represent unique examples of a former Soviet state that emerged to conduct democratic and peaceful government transitions of power. Popular and government support for integration with the West is high in Georgia. Joining the EU and NATO are among the country's top foreign policy goals.

GEOGRAPHY

Location: Southwestern Asia, bordering the Black Sea, between Turkey and Russia, with a sliver of land north of the Caucasus extending into Europe; note—Georgia views itself as part of Europe
Geographic coordinates: 42 00 N, 43 30 E
Map references: Middle East
Area: *total:* 69,700 sq km
country comparison to the world: 121
land: 69,700 sq km
water: 0 sq km
Area—comparative: slightly smaller than South Carolina
Land boundaries: *total:* 1,461 km
border countries: Armenia 164 km, Azerbaijan 322 km, Russia 723 km, Turkey 252 km
Coastline: 310 km
Maritime claims: *territorial sea:* 12 nm
exclusive economic zone: 200 nm
Climate: warm and pleasant; Mediterranean-like on Black Sea coast
Terrain: largely mountainous with Great Caucasus Mountains in the north and Lesser Caucasus Mountains in the south; Kolkhet'is Dablobi (Kolkhida Lowland) opens to the Black Sea in the west; Mtkvari River Basin in the east; good soils in river valley flood plains, foothills of Kolkhida Lowland
Elevation extremes: *lowest point:* Black Sea 0 m
highest point: Mt'a Shkhara 5,201 m
Natural resources: timber, hydropower, manganese deposits, iron ore, copper, minor coal and oil deposits; coastal climate and soils allow for important tea and citrus growth
Land use: *arable land:* 5.94%
permanent crops: 1.65%
other: 92.41% (2011)
Irrigated land: 4,328 sq km (2007)
Total renewable water resources: 63.33 cu km (2011)
Freshwater withdrawal (domestic/industrial/agricultural): *total:* 1.81 cu km/yr (20%/22%/58%)
per capita: 410.6 cu m/yr (2005)
Natural hazards: earthquakes
Environment—current issues: air pollution, particularly in Rust'avi; heavy pollution of Mtkvari River and the Black Sea; inadequate supplies of potable water; soil pollution from toxic chemicals
Environment—international agreements: *party to:* Air Pollution, Biodiversity, Climate Change, Climate Change-Kyoto Protocol, Desertification, Endangered Species, Hazardous Wastes, Law of the Sea, Ozone Layer Protection, Ship Pollution, Wetlands signed, but not ratified: none of the selected agreements
Geography—note: strategically located east of the Black Sea; Georgia controls much of the Caucasus Mountains and the routes through t h e m

PEOPLE AND SOCIETY

Nationality: *noun:* Georgian(s)
adjective: Georgian
Ethnic groups: Georgian 83.8%, Azeri 6.5%, Armenian 5.7%, Russian 1.5%, other 2.5% (2002 census)
Languages: Georgian (official) 71%, Russian 9%, Armenian 7%, Azeri 6%, other 7% note: Abkhaz is the official language in Abkhazia
Religions: Orthodox Christian (official) 83.9%, Muslim 9.9%, Armenian-Gregorian 3.9%,

Catholic 0.8%, other 0.8%, none 0.7% (2002 census)

Population: 4,935,880 (July 2014 est.)
country comparison to the world: 122

Age structure: *0-14 years:* 17.6% (male 459,334/ female 410,494)
15-24 years: 14% (male 359,559/female 332,182)
25-54 years: 40.9% (male 976,129/female 1,042,898)
55-64 years: 15.3% (male 269,367/female 330,386)
65 years and over: 16.2% (male 295,673/female 459,858) (2014 est.)

Dependency ratios:
total dependency ratio: 47.7 %
youth dependency ratio: 26.4 %
elderly dependency ratio: 21.3 %
potential support ratio: 4.7 (2013)

Median age: *total:* 37.7 years
male: 34.9 years
female: 40.4 years (2014 est.)

Population growth rate: -0.11% (2014 est.)
country comparison to the world: 206

Birth rate: 12.93 births/1,000 population (2014 est.)
country comparison to the world: 155

Death rate: 10.77 deaths/1,000 population (2014 est.)
country comparison to the world: 37

Net migration rate: -3.25 migrant(s)/1,000 population (2014 est.)
country comparison to the world: 182

Urbanization: *urban population:* 52.8% of total population (2011)
rate of urbanization: -0.37% annual rate of change (2010-15 est.)

Major urban areas—population: TBILISI (capital) 1.115 million (2009)

Sex ratio: *at birth:* 1.08 male(s)/female
0-14 years: 1.12 male(s)/female
15-24 years: 1.08 male(s)/female
25-54 years: 0.94 male(s)/female
55-64 years: 0.92 male(s)/female
65 years and over: 0.66 male(s)/female
total population: 0.91 male(s)/female (2014 est.)

Mother's mean age at first birth: 23.9 (2010 est.)

Maternal mortality rate: 67 deaths/100,000 live births (2010)
country comparison to the world: 91

Infant mortality rate: *total:* 16.68 deaths/1,000 live births
country comparison to the world: 100
male: 18.86 deaths/1,000 live births
female: 14.32 deaths/1,000 live births (2014 est.)

Life expectancy at birth: *total population:* 75.72 years
country comparison to the world: 90
male: 71.62 years
female: 80.17 years (2014 est.)

Total fertility rate: 1.77 children born/woman (2014 est.)
country comparison to the world: 159

Contraceptive prevalence rate: 53.4%
note: percent of women aged 15-44 (2010)

Health expenditures: 9.4% of GDP (2011)
country comparison to the world: 34

Physicians density: 4.24 physicians/1,000 population (2011)

Hospital bed density: 2.9 beds/1,000 population (2011)

Drinking water source:
improved:
urban: 100% of population
rural: 95.9% of population
total: 98.1% of population
unimproved:
urban: 0% of population
rural: 4.1% of population
total: 1.9% of population (2011 est.)

Sanitation facility access:
improved:
urban: 95.6% of population
rural: 91% of population
total: 93.4% of population
unimproved:
urban: 4.4% of population
rural: 9% of population
total: 6.6% of population (2011 est.)

HIV/AIDS—adult prevalence rate: 0.3% (2012 est.)
country comparison to the world: 93

HIV/AIDS—people living with HIV/AIDS: 6,600 (2012 est.)
country comparison to the world: 119

HIV/AIDS—deaths: 200 (2012 est.)
country comparison to the world: 107

Obesity—adult prevalence rate: 22.1% (2008)
country comparison to the world: 82

Children under the age of 5 years underweight: 1.1% (2009)
country comparison to the world: 132

Education expenditures: 2% of GDP (2012)
country comparison to the world: 167

Literacy: *definition:* age 15 and over can read and write
total population: 99.7%
male: 99.8%
female: 99.7% (2011 est.)

School life expectancy (primary to tertiary education): *total:* 13 years
male: 13 years
female: 13 years (2008)

Child labor—children ages 5-14: total number: 113,106
percentage: 18 % (2005 est.)

Unemployment, youth ages 15-24: total: 33.3% (2012)
country comparison to the world: 23

GOVERNMENT

Country name: *conventional long form:* none
conventional short form: Georgia
local long form: none
local short form: Sak'art'velo
former: Georgian Soviet Socialist Republic

Government type: republic

Capital: *name:* Tbilisi

geographic coordinates: 41 41 N, 44 50 E
time difference: UTC+4 (9 hours ahead of Washington, DC during Standard Time)

Administrative divisions: 9 regions (mkharebi, singular—mkhare), 1 city (k'alak'i), and 2 autonomous republics (avtomnoy respubliki, singular—avtom respublika)
regions: Guria, Imereti, Kakheti, Kvemo Kartli, Mtskheta-Mtianeti, Racha-Lechkhumi and Kvemo Svaneti, Samegrelo and Zemo Svaneti, Samtskhe-Javakheti, Shida Kartli
city: Tbilisi
autonomous republics: Abkhazia or Ap'khazet'is Avtonomiuri Respublika (Sokhumi), Ajaria or Acharis Avtonomiuri Respublika (Bat'umi)
note: the administrative centers of the two autonomous republics are shown in parentheses

Independence: 9 April 1991 (from the Soviet Union); notable earlier date: A.D. 1008 (Georgia unified under King BAGRAT III)

National holiday: Independence Day, 26 May (1918); note—26 May 1918 was the date of independence from Soviet Russia, 9 April 1991 was the date of independence from the Soviet Union

Constitution: previous 1921, 1978 (based on 1977 Soviet Union constitution); latest approved 24 August 1995, effective 17 October 1995; amended several times, last in 2013 (2013)

Legal system: civil law system

International law organization participation: accepts compulsory ICJ jurisdiction; accepts ICCt jurisdiction

Suffrage: 18 years of age; universal

Executive branch: *chief of state:* President Giorgi MARGVELASHVILI (since 17 November 2013)
head of government: Prime Minister Irakli GARIBASHVILI (since 20 November 2013)
cabinet: Cabinet of Ministers (For more information visit the World Leaders website)
elections: president elected by popular vote for a five-year term (eligible for a second term); election last held on 27 October 2013 (next to be held in October 2018)
election results: Giorgi MARGVELASHVILI elected president; percent of vote—Giorgi MARGVELASHVILI 62.1%, Davit BAKRADZE 21.7%, Nino BURJANADZE 10.2%, other 6%

Legislative branch: unicameral Parliament or Parlamenti (150 seats; 77 members elected by proportional representation, 73 elected in single-member constituencies; members to serve four-year terms)
elections: last held on 1 October 2012 (next to be held in 2016)
election results: percent of vote by party—Georgian Dream 55%, United National Movement 40.3%, other 4.7%; seats by party—Georgian Dream 85, United National Movement 65

Judicial branch: *highest court(s):* Supreme Court (organized into several specialized judicial chambers; number of judges determined by the president of Georgia); Constitutional Court (consists of 9 judges) note—the Abkhazian and Ajarian Autonomous republics each have a supreme court and a hierarchy of lower courts
judge selection and term of office: Supreme Court judges nominated by the president and appointed by the Parliament; judges serve not less than 10-year terms; Constitutional Court judges appointed by the president following candidate selection by the Justice Council of Georgia, a 12-member consultative body of high-level judges, and presidential and parliamentary appointees; judges appointed for 10-year terms
subordinate courts: Courts of Appeal; regional (town) and district courts

Political parties and leaders: Christian Democratic Movement [Giorgi AKHVELDIANI]; Conservative Party [Zviad DZIDZIGURI]; European Democrats [Paata DAVITAIA]; For Fair Georgia [Zurab NOGAIDELI]; Free Georgia [Kakha KUKAVA]; Georgian Dream (a six-party coalition composed of Georgian Dream-Democratic Georgia, Republican Party, Our; Georgia-Free Democrats, National Forum, Conservative Party, and Industry Will Save Georgia); Georgian Dream-Democratic

Georgia [Irakli GARIBASHVILI]; Georgian People's Front [Nodar NATADZE]; Georgian Troupe [Jondi BAGHTURIA]; Industry Will Save Georgia (Industrialists) or IWSG [Georgi TOPADZE]; Labor Party [Shalva NATELASHVILI]; National Democratic Party or NDP [Bachuki KARDAVA]; National Forum [Kakhaber SHARTAVA]; New Rights [Pikria CHIKHRADZE]; Our Georgia-Free Democrats (OGFD) [Irakli KADAGIDZE]; People's Party [Koba DAVITASHVILI; Republican Party [Khatuna SAMNIDZE]; Traditionalists [Akaki ASATIANI]; United National Movement or UNM [Vano MERABISHVILI]

Political pressure groups and leaders: separatists in the Russian-occupied regions of Abkhazia and South Ossetia

International organization participation: ADB, BSEC, CD, CE, EAPC, EBRD, FAO, G-11, GCTU, GUAM, IAEA, IBRD, ICAO, ICC (national committees), ICRM, IDA, IFAD, IFC, IFRCS, ILO, IMF, IMO, Interpol, IOC, IOM, IPU, ISO (correspondent), ITSO, ITU, ITUC (NGOs), MIGA, OAS (observer), OIF (observer), OPCW, OSCE, PFP, SELEC (observer), UN, UNCTAD, UNESCO, UNIDO, UNWTO, UPU, WCO, WHO, WIPO, WMO, WTO

Diplomatic representation in the US:
chief of mission: Ambassador Archil GEGESHIDZE (since 12 April 2013)
chancery: 2209 Massachusetts Avenue NW, Washington, DC 20008
telephone: [1] (202) 387-2390
FAX: [1] (202) 387-0864
consulate(s) general: New York

Diplomatic representation from the US:
chief of mission: Ambassador Richard NORLAND (since 25 July 2012)
embassy: 11 George Balanchine Street, T'bilisi 0131
mailing address: 7060 T'bilisi Place, Washington, DC 20521-7060
telephone: [995] (32) 227-70-00
FAX: [995] (32) 253-23-10

Flag description: white rectangle with a central red cross extending to all four sides of the flag; each of the four quadrants displays a small red bolnur-katskhuri cross; sometimes referred to as the Five-Cross Flag; although adopted as the official Georgian flag in 2004, the five-cross design appears to date back to the 14th century

National symbol(s): Saint George; lion

National anthem: *name:* "Tavisupleba" (Liberty)
lyrics/music: Davit MAGRADSE/Zakaria PALIASHVILI (adapted by Joseb KETSCHAKMADSE)
note: adopted 2004; after the Rose Revolution, a new anthem with music based on the operas "Abesalom da Eteri" and "Daisi" was adopted

Economy

Economy—overview: Georgia's main economic activities include cultivation of agricultural products such as grapes, citrus fruits, and hazelnuts; mining of manganese, copper, and gold; and producing alcoholic and nonalcoholic beverages, metals, machinery, and chemicals in small-scale industries. The country imports nearly all its needed supplies of natural gas and oil products. It has sizeable hydropower capacity that now provides most of its energy needs. Georgia has overcome the chronic energy shortages and gas supply interruptions of the past by renovating hydropower plants and by increasingly relying on natural gas imports from Azerbaijan instead of from Russia. Construction of the Baku-T'bilisi-Ceyhan oil pipeline, the South Caucasus gas pipeline, and the Kars-Akhalkalaki Railroad are part of a strategy to capitalize on Georgia's strategic location between Europe and Asia and develop its role as a transit point for gas, oil, and other goods. The expansion of the South Caucasus pipeline, as part of the Shah Deniz II Southern Gas Corridor project, will result in a $2 billion foreign investment in Georgia, the largest ever in the country. Gas from Shah Deniz II is expected to begin flowing in 2019. Georgia's economy sustained GDP growth of more than 10% in 2006-07, based on strong inflows of foreign investment and robust government spending. However, GDP growth slowed following the August 2008 conflict with Russia, and sunk to negative 4% in 2009 as foreign direct investment and workers' remittances declined in the wake of the global financial crisis. The economy rebounded in 2010-13, but FDI inflows, the engine of Georgian economic growth prior to the 2008 conflict, have not recovered fully. Unemployment has also remained high. Georgia has historically suffered from a chronic failure to collect tax revenues; however, since 2004 the government has simplified the tax code, improved tax administration, increased tax enforcement, and cracked down on petty corruption, leading to higher revenues. The country is pinning its hopes for renewed growth on a determined effort to continue to liberalize the economy by reducing regulation, taxes, and corruption in order to attract foreign investment, with a focus on hydropower, agriculture, tourism, and textiles production. The government has received high marks from the World Bank for its anti-corruption efforts. Over the past year the Georgian Dream-led government continued the previous administration's low-regulation, low-tax, free market policies, while modestly increasing social spending, strengthening anti-trust policy, and amending the labor code to comply with International Labor Standards. The government is finalizing its 2020 Economic Development Strategy and has launched the Georgia Co-Investment Fund, a $6 billion private equity fund that will invest in tourism, agriculture, logistics, energy, infrastructure, and manufacturing.

GDP (purchasing power parity): $27.3 billion (2013 est.)
country comparison to the world: 120
$26.64 billion (2012 est.)
$25.1 billion (2011 est.)
note: data are in 2013 US dollars

GDP (official exchange rate): $15.95 billion (2013 est.)

GDP—real growth rate: 2.5% (2013 est.)
country comparison to the world: 131
6.1% (2012 est.)
7.2% (2011 est.)

GDP—per capita (PPP): $6,100 (2013 est.)
country comparison to the world: 151
$5,900 (2012 est.)
$5,600 (2011 est.)
note: data are in 2013 US dollars

Gross national saving: 18% of GDP (2013 est.)
country comparison to the world: 90
17.1% of GDP (2012 est.)
12.6% of GDP (2011 est.)

GDP—composition, by end use:
household consumption: 68.6%
government consumption: 19%
investment in fixed capital: 23.6%
investment in inventories: 3.2%
exports of goods and services: 39.9%
imports of goods and services: -54.4% (2013 est.)

GDP—composition, by sector of origin:
agriculture: 8.5%
industry: 21.6%
services: 69.9% (2013 est.)

Agriculture—products: citrus, grapes, tea, hazelnuts, vegetables; livestock

Industries: steel, machine tools, electrical appliances, mining (manganese, copper, and gold), chemicals, wood products, wine

Industrial production growth rate: 3% (2013 est.)
country comparison to the world: 103

Labor force: 1.959 million (2011 est.)
country comparison to the world: 122

Labor force—by occupation: *agriculture:* 55.6%
industry: 8.9%
services: 35.5% (2006 est.)

Unemployment rate: 15% (2013 est.)
country comparison to the world: 141
15.1% (2011 est.)

Population below poverty line: 9.2% (2010)

Household income or consumption by percentage share: *lowest 10%:* 2%
highest 10%: 31.3% (2008)

Distribution of family income—Gini index: 46 (2011)
country comparison to the world: 35
37.1 (1996)

Budget: *revenues:* $4.834 billion
expenditures: $5.257 billion (2013 est.)

Taxes and other revenues: 30.3% of GDP (2013 est.)
country comparison to the world: 91

Budget surplus (+) or deficit (-): -2.7% of GDP (2013 est.)
country comparison to the world: 113

Public debt: 36.3% of GDP (2012 est.)
country comparison to the world: 103
36.5% of GDP (2011 est.)
note: data cover general government debt, and includes debt instruments issued (or owned) by government entities other than the treasury; the data include treasury debt held by foreign entities; the data include debt issued by subnational entities; Georgia does not maintain intra-governmental debt or social funds

Fiscal year: calendar year

Inflation rate (consumer prices): -0.5% (2013 est.)
country comparison to the world: 4
-0.9% (2012 est.)

Central bank discount rate: 3.75% (15 January 2013)
country comparison to the world: 65
5.25% (31 December 2012)
note: this is the Refinancing Rate, the key monetary policy rate of the National Bank of Georgia

Commercial bank prime lending rate: 20.7% (31 December 2013 est.)
country comparison to the world: 15
22.08% (31 December 2012 est.)

Stock of narrow money: $2.025 billion (31 December 2013 est.)
country comparison to the world: 127
$1.965 billion (31 December 2012 est.)

Stock of broad money: $4.72 billion (31 September 2012 est.)

country comparison to the world: 130
$4.249 billion (31 December 2011 est.)

Stock of domestic credit: $5.96 billion (31 December 2013 est.)
country comparison to the world: 110
$5.518 billion (31 December 2012 est.)

Market value of publicly traded shares: $943.4 million (31 December 2012 est.)
country comparison to the world: 108
$795.7 million (31 December 2011)
$1.06 billion (31 December 2010 est.)

Current account balance: -$1.375 billion (2013 est.)
country comparison to the world: 131
-$1.875 billion (2012 est.)

Exports: $2.618 billion (2013 est.)
country comparison to the world: 135
$2.377 billion (2012 est.)

Exports—commodities: vehicles, ferro-alloys, fertilizers, nuts, scrap metal, gold, copper ores

Exports—partners: Azerbaijan 25%, Armenia 11%, Ukraine 7%, Turkey 6%, Russia 6% (2013 est.)

Imports: $7.064 billion (2013 est.)
country comparison to the world: 114
$7.842 billion (2012 est.)

Imports—commodities: fuels, vehicles, machinery and parts, grain and other foods, pharmaceuticals

Imports—partners: Turkey 17%, Ukraine 8%, Azerbaijan 8%, Russia 7%, China 7% (2013 est.)

Reserves of foreign exchange and gold: $3.317 billion (31 December 2013 est.)
country comparison to the world: 105
$2.873 billion (31 December 2012 est.)

Debt—external: $11.74 billion (31 December 2013 est.)
country comparison to the world: 97
$11.67 billion (31 December 2012 est.)

Stock of direct foreign investment—at home: $11.19 billion (31 December 2013 est.)
country comparison to the world: 83
$10.49 billion (31 December 2012 est.)

Stock of direct foreign investment—abroad: $1.359 billion (31 December 2013 est.)
country comparison to the world: 77
$1.329 billion (31 December 2012 est.)

Exchange rates: laris (GEL) per US dollar—
1.655 (2013 est.)
1.6513 (2012 est.)
1.7823 (2010 est.)
1.6705 (2009 est.)
1.47 (2008 est.)

ENERGY

Electricity—production: 9.694 billion kWh (2012 est.)
country comparison to the world: 9 4

Electricity—consumption: 9.379 billion kWh (2012 est.)
country comparison to the world: 90

Electricity—exports: 1.492 billion kWh (2010 est.)
country comparison to the world: 50

Electricity—imports: 614 million kWh (2012 est.)
country comparison to the world: 73

Electricity—installed generating capacity: 4.538 million kW (2010 est.)
country comparison to the world: 76

Electricity—from fossil fuels: 37.2% of total installed capacity (2010 est.)
country comparison to the world: 172

Electricity—from nuclear fuels: 0% of total installed capacity (2010 est.)
country comparison to the world: 93

Electricity—from hydroelectric plants: 62.8% of total installed capacity (2010 est.)
country comparison to the world: 31

Electricity—from other renewable sources: 0% of total installed capacity (2010 est.)
country comparison to the world: 176

Crude oil—production: 979.5 bbl/day (2012 est.)
country comparison to the world: 111

Crude oil—exports: 531 bbl/day (2012 est.)
country comparison to the world: 71

Crude oil—imports: 0 bbl/day (2013 est.)
country comparison to the world: 190

Crude oil—proved reserves: 35 million bbl (1 January 2013 es)
country comparison to the world: 81

Refined petroleum products—production: 0 bbl/day (2013 est.)
country comparison to the world: 147

Refined petroleum products—consumption: 17,280 bbl/day (2011 est.)
country comparison to the world: 137

Refined petroleum products—exports: 0 bbl/day (2011 est.)
country comparison to the world: 178

Refined petroleum products—imports: 18,500 bbl/day (2010 est.)
country comparison to the world: 108

Natural gas—production: 9.151 million cu m (2012 est.)
country comparison to the world: 92

Natural gas—consumption: 1.97 billion cu m (2012 est.)
country comparison to the world: 79

Natural gas—exports: 0 cu m (2012 est.)
country comparison to the world: 105

Natural gas—imports: 1.96 billion cu m (2012 est.)
country comparison to the world: 50

Natural gas—proved reserves: 8.495 billion cu m (1 January 2013 es)
country comparison to the world: 84

Carbon dioxide emissions from consumption of energy: 5.868 million Mt (2011 est.)
country comparison to the world: 122

COMMUNICATIONS

Telephones—main lines in use: 1.276 million (2012)
country comparison to the world: 6 7

Telephones—mobile cellular: 4.699 million (2012)
country comparison to the world: 116

Telephone system: *general assessment:* fixed-line telecommunications network has limited coverage outside Tbilisi; multiple mobile-cellular providers provide services to an increasing subscribership throughout the country
domestic: cellular telephone networks cover the entire country; mobile-cellular teledensity roughly 100 per 100 people; intercity facilities include a fiber-optic line between T'bilisi and K'ut'aisi
international: country code—995; the Georgia-Russia fiber-optic submarine cable provides connectivity to Russia; international service is available by microwave, landline, and satellite through the Moscow switch; international electronic mail and telex service are available (2011)

Broadcast media: 1 public broadcaster in Tbilisi, 1 state-owned broadcaster in Ajaria Autonomous Republic; 8 privately owned TV stations; state run public broadcaster operates 2 TV stations; dozens of cable TV operators, several major commercial TV stations, and several dozen private radio stations; state run public broadcaster operates 2 radio stations (2012)

Internet country code: .ge

Internet hosts: 357,864 (2012)
country comparison to the world: 59

Internet users: 1.3 million (2009)
country comparison to the world: 90

TRANSPORTATION

Airports: 22 (2013)
country comparison to the world: 135

Airports—with paved runways: *total:* 1 8
over 3,047 m: 1
2,438 to 3,047 m: 7
1,524 to 2,437 m: 3
914 to 1,523 m: 5
under 914 m: 2 (2013)

Airports—with unpaved runways: *total:* 4
1,524 to 2,437 m: 1
914 to 1,523 m: 2
under 914 m: 1 (2013)

Heliports: 2 (2013)

Pipelines: gas 1,596 km; oil 1,175 km (2013)

Railways: *total:* 1,612 km
country comparison to the world: 78
broad gauge: 1,575 km 1.520-m gauge (1,575 km electrified)
narrow gauge: 37 km 0.912-m gauge (37 km electrified) (2008)

Roadways: *total:* 19,109 km
country comparison to the world: 113
paved: 19,109 km (includes 69 km of expressways) (2010)

Merchant marine: *total:* 142
country comparison to the world: 40
by type: bulk carrier 13, cargo 114, chemical tanker 1, container 1, liquefied gas 1, passenger/cargo 1, petroleum tanker 3, refrigerated cargo 1, roll on/roll off 5, vehicle carrier 2
foreign-owned: 95 (Bulgaria 1, China 10, Egypt 7, Hong Kong 3, Israel 1, Italy 2, Latvia 1, Lebanon 1, Romania 7, Russia 6, Syria 24, Turkey 14, UAE 2, UK 5, Ukraine 10, US 1)
registered in other countries: 1 (unknown 1) (2010)

Ports and terminals: *major seaport(s):* Black Sea—Bat'umi, P'ot'i

MILITARY

Military branches: Georgian Armed Forces: Land Forces (include Air and Air Defense Forces); separatist Abkhazia Armed Forces: Ground Forces, Air Forces; separatist South Ossetia Armed Forces *note:* Georgian naval forces have been incorporated into the coast guard, which is not part of the Defense Ministry (2011)

Military service age and obligation: 18 to 34 years of age for compulsory and voluntary active duty military service; conscript service obligation is 18 months (2012)

Manpower available for military service:
males age 16-49: 1,080,840
females age 16-49: 1,122,031 (2010 est.)

Manpower fit for military service:
males age 16-49: 893,003
females age 16-49: 931,683 (2010 est.)

Manpower reaching militarily significant age annually: *male:* 29,723
female: 27,242 (2010 est.)

Military expenditures: 2.88% of GDP (2012)
country comparison to the world: 24
3.25% of GDP (2011)
2.88% of GDP (2010)

TRANSNATIONAL ISSUES

Disputes—international: Russia's military support and subsequent recognition of Abkhazia and South Ossetia independence in 2008 continue to sour relations with Georgia

Refugees and internally displaced persons: *IDPs:* 268,415—280,000 (displaced in the 1990s and 2008 from Abkhazia and South Ossetia) (2012)
stateless persons: 1,156 (2012)

Illicit drugs: limited cultivation of cannabis and opium poppy, mostly for domestic consumption; used as transshipment point for opiates via Central Asia to Western Europe and Russia

GERMANY

INTRODUCTION

Background: As Europe's largest economy and second most populous nation (after Russia), Germany is a key member of the continent's economic, political, and defense organizations. European power struggles immersed Germany in two devastating World Wars in the first half of the 20th century and left the country occupied by the victorious Allied powers of the US, UK, France, and the Soviet Union in 1945. With the advent of the Cold War, two German states were formed in 1949: the western Federal Republic of Germany (FRG) and the eastern German Democratic Republic (GDR). The democratic FRG embedded itself in key Western economic and security organizations, the EC, which became the EU, and NATO, while the communist GDR was on the front line of the Soviet-led Warsaw Pact. The decline of the USSR and the end of the Cold War allowed for German unification in 1990. Since then, Germany has expended considerable funds to bring Eastern productivity and wages up to Western standards. In January 1999, Germany and 10 other EU countries introduced a common European exchange currency, the euro.

GEOGRAPHY

Location: Central Europe, bordering the Baltic Sea and the North Sea, between the Netherlands and Poland, south of Denmark

Geographic coordinates: 51 00 N, 9 00 E

Map references: Europe

Area: *total:* 357,022 sq km
country comparison to the world: 63
land: 348,672 sq km
water: 8,350 sq km

Area—comparative: three times the size of Pennsylvania; slightly smaller than Montana

Land boundaries: *total:* 3,790 km
border countries: Austria 784 km, Belgium 167 km, Czech Republic 815 km, Denmark 68 km, France 451 km, Luxembourg 138 km, Netherlands 577 km, Poland 456 km, Switzerland 334 km

Coastline: 2,389 km

Maritime claims: territorial sea: 12 nm
exclusive economic zone: 200 nm
continental shelf: 200 m depth or to the depth of exploitation

Climate: temperate and marine; cool, cloudy, wet winters and summers; occasional warm mountain (foehn) wind

Terrain: lowlands in north, uplands in center, Bavarian Alps in south

Elevation extremes: *lowest point:* Neuendorf bei Wilster -3.54 m
highest point: Zugspitze 2,963 m

Natural resources: coal, lignite, natural gas, iron ore, copper, nickel, uranium, potash, salt, construction materials, timber, arable land

Land use: *arable land:* 33.25%
permanent crops: 0.56%
other: 66.19% (2011)

Irrigated land: 5,157 sq km (2006)

Total renewable water resources: 154 cu km (2011)

Freshwater withdrawal (domestic/industrial/agricultural): *total:* 32.3 cu km/yr (16%/84%/0%)
per capita: 391.4 cu m/yr (2007)

Natural hazards: flooding

Environment—current issues: emissions from coal-burning utilities and industries contribute to air pollution; acid rain, resulting from sulfur dioxide emissions, is damaging forests; pollution in the Baltic Sea from raw sewage and industrial effluents from rivers in eastern Germany; hazardous waste disposal; government established a mechanism for ending the use of nuclear power over the next 15 years; government working to meet EU commitment to identify nature preservation areas in line with the EU's Flora, Fauna, and Habitat directive

Environment—international agreements: *party to:* Air Pollution, Air Pollution-Nitrogen Oxides, Air Pollution-Persistent Organic Pollutants, Air Pollution-Sulfur 85, Air Pollution-Sulfur 94, Air Pollution-Volatile Organic Compounds, Antarctic-Environmental Protocol, Antarctic-Marine Living Resources, Antarctic Seals, Antarctic Treaty, Biodiversity, Climate Change, Climate Change-Kyoto Protocol, Desertification, Endangered Species, Environmental Modification, Hazardous Wastes, Law of the Sea, Marine Dumping, Ozone Layer Protection, Ship Pollution, Tropical Timber 83, Tropical Timber 94, Wetlands, Whaling
signed, but not ratified: none of the selected agreements

Geography—note: strategic location on North European Plain and along the entrance to the Baltic Sea

PEOPLE AND SOCIETY

Nationality: *noun:* German(s)
adjective: German

Ethnic groups: German 91.5%, Turkish 2.4%, other 6.1% (made up largely of Greek, Italian, Polish, Russian, Serbo-Croatian, Spanish)

Languages: German

Religions: Protestant 34%, Roman Catholic 34%, Muslim 3.7%, unaffiliated or other 28.3%

Population: 80,996,685 (July 2014 est.)
country comparison to the world: 18

Age structure: *0-14 years:* 13% (male 5,386,525/female 5,107,336)
15-24 years: 10.6% (male 4,367,713/female 4,188,566)
25-54 years: 41.7% (male 17,116,346/female 16,664,995)
55-64 years: 21.1% (male 5,463,221/female 5,574,166)
65 years and over: 20.9% (male 7,468,552/female 9,659,265) (2014 est.)

Dependency ratios: *total dependency ratio:* 52 %
youth dependency ratio: 19.9 %
elderly dependency ratio: 32.1 %
potential support ratio: 3.1 (2013)

Median age: *total:* 46.1 years
male: 45.1 years
female: 47.2 years (2014 est.)

Population growth rate: -0.18% (2014 est.)
country comparison to the world: 212

Birth rate: 8.42 births/1,000 population (2014 est.)
country comparison to the world: 219

Death rate: 11.29 deaths/1,000 population (2014 est.)
country comparison to the world: 31

Net migration rate: 1.06 migrant(s)/1,000 population (2014 est.)
country comparison to the world: 60

Urbanization: *urban population:* 74% of total population (2010)
rate of urbanization: 0% annual rate of change (2010-15 est.)

Major urban areas—population: BERLIN (capital) 3.438 million; Hamburg 1.786 million; Munich 1.349 million; Cologne 1.001 million (2009)

Sex ratio: *at birth:* 1.06 male(s)/female
0-14 years: 1.06 male(s)/female
15-24 years: 1.04 male(s)/female
25-54 years: 1.03 male(s)/female
55-64 years: 0.97 male(s)/female
65 years and over: 0.76 male(s)/female
total population: 0.97 male(s)/female (2014 est.)

Mother's mean age at first birth: 28.9
note: data are based on events and not on fertility rates; data refer to first birth within current marriage (2010 est.)

Maternal mortality rate: 7 deaths/100,000 live births (2010)
country comparison to the world: 165

Infant mortality rate: *total:* 3.46 deaths/1,000 live births
country comparison to the world: 209
male: 3.75 deaths/1,000 live births
female: 3.14 deaths/1,000 live births (2014 est.)

Life expectancy at birth: total population: 80.44 years
country comparison to the world: 28
male: 78.15 years
female: 82.86 years (2014 est.)

Total fertility rate: 1.43 children born/woman (2014 est.)
country comparison to the world: 203

Contraceptive prevalence rate: 66.2%
note: percent of women aged 18-49 (2005)

Health expenditures: 11.1% of GDP (2011)
country comparison to the world: 14

Physicians density: 3.69 physicians/1,000 population (2010)

Hospital bed density: 8.3 beds/1,000 population (2010)

Drinking water source:
improved:
urban: 100% of population
rural: 100% of population
total: 100% of population
unimproved:
urban: 0% of population
rural: 0% of population
total: 0% of population (2011 est.)

Sanitation facility access:
improved:
urban: 100% of population
rural: 100% of population
total: 100% of population
unimproved:
urban: 0% of population
rural: 0% of population
total: 0% of population (2011 est.)

HIV/AIDS—adult prevalence rate: 0.1% (2009 est.)
country comparison to the world: 138
HIV/AIDS—people living with HIV/AIDS: 67,000 (2009 est.)
country comparison to the world: 56

HIV/AIDS—deaths: fewer than 1,000 (2009 est.)
country comparison to the world: 79

Obesity—adult prevalence rate: 25.1% (2008)
country comparison to the world: 59

Children under the age of 5 years underweight: 1.1% (2006)
country comparison to the world: 133

Education expenditures: 5.1% of GDP (2010)
country comparison to the world: 74

Literacy: *definition:* age 15 and over can read and write
total population: 99%
male: 99%
female: 99% (2003 est.)

School life expectancy (primary to tertiary education): *total:* 16 years
male: 16 years
female: 16 years (2011)

Unemployment, youth ages 15-24: total: 8.1%
country comparison to the world: 121
male: 8.8%
female: 7.4% (2012)

GOVERNMENT

Country name: conventional long form: Federal Republic of Germany
conventional short form: Germany
local long form: Bundesrepublik Deutschland
local short form: Deutschland
former: German Empire, German Republic, German Reich

Government type: federal republic

Capital: *name:* Berlin
geographic coordinates: 52 31 N, 13 24 E
time difference: UTC+1 (6 hours ahead of Washington, DC during Standard Time)
daylight saving time: +1hr, begins last Sunday in March; ends last Sunday in October

Administrative divisions: 16 states (Laender, singular—Land); Baden-Wuerttemberg, Bayern (Bavaria), Berlin, Brandenburg, Bremen, Hamburg, Hessen (Hesse), Mecklenburg-Vorpommern (Mecklenburg-Western Pomerania), Niedersachsen (Lower Saxony), Nordrhein-Westfalen (North Rhine-Westphalia), Rheinland-Pfalz (Rhineland-Palatinate), Saarland, Sachsen (Saxony), Sachsen-Anhalt (Saxony-Anhalt), Schleswig-Holstein, Thueringen (Thuringia); note—Bayern, Sachsen, and Thueringen refer to themselves as free states (Freistaaten, singular—Freistaat)

Independence: 18 January 1871 (establishment of the German Empire); divided into four zones of occupation (UK, US, USSR, and France) in 1945 following World War II; Federal Republic of Germany (FRG or West Germany) proclaimed on 23 May 1949 and included the former UK, US, and French zones; German Democratic Republic (GDR or East Germany) proclaimed on 7 October 1949 and included the former USSR zone; West Germany and East Germany unified on 3 October 1990; all four powers formally relinquished rights on 15 March 1991; notable earlier dates: 10 August 843 (Eastern Francia established from the division of the Carolingian Empire); 2 February 962 (crowning of OTTO I, recognized as the first Holy Roman Emperor)

National holiday: Unity Day, 3 October (1990)
Constitution: previous 1919 (Weimar Constitution); latest drafted 10 to 23 August 1948, approved 12 May 1949, promulgated 23 May 1949, entered into force 24 May 1949; amended many times, last in 2012 (2012)

Legal system: civil law system

International law organization participation: accepts compulsory ICJ jurisdiction with reservations; accepts ICCt jurisdiction

Suffrage: 18 years of age; universal

Executive branch: *chief of state:* President Joachim GAUCK (since 23 March 2012)
head of government: Chancellor Angela MERKEL (since 22 November 2005)
cabinet: Cabinet or Bundesminister (Federal Ministers) appointed by the president on the recommendation of the chancellor (For more information visit the World Leaders website)
elections: president elected for a five-year term (eligible for a second term) by a Federal Convention, including all members of the Federal Parliament (Bundestag) and an equal number of delegates elected by the state parliaments; election last held on 19 February 2012 (next to be held by June 2017); chancellor elected by an absolute majority of the Federal Parliament for a four-year term; Federal Parliament vote for Chancellor last held on 17 December 2013 (next to be held after the September 2017 elections)
election results: Joachim GAUCK elected president; received 991 votes of the Federal Convention against 126 for Beate KLARSFELD and 3 for Olaf ROSE; Angela MERKEL reelected chancellor; vote by Federal Parliament 462 to 150 with four abstentions

Legislative branch: bicameral legislature consists of the Federal Council or Bundesrat (69 votes; state governments sit in the Council; each has three to six votes in proportion to population and is required to vote as a block) and the Federal Parliament or Bundestag (630 seats; members elected by popular vote for a four-year term under a system of personalized proportional representation; a party must win 5% of the national vote or three direct mandates to gain proportional representation and caucus recognition)
elections: Bundestag—last held on 22 September 2013 (next to be held no later than autumn 2017); most all postwar German governments have been coalitions; note—there are no elections for the Bundesrat; composition is determined by the composition of the state-level governments; the composition of the Bundesrat has the potential to change any time one of the 16 states holds an election
election results: Bundestag—percent of vote by party—CDU/CSU 41.5%, SPD 25.7%, Left 8.6%, Greens 8.4%, FDP 4.8%, other 10.9%; seats by party—CDU/CSU 311, SPD 193, Left 64, Greens 63
Judicial branch: highest court(s): Federal Court of Justice (court consists of 127 judges including the court president, vice-presidents, presiding judges, and other judges, and organized into 25 Senates subdivided into 12 civil panels, 5 criminal panels, and 8 special panels; Federal Constitutional Court or Bundesverfassungsgericht (consists of 2 Senates each subdivided into 3 chambers, each with a chairman and 8 members)
judge selection and term of office: Federal Court of Justice judges selected by the Judges Election Committee, which consists of the Secretaries of Justice from each of the 16 federated States and 16 members appointed by the Federal Parliament; judges appointed by the president of Germany; judges serve until mandatory retirement at age 65; Federal Constitutional Court judges—one-half elected by the House of Representatives and one-half by the Senate; judges appointed for 12-year terms with mandatory retirement at age 68
subordinate courts: Federal Administrative Court; Federal Finance Court; Federal Labor Court; Federal Social Court; each of the 16 German states or Land has its own constitutional court and a hierarchy of ordinary (civil, criminal, family) and specialized (administrative, finance, labor, social) courts

Political parties and leaders: Alliance '90/ Greens [Cem OEZDEMIR and Simone PETER]; Christian Democratic Union or CDU [Angela MERKEL]; Christian Social Union or CSU [Horst SEEHOFER]; Free Democratic Party or FDP [Christian LINDNER]; Left Party or Die Linke [Katia KIPPING and Bernd RIEXINGER]; Social Democratic Party or SPD [Sigmar GABRIEL]

Political pressure groups and leaders: business associations and employers' organizations trade unions; religious, immigrant, expellee, and veterans groups

International organization participation: ADB (nonregional member), AfDB (nonregional member), Arctic Council (observer), Australia Group, BIS, BSEC (observer), CBSS, CD, CDB, CE, CERN, EAPC, EBRD, ECB, EIB, EITI (implementing country), EMU, ESA, EU, FAO, FATF, G-20, G-5, G-7, G-8, G-10, IADB, IAEA, IBRD, ICAO, ICC (national committees), ICRM, IDA, IEA, IFAD, IFC, IFRCS, IGAD (partners), IHO, ILO, IMF, IMO, IMSO, Interpol, IOC, IOM, IPU, ISO, ITSO, ITU, ITUC (NGOs), MIGA, MINUSMA, NATO, NEA, NSG, OAS (observer), OECD, OPCW, OSCE, Paris Club, PCA, Schengen Convention, SELEC (observer), SICA (observer), UN, UNAMID, UNCTAD, UNESCO, UNHCR, UNIDO, UNIFIL, UNMIL, UNMISS, UNRWA, UNWTO, UPU, WCO, WHO, WIPO, WMO, WTO, ZC

Diplomatic representation in the US: *chief of mission:* Ambassador Niels Peter Georg AMMON (since 9 August 2011)
chancery: 2300 M Street NW, Washington, DC 20037
telephone: [1] (202) 298-4000
FAX: [1] (202) 298-4261
consulate(s) general: Atlanta, Boston, Chicago, Houston, Los Angeles, Miami, New York, San Francisco

Diplomatic representation from the US: *chief of mission:* Ambassador John B. EMERSON (since 7 August 2013)
embassy: Pariser Platz 2, 10117 Berlin
mailing address: Unit 5090, Box 1000, DPO AE09265
telephone: [49] (30) 48305-0
FAX: [49] (30) 8305-1215
consulate(s) general: Duesseldorf, Frankfurt am Main, Hamburg, Leipzig, Munich

Flag description: three equal horizontal bands of black (top), red, and gold; these colors have played an important role in German history and can be traced back to the medieval banner of the Holy Roman Emperor—a black eagle with red claws and beak on a gold field

National symbol(s): golden eagle

National anthem: *name:* "Das Lied der Deutschen" (Song of the Germans)
lyrics/music: August Heinrich HOFFMANN VON FALLERSLEBEN/Franz Joseph HAYDN
note: adopted 1922; the anthem, also known as "Deutschlandlied" (Song of Germany), was originally adopted for its connection to the March 1848 liberal revolution; following appropriation by the Nazis of the first verse, specifically the phrase, "Deutschland, Deutschland ueber alles" (Germany, Germany above all) to promote nationalism, it was banned after 1945; in 1952, its third verse was adopted by West Germany as its national anthem; in 1990, it became the national anthem for the reunited Germany

ECONOMY

overview: The German economy—the fifth largest economy in the world in PPP terms and Europe's largest—is a leading exporter of machinery, vehicles, chemicals, and household equipment and benefits from a highly skilled labor force. Like its Western European neighbors, Germany faces significant demographic challenges to sustained long-term growth. Low fertility rates and declining net immigration are increasing pressure on the country's social welfare system and necessitate structural reforms. Reforms launched by the government of Chancellor Gerhard SCHROEDER (1998-2005), deemed necessary to address chronically high unemployment and low average growth, has contributed to strong growth and falling unemployment. These advances, as well as a government subsidized, reduced working hour scheme, help explain the relatively modest increase in unemployment during the 2008-09 recession—the deepest since World War II—and its decrease to 5.3% in 2013. The new German government introduced a minimum wage of $11 per hour to take effect in 2015. Stimulus and stabilization efforts initiated in 2008 and 2009 and tax cuts introduced in Chancellor Angela MERKEL's second term increased Germany's total budget deficit—including federal, state, and municipal—to 4.1% in 2010, but slower spending and higher tax revenues reduced the deficit to 0.8% in 2011 and in 2012 Germany reached a budget surplus of 0.1%. A constitutional amendment approved in 2009 limits the federal government to structural deficits of no more than 0.35% of GDP per annum as of 2016 though the target was already reached in 2012. Following the March 2011 Fukushima nuclear disaster, Chancellor Angela MERKEL announced in May 2011 that eight of the country's 17 nuclear reactors would be shut down immediately and the remaining plants would close by 2022. Germany hopes to replace nuclear power with renewable energy. Before the shutdown of the eight reactors, Germany relied on nuclear power for 23% of its electricity generating capacity and 46% of its base-load electricity production.

GDP (purchasing power parity): $3.227 trillion (2013 est.)
country comparison to the world: 6
$3.211 trillion (2012 est.)
$3.182 trillion (2011 est.)
note: data are in 2013 US dollars

GDP (official exchange rate): $3.593 trillion (2013 est.)

GDP—real growth rate: 0.5% (2013 est.)
country comparison to the world: 183
0.9% (2012 est.)
3.4% (2011 est.)

GDP—per capita (PPP): $39,500 (2013 est.)
country comparison to the world: 29
$39,200 (2012 est.)
$38,900 (2011 est.)
note: data are in 2013 US dollars

Gross national saving: 24.7% of GDP (2013 est.)
country comparison to the world: 51
24.3% of GDP (2012 est.)
24.4% of GDP (2011 est.)

GDP—composition, by end use:
household consumption: 57.6%
government consumption: 19.4%
investment in fixed capital: 17.5%
investment in inventories: 0.1%
exports of goods and services: 49.5%
imports of goods and services: -44.1% (2013 est.)

GDP—composition, by sector of origin:
agriculture: 0.8%
industry: 30.1%
services: 69% (2013 est.)

Agriculture—products: potatoes, wheat, barley, sugar beets, fruit, cabbages; milk products; cattle, pigs, poultry

Industries: among the world's largest and most technologically advanced producers of iron, steel, coal, cement, chemicals, machinery, vehicles, machine tools, electronics, automobiles, food and beverages, shipbuilding, textiles

Industrial production growth rate: -0.3% (2013 est.)
country comparison to the world: 169

Labor force: 44.2 million (2013 est.)
country comparison to the world: 15

Labor force—by occupation: agriculture: 1.6%
industry: 24.6%
services: 73.8% (2011)

Unemployment rate: 5.3% (2013 est.)
country comparison to the world: 52
5.5% (2012 est.)

Population below poverty line: 15.5% (2010 est.)

Household income or consumption by percentage share: *lowest 10%:* 3.6%
highest 10%: 24% (2000)

Distribution of family income—Gini index: 27 (2006)
country comparison to the world: 128
30 (1994)

Budget: *revenues:* $1.626 trillion
expenditures: $1.624 trillion (2013 est.)

Taxes and other revenues: 45.3% of GDP (2013 est.)
country comparison to the world: 20

Budget surplus (+) or deficit (-): 0.1% of GDP (2013 est.)
country comparison to the world: 41

Public debt: 79.9% of GDP (2013 est.)
country comparison to the world: 26
81% of GDP (2012 est.)
note: general government gross debt is defined in the Maastricht Treaty as consolidated general government gross debt at nominal value, outstanding at the end of the year in the following categories of government liabilities (as defined in ESA95): currency and deposits (AF.2), securities other than shares excluding financial derivatives (AF.3, excluding AF.34), and loans (AF.4); the general government sector comprises the sub-sectors of central government, state government, local government and social security funds; the series are presented as a percentage of GDP and in millions of euro; GDP used as a denominator is the gross domestic product at current market prices; data expressed in national currency are converted into euro using end-of-year exchange rates provided by the European Central Bank

Fiscal year: calendar year

Inflation rate (consumer prices): 1.6% (2013 est.)
country comparison to the world: 43
2.1% (2012 est.)

Central bank discount rate: 0.75% (31 December 2013)
country comparison to the world: 120
1.5% (31 December 2010)
note: this is the European Central Bank's rate on the marginal lending facility, which offers overnight credit to banks in the euro area

Commercial bank prime lending rate: 2.8% (31 December 2013 est.)
country comparison to the world: 174
3.07% (31 December 2012 est.)

Stock of narrow money: $2.158 trillion (31 December 2013 est.)
country comparison to the world: 5
$2.025 trillion (31 December 2012 est.)
note: see entry for the European Union for money supply in the euro area; the European Central Bank (ECB) controls monetary policy for the 17 members of the Economic and Monetary Union (EMU); individual members of the EMU do not control the quantity of money circulating within their own borders

Stock of broad money: $4.551 trillion (31 December 2013 est.)
country comparison to the world: 5
$4.342 trillion (31 December 2012 est.)

Stock of domestic credit: $4.457 trillion (31 December 2013 est.)
country comparison to the world: 5
$4.277 trillion (31 December 2012 est.)

Market value of publicly traded shares: $1.486 trillion (31 December 2012 est.)
country comparison to the world: 10
$1.184 trillion (31 December 2011)
$1.43 trillion (31 December 2010 est.)

Current account balance: $257.1 billion (2013 est.)
country comparison to the world: 1
$238.5 billion (2012 est.)

Exports: $1.493 trillion (2013 est.)
country comparison to the world: 4
$1.46 trillion (2012 est.)

Exports—commodities: motor vehicles, machinery, chemicals, computer and electronic products, electrical equipment, pharmaceuticals, metals, transport equipment, foodstuffs, textiles, rubber and plastic products

Exports—partners: France 9.21%, United States 8.1%, United Kingdom 6.53%, Netherlands 6.5%, China 6.1%, Italy 5.05%, Austria 5.03%, Switzerland 4.3%, Belgium 4.04% (2013 est.)

Imports: $1.233 trillion (2013 est.)
country comparison to the world: 4
$1.222 trillion (2012 est.)

Imports—commodities: machinery, data processing equipment, vehicles, chemicals, oil and gas, metals, electric equipment, pharmaceuticals, foodstuffs, agricultural products

Imports—partners: Netherlands 10%, France 7.61%, China 6.25%, Belgium 6.13%, Italy 5.31%, United Kingdom 4.7%, Austria 4.33%, United States 4.19%, Switzerland 4.3%, Austria 4.1%, Poland 4% (2013 est.)

Reserves of foreign exchange and gold: $248.9 billion (31 December 2012 est.)
country comparison to the world: 13
$238.9 billion (31 December 2011 est.)

Debt—external: $5.717 trillion (31 December 2012 est.)
country comparison to the world: 4
$5.338 trillion (31 December 2011)

Stock of direct foreign investment—at home: $1.335 trillion (31 December 2013 est.)
country comparison to the world: 5
$1.307 trillion (31 December 2012 est.)

Stock of direct foreign investment—abroad: $1.871 trillion (31 December 2013 est.)
country comparison to the world: 3
$1.788 trillion (31 December 2012 est.)

Exchange rates: euros (EUR) per US dollar—
0.7634 (2013 est.)
0.7752 (2012 est.)
0.755 (2010 est.)
0.7198 (2009 est.)
0.6827 (2008 est.)

ENERGY

Electricity—production: 526.6 billion kWh (2012 est.)
country comparison to the world: 1 0

Electricity—consumption: 582.5 billion kWh (2012 est.)
country comparison to the world: 7

Electricity—exports: 66.81 billion kWh (2012 est.)
country comparison to the world: 1

Electricity—imports: 46.27 billion kWh (2012 est.)
country comparison to the world: 2

Electricity—installed generating capacity: 178.4 million kW (2012 est.)
country comparison to the world: 7

Electricity—from fossil fuels: 51% of total installed capacity (2012 est.)
country comparison to the world: 154

Electricity—from nuclear fuels: 7% of total installed capacity (2012 est.)
country comparison to the world: 22

Electricity—from hydroelectric plants: 6% of total installed capacity (2012 est.)
country comparison to the world: 123

Electricity—from other renewable sources: 36% of total installed capacity (2012 est.)
country comparison to the world: 3

Crude oil—production: 169,500 bbl/day (2012 est.)
country comparison to the world: 41

Crude oil—exports: 14,260 bbl/day (2010 est.)
country comparison to the world: 56

Crude oil—imports: 1.876 million bbl/day (2010 est.)
country comparison to the world: 7

Crude oil—proved reserves: 254.2 million bbl (1 January 2013 es)
country comparison to the world: 55

Refined petroleum products—production: 2.198 million bbl/day (2010 est.)
country comparison to the world: 8

Refined petroleum products—consumption: 2.4 million bbl/day (2011 est.)
country comparison to the world: 9

Refined petroleum products—exports: 376,600 bbl/day (2010 est.)
country comparison to the world: 19

Refined petroleum products—imports: 758,100 bbl/day (2010 est.)
country comparison to the world: 9

Natural gas—production: 9 billion cu m (2012 est.)
country comparison to the world: 44

Natural gas—consumption: 75.2 billion cu m (2012 est.)
country comparison to the world: 10

Natural gas—exports: 18.17 billion cu m (2012 est.)
country comparison to the world: 19

Natural gas—imports: 87.96 billion cu m (2012 est.)
country comparison to the world: 4

Natural gas—proved reserves: 125 billion cu m (1 January 2013 es)
country comparison to the world: 52

Carbon dioxide emissions from consumption of energy: 814 million Mt (2012 est.)
country comparison to the world: 7

COMMUNICATIONS

Telephones—main lines in use: 50.7 million (2012)
country comparison to the world: 4

Telephones—mobile cellular: 107.7 million (2012)
country comparison to the world: 11

Telephone system: *general assessment:* Germany has one of the world's most technologically advanced telecommunications systems; as a result of intensive capital expenditures since reunification, the formerly backward system of the eastern part of the country, dating back to World War II, has been modernized and integrated with that of the western part
domestic: Germany is served by an extensive system of automatic telephone exchanges connected by modern networks of fiber-optic cable, coaxial cable, microwave radio relay, and a domestic satellite system; cellular telephone service is widely available, expanding rapidly, and includes roaming service to many foreign countries
international: country code—49; Germany's international service is excellent worldwide, consisting of extensive land and undersea cable facilities as well as earth stations in the Inmarsat, Intelsat, Eutelsat, and Intersputnik satellite systems (2011)

Broadcast media: a mixture of publicly operated and privately owned TV and radio stations; national and regional public broadcasters compete with nearly 400 privately owned national and regional TV stations; more than 90% of households have cable or satellite TV; hundreds of radio stations including multiple national radio networks, regional radio networks, and a large number of local radio stations (2008)

Internet country code: .de

Internet hosts: 20.043 million (2012)
country comparison to the world: 6

Internet users: 65.125 million (2009)
country comparison to the world: 5

TRANSPORTATION

Airports: 539 (2013)
country comparison to the world: 1 3

Airports—with paved runways: *total:* 318
over 3,047 m: 14
2,438 to 3,047 m: 49
1,524 to 2,437 m: 60
914 to 1,523 m: 70
under 914 m: 125 (2013)

Airports—with unpaved runways: *total:* 221
1,524 to 2,437 m: 1
914 to 1,523 m: 35
under 914 m: 185 (2013)

Heliports: 23 (2013)

Pipelines: condensate 37 km; gas 26,985 km; oil 2,826 km; refined products 4,479 km; water 8 km (2013)

Railways: *total:* 41,981 km
country comparison to the world: 6
standard gauge: 41,722 km 1.435-m gauge (20,053 km electrified)
narrow gauge: 220 km 1.000-m gauge (75 km electrified); 39 km 0.750-m gauge (24 km electrified) (2008)

Roadways: *total:* 645,000 km
country comparison to the world: 11
paved: 645,000 km (includes 12,800 km of expressways)
note: includes local roads (2010)

Waterways: 7,467 km (Rhine River carries most goods; Main-Danube Canal links North Sea and Black Sea) (2012)
country comparison to the world: 19

Merchant marine: *total:* 427
country comparison to the world: 24
by type: barge carrier 2, bulk carrier 6, cargo 51, carrier 1, chemical tanker 15, container 298, liquefied gas 6, passenger 4, passenger/cargo 24, petroleum tanker 10, refrigerated cargo 3, roll on/roll off 6, vehicle carrier 1

foreign-owned: 6 (Finland 3, Netherlands 1, Switzerland 2)
registered in other countries: 3,420 (Antigua and Barbuda 1094, Australia 2, Bahamas 30, Bermuda 14, Brazil 6, Bulgaria 12, Burma 1, Cayman Islands 3, Cook Islands 1, Curacao 25, Cyprus 192, Denmark 9, Dominica 5, Estonia 1, France 1, Gibraltar 123, Hong Kong 10, Isle of Man 56, Jamaica 10, Liberia 1185, Luxembourg 9, Malta 135, Marshall Islands 248, Morocco 1, Netherlands 86, NZ 2, Panama 24, Papua New Guinea 1, Philippines 2, Portugal 14, Saint Vincent and the Grenadines 3, Singapore 32, Slovakia 3, Spain 4, Sri Lanka 8, Sweden 3, UK 59, US 5, Venezuela 1) (2010)

Ports and terminals: *major seaport(s):* Baltic Sea—Rostock; North Sea—Wilhelmshaven
river port(s): Bremen (Weser); Bremerhaven (Geeste); Duisburg, Karlsruhe, Neuss-Dusseldorf (Rhine); Brunsbuttel, Hamburg (Elbe); Lubeck (Wakenitz)
oil/gas terminal(s): Brunsbuttel Canal terminals
container port(s): Bremen/Bremerhaven (5,915,487), Hamburg (9,014,165)(2011)

MILITARY

Military branches: Federal Armed Forces (Bundeswehr): Army (Heer); Navy (Deutsche Marine, includes naval air arm); Air Force (Luftwaffe); Joint Support Services (Streitkraeftebasis, SKB); Central Medical Service (Zentraler Sanitaetsdienst, ZSanDstBw) (2013)

Military service age and obligation: 17-23 years of age for male and female voluntary military service; conscription ended 1 July 2011; service obligation 8-23 months or 12 years; women have been eligible for voluntary service in all military branches and positions since 2001 (2013)

Manpower available for military service:
males age 16-49: 18,529,299
females age 16-49: 17,888,543 (2010 est.)

Manpower fit for military service:
males age 16-49: 15,027,886
females age 16-49: 14,510,527 (2010 est.)

Manpower reaching militarily significant age annually: *male:* 405,438
female: 384,930 (2010 est.)

Military expenditures: 1.35% of GDP (2012)
country comparison to the world: 77
1.34% of GDP (2011)
1.35% of GDP (2010)

TRANSNATIONAL ISSUES

Disputes—international: none

Refugees and internally displaced persons: *refugees (country of origin):* 113,809 (Serbia); 90,773 (Turkey); 49,829 (Iraq); 40,204 (Russia); 31,746 (Afghanistan); 23,799 (Vietnam); 23,460 (Bosnia and Herzegovina); 21,629 (Iran); 20,059 (Ukraine); 18,165 (Syria); 11,819 (Lebanon); 11,672 (Sri Lanka); 6,575 (Azerbaijan); 6,175 (Macedonia); 5,206 (Democratic Republic of the Congo) (2012)
stateless persons: 5,683 (2012)

Illicit drugs: source of precursor chemicals for South American cocaine processors; transshipment point for and consumer of Southwest Asian heroin, Latin American cocaine, and European-produced synthetic drugs; major financial center

GHANA

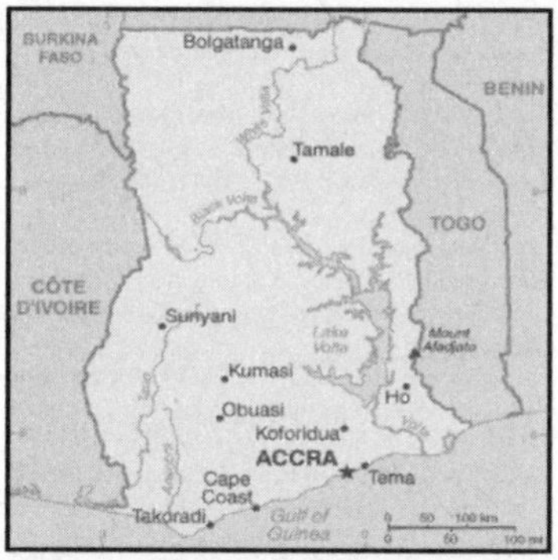

INTRODUCTION

Background: Formed from the merger of the British colony of the Gold Coast and the Togoland trust territory, Ghana in 1957 became the first sub-Saharan country in colonial Africa to gain its independence. Ghana endured a long series of coups before Lt. Jerry RAWLINGS took power in 1981 and banned political parties. After approving a new constitution and restoring multiparty politics in 1992, RAWLINGS won presidential elections in 1992 and 1996 but was constitutionally prevented from running for a third term in 2000. John KUFUOR succeeded him and was reelected in 2004. John Atta MILLS won the 2008 presidential election and took over as head of state, but he died in July 2012 and was constitutionally succeeded by his vice president John Dramani MAHAMA, who subsequently won the December 2012 presidential election.

GEOGRAPHY

Location: Western Africa, bordering the Gulf of Guinea, between Cote d'Ivoire and Togo

Geographic coordinates: 8 00 N, 2 00 W

Map references: Africa

Area: *total:* 238,533 sq km
country comparison to the world: 82
land: 227,533 sq km
water: 11,000 sq km

Area—comparative: slightly smaller than Oregon
Land boundaries:
total: 2,094 km
border countries: Burkina Faso 549 km, Cote d'Ivoire 668 km, Togo 877 km

Coastline: 539 km

Maritime claims: territorial sea: 12 nm
contiguous zone: 24 nm
exclusive economic zone: 200 nm
continental shelf: 200 nm

Climate: tropical; warm and comparatively dry along southeast coast; hot and humid in southwest; hot and dry in north

Terrain: mostly low plains with dissected plateau in south-central area

Elevation extremes: lowest point: Atlantic Ocean 0 m
highest point: Mount Afadjato 885 m

Natural resources: gold, timber, industrial diamonds, bauxite, manganese, fish, rubber, hydropower, petroleum, silver, salt, limestone

Land use: *arable land:* 20.12%
permanent crops: 11.74%
other: 68.14% (2011)

Irrigated land: 309 sq km (2003)

Total renewable water resources: 53.2 cu km (2011)

Freshwater withdrawal (domestic/industrial/agricultural): *total:* 0.98 cu km/yr (24%/10%/66%)
per capita: 48.82 cu m/yr (2000)

Natural hazards: dry, dusty, northeastern harmattan winds from January to March; droughts

Environment—current issues: recurrent drought in north severely affects agricultural activities; deforestation; overgrazing; soil erosion; poaching and habitat destruction threatens wildlife populations; water pollution; inadequate supplies of potable water

Environment—international agreements: *party to:* Biodiversity, Climate Change, Climate Change-Kyoto Protocol, Desertification, Endangered Species, Environmental Modification, Hazardous Wastes, Law of the Sea, Ozone Layer Protection, Ship Pollution, Tropical Timber 83, Tropical Timber 94, Wetlands
signed, but not ratified: Marine Life Conservation

Geography—note: Lake Volta is the world's largest artificial lake by surface area (8,482 sq km; 3,275 sq mi)

PEOPLE AND SOCIETY

Nationality: *noun:* Ghanaian(s)
adjective: Ghanaian

Ethnic groups: Akan 47.5%, Mole-Dagbon 16.6%, Ewe 13.9%, Ga-Dangme 7.4%, Gurma 5.7%, Guan 3.7%, Grusi 2.5%, Mande-Busanga 1.1%, other 1.6% (2010 census)

Languages: Asante 14.8%, Ewe 12.7%, Fante 9.9%, Boron (Brong) 4.6%, Dagomba 4.3%, Dangme 4.3%, Dagarte (Dagaba) 3.7%, Akyem 3.4%, Ga 3.4%, Akuapem 2.9%, other (includes English (official)) 36.1% (2000 census)

Religions: Christian 71.2% (Pentecostal/Charismatic 28.3%, Protestant 18.4%, Catholic 13.1%, other 11.4%), Muslim 17.6%, traditional 5.2%, other 0.8%, none 5.2% (2010 census)

Population: 25,758,108 (July 2014 est.)
country comparison to the world: 49
note: estimates for this country explicitly take into account the effects of excess mortality due to AIDS; this can result in lower life expectancy, higher infant mortality, higher death rates, lower population growth rates, and changes in the distribution of population by age and sex than would otherwise be expected

Age structure: *0-14 years:* 38.6% (male 4,988,823/female 4,943,451)
15-24 years: 18.7% (male 2,403,526/female 2,426,076)
25-54 years: 33.8% (male 4,228,326/female 4,480,090)
55-64 years: 4.1% (male 599,510/female 633,688)
65 years and over: 4.1% (male 489,566/female 565,052) (2014 est.)

Dependency ratios:
total dependency ratio: 72.2 %
youth dependency ratio: 66.2 %
elderly dependency ratio: 6 %
potential support ratio: 16.7 (2013)

Median age: *total:* 20.8 years
male: 20.4 years
female: 21.3 years (2014 est.)

Population growth rate: 2.19% (2014 est.)
country comparison to the world: 44

Birth rate: 31.4 births/1,000 population (2014 est.)
country comparison to the world: 38

Death rate: 7.37 deaths/1,000 population (2014 est.)
country comparison to the world: 118

Net migration rate: -2.13 migrant(s)/1,000 population (2014 est.)
country comparison to the world: 169

Urbanization: *urban population:* 51.9% of total population (2011)
rate of urbanization: 3.5% annual rate of change (2010-15 est.)

Major urban areas—population: ACCRA (capital) 2.269 million; Kumasi 1.773 million (2009)

Sex ratio: *at birth:* 1.03 male(s)/female
0-14 years: 1.01 male(s)/female
15-24 years: 0.99 male(s)/female
25-54 years: 0.94 male(s)/female
55-64 years: 0.97 male(s)/female
65 years and over: 0.88 male(s)/female
total population: 0.98 male(s)/female (2014 est.)

Mother's mean age at first birth: 21.8
note: median age at first birth among women 25-29 (2008 est.)

Maternal mortality rate: 350 deaths/100,000 live births (2010)
country comparison to the world: 32

Infant mortality rate: *total:* 38.52 deaths/1,000 live births
country comparison to the world: 58
male: 42.58 deaths/1,000 live births
female: 34.34 deaths/1,000 live births (2014 est.)

Life expectancy at birth: *total population:* 65.75 years
country comparison to the world: 172
male: 63.38 years
female: 68.19 years (2014 est.)

Total fertility rate: 4.09 children born/woman (2014 est.)
country comparison to the world: 37

Contraceptive prevalence rate: 23.5% (2008)

Health expenditures: 4.8% of GDP (2011)
country comparison to the world: 147

Physicians density: 0.09 physicians/1,000 population (2009)

Hospital bed density: 0.9 beds/1,000 population (2011)

Drinking water source:
improved:
urban: 92.1% of population
rural: 80% of population
total: 86.3% of population
unimproved:
urban: 7.9% of population
rural: 20% of population
total: 13.7% of population (2011 est.)

Sanitation facility access:
improved:
urban: 18.8% of population
rural: 7.7% of population
total: 13.5% of population
unimproved:
urban: 81.2% of population
rural: 92.3% of population
total: 86.5% of population (2011 est.)

HIV/AIDS—adult prevalence rate: 1.4% (2012 est.)
country comparison to the world: 33

HIV/AIDS—people living with HIV/AIDS: 235,800 (2012 est.)
country comparison to the world: 25

HIV/AIDS—deaths: 11,600 (2012 est.)
country comparison to the world: 27

Major infectious diseases: *degree of risk:* very high
food or waterborne diseases: bacterial and protozoal diarrhea, hepatitis A, and typhoid fever
vectorborne diseases: malaria, dengue fever, and yellow fever
water contact disease: schistosomiasis
respiratory disease: meningococcal meningitis
animal contact disease: rabies
note: highly pathogenic H5N1 avian influenza has been identified in this country; it poses a negligible risk with extremely rare cases possible among US citizens who have close contact with birds (2013)

Obesity—adult prevalence rate: 7.5% (2008)
country comparison to the world: 140

Children under the age of 5 years underweight: 14.3% (2008)
country comparison to the world: 53

Education expenditures: 8.1% of GDP (2011)
country comparison to the world: 13

Literacy: *definition:* age 15 and over can read and write
total population: 71.5%
male: 78.3%
female: 65.3% (2010 est.)

School life expectancy (primary to tertiary education): *total:* 12 years
male: 12 years
female: 11 years (2012)

Child labor—children ages 5-14: *total number:* 1,806,750
percentage: 34 % (2006 est.)

Unemployment, youth ages 15-24: *total:* 16.6%
country comparison to the world: 78
male: 16.4%
female: 16.7% (2000)

GOVERNMENT

Country name: *conventional long form:* Republic of Ghana
conventional short form: Ghana
former: Gold Coast

Government type: constitutional democracy

Capital: *name:* Accra
geographic coordinates: 5 33 N, 0 13 W
time difference: UTC 0 (5 hours ahead of Washington, DC during Standard Time)

Administrative divisions: 10 regions; Ashanti, Brong-Ahafo, Central, Eastern, Greater Accra, Northern, Upper East, Upper West, Volta, Western

Independence: 6 March 1957 (from the UK)

National holiday: Independence Day, 6 March (1957)

Constitution: several previous; latest drafted 31 March 1992, approved and promulgated 28 April 1992, entered into force 7 January 1993; amended 1996 (2012)

Legal system: mixed system of English common law and customary law

International law organization participation: has not submitted an ICJ jurisdiction declaration; accepts ICCt jurisdiction

Suffrage: 18 years of age; universal

Executive branch: *chief of state:* President John Dramani MAHAMA (since 24 July 2012); Vice President Kwesi Bekoe AMISSAH-ARTHUR (since 6 August 2012); note—President MAHAMA assumed office due to the death of former president John Atta MILLS and subsequently won the December 2012 presidential election; the *president is both the chief of state and head of government*
head of government: President John Dramani MAHAMA (since 24 July 2012); Vice President Kwesi Bekoe AMISSAH-ARTHUR (since 6 August 2012);
cabinet: Council of Ministers; president nominates members subject to approval by Parliament (For more information visit the World Leaders website)
elections: president and vice president elected on the same ticket by popular vote for four-year terms (eligible for a second term); election last held on 7 December 2012, extended to 8 December because of technical difficulties (next to be held in December 2016)
election results: John Dramani MAHAMA elected president; percent of vote—John Dramani MAHAMA 50.7%, Nana Addo Dankwa AKUFO-ADDO 47.7%, other 1.6%

Legislative branch: unicameral Parliament (275 seats; members elected by direct, popular vote in single-seat constituencies to serve four-year terms)
elections: last held on 7 and 8 December 2012 (next to be held in December 2016)
election results: percent of vote by party—NPP 47.5%, NDC 46.4%, PNC 0.6%, independent 2.5%, other 3.0%; seats by party—NDC 151, NPP 120, PNC 1, independent 3

Judicial branch: *highest court(s):* Supreme Court (consists of a chief justice and 12 justices)
judge selection and term of office: chief justice appointed by the president in consultation with the Council of State (a small advisory body of prominent citizens) and with the approval of Parliament; other justices appointed by the president upon the advice of the Judicial Council (an 18-member independent body of judicial, military and police officials, and presidential nominees)

and on the advice of the Council of State; justices can retire at age 60, with compulsory retirement at age 70
subordinate courts: Court of Appeal; High Court; Circuit Court; District Court; regional tribunals

Political parties and leaders: Convention People's Party or CPP [Samia NKRUMAH]; National Democratic Congress or NDC [Kwabena ADJEI]; New Patriotic Party or NPP [Jake OBETSEBI-LAMPTEY]; People's National Convention or PNC [Alhaji Amed RAMADAN]; note—listed are four of the more popular political parties as of December 2012; there are more than 20; registered parties

Political pressure groups and leaders: Christian Aid (water rights); Committee for Joint Action or CJA (education reform); National Coalition Against the Privatization of Water or CAP (water rights); Oxfam (water rights); Public Citizen (water rights); Students Coalition Against EPA [Kwabena Ososukene OKAI] (education reform); Third World Network (education reform)

International organization participation: ACP, AfDB, AU, C, ECOWAS, EITI (compliant country), FAO, G-24, G-77, IAEA, IBRD, ICAO, ICC (national committees), ICRM, IDA, IFAD, IFC, IFRCS, ILO, IMF, IMO, IMSO, Interpol, IOC, IOM, IPU, ISO, ITSO, ITU, ITUC (NGOs), MIGA, MINURSO, MINUSMA, MONUSCO, NAM, OAS (observer), OIF, OPCW, UN, UNAMID, UNCTAD, UNESCO, UNHCR, UNIDO, UNIFIL, UNISFA, UNMIL, UNMISS, UNOCI, UNWTO, UPU, WCO, WFTU (NGOs), WHO, WIPO, WMO, WTO

Diplomatic representation in the US: *chief of mission:* Ambassador (vacant); Amma Adamaa Twum AMOAH, Charge d'Affaires (since 11 February 2014)
chancery: 3512 International Drive NW, Washington, DC 20008
telephone: [1] (202) 686-4520
FAX: [1] (202) 686-4527
consulate(s) general: New York

Diplomatic representation from the US: *chief of mission:* Ambassador Gene A. CRETZ (since 11 September 2012)
embassy: 24 Fourth Circular Rd., Cantonments, Accra
mailing address: P. O. Box 194, Accra
telephone: [233] 30-2741-000
FAX: [233] 30-2741-389

Flag description: three equal horizontal bands of red (top), yellow, and green, with a large black five-pointed star centered in the yellow band; red symbolizes the blood shed for independence, yellow represents the country's mineral wealth, while green stands for its forests and natural wealth; the black star is said to be the lodestar of African freedom
note: uses the popular Pan-African colors of Ethiopia; similar to the flag of Bolivia, which has a coat of arms centered in the yellow band

National symbol(s): black star; golden eagle

National anthem: *name:* "God Bless Our Homeland Ghana"
lyrics/music: unknown/Philip GBEHO
note: music adopted 1957, lyrics adopted 1966; the lyrics were changed twice, once when a republic was declared in 1960 and again after a 1966 coup

ECONOMY

Economy—overview: Ghana's economy has been strengthened by a quarter century of relatively sound management, a competitive business environment, and sustained reductions in poverty levels. In late 2010, Ghana was recategorized as a lower middle-income country. Ghana is well-endowed with natural resources and agriculture accounts for roughly one-quarter of GDP and employs more than half of the workforce, mainly small landholders. The services sector accounts for 50% of GDP. Gold and cocoa production and individual remittances are major sources of foreign exchange. Oil production at Ghana's offshore Jubilee field began in mid-December 2010,and is producing close to target levels. Additional oil projects are being developed and are expected to come on line in a few years. Estimated oil reserves have jumped to almost 700 million barrels and Ghana's growing oil industry is expected to boost economic growth as the country faces the consequences of two years of loose fiscal policy, high budget and current account deficits, and a depreciating currency. President MAHAMA faces challenges in managing a population that is unhappy with living standards and that perceives they are not reaping the benefits of oil production because of political corruption.

GDP (purchasing power parity): $90.41 billion (2013 est.)
country comparison to the world: 78
$83.79 billion (2012 est.)
$77.64 billion (2011 est.)
note: data are in 2013 US dollars

GDP (official exchange rate): $45.55 billion (2013 est.)

GDP—real growth rate: 7.9% (2013 est.)
country comparison to the world: 13
7.9% (2012 est.)
15% (2011 est.)

GDP—per capita (PPP): $3,500 (2013 est.)
country comparison to the world: 174
$3,400 (2012 est.)
$3,200 (2011 est.)
note: data are in 2013 US dollars

Gross national saving: 21.1% of GDP (2013 est.)
country comparison to the world: 74
17.9% of GDP (2012 est.)
17.5% of GDP (2011 est.)

GDP—composition, by end use:
household consumption: 64.2%
government consumption: 14.2%
investment in fixed capital: 31.7%
investment in inventories: 0.7%
exports of goods and services: 50.2%

imports of goods and services: -61% (2013 est.)

GDP—composition, by sector of origin:
agriculture: 21.5%
industry: 28.7%
services: 49.8% (2013 est.)

Agriculture—products: cocoa, rice, cassava (manioc), peanuts, corn, shea nuts, bananas; timber

Industries: mining, lumbering, light manufacturing, aluminum smelting, food processing, cement, small commercial ship building, petroleum

Industrial production growth rate: 10.5% (2013 est.)
country comparison to the world: 13

Labor force: 12.07 million (2013 est.)
country comparison to the world: 44

Labor force—by occupation: *agriculture:* 56%
industry: 15%
services: 29% (2005 est.)

Unemployment rate: 11% (2000 est.)
country comparison to the world: 116

Population below poverty line: 28.5% (2007 est.)

Household income or consumption by percentage share: *lowest 10%:* 2%
highest 10%: 32.8% (2006)

Distribution of family income—Gini index: 39.4 (2005-06)
country comparison to the world: 63
40.7 (1999)

Budget: *revenues:* $10.56 billion
expenditures: $14.87 billion (2013 est.)

Taxes and other revenues: 23.2% of GDP (2013 est.)
country comparison to the world: 143

Budget surplus (+) or deficit (-):
-9.5% of GDP (2013 est.)
country comparison to the world: 203

Public debt: 53.1% of GDP (2013 est.)
country comparison to the world: 61
50% of GDP (2012 est.)

Fiscal year: calendar year

Inflation rate (consumer prices): 11% (2013 est.)
country comparison to the world: 211
9.2% (2012 est.)

Central bank discount rate: 18% (31 December 2009)
country comparison to the world: 8
17% (31 December 2008)

Commercial bank prime lending rate:
27% (31 December 2013 est.)
country comparison to the world: 13
22.8% (31 December 2012 est.)

Stock of narrow money: $6.256 billion (31 December 2013 est.)
country comparison to the world: 94
$6.153 billion (31 December 2012 est.)

Stock of broad money: $12.59 billion (31 December 2013 est.)
country comparison to the world: 96
$12.17 billion (31 December 2012 est.)

Stock of domestic credit: $13.31 billion (31 December 2013 est.)
country comparison to the world: 91
$12.56 billion (31 December 2012 est.)

Market value of publicly traded shares:
$3.465 billion (31 December 2012 est.)
country comparison to the world: 93
$3.097 billion (31 December 2011)
$3.531 billion (31 December 2010 est.)

Current account balance: -$5.149 billion (2013 est.)
country comparison to the world: 169
-$4.778 billion (2012 est.)

Exports: $13.37 billion (2013 est.)
country comparison to the world: 83
$13.54 billion (2012 est.)

Exports—commodities: oil, gold, cocoa, timber, tuna, bauxite, aluminum, manganese ore, diamonds, horticultural products

Exports—partners: France 13.6%, Italy 12.4%, Netherlands 8.9%, China 7.4%, Germany 4.3% (2012)

Imports: $18.49 billion (2013 est.)
country comparison to the world: 80
$17.76 billion (2012 est.)

Imports—commodities: capital equipment, refined petroleum, foodstuffs

Imports—partners: China 25.6%, Nigeria 11%, US 7%, Netherlands 6.2%, Singapore 4.5%, UK 4.1%, India 4% (2012)

Reserves of foreign exchange and gold: $6.016 billion (31 December 2013 est.)
country comparison to the world: 87
$5.705 billion (31 December 2012 est.)

Debt—external: $14.68 billion (31 December 2013 est.)
country comparison to the world: 90
$12.64 billion (31 December 2012 est.)

Stock of direct foreign investment—at home: $NA

Stock of direct foreign investment—abroad: $NA

Exchange rates: cedis (GHC) per US dollar—
2.018 (2013 est.)
1.796 (2012 est.)
1.431 (2010 est.)
1.409 (2009)
1.1 (2008)

ENERGY

Electricity—production: 8.213 billion kWh (2010 est.)
country comparison to the world: 9 7

Electricity—consumption: 5.311 billion kWh (2010 est.)
country comparison to the world: 113

Electricity—exports: 1.036 billion kWh (2010 est.)
country comparison to the world: 56

Electricity—imports: 106 million kWh (2010 est.)
country comparison to the world: 92

Electricity—installed generating capacity: 1.985 million kW (2010 est.)
country comparison to the world: 102

Electricity—from fossil fuels: 40.6% of total installed capacity (2010 est.)
country comparison to the world: 169

Electricity—from nuclear fuels: 0% of total installed capacity (2010 est.)
country comparison to the world: 94

Electricity—from hydroelectric plants: 59.4% of total installed capacity (2010 est.)
country comparison to the world: 33

Electricity—from other renewable sources: 0% of total installed capacity (2010 est.)
country comparison to the world: 177

Crude oil—production: 79,630 bbl/day (2012 est.)
country comparison to the world: 53

Crude oil—exports: 0 bbl/day (2010 est.)
country comparison to the world: 117

Crude oil—imports: 32,060 bbl/day (2010 est.)
country comparison to the world: 63

Crude oil—proved reserves: 660 million bbl (1 January 2013 es)
country comparison to the world: 45

Refined petroleum products—production: 22,130 bbl/day (2010 est.)
country comparison to the world: 92

Refined petroleum products—consumption: 61,590 bbl/day (2011 est.)
country comparison to the world: 92

Refined petroleum products—exports: 9,977 bbl/day (2010 est.)
country comparison to the world: 85

Refined petroleum products—imports: 37,240 bbl/day (2010 est.)
country comparison to the world: 82

Natural gas—production: 50 million cu m (2010 est.)
country comparison to the world: 87

Natural gas—consumption: 120 million cu m (2010 est.)
country comparison to the world: 105

Natural gas—exports: 0 cu m (2011 est.)
country comparison to the world: 106

Natural gas—imports: 830 million cu m (2011 est.)
country comparison to the world: 60

Natural gas—proved reserves: 22.65 billion cu m (1 January 2013 es)
country comparison to the world: 75

Carbon dioxide emissions from consumption of energy: 9.005 million Mt (2011 est.)
country comparison to the world: 103

COMMUNICATIONS

Telephones—main lines in use: 285,000 (2012)
country comparison to the world: 120

Telephones—mobile cellular: 25.618 million (2012)
country comparison to the world: 42

Telephone system: *general assessment:* primarily microwave radio relay; wireless local loop has been installed; outdated and unreliable fixed-line infrastructure heavily concentrated in Accra
domestic: competition among multiple mobile-cellular providers has spurred growth with a subscribership of more than 80 per 100 persons and rising
international: country code—233; landing point for the SAT-3/WASC, Main One, and GLO-1 fiber-optic submarine cables that provide connectivity to South Africa, Europe, and Asia; satellite earth stations—4 Intelsat (Atlantic Ocean); microwave radio relay link to Panaftel system connects Ghana to its neighbors (2009)

Broadcast media: state-owned TV station, 2 state-owned radio networks; several privately owned TV stations and a large number of privately owned radio stations; transmissions of multiple international broadcasters are accessible; several cable and satellite TV subscription services are obtainable (2007)

Internet country code: .gh

Internet hosts: 59,086 (2012)
country comparison to the world: 93

Internet users: 1.297 million (2009)
country comparison to the world: 93

TRANSPORTATION

Airports: 10 (2013)
country comparison to the world: 156

Airports—with paved runways: *total:* 7
over 3,047 m: 1
2,438 to 3,047 m: 1
1,524 to 2,437 m: 3
914 to 1,523 m: 2 (2013)

Airports—with unpaved runways: *total:* 3
914 to 1,523 m: 3 (2013)

Pipelines: gas 394 km; oil 20 km; refined products 361 km (2013)

Railways: *total:* 947 km
country comparison to the world: 91
narrow gauge: 947 km 1.067-m gauge (2008)

Roadways: *total:* 109,515 km
country comparison to the world: 43
paved: 13,787 km
unpaved: 95,728 km (2009)

Waterways: 1,293 km (168 km for launches and lighters on Volta, Ankobra, and Tano rivers; 1,125 km of arterial and feeder waterways on Lake Volta) (2011)
country comparison to the world: 57

Merchant marine: *total:* 4
country comparison to the world: 131
by type: petroleum tanker 1, refrigerated cargo 3
foreign-owned: 2 (Brazil 1, South Korea 1) (2010)

Ports and terminals: *major seaport(s):* Takoradi, Tema

MILITARY

Military branches: Ghana Army, Ghana Navy, Ghana Air Force (2012)

Military service age and obligation: 18-26 years of age for voluntary military service, with basic education certificate; no conscription; must be HIV/AIDS negative (2012)

Manpower available for military service:
males age 16-49: 6,268,191
females age 16-49: 6,194,339 (2010 est.)

Manpower fit for military service:
males age 16-49: 4,136,406
females age 16-49: 4,220,761 (2010 est.)

Manpower reaching militarily significant age annually: *male:* 267,896
female: 260,992 (2010 est.)

Military expenditures: 0.27% of GDP (2012)
country comparison to the world: 129
0.25% of GDP (2011)
0.27% of GDP (2010)

TRANSNATIONAL ISSUES

Disputes—international: disputed maritime border between Ghana and Cote d'Ivoire

Refugees and internally displaced persons: *refugees (country of origin):* 5,156 (Liberia) (2012); 8,532 (Cote d'Ivoire; flight from 2010 post-election fighting) (2013)

Illicit drugs: illicit producer of cannabis for the international drug trade; major transit hub for Southwest and Southeast Asian heroin and, to a lesser extent, South American cocaine destined for Europe and the US; widespread crime and money laundering problem, but the lack of a well-developed financial infrastructure limits the country's utility as a money laundering center; significant domestic cocaine and cannabis use

GIBRALTAR

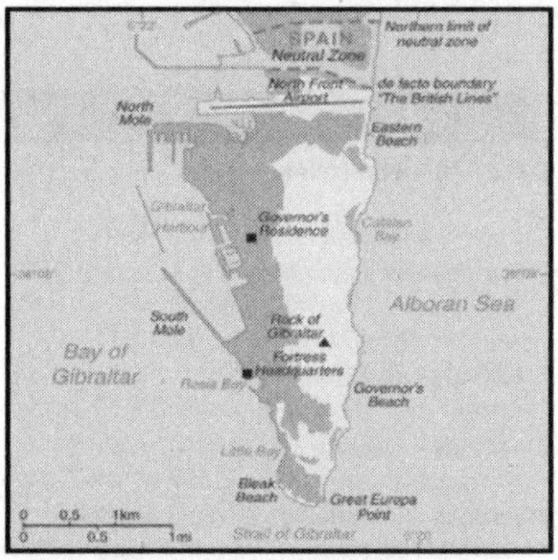

INTRODUCTION

Background: Strategically important, Gibraltar was reluctantly ceded to Great Britain by Spain in the 1713 Treaty of Utrecht; the British garrison was formally declared a colony in 1830. In a referendum held in 1967, Gibraltarians voted overwhelmingly to remain a British dependency. The subsequent granting of autonomy in 1969 by the UK led to Spain closing the border and severing all communication links. Between 1997 and 2002, the UK and Spain held a series of talks on establishing temporary joint sovereignty over Gibraltar. In response to these talks, the Gibraltar Government called a referendum in late 2002 in which the majority of citizens voted overwhelmingly against any sharing of sovereignty with Spain. Since late 2004, Spain, the UK, and Gibraltar have held tripartite talks with the aim of cooperatively resolving problems that affect the local population, and work continues on cooperation agreements in areas such as taxation and financial services; communications and maritime security; policy, legal and customs services; environmental protection; and education and visa services. Throughout 2009, a dispute over Gibraltar's claim to territorial waters extending out three miles gave rise to periodic non-violent maritime confrontations between Spanish and UK naval patrols and in 2013, the British reported a record number of entries by Spanish vessels into waters claimed by Gibraltar following a dispute over Gibraltar's creation of an artificial reef in those waters. A new noncolonial constitution came into effect in 2007, and the European Court of First Instance recognized Gibraltar's right to regulate its own tax regime in December 2008. The UK retains responsibility for defense, foreign relations, internal security, and financial stability.

GEOGRAPHY

Location: Southwestern Europe, bordering the Strait of Gibraltar, which links the Mediterranean Sea and the North Atlantic Ocean, on the southern coast of Spain

Geographic coordinates: 36 08 N, 5 21 W

Map references: Europe

Area: *total:* 6.5 sq km
country comparison to the world: 243
land: 6.5 sq km
water: 0 sq km

Area—comparative: more than 10 times the size of The National Mall in Washington, D.C.

Land boundaries: total: 1.2 km
border countries: Spain 1.2 km

Coastline: 12 km

Maritime claims: *territorial sea:* 3 nm

Climate: Mediterranean with mild winters and warm summers

Terrain: a narrow coastal lowland borders the Rock of Gibraltar

Elevation extremes: *lowest point:* Mediterranean Sea 0 m
highest point: Rock of Gibraltar 426 m

Natural resources: none

Land use: *arable land:* 0%
permanent crops: 0%
other: 100% (2011)

Irrigated land: NA

Natural hazards: NA

Environment—current issues: limited natural freshwater resources: large concrete or natural rock water catchments collect rainwater (no longer used for drinking water) and adequate desalination plant

Geography—note: strategic location on Strait of Gibraltar that links the North Atlantic Ocean and Mediterranean Sea

PEOPLE AND SOCIETY

Nationality: *noun:* Gibraltarian(s)
adjective: Gibraltar

Ethnic groups: Spanish, Italian, English, Maltese, Portuguese, German, North Africans

Languages: English (used in schools and for official purposes), Spanish, Italian, Portuguese

Religions: Roman Catholic 78.1%, Church of England 7%, other Christian 3.2%, Muslim 4%, Jewish 2.1%, Hindu 1.8%, other or unspecified 0.9%, none 2.9% (2001 census)

Population: 29,185 (July 2014 est.)
country comparison to the world: 219

Age structure: *0-14 years:* 20.1% (male 3,009/female 2,862)
15-24 years: 16% (male 2,433/female 2,225)
25-54 years: 38.1% (male 5,593/female 5,524)
55-64 years: 15% (male 1,488/female 1,664)
65 years and over: 14.6% (male 2,156/female 2,231) (2014 est.)

Median age: *total:* 34 years
male: 33.1 years
female: 35 years (2014 est.)

Population growth rate: 0.25% (2014 est.)
country comparison to the world: 176

Birth rate: 14.15 births/1,000 population (2014 est.)
country comparison to the world: 139

Death rate: 8.33 deaths/1,000 population (2014 est.)
country comparison to the world: 88

Net migration rate: -3.29 migrant(s)/1,000 population (2014 est.)
country comparison to the world: 183

Urbanization: *urban population:* 100% of total population (2010)
rate of urbanization: 0.2% annual rate of change (2010-15 est.)

Sex ratio: *at birth:* 1.07 male(s)/female
0-14 years: 1.05 male(s)/female
15-24 years: 1.09 male(s)/female
25-54 years: 1.01 male(s)/female
55-64 years: 1.01 male(s)/female
65 years and over: 0.95 male(s)/female
total population: 1.01 male(s)/female (2014 est.)

Infant mortality rate: *total:* 6.29 deaths/1,000 live births
country comparison to the world: 166
male: 6.99 deaths/1,000 live births
female: 5.53 deaths/1,000 live births (2014 est.)

Life expectancy at birth: *total population:* 79.13 years
country comparison to the world: 46
male: 76.28 years
female: 82.18 years (2014 est.)

Total fertility rate: 1.92 children born/woman (2014 est.)
country comparison to the world: 137

HIV/AIDS—adult prevalence rate: NA

HIV/AIDS—people living with HIV/AIDS: NA

HIV/AIDS—deaths: NA

Education expenditures: NA

Literacy: *definition:* NA
total population: above 80%
male: NA
female: NA

GOVERNMENT

Country name: *conventional long form:* none
conventional short form: Gibraltar

Dependency status: overseas territory of the UK

Government type: NA

Capital: *name:* Gibraltar
geographic coordinates: 36 08 N, 5 21 W
time difference: UTC+1 (6 hours ahead of Washington, DC during Standard Time)
daylight saving time: +1hr, begins last Sunday in March; ends last Sunday in October

Administrative divisions: none (overseas territory of the UK)

Independence: none (overseas territory of the UK)

National holiday: National Day, 10 September (1967); note—day of the national referendum to decide whether to remain with the UK or join Spain

Constitution: previous 1969; latest passed by referendum 30 November 2006, entered into effect 14 December 2006, entered into force 2 January 2007; amended 2009 (2009)

Legal system: the laws of the UK, where applicable, apply

Suffrage: 18 years of age; universal; and British citizens who have been residents six months or more

Executive branch: *chief of state:* Queen ELIZABETH II (since 6 February 1952); represented by Governor Sir James DUTTON (since 6 December 2013)
head of government: Chief Minister Fabian PICARDO (since 9 December 2011)
cabinet: Council of Ministers appointed from among the 17 elected members of the Parliament by the governor in consultation with the chief

minister (For more information visit the World Leaders website)
elections: the monarchy is hereditary; governor appointed by the monarch; following legislative elections, the leader of the majority party or the leader of the majority coalition is usually appointed chief minister by the governor

Legislative branch: unicameral Parliament (18 seats: 17 members elected by popular vote, 1 for the speaker appointed by Parliament; members serve four-year terms)
elections: last held on 8 December 2011 (next to be held not later than 8 December 2015)
election results: percent of vote by party—GSD 48%, GSLP 46.8%, Progressive Democratic Party 4.4%, other 0.8%; seats by party—GSD 10, GSLP 7

Judicial branch: *highest court(s):* Court of Appeal (consists of at least three judges, including the court president); Supreme Court of Gibraltar (consists of the chief justice and 3 judges) note—appeals beyond the Court of Appeal are heard by the Judicial Committee of the Privy Council (in London)
judge selection and term of office: Court of Appeal and Supreme Court judges appointed by the governor upon the advice of the Judicial Service Commission, a 7-member body of judges and appointees of the governor; tenure of the Court of Appeal president based on terms of appointment; Supreme Court chief justice and judge normally appointed until retirement at age 67, but can be extended 3 years
subordinate courts: Court of First Instance; Magistrates' Court; specialized tribunals for issues relating to social security, taxes, and employment

Political parties and leaders: Gibraltar Liberal Party [Joseph GARCIA]; Gibraltar Social Democrats or GSD [Daniel FEETHAM]; Gibraltar Socialist Labor Party or GSLP [Fabian PICARDO]; Progressive Democratic Party [Nick CRUZ]

Political pressure groups and leaders: Chamber of Commerce; Gibraltar Representatives Organization; Women's Association

International organization participation: ICC (NGOs), Interpol (subbureau), UPU

Diplomatic representation in the US: none (overseas territory of the UK)

Diplomatic representation from the US: none (overseas territory of the UK)

Flag description: two horizontal bands of white (top, double width) and red with a three-towered red castle in the center of the white band; hanging from the castle gate is a gold key centered in the red band; the design is that of Gibraltar's coat of arms granted on 10 July 1502 by King Ferdinand and Queen Isabella of Spain; the castle symbolizes Gibraltar as a fortress, while the key represents Gibraltar's strategic importance—the key to the Mediterranean

National symbol(s): Barbary macaque

National anthem: *name:* "Gibraltar Anthem"
lyrics/music: Peter EMBERLEY
note: adopted 1994; serves as a local anthem; as a territory of the United Kingdom, "God Save the Queen" remains official (see United Kingdom)

ECONOMY

Economy—overview: Self-sufficient Gibraltar benefits from an extensive shipping trade, offshore banking, and its position as an international conference center. Tax rates are low to attract foreign investment. The British military presence has been sharply reduced and now contributes about 7% to the local economy, compared with 60% in 1984. The financial sector, tourism (over 11 million visitors in 2012), gaming revenues, shipping services fees, and duties on consumer goods also generate revenue. The financial sector, tourism, and the shipping sector contribute 30%, 30%, and 25%, respectively, of GDP. Telecommunications, e-commerce, and e-gaming account for the remaining 15%. In recent years, Gibraltar has seen major structural change from a public to a private sector economy, but changes in government spending still have a major impact on the level of employment.

GDP (purchasing power parity): $1.275 billion (2008 est.)
country comparison to the world: 201
$1.203 billion (2007 est.)
$1.106 billion (2006 est.)

GDP (official exchange rate): $1.106 billion (2006 est.)

GDP—real growth rate: 6% (2008)
country comparison to the world: 38
8.8% (2007)
0% (2006 est.)

GDP—per capita (PPP): $43,000 (2006 est.)
country comparison to the world: 20
$41,200 (2007 est.)
$38,400 (2006 est.)

GDP—composition, by sector of origin:
agriculture: 0%
industry: 0%
services: 100% (2008 est.)

Agriculture—products: none

Industries: tourism, banking and finance, ship repairing, tobacco

Industrial production growth rate: NA%

Labor force: 12,690 (2001) (2001)
country comparison to the world: 215
Labor force—by occupation: *agriculture:* negligible
industry: 40%
services: 60% (2001)

Unemployment rate: 3% (2005 est.)
country comparison to the world: 23

Population below poverty line: NA%

Household income or consumption by percentage share: *lowest 10%:* NA%
highest 10%: NA%

Budget: *revenues:* $475.8 million
expenditures: $452.3 million (2008 est.)

Taxes and other revenues: 43% of GDP (2008 est.)
country comparison to the world: 25

Budget surplus (+) or deficit (-): 2.1% of GDP (2008 est.)
country comparison to the world: 16

Public debt: 7.5% of GDP (2008 est.)
country comparison to the world: 153
13.5% of GDP (2006 est.)

Fiscal year: 1 July—30 June

Inflation rate (consumer prices): 2.8% (2008)
country comparison to the world: 106
2.6% (2006)

Exports: $271 million (2004 est.)
country comparison to the world: 182

Exports—commodities: (principally reexports) petroleum 51%, manufactured goods

Imports: $2.967 billion (2004 est.)
country comparison to the world: 148

Imports—commodities: fuels, manufactured goods, foodstuffs

Debt—external: $NA

Exchange rates: Gibraltar pounds (GIP) per US dollar—
0.6391 (2013)
0.6307 (2012)
0.6472 (2010)
0.6175 (2009)
0.5302 (2008)

ENERGY

Electricity—production: 166.4 million kWh (2010 est.)
country comparison to the world: 185

Electricity—consumption: 154.7 million kWh (2010 est.)
country comparison to the world: 189

Electricity—exports: 0 kWh (2012 est.)
country comparison to the world: 141

Electricity—imports: 0 kWh (2012 est.)
country comparison to the world: 148

Electricity—installed generating capacity: 43,000 kW (2010 est.)
country comparison to the world: 193

Electricity—from fossil fuels: 100% of total installed capacity (2010 est.)
country comparison to the world: 14

Electricity—from nuclear fuels: 0% of total installed capacity (2010 est.)
country comparison to the world: 95

Electricity—from hydroelectric plants: 0% of total installed capacity (2010 est.)
country comparison to the world: 171

Electricity—from other renewable sources: 0% of total installed capacity (2010 est.)
country comparison to the world: 178

Crude oil—production: 0 bbl/day (2012 est.)
country comparison to the world: 173

Crude oil—exports: 0 bbl/day (2010 est.)
country comparison to the world: 118

Crude oil—imports: 0 bbl/day (2010 est.)
country comparison to the world: 191

Crude oil—proved reserves: 0 bbl (1 January 2013 es)
country comparison to the world: 136

Refined petroleum products—production: 0 bbl/day (2010 est.)
country comparison to the world: 148

Refined petroleum products—consumption: 24,920 bbl/day (2011 est.)
country comparison to the world: 121

Refined petroleum products—exports: 0 bbl/day (2010 est.)
country comparison to the world: 179

Refined petroleum products—imports: 28,380 bbl/day (2008 est.)
country comparison to the world: 93

Natural gas—production: 0 cu m (2011 est.)
country comparison to the world: 135

Natural gas—consumption: 0 cu m (2010 est.)
country comparison to the world: 148

Natural gas—exports: 0 cu m (2011 est.)
country comparison to the world: 107

Natural gas—imports: 0 cu m (2011 est.)
country comparison to the world: 197

Natural gas—proved reserves: 0 cu m (1 January 2013 es)
country comparison to the world: 142

Carbon dioxide emissions from consumption of energy: 4.905 million Mt (2011 est.)
country comparison to the world: 126

COMMUNICATIONS

Telephones—main lines in use: 23,100 (2012)
country comparison to the world: 184

Telephones—mobile cellular: 34,750 (2012)
country comparison to the world: 206

Telephone system: *general assessment:* adequate, automatic domestic system and adequate international facilities
domestic: automatic exchange facilities
international: country code—350; radiotelephone; microwave radio relay; satellite earth station—1 Intelsat (Atlantic Ocean)

Broadcast media: Gibraltar Broadcasting Corporation (GBC) provides TV and radio broadcasting services via 1 TV station and 4 radio stations; British Forces Broadcasting Service (BFBS) operates 1 radio station; broadcasts from Spanish radio and TV stations are accessible (2008)

Internet country code: .gi

Internet hosts: 3,509 (2012)
country comparison to the world: 151

Internet users: 20,200 (2009)
country comparison to the world: 193

TRANSPORTATION

Airports: 1 (2013)
country comparison to the world: 217

Airports—with paved runways: *total:* 1
1,524 to 2,437 m: 1 (2013)

Roadways: *total:* 29 km
country comparison to the world: 220
paved: 29 km (2007)

Merchant marine: *total:* 267
country comparison to the world: 32
by type: bulk carrier 3, cargo 146, chemical tanker 64, container 28, liquefied gas 2, petroleum tanker 14, roll on/roll off 2, vehicle carrier 8
foreign-owned: 254 (Belgium 1, Cyprus 1, Denmark 7, Finland 2, Germany 123, Greece 8, Iceland 1, Italy 4, Jersey 1, Morocco 4, Netherlands 34, Norway 46, Sweden 11, UAE 5, UK 6)
registered in other countries: 6 (Liberia 5, Panama 1) (2010)

Ports and terminals: *major seaport(s):* Gibraltar

MILITARY

Military branches: Royal Gibraltar Regiment (2013)

Manpower available for military service:
males age 16-49: 7,037 (2010 est.)

Manpower fit for military service:
males age 16-49: 6,017
females age 16-49: 5,706 (2010 est.)

Manpower reaching militarily significant age annually: *male:* 228
female: 220 (2010 est.)

Military—note: defense is the responsibility of the UK; the Royal Gibraltar Regiment replaced the last British regular infantry forces in 1992

TRANSNATIONAL ISSUES

Disputes—international: in 2002, Gibraltar residents voted overwhelmingly by referendum to reject any "shared sovereignty" arrangement; the Government of Gibraltar insists on equal participation in talks between the UK and Spain; Spain disapproves of UK plans to grant Gibraltar even greater autonomy

GREECE

INTRODUCTION

Background: Greece achieved independence from the Ottoman Empire in 1830. During the second half of the 19th century and the first half of the 20th century, it gradually added neighboring islands and territories, most with Greek-speaking populations. In World War II, Greece was first invaded by Italy (1940) and subsequently occupied by Germany (1941-44); fighting endured in a protracted civil war between supporters of the king and other anti-communist and communist rebels. Following the latter's defeat in 1949, Greece joined NATO in 1952. In 1967, a group of military officers seized power, establishing a military dictatorship that suspended many political liberties and forced the king to flee the country. In 1974, democratic elections and a referendum created a parliamentary republic and abolished the monarchy. In 1981, Greece joined the EC (now the EU); it became the 12th member of the European Economic and Monetary Union in 2001. In 2010, the prospect of a Greek default on its euro-denominated debt created severe strains within the EMU and raised the question of whether a member country might voluntarily leave the common currency or be removed.

GEOGRAPHY

Location: Southern Europe, bordering the Aegean Sea, Ionian Sea, and the Mediterranean Sea, between Albania and Turkey

Geographic coordinates: 39 00 N, 22 00 E

Map references: Europe

Area: *total:* 131,957 sq km
country comparison to the world: 97
land: 130,647 sq km
water: 1,310 sq km

Area—comparative: slightly smaller than Alabama
Land boundaries:
total: 1,228 km
border countries: Albania 282 km, Bulgaria 494 km, Turkey 206 km, Macedonia 246 km

Coastline: 13,676 km

Maritime claims: territorial sea: 12 nm
continental shelf: 200 m depth or to the depth of exploitation

Climate: temperate; mild, wet winters; hot, dry summers

Terrain: mostly mountains with ranges extending into the sea as peninsulas or chains of islands

Elevation extremes: *lowest point:* Mediterranean Sea 0 m
highest point: Mount Olympus 2,917 m

Natural resources: lignite, petroleum, iron ore, bauxite, lead, zinc, nickel, magnesite, marble, salt, hydropower potential

Land use: arable land: 18.95%
permanent crops: 8.73%
other: 72.32% (2011)

Irrigated land: 15,550 sq km (2007)

Total renewable water resources: 74.25 cu km (2011)

Freshwater withdrawal (domestic/industrial/agricultural): *total:* 9.47 cu km/yr (9%/2%/89%)
per capita: 841.4 cu m/yr (2007)

Natural hazards: severe earthquakes
volcanism: Santorini (elev. 367 m) has been deemed a Decade Volcano by the International Association of Volcanology and Chemistry of the Earth's Interior, worthy of study due to its explosive history and close proximity to human populations; although there have been very few eruptions in recent centuries, Methana and Nisyros in the Aegean are classified as historically active

Environment—current issues: air pollution; water pollution

Environment—international agreements:
party to: Air Pollution, Air Pollution-Nitrogen Oxides, Air Pollution-Sulfur 94, Antarctic-Environmental Protocol, Antarctic-Marine Living Resources, Antarctic Treaty, Biodiversity, Climate Change, Climate Change-Kyoto Protocol, Desertification, Endangered Species, Environmental Modification, Hazardous Wastes, Law of the Sea, Marine Dumping, Ozone Layer Protection, Ship Pollution, Tropical Timber 83, Tropical Timber 94, Wetlands
signed, but not ratified: Air Pollution-Persistent Organic Pollutants, Air Pollution-Volatile Organic Compounds

Geography—note: strategic location dominating the Aegean Sea and southern approach to Turkish Straits; a peninsular country, possessing an archipelago of about 2,000 islands

PEOPLE AND SOCIETY

Nationality: *noun:* Greek(s)
adjective: Greek

Ethnic groups: population: Greek 93%, other (foreign citizens) 7% (2001 census)
note: percents represent citizenship, since Greece does not collect data on ethnicity

Languages: Greek (official) 99%, other (includes English and French) 1%

Religions: Greek Orthodox (official) 98%, Muslim 1.3%, other 0.7%

Population: 10,775,557 (July 2014 est.)
country comparison to the world: 81

Age structure: *0-14 years:* 14.1% (male 781,151/female 735,444)
15-24 years: 9.8% (male 537,849/female 515,359)
25-54 years: 43.2% (male 2,321,709/female 2,337,502)
55-64 years: 20.2% (male 670,270/female 694,399)
65 years and over: 20.1% (male 954,605/female 1,227,269) (2014 est.)

Dependency ratios:
total dependency ratio: 52.3 %
youth dependency ratio: 22.3 %
elderly dependency ratio: 29.9 %
potential support ratio: 3.3 (2013)

Median age: *total:* 43.5 years
male: 42.4 years
female: 44.6 years (2014 est.)

Population growth rate: 0.01% (2014 est.)
country comparison to the world: 192

Birth rate: 8.8 births/1,000 population (2014 est.)
country comparison to the world: 213

Death rate: 11 deaths/1,000 population (2014 est.)
country comparison to the world: 34

Net migration rate: 2.32 migrant(s)/1,000 population (2014 est.)
country comparison to the world: 42

Urbanization: *urban population:* 61% of total population (2010)
rate of urbanization: 0.6% annual rate of change (2010-15 est.)

Major urban areas—population: ATHENS (capital) 3.252 million; Thessaloniki 834,000 (2009)

Sex ratio: *at birth:* 1.06 male(s)/female
0-14 years: 1.06 male(s)/female
15-24 years: 1.04 male(s)/female
25-54 years: 0.99 male(s)/female
55-64 years: 0.96 male(s)/female
65 years and over: 0.78 male(s)/female
total population: 0.96 male(s)/female (2014 est.)

Mother's mean age at first birth: 29.2 (2007 est.)

Maternal mortality rate: 3 deaths/100,000 live births (2010)
country comparison to the world: 183

Infant mortality rate: total: 4.78 deaths/1,000 live births
country comparison to the world: 181
male: 5.24 deaths/1,000 live births
female: 4.28 deaths/1,000 live births (2014 est.)

Life expectancy at birth: *total population:* 80.3 years
country comparison to the world: 30
male: 77.71 years
female: 83.06 years (2014 est.)

Total fertility rate: 1.41 children born/woman (2014 est.)
country comparison to the world: 207

Contraceptive prevalence rate: 76.2%
note: percent of women aged 16-45 (2001)

Health expenditures: 9% of GDP (2011)
country comparison to the world: 45

Physicians density: 6.04 physicians/1,000 population (2008)

Hospital bed density: 4.9 beds/1,000 population (2009)

Drinking water source:
improved:
urban: 100% of population
rural: 99.4% of population
total: 99.8% of population
unimproved:
urban: 0% of population
rural: 0.6% of population
total: 0.2% of population (2011 est.)

Sanitation facility access:
improved:
urban: 99.4% of population
rural: 97.5% of population
total: 98.6% of population
unimproved:
urban: 0.6% of population
rural: 2.5% of population
total: 1.4% of population (2011 est.)

HIV/AIDS—adult prevalence rate: 0.1% (2009 est.)
country comparison to the world: 139

HIV/AIDS—people living with HIV/AIDS: 8,800 (2009 est.)
country comparison to the world: 108

HIV/AIDS—deaths: fewer than 500 (2009 est.)
country comparison to the world: 96

Obesity—adult prevalence rate: 20.1% (2008)
country comparison to the world: 96

Education expenditures: 4.1% of GDP (2005)
country comparison to the world: 111

Literacy: *definition:* age 15 and over can read and write
total population: 97.3%
male: 98.4%
female: 96.3% (2011 est.)

School life expectancy (primary to tertiary education): *total:* 17 years
male: 16 years
female: 17 years (2007)

Unemployment, youth ages 15-24: *total:* 55.3%
country comparison to the world: 3
male: 48.4%
female: 63.2% (2012)

GOVERNMENT

Country name:
conventional long form: Hellenic Republic
conventional short form: Greece
local long form: Elliniki Dimokratia
local short form: Ellas or Ellada
former: Kingdom of Greece

Government type: parliamentary republic

Capital: *name:* Athens
geographic coordinates: 37 59 N, 23 44 E
time difference: UTC+2 (7 hours ahead of Washington, DC during Standard Time)
daylight saving time: +1hr, begins last Sunday in March; ends last Sunday in October

Administrative divisions: 13 regions (perifereies, singular—perifereia) and 1 autonomous monastic state* (aftonomi monastiki politeia); Agion Oros* (Mount Athos), Anatoliki Makedonia kai Thraki (East Macedonia and Thrace), Attiki (Attica), Dytiki Ellada (West Greece), Dytiki Makedonia (West Macedonia), Ionia Nisia (Ionian Islands), Ipeiros (Epirus), Kentriki Makedonia (Central Macedonia), Kriti (Crete), Notio Aigaio (South Aegean), Peloponnisos (Peloponnese), Sterea Ellada (Central Greece), Thessalia (Thessaly), Voreio Aigaio (North Aegean)

Independence: 1830 (from the Ottoman Empire)

National holiday: Independence Day, 25 March (1821)

Constitution: many previous; latest entered into force 11 June 1975; amended 1986, 2001, 2008 (2013)

Legal system: civil legal system based on Roman law

International law organization participation: accepts compulsory ICJ jurisdiction with reservations; accepts ICCt jurisdiction

Suffrage: 18 years of age; universal and compulsory

Executive branch: *chief of state:* President Karolos PAPOULIAS (since 12 March 2005)
head of government: Prime Minister Antonis SAMARAS (since 20 June 2012)
cabinet: Cabinet appointed by the president on the recommendation of the prime minister (For more information visit the World Leaders website)
elections: president elected by parliament for a five-year term (eligible for a second term); election last held on 3 February 2010 (next to be held by February 2015); president appoints leader of the party securing plurality of vote in election to become prime minister and form a government
election results: Karolos PAPOULIAS reelected president; number of parliamentary votes, 266 out of 300

Legislative branch: unicameral Hellenic Parliament or Vouli ton Ellinon (300 seats; members elected by direct popular vote to serve four-year terms)
elections: last held on 17 June 2012 (next scheduled to be held by 2016); note—there was a legislative election on 6 May 2012 in which none of the leaders of the top three parties (New Democracy, Coalition of the Radical Left, and the Panhellenic Socialist Movement) were able to form a government
election results: percent of vote by party—ND 29.7%, SYRIZA 26.9%, PASOK 12.3%, ANEL 7.5%, Golden Dawn 6.9%, DIMAR 6.3%, KKE 4.5%, other 6.0%; seats by party—ND 129, SYRIZA 71, PASOK 33, ANEL 20, Golden Dawn 18, DIMAR 17, KKE 12; note—only parties surpassing a 3% threshold are entitled to parliamentary seats; parties need 10 seats to become formal parliamentary groups, but can retain that status if the party participated in the last election and received the minimum 3% threshold; note—as of 20 January 2014 the composition of the Parliament was ND 126, SYRIZA 71, PASOK 27, ANEL 17, Golden Dawn 18, DIMAR 14, KKE 12, Independent Democratic Deputies 11, independents 4

Judicial branch: *highest court(s):* Hellenic Supreme Court of Civil and Penal Law (consists of 56 judges)
judge selection and term of office: judges selected by the Supreme Judicial Council which includes the president of the Supreme Court, other judges, and the prosecutor of the Supreme Court; judges appointed for life following a 2-year probationary period
subordinate courts: Supreme Administrative Court; Courts of Appeal; Courts of First Instance; Court of Auditors

Political parties and leaders: Anticapitalist Left Cooperation for the Overthrow or ANTARSYA [Petros KONSTANTINOU]; Coalition of the Radical Left or SYRIZA [Alexis TSIPRAS]; Communist Party of Greece or KKE [Dimitris KOUTSOUMBAS]; Democratic Left or DIMAR [Fotis KOUVELIS]; Ecologist Greens [Nikos CHRYSOGELOS]; Golden Dawn [Nikolaos MICHALOLIAKOS]; Independent Greeks or ANEL [Panagiotis (Panos) KAMMENOS]; New Democracy or ND [Antonis SAMARAS]; Panhellenic Socialist Movement or PASOK [Evangelos VENIZELOS]; Popular Orthodox Rally or LAOS [Georgios KARATZAFERIS]

Political pressure groups and leaders: Supreme Administration of Civil Servants Unions or ADEDY [Spyros PAPASPYROS]; Federation of Greek Industries or SEV [Dimitris DASKALOPOULOS]; General Confederation of Greek Workers or GSEE [Ioannis PANAGOPOULOS]

International organization participation: Australia Group, BIS, BSEC, CD, CE, CERN, EAPC, EBRD, ECB, EIB, EMU, ESA, EU, FAO, FATF, IAEA, IBRD, ICAO, ICC (national committees), ICRM, IDA, IEA, IFAD, IFC, IFRCS, IGAD (partners), IHO, ILO, IMF, IMO, IMSO, Interpol, IOC, IOM, IPU, ISO, ITSO, ITU, ITUC (NGOs), MIGA, NATO, NEA, NSG, OAS (observer), OECD, OIF, OPCW, OSCE, PCA, Schengen Convention, SELEC, UN, UNCTAD, UNESCO, UNHCR, UNIDO, UNIFIL, UNMISS, UNWTO, UPU, WCO, WFTU (NGOs), WHO, WIPO, WMO, WTO, ZC

Diplomatic representation in the US:
chief of mission: Ambassador Christos P. PANAGOPOULOUS (since 17 September 2012)
chancery: 2217 Massachusetts Avenue NW, Washington, DC 20008
telephone: [1] (202) 939-1300
FAX: [1] (202) 939-1324
consulate(s) general: Boston, Chicago, Los Angeles, New York, Tampa (FL), San Francisco
consulate(s): Atlanta, Houston, New Orleans

Diplomatic representation from the US:
chief of mission: Ambassador David D. PEARCE (since 5 September 2013)
embassy: 91 Vasillisis Sophias Avenue, 10160 Athens
mailing address: PSC 108, APO AE 09842-0108
telephone: [30] (210) 721-2951
FAX: [30] (210) 645-6282
consulate(s) general: Thessaloniki (2012)

Flag description: nine equal horizontal stripes of blue alternating with white; a blue square bearing a white cross appears in the upper hoist-side corner; the cross symbolizes Greek Orthodoxy, the established religion of the country; there is no agreed upon meaning for the nine stripes or for the colors; the exact shade of blue has never been set by law and has varied from a light to a dark blue over time

National symbol(s): Greek cross (white cross on blue field; arms equal length)

National anthem: *name:* "Ymnos eis tin Eleftherian" (Hymn to Liberty)
lyrics/music: Dionysios SOLOMOS/Nikolaos MANTZAROS
note: adopted 1864; the anthem is based on a 158 verse poem by the same name, which was inspired by the Greek Revolution of 1821 against the Ottomans; Cyprus also uses "Hymn to Liberty" as its anthem

ECONOMY

Economy—overview: Greece has a capitalist economy with a public sector accounting for about 40% of GDP and with per capita GDP about two-thirds that of the leading euro-zone economies. Tourism provides 18% of GDP. Immigrants make up nearly one-fifth of the work force, mainly in agricultural and unskilled jobs. Greece is a major beneficiary of EU aid, equal to about 3.3% of annual GDP. The Greek economy averaged growth of about 4% per year between 2003 and 2007, but the economy went into recession in 2009 as a result of the world financial crisis, tightening credit conditions, and Athens' failure to address a growing budget deficit. By 2013 the economy had contracted 26%, compared with the pre-crisis level of 2007. Greece met the EU's Growth and Stability Pact budget deficit criterion of no more than 3% of GDP in 2007-08, but violated it in 2009, with the deficit reaching 15% of GDP. Austerity measures have reduced the deficit to about 4% in 2013, including government debt payments. Deteriorating public finances, inaccurate and misreported statistics, and consistent underperformance on reforms prompted major credit rating agencies to downgrade Greece's international debt rating in late 2009, and led the country into a financial crisis. Under intense pressure from the EU and international market participants, the government adopted a medium-term austerity program that includes cutting government spending, decreasing tax evasion, overhauling the health-care and pension systems, and reforming the labor and product markets. Athens, however, faces long-term challenges to continue pushing through unpopular reforms in the face of widespread unrest from the country's powerful labor unions and the general public. In April 2010 a leading credit agency assigned Greek debt its lowest possible credit rating; in May 2010, the International Monetary Fund and Euro-Zone governments provided Greece emergency short- and medium-term loans worth $147 billion so that the country could make debt repayments to creditors. In exchange for the largest bailout ever assembled, the government announced combined spending cuts and tax increases totaling $40 billion over three years, on top of the tough austerity measures already taken. Greece, however, struggled to meet 2010 targets set by the EU and the IMF, especially after Eurostat—the EU's statistical office—revised upward Greece's deficit and debt numbers for 2009 and 2010. European leaders and the IMF agreed in October 2011 to provide Athens a second bailout package of $169 billion. The second deal however, called for holders of Greek government bonds to write down a significant portion of their holdings. As Greek banks held a significant portion of sovereign debt, the banking system was adversely affected by the write down and 41 billion of the second bailout package was set aside to ensure the banking system was adequately capitalized. In exchange for the second loan Greece promised to introduce an additional $7.8 billion in austerity measures during 2013-15. However, the massive austerity cuts have prolonged Greece's economic recession and depressed tax revenues. Throughout 2013, Greece's lenders called on Athens to step up efforts to increase tax collection, dismiss public servants, privatize public enterprises, and rein in health spending. In June 2013 Prime Minister Antonis SAMARAS's efforts to meet bailout conditions led to the departure of one party, the Democratic Left, from the governing coalition when his government made the controversial decision to shut down and restructure the state-owned television and radio company. Subsequent reluctance to institute further cuts and delays in meeting public sector reform targets prompted Greek lenders to withhold bailout fund disbursements until December 2013. However, investor confidence began to show signs of strengthening by the end of 2013 as leading macroeconomic indicators suggested the economy's freefall had been arrested.

GDP (purchasing power parity): $267.1 billion (2013 est.)
country comparison to the world: 51
$277.7 billion (2012 est.)
$296.6 billion (2011 est.)
note: data are in 2013 US dollars

GDP (official exchange rate): $243.3 billion (2013 est.)

GDP—real growth rate: -3.8% (2013 est.)
country comparison to the world: 215
-6.4% (2012 est.)
-7.1% (2011 est.)

GDP—per capita (PPP): $23,600 (2013 est.)
country comparison to the world: 63
$24,600 (2012 est.)
$26,200 (2011 est.)
note: data are in 2013 US dollars

Gross national saving: 12.2% of GDP (2013 est.)
country comparison to the world: 128
10.2% of GDP (2012 est.)
6.2% of GDP (2011 est.)

GDP—composition, by end use:
household consumption: 72.7%
government consumption: 17.4%
investment in fixed capital: 12.3%
investment in inventories: 0.9%
exports of goods and services: 28.4%
imports of goods and services: -31.7% (2013 est.)

GDP—composition, by sector of origin:
agriculture: 3.5%
industry: 16%
services: 80.5% (2013 est.)

Agriculture—products: wheat, corn, barley, sugar beets, olives, tomatoes, wine, tobacco, potatoes; beef, dairy products

Industries: tourism, food and tobacco processing, textiles, chemicals, metal products; mining, petroleum

Industrial production growth rate:
-3.5% (2013 est.)
country comparison to the world: 187

Labor force: 4.918 million (2013 est.)
country comparison to the world: 79

Labor force—by occupation: agriculture: 12.4%
industry: 22.4%
services: 65.1% (2005 est.)

Unemployment rate: 27.9% (2013 est.)
country comparison to the world: 177
24.3% (2012 est.)

Population below poverty line: 20% (2009 est.)

Household income or consumption by percentage share: *lowest 10%:* 2.5%
highest 10%: 26% (2000 est.)

Distribution of family income—Gini index: 34.3 (2012 est.)
country comparison to the world: 92
33.5 (2011 est.)

Budget: *revenues:* $106.2 billion
expenditures: $116 billion (2013 est.)

Taxes and other revenues: 43.7% of GDP (2013 est.)
country comparison to the world: 23

Budget surplus (+) or deficit (-): -4% of GDP (2013 est.)
country comparison to the world: 146

Public debt: 175% of GDP (2013 est.)
country comparison to the world: 3
156.9% of GDP (2012 est.)

Fiscal year: calendar year

Inflation rate (consumer prices): -0.8% (2013 est.)
country comparison to the world: 3
1.5% (2012 est.)

Central bank discount rate: 0.75% (31 December 2013)
country comparison to the world: 119
1.5% (31 December 2010)
note: this is the European Central Bank's rate on the marginal lending facility, which offers overnight credit to banks in the euro area

Commercial bank prime lending rate: 7.1% (31 December 2013 est.)
country comparison to the world: 120
7.33% (31 December 2012 est.)

Stock of narrow money: $112.1 billion (31 December 2013 est.)
country comparison to the world: 32
$116.2 billion (31 December 2012 est.)
note: see entry for the European Union for money supply in the euro area; the European Central Bank (ECB) controls monetary policy for the 17 members of the Economic and Monetary Union (EMU); individual members of the EMU do not control the quantity of money circulating within their own borders

Stock of broad money: $247.4 billion (31 December 2013 est.)
country comparison to the world: 34
$250 billion (31 December 2012 est.)

Stock of domestic credit: $325.1 billion (31 December 2013 est.)
country comparison to the world: 33
$343.9 billion (31 December 2012 est.)

Market value of publicly traded shares: $44.58 billion (31 December 2012 est.)
country comparison to the world: 55
$33.65 billion (31 December 2011)
$72.64 billion (31 December 2010 est.)

Current account balance: $2.021 billion (2013 est.)
country comparison to the world: 40
-$5.933 billion (2012 est.)

Exports: $30.39 billion (2013 est.)
country comparison to the world: 65
$28.31 billion (2012 est.)

Exports—commodities: food and beverages, manufactured goods, petroleum products, chemicals, textiles

Exports—partners: Turkey 11.6%, Italy 9.9%, Germany 6.5%, Bulgaria 4.9% (2013 est.)

Imports: $50.58 billion (2013 est.)
country comparison to the world: 56
$53.53 billion (2012 est.)

Imports—commodities: machinery, transport equipment, fuels, chemicals

Imports—partners: Russia 13.8%, Germany 9.5%, Italy 7.9%, Iraq 7.8%, Netherlands 4.7%, France 4.5%, China 4.5% (2013 est.)

Reserves of foreign exchange and gold: $7.255 billion (31 December 2012 est.)
country comparison to the world: 81
$7.255 billion (31 December 2012 est.)

Debt—external: $568.7 billion (30 September 2013 est.)
country comparison to the world: 25
$577.2 billion (2012)

Stock of direct foreign investment—at home: $40.1 billion (31 December 2013 est.)
country comparison to the world: 57
$37.8 billion (31 December 2012 est.)

Stock of direct foreign investment—abroad: $43.31 billion (31 December 2013 est.)
country comparison to the world: 39
$43.46 billion (31 December 2012 est.)

Exchange rates: euros (EUR) per US dollar—
0.7634 (2013 est.)
0.7752 (2012 est.)
0.755 (2010 est.)
0.7198 (2009 est.)
0.6827 (2008 est.)

ENERGY

Electricity—production: 56.2 billion kWh (2012 est.)
country comparison to the world: 46

Electricity—consumption: 56.4 billion kWh (2010 est.)
country comparison to the world: 43

Electricity—exports: 4.122 billion kWh (2012 est.)
country comparison to the world: 31

Electricity—imports: 5.946 billion kWh (2012 est.)
country comparison to the world: 33

Electricity—installed generating capacity: 15.12 million kW (2010 est.)
country comparison to the world: 46

Electricity—from fossil fuels: 69.5% of total installed capacity (2010 est.)
country comparison to the world: 108

Electricity—from nuclear fuels: 0% of total installed capacity (2010 est.)
country comparison to the world: 99

Electricity—from hydroelectric plants: 16.2% of total installed capacity (2010 est.)
country comparison to the world: 98

Electricity—from other renewable sources: 10.5% of total installed capacity (2010 est.)
country comparison to the world: 26

Crude oil—production: 7,497 bbl/day (2012 est.)
country comparison to the world: 94

Crude oil—exports: 17,020 bbl/day (2010 est.)
country comparison to the world: 54

Crude oil—imports: 405,500 bbl/day (2010 est.)
country comparison to the world: 20

Crude oil—proved reserves: 10 million bbl (1 January 2013 es)
country comparison to the world: 91

Refined petroleum products—production: 462,000 bbl/day (2010 est.)
country comparison to the world: 32

Refined petroleum products—consumption: 343,400 bbl/day (2011 est.)
country comparison to the world: 35

Refined petroleum products—exports: 183,100 bbl/day (2010 est.)
country comparison to the world: 34

Refined petroleum products—imports: 133,100 bbl/day (2010 est.)
country comparison to the world: 42

Natural gas—production: 6 million cu m (2011 est.)
country comparison to the world: 93

Natural gas—consumption: 4.2 billion cu m (2012 est.)
country comparison to the world: 66

Natural gas—exports: 0 cu m (2011 est.)
country comparison to the world: 111

Natural gas—imports: 4.376 billion cu m (2012 est.)
country comparison to the world: 37

Natural gas—proved reserves: 991.1 million cu m (1 January 2013 es)
country comparison to the world: 103

Carbon dioxide emissions from consumption of energy: 85.6 million Mt (2012 est.)
country comparison to the world: 43

Communications

Telephones—main lines in use: 5.461 million (2012)
country comparison to the world: 30

Telephones—mobile cellular: 13.354 million (2012)
country comparison to the world: 63

Telephone system: *general assessment:* adequate, modern networks reach all areas; good mobile telephone and international service
domestic: microwave radio relay trunk system; extensive open-wire connections; submarine cable to offshore islands
international: country code—30; landing point for the SEA-ME-WE-3 optical telecommunications submarine cable that provides links to Europe, Middle East, and Asia; a number of smaller submarine cables provide connectivity to various parts of Europe, the Middle East, and Cyprus; tropospheric scatter; satellite earth stations—4 (2 Intelsat—1 Atlantic Ocean and 1 Indian Ocean, 1 Eutelsat, and 1 Inmarsat—Indian Ocean region)

Broadcast media: Broadcast media dominated by the private sector; roughly 150 private TV channels, about ten of which broadcast at the nationwide; 1 government owned terrestrial TV channel with national coverage; 3 privately owned satellite channels; multi-channel satellite and cable TV services available; upwards of 1,500 radio stations, all of them privately owned; government owned broadcaster has 2 national radio stations (2014)

Internet country code: .gr

Internet hosts: 3.201 million (2012)
country comparison to the world: 32

Internet users: 4.971 million (2009)
country comparison to the world: 46

TRANSPORTATION

Airports: 77 (2013)
country comparison to the world: 69

Airports—with paved runways: *total:* 6 8
over 3,047 m: 6
2,438 to 3,047 m: 15
1,524 to 2,437 m: 19
914 to 1,523 m: 18
under 914 m: 10 (2013)

Airports—with unpaved runways: *total:* 9
914 to 1,523 m: 2
under 914 m: 7 (2013)

Heliports: 9 (2013)

Pipelines: gas 1,329 km; oil 94 km (2013)

Railways: *total:* 2,548 km
country comparison to the world: 66
standard gauge: 1,565 km 1.435-m gauge (764 km electrified)
narrow gauge: 961 km 1.000-m gauge; 22 km 0.750-m gauge (2008)

Roadways: total: 116,960 km
country comparison to the world: 40
paved: 41,357 km (includes 1,091 km of expressways)
unpaved: 75,603 km (2010)

Waterways: 6 km (the 6 km long Corinth Canal crosses the Isthmus of Corinth; it shortens a sea voyage by 325 km) (2012)
country comparison to the world: 107

Merchant marine: *total:* 860
country comparison to the world: 12
by type: bulk carrier 262, cargo 49, carrier 1, chemical tanker 68, container 35, liquefied gas 13, passenger 7, passenger/cargo 109, petroleum tanker 302, roll on/roll off 14
foreign-owned: 42 (Belgium 17, Bermuda 3, Cyprus 3, Italy 5, UK 6, US 8)
registered in other countries: 2,459 (Antigua and Barbuda 4, Bahamas 225, Barbados 14, Belize 2, Bermuda 8, Brazil 1, Cabo Verde 1, Cambodia 2, Cayman Islands 9, Comoros 4, Curacao 1, Cyprus 201, Dominica 4, Egypt 8, Gibraltar 8, Honduras 4, Hong Kong 27, Indonesia 1, Isle of Man 62, Italy 7, Jamaica 3, Liberia 505, Malta 469, Marshall Islands 408, Mexico 2, Moldova 1, Panama 379, Philippines 5, Portugal 2, Saint Kitts and Nevis 2, Saint Vincent and the Grenadines 42, Sao Tome and Principe 1, Saudi Arabia 4, Singapore 22, UAE 3, Uruguay 1, Vanuatu 3, Venezuela 4, unknown 10) (2010)

Ports and terminals: *major seaport(s):* Aspropyrgos, Pachi, Piraeus, Thessaloniki
oil/gas terminal(s): Agioi Theodoroi

MILITARY

Military branches: Hellenic Army (Ellinikos Stratos, ES), Hellenic Navy (Elliniko Polemiko Navtiko, EPN), Hellenic Air Force (Elliniki Polemiki Aeroporia, EPA) (2013)

Military service age and obligation: 19-45 years of age for compulsory military service; during wartime the law allows for recruitment beginning January of the year of inductee's 18th birthday, thus including 17 year olds; 18 years of age for volunteers; conscript service obligation is 1 year for the Army and 9 months for the Air Force and Navy; women are eligible for voluntary military service (2012)

Manpower available for military service:
males age 16-49: 2,485,389
females age 16-49: 2,469,854 (2010 est.)

Manpower fit for military service:
males age 16-49: 2,032,378
females age 16-49: 2,016,552 (2010 est.)

Manpower reaching militarily significant age annually: *male:* 52,754
female: 49,485 (2010 est.)

Military expenditures: 1.72% of GDP (2012)
country comparison to the world: 48
2.31% of GDP (2011)
2.63% of GDP (2010)

TRANSNATIONAL ISSUES

Disputes—international: Greece and Turkey continue discussions to resolve their complex maritime, air, territorial, and boundary disputes in the Aegean Sea; Greece rejects the use of the name Macedonia or Republic of Macedonia; the mass migration of unemployed Albanians still remains a problem for developed countries, chiefly Greece and Italy

Refugees and internally displaced persons:
stateless persons: 154 (2012)

Illicit drugs: a gateway to Europe for traffickers smuggling cannabis and heroin from the Middle East and Southwest Asia to the West and precursor chemicals to the East; some South American cocaine transits or is consumed in Greece; money laundering related to drug trafficking and organized crime

GREENLAND

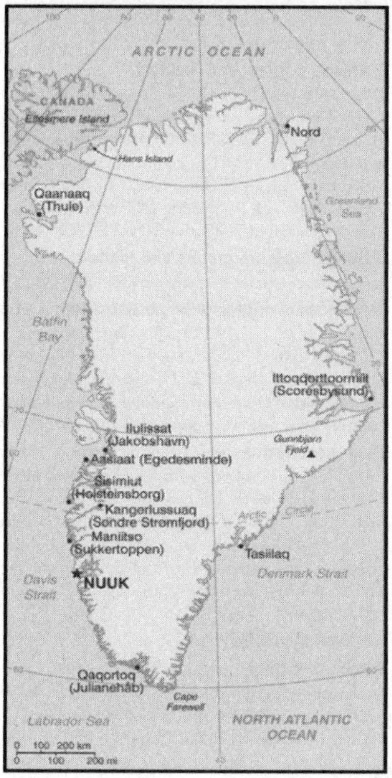

INTRODUCTION

Background: Greenland, the world's largest island, is about 81% ice-capped. Vikings reached the island in the 10th century from Iceland; Danish colonization began in the 18th century, and Greenland was made an integral part of Denmark in 1953. It joined the European Community (now the EU) with Denmark in 1973 but withdrew in 1985 over a dispute centered on stringent fishing quotas. Greenland was granted self-government in 1979 by the Danish parliament; the law went into effect the following year. Greenland voted in favor of increased self-rule in November 2008 and acquired greater responsibility for internal affairs when the Act on Greenland Self-Government was signed into law in June 2009. Denmark, however, continues to exercise control over several policy areas on behalf of Greenland including foreign affairs, security, and financial policy in consultation with Greenland's Self-Rule Government.

GEOGRAPHY

Location: Northern North America, island between the Arctic Ocean and the North Atlantic Ocean, northeast of Canada

Geographic coordinates: 72 00 N, 40 00 W

Map references: North America

Area: total: 2,166,086 sq km
country comparison to the world: 12
land: 2,166,086 sq km (410,449 sq km ice-free, 1,755,637 sq km ice-covered)

Area—comparative: slightly more than three times the size of Texas

Land boundaries: 0 km

Coastline: 44,087 km

Maritime claims: territorial sea: 3 nm
exclusive fishing zone: 200 nm or agreed boundaries or median line
continental shelf: 200 nm or agreed boundaries or median line

Climate: arctic to subarctic; cool summers, cold winters

Terrain: flat to gradually sloping icecap covers all but a narrow, mountainous, barren, rocky coast

Elevation extremes: *lowest point:* Atlantic Ocean 0 m
highest point: Gunnbjorn Fjeld 3,700 m

Natural resources: coal, iron ore, lead, zinc, molybdenum, diamonds, gold, platinum, niobium, tantalite, uranium, fish, seals, whales, hydropower, possible oil and gas

Land use: arable land: 0%
permanent crops: 0%
other: 100% (2011)

Irrigated land: NA

Natural hazards: continuous permafrost over northern two-thirds of the island

Environment—current issues: protection of the arctic environment; preservation of the Inuit traditional way of life, including whaling and seal hunting

Geography—note: dominates North Atlantic Ocean between North America and Europe; sparse population confined to small settlements along coast; close to one-quarter of the population lives in the capital, Nuuk; world's second largest ice cap

PEOPLE AND SOCIETY

Nationality: *noun:* Greenlander(s)
adjective: Greenlandic

Ethnic groups: Inuit 89%, Danish and other 11% (2009)

Languages: Greenlandic (East Inuit) (official), Danish (official), English

Religions: Evangelical Lutheran, traditional Inuit spiritual beliefs

Population: 57,728 (July 2014 est.)
country comparison to the world: 206

Age structure:
0-14 years: 21.5% (male 6,287/female 6,099)
15-24 years: 16.5% (male 4,843/female 4,702)
25-54 years: 42.5% (male 12,928/female 11,590)
55-64 years: 8.3% (male 3,681/female 2,818)
65 years and over: 8.1% (male 2,550/female 2,230) (2014 est.)

Median age: *total:* 33.6 years
male: 34.9 years
female: 32.3 years (2014 est.)

Population growth rate: 0.02% (2014 est.)
country comparison to the world: 190

Birth rate: 14.53 births/1,000 population (2014 est.)
country comparison to the world: 137

Death rate: 8.38 deaths/1,000 population (2014 est.)
country comparison to the world: 86

Net migration rate: -5.98 migrant(s)/1,000 population (2014 est.)
country comparison to the world: 198

Urbanization: *urban population:* 84% of total population (2010)
rate of urbanization: 0.3% annual rate of change (2010-15 est.)

Major urban areas—population: NUUK (capital) 15,000 (2009)

Sex ratio: *at birth:* 1.05 male(s)/female
0-14 years: 1.03 male(s)/female
15-24 years: 1.03 male(s)/female
25-54 years: 1.12 male(s)/female
55-64 years: 1.1 male(s)/female
65 years and over: 1.1 male(s)/female
total population: 1.11 male(s)/female (2014 est.)

Infant mortality rate: total: 9.42 deaths/1,000 live births
country comparison to the world: 144
male: 10.76 deaths/1,000 live births
female: 8.02 deaths/1,000 live births (2014 est.)

Life expectancy at birth: *total population:* 71.82 years
country comparison to the world: 142
male: 69.15 years
female: 74.63 years (2014 est.)

Total fertility rate: 2.06 children born/woman (2014 est.)
country comparison to the world: 116

Physicians density: 1.67 physicians/1,000 population (2009)

Hospital bed density: 5.8 beds/1,000 population (2009)

Drinking water source:
improved:
urban: 100% of population
rural: 100% of population
total: 100% of population
unimproved:
urban: 0% of population
rural: 0% of population
total: 0% of population (2011 est.)

Sanitation facility access:
improved:
urban: 100% of population
rural: 100% of population
total: 100% of population
unimproved:
urban: 0% of population
rural: 0% of population
total: 0% of population (2011 est.)

HIV/AIDS—adult prevalence rate: NA

HIV/AIDS—people living with HIV/AIDS: NA

HIV/AIDS—deaths: NA

Literacy: *definition:* age 15 and over can read and write
total population: 100%
male: 100%
female: 100% (2001 est.)

GOVERNMENT

Country name: *conventional long form:* none
conventional short form: Greenland
local long form: none
local short form: Kalaallit Nunaat

Dependency status: part of the Kingdom of Denmark; self-governing overseas administrative division of Denmark since 1979

Government type: parliamentary democracy within a constitutional monarchy

Capital: *name:* Nuuk (Godthab)
geographic coordinates: 64 11 N, 51 45 W
time difference: UTC-3 (2 hours ahead of Washington, DC during Standard Time)
daylight saving time: +1hr, begins last Sunday in March; ends last Sunday in October
note: Greenland is divided into four time zones

Administrative divisions: 4 municipalities (kommuner, singular kommune); Kujalleq, Qaasuitsup, Qeqqata, Sermersooq
note: the North and East Greenland National Park (Avannaarsuani Tunumilu Nuna Allanngutsaaliugaq) and the Thule Air Base in Pituffik (in northwest Greenland) are two unincorporated areas; the national park's 972,000 sq km—about 46% of the island—make it the largest national park in the world and also the most northerly

Independence: none (extensive self-rule as part of the Kingdom of Denmark; foreign affairs is the responsibility of Denmark, but Greenland actively participates in international agreements relating to Greenland)

National holiday: June 21 (longest day)

Constitution: previous 1953 (Greenland established as a constituency in the Danish constitution), 1979 (Greenland Home Rule Act); latest 21 June 2009 (Greenland Self-Government Act) (2009)

Legal system: the laws of Denmark apply

Suffrage: 18 years of age; universal

Executive branch: *chief of state:* Queen MARGRETHE II of Denmark (since 14 January 1972), represented by High Commissioner Mikaela ENGELL (since April 2011) head of government: Prime Minister Aleqa HAMMOND (since 13 March 2013)
cabinet: Home Rule Government elected by the Parliament (Landsting) on the basis of the strength of parties (For more information visit the World Leaders website)
elections: the monarchy is hereditary; high commissioner appointed by the monarch; prime minister elected by parliament (usually the leader of the majority party)
election results: Aleqa HAMMOND elected prime minister

Legislative branch: unicameral Parliament or Inatsisartut (Landsting) (31 seats; members elected by popular vote on the basis of proportional representation to serve four-year terms)
elections: last held on 13 March 2013 (next to be held by 2017)
election results: percent of vote by party—S 42.8%, IA 34.4%, A 8.1%, PI 6.4%; D 6.2%; other 2.1%; seats by party—S 14, IA 11, A 2, PI 2, D 2
note: two representatives were elected to the Danish Parliament or Folketing on 15 September 2011 (next to be held by September 2015); percent of vote by party—NA; seats by party—Siumut 1, Inuit Ataqatigiit 1 (2013)

Judicial branch: *highest court(s):* High Court of Greenland (consists of the presiding professional judge and 2 lay assessors) note—appeals beyond the High Court of Greenland can be heard by the Supreme Court (in Copenhagen)
judge selection and term of office: judges appointed by the monarch upon the recommendation of the Judicial Appointments Council, a 6-member independent body of judges and lawyers; judges appointed for life with retirement at age 70
subordinate courts: Court of Greenland; 18 district or magistrates' courts

Political parties and leaders: Candidate List (Kattusseqatigiit) or K [Anthon FREDERIKSEN]; Democrats Party (Demokraatit) or D [Jens B. FREDERIKSEN]; Forward Party (Siumut) or S [Aleqa HAMMOND]; Inuit Community (Inuit Ataqatigiit) or IA [Kuupik KLEIST]; Inuit Party (Partii Inuit) or PI [Nikku OLSEN]; Solidarity Party (Atassut) or A [Gerhardt PETERSEN]

Political pressure groups and leaders: conservationists; environmentalists

International organization participation: Arctic Council, ICC, NC, NIB, UPU; Diplomatic representation in the US; none (self-governing overseas administrative division of Denmark); Diplomatic representation from the US; none (self-governing overseas administrative division of Denmark)

Flag description: two equal horizontal bands of white (top) and red with a large disk slightly to the hoist side of center—the top half of the disk is red, the bottom half is white; the design represents the sun reflecting off a field of ice; the colors are the same as those of the Danish flag and symbolize Greenland's links to the Kingdom of Denmark

National symbol(s): polar bear

National anthem: *name:* "Nunarput utoqqarsuanngoravit" ("Our Country, Who's Become So Old" also translated as "You Our Ancient Land")
lyrics/music: Henrik LUND/Jonathan PETERSEN
note: adopted 1916; the government also recognizes "Nuna asiilasooq" as a secondary anthem

ECONOMY

Economy—overview: The economy remains critically dependent on exports of shrimp and fish, income from resource exploration and extraction, and on a substantial subsidy from the Danish Government. The subsidy was budgeted to be about $651 million in 2012, approximately 56% of government revenues that year. The public sector, including publicly owned enterprises and the municipalities, plays the dominant role in Greenland's economy. Greenland's real GDP contracted about 1% in 2009 as a result of the global economic slowdown, but is estimated to have grown marginally in 2010-13. The relative ease with which Greenland has weathered the economic crisis is due to increased hydrocarbon and mineral exploration and extraction activities, a high level of construction activity in the Nuuk area and the increasing price of fish and shrimp. During the last decade the Greenland Home Rule Government (GHRG) pursued conservative fiscal and monetary policies, but public pressure has increased for better schools, health care and retirement systems. The Greenlandic economy has benefited from increasing catches and exports of shrimp, Greenland halibut and, more recently, crabs. Due to Greenland's continued dependence on exports of fish—which accounted for 89% of exports in 2010—the economy remains very sensitive to foreign developments. International consortia are increasingly active in exploring for hydrocarbon resources off Greenland's western coast, and international studies indicate the potential for oil and gas fields in northern and northeastern Greenland. In May 2007 a US aluminum producer concluded a memorandum of understanding with the Greenland Home Rule Government to build an aluminum smelter and a power generation facility, which takes advantage of Greenland's abundant hydropower potential. Within the area of mining, olivine sand continues to be produced and gold production has resumed in south Greenland, while rare-earth and iron ore mineral projects have been proposed or planned elsewhere on the island. Tourism also offers another avenue of economic growth for Greenland, with increasing numbers of cruise lines now operating in Greenland's western and southern waters during the peak summer tourism season.

GDP (purchasing power parity): $2.133 billion (2011 est.)
country comparison to the world: 192
$2.071 billion (2010 est.)
$1.974 billion (2009 est.)
note: data are in 2011 US dollars

GDP (official exchange rate): $2.16 billion (2011 est.)

GDP—real growth rate: 3% (2011 est.)
country comparison to the world: 118
4.9% (2010 est.)
-2.7% (2009 est.)

GDP—per capita (PPP): $38,400 (2008 est.)
country comparison to the world: 30
$36,600 (2007 est.)

GDP—composition, by sector of origin:
agriculture: 4%
industry: 29%
services: 67% (2009 est.)

Agriculture—products: forage crops, garden and greenhouse vegetables; sheep, reindeer; fish

Industries: fish processing (mainly shrimp and Greenland halibut); gold, niobium, tantalite, uranium, iron and diamond mining; handicrafts, hides and skins, small shipyards

Industrial production growth rate: NA%

Labor force: 28,600 (2011)
country comparison to the world: 206

Labor force—by occupation: *agriculture:* 4%
industry: 29%
services: 67% (2009 est.)

Unemployment rate: 9.4% (2013 est.)
country comparison to the world: 102
4.2% (2010 est.)

Population below poverty line: 9.2% (2007 est.)

Household income or consumption by percentage share: *lowest 10%:* NA%
highest 10%: NA%

Budget: *revenues:* $1.72 billion
expenditures: $1.68 billion (2010)

Taxes and other revenues: 79.6% of GDP (2010)
country comparison to the world: 1

Budget surplus (+) or deficit (-):
1.9% of GDP (2010)
country comparison to the world: 19

Fiscal year: calendar year

Inflation rate (consumer prices): 2.8% (2011 est.)
country comparison to the world: 110
1.7% (2010 est.)

Exports: $384.3 million (2010)
country comparison to the world: 179
$358 million (2009)

Exports—commodities: fish and fish products 89%, metals 10% (2008)

Exports—partners: Denmark 60.4%, Japan 14.6%, China 7.9% (2012)

Imports: $814.2 million (2010)
country comparison to the world: 183
$726 million (2009)

Imports—commodities: machinery and transport equipment, manufactured goods, food, petroleum products

Imports—partners: Denmark 65.4%, Sweden 17.5%, Netherlands 5.5% (2012)

Debt—external: $36.4 million (2010)
country comparison to the world: 194
$58 million (2009)

Exchange rates: Danish kroner (DKK) per US dollar—
5.695 (2011)
5.6241 (2012)
5.6241 (2010)
5.361 (2009)
5.0236 (2008)

ENERGY

Electricity—production: 276.6 million kWh (2010 est.)
country comparison to the world: 177

Electricity—consumption: 279 million kWh (2010 est.)
country comparison to the world: 178

Electricity—exports: 0 kWh (2012 est.)
country comparison to the world: 143

Electricity—imports: 0 kWh (2012 est.)
country comparison to the world: 150

Electricity—installed generating capacity: 137,000 kW (2010 est.)
country comparison to the world: 166

Electricity—from fossil fuels: 100% of total installed capacity (2010 est.)
country comparison to the world: 15

Electricity—from nuclear fuels: 0% of total installed capacity (2010 est.)
country comparison to the world: 97

Electricity—from hydroelectric plants: 0% of total installed capacity (2010 est.)
country comparison to the world: 173

Electricity—from other renewable sources: 0% of total installed capacity (2010 est.)
country comparison to the world: 179

Crude oil—production: 0 bbl/day (2012 est.)
country comparison to the world: 175

Crude oil—exports: 0 bbl/day (2010 est.)
country comparison to the world: 120

Crude oil—imports: 0 bbl/day (2010 est.)
country comparison to the world: 193

Crude oil—proved reserves: 0 bbl (1 January 2013 es)
country comparison to the world: 138

Refined petroleum products—production: 0 bbl/day (2010 est.)
country comparison to the world: 150

Refined petroleum products—consumption: 3,897 bbl/day (2011 est.)
country comparison to the world: 175

Refined petroleum products—exports: 919.7 bbl/day (2010 est.)
country comparison to the world: 108

Refined petroleum products—imports: 5,164 bbl/day (2010 est.)
country comparison to the world: 149

Natural gas—production: 0 cu m (2011 est.)
country comparison to the world: 137

Natural gas—consumption: 0 cu m (2010 est.)
country comparison to the world: 150

Natural gas—exports: 0 cu m (2011 est.)
country comparison to the world: 109

Natural gas—imports: 0 cu m (2011 est.)
country comparison to the world: 199

Natural gas—proved reserves: 0 cu m (1 January 2013 es)
country comparison to the world: 144

Carbon dioxide emissions from consumption of energy: 611,100 Mt (2011 est.)
country comparison to the world: 176

COMMUNICATIONS

Telephones—main lines in use: 18,900 (2012)
country comparison to the world: 188

Telephones—mobile cellular: 59,455 (2012)
country comparison to the world: 200

Telephone system: *general assessment:* adequate domestic and international service provided by satellite, cables and microwave radio relay; totally digital since 1995
domestic: microwave radio relay and satellite
international: country code—299; satellite earth stations—15 (12 Intelsat, 1 Eutelsat, 2 Americom GE-2 (all Atlantic Ocean)) (2000)

Broadcast media: the Greenland Broadcasting Company provides public radio and TV services throughout the island with a broadcast station and a series of repeaters; a few private local TV and radio stations; Danish public radio rebroadcasts are available (2007)

Internet country code: .gl

Internet hosts: 15,645 (2012)
country comparison to the world: 123

Internet users: 36,000 (2009)
country comparison to the world: 179

TRANSPORTATION

Airports: 15 (2013)
country comparison to the world: 147

Airports—with paved runways: *total:* 1 0
2,438 to 3,047 m: 2
1,524 to 2,437 m: 1
914 to 1,523 m: 1
under 914 m: 6 (2013)

Airports—with unpaved runways: *total:* 5
1,524 to 2,437 m: 1
914 to 1,523 m: 2
under 914 m: 2 (2013)

Roadways: *note:* although there are short roads in towns, there are no roads between towns; inter-urban transport takes place either by sea or air (2012)

Merchant marine: *registered in other countries:* 1 (Denmark 1) (2010)
country comparison to the world: 149

Ports and terminals: *major seaport(s):* Sisimiut

MILITARY

Military branches: no regular military forces

Manpower available for military service:
males age 16-49: 15,280 (2010 est.)

Manpower fit for military service:
males age 16-49: 10,765
females age 16-49: 11,399 (2010 est.)

Manpower reaching militarily significant age annually: *male:* 488
female: 478 (2010 est.)

Military—note: defense is the responsibility of Denmark

TRANSNATIONAL ISSUES

Disputes—international: managed dispute between Canada and Denmark over Hans Island in the Kennedy Channel between Canada's Ellesmere Island and Greenland; Denmark (Greenland) and Norway have made submissions to the Commission on the Limits of the Continental shelf (CLCS) and Russia is collecting additional data to augment its 2001 CLCS submission

GRENADA

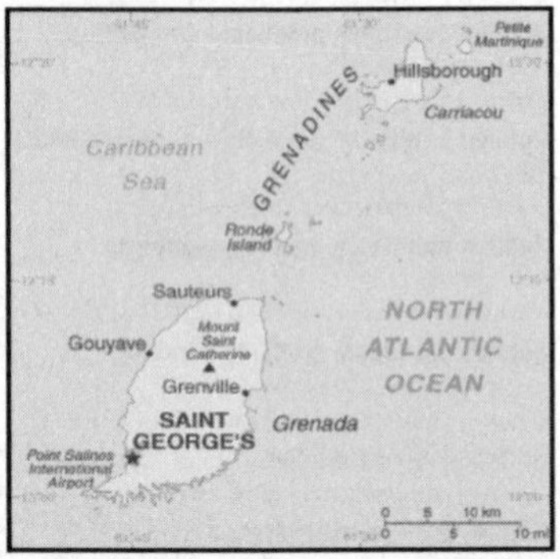

INTRODUCTION

Background: Carib Indians inhabited Grenada when Christopher COLUMBUS discovered the island in 1498, but it remained uncolonized for more than a century. The French settled Grenada in the 17th century, established sugar estates, and imported large numbers of African slaves. Britain took the island in 1762 and vigorously expanded sugar production. In the 19th century, cacao eventually surpassed sugar as the main export crop; in the 20th century, nutmeg became the leading export. In 1967, Britain gave Grenada autonomy over its internal affairs. Full independence was attained in 1974 making Grenada one of the smallest independent countries in the Western Hemisphere. Grenada was seized by a Marxist military council on 19 October 1983. Six days later the island was invaded by US forces and those of six other Caribbean nations, which quickly captured the ringleaders and their hundreds of Cuban advisers. Free elections were reinstituted the following year and have continued since that time. Hurricane Ivan struck Grenada in September of 2004 causing severe damage.

GEOGRAPHY

Location: Caribbean, island between the Caribbean Sea and Atlantic Ocean, north of Trinidad and Tobago

Geographic coordinates: 12 07 N, 61 40 W

Map references: Central America and the Caribbean

Area: *total:* 344 sq km
country comparison to the world: 207
land: 344 sq km
water: 0 sq km

Area—comparative: twice the size of Washington, DC
Land boundaries: 0 km

Coastline: 121 km

Maritime claims: territorial sea: 12 nm
exclusive economic zone: 200 nm

Climate: tropical; tempered by northeast trade winds

Terrain: volcanic in origin with central mountains

Elevation extremes: *lowest point:* Caribbean Sea 0 m
highest point: Mount Saint Catherine 840 m

Natural resources: timber, tropical fruit, deepwater harbors

Land use: arable land: 8.82%
permanent crops: 20.59%
other: 70.59% (2011)

Irrigated land: 2.19 sq km (2003)

Total renewable water resources: NA

Natural hazards: lies on edge of hurricane belt; hurricane season lasts from June to November

Environment—current issues: NA

Environment—international agreements:
party to: Biodiversity, Climate Change, Climate Change-Kyoto Protocol, Desertification, Endangered Species, Law of the Sea, Ozone Layer Protection, Whaling
signed, but not ratified: none of the selected agreements

Geography—note: the administration of the islands of the Grenadines group is divided between Saint Vincent and the Grenadines and Grenada

PEOPLE AND SOCIETY

Nationality: *noun:* Grenadian(s)
adjective: Grenadian

Ethnic groups: black 82%, mixed black and European 13%, European and East Indian 5%, and trace of Arawak/Carib Amerindian

Languages: English (official), French patois

Religions: Roman Catholic 53%, Anglican 13.8%, other Protestant 33.2%

Population: 110,152 (July 2014 est.)
country comparison to the world: 191

Age structure:
0-14 years: 24.5% (male 13,954/female 13,057)
15-24 years: 16.5% (male 9,075/female 9,155)
25-54 years: 40.3% (male 22,765/female 21,628)
55-64 years: 9.4% (male 5,214/female 4,927)
65 years and over: 9.2% (male 4,739/female 5,638) (2014 est.)

Dependency ratios:
total dependency ratio: 51.3 %
youth dependency ratio: 40.5 %
elderly dependency ratio: 10.8 %
potential support ratio: 9.3 (2013)

Median age: *total:* 29.9 years
male: 29.8 years
female: 29.9 years (2014 est.)

Population growth rate: 0.5% (2014 est.)
country comparison to the world: 155

Birth rate: 16.3 births/1,000 population (2014 est.)
country comparison to the world: 120

Death rate: 8.04 deaths/1,000 population (2014 est.)
country comparison to the world: 99

Net migration rate: -3.24 migrant(s)/1,000 population (2014 est.)
country comparison to the world: 181

Urbanization: *urban population:* 39% of total population (2010)
rate of urbanization: 1.6% annual rate of change (2010-15 est.)

Major urban areas—population: SAINT GEORGE'S (capital) 40,000 (2009)

Sex ratio: *at birth:* 1.1 male(s)/female
0-14 years: 1.07 male(s)/female
15-24 years: 0.99 male(s)/female
25-54 years: 1.05 male(s)/female
55-64 years: 1.03 male(s)/female
65 years and over: 0.83 male(s)/female
total population: 1.02 male(s)/female (2014 est.)

Maternal mortality rate: 24 deaths/100,000 live births (2010)
country comparison to the world: 134

Infant mortality rate: total: 10.5 deaths/1,000 live births
country comparison to the world: 137
male: 9.82 deaths/1,000 live births
female: 11.26 deaths/1,000 live births (2014 est.)

Life expectancy at birth: *total population:* 73.8 years
country comparison to the world: 120
male: 71.24 years
female: 76.62 years (2014 est.)

Total fertility rate: 2.09 children born/woman (2014 est.)
country comparison to the world: 109

Contraceptive prevalence rate: 54.3%
note: percent of women aged 15-44 (1990)

Health expenditures: 6.2% of GDP (2011)
country comparison to the world: 101

Physicians density: 0.66 physicians/1,000 population (2006)

Hospital bed density: 3.5 beds/1,000 population (2011)

Drinking water source:
improved:
urban: 94.2% of population
rural: 94.2% of population
total: 94.2% of population
unimproved:
urban: 5.8% of population
rural: 5.8% of population
total: 5.8% of population (2007 est.)

Sanitation facility access:
improved:
urban: 91.6% of population
rural: 91.6% of population
total: 91.6% of population
unimproved:
urban: 8.4% of population
rural: 8.4% of population
total: 8.4% of population (2007 est.)

HIV/AIDS—adult prevalence rate: NA

HIV/AIDS—people living with HIV/AIDS: NA

HIV/AIDS—deaths: NA

Obesity—adult prevalence rate: 22.5% (2008)
country comparison to the world: 78

Education expenditures: 3.9% of GDP (2003)
country comparison to the world: 112

Literacy: *definition:* age 15 and over can read and write
total population: 96%
male: NA
female: NA (2003 est.)

School life expectancy (primary to tertiary education): *total:* 16 years
male: 15 years
female: 16 years (2009)

GOVERNMENT

Country name:
conventional long form: none
conventional short form: Grenada

Government type: parliamentary democracy and a Commonwealth realm

Capital: *name:* Saint George's
geographic coordinates: 12 03 N, 61 45 W
time difference: UTC-4 (1 hour ahead of Washington, DC during Standard Time)

Administrative divisions: 6 parishes and 1 dependency*; Carriacou and Petite Martinique*, Saint Andrew, Saint David, Saint George, Saint John, Saint Mark, Saint Patrick

Independence: 7 February 1974 (from the UK)

National holiday: Independence Day, 7 February (1974)

Constitution: previous 1967; latest presented 19 December 1973, came into operation 7 February 1974, some provisions suspended 1979; amended 1991 (Constitutional Judicature Act, 1991—restored provisions suspended in 1979), 1992 (2008)

Legal system: common law based on English model

International law organization participation: has not submitted an ICJ jurisdiction declaration; non-party state to the ICCt

Suffrage: 18 years of age; universal

Executive branch: *chief of state:* Queen ELIZABETH II (since 6 February 1952); represented by Governor General Cecile LA GRENADE (since 7 May 2013)
head of government: Prime Minister Keith MITCHELL (since 20 February 2013)
cabinet: Cabinet appointed by the governor general on the advice of the prime minister (For more information visit the World Leaders website)
elections: the monarchy is hereditary; governor general appointed by the monarch; following legislative elections, the leader of the majority party or the leader of the majority coalition is usually appointed prime minister by the governor general

Legislative branch: bicameral Parliament consists of the Senate (13 seats, 10 members appointed by the government and 3 by the leader of the opposition) and the House of Representatives (15 seats; members elected by popular vote to serve five-year terms)
elections: last held on 19 February 2013 (next to be held in 2018)
election results: House of Representatives—percent of vote by party—NNP 59%, NDC 41%; seats by party—NNP 15

Judicial branch: *highest court(s):* Supreme Court of Grenada (consists of the High Court with 3 justices and a 2-tier Court of Appeal with NA justices) note—the Eastern Caribbean Supreme Court (ECSC) is the itinerant superior court of record for the 9-member Organization of Eastern Caribbean States to include Grenada; the ECSC—with its headquarters on St. Lucia—is headed by the chief justice and is compri
judge selection and term of office: justice selection and tenure NA
subordinate courts: magistrates' courts; Court of Magisterial Appeals

Political parties and leaders: Grenada United Labor Party or GULP [Wilfred HAYES]; National Democratic Congress or NDC [Tillman THOMAS]; New National Party or NNP [Keith MITCHELL]

Political pressure groups and leaders: Committee for Human Rights in Grenada or CHRG; New Jewel Movement Support Group; The British Grenada Friendship Society; The New Jewel 19 Committee

International organization participation: ACP, AOSIS, C, Caricom, CDB, CELAC, FAO, G-77, IBRD, ICAO, ICRM, IDA, IFAD, IFC, IFRCS, ILO, IMF, IMO, Interpol, IOC, ITU, ITUC, LAES, MIGA, NAM, OAS, OECS, OPANAL, OPCW, Petrocaribe, UN, UNCTAD, UNESCO, UNIDO, UPU, WHO, WIPO, WTO

Diplomatic representation in the US:
chief of mission: Ambassador Ethelstan A. FRIDAY (since 3 September 2013)
chancery: 1701 New Hampshire Avenue NW, Washington, DC 20009
telephone: [1] (202) 265-2561
FAX: [1] (202) 265-2468
consulate(s) general: New York

Diplomatic representation from the US: *chief of mission:* the US does not have an embassy in Grenada; the US Ambassador to Barbados is accredited to Grenada
embassy: Lance-aux-Epines Stretch, Saint George's
mailing address: P. O. Box 54, Saint George's
telephone: [1] (473) 444-1173 through 1177
FAX: [1] (473) 444-4820

Flag description: a rectangle divided diagonally into yellow triangles (top and bottom) and green triangles (hoist side and outer side), with a red border around the flag; there are seven yellow, five-pointed stars with three centered in the top red border, three centered in the bottom red border, and one on a red disk superimposed at the center of the flag; there is also a symbolic nutmeg pod on the hoist-side triangle (Grenada is the world's second-largest producer of nutmeg, after Indonesia); the seven stars stand for the seven administrative divisions, with the central star denoting the capital, St. George; yellow represents the sun and the warmth of the people, green stands for vegetation and agriculture, and red symbolizes harmony, unity, and courage

National anthem: *name:* "Hail Grenada"
lyrics/music: Irva Merle BAPTISTE/Louis Arnold MASANTO
note: adopted 1974

ECONOMY

Economy—overview: Grenada relies on tourism as its main source of foreign exchange especially since the construction of an international airport in 1985. Hurricanes Ivan (2004) and Emily (2005) severely damaged the agricultural sector—particularly nutmeg and cocoa cultivation—which had been a key driver of economic growth. Grenada has rebounded from the devastating effects of the hurricanes but is now saddled with the debt burden from the rebuilding process. Public debt-to-GDP is nearly 110%, leaving the MITCHELL administration limited room to engage in public investments and social spending. MITCHELL in 2013 announced a structural adjustment program that includes a plan to increase tax revenue. Strong performances in construction and manufacturing, together with the development of tourism and an offshore financial industry, have contributed to growth in national output; however, economic growth remained stagnant in 2010-12 after a sizeable contraction in 2009, because of the global economic slowdown's effects on tourism and remittances.

GDP (purchasing power parity): $1.458 billion (2013 est.)
country comparison to the world: 198
$1.447 billion (2012 est.)
$1.458 billion (2011 est.)
note: data are in 2013 US dollars

GDP (official exchange rate): $811 million (2013 est.)

GDP—real growth rate: 0.8% (2013 est.)
country comparison to the world: 179
-0.8% (2012 est.)
1% (2011 est.)

GDP—per capita (PPP): $13,800 (2013 est.)
country comparison to the world: 96
$13,700 (2012 est.)
$13,900 (2011 est.)
note: data are in 2013 US dollars

Gross national saving: -3.6% of GDP (2013 est.)
country comparison to the world: 153
-7.2% of GDP (2012 est.)
-2.1% of GDP (2011 est.)

GDP—composition, by end use:
household consumption: 91.6%
government consumption: 15.8%
investment in fixed capital: 16.8%
investment in inventories: 0%
exports of goods and services: 21.9%
imports of goods and services: -46.1% (2013 est.)

GDP—composition, by sector of origin:
agriculture: 5.6%
industry: 15.8%
services: 78.5% (2013 est.)

Agriculture—products: bananas, cocoa, nutmeg, mace, citrus, avocados, root crops, sugarcane, corn, vegetables

Industries: food and beverages, textiles, light assembly operations, tourism, construction

Industrial production growth rate: -2% (2013 est.)
country comparison to the world: 183

Labor force: 47,580 (2008)
country comparison to the world: 194

Labor force—by occupation: *agriculture:* 11%
industry: 20%
services: 69% (2008 est.)

Unemployment rate: 25% (2008)
country comparison to the world: 174
12.5% (2000)

Population below poverty line: 38% (2008)

Household income or consumption by percentage share: *lowest 10%:* NA%
highest 10%: NA%

Budget: *revenues:* $175.3 million
expenditures: $215.9 million (2009 est.)

Taxes and other revenues: 21.6% of GDP (2009 est.)
country comparison to the world: 151

Budget surplus (+) or deficit (-):
-5% of GDP (2009 est.)
country comparison to the world: 166

Public debt: 110% of GDP (2012 est.)
country comparison to the world: 13

Fiscal year: calendar year

Inflation rate (consumer prices): 2.4% (2013 est.)
country comparison to the world: 90
2.4% (2012 est.)

Central bank discount rate: 6.5% (31 December 2009)
country comparison to the world: 48
6.5% (31 December 2008)

Commercial bank prime lending rate: 9.4% (31 December 2013 est.)
country comparison to the world: 91
9.75% (31 December 2012 est.)

Stock of narrow money: $131.7 million (31 December 2013 est.)
country comparison to the world: 182
$123.3 million (31 December 2012 est.)

Stock of broad money: $697.4 million (31 December 2013 est.)
country comparison to the world: 173
$689.7 million (31 December 2012 est.)

Stock of domestic credit: $744.9 million (31 December 2013 est.)
country comparison to the world: 161
$729.5 million (31 December 2012 est.)

Market value of publicly traded shares: $NA

Current account balance: -$214.4 million (2012 est.)
country comparison to the world: 88
-$204.5 million (2011 est.)

Exports: $40.5 million (2012 est.)
country comparison to the world: 200
$34.9 million (2011 est.)

Exports—commodities: nutmeg, bananas, cocoa, fruit and vegetables, clothing, mace

Exports—partners: Nigeria 40.2%, St. Lucia 10.7%, Antigua and Barbuda 7.3%, US 6.6%, St. Kitts and Nevis 6.5%, Dominica 6.5%, Switzerland 4.3% (2012)

Imports: $297 million (2012 est.)
country comparison to the world: 201
$290.4 million (2011 est.)

Imports—commodities: food, manufactured goods, machinery, chemicals, fuel

Imports—partners: Trinidad and Tobago 44.3%, US 16.4%, China 4.6% (2012)

Debt—external: $538 million (2010 est.)
country comparison to the world: 173
$542 million (2009 est.)

Exchange rates: East Caribbean dollars (XCD) per US dollar—
2.7 (2013 est.)
2.7 (2012 est.)
2.7 (2010 est.)
2.7 (2009)

ENERGY

Electricity—production: 201.4 million kWh (2010 est.)
country comparison to the world: 181

Electricity—consumption: 178.4 million kWh (2010 est.)
country comparison to the world: 188

Electricity—exports: 0 kWh (2012 est.)
country comparison to the world: 142

Electricity—imports: 0 kWh (2012 est.)
country comparison to the world: 149

Electricity—installed generating capacity:
49,700 kW (2010 est.)
country comparison to the world: 189

Electricity—from fossil fuels: 98.6% of total installed capacity (2010 est.)
country comparison to the world: 55

Electricity—from nuclear fuels: 0% of total installed capacity (2010 est.)
country comparison to the world: 96

Electricity—from hydroelectric plants:
0% of total installed capacity (2010 est.)
country comparison to the world: 172

Electricity—from other renewable sources:
1.4% of total installed capacity (2010 est.)
country comparison to the world: 80

Crude oil—production: 0 bbl/day (2012 est.)
country comparison to the world: 174

Crude oil—exports: 0 bbl/day (2010 est.)
country comparison to the world: 119

Crude oil—imports: 0 bbl/day (2010 est.)
country comparison to the world: 192

Crude oil—proved reserves: 0 bbl (1 January 2013 es)
country comparison to the world: 137

Refined petroleum products—production:
0 bbl/day (2010 est.)
country comparison to the world: 149

Refined petroleum products—consumption:
2,803 bbl/day (2011 est.)
country comparison to the world: 183

Refined petroleum products—exports:
0 bbl/day (2010 est.)
country comparison to the world: 180

Refined petroleum products—imports:
2,004 bbl/day (2010 est.)
country comparison to the world: 179

Natural gas—production: 0 cu m (2011 est.)
country comparison to the world: 136

Natural gas—consumption: 0 cu m (2010 est.)
country comparison to the world: 149

Natural gas—exports: 0 cu m (2011 est.)
country comparison to the world: 108

Natural gas—imports: 0 cu m (2011 est.)
country comparison to the world: 198

Natural gas—proved reserves: 0 cu m (1 January 2013 es)
country comparison to the world: 143

Carbon dioxide emissions from consumption of energy: 269,000 Mt (2011 est.)
country comparison to the world: 191

COMMUNICATIONS

Telephones—main lines in use: 28,500 (2012)
country comparison to the world: 178

Telephones—mobile cellular: 128,000 (2012)
country comparison to the world: 189

Telephone system: *general assessment:* automatic, island-wide telephone system
domestic: interisland VHF and UHF radiotelephone links
international: country code—1-473; landing point for the East Caribbean Fiber Optic System (ECFS) submarine cable with links to 13 other islands in the eastern Caribbean extending from the British Virgin Islands to Trinidad; SHF radiotelephone links to Trinidad and Tobago and Saint Vincent; VHF and UHF radio links to Trinidad (2009)

Broadcast media: the Grenada Broadcasting Network, jointly owned by the government and the Caribbean Communications Network of Trinidad and Tobago, operates a TV station and 2 radio stations; multi-channel cable TV subscription service is available; a dozen private radio stations also broadcast (2007)

Internet country code: .gd

Internet hosts: 80 (2012)
country comparison to the world: 212

Internet users: 25,000 (2009)
country comparison to the world: 186

TRANSPORTATION

Airports: 3 (2013)
country comparison to the world: 195

Airports—with paved runways: *total:* 3
2,438 to 3,047 m: 1
1,524 to 2,437 m: 1
under 914 m: 1 (2013)

Roadways: *total:* 1,127 km
country comparison to the world: 183
paved: 687 km
unpaved: 440 km (2001)

Ports and terminals: *major seaport(s):* Saint George's

MILITARY

Military branches: no regular military forces; Royal Grenada Police Force (includes Coast Guard) (2010)

Manpower available for military service:
males age 16-49: 27,468 (2010 est.)

Manpower fit for military service:
males age 16-49: 22,596
females age 16-49: 22,588 (2010 est.)

Manpower reaching militarily significant age annually:
male: 995
female: 1,002 (2010 est.)

TRANSNATIONAL ISSUES

Disputes—international: none

Illicit drugs: small-scale cannabis cultivation; lesser transshipment point for marijuana and cocaine to US

GUAM

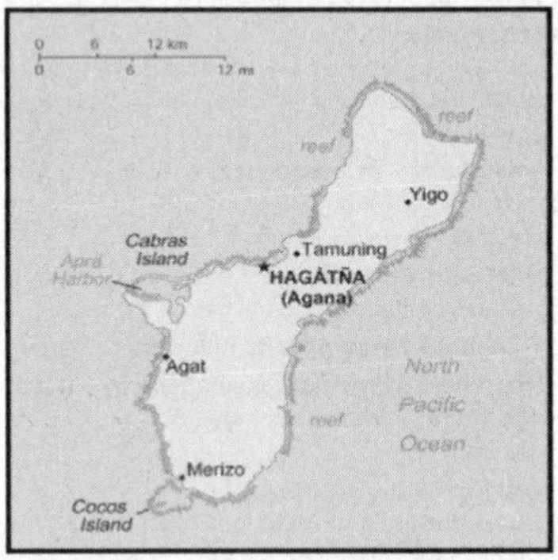

INTRODUCTION

Background: Spain ceded Guam to the US in 1898. Captured by the Japanese in 1941, it was retaken by the US three years later. The military installation on the island is one of the most strategically important US bases in the Pacific.

GEOGRAPHY

Location: Oceania, island in the North Pacific Ocean, about three-quarters of the way from Hawaii to the Philippines

Geographic coordinates: 13 28 N, 144 47 E

Map references: Oceania

Area: *total:* 544 sq km
country comparison to the world: 195
land: 544 sq km
water: 0 sq km

Area—comparative: three times the size of Washington, DC

Land boundaries: 0 km

Coastline: 125.5 km

Maritime claims: territorial sea: 12 nm
exclusive economic zone: 200 nm

Climate: tropical marine; generally warm and humid, moderated by northeast trade winds; dry season (January to June), rainy season (July to December); little seasonal temperature variation

Terrain: volcanic origin, surrounded by coral reefs; relatively flat coralline limestone plateau (source of most fresh water), with steep coastal cliffs and narrow coastal plains in north, low hills in center, mountains in south

Elevation extremes: *lowest point:* Pacific Ocean 0 m
highest point: Mount Lamlam 406 m

Natural resources: aquatic wildlife (supporting tourism), fishing (largely undeveloped)

Land use: arable land: 1.85%
permanent crops: 16.67%
other: 81.48% (2011)

Irrigated land: 2 sq km (2011)

Natural hazards: frequent squalls during rainy season; relatively rare but potentially destructive typhoons (June to December)

Environment—current issues: extirpation of native bird population by the rapid proliferation of the brown tree snake, an exotic, invasive species

Geography—note: largest and southernmost island in the Mariana Islands archipelago; strategic location in western North Pacific Ocean

PEOPLE AND SOCIETY

Nationality: *noun:* Guamanian(s) (US citizens)
adjective: Guamanian

Ethnic groups: Chamorro 37.3%, Filipino 26.3%, white 7.1%, Chuukese 7%, Korean 2.2%, other Pacific Islander 2%, other Asian 2%, Chinese 1.6%, Palauan 1.6%, Japanese 1.5%, Pohnpeian 1.4%, mixed 9.4%, other 0.6% (2010 est.)

Languages: English 43.6%, Filipino 21.2%, Chamorro 17.8%, other Pacific island languages 10%, Asian languages 6.3%, other 1.1% (2010 est.)

Religions: Roman Catholic 85%, other 15% (1999 est.)

Population: 161,001 (July 2014 est.)
country comparison to the world: 188

Age structure:
0-14 years: 26% (male 21,520/female 20,279)
15-24 years: 16.9% (male 14,109/female 13,164)
25-54 years: 39.3% (male 32,285/female 31,058)
55-64 years: 8.5% (male 7,483/female 7,411)
65 years and over: 8.2% (male 6,228/female 7,464) (2014 est.)

Dependency ratios:
total dependency ratio: 52.3 %
youth dependency ratio: 39.9 %
elderly dependency ratio: 12.3 %
potential support ratio: 8.1 (2013)

Median age: *total:* 29.9 years
male: 29.4 years
female: 30.4 years (2014 est.)

Population growth rate: 0.44% (2014 est.)
country comparison to the world: 160

Birth rate: 17.01 births/1,000 population (2014 est.)
country comparison to the world: 110

Death rate: 5.04 deaths/1,000 population (2014 est.)
country comparison to the world: 187

Net migration rate: -7.61 migrant(s)/1,000 population (2014 est.)
country comparison to the world: 205

Urbanization: *urban population:* 93% of total population (2010)
rate of urbanization: 1.2% annual rate of change (2010-15 est.)

Major urban areas—population: HAGATNA (capital) 153,000 (2009)

Sex ratio: *at birth:* 1.06 male(s)/female
0-14 years: 1.06 male(s)/female
15-24 years: 1.07 male(s)/female
25-54 years: 1.04 male(s)/female
55-64 years: 1.03 male(s)/female
65 years and over: 0.84 male(s)/female
total population: 1.03 male(s)/female (2014 est.)

Infant mortality rate: total: 5.51 deaths/1,000 live births
country comparison to the world: 175
male: 5.91 deaths/1,000 live births
female: 5.08 deaths/1,000 live births (2014 est.)

Life expectancy at birth: total population: 78.82 years
country comparison to the world: 50
male: 75.78 years
female: 82.05 years (2014 est.)

Total fertility rate: 2.38 children born/woman (2014 est.)
country comparison to the world: 84

Contraceptive prevalence rate: 66.6%
note: percent of women aged 18-44 (2002)

Drinking water source:
improved:
urban: 99.4% of population
rural: 99.4% of population
total: 99.4% of population
unimproved:
urban: 0.6% of population
rural: 0.6% of population
total: 0.6% of population (2011 est.)

Sanitation facility access:
improved:
urban: 97.4% of population
rural: 97.4% of population
total: 97.4% of population
unimproved:
urban: 2.6% of population
rural: 2.6% of population
total: 2.6% of population (2011 est.)

HIV/AIDS—adult prevalence rate: NA

HIV/AIDS—people living with HIV/AIDS: NA

HIV/AIDS—deaths: NA

Literacy: *definition:* age 15 and over can read and write
total population: 99%
male: 99%
female: 99% (1990 est.)

Unemployment, youth ages 15-24: total: 29.4%
country comparison to the world: 27
male: 29.7%
female: 28.9% (2011)

GOVERNMENT

Country name:
conventional long form: Territory of Guam
conventional short form: Guam
local long form: Guahan
local short form: Guahan

Dependency status: organized, unincorporated territory of the US with policy relations between Guam and the US under the jurisdiction of the Office of Insular Affairs, US Department of the Interior

Government type: NA

Capital: *name:* Hagatna (Agana)
geographic coordinates: 13 28 N, 144 44 E
time difference: UTC+10 (15 hours ahead of Washington, DC during Standard Time)

Administrative divisions: none (territory of the US)

Independence: none (territory of the US)

National holiday: Discovery Day, first Monday in March (1521)

Constitution: effective 1 July 1950; amended many times, last in 2012 (2013)

Legal system: common law modeled on US system; US federal laws apply

Suffrage: 18 years of age; universal; note—Guamanians are US citizens but do not vote in US presidential elections

Executive branch: *chief of state:* President Barack H. OBAMA (since 20 January 2009); Vice President Joseph R. BIDEN (since 20 January 2009)
head of government: Governor Eddie CALVO (since 3 January 2011); Lieutenant Governor Ray TENORIO (since 3 January 2011)
cabinet: heads of executive departments; appointed by the governor with the consent of the Guam legislature (For more information visit the World Leaders website)
elections: under the US Constitution, residents of unincorporated territories, such as Guam, do not vote in elections for US president and vice president; however, they may vote in Democratic and Republican presidential primary elections; governor and lieutenant governor elected on the same ticket by popular vote for a four-year term (can serve two consecutive terms, then must wait a full term before running again); election last held on 2 November 2010 (next to be held in November 2014)
election results: Eddie CALVO elected governor with 50.6% percent of vote against 49.4% for Carl GUTIERREZ; Ray TENORIO elected lieutenant governor

Legislative branch: unicameral Legislature (15 seats; members elected by popular vote to serve two-year terms)
elections: last held on 6 November 2012 (next to be held in November 2014)
election results: percent of vote by party—NA; seats by party—Democratic Party 9, Republican Party 6
note: Guam elects one nonvoting delegate to the US House of Representatives; election last held on 6 November 2012 (next to be held in November 2014); results—percent of vote by party—NA; seats by party—Democratic Party 1

Judicial branch: *highest court(s):* Supreme Court of Guam (consists of 3 justices) note—appeals beyond the Supreme Court of Guam are heard by the US Supreme Court
judge selection and term of office: justices appointed by the governor and confirmed by the Guam legislature; justices appointed for life subject to retention election every 10 years
subordinate courts: Superior Court of Guam—includes several divisions; US Federal District Court for the District of Guam (a US territorial court; appeals beyond this court are heard before the US Court of Appeals for the Ninth Circuit)

Political parties and leaders: Democratic Party [Carlo BRANCH]; Republican Party [Mike BENITO]

Political pressure groups and leaders: Guam Commission on Decolonization; Guam Federation of Teachers' Union; Guam Waterworks Authority Workers; We Are Guahan

International organization participation: IOC, PIF (observer), SPC, UPU

Diplomatic representation in the US: none (territory of the US)

Diplomatic representation from the US: none (territory of the US)

Flag description: territorial flag is dark blue with a narrow red border on all four sides; centered is a red-bordered, pointed, vertical ellipse containing a beach scene, a proa or outrigger canoe with sail, and a palm tree with the word GUAM superimposed in bold red letters; the proa is sailing in Agana Bay with the promontory of Punta Dos Amantes, near the capital, in the background; blue represents the sea and red the blood shed in the struggle against oppression
note: the US flag is the national flag

National symbol(s): coconut tree

National anthem: *name:* "Fanohge Chamoru" (Stand Ye Guamanians)
lyrics/music: Ramon Manalisay SABLAN [English], Lagrimas UNTALAN [Chamoru]/Ramon Manalisay SABLAN
note: adopted 1919; the local anthem is also known as "Guam Hymn"; as a territory of the United States, "The Star-Spangled Banner," which generally follows the playing of "Stand Ye Guamanians," is official (see United States)

ECONOMY

Economy—overview: The economy depends largely on US national defense spending, tourism, other services. Total US grants, wages and salaries, and procurement outlays amounted to approximately $1.6 billion in 2010. Over the past 30 years, tourism has grown to become the largest income source following national defense.

GDP (purchasing power parity): $4.6 billion (2010 est.)
country comparison to the world: 173

GDP (official exchange rate): $4.6 billion (2010 est.)

GDP—real growth rate: 1.3% (2002-10 average est.)
country comparison to the world: 163

GDP—per capita (PPP): $28,700 (2010 est.)
country comparison to the world: 53

GDP—composition, by sector of origin:
agriculture: NA%
industry: NA%
services: NA%

Agriculture—products: fruits, copra, vegetables; eggs, pork, poultry, beef

Industries: national defense, tourism, construction, transshipment services, concrete products, printing and publishing, food processing, textiles

Industrial production growth rate: NA%

Labor force: 69,390
country comparison to the world: 185
note: this number is for the civilian labor force only (2010 est.)

Labor force—by occupation: agriculture: 0.3%
industry: (2004 est.)
services: NA% (2004 est.)

Unemployment rate: 8.2% (2010 est.)
country comparison to the world: 93

Population below poverty line: 23% (2001 est.)

Household income or consumption by percentage share: *lowest* 10%: NA%
highest 10%: NA%

Budget: *revenues:* $942.6 million
expenditures: $1.082 billion (FY10/11 est.)

Taxes and other revenues: 20.5% of GDP (FY10/11 est.)
country comparison to the world: 162

Budget surplus (+) or deficit (-):
-3% of GDP (FY10/11 est.)
country comparison to the world: 124

Fiscal year: 1 October—30 September

Inflation rate (consumer prices): 4% (2011 est.)
country comparison to the world: 137

Exports: $44 million (2011 est.)
country comparison to the world: 198

Exports—commodities: transshipments of refined petroleum products, construction materials, fish, food and beverage products

Imports: $901 million (2011 est.)
country comparison to the world: 179

Imports—commodities: petroleum and petroleum products, food, manufactured goods

Debt—external: $NA

Exchange rates: the US dollar is used

ENERGY

Electricity—production: 1.734 billion kWh (2011 est.)
country comparison to the world: 139

Electricity—consumption: 1.635 billion kWh (2010 est.)
country comparison to the world: 144

Electricity—exports: 0 kWh (2012 est.)
country comparison to the world: 144

Electricity—imports: 0 kWh (2012 est.)
country comparison to the world: 151

Electricity—installed generating capacity: 552,000 kW (2010 est.)
country comparison to the world: 134

Electricity—from fossil fuels: 100% of total installed capacity (2010 est.)
country comparison to the world: 16

Electricity—from nuclear fuels: 0% of total installed capacity (2010 est.)
country comparison to the world: 98

Electricity—from hydroelectric plants: 0% of total installed capacity (2010 est.)
country comparison to the world: 174

Electricity—from other renewable sources: 0% of total installed capacity (2010 est.)
country comparison to the world: 180

Crude oil—production: 0 bbl/day (2012 est.)
country comparison to the world: 176

Crude oil—exports: 0 bbl/day (2010 est.)
country comparison to the world: 121

Crude oil—imports: 0 bbl/day (2010 est.)
country comparison to the world: 194

Crude oil—proved reserves: 0 bbl (1 January 2013 es)
country comparison to the world: 139

Refined petroleum products—production: 0 bbl/day (2010 est.)
country comparison to the world: 151

Refined petroleum products—consumption: 14,490 bbl/day (2011 est.)
country comparison to the world: 145

Refined petroleum products—exports: 0 bbl/day (2010 est.)
country comparison to the world: 181

Refined petroleum products—imports: 6,579 bbl/day (2010 est.)
country comparison to the world: 138

Natural gas—production: 0 cu m (2011 est.)
country comparison to the world: 138

Natural gas—consumption: 0 cu m (2010 est.)
country comparison to the world: 151

Natural gas—exports: 0 cu m (2011 est.)
country comparison to the world: 110

Natural gas—imports: 0 cu m (2011 est.)
country comparison to the world: 200

Natural gas—proved reserves: 0 cu m (1 January 2013 es)
country comparison to the world: 145

Carbon dioxide emissions from consumption of energy: 1.103 million Mt (2011 est.)
country comparison to the world: 164

COMMUNICATIONS

Telephones—main lines in use: 67,000 (2012)
country comparison to the world: 157

Telephones—mobile cellular: 98,000 (2004)
country comparison to the world: 193

Telephone system: *general assessment:* modern system, integrated with US facilities for direct dialing, including free use of 800 numbers
domestic: digital system, including mobile-cellular service and local access to the Internet
international: country code—1-671; major landing point for submarine cables between Asia and the US (Guam is a transpacific communications hub for major carriers linking the US and Asia); satellite earth stations—2 Intelsat (Pacific Ocean) (2011)

Broadcast media: about a dozen TV channels, including digital channels; multi-channel cable TV services are available; roughly 20 radio stations (2009)

Internet country code: .gu

Internet hosts: 23 (2012)
country comparison to the world: 219

Internet users: 90,000 (2009)
country comparison to the world: 163

TRANSPORTATION

Airports: 5 (2013)
country comparison to the world: 182

Airports—with paved runways: *total:* 4
over 3,047 m: 2
2,438 to 3,047 m: 1
914 to 1,523 m: 1 (2013)

Airports—with unpaved runways: *total:* 1
under 914 m:
1 (2013)

Roadways: *total:* 1,045 km (2008)
country comparison to the world: 185

Ports and terminals: *major seaport(s):* Apra Harbor

MILITARY

Manpower fit for military service:
males age 16-49: 38,358
females age 16-49: 36,869 (2010 est.)

Manpower reaching militarily significant age annually: *male:* 1,701
female: 1,608 (2010 est.)

Military—note: defense is the responsibility of the US

TRANSNATIONAL ISSUES

Disputes—international: none

GUATEMALA

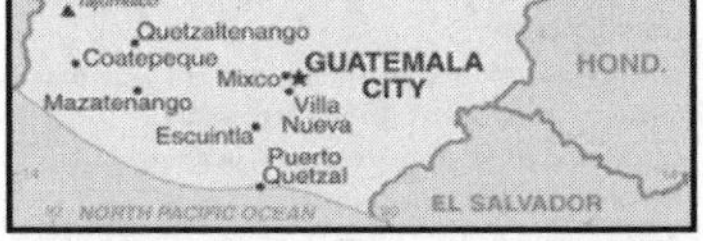

INTRODUCTION

Background: The Maya civilization flourished in Guatemala and surrounding regions during the first millennium A.D. After almost three centuries as a Spanish colony, Guatemala won its independence in 1821. During the second half of the 20th century, it experienced a variety of military and civilian governments, as well as a 36-year guerrilla war. In 1996, the government signed a peace agreement formally ending the conflict, which had left more than 200,000 people dead and had created, by some estimates, about 1 million refugees.

GEOGRAPHY

Location: Central America, bordering the North Pacific Ocean, between El Salvador and Mexico, and bordering the Gulf of Honduras (Caribbean Sea) between Honduras and Belize

Geographic coordinates: 15 30 N, 90 15 W

Map references: Central America and the Caribbean

Area: *total:* 108,889 sq km
country comparison to the world: 107
land: 107,159 sq km
water: 1,730 sq km

Area—comparative: slightly smaller than Pennsylvania

Land boundaries: *total:* 1,687 km
border countries: Belize 266 km, El Salvador 203 km, Honduras 256 km, Mexico 962 km

Coastline: 400 km

Maritime claims: territorial sea: 12 nm
exclusive economic zone: 200 nm
continental shelf: 200 m depth or to the depth of exploitation

Climate: tropical; hot, humid in lowlands; cooler in highlands

Terrain: mostly mountains with narrow coastal plains and rolling limestone plateau

Elevation extremes: *lowest point:* Pacific Ocean 0 m
highest point: Volcan Tajumulco 4,211 m
note: highest point in Central America

Natural resources: petroleum, nickel, rare woods, fish, chicle, hydropower

Land use: *arable land:* 13.78%
permanent crops: 8.68%
other: 77.55% (2011)

Irrigated land: 3,121 sq km (2003)

Total renewable water resources: 111.3 cu km (2011)

Freshwater withdrawal (domestic/industrial/agricultural): *total:* 3.46 cu km/yr (15%/31%/54%)
per capita: 259.1 cu m/yr (2006)

Natural hazards: numerous volcanoes in mountains, with occasional violent earthquakes; Caribbean coast extremely susceptible to hurricanes and other tropical storms
volcanism: significant volcanic activity in the Sierra Madre range; Santa Maria (elev. 3,772 m) has been deemed a Decade Volcano by the International Association of Volcanology and Chemistry of the Earth's Interior, worthy of study due to its explosive history and close proximity to human populations; Pacaya (elev. 2,552 m), which erupted in May 2010 causing an ashfall on

Guatemala City and prompting evacuations, is one of the country's most active volcanoes with frequent eruptions since 1965; other historically active volcanoes include Acatenango, Almolonga, Atitlan, Fuego, and Tacana

Environment—current issues: deforestation in the Peten rainforest; soil erosion; water pollution

Environment—international agreements:
party to: Antarctic Treaty, Biodiversity, Climate Change, Climate Change-Kyoto Protocol, Desertification, Endangered Species, Environmental Modification, Hazardous Wastes, Law of the Sea, Marine Dumping, Ozone Layer Protection, Ship Pollution, Wetlands, Whaling
signed, but not ratified: none of the selected agreements

Geography—note: no natural harbors on west coast

PEOPLE AND SOCIETY

Nationality: *noun:* Guatemalan(s)
adjective: Guatemalan

Ethnic groups: Mestizo (mixed Amerindian-Spanish—in local Spanish called Ladino) and European 59.4%, K'iche 9.1%, Kaqchikel 8.4%, Mam 7.9%, Q'eqchi 6.3%, other Mayan 8.6%, indigenous non-Mayan 0.2%, other 0.1% (2001 census)

Languages: Spanish (official) 60%, Amerindian languages 40%
note: there are 23 officially recognized Amerindian languages, including Quiche, Cakchiquel, Kekchi, Mam, Garifuna, and Xinca

Religions: Roman Catholic, Protestant, indigenous Mayan beliefs

Demographic profile: Guatemala is a predominantly poor country that struggles in several areas of health and development, including infant, child, and maternal mortality, malnutrition, literacy, and contraceptive awareness and use. The large indigenous population is disproportionately affected. Guatemala is the most populous country in Central America and has the highest fertility rate in Latin America. It also has the highest population growth rate in Latin America, which is likely to continue in the long term because of its large reproductive-age population and high birth rate. Almost half of Guatemala's population is under age 19, making it the youngest population in Latin America. Guatemala's total fertility rate has slowly declined during the last few decades due in part to limited government-funded health programs. However, the birth rate is still more than three children per woman and is markedly higher among its rural and indigenous populations. Guatemalans have a history of emigrating legally and illegally to Mexico, the United States, and Canada because of a lack of economic opportunity, political instability, and natural disasters. Emigration, primarily to the United States, escalated during the 1960-1996 civil war and accelerated after a peace agreement was signed. Thousands of Guatemalans who fled to Mexico returned after the war, but labor migration to southern Mexico continues.

Population: 14,647,083 (July 2014 est.)
country comparison to the world: 70

Age structure:
0-14 years: 36.2% (male 2,698,238/female 2,597,026)
15-24 years: 22.1% (male 1,625,139/female 1,615,543)
25-54 years: 32.4% (male 2,251,665/female 2,487,332)
55-64 years: 4.2% (male 362,686/female 393,273)
65 years and over: 4.1% (male 286,041/female 330,140) (2014 est.)

Dependency ratios:
total dependency ratio: 81.8 %
youth dependency ratio: 73.5 %
elderly dependency ratio: 8.3 %
potential support ratio: 12.1 (2013)

Median age: *total:* 21 years
male: 20.4 years
female: 21.7 years (2014 est.)

Population growth rate: 1.86% (2014 est.)
country comparison to the world: 63

Birth rate: 25.46 births/1,000 population (2014 est.)
country comparison to the world: 52

Death rate: 4.82 deaths/1,000 population (2014 est.)
country comparison to the world: 195

Net migration rate: -2 migrant(s)/1,000 population (2014 est.)
country comparison to the world: 166

Urbanization: *urban population:* 49% of total population (2010)
rate of urbanization: 3.4% annual rate of change (2010-15 est.)

Major urban areas—population: GUATEMALA CITY (capital) 1.075 million (2009)

Sex ratio: *at birth:* 1.05 male(s)/female
0-14 years: 1.04 male(s)/female
15-24 years: 1.01 male(s)/female
25-54 years: 0.91 male(s)/female
55-64 years: 0.97 male(s)/female
65 years and over: 0.87 male(s)/female
total population: 0.97 male(s)/female (2014 est.)

Mother's mean age at first birth: 20.3
note: median age at first birth among women 25-29 (2009 est.)

Maternal mortality rate: 120 deaths/100,000 live births (2010)
country comparison to the world: 64

Infant mortality rate: *total:* 23.51 deaths/1,000 live births
country comparison to the world: 77
male: 25.57 deaths/1,000 live births
female: 21.35 deaths/1,000 live births (2014 est.)

Life expectancy at birth: *total population:* 71.74 years
country comparison to the world: 143
male: 69.82 years
female: 73.76 years (2014 est.)

Total fertility rate: 2.99 children born/woman (2014 est.)
country comparison to the world: 56

Contraceptive prevalence rate: 43.3% (2002)

Health expenditures: 6.7% of GDP (2011)
country comparison to the world: 92

Physicians density: 0.93 physicians/1,000 population (2009)

Hospital bed density: 0.7 beds/1,000 population (2011)

Drinking water source:
improved:
urban: 99.1% of population
rural: 88.6% of population
total: 93.8% of population
unimproved:
urban: 0.9% of population
rural: 11.4% of population
total: 6.2% of population (2011 est.)

Sanitation facility access:
improved:
urban: 88.4% of population
rural: 72.1% of population
total: 80.2% of population
unimproved:
urban: 11.6% of population
rural: 27.9% of population
total: 19.8% of population (2011 est.)

HIV/AIDS—adult prevalence rate: 0.7% (2012 est.)
country comparison to the world: 56

HIV/AIDS—people living with HIV/AIDS: 57,800 (2012 est.)
country comparison to the world: 58

HIV/AIDS—deaths: 3,400 (2012 est.)
country comparison to the world: 50

Major infectious diseases: *degree of risk:* high
food or waterborne diseases: bacterial diarrhea, hepatitis A, and typhoid fever
vectorborne disease: dengue fever and malaria (2013)

Obesity—adult prevalence rate: 19.2% (2008)
country comparison to the world: 100

Children under the age of 5 years underweight: 13% (2009)
country comparison to the world: 57

Education expenditures: 3% of GDP (2012)
country comparison to the world: 139

Literacy: *definition:* age 15 and over can read and write
total population: 75.9%
male: 81.2%
female: 71.1% (2011 est.)

School life expectancy (primary to tertiary education): *total:* 11 years
male: 11 years
female: 10 years (2007)

Child labor—children ages 5-14: *total number:* 929,852
percentage: 21 %
note: data represents children ages 5-17 (2006 est.)

Unemployment, youth ages 15-24: *total:* 7.5%
country comparison to the world: 126
male: 4.5%
female: 13.6% (2011)

GOVERNMENT

Country name:
conventional long form: Republic of Guatemala
conventional short form: Guatemala
local long form: Republica de Guatemala
local short form: Guatemala

Government type: constitutional democratic republic

Capital: *name:* Guatemala City
geographic coordinates: 14 37 N, 90 31 W
time difference: UTC-6 (1 hour behind Washington, DC during Standard Time)

Administrative divisions: 22 departments (departamentos, singular—departamento); Alta Verapaz, Baja Verapaz, Chimaltenango, Chiquimula, El Progreso, Escuintla, Guatemala, Huehuetenango, Izabal, Jalapa, Jutiapa, Peten, Quetzaltenango, Quiche, Retalhuleu, Sacatepequez, San Marcos, Santa Rosa, Solola, Suchitepequez, Totonicapan, Zacapa

Independence: 15 September 1821 (from Spain)

National holiday: Independence Day, 15 September (1821)

Constitution: several previous; latest adopted 31 May 1985, effective 14 January 1986; suspended, reinstated, and amended in 1993 (2013)

Legal system: civil law system; judicial review of legislative acts

International law organization participation: has not submitted an ICJ jurisdiction declaration; the Congress ratified Statute of Rome on 18 January 2012, and ICCt jurisdiction entered into force on 23 February 2012

Suffrage: 18 years of age; universal; note—active duty members of the armed forces and police may not vote by law and are restricted to their barracks on election day

Executive branch: *chief of state:* President Otto Fernando PEREZ MOLINA (since 14 January 2012); Vice President Ingrid Roxana BALDETTI Elias (since 14 January 2012); note—the president is both the chief of state and head of government
head of government: President Otto Fernando PEREZ MOLINA (since 14 January 2012); Vice President Ingrid Roxana BALDETTI Elias (since 14 January 2012)
cabinet: Council of Ministers appointed by the president (For more information visit the World Leaders website)
elections: president and vice president elected on the same ticket by popular vote for a four-year term (may not serve consecutive terms); election last held on 11 September 2011; runoff held on 6 November 2011 (next to be held in September 2015)
election results: Otto Fernando PEREZ MOLINA elected president in a runoff election; percent of vote—Otto Fernando PEREZ MOLINA 53.7%, Manuel BALDIZON 46.3%

Legislative branch: unicameral Congress of the Republic or Congreso de la Republica (158 seats; members elected through a party list proportional *representation system)*
elections: last held on 11 September 2011 (next to be held in September 2015)
election results: percent of vote by party—PP 26.62%, UNE-GANA 22.67%, UNC 9.50%, LIDER 8.87%, CREO 8.67%, VIVA-EG 7.87%, Winaq-URNG-ANN 3.23%, PAN 3.12%, FRG 2.74%, PU 2.70%, other 3.59%; seats by party—PP 57, UNE-GANA 48, LIDER 14, UCN 14, CREO 12, VIVA-EG 6, PAN 2, Winaq-URNG-ANN 2, FRG 1, PU 1, Victoria 1; note—changes in party affiliation now reflect the following
seat distribution: as of 15 January 2014—PP 55, LIDER 39, TODOS 18, independents 10, CREO 8, UNE 8, GANA 6, EG 3, PU 2, PRI (formerly FRG) 2, PAN 1, UCN 1, URNG 2, Victoria 1, VIVA 1, Winaq 1

Judicial branch: *highest court(s):* Supreme Court of Justice or Corte Suprema de Justicia (consists of 13 magistrates including the court president and organized into several chambers); note—the court president also supervises trial judges countrywide; Constitutional Court or Corte de Constitcionalidad (consists of 5 judges and 5 alternates)
judge selection and term of office: Supreme Court magistrates elected by the Congress of the Republic from candidates proposed by the Postulation Committee, an independent body of deans of the country's university law schools, representatives of the country's law associations, and representatives of the Court of Appeal and other tribunals; magistrates elected for renewable 5-year terms; Constitutional Court judges—1 elected by the Congress of the Republic, 1 by the Supreme Court president, 1 by the president of the republic, 1 by the University of San Carlos, and one by the BAR association; judges elected for concurrent 5-year terms; the presidency of the court rotates among the magistrates for a single 1-year term
subordinate courts: numerous first instance and appellate courts

Political parties and leaders: Commitment, Renewal, and Order or CREO [Roberto GONZALEZ Diaz-Duran]; Democratic Union or UD [Edwin Armando MARTINEZ Herrera]; Encounter for Guatemala or EG [Nineth MONTENEGRO Cottom]; Everyone Together for Guatemala or TODOS [Felipe ALEJOS]; Grand National Alliance or GANA [Jaime Antonio MARTINEZ Lohayza]; Guatemalan National Revolutionary Unity or URNG [Angel SANCHEZ Viesca]; Guatemalan Republican Front or FRG [Luis Fernando PEREZ]; Institutional Republican Party (formerly the Guatemalan Republican Front) or PRI [Zury RIOS Montt]; National Advancement Party or PAN [Juan GUTIERREZ Strauss]; National Unity for Hope or UNE [Sandra TORRES]; Nationalist Change Union or UCN [Mario ESTRADA]; New National Alternative or ANN [Pablo MONSANTO]; Patriot Party or PP [Ingrid Roxana BALDETTI Elias]; Renewed Democratic Liberty or LIDER [Manuel BALDIZON]; Unionista Party or PU [Alvaro ARZU Irigoyen]; Victoria (Victory) [Amilcar RIVERA]; Vision with Values or VIVA [Harold CABALLEROS] (part of a coalition with EG during the last legislative election); Winaq [Rigoberta MENCHU]

Political pressure groups and leaders: Alliance Against Impunity or AI (which includes among others Center for Legal Action on Human Rights (CALDH), and Family and; Friends of the Disappeared of Guatemala (FAMDEGUA)); Committee for Campesino Unity or CUC; Coordinating Committee of Agricultural, Commercial, Industrial, and Financial Associations or CACIF (which includes among others; the Agrarian Chamber (CAMAGRO) and the Industry Chamber of Guatemala (CIG)); Guatemalan Chamber of Commerce (Camara de Comercio); International Commission Against Impunity in Guatemala or CICIG; Mutual Support Group or GAM; Movimiento PRO-Justicia; National Union of Agriculture Workers or UNAGRO

International organization participation: BCIE, CACM, CD, CELAC, EITI (candidate country), FAO, G-24, G-77, IADB, IAEA, IBRD, ICAO, ICC (national committees), ICRM, IDA, IFAD, IFC, IFRCS, IHO, ILO, IMF, IMO, Interpol, IOC, IOM, IPU, ISO (correspondent), ITSO, ITU, ITUC (NGOs), LAES, LAIA (observer), MIGA, MINUSTAH, MONUSCO, NAM, OAS, OPANAL, OPCW, PCA, Petrocaribe, SICA, UN, UNAMID, UNCTAD, UNESCO, UNIDO, UNIFIL, Union Latina, UNISFA, UNITAR, UNMISS, UNOCI, UNWTO, UPU, WCO, WFTU (NGOs), WHO, WIPO, WMO, WTO

Diplomatic representation in the US:
chief of mission: Ambassador Jose Julio Alejandro LIGORRIA Carballido (since 5 September 2013)
chancery: 2220 R Street NW, Washington, DC 20008
telephone: [1] (202) 745-4952
FAX: [1] (202) 745-1908
consulate(s) general: Atlanta, Chicago, Denver, Houston, McAllen (TX), Miami, New York, Phoenix, San Francisco

Diplomatic representation from the US:
chief of mission: Ambassador Arnold A. CHACON (since 29 August 2011)
embassy: 7-01 Avenida Reforma, Zone 10, Guatemala City
mailing address: DPO AA 34024
telephone: [502] 2326-4000
FAX: [502] 2326-4654

Flag description: three equal vertical bands of light blue (hoist side), white, and light blue, with the coat of arms centered in the white band; the coat of arms includes a green and red quetzal (the national bird) representing liberty and a scroll bearing the inscription LIBERTAD 15 DE SEPTIEMBRE DE 1821 (the original date of independence from Spain) all superimposed on a pair of crossed rifles signifying Guatemala's willingness to defend itself and a pair of crossed swords representing honor and framed by a laurel wreath symbolizing victory; the blue bands stand for the Pacific Ocean and the Caribbean Sea and the sea and sky; the white band denotes peace and purity

National symbol(s): quetzal (bird)

National anthem: *name:* "Himno Nacional de Guatemala" (National Anthem of Guatemala)
lyrics/music: Jose Joaquin PALMA/Rafael Alvarez OVALLE
note: adopted 1897, modified lyrics adopted 1934; Cuban poet Jose Joaquin PALMA anonymously submitted lyrics to a public contest calling for a national anthem; his authorship was not discovered until 1911

ECONOMY

Economy—overview: Guatemala is the most populous country in Central America with a GDP per capita roughly one-half that of the average for Latin America and the Caribbean. The agricultural sector accounts for 13.5% of GDP and 38% of the labor force; key agricultural exports include coffee, sugar, bananas, and vegetables. The 1996 peace accords, which ended 36 years of civil war, removed a major obstacle to foreign investment, and since then Guatemala has pursued important reforms and macroeconomic stabilization. The Dominican Republic-Central American Free Trade Agreement (CAFTA-DR) entered into force in July 2006 spurring increased investment and diversification of exports, with the largest increases in ethanol and non-traditional agricultural exports. While CAFTA-DR has helped improve the investment climate, concerns over security, the lack of skilled workers and poor infrastructure continue to hamper foreign direct investment. The distribution of income remains highly unequal with the richest 20% of the population accounting for more than 51% of Guatemala's overall consumption. More than half of the population is below the national poverty line and 13% of the population lives in extreme poverty. Poverty among indigenous groups, which make up about 40% of the population, averages 73% and extreme poverty rises to 28%. Nearly one-half of Guatemala's children under age five are chronically malnourished, one of the highest malnutrition rates in the world. Given Guatemala's large expatriate community in the United States, it is the top remittance recipient in Central America, with inflows serving as a primary source of foreign income equivalent to nearly two-fifths of exports or one-tenth of GDP.

GDP (purchasing power parity): $81.51 billion (2013 est.)
country comparison to the world: 80
$78.91 billion (2012 est.)
$76.64 billion (2011 est.)
note: data are in 2013 US dollars

GDP (official exchange rate): $53.9 billion (2013 est.)

GDP—real growth rate: 3.3% (2013 est.)
country comparison to the world: 105
3% (2012 est.)
4.2% (2011 est.)

GDP—per capita (PPP): $5,300 (2013 est.)
country comparison to the world: 157
$5,200 (2012 est.)
$5,200 (2011 est.)
note: data are in 2013 US dollars

GDP—composition, by end use:
household consumption: 84.5%
government consumption: 11%
investment in fixed capital: 14.1%
investment in inventories: 0.7%
exports of goods and services: 25.1%
imports of goods and services: -35.3% (2013 est.)

GDP—composition, by sector of origin:
agriculture: 13.5%
industry: 23.8%
services: 62.7% (2013 est.)

Agriculture—products: sugarcane, corn, bananas, coffee, beans, cardamom; cattle, sheep, pigs, chickens

Industries: sugar, textiles and clothing, furniture, chemicals, petroleum, metals, rubber, tourism

Industrial production growth rate: 3.7% (2013 est.)
country comparison to the world: 79

Labor force: 4.465 million (2013 est.)
country comparison to the world: 85

Labor force—by occupation: *agriculture:* 38%
industry: 14%
services: 48% (2011 est.)

Unemployment rate: 4.1% (2011 est.)
country comparison to the world: 33
3.5% (2010 est.)

Population below poverty line: 54% (2011 est.)

Household income or consumption by percentage share: *lowest 10%:* 1.3%
highest 10%: 42.4% (2006)

Distribution of family income—Gini index:
55.1 (2007)
country comparison to the world: 10
55.8 (1998)

Budget: *revenues:* $6.411 billion
expenditures: $7.851 billion (2013 est.)

Taxes and other revenues: 11.9% of GDP (2013 est.)
country comparison to the world: 203

Budget surplus (+) or deficit (-):
-2.7% of GDP (2013 est.)
country comparison to the world: 112

Public debt: 31% of GDP (2013 est.)
country comparison to the world: 117
29.5% of GDP (2012 est.)

Fiscal year: calendar year

Inflation rate (consumer prices): 4.4% (2013 est.)
country comparison to the world: 144
3.8% (2012 est.)

Central bank discount rate: 6.5% (31 December 2010 est.)

Commercial bank prime lending rate: 13.4% (31 December 2013 est.)
country comparison to the world: 56
13.49% (31 December 2012 est.)

Stock of narrow money: $8.461 billion (31 December 2013 est.)
country comparison to the world: 85
$7.975 billion (31 December 2012 est.)

Stock of broad money: $23.83 billion (31 December 2013 est.)
country comparison to the world: 80
$22.3 billion (31 December 2012 est.)

Stock of domestic credit: $22.6 billion (31 December 2013 est.)
country comparison to the world: 79
$20.5 billion (31 December 2012 est.)

Market value of publicly traded shares: $NA

Current account balance: -$1.822 billion (2013 est.)
country comparison to the world: 139
-$1.489 billion (2012 est.)

Exports: $10.29 billion (2013 est.)
country comparison to the world: 94
$10.11 billion (2012 est.)

Exports—commodities: coffee, sugar, petroleum, apparel, bananas, fruits and vegetables, cardamom

Exports—partners: US 40.2%, El Salvador 11.1%, Honduras 8%, Mexico 5.5%, Nicaragua 4.7%, Costa Rica 4.3% (2012)

Imports: $16.7 billion (2013 est.)
country comparison to the world: 84
$15.84 billion (2012 est.)

Imports—commodities: fuels, machinery and transport equipment, construction materials, grain, fertilizers, electricity, mineral products, chemical products, plastic materials and products

Imports—partners: US 38%, Mexico 11.3%, China 7.4%, El Salvador 4.6% (2012)

Reserves of foreign exchange and gold:
$7.118 billion (31 December 2013 est.)
country comparison to the world: 84
$6.694 billion (31 December 2012 est.)

Debt—external: $17.67 billion (31 December 2013 est.)
country comparison to the world: 83
$16.61 billion (31 December 2012 est.)

Exchange rates: quetzales (GTQ) per US dollar—
7.883 (2013 est.)
7.8336 (2012 est.)
8.0578 (2010 est.)
8.1616 (2009)
7.5895 (2008)

ENERGY

Electricity—production: 8.146 billion kWh (2011 est.)
country comparison to the world: 9 8

Electricity—consumption: 8.161 billion kWh (2011 est.)
country comparison to the world: 93

Electricity—exports: 193.3 million kWh (2011 est.)
country comparison to the world: 70

Electricity—imports: 525.6 million kWh (2011 est.)
country comparison to the world: 78

Electricity—installed generating capacity:
2.745 million kW (2010 est.)
country comparison to the world: 91

Electricity—from fossil fuels:
56.5% of total installed capacity (2010 est.)
country comparison to the world: 141

Electricity—from nuclear fuels:
0% of total installed capacity (2010 est.)
country comparison to the world: 100

Electricity—from hydroelectric plants:
31.1% of total installed capacity (2010 est.)
country comparison to the world: 75

Electricity—from other renewable sources:
12.4% of total installed capacity (2010 est.)
country comparison to the world: 20

Crude oil—production: 14,020 bbl/day (2012 est.)
country comparison to the world: 84

Crude oil—exports: 10,960 bbl/day (2010 est.)
country comparison to the world: 57

Crude oil—imports: 0 bbl/day (2010 est.)
country comparison to the world: 195

Crude oil—proved reserves: 83.07 million bbl (1 January 2013 es)
country comparison to the world: 73

Refined petroleum products—production:
1,253 bbl/day (2010 est.)
country comparison to the world: 110

Refined petroleum products—consumption:
80,810 bbl/day (2011 est.)
country comparison to the world: 84

Refined petroleum products—exports:
4,911 bbl/day (2010 est.)
country comparison to the world: 91

Refined petroleum products—imports:
71,390 bbl/day (2010 est.)
country comparison to the world: 59

Natural gas—production: 0 cu m (2011 est.)
country comparison to the world: 139

Natural gas—consumption: 0 cu m (2010 est.)
country comparison to the world: 152

Natural gas—exports: 0 cu m (2011 est.)
country comparison to the world: 112

Natural gas—imports: 0 cu m (2011 est.)
country comparison to the world: 201

Natural gas—proved reserves: 2.96 billion cu m (1 January 2006 es)
country comparison to the world: 96

Carbon dioxide emissions from consumption of energy: 11.71 million Mt (2011 est.)
country comparison to the world: 99

COMMUNICATIONS

Telephones—main lines in use: 1.744 million (2012)
country comparison to the world: 6 3

Telephones—mobile cellular: 20.787 million (2012)
country comparison to the world: 46

Telephone system: *general assessment:* fairly modern network centered in the city of Guatemala

domestic: state-owned telecommunications company privatized in the late 1990s opening the way for competition; fixed-line teledensity roughly 10 per 100 persons; fixed-line investments are being concentrated on improving rural connectivity; mobile-cellular teledensity approaching 150 per 100 persons
international: country code—502; landing point for both the Americas Region Caribbean Ring System (ARCOS-1) and the SAM-1 fiber optic submarine cable system that together provide connectivity to South and Central America, parts of the Caribbean, and the US; connected to Central American Microwave System; satellite earth station—1 Intelsat (Atlantic Ocean) (2011)

Broadcast media: 4 privately owned national terrestrial TV channels dominate TV broadcasting; multi-channel satellite and cable services are available; 1 government-owned radio station and hundreds of privately owned radio stations (2007)

Internet country code: .gt

Internet hosts: 357,552 (2012)
country comparison to the world: 60

Internet users: 2.279 million (2009)
country comparison to the world: 72

TRANSPORTATION

Airports: 291 (2013)
country comparison to the world: 2 3

Airports—with paved runways: *total:* 1 6
2,438 to 3,047 m: 2
1,524 to 2,437 m: 4
914 to 1,523 m: 6
under 914 m: 4 (2013)

Airports—with unpaved runways: *total:* 275
2,438 to 3,047 m: 1
1,524 to 2,437 m: 2
914 to 1,523 m: 77
under 914 m: 195 (2013)

Heliports: 1 (2013)

Pipelines: oil 480 km (2013)

Railways: *total:* 332 km
country comparison to the world: 118
narrow gauge: 332 km 0.914-m gauge (2008)

Roadways: *total:* 11,501 km
country comparison to the world: 130
paved: 6,797 km (includes 127 km of expressways)
unpaved: 4,704 km (2010)

Waterways: 990 km (260 km navigable year round; additional 730 km navigable during high-water season) (2012)
country comparison to the world: 66

Ports and terminals: major seaport(s): Puerto Quetzal, Santo Tomas de Castilla

MILITARY

Military branches: National Army of Guatemala (Ejercito Nacional de Guatemala, ENG; includes Guatemalan Navy (Fuerza de Mar, including Marines), Guatemalan Air Force (Fuerza Aerea Guatemalteca, FAG)) (2013)

Military service age and obligation: all male citizens between the ages of 18 and 50 are liable for military service; in practice, a selective draft system is employed, with only a small portion of 17-21 year-olds conscripted; conscript service obligation varies from 1 to 2 years; women can serve as officers (2013)

Manpower available for military service:
males age 16-49: 3,165,870
females age 16-49: 3,371,217 (2010 est.)

Manpower fit for military service:
males age 16-49: 2,590,843
females age 16-49: 2,926,544 (2010 est.)

Manpower reaching militarily significant age annually: *male:* 171,092
female: 168,151 (2010 est.)

Military expenditures: 0.42% of GDP (2012)
country comparison to the world: 127
0.41% of GDP (2011)
0.42% of GDP (2010)

TRANSNATIONAL ISSUES

Disputes—international: annual ministerial meetings under the Organization of American States-initiated Agreement on the Framework for Negotiations and Confidence Building Measures continue to address Guatemalan land and maritime claims in Belize and the Caribbean Sea; Guatemala persists in its territorial claim to half of Belize, but agrees to Line of Adjacency to keep Guatemalan squatters out of Belize's forested interior; both countries agreed in April 2012 to hold simultaneous referenda, scheduled for 6 October 2013, to decide whether to refer the dispute to the ICJ for binding resolution; Mexico must deal with thousands of impoverished Guatemalans and other Central Americans who cross the porous border looking for work in Mexico and the United States
Refugees and internally displaced persons:
IDPs: undetermined (more than three decades of internal conflict that ended in 1996 displaced mainly the indigenous Maya population and rural peasants; ongoing drug cartel and gang violence) (2011)

Illicit drugs: major transit country for cocaine and heroin; in 2005, cultivated 100 hectares of opium poppy after reemerging as a potential source of opium in 2004; potential production of less than 1 metric ton of pure heroin; marijuana cultivation for mostly domestic consumption; proximity to Mexico makes Guatemala a major staging area for drugs (particularly for cocaine); money laundering is a serious problem; corruption is a major problem

GUERNSEY

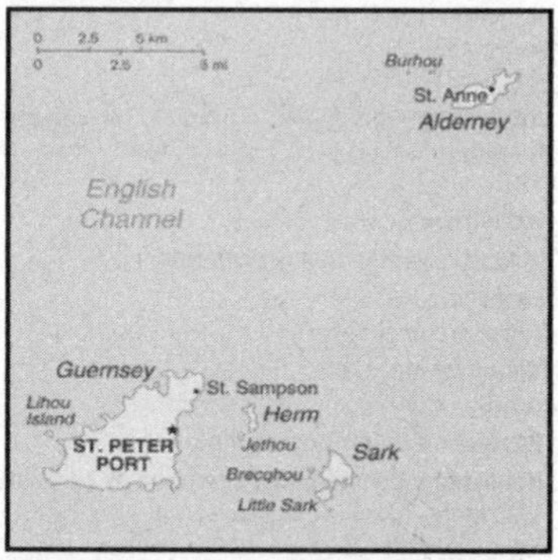

INTRODUCTION

Background: Guernsey and the other Channel Islands represent the last remnants of the medieval Dukedom of Normandy, which held sway in both France and England. The islands were the only British soil occupied by German troops in World War II. Guernsey is a British crown dependency but is not part of the UK or of the European Union. However, the UK Government is constitutionally responsible for its defense and international representation.

GEOGRAPHY

Location: Western Europe, islands in the English Channel, northwest of France

Geographic coordinates: 49 28 N, 2 35 W

Map references: Europe

Area: *total:* 78 sq km
country comparison to the world: 228
land: 78 sq km
water: 0 sq km
note: includes Alderney, Guernsey, Herm, Sark, and some other smaller islands

Area—comparative: about one-half the size of Washington, DC

Land boundaries: 0 km

Coastline: 50 km

Maritime claims: territorial sea: 3 nm
exclusive fishing zone: 12 nm

Climate: temperate with mild winters and cool summers; about 50% of days are overcast

Terrain: mostly level with low hills in southwest

Elevation extremes: lowest point: Atlantic Ocean 0 m
highest point: unnamed elevation on Sark 114 m

Natural resources: cropland

Land use: *arable land:* NA
permanent crops: NA
other: NA

Irrigated land: NA

Natural hazards: NA

Environment—current issues: NA

Geography—note: large, deepwater harbor at Saint Peter Port

PEOPLE AND SOCIETY

Nationality: *noun:* Channel Islander(s)
adjective: Channel Islander

Ethnic groups: British and Norman-French descent with small percentages from other European countries

Languages: English, French, Norman-French dialect spoken in country districts

Religions: Protestant (Anglican, Presbyterian, Baptist, Congregational, Methodist), Roman Catholic

Population: 65,849 (July 2014 est.)
country comparison to the world: 205

Age structure:
0-14 years: 14.6% (male 4,967/female 4,629)
15-24 years: 11.9% (male 3,993/female 3,854)
25-54 years: 42.2% (male 13,991/female 13,800)
55-64 years: 18.4% (male 4,229/female 4,249)
65 years and over: 17.9% (male 5,469/female 6,668) (2014 est.)

Dependency ratios:
total dependency ratio: 46 %
youth dependency ratio: 21.8 %
elderly dependency ratio: 24.2 %
potential support ratio: 4.1
note: data represents the Channel Islands (2013)

Median age: *total:* 43.1 years
male: 41.9 years
female: 44.2 years (2014 est.)

Population growth rate: 0.36% (2014 est.)
country comparison to the world: 164

Birth rate: 9.89 births/1,000 population (2014 est.)
country comparison to the world: 196

Death rate: 8.69 deaths/1,000 population (2014 est.)
country comparison to the world: 74

Net migration rate: 2.4 migrant(s)/1,000 population (2014 est.)
country comparison to the world: 41

Urbanization: *urban population:* 31% of total population (2010)
rate of urbanization: 0.8% annual rate of change (2010-15 est.)

Sex ratio: *at birth:* 1.05 male(s)/female
0-14 years: 1.07 male(s)/female
15-24 years: 1.04 male(s)/female
25-54 years: 1.01 male(s)/female
55-64 years: 0.98 male(s)/female
65 years and over: 0.81 male(s)/female
total population: 0.98 male(s)/female (2014 est.)

Infant mortality rate: total: 3.47 deaths/1,000 live births
country comparison to the world: 208
male: 3.77 deaths/1,000 live births
female: 3.15 deaths/1,000 live births (2014 est.)

Life expectancy at birth: *total population:* 82.39 years
country comparison to the world: 9
male: 79.72 years
female: 85.2 years (2014 est.)

Total fertility rate: 1.55 children born/woman (2014 est.)
country comparison to the world: 186

HIV/AIDS—adult prevalence rate: NA

HIV/AIDS—people living with HIV/AIDS: NA

HIV/AIDS—deaths: NA

Literacy: NA

GOVERNMENT

Country name:
conventional long form: Bailiwick of Guernsey
conventional short form: Guernsey
Dependency status:
British crown dependency

Government type: parliamentary democracy

Capital: *name:* Saint Peter Port
geographic coordinates: 49 27 N, 2 32 W
time difference: UTC 0 (5 hours ahead of Washington, DC during Standard Time)
daylight saving time: +1hr, begins last Sunday in March; ends last Sunday in October

Administrative divisions: none (British crown dependency); there are no first-order administrative divisions as defined by the US Government, but there are 10 parishes: Castel, Forest, Saint Andrew, Saint Martin, Saint Peter Port, Saint Pierre du Bois, Saint Sampson, Saint Saviour, Torteval, Vale

Independence: none (British crown dependency)

National holiday: Liberation Day, 9 May (1945)

Constitution: unwritten; includes royal charters, statutes, and common law and practice

Legal system: customary legal system based on Norman customary law, and includes elements of the French Civil Code and English common law

Suffrage: 16 years of age; universal

Executive branch: *chief of state:* Queen ELIZABETH II (since 6 February 1952), represented by Lieutenant Governor Air Marshall Peter WALKER (since 15 April 2011)
head of government: Chief Minister Jonathan LE TOCQ (since 12 March 2014); Bailiff Richard COLLAS (since 23 March 2012) Chief Minister Peter HARWOOD resigned 25 February 2014
cabinet: Policy Council elected by the States of Deliberation (For more information visit the World Leaders website)
elections: the monarchy is hereditary; lieutenant governor and bailiff appointed by the monarch; chief minister elected by States of Deliberation
election results: Peter HARWOOD elected chief minister, percent of vote NA

Legislative branch: unicameral States of Deliberation (45 seats; members elected by popular vote to serve four-year terms; note—there are also 10 Douzaine representatives—one from each parish, 2 representatives from Alderney and the appointed attorney general and soliciter general); note—Alderney and Sark have parliaments
elections: last held on 18 April 2012 (next to be held in 2016)
election results: percent of vote—NA; seats—all independents

Judicial branch: *highest court(s):* Guernsey Court of Appeal (consists of the Bailiff of Guernsey, who is the ex-officio president of the Guernsey Court of Appeal, and at least 12 judges); Royal Court (organized into 3 divisions—Full Court sits with 1 judge and 7 to 12 jurats acting as judges of fact, Ordinary Court sits with 1 judge and normally 3 jurats, and Matrimonial Causes Division sits with a 1 judge and 4 jurats); note—appeals beyond Guernsey courts are heard by the Judicial Committee of the Privy Council (in London)
judge selection and term of office: Royal Court Balliff, Deputy Balliff and Court of Appeal justices appointed by the British Crown and hold office at Her Majesty's pleasure; jurats elected by the States of Election, a body chaired by the Balliff and a number of jurats
subordinate courts: Court of Alderney; Court of the Seneschal of Sark; Magistrate's Court (includes Juvenile Court); Contracts Court; Ecclesiastical Court; Court of Chief Pleas

Political parties and leaders: none; all independents

Political pressure groups and leaders: Stop Traffic Endangering Pedestrian Safety or STEPS No More Masts [Colin FALLAIZE]

International organization participation: UPU

Diplomatic representation in the US: none (British crown dependency)

Diplomatic representation from the US: none (British crown dependency)

Flag description: white with the red cross of Saint George (patron saint of England) extending to the edges of the flag and a yellow equal-armed cross of William the Conqueror superimposed on the Saint George cross; the red cross represents the old ties with England and the fact that Guernsey is a British Crown dependency; the gold cross is a replica of the one used by Duke William of Normandy at the Battle of Hastings

National symbol(s): Guernsey cow; donkey

National anthem: name: "Sarnia Cherie" (Guernsey Dear)
lyrics/music: George DEIGHTON/Domencio SANTANGELO
note: adopted 1911; serves as a local anthem; as a British crown dependency, "God Save the Queen" remains official (see United Kingdom)

ECONOMY

Economy—overview: Financial services—banking, fund management, insurance—account for about 23% of employment and about 55% of total income in this tiny, prosperous Channel Island economy. Tourism, manufacturing, and horticulture, mainly tomatoes and cut flowers, have been declining. Financial services, construction, retail, and the public sector have been growing. Light tax and death duties make Guernsey a popular tax haven. In January 2013, Guernsey signed a tax agreement with Jersey and the Isle of Man, in order to enable the islands' authorities to end tax avoidance and evasion. The evolving economic integration of the EU nations is changing the environment under which Guernsey operates.

GDP (purchasing power parity): $2.742 billion (2005)
country comparison to the world: 185

GDP (official exchange rate): $2.742 billion (2005)

GDP—real growth rate: 3% (2005 est.)
country comparison to the world: 117

GDP—per capita (PPP): $44,600 (2005)
country comparison to the world: 16

GDP—composition, by sector of origin:
agriculture: 3%
industry: 10%
services: 87% (2000)

Agriculture—products: tomatoes, greenhouse flowers, sweet peppers, eggplant, fruit; Guernsey cattle

Industries: tourism, banking

Industrial production growth rate: NA%

Labor force: 31,470 (March 2006)
country comparison to the world: 204

Unemployment rate: 0.9% (March 2006 est.)
country comparison to the world: 5

Population below poverty line: NA%

Household income or consumption by percentage share: *lowest 10%:* NA%
highest 10%: NA%

Budget: *revenues:* $563.6 million
expenditures: $530.9 million (2005)

Taxes and other revenues: 20.6% of GDP (2005)
country comparison to the world: 160

Budget surplus (+) or deficit (-):
1.2% of GDP (2005)
country comparison to the world: 23

Fiscal year: calendar year

Inflation rate (consumer prices): 3.4% (June 2006)
country comparison to the world: 121

Exports: $NA

Exports—commodities: tomatoes, flowers and ferns, sweet peppers, eggplant, other vegetables

Imports: $NA

Imports—commodities: coal, gasoline, oil, machinery and equipment

Debt—external: $NA

Exchange rates: Guernsey pound
0.6391 (2013)
0.6307 (2012)
0.6472 (2010)
0.6175 (2009)
0.5302 (2008)

COMMUNICATIONS

Telephones—main lines in use: 45,100 (2010)
country comparison to the world: 165

Telephones—mobile cellular: 43,800 (2004)
country comparison to the world: 203

Telephone system: *domestic:* fixed-line and mobile-cellular services widely available; combined fixed and mobile-cellular teledensity exceeds 100 per 100 persons
international: country code—44; 1 submarine cable (2011)

Broadcast media: multiple UK terrestrial TV broadcasts are received via a transmitter in Jersey with relays in Jersey, Guernsey, and Alderney; satellite packages are available; BBC Radio Guernsey and 1 other radio station operating (2009)

Internet country code: .gg

Internet hosts: 239 (2012)
country comparison to the world: 196

Internet users: 48,300 (2009)
country comparison to the world: 175

TRANSPORTATION

Airports: 2 (2013)
country comparison to the world: 200

Airports—with paved runways: total: 2
1,524 to 2,437 m: 1
under 914 m: 1 (2013)

Ports and terminals: *major seaport(s):* Braye Bay, Saint Peter Port

MILITARY

Manpower fit for military service:
males age 16-49: 12,493
females age 16-49: 12,272 (2010 est.)

Manpower reaching militarily significant age annually: *male:* 354
female: 342 (2010 est.)

Military—note: defense is the responsibility of the UK

TRANSNATIONAL ISSUES

Disputes—international: none

GUINEA

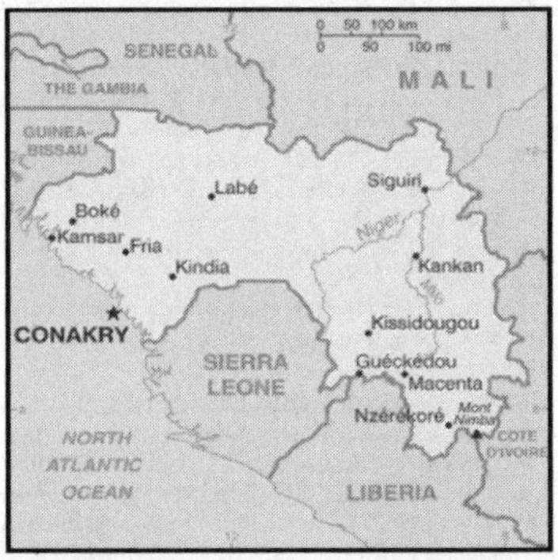

INTRODUCTION

Background: Guinea is at a turning point after decades of authoritarian rule since gaining its independence from France in 1958. Guinea held its first free and competitive democratic presidential and legislative elections in 2010 and 2013 respectively. Alpha CONDE was elected to a five year term as president in 2010, and the National Assembly was seated in January 2014. CONDE's cabinet is the first all-civilian government in Guinea. Previously, Sekou TOURE ruled the country as president from independence to his death in 1984. Lansana CONTE came to power in 1984 when the military seized the government after TOURE's death. Gen. CONTE organized and won presidential elections in 1993, 1998, and 2003, though all the polls were rigged. Upon CONTE's death in December 2008, Capt. Moussa Dadis CAMARA led a military coup, seizing power and suspending the constitution. His unwillingness to yield to domestic and international pressure to step down led to heightened political tensions that culminated in September 2009 when presidential guards opened fire on an opposition rally killing more than 150 people, and in early December 2009 when CAMARA was wounded in an assassination attempt and exiled to Burkina Faso. A transitional government led by Gen. Sekouba KONATE paved the way for Guinea's transition to a fledgling democracy.

GEOGRAPHY

Location: Western Africa, bordering the North Atlantic Ocean, between Guinea-Bissau and Sierra Leone

Geographic coordinates: 11 00 N, 10 00 W

Map references: Africa

Area: *total:* 245,857 sq km
country comparison to the world: 79
land: 245,717 sq km
water: 140 sq km

Area—comparative: slightly smaller than Oregon

Land boundaries: *total:* 3,399 km
border countries: Cote d'Ivoire 610 km, Guinea-Bissau 386 km, Liberia 563 km, Mali 858 km, Senegal 330 km, Sierra Leone 652 km

Coastline: 320 km

Maritime claims: *territorial sea:* 12 nm
exclusive economic zone: 200 nm

Climate: generally hot and humid; monsoonal-type rainy season (June to November) with southwesterly winds; dry season (December to May) with northeasterly harmattan winds

Terrain: generally flat coastal plain, hilly to mountainous interior
Elevation extremes: lowest point: Atlantic Ocean 0 m
highest point: Mont Nimba 1,752 m

Natural resources: bauxite, iron ore, diamonds, gold, uranium, hydropower, fish, salt

Land use: *arable land:* 11.59%
permanent crops: 2.81%
other: 85.6% (2011)

Irrigated land: 949.2 sq km (2003)

Total renewable water resources: 226 cu km (2011)

Freshwater withdrawal (domestic/industrial/agricultural): *total:* 0.55 cu km/yr (39%/10%/51%)
per capita: 64.3 cu m/yr (2005)

Natural hazards: hot, dry, dusty harmattan haze may reduce visibility during dry season

Environment—current issues: deforestation; inadequate supplies of potable water; desertification; soil contamination and erosion; overfishing, overpopulation in forest region; poor mining practices have led to environmental damage

Environment—international agreements:
party to: Biodiversity, Climate Change, Climate Change-Kyoto Protocol, Desertification, Endangered Species, Hazardous Wastes, Law of the Sea, Ozone Layer Protection, Ship Pollution, Wetlands, Whaling
signed, but not ratified: none of the selected agreements

Geography—note: the Niger and its important tributary the Milo have their sources in the Guinean highlands

PEOPLE AND SOCIETY

Nationality: *noun:* Guinean(s)
adjective: Guinean

Ethnic groups: Peuhl 40%, Malinke 30%, Soussou 20%, smaller ethnic groups 10%

Languages: French (official)
note: each ethnic group has its own language

Religions: Muslim 85%, Christian 8%, indigenous beliefs 7%

Population: 11,474,383 (July 2014 est.)
country comparison to the world: 76

Age structure:
0-14 years: 42% (male 2,437,142/female 2,387,105)
15-24 years: 19.5% (male 1,130,432/female 1,108,834)
25-54 years: 30.4% (male 1,748,867/female 1,739,881)
55-64 years: 3.6% (male 243,032/female 266,578)
65 years and over: 3.6% (male 182,084/female 230,428) (2014 est.)

Dependency ratios:
total dependency ratio: 83.2 %
youth dependency ratio: 77.5 %
elderly dependency ratio: 5.7 %
potential support ratio: 17.5 (2013)

Median age: *total:* 18.7 years
male: 18.4 years
female: 18.9 years (2014 est.)

Population growth rate: 2.63% (2014 est.)
country comparison to the world: 24

Birth rate: 36.02 births/1,000 population (2014 est.)
country comparison to the world: 21

Death rate: 9.69 deaths/1,000 population (2014 est.)
country comparison to the world: 53

Net migration rate: 0 migrant(s)/1,000 population (2014 est.)
country comparison to the world: 109

Urbanization: *urban population:* 35.4% of total population (2011)
rate of urbanization: 3.86% annual rate of change (2010-15 est.)

Major urban areas—population: CONAKRY (capital) 1.597 million (2009)

Sex ratio: *at birth:* 1.03 male(s)/female
0-14 years: 1.02 male(s)/female
15-24 years: 1.02 male(s)/female
25-54 years: 1.01 male(s)/female
55-64 years: 1 male(s)/female
65 years and over: 0.79 male(s)/female
total population: 1 male(s)/female (2014 est.)

Mother's mean age at first birth: 18.8 (2005 est.)

Maternal mortality rate: 610 deaths/100,000 live births (2010)
country comparison to the world: 13

Infant mortality rate: *total:* 55.24 deaths/1,000 live births
country comparison to the world: 30
male: 58.17 deaths/1,000 live births
female: 52.22 deaths/1,000 live births (2014 est.)

Life expectancy at birth: *total population:* 59.6 years
country comparison to the world: 195
male: 58.08 years
female: 61.17 years (2014 est.)

Total fertility rate: 4.93 children born/woman (2014 est.)
country comparison to the world: 18

Contraceptive prevalence rate: 5.6% (2012)

Health expenditures: 6% of GDP (2011)
country comparison to the world: 111

Physicians density: 0.1 physicians/1,000 population (2005)

Hospital bed density: 0.3 beds/1,000 population (2011)

Drinking water source:
improved:
urban: 89.8% of population
rural: 64.8% of population
total: 73.6% of population
unimproved:
urban: 10.2% of population
rural: 35.2% of population
total: 26.4% of population (2011 est.)

Sanitation facility access:
improved:
urban: 32.2% of population
rural: 10.9% of population
total: 18.5% of population
unimproved:
urban: 67.8% of population
rural: 89.1% of population
total: 81.5% of population (2011 est.)

HIV/AIDS—adult prevalence rate: 1.7% (2012 est.)
country comparison to the world: 28

HIV/AIDS—people living with HIV/AIDS: 118,100 (2012 est.)
country comparison to the world: 41

HIV/AIDS—deaths: 5,100 (2012 est.)
country comparison to the world: 39

Major infectious diseases: *degree of risk:* very high
food or waterborne diseases: bacterial and protozoal diarrhea, hepatitis A, and typhoid fever
vectorborne diseases: malaria, dengue fever, and yellow fever
water contact disease: schistosomiasis aerosolized dust or soil contact disease: Lassa fever
animal contact disease: rabies (2013)

Obesity—adult prevalence rate: 4.4% (2008)
country comparison to the world: 165

Children under the age of 5 years underweight: 16.3% (2012)
country comparison to the world: 43

Education expenditures: 2.5% of GDP (2012)
country comparison to the world: 156

Literacy: *definition:* age 15 and over can read and write
total population: 41%
male: 52%
female: 30% (2010 est.)

School life expectancy (primary to tertiary education): *total:* 9 years
male: 10 years
female: 7 years (2011)

Child labor—children ages 5-14: *total number:* 571,774
percentage: 25 % (2003 est.)

GOVERNMENT

Country name:
conventional long form: Republic of Guinea
conventional short form: Guinea
local long form: Republique de Guinee
local short form: Guinee
former: French Guinea

Government type: republic

Capital: *name:* Conakry
geographic coordinates: 9 30 N, 13 42 W
time difference: UTC 0 (5 hours ahead of Washington, DC during Standard Time)

Administrative divisions: 7 regions and 1 governate*; Boke, Conakry*, Faranah, Kankan, Kindia, Labe, Mamou, N'Zerekore

Independence: 2 October 1958 (from France)

National holiday: Independence Day, 2 October (1958)

Constitution: previous 1958, 1990; latest promulgated 19 April 2010, approved 7 May 2010 (2010)

Legal system: civil law system based on the French model

International law organization participation: accepts compulsory ICJ jurisdiction with reservations; accepts ICCt jurisdiction

Suffrage: 18 years of age; universal

Executive branch: *chief of state:* President Alpha CONDE (since 21 December 2010)
head of government: Prime Minister Prime Minister Mohamed Said FOFANA (since 24 December 2010)
cabinet: Council of Ministers appointed by the president (For more information visit the World Leaders website)
elections: president elected by popular vote for a five-year term (eligible for a second term); candidate must receive a majority of the votes cast to be elected president; election last held on 27 June 2010 with a runoff election held on 7 November 2010
election results: Alpha CONDE elected president in a runoff election; percent of vote Alpha CONDE 52.5%, Cellou Dalein DIALLO 47.5%

Legislative branch: unicameral People's National Assembly or Assemblee Nationale Populaire (114 seats; members elected by a mixed system of direct popular vote and proportional party lists)
note: the legislature was dissolved by junta leader Moussa Dadis CAMARA in December 2008 and in February 2010, the Transition Government appointed a 155 member National Transition Council (CNT) that has since acted in the legislature's place pending elections finally held on 28 September 2013; the Assembly can be dissolved one time by the President, with snap elections required within 90 days
elections: last held on 28 September 2013 (next election scheduled for 2018)
election results: percent of vote by party—NA; seats by party—RPG 53, UFDG 37, UFR 10, others 14

Judicial branch: *highest court(s):* Supreme Court or Cour Supreme (organized into Constitutional, Civil, Penal, Commercial, and Administrative Chambers, and Chamber of Accounts; court consists of the first president, chamber presidents, and NA members); note—the court is due to be reorganized by the New National Assembly in accordance with the 2010 constitution and democratic transition
judge selection and term of office: court first president appointed by the national president after consultation with the National Assembly; other members appointed by presidential decree; member tenure NA
subordinate courts: Courts of Appeal or Cour d'Appel; courts of first instance or Tribunal de Premiere Instance; High Court of Justice or Cour d'Assises; labor court; military tribunal; justices of the peace

Political parties and leaders: National Party for Hope and Development or PEDN [Lansana KOUYATE]; Rally for the Guinean People or RPG [Alpha CONDE]; Union for the Progress of Guinea or UPG [Jean Marie DORE]; Union of Democratic Forces of Guinea or UFDG [Cellou Dalein DIALLO]; Union of Republican Forces or UFR [Sidya TOURE]
note: listed are the five most popular parties as of January 2014; overall, there are more than 140 registered parties

Political pressure groups and leaders: National Confederation of Guinean Workers-Labor Union of Guinean Workers or CNTG-USTG Alliance; (includes National Confederation of Guinean Workers or CNTG and Labor Union of Guinean Workers or USTG); Syndicate of Guinean Teachers and Researchers or SLECG

International organization participation: ACP, AfDB, AU, ECOWAS, EITI (candidate country), FAO, G-77, IBRD, ICAO, ICRM, IDA, IDB, IFAD, IFC, IFRCS, ILO, IMF, IMO, Interpol, IOC, IOM, ISO (correspondent), ITSO, ITU, ITUC (NGOs), MIGA, MINURSO, MINUSMA, NAM, OIC, OIF, OPCW, UN, UNCTAD, UNESCO, UNHCR, UNIDO, UNISFA, UNMISS, UNOCI, UNWTO, UPU, WCO, WFTU (NGOs), WHO, WIPO, WMO, WTO

Diplomatic representation in the US:
chief of mission: Ambassador Blaise CHERIF (since 2 September 2011)
chancery: 2112 Leroy Place NW, Washington, DC 20008
telephone: [1] (202) 986-4300
FAX: [1] (202) 478-3010

Diplomatic representation from the US:
chief of mission: Ambassador Alexander Mark LASKARIS (since 10 September 2012)
embassy: Koloma, Conakry, east of Hamdallaye Circle
mailing address: B. P. 603, Transversale No. 2, Centre Administratif de Koloma, Commune de Ratoma, Conakry
telephone: [224] 655-10-40-00
FAX: [224] 655-10-42-97

Flag description: three equal vertical bands of red (hoist side), yellow, and green; red represents the people's sacrifice for liberation and work; yellow stands for the sun, for the riches of the earth, and for justice; green symbolizes the country's vegetation and unity
note: uses the popular Pan-African colors of Ethiopia; the colors from left to right are the reverse of those on the flags of neighboring Mali and Senegal

National anthem: *name:* "Liberte" (Liberty)
lyrics/music: unknown/Fodeba KEITA
note: adopted 1958

ECONOMY

Economy—overview: Guinea is a poor country that possesses major mineral, hydropower, solar power, and agricultural resources. Guinea has historically been an exporter of agricultural commodities, but in recent years has shifted to importing the majority of food crops. Bauxite is Guinea's main mineral resource as well as its main source of foreign currency. Guinea is the second largest producer of bauxite in the world and has the largest reserves of bauxite, estimated at 29 billion tons. The country also has significant iron ore, gold, and diamond reserves. However, Guinea has been unable to profit from this potential, as rampant corruption, dilapidated infrastructure, and political uncertainty have drained investor confidence. In the time since a 2008 coup following the death of long-term President Lansana CONTE, international donors, including the G-8, the IMF, and the World Bank, significantly curtailed their development programs but, following the December 2010 presidential elections, the IMF approved a new 3-year ECF arrangement in 2012. Guinea in September 2012 reached HIPC completion point status. Further international assistance and investment are contingent on the ability of the government to be transparent, combat corruption, reform its banking system, improve its business environment, and build infrastructure. International investors have expressed keen interest in Guinea's vast iron ore reserves, which could propel the country's growth. The government in April 2013 amended the September 2011 mining code to reduce taxes and royalties. Longer range plans to deploy broadband Internet throughout the country could spur economic growth as well. The biggest threats to Guinea's economy are political instability and low international commodity prices.

GDP (purchasing power parity): $12.56 billion (2013 est.)
country comparison to the world: 151
$12.21 billion (2012 est.)
$11.74 billion (2011 est.)
note: data are in 2013 US dollars

GDP (official exchange rate): $6.544 billion (2013 est.)

GDP—real growth rate: 2.9% (2013 est.)
country comparison to the world: 120
3.9% (2012 est.)
3.9% (2011 est.)

GDP—per capita (PPP): $1,100 (2013 est.)
country comparison to the world: 215
$1,100 (2012 est.)
$1,100 (2011 est.)
note: data are in 2013 US dollars

Gross national saving: NA% (2012 est.)
-6.4% of GDP (2011 est.)
-6.4% of GDP (2011 est.)

GDP—composition, by end use:
household consumption: 84.7%
government consumption: 12.4%
investment in fixed capital: 37.1%
investment in inventories: 0%
exports of goods and services: 22.8%
imports of goods and services: -57% (2013 est.)

GDP—composition, by sector of origin:
agriculture: 22.9%
industry: 46.5%
services: 30.5% (2013 est.)

Agriculture—products: rice, coffee, pineapples, palm kernels, cassava (manioc), bananas, sweet potatoes; cattle, sheep, goats; timber

Industries: bauxite, gold, diamonds, iron ore; alumina refining; light manufacturing, and agricultural processing

Industrial production growth rate: 4.6% (2013 est.)
country comparison to the world: 62

Labor force: 5.409 million (2013 est.)
country comparison to the world: 69

Labor force—by occupation: agriculture: 76%
industry and services: 24% (2006 est.)

Unemployment rate: NA%

Population below poverty line: 47% (2006 est.)

Household income or consumption by percentage share: *lowest 10%:* 2.7%
highest 10%: 30.3% (2007)

Distribution of family income—Gini index:
39.4 (2007)
country comparison to the world: 64
40.3 (1994)

Budget: *revenues:* $1.508 billion
expenditures: $1.839 billion (2013 est.)

Taxes and other revenues: 23% of GDP (2013 est.)
country comparison to the world: 147

Budget surplus (+) or deficit (-):
-5.1% of GDP (2013 est.)
country comparison to the world: 170

Fiscal year: calendar year
Inflation rate (consumer prices):
11.9% (2013 est.)
country comparison to the world: 214
15.2% (2012 est.)

Central bank discount rate: NA% (31 December 2010 est.)
country comparison to the world: 6
22.25% (31 December 2005)

Commercial bank prime lending rate:
26% (31 December 2013 est.)
country comparison to the world: 9
27% (31 December 2012 est.)

Stock of narrow money: $1.533 billion (31 December 2013 est.)
country comparison to the world: 138
$1.492 billion (31 December 2012 est.)

Stock of broad money: $1.881 billion (31 December 2013 est.)
country comparison to the world: 153
$1.818 billion (31 December 2012 est.)

Stock of domestic credit: $1.518 billion (31 December 2013 est.)
country comparison to the world: 145
$1.539 billion (31 December 2012 est.)

Market value of publicly traded shares: $NA

Current account balance: -$1.754 billion (2012 est.)
country comparison to the world: 137
-$1.215 billion (2011 est.)

Exports: $1.31 billion (2013 est.)
country comparison to the world: 152
$1.348 billion (2012 est.)

Exports—commodities: bauxite, alumina, gold, diamonds, coffee, fish, agricultural products

Exports—partners: India 10.6%, Spain 9.6%, Chile 9.4%, US 7.1%, Ireland 6.3%, Germany 6.3%, Ukraine 5.7%, France 5% (2012)

Imports: $2.384 billion (2013 est.)
country comparison to the world: 159
$2.606 billion (2012 est.)

Imports—commodities: petroleum products, metals, machinery, transport equipment, textiles, grain and other foodstuffs

Imports—partners: China 14.2%, Netherlands 7.6% (2012)

Reserves of foreign exchange and gold:
$183.1 million (31 December 2013 est.)
country comparison to the world: 161
$174.3 million (31 December 2012 est.)

Debt—external: $2.584 billion (31 December 2012 est.)
country comparison to the world: 140
$3.139 billion (31 December 2011 est.)

Stock of direct foreign investment—abroad:
$145 million (31 December 2013 est.)
country comparison to the world: 85
$145 million

Exchange rates: Guinean francs (GNF) per US dollar—
6,875 (2013 est.)
6,986 (2012 est.)
5,726.1 (2010 est.)
5,500 (2009)
5,500 (2008)

ENERGY

Electricity—production: 969 million kWh (2010 est.)
country comparison to the world: 148

Electricity—consumption: 901.2 million kWh (2010 est.)
country comparison to the world: 153

Electricity—exports: 0 kWh (2012 est.)
country comparison to the world: 145

Electricity—imports: 0 kWh (2012 est.)
country comparison to the world: 152

Electricity—installed generating capacity:
395,000 kW (2010 est.)
country comparison to the world: 146

Electricity—from fossil fuels: 68.4% of total installed capacity (2010 est.)
country comparison to the world: 111

Electricity—from nuclear fuels: 0% of total installed capacity (2010 est.)
country comparison to the world: 101

Electricity—from hydroelectric plants: 31.6% of total installed capacity (2010 est.)
country comparison to the world: 74

Electricity—from other renewable sources:
0% of total installed capacity (2010 est.)
country comparison to the world: 181

Crude oil—production: 0 bbl/day (2012 est.)
country comparison to the world: 177

Crude oil—exports: 0 bbl/day (2010 est.)
country comparison to the world: 122

Crude oil—imports: 0 bbl/day (2010 est.)
country comparison to the world: 196

Crude oil—proved reserves: 0 bbl (1 January 2013 es)
country comparison to the world: 140

Refined petroleum products—production:
0 bbl/day (2010 est.)
country comparison to the world: 152

Refined petroleum products—consumption:
8,671 bbl/day (2011 est.)
country comparison to the world: 156

Refined petroleum products—exports:
0 bbl/day (2010 est.)
country comparison to the world: 182

Refined petroleum products—imports:
9,089 bbl/day (2010 est.)
country comparison to the world: 133

Natural gas—production: 0 cu m (2011 est.)
country comparison to the world: 140

Natural gas—consumption: 0 cu m (2010 est.)
country comparison to the world: 153

Natural gas—exports: 0 cu m (2011 est.)
country comparison to the world: 113

Natural gas—imports: 0 cu m (2011 est.)
country comparison to the world: 202

Natural gas—proved reserves: 0 cu m (1 January 2013 es)
country comparison to the world: 146

Carbon dioxide emissions from consumption of energy: 1.419 million Mt (2011 est.)
country comparison to the world: 158

COMMUNICATIONS

Telephones—main lines in use: 18,000 (2012)
country comparison to the world: 192

Telephones—mobile cellular: 4.781 million (2012)
country comparison to the world: 115

Telephone system: *general assessment:* inadequate system of open-wire lines, small radiotelephone communication stations, and new microwave radio relay system
domestic: Conakry reasonably well-served; coverage elsewhere remains inadequate and large companies tend to rely on their own systems for nationwide links; fixed-line teledensity less than 1 per 100 persons; mobile-cellular subscribership is expanding and exceeds 40 per 100 persons
international: country code—224; satellite earth station—1 Intelsat (Atlantic Ocean) (2011)

Broadcast media: government maintains marginal control over broadcast media; single state-run TV station; state-run radio broadcast station also operates several stations in rural areas; a steadily increasing number of privately owned radio stations, nearly all in Conakry, and about a dozen community radio stations; foreign TV programming available via satellite and cable subscription services (2011)

Internet country code: .gn

Internet hosts: 15 (2012)
country comparison to the world: 223

Internet users: 95,000 (2009)
country comparison to the world: 161

TRANSPORTATION

Airports: 16 (2013)
country comparison to the world: 144

Airports—with paved runways: *total:* 4
over 3,047 m: 1
1,524 to 2,437 m: 3 (2013)

Airports—with unpaved runways: *total:* 1 2
1,524 to 2,437 m: 7
914 to 1,523 m: 3
under 914 m: 2 (2013)

Railways: *total:* 1,185 km
country comparison to the world: 87
standard gauge: 238 km 1.435-m gauge
narrow gauge: 947 km 1.000-m gauge (2008)

Roadways: *total:* 44,348 km
country comparison to the world: 80
paved: 4,342 km
unpaved: 40,006 km (2003)

Waterways: 1,300 km (navigable by shallow-draft native craft in the northern part of the Niger system) (2011)
country comparison to the world: 55

Ports and terminals: *major seaport(s):* Conakry, Kamsar

MILITARY

Military branches: National Armed Forces: Army, Guinean Navy (Armee de Mer or Marine Guineenne, includes Marines), Guinean Air Force (Force Aerienne de Guinee) (2009)

Military service age and obligation: 18-25 years of age for compulsory and voluntary military service; 18-month conscript service obligation (2012)

Manpower available for military service:
males age 16-49: 2,359,203
females age 16-49: 2,329,784 (2010 est.)

Manpower fit for military service:
males age 16-49: 1,493,991
females age 16-49: 1,535,418 (2010 est.)

Manpower reaching militarily significant age annually: *male:* 118,443
female: 115,901 (2010 est.)

TRANSNATIONAL ISSUES

Disputes—international: conflicts among rebel groups, warlords, and youth gangs in neighboring states have spilled over into Guinea resulting in domestic instability; Sierra Leone considers Guinea's definition of the flood plain limits to define the left bank boundary of the Makona and Moa rivers excessive and protests Guinea's continued occupation of these lands, including the hamlet of Yenga, occupied since 1998

Refugees and internally displaced persons: *refugees (country of origin):* 6,552 (Cote d'Ivoire) (2012)

Trafficking in persons: *current situation:* Guinea is a source, transit, and, to a lesser extent, a destination country for men, women, and children subjected to forced labor and sex trafficking; the majority of trafficking victims are Guinean children; Guinean girls are subjected to domestic servitude and commercial sexual exploitation, while boys are forced to beg, work as street vendors or shoe shiners, or miners; some Guinean children are forced to mine in Senegal, Mali, and possibly other West African countries; Guinean women and girls are subjected to domestic servitude and sex trafficking in Nigeria, Cote d'Ivoire, Benin, Senegal, Greece, and Spain, while Chinese and Vietnamese women are reportedly forced into prostitution in Guinea

tier rating: Tier 2 Watch List—Guinea does not fully comply with the minimum standards for the elimination of trafficking; however, it is making significant efforts to do so; a new police unit has been created to focus on human trafficking and child labor; the government has initiated five new trafficking investigations but has failed to prosecute or convict any trafficking offenders, which represents a decrease in anti-trafficking law enforcement over the previous year; the government fails to provide victims with protective services and has not supported NGOs that assist victims but continues to refer child victims to NGOs on an ad hoc basis; Guinean law does not prohibit all forms of trafficking, excluding, for example, forced prostitution of adults and debt bondage, which are not criminalized (2013)

GUINEA-BISSAU

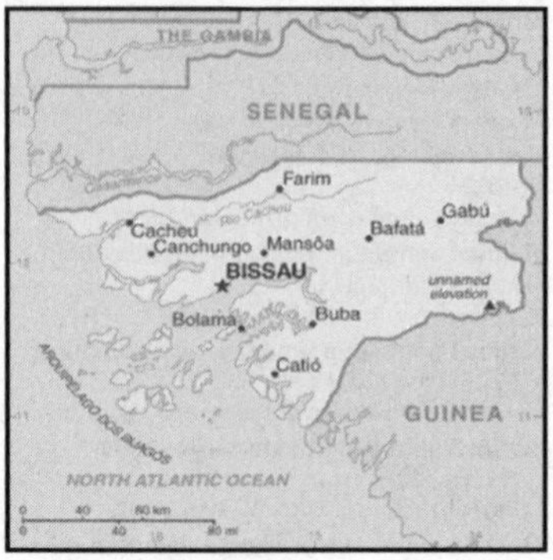

INTRODUCTION

Background: Since independence from Portugal in 1974, Guinea-Bissau has experienced considerable political and military upheaval. In 1980, a military coup established authoritarian dictator Joao Bernardo 'Nino' VIEIRA as president. Despite setting a path to a market economy and multiparty system, VIEIRA's regime was characterized by the suppression of political opposition and the purging of political rivals. Several coup attempts through the 1980s and early 1990s failed to unseat him. In 1994 VIEIRA was elected president in the country's first free elections. A military mutiny and resulting civil war in 1998 eventually led to VIEIRA's ouster in May 1999. In February 2000, a transitional government turned over power to opposition leader Kumba YALA after he was elected president in transparent polling. In September 2003, after only three years in office, YALA was overthrown in a bloodless military coup, and businessman Henrique ROSA was sworn in as interim president. In 2005, former President VIEIRA was re-elected president pledging to pursue economic development and national reconciliation; he was assassinated in March 2009. Malam Bacai SANHA was elected in an emergency election held in June 2009, but he passed away in January 2012 from an existing illness. A military coup in April 2012 prevented Guinea-Bissau's second-round presidential election—to determine SANHA's successor—from taking place.

GEOGRAPHY

Location: Western Africa, bordering the North Atlantic Ocean, between Guinea and Senegal

Geographic coordinates: 12 00 N, 15 00 W

Map references: Africa

Area: total: 36,125 sq km
country comparison to the world: 138
land: 28,120 sq km
water: 8,005 sq km

Area—comparative: slightly less than three times the size of Connecticut

Land boundaries: *total:* 724 km
border countries: Guinea 386 km, Senegal 338 km

Coastline: 350 km

Maritime claims: territorial sea: 12 nm
exclusive economic zone: 200 nm

Climate: tropical; generally hot and humid; monsoonal-type rainy season (June to November) with southwesterly winds; dry season (December to May) with northeasterly harmattan winds

Terrain: mostly low-lying coastal plain with a deeply indented estuarine coastline rising to savanna in east; numerous off-shore islands including the Arquipelago Dos Bijagos consisting of 18 main islands and many small islets

Elevation extremes: lowest point: Atlantic Ocean 0 m
highest point: unnamed elevation in the eastern part of the country 300 m

Natural resources: fish, timber, phosphates, bauxite, clay, granite, limestone, unexploited deposits of petroleum

Land use: arable land: 8.3%
permanent crops: 6.92%
other: 84.78% (2011)

Irrigated land: 225.6 sq km (2003)

Total renewable water resources: 31 cu km (2011)

Freshwater withdrawal (domestic/industrial/agricultural): *total:* 0.18 cu km/yr (18%/6%/76%)
per capita: 135.7 cu m/yr (2005)

Natural hazards: hot, dry, dusty harmattan haze may reduce visibility during dry season; brush fires

Environment—current issues: deforestation; soil erosion; overgrazing; overfishing

Environment—international agreements:
party to: Biodiversity, Climate Change, Climate Change-Kyoto Protocol, Desertification, Endangered Species, Hazardous Wastes, Law of the Sea, Ozone Layer Protection, Wetlands
signed, but not ratified: none of the selected agreements

Geography—note: this small country is swampy along its western coast and low-lying inland

PEOPLE AND SOCIETY

Nationality: *noun:* Bissau-Guinean(s)
adjective: Bissau-Guinean

Ethnic groups: African 99% (includes Balanta 30%, Fula 20%, Manjaca 14%, Mandinga 13%, Papel 7%), European and mulatto less than 1%

Languages: Portuguese (official), Crioulo, African languages

Religions: Muslim 50%, indigenous beliefs 40%, Christian 10%

Population: 1,693,398 (July 2014 est.)
country comparison to the world: 153

Age structure:
0-14 years: 39.8% (male 336,053/female 337,270)
15-24 years: 20.2% (male 169,574/female 172,221)
25-54 years: 32.1% (male 270,432/female 273,053)
55-64 years: 3.3% (male 29,112/female 50,083)
65 years and over: 3.2% (male 21,236/female 34,364) (2014 est.)

Dependency ratios:
total dependency ratio: 79.7 %
youth dependency ratio: 74.5 %
elderly dependency ratio: 5.2 %
potential support ratio: 19.3 (2013)

Median age: *total:* 19.8 years
male: 19.3 years
female: 20.3 years (2014 est.)

Population growth rate: 1.93% (2014 est.)
country comparison to the world: 56

Birth rate: 33.83 births/1,000 population (2014 est.)
country comparison to the world: 31

Death rate: 14.54 deaths/1,000 population (2014 est.)
country comparison to the world: 5

Net migration rate: 0 migrant(s)/1,000 population (2014 est.)
country comparison to the world: 91

Urbanization: *urban population:* 43.9% of total population (2011)
rate of urbanization: 3.59% annual rate of change (2010-15 est.)

Major urban areas—population: BISSAU (capital) 302,000 (2009)

Sex ratio: *at birth:* 1.03 male(s)/female
0-14 years: 1 male(s)/female
15-24 years: 0.99 male(s)/female
25-54 years: 0.99 male(s)/female
55-64 years: 0.95 male(s)/female
65 years and over: 0.64 male(s)/female
total population: 0.95 male(s)/female (2014 est.)

Maternal mortality rate: 790 deaths/100,000 live births (2010)
country comparison to the world: 7

Infant mortality rate: *total:* 90.92 deaths/1,000 live births
country comparison to the world: 5
male: 100.59 deaths/1,000 live births
female: 80.97 deaths/1,000 live births (2014 est.)

Life expectancy at birth: total population: 49.87 years
country comparison to the world: 221
male: 47.87 years
female: 51.93 years (2014 est.)

Total fertility rate: 4.3 children born/woman (2014 est.)
country comparison to the world: 32

Contraceptive prevalence rate: 14% (2010)

Health expenditures: 6.3% of GDP (2011)
country comparison to the world: 99

Physicians density: 0.07 physicians/1,000 population (2009)

Hospital bed density: 1 beds/1,000 population (2009)

Drinking water source:
improved:
urban: 93.8% of population
rural: 54.5% of population
total: 71.7% of population
unimproved:
urban: 6.2% of population
rural: 45.5% of population
total: 28.3% of population (2011 est.)

Sanitation facility access:
improved:
urban: 33% of population
rural: 8.1% of population
total: 19% of population
unimproved:
urban: 67% of population
rural: 91.9% of population
total: 81% of population (2011 est.)

HIV/AIDS—adult prevalence rate: 3.9% (2012 est.)
country comparison to the world: 17

HIV/AIDS—people living with HIV/AIDS: 41,300 (2012 est.)
country comparison to the world: 66

HIV/AIDS—deaths: 2,300 (2012 est.)
country comparison to the world: 57

Major infectious diseases: *degree of risk:* very high
food or waterborne diseases: bacterial and protozoal diarrhea, hepatitis A, and typhoid fever
vectorborne diseases: malaria, dengue fever, and yellow fever
water contact disease: schistosomiasis
animal contact disease: rabies (2013)

Obesity—adult prevalence rate: 4.9% (2008)
country comparison to the world: 159

Children under the age of 5 years underweight: 16.6% (2008)
country comparison to the world: 40

Education expenditures: NA

Literacy: *definition:* age 15 and over can read and write
total population: 55.3%
male: 68.9%
female: 42.1% (2011 est.)

School life expectancy (primary to tertiary education): *total:* 9 years (2006)

Child labor—children ages 5-14: *total number:* 226,316
percentage: 57 % (2010 est.)

GOVERNMENT

Country name: *conventional long form:* Republic of Guinea-Bissau
conventional short form: Guinea-Bissau
local long form: Republica da Guine-Bissau
local short form: Guine-Bissau
former: Portuguese Guinea

Government type: republic

Capital: *name:* Bissau
geographic coordinates: 11 51 N, 15 35 W
time difference: UTC 0 (5 hours ahead of Washington, DC during Standard Time)

Administrative divisions: 9 regions (regioes, singular—regiao); Bafata, Biombo, Bissau, Bolama, Cacheu, Gabu, Oio, Quinara, Tombali; note—Bolama may have been renamed Bolama-Bijagos

Independence: 24 September 1973 (declared); 10 September 1974 (from Portugal)

National holiday: Independence Day, 24 September (1973)

Constitution: promulgated 16 May 1984; amended several times, last in 1996; note—constitution suspended following military coup in April 2012 (2013)

Legal system: mixed legal system of civil law (influenced by the early French Civil Code) and customary law

International law organization participation: accepts compulsory ICJ jurisdiction; non-party state to the ICCt

Suffrage: 18 years of age; universal

Executive branch: *chief of state:* [transitional] President Manuel Serifo NHAMADJO (since 11 May 2012)
head of government: transitional Prime Minister Rui Duarte BARROS (since 16 May 2012)
cabinet: NA (For more information visit the World Leaders website)
elections: president elected by absolute majority vote in two rounds for a 5-year term (no term limits); election—first round held on 13 April 2014; prime minister appointed by the president after consultation with party leaders in the National People's Assembly
election results: 13 April 2014 first round results—Jose Mario VAZ 41%, Nuno Gomez NABIAM 25.1%, other 33.9%; runoff scheduled for 18 May 2014

Legislative branch: unicameral National People's Assembly or Assembleia Nacional Popular (102 seats including 2 seats reserved for diaspora; members elected by popular vote to serve four-year terms)
elections: last held on 13 April 2014 (next to be held in 2018)
election results: percent of vote by party—PAIGC 47.3%, PRS 31.1%, other 21.6%; seats by party—PAIGC 55, PRS 41, other 4; note—2 diaspora seats unfilled

Judicial branch: *highest court(s):* Supreme Court of Justice (consists of 9 judges and organized into Civil, Criminal, and Social and Administrative Disputes Chambers) note—the Supreme Court has both appellate and constitutional jurisdiction
judge selection and term of office: judges nominated by the Higher Council of the Magistrate, a major government organ responsible for judge appointments, dismissals, and discipline of the judiciary; judges appointed by the president with tenure for life
subordinate courts: Appeal Court; regional (first instance) courts; military court

Political parties and leaders: African Party for the Independence of Guinea-Bissau and Cabo Verde or PAIGC [Rui Dia de SOUSA]; Democratic Alliance or AD [Victor MANDINGA]; New Democracy Party or PND; Party for Social Renewal or PRS [Kumba YALA]; Republican Party for Independence and Development or PRID [Aristides GOMES]

Political pressure groups and leaders: NA

International organization participation: ACP, AfDB, AOSIS, AU (suspended), CPLP, ECOWAS, FAO, FZ, G-77, IBRD, ICAO, ICRM, IDA, IDB, IFAD, IFC, IFRCS, ILO, IMF, IMO, Interpol, IOC, IOM, IPU, ITSO, ITU, ITUC (NGOs), MIGA, MINUSMA, NAM, OIC, OIF, OPCW, UN, UNCTAD, UNESCO, UNIDO, Union Latina, UNWTO, UPU, WADB (regional), WAEMU, WCO, WFTU (NGOs), WHO, WIPO, WMO, WTO

Diplomatic representation in the US: *chief of mission:* none; note—Guinea-Bissau does not have official representation in Washington, DC

Diplomatic representation from the US: the US Embassy suspended operations on 14 June 1998 in the midst of violent conflict between forces loyal to then President VIEIRA and military-led junta; the US Ambassador to Senegal, currently Ambassador Lewis LUKENS, is accredited to Guinea-Bissau

Flag description: two equal horizontal bands of yellow (top) and green with a vertical red band on the hoist side; there is a black five-pointed star centered in the red band; yellow symbolizes the sun; green denotes hope; red represents blood shed during the struggle for independence; the black star stands for African unity
note: uses the popular Pan-African colors of Ethiopia; the flag design was heavily influenced by the Ghanaian flag

National anthem: name: "Esta e a Nossa Patria Bem Amada" (This Is Our Beloved Country)
lyrics/music: Amilcar Lopes CABRAL/XIAO He
note: adopted 1974; a delegation from Portuguese Guinea visited China in 1963 and heard music by XIAO He; Amilcar Lopes CABRA, the leader of Guinea-Bissau's independence movement, asked the composer to create a piece that would inspire his people to struggle for independence

ECONOMY

Economy—overview: Guinea-Bissau's legal economy is based on farming and fishing, but trafficking in narcotics is probably the most lucrative economic activity. The combination of limited economic prospects, a weak and faction-ridden government, and favorable geography have made this West African country a way station for drugs bound for Europe. Cashew nuts are the main source of income for rural communities and the country's main export crop. Cashew sector performance helps to determine the overall macroeconomic situation of the country and food security status of rural areas. In 2013 cashew production and exports were disrupted as a result of the March 2012 coup. Guinea-Bissau is heavily reliant on foreign aid, which has not recovered to pre-coup levels.

GDP (purchasing power parity): $2.005 billion (2013 est.)
country comparison to the world: 193
$1.937 billion (2012 est.)
$1.965 billion (2011 est.)
note: data are in 2013 US dollars

GDP (official exchange rate): $880 million (2013 est.)

GDP—real growth rate: 3.5% (2013 est.)
country comparison to the world: 95
-1.5% (2012 est.)
5.3% (2011 est.)

GDP—per capita (PPP): $1,200 (2013 est.)
country comparison to the world: 213
$1,200 (2012 est.)
$1,300 (2011 est.)
note: data are in 2013 US dollars

GDP—composition, by end use:
household consumption: 81.3%
government consumption: 13%
investment in fixed capital: 12.9%
investment in inventories: 0%
exports of goods and services: 25.5%
imports of goods and services: -32.7% (2013 est.)

GDP—composition, by sector of origin:
agriculture: 58%
industry: 13.5%
services: 28.5% (2013 est.)

Agriculture—products: rice, corn, beans, cassava (manioc), cashew nuts, peanuts, palm kernels, cotton; timber; fish

Industries: agricultural products processing, beer, soft drinks

Industrial production growth rate: 1.2% (2013 est.)
country comparison to the world: 143

Labor force: 632,700 (2007)
country comparison to the world: 154

Labor force—by occupation: agriculture: 82%
industry and services: 18% (2000 est.)

Unemployment rate: NA%

Population below poverty line: NA%

Household income or consumption by percentage share: *lowest 10%:* 2.9%
highest 10%: 28% (2002)

Budget: *revenues:* $142 million
expenditures: $157.7 million (2013 est.)

Taxes and other revenues: 16.1% of GDP (2013 est.)
country comparison to the world: 188

Budget surplus (+) or deficit (-):
-1.8% of GDP (2013 est.)
country comparison to the world: 80

Fiscal year: calendar year

Inflation rate (consumer prices): 1.9% (2013 est.)
country comparison to the world: 60
2.1% (2012 est.)

Central bank discount rate: 4.25% (31 December 2009)
country comparison to the world: 75
4.75% (31 December 2008)

Commercial bank prime lending rate: 15% (31 December 2013 est.)
country comparison to the world: 42
15% (31 December 2012 est.)

Stock of narrow money: $242.8 million (31 December 2013 est.)
country comparison to the world: 173
$264.9 million (31 December 2012 est.)

Stock of broad money: $338.1 million (31 December 2013 est.)
country comparison to the world: 184
$327.5 million (31 December 2012 est.)

Stock of domestic credit: $173.3 million (31 December 2013 est.)
country comparison to the world: 175
$171.8 million (31 December 2012 est.)

Market value of publicly traded shares: $NA

Current account balance: -$47.3 million (2013 est.)
country comparison to the world: 69
-$47.4 million (2012 est.)

Exports: $147.6 million (2013 est.)
country comparison to the world: 186
$127.9 million (2012 est.)

Exports—commodities: fish, shrimp; cashew nuts, peanuts, palm kernels, sawn lumber

Exports—partners: India 56.5%, Nigeria 27.1%, Togo 5.9% (2012)

Imports: $206.4 million (2013 est.)
country comparison to the world: 206
$189.8 million (2012 est.)

Imports—commodities: foodstuffs, machinery and transport equipment, petroleum products

Imports—partners: Portugal 28.8%, Senegal 17.5%, US 7.3%, China 5% (2012)

Debt—external: $1.095 billion (31 December 2010 est.)
country comparison to the world: 159
$941.5 million (31 December 2000 est.)

Exchange rates: Communaute Financiere Africaine francs (XOF) per US dollar—

500.7 (2013 est.)
510.53 (2012 est.)
495.28 (2010 est.)
472.19 (2009)
447.81 (2008)

ENERGY

Electricity—production: 67 million kWh (2010 est.)
country comparison to the world: 203

Electricity—consumption: 62.31 million kWh (2010 est.)
country comparison to the world: 203

Electricity—exports: 0 kWh (2012 est.)
country comparison to the world: 184

Electricity—imports: 0 kWh (2012 est.)
country comparison to the world: 187

Electricity—installed generating capacity: 26,000 kW (2010 est.)
country comparison to the world: 201

Electricity—from fossil fuels: 100% of total installed capacity (2010 est.)
country comparison to the world: 28

Electricity—from nuclear fuels: 0% of total installed capacity (2010 est.)
country comparison to the world: 165

Electricity—from hydroelectric plants: 0% of total installed capacity (2010 est.)
country comparison to the world: 191

Electricity—from other renewable sources: 0% of total installed capacity (2010 est.)
country comparison to the world: 114

Crude oil—production: 0 bbl/day (2012 est.)
country comparison to the world: 206

Crude oil—exports: 0 bbl/day (2010 est.)
country comparison to the world: 170

Crude oil—imports: 0 bbl/day (2010 est.)
country comparison to the world: 110

Crude oil—proved reserves: 0 bbl (1 January 2013 es)
country comparison to the world: 178

Refined petroleum products—production: 0 bbl/day (2010 est.)
country comparison to the world: 186

Refined petroleum products—consumption: 2,922 bbl/day (2011 est.)
country comparison to the world: 181

Refined petroleum products—exports: 0 bbl/day (2010 est.)
country comparison to the world: 208

Refined petroleum products—imports: 2,661 bbl/day (2010 est.)
country comparison to the world: 174

Natural gas—production: 0 cu m (2011 est.)
country comparison to the world: 182

Natural gas—consumption: 0 cu m (2010 est.)
country comparison to the world: 187

Natural gas—exports: 0 cu m (2011 est.)
country comparison to the world: 168

Natural gas—imports: 0 cu m (2011 est.)
country comparison to the world: 119

Natural gas—proved reserves: 0 cu m (1 January 2013 es)
country comparison to the world: 185

Carbon dioxide emissions from consumption of energy: 459,800 Mt (2011 est.)
country comparison to the world: 180

COMMUNICATIONS

Telephones—main lines in use: 5,000 (2012)
country comparison to the world: 210

Telephones—mobile cellular: 1.1 million (2012)
country comparison to the world: 156

Telephone system: *general assessment:* small system including a combination of microwave radio relay, open-wire lines, radiotelephone, and mobile-cellular communications
domestic: fixed-line teledensity less than 1 per 100 persons; mobile-cellular teledensity is roughly 50 per 100 persons
international: country code—245 (2011)

Broadcast media: 1 state-owned TV station and a second station, Radio e Televisao de Portugal (RTP) Africa, is operated by Portuguese public broadcaster (RTP); 1 state-owned radio station, several private radio stations, and some community radio stations; multiple international broadcasters are available (2007)

Internet country code: .gw

Internet hosts: 90 (2012)
country comparison to the world: 211

Internet users: 37,100 (2009)
country comparison to the world: 177

TRANSPORTATION

Airports: 8 (2013)
country comparison to the world: 161

Airports—with paved runways: *total:* 2
over 3,047 m: 1
1,524 to 2,437 m: 1 (2013)

Airports—with unpaved runways: total: 6
1,524 to 2,437 m: 1
914 to 1,523 m: 2
under 914 m: 3 (2013)

Roadways: *total:* 3,455 km
country comparison to the world: 161
paved: 965 km
unpaved: 2,490 km (2002)

Waterways: (rivers are navigable for some distance; many inlets and creeks give shallow-water access to much of interior) (2012)

Ports and terminals: *major seaport(s):* Bissau, Buba, Cacheu, Farim

MILITARY

Military branches: People's Revolutionary Armed Force (FARP): Army, Navy, National Air Force (Forca Aerea Nacional); Presidential Guard (2012)

Military service age and obligation: 18-25 years of age for selective compulsory military service (Air Force service is voluntary); 16 years of age or younger, with parental consent, for voluntary service (2013)

Manpower available for military service:
males age 16-49: 370,790
females age 16-49: 372,171 (2010 est.)

Manpower fit for military service: males age 16-49: 205,460
females age 16-49: 212,277 (2010 est.)

Manpower reaching militarily significant age annually: *male:* 17,639
female: 17,865 (2010 est.)

Military expenditures: 1.85% of GDP (2012)
country comparison to the world: 47
1.81% of GDP (2011)
1.85% of GDP (2010)

TRANSNATIONAL ISSUES

Disputes—international: in 2006, political instability within Senegal's Casamance region resulted in thousands of Senegalese refugees, cross-border raids, and arms smuggling into Guinea-Bissau

Refugees and internally displaced persons: *refugees (country of origin):* 7,700 (Senegal) (2012)

Trafficking in persons: *current situation:* Guinea-Bissau is a country of origin and destination for children subjected to forced labor and sex trafficking; the scope of the problem of trafficking women or men for forced labor or forced prostitution is unknown; boys reportedly are transported to southern Senegal for forced manual and agricultural labor; girls may be subjected to forced domestic service and child prostitution in Senegal and Guinea; both boys and girls are forced to work as street vendors in cities in Guinea-Bissau and Senegal

tier rating: Tier 3—the government of Guinea-Bissau does not fully comply with the minimum standards for the elimination of trafficking and is not making significant efforts to do so; despite enacting an anti-trafficking law and finalizing and adopting a national action plan in 2011, authorities have not conducted any investigations or prosecutions of trafficking offenses; the government has not provided adequate protection to identified trafficking victims, conducted any tangible prevention activities in 2012, or made progress on the implementation of its national action plan (2013)
Illicit drugs: increasingly important transit country for South American cocaine en route to Europe; enabling environment for trafficker operations thanks to pervasive corruption; archipelago-like geography around the capital facilitates drug smuggling

GUYANA

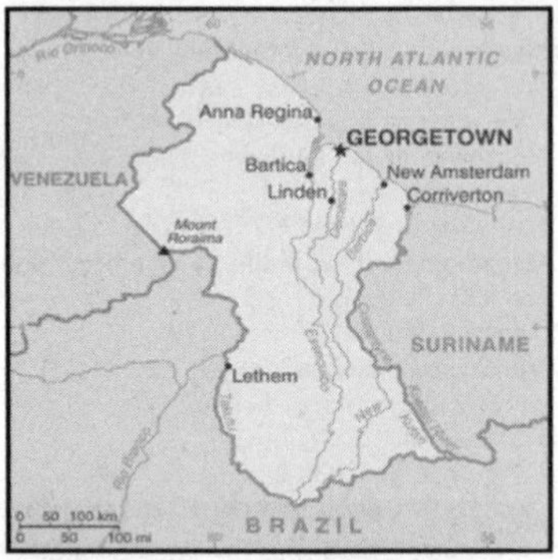

INTRODUCTION

Background: Originally a Dutch colony in the 17th century, by 1815 Guyana had become a British possession. The abolition of slavery led to black settlement of urban areas and the importation of indentured servants from India to work the sugar plantations. The resulting ethnocultural divide has persisted and has led to turbulent politics. Guyana achieved independence from the UK in 1966, and since then it has been ruled mostly by socialist-oriented governments. In 1992, Cheddi JAGAN was elected president in what is considered the country's first free and fair election since independence. After his death five years later, his wife, Janet JAGAN, became president but resigned in 1999 due to poor health. Her successor, Bharrat JAGDEO, was reelected in 2001 and again in 2006. Donald RAMOTAR was elected president in 2011.

GEOGRAPHY

Location: Northern South America, bordering the North Atlantic Ocean, between Suriname and Venezuela

Geographic coordinates: 5 00 N, 59 00 W

Map references: South America

Area: *total:* 214,969 sq km
country comparison to the world: 85
land: 196,849 sq km
water: 18,120 sq km

Area—comparative: slightly smaller than Idaho

Land boundaries: total: 2,949 km
border countries: Brazil 1,606 km, Suriname 600 km, Venezuela 743 km

Coastline: 459 km

Maritime claims: territorial sea: 12 nm
exclusive economic zone: 200 nm
continental shelf: 200 nm or to the outer edge of the continental margin

Climate: tropical; hot, humid, moderated by northeast trade winds; two rainy seasons (May to August, November to January)

Terrain: mostly rolling highlands; low coastal plain; savanna in south

Elevation extremes: *lowest point:* Atlantic Ocean 0 m
highest point: Mount Roraima 2,835 m

Natural resources: bauxite, gold, diamonds, hardwood timber, shrimp, fish

Land use: *arable land:* 1.95%
permanent crops: 0.13%
other: 97.92% (2011)

Irrigated land: 1,501 sq km (2003)

Total renewable water resources: 241 cu km (2011)

Freshwater withdrawal (domestic/industrial/agricultural): *total:* 1.64 cu km/yr (4%/1%/94%)
per capita: 2,222 cu m/yr (2010)

Natural hazards: flash flood threat during rainy seasons

Environment—current issues: water pollution from sewage and agricultural and industrial chemicals; deforestation

Environment—international agreements:
party to: Biodiversity, Climate Change, Climate Change-Kyoto Protocol, Desertification, Endangered Species, Hazardous Wastes, Law of the Sea, Ozone Layer Protection, Ship Pollution, Tropical Timber 83, Tropical Timber 94
signed, but not ratified: none of the selected agreements

Geography—note: the third-smallest country in South America after Suriname and Uruguay; substantial portions of its western and eastern territories are claimed by Venezuela and Suriname respectively

PEOPLE AND SOCIETY

Nationality: noun: Guyanese (singular and plural)
adjective: Guyanese

Ethnic groups: East Indian 43.5%, black (African) 30.2%, mixed 16.7%, Amerindian 9.1%, other 0.5% (2002 census)

Languages: English, Amerindian dialects, Creole, Caribbean Hindustani (a dialect of Hindi), Urdu

Religions: Protestant 30.5% (Pentecostal 16.9%, Anglican 6.9%, Seventh-Day Adventist 5%, Methodist 1.7%), Hindu 28.4%, Roman Catholic 8.1%, Jehovah's Witnesses 1.1%, Muslim 7.2%, other Christian 17.7%, other 4.3%, none 4.3% (2002 census)

Demographic profile: Guyana is the only English-speaking country in South America and shares cultural and historical bonds with the Anglophone Caribbean. Guyana's two largest ethnic groups are the Afro-Guyanese (descendants of African slaves) and the Indo-Guyanese (descendants of Indian indentured laborers), which together comprise about three quarters of Guyana's population. Tensions periodically have boiled over between the two groups, which back ethnically based political parties and vote along ethnic lines. Poverty reduction has stagnated since the late 1990s. About one-third of the Guyanese population lives below the poverty line; indigenous people are disproportionately affected. Although Guyana's literacy rate is reported to be among the highest in the Western Hemisphere, the level of functional literacy is considerably lower, which has been attributed to poor education quality, teacher training, and infrastructure. Guyana's emigration rate is among the highest in the world—more than 55% of its citizens reside abroad—and it is one of the largest recipients of remittances relative to GDP among Latin American and Caribbean counties. Although remittances are a vital source of income for most citizens, the pervasive emigration of skilled workers deprives Guyana of professionals in healthcare and other key sectors. More than 80% of Guyanese nationals with tertiary level educations have emigrated. Brain drain and the concentration of limited medical resources in Georgetown hamper Guyana's ability to meet the health needs of its predominantly rural population. Guyana has one of the highest HIV prevalence rates in the region and continues to rely on international support for its HIV treatment and prevention programs.

Population: 735,554 (July 2014 est.)
country comparison to the world: 165
note: estimates for this country explicitly take into account the effects of excess mortality due to AIDS; this can result in lower life expectancy, higher infant mortality, higher death rates, lower population growth rates, and changes in the distribution of population by age and sex than would otherwise be expected

Age structure:
0-14 years: 29% (male 108,703/female 104,793)
15-24 years: 21% (male 79,354/female 74,921)
25-54 years: 37.2% (male 142,348/female 131,108)
55-64 years: 5.3% (male 24,677/female 30,562)
65 years and over: 5.1% (male 16,318/female 22,770) (2014 est.)

Dependency ratios:
total dependency ratio: 65.3 %
youth dependency ratio: 59.6 %
elderly dependency ratio: 5.7 %
potential support ratio: 17.7 (2013)

Median age: *total:* 25 years
male: 24.6 years
female: 25.4 years (2014 est.)

Population growth rate: -0.11% (2014 est.)
country comparison to the world: 204

Birth rate: 15.9 births/1,000 population (2014 est.)
country comparison to the world: 125

Death rate: 7.3 deaths/1,000 population (2014 est.)
country comparison to the world: 123

Net migration rate: -9.67 migrant(s)/1,000 population (2014 est.)
country comparison to the world: 214

Urbanization: *urban population:* 29% of total population (2010)
rate of urbanization: 0.5% annual rate of change (2010-15 est.)

Major urban areas—population: GEORGETOWN (capital) 132,000 (2009)

Sex ratio: *at birth:* 1.05 male(s)/female
0-14 years: 1.04 male(s)/female
15-24 years: 1.06 male(s)/female
25-54 years: 1.09 male(s)/female
55-64 years: 1.02 male(s)/female
65 years and over: 0.69 male(s)/female
total population: 0.99 male(s)/female (2014 est.)

Mother's mean age at first birth: 20.8
note: median age at first birth among women 25-29 (2009 est.)

Maternal mortality rate: 280 deaths/100,000 live births (2010)
country comparison to the world: 43

Infant mortality rate: total: 33.56 deaths/1,000 live births
country comparison to the world: 65
male: 37.57 deaths/1,000 live births
female: 29.36 deaths/1,000 live births (2014 est.)

Life expectancy at birth: *total population:* 67.81 years
country comparison to the world: 162
male: 64.82 years
female: 70.96 years (2014 est.)

Total fertility rate: 2.14 children born/woman (2014 est.)
country comparison to the world: 106

Contraceptive prevalence rate: 42.5% (2009)

Health expenditures: 5.9% of GDP (2011)
country comparison to the world: 114

Physicians density: 0.21 physicians/1,000 population (2010)

Hospital bed density: 2 beds/1,000 population (2009)

Drinking water source:
improved:
urban: 97.9% of population
rural: 93.2% of population
total: 94.5% of population
unimproved:
urban: 2.1% of population
rural: 6.8% of population
total: 5.5% of population (2011 est.)

Sanitation facility access:
improved:
urban: 87.7% of population
rural: 82.4% of population
total: 83.9% of population
unimproved:
urban: 12.3% of population
rural: 17.6% of population
total: 16.1% of population (2011 est.)

HIV/AIDS—adult prevalence rate: 1.3% (2012 est.)
country comparison to the world: 37

HIV/AIDS—people living with HIV/AIDS: 7,200 (2012 est.)
country comparison to the world: 116

HIV/AIDS—deaths: 100 (2012 est.)
country comparison to the world: 134

Major infectious diseases: *degree of risk:* very high
food or waterborne diseases: bacterial and protozoal diarrhea, hepatitis A, and typhoid fever
vectorborne diseases: dengue fever and malaria (2013)

Obesity—adult prevalence rate: 17.2% (2008)
country comparison to the world: 113

Children under the age of 5 years underweight: 11.1% (2009)
country comparison to the world: 66

Education expenditures: 3.2% of GDP (2012)
country comparison to the world: 136

Literacy: *definition:* age 15 and over has ever attended school
total population: 91.8%
male: 92%
female: 91.6% (2002 Census)

School life expectancy (primary to tertiary education): *total:* 10 years
male: 9 years
female: 11 years (2012)

Child labor—children ages 5-14: total number: 30,255
percentage: 16 % (2006 est.)

Unemployment, youth ages 15-24: total: 46.05%
country comparison to the world: 8
male: 43.59%
female: 50% (2011)

GOVERNMENT

Country name:
conventional long form: Cooperative Republic of Guyana
conventional short form: Guyana
former: British Guiana

Government type: republic

Capital: name: Georgetown
geographic coordinates: 6 48 N, 58 09 W
time difference: UTC-4 (1 hour ahead of Washington, DC during Standard Time)

Administrative divisions: 10 regions; Barima-Waini, Cuyuni-Mazaruni, Demerara-Mahaica, East Berbice-Corentyne, Essequibo Islands-West Demerara, Mahaica-Berbice, Pomeroon-Supenaam, Potaro-Siparuni, Upper Demerara-Berbice, *Upper Takutu-Upper Essequibo*

Independence: 26 May 1966 (from the UK)

National holiday: Republic Day, 23 February (1970)

Constitution: several previous; latest promulgated 6 October 1980; amended many times, last in 2007 (2013)

Legal system: common law system, based on the English model, with some Roman-Dutch civil law influence

International law organization participation: has not submitted an ICJ jurisdiction declaration; accepts ICCt jurisdiction

Suffrage: 18 years of age; universal

Executive branch: *chief of state:* President Donald RAMOTAR (since 03 December 2011);
head of government: Prime Minister Samuel HINDS (since October 1992, except for a period as chief of state after the death of President Cheddi JAGAN on 6 March 1997)
cabinet: Cabinet of Ministers appointed by the president, responsible to the legislature (For more information visit the World Leaders website)
elections: president elected by popular vote as leader of a party list in parliamentary elections, which must be held at least every five years (no term limits); elections last held on 28 November 2011 (next to be called by December 2016); prime minister appointed by the president
election results: Donald RAMOTAR elected president, percent of vote 48.6%

Legislative branch: unicameral National Assembly (65 seats; members elected by popular vote, also not more than 4 non-elected non-voting ministers and 2 non-elected non-voting parliamentary secretaries appointed by the president; members to serve five-year terms)
elections: last held on 28 November 2011 (next to be held by November 2016)
election results: percent of vote by party—PPP/C 48.6%, APNU 40%, AFC 10.3%, other 1.1%; seats by party—PPP/C 32, APNU 26, AFC 7

Judicial branch: *highest court(s):* Supreme Court of Judicature (consists of the Court of Appeal with a chief justice and 3 justices, and the High Court with a chief justice and 10 justices organized into 3- or 5-judge panels) note—in 2009, Guyana ceased final appeals in civil and criminal cases to the Judicial Committee of the Privy Council (in London), replacing it with the Caribbean Court of Justice, the judicial organ of the Caribbean Community
judge selection and term of office: Court of Appeal and High Court chief justices appointed by the president; other judges of both courts appointed by the Judicial Service Commission, a body appointed by the president; judges appointed for life with retirement at age 65
subordinate courts: Land Court; magistrates' courts

Political parties and leaders: Alliance for Change or AFC [Khemraj RAMJATTAN] Justice for All Party [C.N. SHARMA] A Partnership for National Unity or APNU [David GRANGER] People's Progressive Party/Civic or PPP/C [Donald RAMOTAR] Rise, Organize, and Rebuild or ROAR [Ravi DEV] The United Force or TUF [Manzoor NADIR] The Unity Party [Joey JAGAN] Vision Guyana [Peter RAMSAROOP]

Political pressure groups and leaders: Amerindian People's Association Guyana Bar Association Guyana Citizens Initiative Guyana Human Rights Association Guyana Public Service Union or GPSU Private Sector Commission Trades Union Congress

International organization participation: ACP, AOSIS, C, Caricom, CD, CDB, CELAC, FAO, G-77, IADB, IBRD, ICAO, ICRM, IDA, IFAD, IFC, IFRCS, ILO, IMF, IMO, Interpol, IOC, IOM, ISO (correspondent), ITU, LAES, MIGA, NAM, OAS, OIC, OPANAL, OPCW, PCA, Petrocaribe, UN, UNASUR, UNCTAD, UNESCO, UNIDO, UPU, WCO, WFTU (NGOs), WHO, WIPO, WMO, WTO

Diplomatic representation in the US:
chief of mission: Ambassador Bayney KARRAN (since 4 December 2003)
chancery: 2490 Tracy Place NW, Washington, DC 20008
telephone: [1] (202) 265-6900
FAX: [1] (202) 232-1297
consulate(s) general: New York

Diplomatic representation from the US:
chief of mission: Ambassador D. Brent HARDT (since 19 August 2011)
embassy: US Embassy, 100 Young and Duke Streets, Kingston, Georgetown
mailing address: P. O. Box 10507, Georgetown; US Embassy, 3170 Georgetown Place, Washington DC 20521-3170
telephone: [592] 225-4900 through 4909
FAX: [592] 225-8497

Flag description: green, with a red isosceles triangle (based on the hoist side) superimposed on a long, yellow arrowhead; there is a narrow, black border between the red and yellow, and a narrow, white border between the yellow and the green; green represents forest and foliage; yellow stands for mineral resources and a bright future; white symbolizes Guyana's rivers; red signifies zeal and the sacrifice of the people; black indicates perseverance

National symbol(s): Canje pheasant (hoatzin); jaguar

National anthem: *name:* "Dear Land of Guyana, of Rivers and Plains"
lyrics/music: Archibald Leonard LUKERL/Robert Cyril Gladstone POTTER
note: adopted 1966

ECONOMY

Economy—overview: The Guyanese economy exhibited moderate economic growth in recent years and is based largely on agriculture and extractive industries. The economy is heavily dependent upon the export of six commodities—sugar, gold, bauxite, shrimp, timber, and rice—which represent nearly 60% of the country's GDP and are highly susceptible to adverse weather conditions and fluctuations in commodity prices. Guyana's entrance into the Caricom Single Market and Economy (CSME) in January 2006 has broadened the country's export market, primarily in the raw materials sector. Guyana has experienced positive growth almost every year over the past decade. Inflation has been kept under control. Recent years have seen the government's stock of debt reduced significantly—with external debt now less than half of what it was in the early 1990s. Chronic problems include a shortage of skilled labor and a deficient infrastructure. Despite recent improvements, the government is still juggling a sizable external debt against the urgent need for expanded public investment. In March 2007, the Inter-American Development Bank, Guyana's principal donor, canceled Guyana's nearly $470 million debt, equivalent to 21% of GDP, which along with other Highly Indebted Poor Country (HIPC) debt forgiveness brought the debt-to-GDP ratio down from 183% in 2006 to 60% in 2013. Guyana had become heavily indebted as a result of the inward-looking, state-led development model pursued in the 1970s and 1980s. Much of Guyana's growth in recent years has come from a surge in gold production in response to global prices, although downward trends in gold prices may threaten future growth. In 2013, production of sugar dropped to a 23-year low.

GDP (purchasing power parity): $6.593 billion (2013 est.)
country comparison to the world: 163
$6.26 billion (2012 est.)
$5.972 billion (2011 est.)
note: data are in 2013 US dollars

GDP (official exchange rate): $3.02 billion (2013 est.)

GDP—real growth rate: 5.3% (2013 est.)
country comparison to the world: 49
4.8% (2012 est.)
5.4% (2011 est.)

GDP—per capita (PPP): $8,500 (2013 est.)
country comparison to the world: 129
$8,100 (2012 est.)
$7,700 (2011 est.)
note: data are in 2013 US dollars

Gross national saving: 6.2% of GDP (2013 est.)
country comparison to the world: 146
8.3% of GDP (2012 est.)
9.4% of GDP (2011 est.)

GDP—composition, by end use:
household consumption: 85.6%
government consumption: 16.3%
investment in fixed capital: 22.5%
investment in inventories: -13.5%
exports of goods and services: 59.9%
imports of goods and services: -70.8% (2013 est.)

GDP—composition, by sector of origin:
agriculture: 20.7%
industry: 38.5%
services: 40.8% (2013 est.)

Agriculture—products: sugarcane, rice, edible oils; beef, pork, poultry; shrimp, fish

Industries: bauxite, sugar, rice milling, timber, textiles, gold mining

Industrial production growth rate: 13.5% (2013 est.)
country comparison to the world: 5

Labor force: 313,100 (2009 est.)
country comparison to the world: 164

Labor force—by occupation: agriculture: NA%
industry: NA%
services: NA%

Unemployment rate: 11% (2007)
country comparison to the world: 117

Population below poverty line: 35% (2006)

Household income or consumption by percentage share: *lowest 10%:* 1.3%
highest 10%: 33.8% (1999)

Distribution of family income—Gini index: 44.6 (2007)
country comparison to the world: 44
43.2 (1999)

Budget: *revenues:* $756.7 million
expenditures: $948.5 million (2013 est.)

Taxes and other revenues: 25.1% of GDP (2013 est.)
country comparison to the world: 126

Budget surplus (+) or deficit (-): -6.4% of GDP (2013 est.)
country comparison to the world: 183

Public debt: 59.9% of GDP (2013 est.)
country comparison to the world: 48
59.5% of GDP (2012 est.)

Fiscal year: calendar year

Inflation rate (consumer prices): 3.9% (2013 est.)
country comparison to the world: 129
2.4% (2012 est.)

Central bank discount rate: 5.5% (31 December 2011 est.)
country comparison to the world: 91
4.25% (31 December 2010 est.)

Commercial bank prime lending rate: 13.8% (31 December 2013 est.)
country comparison to the world: 53
13.86% (31 December 2012 est.)

Stock of narrow money: $601.8 million (31 December 2013 est.)
country comparison to the world: 156
$550.4 million (31 December 2012 est.)

Stock of broad money: $1.617 billion (31 December 2013 est.)
country comparison to the world: 157
$1.49 billion (31 December 2012 est.)

Stock of domestic credit: $1.352 billion (31 December 2013 est.)
country comparison to the world: 148
$1.223 billion (31 December 2012 est.)

Market value of publicly traded shares:
$610.9 million (31 December 2012 est.)
country comparison to the world: 111
$440.4 million (31 December 2011)
$339.8 million (31 December 2010 est.)

Current account balance: -$510.7 million (2013 est.)
country comparison to the world: 102
-$394.8 million (2012 est.)

Exports: $1.337 billion (2013 est.)
country comparison to the world: 150
$1.396 billion (2012 est.)

Exports—commodities: sugar, gold, bauxite, alumina, rice, shrimp, molasses, rum, timber

Exports—partners: US 30.8%, Canada 28.9%, UK 6.2% (2012)

Imports: $2.039 billion (2013 est.)
country comparison to the world: 165
$1.978 billion (2012 est.)

Imports—commodities: manufactures, machinery, petroleum, food

Imports—partners: US 22.2%, Trinidad and Tobago 21.9%, China 12.3%, Cuba 6.1%, Suriname 4% (2012)

Reserves of foreign exchange and gold:
$854.7 million (31 December 2013 est.)
country comparison to the world: 139
$864 million (31 December 2012 est.)

Debt—external: $1.846 billion (31 December 2011 est.)
country comparison to the world: 144
$1.846 billion (31 December 2011 est.)

Exchange rates: Guyanese dollars (GYD) per US dollar—
205.9 (2013 est.)
204.36 (2012 est.)
203.64 (2010 est.)
203.95 (2009)
203.86 (2008)

ENERGY

Electricity—production: 700 million kWh (2010 est.)
country comparison to the world: 155

Electricity—consumption: 512 million kWh (2010 est.)
country comparison to the world: 169

Electricity—exports: 0 kWh (2012 est.)
country comparison to the world: 146

Electricity—imports: 0 kWh (2012 est.)
country comparison to the world: 153

Electricity—installed generating capacity:
362,500 kW (2010 est.)
country comparison to the world: 147

Electricity—from fossil fuels: 96% of total installed capacity (2010 est.)
country comparison to the world: 67

Electricity—from nuclear fuels: 0% of total installed capacity (2010 est.)
country comparison to the world: 102

Electricity—from hydroelectric plants: 0.3% of total installed capacity (2010 est.)
country comparison to the world: 146

Electricity—from other renewable sources: 3.7% of total installed capacity (2010 est.)
country comparison to the world: 50

Crude oil—production: 0 bbl/day (2012 est.)
country comparison to the world: 178

Crude oil—exports: 0 bbl/day (2010 est.)
country comparison to the world: 123

Crude oil—imports: 0 bbl/day (2010 est.)
country comparison to the world: 197

Crude oil—proved reserves: 0 bbl (1 January 2013 es)
country comparison to the world: 141

Refined petroleum products—production: 0 bbl/day (2010 est.)
country comparison to the world: 153

Refined petroleum products—consumption: 10,910 bbl/day (2011 est.)
country comparison to the world: 151

Refined petroleum products—exports: 0 bbl/day (2010 est.)
country comparison to the world: 183

Refined petroleum products—imports: 10,780 bbl/day (2010 est.)
country comparison to the world: 129

Natural gas—production: 0 cu m (2011 est.)
country comparison to the world: 141

Natural gas—consumption: 0 cu m (2010 est.)
country comparison to the world: 154

Natural gas—exports: 0 cu m (2011 est.)
country comparison to the world: 114

Natural gas—imports: 0 cu m (2011 est.)
country comparison to the world: 203

Natural gas—proved reserves: 0 cu m (1 January 2013 es)
country comparison to the world: 147

Carbon dioxide emissions from consumption of energy: 1.673 million Mt (2011 est.)
country comparison to the world: 152

COMMUNICATIONS

Telephones—main lines in use: 154,200 (2012)
country comparison to the world: 136

Telephones—mobile cellular: 547,000 (2012)
country comparison to the world: 167

Telephone system: *general assessment:* fair system for long-distance service; microwave radio relay network for trunk lines; many areas still lack fixed-line telephone services
domestic: fixed-line teledensity is about 20 per 100 persons; mobile-cellular teledensity about 70 per 100 persons in 2011
international: country code—592; tropospheric scatter to Trinidad; satellite earth station—1 Intelsat (Atlantic Ocean) (2011)

Broadcast media: government-dominated broadcast media; the National Communications Network (NCN) TV is state-owned; a few private TV stations relay satellite services; the state owns and operates 2 radio stations broadcasting on multiple frequencies capable of reaching the entire country; government limits on licensing of new private radio stations continue to constrain competition in broadcast media (2007)

Internet country code: .gy

Internet hosts: 24,936 (2012)
country comparison to the world: 112

Internet users: 189,600 (2009)
country comparison to the world: 142

TRANSPORTATION

Airports: 117 (2013)
country comparison to the world: 5 0

Airports—with paved runways: total: 1 1
1,524 to 2,437 m: 2
914 to 1,523 m: 1
under 914 m: 8 (2013)

Airports—with unpaved runways: *total:* 106
1,524 to 2,437 m: 1
914 to 1,523 m: 16
under 914 m: 89 (2013)

Roadways: *total:* 7,970 km
country comparison to the world: 141
paved: 590 km
unpaved: 7,380 km (2000)

Waterways: 330 km (the Berbice, Demerara, and Essequibo rivers are navigable by oceangoing vessels for 150 km, 100 km, and 80 km respectively) (2012)
country comparison to the world: 92

Merchant marine: *total:* 1 0
country comparison to the world: 114
by type: cargo 7, petroleum tanker 2, refrigerated cargo 1
registered in other countries: 3 (Saint Vincent and the Grenadines 2, unknown 1) (2010)

Ports and terminals: *major seaport(s):* Georgetown

MILITARY

Military branches: Guyana Defense Force: Army (includes Air Corps, Coast Guard) (2012)

Military service age and obligation: 16 years of age or younger for voluntary military service; no conscription (2013)

Manpower available for military service:
males age 16-49: 189,840 (2010 est.)

Manpower fit for military service:
males age 16-49: 133,239
females age 16-49: 147,719 (2010 est.)

Manpower reaching militarily significant age annually: *male:* 8,849
female: 8,460 (2010 est.)

Military expenditures: 1.09% of GDP (2012)
country comparison to the world: 94
1.17% of GDP (2011)
1.09% of GDP (2010)

TRANSNATIONAL ISSUES

Disputes—international: all of the area west of the Essequibo River is claimed by Venezuela preventing any discussion of a maritime boundary; Guyana has expressed its intention to join Barbados in asserting claims before UN Convention on the Law of the Sea (UNCLOS) that Trinidad and Tobago's maritime boundary with Venezuela extends into their waters; Suriname claims a triangle of land between the New and Kutari/Koetari rivers in a historic dispute over the headwaters of the Courantyne; Guyana seeks arbitration under provisions of the UNCLOS to resolve the long-standing dispute with Suriname over the axis of the territorial sea boundary in potentially oil-rich waters

Trafficking in persons: current situation: Guyana is a source and destination country for men, women, and children subjected to sex trafficking and forced labor; Guyanese and foreign women and girls are forced into prostitution in Guyana; experts are concerned that Guyanese children are subjected to exploitive labor practices in the mining, agriculture, and forestry sectors; Indonesian workers are victims of forced labor on Guyanese-flagged fishing boats

tier rating: Tier 2 Watch List—Guyana does not fully comply with the minimum standards for the elimination of trafficking; however, it is making significant efforts to do so; despite some progress in identifying and assisting some trafficking victims, the government has failed to increase its efforts to hold trafficking offenders accountable with jail time, creating an enabling environment for human trafficking; public comments from the government downplaying the scope of Guyana's trafficking problem diminishes the potential impact of its awareness campaigns; authorities operate a hotline for trafficking victims and conduct several awareness and sensitization sessions that target vulnerable communities (2013)

Illicit drugs: transshipment point for narcotics from South America—primarily Venezuela—to Europe and the US; producer of cannabis; rising money laundering related to drug trafficking and human smuggling

HAITI

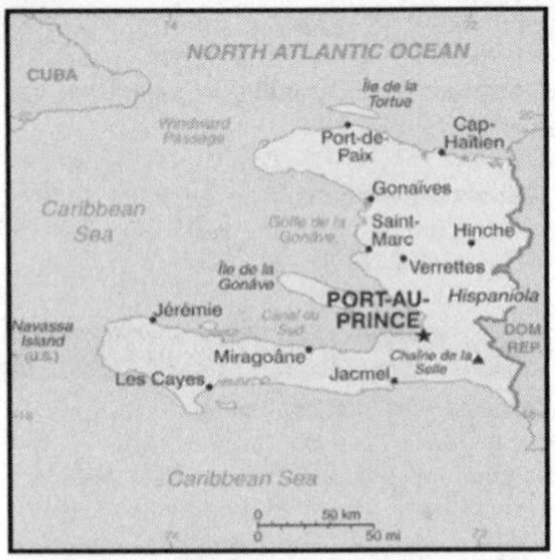

INTRODUCTION

Background: The native Taino—who inhabited the island of Hispaniola when it was discovered by Christopher COLUMBUS in 1492—were virtually annihilated by Spanish settlers within 25 years. In the early 17th century, the French established a presence on Hispaniola. In 1697, Spain ceded to the French the western third of the island, which later became Haiti. The French colony, based on forestry and sugar-related industries, became one of the wealthiest in the Caribbean but only through the heavy importation of African slaves and considerable environmental degradation. In the late 18th century, Haiti's nearly half million slaves revolted under Toussaint L'OUVERTURE. After a prolonged struggle, Haiti became the first post-colonial black-led nation in the world, declaring its independence in 1804. Currently the poorest country in the Western Hemisphere, Haiti has experienced political instability for most of its history. After an armed rebellion led to the forced resignation and exile of President Jean-Bertrand ARISTIDE in February 2004, an interim government took office to organize new elections under the auspices of the United Nations. Continued instability and technical delays prompted repeated postponements, but Haiti inaugurated a democratically elected president and parliament in May of 2006. This was followed by contested elections in 2010 that resulted in the election of Haiti's current President, Michel MARTELLY. A massive magnitude 7.0 earthquake struck Haiti in January 2010 with an epicenter about 25 km (15 mi) west of the capital, Port-au-Prince. Estimates are that over 300,000 people were killed and some 1.5 million left homeless. The earthquake was assessed as the worst in this region over the last 200 years.

GEOGRAPHY

Location: Caribbean, western one-third of the island of Hispaniola, between the Caribbean Sea and the North Atlantic Ocean, west of the Dominican Republic

Geographic coordinates: 19 00 N, 72 25 W

Map references: Central America and the Caribbean

Area: *total:* 27,750 sq km
country comparison to the world: 148
land: 27,560 sq km
water: 190 sq km

Area—comparative: slightly smaller than Maryland

Land boundaries: *total:* 360 km
border countries: Dominican Republic 360 km

Coastline: 1,771 km

Maritime claims: *territorial sea:* 12 nm
contiguous zone: 24 nm
exclusive economic zone: 200 nm
continental shelf: to depth of exploitation

Climate: tropical; semiarid where mountains in east cut off trade winds

Terrain: mostly rough and mountainous

Elevation extremes: *lowest point:* Caribbean Sea 0 m
highest point: Chaine de la Selle 2,680 m

Natural resources: bauxite, copper, calcium carbonate, gold, marble, hydropower

Land use: *arable land:* 36.04%
permanent crops: 10.09%
other: 53.87% (2011)

Irrigated land: 970 sq km (2009)

Total renewable water resources: 14.03 cu km (2011)

Freshwater withdrawal (domestic/industrial/agricultural): *total:* 1.2 cu km/yr (17%/3%/80%)
per capita: 134.3 cu m/yr (2009)

Natural hazards: lies in the middle of the hurricane belt and subject to severe storms from June to October; occasional flooding and earthquakes; *periodic droughts*

Environment—current issues: extensive deforestation (much of the remaining forested land is being cleared for agriculture and used as fuel); soil erosion; inadequate supplies of potable water

Environment—international agreements: *party to:* Biodiversity, Climate Change, Climate Change-Kyoto Protocol, Desertification, Law of the Sea, Marine Dumping, Marine Life Conservation, Ozone Layer Protection signed, but not ratified: Hazardous Wastes

Geography—note: shares island of Hispaniola with Dominican Republic (western one-third is Haiti, eastern two-thirds is the Dominican Republic)

PEOPLE AND SOCIETY

Nationality: *noun:* Haitian(s)
adjective: Haitian

Ethnic groups: black 95%, mulatto and white 5%

Languages: French (official), Creole (official)

Religions: Roman Catholic 80%, Protestant 16% (Baptist 10%, Pentecostal 4%, Adventist 1%, other 1%), none 1%, other 3%
note: roughly half of the population practices voodoo

Population: 9,996,731 (July 2014 est.)
country comparison to the world: 89
note: estimates for this country explicitly take into account the effects of excess mortality due to AIDS; this can result in lower life expectancy, higher infant mortality, higher death rates, lower population growth rates, and changes in the distribution of population by age and sex than would otherwise be expected

Age structure:
0-14 years: 34% (male 1,701,559/female 1,693,236)
15-24 years: 21.6% (male 1,078,994/female 1,081,005)
25-54 years: 35.3% (male 1,755,722/female 1,770,386)
55-64 years: 4.1% (male 241,174/female 263,369)
65 years and over: 4.1% (male 183,627/female 227,659) (2014 est.)

Dependency ratios:
total dependency ratio: 65.2 %
youth dependency ratio: 57.8 %
elderly dependency ratio: 7.5 %
potential support ratio: 13.4 (2013)

Median age: *total:* 22.2 years
male: 22 years
female: 22.4 years (2014 est.)

Population growth rate: 1.08%
country comparison to the world: 113
note: the preliminary 2011 numbers differ significantly from those of 2010, which were strongly influenced by the demographic effect of the January 2010 earthquake; the latest figures more closely correspond to those of 2009 (2014 est.)

Birth rate: 22.83 births/1,000 population (2014 est.)
country comparison to the world: 73

Death rate: 7.91 deaths/1,000 population (2014 est.)
country comparison to the world: 104

Net migration rate: -4.12 migrant(s)/1,000 population (2014 est.)
country comparison to the world: 191

Urbanization: *urban population:* 52% of total population (2010)
rate of urbanization: 3.9% annual rate of change (2010-15 est.)

Major urban areas—population: PORT-AU-PRINCE (capital) 2.143 million (2010)

Sex ratio: *at birth:* 1.01 male(s)/female
0-14 years: 1.01 male(s)/female
15-24 years: 1 male(s)/female
25-54 years: 0.99 male(s)/female
55-64 years: 0.99 male(s)/female
65 years and over: 0.8 male(s)/female
total population: 0.98 male(s)/female (2014 est.)

Mother's mean age at first birth: 22.7
note: median age at first birth among women 25-29 (2012)

Maternal mortality rate: 350 deaths/100,000 live births (2010)
country comparison to the world: 31

Infant mortality rate: *total:* 49.43 deaths/1,000 live births
country comparison to the world: 40
male: 53.26 deaths/1,000 live births
female: 45.56 deaths/1,000 live births
note: the preliminary 2011 numbers differ significantly from those of 2010, which were strongly influenced by the demographic effect of the January 2010 earthquake; the latest figures more closely correspond to those of 2009 (2014 est.)

Life expectancy at birth: *total population:* 63.18 years
country comparison to the world: 186
male: 61.77 years
female: 64.6 years
note: the preliminary 2011 numbers differ significantly from those of 2010, which were strongly influenced by the demographic effect of the January 2010 earthquake; the latest figures more closely correspond to those of 2009 (2014 est.)

Total fertility rate: 2.79 children born/woman (2014 est.)
country comparison to the world: 68

Contraceptive prevalence rate: 34.5% (2012)

Health expenditures: 7.9% of GDP (2011)
country comparison to the world: 65

Physicians density: 0.25 physicians/1,000 population (1998)

Hospital bed density: 1.3 beds/1,000 population (2007)

Drinking water source:
improved:

urban: 77.5% of population
rural: 48.5% of population
total: 64% of population
unimproved:
urban: 22.5% of population
rural: 51.5% of population
total: 36% of population (2011 est.)

Sanitation facility access:
improved:
urban: 33.7% of population
rural: 17.4% of population
total: 26.1% of population
unimproved:
urban: 66.3% of population
rural: 82.6% of population
total: 73.9% of population (2011 est.)

HIV/AIDS—adult prevalence rate: 2.1% (2012 est.)
country comparison to the world: 27

HIV/AIDS—people living with HIV/AIDS: 146,000 (2012 est.)
country comparison to the world: 36

HIV/AIDS—deaths: 7,500 (2012 est.)
country comparison to the world: 29

Major infectious diseases: *degree of risk:* high
food or waterborne diseases: bacterial and protozoal diarrhea, hepatitis A and E, and typhoid fever
vectorborne diseases: dengue fever and malaria (2013)

Obesity—adult prevalence rate: 7.9% (2008)
country comparison to the world: 137

Children under the age of 5 years underweight: 18.9% (2006)
country comparison to the world: 33

Education expenditures: NA

Literacy: *definition:* age 15 and over can read and write
total population: 48.7%
male: 53.4%
female: 44.6% (2006 est.)

Child labor—children ages 5-14: total number: 2,587,205
percentage: 21 % (2006 est.)

GOVERNMENT

Country name: *conventional long form:* Republic of Haiti
conventional short form: Haiti
local long form: Republique d'Haiti/Repiblik d' Ayiti
local short form: Haiti/Ayiti

Government type: republic

Capital: name: Port-au-Prince
geographic coordinates: 18 32 N, 72 20 W
time difference: UTC-5 (same time as Washington, DC during Standard Time)
daylight saving time: +1hr, begins second Sunday in March; ends first Sunday in November

Administrative divisions: 10 departments (departements, singular—departement); Artibonite, Centre, Grand'Anse, Nippes, Nord, Nord-Est, Nord-Ouest, Ouest, Sud, Sud-Est

Independence: 1 January 1804 (from France)

National holiday: Independence Day, 1 January (1804)

Constitution: many previous (23 total); latest adopted 10 March 1987; amended 2012 (2013)

Legal system: civil law system strongly influenced by Napoleonic Code

International law organization participation: accepts compulsory ICJ jurisdiction; non-party state to the ICCt

Suffrage: 18 years of age; universal

Executive branch: *chief of state:* President Michel MARTELLY (since 14 May 2011)
head of government: Prime Minister Laurent LAMOTHE (since 16 May 2012)
cabinet: Cabinet chosen by the prime minister in consultation with the president (For more information visit the World Leaders website)
elections: president elected by popular vote for a five-year term (may not serve consecutive terms); election last held on 28 November 2010; runoff on 20 March 2011 (next to be held in 2015); prime minister appointed by the president, ratified by the National Assembly
election results: Michel MARTELLY won the runoff election held on 20 March 2011 with 67.6% of the vote against 31.7% for Mirlande MANIGAT

Legislative branch: bicameral National Assembly or Assemblee Nationale consists of the Senate (30 seats; members elected by popular vote to serve six-year terms; one-third elected every two years) and the Chamber of Deputies (99 seats; members elected by popular vote to serve four-year terms);
elections: Senate—last held on 28 November 2010 with run-off elections on 20 March 2011 (next regular election, for one third of seats, scheduled for 2012 but delayed); Chamber of Deputies—last held on 28 November 2010 with run-off elections on 20 March 2011 (next regular election to be held in 2014)
election results: 2010 Senate—percent of vote by party—NA; seats by party—Inite 6, ALTENATIV 4, LAVNI 1; 2010 Chamber of Deputies—percent of vote by party—NA; seats by party—Inite 32, Altenativ 11, Ansanm Nou Fo 10, AAA 8, LAVNI 7, RASANBLE 4, KONBIT 3, MOCHRENA 3, Platforme Liberation 3, PONT 3, Repons Peyizan 3, Independent 2, MAS 2, MODELH-PRDH 1, PLAPH 1, RESPE 1, Veye Yo 1, vacant 4

Judicial branch: *highest court(s):* Supreme Court or Cour de Cassation (consists of a chief judge and other judges) note—Haiti is a member of the Caribbean Court of Justice
judge selection and term of office: judges appointed by the president from candidate lists submitted by the Senate of the National Assembly; note—Article 174 of the Haiti Constitution states "Judges of the Supreme Court.... are appointed for 10 years." whereas Article 177 states "Judges of the Supreme Court..... are appointed for life."
subordinate courts: Courts of Appeal; Courts of First Instance; magistrates' courts; special courts

Political parties and leaders: Assembly of Progressive National Democrats or RDNP [Mirlande MANIGAT]; Christian and Citizen For Haiti's Reconstruction or ACCRHA [Chavannes JEUNE]; Convention for Democratic Unity or KID [Evans PAUL]; Cooperative Action to Rebuild Haiti or KONBA [Jean William JEANTY]; December 16 Platform or Platfom 16 Desanm [Dr. Gerard BLOT]; Democratic Alliance or ALYANS [Evans PAUL] (coalition composed of KID and PPRH); Democratic Centers's National Council or CONACED [Osner FEVRY]; Democratic Movement for the Liberation of Haiti-Revolutionary Party of Haiti or MODELH-PRDH; Effort and Solidarity to Create an Alternative for the People or ESKAMP [Joseph JASME]; Fanmi Lavalas or FL [Jean-Bertrand ARISTIDE]; For Us All or PONT [Jean-Marie CHERESTAL]; Grouping of Citizens for Hope or RESPE [Charles-Henri BAKER]; Haiti in Action or AAA [Youri LATORTUE]; Haitians for Haiti [Yvon NEPTUNE]; Independent Movement for National Reconstruction or MIRN [Luc FLEURINORD]; Konbit Pou refe Ayiti or KONBIT; Lavni Organization or LAVNI [Yves CRISTALIN]; Liberal Party of Haiti or PLH [Jean Andre VICTOR]; Liberation Platform or PLATFORME LIBERATION; Love Haiti or Renmen Ayiti [Jean-Henry CEANT and Camille LEBLANC]; Merging of Haitian Social Democratics or FUSION [Edmonde Supplice BEAUZILE] (coalition of Ayiti Capable, Haitian National; Revolutionary Party, and National Congress of Democratic Movements); Mobilization for National Development or MDN [Hubert de RONCERAY]; National Front for the Reconstruction of Haiti or FRN [Guy PHILIPPE]; New Christian Movement for a New Haiti or MOCHRENA [Luc MESADIEU]; Peasant's Response or Repons Peyizan [Michel MARTELLY]; Platform Alternative for Progress and Democracy or ALTENATIV [Victor BENOIT and Evans PAUL]; Platform of Haitian Patriots or PLAPH [Dejean BELISAIRE and Himmler REBU]; Popular Party for the Renewal of Haiti or PPRH [Claude ROMAIN]; Rally or RASAMBLE; Respect or RESPE; Socialist Action Movement or MAS; Strength in Unity or Ansanm Nou Fo [Leslie VOLTAIRE]; Struggling People's Organization or OPL [Sauveur PIERRE-ETIENNE]; Union [Chavannes JEUNE]; Union of Haitian Citizens for Democracy, Development, and Education or UCADDE [Jeantel JOSEPH]; Union of Haitian Citizens for Democracy, Development, and Education or UCADDE [Jeantel JOSEPH]; Union of Nationalist and Progressive Haitians or UNPH [Edouard FRANCISQUE]; Unity or Inite [Levaillant LOUIS-JEUNE] (coalition that includes Front for Hope or L'ESPWA); Vigilance or Veye Yo [Lavarice GAUDIN]; Youth for People's Power or JPP [Rene CIVIL]

Political pressure groups and leaders: Autonomous Organizations of Haitian Workers or CATH [Fignole ST-CYR]; Confederation of Haitian Workers or CTH; Economic Forum of the Private Sector or EF [Reginald BOULOS]; Federation of Workers Trade Unions or FOS; General Organization of Independent Haitian Workers [Patrick NUMAS]; Grand-Anse Resistance Committee, or KOREGA; The Haitian Association of Industries or ADIH [Georges SASSINE]; National Popular Assembly or APN; Papaye Peasants Movement or MPP [Chavannes JEAN-BAPTISTE]; Popular Organizations Gathering Power or PROP; Protestant Federation of Haiti; Roman Catholic Church

International organization participation: ACP, AOSIS, Caricom, CD, CDB, CELAC, FAO, G-77, IADB, IAEA, IBRD, ICAO, ICRM, IDA, IFAD, IFC, IFRCS, ILO, IMF, IMO, Interpol, IOC, IOM, IPU, ITSO, ITU, ITUC (NGOs), LAES, MIGA, NAM, OAS, OIF, OPANAL, OPCW, PCA, Petrocaribe, UN, UNCTAD, UNESCO, UNIDO, Union Latina, UNWTO, UPU, WCO, WFTU (NGOs), WHO, WIPO, WMO, WTO

Diplomatic representation in the US:
chief of mission: Ambassador Paul Getty ALTIDOR (since 17 April 2012)
chancery: 2311 Massachusetts Avenue NW, Washington, DC 20008
telephone: [1] (202) 332-4090
FAX: [1] (202) 745-7215
consulate(s) general: Atlanta, Boston, Chicago, Miami, New York, San Juan (Puerto Rico)
consulate(s): Orlando (FL)

Diplomatic representation from the US:
chief of mission: Ambassador Pamela A. WHITE (since 18 July 2012)
embassy: Tabarre 41, Route de Tabarre, Port-au-Prince
mailing address: (in Haiti) P.O. Box 1634, Port-au-Prince, Haiti; (from abroad) 3400 Port-au-Prince, State Department, Washington, DC 20521-3400
telephone: [509] 2229-8000
FAX: [509] 229-8028

Flag description: two equal horizontal bands of blue (top) and red with a centered white rectangle bearing the coat of arms, which contains a palm tree flanked by flags and two cannons above a scroll bearing the motto L'UNION FAIT LA FORCE (Union Makes Strength); the colors are taken from the French Tricolor and represent the union of blacks and mulattoes

National symbol(s): Hispaniolan trogon (bird)
National anthem: name: "La Dessalinienne" (The Dessalines Song)
lyrics/music: Justin LHERISSON/Nicolas GEFFRARD
note: adopted 1904; the anthem is named for Jean-Jacques DESSALINES, a leader in the Haitian Revolution and first ruler of an independent Haiti

ECONOMY

Economy—overview: Haiti is a free market economy that enjoys the advantages of low labor costs and tariff-free access to the US for many of its exports. Poverty, corruption, vulnerability to natural disasters, and low levels of education for much of the population are among Haiti's most serious impediments to economic growth. Haiti's economy suffered a severe setback in January 2010 when a 7.0 magnitude earthquake destroyed much of its capital city, Port-au-Prince, and neighboring areas. Currently the poorest country in the Western Hemisphere with 80% of the population living under the poverty line and 54% in abject poverty, the earthquake further inflicted $7.8 billion in damage and caused the country's GDP to contract. In 2011, the Haitian economy began recovering from the earthquake. However, two hurricanes adversely affected agricultural output and the low public capital spending slowed the recovery in 2012. Two-fifths of all Haitians depend on the agricultural sector, mainly small-scale subsistence farming, and remain vulnerable to damage from frequent natural disasters, exacerbated by the country's widespread deforestation. US economic engagement under the Caribbean Basin Trade Preference Agreement (CBTPA) and the 2008 Haitian Hemispheric Opportunity through Partnership Encouragement (HOPE II) Act helped increase apparel exports and investment by providing duty-free access to the US. Congress voted in 2010 to extend the CBTPA and HOPE II until 2020 under the Haiti Economic Lift Program (HELP) Act; the apparel sector accounts for about 90% of Haitian exports and nearly one-twentieth of GDP. Remittances are the primary source of foreign exchange, equaling one-fifth of GDP and representing more than five times the earnings from exports in 2012. Haiti suffers from a lack of investment, partly because of weak infrastructure such as access to electricity. Haiti's outstanding external debt was cancelled by donor countries following the 2010 earthquake, but has since risen to $1.1 billion as of December 2013. The government relies on formal international economic assistance for fiscal sustainability, with over half of its annual budget coming from outside sources. The MARTELLY administration in 2011 launched a campaign aimed at drawing foreign investment into Haiti as a means for sustainable development. To that end, the MARTELLY government in 2012 created a Commission for Commercial Code Reform, effected reforms to the justice sector, and inaugurated the Caracol industrial park in Haiti's north coast. In 2012, private investment exceeded donor assistance for the first time since the 2010 earthquake.

GDP (purchasing power parity): $13.42 billion (2013 est.)
country comparison to the world: 148
$12.98 billion (2012 est.)
$12.62 billion (2011 est.)
note: data are in 2013 US dollars

GDP (official exchange rate): $8.287 billion (2013 est.)

GDP—real growth rate: 3.4% (2013 est.)
country comparison to the world: 102
2.8% (2012 est.)
5.6% (2011 est.)

GDP—per capita (PPP): $1,300 (2013 est.)
country comparison to the world: 210
$1,200 (2012 est.)
$1,200 (2011 est.)
note: data are in 2013 US dollars

Gross national saving: 3.7% of GDP (2011 est.)
country comparison to the world: 149
3.7% of GDP (2011 est.)
3.7% of GDP

GDP—composition, by sector of origin:
agriculture: 24.1%
industry: 19.9%
services: 56% (2013 est.)

Agriculture—products: coffee, mangoes, cocoa, sugarcane, rice, corn, sorghum; wood, vetiver

Industries: textiles, sugar refining, flour milling, cement, light assembly based on imported parts

Industrial production growth rate: 6% (2013 est.)
country comparison to the world: 43

Labor force: 4.81 million
country comparison to the world: 82
note: shortage of skilled labor, unskilled labor abundant (2010 est.)

Labor force—by occupation: *agriculture:* 38.1%
industry: 11.5%
services: 50.4% (2010)

Unemployment rate: 40.6% (2010 est.)
country comparison to the world: 191
note: widespread unemployment and underemployment; more than two-thirds of the labor force do not have formal jobs

Population below poverty line: 80% (2003 est.)

Household income or consumption by percentage share: *lowest 10%:* 0.7%
highest 10%: 47.7% (2001)

Distribution of family income—Gini index: 59.2 (2001)
country comparison to the world: 7

Budget: *revenues:* $1.989 billion
expenditures: $2.437 billion (2013 est.)

Taxes and other revenues: 24% of GDP (2013 est.)
country comparison to the world: 137

Budget surplus (+) or deficit (-):
-5.4% of GDP (2013 est.)
country comparison to the world: 174

Fiscal year: 1 October—30 September

Inflation rate (consumer prices): 6.3% (2013 est.)
country comparison to the world: 180
6.3% (2012 est.)

Commercial bank prime lending rate: 9.2% (31 December 2013 est.)
country comparison to the world: 103
8.93% (31 December 2012 est.)

Stock of narrow money: $1.151 billion (31 December 2013 est.)
country comparison to the world: 146
$1.107 billion (31 December 2012 est.)

Stock of broad money: $3.509 billion (31 October 2012 est.)
country comparison to the world: 139
$3.43 billion (31 December 2011 est.)

Stock of domestic credit: $1.725 billion (31 December 2013 est.)
country comparison to the world: 136
$1.515 billion (31 December 2012 est.)

Market value of publicly traded shares: $NA

Current account balance: -$1.278 billion (2013 est.)
country comparison to the world: 127
-$1.358 billion (2012 est.)

Exports: $876.8 million (2013 est.)
country comparison to the world: 164
$785 million (2012 est.)

Exports—commodities: apparel, manufactures, oils, cocoa, mangoes, coffee

Exports—partners: US 81.7% (2012)

Imports: $2.697 billion (2013 est.)
country comparison to the world: 153
$2.679 billion (2012 est.)

Imports—commodities: food, manufactured goods, machinery and transport equipment, fuels, raw materials

Imports—partners: Dominican Republic 34.5%, US 26.2%, Netherlands Antilles 9.4%, China 7% (2012)

Reserves of foreign exchange and gold:
$1.335 billion (31 December 2013 est.)
country comparison to the world: 129
$1.287 billion (31 December 2012 est.)

Debt—external: $1.118 billion (31 December 2013 est.)
country comparison to the world: 158
$957.6 million (31 December 2012 est.)

Stock of direct foreign investment—at home:
$1.123 billion (31 December 2013 est.)
country comparison to the world: 100
$963.1 million (31 December 2012 est.)

Exchange rates: gourdes (HTG) per US dollar—
43.53 (2013 est.)
41.95 (2012 est.)
39.8 (2010 est.)
42.02 (2009)
39.216 (2008)

ENERGY

Electricity—production: 726 million kWh (2012 est.)
country comparison to the world: 153

Electricity—consumption: 208.5 million kWh (2012 est.)
country comparison to the world: 185

Electricity—exports: 0 kWh (2012 est.)
country comparison to the world: 148

Electricity—imports: 0 kWh (2012 est.)
country comparison to the world: 154

Electricity—installed generating capacity:
130,000 kW (2012 est.)
country comparison to the world: 170

Electricity—from fossil fuels: 79% of total installed capacity (2011 est.)
country comparison to the world: 92

Electricity—from nuclear fuels: 0% of total installed capacity (2011 est.)
country comparison to the world: 103

Electricity—from hydroelectric plants:
21% of total installed capacity (2011 est.)
country comparison to the world: 89

Electricity—from other renewable sources:
0% of total installed capacity (2011 est.)
country comparison to the world: 182

Crude oil—production: 0 bbl/day (2012 est.)
country comparison to the world: 179

Crude oil—exports: 0 bbl/day (2010 est.)
country comparison to the world: 124

Crude oil—imports: 0 bbl/day (2010 est.)
country comparison to the world: 198

Crude oil—proved reserves: 0 bbl (1 January 2013 es)
country comparison to the world: 143

Refined petroleum products—production: 0 bbl/day (2011 est.)
country comparison to the world: 154

Refined petroleum products—consumption: 14,000 bbl/day (2011 est.)
country comparison to the world: 147

Refined petroleum products—exports: 0 bbl/day (2012 est.)
country comparison to the world: 184

Refined petroleum products—imports: 15,130 bbl/day (2011 est.)
country comparison to the world: 120

Natural gas—production: 0 cu m (2011 est.)
country comparison to the world: 142

Natural gas—consumption: 0 cu m (2010 est.)
country comparison to the world: 155

Natural gas—exports: 0 cu m (2011 est.)
country comparison to the world: 115

Natural gas—imports: 0 cu m (2011 est.)
country comparison to the world: 204

Natural gas—proved reserves: 0 cu m (1 January 2013 es)
country comparison to the world: 148

Carbon dioxide emissions from consumption of energy: 2.103 million Mt (2011 est.)
country comparison to the world: 147

COMMUNICATIONS

Telephones—main lines in use: 50,000 (2012)
country comparison to the world: 163

Telephones—mobile cellular: 6.095 million (2012)
country comparison to the world: 102

Telephone system: *general assessment:* telecommunications infrastructure is among the least developed in Latin America and the Caribbean; domestic facilities barely adequate; international facilities slightly better
domestic: mobile-cellular telephone services are expanding rapidly due, in part, to the introduction of low-cost GSM phones; mobile-cellular teledensity exceeds 40 per 100 persons
international: country code—509; satellite earth station—1 Intelsat (Atlantic Ocean) (2010)

Broadcast media: several TV stations, including 1 government-owned; cable TV subscription service available; government-owned radio network; more than 250 private and community radio stations with about 50 FM stations in Port-au-Prince alone (2007)

Internet country code: .ht

Internet hosts: 555 (2012)
country comparison to the world: 181

Internet users: 1 million (2009)
country comparison to the world: 98

TRANSPORTATION

Airports: 14 (2013)
country comparison to the world: 148

Airports—with paved runways: *total:* 4
2,438 to 3,047 m: 2
914 to 1,523 m: 2 (2013)

Airports—with unpaved runways: *total:* 10
914 to 1,523 m: 2
under 914 m:
8 (2013)

Roadways: *total:* 4,266 km
country comparison to the world: 155
paved: 768 km
unpaved: 3,498 km (2009)

Ports and terminals: *major seaport(s):* Cap-Haitien, Gonaives, Jacmel, Port-au-Prince

MILITARY

Military branches: no regular military forces—small Coast Guard; a Ministry of National Defense established May 2012; the regular Haitian Armed Forces (FAdH)—Army, Navy, and Air Force—have been demobilized but still exist on paper until or unless they are constitutionally abolished (2011)

Manpower available for military service:
males age 16-49: 2,398,804
females age 16-49: 2,415,039 (2010 est.)

Manpower fit for military service:
males age 16-49: 1,666,324
females age 16-49: 1,704,364 (2010 est.)

Manpower reaching militarily significant age annually: *male:* 115,246
female: 115,282 (2010 est.)

TRANSNATIONAL ISSUES

Disputes—international: since 2004, peacekeepers from the UN Stabilization Mission in Haiti have assisted in maintaining civil order in Haiti; the mission currently includes 6,685 military, 2,607 police, and 443 civilian personnel; despite efforts to control illegal migration, Haitians cross into the Dominican Republic and sail to neighboring countries; Haiti claims US-administered Navassa Island

Refugees and internally displaced persons: *IDPs:* 137,000 (includes only IDPs from the 2010 earthquake living in camps or camp-like situations; information is lacking about IDPs living outside camps or who have left camps) (2014)

Trafficking in persons: current situation: Haiti is a source, transit, and destination country for men, women, and children subjected to forced labor and sex trafficking; many of Haiti's trafficking cases involve children recruited to live with families in other towns in the hope of going to school but who instead become forced domestic servants known as restaveks; restaveks are vulnerable to abuse and make up a large proportion of Haiti's population of street children, who are forced into prostitution, begging, and street crime by violent gangs; Haitians are exploited in forced labor in the Dominican Republic, elsewhere in the Caribbean, and the US, and some Dominican women are forced into prostitution in Haiti; women and children living in camps for internally displaced people are at increased risk of sex trafficking and forced labor
tier rating: Tier 2 Watch List—Haiti does not fully comply with the minimum standards for the elimination of trafficking; however, it is making significant efforts to do so; the government has made no discernible progress in prosecuting trafficking offenders largely because Haiti does not have a law specifically prohibiting human trafficking; the government does not provide direct or specialized services for trafficking victims and refers suspected victims to donor-funded NGOs, which provide shelter, food, medical, and psychosocial support; no proactive identification or assistance for adult victims was reported; an inter-ministerial working-group on human trafficking and a national commission for the elimination of the worst forms of child labor hae been created (2013)

Illicit drugs: Caribbean transshipment point for cocaine en route to the US and Europe; substantial bulk cash smuggling activity; Colombian narcotics traffickers favor Haiti for illicit financial transactions; pervasive corruption; significant consumer of cannabis

HEARD ISLAND AND MCDONALD ISLANDS

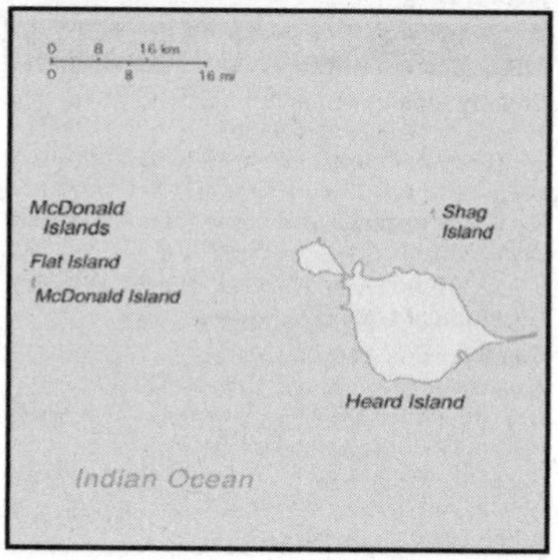

INTRODUCTION

Background: The United Kingdom transferred these uninhabited, barren, sub-Antarctic islands to Australia in 1947. Populated by large numbers of seal and bird species, the islands have been designated a nature preserve.

GEOGRAPHY

Location: islands in the Indian Ocean, about two-thirds of the way from Madagascar to Antarctica

Geographic coordinates: 53 06 S, 72 31 E

Map references: Antarctic Region

Area: *total:* 412 sq km
country comparison to the world: 203
land: 412 sq km
water: 0 sq km

Area—comparative: slightly more than two times the size of Washington, DC

Land boundaries: 0 km

Coastline: 101.9 km

Maritime claims: territorial sea: 12 nm
exclusive fishing zone: 200 nm

Climate: antarctic

Terrain: Heard Island—80% ice-covered, bleak and mountainous, dominated by a large massif (Big Ben) and an active volcano (Mawson Peak); McDonald Islands—small and rocky

Elevation extremes: *lowest point:* Indian Ocean 0 m
highest point: Mawson Peak on Big Ben volcano 2,745 m

Natural resources: fish

Land use: arable land: 0%
permanent crops: 0%
other: 100% (2011)

Irrigated land: 0 sq km (2011)

Natural hazards: Mawson Peak, an active volcano, is on Heard Island

Environment—current issues: NA

Geography—note: Mawson Peak on Heard Island is the highest Australian mountain (at 2,745 meters, it is taller than Mt. Kosciuszko in Australia proper), and one of only two active volcanoes located in Australian territory, the other being McDonald Island; in 1992, McDonald Island broke its dormancy and began erupting; it has erupted several times since, most recently in 2005

PEOPLE AND SOCIETY

Population: uninhabited

GOVERNMENT

Country name: *conventional long form:* Territory of Heard Island and McDonald Islands
conventional short form: Heard Island and McDonald Islands
abbreviation: HIMI

Dependency status: *territory of Australia;* administered from Canberra by the Department of *Sustainability, Environment, Water, Population and Communities (Australian Antarctic Division)*

Legal system: the laws of Australia, where applicable, apply

Diplomatic representation in the US: none (territory of Australia)

Diplomatic representation from the US: none (territory of Australia)

Flag description: the flag of Australia is used

ECONOMY

Economy—overview: The islands have no indigenous economic activity, but the Australian Government allows limited fishing in the surrounding waters. Visits to Heard Island typically focus on terrestrial and marine research and infrequent private expeditions.

COMMUNICATIONS

Internet country code: .hm

Internet hosts: 102 (2012)
country comparison to the world: 208

TRANSPORTATION

Ports and terminals: *none;* offshore anchorage only

MILITARY

Military—note: defense is the responsibility of Australia; Australia conducts fisheries patrols

TRANSNATIONAL ISSUES

Disputes—international: none

HOLY SEE (VATICAN CITY)

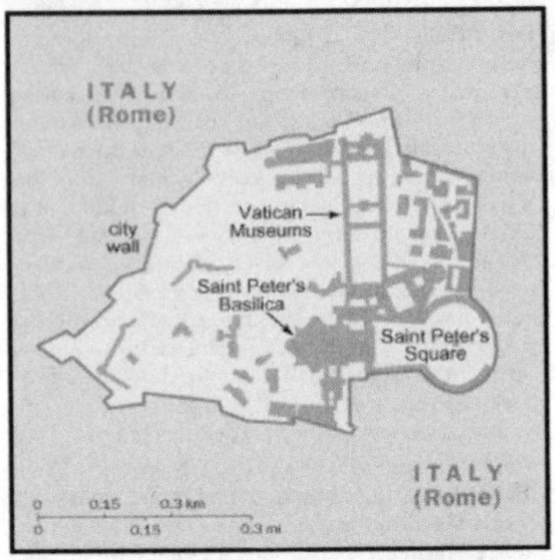

INTRODUCTION

Background: Popes in their secular role ruled portions of the Italian peninsula for more than a thousand years until the mid 19th century, when many of the Papal States were seized by the newly united Kingdom of Italy. In 1870, the pope's holdings were further circumscribed when Rome itself was annexed. Disputes between a series of "prisoner" popes and Italy were resolved in 1929 by three Lateran Treaties, which established the independent state of Vatican City and granted Roman Catholicism special status in Italy. In 1984, a concordat between the Holy See and Italy modified certain of the earlier treaty provisions, including the primacy of Roman Catholicism as the Italian state religion. Present concerns of the Holy See include religious freedom, threats against minority Christian communities in Africa and the Middle East, sexual misconduct by clergy, international development, interreligious dialogue and reconciliation, and the application of church doctrine in an era of rapid change and globalization. About 1.2 billion people worldwide profess Catholicism—the world's largest Christian faith.

GEOGRAPHY

Location: Southern Europe, an enclave of Rome (Italy)

Geographic coordinates: 41 54 N, 12 27 E

Map references: Europe

Area: *total:* 0.44 sq km
country comparison to the world: 252
land: 0.44 sq km
water: 0 sq km

Area—comparative: about 0.7 times the size of The National Mall in Washington, DC

Land boundaries: *total:* 3.2 km
border countries: Italy 3.2 km

Coastline: 0 km (landlocked)

Maritime claims: none (landlocked)

Climate: temperate; mild, rainy winters (September to May) with hot, dry summers (May to September)

Terrain: urban; low hill

Elevation extremes: *lowest point:* unnamed location 19 m
highest point: unnamed elevation 75 m

Natural resources: none

Land use: arable land:
permanent crops: 0%
other: 100% (urban area) (2011)

Irrigated land: 0 sq km (2011)

Natural hazards: NA

Environment—current issues: NA

Environment—international agreements: *party to:* Ozone Layer Protection
signed, but not ratified: Air Pollution, Environmental Modification

Geography—note: landlocked; enclave in Rome, Italy; world's smallest state; beyond the territorial boundary of Vatican City, the Lateran Treaty of 1929 grants the Holy See extraterritorial authority over 23 sites in Rome and five outside of Rome, including the Pontifical Palace at Castel Gandolfo (the Pope's summer residence)

PEOPLE AND SOCIETY

Nationality: *noun:* none
adjective: none

Ethnic groups: Italians, Swiss, other

Languages: Italian, Latin, French, various other languages

Religions: Roman Catholic

Population: 842 (July 2014 est.)
country comparison to the world: 238

Population growth rate: 0% (2014 est.)
country comparison to the world: 195

Urbanization: *urban population:* 100% of total population (2010)
rate of urbanization: 0.1% annual rate of change (2010-15 est.)

HIV/AIDS—adult prevalence rate: NA

HIV/AIDS—people living with HIV/AIDS: NA

HIV/AIDS—deaths: NA

Education expenditures: NA

Literacy: *definition:* age 15 and over can read and write
total population: 100%
male: 100%
female: 100%

GOVERNMENT

Country name: *conventional long form:* The Holy See (Vatican City State)
conventional short form: Holy See (Vatican City)
local long form: La Santa Sede (Stato della Citta del Vaticano)
local short form: Santa Sede (Citta del Vaticano)

Government type: ecclesiastical

Capital: name: Vatican City
geographic coordinates: 41 54 N, 12 27 E
time difference: UTC+1 (6 hours ahead of Washington, DC during Standard Time)
daylight saving time: +1hr, begins last Sunday in March; ends last Sunday in October

Administrative divisions: none

Independence: 11 February 1929 (from Italy); note—the three treaties signed with Italy on 11 February 1929 acknowledged, among other things, the full sovereignty of the Holy See and established its territorial extent; however, the origin of the Papal States, which over centuries varied considerably in extent, may be traced back to 754

National holiday: Election Day of Pope FRANCIS, 13 March (2013)

Constitution: previous 1929, 1963; latest adopted 26 November 2000, effective 22 February 2001 (Fundamental Law by Pope JOHN PAUL II); note—Pope Francis in October 2013 appointed a group of cardinals to revise the constitution (2013)

Legal system: religious legal system based on canon (religious) law

International law organization participation: has not submitted an ICJ jurisdiction declaration; non-party state to the ICCt

Suffrage: election of the pope is limited to cardinals less than 80 years old

Executive branch: *chief of state:* Pope FRANCIS (since 13 March 2013)
head of government: Secretary of State Archbishop Pietro PAROLIN (since 15 October 2013); note—previous Secretary of State Cardinal Tarcisio BERTONE will remain as Camerlengo, a position he has held since 4 April 2007
cabinet: Pontifical Commission for the State of Vatican City appointed by the pope (For more information visit the World Leaders website)
elections: pope elected for life, or until voluntary resignation, by the College of Cardinals; election last held on 13 March 2013 (next to be held after the death or resignation of the current pope); Secretary of State appointed by the pope
election results: Jorge Mario BERGOGLIO elected Pope FRANCIS

Legislative branch: unicameral Pontifical Commission for Vatican City State

Judicial branch: *highest court(s):* Supreme Court or Supreme Tribunal of the Apostolic Signatura (consists of the cardinal prefect, who serves as ex-officio president of the court, and 2 other cardinals of the Prefect Signatura) note—judicial duties were established by the Motu Proprio, papal directive, of Pope PIUS XII on 1 May 1946; note 2: most Vatican City criminal matters are handled by the Republic of Italy courts
judge selection and term of office: cardinal prefect appointed by the Pope; the other 2 cardinals of the court appointed by the cardinal prefect on a yearly basis
subordinate courts: Appellate Court of Vatican City; Tribunal of Vatican City

Political parties and leaders: none

Political pressure groups and leaders: none (exclusive of influence exercised by church officers)

International organization participation: CE (observer), IAEA, Interpol, IOM, ITSO, ITU, ITUC (NGOs), OAS (observer), OPCW, OSCE, Schengen Convention (de facto member), UN (observer), UNCTAD, UNHCR, Union Latina (observer), UNWTO (observer), UPU, WIPO, WTO (observer)

Diplomatic representation in the US:
chief of mission: Apostolic Nuncio Carlo Maria VIGANO (since 16 November 2011)
chancery: 3339 Massachusetts Avenue NW, Washington, DC 20008
telephone: [1] (202) 333-7121
FAX: [1] (202) 337-4036

Diplomatic representation from the US:
chief of mission: Ambassador Kenneth F. HACKETT (since 20 August 2013)
embassy: Villa Domiziana, Via delle Terme Deciane 26, 00153 Rome
mailing address: Unit 5660, Box 66, DPO AE 09624-0066
telephone: [39] (06) 4674-3428
FAX: [39] (06) 575-8346

Flag description: two vertical bands of yellow (hoist side) and white with the arms of the Holy See, consisting of the crossed keys of Saint Peter surmounted by the three-tiered papal tiara, centered in the white band; the yellow color represents the pope's spiritual power, the white his worldly power

National symbol(s): crossed keys

National anthem: *name:* "Inno e Marcia Pontificale" (Hymn and Pontifical March); often called The Pontifical Hymn
lyrics/music: Raffaello LAVAGNA/Charles-Francois GOUNOD
note: adopted 1950

ECONOMY

Economy—overview: The Holy See is supported financially by a variety of sources, including investments, real estate income, and donations from Catholic individuals, dioceses, and institutions; these help fund the Roman Curia (Vatican bureaucracy), diplomatic missions, and media outlets. Moreover, an annual collection taken up in dioceses and from direct donations go to a non-budgetary fund, known as Peter's Pence, which is used directly by the Pope for charity, disaster relief, and aid to churches in developing nations. Donations increased between 2010 and 2011. The separate Vatican City State budget includes the Vatican museums and post office and is supported financially by the sale of stamps, coins, medals, and tourist mementos; by fees for admission to museums; and by publication sales. Its revenues increased between 2010 and 2011 because of expanded opening hours and a growing number of visitors. However, the Holy See has not escaped the financial difficulties engulfing other European countries; in 2012 it started a spending review to determine where to cut costs to reverse its 2011 budget deficit of 15 million euros. Most public expenditures go to wages and other personnel costs; the incomes and living standards of lay workers are comparable to those of counterparts who work in the city of Rome.

GDP (purchasing power parity): $NA

Industries: printing; production of coins, medals, postage stamps; mosaics and staff uniforms; worldwide banking and financial activities

Labor force: 2,832 (December 2011)
country comparison to the world: 227

Labor force—by occupation: *note:* essentially services with a small amount of industry; nearly all dignitaries, priests, nuns, guards, and the approximately 3,000 lay workers live outside the Vatican

Population below poverty line: NA%

Budget: revenues: $308 million
expenditures: $326.4 million (2011)

Fiscal year: calendar year

Exchange rates: euros (EUR) per US dollar—
0.7634 (2013 est.)
0.7752 (2012 est.)
0.755 (2010 est.)
0.7198 (2009 est.)
0.6827 (2008 est.)

COMMUNICATIONS

Telephone system: *general assessment:* automatic digital exchange
domestic: connected via fiber optic cable to Telecom Italia network
international: country code—39; uses Italian system (2012)

Broadcast media: the Vatican Television Center (CTV) transmits live broadcasts of the Pope's Sunday and Wednesday audiences, as well as the Pope's public celebrations; CTV also produces documentaries; Vatican Radio is the Holy See's official broadcasting service broadcasting via shortwave, AM and FM frequencies, and via satellite and Internet connections (2008)

Internet country code: .va

Internet hosts: 107 (2012)
country comparison to the world: 207

MILITARY

Military branches: Pontifical Swiss Guard Corps (Corpo della Guardia Svizzera Pontificia) (2013)

Military service age and obligation: Pontifical Swiss Guard Corps (Corpo della Guardia Svizzera Pontificia): 19-30 years of age for voluntary military service; no conscription; must be Roman Catholic, a Swiss citizen, with a secondary education (2013)

Military—note: defense is the responsibility of Italy; ceremonial and limited security duties performed by Pontifical Swiss Guard

TRANSNATIONAL ISSUES

Disputes—international: none

HONDURAS

INTRODUCTION

Background: Once part of Spain's vast empire in the New World, Honduras became an independent nation in 1821. After two and a half decades of mostly military rule, a freely elected civilian government came to power in 1982. During the 1980s, Honduras proved a haven for anti-Sandinista contras fighting the Marxist Nicaraguan Government and an ally to Salvadoran Government forces fighting leftist guerrillas. The country was devastated by Hurricane Mitch in 1998, which killed about 5,600 people and caused approximately $2 billion in damage. Since then, the economy has slowly rebounded.

GEOGRAPHY

Location: Central America, bordering the Caribbean Sea, between Guatemala and Nicaragua and bordering the Gulf of Fonseca (North Pacific Ocean), between El Salvador and Nicaragua

Geographic coordinates: 15 00 N, 86 30 W

Map references: Central America and the Caribbean

Area: *total:* 112,090 sq km
country comparison to the world: 103
land: 111,890 sq km
water: 200 sq km

Area—comparative: slightly larger than Tennessee

Land boundaries: total: 1,520 km
border countries: Guatemala 256 km, El Salvador 342 km, Nicaragua 922 km

Coastline: Caribbean Sea 669 km; Gulf of Fonseca 163 km

Maritime claims: *territorial sea:* 12 nm
contiguous zone: 24 nm
exclusive economic zone: 200 nm
continental shelf: natural extension of territory or to 200 nm

Climate: subtropical in lowlands, temperate in mountains

Terrain: mostly mountains in interior, narrow coastal plains

Elevation extremes: *lowest point:* Caribbean Sea 0 m
highest point: Cerro Las Minas 2,870 m

Natural resources: timber, gold, silver, copper, lead, zinc, iron ore, antimony, coal, fish, hydropower

Land use: *arable land:* 9.07%
permanent crops: 3.91%
other: 87.02% (2011)

Irrigated land: 878.5 sq km (2007)

Total renewable water resources: 95.93 cu km (2011)

Freshwater withdrawal (domestic/industrial/agricultural): *total:* 2.12 cu km/yr (16%/23%/61%)
per capita: 295.6 cu m/yr (2006)

Natural hazards: frequent, but generally mild, earthquakes; extremely susceptible to damaging hurricanes and floods along the Caribbean coast

Environment—current issues: urban population expanding; deforestation results from logging and the clearing of land for agricultural purposes; further land degradation and soil erosion hastened by uncontrolled development and improper land use practices such as farming of marginal lands; mining activities polluting Lago de Yojoa (the country's largest source of fresh water), as well as several rivers and streams, with heavy metals

Environment—international agreements:
party to: Biodiversity, Climate Change, Climate Change-Kyoto Protocol, Desertification, Endangered Species, Hazardous Wastes, Law of the Sea, Marine Dumping, Ozone Layer Protection, Ship Pollution, Tropical Timber 83, Tropical Timber 94, Wetlands
signed, but not ratified: none of the selected agreements

Geography—note: has only a short Pacific coast but a long Caribbean shoreline, including the virtually uninhabited eastern Mosquito Coast

PEOPLE AND SOCIETY

Nationality: *noun:* Honduran(s)
adjective: Honduran

Ethnic groups: mestizo (mixed Amerindian and European) 90%, Amerindian 7%, black 2%, white 1%

Languages: Spanish (official), Amerindian dialects

Religions: Roman Catholic 97%, Protestant 3%

Demographic profile: Honduras is one of the poorest countries in Latin America and has the world's highest murder rate. More than half of the population lives in poverty and per capita income is one of the lowest in the region. Poverty rates are higher among rural and indigenous people and in the south, west, and along the eastern border than in the north and central areas where most of Honduras' industries and infrastructure are concentrated. The increased productivity needed to break Honduras' persistent high poverty rate depends, in part, on further improvements in educational attainment. Although primary-school enrollment is near 100%, educational quality is poor, the dropout rate and grade repetition remain high, and teacher and school accountability is low. Honduras' population growth rate has slowed since the 1990s, but it remains high at nearly 2% annually because the birth rate averages approximately three children per woman and more among rural, indigenous, and poor women. Consequently, Honduras' young adult population—ages 15 to 29—is projected to continue growing rapidly for the next three decades and then stabilize or slowly shrink. Population growth and limited job prospects outside of agriculture will continue to drive emigration. Remittances represent about a fifth of GDP.

Population: 8,598,561 (July 2014 est.)
country comparison to the world: 94
note: estimates for this country explicitly take into account the effects of excess mortality due to AIDS; this can result in lower life expectancy, higher infant mortality, higher death rates, lower population growth rates, and changes in the distribution of population by age and sex than would otherwise be expected

Age structure:
0-14 years: 34.8% (male 1,529,578/female 1,465,188)
15-24 years: 21.2% (male 928,756/female 892,629)
25-54 years: 35.3% (male 1,530,429/female 1,502,916)
55-64 years: 4% (male 187,771/female 217,093)
65 years and over: 3.9% (male 150,681/female 193,520) (2014 est.)

Dependency ratios:
total dependency ratio: 65.8 %
youth dependency ratio: 58.4 %
elderly dependency ratio: 7.4 %
potential support ratio: 13.6 (2013)

Median age: *total:* 21.9 years
male: 21.6 years
female: 22.3 years (2014 est.)

Population growth rate: 1.74% (2014 est.)
country comparison to the world: 71

Birth rate: 23.66 births/1,000 population (2014 est.)
country comparison to the world: 65

Death rate: 5.13 deaths/1,000 population (2014 est.)
country comparison to the world: 184

Net migration rate: -1.18 migrant(s)/1,000 population (2014 est.)
country comparison to the world: 153

Urbanization: *urban population:* 52% of total population (2010)
rate of urbanization: 3.1% annual rate of change (2010-15 est.)

Major urban areas—population: TEGUCIGALPA (capital) 1 million (2009)

Sex ratio: *at birth:* 1.05 male(s)/female
0-14 years: 1.04 male(s)/female
15-24 years: 1.04 male(s)/female
25-54 years: 1.02 male(s)/female
55-64 years: 1.01 male(s)/female
65 years and over: 0.79 male(s)/female
total population: 1.01 male(s)/female (2014 est.)

Mother's mean age at first birth: 21.1
note: median age a first birth among women 25-29 (2011-12)

Maternal mortality rate: 100 deaths/100,000 live births (2010)
country comparison to the world: 69

Infant mortality rate: *total:* 18.72 deaths/1,000 live births
country comparison to the world: 96
male: 21.2 deaths/1,000 live births
female: 16.13 deaths/1,000 live births (2014 est.)

Life expectancy at birth: *total population:* 70.91 years
country comparison to the world: 147
male: 69.24 years
female: 72.65 years (2014 est.)

Total fertility rate: 2.86 children born/woman (2014 est.)
country comparison to the world: 65

Contraceptive prevalence rate: 65.2% (2005/06)

Health expenditures: 9.1% of GDP (2009)
country comparison to the world: 40

Physicians density: 0.37 physicians/1,000 population (2005)

Hospital bed density: 0.7 beds/1,000 population (2011)

Drinking water source:
improved:
urban: 96.5% of population
rural: 80.7% of population
total: 88.9% of population
unimproved:
urban: 3.5% of population
rural: 19.3% of population
total: 11.1% of population (2011 est.)

Sanitation facility access:
improved:
urban: 86.3% of population
rural: 74.4% of population
total: 80.6% of population
unimproved:
urban: 13.7% of population
rural: 25.6% of population
total: 19.4% of population (2011 est.)

HIV/AIDS—adult prevalence rate: 0.5% (2012 est.)
country comparison to the world: 70

HIV/AIDS—people living with HIV/AIDS: 25,600 (2012 est.)
country comparison to the world: 75

HIV/AIDS—deaths: 1,700 (2012 est.)
country comparison to the world: 63

Major infectious diseases: *degree of risk:* high
food or waterborne diseases: bacterial diarrhea, hepatitis A, and typhoid fever
vectorborne diseases: dengue fever and malaria (2013)

Obesity—adult prevalence rate: 18.4% (2008)
country comparison to the world: 106

Children under the age of 5 years underweight: 8.6% (2006)
country comparison to the world: 73

Education expenditures: NA

Literacy: *definition:* age 15 and over can read and write
total population: 85.1%
male: 85.3%
female: 84.9% (2011 est.)

School life expectancy (primary to tertiary education): *total:* 11 years
male: 11 years
female: 12 years (2012)

Child labor—children ages 5-14: total number: 280,809
percentage: 16 % (2002 est.)

Unemployment, youth ages 15-24: total: 8%
country comparison to the world: 122
male: 5.5%
female: 13.8% (2011)

GOVERNMENT

Country name: *conventional long form:* Republic of Honduras
conventional short form: Honduras
local long form: Republica de Honduras
local short form: Honduras

Government type: democratic constitutional republic

Capital: *name:* Tegucigalpa
geographic coordinates: 14 06 N, 87 13 W
time difference: UTC-6 (1 hour behind Washington, DC during Standard Time)
daylight saving time: none scheduled for 2013

Administrative divisions: 18 departments (departamentos, singular—departamento); Atlantida, Choluteca, Colon, Comayagua, Copan, Cortes, El Paraiso, Francisco Morazan, Gracias a Dios, Intibuca, Islas de la Bahia, La Paz, Lempira, Ocotepeque, Olancho, Santa Barbara, Valle, Yoro

Independence: 15 September 1821 (from Spain)

National holiday: Independence Day, 15 September (1821)

Constitution: several previous; latest approved 11 January 1982, effective 20 January 1982; amended many times, last in 2012 (2013)

Legal system: civil law system

International law organization participation: accepts compulsory ICJ jurisdiction with reservations; accepts ICCt jurisdiction

Suffrage: 18 years of age; universal and compulsory

Executive branch: *chief of state:* President Juan Orlando HERNANDEZ Alvarado (since 27 January 2014); Vice Presidents Ricardo ALVAREZ, Rossana GUEVARA, and Lorena HERRERA (since 27 January 2014); note—the president is both the chief of state and head of government
head of government: President Juan Orlando HERNANDEZ Alvarado (since 27 January 2014); Vice Presidents Ricardo ALVAREZ, Rossana GUEVARA, and Lorena HERRERA (since 27 January 2014)
cabinet: Cabinet appointed by president (For more information visit the World Leaders website)
elections: president elected by popular vote for a four-year term; election last held on 24 November 2013 (next to be held in November 2017)
election results: Juan Orlando HERNANDEZ Alvarado elected president; percent of vote—Juan Orlando HERNANDEZ Alvarado 36.9%, Xiomara CASTRO 28.8%, Mauricio VILLEDA 20.3%, Salvador NASRALLA 13.4%

Legislative branch: unicameral National Congress or Congreso Nacional (128 seats; members elected proportionally by department to serve four-year terms)
elections: last held on 24 November 2013 (next to be held in November 2017)
election results: percent of vote by party—NA; seats by party—PNH 48, PLR 37, PL 27, PAC 13, DC 1, UD 1, PINU 1

Judicial branch: *highest court(s):* Supreme Court of Justice or Corte Suprema de Justicia (9 principal judges—including the court president—and 7 alternates; court organized into civil, criminal, and labor chambers); note—the court has both judicial and constitutional jurisdiction
judge selection and term of office: court president elected by his peers; judges elected by the National Congress from candidates proposed by the Nominating Board, a diverse 7-member group of judicial officials, other government and non-government officials selected by each of their organizations; judges elected by Congress for renewable, 7-year terms
subordinate courts: courts of appeal; courts of first instance; peace courts

Political parties and leaders: Anti-Corruption Party or PAC [Salvador NASRALLA]; Christian Democratic Party or DC [Felicito AVILA Ordonez]; Broad Political Electoral Front in Resistance or FAPER [Andres PAVON]; Democratic Unification Party or UD [Cesar HAM]; Freedom and Refounding Party or LIBRE [Jose Manuel ZELAYA Rosales]; Liberal Party or PL [Elvin SANTOS Brito]; National Party of Honduras or PNH [Ricardo ALVAREZ]; Social Democratic Innovation and Unity Party or PINU [Jorge Rafael AGUILAR Paredes]

Political pressure groups and leaders: Beverage and Related Industries Syndicate or STIBYS; Committee for the Defense of Human Rights in Honduras or CODEH; Confederation of Honduran Workers or CTH; Coordinating Committee of Popular Organizations or CCOP; General Workers Confederation or CGT; Honduran Council of Private Enterprise or COHEP; National Association of Honduran Campesinos or ANACH; National Union of Campesinos or UNC; Popular Bloc or BP; United Confederation of Honduran Workers or CUTH; United Farm Workers' Movement of the Aguan (MUCA)

International organization participation: BCIE, CACM, CD, CELAC, FAO, G-11, G-77, IADB, IAEA, IBRD, ICAO, ICRM, IDA, IFAD, IFC, IFRCS, ILO, IMF, IMO, Interpol, IOC (suspended), IOM, IPU, ISO (subscriber), ITSO, ITU, ITUC (NGOs), LAES, LAIA (observer), MIGA, MINURSO, NAM, OAS (suspended), OPANAL, OPCW, PCA, Petrocaribe, SICA, UN, UNCTAD, UNESCO, UNIDO, Union Latina, UNWTO, UPU, WCO (suspended), WFTU (NGOs), WHO, WIPO, WMO, WTO

Diplomatic representation in the US: *chief of mission:* Ambassador Jorge Ramon HERNANDEZ-Alcerro (since 9 June 2010)
chancery: Suite 4-M, 3007 Tilden Street NW, Washington, DC 20008
telephone: [1] (202) 966-2604
FAX: [1] (202) 966-9751
consulate(s) general: Atlanta, Belmont (MA), Chicago, Houston, Los Angeles, Miami, New Orleans, New York, Phoenix, San Francisco

Diplomatic representation from the US:
chief of mission: Ambassador Lisa J. KUBISKE (since 26 July 2011)
embassy: Avenida La Paz, Apartado Postal No. 3453, Tegucigalpa
mailing address: American Embassy, APO AA 34022, Tegucigalpa
telephone: [504] 2236-9320, 2238-5114
FAX: [504] 2236-9037

Flag description: three equal horizontal bands of blue (top), white, and blue, with five blue, five-pointed stars arranged in an X pattern centered in the white band; the stars represent the members of the former Federal Republic of Central America—Costa Rica, El Salvador, Guatemala, Honduras, and Nicaragua; the blue bands symbolize the Pacific Ocean and the Caribbean Sea; the white band represents the land between the two bodies of water and the peace and prosperity of its people
note: similar to the flag of El Salvador, which features a round emblem encircled by the words REPUBLICA DE EL SALVADOR EN LA AMERICA CENTRAL centered in the white band; also similar to the flag of Nicaragua, which features a triangle encircled by the words REPUBLICA DE NICARAGUA on top and AMERICA CENTRAL on the bottom, centered in the white band

National symbol(s): scarlet macaw; white-tailed deer

National anthem: *name:* "Himno Nacional de Honduras" (National Anthem of Honduras)
lyrics/music: Augusto Constancio COELLO/Carlos HARTLING
note: adopted 1915; the anthem's seven verses chronicle Honduran history; on official occasions, only the chorus and last verse are sung

ECONOMY

Economy—overview: Honduras, the second poorest country in Central America, suffers from extraordinarily unequal distribution of income, as well as high underemployment. While historically dependent on the export of bananas and coffee, Honduras has diversified its export base to include apparel and automobile wire harnessing. Nearly half of Honduras's economic activity is directly tied to the US, with exports to the US accounting for 30% of GDP and remittances for another 20%. The US-Central America-Dominican Republic Free Trade Agreement (CAFTA-DR) came into force in 2006 and has helped foster foreign direct investment, but physical and political insecurity, as well as crime and perceptions of corruption, may deter potential investors; about 70% of FDI is from US firms. The economy registered modest economic growth of 3.0%-4.0% from 2010 to 2012, insufficient to improve living standards for the nearly 65% of the population in poverty. An 18-month IMF Standby Arrangement expired in March 2012 and was not renewed, due to the country's growing budget deficit and weak current account performance. Public sector workers complained of not receiving their salaries in November and December 2012, and government suppliers are owed at least several hundred million dollars in unpaid contracts. The government announced in January 2013 that loss-making public enterprises will be forced to submit financial rescue plans before receiving their budget allotments for 2013.

GDP (purchasing power parity): $39.23 billion (2013 est.)
country comparison to the world: 108
$38.16 billion (2012 est.)
$36.74 billion (2011 est.)
note: data are in 2013 US dollars

GDP (official exchange rate): $18.88 billion (2013 est.)

GDP—real growth rate: 2.8% (2013 est.)
country comparison to the world: 122
3.9% (2012 est.)
3.8% (2011 est.)

GDP—per capita (PPP): $4,800 (2013 est.)
country comparison to the world: 163
$4,800 (2012 est.)
$4,700 (2011 est.)
note: data are in 2013 US dollars

Gross national saving: 17.7% of GDP (2013 est.)
country comparison to the world: 92
16.4% of GDP (2012 est.)
17.5% of GDP (2011 est.)

GDP—composition, by end use:
household consumption: 79.5%
government consumption: 16.4%
investment in fixed capital: 25.2%
investment in inventories: 1.2%
exports of goods and services: 51.5%
imports of goods and services: -73.8% (2013 est.)

GDP—composition, by sector of origin:
agriculture: 14%
industry: 28.2%
services: 57.8% (2013 est.)

Agriculture—products: bananas, coffee, citrus, corn, African palm; beef; timber; shrimp, tilapia, lobster

Industries: sugar, coffee, woven and knit apparel, wood products, cigars

Industrial production growth rate: 4.6% (2013 est.)
country comparison to the world: 61

Labor force: 3.507 million (2013 est.)
country comparison to the world: 97

Labor force—by occupation: agriculture: 39.2%
industry: 20.9%
services: 39.8% (2005 est.)

Unemployment rate: 4.5% (2013 est.)
country comparison to the world: 41
4.4% (2012 est.)
note: about one-third of the people are underemployed

Population below poverty line: 60% (2010 est.)

Household income or consumption by percentage share: *lowest 10%:* 0.4%
highest 10%: 42.4% (2009 est.)

Distribution of family income—Gini index:
57.7 (2007)
country comparison to the world: 8
53.8 (2003)

Budget: *revenues:* $3.113 billion
expenditures: $4.285 billion (2013 est.)

Taxes and other revenues: 16.5% of GDP (2013 est.)
country comparison to the world: 184

Budget surplus (+) or deficit (-):
-6.2% of GDP (2013 est.)
country comparison to the world: 182

Public debt: 40.6% of GDP (2013 est.)
country comparison to the world: 87
35.8% of GDP (2012 est.)

Fiscal year: calendar year

Inflation rate (consumer prices): 5.2% (2013 est.)
country comparison to the world: 157
5.2% (2012 est.)

Central bank discount rate: 6.25% (31 December 2010 est.)
NA% (31 December 2009 est.)

Commercial bank prime lending rate:
17.8% (31 December 2013 est.)
country comparison to the world: 22
18.45% (31 December 2012 est.)

Stock of narrow money: $1.781 billion (31 December 2013 est.)
country comparison to the world: 131
$1.913 billion (31 December 2012 est.)

Stock of broad money: $6.845 billion (31 December 2013 est.)
country comparison to the world: 117
$6.801 billion (31 December 2012 est.)

Stock of domestic credit: $10.5 billion (31 December 2013 est.)
country comparison to the world: 98
$10.43 billion (31 December 2012 est.)

Market value of publicly traded shares: $NA

Current account balance: -$1.636 billion (2013 est.)
country comparison to the world: 136
-$1.744 billion (2012 est.)

Exports: $7.881 billion (2013 est.)
country comparison to the world: 102
$7.931 billion (2012 est.)

Exports—commodities: apparel, coffee, shrimp, automobile wire harnesses, cigars, bananas, gold, palm oil, fruit, lobster, lumber

Exports—partners: US 34.5%, Germany 11.6%, Belgium 6.8%, El Salvador 6.6%, Guatemala 4.9%, Nicaragua 4.6% (2012)

Imports: $11.34 billion (2013 est.)
country comparison to the world: 95
$11.18 billion (2012 est.)

Imports—commodities: machinery and transport equipment, industrial raw materials, chemical products, fuels, foodstuffs

Imports—partners: US 44.3%, Guatemala 8.5%, El Salvador 5.7%, Mexico 5.6%, China 4.7%, Costa Rica 4.1% (2012)

Reserves of foreign exchange and gold:
$2.414 billion (31 December 2013 est.)
country comparison to the world: 116
$2.533 billion (31 December 2012 est.)

Debt—external: $6.173 billion (31 December 2013 est.)
country comparison to the world: 116
$5.233 billion (31 December 2012 est.)

Exchange rates: lempiras (HNL) per US dollar—
20.53 (2013 est.)
19.638 (2012 est.)
18.9 (2010 est.)
18.9 (2009)
18.983 (2008)

ENERGY

Electricity—production: 6.486 billion kWh (2010 est.)
country comparison to the world: 111

Electricity—consumption: 4.85 billion kWh (2010 est.)
country comparison to the world: 115

Electricity—exports: 22 million kWh (2010 est.)
country comparison to the world: 87

Electricity—imports: 22 million kWh (2010 est.)
country comparison to the world: 103

Electricity—installed generating capacity:
1.701 million kW (2010 est.)
country comparison to the world: 108

Electricity—from fossil fuels: 63.7% of total installed capacity (2010 est.)
country comparison to the world: 125

Electricity—from nuclear fuels: 0% of total installed capacity (2010 est.)
country comparison to the world: 105

Electricity—from hydroelectric plants:
30.9% of total installed capacity (2010 est.)
country comparison to the world: 78

Electricity—from other renewable sources:
5.4% of total installed capacity (2010 est.)
country comparison to the world: 41

Crude oil—production: 20 bbl/day (2012 est.)
country comparison to the world: 127

Crude oil—exports: 0 bbl/day (2010 est.)
country comparison to the world: 126

Crude oil—imports: 0 bbl/day (2010 est.)
country comparison to the world: 200

Crude oil—proved reserves: 0 bbl (1 January 2013 es)
country comparison to the world: 145

Refined petroleum products—production:
0 bbl/day (2010 est.)
country comparison to the world: 156

Refined petroleum products—consumption:
58,150 bbl/day (2011 est.)
country comparison to the world: 95

Refined petroleum products—exports:
0 bbl/day (2010 est.)
country comparison to the world: 185

Refined petroleum products—imports:
46,370 bbl/day (2010 est.)
country comparison to the world: 73

Natural gas—production: 0 cu m (2011 est.)
country comparison to the world: 144

Natural gas—consumption: 0 cu m (2010 est.)
country comparison to the world: 156

Natural gas—exports: 0 cu m (2011 est.)
country comparison to the world: 117

Natural gas—imports: 0 cu m (2011 est.)
country comparison to the world: 205

Natural gas—proved reserves: 0 cu m (1 January 2013 es)
country comparison to the world: 150

Carbon dioxide emissions from consumption of energy: 7.975 million Mt (2011 est.)
country comparison to the world: 109

COMMUNICATIONS

Telephones—main lines in use: 610,000 (2012)
country comparison to the world: 9 1

Telephones—mobile cellular: 7.37 million (2012)
country comparison to the world: 93

Telephone system: *general assessment:* fixed-line connections are increasing but still limited; competition among multiple providers of mobile-cellular services is contributing to a sharp increase in subscribership
domestic: beginning in 2003, private sub-operators allowed to provide fixed-lines in order to expand telephone coverage contributing to a small increase in fixed-line teledensity; mobile-cellular subscribership is roughly 100 per 100 persons
international: country code—504; landing point for both the Americas Region Caribbean Ring System (ARCOS-1) and the MAYA-1 fiber-optic submarine cable system that together provide connectivity to South and Central America, parts of the Caribbean, and the US; satellite earth stations—2 Intelsat (Atlantic Ocean); connected to Central American Microwave System (2011)

Broadcast media: multiple privately owned terrestrial TV networks, supplemented by multiple cable TV networks; Radio Honduras is the lone government-owned radio network; roughly 300 privately owned radio stations (2007)

Internet country code: . h n

Internet hosts: 30,955 (2012)
country comparison to the world: 107

Internet users: 731,700 (2009)
country comparison to the world: 108

TRANSPORTATION

Airports: 103 (2013)
country comparison to the world: 5 4

Airports—with paved runways: *total:* 1 3
2,438 to 3,047 m: 3
1,524 to 2,437 m: 3
914 to 1,523 m: 4
under 914 m: 3 (2013)

Airports—with unpaved runways: *total:* 9 0
1,524 to 2,437 m: 1
914 to 1,523 m: 16
under 914 m: 73 (2013)
Railways: total: 44 km
country comparison to the world: 131
narrow gauge: 44 km 1.067-m gauge
note: (4 km are in use) (2012)

Roadways: *total:* 14,742 km
country comparison to the world: 123
paved: 3,367 km
unpaved: 11,375 km (1,543 km summer only)
note: there are another 8,951 km of non-offical roads used by the coffee industry (2012)

Waterways: 465 km (most navigable only by small craft) (2012)
country comparison to the world: 85

Merchant marine: total: 8 8
country comparison to the world: 55
by type: bulk carrier 5, cargo 39, carrier 2, chemical tanker 5, container 1, passenger 4, passenger/cargo 1, petroleum tanker 21, refrigerated cargo 7, roll on/roll off 3
foreign-owned: 47 (Bahrain 5, Canada 1, Chile 1, China 2, Egypt 2, Greece 4, Israel 1, Japan 4, Lebanon 2, Montenegro 1, Panama 1, Singapore 11, South Korea 6, Taiwan 1, Thailand 2, UAE 1, UK 1, US 1) (2010)

Ports and terminals: *major seaport(s):* La Ceiba, Puerto Cortes, San Lorenzo, Tela

MILITARY

Military branches: Honduran Armed Forces (Fuerzas Armadas de Honduras, FFAA): Army, Navy (includes Naval Infantry), Honduran Air Force (Fuerza Aerea Hondurena, FAH) (2012)

Military service age and obligation: 18 years of age for voluntary 2- to 3-year military service; no conscription (2012)

Manpower available for military service:
males age 16-49: 2,045,914
females age 16-49: 1,991,418 (2010 est.)

Manpower fit for military service:
males age 16-49: 1,525,578
females age 16-49: 1,539,688 (2010 est.)

Manpower reaching militarily significant age annually: *male:* 95,895
female: 92,087 (2010 est.)

Military expenditures: 1.05% of GDP (2012)
country comparison to the world: 97
1.13% of GDP (2011)
1.05% of GDP (2010)

TRANSNATIONAL ISSUES

Disputes—international: International Court of Justice (ICJ) ruled on the delimitation of "bolsones" (disputed areas) along the El Salvador-Honduras border in 1992 with final settlement by the parties in 2006 after an Organization of American States survey and a further ICJ ruling in 2003; the 1992 ICJ ruling advised a tripartite resolution to a maritime boundary in the Gulf of Fonseca with consideration of Honduran access to the Pacific; El Salvador continues to claim tiny Conejo Island, not mentioned in the ICJ ruling, off Honduras in the Gulf of Fonseca; Honduras claims the Belizean-administered Sapodilla Cays off the coast of Belize in its constitution, but agreed to a joint ecological park around the cays should Guatemala consent to a maritime corridor in the Caribbean under the OAS-sponsored 2002 *Belize-Guatemala Differendum*

Trafficking in persons: *current situation:* Honduras is a source and transit country for men, women, and children subjected to sex trafficking and forced labor; Honduran women and girls, and, to a lesser extent, women and girls from neighboring countries, are forced into prostitution in urban and tourist centers; Honduran women and girls are also exploited in sex trafficking in other countries in the region, including Mexico, Guatemala, El Salvador, and the US; Honduran adults and children are subjected to forced labor in Guatemala, Mexico, and the US and domestically in agriculture and domestic service; gangs coerce some young men to transport drugs or be hit men
tier rating: Tier 2 Watch List—Honduras does not fully comply with the minimum standards for the elimination of trafficking; however, it is making significant efforts to do so; the government maintains limited law enforcement efforts against child sex trafficking offenders but has held no offenders accountable for the forced labor or forced prostitution of adults; most trafficking offenders are prosecuted under non-trafficking statutes that prescribe lower penalties; government efforts to identify, refer, and assist trafficking victims are inadequate, and most services for victims are provided by NGOs without government funding (2013)

Illicit drugs: transshipment point for drugs and narcotics; illicit producer of cannabis, cultivated on small plots and used principally for local consumption; corruption is a major problem; some money-laundering activity

HONG KONG

INTRODUCTION

Background: Occupied by the UK in 1841, Hong Kong was formally ceded by China the following year; various adjacent lands were added later in the 19th century. Pursuant to an agreement signed by China and the UK on 19 December 1984, Hong Kong became the Hong Kong Special Administrative Region (SAR) of the People's Republic of China on 1 July 1997. In this agreement, China promised that, under its "one country, two systems" formula, China's socialist economic system would not be imposed on Hong Kong and that Hong Kong would enjoy a "high degree of autonomy" in all matters except foreign and defense affairs for the subsequent 50 years.

GEOGRAPHY

Location: Eastern Asia, bordering the South China Sea and China

Geographic coordinates: 22 15 N, 114 10 E

Map references: Southeast Asia

Area: *total:* 1,104 sq km
country comparison to the world: 184
land: 1,054 sq km
water: 50 sq km

Area—comparative: six times the size of Washington, DC

Land boundaries: *total:* 30 km
regional border: China 30 km

Coastline: 733 km

Maritime claims: *territorial sea:* 3 nm

Climate: subtropical monsoon; cool and humid in winter, hot and rainy from spring through summer, warm and sunny in fall

Terrain: hilly to mountainous with steep slopes; lowlands in north

Elevation extremes: *lowest point:* South China Sea 0 m
highest point: Tai Mo Shan 958 m

Natural resources: outstanding deepwater harbor, feldspar

Land use: *arable land:* 5.05%
permanent crops: 1.01%
other: 93.94% (2011)

Irrigated land: NA; note—included in the total for China

Natural hazards: occasional typhoons

Environment—current issues: air and water pollution from rapid urbanization

Environment—international agreements:
party to: Marine Dumping (associate member), Ship Pollution (associate member)

Geography—note: composed of more than 200 islands

PEOPLE AND SOCIETY

Nationality: *noun:* Chinese/Hong Konger
adjective: Chinese/Hong Kong

Ethnic groups: Chinese 93.1%, Indonesian 1.9%, Filipino 1.9%, other 3% (2011 est.)

Languages: Cantonese (official) 89.5%, English (official) 3.5%, Putonghua (Mandarin) 1.4%, other Chinese dialects 4%, other 1.6% (2011 est.)

Religions: eclectic mixture of local religions 90%, Christian 10%

Population: 7,112,688 (July 2014 est.)
country comparison to the world: 102

Age structure: 0-14 years: 12.1% (male 456,638/female 402,462)
15-24 years: 11.5% (male 417,300/female 398,270)
25-54 years: 46.9% (male 1,430,036/female 1,905,585)
55-64 years: 14.7% (male 517,045/female 537,290)
65 years and over: 14.4% (male 493,399/female 554,663) (2014 est.)

Dependency ratios:
total dependency ratio: 34.6 %
youth dependency ratio: 15.8 %
elderly dependency ratio: 18.9 %
potential support ratio: 5.3 (2013)

Median age: *total:* 43.2 years
male: 42.8 years
female: 43.4 years (2014 est.)

Population growth rate: 0.41% (2014 est.)
country comparison to the world: 162

Birth rate: 9.38 births/1,000 population (2014 est.)
country comparison to the world: 204

Death rate: 6.93 deaths/1,000 population (2014 est.)
country comparison to the world: 137

Net migration rate: 1.69 migrant(s)/1,000 population (2014 est.)
country comparison to the world: 51

Urbanization: *urban population:* 100% of total population (2011)
rate of urbanization: 1.04% annual rate of change (2010-15 est.)

Sex ratio: *at birth:* 1.13 male(s)/female
0-14 years: 1.14 male(s)/female
15-24 years: 1.05 male(s)/female
25-54 years: 0.75 male(s)/female
55-64 years: 0.87 male(s)/female
65 years and over: 0.88 male(s)/female
total population: 0.94 male(s)/female (2014 est.)

Mother's mean age at first birth: 29.8 (2008 est.)

Infant mortality rate: *total:* 2.73 deaths/1,000 live births
country comparison to the world: 217
male: 2.97 deaths/1,000 live births
female: 2.46 deaths/1,000 live births (2014 est.)

Life expectancy at birth: *total population:* 82.78 years
country comparison to the world: 6
male: 80.18 years
female: 85.71 years (2014 est.)

Total fertility rate: 1.17 children born/woman (2014 est.)
country comparison to the world: 221

Contraceptive prevalence rate: 79.5% (2007)

HIV/AIDS—adult prevalence rate: 0.1% (2003 est.)
country comparison to the world: 117

HIV/AIDS—people living with HIV/AIDS: 2,600 (2003 est.)
country comparison to the world: 136

HIV/AIDS—deaths: fewer than 200 (2003 est.)
country comparison to the world: 114

Education expenditures: 3.5% of GDP (2012)
country comparison to the world: 124

Literacy: *definition:* age 15 and over has ever attended school
total population: 93.5%
male: 96.9%
female: 89.6% (2002)

School life expectancy (primary to tertiary education): *total:* 16 years
male: 15 years
female: 15 years (2012)

Unemployment, youth ages 15-24: *total:* 9.3%
country comparison to the world: 115
male: 10.9%
female: 7.8% (2012)

GOVERNMENT

Country name: *conventional long form:* Hong Kong Special Administrative Region
conventional short form: Hong Kong
official long form: Xianggang Tebie Xingzhengqu
official short form: Xianggang
abbreviation: HK

Dependency status: special administrative region of China

Government type: limited democracy

Administrative divisions: none (special administrative region of China)

Independence: none (special administrative region of China)

National holiday: National Day (Anniversary of the Founding of the People's Republic of China), 1 October (1949); note—1 July 1997 is celebrated as Hong Kong Special Administrative Region Establishment Day

Constitution: several previous (governance documents while under British authority); latest drafted April 1988 to February 1989, approved March 1990, promulgated 4 April 1990 (Basic Law of the Hong Kong Special Administrative Region of the People's Republic of China serves as the constitution); note—since 1990, China's National People's Congress has interpreted specific articles of the Basic Law (2013)

Legal system: mixed legal system of common law based on the English model and Chinese customary law (in matters of family and land tenure)

Suffrage: 18 years of age in direct elections for half the legislature and a majority of seats in 18 district councils; universal for permanent residents living in the territory of Hong Kong for the past seven years; note—in indirect elections, suffrage is limited to about 220,000 members of functional constituencies for the other half of the legislature and an 1,200-member election committee for the chief executive drawn from broad sectoral groupings, central government bodies, municipal organizations, and elected Hong Kong officials

Executive branch: *chief of state:* President of China XI Jinping (since 14 March 2013)
head of government: Chief Executive LEUNG Chun-ying [C.Y. LEUNG] (since 1 July 2012)
cabinet: Executive Council or ExCo consists of 15 official members and 14 non-official members (For more information visit the World Leaders website)
elections: chief executive elected for five-year term by a 1,200-member election committee; on 25 March 2012 LEUNG Chun-ying [C.Y.LEUNG] was elected chief executive by a 1,193-member election committee; he took office on 1 July 2012; (next to be held in March 2017)
note: the Legislative Council voted in June 2010 to expand the electoral committee to 1,200 seats for the 2012 selection
election results: LEUNG Chun-ying was selected with 689 votes; Henry TANG received 285 votes, and Albert HO received 76 of the 1,132 votes cast; 82 ballots were deemed invalid; most were blank

Legislative branch: unicameral Legislative Council or LegCo (70 seats; 35 members indirectly elected by functional constituencies, 35 elected by popular vote; members serve four-year terms)
note: the LegCo voted in June 2010 to expand to 70 seats for the 2012 election; the measure was approved by the National People's Congress Standing Committee in August 2010
elections: last held on 9 September 2012 (next to be held in September 2016)
election results: percent of vote by block—pro-democracy 56%; pro-Beijing 41%, independent 3%; seats by parties—(pro-Beijing 43) DAB 13, BPA 7, FTU 6, Liberal Party 5, NPP 2, others 10; (pro-democracy 27) Democratic Party 6, Civic Party 6, Labor Party 4, People Power 3, Professional Commons 2, League of Social Democrats 1, ADPL 1, PTU 1, Neo Democrats 1, NWSC 1; independent 2

Judicial branch: *highest court(s):* Court of Final Appeal (consists of the chief justice, 3 permanent judges and 20 non-permanent judges); note—a sitting bench consists of the chief justice and 3 permanent and 1 non-permanent judges
judge selection and term of office: all judges appointed by the Hong Kong Chief Executive upon the recommendation of the Judicial Officers Recommendation Commission, an independent body consisting of the Secretary for Justice and other judges, judicial and legal professionals; permanent judges appointed until normal retirement at age 65, but can be extended; non-permanent judges appointed for renewable 3-year terms without age limit
subordinate courts: High Court (consists of the Court of Appeal and Court of First Instance); District Courts (includes Family and Land Courts); magistrates' courts; specialized tribunals

Political parties and leaders:
parties:
Association for Democracy and People's Livelihood or ADPL [Bruce LIU Sing-lee]; Business and Professional Alliance or BPA [Andrew LEUNG]; Civic Party [EU Audrey]; Democratic Alliance for the Betterment and Progress of Hong Kong or DAB [TAM Yiu-chung]; Democratic Party [Emily LAU]; Labor Party [LEE Cheuk-yan]; League of Social Democrats or LSD [LEUNG Kwok-hung]; Liberal Party [James TIEN]; Neo Democrats [joint leaders]; New People's Party [Regina IP Lau Suyee]; People Power [Erica YUEN Mi-ming]
others: Confederation of Trade Unions or CTU; Federation of Trade Unions or FTU; Neighborhood and Workers Service Center or NWSC; Professional Commons (think tank) [Charles Peter MOK]; Professional Teachers Union or PTU;
note: political blocs include: pro-democracy—ADPL, Civic Party, Democratic Party, Labor Party, LSD, People Power, Professional Commons; pro-Beijing—DAB, FTU, Liberal Party, New People's Party, BPA; there is no political party ordinance, so there are no registered political parties; politically active groups register as societies or companies

Political pressure groups and leaders: Chinese General Chamber of Commerce (pro-China); Chinese Manufacturers' Association of Hong Kong; Confederation; of Trade Unions or CTU (pro-democracy) [LEE Cheuk-yan, general secretary]; Federation of Hong Kong Industries; Federation of Trade Unions or FTU (pro-China) [CHENG Yiu-tong, executive councilor]; Hong Kong Alliance in Support; of the Patriotic Democratic Movement in China [LEE Cheuk-yan, chairman]; Hong Kong and Kowloon Trade Union; Council (pro-Taiwan); Hong Kong General Chamber of Commerce; Hong Kong Professional Teachers' Union [FUNG; Wai-wah, president]; Neighborhood and Workers' Service Center or NWSC [LEUNG Yiu-chung, LegCo member]; (pro-democracy); Civic Act-up [Cyd HO Sau-lan, LegCo member] (pro-democracy)

International organization participation: ADB, APEC, BIS, FATF, ICC (national committees), IHO, IMF, IMO (associate), Interpol (subbureau), IOC, ISO (correspondent), ITUC (NGOs), UNWTO (associate), UPU, WCO, WTO

Diplomatic representation in the US: none (Special Administrative Region of China); Hong Kong Economic and Trade Office (HKETO) carries out normal liaison and communication with the US Government and other US entities
commissioner: Clement C.M. LEUNG
office: 1520 18th Street NW, Washington, DC 20036
telephone: [1] 202 331-8947
FAX: [1] 202 331-8958
HKETO offices: New York, San Francisco

Diplomatic representation from the US:
chief of mission: Consul General Clifford A. HART Jr. (since 30 July 2013); note—also accredited to Macau
consulate(s) general: 26 Garden Road, Hong Kong
mailing address: Unit 8000, Box 1, DPO AP 96521-0006
telephone: [852] 2523-9011
FAX: [852] 2845-1598

Flag description: red with a stylized, white, five-petal Bauhinia flower in the center; each petal contains a small, red, five-pointed star in its middle; the red color is the same as that on the Chinese flag and represents the motherland; the fragrant Bauhinia-developed in Hong Kong the late 19th century—has come to symbolize the region; the five stars echo those on the flag of China

National symbol(s): orchid tree flower

National anthem: *note:* as a Special Administrative Region of China, "Yiyongjun Jinxingqu" is the official anthem (see China)

ECONOMY

Economy—overview: Hong Kong has a free market economy, highly dependent on international trade and finance—the value of goods and services trade, including the sizable share of re-exports, is about four times GDP. Hong Kong has no tariffs on imported goods, and it levies excise duties on only four commodities, whether imported or produced locally: hard alcohol, tobacco, hydrocarbon oil, and methyl alcohol. There are no quotas or dumping laws. Hong Kong's open economy left it exposed to the global economic slowdown that began in 2008. Although increasing integration with China, through trade, tourism, and financial links, helped it to make an initial recovery more quickly than many observers anticipated, its continued reliance on foreign trade and investment leaves it vulnerable to renewed global financial market volatility or a slowdown in the global economy. The Hong Kong government is promoting the Special Administrative Region (SAR) as the site for Chinese renminbi (RMB) internationalization. Hong Kong residents are allowed to establish RMB-denominated savings accounts; RMB-denominated corporate and Chinese government bonds have been issued in Hong Kong; and RMB trade settlement is allowed. The territory far exceeded the RMB conversion quota set by Beijing for trade settlements in 2010 due to the growth of earnings from exports to the mainland. RMB quota set by Beijing for trade settlements in 2010 due to the growth of earnings from exports to the mainland. RMB deposits grew to roughly 12% of total system deposits in Hong Kong by the end of 2013. The government is pursuing efforts to introduce additional use of RMB in Hong Kong financial markets and is seeking to expand the RMB quota. The mainland has long been Hong Kong's largest trading partner, accounting for about half of Hong Kong's total trade by value. Hong Kong's natural resources are limited, and food and raw materials must be imported. As a result of China's easing of travel restrictions, the number of mainland tourists to the territory has surged from 4.5 million in 2001 to 34.9 million in 2012, outnumbering visitors from all other countries combined. Hong Kong has also established itself as the premier stock market for Chinese firms seeking to list abroad. In 2012 mainland Chinese companies constituted about 46.6% of the firms listed on the Hong Kong Stock Exchange and accounted for about 57.4% of the Exchange's market capitalization. During the past decade, as Hong Kong's manufacturing industry moved to the mainland, its service industry has grown rapidly. Credit expansion and tight housing supply conditions have caused Hong Kong property prices to rise rapidly; consumer prices increased by more than 4% in 2013. Lower and middle income segments of the population are increasingly unable to afford adequate housing. Hong Kong continues to link its currency closely to the US dollar, maintaining an arrangement established in 1983. In 2013, Hong Kong and China signed new agreements under the Closer Economic Partnership Agreement, adopted in 2003 to forge closer ties between Hong Kong and the mainland. The new measures, effective from January 2014, cover services and trade facilitation, and will improve access to the mainland's service sector for Hong Kong-based companies.

GDP (purchasing power parity): $381.7 billion (2013 est.)
country comparison to the world: 36
$370.6 billion (2012 est.)
$365.1 billion (2011 est.)
note: data are in 2013 US dollars

GDP (official exchange rate): $279.7 billion (2013 est.)

GDP—real growth rate: 3% (2013 est.)
country comparison to the world: 116
1.5% (2012 est.)
4.9% (2011 est.)

GDP—per capita (PPP): $52,700 (2013 est.)
country comparison to the world: 14
$51,600 (2012 est.)
$51,300 (2011 est.)
note: data are in 2013 US dollars

Gross national saving: 28.6% of GDP (2013 est.)
country comparison to the world: 32
28.3% of GDP (2012 est.)
29.7% of GDP (2011 est.)

GDP—composition, by end use:
household consumption: 64%
government consumption: 9.3%
investment in fixed capital: 24.8%
investment in inventories: 0.2%
exports of goods and services: 222.6%
imports of goods and services: -220.9% (2013 est.)

GDP—composition, by sector of origin:
agriculture: 0%
industry: 6.9%
services: 93% (2013 est.)

Agriculture—products: fresh vegetables and fruit; poultry, pork; fish

Industries: textiles, clothing, tourism, banking, shipping, electronics, plastics, toys, watches, clocks

Industrial production growth rate: 0% (2013 est.)
country comparison to the world: 168

Labor force: 3.843 million (2013 est.)
country comparison to the world: 93

Labor force—by occupation: *manufacturing:* 4%
construction: 2.7%
wholesale and retail trade, restaurants, and hotels: 40.9%
financing, insurance, and real estate: 12.5%
transport and communications: 9.9%
community and social services: 16.9%
note: above data exclude public sector (2012 est.)

Unemployment rate: 3.1% (2013 est.)
country comparison to the world: 25
3.3% (2012 est.)

Population below poverty line: NA%

Household income or consumption by percentage share: *lowest 10%:* NA%
highest 10%: NA%

Distribution of family income—Gini index:
53.7 (2011)
country comparison to the world: 11
53.3 (2007)

Budget: *revenues:* $59.33 billion
expenditures: $54.23 billion (2013 est.)

Taxes and other revenues: 21.2% of GDP (2013 est.)
country comparison to the world: 154

Budget surplus (+) or deficit (-):
1.8% of GDP (2013 est.)
country comparison to the world: 20

Public debt: 35.6% of GDP (2013 est.)
country comparison to the world: 106
37.8% of GDP (2012 est.)

Fiscal year: 1 April—31 March

Inflation rate (consumer prices): 4.3% (2013 est.)
country comparison to the world: 142
4.1% (2012 est.)

Central bank discount rate: 0.5% (31 December 2012)
country comparison to the world: 138
0.5% (31 December 2011)

Commercial bank prime lending rate: 5% (31 December 2013 est.)
country comparison to the world: 158
5% (31 December 2012 est.)

Stock of narrow money: $199.8 billion (31 December 2013 est.)
country comparison to the world: 20
$177.7 billion (31 December 2012 est.)

Stock of broad money: $1.256 trillion (31 December 2013 est.)
country comparison to the world: 15
$1.155 trillion (31 December 2012 est.)

Stock of domestic credit: $714 billion (31 December 2012 est.)
country comparison to the world: 20
$651.4 billion (31 December 2011 est.)

Market value of publicly traded shares:
$1.108 trillion (31 December 2012 est.)
country comparison to the world: 15
$889.6 billion (31 December 2011)
$1.08 trillion (31 December 2010 est.)

Current account balance: $10.22 billion (2013 est.)
country comparison to the world: 24
$4.412 billion (2012 est.)

Exports: $486.1 billion (2013 est.)
country comparison to the world: 10
$493 billion (2012 est.)

Exports—commodities: electrical machinery and appliances, textiles, apparel, footwear, watches and clocks, toys, plastics, precious stones, printed material

Exports—partners: China 57.7%, US 8.9%, Japan 4.2% (2012 est.)

Imports: $514.5 billion (2013 est.)
country comparison to the world: 9
$554.2 billion (2012 est.)

Imports—commodities: raw materials and semi-manufactures, consumer goods, capital goods, foodstuffs, fuel (most is reexported)

Imports—partners: China 44.5%, Japan 8%, Taiwan 6.8%, South Korea 5.5%, US 4.9% (2012 est.)

Reserves of foreign exchange and gold:
$309 billion (31 December 2013 est.)
country comparison to the world: 10
$317.4 billion (31 December 2012 est.)

Debt—external: $1.109 trillion (31 December 2013 est.)
country comparison to the world: 17
$1.03 trillion (31 December 2012 est.)

Stock of direct foreign investment—at home:
$1.502 trillion (31 December 2013 est.)
country comparison to the world: 2
$1.355 trillion (31 December 2012 est.)

Stock of direct foreign investment—abroad:
$1.392 trillion (31 December 2013 est.)
country comparison to the world: 6
$1.273 trillion (31 December 2012 est.)

Exchange rates: Hong Kong dollars (HKD) per US dollar—
7.772 (2013 est.)
7.756 (2012 est.)
7.77 (2010 est.)
7.75 (2009)
7.751 (2008)

ENERGY

Electricity—production: 41.3 billion kWh (2012 est.)
country comparison to the world: 5 8

Electricity—consumption: 45.07 billion kWh (2012 est.)
country comparison to the world: 50

Electricity—exports: 497.4 million kWh (2012 est.)
country comparison to the world: 64

Electricity—imports: 11.15 billion kWh (2012 est.)
country comparison to the world: 20

Electricity—installed generating capacity: 10.66 million kW (2012 est.)
country comparison to the world: 52

Electricity—from fossil fuels: 100% of total installed capacity (2012 est.)
country comparison to the world: 17

Electricity—from nuclear fuels: 0% of total installed capacity (2012 est.)
country comparison to the world: 104

Electricity—from hydroelectric plants: 0% of total installed capacity (2012 est.)
country comparison to the world: 175

Electricity—from other renewable sources: 0% of total installed capacity (2012 est.)
country comparison to the world: 183

Crude oil—production: 100 bbl/day (2012 est.)
country comparison to the world: 123

Crude oil—exports: 0 bbl/day (2012 est.)
country comparison to the world: 125

Crude oil—imports: 0 bbl/day (2012 est.)
country comparison to the world: 199

Crude oil—proved reserves: 0 bbl (1 January 2013 es)
country comparison to the world: 144

Refined petroleum products—production: 0 bbl/day (2012 est.)
country comparison to the world: 155

Refined petroleum products—consumption: 337,600 bbl/day (2012 est.)
country comparison to the world: 37

Refined petroleum products—exports: 16,520 bbl/day (2012)
country comparison to the world: 76

Refined petroleum products—imports: 354,100 bbl/day (2012 est.)
country comparison to the world: 18

Natural gas—production: 0 cu m (2012 est.)
country comparison to the world: 143

Natural gas—consumption: 2.79 billion cu m (2012 est.)
country comparison to the world: 75

Natural gas—exports: 0 cu m (2012 est.)
country comparison to the world: 116

Natural gas—imports: 2.79 billion cu m (2012 est.)
country comparison to the world: 43

Natural gas—proved reserves: 0 cu m (1 January 2013 es)
country comparison to the world: 149

Carbon dioxide emissions from consumption of energy: 92.91 million Mt (2011 est.)
country comparison to the world: 41

COMMUNICATIONS

Telephones—main lines in use: 4.362 million (2012)
country comparison to the world: 3 9

Telephones—mobile cellular: 16.403 million (2012)
country comparison to the world: 57

Telephone system: *general assessment:* modern facilities provide excellent domestic and international services
domestic: microwave radio relay links and extensive fiber-optic network
international: country code—852; multiple international submarine cables provide connections to Asia, US, Australia, the Middle East, and Western Europe; satellite earth stations—3 Intelsat (1 Pacific Ocean and 2 Indian Ocean); coaxial cable to Guangzhou, China (2012)

Broadcast media: 2 commercial terrestrial TV networks each with multiple stations; multi-channel satellite and cable TV systems available; 3 radio networks, one of which is government-funded, operate about 15 radio stations (2012)

Internet country code: .hk

Internet hosts: 870,041 (2012)
country comparison to the world: 48

Internet users: 4.873 million (2009)
country comparison to the world: 47

TRANSPORTATION

Airports: 2 (2013)
country comparison to the world: 201

Airports—with paved runways: *total:* 2
over 3,047 m: 1
1,524 to 2,437 m: 1 (2013)

Heliports: 9 (2013)

Roadways: total: 2,090 km
country comparison to the world: 174
paved: 2,090 km (2012)

Merchant marine: *total:* 1,644
country comparison to the world: 5
by type: barge carrier 2, bulk carrier 785, cargo 198, carrier 10, chemical tanker 149, container 288, liquefied gas 31, passenger 4, passenger/cargo 9, petroleum tanker 156, roll on/roll off 5, vehicle carrier 7
foreign-owned: 976 (Bangladesh 1, Belgium 26, Bermuda 20, Canada 77, China 500, Cyprus 3, Denmark 42, France 4, Germany 10, Greece 27, Indonesia 10, Iran 3, Japan 79, Libya 1, Norway 48, Russia 1, Singapore 13, South Korea 3, Switzerland 5, Taiwan 25, UAE 1, UK 33, US 44)
registered in other countries: 341 (Bahamas 3, Bermuda 4, Cambodia 10, China 18, Curacao 1, Cyprus 2, Georgia 3, India 2, Kiribati 2, Liberia 48, Malaysia 8, Malta 4, Marshall Islands 3, NZ 1, Panama 144, Saint Vincent and the Grenadines 5, Seychelles 1, Sierra Leone 7, Singapore 46, Thailand 1, UK 12, unknown 16) (2010)

Ports and terminals: *major seaport(s):* Hong Kong

MILITARY

Military branches: no regular indigenous military forces; Hong Kong garrison of China's People's Liberation Army (PLA) includes elements of the PLA Ground Forces, PLA Navy, and PLA Air Force; these forces are under the direct leadership of the Central Military Commission in Beijing and under administrative control of the adjacent Guangzhou Military Region (2012)

Manpower available for military service:
males age 16-49: 1,704,090
females age 16-49: 1,873,175 (2010 est.)

Manpower fit for military service:
males age 16-49: 1,387,213
females age 16-49: 1,505,875 (2010 est.)

Manpower reaching militarily significant age annually: *male:* 39,579
female: 36,554 (2010 est.)

Military—note: defense is the responsibility of China

TRANSNATIONAL ISSUES

Disputes—international: none

Illicit drugs: despite strenuous law enforcement efforts, faces difficult challenges in controlling transit of heroin and methamphetamine to regional and world markets; modern banking system provides conduit for money laundering; rising indigenous use of synthetic drugs, especially among young people

HOWLAND ISLAND

INTRODUCTION

Background: Discovered by the US early in the 19th century, the island was officially claimed by the US in 1857. Both US and British companies mined for guano until about 1890. Earhart Light is a day beacon near the middle of the west coast that was partially destroyed during World War II, but subsequently rebuilt; it is named in memory of the famed aviatrix Amelia EARHART. The island is administered by the US Department of the Interior as a National Wildlife Refuge.

GEOGRAPHY

Location: Oceania, island in the North Pacific Ocean, about half way between Hawaii and Australia

Geographic coordinates: 0 48 N, 176 38 W

Map references: Oceania

Area: *total:* 1.6 sq km
country comparison to the world: 251
land: 1.6 sq km
water: 0 sq km

Area—comparative: about three times the size of The Mall in Washington, DC

Land boundaries: 0 km

Coastline: 6.4 km

Maritime claims: *territorial sea:* 12 nm
exclusive economic zone: 200 nm

Climate: equatorial; scant rainfall, constant wind, burning sun

Terrain: low-lying, nearly level, sandy, coral island surrounded by a narrow fringing reef; depressed central area

Elevation extremes: *lowest point:* Pacific Ocean 0 m
highest point: unnamed location 3 m

Natural resources: guano (deposits worked until late 1800s), terrestrial and aquatic wildlife

Land use: *arable land:* 0%
permanent crops: 0%
other: 100% (2001)

Irrigated land: 0 sq km

Natural hazards: the narrow fringing reef surrounding the island can be a maritime hazard

Environment—current issues: no natural fresh water resources

Geography—note: almost totally covered with grasses, prostrate vines, and low-growing shrubs; small area of trees in the center; primarily a nesting, roosting, and foraging habitat for seabirds, shorebirds, and marine wildlife

PEOPLE AND SOCIETY

Population: uninhabited
note: American civilians evacuated in 1942 after Japanese air and naval attacks during World War II; occupied by US military during World War II, but abandoned after the war; public entry is by special-use permit from US Fish and Wildlife Service only and generally restricted to scientists and educators; visited annually by US Fish and Wildlife Service

GOVERNMENT

Country name: *conventional long form:* none
conventional short form: Howland Island

Dependency status: unincorporated territory of the US; administered from Washington, DC, by the Fish and Wildlife Service of the US Department of the Interior as part of the National Wildlife Refuge system

Legal system: the laws of the US, where applicable, apply

Flag description: the flag of the US is used

TRANSPORTATION

Ports and terminals: none; offshore anchorage only; note—there is one small boat landing area along the middle of the west coast

Transportation—note: Earhart Light, a day beacon near the middle of the west coast, was partially destroyed during World War II but rebuilt during the 1960s; today it is crumbling and in poor repair; named in memory of famed aviatrix Amelia EARHART

MILITARY

Military—note: defense is the responsibility of the US; visited annually by the US Coast Guard

TRANSNATIONAL ISSUES

Disputes—international: none

HUNGARY

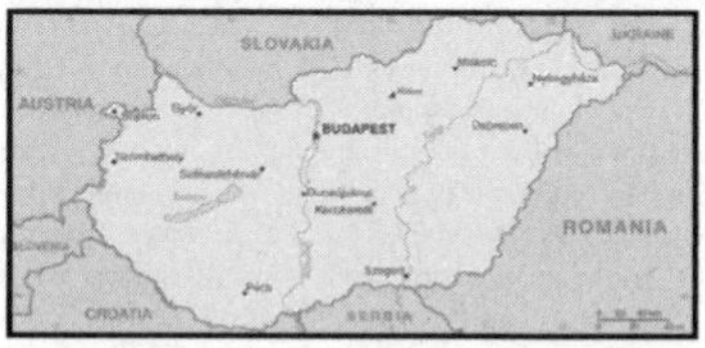

INTRODUCTION

Background: Hungary became a Christian kingdom in A.D. 1000 and for many centuries served as a bulwark against Ottoman Turkish expansion in Europe. The kingdom eventually became part of the polyglot Austro-Hungarian Empire, which collapsed during World War I. The country fell under communist rule following World War II. In 1956, a revolt and an announced withdrawal from the Warsaw Pact were met with a massive military intervention by Moscow. Under the leadership of Janos KADAR in 1968, Hungary began liberalizing its economy, introducing so-called "Goulash Communism." Hungary held its first multiparty elections in 1990 and initiated a free market economy. It joined NATO in 1999 and the EU five years later. In 2011, Hungary assumed the six-month rotating presidency of the EU for the first time.

GEOGRAPHY

Location: Central Europe, northwest of Romania

Geographic coordinates: 47 00 N, 20 00 E

Map references: Europe

Area: *total:* 93,028 sq km
country comparison to the world: 110
land: 89,608 sq km
water: 3,420 sq km

Area—comparative: slightly smaller than Indiana

Land boundaries: *total:* 2,185 km
border countries: Austria 366 km, Croatia 329 km, Romania 443 km, Serbia 166 km, Slovakia 676 km, Slovenia 102 km, Ukraine 103 km

Coastline: 0 km (landlocked)

Maritime claims: none (landlocked)

Climate: temperate; cold, cloudy, humid winters; warm summers

Terrain: mostly flat to rolling plains; hills and low mountains on the Slovakian border

Elevation extremes: *lowest point:* Tisza River 78 m
highest point: Kekes 1,014 m

Natural resources: bauxite, coal, natural gas, fertile soils, arable land

Land use: *arable land:* 47.24%
permanent crops: 1.97%
other: 50.79% (2011)

Irrigated land: 1,409 sq km (2007)

Total renewable water resources: 104 cu km (2011)

Freshwater withdrawal (domestic/industrial/agricultural): *total:* 5.58 cu km/yr (12%/83%/5%)
per capita: 555.9 cu m/yr (2007)

Environment—current issues: the upgrading of Hungary's standards in waste management, energy efficiency, and air, soil, and water pollution to meet EU requirements will require large investments

Environment—international agreements: *party to:* Air Pollution, Air Pollution-Nitrogen Oxides, Air Pollution-Persistent Organic Pollutants, Air Pollution-Sulfur 85, Air Pollution-Sulfur 94, Air Pollution-Volatile Organic Compounds, Antarctic Treaty, Biodiversity, Climate Change, Climate Change-Kyoto Protocol, Desertification, Endangered Species, Environmental Modification, Hazardous Wastes, Law of the Sea, Marine Dumping, Ozone Layer Protection, Ship Pollution, Wetlands, Whaling
signed, but not ratified: none of the selected agreements

Geography—note: landlocked; strategic location astride main land routes between Western Europe and Balkan Peninsula as well as between Ukraine and Mediterranean basin; the north-south flowing Duna (Danube) and Tisza Rivers divide the country into three large regions

PEOPLE AND SOCIETY

Nationality: *noun:* Hungarian(s)
adjective: Hungarian

Ethnic groups: Hungarian 92.3%, Roma 1.9%, other or unknown 5.8% (2001 census)

Languages: Hungarian 84.6%, other or unspecified 16.4% (2011 est.)

Religions: Roman Catholic 37.2%, Calvinist 11.6%, Lutheran 2.2%, Greek Catholic 1.8%, other 1.9%, none 18.2%, unspecified 27.2% (2011 est.)

Population: 9,919,128 (July 2014 est.)
country comparison to the world: 90

Age structure:
0-14 years: 14.8% (male 757,868/female 712,908)
15-24 years: 11.7% (male 596,005/female 561,606)
25-54 years: 41.6% (male 2,071,845/female 2,056,611)
55-64 years: 17.8% (male 639,298/female 754,129)
65 years and over: 17.5% (male 661,256/female 1,107,602) (2014 est.)

Dependency ratios:
total dependency ratio: 46.8 %
youth dependency ratio: 21.5 %
elderly dependency ratio: 25.3 %
potential support ratio: 4 (2013)

Median age: *total:* 41.1 years
male: 39.1 years
female: 43.5 years (2014 est.)

Population growth rate: -0.21% (2014 est.)
country comparison to the world: 214

Birth rate: 9.26 births/1,000 population (2014 est.)
country comparison to the world: 207

Death rate: 12.72 deaths/1,000 population (2014 est.)

country comparison to the world: 23

Net migration rate: 1.34 migrant(s)/1,000 population (2014 est.)
country comparison to the world: 55

Urbanization: *urban population:* 69.5% of total population (2011)
rate of urbanization: 0.51% annual rate of change (2010-15 est.)

Major urban areas—population: BUDAPEST (capital) 1.705 million (2009)

Sex ratio: *at birth:* 1.06 male(s)/female
0-14 years: 1.06 male(s)/female
15-24 years: 1.06 male(s)/female
25-54 years: 1.01 male(s)/female
55-64 years: 0.91 male(s)/female
65 years and over: 0.59 male(s)/female
total population: 0.91 male(s)/female (2014 est.)

Mother's mean age at first birth: 28.2 (2010 est.)

Maternal mortality rate:
21 deaths/100,000 live births (2010)
country comparison to the world: 135

Infant mortality rate: *total:* 5.09 deaths/1,000 live births
country comparison to the world: 179
male: 5.36 deaths/1,000 live births
female: 4.81 deaths/1,000 live births (2014 est.)

Life expectancy at birth: *total population:* 75.46 years
country comparison to the world: 93
male: 71.73 years
female: 79.41 years (2014 est.)

Total fertility rate: 1.42 children born/woman (2014 est.)
country comparison to the world: 206

Contraceptive prevalence rate: 80.6%
note: percent of women aged 18-41 (1992/93)

Health expenditures: 7.7% of GDP (2011)
country comparison to the world: 72

Physicians density: 3.41 physicians/1,000 population (2010)

Hospital bed density: 7.2 beds/1,000 population (2010)

Drinking water source:
improved: *urban:* 100% of population
rural: 100% of population
total: 100% of population
unimproved: *urban:* 0% of population
rural: 0% of population
total: 0% of population (2011 est.)

Sanitation facility access:
improved: *urban:* 100% of population
rural: 100% of population
total: 100% of population
unimproved: *urban:* 0% of population
rural: 0% of population
total: 0% of population (2011 est.)

HIV/AIDS—adult prevalence rate: less than 0.1% (2009 est.)
country comparison to the world: 118

HIV/AIDS—people living with HIV/AIDS:
3,000 (2009 est.)
country comparison to the world: 133

HIV/AIDS—deaths: fewer than 200 (2009 est.)
country comparison to the world: 112

Major infectious diseases: *degree of risk:* intermediate
vectorborne diseases: tickborne encephalitis (2013)

Obesity—adult prevalence rate: 27.6% (2008)
country comparison to the world: 37

Education expenditures: 4.9% of GDP (2010)
country comparison to the world: 81

Literacy: *definition:* age 15 and over can read and write
total population: 99%
male: 99.2%
female: 98.9% (2011 est.)

School life expectancy (primary to tertiary education): *total:* 15 years
male: 15 years
female: 16 years (2011)

Unemployment, youth ages 15-24: *total:* 28.1%
country comparison to the world: 33
male: 28.8%
female: 27.3% (2012)

GOVERNMENT

Country name: *conventional long form:* none
conventional short form: Hungary
local long form: none
local short form: Magyarorszag

Government type: parliamentary democracy

Capital: *name:* Budapest
geographic coordinates: 47 30 N, 19 05 E
time difference: UTC+1 (6 hours ahead of Washington, DC during Standard Time)
daylight saving time: +1hr, begins last Sunday in March; ends last Sunday in October

Administrative divisions: 19 counties (megyek, singular—megye), 23 urban counties (singular—megyei varos), and 1 capital city (fovaros)
counties: Bacs-Kiskun, Baranya, Bekes, Borsod-Abauj-Zemplen, Csongrad, Fejer, Gyor-Moson-Sopron, Hajdu-Bihar, Heves, Jasz-Nagykun-Szolnok, Komarom-Esztergom, Nograd, Pest, Somogy, Szabolcs-Szatmar-Bereg, Tolna, Vas, Veszprem, Zala
urban counties: Bekescsaba, Debrecen, Dunaujvaros, Eger, Erd, Gyor, Hodmezovasarhely, Kaposvar, Kecskemet, Miskolc, Nagykanizsa, Nyiregyhaza, Pecs, Salgotarjan, Sopron, Szeged, Szekesfehervar, Szekszard, Szolnok, Szombathely, Tatabanya, Veszprem, Zalaegerszeg
capital city: Budapest

Independence: 16 November 1918 (republic proclaimed); notable earlier dates: 25 December 1000 (crowning of King STEPHEN I, traditional founding date); 30 March 1867 (Austro-Hungarian dual monarchy established)

National holiday: Saint Stephen's Day, 20 August; note—commemorates the date when his remains were transferred to Buda (now Budapest)

Constitution: previous 1949 (heavily amended in 1989 following collapse of communism); latest approved 18 April 2011, signed 25 April 2011, effective 1 January 2012; amended several times, last in 2013 (2013)

Legal system: civil legal system influenced by the German model

International law organization participation:
accepts compulsory ICJ jurisdiction with reservations; accepts ICCt jurisdiction

Suffrage: 18 years of age, 16 if married; universal

Executive branch: *chief of state:* Janos ADER (since 10 May 2012)
head of government: Prime Minister Viktor ORBAN (since 29 May 2010)
cabinet: Cabinet of Ministers prime minister elected by the National Assembly on the recommendation of the president; other ministers proposed by the prime minister and appointed and relieved of their duties by the president (For more information visit the World Leaders website)
elections: president elected by the National Assembly for a five-year term (eligible for a second term); election last held on 2 May 2012 (next to be held by May 2017); prime minister elected by the National Assembly on the recommendation of the president; election last held 29 May 2010
election results: Janos ADER elected president, National Assembly vote—262 to 40; Viktor ORBAN elected prime minister, National Assembly vote—261 to 107
note: to be elected, the president must win two-thirds of legislative vote in the first round or a simple majority in the second round

Legislative branch: unicameral National Assembly or Orszaggyules (199 seats; 106 single-round, single-member district vote, 93 nationwide party list vote; members serve four-year terms)
elections: last held on 6 April 2014 (next to be held in April 2018)
election results: percent of vote by party—Fidesz-KNDP 66.8%, Unity 19.1%, Jobbik 11.6%, LMP 2.5%; seats by party—Fidesz-KNDP 133, Unity 38, Jobbik 23, LMP 5

Judicial branch: *highest court(s):* Curia or Supreme Judicial Court (consists of Curia president and 8 judges); Constitutional Court (consists of 15 members)
judge selection and term of office: Curia president elected from among its members for 9 years by the National Assembly on the recommendation of the president of the republic; other Curia judges appointed by the president upon the recommendation of the National Council of Justice, a separate 15-member administrative body; all judges serve until the normal retirement age; Constitutional Court members elected by two-thirds vote of the National Assembly; members serve 12-year terms
subordinate courts: regional courts of appeal; county courts, including the Municipal Court of Budapest; local courts

Political parties and leaders: Christian Democratic People's Party or KDNP [Zsolt SEMJEN]; Democratic Coalition or DK [Ferenc GYURCSANY]; Dialogue for Hungary or PM [Benedek JAVOR, Timea SZABO, co-chairs]; Fidesz-Hungarian Civic Alliance or Fidesz [Viktor ORBAN, chairman]; Hungarian Liberal Party or MLP [Gabor FODOR]; Hungarian Socialist Party or MSZP [Attila MESTERHAZY]; Movement for a Better Hungary or Jobbik [Gabor VONA]; Politics Can Be Different or LMP [Andras SCHIFFER, Bernadett SZEL]; Together or Egyutt [Gordon BAJNAI]; Unity [a coalition of MSZP, Egyutt, DK, PM, and MLP]

Political pressure groups and leaders: Air Work Group (works to reduce air pollution in towns and cities); Danube Circle (protests the building of the Gabchikovo-Nagymaros dam); Fourth Republic (Negyedik Koztarsasag) or 4K! (anti-Orban, pro-democracy Facebook movement emerged from a Facebook group, One Million for Freedom of the Press or "Milla"); Green Future (protests the impact of lead contamination of local factory on health of the people); Hungarian Civil Liberties Union (Tarsasag a Szabadsagjogokert) or TASZ (freedom of expression, information privacy); Hungarian Helsinki Committee (asylum seekers' rights, human rights in law enforcement and the judicial system); Szolidaritas ("Solidarity," formed in October 2011 by three trade unions and an NGO—anti-Orban government); "Egyutt 2014-Parbeszed Magyarorszagert" ("Together

2014-Dialogue for Hungary," a political electoral alliance bringing together Milla, Szolidaritas, and "Haza es Haladas," an association headed by former PM Gordon BAJNAI, to contest Fidesz and Viktor ORBAN in the; 2014 parliamentary elections); Civil Osszefogas Forum ("Civil Unity Forum," nominally independent organization that serves as the steering committee for the; pro-government mass organization Bekemenet (Peace March), supporting ORBAN government's policies)
environmentalists: Hungarian Ornithological and Nature Conservation Society (Magyar Madartani Egyesulet) or MME; Green Alternative (Zold Alternativa)

International organization participation: Australia Group, BIS, CD, CE, CEI, CERN, EAPC, EBRD, EIB, ESA (cooperating state), EU, FAO, G-9, IAEA, IBRD, ICAO, ICC (national committees), ICRM, IDA, IEA, IFAD, IFC, IFRCS, ILO, IMF, IMO, IMSO, Interpol, IOC, IOM, IPU, ISO, ITSO, ITU, ITUC (NGOs), MIGA, MINURSO, NATO, NEA, NSG, OAS (observer), OECD, OIF (observer), OPCW, OSCE, PCA, Schengen Convention, SELEC, UN, UNCTAD, UNESCO, UNFICYP, UNHCR, UNIDO, UNIFIL, UNWTO, UPU, WCO, WFTU (NGOs), WHO, WIPO, WMO, WTO, ZC

Diplomatic representation in the US:
chief of mission: Ambassador Gyorgy SZAPARY (since 31 January 2011)
chancery: 3910 Shoemaker Street NW, Washington, DC 20008
telephone: [1] (202) 362-6730
FAX: [1] (202) 966-8135
consulate(s) general: Chicago, Los Angeles, New York

Diplomatic representation from the US:
chief of mission: Ambassador (vacant); Charge d'Affaires M. Andre GOODFRIEND (since August 2013)
embassy: Szabadsag ter 12, H-1054 Budapest
mailing address: pouch: American Embassy Budapest, 5270 Budapest Place, US Department of State, Washington, DC 20521-5270
telephone: [36] (1) 475-4400
FAX: [36] (1) 475-4764

Flag description: three equal horizontal bands of red (top), white, and green; the flag dates to the national movement of the 18th and 19th centuries, and fuses the medieval colors of the Hungarian coat of arms with the revolutionary tricolor form of the French flag; folklore attributes virtues to the colors: red for strength, white for faithfulness, and green for hope; alternatively, the red is seen as being for the blood spilled in defense of the land, white for freedom, and green for the pasturelands that make up so much of the country

National symbol(s): Holy Crown of Hungary (Crown of Saint Stephen); turul (falcon)

National anthem: *name:* "Himnusz" (Hymn)
lyrics/music: Ferenc KOLCSEY/Ferenc ERKEL
note: adopted 1844

ECONOMY

Economy—overview: Hungary has made the transition from a centrally planned to a market economy, with a per capita income nearly two-thirds that of the EU-28 average. In late 2008, Hungary's impending inability to service its short-term debt—brought on by the global financial crisis - led Budapest to obtain an IMF/EU/World Bank-arranged financial assistance package worth over $25 billion. The global economic downturn, declining exports, and low domestic consumption and fixed asset accumulation, dampened by government austerity measures, resulted in a severe economic contraction in 2009. In 2010 the new government implemented a number of changes including cutting business and personal income taxes, but imposed "crisis taxes" on financial institutions, energy and telecom companies, and retailers. The IMF/EU bail-out program lapsed at the end of the year and was replaced by Post Program Monitoring and Article IV Consultations on overall economic and fiscal processes. At the end of 2011 the government turned to the IMF and the EU to obtain financial backstop to support its efforts to refinance foreign currency debt and bond obligations in 2012 and beyond, but Budapest's rejection of EU and IMF economic policy recommendations led to a breakdown in talks with the lenders in late 2012. Global demand for high yield has since helped Hungary to obtain funds on international markets. Hungary's progress reducing its deficit to under 3% of GDP led the European Commission in 2013 to permit Hungary for the first time since joining the EU in 2004 to exit the Excessive Deficit Procedure.

GDP (purchasing power parity): $196.6 billion (2013 est.)
country comparison to the world: 57
$196.3 billion (2012 est.)
$199.8 billion (2011 est.)
note: data are in 2013 US dollars

GDP (official exchange rate): $130.6 billion (2013 est.)

GDP—real growth rate: 0.2% (2013 est.)
country comparison to the world: 191
-1.7% (2012 est.)
1.6% (2011 est.)

GDP—per capita (PPP): $19,800 (2013 est.)
country comparison to the world: 71
$19,800 (2012 est.)
$20,000 (2011 est.)
note: data are in 2013 US dollars

Gross national saving: 17.1% of GDP (2013 est.)
country comparison to the world: 98
19.3% of GDP (2012 est.)
20.4% of GDP (2011 est.)

GDP—composition, by end use:
household consumption: 55.5%
government consumption: 20.4%
investment in fixed capital: 16.4%
investment in inventories: -0.7%
exports of goods and services: 97.2%
imports of goods and services: -88.8% (2013 est.)

GDP—composition, by sector of origin:
agriculture: 3.4%
industry: 28%
services: 68.7% (2013 est.)

Agriculture—products: wheat, corn, sunflower seed, potatoes, sugar beets; pigs, cattle, poultry, dairy products

Industries: mining, metallurgy, construction materials, processed foods, textiles, chemicals (especially pharmaceuticals), motor vehicles

Industrial production growth rate: 1.8% (2013 est.)
country comparison to the world: 130

Labor force: 4.263 million (2013 est.)
country comparison to the world: 88

Labor force—by occupation: *agriculture:* 7.1%
industry: 29.7%
services: 63.2% (2011)

Unemployment rate: 10.5% (2013 est.)
country comparison to the world: 112
10.7% (2012 est.)

Population below poverty line: 14% (2012)

Household income or consumption by percentage share: *lowest 10%:* 3.1%
highest 10%: 22.6% (2009)

Distribution of family income—Gini index:
24.7 (2009)
country comparison to the world: 136
24.4 (1998)

Budget: *revenues:* $62.24 billion
expenditures: $66.01 billion (2013 est.)

Taxes and other revenues: 47.7% of GDP (2013 est.)
country comparison to the world: 16

Budget surplus (+) or deficit (-):
-2.9% of GDP
country comparison to the world: 118
note: Hungary has been under the EU Excessive Deficit Procedure since it joined the EU in 2004; in March 2012 the EU elevated its Excessive Deficit Procedure against Hungary and proposed freezing 30% of the country's Cohesion Funds because 2011 deficit reductions were not achieved in a sustainable manner; in June 2012, the EU lifted the freeze, reognizing that steps had been taken to reduce the deficit; the latest EC forecasts project the Hungarian deficit to increase above 3% both in 2013 and in 2014 due to sluggish growth and the government's fiscal tightening (2013 est.)

Public debt: 79.8% of GDP (2013 est.)
country comparison to the world: 27
79.3% of GDP (2012 est.)
note: general government gross debt is defined in the Maastricht Treaty as consolidated general government gross debt at nominal value, outstanding at the end of the year in the following categories of government liabilities: currency and deposits, securities other than shares excluding financial derivatives, and government, state government, local government, and social security funds.

Fiscal year: calendar year

Inflation rate (consumer prices): 1.9% (2013 est.)
country comparison to the world: 61
5.7% (2012 est.)

Central bank discount rate: 5.75% (19 December 2012)
country comparison to the world: 39
7% (31 December 2011)

Commercial bank prime lending rate: 6.5% (31 December 2013 est.)
country comparison to the world: 101
9.02% (31 December 2012 est.)

Stock of narrow money: $34.75 billion (31 December 2013 est.)
country comparison to the world: 57
$33.03 billion (31 December 2012 est.)

Stock of broad money: $67.47 billion (31 December 2013 est.)
country comparison to the world: 64
$68.7 billion (31 December 2012 est.)

Stock of domestic credit: $77.79 billion (31 December 2013 est.)
country comparison to the world: 59
$87.27 billion (31 December 2012 est.)

Market value of publicly traded shares:
$22.9 billion (31 December 2012 est.)
country comparison to the world: 61
$22.8 billion (31 December 2011)
$27.71 billion (31 December 2010 est.)

Current account balance: $1.722 billion (2013 est.)
country comparison to the world: 46
$2.087 billion (2012 est.)

Exports: $92.98 billion (2013 est.)
country comparison to the world: 39
$90.23 billion (2012 est.)

Exports—commodities: machinery and equipment 53.5%, other manufactures 31.2%, food products 8.7%, raw materials 3.4%, fuels and electricity 3.9% (2012)

Exports—partners: Germany 25.6%, Romania 6.2%, Slovakia 6.1%, Austria 6%, Italy 4.8%, France 4.8%, UK 4.2% (2012)

Imports: $89.52 billion (2013 est.)
country comparison to the world: 37
$87.37 billion (2012 est.)

Imports—commodities: machinery and equipment 45.4%, other manufactures 34.3%, fuels and electricity 12.6%, food products 5.3%, raw materials 2.5% (2012)

Imports—partners: Germany 25.1%, Russia 8.8%, China 7.4%, Austria 7.1%, Slovakia 5.6%, Poland 4.8%, Italy 4.5%, Netherlands 4.2% (2012)

Reserves of foreign exchange and gold:
$38.49 billion (31 December 2013 est.)
country comparison to the world: 47
$44.67 billion (31 December 2012 est.)

Debt—external: $170.3 billion (31 December 2013 est.)
country comparison to the world: 34
$169.3 billion (31 December 2012 est.)

Stock of direct foreign investment—at home:
$112 billion (31 December 2013 est.)
country comparison to the world: 40
$107 billion (31 December 2012 est.)

Stock of direct foreign investment—abroad:
$45.95 billion (31 December 2013 est.)
country comparison to the world: 38
$41.82 billion (31 December 2012 est.)

Exchange rates: forints (HUF) per US dollar—
227.8 (2013 est.)
225.1 (2012 est.)
207.94 (2010 est.)
202.34 (2009)
171.8 (2008)

ENERGY

Electricity—production: 34.28 billion kWh (2012 est.)
country comparison to the world: 6 2

Electricity—consumption: 36.13 billion kWh (2012 est.)
country comparison to the world: 55

Electricity—exports: 9 billion kWh (2012 est.)
country comparison to the world: 22

Electricity—imports: 16.97 billion kWh (2012 est.)
country comparison to the world: 9

Electricity—installed generating capacity:
9.9 million kW (2011 est.)
country comparison to the world: 57

Electricity—from fossil fuels: 72% of total installed capacity (2011 est.)
country comparison to the world: 103

Electricity—from nuclear fuels: 20% of total installed capacity (2011 est.)
country comparison to the world: 8

Electricity—from hydroelectric plants:
1% of total installed capacity (2011 est.)
country comparison to the world: 142

Electricity—from other renewable sources:
7% of total installed capacity (2011 est.)
country comparison to the world: 34

Crude oil—production: 27,990 bbl/day (2012 est.)
country comparison to the world: 70

Crude oil—exports: 0 bbl/day (2010 est.)
country comparison to the world: 128

Crude oil—imports: 114,800 bbl/day (2010 est.)
country comparison to the world: 48

Crude oil—proved reserves: 27.32 million bbl (1 January 2013 es)
country comparison to the world: 83

Refined petroleum products—production:
177,500 bbl/day (2010 est.)
country comparison to the world: 59

Refined petroleum products—consumption:
141,100 bbl/day (2011 est.)
country comparison to the world: 70

Refined petroleum products—exports:
59,110 bbl/day (2010 est.)
country comparison to the world: 59

Refined petroleum products—imports:
171,600 bbl/day (2010 est.)
country comparison to the world: 33

Natural gas—production: 2.462 billion cu m (2012 est.)
country comparison to the world: 57

Natural gas—consumption: 11.9 billion cu m (2012 est.)
country comparison to the world: 44

Natural gas—exports: 2.837 billion cu m (2012 est.)
country comparison to the world: 41

Natural gas—imports: 10.18 billion cu m (2012 est.)
country comparison to the world: 30

Natural gas—proved reserves: 8.098 billion cu m (1 January 2013 es)
country comparison to the world: 85

Carbon dioxide emissions from consumption of energy: 49.56 million Mt (2011 est.)
country comparison to the world: 65

COMMUNICATIONS

Telephones—main lines in use: 2.96 million (2012)
country comparison to the world: 5 1

Telephones—mobile cellular: 11.58 million (2012)
country comparison to the world: 72

Telephone system: *general assessment:* the telephone system has been modernized; the system is digital and highly automated; trunk services are carried by fiber-optic cable and digital microwave radio relay; a program for fiber-optic subscriber connections was initiated in 1996
domestic: competition among mobile-cellular service providers has led to a sharp increase in the use of mobile-cellular phones since 2000 and a decrease in the number of fixed-line connections
international: country code—36; Hungary has fiber-optic cable connections with all neighboring countries; the international switch is in Budapest; satellite earth stations—2 Intelsat (Atlantic Ocean and Indian Ocean regions), 1 Inmarsat, 1 very small aperture terminal (VSAT) system of ground terminals (2011)

Broadcast media: mixed system of state-supported public service broadcast media and private broadcasters; the 3 publicly owned TV channels and the 2 main privately owned TV stations are the major national broadcasters; a large number of special interest channels; highly developed market for satellite and cable TV services with about two-thirds of viewers utilizing their services; 3 state-supported public-service radio networks and 2 major national commercial stations; a large number of local stations including commercial, public service, nonprofit, and community radio stations; digital transition postponed to the end of 2014 (2007)

Internet country code: . h u

Internet hosts: 3.145 million (2012)
country comparison to the world: 33

Internet users: 6.176 million (2009)
country comparison to the world: 41

TRANSPORTATION

Airports: 41 (2013)
country comparison to the world: 104

Airports—with paved runways: *total:* 2 0
over 3,047 m: 2
2,438 to 3,047 m: 6
1,524 to 2,437 m: 6
914 to 1,523 m: 5
under 914 m: 1 (2013)

Airports—with unpaved runways: *total:* 2 1
1,524 to 2,437 m: 2
914 to 1,523 m: 8
under 914 m: 11 (2013)

Heliports: 3 (2013)

Pipelines: gas 19,028 km; oil 1,007 km; refined products 842 km (2013)

Railways: *total:* 8,057 km
country comparison to the world: 26
broad gauge: 36 km 1.524-m gauge
standard gauge: 7,802 km 1.435-m gauge (2,911 km electrified)
narrow gauge: 219 km 0.760-m gauge (2009)

Roadways: *total:* 199,567 km
country comparison to the world: 25
paved: 76,075 km (includes 1,477 km of expressways)
unpaved: 123,492 km (2010)

Waterways: 1,622 km (most on Danube River) (2011)
country comparison to the world: 48

Ports and terminals: Budapest, Dunaujvaros, Gyor-Gonyu, Csepel, Baja, Mohacs

MILITARY

Military branches: Hungarian Defense Forces: Land Forces, Hungarian Air Force (Magyar Legiero, ML) (2011)

Military service age and obligation: 18-25 years of age for voluntary military service; no conscription; 6-month service obligation (2012)

Manpower available for military service:
males age 16-49: 2,349,948
females age 16-49: 2,290,568 (2010 est.)

Manpower fit for military service: males age 16-49: 1,902,639
females age 16-49: 1,897,378 (2010 est.)

Manpower reaching militarily significant age annually: *male:* 59,237
female: 55,533 (2010 est.)

Military expenditures: 0.83% of GDP (2012)
country comparison to the world: 113
0.99% of GDP (2011)
0.83% of GDP (2010)

TRANSNATIONAL ISSUES

Disputes—international: bilateral government, legal, technical and economic working group negotiations continue in 2006 with Slovakia over Hungary's failure to complete its portion of the Gabcikovo-Nagymaros hydroelectric dam project along the Danube; as a member state that forms part of the EU's external border, Hungary has implemented the strict Schengen border rules

Refugees and internally displaced persons:
stateless persons: 111 (2012)

Illicit drugs: transshipment point for Southwest Asian heroin and cannabis and for South American cocaine destined for Western Europe; limited producer of precursor chemicals, particularly for amphetamine and methamphetamine; efforts to counter money laundering, related to organized crime and drug trafficking are improving but remain vulnerable; significant consumer of ecstasy

ICELAND

INTRODUCTION

Background: Settled by Norwegian and Celtic (Scottish and Irish) immigrants during the late 9th and 10th centuries A.D., Iceland boasts the world's oldest functioning legislative assembly, the Althing, established in 930. Independent for over 300 years, Iceland was subsequently ruled by Norway and Denmark. Fallout from the Askja volcano of 1875 devastated the Icelandic economy and caused widespread famine. Over the next quarter century, 20% of the island's population emigrated, mostly to Canada and the US. Denmark granted limited home rule in 1874 and complete independence in 1944. The second half of the 20th century saw substantial economic growth driven primarily by the fishing industry. The economy diversified greatly after the country joined the European Economic Area in 1994, but Iceland was especially hard hit by the global financial crisis in the years following 2008. Literacy, longevity, and social cohesion are first rate by world standards.

GEOGRAPHY

Location: Northern Europe, island between the Greenland Sea and the North Atlantic Ocean, northwest of the United Kingdom

Geographic coordinates: 65 00 N, 18 00 W

Map references: Europe

Area: *total:* 103,000 sq km
country comparison to the world: 108
land: 100,250 sq km
water: 2,750 sq km

Area—comparative: slightly smaller than Kentucky

Land boundaries: 0 km

Coastline: 4,970 km

Maritime claims: territorial sea: 12 nm
exclusive economic zone: 200 nm
continental shelf: 200 nm or to the edge of the continental margin

Climate: temperate; moderated by North Atlantic Current; mild, windy winters; damp, cool summers

Terrain: mostly plateau interspersed with mountain peaks, icefields; coast deeply indented by bays and fiords

Elevation extremes: *lowest point:* Atlantic Ocean 0 m
highest point: Hvannadalshnukur 2,110 m (at Vatnajokull glacier)

Natural resources: fish, hydropower, geothermal power, diatomite

Land use: *arable land:* 1.19%
permanent crops: 0%
other: 98.81% (2011)

Irrigated land: NA

Total renewable water resources: 170 cu km (2011)

Freshwater withdrawal (domestic/industrial/agricultural): *total:* 0.17 cu km/yr (49%/8%/42%)
per capita: 539.2 cu m/yr (2005)

Natural hazards: earthquakes and volcanic activity
volcanism: Iceland, situated on top of a hotspot, experiences severe volcanic activity; Eyjafjallajokull (elev. 1,666 m) erupted in 2010, sending ash high into the atmosphere and seriously disrupting European air traffic; scientists continue to monitor nearby Katla (elev. 1,512 m), which has a high probability of eruption in the very near future, potentially disrupting air traffic; Grimsvoetn and Hekla are Iceland's most active volcanoes; other historically active volcanoes include Askja, Bardarbunga, Brennisteinsfjoll, Esjufjoll, Hengill, Krafla, Krisuvik, Kverkfjoll, Oraefajokull, Reykjanes, Torfajokull, and Vestmannaeyjar

Environment—current issues: water pollution from fertilizer runoff; inadequate wastewater treatment

Environment—international agreements:
party to: Air Pollution, Air Pollution-Persistent Organic Pollutants, Biodiversity, Climate Change, Climate Change-Kyoto Protocol, Desertification, Endangered Species, Hazardous Wastes, Kyoto Protocol, Law of the Sea, Marine Dumping, Ozone Layer Protection, Ship Pollution, Transboundary Air Pollution, Wetlands, Whaling
signed, but not ratified: Environmental Modification, Marine Life Conservation

Geography—note: strategic location between Greenland and Europe; westernmost European country; Reykjavik is the northernmost national capital in the world; more land covered by glaciers than in all of continental Europe

PEOPLE AND SOCIETY

Nationality: *noun:* Icelander(s)
adjective: Icelandic

Ethnic groups: homogeneous mixture of descendants of Norse and Celts 94%, population of foreign origin 6%

Languages: Icelandic, English, Nordic languages, German widely spoken

Religions: Evangelical Lutheran Church of Iceland (official) 76.2%, Roman Catholic 3.4%, Reykjavik Free Church 2.9%, Hafnarfjorour Free Church 1.9%, The Independent Congregation 1%, other religions 3.6% (includes Pentecostal and Asatru Association), none 5.2%, other or unspecified 5.9% (2013 est.)

Population: 317,351 (July 2014 est.)
country comparison to the world: 180

Age structure:
0-14 years: 19.7% (male 31,660/female 30,720)
15-24 years: 14.5% (male 23,116/female 22,742)
25-54 years: 40.7% (male 65,218/female 64,102)
55-64 years: 13.5% (male 18,644/female 18,225)
65 years and over: 13.2% (male 19,754/female 23,170) (2014 est.)

Dependency ratios:
total dependency ratio: 50.4 %
youth dependency ratio: 31.1 %
elderly dependency ratio: 19.3 %
potential support ratio: 5.2 (2013)

Median age: *total:* 36.4 years
male: 35.9 years
female: 36.9 years (2014 est.)

Population growth rate: 0.65% (2014 est.)
country comparison to the world: 149

Birth rate: 13.09 births/1,000 population (2014 est.)
country comparison to the world: 153

Death rate: 7.13 deaths/1,000 population (2014 est.)
country comparison to the world: 127

Net migration rate: 0.52 migrant(s)/1,000 population (2014 est.)
country comparison to the world: 69

Urbanization: *urban population:* 93% of total population (2010)
rate of urbanization: 1.5% annual rate of change (2010-15 est.)

Major urban areas—population: REYKJAVIK (capital) 198,000 (2009)

Sex ratio: *at birth:* 1.04 male(s)/female
0-14 years: 1.03 male(s)/female
15-24 years: 1.02 male(s)/female
25-54 years: 1.02 male(s)/female
55-64 years: 1 male(s)/female
65 years and over: 0.85 male(s)/female
total population: 1 male(s)/female (2014 est.)

Mother's mean age at first birth: 27 (2011 est.)

Maternal mortality rate: 5 deaths/100,000 live births (2010)
country comparison to the world: 177

Infant mortality rate: *total:* 3.15 deaths/1,000 live births
country comparison to the world: 215
male: 3.3 deaths/1,000 live births
female: 3 deaths/1,000 live births (2014 est.)

Life expectancy at birth: *total population:* 81.22 years
country comparison to the world: 20
male: 78.98 years
female: 83.54 years (2014 est.)

Total fertility rate: 1.88 children born/woman (2014 est.)
country comparison to the world: 143

Health expenditures: 9.1% of GDP (2011)
country comparison to the world: 41

Physicians density: 3.46 physicians/1,000 population (2011)

Hospital bed density: 5.8 beds/1,000 population (2007)

Drinking water source:
improved:
urban: 100% of population
rural: 100% of population
total: 100% of population
unimproved:
urban: 0% of population
rural: 0% of population
total: 0% of population (2011 est.)

Sanitation facility access:
improved:
urban: 100% of population
rural: 100% of population
total: 100% of population
unimproved:
urban: 0% of population
rural: 0% of population
total: 0% of population (2011 est.)

HIV/AIDS—adult prevalence rate: 0.3% (2009 est.)
country comparison to the world: 85

HIV/AIDS—people living with HIV/AIDS: fewer than 1,000 (2009 est.)
country comparison to the world: 147

HIV/AIDS—deaths: fewer than 100 (2009 est.)
country comparison to the world: 118

Obesity—adult prevalence rate: 23.2% (2008)

country comparison to the world: 76

Education expenditures: 7.6% of GDP (2010)
country comparison to the world: 14

Literacy: *definition:* age 15 and over can read and write
total population: 99%
male: 99%
female: 99% (2003 est.)

School life expectancy (primary to tertiary education): *total:* 19 years
male: 18 years
female: 20 years (2011)

Unemployment, youth ages 15-24: total: 13.6%
country comparison to the world: 93
male: 14.7%
female: 12.4% (2012)

GOVERNMENT

Country name: *conventional long form:* Republic of Iceland
conventional short form: Iceland
local long form: Lydveldid Island
local short form: Island

Government type: constitutional republic

Capital: *name:* Reykjavik
geographic coordinates: 64 09 N, 21 57 W
time difference: UTC 0 (5 hours ahead of Washington, DC during Standard Time)

Administrative divisions: 8 regions; Austurland, Hofudhborgarsvaedhi, Nordhurland Eystra, Nordhurland Vestra, Sudhurland, Sudhurnes, Vestfirdhir, Vesturland

Independence: 1 December 1918 (became a sovereign state under the Danish Crown); 17 June 1944 (from Denmark; birthday of Jon SIGURDSSON leader of Iceland's 19th Century independence movement)

National holiday: Independence Day, 17 June (1944)

Constitution: several previous; latest ratified 16 June 1944, effective 17 June 1944 (at independence); amended many times, last in 2013; note—a new constitution drafted in 2012 in the aftermath of the country's banking collapse was voted down in April 2013 by the recently elected parliament, though several amendments were passed (2013)

Legal system: civil law system influenced by the Danish model

International law organization participation: has not submitted an ICJ jurisdiction declaration; accepts ICCt jurisdiction

Suffrage: 18 years of age; universal

Executive branch: *chief of state:* President Olafur Ragnar GRIMSSON (since 1 August 1996)
head of government: Prime Minister Sigmundur David GUNNLAUGSSON (since 23 May 2013)
cabinet: Cabinet appointed by the prime minister (For more information visit the World Leaders website)
elections: president is elected by popular vote for a four-year term (no term limits); election last held on 30 June 2012 (next to be held in June 2016); note—following legislative elections, the leader of the majority party or the leader of the majority coalition is usually the prime minister
election results: Olafur Ragnar GRIMSSON elected president; percent of vote—Olafur Ragnar GRIMSSON 52.8%, Thora ARNORSDOTTIR 33.2%, Ari Trausti GUDMUNDSSON 8.6%, other 5.4%

Legislative branch: unicameral Althingi (parliament) (63 seats; members elected by popular vote to serve four-year terms)
elections: last held on 27 April 2013 (next to be held in 2017)
election results: percent of vote by party—SDA 30.16%, IP 25.4%, LGM 17.46%, PP 14.29%, Bright Future 3.18%, Dawn 3.18%, Rainbow 3.18%, Pirate Party 1.59%, Solidarity 1.59%; seats by party—SDA 19, IP 16, LGM 11, PP 9, Bright Future 2, Dawn 2, Rainbow 2, Pirate Party 1, Solidarity 1

Judicial branch: *highest court(s):* Supreme Court or Haestirettur (consists of 9 judges)
judge selection and term of office: judges proposed by Ministry of Interior selection committee and appointed by the president; judges appointed for an indefinite period
subordinate courts: 8 district courts; Labor Court

Political parties and leaders: Bright Future (Bjort Framtid) or BF [Gudmundur STEINGRIMSSON]; Dawn (Dogun) [Benedikt SIGURDARSON]; Independence Party (Sjalfstaedisflokkurinn) or IP [Bjarni BENEDIKTSSON]; Left-Green Movement (Vinstrihreyfingin) or LGM [Katrin JAKOBSDOTTIR]; Pirate Party [Birgitta JONSDOTTIR]; Progressive Party (Framsoknarflokkurinn) or PP [Sigmundur David GUNNLAUGSSON]; Rainbow [Atli GISLASON] [Jon BJARNASON]; Social Democratic Alliance (Samfylkingin) or SDA [Arni Pall ARNASON]; Solidarity (Samstada) [Lilja MOSESDOTTIR]

International organization participation: Arctic Council, Australia Group, BIS, CBSS, CD, CE, EAPC, EBRD, EFTA, EU (candidate country), FAO, FATF, IAEA, IBRD, ICAO, ICC (national committees), ICRM, IDA, IFAD, IFC, IFRCS, IHO, ILO, IMF, IMO, IMSO, Interpol, IOC, IPU, ISO, ITSO, ITU, ITUC (NGOs), MIGA, NATO, NC, NEA, NIB, NSG, OAS (observer), OECD, OPCW, OSCE, PCA, Schengen Convention, UN, UNCTAD, UNESCO, UPU, WCO, WHO, WIPO, WMO, WTO

Diplomatic representation in the US:
chief of mission: Ambassador Gudmundur A. STEFANSSON (since 12 October 2011)
chancery: House of Sweden, 2900 K Street NW #509, Washington, DC 20007
telephone: [1] (202) 265-6653
FAX: [1] (202) 265-6656
consulate(s) general: New York

Diplomatic representation from the US:
chief of mission: Ambassador (vacant); Charge d'Affaires Paul O'Friel (since 24 November 2013)
embassy: Laufasvegur 21, 101 Reykjavik
mailing address: US Department of State, 5640 Reykjavik Place, Washington, D.C. 20521-5640
telephone: [354] 595-22 00
FAX: [354] 562-9118

Flag description: blue with a red cross outlined in white extending to the edges of the flag; the vertical part of the cross is shifted to the hoist side in the style of the Dannebrog (Danish flag); the colors represent three of the elements that make up the island: red is for the island's volcanic fires, white recalls the snow and ice fields of the island, and blue is for the surrounding ocean

National symbol(s): gyrfalcon
National anthem: name: "Lofsongur" (Song of Praise)
lyrics/music: Matthias JOCHUMSSON/Sveinbjorn SVEINBJORNSSON
note: adopted 1944; the anthem, also known as "O, Gud vors lands" (O, God of Our Land), was originally written and performed in 1874

ECONOMY

Economy—overview: Iceland's Scandinavian-type social-market economy combines a capitalist structure and free-market principles with an extensive welfare system. Prior to the 2008 crisis, Iceland had achieved high growth, low unemployment, and a remarkably even distribution of income. The economy depends heavily on the fishing industry, which provides 40% of export earnings, more than 12% of GDP, and employs nearly 5% of the work force. It remains sensitive to declining fish stocks as well as to fluctuations in world prices for its main exports: fish and fish products, aluminum, and ferrosilicon. Iceland's economy has been diversifying into manufacturing and service industries in the last decade, particularly within the fields of software production, biotechnology, and tourism. In fall 2013, the Icelandic government approved a joint application by Icelandic, Chinese and Norwegian energy firms to conduct oil exploration off Iceland's northeast coast. Abundant geothermal and hydropower sources have attracted substantial foreign investment in the aluminum sector, boosted economic growth, and sparked some interest from high-tech firms looking to establish data centers using cheap green energy, although the financial crisis has put several investment projects on hold. Much of Iceland's economic growth in recent years came as the result of a boom in domestic demand following the rapid expansion of the country's financial sector. Domestic banks expanded aggressively in foreign markets, and consumers and businesses borrowed heavily in foreign currencies, following the privatization of the banking sector in the early 2000s. Worsening global financial conditions throughout 2008 resulted in a sharp depreciation of the krona vis-a-vis other major currencies. The foreign exposure of Icelandic banks, whose loans and other assets totaled more than 10 times the country's GDP, became unsustainable. Iceland's three largest banks collapsed in late 2008. The country secured over $10 billion in loans from the IMF and other countries to stabilize its currency and financial sector, and to back government guarantees for foreign deposits in Icelandic banks. GDP fell 6.8% in 2009, and unemployment peaked at 9.4% in February 2009. Since the collapse of Iceland's financial sector, government economic priorities have included: stabilizing the krona, implementing capital controls, reducing Iceland's high budget deficit, containing inflation, addressing high household debt, restructuring the financial sector, and diversifying the economy. Three new banks were established to take over the domestic assets of the collapsed banks. Two of them have foreign majority ownership, while the State holds a majority of the shares of the third. Iceland began making payments to the UK, the Netherlands, and other claimants in late 2011 following Iceland's Supreme Court ruling that upheld 2008 emergency legislation that gives priority to depositors for compensation from failed Icelandic banks. Iceland owes British and Dutch authorities approximately $5.5 billion for compensating British and Dutch citizens who lost deposits in Icesave when parent bank Landsbanki failed in 2008. Iceland began accession negotiations with the EU in July 2010, but decided in mid-2013 to suspend negotiations with the EU because of concern about losing control over fishing resources and worries over the ongoing Eurozone crisis.

GDP (purchasing power parity): $13.11 billion (2013 est.)
country comparison to the world: 150
$12.87 billion (2012 est.)
$12.66 billion (2011 est.)
note: data are in 2013 US dollars

GDP (official exchange rate): $14.59 billion (2013 est.)

GDP—real growth rate: 1.9% (2013 est.)
country comparison to the world: 146
1.6% (2012 est.)
2.9% (2011 est.)

GDP—per capita (PPP): $40,700 (2013 est.)

country comparison to the world: 27
$40,300 (2012 est.)
$39,800 (2011 est.)
note: data are in 2013 US dollars

Gross national saving: 15.4% of GDP (2013 est.)
country comparison to the world: 109
9.3% of GDP (2012 est.)
8.1% of GDP (2011 est.)

GDP—composition, by end use:
household consumption: 53.3%
government consumption: 24.9%
investment in fixed capital: 13.8%
investment in inventories: 2%
exports of goods and services: 56.4%
imports of goods and services: -50.4% (2013 est.)

GDP—composition, by sector of origin:
agriculture: 5.9%
industry: 22.9%
services: 71.2% (2013 est.)

Agriculture—products: potatoes, green vegetables; mutton, chicken, pork, beef, dairy products; fish

Industries: fish processing; aluminum smelting, ferrosilicon production; geothermal power, hydropower, tourism

Industrial production growth rate: -1% (2013 est.)
country comparison to the world: 179

Labor force: 181,100 (2013 est.)
country comparison to the world: 175

Labor force—by occupation:
agriculture: 4.8%
industry: 22.2%
services: 73% (2008)

Unemployment rate: 4.5% (2013 est.)
country comparison to the world: 40
5.8% (2012 est.)

Population below poverty line: NA%
note: 332,100 families (2011 est.)

Household income or consumption by percentage share: *lowest 10%:* NA%
highest 10%: NA%

Distribution of family income—Gini index:
28 (2006)
country comparison to the world: 125
25 (2005)

Budget: *revenues:* $6.231 billion
expenditures: $6.448 billion (2013 est.)

Taxes and other revenues: 42.7% of GDP (2013 est.)
country comparison to the world: 26

Budget surplus (+) or deficit (-):
-1.5% of GDP (2013 est.)
country comparison to the world: 71

Public debt: 130.5% of GDP (2013 est.)
country comparison to the world: 5
131.8% of GDP (2012 est.)

Fiscal year: calendar year

Inflation rate (consumer prices): 3.9% (2013 est.)
country comparison to the world: 130
5.2% (2012 est.)

Central bank discount rate: 5.4% (31 January 2012 est.)
country comparison to the world: 63
5.75% (31 December 2010 est.)

Commercial bank prime lending rate: 9.3% (31 December 2013 est.)
country comparison to the world: 112
8.33% (31 December 2012 est.)

Stock of narrow money: $3.876 billion (31 December 2013 est.)
country comparison to the world: 110
$3.562 billion (31 December 2012 est.)

Stock of broad money: $7.152 billion (31 December 2012 est.)
country comparison to the world: 115
$7.006 billion (31 December 2012 est.)

Stock of domestic credit: $19.35 billion (31 December 2013 est.)
country comparison to the world: 83
$18.96 billion (31 December 2012 est.)

Market value of publicly traded shares: $2.825 billion (31 December 2012 est.)
country comparison to the world: 98
$2.021 billion (31 December 2011)
$1.996 billion (31 December 2010 est.)

Current account balance: -$100 million (2013 est.)
country comparison to the world: 75
-$740 million (2012 est.)

Exports: $5.2 billion (2013 est.)
country comparison to the world: 113
$5.06 billion (2012 est.)

Exports—commodities: fish and fish products 40%, aluminum, animal products, ferrosilicon, diatomite

Exports—partners: Netherlands 30%, Germany 12.9%, UK 9.8%, Norway 5.1%, US 4.5%, France 4.4% (2012)

Imports: $4.526 billion (2013 est.)
country comparison to the world: 135
$4.441 billion (2012 est.)

Imports—commodities: machinery and equipment, petroleum products, foodstuffs, textiles

Imports—partners: Norway 16.6%, US 10.2%, Germany 9.2%, China 7.2%, Brazil 6.7%, Netherlands 6%, Denmark 5.7%, UK 4.6% (2012)

Reserves of foreign exchange and gold:
$5.604 billion (31 December 2013 est.)
country comparison to the world: 90
$4.192 billion (31 December 2012 est.)

Debt—external: $102 billion (31 December 2012 est.)
country comparison to the world: 46
$110.8 billion (31 December 2011 est.)

Stock of direct foreign investment—at home:
$NA
$9.2 billion (31 December 2008)

Stock of direct foreign investment—abroad:
$NA
$8.8 billion (31 December 2008)

Exchange rates: Icelandic kronur (ISK) per US dollar—
123.7 (2013 est.)
125.08 (2012 est.)
122.24 (2010 est.)
123.64 (2009)
85.619 (2008)

ENERGY

Electricity—production: 17.08 billion kWh (2011 est.)
country comparison to the world: 7 9

Electricity—consumption: 16.23 billion kWh (2010 est.)
country comparison to the world: 74

Electricity—exports: 0 kWh (2012 est.)
country comparison to the world: 149

Electricity—imports: 0 kWh (2012 est.)
country comparison to the world: 155

Electricity—installed generating capacity:
2.579 million kW (2010 est.)
country comparison to the world: 94

Electricity—from fossil fuels: 4.7% of total installed capacity (2010 est.)
country comparison to the world: 199

Electricity—from nuclear fuels: 0% of total installed capacity (2010 est.)
country comparison to the world: 107

Electricity—from hydroelectric plants: 73% of total installed capacity (2010 est.)
country comparison to the world: 19

Electricity—from other renewable sources:
22.3% of total installed capacity (2010 est.)
country comparison to the world: 7

Crude oil—production: 0 bbl/day (2012 est.)
country comparison to the world: 180

Crude oil—exports: 0 bbl/day (2010 est.)
country comparison to the world: 129

Crude oil—imports: 0 bbl/day (2010 est.)
country comparison to the world: 201

Crude oil—proved reserves: 0 bbl (1 January 2013 es)
country comparison to the world: 146

Refined petroleum products—production:
0 bbl/day (2010 est.)
country comparison to the world: 157

Refined petroleum products—consumption:
20,770 bbl/day (2011 est.)
country comparison to the world: 126

Refined petroleum products—exports:
1,420 bbl/day (2010 est.)
country comparison to the world: 103

Refined petroleum products—imports:
14,160 bbl/day (2010 est.)
country comparison to the world: 122

Natural gas—production: 0 cu m (2011 est.)
country comparison to the world: 145

Natural gas—consumption: 0 cu m (2010 est.)
country comparison to the world: 157

Natural gas—exports: 0 cu m (2011 est.)
country comparison to the world: 118

Natural gas—imports: 0 cu m (2011 est.)
country comparison to the world: 206

Natural gas—proved reserves: 0 cu m (1 January 2013 es)
country comparison to the world: 151

Carbon dioxide emissions from consumption of energy: 3.809 million Mt (2011 est.)
country comparison to the world: 134

COMMUNICATIONS

Telephones—main lines in use: 189,000 (2012)
country comparison to the world: 128

Telephones—mobile cellular: 346,000 (2012)
country comparison to the world: 173

Telephone system: *general assessment:* telecommunications infrastructure is modern and fully digitized, with satellite-earth stations, fiber-optic cables, and an extensive broadband network
domestic: liberalization of the telecommunications sector beginning in the late 1990s has led to increased competition especially in the mobile services segment of the market
international: country code—354; the CANTAT-3 and FARICE-1 submarine cable systems provide connectivity to Canada, the Faroe Islands, UK, Denmark, and Germany; a planned new section of the Hibernia-Atlantic submarine cable will provide additional connectivity to Canada, US, and Ireland; satellite earth stations—2 Intelsat (Atlantic Ocean), 1 Inmarsat (Atlantic and Indian Ocean regions); note—Iceland shares the Inmarsat earth station with the other Nordic countries (Denmark, Finland, Norway, and Sweden) (2011)

Broadcast media: state-owned public TV broadcaster operates 1 TV channel nationally; several privately owned TV stations broadcast nationally and roughly another half-dozen operate locally; about one-half the households utilize multi-channel cable or satellite TV services; state-owned public radio broadcaster operates 2 national networks and 4 regional stations; 2 privately owned radio stations operate nationally and another 15 provide more limited coverage (2007)

Internet country code: .is

Internet hosts: 369,969 (2012)
country comparison to the world: 56

Internet users: 301,600 (2009)
country comparison to the world: 129

TRANSPORTATION

Airports: 96 (2013)
country comparison to the world: 59

Airports—with paved runways: *total:* 7
over 3,047 m: 1
1,524 to 2,437 m: 3
914 to 1,523 m: 3 (2013)

Airports—with unpaved runways: *total:* 89
1,524 to 2,437 m: 3
914 to 1,523 m: 26
under 914 m: 60 (2013)

Roadways: *total:* 12,890 km
country comparison to the world: 126
paved/oiled gravel: 4,782 km (does not include urban roads)
unpaved: 8,108 km (2012)

Merchant marine: *total:* 2
country comparison to the world: 144
by type: passenger/cargo 2
registered in other countries: 19 (Antigua and Barbuda 10, Belize 1, Faroe Islands 4, Finland 1, Gibraltar 1, Norway 2) (2010)

Ports and terminals: major seaport(s): Grundartangi, Hafnarfjordur, Reykjavik

MILITARY

Military branches: no regular military forces; Icelandic National Police; Icelandic Coast Guard (2013)

Manpower available for military service:
males age 16-49: 75,337 (2010 est.)

Manpower fit for military service:
males age 16-49: 62,781
females age 16-49: 61,511 (2010 est.)

Manpower reaching militarily significant age annually: *male:* 2,277
female: 2,200 (2010 est.)

Military expenditures: 0.13% of GDP (2012)
country comparison to the world: 131
0.14% of GDP (2011)
0.13% of GDP (2010)

Military—note: Iceland has no standing military force; all US military forces in Iceland were withdrawn as of October 2006; defense of Iceland remains a NATO commitment and NATO maintains an air policing presence in Icelandic airspace; Iceland participates in international peacekeeping missions with the civilian-manned Icelandic Crisis Response Unit (ICRU) (2011)

TRANSNATIONAL ISSUES

Disputes—international: Iceland, the UK, and Ireland dispute Denmark's claim that the Faroe Islands' continental shelf extends beyond 200 nm; the European Free Trade Association Surveillance Authority filed a suit against Iceland, claiming the country violated the European Economic Area agreement in failing to pay minimum compensation to Icesave depositors

Refugees and internally displaced persons:
stateless persons: 119 (2012)

INDIA

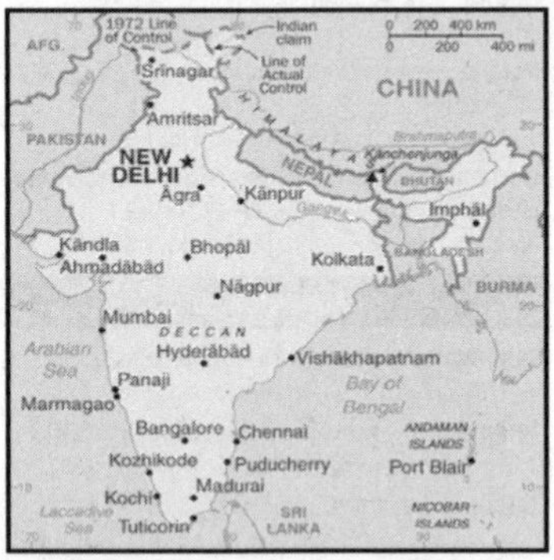

INTRODUCTION

Background: The Indus Valley civilization, one of the world's oldest, flourished during the 3rd and 2nd millennia B.C. and extended into northwestern India. Aryan tribes from the northwest infiltrated the Indian subcontinent about 1500 B.C.; their merger with the earlier Dravidian inhabitants created the classical Indian culture. The Maurya Empire of the 4th and 3rd centuries B.C.—which reached its zenith under ASHOKA—united much of South Asia. The Golden Age ushered in by the Gupta dynasty (4th to 6th centuries A.D.) saw a flowering of Indian science, art, and culture. Islam spread across the subcontinent over a period of 700 years. In the 10th and 11th centuries, Turks and Afghans invaded India and established the Delhi Sultanate. In the early 16th century, the Emperor BABUR established the Mughal Dynasty which ruled India for more than three centuries. European explorers began establishing footholds in India during the 16th century. By the 19th century, Great Britain had become the dominant political power on the subcontinent. The British Indian Army played a vital role in both World Wars. Years of nonviolent resistance to British rule, led by Mohandas GANDHI and Jawaharlal NEHRU, eventually resulted in Indian independence, which was granted in 1947. Large-scale communal violence took place before and after the subcontinent partition into two separate states—India and Pakistan. The neighboring nations have fought three wars since independence, the last of which was in 1971 and resulted in East Pakistan becoming the separate nation of Bangladesh. India's nuclear weapons tests in 1998 emboldened Pakistan to conduct its own tests that same year. In November 2008, terrorists originating from Pakistan conducted a series of coordinated attacks in Mumbai, India's financial capital. Despite pressing problems such as significant overpopulation, environmental degradation, extensive poverty, and widespread corruption, economic growth following the launch of economic reforms in 1991 and a massive youthful population are driving India's emergence as a regional and global power.

GEOGRAPHY

Location: Southern Asia, bordering the Arabian Sea and the Bay of Bengal, between Burma and Pakistan

Geographic coordinates: 20 00 N, 77 00 E

Map references: Asia

Area: *total:* 3,287,263 sq km
country comparison to the world: 7
land: 2,973,193 sq km
water: 314,070 sq km

Area—comparative: slightly more than one-third the size of the US

Land boundaries: *total:* 14,103 km
border countries: Bangladesh 4,053 km, Bhutan 605 km, Burma 1,463 km, China 3,380 km, Nepal 1,690 km, Pakistan 2,912 km

Coastline: 7,000 km

Maritime claims: *territorial sea:* 12 nm
contiguous zone: 24 nm
exclusive economic zone: 200 nm
continental shelf: 200 nm or to the edge of the continental margin

Climate: varies from tropical monsoon in south to temperate in north

Terrain: upland plain (Deccan Plateau) in south, flat to rolling plain along the Ganges, deserts in west, Himalayas in north

Elevation extremes: *lowest point:* Indian Ocean 0 m
highest point: Kanchenjunga 8,598 m

Natural resources: coal (fourth-largest reserves in the world), iron ore, manganese, mica, bauxite, rare earth elements, titanium ore, chromite, natural gas, diamonds, petroleum, limestone, arable land

Land use: *arable land:* 47.87%

permanent crops: 3.74%
other: 48.39% (2011)

Irrigated land: 663,340 sq km (2008)

Total renewable water resources: 1,911 cu km (2011)

Freshwater withdrawal (domestic/industrial/agricultural): *total:* 761 cu km/yr (7%/2%/90%)
per capita: 613 cu m/yr (2010)

Natural hazards: droughts; flash floods, as well as widespread and destructive flooding from monsoonal rains; severe thunderstorms; earthquakes
volcanism: Barren Island (elev. 354 m) in the Andaman Sea has been active in recent years

Environment—current issues: deforestation; soil erosion; overgrazing; desertification; air pollution from industrial effluents and vehicle emissions; water pollution from raw sewage and runoff of agricultural pesticides; tap water is not potable throughout the country; huge and growing population is overstraining natural resources

Environment—international agreements:
party to: Antarctic-Environmental Protocol, Antarctic-Marine Living Resources, Antarctic Treaty, Biodiversity, Climate Change, Climate Change-Kyoto Protocol, Desertification, Endangered Species, Environmental Modification, Hazardous Wastes, Law of the Sea, Ozone Layer Protection, Ship Pollution, Tropical Timber 83, Tropical Timber 94, Wetlands, Whaling
signed, but not ratified: none of the selected agreements

Geography—note: dominates South Asian subcontinent; near important Indian Ocean trade routes; Kanchenjunga, third tallest mountain in the world, lies on the border with Nepal

PEOPLE AND SOCIETY

Nationality: *noun:* Indian(s)
adjective: Indian

Ethnic groups: Indo-Aryan 72%, Dravidian 25%, Mongoloid and other 3% (2000)

Languages: Hindi 41%, Bengali 8.1%, Telugu 7.2%, Marathi 7%, Tamil 5.9%, Urdu 5%, Gujarati 4.5%, Kannada 3.7%, Malayalam 3.2%, Oriya 3.2%, Punjabi 2.8%, Assamese 1.3%, Maithili 1.2%, other 5.9%
note: English enjoys the status of subsidiary official language but is the most important language for national, political, and commercial communication; Hindi is the most widely spoken language and primary tongue of 41% of the people; there are 14 other official languages: Bengali, Telugu, Marathi, Tamil, Urdu, Gujarati, Malayalam, Kannada, Oriya, Punjabi, Assamese, Kashmiri, Sindhi, and Sanskrit; Hindustani is a popular variant of Hindi/Urdu spoken widely throughout northern India but is not an official language (2001 census)

Religions: Hindu 80.5%, Muslim 13.4%, Christian 2.3%, Sikh 1.9%, other 1.8%, unspecified 0.1% (2001 census)

Population: 1,236,344,631 (July 2014 est.)
country comparison to the world: 2

Age structure:
0-14 years: 28.5% (male 187,016,401/female 165,048,695)
15-24 years: 18.1% (male 118,696,540/female 105,342,764)
25-54 years: 40.6% (male 258,202,535/female 243,293,143)
55-64 years: 5.8% (male 43,625,668/female 43,175,111)
65 years and over: 5.7% (male 34,133,175/female 37,810,599) (2014 est.)

Dependency ratios:
total dependency ratio: 52.4 %
youth dependency ratio: 44.3 %
elderly dependency ratio: 8 %
potential support ratio: 12.4 (2013)

Median age: *total:* 27 years
male: 26.4 years
female: 27.7 years (2014 est.)

Population growth rate: 1.25% (2014 est.)
country comparison to the world: 94

Birth rate: 19.89 births/1,000 population (2014 est.)
country comparison to the world: 86

Death rate: 7.35 deaths/1,000 population (2014 est.)
country comparison to the world: 119

Net migration rate: -0.05 migrant(s)/1,000 population (2014 est.)
country comparison to the world: 112

Urbanization: *urban population:* 31.3% of total population (2011)
rate of urbanization: 2.47% annual rate of change (2010-15 est.)

Major urban areas—population: NEW DELHI (capital) 21.72 million; Mumbai 19.695 million; Kolkata 15.294 million; Chennai 7.416 million; Bangalore 7.079 million (2009)

Sex ratio: *at birth:* 1.12 male(s)/female
0-14 years: 1.13 male(s)/female
15-24 years: 1.13 male(s)/female
25-54 years: 1.06 male(s)/female
55-64 years: 1.08 male(s)/female
65 years and over: 0.91 male(s)/female
total population: 1.08 male(s)/female (2014 est.)

Mother's mean age at first birth: 19.9 (2006 est.)

Maternal mortality rate: 200 deaths/100,000 live births (2010)
country comparison to the world: 55

Infant mortality rate: total: 43.19 deaths/1,000 live births
country comparison to the world: 50
male: 41.9 deaths/1,000 live births
female: 44.63 deaths/1,000 live births (2014 est.)

Life expectancy at birth: *total population:* 67.8 years
country comparison to the world: 163
male: 66.68 years
female: 69.06 years (2014 est.)

Total fertility rate: 2.51 children born/woman (2014 est.)
country comparison to the world: 81

Contraceptive prevalence rate: 54.8% (2007/08)

Health expenditures: 3.9% of GDP (2011)
country comparison to the world: 167

Physicians density: 0.65 physicians/1,000 population (2009)

Hospital bed density: 0.9 beds/1,000 population (2005)

Drinking water source:
improved:
urban: 96.3% of population
rural: 89.5% of population
total: 91.6% of population
unimproved:
urban: 3.7% of population
rural: 10.5% of population
total: 8.4% of population (2011 est.)

Sanitation facility access:
improved:
urban: 59.7% of population
rural: 23.9% of population
total: 35.1% of population
unimproved:
urban: 40.3% of population
rural: 76.1% of population
total: 64.9% of population (2011 est.)

HIV/AIDS—adult prevalence rate:
0.3% (2012 est.)
country comparison to the world: 101

HIV/AIDS—people living with HIV/AIDS:
2.085 million (2012 est.)
country comparison to the world: 3

HIV/AIDS—deaths: 135,500 (2012 est.)
country comparison to the world: 3

Major infectious diseases: *degree of risk:* very high
food or waterborne diseases: bacterial diarrhea, hepatitis A and E, and typhoid fever
vectorborne diseases: dengue fever, Japanese encephalitis, and malaria
water contact disease: leptospirosis
animal contact disease: rabies
note: highly pathogenic H5N1 avian influenza has been identified in this country; it poses a negligible risk with extremely rare cases possible among US citizens who have close contact with birds (2013)

Obesity—adult prevalence rate: 1.9% (2008)
country comparison to the world: 184

Children under the age of 5 years underweight:
43.5% (2006)
country comparison to the world: 2

Education expenditures: 3.2% of GDP (2011)
country comparison to the world: 134

Literacy: *definition:* age 15 and over can read and write
total population: 62.8%
male: 75.2%
female: 50.8% (2006 est.)

School life expectancy (primary to tertiary education): *total:* 12 years
male: 12 years
female: 11 years (2011)

Child labor—children ages 5-14: *total number:* 26,965,074
percentage: 12 % (2006 est.)

Unemployment, youth ages 15-24: *total:* 10.7%
country comparison to the world: 107
male: 10.4%
female: 11.6% (2012)

GOVERNMENT

Country name: *conventional long form:* Republic of India
conventional short form: India
local long form: Republic of India/Bharatiya Ganarajya
local short form: India/Bharat

Government type: federal republic

Capital: *name:* New Delhi
geographic coordinates: 28 36 N, 77 12 E

time difference: UTC+5.5 (10.5 hours ahead of Washington, DC during Standard Time)

Administrative divisions: 28 states and 7 union territories*; Andaman and Nicobar Islands*, Andhra Pradesh, Arunachal Pradesh, Assam, Bihar, Chandigarh*, Chhattisgarh, Dadra and Nagar Haveli*, Daman and Diu*, Delhi*, Goa, Gujarat, Haryana, Himachal Pradesh, Jammu and Kashmir, Jharkhand, Karnataka, Kerala, Lakshadweep*, Madhya Pradesh, Maharashtra, Manipur, Meghalaya, Mizoram, Nagaland, Odisha, Puducherry*, Punjab, Rajasthan, Sikkim, Tamil Nadu, Tripura, Uttar Pradesh, Uttarakhand, West Bengal
note: although its status is that of a union territory, the official name of Delhi is National Capital Territory of Delhi

Independence: 15 August 1947 (from the UK)

National holiday: Republic Day, 26 January (1950)

Constitution: previous 1935 (preindependence); latest draft completed 4 November 1949, adopted 26 November 1949, effective 26 January 1950; amended many times, last in 2013 (2013)

Legal system: common law system based on the English model; separate personal law codes apply to Muslims, Christians, and Hindus; judicial review of legislative acts International law organization participation: accepts compulsory ICJ jurisdiction with reservations; non-party state to the ICCt

Suffrage: 18 years of age; universal

Executive branch: *chief of state:* President Pranab MUKHERJEE (since 22 July 2012); Vice President Mohammad Hamid ANSARI (since 11 August 2007)
head of government: Prime Minister Manmohan SINGH (since 22 May 2004)
cabinet: Union Council of Ministers appointed by the president on the recommendation of the prime minister (For more information visit the World Leaders website)
elections: president elected by an electoral college consisting of elected members of both houses of Parliament and the legislatures of the states for a five-year term (no term limits); election last held in July 2012 (next to be held in July 2017); vice president elected by both houses of Parliament for a five-year term; election last held in August 2012 (next to be held in August 2017); prime minister chosen by parliamentary members of the majority party following legislative elections; election last held April—May 2009 (next to be held no later than May 2014)
election results: Pranab MUKHERJEE elected president; percent of vote—Pranab MUKHERJEE *69.31%, Purno SANGMA—30.69%*

Legislative branch: bicameral Parliament or Sansad consists of the Council of States or Rajya Sabha (a body consisting of 245 seats up to 12 of which are appointed by the president, the remainder chosen in staggered elections by the elected members of the state and territorial assemblies; members serve six-year terms) and the People's Assembly or Lok Sabha (545 seats; 543 members elected by popular vote, 2 appointed by the president; members serve five-year terms)
elections: People's Assembly—being held in 9 phases from 7 April through 12 May 2014 (next must be held by May 2019)
election results: People's Assembly—2014 percent of vote by party—NA; seats by party—NA; note—2014 results expected on 16 May 2014

Judicial branch: *highest court(s):* Supreme Court (the chief justice and 25 associate justices); note—parliament approved an additional 5 judges in 2008 note—in mid-2011 India's Cabinet approved the program, National Mission for Justice Delivery and Legal Reform, to eliminate judicial corruption and reduce the backlog of cases
judge selection and term of office: justices appointed by the president to serve until age 65
subordinate courts: High Courts; District Courts; Labour Court

Political parties and leaders: Aam Aadmi Party or AAP [Arvind KEJRIWAL]; All India Anna Dravida Munnetra Kazhagam or AIADMK [J. JAYALALITHAA]; All India Trinamool Congress or TMC [Mamata BANERJEE]; Bahujan Samaj Party or BSP [MAYAWATI]; Bharatiya Janata Party or BJP [Rajnath SINGH]; Biju Janata Dal or BJD [Naveen PATNAIK]; Communist Party of India or CPI [Suravaram Sudhakar REDDY, Secretary-General]; Communist Party of India-Marxist or CPI(M) [Prakash KARAT]; Dravida Munnetra Kazhagam or DMK [M.KARUNANIDHI]; Indian National Congress or INC [Sonia GANDHI]; Janata Dal (United) or JD(U) [Sharad YADAV]; Nationalist Congress Party or NCP [Sharad PAWAR]; Rashtriya Janata Dal or RJD [Lalu Prasad YADAV]; Rashtriya Lok Dal or RLD [Ajit SINGH]; Samajwadi Party or SP [Mulayam Singh YADAV]; Shiromani Akali Dal or SAD [Parkash Singh BADAL]; Shiv Sena or SS [Uddhav THACKERAY]; Telugu Desam Party or TDP [Chandrababu NAIDU]
note: India has dozens of national and regional political parties

Political pressure groups and leaders: All Parties Hurriyat Conference in the Kashmir Valley (separatist group); Bajrang Dal (religious organization); India Against Corruption [Anna HAZARE]; Jamiat Ulema-e Hind (religious organization); Rashtriya Swayamsevak Sangh [Mohan BHAGWAT] (religious organization); Vishwa Hindu Parishad [Ashok SINGHAL] (religious organization)
other: numerous religious or militant/chauvinistic organizations hundreds of social reform, anti-corruption, and environmental groups at state and local level various separatist groups seeking greater communal and/or regional autonomy

International organization participation: ABEDA, ADB, AfDB (nonregional member), ARF, ASEAN (dialogue partner), BIMSTEC, BIS, BRICS, C, CD, CERN (observer), CICA, CP, EAS, FAO, FATF, G-15, G-20, G-24, G-77, IAEA, IBRD, ICAO, ICC; (national committees), ICRM, IDA, IFAD, IFC, IFRCS, IHO, ILO, IMF, IMO, IMSO, Interpol, IOC, IOM, IPU, ISO, ITSO, ITU, ITUC (NGOs), LAS (observer), MIGA, MONUSCO, NAM, OAS (observer), OECD, OPCW, PCA, PIF (partner), SAARC, SACEP, SCO (observer), UN, UNCTAD, UNDOF, UNESCO, UNHCR, UNIDO, UNIFIL, UNISFA, UNITAR, UNMISS, UNOCI, UNSC (temporary), UNWTO, UPU, WCO, WFTU; (NGOs), WHO, WIPO, WMO, WTO

Diplomatic representation in the US:
chief of mission: Ambassador Subrahmanyam JAISHANKAR (since 26 December 2013)
chancery: 2107 Massachusetts Avenue NW, Washington, DC 20008; note—Consular Wing located at 2536 Massachusetts Avenue NW, Washington, DC 20008
telephone: [1] (202) 939-7000
FAX: [1] (202) 265-4351
consulate(s) general: Atlanta, Chicago, Houston, New York, San Francisco

Diplomatic representation from the US:
chief of mission: Ambassador Nancy J. POWELL (since 19 April 2012)
embassy: Shantipath, Chanakyapuri, New Delhi 110021
mailing address: use embassy street address
telephone: [91] (11) 2419-8000
FAX: [91] (11) 2419-0017
consulate(s) general: Chennai (Madras), Hyderabad; Kolkata (Calcutta), Mumbai (Bombay)

Flag description: three equal horizontal bands of saffron (subdued orange) (top), white, and green, with a blue; chakra (24-spoked wheel) centered in the white band; saffron represents courage, sacrifice, and; the spirit of renunciation; white signifies purity and truth; green stands for faith and fertility; the; blue chakra symbolizes the wheel of life in movement and death in stagnation
note: similar to the flag of Niger, which has a small orange disk centered in the white band

National symbol(s): the Lion Capital of Ashoka, which depicts four Asiatic lions standing back to back mounted on a circular abacus, is the official emblem; the Bengal tiger is the national animal; the lotus is the national flower

National anthem: name: "Jana-Gana-Mana" (Thou Art the Ruler of the Minds of All People)
lyrics/music: Rabindranath TAGORE
note: adopted 1950; Rabindranath TAGORE, a Nobel laureate, also wrote Bangladesh's national anthem

ECONOMY

Economy—overview: India is developing into an open-market economy, yet traces of its past autarkic policies remain. Economic liberalization measures, including industrial deregulation, privatization of state-owned enterprises, and reduced controls on foreign trade and investment, began in the early 1990s and served to accelerate the country's growth, which averaged under 7% per year from 1997 to 2011. India's diverse economy encompasses traditional village farming, modern agriculture, handicrafts, a wide range of modern industries, and a multitude of services. Slightly less than half of the work force is in agriculture, but, services are the major source of economic growth, accounting for nearly two-thirds of India's output with less than one-third of its labor force. India has capitalized on its large educated English-speaking population to become a major exporter of information technology services, business outsourcing services, and software workers. India's economic growth began slowing in 2011 because of a decline in investment, caused by high interest rates, rising inflation, and investor pessimism about the government's commitment to further economic reforms and about the global situation. In late 2012, the Indian Government announced additional reforms and deficit reduction measures, including allowing higher levels of foreign participation in direct investment in the economy. The outlook for India's long-term growth is moderately positive due to a young population and corresponding low dependency ratio, healthy savings and investment rates, and increasing integration into the global economy. However, India has many challenges that it has yet to fully address, including poverty, corruption, violence and discrimination against women and girls, an inefficient power generation and distribution system, ineffective enforcement of intellectual property rights, decades-long civil litigation dockets, inadequate transport and agricultural infrastructure, limited non-agricultural employment opportunities, high spending and poorly-targeted subsidies, inadequate availability of quality basic and higher education, and accommodating rural-to-urban migration. Growth in 2013 fell to a decade low based on weak fundamentals, and India's economic leaders are now struggling to improve the country's wide fiscal and current account deficits. Improving conditions in Western countries have led investors to shift investment away from India and prompted a severe depreciation in the rupee.

GDP (purchasing power parity): $4.962 trillion (2013 est.)
country comparison to the world: 4
$4.78 trillion (2012 est.)
$4.63 trillion (2011 est.)
note: data are in 2013 US dollars

GDP (official exchange rate): $1.758 trillion (2013 est.)

GDP—real growth rate: 4.7% (2013 est.)
country comparison to the world: 64
5.1% (2012 est.)
7.5% (2011 est.)

GDP—per capita (PPP): $4,000 (2013 est.)
country comparison to the world: 168
$3,900 (2012 est.)
$3,800 (2011 est.)
note: data are in 2013 US dollars

Gross national saving: 28.8% of GDP (2013 est.)
country comparison to the world: 29
28.8% of GDP (2012 est.)
30.3% of GDP (2011 est.)

GDP—composition, by end use:
household consumption: 56.4%
government consumption: 12.4%
investment in fixed capital: 29.6%
investment in inventories: 8.2%
exports of goods and services: 25.2%
imports of goods and services: -31.8% (2013 est.)

GDP—composition, by sector of origin:
agriculture: 16.9%
industry: 17%
services: 66.1% (2013 est.)

Agriculture—products: rice, wheat, oilseed, cotton, jute, tea, sugarcane, lentils, onions, potatoes; dairy products, sheep, goats, poultry; fish

Industries: textiles, chemicals, food processing, steel, transportation equipment, cement, mining, petroleum, machinery, software, pharmaceuticals

Industrial production growth rate: 0.9% (2013 est.)
country comparison to the world: 156

Labor force: 487.3 million (2013 est.)
country comparison to the world: 2

Labor force—by occupation: *agriculture:* 49%
industry: 20%
services: 31% (2012 est.)

Unemployment rate: 8.8% (2013 est.)
country comparison to the world: 98
8.5% (2012 est.)

Population below poverty line: 29.8% (2010 est.)

Household income or consumption by percentage share: *lowest 10%:* 3.6%
highest 10%: 31.1% (2005)

Distribution of family income—Gini index: 36.8 (2004)
country comparison to the world: 80
37.8 (1997)

Budget: *revenues:* $181.3 billion
expenditures: $281.6 billion (2013 est.)

Taxes and other revenues: 10.3% of GDP (2013 est.)
country comparison to the world: 208

Budget surplus (+) or deficit (-): -5.7% of GDP (2013 est.)
country comparison to the world: 177

Public debt: 51.8% of GDP (2013 est.)
country comparison to the world: 63
51.7% of GDP (2012 est.)
note: data cover central government debt, and exclude debt instruments issued (or owned) by government entities other than the treasury; the data include treasury debt held by foreign entities; the data exclude debt issued by subnational entities, as well as intra-governmental debt; intra-governmental debt consists of treasury borrowings from surpluses in the social funds, such as for retirement, medical care, and unemployment; debt instruments for the social funds are not sold at public auctions

Fiscal year: 1 April—31 March

Inflation rate (consumer prices): 9.6% (2013 est.)
country comparison to the world: 208
9.7% (2012 est.)

Central bank discount rate: 7.75% (31 December 2013 est.)
country comparison to the world: 33
8% (31 December 2010 est.)
note: this is the Indian central bank's policy rate—the repurchase rate

Commercial bank prime lending rate: 10.6% (31 December 2013 est.)
country comparison to the world: 82
10.63% (31 December 2012 est.)

Stock of narrow money: $303.1 billion (31 December 2013 est.)
country comparison to the world: 16
$317.4 billion (31 December 2012 est.)

Stock of broad money: $1.376 trillion (31 December 2013 est.)
country comparison to the world: 13
$1.396 trillion (31 December 2012 est.)

Stock of domestic credit: $1.379 trillion (31 December 2013 est.)
country comparison to the world: 15
$1.401 trillion (31 December 2012 est.)

Market value of publicly traded shares:
$1.263 trillion (31 December 2012 est.)
country comparison to the world: 13
$1.015 trillion (31 December 2011)
$1.616 trillion (31 December 2010 est.)

Current account balance: -$74.79 billion (2013 est.)
country comparison to the world: 190
-$91.47 billion (2012 est.)

Exports: $313.2 billion (2013 est.)
country comparison to the world: 19
$296.8 billion (2012 est.)

Exports—commodities: petroleum products, precious stones, machinery, iron and steel, chemicals, vehicles, apparel

Exports—partners: UAE 12.3%, US 12.2%, China 5%, Singapore 4.9%, Hong Kong 4.1% (2012)

Imports: $467.5 billion (2013 est.)
country comparison to the world: 12
$488.9 billion (2012 est.)

Imports—commodities: crude oil, precious stones, machinery, fertilizer, iron and steel, chemicals

Imports—partners: China 10.7%, UAE 7.8%, Saudi Arabia 6.8%, Switzerland 6.2%, US 5.1% (2012)

Reserves of foreign exchange and gold:
$295 billion (31 December 2013 est.)
country comparison to the world: 11
$296 billion (28 December 2012 est.)

Debt—external: $412.2 billion (31 December 2013 est.)
country comparison to the world: 29
$378.9 billion (31 December 2012 est.)

Stock of direct foreign investment—at home:
$310 billion (30 November 2013 est.)
country comparison to the world: 20
$225.1 billion (31 December 2012 est.)

Stock of direct foreign investment—abroad:
$120.1 billion (31 December 2013 est.)
country comparison to the world: 28
$118.1 billion (31 December 2012 est.)

Exchange rates: Indian rupees (INR) per US dollar—
58.68 (2013 est.)
53.437 (2012 est.)
45.726 (2010 est.)
48.405 (2009)
43.319 (2008)

ENERGY

Electricity—production: 985.4 billion kWh (2011 est.)
country comparison to the world: 5

Electricity—consumption: 698.8 billion kWh (2010 est.)
country comparison to the world: 6

Electricity—exports: 62 million kWh (2011 est.)
country comparison to the world: 81

Electricity—imports: 5.7 billion kWh (2011 est.)
country comparison to the world: 35

Electricity—installed generating capacity:
208.1 million kW (2010 est.)
country comparison to the world: 6

Electricity—from fossil fuels: 70.8% of total installed capacity (2010 est.)
country comparison to the world: 104

Electricity—from nuclear fuels: 2.2% of total installed capacity (2010 est.)
country comparison to the world: 26

Electricity—from hydroelectric plants:
19.5% of total installed capacity (2010 est.)
country comparison to the world: 92

Electricity—from other renewable sources:
7.5% of total installed capacity (2010 est.)
country comparison to the world: 33

Crude oil—production: 990,200 bbl/day (2012 est.)
country comparison to the world: 22

Crude oil—exports: 0 bbl/day (2010 est.)
country comparison to the world: 130

Crude oil—imports: 3.272 million bbl/day (2010 est.)
country comparison to the world: 5

Crude oil—proved reserves: 5.476 billion bbl (1 January 2013 es)
country comparison to the world: 23

Refined petroleum products—production: 4.216 million bbl/day (2010 est.)
country comparison to the world: 5

Refined petroleum products—consumption: 3.292 million bbl/day (2011 est.)
country comparison to the world: 5

Refined petroleum products—exports: 1.247 million bbl/day (2010 est.)
country comparison to the world: 6

Refined petroleum products—imports: 379,600 bbl/day (2010 est.)
country comparison to the world: 16

Natural gas—production: 40.38 billion cu m (2012 est.)
country comparison to the world: 23

Natural gas—consumption: 64.49 billion cu m (2010 est.)
country comparison to the world: 12

Natural gas—exports: 0 cu m (2011 est.)
country comparison to the world: 119

Natural gas—imports: 16.39 billion cu m (2011 est.)
country comparison to the world: 23

Natural gas—proved reserves: 1.241 trillion cu m (1 January 2013 es)
country comparison to the world: 23

Carbon dioxide emissions from consumption of energy: 1.726 billion Mt (2011 est.)
country comparison to the world: 5

COMMUNICATIONS

Telephones—main lines in use: 31.08 million (2012)
country comparison to the world: 1 0

Telephones—mobile cellular: 893.862 million (2013)
country comparison to the world: 2

Telephone system: *general assessment:* supported by recent deregulation and liberalization of telecommunications laws and policies, India has emerged as one of the fastest growing telecom markets in the world; total telephone subscribership base exceeded 900 million in 2011, an overall teledensity of roughly 75%, and subscribership is currently growing more than 20 million per month; urban teledensity now exceeds 100% and rural teledensity is steadily growing
domestic: mobile cellular service introduced in 1994 and organized nationwide into four metropolitan areas and 19 telecom circles each with multiple private service providers and one or more state-owned service providers; in recent years significant trunk capacity added in the form of fiber-optic cable and one of the world's largest domestic satellite systems, the Indian National Satellite system (INSAT), with 6 satellites supporting 33,000 very small aperture terminals (VSAT)
international: country code—91; a number of major international submarine cable systems, including Sea-Me-We-3 with landing sites at Cochin and Mumbai (Bombay), Sea-Me-We-4 with a landing site at Chennai, Fiber-Optic Link Around the Globe (FLAG) with a landing site at Mumbai (Bombay), South Africa—Far East (SAFE) with a landing site at Cochin, the i2i cable network linking to Singapore with landing sites at Mumbai (Bombay) and Chennai (Madras), and Tata Indicom linking Singapore and Chennai (Madras), provide a significant increase in the bandwidth available for both voice and data traffic; satellite earth stations—8 Intelsat (Indian Ocean) and 1 Inmarsat (Indian Ocean region); 9 gateway exchanges operating from Mumbai (Bombay), New Delhi, Kolkata (Calcutta), Chennai (Madras), Jalandhar, Kanpur, Gandhinagar, Hyderabad, and Ernakulam (2011)

Broadcast media: Doordarshan, India's public TV network, operates about 20 national, regional, and local services; a large and increasing number of privately owned TV stations are distributed by cable and satellite service providers; by 2011, more than 100 million homes had access to cable and satellite TV offering more than 700 TV channels; government controls AM radio with All India Radio operating domestic and external networks; news broadcasts via radio are limited to the All India Radio Network; since 2000, privately-owned FM stations have been permitted and their numbers have increased rapidly (2007)

Internet country code: .in

Internet hosts: 6.746 million (2012)
country comparison to the world: 17

Internet users: 61.338 million (2009)
country comparison to the world: 6

TRANSPORTATION

Airports: 346 (2013)
country comparison to the world: 2 1

Airports—with paved runways: *total:* 253
over 3,047 m: 22
2,438 to 3,047 m: 59
1,524 to 2,437 m: 76
914 to 1,523 m: 82
under 914 m: 14 (2013)

Airports—with unpaved runways: *total:* 9 3
over 3,047 m: 1
2,438 to 3,047 m: 3
1,524 to 2,437 m: 6
914 to 1,523 m: 38
under 914 m: 45 (2013)

Heliports: 45 (2013)

Pipelines: condensate/gas 9 km; gas 13,581 km; liquid petroleum gas 2,054 km; oil 8,943 km; oil/gas/water 20 km; refined products 11,069 km (2013)

Railways: *total:* 63,974 km
country comparison to the world: 4
broad gauge: 54,257 km 1.676-m gauge (18,927 km electrified)
narrow gauge: 7,180 km 1.000-m gauge; 2,537 km 0.762-m gauge and 0.610-m gauge (2009)

Roadways: *total:* 4,689,842 km
country comparison to the world: 2
note: includes 79,116 km of national highways and expressways, 155,716 km of state highways, and 4,455,010 km of other roads (2013)

Waterways: 14,500 km (5,200 km on major rivers and 485 km on canals suitable for mechanized vessels) (2012)
country comparison to the world: 9

Merchant marine: *total:* 340
country comparison to the world: 29
by type: bulk carrier 104, cargo 78, chemical tanker 22, container 14, liquefied gas 11, passenger 4, passenger/cargo 15, petroleum tanker 92
foreign-owned: 10 (China 1, Hong Kong 2, Jersey 2, Malaysia 1, UAE 4)
registered in other countries: 76 (Cyprus 4, Dominica 2, Liberia 8, Malta 3, Marshall Islands 10, Nigeria 1, Panama 24, Saint Kitts and Nevis 2, Singapore 21, unknown 1) (2010)

Ports and terminals: *major seaport(s):* Chennai, Jawaharal Nehru Port, Kandla, Kolkata (Calcutta), Mumbai (Bombay), Sikka, Vishakhapatnam
container port(s) (TEUs): Chennai (1,558,343), Jawaharal Nehru Port (4,307,622)

MILITARY

Military branches: Army; Navy (includes naval air arm); Air Force; Coast Guard (2011)

Military service age and obligation: 16-18 years of age for voluntary military service (Army 17 1/2, Air Force 17, Navy 16 1/2); no conscription; women may join as officers, but for noncombat roles only (2012)

Manpower available for military service:
males age 16-49: 319,129,420
females age 16-49: 296,071,637 (2010 est.)

Manpower fit for military service: males age 16-49: 249,531,562
females age 16-49: 240,039,958 (2010 est.)

Manpower reaching militarily significant age annually: *male:* 12,151,065
female: 10,745,891 (2010 est.)

Military expenditures: 2.43% of GDP (2012)
country comparison to the world: 30
2.58% of GDP (2011)
2.43% of GDP (2010)

TRANSNATIONAL ISSUES

Disputes—international: since China and India launched a security and foreign policy dialogue in 2005, consolidated discussions related to the dispute over most of their rugged, militarized boundary, regional nuclear proliferation, Indian claims that China transferred missiles to Pakistan, and other matters continue; Kashmir remains the site of the world's largest and most militarized territorial dispute with portions under the de facto administration of China (Aksai Chin), India (Jammu and Kashmir), and Pakistan (Azad Kashmir and Northern Areas); India and Pakistan resumed bilateral dialogue in February 2011 after a two-year hiatus, have maintained the 2003 cease-fire in Kashmir, and continue to have disputes over water sharing of the Indus River and its tributaries; UN Military Observer Group in India and Pakistan has maintained a small group of peacekeepers since 1949; India does not recognize Pakistan's ceding historic Kashmir lands to China in 1964; to defuse tensions and prepare for discussions on a maritime boundary, India and Pakistan seek technical resolution of the disputed boundary in Sir Creek estuary at the mouth of the Rann of Kutch in the Arabian Sea; Pakistani maps continue to show its Junagadh claim in Indian Gujarat State; Prime Minister Singh's September 2011 visit to Bangladesh resulted in the signing of a Protocol to the 1974 Land Boundary Agreement between India and Bangladesh, which had called for the settlement of longstanding boundary disputes over undemarcated areas and the exchange of territorial enclaves, but which had never been implemented; Bangladesh referred its maritime boundary claims with Burma and India to the International Tribunal on the Law of the Sea; Joint Border Committee with Nepal continues to examine contested boundary sections, including the 400 square kilometer dispute over the source of the Kalapani River; India maintains a strict border regime to keep out Maoist insurgents and control illegal cross-border activities from Nepal

Refugees and internally displaced persons: *refugees (country of origin)*: 100,003 (Tibet/China); 67,165 (Sri Lanka); 9,633 (Afghanistan); 7,671 (Burma) (2012)
IDPs: at least 540,000 (about 250,000 are Kashmiri Pandits from Jammu and Kashmir) (2012)

Illicit drugs: world's largest producer of licit opium for the pharmaceutical trade, but an undetermined quantity of opium is diverted to illicit international drug markets; transit point for illicit narcotics produced in neighboring countries and throughout Southwest Asia; illicit producer of methaqualone; vulnerable to narcotics money laundering through the hawala system; licit ketamine and precursor production

INDIAN OCEAN

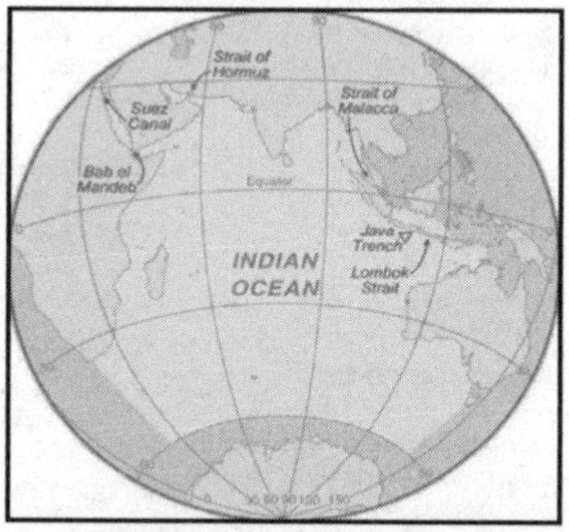

INTRODUCTION

Background: The Indian Ocean is the third largest of the world's five oceans (after the Pacific Ocean and Atlantic Ocean, but larger than the Southern Ocean and Arctic Ocean). Four critically important access waterways are the Suez Canal (Egypt), Bab el Mandeb (Djibouti-Yemen), Strait of Hormuz (Iran-Oman), and Strait of Malacca (Indonesia-Malaysia). The decision by the International Hydrographic Organization in the spring of 2000 to delimit a fifth ocean, the Southern Ocean, removed the portion of the Indian Ocean south of 60 degrees south latitude.

GEOGRAPHY

Location: body of water between Africa, the Southern Ocean, Asia, and Australia

Geographic coordinates: 20 00 S, 80 00 E

Map references: Political Map of the World

Area: *total*: 68.556 million sq km
note: includes Andaman Sea, Arabian Sea, Bay of Bengal, Flores Sea, Great Australian Bight, Gulf of Aden, Gulf of Oman, Java Sea, Mozambique Channel, Persian Gulf, Red Sea, Savu Sea, Strait of Malacca, Timor Sea, and other tributary water bodies

Area—comparative: about 5.5 times the size of the US

Coastline: 66,526 km

Climate: northeast monsoon (December to April), southwest monsoon (June to October); tropical cyclones occur during May/June and October/November in the northern Indian Ocean and January/February in the southern Indian Ocean

Terrain: surface dominated by counterclockwise gyre (broad, circular system of currents) in the southern Indian Ocean; unique reversal of surface currents in the northern Indian Ocean; low atmospheric pressure over southwest Asia from hot, rising, summer air results in the southwest monsoon and southwest-to-northeast winds and currents, while high pressure over northern Asia from cold, falling, winter air results in the northeast monsoon and northeast-to-southwest winds and currents; ocean floor is dominated by the Mid-Indian Ocean Ridge and subdivided by the Southeast Indian Ocean Ridge, Southwest Indian Ocean Ridge, and Ninetyeast Ridge

Elevation extremes: *lowest point*: Java Trench -7,258 m
highest point: sea level 0 m

Natural resources: oil and gas fields, fish, shrimp, sand and gravel aggregates, placer deposits, polymetallic nodules

Natural hazards: occasional icebergs pose navigational hazard in southern reaches

Environment—current issues: endangered marine species include the dugong, seals, turtles, and whales; oil pollution in the Arabian Sea, Persian Gulf, and Red Sea

Geography—note: major chokepoints include Bab el Mandeb, Strait of Hormuz, Strait of Malacca, southern access to the Suez Canal, and the Lombok Strait

ECONOMY

Economy—overview: The Indian Ocean provides major sea routes connecting the Middle East, Africa, and East Asia with Europe and the Americas. It carries a particularly heavy traffic of petroleum and petroleum products from the oilfields of the Persian Gulf and Indonesia. Its fish are of great and growing importance to the bordering countries for domestic consumption and export. Fishing fleets from Russia, Japan, South Korea, and Taiwan also exploit the Indian Ocean, mainly for shrimp and tuna. Large reserves of hydrocarbons are being tapped in the offshore areas of Saudi Arabia, Iran, India, and western Australia. An estimated 40% of the world's offshore oil production comes from the Indian Ocean. Beach sands rich in heavy minerals and offshore placer deposits are actively exploited by bordering countries, particularly India, South Africa, Indonesia, Sri Lanka, and Thailand.

TRANSPORTATION

Ports and terminals: *major seaport(s)*: Chennai (Madras, India); Colombo (Sri Lanka); Durban (South Africa); Jakarta (Indonesia); Kolkata (Calcutta, India); Melbourne (Australia); Mumbai (Bombay, India); Richards Bay (South Africa)

Transportation—note: although the number of reported incidents of piracy have dropped dramatically in 2012, the International Maritime Bureau continues to report the territorial waters of littoral states and offshore waters as high risk for piracy and armed robbery against ships, particularly in the Gulf of Aden, along the east coast of Africa, the Bay of Bengal, and the Strait of Malacca; the presence of several naval task forces in the Gulf of Aden and additional anti-piracy measures on the part of ship operators, including the use of on-board armed security teams, have reduced incidents of piracy; in response, Somali-based pirates, using hijacked fishing trawlers as "mother ships" to extend their range, shifted operations as far south as the Mozambique Channel, eastward to the vicinity of the Maldives, and northeastward to the Strait of Hormuz Transnational Issues :: Indian Ocean

Disputes—international: some maritime disputes (see littoral states)

INDONESIA

INTRODUCTION

Background: The Dutch began to colonize Indonesia in the early 17th century; Japan occupied the islands from 1942 to 1945. Indonesia declared its independence shortly before Japan's surrender, but it required four years of sometimes brutal fighting, intermittent negotiations, and UN mediation before the Netherlands agreed to transfer sovereignty in 1949. A period of sometimes unruly parliamentary democracy ended in 1957 when President SOEKARNO declared martial law and instituted "Guided Democracy." After an abortive coup in 1965 by alleged communist sympathizers, SOEKARNO was gradually eased from power. From 1967 until 1988, President SUHARTO ruled Indonesia with his "New Order" government. After rioting toppled Suharto in 1998, free and fair legislative elections took place in 1999. Indonesia is now the world's third most populous democracy, the world's largest archipelagic state, and the world's largest Muslim-majority nation. Current issues include: alleviating poverty, improving education, preventing terrorism, consolidating democracy after four decades of authoritarianism, implementing economic and financial reforms, stemming corruption, reforming the criminal justice system, holding the military and police accountable for human rights violations, addressing climate change, and controlling infectious diseases, particularly those of global and regional importance. In 2005, Indonesia reached a historic peace agreement with armed separatists in Aceh, which led to democratic elections in Aceh in December 2006. Indonesia continues to face low intensity armed resistance in Papua by the separatist Free Papua Movement.

GEOGRAPHY

Location: Southeastern Asia, archipelago between the Indian Ocean and the Pacific Ocean

Geographic coordinates: 5 00 S, 120 00 E

Map references: Southeast Asia

Area: *total:* 1,904,569 sq km
country comparison to the world: 15
land: 1,811,569 sq km
water: 93,000 sq km

Area—comparative: slightly less than three times the size of Texas

Land boundaries: *total:* 2,830 km
border countries: Timor-Leste 228 km, Malaysia 1,782 km, Papua New Guinea 820 km

Coastline: 54,716 km

Maritime claims: measured from claimed archipelagic straight baselines
territorial sea: 12 nm
exclusive economic zone: 200 nm

Climate: tropical; hot, humid; more moderate in highlands

Terrain: mostly coastal lowlands; larger islands have interior mountains

Elevation extremes: *lowest point:* Indian Ocean 0 m
highest point: Puncak Jaya 4,884 m

Natural resources: petroleum, tin, natural gas, nickel, timber, bauxite, copper, fertile soils, coal, gold, silver

Land use: *arable land:* 12.34%
permanent crops: 10.5%
other: 77.16% (2011)

Irrigated land: 67,220 sq km (2005)

Total renewable water resources: 2,019 cu km (2011)

Freshwater withdrawal (domestic/industrial/agricultural): *total:* 113.3 cu km/yr (11%/19%/71%)
per capita: 517.3 cu m/yr (2005)

Natural hazards: occasional floods; severe droughts; tsunamis; earthquakes; volcanoes; forest fires
volcanism: Indonesia contains the most volcanoes of any country in the world—some 76 are historically active; significant volcanic activity occurs on Java, Sumatra, the Sunda Islands, Halmahera Island, Sulawesi Island, Sangihe Island, and in the Banda Sea; Merapi (elev. 2,968 m), Indonesia's most active volcano and in eruption since 2010, has been deemed a Decade Volcano by the International Association of Volcanology and Chemistry of the Earth's Interior, worthy of study due to its explosive history and close proximity to human populations; other notable historically active volcanoes include Agung, Awu, Karangetang, Krakatau (Krakatoa), Makian, Raung, and Tambora

Environment—current issues: deforestation; water pollution from industrial wastes, sewage; air pollution in urban areas; smoke and haze from forest fires

Environment—international agreements:
party to: Biodiversity, Climate Change, Climate Change-Kyoto Protocol, Desertification, Endangered Species, Hazardous Wastes, Law of the Sea, Ozone Layer Protection, Ship Pollution, Tropical Timber 83, Tropical Timber 94, Wetlands
signed, but not ratified: Marine Life Conservation

Geography—note: archipelago of 17,508 islands, some 6,000 of which are inhabited (Indonesia is the world's largest country comprised solely of islands); straddles equator; strategic location astride or along major sea lanes from Indian Ocean to Pacific Ocean

PEOPLE AND SOCIETY

Nationality: *noun:* Indonesian(s)
adjective: Indonesian

Ethnic groups: Javanese 40.1%, Sundanese 15.5%, Malay 3.7%, Batak 3.6%, Madurese 3%, Betawi 2.9%, Minangkabau 2.7%, Buginese 2.7%, Bantenese 2%, Banjarese 1.7%, Balinese 1.7%, Acehnese 1.4%, Dayak 1.4%, Sasak 1.3%, Chinese 1.2%, other 15% (2010 est.)

Languages: Bahasa Indonesia (official, modified form of Malay), English, Dutch, local dialects (of which the most widely spoken is Javanese)
note: more than 700 languages are used in Indonesia

Religions: Muslim 87.2%, Christian 7%, Roman Catholic 2.9%, Hindu 1.7%, other 0.9% (includes Buddhist and Confucian), unspecified 0.4% (2010 est.)

Population: 253,609,643 (July 2014 est.)
country comparison to the world: 5

Age structure: 0-14 years: 26.2% (male 33,854,520/female 32,648,568)
15-24 years: 17.1% (male 22,067,716/female 21,291,548)
25-54 years: 42.3% (male 54,500,650/female 52,723,359)
55-64 years: 6.5% (male 9,257,637/female 10,780,724)
65 years and over: 6.4% (male 7,176,865/female 9,308,056) (2014 est.)

Dependency ratios:
total dependency ratio: 51.8 %
youth dependency ratio: 43.8 %
elderly dependency ratio: 7.9 %
potential support ratio: 12.6 (2013)

Median age: *total:* 29.2 years
male: 28.7 years
female: 29.8 years (2014 est.)

Population growth rate: 0.95% (2014 est.)
country comparison to the world: 124

Birth rate: 17.04 births/1,000 population (2014 est.)
country comparison to the world: 108

Death rate: 6.34 deaths/1,000 population (2014 est.)
country comparison to the world: 157

Net migration rate:
-1.18 migrant(s)/1,000 population (2014 est.)
country comparison to the world: 154

Urbanization: *urban population:* 50.7% of total population (2011)
rate of urbanization: 2.45% annual rate of change (2010-15 est.)

Major urban areas—population: JAKARTA (capital) 9.121 million; Surabaya 2.509 million; Bandung 2.412 million; Medan 2.131 million; Semarang 1.296 million (2009)

Sex ratio: *at birth:* 1.05 male(s)/female
0-14 years: 1.04 male(s)/female
15-24 years: 1.04 male(s)/female
25-54 years: 1.03 male(s)/female
55-64 years: 1 male(s)/female
65 years and over: 0.78 male(s)/female
total population: 1 male(s)/female (2014 est.)

Mother's mean age at first birth: 22.8
note: median age at first birth among women 25-29 (2012 est.)

Maternal mortality rate: 220 deaths/100,000 live births (2010)
country comparison to the world: 52

Infant mortality rate: *total:* 25.16 deaths/1,000 live births
country comparison to the world: 71
male: 29.45 deaths/1,000 live births
female: 20.66 deaths/1,000 live births (2014 est.)

Life expectancy at birth: *total population:* 72.17 years
country comparison to the world: 137
male: 69.59 years
female: 74.88 years (2014 est.)

Total fertility rate: 2.18 children born/woman (2014 est.)
country comparison to the world: 102

Contraceptive prevalence rate: 61.9% (2012)
Health expenditures:
2.7% of GDP (2011)
country comparison to the world: 181

Physicians density: 0.2 physicians/1,000 population (2012)

Hospital bed density: 0.6 beds/1,000 population (2010)

Drinking water source:
improved:
urban: 92.8% of population
rural: 75.5% of population
total: 84.3% of population
unimproved:
urban: 7.2% of population
rural: 24.5% of population
total: 15.7% of population (2011 est.)

Sanitation facility access:
improved:
urban: 73.4% of population
rural: 43.5% of population
total: 58.7% of population
unimproved:
urban: 26.6% of population
rural: 56.5% of population
total: 41.3% of population (2011 est.)

HIV/AIDS—adult prevalence rate: 0.4% (2012 est.)
country comparison to the world: 74

HIV/AIDS—people living with HIV/AIDS: 605,500 (2012 est.)
country comparison to the world: 15

HIV/AIDS—deaths: 26,800 (2012 est.)
country comparison to the world: 15

Major infectious diseases: *degree of risk:* very high
food or waterborne diseases: bacterial diarrhea, hepatitis A, and typhoid fever
vectorborne diseases: dengue fever and malaria
note: highly pathogenic H5N1 avian influenza has been identified in this country; it poses a negligible risk with extremely rare cases possible among US citizens who have close contact with birds (2013)

Obesity—adult prevalence rate: 4.8% (2008)
country comparison to the world: 160

Children under the age of 5 years underweight: 18.6% (2010)
country comparison to the world: 36

Education expenditures: 2.8% of GDP (2011)
country comparison to the world: 143

Literacy: *definition:* age 15 and over can read and write
total population: 92.8%
male: 95.6%
female: 90.1% (2011 est.)

School life expectancy (primary to tertiary education): *total:* 13 years
male: 13 years
female: 13 years (2011)

Child labor—children ages 5-14: total number: 4,026,285
percentage: 7 %
note: data represents children ages 5-17 (2009 est.)

Unemployment, youth ages 15-24: *total:* 22.2%
country comparison to the world: 52
male: 21.6%
female: 23% (2009)

GOVERNMENT

Country name: *conventional long form:* Republic of Indonesia
conventional short form: Indonesia
local long form: Republik Indonesia
local short form: Indonesia
former: Netherlands East Indies, Dutch East Indies

Government type: republic

Capital: *name:* Jakarta
geographic coordinates: 6 10 S, 106 49 E
time difference: UTC+7 (12 hours ahead of Washington, DC during Standard Time)
note: Indonesia is divided into three time zones

Administrative divisions: 31 provinces (provinsi-provinsi, singular—provinsi), 1 autonomous province*, 1 special region** (daerah-daerah istimewa, singular—daerah istimewa), and 1 national capital district*** (daerah khusus ibukota); Aceh*, Bali, Banten, Bengkulu, Gorontalo, Jakarta Raya***, Jambi, Jawa Barat (West Java), Jawa Tengah (Central Java), Jawa Timur (East Java), Kalimantan Barat (West Kalimantan), Kalimantan Selatan (South Kalimantan), Kalimantan Utara (North Kalimantan), Kalimantan Tengah (Central Kalimantan), Kalimantan Timur (East Kalimantan), Kepulauan Bangka Belitung (Bangka Belitung Islands), Kepulauan Riau (Riau Islands), Lampung, Maluku, Maluku Utara (North Maluku), Nusa Tenggara Barat (West Nusa Tenggara), Nusa Tenggara Timur (East Nusa Tenggara), Papua, Papua Barat (West Papua), Riau, Sulawesi Barat (West Sulawesi), Sulawesi Selatan (South Sulawesi), Sulawesi Tengah (Central Sulawesi), Sulawesi Tenggara (Southeast Sulawesi), Sulawesi Utara (North Sulawesi), Sumatera Barat (West Sumatra), Sumatera Selatan (South Sumatra), Sumatera Utara (North Sumatra), Yogyakarta**
note: following the implementation of decentralization beginning on 1 January 2001, regencies and municipalities have become the key administrative units responsible for providing most government services

Independence: 17 August 1945 (declared)

National holiday: Independence Day, 17 August (1945)

Constitution: drafted July to August 1945, effective 17 August 1945, abrogated by 1949 and 1950 constitutions, 1945 constitution restored 5 July 1959; amended several times, last in 2002 (2013)

Legal system: civil law system based on the Roman-Dutch model and influenced by customary law

International law organization participation: has not submitted an ICJ jurisdiction declaration; non-party state to the ICCt

Suffrage: 17 years of age; universal and married persons regardless of age

Executive branch: *chief of state:* President Susilo Bambang YUDHOYONO (since 20 October 2004); Vice President BOEDIONO (since 20 October 2009); note—the president is both the chief of state and head of government
head of government: President Susilo Bambang YUDHOYONO (since 20 October 2004); Vice President BOEDIONO (since 20 October 2009)
cabinet: Cabinet appointed by the president (For more information visit the World Leaders website)
elections: president and vice president elected for five-year terms (eligible for a second term) by direct vote of the citizenry; presidential election last held on 8 July 2009 (next to be held in 2014)
election results: Susilo Bambang YUDHOYONO elected president; percent of vote—Susilo Bambang YUDHOYONO 60.8%, MEGAWATI Sukarnoputri 26.8%, Jusuf KALLA 12.4%

Legislative branch: People's Consultative Assembly (Majelis Permusyawaratan Rakyat or MPR) is the upper house; it consists of members of the DPR and DPD and has role in inaugurating and impeaching the president and in amending the constitution but does not formulate national policy; House of Representatives or Dewan Perwakilan Rakyat (DPR) (560 seats, members elected to serve five-year terms), formulates and passes legislation at the national level; House of Regional Representatives (Dewan Perwakilan Daerah or DPD), constitutionally mandated role includes providing legislative input to DPR on issues affecting regions (132 members, four from each of Indonesia's origianal 30 provinces, two special regions, and one special capital city district)
elections: last held on 9 April 2009 (next to be held in 2014)
election results: percent of vote by party—PD 20.9%, GOLKAR 14.5%, PDI-P 14.0%, PKS 7.9%, PAN 6.0%, PPP 5.3%, PKB 4.9%, GERINDRA 4.5%, HANURA 3.8%, others 18.2%; seats by party—PD 148, GOLKAR 107, PDI-P 94, PKS 57, PAN 46, PPP 37, PKB 28, GERINDRA 26, HANURA 17
note: 29 other parties received less than 2.5% of the vote so did not obtain any seats; because of election rules, the number of seats won does not always follow the percentage of votes received by parties

Judicial branch: *highest court(s):* Supreme Court or Mahkamah Agung (51 judges divided into 8 chambers); Constitutional Court (consists of 9 judges)
judge selection and term of office: Supreme Court judges nominated by Judicial Commission, appointed by president with concurrence of parliament; judges serve until retirement age; Constitutional Court judges—3 nominated by president, 3 by Supreme Court, and 3 by parliament; judges appointed by the president; judges serve until mandatory retirement at age 70
subordinate courts: High Courts of Appeal, district courts, religious courts

Political parties and leaders: Democrat Party or PD [Susilo Bambang YUDHOYONO]; Functional Groups Party or GOLKAR [Aburizal BAKRIE]; Great Indonesia Movement Party or GERINDRA [SUHARDI]; Indonesia Democratic Party-Struggle or PDI-P [MEGAWATI Sukarnoputri]; National Awakening Party or PKB [Muhaiman ISKANDAR]; National Mandate Party or PAN [Hatta RAJASA]; People's Conscience Party or HANURA [WIRANTO]; Prosperous Justice Party or PKS [Anis MATTA]; United Development Party or PPP [Suryadharma ALI]

Political pressure groups and leaders: Commission for the "Disappeared" and Victims of Violence or KontraS; Indonesia Corruption Watch or ICW; Indonesian Forum for the Environment or WALHI

International organization participation: ADB, APEC, ARF, ASEAN, BIS, CD, CICA (observer), CP, D-8, EAS, EITI (candidate country), FAO, G-11, G-15, G-20, G-77, IAEA, IBRD, ICAO, ICC (national committees), ICRM, IDA, IDB, IFAD, IFC, IFRCS, IHO, ILO, IMF, IMO, IMSO, Interpol, IOC, IOM (observer), IPU, ISO, ITSO, ITU, ITUC (NGOs), MIGA, MONUSCO, NAM, OECD (Enhanced Engagement, OIC, OPCW, PIF (partner), UN, UNAMID, UNCTAD, UNESCO, UNIDO, UNIFIL, UNISFA, UNMIL, UNMISS, UNWTO, UPU, WCO, WFTU (NGOs), WHO, WIPO, WMO, WTO

Diplomatic representation in the US:
chief of mission: Ambassador (vacant); Budi BOWOLEKSONO (nominated)
chancery: 2020 Massachusetts Avenue NW, Washington, DC 20036
telephone: [1] (202) 775-5200
FAX: [1] (202) 775-5365
consulate(s) general: Chicago, Houston, Los Angeles, New York, San Francisco

Diplomatic representation from the US:
chief of mission: Ambassador-designate Robert O. BLAKE (since 21 November 2013); Charge d'Affaires Kristen F. BAUER (since 18 July 2013)
embassy: Jalan Medan Merdeka Selatan 3-5, Jakarta 10110
mailing address: Unit 8129, Box 1, FPO AP 96520
telephone: [62] (21) 3435-9000
FAX: [62] (21) 386-2259
consulate general: Surabaya
presence post: Medan
consular agency: Bali
Flag description: two equal horizontal bands of red (top) and white; the colors derive from the banner of the Majapahit Empire of the 13th-15th centuries; red symbolizes courage, white represents purity
note: similar to the flag of Monaco, which is shorter; also similar to the flag of Poland, which is white (top) and red

National symbol(s): garuda (mythical bird)

National anthem: *name:* "Indonesia Raya" (Great Indonesia)
lyrics/music: Wage Rudolf SOEPRATMAN
note: adopted 1945

ECONOMY

Economy—overview: Indonesia, a vast polyglot nation, has grown strongly since 2010. During the global financial crisis, Indonesia outperformed its regional neighbors and joined China and India as the only G20 members posting growth. The government has promoted fiscally conservative policies, resulting in a debt-to-GDP ratio of less than 25% and historically low rates of inflation. Fitch and Moody's upgraded Indonesia's credit rating to investment grade in December 2011. Indonesia still struggles with poverty and unemployment, inadequate infrastructure, corruption, a complex regulatory environment, and unequal resource distribution among regions. The government also faces the challenges of quelling labor unrest and reducing fuel subsidies in the face of high oil prices.

GDP (purchasing power parity): $1.285 trillion (2013 est.)
country comparison to the world: 16
$1.22 trillion (2012 est.)
$1.149 trillion (2011 est.)
note: data are in 2013 US dollars

GDP (official exchange rate): $867.5 billion (2013 est.)

GDP—real growth rate: 5.3% (2013 est.)
country comparison to the world: 48
6.2% (2012 est.)
6.5% (2011 est.)

GDP—per capita (PPP): $5,200 (2013 est.)
country comparison to the world: 158
$5,000 (2012 est.)
$4,800 (2011 est.)
note: data are in 2013 US dollars

Gross national saving: 31.5% of GDP (2013 est.)
country comparison to the world: 22
32.6% of GDP (2012 est.)
33.1% of GDP (2011 est.)

GDP—composition, by end use:
household consumption: 56%
government consumption: 9.4%
investment in fixed capital: 32.7%
investment in inventories: 2%
exports of goods and services: 23.5%
imports of goods and services: -25.8% (2013 est.)

GDP—composition, by sector of origin:
agriculture: 14.3%
industry: 46.6%
services: 39.1% (2013 est.)

Agriculture—products: rubber and similar products, palm oil, poultry, beef, forest products, shrimp, cocoa, coffee, medicinal herbs, essential oil, fish and its similar products, and spices

Industries: petroleum and natural gas, textiles, automotive, electrical appliances, apparel, footwear, mining, cement, medical instuments and appliances, handicrafts, chemical fertilizers, plywood, rubber, processed food, jewelry, and tourism

Industrial production growth rate: 4.3% (2013 est.)
country comparison to the world: 66

Labor force: 120 million (2013 est.)
country comparison to the world: 5

Labor force—by occupation: *agriculture:* 38.9%
industry: 22.2%
services: 47.9% (2012 est.)

Unemployment rate: 6.6% (2013 est.)
country comparison to the world: 69
6.1% (2012 est.)

Population below poverty line: 11.7% (2012 est.)

Household income or consumption by percentage share: *lowest 10%:* 3.3%
highest 10%: 29.9% (2009)

Distribution of family income—Gini index: 36.8 (2009)
country comparison to the world: 82
39.4 (2005)

Budget: *revenues:* $137.5 billion
expenditures: $166 billion (2013 est.)

Taxes and other revenues: 15.8% of GDP (2013 est.)
country comparison to the world: 189

Budget surplus (+) or deficit (-): -3.3% of GDP (2013 est.)
country comparison to the world: 133

Public debt: 24.2% of GDP (2013 est.)
country comparison to the world: 129
23% of GDP (2012 est.)

Fiscal year: calendar year

Inflation rate (consumer prices): 7.7% (2013 est.)
country comparison to the world: 193
4.3% (2012 est.)

Central bank discount rate: 6.37% (31 December 2010)
country comparison to the world: 57
6.46% (31 December 2009)
note: this figure represents the 3-month SBI rate; the Bank of Indonesia has not employed the one-month SBI since September 2010

Commercial bank prime lending rate: 12.1% (31 December 2013 est.)
country comparison to the world: 71
11.8% (31 December 2012 est.)
note: these figures represent the average annualized rate on working capital loans

Stock of narrow money: $82.99 billion (31 December 2013 est.)
country comparison to the world: 40
$87.04 billion (31 December 2012 est.)

Stock of broad money: $325 billion (31 December 2013 est.)
country comparison to the world: 29
$342 billion (31 December 2012 est.)

Stock of domestic credit: $336.2 billion (31 December 2013 est.)
country comparison to the world: 32
$350 billion (31 December 2012 est.)

Market value of publicly traded shares: $396.8 billion (31 December 2012 est.)
country comparison to the world: 24
$390.1 billion (31 December 2011)
$360.4 billion (31 December 2010 est.)

Current account balance: -$28.72 billion (2013 est.)
country comparison to the world: 184
-$24.07 billion (2012 est.)

Exports: $178.9 billion (2013 est.)
country comparison to the world: 29
$187.3 billion (2012 est.)

Exports—commodities: oil and gas, electrical appliances, plywood, textiles, rubber

Exports—partners: Japan 15.9%, China 11.4%, Singapore 9%, South Korea 7.9%, US 7.8%, India 6.6%, Malaysia 5.9% (2012)

Imports: $178.6 billion (2013 est.)
country comparison to the world: 28
$178.7 billion (2012 est.)

Imports—commodities: machinery and equipment, chemicals, fuels, foodstuffs

Imports—partners: China 15.3%, Singapore 13.6%, Japan 11.9%, Malaysia 6.4%, South Korea 6.2%, US 6.1%, Thailand 6% (2012)

Reserves of foreign exchange and gold: $83.45 billion (31 December 2013 est.)
country comparison to the world: 27
$112.8 billion (31 December 2012 est.)

Debt—external: $223.8 billion (31 December 2013 est.)
country comparison to the world: 33
$224.1 billion (31 December 2012 est.)

Stock of direct foreign investment—at home: $207.2 billion (31 December 2013 est.)
country comparison to the world: 27
$192.7 billion (31 December 2012 est.)

Stock of direct foreign investment—abroad: $17.41 billion (31 December 2013 est.)
country comparison to the world: 48
$14.81 billion (31 December 2012 est.)

Exchange rates: Indonesian rupiah (IDR) per US dollar—
10,341.6 (2013 est.)
9,386.63 (2012 est.)
9,090.4 (2010 est.)
10,389.9 (2009)
9,698.9 (2008)

ENERGY

Electricity—production: 173.8 billion kWh (2011 est.)
country comparison to the world: 2 3

Electricity—consumption: 158 billion kWh (2011 est.)
country comparison to the world: 24

Electricity—exports: 0 kWh (2012 est.)
country comparison to the world: 150

Electricity—imports: 2.542 billion kWh (2011 est.)
country comparison to the world: 51

Electricity—installed generating capacity: 39.9 million kW (2011 est.)
country comparison to the world: 23

Electricity—from fossil fuels: 87% of total installed capacity (2011 est.)
country comparison to the world: 85

Electricity—from nuclear fuels: 0% of total installed capacity (2011 est.)
country comparison to the world: 108

Electricity—from hydroelectric plants: 9.9% of total installed capacity (2011 est.)
country comparison to the world: 115

Electricity—from other renewable sources: 3.1% of total installed capacity (2011 est.)
country comparison to the world: 57

Crude oil—production: 974,300 bbl/day (2012 est.)
country comparison to the world: 23

Crude oil—exports: 338,100 bbl/day (2010 est.)
country comparison to the world: 23

Crude oil—imports: 388,400 bbl/day (2010 est.)
country comparison to the world: 23

Crude oil—proved reserves: 4.03 billion bbl (1 January 2013 es)
country comparison to the world: 27

Refined petroleum products—production: 935,300 bbl/day (2011 est.)
country comparison to the world: 20

Refined petroleum products—consumption: 1.322 million bbl/day (2011 est.)
country comparison to the world: 18

Refined petroleum products—exports: 142,400 bbl/day (2010 est.)
country comparison to the world: 40

Refined petroleum products—imports: 473,400 bbl/day (2011 est.)
country comparison to the world: 13

Natural gas—production: 76.25 billion cu m (2011 est.)
country comparison to the world: 12

Natural gas—consumption: 39.56 billion cu m (2010 est.)
country comparison to the world: 24

Natural gas—exports: 38.67 billion cu m (2011 est.)
country comparison to the world: 12

Natural gas—imports: 0 cu m (2011 est.)
country comparison to the world: 207

Natural gas—proved reserves: 3.069 trillion cu m (1 January 2013 es)
country comparison to the world: 13

Carbon dioxide emissions from consumption of energy: 426.8 million Mt (2011 est.)
country comparison to the world: 16

COMMUNICATIONS

Telephones—main lines in use: 37.983 million (2012)
country comparison to the world: 8

Telephones—mobile cellular: 281.96 million (2012)
country comparison to the world: 4

Telephone system: *general assessment:* domestic service includes an interisland microwave system, an HF radio police net, and a domestic satellite communications system; international service good
domestic: coverage provided by existing network has been expanded by use of over 200,000 telephone kiosks many located in remote areas; mobile-cellular subscribership growing rapidly
international: country code—62; landing point for both the SEA-ME-WE-3 and SEA-ME-WE-4 submarine cable networks that provide links throughout Asia, the Middle East, and Europe; satellite earth stations—2 Intelsat (1 Indian Ocean and 1 Pacific Ocean) (2011)

Broadcast media: mixture of about a dozen national TV networks—2 public broadcasters, the remainder private broadcasters—each with multiple transmitters; more than 100 local TV stations; widespread use of satellite and cable TV systems; public radio broadcaster operates 6 national networks as well as regional and local stations; overall, more than 700 radio stations with more than 650 privately operated (2008)

Internet country code: .id

Internet hosts: 1.344 million (2012)
country comparison to the world: 42

Internet users: 20 million (2009)
country comparison to the world: 22

TRANSPORTATION

Airports: 673 (2013)
country comparison to the world: 1 0

Airports—with paved runways: *total:* 186
over 3,047 m: 5
2,438 to 3,047 m: 21
1,524 to 2,437 m: 51
914 to 1,523 m: 72
under 914 m: 37 (2013)

Airports—with unpaved runways: total: 487
1,524 to 2,437 m: 4
914 to 1,523 m: 23
under 914 m: 460 (2013)

Heliports: 76 (2013)

Pipelines: condensate 1,064 km; condensate/gas 150 km; gas 11,702 km; liquid petroleum gas 119 km; oil 7,767 km; oil/gas/water 77 km; refined products 728 km; unknown 53 km; water 44 km (2013)

Railways: *total:* 5,042 km
country comparison to the world: 35
narrow gauge: 5,042 km 1.067-m gauge (565 km electrified) (2008)

Roadways: *total:* 496,607 km
country comparison to the world: 13
paved: 283,102 km
unpaved: 213,505 km (2011)

Waterways: 21,579 km (2011)
country comparison to the world: 7

Merchant marine: *total:* 1,340
country comparison to the world: 8
by type: bulk carrier 105, cargo 618, chemical tanker 69, container 120, liquefied gas 28, passenger 49, passenger/cargo 77, petroleum tanker 244, refrigerated cargo 6, roll on/roll off 12, specialized tanker 1, vehicle carrier 11
foreign-owned: 69 (China 1, France 1, Greece 1, Japan 8, Jordan 1, Malaysia 1, Norway 3, Singapore 46, South Korea 2, Taiwan 1, UK 2, US 2)
registered in other countries: 95 (Bahamas 2, Cambodia 2, China 2, Hong Kong 10, Liberia 4, Marshall Islands 1, Mongolia 2, Panama 10, Singapore 60, Tuvalu 1, unknown 1) (2010)

Ports and terminals: *major seaport(s):* Banjarmasin, Belawan, Kotabaru, Krueg Geukueh, Palembang, Panjang, Sungai Pakning, Tanjung Perak, Tanjung Priok
container port(s) (TEUs): Tanjung Priok (5,617,562)

Transportation—note: the International Maritime Bureau continues to report the territorial and offshore waters in the Strait of Malacca and South China Sea as high risk for piracy and armed robbery against ships; attacks have increased yearly since 2009; in 2012, 73 commercial vessels were boarded and 47 crew members taken hostage; hijacked vessels are often disguised and cargo diverted to ports in East Asia; crews have been murdered or cast adrift

MILITARY

Military branches: Indonesian Armed Forces (Tentara Nasional Indonesia, TNI): Army (TNI-Angkatan Darat (TNI-AD)), Navy (TNI-Angkatan Laut (TNI-AL); includes marines (Korps Marinir, KorMar), naval air arm), Air Force (TNI-Angkatan Udara (TNI-AU)), National Air Defense Command (Kommando Pertahanan Udara Nasional (Kohanudnas)) (2013)

Military service age and obligation: 18-45 years of age for voluntary military service, with selective conscription authorized; 2-year service obligation, with reserve obligation to age 45 (officers); Indonesian citizens only (2012)

Manpower available for military service: *males age 16-49:* 65,847,171
females age 16-49: 63,228,017 (2010 est.)

Manpower fit for military service: *males age 16-49:* 54,264,299
females age 16-49: 53,274,361 (2010 est.)

Manpower reaching militarily significant age annually: *male:* 2,263,892
female: 2,191,267 (2010 est.)

Military expenditures: 0.78% of GDP (2012)
country comparison to the world: 116
0.67% of GDP (2011)
0.78% of GDP (2010)

TRANSNATIONAL ISSUES

Disputes—international: Indonesia has a stated foreign policy objective of establishing stable fixed land and maritime boundaries with all of its neighbors; three stretches of land borders with Timor-Leste have yet to be delimited, two of which are in the Oecussi exclave area, and no maritime or Exclusive Economic Zone (EEZ) boundaries have been established between the countries; many refugees from Timor-Leste who left in 2003 still reside in Indonesia and refuse repatriation; all borders between Indonesia and Australia have been agreed upon bilaterally, but a 1997 treaty that would settle the last of their maritime and EEZ boundary has yet to be ratified by Indonesia's legislature; Indonesian groups challenge Australia's claim to Ashmore Reef; Australia has closed parts of the Ashmore and Cartier Reserve to Indonesian traditional fishing and placed restrictions on certain catches; land and maritime negotiations with Malaysia are ongoing, and disputed areas include the controversial Tanjung Datu and Camar Wulan border area in Borneo and the maritime boundary in the Ambalat oil block in the Celebes Sea; Indonesia and Singapore continue to work on finalizing their 1973 maritime boundary agreement by defining unresolved areas north of Indonesia's Batam Island; Indonesian secessionists, squatters, and illegal migrants create repatriation problems for Papua New Guinea; maritime delimitation talks continue with Palau; EEZ negotiations with Vietnam are ongoing, and the two countries in Fall 2011 agreed to work together to reduce illegal fishing along their maritime boundary

Refugees and internally displaced persons: *IDPs:* 180,000 (government offensives against rebels in Aceh; most IDPs in Aceh, Central Kalimantan, Central Sulawesi Provinces, and Maluku) (2011)

Illicit drugs: illicit producer of cannabis largely for domestic use; producer of methamphetamine and ecstasy

IRAN

INTRODUCTION

Background: Known as Persia until 1935, Iran became an Islamic republic in 1979 after the ruling monarchy was overthrown and Shah Mohammad Reza PAHLAVI was forced into exile. Conservative clerical forces led by Ayatollah Ruhollah KHOMEINI established a theocratic system of government with ultimate political authority vested in a learned religious scholar referred to commonly as the Supreme Leader who, according to the constitution, is accountable only to the Assembly of Experts—a popularly elected 86-member body of clerics. US-Iranian relations became strained when a group of Iranian students seized the US Embassy in Tehran in November 1979 and held embassy personnel hostages until mid-January 1981. The US cut off diplomatic relations with Iran in April 1980. During the period 1980-88, Iran fought a bloody, indecisive war with Iraq that eventually expanded into the Persian Gulf and led to clashes between US Navy and Iranian military forces. Iran has been designated a state sponsor of terrorism for its activities in Lebanon and elsewhere in the world and remains subject to US, UN, and EU economic sanctions and export controls because of its continued involvement in terrorism and concerns over possible military dimensions of its nuclear program. Following the election of reformer Hojjat ol-Eslam Mohammad KHATAMI as president in 1997 and a reformist Majles (legislature) in 2000, a campaign to foster political reform in response to popular dissatisfaction was initiated. The movement floundered as conservative politicians, supported by the Supreme Leader, unelected institutions of authority like the Council of Guardians, and the security services reversed and blocked reform measures while increasing security repression. Starting with nationwide municipal elections in 2003 and continuing through Majles elections in 2004, conservatives reestablished control over Iran's elected government institutions, which culminated with the August 2005 inauguration of hardliner Mahmud AHMADI-NEJAD as president. His controversial reelection in June 2009 sparked nationwide protests over allegations of electoral fraud. These protests were quickly suppressed, and the political opposition that arouse as a consequence of AHMADI-NEJAD's election was repressed. Deteriorating economic conditions due primarily to government mismanagement and international sanctions prompted at least two major economically based protests in July and October 2012, but Iran's internal security situation remained stable. President AHMADI-NEJAD's independent streak angered regime establishment figures, including the Supreme Leader, leading to conservative opposition to his agenda for the last year of his presidency, and an alienation of his political supporters. In June 2013 Iranians elected a moderate conservative cleric, Dr. Hasan Fereidun RUHANI to the presidency. He is a long-time senior member in the regime, but has made promises of reforming society and Iran's foreign policy. The UN Security Council has passed a number of resolutions calling for Iran to suspend its uranium enrichment and reprocessing activities and comply with its IAEA obligations and responsibilities, but in November 2013 the five permanent members, plus Germany, (P5+1) signed a joint plan with Iran to provide the country with incremental relief from international pressure for positive steps toward transparency of their nuclear program.

GEOGRAPHY

Location: Middle East, bordering the Gulf of Oman, the Persian Gulf, and the Caspian Sea, between Iraq and Pakistan

Geographic coordinates: 32 00 N, 53 00 E

Map references: Middle East

Area: *total:* 1,648,195 sq km
country comparison to the world: 18
land: 1,531,595 sq km
water: 116,600 sq km

Area—comparative: almost two and a half times the size of Teas; slightly smaller than Alaska

Land boundaries: *total:* 5,440 km
border countries: Afghanistan 936 km, Armenia 35 km, Azerbaijan-proper 432 km, Azerbaijan-Naxcivan exclave 179 km, Iraq 1,458 km, Pakistan 909 km, Turkey 499 km, Turkmenistan 992 km

Coastline: 2,440 km; note—Iran also borders the Caspian Sea (740 km)

Maritime claims: *territorial sea:* 12 nm
contiguous zone: 24 nm
exclusive economic zone: bilateral agreements or median lines in the Persian Gulf
continental shelf: natural prolongation

Climate: mostly arid or semiarid, subtropical along Caspian coast

Terrain: rugged, mountainous rim; high, central basin with deserts, mountains; small, discontinuous plains along both coasts

Elevation extremes: *lowest point:* Caspian Sea -28 m
highest point: Kuh-e Damavand 5,671 m

Natural resources: petroleum, natural gas, coal, chromium, copper, iron ore, lead, manganese, zinc, sulfur

Land use: *arable land:* 10.05%
permanent crops: 1.08%
other: 88.86% (2011)

Irrigated land: 87,000 sq km (2009)

Total renewable water resources: 137 cu km (2011)

Freshwater withdrawal (domestic/industrial/agricultural): *total:* 93.3 cu km/yr (7%/1%/92%)
per capita: 1,306 cu m/yr (2004)

Natural hazards: periodic droughts, floods; dust storms, sandstorms; earthquakes

Environment—current issues: air pollution, especially in urban areas, from vehicle emissions, refinery operations, and industrial effluents; deforestation; overgrazing; desertification; oil pollution in the Persian Gulf; wetland losses from drought; soil degradation (salination); inadequate supplies of potable water; water pollution from raw sewage and industrial waste; urbanization

Environment—international agreements: *party to:* Biodiversity, Climate Change, Climate Change-Kyoto Protocol, Desertification, Endangered Species, Hazardous Wastes, Marine Dumping, Ozone Layer Protection, Ship Pollution, Wetlands
signed, but not ratified: Environmental Modification, Law of the Sea, Marine Life Conservation

Geography—note: strategic location on the Persian Gulf and Strait of Hormuz, which are vital maritime pathways for crude oil transport

PEOPLE AND SOCIETY

Nationality: *noun:* Iranian(s)
adjective: Iranian

Ethnic groups: Persian 61%, Azeri 16%, Kurd 10%, Lur 6%, Baloch 2%, Arab 2%, Turkmen and Turkic tribes 2%, other 1%

Languages: Persian (official) 53%, Azeri Turkic and Turkic dialects 18%, Kurdish 10%, Gilaki and Mazandarani 7%, Luri 6%, Balochi 2%, Arabic 2%, other 2%

Religions: Muslim (official) 99.4% (Shia 90-95%, Sunni 5-10%), other (includes Zoroastrian, Jewish, and Christian) 0.3%, unspecified 0.4% (2011 est.)

Population: 80,840,713 (July 2014 est.)
country comparison to the world: 19

Age structure:
0-14 years: 23.7% (male 9,834,866/female 9,350,017)
15-24 years: 18.7% (male 7,757,256/female 7,341,309)
25-54 years: 46.1% (male 18,955,874/female 18,289,849)
55-64 years: 5.2% (male 2,519,630/female 2,603,458)
65 years and over: 5.1% (male 1,941,692/female 2,246,762) (2014 est.)

Dependency ratios:
total dependency ratio: 41 %
youth dependency ratio: 33.6 %
elderly dependency ratio: 7.5 %
potential support ratio: 13.4 (2013)

Median age: *total:* 28.3 years
male: 28 years
female: 28.6 years (2014 est.)

Population growth rate: 1.22% (2014 est.)
country comparison to the world: 97

Birth rate: 18.23 births/1,000 population (2014 est.)
country comparison to the world: 105

Death rate: 5.94 deaths/1,000 population (2014 est.)
country comparison to the world: 169

Net migration rate: -0.08 migrant(s)/1,000 population (2014 est.)
country comparison to the world: 115

Urbanization: *urban population:* 69.1% of total population (2011)
rate of urbanization: 1.25% annual rate of change (2010-15 est.)

Major urban areas—population: TEHRAN (capital) 7.19 million; Mashhad 2.592 million; Esfahan 1.704 million; Karaj 1.531 million; Tabriz 1.459 million (2009)

Sex ratio: *at birth:* 1.05 male(s)/female
0-14 years: 1.05 male(s)/female
15-24 years: 1.06 male(s)/female
25-54 years: 1.04 male(s)/female
55-64 years: 1.03 male(s)/female
65 years and over: 0.89 male(s)/female
total population: 1.03 male(s)/female (2014 est.)

Maternal mortality rate: 21 deaths/100,000 live births (2010)
country comparison to the world: 137

Infant mortality rate: total: 39 deaths/1,000 live births
country comparison to the world: 55
male: 39.53 deaths/1,000 live births
female: 38.45 deaths/1,000 live births (2014 est.)

Life expectancy at birth: *total population:* 70.89 years
country comparison to the world: 148
male: 69.32 years
female: 72.53 years (2014 est.)

Total fertility rate: 1.85 children born/woman (2014 est.)
country comparison to the world: 146

Contraceptive prevalence rate: 73.3% (2002)

Health expenditures: 6% of GDP (2011)
country comparison to the world: 110

Physicians density: 0.89 physicians/1,000 population (2005)

Hospital bed density: 1.7 beds/1,000 population (2009)

Drinking water source:
improved:
urban: 97.5% of population
rural: 90.3% of population
total: 95.3% of population
unimproved:
urban: 2.5% of population
rural: 9.7% of population
total: 4.7% of population (2011 est.)

Sanitation facility access:
improved:
urban: 100% of population
rural: 98.7% of population
total: 99.6% of population
unimproved:
urban: 0% of population
rural: 1.3% of population
total: 0.4% of population (2011 est.)

HIV/AIDS—adult prevalence rate: 0.2% (2012 est.)
country comparison to the world: 102

HIV/AIDS—people living with HIV/AIDS: 70,900 (2012 est.)
country comparison to the world: 54

HIV/AIDS—deaths: 4,600 (2012 est.)
country comparison to the world: 43

Major infectious diseases: *degree of risk:* intermediate
food or waterborne diseases: bacterial diarrhea
vectorborne diseases: Crimean-Congo hemorrhagic fever
note: highly pathogenic H5N1 avian influenza has been identified in this country; it poses a negligible risk with extremely rare cases possible among US citizens who have close contact with birds (2013)

Obesity—adult prevalence rate: 19.4% (2008)
country comparison to the world: 99

Children under the age of 5 years underweight: 4.6% (2004)
country comparison to the world: 92

Education expenditures: 3.7% of GDP (2012)
country comparison to the world: 119

Literacy: *definition:* age 15 and over can read and write
total population: 85%
male: 89.3%
female: 80.7% (2008 est.)

School life expectancy (primary to tertiary education): *total:* 15 years
male: 15 years
female: 15 years (2012)

Unemployment, youth ages 15-24: *total:* 23%
country comparison to the world: 48
male: 20.2%
female: 33.9% (2008)

GOVERNMENT

Country name: *conventional long form:* Islamic Republic of Iran
conventional short form: Iran
local long form: Jomhuri-ye Eslami-ye Iran
local short form: Iran
former: Persia

Government type: theocratic republic

Capital: *name:* Tehran
geographic coordinates: 35 42 N, 51 25 E
time difference: UTC+3.5 (8.5 hours ahead of Washington, DC during Standard Time)
daylight saving time: +1hr, begins fourth Tuesday in March; ends fourth Thursday in September

Administrative divisions: 31 provinces (ostanha, singular—ostan); Alborz, Ardabil, Azarbayjan-e Gharbi (West Azerbaijan), Azarbayjan-e Sharqi (East Azerbaijan), Bushehr, Chahar Mahal va Bakhtiari, Esfahan, Fars, Gilan, Golestan, Hamadan, Hormozgan, Ilam, Kerman, Kermanshah, Khorasan-e Jonubi (South Khorasan), Khorasan-e Razavi (Razavi Khorasan), Khorasan-e Shomali (North Khorasan), Khuzestan, Kohgiluyeh va Bowyer Ahmad, Kordestan, Lorestan, Markazi, Mazandaran, Qazvin, Qom, Semnan, Sistan va Baluchestan, Tehran, Yazd, Zanjan

Independence: 1 April 1979 (Islamic Republic of Iran proclaimed); notable earlier dates: 16 January 1979 (Shah Reza PAHLAVI flees Iran to escape popular political revolt against his rule); 12 December 1925 (modern Iran established under the PAHLAVI Dynasty); 1905-1907 (constitutional revolution resulting in establishment of a parliament); A.D. 1501 (Iran reunified under the Safavid Dynasty)

National holiday: Republic Day, 1 April (1979)

Constitution: previous 1906; latest adopted 24 October 1979, effective 3 December 1979; amended 1989 (2013)

Legal system: religious legal system based on secular and Islamic law

International law organization participation: has not submitted an ICJ jurisdiction declaration; non-party state to the ICCt

Suffrage: 18 years of age; universal

Executive branch: *chief of state:* Supreme Leader Ali Hoseini-KHAMENEI (since 4 June 1989)
head of government: President Hasan Fereidun RUHANI (since 3 August 2013); First Vice President Eshaq JAHANGIRI (since 5 August 2013)
cabinet: Council of Ministers selected by the president with legislative approval; the Supreme Leader has some control over appointments to the more sensitive ministries (For more information visit the World Leaders website)
note: also considered part of the Executive branch of government are three oversight bodies: 1) Council of Guardians of the Constitution or Council of Guardians or Guardians Council (Shora-ye Negban-e Qanon-e Asasi) determines whether proposed legislation is both constitutional and faithful to Islamic law, vets candidates in popular elections for suitability, and supervises national elections; 2) Assembly of Experts (Majles-e Khoebregan), an elected consultative body of senior clerics constitutionally mandated to select, appoint, supervise,

and dismiss the Supreme Leader; 3) Expediency Council or the Council for the Discernment of Expediency (Majma-ye- Tashkhis-e -Maslahat-e-Nezam) resolves legislative issues when the Majles and the Council of Guardians disagree and since 1989 has been used to advise national religious leaders on matters of national policy; in 2005 the Council's powers were expanded to act as a supervisory body for the government
elections: supreme leader appointed for life by the Assembly of Experts; president elected by popular vote for a four-year term (eligible for a second term and additional nonconsecutive term); election last held on 14 June 2013 (next presidential election to be held in June 2017)
election results: Hasan Fereidun RUHANI 50.7%, Mohammad Baqer QALIBAF 16.5%, Saeed JALILI 11.4%, Mohsen REZAI 10.6%, Ali Akber VELAYATI 6.2%, other 4.6%

Legislative branch: unicameral Islamic Consultative Assembly or Majles-e Shura-ye Eslami or Majles (290 seats; members elected by popular vote from single and multimember districts to serve four-year terms)
elections: last held on 2 March 2012 (first round); second round held on 4 May 2012; (next election to be held in 2016)
election results: percent of vote by party—NA; seats by party—NA

Judicial branch: *highest court(s):* Supreme Court (consists of a president and NA judges)
judge selection and term of office: Supreme Court president appointed by the head of the Supreme Judicial Council in consultation with judges of the Supreme Court; president appointed for a 5-year term; other judge appointments and tenure NA
subordinate courts: Penal Courts I and II; Islamic Revolutionary Courts; Courts of Peace; Special Clerical Court (functions outside the judicial system and handles cases involving clerics); military courts

Political parties and leaders:
note: formal political parties are a relatively new phenomenon in Iran and most conservatives still prefer to work through political pressure groups rather than parties; often political parties or coalitions are formed prior to elections and disbanded soon thereafter; a loose pro-reform coalition called the 2nd Khordad Front, which includes political parties as well as less formal groups and organizations, achieved considerable success in elections for the sixth Majles in early 2000; groups in the coalition included the Islamic Iran Participation Front (IIPF), Executives of Construction Party (Kargozaran), Solidarity Party, Islamic Labor Party, Mardom Salari, Mojahedin of the Islamic Revolution Organization (MIRO), and Militant Clerics Society (MCS; Ruhaniyun); the coalition participated in the seventh Majles elections in early 2004 but boycotted them after 80 incumbent reformists were disqualified; following his defeat in the 2005 presidential elections, former MCS Secretary General and sixth Majles Speaker Mehdi KARUBI formed the National Trust Party; a new conservative group, Islamic Iran Developers Coalition (Abadgaran), took a leading position in the new Majles after winning a majority of the seats in February 2004; ahead of the 2008 Majles elections, traditional and hardline conservatives attempted to close ranks under the United Front of Principlists and the Broad Popular Coalition of Principlists; several reformist groups, such as the MIRO and the IIPF, also came together as a reformist coalition in advance of the 2008 Majles elections; the IIPF has repeatedly complained that the overwhelming majority of its candidates were unfairly disqualified from the 2008 elections

Political pressure groups and leaders: *groups that generally support the Islamic Republic:* Ansar-e Hizballah; Followers of the Line of the Imam and the Leader; Islamic Coalition Party (Motalefeh); Islamic Engineers Society; Tehran Militant Clergy Association (MCA; Ruhaniyat)
active pro-reform student group: Office of Strengthening Unity (OSU)
opposition groups: Freedom Movement of Iran; Green Path movement [Mehdi KARUBI, Mir-Hosein MUSAVI]; Marz-e Por Gohar; National Front; various ethnic and monarchist organizations
armed political groups repressed by the government: Democratic Party of Iranian Kurdistan (KDPI); Harekat-e Ansar-e Iran (splinter faction of Jundallah); Jaysh l-Adl (formerly known as Jundallah); Komala; Mojahedin-e Khalq Organization (MEK or MKO); People's Fedayeen; People's Free Life Party of Kurdistan (PJAK)

International organization participation: CICA, CP, D-8, ECO, FAO, G-15, G-24, G-77, IAEA, IBRD, ICAO, ICC (national committees), ICRM, IDA, IDB, IFAD, IFC, IFRCS, IHO, ILO, IMF, IMO, IMSO, Interpol, IOC, IOM, IPU, ISO, ITSO, ITU, MIGA, NAM, OIC, OPCW, OPEC, PCA, SAARC (observer), SCO (observer), UN, UNAMID, UNCTAD, UNESCO, UNHCR, UNIDO, UNITAR, UNWTO, UPU, WCO, WFTU (NGOs), WHO, WIPO, WMO, WTO (observer)

Diplomatic representation in the US: none; note—Iran has an Interests Section in the Pakistani Embassy; address: Iranian Interests Section, Pakistani Embassy, 2209 Wisconsin Avenue NW, Washington, DC 20007;
telephone: [1] (202) 965-4990;
FAX [1] (202) 965-1073

Diplomatic representation from the US: none; note—the US Interests Section is located in the Embassy of Switzerland No. 39 Shahid Mousavi (Golestan 5th), Pasdaran Ave., Tehran, Iran; telephone [98] 21 2254 2178/2256 5273; FAX [98] 21 2258 0432

Flag description: three equal horizontal bands of green (top), white, and red; the national emblem (a stylized representation of the word Allah in the shape of a tulip, a symbol of martyrdom) in red is centered in the white band; ALLAH AKBAR (God is Great) in white Arabic script is repeated 11 times along the bottom edge of the green band and 11 times along the top edge of the red band; green is the color of Islam and also represents growth, white symbolizes honesty and peace, red stands for bravery and martyrdom

National symbol(s): lion

National anthem: *name:* "Soroud-e Melli-ye Jomhouri-ye Eslami-ye Iran" (National Anthem of the Islamic Republic of Iran)
lyrics/music: multiple authors/Hassan RIAHI
note: adopted 1990

ECONOMY

Economy—overview: Iran's economy is marked by statist policies, an inefficient state sector, and reliance on oil, a major source of government revenues. Price controls, subsidies, and other distortions weigh down the economy, undermining the potential for private-sector-led growth. Private sector activity is typically limited to small-scale workshops, farming, some manufacturing, and services. Significant informal market activity flourishes and corruption is widespread. New fiscal and monetary constraints on Tehran, following the expansion of international sanctions in 2012 against Iran's Central Bank and oil exports, significantly reduced Iran's oil revenue, forced government spending cuts, and fueled a 60% currency depreciation. Economic growth turned negative in 2012 and 2013, for the first time in two decades. Iran continues to suffer from double-digit unemployment and underemployment. Lack of job opportunities has convinced many educated Iranian youth to seek jobs overseas, resulting in a significant "brain drain." However, the election of President Hasan RUHANI in June 2013 brought about widespread expectations of economic improvements and greater international engagement among the Iranian public, and early in Ruhani's term the country saw a strengthened national currency and a historic boost to market values at the Tehran Stock Exchange.

GDP (purchasing power parity): $987.1 billion (2013 est.)
country comparison to the world: 19
$1.002 trillion (2012 est.)
$1.021 trillion (2011 est.)
note: data are in 2013 US dollars

GDP (official exchange rate): $411.9 billion (2013 est.)

GDP—real growth rate: -1.5% (2013 est.)
country comparison to the world: 207
-1.9% (2012 est.)
3% (2011 est.)

GDP—per capita (PPP): $12,800 (2013 est.)
country comparison to the world: 103
$13,200 (2012 est.)
$13,600 (2011 est.)
note: data are in 2013 US dollars

Gross national saving: 30.3% of GDP (2013 est.)
country comparison to the world: 26
30.3% of GDP (2012 est.)
36.6% of GDP (2011 est.)

GDP—composition, by end use:
household consumption: 45.4%
government consumption: 14.1%
investment in fixed capital: 31.1%
investment in inventories: 1.2%
exports of goods and services: 20.8%
imports of goods and services: -12.7% (2013 est.)

GDP—composition, by sector of origin:
agriculture: 10.6%
industry: 44.9%
services: 44.5% (2013 est.)

Agriculture—products: wheat, rice, other grains, sugar beets, sugarcane, fruits, nuts, cotton; dairy products, wool; caviar

Industries: petroleum, petrochemicals, fertilizers, caustic soda, textiles, cement and other construction materials, food processing (particularly sugar refining and vegetable oil production), ferrous and non-ferrous metal fabrication, armaments

Industrial production growth rate: -5.2% (2013 est.)
country comparison to the world: 191

Labor force: 27.72 million
country comparison to the world: 23
note: shortage of skilled labor (2013 est.)

Labor force—by occupation: *agriculture:* 16.9%
industry: 34.4%
services: 48.7% (2012 est.)

Unemployment rate: 16% (2013 est.)
country comparison to the world: 145
15.5% (2012 est.)
note: data are according to the Iranian Government

Population below poverty line: 18.7% (2007 est.)

Household income or consumption by percentage share: *lowest 10%:* 2.6%
highest 10%: 29.6% (2005)

Distribution of family income—Gini index: 44.5 (2006)
country comparison to the world: 45

Budget: *revenues:* $47.84 billion
expenditures: $66.38 billion (2013 est.)

Taxes and other revenues: 11.6% of GDP (2013 est.)
country comparison to the world: 204

Budget surplus (+) or deficit (-):
-4.5% of GDP (2013 est.)
country comparison to the world: 159

Public debt: 18.7% of GDP (2013 est.)
country comparison to the world: 136
18.6% of GDP (2012 est.)
note: includes publicly guaranteed debt

Fiscal year: 21 March—20 March

Inflation rate (consumer prices): 42.3% (2013 est.)
country comparison to the world: 221
30.5% (2012 est.)
note: official Iranian estimate

Central bank discount rate: NA%

Commercial bank prime lending rate: 12% (2013 est.)
country comparison to the world: 79
11% (31 December 2012 est.)

Stock of narrow money: $26.3 billion (31 December 2013 est.)
country comparison to the world: 62
$42.91 billion (31 December 2012 est.)

Stock of broad money: $65.02 billion (31 December 2013 est.)
country comparison to the world: 65
$104.6 billion (31 December 2012 est.)

Stock of domestic credit: $42.32 billion (31 December 2013 est.)
country comparison to the world: 64
$77.74 billion (31 December 2012 est.)

Market value of publicly traded shares:
$172 billion (31 December 2013 est.)
country comparison to the world: 37
$140.8 billion (31 December 2012)
$107.2 billion (31 December 2011 est.)

Current account balance: -$8.659 billion (2013 est.)
country comparison to the world: 174
-$9.333 billion (2012 est.)

Exports: $61.22 billion (2013 est.)
country comparison to the world: 53
$67.04 billion (2012 est.)

Exports—commodities: petroleum 80%, chemical and petrochemical products, fruits and nuts, carpets

Exports—partners: China 22.1%, India 11.9%, Turkey 10.6%, South Korea 7.6%, Japan 7.1% (2012)

Imports: $64.42 billion (2013 est.)
country comparison to the world: 46
$70.03 billion (2012 est.)

Imports—commodities: industrial supplies, capital goods, foodstuffs and other consumer goods, technical services

Imports—partners: UAE 33.2%, China 13.8%, Turkey 11.8%, South Korea 7.4% (2012)

Reserves of foreign exchange and gold:
$68.06 billion (31 December 2013 est.)
country comparison to the world: 31
$74.06 billion (31 December 2012 est.)

Debt—external: $15.64 billion (2013 est.)
country comparison to the world: 87
$17.25 billion (31 December 2012 est.)

Stock of direct foreign investment—at home:
$41.45 billion (31 December 2013 est.)
country comparison to the world: 56
$37.31 billion (31 December 2012 est.)

Stock of direct foreign investment—abroad:
$3.645 billion (31 December 2013 est.)
country comparison to the world: 66
$3.345 billion (31 December 2012 est.)

Exchange rates: Iranian rials (IRR) per US dollar—
18,517.2 (2013 est.)
12,175.5 (2012 est.)
10,254.18 (2010 est.)
9,864.3 (2009)
9,142.8 (2008)
note: Iran devalued its currency in July 2013

ENERGY

Electricity—production: 239.7 billion kWh (2011 est.)
country comparison to the world: 1 8

Electricity—consumption: 199.8 billion kWh (2011 est.)
country comparison to the world: 19

Electricity—exports: 6.707 billion kWh (2010 est.)
country comparison to the world: 24

Electricity—imports: 3.015 billion kWh (2010 est.)
country comparison to the world: 46

Electricity—installed generating capacity:
62.09 million kW (2010 est.)
country comparison to the world: 15

Electricity—from fossil fuels: 86.2% of total installed capacity (2010 est.)
country comparison to the world: 86

Electricity—from nuclear fuels: 0% of total installed capacity (2010 est.)
country comparison to the world: 109

Electricity—from hydroelectric plants: 13.7% of total installed capacity (2010 est.)
country comparison to the world: 105

Electricity—from other renewable sources:
0.2% of total installed capacity (2010 est.)
country comparison to the world: 96

Crude oil—production: 3.594 million bbl/day (2012 est.)
country comparison to the world: 6

Crude oil—exports: 2.445 million bbl/day (2011 est.)
country comparison to the world: 3

Crude oil—imports: 15,600 bbl/day (2010 est.)
country comparison to the world: 72

Crude oil—proved reserves: 154.6 billion bbl (1 January 2013 es)
country comparison to the world: 4

Refined petroleum products—production:
1.718 million bbl/day (2011 est.)
country comparison to the world: 12

Refined petroleum products—consumption:
1.709 million bbl/day (2012 est.)
country comparison to the world: 14

Refined petroleum products—exports:
330,800 bbl/day (2010 est.)
country comparison to the world: 22

Refined petroleum products—imports:
180,400 bbl/day (2010 est.)
country comparison to the world: 29

Natural gas—production: 162.6 billion cu m (2012 est.)
country comparison to the world: 4

Natural gas—consumption: 144.6 billion cu m (2010 est.)
country comparison to the world: 4

Natural gas—exports: 9.05 billion cu m (2011 est.)
country comparison to the world: 27

Natural gas—imports: 10.59 billion cu m (2011 est.)
country comparison to the world: 29

Natural gas—proved reserves: 33.61 trillion cu m (1 January 2013 es)
country comparison to the world: 2

Carbon dioxide emissions from consumption of energy: 624.9 million Mt (2011 est.)
country comparison to the world: 8

COMMUNICATIONS

Telephones—main lines in use: 28.76 million (2012)
country comparison to the world: 1 2

Telephones—mobile cellular: 58.16 million (2012)
country comparison to the world: 24

Telephone system: *general assessment:* currently being modernized and expanded with the goal of not only improving the efficiency and increasing the volume of the urban service but also bringing telephone service to several thousand villages, not presently connected
domestic: the addition of new fiber cables and modern switching and exchange systems installed by Iran's state-owned telecom company have improved and expanded the fixed-line network greatly; fixed-line availability has more than doubled to more than 27 million lines since 2000; additionally, mobile-cellular service has increased dramatically serving roughly 56 million subscribers in 2011; combined fixed and mobile-cellular subscribership now exceeds 100 per 100 persons
international: country code—98; submarine fiber-optic cable to UAE with access to Fiber-Optic Link Around the Globe (FLAG);

Trans-Asia-Europe (TAE) fiber-optic line runs from Azerbaijan through the northern portion of Iran to Turkmenistan with expansion to Georgia and Azerbaijan; HF radio and microwave radio relay to Turkey, Azerbaijan, Pakistan, Afghanistan, Turkmenistan, Syria, Kuwait, Tajikistan, and Uzbekistan; satellite earth stations—13 (9 Intelsat and 4 Inmarsat) (2011)

Broadcast media: state-run broadcast media with no private, independent broadcasters; Islamic Republic of Iran Broadcasting (IRIB), the state-run TV broadcaster, operates 5 nationwide channels, a news channel, about 30 provincial channels, and several international channels; about 20 foreign Persian-language TV stations broadcasting on satellite TV are capable of being seen in Iran; satellite dishes are illegal and, while their use had been tolerated, authorities began confiscating satellite dishes following the unrest stemming from the 2009 presidential election; IRIB operates 8 nationwide radio networks, a number of provincial stations, and an external service; most major international broadcasters transmit to Iran (2009)

Internet country code: .ir

Internet hosts: 197,804 (2012)
country comparison to the world: 72

Internet users: 8.214 million (2009)
country comparison to the world: 35

TRANSPORTATION

Airports: 319 (2013)
country comparison to the world: 2 2

Airports—with paved runways: *total:* 140
over 3,047 m: 42
2,438 to 3,047 m: 29
1,524 to 2,437 m: 26
914 to 1,523 m: 36
under 914 m: 7 (2013)

Airports—with unpaved runways: *total:* 179
over 3,047 m: 1
2,438 to 3,047 m: 2
1,524 to 2,437 m: 9
914 to 1,523 m: 135
under 914 m: 32 (2013)

Heliports: 26 (2013)

Pipelines: condensate 7 km; condensate/gas 973 km; gas 20,794 km; liquid petroleum gas 570 km; oil 8,625 km; refined products 7,937 km (2013)

Railways: *total:* 8,442 km
country comparison to the world: 24
broad gauge: 94 km 1.676-m gauge
standard gauge: 8,348 km 1.435-m gauge (148 km electrified) (2008)

Roadways: *total:* 198,866 km
country comparison to the world: 26
paved: 160,366 km (includes 1,948 km of expressways)
unpaved: 38,500 km (2010)

Waterways: 850 km (on Karun River; some navigation on Lake Urmia) (2012)
country comparison to the world: 70

Merchant marine: *total:* 7 6
country comparison to the world: 60
by type: bulk carrier 8, cargo 51, chemical tanker 3, container 4, liquefied gas 1, passenger/cargo 3, petroleum tanker 2, refrigerated cargo 2, roll on/roll off 2
foreign-owned: 2 (UAE 2)
registered in other countries: 71 (Barbados 5, Cyprus 10, Hong Kong 3, Malta 48, Panama 5) (2010)

Ports and terminals: *major seaport(s):* Bandar-e Asaluyeh, Bandar Abbas
river port(s): Bandar Emam Khomeyni (Shatt al-Arab)
container port(s) (TEUs): Bandar Abbas (2,752,460)

MILITARY

Military branches: Islamic Republic of Iran Regular Forces (Artesh): Ground Forces, Navy, Air Force (IRIAF), Khatemolanbia Air Defense Headquarters; Islamic Revolutionary Guard Corps (Sepah-e Pasdaran-e Enqelab-e Eslami, IRGC): Ground Resistance Forces, Navy, Aerospace Force, Quds Force (special operations); Law Enforcement Forces (2011)

Military service age and obligation: 18 years of age for compulsory military service; 16 years of age for volunteers; 17 years of age for Law Enforcement Forces; 15 years of age for Basij Forces (Popular Mobilization Army); conscript military service obligation is 18 months; women exempt from military service (2012)

Manpower available for military service:
males age 16-49: 23,619,215
females age 16-49: 22,628,341 (2010 est.)

Manpower fit for military service:
males age 16-49: 20,149,222
females age 16-49: 19,417,275 (2010 est.)

Manpower reaching militarily significant age annually: *male:* 715,111
female: 677,372 (2010 est.)

TRANSNATIONAL ISSUES

Disputes—international: Iran protests Afghanistan's limiting flow of dammed Helmand River tributaries during drought; Iraq's lack of a maritime boundary with Iran prompts jurisdiction disputes beyond the mouth of the Shatt al Arab in the Persian Gulf; Iran and UAE dispute Tunb Islands and Abu Musa Island, which are occupied by Iran; Azerbaijan, Kazakhstan, and Russia ratified Caspian seabed delimitation treaties based on equidistance, while Iran continues to insist on a one-fifth slice of the sea; Afghan and Iranian commissioners have discussed boundary monument densification and resurvey

Refugees and internally displaced persons: *refugees (country of origin):* 42,500 (Iraq) (2013); 2.4 million (1 million registered, 1.4 million undocumented) (Afghanistan) (2014)

Trafficking in persons: *current situation:* Iran is a presumed source, transit, and destination country for men, women, and children subjected to sex trafficking and forced labor; Iranian and Afghan boys and girls are forced into prostitution domestically; Iranian women are subjected to sex trafficking in Iran, Pakistan, the Persian Gulf, and Europe; Azerbaijani women and children are also sexually exploited in Iran; Afghan migrants and refugees and Pakistani men and women are subjected to conditions of forced labor in Iran; NGO reports indicate that criminal organizations play a significant role in human trafficking in Iran

tier rating: Tier 3—Iran does not comply with the minimum standards for the elimination of trafficking, and is not making significant efforts to do so; the government does not share information on its anti-trafficking efforts, making it difficult to assess the country's human trafficking problem or the government's attempts to curb it; NGOs report that laws against human trafficking, forced labor, and debt bondage remain unenforced because of a lack of political will and widespread political corruption; there is no evidence that the government has a process to identify trafficking victims, refers victims to protective services, or has made efforts to prevent human trafficking (2013)

Illicit drugs: despite substantial interdiction efforts and considerable control measures along the border with Afghanistan, Iran remains one of the primary transshipment routes for Southwest Asian heroin to Europe; suffers one of the highest opiate addiction rates in the world, and has an increasing problem with synthetic drugs; lacks anti-money laundering laws; has reached out to neighboring countries to share counter-drug intelligence

IRAQ

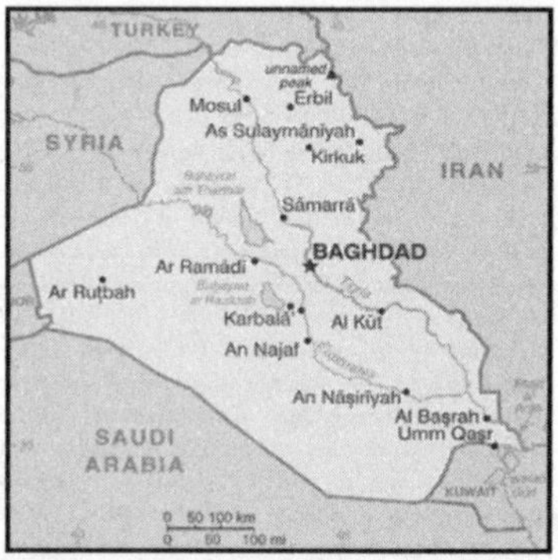

INTRODUCTION

Background: Formerly part of the Ottoman Empire, Iraq was occupied by Britain during the course of World War I; in 1920, it was declared a League of Nations mandate under UK administration. In stages over the next dozen years, Iraq attained its independence as a kingdom in 1932. A "republic" was proclaimed in 1958, but in actuality a series of strongmen ruled the country until 2003. The last was SADDAM Husayn. Territorial disputes with Iran led to an inconclusive and costly eight-year war (1980-88). In August 1990, Iraq seized Kuwait but was expelled by US-led, UN coalition forces during the Gulf War of January-February 1991. Following Kuwait's liberation, the UN Security Council (UNSC) required Iraq to scrap all weapons of mass destruction and long-range missiles and to allow UN verification inspections. Continued Iraqi noncompliance with UNSC resolutions over a period of 12 years led to the US-led invasion of Iraq in March 2003 and the ouster of the SADDAM Husayn regime. US forces remained in Iraq under a UNSC mandate through 2009 and under a bilateral security agreement thereafter, helping to provide security and to train and mentor Iraqi security forces. In October 2005, Iraqis approved a constitution in a national referendum and, pursuant to this document, elected a 275-member Council of Representatives (COR) in December 2005. The COR approved most cabinet ministers in May 2006, marking the transition to Iraq's first constitutional government in nearly a half century. In January 2009, Iraq held elections for provincial councils in all governorates except for the three governorates comprising the Kurdistan Regional Government and Kirkuk Governorate. Iraq held a national legislative election in March 2010—choosing 325 legislators in an expanded COR—and, after nine months of deadlock the COR approved the new government in December 2010. Nearly nine years after the start of the Second Gulf War in Iraq, US military operations there ended in mid-December 2011.

GEOGRAPHY

Location: Middle East, bordering the Persian Gulf, between Iran and Kuwait

Geographic coordinates: 33 00 N, 44 00 E

Map references: Middle East

Area: *total:* 438,317 sq km
country comparison to the world: 59
land: 437,367 sq km
water: 950 sq km

Area—comparative: slightly more than twice the size of Idaho

Land boundaries: *total:* 3,650 km
border countries: Iran 1,458 km, Jordan 181 km, Kuwait 240 km, Saudi Arabia 814 km, Syria 605 km, Turkey 352 km

Coastline: 58 km

Maritime claims: *territorial sea:* 12 nm
continental shelf: not specified

Climate: mostly desert; mild to cool winters with dry, hot, cloudless summers; northern mountainous regions along Iranian and Turkish borders experience cold winters with occasionally heavy snows that melt in early spring, sometimes causing extensive flooding in central and southern Iraq

Terrain: mostly broad plains; reedy marshes along Iranian border in south with large flooded areas; mountains along borders with Iran and Turkey

Elevation extremes: *lowest point:* Persian Gulf 0 m
highest point: unnamed peak; 3,611 m; note—this peak is neither Gundah Zhur 3,607 m nor Kuh-e Hajji-Ebrahim 3,595 m

Natural resources: petroleum, natural gas, phosphates, sulfur

Land use: *arable land:* 9.19%
permanent crops: 0.48%
other: 90.33% (2011)

Irrigated land: 35,250 sq km (2003)

Total renewable water resources: 89.86 cu km (2011)

Freshwater withdrawal (domestic/industrial/agricultural): *total:* 66 cu km/yr (7%/15%/79%)
per capita: 2,616 cu m/yr (2000)

Natural hazards: dust storms; sandstorms; floods

Environment—current issues: government water control projects have drained most of the inhabited marsh areas east of An Nasiriyah by drying up or diverting the feeder streams and rivers; a once sizable population of Marsh Arabs, who inhabited these areas for thousands of years, has been displaced; furthermore, the destruction of the natural habitat poses serious threats to the area's wildlife populations; inadequate supplies of potable water; development of the Tigris and Euphrates rivers system contingent upon agreements with upstream riparian Turkey; air and water pollution; soil degradation (salination) and erosion; desertification

Environment—international agreements:
party to: Biodiversity, Law of the Sea, Ozone Layer Protection
signed, but not ratified: Environmental Modification

Geography—note: strategic location on Shatt al Arab waterway and at the head of the Persian Gulf

PEOPLE AND SOCIETY

Nationality: *noun:* Iraqi(s)
adjective: Iraqi

Ethnic groups: Arab 75%-80%, Kurdish 15%-20%, Turkoman, Assyrian, or other 5%

Languages: Arabic (official), Kurdish (official), Turkmen (a Turkish dialect) and Assyrian (Neo-Aramaic) are official in areas where they constitute a majority of the population), Armenian

Religions: Muslim (official) 97% (Shia 60%-65%, Sunni 32%-37%), Christian or other 3%
note: while there has been voluntary relocation of many Christian families to northern Iraq, recent reporting indicates that the overall Christian population may have dropped by as much as 50 percent since the fall of the Saddam HUSSEIN regime in 2003, with many fleeing to Syria, Jordan, and Lebanon

Population: 31,858,481 (July 2013 est.)
country comparison to the world: 40

Age structure:
0-14 years: 37.2% (male 6,029,869/female 5,818,752)
15-24 years: 19.6% (male 3,175,754/female 3,082,880)
25-54 years: 35.8% (male 5,823,608/female 5,585,217)
55-64 years: 4.2% (male 637,889/female 698,691)
65 years and over: 3.2% (male 467,858/female 537,963) (2013 est.)

Dependency ratios:
total dependency ratio: 76.2 %
youth dependency ratio: 70.6 %
elderly dependency ratio: 5.6 %
potential support ratio: 17.8 (2013)

Median age: total: 21.3 years
male: 21.2 years
female: 21.4 years (2013 est.)

Population growth rate: 2.29% (2013 est.)
country comparison to the world: 39

Birth rate: 27.51 births/1,000 population (2013 est.)
country comparison to the world: 46

Death rate: 4.65 deaths/1,000 population (2013 est.)
country comparison to the world: 198

Net migration rate: 0 migrant(s)/1,000 population (2013 est.)
country comparison to the world: 90

Urbanization: *urban population:* 66.5% of total population (2011)
rate of urbanization: 3.05% annual rate of change (2010-15 est.)

Major urban areas—population: BAGHDAD (capital) 5.751 million; Mosul 1.447 million; Erbil 1.009 million; Basra 923,000; As Sulaymaniyah 836,000 (2009)

Sex ratio: *at birth:* 1.05 male(s)/female
0-14 years: 1.04 male(s)/female
15-24 years: 1.03 male(s)/female
25-54 years: 1.04 male(s)/female
55-64 years: 0.91 male(s)/female
65 years and over: 0.87 male(s)/female
total population: 1.03 male(s)/female (2013 est.)

Maternal mortality rate: 63 deaths/100,000 live births (2010)
country comparison to the world: 99

Infant mortality rate: total: 38.86 deaths/1,000 live births
country comparison to the world: 62
male: 42.98 deaths/1,000 live births
female: 34.55 deaths/1,000 live births (2013 est.)

Life expectancy at birth: *total population:* 71.14 years
country comparison to the world: 147
male: 69.67 years
female: 72.67 years (2013 est.)

Total fertility rate: 3.5 children born/woman (2013 est.)
country comparison to the world: 46

Contraceptive prevalence rate: 51.2% (2011)

Health expenditures: 8.4% of GDP (2010)
country comparison to the world: 53

Physicians density: 0.69 physicians/1,000 population (2009)

Hospital bed density: 1.3 beds/1,000 population (2010)

Drinking water source:
improved:
urban: 91% of population
rural: 56% of population
total: 79% of population
unimproved:
urban: 9% of population
rural: 44% of population
total: 21% of population (2010 est.)

Sanitation facility access:
improved:
urban: 76% of population
rural: 67% of population
total: 73% of population
unimproved:
urban: 24% of population
rural: 33% of population
total: 27% of population (2010 est.)

HIV/AIDS—adult prevalence rate:
less than 0.1% (2001 est.)
country comparison to the world: 159

HIV/AIDS—people living with HIV/AIDS:
fewer than 500 (2003 est.)
country comparison to the world: 151

HIV/AIDS—deaths: NA

Major infectious diseases: *degree of risk:* intermediate
food or waterborne diseases: bacterial diarrhea, hepatitis A, and typhoid fever
note: highly pathogenic H5N1 avian influenza has been identified in this country; it poses a negligible risk with extremely rare cases possible among US citizens who have close contact with birds (2013)

Obesity—adult prevalence rate: 27% (2008)
country comparison to the world: 42

Children under the age of 5 years underweight:
7.1% (2006)
country comparison to the world: 75

Education expenditures: NA

Literacy: *definition:* age 15 and over can read and write
total population: 78.5%
male: 86%
female: 71.2% (2011 est.)

School life expectancy (primary to tertiary education): *total:* 10 years
male: 11 years
female: 9 years (2004)

Child labor—children ages 5-14: *total number:* 715,737
percentage: 11 % (2006 est.)

GOVERNMENT

Country name: *conventional long form:* Republic of Iraq
conventional short form: Iraq
local long form: Jumhuriyat al-Iraq/Komar-i Eraq
local short form: Al Iraq/Eraq

Government type: parliamentary democracy

Capital: *name:* Baghdad
geographic coordinates: 33 20 N, 44 24 E
time difference: UTC+3 (8 hours ahead of Washington, DC during Standard Time)

Administrative divisions: 18 governorates (muhafazat, singular—muhafazah (Arabic); parezgakan, singular—parezga (Kurdish)) and 1 region*; Al Anbar; Al Basrah; Al Muthanna; Al Qadisiyah (Ad Diwaniyah); An Najaf; Arbil (Erbil) (Arabic), Hewler (Kurdish); As Sulaymaniyah (Arabic), Slemani (Kurdish); Babil; Baghdad; Dahuk (Arabic), Dihok (Kurdish); Dhi Qar; Diyala; Karbala'; Kirkuk; Kurdistan Regional Government*; Maysan; Ninawa; Salah ad Din; Wasit

Independence: 3 October 1932 (from League of Nations mandate under British administration); note—on 28 June 2004 the Coalition Provisional Authority transferred sovereignty to the Iraqi Interim Government

National holiday: Republic Day, July 14 (1958); note—the Government of Iraq has yet to declare an official national holiday but still observes Republic Day

Constitution: ratified 15 October 2005 (subject to review by the Constitutional Review Committee and a possible public referendum)

Legal system: mixed legal system of civil and Islamic law

International law organization participation:
has not submitted an ICJ jurisdiction declaration; non-party state to the ICCt

Suffrage: 18 years of age; universal

Executive branch: *chief of state:* President Jalal TALABANI (since 6 April 2005)
head of government: Prime Minister Nuri al-MALIKI (since 20 May 2006)
cabinet: The Council of Ministers consists of the prime minister and cabinet ministers the prime minister proposes; approved by an absolute majority vote by the Council of Representatives (For more information visit the World Leaders website)
elections: president elected by Council of Representatives (parliament) to serve a four-year term (eligible for a second term); presidential election in parliament last held on 11 November 2010 (next to be held in 2014)
election results: President Jalal TALABANI reelected on 11 November 2010; Council of Representatives vote count on second ballot—195 votes; Nuri al-MALIKI reelected prime minister

Legislative branch: unicameral Council of Representatives (325 seats consisting of 317 members elected by an optional open-list and representing a specific governorate, proportional representation system and 8 seats reserved for minorities; members serve four-year terms); note—Iraq's Constitution calls for the establishment of an upper house, the Federation Council
elections: last held on 7 March 2010 for an enlarged 325-seat parliament (next to be held in 2014)
election results: Council of Representatives—percent of vote by coalition—Iraqi National Movement 25.9%, State of Law coalition 25.8%, Iraqi National Alliance 19.4%, Kurdistan Alliance 15.3%, Goran (Change) List 4.4%, Tawafuq Front 2.7%, Iraqi Unity Alliance 2.9%, Kurdistan Islamic Union 2.3%, Kurdistan Islamic Group 1.4%; seats by coalition—NA

Judicial branch: *highest court(s):* Federal Supreme Court or FSC (consists of 9 judges); note—court jurisdiction limited to constitutional issues); Court of Cassation (consists of a court president, 5 vice-presidents, and at least 24 judges)
judge selection and term of office: Federal Supreme Court and Court of Cassation judges appointed by the Higher Juridical Council, a 26-member independent committee of judicial officials; FSC members appointed for life ; Court of Cassation judges appointed for 1-year probationary period and upon satisfactory performance may be confirmed for permanent tenure until retirement at age 63
subordinate courts: Courts of Appeal (governorate level); courts of first instance; personal status, labor, criminal, juvenile, and religious courts

Political parties and leaders: Badr Organization [Hadi al-AMIRI]; Da'wa Party (Islamic) [Prime Minister Nuri al-MALIKI]; Da'wa Tanzim [Hashim al-MUSAWI branch]; Da-wa Tanzim [Abd al-Karim al-ANZI branch]; Fadilah Party [Hasan al-SHAMMARI and Ammar TUAMA]; Goran (Change) List (also known as the Movement for Change) [Nushirwan MUSTAFA]; Iraqi Covenant Gathering [Ahmad Abd al-Ghafur al-SAMARRAI]; Iraqi Constitutional Party [Jawad al-BULANI]; Iraqi Front for National Dialogue [Deputy Prime Minister Salih al-MUTLAQ]; Iraqi Islamic Party or IIP [Usama al-TIKRITI]; Iraqi Justice and Reform Movement [Shaykh Abdallah al-YAWR]; Iraqi National Accord or INA [Ayad ALLAWI]; Iraqi National Alliance [Ibrahim al-JAFARI]; Iraqi National Congress or INC [Ahmad CHALABI]; Iraqi National Movement (see Iraqi National Accord); Iraqi Unity Alliance [Nauaf Saud ZAID]; Islamic Supreme Council of Iraq or ISCI [Ammar al-HAKIM]; Kurdistan Alliance; Kurdistan Democratic Party or KDP [Kurdistan Regional Government President Masud BARZANI]; Kurdistan Islamic Group (also called Islamic Group of Kurdistan) [Ali BAPIR]; Kurdistan Islamic Union [Mohammed FARAI]; Future National Gathering [Finance Minister Rafi al-ISSAWI]; National Iraqiyun Gathering [Usama al-NUJAYFI]; National Movement for Reform and Development [Jamal al-KARBULI]; National Reform Trend (part of the National Iraqi Alliance) [former Prime Minister Ibrahim; al-JAFARI]; Patriotic Union of Kurdistan or PUK [President Jalal TALABANI]; Renewal List [Vice President Tariq al-HASHIMI]; Sadrist Trend [Muqtada al-SADR]; Sahawa al-Iraq [Ahmad al-RISHAWI]; State of Law Coalition [Nouri al-MALIKI]; Tawafuq Front (also known as the Iraqi Accord Front)
note: numerous smaller local, tribal, and minority parties

Political pressure groups and leaders: Sunni militias; Shia militias, some associated with political parties

International organization participation: ABEDA, AFESD, AMF, CAEU, CICA, EITI (candidate country), FAO, G-77, IAEA, IBRD, ICAO, ICRM, IDA, IDB, IFAD, IFC, IFRCS, ILO, IMF, IMO, IMSO, Interpol, IOC, IPU, ISO, ITSO, ITU, LAS, MIGA, NAM, OAPEC, OIC, OPCW, OPEC, PCA, UN, UNCTAD, UNESCO, UNIDO, UNWTO, UPU, WCO, WFTU (NGOs), WHO, WIPO, WMO, WTO (observer)

Diplomatic representation in the US:
chief of mission: Ambassador Luqman Abd al-Rahim FAYLI
chancery: 3421 Massachusetts Ave, NW, Washington, DC 20007
telephone: [1] (202) 742-1600
FAX: [1] (202) 333-1129
consulate(s) general: Chicago, Houston, Los Angeles, New York, San Francisco

Diplomatic representation from the US:
chief of mission: Ambassador Robert Stephen BEECROFT
embassy: Al-Kindi Street, International Zone, Baghdad
mailing address: APO AE 09316
telephone: 0760-030-3000
FAX: NA

Flag description: three equal horizontal bands of red (top), white, and black; the Takbir (Arabic expression meaning "God is great") in green Arabic script is centered in the white band; the band colors derive from the Arab Liberation flag and represent oppression (black), overcome through bloody struggle (red), to be replaced by a bright future (white); the Council of Representatives approved this flag in 2008 as a compromise temporary replacement for the Ba'athist Saddam-era flag
note: similar to the flag of Syria, which has two stars but no script, Yemen, which has a plain white band, and that of Egypt, which has a gold Eagle of Saladin centered in the white band

National symbol(s): golden eagle

National anthem: *name:* "Mawtini" (My Homeland)
lyrics/music: Ibrahim TOUQAN/Mohammad FLAYFEL
note: adopted 2004; following the ousting of Saddam HUSSEIN, Iraq adopted "Mawtini," a popular folk song throughout the Arab world, which also serves as an unofficial anthem of the Palestinian people

ECONOMY

Economy—overview: An improving security environment and foreign investment are helping to spur economic activity, particularly in the energy, construction, and retail sectors. Broader economic development, long-term fiscal health, and sustained improvements in the overall standard of living still depend on the central government passing major policy reforms. Iraq's largely state-run economy is dominated by the oil sector, which provides more than 90% of government revenue and 80% of foreign exchange earnings. Iraq in 2012 boosted oil exports to a 30-year high of 2.6 million barrels per day, a significant increase from Iraq's average of 2.2 million in 2011. Government revenues increased as global oil prices remained persistently high for much of 2012. Iraq's contracts with major oil companies have the potential to further expand oil exports and revenues, but Iraq will need to make significant upgrades to its oil processing, pipeline, and export infrastructure to enable these deals to reach their economic potential. The Iraqi Kurdistan Region's (IKR) autonomous Kurdistan Regional Government (KRG) passed its own oil law in 2007, and has directly signed about 50 contracts to develop IKR energy reserves. The federal government has disputed the legal authority of the KRG to conclude most of these contracts, some of which are also in areas with unresolved administrative boundaries in dispute between the federal and regional government. Iraq is making slow progress enacting laws and developing the institutions needed to implement economic policy, and political reforms are still needed to assuage investors' concerns regarding the uncertain business climate, which may have been harmed by the November 2012 standoff between Baghdad and Erbil and the removal of the Central Bank Governor in October 2012. The government of Iraq is eager to attract additional foreign direct investment, but it faces a number of obstacles including a tenuous political system and concerns about security and societal stability. Rampant corruption, outdated infrastructure, insufficient essential services, skilled labor shortages, and antiquated commercial laws stifle investment and continue to constrain growth of private, nonoil sectors. Iraq is considering a package of laws to establish a modern legal framework for the oil sector and a mechanism to equitably divide oil revenues within the nation, although these reforms are still under contentious and sporadic negotiation. Under the Iraqi Constitution, some competencies relevant to the overall investment climate are either shared by the federal government and the regions or are devolved entirely to the regions. Investment in the IKR operates within the framework of the Kurdistan Region Investment Law (Law 4 of 2006) and the Kurdistan Board of Investment, which is designed to provide incentives to help economic development in areas under the authority of the KRG. Inflation has remained under control since 2006 as security improved. However, Iraqi leaders remain hard pressed to translate macroeconomic gains into an improved standard of living for the Iraqi populace. Unemployment remains a problem throughout the country despite a bloated public sector. Encouraging private enterprise through deregulation would make it easier for Iraqi citizens and foreign investors to start new businesses. Rooting out corruption and implementing reforms—such as restructuring banks and developing the private sector—would be important steps in this direction.

GDP (purchasing power parity): $242.5 billion (2012 est.)
country comparison to the world: 53
$223.7 billion (2011 est.)
$206 billion (2010 est.)
note: data are in 2012 US dollars

GDP (official exchange rate): $212.5 billion (2012 est.)

GDP—real growth rate: 8.4% (2012 est.)
country comparison to the world: 14
8.6% (2011 est.)
5.9% (2010 est.)

GDP—per capita (PPP): $7,200 (2012 est.)
country comparison to the world: 141
$6,800 (2011 est.)
$6,500 (2010 est.)
note: data are in 2012 US dollars

GDP—composition, by sector of origin:
agriculture: 3.4%
industry: 64.9%
services: 31.7% (2012 est.)

Agriculture—products: wheat, barley, rice, vegetables, dates, cotton; cattle, sheep, poultry

Industries: petroleum, chemicals, textiles, leather, construction materials, food processing, fertilizer, metal fabrication/processing

Industrial production growth rate: 11.3% (2012 est.)
country comparison to the world: 7

Labor force: 8.9 million (2010 est.)
country comparison to the world: 53

Labor force—by occupation: agriculture: 21.6%
industry: 18.7%
services: 59.8% (2008 est.)

Unemployment rate: 16% (2012 est.)
country comparison to the world: 150
15% (2010 est.)

Population below poverty line: 25% (2008 est.)

Household income or consumption by percentage share: *lowest 10%:* 3.6%
highest 10%: 25.7% (2007 est.)

Budget: *revenues:* $103.4 billion
expenditures: $88.34 billion (2012 est.)

Taxes and other revenues: 48.7% of GDP (2012 est.)
country comparison to the world: 15

Budget surplus (+) or deficit (-):
7.1% of GDP (2012 est.)
country comparison to the world: 9

Fiscal year: calendar year
Inflation rate (consumer prices):
6.1% (2012 est.)
country comparison to the world: 164
5.6% (2011 est.)

Central bank discount rate: 6% (December 2012)
country comparison to the world: 59
6% (December 2011)

Commercial bank prime lending rate:
6% (31 December 2012 est.)
country comparison to the world: 142
6% (31 December 2011 est.)

Stock of narrow money: $54.68 billion (31 December 2012 est.)
country comparison to the world: 45
$53.4 billion (31 December 2011 est.)

Stock of broad money: $71.48 billion (31 December 2012 est.)
country comparison to the world: 61
$61.81 billion (31 December 2011 est.)

Stock of domestic credit: $1.779 billion (31 December 2011 est.)
country comparison to the world: 139
$1.727 billion (31 December 2010 est.)

Market value of publicly traded shares:
$4 billion (9 December 2011)
country comparison to the world: 93
$2.6 billion (31 July 2010)
$2 billion (31 July 2009 est.)

Current account balance: $20.63 billion (2012 est.)
country comparison to the world: 17
$21.68 billion (2011 est.)

Exports: $93.91 billion (2012 est.)
country comparison to the world: 41
$79.68 billion (2011 est.)

Exports—commodities: crude oil 84%, crude materials excluding fuels, food and live animals

Exports—partners: US 21.4%, India 21.1%, China 13.8%, South Korea 11.2%, Canada 4.8%, Italy 4.5%, Spain 4.3% (2012)

Imports: $56.89 billion (2012 est.)
country comparison to the world: 51
$40.63 billion (2011 est.)

Imports—commodities: food, medicine, manufactures

Imports—partners: Turkey 27.8%, Syria 15.9%, China 12.6%, US 5.2%, South Korea 4.8% (2012)

Reserves of foreign exchange and gold:
$70.33 billion (31 December 2012 est.)
country comparison to the world: 29
$61.04 billion (31 December 2011 est.)

Debt—external: $50.26 billion (31 December 2012 est.)
country comparison to the world: 63
$50.79 billion (31 December 2011 est.)

Exchange rates: Iraqi dinars (IQD) per US dollar—
1,166 (2012 est.)
1,170 (2011 est.)
1,170 (2010 est.)
1,170 (2009)
1,176 (2008)

ENERGY

Electricity—production: 47.4 billion kWh (2010 est.)
country comparison to the world: 5 2

Electricity—consumption: 35.12 billion kWh (2010 est.)
country comparison to the world: 56

Electricity—exports: 0 kWh (2012 est.)
country comparison to the world: 209

Electricity—imports: 12.28 billion kWh (2012 est.)
country comparison to the world: 15

Electricity—installed generating capacity:
10.11 million kW (2012 est.)
country comparison to the world: 55

Electricity—from fossil fuels: 69% of total installed capacity (2012 est.)
country comparison to the world: 110

Electricity—from nuclear fuels:
0% of total installed capacity (2012 est.)
country comparison to the world: 113

Electricity—from hydroelectric plants:
31% of total installed capacity (2012 est.)
country comparison to the world: 73

Electricity—from other renewable sources:
0% of total installed capacity (2012 est.)
country comparison to the world: 140

Crude oil—production: 2.9 million bbl/day (2012 est.)
country comparison to the world: 9

Crude oil—exports: 2.6 million bbl/day (2012 est.)
country comparison to the world: 3

Crude oil—imports: 0 bbl/day (2012 est.)
country comparison to the world: 201

Crude oil—proved reserves: 143.1 billion bbl (1 January 2012 est.)
country comparison to the world: 5

Refined petroleum products—production:
410,500 bbl/day (2008 est.)
country comparison to the world: 37

Refined petroleum products—consumption:
818,000 bbl/day (2011 est.)
country comparison to the world: 22

Refined petroleum products—exports:
0 bbl/day (2008 est.)
country comparison to the world: 186

Refined petroleum products—imports:
144,100 bbl/day (2008 est.)
country comparison to the world: 39

Natural gas—production: 1.303 billion cu m (2010 est.)
country comparison to the world: 62

Natural gas—consumption: 1.3 billion cu m (2010 est.)
country comparison to the world: 84

Natural gas—exports: 0 cu m (2010 est.)
country comparison to the world: 120

Natural gas—imports: 0 cu m (2010 est.)
country comparison to the world: 209

Natural gas—proved reserves: 3.171 trillion cu m (1 January 2012 est.)
country comparison to the world: 13

Carbon dioxide emissions from consumption of energy: 118.3 million Mt (2010 est.)
country comparison to the world: 35

COMMUNICATIONS

Telephones—main lines in use: 1.794 million (2011)
country comparison to the world: 6 2

Telephones—mobile cellular: 27 million (2012)
country comparison to the world: 38

Telephone system: *general assessment:* the 2003 liberation of Iraq severely disrupted telecommunications throughout Iraq including international connections; widespread government efforts to rebuild domestic and international communications through fiber optic links are in progress; the mobile cellular market has expanded rapidly to some 27 million subscribers by the end of 2012
domestic: repairs to switches and lines destroyed during 2003 continue; additional switching capacity is improving access; 3 GSM operators since 2007 have expanded beyond their regional roots and offer near country-wide access to second-generation services; third-generation mobile services are not available nationwide; wireless local loop is available in some metropolitan areas and additional licenses have been issued with the hope of overcoming the lack of fixed-line infrastructure
international: country code—964; satellite earth stations—4 (2 Intelsat—1 Atlantic Ocean and 1 Indian Ocean, 1 Intersputnik—Atlantic Ocean region, and 1 Arabsat (inoperative)); local microwave radio relay connects border regions to Jordan, Kuwait, Syria, and Turkey; international terrestrial fiber-optic connections have been established with Saudi Arabia, Turkey, Kuwait, Jordan, and Iran; links to the Fiber-Optic Link Around the Globe (FLAG) and the Gulf Bridge International (GBI) submarine fiber-optic cables have been established (2011)

Broadcast media: the number of private radio and TV stations has increased rapidly since 2003; government-owned TV and radio stations are operated by the publicly funded Iraqi Public Broadcasting Service; private broadcast media are mostly linked to political, ethnic, or religious groups; satellite TV is available to an estimated 70% of viewers and many of the broadcasters are based abroad; transmissions of multiple international radio broadcasters are accessible (2007)

Internet country code: .iq

Internet hosts: 26 (2012)
country comparison to the world: 218

Internet users: 325,900 (2009)
country comparison to the world: 126

TRANSPORTATION

Airports: 102 (2013)
country comparison to the world: 5 5

Airports—with paved runways: *total:* 7 2
over 3,047 m: 20
2,438 to 3,047 m: 34
1,524 to 2,437 m: 4
914 to 1,523 m: 7
under 914 m: 7 (2013)

Airports—with unpaved runways: *total:* 3 0
over 3,047 m: 3
2,438 to 3,047 m: 5
1,524 to 2,437 m: 3
914 to 1,523 m: 13
under 914 m: 6 (2013)

Heliports: 16 (2013)

Pipelines: gas 2,455 km; liquid petroleum gas 913 km; oil 5,432 km; refined products 1,637 km (2013)

Railways: *total:* 2,370 km
country comparison to the world: 66
standard gauge: 2,370 km 1.435-m gauge (2012)

Roadways: *total:* 59,623 km
country comparison to the world: 73
paved: 59,623 km (includes Kurdistan Region) (2012)

Waterways: 5,279 km (the Euphrates River (2,815 km), Tigris River (1,899 km), and Third River (565 km) are the principal waterways) (2012)
country comparison to the world: 23

Merchant marine: *total:* 2
country comparison to the world: 142
by type: petroleum tanker 2
registered in other countries: 2 (Marshall Islands 2) (2010)

Ports and terminals: Al Basrah, Khawr az Zubayr, Umm Qasr

MILITARY

Military branches: Counterterrorism Service Forces: Counterterrorism Command; Iraqi Special Operations Forces (ISOF); Ministry of Defense Forces: Iraqi Army (includes Army Aviation Directorate, former National Guard Iraqi Intervention Forces, and Strategic Infrastructure Battalions), Iraqi Navy (former Iraqi Coastal Defense Force, includes Iraq Marine Force), Iraqi Air Force (Al-Quwwat al-Jawwiya al-Iraqiya) (2011)

Military service age and obligation: 18-40 years of age for voluntary military service; no conscription (2013)

Manpower available for military service:
males age 16-49: 7,767,329
females age 16-49: 7,461,766 (2010 est.)

Manpower fit for military service:
males age 16-49: 6,591,185
females age 16-49: 6,421,717 (2010 est.)

Manpower reaching militarily significant age annually: *male:* 332,194
female: 322,010 (2010 est.)

Military expenditures: 8.6% of GDP (2006)
country comparison to the world: 6

TRANSNATIONAL ISSUES

Disputes—international: approximately two million Iraqis have fled the conflict in Iraq, with the majority taking refuge in Syria and Jordan, and lesser numbers to Egypt, Lebanon, Iran, and Turkey; Iraq's lack of a maritime boundary with Iran prompts jurisdiction disputes beyond the mouth of the Shatt al Arab in the Persian Gulf; Turkey has expressed concern over the autonomous status of Kurds in Iraq

Refugees and internally displaced persons: *refugees (country of origin):* 15,496 (Turkey); 11,467 (West Bank and Gaza Strip); 8,259 (Iran) (2012); 183,195 (Syria) (2013)
IDPs: 1.1 million (since 2006 from ethno-sectarian violence) (2013)
stateless persons: 120,000 (2012); note—in the 1970s and 1980s under Saddam Hussein's administration, thousands of Iraq's Faili Kurds, followers of Shia Islam, were stripped of their Iraqi citizenship, had their property seized by the government, and many were deported; some Faili Kurds had their citizenship reinstated under the 2006 Iraqi Nationality Law, but others lack the documentation to prove their Iraqi origins; some Palestinian refugees, who were also persecuted under the Saddam Hussein regime, still remain stateless in Iraq

IRELAND

INTRODUCTION

Background: Celtic tribes arrived on the island between 600 and 150 B.C. Invasions by Norsemen that began in the late 8th century were finally ended when King Brian BORU defeated the Danes in 1014. English invasions began in the 12th century and set off more than seven centuries of Anglo-Irish struggle marked by fierce rebellions and harsh repressions. A failed 1916 Easter Monday Rebellion touched off several years of guerrilla warfare that in 1921 resulted in independence from the UK for 26 southern counties; six northern (Ulster) counties remained part of the UK. In 1949, Ireland withdrew from the British Commonwealth; it joined the European Community in 1973. Irish governments have sought the peaceful unification of Ireland and have cooperated with Britain against terrorist groups. A peace settlement for Northern Ireland is gradually being implemented despite some difficulties. In 2006, the Irish and British governments developed and began to implement the St. Andrews Agreement, building on the Good Friday Agreement approved in 1998. In 2010, the most recent phase of the peace process was implemented with the Hillsborough Castle Agreement, which paved the way for the devolution of justice and policing powers to the province.

GEOGRAPHY

Location: Western Europe, occupying five-sixths of the island of Ireland in the North Atlantic Ocean, west of Great Britain

Geographic coordinates: 53 00 N, 8 00 W

Map references: Europe

Area: *total:* 70,273 sq km
country comparison to the world: 120
land: 68,883 sq km
water: 1,390 sq km

Area—comparative: slightly larger than West Virginia

Land boundaries: *total:* 360 km
border countries: UK 360 km

Coastline: 1,448 km

Maritime claims: territorial sea: 12 nm
exclusive fishing zone: 200 nm

Climate: temperate maritime; modified by North Atlantic Current; mild winters, cool summers; consistently humid; overcast about half the time

Terrain: mostly level to rolling interior plain surrounded by rugged hills and low mountains; sea cliffs on west coast

Elevation extremes: *lowest point:* Atlantic Ocean 0 m
highest point: Carrauntoohil 1,041 m

Natural resources: natural gas, peat, copper, lead, zinc, silver, barite, gypsum, limestone, dolomite

Land use: *arable land:* 15.11%
permanent crops: 0.01%
other: 84.87% (2011)

Irrigated land: 11 sq km (2003)

Total renewable water resources: 52 cu km (2011)

Freshwater withdrawal (domestic/industrial/agricultural): *total:* 0.79 cu km/yr (94%/6%/0%)
per capita: 226.9 cu m/yr (2007)

Natural hazards: NA

Environment—current issues: water pollution, especially of lakes, from agricultural runoff

Environment—international agreements: *party to:* Air Pollution, Air Pollution-Nitrogen Oxides, Air Pollution-Sulfur 94, Biodiversity, Climate Change, Climate Change-Kyoto Protocol, Desertification, Endangered Species, Environmental Modification, Hazardous Wastes, Law of the Sea, Marine Dumping, Ozone Layer Protection, Ship Pollution, Tropical Timber 83, Tropical Timber 94, Wetlands, Whaling
signed, but not ratified: Air Pollution-Persistent Organic Pollutants, Marine Life Conservation

Geography—note: strategic location on major air and sea routes between North America and northern Europe; over 40% of the population resides within 100 km of Dublin

PEOPLE AND SOCIETY

Nationality: *noun:* Irishman(men), Irishwoman (women), Irish (collective plural)
adjective: Irish

Ethnic groups: Irish 84.5%, other white 9.8%, Asian 1.9%, black 1.4%, mixed and other 0.9%, unspecified 1.6% (2011 est.)

Languages: English (official, the language generally used), Irish (Gaelic or Gaeilge) (official, spoken mainly in areas along the western coast)

Religions: Roman Catholic 84.7%, Church of Ireland 2.7%, other Christian 2.7%, Muslim 1.1%, other 1.7%, unspecified 1.5%, none 5.7% (2011 est.)

Population: 4,832,765 (July 2014 est.)
country comparison to the world: 123

Age structure:
0-14 years: 21.4% (male 529,140/female 506,857)
15-24 years: 11.9% (male 292,962/female 283,127)
25-54 years: 44.1% (male 1,070,875/female 1,061,396)
55-64 years: 12.4% (male 245,913/female 244,345)
65 years and over: 12.1% (male 275,114/female 323,036) (2014 est.)

Dependency ratios:
total dependency ratio: 50.8 %
youth dependency ratio: 32.6 %
elderly dependency ratio: 18.2 %
potential support ratio: 5.5 (2013)

Median age: *total:* 35.7 years
male: 35.4 years
female: 36.1 years (2014 est.)

Population growth rate: 1.2% (2014 est.)
country comparison to the world: 99

Birth rate: 15.18 births/1,000 population (2014 est.)
country comparison to the world: 132

Death rate: 6.45 deaths/1,000 population (2014 est.)
country comparison to the world: 155

Net migration rate: 3.31 migrant(s)/1,000 population (2014 est.)
country comparison to the world: 34

Urbanization: *urban population:* 62% of total population (2010)
rate of urbanization: 1.8% annual rate of change (2010-15 est.)

Major urban areas—population: DUBLIN (capital) 1.084 million (2009)

Sex ratio: *at birth:* 1.06 male(s)/female
0-14 years: 1.04 male(s)/female
15-24 years: 1.04 male(s)/female
25-54 years: 1.01 male(s)/female
55-64 years: 1 male(s)/female
65 years and over: 0.84 male(s)/female
total population: 1 male(s)/female (2014 est.)

Mother's mean age at first birth: 29.8 (2011 est.)

Maternal mortality rate: 6 deaths/100,000 live births (2010)

country comparison to the world: 169
Infant mortality rate: total: 3.74 deaths/1,000 live births
country comparison to the world: 202
male: 4.11 deaths/1,000 live births
female: 3.35 deaths/1,000 live births (2014 est.)
Life expectancy at birth: *total population:* 80.56 years
country comparison to the world: 27
male: 78.28 years
female: 82.97 years (2014 est.)
Total fertility rate: 2 children born/woman (2014 est.)
country comparison to the world: 125
Contraceptive prevalence rate: 64.8%
note: percent of women aged 18-49 (2004/05)
Health expenditures: 9.4% of GDP (2011)
country comparison to the world: 35
Physicians density: 3.19 physicians/1,000 population (2008)
Hospital bed density: 3.2 beds/1,000 population (2010)
Drinking water source:
improved:
urban: 100% of population
rural: 99.7% of population
total: 99.9% of population
unimproved:
urban: 0% of population
rural: 0.3% of population
total: 0.1% of population (2011 est.)
Sanitation facility access:
improved:
urban: 99.6% of population
rural: 97.9% of population
total: 99% of population
unimproved:
urban: 0.4% of population
rural: 2.1% of population
total: 1% of population (2011 est.)
HIV/AIDS—adult prevalence rate: 0.2% (2009 est.)
country comparison to the world: 116
HIV/AIDS—people living with HIV/AIDS: 6,900 (2009 est.)
country comparison to the world: 118
HIV/AIDS—deaths: fewer than 100 (2009 est.)
country comparison to the world: 119
Obesity—adult prevalence rate: 25.2% (2008)
country comparison to the world: 57
Education expenditures: 6.4% of GDP (2010)
country comparison to the world: 31
Literacy: *definition:* age 15 and over can read and write
total population: 99%
male: 99%
female: 99% (2003 est.)
School life expectancy (primary to tertiary education): *total:* 19 years
male: 19 years
female: 19 years (2011)
Unemployment, youth ages 15-24: total: 24%
country comparison to the world: 42
male: 36.4%
female: 24% (2012)

GOVERNMENT

Country name: *conventional long form:* none
conventional short form: Ireland
local long form: none
local short form: Eire
Government type: republic, parliamentary democracy
Capital: *name:* Dublin
geographic coordinates: 53 19 N, 6 14 W
time difference: UTC 0 (5 hours ahead of Washington, DC during Standard Time)
daylight saving time: +1hr, begins last Sunday in March; ends last Sunday in October
Administrative divisions: 29 counties and 5 cities*; Carlow, Cavan, Clare, Cork, Cork*, Donegal, Dublin*, Dun Laoghaire-Rathdown, Fingal, Galway, Galway*, Kerry, Kildare, Kilkenny, Laois, Leitrim, Limerick, Limerick*, Longford, Louth, Mayo, Meath, Monaghan, North Tipperary, Offaly, Roscommon, Sligo, South Dublin, South Tipperary, Waterford, Waterford*, Westmeath, Wexford, Wicklow Independence: 6 December 1921 (from the UK by treaty)
National holiday: Saint Patrick's Day, 17 March
Constitution: previous 1922; latest drafted 14 June 1937, adopted by plebiscite 1 July 1937, effective 29 December 1937; amended many times, last in 2012 (2012)
Legal system: common law system based on the English model but substantially modified by customary law; judicial review of legislative acts in Supreme Court
International law organization participation: has not submitted an ICJ jurisdiction declaration; accepts ICCt jurisdiction
Suffrage: 18 years of age; universal
Executive branch: *chief of state:* President Michael D. HIGGINS (since 29 October 2011)
head of government: Taoiseach (Prime Minister) Enda KENNY (since 9 March 2011)
cabinet: Cabinet appointed by the president with previous nomination by the prime minister and approval of the lower house of Parliament (For more information visit the World Leaders website)
elections: president elected by popular vote for a seven-year term (eligible for a second term); election last held on 29 October 2011 (next to be held in October 2018); taoiseach (prime minister) nominated by the House of Representatives (Dail Eireann) and appointed by the president
election results: Michael D. HIGGINS elected president; percent of vote—Michael D. HIGGINS 39.6%, Sean GALLAGHER 28.5%, Martin MCGUINNESS 13.7%, Gay MITCHELL 6.4%, David NORRIS 6.2%, other 5.6%
Legislative branch: bicameral Parliament or Oireachtas consists of the Senate or Seanad Eireann (60 seats; 49 members elected by the universities and from candidates put forward by five vocational panels, 11 are nominated by the prime minister; members serve five-year terms) and the lower house of Parliament or Dail Eireann (166 seats; members elected by popular vote on the basis of proportional representation to serve five-year terms)
elections: Senate—last held in 27 April 2011 (next to be held 2016); House of Representatives—last held on 25 February 2011 (next to be held probably in 2016)
election results: Senate—percent of vote by party—NA; seats by party—Fine Gael 19, Fianna Fail 14, Labor Party 12, Sinn Fein 3, independents 12; House of Representatives—percent of vote by party—Fine Gael 45.8%, Labor Party 22.3%, Fianna Fail 12.0%, Sinn Fein 8.4%, United Left Alliance 3.0%, New Vision 0.6%, independents 7.8%; seats by party—Fine Gael 76, Labor Party 37, Fianna Fail 20, Sinn Fein 14, United Left Alliance 5, New Vision 1, independents 13; note—after November 2009 disbandment of the Progressive Democrats, the two members of the Senate continued as independent DPs note: on 8 November 2008, delegates voted to disband the Progressive Democrats, and in November 2009 it officially stopped operating as a political party
Judicial branch: *highest court(s):* Supreme Court or Court of Final Appeal (consists of the chief justice and 7 judges)
judge selection and term of office: judges nominated by the prime minister and Cabinet and appointed by the president; judges serve till age 70
subordinate courts: High Court, Court of Criminal Appeal; circuit and district courts
Political parties and leaders: Fianna Fail [Micheal MARTIN]; Fine Gael [Enda KENNY]; Green Party [Eamon RYAN]; Labor Party [Eamon GILMORE]; New Vision; Sinn Fein [Gerry ADAMS]; Socialist Party [Collective Leadership]; The Workers' Party [Michael FINNEGAN]; United Left Alliance
Political pressure groups and leaders: Families Acting for Innocent Relatives or FAIR [Brian MCCONNELL] (seek compensation for victims of; violence); Iona Institute [David QUINN] (a conservative Catholic think tank); Irish Anti-War Movement [Richard BOYD BARRETT] (campaigns against wars around the world); Oglaigh na hEireann (terrorist group); Continuity IRA (terrorist group); Republican Action Against Drugs, and other unaffiliated republican paramilitary groups); New Irish Republican Army (terrorist group combining elements of the Real IRA); Keep Ireland Open (environmental group); Midland Railway Action Group or MRAG [Willie ALLEN] (transportation promoters); Peace and Neutrality Alliance [Roger COLE] (campaigns to protect Irish neutrality); Rail Users Ireland (formerly the Platform 11—transportation promoters); 32 Country Sovereignty Movement or 32CSM (supports unifying Northern Ireland with the rest of the island under Irish government sovereignty);
International organization participation: ADB (nonregional member), Australia Group, BIS, CD, CE, EAPC, EBRD, ECB, EIB, EMU, ESA, EU, FAO, FATF, IAEA, IBRD, ICAO, ICC (national committees), ICRM, IDA, IEA, IFAD, IFC, IFRCS, IGAD (partners), IHO, ILO, IMF, IMO, Interpol, IOC, IOM, IPU, ISO, ITSO, ITU, ITUC (NGOs), MIGA, MINURSO, MONUSCO, NEA, NSG, OAS (observer), OECD, OPCW, OSCE, Paris Club, PCA, PFP, UN, UNCTAD, UNESCO, UNHCR, UNIDO, UNIFIL, UNITAR, UNOCI, UNRWA, UNTSO, UPU, WCO, WHO, WIPO, WMO, WTO, ZC
Diplomatic representation in the US:
chief of mission: Ambassador Anne Colette ANDERSON (since 28 August 2013)
chancery: 2234 Massachusetts Avenue NW, Washington, DC 20008
telephone: [1] (202) 462-3939
FAX: [1] (202) 232-5993
consulate(s) general: Atlanta, Boston, Chicago, New York, San Francisco
Diplomatic representation from the US:

chief of mission: Ambassador (vacant); Charge d'Affaires Stuart DWYER (since 5 September 2013)
embassy: 42 Elgin Road, Ballsbridge, Dublin 4
mailing address: use embassy street address
telephone: [353] (1) 668-8777
FAX: [353] (1) 668-9946

Flag description: three equal vertical bands of green (hoist side), white, and orange; officially the flag colors have no meaning, but a common interpretation is that the green represents the Irish nationalist (Gaelic) tradition of Ireland; orange represents the Orange tradition (minority supporters of William of Orange); white symbolizes peace (or a lasting truce) between the green and the orange note: similar to the flag of Cote d'Ivoire, which is shorter and has the colors reversed—orange (hoist side), white, and green; also similar to the flag of Italy, which is shorter and has colors of green (hoist side), white, and red

National symbol(s): harp, shamrock (trefoil)

National anthem: *name:* "Amhran na bhFiann" (The Soldier's Song)
lyrics/music: Peadar KEARNEY [English], Liam O RINN [Irish]/Patrick HEENEY and Peadar KEARNEY
note: adopted 1926; instead of "Amhran na bhFiann," the song "Ireland's Call" is often used in athletic events where citizens of the Republic of Ireland and Northern Ireland compete as a unified team

ECONOMY

Economy—overview: Ireland is a small, modern, trade-dependent economy. Ireland was among the initial group of 12 EU nations that began circulating the euro on 1 January 2002. GDP growth averaged 6% in 1995-2007, but economic activity has dropped sharply since the onset of the world financial crisis. Ireland entered into a recession in 2008 for the first time in more than a decade, with the subsequent collapse of its domestic property market and construction industry. Property prices rose more rapidly in Ireland in the decade up to 2007 than in any other developed economy. Since their 2007 peak, average house prices have fallen 47%. In the wake of the collapse of the construction sector and the downturn in consumer spending and business investment, the export sector, dominated by foreign multinationals, has become an even more important component of Ireland's economy. Agriculture, once the most important sector, is now dwarfed by industry and services. In 2008 the former COWEN government moved to guarantee all bank deposits, recapitalize the banking system, and establish partly-public venture capital funds in response to the country's economic downturn. In 2009, in continued efforts to stabilize the banking sector, the Irish Government established the National Asset Management Agency (NAMA) to acquire problem commercial property and development loans from Irish banks. Faced with sharply reduced revenues and a burgeoning budget deficit, the Irish Government introduced the first in a series of draconian budgets in 2009. In addition to across-the-board cuts in spending, the 2009 budget included wage reductions for all public servants. These measures were not sufficient to stabilize Ireland's public finances. In 2010, the budget deficit reached 32.4% of GDP—the world's largest deficit, as a percentage of GDP—because of additional government support for the country's deeply troubled banking sector. In late 2010, the former COWEN government agreed to a $92 billion loan package from the EU and IMF to help Dublin recapitalize Ireland's fragile banking sector and avoid defaulting on its sovereign debt. Since entering office in March 2011, the new KENNY government has intensified austerity measures to try to meet the deficit targets under Ireland's EU-IMF program. Ireland has grown slowly since 2011, but managed to reduce the budget deficit to 7.2% of GDP in 2013. In late 2013, Ireland formally exited its EU-IMF bailout program, benefiting from its strict adherence to deficit-reduction targets and success in refinancing a large amount of banking-related debt.

GDP (purchasing power parity): $190.4 billion (2013 est.)
country comparison to the world: 59
$189.3 billion (2012 est.)
$189 billion (2011 est.)
note: data are in 2013 US dollars

GDP (official exchange rate): $220.9 billion (2013 est.)

GDP—real growth rate: 0.6% (2013 est.)
country comparison to the world: 182
0.2% (2012 est.)
2.2% (2011 est.)

GDP—per capita (PPP): $41,300 (2013 est.)
country comparison to the world: 25
$41,300 (2012 est.)
$41,300 (2011 est.)
note: data are in 2013 US dollars

Gross national saving: 13.4% of GDP (2013 est.)
country comparison to the world: 118
15.3% of GDP (2012 est.)
12.5% of GDP (2011 est.)

GDP—composition, by end use:
household consumption: 50.2%
government consumption: 14.8%
investment in fixed capital: 10%
investment in inventories: 0%
exports of goods and services: 106.8%
imports of goods and services: -81.9% (2013 est.)

GDP—composition, by sector of origin:
agriculture: 1.6%
industry: 28%
services: 70.4% (2013 est.)

Agriculture—products: barley, potatoes, wheat; beef, dairy products

Industries: pharmaceuticals, chemicals, computer hardware and software, food products, beverages and brewing; medical devices

Industrial production growth rate: 0.2% (2013 est.)
country comparison to the world: 165

Labor force: 2.161 million (2013 est.)
country comparison to the world: 120

Labor force—by occupation: *agriculture:* 5%
industry: 19%
services: 76% (2011 est.)

Unemployment rate: 13.5% (2013 est.)
country comparison to the world: 132
14.7% (2012 est.)

Population below poverty line: 5.5% (2009)

Household income or consumption by percentage share: *lowest 10%:* 2.9%
highest 10%: 27.2% (2000)

Distribution of family income—Gini index: 33.9 (2010)
country comparison to the world: 96
35.9 (1987)

Budget: *revenues:* $75.32 billion
expenditures: $91.3 billion (2013 est.)

Taxes and other revenues: 34.1% of GDP (2013 est.)
country comparison to the world: 69

Budget surplus (+) or deficit (-): -7.2% of GDP (2013 est.)
country comparison to the world: 188

Public debt: 124.2% of GDP (2013 est.)
country comparison to the world: 7
117.6% of GDP (2012 est.)
note: data cover general government debt, and includes debt instruments issued (or owned) by government entities other than the treasury; the data include treasury debt held by foreign entities; the data include debt issued by subnational entities, as well as intra-governmental debt; intra-governmental debt consists of treasury borrowings from surpluses in the social funds, such as for retirement, medical care, and unemployment; debt instruments for the social funds are not sold at public auctions

Fiscal year: calendar year

Inflation rate (consumer prices): 0.6% (2013 est.)
country comparison to the world: 15
1.7% (2012 est.)

Central bank discount rate: 0.75% (31 December 2013)
country comparison to the world: 123
1.5% (31 December 2010)
note: this is the European Central Bank's rate on the marginal lending facility, which offers overnight credit to banks in the euro area

Commercial bank prime lending rate: 3.2% (31 December 2013 est.)
country comparison to the world: 170
3.55% (31 December 2012 est.)

Stock of narrow money: $121.3 billion (31 December 2013 est.)
country comparison to the world: 31
$122.3 billion (31 December 2012 est.)
note: see entry for the European Union for money supply in the euro area; the European Central Bank (ECB) controls monetary policy for the 17 members of the Economic and Monetary Union (EMU); individual members of the EMU do not control the quantity of money circulating within their own borders

Stock of broad money: $238 billion (31 December 2013 est.)
country comparison to the world: 35
$238.7 billion (31 December 2012 est.)

Stock of domestic credit: $425.4 billion (31 December 2013 est.)
country comparison to the world: 28
$433.1 billion (31 December 2012 est.)

Market value of publicly traded shares: $109 billion (31 December 2012 est.)
country comparison to the world: 41
$108.1 billion (31 December 2011)
$60.45 billion (31 December 2010 est.)

Current account balance: $7.3 billion (2013 est.)
country comparison to the world: 27
$9.245 billion (2012 est.)

Exports: $113.6 billion (2013 est.)
country comparison to the world: 35
$119.3 billion (2012 est.)

Exports—commodities: machinery and equipment, computers, chemicals, medical devices, pharmaceuticals; food products, animal products

Exports—partners: US 17.9%, UK 17.3%, Belgium 15.6%, Germany 8.4%, Switzerland 5.8%, France 5% (2012)

Imports: $61.51 billion (2013 est.)

country comparison to the world: 48
$63.63 billion (2012 est.)

Imports—commodities: data processing equipment, other machinery and equipment, chemicals, petroleum and petroleum products, textiles, clothing

Imports—partners: UK 39.8%, US 13.2%, Germany 7.6%, Netherlands 5.7% (2012)

Reserves of foreign exchange and gold:
$1.707 billion (31 December 2012 est.)
country comparison to the world: 126
$1.703 billion (31 December 2011 est.)

Debt—external: $2.164 trillion (31 December 2012 est.)
country comparison to the world: 11
$2.213 trillion (31 December 2011)

Stock of direct foreign investment—at home:
$777.3 billion (31 December 2013 est.)
country comparison to the world: 12
$725.8 billion (31 December 2012 est.)

Stock of direct foreign investment—abroad:
$792.6 billion (31 December 2013 est.)
country comparison to the world: 11
$766 billion (31 December 2012 est.)

Exchange rates: euros (EUR) per US dollar—
0.7634 (2013 est.)
0.7752 (2012 est.)
0.755 (2010 est.)
0.7198 (2009 est.)
0.6827 (2008 est.)

ENERGY

Electricity—production: 26.04 billion kWh (2011 est.)
country comparison to the world: 6 7

Electricity—consumption: 26.1 billion kWh (2011 est.)
country comparison to the world: 65

Electricity—exports: 370 million kWh (2012 est.)
country comparison to the world: 68

Electricity—imports: 724 million kWh (2012 est.)
country comparison to the world: 69

Electricity—installed generating capacity:
8.316 million kW (2010 est.)
country comparison to the world: 63

Electricity—from fossil fuels: 76.2% of total installed capacity (2010 est.)
country comparison to the world: 97

Electricity—from nuclear fuels: 0% of total installed capacity (2010 est.)
country comparison to the world: 81

Electricity—from hydroelectric plants:
2.9% of total installed capacity (2010 est.)
country comparison to the world: 129

Electricity—from other renewable sources:
17.4% of total installed capacity (2010 est.)
country comparison to the world: 9

Crude oil—production: 725.6 bbl/day (2012 est.)
country comparison to the world: 112

Crude oil—exports: 1,858 bbl/day (2010 est.)
country comparison to the world: 68

Crude oil—imports: 62,070 bbl/day (2010 est.)
country comparison to the world: 54

Crude oil—proved reserves: 0 bbl (1 January 2013 es)
country comparison to the world: 126

Refined petroleum products—production:
59,630 bbl/day (2010 est.)
country comparison to the world: 81

Refined petroleum products—consumption:
144,000 bbl/day (2011 est.)
country comparison to the world: 69

Refined petroleum products—exports:
26,120 bbl/day (2010 est.)
country comparison to the world: 71

Refined petroleum products—imports:
166,000 bbl/day (2010 est.)
country comparison to the world: 34

Natural gas—production: 373 million cu m (2012 est.)
country comparison to the world: 74

Natural gas—consumption: 5.506 billion cu m (2010 est.)
country comparison to the world: 58

Natural gas—exports: 0 cu m (2011 est.)
country comparison to the world: 93

Natural gas—imports: 4.522 billion cu m (2012 est.)
country comparison to the world: 36

Natural gas—proved reserves: 9.911 billion cu m (1 January 2013 es)
country comparison to the world: 83

Carbon dioxide emissions from consumption of energy: 36.57 million Mt (2011 est.)
country comparison to the world: 72

COMMUNICATIONS

Telephones—main lines in use: 2.007 million (2012)
country comparison to the world: 5 7

Telephones—mobile cellular: 4.906 million (2012)
country comparison to the world: 114

Telephone system: *general assessment:* modern digital system using cable and microwave radio relay
domestic: system privatized but dominated by former state monopoly operator; increasing levels of *broadband access particularly in urban areas*
international: country code—353; landing point for the Hibernia-Atlantic submarine cable with links to the US, Canada, and UK; satellite earth station—1 Intelsat (Atlantic Ocean) (2011)

Broadcast media: publicly owned broadcaster Radio Telefis Eireann (RTE) operates 2 TV stations; commercial TV stations are available; about 75% of households utilize multi-channel satellite and TV services that provide access to a wide range of stations; RTE operates 4 national radio stations and has launched digital audio broadcasts on several stations; a number of commercial broadcast stations operate at the national, regional, and local levels (2007)

Internet country code: .ie

Internet hosts: 1.387 million (2012)
country comparison to the world: 40

Internet users: 3.042 million (2009)
country comparison to the world: 67

TRANSPORTATION

Airports: 40 (2013)
country comparison to the world: 105

Airports—with paved runways: *total:* 1 6
over 3,047 m: 1
2,438 to 3,047 m: 1
1,524 to 2,437 m: 4
914 to 1,523 m: 5
under 914 m: 5 (2013)

Airports—with unpaved runways: *total:* 2 4
2,438 to 3,047 m: 1
914 to 1,523 m: 2
under 914 m: 21 (2013)

Pipelines: gas 2,147 km (2013)

Railways: *total:* 3,237 km
country comparison to the world: 54
broad gauge: 1,872 km 1.600-m gauge (37 km electrified)
narrow gauge: 1,365 km 0.914-m gauge (operated by the Irish Peat Board to transport peat to power *stations and briquetting plants) (2008)*

Roadways: *total:* 96,036 km
country comparison to the world: 49
paved: 96,036 km (includes 1,224 km of expressways) (2010)

Waterways: 956 km (pleasure craft only) (2010)
country comparison to the world: 68

Merchant marine: *total:* 3 1
country comparison to the world: 83
by type: cargo 28, chemical tanker 2, container 1
foreign-owned: 5 (France 2, Spain 1, US 2)
registered in other countries: 33 (Bahamas 3, Bermuda 1, Cambodia 1, Cyprus 3, Isle of Man 1, Kazakhstan 1, Malta 4, Marshall Islands 6, Netherlands 8, Panama 1, Russia 1, Slovakia 1, Sweden 1, UK 1) (2010)

Ports and terminals: *major seaport(s):* Dublin, Shannon Foynes,
river port(s): Cork (Lee), Waterford (Suir)
container port(s) (TEUs): Dublin (1,931,001)

MILITARY

Military branches: Irish Defense Forces (Oglaigh na h-Eireannn), Permanent Defence Force: Army, Naval Service, Air Corps (2012)

Military service age and obligation: 17-25 years of age for male and female voluntary military service (17-27 years of age for the Naval Service); enlistees 16 years of age can be recruited for apprentice specialist positions; 17-35 years of age for the Reserve Defense Forces (RDF); maximum obligation 12 years (5 years IDF, 7 years RDF); EU *citizenship or 5-year residence in Ireland required (2012)*

Manpower available for military service:
males age 16-49: 1,179,125
females age 16-49: 1,163,728 (2010 est.)

Manpower fit for military service:
males age 16-49: 977,631
females age 16-49: 965,900 (2010 est.)

Manpower reaching militarily significant age annually: *male:* 28,564
female: 27,197 (2010 est.)

Military expenditures: 0.55% of GDP (2012)
country comparison to the world: 125
0.59% of GDP (2011)
0.55% of GDP (2010)

TRANSNATIONAL ISSUES

Disputes—international: Ireland, Iceland, and the UK dispute Denmark's claim that the Faroe Islands' continental shelf extends beyond 200 nm

Refugees and internally displaced persons:
stateless persons: 73 (2012)

Illicit drugs: transshipment point for and consumer of hashish from North Africa to the UK and Netherlands and of European-produced synthetic drugs; increasing consumption of South American cocaine; minor transshipment point for heroin and cocaine destined for Western Europe; despite recent legislation, narcotics-related money laundering—using bureaux de change, trusts, and shell companies involving the offshore financial community—remains a concern

ISLE OF MAN

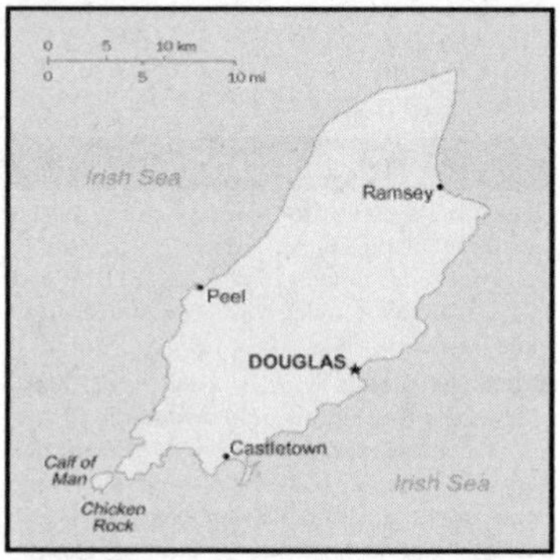

INTRODUCTION

Background: Part of the Norwegian Kingdom of the Hebrides until the 13th century when it was ceded to Scotland, the isle came under the British crown in 1765. Current concerns include reviving the almost extinct Manx Gaelic language. Isle of Man is a British crown dependency but is not part of the UK or of the European Union. However, the UK Government remains constitutionally responsible for its defense and international representation.

GEOGRAPHY

Location: Western Europe, island in the Irish Sea, between Great Britain and Ireland

Geographic coordinates: 54 15 N, 4 30 W

Map references: Europe

Area: *total:* 572 sq km
country comparison to the world: 194
land: 572 sq km
water: 0 sq km

Area—comparative: slightly more than three times the size of Washington, DC

Land boundaries: 0 km

Coastline: 160 km

Maritime claims: territorial sea: 12 nm
exclusive fishing zone: 12 nm

Climate: temperate; cool summers and mild winters; overcast about a third of the time

Terrain: hills in north and south bisected by central valley

Elevation extremes: *lowest point:* Irish Sea 0 m
highest point: Snaefell 621 m

Natural resources: none

Land use: *arable land:* 43.86%
permanent crops: 0%
other: 56.14% (permanent pastures, forests, mountain, and heathland) (2011)

Irrigated land: 0 sq km (2011)

Natural hazards: NA

Environment—current issues: waste disposal (both household and industrial); transboundary air pollution

Geography—note: one small islet, the Calf of Man, lies to the southwest and is a bird sanctuary

PEOPLE AND SOCIETY

Nationality: *noun:* Manxman (men), Manxwoman (women)
adjective: Manx

Ethnic groups: white 96.5%, Asian/Asian British 1.9%, other 1.5% (2011 est.)

Languages: English, Manx Gaelic (about 2% of the population has some knowledge)

Religions: Protestant (Anglican, Methodist, Baptist, Presbyterian, Society of Friends), Roman Catholic

Population: 86,866 (July 2014 est.)
country comparison to the world: 200

Age structure:
0-14 years: 16.3% (male 7,457/female 6,721)
15-24 years: 11.9% (male 5,371/female 4,990)
25-54 years: 39.5% (male 17,110/female 17,209)
55-64 years: 19.4% (male 5,605/female 5,519)
65 years and over: 19.1% (male 7,839/female 9,045) (2014 est.)

Median age: *total:* 43.4 years
male: 42.7 years
female: 44.1 years (2014 est.)

Population growth rate: 0.8% (2014 est.)
country comparison to the world: 138

Birth rate: 11.17 births/1,000 population (2014 est.)
country comparison to the world: 176

Death rate: 10.03 deaths/1,000 population (2014 est.)
country comparison to the world: 50

Net migration rate: 6.84 migrant(s)/1,000 population (2014 est.)
country comparison to the world: 20

Urbanization: *urban population:* 51% of total population (2010)
rate of urbanization: 0% annual rate of change (2010-15 est.)

Major urban areas—population: DOUGLAS (capital) 26,000 (2009)

Sex ratio: *at birth:* 1.08 male(s)/female
0-14 years: 1.11 male(s)/female
15-24 years: 1.08 male(s)/female
25-54 years: 0.99 male(s)/female
55-64 years: 1 male(s)/female
65 years and over: 0.85 male(s)/female
total population: 0.99 male(s)/female (2014 est.)

Infant mortality rate: *total:* 4.17 deaths/1,000 live births
country comparison to the world: 195
male: 4.12 deaths/1,000 live births
female: 4.21 deaths/1,000 live births (2014 est.)

Life expectancy at birth: *total population:* 80.98 years
country comparison to the world: 25
male: 79.33 years
female: 82.75 years (2014 est.)

Total fertility rate: 1.94 children born/woman (2014 est.)
country comparison to the world: 135

HIV/AIDS—adult prevalence rate: NA

HIV/AIDS—people living with HIV/AIDS: NA

HIV/AIDS—deaths: NA

Literacy: NA

Unemployment, youth ages 15-24: *total:* 7.2%
country comparison to the world: 128
male: 9.5%
female: 5.1% (2006)

GOVERNMENT

Country name: *conventional long form:* none
conventional short form: Isle of Man
abbreviation: I.O.M.

Dependency status: British crown dependency

Government type: parliamentary democracy

Capital: *name:* Douglas
geographic coordinates: 54 09 N, 4 29 W
time difference: UTC 0 (5 hours ahead of Washington, DC during Standard Time)
daylight saving time: +1hr, begins last Sunday in March; ends last Sunday in October

Administrative divisions: none; there are no first-order administrative divisions as defined by the US Government, but there are 24 local authorities each with its own elections

Independence: none (British crown dependency)

National holiday: Tynwald Day, 5 July

Constitution: several previous; latest announced 16 October 2006 (Isle of Man Constitution Act 2006) (2006)

Legal system: the laws of the UK where applicable apply and include Manx statutes

Suffrage: 16 years of age; universal

Executive branch: *chief of state:* Lord of Mann Queen ELIZABETH II (since 6 February 1952); represented by Lieutenant Governor Adam WOOD (since 7 April 2011)
head of government: Chief Minister Allan BELL (since 11 October 2011) cabinet: Council of Ministers (For more information visit the World Leaders website)
elections: the monarchy is hereditary; lieutenant governor appointed by the monarch; the chief minister elected by the Tynwald for a five-year term; election last held on 11 October 2011 (next to be held in December 2016)
election results: House of Keys speaker Allan BELL elected chief minister by the Tynwald with 27 votes out of 30

Legislative branch: bicameral Tynwald consists of the Legislative Council (11 seats; members composed of the President of Tynwald, the Lord Bishop of Sodor and Man, a nonvoting attorney general, and 8 others named by the House of Keys) and the House of Keys (24 seats; members elected by popular vote to serve five-year terms)
elections: House of Keys—last held on 29 September 2011 (next to be held in September 2016)
election results: House of Keys—percent of vote by party—NA; seats by party—Liberal Vannin Party 3, independents 21

Judicial branch: *highest court(s):* Isle of Man High Courts of Justice (consists of 3 permanent judges called "deemsters" and 1 judge of appeal; organized into the Staff of Government Division

or Court of Appeal and the Civil Division) note—appeals beyond the High Court of Justice are referred to the Judicial Committee of the Privy Council (in London)
judge selection and term of office: judges appointed by the Lord Chancellor of England on the nomination of the lieutenant governor; judge tenure NA
subordinate courts: High Court; Court of Summary Gaol Delivery; Summary Courts; magistrate's Court; specialized courts

Political parties and leaders: Alliance for Progressive Government; Liberal Vannin Party [Peter KARRAN]; Manx Labor Party; Mec Vannin [Bernard MOFFATT]; note—sometimes referred to as the Manx Nationalist Party
note: most members sit as independents

Political pressure groups and leaders: Alliance for Progressive Government or APG (a government watchdog); Mec Vannin (political party advocating a sovereign state and environment policies); note—has only had one member elected to the Tynwald

International organization participation: UPU

Diplomatic representation in the US: none (British crown dependency)

Diplomatic representation from the US: none (British crown dependency)

Flag description: red with the Three Legs of Man emblem (triskelion), in the center; the three legs are joined at the thigh and bent at the knee; in order to have the toes pointing clockwise on both sides of the flag, a two-sided emblem is used; the flag is based on the coat-of-arms of the last recognized Norse King of Mann, Magnus III (r. 1252-65); the triskelion has its roots in an early Celtic sun symbol

National symbol(s): triskelion (a motif of three legs)

National anthem: *name:* "Arrane Ashoonagh dy Vannin" (O Land of Our Birth)
lyrics/music: William Henry GILL [English], John J. KNEEN [Manx]/traditional
note: adopted 2003, in use since 1907; serves as a local anthem; as a British crown dependency, "God Save the Queen" is official (see United Kingdom) and is played when the sovereign, members of the royal family, or the lieutenant governor are present

ECONOMY

Economy—overview: Offshore banking, manufacturing, and tourism are key sectors of the economy. The government offers low taxes and other incentives to high-technology companies and financial institutions to locate on the island; this has paid off in expanding employment opportunities in high-income industries. As a result, agriculture and fishing, once the mainstays of the economy, have declined in their contributions to GDP. The Isle of Man also attracts online gambling sites and the film industry. Trade is mostly with the UK. In January 2013, the Isle of Man signed a tax agreement with Guernsey and Jersey, in order to enable the islands' authorities to end tax avoidance and evasion. The Isle of Man enjoys free access to EU markets.

GDP (purchasing power parity): $4.076 billion (2007 est.)
country comparison to the world: 176
$2.719 billion (2005 est.)

GDP (official exchange rate): $4.076 billion (2007 est.)

GDP—real growth rate: 5.2% (2005)
country comparison to the world: 51

GDP—per capita (PPP): $53,800 (2007 est.)
country comparison to the world: 12
$35,000 (2005 est.)

GDP—composition, by sector of origin:
agriculture: 1%
industry: 11%
services: 88% (FY08/09 est.)

Agriculture—products: cereals, vegetables; cattle, sheep, pigs, poultry

Industries: financial services, light manufacturing, tourism

Labor force: 41,790 (2006)
country comparison to the world: 195

Labor force—by occupation: *agriculture, forestry, and fishing:* 2%
manufacturing: 5%
construction: 8%
gas, electricity, and water: 1%
transport and communication: 9%
wholesale and retail distribution: 11%
professional and scientific services: 20%
public administration: 7%
banking and finance: 23%
tourism: 1%
entertainment and catering: 5%
miscellaneous services: 8% (2006)

Unemployment rate: 2% (April 2011 est.)
country comparison to the world: 13
1.8% (October 2010 est.)

Population below poverty line: NA%

Household income or consumption by percentage share: *lowest 10%:* NA%
highest 10%: NA%

Budget: *revenues:* $965 million
expenditures: $943 million (FY05/06 est.)

Taxes and other revenues: 23.7% of GDP (FY05/06 est.)
country comparison to the world: 138

Budget surplus (+) or deficit (-):
0.5% of GDP (FY05/06 est.)
country comparison to the world: 34

Fiscal year: 1 April—31 March

Inflation rate (consumer prices): 5% (2010 est.)
country comparison to the world: 154
3.1% (2006)

Market value of publicly traded shares: $NA

Exports: $NA

Exports—commodities: tweeds, herring, processed shellfish, beef, lamb

Imports: $NA

Imports—commodities: timber, fertilizers, fish

Debt—external: $NA

Exchange rates: Manx pounds (IMP) per US dollar—
0.6391 (2011)
0.6472 (2012)
0.6472 (2010)
0.6175 (2009)
0.5302 (2008)

COMMUNICATIONS

Telephone system: domestic: landline, telefax, mobile cellular telephone system
international: country code—44; fiber-optic cable, microwave radio relay, satellite earth station, submarine cable

Broadcast media: national public radio broadcasts over 3 FM stations and 1 AM station; 2 commercial broadcasters operating with 1 having multiple FM stations; receives radio and TV services via relays from British TV and radio broadcasters (2008)

Internet country code: .im

Internet hosts: 895 (2012)
country comparison to the world: 174

TRANSPORTATION

Airports: 1 (2013)
country comparison to the world: 219

Airports—with paved runways: *total:* 1
1,524 to 2,437 m: 1 (2013)

Railways: *total:* 63 km
country comparison to the world: 128
narrow gauge: 6 km 1.076-m gauge (6 km electrified); 57 km 0.914-m gauge (29 km electrified)
note: primarily summer tourist attractions (2008)

Roadways: *total:* 500 km (2008)
country comparison to the world: 195

Merchant marine: *total:* 321
country comparison to the world: 30
by type: bulk carrier 59, cargo 55, chemical tanker 52, container 7, liquefied gas 43, passenger/cargo 2, petroleum tanker 93, roll on/roll off 5, vehicle carrier 5
foreign-owned: 223 (Bermuda 7, Chile 9, Denmark 30, Germany 56, Greece 62, Ireland 1, Japan 19, Malaysia 6, Norway 30, South Africa 2, US 1) (2010)

Ports and terminals: *major seaport(s):* Douglas, Ramsey

MILITARY

Manpower fit for military service:
males age 16-49: 15,206
females age 16-49: 15,127 (2010 est.)

Manpower reaching militarily significant age annually: *male:* 507
female: 494 (2010 est.)

Military—note: defense is the responsibility of the UK

TRANSNATIONAL ISSUES

Disputes—international: none

ISRAEL

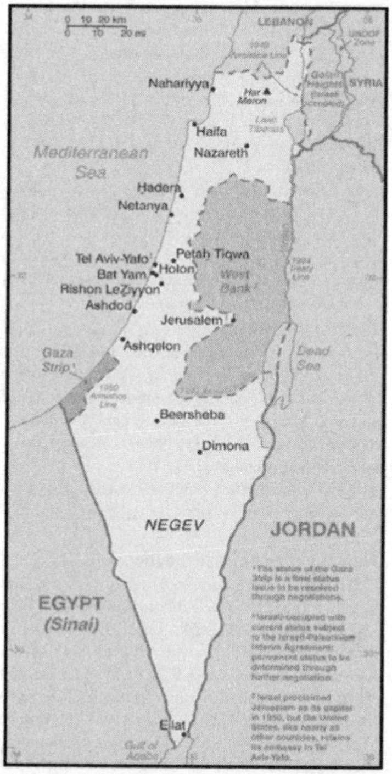

INTRODUCTION

Background: Following World War II, the British withdrew from their mandate of Palestine, and the UN proposed partitioning the area into Arab and Jewish states, an arrangement rejected by the Arabs. Subsequently, the Israelis defeated the Arabs in a series of wars without ending the deep tensions between the two sides. (The territories Israel occupied since the 1967 war are not included in the Israel country profile, unless otherwise noted.) On 25 April 1982, Israel withdrew from the Sinai pursuant to the 1979 Israel-Egypt Peace Treaty. In keeping with the framework established at the Madrid Conference in October 1991, bilateral negotiations were conducted between Israel and Palestinian representatives and Syria to achieve a permanent settlement. Israel and Palestinian officials signed on 13 September 1993 a Declaration of Principles (also known as the "Oslo Accords"), enshrining the idea of a two-state solution to their conflict and guiding an interim period of Palestinian self-rule. Outstanding territorial and other disputes with Jordan were resolved in the 26 October 1994 Israel-Jordan Treaty of Peace. Progress toward a permanent status agreement with the Palestinians was undermined by Israeli-Palestinian violence between 2001 and February 2005. Israel in 2005 unilaterally disengaged from the Gaza Strip, evacuating settlers and its military while retaining control over most points of entry into the Gaza Strip. The election of HAMAS to head the Palestinian Legislative Council in 2006 froze relations between Israel and the Palestinian Authority (PA). In 2006 Israel engaged in a 34-day conflict with Hizballah in Lebanon in June-August 2006 and a 23-day conflict with HAMAS in the Gaza Strip during December 2008 and January 2009. Direct talks with the Palestinians launched in September 2010 collapsed following the expiration of Israel's 10-month partial settlement construction moratorium in the West Bank. In November 2012, Israel engaged in a seven-day conflict with HAMAS in the Gaza Strip. Prime Minister Binyamin NETANYAHU formed a coalition government in March 2013 following general elections in January 2013. Direct talks with the Palestinians resumed in July 2013 and are ongoing.

GEOGRAPHY

Location: Middle East, bordering the Mediterranean Sea, between Egypt and Lebanon

Geographic coordinates: 31 30 N, 34 45 E

Map references: Middle East

Area: *total:* 20,770 sq km
country comparison to the world: 154
land: 20,330 sq km
water: 440 sq km

Area—comparative: slightly larger than New Jersey

Land boundaries: *total:* 1,017 km
border countries: Egypt 266 km, Gaza Strip 51 km, Jordan 238 km, Lebanon 79 km, Syria 76 km, West Bank 307 km

Coastline: 273 km

Maritime claims: territorial sea: 12 nm
continental shelf: to depth of exploitation

Climate: temperate; hot and dry in southern and eastern desert areas

Terrain: Negev desert in the south; low coastal plain; central mountains; Jordan Rift Valley

Elevation extremes: *lowest point:* Dead Sea -408 m
highest point: Har Meron 1,208 m

Natural resources: timber, potash, copper ore, natural gas, phosphate rock, magnesium bromide, clays, sand

Land use: *arable land:* 13.68%
permanent crops: 3.69%
other: 82.62% (2011)

Irrigated land: 2,250 sq km (2004)

Total renewable water resources: 1.78 cu km (2011)

Freshwater withdrawal (domestic/industrial/agricultural): *total:* 1.95 cu km/yr (39%/6%/55%)
per capita: 282.4 cu m/yr (2009)

Natural hazards: sandstorms may occur during spring and summer; droughts; periodic earthquakes

Environment—current issues: limited arable land and natural freshwater resources pose serious constraints; desertification; air pollution from industrial and vehicle emissions; groundwater pollution from industrial and domestic waste, chemical fertilizers, and pesticides

Environment—international agreements: party to: Biodiversity, Climate Change, Climate Change-Kyoto Protocol, Desertification, Endangered Species, Hazardous Wastes, Ozone Layer Protection, Ship Pollution, Wetlands, Whaling
signed, but not ratified: Marine Life Conservation

Geography—note: Lake Tiberias (Sea of Galilee) is an important freshwater source; the Dead Sea is the second saltiest body of water in the world (after Lake Assal in Djibouti); there are about 355 Israeli civilian sites including about 145 small outpost communities in the West Bank, 41 sites in theGolan Heights, and 32 in East Jerusalem (2010 est.)

PEOPLE AND SOCIETY

Nationality: *noun:* Israeli(s)
adjective: Israeli

Ethnic groups: Jewish 75.1% (of which Israel-born 73.6%, Europe/America/Oceania-born 17.9%, Africa-born 5.2%, Asia-born 3.2%), non-Jewish 24.9% (mostly Arab) (2012 est.)

Languages: Hebrew (official), Arabic (used officially for Arab minority), English (most commonly used foreign language)

Religions: Jewish 75.1%, Muslim 17.4%, Christian 2%, Druze 1.6%, other 3.9% (2012 est.)

Population: 7,821,850 (July 2014 est.)
country comparison to the world: 99
note: approximately 341,400 Israeli settlers live in the West Bank (2012); approximately 18,900 Israeli settlers live in the Golan Heights (2012); approximately 196,400 Israeli settlers live in East Jerusalem (2011)

Age structure:
0-14 years: 27.1% (male 1,084,748/female 1,035,525)
15-24 years: 15.7% (male 628,205/female 599,871)
25-54 years: 37.8% (male 1,508,860/female 1,443,898)
55-64 years: 10.7% (male 333,453/female 352,302)
65 years and over: 10.5% (male 368,318/female 466,670) (2014 est.)

Dependency ratios:
total dependency ratio: 62.5 %
youth dependency ratio: 45.1 %
elderly dependency ratio: 17.4 %
potential support ratio: 5.7 (2013)

Median age: *total:* 29.9 years
male: 29.2 years
female: 30.6 years (2014 est.)

Population growth rate: 1.46% (2014 est.)
country comparison to the world: 84

Birth rate: 18.44 births/1,000 population (2014 est.)
country comparison to the world: 101

Death rate: 5.54 deaths/1,000 population (2014 est.)
country comparison to the world: 176

Net migration rate: 1.68 migrant(s)/1,000 population (2014 est.)
country comparison to the world: 53

Urbanization: *urban population:* 91.9% of total population (2011)
rate of urbanization: 1.73% annual rate of change (2010-15 est.)

Major urban areas—population: Tel Aviv-Yafo 3.219 million; Haifa 1.027 million; JERUSALEM (capital) 768,000 (2009)

Sex ratio: *at birth:* 1.05 male(s)/female
0-14 years: 1.05 male(s)/female

15-24 years: 1.05 male(s)/female
25-54 years: 1.05 male(s)/female
55-64 years: 1.01 male(s)/female
65 years and over: 0.78 male(s)/female
total population: 1.01 male(s)/female (2014 est.)

Mother's mean age at first birth: 27.3 (2011 est.)

Maternal mortality rate: 7 deaths/100,000 live births (2010)
country comparison to the world: 168

Infant mortality rate: *total:* 3.98 deaths/1,000 live births
country comparison to the world: 199
male: 4.16 deaths/1,000 live births
female: 3.8 deaths/1,000 live births (2014 est.)

Life expectancy at birth: *total population:* 81.28 years
country comparison to the world: 19
male: 79.05 years
female: 83.61 years (2014 est.)

Total fertility rate: 2.62 children born/woman (2014 est.)
country comparison to the world: 75

Health expenditures: 7.7% of GDP (2011)
country comparison to the world: 71

Physicians density: 3.11 physicians/1,000 population (2011)

Hospital bed density: 3.4 beds/1,000 population (2011)

Drinking water source:
improved:
urban: 100% of population
rural: 100% of population
total: 100% of population
unimproved:
urban: 0% of population
rural: 0% of population
total: 0% of population (2011 est.)

Sanitation facility access:
improved:
urban: 100% of population
rural: 100% of population
total: 100% of population
unimproved:
urban: 0% of population
rural: 0% of population
total: 0% of population (2011 est.)

HIV/AIDS—adult prevalence rate: 0.2% (2009 est.)
country comparison to the world: 104

HIV/AIDS—people living with HIV/AIDS: 7,500 (2009 est.)
country comparison to the world: 115

HIV/AIDS—deaths: fewer than 100 (2009 est.)
country comparison to the world: 120

Obesity—adult prevalence rate: 26.2% (2008)
country comparison to the world: 49

Education expenditures: 5.6% of GDP (2011)
country comparison to the world: 57

Literacy: *definition:* age 15 and over can read and write
total population: 97.1%
male: 98.5%
female: 95.9% (2004 est.)

School life expectancy (primary to tertiary education): *total:* 16 years
male: 15 years
female: 16 years (2009)

Unemployment, youth ages 15-24: *total:* 12.1%
country comparison to the world: 98
male: 11.6%
female: 12.7% (2012)

GOVERNMENT

Country name: *conventional long form:* State of Israel
conventional short form: Israel
local long form: Medinat Yisra'el
local short form: Yisra'el

Government type: parliamentary democracy

Capital: *name:* Jerusalem
geographic coordinates: 31 46 N, 35 14 E
time difference: UTC+2 (7 hours ahead of Washington, DC during Standard Time)
daylight saving time: +1hr, begins Friday before the last Sunday in March; ends the last Sunday in October
note: Israel proclaimed Jerusalem as its capital in 1950, but the US, like all other countries, maintains its Embassy in Tel Aviv

Administrative divisions: 6 districts (mehozot, singular—mehoz); Central, Haifa, Jerusalem, Northern, Southern, Tel Aviv

Independence: 14 May 1948 (from League of Nations mandate under British administration)

National holiday: Independence Day, 14 May (1948); note—Israel declared independence on 14 May 1948, but the Jewish calendar is lunar and the holiday may occur in April or May

Constitution: no formal constitution; some functions of a constitution are filled by the Declaration of Establishment (1948), the Basic Laws of the Parliament (Knesset), and the Israeli citizenship law (2013)

Legal system: mixed legal system of English common law, British Mandate regulations, and Jewish, Christian, and Muslim religious laws

International law organization participation: has not submitted an ICJ jurisdiction declaration; withdrew acceptance of ICCt jurisdiction in 2002

Suffrage: 18 years of age; universal

Executive branch: *chief of state:* President Shimon PERES (since 15 July 2007)
head of government: Prime Minister Binyamin NETANYAHU (since 31 March 2009)
cabinet: Cabinet selected by prime minister and approved by the Knesset (For more information visit the World Leaders website)
elections: president largely a ceremonial role and is elected by the Knesset for a seven-year term (one-term limit); election last held 13 June 2007 (next to be held in 2014 but can be called earlier); following legislative elections, the president, in consultation with party leaders, assigns the task of forming a governing coalition to a Knesset member whom he or she determines is most likely to accomplish that task
election results: Shimon PERES elected president; number of votes in first round—Shimon PERES 58, Reuven RIVLIN 37, Colette AVITAL 21; PERES elected president in second round with 86 votes (unopposed)

Legislative branch: unicameral Knesset (120 seats; political parties are elected by popular vote and assigned seats for members on a proportional basis; members serve 4-year terms)
elections: last held on 22 January 2013 (next to be held in 2017)
election results: percent of vote by party—Likud-Beiteinu (combined for electoral purposes only) 23.3%, Yesh Atid 14.3%, Labor 11.4%, The Jewish Home 9.1%, SHAS 8.7%, United Torah Judaism 5.2%, The Movement 5%, The New Movement-Meretz 4.5%, United Arab List-Ta'al 3.6%, HADASH 3%, Balad 2.6%, Kadima 2.1%; other 7.2%; seats by party—Likud-Beiteinu 31, Yesh Atid 19, Labor 15, The Jewish Home 12, SHAS 11, United Torah Judaism 7, The Movement 6, Meretz 6, United Arab List-Ta'al 4, HADASH 4, Balad 3, Kadima 2
note: Ehud BARAK and four others on 17 January 2011 split from the Labor Party and formed the Atzmaut (Independence) Party; the Labor Party holds 8 seats in the Knesset and the Independence Party holds 5 seats; Aztmaut did not submit a candidate list for the election on 22 January 2013

Judicial branch: *highest court(s):* Supreme Court (consists of the chief justice and 14 judges)
judge selection and term of office: judges selected by the Judicial Selection Committee, made up of all three branches of the government and chaired by the Minister of Justice; judges can serve up to mandatory retirement age of 70
subordinate courts: district and magistrate courts; national and regional labor courts; special and religious courts

Political parties and leaders: Balad [Jamal ZAHALKA]; Democratic Front for Peace and Equality (HADASH) [Muhammad BARAKEH]; Kadima [Shaul MOFAZ]; Labor Party [Yitzhak HERZOG]; Likud [Binyamin NETANYAHU]; National Union [Uri ARIEL]; SHAS [Eliyahu YISHAI]; The Jewish Home (HaBayit HaYehudi) [Naftali BENNETT]; The Movement (Hatnuah) [Tzipora "Tzipi" LIVNI]; The New Movement-Meretz [Haim ORON]; United Arab List-Ta'al [Ibrahim SARSUR]; United Torah Judaism or UTJ [Yaakov LITZMAN] (a conglomerate of three parties); Yesh Atid [Yair LAPID]; Yisrael Beiteinu or YB [Avigdor LIEBERMAN]

Political pressure groups and leaders: B'Tselem [Jessica MONTELL, Executive Director] monitors human rights abuses; Peace Now [Yariv OPPENHEIMER, Secretary General] supports territorial concessions in the West Bank and Gaza Strip; YESHA Council [Danny DAYAN, Chairman] promotes settler interests and opposes territorial compromise; Breaking the Silence [Yehuda SHAUL, Executive Director] collects testimonies from soldiers who served in the West Bank and Gaza Strip

International organization participation: BIS, BSEC (observer), CE (observer), CICA, EBRD, FAO, IADB, IAEA, IBRD, ICAO, ICC (national committees), ICRM, IDA, IFAD, IFC, IFRCS, ILO, IMF, IMO, IMSO, Interpol, IOC, IOM, IPU, ISO, ITSO, ITU, ITUC (NGOs), MIGA, OAS (observer), OECD, OPCW (signatory), OSCE (partner), Paris Club (associate), PCA, SELEC (observer), UN, UNCTAD, UNESCO, UNHCR, UNIDO, UNWTO, UPU, WCO, WHO, WIPO, WMO, WTO

Diplomatic representation in the US:
chief of mission: Ambassador Ron DERMER (since 3 December 2013)
chancery: 3514 International Drive NW, Washington, DC 20008
telephone: [1] (202) 364-5500
FAX: [1] (202) 364-5647

consulate(s) general: Atlanta, Boston, Chicago, Houston, Los Angeles, Miami, New York, Philadelphia, San Francisco

Diplomatic representation from the US:
chief of mission: Ambassador Daniel B. SHAPIRO (since 8 July 2011)
embassy: 71 Hayarkon Street, Tel Aviv 63903
telephone: [972] (3) 519-7475
FAX: [972] (3) 516-4390
consulate(s) general: Jerusalem; note—an independent US mission, established in 1928, whose members are not accredited to a foreign government

Flag description: white with a blue hexagram (six-pointed linear star) known as the Magen David (Star of David or Shield of David) centered between two equal horizontal blue bands near the top and bottom edges of the flag; the basic design resembles a traditional Jewish prayer shawl (tallit), which is white with blue stripes; the hexagram as a Jewish symbol dates back to medieval times

National symbol(s): Star of David (Magen David)

National anthem: *name:* "Hatikvah" (The Hope)
lyrics/music: Naftali Herz IMBER/traditional, arranged by Samuel COHEN
note: adopted 2004, unofficial since 1948; used as the anthem of the Zionist movement since 1897; the 1888 arrangement by Samuel COHEN is thought to be based on the Romanian folk song "Carul cu boi" (The Ox Driven Cart)

ECONOMY

Economy—overview: Israel has a technologically advanced market economy. Cut diamonds, high-technology equipment, and pharmaceuticals are among the leading exports. Its major imports include crude oil, grains, raw materials, and military equipment. Israel usually posts sizable trade deficits, which are covered by tourism and other service exports, as well as significant foreign investment inflows. Between 2004 and 2011, growth averaged nearly 5% per year, led by exports. The global financial crisis of 2008-09 spurred a brief recession in Israel, but the country entered the crisis with solid fundamentals, following years of prudent fiscal policy and a resilient banking sector. In 2010, Israel formally acceded to the OECD. Israel's economy also has weathered the Arab Spring because strong trade ties outside the Middle East have insulated the economy from spillover effects. The economy has recovered better than most advanced, comparably sized economies, but slowing demand domestically and internationally, and a strong shekel, have reduced forecasts for the next decade to the 3% level. Natural gas fields discovered off Israel's coast since 2009 have brightened Israel's energy security outlook. The Tamar and Leviathan fields were some of the world's largest offshore natural gas finds this past decade. The massive Leviathan field is not due to come online until 2018, but production from Tamar provided a one percentage point boost to Israel's GDP in 2013 and is expected to contribute 0.5% growth in 2014. In mid-2011, public protests arose around income inequality and rising housing and commodity prices. Israel's income inequality and poverty rates are among the highest of OECD countries and there is a broad perception among the public that a small number of "tycoons" have a cartel-like grip over the major parts of the economy. The government formed committees to address some of the grievances but has maintained that it will not engage in deficit spending to satisfy populist demands. In May 2013 the Israeli government, in a politically difficult process, passed an austerity budget to reign in the deficit and restore confidence in the government's fiscal position. Over the long term, Israel faces structural issues, including low labor participation rates for its fastest growing social segments—the ultra-orthodox and Arab-Israeli communities. Also, Israel's progressive, globally competitive, knowledge-based technology sector employs only 9% of the workforce, with the rest employed in manufacturing and services—sectors which face downward wage pressures from global competition.

GDP (purchasing power parity): $274.5 billion (2013 est.)
country comparison to the world: 49
$264.5 billion (2012 est.)
$255.9 billion (2011 est.)
note: data are in 2013 US dollars

GDP (official exchange rate): $272.7 billion (2013 est.)

GDP—real growth rate: 3.8% (2013 est.)
country comparison to the world: 84
3.4% (2012 est.)
4.6% (2011 est.)

GDP—per capita (PPP): $34,900 (2013 est.)
country comparison to the world: 40
$34,300 (2012 est.)
$34,000 (2011 est.)
note: data are in 2013 US dollars

Gross national saving: 22.2% of GDP (2013 est.)
country comparison to the world: 66
21% of GDP (2012 est.)
21.4% of GDP (2011 est.)

GDP—composition, by end use:
household consumption: 56.1%
government consumption: 22.7%
investment in fixed capital: 19.6%
investment in inventories: 0.7%
exports of goods and services: 34.4%
imports of goods and services: -33.5% (2013 est.)

GDP—composition, by sector of origin:
agriculture: 2.4%
industry: 31.2%
services: 66.4% (2013 est.)

Agriculture—products: citrus, vegetables, cotton; beef, poultry, dairy products

Industries: high-technology products (including aviation, communications, computer-aided design and manufactures, medical electronics, fiber optics), wood and paper products, potash and phosphates, food, beverages, and tobacco, caustic soda, cement, construction, metals products, chemical products, plastics, cut diamonds, textiles, footwear

Industrial production growth rate: 5.5% (2013 est.)
country comparison to the world: 51

Labor force: 3.692 million (2013 est.)
country comparison to the world: 95

Labor force—by occupation: agriculture: 2%
industry: 16%
services: 82% (September 2008)

Unemployment rate: 6.8% (2013 est.)
country comparison to the world: 72
6.9% (2012 est.)

Population below poverty line: 21%
note: Israel's poverty line is $7.30 per person per day (2012)

Household income or consumption by percentage share: *lowest 10%:* 2.5%
highest 10%: 24.3% (2008)

Distribution of family income—Gini index: 37.6 (2012)
country comparison to the world: 75
39.2 (2008)

Budget: *revenues:* $72.55 billion
expenditures: $82.66 billion (2013 est.)

Taxes and other revenues: 26.6% of GDP (2013 est.)
country comparison to the world: 112

Budget surplus (+) or deficit (-):
-3.7% of GDP (2013 est.)
country comparison to the world: 139

Public debt: 67.1% of GDP (2013 est.)
country comparison to the world: 39
66.9% of GDP (2012 est.)

Fiscal year: calendar year

Inflation rate (consumer prices): 1.7% (2013 est.)
country comparison to the world: 51
1.7% (2012 est.)

Central bank discount rate: 1% (31 December 2013 est.)
country comparison to the world: 115
1.75% (31 December 2012 est.)

Commercial bank prime lending rate: 3.8% (31 December 2013 est.)
country comparison to the world: 156
5.16% (31 December 2012 est.)

Stock of narrow money: $37.09 billion (31 December 2013 est.)
country comparison to the world: 56
$32.48 billion (31 December 2012 est.)

Stock of broad money: $151.2 billion (31 December 2013 est.)
country comparison to the world: 46
$136.2 billion (31 December 2012 est.)

Stock of domestic credit: $207.7 billion (31 December 2013 est.)
country comparison to the world: 40
$192.3 billion (31 December 2012 est.)

Market value of publicly traded shares:
$148.4 billion (31 December 2012 est.)
country comparison to the world: 35
$145 billion (31 December 2011)
$218.1 billion (31 December 2010 est.)

Current account balance: $5.259 billion (2013 est.)
country comparison to the world: 30
$609 million (2012 est.)

Exports: $60.67 billion (2013 est.)
country comparison to the world: 55
$62.32 billion (2012 est.)

Exports—commodities: machinery and equipment, software, cut diamonds, agricultural products, chemicals, textiles and apparel

Exports—partners: US 27.8%, Hong Kong 7.7%, UK 5.7%, Belgium 4.6%, China 4.3% (2012)

Imports: $67.03 billion (2013 est.)
country comparison to the world: 44
$71.67 billion (2012 est.)

Imports—commodities: raw materials, military equipment, investment goods, rough diamonds, fuels, grain, consumer goods

Imports—partners: US 12.9%, China 7.3%, Germany 6.3%, Switzerland 5.5%, Belgium 4.8% (2012)

Reserves of foreign exchange and gold:
$80.74 billion (31 December 2013 est.)
country comparison to the world: 28
$75.91 billion (31 December 2012 est.)

Debt—external: $96.3 billion (31 December 2013 est.)
country comparison to the world: 48
$93.98 billion (31 December 2012 est.)

Stock of direct foreign investment—at home: $86.04 billion (31 December 2013 est.)
country comparison to the world: 43
$75.94 billion (31 December 2012 est.)

Stock of direct foreign investment—abroad: $80.85 billion (31 December 2013 est.)
country comparison to the world: 31
$74.75 billion (31 December 2012 est.)

Exchange rates: new Israeli shekels (ILS) per US dollar—
3.621 (2013 est.)
3.8559 (2012 est.)
3.739 (2010 est.)
3.93 (2009)
3.588 (2008)

ENERGY

Electricity—production: 55.77 billion kWh (2011 est.)
country comparison to the world: 47

Electricity—consumption: 48.73 billion kWh (2010 est.)
country comparison to the world: 47

Electricity—exports: 4.224 billion kWh (2011 est.)
country comparison to the world: 30

Electricity—imports: 0 kWh (2012 est.)
country comparison to the world: 156

Electricity—installed generating capacity: 15.33 million kW (2010 est.)
country comparison to the world: 45

Electricity—from fossil fuels: 98.1% of total installed capacity (2010 est.)
country comparison to the world: 58

Electricity—from nuclear fuels: 0% of total installed capacity (2010 est.)
country comparison to the world: 110

Electricity—from hydroelectric plants: 0% of total installed capacity (2010 est.)
country comparison to the world: 176

Electricity—from other renewable sources: 1.8% of total installed capacity (2010 est.)
country comparison to the world: 73

Crude oil—production: 5,839 bbl/day (2012 est.)
country comparison to the world: 96

Crude oil—exports: 0 bbl/day (2010 est.)
country comparison to the world: 131

Crude oil—imports: 260,600 bbl/day (2010 est.)
country comparison to the world: 28

Crude oil—proved reserves: 11.5 million bbl (1 January 2013 es)
country comparison to the world: 90

Refined petroleum products—production: 278,400 bbl/day (2010 est.)
country comparison to the world: 46

Refined petroleum products—consumption: 238,400 bbl/day (2011 est.)
country comparison to the world: 53

Refined petroleum products—exports: 83,700 bbl/day (2010 est.)
country comparison to the world: 48

Refined petroleum products—imports: 56,420 bbl/day (2010 est.)
country comparison to the world: 65

Natural gas—production: 6.86 billion cu m (2013 est.)
country comparison to the world: 49

Natural gas—consumption: 6.86 billion cu m (2013 est.)
country comparison to the world: 54

Natural gas—exports: 0 cu m (2011 est.)
country comparison to the world: 120

Natural gas—imports: 720 million cu m (2011 est.)
country comparison to the world: 63

Natural gas—proved reserves: 268.5 billion cu m (1 January 2013 es)
country comparison to the world: 43

Carbon dioxide emissions from consumption of energy: 72.1 million Mt (2011 est.)
country comparison to the world: 48

COMMUNICATIONS

Telephones—main lines in use: 3.594 million (2012)
country comparison to the world: 44

Telephones—mobile cellular: 9.225 million (2012)
country comparison to the world: 84

Telephone system: *general assessment:* most highly developed system in the Middle East
domestic: good system of coaxial cable and microwave radio relay; all systems are digital; four privately owned mobile-cellular service providers with countrywide coverage
international: country code—972; submarine cables provide links to Europe, Cyprus, and parts of the Middle East; satellite earth stations—3 Intelsat (2 Atlantic Ocean and 1 Indian Ocean) (2011)

Broadcast media: state broadcasting network, operated by the Israel Broadcasting Authority (IBA), broadcasts on 2 channels, one in Hebrew and the other in Arabic; 5 commercial channels including a channel broadcasting in Russian, a channel broadcasting Knesset proceedings, and a music channel supervised by a public body; multichannel satellite and cable TV packages provide access to foreign channels; IBA broadcasts on 8 radio networks with multiple repeaters and Israel Defense Forces Radio broadcasts over multiple stations; about 15 privately owned radio stations; overall more than 100 stations and repeater stations (2008)

Internet country code: .il

Internet hosts: 2.483 million (2012)
country comparison to the world: 36

Internet users: 4.525 million (2009)
country comparison to the world: 51

TRANSPORTATION

Airports: 47 (2013)
country comparison to the world: 95

Airports—with paved runways: *total:* 29
over 3,047 m: 2
2,438 to 3,047 m: 5
1,524 to 2,437 m: 6
914 to 1,523 m: 11
under 914 m: 5 (2013)

Airports—with unpaved runways: *total:* 18
1,524 to 2,437 m: 1
914 to 1,523 m: 3
under 914 m: 14 (2013)

Heliports: 3 (2013)

Pipelines: gas 763 km; oil 442 km; refined products 261 km (2013)

Railways: *total:* 975 km
country comparison to the world: 89
standard gauge: 975 km 1.435-m gauge (2008)

Roadways: *total:* 18,566 km
country comparison to the world: 115
paved: 18,566 km (includes 449 km of expressways) (2011)

Merchant marine: *total:* 8
country comparison to the world: 120
by type: cargo 1, container 7
registered in other countries: 48 (Bermuda 3, Georgia 1, Honduras 1, Liberia 34, Malta 3, Moldova 2, Panama 1, Saint Vincent and the Grenadines 3) (2010)

Ports and terminals: *major seaport(s):* Ashdod, Elat (Eilat), Hadera, Haifa
container port(s) TEUs): Ashdod (1,176,000), Haifa (1,238,000)

MILITARY

Military branches: Israel Defense Forces (IDF), Israel Naval Force (IN), Israel Air Force (IAF) (2010)

Military service age and obligation: 18 years of age for compulsory (Jews, Druzes) military service; 17 years of age for voluntary (Christians, Muslims, Circassians) military service; both sexes are obligated to military service; conscript service obligation—36 months for enlisted men, 21 months for enlisted women, 48 months for officers; pilots commit to 9 years service; reserve obligation to age 41-51 (men), 24 (women) (2013)

Manpower available for military service:
males age 16-49: 1,797,960
females age 16-49: 1,713,230 (2010 est.)

Manpower fit for military service:
males age 16-49: 1,517,510
females age 16-49: 1,446,132 (2010 est.)

Manpower reaching militarily significant age annually: *male:* 62,304
female: 59,418 (2010 est.)

Military expenditures: 5.69% of GDP (2012)
country comparison to the world: 4
5.87% of GDP (2011)
5.69% of GDP (2010)

TRANSNATIONAL ISSUES

Disputes—international: West Bank and Gaza Strip are Israeli-occupied with current status subject to the Israeli-Palestinian Interim Agreement—permanent status to be determined through further negotiation; Israel continues construction of a "seam line" separation barrier along parts of the Green Line and within the West Bank; Israel withdrew its settlers and military from the Gaza Strip and from four settlements in the West Bank in August 2005; Golan Heights is Israeli-occupied (Lebanon claims the Shab'a Farms area of Golan Heights); since 1948, about 350 peacekeepers from the UN Truce Supervision Organization headquartered in Jerusalem monitor ceasefires, supervise armistice agreements, prevent isolated incidents from escalating, and assist other UN personnel in the region

Refugees and internally displaced persons: *refugees (country of origin):* 37,347 (Eritrea); 10,743 (Sudan) (2012)
stateless persons: 14 (2012)

Illicit drugs: increasingly concerned about ecstasy, cocaine, and heroin abuse; drugs arrive in country from Lebanon and, increasingly, from Jordan; money-laundering center

ITALY

INTRODUCTION

Background: Italy became a nation-state in 1861 when the regional states of the peninsula, along with Sardinia and Sicily, were united under King Victor EMMANUEL II. An era of parliamentary government came to a close in the early 1920s when Benito MUSSOLINI established a Fascist dictatorship. His alliance with Nazi Germany led to Italy's defeat in World War II. A democratic republic replaced the monarchy in 1946 and economic revival followed. Italy is a charter member of NATO and the European Economic Community (EEC). It has been at the forefront of European economic and political unification, joining the Economic and Monetary Union in 1999. Persistent problems include sluggish economic growth, high youth and female unemployment, organized crime, corruption, and economic disparities between southern Italy and the more prosperous north.

GEOGRAPHY

Location: Southern Europe, a peninsula extending into the central Mediterranean Sea, northeast of Tunisia

Geographic coordinates: 42 50 N, 12 50 E

Map references: Europe

Area: *total:* 301,340 sq km
country comparison to the world: 72
land: 294,140 sq km
water: 7,200 sq km
note: includes Sardinia and Sicily

Area—comparative: almost twice the size of Georgia; slightly larger than Arizona

Land boundaries: *total:* 1,899.2 km
border countries: Austria 430 km, France 488 km, Holy See (Vatican City) 3.2 km, San Marino 39 km, Slovenia 199 km, Switzerland 740 km

Coastline: 7,600 km

Maritime claims: territorial sea: 12 nm
continental shelf: 200 m depth or to the depth of exploitation

Climate: predominantly Mediterranean; Alpine in far north; hot, dry in south

Terrain: mostly rugged and mountainous; some plains, coastal lowlands

Elevation extremes: *lowest point:* Mediterranean Sea 0 m
highest point: Mont Blanc (Monte Bianco) de Courmayeur 4,748 m (a secondary peak of Mont Blanc)

Natural resources: coal, mercury, zinc, potash, marble, barite, asbestos, pumice, fluorspar, feldspar, pyrite (sulfur), natural gas and crude oil reserves, fish, arable land

Land use: *arable land:* 22.57%
permanent crops: 8.37%
other: 69.07% (2011)

Irrigated land: 39,510 sq km (2007)

Total renewable water resources: 191.3 cu km (2011)

Freshwater withdrawal (domestic/industrial/agricultural): *total:* 45.41 cu km/yr (24%/43%/34%)
per capita: 789.8 cu m/yr (2008)

Natural hazards: regional risks include landslides, mudflows, avalanches, earthquakes, volcanic eruptions, flooding; land subsidence in Venice
volcanism: significant volcanic activity; Etna (elev. 3,330 m), which is in eruption as of 2010, is Europe's most active volcano; flank eruptions pose a threat to nearby Sicilian villages; Etna, along with the famous Vesuvius, which remains a threat to the millions of nearby residents in the Bay of Naples area, have both been deemed Decade Volcanoes by the International Association of Volcanology and Chemistry of the Earth's Interior, worthy of study due to their explosive history and close proximity to human populations; Stromboli, on its namesake island, has also been continuously active with moderate volcanic activity; other historically active volcanoes include Campi Flegrei, Ischia, Larderello, Pantelleria, Vulcano, and Vulsini

Environment—current issues: air pollution from industrial emissions such as sulfur dioxide; coastal and inland rivers polluted from industrial and agricultural effluents; acid rain damaging lakes; inadequate industrial waste treatment and disposal facilities

Environment—international agreements:
party to: Air Pollution, Air Pollution-Nitrogen Oxides, Air Pollution-Persistent Organic Pollutants, Air Pollution-Sulfur 85, Air Pollution-Sulfur 94, Air Pollution-Volatile Organic Compounds, Antarctic-Environmental Protocol, Antarctic-Marine Living Resources, Antarctic Seals, Antarctic Treaty, Biodiversity, Climate Change, Climate Change-Kyoto Protocol, Desertification, Endangered Species, Environmental Modification, Hazardous Wastes, Law of the Sea, Marine Dumping, Ozone Layer Protection, Ship Pollution, Tropical Timber 83, Tropical Timber 94, Wetlands, Whaling
signed, but not ratified: none of the selected agreements

Geography—note: strategic location dominating central Mediterranean as well as southern sea and air approaches to Western Europe

PEOPLE AND SOCIETY

Nationality: *noun:* Italian(s)
adjective: Italian

Ethnic groups: Italian (includes small clusters of German-, French-, and Slovene-Italians in the north and Albanian-Italians and Greek-Italians in the south)

Languages: Italian (official), German (parts of Trentino-Alto Adige region are predominantly German-speaking), French (small French-speaking minority in Valle d'Aosta region), Slovene (Slovene-speaking minority in the Trieste-Gorizia area)

Religions: Christian 80% (overwhelmingly Roman Catholic with very small groups of Jehovah's Witnesses and Protestants), Muslim (about 800,000 to 1 million), Atheist and Agnostic 20%

Population: 61,680,122 (July 2014 est.)
country comparison to the world: 24

Age structure:
0-14 years: 13.8% (male 4,340,943/female 4,154,547)
15-24 years: 9.8% (male 3,046,202/female 3,028,190)
25-54 years: 43% (male 13,107,098/female 13,405,812)
55-64 years: 21% (male 3,703,329/female 3,942,261)
65 years and over: 20.8% (male 5,548,047/female 7,403,693) (2014 est.)

Dependency ratios:
total dependency ratio: 54.3 %
youth dependency ratio: 21.7 %
elderly dependency ratio: 32.6 %
potential support ratio: 3.1 (2013)

Median age: *total:* 44.5 years
male: 43.3 years
female: 45.6 years (2014 est.)

Population growth rate: 0.3% (2014 est.)
country comparison to the world: 171

Birth rate: 8.84 births/1,000 population (2014 est.)
country comparison to the world: 212

Death rate: 10.1 deaths/1,000 population (2014 est.)
country comparison to the world: 49

Net migration rate: 4.29 migrant(s)/1,000 population (2014 est.)
country comparison to the world: 29

Urbanization: *urban population:* 68% of total population (2010)
rate of urbanization: 0.5% annual rate of change (2010-15 est.)

Major urban areas—population: ROME (capital) 3.357 million; Milan 2.962 million; Naples 2.27 million; Turin 1.662 million; Palermo 872,000 (2009)

Sex ratio: *at birth:* 1.06 male(s)/female
0-14 years: 1.05 male(s)/female
15-24 years: 1.01 male(s)/female
25-54 years: 0.98 male(s)/female
55-64 years: 0.93 male(s)/female
65 years and over: 0.74 male(s)/female
total population: 0.93 male(s)/female (2014 est.)

Mother's mean age at first birth: 27.7 (2010 est.)

Maternal mortality rate: 4 deaths/100,000 live births (2010)
country comparison to the world: 180

Infant mortality rate: total: 3.31 deaths/1,000 live births
country comparison to the world: 213
male: 3.51 deaths/1,000 live births
female: 3.1 deaths/1,000 live births (2014 est.)

Life expectancy at birth: *total population:* 82.03 years
country comparison to the world: 11
male: 79.4 years
female: 84.82 years (2014 est.)

Total fertility rate: 1.42 children born/woman (2014 est.)
country comparison to the world: 205

Contraceptive prevalence rate: 62.7%
note: percent of women aged 20-49 (1995/96)

Health expenditures: 9.5% of GDP (2011)
country comparison to the world: 33

Physicians density: 3.8 physicians/1,000 population (2009)

Hospital bed density: 3.5 beds/1,000 population (2010)

Drinking water source:
improved:
urban: 100% of population
rural: 100% of population
total: 100% of population
unimproved:
urban: 0% of population
rural: 0% of population
total: 0% of population (2011 est.)

HIV/AIDS—adult prevalence rate: 0.3% (2009 est.)
country comparison to the world: 87

HIV/AIDS—people living with HIV/AIDS: 140,000 (2009 est.)
country comparison to the world: 37

HIV/AIDS—deaths: fewer than 1,000 (2009 est.)
country comparison to the world: 77

Obesity—adult prevalence rate: 19.8% (2008)
country comparison to the world: 97

Education expenditures: 4.5% of GDP (2010)
country comparison to the world: 93

Literacy: *definition:* age 15 and over can read and write
total population: 99%
male: 99.2%
female: 98.7% (2011 est.)

School life expectancy (primary to tertiary education): *total:* 16 years
male: 16 years
female: 17 years (2011)

Unemployment, youth ages 15-24: *total:* 35.3%
country comparison to the world: 18
male: 33.7%
female: 37.5% (2012)

GOVERNMENT

Country name: *conventional long form:* Italian Republic
conventional short form: Italy
local long form: Repubblica Italiana
local short form: Italia
former: Kingdom of Italy

Government type: republic

Capital: *name:* Rome
geographic coordinates: 41 54 N, 12 29 E
time difference: UTC+1 (6 hours ahead of Washington, DC during Standard Time)
daylight saving time: +1hr, begins last Sunday in March; ends last Sunday in October

Administrative divisions: 15 regions (regioni, singular—regione) and 5 autonomous regions (regioni autonome, singular—regione autonoma)
regions: Abruzzo, Basilicata, Calabria, Campania, Emilia-Romagna, Lazio (Latium), Liguria, Lombardia, Marche, Molise, Piemonte (Piedmont), Puglia (Apulia), Toscana (Tuscany), Umbria, Veneto (Venetia)
autonomous regions: Friuli-Venezia Giulia; Sardegna (Sardinia); Sicilia (Sicily); Trentino-Alto Adige (Trentino-South Tyrol) or Trentino-Suedtirol (German); Valle d'Aosta (Aosta Valley) or Vallee d'Aoste (French)

Independence: 17 March 1861 (Kingdom of Italy proclaimed; Italy was not finally unified until 1870)

National holiday: Republic Day, 2 June (1946)

Constitution: previous 1848 (originally for Kingdom of Sardinia and adopted by Kingdom of Italy in 1861); latest enacted 22 December 1947, adopted 27 December 1947, entered into force 1 January 1948; amended many times, last in 2012 (2013)

Legal system: civil law system; judicial review under certain conditions in Constitutional Court

International law organization participation: has not submitted an ICJ jurisdiction declaration; accepts ICCt jurisdiction

Suffrage: 18 years of age; universal (except in senatorial elections, where minimum age is 25)

Executive branch: *chief of state:* President Giorgio NAPOLITANO (since 15 May 2006)
head of government: Prime Minister Matteo RENZI (since 22 February 2014); note—the prime minister is referred to as the President of the Council of Ministers
cabinet: Council of Ministers proposed by the prime minister and nominated by the President of the Republic (For more information visit the World Leaders website)
elections: president elected by an electoral college consisting of both houses of parliament and 58 regional representatives for a seven-year term (no term limits); election last held on 18-20 April 2013 (next scheduled for 2020); prime minister appointed by the president and confirmed by parliament; national parliamentary elections were last held on 24-25 February 2013
election results: Giorgio NAPOLITANO elected president on the sixth round of voting; electoral college vote—738 out of a possible 1,007 (504 votes required); Enrico LETTA sworn in as Prime Minister on 28 April 2013 following formal talks between the center-left Democratic Party (PD), the center-right People of Freedom party (PdL), the centrist Civic Choice, and President NAPOLITANO that also led to the creation of a broad coalition government; the talks coming after the February 2013 legislative election produced a stalemate that impeded government formation; the PdL split into the Forza Italia and the New Center Right (NCD) in November 2013 and only the NCD remained in the governing coalition

Legislative branch: bicameral Parliament or Parlamento consists of the Senate or Senato della Repubblica (321 seats; members elected by proportional vote with the winning coalition in each region receiving 55% of seats from that region; members to serve five-year terms; and up to 5 senators for life appointed by the president of the Republic) and the Chamber of Deputies or Camera dei Deputati (630 seats; members elected by popular vote with the winning national coalition receiving 54% of chamber seats; members to serve five-year terms); note—it has not been clarified if each president has the power to designate up to five senators or if five is the number of senators for life who might sit in the Senate
elections: Senate—last held on 24-25 February 2013 (next to be held in 2018); Chamber of Deputies—last held on 24-25 February 2013 (next to be held in 2018)
election results: Senate—percent of vote by party—NA; seats by party—center-left coalition [Pier Luigi BERSANI] 123 (PD 111, SEL 7, SVP 2, other 3), center-right coalition [Silvio BERLUSCONI] 117 (PdL 98, LN 18, other 1), M5S 54, centrist coalition [Mario MONTI] 19, other 2; Chamber of Deputies—percent of vote by party—NA; seats by party—center-left coalition [Pier Luigi BERSANI] 345 (PD 297, SEL 37, CD 6 SVP 5), center-right coalition [Silvio BERLUSCONI] 125 (PdL 98, LN 18, FdI 9), M5S 109, centrist coalition [Mario MONTI] 47, other 4; note—President NAPOLITANO dissolved Parliament on 22 December 2012

Judicial branch: *highest court(s):* Supreme Court of Cassation or Corte Suprema di Cassazione (organized into penal, civil, administrative, and military divisions, each with a president and several judges); Constitutional Court or Corte Costituzionale (consists of 15 judges)
judge selection and term of office: Supreme Court judges appointed by the Superior Council of the Judiciary, headed by the president, to serve NA terms; Constitutional Court judges—5 appointed by the president, 5 elected by parliament, 5 elected by select higher courts; judges serve up to 9 years)
subordinate courts: various lower civil and criminal courts (primary and secondary tribunals, courts, and courts of appeal)

Political parties and leaders:
Center-right parties: Forza Italia [Silvio BERLUSCONI]; The New Center-Right or NCD [Angelino ALFANO]; Northern League or LN [Roberto MARONI]; Brothers of Italy or FdI [Giorgia MELONI, Ignazio LA RUSSA, and Guido CROSETTO]; The Right or LD [Francesco STORACE]; other minor parties
Center-left parties: Democratic Party or PD [Matteo RENZI]; Left Ecology Freedom or SEL [Nichi VENDOLA]; Italian Socialist Party or PSI [Riccardo NENCINI]; Democratic Centre or CD [Bruno TABACCI and Massimo DONADI]; South Tyrolean People's Party or SVP [Arno KOMPATSCHER]
Centrist parties: Civic Choice or SC [Alberto BOMBASSEI]; Union of the Center or UdC [Pier Ferdinando CASINI]; Future and Freedom for Italy or FLI [vacant]
other coalitions and parties: Five Star Movment or M5S [Beppe GRILLO]; Civil Revolution or RC [Antonio INGROIA]; Act to Stop the Decline or FiD [Michele BOLDRIN]

Political pressure groups and leaders: manufacturers and merchants associations—Confcommercio; Confindustria; organized farm groups—Confcoltivatori; Confagricoltura; Roman Catholic Church three major trade union confederations—Confederazione Generale Italiana del Lavoro or CGIL [Susanna CAMUSSO] which is left wing; Confederazione Italiana dei Sindacati Lavoratori or CISL [Raffaele BONANNI], which is Roman Catholic centrist; Unione Italiana del Lavoro or UIL [Luigi ANGELETTI] which is lay centrist

International organization participation: ADB (nonregional member), AfDB (nonregional member), Australia Group, BIS, BSEC (observer), CBSS (observer), CD, CDB, CE, CEI, CERN, EAPC, EBRD, ECB, EIB, EITI (implementing country), EMU, ESA, EU, FAO, FATF, G-20, G-7, G-8, G-10, IADB, IAEA, IBRD, ICAO, ICC (national committees), ICRM, IDA, IEA, IFAD, IFC, IFRCS, IGAD (partners), IHO, ILO, IMF, IMO, IMSO, Interpol, IOC, IOM, IPU, ISO, ITSO, ITU, ITUC (NGOs), LAIA (observer), MIGA, MINURSO, MINUSMA, NATO, NEA, NSG, OAS (observer), OECD, OPCW, OSCE, Paris Club, PCA, PIF (partner), Schengen Convention, SELEC (observer), SICA (observer), UN, UNAMID, UNCTAD, UNESCO, UNHCR, UNIDO, UNIFIL, Union Latina, UNMISS, UNMOGIP, UNRWA, UNTSO, UNWTO, UPU, WCO, WHO, WIPO, WMO, WTO, ZC

Diplomatic representation in the US:
chief of mission: Ambassador Claudio BISOGNIERO (since 13 January 2012)
chancery: 3000 Whitehaven Street NW, Washington, DC 20008
telephone: [1] (202) 612-4400
FAX: [1] (202) 518-2154
consulate(s) general: Boston, Chicago, Houston, Miami, New York, Los Angeles, Philadelphia, San Francisco
consulate(s): Detroit, Newark (NJ), San Francisco

Diplomatic representation from the US:
chief of mission: Ambassador John R. PHILLIPS (since 16 August 2013); note—also accredited to San Marino
embassy: Via Vittorio Veneto 121, 00187-Rome
mailing address: PSC 59, Box 100, APO AE 09624
telephone: [39] (06) 46741
FAX: [39] (06) 4674-2244
consulate(s) general: Florence, Milan, Naples

Flag description: three equal vertical bands of green (hoist side), white, and red; design inspired by the French flag brought to Italy by Napoleon in 1797; colors are those of Milan (red and white) combined with the green uniform color of the Milanese civic guard note: similar to the flag of Mexico, which is longer, uses darker shades of red and green, and has its coat of arms centered on the white band; Ireland, which is longer and is green (hoist side), white, and orange; also similar to the flag of the Cote d'Ivoire, which has the colors reversed—orange (hoist side), white, and green

National symbol(s): white, five-pointed star (Stella d'Italia)

National anthem: *name:* "Il Canto degli Italiani" (The Song of the Italians)
lyrics/music: Goffredo MAMELI/Michele NOVARO
note: adopted 1946; the anthem, originally written in 1847, is also known as "L'Inno di Mameli" (Mameli's Hymn), and "Fratelli D'Italia" (Brothers of Italy)

ECONOMY

Economy—overview: Italy has a diversified industrial economy, which is divided into a developed industrial north, dominated by private companies, and a less-developed, highly subsidized, agricultural south, where unemployment is higher. The Italian economy is driven in large part by the manufacture of high-quality consumer goods produced by small and medium-sized enterprises, many of them family-owned. Italy also has a sizable underground economy, which by some estimates accounts for as much as 17% of GDP. These activities are most common within the agriculture, construction, and service sectors. Italy is the third-largest economy in the euro-zone, but its exceptionally high public debt and structural impediments to growth have rendered it vulnerable to scrutiny by financial markets. Public debt has increased steadily since 2007, topping 133% of GDP in 2013, but investor concerns about Italy and the broader euro-zone crisis eased in 2013, bringing down Italy's borrowing costs on sovereign government debt from euro-era records. The government still faces pressure from investors and European partners to sustain its efforts to address Italy's long-standing structural impediments to growth, such as labor market inefficiencies and widespread tax evasion. In 2013 economic growth and labor market conditions deteriorated, with growth at -1.8% and unemployment rising to 12.4%, with youth unemployment around 40%. Italy's GDP is now 8% below its 2007 pre-crisis level.

GDP (purchasing power parity): $1.805 trillion (2013 est.)
country comparison to the world: 12
$1.838 trillion (2012 est.)
$1.883 trillion (2011 est.)
note: data are in 2013 US dollars

GDP (official exchange rate): $2.068 trillion (2013 est.)

GDP—real growth rate: -1.8% (2013 est.)
country comparison to the world: 210
-2.4% (2012 est.)
0.4% (2011 est.)

GDP—per capita (PPP): $29,600 (2013 est.)
country comparison to the world: 51
$29,800 (2012 est.)
$30,100 (2011 est.)
note: data are in 2013 US dollars

Gross national saving: 17.4% of GDP (2013 est.)
country comparison to the world: 94
16.9% of GDP (2012 est.)
16.4% of GDP (2011 est.)

GDP—composition, by end use:
household consumption: 60%
government consumption: 20.6%
investment in fixed capital: 17.6%
investment in inventories: -0.3%
exports of goods and services: 30.1%
imports of goods and services: -27.9% (2013 est.)

GDP—composition, by sector of origin:
agriculture: 2%
industry: 24.4%
services: 73.5% (2013 est.)

Agriculture—products: fruits, vegetables, grapes, potatoes, sugar beets, soybeans, grain, olives; beef, dairy products; fish

Industries: tourism, machinery, iron and steel, chemicals, food processing, textiles, motor vehicles, clothing, footwear, ceramics

Industrial production growth rate: -2.7% (2013 est.)
country comparison to the world: 184

Labor force: 25.74 million (2013 est.)
country comparison to the world: 26

Labor force—by occupation: *agriculture:* 3.9%
industry: 28.3%
services: 67.8% (2011)

Unemployment rate: 12.4% (2013 est.)
country comparison to the world: 125
10.7% (2012 est.)

Population below poverty line: 29.9% (2012)

Household income or consumption by percentage share: *lowest 10%:* 2.3%
highest 10%: 26.8% (2000)

Distribution of family income—Gini index:
31.9 (2012 est.)
country comparison to the world: 110
27.3 (1995)

Budget: *revenues:* $984 billion
expenditures: $1.052 trillion (2013 est.)

Taxes and other revenues: 47.6% of GDP (2013 est.)
country comparison to the world: 17

Budget surplus (+) or deficit (-):
-3.3% of GDP (2013 est.)
country comparison to the world: 132

Public debt: 133% of GDP (2013 est.)
country comparison to the world: 4
126.9% of GDP (2012 est.)
note: Italy reports its data on public debt according to guidelines set out in the Maastricht Treaty; general government gross debt is defined in the Maastricht Treaty as consolidated general government gross debt at nominal value, outstanding at the end of the year, in the following categories of government liabilities (as defined in ESA95): currency and deposits (AF.2), securities other than shares excluding financial derivatives (AF.3, excluding AF.34), and loans (AF.4); the general government sector comprises the central government, state government, local government and social security funds

Fiscal year: calendar year

Inflation rate (consumer prices): 1.2% (2013 est.)
country comparison to the world: 29
3% (2012 est.)

Central bank discount rate: 0.25% (31 December 2013)
country comparison to the world: 134
0.75% (31 December 2012)
note: this is the European Central Bank's rate on the marginal lending facility, which offers overnight credit to banks in the euro area

Commercial bank prime lending rate: 5.2% (31 December 2013 est.)
country comparison to the world: 155
5.22% (31 December 2012 est.)

Stock of narrow money: $1.138 trillion (31 December 2013 est.)
country comparison to the world: 6
$1.162 trillion (31 December 2012 est.)
note: see entry for the European Union for money supply in the euro area; the European Central Bank (ECB) controls monetary policy for the 17 members of the Economic and Monetary Union (EMU); individual members of the EMU do not control the quantity of money circulating within their own borders

Stock of broad money: $2.15 trillion (31 December 2013 est.)
country comparison to the world: 8
$2.134 trillion (31 December 2012 est.)

Stock of domestic credit: $3.407 trillion (31 December 2013 est.)
country comparison to the world: 8
$3.438 trillion (31 December 2012 est.)

Market value of publicly traded shares: $480.5 billion (31 December 2012 est.)
country comparison to the world: 21
$431.5 billion (31 December 2011)
$318.1 billion (31 December 2010 est.)

Current account balance: -$2.4 billion (2013 est.)
country comparison to the world: 151
-$14.88 billion (2012 est.)

Exports: $474 billion (2013 est.)
country comparison to the world: 12
$478.9 billion (2012 est.)

Exports—commodities: engineering products, textiles and clothing, production machinery, motor vehicles, transport equipment, chemicals; food, beverages and tobacco; minerals, nonferrous metals

Exports—partners: Germany 12.63%, France 11.11%, United States 6.84%, Switzerland 5.72%, United Kingdom 4.72%, Spain 4.48% (2013 est.)

Imports: $435.8 billion (2013 est.)
country comparison to the world: 13
$453.5 billion (2012 est.)

Imports—commodities: engineering products, chemicals, transport equipment, energy products, minerals and nonferrous metals, textiles and clothing; food, beverages, and tobacco

Imports—partners: Germany 14.73%, France 8.4%, China 8.4%, Russia 6.35%, Netherlands 5.85%, Spain 4.54%, Belgium 4.09% (2013 est.)

Reserves of foreign exchange and gold:
$181.7 billion (31 December 2012 est.)
country comparison to the world: 16

$173.3 billion (31 December 2011 est.)
Debt—external: $2.604 trillion (31 December 2013 est.)
country comparison to the world: 8
$2.516 trillion (31 December 2012 est.)
Stock of direct foreign investment—at home: $466.3 billion (31 December 2013 est.)
country comparison to the world: 18
$457.8 billion (31 December 2012 est.)
Stock of direct foreign investment—abroad: $683.6 billion (31 December 2013 est.)
country comparison to the world: 13
$653.3 billion (31 December 2012 est.)
Exchange rates: euros (EUR) per US dollar—
0.7634 (2013 est.)
0.7752 (2012 est.)
0.755 (2010 est.)
0.7198 (2009 est.)
0.6827 (2008 est.)

ENERGY

Electricity—production: 299.3 billion kWh (2012 est.)
country comparison to the world: 1 3
Electricity—consumption: 307.2 billion kWh (2012 est.)
country comparison to the world: 13
Electricity—exports: 2.304 billion kWh (2012 est.)
country comparison to the world: 41
Electricity—imports: 45.41 billion kWh (2012 est.)
country comparison to the world: 3
Electricity—installed generating capacity: 124.2 million kW (2012 est.)
country comparison to the world: 10
Electricity—from fossil fuels: 65% of total installed capacity (2011 est.)
country comparison to the world: 121
Electricity—from nuclear fuels: 0% of total installed capacity (2012 est.)
country comparison to the world: 111
Electricity—from hydroelectric plants: 18% of total installed capacity (2011 est.)
country comparison to the world: 96
Electricity—from other renewable sources: 15.8% of total installed capacity (2011 est.)
country comparison to the world: 13
Crude oil—production: 112,000 bbl/day (2012 est.)
country comparison to the world: 47
Crude oil—exports: 6,300 bbl/day (2010 est.)
country comparison to the world: 63
Crude oil—imports: 1.591 million bbl/day (2010 est.)
country comparison to the world: 8
Crude oil—proved reserves: 521.3 million bbl (1 January 2013 es)
country comparison to the world: 50
Refined petroleum products—production: *6,600 bbl/day (2011 est.)*
country comparison to the world: 107
Refined petroleum products—consumption: *1.454 million bbl/day (2011 est.)*
country comparison to the world: 16
Refined petroleum products—exports: 628,000 bbl/day (2010 est.)
country comparison to the world: 13
Refined petroleum products—imports: 393,300 bbl/day (2010 est.)
country comparison to the world: 15
Natural gas—production: 7.8 billion cu m (2012 est.)
country comparison to the world: 47
Natural gas—consumption: 68.7 billion cu m (2012 est.)
country comparison to the world: 11
Natural gas—exports: 324 million cu m (2012 est.)
country comparison to the world: 48
Natural gas—imports: 67.8 billion cu m (2012 est.)
country comparison to the world: 5
Natural gas—proved reserves: 62.35 billion cu m (1 January 2013 es)
country comparison to the world: 62
Carbon dioxide emissions from consumption of energy: 400.9 million Mt (2011 est.)
country comparison to the world: 17

COMMUNICATIONS

Telephones—main lines in use: 21.656 million (2012)
country comparison to the world: 1 3
Telephones—mobile cellular: 97.225 million (2012)
country comparison to the world: 14
Telephone system: *general assessment:* modern, well-developed, fast; fully automated telephone, telex, and data services
domestic: high-capacity cable and microwave radio relay trunks
international: country code—39; a series of submarine cables provide links to Asia, Middle East, Europe, North Africa, and US; satellite earth stations—3 Intelsat (with a total of 5 antennas—3 for Atlantic Ocean and 2 for Indian Ocean), 1 Inmarsat (Atlantic Ocean region), and NA Eutelsat (2011)
Broadcast media: two Italian media giants dominate—the publicly owned Radiotelevisione Italiana (RAI) with 3 national terrestrial stations and privately owned Mediaset with 3 national terrestrial stations; a large number of private stations and Sky Italia—a satellite TV network; RAI operates 3 AM/FM nationwide radio stations; some 1,300 commercial radio stations (2007)
Internet country code: .it
Internet hosts: 25.662 million (2012)
country comparison to the world: 4
Internet users: 29.235 million (2009)
country comparison to the world: 13

TRANSPORTATION

Airports: 129 (2013)
country comparison to the world: 4 5
Airports—with paved runways: *total:* 9 8
over 3,047 m: 9
2,438 to 3,047 m: 31
1,524 to 2,437 m: 18
914 to 1,523 m: 29
under 914 m: 11 (2013)
Airports—with unpaved runways: *total:* 3 1
1,524 to 2,437 m: 1
914 to 1,523 m: 10
under 914 m: 20 (2013)
Heliports: 5 (2013)
Pipelines: gas 20,223 km; oil 1,393 km; refined products 1,574 km (2013)
Railways: *total:* 20,255 km
country comparison to the world: 13
standard gauge: 18,611 km 1.435-m gauge (12,662 km electrified)
narrow gauge: 123 km 1.000-m gauge (123 km electrified); 1,290 km 0.950-m gauge (151 km electrified);
231 km 0.850-m gauge (2008)
Roadways: *total:* 487,700 km
country comparison to the world: 14
paved: 487,700 km (includes 6,700 km of expressways) (2007)
Waterways: 2,400 km (used for commercial traffic; of limited overall value compared to road and rail) (2012)
country comparison to the world: 37
Merchant marine: *total:* 681
country comparison to the world: 17
by type: bulk carrier 105, cargo 42, carrier 1, chemical tanker 164, container 21, liquefied gas 28, passenger 25, passenger/cargo 154, petroleum tanker 59, refrigerated cargo 4, roll on/roll off 39, specialized tanker 9, vehicle carrier 30
foreign-owned: 90 (Denmark 4, France 2, Greece 7, Luxembourg 14, Netherlands 2, Nigeria 1, Norway 6, Singapore 1, Sweden 1, Switzerland 13, Taiwan 10, Turkey 4, UK 2, US 23)
registered in other countries: 201 (Bahamas 1, Belize 3, Cayman Islands 7, Cyprus 6, Georgia 2, Gibraltar 4, Greece 5, Liberia 47, Malta 45, Marshall Islands 1, Morocco 1, Netherlands 6, Panama 25, Portugal 12, Russia 14, Saint Vincent and the Grenadines 4, Singapore 5, Slovakia 2, Spain 1, Sweden 5, Turkey 1, UK 3, unknown 1) (2010)
Ports and terminals: *major seaport(s):* Augusta, Cagliari, Genoa, Livorno, Taranto, Trieste, Venice
oil terminals: Melilli (Santa Panagia) oil terminal, Sarroch oil terminal
container port(s) (TEUs): Genoa (1,847,648), Gioia Tauro (2,264,798), La Spezia (1,307,274)

MILITARY

Military branches: Italian Armed Forces: Army (Esercito Italiano, EI), Navy (Marina Militare Italiana, MMI), Italian Air Force (Aeronautica Militare Italiana, AMI), Carabinieri Corps (Arma dei Carabinieri, CC) (2011)
Military service age and obligation: 18-25 years of age for voluntary military service; women may serve in any military branch; Italian *citizenship required; 12-month service obligation (2013)*
Manpower available for military service: *males age 16-49:* 13,865,688
females age 16-49: 14,003,755 (2010 est.)
Manpower fit for military service: *males age 16-49:* 11,247,446
females age 16-49: 11,348,695 (2010 est.)
Manpower reaching militarily significant age annually: *male:* 288,188
female: 281,671 (2010 est.)
Military expenditures: 1.69% of GDP (2012)
country comparison to the world: 53
1.72% of GDP (2011)
1.69% of GDP (2010)

TRANSNATIONAL ISSUES

Disputes—international: Italy's long coastline and developed economy entices tens of thousands of illegal immigrants from southeastern Europe and northern Africa
Refugees and internally displaced persons: *refugees (country of origin):* 11,345 (Eritrea); 9,284 (Somalia); 5,058 (Afghanistan) (2012)
stateless persons: 470 (2012)
Illicit drugs: important gateway for and consumer of Latin American cocaine and Southwest Asian heroin entering the European market; money laundering by organized crime and from smuggling

JAMAICA

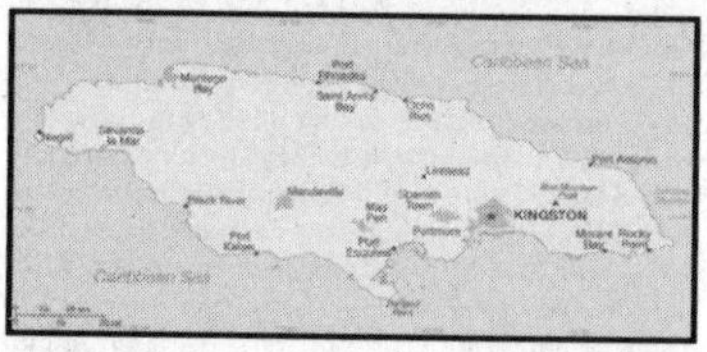

INTRODUCTION

Background: The island—discovered by Christopher COLUMBUS in 1494—was settled by the Spanish early in the 16th century. The native Taino, who had inhabited Jamaica for centuries, were gradually exterminated and replaced by African slaves. England seized the island in 1655 and established a plantation economy based on sugar, cocoa, and coffee. The abolition of slavery in 1834 freed a quarter million slaves, many of whom became small farmers. Jamaica gradually increased its independence from Britain. In 1958 it joined other British Caribbean colonies in forming the Federation of the West Indies. Jamaica gained full independence when it withdrew from the Federation in 1962. Deteriorating economic conditions during the 1970s led to recurrent violence as rival gangs affiliated with the major political parties evolved into powerful organized crime networks involved in international drug smuggling and money laundering. Violent crime, drug trafficking, and poverty pose significant challenges to the government today. Nonetheless, many rural and resort areas remain relatively safe and contribute substantially to the economy.

GEOGRAPHY

Location: Caribbean, island in the Caribbean Sea, south of Cuba

Geographic coordinates: 18 15 N, 77 30 W

Map references: Central America and the Caribbean

Area: *total:* 10,991 sq km
country comparison to the world: 168
land: 10,831 sq km
water: 160 sq km

Area—comparative: slightly smaller than Connecticut

Land boundaries: 0 km

Coastline: 1,022 km

Maritime claims: measured from claimed archipelagic straight baselines
territorial sea: 12 nm
contiguous zone: 24 nm
exclusive economic zone: 200 nm
continental shelf: 200 nm or to edge of the continental margin

Climate: tropical; hot, humid; temperate interior

Terrain: mostly mountains, with narrow, discontinuous coastal plain

Elevation extremes: *lowest point:* Caribbean Sea 0 m
highest point: Blue Mountain Peak 2,256 m

Natural resources: bauxite, gypsum, limestone

Land use: *arable land:* 10.92%
permanent crops: 9.1%
other: 79.98% (2011)

Irrigated land: 252.2 sq km (2003)

Total renewable water resources: 9.4 cu km (2011)

Freshwater withdrawal (domestic/industrial/agricultural): *total:* 0.93 cu km/yr (32%/16%/52%)
per capita: 369.9 cu m/yr (2009)

Natural hazards: hurricanes (especially July to November)

Environment—current issues: heavy rates of deforestation; coastal waters polluted by industrial waste, sewage, and oil spills; damage to coral reefs; air pollution in Kingston from vehicle emissions

Environment—international agreements: *party to:* Biodiversity, Climate Change, Climate Change-Kyoto Protocol, Desertification, Endangered Species, Hazardous Wastes, Law of the Sea, Marine Dumping, Marine Life Conservation, Ozone Layer Protection, Ship Pollution, Wetlands
signed, but not ratified: none of the selected agreements

Geography—note: strategic location between Cayman Trench and Jamaica Channel, the main sea lanes for the Panama Canal

PEOPLE AND SOCIETY

Nationality: *noun:* Jamaican(s)
adjective: Jamaican

Ethnic groups: black 92.1%, mixed 6.1%, East Indian 0.8%, other 0.4%, unspecified 0.7% (2011 est.)

Languages: English, English patois

Religions: Protestant 64.8% (includes Seventh Day Adventist 12.0%, Pentecostal 11.0%, Other Church of God 9.2%, New Testament Church of God 7.2%, Baptist 6.7%, Church of God in Jamaica 4.8%, Church of God of Prophecy 4.5%, Anglican 2.8%, United Church 2.1%, Methodist 1.6%, Revived 1.4%, Brethren .9%, and Moravian .7%), Roman Catholic 2.2%, Jehovah's Witness 1.9%, Rastafarian 1.1%, other 6.5%, none 21.3%, unspecified 2.3% (2011 est.)

Population: 2,930,050 (July 2014 est.)
country comparison to the world: 140

Age structure:
0-14 years: 28.4% (male 423,855/female 409,651)
15-24 years: 21.7% (male 319,291/female 316,773)
25-54 years: 36.4% (male 525,288/female 542,015)
55-64 years: 7.8% (male 79,875/female 84,562)
65 years and over: 7.7% (male 102,377/female 126,363) (2014 est.)

Dependency ratios:
total dependency ratio: 54 %
youth dependency ratio: 41.8 %
elderly dependency ratio: 12.2 %
potential support ratio: 8.2 (2013)

Median age: *total:* 24.9 years
male: 24.4 years
female: 25.4 years (2014 est.)

Population growth rate: 0.69% (2014 est.)
country comparison to the world: 146

Birth rate: 18.41 births/1,000 population (2014 est.)
country comparison to the world: 102

Death rate: 6.67 deaths/1,000 population (2014 est.)
country comparison to the world: 143

Net migration rate: -4.83 migrant(s)/1,000 population (2014 est.)
country comparison to the world: 193

Urbanization: *urban population:* 52% of total population (2010)
rate of urbanization: 0.6% annual rate of change (2010-15 est.)

Major urban areas—population: KINGSTON (capital) 580,000 (2009)

Sex ratio: *at birth:* 1.05 male(s)/female
0-14 years: 1.04 male(s)/female
15-24 years: 1.01 male(s)/female
25-54 years: 0.97 male(s)/female
55-64 years: 0.98 male(s)/female
65 years and over: 0.81 male(s)/female
total population: 0.98 male(s)/female (2014 est.)

Mother's mean age at first birth: 21.2
note: median age at first birth among women 25-29 (2008 est.)

Maternal mortality rate: 110 deaths/100,000 live births (2010)
country comparison to the world: 65

Infant mortality rate: total: 13.69 deaths/1,000 live births
country comparison to the world: 114
male: 14.27 deaths/1,000 live births
female: 13.08 deaths/1,000 live births (2014 est.)

Life expectancy at birth: *total population:* 73.48 years
country comparison to the world: 121
male: 71.87 years
female: 75.17 years (2014 est.)

Total fertility rate: 2.05 children born/woman (2014 est.)
country comparison to the world: 118

Contraceptive prevalence rate: 69% (2002/03)

Health expenditures: 5.2% of GDP (2010)
country comparison to the world: 139

Physicians density: 0.41 physicians/1,000 population (2008)

Hospital bed density: 1.8 beds/1,000 population (2010)

Drinking water source:
improved:
urban: 97.1% of population
rural: 88.8% of population
total: 93.1% of population
unimproved:
urban: 2.9% of population
rural: 11.2% of population
total: 6.9% of population (2011 est.)

Sanitation facility access:
improved:
urban: 78.4% of population
rural: 82.2% of population
total: 80.2% of population
unimproved:
urban: 21.6% of population
rural: 17.8% of population
total: 19.8% of population (2011 est.)

HIV/AIDS—adult prevalence rate: 1.7% (2012 est.)
country comparison to the world: 29

HIV/AIDS—people living with HIV/AIDS: 28,400 (2012 est.)
country comparison to the world: 73

HIV/AIDS—deaths: 1,300 (2012 est.)
country comparison to the world: 66

Obesity—adult prevalence rate: 24.1% (2008)
country comparison to the world: 67

Children under the age of 5 years underweight: 3.2% (2010)
country comparison to the world: 112

Education expenditures: 6.1% of GDP (2012)
country comparison to the world: 40

Literacy: *definition:* age 15 and over has ever attended school
total population: 87%
male: 82.1%
female: 91.8% (2011 est.)

School life expectancy (primary to tertiary education): *total:* 12 years
male: 12 years
female: 12 years (2002)

Child labor—children ages 5-14: *total number:* 38,516
percentage: 6 % (2005 est.)

Unemployment, youth ages 15-24: *total:* 34%
country comparison to the world: 20
male: 27.1%
female: 42.6% (2012)

GOVERNMENT

Country name: *conventional long form:* none
conventional short form: Jamaica

Government type: constitutional parliamentary democracy and a Commonwealth realm

Capital: *name:* Kingston
geographic coordinates: 18 00 N, 76 48 W
time difference: UTC-5 (same time as Washington, DC during Standard Time)

Administrative divisions: 14 parishes; Clarendon, Hanover, Kingston, Manchester, Portland, Saint Andrew, Saint Ann, Saint Catherine, Saint Elizabeth, Saint James, Saint Mary, Saint Thomas, Trelawny, Westmoreland
note: for local government purposes, Kingston and Saint Andrew were amalgamated in 1923 into the present single corporate body known as the Kingston and Saint Andrew Corporation

Independence: 6 August 1962 (from the UK)

National holiday: Independence Day, 6 August (1962)

Constitution: several previous (preindependence); latest drafted 1961-62, submitted to British Parliament 24 July 1962, entered into force 6 August 1962 (at independence); amended many times, last in 2011 (2011)

Legal system: common law system based on the English model

International law organization participation: has not submitted an ICJ jurisdiction declaration; non-party state to the ICCt

Suffrage: 18 years of age; universal

Executive branch: *chief of state:* Queen ELIZABETH II (since 6 February 1952); represented by Governor General Dr. Patrick L. ALLEN (since 26 February 2009)
head of government: Prime Minister Portia SIMPSON-MILLER (since 5 January 2012)
cabinet: Cabinet is appointed by the governor general on the advice of the prime minister (For more information visit the World Leaders website)
elections: the monarchy is hereditary; governor general appointed by the monarch on the recommendation of the prime minister; following legislative elections, the leader of the majority party or the leader of the majority coalition in the House of Representatives is appointed prime minister by the governor general

Legislative branch: bicameral Parliament consists of the Senate (a 21-member body appointed by the governor general on the recommendations of the prime minister and the leader of the opposition; ruling party is allocated 13 seats, and the opposition is allocated 8 seats) and the House of Representatives (63 seats; members elected by popular vote to serve five-year terms)
elections: last held on 29 December 2011 (next to be held no later than December 2016)
election results: percent of vote by party—PNP 53.3%, JLP 46.6%; seats by party—PNP 41, JLP 22

Judicial branch: *highest court(s):* Court of Appeal (consists of president of the court and a minimum of 4 judges; Supreme Court (40 judges organized in specialized divisions) note—appeals beyond Jamicia's highest courts are submitted to the Judicial Committee of the Privy Council (in London) rather than to the Caribbean Court of Justice (the appellate court implemented for member states of the Caribbean Community)
judge selection and term of office: chief justice of the Supreme Court and president of the Court of Appeal appointed by the governor-general on the advice of the prime minister; other judges of both courts appointed by the governor-general on the advice of the Judicial Service Commission; judges of both courts serve till age 70
subordinate courts: resident magistrate courts, district courts, and petty sessions courts

Political parties and leaders: Jamaica Labor Party or JLP [Andrew HOLNESS]; People's National Party or PNP [Portia SIMPSON-MILLER]; National Democratic Movement or NDM [Michael WILLIAMS]

Political pressure groups and leaders: New Beginnings Movement or NBM; Rastafarians (black religious/racial cultists, pan-Africanists)

International organization participation: ACP, AOSIS, C, Caricom, CDB, CELAC, FAO, G-15, G-77, IADB, IAEA, IBRD, ICAO, ICRM, IDA, IFAD, IFC, IFRCS, IHO, ILO, IMF, IMO, Interpol, IOC, IOM, ISO, ITSO, ITU, LAES, MIGA, NAM, OAS, OPANAL, OPCW, Petrocaribe, UN, UNCTAD, UNESCO, UNIDO, UNITAR, UNWTO, UPU, WCO, WFTU (NGOs), WHO, WIPO, WMO, WTO

Diplomatic representation in the US:
chief of mission: Ambassador Stephen C. VASCIANNIE (since 20 July 2012)
chancery: 1520 New Hampshire Avenue NW, Washington, DC 20036
telephone: [1] (202) 452-0660
FAX: [1] (202) 452-0081
consulate(s) general: Miami, New York

Diplomatic representation from the US:
chief of mission: Ambassador Pamela E. BRIDGEWATER (since 1 December 2010)
embassy: 142 Old Hope Road, Kingston 6
mailing address: P.O. Box 541, Kingston 5
telephone: [1] (876) 702-6000
FAX: [1] (876) 702-6001

Flag description: diagonal yellow cross divides the flag into four triangles—green (top and bottom) and black (hoist side and outer side); green represents hope, vegetation, and agriculture, black reflects hardships overcome and to be faced, and yellow recalls golden sunshine and the island's natural resources

National symbol(s): green-and-black streamertail (bird)

National anthem: *name:* "Jamaica, Land We Love"
lyrics/music: Hugh Braham SHERLOCK/Robert Charles LIGHTBOURNE
note: adopted 1962

ECONOMY

Economy—overview: The Jamaican economy is heavily dependent on services, which accounted for more than 60% of GDP in 2013. The country continues to derive most of its foreign exchange from tourism, remittances, and bauxite/alumina. Remittances account for nearly 15% of GDP and exports of bauxite and alumina make up roughly 5%. The bauxite/alumina sector was most affected by the global downturn while the tourism industry was resilient. Tourism revenues account for roughly 5% of GDP in 2011. Jamaica's economy faces many challenges to growth: high crime and corruption, large-scale unemployment and underemployment, and a debt-to-GDP ratio of nearly 125%. Jamaica's onerous public debt burden is the result of government bailouts to ailing sectors of the economy, most notably to the financial sector. In early 2010, the Jamaican Government created the Jamaica Debt Exchange in order to retire high-priced domestic bonds and significantly reduce annual debt servicing. Despite the improvement, debt servicing costs still hinder the government's ability to spend on infrastructure and social programs, particularly as job losses rise in a shrinking economy. Jamaica was hard hit by the effects of the global economic crisis and growth remains low. The SIMPSON-MILLER administration faces the difficult prospect of having to achieve fiscal discipline in order to maintain debt payments, while simultaneously attacking a serious crime problem that is hampering economic growth. High unemployment exacerbates the crime problem, including gang violence that is fueled by the drug trade. The SIMPSON-MILLER government negotiated a new IMF Stand-by agreement to gain access to additional funds in 2013, although the deal will require the government to raise taxes and decrease public sector wages.

GDP (purchasing power parity): $25.13 billion (2013 est.)
country comparison to the world: 126
$25.03 billion (2012 est.)
$25.15 billion (2011 est.)
note: data are in 2013 US dollars

GDP (official exchange rate): $14.39 billion (2013 est.)

GDP—real growth rate: 0.4% (2013 est.)
country comparison to the world: 188
-0.5% (2012 est.)
1.4% (2011 est.)

GDP—per capita (PPP): $9,000 (2013 est.)
country comparison to the world: 125
$9,000 (2012 est.)
$9,100 (2011 est.)
note: data are in 2013 US dollars

Gross national saving: 10.8% of GDP (2013 est.)
country comparison to the world: 131
8.7% of GDP (2012 est.)
7% of GDP (2011 est.)

GDP—composition, by end use:
household consumption: 86.6%
government consumption: 15.7%
investment in fixed capital: 21.2%
investment in inventories: 0.5%
exports of goods and services: 34.5%
imports of goods and services: -58.4% (2013 est.)

GDP—composition, by sector of origin:
agriculture: 6.5%
industry: 29.4%
services: 64.1% (2013 est.)

Agriculture—products: sugarcane, bananas, coffee, citrus, yams, ackees, vegetables; poultry, goats, milk; shellfish

Industries: tourism, bauxite/alumina, agro-processing, light manufactures, rum, cement, metal, paper, chemical products, telecommunications

Industrial production growth rate: 1.5% (2013 est.)
country comparison to the world: 138

Labor force: 1.261 million (2013 est.)
country comparison to the world: 138

Labor force—by occupation:
agriculture: 17%
industry: 19%
services: 64% (2006)

Unemployment rate: 16.3% (2013 est.)
country comparison to the world: 148
13.7% (2012 est.)

Population below poverty line: 16.5% (2009 est.)

Household income or consumption by percentage share: *lowest 10%:* 2.1%
highest 10%: 35.8% (2004)

Distribution of family income—Gini index: 45.5 (2004)

country comparison to the world: 38
37.9 (2000)

Budget: *revenues:* $3.826 billion
expenditures: $4.088 billion (2013 est.)

Taxes and other revenues: 26.6% of GDP (2013 est.)
country comparison to the world: 113

Budget surplus (+) or deficit (-):
-1.8% of GDP (2013 est.)
country comparison to the world: 82

Public debt: 123.6% of GDP (2013 est.)
country comparison to the world: 8
132.9% of GDP (2012 est.)

Fiscal year: 1 April—31 March

Inflation rate (consumer prices): 9.4% (2013 est.)
country comparison to the world: 206
6.9% (2012 est.)

Central bank discount rate: 2% (31 December 2010 est.)
NA% (31 December 2009 est.)

Commercial bank prime lending rate: 17% (31 December 2013 est.)
country comparison to the world: 26
17.63% (31 December 2012 est.)

Stock of narrow money: $1.671 billion (31 December 2013 est.)
country comparison to the world: 133
$1.723 billion (31 December 2012 est.)

Stock of broad money: $5.928 billion (31 December 2013 est.)
country comparison to the world: 124
$6.239 billion (31 December 2012 est.)

Stock of domestic credit:
$7.197 billion (31 December 2013 est.)
country comparison to the world: 108
$7.351 billion (31 December 2012 est.)

Market value of publicly traded shares:
$6.39 billion (31 December 2012 est.)
country comparison to the world: 78
$7.223 billion (31 December 2011)
$6.626 billion (31 December 2010 est.)

Current account balance: -$1.583 billion (2013 est.)
country comparison to the world: 135
-$1.905 billion (2012 est.)

Exports: $1.775 billion (2013 est.)
country comparison to the world: 143
$1.747 billion (2012 est.)

Exports—commodities: alumina, bauxite, sugar, rum, coffee, yams, beverages, chemicals, wearing apparel, mineral fuels

Exports—partners: US 48%, Canada 7.2%, Slovenia 4.2%, Netherlands 4.1%, UAE 4.1% (2012)
Imports:
$5.559 billion (2013 est.)
country comparison to the world: 123
$5.905 billion (2012 est.)

Imports—commodities: food and other consumer goods, industrial supplies, fuel, parts and accessories of capital goods, machinery and transport equipment, construction materials

Imports—partners: US 36.1%, Venezuela 15.6%, Trinidad and Tobago 10.8%, China 4.8%, Mexico 4% (2012)

Reserves of foreign exchange and gold:
$1.9 billion (31 December 2013 est.)
country comparison to the world: 122
$1.981 billion (31 December 2012 est.)

Debt—external: $13.82 billion (31 December 2013 est.)
country comparison to the world: 93
$14.09 billion (31 December 2012 est.)

Exchange rates: Jamaican dollars (JMD) per US dollar—
99.83 (2013 est.)
88.751 (2012 est.)
87.196 (2010 est.)
87.89 (2009)
72.236 (2008)

ENERGY

Electricity—production: 3.957 billion kWh (2010 est.)
country comparison to the world: 123

Electricity—consumption: 3.066 billion kWh (2010 est.)
country comparison to the world: 131

Electricity—exports: 0 kWh (2012 est.)
country comparison to the world: 153

Electricity—imports: 0 kWh (2012 est.)
country comparison to the world: 159

Electricity—installed generating capacity:
1.175 million kW (2010 est.)
country comparison to the world: 120

Electricity—from fossil fuels: 94.8% of total installed capacity (2010 est.)
country comparison to the world: 68

Electricity—from nuclear fuels: 0% of total installed capacity (2010 est.)
country comparison to the world: 114

Electricity—from hydroelectric plants: 2.1% of total installed capacity (2010 est.)
country comparison to the world: 135

Electricity—from other renewable sources:
3% of total installed capacity (2010 est.)
country comparison to the world: 62

Crude oil—production: 2,120 bbl/day (2012 est.)
country comparison to the world: 104

Crude oil—exports: 0 bbl/day (2010 est.)
country comparison to the world: 133

Crude oil—imports: 22,940 bbl/day (2010 est.)
country comparison to the world: 67

Crude oil—proved reserves: 0 bbl (1 January 2013 es)
country comparison to the world: 147

Refined petroleum products—production:
23,120 bbl/day (2010 est.)
country comparison to the world: 89

Refined petroleum products—consumption:
78,520 bbl/day (2011 est.)
country comparison to the world: 87

Refined petroleum products—exports:
0 bbl/day (2010 est.)
country comparison to the world: 186

Refined petroleum products—imports:
32,920 bbl/day (2010 est.)
country comparison to the world: 88

Natural gas—production: 0 cu m (2011 est.)
country comparison to the world: 146

Natural gas—consumption: 0 cu m (2010 est.)
country comparison to the world: 158

Natural gas—exports: 0 cu m (2011 est.)
country comparison to the world: 124

Natural gas—imports: 0 cu m (2011 est.)
country comparison to the world: 210

Natural gas—proved reserves: 0 cu m (1 January 2013 es)
country comparison to the world: 152

Carbon dioxide emissions from consumption of energy: 9.557 million Mt (2011 est.)
country comparison to the world: 101

COMMUNICATIONS

Telephones—main lines in use: 265,000 (2011)
country comparison to the world: 123

Telephones—mobile cellular: 2.665 million (2012)
country comparison to the world: 135

Telephone system: *general assessment:* fully automatic domestic telephone network
domestic: the 1999 agreement to open the market for telecommunications services resulted in rapid growth in mobile-cellular telephone usage while the number of fixed-lines in use has declined; combined mobile-cellular teledensity exceeded 110 per 100 persons in 2011
international: country code—1-876; the Fibralink submarine cable network provides enhanced delivery of business and broadband traffic and is linked to the Americas Region Caribbean Ring System (ARCOS-1) submarine cable in the Dominican Republic; the link to ARCOS-1 provides seamless connectivity to US, parts of the Caribbean, Central America, and South America; the ALBA-1 fiber-optic submarine cable links Jamaica, Cuba, and Venezuela; satellite earth stations—2 Intelsat (Atlantic Ocean) (2010)

Broadcast media: 3 free-to-air TV stations, subscription cable services, and roughly 30 radio stations (2013)

Internet country code: .jm

Internet hosts: 3,906 (2012)
country comparison to the world: 149

Internet users: 1.581 million (2009)
country comparison to the world: 80

TRANSPORTATION

Airports: 28 (2013)
country comparison to the world: 123

Airports—with paved runways: *total:* 1 1
2,438 to 3,047 m: 2
914 to 1,523 m: 4
under 914 m: 5 (2013)

Airports—with unpaved runways: *total:* 1 7
914 to 1,523 m: 1
under 914 m: 16 (2013)

Roadways: total: 22,121 km (includes 44 km of expressways)
country comparison to the world: 103
paved: 16,148 km
unpaved: 5,973 km (2011)

Merchant marine: *total:* 1 4
country comparison to the world: 102
by type: bulk carrier 4, cargo 5, container 4, roll on/roll off 1
foreign-owned: 14 (Denmark 1, Germany 10, Greece 3) (2010)

Ports and terminals: *major seaport(s):* Discovery Bay (Port Rhoades), Kingston, Montego Bay, Port Antonio, Port Esquivel, Port Kaiser, Rocky Point
container port(s) (TEUs): Kingston (1,724,928)

MILITARY

Military branches: Jamaica Defense Force: Ground Forces, Coast Guard, Air Wing (2010)

Military service age and obligation:
17 1/2 is the legal minimum age for voluntary military service; no conscription (2012)

Manpower available for military service:
males age 16-49: 726,263
females age 16-49: 742,958 (2010 est.)

Manpower fit for military service:
males age 16-49: 590,673
females age 16-49: 596,414 (2010 est.)

Manpower reaching militarily significant age annually: *male:* 33,369
female: 32,702 (2010 est.)

Military expenditures: 0.86% of GDP (2012)
country comparison to the world: 112
0.92% of GDP (2011)
0.86% of GDP (2010)

TRANSNATIONAL ISSUES

Disputes—international: none

Illicit drugs: transshipment point for cocaine from South America to North America and Europe; illicit cultivation and consumption of cannabis; government has an active manual cannabis eradication program; corruption is a major concern; substantial money-laundering activity; Colombian narcotics traffickers favor Jamaica for illicit financial transactions

JAN MAYEN

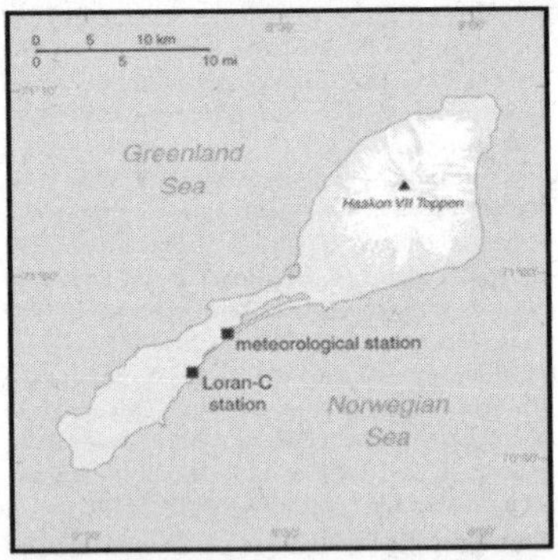

INTRODUCTION

Background: This desolate, arctic, mountainous island was named after a Dutch whaling captain who indisputably discovered it in 1614 (earlier claims are inconclusive). Visited only occasionally by seal hunters and trappers over the following centuries, the island came under Norwegian sovereignty in 1929. The long dormant Beerenberg volcano, the northernmost active volcano on earth, resumed activity in 1970 and the most recent eruption occurred in 1985.

GEOGRAPHY

Location: Northern Europe, island between the Greenland Sea and the Norwegian Sea, northeast of Iceland

Geographic coordinates: 71 00 N, 8 00 W

Map references: Europe

Area: *total:* 377 sq km
country comparison to the world: 205
land: 377 sq km
water: 0 sq km

Area—comparative: slightly more than twice the size of Washington, DC

Land boundaries: 0 km

Coastline: 124.1 km

Maritime claims: *territorial sea:* 4 nm
contiguous zone: 10 nm
exclusive economic zone: 200 nm
continental shelf: 200 m depth or to the depth of exploitation

Climate: arctic maritime with frequent storms and persistent fog

Terrain: volcanic island, partly covered by glaciers

Elevation extremes: *lowest point:* Norwegian Sea 0 m
highest point: Haakon VII Toppen on Beerenberg 2,277 m
note: Beerenberg volcano has numerous peaks; the highest point on the volcano rim is named Haakon VII Toppen, after Norway's first king following the reestablishment of Norwegian independence in 1905

Natural resources: none

Land use: *arable land:* 0%
permanent crops: 0%
other: 100% (2011)

Irrigated land: 0 sq km (2011)

Natural hazards: dominated by the volcano Beerenberg
volcanism: Beerenberg (elev. 2,227 m) is Norway's only active volcano; volcanic activity resumed in 1970; the most recent eruption occurred in 1985

Environment—current issues: NA

Geography—note: barren volcanic island with some moss and grass

PEOPLE AND SOCIETY

Population: no indigenous inhabitants
note: personnel operate the Long Range Navigation (Loran-C) base and the weather and coastal services radio station

GOVERNMENT

Country name: *conventional long form:* none
conventional short form: Jan Mayen

Dependency status: territory of Norway; since August 1994, administered from Oslo through the county governor (fylkesmann) of Nordland; however, authority has been delegated to a station commander of the Norwegian Defense Communication Service

Legal system: the laws of Norway, where applicable, apply

Flag description: the flag of Norway is used

ECONOMY

Economy—overview: Jan Mayen is a volcanic island with no exploitable natural resources, although surrounding waters contain substantial fish stocks and potential untapped petroleum resources. Economic activity is limited to providing services for employees of Norway's radio and meteorological stations on the island.

COMMUNICATIONS

Broadcast media: a coastal radio station has been remotely operated since 1994 (2008)

TRANSPORTATION

Airports: 1 (2013)
country comparison to the world: 222

Airports—with unpaved runways: *total:* 1
1,524 to 2,437 m: 1 (2013)

Ports and terminals: none; offshore anchorage only

MILITARY

Military—note: defense is the responsibility of Norway

TRANSNATIONAL ISSUES

Disputes—international: none

JAPAN

INTRODUCTION

Background: In 1603, after decades of civil warfare, the Tokugawa shogunate (a military-led, dynastic government) ushered in a long period of relative political stability and isolation from foreign influence. For more than two centuries this policy enabled Japan to enjoy a flowering of its indigenous culture. Japan opened its ports after signing the Treaty of Kanagawa with the US in 1854 and began to intensively modernize and industrialize. During the late 19th and early 20th centuries, Japan became a regional power that was able to defeat the forces of both China and Russia. It occupied Korea, Formosa (Taiwan), and southern Sakhalin Island. In 1931-32 Japan occupied Manchuria, and in 1937 it launched a full-scale invasion of China. Japan attacked US forces in 1941—triggering America's entry into World War II—and soon occupied much of East and Southeast Asia. After its defeat in World War II, Japan recovered to become an economic power and an ally of the US. While the emperor retains his throne as a symbol of national unity, elected

politicians hold actual decision-making power. Following three decades of unprecedented growth, Japan's economy experienced a major slowdown starting in the 1990s, but the country remains a major economic power. In March 2011, Japan's strongest-ever earthquake, and an accompanying tsunami, devastated the northeast part of Honshu island, killing thousands and damaging several nuclear power plants. The catastrophe hobbled the country's economy and its energy infrastructure, and tested its ability to deal with humanitarian disasters.

GEOGRAPHY

Location: Eastern Asia, island chain between the North Pacific Ocean and the Sea of Japan, east of the Korean Peninsula

Geographic coordinates: 36 00 N, 138 00 E

Map references: Asia

Area: *total:* 377,915 sq km
country comparison to the world: 62
land: 364,485 sq km
water: 13,430 sq km
note: includes Bonin Islands (Ogasawara-gunto), Daito-shoto, Minami-jima, Okino-tori-shima, Ryukyu Islands (Nansei-shoto), and Volcano Islands (Kazan-retto)

Area—comparative: slightly smaller than California

Land boundaries: 0 km

Coastline: 29,751 km

Maritime claims: territorial sea: 12 nm; between 3 nm and 12 nm in the international straits—La Perouse or Soya, Tsugaru, Osumi, and Eastern and Western Channels of the Korea or Tsushima Strait
contiguous zone: 24 nm
exclusive economic zone: 200 nm

Climate: varies from tropical in south to cool temperate in north

Terrain: mostly rugged and mountainous

Elevation extremes: *lowest point:* Hachiro-gata -4 m
highest point: Fujiyama 3,776 m

Natural resources: negligible mineral resources, fish
note: with virtually no energy natural resources, Japan is the world's largest importer of coal and liquefied natural gas, as well as the second largest importer of oil

Land use: *arable land:* 11.26%
permanent crops: 0.81%
other: 87.93% (2011)

Irrigated land: 25,000 sq km (2010)

Total renewable water resources: 430 cu km (2011)

Freshwater withdrawal (domestic/industrial/agricultural): *total:* 90.04 cu km/yr (20%/18%/62%)
per capita: 714.3 cu m/yr (2007)

Natural hazards: many dormant and some active volcanoes; about 1,500 seismic occurrences (mostly tremors but occasional severe earthquakes) every year; tsunamis; typhoons
volcanism: both Unzen (elev. 1,500 m) and Sakura-jima (elev. 1,117 m), which lies near the densely populated city of Kagoshima, have been deemed Decade Volcanoes by the International Association of Volcanology and Chemistry of the Earth's Interior, worthy of study due to their explosive history and close proximity to human populations; other notable historically active volcanoes include Asama, Honshu Island's most active volcano, Aso, Bandai, Fuji, Iwo-Jima, Kikai, Kirishima, Komaga-take, Oshima, Suwanosejima, Tokachi, Yake-dake, and Usu

Environment—current issues: air pollution from power plant emissions results in acid rain; acidification of lakes and reservoirs degrading water quality and threatening aquatic life; Japan is one of the largest consumers of fish and tropical timber, *contributing to the depletion of these resources in Asia and elsewhere*

Environment—international agreements:
party to: Antarctic-Environmental Protocol, Antarctic-Marine Living Resources, Antarctic Seals, Antarctic Treaty, Biodiversity, Climate Change, Climate Change-Kyoto Protocol, Desertification, Endangered Species, Environmental Modification, Hazardous Wastes, Law of the Sea, Marine Dumping, Ozone Layer Protection, Ship Pollution, Tropical Timber 83, Tropical Timber 94, Wetlands, Whaling
signed, but not ratified: none of the selected agreements

Geography—note: strategic location in northeast Asia

PEOPLE AND SOCIETY

Nationality: *noun:* Japanese (singular and plural)
adjective: Japanese

Ethnic groups: Japanese 98.5%, Koreans 0.5%, Chinese 0.4%, other 0.6%
note: up to 230,000 Brazilians of Japanese origin migrated to Japan in the 1990s to work in industries; some have returned to Brazil (2004)

Languages: Japanese

Religions: Shintoism 83.9%, Buddhism 71.4%, Christianity 2%, other 7.8%
note: total adherents exceeds 100% because many people belong to both Shintoism and Buddhism (2005)

Population: 127,103,388 (July 2014 est.)
country comparison to the world: 11

Age structure:
0-14 years: 13.2% (male 8,681,728/female 8,132,809)
15-24 years: 9.7% (male 6,429,429/female 5,890,991)
25-54 years: 38.1% (male 23,953,643/female 24,449,655)
55-64 years: 25.8% (male 8,413,872/female 8,400,953)
65 years and over: 24.8% (male 14,218,655/female 18,531,653) (2014 est.)

Dependency ratios:
total dependency ratio: 61.6 %
youth dependency ratio: 21.1 %
elderly dependency ratio: 40.5 %
potential support ratio: 2.5 (2013)

Median age: *total:* 46.1 years
male: 44.8 years
female: 47.5 years (2014 est.)

Population growth rate: -0.13% (2014 est.)
country comparison to the world: 210

Birth rate: 8.07 births/1,000 population (2014 est.)
country comparison to the world: 222

Death rate: 9.38 deaths/1,000 population (2014 est.)
country comparison to the world: 59

Net migration rate: 0 migrant(s)/1,000 population (2014 est.)
country comparison to the world: 93

Urbanization: *urban population:* 91.3% of total population (2011)
rate of urbanization: 0.57% annual rate of change (2010-15 est.)

Major urban areas—population: TOKYO (capital) 36.507 million; Osaka-Kobe 11.325 million; Nagoya 3.257 million; Fukuoka-Kitakyushu 2.809 million; Sapporo 2.673 million (2009)

Sex ratio: *at birth:* 1.06 male(s)/female
0-14 years: 1.07 male(s)/female
15-24 years: 1.09 male(s)/female
25-54 years: 0.98 male(s)/female
55-64 years: 0.94 male(s)/female
65 years and over: 0.76 male(s)/female
total population: 0.95 male(s)/female (2014 est.)

Mother's mean age at first birth: 29.4 (2007 est.)

Maternal mortality rate: 5 deaths/100,000 live births (2010)
country comparison to the world: 176

Infant mortality rate: *total:* 2.13 deaths/1,000 live births
country comparison to the world: 223
male: 2.35 deaths/1,000 live births
female: 1.88 deaths/1,000 live births (2014 est.)

Life expectancy at birth: *total population:* 84.46 years
country comparison to the world: 3
male: 81.13 years
female: 87.99 years (2014 est.)

Total fertility rate: 1.4 children born/woman (2014 est.)
country comparison to the world: 208

Contraceptive prevalence rate: 54.3%
note: percent of women aged 20-49 (2005)

Health expenditures: 9.3% of GDP (2011)
country comparison to the world: 38

Physicians density: 2.14 physicians/1,000 population (2008)

Hospital bed density: 13.7 beds/1,000 population (2009)

Drinking water source:
improved:
urban: 100% of population
rural: 100% of population
total: 100% of population
unimproved:
urban: 0% of population
rural: 0% of population
total: 0% of population (2011 est.)

Sanitation facility access:
improved:
urban: 100% of population
rural: 100% of population
total: 100% of population
unimproved:
urban: 0% of population
rural: 0% of population
total: 0% of population (2011 est.)

HIV/AIDS—adult prevalence rate:
less than 0.1% (2009 est.)
country comparison to the world: 120

HIV/AIDS—people living with HIV/AIDS:
8,100 (2009 est.)
country comparison to the world: 112

HIV/AIDS—deaths: fewer than 100 (2009 est.)
country comparison to the world: 121

Obesity—adult prevalence rate: 5% (2008)
country comparison to the world: 157

Education expenditures: 3.8% of GDP (2011)
country comparison to the world: 115

Literacy: *definition:* age 15 and over can read and write
total population: 99%
male: 99%
female: 99% (2002)

School life expectancy (primary to tertiary education): *total:* 15 years
male: 15 years
female: 15 years (2011)

Unemployment, youth ages 15-24: *total:* 7.9%
country comparison to the world: 123
male: 8.7%
female: 7.1% (2012)

GOVERNMENT

Country name: *conventional long form:* none
conventional short form: Japan
local long form: Nihon-koku/Nippon-koku
local short form: Nihon/Nippon

Government type: a parliamentary government with a constitutional monarchy

Capital: *name:* Tokyo
geographic coordinates: 35 41 N, 139 45 E
time difference: UTC+9 (14 hours ahead of Washington, DC during Standard Time)

Administrative divisions: 47 prefectures; Aichi, Akita, Aomori, Chiba, Ehime, Fukui, Fukuoka, Fukushima, Gifu, Gunma, Hiroshima, Hokkaido, Hyogo, Ibaraki, Ishikawa, Iwate, Kagawa, Kagoshima, Kanagawa, Kochi, Kumamoto, Kyoto, Mie, Miyagi, Miyazaki, Nagano, Nagasaki, Nara, Niigata, Oita, Okayama, Okinawa, Osaka, Saga, Saitama, Shiga, Shimane, Shizuoka, Tochigi, Tokushima, Tokyo, Tottori, Toyama, Wakayama, Yamagata, Yamaguchi, Yamanashi

Independence: 3 May 1947 (current constitution adopted as amendment to Meiji Constitution); notable earlier dates: 660 B.C. (traditional date of the founding of the nation by Emperor JIMMU); 29 November 1890 (Meiji Constitution provides for constitutional monarchy)

National holiday: Birthday of Emperor AKIHITO, 23 December (1933)

Constitution: previous 1890; latest approved 6 October 1946, adopted 3 November 1946, effective 3 May 1947 (2013)

Legal system: civil law system based on German model; system also reflects Anglo-American influence and Japanese traditions; judicial review of legislative acts in the Supreme Court

International law organization participation: accepts compulsory ICJ jurisdiction with reservations; accepts ICCt jurisdiction

Suffrage: 20 years of age; universal

Executive branch: *chief of state:* Emperor AKIHITO (since 7 January 1989)
head of government: Prime Minister Shinzo ABE (since 26 December 2012); Deputy Prime Minister Taro ASO (since 26 December 2012)
cabinet: Cabinet is appointed by the prime minister (For more information visit the World Leaders website)
elections: Diet, the bicameral legislature, designates the prime minister; constitution requires that the prime minister commands parliamentary majority; following legislative elections, the leader of majority party or leader of majority coalition in House of Representatives usually becomes prime minister; the monarchy is hereditary

Legislative branch: bicameral Diet or Kokkai consists of the House of Councillors or Sangi-in (242 seats—members elected for fixed six-year terms; 146 members in multi-seat constituencies and 96 by proportional representation) half elected every three years; and the House of Representatives or Shugi-in (480 seats—members elected for maximum four-year terms; 300 in single-seat constituencies; 180 members by proportional representation in 11 regional blocs); the prime minister has the right to dissolve the House of Representatives at any time with the concurrence of the cabinet
elections: House of Councillors—last held on 21 July 2013 (next to be held in July 2016); House of *Representatives—last held on 16 December 2012 (next to be held by 15 December 2016)*
election results: House of Councillors—percent of vote by party—NA; seats by party—LPD 115, DPJ 59, New Komeito 20, Your Party 18, JCP 11, JRP 9, SDP 3, others 4, independents 3 House of Representatives—percent of vote by party (by proportional representation)—LDP 31.6%, DPJ 16.6%, JRP 22.2%, New Komeito 12.2%, Your Party 7.7%, JCP 4.4%, TRP 3.9%, others 1.4%; seats by party LDP 294, DPJ 57, JRP 54, New Komeito 31, Your Party 18, TPJ 9, JCP 8, others 4, independents 5

Judicial branch: *highest court(s):* Supreme Court or Saiko saibansho (consists of the chief justice and 14 associate justices) note—the Supreme Court has jurisdiction in constitutional issues
judge selection and term of office: Supreme Court chief justice designated by the Cabinet and appointed by the monarch; associate justices appointed by the Cabinet and confirmed by the monarch; all justices are reviewed in a popular referendum at the first general election of the House of Representatives following each judge's appointment and every 10 years afterward
subordinate courts: 8 High Courts (Koto-saibansho), each with a Family Court (Katei-saiban-sho); 50 District Courts (Chiho saibansho), with 203 additional branches; 438 Summary Courts (Kani saibansho)

Political parties and leaders: Democratic Party of Japan or DPJ [Banri KAIEDA]; Japan Communist Party or JCP [Kazuo SHII]; Japan Restoration Party or JRP [Shintaro ISHIHARA]; Liberal Democratic Party or LDP [Shinzo ABE]; New Komeito or NK [Natsuo YAMAGUCHI]; People's Life Party or PF [Ichiro OZAWA]; Social Democratic Party or SDP [Tadatomo YOSHIDA]; Tomorrow Party of Japan or TPJ [Tomoko ABE]; Your Party or YP [Yoshimi WATANABE]

Political pressure groups and leaders: *other:* business groups; trade unions

International organization participation: ADB, AfDB (nonregional member), APEC, ARF, ASEAN (dialogue partner), Australia Group, BIS, CD, CE (observer), CERN (observer), CICA (observer), CP, EAS, EBRD, EITI (implementing country), FAO, FATF, G-20, G-5, G-7, G-8, G-10, IADB, IAEA, IBRD, ICAO, ICC (national committees), ICRM, IDA, IEA, IFAD, IFC, IFRCS, IGAD (partners), IHO, ILO, IMF, IMO, IMSO, Interpol, IOC, IOM, IPU, ISO, ITSO, ITU, ITUC (NGOs), LAIA (observer), MIGA, NEA, NSG, OAS (observer), OECD, OPCW, OSCE (partner), Paris Club, PCA, PIF (partner), SAARC (observer), SELEC (observer), SICA (observer), UN, UNCTAD, UNDOF, UNESCO, UNHCR, UNIDO, UNMISS, UNRWA, UNWTO, UPU, WCO, WFTU (NGOs), WHO, WIPO, WMO, WTO, ZC

Diplomatic representation in the US:
chief of mission: Ambassador Kenichiro SASAE (since 19 November 2012)
chancery: 2520 Massachusetts Avenue NW, Washington, DC 20008
telephone: [1] (202) 238-6700
FAX: [1] (202) 328-2187
consulate(s) general: Atlanta, Boston, Chicago, Denver, Detroit, Agana (Guam), Honolulu, Houston, Los Angeles, Miami, Nashville (TN), New York, Portland (OR), San Francisco, Seattle
consulate(s): Anchorage (AK), Saipan (Northern Mariana Islands)

Diplomatic representation from the US:
chief of mission: Ambassador Caroline Bouvier KENNEDY (since 19 November 2013)
embassy: 1-10-5 Akasaka, Minato-ku, Tokyo 107-8420
mailing address: Unit 9800, Box 300, APO AP 96303-0300
telephone: [81] (03) 3224-5000
FAX: [81] (03) 3505-1862
consulate(s) general: Naha (Okinawa), Osaka-Kobe, Sapporo
consulate(s): Fukuoka, Nagoya

Flag description: white with a large red disk (representing the sun without rays) in the center

National symbol(s): red sun disc; chrysanthemum

National anthem: *name:* "Kimigayo" (The Emperor's Reign)
lyrics/music: unknown/Hiromori HAYASHI
note: adopted 1999; in use as unofficial national anthem since 1883; oldest anthem lyrics in the world, dating to the 10th century or earlier; there is some opposition to the anthem because of its association with militarism and worship of the emperor

ECONOMY

Economy—overview: In the years following World War II, government-industry cooperation, a strong work ethic, mastery of high technology, and a comparatively small defense allocation (1% of GDP) helped Japan develop a technologically advanced economy. Two notable characteristics of the post-war economy were the close interlocking structures of manufacturers, suppliers, and distributors, known as keiretsu, and the guarantee of lifetime employment for a substantial portion of the urban labor force. Both features are now eroding under the dual pressures of global competition and domestic demographic change. Japan's industrial sector is heavily dependent on imported raw materials and fuels. A small agricultural sector is highly subsidized and protected, with crop yields among the highest in the world. While self-sufficient in rice production, Japan imports about 60% of its food on a caloric basis. For three decades, overall real economic growth had been spectacular—a 10% average in the 1960s, a 5% average in the 1970s, and a 4% average in the 1980s. Growth slowed markedly in the 1990s, averaging just 1.7%, largely because of the after effects of inefficient investment and an asset price bubble in the late 1980s that required a protracted period of time for firms to reduce excess debt, capital, and labor. Modest economic growth continued after 2000, but the economy has fallen into recession three times since 2008. A sharp downturn in business investment and global demand for Japan's exports in late 2008 pushed Japan into recession. Government stimulus spending helped the economy recover in late 2009 and 2010, but the economy contracted again in 2011 as the massive 9.0 magnitude earthquake and the ensuing tsunami in March disrupted manufacturing. The economy has largely recovered in the two years since the disaster, but reconstruction in the Tohoku region has been uneven. Prime Minister Shinzo ABE has declared the economy his government's top priority; he has overturned his predecessor's plan to permanently close nuclear power plants and is pursuing an economic revitalization agenda of fiscal stimulus, monetary easing, and structural reform. Japan joined the Trans Pacific Partnership negotiations in 2013, a pact that would open Japan's economy to increased foreign competition and create new export opportunities for Japanese businesses. Measured on a purchasing power parity (PPP) basis that adjusts for price differences, Japan in 2013 stood as the fourth-largest economy in the world after second-place China, which surpassed Japan in 2001, and third-place India, which edged out Japan in 2012. The new government will continue a longstanding debate on restructuring the economy and reining in Japan's huge government debt, which is exceeding 230% of GDP. To help raise government revenue and reduce public debt, Japan decided in 2013 to gradually increase the consumption tax to a total of 10% by the year 2015. Japan is making progress on ending deflation due to a weaker yen and higher energy costs, but reliance on exports to drive growth and an aging, shrinking population pose other major long-term challenges for the economy.

GDP (purchasing power parity): $4.729 trillion (2013 est.)
country comparison to the world: 5
$4.638 trillion (2012 est.)
$4.549 trillion (2011 est.)
note: data are in 2013 US dollars

GDP (official exchange rate): $5.007 trillion (2013 est.)

GDP—real growth rate: 2% (2013 est.)
country comparison to the world: 138
2% (2012 est.)
-0.6% (2011 est.)

GDP—per capita (PPP): $37,100 (2013 est.)
country comparison to the world: 36
$36,300 (2012 est.)
$35,600 (2011 est.)
note: data are in 2013 US dollars

Gross national saving: 22.1% of GDP (2013 est.)
country comparison to the world: 68
21.6% of GDP (2012 est.)
22% of GDP (2011 est.)

GDP—composition, by end use:
household consumption: 61%
government consumption: 20.7%
investment in fixed capital: 21.6%
investment in inventories: -0.6%
exports of goods and services: 15.8%
imports of goods and services: -18.4% (2013 est.)

GDP—composition, by sector of origin:
agriculture: 1.1%
industry: 25.6%
services: 73.2% (2013 est.)

Agriculture—products: rice, sugar beets, vegetables, fruit; pork, poultry, dairy products, eggs; fish

Industries: among world's largest and technologically advanced producers of motor vehicles, electronic equipment, machine tools, steel and nonferrous metals, ships, chemicals, textiles, processed foods

Industrial production growth rate: 1% (2013 est.)
country comparison to the world: 153

Labor force: 65.62 million (2013 est.)
country comparison to the world: 9

Labor force—by occupation: *agriculture:* 3.9%
industry: 26.2%
services: 69.8% (2010 est.)

Unemployment rate: 4.1% (2013 est.)
country comparison to the world: 32
4.4% (2012 est.)

Population below poverty line: 16% (2010)

Household income or consumption by percentage share: *lowest 10%:* 1.9%
highest 10%: 27.5% (2008)

Distribution of family income—Gini index:
37.6 (2008)
country comparison to the world: 76
24.9 (1993)

Budget: *revenues:* $1.739 trillion
expenditures: $2.149 trillion (2013 est.)

Taxes and other revenues: 34.7% of GDP (2013 est.)
country comparison to the world: 68

Budget surplus (+) or deficit (-):
-8.2% of GDP (2013 est.)
country comparison to the world: 198

Public debt: 226.1% of GDP (2013 est.)
country comparison to the world: 1
219.1% of GDP (2012 est.)

Fiscal year: 1 April—31 March
Inflation rate (consumer prices):
0.2% (2013 est.)
country comparison to the world: 13
0% (2012 est.)

Central bank discount rate: 0.1% (31 December 2012)
country comparison to the world: 140
0.3% (31 December 2009)

Commercial bank prime lending rate: 1.5% (31 December 2013 est.)
country comparison to the world: 181
1.48% (31 December 2012 est.)

Stock of narrow money: $5.604 trillion (31 December 2013 est.)
country comparison to the world: 2
$6.176 trillion (31 December 2012 est.)

Stock of broad money: $13.12 trillion (31 December 2011 est.)
country comparison to the world: 2
$13.41 trillion (31 December 2010 est.)

Stock of domestic credit: $12.39 trillion (31 December 2013 est.)
country comparison to the world: 3
$13.72 trillion (31 December 2012 est.)

Market value of publicly traded shares:
$3.681 trillion (31 December 2012 est.)
country comparison to the world: 4
$3.541 trillion (31 December 2011)
$4.1 trillion (31 December 2010 est.)

Current account balance: $56.6 billion (2013 est.)
country comparison to the world: 10
$60.8 billion (2012 est.)

Exports: $697 billion (2013 est.)
country comparison to the world: 5
$776.6 billion (2012 est.)

Exports—commodities: motor vehicles 13.6%; semiconductors 6.2%; iron and steel products 5.5%; auto parts 4.6%; plastic materials 3.5%; power generating machinery 3.5%

Exports—partners: China 18.1%, US 17.8%, South Korea 7.7%, Thailand 5.5%, Hong Kong 5.1% (2012)

Imports: $766.6 billion (2013 est.)
country comparison to the world: 5
$830.1 billion (2012 est.)

Imports—commodities: petroleum 15.5%; liquid natural gas 5.7%; clothing 3.9%; semiconductors 3.5%; coal 3.5%; audio and visual apparatus 2.7% (2011 est.)

Imports—partners: China 21.3%, US 8.8%, Australia 6.4%, Saudi Arabia 6.2%, UAE 5%, South Korea 4.6%, Qatar 4% (2012)

Reserves of foreign exchange and gold:
$1.268 trillion (31 December 2012 est.)
country comparison to the world: 2
$1.296 trillion (31 December 2011 est.)

Debt—external: $3.017 trillion (31 December 2012 est.)
country comparison to the world: 6
$3.115 trillion (31 December 2011)

Stock of direct foreign investment—at home:
$231.2 billion (31 December 2013 est.)
country comparison to the world: 25
$222.2 billion (31 December 2012 est.)

Stock of direct foreign investment—abroad:
$1.179 trillion (31 December 2013 est.)
country comparison to the world: 8
$1.054 trillion (31 December 2012 est.)

Exchange rates: yen (JPY) per US dollar—
97.44 (2013 est.)
79.79 (2012 est.)
87.78 (2010 est.)
93.57 (2009)
103.58 (2008)

ENERGY

Electricity—production: 936.2 billion kWh (2012 est.)
country comparison to the world: 6

Electricity—consumption: 859.7 billion kWh (2012 est.)
country comparison to the world: 5

Electricity—exports: 0 kWh (2012 est.)
country comparison to the world: 152

Electricity—imports: 0 kWh (2012 est.)
country comparison to the world: 158

Electricity—installed generating capacity:
287 million kW (2010 est.)
country comparison to the world: 4

Electricity—from fossil fuels: 63.5% of total installed capacity (2010 est.)
country comparison to the world: 127

Electricity—from nuclear fuels: 17.1% of total installed capacity (2010 est.)
country comparison to the world: 13

Electricity—from hydroelectric plants: 7.8% of total installed capacity (2010 est.)
country comparison to the world: 119

Electricity—from other renewable sources:
2.8% of total installed capacity (2010 est.)
country comparison to the world: 63

Crude oil—production: 135,500 bbl/day (2012 est.)
country comparison to the world: 45

Crude oil—exports: 0 bbl/day (2010 est.)
country comparison to the world: 132

Crude oil—imports: 3.472 million bbl/day (2010 est.)
country comparison to the world: 4

Crude oil—proved reserves: 44.12 million bbl (1 January 2013 es)
country comparison to the world: 79

Refined petroleum products—production:
3.862 million bbl/day (2010 est.)
country comparison to the world: 6

Refined petroleum products—consumption:
4.464 million bbl/day (2011 est.)
country comparison to the world: 4

Refined petroleum products—exports:
349,900 bbl/day (2010 est.)
country comparison to the world: 20

Refined petroleum products—imports:
1.311 million bbl/day (2010 est.)
country comparison to the world: 6

Natural gas—production: 3.273 billion cu m (2012 est.)
country comparison to the world: 56

Natural gas—consumption: 112.6 billion cu m (2011 est.)
country comparison to the world: 6

Natural gas—exports: 0 cu m (2012 est.)
country comparison to the world: 123

Natural gas—imports: 122.2 billion cu m (2012 est.)
country comparison to the world: 2

Natural gas—proved reserves: 20.9 billion cu m (1 January 2013 es)
country comparison to the world: 77

Carbon dioxide emissions from consumption of energy: 1.181 billion Mt (2011 est.)
country comparison to the world: 6

COMMUNICATIONS

Telephones—main lines in use: 64.273 million (2012)
country comparison to the world: 3

Telephones—mobile cellular: 138.363 million (2011)
country comparison to the world: 7

Telephone system: *general assessment:* excellent domestic and international service
domestic: high level of modern technology and excellent service of every kind
international: country code—81; numerous submarine cables provide links throughout Asia, Australia, the Middle East, Europe, and US; satellite earth stations—7 Intelsat (Pacific and Indian Oceans), 1 Intersputnik (Indian Ocean region), 2 Inmarsat (Pacific and Indian Ocean regions), and 8 SkyPerfect JSAT (2012)

Broadcast media: a mixture of public and commercial broadcast TV and radio stations; 6 national terrestrial TV networks including 1 public broadcaster; the large number of radio and TV stations available provide a wide range of choices; satellite and cable services provide access to international channels (2012)

Internet country code: .jp

Internet hosts: 64.453 million (2012)
country comparison to the world: 2

Internet users: 99.182 million (2009)
country comparison to the world: 3

TRANSPORTATION

Airports: 175 (2013)
country comparison to the world: 3 3

Airports—with paved runways: *total:* 142
over 3,047 m: 6
2,438 to 3,047 m: 45
1,524 to 2,437 m: 38
914 to 1,523 m: 28
under 914 m: 25 (2013)

Airports—with unpaved runways: *total:* 3 3
914 to 1,523 m: 5
under 914 m: 28 (2013)

Heliports: 16 (2013)

Pipelines: gas 4,456 km; oil 174 km; oil/gas/water 104 km (2013)

Railways: *total:* 27,182 km
country comparison to the world: 11
standard gauge: 4,251 km 1.435-m gauge (4,251 km electrified)
dual gauge: 486 km 1.435-1.067-m gauge (486 km electrified)
narrow gauge: 96 km 1.372-m gauge (96 km electrified); 22,301 km 1.067-m gauge (15,222 km electrified);
48 km 0.762-m gauge (48 km electrified) (2009)

Roadways: *total:* 1,210,251 km
country comparison to the world: 6
paved: 973,234 km (includes 7,803 km of expressways)
unpaved: 237,017 km (2010)

Waterways: 1,770 km (seagoing vessels use inland seas) (2010)
country comparison to the world: 45

Merchant marine: *total:* 684
country comparison to the world: 16
by type: bulk carrier 168, cargo 34, carrier 3, chemical tanker 29, container 2, liquefied gas 58, passenger 11, passenger/cargo 117, petroleum tanker 152, refrigerated cargo 4, roll on/roll off 52, vehicle carrier 54
registered in other countries: 3,122 (Bahamas 88, Bermuda 2, Burma 1, Cambodia 1, Cayman Islands 23, China 2, Cyprus 16, Honduras 4, Hong Kong 79, Indonesia 8, Isle of Man 19, Liberia 110, Luxembourg 3, Malaysia 2, Malta 5, Marshall Islands 59, Mongolia 2, Netherlands 1, Panama 2372, Philippines 77, Portugal 9, Saint Kitts and Nevis 2, Saint Vincent and the Grenadines 3, Sierra Leone 4, Singapore 164, South Korea 14, Tanzania 1, UK 5, Vanuatu 39, unknown 7) (2010)

Ports and terminals: *major seaport(s):* Chiba, Kawasaki, Kobe, Mizushima, Moji, Nagoya, Osaka, Tokyo, Tomakomai, Yokohama
container port(s) (TEUs): Kobe (2,725,304), Nagoya (2,471,821), Osaka (2,172,797), Tokyo (4,416,119), Yokohama (2,992,517)

MILITARY

Military branches: Japanese Ministry of Defense (MOD): Ground Self-Defense Force (Rikujou Jieitai, GSDF); Maritime Self-Defense Force (Kaijou Jieitai, MSDF); Air Self-Defense Force (Koukuu Jieitai, ASDF) (2011)

Military service age and obligation: 18 years of age for voluntary military service; no conscription; mandatory retirement at age 53 for senior enlisted personnel and at 62 years for senior service officers (2012)

Manpower available for military service:
males age 16-49: 27,301,443
females age 16-49: 26,307,003 (2010 est.)

Manpower fit for military service:
males age 16-49: 22,390,431
females age 16-49: 21,540,322 (2010 est.)

Manpower reaching militarily significant age annually: *male:* 623,365
female: 591,253 (2010 est.)

Military expenditures: 0.99% of GDP (2012)
country comparison to the world: 103
1.01% of GDP (2011)
0.99% of GDP (2010)

TRANSNATIONAL ISSUES

Disputes—international: the sovereignty dispute over the islands of Etorofu, Kunashiri, and Shikotan, and the Habomai group, known in Japan as the "Northern Territories" and in Russia as the "Southern Kuril Islands," occupied by the Soviet Union in 1945, now administered by Russia and claimed by Japan, remains the primary sticking point to signing a peace treaty formally ending World War II hostilities; Japan and South Korea claim Liancourt Rocks (Take-shima/Tok-do) occupied by South Korea since 1954; China and Taiwan dispute both Japan's claims to the uninhabited islands of the Senkaku-shoto (Diaoyu Tai) and Japan's unilaterally declared exclusive economic zone in the East China Sea, the site of intensive hydrocarbon prospecting

Refugees and internally displaced persons: *stateless persons:* 1,100 (2012)

JARVIS ISLAND

INTRODUCTION

Background: First discovered by the British in 1821, the uninhabited island was annexed by the US in 1858 but abandoned in 1879 after tons of guano deposits had been removed for use in producing fertilizer. The UK annexed the island in 1889 but never carried out plans for further exploitation. The US occupied and reclaimed the island in 1935. Abandoned after World War II, the island is currently a National Wildlife Refuge administered by the US Department of the Interior.

GEOGRAPHY

Location: Oceania, island in the South Pacific Ocean, about half way between Hawaii and the Cook Islands

Geographic coordinates: 0 22 S, 160 01 W

Map references: Oceania

Area: *total:* 4.5 sq km
land: 4.5 sq km
water: 0 sq km

Area—comparative: about eight times the size of The Mall in Washington, DC

Land boundaries: 0 km

Coastline: 8 km

Maritime claims: *territorial sea:* 12 nm
exclusive economic zone: 200 nm

Climate: tropical; scant rainfall, constant wind, burning sun

Terrain: sandy, coral island surrounded by a narrow fringing reef

Elevation extremes: *lowest point:* Pacific Ocean 0 m
highest point: unnamed location 7 m

Natural resources: guano (deposits worked until late 1800s), terrestrial and aquatic wildlife

Land use: *arable land:* 0%
permanent crops: 0%
other: 100% (2011)

Irrigated land: 0 sq km (2011)

Natural hazards: the narrow fringing reef surrounding the island poses a maritime hazard

Environment—current issues: no natural fresh water resources

Geography—note: sparse bunch grass, prostrate vines, and low-growing shrubs; primarily a nesting, roosting, and foraging habitat for seabirds, shorebirds, and marine wildlife

PEOPLE AND SOCIETY

Population: uninhabited
note: Millersville settlement on western side of island occasionally used as a weather station from 1935 until World War II, when it was abandoned;

reoccupied in 1957 during the International Geophysical Year by scientists who left in 1958; public entry is by special-use permit from US Fish and Wildlife Service only and generally restricted to scientists and educators; visited annually by US Fish and Wildlife Service

GOVERNMENT

Country name: *conventional long form:* none
conventional short form: Jarvis Island

Dependency status: unincorporated territory of the US; administered from Washington, DC, by the Fish and Wildlife Service of the US Department of the Interior as part of the National Wildlife Refuge system

Legal system: the laws of the US, where applicable, apply

Flag description: the flag of the US is used

TRANSPORTATION

Ports and terminals: none; offshore anchorage only; note—there is one small boat landing area in the middle of the west coast and another near the southwest corner of the island

Transportation—note: there is a day beacon near the middle of the west coast

MILITARY

Military—note: defense is the responsibility of the US; visited annually by the US Coast Guard

TRANSNATIONAL ISSUES

Disputes—international: none

JERSEY

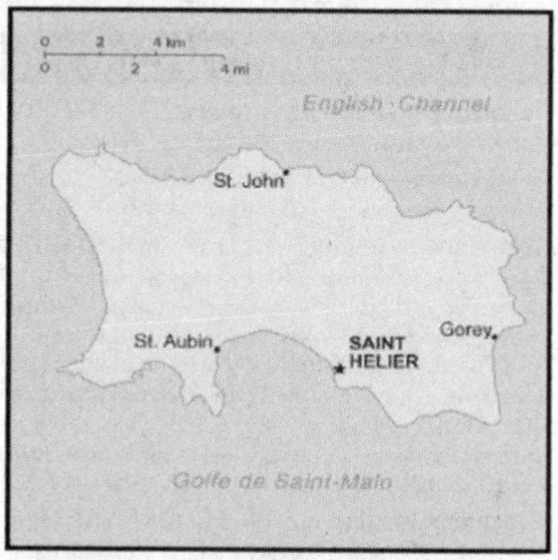

INTRODUCTION

Background: Jersey and the other Channel Islands represent the last remnants of the medieval Dukedom of Normandy that held sway in both France and England. These islands were the only British soil occupied by German troops in World War II. Jersey is a British crown dependency but is not part of the UK or of the European Union. However, the UK Government is constitutionally responsible for its defense and international representation.

GEOGRAPHY

Location: Western Europe, island in the English Channel, northwest of France

Geographic coordinates: 49 15 N, 2 10 W

Map references: Europe

Area: *total:* 116 sq km
country comparison to the world: 225
land: 116 sq km
water: 0 sq km

Area—comparative: about two-thirds the size of Washington, DC

Land boundaries: 0 km

Coastline: 70 km

Maritime claims: *territorial sea:* 3 nm
exclusive fishing zone: 12 nm

Climate: temperate; mild winters and cool summers

Terrain: gently rolling plain with low, rugged hills along north coast

Elevation extremes: lowest point: Atlantic Ocean 0 m
highest point: unnamed elevation 143 m

Natural resources: *arable land*

Land use: *arable land:* NA
permanent crops: NA
other: NA

Irrigated land: NA

Natural hazards: NA
Environment—current issues:
NA

Geography—note: largest and southernmost of Channel Islands; about 30% of population concentrated in Saint Helier

PEOPLE AND SOCIETY

Nationality: *noun:* Channel Islander(s)
adjective: Channel Islander

Ethnic groups: Jersey 46.4%, British 32.7%, Portuguese/Madeiran 8.2%, Polish 3.3%, Irish, French, and other white 7.1%, other 2.4% (2011 est.)

Languages: English 94.5% (official), Portuguese 4.6%, other 0.9% (2001 census)

Religions: Protestant (Anglican, Baptist, Congregational New Church, Methodist, Presbyterian), Roman Catholic

Population: 96,513 (July 2014 est.)
country comparison to the world: 197

Age structure:
0-14 years: 16% (male 8,001/female 7,456)
15-24 years: 14.8% (male 7,271/female 6,972)
25-54 years: 41.4% (male 20,000/female 19,927)
55-64 years: 15.7% (male 5,690/female 6,055)
65 years and over: 15.4% (male 6,464/female 8,677) (2014 est.)

Dependency ratios:
total dependency ratio: 46 %
youth dependency ratio: 21.8 %
elderly dependency ratio: 24.2 %
potential support ratio: 4.1
note: data represents the Channel Islands (2013)

Median age: *total:* 39.5 years
male: 37.1 years
female: 41.6 years (2014 est.)

Population growth rate: 0.81% (2014 est.)
country comparison to the world: 136

Birth rate: 11.65 births/1,000 population (2014 est.)
country comparison to the world: 170

Death rate: 7.63 deaths/1,000 population (2014 est.)
country comparison to the world: 114

Net migration rate: 4.08 migrant(s)/1,000 population (2014 est.)
country comparison to the world: 30

Urbanization: *urban population:* 31% of total population (2010)
rate of urbanization: 0.8% annual rate of change (2010-15 est.)

Sex ratio: *at birth:* 1.06 male(s)/female
0-14 years: 1.07 male(s)/female
15-24 years: 1.04 male(s)/female
25-54 years: 1 male(s)/female
55-64 years: 0.97 male(s)/female
65 years and over: 0.74 male(s)/female
total population: 0.96 male(s)/female (2014 est.)

Infant mortality rate: *total:* 3.86 deaths/1,000 live births
country comparison to the world: 201
male: 4.08 deaths/1,000 live births
female: 3.63 deaths/1,000 live births (2014 est.)

Life expectancy at birth: *total population:* 81.66 years
country comparison to the world: 16
male: 79.22 years
female: 84.26 years (2014 est.)

Total fertility rate: 1.66 children born/woman (2014 est.)
country comparison to the world: 175

HIV/AIDS—adult prevalence rate: NA

HIV/AIDS—people living with HIV/AIDS: NA

HIV/AIDS—deaths: NA

Literacy: NA

GOVERNMENT

Country name: *conventional long form:* Bailiwick of Jersey
conventional short form: Jersey

Dependency status: British crown dependency

Government type: parliamentary democracy

Capital: *name:* Saint Helier
geographic coordinates: 49 11 N, 2 06 W
time difference: UTC 0 (5 hours ahead of Washington, DC during Standard Time)
daylight saving time: +1hr, begins last Sunday in March; ends last Sunday in October

Administrative divisions: none (British crown dependency); there are no first-order administrative divisions as defined by the US Government, but there are 12 parishes: Grouville, Saint Brelade, Saint Clement, Saint Helier, Saint John, Saint Lawrence, Saint Martin, Saint Mary, Saint Ouen, Saint Peter, Saint Saviour, and Trinity

Independence: none (British crown dependency)

National holiday: Liberation Day, 9 May (1945)

Constitution: unwritten; partly statutes, partly common law and practice (2013)

Legal system: the laws of the UK, where applicable, apply; local statutes

Suffrage: 16 years of age; universal

Executive branch: *chief of state:* Queen ELIZABETH II (since 6 February 1952); represented by Lieutenant Governor Sir John MCCOLL (since 26 September 2011)
head of government: Chief Minister Ian GORST (18 December 2011); Bailiff Michael BIRT (since 9 July 2009)
cabinet: Cabinet (since December 2005) (For more information visit the World Leaders website)
elections: ministers of the Cabinet including the chief minister are elected by the Assembly of States; the monarchy is hereditary; lieutenant governor and bailiff appointed by the monarch

Legislative branch: unicameral Assembly of the States of Jersey (58 seats; 53 are voting members, of which 12 are senators elected for six-year terms, 12 are constables or heads of parishes elected for three-year terms, 29 are deputies elected for three-year terms; the 5 non-voting members include the bailiff and the deputy bailiff, the Dean of Jersey, the Attorney General, and the Solicitor General appointed by the monarch)
elections: last held on 27 April 2011 (next to be held in 2014)
election results: percent of vote—NA; seats—independents 53; note—starting with the 2014 elections, the number of Senators will be reduced to 8

Judicial branch: *highest court(s):* Jersey Court of Appeal (consists of the bailiff, deputy bailiff, and 12 judges and organized into Heritage, Family, Probate, and Civil and Criminal Divisions); Royal Court (consists of the bailiff, deputy bailiff, 6 commissioners—part-time judges, and NA lay people referred to as jurats)
judge selection and term of office: Jersey Court of Appeal bailiffs and judges appointed by the Crown upon the advice of the Secretary of State for Justice; bailiffs and judges appointed for extent of good behavior; Royal Court bailiffs appointed by the Crown upon the advice of the Secretary of State for Justice; commissioners appointed by the bailiff; jurats appointed by the Electoral College; bailiffs and commissioners appointed for extent of good behavior; jurats appointed until retirement at age 72
subordinate courts: Magistrate's Court; Youth Court; Petty Debts Court; Parish Hall Enquires (a process of preliminary investigation into youth and minor adult offenses to determine need for presentation before a court)

Political parties and leaders: one declared parties; Jersey Democratic Alliance
note: all senators and deputies elected in 2008 were independents

Political pressure groups and leaders: Institute of Directors, Jersey branch (provides business support); Jersey Hospitality Association [Robert JONES] (trade association); Jersey Rights Association [David ROTHERHAM] (human rights); La Societe Jersiaise (education and conservation group); Progress Jersey [Daren O'TOOLE, Gino RISOLI] (human rights); Royal Jersey Agriculture and Horticultural Society or RJA&HS (development and management of the Jersey; breed of cattle); Save Jersey's Heritage (protects heritage through building preservation)

Diplomatic representation in the US:
none (British crown dependency)

Diplomatic representation from the US:
none (British crown dependency)

Flag description: white with a diagonal red cross extending to the corners of the flag; in the upper quadrant, surmounted by a yellow crown, a red shield with three lions in yellow; according to tradition, the ships of Jersey—in an attempt to differentiate themselves from English ships flying the horizontal cross of St. George—rotated the cross to the "X" (saltire) configuration; because this arrangement still resembled the Irish cross of St. Patrick, the yellow Plantagenet crown and Jersey coat of arms were added

National symbol(s): Jersey cow

National anthem: *name:* "Isle de Siez Nous" (Island Home)
lyrics/music: Gerard LE FEUVRE
note: adopted 2008; serves as a local anthem; as a British crown dependency, "God Save the Queen" is official (see United Kingdom)

ECONOMY

Economy—overview: Jersey's economy is based on international financial services, agriculture, and tourism. In 2010 the financial services sector accounted for about 50% of the island's output. Potatoes, cauliflower, tomatoes, and especially flowers are important export crops, shipped mostly to the UK. The Jersey breed of dairy cattle is known worldwide and represents an important export income earner. Milk products go to the UK and other EU countries. Tourism accounts for one-quarter of GDP. In recent years, the government has encouraged light industry to locate in Jersey with the result that an electronics industry has developed, displacing more traditional industries. All raw material and energy requirements are imported as well as a large share of Jersey's food needs. Light taxes and death duties make the island a popular tax haven. In January 2013, Jersey signed a tax agreement with Guernsey and the Isle of Man, in order to enable the islands' authorities to end tax avoidance and evasion. Living standards come close to those of the UK.

GDP (purchasing power parity): $5.1 billion (2005 est.)
country comparison to the world: 171

GDP (official exchange rate): $5.1 billion (2005 est.)

GDP—real growth rate: NA%

GDP—per capita (PPP): $57,000 (2005 est.)
country comparison to the world: 8

GDP—composition, by sector of origin:
agriculture: 2%
industry: 2%
services: 96% (2010)

Agriculture—products: potatoes, cauliflower, tomatoes; beef, dairy products

Industries: tourism, banking and finance, dairy, electronics

Industrial production growth rate: NA%

Labor force: 53,380 (June 2012)
country comparison to the world: 188

Unemployment rate: 1.7% (2012 est.)
country comparison to the world: 8
2.2% (2006 est.)

Population below poverty line: NA%

Household income or consumption by percentage share: *lowest 10%:* NA%
highest 10%: NA%

Budget: *revenues:* $829 million
expenditures: $851 million (2005)

Taxes and other revenues: 16.3% of GDP (2005)
country comparison to the world: 186

Budget surplus (+) or deficit (-):
-0.4% of GDP (2005)
country comparison to the world: 54

Fiscal year: 1 April—31 March

Inflation rate (consumer prices): 3.7% (2006)
country comparison to the world: 125

Market value of publicly traded shares: $NA

Exports: $NA

Exports—commodities: light industrial and electrical goods, dairy cattle, foodstuffs, textiles, flowers

Imports: $NA

Imports—commodities: machinery and transport equipment, manufactured goods, foodstuffs, mineral fuels, chemicals

Debt—external: $NA

Exchange rates: Jersey pounds (JEP) per US dollar
0.6391 (2012)
0.6307 (2012)
0.6472 (2010)
0.6175 (2009)
0.5302 (2008)

ENERGY

Electricity—consumption: 630.1 million kWh (2004 est.)
country comparison to the world: 163

COMMUNICATIONS

Telephones—main lines in use: 73,800 (2010)
country comparison to the world: 153

Telephones—mobile cellular: 108,000 (2010)
country comparison to the world: 192

Telephone system: *general assessment:* increasingly modern system, with broadband access
domestic: digital telephone system launch announced in 2006 now implemented; fixed-line and mobile-cellular services widely available; combined fixed and mobile-cellular density exceeds 100 per 100 persons
international: country code—44; submarine cable connectivity to Guernsey, the UK, and France (2010)

Broadcast media: multiple UK terrestrial television broadcasts are received via a transmitter in Jersey; satellite packages available; BBC Radio Jersey and 1 other radio station operating (2009)

Internet country code: .je

Internet hosts: 264 (2012)
country comparison to the world: 193

Internet users: 29,500 (2009)
country comparison to the world: 182

TRANSPORTATION

Airports: 1 (2013)
country comparison to the world: 221

Airports—with paved runways: *total:* 1
1,524 to 2,437 m: 1 (2013)

Roadways: *total:* 576 km (2010)
country comparison to the world: 191

Merchant marine:
registered in other countries: 14 (Gibraltar 1, India 2, Marshall Islands 11) (2010)
country comparison to the world: 103

Ports and terminals: *major seaport(s):* Gorey, Saint Aubin, Saint Helier

MILITARY

Manpower fit for military service:
males age 16-49: 18,688
females age 16-49: 18,615 (2010 est.)

Manpower reaching militarily significant age annually: *male:* 664
female: 590 (2010 est.)

Military—note: defense is the responsibility of the UK

TRANSNATIONAL ISSUES

Disputes—international: none

JOHNSTON ATOLL

INTRODUCTION

Background: Both the US and the Kingdom of Hawaii annexed Johnston Atoll in 1858, but it was the US that mined the guano deposits until the late 1880s. Johnston Island and Sand Island were designated wildlife refuges in 1926. The US Navy took over the atoll in 1934, and subsequently the US Air Force assumed control in 1948. The site was used for high-altitude nuclear tests in the 1950s and 1960s, and until late in 2000 the atoll was maintained as a storage and disposal site for chemical weapons. Cleanup and closure of the weapons facility ended in May 2005.

GEOGRAPHY

Location: Oceania, atoll in the North Pacific Ocean 717 nm (1328 km) southwest of Honolulu, Hawaii, about one-third of the way from Hawaii to the Marshall Islands

Geographic coordinates: 16 45 N, 169 31 W

Map references: Oceania

Area: *total:* 2.63 sq km
land: 2.63 sq km
water: 0 sq km

Area—comparative: about 4.7 times the size of The Mall in Washington, DC

Land boundaries: 0 km

Coastline: 34 km

Maritime claims: *territorial sea:* 12 nm
exclusive economic zone: 200 nm

Climate: tropical, but generally dry; consistent northeast trade winds with little seasonal temperature variation

Terrain: mostly flat

Elevation extremes: *lowest point:* Pacific Ocean 0 m
highest point: Summit Peak 5 m

Natural resources: guano deposits (worked until depletion about 1890), terrestrial and aquatic wildlife

Land use: *arable land:* 0%
permanent crops: 0%
other: 100% (2011)

Irrigated land: 0 sq km (2011)

Natural hazards: NA

Environment—current issues: no natural fresh water resources

Geography—note: strategic location in the North Pacific Ocean; Johnston Island and Sand Island are natural islands, which have been expanded by coral dredging; North Island (Akau) and East Island (Hikina) are manmade islands formed from coral dredging; the egg-shaped reef is 34 km in circumference; closed to the public; a former US nuclear weapons test site; site of now-closed Johnston Atoll Chemical Agent Disposal System (JACADS); most facilities dismantled and cleanup complete in 2004; some low-growing vegetation

PEOPLE AND SOCIETY

Population: 315 uninhabited
note: in previous years, there was an average of 1,100 US military and civilian contractor personnel present; as of September 2001, population had decreased significantly when US Army Chemical Activity Pacific (USACAP) departed; as of May 2005 all US government personnel had left the island (July 2010 est.)

GOVERNMENT

Country name: *conventional long form:* none
conventional short form: Johnston Atoll

Dependency status: unincorporated territory of the US; administered from Honolulu, HI, by Pacific Air Forces, Hickam Air Force Base, and the Fish and Wildlife Service of the US Department of the Interior as part of the National Wildlife Refuge system

Legal system: the laws of the US, where applicable, apply

Flag description: the flag of the US is used

TRANSPORTATION

Airports—with paved runways: *total:* 1
2,438 to 3,047 m: 1 (2013)

Ports and terminals: Johnston Island

MILITARY

Military—note: defense is the responsibility of the US

TRANSNATIONAL ISSUES

Disputes—international: none

JORDAN

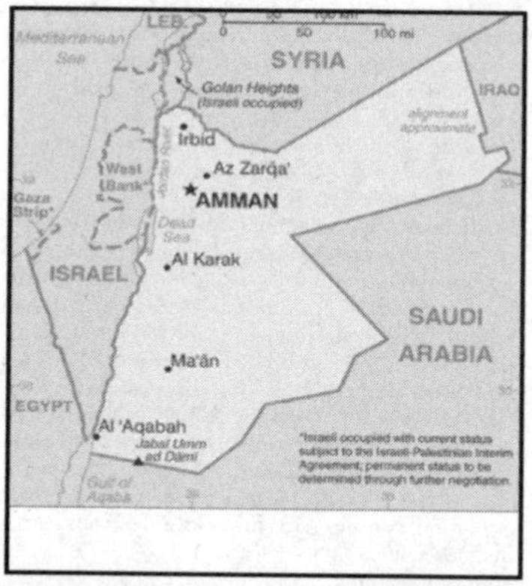

INTRODUCTION

Background: Following World War I and the dissolution of the Ottoman Empire, the League of Nations awarded Britain the mandate to govern much of the Middle East. Britain demarcated a semi-autonomous region of Transjordan from Palestine in the early 1920s. The area gained its independence in 1946 and thereafter became The Hashemite Kingdom of Jordan. The country's long-time ruler, King HUSSEIN (1953-99), successfully navigated competing pressures from the major powers (US, USSR, and UK), various Arab states, Israel, and a large internal Palestinian population. Jordan lost the West Bank to Israel in the 1967 Six-Day War. King HUSSEIN in 1988 permanently relinquished Jordanian claims to the West Bank; in 1994 he signed a peace treaty with Israel. King ABDALLAH II, King HUSSEIN's eldest son, assumed the throne following his father's death in 1999. He implemented modest political and economic reforms, but in the wake of the "Arab Revolution" across the Middle East, Jordanians continue to press for further political liberalization, government reforms, and economic improvements. In January 2014, Jordan assumed a nonpermanent seat on the UN Security Council for the 2014-15 term.

GEOGRAPHY

Location: Middle East, northwest of Saudi Arabia, between Israel (to the west) and Iraq

Geographic coordinates: 31 00 N, 36 00 E

Map references: Middle East

Area: *total:* 89,342 sq km
country comparison to the world: 112
land: 88,802 sq km
water: 540 sq km

Area—comparative: slightly smaller than Indiana

Land boundaries: *total:* 1,635 km
border countries: Iraq 181 km, Israel 238 km, Saudi Arabia 744 km, Syria 375 km, West Bank 97 km

Coastline: 26 km

Maritime claims: *territorial sea:* 3 nm

Climate: mostly arid desert; rainy season in west (November to April)

Terrain: mostly desert plateau in east, highland area in west; Great Rift Valley separates East and West Banks of the Jordan River

Elevation extremes: *lowest point:* Dead Sea -408 m
highest point: Jabal Umm ad Dami 1,854 m

Natural resources: phosphates, potash, shale oil

Land use: *arable land:* 1.97%
permanent crops: 0.95%
other: 97.08% (2011)

Irrigated land: 788.6 sq km (2004)

Total renewable water resources: 0.94 cu km (2011)

Freshwater withdrawal (domestic/industrial/agricultural): *total:* 0.94 cu km/yr (31%/4%/65%)
per capita: 166 cu m/yr (2005)

Natural hazards: droughts; periodic earthquakes

Environment—current issues:
limited natural freshwater resources; deforestation; overgrazing; soil erosion; desertification

Environment—international agreements:
party to: Biodiversity, Climate Change, Climate Change-Kyoto Protocol, Desertification, Endangered Species, Hazardous Wastes, Law of the

Sea, Marine Dumping, Ozone Layer Protection, Wetlands
signed, but not ratified: none of the selected agreements

Geography—note: strategic location at the head of the Gulf of Aqaba and as the Arab country that shares the longest border with Israel and the occupied West Bank

PEOPLE AND SOCIETY

Nationality: *noun:* Jordanian(s)
adjective: Jordanian

Ethnic groups: Arab 98%, Circassian 1%, Armenian 1%
Languages: Arabic (official), English (widely understood among upper and middle classes)

Religions: Muslim 97.2% (official; predominantly Sunni), Christian 2.2% (majority Greek Orthodox, but some Greek and Roman Catholics, Syrian Orthodox, Coptic Orthodox, Armenian Orthodox, and Protestant denominations), Buddhist 0.4%, Hindu 0.1%, Jewish

Population: 7,930,491 (July 2014 est.)
country comparison to the world: 98

Age structure:
0-14 years: 35.8% (male 1,457,174/female 1,385,604)
15-24 years: 20.4% (male 826,482/female 788,950)
25-54 years: 35.7% (male 1,421,634/female 1,412,888)
55-64 years: 3.9% (male 160,224/female 169,965)
65 years and over: 5.1% (male 145,515/female 162,055) (2014 est.)

Dependency ratios:
total dependency ratio: 60.2 %
youth dependency ratio: 54.5 %
elderly dependency ratio: 5.7 %
potential support ratio: 17.6 (2013)

Median age: *total:* 21.8 years
male: 21.5 years
female: 22.1 years (2014 est.)

Population growth rate: 3.86% (2014 est.)
country comparison to the world: 4

Birth rate: 25.23 births/1,000 population (2014 est.)
country comparison to the world: 53

Death rate: 3.8 deaths/1,000 population (2014 est.)
country comparison to the world: 213

Net migration rate: 17.22 migrant(s)/1,000 population (2014 est.)
country comparison to the world: 5

Urbanization: *urban population:* 82.7% of total population (2011)
rate of urbanization: 2.17% annual rate of change (2010-15 est.)

Major urban areas—population: AMMAN (capital) 1.088 million (2009)

Sex ratio: *at birth:* 1.06 male(s)/female
0-14 years: 1.05 male(s)/female
15-24 years: 1.05 male(s)/female
25-54 years: 1.01 male(s)/female
55-64 years: 1.02 male(s)/female
65 years and over: 0.95 male(s)/female
total population: 1.03 male(s)/female (2014 est.)

Mother's mean age at first birth: 24.7
note: median age at first birth among women 25-29 (2012 est.)

Maternal mortality rate: 63 deaths/100,000 live births (2010)
country comparison to the world: 97

Infant mortality rate: *total:* 15.73 deaths/1,000 live births
country comparison to the world: 104
male: 16.63 deaths/1,000 live births
female: 14.79 deaths/1,000 live births (2014 est.)

Life expectancy at birth: *total population:* 74.1 years
country comparison to the world: 117
male: 72.79 years
female: 75.5 years (2014 est.)

Total fertility rate: 3.16 children born/woman (2014 est.)
country comparison to the world: 52

Contraceptive prevalence rate: 59.3% (2009)

Health expenditures: 8.4% of GDP (2011)
country comparison to the world: 55

Physicians density: 2.56 physicians/1,000 population (2010)

Hospital bed density: 1.8 beds/1,000 population (2010)

Drinking water source:
improved:
urban: 97.3% of population
rural: 90.5% of population
total: 96.2% of population
unimproved:
urban: 2.7% of population
rural: 9.5% of population
total: 3.8% of population (2011 est.)

Sanitation facility access:
improved:
urban: 98.1% of population
rural: 98% of population
total: 98.1% of population
unimproved:
urban: 1.9% of population
rural: 2% of population
total: 1.9% of population (2011 est.)

HIV/AIDS—adult prevalence rate:
less than 0.1% (2001 est.)
country comparison to the world: 152

HIV/AIDS—people living with HIV/AIDS:
600 (2007 est.)
country comparison to the world: 154

HIV/AIDS—deaths: fewer than 500 (2003 est.)
country comparison to the world: 89

Obesity—adult prevalence rate: 30% (2008)
country comparison to the world: 28

Children under the age of 5 years underweight:
1.9% (2009)
country comparison to the world: 123

Education expenditures: NA

Literacy: *definition:* age 15 and over can read and write
total population: 95.9%
male: 97.7%
female: 93.9% (2011 est.)

School life expectancy (primary to tertiary education): *total:* 13 years
male: 13 years
female: 14 years (2011)

Unemployment, youth ages 15-24: *total:* 29.3%
country comparison to the world: 28
male: 25.2%
female: 48.8% (2012)

GOVERNMENT

Country name: *conventional long form:* Hashemite Kingdom of Jordan
conventional short form: Jordan
local long form: Al Mamlakah al Urduniyah al Hashimiyah
local short form: Al Urdun
former: Transjordan

Government type: constitutional monarchy

Capital: *name:* Amman
geographic coordinates: 31 57 N, 35 56 E
time difference: UTC+2 (7 hours ahead of Washington, DC during Standard Time)
daylight saving time: +1hr, begins last Friday in March; ends last Friday in October

Administrative divisions: 12 governorates (muhafazat, singular—muhafazah); 'Ajlun, Al 'Aqabah, Al Balqa', Al Karak, Al Mafraq, 'Amman, At Tafilah, Az Zarqa', Irbid, Jarash, Ma'an, Madaba

Independence: 25 May 1946 (from League of Nations mandate under British administration)

National holiday: Independence Day, 25 May (1946)

Constitution: previous 1928 (preindependence); latest initially adopted 28 November 1947, revised and ratified 1 January 1952; amended several times, last in 2011 (2012)

Legal system: mixed legal system of civil law and Islamic religious law; judicial review of legislative acts in a specially provided High Tribunal

International law organization participation: has not submitted an ICJ jurisdiction declaration; accepts ICCt jurisdiction

Suffrage: 18 years of age; universal

Executive branch: *chief of state:* King ABDALLAH II (since 7 February 1999); Crown Prince HUSSEIN (born 28 June 1994), eldest son of King ABDALLAH II
head of government: Prime Minister Abdullah NSOUR (since 11 October 2012)
cabinet: Cabinet appointed by the prime minister in consultation with the monarch; note—a new cabinet was sworn in 21 August 2013 and includes 13 new ministers, enlarging the government as part of promised reforms (For more information visit the World Leaders website)
elections: the monarchy is hereditary; prime minister appointed by the monarch

Legislative branch: bicameral National Assembly or Majlis al-'Umma consists of the Senate, also called the House of Notables or Majlis al-Ayan (60 seats; members appointed by the monarch to serve four-year terms) and the Chamber of Deputies, also called the House of Representatives or Majlis al-Nuwaab (150 seats; 123 members elected using the single, non-transferable vote system in multi-member districts, and 27 seats elected using a closed national list system based on proportional representation; all legislators serve four-year terms); note—the new electoral law enacted in July 2012 allocated an additional 10 seats (6 seats added to the number reserved for women, bringing the total to 15; 2 additional seats for Amman; and 1 seat each for the cities of Zarqa and Irbid; unchanged are 9 seats reserved for Christian candidates, 9 for Bedouin candidates, and 3 for Jordanians of Chechen or Circassian descent
elections: Chamber of Deputies—last held on 23 January 2013 (next election 2017); note—the King dissolved the previous Chamber of Deputies in November 2012, midway through the parliamentary term
election results: Chamber of Deputies—percent of vote by party—NA; seats by party—27 elected on closed national list to include: Islamic Centrist Party 3, Nation 2, National Union 2, Stronger Jordan 2, Ahl al-Himma 1, Al-Bayyan 1, Citizenship 1, Construction 1, Cooperation 1, Dawn 1, Dignity 1, Free Voice 1, Labor and Trade 1, National Accord Youth Block 1, National Action 1, National Current 1 (member resigned in February 2013), National Unity 1, Nobel Jerusalem 1, Salvation 1, The People 1, Unified Front 1, Voice of Nation 1; other 123; note—the IAF boycotted the election

Judicial branch: *highest court(s):* Court of Cassation or Supreme Court (consists of 7 judges including the chief justice; 7-judge panels for important cases and 5 judge panels for most appeals cases)
judge selection and term of office: chief justice appointed by the king; other judges nominated by the Higher Judicial Council and approved by the king; judge tenure NA
subordinate courts: courts of appeal; magistrate courts; courts of first instance; religious courts; State Security Court

Political parties and leaders: Ahl al-Himma; Al-Bayyan; Al-Hayah Jordanian Party [Zahier AMR]; Arab Ba'ath Socialist Party [Akram al-HIMSI]; Ba'ath Arab Progressive Party [Fuad DABBOUR]; Citizenship; Construction; Cooperation; Dawn; Democratic People's Party [Ablah ABU ULBAH]; Democratic Popular Unity Party [Sa'id DIAB]; Dignity; Du'a Party [Muhammed ABU BAKR]; Free Voice; Islamic Action Front or IAF [Hamzah MANSOUR]; Islamic Centrist Party [Muhammad al-HAJ]; Jordanian Communist Party [Munir HAMARNAH]; Jordanian National Party [Muna ABU BAKR]; Jordanian United Front [Amjad al-MAJALI]; Labor and Trade; Nation; National Accord Youth Block; National Action; National Constitution Party [Ahmad al-SHUNAQ]; National Current Party [Abd al-Hadi al-MAJALI]; National Movement for Direct Democracy [Muhammad al-QAQ]; National Union; National Unity; Nobel Jerusalem; Risalah Party [Hazem QASHOU]; Salvation; Stronger Jordan; The Direct Democratic Nationalists Movement Party [Nash'at KHALIFAH]; The People; Unified Front; United Front; Voice of the Nation

Political pressure groups and leaders: 15 April Movement [Mohammad SUNEID, chairman]; 24 March Movement [Mu'az al-KHAWALIDAH, Abdel Rahman HASANEIN, spokespersons]; 1952 Constitution Movement; Anti-Normalization Committee [Hamzah MANSOUR, chairman]; Economic and Social Association of Retired Servicemen and Veterans or ESARSV [Abdulsalam; al-HASSANAT, chairman]; Group of 36; Higher Coordination Committee of Opposition Parties [Said DIAB]; Higher National Committee for Military Retirees or HNCMR [Ali al-HABASHNEH, chairman]; Hirak; Jordan Bar Association [Saleh al-ARMUTI, chairman]; Jordanian Campaign for Change or Jayin; Jordanian Muslim Brotherhood [Dr. Hamam SAID, controller general]; Jordanian Press Association [Sayf al-SHARIF, president]; National Front for Reform or NFR [Ahmad OBEIDAT, chairman]; Popular Gathering for Reform; Professional Associations Council [Abd al-Hadi al-FALAHAT, chairman]; Sons of Jordan

International organization participation: ABEDA, AFESD, AMF, CAEU, CD, CICA, EBRD, FAO, G-11, G-77, IAEA, IBRD, ICAO, ICC (national committees), ICRM, IDA, IDB, IFAD, IFC, IFRCS, ILO, IMF, IMO, Interpol, IOC, IOM, IPU, ISO, ITSO, ITU, ITUC (NGOs), LAS, MIGA, MINUSTAH, MINUSMA, MONUSCO, NAM, OIC, OPCW, OSCE (partner), PCA, UN, UN Security Council (temporary), UNAMID, UNCTAD, UNESCO, UNHCR, UNIDO, UNISFA, UNMIL, UNMISS, UNOCI, UNRWA, UNWTO, UPU, WCO, WFTU (NGOs), WHO, WIPO, WMO, WTO

Diplomatic representation in the US:
chief of mission: Ambassador Alia Hatough BOURAN (since 14 September 2010)
chancery: 3504 International Drive NW, Washington, DC 20008
telephone: [1] (202) 966-2664
FAX: [1] (202) 966-3110

Diplomatic representation from the US:
chief of mission: Ambassador Stuart E. JONES (since 21 July 2011)
embassy: Abdoun, Al-Umawyeen St., Amman
mailing address: P. O. Box 354, Amman 11118 Jordan; Unit 70200, Box 5, DPO AE 09892-0200
telephone: [962] (6) 590-6000
FAX: [962] (6) 592-0163

Flag description: three equal horizontal bands of black (top), representing the Abbassid Caliphate, white, representing the Ummayyad Caliphate, and green, representing the Fatimid Caliphate; a red isosceles triangle on the hoist side, representing the Great Arab Revolt of 1916, and bearing a small white seven-pointed star symbolizing the seven verses of the opening Sura (Al-Fatiha) of the Holy Koran; the seven points on the star represent faith in One God, humanity, national spirit, humility, social justice, virtue, and aspirations; design is based on the Arab Revolt flag of World War I

National symbol(s): eagle

National anthem: *name:* "As-salam al-malaki al-urdoni" (Long Live the King of Jordan)
lyrics/music: Abdul-Mone'm al-RIFAI'/Abdul-Qader al-TANEER
note: adopted 1946; the shortened version of the anthem is used most commonly, while the full version is reserved for special occasions

ECONOMY

Economy—overview: Jordan's economy is among the smallest in the Middle East, with insufficient supplies of water, oil, and other natural resources underlying the government's heavy reliance on foreign assistance. Other economic challenges for the government include chronic high rates of poverty, unemployment, inflation, and a large budget deficit. Since assuming the throne in 1999, King ABDALLAH has implemented significant economic reforms, such as opening the trade regime, privatizing state-owned companies, and eliminating some fuel subsidies, which in the last decade spurred economic growth by attracting foreign investment and creating some jobs. The global economic slowdown and regional turmoil, however, have depressed Jordan's GDP growth, impacting export-oriented sectors, construction, and tourism. In 2011 and 2012, the government approved two economic relief packages and a budgetary supplement, meant to improve the living conditions for the middle and poor classes. Jordan's finances have also been strained by a series of natural gas pipeline attacks in Egypt, causing Jordan to substitute more expensive diesel imports, primarily from Saudi Arabia, to generate electricity. Jordan is currently exploring nuclear power generation in addition to the exploitation of abundant oil shale reserves and renewable technologies to forestall energy shortfalls. In 2012, to correct budgetary and balance of payments imbalances, Jordan entered into a $2.1 billion, multiple year International Monetary Fund Stand-By Arrangement. Jordan's financial sector has been relatively isolated from the international financial crisis because of its limited exposure to overseas capital markets. In 2013, Jordan depended heavily on foreign assistance to finance the budget deficit, as the influx of about 600,000 Syrian refugees put additional pressure on expenditures.

GDP (purchasing power parity): $40.02 billion (2013 est.)
country comparison to the world: 105
$38.76 billion (2012 est.)
$37.71 billion (2011 est.)
note: data are in 2013 US dollars

GDP (official exchange rate): $34.08 billion (2013 est.)

GDP—real growth rate: 3.3% (2013 est.)
country comparison to the world: 106
2.8% (2012 est.)
2.6% (2011 est.)

GDP—per capita (PPP): $6,100 (2013 est.)
country comparison to the world: 150
$6,100 (2012 est.)
$6,000 (2011 est.)
note: data are in 2013 US dollars

Gross national saving: 29.1% of GDP (2013 est.)
country comparison to the world: 28
24.7% of GDP (2012 est.)
28.5% of GDP (2011 est.)

GDP—composition, by end use:
household consumption: 73.1%
government consumption: 21%
investment in fixed capital: 26.2%
investment in inventories: 17%
exports of goods and services: 44.1%
imports of goods and services: -81.4% (2013 est.)

GDP—composition, by sector of origin:
agriculture: 3.2%
industry: 29.9%
services: 67% (2013 est.)

Agriculture—products: citrus, tomatoes, cucumbers, olives, strawberries, stone fruits; sheep, poultry, dairy

Industries: clothing, fertilizers, potash, phosphate mining, pharmaceuticals, petroleum refining, cement, inorganic chemicals, light manufacturing, tourism

Industrial production growth rate: 2.8% (2013 est.)
country comparison to the world: 110

Labor force: 1.898 million (2013 est.)
country comparison to the world: 123

Labor force—by occupation:
agriculture: 2.7%
industry: 20%
services: 77.4% (2007 est.)

Unemployment rate: 14% (2013 est.)
country comparison to the world: 135
12.5% (2012 est.)
note: official rate; unofficial rate is approximately 30%

Population below poverty line: 14.2% (2002)

Household income or consumption by percentage share: *lowest 10%:* 3.4%
highest 10%: 28.7% (2010 est.)

Distribution of family income—Gini index: 39.7 (2007)
country comparison to the world: 61
36.4 (1997)

Budget: *revenues:* $6.868 billion
expenditures: $10.71 billion (2013 est.)

Taxes and other revenues: 20.2% of GDP (2013 est.)
country comparison to the world: 165

Budget surplus (+) or deficit (-):
-11.3% of GDP (2013 est.)
country comparison to the world: 208

Public debt: 79.1% of GDP (2013 est.)
country comparison to the world: 28
75.5% of GDP (2012 est.)
note: data cover central government debt, and include debt instruments issued (or owned) by government entities other than the treasury; the data include treasury debt held by foreign entities; the data exclude debt issued by subnational entities, as well as intra-governmental debt; intra-governmental debt consists of treasury borrowings from surpluses in the social funds, such as for retirement, medical care, and unemployment; debt instruments for the social funds are not sold at public auctions

Fiscal year: calendar year

Inflation rate (consumer prices): 5.9% (2013 est.)
country comparison to the world: 168
4.8% (2012 est.)

Central bank discount rate: 0.3% (31 December 2010 est.)
country comparison to the world: 76
4.75% (31 December 2009 est.)

Commercial bank prime lending rate: 8.9% (31 December 2013 est.)
country comparison to the world: 102
8.95% (31 December 2012 est.)

Stock of narrow money: $10.68 billion (31 December 2013 est.)
country comparison to the world: 76
$10.17 billion (31 December 2012 est.)

Stock of broad money: $37.19 billion (31 December 2013 est.)
country comparison to the world: 73
$35.18 billion (31 December 2012 est.)

Stock of domestic credit: $38.3 billion (31 December 2013 est.)
country comparison to the world: 65
$35.39 billion (31 December 2012 est.)

Market value of publicly traded shares: $27 billion (31 December 2012 est.)
country comparison to the world: 57
$27.18 billion (31 December 2011)
$30.86 billion (31 December 2010 est.)

Current account balance: -$4.766 billion (2013 est.)
country comparison to the world: 166
-$5.37 billion (2012 est.)

Exports: $7.914 billion (2013 est.)
country comparison to the world: 101
$7.898 billion (2012 est.)

Exports—commodities: clothing, fertilizers, potash, phosphates, vegetables, pharmaceuticals

Exports—partners: US 16.6%, Iraq 15.1%, Saudi Arabia 11%, India 10.5%, Indonesia 4.2% (2012)

Imports: $18.61 billion (2013 est.)
country comparison to the world: 79
$18.46 billion (2012 est.)

Imports—commodities: crude oil, machinery, transport equipment, iron, cereals

Imports—partners: Saudi Arabia 23.6%, China 9.4%, US 6.7%, Italy 4.7%, Turkey 4.6% (2012)

Reserves of foreign exchange and gold: $11.83 billion (31 December 2013 est.)
country comparison to the world: 71
$8.829 billion (31 December 2012 est.)

Debt—external: $22.04 billion (31 December 2013 est.)
country comparison to the world: 80
$19.67 billion (31 December 2012 est.)

Stock of direct foreign investment—at home: $26.69 billion (31 December 2013 est.)
country comparison to the world: 65
$24.78 billion (31 December 2012 est.)

Stock of direct foreign investment—abroad: $549 million (31 December 2013 est.)
country comparison to the world: 80
$509 million (31 December 2012 est.)

Exchange rates: Jordanian dinars (JOD) per US dollar—
0.709 (2013 est.)
0.709 (2012 est.)
0.71 (2010 est.)
0.709 (2009)
0.709 (2008)

ENERGY

Electricity—production: 14.64 billion kWh (2011 est.)
country comparison to the world: 8 5

Electricity—consumption: 13.54 billion kWh (2011 est.)
country comparison to the world: 81

Electricity—exports: 86 million kWh (2011 est.)
country comparison to the world: 78

Electricity—imports: 1.738 billion kWh (2011 est.)
country comparison to the world: 56

Electricity—installed generating capacity: 3.138 million kW (2010 est.)
country comparison to the world: 87

Electricity—from fossil fuels: 99.4% of total installed capacity (2010 est.)
country comparison to the world: 51

Electricity—from nuclear fuels: 0% of total installed capacity (2010 est.)
country comparison to the world: 115

Electricity—from hydroelectric plants: 0.4% of total installed capacity (2010 est.)
country comparison to the world: 145

Electricity—from other renewable sources: 0.2% of total installed capacity (2010 est.)
country comparison to the world: 95

Crude oil—production: 164.8 bbl/day (2012 est.)
country comparison to the world: 120

Crude oil—exports: 0 bbl/day (2010 est.)
country comparison to the world: 134

Crude oil—imports: 68,320 bbl/day (2010 est.)
country comparison to the world: 53

Crude oil—proved reserves: 1 million bbl (1 January 2013 es)
country comparison to the world: 97

Refined petroleum products—production: 72,190 bbl/day (2010 est.)
country comparison to the world: 78

Refined petroleum products—consumption: 107,000 bbl/day (2011 est.)
country comparison to the world: 75

Refined petroleum products—exports: 0 bbl/day (2010 est.)
country comparison to the world: 187

Refined petroleum products—imports: 35,600 bbl/day (2010 est.)
country comparison to the world: 85

Natural gas—production: 230 million cu m (2011 est.)
country comparison to the world: 77

Natural gas—consumption: 1.4 billion cu m (2011 est.)
country comparison to the world: 84

Natural gas—exports: 0 cu m (2011 est.)
country comparison to the world: 125

Natural gas—imports: 830 million cu m (2011 est.)
country comparison to the world: 61

Natural gas—proved reserves: 6.031 billion cu m (1 January 2013 es)
country comparison to the world: 90

Carbon dioxide emissions from consumption of energy: 18.55 million Mt (2011 est.)
country comparison to the world: 88

COMMUNICATIONS

Telephones—main lines in use: 435,000 (2012)
country comparison to the world: 100

Telephones—mobile cellular: 8.984 million (2012)
country comparison to the world: 87

Telephone system: *general assessment:* service has improved recently with increased use of digital switching equipment; microwave radio relay transmission and coaxial and fiber-optic cable are employed on trunk lines; growing mobile-cellular usage in both urban and rural areas is reducing use of fixed-line services
domestic: 1995 telecommunications law opened all non-fixed-line services to private competition; in 2005, monopoly over fixed-line services terminated and the entire telecommunications sector was opened to competition; currently multiple mobile-cellular providers with subscribership reaching 115 per 100 persons in 2011
international: country code—962; landing point for the Fiber-Optic Link Around the Globe (FLAG) FEA and FLAG Falcon submarine cable networks; satellite earth stations—33 (3 Intelsat, 1 Arabsat, and 29 land and maritime Inmarsat terminals); fiber-optic cable to Saudi Arabia and microwave radio relay link with Egypt maritime Inmarsat terminals); fiber-optic cable to Saudi Arabia and microwave radio relay link with Egypt and Syria; participant in Medarabtel (2011)

Broadcast media: radio and TV dominated by the government-owned Jordan Radio and Television Corporation (JRTV) that operates a main network, a sports network, a film network, and a satellite channel; first independent TV broadcaster aired in 2007; international satellite TV and Israeli and Syrian TV broadcasts are available; roughly 30 radio stations with JRTV operating the main government-owned station; transmissions of multiple international radio broadcasters are available (2007)

Internet country code: .jo

Internet hosts: 69,473 (2012)
country comparison to the world: 89

Internet users: 1.642 million (2009)
country comparison to the world: 78

TRANSPORTATION

Airports: 18 (2013)
country comparison to the world: 140

Airports—with paved runways: *total:* 1 6
over 3,047 m: 8
2,438 to 3,047 m: 5
1,524 to 2,437 m: 2
914 to 1,523 m: 1 (2013)

Airports—with unpaved runways: *total:* 2
under 914 m: 2 (2013)

Heliports: 1 (2012)

Pipelines: gas 473 km; oil 49 km (2013)

Railways: *total:* 507 km
country comparison to the world: 111
narrow gauge: 507 km 1.050-m gauge (2008)

Roadways: *total:* 7,203 km
country comparison to the world: 144
paved: 7,203 km (2011)

Merchant marine: *total:* 1 2
country comparison to the world: 107
by type: cargo 4, passenger/cargo 6, petroleum tanker 1, roll on/roll off 1
foreign-owned: 2 (UAE 2)
registered in other countries: 16 (Bahamas 2, Egypt 2, Indonesia 1, Panama 11) (2010)

Ports and terminals: *major seaport(s):* Al 'Aqabah

MILITARY

Military branches: Jordanian Armed Forces (JAF): Royal Jordanian Land Force (RJLF), Royal Jordanian Navy, Royal Jordanian Air Force (Al-Quwwat al-Jawwiya al-Malakiya al-Urduniya, RJAF), Special Operations Command (Socom); Public Security Directorate (normally falls under Ministry of Interior, but comes under JAF in wartime or crisis) (2013)

Military service age and obligation: 17 years of age for voluntary male military service; initial service term 2 years, with option to reenlist for 18 years; conscription at age 18 suspended in 1999; women not subject to conscription, but can volunteer to serve in noncombat military positions in the Royal Jordanian Arab Army Women's Corps and RJAF (2013)

Manpower available for military service:
males age 16-49: 1,674,260
females age 16-49: 1,611,315 (2010 est.)

Manpower fit for military service:
males age 16-49: 1,439,192
females age 16-49: 1,384,500 (2010 est.)

Manpower reaching militarily significant age annually: *male:* 73,574
female: 69,420 (2010 est.)

Military expenditures: 4.65% of GDP (2012)
country comparison to the world: 6
4.64% of GDP (2011)
4.65% of GDP (2010)

TRANSNATIONAL ISSUES

Disputes—international: 2004 Agreement settles border dispute with Syria pending demarcation

Refugees and internally displaced persons: *refugees (country of origin):* 63,037 (Iraq) (2012); 2,054,527 (Palestinian refugees (UNRWA)) (2013); 589,792 (Syria) (2014)

KAZAKHSTAN

INTRODUCTION

Background: Ethnic Kazakhs, a mix of Turkic and Mongol nomadic tribes who migrated to the region by the 13th century, were rarely united as a single nation. The area was conquered by Russia in the 18th century, and Kazakhstan became a Soviet Republic in 1936. During the 1950s and 1960s agricultural "Virgin Lands" program, Soviet citizens were encouraged to help cultivate Kazakhstan's northern pastures. This influx of immigrants (mostly Russians, but also some other deported nationalities) skewed the ethnic mixture and enabled non-ethnic Kazakhs to outnumber natives. Non-Muslim ethnic minorities departed Kazakhstan in large numbers from the mid-1990s through the mid-2000s and a national program has repatriated about a million ethnic Kazakhs back to Kazakhstan. These trends have allowed Kazakhs to become the titular majority again. This dramatic demographic shift has also undermined the previous religious diversity and made the country more than 70 percent Muslim. Kazakhstan's economy is larger than those of all the other Central Asian states largely due to the country's vast natural resources. Current issues include: developing a cohesive national identity; managing Islamic revivalism; expanding the development of the country's vast energy resources and exporting them to world markets; diversifying the economy outside the oil, gas, and mining sectors; enhancing Kazakhstan's economic competitiveness; developing a multiparty parliament and advancing political and social reform; and strengthening relations with neighboring states and other foreign powers.

GEOGRAPHY

Location: Central Asia, northwest of China; a small portion west of the Ural (Zhayyq) River in eastern-most Europe

Geographic coordinates: 48 00 N, 68 00 E

Map references: Asia

Area: *total:* 2,724,900 sq km
country comparison to the world: 9
land: 2,699,700 sq km
water: 25,200 sq km

Area—comparative: slightly less than four times the size of Texas

Land boundaries: *total:* 12,185 km
border countries: China 1,533 km, Kyrgyzstan 1,224 km, Russia 6,846 km, Turkmenistan 379 km, Uzbekistan 2,203 km

Coastline: 0 km (landlocked); note—Kazakhstan borders the Aral Sea, now split into two bodies of water (1,070 km), and the Caspian Sea (1,894 km)

Maritime claims: none (landlocked)

Climate: continental, cold winters and hot summers, arid and semiarid

Terrain: vast flat steppe extending from the Volga in the west to the Altai Mountains in the east and from the plains of western Siberia in the north to oases and deserts of Central Asia in the south

Elevation extremes: *lowest point:* Vpadina Kaundy—132 m
highest point: Khan Tangiri Shyngy (Pik Khan-Tengri) 6,995 m

Natural resources: major deposits of petroleum, natural gas, coal, iron ore, manganese, chrome ore, nickel, cobalt, copper, molybdenum, lead, zinc, bauxite, gold, uranium

Land use: *arable land:* 8.82%
permanent crops: 0.03%
other: 91.15% (2011)

Irrigated land: 20,660 sq km (2010)

Total renewable water resources: 107.5 cu km (2011)

Freshwater withdrawal (domestic/industrial/agricultural): *total:* 21.14 cu km/yr (4%/30%/66%)
per capita: 1,304 cu m/yr (2010)

Natural hazards: earthquakes in the south; mudslides around Almaty

Environment—current issues: radioactive or toxic chemical sites associated with former defense industries and test ranges scattered throughout the country pose health risks for humans and animals; industrial pollution is severe in some cities; because the two main rivers that flowed into the Aral Sea have been diverted for irrigation, it is drying up and leaving behind a harmful layer of chemical pesticides and natural salts; these substances are then picked up by the wind and blown into noxious dust storms; pollution in the Caspian Sea; soil pollution from overuse of agricultural chemicals and salination from poor infrastructure and wasteful irrigation practices

Environment—international agreements:
party to: Air Pollution, Biodiversity, Climate Change, Desertification, Endangered Species, Environmental Modification, Hazardous Wastes, Ozone Layer Protection, Ship Pollution, Wetlands
signed, but not ratified: Climate Change-Kyoto Protocol

Geography—note: landlocked; Russia leases approximately 6,000 sq km of territory enclosing the Baykonur Cosmodrome; in January 2004, Kazakhstan and Russia extended the lease to 2050

PEOPLE AND SOCIETY

Nationality: *noun:* Kazakhstani(s)
adjective: Kazakhstani

Ethnic groups: Kazakh (Qazaq) 63.1%, Russian 23.7%, Uzbek 2.8%, Ukrainian 2.1%, Uighur 1.4%, Tatar 1.3%, German 1.1%, other 4.5% (2009 census)

Languages: Kazakh (Qazaq, state language) 64.4%, Russian (official, used in everyday business, designated the "language of interethnic communication") 95% (2001 est.)

Religions: Muslim 70.2%, Christian 26.2% (Russian Orthodox 23.9%, other Christian 2.3%), Buddhist 0.1%, other 0.2%, atheist 2.8%, unspecified 0.5% (2009 Census)

Population: 17,948,816 (July 2014 est.)
country comparison to the world: 62

Age structure:
0-14 years: 25.1% (male 2,247,628/female 2,254,744)
15-24 years: 16.1% (male 1,469,275/female 1,418,175)
25-54 years: 42.6% (male 3,720,498/female 3,927,626)
55-64 years: 7% (male 724,683/female 935,416)
65 years and over: 6.8% (male 429,565/female 821,206) (2014 est.)

Dependency ratios:
total dependency ratio: 48 %
youth dependency ratio: 38.1 %
elderly dependency ratio: 9.9 %
potential support ratio: 10.1 (2013)

Median age: *total:* 29.7 years
male: 28.4 years
female: 31.1 years (2014 est.)

Population growth rate: 1.17% (2014 est.)
country comparison to the world: 103

Birth rate: 19.61 births/1,000 population (2014 est.)
country comparison to the world: 88

Death rate: 8.31 deaths/1,000 population (2014 est.)
country comparison to the world: 89

Net migration rate: 0.42 migrant(s)/1,000 population (2014 est.)
country comparison to the world: 72

Urbanization: *urban population:* 53.6% of total population (2011)
rate of urbanization: 0.87% annual rate of change (2010-15 est.)

Major urban areas—population: Almaty 1.383 million; ASTANA (capital) 650,000 (2009)

Sex ratio: *at birth:* 0.94 male(s)/female
0-14 years: 1 male(s)/female
15-24 years: 1.04 male(s)/female
25-54 years: 0.95 male(s)/female
55-64 years: 0.92 male(s)/female
65 years and over: 0.52 male(s)/female
total population: 0.92 male(s)/female (2014 est.)

Mother's mean age at first birth: 27.6 (2010 est.)

Maternal mortality rate: 51 deaths/100,000 live births (2010)
country comparison to the world: 107

Infant mortality rate: *total:* 21.61 deaths/1,000 live births
country comparison to the world: 83
male: 24.34 deaths/1,000 live births
female: 19.06 deaths/1,000 live births (2014 est.)

Life expectancy at birth: *total population:* 70.24 years
country comparison to the world: 150
male: 64.98 years
female: 75.17 years (2014 est.)

Total fertility rate: 2.34 children born/woman (2014 est.)
country comparison to the world: 91

Contraceptive prevalence rate: 51% (2011)

Health expenditures: 3.9% of GDP (2011)
country comparison to the world: 165

Physicians density: 3.84 physicians/1,000 population (2011)

Hospital bed density: 7.6 beds/1,000 population (2009)

Drinking water source:
improved:
urban: 98.7% of population
rural: 90.4% of population

total: 94.8% of population
unimproved:
urban: 1.3% of population
rural: 9.6% of population
total: 5.2% of population (2011 est.)

Sanitation facility access:
improved:
urban: 96.8% of population
rural: 97.9% of population
total: 97.3% of population
unimproved:
urban: 3.2% of population
rural: 2.1% of population
total: 2.7% of population (2011 est.)

HIV/AIDS—adult prevalence rate: 0.1% (2009 est.)
country comparison to the world: 153

HIV/AIDS—people living with HIV/AIDS: 13,000 (2009 est.)
country comparison to the world: 97

HIV/AIDS—deaths: fewer than 500 (2009 est.)
country comparison to the world: 90

Obesity—adult prevalence rate: 23.7% (2008)
country comparison to the world: 74

Children under the age of 5 years underweight: 3.7% (2011)
country comparison to the world: 100

Education expenditures: 3.1% of GDP (2009)
country comparison to the world: 138

Literacy: *definition:* age 15 and over can read and write
total population: 99.7%
male: 99.8%
female: 99.7% (2009 est.)

School life expectancy (primary to tertiary education): *total:* 15 years
male: 15 years
female: 15 years (2012)

Child labor—children ages 5-14: *total number:* 59,254
percentage: 2 % (2006 est.)

Unemployment, youth ages 15-24: *total:* 3.9%
country comparison to the world: 139
male: 2.9%
female: 5.1% (2012)

GOVERNMENT

Country name: *conventional long form:* Republic of Kazakhstan
conventional short form: Kazakhstan
local long form: Qazaqstan Respublikasy
local short form: Qazaqstan
former: Kazakh Soviet Socialist Republic

Government type: republic; authoritarian presidential rule, with little power outside the executive branch

Capital: *name:* Astana
geographic coordinates: 51 10 N, 71 25 E
time difference: UTC+6 (11 hours ahead of Washington, DC during Standard Time)
note: Kazakhstan is divided into two time zones

Administrative divisions: 14 provinces (oblystar, singular—oblys) and 3 cities* (qalalar, singular—qala); Almaty Oblysy, Almaty Qalasy*, Aqmola Oblysy (Astana), Aqtobe Oblysy, Astana Qalasy*, Atyrau Oblysy, Batys Qazaqstan Oblysy [West Kazakhstan] (Oral), Bayqongyr Qalasy [Baykonur]*, Mangghystau Oblysy (Aqtau), Ongtustik Qazaqstan Oblysy [South Kazakhstan] (Shymkent), Pavlodar Oblysy, Qaraghandy Oblysy, Qostanay Oblysy, Qyzylorda Oblysy, Shyghys Qazaqstan Oblysy [East Kazakhstan] (Oskemen), Soltustik Qazaqstan Oblysy [North Kazakhstan] (Petropavlovsk), Zhambyl Oblysy (Taraz)
note: administrative divisions have the same names as their administrative centers (exceptions have the administrative center name following in parentheses); in 1995, the Governments of Kazakhstan and Russia entered into an agreement whereby Russia would lease for a period of 20 years an area of 6,000 sq km enclosing the Baykonur space launch facilities and the city of Bayqongyr (Baykonur, formerly Leninsk); in 2004, a new agreement extended the lease to 2050

Independence: 16 December 1991 (from the Soviet Union)

National holiday: Independence Day, 16 December (1991)

Constitution: previous 1937, 1978 (preindependence); latest adopted 28 January 1993, approved by referendum 30 August 1995, effective 5 September 1995; amended 1998, 2007, 2011 (2012)

Legal system: civil law system influenced by Roman-Germanic law and by the theory and practice of the Russian Federation

International law organization participation: has not submitted an ICJ jurisdiction declaration; non-party state to the ICCt

Suffrage: 18 years of age; universal

Executive branch: *chief of state:* President Nursultan Abishuly NAZARBAYEV (chairman of the Supreme Soviet from 22 February 1990, elected president 1 December 1991)
head of government: Prime Minister Karim MASIMOV (since 2 April 2014); First Deputy Prime Minister Bakytzhan SAGINTAYEV (since 16 January 2013); Deputy Prime Ministers Gulshara ABDYKALIKOVA (since 28 November 2013), Aset ISEKESHEV (since 25 September 2012); Bakyt SULTANOV (since 6 November 2013)
cabinet: Council of Ministers appointed by the president (For more information visit the World Leaders website)
elections: president elected by popular vote for a five-year term; election last held on 3 April 2011 (next to be held in 2016); prime minister and deputy prime ministers appointed by the president, with Mazhilis approval; note—constitutional amendments of May 2007 shortened the presidential term from seven years to five years and established a two-consecutive-term limit; NAZARBAYEV has official status as the "First President of Kazakhstan" and is allowed an unlimited amount of terms
note: constitutional amendments of February 2011 moved election date from 2012 to April 2011 but kept five-year term; subsequent election to take place in 2016
election results: Nursultan Abishuly NAZARBAYEV reelected president; percent of vote—Nursultan Abishuly NAZARBAYEV 95.5%, *other 4.5%*
Legislative branch: bicameral Parliament consists of the Senate (47 seats; 15 members are appointed by the president; 32 members elected by local assemblies; members serve six-year terms, but elections are staggered with half of the members up for re-election every three years) and the Mazhilis (107 seats; 9 out of the 107 Mazhilis members elected by the Assembly of the People of Kazakhstan, a presidentially appointed advisory body designed to represent the country's ethnic minorities; non-appointed members are popularly elected to serve five-year terms)
elections: Senate—(indirect) last held in August 2011 (next to be held in 2014); Mazhilis—last held on 15 January 2012 (next to be held in 2017)
election results: Senate—percent of vote by party—NA; seats by party—Nur Otan 16; Mazhilis—percent of vote by party—Nur-Otan 81%, Ak Zhol 7.5%, Communist People's Party 7.2%, other 4.3%; seats by party—Nur-Otan 83, Ak Zhol 8, Communist People's Party 7

Judicial branch: *highest court(s):* Supreme Court of the Republic (consists of 44 members); Constitutional Council (consists of 7 members)
judge selection and term of office: Supreme Court judges proposed by the president of ther epublic on recommendation of the Supreme Judicial Council, and confirmed by the Senate; judge tenure NA; Constitutional Council—the president of the republic, the Senate chairperson, the Majilis chairperson each appoints one member for a 3-year term and each appoints one member for a 6-year term; chairperson of the Constitutional Council appointed by the president of the republic for a 6-year term
subordinate courts: regional and local courts

Political parties and leaders: Ak Zhol Party (Bright Path) [Azat PERUASHEV]; Alga [Vladimir KOZLOV] (unregistered and banned as extremist in November 2012); Auyl (Village) [Gani KALIYEV]; Azat (Freedom) Party [Bolat ABILOV] (formerly True Ak Zhol Party); Birlik (Unity) [Seril SULTANGALI] (Birlik is an April 2013 merger of Adilet (Justice; formerly Democratic Party of Kazakhstan) and; Rukhaniyat (Spirituality)); NSDP [Zharmakhan TUYAKBAY]; Communist Party of Kazakhstan or KPK [Serikbolsyn ABDILDIN] (suspended by court decision); Communist People's Party of Kazakhstan [Vladislav KOSAREV]; National Social Democratic Party or NSDP [Zharmakhan TUYAKBAY]; Nur Otan (Fatherland's Ray of Light) [Nursultan NAZARBAYEV, Nurlan NIGMATULIN] (the Agrarian, Asar, and Civic parties merged with; Otan); Patriots' Party [Gani KASYMOV]

Political pressure groups and leaders: Adil-Soz [Tamara KALEYEVA]; Almaty Helsinki Committee [Ninel FOKINA]; Confederation of Free Trade Unions [Sergei BELKIN]; For Fair Elections [Yevgeniy ZHOVTIS, Sabit ZHUSUPOV, Sergey DUVANOV, Ibrash NUSUPBAYEV]; Kazakhstan International Bureau on Human Rights [Yevgeniy ZHOVTIS, Chairman of Bureau's Council, Roza AKYLBEKOVA, director] Khalyk Maidany (Peoples' Front)—an informal union between the unregistered Alga Party, the unregistered Communist Party of; Kazakhstan, and several opposition-oriented civil society groups, banned in November 2012 [no formal leader]; Pan-National Social Democratic Party of Kazakhstan [Zharmakhan TUYAKBAY]; Pensioners Movement or Pokoleniye [Irina SAVOSTINA, chairwoman]; Republican Network of International Monitors [Daniyar LIVAZOV]; Transparency International [Sergey ZLOTNIKOV]

International organization participation: ADB, CICA, CIS, CSTO, EAEC, EAPC, EBRD, ECO, EITI (candidate country), FAO, GCTU, IAEA, IBRD, ICAO, ICC (NGOs), ICRM, IDA, IDB, IFAD, IFC, IFRCS, ILO, IMF, IMO, Interpol, IOC, IOM, IPU, ISO, ITSO, ITU, MIGA, NAM (observer), NSG, OAS (observer), OIC, OPCW, OSCE, PFP, SCO, UN, UNCTAD, UNESCO, UNIDO, UNWTO, UPU, WCO, WFTU (NGOs), WHO, WIPO, WMO, WTO (observer), ZC

Diplomatic representation in the US:
chief of mission: Ambassador Kayrat UMAROV (since 14 January 2013)
chancery: 1401 16th Street NW, Washington, DC 20036
telephone: [1] (202) 232-5488
FAX: [1] (202) 232-5845
consulate(s) general: New York

Diplomatic representation from the US:
chief of mission: Ambassador (vacant); Charge d'Affaires John ORDWAY
embassy: Rakhymzhan Koshkarbayev Ave. No 3, Astana 010010
mailing address: use embassy street address
telephone: [7] (7172) 70-21-00
FAX: [7] (7172) 54-09-14

Flag description: a gold sun with 32 rays above a soaring golden steppe eagle, both centered on a sky blue background; the hoist side displays a national ornamental pattern "koshkar-muiz" (the horns of the ram) in gold; the blue color is of religious significance to the Turkic peoples of the country, and so symbolizes cultural and ethnic unity; it also represents the endless sky as well as water; the sun, a source of life and energy, exemplifies wealth and plenitude; the sun's rays are shaped like grain, which is the basis of abundance and prosperity; the eagle has appeared on the flags of Kazakh tribes for centuries and represents freedom, power, and the flight to the future

National symbol(s): golden eagle

National anthem: *name:* "Menin Qazaqstanim" (My Kazakhstan)
lyrics/music: Zhumeken NAZHIMEDENOV and Nursultan NAZARBAYEV/Shamshi KALDAYAKOV
note: adopted 2006; President Nursultan NAZARBAYEV played a role in revising the lyrics

Economy

Economy—overview: Kazakhstan, geographically the largest of the former Soviet republics, excluding Russia, possesses enormous fossil fuel reserves and plentiful supplies of other minerals and metals, such as uranium, copper, and zinc. It also has a large agricultural sector featuring livestock and grain. In 2002 Kazakhstan became the first country in the former Soviet Union to receive an investment-grade credit rating. Extractive industries have been and will continue to be the engine of Kazakhstan's growth, although the country is aggressively pursuing diversification strategies. Landlocked, with restricted access to the high seas, Kazakhstan relies on its neighbors to export its products, especially oil and grain. Although its Caspian Sea ports, pipelines, and rail lines carrying oil have been upgraded, civil aviation and roadways continue to need attention. Telecoms are improving, but require considerable investment, as does the information technology base. Supply and distribution of electricity can be erratic because of regional dependencies, but the country is moving forward with plans to improve reliability of electricity and gas supply to its population. At the end of 2007, global financial markets froze up and the loss of capital inflows to Kazakhstani banks caused a credit crunch. The subsequent and sharp fall of oil and commodity prices in 2008 aggravated the economic situation, and Kazakhstan plunged into recession. While the global financial crisis took a significant toll on Kazakhstan's economy, it has rebounded well, helped by prudent government measures. Rising commodity prices have helped the recovery. Despite solid macroeconomic indicators, the government realizes that its economy suffers from an overreliance on oil and extractive industries, the so-called "Dutch disease." In response, Kazakhstan has embarked on an ambitious diversification program, aimed at developing targeted sectors like transport, pharmaceuticals, telecommunications, petrochemicals and food processing. In 2010 Kazakhstan joined the Belarus-Kazakhstan-Russia Customs Union in an effort to boost foreign investment and improve trade relationships.

GDP (purchasing power parity): $243.6 billion (2013 est.)
country comparison to the world: 53
$231.9 billion (2012 est.)
$220.6 billion (2011 est.)
note: data are in 2013 US dollars

GDP (official exchange rate): $224.9 billion (2013 est.)

GDP—real growth rate: 5% (2013 est.)
country comparison to the world: 60
5.1% (2012 est.)
7.5% (2011 est.)

GDP—per capita (PPP): $14,100 (2013 est.)
country comparison to the world: 95
$13,700 (2012 est.)
$13,200 (2011 est.)
note: data are in 2013 US dollars

Gross national saving: 28.8% of GDP (2013 est.)
country comparison to the world: 30
23.9% of GDP (2012 est.)
28.4% of GDP (2011 est.)

GDP—composition, by end use:
household consumption: 51%
government consumption: 12.4%
investment in fixed capital: 22.1%
investment in inventories: 2.5%
exports of goods and services: 44.6%
imports of goods and services: -32.6% (2013 est.)

GDP—composition, by sector of origin:
agriculture: 5.2%
industry: 37.9%
services: 56.9% (2011 est.)

Agriculture—products: grain (mostly spring wheat and barley), potatoes, vegetables, melons; livestock

Industries: oil, coal, iron ore, manganese, chromite, lead, zinc, copper, titanium, bauxite, gold, silver, phosphates, sulfur, uranium, iron and steel; tractors and other agricultural machinery, electric motors, construction materials

Industrial production growth rate:
2.1% (2013 est.)
country comparison to the world: 123

Labor force: 9.022 million (2013 est.)
country comparison to the world: 52

Labor force—by occupation: *agriculture:* 25.8%
industry: 11.9%
services: 62.3% (2012)

Unemployment rate: 5.3% (2013 est.)
country comparison to the world: 51
5.3% (2012 est.)

Population below poverty line: 5.3% (2011 est.)

Household income or consumption by percentage share: *lowest 10%:* 3.9%
highest 10%: 23.7% (2011 est.)

Distribution of family income—Gini index:
28.9 (2011)
country comparison to the world: 122
31.5 (2003)

Budget: *revenues:* $43.88 billion
expenditures: $49 billion (2013 est.)

Taxes and other revenues: 19.5% of GDP (2013 est.)
country comparison to the world: 170

Budget surplus (+) or deficit (-):
-2.3% of GDP (2013 est.)
country comparison to the world: 94

Public debt: 15.6% of GDP (2013 est.)
country comparison to the world: 142
13.2% of GDP (2012 est.)

Fiscal year: calendar year

Inflation rate (consumer prices): 5.8% (2013 est.)
country comparison to the world: 165
5.1% (2012 est.)

Central bank discount rate: 5.5% (31 December 2012 est.)
country comparison to the world: 36
7.5% (31 December 2011 est.)

Commercial bank prime lending rate: 6.3% (31 December 2013 est.)
country comparison to the world: 132
6.6% (31 December 2012 est.)

Stock of narrow money: $24.51 billion (31 December 2013 est.)
country comparison to the world: 63
$25.82 billion (31 December 2012 est.)

Stock of broad money: $70.36 billion (31 December 2012 est.)
country comparison to the world: 62
$65.71 billion (31 December 2011 est.)

Stock of domestic credit: $87.05 billion (31 December 2013 est.)
country comparison to the world: 56
$83.08 billion (31 December 2012 est.)

Market value of publicly traded shares:
$23.5 billion (31 December 2012 est.)
country comparison to the world: 53
$43.3 billion (31 December 2011)
$60.74 billion (31 December 2010 est.)

Current account balance: $1.965 billion (2013 est.)
country comparison to the world: 42
$640.5 million (2012 est.)

Exports: $87.23 billion (2013 est.)
country comparison to the world: 43
$86.93 billion (2012 est.)

Exports—commodities: oil and oil products, natural gas, ferrous metals, chemicals, machinery, grain, wool, meat, coal

Exports—partners: China 19.3%, Italy 18.1%, Netherlands 8.8%, France 6.6%, Switzerland 5.8%, Austria 5.8% (2012)

Imports: $52.03 billion (2013 est.)
country comparison to the world: 55
$49.08 billion (2012 est.)

Imports—commodities: machinery and equipment, metal products, foodstuffs

Imports—partners: China 28%, Ukraine 10.9%, Germany 8.5%, US 7.9% (2012)

Reserves of foreign exchange and gold: $29.34 billion (31 December 2013 est.)
country comparison to the world: 53
$28.28 billion (31 December 2012 est.)

Debt—external: $131.3 billion (31 December 2013 est.)
country comparison to the world: 41
$133.5 billion (31 December 2012 est.)

Stock of direct foreign investment—at home:
$123.5 billion (31 December 2013 est.)
country comparison to the world: 37
$111.5 billion (31 December 2012 est.)

Stock of direct foreign investment—abroad:
$26.53 billion (31 December 2013 est.)

country comparison to the world: 44
$25.53 billion (31 December 2012 est.)

Exchange rates: tenge (KZT) per US dollar—
151.8 (2013 est.)
149.11 (2012 est.)
147.36 (2010 est.)
147.5 (2009)
120.25 (2008)

ENERGY

Electricity—production: 90.53 billion kWh (2012 est.)
country comparison to the world: 3 6

Electricity—consumption: 88.11 billion kWh (2011 est.)
country comparison to the world: 33

Electricity—exports: 1.8 billion kWh (2011 est.)
country comparison to the world: 43

Electricity—imports: 3.7 billion kWh (2011 est.)
country comparison to the world: 43

Electricity—installed generating capacity: 18.73 million kW (2010 est.)
country comparison to the world: 39

Electricity—from fossil fuels: 88.2% of total installed capacity (2010 est.)
country comparison to the world: 81

Electricity—from nuclear fuels: 0% of total installed capacity (2010 est.)
country comparison to the world: 121

Electricity—from hydroelectric plants: 11.8% of total installed capacity (2010 est.)
country comparison to the world: 110

Electricity—from other renewable sources: 0% of total installed capacity (2010 est.)
country comparison to the world: 190

Crude oil—production: 1.606 million bbl/day (2012 est.)
country comparison to the world: 18

Crude oil—exports: 1.406 million bbl/day (2010 est.)
country comparison to the world: 12

Crude oil—imports: 119,600 bbl/day (2010 est.)
country comparison to the world: 47

Crude oil—proved reserves: 30 billion bbl (1 January 2013 es)
country comparison to the world: 11

Refined petroleum products—production: *288,600 bbl/day (2010 est.)*
country comparison to the world: 43

Refined petroleum products—consumption: 244,200 bbl/day (2011 est.)
country comparison to the world: 52

Refined petroleum products—exports: 149,800 bbl/day (2011 est.)
country comparison to the world: 38

Refined petroleum products—imports: 94,430 bbl/day (2010 est.)
country comparison to the world: 52

Natural gas—production: 20.2 billion cu m (2011 est.)
country comparison to the world: 31

Natural gas—consumption: 10.2 billion cu m (2011 est.)
country comparison to the world: 45

Natural gas—exports: 9.7 billion cu m (2011 est.)
country comparison to the world: 25

Natural gas—imports: 10.7 billion cu m (2011 est.)
country comparison to the world: 28

Natural gas—proved reserves: 2.407 trillion cu m (1 January 2013 es)
country comparison to the world: 14

Carbon dioxide emissions from consumption of energy: 195.4 million Mt (2011 est.)
country comparison to the world: 30

COMMUNICATIONS

Telephones—main lines in use: 4.34 million (2012)
country comparison to the world: 4 0

Telephones—mobile cellular: 28.731 million (2012)
country comparison to the world: 37

Telephone system: general assessment: inherited an outdated telecommunications network from the Soviet era requiring modernization
domestic: intercity by landline and microwave radio relay; number of fixed-line connections is gradually increasing and fixed-line teledensity now roughly 25 per 100 persons; mobile-cellular usage has increased rapidly and the subscriber base now exceeds 140 per 100 persons
international: country code—7; international traffic with other former Soviet republics and China carried by landline and microwave radio relay and with other countries by satellite and by the Trans-Asia-Europe (TAE) fiber-optic cable; satellite earth stations—2 Intelsat (2008)

Broadcast media: state owns nearly all radio and TV transmission facilities and operates national TV and radio networks; nearly all nationwide TV networks are wholly or partly owned by the government; some former state-owned media outlets have been privatized; households with satellite dishes have access to foreign media; a small number of commercial radio stations operate along with state-run radio stations; recent legislation requires all media outlets to register with the government and all TV providers to broadcast in digital format by 2015 (2008)

Internet country code: . k z

Internet hosts: 67,464 (2012)
country comparison to the world: 90

Internet users: 5.299 million (2009)
country comparison to the world: 44

TRANSPORTATION

Airports: 96 (2013) country comparison to the world: 6 0

Airports—with paved runways: *total:* 6 3
over 3,047 m: 10
2,438 to 3,047 m: 25
1,524 to 2,437 m: 15
914 to 1,523 m: 5
under 914 m: 8 (2013)

Airports—with unpaved runways: *total:* 3 3
over 3,047 m: 5
2,438 to 3,047 m: 7
1,524 to 2,437 m: 3
914 to 1,523 m: 5
under 914 m: 13 (2013)

Heliports: 3 (2013)

Pipelines: condensate 658 km; gas 12,432 km; oil 11,313 km; refined products 1,095 km; water 1,465 km (2013)

Railways: *total:* 15,333 km
country comparison to the world: 18
broad gauge: 15,333 km 1.520-m gauge (4,000 km electrified) (2012)

Roadways: *total:* 97,418 km
country comparison to the world: 46
paved: 87,140 km
unpaved: 10,278 km (2012)

Waterways: 4,000 km (on the Ertis (Irtysh) River (80%) and Syr Darya (Syrdariya) River) (2010)
country comparison to the world: 27

Merchant marine: *total:* 1 1
country comparison to the world: 111
by type: cargo 1, petroleum tanker 8, refrigerated cargo 1, specialized tanker 1
foreign-owned: 3 (Austria 1, Ireland 1, Turkey 1) (2010)

Ports and terminals: *major seaport(s):* Aqtau (Shevchenko), Atyrau (Gur'yev)
river port(s): Oskemen (Ust-Kamenogorsk), Pavlodar, Semey (Semipalatinsk) (Irtysh River)

MILITARY

Military branches: Kazakhstan Armed Forces: Ground Forces, Navy, Air Mobile Forces, Air Defense Forces (2013)

Military service age and obligation: 18 is the legal minimum age for compulsory military service; conscript service obligation is 2 years, but Kazakhstan may be transitioning to a contract force; 19 is the legal minimum age for voluntary service; military cadets in intermediate (ages 15-17) and higher (ages 17-21) education institutes are classified as military service personnel (2012)

Manpower available for military service:
males age 16-49: 4,163,629
females age 16-49: 4,179,051 (2010 est.)

Manpower fit for military service:
males age 16-49: 2,909,999
females age 16-49: 3,528,169 (2010 est.)

Manpower reaching militarily significant age annually: *male:* 125,322
female: 119,541 (2010 est.)

Military expenditures: 1.21% of GDP (2012)
country comparison to the world: 84
0.97% of GDP (2011)
1.21% of GDP (2010)

TRANSNATIONAL ISSUES

Disputes—international: Kyrgyzstan has yet to ratify the 2001 boundary delimitation with Kazakhstan; field demarcation of the boundaries commenced with Uzbekistan in 2004 and with Turkmenistan in 2005; ongoing demarcation with Russia began in 2007; demarcation with China was completed in 2002; creation of a seabed boundary with Turkmenistan in the Caspian Sea remains under discussion; Azerbaijan, Kazakhstan, and Russia ratified Caspian seabed delimitation treaties based on equidistance, while Iran continues to insist on a one-fifth slice of the sea

Refugees and internally displaced persons: *stateless persons:* 6,935 (2012)

Illicit drugs: significant illicit cultivation of cannabis for CIS markets, as well as limited cultivation of opium poppy and ephedra (for the drug ephedrine); limited government eradication of illicit crops; transit point for Southwest Asian narcotics bound for Russia and the rest of Europe; significant consumer of opiates

KENYA

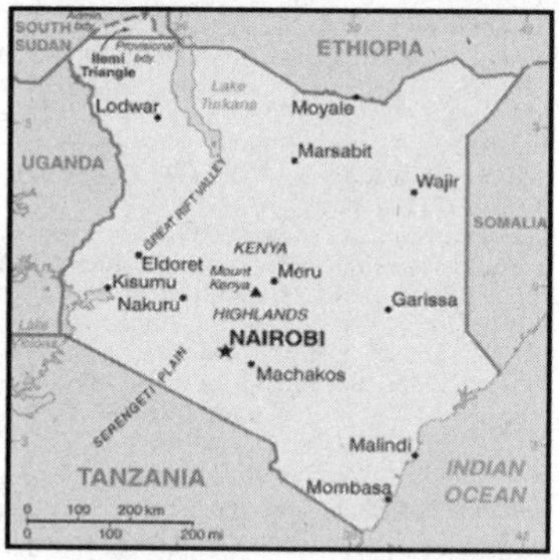

INTRODUCTION

Background: Founding president and liberation struggle icon Jomo KENYATTA led Kenya from independence in 1963 until his death in 1978, when President Daniel MOI took power in a constitutional succession. The country was a de facto one-party state from 1969 until 1982 when the ruling Kenya African National Union (KANU) made itself the sole legal party in Kenya. MOI acceded to internal and external pressure for political liberalization in late 1991. The ethnically fractured opposition failed to dislodge KANU from power in elections in 1992 and 1997, which were marred by violence and fraud, but were viewed as having generally reflected the will of the Kenyan people. President MOI stepped down in December 2002 following fair and peaceful elections. Mwai KIBAKI, running as the candidate of the multiethnic, united opposition group, the National Rainbow Coalition (NARC), defeated KANU candidate Uhuru KENYATTA and assumed the presidency following a campaign centered on an anticorruption platform. KIBAKI's NARC coalition splintered in 2005 over a constitutional review process. Government defectors joined with KANU to form a new opposition coalition, the Orange Democratic Movement (ODM), which defeated the government's draft constitution in a popular referendum in November 2005. KIBAKI's reelection in December 2007 brought charges of vote rigging from ODM candidate Raila ODINGA and unleashed two months of violence in which as many as 1,500 people died. African Union-sponsored mediation led by former UN Secretary General Kofi ANNAN in late February 2008 resulted in a power-sharing accord bringing ODINGA into the government in the restored position of prime minister. The power sharing accord included a broad reform agenda, the centerpiece of which was constitutional reform. In August 2010, Kenyans overwhelmingly adopted a new constitution in a national referendum. The new constitution introduced additional checks and balances to executive power and significant devolution of power and resources to 47 newly created counties. It also eliminated the position of prime minister following the first presidential election under the new constitution, which occurred on 4 March 2013. Uhuru KENYATTA, the son of founding president Jomo KENYATTA, won the March elections in the first round by a close margin and was sworn into office on 9 April 2013.

GEOGRAPHY

Location: Eastern Africa, bordering the Indian Ocean, between Somalia and Tanzania

Geographic coordinates: 1 00 N, 38 00 E

Map references: Africa

Area: *total:* 580,367 sq km
country comparison to the world: 49
land: 569,140 sq km
water: 11,227 sq km

Area—comparative: five times the size of Ohio; slightly more than twice the size of Nevada

Land boundaries: *total:* 3,477 km
border countries: Ethiopia 861 km, Somalia 682 km, South Sudan 232 km, Tanzania 769 km, Uganda 933 km

Coastline: 536 km

Maritime claims: *territorial sea:* 12 nm
exclusive economic zone: 200 nm
continental shelf: 200 m depth or to the depth of exploitation

Climate: varies from tropical along coast to arid in interior

Terrain: low plains rise to central highlands bisected by Great Rift Valley; fertile plateau in west

Elevation extremes: *lowest point:* Indian Ocean 0 m
highest point: Mount Kenya 5,199 m

Natural resources: limestone, soda ash, salt, gemstones, fluorspar, zinc, diatomite, gypsum, wildlife, hydropower

Land use: *arable land:* 9.48%
permanent crops: 1.12%
other: 89.4% (2011)

Irrigated land: 1,032 sq km (2003)

Total renewable water resources: 30.7 cu km (2011)

Freshwater withdrawal (domestic/industrial/agricultural): *total:* 2.74 cu km/yr (17%/4%/79%)
per capita: 72.96 cu m/yr (2003)

Natural hazards: recurring drought; flooding during rainy seasons
volcanism: limited volcanic activity; the Barrier (elev. 1,032 m) last erupted in 1921; South Island is the only other historically active volcano

Environment—current issues: water pollution from urban and industrial wastes; degradation of water quality from increased use of pesticides and fertilizers; water hyacinth infestation in Lake Victoria; deforestation; soil erosion; desertification; poaching

Environment—international agreements:
party to: Biodiversity, Climate Change, Climate Change-Kyoto Protocol, Desertification, Endangered Species, Hazardous Wastes, Law of the Sea, Marine Dumping, Marine Life Conservation, Ozone Layer Protection, Ship Pollution, Wetlands, Whaling
signed, but not ratified: none of the selected agreements

Geography—note: the Kenyan Highlands comprise one of the most successful agricultural production regions in Africa; glaciers are found on Mount Kenya, Africa's second highest peak; unique physiography supports abundant and varied wildlife of scientific and economic value

PEOPLE AND SOCIETY

Nationality: *noun:* Kenyan(s)
adjective: Kenyan

Ethnic groups: Kikuyu 22%, Luhya 14%, Luo 13%, Kalenjin 12%, Kamba 11%, Kisii 6%, Meru 6%, other African 15%, non-African (Asian, European, and Arab) 1%

Languages: English (official), Kiswahili (official), numerous indigenous languages

Religions: Christian 82.5% (Protestant 47.4%, Catholic 23.3%, other 11.8%), Muslim 11.1%, Traditionalists 1.6%, other 1.7%, none 2.4%, unspecified 0.7% (2009 census)

Population: 45,010,056 (July 2014 est.)
country comparison to the world: 31
note: estimates for this country explicitly take into account the effects of excess mortality due to AIDS; this can result in lower life expectancy, higher infant mortality, higher death rates, lower population growth rates, and changes in the distribution of population by age and sex than would otherwise be expected

Age structure:
0-14 years: 42.1% (male 9,494,983/female 9,435,795)
15-24 years: 18.7% (male 4,197,382/female 4,202,399)
25-54 years: 32.8% (male 7,458,665/female 7,302,534)
55-64 years: 2.8% (male 751,296/female 910,523)
65 years and over: 2.7% (male 548,431/female 708,048) (2014 est.)

Dependency ratios:
total dependency ratio: 81.5 %
youth dependency ratio: 76.6 %
elderly dependency ratio: 4.9 %
potential support ratio: 20.6 (2013)

Median age: *total:* 19.1 years
male: 18.9 years
female: 19.2 years (2014 est.)

Population growth rate: 2.11% (2014 est.)
country comparison to the world: 47

Birth rate: 28.27 births/1,000 population (2014 est.)
country comparison to the world: 45

Death rate: 7 deaths/1,000 population (2014 est.)
country comparison to the world: 133

Net migration rate: -0.22 migrant(s)/1,000 population (2014 est.)
country comparison to the world: 121

Urbanization: *urban population:* 24% of total population (2011)
rate of urbanization: 4.36% annual rate of change (2010-15 est.)

Major urban areas—population: NAIROBI (capital) 3.375 million; Mombassa 966,000 (2009)

Sex ratio: *at birth:* 1.02 male(s)/female
0-14 years: 1.01 male(s)/female
15-24 years: 1 male(s)/female
25-54 years: 1.02 male(s)/female
55-64 years: 1 male(s)/female
65 years and over: 0.79 male(s)/female
total population: 1 male(s)/female (2014 est.)

Mother's mean age at first birth: 19.8

note: median age at first birth among women 25-29 (2009 est.)

Maternal mortality rate: 360 deaths/100,000 live births (2010)
country comparison to the world: 30

Infant mortality rate: *total:* 40.71 deaths/1,000 live births
country comparison to the world: 52
male: 45.33 deaths/1,000 live births
female: 35.99 deaths/1,000 live births (2014 est.)

Life expectancy at birth: *total population:* 63.52 years
country comparison to the world: 180
male: 62.06 years
female: 65.01 years (2014 est.)

Total fertility rate: 3.54 children born/woman (2014 est.)
country comparison to the world: 45

Contraceptive prevalence rate: 45.5% (2008/09)

Health expenditures: 4.5% of GDP (2011)
country comparison to the world: 151

Physicians density: 0.18 physicians/1,000 population (2011)

Hospital bed density: 1.4 beds/1,000 population (2010)

Drinking water source:
improved:
urban: 82.7% of population
rural: 54% of population
total: 60.9% of population
unimproved:
urban: 17.3% of population
rural: 46% of population
total: 39.1% of population (2011 est.)

Sanitation facility access:
improved:
urban: 31.1% of population
rural: 28.8% of population
total: 29.4% of population
unimproved:
urban: 68.9% of population
rural: 71.2% of population
total: 70.6% of population (2011 est.)

HIV/AIDS—adult prevalence rate: 6.1% (2012 est.)
country comparison to the world: 12

HIV/AIDS—people living with HIV/AIDS: 1.646 million (2012 est.)
country comparison to the world: 4

HIV/AIDS—deaths: 57,500 (2012 est.)
country comparison to the world: 7

Major infectious diseases: *degree of risk:* high
food or waterborne diseases: bacterial and protozoal diarrhea, hepatitis A, and typhoid fever
vectorborne disease: malaria, dengue fever, and Rift Valley fever
water contact disease: schistosomiasis
animal contact disease: rabies (2013)

Obesity—adult prevalence rate: 4.2% (2008)
country comparison to the world: 171

Children under the age of 5 years underweight: 16.4% (2009)
country comparison to the world: 42

Education expenditures: 6.7% of GDP (2010)
country comparison to the world: 28

Literacy: *definition:* age 15 and over can read and write
total population: 87.4%
male: 90.6%
female: 84.2% (2010 est.)

School life expectancy (primary to tertiary education): *total:* 11 years
male: 11 years
female: 11 years (2009)

Child labor—children ages 5-14: *total number:* 2,146,058
percentage: 26 % (2000 est.)

GOVERNMENT

Country name: *conventional long form:* Republic of Kenya
conventional short form: Kenya
local long form: Republic of Kenya/Jamhuri ya Kenya
local short form: Kenya
former: British East Africa

Government type: republic

Capital: *name:* Nairobi
geographic coordinates: 1 17 S, 36 49 E
time difference: UTC+3 (8 hours ahead of Washington, DC during Standard Time)

Administrative divisions: 47 counties; Baringo, Bomet, Bungoma, Busia, Elgeyo/Marakwet, Embu, Garissa, Homa Bay, Isiolo, Kajiado, Kakamega, Kericho, Kiambu, Kilifi, Kirinyaga, Kisii, Kisumu, Kitui, Kwale, Laikipia, Lamu, Machakos, Makueni, Mandera, Marsabit, Meru, Migori, Mombasa, Murang'a, Nairobi City, Nakuru, Nandi, Narok, Nyamira, Nyandarua, Nyeri, Samburu, Siaya, Taita/Taveta, Tana River, Tharaka-Nithi, Trans Nzoia, Turkana, Uasin Gishu, Vihiga, Wajir, West Pokot

Independence: 12 December 1963 (from the UK)
National holiday: Independence Day, 12 December (1963); Madaraka Day, 1 June (1963); Mashujaa Day, 20 October (2010)

Constitution: previous 1963, 1969; latest drafted 6 May 2010, passed by referendum 4 August 2010, promulgated 27 August 2010 (2013)

Legal system: mixed legal system of English common law, Islamic law, and customary law; judicial review in a new Supreme Court established pursuant to the new constitution

International law organization participation: accepts compulsory ICJ jurisdiction with reservations; accepts ICCt jurisdiction

Suffrage: 18 years of age; universal

Executive branch: *chief of state:* President Uhuru KENYATTA (since 9 April 2013); Deputy President William RUTO (since 9 April 2013); note—the president is both the chief of state and head of government
head of government: President Uhuru KENYATTA (since 9 April 2013); Deputy President William RUTO (since 9 April 2013); note—according to the 2008 power sharing agreement the position of prime minister was created though not well defined, consistent with the new constitution the position was then abolished after the March 2013 elections
cabinet: Cabinet appointed by the president (For more information visit the World Leaders website)
elections: president and running mate, to serve as deputy president, elected by popular vote for a five-year term (eligible for a second term); in addition to receiving a simple majority of votes, the presidential candidate must also win 25% or more of the votes cast in each of more than half of the 47 counties to avoid a runoff; election last held on 4 March 2013 (next to be held in 2017 or 2018); note—the new constitution had set elections for August 2011 but elections were delayed to 2013
election results: President Uhuru KENYATTA elected in first round; percent of vote—Uhuru KENYATTA 50.1%, Raila ODINGA 43.7%, Musalia MUDAVADI 4.0%, other 2.2%

Legislative branch: bicameral parliament consists of a Senate (67 seats of which 47 are elected and 20 are appointed) and a National Assembly (349 seats of which 290 are elected and 59 are appointed); members to serve five-year terms
elections: last held on 4 March 2013 (next to be held in 2017 or 2018)
election results: Senate—percent of vote by party—NA; seats by party—Jubilee coalition TNA 17, URP 12, NARC 1; CORD coalition ODM 17, Ford-K 5, WDM 5, FPK 1; Amani coalition KANU 3, UDF 3; unaffiliated APK 3; National Assembly—percent of vote by party—NA; seats by party—ODM 96, TNA 89, URP 75, WDM-K 26, UDF 12, FORD-K 10, KANU 6, NFK 6, APK 5, FORD-P 4, independents 4, other 16

Judicial branch: *highest court(s):* Supreme Court (consists of chief and deputy chief justices and five judges)
judge selection and term of office: chief and deputy chief justices nominated by Judicial Service Commission (JSC) and appointed by president with approval of the National Assembly; other judges nominated by the JSC and appointed by president; chief justice serves nonrenewable 10-year terms or till age 70 whichever comes first; other judges serve till age 70
subordinate courts: High Court; Court of Appeal; courts martial; magistrates' courts; religious courts

Political parties and leaders: Federal Party of Kenya or FPK; Kenya African National Union or KANU [Gideon MOI]; The National Party Alliance or TNA [Uhuru KENYATTA]; National Rainbow Coalition-Kenya or NARC-Kenya [Martha KARUA]; Orange Democratic Movement of Kenya or ODM [Raila ODINGA]; Orange Democratic Movement-Kenya or ODM-K [Kalonzo MUSYOKA]; United Democratic Forum Party or UDF [Musalia MUDAVADI]; United Republican Party or URP [William RUTO]; Wiper Democratic Movement or WDM [Kalonzo MUSYOKA]

Political pressure groups and leaders: Council of Islamic Preachers of Kenya or CIPK [Sheikh Idris MOHAMMED]; Kenya Human Rights Commission [L. Muthoni WANYEKI]; Muslim Human Rights Forum [Ali-Amin KIMATHI]; National Muslim Leaders Forum or NAMLEF [Abdullahi ABDI]; Protestant National Council of Churches of Kenya or NCCK [Canon Peter Karanja MWANGI]; Roman Catholic and other Christian churches; Supreme Council of Kenya Muslims or SUPKEM [Shaykh Abdul Gafur al-BUSAIDY]; other: labor unions, Kenya Association of Manufacturers, Kenya Private Sector Alliance

International organization participation: ACP, AfDB, AU, C, CD, COMESA, EAC, EADB, FAO, G-15, G-77, IAEA, IBRD, ICAO, ICC (national committees), ICRM, IDA, IFAD, IFC, IFRCS, IGAD, ILO, IMF, IMO, IMSO, Interpol, IOC, IOM, IPU, ISO, ITSO, ITU, ITUC (NGOs), MIGA, MINUSMA, MONUSCO, NAM, OPCW, PCA, UN, UNAMID, UNCTAD, UNESCO, UNHCR, UNIDO, UNIFIL, UNMISS, UNWTO, UPU, WCO, WHO, WIPO, WMO, WTO

Diplomatic representation in the US:
chief of mission: Ambassador (vacant); Charge d'Affaires Jean KAMAU
chancery: 2249 R Street NW, Washington, DC 20008
telephone: [1] (202) 387-6101
FAX: [1] (202) 462-3829
consulate(s) general: Los Angeles
consulate(s): New York

Diplomatic representation from the US:
chief of mission: Ambassador Robert F. GODEC (since 16 January 2013)
embassy: US Embassy, United Nations Avenue, Nairobi; P. O. Box 606 Village Market, Nairobi 00621
mailing address: American Embassy Nairobi, U.S. Department of State, Washington, DC 20521-8900
telephone: [254] (20) 363-6000
FAX: [254] (20) 363-6157

Flag description: three equal horizontal bands of black (top), red, and green; the red band is edged in white; a large Maasai warrior's shield covering crossed spears is superimposed at the center; black symbolizes the majority population, red the blood shed in the struggle for freedom, green stands for natural wealth, and white for peace; the shield and crossed spears symbolize the defense of freedom

National symbol(s): lion

National anthem: *name:* "Ee Mungu Nguvu Yetu" (Oh God of All Creation)
lyrics/music: Graham HYSLOP, Thomas KALUME, Peter KIBUKOSYA, Washington OMONDI, and George W. SENOGA-ZAKE/traditional, adapted by Graham HYSLOP, Thomas KALUME, Peter KIBUKOSYA, Washington OMONDI, and George W. SENOGA-ZAKE
note: adopted 1963; the anthem is based on a traditional Kenyan folk song

ECONOMY

Economy—overview: Kenya hKenya has been hampered by corruption and by reliance upon several primary goods whose prices have remained low. Low infrastructure investment threatens Kenya's long-term position as the largest East African economy, although the Kenyatta administration has prioritized infrastructure development. International financial lenders and donors remain important to Kenya's economic growth and development. Unemployment is high at around 40%. The country has chronic budget deficits. Inflationary pressures and sharp currency depreciation peaked in early 2012 but have since abated following low global food and fuel prices and monetary interventions by the Central Bank. Recent terrorism in Kenya and the surrounding region threatens Kenya's important tourism industry. Kenya, in conjunction with neighboring Ethiopia and South Sudan, intends to begin construction on a transport corridor and oil pipeline into the port of Lamu in 2014.

GDP (purchasing power parity): $79.9 billion (2013 est.)
country comparison to the world: 82
$76.03 billion (2012 est.)
$72.71 billion (2011 est.)
note: data are in 2013 US dollars

GDP (official exchange rate): $45.31 billion (2013 est.)

GDP—real growth rate: 5.1% (2013 est.)
country comparison to the world: 56
4.6% (2012 est.)
4.4% (2011 est.)

GDP—per capita (PPP): $1,800 (2013 est.)
country comparison to the world: 198
$1,700 (2013 est.)
$1,700 (2011 est.)
note: data are in 2013 US dollars

Gross national saving: 10.6% of GDP (2013 est.)
country comparison to the world: 132
9.5% of GDP (2012 est.)
10.8% of GDP (2011 est.)

GDP—composition, by end use:
household consumption: 79.2%
government consumption: 18.2%
investment in fixed capital: 21.3%
investment in inventories: -0.3%
exports of goods and services: 28.5%
imports of goods and services: -47% (2013 est.)

GDP—composition, by sector of origin:
agriculture: 29.3%
industry: 17.4%
services: 53.3% (2013 est.)

Agriculture—products: tea, coffee, corn, wheat, sugarcane, fruit, vegetables; dairy products, beef, fish, pork, poultry, eggs

Industries: small-scale consumer goods (plastic, furniture, batteries, textiles, clothing, soap, cigarettes, flour), agricultural products, horticulture, oil refining; aluminum, steel, lead; cement, commercial ship repair, tourism

Industrial production growth rate: 5.1% (2013 est.)
country comparison to the world: 54

Labor force: 19.67 million (2013 est.)
country comparison to the world: 31

Labor force—by occupation: *agriculture:* 75%
industry and services: 25% (2007 est.)

Unemployment rate: 40% (2008 est.)
country comparison to the world: 189
40% (2001 est.)

Population below poverty line: 43.4% (2012 est.)

Household income or consumption by percentage share: *lowest 10%:* 1.8%
highest 10%: 37.8% (2005)

Distribution of family income—Gini index: 42.5 (2008 est.)
country comparison to the world: 48
44.9 (1997)

Budget: *revenues:* $7.866 billion
expenditures: $9.742 billion (2013 est.)

Taxes and other revenues: 17.4% of GDP (2013 est.)
country comparison to the world: 179

Budget surplus (+) or deficit (-): -4.1% of GDP (2013 est.)
country comparison to the world: 150

Public debt: 53.5% of GDP (2013 est.)
country comparison to the world: 60
52.5% of GDP (2012 est.)

Fiscal year: 1 July—30 June

Inflation rate (consumer prices): 5.8% (2013 est.)
country comparison to the world: 167
9.4% (2012 est.)

Central bank discount rate: 7% (31 December 2010 est.)
NA% (31 December 2009 est.)

Commercial bank prime lending rate: 17.1% (31 December 2013 est.)
country comparison to the world: 17
19.7% (31 December 2012 est.)

Stock of narrow money: $9.198 billion (31 December 2013 est.)
country comparison to the world: 81
$8.264 billion (31 December 2012 est.)

Stock of broad money: $19.37 billion (31 December 2013 est.)
country comparison to the world: 87
$17.08 billion (31 December 2012 est.)

Stock of domestic credit: $23.1 billion (31 December 2013 est.)
country comparison to the world: 76
$20.93 billion (31 December 2012 est.)

Market value of publicly traded shares: $14.79 billion (31 December 2012 est.)
country comparison to the world: 70
$10.2 billion (31 December 2011)
$14.46 billion (31 December 2010 est.)

Current account balance: -$4.495 billion (2013 est.)
country comparison to the world: 164
-$4.31 billion (2012 est.)

Exports: $6.58 billion (2013 est.)
country comparison to the world: 106
$6.228 billion (2012 est.)

Exports—commodities: tea, horticultural products, coffee, petroleum products, fish, cement

Exports—partners: Uganda 10.3%, Tanzania 10%, Netherlands 7.7%, UK 7.2%, US 6.3%, Egypt 4.8%, Democratic Republic of the Congo 4.4% (2012)

Imports: $15.86 billion (2013 est.)
country comparison to the world: 86
$15.1 billion (2011 est.)

Imports—commodities: machinery and transportation equipment, petroleum products, motor vehicles, iron and steel, resins and plastics

Imports—partners: India 20.9%, China 15.4%, UAE 9.8%, Saudi Arabia 6.9% (2012)

Reserves of foreign exchange and gold: $5.541 billion (31 December 2013 est.)
country comparison to the world: 91
$5.712 billion (31 December 2012 est.)

Debt—external: $11.96 billion (31 December 2013 est.)
country comparison to the world: 96
$11.06 billion (31 December 2012 est.)

Stock of direct foreign investment—at home: $3.273 billion (31 December 2013 est.)
country comparison to the world: 93
$2.877 billion (31 December 2012 est.)

Stock of direct foreign investment—abroad: $335.4 million (31 December 2013 est.)
country comparison to the world: 82
$315.4 million (31 December 2012 est.)

Exchange rates: Kenyan shillings (KES) per US dollar—
86.73 (2013 est.)
84.53 (2012 est.)
79.233 (2010 est.)
77.352 (2009)
68.358 (2008)

ENERGY

Electricity—production: 7.33 billion kWh (2010 est.)
country comparison to the world: 105

Electricity—consumption: 6.15 billion kWh (2010 est.)
country comparison to the world: 106

Electricity—exports: 31 million kWh (2010 est.)
country comparison to the world: 85

Electricity—imports: 31 million kWh (2010 est.)
country comparison to the world: 100

Electricity—installed generating capacity: 1.698 million kW (2010 est.)
country comparison to the world: 109

Electricity—from fossil fuels: 41.9% of total installed capacity (2010 est.)
country comparison to the world: 168

Electricity—from nuclear fuels: 0% of total installed capacity (2010 est.)
country comparison to the world: 116

Electricity—from hydroelectric plants: 44.8% of total installed capacity (2010 est.)
country comparison to the world: 52

Electricity—from other renewable sources: 13.3% of total installed capacity (2010 est.)
country comparison to the world: 17

Crude oil—production: 0 bbl/day (2011 est.)
country comparison to the world: 181

Crude oil—exports: 0 bbl/day (2010 est.)
country comparison to the world: 135

Crude oil—imports: 31,040 bbl/day (2010 est.)
country comparison to the world: 64

Crude oil—proved reserves: 0 bbl (1 January 2013 es)
country comparison to the world: 148

Refined petroleum products—production: 32,240 bbl/day (2010 est.)
country comparison to the world: 87

Refined petroleum products—consumption: 79,410 bbl/day (2011 est.)
country comparison to the world: 86

Refined petroleum products—exports: 1,266 bbl/day (2010 est.)
country comparison to the world: 104

Refined petroleum products—imports: 52,160 bbl/day (2010 est.)
country comparison to the world: 68

Natural gas—production: 0 cu m (2011 est.)
country comparison to the world: 147

Natural gas—consumption: 0 cu m (2010 est.)
country comparison to the world: 159

Natural gas—exports: 0 cu m (2011 est.)
country comparison to the world: 126

Natural gas—imports: 0 cu m (2011 est.)
country comparison to the world: 211

Natural gas—proved reserves: 0 cu m (1 January 2013 es)
country comparison to the world: 153

Carbon dioxide emissions from consumption of energy: 12.62 million Mt (2011 est.)
country comparison to the world: 96

COMMUNICATIONS

Telephones—main lines in use: 251,600 (2012)
country comparison to the world: 124

Telephones—mobile cellular: 30.732 million (2012)
country comparison to the world: 33

Telephone system: *general assessment:* inadequate; fixed-line telephone system is small and inefficient; trunks are primarily microwave radio relay; business data commonly transferred by a very small aperture terminal (VSAT) system
domestic: sole fixed-line provider, Telkom Kenya, is slated for privatization; multiple providers in the mobile-cellular segment of the market fostering a boom in mobile-cellular telephone usage with teledensity reaching 65 per 100 persons in 2011
international: country code—254; landing point for the EASSy, TEAMS and SEACOM fiber-optic submarine cable systems; satellite earth stations—4 Intelsat (2011)

Broadcast media: about a half-dozen large-scale privately owned media companies with TV and radio stations as well as a state-owned TV broadcaster provide service nation-wide; satellite and cable TV subscription services available; state-owned radio broadcaster operates 2 national radio channels and provides regional and local radio services in multiple languages; a large number of private radio stations broadcast on a national level along with over 100 private and non-profit provincial stations broadcasting in local languages; transmissions of several international broadcasters available (2014)

Internet country code: .ke

Internet hosts: 71,018 (2012)
country comparison to the world: 88

Internet users: 3.996 million (2009)
country comparison to the world: 59

TRANSPORTATION

Airports: 197 (2013)
country comparison to the world: 2 8

Airports—with paved runways: *total:* 1 6
over 3,047 m: 5
2,438 to 3,047 m: 2
1,524 to 2,437 m: 2
914 to 1,523 m: 6
under 914 m: 1 (2013)

Airports—with unpaved runways: *total:* 181
1,524 to 2,437 m: 14
914 to 1,523 m: 107
under 914 m: 60 (2013)

Pipelines: oil 4 km; refined products 928 km (2013)

Railways: *total:* 2,066 km
country comparison to the world: 71
narrow gauge: 2,066 km 1.000-m gauge (2008)

Roadways: *total:* 160,878 km
country comparison to the world: 30
paved: 11,189 km
unpaved: 149,689 km
note: includes 98.941 km of urban and other roads (2013)

Waterways: none specifically, the only significant inland waterway in the country is the part of Lake Victoria within the boundaries of Kenya; Kisumu is the main port and has ferry connections to Uganda and Tanzania (2011)

Merchant marine: registered in other countries: 5 (Comoros 2, Saint Vincent and the Grenadines 2, unknown 1) (2010)
country comparison to the world: 124

Ports and terminals: *major seaport(s):* Kisumu, Mombasa

MILITARY

Military branches: Kenya Defence Forces: Kenya Army, Kenya Air Force, Kenya Navy (2012)

Military service age and obligation: 18-26 years of age for male and female voluntary service (under 18 with parental consent), with a 9-year obligation (7 years for Kenyan Navy); applicants must be Kenyan citizens and provide a national identity card (obtained at age 18) and a school-leaving certificate; women serve under the same terms and conditions as men; mandatory retirement at age 55 (2012)

Manpower available for military service:
males age 16-49: 9,768,140
females age 16-49: 9,466,257 (2010 est.)

Manpower fit for military service: males age 16-49: 6,361,268
females age 16-49: 6,106,870 (2010 est.)

Manpower reaching militarily significant age annually: *male:* 422,104
female: 416,927 (2010 est.)

Military expenditures: 1.96% of GDP (2012)
country comparison to the world: 42
1.88% of GDP (2011)
1.96% of GDP (2010)

Transnational Issues

Disputes—international: Kenya served as an important mediator in brokering Sudan's north-south separation in February 2005; Kenya provides shelter to almost a quarter million refugees, including Ugandans who flee across the border periodically to seek protection from Lord's Resistance Army rebels; Kenya works hard to prevent the clan and militia fighting in Somalia from spreading across the border, which has long been open to nomadic pastoralists; the boundary that separates Kenya's and Sudan's sovereignty is unclear in the "Ilemi Triangle," which Kenya has administered since colonial times

Refugees and internally displaced persons: *refugees (country of origin):* 430,513 (Somalia); 34,301 (South Sudan); 30,251 (Ethiopia); 14,490 (Democratic Republic of Congo); 7,961 (Sudan); 5,457 (Burundi) (2014)
IDPs: at least 300,000 (2007-08 post-election violence; the status of the estimated 300,000 IDPs from the 2007-08 post-election violence who found refuge in host communities rather than camps—and IDPs displaced through natural disasters, drought, development and environmental projects, land disputes, cattle rustling, and inter-communal violence—is not captured in Kenya's national database; in 2012, inter-communal violence displaced approximately 118,000 people and floods displaced an estimated 100,000) (2012)
stateless persons: 20,000 (2012); note—the stateless population is composed of Nubians, Kenyan Somalis, and coastal Arabs; the Nubians are descendants of Sudanese soldiers recruited by the British to fight for them in East Africa more than a century ago; they did not receive Kenyan citizenship when the country became independent in 1963; only recently have Nubians become a formally recognized tribe and had less trouble obtaining national IDs; Galjeel and other Somalis who have lived in Kenya for decades are lumped in *with more recent Somali refugees and denied ID cards*

Trafficking in persons: current situation: Kenya is a source, transit, and destination country for adults and children subjected to forced labor and sex trafficking; Kenyan children are forced to work in domestic service, agriculture, fishing, cattle herding, street vending, begging, and prostitution; Kenyan economic migrants to other East African countries, South Sudan, Europe, the US, and the Middle East are at times exploited in domestic servitude, massage parlors or brothels, or forced manual labor; children from Burundi, Ethiopia, Somalia, South Sudan, Tanzania, and Uganda are subjected to forced labor and prostitution in Kenya; Somali refugees living in the Dadaab complex may be forced into prostitution or work on tobacco farms

tier rating: Tier 2 Watch List—Kenya does not fully comply with the minimum standards for the elimination of trafficking; the government enacted the Counter-Trafficking in Persons Act in October 2012 but has not launched and implemented its national plan of action, convened the Counter-Trafficking in Persons Advisory Committee, taken tangible action against trafficking complicity among law enforcement officials, provided shelter and other protective services for adult victims, monitor the work of overseas labor recruitment agencies, or provide wide-scale anti-trafficking training to its officials; efforts to assist and care for child victims remain strong; corruption among officials continue to hamper efforts to bring traffickers to justice (2013)

Illicit drugs: widespread harvesting of small plots of marijuana; transit country for South Asian heroin destined for Europe and North America; Indian methaqualone also transits on way to South Africa; significant potential for money-laundering activity given the country's status as a regional financial center; massive corruption, and relatively high levels of narcotics-associated activities

KINGMAN REEF

INTRODUCTION

Background: The US annexed the reef in 1922. Its sheltered lagoon served as a way station for flying boats on Hawaii-to-American Samoa flights during the late 1930s. There are no terrestrial plants on the reef, which is frequently awash, but it does support abundant and diverse marine fauna and flora. In 2001, the waters surrounding the reef out to 12 nm were designated a US National Wildlife Refuge.

GEOGRAPHY

Location: Oceania, reef in the North Pacific Ocean, about half way between Hawaii and American Samoa

Geographic coordinates: 6 24 N, 162 22 W

Map references: Oceania

Area: *total:* 1 sq km
land: 1 sq km
water: 0 sq km

Area—comparative: about 1.7 times the size of The Mall in Washington, DC

Land boundaries: 0 km

Coastline: 3 km

Maritime claims: *territorial sea:* 12 nm
exclusive economic zone: 200 nm

Climate: tropical; moderated by prevailing winds

Terrain: low and nearly level

Elevation extremes: *lowest point:* Pacific Ocean 0 m
highest point: unnamed location 1 m

Natural resources: terrestrial and aquatic wildlife

Land use: *arable land:* 0%
permanent crops: 0%
other: 100% (2011)

Natural hazards: wet or awash most of the time, maximum elevation of about 1 meter makes Kingman Reef a maritime hazard

Environment—current issues: none

Geography—note: barren coral atoll with deep interior lagoon; closed to the public

PEOPLE AND SOCIETY

Population: uninhabited (July 2007 est.)

GOVERNMENT

Country name: *conventional long form:* none
conventional short form: Kingman Reef

Dependency status: unincorporated territory of the US; administered from Washington, DC by the US Fish and Wildlife Service of the Department of the Interior
note: on 1 September 2000, the Department of the Interior accepted restoration of its administrative jurisdiction over Kingman Reef from the Department of the Navy; Executive Order 3223 signed 18 January 2001 established Kingman Reef National Wildlife Refuge to be administered by the Director, US Fish and Wildlife Service; this refuge is managed to protect the terrestrial and aquatic wildlife of Kingman Reef out to the 12 nm territorial sea limit

Legal system: the laws of the US, where applicable, apply

Flag description: the flag of the US is used

TRANSPORTATION

Ports and terminals: none; offshore anchorage only

MILITARY

Military—note: defense is the responsibility of the US

TRANSNATIONAL ISSUES

Disputes—international: none

KIRIBATI

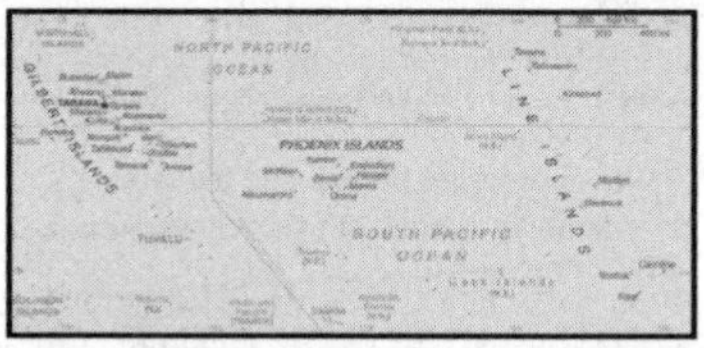

INTRODUCTION

Background: The Gilbert Islands became a British protectorate in 1892 and a colony in 1915; they were captured by the Japanese in the Pacific War in 1941. The islands of Makin and Tarawa were the sites of major US amphibious victories over entrenched Japanese garrisons in 1943. The Gilbert Islands were granted self-rule by the UK in 1971 and complete independence in 1979 under the new name of Kiribati. The US relinquished all claims to the sparsely inhabited Phoenix and Line Island groups in a 1979 treaty of friendship with Kiribati.

GEOGRAPHY

Location: Oceania, group of 33 coral atolls in the Pacific Ocean, straddling the Equator; the capital Tarawa is about half way between Hawaii and Australia

Geographic coordinates: 1 25 N, 173 00 E

Map references: Oceania

Area: *total:* 811 sq km
country comparison to the world: 187
land: 811 sq km
water: 0 sq km
note: includes three island groups—Gilbert Islands, Line Islands, Phoenix Islands

Area—comparative: four times the size of Washington, DC

Land boundaries: 0 km

Coastline: 1,143 km

Maritime claims: *territorial sea:* 12 nm
exclusive economic zone: 200 nm

Climate: tropical; marine, hot and humid, moderated by trade winds

Terrain: mostly low-lying coral atolls surrounded by extensive reefs

Elevation extremes: *lowest point:* Pacific Ocean 0 m
highest point: unnamed elevation on Banaba 81 m

Natural resources: phosphate (production discontinued in 1979)

Land use: *arable land:* 2.47%
permanent crops: 39.51%
other: 58.02% (2011)

Irrigated land: NA

Natural hazards: typhoons can occur any time, but usually November to March; occasional tornadoes; low level of some of the islands make them sensitive to changes in sea level

Environment—current issues: heavy pollution in lagoon of south Tarawa atoll due to heavy migration mixed with traditional practices such as lagoon latrines and open-pit dumping; ground water at risk

Environment—international agreements:
party to: Biodiversity, Climate Change, Climate Change-Kyoto Protocol, Desertification, Hazardous Wastes, Law of the Sea, Marine Dumping, Ozone Layer Protection, Whaling
signed, but not ratified: none of the selected agreements

Geography—note: 21 of the 33 islands are inhabited; Banaba (Ocean Island) in Kiribati is one of the three great phosphate rock islands in the Pacific Ocean—the others are Makatea in French Polynesia, and Nauru; Kiribati is the only country in the world to fall into all four hemispheres (northern, southern, eastern, and western)

PEOPLE AND SOCIETY

Nationality: *noun:* I-Kiribati (singular and plural)
adjective: I-Kiribati

Ethnic groups: I-Kiribati 89.5%, I-Kiribati/mixed 9.7%, Tuvaluan 0.1%, other 0.8% (2010 est.)

Languages: I-Kiribati, English (official)

Religions: Roman Catholic 55.8%, Kempsville Presbyterian Church 33.5%, Mormon 4.7%, Baha'i 2.3%, Seventh-Day Adventist 2%, other 1.5%, none 0.2%, unspecified 0.05% (2010 est.)

Population: 104,488 (July 2014 est.)
country comparison to the world: 194

Age structure:
0-14 years: 31.5% (male 16,779/female 16,151)
15-24 years: 21.3% (male 11,099/female 11,122)
25-54 years: 37.8% (male 18,978/female 20,477)
55-64 years: 4% (male 2,605/female 3,137)
65 years and over: 3.9% (male 1,630/female 2,510) (2014 est.)

Dependency ratios:

total dependency ratio: 56.2 %
youth dependency ratio: 49.8 %
elderly dependency ratio: 6.5 %
potential support ratio: 15.5 (2013)

Median age: *total:* 23.6 years
male: 22.7 years
female: 24.4 years (2014 est.)

Population growth rate: 1.18% (2014 est.)
country comparison to the world: 102

Birth rate: 21.85 births/1,000 population (2014 est.)
country comparison to the world: 75

Death rate: 7.18 deaths/1,000 population (2014 est.)
country comparison to the world: 126

Net migration rate: -2.86 migrant(s)/1,000 population (2014 est.)
country comparison to the world: 176

Urbanization: *urban population:* 44% of total population (2010)
rate of urbanization: 1.9% annual rate of change (2010-15 est.)

Major urban areas—population: TARAWA (capital) 43,000 (2009)

Sex ratio: *at birth:* 1.05 male(s)/female
0-14 years: 1.04 male(s)/female
15-24 years: 1 male(s)/female
25-54 years: 0.93 male(s)/female
55-64 years: 0.96 male(s)/female
65 years and over: 0.64 male(s)/female
total population: 0.96 male(s)/female (2014 est.)

Maternal mortality rate: 9 deaths/100,000 live births (2008)
country comparison to the world: 155

Infant mortality rate: total: 35.37 deaths/1,000 live births
country comparison to the world: 63
male: 36.59 deaths/1,000 live births
female: 34.08 deaths/1,000 live births (2014 est.)

Life expectancy at birth: *total population:* 65.47 years
country comparison to the world: 173
male: 63.03 years
female: 68.02 years (2014 est.)

Total fertility rate: 2.56 children born/woman (2014 est.)
country comparison to the world: 77

Contraceptive prevalence rate: 22.3% (2009)

Health expenditures: 10.1% of GDP (2011)
country comparison to the world: 25

Physicians density: 0.38 physicians/1,000 population (2010)

Hospital bed density: 1.3 beds/1,000 population (2011)

Drinking water source:
improved:
urban: 86.8% of population
rural: 49.9% of population
total: 66.1% of population
unimproved:
urban: 13.2% of population
rural: 50.1% of population
total: 33.9% of population (2011 est.)

Sanitation facility access:
improved:
urban: 50.8% of population
rural: 30.1% of population
total: 39.2% of population
unimproved:
urban: 49.2% of population
rural: 69.9% of population
total: 60.8% of population (2011 est.)

HIV/AIDS—adult prevalence rate: NA

HIV/AIDS—people living with HIV/AIDS: NA

HIV/AIDS—deaths: NA

Obesity—adult prevalence rate: 46% (2008)
country comparison to the world: 8

Education expenditures: 12% of GDP (2001)
country comparison to the world: 4

Literacy: NA

School life expectancy (primary to tertiary education): *total:* 12 years
male: 12 years
female: 13 years (2008)

GOVERNMENT

Country name: *conventional long form:* Republic of Kiribati
conventional short form: Kiribati
local long form: Republic of Kiribati
local short form: Kiribati
note: pronounced keer-ree-bahss
former: Gilbert Islands

Government type: republic

Capital: *name:* Tarawa
geographic coordinates: 1 21 N, 173 02 E
time difference: UTC+12 (17 hours ahead of Washington, DC during Standard Time)
note: on 1 January 1995, Kiribati proclaimed that all of its territory was in the same time zone as its Gilbert Islands group (UTC +12) even though the Phoenix Islands and the Line Islands under its jurisdiction were on the other side of the International Date Line

Administrative divisions: 3 geographical units: Gilbert Islands, Line Islands, Phoenix Islands; note—there are no first-order administrative divisions but there are 6 districts (Banaba, Central Gilberts, Line Islands, Northern Gilberts, Southern Gilberts, Tarawa) and 21 island councils—one for each of the inhabited islands (Abaiang, Abemama, Aranuka, Arorae, Banaba, Beru, Butaritari, Kanton, Kiritimati, Kuria, Maiana, Makin, Marakei, Nikunau, Nonouti, Onotoa, Tabiteuea, Tabuaeran, Tamana, Tarawa, Teraina)

Independence: 12 July 1979 (from the UK)

National holiday: Independence Day, 12 July (1979)

Constitution: preindependence—The Gilbert and Ellice Islands Order in Council 1915, The Gilbert Islands Order in Council 1975; latest promulgated 12 July 1979 (at independence); amended 1995 (2013)

Legal system: English common law supplemented by customary law

International law organization participation: has not submitted an ICJ jurisdiction declaration; non-party state to the ICCt

Suffrage: 18 years of age; universal

Executive branch: *chief of state:* President Anote TONG (since 10 July 2003); Vice President Teima ONORIO; note—the president is both the chief of state and head of government
head of government: President Anote TONG (since 10 July 2003); Vice President Teima ONORIO
cabinet: 12-member cabinet appointed by the president from among the members of the House of Parliament (For more information visit the World Leaders website)
elections: the House of Parliament nominates the presidential candidates from among its members following parliamentary elections and then those candidates compete in a general election; president elected by popular vote for a four-year term (eligible for two more terms); election last held on 13 January 2012 (next to be held in 2015); vice president appointed by the president
election results: Anote TONG 42.2%, Tetaua TAITAI 35%, Rimeta BENIAMINA 22.8%

Legislative branch: unicameral House of Parliament or Maneaba Ni Maungatabu (46 seats; 44 members elected by popular vote, 1 ex officio member—the attorney general, 1 nominated by the Rabi Council of Leaders (representing Banaba Island); members serve four-year terms)
elections: legislative elections were held in two rounds—the first round on 21 October 2011 and the second round on 28 October 2011 (next to be held in 2015)
election results: percent of vote by party—NA; seats by party—NA, other 2 (includes attorney general)

Judicial branch: *highest court(s):* High Court (consists of a chief justice and other judges as prescribed by the president)
note—the High Court has jurisdiction on constitutional issues
judge selection and term of office: chief justice appointed by the president on the advice of the cabinet in consultation with the Public Service Commission (PSC); other judges appointed by the president on the advice of the chief justice along with the PSC
subordinate courts: Court of Appeal; magistrates' courts

Political parties and leaders: Boutokaan Te Koaua Party or BTK [Anote TONG]; Kamaeuraoan Te I-Kiribati Party or KTK [Tetaua TAITAI]; Maurin Kiribati Pati or MKP [Rimeta BENIAMINA]
note: there is no tradition of formally organized political parties in Kiribati; they more closely resemble factions or interest groups because they have no party headquarters, formal platforms, or party structures

Political pressure groups and leaders: NA

International organization participation: ACP, ADB, AOSIS, C, FAO, IBRD, ICAO, ICRM, IDA, IFAD, IFC, IFRCS, ILO, IMF, IMO, IOC, ITU, ITUC (NGOs), OPCW, PIF, Sparteca, SPC, UN, UNCTAD, UNESCO, UPU, WHO, WMO

Diplomatic representation in the US: Kiribati does not have an embassy in the US; there is an honorary consulate in Honolulu

Diplomatic representation from the US: the US does not have an embassy in Kiribati; the US ambassador to Fiji, currently Ambassador Frankie A. REED, is accredited to Kiribati

Flag description: the upper half is red with a yellow frigatebird flying over a yellow rising sun, and the lower half is blue with three horizontal wavy white stripes to represent the Pacific ocean; the white stripes represent the three island groups—the Gilbert, Line, and Phoenix Islands; the 17 rays of the sun represent the 16 Gilbert Islands and Banaba (formerly Ocean Island); the frigatebird symbolizes authority and freedom

National symbol(s): frigatebird

National anthem: *name:* "Teirake kaini Kiribati" (Stand Up, Kiribati)
lyrics/music: Urium Tamuera IOTEBA
note: adopted 1979

ECONOMY

Economy—overview: A remote country of 33 scattered coral atolls, Kiribati has few natural resources and is one of the least developed Pacific

Islands. Commercially viable phosphate deposits were exhausted at the time of independence from the UK in 1979. Copra and fish now represent the bulk of production and exports. The economy has fluctuated widely in recent years. Economic development is constrained by a shortage of skilled workers, weak infrastructure, and remoteness from international markets. Tourism provides more than one-fifth of GDP. Private sector initiatives and a financial sector are in the early stages of development. Foreign financial aid from the EU, UK, US, Japan, Australia, New Zealand, Canada, UN agencies, and Taiwan accounts for 20-25% of GDP. Remittances from seamen on merchant ships abroad account for more than $5 million each year. Kiribati receives around $15 million annually for the government budget from an Australian trust fund.

GDP (purchasing power parity): $698 million (2013 est.)
country comparison to the world: 212
$678.2 million (2012 est.)
$660.1 million (2011 est.)
note: data are in 2013 US dollars

GDP (official exchange rate): $173 million (2013 est.)

GDP—real growth rate: 2.9% (2013 est.)
country comparison to the world: 119
2.8% (2012 est.)
2.7% (2011 est.)

GDP—per capita (PPP): $6,400 (2013 est.)
country comparison to the world: 146
$6,300 (2012 est.)
$6,300 (2011 est.)
note: data are in 2013 US dollars

GDP—composition, by sector of origin:
agriculture: 24.3%
industry: 7.9%
services: 67.8% (2010 est.)

Agriculture—products: copra, taro, breadfruit, sweet potatoes, vegetables; fish

Industries: fishing, handicrafts

Industrial production growth rate: NA%

Labor force: 7,870
country comparison to the world: 218
note: economically active, not including subsistence farmers (2001)

Labor force—by occupation: *agriculture:* 2.7%
industry: 32%
services: 65.3% (2000)

Unemployment rate: 2% (1992 est.)
country comparison to the world: 12

Population below poverty line: NA%

Household income or consumption by percentage share: *lowest* 10%: NA%
highest 10%: NA%

Budget: *revenues:* $55.52 million
expenditures: $107.1 million (2010 est.)

Taxes and other revenues: 32.1% of GDP (2010 est.)
country comparison to the world: 81

Budget surplus (+) or deficit (-):
-29.8% of GDP (2010 est.)
country comparison to the world: 215

Fiscal year: NA

Inflation rate (consumer prices): 0.2% (2007 est.)
country comparison to the world: 10

Market value of publicly traded shares: $NA

Current account balance: -$35.01 million (2010 est.)
country comparison to the world: 66
-$21 million (2007 est.)

Exports: $7.066 million (2010 est.)
country comparison to the world: 215
$17 million (2004 est.)
Exports—commodities: copra 62%, coconuts, seaweed, fish

Imports: $80.09 million (2010 est.)
country comparison to the world: 216
$62 million (2004 est.)

Imports—commodities: foodstuffs, machinery and equipment, miscellaneous manufactured goods, fuel

Reserves of foreign exchange and gold: $8.37 million (2010 est.)

Debt—external: $10 million (1999 est.)
country comparison to the world: 197

Exchange rates: Australian dollars (AUD) per US dollar—
1.031 (2011)
0.9695 (2011 est.)
1.2822 (2009)
1.2059 (2008)

ENERGY

Electricity—production: 25 million kWh (2010 est.)
country comparison to the world: 212

Electricity—consumption: 23.25 million kWh (2010 est.)
country comparison to the world: 212

Electricity—exports: 0 kWh (2012 est.)
country comparison to the world: 155

Electricity—imports: 0 kWh (2012 est.)
country comparison to the world: 162

Electricity—installed generating capacity: 5,000 kW (2010 est.)
country comparison to the world: 209

Electricity—from fossil fuels: 100% of total installed capacity (2010 est.)
country comparison to the world: 18

Electricity—from nuclear fuels: 0% of total installed capacity (2010 est.)
country comparison to the world: 119

Electricity—from hydroelectric plants: 0% of total installed capacity (2010 est.)
country comparison to the world: 177

Electricity—from other renewable sources: 0% of total installed capacity (2010 est.)
country comparison to the world: 188

Crude oil—production: 0 bbl/day (2012 est.)
country comparison to the world: 183

Crude oil—exports: 0 bbl/day (2010 est.)
country comparison to the world: 138

Crude oil—imports: 0 bbl/day (2010 est.)
country comparison to the world: 204

Crude oil—proved reserves: 0 bbl (1 January 2013 es)
country comparison to the world: 150

Refined petroleum products—production: 0 bbl/day (2010 est.)
country comparison to the world: 159

Refined petroleum products—consumption: 300 bbl/day (2011 est.)
country comparison to the world: 209

Refined petroleum products—exports: 0 bbl/day (2010 est.)
country comparison to the world: 189

Refined petroleum products—imports: 420.2 bbl/day (2010 est.)
country comparison to the world: 206

Natural gas—production: 0 cu m (2011 est.)
country comparison to the world: 149

Natural gas—consumption: 0 cu m (2010 est.)
country comparison to the world: 160

Natural gas—exports: 0 cu m (2011 est.)
country comparison to the world: 129

Natural gas—imports: 0 cu m (2011 est.)
country comparison to the world: 85

Natural gas—proved reserves: 0 cu m (1 January 2013 es)
country comparison to the world: 155

Carbon dioxide emissions from consumption of energy: 59,340 Mt (2011 est.)
country comparison to the world: 208

COMMUNICATIONS

Telephones—main lines in use: 9,000 (2012)
country comparison to the world: 201

Telephones—mobile cellular: 16,000 (2012)
country comparison to the world: 211

Telephone system: *general assessment:* generally good quality national and international service
domestic: wire line service available on Tarawa and Kiritimati (Christmas Island); connections to outer islands by HF/VHF radiotelephone; wireless service available in Tarawa since 1999
international: country code—686; Kiribati is being linked to the Pacific Ocean Cooperative Telecommunications Network, which should improve telephone service; satellite earth station—1 Intelsat (Pacific Ocean) (2010)
Broadcast media: 1 TV broadcast station that provides about 1 hour of local programming Monday-Friday; multi-channel TV packages provide access to Australian and US stations; 1 government-operated radio station broadcasts on AM, FM, and shortwave (2009)

Internet country code: .ki

Internet hosts: 327 (2012)
country comparison to the world: 188

Internet users: 7,800 (2009)
country comparison to the world: 204

TRANSPORTATION

Airports: 19 (2013)
country comparison to the world: 137

Airports—with paved runways: *total:* 4
1,524 to 2,437 m: 4 (2013)

Airports—with unpaved runways: *total:* 1 5
914 to 1,523 m: 10
under 914 m:
5 (2013)

Roadways: *total:* 670 km (2011)
country comparison to the world: 190

Waterways: 5 km (small network of canals in Line Islands) (2012)
country comparison to the world: 108

Merchant marine: *total:* 7 7
country comparison to the world: 58
by type: bulk carrier 7, cargo 35, chemical tanker 6, passenger 1, passenger/cargo 1, petroleum tanker 12, refrigerated cargo 15
foreign-owned: 43 (China 26, Hong Kong 2, Russia 1, Singapore 9, South Korea 1, Taiwan 2, Vietnam 2) (2010)

Ports and terminals: *major seaport(s):* Betio (Tarawa Atoll), Canton Island, English Harbor

MILITARY

Military branches: no regular military forces (establishment prevented by the constitution); Police Force (2011)

Manpower available for military service:
males age 16-49: 25,190 (2010 est.)
Manpower fit for military service:
males age 16-49: 18,364
females age 16-49: 20,302 (2010 est.)
Manpower reaching militarily significant age annually: *male:* 1,132
female: 1,120 (2010 est.)
Military—note: Kiribati does not have military forces; defense assistance is provided by Australia and NZ

TRANSNATIONAL ISSUES

Disputes—international: none

KOREA, NORTH

INTRODUCTION

Background: An independent kingdom for much of its long history, Korea was occupied by Japan beginning in 1905 following the Russo-Japanese War. Five years later, Japan formally annexed the entire peninsula. Following World War II, Korea was split with the northern half coming under Soviet-sponsored communist control. After failing in the Korean War (1950-53) to conquer the US-backed Republic of Korea (ROK) in the southern portion by force, North Korea (DPRK), under its founder President KIM Il Sung, adopted a policy of ostensible diplomatic and economic "self-reliance" as a check against outside influence. The DPRK demonized the US as the ultimate threat to its social system through state-funded propaganda, and molded political, economic, and military policies around the core ideological objective of eventual unification of Korea under Pyongyang's control. KIM Il Sung's son, KIM Jong Il, was officially designated as his father's successor in 1980, assuming a growing political and managerial role until the elder KIM's death in 1994. KIM Jong Un was publicly unveiled as his father's successor in September 2010. Following KIM Jong Il's death in December 2011, the regime began to take actions to transfer power to KIM Jong Un and KIM has now assumed many his father's former titles and duties. After decades of economic mismanagement and resource misallocation, the DPRK since the mid-1990s has relied heavily on international aid to feed its population. The DPRK began to ease restrictions to allow semi-private markets, starting in 2002, but then sought to roll back the scale of economic reforms in 2005 and 2009. North Korea's history of regional military provocations; proliferation of military-related items; long-range missile development; WMD programs including tests of nuclear devices in 2006, 2009, and 2013; and massive conventional armed forces are of major concern to the international community. The regime in 2013 announced a new policy calling for the simultaneous development of the North's nuclear weapons program and its economy.

GEOGRAPHY

Location: Eastern Asia, northern half of the Korean Peninsula bordering the Korea Bay and the Sea of Japan, between China and South Korea
Geographic coordinates: 40 00 N, 127 00 E
Map references: Asia
Area: *total:* 120,538 sq km
country comparison to the world: 99
land: 120,408 sq km
water: 130 sq km
Area—comparative: slightly larger than Virginia; slightly smaller than Mississippi
Land boundaries: *total:* 1,671.5 km
border countries: China 1,416 km, South Korea 238 km, Russia 17.5 km
Coastline: 2,495 km
Maritime claims: *territorial sea:* 12 nm
exclusive economic zone: 200 nm
note: military boundary line 50 nm in the Sea of Japan and the exclusive economic zone limit in the Yellow Sea where all foreign vessels and aircraft without permission are banned
Climate: temperate with rainfall concentrated in summer
Terrain: mostly hills and mountains separated by deep, narrow valleys; coastal plains wide in west, discontinuous in east
Elevation extremes: *lowest point:* Sea of Japan 0 m
highest point: Paektu-san 2,744 m
Natural resources: coal, lead, tungsten, zinc, graphite, magnesite, iron ore, copper, gold, pyrites, salt, fluorspar, hydropower
Land use: *arable land:* 19.08%
permanent crops: 1.7%
other: 79.22% (2011)
Irrigated land: 14,600 sq km (2003)
Total renewable water resources: 77.15 cu km (2011)
Freshwater withdrawal (domestic/industrial/agricultural): *total:* 8.66 cu km/yr (10%/13%/76%)
per capita: 360.6 cu m/yr (2005)
Natural hazards: late spring droughts often followed by severe flooding; occasional typhoons during the early fall
volcanism: Changbaishan (elev. 2,744 m) (also known as Baitoushan, Baegdu or P'aektu-san), on the Chinese border, is considered historically active
Environment—current issues: water pollution; inadequate supplies of potable water; waterborne disease; deforestation; soil erosion and degradation
Environment—international agreements:
party to: Antarctic Treaty, Biodiversity, Climate Change, Climate Change-Kyoto Protocol, Desertification, Environmental Modification, Hazardous Wastes, Ozone Layer Protection, Ship Pollution
signed, but not ratified: Law of the Sea
Geography—note: strategic location bordering China, South Korea, and Russia; mountainous interior is isolated and sparsely populated

PEOPLE AND SOCIETY

Nationality: *noun:* Korean(s)
adjective: Korean
Ethnic groups: racially homogeneous; there is a small Chinese community and a few ethnic Japanese
Languages: Korean
Religions: traditionally Buddhist and Confucianist, some Christian and syncretic Chondogyo (Religion of the Heavenly Way)
note: autonomous religious activities now almost nonexistent; government-sponsored religious groups exist to provide illusion of religious freedom
Population: 24,851,627 (July 2014 est.)
country comparison to the world: 50
Age structure:
0-14 years: 21.5% (male 2,709,580/female 2,628,456)
15-24 years: 16.3% (male 2,041,861/female 1,997,413)
25-54 years: 44% (male 5,465,889/female 5,456,850)
55-64 years: 9.7% (male 1,007,667/female 1,127,455)
65 years and over: 9.5% (male 826,175/female 1,590,281) (2014 est.)
Dependency ratios:
total dependency ratio: 45.2 %
youth dependency ratio: 31.5 %
elderly dependency ratio: 13.7 %
potential support ratio: 7.3 (2013)
Median age: *total:* 33.4 years
male: 31.8 years
female: 35 years (2014 est.)
Population growth rate: 0.53% (2014 est.)
country comparison to the world: 153
Birth rate: 14.51 births/1,000 population (2014 est.)
country comparison to the world: 138
Death rate: 9.18 deaths/1,000 population (2014 est.)
country comparison to the world: 65
Net migration rate: -0.04 migrant(s)/1,000 population (2014 est.)
country comparison to the world: 111
Urbanization: *urban population:* 60.3% of total population (2011)
rate of urbanization: 0.63% annual rate of change (2010-15 est.)
Major urban areas—population: PYONGYANG (capital) 2.843 million (2011)

Sex ratio: *at birth:* 1.05 male(s)/female
0-14 years: 1.03 male(s)/female
15-24 years: 1.02 male(s)/female
25-54 years: 1 male(s)/female
55-64 years: 0.94 male(s)/female
65 years and over: 0.51 male(s)/female
total population: 0.94 male(s)/female (2014 est.)

Maternal mortality rate: 81 deaths/100,000 live births (2010)
country comparison to the world: 82

Infant mortality rate: *total:* 24.5 deaths/1,000 live births
country comparison to the world: 75
male: 27.18 deaths/1,000 live births
female: 21.68 deaths/1,000 live births (2014 est.)

Life expectancy at birth: *total population:* 69.81 years
country comparison to the world: 154
male: 65.96 years
female: 73.86 years (2014 est.)

Total fertility rate: 1.98 children born/woman (2014 est.)
country comparison to the world: 129

Contraceptive prevalence rate: 68.6% (2002)

Physicians density: 3.29 physicians/1,000 population (2003)

Hospital bed density: 13.2 beds/1,000 population (2002)

Drinking water source:
improved:
urban: 98.9% of population
rural: 96.9% of population
total: 98.1% of population
unimproved:
urban: 1.1% of population
rural: 3.1% of population
total: 1.9% of population (2011 est.)

Sanitation facility access:
improved:
urban: 87.9% of population
rural: 72.5% of population
total: 81.8% of population
unimproved:
urban: 12.1% of population
rural: 27.5% of population
total: 18.2% of population (2011 est.)

HIV/AIDS—adult prevalence rate: NA

HIV/AIDS—people living with HIV/AIDS: NA

HIV/AIDS—deaths: NA

Obesity—adult prevalence rate: 3.9% (2008)
country comparison to the world: 173

Children under the age of 5 years underweight: 18.8% (2009)
country comparison to the world: 34

Education expenditures: NA

Literacy: *definition:* age 15 and over can read and write
total population: 100%
male: 100%
female: 100% (2008 est.)

GOVERNMENT

Country name: *conventional long form:* Democratic People's Republic of Korea
conventional short form: North Korea
local long form: Choson-minjujuui-inmin-konghwaguk
local short form: Choson
abbreviation: DPRK

Government type: Communist state one-man dictatorship

Capital: *name:* Pyongyang
geographic coordinates: 39 01 N, 125 45 E
time difference: UTC+9 (14 hours ahead of Washington, DC during Standard Time)

Administrative divisions: 9 provinces (do, singular and plural) and 2 municipalities (si, singular and plural) provinces: Chagang-do (Chagang), Hamgyong-bukto (North Hamgyong), Hamgyong-namdo (South Hamgyong), Hwanghae-bukto (North Hwanghae), Hwanghae-namdo (South Hwanghae), Kangwon-do (Kangwon), P'yongan-bukto (North P'yongan), P'yongan-namdo (South P'yongan), Yanggang-do (Yanggang) municipalities: Nason-si, P'yongyang-si (Pyongyang)

Independence: 15 August 1945 (from Japan)

National holiday: Founding of the Democratic People's Republic of Korea (DPRK), 9 September (1948)

Constitution: previous 1948, 1972 (revised several times); latest adopted 1998 (during KIM Jong Il era); revised 2009, 2012 (2012)

Legal system: civil law system based on the Prussian model; system influenced by Japanese traditions and Communist legal theory

International law organization participation: has not submitted an ICJ jurisdiction declaration; non-party state to the ICCt

Suffrage: 17 years of age; universal

Executive branch: *chief of state:* KIM Jong Un (since 17 December 2011); note—the rubberstamp Supreme People's Assembly (SPA) reelected KIM Yong Nam in 2014 president of its Presidium with responsibility of representing state and receiving diplomatic credentials
head of government: Premier PAK Pong Ju (since 2 April 2013); Vice Premiers: KIM Yong Jin (since 6 January 2012), RI Chol Man (since 13 April 2012), RI Mu Yong (since 31 May 2011), RO Tu Chol (since 3 September 2003)
cabinet: Naegak (cabinet) members, except for Minister of People's Armed Forces, are appointed by SPA (For more information visit the World Leaders website)
elections: last election on 9 March 2014; date of next election NA
election results: KIM Jong Un elected unopposed
note: the Korean Workers' Party continues to list deceased leaders KIM Il Sung and KIM Jong Il as Eternal President and Eternal General Secretary respectively

Legislative branch: unicameral Supreme People's Assembly or Ch'oego Inmin Hoeui (687 seats; members elected by popular vote to serve five-year terms)
elections: last held on 9 March 2014 (next to be held in March 2019)
election results: percent of vote by party—NA; seats by party—NA; ruling party approves a list of candidates who are elected without opposition; a token number of seats are reserved for minor parties

Judicial branch: *highest court(s):* Supreme Court or Central Court (consists of the chief justice and two "People's Assessors" and for some cases, 3 judges)
judge selection and term of office: judges elected by the Supreme People's Assembly for 5-year terms
subordinate courts: provincial, municipal, military, special courts; people' courts (lowest level)

Political parties and leaders:
major party: Korean Workers' Party or KWP [KIM Jong Un]
minor parties: Chondoist Chongu Party [RYU Mi Yong] (under KWP control); Social Democratic Party [KIM Yong Dae] (under KWP control)

Political pressure groups and leaders: none

International organization participation: ARF, FAO, G-77, ICAO, ICC (NGOs), ICRM, IFAD, IFRCS, IHO, IMO, IOC, IPU, ISO, ITSO, ITU, NAM, UN, UNCTAD, UNESCO, UNIDO, UNWTO, UPU, WFTU (NGOs), WHO, WIPO, WMO

Diplomatic representation in the US: none; North Korea has a Permanent Mission to the UN in New York

Diplomatic representation from the US: none; note—Swedish Embassy in Pyongyang represents the US as consular protecting power

Flag description: three horizontal bands of blue (top), red (triple width), and blue; the red band is edged in white; on the hoist side of the red band is a white disk with a red five-pointed star; the broad red band symbolizes revolutionary traditions; the narrow white bands stands for purity, strength, and dignity; the blue bands signify sovereignty, peace, and friendship; the red star represents socialism

National symbol(s): red star

National anthem: *name:* "Aegukka" (Patriotic Song)
lyrics/music: PAK Se Yong/KIM Won Gyun
note: adopted 1947; both North Korea and South Korea's anthems share the same name and have a vaguely similar melody but have different lyrics; the North Korean anthem is also known as "Ach'imun pinnara" (Let Morning Shine)

ECONOMY

Economy—overview: North Korea, one of the world's most centrally directed and least open economies, faces chronic economic problems. Industrial capital stock is nearly beyond repair as a result of years of underinvestment, shortages of spare parts, and poor maintenance. Large-scale military spending draws off resources needed for investment and civilian consumption. Industrial and power output have stagnated for years at a fraction of pre-1990 levels. Frequent weather-related crop failures aggravated chronic food shortages caused by on-going systemic problems, including a lack of arable land, collective farming practices, poor soil quality, insufficient fertilization, and persistent shortages of tractors and fuel. Large-scale international food aid deliveries have allowed the people of North Korea to escape widespread starvation since famine threatened in 1995, but the population continues to suffer from prolonged malnutrition and poor living conditions. Since 2002, the government has allowed private "farmers' markets" to begin selling a wider range of goods. It also permitted some private farming—on an experimental basis—in an effort to boost agricultural output. In December 2009, North Korea carried out a redenomination of its currency, capping the amount of North Korean won that could be exchanged for the new notes, and limiting the exchange to a one-week window. A concurrent crackdown on markets and foreign currency use yielded severe shortages and inflation, forcing Pyongyang to ease the restrictions by

February 2010. In response to the sinking of the South Korean warship Cheonan and the shelling of Yeonpyeong Island, South Korea's government cut off most aid, trade, and bilateral cooperation activities, with the exception of operations at the Kaesong Industrial Complex. In preparation for the 100th anniversary of KIM Il-sung's birthday in 2012, North Korea continued efforts to develop special economic zones with China and expressed willingness to permit construction of a trilateral gas pipeline that would carry Russian natural gas to South Korea. The North Korean government often highlights its goal of becoming a "strong and prosperous" nation and attracting foreign investment, a key factor for improving the overall standard of living. In this regard, in 2013 the regime rolled out 14 new Special Economic Zones set up for foreign investors, though the initiative remains in its infancy. Nevertheless, firm political control remains the government's overriding concern, which likely will inhibit changes to North Korea's current economic system.

GDP (purchasing power parity): $40 billion (2012 est.)
country comparison to the world: 106
$40 billion (2011 est.)
$40 billion (2010 est.)
note: data are in 2011 US dollars;
North Korea does not publish reliable National Income Accounts data; the data shown here are derived from purchasing power parity (PPP) GDP estimates for North Korea that were made by Angus MADDISON in a study conducted for the OECD; his figure for 1999 was extrapolated to 2011 using estimated real growth rates for North Korea's GDP and an inflation factor based on the US GDP deflator; the results were rounded to the nearest $10 billion.

GDP (official exchange rate): $28 billion (2009 est.)

GDP—real growth rate: 1.3% (2012 est.)
country comparison to the world: 164
0.8% (2011 est.)
-0.5% (2010 est.)

GDP—per capita (PPP): $1,800 (2011 est.)
country comparison to the world: 197
$1,800 (2010 est.)
$1,900 (2009 est.)
note: data are in 2011 US dollars

GDP—composition, by sector of origin:
agriculture: 23.4%
industry: 47.2%
services: 29.4% (2012 est.)

Agriculture—products: rice, corn, potatoes, soybeans, pulses; cattle, pigs, pork, eggs

Industries: military products; machine building, electric power, chemicals; mining (coal, iron ore, limestone, magnesite, graphite, copper, zinc, lead, and precious metals), metallurgy; textiles, food processing; tourism

Industrial production growth rate: 0.5%
country comparison to the world: 159

Labor force: 12.6 million
country comparison to the world: 42
note: estimates vary widely (2012 est.)

Labor force—by occupation: agriculture: 35%
industry and services: 65% (2008 est.)

Unemployment rate: NA%

Population below poverty line: NA%

Household income or consumption by percentage share:
lowest 10%: NA%
highest 10%: NA%

Budget: *revenues:* $3.2 billion
expenditures: $3.3 billion (2007 est.)

Taxes and other revenues: 11.4% of GDP
country comparison to the world: 205
note: excludes earnings from state-operated enterprises (2007 est.)

Budget surplus (+) or deficit (-):
-0.4% of GDP (2007 est.)
country comparison to the world: 52

Fiscal year: calendar year

Inflation rate (consumer prices): NA%

Exports: $3.954 billion (2012 est.)
country comparison to the world: 122
$3.703 billion (2011 est.)

Exports—commodities: minerals, metallurgical products, manufactures (including armaments), textiles, agricultural and fishery products

Exports—partners: China 63%, South Korea 27% (2012 est.)

Imports: $4.828 billion (2012 est.)
country comparison to the world: 130
$4.367 billion

Imports—commodities: petroleum, coking coal, machinery and equipment, textiles, grain

Imports—partners: China 73%, South Korea 19% (2012 est.)

Debt—external: $3 billion (2012 est.)
country comparison to the world: 137

Exchange rates: North Korean won (KPW) per US dollar (market rate)
157 (2013 est.)
155.5 (2012 est.)
145 (2010 est.)
3,630 (December 2008)
140 (2007)

ENERGY

Electricity—production: 21.04 billion kWh (2010 est.)

country comparison to the world: 7 2

Electricity—consumption: 17.62 billion kWh (2010 est.)
country comparison to the world: 71

Electricity—exports: 0 kWh (2012 est.)
country comparison to the world: 154

Electricity—imports: 0 kWh (2012 est.)
country comparison to the world: 161

Electricity—installed generating capacity: 9.5 million kW (2011 est.)
country comparison to the world: 59

Electricity—from fossil fuels: 47.4% of total installed capacity (2011 est.)
country comparison to the world: 160

Electricity—from nuclear fuels: 0% of total installed capacity (2011 est.)
country comparison to the world: 118

Electricity—from hydroelectric plants: 52.6% of total installed capacity (2011 est.)
country comparison to the world: 41

Electricity—from other renewable sources: 0% of total installed capacity (2011 est.)
country comparison to the world: 187

Crude oil—production: 0 bbl/day (2012 est.)
country comparison to the world: 182

Crude oil—exports: 0 bbl/day (2010 est.)
country comparison to the world: 137

Crude oil—imports: 10,500 bbl/day (2012 est.)
country comparison to the world: 77

Crude oil—proved reserves: 0 bbl (1 January 2013 es)
country comparison to the world: 149

Refined petroleum products—production: 6,965 bbl/day (2010 est.)
country comparison to the world: 106

Refined petroleum products—consumption: 15,000 bbl/day (2012 est.)
country comparison to the world: 143

Refined petroleum products—exports: 0 bbl/day (2012 est.)
country comparison to the world: 188

Refined petroleum products—imports: 4,000 bbl/day (2010 est.)
country comparison to the world: 162

Natural gas—production: 0 cu m (2011 est.)
country comparison to the world: 148

Natural gas—consumption: 1 cu m (2011 est.)
country comparison to the world: 114

Natural gas—exports: 0 cu m (2011 est.)
country comparison to the world: 128

Natural gas—imports: 0 cu m (2011 est.)
country comparison to the world: 212

Natural gas—proved reserves: 0 cu m (1 January 2013 es)
country comparison to the world: 154

Carbon dioxide emissions from consumption of energy: 65.96 million Mt (2011 est.)
country comparison to the world: 52

COMMUNICATIONS

Telephones—main lines in use: 1.18 million (2011)
country comparison to the world: 7 0

Telephones—mobile cellular: 1.7 million (2012)
country comparison to the world: 148

Telephone system: *general assessment:* adequate system; nationwide fiber-optic network; mobile-cellular service expanding beyond Pyongyang
domestic: fiber-optic links installed down to the county level; telephone directories unavailable; GSM mobile-cellular service initiated in 2002 but suspended in 2004; Orascom Telecom Holding, an Egyptian company, launched W-CDMA mobile service on 15 December 2008 for the Pyongyang area, has expanded service to several large cities and now has a 1-million-person subscriber base
international: country code—850; satellite earth stations—2 (1 Intelsat—Indian Ocean, 1 Russian—Indian Ocean region); other international connections through Moscow and Beijing (2011)

Broadcast media: no independent media; radios and TVs are pre-tuned to government stations; 4 government-owned TV stations; the Korean Workers' Party owns and operates the Korean Central Broadcasting Station, and the state-run Voice of Korea operates an external broadcast service; the government prohibits listening to and jams foreign broadcasts (2008)

Internet country code: .kp

Internet hosts: 8 (2012)
country comparison to the world: 226

TRANSPORTATION

Airports: 82 (2013)
country comparison to the world: 6 7

Airports—with paved runways: *total:* 3 9
over 3,047 m: 3
2,438 to 3,047 m: 22
1,524 to 2,437 m: 8
914 to 1,523 m: 2
under 914 m: 4 (2013)

Airports—with unpaved runways: *total:* 4 3

2,438 to 3,047 m: 3
1,524 to 2,437 m: 17
914 to 1,523 m: 15
under 914 m: 8 (2013)

Heliports: 23 (2013)

Pipelines: oil 6 km (2013)

Railways: *total:* 5,242 km
country comparison to the world: 33
standard gauge: 5,242 km 1.435-m gauge (3,500 km electrified) (2009)

Roadways: *total:* 25,554 km
country comparison to the world: 100
paved: 724 km
unpaved: 24,830 km (2006)

Waterways: 2,250 km (most navigable only by small craft) (2011)
country comparison to the world: 38

Merchant marine: *total:* 158

country comparison to the world: 37
by type: bulk carrier 6, cargo 131, carrier 1, chemical tanker 1, container 4, passenger/cargo 1, petroleum tanker 12, refrigerated cargo 2
foreign-owned: 13 (Belgium 1, China 3, Nigeria 1, Singapore 1, South Korea 1, Syria 4, UAE 2)
registered in other countries: 6 (Mongolia 1, Sierra Leone 2, unknown 3) (2010)

Ports and terminals: *major seaport(s):* Ch'ongjin, Haeju, Hungnam (Hamhung), Namp'o, Senbong, Songnim, Sonbong (formerly Unggi), Wonsan

MILITARY

Military branches: North Korean People's Army: Ground Forces, Navy, Air Force; civil security forces (2005)

Military service age and obligation: 18 is presumed to be the legal minimum age for compulsory military service; 16-17 is the presumed legal minimum age for voluntary service (2012)

Manpower available for military service:
males age 16-49: 6,515,279
females age 16-49: 6,418,693 (2010 est.)

Manpower fit for military service:
males age 16-49: 4,836,567
females age 16-49: 5,230,137 (2010 est.)

Manpower reaching militarily significant age annually: *male:* 207,737
female: 204,553 (2010 est.)

TRANSNATIONAL ISSUES

Disputes—international: risking arrest, imprisonment, and deportation, tens of thousands of North Koreans cross into China to escape famine, economic privation, and political oppression; North Korea and China dispute the sovereignty of certain islands in Yalu and Tumen rivers; Military Demarcation Line within the 4-km-wide Demilitarized Zone has separated North from South Korea since 1953; periodic incidents in the Yellow Sea with South Korea which claims the Northern Limiting Line as a maritime boundary; North Korea supports South Korea in rejecting Japan's claim to Liancourt Rocks (Tok-do/Take-shima)

Refugees and internally displaced persons:
IDPs: undetermined (periodic flooding and famine during mid-1990s) (2007)

Trafficking in persons: *current situation:* North Korea is a source country for men, women, and children who are subjected to forced labor, forced marriage, and sex trafficking; in the recent past, many North Korean women and girls lured by promises of food, jobs, and freedom migrated to China illegally to escape poor social and economic conditions only to be forced into prostitution, marriage, or exploitative labor arrangements; North Koreans do not have a choice in the work the government assigns them and are not free to change jobs at will; many North Korean workers recruited to work abroad under bilateral contracts with foreign governments are subjected to forced labor and reportedly face government reprisals if they try to escape or complain to outsiders; thousands of North Koreans, including children, are subjected to forced labor in prison camps

tier rating: Tier 3—North Korea does not fully comply with minimum standards for the elimination of trafficking and is not making significant efforts to do so; the government has conducted no known investigations, prosecutions, or convictions of trafficking offenders or officials complicit in forced labor or forced prostitution; the government also has reported no efforts to identify or assist trafficking victims and continues to deny human trafficking is a problem; authorities provide no discernible protection services to trafficking victims and does not permit NGOs to assist victims (2013)

Illicit drugs: for years, from the 1970s into the 2000s, citizens of the Democratic People's Republic of (North) Korea (DPRK), many of them diplomatic employees of the government, were apprehended abroad while trafficking in narcotics, including two in Turkey in December 2004; police investigations in Taiwan and Japan in recent years have linked North Korea to large illicit shipments of heroin and methamphetamine, including an attempt by the North Korean merchant ship Pong Su to deliver 150 kg of heroin to Australia in April 2003

KOREA, SOUTH

INTRODUCTION

Background: An independent kingdom for much of its long history, Korea was occupied by Japan beginning in 1905 following the Russo-Japanese War. In 1910, Tokyo formally annexed the entire Peninsula. Korea regained its independence following Japan's surrender to the United States in 1945. After World War II, a democratic-based government (Republic of Korea, ROK) was set up in the southern half of the Korean Peninsula while a communist-style government was installed in the north (Democratic People's Republic of Korea, DPRK). During the Korean War (1950-53), US troops and UN forces fought alongside ROK soldiers to defend South Korea from a DPRK invasion supported by China and the Soviet Union. A 1953 armistice split the peninsula along a demilitarized zone at about the 38th parallel. PARK Chung-hee took over leadership of the country in a 1961 coup. During his regime, from 1961 to 1979, South Korea achieved rapid economic growth, with per capita income rising to roughly 17 times the level of North Korea. South Korea held its first free presidential election under a revised democratic constitution in 1987, with former ROK Army general ROH Tae-woo winning a close race. In 1993, KIM Young-sam (1993-98) became the first civilian president of South Korea's new democratic era. President KIM Dae-jung (1998-2003) won the Nobel Peace Prize in 2000 for his contributions to South Korean democracy and his "Sunshine" policy of engagement with North Korea. President PARK Geun-hye, daughter of former ROK President PARK Chung-hee, took office in February 2013 and is South Korea's first female leader. South Korea holds a non-permanent seat (2013-14) on the UN Security Council and will host the 2018 Winter Olympic Games. Serious tensions with North Korea have punctuated inter-Korean relations in recent years, including the North's attacks on a South Korean ship and island in 2010, nuclear and missile tests, and its temporary closure of the inter-Korean Kaesong Industrial Complex in 2013.

GEOGRAPHY

Location: Eastern Asia, southern half of the Korean Peninsula bordering the Sea of Japan and the Yellow Sea

Geographic coordinates: 37 00 N, 127 30 E

Map references: Asia

Area: *total:* 99,720 sq km
country comparison to the world: 109
land: 96,920 sq km
water: 2,800 sq km

Area—comparative: slightly smaller than Pennsylvania; slightly larger than Indiana

Land boundaries: *total:* 238 km
border countries: North Korea 238 km

Coastline: 2,413 km

Maritime claims: territorial sea: 12 nm; between 3 nm and 12 nm in the Korea Strait
contiguous zone: 24 nm
exclusive economic zone: 200 nm
continental shelf: not specified

Climate: temperate, with rainfall heavier in summer than winter

Terrain: mostly hills and mountains; wide coastal plains in west and south

Elevation extremes: *lowest point:* Sea of Japan 0 m
highest point: Halla-san 1,950 m

Natural resources: coal, tungsten, graphite, molybdenum, lead, hydropower potential

Land use: *arable land:* 14.93%
permanent crops: 2.06%

other: 83% (2011)

Irrigated land: 8,804 sq km (2003)

Total renewable water resources: 69.7 cu km (2011)

Freshwater withdrawal (domestic/industrial/agricultural): *total:* 25.47 cu km/yr (26%/12%/62%)
per capita: 548.7 cu m/yr (2003)

Natural hazards: occasional typhoons bring high winds and floods; low-level seismic activity common in southwest
volcanism: Halla (elev. 1,950 m) is considered historically active although it has not erupted in many centuries

Environment—current issues: air pollution in large cities; acid rain; water pollution from the discharge of sewage and industrial effluents; drift net fishing

Environment—international agreements: *party to:* Antarctic-Environmental Protocol, Antarctic-Marine Living Resources, Antarctic Treaty, Biodiversity, Climate Change, Climate Change-Kyoto Protocol, Desertification, Endangered Species, Environmental Modification, Hazardous Wastes, Law of the Sea, Marine Dumping, Ozone Layer Protection, Ship Pollution, Tropical Timber 83, Tropical Timber 94, Wetlands, Whaling
signed, but not ratified: none of the selected agreements

Geography—note: strategic location on Korea Strait

PEOPLE AND SOCIETY

Nationality: *noun:* Korean(s)
adjective: Korean

Ethnic groups: homogeneous (except for about 20,000 Chinese)

Languages: Korean, English (widely taught in junior high and high school)

Religions: Christian 31.6% (Protestant 24%, Roman Catholic 7.6%), Buddhist 24.2%, other or unknown 0.9%, none 43.3% (2010 survey)

Population: 49,039,986 (July 2014 est.)
country comparison to the world: 27

Age structure:
0-14 years: 14.1% (male 3,603,943/female 3,328,634)
15-24 years: 13.5% (male 3,515,271/female 3,113,257)
25-54 years: 47.3% (male 11,814,872/female 11,360,962)
55-64 years: 12.7% (male 3,012,051/female 3,081,480)
65 years and over: 12.3% (male 2,570,433/female 3,639,083) (2014 est.)

Dependency ratios:
total dependency ratio: 37.1 %
youth dependency ratio: 20.4 %
elderly dependency ratio: 16.7 %
potential support ratio: 6 (2013)
Median age: *total:* 40.2 years
male: 38.7 years
female: 41.6 years (2014 est.)

Population growth rate: 0.16% (2014 est.)
country comparison to the world: 183

Birth rate: 8.26 births/1,000 population (2014 est.)
country comparison to the world: 220

Death rate: 6.63 deaths/1,000 population (2014 est.)
country comparison to the world: 144

Net migration rate: 0 migrant(s)/1,000 population (2014 est.)
country comparison to the world: 85

Urbanization: *urban population:* 83.2% of total population (2011)
rate of urbanization: 0.71% annual rate of change (2010-15 est.)

Major urban areas—population: SEOUL (capital) 9.778 million; Busan (Pusan) 3.439 million; Incheon (Inch'on) 2.572 million; Daegu (Taegu) 2.458 million; Daejon (Taejon) 1.497 million (2009)

Sex ratio: *at birth:* 1.07 male(s)/female
0-14 years: 1.08 male(s)/female
15-24 years: 1.13 male(s)/female
25-54 years: 1.04 male(s)/female
55-64 years: 1 male(s)/female
65 years and over: 0.69 male(s)/female
total population: 1 male(s)/female (2014 est.)

Mother's mean age at first birth: 29.6 (2008 est.)

Maternal mortality rate: 16 deaths/100,000 live births (2010)
country comparison to the world: 143

Infant mortality rate: *total:* 3.93 deaths/1,000 live births
country comparison to the world: 200
male: 4.13 deaths/1,000 live births
female: 3.73 deaths/1,000 live births (2014 est.)

Life expectancy at birth: *total population:* 79.8 years
country comparison to the world: 39
male: 76.67 years
female: 83.13 years (2014 est.)

Total fertility rate: 1.25 children born/woman (2014 est.)
country comparison to the world: 220

Contraceptive prevalence rate: 80%
note: percent of women aged 15-44 (2009)

Health expenditures: 7.2% of GDP (2011)
country comparison to the world: 83

Physicians density: 2.02 physicians/1,000 population (2010)

Hospital bed density: 10.3 beds/1,000 population (2009)

Drinking water source:
improved:
urban: 99.7% of population
rural: 87.9% of population
total: 97.8% of population
unimproved:
urban: 0.3% of population
rural: 12.1% of population
total: 2.2% of population (2011 est.)

Sanitation facility access:
improved:
urban: 100% of population
rural: 100% of population
total: 100% of population
0% of population
0% of population
0% of population (2011 est.)

HIV/AIDS—adult prevalence rate: less than 0.1% (2009 est.)
country comparison to the world: 154

HIV/AIDS—people living with HIV/AIDS: 9,500 (2009 est.)
country comparison to the world: 107

HIV/AIDS—deaths: fewer than 500 (2009 est.)
country comparison to the world: 91

Obesity—adult prevalence rate: 7.7% (2008)
country comparison to the world: 139

Education expenditures: 5% of GDP (2009)
country comparison to the world: 75

Literacy: *definition:* age 15 and over can read and write
total population: 97.9%
male: 99.2%
female: 96.6% (2002)

School life expectancy (primary to tertiary education): *total:* 17 years
male: 18 years
female: 16 years (2011)

Unemployment, youth ages 15-24: *total:* 9%
country comparison to the world: 116
male: 9.7%
female: 8.5% (2012)

GOVERNMENT

Country name: *conventional long form:* Republic of Korea
conventional short form: South Korea
local long form: Taehan-min'guk
local short form: Han'guk
abbreviation: ROK

Government type: republic

Capital: *name:* Seoul

geographic coordinates: 37 33 N, 126 59 E
time difference: UTC+9 (14 hours ahead of Washington, DC during Standard Time)

Administrative divisions: 9 provinces (do, singular and plural), 6 metropolitan cities (gwangyoksi, singular and plural), 1 special city, and 1 special self-governing city
provinces: Chungbuk (North Chungcheong), Chungnam (South Chungcheong), Gangwon, Gyeonggi, Gyeongbuk (North Gyeongsang), Gyeongnam (South Gyeongsang), Jeju, Jeonbuk (North Jeolla), Jeonnam (South Jeolla)
metropolitan cities: Busan (Pusan), Daegu (Taegu), Daejeon (Taejon), Gwangju (Kwangju), Incheon (Inch'on), Ulsan
special city: Seoul
special self-governing city: Sejong

Independence: 15 August 1945 (from Japan)

National holiday: Liberation Day, 15 August (1945)

Constitution: effective 17 July 1948; amended several times, last in 1987 (2013)

Legal system: mixed legal system combining European civil law, Anglo-American law, and Chinese classical thought

International law organization participation: has not submitted an ICJ jurisdiction declaration; accepts ICCt jurisdiction

Suffrage: 19 years of age; universal

Executive branch: *chief of state:* President PARK Geun-hye (since 25 February 2013)
head of government: [vacant]; note—Prime Minister CHUNG Hong-won resigned 27 April 2014; Deputy Prime Minister HYUN Oh-seok (since 26 June 2013)
cabinet: State Council appointed by the president on the prime minister's recommendation (For more information visit the World Leaders website)
elections: president elected by popular vote for a single five-year term; PARK Geun-hye elected on 19 December 2012; next election to be held in December 2017; prime minister appointed by president with consent of National Assembly
election results: PARK Geun-Hye elected president on 19 December 2012; percent of vote—PARK Geun-Hye (NFP) 51.6%, MOON Jae-In (DUP) 48%, others 0.4%

Legislative branch: unicameral National Assembly or Gukhoe (300 seats; 246 members elected in single-seat constituencies, 54 elected by proportional representation; members serve four-year terms)
elections: last held on 11 April 2012 (next to be held in April 2016)
election results: percent of vote by party—NFP 42.8%, DUP 36.5%, UPP 10.3%, LFP 3.2%, others

7.2%; seats by party—NFP 152, DUP 127, UPP 13, LFP 5, independents 3
note: seats by negotiation group as of April 2014—NFP 156, NPAD 130, UPP 6, Justice Party 5, Independents 1; note—2 seats are vacant

Judicial branch: *highest court(s):* Supreme Court of South Korea (consists of a chief justice and 13 justices); Constitutional Court (consists of a court head and 8 justices)
judge selection and term of office: Supreme Court chief justice appointed by the president with the consent of the National Assembly; other justices appointed by the president upon the recommendation of the chief justice and consent of the National Assembly; position of the chief justice is a 6-year non-renewable term; other justices serve 6-year renewable terms; Constitutional Court justices appointed—3 by the president, 3 by the National Assembly, and 3 by the Supreme Court chief justice; court head serves until retirement at age 70, while other justices serve 6-year renewable terms with mandatory retirement at age 65
subordinate courts: High Courts; District Courts; Branch Courts (organized undeer the Branch Courts); specialized courts for family and administrative issues

Political parties and leaders: Justice Party [CHEON Ho-sun]; Liberty Forward Party or LFP (merged with NFP in October 2012); New Frontier Party (NFP) or Saenuri (formerly Grand National Party) [HWANG Woo-yea]; New Politics Alliance for Diplomacy or NPAD [KIM Han-gil and AHN Cheol-soo] (merger of the Democratic; Party or DP (formerly DUP) [Kim Han-gil] and the New Political Vision Party or NPVP [AHN Cheol-soo] in; March 2014); Progressive Justice Party or PJP [ROH Hoe-chan and CHO Joon-ho]; Unified Progressive Party or UPP [LEE Jung-hee]

Political pressure groups and leaders: Catholic Priests' Association for Justice; Citizen's Coalition for Economic Justice; Federation of Korean Industries; Federation of Korean Trade Unions; Korean Confederation of Trade Unions; Korean Veterans' Association; Lawyers for a Democratic Society; National Council of Churches; People's Solidarity for Participatory Democracy

International organization participation: ADB, AfDB (nonregional member), APEC, ARF, ASEAN (dialogue partner), Australia Group, BIS, CD, CICA, CP, EAS, EBRD, FAO, FATF, G-20, IADB, IAEA, IBRD, ICAO, ICC (national committees), ICRM, IDA, IEA, IFAD, IFC, IFRCS, IHO, ILO, IMF, IMO, IMSO, Interpol, IOC, IOM, IPU, ISO, ITSO, ITU, ITUC (NGOs), LAIA (observer), MIGA, MINURSO, NEA, NSG, OAS (observer), OECD, OPCW, OSCE (partner), Paris Club (associate), PCA, PIF (partner), SAARC (observer), SICA (observer), UN, UN Security Council (temporary), UNAMID, UNCTAD, UNESCO, UNHCR, UNIDO, UNIFIL, UNISFA, UNMIL, UNMISS, UNMOGIP, UNOCI, UNWTO, UPU, WCO, WHO, WIPO, WMO, WTO, ZC

Diplomatic representation in the US: *chief of mission:* Ambassador AHN Ho-young (since 7 June 2013)
chancery: 2450 Massachusetts Avenue NW, Washington, DC 20008
telephone: [1] (202) 939-5600
FAX: [1] (202) 797-0595
consulate(s) general: Agana (Guam), Atlanta, Boston, Chicago, Honolulu, Houston, Los Angeles, New York, San Francisco, Seattle
consulate(s): Anchorage (AK), Dallas, Hagatna (Guam)

Diplomatic representation from the US: *chief of mission:* Ambassador Sung Y. KIM (since 3 November 2011)
embassy: 188 Sejong-daero, Jongno-gu, Seoul 110-710
mailing address: US Embassy Seoul, Unit 15550, APO AP 96205-5550
telephone: [82] (2) 397-4114
FAX: [82] (2) 725-0152

Flag description: white with a red (top) and blue yin-yang symbol in the center; there is a different black trigram from the ancient I Ching (Book of Changes) in each corner of the white field; the South Korean national flag is called Taegukki; white is a traditional Korean color and represents peace and purity; the blue section represents the negative cosmic forces of the yin, while the red symbolizes the opposite positive forces of the yang; each trigram (kwae) denotes one of the four universal elements, which together express the principle of movement and harmony

National symbol(s): taegeuk (yin yang symbol)

National anthem: *name:* "Aegukga" (Patriotic Song)
lyrics/music: YUN Ch'i-Ho or AN Ch'ang-Ho/ AHN Eaktay
note: adopted 1948, well-known by 1910; both North Korea and South Korea's anthems share the same name and have a vaguely similar melody but have different lyrics

ECONOMY

Economy—overview: South Korea over the past four decades has demonstrated incredible growth and global integration to become a high-tech industrialized economy. In the 1960s, GDP per capita was comparable with levels in the poorer countries of Africa and Asia. In 2004, South Korea joined the trillion-dollar club of world economies, and is currently the world's 12th largest economy. Initially, a system of close government and business ties, including directed credit and import restrictions, made this success possible. The government promoted the import of raw materials and technology at the expense of consumer goods, and encouraged savings and investment over consumption. The Asian financial crisis of 1997-98 exposed longstanding weaknesses in South Korea's development model including high debt/equity ratios and massive short-term foreign borrowing. GDP plunged by 6.9% in 1998, and then recovered by 9% in 1999-2000. South Korea adopted numerous economic reforms following the crisis, including greater openness to foreign investment and imports. Growth moderated to about 4% annually between 2003 and 2007. South Korea's export focused economy was hit hard by the 2008 global economic downturn, but quickly rebounded in subsequent years, reaching 6.3% growth in 2010. The US-Korea Free Trade Agreement was ratified by both governments in 2011 and went into effect in March 2012. Throughout 2012 and 2013 the economy experienced sluggish growth because of market slowdowns in the United States, China, and the Eurozone. The administration in 2014 is likely to face the challenge of balancing heavy reliance on exports with developing domestic-oriented sectors, such as services. The South Korean economy's long term challenges include a rapidly aging population, inflexible labor market, dominance of large conglomerates (chaebols), and heavy reliance on exports, which comprise about half of GDP.

GDP (purchasing power parity): $1.666 trillion (2013 est.)
country comparison to the world: 13
$1.62 trillion (2012 est.)
$1.587 trillion (2011 est.)
note: data are in 2013 US dollars

GDP (official exchange rate): $1.198 trillion (2013 est.)

GDP—real growth rate: 2.8% (2013 est.)
country comparison to the world: 123
2% (2012 est.)
3.7% (2011 est.)

GDP—per capita (PPP): $33,200 (2013 est.)
country comparison to the world: 42
$32,400 (2012 est.)
$31,900 (2011 est.)
note: data are in 2013 US dollars

Gross national saving: 31.9% of GDP (2013 est.)
country comparison to the world: 21
31.4% of GDP (2012 est.)
31.9% of GDP (2011 est.)

GDP—composition, by end use:
household consumption: 53.1%
government consumption: 15.9%
investment in fixed capital: 27%
investment in inventories: 0.3%
exports of goods and services: 54.6%
imports of goods and services: -50.8% (2013 est.)

GDP—composition, by sector of origin:
agriculture: 2.6%
industry: 39.2%
services: 58.2% (2013 est.)

Agriculture—products: rice, root crops, barley, vegetables, fruit; cattle, pigs, chickens, milk, eggs; fish

Industries: electronics, telecommunications, automobile production, chemicals, shipbuilding, steel

Industrial production growth rate: 2.5% (2013 est.)
country comparison to the world: 121

Labor force: 25.86 million (2013 est.)
country comparison to the world: 25
Labor force—by occupation:
agriculture: 6.9%
industry: 23.6%
services: 69.4% (October 2013 est.)

Unemployment rate: 3.2% (2013 est.)
country comparison to the world: 26
3.2% (2012 est.)

Population below poverty line: 16% (2009 est.)
Household income or consumption by percentage share: *lowest 10%:* 6.4%
highest 10%: 37.7% (2011)

Distribution of family income—Gini index: 31.1 (2011 est.)
country comparison to the world: 112
35.8 (2000)

Budget: *revenues:* $296.1 billion
expenditures: $287.2 billion (2013 est.)

Taxes and other revenues: 24.7% of GDP (2013 est.)
country comparison to the world: 133

Budget surplus (+) or deficit (-):
0.7% of GDP (2013 est.)
country comparison to the world: 30

Public debt: 35.8% of GDP (2013 est.)
country comparison to the world: 105
35.5% of GDP (2012 est.)

Fiscal year: calendar year

Inflation rate (consumer prices): 1.1% (2013 est.)
country comparison to the world: 27
2.2% (2012 est.)

Central bank discount rate: 2.5% (31 December 2013)
country comparison to the world: 109
2.75% (31 December 2012)

Commercial bank prime lending rate: 4.7% (31 December 2013 est.)
country comparison to the world: 149
5.39% (31 December 2012 est.)

Stock of narrow money: $465.2 billion (31 December 2013 est.)
country comparison to the world: 12
$426 billion (31 December 2012 est.)

Stock of broad money: $1.764 trillion (31 December 2013 est.)
country comparison to the world: 10
$1.664 trillion (31 December 2012 est.)

Stock of domestic credit: $1.266 trillion (31 December 2013 est.)
country comparison to the world: 16
$1.183 trillion (31 December 2012 est.)

Market value of publicly traded shares: $1.068 trillion (31 December 2013 est.)
country comparison to the world: 11
$1.078 trillion (28 December 2012)
$904.7 billion (29December 2011 est.)

Current account balance: $55.69 billion (2013 est.)
country comparison to the world: 11
$43.34 billion (2012 est.)

Exports: $557.3 billion (2013 est.)
country comparison to the world: 7
$547.9 billion (2012 est.)

Exports—commodities: semiconductors, wireless telecommunications equipment, motor vehicles, auto parts, computers, display, home appliances, wire telecommunication equipment, steel, ships, petrochemicals

Exports—partners: China 24.5%, US 10.7%, Japan 7.1%, Hong Kong 6%, Singapore 4.2% (2012 est.)

Imports: $516.6 billion (2013 est.)
country comparison to the world: 8
$519.6 billion (2012 est.)

Imports—commodities: machinery, electronics and electronic equipment, oil, steel, optical instruments, transport equipment, organic chemicals, plastics

Imports—partners: China 15.6%, Japan 12.4%, US 8.3%, Saudi Arabia 7.6%, Australia 5%, Australia 4.4% (2012 est.)

Reserves of foreign exchange and gold: $341.8 billion (31 December 2013 est.)
country comparison to the world: 9
$327 billion (31 December 2012 est.)

Debt—external: $430.9 billion (31 December 2013 est.)
country comparison to the world: 28
$425.1 billion (31 December 2012 est.)

Stock of direct foreign investment—at home: $152.3 billion (31 December 2013 est.)
country comparison to the world: 30
$147.2 billion (31 December 2012 est.)

Stock of direct foreign investment—abroad: $223.2 billion (31 December 2013 est.)

country comparison to the world: 23
$196.4 billion (31 December 2012 est.)

Exchange rates: South Korean won (KRW) per US dollar—
1,107.3 (2013 est.)
1,126.47 (2012 est.)
1,156.1 (2010 est.)
1,276.93 (2009)
1,101.7 (2008)

ENERGY

Electricity—production: 485.1 billion kWh (2011 est.)
country comparison to the world: 1 1

Electricity—consumption: 449.5 billion kWh (2010 est.)
country comparison to the world: 11

Electricity—exports: 0 kWh (2012 est.)
country comparison to the world: 156

Electricity—imports: 0 kWh (2012 est.)
country comparison to the world: 163

Electricity—installed generating capacity: 84.66 million kW (2010 est.)
country comparison to the world: 14

Electricity—from fossil fuels: 74.5% of total installed capacity (2010 est.)
country comparison to the world: 102

Electricity—from nuclear fuels: 21.9% of total installed capacity (2010 est.)
country comparison to the world: 6

Electricity—from hydroelectric plants: 2% of total installed capacity (2010 est.)
country comparison to the world: 137

Electricity—from other renewable sources: 1.5% of total installed capacity (2010 est.)
country comparison to the world: 79

Crude oil—production: 0 bbl/day (2012 est.)
country comparison to the world: 184

Crude oil—exports: 0 bbl/day (2010 est.)
country comparison to the world: 139

Crude oil—imports: 2.59 million bbl/day (2012 est.)
country comparison to the world: 6

Crude oil—proved reserves: 0 bbl
country comparison to the world: 151

Refined petroleum products—production: 2.83 million bbl/day (2012 est.)
country comparison to the world: 7

Refined petroleum products—consumption: 2.301 million bbl/day (2012 est.)
country comparison to the world: 10

Refined petroleum products—exports: 944,700 bbl/day (2010 est.)
country comparison to the world: 9

Refined petroleum products—imports: 794,000 bbl/day (2010 est.)
country comparison to the world: 8

Natural gas—production: 424.9 million cu m (2012 est.)
country comparison to the world: 72

Natural gas—consumption: 49.66 billion cu m (2012 est.)
country comparison to the world: 17

Natural gas—exports: 0 cu m (2012 est.)
country comparison to the world: 130

Natural gas—imports: 47.34 billion cu m (2012 est.)
country comparison to the world: 9

Natural gas—proved reserves: 5.269 billion cu m (1 January 2013 es)
country comparison to the world: 95

Carbon dioxide emissions from consumption of energy: 611 million Mt (2011 est.)
country comparison to the world: 9

COMMUNICATIONS

Telephones—main lines in use: 30.1 million (2012)
country comparison to the world: 1 1

Telephones—mobile cellular: 53.625 million (2012)
country comparison to the world: 25

Telephone system: *general assessment:* excellent domestic and international services featuring rapid incorporation of new technologies
domestic: fixed-line and mobile-cellular services widely available with a combined telephone subscribership of roughly 170 per 100 persons; rapid assimilation of a full range of telecommunications technologies leading to a boom in e-commerce
international: country code—82; numerous submarine cables provide links throughout Asia, Australia, the Middle East, Europe, and US; satellite earth stations—66 (2011)

Broadcast media: multiple national TV networks with 2 of the 3 largest networks publicly operated; the largest privately owned network, Seoul Broadcasting Service (SBS), has ties with other commercial TV networks; cable and satellite TV subscription services available; publicly operated radio broadcast networks and many privately owned radio broadcasting networks, each with multiple affiliates, and independent local stations (2010)

Internet country code: .kr

Internet hosts: 315,697 (2012)
country comparison to the world: 62

Internet users: 39.4 million (2009)
country comparison to the world: 11

TRANSPORTATION

Airports: 111 (2013)
country comparison to the world: 5 3

Airports—with paved runways: *total:* 7 1
over 3,047 m: 4
2,438 to 3,047 m: 19
1,524 to 2,437 m: 12
914 to 1,523 m: 13
under 914 m: 23 (2013)

Airports—with unpaved runways: *total:* 4 0
914 to 1,523 m: 2
under 914 m: 38 (2013)

Heliports: 466 (2013)

Pipelines: gas 2,216 km; oil 16 km; refined products 889 km (2013)

Railways: *total:* 3,381 km
country comparison to the world: 52
standard gauge: 3,381 km 1.435-m gauge (1,843 km electrified) (2008)

Roadways: *total:* 104,983 km
country comparison to the world: 44
paved: 83,199 km (includes 3,779 km of expressways)
unpaved: 21,784 km (2009)

Waterways: 1,600 km (most navigable only by small craft) (2011)
country comparison to the world: 51

Merchant marine: *total:* 786
country comparison to the world: 14
by type: bulk carrier 191, cargo 235, carrier 8, chemical tanker 130, container 72, liquefied gas 44, passenger 5, passenger/cargo 15, petroleum tanker 55, refrigerated cargo 15, roll on/roll off 10, vehicle carrier 6
foreign-owned: 31 (China 6, France 2, Japan 14, Taiwan 1, US 8)
registered in other countries: 457 (Bahamas 1, Cambodia 10, Ghana 1, Honduras 6, Hong Kong 3, Indonesia 2, Kiribati 1, Liberia 2, Malta 2, Marshall Islands 41, North Korea 1, Panama 373, Philippines 1, Russia 1, Singapore 3, Tuvalu 1, unknown 8) (2010)

Ports and terminals: *major seaport(s)*: Incheon, Pohang, Busan, Ulsan, Yeosu
container port(s) (TEUs): Busan (16,163,842), Kwangyang (2,061,958), Incheon (1,924,644)

MILITARY

Military branches: Republic of Korea Army; Navy (includes Marine Corps); Air Force (2011)

Military service age and obligation: 20-30 years of age for compulsory military service, with middle school education required; conscript service obligation—21 months (Army, Marines), 23 months (Navy), 24 months (Air Force); 18-26 years of age for voluntary military service; women, in service since 1950, admitted to 7 service branches, including infantry, but excluded from artillery, armor, anti-air, and chaplaincy corps; HIV-positive individuals are exempt from military service (2012)

Manpower available for military service:
males age 16-49: 13,185,794
females age 16-49: 12,423,496 (2010 est.)

Manpower fit for military service:
males age 16-49: 10,864,566
females age 16-49: 10,168,709 (2010 est.)

Manpower reaching militarily significant age annually: *male:* 365,760
female: 321,225 (2010 est.)

Military expenditures: 2.8% of GDP (2012)
country comparison to the world: 26
2.77% of GDP (2011)
2.8% of GDP (2010)

TRANSNATIONAL ISSUES

Disputes—international: Military Demarcation Line within the 4-km-wide Demilitarized Zone has separated North from South Korea since 1953; periodic incidents with North Korea in the Yellow Sea over the Northern Limit Line, which South Korea claims as a maritime boundary; South Korea and Japan claim Liancourt Rocks (Tok-do/Takeshima), occupied by South Korea since 1954

Refugees and internally displaced persons:
stateless persons: 179 (2012)

KOSOVO

INTRODUCTION

Background: The central Balkans were part of the Roman and Byzantine Empires before ethnic Serbs migrated to the territories of modern Kosovo in the 7th century. During the medieval period, Kosovo became the center of a Serbian Empire and saw the construction of many important Serb religious sites, including many architecturally significant Serbian Orthodox monasteries. The defeat of Serbian forces at the Battle of Kosovo in 1389 led to five centuries of Ottoman rule during which large numbers of Turks and Albanians moved to Kosovo. By the end of the 19th century, Albanians replaced the Serbs as the dominant ethnic group in Kosovo. Serbia reacquired control over Kosovo from the Ottoman Empire during the First Balkan War of 1912. After World War II, Kosovo became an autonomous province of Serbia in the Socialist Federal Republic of Yugoslavia (S.F.R.Y.) with status almost equivalent to that of a republic under the 1974 S.F.R.Y. constitution. Despite legislative concessions, Albanian nationalism increased in the 1980s, which led to riots and calls for Kosovo's independence. At the same time, Serb nationalist leaders, such as Slobodan MILOSEVIC, exploited Kosovo Serb claims of maltreatment to secure votes from supporters, many of whom viewed Kosovo as their cultural heartland. Under MILOSEVIC's leadership, Serbia instituted a new constitution in 1989 that revoked Kosovo's status as an autonomous province of Serbia. Kosovo's Albanian leaders responded in 1991 by organizing a referendum that declared Kosovo independent. Under MILOSEVIC, Serbia carried out repressive measures against the Kosovar Albanians in the early 1990s as the unofficial Kosovo government, led by Ibrahim RUGOVA, used passive resistance in an attempt to try to gain international assistance and recognition of an independent Kosovo. Albanians dissatisfied with RUGOVA's passive strategy in the 1990s created the Kosovo Liberation Army and launched an insurgency. Starting in 1998, Serbian military, police, and paramilitary forces under MILOSEVIC conducted a brutal counterinsurgency campaign that resulted in massacres and massive expulsions of ethnic Albanians. Approximately 800,000 ethnic Albanians were forced from their homes in Kosovo during this time. International attempts to mediate the conflict failed, and MILOSEVIC's rejection of a proposed settlement led to a three-month NATO military operation against Serbia beginning in March 1999 that forced Serbia to agree to withdraw its military and police forces from Kosovo. UN Security Council Resolution 1244 (1999) placed Kosovo under a transitional administration, the UN Interim Administration Mission in Kosovo (UNMIK), pending a determination of Kosovo's future status. A UN-led process began in late 2005 to determine Kosovo's final status. The negotiations ran in stages between 2006 and 2007, but ended without agreement between Belgrade and Pristina. On 17 February 2008, the Kosovo Assembly declared Kosovo independent. Since then, over 100 countries have recognized Kosovo, and it has joined the International Monetary Fund, World Bank, European Bank for Reconstruction and Development, the Council of Europe Development Bank, and signed a framework agreement with the European Investment Bank (EIB). In October 2008, Serbia sought an advisory opinion from the International Court of Justice (ICJ) on the legality under international law of Kosovo's declaration of independence. The ICJ released the advisory opinion in July 2010 affirming that Kosovo's declaration of independence did not violate general principles of international law, UN Security Council Resolution 1244, or the Constitutive Framework. The opinion was closely tailored to Kosovo's unique history and circumstances. Serbia continues to reject Kosovo's independence, but the two countries reached an agreement to normalize their relations in April 2013 through EU-facilitated talks and are currently engaged in the implementation process.

GEOGRAPHY

Location: Southeast Europe, between Serbia and Macedonia

Geographic coordinates: 42 35 N, 21 00 E

Map references: Europe

Area: *total:* 10,887 sq km
country comparison to the world: 169
land: 10,887 sq km
water: 0 sq km

Area—comparative: slightly larger than Delaware

Land boundaries: *total:* 702 km
border countries: Albania 112 km, Macedonia 159 km, Montenegro 79 km, Serbia 352 km

Coastline: 0 km (landlocked)

Maritime claims: none (landlocked)

Climate: influenced by continental air masses resulting in relatively cold winters with heavy snowfall and hot, dry summers and autumns; Mediterranean and alpine influences create regional variation; maximum rainfall between October and December

Terrain: flat fluvial basin with an elevation of 400-700 m above sea level surrounded by several high mountain ranges with elevations of 2,000 to 2,500 m

Elevation extremes: *lowest point:* Drini i Bardhe/Beli Drim 297 m (located on the border with Albania)
highest point: Gjeravica/Deravica 2,656 m

Natural resources: nickel, lead, zinc, magnesium, lignite, kaolin, chrome, bauxite

PEOPLE AND SOCIETY

Nationality: *noun:* Kosovar (Albanian), Kosovac (Serbian)
adjective: Kosovar (Albanian), Kosovski (Serbian)
note: Kosovan, a neutral term, is sometimes also used as a noun or adjective

Ethnic groups: Albanians 92%, other (Serb, Bosniak, Gorani, Roma, Turk, Ashkali, Egyptian) 8% (2008)

Languages: Albanian (official), Serbian (official), Bosnian, Turkish, Roma

Religions: Muslim, Serbian Orthodox, Roman Catholic

Population: 1,859,203 (July 2014 est.)
country comparison to the world: 151

Age structure:
0-14 years: 26.3% (male 253,876/female 234,810)
15-24 years: 18.1% (male 176,738/female 159,455)
25-54 years: 41.5% (male 407,347/female 365,029)
55-64 years: 6.9% (male 65,762/female 67,243)
65 years and over: 6.9% (male 54,059/female 74,884) (2014 est.)

Median age: *total:* 27.8 years
male: 27.4 years
female: 28.2 years (2014 est.)

Sex ratio: *at birth:* 1.08 male(s)/female
0-14 years: 1.08 male(s)/female
15-24 years: 1.11 male(s)/female
25-54 years: 1.12 male(s)/female
55-64 years: 1.06 male(s)/female
65 years and over: 0.73 male(s)/female
total population: 1.06 male(s)/female (2014 est.)

Education expenditures: 4.3% of GDP (2008)
country comparison to the world: 98

Literacy: *definition:* age 15 and over can read and write
total population: 91.9%

male: 96.6%
female: 87.5% (2007 Census)

Unemployment, youth ages 15-24: *total:* 55.3%
country comparison to the world: 2
male: 52%
female: 63.8% (2012)

GOVERNMENT

Country name: *conventional long form:* Republic of Kosovo
conventional short form: Kosovo
local long form: Republika e Kosoves (Republika Kosovo)
local short form: Kosova (Kosovo)

Government type: republic

Capital: *name:* Pristina (Prishtine, Prishtina)
geographic coordinates: 42 40 N, 21 10 E
time difference: UTC+1 (6 hours ahead of Washington, DC during Standard Time)
daylight saving time: +1hr, begins last Sunday in March; ends last Sunday in October

Administrative divisions: 37 municipalities (komunat, singular—komuna (Albanian); opstine, singular—opstina (Serbian)); Decan (Decani), Dragash (Dragas), Ferizaj (Urosevac), Fushe Kosove (Kosovo Polje), Gjakove (Dakovica), Gjilan (Gnjilane), Gllogovc (Glogovac), Gracanice (Gracanica), Hani i Elezit (Deneral Jankovic), Istog (Istok), Junik, Kacanik, Kamenice/Dardana (Kamenica), Kline (Klina), Kllokot (Klokot), Leposaviq (Leposavic), Lipjan (Lipljan), Malisheve (Malisevo), Mamushe (Mamusa), Mitrovice (Mitrovica), Novoberde (Novo Brdo), Obiliq (Obilic), Partesh (Partes), Peje (Pec), Podujeve (Podujevo), Prishtine (Pristina), Prizren, Rahovec (Orahovac), Ranillug (Ranilug), Shterpce (Strpce), Shtime (Stimlje), Skenderaj (Srbica), Suhareke (Suva Reka), Viti (Vitina), Vushtrri (Vucitrn), Zubin Potok, Zvecan; note—a 38th municipality (Mitrovica e Veriut/Severna Mitrovica (Mitrovica North)) may have been created; when/if approved by the US Board on Geographic Names it will be added to the above listing

Independence: 17 February 2008 (from Serbia)

National holiday: Independence Day, 17 February (2008)

Constitution: previous 1974, 1990; latest (postindependence) draft finalized 2 April 2008, signed 7 April 2008, ratified 8 April 2008, entered into force 15 June 2008; amended 2013 (2013)

Legal system: evolving legal system; mixture of applicable Kosovo law, UNMIK laws and regulations, and applicable laws of the Former Socialist Republic of Yugoslavia that were in effect in Kosovo as of 22 March 1989

International law organization participation: has not submitted an ICJ jurisdiction declaration; non-party state to the ICCt

Suffrage: 18 years of age; universal

Executive branch: *chief of state:* President Atifete JAHJAGA (since 7 April 2011);
head of government: Prime Minister Hashim THACI (since 9 January 2008)
cabinet: ministers; elected by the Kosovo Assembly (For more information visit the World Leaders website)
elections: the president is elected for a five-year term by the Kosovo Assembly; election last held on 7 April 2011; note—the prime minister elected by the Kosovo Assembly
election results: Atifete JAHJAGA elected in one round (Atifete JAHJAGA 80, Suzana NOVOBERDALIU 10); Hashim THACI reelected prime minister by the Assembly

Legislative branch: unicameral national Assembly (120 seats; 100 seats directly elected, 10 seats guaranteed for ethnic Serbs, 10 seats guaranteed for other ethnic minorities; members to serve three-year terms)
elections: last held on 12 December 2010 with runoff elections in a few municipalities in January 2011 (next expected to be held in June 2014)
election results: percent of vote by party/coalition—PDK 32.1%, LDK 24.7%, VV 12.7%, AAK 11.0%, KKR 7.3%, SLS 2.1%, KDTP 1.2%, and others 8.9; seats by party/coalition—PDK 34, LDK 27, VV 14, AAK 12, KKR 8, SLS 8, JSL 4, KDTP 3, VAKAT 2, PDAK 1, NDS 1, BSDAK 1, IRDK, 1, PAI 1, SDSKIM 1, GIG 1, PREBK 1

Judicial branch: *highest court(s):* Supreme Court (consists of the court president and at least 15 percent of judges to reflect Kosovo's territorial ethnic composition); Constitutional Court (consists of the court president, vice president, and 7 judges) note—Kosovo initiated a new judicial system in January 2013
judge selection and term of office: Supreme Court judges nominated by the Kosovo Judicial Council, an independent body staffed by judges and lay members, and also responsible for overall administration of Kosovo's judicial system; judges appointed by the president of the Republic of Kosovo; judges appointed until mandatory retirement age; Constitutional Court members nominated by the Kosovo Assembly and appointed by the president of the republic to serve single, 9-year terms
subordinate courts: Court of Appeals (organized into 4 departments: General, Serious Crime, Commercial Matters), and Administrative Matters; Basic Court (located in 9 municipalities, each with several branches)

Political parties and leaders: Albanian Christian Democratic Party of Kosovo or PSHDK [Uke BERISHA]; Alliance for a New Kosovo or AKR [Behgjet PACOLLI]; Alliance for the Future of Kosovo or AAK [Ramush HARADINAJ]; Ashkali Party for Integration or PAI; Bosniak Party of Democratic Action of Kosovo or BSDAK; Citizens' Initiative of Gora or GIG [Murselj HALJILJI]; Coalition for New Kosovo or KKR (includes AKR, Justice Party, Social Democratic Party, Pensionists and; Disabled Party, Pensionists of Kosovo, PNDSH, and the Green Party of Kosovo); Democratic Action Party or SDA [Numan BALIC]; Democratic League of Dardania or LDD [Nexhat DACI]; Democratic League of Kosovo or LDK [Isa MUSTAFA]; Democratic Party of Ashkali of Kosovo or PDAK [Berat QERIMI]; Democratic Party of Kosovo or PDK [Hashim THACI]; Independent Liberal Party or SLS [Slobadan PETROVIC]; Kosovo Democratic Turkish Party or KDTP [Mahir YAGCILAR]; Movement for Self-Determination (Vetevendosje) or VV [Albin KURTI]; Movement for Unification or LB [Avni KLINAKU]; National Democratic Party of Albania or PNDSH [Bujar ABDULLAHU]; New Democratic Initiative of Kosovo or IRDK [Xhevdet NEZIRAJ]; New Democratic Party or NDS [Predrag JOVIC]; Serb People's Party or SNS [Mihailo SCEPANOVIC]; Serb People's Party of Kosovo or SNPK; Serbian Democratic Party of Kosovo and Metohija or SDSKiM [Sasa DJOKIC]; Serbian Kosovo and Metohija Party or SKMS [Dragisa MIRIC]; Serbian National Council of Northern Kosovo and Metohija or SNV [Milan IVANOVIC]; Serbian Social Democratic Party or SSDS; Social Democratic Party of Kosovo or PSDK; Socialist Party of Kosovo or PSK [Ilaz KADOLLI]; Union of Independent Social Democrats of Kosovo and Metohija or SNSKiM [Ljubisa ZIVIC]; United Roma Party of Kosovo or PREBK [Haxhi Zylfi MERXHA]; United Serb List or JSL; Vakat Coalition or VAKAT [Sadik IDRIZI]

Political pressure groups and leaders: Council for the Defense of Human Rights and Freedom (human rights); Organization for Democracy, Anti-Corruption and Dignity Rise! [Avni ZOGIANI]; Serb National Council (SNV); The Speak Up Movement [Ramadan ILAZI]

International organization participation: IBRD, IDA, IFC, IMF, ITUC (NGOs), MIGA

Diplomatic representation in the US: *chief of mission:* Ambassador Akan ISMAILI (since 23 April 2012)
chancery: 1101 30th Street NW, Suites 330/340, Washington, DC 20007
telephone: 202-380-3581
FAX: 202-380-3628
consulate(s) general: New York

Diplomatic representation from the US: *chief of mission:* Ambassador Tracey Ann JACOBSON (since 26 July 2012)
embassy: Arberia/Dragodan, Nazim Hikmet 30, Pristina, Kosovo
mailing address: use embassy street address
telephone: [381] 38 59 59 3000
FAX: [381] 38 549 890

Flag description: centered on a dark blue field is the geographical shape of Kosovo in a gold color surmounted by six white, five-pointed stars arrayed in a slight arc; each star represents one of the major ethnic groups of Kosovo: Albanians, Serbs, Turks, Gorani, Roma, and Bosniaks

National anthem: *name:* "Europe"
lyrics/music: none/Mendi MENGJIQI
note: adopted 2008; Kosovo chose to not include lyrics in its anthem so as not to offend minority ethnic groups in the country

ECONOMY

Economy—overview: Kosovo's economy has shown significant progress in transitioning to a market-based system and maintaining macroeconomic stability, but it is still highly dependent on the international community and the diaspora for financial and technical assistance. Kosovo's citizens are the poorest in Europe with a per capita GDP (PPP) of $7,600 in 2013. An unemployment rate of 45% encourages emigration and fuels a significant informal, unreported economy. Remittances from the diaspora—located mainly in Germany, Switzerland, and the Nordic countries—are estimated to account for about 15% of GDP, and donor-financed activities and aid for approximately 10%. Most of Kosovo's population lives in rural towns outside of the capital, Pristina. Inefficient, near-subsistence farming is common—the result of small plots, limited mechanization, and lack of technical expertise. With international assistance, Kosovo has been able to privatize a majority of its state-owned-enterprises. Minerals and metals—including lignite, lead, zinc, nickel, chrome, aluminum, magnesium, and a wide variety of construction materials—once formed the backbone of industry, but output has declined because of ageing equipment and insufficient investment. A limited and unreliable electricity supply due to technical and financial problems is a major impediment to economic development, but Kosovo has received technical assistance to help improve accounting and controls and, in 2012, privatized its distribution network. The US Government is cooperating with the Ministry for

Energy and Mines and the World Bank to prepare commercial tenders for the construction of a new power plant, rehabilitation of an old plant, and the development of a coal mine that could supply both. In July 2008, Kosovo received pledges of $1.9 billion from 37 countries in support of its reform priorities, but the global financial crisis has limited this assistance and also negatively affected remittance inflows. In June 2009, Kosovo joined the World Bank and International Monetary Fund, and Kosovo began servicing its share of the former Yugoslavia's debt. In order to help integrate Kosovo into regional economic structures, UNMIK signed (on behalf of Kosovo) its accession to the Central Europe Free Trade Area (CEFTA) in 2006. Serbia and Bosnia previously had refused to recognize Kosovo's customs stamp or extend reduced tariff privileges for Kosovo products under CEFTA, but both countries resumed trade with Kosovo in 2011. The official currency of Kosovo is the euro, but the Serbian dinar is also used illegally in Serb enclaves. Kosovo's tie to the euro has helped keep core inflation low. Kosovo maintained a budget surplus until 2011, when government expenditures climbed sharply. In 2013 Kosovo signed a Free Trade Agreement with Turkey and is negotiating liberalization of trade with EU as part of a Stabilization and Association Agreement.

GDP (purchasing power parity): $14.11 billion (2013 est.)
country comparison to the world: 146
$13.77 billion (2012 est.)
$13.43 billion (2011 est.)
note: data are in 2013 US dollars

GDP (official exchange rate): $7.15 billion (2013 est.)

GDP—real growth rate: 2.5% (2013 est.)
country comparison to the world: 129
2.5% (2012 est.)
4.4% (2011 est.)

GDP—per capita (PPP): $7,600 (2013 est.)
country comparison to the world: 136
$7,500 (2012 est.)
$7,400 (2011 est.)
note: data are in 2013 US dollars

Gross national saving: 12.7% of GDP
country comparison to the world: 122
12.5% of GDP
12.4% of GDP

GDP—composition, by end use:
household consumption: 90.5%
government consumption: 16%
investment in fixed capital: 28.2%
investment in inventories: 3%
exports of goods and services: 18.8%
imports of goods and services: -53.9% (2012 est.)

GDP—composition, by sector of origin:
agriculture: 12.9%
industry: 22.6%
services: 64.5% (2009 est.)

Agriculture—products: wheat, corn, berries, potatoes, peppers, fruit; dairy, livestock; fish

Industries: mineral mining, construction materials, base metals, leather, machinery, appliances, foodstuffs and beverages, textiles

Labor force: 800,000
country comparison to the world: 149
note: includes those estimated to be employed in the grey economy (2011 est.)

Labor force—by occupation:
agriculture: 23.6%
industry: NA%
services: NA% (2010)

Unemployment rate: 30.9% (2013 est.)
country comparison to the world: 185
45% (1)
note: Kosovo has a large informal sector that may not be reflected in these data

Population below poverty line: 30% (2013 est.)

Distribution of family income—Gini index: 30 (FY05/06)
country comparison to the world: 120

Budget: *revenues:* $1.916 billion
expenditures: $2.048 billion (2013 est.)

Taxes and other revenues: 26.8% of GDP (2013 est.)
country comparison to the world: 110

Budget surplus (+) or deficit (-):
-1.8% of GDP (2013 est.)
country comparison to the world: 81

Public debt: 9.1% of GDP (2013)
country comparison to the world: 149
8.4% of GDP (2012)

Inflation rate (consumer prices): 1.8% (2013 est.)
country comparison to the world: 54
2.5% (2012 est.)

Commercial bank prime lending rate: 12.8% (30 June 2013 est.)
country comparison to the world: 54
13.7% (31 December 2012 est.)

Stock of broad money: $2.773 billion
country comparison to the world: 145
$2.637 billion

Stock of domestic credit: $2.505 billion
country comparison to the world: 131
$2.445 billion

Current account balance: -$919.7 million (2013 est.)
country comparison to the world: 118
-$1.083 billion (2012 est.)

Exports: $408 million (2013 est.)
country comparison to the world: 178
$382.8 million (2012 est.)

Exports—commodities: mining and processed metal products, scrap metals, leather products, machinery, appliances, prepared foodstuffs, beverages and tobacco, vegetable products, textile and textile articles

Exports—partners: Italy 25.8%, Albania 14.6%, Macedonia 9.6%, China 5.5%, Gernamy 5.4%, Switzerland 5.4%, Turkey 4.1% (2012 est.)

Imports: $3.398 billion (2013 est.)
country comparison to the world: 141
$3.477 billion (2012 est.)

Imports—commodities: foodstuffs, livestock, wood, petroleum, chemicals, machinery, minerals, textiles, stone, ceramic and glass products, electrical equipment

Imports—partners: Germany 11.9%, Macedonia 11.5%, Serbia 11.1%, Italy 8.5%, Turkey 9%, China 6.4%, Albania 4.4% (2012 est.)

Reserves of foreign exchange and gold: $NA

Debt—external: $448.2 million (2013 est.)
country comparison to the world: 176
$466 million (2012 est.)

Stock of direct foreign investment—at home:
$21.2 billion (31 December 2013 est.)
country comparison to the world: 71
$25.8 million (31 December 2012 est.)

Exchange rates: euros (EUR) per US dollar—
0.7634 (2013 est.)
0.7752 (2012 est.)
0.755 (2010 est.)
0.7198 (2009 est.)
0.6827 (2008 est.)

ENERGY

Electricity—production: 5.847 billion kWh (2012)
country comparison to the world: 113

Electricity—consumption: 5.467 billion kWh (2012)
country comparison to the world: 112

Electricity—exports: 371.3 million kWh
country comparison to the world: 67

Electricity—imports: 625.1 million kWh
country comparison to the world: 72

Electricity—installed generating capacity: 1.526 million kW
country comparison to the world: 115

Crude oil—proved reserves: NA bbl

Refined petroleum products—production: 0 bbl/day (2007)
country comparison to the world: 160

Refined petroleum products—consumption: NA bbl/day (2011 est.)

Natural gas—production: 0 cu m (2007)
country comparison to the world: 150

Natural gas—consumption: 0 cu m (2007)
country comparison to the world: 161

Natural gas—proved reserves: NA cu m

COMMUNICATIONS

Telephones—main lines in use: 106,300 (2006)
country comparison to the world: 144

Telephones—mobile cellular: 562,000 (2007)
country comparison to the world: 164

TRANSPORTATION

Airports: 6 (2013)
country comparison to the world: 173

Airports—with paved runways: *total:* 3
2,438 to 3,047 m: 1
1,524 to 2,437 m: 1
under 914 m: 1 (2013)

Airports—with unpaved runways: *total:* 3
under 914 m: 3 (2013)

Heliports: 2 (2013)

Railways: *total:* 430 km
country comparison to the world: 114
standard gauge: 430 km 1.435-m gauge (2007)

Roadways: *total:* 6,955 km
country comparison to the world: 146
paved: 1,843 km (includes 38 km of expessways)
unpaved: 5,112 km (2012)

MILITARY

Military branches: Kosovo Security Force (FSK) (2010)

Manpower fit for military service:
males age 16-49: 430,926
females age 16-49: 389,614 (2010 est.)

TRANSNATIONAL ISSUES

Disputes—international: Serbia with several other states protest the US and other states'

recognition of Kosovo's declaration of its status as a sovereign and independent state in February 2008; ethnic Serbian municipalities along Kosovo's northern border challenge final status of Kosovo-Serbia boundary; several thousand NATO-led Kosovo Force peacekeepers under United Nations Interim Administration Mission in Kosovo authority continue to keep the peace within Kosovo between the ethnic Albanian majority and the Serb minority in Kosovo; Kosovo and Macedonia completed demarcation of their boundary in September 2008

Refugees and internally displaced persons: *IDPs:* 17,853 (primarily ethnic Serbs displaced during the 1998-1999 war; IDPs consist of an estimated 54% Serbs, 40% Albanians, and 5% Roma, Ashkalis, and Egyptians) (2012)

KUWAIT

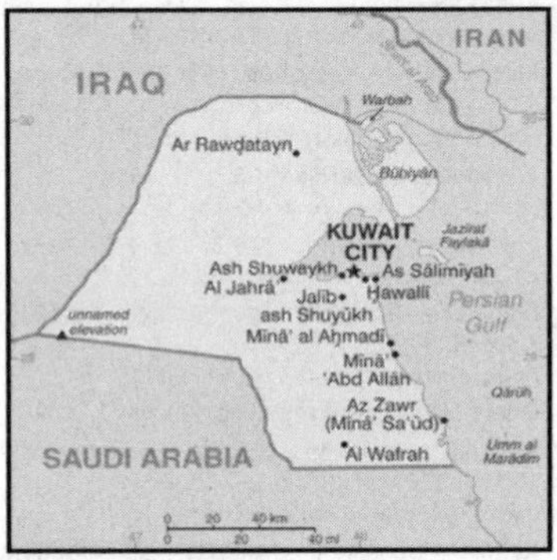

INTRODUCTION

Background: Britain oversaw foreign relations and defense for the ruling Kuwaiti AL-SABAH dynasty from 1899 until independence in 1961. Kuwait was attacked and overrun by Iraq on 2 August 1990. Following several weeks of aerial bombardment, a US-led, UN coalition began a ground assault on 23 February 1991 that liberated Kuwait in four days. Kuwait spent more than $5 billion to repair oil infrastructure damaged during 1990-91. The AL-SABAH family has ruled since returning to power in 1991 and reestablished an elected legislature that in recent years has become increasingly assertive. The country witnessed the historic election in 2009 of four women to its National Assembly. Amid the 2010-11 uprisings and protests across the Arab world, stateless Arabs, known as bidun, staged small protests in February and March 2011 demanding citizenship, jobs, and other benefits available to Kuwaiti nationals. Youth activist groups—supported by opposition legislators—rallied repeatedly in 2011 for the prime minister's dismissal amid allegations of widespread government corruption. Demonstrators forced the prime minister to resign in late 2011. In late 2012, Kuwait witnessed unprecedented protests in response to the Amir's changes to the electoral law by decree reducing the number of votes per person from four to one. The opposition, led by a coalition of Sunni Islamists, tribalists, some liberals, and myriad youth groups, largely boycotted legislative elections in 2012 and 2013 ushering in legislatures more amenable to the government's agenda. Since 2006, the Amir has dissolved the National Assembly on five occasions (the Constitutional Court annulled the Assembly in June 2012 and again in June 2013) and shuffled the cabinet over a dozen times, usually citing political stagnation and gridlock between the legislature and the government.

GEOGRAPHY

Location: Middle East, bordering the Persian Gulf, between Iraq and Saudi Arabia

Geographic coordinates: 29 30 N, 45 45 E

Map references: Middle East

Area: *total:* 17,818 sq km
country comparison to the world: 158
land: 17,818 sq km
water: 0 sq km

Area—comparative: slightly smaller than New Jersey

Land boundaries: *total:* 462 km
border countries: Iraq 240 km, Saudi Arabia 222 km

Coastline: 499 km

Maritime claims: *territorial sea:* 12 nm

Climate: dry desert; intensely hot summers; short, cool winters

Terrain: flat to slightly undulating desert plain

Elevation extremes: *lowest point:* Persian Gulf 0 m
highest point: unnamed elevation 306 m

Natural resources: petroleum, fish, shrimp, natural gas

Land use: *arable land:* 0.62%
permanent crops: 0.28%
other: 99.1% (2011)

Irrigated land: 86 sq km (2007)

Total renewable water resources: 0.02 cu km (2011)

Freshwater withdrawal (domestic/industrial/agricultural): *total:* 0.91 cu km/yr (47%/2%/51%)
per capita: 441.2 cu m/yr (2005)

Natural hazards: sudden cloudbursts are common from October to April and bring heavy rain, which can damage roads and houses; sandstorms and dust storms occur throughout the year but are most common between March and August

Environment—current issues: limited natural freshwater resources; some of world's largest and most sophisticated desalination facilities provide much of the water; air and water pollution; desertification

Environment—international agreements: *party to:* Biodiversity, Climate Change, Climate Change-Kyoto Protocol, Desertification, Endangered Species, Environmental Modification, Hazardous Wastes, Law of the Sea, Ozone Layer Protection
signed, but not ratified: Marine Dumping

Geography—note: strategic location at head of Persian Gulf

PEOPLE AND SOCIETY

Nationality: *noun:* Kuwaiti(s)
adjective: Kuwaiti

Ethnic groups: Kuwaiti 31.3%, other Arab 27.9%, Asian 37.8%, African 1.9%, other 0.6% (includes European, North American, South American, and Australian) (2013 est.)

Languages: Arabic (official), English widely spoken

Religions: Muslim (official) 76.7%, Christian 17.3%, other and unspecified 5.9%

note: represents the total population; about 69% of the population consists of immigrants (2013 est.)

Population: 2,742,711 (July 2014 est.)
country comparison to the world: 141
note: Kuwait's Public Authority for Civil Information estimates the country's total population to be 3,996,899 for 2014, with immigrants accounting for almost 69%

Age structure:
0-14 years: 25.4% (male 363,001/female 334,851)
15-24 years: 15.3% (male 230,628/female 188,892)
25-54 years: 52.3% (male 910,832/female 524,690)
55-64 years: 2.2% (male 73,816/female 54,678)
65 years and over: 2.1% (male 29,312/female 32,011) (2014 est.)

Dependency ratios:
total dependency ratio: 37.2 %
youth dependency ratio: 34 %
elderly dependency ratio: 3.2 %
potential support ratio: 31.3 (2013)

Median age: *total:* 28.9 years
male: 30.1 years
female: 26.8 years (2014 est.)

Population growth rate: 1.7%
country comparison to the world: 73
note: this rate reflects a return to pre-Gulf crisis immigration of expatriates (2014 est.)

Birth rate: 20.26 births/1,000 population (2014 est.)
country comparison to the world: 84

Death rate: 2.16 deaths/1,000 population (2014 est.)
country comparison to the world: 224

Net migration rate: -1.11 migrant(s)/1,000 population (2014 est.)
country comparison to the world: 151

Urbanization: *urban population:* 98.3% of total population (2011)
rate of urbanization: 2.42% annual rate of change (2010-15 est.)

Major urban areas—population: KUWAIT (capital) 2.23 million (2009)

Sex ratio: *at birth:* 1.05 male(s)/female
0-14 years: 1.08 male(s)/female
15-24 years: 1.22 male(s)/female
25-54 years: 1.74 male(s)/female
55-64 years: 1.42 male(s)/female
65 years and over: 0.96 male(s)/female
total population: 1.43 male(s)/female (2014 est.)

Maternal mortality rate: 14 deaths/100,000 live births (2010)
country comparison to the world: 145

Infant mortality rate: *total:* 7.51 deaths/1,000 live births
country comparison to the world: 159
male: 7.26 deaths/1,000 live births
female: 7.76 deaths/1,000 live births (2014 est.)

Life expectancy at birth: *total population:* 77.64 years
country comparison to the world: 64

male: 76.37 years
female: 78.96 years (2014 est.)

Total fertility rate: 2.53 children born/woman (2014 est.)
country comparison to the world: 79

Contraceptive prevalence rate: 52% (1999)

Health expenditures: 2.7% of GDP (2011)
country comparison to the world: 182

Physicians density: 1.79 physicians/1,000 population (2009)

Hospital bed density: 2 beds/1,000 population (2009)

Drinking water source:
improved:
urban: 99% of population
rural: 99% of population
total: 99% of population
unimproved:
urban: 1% of population
rural: 1% of population
total: 1% of population (2011 est.)

Sanitation facility access: improved:
urban: 100% of population
rural: 100% of population
total: 100% of population
0% of population
0% of population
0% of population (2011 est.)

HIV/AIDS—adult prevalence rate: 0.1% (2001 est.)
country comparison to the world: 155

HIV/AIDS—people living with HIV/AIDS: NA

HIV/AIDS—deaths: NA

Obesity—adult prevalence rate: 42% (2008)
country comparison to the world: 10

Children under the age of 5 years underweight: 2.2% (2012)
country comparison to the world: 120

Education expenditures: 3.8% of GDP (2006)
country comparison to the world: 116

Literacy: *definition:* age 15 and over can read and write
total population: 93.9%
male: 95%
female: 91.8% (2008 est.)

School life expectancy (primary to tertiary education): *total:* 15 years
male: 14 years
female: 15 years (2004)

Unemployment, youth ages 15-24: *total:* 11.3%
country comparison to the world: 103
male: 11.8%
female: 10% (2005)

GOVERNMENT

Country name: *conventional long form:* State of Kuwait
conventional short form: Kuwait
local long form: Dawlat al Kuwayt
local short form: Al Kuwayt

Government type: constitutional emirate

Capital: *name:* Kuwait City
geographic coordinates: 29 22 N, 47 58 E
time difference: UTC+3 (8 hours ahead of Washington, DC during Standard Time)

Administrative divisions: 6 governorates (muhafazat, singular—muhafazah); Al Ahmadi, Al 'Asimah, Al Farwaniyah, Al Jahra', Hawalli, Mubarak al Kabir

Independence: 19 June 1961 (from the UK)

National holiday: National Day, 25 February (1950)

Constitution: approved and promulgated 11 November 1962 (2013)

Legal system: mixed legal system consisting of English common law, French civil law, and Islamic religious law International organization participation: has not submitted an ICJ jurisdiction declaration; non-party state to the ICCt

Suffrage: 21 years of age; universal; note—members of the military or police are by law not allowed to vote; all voters must have been citizens for 20 years

Executive branch: *chief of state:* Amir SABAH al-Ahmad al-Jabir al-Sabah (since 29 January 2006); Crown Prince NAWAF al-Ahmad al-Jabir al-Sabah (born 25 June 1937)
head of government: Prime Minister JABIR AL-MUBARAK al-Hamad al-Sabah (since 30 November 2011); First Deputy Prime Minister SABAH Khaled al-Hamad al-Sabah; Deputy Prime Ministers KHALD al-Jarrah al-Sabah, MUHAMMAD AL-KHALID al-Hamad al-Sabah, Abdulmohsen MUDEJ
cabinet: Council of Ministers appointed by the prime minister and approved by the amir; new cabinet formed in January 2014 (For more information visit the World Leaders website)
elections: none; the amir is chosen from within the ruling family and confirmed by parliamentary vote; the amir appoints the prime minister and deputy prime ministers

Legislative branch: unicameral National Assembly or Majlis al-Umma (65 seats; 50 members elected by popular vote to serve 4-year terms and 16 cabinet ministers serve as ex officio members on most issues, two of whom are also elected MPs, appointed by the prime minister)
elections: last held 27 July 2013 (next to be held in July 2017)
election results: voter turnout 52%; seats won—pro-government 30, liberals 9, Shiites 8, Sunni 3

Judicial branch: *highest court(s):* Constitutional Court (five judges); Supreme Court or Court of Cassation (organized into several circuits, each with five judges)
judge selection and term of office: all Kuwaiti judges appointed by the Amir upon recommendation of the Supreme Judicial Council, a consultative body comprised of Kuwaiti judges and Ministry of Justice officials
subordinate courts: High Court of Appeal; Court of First Instance; Summary Court

Political parties and leaders: none; while the formation of political parties is not permitted, they are not forbidden by law

Political pressure groups and leaders: *other:* Islamists; merchants; political groups; secular liberals and pro-governmental deputies; Shia activists; tribal groups

International organization participation: ABEDA, AfDB (nonregional member), AFESD, AMF, BDEAC, CAEU, CD, FAO, G-77, GCC, IAEA, IBRD, ICAO, ICC (national committees), ICRM, IDA, IDB, IFAD, IFC, IFRCS, IHO, ILO, IMF, IMO, IMSO, Interpol, IOC, IPU, ISO, ITSO, ITU, ITUC (NGOs), LAS, MIGA, NAM, OAPEC, OIC, OPCW, OPEC, Paris Club (associate), PCA, UN, UNCTAD, UNESCO, UNIDO, UNRWA, UNWTO, UPU, WCO, WFTU (NGOs), WHO, WIPO, WMO, WTO

Diplomatic representation in the US: *chief of mission:* Ambassador SALIM al-Abdallah al-Jabir al-Sabah (since 10 October 2001)
chancery: 2940 Tilden Street NW, Washington, DC 20008
telephone: [1] (202) 966-0702
FAX: [1] (202) 364-2868
consulate(s) general: Los Angeles

Diplomatic representation from the US: *chief of mission:* Ambassador Matthew H. TUELLER (since 9 September 2011)
embassy: Bayan 36302, Block 13, Al-Masjed Al-Aqsa Street (near the Bayan palace), Kuwait City
mailing address: P. O. Box 77 Safat 13001 Kuwait; or PSC 1280 APO AE 09880-9000
telephone: [965] 2259-1001
FAX: [965] 2538-0282

Flag description: three equal horizontal bands of green (top), white, and red with a black trapezoid based on the hoist side; colors and design are based on the Arab Revolt flag of World War I; green represents fertile fields, white stands for purity, red denotes blood on Kuwaiti swords, black signifies the defeat of the enemy

National symbol(s): golden falcon

National anthem: *name:* "Al-Nasheed Al-Watani" (National Anthem)
lyrics/music: Ahmad MUSHARI al-Adwani/Ibrahim Nasir al-SOULA
note: adopted 1978; the anthem is only used on formal occasions

ECONOMY

Economy—overview: Kuwait has a geographically small, but wealthy, relatively open economy with crude oil reserves of about 102 billion barrels—more than 6% of world reserves. Petroleum accounts for nearly half of GDP, 95% of export revenues, and 95% of government income. Kuwaiti officials have committed to increasing oil production to 4 million barrels per day by 2020. Budget surpluses have stayed around 30% of GDP, which has led to higher budget expenditures, particularly wage hikes for many public sector employees, as well as increased allotments to Kuwait's Future Generations Fund. Kuwait has done little to diversify its economy, in part, because of this positive fiscal situation, and, in part, due to the poor business climate and the historically acrimonious relationship between the National Assembly and the executive branch, which has stymied most movement on economic reforms. In 2010, Kuwait passed an economic development plan that pledges to spend up to $130 billion over five years to diversify the economy away from oil, attract more investment, and boost private sector participation in the economy, though much of these funds have yet to be allocated.

GDP (purchasing power parity): $165.8 billion (2013 est.)
country comparison to the world: 61
$159.6 billion (2012 est.)
$144.8 billion (2011 est.)
note: data are in 2013 US dollars

GDP (official exchange rate): $179.5 billion (2013 est.)

GDP—real growth rate: 2.3% (2013 est.)
country comparison to the world: 135
8.3% (2012 est.)
10.2% (2011 est.)

GDP—per capita (PPP): $42,100 (2013 est.)
country comparison to the world: 23
$41,800 (2012 est.)
$39,200 (2011 est.)
note: data are in 2013 US dollars

Gross national saving: 54.8% of GDP (2013 est.)
country comparison to the world: 2
58.9% of GDP (2012 est.)

58.2% of GDP (2011 est.)

GDP—composition, by end use:
household consumption: 23.9%
government consumption: 16.4%
investment in fixed capital: 16.2%
investment in inventories: 0%
exports of goods and services: 68.5%
imports of goods and services: -25.1% (2013 est.)

GDP—composition, by sector of origin:
agriculture: 0.3%
industry: 50.6%
services: 49.1% (2013 est.)

Agriculture—products: fish

Industries: petroleum, petrochemicals, cement, shipbuilding and repair, water desalination, food processing, construction materials

Industrial production growth rate: 4.1% (2013 est.)
country comparison to the world: 70

Labor force: 2.38 million
country comparison to the world: 114
note: non-Kuwaitis represent about 60% of the labor force (2013 est.)

Labor force—by occupation: *agriculture:* NA%
industry: NA%
services: NA%

Unemployment rate: 3.4% (2011 est.)
country comparison to the world: 27
2.9% (2010)

Population below poverty line: NA%

Household income or consumption by percentage share: *lowest 10%:* NA%
highest 10%: NA%

Budget: *revenues:* $114.1 billion
expenditures: $61.81 billion (2013 est.)

Taxes and other revenues: 63.6% of GDP (2013 est.)
country comparison to the world: 3

Budget surplus (+) or deficit (-):
29.2% of GDP (2013 est.)
country comparison to the world: 2

Public debt: 6.4% of GDP (2013 est.)
country comparison to the world: 155
6.3% of GDP (2012 est.)

Fiscal year: 1 April—31 March

Inflation rate (consumer prices): 2.8% (2013 est.)
country comparison to the world: 104
2.9% (2012 est.)

Central bank discount rate: 1.25% (31 December 2010 est.)
country comparison to the world: 104
3% (31 December 2009 est.)

Commercial bank prime lending rate: 4.9% (31 December 2013 est.)
country comparison to the world: 157
5% (31 December 2012 est.)

Stock of narrow money: $31.68 billion (31 December 2013 est.)
country comparison to the world: 59
$27.55 billion (31 December 2012 est.)

Stock of broad money: $110.1 billion (31 December 2013 est.)
country comparison to the world: 51
$105.9 billion (31 December 2012 est.)

Stock of domestic credit: $90.63 billion (31 December 2013 est.)
country comparison to the world: 55
$89.13 billion (31 December 2012 est.)

Market value of publicly traded shares:
$97.09 billion (31 December 2012 est.)
country comparison to the world: 42
$100.9 billion (31 December 2011)
$119.6 billion (31 December 2010 est.)

Current account balance: $69.13 billion (2013 est.)
country comparison to the world: 6
$80.33 billion (2012 est.)

Exports: $112 billion (2013 est.)
country comparison to the world: 36
$121 billion (2012 est.)

Exports—commodities: oil and refined products, fertilizers

Exports—partners: South Korea 16.1%, India 15.7%, Japan 13.4%, US 11.7%, China 9.2%, Singapore 4.2% (2013 est.)

Imports: $24.42 billion (2013 est.)
country comparison to the world: 74
$22.79 billion (2012 est.)

Imports—commodities: food, construction materials, vehicles and parts, clothing

Imports—partners: US 11.8%, China 9.2%, Saudi Arabia 8.6%, Japan 8.2%, South Korea 6.9%, German 5.1%, India 4.6%, UAE 4.4% (2013 est.)

Reserves of foreign exchange and gold:
$34.35 billion (31 December 2013 est.)
country comparison to the world: 49
$29 billion (31 December 2012 est.)

Debt—external: $34.41 billion (2013 est.)
country comparison to the world: 69
$35.29 billion (2012 est.)

Stock of direct foreign investment—at home:
$5.677 billion (31 December 2013 est.)
country comparison to the world: 88
$5.212 billion (31 December 2012 est.)

Stock of direct foreign investment—abroad:
$60.76 billion (31 December 2013 est.)
country comparison to the world: 36
$52.59 billion (31 December 2012 est.)

Exchange rates: Kuwaiti dinars (KD) per US dollar—
0.2838 (2013 est.)
0.2799 (2012 est.)
0.2866 (2010 est.)
0.2877 (2009)
0.2679 (2008)

ENERGY

Electricity—production: 55.55 billion kWh (2011 est.)
country comparison to the world: 4 8

Electricity—consumption: 46.71 billion kWh (2010 est.)
country comparison to the world: 48

Electricity—exports: 0 kWh (2012 est.)
country comparison to the world: 157

Electricity—imports: 0 kWh (2012 est.)
country comparison to the world: 164

Electricity—installed generating capacity: 13.5 million kW (2011 est.)
country comparison to the world: 49

Electricity—from fossil fuels: 100% of total installed capacity (2010 est.)
country comparison to the world: 19

Electricity—from nuclear fuels: 0% of total installed capacity (2010 est.)
country comparison to the world: 120

Electricity—from hydroelectric plants: 0% of total installed capacity (2010 est.)
country comparison to the world: 178

Electricity—from other renewable sources: 0% of total installed capacity (2010 est.)
country comparison to the world: 189

Crude oil—production: 2.797 million bbl/day (2012 est.)
country comparison to the world: 10

Crude oil—exports: 1.395 million bbl/day (2010 est.)
country comparison to the world: 13

Crude oil—imports: 0 bbl/day (2010 est.)
country comparison to the world: 205

Crude oil—proved reserves: 104 billion bbl (1 January 2013 es)
country comparison to the world: 6

Refined petroleum products—production:
915,900 bbl/day (2010 est.)
country comparison to the world: 22

Refined petroleum products—consumption:
339,000 bbl/day (2011 est.)
country comparison to the world: 36

Refined petroleum products—exports:
656,100 bbl/day (2010 est.)
country comparison to the world: 11

Refined petroleum products—imports:
0 bbl/day (2010 est.)
country comparison to the world: 212

Natural gas—production: 13.53 billion cu m (2011 est.)
country comparison to the world: 36

Natural gas—consumption: 14.22 billion cu m (2011 est.)
country comparison to the world: 40

Natural gas—exports: 0 cu m (2011 est.)
country comparison to the world: 131

Natural gas—imports: 688 million cu m (2011 est.)
country comparison to the world: 64

Natural gas—proved reserves: 1.798 trillion cu m (1 January 2013 es)
country comparison to the world: 21

Carbon dioxide emissions from consumption of energy: 82.37 million Mt (2011 est.)
country comparison to the world: 44

COMMUNICATIONS

Telephones—main lines in use: 510,000 (2012)
country comparison to the world: 9 6

Telephones—mobile cellular: 5.526 million (2012)
country comparison to the world: 105

Telephone system: *general assessment:* the quality of service is excellent
domestic: new telephone exchanges provide a large capacity for new subscribers; trunk traffic is carried by microwave radio relay, coaxial cable, and open-wire and fiber-optic cable; a mobile-cellular telephone system operates throughout Kuwait, and the country is well supplied with pay telephones
international: country code—965; linked to international submarine cable Fiber-Optic Link Around the Globe (FLAG); linked to Bahrain, Qatar, UAE via the Fiber-Optic Gulf (FOG) cable; coaxial cable and microwave radio relay to Saudi Arabia; satellite earth stations—6 (3 Intelsat—1 Atlantic Ocean and 2 Indian Ocean, 1 Inmarsat—Atlantic Ocean, and 2 Arabsat) (2011)

Broadcast media: state-owned TV broadcaster operates 4 networks and a satellite channel; several private TV broadcasters have emerged since 2003; satellite TV available with pan-Arab TV stations especially popular; state-owned Radio Kuwait broadcasts on a number of channels in Arabic and English; first private radio station emerged in 2005; transmissions of at least 2 international radio broadcasters are available (2007)

Internet country code: .kw

Internet hosts: 2,771 (2012)
country comparison to the world: 156

Internet users: 1.1 million (2009)
country comparison to the world: 96

TRANSPORTATION

Airports: 7 (2013)
country comparison to the world: 168

Airports—with paved runways: *total:* 4
over 3,047 m: 1
2,438 to 3,047 m: 2
914 to 1,523 m: 1 (2013)

Airports—with unpaved runways: *total:* 3
1,524 to 2,437 m: 1
under 914 m: 2 (2013)

Heliports: 4 (2013)

Pipelines: gas 261 km; oil 540 km; refined products 57 km (2013)

Roadways: *total:* 6,608 km (2010)
country comparison to the world: 148

Merchant marine: *total:* 3 4
country comparison to the world: 82
by type: bulk carrier 2, carrier 3, container 6, liquefied gas 4, petroleum tanker 19
registered in other countries: 45 (Bahamas 1, Bahrain 5, Comoros 1, Libya 1, Malta 3, Marshall Islands 2, Panama 12, Qatar 6, Saudi Arabia 4, UAE 10) (2010)

Ports and terminals: *major seaport(s):* Ash Shu'aybah, Ash Shuwaykh, Az Zawr (Mina' Sa'ud), Mina' 'Abd Allah, Mina' al Ahmadi

MILITARY

Military branches: Kuwaiti Land Forces (KLF), Kuwaiti Navy, Kuwaiti Air Force (Al-Quwwat al-Jawwiya al-Kuwaitiya; includes Kuwaiti Air Defense Force, KADF), Kuwaiti National Guard (KNG) (2013)

Military service age and obligation: 17-21 years of age for voluntary military service; conscription suspended (2012)

Manpower available for military service:
males age 16-49: 1,002,480
females age 16-49: 616,958 (2010 est.)

Manpower fit for military service:
males age 16-49: 840,912
females age 16-49: 523,206 (2010 est.)

Manpower reaching militarily significant age annually: *male:* 17,653
female: 16,232 (2010 est.)

Military expenditures: 0% of GDP (2012)
country comparison to the world: 132
3.35% of GDP (2011)
0% of GDP (2010)

TRANSNATIONAL ISSUES

Disputes—international: Kuwait and Saudi Arabia continue negotiating a joint maritime boundary with Iran; no maritime boundary exists with Iraq in the Persian Gulf

Refugees and internally displaced persons: *stateless persons:* 93,000 (2012); note—Kuwait's 1959 Nationality Law defined citizens as persons who settled in the country before 1920 and who had maintained normal residence since then; one-third of the population, descendants of Bedouin tribes, missed the window of opportunity to register for nationality rights after Kuwait became independent in 1961 and were classified as bidun (meaning without); since the 1980s Kuwait's bidun have progressively lost their rights, including opportunities for employment and education, amid official claims that they are nationals of other countries who have destroyed their identification documents in hopes of gaining Kuwaiti citizenship; Kuwaiti authorities have delayed processing citizenship applications and labeled biduns as "illegal residents," denying them access to civil documentation, such as birth and marriage certificates; 2011 bidun demonstrations for the recognition of their Kuwaiti nationality led to several arrests

Trafficking in persons: *current situation:* Kuwait is a destination country for men and women subjected to forced labor and, to a lesser degree, forced prostitution; men and women migrate from India, Egypt, Bangladesh, Syria, Pakistan, the Philippines, Sri Lanka, Indonesia, Nepal, Iran, Jordan, Ethiopia, and Iraq to work in Kuwait, most of them in the domestic service, construction, and sanitation sectors; although most of these migrants enter Kuwait voluntarily, upon arrival some are subjected to conditions of forced labor by their sponsors and labor agents, including nonpayment of wages, long working hours without rest, deprivation of food, threats, physical or sexual abuse, and restrictions on movement, such as the withholding of passports or confinement to the workplace

tier rating: Tier 3—Kuwait does not fully comply with the minimum standards for the elimination of trafficking and is not making sufficient efforts to do so; the government enacted comprehensive anti-trafficking legislation in 2013 but did not report any arrests, prosecutions, convictions, or sentences of traffickers for either forced labor or sex trafficking in the last year; Kuwait's victim protection measures remain weak, particularly due to its lack of proactive victim identification procedures and continued reliance on the sponsorship system, which causes victims of trafficking to be punished for immigration violations rather than protected (2013)

KYRGYZSTAN

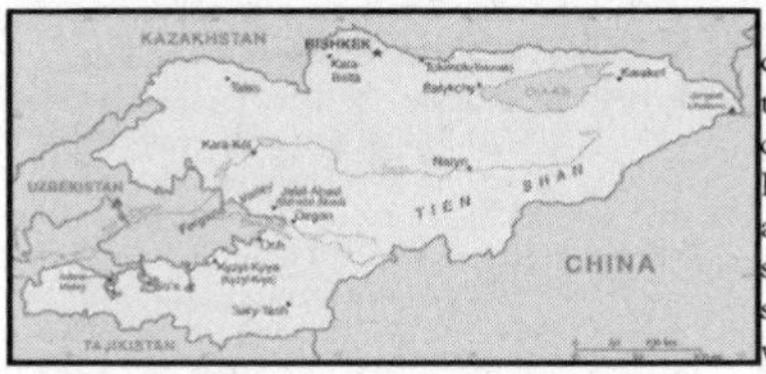

INTRODUCTION

Background: A Central Asian country of incredible natural beauty and proud nomadic traditions, most of Kyrgyzstan was formally annexed to Russia in 1876. The Kyrgyz staged a major revolt against the Tsarist Empire in 1916 in which almost one-sixth of the Kyrgyz population was killed. Kyrgyzstan became a Soviet republic in 1936 and achieved independence in 1991 when the USSR dissolved. Nationwide demonstrations in the spring of 2005 resulted in the ouster of President Askar AKAEV, who had run the country since 1990. Former prime minister Kurmanbek BAKIEV overwhelmingly won the presidential election in the summer of 2005. Over the next few years, he manipulated the parliament to accrue new powers for the presidency. In July 2009, after months of harassment against his opponents and media critics, BAKIEV won re-election in a presidential campaign that the international community deemed flawed. In April 2010, violent protests in Bishkek led to the collapse of the BAKIEV regime and his eventual fleeing to Minsk, Belarus. His successor, Roza OTUNBAEVA, served as transitional president until Almazbek ATAMBAEV was inaugurated in December 2011, marking the first peaceful transfer of presidential power in independent Kyrgyzstan's history. Continuing concerns include: the trajectory of democratization, endemic corruption, poor interethnic relations, and terrorism.

GEOGRAPHY

Location: Central Asia, west of China, south of Kazakhstan

Geographic coordinates: 41 00 N, 75 00 E

Map references: Asia

Area: *total:* 199,951 sq km
country comparison to the world: 87
land: 191,801 sq km
water: 8,150 sq km

Area—comparative: slightly smaller than South Dakota

Land boundaries: *total:* 3,051 km
border countries: China 858 km, Kazakhstan 1,224 km, Tajikistan 870 km, Uzbekistan 1,099 km

Coastline: 0 km (landlocked)

Maritime claims: none (landlocked)

Climate: dry continental to polar in high Tien Shan Mountains; subtropical in southwest (Fergana Valley); temperate in northern foothill zone

Terrain: peaks of Tien Shan and associated valleys and basins encompass entire nation

Elevation extremes: *lowest point:* Kara-Daryya (Karadar'ya) 132 m
highest point: Jengish Chokusu (Pik Pobedy) 7,439 m

Natural resources: abundant hydropower; significant deposits of gold and rare earth metals; locally exploitable coal, oil, and natural gas; other deposits of nepheline, mercury, bismuth, lead, and zinc

Land use: *arable land:* 6.38%
permanent crops: 0.37%
other: 93.24%
note: Kyrgyzstan has the world's largest natural-growth walnut forest (2011)

Irrigated land: 10,210 sq km (2005)

Total renewable water resources: 23.62 cu km (2011)

Freshwater withdrawal (domestic/industrial/agricultural): *total:* 8.01 cu km/yr (3%/4%/93%)
per capita: 1,558 cu m/yr (2006)

Natural hazards: NA

Environment—current issues: water pollution; many people get their water directly from contaminated streams and wells; as a result, water-borne diseases are prevalent; increasing soil salinity from faulty irrigation practices

Environment—international agreements: *party to:* Air Pollution, Biodiversity, Climate Change, Climate Change-Kyoto Protocol, Desertification, Hazardous Wastes, Ozone Layer Protection, Wetlands
signed, but not ratified: none of the selected agreements

Geography—note: landlocked; entirely mountainous, dominated by the Tien Shan range; 94% of the country is 1,000 m above sea level with an average elevation of 2,750 m; many tall peaks, glaciers, and high-altitude lakes

PEOPLE AND SOCIETY

Nationality: *noun:* Kyrgyzstani(s)
adjective: Kyrgyzstani

Ethnic groups: Kyrgyz 64.9%, Uzbek 13.8%, Russian 12.5%, Dungan 1.1%, Ukrainian 1%, Uighur 1%, other 5.7% (1999 census)

Languages: Kyrgyz (official) 64.7%, Uzbek 13.6%, Russian (official) 12.5%, Dungun 1%, other 8.2% (1999 census)

Religions: Muslim 75%, Russian Orthodox 20%, other 5%

Population: 5,604,212 (July 2014 est.)
country comparison to the world: 114

Age structure:
0-14 years: 29.8% (male 854,029/female 815,300)
15-24 years: 18.8% (male 536,355/female 519,440)
25-54 years: 39.4% (male 1,079,691/female 1,127,520)
55-64 years: 4.9% (male 171,960/female 224,450)
65 years and over: 4.9% (male 105,651/female 169,816) (2014 est.)

Dependency ratios:
total dependency ratio: 52.7 %
youth dependency ratio: 46.4 %
elderly dependency ratio: 6.4 %
potential support ratio: 15.7 (2013)

Median age: *total:* 25.7 years
male: 24.7 years
female: 26.7 years (2014 est.)

Population growth rate: 1.04% (2014 est.)
country comparison to the world: 115

Birth rate: 23.33 births/1,000 population (2014 est.)
country comparison to the world: 69

Death rate: 6.74 deaths/1,000 population (2014 est.)
country comparison to the world: 142

Net migration rate: -6.16 migrant(s)/1,000 population (2014 est.)
country comparison to the world: 199

Urbanization: *urban population:* 35.3% of total population (2011)
rate of urbanization: 1.31% annual rate of change (2010-15 est.)

Major urban areas—population: BISHKEK (capital) 854,000 (2009)

Sex ratio: *at birth:* 1.07 male(s)/female
0-14 years: 1.05 male(s)/female
15-24 years: 1.03 male(s)/female
25-54 years: 0.96 male(s)/female
55-64 years: 0.96 male(s)/female
65 years and over: 0.63 male(s)/female
total population: 0.96 male(s)/female (2014 est.)

Mother's mean age at first birth: 23.6 (2010 est.)

Maternal mortality rate: 71 deaths/100,000 live births (2010)
country comparison to the world: 86

Infant mortality rate: *total:* 28.71 deaths/1,000 live births
country comparison to the world: 67
male: 32.98 deaths/1,000 live births
female: 24.16 deaths/1,000 live births (2014 est.)

Life expectancy at birth: *total population:* 70.06 years
country comparison to the world: 153
male: 65.89 years
female: 74.51 years (2014 est.)

Total fertility rate: 2.68 children born/woman (2014 est.)
country comparison to the world: 72

Contraceptive prevalence rate: 47.8% (2005/06)

Health expenditures: 6.2% of GDP (2010)
country comparison to the world: 102

Physicians density: 2.47 physicians/1,000 population (2011)

Hospital bed density: 4.8 beds/1,000 population (2011)

Drinking water source:
improved:
urban: 96% of population
rural: 84.7% of population
total: 88.7% of population
unimproved:
urban: 4% of population
rural: 15.3% of population
total: 11.3% of population (2011 est.)

Sanitation facility access:
improved:
urban: 93.6% of population
rural: 93.1% of population
total: 93.3% of population
unimproved:
urban: 6.4% of population
rural: 6.9% of population
total: 6.7% of population (2011 est.)

HIV/AIDS—adult prevalence rate: 0.3% (2012 est.)
country comparison to the world: 95

HIV/AIDS—people living with HIV/AIDS: 8,700 (2012 est.)
country comparison to the world: 109

HIV/AIDS—deaths: 300 (2012 est.)
country comparison to the world: 101

Obesity—adult prevalence rate: 15.5% (2008)
country comparison to the world: 118

Children under the age of 5 years underweight: 2.7% (2006)
country comparison to the world: 116

Education expenditures: 6.8% of GDP (2011)
country comparison to the world: 25

Literacy: *definition:* age 15 and over can read and write
total population: 99.2%
male: 99.5%
female: 99% (2009 est.)

School life expectancy (primary to tertiary education): *total:* 13 years
male: 12 years
female: 13 years (2011)

Child labor—children ages 5-14: *total number:* 563,920
percentage: 40.3 %
note: data represents children ages 5-17 (2007 est.)

Unemployment, youth ages 15-24: *total:* 14.6%
country comparison to the world: 86
male: 13.6%
female: 16.2% (2006)

GOVERNMENT

Country name: *conventional long form:* Kyrgyz Republic
conventional short form: Kyrgyzstan
local long form: Kyrgyz Respublikasy
local short form: Kyrgyzstan
former: Kirghiz Soviet Socialist Republic

Government type: republic

Capital: *name:* Bishkek
geographic coordinates: 42 52 N, 74 36 E
time difference: UTC+6 (11 hours ahead of Washington, DC during Standard Time)

Administrative divisions: 7 provinces (oblustar, singular—oblus) and 2 cities* (shaarlar, singular—shaar); Batken Oblusu, Bishkek Shaary*, Chuy Oblusu (Bishkek), Jalal-Abad Oblusu, Naryn Oblusu, Osh Oblusu, Osh Shaary*, Talas Oblusu, Ysyk-Kol Oblusu (Karakol)
note: administrative divisions have the same names as their administrative centers (exceptions have the administrative center name following in parentheses)

Independence: 31 August 1991 (from the Soviet Union)

National holiday: Independence Day, 31 August (1991)

Constitution: previous 1993; latest adopted 27 June 2010, effective 2 July 2010 (2010)

Legal system: civil law system which includes features of French civil law and Russian Federation laws

International law organization participation: has not submitted an ICJ jurisdiction declaration; non-party state to the ICCt

Suffrage: 18 years of age; universal

Executive branch: *chief of state:* President Almazbek ATAMBAEV (since 1 December 2011)
head of government: Prime Minister Joomart OTORBAEV (since 2 April 2014, acting since 26 March 2014); First Deputy Prime Minister - Tayyrbek SARPASHEV (since 2 April 2014); Deputy Prime Ministers—Valeriy DIL, Abdyrakhman MAMATALIEV, Elvira SARIEVA (all since 2 April 2014)
cabinet: Cabinet of Ministers proposed by the prime minister, appointed by the president; ministers in charge of defense and security are appointed solely by the president (For more information visit the World Leaders website)
elections: president elected by popular vote for one six-year term; election last held on 30 October 2011 (next to be held in 2017); prime minister nominated by the parliamentary party holding more than 50% of the seats; if no such party exists, the president selects the party that will form a coalition majority and government
election results: Almazbek ATAMBAEV elected president; percent of vote—Almazbek ATAMBAEV 63.2%, Adakhan MADUMAROV 14.7%, Kamchybek TASHIEV 14.3%, other 7.8%; Jantoro SATYBALDIEV elected prime minister; parliamentary vote—111-2

Legislative branch: unicameral Supreme Council or Jogorku Kengesh (120 seats; members elected by popular vote to serve five-year terms)
elections: last held on 10 October 2010 (next to be held in 2015)
election results: Supreme Council—percent of vote by party—NA; seats by party—Ata-Jurt 28, SDPK 26, Ar-Namys 25, Respublika 23, Ata-Meken 18

Judicial branch: *highest court(s):* Supreme Court (consists of 25 judges); Constitutional Court (consists of 9 judges)
judge selection and term of office: Supreme Court and Constitutional Court judges appointed by the Supreme Council on the recommendation of the president; Supreme Court judges serve for 10 years, Constitutional Court judges serve for 15 years; mandatory retirement at age 70 for judges of both courts
subordinate courts: Higher Court of Arbitration; oblast (provincial) and city courts

Political parties and leaders: Ar-Namys (Dignity) Party [Feliks KULOV]; Ata-Jurt (Homeland) [Kamchybek TASHIEV, Akhmat KELDIBEKOV, Sadyr JAPAROV]; Ata-Meken (Fatherland) [Omurbek TEKEBAEV]; Butun Kyrgyzstan (All Kyrgyzstan) [Adakhan MADUMAROV]; Respublika [Omurbek BABANOV]; Social-Democratic Party of Kyrgyzstan (SDPK) [Almazbek ATAMBAEV]

Political pressure groups and leaders: Adilet (Justice) Legal Clinic [Cholpon JAKUPOVA]; Citizens Against Corruption [Tolekan ISMAILOVA]; Coalition for Democracy and Civil Society [Dinara OSHURAKHUNOVA]; Kylym Shamy (Torch of the Century) [Aziza ABDIRASULOVA]; Precedent Partnership Group [Nurbek TOKTAKUNOV]; Societal Analysis Public Association [Rita KARASARTOVA]; Union of True Muslims [Nurlan MOTUEV]

International organization participation: ADB, CICA, CIS, CSTO, EAEC, EAPC, EBRD, ECO, EITI (compliant country), FAO, GCTU, IAEA, IBRD, ICAO, ICC (NGOs), ICRM, IDA, IDB, IFAD, IFC, IFRCS, ILO, IMF, Interpol, IOC, IOM, IPU, ISO (correspondent), ITSO, ITU, MIGA, NAM (observer), OIC, OPCW, OSCE, PCA, PFP, SCO, UN, UNCTAD, UNESCO, UNIDO, UNISFA, UNMIL, UNMISS, UNWTO, UPU, WCO, WFTU (NGOs), WHO, WIPO, WMO, WTO

Diplomatic representation in the US: *chief of mission:* Ambassador Mukhtar JUMALIEV (since 7 December 2010)
chancery: 2360 Massachusetts Ave. NW, Washington, DC 20008
telephone: [1] (202) 449-9822
FAX: [1] (202) 386-7550
consulate(s): New York

Diplomatic representation from the US: *chief of mission:* Ambassador Pamela L. SPRATLEN (since 15 April 2011)
embassy: 171 Prospect Mira, Bishkek 720016
mailing address: use embassy street address
telephone: [996] (312) 551-241, (517) 777-217
FAX: [996] (312) 551-264

Flag description: red field with a yellow sun in the center having 40 rays representing the 40 Kyrgyz tribes; on the obverse side the rays run counterclockwise, on the reverse, clockwise; in the center of the sun is a red ring crossed by two sets of three lines, a stylized representation of a "tunduk"—the crown of a traditional Kyrgyz yurt; red symbolizes bravery and valor, the sun evinces peace and wealth

National symbol(s): gyrfalcon

National anthem: *name:* "Kyrgyz Respublikasynyn Mamlekettik Gimni" (National Anthem of the Kyrgyz Republic)
lyrics/music: Djamil SADYKOV and Eshmambet KULUEV/Nasyr DAVLESOV and Kalyi MOLDOBASANOV
note: adopted 1992

ECONOMY

Economy—overview: Kyrgyzstan is a poor, mountainous country with a dominant agricultural sector. Cotton, tobacco, wool, and meat are the main agricultural products, although only tobacco and cotton are exported in any quantity. Industrial exports include gold, mercury, uranium, natural gas, and electricity. The economy depends heavily on gold exports—mainly from output at the Kumtor gold mine - and on remittances from Kyrgyzstani migrant workers primarily in Russia. Following independence, Kyrgyzstan was progressive in carrying out market reforms, such as an improved regulatory system and land reform. Kyrgyzstan was the first Commonwealth of Independent States (CIS) country to be accepted into the World Trade Organization. Much of the government's stock in enterprises has been sold. Drops in production had been severe after the breakup of the Soviet Union in December 1991, but by mid-1995, production began to recover and exports began to increase. The overthrow of President BAKIEV in April 2010 and subsequent ethnic clashes left hundreds dead and damaged infrastructure. Under President ATAMBAYEV, Kyrgyzstan has developed a plan for economic development in coordination with international donors, and has also expressed its intent to join the Customs Union of Russia, Belarus, and Kazakhstan. Progress in fighting corruption, improving transparency in licensing, business permits and taxations, restructuring domestic industry, and attracting foreign aid and investment are key to future growth.

GDP (purchasing power parity): $14.3 billion (2013 est.)
country comparison to the world: 145
$13.32 billion (2012 est.)
$13.44 billion (2011 est.)
note: data are in 2013 US dollars

GDP (official exchange rate): $7.234 billion (2013 est.)

GDP—real growth rate: 7.4% (2013 est.)
country comparison to the world: 17
-0.9% (2012 est.)
6% (2011 est.)

GDP—per capita (PPP): $2,500 (2013 est.)
country comparison to the world: 185
$2,400 (2012 est.)
$2,400 (2011 est.)
note: data are in 2013 US dollars

Gross national saving: 9.1% of GDP (2013 est.)
country comparison to the world: 140
2.4% of GDP (2012 est.)
15% of GDP (2011 est.)

GDP—composition, by end use:
household consumption: 78.1%
government consumption: 17.6%
investment in fixed capital: 25.3%
investment in inventories: 8%
exports of goods and services: 51.2%
imports of goods and services: -80.2% (2013 est.)

GDP—composition, by sector of origin:
agriculture: 20.8%
industry: 34.4%
services: 44.8% (2013 est.)

Agriculture—products: tobacco, cotton, potatoes, vegetables, grapes, fruits and berries; sheep, goats, cattle, wool

Industries: small machinery, textiles, food processing, cement, shoes, sawn logs, refrigerators, furniture, electric motors, gold, rare earth metals

Industrial production growth rate: 12% (2013 est.)
country comparison to the world: 6

Labor force: 2.344 million (2007)
country comparison to the world: 115

Labor force—by occupation: *agriculture:* 48%
industry: 12.5%
services: 39.5% (2005 est.)

Unemployment rate: 8.6% (2011 est.)
country comparison to the world: 95
18% (2004 est.)

Population below poverty line: 33.7% (2011 est.)

Household income or consumption by percentage share: *lowest* 10%: 2.8%
highest 10%: 27.8% (2009 est.)

Distribution of family income—Gini index: 33.4 (2007)
country comparison to the world: 98
29 (2001)

Budget: *revenues:* $2.128 billion
expenditures: $2.458 billion (2013 est.)

Taxes and other revenues: 29.4% of GDP (2013 est.)
country comparison to the world: 94

Budget surplus (+) or deficit (-): -4.6% of GDP (2013 est.)
country comparison to the world: 160

Fiscal year: calendar year

Inflation rate (consumer prices): 6.8% (2013 est.)
country comparison to the world: 183
2.7% (2012 est.)

Central bank discount rate: 13.73% (22 December 2011 est.)
country comparison to the world: 110
2.5% (31 December 2010 est.)

Commercial bank prime lending rate: 25% (31 December 2013 est.)
country comparison to the world: 7
28.43% (31 December 2012 est.)

Stock of narrow money: $1.479 billion (31 December 2013 est.)
country comparison to the world: 140
$1.372 billion (31 December 2012 est.)

Stock of broad money: $1.776 billion (31 December 2013 est.)
country comparison to the world: 155
$1.634 billion (31 December 2012 est.)

Stock of domestic credit: $1.011 billion (31 December 2013 est.)
country comparison to the world: 154
$932.5 million (31 December 2012 est.)

Market value of publicly traded shares: $165 million (31 December 2012 est.)
country comparison to the world: 117
$165 million (31 December 2011)
$79 million (31 December 2010 est.)

Current account balance: -$1.125 billion (2013 est.)
country comparison to the world: 122
-$1.497 billion (2012 est.)

Exports: $1.881 billion (2013 est.)
country comparison to the world: 142
$1.921 billion (2012 est.)

Exports—commodities: gold, cotton, wool, garments, meat, tobacco; mercury, uranium, electricity; machinery; shoes

Exports—partners: Kazakhstan 26.2%, Uzbekistan 26.1%, Russia 14.6%, China 7%, UAE 6.1%, Afghanistan 5.2% (2012)

Imports: $5.082 billion (2013 est.)
country comparison to the world: 127
$4.967 billion (2012 est.)

Imports—commodities: oil and gas, machinery and equipment, chemicals, foodstuffs

Imports—partners: China 55.2%, Russia 17.4%, Kazakhstan 7.9% (2012)

Reserves of foreign exchange and gold:
$2.199 billion (31 December 2013 est.)
country comparison to the world: 120
$2.066 billion (31 December 2012 est.)

Debt—external: $3.859 billion (31 December 2013 est.)
country comparison to the world: 129
$3.746 billion (31 December 2012 est.)

Stock of direct foreign investment—at home:
$2.005 billion (31 December 2013 est.)
country comparison to the world: 98
$1.685 billion (31 December 2012 est.)

Stock of direct foreign investment—abroad:
$39.6 million (31 December 2013 est.)
country comparison to the world: 90
$39.6 million (31 December 2012 est.)

Exchange rates: soms (KGS) per US dollar—
48.87 (2013 est.)
47.005 (2012 est.)
45.964 (2010 est.)
42.905 (2009)
36.108 (2008)

ENERGY

Electricity—production: 14.9 billion kWh (2011 est.)
country comparison to the world: 8 2

Electricity—consumption: 7.326 billion kWh (2010 est.)
country comparison to the world: 98

Electricity—exports: 2.62 billion kWh (2011 est.)
country comparison to the world: 38

Electricity—imports: 0 kWh (2010 est.)
country comparison to the world: 160

Electricity—installed generating capacity: 3.64 million kW (2010 est.)
country comparison to the world: 83

Electricity—from fossil fuels: 20.1% of total installed capacity (2010 est.)
country comparison to the world: 191

Electricity—from nuclear fuels: 0% of total installed capacity (2010 est.)
country comparison to the world: 117

Electricity—from hydroelectric plants: 79.9% of total installed capacity (2010 est.)
country comparison to the world: 15

Electricity—from other renewable sources: 0% of total installed capacity (2010 est.)
country comparison to the world: 186

Crude oil—production: 1,000 bbl/day (2011 est.)
country comparison to the world: 109

Crude oil—exports: 0 bbl/day (2010 est.)
country comparison to the world: 136

Crude oil—imports: 0 bbl/day (2010 est.)
country comparison to the world: 203

Crude oil—proved reserves: 40 million bbl (1 January 2013 es)
country comparison to the world: 80

Refined petroleum products—production: 0 bbl/day (2010 est.)
country comparison to the world: 158

Refined petroleum products—consumption:
16,640 bbl/day (2011 est.)
country comparison to the world: 139

Refined petroleum products—exports: 2,433 bbl/day (2010 est.)
country comparison to the world: 99

Refined petroleum products—imports: 35,040 bbl/day (2010 est.)
country comparison to the world: 86

Natural gas—production: 10 million cu m (2011 est.)
country comparison to the world: 90

Natural gas—consumption: 462.5 million cu m (2010 est.)
country comparison to the world: 98

Natural gas—exports: 0 cu m (2011 est.)
country comparison to the world: 127

Natural gas—imports: 390 million cu m (2011 est.)
country comparison to the world: 66

Natural gas—proved reserves: 5.663 billion cu m (1 January 2013 es)
country comparison to the world: 94

Carbon dioxide emissions from consumption of energy: 7.793 million Mt (2011 est.)
country comparison to the world: 110

COMMUNICATIONS

Telephones—main lines in use: 489,000 (2012)
country comparison to the world: 9 8

Telephones—mobile cellular: 6.8 million (2012)
country comparison to the world: 94

Telephone system: *general assessment:* telecommunications infrastructure is being upgraded; loans from the European Bank for Reconstruction and Development (EBRD) are being used to install a digital network, digital radio-relay stations, and fiber-optic links
domestic: fixed-line penetration remains low and concentrated in urban areas; multiple mobile-cellular service providers with growing coverage; mobile-cellular subscribership was about 115 per 100 persons in 2011
international: country code—996; connections with other CIS countries by landline or microwave radio relay and with other countries by leased connections with Moscow international gateway switch and by satellite; satellite earth stations—2 (1 Intersputnik, 1 Intelsat); connected internationally by the Trans-Asia-Europe (TAE) fiber-optic line (2011)

Broadcast media: state-run TV broadcaster operates 2 nationwide networks and 6 regional stations; roughly 20 private TV stations operating with most rebroadcasting other channels; state-run radio broadcaster operates 2 networks; about 20 private radio stations (2007)

Internet country code: .kg

Internet hosts: 115,573 (2012)
country comparison to the world: 81

Internet users: 2.195 million (2009)
country comparison to the world: 74

TRANSPORTATION

Airports: 28 (2013)
country comparison to the world: 122

Airports—with paved runways: *total:* 1 8
over 3,047 m: 1
2,438 to 3,047 m: 3
1,524 to 2,437 m: 11
under 914 m: 3 (2013)

Airports—with unpaved runways: *total:* 1 0
1,524 to 2,437 m: 1
914 to 1,523 m: 1
under 914 m: 8 (2013)

Pipelines: gas 480 km; oil 16 km (2013)

Railways: *total:* 470 km
country comparison to the world: 112
broad gauge: 470 km 1.520-m gauge (2008)

Roadways: *total:* 34,000 km (2007)
country comparison to the world: 94

Waterways: 600 km (2010)
country comparison to the world: 79

Ports and terminals: *lake port(s):* Balykchy (Ysyk-Kol or Rybach'ye)(Lake Ysyk-Kol)

MILITARY

Military branches: Ground Forces, Air Force (includes Air Defense Forces) (2013)

Military service age and obligation: 18-27 years of age for compulsory or voluntary male military service in the Armed Forces or Interior Ministry; service obligation—1 year, with optional fee-based 3-year service in the callup mobilization reserve; women may volunteer at age 19; 16-17 years of age for military cadets, who cannot take part in military operations (2013)

Manpower available for military service:
males age 16-49: 1,456,881
females age 16-49: 1,470,317 (2010 est.)

Manpower fit for military service:
males age 16-49: 1,119,224
females age 16-49: 1,257,263 (2010 est.)

Manpower reaching militarily significant age annually: *male:* 56,606
female: 54,056 (2010 est.)

Military expenditures: NA% (2012)
3.74% of GDP (2011)
NA% (2010)

TRANSNATIONAL ISSUES

Disputes—international: Kyrgyzstan has yet to ratify the 2001 boundary delimitation with Kazakhstan; disputes in Isfara Valley delay completion of delimitation with Tajikistan; delimitation of 130 km of border with Uzbekistan is hampered by serious disputes over enclaves and other areas

Refugees and internally displaced persons: *IDPs:* 172,000 (June 2010 violence in southern Kyrgyzstan between the Kyrgyz majority and the Uzbek minority) (2012)
stateless persons: 15,473 (2012); note—most stateless people were born in Kyrgystan, have lived there many years, or are married to a Kyrgyz citizen; in 2009, Kyrgyzstan adopted a national action plan to speed up the exchange of old Soviet passports for Kyrgyz ones; stateless people are unable to register marriages and births, to travel within the country or abroad, to own property, or to receive social benefits

Illicit drugs: limited illicit cultivation of cannabis and opium poppy for CIS markets; limited government eradication of illicit crops; transit point for Southwest Asian narcotics bound for Russia and the rest of Europe; major consumer of opiates

LAOS

INTRODUCTION

Background: Modern-day Laos has its roots in the ancient Lao kingdom of Lan Xang, established in the 14th century under King FA NGUM. For 300 years Lan Xang had influence reaching into present-day Cambodia and Thailand, as well as over all of what is now Laos. After centuries of gradual decline, Laos came under the domination of Siam (Thailand) from the late 18th century until the late 19th century when it became part of French Indochina. The Franco-Siamese Treaty of 1907 defined the current Lao border with Thailand. In 1975, the communist Pathet Lao took control of the government ending a six-century-old monarchy and instituting a strict socialist regime closely aligned to Vietnam. A gradual, limited return to private enterprise and the liberalization of foreign investment laws began in 1988. Laos became a member of ASEAN in 1997 and the WTO in 2013.

GEOGRAPHY

Location: Southeastern Asia, northeast of Thailand, west of Vietnam

Geographic coordinates: 18 00 N, 105 00 E

Map references: Southeast Asia

Area: *total:* 236,800 sq km
country comparison to the world: 84
land: 230,800 sq km
water: 6,000 sq km

Area—comparative: slightly larger than Utah

Land boundaries: *total:* 5,083 km
border countries: Burma 235 km, Cambodia 541 km, China 423 km, Thailand 1,754 km, Vietnam 2,130 km

Coastline: 0 km (landlocked)

Maritime claims: none (landlocked)

Climate: tropical monsoon; rainy season (May to November); dry season (December to April)

Terrain: mostly rugged mountains; some plains and plateaus

Elevation extremes: *lowest point:* Mekong River 70 m
highest point: Phu Bia 2,817 m

Natural resources: timber, hydropower, gypsum, tin, gold, gemstones
Land use: *arable land:* 5.91%
permanent crops: 0.42%
other: 93.67% (2011)

Irrigated land: 3,100 sq km (2005)

Total renewable water resources: 333.5 cu km (2011)

Freshwater withdrawal (domestic/industrial/agricultural): *total:* 3.49 cu km/yr (4%/5%/91%)
per capita: 588.9 cu m/yr (2005)

Natural hazards: floods, droughts

Environment—current issues: unexploded ordnance; deforestation; soil erosion; most of the population does not have access to potable water

Environment—international agreements: *party to:* Biodiversity, Climate Change, Climate Change-Kyoto Protocol, Desertification, Endangered Species, Environmental Modification, Law of the Sea, Ozone Layer Protection
signed, but not ratified: none of the selected agreements

Geography—note: landlocked; most of the country is mountainous and thickly forested; the Mekong River forms a large part of the western boundary with Thailand

PEOPLE AND SOCIETY

Nationality: noun: Lao(s) or Laotian(s)
adjective: Lao or Laotian

Ethnic groups: Lao 55%, Khmou 11%, Hmong 8%, other (over 100 minor ethnic groups) 26% (2005 census)

Languages: Lao (official), French, English, various ethnic languages

Religions: Buddhist 67%, Christian 1.5%, other and unspecified 31.5% (2005 census)

Population: 6,803,699 (July 2014 est.)
country comparison to the world: 104

Age structure:
0-14 years: 34.8% (male 1,195,364/female 1,173,520)
15-24 years: 21.3% (male 719,205/female 728,729)
25-54 years: 35% (male 1,176,018/female 1,208,452)
55-64 years: 3.8% (male 169,291/female 175,815)
65 years and over: 3.7% (male 116,299/female 141,006) (2014 est.)

Dependency ratios:
total dependency ratio: 63.8 %
youth dependency ratio: 57.6 %
elderly dependency ratio: 6.2 %
potential support ratio: 16.1 (2013)

Median age: *total:* 22 years
male: 21.7 years
female: 22.3 years (2014 est.)

Population growth rate: 1.59% (2014 est.)
country comparison to the world: 78

Birth rate: 24.76 births/1,000 population (2014 est.)
country comparison to the world: 58

Death rate: 7.74 deaths/1,000 population (2014 est.)
country comparison to the world: 110

Net migration rate: -1.1 migrant(s)/1,000 population (2014 est.)
country comparison to the world: 150

Urbanization: *urban population:* 34.3% of total population (2011)
rate of urbanization: 4.41% annual rate of change (2010-15 est.)

Major urban areas—population: VIENTIANE (capital) 799,000 (2009)

Sex ratio: *at birth:* 1.04 male(s)/female
0-14 years: 1.02 male(s)/female
15-24 years: 0.99 male(s)/female
25-54 years: 0.97 male(s)/female
55-64 years: 0.99 male(s)/female
65 years and over: 0.82 male(s)/female
total population: 0.99 male(s)/female (2014 est.)

Maternal mortality rate: 470 deaths/100,000 live births (2010)
country comparison to the world: 21

Infant mortality rate: *total:* 54.53 deaths/1,000 live births
country comparison to the world: 33
male: 60.19 deaths/1,000 live births
female: 48.64 deaths/1,000 live births (2014 est.)

Life expectancy at birth: *total population:* 63.51 years
country comparison to the world: 182
male: 61.54 years
female: 65.56 years (2014 est.)

Total fertility rate: 2.9 children born/woman (2014 est.)
country comparison to the world: 60

Contraceptive prevalence rate: 38.4% (2005)

Health expenditures: 2.8% of GDP (2011)
country comparison to the world: 180

Physicians density: 0.19 physicians/1,000 population (2009)

Hospital bed density: 0.7 beds/1,000 population (2010)

Drinking water source:
improved:
urban: 82.8% of population
rural: 62.7% of population
total: 69.6% of population
unimproved:
urban: 17.2% of population
rural: 37.3% of population
total: 30.4% of population (2011 est.)

Sanitation facility access:
improved:
urban: 87.5% of population
rural: 48% of population
total: 61.5% of population
unimproved:
urban: 12.5% of population
rural: 52% of population
total: 38.5% of population (2011 est.)

HIV/AIDS—adult prevalence rate: 0.3% (2012 est.)
country comparison to the world: 96

HIV/AIDS—people living with HIV/AIDS: 11,500 (2012 est.)
country comparison to the world: 99

HIV/AIDS—deaths: 400 (2012 est.)
country comparison to the world: 98

Major infectious diseases: *degree of risk:* very high
food or waterborne diseases: bacterial and protozoal diarrhea, hepatitis A, and typhoid fever
vectorborne diseases: dengue fever and malaria
note: highly pathogenic H5N1 avian influenza has been identified in this country; it poses a negligible

risk with extremely rare cases possible among US citizens who have close contact with birds (2013)

Obesity—adult prevalence rate: 2.6% (2008)
country comparison to the world: 179

Children under the age of 5 years underweight: 31.6% (2006)
country comparison to the world: 13

Education expenditures: 2.8% of GDP (2010)
country comparison to the world: 147

Literacy: *definition:* age 15 and over can read and write
total population: 72.7%
male: 82.5%
female: 63.2% (2005 est.)

School life expectancy (primary to tertiary education): *total:* 10 years
male: 11 years
female: 10 years (2012)

Child labor—children ages 5-14: *total number:* 175,138
percentage: 11 % (2006 est.)

GOVERNMENT

Country name: *conventional long form:* Lao People's Democratic Republic
conventional short form: Laos
local long form: Sathalanalat Paxathipatai Paxaxon Lao
local short form: Pathet Lao (unofficial)

Government type: Communist state

Capital: *name:* Vientiane (Viangchan)
geographic coordinates: 17 58 N, 102 36 E
time difference: UTC+7 (12 hours ahead of Washington, DC during Standard Time)

Administrative divisions: 16 provinces (khoueng, singular and plural) and 1 capital city* (nakhon luang, singular and plural); Attapu, Bokeo, Bolikhamxai, Champasak, Houaphan, Khammouan, Louangnamtha, Louangphabang, Oudomxai, Phongsali, Salavan, Savannakhet, Viangchan (Vientiane)*, Viangchan, Xaignabouli, Xekong, Xiangkhouang

Independence: 19 July 1949 (from France)

National holiday: Republic Day, 2 December (1975)

Constitution: previous 1947 (preindependence); latest promulgated 13-15 August 1991; amended 2003 (2003)

Legal system: civil law system similar in form to the French system

International law organization participation: has not submitted an ICJ jurisdiction declaration; non-party state to the ICCt

Suffrage: 18 years of age; universal

Executive branch: *chief of state:* President Lt. Gen. CHOUMMALI Saignason (since 8 June 2006); Vice President BOUN-GNANG Volachit (since 8 June 2006)
head of government: Prime Minister THONGSING Thammavong (since 24 December 2010); First Deputy Prime Minister Maj. Gen. ASANG Laoli (since May 2002), Deputy Prime Ministers Maj. Gen. DOUANGCHAI Phichit (since 8 June 2006), SOMSAVAT Lengsavat (since 26 February 1998), and THONGLOUN Sisoulit (since 27 March 2001)
cabinet: Ministers appointed by president, approved by National Assembly (For more information visit the World Leaders website)
elections: president and vice president elected by National Assembly for five-year terms; election last held on 30 April 2011 (next to be held in 2016); prime minister nominated by the president and elected by the National Assembly for five-year term
election results: CHOUMMALI Saignason elected president; BOUN-GNANG Volachit elected vice president; percent of National Assembly vote—NA; THONGSING Thammavong elected prime minister; percent of National Assembly vote—NA

Legislative branch: unicameral National Assembly (132 seats; members elected by popular vote from a list of candidates selected by the Lao People's Revolutionary Party to serve five-year terms)
elections: last held on 30 April 2011 (next to be held in 2016)
election results: percent of vote by party—NA; seats by party—LPRP 128, independents 4

Judicial branch: *highest court(s):* People's Supreme Court (consists of NA judges)
judge selection and term of office: president of People's Supreme Court elected by National Assembly on recommendation of National Assembly Standing Committee; vice president of People's Supreme Court and judges appointed by National Assembly Standing Committee; term of office NA
subordinate courts: provincial, municipal, district, and military courts

Political parties and leaders: Lao People's Revolutionary Party or LPRP [CHOUMMALI Saignason]; other parties proscribed

Political pressure groups and leaders: NA

International organization participation: ADB, ARF, ASEAN, CP, EAS, FAO, G-77, IAEA, IBRD, ICAO, ICRM, IDA, IFAD, IFC, IFRCS, ILO, IMF, Interpol, IOC, IPU, ISO (subscriber), ITU, MIGA, NAM, OIF, OPCW, PCA, UN, UNCTAD, UNESCO, UNIDO, UNWTO, UPU, WCO, WFTU (NGOs), WHO, WIPO, WMO, WTO

Diplomatic representation in the US: *chief of mission:* Ambassador SENG Soukhathivong (since 4 June 2010)
chancery: 2222 S Street NW, Washington, DC 20008
telephone: [1] (202) 332-6416
FAX: [1] (202) 332-4923

Diplomatic representation from the US: *chief of mission:* Ambassador David A. CLUNE (since 16 September 2013)
embassy: 19 Rue Bartholonie, That Dam, Vientiane
mailing address: American Embassy Vientiane, APO AP 96546
telephone: [856] 21-26-7000
FAX: [856] 21-26-7190

Flag description: three horizontal bands of red (top), blue (double width), and red with a large white disk centered in the blue band; the red bands recall the blood shed for liberation; the blue band represents the Mekong River and prosperity; the white disk symbolizes the full moon against the Mekong River, but also signifies the unity of the people under the Lao People's Revolutionary Party, as well as the country's bright future

National symbol(s): elephant

National anthem: *name:* "Pheng Xat Lao" (Hymn of the Lao People)
lyrics/music: SISANA Sisane/THONGDY Sounthonevichit
note: music adopted 1945, lyrics adopted 1975; the anthem's lyrics were changed following the 1975 Communist revolution that overthrew the monarchy

ECONOMY

Economy—overview: The government of Laos, one of the few remaining one-party communist states, began decentralizing control and encouraging private enterprise in 1986. The results, starting from an extremely low base, were striking—growth averaged 6% per year from 1988-2008 except during the short-lived drop caused by the Asian financial crisis that began in 1997. Laos' growth exceeded 7% per year during 2008-13. Despite this high growth rate, Laos remains a country with an underdeveloped infrastructure, particularly in rural areas. It has a basic, but improving, road system, and limited external and internal land-line telecommunications. Electricity is available in 83 % of the country. Laos' economy is heavily dependent on capital-intensive natural resource exports. The labor force, however, still relies on agriculture, dominated by rice cultivation in lowland areas, which accounts for about 25% of GDP and 73% of total employment. Economic growth has reduced official poverty rates from 46% in 1992 to 26% in 2010. The economy also has benefited from high-profile foreign direct investment in hydropower, copper and gold mining, logging, and construction though some projects in these industries have drawn criticism for their environmental impacts. Laos gained Normal Trade Relations status with the US in 2004 and applied for Generalized System of Preferences trade benefits in 2013 after being admitted to the World Trade Organization earlier in the year. Laos is in the process of implementing a value-added tax system. Simplified investment procedures and expanded bank credits for small farmers and small entrepreneurs will improve Laos' economic prospects. The government appears committed to raising the country's profile among investors, but suffered through a fiscal crisis in 2013 brought about by public sector wage increases, fiscal mismanagement, and revenue shortfalls. The World Bank has declared that Laos' goal of graduating from the UN Development Program's list of least-developed countries by 2020 is achievable, and the country is preparing to enter the ASEAN Economic Community in 2015.

GDP (purchasing power parity): $20.78 billion (2013 est.)
country comparison to the world: 132
$19.18 billion (2012 est.)
$17.78 billion (2011 est.)
note: data are in 2013 US dollars

GDP (official exchange rate): $10.1 billion (2013 est.)

GDP—real growth rate: 8.3% (2013 est.)
country comparison to the world: 9
7.9% (2012 est.)
8% (2011 est.)

GDP—per capita (PPP): $3,100 (2013 est.)
country comparison to the world: 177
$2,900 (2012 est.)
$2,700 (2011 est.)
note: data are in 2013 US dollars

Gross national saving: 27.4% of GDP (2013 est.)
country comparison to the world: 37
26.2% of GDP (2012 est.)
25.2% of GDP (2011 est.)

GDP—composition, by end use:
household consumption: 66.9%
government consumption: 9.8%
investment in fixed capital: 31.7%
investment in inventories: -1.3%
exports of goods and services: 40%
imports of goods and services: -48.4% (2013 est.)

GDP—composition, by sector of origin:
agriculture: 24.8%
industry: 32%
services: 37.5% (2013 est.)

Agriculture—products: sweet potatoes, vegetables, corn, coffee, sugarcane, tobacco, cotton, tea, peanuts, rice; cassava (manioc), water buffalo, pigs, cattle, poultry

Industries: mining (copper, tin, gold, and gypsum); timber, electric power, agricultural processing, rubber, construction, garments, cement, tourism

Industrial production growth rate: 11% (2013 est.)
country comparison to the world: 12

Labor force: 3.373 million (2013 est.)
country comparison to the world: 100

Labor force—by occupation: *agriculture:* 75.1%
industry and services: NA (2010 est.)

Unemployment rate: 2.5% (2009 est.)
country comparison to the world: 19
2.4% (2005 est.)

Population below poverty line: 26% (2010 est.)

Household income or consumption by percentage share: *lowest 10%:* 3.3%
highest 10%: 30.3% (2008)

Distribution of family income—Gini index: 36.7 (2008)
country comparison to the world: 83
34.6 (2002)

Budget: *revenues:* $2.481 billion
expenditures: $2.642 billion (2013 est.)

Taxes and other revenues: 24.6% of GDP (2013 est.)
country comparison to the world: 135

Budget surplus (+) or deficit (-): -1.6% of GDP (2013 est.)
country comparison to the world: 73

Public debt: 46.3% of GDP (2013 est.)
country comparison to the world: 78
49.1% of GDP (2012 est.)

Fiscal year: 1 October—30 September

Inflation rate (consumer prices): 6.5% (2013 est.)
country comparison to the world: 181
4.3% (2012 est.)

Central bank discount rate: 4.3% (31 December 2010)
country comparison to the world: 95
4% (31 December 2009)

Commercial bank prime lending rate: 23.2% (31 December 2013 est.)
country comparison to the world: 14
22.3% (31 December 2012 est.)

Stock of narrow money: $1.389 billion (31 December 2013 est.)
country comparison to the world: 142
$1.154 billion (31 December 2012 est.)

Stock of broad money: $4.071 billion (31 December 2013 est.)
country comparison to the world: 135
$3.673 billion (31 December 2012 est.)

Stock of domestic credit: $4.716 billion (31 December 2013 est.)
country comparison to the world: 116
$4.034 billion (31 December 2012 est.)

Current account balance: -$484.3 million (2013 est.)
country comparison to the world: 98
-$315.5 million (2012 est.)

Exports: $2.313 billion (2013 est.)
country comparison to the world: 140
$1.984 billion (2012 est.)

Exports—commodities: wood products, coffee, electricity, tin, copper, gold, cassava

Exports—partners: Thailand 34%, China 21.5%, Vietnam 12.2% (2012)

Imports: $3.238 billion (2013 est.)
country comparison to the world: 145
$2.744 billion (2012 est.)

Imports—commodities: machinery and equipment, vehicles, fuel, consumer goods

Imports—partners: Thailand 62.1%, China 16.2%, Vietnam 7.3% (2012)

Reserves of foreign exchange and gold: $845.4 million (31 December 2013 est.)
country comparison to the world: 141
$796.9 million (31 December 2012 est.)

Debt—external: $6.69 billion (31 December 2013 est.)
country comparison to the world: 112
$6.288 billion (31 December 2012 est.)

Exchange rates: kips (LAK) per US dollar—
7,875.9 (2013 est.)
8,007.3 (2012 est.)
8,258.8 (2010 est.)
8,516.04 (2009)
8,760.69 (2008)

ENERGY

Electricity—production: 3.629 billion kWh (2010 est.)
country comparison to the world: 127

Electricity—consumption: 2.355 billion kWh (2010 est.)
country comparison to the world: 137

Electricity—exports: 2.02 billion kWh (2010 est.)
country comparison to the world: 42

Electricity—imports: 1 billion kWh (2010 est.)
country comparison to the world: 64

Electricity—installed generating capacity: 1.895 million kW (2010 est.)
country comparison to the world: 105

Electricity—from fossil fuels: 2.6% of total installed capacity (2010 est.)
country comparison to the world: 201

Electricity—from nuclear fuels: 0% of total installed capacity (2010 est.)
country comparison to the world: 122

Electricity—from hydroelectric plants: 97.4% of total installed capacity (2010 est.)
country comparison to the world: 9

Electricity—from other renewable sources: 0% of total installed capacity (2010 est.)
country comparison to the world: 191

Crude oil—production: 0 bbl/day (2012 est.)
country comparison to the world: 185

Crude oil—exports: 0 bbl/day (2010 est.)
country comparison to the world: 140

Crude oil—imports: 0 bbl/day (2010 est.)
country comparison to the world: 206

Crude oil—proved reserves: 0 bbl (1 January 2013 es)
country comparison to the world: 152

Refined petroleum products—production: 0 bbl/day (2010 est.)
country comparison to the world: 161

Refined petroleum products—consumption: 3,391 bbl/day (2011 est.)
country comparison to the world: 177

Refined petroleum products—exports: 0 bbl/day (2010 est.)
country comparison to the world: 190

Refined petroleum products—imports: 3,160 bbl/day (2010 est.)
country comparison to the world: 170

Natural gas—production: 0 cu m (2011 est.)
country comparison to the world: 151

Natural gas—consumption: 0 cu m (2010 est.)
country comparison to the world: 162

Natural gas—exports: 0 cu m (2011 est.)
country comparison to the world: 132

Natural gas—imports: 0 cu m (2011 est.)
country comparison to the world: 86

Natural gas—proved reserves: 0 cu m (1 January 2013 es)
country comparison to the world: 156

Carbon dioxide emissions from consumption of energy: 1.404 million Mt (2011 est.)
country comparison to the world: 159

COMMUNICATIONS

Telephones—main lines in use: 112,000 (2012)
country comparison to the world: 143

Telephones—mobile cellular: 6.492 million (2012)
country comparison to the world: 99

Telephone system: *general assessment:* service to general public is improving; the government relies on a radiotelephone network to communicate with remote areas
domestic: 4 service providers with mobile cellular usage growing very rapidly
international: country code—856; satellite earth station—1 Intersputnik (Indian Ocean region) and a second to be developed by China (2012)

Broadcast media: 6 TV stations operating out of Vientiane—3 government-operated and the others commercial; 17 provincial stations operating with nearly all programming relayed via satellite from the government-operated stations in Vientiane; Chinese and Vietnamese programming relayed via satellite from Lao National TV; broadcasts available from stations in Thailand and Vietnam in border areas; multi-channel satellite and cable TV systems provide access to a wide range of foreign stations; state-controlled radio with state-operated Lao National Radio (LNR) broadcasting on 5 frequencies—1 AM, 1 SW, and 3 FM; LNR's AM and FM programs are relayed via satellite constituting a large part of the programming schedules of the provincial radio stations; Thai radio broadcasts available in border areas and transmissions of multiple international broadcasters are also accessible (2012)

Internet country code: .la

Internet hosts: 1,532 (2012)
country comparison to the world: 166

Internet users: 300,000 (2009)
country comparison to the world: 130

TRANSPORTATION

Airports: 41 (2013)
country comparison to the world: 103

Airports—with paved runways: *total:* 8
2,438 to 3,047 m: 3
1,524 to 2,437 m: 4
914 to 1,523 m: 1 (2013)

Airports—with unpaved runways: *total:* 3 3
1,524 to 2,437 m: 2
914 to 1,523 m: 9
under 914 m: 22 (2013)

Pipelines: refined products 540 km (2013)

Roadways: *total:* 39,568 km
country comparison to the world: 89
paved: 530 km
unpaved: 39,038 km (2007)

Waterways: 4,600 km (primarily on the Mekong River and its tributaries; 2,900 additional km are intermittently navigable by craft drawing less than 0.5 m) (2012)
country comparison to the world: 24

MILITARY

Military branches: Lao People's Armed Forces (LPAF): Lao People's Army (LPA; includes Riverine Force), Air Force (2011)

Military service age and obligation: 18 years of age for compulsory or voluntary military service; conscript service obligation—minimum 18-months (2012)

Manpower available for military service: *males age 16-49:* 1,574,362
females age 16-49: 1,607,856 (2010 est.)

Manpower fit for military service: *males age 16-49:* 1,111,629
females age 16-49: 1,190,035 (2010 est.)

Manpower reaching militarily significant age annually: *male:* 71,400
female: 73,038 (2010 est.)

Military expenditures: NA% (2012)
0.23% of GDP (2011)
NA% (2010)

Military—note: serving one of the world's least developed countries, the Lao People's Armed Forces (LPAF) is small, poorly funded, and ineffectively resourced; its mission focus is border and internal security, primarily in countering ethnic Hmong insurgent groups; together with the Lao People's Revolutionary Party and the government, the Lao People's Army (LPA) is the third pillar of state machinery, and as such is expected to suppress political and civil unrest and similar national emergencies, but the LPA also has upgraded skills to respond to avian influenza outbreaks; there is no perceived external threat to the state and the LPA maintains strong ties with the neighboring Vietnamese military (2008)

TRANSNATIONAL ISSUES

Disputes—international: southeast Asian states have enhanced border surveillance to check the spread of avian flu; talks continue on completion of demarcation with Thailand but disputes remain over islands in the Mekong River; concern among Mekong River Commission members that China's construction of dams on the Mekong River and its tributaries will affect water levels; Cambodia and Vietnam are concerned about Laos' extensive upstream dam construction

Illicit drugs: estimated opium poppy cultivation in 2008 was 1,900 hectares, about a 73% increase from 2007; estimated potential opium production in 2008 more than tripled to 17 metric tons; unsubstantiated reports of domestic methamphetamine production; growing domestic methamphetamine problem (2007)

LATVIA

INTRODUCTION

Background: The name "Latvia" originates from the ancient Latgalians, one of four eastern Baltic tribes that formed the ethnic core of the Latvian people (ca. 8th-12th centuries A.D.). The region subsequently came under the control of Germans, Poles, Swedes, and finally, Russians. A Latvian republic emerged following World War I, but it was annexed by the USSR in 1940—an action never recognized by the US and many other countries. Latvia reestablished its independence in 1991 following the breakup of the Soviet Union. Although the last Russian troops left in 1994, the status of the Russian minority (some 28% of the population) remains of concern to Moscow. Latvia acceded to both NATO and the EU in the spring of 2004; it joined the eurozone in 2014.

GEOGRAPHY

Location: Eastern Europe, bordering the Baltic Sea, between Estonia and Lithuania

Geographic coordinates: 57 00 N, 25 00 E

Map references: Europe

Area: *total:* 64,589 sq km
country comparison to the world: 124
land: 62,249 sq km
water: 2,340 sq km

Area—comparative: slightly larger than West Virginia

Land boundaries: *total:* 1,382 km
border countries: Belarus 171 km, Estonia 343 km, Lithuania 576 km, Russia 292 km

Coastline: 498 km

Maritime claims: *territorial sea:* 12 nm
exclusive economic zone: 200 nm
continental shelf: 200 m depth or to the depth of exploitation

Climate: maritime; wet, moderate winters

Terrain: low plain

Elevation extremes: *lowest point:* Baltic Sea 0 m
highest point: Gaizina Kalns 312 m

Natural resources: peat, limestone, dolomite, amber, hydropower, timber, arable land

Land use: *arable land:* 17.96%
permanent crops: 0.11%
other: 81.93% (2011)

Irrigated land: 8.3 sq km
note: land in Latvia is often too wet and in need of drainage not irrigation; approximately 16,000 sq km or 85% of agricultural land has been improved by drainage (2007)

Total renewable water resources: 35.45 cu km (2011)

Freshwater withdrawal (domestic/industrial/agricultural): *total:* 0.42 cu km/yr (42%/45%/13%)
per capita: 177.9 cu m/yr (2007)

Natural hazards: NA

Environment—current issues: Latvia's environment has benefited from a shift to service industries after the country regained independence; the main environmental priorities are improvement of drinking water quality and sewage system, household, and hazardous waste management, as well as reduction of air pollution; in 2001, Latvia closed the EU accession negotiation chapter on environment committing to full enforcement of EU environmental directives by 2010

Environment—international agreements: *party to:* Air Pollution, Air Pollution-Persistent Organic Pollutants, Biodiversity, Climate Change, Climate Change-Kyoto Protocol, Desertification, Endangered Species, Hazardous Wastes, Law of the Sea, Ozone Layer Protection, Ship Pollution, Wetlands
signed, but not ratified: none of the selected agreements

Geography—note: most of the country is composed of fertile low-lying plains with some hills in the east

PEOPLE AND SOCIETY

Nationality: *noun:* Latvian(s)
adjective: Latvian

Ethnic groups: Latvian 61.1%, Russian 26.2%, Belarusian 3.5%, Ukrainian 2.3%, Polish 2.2%, Lithuanian 1.3%, other 3.4% (2013 est.)

Languages: Latvian (official) 56.3%, Russian 33.8%, other 0.6% (includes Polish, Ukrainian, and Belarusian), unspecified 9.4% (2011 est.)

Religions: Lutheran 19.6%, Orthodox 15.3%, other Christian 1%, other 0.4%, unspecified 63.7% (2006)

Population: 2,165,165 (July 2014 est.)
country comparison to the world: 144

Age structure:
0-14 years: 14.2% (male 156,851/female 150,074)
15-24 years: 11% (male 121,435/female 116,602)
25-54 years: 44.8% (male 481,336/female 487,991)
55-64 years: 17.2% (male 122,544/female 155,114)
65 years and over: 17.1% (male 121,668/female 251,550) (2014 est.)

Dependency ratios:
total dependency ratio: 50.2 %
youth dependency ratio: 22.3 %
elderly dependency ratio: 27.9 %
potential support ratio: 3.6 (2013)

Median age: *total:* 41.4 years
male: 38.4 years
female: 44.3 years (2014 est.)

Population growth rate: -0.62% (2014 est.)
country comparison to the world: 225

Birth rate: 9.79 births/1,000 population (2014 est.)
country comparison to the world: 198

Death rate: 13.6 deaths/1,000 population (2014 est.)
country comparison to the world: 14

Net migration rate: -2.37 migrant(s)/1,000 population (2014 est.)
country comparison to the world: 172

Urbanization: *urban population:* 68% of total population (2010)
rate of urbanization: -0.4% annual rate of change (2010-15 est.)

Major urban areas—population: RIGA (capital) 711,000 (2009)

Sex ratio: *at birth:* 1.05 male(s)/female
0-14 years: 1.05 male(s)/female
15-24 years: 1.04 male(s)/female
25-54 years: 0.99 male(s)/female
55-64 years: 0.86 male(s)/female
65 years and over: 0.48 male(s)/female
total population: 0.86 male(s)/female (2014 est.)

Mother's mean age at first birth: 26.4 (2010 est.)

Maternal mortality rate: 34 deaths/100,000 live births (2010)
country comparison to the world: 120

Infant mortality rate: *total:* 7.91 deaths/1,000 live births
country comparison to the world: 156
male: 9.6 deaths/1,000 live births
female: 6.13 deaths/1,000 live births (2014 est.)

Life expectancy at birth: *total population:* 73.44 years
country comparison to the world: 123
male: 68.41 years
female: 78.75 years (2014 est.)

Total fertility rate: 1.35 children born/woman (2014 est.)
country comparison to the world: 211

Contraceptive prevalence rate: 67.8%
note: percent of women aged 18-49 (1995)

Health expenditures: 6.7% of GDP (2010)
country comparison to the world: 93

Physicians density: 2.9 physicians/1,000 population (2010)

Hospital bed density: 5.3 beds/1,000 population (2010)

Drinking water source:
improved:
urban: 99.6% of population
rural: 95.8% of population
total: 98.4% of population
unimproved:
urban: 0.4% of population
rural: 4.2% of population
total: 1.6% of population (2011 est.)

Sanitation facility access:
improved:
urban: 82.1% of population
rural: 71.1% of population
total: 78.6% of population
unimproved:
urban: 17.9% of population
rural: 28.9% of population
total: 21.4% of population (2009 est.)

HIV/AIDS—adult prevalence rate: 0.7% (2009 est.)
country comparison to the world: 58

HIV/AIDS—people living with HIV/AIDS: 8,600 (2009 est.)
country comparison to the world: 110

HIV/AIDS—deaths: fewer than 1,000 (2009 est.)
country comparison to the world: 74

Major infectious diseases: *degree of risk:* intermediate
vectorborne diseases: tickborne encephalitis (2013)

Obesity—adult prevalence rate: 24.9% (2008)
country comparison to the world: 62

Education expenditures: 5% of GDP (2010)
country comparison to the world: 77

Literacy: *definition:* age 15 and over can read and write
total population: 99.8%
male: 99.8%
female: 99.8% (2011 est.)

School life expectancy (primary to tertiary education): *total:* 16 years
male: 15 years
female: 16 years (2011)

Unemployment, youth ages 15-24: *total:* 28.4%
country comparison to the world: 29
male: 27.6%
female: 29.3% (2012)

GOVERNMENT

Country name: *conventional long form:* Republic of Latvia
conventional short form: Latvia
local long form: Latvijas Republika
local short form: Latvija
former: Latvian Soviet Socialist Republic

Government type: parliamentary democracy

Capital: *name:* Riga

geographic coordinates: 56 57 N, 24 06 E
time difference: UTC+2 (7 hours ahead of Washington, DC during Standard Time)
daylight saving time: +1hr, begins last Sunday in March; ends last Sunday in October

Administrative divisions: 110 municipalities (novadi, singular—novads) and 9 cities
municipalities: Adazu Novads, Aglonas Novads, Aizkraukles Novads, Aizputes Novads, Aknistes Novads, Alojas Novads, Alsungas Novads, Aluksnes Novads, Amatas Novads, Apes Novads, Auces Novads, Babites Novads, Baldones Novads, Baltinavas Novads, Balvu Novads, Bauskas Novads, Beverinas Novads, Brocenu Novads, Burtnieku Novads, Carnikavas Novads, Cesu Novads, Cesvaines Novads, Ciblas Novads, Dagdas Novads, Daugavpils Novads, Dobeles Novads, Dundagas Novads, Durbes Novads, Engures Novads, Erglu Novads, Garkalnes Novads, Grobinas Novads, Gulbenes Novads, Iecavas Novads, Ikskiles Novads, Ilukstes Novads, Incukalna Novads, Jaunjelgavas Novads, Jaunpiebalgas Novads, Jaunpils Novads, Jekabpils Novads, Jelgavas Novads, Kandavas Novads, Karsavas Novads, Keguma Novads, Kekavas Novads, Kocenu Novads, Kokneses Novads, Kraslavas Novads, Krimuldas Novads, Krustpils Novads, Kuldigas Novads, Lielvardes Novads, Ligatnes Novads, Limbazu Novads, Livanu Novads, Lubanas Novads, Ludzas Novads, Madonas Novads, Malpils Novads, Marupes Novads, Mazsalacas Novads, Mersraga Novads, Nauksenu Novads, Neretas Novads, Nicas Novads, Ogres Novads, Olaines Novads, Ozolnieku Novads, Pargaujas Novads, Pavilostas Novads, Plavinu Novads, Preilu Novads, Priekules Novads, Priekulu Novads, Raunas Novads, Rezeknes Novads, Riebinu Novads, Rojas Novads, Ropazu Novads, Rucavas Novads, Rugaju Novads, Rujienas Novads, Rundales Novads, Salacgrivas Novads, Salas Novads, Salaspils Novads, Saldus Novads, Saulkrastu Novads, Sejas Novads, Siguldas Novads, Skriveru Novads, Skrundas Novads, Smiltenes Novads, Stopinu Novads, Strencu Novads, Talsu Novads, Tervetes Novads, Tukuma Novads, Vainodes Novads, Valkas Novads, Varaklanu Novads, Varkavas Novads, Vecpiebalgas Novads, Vecumnieku Novads, Ventspils Novads, Viesites Novads, Vilakas Novads, Vilanu Novads, Zilupes Novads
cities: Daugavpils, Jekabpils, Jelgava, Jurmala, Liepaja, Rezekne, Riga, Valmiera, Ventspils

Independence: 4 May 1990 (declared); 6 September 1991 (recognized by the Soviet Union)

National holiday: Independence Day, 18 November (1918); note—18 November 1918 was the date Latvia declared independence from Soviet Russia and established its statehood; 4 May 1990 was the date it declared its independence from the Soviet Union

Constitution: several previous (preindependence); note—at independence, parts of the 1922 constitution were reinforced and fully reinforced 6 July 1993; amended several times, last in 2009 (2009)

Legal system: civil law system with traces of socialist legal traditions and practices

International law organization participation: has not submitted an ICJ jurisdiction declaration; accepts ICCt jurisdiction

Suffrage: 18 years of age; universal for Latvian citizens

Executive branch: *chief of state:* President Andris BERZINS (since 8 July 2011)
head of government: Prime Minister Laimdota STRAUJUMA (since 22 January 2014)
cabinet: Cabinet of Ministers nominated by the prime minister and appointed by Parliament (For more information visit the World Leaders website)
elections: president elected by Parliament for a four-year term (eligible for a second term); election last held on 2 June 2011 (next to be held in 2015); prime minister appointed by the president, confirmed by Parliament
election results: Andris BERZINS elected president; parliamentary vote—Andris BERZINS 53, Valdis ZATLERS 41

Legislative branch: unicameral Parliament or Saeima (100 seats; members elected by proportional representation from party lists by popular vote to serve four-year terms)
elections: last held on 17 September 2011 (next to be held in October 2014)
election results: percent of vote by party—SC 28.4%, Reform 20.8%, Unity 18.8%, National Alliance 13.9%, ZZS 12.2%, other 5.9%; seats by party—SC 31, Unity 20, Reform 16, National Alliance 14, ZZS 13, unaffiliated 6

Judicial branch: *highest court(s):* Supreme Court (consists of the Senate with 27 judges and Supreme Court of Chambers with 22 judges); Constitutional Court (consists of 7 judges)
judge selection and term of office: Supreme Court judges nominated by chief justice and confirmed by the Saeima; judges serve until age 70, but term can be extended 2 years; Constitutional Court judges—3 nominated by Saeima members, 2 by Cabinet ministers, and 2 by plenum of Supreme Court; all judges confirmed by Saeima majority vote; Constitutional Court president and vice president serve in their positions for 3 years; all judges serve 10-year terms; mandatory retirement at age 70
subordinate courts: district (city) and regional courts

Political parties and leaders: Union of Greens and Farmers or ZZS [Raimonds VEJONIS]; Harmony Center or SC [Nils USAKOVS]; National Alliance "All For Latvia!"-"For Fatherland and Freedom/LNNK" or NA [Gaidis BERZINS, Raivis; DZINTARS]; Unity [Solvita ABOLTINA]; Reform Party or RP [Edmunds DEMITERS]

Political pressure groups and leaders: Free Trade Union Confederation of Latvia [Peteris KRIGERS]; Employers' Confederation of Latvia [Vitalijs GAVRILOVS]; Farmers' Parliament [Juris LAZDINS]

International organization participation: Australia Group, BA, BIS, CBSS, CD, CE, EAPC, EBRD, EIB, EU, FAO, IAEA, IBRD, ICAO, ICC (NGOs), ICRM, IDA, IFC, IFRCS, IHO, ILO, IMF, IMO, IMSO, Interpol, IOC, IOM, IPU, ISO (correspondent), ITU, ITUC (NGOs), MIGA, NATO, NIB, NSG, OAS (observer), OIF (observer), OPCW, OSCE, PCA, Schengen Convention, UN, UNCTAD, UNESCO, UNWTO, UPU, WCO, WHO, WIPO, WMO, WTO

Diplomatic representation in the US: *chief of mission:* Ambassador Andris RAZANS (since 27 July 2012)
chancery: 2306 Massachusetts Ave. NW, Washington, DC 20008
telephone: [1] (202) 328-2840
FAX: [1] (202) 328-2860

Diplomatic representation from the US: *chief of mission:* Ambassador Mark A. PEKALA (since 10 July 2012)
embassy: 1 Samnera Velsa St, Riga LV-1510
mailing address: Embassy of the United States of America, 1 Samnera Velsa St, Riga, LV-1510, Latvia
telephone: [371] 6710-7000
FAX: [371] 6710-7050

Flag description: three horizontal bands of maroon (top), white (half-width), and maroon; the flag is one of the older banners in the world; a medieval chronicle mentions a red standard with a white stripe being used by Latvian tribes in about 1280

National symbol(s): white wagtail (bird)

National anthem: *name:* "Dievs, sveti Latviju!" (God Bless Latvia)
lyrics/music: Karlis BAUMANIS
note: adopted 1920, restored 1990; the song was first performed in 1873 while Latvia was a part of Russia; the anthem was banned during the Soviet occupation from 1940 to 1990

ECONOMY

Economy—overview: Latvia is a small, open economy with exports contributing nearly a third of GDP. Due to its geographical location, transit services are highly-developed, along with timber and wood-processing, agriculture and food products, and manufacturing of machinery and electronics industries. Corruption continues to be an impediment to attracting foreign direct investment and Latvia's low birth rate and decreasing population are major challenges to its long-term economic vitality. Latvia's economy experienced GDP growth of more than 10% per year during 2006-07, but entered a severe recession in 2008 as a result of an unsustainable current account deficit and large debt exposure amid the softening world economy. Triggered by the collapse of the second largest bank, GDP plunged 18% in 2009. The economy has not returned to pre-crisis levels despite strong growth, especially in the export sector in 2011-12. The IMF, EU, and other international donors provided substantial financial assistance to Latvia as part of an agreement to defend the currency's peg to the euro in exchange for the government's commitment to stringent austerity measures. The IMF/EU program successfully concluded in December 2011. The government of Prime Minister Valdis DOMBROVSKIS remains committed to fiscal prudence and reducing the fiscal deficit. The majority of companies, banks, and real estate have been privatized, although the state still holds sizable stakes in a few large enterprises, including 99.8% ownership of the Latvian national airline. Latvia officially joined the World Trade Organization in February 1999 and the EU in May 2004. Latvia intends to join the euro zone in 2014.

GDP (purchasing power parity): $38.87 billion (2013 est.)
country comparison to the world: 109
$37.38 billion (2012 est.)
$35.4 billion (2011 est.)
note: data are in 2013 US dollars

GDP (official exchange rate): $30.38 billion (2013 est.)

GDP—real growth rate: 4% (2013 est.)
country comparison to the world: 79
5.6% (2012 est.)
5.5% (2011 est.)

GDP—per capita (PPP): $19,100 (2013 est.)
country comparison to the world: 73
$18,300 (2012 est.)
$17,100 (2011 est.)
note: data are in 2013 US dollars

Gross national saving: 23.2% of GDP (2013 est.)
country comparison to the world: 62
24.6% of GDP (2012 est.)
22.7% of GDP (2011 est.)

GDP—composition, by end use:
household consumption: 62.4%
government consumption: 15%
investment in fixed capital: 22.5%
investment in inventories: 2.8%
exports of goods and services: 61.3%
imports of goods and services: -63.9% (2013 est.)

GDP—composition, by sector of origin:
agriculture: 4.9%
industry: 25.7%
services: 69.4% (2013 est.)

Agriculture—products: grain, rapeseed, potatoes, vegetables; pork, poultry, milk, eggs; fish

Industries: processed foods, processed wood products, textiles, processed metals, pharmaceuticals, railroad cars, synthetic fibers, electronics

Industrial production growth rate: 4.2% (2013 est.)
country comparison to the world: 68

Labor force: 1.022 million (2013 est.)
country comparison to the world: 143

Labor force—by occupation: *agriculture:* 8.8%
industry: 24%
services: 67.2% (2010 est.)

Unemployment rate: 9.8% (2013 est.)
country comparison to the world: 106
11.4% (2012 est.)

Population below poverty line: NA%

Household income or consumption by percentage share: *lowest 10%:* 2.7%
highest 10%: 27.6% (2008)

Distribution of family income—Gini index: 35.2 (2010)
country comparison to the world: 90
32 (1999)

Budget: *revenues:* $10.9 billion
expenditures: $10.95 billion (2013 est.)

Taxes and other revenues: 35.9% of GDP (2013 est.)
country comparison to the world: 60

Budget surplus (+) or deficit (-):
-0.2% of GDP (2013 est.)
country comparison to the world: 48

Public debt: 39.2% of GDP (2013 est.)
country comparison to the world: 92
40.7% of GDP (2012 est.)
note: data cover general government debt, and includes debt instruments issued (or owned) by government entities, including sub-sectors of central government, state government, local government, and social security funds

Fiscal year: calendar year

Inflation rate (consumer prices): 0.2% (2013 est.)
country comparison to the world: 11
2.3% (2012 est.)

Central bank discount rate: 3.5% (31 December 2011 est.)
country comparison to the world: 99
3.5% (31 December 2010 est.)

Commercial bank prime lending rate: 5% (31 December 2013 est.)
country comparison to the world: 146
5.52% (31 December 2012 est.)

Stock of narrow money: $9.865 billion (31 December 2013 est.)
country comparison to the world: 79
$9.099 billion (31 December 2012 est.)

Stock of broad money: $12.57 billion (31 December 2013 est.)
country comparison to the world: 97
$12.63 billion (31 December 2012 est.)

Stock of domestic credit: $17.39 billion (31 December 2013 est.)
country comparison to the world: 86
$18.39 billion (31 December 2012 est.)

Market value of publicly traded shares:
$1.115 billion (31 December 2012 est.)
country comparison to the world: 106
$1.076 billion (31 December 2011)
$1.252 billion (31 December 2010 est.)

Current account balance: -$613.9 million (2013 est.)
country comparison to the world: 107
-$473.4 million (2012 est.)

Exports: $12.67 billion (2013 est.)
country comparison to the world: 88
$12.23 billion (2012 est.)

Exports—commodities: food products, wood and wood products, metals, machinery and equipment, textiles

Exports—partners: Russia 18.2%, Lithuania 14.9%, Estonia 12.1%, Germany 7.5%, Poland 5.6%, Sweden 4.8% (2012)

Imports: $15.56 billion (2013 est.)
country comparison to the world: 87
$15.15 billion (2012 est.)

Imports—commodities: machinery and equipment, consumer goods, chemicals, fuels, vehicles

Imports—partners: Lithuania 19.1%, Germany 11.6%, Russia 9.2%, Poland 8.2%, Estonia 7.6%, Italy 4.6%, Finland 4.4% (2012)

Reserves of foreign exchange and gold:
$7.22 billion (31 December 2013 est.)
country comparison to the world: 82
$7.523 billion (31 December 2012 est.)

Debt—external: $39.87 billion (31 December 2013 est.)
country comparison to the world: 66
$39.43 billion (31 December 2012 est.)

Stock of direct foreign investment—at home:
$15.49 billion (31 December 2013 est.)
country comparison to the world: 80
$14.14 billion (31 December 2012 est.)

Stock of direct foreign investment—abroad:
$2.212 billion (31 December 2013 est.)
country comparison to the world: 72
$1.992 billion (31 December 2012 est.)

Exchange rates: lati (LVL) per US dollar—
0.5313 (2013 est.)
0.5469 (2012 est.)
0.5305 (2010 est.)
0.5056 (2009)
0.4701 (2008)
note: Latvia joined the EMU and adopted the euro as its currency on 1 January 2014

ENERGY

Electricity—production: 6.412 billion kWh (2010 est.)
country comparison to the world: 112

Electricity—consumption: 6.56 billion kWh (2010 est.)
country comparison to the world: 102

Electricity—exports: 2.764 billion kWh (2011 est.)
country comparison to the world: 36

Electricity—imports: 4.009 billion kWh (2011 est.)
country comparison to the world: 40

Electricity—installed generating capacity:
2.166 million kW (2010 est.)
country comparison to the world: 98

Electricity—from fossil fuels: 27.2% of total installed capacity (2010 est.)
country comparison to the world: 186

Electricity—from nuclear fuels: 0% of total installed capacity (2010 est.)
country comparison to the world: 124

Electricity—from hydroelectric plants: 70.9% of total installed capacity (2010 est.)
country comparison to the world: 22

Electricity—from other renewable sources: 1.9% of total installed capacity (2010 est.)
country comparison to the world: 69

Crude oil—production: 1,000 bbl/day (2012 est.)
country comparison to the world: 110

Crude oil—exports: 0 bbl/day (2010 est.)
country comparison to the world: 142

Crude oil—imports: 0 bbl/day (2010 est.)
country comparison to the world: 208

Crude oil—proved reserves: 0 bbl (1 January 2013 es)
country comparison to the world: 154

Refined petroleum products—production: 0 bbl/day (2010 est.)
country comparison to the world: 163

Refined petroleum products—consumption: 31,340 bbl/day (2011 est.)
country comparison to the world: 112

Refined petroleum products—exports: 6,146 bbl/day (2010 est.)
country comparison to the world: 89

Refined petroleum products—imports: 35,930 bbl/day (2010 est.)
country comparison to the world: 84

Natural gas—production: 0 cu m (2011 est.)
country comparison to the world: 153

Natural gas—consumption: 1.52 billion cu m (2010 est.)
country comparison to the world: 82

Natural gas—exports: 0 cu m (2011 est.)
country comparison to the world: 134

Natural gas—imports: 1.58 billion cu m (2011 est.)
country comparison to the world: 53

Natural gas—proved reserves: 0 cu m (1 January 2013 es)
country comparison to the world: 158

Carbon dioxide emissions from consumption of energy: 8.475 million Mt (2011 est.)
country comparison to the world: 106

COMMUNICATIONS

Telephones—main lines in use: 501,000 (2012)
country comparison to the world: 9 7

Telephones—mobile cellular: 2.31 million (2012)
country comparison to the world: 139

Telephone system: *general assessment:* recent efforts focused on bringing competition to the telecommunications sector; the number of fixed lines is decreasing as mobile-cellular telephone service expands
domestic: number of telecommunications operators has grown rapidly since the fixed-line market opened to competition in 2003; combined fixed-line and mobile-cellular subscribership roughly 150 per 100 persons
international: country code—371; the Latvian network is now connected via fiber optic cable to Estonia, Finland, and Sweden (2008)

Broadcast media: several national and regional commercial TV stations are foreign-owned, 2 national TV stations are publicly owned; system supplemented by privately owned regional and local TV stations; cable and satellite multi-channel TV services with domestic and foreign broadcasts available; publicly owned broadcaster operates 4 radio networks with dozens of stations throughout the country; dozens of private broadcasters also operate radio stations (2007)

Internet country code: .lv

Internet hosts: 359,604 (2012)
country comparison to the world: 58

Internet users: 1.504 million (2009)
country comparison to the world: 81

TRANSPORTATION

Airports: 42 (2013)
country comparison to the world: 101

Airports—with paved runways: *total:* 1 8
over 3,047 m: 1
2,438 to 3,047 m: 3
1,524 to 2,437 m: 4
914 to 1,523 m: 3
under 914 m: 7 (2013)

Airports—with unpaved runways: *total:* 2 4
under 914 m: 24 (2013)

Heliports: 1 (2013)

Pipelines: gas 928 km; refined products 415 km (2013)

Railways: *total:* 2,239 km
country comparison to the world: 68
broad gauge: 2,206 km 1.520-m gauge
narrow gauge: 33 km 0.750-m gauge (2008)

Roadways: *total:* 72,440 km
country comparison to the world: 64
paved: 14,707 km
unpaved: 57,733 km (2013)

Waterways: 300 km (navigable year round) (2010)
country comparison to the world: 93

Merchant marine: *total:* 1 1
country comparison to the world: 113
by type: cargo 3, chemical tanker 1, passenger/cargo 4, petroleum tanker 2, roll on/roll off 1
foreign-owned: 3 (Estonia 3)
registered in other countries: 79 (Antigua and Barbuda 16, Belize 9, Comoros 2, Dominica 2, Georgia 1, Liberia 5, Malta 8, Marshall Islands 19, Russia 2, Saint Vincent and the Grenadines 15) (2010)

Ports and terminals: *major seaport(s):* Riga, Ventspils

MILITARY

Military branches: National Armed Forces (Nacionalo Brunoto Speku): Land Forces (Latvijas Sauszemes Speki), Navy (Latvijas Juras Speki; includes Coast Guard (Latvijas Kara Flotes)), Latvian Air Force (Latvijas Gaisa Speki), Latvian Home Guard (Latvijas Zemessardze) (2011)

Military service age and obligation: 18 years of age for voluntary male and female military service; no conscription; under current law, every citizen is entitled to serve in the armed forces for life (2012)

Manpower available for military service:
males age 16-49: 546,090
females age 16-49: 540,810 (2010 est.)

Manpower fit for military service:
males age 16-49: 401,691
females age 16-49: 447,638 (2010 est.)

Manpower reaching militarily significant age annually: *male:* 10,482
female: 9,858 (2010 est.)

Military expenditures: 0.92% of GDP (2012)
country comparison to the world: 106
1.05% of GDP (2011)
0.92% of GDP (2010)

TRANSNATIONAL ISSUES

Disputes—international: Russia demands better Latvian treatment of ethnic Russians in Latvia; boundary demarcated with Latvia and Lithuania; the Latvian parliament has not ratified its 1998 maritime boundary treaty with Lithuania, primarily due to concerns over oil exploration rights; as a member state that forms part of the EU's external border, Latvia has implemented the strict Schengen border rules with Russia

Refugees and internally displaced persons: *stateless persons:* 280,759 (2012); note—individuals who were Latvian citizens prior to the 1940 Soviet occupation and their descendants were recognized as Latvian citizens when the country's independence was restored in 1991; citizens of the former Soviet Union residing in Latvia who have neither Latvian nor other citizenship are considered non-citizens (officially there is no statelessness in Latvia) and are entitled to non-citizen passports; children born after Latvian independence to stateless parents are entitled to Latvian citizenship upon their parents' request; non-citizens cannot vote or hold certain government jobs and are exempt from military service but can travel visa-free in the EU under the Schengen accord like Latvian citizens; non-citizens can obtain naturalization if they have been permanent residents of Latvia for at least five years, pass tests in Latvian language and history, and know the words of the Latvian national anthem

Illicit drugs: transshipment and destination point for cocaine, synthetic drugs, opiates, and cannabis from Southwest Asia, Western Europe, Latin America, and neighboring Balkan countries; despite improved legislation, vulnerable to money laundering due to nascent enforcement capabilities and comparatively weak regulation of offshore companies and the gaming industry; CIS organized crime (including counterfeiting, corruption, extortion, stolen cars, and prostitution) accounts for most laundered proceeds

LEBANON

INTRODUCTION

Background: Following World War I, France acquired a mandate over the northern portion of the former Ottoman Empire province of Syria. The French demarcated the region of Lebanon in 1920 and granted this area independence in 1943. Since independence the country has been marked by periods of political turmoil interspersed with prosperity built on its position as a regional center for finance and trade. The country's 1975-90 civil war that resulted in an estimated 120,000 fatalities, was followed by years of social and political instability. Sectarianism is a key element of Lebanese political life. Neighboring Syria has long influenced Lebanon's foreign policy and internal policies, and its military occupied Lebanon from 1976 until 2005. The Lebanon-based Hizballah militia and Israel continued attacks and counterattacks against each other after Syria's withdrawal, and fought a brief war in 2006. Lebanon's borders with Syria and Israel remain unresolved.

GEOGRAPHY

Location: Middle East, bordering the Mediterranean Sea, between Israel and Syria

Geographic coordinates: 33 50 N, 35 50 E

Map references: Middle East

Area: *total:* 10,400 sq km
country comparison to the world: 170
land: 10,230 sq km
water: 170 sq km

Area—comparative: about one-third the size of Maryland

Land boundaries: *total:* 454 km
border countries: Israel 79 km, Syria 375 km

Coastline: 225 km

Maritime claims: *territorial sea:* 12 nm

Climate: Mediterranean; mild to cool, wet winters with hot, dry summers; Lebanon mountains experience heavy winter snows

Terrain: narrow coastal plain; El Beqaa (Bekaa Valley) separates Lebanon and Anti-Lebanon Mountains

Elevation extremes: *lowest point:* Mediterranean Sea 0 m
highest point: Qornet es Saouda 3,088 m

Natural resources: limestone, iron ore, salt, water-surplus state in a water-deficit region, arable land

Land use: *arable land:* 10.72%
permanent crops: 12.06%
other: 77.22% (2011)

Irrigated land: 1,040 sq km (2003)

Total renewable water resources: 4.5 cu km (2011)

Freshwater withdrawal (domestic/industrial/agricultural): *total:* 1.31 cu km/yr (29%/11%/60%)
per capita: 316.8 cu m/yr (2005)

Natural hazards: dust storms, sandstorms

Environment—current issues: deforestation; soil erosion; desertification; air pollution in Beirut from vehicular traffic and the burning of industrial wastes; pollution of coastal waters from raw sewage and oil spills

Environment—international agreements: *party to:* Biodiversity, Climate Change, Climate Change-Kyoto Protocol, Desertification, Hazardous Wastes, Law of the Sea, Ozone Layer Protection, Ship Pollution, Wetlands
signed, but not ratified: Environmental Modification, Marine Life Conservation

Geography—note: Nahr el Litani is the only major river in Near East not crossing an international boundary; rugged terrain historically helped isolate, protect, and develop numerous factional groups based on religion, clan, and ethnicity

PEOPLE AND SOCIETY

Nationality: *noun:* Lebanese (singular and plural)
adjective: Lebanese

Ethnic groups: Arab 95%, Armenian 4%, other 1%
note: many Christian Lebanese do not identify themselves as Arab but rather as descendents of the ancient Canaanites and prefer to be called Phoenicians

Languages: Arabic (official), French, English, Armenian

Religions: Muslim 54% (27% Sunni, 27% Shia), Christian 40.5% (includes 21% Maronite Catholic, 8% Greek Orthodox, 5% Greek Catholic, 6.5% other Christian), Druze 5.6%, very small numbers of Jews, Baha'is, Buddhists, Hindus, and Mormons
note: 18 religious sects recognized (2012 est.)

Population: 5,882,562 (July 2014 est.)
country comparison to the world: 110

Age structure: 0-14 years: 25.2% (male 758,153/female 723,619)
15-24 years: 17.2% (male 515,591/female 493,879)
25-54 years: 44.1% (male 1,309,544/female 1,283,074)
55-64 years: 6.7% (male 185,503/female 219,242)
65 years and over: 9.4% (male 175,911/female 218,046) (2014 est.)

Dependency ratios:
total dependency ratio: 41.8 %
youth dependency ratio: 29.5 %
elderly dependency ratio: 12.3 %
potential support ratio: 8.1 (2013)

Median age: *total:* 29.3 years
male: 28.7 years
female: 29.8 years (2014 est.)

Population growth rate: 9.37% (2014 est.)
country comparison to the world: 1

Birth rate: 14.8 births/1,000 population (2014 est.)
country comparison to the world: 133

Death rate: 4.95 deaths/1,000 population (2014 est.)
country comparison to the world: 190

Net migration rate: 83.82 migrant(s)/1,000 population (2014 est.)
country comparison to the world: 1

Urbanization: *urban population:* 87.2% of total population (2011)
rate of urbanization: 0.86% annual rate of change (2010-15 est.)

Major urban areas—population: BEIRUT (capital) 1.909 million (2009)

Sex ratio: *at birth:* 1.05 male(s)/female
0-14 years: 1.05 male(s)/female
15-24 years: 1.04 male(s)/female
25-54 years: 1.02 male(s)/female
55-64 years: 1 male(s)/female
65 years and over: 0.86 male(s)/female
total population: 0.96 male(s)/female (2014 est.)

Maternal mortality rate: 25 deaths/100,000 live births (2010)
country comparison to the world: 130

Infant mortality rate: *total:* 7.98 deaths/1,000 live births
country comparison to the world: 155
male: 8.4 deaths/1,000 live births
female: 7.53 deaths/1,000 live births (2014 est.)

Life expectancy at birth: *total population:* 77.22 years
country comparison to the world: 69
male: 76.03 years
female: 78.46 years (2014 est.)

Total fertility rate: 1.74 children born/woman (2014 est.)
country comparison to the world: 167

Contraceptive prevalence rate: 58% (2004)

Health expenditures: 6.3% of GDP (2011)
country comparison to the world: 100

Physicians density: 3.54 physicians/1,000 population (2009)

Hospital bed density: 3.5 beds/1,000 population (2009)

Drinking water source:
improved:
urban: 100% of population
rural: 100% of population
total: 100% of population
unimproved:
urban: 0% of population
rural: 0% of population
total: 0% of population (2011 est.)

Sanitation facility access:
improved:
urban: 100% of population
rural: 87% of population
total: 98.3% of population
unimproved:
urban: 0% of population
rural: 13% of population
total: 1.7% of population (2005 est.)

HIV/AIDS—adult prevalence rate: 0.1% (2009 est.)
country comparison to the world: 156

HIV/AIDS—people living with HIV/AIDS: 3,600 (2009 est.)
country comparison to the world: 129

HIV/AIDS—deaths: fewer than 500 (2009 est.)
country comparison to the world: 92

Obesity—adult prevalence rate: 27.4% (2008)
country comparison to the world: 40

Children under the age of 5 years underweight: 4.2% (2004)
country comparison to the world: 98

Education expenditures: 2.2% of GDP (2012)
country comparison to the world: 162

Literacy: *definition:* age 15 and over can read and write
total population: 89.6%
male: 93.4%
female: 86% (2007 est.)

School life expectancy (primary to tertiary education): *total:* 13 years
male: 13 years
female: 13 years (2012)

Child labor—children ages 5-14: *total number:* 54,387
percentage: 7 % (2000 est.)

Unemployment, youth ages 15-24: *total:* 16.8%
country comparison to the world: 76
male: 14.6%
female: 22.3% (2009)

GOVERNMENT

Country name: *conventional long form:* Lebanese Republic
conventional short form: Lebanon
local long form: Al Jumhuriyah al Lubnaniyah
local short form: Lubnan
former: Greater Lebanon

Government type: republic

Capital: *name:* Beirut

geographic coordinates: 33 52 N, 35 30 E
time difference: UTC+2 (7 hours ahead of Washington, DC during Standard Time)
daylight saving time: +1hr, begins last Sunday in March; ends last Sunday in October

Administrative divisions: 6 governorates (mohafazat, singular—mohafazah); Beqaa, Beyrouth (Beirut), Liban-Nord, Liban-Sud, Mont-Liban, Nabatiye *note:* two new governorates—Aakkar and Baalbek-Hermel—have been legislated but not yet implemented

Independence: 22 November 1943 (from League of Nations mandate under French administration)

National holiday: Independence Day, 22 November (1943)

Constitution: drafted 15 May 1926, adopted 23 May 1926; amended several times, last in 2004 (2013)

Legal system: mixed legal system of civil law based on the French civil code, Ottoman legal tradition, and religious laws covering personal status, marriage, divorce, and other family relations of the Jewish, Islamic, and Christian communities

International law organization participation: has not submitted an ICJ jurisdiction declaration; non-party state to the ICCt

Suffrage: 21 years of age; compulsory for all males; authorized for women at age 21 with elementary education; excludes military personnel

Executive branch:
note: following Prime Minister Tamam SALAM's formation of his Cabinet on 15 February 2014, the government is in caretaker status until it receives a vote of confidence in the National Assembly
chief of state: President Michel SULAYMAN (since 25 May 2008)
head of government: Prime Minister Tamam SALAM (since 6 April 2013), Deputy Prime Minister Samir MOQBIL (since 7 July 2011)
cabinet: Cabinet chosen by the prime minister in consultation with the president and members of the National Assembly (For more information visit the World Leaders website)
elections: president elected by the National Assembly for a six-year term (may not serve consecutive terms); election last held on 25 May 2008 (next to be held in 2014); the prime minister and deputy prime minister appointed by the president in consultation with the National Assembly
election results: Michel SULAYMAN elected president; National Assembly vote—118 for, 6 abstentions, 3 invalidated; 1 seat unfilled due to death of incumbent

Legislative branch: unicameral National Assembly or Majlis al-Nuwab (Arabic) or Assemblee Nationale (French) (128 seats; members elected by popular vote on the basis of sectarian proportional representation to serve four-year terms)
elections: last held on 7 June 2009 (next to be held in 2013)
election results: percent of vote by group—March 8 Coalition 54.7%, March 14 Coalition 45.3%; seats by group—March 14 Coalition 71; March 8 Coalition 57; seats by party following 16 July 2012 byelection held to fill one seat—March 14 Coalition 72, March 8 Coalition 56

Judicial branch: *highest court(s):* Court of Cassation or Supreme Court (organized into 4 divisions, each with a presiding judge and 2 associate judges); Constitutional Council (consists of 10 members)
judge selection and term of office: Court of Cassation judges appointed by Supreme Judicial Council, headed by the chief justice, and includes other judicial officials; judge tenure NA; Constitutional Council members appointed—5 by the Council of Ministers and 5 by parliament; members serve 5-year terms
subordinate courts: Courts of Appeal (6); Courts of First Instance; specialized tribunals, religious courts; military courts

Political parties and leaders:
14 March Coalition: Democratic Left [Ilyas ATALLAH]; Democratic Renewal Movement [Nassib LAHUD]; Future Movement Bloc [Sa'ad al-HARIRI]; Kataeb Party [Amine GEMAYEL]; Lebanese Forces [Samir JA'JA]; Tripoli Independent Bloc
8 March Coalition: Development and Resistance Bloc [Nabih BERRI, leader of Amal Movement]; Free Patriotic Movement [Michel AWN]; Loyalty to the Resistance Bloc [Mohammad RA'AD] (includes Hizballah [Hassan NASRALLAH]); Nasserite Popular Movement [Usama SAAD]; Popular Bloc [Elias SKAFF]; Syrian Ba'th Party [Sayez SHUKR]; Syrian Social Nationalist Party [Ali QANSO]; Tashnaq [Hovig MEKHITIRIAN]
Independent: Democratic Gathering Bloc [Walid JUNBLATT, leader of Progressive Socialist Party]; Metn Bloc [Michel MURR]

Political pressure groups and leaders: Maronite Church [Patriarch Bishara al-Ra'i]
other: note—most sects retain militias and a number of militant groups operate in Palestinian refugee camps

International organization participation: ABEDA, AFESD, AMF, CAEU, FAO, G-24, G-77, IAEA, IBRD, ICAO, ICC (national committees), ICRM, IDA, IDB, IFAD, IFC, IFRCS, ILO, IMF, IMO, IMSO, Interpol, IOC, IPU, ISO, ITSO, ITU, LAS, MIGA, NAM, OAS (observer), OIC, OIF, OPCW, PCA, UN, UNCTAD, UNESCO, UNHCR, UNIDO, UNRWA, UNWTO, UPU, WCO, WFTU (NGOs), WHO, WIPO, WMO, WTO (observer)

Diplomatic representation in the US: *chief of mission:* Ambassador Antoine CHEDID (since 4 June 2008)
chancery: 2560 28th Street NW, Washington, DC 20008
telephone: [1] (202) 939-6300
FAX: [1] (202) 939-6324
consulate(s) general: Detroit, New York, Los Angeles

Diplomatic representation from the US: *chief of mission:* Ambassador David HALE (since 6 September 2013)
embassy: Awkar, Lebanon (Awkar facing the Municipality)
mailing address: P. O. Box 70-840, Antelias, Lebanon; from US: US Embassy Beirut, 6070 Beirut Place, Washington, DC 20521-6070
telephone: [961] (4) 542600, 543600
FAX: [961] (4) 544136

Flag description: three horizontal bands consisting of red (top), white (middle, double width), and red (bottom) with a green cedar tree centered in the white band; the red bands symbolize blood shed for liberation, the white band denotes peace, the snow of the mountains, and purity; the green cedar tree is the symbol of Lebanon and represents eternity, steadiness, happiness, and prosperity

National symbol(s): cedar tree

National anthem: *name:* "Kulluna lil-watan" (All Of Us, For Our Country!)
lyrics/music: Rachid NAKHLE/Wadih SABRA
note: adopted 1927; the anthem was chosen following a nationwide competition

ECONOMY

Economy—overview: Lebanon has a free-market economy and a strong laissez-faire commercial tradition. The government does not restrict foreign investment; however, the investment climate suffers from red tape, corruption, arbitrary licensing decisions, complex customs procedures, high taxes, tariffs, and fees, archaic legislation, and weak intellectual property rights. The Lebanese economy is service-oriented; main growth sectors include banking and tourism. The 1975-90 civil war seriously damaged Lebanon's economic infrastructure, cut national output by half, and derailed Lebanon's position as a Middle Eastern entrepot and banking hub. Following the civil war, Lebanon rebuilt much of its war-torn physical and financial infrastructure by borrowing heavily, mostly from domestic banks, which saddled the government with a huge debt burden. Pledges of economic and financial reforms made at separate international donor conferences during the 2000s have mostly gone unfulfilled, including those made during the Paris III Donor Conference in 2007 following the July 2006 war. The collapse of the MIKATI government in early 2011 over its backing of the Special Tribunal for Lebanon and the conflict in neighboring Syria slowed economic growth to the 1-2% range in 2011-13, after four years of 8% average growth. In September 2011 the Cabinet endorsed a bill that would provide $1.2 billion in funding to improve Lebanon's downtrodden electricity sector, but fiscal limitations will test the government's ability to invest in other areas, such as water.

GDP (purchasing power parity): $64.31 billion (2013 est.)
country comparison to the world: 88
$63.36 billion (2012 est.)
$62.42 billion (2011 est.)
note: data are in 2013 US dollars

GDP (official exchange rate): $43.49 billion (2013 est.)

GDP—real growth rate: 1.5% (2013 est.)
country comparison to the world: 157
1.5% (2012 est.)
1.5% (2011 est.)

GDP—per capita (PPP): $15,800 (2013 est.)
country comparison to the world: 87
$15,800 (2012 est.)
$15,800 (2011 est.)
note: data are in 2013 US dollars

Gross national saving: 24.6% of GDP (2013 est.)
country comparison to the world: 53
29.2% of GDP (2012 est.)
22.3% of GDP (2011 est.)

GDP—composition, by end use:
household consumption: 82.3%
government consumption: 14.9%
investment in fixed capital: 31.2%
exports of goods and services: 18.6%
imports of goods and services: -47% (2013 est.)

GDP—composition, by sector of origin:
agriculture: 4.6%
industry: 20%
services: 75.4% (2013 est.)

Agriculture—products: citrus, grapes, tomatoes, apples, vegetables, potatoes, olives, tobacco; sheep, goats

Industries: banking, tourism, food processing, wine, jewelry, cement, textiles, mineral and chemical products, wood and furniture products, oil refining, metal fabricating

Industrial production growth rate: 3% (2013 est.)
country comparison to the world: 102

Labor force: 1.481 million
country comparison to the world: 130
note: in addition, there are as many as 1 million foreign workers (2007 est.)

Labor force—by occupation:
agriculture: NA%
industry: NA%
services: NA%

Unemployment rate: NA%

Population below poverty line: 28% (1999 est.)

Household income or consumption by percentage share: *lowest* 10%: NA%
highest 10%: NA%

Budget: *revenues:* $9.487 billion
expenditures: $13.56 billion (2013 est.)

Taxes and other revenues: 21.8% of GDP (2013 est.)
country comparison to the world: 150

Budget surplus (+) or deficit (-):
-9.4% of GDP (2013 est.)
country comparison to the world: 202

Public debt: 120% of GDP (2013 est.)
country comparison to the world: 9
119.6% of GDP (2012 est.)
note: data cover central government debt, and exclude debt instruments issued (or owned) by government entities other than the treasury; the data include treasury debt held by foreign entities; the data include debt issued by subnational entities, as well as intra-governmental debt; intragovernmental debt consists of treasury borrowings from surpluses in the social funds, such as for retirement, medical care, and unemployment

Fiscal year: calendar year

Inflation rate (consumer prices): 5% (2013 est.)
country comparison to the world: 152
6.4% (2012 est.)

Central bank discount rate: 3.5% (31 December 2010 est.)
country comparison to the world: 26
10% (31 December 2009 est.)

Commercial bank prime lending rate: 7.5% (31 December 2013 est.)
country comparison to the world: 121
7.25% (31 December 2012 est.)

Stock of narrow money: $5.419 billion (31 December 2013 est.)
country comparison to the world: 97
$4.712 billion (31 December 2012 est.)

Stock of broad money: $97.04 billion (31 December 2011 est.)
country comparison to the world: 54
$92 billion (31 December 2010 est.)

Stock of domestic credit: $80.3 billion (31 December 2013 est.)
country comparison to the world: 58
$75.76 billion (31 December 2012 est.)

Market value of publicly traded shares: $10.3 billion (31 December 2012 est.)
country comparison to the world: 71
$10.16 billion (31 December 2011)
$12.59 billion (31 December 2010 est.)

Current account balance: -$3.224 billion (2013 est.)
country comparison to the world: 159
-$1.663 billion (2012 est.)

Exports: $5.826 billion (2013 est.)
country comparison to the world: 110
$5.615 billion (2012 est.)

Exports—commodities: jewelry, base metals, chemicals, miscellaneous consumer goods, fruit and vegetables, tobacco, construction minerals, electric power machinery and switchgear, textile fibers, paper

Exports—partners: South Africa 19.3%, Switzerland 12.2%, Saudi Arabia 8%, UAE 7.9%, Syria 6.6%, Iraq 4.7% (2012)

Imports: $20.97 billion (2013 est.)
country comparison to the world: 77
$20.33 billion (2012 est.)

Imports—commodities: petroleum products, cars, medicinal products, clothing, meat and live animals, consumer goods, paper, textile fabrics, tobacco, electrical machinery and equipment, chemicals

Imports—partners: US 11.2%, Italy 8.6%, China 8.3%, France 7.2%, Germany 5.6%, Turkey 4.5%, Greece 4.2% (2012)

Reserves of foreign exchange and gold:
$51.95 billion (31 December 2013 est.)
country comparison to the world: 38
$52.5 billion (31 December 2012 est.)

Debt—external: $26.74 billion (31 December 2013 est.)
country comparison to the world: 77
$25.16 billion (31 December 2012 est.)

Stock of direct foreign investment—at home:
$NA

Stock of direct foreign investment—abroad:
$NA

Exchange rates: Lebanese pounds (LBP) per US dollar—
1,507.5 (2013 est.)
1,507.5 (2012 est.)
1,507.5 (2010 est.)
1,507.5 (2009)
1,507.5 (2008)

ENERGY

Electricity—production: 14.81 billion kWh (2010 est.)
country comparison to the world: 84

Electricity—consumption: 14.19 billion kWh (2010 est.)
country comparison to the world: 78

Electricity—exports: 0 kWh (2012 est.)
country comparison to the world: 158

Electricity—imports: 1.245 billion kWh (2010 est.)
country comparison to the world: 60

Electricity—installed generating capacity: 2.314 million kW (2010 est.)
country comparison to the world: 97

Electricity—from fossil fuels: 87.9% of total installed capacity (2010 est.)
country comparison to the world: 82

Electricity—from nuclear fuels: 0% of total installed capacity (2010 est.)
country comparison to the world: 123

Electricity—from hydroelectric plants: 12.1% of total installed capacity (2010 est.)
country comparison to the world: 109

Electricity—from other renewable sources:
0% of total installed capacity (2010 est.)
country comparison to the world: 192

Crude oil—production: 0 bbl/day (2012 est.)
country comparison to the world: 186

Crude oil—exports: 0 bbl/day (2010 est.)
country comparison to the world: 141

Crude oil—imports: 0 bbl/day (2010 est.)
country comparison to the world: 207

Crude oil—proved reserves: 0 bbl (1 January 2013 es)
country comparison to the world: 153

Refined petroleum products—production: 0 bbl/day (2010 est.)
country comparison to the world: 162

Refined petroleum products—consumption:
106,700 bbl/day (2011 est.)
country comparison to the world: 76

Refined petroleum products—exports:
0 bbl/day (2010 est.)
country comparison to the world: 191

Refined petroleum products—imports:
120,400 bbl/day (2010 est.)
country comparison to the world: 45

Natural gas—production: 0 cu m (2011 est.)
country comparison to the world: 152

Natural gas—consumption: 150 million cu m (2010 est.)
country comparison to the world: 103

Natural gas—exports: 0 cu m (2011 est.)
country comparison to the world: 133

Natural gas—imports: 150 million cu m (2010 est.)
country comparison to the world: 72

Natural gas—proved reserves: 0 cu m (1 January 2013 es)
country comparison to the world: 157

Carbon dioxide emissions from consumption of energy: 19.45 million Mt (2011 est.)
country comparison to the world: 86

COMMUNICATIONS

Telephones—main lines in use: 878,000 (2012)
country comparison to the world: 81

Telephones—mobile cellular: 4 million (2012)
country comparison to the world: 122

Telephone system: *general assessment:* repair of the telecommunications system, severely damaged during the civil war, now complete
domestic: two mobile-cellular networks provide good service; combined fixed-line and mobile-cellular subscribership roughly 100 per 100 persons
international: country code—961; submarine cable links to Cyprus, Egypt, and Syria; satellite earth stations—2 Intelsat (1 Indian Ocean and 1 Atlantic Ocean); coaxial cable to Syria (2011)

Broadcast media: 7 TV stations, 1 of which is state-owned; more than 30 radio stations, 1 of which is state-owned; satellite and cable TV services available; transmissions of at least 2 international broadcasters are accessible through partner stations (2007)

Internet country code: .lb

Internet hosts: 64,926 (2012)
country comparison to the world: 91

Internet users: 1 million (2009)
country comparison to the world: 99

TRANSPORTATION

Airports: 8 (2013)
country comparison to the world: 160

Airports—with paved runways: *total:* 5
over 3,047 m: 1
2,438 to 3,047 m: 2
1,524 to 2,437 m: 1
under 914 m: 1 (2013)

Airports—with unpaved runways: *total:* 3
914 to 1,523 m: 2
under 914 m: 1 (2013)

Heliports: 1 (2013)

Pipelines: gas 88 km (2013)

Railways: *total:* 401 km
country comparison to the world: 116
standard gauge: 319 km 1.435-m gauge
narrow gauge: 82 km 1.050-m gauge
note: rail system unusable because of the damage done during fighting in the 1980s and in 2006 (2008)

Roadways: *total:* 6,970 km (includes 170 km of expressways) (2005)
country comparison to the world: 145

Merchant marine: *total:* 29
country comparison to the world: 85
by type: bulk carrier 4, cargo 7, carrier 17, vehicle carrier 1
foreign-owned: 2 (Syria 2)
registered in other countries: 34 (Barbados 2, Cambodia 5, Comoros 2, Egypt 1, Georgia 1, Honduras 2, Liberia 1, Malta 6, Moldova 1, Panama 2, Saint Vincent and the Grenadines 2, Sierra Leone 2, Togo 6, unknown 1) (2010)

Ports and terminals: *major seaport(s):* Beirut, Tripoli
container port(s) (TEUs): Beirut (1,034,249)

MILITARY

Military branches: Lebanese Armed Forces (LAF): Lebanese Army ((Al Jaysh al Lubnani) includes Lebanese Navy (Al Quwwat al Bahiriyya al Lubnaniya), Lebanese Air Force (Al Quwwat al Jawwiya al Lubnaniya)) (2013)

Military service age and obligation: 17-30 years of age for voluntary military service; 18-24 years of age for officer candidates; no conscription (2013)

Manpower available for military service:
males age 16-49: 1,081,016
females age 16-49: 1,115,349 (2010 est.)

Manpower fit for military service:
males age 16-49: 920,825
females age 16-49: 941,806 (2010 est.)

Manpower reaching militarily significant age annually: *male:* 36,856
female: 35,121 (2010 est.)

Military expenditures: 4.04% of GDP (2012)
country comparison to the world: 10
4.06% of GDP (2011)
4.04% of GDP (2010)

TRANSNATIONAL ISSUES

Disputes—international: lacking a treaty or other documentation describing the boundary, portions of the Lebanon-Syria boundary are unclear with several sections in dispute; since 2000, Lebanon has claimed Shab'a Farms area in the Israeli-occupied Golan Heights; the roughly 2,000-strong UN Interim Force in Lebanon has been in place since 1978

Refugees and internally displaced persons: *refugees (country of origin):* 6,516 (Iraq) (2012); 444,480 (Palestinian refugees (UNRWA)) (2013); 1,029,473 (Syria) (2014)
IDPs: at least 47,000 (1975-90 civil war, 2007 Lebanese security forces' destruction of Palestinian refugee camp) (2011)

Trafficking in persons: *current situation:* Lebanon is a source, transit, and destination country for women and children subjected to forced labor and sex trafficking; Eastern European women and children are transported through Lebanon for sexual exploitation in other Middle Eastern countries; women from Sri Lanka, the Philippines, Ethiopia, Kenya, Bangladesh, Nepal, Madagascar, Congo, Togo, Cameroon, and Nigeria are recruited by agencies to work in domestic service but are often subject to conditions indicative of forced labor, including the withholding of passports, nonpayment of wages, restricted movement, threats, and abuse; Lebanon's artiste visa program enabling women to work as dancers for three months in the adult entertainment industry sustains a significant sex trade; anecdotal information indicates some Lebanese children are victims of forced labor, such as street begging and commercial sexual exploitation; Syrian refugee women and children in Lebanon are at increased risk of sex trafficking
tier rating: Tier 2 Watch List—Lebanon does not fully comply with the minimum standards for the elimination of trafficking; however, it is making significant efforts to do so; the government conducts investigations of human trafficking and possibly some prosecutions but for another year did not report convicting any trafficking offenders or officials complicit in human trafficking; the government continues to lack a formal system for identifying victims and does not have a policy to protect victims from being punished for crimes committed as a direct result of being trafficked; NGOs, rather than the government, provide victim assistance and protection (2013)

Illicit drugs: cannabis cultivation dramatically reduced to 2,500 hectares in 2002 despite continued significant cannabis consumption; opium poppy cultivation minimal; small amounts of Latin American cocaine and Southwest Asian heroin transit country on way to European markets and for Middle Eastern consumption; money laundering of drug proceeds fuels concern that extremists are benefiting from drug trafficking

LESOTHO

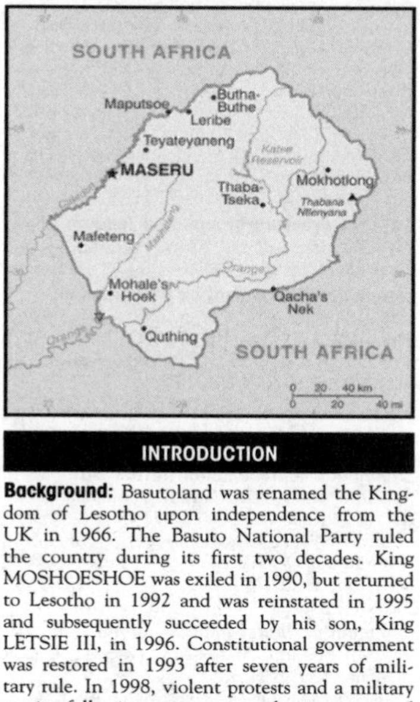

INTRODUCTION

Background: Basutoland was renamed the Kingdom of Lesotho upon independence from the UK in 1966. The Basuto National Party ruled the country during its first two decades. King MOSHOESHOE was exiled in 1990, but returned to Lesotho in 1992 and was reinstated in 1995 and subsequently succeeded by his son, King LETSIE III, in 1996. Constitutional government was restored in 1993 after seven years of military rule. In 1998, violent protests and a military mutiny following a contentious election prompted a brief but bloody intervention by South African and Batswana military forces under the aegis of the Southern African Development Community. Subsequent constitutional reforms restored relative political stability. Peaceful parliamentary elections were held in 2002, but the National Assembly elections of February 2007 were hotly contested and aggrieved parties disputed how the electoral law was applied to award proportional seats in the Assembly. In May 2012, competitive elections involving 18 parties saw Prime Minister Motsoahae Thomas THABANE form a coalition government—the first in the country's history—that ousted the 14-year incumbent, Pakalitha MOSISILI, who peacefully transferred power the following month.

GEOGRAPHY

Location: Southern Africa, an enclave of South Africa

Geographic coordinates: 29 30 S, 28 30 E

Map references: Africa

Area: *total:* 30,355 sq km
country comparison to the world: 142
land: 30,355 sq km
water: 0 sq km

Area—comparative: slightly smaller than Maryland

Land boundaries: *total:* 909 km
border countries: South Africa 909 km

Coastline: 0 km (landlocked)

Maritime claims: none (landlocked)

Climate: temperate; cool to cold, dry winters; hot, wet summers

Terrain: mostly highland with plateaus, hills, and mountains

Elevation extremes: *lowest point:* junction of the Orange and Makhaleng Rivers 1,400 m
highest point: Thabana Ntlenyana 3,482 m

Natural resources: water, agricultural and grazing land, diamonds, sand, clay, building stone

Land use: *arable land:* 10.14%
permanent crops: 0.13%
other: 89.72% (2011)

Irrigated land: 26.37 sq km (2003)

Total renewable water resources: 3.02 cu km (2011)

Freshwater withdrawal (domestic/industrial/agricultural): *total:* 0.04 cu km/yr (46%/46%/9%)
per capita: 21.79 cu m/yr (2000)

Natural hazards: periodic droughts

Environment—current issues: population pressure forcing settlement in marginal areas results in overgrazing, severe soil erosion, and soil exhaustion; desertification; Highlands Water Project controls, stores, and redirects water to South Africa

Environment—international agreements: *party to:* Biodiversity, Climate Change, Climate Change-Kyoto Protocol, Desertification, Endangered Species, Hazardous Wastes, Law of the Sea, Marine Life Conservation, Ozone Layer Protection, Wetlands
signed, but not ratified: none of the selected agreements

Geography—note: landlocked, completely surrounded by South Africa; mountainous, more than 80% of the country is 1,800 m above sea level

PEOPLE AND SOCIETY

Nationality: noun: Mosotho (singular), Basotho (plural)
adjective: Basotho

Ethnic groups: Sotho 99.7%, Europeans, Asians, and other 0.3%,

Languages: Sesotho (official) (southern Sotho), English (official), Zulu, Xhosa

Religions: Christian 80%, indigenous beliefs 20%

Population: 1,942,008 (July 2014 est.)
country comparison to the world: 149
note: estimates for this country explicitly take into account the effects of excess mortality due to AIDS; this can result in lower life expectancy, higher infant mortality, higher death rates, lower population growth rates, and changes in the distribution of population by age and sex than would otherwise be expected

Age structure: *0-14 years:* 32.9% (male 321,017/female 318,265)
15-24 years: 19.9% (male 184,006/female 203,336)
25-54 years: 36.8% (male 349,365/female 364,970)
55-64 years: 5.4% (male 51,274/female 44,847)
65 years and over: 5.4% (male 52,955/female 51,973) (2014 est.)

Dependency ratios:
total dependency ratio: 68.3 %
youth dependency ratio: 61.2 %
elderly dependency ratio: 7.1 %
potential support ratio: 14.1 (2013)

Median age: *total:* 23.6 years
male: 23.6 years

female: 23.6 years (2014 est.)

Population growth rate: 0.34% (2014 est.)
country comparison to the world: 167

Birth rate: 25.92 births/1,000 population (2014 est.)
country comparison to the world: 49

Death rate: 14.91 deaths/1,000 population (2014 est.)
country comparison to the world: 3

Net migration rate: -7.62 migrant(s)/1,000 population (2014 est.)
country comparison to the world: 206

Urbanization: *urban population:* 27.6% of total population (2011)
rate of urbanization: 3.57% annual rate of change (2010-15 est.)

Major urban areas—population: MASERU (capital) 220,000 (2009)

Sex ratio: *at birth:* 1.03 male(s)/female
0-14 years: 1.01 male(s)/female
15-24 years: 0.91 male(s)/female
25-54 years: 0.96 male(s)/female
55-64 years: 0.98 male(s)/female
65 years and over: 0.99 male(s)/female
total population: 0.97 male(s)/female (2014 est.)

Mother's mean age at first birth: 21.2
note: median age at first birth among women 25-29 (2009 est.)

Maternal mortality rate: 620 deaths/100,000 live births (2010)
country comparison to the world: 12

Infant mortality rate: *total:* 50.48 deaths/1,000 live births
country comparison to the world: 37
male: 54.38 deaths/1,000 live births
female: 46.45 deaths/1,000 live births (2014 est.)

Life expectancy at birth: *total population:* 52.65 years
country comparison to the world: 211
male: 52.55 years
female: 52.75 years (2014 est.)

Total fertility rate: 2.78 children born/woman (2014 est.)
country comparison to the world: 70

Contraceptive prevalence rate: 47% (2009/10)

Health expenditures: 12.8% of GDP (2011)
country comparison to the world: 8

Physicians density: 0.05 physicians/1,000 population (2003)

Hospital bed density: 1.3 beds/1,000 population (2006)

Drinking water source:
improved:
urban: 90.8% of population
rural: 72.7% of population
total: 77.7% of population
unimproved:
urban: 9.2% of population
rural: 27.3% of population
total: 22.3% of population (2011 est.)

Sanitation facility access:
improved:
urban: 32% of population
rural: 24.2% of population
total: 26.3% of population
unimproved:
urban: 68% of population
rural: 75.8% of population
total: 73.7% of population (2011 est.)

HIV/AIDS—adult prevalence rate: 23.1% (2012 est.)
country comparison to the world: 2

HIV/AIDS—people living with HIV/AIDS: 358,700 (2012 est.)
country comparison to the world: 20

HIV/AIDS—deaths: 15,500 (2012 est.)
country comparison to the world: 20

Obesity—adult prevalence rate: 14.6% (2008)
country comparison to the world: 120

Children under the age of 5 years underweight: 13.5% (2010)
country comparison to the world: 56

Education expenditures: 13% of GDP (2008)

country comparison to the world: 1

Literacy: *definition:* age 15 and over can read and write
total population: 89.6%
male: 83.3%
female: 95.6% (2010 est.)

School life expectancy (primary to tertiary education): *total:* 11 years
male: 11 years
female: 12 years (2012)

Child labor—children ages 5-14: *total number:* 103,020
percentage: 23 % (2000 est.)

Unemployment, youth ages 15-24: *total:* 34.4%
country comparison to the world: 19
male: 29%
female: 41.9% (2008)

GOVERNMENT

Country name: *conventional long form:* Kingdom of Lesotho
conventional short form: Lesotho
local long form: Kingdom of Lesotho
local short form: Lesotho
former: Basutoland

Government type: parliamentary constitutional monarchy

Capital: *name:* Maseru

geographic coordinates: 29 19 S, 27 29 E
time difference: UTC+2 (7 hours ahead of Washington, DC during Standard Time)

Administrative divisions: 10 districts; Berea, Butha-Buthe, Leribe, Mafeteng, Maseru, Mohale's Hoek, Mokhotlong, Qacha's Nek, Quthing, Thaba-Tseka

Independence: 4 October 1966 (from the UK)

National holiday: Independence Day, 4 October (1966)

Constitution: previous 1959, 1967; latest adopted 2 April 1993 (effectively restoring the 1967 version); amended 2001 (2013)

Legal system: mixed legal system of English common law and Roman-Dutch law; judicial review of legislative acts in High Court and Court of Appeal

International law organization participation: accepts compulsory ICJ jurisdiction with reservations; accepts ICCt jurisdiction

Suffrage: 18 years of age; universal

Executive branch: *chief of state:* King LETSIE III (since 7 February 1996); note—King LETSIE III formerly occupied the throne from November 1990 to February 1995 while his father was in exile
head of government: Prime Minister Motsoahae Thomas THABANE (since 8 June 2012)
cabinet: Cabinet (For more information visit the World Leaders website)
elections: according to the constitution, the leader of the majority party, or coalition of parties, in the Assembly automatically becomes prime minister; the monarchy is hereditary, but, under the terms of the constitution that came into effect after the March 1993 election, the monarch is a "living symbol of national unity" with no executive or legislative powers; under traditional law the college of chiefs has the power to depose the monarch, determine who is next in the line of succession, or who shall serve as regent in the event that the successor is not of mature age

Legislative branch: bicameral Parliament consists of the Senate (33 members—22 principal chiefs and 11 other members appointed by the ruling party) and the Assembly (120 seats, 80 by popular vote and 40 by proportional vote; members elected by popular vote to serve five-year terms)
elections: last held on 26 May 2012 (next to be held in 2017)
election results: percent of vote by party—NA; seats by party—DC 48, ABC 30, LCD 26, BNP 5, PFD 3, NIP 2, other 6

Judicial branch: *highest court(s):* Court of Appeal (consists of the court president, such number of justices of appeal as set by Parliament, and the Chief Justice and the puisne judges of the High Court ex officio); High Court (consists of the chief justice and such number of puisne judges as set by Parliament); note—both the Court of Appeal and the High Court have jurisdiction in constitutional issues
judge selection and term of office: Court of Appeal president and High Court chief justice appointed by the monarch on the advice of the prime minister; puisne judges appointed by the monarch on advice of the Judicial Service Commission, an independent body of judicial officers and officials designated by the monarch; judges of both courts can serve until age 75
subordinate courts: Magistrate Courts; customary or traditional courts; Courts Martial

Political parties and leaders: All Basotho Convention or ABC [Motsoahae Thomas THABANE]; Basotho Batho Democratic Party or BBDP [Geremane RAMATHEBANE]; Basotho Congress Party or BCP [Thulo MAHLAKENG]; Basotho Democratic National Party or BDNP [Thabang NYEOE]; Basotho National Party or BNP [Thesele 'MASERIBANE]; Democratic Congress or DC [Pakalitha MOSISILI]; Lesotho Congress for Democracy or LCD [Mothetjoa METSING]; Lesotho Peoples Congress or LPC [Kelebone MAOPE]; Lesotho Workers Party or LWP [Macaefa BILLY]; Marematlou Freedom Party or MFP [Vincent MALEBO]; National Independent Party or NIP [Kimetso MATHABA]

Political pressure groups and leaders: Media Institute of Southern Africa, Lesotho chapter [Tsebo MATŠASA] (pushes for media freedom)

International organization participation: ACP, AfDB, AU, C, CD, FAO, G-77, IAEA, IBRD, ICAO, ICRM, IDA, IFAD, IFC, IFRCS, ILO, IMF, Interpol, IOC, IOM, IPU, ISO (correspondent), ITU, MIGA, NAM, OPCW, SACU, SADC, UN, UNAMID, UNCTAD, UNESCO, UNHCR, UNIDO, UNWTO, UPU, WCO, WFTU (NGOs), WHO, WIPO, WMO, WTO

Diplomatic representation in the US: *chief of mission:* Ambassador Eliachim Molapi SEBATANE (since 2 November 2011)
chancery: 2511 Massachusetts Avenue NW, Washington, DC 20008
telephone: [1] (202) 797-5533
FAX: [1] (202) 234-6815

Diplomatic representation from the US: *chief of mission:* Ambassador (vacant); Charge d'Affaires Carl B. FOX
embassy: 254 Kingsway Road, Maseru West (Consular Section)
mailing address: P. O. Box 333, Maseru 100, Lesotho
telephone: [266] 22 312666
FAX: [266] 22 310116

Flag description: three horizontal stripes of blue (top), white, and green in the proportions of 3:4:3; the colors represent rain, peace, and prosperity respectively; centered in the white stripe is a black Basotho hat representing the indigenous people; the flag was unfurled in October 2006 to celebrate 40 years of independence

National symbol(s): Basotho hat

National anthem: *name:* "Lesotho fatse la bo ntat'a rona" (Lesotho, Land of Our Fathers)

lyrics/music: Francois COILLARD/Ferdinand-Samuel LAUR
note: adopted 1967; the anthem's music derives from an 1823 Swiss songbook

ECONOMY

Economy—overview: Small, mountainous, and completely landlocked by South Africa, Lesotho is a least developed country in which about three-fourths of the people live in rural areas and engage in subsistence agriculture. Lesotho produces less than 20% of the nation's demand for food. Rain-fed agriculture is vulnerable to weather and climate variability; an estimated 725,500 people will require food assistance in 2012/13. The distribution of income in Lesotho remains inequitable. Lesotho relies on South Africa for much of its economic activity. Lesotho imports 90% of the goods it consumes from South Africa, including most agricultural inputs. Households depend heavily on remittances from family members working in South Africa, in mines, on farms and as domestic workers, though mining employment has declined substantially since the 1990s. Government revenue depends heavily on transfers from South Africa. Customs duties from the Southern Africa Customs Union accounted for 44% of government revenue in 2012. The South African Government also pays royalties for water transferred to South Africa from a dam and reservoir system in Lesotho. However, the government continues to strengthen its tax system to reduce dependency on customs duties and other transfers. Access to credit remains a problem for the private sector. The government maintains a large presence in the economy—government consumption accounted for 39% of GDP in 2013 and the government remains Lesotho's largest employer. Lesotho's largest private employer is the textile and garment industry—approximately 36,000 Basotho, mainly women, work in factories producing garments for export to South Africa and the US. Diamond mining in Lesotho has grown in recent years and may contribute 8.5% to GDP by 2015, according to current forecasts. Lesotho's $362.5 million Millennium Challenge Account Compact, which focused on strengthening the healthcare system, developing the private sector, and providing access to improved water supplies and sanitation facilities, will end in September 2013. Despite the 2008/09 global economic crisis, the economy has had strong, but declining growth since 2010.

GDP (purchasing power parity): $4.265 billion (2013 est.)
country comparison to the world: 175
$4.096 billion (2012 est.)
$3.918 billion (2011 est.)
note: data are in 2013 US dollars

GDP (official exchange rate): $2.457 billion (2013 est.)

GDP—real growth rate: 4.1% (2013 est.)
country comparison to the world: 74
4.5% (2012 est.)
5.7% (2011 est.)

GDP—per capita (PPP): $2,200 (2013 est.)
country comparison to the world: 192
$2,200 (2012 est.)
$2,100 (2011 est.)
note: data are in 2013 US dollars

Gross national saving: 11.4% of GDP (2013 est.)
country comparison to the world: 130
7.8% of GDP (2012 est.)
7.8% of GDP (2011 est.)

GDP—composition, by end use:
household consumption: 86%
government consumption: 39.4%
investment in fixed capital: 33.7%
investment in inventories: 1.2%
exports of goods and services: 47.9%
imports of goods and services: -108.2% (2013 est.)

GDP—composition, by sector of origin:
agriculture: 7.4%
industry: 34.5%
services: 58.2% (2013 est.)

Agriculture—products: corn, wheat, pulses, sorghum, barley; livestock

Industries: food, beverages, textiles, apparel assembly, handicrafts, construction, tourism

Industrial production growth rate: 4.3% (2013 est.)
country comparison to the world: 67

Labor force: 874,200 (2013 est.)
country comparison to the world: 148

Labor force—by occupation:
agriculture: 86%
industry and services: 14%
note: most of resident population engaged in subsistence agriculture; roughly 35% of the active male wage earners work in South Africa (2002 est.)

Unemployment rate: 25% (2008 est.)
country comparison to the world: 175
45% (2002 est.)

Population below poverty line: 49% (1999)

Household income or consumption by percentage share: *lowest 10%:* 1%
highest 10%: 39.4% (2003)

Distribution of family income—Gini index: 63.2 (1995)
country comparison to the world: 1
56 (1986-87)

Budget: *revenues:* $1.462 billion
expenditures: $1.483 billion (2013 est.)

Taxes and other revenues: 59.5% of GDP (2013 est.)
country comparison to the world: 4

Budget surplus (+) or deficit (-): -0.9% of GDP (2013 est.)
country comparison to the world: 62

Public debt: NA

Fiscal year: 1 April—31 March

Inflation rate (consumer prices): 5% (2013 est.)
country comparison to the world: 153
6.1% (2012 est.)

Central bank discount rate: 9.36% (31 December 2012 est.)
country comparison to the world: 27
10% (31 December 2010 est.)

Commercial bank prime lending rate: 10% (31 December 2013 est.)
country comparison to the world: 87
10.12% (31 December 2012 est.)

Stock of narrow money: $425.1 million (31 December 2013 est.)
country comparison to the world: 162
$408.9 million (31 December 2012 est.)

Stock of broad money: $903.4 million (31 December 2013 est.)
country comparison to the world: 170
$840.9 million (31 December 2012 est.)

Stock of domestic credit: $85,420 (31 December 2013 est.)
country comparison to the world: 181
$75,280 (31 December 2012 est.)

Current account balance: -$518.4 million (2013 est.)
country comparison to the world: 103
-$587.4 million (2012 est.)

Exports: $941.2 million (2013 est.)
country comparison to the world: 162
$972.4 million (2012 est.)

Exports—commodities: manufactures (clothing, footwear), wool and mohair, food and live animals, electricity, water, diamonds

Imports: $2.148 billion (2013 est.)
country comparison to the world: 163
$2.239 billion (2012 est.)

Imports—commodities: food; building materials, vehicles, machinery, medicines, petroleum products

Reserves of foreign exchange and gold: $857.9 million (31 December 2013 est.)
country comparison to the world: 138
$749.4 million (31 December 2012 est.)

Debt—external: $794 million (31 December 2013 est.)
country comparison to the world: 167
$779.8 million (31 December 2012 est.)

Stock of direct foreign investment—at home: $635.7 million (31 December 2013 est.)
country comparison to the world: 102
$398 million (31 December 2012 est.)

Exchange rates: maloti (LSL) per US dollar—
9.575 (2013 est.)
8.2 (2012 est.)
7.32 (2010 est.)
8.47 (2009)
7.75 (2008)

ENERGY

Electricity—production: 200 million kWh (2010 est.)
country comparison to the world: 183

Electricity—consumption: 307 million kWh (2010 est.)
country comparison to the world: 174

Electricity—exports: 0 kWh (2012 est.)
country comparison to the world: 160

Electricity—imports: 247 million kWh (2011 est.)
country comparison to the world: 84

Electricity—installed generating capacity: 76,000 kW (2010 est.)
country comparison to the world: 179

Electricity—from fossil fuels: 0% of total installed capacity (2010 est.)
country comparison to the world: 210

Electricity—from nuclear fuels: 0% of total installed capacity (2010 est.)
country comparison to the world: 127

Electricity—from hydroelectric plants: 100% of total installed capacity (2010 est.)
country comparison to the world: 1

Electricity—from other renewable sources: 0% of total installed capacity (2010 est.)
country comparison to the world: 194

Crude oil—production: 0 bbl/day (2012 est.)
country comparison to the world: 188

Crude oil—exports: 0 bbl/day (2010 est.)
country comparison to the world: 144

Crude oil—imports: 0 bbl/day (2010 est.)
country comparison to the world: 210

Crude oil—proved reserves: 0 bbl (1 January 2013 es)
country comparison to the world: 156

Refined petroleum products—production: 0 bbl/day (2010 est.)
country comparison to the world: 165

Refined petroleum products—consumption: 1,777 bbl/day (2011 est.)
country comparison to the world: 191

Refined petroleum products—exports: 0 bbl/day (2010 est.)
country comparison to the world: 192
Refined petroleum products—imports: 3,711 bbl/day (2010 est.)
country comparison to the world: 164

Natural gas—production: 0 cu m (2011 est.)
country comparison to the world: 156

Natural gas—consumption: 0 cu m (2010 est.)
country comparison to the world: 164

Natural gas—exports: 0 cu m (2011 est.)
country comparison to the world: 137

Natural gas—imports: 0 cu m (2011 est.)
country comparison to the world: 88

Natural gas—proved reserves: 0 cu m (1 January 2013 es)
country comparison to the world: 161

Carbon dioxide emissions from consumption of energy: 445,600 Mt (2011 est.)
country comparison to the world: 181

COMMUNICATIONS

Telephones—main lines in use: 43,100 (2012)
country comparison to the world: 168

Telephones—mobile cellular: 1.312 million (2012)
country comparison to the world: 153

Telephone system: *general assessment:* rudimentary system consisting of a modest number of landlines, a small microwave radio relay system, and a small radiotelephone communication system; mobile-cellular telephone system is expanding
domestic: privatized in 2001, Telecom Lesotho was tasked with providing an additional 50,000 fixed-line connections within five years, a target not met; mobile-cellular service dominates the market and is expanding with a subscribership roughly 65 per 100 persons in 2011; rural services are scant
international: country code—266; satellite earth station—1 Intelsat (Atlantic Ocean) (2011)

Broadcast media: 1 state-owned TV station and 2 state-owned radio stations; government controls most private broadcast media; satellite TV subscription service available; transmissions of multiple international broadcasters obtainable (2008)

Internet country code: .ls

Internet hosts: 11,030 (2012)
country comparison to the world: 131

Internet users: 76,800 (2009)
country comparison to the world: 168

TRANSPORTATION

Airports: 24 (2013)
country comparison to the world: 132

Airports—with paved runways: *total:* 3
over 3,047 m: 1
914 to 1,523 m: 1
under 914 m: 1 (2013)

Airports—with unpaved runways: *total:* 21
914 to 1,523 m: 5
under 914 m: 16 (2013)

Roadways: *total:* 5,940 km
country comparison to the world: 150
paved: 1,069 km
unpaved: 4,871 km (2011)

MILITARY

Military branches: Lesotho Defense Force (LDF): Army (includes Air Wing) (2012)

Military service age and obligation: 18-24 years of age for voluntary military service; no conscription; women serve as commissioned officers (2012)

Manpower available for military service:
males age 16-49: 472,456
females age 16-49: 508,953 (2010 est.)

Manpower fit for military service:
males age 16-49: 270,184
females age 16-49: 275,734 (2010 est.)

Manpower reaching militarily significant age annually: *male:* 19,110
female: 20,037 (2010 est.)

Military expenditures: 1.94% of GDP (2012)
country comparison to the world: 44
2.3% of GDP (2011)
1.94% of GDP (2010)

Military—note: Lesotho's declared policy is maintenance of its independent sovereignty and preservation of internal security; in practice, external security is guaranteed by South Africa; restructuring of the Lesotho Defense Force (LDF) and Ministry of Defense and Public Service over the past five years has focused on subordinating the defense apparatus to civilian control and restoring the LDF's cohesion; the restructuring has considerably improved capabilities and professionalism, but the LDF is disproportionately large for a small, poor country; the government has outlined a reduction to a planned 1,500-man strength, but these plans have met with vociferous resistance from the political opposition and from inside the LDF (2008)

TRANSNATIONAL ISSUES

Disputes—international: South Africa has placed military units to assist police operations along the border of Lesotho, Zimbabwe, and Mozambique to control smuggling, poaching, and illegal migration

Trafficking in persons: *current situation:* Lesotho is a source, transit, and destination country for women and children subjected to forced labor and sex trafficking and for men subjected to forced labor; Basotho women and children are subjected to domestic servitude and children, to a lesser extent, commercial sexual exploitation within Lesotho and South Africa; some Basotho women willingly migrate to South Africa seeking work in domestic service only to be forced into prostitution; some Basotho men who voluntarily migrate to South Africa for work become victims of forced labor in agriculture and mining or are coerced into committing crimes

tier rating: Tier 2 Watch List—Lesotho does not fully comply with the minimum standards for the elimination of trafficking; however, it is making significant efforts to do so; the government has decreased its anti-trafficking law enforcement and victim protection efforts during 2012; authorities have initiated fewer prosecutions, ceased arresting suspected trafficking offenders due to a backlog of prosecutions, and stopped referring victims to NGO centers for care; the government has not implemented key portions of the 2011 anti-trafficking act, including failing to develop formal referral procedures, establish victim care centers, and complete a national action plan (2013)

LIBERIA

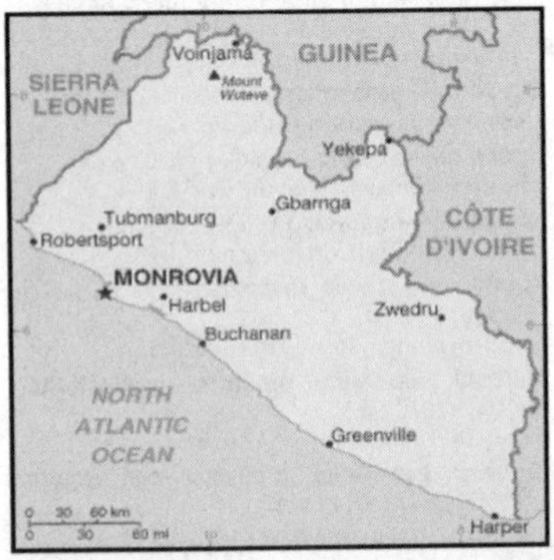

INTRODUCTION

Background: Settlement of freed slaves from the US in what is today Liberia began in 1822; by 1847, the Americo-Liberians were able to establish a republic. William TUBMAN, president from 1944-71, did much to promote foreign investment and to bridge the economic, social, and political gaps between the descendants of the original settlers and the inhabitants of the interior. In 1980, a military coup led by Samuel DOE ushered in a decade of authoritarian rule. In December 1989, Charles TAYLOR launched a rebellion against DOE's regime that led to a prolonged civil war in which DOE was killed. A period of relative peace in 1997 allowed for elections that brought TAYLOR to power, but major fighting resumed in 2000. An August 2003 peace agreement ended the war and prompted the resignation of former president Charles TAYLOR, who faces war crimes charges in The Hague related to his involvement in Sierra Leone's civil war. After two years of rule by a transitional government, democratic elections in late 2005 brought President Ellen JOHNSON SIRLEAF to power. She subsequently won reelection in 2011 in a second round vote that was boycotted by the opposition and remains challenged to build Liberia's economy and reconcile a nation still recovering from 14 years of fighting. The United Nations Security Council in September 2012 passed Resolution 2066 which calls for a reduction of UN troops in Liberia by half by 2015, bringing the troop total down to fewer than 4000, and challenging Liberia's security sector to fill the gaps.

GEOGRAPHY

Location: Western Africa, bordering the North Atlantic Ocean, between Cote d'Ivoire and Sierra Leone

Geographic coordinates: 6 30 N, 9 30 W

Map references: Africa

Area: *total:* 111,369 sq km
country comparison to the world: 104
land: 96,320 sq km
water: 15,049 sq km

Area—comparative: slightly larger than Tennessee

Land boundaries: *total:* 1,585 km
border countries: Guinea 563 km, Cote d'Ivoire 716 km, Sierra Leone 306 km

Coastline: 579 km

Maritime claims: *territorial sea:* 200 nm

Climate: tropical; hot, humid; dry winters with hot days and cool to cold nights; wet, cloudy summers with frequent heavy showers

Terrain: mostly flat to rolling coastal plains rising to rolling plateau and low mountains in northeast

Elevation extremes: *lowest point:* Atlantic Ocean 0 m
highest point: Mount Wuteve 1,380 m

Natural resources: iron ore, timber, diamonds, gold, hydropower

Land use: *arable land:* 4.04%
permanent crops: 1.62%
other: 94.34% (2011)

Irrigated land: 21 sq km (2003)

Total renewable water resources: 232 cu km (2011)

Freshwater withdrawal (domestic/industrial/agricultural): *total:* 0.13 cu km/yr (55%/37%/8%)
per capita: 43.66 cu m/yr (2005)

Natural hazards: dust-laden harmattan winds blow from the Sahara (December to March)

Environment—current issues: tropical rain forest deforestation; soil erosion; loss of biodiversity; pollution of coastal waters from oil residue and raw sewage

Environment—international agreements: *party to:* Biodiversity, Climate Change, Climate Change-Kyoto Protocol, Desertification, Endangered Species, Hazardous Wastes, Law of the Sea, Ozone Layer Protection, Ship Pollution, Tropical Timber 83, Tropical Timber 94, Wetlands
signed, but not ratified: Environmental Modification, Marine Life Conservation

Geography—note: facing the Atlantic Ocean, the coastline is characterized by lagoons, mangrove swamps, and river-deposited sandbars; the inland grassy plateau supports limited agriculture

PEOPLE AND SOCIETY

Nationality: *noun:* Liberian(s)
adjective: Liberian

Ethnic groups: Kpelle 20.3%, Bassa 13.4%, Grebo 10%, Gio 8%, Mano 7.9%, Kru 6%, Lorma 5.1%, Kissi 4.8%, Gola 4.4%, other 20.1% (2008 Census)

Languages: English 20% (official), some 20 ethnic group languages few of which can be written or used in correspondence

Religions: Christian 85.6%, Muslim 12.2%, Traditional 0.6%, other 0.2%, none 1.4% (2008 Census)

Population: 4,092,310 (July 2014 est.)
country comparison to the world: 128

Age structure: *0-14 years:* 43.2% (male 891,002/female 876,655)
15-24 years: 17.9% (male 357,952/female 375,708)
25-54 years: 31.5% (male 642,835/female 646,104)
55-64 years: 3.1% (male 85,906/female 89,943)
65 years and over: 3% (male 62,475/female 63,730) (2014 est.)

Dependency ratios:
total dependency ratio: 84.9 %
youth dependency ratio: 79.3 %
elderly dependency ratio: 5.6 %
potential support ratio: 17.8 (2013)

Median age: *total:* 17.9 years
male: 17.7 years
female: 18.1 years (2014 est.)

Population growth rate: 2.52% (2014 est.)
country comparison to the world: 29

Birth rate: 35.07 births/1,000 population (2014 est.)
country comparison to the world: 26

Death rate: 9.9 deaths/1,000 population (2014 est.)
country comparison to the world: 51

Net migration rate: 0 migrant(s)/1,000 population (2014 est.)
country comparison to the world: 86

Urbanization: *urban population:* 48.2% of total population (2011)
rate of urbanization: 3.43% annual rate of change (2010-15 est.)

Major urban areas—population: MONROVIA (capital) 882,000 (2009)

Sex ratio: *at birth:* 1.03 male(s)/female
0-14 years: 1.02 male(s)/female
15-24 years: 0.95 male(s)/female
25-54 years: 1 male(s)/female
55-64 years: 0.99 male(s)/female
65 years and over: 1.01 male(s)/female
total population: 1 male(s)/female (2014 est.)

Mother's mean age at first birth: 19.1 (2007 est.)

Maternal mortality rate: 770 deaths/100,000 live births (2010)
country comparison to the world: 8

Infant mortality rate: *total:* 69.19 deaths/1,000 live births
country comparison to the world: 15
male: 73.46 deaths/1,000 live births
female: 64.79 deaths/1,000 live births (2014 est.)

Life expectancy at birth: *total population:* 58.21 years
country comparison to the world: 199
male: 56.56 years
female: 59.9 years (2014 est.)

Total fertility rate: 4.81 children born/woman (2014 est.)
country comparison to the world: 21

Contraceptive prevalence rate: 11.4% (2007)

Health expenditures: 19.5% of GDP (2011)
country comparison to the world: 1

Physicians density: 0.01 physicians/1,000 population (2008)

Hospital bed density: 0.8 beds/1,000 population (2010)

Drinking water source:
improved:
urban: 89.4% of population
rural: 60.5% of population
total: 74.4% of population
unimproved:
urban: 10.6% of population
rural: 39.5% of population
total: 25.6% of population (2011 est.)

Sanitation facility access:
improved:
urban: 30.1% of population
rural: 7.2% of population
total: 18.2% of population
unimproved:
urban: 69.9% of population
rural: 92.8% of population
total: 81.8% of population (2011 est.)

HIV/AIDS—adult prevalence rate: 0.9% (2012 est.)
country comparison to the world: 51

HIV/AIDS—people living with HIV/AIDS: 21,800 (2012 est.)
country comparison to the world: 80

HIV/AIDS—deaths: 1,700 (2012 est.)
country comparison to the world: 61

Major infectious diseases: *degree of risk:* very high
food or waterborne diseases: bacterial and protozoal diarrhea, hepatitis A, and typhoid fever
vectorborne diseases: malaria, dengue fever, and yellow fever
water contact disease: schistosomiasis
aerosolized dust or soil contact disease: Lassa fever
animal contact disease: rabies (2013)

Obesity—adult prevalence rate: 4.8% (2008)
country comparison to the world: 161

Children under the age of 5 years underweight: 20.4% (2007)
country comparison to the world: 29

Education expenditures: 2.8% of GDP (2012)
country comparison to the world: 144

Literacy: *definition:* age 15 and over can read and write
total population: 60.8%
male: 64.8%
female: 56.8% (2010 est.)

School life expectancy (primary to tertiary education): *total:* 11 years
male: 12 years
female: 9 years (2000)

Child labor—children ages 5-14: *total number:* 177,160
percentage: 21 % (2007 est.)

Unemployment, youth ages 15-24: *total:* 5.1%
country comparison to the world: 137
male: 3.4%
female: 6.6% (2010)

GOVERNMENT

Country name: *conventional long form:* Republic of Liberia
conventional short form: Liberia

Government type: republic

Capital: *name:* Monrovia

geographic coordinates: 6 18 N, 10 48 W
time difference: UTC 0 (5 hours ahead of Washington, DC during Standard Time)

Administrative divisions: 15 counties; Bomi, Bong, Gbarpolu, Grand Bassa, Grand Cape Mount, Grand Gedeh, Grand Kru, Lofa, Margibi, Maryland, Montserrado, Nimba, River Cess, River Gee, Sinoe

Independence: 26 July 1847

National holiday: Independence Day, 26 July (1847)

Constitution: previous 1847 (at independence); latest drafted 19 October 1983, revised version adopted by referendum 3 July 1984, effective 6 January 1986; amended 2011 (2011)

Legal system: mixed legal system of common law (based on Anglo-American law) and customary law

International law organization participation: accepts compulsory ICJ jurisdiction with reservations; accepts ICCt jurisdiction

Suffrage: 18 years of age; universal

Executive branch: *chief of state:* President Ellen JOHNSON SIRLEAF (since 16 January 2006); Vice President Joseph BOAKAI (since 16 January 2006); note—the president is both the chief of state and head of government
head of government: President Ellen JOHNSON SIRLEAF (since 16 January 2006); Vice President Joseph BOAKAI (since 16 January 2006)
cabinet: Cabinet appointed by the president and confirmed by the Senate (For more information visit the World Leaders website)
elections: president elected by popular vote for a six-year term (eligible for a second term); elections last held on 11 October and 8 November 2011 (next to be held in 2017)
election results: Ellen JOHNSON SIRLEAF reelected president; percent of vote, second round—Ellen JOHNSON SIRLEAF 90.7%, Winston TUBMAN 9.3%

Legislative branch: bicameral National Assembly consists of the Senate (30 seats; members elected by popular vote to serve nine-year terms) and the House of Representatives (73 seats; members elected by popular vote to serve six-year terms)
elections: Senate—last held on 11 October 2011 (next to be held in 2014); House of Representatives—last held on 11 October 2011 (next to be held in 2017)
election results: Senate—percent of vote by party—NA; seats by party—UP 10, NPP 6, CDC 3, APD 2, NUDP 2, LDP 1, LP 1, NDC 1, NDPL 1, independents 3; House of Representatives—percent of vote by party—NA; seats by party—UP 24 CDC 11, LP 7, NUDP 6, NDC 5, APD 3, NPP 3, MPC 2, LDP 1, LTP 1, NRP 1, independents 9

Judicial branch: *highest court(s):* Supreme Court (consists of a chief Justice and 4 associate justices) note—the Supreme Court has jurisdiction for all constitutional cases
judge selection and term of office: chief justice and associate justices appointed by the president of Liberia with consent of the Senate; judges can serve until age 70
subordinate courts: judicial circuit courts; special courts including criminal, civil, labor, traffic; magistrate and traditional or customary courts

Political parties and leaders: Alliance for Peace and Democracy or APD [Marcus S. G. DAHN]; Alternative National Congress or ANC [Orishil GOULD]; Congress for Democratic Change or CDC [George WEAH]; Liberia Destiny Party or LDP [Nathaniel BARNES]; Liberty Party or LP [J. Fonati KOFFA]; Liberia Transformation Party or LTP [Julius SUKU]; Movement for Progressive Change or MPC [Simeon FREEMAN]; National Democratic Coalition or NDC [Dew MAYSON]; National Democratic Party of Liberia or NDPL [D. Nyandeh SIEH]; National Patriotic Party or NPP [Theophilus C. GOULD]; National Reformist Party or NRP [Maximillian T. W. DIABE]; National Union for Democratic Progress or NUDP [Victor BARNEY]; Unity Party or UP [Varney SHERMAN]

Political pressure groups and leaders:
other: demobilized former military officers

International organization participation: ACP, AfDB, AU, ECOWAS, EITI (compliant country), FAO, G-77, IAEA, IBRD, ICAO, ICC (NGOs), ICRM, IDA, IFAD, IFC, IFRCS, ILO, IMF, IMO, IMSO, Interpol, IOC, IOM, ISO (correspondent), ITU, ITUC (NGOs), MIGA, MINUSMA, NAM, OPCW, UN, UNCTAD, UNESCO, UNIDO, UNWTO, UPU, WCO, WFTU (NGOs), WHO, WIPO, WMO, WTO (observer)

Diplomatic representation in the US: *chief of mission:* Ambassador Jeremiah Congbeh SULUNTEH (since 25 April 2012)
chancery: 5201 16th Street NW, Washington, DC 20011
telephone: [1] (202) 723-0437
FAX: [1] (202) 723-0436
consulate(s) general: New York

Diplomatic representation from the US: *chief of mission:* Ambassador Deborah R. MALAC (since 26 July 2012)
embassy: U.S. Embassy, P.O. Box 98, 502 Benson Street, Monrovia
mailing address: P.O. Box 98, Monrovia
telephone: [231] 77-677-7000
FAX: [231] 77-677-7370

Flag description: 11 equal horizontal stripes of red (top and bottom) alternating with white; a white five-pointed star appears on a blue square in the upper hoist-side corner; the stripes symbolize the signatories of the Liberian Declaration of Independence; the blue square represents the African mainland, and the star represents the freedom granted to the ex-slaves; according to the constitution, the blue color signifies liberty, justice, and fidelity, the white color purity, cleanliness, and guilelessness, and the red color steadfastness, valor, and fervor
note: the design is based on the US flag

National symbol(s): white star

National anthem: *name:* "All Hail, Liberia Hail!"
lyrics/music: Daniel Bashiel WARNER/Olmstead LUCA
note: lyrics adopted 1847, music adopted 1860; the anthem's author would become the third president of Liberia

ECONOMY

Economy—overview: Liberia is a low income country that relies heavily on foreign assistance. Civil war and government mismanagement destroyed much of Liberia's economy, especially the infrastructure in and around the capital, Monrovia. Many businesses fled the country, taking capital and expertise with them, but with the conclusion of fighting and the installation of a democratically elected government in 2006, several have returned. Liberia is richly endowed with water, mineral resources, forests, and a climate favorable to agriculture, and iron ore and rubber have driven growth in recent years. Liberia is also reviving its raw timber sector and is encouraging oil exploration. President JOHNSON SIRLEAF, a Harvard-educated banker and administrator, has taken steps to reduce corruption, build support from international donors, and encourage private investment. Rebuilding infrastructure and raising incomes will depend on financial and technical assistance from donor countries and foreign investment in key sectors, such as infrastructure and power generation. The country achieved high growth during 2010-13 due to favorable world prices for its commodities. In the future, growth will depend on global commodity prices, on sustained foreign aid, trade, investment, and remittances, on the development of infrastructure and institutions, but mostly on maintaining political stability and security.

GDP (purchasing power parity): $2.898 billion (2013 est.)
country comparison to the world: 183
$2.681 billion (2012 est.)
$2.475 billion (2011 est.)
note: data are in 2013 US dollars

GDP (official exchange rate): $1.977 billion (2013 est.)

GDP—real growth rate: 8.1% (2013 est.)
country comparison to the world: 11
8.3% (2012 est.)
7.9% (2011 est.)

GDP—per capita (PPP): $700 (2013 est.)
country comparison to the world: 223
$700 (2012 est.)
$600 (2011 est.)
note: data are in 2013 US dollars

Gross national saving: NA (2012 est.)
-36.6% of GDP (2011 est.)
-36.6% of GDP (2011 est.)

GDP—composition, by end use:
household consumption: 125.6%
government consumption: 15.2%
investment in fixed capital: 25%
investment in inventories: 0%
exports of goods and services: 27.5% imports of goods and services: -93.3% (2011 est.)

GDP—composition, by sector of origin:
agriculture: 76.9%
industry: 5.4%
services: 17.7% (2002 est.)

Agriculture—products: rubber, coffee, cocoa, rice, cassava (manioc), palm oil, sugarcane, bananas; sheep, goats; timber

Industries: mining (iron ore), rubber processing, palm oil processing, timber, diamonds

Industrial production growth rate: NA%

Labor force: 1.372 million (2007)
country comparison to the world: 134

Labor force—by occupation: *agriculture:* 70%
industry: 8%
services: 22% (2000 est.)

Unemployment rate: 85% (2003 est.)
country comparison to the world: 201

Population below poverty line: 80% (2000 est.)

Household income or consumption by percentage share: *lowest 10%:* 2.4%
highest 10%: 30.1% (2007)

Budget: *revenues:* $465 million
expenditures: $521.7 million (2013 est.)

Taxes and other revenues: 23.5% of GDP (2013 est.)
country comparison to the world: 141

Budget surplus (+) or deficit (-):
-2.9% of GDP (2013 est.)
country comparison to the world: 116

Public debt: 3.3% of GDP (2013 est.)
country comparison to the world: 160
0.4% of GDP (2012 est.)

Fiscal year: calendar year

Inflation rate (consumer prices): 5.2% (2013 est.)
country comparison to the world: 158
6.8% (2012 est.)

Commercial bank prime lending rate: 14% (31 December 2013 est.)
country comparison to the world: 55
13.52% (31 December 2012 est.)

Stock of narrow money: $419.4 million (31 December 2013 est.)
country comparison to the world: 164
$408.2 million (31 December 2012 est.)

Stock of broad money: $799.5 million (31 December 2013 est.)
country comparison to the world: 172
$591.3 million (31 December 2012 est.)

Stock of domestic credit: $705.4 million (31 December 2013 est.)
country comparison to the world: 163
$521.9 million (31 December 2012 est.)

Market value of publicly traded shares: $NA

Current account balance: -$742.4 million (2013 est.)
country comparison to the world: 113
-$918.8 million (2012 est.)

Exports: $929.8 million (2013 est.)
country comparison to the world: 163
$774.8 million (2012 est.)

Exports—commodities: rubber, timber, iron, diamonds, cocoa, coffee

Exports—partners: China 24%, US 15.3%, Spain 11%, Algeria 6.5%, Thailand 4.5%, Malaysia 4.1%, France 4% (2012)

Imports: $2.457 billion (2013 est.)
country comparison to the world: 156
$2.275 billion (2012 est.)

Imports—commodities: fuels, chemicals, machinery, transportation equipment, manufactured goods; foodstuffs

Imports—partners: South Korea 26.7%, China 24.4%, Singapore 23.2%, Japan 16.1% (2012)

Debt—external: $438.1 million (31 December 2013 est.)
country comparison to the world: 179
$349.2 million (31 December 2012 est.)

Stock of direct foreign investment—at home:
$4.241 billion (31 December 2013 est.)
country comparison to the world: 91
$3.574 billion (31 December 2012 est.)

Stock of direct foreign investment—abroad:
$NA (31 December 2013 est.)
$NA (31 December 2012 est.)

Exchange rates: Liberian dollars (LRD) per US dollar—
77.63 (2013 est.)
73.515 (2012 est.)
71.403 (2010 est.)

ENERGY

Electricity—production: 335 million kWh (2010 est.)
country comparison to the world: 168

Electricity—consumption: 311.6 million kWh (2010 est.)
country comparison to the world: 173

Electricity—exports: 0 kWh (2012 est.)
country comparison to the world: 159

Electricity—imports: 0 kWh (2012 est.)
country comparison to the world: 165

Electricity—installed generating capacity: 197,000 kW (2010 est.)
country comparison to the world: 158

Electricity—from fossil fuels: 100% of total installed capacity (2010 est.)
country comparison to the world: 20

Electricity—from nuclear fuels: 0% of total installed capacity (2010 est.)
country comparison to the world: 126

Electricity—from hydroelectric plants: 0% of total installed capacity (2010 est.)
country comparison to the world: 179

Electricity—from other renewable sources: 0% of total installed capacity (2010 est.)
country comparison to the world: 193

Crude oil—production: 0 bbl/day (2012 est.)
country comparison to the world: 187

Crude oil—exports: 0 bbl/day (2010 est.)
country comparison to the world: 143

Crude oil—imports: 0 bbl/day (2010 est.)
country comparison to the world: 209

Crude oil—proved reserves: 0 bbl (1 January 2013 es)
country comparison to the world: 155

Refined petroleum products—production: 0 bbl/day (2010 est.)
country comparison to the world: 164

Refined petroleum products—consumption: 3,533 bbl/day (2011 est.)
country comparison to the world: 176

Refined petroleum products—exports: 23.37 bbl/day (2010 est.)
country comparison to the world: 125

Refined petroleum products—imports: 3,673 bbl/day (2010 est.)
country comparison to the world: 165

Natural gas—production: 0 cu m (2011 est.)
country comparison to the world: 155

Natural gas—consumption: 0 cu m (2010 est.)
country comparison to the world: 163

Natural gas—exports: 0 cu m (2011 est.)
country comparison to the world: 136

Natural gas—imports: 0 cu m (2011 est.)
country comparison to the world: 87

Natural gas—proved reserves: 0 cu m (1 January 2013 es)
country comparison to the world: 160

Carbon dioxide emissions from consumption of energy: 588,000 Mt (2011 est.)
country comparison to the world: 178

COMMUNICATIONS

Telephones—main lines in use: 3,200 (2011)
country comparison to the world: 213

Telephones—mobile cellular: 2.394 million (2012)
country comparison to the world: 138

Telephone system: *general assessment:* the limited services available are found almost exclusively in the capital Monrovia; fixed-line service stagnant and extremely limited; telephone coverage extended to a number of other towns and rural areas by four mobile-cellular network operators
domestic: mobile-cellular subscription base growing and teledensity reached 50 per 100 persons in 2011

international: country code—231; satellite earth station—1 Intelsat (Atlantic Ocean) (2010)

Broadcast media: 3 private TV stations; satellite TV service available; 1 state-owned radio station; about 15 independent radio stations broadcasting in Monrovia, with another 25 local stations operating in other areas; transmissions of 2 international broadcasters are available (2007)

Internet country code: .lr

Internet hosts: 7 (2012)
country comparison to the world: 228

Internet users: 20,000 (2009)
country comparison to the world: 194

TRANSPORTATION

Airports: 29 (2013)
country comparison to the world: 117

Airports—with paved runways: *total:* 2
over 3,047 m: 1
1,524 to 2,437 m: 1 (2013)

Airports—with unpaved runways: *total:* 2 7
1,524 to 2,437 m: 5
914 to 1,523 m: 8
under 914 m: 14 (2013)

Pipelines: oil 4 km (2013)

Railways: *total:* 429 km
country comparison to the world: 115
standard gauge: 345 km 1.435-m gauge
narrow gauge: 84 km 1.067-m gauge
note: most sections of the railways were inoperable because of damage suffered during the civil wars from 1980 to 2003, but many are being rebuilt (2008)

Roadways: *total:* 10,600 km
country comparison to the world: 134
paved: 657 km
unpaved: 9,943 km (2000)

Merchant marine: *total:* 2,771
country comparison to the world: 2
by type: barge carrier 5, bulk carrier 662, cargo 143, carrier 2, chemical tanker 248, combination ore/oil 8, container 937, liquefied gas 92, passenger 2, passenger/cargo 2, petroleum tanker 526, refrigerated cargo 102, roll on/roll off 5, specialized tanker 10, vehicle carrier 27
foreign-owned: 2,581 (Angola 1, Argentina 1, Australia 1, Belgium 1, Bermuda 4, Brazil 20, Canada 2, Chile 9, China 4, Croatia 1, Cyprus 9, Denmark 8, Egypt 3, Germany 1185, Gibraltar 5, Greece 505, Hong Kong 48, India 8, Indonesia 4, Israel 34, Italy 47, Japan 110, Latvia 5, Lebanon 1, Monaco 8, Netherlands 31, Nigeria 4, Norway 38, Poland 13, Qatar 5, Romania 3, Russia 109, Saudi Arabia 20, Singapore 22, Slovenia 7, South Korea 2, Sweden 12, Switzerland 25, Syria 1, Taiwan 94, Turkey 16, UAE 37, UK 32, UK 22, Ukraine 10, Uruguay 1, US 53) (2010)

Ports and terminals: *major seaport(s):* Buchanan, Monrovia

MILITARY

Military branches: Armed Forces of Liberia (AFL): Army, Navy, Air Force

Military service age and obligation: 18 years of age for voluntary military service; no conscription (2012)

Manpower available for military service:
males age 16-49: 815,826
females age 16-49: 828,484 (2010 est.)

Manpower fit for military service:
males age 16-49: 524,243
females age 16-49: 544,349 (2010 est.)

Manpower reaching militarily significant age annually: *male:* 36,585
female: 38,516 (2010 est.)

Military expenditures: 0.82% of GDP (2012)
country comparison to the world: 114
0.86% of GDP (2011)
0.82% of GDP (2010)

TRANSNATIONAL ISSUES

Disputes—international: although civil unrest continues to abate with the assistance of 18,000 UN Mission in Liberia peacekeepers, as of January 2007, Liberian refugees still remain in Guinea, Cote d'Ivoire, Sierra Leone, and Ghana; Liberia, in turn, shelters refugees fleeing turmoil in Cote d'Ivoire; despite the presence of over 9,000 UN forces in Cote d'Ivoire since 2004, ethnic conflict continues to spread into neighboring states who can no longer send their migrant workers to Ivorian cocoa plantations; UN sanctions ban Liberia from exporting diamonds and timber

Refugees and internally displaced persons: *refugees (country of origin):* 43,618 (Cote d'Ivoire) (2014)
IDPs: undetermined (civil war from 1990-2004; post-election violence in March and April 2011; unclear how many have found durable solutions; many dwell in slums in Monrovia) (2012)

Trafficking in persons: *current situation:* Liberia is a source, transit, and destination country for men, women, and children subjected to forced labor and sex trafficking; most victims are Liberian and are exploited within the country, where they are forced into domestic servitude, begging, prostitution, street vending, agricultural work, and diamond mining; a small number of Liberian men, women, and children are trafficked to Cote d'Ivoire, Guinea, Sierra Leone, Nigeria, and the US, while trafficking victims are brought to Liberia from neighboring West African countries, including Sierra Leone, Guinea, Cote d'Ivoire, and Nigeria

tier rating: Tier 2 Watch List—Liberia does not fully comply with the minimum standards for the elimination of trafficking; however, it is making significant efforts to do so; the government has increased its anti-trafficking law enforcement efforts and achieved its first conviction under its 2005 anti-trafficking law; the government has failed to make adequate efforts to identify and protect trafficking victims and has not adopted or implemented the standard operating procedures for assisting victims finalized by the anti-trafficking secretariat in 2012; the referral of victims to NGOs for protective services is inconsistent (2013)

Illicit drugs: transshipment point for Southeast and Southwest Asian heroin and South American cocaine for the European and US markets; corruption, criminal activity, arms-dealing, and diamond trade provide significant potential for money laundering, but the lack of well-developed financial system limits the country's utility as a major money-laundering center

LIBYA

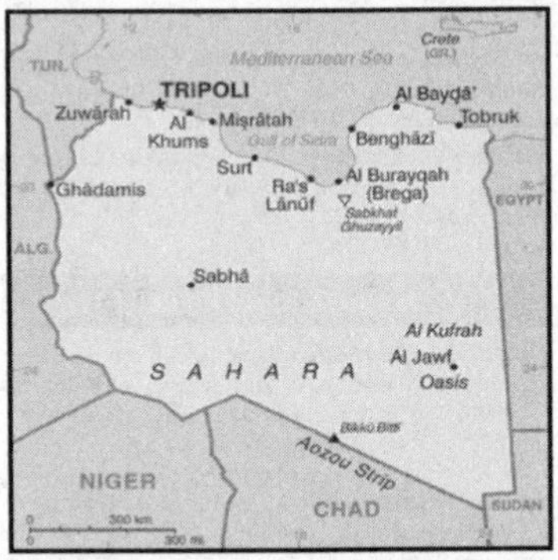

INTRODUCTION

Background: The Italians supplanted the Ottoman Turks in the area around Tripoli in 1911 and did not relinquish their hold until 1943 when defeated in World War II. Libya then passed to UN administration and achieved independence in 1951. Following a 1969 military coup, Col. Muammar al-QADHAFI assumed leadership and began to espouse his political system at home, which was a combination of socialism and Islam. During the 1970s, QADHAFI used oil revenues to promote his ideology outside Libya, supporting subversive and terrorist activities that included the downing of two airliners—one over Scotland, another in Northern Africa—and a discotheque bombing in Berlin. UN sanctions in 1992 isolated QADHAFI politically and economically following the attacks; sanctions were lifted in 2003 following Libyan acceptance of responsibility for the bombings and agreement to claimant compensation. QADHAFI also agreed to end Libya's program to develop weapons of mass destruction, and he made significant strides in normalizing relations with Western nations. Unrest that began in several Middle Eastern and North African countries in late 2010 erupted in Libyan cities in early 2011. QADHAFI's brutal crackdown on protesters spawned a civil war that triggered UN authorization of air and naval intervention by the international community. After months of seesaw fighting between government and opposition forces, the QADHAFI regime was toppled in mid-2011 and replaced by a transitional government. Libya in 2012 formed a new parliament and elected a new prime minister.

GEOGRAPHY

Location: Northern Africa, bordering the Mediterranean Sea, between Egypt, Tunisia, and Algeria

Geographic coordinates: 25 00 N, 17 00 E

Map references: Africa

Area: *total:* 1,759,540 sq km
country comparison to the world: 17
land: 1,759,540 sq km
water: 0 sq km

Area—comparative: about 2.5 times the size of Texas; slightly larger than Alaska

Land boundaries: *total:* 4,348 km
border countries: Algeria 982 km, Chad 1,055 km, Egypt 1,115 km, Niger 354 km, Sudan 383 km, Tunisia 459 km

Coastline: 1,770 km

Maritime claims: *territorial sea:* 12 nm
note: Gulf of Sidra closing line—32 degrees, 30 minutes north
exclusive fishing zone: 62 nm

Climate: Mediterranean along coast; dry, extreme desert interior

Terrain: mostly barren, flat to undulating plains, plateaus, depressions

Elevation extremes: *lowest point:* Sabkhat Ghuzayyil -47 m
highest point: Bikku Bitti 2,267 m

Natural resources: petroleum, natural gas, gypsum

Land use: *arable land:* 0.99%
permanent crops: 0.19%
other: 98.82% (2011)

Irrigated land: 4,700 sq km (2003)

Total renewable water resources: 0.7 cu km (2011)

Freshwater withdrawal (domestic/industrial/agricultural): *total:* 4.33 cu km/yr (14%/3%/83%)
per capita: 796.1 cu m/yr (2000)

Natural hazards: hot, dry, dust-laden ghibli is a southern wind lasting one to four days in spring and fall; dust storms, sandstorms

Environment—current issues: desertification; limited natural freshwater resources; the Great Manmade River Project, the largest water development scheme in the world, brings water from large aquifers under the Sahara to coastal cities

Environment—international agreements: *party to:* Biodiversity, Climate Change, Climate Change-Kyoto Protocol, Desertification, Endangered Species, Hazardous Wastes, Marine Dumping, Ozone Layer Protection, Ship Pollution, Wetlands
signed, but not ratified: Law of the Sea

Geography—note: more than 90% of the country is desert or semidesert

PEOPLE AND SOCIETY

Nationality: *noun:* Libyan(s)
adjective: Libyan

Ethnic groups: Berber and Arab 97%, other 3% (includes Greeks, Maltese, Italians, Egyptians, Pakistanis, Turks, Indians, and Tunisians)

Languages: Arabic (official), Italian, English (all widely understood in the major cities); Berber (Nafusi, Ghadamis, Suknah, Awjilah, Tamasheq)

Religions: Muslim (official; virtually all Sunni) 96.6%, Christian 2.7%, Buddhist 0.3%, Hindu
note: non-Sunni Muslims include native Ibadhi Muslims (

Population: 6,244,174 (July 2014 est.)
country comparison to the world: 108
note: immigrants make up just over 12% of the total population, according to UN data (2013)

Age structure: *0-14 years:* 26.9% (male 859,016/female 820,643)
15-24 years: 18.2% (male 586,749/female 546,602)
25-54 years: 46.1% (male 1,509,108/female 1,370,709)
55-64 years: 4% (male 154,847/female 145,330)
65 years and over: 3.9% (male 126,691/female 124,479) (2014 est.)

Dependency ratios:
total dependency ratio: 52.1 %
youth dependency ratio: 44.8 %
elderly dependency ratio: 7.3 %
potential support ratio: 13.7 (2013)

Median age: *total:* 27.5 years
male: 27.7 years
female: 27.4 years (2014 est.)

Population growth rate: 3.08% (2014 est.)
country comparison to the world: 10

Birth rate: 18.4 births/1,000 population (2014 est.)
country comparison to the world: 104

Death rate: 3.57 deaths/1,000 population (2014 est.)
country comparison to the world: 215

Net migration rate: 16.01 migrant(s)/1,000 population (2014 est.)
country comparison to the world: 6

Urbanization: *urban population:* 77.7% of total population (2011)
rate of urbanization: 1% annual rate of change (2010-15 est.)

Major urban areas—population: TRIPOLI (capital) 1.095 million (2009)

Sex ratio: *at birth:* 1.05 male(s)/female
0-14 years: 1.05 male(s)/female
15-24 years: 1.07 male(s)/female
25-54 years: 1.1 male(s)/female
55-64 years: 1.08 male(s)/female
65 years and over: 1.04 male(s)/female
total population: 1.08 male(s)/female (2014 est.)

Maternal mortality rate: 58 deaths/100,000 live births (2010)
country comparison to the world: 102

Infant mortality rate: *total:* 11.87 deaths/1,000 live births
country comparison to the world: 126
male: 12.83 deaths/1,000 live births
female: 10.85 deaths/1,000 live births (2014 est.)

Life expectancy at birth: *total population:* 76.04 years
country comparison to the world: 86
male: 74.36 years
female: 77.82 years (2014 est.)

Total fertility rate: 2.07 children born/woman (2014 est.)
country comparison to the world: 114

Contraceptive prevalence rate: 45.2% (1995)

Health expenditures: 4.4% of GDP (2011)
country comparison to the world: 153

Physicians density: 1.9 physicians/1,000 population (2009)

Hospital bed density: 3.7 beds/1,000 population (2009)

Drinking water source:
improved:
urban: 54.2% of population
rural: 54.9% of population
total: 54.4% of population
unimproved:
urban: 45.8% of population
rural: 45.1% of population
total: 54.4% of population (2000 est.)

Sanitation facility access:
improved:
urban: 96.8% of population

rural: 95.7% of population
total: 96.6% of population
unimproved:
urban: 3.2% of population
rural: 4.3% of population
total: 3.4% of population (2011 est.)

HIV/AIDS—adult prevalence rate: 0.3% (2001 est.)
country comparison to the world: 97

HIV/AIDS—people living with HIV/AIDS: 10,000 (2001 est.)
country comparison to the world: 103

HIV/AIDS—deaths: NA

Obesity—adult prevalence rate: 27.8% (2008)
country comparison to the world: 35

Children under the age of 5 years underweight: 5.6% (2007)
country comparison to the world: 86

Education expenditures: NA

Literacy: *definition:* age 15 and over can read and write
total population: 89.5%
male: 95.8%
female: 83.3% (2011 est.)

School life expectancy (primary to tertiary education): *total:* 16 years
male: 16 years
female: 16 years (2003)

GOVERNMENT

Country name: *conventional long form:* none
conventional short form: Libya
local long form: none
local short form: Libiya

Government type: operates under a transitional government

Capital: *name:* Tripoli (Tarabulus)

geographic coordinates: 32 53 N, 13 10 E
time difference: UTC+1 (6 hours ahead of Washington, DC during Standard Time)
daylight saving time: +1hr, begins last Friday in March; ends last Friday in October
note: on 10 November 2012, Libya changed its standard time from UTC+2 to UTC+1

Administrative divisions: 22 districts (shabiyat, singular—shabiyat); Al Butnan, Al Jabal al Akhdar, Al Jabal al Gharbi, Al Jafarah, Al Jufrah, Al Kufrah, Al Marj, Al Marqab, Al Wahat, An Nuqat al Khams, Az Zawiyah, Banghazi, Darnah, Ghat, Misratah, Murzuq, Nalut, Sabha, Surt, Tarabulus, Wadi al Hayat, Wadi ash Shati

Independence: 24 December 1951 (from UN trusteeship)

National holiday: Liberation Day, 23 October (2011)

Constitution: previous 1951, 1977; latest 2011 (interim); note—in mid-July 2013, Libya's legislative body agreed on steps for drafting a new constitution (2013)

Legal system: Libya's post-revolution legal system is in flux and driven by state and non-state entities

International law organization participation: has not submitted an ICJ jurisdiction declaration; non-party state to the ICCt

Suffrage: 18 years of age, universal

Executive branch: *chief of state:* President, General National Congress Nuri Abu SAHMAYN
head of government: Prime Minister (vacant); Deputy Prime Ministers Awad Ibrik Ibrahim al-BARASI, Sadiq Abd al-Karim Abd al-Rahman KARIM, Abd-al-Salam Muhammad al-Mahdi al-QADI
cabinet: new cabinet approved by the National Congress on 31 October 2012 (For more information visit the World Leaders website)
elections: prime minister and National Congress president elected by the National Congress
election results: NA

Legislative branch: unicameral General National Congress (200 seats; 120 individual seats elected from 69 constituencies and 80 party list seats elected from 20 constituencies; member term NA)
elections: first General National Congress election held on 7 July 2012 (next to be held NA)
election results: percent of vote for party list seats only—NFA 48.7%, JCP 21.3%, other parties 30%; list and constituent seats—NFA 39, JCP 17, other 24, independents 120

Judicial branch: *highest court(s):* NA; note—government in transition

Political parties and leaders: Al-Watan (Homeland) Party; Justice and Construction Party or JCP [Muhammad SAWAN]; National Front (initially the National Front for the Salvation of Libya, formed in 1981 as a diaspora opposition group); National Forces Alliance or NFA [Mahmoud JIBRIL, founder] (includes many political organizations, NGOs, and independents); Union for the Homeland [Abd al-Rahman al-SUWAYHILI]
note: list includes some of the larger political parties and leaders

Political pressure groups and leaders: NA

International organization participation: ABEDA, AfDB, AFESD, AMF, AMU, AU, BDEAC, CAEU, COMESA, FAO, G-77, IAEA, IBRD, ICAO, ICC (NGOs), ICRM, IDA, IDB, IFAD, IFC, IFRCS, ILO, IMF, IMO, IMSO, Interpol, IOC, IOM, IPU, ISO, ITSO, ITU, LAS, MIGA, NAM, OAPEC, OIC, OPCW, OPEC, PCA, UN, UNCTAD, UNESCO, UNIDO, UNWTO, UPU, WCO, WFTU (NGOs), WHO, WIPO, WMO, WTO (observer)

Diplomatic representation in the US: *chief of mission:* Ambassador (vacant); Charge d'Affaires Suleiman ABULHI
chancery: 2600 Virginia Avenue NW, Suite 705, Washington, DC 20037
telephone: [1] (202) 944-9601
FAX: [1] (202) 944-9606

Diplomatic representation from the US: *chief of mission:* Ambassador Deborah K. JONES (since 11 June 2013)
note: on 11 September 2012, US Ambassador Christopher STEVENS and three other American diplomats were killed in an attack by heavily armed militants on a US diplomatic post in the eastern city of Benghazi embassy: Sidi Slim Area/ Walie Al-Ahed Road, Tripoli
mailing address: US Embassy, 8850 Tripoli Place, Washington, DC 20521-8850
telephone: [218] (0) 91-220-3239

Flag description: three horizontal bands of red (top), black (double width), and green with a white crescent and star centered on the black stripe; the National Transitional Council reintroduced this flag design of the former Kingdom of Libya (1951-1969) on 27 February 2011; it replaced the former all-green banner promulgated by the QADHAFI regime in 1977; the colors represent the three major regions of the country: red stands for Fezzan, black symbolizes Cyrenaica, and green denotes Tripolitania; the crescent and star represent Islam, the main religion of the country

National symbol(s): star and crescent; hawk

National anthem: *name:* "Allahu Akbar" (God Is Greatest)
lyrics/music: Mahmoud el-SHERIF/Abdalla Shams el-DIN
note: adopted 1969; the anthem was originally a battle song for the Egyptian Army in the 1956 Suez War

ECONOMY

Economy—overview: Libya's economy is structured primarily around the nation's energy sector, which generates about 95% of export earnings, 80% of GDP, and 99% of government income. Substantial revenue from the energy sector coupled with a small population give Libya one of the highest per capita GDPs in Africa, but Tripoli largely has not used its significant financial resources to develop national infrastructure or the economy, leaving many citizens poor. In the final five years of QADHAFI's rule, Libya made some progress on economic reform as part of a broader campaign to reintegrate the country into the international fold. This effort picked up steam after UN sanctions were lifted in September 2003 and after Libya announced in December 2003 that it would abandon programs to build weapons of mass destruction. The process of lifting US unilateral sanctions began in the spring of 2004; all sanctions were removed by June 2006, helping Libya attract greater foreign direct investment, especially in the energy and banking sectors. Libyan oil and gas licensing rounds drew high international interest, but new rounds are unlikely to be successful until Libya establishes a more permanent government and is able to offer more attractive financial terms on contracts and increase security. Libya faces a long road ahead in liberalizing its primarily socialist economy, but the revolution has unleashed previously restrained entrepreneurial activity and increased the potential for the evolution of a more market-based economy. The service and construction sectors expanded over the past five years and could become a larger share of GDP if Tripoli prioritizes capital spending on development projects once political and security uncertainty subside. Climatic conditions and poor soils severely limit agricultural output, and Libya imports about 80% of its food. Libya's primary agricultural water source is the Great Manmade River Project.

GDP (purchasing power parity): $73.6 billion (2013 est.)
country comparison to the world: 85
$77.57 billion (2012 est.)
$37.94 billion (2011 est.)
note: data are in 2013 US dollars

GDP (official exchange rate): $70.92 billion (2013 est.)

GDP—real growth rate: -5.1% (2013 est.)
country comparison to the world: 216
104.5% (2012 est.)
-62.1% (2011 est.)

GDP—per capita (PPP): $11,300 (2013 est.)
country comparison to the world: 109
$12,100 (2012 est.)
$6,000 (2011 est.)
note: data are in 2013 US dollars

Gross national saving: 14% of GDP (2013 est.)
country comparison to the world: 115
44.4% of GDP (2012 est.)
-3.5% of GDP (2011 est.)

GDP—composition, by end use:
household consumption: 58%
government consumption: 20.2%
investment in fixed capital: 8.6%
investment in inventories: 0.5%
exports of goods and services: 54.5%
imports of goods and services: -41.9% (2013 est.)

GDP—composition, by sector of origin:
agriculture: 2%

industry: 58.3%
services: 39.7% (2013 est.)
Agriculture—products: wheat, barley, olives, dates, citrus, vegetables, peanuts, soybeans; cattle
Industries: petroleum, petrochemicals, aluminum, iron and steel, food processing, textiles, handicrafts, cement
Industrial production growth rate: 9.6% (2013 est.)
country comparison to the world: 16
Labor force: 1.644 million (2013 est.)
country comparison to the world: 127
Labor force—by occupation: *agriculture:* 17%
industry: 23%
services: 59% (2004 est.)
Unemployment rate: 30% (2004 est.)
country comparison to the world: 182
Population below poverty line: NA%
note: about one-third of Libyans live at or below the national poverty line
Household income or consumption by percentage share: *lowest 10%:* NA%
highest 10%: NA%
Budget: *revenues:* $41.54 billion
expenditures: $41.87 billion (2013 est.)
Taxes and other revenues: 58.6% of GDP (2013 est.)
country comparison to the world: 5
Budget surplus (+) or deficit (-):
-0.5% of GDP (2013 est.)
country comparison to the world: 55
Public debt: 4.8% of GDP (2013 est.)
country comparison to the world: 158
4.1% of GDP (2012 est.)
Fiscal year: calendar year
Inflation rate (consumer prices): 3.2% (2013 est.)
country comparison to the world: 119
6.1% (2012 est.)
Central bank discount rate: 9.52% (31 December 2010 est.)
country comparison to the world: 103
3% (31 December 2009 est.)
Commercial bank prime lending rate: 6% (31 December 2013 est.)
country comparison to the world: 139
6% (31 December 2012 est.)
Stock of narrow money: $47.25 billion (31 December 2013 est.)
country comparison to the world: 48
$45.2 billion (31 December 2012 est.)
Stock of broad money: $51.86 billion (31 December 2013 est.)
country comparison to the world: 68
$49.28 billion (31 December 2012 est.)
Stock of domestic credit: $-54.04 billion (31 December 2013 est.)
country comparison to the world: 191
$-47.25 billion (31 December 2012 est.)
Market value of publicly traded shares: $NA
Current account balance: $2.727 billion (2013 est.)
country comparison to the world: 35
$27.17 billion (2012 est.)
Exports: $38.45 billion (2013 est.)
country comparison to the world: 61
$52.02 billion (2012 est.)
Exports—commodities: crude oil, refined petroleum products, natural gas, chemicals
Exports—partners: Italy 23.3%, Germany 12.4%, China 11.2%, France 9.7%, Spain 7.6%, UK 4.7%, US 4.5% (2012)
Imports: $27.15 billion (2013 est.)
country comparison to the world: 69
$18.1 billion (2012 est.)
Imports—commodities: machinery, semi-finished goods, food, transport equipment, consumer products
Imports—partners: China 13%, Turkey 11.6%, Italy 8.2%, Egypt 7.7%, Tunisia 6.6%, South Korea 5.8%, Greece 5.4%, Germany 4.6% (2012)
Reserves of foreign exchange and gold:
$120.9 billion (31 December 2013 est.)
country comparison to the world: 21
$118.6 billion (31 December 2012 est.)
Debt—external: $6.319 billion (31 December 2013 est.)
country comparison to the world: 113
$5.278 billion (31 December 2012 est.)
Stock of direct foreign investment—at home:
$17.92 billion (31 December 2013 est.)
country comparison to the world: 74
$16.84 billion (31 December 2012 est.)
Stock of direct foreign investment—abroad:
$17.82 billion (31 December 2013 est.)
country comparison to the world: 47
$17.21 billion (31 December 2012 est.)
Exchange rates: Libyan dinars (LYD) per US dollar—
1.277 (2013 est.)
1.2617 (2012 est.)
1.2668 (2010 est.)
1.2535 (2009)
1.2112 (2008)

ENERGY

Electricity—production: 29.72 billion kWh (2010 est.)
country comparison to the world: 6 6
Electricity—consumption: 25.24 billion kWh (2010 est.)
country comparison to the world: 66
Electricity—exports: 129 million kWh (2010 est.)
country comparison to the world: 74
Electricity—imports: 76 million kWh (2010 est.)
country comparison to the world: 95
Electricity—installed generating capacity:
6.766 million kW (2010 est.)
country comparison to the world: 68
Electricity—from fossil fuels: 100% of total installed capacity (2010 est.)
country comparison to the world: 21
Electricity—from nuclear fuels: 0% of total installed capacity (2010 est.)
country comparison to the world: 129
Electricity—from hydroelectric plants:
0% of total installed capacity (2010 est.)
country comparison to the world: 180
Electricity—from other renewable sources:
0% of total installed capacity (2010 est.)
country comparison to the world: 195
Crude oil—production: 1.483 million bbl/day (2012 est.)
country comparison to the world: 20
Crude oil—exports: 1.378 million bbl/day (2010 est.)
country comparison to the world: 15
Crude oil—imports: 0 bbl/day (2010 est.)
country comparison to the world: 84
Crude oil—proved reserves: 48.01 billion bbl (1 January 2013 es)
country comparison to the world: 9
Refined petroleum products—production:
388,300 bbl/day (2010 est.)
country comparison to the world: 37
Refined petroleum products—consumption:
314,000 bbl/day (2011 est.)
country comparison to the world: 43
Refined petroleum products—exports:
119,000 bbl/day (2010 est.)
country comparison to the world: 41
Refined petroleum products—imports:
575.3 bbl/day (2010 est.)
country comparison to the world: 202
Natural gas—production: 7.855 billion cu m (2011 est.)
country comparison to the world: 46
Natural gas—consumption: 6.844 billion cu m (2010 est.)
country comparison to the world: 55
Natural gas—exports: 3.666 billion cu m (2011 est.)
country comparison to the world: 37
Natural gas—imports: 0 cu m (2011 est.)
country comparison to the world: 89
Natural gas—proved reserves: 1.547 trillion cu m (1 January 2013 es)
country comparison to the world: 22
Carbon dioxide emissions from consumption of energy: 49.67 million Mt (2011 est.)
country comparison to the world: 64

COMMUNICATIONS

Telephones—main lines in use: 814,000 (2012)
country comparison to the world: 8 5
Telephones—mobile cellular: 9.59 million (2012)
country comparison to the world: 81
Telephone system: *general assessment:* telecommunications system is state-owned and service is poor, but investment is being made to upgrade; state retains monopoly in fixed-line services; mobile-cellular telephone system became operational in 1996
domestic: multiple providers for a mobile telephone system that is growing rapidly; combined fixed-line and mobile-cellular teledensity has soared
international: country code—218; satellite earth stations—4 Intelsat, NA Arabsat, and NA Intersputnik; submarine cable to France and Italy; microwave radio relay to Tunisia and Egypt; tropospheric scatter to Greece; participant in Medarabtel (2010)
Broadcast media: state-funded and private TV stations; some provinces operate local TV stations; pan-Arab satellite TV stations are available; state-funded radio (2012)
Internet country code: .ly
Internet hosts: 17,926 (2012)
country comparison to the world: 121
Internet users: 353,900 (2009)
country comparison to the world: 124

TRANSPORTATION

Airports: 146 (2013)
country comparison to the world: 4 1
Airports—with paved runways: *total:* 6 8
over 3,047 m: 23
2,438 to 3,047 m: 7
1,524 to 2,437 m: 30
914 to 1,523 m: 7

under 914 m: 1 (2013)

Airports—with unpaved runways: *total:* 7 8
over 3,047 m: 2
2,438 to 3,047 m: 5
1,524 to 2,437 m: 14
914 to 1,523 m: 37
under 914 m: 20 (2013)

Heliports: 2 (2013)

Pipelines: condensate 882 km; gas 3,743 km; oil 7,005 km (2013)

Roadways: *total:* 100,024 km
country comparison to the world: 45
paved: 57,214 km
unpaved: 42,810 km (2003)

Merchant marine: *total:* 2 3
country comparison to the world: 91
by type: cargo 2, chemical tanker 4, liquefied gas 3, petroleum tanker 13, roll on/roll off 1
foreign-owned: 2 (Kuwait 1, Norway 1)
registered in other countries: 6 (Hong Kong 1, Malta 5) (2010)

Ports and terminals: *major seaport(s):* Marsa al Burayqah (Marsa el Brega), Tripoli
oil terminal(s): Az Zawiyah, Ra's Lanuf

MILITARY

Military branches: note—in transition; government attempting to staff a new national army with anti-QADAFI militia fighters and former members of QADAFI's military (2008)

Military service age and obligation: 18 years of age for mandatory or voluntary service (2012)

Manpower available for military service:
males age 16-49: 1,775,078
females age 16-49: 1,714,194 (2010 est.)

Manpower fit for military service:
males age 16-49: 1,511,144
females age 16-49: 1,458,934 (2010 est.)

Manpower reaching militarily significant age annually: *male:* 59,547
female: 57,070 (2010 est.)

TRANSNATIONAL ISSUES

Disputes—international: dormant disputes include Libyan claims of about 32,000 sq km still reflected on its maps of southeastern Algeria and the FLN's assertions of a claim to Chirac Pastures in southeastern Morocco; various Chadian rebels from the Aozou region reside in southern Libya

Refugees and internally displaced persons: *IDPs:* 74,000 (conflict between pro-Qadhafi and anti-Qadhafi forces; figure does not include displaced third-country nationals) (2012)

Trafficking in persons: *current situation:* Libya is a destination and transit country for men and women from sub-Saharan Africa and Asia subjected to forced labor and forced prostitution; migrants who seek employment in Libya as laborers and domestic workers or transit Libya en route to Europe may be subject to forced labor; private employers also recruit migrants from detention centers as forced laborers on farms and construction sites; some sub-Saharan women are reportedly forced to work in Libyan brothels
tier rating: Tier 3—the Libyan Government does not fully comply with the minimum standards for the elimination of trafficking and is not making significant efforts to do so; the government has failed to demonstrate significant efforts to investigate and prosecute trafficking offenders or to protect trafficking victims; policies and practices with respect to undocumented migrant workers has resulted in Libyan authorities detaining and punishing trafficking victims for unlawful acts that were committed as a result of being trafficked; no public anti-trafficking awareness campaigns are conducted; officials receive no training on trafficking issues (2013)

LIECHTENSTEIN

INTRODUCTION

Background: The Principality of Liechtenstein was established within the Holy Roman Empire in 1719. Occupied by both French and Russian troops during the Napoleonic Wars, it became a sovereign state in 1806 and joined the Germanic Confederation in 1815. Liechtenstein became fully independent in 1866 when the Confederation dissolved. Until the end of World War I, it was closely tied to Austria, but the economic devastation caused by that conflict forced Liechtenstein to enter into a customs and monetary union with Switzerland. Since World War II (in which Liechtenstein remained neutral), the country's low taxes have spurred outstanding economic growth. In 2000, shortcomings in banking regulatory oversight resulted in concerns about the use of financial institutions for money laundering. However, Liechtenstein implemented anti-money laundering legislation and a Mutual Legal Assistance Treaty with the US that went into effect in 2003.

GEOGRAPHY

Location: Central Europe, between Austria and Switzerland

Geographic coordinates: 47 16 N, 9 32 E

Map references: Europe

Area: *total:* 160 sq km
country comparison to the world: 219
land: 160 sq km
water: 0 sq km

Area—comparative: about 0.9 times the size of Washington, DC

Land boundaries: *total:* 76 km
border countries: Austria 34.9 km, Switzerland 41.1 km

Coastline: 0 km (doubly landlocked)

Maritime claims: none (landlocked)

Climate: continental; cold, cloudy winters with frequent snow or rain; cool to moderately warm, cloudy, humid summers

Terrain: mostly mountainous (Alps) with Rhine Valley in western third

Elevation extremes: *lowest point:* Ruggeller Riet 430 m
highest point: Vorder-Grauspitz 2,599 m

Natural resources: hydroelectric potential, arable land

Land use: *arable land:* 21.88%
permanent crops: 0%
other: 78.12% (2011)

Irrigated land: NA

Natural hazards: NA

Environment—current issues: NA

Environment—international agreements: *party to:* Air Pollution, Air Pollution-Nitrogen Oxides, Air Pollution-Persistent Organic Pollutants, Air Pollution-Sulfur 85, Air Pollution-Sulfur 94, Air Pollution-Volatile Organic Compounds, Biodiversity, Climate Change, Climate Change-Kyoto Protocol, Desertification, Endangered Species, Hazardous Wastes, Ozone Layer Protection, Wetlands
signed, but not ratified: Law of the Sea

Geography—note: along with Uzbekistan, one of only two doubly landlocked countries in the world; variety of microclimatic variations based on elevation

PEOPLE AND SOCIETY

Nationality: *noun:* Liechtensteiner(s)
adjective: Liechtenstein

Ethnic groups: Liechtensteiner 65.6%, other 34.4% (2000 census)

Languages: German 94.5% (official) (Alemannic is the main dialect), Italian 1.1%, other 4.3% (2010 est.)

Religions: Roman Catholic (official) 75.9%, Protestant Reformed 6.5%, Muslim 5.4%, Lutheran 1.3%, other 1.8%, none 5.4%, unspecified 2.6% (2010 est.)

Population: 37,313 (July 2014 est.)
country comparison to the world: 214

Age structure: *0-14 years:* 15.7% (male 3,130/female 2,744)
15-24 years: 11.7% (male 2,160/female 2,197)
25-54 years: 43.1% (male 8,029/female 8,069)
55-64 years: 16% (male 2,479/female 2,535)

65 years and over: 15.4% (male 2,713/female 3,257) (2014 est.)

Median age: *total:* 42.4 years
male: 41.3 years
female: 43.5 years (2014 est.)

Population growth rate: 0.82% (2014 est.)
country comparison to the world: 134

Birth rate: 10.53 births/1,000 population (2014 est.)
country comparison to the world: 183

Death rate: 7.02 deaths/1,000 population (2014 est.)
country comparison to the world: 132

Net migration rate: 4.72 migrant(s)/1,000 population (2014 est.)
country comparison to the world: 27

Urbanization: *urban population:* 14% of total population (2010)
rate of urbanization: 0.9% annual rate of change (2010-15 est.)

Major urban areas—population: VADUZ (capital) 5,000 (2009)

Sex ratio: *at birth:* 1.26 male(s)/female
0-14 years: 1.14 male(s)/female
15-24 years: 0.98 male(s)/female
25-54 years: 1 male(s)/female
55-64 years: 0.99 male(s)/female
65 years and over: 0.81 male(s)/female
total population: 0.98 male(s)/female (2014 est.)

Infant mortality rate: *total:* 4.33 deaths/1,000 live births
country comparison to the world: 192
male: 4.62 deaths/1,000 live births
female: 3.96 deaths/1,000 live births (2014 est.)

Life expectancy at birth: *total population:* 81.68 years
country comparison to the world: 13
male: 79.52 years
female: 84.4 years (2014 est.)

Total fertility rate: 1.69 children born/woman (2014 est.)
country comparison to the world: 173

HIV/AIDS—adult prevalence rate: NA

HIV/AIDS—people living with HIV/AIDS: NA

HIV/AIDS—deaths: NA

Education expenditures: 2.1% of GDP (2008)
country comparison to the world: 166

Literacy: *definition:* age 10 and over can read and write
total population: 100%
male: 100%
female: 100%

School life expectancy (primary to tertiary education): *total:* 15 years
male: 16 years
female: 14 years (2011)

GOVERNMENT

Country name: *conventional long form:* Principality of Liechtenstein
conventional short form: Liechtenstein
local long form: Fuerstentum Liechtenstein
local short form: Liechtenstein

Government type: hereditary constitutional monarchy

Capital: *name:* Vaduz

geographic coordinates: 47 08 N, 9 31 E
time difference: UTC+1 (6 hours ahead of Washington, DC during Standard Time)
daylight saving time: +1hr, begins last Sunday in March; ends last Sunday in October

Administrative divisions: 11 communes (Gemeinden, singular—Gemeinde); Balzers, Eschen, Gamprin, Mauren, Planken, Ruggell, Schaan, Schellenberg, Triesen, Triesenberg, Vaduz

Independence: 23 January 1719 (Principality of Liechtenstein established); 12 July 1806 (independence from the Holy Roman Empire); 24 August 1866 (independence from the German Confederation)

National holiday: Assumption Day, 15 August

Constitution: previous 1862; latest adopted 5 October 1921; amended many times, last in 2011 (2013)

Legal system: civil law system influenced by Swiss, Austrian, and German law

International law organization participation: accepts compulsory ICJ jurisdiction with reservations; accepts ICCt jurisdiction

Suffrage: 18 years of age; universal

Executive branch: *chief of state:* Prince HANS ADAM II (since 13 November 1989, assumed executive powers on 26 August 1984); Heir Apparent Prince ALOIS, son of the monarch (born 11 June 1968); note—on 15 August 2004, HANS ADAM transferred the official duties of the ruling prince to ALOIS, but HANS ADAM retains status of chief of state
head of government: Head of Government (Prime Minister) Adrian HASLER (since 27 March 2013)
cabinet: Cabinet elected by the Parliament, confirmed by the monarch (For more information visit the World Leaders website)
elections: the monarchy is hereditary; following legislative elections, the leader of the majority party in the Landtag usually appointed the head of government by the monarch and the leader of the largest minority party in the Landtag usually appointed the deputy head of government by the monarch if there is a coalition government

Legislative branch: unicameral Parliament or Landtag (25 seats; members elected by popular vote under proportional representation to serve four-year terms)
elections: last held on 3 February 2013 (next to be held in February 2017)
election results: percent of vote by party—FBP 40.0%, VU 33.5%, DU 15.3% FL 11.1%; seats by party—FBP 10, VU 8, DU 4, FL 3

Judicial branch: *highest court(s):* Supreme Court or Oberster Gerichtshof (consists of 5 judges); Constitutional Court or Verfassungsgericht (consists of 5 judges and 5 alternates)
judge selection and term of office: judges of both courts elected by the Landtag and appointed by the monarch; Supreme Court judges serve 4-year renewable terms; Constitutional Court judge tenure NA
subordinate courts: Court of Appeal or Obergericht (second instance), Court of Justice (first instance), Administrative Court, county courts

Political parties and leaders: The Free List (Die Freie Liste) or FL [Wolfgang MARXER]; the independents (Die Unabhaengigen) or DU [Harry QUADERER]; Progressive Citizens' Party (Fortschrittliche Buergerpartei) or FBP [Alexander BATLINER]; Fatherland Union (Vaterlaendische Union) or VU [Jakob BUECHEL]

Political pressure groups and leaders: NA

International organization participation: CD, CE, EBRD, EFTA, IAEA, ICRM, IFRCS, Interpol, IOC, IPU, ITSO, ITU, ITUC (NGOs), OPCW, OSCE, PCA, Schengen Convention, UN, UNCTAD, UPU, WIPO, WTO

Diplomatic representation in the US: *chief of mission:* Ambassador Claudia FRITSCHE (since 7 December 2000)
chancery: 2900 K Street, NW, Suite 602B, Washington, DC 20007
telephone: [1] (202) 331-0590
FAX: [1] (202) 331-3221

Diplomatic representation from the US: the US does not have an embassy in Liechtenstein; the US Ambassador to Switzerland, currently Charge d'Affaires Jeffrey R. CELLARS, is accredited to Liechtenstein

Flag description: two equal horizontal bands of blue (top) and red with a gold crown on the hoist side of the blue band; the colors may derive from the blue and red livery design used in the principality's household in the 18th century; the prince's crown was introduced in 1937 to distinguish the flag from that of Haiti

National anthem: *name:* "Oben am jungen Rhein" (High Above the Young Rhine)
lyrics/music: Jakob Joseph JAUCH/Josef FROMMELT
note: adopted 1850, revised 1963; the anthem uses the tune of "God Save the Queen"

ECONOMY

Economy—overview: Despite its small size and limited natural resources, Liechtenstein has developed into a prosperous, highly industrialized, free-enterprise economy with a vital financial service sector and likely the second highest per capita income in the world. The Liechtenstein economy is widely diversified with a large number of small businesses. Low business taxes—the maximum tax rate is 20%—and easy incorporation rules have induced many holding companies to establish nominal offices in Liechtenstein providing 30% of state revenues. The country participates in a customs union with Switzerland and uses the Swiss franc as its national currency. It imports more than 90% of its energy requirements. Liechtenstein has been a member of the European Economic Area (an organization serving as a bridge between the European Free Trade Association (EFTA) and the EU) since May 1995. The government is working to harmonize its economic policies with those of an integrated Europe. Since 2008, Liechtenstein has faced renewed international pressure—particularly from Germany—to improve transparency in its banking and tax systems. In December 2008, Liechtenstein signed a Tax Information Exchange Agreement with the US. Upon Liechtenstein's conclusion of 12 bilateral information-sharing agreements, the OECD in October 2009 removed the principality from its "grey list" of countries that had yet to implement the organization's Model Tax Convention. By the end of 2010, Liechtenstein had signed 25 Tax Information Exchange Agreements or Double Tax Agreements. In 2011 Liechtenstein joined the Schengen area, which allows passport-free travel across 26 European countries.

GDP (purchasing power parity): $3.2 billion (2009)
country comparison to the world: 179
$3.216 billion (2008)
$3.159 billion (2007)

GDP (official exchange rate): $5.113 billion (2010)

GDP—real growth rate: -0.5% (2009 est.)
country comparison to the world: 200
1.8% (2008 est.)
3.1% (2007 est.)

GDP—per capita (PPP): $89,400 (2009 est.)

country comparison to the world: 2
$90,600 (2008 est.)
$89,700 (2007 est.)

GDP—composition, by sector of origin:
agriculture: 8%
industry: 37%
services: 55% (2009)

Agriculture—products: wheat, barley, corn, potatoes; livestock, dairy products

Industries: electronics, metal manufacturing, dental products, ceramics, pharmaceuticals, food products, precision instruments, tourism, optical instruments

Industrial production growth rate: NA%

Labor force: 35,250 (2012)
country comparison to the world: 202
note: 51% of the labor force in Liechtenstein commuted daily from Austria, Switzerland, or Germany (2012)

Labor force—by occupation:
agriculture: 0.8%
industry: 39.4%
services: 59.9% (2010)

Unemployment rate: 2.5% (2011)
country comparison to the world: 18
2.2% (2010)

Population below poverty line: NA%

Household income or consumption by percentage share: *lowest 10%:* NA%
highest 10%: NA%

Budget: *revenues:* $1.29 billion
expenditures: $1.372 billion (2011 est.)

Taxes and other revenues: 25.2% of GDP (2011 est.)
country comparison to the world: 124

Budget surplus (+) or deficit (-):
-1.6% of GDP (2011 est.)
country comparison to the world: 75

Fiscal year: calendar year

Inflation rate (consumer prices): 0.2% (2011)
country comparison to the world: 12
0.7% (2010)

Market value of publicly traded shares: $NA

Exports: $3.76 billion (2011 est.)
country comparison to the world: 126
$3.191 billion (2010 est.)
note: trade data exclude trade with Switzerland

Exports—commodities: small specialty machinery, connectors for audio and video, parts for motor vehicles, dental products, hardware, prepared foodstuffs, electronic equipment, optical products

Imports: $2.218 billion (2011 est.)
country comparison to the world: 161
$1.806 billion (2010 est.)
note: trade data exclude trade with Switzerland

Imports—commodities: agricultural products, raw materials, energy products, machinery, metal goods, textiles, foodstuffs, motor vehicles

Debt—external: $0 (2001)
country comparison to the world: 202

Exchange rates: Swiss francs (CHF) per US dollar—
0.9542 (2013)
0.9374 (2012)
1.0429 (2010)
1.0881 (2009)
1.0774 (2008)

COMMUNICATIONS

Telephones—main lines in use: 20,000 (2012)
country comparison to the world: 185

Telephones—mobile cellular: 38,000 (2012)
country comparison to the world: 204

Telephone system: *general assessment:* automatic telephone system
domestic: fixed-line and mobile-cellular services widely available; combined telephone service subscribership exceeds 150 per 100 persons
international: country code—423; linked to Swiss networks by cable and microwave radio relay (2011)

Broadcast media: relies on foreign terrestrial and satellite broadcasters for most broadcast media services; first Liechtenstein-based TV station established August 2008; Radio Liechtenstein operates multiple radio stations; a Swiss-based broadcaster operates several radio stations in Liechtenstein (2008)

Internet country code: .li

Internet hosts: 14,278 (2012)
country comparison to the world: 128

Internet users: 23,000 (2009)
country comparison to the world: 190

TRANSPORTATION

Pipelines: gas 20 km (2013)

Railways: *total:* 9 km
country comparison to the world: 134
standard gauge: 9 km 1.435-m gauge (electrified)
note: belongs to the Austrian Railway System connecting Austria and Switzerland (2008)

Roadways: *total:* 380 km
country comparison to the world: 201
paved: 380 km (2012)

Waterways: 28 km (2010)
country comparison to the world: 106

MILITARY

Military branches: no regular military forces; National Police maintains close relations with neighboring forces (2013)

Manpower available for military service:
males age 16-49: 8,009 (2010 est.)

Manpower fit for military service:
males age 16-49: 6,538
females age 16-49: 6,746 (2010 est.)

Manpower reaching militarily significant age annually: *male:* 219
female: 211 (2010 est.)

Military—note: Liechtenstein has no military forces, but the modern National Police maintains close relations with neighboring forces. (2013)

TRANSNATIONAL ISSUES

Disputes—international: none

Refugees and internally displaced persons:
stateless persons: 5 (2012)

Illicit drugs: has strengthened money laundering controls, but money laundering remains a concern due to Liechtenstein's sophisticated offshore financial services sector

LITHUANIA

INTRODUCTION

Background: Lithuanian lands were united under MINDAUGAS in 1236; over the next century, through alliances and conquest, Lithuania extended its territory to include most of present-day Belarus and Ukraine. By the end of the 14th century Lithuania was the largest state in Europe. An alliance with Poland in 1386 led the two countries into a union through the person of a common ruler. In 1569, Lithuania and Poland formally united into a single dual state, the Polish-Lithuanian Commonwealth. This entity survived until 1795 when its remnants were partitioned by surrounding countries. Lithuania regained its independence following World War I but was annexed by the USSR in 1940—an action never recognized by the US and many other countries. On 11 March 1990, Lithuania became the first of the Soviet republics to declare its independence, but Moscow did not recognize this proclamation until September of 1991 (following the abortive coup in Moscow). The last Russian troops withdrew in 1993. Lithuania subsequently restructured its economy for integration into Western European institutions; it joined both NATO and the EU in the spring of 2004. In January 2014, Lithuania assumed a nonpermanent seat on the UN Security Council for the 2014-15 term.

GEOGRAPHY

Location: Eastern Europe, bordering the Baltic Sea, between Latvia and Russia

Geographic coordinates: 56 00 N, 24 00 E

Map references: Europe

Area: *total:* 65,300 sq km
country comparison to the world: 123
land: 62,680 sq km
water: 2,620 sq km

Area—comparative: slightly larger than West Virginia

Land boundaries: *total:* 1,574 km
border countries: Belarus 680 km, Latvia 576 km, Poland 91 km, Russia (Kaliningrad) 227 km

Coastline: 90 km

Maritime claims: *territorial sea:* 12 nm

Climate: transitional, between maritime and continental; wet, moderate winters and summers

Terrain: lowland, many scattered small lakes, fertile soil

Elevation extremes: *lowest point:* Baltic Sea 0 m
highest point: Aukstojas 294 m

Natural resources: peat, arable land, amber

Land use: *arable land:* 33.48%
permanent crops: 0.47%
other: 66.05% (2011)

Irrigated land: 13.4 sq km (2007)

Total renewable water resources: 24.9 cu km (2011)

Freshwater withdrawal (domestic/industrial/agricultural): *total:* 2.38 cu km/yr (7%/90%/3%)
per capita: 703.8 cu m/yr (2009)

Natural hazards: NA

Environment—current issues: contamination of soil and groundwater with petroleum products and chemicals at military bases

Environment—international agreements: *party to:* Air Pollution, Air Pollution-Nitrogen Oxides, Air Pollution-Persistent Organic Pollutants, Air Pollution-Sulphur 85, Air Pollution-Sulphur 94, Air Pollution-Volatile Organic Compounds, Biodiversity, Climate Change, Climate Change-Kyoto Protocol, Desertification, Endangered Species, Environmental Modification, Hazardous Wastes, Law of the Sea, Ozone Layer Protection, Ship Pollution, Wetlands
signed, but not ratified: none of the selected agreements

Geography—note: fertile central plains are separated by hilly uplands that are ancient glacial deposits

PEOPLE AND SOCIETY

Nationality: *noun:* Lithuanian(s)
adjective: Lithuanian

Ethnic groups: Lithuanian 84.1%, Polish 6.6%, Russian 5.8%, Belarusian 1.2%, other 1.1%, unspecified 1.2% (2011 est.)

Languages: Lithuanian (official) 82%, Russian 8%, Polish 5.6%, other 0.9%, unspecified 3.5% (2011 est.)

Religions: Roman Catholic 77.2%, Russian Orthodox 4.1%, Old Believer 0.8%, Evangelical Lutheran 0.6%, Evangelical Reformist 0.2%, other (including Sunni Muslim, Jewish, Greek Catholic, and Karaite) 0.8%, none 6.1%, unspecified 10.1% (2011 est.)

Population: 3,505,738 (July 2014 est.)
country comparison to the world: 134
note: Statistics Lithuania (the national statistical agency of Lithuania) estimates the country's total population at the start of 2013 to be 2,971,905, which takes into account the findings of Lithuania's 2011 census and the high rate of net outmigration since the country joined the EU in 2004

Age structure: *0-14 years:* 13.5% (male 243,001/female 230,674)
15-24 years: 12.5% (male 224,584/female 214,184)
25-54 years: 44.7% (male 782,238/female 785,521)
55-64 years: 17% (male 193,374/female 235,595)
65 years and over: 16.8% (male 207,222/female 389,345) (2014 est.)

Dependency ratios: *total dependency ratio:* 44.6 %
youth dependency ratio: 22 %
elderly dependency ratio: 22.7 %
potential support ratio: 4.4 (2013)

Median age: *total:* 41.2 years
male: 38.5 years
female: 43.7 years (2014 est.)

Population growth rate: -0.29% (2014 est.)
country comparison to the world: 218

Birth rate: 9.36 births/1,000 population (2014 est.)
country comparison to the world: 205

Death rate: 11.55 deaths/1,000 population (2014 est.)
country comparison to the world: 30

Net migration rate: -0.73 migrant(s)/1,000 population (2014 est.)
country comparison to the world: 143

Urbanization: *urban population:* 67% of total population (2010)
rate of urbanization: -0.5% annual rate of change (2010-15 est.)

Major urban areas—population: VILNIUS (capital) 546,000 (2009)

Sex ratio: *at birth:* 1.06 male(s)/female
0-14 years: 1.05 male(s)/female
15-24 years: 1.05 male(s)/female
25-54 years: 1 male(s)/female
55-64 years: 0.89 male(s)/female
65 years and over: 0.53 male(s)/female
total population: 0.89 male(s)/female (2014 est.)

Mother's mean age at first birth: 26.6 (2010 est.)

Maternal mortality rate: 8 deaths/100,000 live births (2010)
country comparison to the world: 163

Infant mortality rate: *total:* 6 deaths/1,000 live births
country comparison to the world: 171
male: 7.14 deaths/1,000 live births
female: 4.78 deaths/1,000 live births (2014 est.)

Life expectancy at birth: *total population:* 75.98 years
country comparison to the world: 87
male: 71.2 years
female: 81.02 years (2014 est.)

Total fertility rate: 1.29 children born/woman (2014 est.)
country comparison to the world: 217

Contraceptive prevalence rate: 62.9%
note: percent of women aged 18-49 (2006)

Health expenditures: 7% of GDP (2010)
country comparison to the world: 85

Physicians density: 3.64 physicians/1,000 population (2010)

Hospital bed density: 6.8 beds/1,000 population (2010)

Drinking water source:
improved:
urban: 97.6% of population
rural: 80.7% of population
total: 92% of population
unimproved:
urban: 2.4% of population
rural: 19.3% of population
total: 8% of population (2009 est.)

Sanitation facility access:
improved:
urban: 95.4% of population
rural: 69.1% of population
total: 86.7% of population
unimproved:
urban: 4.6% of population
rural: 30.9% of population
total: 13.3% of population (2009 est.)

HIV/AIDS—adult prevalence rate: 0.1% (2009 est.)
country comparison to the world: 157

HIV/AIDS—people living with HIV/AIDS: 1,200 (2009 est.)
country comparison to the world: 142

HIV/AIDS—deaths: fewer than 100 (2009 est.)
country comparison to the world: 145

Major infectious diseases: *degree of risk:* intermediate
vectorborne diseases: tickborne encephalitis (2013)

Obesity—adult prevalence rate: 27.6% (2008)
country comparison to the world: 38

Education expenditures: 5.4% of GDP (2010)
country comparison to the world: 61

Literacy: *definition:* age 15 and over can read and write
total population: 99.7%
male: 99.7%
female: 99.7% (2011 est.)

School life expectancy (primary to tertiary education): *total:* 17 years
male: 16 years
female: 17 years (2011)

Unemployment, youth ages 15-24: *total:* 26.4%
country comparison to the world: 37
male: 29.9%
female: 21.8% (2012)

GOVERNMENT

Country name: *conventional long form:* Republic of Lithuania
conventional short form: Lithuania
local long form: Lietuvos Respublika
local short form: Lietuva
former: Lithuanian Soviet Socialist Republic

Government type: parliamentary democracy

Capital: *name:* Vilnius
geographic coordinates: 54 41 N, 25 19 E
time difference: UTC+2 (7 hours ahead of Washington, DC during Standard Time)
daylight saving time: +1hr, begins last Sunday in March; ends last Sunday in October

Administrative divisions: 10 counties (apskritys, singular—apskritis); Alytaus, Kauno, Klaipedos, Marijampoles, Panevezio, Siauliu, Taurages, Telsiu, Utenos, Vilniaus

Independence: 11 March 1990 (declared); 6 September 1991 (recognized by the Soviet Union); notable earlier dates: 6 July 1253 (coronation of MINDAUGAS, traditional founding date), 1 July 1569 (Polish-Lithuanian Commonwealth created)

National holiday: Independence Day, 16 February (1918); note—16 February 1918 was the date Lithuania declared its independence from Soviet Russia and established its statehood; 11 March 1990 was the date it declared its independence from the Soviet Union

Constitution: several previous; latest adopted by referendum 25 October 1992, entered into force 2 November 1992; amended 2003 (2012)

Legal system: civil law system; legislative acts can be appealed to the constitutional court

International law organization participation: has not submitted an ICJ jurisdiction declaration; accepts ICCt jurisdiction

Suffrage: 18 years of age; universal

Executive branch: *chief of state:* President Dalia GRYBAUSKAITE (since 12 July 2009)
head of government: Prime Minister Algirdas BUTKEVICIUS (since 22 November 2012)
cabinet: Council of Ministers appointed by the president on the nomination of the prime minister and approval of the Parliament (For more information visit the World Leaders website)
elections: president elected by popular vote for a five-year term (eligible for a second term); election last held on 17 May 2009 (next to be held in May 2014); prime minister appointed by the president on the approval of the Parliament

election results: Dalia GRYBAUSKAITE elected president; percent of vote—Dalia GRYBAUSKAITE 69.1%, Algirdas BUTKEVICIUS 11.8%, Valentinas MAZURONIS 6.2%, others 12.9%; Algirdas BUTKEVICIUS approved by Parliament 90-40

Legislative branch: unicameral Parliament or Seimas (141 seats; 71 members elected in single-member districts, 70 elected by proportional representation; members to serve four-year terms)
elections: last held on 14 and 28 October 2012 (next to be held in October 2016)
election results: percent of vote by party (proportional vote)—DP 19.8%, LSDP 18.4%, TS-LKD 15.1%, LS 8.6%, DK 8%, TT 7.3%, LLRA 5.8%, LVZS 3.9%, other parties 13.1%; seats by party—LSDP 38, TS-LKD 33, DP 29, TT 11, LS 10, LLRA 8, DK 7, unaffiliated 4, vacant 1

Judicial branch: *highest court(s):* Supreme Court (consists of 37 judges); Constitutional Court (consists of 9 judges)
judge selection and term of office: Supreme Court judges nominated by the president and appointed by the Seimas; judges serve 5-year renewable terms; Constitutional Court judges selected by Seimas from among nominations by the president, by the Seimas chairperson, and Supreme Court chairperson; judges serve 9-year, nonrenewable terms; note—one-third of court judges reconstituted every 3 years
subordinate courts: Court of Appeals; district and local courts

Political parties and leaders: Christian Party or KP [Gediminas VAGNORIUS]; Civil Democracy Party or PDP [Algimantas MATULEVICIUS]; Democratic Labor and Unity Party or DDVP [Kristina BRAZAUSKIENE]; Electoral Action of Lithuanian Poles or LLRA [Valdemar TOMASEVSKI]; Emigrants Party or EP [Juozas MURAUSKAS]; Homeland Union-Lithuanian Christian Democrats or TS-LKD [Andrius KUBILIUS]; Labor Party or DP [Loreta GRAUZINIENE]; Liberal and Center Union or LCS [Arturas MELIANAS]; Liberal Movement or LS or LRLS [Eligijus MASIULIS]; Lithuanian People's Party or LLP [Kazimiera PRUNSKIENE]; Lithuanian People's Party or LZP [Joana SIMANAUSKIENE]; Lithuanian Russian Union or LRS [Sergejus DMITRIJEVAS]; Lithuanian Social Democratic Party or LSDP [Algirdas BUTKEVICIUS]; Nationalist Union or TS [Gintaras SONGAILA]; Order and Justice Party or TT [Rolandas PAKSAS]; Peasant and Greens Union or LVZS [Ramunas KARBAUSKIS]; Republican Party or RP [Valdemaras VALKIUNAS]; Russian Alliance or RA [Tamara LOCHANKINA]; Socialist People's Front or SLF [Algirdas PALECKIS]; Way of Courage or DK [Jonas VARKALA]; YES-Homeland Revival and Perspective or YES Union or TAIP Union or TAIP [Arturas ZUOKAS]; Young Lithuania Party or PJL [Stanislovas BUSKEVICIUS]

International organization participation: Australia Group, BA, BIS, CBSS, CD, CE, EAPC, EBRD, EIB, EU, FAO, IAEA, IBRD, ICAO, ICC (national committees), ICRM, IDA, IFC, IFRCS, ILO, IMF, IMO, Interpol, IOC, IOM, IPU, ISO, ITU, ITUC (NGOs), MIGA, NATO, NIB, NSG, OAS (observer), OIF (observer), OPCW, OSCE, PCA, Schengen Convention, UN, UN Security Council (temporary), UNCTAD, UNESCO, UNIDO, UNWTO, UPU, WCO, WHO, WIPO, WMO, WTO

Diplomatic representation in the US: *chief of mission:* Ambassador Zygimantas PAVILIONIS (since 5 August 2010)
chancery: 2622 16th Street NW, Washington, DC 20009
telephone: [1] (202) 234-5860
FAX: [1] (202) 328-0466
consulate(s) general: Chicago, New York

Diplomatic representation from the US: *chief of mission:* Ambassador Deborah A. MCCARTHY (since 5 February 2013)
embassy: Akmenu gatve 6, Vilnius, LT-03106
mailing address: American Embassy, Akmenu Gatve 6, Vilnius LT-03106
telephone: [370] (5) 266-5500
FAX: [370] (5) 266-5510

Flag description: three equal horizontal bands of yellow (top), green, and red; yellow symbolizes golden fields, as well as the sun, light, and goodness; green represents the forests of the countryside, in addition to nature, freedom, and hope; red stands for courage and the blood spilled in defense of the homeland

National symbol(s): mounted knight known as Vytis (the Chaser)

National anthem: *name:* "Tautiska giesme" (The National Song)
lyrics/music: Vincas KUDIRKA
note: adopted 1918, restored 1990; the anthem was written in 1898 while Lithuania was a part of Russia; it was banned during the Soviet occupation from 1940 to 1990

ECONOMY

Economy—overview: Lithuania gained membership in the World Trade Organization and joined the EU in May 2004. Despite its EU accession, Lithuania's trade with its Central and Eastern European neighbors, and Russia in particular, accounts for a significant share of total trade. Foreign investment and business support have helped in the transition from the old command economy to a market economy. The three former Soviet Baltic republics were among the hardest hit by the 2008-09 financial crisis. The government's efforts to attract foreign investment, to develop export markets, and to pursue broad economic reforms has been key to Lithuania's quick recovery from a deep recession, making Lithuania one of the fastest growing economies in the EU. Lithuania is committed to meeting the Maastricht criteria to join the euro zone, which the government expects to achieve by 2015. Under the Conservative Party's leadership, Lithuania raised the monthly minimum wage in January 2012 nearly 25% over 2011. In January 2013, the new Social Democrat-led government increased the minimum wage another 25% over January 2012. Despite government efforts, unemployment remains high.

GDP (purchasing power parity): $67.43 billion (2013 est.)
country comparison to the world: 86
$65.19 billion (2012 est.)
$62.92 billion (2011 est.)
note: data are in 2013 US dollars

GDP (official exchange rate): $46.71 billion (2013 est.)

GDP—real growth rate: 3.4% (2013 est.)
country comparison to the world: 101
3.6% (2012 est.)
5.9% (2011 est.)

GDP—per capita (PPP): $22,600 (2013 est.)
country comparison to the world: 65
$21,700 (2012 est.)
$20,800 (2011 est.)
note: data are in 2013 US dollars

Gross national saving: 16.5% of GDP (2013 est.)
country comparison to the world: 101
17.2% of GDP (2012 est.)
18.9% of GDP (2011 est.)

GDP—composition, by end use:
household consumption: 64.4%
government consumption: 17.2%
investment in fixed capital: 16.8%
investment in inventories: 0.9%
exports of goods and services: 85.4%
imports of goods and services: -84.7% (2013 est.)

GDP—composition, by sector of origin:
agriculture: 3.7%
industry: 28.3%
services: 68% (2013 est.)

Agriculture—products: grain, potatoes, sugar beets, flax, vegetables; beef, milk, eggs; fish

Industries: metal-cutting machine tools, electric motors, television sets, refrigerators and freezers, petroleum refining, shipbuilding (small ships), furniture making, textiles, food processing, fertilizers, agricultural machinery, optical equipment, electronic components, computers, amber jewelry

Industrial production growth rate: 2% (2013 est.)
country comparison to the world: 125

Labor force: 1.452 million (2013 est.)
country comparison to the world: 131

Labor force—by occupation:
agriculture: 7.9%
industry: 19.6%
services: 72.5% (2012 est.)

Unemployment rate: 12.4% (2013 est.)
country comparison to the world: 126
13.2% (2012 est.)

Population below poverty line: 4% (2008)

Household income or consumption by percentage share: *lowest 10%:* 2.6%
highest 10%: 29.1% (2008)

Distribution of family income—Gini index: 35.5 (2009)
country comparison to the world: 88
34 (1999)

Budget: *revenues:* $14.5 billion
expenditures: $15.43 billion (2013 est.)

Taxes and other revenues: 31% of GDP (2013 est.)
country comparison to the world: 88

Budget surplus (+) or deficit (-): -2% of GDP (2013 est.)
country comparison to the world: 86

Public debt: 40.2% of GDP (2013 est.)
country comparison to the world: 89
41% of GDP (2012 est.)
note: official data; data cover general government debt, and includes debt instruments issued (or owned) by government entities other than the treasury; the data include treasury debt held by foreign entities, debt issued by subnational entities, as well as intra-governmental debt; intragovernmental debt consists of treasury borrowings from surpluses in the social funds, such as for retirement, medical care, and unemployment; debt instruments for the social funds are sold at public auctions

Fiscal year: calendar year

Inflation rate (consumer prices): 1.2% (2013 est.)
country comparison to the world: 31
3.1% (2012 est.)

Central bank discount rate: 3% (31 December 2010 est.)
country comparison to the world: 113
2.06% (31 December 2009 est.)

Commercial bank prime lending rate: 4.5% (31 December 2013 est.)
country comparison to the world: 153
5.28% (31 December 2012 est.)

Stock of narrow money: $13.83 billion (31 December 2013 est.)

country comparison to the world: 71
$13.77 billion (31 December 2012 est.)

Stock of broad money: $20.59 billion (31 December 2013 est.)
country comparison to the world: 84
$20.58 billion (31 December 2012 est.)

Stock of domestic credit: $22.02 billion (31 December 2013 est.)
country comparison to the world: 81
$22.69 billion (31 December 2012 est.)

Market value of publicly traded shares:
$3.964 billion (31 December 2012 est.)
country comparison to the world: 88
$4.075 billion (31 December 2011)
$5.661 billion (31 December 2010 est.)

Current account balance: -$567 million (2013 est.)
country comparison to the world: 104
-$231 million (2012 est.)

Exports: $30.4 billion (2013 est.)
country comparison to the world: 64
$28.76 billion (2012 est.)

Exports—commodities: mineral products, machinery and equipment, chemicals, textiles , foodstuffs, plastics

Exports—partners: Russia 19%, Latvia 11%, Germany 7.9%, Estonia 7.8%, UK 6.4%, Poland 6.1%, Netherlands 5.9%, Belarus 4.5% (2012)

Imports: $32.52 billion (2013 est.)
country comparison to the world: 66
$30.44 billion (2012 est.)

Imports—commodities: mineral products, machinery and equipment, transport equipment, chemicals, textiles and clothing, metals

Imports—partners: Russia 31.6%, Germany 10%, Poland 9.9%, Latvia 6.2%, Netherlands 5.6% (2012)

Reserves of foreign exchange and gold:
$10.37 billion (31 December 2013 est.)
country comparison to the world: 75
$8.529 billion (31 December 2012 est.)

Debt—external: $29.55 billion (31 December 2013 est.)
country comparison to the world: 73
$32.84 billion (31 December 2012 est.)

Stock of direct foreign investment—at home:
$16.57 billion (31 December 2013 est.)
country comparison to the world: 79
$15.56 billion (31 December 2012 est.)

Stock of direct foreign investment—abroad:
$3.029 billion (31 December 2013 est.)
country comparison to the world: 69
$2.729 billion (31 December 2012 est.)

Exchange rates: litai (LTL) per US dollar—
2.658 (2013 est.)
2.685 (2012 est.)
2.6063 (2010 est.)
2.4787 (2009)
2.3251 (2008)

ENERGY

Electricity—production: 12.27 billion kWh (2012 est.)
country comparison to the world: 9 0

Electricity—consumption: 10.3 billion kWh (2012 est.)
country comparison to the world: 88

Electricity—exports: 186 million kWh (2012 est.)
country comparison to the world: 71

Electricity—imports: 1.17 billion kWh (2012 est.)
country comparison to the world: 62

Electricity—installed generating capacity:
3.82 million kW (2011 est.)
country comparison to the world: 81

Electricity—from fossil fuels: 70.6% of total installed capacity (2010 est.)
country comparison to the world: 105

Electricity—from nuclear fuels: 0% of total installed capacity (2010 est.)
country comparison to the world: 125

Electricity—from hydroelectric plants: 3.2% of total installed capacity (2010 est.)
country comparison to the world: 128

Electricity—from other renewable sources: 5% of total installed capacity (2010 est.)
country comparison to the world: 44

Crude oil—production: 9,111 bbl/day (2012 est.)
country comparison to the world: 93

Crude oil—exports: 2,181 bbl/day (2010 est.)
country comparison to the world: 67

Crude oil—imports: 190,100 bbl/day (2010 est.)
country comparison to the world: 34

Crude oil—proved reserves: 12 million bbl (1 January 2013 es)
country comparison to the world: 89

Refined petroleum products—production: 197,400 bbl/day (2010 est.)
country comparison to the world: 55

Refined petroleum products—consumption: 70,390 bbl/day (2011 est.)
country comparison to the world: 91

Refined petroleum products—exports: 155,000 bbl/day (2010 est.)
country comparison to the world: 37

Refined petroleum products—imports: 16,110 bbl/day (2010 est.)
country comparison to the world: 117

Natural gas—production: 0 cu m (2011 est.)
country comparison to the world: 154

Natural gas—consumption: 3.3 billion cu m (2012 est.)
country comparison to the world: 68

Natural gas—exports: 0 cu m (2012 est.)
country comparison to the world: 135

Natural gas—imports: 3.4 billion cu m (2011 est.)
country comparison to the world: 40

Natural gas—proved reserves: 0 cu m (1 January 2013 es)
country comparison to the world: 159

Carbon dioxide emissions from consumption of energy: 16.05 million Mt (2011 est.)
country comparison to the world: 90

COMMUNICATIONS

Telephones—main lines in use: 667,300 (2012)
country comparison to the world: 8 9

Telephones—mobile cellular: 5 million (2012)
country comparison to the world: 110

Telephone system: *general assessment:* adequate; being modernized to provide improved international capability and better residential access
domestic: rapid expansion of mobile-cellular services has resulted in a steady decline in the number of fixed-line connections; mobile-cellular teledensity stands at about 140 per 100 persons
international: country code—370; major international connections to Denmark, Sweden, and Norway by submarine cable for further transmission by satellite; landline connections to Latvia and Poland (2010)

Broadcast media: public broadcaster operates 3 channels with the third channel—a satellite channel—introduced in 2007; various privately owned commercial TV broadcasters operate national and multiple regional channels; many privately owned local TV stations; multi-channel cable and satellite TV services available; publicly owned broadcaster operates 3 radio networks; many privately owned commercial broadcasters, many with repeater stations in various regions throughout the country (2007)

Internet country code: .lt

Internet hosts: 1.205 million (2012)
country comparison to the world: 43

Internet users: 1.964 million (2009)
country comparison to the world: 75

TRANSPORTATION

Airports: 61 (2013)
country comparison to the world: 8 1

Airports—with paved runways: *total:* 2 2
over 3,047 m: 3
2,438 to 3,047 m: 1
1,524 to 2,437 m: 7
914 to 1,523 m: 2
under 914 m: 9 (2013)

Airports—with unpaved runways: *total:* 3 9
over 3,047 m: 1
914 to 1,523 m: 2
under 914 m: 36 (2013)

Pipelines: gas 1,921 km; refined products 121 km (2013)

Railways: *total:* 1,767 km
country comparison to the world: 76
broad gauge: 1,745 km 1.524-m gauge (122 km electrified)
standard gauge: 22 km 1.435-m gauge (2011)

Roadways: *total:* 84,166 km
country comparison to the world: 56
paved: 72,297 km (includes 312 km of expressways)
unpaved: 11,869 km (2012)

Waterways: 441 km (navigable year round) (2007)
country comparison to the world: 87

Merchant marine: *total:* 3 8
country comparison to the world: 76
by type: cargo 20, container 1, passenger/cargo 6, refrigerated cargo 9, roll on/roll off 2
foreign-owned: 8 (Denmark 8)
registered in other countries: 22 (Antigua and Barbuda 3, Belize 1, Comoros 1, Cook Islands 1, Norway 1, Panama 3, Saint Vincent and the Grenadines 9, unknown 3) (2010)

Ports and terminals: *major seaport(s):* Klaipeda
oil terminals: Butinge oil terminal

MILITARY

Military branches: Lithuanian Armed Forces (Lietuvos Ginkluotosios Pajegos): Land Forces (Sausumos Pajegos), Naval Forces (Karines Juru Pajegos), Air Forces (Karines Oro Pajegos) (2013)

Military service age and obligation: 18 years of age for voluntary military service; service obligation 1 year; Lithuania converted to a professional military in the fall of 2008, although the decision continues under judicial review (2012)

Manpower available for military service:
males age 16-49: 890,074
females age 16-49: 875,780 (2010 est.)

Manpower fit for military service:
males age 16-49: 669,111
females age 16-49: 724,803 (2010 est.)

Manpower reaching militarily significant age annually: *male:* 20,425
female: 19,527 (2010 est.)

Military expenditures: 0.97% of GDP (2012)
country comparison to the world: 104

1.04% of GDP (2011)
0.97% of GDP (2010)

TRANSNATIONAL ISSUES

Disputes—international: Lithuania and Russia committed to demarcating their boundary in 2006 in accordance with the land and maritime treaty ratified by Russia in May 2003 and by Lithuania in 1999; Lithuania operates a simplified transit regime for Russian nationals traveling from the Kaliningrad coastal exclave into Russia, while still conforming, as a EU member state having an external border with a non-EU member, to strict Schengen border rules; boundary demarcated with Latvia and Lithuania; as of January 2007, ground demarcation of the boundary with Belarus was complete and mapped with final ratification documents in preparation

Refugees and internally displaced persons: *stateless persons:* 4,130 (2012)

Illicit drugs: transshipment and destination point for cannabis, cocaine, ecstasy, and opiates from Southwest Asia, Latin America, Western Europe, and neighboring Baltic countries; growing production of high-quality amphetamines, but limited production of cannabis, methamphetamines; susceptible to money laundering despite changes to banking legislation

LUXEMBOURG

INTRODUCTION

Background: Founded in 963, Luxembourg became a grand duchy in 1815 and an independent state under the Netherlands. It lost more than half of its territory to Belgium in 1839 but gained a larger measure of autonomy. Full independence was attained in 1867. Overrun by Germany in both world wars, it ended its neutrality in 1948 when it entered into the Benelux Customs Union and when it joined NATO the following year. In 1957, Luxembourg became one of the six founding countries of the European Economic Community (later the European Union), and in 1999 it joined the euro currency area. In January 2013, Luxembourg assumed a nonpermanent seat on the UN Security Council for the 2013-14 term.

GEOGRAPHY

Location: Western Europe, between France and Germany

Geographic coordinates: 49 45 N, 6 10 E

Map references: Europe

Area: *total:* 2,586 sq km
country comparison to the world: 179
land: 2,586 sq km
water: 0 sq km

Area—comparative: slightly smaller than Rhode Island

Land boundaries: *total:* 359 km
border countries: Belgium 148 km, France 73 km, Germany 138 km

Coastline: 0 km (landlocked)

Maritime claims: none (landlocked)

Climate: modified continental with mild winters, cool summers

Terrain: mostly gently rolling uplands with broad, shallow valleys; uplands to slightly mountainous in the north; steep slope down to Moselle flood plain in the southeast

Elevation extremes: *lowest point:* Moselle River 133 m
highest point: Buurgplaatz 559 m

Natural resources: iron ore (no longer exploited), arable land

Land use: *arable land:* 23.9%
permanent crops: 0.58%
other: 75.52% (includes Belgium) (2011)

Irrigated land: NA

Total renewable water resources: 3.1 cu km (2011)

Freshwater withdrawal (domestic/industrial/agricultural): *total:* 0.06 cu km/yr (65%/33%/1%)
per capita: 135.9 cu m/yr (2010)

Natural hazards: NA

Environment—current issues: air and water pollution in urban areas, soil pollution of farmland

Environment—international agreements: *party to:* Air Pollution, Air Pollution-Nitrogen Oxides, Air Pollution-Persistent Organic Pollutants, Air Pollution-Sulfur 85, Air Pollution-Sulfur 94, Air Pollution-Volatile Organic Compounds, Biodiversity, Climate Change, Climate Change-Kyoto Protocol, Desertification, Endangered Species, Hazardous Wastes, Law of the Sea, Marine Dumping, Ozone Layer Protection, Ship Pollution, Tropical Timber 83, Tropical Timber 94, Wetlands
signed, but not ratified: Environmental Modification

Geography—note: landlocked; the only Grand Duchy in the world

PEOPLE AND SOCIETY

Nationality: *noun:* Luxembourger(s)
adjective: Luxembourg

Ethnic groups: Luxembourger 63.1%, Portuguese 13.3%, French 4.5%, Italian 4.3%, German 2.3%, other EU 7.3%, other 5.2% (2000 census)

Languages: Luxembourgish (official administrative language and national language (spoken vernacular)), French (official administrative language), German (official administrative language)

Religions: Roman Catholic 87%, other (includes Protestant, Jewish, and Muslim) 13% (2000)

Population: 520,672 (July 2014 est.)
country comparison to the world: 174

Age structure: *0-14 years:* 17.9% (male 47,968/female 45,100)
15-24 years: 12.7% (male 33,657/female 32,212)
25-54 years: 42.1% (male 109,528/female 109,662)
55-64 years: 15.4% (male 31,076/female 31,212)
65 years and over: 15.2% (male 33,892/female 46,365) (2014 est.)

Dependency ratios: *total dependency ratio:* 46.5 %
youth dependency ratio: 25.7 %
elderly dependency ratio: 20.8 %
potential support ratio: 4.8 (2013)

Median age: *total:* 39.6 years
male: 38.5 years
female: 40.7 years (2014 est.)

Population growth rate: 1.12% (2014 est.)
country comparison to the world: 109

Birth rate: 11.75 births/1,000 population (2014 est.)
country comparison to the world: 169

Death rate: 8.53 deaths/1,000 population (2014 est.)
country comparison to the world: 77

Net migration rate: 7.97 migrant(s)/1,000 population (2014 est.)
country comparison to the world: 17

Urbanization: *urban population:* 85% of total population (2010)
rate of urbanization: 1.4% annual rate of change (2010-15 est.)

Major urban areas—population: LUXEMBOURG (capital) 90,000 (2009)

Sex ratio: *at birth:* 1.07 male(s)/female
0-14 years: 1.06 male(s)/female
15-24 years: 1.05 male(s)/female
25-54 years: 1 male(s)/female
55-64 years: 0.97 male(s)/female
65 years and over: 0.71 male(s)/female
total population: 0.97 male(s)/female (2014 est.)

Mother's mean age at first birth: 29.3 (2008 est.)

Maternal mortality rate: 20 deaths/100,000 live births (2010)
country comparison to the world: 141

Infant mortality rate: *total:* 4.28 deaths/1,000 live births
country comparison to the world: 193
male: 4.32 deaths/1,000 live births
female: 4.24 deaths/1,000 live births (2014 est.)

Life expectancy at birth: *total population:* 80.01 years
country comparison to the world: 35
male: 76.77 years
female: 83.46 years (2014 est.)

Total fertility rate: 1.77 children born/woman (2014 est.)
country comparison to the world: 158

Health expenditures: 7.7% of GDP (2011)
country comparison to the world: 70

Physicians density: 2.78 physicians/1,000 population (2011)

Hospital bed density: 5.4 beds/1,000 population (2010)

Drinking water source:
improved:
urban: 100% of population
rural: 100% of population
total: 100% of population
unimproved:
urban: 0% of population
rural: 0% of population
total: 0% of population (2011 est.)

Sanitation facility access:
improved:
urban: 100% of population
rural: 100% of population
total: 100% of population

unimproved:
urban: 0% of population
rural: 0% of population
total: 0% of population (2011 est.)

HIV/AIDS—adult prevalence rate: 0.3% (2009 est.)
country comparison to the world: 98

HIV/AIDS—people living with HIV/AIDS: fewer than 1,000 (2009 est.)
country comparison to the world: 148

HIV/AIDS—deaths: fewer than 100 (2009 est.)
country comparison to the world: 144

Obesity—adult prevalence rate: 26% (2008)
country comparison to the world: 50

Education expenditures: 3.7% of GDP (2001)
country comparison to the world: 118

Literacy: *definition:* age 15 and over can read and write
total population: 100%
male: 100%
female: 100% (2000 est.)

School life expectancy (primary to tertiary education): *total:* 14 years
male: 14 years
female: 14 years (2010)

Unemployment, youth ages 15-24: *total:* 18.8%
country comparison to the world: 64
male: 18.9%
female: 18.6% (2012)

GOVERNMENT

Country name: *conventional long form:* Grand Duchy of Luxembourg
conventional short form: Luxembourg
local long form: Grand Duche de Luxembourg
local short form: Luxembourg

Government type: constitutional monarchy

Capital: *name:* Luxembourg

geographic coordinates: 49 36 N, 6 07 E
time difference: UTC+1 (6 hours ahead of Washington, DC during Standard Time)
daylight saving time: +1hr, begins last Sunday in March; ends last Sunday in October

Administrative divisions: 3 districts; Diekirch, Grevenmacher, Luxembourg

Independence: 1839 (from the Netherlands)

National holiday: National Day (Birthday of Grand Duchess Charlotte) 23 June; note—the actual date of birth was 23 January 1896, but the festivities were shifted by five months to allow observance during a more favorable time of year

Constitution: previous 1842 (heavily amended 1848, 1856); latest effective 17 October 1968; amended many times, last in 2008 (2008)

Legal system: civil law system

International law organization participation: accepts compulsory ICJ jurisdiction; accepts ICCt jurisdiction

Suffrage: 18 years of age; universal and compulsory

Executive branch: *chief of state:* Grand Duke HENRI (since 7 October 2000); Heir Apparent Prince GUILLAUME (son of the monarch, born 11 November 1981)
head of government: Prime Minister Xavier BETTEL (since 4 December 2013); Deputy Prime Minister Etienne SCHNEIDER (since 4 December 2013)
cabinet: Council of Ministers recommended by the prime minister and appointed by the monarch (For more information visit the World Leaders website)
elections: the monarchy is hereditary; following popular elections to the Chamber of Deputies, the leader of the majority party or the leader of the majority coalition usually appointed prime minister by the monarch; the deputy prime minister appointed by the monarch; they are responsible to the Chamber of Deputies
note: government coalition—DP, LSAP, and the Green Party (first time since 1979 that the CSV is in opposition)

Legislative branch: unicameral Chamber of Deputies or Chambre des Deputes (60 seats; members elected by popular vote to serve five-year terms)
elections: last held on 20 October 2013 (next to be held by June 2018)
election results: percent of vote by party—CSV 33.7%, LSAP 20.3%, DP 18.3%, Green Party 10.1%, ADR 6.6%, The Left 4.5%, other 6.1%; seats by party—CSV 23, LSAP 13, DP 13, Green Party 6, ADR 3, The Left 2
note: there is also a Council of State that serves as an advisory body to the Chamber of Deputies; the Council of State has 21 members appointed by the Grand Duke on the advice of the prime minister

Judicial branch: *highest court(s):* Superior Court of Justice includes Court of Appeal and Court of Cassation (consists of 27 judges on 9 benches); Constitutional Court (consists of 9 members)
judge selection and term of office: judges of both courts appointed by the monarch for life
subordinate courts: district and local tribunals and courts

Political parties and leaders: Alternative Democratic Reform Party or ADR [Jean SCHOOS]; Christian Social People's Party or CSV [Michel WOLTER]; The Left (dei Lenk/la Gauche) [Serge URBANY]; Democratic Party or DP [Xavier BETTEL]; Green Party [Sam TANSON and Christian KMIOTEK]; Luxembourg Socialist Workers' Party or LSAP [Alex BODRY]; other minor parties

Political pressure groups and leaders: ABBL (bankers' association) [Ernst Wilhelm CONTZEN]; ALEBA (financial sector trade union) [Marc GLESENER]; Centrale Paysanne (federation of agricultural producers) [Marc FISCH]; CEP (professional sector chamber) [Stephane LIA]; CGFP (trade union representing civil service) [Joseph DALEIDEN]; Chamber of Commerce (Chambre de Commerce) [Carlo THELEN]; Chamber of Artisans (Chambre des Metiers) [Roland KUHN]; FEDIL (federation of industrialists) [Nicolas SOISSON]; Greenpeace (environment protection) [Kumi NAIDOO]; LCGP (center-right trade union) [Patrick DURY]; Mouvement Ecologique (environment protection) [Blanche WEBER]; OGBL (center-left trade union) [Jean-Claude REDING]

International organization participation: ADB (nonregional member), Australia Group, Benelux, BIS, CD, CE, EAPC, EBRD, ECB, EIB, EMU, ESA, EU, FAO, FATF, IAEA, IBRD, ICAO, ICC (national committees), ICRM, IDA, IEA, IFAD, IFC, IFRCS, ILO, IMF, IMO, Interpol, IOC, IOM, IPU, ISO, ITSO, ITU, ITUC (NGOs), MIGA, NATO, NEA, NSG, OAS (observer), OECD, OIF, OPCW, OSCE, PCA, Schengen Convention, UN, UN Security Council (temporary), UNCTAD, UNESCO, UNHCR, UNIDO, UNIFIL, UNRWA, UPU, WCO, WHO, WIPO, WMO, WTO, ZC

Diplomatic representation in the US: *chief of mission:* Ambassador Jean-Louis WOLZFELD (since 11 September 2012)
chancery: 2200 Massachusetts Avenue NW, Washington, DC 20008
telephone: [1] (202) 265-4171 through 72
FAX: [1] (202) 328-8270
consulate(s) general: New York, San Francisco

Diplomatic representation from the US: *chief of mission:* Ambassador Robert MANDELL (since 25 October 2011)
embassy: 22 Boulevard Emmanuel Servais, L-2535 Luxembourg City
mailing address: American Embassy Luxembourg, Unit 1410, APO AE 09126-1410 (official mail); American Embassy Luxembourg, PSC 9, Box 9500, APO AE 09123 (personal mail)
telephone: [352] 46-01-23
FAX: [352] 46-14-01

Flag description: three equal horizontal bands of red (top), white, and light blue; similar to the flag of the Netherlands, which uses a darker blue and is shorter; the coloring is derived from the Grand Duke's coat of arms (a red lion on a white and blue striped field)

National symbol(s): lion

National anthem: *name:* "Ons Heemecht" (Our Motherland); "De Wilhelmus" (The William)
lyrics/music: Michel LENTZ/Jean-Antoine ZINNEN; Nikolaus WELTER/unknown
note: "Ons Heemecht," adopted 1864, is the national anthem, while "De Wilhelmus," adopted 1919, serves as a royal anthem for use when members of the grand ducal family enter or exit a ceremony in Luxembourg

ECONOMY

Economy—overview: This small, stable, high-income economy—benefiting from its proximity to France, Belgium, and Germany - has historically featured solid growth, low inflation, and low unemployment. The industrial sector, initially dominated by steel, has become increasingly diversified to include chemicals, rubber, and other products. Growth in the financial sector, which now accounts for about 27% of GDP, has more than compensated for the decline in steel. Most banks are foreign-owned and have extensive foreign dealings, but Luxembourg has lost some of its advantages as a favorable tax location because of OECD and EU pressure. The economy depends on foreign and cross-border workers for about 40% of its labor force. Luxembourg, like all EU members, suffered from the global economic crisis that began in late 2008, but unemployment has trended below the EU average. Following strong expansion from 2004 to 2007, Luxembourg's economy contracted 3.6% in 2009, but rebounded in 2010-11 before slowing again in 2012. The country continues to enjoy an extraordinarily high standard of living—GDP per capita ranks among the highest in the world, and is the highest in the euro zone. Turmoil in the world financial markets and lower global demand during 2008-09 prompted the government to inject capital into the banking sector and implement stimulus measures to boost the economy. Government stimulus measures and support for the banking sector, however, led to a 5% government budget deficit in 2009. Nevertheless, the deficit was cut to 1.1% in 2011 and 0.9% in 2012. Even during the financial crisis and recovery, Luxembourg retained the highest current account surplus as a share of GDP in the euro zone, owing largely to their strength in financial services. Public debt remains among the lowest of the region although it has more than doubled since 2007 as percentage of GDP. Luxembourg's economy, while stabile, grew slowly in 2012 due to ongoing weak growth in the euro area. Authorities have strengthened supervision of domestic banks because of their exposure to the activities of foreign banks.

GDP (purchasing power parity): $42.67 billion (2013 est.)
country comparison to the world: 103
$42.44 billion (2012 est.)
$42.3 billion (2011 est.)
note: data are in 2013 US dollars

GDP (official exchange rate): $60.54 billion (2013 est.)

GDP—real growth rate: 0.5% (2013 est.)
country comparison to the world: 184
0.3% (2012 est.)
1.7% (2011 est.)

GDP—per capita (PPP): $77,900 (2013 est.)
country comparison to the world: 5
$79,000 (2012 est.)
$81,400 (2011 est.)
note: data are in 2013 US dollars

GDP—composition, by end use:
household consumption: 32.3%
government consumption: 17.5%
investment in fixed capital: 22.2%
investment in inventories: -2.4%
exports of goods and services: 170.5%
imports of goods and services: -140.1% (2013 est.)

GDP—composition, by sector of origin:
agriculture: 0.3%
industry: 13.3%
services: 86.4% (2013 est.)

Agriculture—products: grapes, barley, oats, potatoes, wheat, fruits; dairy and livestock products

Industries: banking and financial services, iron and steel, information technology, telecommunications, cargo transportation, food processing, chemicals, metal products, engineering, tires, glass, aluminum, tourism

Industrial production growth rate: -1% (2013 est.)
country comparison to the world: 176

Labor force: 208,800
country comparison to the world: 168
note: data exclude foreign workers; in addition to the figure for domestic labor force, about 150,000 workers commute daily from France, Belgium, and Germany (2013 est.)

Labor force—by occupation: *agriculture:* 2.2%
industry: 17.2%
services: 80.6% (2007 est.)

Unemployment rate: 4.9% (2013 est.)
country comparison to the world: 46
6.1% (2012 est.)

Population below poverty line: NA%

Household income or consumption by percentage share: *lowest* 10%: 3.5%
highest 10%: 23.8% (2000)

Distribution of family income—Gini index: 26 (2005)
country comparison to the world: 131

Budget: *revenues:* $23.91 billion
expenditures: $24.94 billion (2013 est.)

Taxes and other revenues: 39.5% of GDP (2013 est.)
country comparison to the world: 46

Budget surplus (+) or deficit (-):
-1.7% of GDP (2013 est.)
country comparison to the world: 76

Public debt: 22.9% of GDP (2013 est.)
country comparison to the world: 133
20.8% of GDP (2012 est.)
note: data cover general government debt, and includes debt instruments issued (or owned) by government entities other than the treasury; the data include treasury debt held by foreign entities; the data include debt issued by subnational entities, as well as intra-governmental debt; intra-governmental debt consists of treasury borrowings from surpluses in the social funds, such as for retirement, medical care, and unemployment; debt instruments for the social funds are not sold at public auctions

Fiscal year: calendar year

Inflation rate (consumer prices): 2% (2013 est.)
country comparison to the world: 67
2.7% (2012 est.)

Central bank discount rate: 0.75% (31 December 2013)
country comparison to the world: 118
1.5% (31 December 2010)
note: this is the European Central Bank's rate on the marginal lending facility, which offers overnight credit to banks in the euro area

Stock of narrow money: $84.91 billion (31 December 2013 est.)
country comparison to the world: 39
$89.87 billion (31 December 2012 est.)
note: see entry for the European Union for money supply in the euro area; the European Central Bank (ECB) controls monetary policy for the 17 members of the Economic and Monetary Union (EMU); individual members of the EMU do not control the quantity of money circulating within their own borders

Stock of broad money: $235.8 billion (31 December 2013 est.)
country comparison to the world: 36
$238.2 billion

Stock of domestic credit: $97.73 billion (31 December 2013 est.)
country comparison to the world: 52
$97.39 billion (31 December 2012 est.)

Market value of publicly traded shares: $70.34 billion (31 December 2012 est.)
country comparison to the world: 46
$67.63 billion (31 December 2011)
$101.1 billion (31 December 2010 est.)

Current account balance: $2.7 billion (2013 est.)
country comparison to the world: 36
$3.272 billion (2012 est.)

Exports: $15.8 billion (2013 est.)
country comparison to the world: 77
$15.93 billion (2012 est.)

Exports—commodities: machinery and equipment, steel products, chemicals, rubber products, glass

Exports—partners: Germany 21.5%, France 15.5%, Belgium 14.5%, UK 5.8%, Italy 5.6%, Switzerland 4.7% (2012)

Imports: $23.12 billion (2013 est.)
country comparison to the world: 75
$23.78 billion (2012 est.)

Imports—commodities: minerals, metals, foodstuffs, quality consumer goods

Imports—partners: Belgium 30.6%, Germany 23.6%, France 10.4%, US 8.3%, China 7.2%, Netherlands 5.1% (2012)

Reserves of foreign exchange and gold: $991 million (31 December 2012 est.)
country comparison to the world: 136
$1.014 billion (31 December 2011 est.)

Debt—external: $2.935 trillion (31 December 2012 est.)
country comparison to the world: 7
$2.084 trillion (31 December 2011)

Stock of direct foreign investment—at home: $NA
$11.21 billion (31 December 2008 est.)

Stock of direct foreign investment—abroad: $NA

Exchange rates: euros (EUR) per US dollar—
0.7634 (2013 est.)
0.7752 (2012 est.)
0.755 (2010 est.)
0.7198 (2009 est.)
0.6827 (2008 est.)

ENERGY

Electricity—production: 2.07 billion kWh (2011 est.)
country comparison to the world: 134

Electricity—consumption: 6.445 billion kWh (2010 est.)
country comparison to the world: 103

Electricity—exports: 2.623 billion kWh (2012 est.)
country comparison to the world: 37

Electricity—imports: 6.684 billion kWh (2012 est.)
country comparison to the world: 32

Electricity—installed generating capacity: 1.723 million kW (2010 est.)

country comparison to the world: 106

Electricity—from fossil fuels: 28.3% of total installed capacity (2010 est.)
country comparison to the world: 183

Electricity—from nuclear fuels: 0% of total installed capacity (2010 est.)
country comparison to the world: 128

Electricity—from hydroelectric plants: 2% of total installed capacity (2010 est.)
country comparison to the world: 136

Electricity—from other renewable sources: 5.9% of total installed capacity (2010 est.)
country comparison to the world: 38

Crude oil—production: 0 bbl/day (2012 est.)
country comparison to the world: 189

Crude oil—exports: 0 bbl/day (2010 est.)
country comparison to the world: 145

Crude oil—imports: 0 bbl/day (2010 est.)
country comparison to the world: 83

Crude oil—proved reserves: 0 bbl (1 January 2013 es)
country comparison to the world: 157

Refined petroleum products—production: 0 bbl/day (2010 est.)
country comparison to the world: 166

Refined petroleum products—consumption: 61,380 bbl/day (2011 est.)
country comparison to the world: 93

Refined petroleum products—exports: 52.22 bbl/day (2010 est.)
country comparison to the world: 122

Refined petroleum products—imports: 56,780 bbl/day (2010 est.)
country comparison to the world: 64

Natural gas—production: 0 cu m (2011 est.)
country comparison to the world: 157

Natural gas—consumption: 1.364 billion cu m (2010 est.)
country comparison to the world: 85

Natural gas—exports: 0 cu m (2011 est.)
country comparison to the world: 138

Natural gas—imports: 1.206 billion cu m (2012 est.)
country comparison to the world: 54

Natural gas—proved reserves: 0 cu m (1 January 2013 es)
country comparison to the world: 162

Carbon dioxide emissions from consumption of energy: 11.87 million Mt (2011 est.)
country comparison to the world: 97

COMMUNICATIONS

Telephones—main lines in use: 266,700 (2012)
country comparison to the world: 122

Telephones—mobile cellular: 761,300 (2012)
country comparison to the world: 161

Telephone system: *general assessment:* highly developed, completely automated and efficient system, mainly buried cables
domestic: fixed line teledensity over 50 per 100 persons; nationwide mobile-cellular telephone system with market for mobile-cellular phones virtually saturated

international: country code—352 (2010)

Broadcast media: Luxembourg has a long tradition of operating radio and TV services to pan-European audiences and is home to Europe's largest privately owned broadcast media group, the RTL group, which operates 46 TV stations and 29 radio stations in Europe; also home to Europe's largest satellite operator, Societe Europeenne des Satellites (SES); domestically, the RTL group operates TV and radio networks; other domestic private radio and TV operators and French and German stations available; satellite and cable TV services available (2008)

Internet country code: .lu

Internet hosts: 250,900 (2012)
country comparison to the world: 68

Internet users: 424,500 (2009)
country comparison to the world: 121

TRANSPORTATION

Airports: 2 (2013)
country comparison to the world: 202

Airports—with paved runways: *total:* 1
over 3,047 m: 1 (2013)

Airports—with unpaved runways: *total:* 1
under 914 m: 1 (2013)

Heliports: 1 (2013)

Pipelines: gas 142 km; refined products 27 km (2013)

Railways: *total:* 275 km
country comparison to the world: 123
standard gauge: 275 km 1.435-m gauge (243 km electrified) (2008)

Roadways: *total:* 2,899 km
country comparison to the world: 167
paved: 2,899 km (includes 152 km of expressways) (2011)

Waterways: 37 km (on Moselle River) (2010)
country comparison to the world: 105

Merchant marine: *total:* 4 9
country comparison to the world: 71
by type: bulk carrier 2, cargo 3, chemical tanker 20, container 10, petroleum tanker 2, roll on/roll off 12
foreign-owned: 48 (Belgium 11, Denmark 1, France 15, Germany 9, Japan 3, Netherlands 3, Switzerland 1, UK 5)
registered in other countries: 18 (Italy 14, Malta 3, Panama 1) (2010)

Ports and terminals: *river port(s):* Mertert (Moselle)

MILITARY

Military branches: Luxembourg Army (L'Armee Luxembourgeoises) (2013)

Military service age and obligation: 18-24 years of age for male and female voluntary military service; no conscription; Luxembourg citizen or EU citizen with 3-year residence in Luxembourg (2012)

Manpower available for military service:
males age 16-49: 118,665
females age 16-49: 117,456 (2010 est.)
Manpower fit for military service:
males age 16-49: 97,290
females age 16-49: 96,361 (2010 est.)

Manpower reaching militarily significant age annually: *male:* 3,263
female: 3,084 (2010 est.)

Military expenditures: 0.6% of GDP (2012)
country comparison to the world: 123
0.61% of GDP (2011)
0.6% of GDP (2010)

TRANSNATIONAL ISSUES

Disputes—international: none

Refugees and internally displaced persons: *stateless persons:* 177 (2012)

MACAU

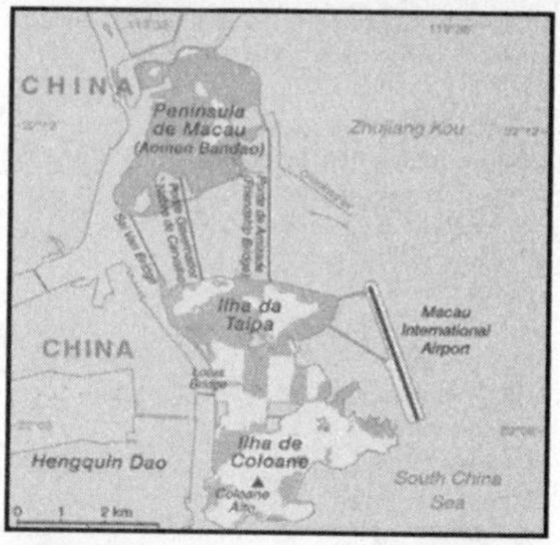

INTRODUCTION

Background: Colonized by the Portuguese in the 16th century, Macau was the first European settlement in the Far East. Pursuant to an agreement signed by China and Portugal on 13 April 1987, Macau became the Macau Special Administrative Region (SAR) of the People's Republic of China on 20 December 1999. In this agreement, China promised that, under its "one country, two systems" formula, China's political and economic system would not be imposed on Macau, and that Macau would enjoy a "high degree of autonomy" in all matters except foreign affairs and defense for the subsequent 50 years.

GEOGRAPHY

Location: Eastern Asia, bordering the South China Sea and China

Geographic coordinates: 22 10 N, 113 33 E

Map references: Southeast Asia

Area: *total:* 28.2 sq km
country comparison to the world: 237
land: 28.2 sq km
water: 0 sq km

Area—comparative: less than one-sixth the size of Washington, DC

Land boundaries: *total:* 0.34 km
regional border: China 0.34 km

Coastline: 41 km

Maritime claims: not specified

Climate: subtropical; marine with cool winters, warm summers

Terrain: generally flat

Elevation extremes: *lowest point:* South China Sea 0 m
highest point: Coloane Alto 172 m

Natural resources: NEGL

Land use: *arable land:* 0%
permanent crops: 0%
other: 100% (2011)

Irrigated land: NA; note—included in the total for China

Natural hazards: typhoons

Environment—current issues: NA

Environment—international agreements: party to: Marine Dumping (associate member), Ship Pollution (associate member)

Geography—note: essentially urban; an area of land reclaimed from the sea measuring 5.2 sq km and known as Cotai now connects the islands of Coloane and Taipa; the island area is connected to the mainland peninsula by three bridges

PEOPLE AND SOCIETY

Nationality: *noun:* Chinese
adjective: Chinese

Ethnic groups: Chinese 92.4%, Portuguese 0.6%, mixed 1.1%, other 5.9% (includes Macanese—mixed Portuguese and Asian ancestry) (2011 est.)

Languages: Cantonese 83.3%, Mandarin 5%, Hokkien 3.7%, English 2.3%, other Chinese dialects 2%, Tagalog 1.7%, Portuguese 0.7%, other 1.3%
note: Chinese and Portuguese are official languages (2011 est.)

Religions: Buddhist 50%, Roman Catholic 15%, none or other 35% (1997 est.)

Population: 587,914
country comparison to the world: 170
note: Macau's statistical agency estimated the total population to be approximately 607,500 as of 31 December 2013 (July 2014 est.)

Age structure: *0-14 years:* 14.4% (male 44,350/female 40,272)
15-24 years: 13.7% (male 41,941/female 38,697)
25-54 years: 50.9% (male 133,612/female 165,735)
55-64 years: 9.2% (male 35,011/female 34,372)
65 years and over: 8.8% (male 25,254/female 28,670) (2014 est.)

Dependency ratios:
total dependency ratio: 25.8 %
youth dependency ratio: 15.6 %
elderly dependency ratio: 10.2 %
potential support ratio: 9.8 (2013)

Median age: *total:* 37.7 years
male: 38.3 years
female: 37.3 years (2014 est.)

Population growth rate: 0.83% (2014 est.)
country comparison to the world: 133

Birth rate: 8.98 births/1,000 population (2014 est.)
country comparison to the world: 209

Death rate: 4.1 deaths/1,000 population (2014 est.)
country comparison to the world: 210

Net migration rate: 3.4 migrant(s)/1,000 population (2014 est.)
country comparison to the world: 33

Urbanization: *urban population:* 100% of total population (2011)
rate of urbanization: 2.01% annual rate of change (2010-15 est.)

Sex ratio: *at birth:* 1.05 male(s)/female
0-14 years: 1.1 male(s)/female
15-24 years: 1.08 male(s)/female
25-54 years: 0.81 male(s)/female
55-64 years: 0.91 male(s)/female
65 years and over: 0.88 male(s)/female
total population: 0.91 male(s)/female (2014 est.)

Infant mortality rate: *total:* 3.13 deaths/1,000 live births
country comparison to the world: 216
male: 3.29 deaths/1,000 live births
female: 2.97 deaths/1,000 live births (2014 est.)

Life expectancy at birth: *total population:* 84.48 years
country comparison to the world: 2
male: 81.52 years
female: 87.59 years (2014 est.)

Total fertility rate: 0.93 children born/woman (2014 est.)
country comparison to the world: 223

HIV/AIDS—adult prevalence rate: NA

HIV/AIDS—people living with HIV/AIDS: NA

HIV/AIDS—deaths: NA

Education expenditures: 2.7% of GDP (2011)
country comparison to the world: 148

Literacy: *definition:* age 15 and over can read and write
total population: 95.6%
male: 97.8%
female: 93.7% (2011 est.)

School life expectancy (primary to tertiary education): *total:* 14 years
male: 15 years
female: 14 years (2008)

Unemployment, youth ages 15-24: total: 5.8%
country comparison to the world: 134
male: 7%
female: 4.7% (2011)

GOVERNMENT

Country name: *conventional long form:* Macau Special Administrative Region
conventional short form: Macau
official long form: Aomen Tebie Xingzhengqu (Chinese); Regiao Administrativa Especial de Macau (Portuguese)
official short form: Aomen (Chinese); Macau (Portuguese)

Dependency status: special administrative region of the People's Republic of China

Government type: limited democracy

Administrative divisions: none (special administrative region of the People's Republic of China)

Independence: none (special administrative region of China)

National holiday: National Day (Anniversary of the Founding of the People's Republic of China), 1 October (1949); note—20 December 1999 is celebrated as Macau Special Administrative Region Establishment Day

Constitution: previous 1976 (Organic Statute of Macau, by Portugal); latest adopted 31 March 1993, effective 20 December 1999 (Basic Law of the Macau Special Administrative Region, by the People's Republic of China, serves as Macau's constitution) (2013)

Legal system: civil law system based on the Portuguese model

Suffrage: 18 years of age in direct elections for some legislative positions, universal for permanent residents living in Macau for the past seven years; note—indirect elections are limited to organizations registered as "corporate voters" (973 were registered in the 2009 legislative elections) and a 400-member Election Committee for the Chief Executive (CE) drawn from broad regional groupings, municipal organizations, central government bodies, and elected Macau officials

Executive branch: *chief of state:* President of China XI Jinping (since 14 March 2013)
head of government: Chief Executive Fernando CHUI Sai On (since 20 December 2009)
cabinet: Executive Council consists of 1 government secretary, 3 legislators, 4 businessmen, 2 pro-Beijing unionists, and 1 professional (For more information visit the World Leaders website)
elections: chief executive chosen by a 400-member Election Committee for a five-year term (current chief executive is eligible for a second term); election last held on 26 July 2009 (next to be held in August 2014)
note: the Legislative Assembly voted in August 2012 to expand the electoral committee from 300 to 400 seats for the 2014 election.
election results: Fernando CHUI Sai On elected in 2009 with 282 votes, took office on 20 December 2009

Legislative branch: unicameral Legislative Assembly (33 seats; 14 geographical constituency seats elected by popular vote, 12 functional constituency seats elected by indirect vote, and 7 seats appointed by the chief executive; members serve four-year terms)
elections: last held on 15 September 2013 (next to be held in September 2017)
election results: percent of vote—ACUM 18.0%, UMG 11.1%, UPP 10.8%, NE 9.0%, NUDM 8.9%, UPD 8.2%, APMD 7.5%, ANMD 6.0%, APM 6.0%, others 14.5%; seats by political group—ACUM 3, UMG 2, UPP 2, NE 2, NUDM 1, UPD 1, APMD 1, ANMD 1, APM 1; 12 seats filled by professional and business groups; 7 members appointed by the chief executive

Judicial branch: *highest court(s):* Court of Final Appeal of Macau Special Administrative Region (consists of the court president and 2 associate justices)
judge selection and term of office: justices appointed by the Macau chief executive upon the recommendation of an independent commission of judges, lawyers, and "eminent" persons; judge tenure NA
subordinate courts: Court of Second Instance; Court of First instance; Lower Court; Administrative Court

Political parties and leaders: Alliance for Change or APM [Melinda CHAN Mei-yi]; Macau-Guangdong Union or UMG [MAK Soi-kun]; New Democratic Macau Association or ANMD (an electoral list of New Macau Association [Jason CHAO; Teng-hei]; New Hope or NE [Jose Maria Pereira COUTINHO]; New Macau Association or AMN [Jason CHAO Teng-hei]; New Union for Macau's Development or NUDM [Angela LEONG On-kei]; Prosperous Democratic Macau Association or APMD (an electoral list of New Macau Association [Jason; CHAO Teng-hei]; Union for Development or UPD [KWAN Tsui-hang]; Union for Promoting Progress or UPP [HO Ion-sang]; United Citizens Association of Macau or ACUM [CHAN Meng-kam]
note: there is no political party ordinance, so there are no registered political parties; politically active groups register as societies or companies

Political pressure groups and leaders: Civic Power [Agnes LAM lok-fong]; Democratic Action [LEE Kin-yun]; Bar-Bending Workers' Association [WONG Wai-Man]; Macau New Chinese Youth Association [LEONG Sin-man]; Macau Worker's Union [HO Heng-kuok]; New Macau Association [Antonio NG Kuok-cheong]; Workers' Self-Help Union [CHEONG Weng-fat]

International organization participation: ICC (national committees), IHO, IMF, IMO (associate), Interpol (subbureau), ISO (correspondent), UNESCO (associate), UNWTO (associate), UPU, WCO, WTO

Diplomatic representation in the US: none (Special Administrative Region of China)

Diplomatic representation from the US: the US has no offices in Macau; US Consulate General in Hong Kong, currently Consul General Clifford A. HART Jr., is accredited to Macau

Flag description: green with a lotus flower above a stylized bridge and water in white, beneath an arc of five gold, five-pointed stars: one large in the center of the arc and two smaller on either side; the lotus is the floral emblem of Macau, the three petals represent the peninsula and two islands that make up Macau; the five stars echo those on the flag of China

National symbol(s): lotus blossom

National anthem: *note:* as a Special Administrative Region of China, "Yiyongjun Jinxingqu" is the official anthem (see China)

ECONOMY

Economy—overview: Since opening up its locally-controlled casino industry to foreign competition in 2001, Macau has attracted tens of billions of dollars in foreign investment, transforming the territory into one of the world's largest gaming centers. Macau's gaming and tourism businesses were fueled by China"s decision to relax travel restrictions on Chinese citizens wishing to visit Macau.—In 2013, Macau's gaming-related taxes accounted for more than 85% of total government revenue. Macau"s economy slowed dramatically in 2009 as a result of the global economic slowdown, but strong growth resumed in 2010-13, largely on the back of tourism from mainland China and the gaming sectors. In 2013, this city of 607,500 hosted nearly 29.3 million visitors. Almost 64% came from mainland China. Macau"s traditional manufacturing industry has slowed greatly since the termination of the Multi-Fiber Agreement in 2005. China is Macau"s second largest goods export market, behind Hong Kong, and followed by the United States. In 2013, exports were US$1.1 billion, while gaming receipts were US$45.2 billion, an 18.6% increase over 2012. Macau"s economy expanded by 11.9% in 2013; although impressive, it was a slower growth rate than in previous years. Macau continues to face the challenges of managing its growing casino industry, money-laundering, and the need to diversify the economy away from heavy dependence on gaming revenues. Macau"s currency, the pataca, is closely tied to the Hong Kong dollar, which is also freely accepted in the territory.

GDP (purchasing power parity): $47.19 billion (2011 est.)
country comparison to the world: 99
$42.9 billion (2011 est.)
$39 billion (2010 est.)
note: data are in 2013 US dollars

GDP (official exchange rate): $44.3 billion (2012 est.)

GDP—real growth rate: 10% (2012 est.)
country comparison to the world: 7
20.7% (2012 est.)
27% (2010 est.)

GDP—per capita (PPP): $82,400 (2011 est.)
country comparison to the world: 4
$75,500 (2010 est.)
$69,700 (2009 est.)

GDP—composition, by end use:
household consumption: 19.2%
government consumption: 6.3%
investment in fixed capital: 13.3%
investment in inventories: 0%
exports of goods and services: 107.5%
imports of goods and services: -46.4% (2013 est.)

GDP—composition, by sector of origin:
agriculture: 0%
industry: 6.5%
services: 93.5% (2013 est.)

Agriculture—products: only 2% of land area is cultivated, mainly by vegetable growers; fishing, mostly for crustaceans, is important; some of the catch is exported to Hong Kong

Industries: tourism, gambling, clothing, textiles, electronics, footwear, toys

Industrial production growth rate: 13.5% (2013 est.)
country comparison to the world: 4

Labor force: 364,300 (2013 est.)
country comparison to the world: 160

Labor force—by occupation:
manufacturing: 3%
construction: 6.6%
transport and communications: 4.3%
wholesale and retail trade: 12.7%
restaurants and hotels: 15.5%
gambling: 15.1%
public sector: 7.1%
financial services: 2.2%
other services: 33.5% (2012 est.)

Unemployment rate: 1.9% (2013 est.)
country comparison to the world: 10
2% (2012 est.)

Population below poverty line: NA%

Household income or consumption by percentage share: *lowest 10%:* NA%
highest 10%: NA%

Budget: *revenues:* $18.5 billion
expenditures: $4.975 billion (2013 est.)

Taxes and other revenues: 41.8% of GDP (2013 est.)
country comparison to the world: 31

Budget surplus (+) or deficit (-):
30.5% of GDP (2013 est.)
country comparison to the world: 1

Fiscal year: calendar year

Inflation rate (consumer prices): 5.4% (2013 est.)
country comparison to the world: 161
6.1% (2012 est.)

Commercial bank prime lending rate: 5.3% (31 December 2013 est.)
country comparison to the world: 154
5.25% (31 December 2012 est.)

Stock of narrow money: $8.263 billion (31 December 2013 est.)
country comparison to the world: 86
$5.862 billion (31 December 2012 est.)

Stock of broad money: $57.9 billion (31 December 2013 est.)

country comparison to the world: 67
$46.93 billion (31 December 2012 est.)

Stock of domestic credit: $-6.513 billion (31 December 2013 est.)
country comparison to the world: 189
$-5.689 billion (31 December 2012 est.)

Market value of publicly traded shares: $85.5 billion (2 March 2012 est.)
country comparison to the world: 51
$46.1 billion (31 February 2011)
$2.3 billion (31 December 2008 est.)

Current account balance: $17.01 billion (2011 est.)
country comparison to the world: 17
$12.06 billion (2010 est.)

Exports: $1.02 billion (2012 est.)
country comparison to the world: 159
$871 million (2011 est.)
note: includes reexports

Exports—commodities: clothing, textiles, footwear, toys, electronics, machinery and parts

Exports—partners: Hong Kong 50.3%, China 16.8%, US 6.2% (2012)

Imports: $8.866 billion (2012 est.)
country comparison to the world: 107
$7.786 billion (2011 est.)

Imports—commodities: raw materials and semi-manufactured goods, consumer goods (foodstuffs, beverages, tobacco, garments and footwear, motor vehicles), capital goods, mineral fuels and oils

Imports—partners: China 32.2%, Hong Kong 11.6%, France 8.8%, Switzerland 8.6%, Italy 7.5%, Japan 5.9%, US 5.2% (2012)

Reserves of foreign exchange and gold: $16.6 billion (31 December 2012 est.)
country comparison to the world: 65
$34.03 billion (31 December 2011 est.)
note: the Fiscal Reserves Act that came into force on 1 January 2012 requires the fiscal reserve to be separated from the foreign exchange reserves and to be managed separately; the transfer of assets took place in February 2012

Debt—external: $0 (2012)
country comparison to the world: 205

Stock of direct foreign investment—at home: $14.9 billion (2010 est.)
country comparison to the world: 81
$13.6 billion (#REF! est.)

Stock of direct foreign investment—abroad: $672.1 million (2011 est.)
country comparison to the world: 79
$550.6 million (2010)

Exchange rates: patacas (MOP) per US dollar—
8 (2013 est.)
7.9899 (2012 est.)
8.0022 (2010 est.)
7.983 (2008)
8.011 (2007)

ENERGY

Electricity—production: 561 million kWh (2012 est.)
country comparison to the world: 160

Electricity—consumption: 4.214 billion kWh (2012 est.)
country comparison to the world: 121

Electricity—exports: 0 kWh (2012 est.)
country comparison to the world: 162

Electricity—imports: 3.86 billion kWh (2012 est.)
country comparison to the world: 42

Electricity—installed generating capacity: 472,000 kW (2012 est.)
country comparison to the world: 141

Electricity—from fossil fuels: 100% of total installed capacity (2012 est.)
country comparison to the world: 22

Electricity—from nuclear fuels: 0% of total installed capacity (2012 est.)
country comparison to the world: 131

Electricity—from hydroelectric plants: 0% of total installed capacity (2012 est.)
country comparison to the world: 181

Electricity—from other renewable sources: 0% of total installed capacity (2012 est.)
country comparison to the world: 197

Crude oil—production: 0 bbl/day (2012 est.)
country comparison to the world: 191

Crude oil—exports: 0 bbl/day (2012 est.)
country comparison to the world: 147

Crude oil—imports: 0 bbl/day (2012 est.)
country comparison to the world: 86

Crude oil—proved reserves: 0 bbl (1 January 2013 es)
country comparison to the world: 159

Refined petroleum products—production: 0 bbl/day (2012 est.)
country comparison to the world: 168

Refined petroleum products—consumption: 7,522 bbl/day (2012 est.)
country comparison to the world: 160

Refined petroleum products—exports: 0 bbl/day (2012 est.)
country comparison to the world: 193

Refined petroleum products—imports: 5,948 bbl/day (2012 est.)
country comparison to the world: 144

Natural gas—production: 0 cu m (2012 est.)
country comparison to the world: 159

Natural gas—consumption: 0 cu m (2012)
country comparison to the world: 166

Natural gas—exports: 0 cu m (2012 est.)
country comparison to the world: 140

Natural gas—imports: 0 cu m (2012 est.)
country comparison to the world: 91

Natural gas—proved reserves: 0 cu m (1 January 2013 es)
country comparison to the world: 163

Carbon dioxide emissions from consumption of energy: 1.805 million Mt (2011 est.)
country comparison to the world: 150

COMMUNICATIONS

Telephones—main lines in use: 162,500 (2012)
country comparison to the world: 132

Telephones—mobile cellular: 1.613 million (2012)
country comparison to the world: 150

Telephone system: *general assessment:* fairly modern communication facilities maintained for domestic and international services
domestic: termination of monopoly over mobile-cellular telephone services in 2001 spurred sharp increase in subscriptions with mobile-cellular teledensity exceeding 200 per 100 persons; fixed-line subscribership appears to have peaked and is now in decline
international: country code—853; landing point for the SEA-ME-WE-3 submarine cable network that provides links to Asia, the Middle East, and Europe; HF radiotelephone communication facility; satellite earth station—1 Intelsat (Indian Ocean) (2011)

Broadcast media: local government dominates broadcast media; 2 television stations operated by the government with one broadcasting in Portuguese and the other in Cantonese and Mandarin; 1 cable TV and 4 satellite TV services available; 3 radio stations broadcasting, of which 2 are government-operated (2012)

Internet country code: .mo

Internet hosts: 327 (2012)
country comparison to the world: 189

Internet users: 270,200 (2009)
country comparison to the world: 134

TRANSPORTATION

Airports: 1 (2013)
country comparison to the world: 224

Airports—with paved runways: *total:* 1
over 3,047 m: 1 (2013)

Heliports: 2 (2013)

Roadways: *total:* 413 km
country comparison to the world: 199
paved: 413 km (2009)

Ports and terminals: *major seaport(s):* Macau

MILITARY

Military branches: no regular indigenous military forces

Manpower available for military service:
males age 16-49: 150,780 (2010 est.)

Manpower fit for military service:
males age 16-49: 124,189
females age 16-49: 149,514 (2010 est.)

Manpower reaching militarily significant age annually: *male:* 4,274
female: 3,674 (2010 est.)

Military—note: defense is the responsibility of China

TRANSNATIONAL ISSUES

Disputes—international: none

Illicit drugs: transshipment point for drugs going into mainland China; consumer of opiates and amphetamines

MACEDONIA

INTRODUCTION

Background: Macedonia gained its independence peacefully from Yugoslavia in 1991. Greece's objection to the new state's use of what it considered a Hellenic name and symbols delayed international recognition, which occurred under the provisional designation of "the Former Yugoslav Republic of Macedonia." In 1995, Greece lifted a 20-month trade embargo and the two countries agreed to normalize relations, but the issue of the name remained unresolved and negotiations for a solution are ongoing. Since 2004, the US and over 130 other nations have recognized Macedonia by its constitutional name, Republic of Macedonia. Ethnic Albanian grievances over perceived political and economic inequities escalated into an insurgency in 2001 that eventually led to the internationally brokered Ohrid Framework Agreement, which ended the fighting and established guidelines for constitutional amendments and the creation of new laws that enhanced the rights of minorities. Although Macedonia became an EU candidate in 2005, the country still faces challenges, including fully implementing the Framework Agreement, improving relations with Bulgaria, carrying out democratic reforms, and stimulating economic growth and development. Macedonia's membership in NATO was blocked by Greece at the Alliance's Summit of Bucharest in 2008.

GEOGRAPHY

Location: Southeastern Europe, north of Greece

Geographic coordinates: 41 50 N, 22 00 E

Map references: Europe

Area: *total:* 25,713 sq km
country comparison to the world: 150
land: 25,433 sq km
water: 280 sq km

Area—comparative: slightly larger than Vermont

Land boundaries: *total:* 766 km
border countries: Albania 151 km, Bulgaria 148 km, Greece 246 km, Kosovo 159 km, Serbia 62 km

Coastline: 0 km (landlocked)

Maritime claims: none (landlocked)

Climate: warm, dry summers and autumns; relatively cold winters with heavy snowfall

Terrain: mountainous territory covered with deep basins and valleys; three large lakes, each divided by a frontier line; country bisected by the Vardar River

Elevation extremes: *lowest point:* Vardar River 50 m
highest point: Golem Korab (Maja e Korabit) 2,764 m

Natural resources: low-grade iron ore, copper, lead, zinc, chromite, manganese, nickel, tungsten, gold, silver, asbestos, gypsum, timber, arable land

Land use: *arable land:* 16.1%
permanent crops: 1.36%
other: 82.54% (2011)

Irrigated land: 1,278 sq km (2004)

Total renewable water resources: 6.4 cu km (2011)

Freshwater withdrawal (domestic/industrial/agricultural): *total:* 1.03 cu km/yr (21%/67%/12%)
per capita: 502 cu m/yr (2007)

Natural hazards: high seismic risks

Environment—current issues: air pollution from metallurgical plants

Environment—international agreements: *party to:* Air Pollution, Biodiversity, Climate Change, Climate Change-Kyoto Protocol, Desertification, Endangered Species, Hazardous Wastes, Law of the Sea, Ozone Layer Protection, Wetlands
signed, but not ratified: none of the selected agreements

Geography—note: landlocked; major transportation corridor from Western and Central Europe to Aegean Sea and Southern Europe to Western Europe

PEOPLE AND SOCIETY

Nationality: *noun:* Macedonian(s)
adjective: Macedonian

Ethnic groups: Macedonian 64.2%, Albanian 25.2%, Turkish 3.9%, Roma (Gypsy) 2.7%, Serb 1.8%, other 2.2% (2002 census)

Languages: Macedonian (official) 66.5%, Albanian (official) 25.1%, Turkish 3.5%, Roma 1.9%, Serbian 1.2%, other 1.8% (2002 census)

Religions: Macedonian Orthodox 64.7%, Muslim 33.3%, other Christian 0.37%, other and unspecified 1.63% (2002 census)

Population: 2,091,719 (July 2014 est.)
country comparison to the world: 147

Age structure: *0-14 years:* 17.7% (male 191,682/female 178,510)
15-24 years: 14.1% (male 151,901/female 142,679)
25-54 years: 43.8% (male 464,392/female 451,038)
55-64 years: 12.4% (male 123,272/female 129,081)
65 years and over: 12.1% (male 111,090/female 148,074) (2014 est.)

Dependency ratios: *total dependency ratio:* 40.9 %
youth dependency ratio: 23.5 %
elderly dependency ratio: 17.4 %
potential support ratio: 5.7 (2013)

Median age: *total:* 36.8 years
male: 35.7 years
female: 37.9 years (2014 est.)

Population growth rate: 0.21% (2014 est.)
country comparison to the world: 180

Birth rate: 11.64 births/1,000 population (2014 est.)
country comparison to the world: 171

Death rate: 9.04 deaths/1,000 population (2014 est.)
country comparison to the world: 67

Net migration rate: -0.48 migrant(s)/1,000 population (2014 est.)
country comparison to the world: 135

Urbanization: *urban population:* 59% of total population (2010)
rate of urbanization: 0.3% annual rate of change (2010-15 est.)

Major urban areas—population: SKOPJE (capital) 480,000 (2009)

Sex ratio: *at birth:* 1.08 male(s)/female
0-14 years: 1.07 male(s)/female
15-24 years: 1.07 male(s)/female
25-54 years: 1.03 male(s)/female
55-64 years: 0.99 male(s)/female
65 years and over: 0.75 male(s)/female
total population: 0.99 male(s)/female (2014 est.)

Mother's mean age at first birth: 26 (2010 est.)

Maternal mortality rate: 10 deaths/100,000 live births (2010)
country comparison to the world: 153

Infant mortality rate: *total:* 7.9 deaths/1,000 live births
country comparison to the world: 157
male: 8.16 deaths/1,000 live births
female: 7.63 deaths/1,000 live births (2014 est.)

Life expectancy at birth: *total population:* 75.8 years
country comparison to the world: 89
male: 73.23 years
female: 78.56 years (2014 est.)

Total fertility rate: 1.59 children born/woman (2014 est.)
country comparison to the world: 180

Health expenditures: 6.6% of GDP (2011)
country comparison to the world: 94

Physicians density: 2.62 physicians/1,000 population (2009)

Hospital bed density: 4.6 beds/1,000 population (2010)

Drinking water source:
improved:
urban: 100% of population
rural: 99% of population
total: 99.6% of population
unimproved:
urban: 0% of population
rural: 1% of population
total: 0.4% of population (2011 est.)

Sanitation facility access:
improved:
urban: 97% of population
rural: 83.1% of population
total: 91.3% of population
unimproved:
urban: 3% of population
rural: 16.9% of population
total: 8.7% of population (2011 est.)

HIV/AIDS—adult prevalence rate: less than 0.1% (2007 est.)
country comparison to the world: 158

HIV/AIDS—people living with HIV/AIDS: fewer than 200 (2007 est.)
country comparison to the world: 163

HIV/AIDS—deaths: fewer than 100 (2003 est.)
country comparison to the world: 143

Obesity—adult prevalence rate: 21.1% (2008)
country comparison to the world: 92

Children under the age of 5 years underweight: 1.8% (2005)
country comparison to the world: 124

Literacy: *definition:* age 15 and over can read and write

total population: 97.4% *male:* 98.7%
female: 96% (2011 est.)

School life expectancy (primary to tertiary education): *total:* 13 years
male: 13 years
female: 13 years (2010)

Child labor—children ages 5-14: *total number:* 16,782
percentage: 6 % (2005 est.)

Unemployment, youth ages 15-24: *total:* 53.9%
country comparison to the world: 4
male: 55.2%
female: 51.7% (2012)

GOVERNMENT

Country name: *conventional long form:* Republic of Macedonia
conventional short form: Macedonia
local long form: Republika Makedonija
local short form: Makedonija
note: the provisional designation used by the UN, EU, and NATO is the "former Yugoslav Republic of Macedonia" (FYROM)
former: People's Republic of Macedonia, Socialist Republic of Macedonia

Government type: parliamentary democracy

Capital: *name:* Skopje

geographic coordinates: 42 00 N, 21 26 E
time difference: UTC+1 (6 hours ahead of Washington, DC during Standard Time)
daylight saving time: +1hr, begins last Sunday in March; ends last Sunday in October

Administrative divisions: 71 municipalities (opstini, singular—opstina); Aracinovo, Berovo, Bitola, Bogdanci, Bogovinje, Bosilovo, Brvenica, Caska, Centar Zupa, Cesinovo-Oblesevo, Cucer Sandevo, Debar, Debarca, Delcevo, Demir Hisar, Demir Kapija, Dojran, Dolneni, Gevgelija, Gostivar, Grad Skopje, Gradsko, Ilinden, Jegunovce, Karbinci, Kavadarci, Kicevo, Kocani, Konce, Kratovo, Kriva Palanka, Krivogastani, Krusevo, Kumanovo, Lipkovo, Lozovo, Makedonska Kamenica, Makedonski Brod, Mavrovo i Rostusa, Mogila, Negotino, Novaci, Novo Selo, Ohrid, Pehcevo, Petrovec, Plasnica, Prilep, Probistip, Radovis, Rankovce, Resen, Rosoman, Sopiste, Staro Nagoricane, Stip, Struga, Strumica, Studenicani, Sveti Nikole, Tearce, Tetovo, Valandovo, Vasilevo, Veles, Vevcani, Vinica, Vrapciste, Zelenikovo, Zelino, Zrnovci

Independence: 8 September 1991 (referendum by registered voters endorsed independence from Yugoslavia)

National holiday: Independence Day, 8 September (1991); also known as National Day

Constitution: several previous; latest adopted 17 November 1991, effective 20 November 1991; amended several times, last in 2011 (2011)

Legal system: civil law system; judicial review of legislative acts

International law organization participation: has not submitted an ICJ jurisdiction declaration; accepts ICCt jurisdiction

Suffrage: 18 years of age; universal

Executive branch: *chief of state:* President Gjorge IVANOV (since 12 May 2009)
head of government: Prime Minister Nikola GRUEVSKI (since 26 August 2006)
cabinet: Council of Ministers elected by the majority vote of all the deputies in the Assembly; note—current cabinet formed by the government coalition parties VMRO-DPMNE, DUI, and several small parties (For more information visit the World Leaders website)
elections: president elected by popular vote for a five-year term (eligible for a second term); two-round
election: first round held on 13 April 2014, second round to be held on 27 April 2009; prime minister elected by the Assembly following legislative elections; the leader of the majority party or majority coalition usually elected prime minister
election results: Gjorge IVANOV elected president on second-round ballot in 2009; percent of vote—Gjorge IVANOV 63.1%, Ljubomir FRCKOSKI 36.9%; note—13 April 2014 first round results—Gjorge IVANOV 51.7%, Stevo PENDAROVSKI 37.5%; second round to be held on 27 April 2014

Legislative branch: unicameral Assembly or Sobranie (123 seats; all members elected by popular vote from party lists based on the percentage of the overall vote the parties gain in each of the six domestic and three diaspora electoral districts; members serve four-year terms)
elections: last held on 5 June 2011 (next to be held on 27 April 2014)
election results: percent of vote by party—VMRO-DPMNE-led block 39%, SDSM-led block 32.8%, DUI 10.2%, DPA 5.9%, other 12.1%; seats by party—VMRO-DPMNE-led block 56, SDSM-led block 42, DUI 15, DPA 8, NDR 2

Judicial branch: *highest court(s):* Supreme Court (consist of NA judges); Constitutional Court (consists of 9 judges)
judge selection and term of office: Supreme Court judges nominated by the Judicial Council, a 7-member body of legal professionals, and appointed by the Assembly; judge tenure NA; Constitutional Court judges appointed by the legislature for nonrenewable, 9-year terms
subordinate courts: Courts of Appeal; Basic Courts

Political parties and leaders: Albanian Democratic Union or BDSH [Bardhyl MAHMUTI]; Alliance for Positive Macedonia or APM [Ljupco ZIKOV]; Citizens Option for Macedonia or GROM [Stevco JAKIMOVSKI]; Democratic League of Bosniaks in Macedonia [Rafet MUMINOVIK]; Democratic Party of Serbs in Macedonia or DPSM [Ivan STOILJKOVIC]; Democratic Party of the Albanians or DPA [Menduh THACI]; Democratic Party of Turks of Macedonia or DPTM [Kenan HASIPI]; Democratic Renewal of Macedonia or DOM [Liljana POPOVSKA]; Democratic Union or DS [Pavle TRAJANOV]; Democratic Union for Integration or DUI [Ali AHMETI]; Dosoinstvo (Diginity) [Stojance ANGELOV]; Internal Macedonian Revolutionary Organization—Democratic Party for Macedonian National Unity or VMRO-DPMNE [Nikola GRUEVSKI]; Internal Macedonian Revolutionary Organization—People's Party or VMRO-NP [Ljubco GEORGIEVSKI]; Liberal Democratic Party or LDP [Andrej ZERNOVSKI]; Liberal Party of Macedonia or LP [Ivon VELICKOVSKI]; Movement for Turkish National Union [Erdogan SARAC]; National Democratic Revival or NDR [Rufi OSMANI]; New Democracy or DR [Kastriot HAXHIREXHA]; New Social-Democratic Party or NSDP [Tito PETKOVSKI]; Party for a European Future or PEI [Fijat CANOSKI]; Party for Democratic Action of Macedonia or SDA [Avdija PEPIC]; Party for Democratic Prosperity [Arben RUSI]; Party for the Total Emancipation of Roma or PCER [Samka IBRAIMOVSKI]; Party of United Democrats of Macedonia or PODEM [Zivko JANKULOVSKI]; SDSM-led block [Zoran ZAEV] (includes SDSM, LP, NSDP, PEI); Serbian Progressive Party in Macedonia or SPSM [Dragisha MILETIC]; Social Democratic Union of Macedonia or SDSM [Zoran ZAEV]; Socialist Party of Macedonia or SP [Ljubisav IVANOV DZINGO]; Union of Roma of Macedonia or SR [Amdi BAJRAM]; United for Macedonia or OM [Ljube BOSKOSKI]; VMRO-DPMNE-led block [includes Nikola GRUEVSI] (includes VMRO-DPMNE, DPSM, DPTM, DOM, DS, SP, SR)

Political pressure groups and leaders: Federation of Free Trade Unions [Mirjana ANDREVSKA]; Federation of Trade Unions [Zivko MITREVSKI]; Trade Union of Education, Science and Culture [Jakim NEDELKOV]

International organization participation: BIS, CD, CE, CEI, EAPC, EBRD, EU (candidate country), FAO, IAEA, IBRD, ICAO, ICC (NGOs), ICRM, IDA, IFAD, IFC, IFRCS, ILO, IMF, IMO, Interpol, IOC, IOM (observer), IPU, ISO, ITU, ITUC (NGOs), MIGA, OAS (observer), OIF, OPCW, OSCE, PCA, PFP, SELEC, UN, UNCTAD, UNESCO, UNHCR, UNIDO, UNIFIL, UNWTO, UPU, WCO, WHO, WIPO, WMO, WTO

Diplomatic representation in the US: *chief of mission:* Ambassador Zoran JOLEVSKI (since 22 March 2007)
chancery: 2129 Wyoming Avenue NW, Washington, DC 20008
telephone: [1] (202) 667-0501
FAX: [1] (202) 667-2131
consulate(s) general: Chicago, New York, Southfield (MI)

Diplomatic representation from the US: *chief of mission:* Ambassador Paul D. WOHLERS (since 11 August 2011)
embassy: Str. Samolilova, Nr. 21, 1000 Skopje
mailing address: American Embassy Skopje, US Department of State, 7120 Skopje Place, Washington, DC 20521-7120 (pouch)
telephone: [389] (2) 310-2000
FAX: [389] (2) 310-2499

Flag description: a yellow sun (the Sun of Liberty) with eight broadening rays extending to the edges of the red field; the red and yellow colors have long been associated with Macedonia National symbol(s): eight-rayed sun

National anthem: *name:* "Denes Nad Makedonija" (Today Over Macedonia)
lyrics/music: Vlado MALESKI/Todor SKALOVSKI
note: adopted 1991; the song, written in 1943, previously served as the anthem of the Socialist Republic of Macedonia while part of Yugoslavia

ECONOMY

Economy—overview: Since its independence in 1991, Macedonia has made significant progress in liberalizing its economy and improving its business environment, but has lagged the Balkan region in attracting foreign investment. Unemployment has remained consistently high at more than 30% since 2008, but may be overstated based on the existence of an extensive gray market, estimated to be between 20% and 45% of GDP, that is not captured by official statistics. Macedonia's economy is closely linked to Europe as a customer for exports and source of investment, and has suffered as a result of prolonged weakness in the euro zone. Macedonia maintained macroeconomic stability through the global financial crisis by conducting prudent monetary policy, which keeps the domestic currency pegged against the euro, and by limiting fiscal deficits. The government has been loosening fiscal policy, however, and the budget deficit expanded to 4.2% of GDP in 2013. Macedonia achieved modest GDP growth in 2013 after a small contraction in 2012; inflation is under control.

GDP (purchasing power parity): $22.57 billion (2013 est.)
country comparison to the world: 127
$21.89 billion (2012 est.)
$21.98 billion (2011 est.)
note: data are in 2013 US dollars; Macedonia has a large informal sector that may not be reflected in these data

GDP (official exchange rate): $10.65 billion (2013 est.)

GDP—real growth rate: 3.1% (2013 est.)
country comparison to the world: 112
-0.4% (2012 est.)
2.9% (2011 est.)

GDP—per capita (PPP): $10,800 (2013 est.)
country comparison to the world: 113
$10,600 (2012 est.)
$10,700 (2011 est.)
note: data are in 2013 US dollars

Gross national saving: 23.2% of GDP (2013 est.)
country comparison to the world: 61
24.7% of GDP (2012 est.)
23.2% of GDP (2011 est.)

GDP—composition, by end use:
household consumption: 77.5%
government consumption: 15.3%
investment in fixed capital: 22.5%
investment in inventories: 3.1%
exports of goods and services: 47.7%
imports of goods and services: -66.1% (2013 est.)

GDP—composition, by sector of origin:
agriculture: 10.2%
industry: 27.5%
services: 62.3% (2013 est.)

Agriculture—products: grapes, tobacco, vegetables, fruits; milk, eggs

Industries: food processing, beverages, textiles, chemicals, iron, steel, cement, energy, pharmaceuticals

Industrial production growth rate: 3.2% (2013 est.)
country comparison to the world: 92

Labor force: 960,700 (2013 est.)
country comparison to the world: 145

Labor force—by occupation: *agriculture:* 18.8%
industry: 27.5%
services: 53.7% (31 September 2013)

Unemployment rate: 28.6% (2013 est.)
country comparison to the world: 179
31% (2012 est.)

Population below poverty line: 30.4% (2011)

Household income or consumption by percentage share: *lowest 10%:* 2.2%
highest 10%: 34.5% (2009 est.)

Distribution of family income—Gini index: 39.2 (2011)
country comparison to the world: 65
43.2 (2009)

Budget: *revenues:* $3.023 billion
expenditures: $3.438 billion (2013 est.)

Taxes and other revenues: 30.6% of GDP (2013 est.)
country comparison to the world: 89

Budget surplus (+) or deficit (-):
-4.1% of GDP (2013 est.)
country comparison to the world: 151

Public debt: 34.3% of GDP (2013 est.)
country comparison to the world: 107
34.1% of GDP (2012 est.)
note: official data from Ministry of Finance; data cover central government debt; this data excludes debt instruments issued (or owned) by government entities other than the treasury; includes treasury debt held by foreign entitites; excludes debt issued by sub-national entities, as well as intra-governmental debt; there are no debt instruments sold for social funds

Fiscal year: calendar year

Inflation rate (consumer prices): 2.8% (2013 est.)
country comparison to the world: 103
3.3% (2012 est.)

Central bank discount rate:
3.25% (31 December 2013 est.)
country comparison to the world: 97
3.75% (31 December 2012 est.)
note: series discontinued in January 2010; the discount rate has been replaced by a referent rate for calculating the penalty rate

Commercial bank prime lending rate: 6.4% (31 December 2013 est.)
country comparison to the world: 130
6.8% (31 December 2012 est.)

Stock of narrow money: $1.57 billion (31 December 2013 est.)
country comparison to the world: 136
$1.414 billion (31 December 2012 est.)

Stock of broad money: $6.286 billion (31 December 2013 est.)
country comparison to the world: 121
$5.708 billion (31 December 2012 est.)

Stock of domestic credit: $5.211 billion (31 December 2013 est.)
country comparison to the world: 114
$4.681 billion (31 December 2012 est.)

Market value of publicly traded shares: $2.214 billion (31 December 2013)
country comparison to the world: 97
$2.423 billion (31 December 2012)
$2.495 billion (31 December 2011)

Current account balance: -$194.1 million (2013 est.)
country comparison to the world: 84
-$385.2 million (2012 est.)

Exports: $4.267 billion (2013 est.)
country comparison to the world: 118
$4.002 billion (2012 est.)

Exports—commodities: food, beverages, tobacco; textiles, miscellaneous manufactures, iron, steel; automotive parts

Exports—partners: Germany 36.9%, Bulgaria 7.6%, Italy 6.5%, Kosovo 6.5%, Serbia 6.3%, Greece 5% (2012 est.)

Imports: $6.6 billion (2013 est.)
country comparison to the world: 117
$6.511 billion (2012 est.)

Imports—commodities: machinery and equipment, automobiles, chemicals, fuels, food products

Imports—partners: Great Britain 11%, Greece 10.6%, Germany 10.5%, Serbia 7.9%, Italy 6.5%, China 5.8%, Bulgaria 5.5%, Turkey 4.8% (2012 est.)

Reserves of foreign exchange and gold: $2.747 billion (31 December 2013 est.)
country comparison to the world: 112
$2.891 billion (31 December 2012 est.)

Debt—external: $7.451 billion (30 September 2013 est.)
country comparison to the world: 108
$6.818 billion (31 December 2012 est.)

Stock of direct foreign investment—at home: $4.695 billion (31 December 2013 est.)
country comparison to the world: 89
$4.361 billion (31 December 2012 est.)

Stock of direct foreign investment—abroad: $NA
$564 million (31 December 2009 est.)

Exchange rates: Macedonian denars (MKD) per US dollar—
46.398 (2013 est.)
47.885 (2012 est.)
46.485 (2010 est.)
44.1 (2009)
41.414 (2008)

ENERGY

Electricity—production: 5.676 billion kWh (2013 est.)
country comparison to the world: 117

Electricity—consumption: 6.989 billion kWh (2013 est.)
country comparison to the world: 100

Electricity—exports: 62.36 million kWh (2013 est.)
country comparison to the world: 80

Electricity—imports: 2.491 billion kWh (2013 est.)
country comparison to the world: 53

Electricity—installed generating capacity: 1.953 million kW (2013 est.)
country comparison to the world: 104

Electricity—from fossil fuels: 66.4% of total installed capacity (2013 est.)
country comparison to the world: 117

Electricity—from nuclear fuels: 0% of total installed capacity (2013 est.)
country comparison to the world: 137

Electricity—from hydroelectric plants: 33.2% of total installed capacity (2013 est.)
country comparison to the world: 69

Electricity—from other renewable sources: 0.4% of total installed capacity (2013 est.)
country comparison to the world: 88

Crude oil—production: 0 bbl/day (2013 est.)
country comparison to the world: 194

Crude oil—exports: 0 bbl/day (2013)

country comparison to the world: 152

Crude oil—imports: 51.51 million bbl/day (2013 est.)
country comparison to the world: 1

Crude oil—proved reserves: 0 bbl (1 January 2013 es)
country comparison to the world: 163

Refined petroleum products—production: 17,030 bbl/day (2010 est.)
country comparison to the world: 96

Refined petroleum products—consumption: 17,490 bbl/day (2011 est.)
country comparison to the world: 135

Refined petroleum products—exports: 6,750 bbl/day (2010 est.)
country comparison to the world: 88

Refined petroleum products—imports: 21,530 bbl/day (2010 est.)
country comparison to the world: 103

Natural gas—production: 0 cu m (2013)
country comparison to the world: 165

Natural gas—consumption: 158.6 million cu m (2013 est.)
country comparison to the world: 102

Natural gas—exports: 0 cu m (2013)
country comparison to the world: 146

Natural gas—imports: 158.6 million cu m (2013 est.)
country comparison to the world: 71

Natural gas—proved reserves: 0 cu m (1 January 2013 es)
country comparison to the world: 169

Carbon dioxide emissions from consumption of energy: 6.947 million Mt (2011 est.)
country comparison to the world: 113

COMMUNICATIONS

Telephones—main lines in use: 407,900 (2012)
country comparison to the world: 103

Telephones—mobile cellular: 2.235 million (2012)
country comparison to the world: 142

Telephone system: *general assessment:* competition from the mobile-cellular segment of the telecommunications market has led to a drop in fixed-line telephone subscriptions
domestic: combined fixed-line and mobile-cellular telephone subscribership about 130 per 100 persons
international: country code—389 (2012)

Broadcast media: public TV broadcaster operates 3 national channels and a satellite network; 5 privately owned TV channels broadcast nationally using terrestrial transmitters and about 15 broadcast on national level via satellite; roughly 75 local commercial TV stations; large number of cable operators offering domestic and international programming; public radio broadcaster operates over multiple stations; 3 privately owned radio stations broadcast nationally; about 70 local commercial radio stations (2012)

Internet country code: .mk

Internet hosts: 62,826 (2012)
country comparison to the world: 92

Internet users: 1.057 million (2009)
country comparison to the world: 97

TRANSPORTATION

Airports: 10 (2013)
country comparison to the world: 155

Airports—with paved runways: *total:* 8
2,438 to 3,047 m: 2
under 914 m: 6 (2013)

Airports—with unpaved runways: *total:* 2
914 to 1,523 m: 1
under 914 m: 1 (2013)

Pipelines: gas 268 km; oil 120 km (2013)

Railways: *total:* 699 km
country comparison to the world: 100
standard gauge: 699 km 1.435-m gauge (234 km electrified) (2012)

Roadways: *total:* 14,038 km (includes 259 km of expressways)
country comparison to the world: 124
paved: 9,489 km
unpaved: 4,549 km (2012)

MILITARY

Military branches: Army of the Republic of Macedonia (ARM; includes General Staff and subordinate Joint Operational Command, Training and Doctrine Command, Special Operations Regiment) (2012)

Military service age and obligation: 18 years of age for voluntary military service; conscription abolished in 2008 (2013)

Manpower available for military service:
males age 16-49: 532,196
females age 16-49: 511,964 (2010 est.)

Manpower fit for military service:
males age 16-49: 443,843
females age 16-49: 426,251 (2010 est.)

Manpower reaching militarily significant age annually: *male:* 16,144

female: 14,920 (2010 est.)

Military expenditures: 1.38% of GDP (2012)
country comparison to the world: 74
1.27% of GDP (2011)
1.38% of GDP (2010)

TRANSNATIONAL ISSUES

Disputes—international: Kosovo and Macedonia completed demarcation of their boundary in September 2008; Greece continues to reject the use of the name Macedonia or Republic of Macedonia

Refugees and internally displaced persons: *stateless persons:* 905 (2012)

Illicit drugs: major transshipment point for Southwest Asian heroin and hashish; minor transit point for South American cocaine destined for Europe; although not a financial center and most criminal activity is thought to be domestic, money laundering is a problem due to a mostly cash-based economy and weak enforcement

MADAGASCAR

INTRODUCTION

Background: Formerly an independent kingdom, Madagascar became a French colony in 1896 but regained independence in 1960. During 1992-93, free presidential and National Assembly elections were held ending 17 years of single-party rule. In 1997, in the second presidential race, Didier RATSIRAKA, the leader during the 1970s and 1980s, was returned to the presidency. The 2001 presidential election was contested between the followers of Didier RATSIRAKA and Marc RAVALOMANANA, nearly causing secession of half of the country. In April 2002, the High Constitutional Court announced RAVALOMANANA the winner. RAVALOMANANA achieved a second term following a landslide victory in the generally free and fair presidential elections of 2006. In early 2009, protests over increasing restrictions on opposition press and activities resulted in RAVALOMANANA handing over power to the military, which then conferred the presidency on the mayor of Antananarivo, Andry RAJOELINA, in what amounted to a coup d'etat. Following a lengthy mediation process led by the Southern African Development Community (SADC), Madagascar held UN-supported presidential and parliamentary elections in 2013. Former de facto finance minister Hery RAJAONARIMAMPIANINA defeated RAVALOMANANA's favored candidate Jean-Louis ROBINSON in a presidential runoff and was inaugurated in January 2014. Most international observers, while noting some irregularities, declared polls to be a credible reflection of the Malagasy public's will.

GEOGRAPHY

Location: Southern Africa, island in the Indian Ocean, east of Mozambique

Geographic coordinates: 20 00 S, 47 00 E

Map references: Africa

Area: *total:* 587,041 sq km
country comparison to the world: 47
land: 581,540 sq km
water: 5,501 sq km

Area—comparative: slightly less than twice the size of Arizona

Land boundaries: 0 km

Coastline: 4,828 km

Maritime claims: *territorial sea:* 12 nm
contiguous zone: 24 nm
exclusive economic zone: 200 nm
continental shelf: 200 nm or 100 nm from the 2,500-m isobath

Climate: tropical along coast, temperate inland, arid in south

Terrain: narrow coastal plain, high plateau and mountains in center

Elevation extremes: *lowest point:* Indian Ocean 0 m
highest point: Maromokotro 2,876 m

Natural resources: graphite, chromite, coal, bauxite, rare earth elements, salt, quartz, tar sands, semiprecious stones, mica, fish, hydropower

Land use: *arable land:* 5.96%
permanent crops: 1.02%
other: 93.02% (2011)

Irrigated land: 10,860 sq km (2003)

Total renewable water resources: 337 cu km (2011)

Freshwater withdrawal (domestic/industrial/agricultural): *total:* 16.5 cu km/yr (2%/1%/97%)
per capita: 1,010 cu m/yr (2005)

Natural hazards: periodic cyclones; drought; and locust infestation
volcanism: Madagascar's volcanoes have not erupted in historical times

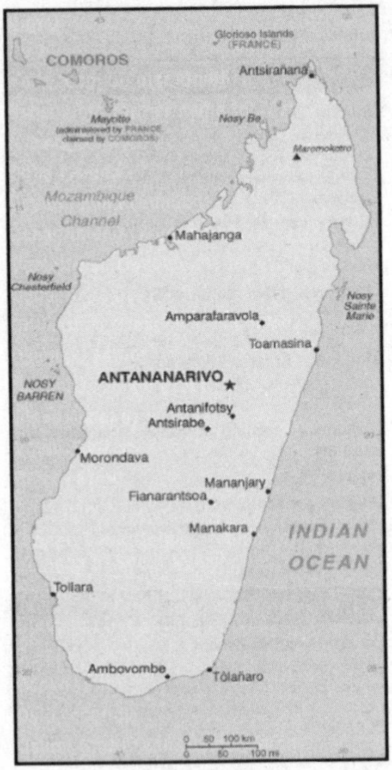

Environment—current issues: soil erosion results from deforestation and overgrazing; desertification; surface water contaminated with raw sewage and other organic wastes; several endangered species of flora and fauna unique to the island

Environment—international agreements: *party to:* Biodiversity, Climate Change, Climate Change-Kyoto Protocol, Desertification, Endangered Species, Hazardous Wastes, Law of the Sea, Marine Life Conservation, Ozone Layer Protection, Ship Pollution, Wetlands
signed, but not ratified: none of the selected agreements

Geography—note: world's fourth-largest island; strategic location along Mozambique Channel

PEOPLE AND SOCIETY

Nationality: *noun:* Malagasy (singular and plural)
adjective: Malagasy

Ethnic groups: Malayo-Indonesian (Merina and related Betsileo), Cotiers (mixed African, Malayo-Indonesian, and Arab ancestry—Betsimisaraka, Tsimihety, Antaisaka, Sakalava), French, Indian, Creole, Comoran

Languages: French (official), Malagasy (official), English

Religions: indigenous beliefs 52%, Christian 41%, Muslim 7%

Population: 23,201,926 (July 2014 est.)
country comparison to the world: 53

Age structure: *0-14 years:* 40.7% (male 4,765,523/female 4,685,298)
15-24 years: 20.6% (male 2,394,146/female 2,384,564)
25-54 years: 31.3% (male 3,635,506/female 3,629,204)
55-64 years: 3.2% (male 466,263/female 503,375)
65 years and over: 3.1% (male 334,533/female 403,514) (2014 est.)

Dependency ratios:
total dependency ratio: 82.5 %
youth dependency ratio: 77.4 %
elderly dependency ratio: 5.1 %
potential support ratio: 19.5 (2013)

Median age: *total:* 19.2 years
male: 19 years
female: 19.4 years (2014 est.)

Population growth rate: 2.62% (2014 est.)
country comparison to the world: 25

Birth rate: 33.12 births/1,000 population (2014 est.)
country comparison to the world: 33

Death rate: 6.95 deaths/1,000 population (2014 est.)
country comparison to the world: 136

Net migration rate: 0 migrant(s)/1,000 population (2014 est.)
country comparison to the world: 87

Urbanization: *urban population:* 32.6% of total population (2011)
rate of urbanization: 4.73% annual rate of change (2010-15 est.)

Major urban areas—population: ANTANANARIVO (capital) 1.816 million (2009)

Sex ratio: *at birth:* 1.03 male(s)/female
0-14 years: 1.02 male(s)/female
15-24 years: 1 male(s)/female
25-54 years: 1 male(s)/female
55-64 years: 1 male(s)/female
65 years and over: 0.83 male(s)/female
total population: 1 male(s)/female (2014 est.)

Mother's mean age at first birth: 19.5
note: median age at first birth among women 25-29 (2009 est.)

Maternal mortality rate: 240 deaths/100,000 live births (2010)
country comparison to the world: 48

Infant mortality rate: *total:* 44.88 deaths/1,000 live births
country comparison to the world: 48
male: 48.86 deaths/1,000 live births
female: 40.78 deaths/1,000 live births (2014 est.)

Life expectancy at birth: *total population:* 65.2 years
country comparison to the world: 174
male: 63.77 years
female: 66.67 years (2014 est.)

Total fertility rate: 4.28 children born/woman (2014 est.)
country comparison to the world: 33

Contraceptive prevalence rate: 39.9% (2008/09)

Health expenditures: 4.1% of GDP (2011)
country comparison to the world: 161

Physicians density: 0.16 physicians/1,000 population (2007)

Hospital bed density: 0.2 beds/1,000 population (2010)

Drinking water source:
improved:
urban: 77.7% of population
rural: 33.8% of population
total: 48.1% of population
unimproved:
urban: 22.3% of population
rural: 66.2% of population
total: 51.9% of population (2011 est.)

Sanitation facility access:
improved:
urban: 19% of population
rural: 11.1% of population
total: 13.7% of population
unimproved:
urban: 81% of population
rural: 88.9% of population
total: 86.3% of population (2011 est.)

HIV/AIDS—adult prevalence rate: 0.5% (2012 est.)
country comparison to the world: 73

HIV/AIDS—people living with HIV/AIDS: 58,800 (2012 est.)
country comparison to the world: 57

HIV/AIDS—deaths: 6,200 (2012 est.)
country comparison to the world: 32

Major infectious diseases: *degree of risk:* very high
food or waterborne diseases: bacterial diarrhea, hepatitis A, and typhoid fever
vectorborne diseases: malaria and dengue fever
water contact disease: schistosomiasis
animal contact disease: rabies (2013)

Obesity—adult prevalence rate: 1.6% (2008)
country comparison to the world: 187

Children under the age of 5 years underweight: 36.8% (2004)
country comparison to the world: 6

Education expenditures: 2.7% of GDP (2012)
country comparison to the world: 150

Literacy: *definition:* age 15 and over can read and write
total population: 64.5%
male: 67.4%
female: 61.6% (2009 est.)

School life expectancy (primary to tertiary education): *total:* 10 years
male: 11 years
female: 10 years (2012)

Child labor—children ages 5-14:
total number: 1,827,423
percentage: 28 %
note: data represents children ages 5-17 (2007 est.)

Unemployment, youth ages 15-24: *total:* 2.3%
country comparison to the world: 145
male: 1.7%
female: 2.8% (2005)

GOVERNMENT

Country name: *conventional long form:* Republic of Madagascar
conventional short form: Madagascar
local long form: Republique de Madagascar/ Repoblikan'i Madagasikara
local short form: Madagascar/Madagasikara
former: Malagasy Republic

Government type: republic

Capital: *name:* Antananarivo

geographic coordinates: 18 55 S, 47 31 E
time difference: UTC+3 (8 hours ahead of Washington, DC during Standard Time)

Administrative divisions: Hi Trent,6 provinces (faritany); Antananarivo, Antsiranana, Fianarantsoa, Mahajanga, Toamasina, Toliara

Independence: 26 June 1960 (from France)

National holiday: Independence Day, 26 June (1960)

Constitution: previous 1992; latest passed by referendum 17 November 2010, promulgated 11 December 2010 (2012)

Legal system: civil law system based on the old French civil code and customary law in matters of marriage, family, and obligation

International law organization participation: accepts compulsory ICJ jurisdiction with reservations; accepts ICCt jurisdiction

Suffrage: 18 years of age; universal

Executive branch: *chief of state:* President Hery Martial RAJAONARIMAMPIANINA Rakotoarimana (since 25 January 2014)
head of government: Prime Minister Roger Laurent Christophe KOLO, M.D. (since 11 April 2014)
cabinet: Council of Ministers appointed by the prime minister (For more information visit the World Leaders website)

elections: president elected by popular vote for a five-year term (eligible for a second term); election last held on 20 December 2013 (next to be held in 2018); prime minister nominated by the National Assembly and appointed by the president
election results: percent of vote—Hery RAJAONARIMAMPIANINA 53.5%, Jean Louis ROBINSON 46.5%; note—results of second round; first round on 25 October 2013 produced no outright winner)
note: on 17 March 2009, democratically elected President Marc RAVALOMANANA stepped down handing the government over to the military, which in turn conferred the presidency on opposition leader and Antananarivo mayor Andry RAJOELINA; a power-sharing agreement established a 15-month transition period to conclude with general elections in 2010, which failed to occur; a subsequent agreement aimed for elections in early 2013—the first round was held 25 October 2013 and the second round on 20 December 2013

Legislative branch: bicameral legislature consists of a Senate or Senat (33 seats; 22 elected from each of the 22 regions; the remaining 11 appointed by the president; members to serve six-year terms) and a National Assembly or Assemblee Nationale (151 seats in the December 2013 election; reduced from 160 seats to 127 seats by an April 2007 national referendum—never used; members elected by popular vote to serve four-year terms)
elections: National Assembly—last held on 20 December 2013 (next to be held in 2017); note—a power-sharing agreement in the summer of 2009 established a 15-month transition, concluding in general elections scheduled for late 2013 after repeated delays
election results: National Assembly—percent of vote by party—Party of Andry Rajoelina 17.3%, Ravalomannana Movement 10.8%, Vondrona Politika 8.2%, independents and others 63.7%; seats by party—Party of Andry Rajoelina 49, the Ravalomannana Movement 20, Malagasy Miara Mianinga 13, independents 25, seats with delayed elections 4, other 40

Judicial branch: *highest court(s):* Supreme Court or Cour Supreme (consists of 11 members; addresses judicial administration issues only); High Constitutional Court or Haute Cour Constitutionnelle (consists of 9 members) note—the judiciary includes a High Court of Justice responsible for adjudicating crimes and misdemeanors by government officials including the president
judge selection and term of office: Supreme Court heads elected by the president and judiciary officials to serve single-renewable, 3-year terms; High Constitutional Court members appointed—3 each by the president, by both legislative bodies, and by the Council of Magistrates; members serve single, 6-year terms
subordinate courts: Courts of Appeal; provincial and city tribunals

Political parties and leaders: AVANA Party [Jean-Louis ROBINSON]; Economic Liberalism and Democratic Action for National Recovery or LEADER/Fanilo [Jean-Max; RAKOTOMAMONJY]; Green Party or Parti Vert [Sarah Georget RABEHARISOA]; I Love Madagascar or TIM [Marc RAVALOMANANA]; Judged by Your Work or AVI [Norbert RATSIRAHONANA]; Malagasy Miara-Miainga or MMM [Hajo ANDRIANAINARIVELO]; Malagasy Tonga Saina or MTS [Roland RATSIRAKA]; Movement for Democracy in Madagascar or MDM [Pierrot RAJAONARIVELO]; New Force for Madagascar of FIDIO [Hery RAJAONARIMAMPIANINA]; Renewal of the Social Democratic Party or RPSD [Evariste MARSON]; Socialist and Democratic Party for the Unity of Madagascar or PSDUM [Jean LAHINIRIKO]; Union Party or Tambatra [Albert Camille VITAL]; Young Malagasies Determined or TGV [Andry RAJOELINA]

Political pressure groups and leaders: Committee for the Defense of Truth and Justice or KMMR; Committee for National Reconciliation or CRN [Albert Zafy]; National Council of Christian Churches or FFKM

International organization participation: ACP, AfDB, AU, CD, COMESA, EITI (candidate country), FAO, G-77, IAEA, IBRD, ICAO, ICC (national committees), ICRM, IDA, IFAD, IFC, IFRCS, ILO, IMF, IMO, InOC, Interpol, IOC, IOM, ISO (correspondent), ITSO, ITU, ITUC (NGOs), MIGA, NAM, OIF, OPCW, PCA, SADC, UN, UNCTAD, UNESCO, UNHCR, UNIDO, UNWTO, UPU, WCO, WFTU (NGOs), WHO, WIPO, WMO, WTO

Diplomatic representation in the US: *chief of mission:* Ambassador (vacant); Charge d'Affaires Velotiana Rakotoanosy RAOBELINA
chancery: 2374 Massachusetts Avenue NW, Washington, DC 20008
telephone: [1] (202) 265-5525 through 5526
FAX: [1] (202) 265-3034
consulate(s) general: New York

Diplomatic representation from the US: *chief of mission:* Ambassador (vacant); Charge d'Affaires Eric WONG note—also accredited to Comoros
embassy: Lot 207A, Point Liberty, Andranoro, Antehiroka, 105 Antananarivo
mailing address: B. P. 620, Antsahavola, Antananarivo
telephone: [261] (23) 480 00/01
FAX: [261] (23) 480 35

Flag description: two equal horizontal bands of red (top) and green with a vertical white band of the same width on hoist side; by tradition, red stands for sovereignty, green for hope, white for purity

National anthem: *name:* "Ry Tanindraza nay malala o" (Oh, Our Beloved Fatherland)
lyrics/music: Pasteur RAHAJASON/Norbert RAHARISOA
note: adopted 1959

ECONOMY

Economy—overview: After discarding socialist economic policies in the mid-1990s, Madagascar followed a World Bank- and IMF-led policy of privatization and liberalization that has been undermined since the start of the political crisis. This strategy placed the country on a slow and steady growth path from an extremely low level. Agriculture, including fishing and forestry, is a mainstay of the economy, accounting for more than one-fourth of GDP and employing 80% of the population. Exports of apparel boomed in recent years primarily due to duty-free access to the US; however, Madagascar's failure to comply with the requirements of the African Growth and Opportunity Act (AGOA) led to the termination of the country's duty-free access in January 2010 and a sharp fall in textile production. Deforestation and erosion, aggravated by the use of firewood as the primary source of fuel, are serious concerns. The current political crisis, which began in early 2009, has dealt additional blows to the economy. Tourism dropped more than 50% in 2009 compared with the previous year, and many investors are wary of entering the uncertain investment environment. Growth was slow during 2010 to 2013 although expansion in mining and agricultural sectors is expected to contribute to more growth in 2014. International organizations and foreign donors are expected to resume development aid to Madagascar once RAJAONARIMAMPIANINA appoints a new government.

GDP (purchasing power parity): $22.03 billion (2013 est.)
country comparison to the world: 129
$21.47 billion (2012 est.)
$21.06 billion (2011 est.)
note: data are in 2013 US dollars

GDP (official exchange rate): $10.53 billion (2013 est.)

GDP—real growth rate: 2.6% (2013 est.)
country comparison to the world: 126
1.9% (2012 est.)
1.8% (2011 est.)

GDP—per capita (PPP): $1,000 (2013 est.)
country comparison to the world: 219
$1,000 (2012 est.)
$1,000 (2011 est.)
note: data are in 2013 US dollars

Gross national saving: -3.7% of GDP (2013 est.)
country comparison to the world: 154
-5.8% of GDP (2012 est.)
-7.2% of GDP (2011 est.)

GDP—composition, by end use:
household consumption: 84%
government consumption: 12.7%
investment in fixed capital: 14%
investment in inventories: 0%
exports of goods and services: 24.7%
imports of goods and services: -35.3% (2013 est.)

GDP—composition, by sector of origin:
agriculture: 27.3%
industry: 16.4%
services: 56.3% (2013 est.)

Agriculture—products: coffee, vanilla, sugarcane, cloves, cocoa, rice, cassava (tapioca), beans, bananas, peanuts; livestock products

Industries: meat processing, seafood, soap, breweries, tanneries, sugar, textiles, glassware, cement, automobile assembly plant, paper, petroleum, tourism

Industrial production growth rate: 4% (2013 est.)
country comparison to the world: 72

Labor force: 9.504 million (2007)
country comparison to the world: 50

Population below poverty line: 50% (2004 est.)

Household income or consumption by percentage share: *lowest 10%:* 2.2%
highest 10%: 34.7% (2010 est.)

Distribution of family income—Gini index: 47.5 (2001)
country comparison to the world: 29
38.1 (1999)

Budget: *revenues:* $2.113 billion
expenditures: $2.356 billion (2013 est.)

Taxes and other revenues: 20.1% of GDP (2013 est.)
country comparison to the world: 167

Budget surplus (+) or deficit (-): -2.3% of GDP (2013 est.)
country comparison to the world: 95

Fiscal year: calendar year

Inflation rate (consumer prices): 8.8% (2013 est.)
country comparison to the world: 201
6.4% (2012 est.)

Central bank discount rate: 5% (31 December 2010 est.)
NA% (31 December 2009 est.)

Commercial bank prime lending rate: 44% (31 December 2013 est.)
country comparison to the world: 1
56.25% (31 December 2012 est.)

Stock of narrow money: $1.839 billion (31 December 2013 est.)
country comparison to the world: 129
$1.492 billion (31 December 2012 est.)

Stock of broad money: $3.163 billion (31 December 2013 est.)
country comparison to the world: 142
$2.357 billion (31 December 2012 est.)

Stock of domestic credit: $1.663 billion (31 December 2013 est.)
country comparison to the world: 139
$1.245 billion (31 December 2012 est.)

Market value of publicly traded shares: $NA

Current account balance: -$1.945 billion (2013 est.)
country comparison to the world: 142
-$1.989 billion (2012 est.)

Exports: $644.4 million (2013 est.)
country comparison to the world: 169
$592.1 million (2012 est.)

Exports—commodities: coffee, vanilla, shellfish, sugar, cotton cloth, clothing, chromite, petroleum products

Exports—partners: France 23.4%, China 6.6%, US 6.6%, Singapore 5.9%, Canada 5.5%, Germany 5.4%, Indonesia 5.3%, India 5.2%, South Africa 4.5% (2012)

Imports: $2.794 billion (2013 est.)
country comparison to the world: 151
$2.755 billion (2012 est.)

Imports—commodities: capital goods, petroleum, consumer goods, food

Imports—partners: China 17.7%, France 12.4%, South Africa 5.3%, India 5.1%, Mauritius 5%, Bahrain 4.7%, Kuwait 4.6% (2012)

Reserves of foreign exchange and gold: $1.249 billion (31 December 2013 est.)
country comparison to the world: 131
$1.191 billion (31 December 2012 est.)

Debt—external: $3.361 billion (31 December 2013 est.)
country comparison to the world: 132
$3.116 billion (31 December 2012 est.)

Stock of direct foreign investment—at home: $NA

Stock of direct foreign investment—abroad: $NA

Exchange rates: Malagasy ariary (MGA) per US dollar—
2,227.8 (2013 est.)
2,195 (2012 est.)
2,090 (2010 est.)
1,956.2 (2009)
1,654.78 (2008)

ENERGY

Electricity—production: 1.211 billion kWh (2010 est.)
country comparison to the world: 142

Electricity—consumption: 1.126 billion kWh (2010 est.)
country comparison to the world: 148

Electricity—exports: 0 kWh (2012 est.)
country comparison to the world: 161

Electricity—imports: 0 kWh (2012 est.)
country comparison to the world: 166

Electricity—installed generating capacity: 430,000 kW (2010 est.)
country comparison to the world: 143

Electricity—from fossil fuels: 65.6% of total installed capacity (2010 est.)
country comparison to the world: 120

Electricity—from nuclear fuels: 0% of total installed capacity (2010 est.)
country comparison to the world: 130

Electricity—from hydroelectric plants: 34.4% of total installed capacity (2010 est.)
country comparison to the world: 64

Electricity—from other renewable sources: 0% of total installed capacity (2010 est.)
country comparison to the world: 196

Crude oil—production: 0 bbl/day (2012 est.)
country comparison to the world: 190

Crude oil—exports: 0 bbl/day (2010 est.)
country comparison to the world: 146

Crude oil—imports: 0 bbl/day (2010 est.)
country comparison to the world: 85

Crude oil—proved reserves: 0 bbl (1 January 2013 es)
country comparison to the world: 158

Refined petroleum products—production: 0 bbl/day (2010 est.)
country comparison to the world: 167

Refined petroleum products—consumption: 17,480 bbl/day (2011 est.)
country comparison to the world: 136

Refined petroleum products—exports: 364.9 bbl/day (2010 est.)
country comparison to the world: 116

Refined petroleum products—imports: 12,120 bbl/day (2010 est.)
country comparison to the world: 127

Natural gas—production: 0 cu m (2011 est.)
country comparison to the world: 158

Natural gas—consumption: 0 cu m (2010 est.)
country comparison to the world: 165

Natural gas—exports: 0 cu m (2011 est.)
country comparison to the world: 139

Natural gas—imports: 0 cu m (2011 est.)
country comparison to the world: 90

Natural gas—proved reserves: 2.01 billion cu m (1 January 2012 es)
country comparison to the world: 99

Carbon dioxide emissions from consumption of energy: 1.843 million Mt (2011 est.)
country comparison to the world: 149

COMMUNICATIONS

Telephones—main lines in use: 143,700 (2012)
country comparison to the world: 138

Telephones—mobile cellular: 8.564 million (2012)
country comparison to the world: 89

Telephone system: *general assessment:* system is above average for the region; Antananarivo's main telephone exchange modernized in the late 1990s, but the rest of the analogue-based telephone system is poorly developed
domestic: combined fixed-line and mobile-cellular teledensity about 40 per 100 persons
international: country code—261; landing point for the EASSy, SEACOM, and LION fiber-optic submarine cable systems; satellite earth stations—2 (1 Intelsat—Indian Ocean, 1 Intersputnik—Atlantic Ocean region) (2010)

Broadcast media: state-owned Radio Nationale Malagasy (RNM) and Television Malagasy (TVM) have an extensive national network reach; privately owned radio and TV broadcasters in cities and major towns; state-run radio dominates in rural areas; relays of 2 international broadcasters are available in Antananarivo (2007)

Internet country code: .mg

Internet hosts: 38,392 (2012)
country comparison to the world: 102

Internet users: 319,900 (2009)
country comparison to the world: 127

TRANSPORTATION

Airports: 83 (2013)
country comparison to the world: 6 6

Airports—with paved runways: *total:* 2 6
over 3,047 m: 1
2,438 to 3,047 m: 2
1,524 to 2,437 m: 6
914 to 1,523 m: 16
under 914 m: 1 (2013)

Airports—with unpaved runways: *total:* 5 7
1,524 to 2,437 m: 1
914 to 1,523 m: 38
under 914 m: 18 (2013)

Railways: *total:* 854 km
country comparison to the world: 97
narrow gauge: 854 km 1.000-m gauge (2008)

Roadways: *total:* 34,476 km
country comparison to the world: 92
paved: 5,613 km
unpaved: 2,886 km (2010)

Waterways: 600 km (432 km navigable) (2011)
country comparison to the world: 80

Merchant marine: *total:* 1
country comparison to the world: 156
by type: cargo 1
registered in other countries: 1 (unknown 1) (2010)

Ports and terminals: *major seaport(s):* Antsiranana (Diego Suarez), Mahajanga, Toamasina, Toliara (Tulear)

MILITARY

Military branches: People's Armed Forces: Intervention Force, Development Force, and Aeronaval Force (navy and air); National Gendarmerie

Military service age and obligation: 18-25 years of age for male-only voluntary military service; no conscription; service obligation is 18 months for military or equivalent civil service; 20-30 years of age for National Gendarmerie recruits and 35 years of age for those with military experience (2012)

Manpower available for military service:
males age 16-49: 4,900,729
females age 16-49: 4,909,061 (2010 est.)

Manpower fit for military service:
males age 16-49: 3,390,071
females age 16-49: 3,682,180 (2010 est.)

Manpower reaching militarily significant age annually: *male:* 248,184
female: 246,769 (2010 est.)

Military expenditures: 0.69% of GDP (2012)
country comparison to the world: 119
0.73% of GDP (2011)
0.69% of GDP (2010)

TRANSNATIONAL ISSUES

Disputes—international: claims Bassas da India, Europa Island, Glorioso Islands, and Juan de Nova Island (all administered by France); the vegetated drying cays of Banc du Geyser, which were claimed by Madagascar in 1976, also fall within the EEZ claims of the Comoros and France (Glorioso Islands, part of the French Southern and Antarctic Lands)

Trafficking in persons: *current situation:* Madagascar is a source country for men, women, and children subjected to forced labor and women and children subjected to sex trafficking; poor Malagasy women hired as domestic workers in Lebanon and Kuwait are vulnerable to abuse by recruitment agencies and employers; an increasing number of Malagasy men were victimized by labor trafficking abroad in 2012; Malagasy children are subjected to domestic servitude, prostitution, forced begging, and forced labor within the country, often with the complicity of family members; coastal cities have child sex tourism trades, with Malagasy men being the main clients

tier rating: Tier 2 Watch List—Madagascar does not fully comply with the minimum standards for the elimination of trafficking; however, it is making significant efforts to do so; law enforcement authorities have made a significant increase in efforts in 2012, resulting in 30 trafficking-related prosecutions and two convictions; public officials complicity in human trafficking, however, remains a significant problem; the government has failed to identify and refer victims to protective services and has not supported NGO-run care facilities; the government also has not engaged any Middle Eastern governments regarding the protection of and legal remedies for Malagasy workers exploited abroad (2013)

Illicit drugs: illicit producer of cannabis (cultivated and wild varieties) used mostly for domestic consumption; transshipment point for heroin

MALAWI

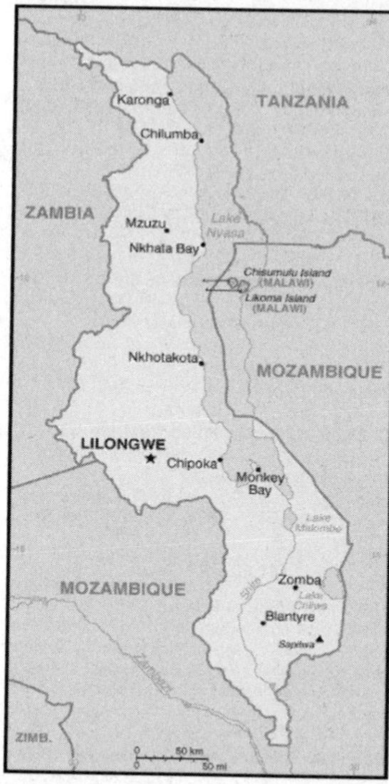

INTRODUCTION

Background: Established in 1891, the British protectorate of Nyasaland became the independent nation of Malawi in 1964. After three decades of one-party rule under President Hastings Kamuzu BANDA the country held multiparty elections in 1994, under a provisional constitution that came into full effect the following year. President Bingu wa MUTHARIKA, elected in May 2004 after a failed attempt by the previous president to amend the constitution to permit another term, struggled to assert his authority against his predecessor and subsequently started his own party, the Democratic Progressive Party (DPP) in 2005. MUTHARIKA was reelected to a second term in May 2009. He oversaw some economic improvement in his first term, but was accused of economic mismanagement and poor governance in his second term. He died abruptly in April 2012 and was succeeded by his vice president, Joyce BANDA, who had earlier started her own party, the People's Party (PP). Population growth, increasing pressure on agricultural lands, corruption, and the scourge of HIV/AIDS pose major problems for Malawi.

GEOGRAPHY

Location: Southern Africa, east of Zambia, west and north of Mozambique

Geographic coordinates: 13 30 S, 34 00 E

Map references: Africa

Area: *total:* 118,484 sq km
country comparison to the world: 100
land: 94,080 sq km
water: 24,404 sq km

Area—comparative: slightly smaller than Pennsylvania

Land boundaries: *total:* 2,881 km
border countries: Mozambique 1,569 km, Tanzania 475 km, Zambia 837 km

Coastline: 0 km (landlocked)

Maritime claims: none (landlocked)

Climate: sub-tropical; rainy season (November to May); dry season (May to November)

Terrain: narrow elongated plateau with rolling plains, rounded hills, some mountains
Elevation extremes: lowest point: junction of the Shire River and international boundary with Mozambique 37 m
highest point: Sapitwa (Mount Mlanje) 3,002 m

Natural resources: limestone, arable land, hydropower, unexploited deposits of uranium, coal, and bauxite

Land use: *arable land:* 30.38%
permanent crops: 1.1%
other: 68.52% (2011)

Irrigated land: 735 sq km (2006)

Total renewable water resources: 17.28 cu km (2011)

Freshwater withdrawal (domestic/industrial/agricultural): *total:* 1.36 cu km/yr (11%/4%/86%)
per capita: 99.86 cu m/yr (2005)

Natural hazards: NA

Environment—current issues: deforestation; land degradation; water pollution from agricultural runoff, sewage, industrial wastes; siltation of spawning grounds endangers fish populations

Environment—international agreements:
party to: Biodiversity, Climate Change, Climate Change-Kyoto Protocol, Desertification, Endangered Species, Environmental Modification, Hazardous Wastes, Marine Life Conservation, Ozone Layer Protection, Ship Pollution, Wetlands
signed, but not ratified: Law of the Sea

Geography—note: landlocked; Lake Nyasa, some 580 km long, is the country's most prominent physical feature; it contains more fish species than any other lake on earth

PEOPLE AND SOCIETY

Nationality: *noun:* Malawian(s)
adjective: Malawian

Ethnic groups: Chewa 32.6%, Lomwe 17.6%, Yao 13.5%, Ngoni 11.5%, Tumbuka 8.8%, Nyanja 5.8%, Sena 3.6%, Tonga 2.1%, Ngonde 1%, other 3.5%

Languages: English (official), Chichewa (common), Chinyanja, Chiyao, Chitumbuka, Chilomwe, Chinkhonde, Chingoni, Chisena, Chitonga, Chinyakyusa, Chilambya

Religions: Christian 82.6%, Muslim 13%, other 1.9%, none 2.5% (2008 est.)

Population: 17,377,468 (July 2014 est.)
country comparison to the world: 64
note: estimates for this country explicitly take into account the effects of excess mortality due to AIDS; this can result in lower life expectancy, higher infant mortality, higher death rates, lower population growth rates, and changes in the distribution of population by age and sex than would otherwise be expected

Age structure: *0-14 years:* 46.9% (male 4,056,810/female 4,100,841)
15-24 years: 20.2% (male 1,748,919/female 1,765,212)
25-54 years: 27.1% (male 2,329,952/female 2,371,274)
55-64 years: 2.7% (male 256,034/female 280,997)
65 years and over: 2.7% (male 206,923/female 260,506) (2014 est.)

Dependency ratios:
total dependency ratio: 94.1 %
youth dependency ratio: 87.9 %
elderly dependency ratio: 6.2 %
potential support ratio: 16.1 (2013)

Median age: *total:* 16.3 years
male: 16.2 years
female: 16.4 years (2014 est.)

Population growth rate: 3.33% (2014 est.)
country comparison to the world: 6

Birth rate: 41.8 births/1,000 population (2014 est.)
country comparison to the world: 7

Death rate: 8.74 deaths/1,000 population (2014 est.)
country comparison to the world: 72

Net migration rate: 0.25 migrant(s)/1,000 population (2014 est.)
country comparison to the world: 75

Urbanization: *urban population:* 15.7% of total population (2011)
rate of urbanization: 4.2% annual rate of change (2010-15 est.)

Major urban areas—population: Blantyre 856,000; LILONGWE (capital) 821,000 (2009)

Sex ratio: *at birth:* 1.02 male(s)/female
0-14 years: 0.99 male(s)/female
15-24 years: 0.99 male(s)/female
25-54 years: 0.98 male(s)/female
55-64 years: 0.98 male(s)/female
65 years and over: 0.75 male(s)/female
total population: 0.99 male(s)/female (2014 est.)

Mother's mean age at first birth: 18.9
note: median age at first birth among women 25-29 (2010 est.)

Maternal mortality rate: 460 deaths/100,000 live births (2010)
country comparison to the world: 24

Infant mortality rate: *total:* 48.01 deaths/1,000 live births
country comparison to the world: 42
male: 54.94 deaths/1,000 live births
female: 40.98 deaths/1,000 live births (2014 est.)

Life expectancy at birth: total population: 59.99 years
country comparison to the world: 194
male: 58.04 years
female: 61.97 years (2014 est.)

Total fertility rate: 5.66 children born/woman (2014 est.)
country comparison to the world: 8

Contraceptive prevalence rate: 46.1% (2010)

Health expenditures: 8.4% of GDP (2011)
country comparison to the world: 56

Physicians density: 0.02 physicians/1,000 population (2008)

Hospital bed density: 1.3 beds/1,000 population (2011)

Drinking water source:
improved:
urban: 94.6% of population
rural: 81.7% of population
total: 83.7% of population

unimproved:
urban: 5.4% of population
rural: 18.3% of population
total: 16.3% of population (2011 est.)

Sanitation facility access:
improved:
urban: 49.6% of population
rural: 53.5% of population
total: 52.9% of population
unimproved:
urban: 50.4% of population
rural: 46.5% of population
total: 47.1% of population (2011 est.)

HIV/AIDS—adult prevalence rate: 10.8% (2012 est.)
country comparison to the world: 9

HIV/AIDS—people living with HIV/AIDS: 1,129,800 (2012 est.)
country comparison to the world: 10

HIV/AIDS—deaths: 45,600 (2012 est.)
country comparison to the world: 9

Major infectious diseases: *degree of risk:* very high
food or waterborne diseases: bacterial and protozoal diarrhea, hepatitis A, and typhoid fever
vectorborne diseases: malaria and dengue fever
water contact disease: schistosomiasis
animal contact disease: rabies (2013)

Obesity—adult prevalence rate: 4.3% (2008)
country comparison to the world: 168

Children under the age of 5 years underweight: 13.8% (2010)
country comparison to the world: 55

Education expenditures: 5.4% of GDP (2011)
country comparison to the world: 60

Literacy: *definition:* age 15 and over can read and write
total population: 74.8%
male: 81.1%
female: 68.5% (2010 est.)

School life expectancy (primary to tertiary education): *total:* 11 years
male: 11 years
female: 11 years (2011)

Child labor—children ages 5-14: *total number:* 993,318
percentage: 26 % (2006 est.)

GOVERNMENT

Country name: *conventional long form:* Republic of Malawi
conventional short form: Malawi
local long form: Dziko la Malawi
local short form: Malawi
former: British Central African Protectorate, Nyasaland Protectorate, Nyasaland

Government type: multiparty democracy

Capital: *name:* Lilongwe

geographic coordinates: 13 58 S, 33 47 E
time difference: UTC+2 (7 hours ahead of Washington, DC during Standard Time)

Administrative divisions: 28 districts; Balaka, Blantyre, Chikwawa, Chiradzulu, Chitipa, Dedza, Dowa, Karonga, Kasungu, Likoma, Lilongwe, Machinga, Mangochi, Mchinji, Mulanje, Mwanza, Mzimba, Neno, Ntcheu, Nkhata Bay, Nkhotakota, Nsanje, Ntchisi, Phalombe, Rumphi, Salima, Thyolo, Zomba

Independence: 6 July 1964 (from the UK)

National holiday: Independence Day (Republic Day), 6 July (1964)

Constitution: previous 1953 (preindependence), 1966; latest drafted January to May 1994, approved 16 May 1994, entered into force 18 May 1995; amended several times, last in 2013 (2007)

Legal system: mixed legal system of English common law and customary law; judicial review of legislative acts in the Supreme Court of Appeal

International law organization participation: accepts compulsory ICJ jurisdiction with reservations; accepts ICCt jurisdiction

Suffrage: 18 years of age; universal

Executive branch: *chief of state:* President Joyce BANDA (since 7 April 2012); Vice President Khumbo Hastings KACHALI (since 11 April 2012); note—the president is both the chief of state and head of government; former President Bingu wa MUTHARIKA died on 5 April 2012, Vice President Joyce BANDA was subsequently sworn in on 7 April 2012
head of government: President Joyce BANDA (since 7 April 2012); Vice President Khumbo Hastings KACHALI (since 11 April 2012)
cabinet: 26-32-member Cabinet named by the president (For more information visit the World Leaders website)
elections: president elected by popular vote for a five-year term (eligible for a second term); election last held on 19 May 2009 (next to be held 20 May 2014)
election results: Bingu wa MUTHARIKA elected president; percent of vote—Bingu wa MUTHARIKA 66%, John TEMBO 30.7%, other 3.3%; note—MUTHARIKA passed away on 5 April 2012 and was succeeded by then vice president Joyce BANDA

Legislative branch: unicameral National Assembly (193 seats; members elected by popular vote to serve five-year terms)
elections: last held on 19 May 2009 (next to be held 20 May 2014)
election results: percent of vote by party—NA; seats by party—DPP 114, MCP 26, UDF 17, independents 32, other 4

Judicial branch: *highest court(s):* Supreme Court of Appeal (consists of the chief justice and at least 3 judges)
judge selection and term of office: Supreme Court chief justice appointed by the president and confirmed by the National Assembly; other judges appointed by the president upon recommendation of the Judicial Service Commission, which regulates judicial officers; judges serve until age 65
subordinate courts: High Court; magistrate courts; Industrial Relations Court; district and city traditional or local courts

Political parties and leaders: Alliance for Democracy or AFORD [Godfrey SHAWA]; Chipani Cha Fuko or CCP [Davis KATSONGA PHIRI]; Christian Liberation Party or CONU [Sylvester CHABUKA]; Democratic Progressive Party or DPP [Peter MUTHARIKA]; Malawi Congress Party or MCP [Lazarous CHAKWERA]; Malawi Democratic Party or MDP [Kampelo KALUA]; Malawi Forum for Unity and Development or MAFUNDE [George MNESA]; National Rainbow Coalition or NARC [Loveness GONDWE]; National Salvation Front or NASAF [James NYONDO]; Nthanda Congress Party or NCP [Dr. Chakhumbila KHAILA]; New Labour Party or NLP [Friday JUMBE]; New Republican Party [Gwanda CHAKUWAMBA]; People's Party or PP [Joyce BANDA]; People's Progressive Movement or PPM [Mark Katsonga PHIRI]; People's Transformation Movement or PETRA [Kamuzu CHIBAMBO]; Umodzi Party or UP [John CHISI, Interim president]; United Democratic Front or UDF [Atupele MULUZI]; United Independent Party or UIP [Helen SINGH]

Political pressure groups and leaders: Council for NGOs in Malawi or CONGOMA (human rights, democracy, and development); Human Rights Consultative Committee or HRCC (human rights); Malawi Economic Justice Network or MEJN (pro economic growth, development, government accountability); Malawi Law Society (an umbrella organization of all lawyers in Malawi); Public Affairs Committee or PAC (promotes democracy, development, peace and unity)

International organization participation: ACP, AfDB, AU, C, CD, COMESA, FAO, G-77, IAEA, IBRD, ICAO, ICRM, IDA, IFAD, IFC, IFRCS, ILO, IMF, IMO, Interpol, IOC, IPU, ISO (correspondent), ITSO, ITU, ITUC (NGOs), MIGA, MINURSO, MONUSCO, NAM, OPCW, SADC, UN, UNAMID, UNCTAD, UNESCO, UNIDO, UNOCI, UNWTO, UPU, WCO, WFTU (NGOs), WHO, WIPO, WMO, WTO

Diplomatic representation in the US: *chief of mission:* Ambassador Stephen Dick Tennyson MATENSE (since 10 September 2010)
chancery: 2408 Massachusetts Avenue NW, Washington, DC 20008
telephone: [1] (202) 721-0270
FAX: [1] (202) 721-0288

Diplomatic representation from the US: *chief of mission:* Ambassador Jeanine E. JACKSON (since 11 September 2011)
embassy: 16 Jomo Kenyatta Road, Lilongwe 3
mailing address: P. O. Box 30016, Lilongwe 3, Malawi
telephone: [265] (1) 773-166
FAX: [265] (1) 770-471

Flag description: three equal horizontal bands of black (top), red, and green with a radiant, rising, red sun centered on the black band; black represents the native peoples, red the blood shed in their struggle for freedom, and green the color of nature; the rising sun represents the hope of freedom for the continent of Africa

National anthem: *name:* "Mulungu dalitsa Malawi" (Oh God Bless Our Land of Malawi)
lyrics/music: Michael-Fredrick Paul SAUKA
note: adopted 1964

ECONOMY

Economy—overview: Landlocked Malawi ranks among the world's most densely populated and least developed countries. The economy is predominately agricultural with about 80% of the population living in rural areas. Agriculture, which has benefited from fertilizer subsidies since 2006, accounts for one-third of GDP and 90% of export revenues. The performance of the tobacco sector is key to short-term growth as tobacco accounts for more than half of exports. The economy depends on substantial inflows of economic assistance from the IMF, the World Bank, and individual donor nations. In 2006, Malawi was approved for relief under the Heavily Indebted Poor Countries (HIPC) program. In December 2007, the US granted Malawi eligibility status to receive financial support within the Millennium Challenge Corporation (MCC) initiative. The government faces many challenges including developing a market economy, improving educational facilities, facing up to environmental problems, dealing with the rapidly growing problem of HIV/AIDS, and satisfying foreign donors that fiscal discipline is being tightened. Between 2005 and 2009 President BANDA'S government exhibited improved financial discipline under the guidance of Finance Minister Goodall GONDWE and signed a three year IMF Poverty Reduction and Growth Facility (PRGF) worth $56 million. The government announced infrastructure projects that could yield improvements, such as a new oil pipeline for better fuel access, and the potential for a waterway link through Mozambican rivers to the ocean for better transportation options. Since 2009, however, Malawi has experienced some setbacks, including a general shortage of foreign exchange, which has damaged its ability to pay for imports, and fuel shortages that hinder transportation and productivity. Investment has fallen continuously for several years and in 2013 amounted to just 13% of GDP. The government has failed to address barriers to investment such as unreliable power, water shortages, poor telecommunications infrastructure, and the high costs of services. Donors, who provided an average of 36% of government revenue in the past five years, suspended general budget support for Malawi in 2011 due to a negative IMF review and governance issues.

GDP (purchasing power parity): $15.02 billion (2013 est.)
country comparison to the world: 143
$14.3 billion (2012 est.)
$14.04 billion (2011 est.)
note: data are in 2013 US dollars

GDP (official exchange rate): $3.683 billion (2013 est.)

GDP—real growth rate: 5% (2013 est.)
country comparison to the world: 59
1.9% (2012 est.)
4.3% (2011 est.)

GDP—per capita (PPP): $900 (2013 est.)
country comparison to the world: 221
$900 (2012 est.)
$900 (2011 est.)
note: data are in 2013 US dollars

Gross national saving: 8.2% of GDP (2013 est.)
country comparison to the world: 145
8.2% of GDP (2012 est.)
1.9% of GDP (2011 est.)

GDP—composition, by end use:
household consumption: 73.6%
government consumption: 20.7%
investment in fixed capital: 13%
investment in inventories: 1.9%
exports of goods and services: 29.2%
imports of goods and services: -38.4% (2013 est.)

GDP—composition, by sector of origin:
agriculture: 29.4%
industry: 18.9%
services: 51.7% (2013 est.)

Agriculture—products: tobacco, sugarcane, cotton, tea, corn, potatoes, cassava (tapioca), sorghum, pulses, groundnuts, Macadamia nuts; cattle, goats

Industries: tobacco, tea, sugar, sawmill products, cement, consumer goods

Industrial production growth rate: 2.8% (2013 est.)
country comparison to the world: 109

Labor force: 5.747 million (2007 est.)
country comparison to the world: 68

Labor force—by occupation: *agriculture:* 90%
industry and services: 10% (2003 est.)

Unemployment rate: NA%

Population below poverty line: 53% (2004)

Household income or consumption by percentage share: *lowest 10%:* 3%
highest 10%: 31.9% (2004)

Distribution of family income—Gini index: 39 (2004)
country comparison to the world: 68

Budget: *revenues:* $1.347 billion
expenditures: $1.4 billion (2013 est.)

Taxes and other revenues: 36.6% of GDP (2013 est.)
country comparison to the world: 58

Budget surplus (+) or deficit (-): -1.4% of GDP (2013 est.)
country comparison to the world: 69

Public debt: 50.8% of GDP (2013 est.)
country comparison to the world: 66
62.7% of GDP (2012 est.)

Fiscal year: 1 July—30 June

Inflation rate (consumer prices): 26.9% (2013 est.)
country comparison to the world: 220
21.4% (2012 est.)

Central bank discount rate: 15% (31 December 2009)
country comparison to the world: 10
15% (31 December 2008)

Commercial bank prime lending rate: 29.5% (31 December 2013 est.)
country comparison to the world: 3
32.4% (31 December 2012 est.)

Stock of narrow money: $585.3 million (31 December 2013 est.)
country comparison to the world: 157
$457.6 million (31 December 2012 est.)

Stock of broad money: $1.494 billion (31 December 2013 est.)
country comparison to the world: 158
$1.153 billion (31 December 2012 est.)

Stock of domestic credit: $1.243 billion (31 December 2013 est.)
country comparison to the world: 151
$1.128 billion (31 December 2012 est.)

Market value of publicly traded shares: $753.6 million (31 December 2012 est.)
country comparison to the world: 104
$1.384 billion (31 December 2011)
$1.363 billion (31 December 2010 est.)

Current account balance: -$280.1 million (2013 est.)
country comparison to the world: 91
-$315.1 million (2012 est.)

Exports: $1.427 billion (2013 est.)
country comparison to the world: 149
$1.224 billion (2012 est.)

Exports—commodities: tobacco 53%, tea, sugar, cotton, coffee, peanuts, wood products, apparel

Exports—partners: Canada 10.6%, Zimbabwe 9.3%, Germany 7.3%, South Africa 6.6%, Russia 6.5%, US 6.1%, China 4.2% (2012)

Imports: $2.42 billion (2013 est.)
country comparison to the world: 157
$2.151 billion (2012 est.)

Imports—commodities: food, petroleum products, semi-manufactures, consumer goods, transportation equipment

Imports—partners: South Africa 27%, China 16.6%, India 8.7%, Zambia 8.5%, Tanzania 5.1%, US 4.3% (2012)

Reserves of foreign exchange and gold: $364.2 million (31 December 2013 est.)
country comparison to the world: 152
$246 million (31 December 2012 est.)

Debt—external: $1.556 billion (31 December 2013 est.)
country comparison to the world: 149
$1.354 billion (31 December 2012 est.)

Stock of direct foreign investment—at home: $NA

Stock of direct foreign investment—abroad: $NA

Exchange rates: Malawian kwachas (MWK) per US dollar—
342.1 (2013 est.)
249.11 (2012 est.)
150.49 (2010 est.)
141.14 (2009)
142.41 (2008)

ENERGY

Electricity—production: 1.973 billion kWh (2010 est.)
country comparison to the world: 136

Electricity—consumption: 1.835 billion kWh (2010 est.)
country comparison to the world: 141

Electricity—exports: 0 kWh (2012 est.)
country comparison to the world: 165

Electricity—imports: 0 kWh (2012 est.)
country comparison to the world: 168

Electricity—installed generating capacity: 287,000 kW (2010 est.)
country comparison to the world: 151

Electricity—from fossil fuels: 0.3% of total installed capacity (2010 est.)
country comparison to the world: 207

Electricity—from nuclear fuels: 0% of total installed capacity (2010 est.)
country comparison to the world: 135

Electricity—from hydroelectric plants: 99.7% of total installed capacity (2010 est.)
country comparison to the world: 4

Electricity—from other renewable sources: 0% of total installed capacity (2010 est.)
country comparison to the world: 200

Crude oil—production: 200 bbl/day (2012 est.)
country comparison to the world: 118

Crude oil—exports: 0 bbl/day (2010 est.)
country comparison to the world: 150

Crude oil—imports: 0 bbl/day (2010 est.)
country comparison to the world: 90

Crude oil—proved reserves: 0 bbl (1 January 2013 es)
country comparison to the world: 161

Refined petroleum products—production: 0 bbl/day (2010 est.)
country comparison to the world: 171

Refined petroleum products—consumption: 12,060 bbl/day (2011 est.)
country comparison to the world: 150

Refined petroleum products—exports: 0 bbl/day (2010 est.)
country comparison to the world: 196

Refined petroleum products—imports: 6,059 bbl/day (2010 est.)
country comparison to the world: 142

Natural gas—production: 0 cu m (2011 est.)
country comparison to the world: 163

Natural gas—consumption: 0 cu m (2010 est.)
country comparison to the world: 169

Natural gas—exports: 0 cu m (2011 est.)
country comparison to the world: 144

Natural gas—imports: 0 cu m (2011 est.)
country comparison to the world: 94

Natural gas—proved reserves: 0 cu m (1 January 2013 es)
country comparison to the world: 167

Carbon dioxide emissions from consumption of energy: 956,900 Mt (2011 est.)
country comparison to the world: 168

COMMUNICATIONS

Telephones—main lines in use: 227,300 (2012)

country comparison to the world: 126

Telephones—mobile cellular: 4.42 million (2012)
country comparison to the world: 117

Telephone system: *general assessment:* rudimentary; privatization of Malawi Telecommunications (MTL), a necessary step in bringing improvement to telecommunications services, completed in 2006
domestic: limited fixed-line subscribership of about 1 per 100 persons; mobile-cellular services are expanding but network coverage is limited and is based around the main urban areas; mobile-cellular subscribership about 25 per 100 persons
international: country code—265; satellite earth stations—2 Intelsat (1 Indian Ocean, 1 Atlantic Ocean) (2010)

Broadcast media: radio is the main broadcast medium; state-run radio has the widest geographic broadcasting reach, but about a dozen privately owned radio stations broadcast in major urban areas; the single TV network is government-owned; relays of multiple international broadcasters are available (2007)

Internet country code: .mw

Internet hosts: 1,099 (2012)
country comparison to the world: 171

Internet users: 716,400 (2009)
country comparison to the world: 109

TRANSPORTATION

Airports: 32 (2013)
country comparison to the world: 113

Airports—with paved runways: *total:* 7
over 3,047 m: 1
1,524 to 2,437 m: 2
914 to 1,523 m: 4 (2013)

Airports—with unpaved runways: *total:* 2 5
1,524 to 2,437 m: 1
914 to 1,523 m: 11
under 914 m: 13 (2013)

Railways: *total:* 797 km
country comparison to the world: 99
narrow gauge: 797 km 1.067-m gauge (2008)

Roadways: *total:* 15,450 km
country comparison to the world: 120
paved: 6,951 km
unpaved: 8,499 km (2011)

Waterways: 700 km (on Lake Nyasa [Lake Malawi] and Shire River) (2010)
country comparison to the world: 76

Ports and terminals: *lake port(s):* Chipoka, Monkey Bay, Nkhata Bay, Nkhotakota, Chilumba

MILITARY

Military branches: Malawi Defense Forces (MDF): Army (includes Air Wing, Marine Unit) (2012)

Military service age and obligation: 18 years of age for voluntary military service; high school equivalent required for enlisted recruits and college equivalent for officer recruits; initial engagement is 7 years for enlisted personnel and 10 years for officers (2014)

Manpower available for military service:
males age 16-49: 3,514,809 (2010 est.)

Manpower fit for military service:
males age 16-49: 2,132,909
females age 16-49: 2,043,925 (2010 est.)

Manpower reaching militarily significant age annually: *male:* 183,683
female: 183,028 (2010 est.)

Military expenditures: 0.93% of GDP (2012)
country comparison to the world: 105
0.79% of GDP (2011)
0.93% of GDP (2010)

TRANSNATIONAL ISSUES

Disputes—international: disputes with Tanzania over the boundary in Lake Nyasa (Lake Malawi) and the meandering Songwe River remain dormant

MALAYSIA

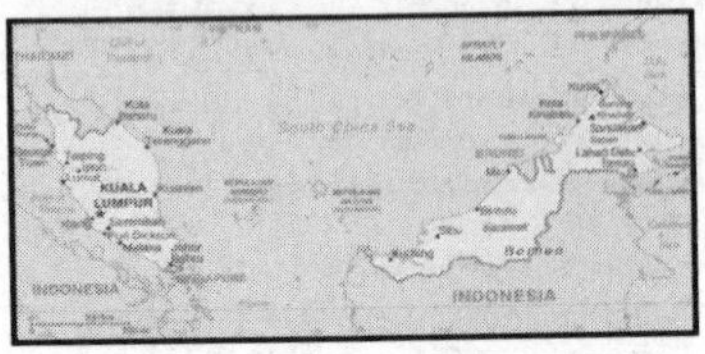

INTRODUCTION

Background: During the late 18th and 19th centuries, Great Britain established colonies and protectorates in the area of current Malaysia; these were occupied by Japan from 1942 to 1945. In 1948, the British-ruled territories on the Malay Peninsula except Singapore formed the Federation of Malaya, which became independent in 1957. Malaysia was formed in 1963 when the former British colonies of Singapore, as well as Sabah and Sarawak on the northern coast of Borneo, joined the Federation. The first several years of the country's independence were marred by a communist insurgency, Indonesian confrontation with Malaysia, Philippine claims to Sabah, and Singapore's withdrawal in 1965. During the 22-year term of Prime Minister MAHATHIR bin Mohamad (1981-2003), Malaysia was successful in diversifying its economy from dependence on exports of raw materials to the development of manufacturing, services, and tourism. Prime Minister Mohamed NAJIB bin Abdul Razak (in office since April 2009) has continued these pro-business policies and has introduced some civil reforms.

GEOGRAPHY

Location: Southeastern Asia, peninsula bordering Thailand and northern one-third of the island of Borneo, bordering Indonesia, Brunei, and the South China Sea, south of Vietnam

Geographic coordinates: 2 30 N, 112 30 E

Map references: Southeast Asia

Area: *total:* 329,847 sq km
country comparison to the world: 67
land: 328,657 sq km
water: 1,190 sq km

Area—comparative: slightly larger than New Mexico

Land boundaries: *total:* 2,669 km
border countries: Brunei 381 km, Indonesia 1,782 km, Thailand 506 km

Coastline: 4,675 km (Peninsular Malaysia 2,068 km, East Malaysia 2,607 km)

Maritime claims: *territorial sea:* 12 nm
exclusive economic zone: 200 nm
continental shelf: 200 m depth or to the depth of exploitation; specified boundary in the South China Sea

Climate: tropical; annual southwest (April to October) and northeast (October to February) monsoons

Terrain: coastal plains rising to hills and mountains

Elevation extremes: *lowest point:* Indian Ocean 0 m
highest point: Gunung Kinabalu 4,100 m

Natural resources: tin, petroleum, timber, copper, iron ore, natural gas, bauxite

Land use: *arable land:* 5.44%
permanent crops: 17.49%
other: 77.07% (2011)

Irrigated land: 3,800 sq km (2009)

Total renewable water resources: 580 cu km (2011)

Freshwater withdrawal (domestic/industrial/agricultural): *total:* 11.2 cu km/yr (35%/43%/22%)
per capita: 414 cu m/yr (2005)

Natural hazards: flooding; landslides; forest fires

Environment—current issues: air pollution from industrial and vehicular emissions; water pollution from raw sewage; deforestation; smoke/haze from Indonesian forest fires

Environment—international agreements:
party to: Biodiversity, Climate Change, Climate Change-Kyoto Protocol, Desertification, Endangered Species, Hazardous Wastes, Law of the Sea, Marine Life Conservation, Ozone Layer Protection, Ship Pollution, Tropical Timber 83, Tropical Timber 94, Wetlands
signed, but not ratified: none of the selected agreements

Geography—note: strategic location along Strait of Malacca and southern South China Sea

PEOPLE AND SOCIETY

Nationality: *noun:* Malaysian(s)
adjective: Malaysian

Ethnic groups: Malay 50.1%, Chinese 22.6%, indigenous 11.8%, Indian 6.7%, other 0.7%, non-citizens 8.2% (2010 est.)

Languages: Bahasa Malaysia (official), English, Chinese (Cantonese, Mandarin, Hokkien, Hakka, Hainan, Foochow), Tamil, Telugu, Malayalam, Panjabi, Thai *note:* in East Malaysia there are several indigenous languages; most widely spoken are Iban and Kadazan

Religions: Muslim (official) 61.3%, Buddhist 19.8%, Christian 9.2%, Hindu 6.3%, Confucianism, Taoism, other traditional Chinese religions 1.3%, other 0.4%, none 0.8%, unspecified 1% (2010 est.)

Population: 30,073,353 (July 2014 est.)
country comparison to the world: 44

Age structure: *0-14 years:* 28.8% (male 4,456,033/female 4,206,727)
15-24 years: 16.9% (male 2,580,486/female 2,511,579)
25-54 years: 41.2% (male 6,277,694/female 6,114,312)
55-64 years: 5.5% (male 1,163,861/female 1,122,746)
65 years and over: 5.3% (male 777,338/female 862,577) (2014 est.)

Dependency ratios:
total dependency ratio: 45.9 %
youth dependency ratio: 38.1 %
elderly dependency ratio: 7.8 %
potential support ratio: 12.8 (2013)

Median age: *total:* 27.7 years
male: 27.4 years
female: 27.9 years (2014 est.)

Population growth rate: 1.47% (2014 est.)
country comparison to the world: 83

Birth rate: 20.06 births/1,000 population (2014 est.)
country comparison to the world: 85

Death rate: 5 deaths/1,000 population (2014 est.)
country comparison to the world: 188

Net migration rate: -0.34 migrant(s)/1,000 population
country comparison to the world: 131
note: does not reflect net flow of an unknown number of illegal immigrants from other countries in the region (2014 est.)

Urbanization: *urban population:* 72.8% of total population (2011)
rate of urbanization: 2.49% annual rate of change (2010-15 est.)

Major urban areas—population: KUALA LUMPUR (capital) 1.493 million; Klang 1.071 million; Johor Bahru 958,000 (2009)

Sex ratio: *at birth:* 1.07 male(s)/female
0-14 years: 1.06 male(s)/female
15-24 years: 1.03 male(s)/female
25-54 years: 1.03 male(s)/female
55-64 years: 1.03 male(s)/female
65 years and over: 0.89 male(s)/female
total population: 1.03 male(s)/female (2014 est.)

Maternal mortality rate: 29 deaths/100,000 live births (2010)
country comparison to the world: 125

Infant mortality rate: *total:* 13.69 deaths/1,000 live births
country comparison to the world: 115
male: 15.82 deaths/1,000 live births
female: 11.42 deaths/1,000 live births (2014 est.)

Life expectancy at birth: *total population:* 74.52 years
country comparison to the world: 110
male: 71.74 years
female: 77.48 years (2014 est.)

Total fertility rate: 2.58 children born/woman (2014 est.)
country comparison to the world: 76

Contraceptive prevalence rate: 49% (2004)

Health expenditures: 3.6% of GDP (2011)
country comparison to the world: 175

Physicians density: 1.2 physicians/1,000 population (2010)

Hospital bed density: 1.8 beds/1,000 population (2011)

Drinking water source:
improved:
urban: 100% of population
rural: 98.5% of population
total: 99.6% of population
unimproved:
urban: 0% of population
rural: 1.5% of population
total: 0.4% of population (2011 est.)

Sanitation facility access:
improved:
urban: 96.1% of population
rural: 94.6% of population
total: 95.7% of population
unimproved:
urban: 3.9% of population
rural: 5.4% of population
total: 4.3% of population (2011 est.)

HIV/AIDS—adult prevalence rate: 0.4% (2012 est.)
country comparison to the world: 82

HIV/AIDS—people living with HIV/AIDS: 82,000 (2012 est.)
country comparison to the world: 49

HIV/AIDS—deaths: 5,200 (2009 est.)
country comparison to the world: 38

Major infectious diseases: *degree of risk:* intermediate
food or waterborne diseases: bacterial diarrhea
vectorborne diseases: dengue fever
water contact disease: leptospirosis
note: highly pathogenic H5N1 avian influenza has been identified in this country; it poses a negligible risk with extremely rare cases possible among US citizens who have close contact with birds (2013)

Obesity—adult prevalence rate: 14% (2008)
country comparison to the world: 123

Children under the age of 5 years underweight: 12.9% (2006)
country comparison to the world: 58

Education expenditures: 5.9% of GDP (2011)
country comparison to the world: 46

Literacy: *definition:* age 15 and over can read and write
total population: 93.1%
male: 95.4%
female: 90.7% (2010 est.)

School life expectancy (primary to tertiary education): *total:* 13 years
male: 13 years
female: 13 years (2005)

Unemployment, youth ages 15-24: *total:* 10.3%
country comparison to the world: 109
male: 9.8%
female: 11% (2012)

GOVERNMENT

Country name: *conventional long form:* none
conventional short form: Malaysia
local long form: none
local short form: Malaysia
former: Federation of Malaya

Government type: constitutional monarchy
note: nominally headed by paramount ruler (commonly referred to as the king) and a bicameral Parliament consisting of a nonelected upper house and an elected lower house; all Peninsular Malaysian states have hereditary rulers (commonly referred to as sultans) except Melaka (Malacca) and Pulau Pinang (Penang); those two states along with Sabah and Sarawak in East Malaysia have governors appointed by government; powers of state governments are limited by federal constitution; under terms of federation, Sabah and Sarawak retain certain constitutional prerogatives (e.g., right to maintain their own immigration controls)

Capital: *name:* Kuala Lumpur
geographic coordinates: 3 10 N, 101 42 E
time difference: UTC+8 (13 hours ahead of Washington, DC during Standard Time)
note: Putrajaya is referred to as an administrative center not the capital; Parliament meets in Kuala Lumpur

Administrative divisions: 13 states (negeri-negeri, singular—negeri); Johor, Kedah, Kelantan, Melaka, Negeri Sembilan, Pahang, Perak, Perlis, Pulau Pinang, Sabah, Sarawak, Selangor, Terengganu; and 1 federal territory (Wilayah Persekutuan) with 3 components, Kuala Lumpur, Labuan, and Putrajaya

Independence: 31 August 1957 (from the UK)

National holiday: Independence Day 31 August (1957) (independence of Malaya); Malaysia Day 16 September (1963) (formation of Malaysia)

Constitution: previous 1948; latest drafted 21 February 1957, effective 27 August 1957; amended many times, last in 2007 (2010)

Legal system: mixed legal system of English common law, Islamic law, and customary law; judicial review of legislative acts in the Supreme Court at request of supreme head of the federation

International law organization participation: has not submitted an ICJ jurisdiction declaration; non-party state to the ICCt

Suffrage: 21 years of age; universal

Executive branch: *chief of state:* King Tuanku ABDUL HALIM Mu'adzam Shah (selected on 13 December 2011; installed on 11 April 2012); the position of the king is primarily ceremonial
head of government: Prime Minister Mohamed NAJIB bin Abdul Najib Razak (since 3 April 2009); Deputy Prime Minister MUHYIDDIN bin Mohamed Yassin (since 9 April 2009)
cabinet: Cabinet appointed by the prime minister from among the members of Parliament with consent of the king (For more information visit the World Leaders website)
elections: kings are elected by and from the hereditary rulers of nine of the states for five-year terms; selection is based on the principle of rotation among rulers of states; elections were last held on 14 October 2011 (next to be held in 2016); prime ministers are designated from among the members of the House of Representatives; following legislative elections, the leader who commands the support of the majority of members in the House becomes prime minister (since independence this has been the leader of the UMNO party)
election results: Tuanku ABDUL HALIM Mu'adzam Shah elected king by fellow hereditary rulers of nine states; Mohamed NAJIB bin Abdul Najib Razak was sworn in as prime minister the

day after his National Front (BN) coalition won a majority of seats during the 5 May 2013 national election; NAJIB was re-elected uncontested as UMNO president on 19 October 2013

Legislative branch: bicameral Parliament or Parlimen consists of Senate or Dewan Negara (70 seats; 44 members appointed by the king, 26 elected by 13 state legislatures to serve three-year terms with a two term limit) and House of Representatives or Dewan Rakyat (222 seats; members elected in 222 constituencies in a first-pass-the-post system to serve up to five-year terms)
elections: House of Representatives—last held on 5 May 2013 (next to be held by May 2018)
election results: House of Representatives—percent of vote—BN coalition 47.4%, opposition parties 50.9%, others 1.7%; seats—BN coalition 133, opposition parties 89

Judicial branch: *highest court(s)*: Federal Court (consists of the chief justice and 4 judges) note—Malaysia has a dual judicial hierarchy of civil and religious (sharia) courts
judge selection and term of office: Federal Court justices appointed by the monarch on advice of the prime minister; judges serve till age 65
subordinate courts: Court of Appeal; High Court; Sessions Court; Magistrates' Court

Political parties and leaders: National Front (Barisan Nasional) or BN (ruling coalition) consists of the following parties; Gerakan Rakyat Malaysia Party or GERAKAN [KOH Tsu Koon]; Liberal Democratic Party (Parti Liberal Demokratik—Sabah) or LDP [LIEW Vui Keong]; Malaysian Chinese Association (Persatuan China Malaysia) or MCA [CHUA Soi Lek]; Malaysian Indian Congress (Kongres India Malaysia) or MIC [Govindasamy PALANIVEL]; Parti Bersatu Rakyat Sabah or PBRS [Joseph KURUP]; Parti Bersatu Sabah or PBS [Joseph PAIRIN Kitingan]; Parti Pesaka Bumiputera Bersatu or PBB [Abdul TAIB Mahmud]; Parti Rakyat Sarawak or PRS [James MASING]; Sarawak Progressive Democratic Party or SPDP [Tan Sri William MAKAN Ikom]; Sarawak United People's Party (Parti Bersatu Rakyat Sarawak) or SUPP [Peter CHIN Fah Kui]; United Malays National Organization or UMNO [NAJIB bin Abdul Razak]; United Pasokmomogun Kadazandusun Murut Organization (Pertubuhan Pasko Momogun Kadazan Dusun Bersatu) or UPKO [Bernard; DOMPOK]; People's Progressive Party (Parti Progresif Penduduk Malaysia) or PPP [M.Kayveas]; People's Alliance (Pakatan Rakyat) or PR (opposition coalition) consists of the following parties:; Democratic Action Party (Parti Tindakan Demokratik) or DAP [KARPAL Singh]; Islamic Party of Malaysia (Parti Islam se Malaysia) or PAS [Abdul HADI Awang; People's Justice Party (Parti Keadilan Rakyat) or PKR [WAN AZIZAH Wan Ismail]; Sarawak National Party or SNAP [Edwin DUNDANG]; notable independent parties; Sabah Progressive Party (Parti Progresif Sabah) or SAPP [YONG Teck Lee]; State Reform Pary (Parti Reformasi Negeri) or STAR [Jeffery KITINGAN]

Political pressure groups and leaders: Bar Council; BERSIH (electoral reform coalition); PEMBELA (Muslim NGO coalition); PERKASA (defense of Malay rights)
other: religious groups; women's groups; youth groups

International organization participation: ADB, APEC, ARF, ASEAN, BIS, C, CICA (observer), CP, D-8, EAS, FAO, G-15, G-77, IAEA, IBRD, ICAO, ICC (national committees), ICRM, IDA, IDB, IFAD, IFC, IFRCS, IHO, ILO, IMF, IMO, IMSO, Interpol, IOC, IPU, ISO, ITSO, ITU, ITUC (NGOs), MIGA, MINURSO, MONUSCO, NAM, OIC, OPCW, PCA, PIF (partner), UN, UNAMID, UNCTAD, UNESCO, UNIDO, UNIFIL, UNMIL, UNWTO, UPU, WCO, WFTU (NGOs), WHO, WIPO, WMO, WTO

Diplomatic representation in the US: *chief of mission:* Ambassador (vacant); Charge d'Affaires IKRAM Bin Mohammad Ibrahim (since 17 December 2013)
chancery: 3516 International Court NW, Washington, DC 20008
telephone: [1] (202) 572-9700
FAX: [1] (202) 572-9882
consulate(s) general: Los Angeles, New York

Diplomatic representation from the US: *chief of mission:* Ambassador Joseph Y. YUN (since 12 September 2013)
embassy: 376 Jalan Tun Razak, 50400 Kuala Lumpur
mailing address: US Embassy Kuala Lumpur, APO AP 96535-8152
telephone: [60] (3) 2168-5000
FAX: [60] (3) 2142-2207

Flag description: 14 equal horizontal stripes of red (top) alternating with white (bottom); there is a blue rectangle in the upper hoist-side corner bearing a yellow crescent and a yellow 14-pointed star; the flag is often referred to as Jalur Gemilang (Stripes of Glory); the 14 stripes stand for the equal status in the federation of the 13 member states and the federal government; the 14 points on the star represent the unity between these entities; the crescent is a traditional symbol of Islam; blue symbolizes the unity of the Malay people and yellow is the royal color of Malay rulers
note: the design is based on the flag of the US

National symbol(s): tiger

National anthem: *name:* "Negaraku" (My Country)
lyrics/music: collective, led by Tunku ABDUL RAHMAN/Pierre Jean DE BERANGER
note: adopted 1957; the full version is only performed in the presence of the king; the tune, which was adopted from a popular French melody titled "La Rosalie," was originally the anthem of the state of Perak

ECONOMY

Economy—overview: Malaysia, a middle-income country, has transformed itself since the 1970s from a producer of raw materials into an emerging multi-sector economy. Under current Prime Minister NAJIB, Malaysia is attempting to achieve high-income status by 2020 and to move farther up the value-added production chain by attracting investments in Islamic finance, high technology industries, biotechnology, and services. NAJIB's Economic Transformation Program (ETP) is a series of projects and policy measures intended to accelerate the country's economic growth. The government has also taken steps to liberalize some services sub-sectors. The NAJIB administration also is continuing efforts to boost domestic demand and reduce the economy's dependence on exports. Nevertheless, exports - particularly of electronics, oil and gas, palm oil and rubber—remain a significant driver of the economy. As an oil and gas exporter, Malaysia has profited from higher world energy prices, although the rising cost of domestic gasoline and diesel fuel, combined with sustained budget deficits, has forced Kuala Lumpur to begin to address fiscal shortfalls, through initial reductions in energy and sugar subsidies and the announcement of the 2015 implementation of a 6% goods and services tax. The government is also trying to lessen its dependence on state oil producer Petronas. The oil and gas sector supplies about 32% of government revenue in 2013. Bank Negara Malaysia (central bank) maintains healthy foreign exchange reserves, and a well-developed regulatory regime has limited Malaysia's exposure to riskier financial instruments and the global financial crisis. Nevertheless, Malaysia could be vulnerable to a fall in commodity prices or a general slowdown in global economic activity because exports are a major component of GDP. In order to attract increased investment, NAJIB earlier raised possible revisions to the special economic and social preferences accorded to ethnic Malays under the New Economic Policy of 1970, but retreated in 2013 after he encountered significant opposition from Malay nationalists and other vested interests. In September 2013 NAJIB launched the new Bumiputra Economic Empowerment Program (BEEP), policies that favor and advance the economic condition of ethnic Malays.

GDP (purchasing power parity): $525 billion (2013 est.)
country comparison to the world: 30
$501.5 billion (2012 est.)
$474.7 billion (2011 est.)
note: data are in 2013 US dollars

GDP (official exchange rate): $312.4 billion (2013 est.)

GDP—real growth rate: 4.7% (2013 est.)
country comparison to the world: 63
5.6% (2012 est.)
5.1% (2011 est.)

GDP—per capita (PPP): $17,500 (2013 est.)
country comparison to the world: 79
$17,000 (2012 est.)
$16,400 (2011 est.)
note: data are in 2013 US dollars

Gross national saving: 32.3% of GDP (2013 est.)
country comparison to the world: 18
31.9% of GDP (2012 est.)
34.9% of GDP (2011 est.)

GDP—composition, by end use:
household consumption: 50.1%
government consumption: 13.9%
investment in fixed capital: 26.2%
investment in inventories: 0.8%
exports of goods and services: 84.1%
imports of goods and services: -75.2% (2013 est.)

GDP—composition, by sector of origin:
agriculture: 11.2%
industry: 40.6%
services: 48.1% (2013 est.)

Agriculture—products: Peninsular Malaysia—palm oil, rubber, cocoa, rice; Sabah—palm oil, subsistence crops; rubber, timber; Sarawak—palm oil, rubber, timber; pepper

Industries: Peninsular Malaysia—rubber and oil palm processing and manufacturing, petroleum and natural gas, light manufacturing, pharmaceuticals, medical technology, electronics and semiconductors, timber processing; Sabah—logging, petroleum and natural gas production; Sarawak—agriculture processing, petroleum and natural gas production, logging

Industrial production growth rate: 5% (2013 est.)
country comparison to the world: 56

Labor force: 13.19 million (2013 est.)
country comparison to the world: 41

Labor force—by occupation: *agriculture:* 11.1%
industry: 36%
services: 53.5% (2012 est.)

Unemployment rate: 3.1% (2013 est.)
country comparison to the world: 24
3% (2012 est.)

Population below poverty line: 3.8% (2009 est.)

Household income or consumption by percentage share: *lowest* 10%: 1.8%
highest 10%: 34.7% (2009 est.)

Distribution of family income—Gini index: 46.2 (2009)
country comparison to the world: 34
49.2 (1997)

Budget: *revenues:* $65.72 billion
expenditures: $79.4 billion (2013 est.)

Taxes and other revenues: 21% of GDP (2013 est.)
country comparison to the world: 157

Budget surplus (+) or deficit (-):
-4.4% of GDP (2013 est.)
country comparison to the world: 158

Public debt: 54.6% of GDP (2013 est.)
country comparison to the world: 59
53.3% of GDP (2012 est.)
note: this figure is based on the amount of federal government debt, RM501.6 billion ($167.2 billion) in 2012; this includes Malaysian Treasury bills and other government securities, as well as loans raised externally and bonds and notes issued overseas; this figure excludes debt issued by non-financial public enterprises and guaranteed by the federal government, which was an additional $47.7 billion in 2012

Fiscal year: calendar year

Inflation rate (consumer prices): 2.2% (2013 est.)
country comparison to the world: 76
1.7% (2012 est.)
note: approximately 30% of goods are price-controlled

Central bank discount rate: 3% (31 December 2011)
country comparison to the world: 108
2.83% (31 December 2010)

Commercial bank prime lending rate: 4.5% (31 December 2013 est.)
country comparison to the world: 162
4.7% (31 December 2012 est.)

Stock of narrow money: $97.03 billion (31 December 2013 est.)
country comparison to the world: 35
$93.89 billion (31 December 2012 est.)

Stock of broad money: $439.7 billion (31 December 2013 est.)
country comparison to the world: 23
$435.2 billion (31 December 2012 est.)

Stock of domestic credit: $421 billion (31 December 2013 est.)
country comparison to the world: 29
$412.4 billion (31 December 2012 est.)

Market value of publicly traded shares: $476.3 billion (31 December 2012 est.)
country comparison to the world: 23
$395.1 billion (31 December 2011)
$410.5 billion (31 December 2010 est.)

Current account balance: $16.67 billion (2013 est.)
country comparison to the world: 18
$18.64 billion (2012 est.)

Exports: $230.7 billion (2013 est.)
country comparison to the world: 25
$227.7 billion (2012 est.)

Exports—commodities: semiconductors and electronic equipment, palm oil, petroleum and liquefied natural gas, wood and wood products, palm oil, rubber, textiles, chemicals, solar panels

Exports—partners: Singapore 13.6%, China 12.6%, Japan 11.8%, US 8.7%, Thailand 5.4%, Hong Kong 4.3%, India 4.2%, Australia 4.1% (2012)

Imports: $192.9 billion (2013 est.)
country comparison to the world: 27
$186.9 billion (2012 est.)

Imports—commodities: electronics, machinery, petroleum products, plastics, vehicles, iron and steel products, chemicals

Imports—partners: China 15.1%, Singapore 13.3%, Japan 10.3%, US 8.1%, Thailand 6%, Indonesia 5.1%, South Korea 4.1% (2012)

Reserves of foreign exchange and gold: $139.4 billion (31 December 2013 est.)
country comparison to the world: 20
$139.7 billion (31 December 2012 est.)

Debt—external: $100.1 billion (31 December 2013 est.)
country comparison to the world: 47
$98.82 billion (31 December 2012 est.)

Stock of direct foreign investment—at home: $143.4 billion (31 December 2013 est.)
country comparison to the world: 33
$132.4 billion (31 December 2012 est.)

Stock of direct foreign investment—abroad: $133.5 billion (31 December 2013 est.)
country comparison to the world: 27
$120.4 billion (31 December 2012 est.)

Exchange rates: ringgits (MYR) per US dollarc
3.174 (2013 est.)
3.09 (2012 est.)
3.22 (2010 est.)
3.52 (2009)
3.33 (2008)

ENERGY

Electricity—production: 118 billion kWh (2012 est.)
country comparison to the world: 3 1

Electricity—consumption: 112 billion kWh (2012 est.)
country comparison to the world: 29

Electricity—exports: 151 million kWh (2010 est.)
country comparison to the world: 72

Electricity—imports: 33 million kWh (2010 est.)
country comparison to the world: 99

Electricity—installed generating capacity: 25.39 million kW (2010 est.)
country comparison to the world: 33

Electricity—from fossil fuels: 91.7% of total installed capacity (2010 est.)
country comparison to the world: 72

Electricity—from nuclear fuels: 0% of total installed capacity (2010 est.)
country comparison to the world: 145

Electricity—from hydroelectric plants: 8.3% of total installed capacity (2010 est.)
country comparison to the world: 118

Electricity—from other renewable sources: 0% of total installed capacity (2010 est.)
country comparison to the world: 205

Crude oil—production: 642,700 bbl/day (2012 est.)
country comparison to the world: 29

Crude oil—exports: 269,000 bbl/day (2012 est.)
country comparison to the world: 28

Crude oil—imports: 160,500 bbl/day (2010 est.)
country comparison to the world: 38

Crude oil—proved reserves: 4 billion bbl (1 January 2013 es)
country comparison to the world: 28

Refined petroleum products—production: 568,800 bbl/day (2010 est.)
country comparison to the world: 30

Refined petroleum products—consumption: 542,900 bbl/day (2011 est.)
country comparison to the world: 33

Refined petroleum products—exports: 176,500 bbl/day (2010 est.)
country comparison to the world: 35

Refined petroleum products—imports: 175,100 bbl/day (2010 est.)
country comparison to the world: 31

Natural gas—production: 61.73 billion cu m (2011 est.)
country comparison to the world: 15

Natural gas—consumption: 32.62 billion cu m (2010 est.)
country comparison to the world: 28

Natural gas—exports:
33.1 billion cu m (2011 est.)

country comparison to the world: 14

Natural gas—imports: 1.99 billion cu m (2011 est.)
country comparison to the world: 49

Natural gas—proved reserves: 2.35 trillion cu m (1 January 2013 es)
country comparison to the world: 15

Carbon dioxide emissions from consumption of energy: 191.4 million Mt (2011 est.)
country comparison to the world: 31

COMMUNICATIONS

Telephones—main lines in use: 4.589 million (2012)
country comparison to the world: 3 4

Telephones—mobile cellular: 41.325 million (2012)
country comparison to the world: 30

Telephone system: *general assessment:* modern system featuring good intercity service on Peninsular Malaysia provided mainly by microwave radio relay and an adequate intercity microwave radio relay network between Sabah and Sarawak via Brunei; international service excellent
domestic: domestic satellite system with 2 earth stations; combined fixed-line and mobile-cellular teledensity roughly 140 per 100 persons

international: country code—60; landing point for several major international submarine cable networks that provide connectivity to Asia, Middle East, and Europe; satellite earth stations—2 Intelsat (1 Indian Ocean, 1 Pacific Ocean) (2011)

Broadcast media: state-owned TV broadcaster operates 2 TV networks with relays throughout the country, and the leading private commercial media group operates 4 TV stations with numerous relays throughout the country; satellite TV subscription service is available; state-owned radio broadcaster operates multiple national networks as well as regional and local stations; many private commercial radio broadcasters and some subscription satellite radio services are available; about 55 radio stations overall (2012)

Internet country code: .my

Internet hosts: 422,470 (2012)
country comparison to the world: 53

Internet users: 15.355 million (2009)
country comparison to the world: 26

TRANSPORTATION

Airports: 114 (2013)
country comparison to the world: 5 1

Airports—with paved runways: *total:* 3 9
over 3,047 m: 8
2,438 to 3,047 m: 8
1,524 to 2,437 m: 7
914 to 1,523 m: 8
under 914 m: 8 (2013)

Airports—with unpaved runways: *total:* 7 5
914 to 1,523 m: 6
under 914 m: 69 (2013)

Heliports: 4 (2013)

Pipelines: condensate 354 km; gas 6,439 km; liquid petroleum gas 155 km; oil 1,937 km; oil/gas/water 43 km; refined products 114 km; water 26 km (2013)

Railways: *total:* 1,849 km
country comparison to the world: 75
standard gauge: 57 km 1.435-m gauge (57 km electrified)
narrow gauge: 1,792 km 1.000-m gauge (150 km electrified) (2010)

Roadways: *total:* 144,403 km (does not include local roads)
country comparison to the world: 33
paved: 116,169 km (includes 1,821 km of expressways)
unpaved: 28,234 km (2010)

Waterways: 7,200 km (Peninsular Malaysia 3,200 km; Sabah 1,500 km; Sarawak 2,500 km) (2011)
country comparison to the world: 20

Merchant marine: *total:* 315
country comparison to the world: 31
by type: bulk carrier 11, cargo 83, carrier 2, chemical tanker 47, container 41, liquefied gas 34, passenger/cargo 4, petroleum tanker 86, roll on/roll off 2, vehicle carrier 5
foreign-owned: 26 (Denmark 1, Hong Kong 8, Japan 2, Russia 2, Singapore 13)
registered in other countries: 82 (Bahamas 13, India 1, Indonesia 1, Isle of Man 6, Malta 1, Marshall Islands 11, Panama 12, Papua New Guinea 1, Philippines 1, Saint Kitts and Nevis 1, Singapore 27, Thailand 3, US 2, unknown 2) (2010)

Ports and terminals: *major seaport(s):* Bintulu, Johor Bahru, George Town (Penang), Port Kelang (Port Klang), Tanjung Pelepas
container port(s) (TEUs): George Town (Penang) (1,202,180), Port Kelang (Port Klang)(9,435,403), Tanjung Pelepas (7,302,461)

Transportation—note: the International Maritime Bureau reports that the territorial and offshore waters in the Strait of Malacca and South China Sea remain high risk for piracy and armed robbery against ships; in the past, commercial vessels have been attacked and hijacked both at anchor and while underway; hijacked vessels are often disguised and cargo diverted to ports in East Asia; crews have been murdered or cast adrift; increased naval patrols since 2005 in the Strait of Malacca resulted in no reported incidents in 2010

MILITARY

Military branches: Malaysian Armed Forces (Angkatan Tentera Malaysia, ATM): Malaysian Army (Tentera Darat Malaysia), Royal Malaysian Navy (Tentera Laut Diraja Malaysia, TLDM), Royal Malaysian Air Force (Tentera Udara Diraja Malaysia, TUDM) (2013)

Military service age and obligation: 17 years 6 months of age for voluntary military service (younger with parental consent and proof of age); mandatory retirement age 60; women serve in the Malaysian Armed Forces; no conscription (2013)

Manpower available for military service:
males age 16-49: 7,501,518
females age 16-49: 7,315,999 (2010 est.)

Manpower fit for military service:
males age 16-49: 6,247,306
females age 16-49: 6,175,274 (2010 est.)

Manpower reaching militarily significant age annually: *male:* 265,008
female: 254,812 (2010 est.)

Military expenditures: 1.55% of GDP (2012)
country comparison to the world: 59
1.67% of GDP (2011)
1.55% of GDP (2010)

TRANSNATIONAL ISSUES

Disputes—international: while the 2002 "Declaration on the Conduct of Parties in the South China Sea" has eased tensions over the Spratly Islands, it is not the legally binding "code of conduct" sought by some parties; Malaysia was not party to the March 2005 joint accord among the national oil companies of China, the Philippines, and Vietnam on conducting marine seismic activities in the Spratly Islands; disputes continue over deliveries of fresh water to Singapore, Singapore's land reclamation, bridge construction, and maritime boundaries in the Johor and Singapore Straits; in 2008, ICJ awarded sovereignty of Pedra Branca (Pulau Batu Puteh/Horsburgh Island) to Singapore, and Middle Rocks to Malaysia, but did not rule on maritime regimes, boundaries, or disposition of South Ledge; land and maritime negotiations with Indonesia are ongoing, and disputed areas include the controversial Tanjung Datu and Camar Wulan border area in Borneo and the maritime boundary in the Ambalat oil block in the Celebes Sea; separatist violence in Thailand's predominantly Muslim southern provinces prompts measures to close and monitor border with Malaysia to stem terrorist activities; Philippines retains a dormant claim to Malaysia's Sabah State in northern Borneo; per Letters of Exchange signed in 2009, Malaysia in 2010 ceded two hydrocarbon concession blocks to Brunei in exchange for Brunei's sultan dropping claims to the Limbang corridor, which divides Brunei; piracy remains a problem in the Malacca Strait

Refugees and internally displaced persons: *refugees (country of origin):* 84,671 (Burma) (2012)
stateless persons: 40,001 (2012); note—Malaysia's stateless population consists of Rohingya refugees from Burma, ethnic Indians, and the children of Filipino and Indonesian illegal migrants; Burma stripped the Rohingya of their nationality in 1982; Filipino and Indonesian children who have not have been registered for birth certificates by their parents or who received birth certificates stamped "foreigner" are not eligible to go to government schools; these children are vulnerable to statelessness should they not be able to apply to their parents' country of origin for a passport

Trafficking in persons: *current situation:* Malaysia is a destination and, to a lesser extent, a source and transit country for women and children subjected to conditions of forced labor and women and children subjected to sex trafficking; Malaysia is mainly a destination country for foreign workers who migrate willingly from countries including Indonesia, Nepal, India, Thailand, China, the Philippines, Burma, Cambodia, Laos, Bangladesh, Pakistan, and Vietnam but subsequently encounter forced labor or debt bondage at the hands of their employers in the domestic, agricultural, construction, plantation, and industrial sectors; a small number of Malaysian citizens were reportedly trafficked internally and abroad to Singapore, China, and Japan for commercial sexual exploitation; refugees are also vulnerable to trafficking; some officials are reportedly complicit in facilitating trafficking

tier rating: Tier 2 Watch List—Malaysia does not fully comply with the minimum standards for the elimination of trafficking; however, it is making significant efforts to do so; the government has made no tangible improvements to its inadequate system for identifying and protecting trafficking victims, such as amending its laws to allow victims to reside in NGO shelters; trafficking victims identified by Malaysian authorities are forcibly detained in government facilities, where they are provided with limited, if any, access to legal or psychological assistance by the government or NGOs; increasing efforts are being made to investigate and prosecute trafficking offenders, notably in the area of labor trafficking, though convictions of sex trafficking offenders has decreased; many front-line officials continue to lack the ability to recognize indicators of human trafficking, hindering the investigation of cases and the identification of victims; although the confiscation of passports by employers is illegal, the government has not prosecuted any employers who confiscated migrants' passports or travel documents or confined them to the workplace (2013)

Illicit drugs: drug trafficking prosecuted vigorously and carries severe penalties; heroin still primary drug of abuse, but synthetic drug demand remains strong; continued ecstasy and methamphetamine producer for domestic users and, to a lesser extent, the regional drug market

MALDIVES

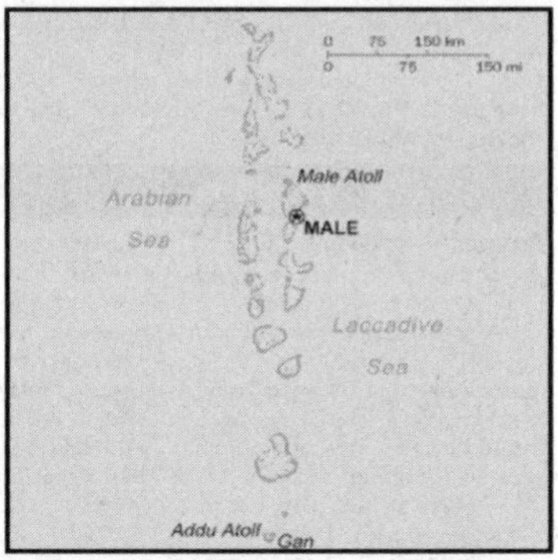

INTRODUCTION

Background: A sultanate since the 12th century, the Maldives became a British protectorate in 1887. It became a republic in 1968, three years after independence. President Maumoon Abdul GAYOOM dominated the islands' political scene for 30 years, elected to six successive terms by single-party referendums. Following political demonstrations in the capital Male in August 2003, the president and his government pledged to embark upon a process of liberalization and democratic reforms, including a more representative political system and expanded political freedoms. Progress was sluggish, however, and many promised reforms were slow to be realized. Nonetheless, political parties were legalized in 2005. In June 2008, a constituent assembly - termed the "Special Majlis"—finalized a new constitution, which was ratified by the president in August. The first-ever presidential elections under a multi-candidate, multi-party system were held in October 2008. GAYOOM was defeated in a runoff poll by Mohamed NASHEED, a political activist who had been jailed several years earlier by the former regime. President NASHEED faced a number of challenges including strengthening democracy and combating poverty and drug abuse. In early February 2012, after several weeks of street protests following his sacking of a top judge, NASHEED resigned the presidency and handed over power to Vice President Mohammed WAHEED Hassan Maniku. In mid-2012, a Commission of National Inquiry was set by the government to probe events leading up to NASHEED's resignation. Though the commission found no evidence of a coup, the report recommended the need to strengthen the country's democratic institutions to avert similar events in the future, and to further investigate alleged police misconduct during the crisis. Maldivian officials have played a prominent role in international climate change discussions (due to the islands' low elevation and the threat from sea-level rise) on the UN Human Rights Council and in other international forums, as well as in encouraging regional cooperation, especially between India and Pakistan.

GEOGRAPHY

Location: Southern Asia, group of atolls in the Indian Ocean, south-southwest of India

Geographic coordinates: 3 15 N, 73 00 E

Map references: Asia

Area: *total:* 298 sq km
country comparison to the world: 210
land: 298 sq km
water: 0 sq km

Area—comparative: about 1.7 times the size of Washington, DC

Land boundaries: 0 km

Coastline: 644 km

Maritime claims: measured from claimed archipelagic straight baselines
territorial sea: 12 nm
contiguous zone: 24 nm
exclusive economic zone: 200 nm

Climate: tropical; hot, humid; dry, northeast monsoon (November to March); rainy, southwest monsoon (June to August)

Terrain: flat, with white sandy beaches

Elevation extremes: *lowest point:* Indian Ocean 0 m
highest point: unnamed location on Viligili in the Addu Atholhu 2.4 m

Natural resources: fish

Land use: *arable land:* 10%
permanent crops: 10%
other: 80% (2011)

Irrigated land: 0 sq km NA (2003)

Total renewable water resources: 0.03 cu km (2011)

Freshwater withdrawal (domestic/industrial/agricultural): *total:* 0.01 cu km/yr (95%/5%/0%)
per capita: 18.44 cu m/yr (2008)

Natural hazards: tsunamis; low elevation of islands makes them sensitive to sea level rise

Environment—current issues: depletion of freshwater aquifers threatens water supplies; global warming and sea level rise; coral reef bleaching

Environment—international agreements:
party to: Biodiversity, Climate Change, Climate Change-Kyoto Protocol, Desertification, Hazardous Wastes, Law of the Sea, Ozone Layer Protection, Ship Pollution
signed, but not ratified: none of the selected agreements

Geography—note: 1,190 coral islands grouped into 26 atolls (200 inhabited islands, plus 80 islands with tourist resorts); archipelago with strategic location astride and along major sea lanes in Indian Ocean

PEOPLE AND SOCIETY

Nationality: *noun:* Maldivian(s)
adjective: Maldivian

Ethnic groups: South Indians, Sinhalese, Arabs

Languages: Dhivehi (official, dialect of Sinhala, script derived from Arabic), English (spoken by most government officials)

Religions: Sunni Muslim (official)

Population: 393,595 (July 2014 est.)
country comparison to the world: 177

Age structure: *0-14 years:* 21% (male 42,154/female 40,490)
15-24 years: 23.4% (male 53,760/female 38,385)
25-54 years: 46.5% (male 107,703/female 75,360)
55-64 years: 4.3% (male 9,782/female 9,180)
65 years and over: 4.2% (male 7,974/female 8,807) (2014 est.)

Dependency ratios:
total dependency ratio: 50.8 %
youth dependency ratio: 43.3 %
elderly dependency ratio: 7.4 %
potential support ratio: 13.4 (2013)

Median age: *total:* 27.1 years
male: 27.3 years
female: 26.7 years (2014 est.)

Population growth rate: -0.09% (2014 est.)
country comparison to the world: 202

Birth rate: 15.59 births/1,000 population (2014 est.)
country comparison to the world: 127

Death rate: 3.84 deaths/1,000 population (2014 est.)
country comparison to the world: 212

Net migration rate: -12.67 migrant(s)/1,000 population (2014 est.)
country comparison to the world: 217

Urbanization: *urban population:* 41.2% of total population (2011)
rate of urbanization: 3.91% annual rate of change (2010-15 est.)

Major urban areas—population: MALE (capital) 120,000 (2009)

Sex ratio: *at birth:* 1.05 male(s)/female
0-14 years: 1.04 male(s)/female
15-24 years: 1.4 male(s)/female
25-54 years: 1.43 male(s)/female
55-64 years: 1.29 male(s)/female
65 years and over: 0.94 male(s)/female
total population: 1.34 male(s)/female (2014 est.)

Mother's mean age at first birth: 23.9
note: median age at first birth among women 25-29 (2009 est.)

Maternal mortality rate: 60 deaths/100,000 live births (2010)
country comparison to the world: 100

Infant mortality rate: *total:* 24.59 deaths/1,000 live births
country comparison to the world: 73
male: 27.01 deaths/1,000 live births
female: 22.04 deaths/1,000 live births (2014 est.)

Life expectancy at birth: *total population:* 75.15 years
country comparison to the world: 99
male: 72.86 years
female: 77.55 years (2014 est.)

Total fertility rate: 1.76 children born/woman (2014 est.)
country comparison to the world: 164

Contraceptive prevalence rate: 34.7% (2009)

Health expenditures: 8.5% of GDP (2011)
country comparison to the world: 53

Physicians density: 1.6 physicians/1,000 population (2007)

Hospital bed density: 4.3 beds/1,000 population (2009)

Drinking water source:
improved:
urban: 99.5% of population
rural: 97.9% of population
total: 98.6% of population
unimproved:
urban: 0.5% of population
rural: 2.1% of population
total: 1.4% of population (2011 est.)

Sanitation facility access:
improved:
urban: 97.5% of population
rural: 98.3% of population
total: 98% of population
unimproved:
urban: 2.5% of population
rural: 1.7% of population
total: 2% of population (2011 est.)

HIV/AIDS—adult prevalence rate: 0.1% (2012 est.)
country comparison to the world: 159

HIV/AIDS—people living with HIV/AIDS: NA

HIV/AIDS—deaths: fewer than 100 (2009 est.)
country comparison to the world: 142

Obesity—adult prevalence rate: 12.9% (2008)

country comparison to the world: 126

Children under the age of 5 years underweight: 17.8% (2009)
country comparison to the world: 38

Education expenditures: 6.8% of GDP (2011)
country comparison to the world: 26

Literacy: *definition:* age 15 and over can read and write
total population: 98.4%
male: 98.4%
female: 98.4% (2006 est.)

School life expectancy (primary to tertiary education): *total:* 13 years
male: 13 years
female: 13 years (2003)

Unemployment, youth ages 15-24: *total:* 22.2%
country comparison to the world: 51
male: 15.5%
female: 30.5% (2006)

GOVERNMENT

Country name: *conventional long form:* Republic of Maldives
conventional short form: Maldives
local long form: Dhivehi Raajjeyge Jumhooriyyaa
local short form: Dhivehi Raajje

Government type: republic

Capital: *name:* Male

geographic coordinates: 4 10 N, 73 30 E
time difference: UTC+5 (10 hours ahead of Washington, DC during Standard Time)

Administrative divisions: 7 provinces and 1 municipality*; Dhekunu (South), Maale*, Mathi Dhekunu (Upper South), Mathi Uthuru (Upper North), Medhu (Central), Medhu Dhekunu (South Central), Medhu Uthuru (North Central), Uthuru (North)

Independence: 26 July 1965 (from the UK)

National holiday: Independence Day, 26 July (1965)

Constitution: many previous; latest ratified 7 August 2008 (2010)

Legal system: Islamic religious legal system with English common law influences, primarily in commercial matters

International law organization participation: has not submitted an ICJ jurisdiction declaration; non-party state to the ICCt

Suffrage: 18 years of age; universal

Executive branch: *chief of state:* President Abdulla YAMEEN Abdul Gayoom (since 17 November 2013); Vice President Mohamed JAMEEL Ahmed (since 17 November 2013) note—the president is both chief of state and head of government
head of government: President Abdulla YAMEEN Abdul Gayoom (since 17 November 2013); Vice President Mohamed JAMEEL Ahmed (since 17 November 2013)
cabinet: Cabinet of Ministers is appointed by the president (For more information visit the World Leaders website)
elections: president elected by direct vote for a five-year term (eligible for a second term); election held on 7 September 2013 was annulled by the Supreme Court; rerun of first round held on 9 November 2013 and runoff held on 16 November (next election to be held in 2018)
election results: first round (9 November 2013); percent of vote—Mohamed NASHEED 46.9%, Abdulla YAMEEN Abdul Gayoom 29.7%, Qasim IBRAHIM 23.3%; runoff (postponed to 16 November 2013); percent of vote—Abdulla YAMEEN Abdul Gayoom elected president 51.4%, Mohamed NASHEED 48.6%

Legislative branch: unicameral Parliament or People's Majlis (85 seats; members elected by direct vote to serve 5-year terms); note—the Elections Commission in December 2013 increased the number of seats to 85 from 77
elections: last held on 22 March 2014 (next to be held in 2019)
election results: percent of vote—PPM 40%, MDP 28.2%, JP 18.8%, MDA 5.9%, other 1.2%, independents 5.9%; seats by party—PPM 33, MDP 26, JP 15, MDA 5, other 1, independents 5

Judicial branch: *highest court(s):* Supreme Court (consists of the chief justice and 6 judges)
judge selection and term of office: Supreme Court judges appointed by the president in consultation with the Judicial Service Commission—a separate 10-member body of selected high government officials and the public—and upon confirmation by voting members of the People's Majlis; judges serve until mandatory retirement at age 70
subordinate courts: High Court; Criminal, Civil, Family, Juvenile, and Drug Courts; Magistrate Courts (on each of the inhabited islands)

Political parties and leaders:
note: political parties with an asterisk were dissolved on 7 February 2014 by the Elections Commission under the Political Parties Act, which requires a minimum membership; the status of these parties is unresolved, as the Supreme Court later ruled the dissolution invalid
Adhaalath (Justice) Party or AP [Sheikh Imran ABDULLA]; Dhivehi Qaumee Party or DQP [Hassan SAEED]*; Dhivehi Rayyithunge Party (Maldivian People's Party) or DRP; Gaumee Itthihaad Party (National Unity Party) or GIP [Mohamed WAHEED]; Islamic Democratic Party or IDP*; Maldives Development Alliance or MDA [Ahmed SIYAM]; Maldives National Congress or MNC [Ali AMJAD]*; Maldives Reform Movement or MRM [Mohamed MUNAWWAR]; Maldivian Democratic Party or MDP [Reeko Moosa MANIKU]; Maldivian Labor Party or MLP [Ahmed MOOSA]*; Maldivian Social Democratic Party or MSDP [Reeko Ibrahim MANIKU]*; Meedhu Dhaaira; People's Alliance or PA [Moosa ZAMEERI]*; People's Party or PP [Ahmed RIYAZ]*; Poverty Alleviation Party or PAP; Progressive Party of Maldives or PPM [Maumoon Abdul GAYOOM]; Republican (Jumhooree) Party or JP [Qasim IBRAHIM]; Social Liberal Party or SLP [Mazian RASHEED]*

Political pressure groups and leaders: *other:* various unregistered political parties

International organization participation: ADB, AOSIS, C, CP, FAO, G-77, IBRD, ICAO, ICC (NGOs), IDA, IDB, IFAD, IFC, IFRCS, ILO, IMF, IMO, Interpol, IOC, IOM, IPU, ITU, MIGA, NAM, OIC, OPCW, SAARC, SACEP, UN, UNCTAD, UNESCO, UNIDO, UNWTO, UPU, WCO, WHO, WIPO, WMO, WTO

Diplomatic representation in the US: *chief of mission:* Ambassador Ahmed SAREER (since 11 January 2013)
chancery: 800 2nd Avenue, Suite 400E, New York, NY 10017
telephone: [1] (212) 599-6194
FAX: [1] (212) 599-6195

Diplomatic representation from the US: the US does not have an embassy in Maldives; the US Ambassador to Sri Lanka, currently Ambassador Michele J. SISON, is accredited to Maldives and makes periodic visits

Flag description: red with a large green rectangle in the center bearing a vertical white crescent moon; the closed side of the crescent is on the hoist side of the flag; red recalls those who have sacrificed their lives in defense of their country, the green rectangle represents peace and prosperity, and the white crescent signifies Islam

National symbol(s): coconut palm, yellowfin tuna

National anthem: *name:* "Gaumee Salaam" (National Salute)
lyrics/music: Mohamed Jameel DIDI/Wannakuwattawaduge DON AMARADEVA
note: lyrics adopted 1948, music adopted 1972; between 1948 and 1972, the lyrics were sung to the tune of "Auld Lang Syne"

ECONOMY

Economy—overview: Tourism, Maldives' largest economic activity, accounts for nearly 30% of GDP and more than 60% of foreign exchange receipts. Fishing is the second leading sector, but the fish catch has dropped sharply in recent years. Agriculture and manufacturing continue to play a lesser role in the economy, constrained by the limited availability of cultivable land and the shortage of domestic labor. Lower than expected tourist arrivals and fish exports, combined with high government spending on social needs, subsidies, and civil servant salaries contributed to a balance of payments crisis, which was temporarily eased with a $79.3 million IMF Stand-By agreement. However, after the first two disbursements, the IMF withheld subsequent disbursements due to concerns over Maldives' growing budget deficit, and the government has been seeking other sources of budgetary support ever since. A new Goods and Services Tax (GST) on tourism introduced in January 2011, on general goods and services in October 2011, and a new Business Profit Tax introduced in July 2011 have provided a boost to revenue. In recent years, gross foreign reserves have hovered around $300 million, sufficient to finance about two to three months of imports. Diversifying the economy beyond tourism and fishing, reforming public finance, increasing employment opportunities, and combating corruption, cronyism, and a growing drug problem are other near-term challenges facing the government. Over the longer term Maldivian authorities worry about the impact of erosion and possible global warming on their low-lying country; 80% of the area is 1 meter or less above sea level.

GDP (purchasing power parity): $3.073 billion (2013 est.)
country comparison to the world: 182
$2.97 billion (2012 est.)
$2.945 billion (2011 est.)
note: data are in 2013 US dollars

GDP (official exchange rate): $2.27 billion (2013 est.)

GDP—real growth rate: 3.5% (2013 est.)
country comparison to the world: 92
0.9% (2012 est.)
6.5% (2011 est.)

GDP—per capita (PPP): $9,100 (2013 est.)
country comparison to the world: 124
$9,000 (2012 est.)
$9,000 (2011 est.)
note: data are in 2013 US dollars

GDP—composition, by sector of origin:
agriculture: 3%
industry: 17%
services: 80% (2012 est.)

Agriculture—products: coconuts, corn, sweet potatoes; fish

Industries: tourism, fish processing, shipping, boat building, coconut processing, woven mats, rope, handicrafts, coral and sand mining

Industrial production growth rate: 14% (2012 est.)
country comparison to the world: 2

Labor force: 159,700 (2012)
country comparison to the world: 177

Labor force—by occupation: *agriculture:* 15%

industry: 15%
services: 70% (2010 est.)

Unemployment rate: 28% (2012 est.)
country comparison to the world: 178
14.5% (2010 est.)

Population below poverty line: 16% (2008)

Household income or consumption by percentage share: *lowest* 10%: 1.2%
highest 10%: 33.3% (FY09/10)

Distribution of family income—Gini index: 37.4
country comparison to the world: 79

Budget: *revenues:* $638 million
expenditures: $917 million (2012 est.)

Taxes and other revenues: 28.1% of GDP (2012 est.)
country comparison to the world: 104

Budget surplus (+) or deficit (-): -12.3% of GDP (2012 est.)
country comparison to the world: 210

Fiscal year: calendar year

Inflation rate (consumer prices): 5.1% (2012 est.)
country comparison to the world: 156
16.7% (2011 est.)

Central bank discount rate: 7% (31 December 2012 est.)
country comparison to the world: 44
6.96% (31 December 2011 est.)

Commercial bank prime lending rate: 10.5% (31 December 2012 est.)
country comparison to the world: 85
10.2% (31 December 2011 est.)

Stock of narrow money: $547.1 million (31 December 2012 est.)
country comparison to the world: 160
$531.4 million (31 December 2011 est.)

Stock of broad money: $1.298 billion (31 December 2012 est.)
country comparison to the world: 162
$1.237 billion (31 December 2011 est.)

Stock of domestic credit: $1.559 billion (31 December 2012 est.)
country comparison to the world: 143
$1.601 billion (31 December 2011 est.)

Market value of publicly traded shares: $555 million (31 December 2011 est.)

Current account balance: -$600 million (2012 est.)
country comparison to the world: 106
$437 million (2011 est.)

Exports: $283 million (2012 est.)
country comparison to the world: 181
$316 million (2011 est.)

Exports—commodities: fish

Exports—partners: France 18.9%, Thailand 15.8%, UK 11.4%, US 9.4%, Sri Lanka 8.6%, Italy 8.1%, Germany 6.4% (2012)

Imports: $1.406 billion (2012 est.)
country comparison to the world: 174
$1.314 billion (2011 est.)

Imports—commodities: petroleum products, clothing, intermediate and capital goods

Imports—partners: Singapore 21.7%, UAE 20.9%, India 9.6%, Malaysia 7.6%, China 6%, Thailand 5.6%, Sri Lanka 4% (2012)

Reserves of foreign exchange and gold: $356 million (30 November 2012 est.)
country comparison to the world: 154
$326 million (30 November 2011 est.)

Debt—external: $890.8 million (2012 est.)
country comparison to the world: 163
$684.2 million (2011 est.)

Exchange rates: rufiyaa (MVR) per US dollar—
15.365 (2011)
14.602 (2011)
12.8 (2008)
12.8 (2007)

ENERGY

Electricity—production: 301.1 million kWh (2010 est.)
country comparison to the world: 172

Electricity—consumption: 280 million kWh (2010 est.)
country comparison to the world: 177

Electricity—exports: 0 kWh (2012 est.)
country comparison to the world: 172

Electricity—imports: 0 kWh (2012 est.)
country comparison to the world: 174

Electricity—installed generating capacity: 62,080 kW (2010 est.)
country comparison to the world: 180

Electricity—from fossil fuels: 99.9% of total installed capacity (2010 est.)
country comparison to the world: 45

Electricity—from nuclear fuels: 0% of total installed capacity (2010 est.)
country comparison to the world: 144

Electricity—from hydroelectric plants: 0% of total installed capacity (2010 est.)
country comparison to the world: 186

Electricity—from other renewable sources: 0.1% of total installed capacity (2010 est.)
country comparison to the world: 101

Crude oil—production: 0 bbl/day (2012 est.)
country comparison to the world: 198

Crude oil—exports: 0 bbl/day (2012 est.)
country comparison to the world: 157

Crude oil—imports: 0 bbl/day (2012 est.)
country comparison to the world: 97

Crude oil—proved reserves: 0 bbl (1 January 2013 es)
country comparison to the world: 167

Refined petroleum products—production: 0 bbl/day (2012 est.)
country comparison to the world: 177

Refined petroleum products—consumption: 6,875 bbl/day (2011 est.)
country comparison to the world: 162

Refined petroleum products—exports: 0 bbl/day (2009 est.)
country comparison to the world: 200

Refined petroleum products—imports: 6,088 bbl/day (2012 est.)
country comparison to the world: 141

Natural gas—production: 0 cu m (2012 est.)
country comparison to the world: 170

Natural gas—consumption: 0 cu m (2012 est.)
country comparison to the world: 175

Natural gas—exports: 0 cu m (2012 est.)
country comparison to the world: 152

Natural gas—imports: 0 cu m (2012 est.)
country comparison to the world: 100

Natural gas—proved reserves: 0 cu m (1 January 2013 es)
country comparison to the world: 173

Carbon dioxide emissions from consumption of energy: 1.071 million Mt (2011 est.)
country comparison to the world: 166

COMMUNICATIONS

Telephones—main lines in use: 23,140 (2012)
country comparison to the world: 183

Telephones—mobile cellular: 560,000 (2012)
country comparison to the world: 166

Telephone system: *general assessment:* telephone services have improved; inter-atoll communication through microwave links; all inhabited islands and resorts are connected with telephone and fax service
domestic: each island now has at least 1 public telephone, and there are mobile-cellular networks with a rapidly expanding subscribership that has reached 135 per 100 persons
international: country code—960; linked to international submarine cable Fiber-Optic Link Around the Globe (FLAG); satellite earth station—3 Intelsat (Indian Ocean) (2011)

Broadcast media: state-owned radio and TV monopoly until recently; state-owned TV operates 2 channels; 3 privately owned TV stations; state owns Voice of Maldives and operates both an entertainment and a music-based station; 5 privately owned radio stations (2012)

Internet country code: .mv

Internet hosts: 3,296 (2012)
country comparison to the world: 153

Internet users: 86,400 (2009)
country comparison to the world: 164

TRANSPORTATION

Airports: 9 (2013)
country comparison to the world: 159

Airports—with paved runways: *total:* 7
over 3,047 m: 1
2,438 to 3,047 m: 1
1,524 to 2,437 m: 1
914 to 1,523 m: 4 (2013)

Airports—with unpaved runways: *total:* 2
914 to 1,523 m: 2 (2013)

Roadways: *total:* 88 km
country comparison to the world: 215
paved roads: 88 km—60 km in Male; 14 km on Addu Atolis; 14 km on Laamu
note: island roads are mainly compacted coral (2013)

Merchant marine: *total:* 1 8
country comparison to the world: 97
by type: bulk carrier 1, cargo 14, petroleum tanker 1, refrigerated cargo 2
foreign-owned: 4 (Singapore 4)
registered in other countries: 4 (Panama 2, Tuvalu 1, unknown 1) (2010)

Ports and terminals: *major seaport(s):* Male

MILITARY

Military branches: Maldives National Defense Force (MNDF): Marine Corps, Security Protection Group, Coast Guard (2010)

Military service age and obligation: 18-28 years of age for voluntary service; no conscription; 10th grade or equivalent education required; must not be a member of a political party (2012)

Manpower available for military service:
males age 16-49: 156,319
females age 16-49: 98,815 (2010 est.)

Manpower fit for military service:
males age 16-49: 135,374
females age 16-49: 85,181 (2010 est.)

Manpower reaching militarily significant age annually: *male:* 4,167

female: 3,595 (2010 est.)

Military—note: the Maldives National Defense Force (MNDF), with its small size and with little serviceable equipment, is inadequate to prevent external aggression and is primarily tasked to reinforce the Maldives Police Service (MPS) and ensure security in the exclusive economic zone (2008)

TRANSNATIONAL ISSUES

Disputes—international: none

Trafficking in persons: *current situation*: Maldives is a destination country for men, women, and children subjected to forced labor and sex trafficking and a source country for Maldivian children subjected to human trafficking within the country; Bangladeshi and Indian migrants working both legally and illegally in the construction and service sectors face conditions of forced labor, including fraudulent recruitment, confiscation of identity and travel documents, nonpayment of wages, and debt bondage; a small number of women from Sri Lanka, Thailand, India, China, the Philippines, Bangladesh, Eastern Europe, and former Soviet states are trafficked to Maldives for sexual exploitation; some Maldivian children are transported to the capital for forced domestic service, where they may also be sexually abused

tier rating: Tier 2 Watch List—Maldives does not fully comply with the minimum standards for the elimination of trafficking; the government does not have laws prohibiting all human trafficking offenses but introduced an anti-trafficking law to the legislature in December 2012, approved an anti-trafficking plan for 2012-13, and formed an anti-trafficking steering committee in May 2012; the government reported that it prosecuted some sex trafficking cases but did not take concrete actions to protect trafficking victims and prevent trafficking; the government continues to lack systematic procedures for identifying trafficking victims among vulnerable populations and referring them to protective services; officials continue to confuse human trafficking with human smuggling and the presence of undocumented migrants (2013)

MALI

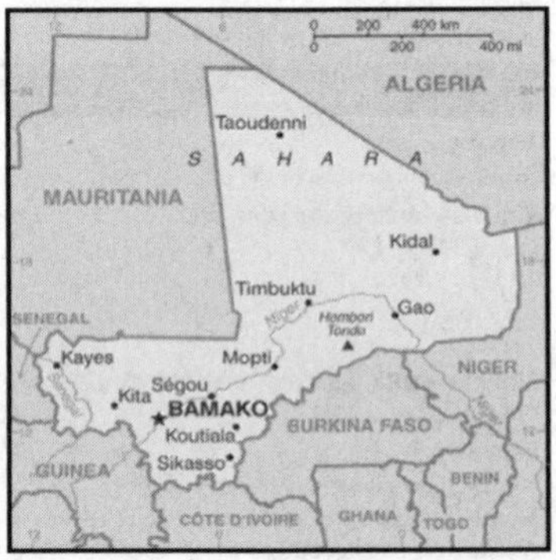

INTRODUCTION

Background: The Sudanese Republic and Senegal became independent of France in 1960 as the Mali Federation. When Senegal withdrew after only a few months, what formerly made up the Sudanese Republic was renamed Mali. Rule by dictatorship was brought to a close in 1991 by a military coup that ushered in a period of democratic rule. President Alpha KONARE won Mali's first two democratic presidential elections in 1992 and 1997. In keeping with Mali's two-term constitutional limit, he stepped down in 2002 and was succeeded by Amadou Toumani TOURE, who was elected to a second term in 2007 elections that were widely judged to be free and fair. Malian returnees from Libya in 2011 exacerbated tensions in northern Mali, and Tuareg ethnic militias started a rebellion in January 2012. Low- and mid-level soldiers, frustrated with the poor handling of the rebellion overthrew TOURE on 22 March. Intensive mediation efforts led by the Economic Community of West African States (ECOWAS) returned power to a civilian administration in April with the appointment of interim President Dioncounda TRAORE. The post-coup chaos led to rebels expelling the Malian military from the three northern regions of the country and allowed Islamic militants to set up strongholds. Hundreds of thousands of northern Malians fled the violence to southern Mali and neighboring countries, exacerbating regional food insecurity in host communities. An international military intervention to retake the three northern regions began in January 2013 and within a month most of the north had been retaken. In a democratic presidential election conducted in July and August of 2013, Ibrahim Boubacar KEITA was elected president in the second round.

GEOGRAPHY

Location: interior Western Africa, southwest of Algeria, north of Guinea, Cote d'Ivoire, and Burkina Faso, west of Niger

Geographic coordinates: 17 00 N, 4 00 W

Map references: Africa

Area: *total:* 1,240,192 sq km
country comparison to the world: 24
land: 1,220,190 sq km
water: 20,002 sq km

Area—comparative: slightly less than twice the size of Texas

Land boundaries: *total:* 7,243 km
border countries: Algeria 1,376 km, Burkina Faso 1,000 km, Guinea 858 km, Cote d'Ivoire 532 km, Mauritania 2,237 km, Niger 821 km, Senegal 419 km

Coastline: 0 km (landlocked)

Maritime claims: none (landlocked)

Climate: subtropical to arid; hot and dry (February to June); rainy, humid, and mild (June to November); cool and dry (November to February)

Terrain: mostly flat to rolling northern plains covered by sand; savanna in south, rugged hills in northeast

Elevation extremes: *lowest point:* Senegal River 23 m
highest point: Hombori Tondo 1,155 m

Natural resources: gold, phosphates, kaolin, salt, limestone, uranium, gypsum, granite, hydropower
note: bauxite, iron ore, manganese, tin, and copper deposits are known but not exploited

Land use: *arable land:* 5.53%
permanent crops: 0.1%
other: 94.37% (2011)

Irrigated land: 2,358 sq km (2003)

Total renewable water resources: 100 cu km (2011)

Freshwater withdrawal (domestic/industrial/agricultural): *total:* 6.55 cu km/yr (9%/1%/90%)
per capita: 545.4 cu m/yr (2000)

Natural hazards: hot, dust-laden harmattan haze common during dry seasons; recurring droughts; occasional Niger River flooding

Environment—current issues: deforestation; soil erosion; desertification; inadequate supplies of potable water; poaching

Environment—international agreements: *party to:* Biodiversity, Climate Change, Climate Change-Kyoto Protocol, Desertification, Endangered Species, Hazardous Wastes, Law of the Sea, Ozone Layer Protection, Wetlands, Whaling
signed, but not ratified: none of the selected agreements

Geography—note: landlocked; divided into three natural zones: the southern, cultivated Sudanese; the central, semiarid Sahelian; and the northern, arid Saharan

PEOPLE AND SOCIETY

Nationality: *noun:* Malian(s)
adjective: Malian

Ethnic groups: Mande 50% (Bambara, Malinke, Soninke), Peul 17%, Voltaic 12%, Songhai 6%, Tuareg and Moor 10%, other 5%

Languages: French (official), Bambara 46.3%, Peul/foulfoulbe 9.4%, Dogon 7.2%, Maraka/soninke 6.4%, Malinke 5.6%, Sonrhai/djerma 5.6%, Minianka 4.3%, Tamacheq 3.5%, Senoufo 2.6%, unspecified 0.6%, other 8.5%
note: Mali has 13 national languages in addition to its official language

Religions: Muslim 94.8%, Christian 2.4%, Animist 2%, none 0.5%, unspecified 0.3% (2009 Census)

Population: 16,455,903 (July 2014 est.)
country comparison to the world: 67
Age structure: *0-14 years:* 47.6% (male 3,931,818/female 3,899,535)
15-24 years: 19% (male 1,489,830/female 1,638,995)
25-54 years: 26.7% (male 2,042,666/female 2,348,337)
55-64 years: 3% (male 307,167/female 306,470)
65 years and over: 3% (male 246,084/female 245,001) (2014 est.)

Dependency ratios:
total dependency ratio: 100.7 %
youth dependency ratio: 95.1 %
elderly dependency ratio: 5.6 %
potential support ratio: 17.9 (2013)

Median age: *total:* 16 years
male: 15.4 years
female: 16.7 years (2014 est.)

Population growth rate: 3% (2014 est.)
country comparison to the world: 12

Birth rate: 45.53 births/1,000 population (2014 est.)
country comparison to the world: 2

Death rate: 13.22 deaths/1,000 population (2014 est.)
country comparison to the world: 18

Net migration rate: -2.33 migrant(s)/1,000 population (2014 est.)
country comparison to the world: 171

Urbanization: *urban population:* 34.9% of total population (2011)
rate of urbanization: 4.77% annual rate of change (2010-15 est.)

Major urban areas—population: BAMAKO (capital) 1.628 million (2009)

Sex ratio: *at birth:* 1.03 male(s)/female
0-14 years: 1.01 male(s)/female
15-24 years: 0.91 male(s)/female
25-54 years: 0.87 male(s)/female
55-64 years: 0.95 male(s)/female
65 years and over: 1.01 male(s)/female
total population: 0.95 male(s)/female (2014 est.)

Mother's mean age at first birth: 18.6 (2006 est.)

Maternal mortality rate: 540 deaths/100,000 live births (2010)
country comparison to the world: 18

Infant mortality rate: *total:* 104.34 deaths/1,000 live births
country comparison to the world: 2
male: 111.04 deaths/1,000 live births
female: 97.44 deaths/1,000 live births (2014 est.)

Life expectancy at birth: *total population:* 54.95 years
country comparison to the world: 206
male: 53.12 years
female: 56.83 years (2014 est.)

Total fertility rate: 6.16 children born/woman (2014 est.)
country comparison to the world: 2

Contraceptive prevalence rate: 8.2% (2006)

Health expenditures: 6.8% of GDP (2011)
country comparison to the world: 88

Physicians density: 0.08 physicians/1,000 population (2010)

Hospital bed density: 0.1 beds/1,000 population (2010)

Drinking water source:
improved:
urban: 89.2% of population
rural: 52.6% of population
total: 65.4% of population
unimproved:
urban: 10.8% of population
rural: 47.4% of population
total: 65.4% of population (2011 est.)

Sanitation facility access:
improved:
urban: 35.2% of population
rural: 14.3% of population
total: 21.6% of population
unimproved:
urban: 64.8% of population
rural: 85.7% of population
total: 78.4% of population (2011 est.)

HIV/AIDS—adult prevalence rate: 0.9% (2012 est.)
country comparison to the world: 50

HIV/AIDS—people living with HIV/AIDS: 100,300 (2012 est.)
country comparison to the world: 44

HIV/AIDS—deaths: 4,900 (2012 est.)
country comparison to the world: 41

Major infectious diseases: *degree of risk:* very high
food or waterborne diseases: bacterial and protozoal diarrhea, hepatitis A, and typhoid fever
vectorborne diseases: malaria and dengue fever
water contact disease: schistosomiasis
respiratory disease: meningococcal meningitis
animal contact disease: rabies (2013)

Obesity—adult prevalence rate: 4.3% (2008)
country comparison to the world: 166

Children under the age of 5 years underweight: 27.9% (2006)
country comparison to the world: 23

Education expenditures: 4.8% of GDP (2011)
country comparison to the world: 83

Literacy: *definition:* age 15 and over can read and write
total population: 33.4%
male: 43.1%
female: 24.6% (2011 est.)

School life expectancy (primary to tertiary education): *total:* 9 years
male: 10 years
female: 8 years (2012)

Child labor—children ages 5-14:
total number: 1,485,027
percentage: 36 % (2010 est.)

GOVERNMENT

Country name: *conventional long form:* Republic of Mali
conventional short form: Mali
local long form: Republique de Mali
local short form: Mali
former: French Sudan and Sudanese Republic

Government type: republic

Capital: *name:* Bamako
geographic coordinates: 12 39 N, 8 00 W
time difference: UTC 0 (5 hours ahead of Washington, DC during Standard Time)

Administrative divisions: 8 regions (regions, singular—region), 1 district*; District de Bamako*, Gao, Kayes, Kidal, Koulikoro, Mopti, Segou, Sikasso, Tombouctou (Timbuktu)

Independence: 22 September 1960 (from France)

National holiday: Independence Day, 22 September (1960)

Constitution: several previous; latest drafted August 1991, approved by referendum 12 January 1992, effective 25 February 1992; amended 1999; note—suspended briefly in 2012 (2011)

Legal system: civil law system based on the French civil law model and influenced by customary law; judicial review of legislative acts in Constitutional Court

International law organization participation: has not submitted an ICJ jurisdiction declaration; accepts ICCt jurisdiction

Suffrage: 18 years of age; universal

Executive branch: *chief of state:* President Ibrahim Boubacar KEITA (since 4 September 2013)
head of government: Prime Minister Moussa MARA (since 5 April 2014)
cabinet: Council of Ministers appointed by the prime minister (For more information visit the World Leaders website)
elections: president elected by popular vote for a five-year term (eligible for a second term); the election scheduled for 29 April 2012 and delayed following the March 2012 coup took place 28 July 2013 and a runoff election was held on 11 August 2013; prime minister appointed by the president
election results: Ibrahim Boubacar KEITA elected president in a runoff election; percent of vote Ibrahim Boubacar KEITA 77.6%, Soumaila CISSE 22.4%

Legislative branch: unicameral National Assembly or Assemblee Nationale (160 seats: 147 seats elected in single seat constituencies and 13 seats elected by Malians abroad; members elected by popular vote to serve five-year terms)
elections: last held in two rounds on 24 November 2013 and on 15 December 2013 (next to be held in 2017); note the scheduled July 2012 election was cancelled due to a coup d'etat and the Tuareg Rebellion
election results: percent of vote by party—NA; seats by party—FDR coalition 64 (RPM 61, PARENA 3), ADP coalition 42 (ADEMA 20, URD 18, CNID 4), FARE 5, CODEM 5, SADI 4, ASMA-CFP 4, Yelema 2, independents 16, other 5; note—13 seats were from voters abroad

Judicial branch: *highest court(s):* Supreme Court or Cour Supreme (consists of 19 members organized into 3 civil chambers and a criminal chamber); Constitutional Court (consists of 9 members)
judge selection and term of office: Supreme Court members appointed by the Ministry of Justice to serve 5-year terms; Constitutional Court members selected—3 each by the president, the National Assembly, and the Supreme Council of the Magistracy; members serve single renewable 7-year terms
subordinate courts: High Court of Justice (jurisdiction limited to cases of high treason or criminal offenses by the president or ministers while in office)

Political parties and leaders: African Solidarity for Democracy and Independence or SADI [Oumar MARIKO, secretary general]; Alliance for Democracy or ADEMA [Dionconda TRAORE]; Alliance for Democracy and Progress or ADP (a coalition of political parties including ADEMA and URD; formed in December 2006 to support the presidential candidacy of Amadou TOURE); Alliance for Democratic Change (political group comprised mainly of Tuareg from Mali's northern region); Alliance for the Solidarity of Mali-Convergence of Patriotic Forces or ASMA-CFP [Soumeylou Boubeye; MAIGA]; Alternative Forces for Renewal and Emergence or FARE [Modibo SIDIBE]; Convergence for the development of Mali or CODEM [Housseyni GUINDO]; Economic and Social Development Party or PDES [Jamille BITTAR]; Front for Democracy and the Republic or FDR (a coalition of political parties including RPM and PARENA; formed to oppose the presidential candidacy of Amadou

TOURE); Movement for a Common Destiny or MODEC [Koniba SIDIBE]; National Congress for Democratic Initiative or CNID [Mountaga TALL]; Party for Democracy and Progress or PDP [Mady KONATE]; Party for National Renewal or PARENA [Tiebile DRAME]; Patriotic Movement for Renewal or MPR [Choguel Kokalla MAIGA]; Rally for Democracy and Labor or RDT [Amadou Ali NIANGADOU]; Rally for Mali or RPM [Ibrahim Boubacar KEITA]; Sudanese Union/African Democratic Rally or US/RDA [Mamadou Bamou TOURE]; Union for Democracy and Development or UDD [Tieman Hubert COULIBALY]; Union for Republic and Democracy or URD [Younoussi TOURE]; Yelema [Moussa Mara]

Political pressure groups and leaders:
other: the army; Islamic authorities; state-run cotton company CMDT

International organization participation: ACP, AfDB, AU, CD, ECOWAS, EITI (compliant country), FAO, FZ, G-77, IAEA, IBRD, ICAO, ICRM, IDA, IDB, IFAD, IFC, IFRCS, ILO, IMF, Interpol, IOC, IOM, IPU, ISO, ITSO, ITU, ITUC (NGOs), MIGA, MONUSCO, NAM, OIC, OIF, OPCW, UN, UNAMID, UNCTAD, UNESCO, UNIDO, UNMIL, UNMISS, UNWTO, UPU, WADB (regional), WAEMU, WCO, WFTU (NGOs), WHO, WIPO, WMO, WTO

Diplomatic representation in the US:
chief of mission: Ambassador Al Maamoun Baba Lamine KEITA (since 8 January 2013)
chancery: 2130 R Street NW, Washington, DC 20008
telephone: [1] (202) 332-2249, 939-8950
FAX: [1] (202) 332-6603

Diplomatic representation from the US:
chief of mission: Ambassador Mary Beth LEONARD (since 7 November 2011)
embassy: located just off the Roi Bin Fahad Aziz Bridge just west of the Bamako central district
mailing address: ACI 2000, Rue 243, Porte 297, Bamako
telephone: [223] 2070-2300
FAX: [223] 2070-2479

Flag description: three equal vertical bands of green (hoist side), yellow, and red
note: uses the popular Pan-African colors of Ethiopia; the colors from left to right are the same as those of neighboring Senegal (which has an additional green central star) and the reverse of those on the flag of neighboring Guinea

National anthem: *name:* "Le Mali" (Mali)
lyrics/music: Seydou Badian KOUYATE/Banzoumana SISSOKO
note: adopted 1962; the anthem is also known as "Pour L'Afrique et pour toi, Mali" (For Africa and for You, Mali) and "A ton appel Mali" (At Your Call, Mali)

ECONOMY

Economy—overview: Among the 25 poorest countries in the world, Mali is a landlocked country that depends on gold mining and agricultural exports for revenue. Economic activity is largely confined to the riverine area irrigated by the Niger River and about 65% of its land area is desert or semidesert. About 10% of the population is nomadic and about 80% of the labor force is engaged in farming and fishing. Mali remains dependent on foreign aid. The country's fiscal status fluctuates with gold and agricultural commodity prices and the harvest; cotton and gold exports make up around 80% of export earnings. Industrial activity is concentrated on processing farm commodities. Mali is developing its iron ore extraction industry to diversify foreign exchange earnings away from gold. Mali has invested in tourism but security issues hurt the industry. Mali experienced economic growth of about 5% per year between 1996-2011, but the global recession, a military coup, and terrorist activity in the north of the country caused a decline in output in 2012; growth resumed at a slow pace in 2013. The main threat to Mali's economy is a return to physical insecurity. Other long term threats to the economy include high population growth, corruption, a weak infrastructure, and low levels of human capital.

GDP (purchasing power parity): $18.9 billion (2013 est.)
country comparison to the world: 138
$18.03 billion (2012 est.)
$18.25 billion (2011 est.)
note: data are in 2013 US dollars

GDP (official exchange rate): $11.37 billion (2013 est.)

GDP—real growth rate: 4.8% (2013 est.)
country comparison to the world: 61
-1.2% (2012 est.)
2.7% (2011 est.)

GDP—per capita (PPP): $1,100 (2013 est.)
country comparison to the world: 217
$1,100 (2012 est.)
$1,200 (2011 est.)
note: data are in 2013 US dollars

Gross national saving: 15.8% of GDP (2013 est.)
country comparison to the world: 107
21.6% of GDP (2012 est.)
12.1% of GDP (2011 est.)

GDP—composition, by end use:
household consumption: 68.8%
government consumption: 18.6%
investment in fixed capital: 23.5%
investment in inventories: 0.6%
exports of goods and services: 22.5%
imports of goods and services: -34%
(2013 est.)

GDP—composition, by sector of origin:
agriculture: 38.5%
industry: 24.4%
services: 37% (2013 est.)

Agriculture—products: cotton, millet, rice, corn, vegetables, peanuts; cattle, sheep, goats

Industries: food processing; construction; phosphate and gold mining

Industrial production growth rate: 7%
country comparison to the world: 32

Labor force: 3.241 million (2007 est.)
country comparison to the world: 101

Labor force—by occupation:
agriculture: 80%
industry and services: 20% (2005 est.)

Unemployment rate: 30% (2004 est.)
country comparison to the world: 183

Population below poverty line: 36.1% (2005 est.)

Household income or consumption by percentage share: *lowest 10%:* 3.5%
highest 10%: 25.8% (2010 est.)

Distribution of family income—Gini index: 40.1 (2001)
country comparison to the world: 58
50.5 (1994)

Budget: *revenues:* $2.868 billion
expenditures: $2.948 billion (2013 est.)

Taxes and other revenues: 25.2% of GDP (2013 est.)
country comparison to the world: 123

Budget surplus (+) or deficit (-):
-0.7% of GDP (2013 est.)
country comparison to the world: 59

Public debt: 30.5% of GDP (2013 est.)
country comparison to the world: 122
27.5% of GDP (2012 est.)

Fiscal year: calendar year

Inflation rate (consumer prices): 0.1% (2013 est.)
country comparison to the world: 7
5.4% (2012 est.)

Central bank discount rate: 16% (31 December 2010 est.)
country comparison to the world: 87
4.25% (31 December 2009 est.)

Commercial bank prime lending rate: 9.3% (31 December 2013 est.)
country comparison to the world: 98
9.3% (31 December 2012 est.)

Stock of narrow money: $2.848 billion (31 December 2013 est.)
country comparison to the world: 118
$2.583 billion (31 December 2012 est.)

Stock of broad money: $3.942 billion (31 December 2013 est.)
country comparison to the world: 138
$3.446 billion (31 December 2012 est.)

Stock of domestic credit: $2.234 billion (31 December 2013 est.)
country comparison to the world: 132
$2.102 billion (31 December 2012 est.)

Market value of publicly traded shares: $NA

Current account balance: -$918 million (2013 est.)
country comparison to the world: 117
-$737.5 million (2012 est.)

Exports: $2.577 billion (2013 est.)
country comparison to the world: 136
$2.756 billion (2012 est.)

Exports—commodities: cotton, gold, livestock

Exports—partners: China 52.9%, Malaysia 11%, Indonesia 5.3%, India 4.1% (2012)

Imports: $2.895 billion (2013 est.)
country comparison to the world: 150
$2.794 billion (2012 est.)

Imports—commodities: petroleum, machinery and equipment, construction materials, foodstuffs, textiles

Imports—partners: France 11.2%, Senegal 9.9%, Cote dIvoire 8.7%, China 8.6% (2012)

Debt—external: $3.349 billion (31 December 2013 est.)
country comparison to the world: 133
$3.041 billion (31 December 2012 est.)

Stock of direct foreign investment—at home: $2.75 billion (31 December 2013 est.)
country comparison to the world: 95
$2.545 billion (31 December 2012 est.)

Stock of direct foreign investment—abroad:

$NA (31 December 2013 est.)
$848.2 million (31 December 2012 est.)
Exchange rates: Communaute Financiere Africaine francs (XOF) per US dollar—
500.7 (2013 est.)
510.53 (2012 est.)
495.28 (2010 est.)
472.19 (2009)
447.81 (2008)

ENERGY

Electricity—production: 520 million kWh (2010 est.)
country comparison to the world: 163

Electricity—consumption: 483.6 million kWh (2010 est.)
country comparison to the world: 170

Electricity—exports: 0 kWh (2012 est.)
country comparison to the world: 166

Electricity—imports: 0 kWh (2012 est.)
country comparison to the world: 169

Electricity—installed generating capacity: 304,000 kW (2010 est.)
country comparison to the world: 150

Electricity—from fossil fuels: 48.4% of total installed capacity (2010 est.)
country comparison to the world: 159

Electricity—from nuclear fuels: 0% of total installed capacity (2010 est.)
country comparison to the world: 138

Electricity—from hydroelectric plants: 51.6% of total installed capacity (2010 est.)
country comparison to the world: 42

Electricity—from other renewable sources: 0% of total installed capacity (2010 est.)
country comparison to the world: 202

Crude oil—production: 0 bbl/day (2012 est.)
country comparison to the world: 195

Crude oil—exports: 0 bbl/day (2010 est.)
country comparison to the world: 153

Crude oil—imports: 0 bbl/day (2010 est.)
country comparison to the world: 92

Crude oil—proved reserves: 0 bbl (1 January 2013 es)
country comparison to the world: 164

Refined petroleum products—production: 0 bbl/day (2010 est.)
country comparison to the world: 173

Refined petroleum products—consumption: 4,994 bbl/day (2011 est.)
country comparison to the world: 169

Refined petroleum products—exports: 0 bbl/day (2010 est.)
country comparison to the world: 197

Refined petroleum products—imports: 4,698 bbl/day (2010 est.)
country comparison to the world: 156

Natural gas—production: 0 cu m (2011 est.)
country comparison to the world: 166

Natural gas—consumption: 0 cu m (2010 est.)
country comparison to the world: 171

Natural gas—exports: 0 cu m (2011 est.)
country comparison to the world: 147

Natural gas—imports: 0 cu m (2011 est.)
country comparison to the world: 96

Natural gas—proved reserves: 0 cu m (1 January 2013 es)
country comparison to the world: 170

Carbon dioxide emissions from consumption of energy: 742,300 Mt (2011 est.)
country comparison to the world: 173

COMMUNICATIONS

Telephones—main lines in use: 112,000 (2012)
country comparison to the world: 142

Telephones—mobile cellular: 14.613 million (2012)
country comparison to the world: 59

Telephone system: *general assessment*: domestic system unreliable but improving; increasing use of local radio loops to extend network coverage to remote areas
domestic: fixed-line subscribership remains less than 1 per 100 persons; mobile-cellular subscribership has increased sharply to about 70 per 100 persons
international: country code—223; satellite communications center and fiber-optic links to neighboring countries; satellite earth stations—2 Intelsat (1 Atlantic Ocean, 1 Indian Ocean) (2010)

Broadcast media: national public TV broadcaster; 2 privately owned companies provide subscription services to foreign multi-channel TV packages; national public radio broadcaster supplemented by a large number of privately owned and community broadcast stations; transmissions of multiple international broadcasters are available (2007)

Internet country code: .ml

Internet hosts: 437 (2012)
country comparison to the world: 186

Internet users: 249,800 (2009)
country comparison to the world: 135

TRANSPORTATION

Airports: 25 (2013)
country comparison to the world: 129

Airports—with paved runways: *total:* 8
over 3,047 m: 1
2,438 to 3,047 m: 4
1,524 to 2,437 m: 2
914 to 1,523 m: 1 (2013)

Airports—with unpaved runways: *total:* 1 7
1,524 to 2,437 m: 3
914 to 1,523 m: 9
under 914 m: 5 (2013)

Heliports: 2 (2013)

Railways: *total:* 593 km
country comparison to the world: 109
narrow gauge: 593 km 1.000-m gauge (2008)

Roadways: *total:* 22,474 km
country comparison to the world: 102
paved: 5,522 km
unpaved: 16,952 km (2009)

Waterways: 1,800 km (downstream of Koulikoro; low water levels on the River Niger cause problems in dry years; in the months before the rainy season the river is not navigable by commercial vessels) (2011)
country comparison to the world: 44

Ports and terminals: *river port(s):* Koulikoro (Niger)

MILITARY

Military branches: *Malian Armed Forces:* Army (Armee de Terre), Republic of Mali Air Force (Force Aerienne de la Republique du Mali, FARM), National Guard (Garde National du Mali) (2013)

Military service age and obligation: 18 years of age for selective compulsory and voluntary military service; conscript service obligation—2 years (2012)

Manpower available for military service:
males age 16-49: 2,848,412
females age 16-49: 2,981,106 (2010 est.)

Manpower fit for military service:
males age 16-49: 1,825,779
females age 16-49: 1,968,563 (2010 est.)

Manpower reaching militarily significant age annually: *male:* 158,031
female: 159,733 (2010 est.)

Military expenditures: 1.44% of GDP (2012)
country comparison to the world: 69
1.51% of GDP (2011)
1.44% of GDP (2010)

TRANSNATIONAL ISSUES

Disputes—international: demarcation is underway with Burkina Faso

Refugees and internally displaced persons:
refugees (country of origin): 12,904 (Mauritania) (2012)
IDPs: 187,000 (Tuareg rebellion since 2012) (2014)

Trafficking in persons: *current situation:* Mali is a source, transit, and destination country for men, women, and children subjected to forced labor and sex trafficking; women and girls are forced into domestic servitude, agricultural labor, and support roles in gold mines, as well as subjected to sex trafficking; Malian boys are found in conditions of forced labor in agricultural settings, gold mines, and the informal commercial sector, as well as forced begging both within Mali and neighboring countries; Malians and other Africans who travel through Mali to Mauritania, Algeria, or Libya in hopes of reaching Europe are particularly at risk of becoming victims of human trafficking; men and boys, primarily of Songhai ethnicity, are subjected to the longstanding practice of debt bondage in the salt mines of Taoudenni in northern Mali; some members of Mali's black Tamachek community are subjected to traditional slavery-related practices, and this involuntary servitude reportedly has extended to their children; reports indicate that non-governmental armed groups operating in northern Mali recruited children as combatants, cooks, porters, guards, spies, and sex slaves

tier rating: Tier 2 Watch List—Mali does not fully comply with the minimum standards for the elimination of trafficking; however, it is making significant efforts to do so; although the government enacted a comprehensive anti-trafficking law in 2012, it did not demonstrate evidence of overall increasing efforts to address human trafficking over the previous year; the government has failed to prosecute or convict any trafficking offenders, has not provided any direct services to victims, and has not made any tangible prevention efforts; the government continues to cite a lack of personnel and resources as reasons for its inability to adequately identify and rescue child victims of forced labor in the mining industry (2013)

MALTA

INTRODUCTION

Background: Great Britain formally acquired possession of Malta in 1814. The island staunchly supported the UK through both world wars and remained in the Commonwealth when it became independent in 1964. A decade later Malta became a republic. Since about the mid-1980s, the island has transformed itself into a freight transshipment point, a financial center, and a tourist destination. Malta became an EU member in May 2004 and began using the euro as currency in 2008.

GEOGRAPHY

Location: Southern Europe, islands in the Mediterranean Sea, south of Sicily (Italy)

Geographic coordinates: 35 50 N, 14 35 E

Map references: Europe

Area: *total:* 316 sq km
country comparison to the world: 208
land: 316 sq km
water: 0 sq km

Area—comparative: slightly less than twice the size of Washington, DC

Land boundaries: 0 km

Coastline: 196.8 km (excludes 56 km for the island of Gozo)

Maritime claims: *territorial sea:* 12 nm
contiguous zone: 24 nm
continental shelf: 200 m depth or to the depth of exploitation
exclusive fishing zone: 25 nm

Climate: Mediterranean; mild, rainy winters; hot, dry summers

Terrain: mostly low, rocky, flat to dissected plains; many coastal cliffs

Elevation extremes: *lowest point:* Mediterranean Sea 0 m
highest point: Ta'Dmejrek 253 m (near Dingli)

Natural resources: limestone, salt, arable land

Land use: *arable land:* 28.12%
permanent crops: 4.06%
other: 67.81% (2011)

Irrigated land: 32 sq km (2007)

Total renewable water resources: 0.05 cu km (2011)

Freshwater withdrawal (domestic/industrial/agricultural): *total:* 0.05 cu km/yr (64%/1%/35%)
per capita: 134.1 cu m/yr (2009)

Natural hazards: NA

Environment—current issues: limited natural freshwater resources; increasing reliance on desalination

Environment—international agreements: *party to:* Air Pollution, Biodiversity, Climate Change, Climate Change-Kyoto Protocol, Desertification, Endangered Species, Hazardous Wastes, Law of the Sea, Marine Dumping, Ozone Layer Protection, Ship Pollution, Wetlands
signed, but not ratified: none of the selected agreements

Geography—note: the country comprises an archipelago, with only the three largest islands (Malta, Ghawdex or Gozo, and Kemmuna or Comino) being inhabited; numerous bays provide good harbors; Malta and Tunisia are discussing the commercial exploitation of the continental shelf between their countries, particularly for oil exploration

PEOPLE AND SOCIETY

Nationality: *noun:* Maltese (singular and plural)
adjective: Maltese

Ethnic groups: Maltese (descendants of ancient Carthaginians and Phoenicians with strong elements of Italian and other Mediterranean stock)

Languages: Maltese (official) 90.1%, English (official) 6%, multilingual 3%, other 0.9% (2005 est.)

Religions: Roman Catholic (official) 98%

Population: 412,655 (July 2014 est.)
country comparison to the world: 176

Age structure:
0-14 years: 15.1% (male 32,021/female 30,432)
15-24 years: 12.6% (male 26,680/female 25,201)
25-54 years: 40.4% (male 85,109/female 81,577)
55-64 years: 17.9% (male 28,751/female 29,113)
65 years and over: 17.2% (male 32,903/female 40,868) (2014 est.)

Dependency ratios:
total dependency ratio: 44.9 %
youth dependency ratio: 21.3 %
elderly dependency ratio: 23.6 %
potential support ratio: 4.2 (2013)

Median age: *total:* 40.9 years
male: 39.7 years
female: 42.1 years (2014 est.)

Population growth rate: 0.33% (2014 est.)
country comparison to the world: 170

Birth rate: 10.24 births/1,000 population (2014 est.)
country comparison to the world: 189

Death rate: 8.96 deaths/1,000 population (2014 est.)
country comparison to the world: 70

Net migration rate: 1.99 migrant(s)/1,000 population (2014 est.)
country comparison to the world: 47

Urbanization: *urban population:* 95% of total population (2010)
rate of urbanization: 0.5% annual rate of change (2010-15 est.)

Major urban areas—population: VALLETTA (capital) 199,000 (2009)

Sex ratio: *at birth:* 1.06 male(s)/female
0-14 years: 1.05 male(s)/female
15-24 years: 1.06 male(s)/female
25-54 years: 1.04 male(s)/female
55-64 years: 0.99 male(s)/female
65 years and over: 0.79 male(s)/female
total population: 0.99 male(s)/female (2014 est.)

Mother's mean age at first birth: 26.5 (2008 est.)

Maternal mortality rate: 8 deaths/100,000 live births (2010)
country comparison to the world: 161

Infant mortality rate: *total:* 3.59 deaths/1,000 live births
country comparison to the world: 207
male: 4 deaths/1,000 live births
female: 3.16 deaths/1,000 live births (2014 est.)

Life expectancy at birth: *total population:* 80.11 years
country comparison to the world: 33
male: 77.8 years
female: 82.56 years (2014 est.)

Total fertility rate: 1.54 children born/woman (2014 est.)
country comparison to the world: 187

Contraceptive prevalence rate: 85.8%
note: percent of women aged 20-45 (1993)

Health expenditures: 8.5% of GDP (2010)
country comparison to the world: 51

Physicians density: 3.23 physicians/1,000 population (2011)

Hospital bed density: 4.4 beds/1,000 population (2011)

Drinking water source:
improved:
urban: 100% of population
rural: 100% of population
total: 100% of population
unimproved:
urban: 0% of population
rural: 0% of population
total: 0% of population (2011 est.)

Sanitation facility access:
improved:
urban: 100% of population
rural: 100% of population
total: 100% of population
unimproved:
urban: 0% of population
rural: 0% of population
total: 0% of population (2011 est.)

HIV/AIDS—adult prevalence rate: 0.1% (2009 est.)
country comparison to the world: 160

HIV/AIDS—people living with HIV/AIDS: fewer than 500 (2009 est.)
country comparison to the world: 159

HIV/AIDS—deaths: fewer than 100 (2009 est.)
country comparison to the world: 141

Obesity—adult prevalence rate: 28.8% (2008)
country comparison to the world: 32

Education expenditures: 6.9% of GDP (2010)
country comparison to the world: 23

Literacy: *definition:* age 15 and over can read and write
total population: 92.4%
male: 91.2%
female: 93.5% (2005 est.)

School life expectancy (primary to tertiary education): *total:* 15 years
male: 14 years

female: 15 years (2011)

Unemployment, youth ages 15-24: *total:* 14.2%
country comparison to the world: 91
male: 14%
female: 14.5% (2012)

GOVERNMENT

Country name: *conventional long form:* Republic of Malta
conventional short form: Malta
local long form: Repubblika ta' Malta
local short form: Malta

Government type: republic

Capital: *name:* Valletta

geographic coordinates: 35 53 N, 14 30 E
time difference: UTC+1 (6 hours ahead of Washington, DC during Standard Time)
daylight saving time: +1hr, begins last Sunday in March; ends last Sunday in October

Administrative divisions: 68 localities (Il-lokalita); Attard, Balzan, Birgu, Birkirkara, Birzebbuga, Bormla, Dingli, Fgura, Floriana, Fontana, Ghajnsielem, Gharb, Gharghur, Ghasri Ghaxaq, Gudja, Gzira, Hamrun, Iklin, Imdina, Imgarr, Imqabba, Imsida, Imtarfa, Isla, Kalkara, Kercem, Kirkop, Lija, Luqa, Marsa, Marsaskala, Marsaxlokk, Mellieha, Mosta, Munxar, Nadur, Naxxar, Paola, Pembroke, Pieta, Qala, Qormi, Qrendi, Rabat, Rabat (Ghawdex), Safi, San Giljan/Saint Julian, San Gwann/Saint John, San Lawrenz/Saint Lawrence, Sannat, San Pawl il-Bahar/Saint Paul's Bay, Santa Lucija/Saint Lucia, Santa Venera/Saint Venera, Siggiewi, Sliema, Swieqi, Tarxien, Ta' Xbiex, Valletta, Xaghra, Xewkija, Xghajra, Zabbar, Zebbug, Zebbug (Ghawdex), Zejtun, Zurrieq

Independence: 21 September 1964 (from the UK)

National holiday: Independence Day, 21 September (1964); Republic Day, 13 December (1974)

Constitution: many previous; latest adopted 21 September 1964; amended many times, last in 2011 (2011)

Legal system: mixed legal system of English common law and civil law (based on the Roman and Napoleonic civil codes)

International law organization participation: accepts compulsory ICJ jurisdiction with reservations; accepts ICCt jurisdiction

Suffrage: 18 years of age; universal

Executive branch: *chief of state:* President Marie-Louise Coleiro PRECA (since 4 April 2014)
head of government: Prime Minister Joseph MUSCAT (since 11 March 2013)
cabinet: Cabinet appointed by the president on the advice of the prime minister (For more information visit the World Leaders website)
elections: president appointed by a resolution of the House of Representatives for a five-year term; appointment last held on 4 April 2014 (next to be held by April 2019); following legislative elections, the leader of the majority party or leader of a majority coalition usually appointed prime minister by the president for a five-year term; the deputy prime minister appointed by the president on the advice of the prime minister
election results: Marie-Louise Coleiro PRECA appointed president; Joseph MUSCAT elected prime minister

Legislative branch: unicameral House of Representatives (normally 65 seats; members are elected by popular vote on the basis of proportional representation by the Single Transferrable Vote (STV) to serve five-year terms; note—the parliament elected in 2013 is composed of 69 seats; when the political party winning an absolute majority of first-count votes (or a plurality of first-count votes in an election where only two parties are represented in parliament) does not win an absolute majority of seats, the constitution provides for the winning party to be awarded additional number of seats in parliament to guarantee it an absolute majority; in the event that more than two parties are represented in parliament, with none acquiring the absolute majority of votes, the party winning the majority of seats prevails
elections: last held on 9 March 2013 (next to be held by March 2018)
election results: percent of vote by party—PL 54.8%, PN 43.3%, other 1.9%; seats by party—PL 39, PN 30
note: in 2009, provisions in the law were made for communities with elected representatives to be
note: in 2009, provisions in the law were made for communities with elected representatives to be established within localities and for an elected chairperson to sit in on council meetings

Judicial branch: *highest court(s):* Court of Appeal (consists of either 1 or 3 judges); Constitutional Court (consists of 3 judges); Court of Criminal Appeal (consists of either 1 or 3 judges)

judge selection and term of office: Court of Appeal and Constitutional Court judges appointed by the president, usually upon the advice of the prime minister; judges of both courts serve until age 65
subordinate courts: Civil Court (divided into the General Jurisdiction Section, Family Section, and Voluntary Section); Criminal Court; Court of Magistrates; Gozo Courts (for the islands of Gozo and Comino)

Political parties and leaders: Alternativa Demokratika/Alliance for Social Justice or AD (Green Party) [Arnold CASSOLA]; Labor Party or PL [Joseph MUSCAT]; Nationalist Party or PN [Simon BUSUTTIL]; Political pressure groups and leaders; Alliance of Liberal Democrats Malta (Alleanza Liberali-Demokratika Malta) of ALDM (for divorce, abortion, gay marriage, women's rights); Together for a Better Environment (Flimkien Ghal-Ambjent Ahjar) or FAA (pro-environment)
other: environmentalists

International organization participation: Australia Group, C, CD, CE, EAPC, EBRD, ECB, EIB, EMU, EU, FAO, IAEA, IBRD, ICAO, ICC (NGOs), ICRM, IDA, IFAD, IFC, IFRCS, ILO, IMF, IMO, IMSO, Interpol, IOC, IOM, IPU, ISO, ITSO, ITU, ITUC (NGOs), MIGA, NSG, OAS (observer), OPCW, OSCE, PCA, PFP, Schengen Convention, UN, UNCTAD, UNESCO, UNIDO, Union Latina (observer), UNWTO, UPU, WCO, WHO, WIPO, WMO, WTO

Diplomatic representation in the US:
chief of mission: Ambassador Marisa Maria Louise MICALLEF (since 22 August 2013)
chancery: 2017 Connecticut Avenue NW, Washington, DC 20008
telephone: [1] (202) 462-3611 through 3612
FAX: [1] (202) 387-5470
consulate(s): New York

Diplomatic representation from the US:
chief of mission: Ambassador Gina ABERCROMBIE-WINSTANLEY (since 18 April 2012)
embassy: Ta' Qali National Park, Attard, ATD 4000
mailing address: 5800 Valetta Place, Dulles, VA 20189
telephone: [356] 2561 4000
FAX: [356] 2124 3229

Flag description: two equal vertical bands of white (hoist side) and red; in the upper hoist-side corner is a representation of the George Cross, edged in red; according to legend, the colors are taken from the red and white checkered banner of Count Roger of Sicily who removed a bi-colored corner and granted it to Malta in 1091; an uncontested explanation is that the colors are those of the Knights of Saint John who ruled Malta from 1530 to 1798; in 1942, King George VI of the United Kingdom awarded the George Cross to the islanders for their exceptional bravery and gallantry in World War II; since independence in 1964, the George Cross bordered in red has appeared directly on the white field

National symbol(s): Maltese cross

National anthem: *name:* "L-Innu Malti" (The Maltese Anthem)
lyrics/music: Dun Karm PSAILA/Robert SAMMUT
note: adopted 1945; the anthem is written in the form of a prayer

ECONOMY

Economy—overview: Malta—the smallest economy in the euro zone—produces only about 20% of its food needs, has limited fresh water supplies, and has few domestic energy sources. Malta's geographic position between Europe and North Africa makes it a target for irregular migration, which has strained Malta's political and economic resources. Malta's fertility rate is below the EU average, and population growth in recent years has largely been from immigration, putting increasing pressure on the pension system. Malta adopted the euro on 1 January 2008. Malta's economy is dependent on foreign trade, manufacturing, and tourism, and was hurt by the global economic downturn, but fared better than most other EU member states. Malta has low unemployment relative to other European countries, and growth has recovered since the 2009 recession. Malta's financial services industry has grown in recent years and it has avoided contagion from the European financial crisis, largely because its debt is mostly held domestically and its banks have low exposure to the sovereign debt of peripheral European countries. The EU reopened an excessive deficit procedure against Malta in June 2013, having found that its forecasted deficit for the year was likely to exceed 3% of GDP.

GDP (purchasing power parity): $11.46 billion (2013 est.)
country comparison to the world: 152
$11.19 billion (2012 est.)
$10.89 billion (2011 est.)
note: data are in 2013 US dollars

GDP (official exchange rate): $9.315 billion (2013 est.)

GDP—real growth rate: 1.1% (2013 est.)
country comparison to the world: 170
1% (2012 est.)
1.8% (2011 est.)

GDP—per capita (PPP): $27,500 (2013 est.)
country comparison to the world: 54
$26,900 (2012 est.)
$26,200 (2011 est.)
note: data are in 2013 US dollars

Gross national saving: 13.7% of GDP (2013 est.)
country comparison to the world: 116
13.5% of GDP (2012 est.)
12.8% of GDP (2011 est.)

GDP—composition, by end use:
household consumption: 58%

government consumption: 21.6%
investment in fixed capital: 13.2%
investment in inventories: -0.1%
exports of goods and services: 94.2%
imports of goods and services: -86.9% (2013 est.)

GDP—composition, by sector of origin:
agriculture: 1.5%
industry: 13.4%
services: 85.1% (2012 est.)

Agriculture—products: potatoes, cauliflower, grapes, wheat, barley, tomatoes, citrus, cut flowers, green peppers; pork, milk, poultry, eggs

Industries: tourism, electronics, ship building and repair, construction, food and beverages, pharmaceuticals, footwear, clothing, tobacco, aviation services, financial services, information technology services

Industrial production growth rate: NA%

Labor force: 185,600 (2012 est.)
country comparison to the world: 174

Labor force—by occupation: *agriculture:* 1%
industry: 23%
services: 76% (2012)

Unemployment rate: 6.4% (2013 est.)
country comparison to the world: 66
6.3% (2012 est.)

Population below poverty line: 15.4% (2011)

Household income or consumption by percentage share: *lowest* 10%: NA%
highest 10%: NA%

Distribution of family income—Gini index: 27.4 (2011)
country comparison to the world: 126
26 (2007)

Budget: *revenues:* $3.791 billion
expenditures: $4.096 billion (2013 est.)

Taxes and other revenues: 40.7% of GDP (2013 est.)
country comparison to the world: 36

Budget surplus (+) or deficit (-):
-3.3% of GDP (2013 est.)
country comparison to the world: 130

Public debt: 73.4% of GDP (2013 est.)
country comparison to the world: 34
71.6% of GDP (2012 est.)
note: Malta reports public debt at nominal value outstanding at the end of the year, according to guidelines set out in the Maastricht Treaty for general government gross debt; the data include the following categories of government liabilities (as defined in ESA95): currency and deposits (AF.2), securities other than shares excluding financial derivatives (AF.3, excluding AF.34), and loans (AF.4); general government comprises the central government, state government, local government and social security funds

Fiscal year: calendar year

Inflation rate (consumer prices): 1.7% (2013 est.)
country comparison to the world: 49
2.4% (2012 est.)

Central bank discount rate: 1.23% (31 December 2013)
country comparison to the world: 131
0.82% (31 December 2010)
note: this is the European Central Bank's rate on the marginal lending facility, which offers overnight credit to banks in the euro area

Commercial bank prime lending rate: 4.8% (31 December 2013 est.)
country comparison to the world: 161
4.7% (31 December 2012 est.)

Stock of narrow money: $5.304 billion (31 December 2013 est.)
country comparison to the world: 99
$5.336 billion (31 December 2012 est.)
note: see entry for the European Union for money supply in the euro area; the European Central Bank (ECB) controls monetary policy for the 17 members of the EMU; individual members of the EMU do not control the quantity of money circulating within their own borders

Stock of broad money: $12.88 billion (31 December 2013 est.)
country comparison to the world: 93
$12.88 billion (31 December 2012 est.)

Stock of domestic credit: $13.12 billion (31 December 2013 est.)
country comparison to the world: 92
$13.38 billion (31 December 2012 est.)

Market value of publicly traded shares: $3.631 billion (31 December 2012 est.)
country comparison to the world: 91
$3.424 billion (31 December 2011)
$2.399 billion (31 December 2010 est.)

Current account balance: $105 million (2013 est.)
country comparison to the world: 57
$95 million (2012 est.)

Exports: $4.127 billion (2013 est.)
country comparison to the world: 121
$4.328 billion (2012 est.)

Exports—commodities: machinery and mechanical appliances; mineral fuels, oils and products; pharmaceutical products; printed books and newspapers; aircraft/spacecraft and parts; toys, games, and sports equipment

Exports—partners: Germany 14.9%, France 12.3%, Italy 7.2%, UK 5.2%, Libya 5%, Netherlands 4.1% (2012)

Imports: $5.232 billion (2013 est.)
country comparison to the world: 126
$5.551 billion (2012 est.)

Imports—commodities: mineral fuels, oils and products; electrical machinery; aircraft/spacecraft and parts thereof; machinery and mechanical appliances; plastic and other semi-manufactured goods; vehicles and parts thereof

Imports—partners: Italy 39.2%, UK 7.3%, France 7.3%, Germany 6.4%, Spain 4.1% (2012)

Reserves of foreign exchange and gold: $582.7 million (31 December 2013 est.)
country comparison to the world: 146
$704.9 million (31 December 2012 est.)

Debt—external: $46.22 billion (31 December 2012 est.)
country comparison to the world: 64
$43.16 billion (31 December 2011)

Stock of direct foreign investment—at home: $17.25 billion (31 December 2010)
country comparison to the world: 77
$9.019 billion (31 December 2009)

Stock of direct foreign investment—abroad: $1.213 billion (2010 est.)
country comparison to the world: 78

Exchange rates: euros (EUR) per US dollar—
0.7634 (2013 est.)
0.7752 (2012 est.)
0.755 (2010 est.)
0.7198 (2009 est.)
0.6827 (2008 est.)

ENERGY

Electricity—production: 2.168 billion kWh (2011)
country comparison to the world: 133

Electricity—consumption: 1.602 billion kWh (2010 est.)
country comparison to the world: 145

Electricity—exports: 0 kWh (2012 est.)
country comparison to the world: 170

Electricity—imports: 0 kWh (2012 est.)
country comparison to the world: 172

Electricity—installed generating capacity: 572,600 kW (2010 est.)
country comparison to the world: 132

Electricity—from fossil fuels: 99.7% of total installed capacity (2010 est.)
country comparison to the world: 50

Electricity—from nuclear fuels: 0% of total installed capacity (2010 est.)
country comparison to the world: 142

Electricity—from hydroelectric plants: 0% of total installed capacity (2010 est.)
country comparison to the world: 184

Electricity—from other renewable sources: 0.3% of total installed capacity (2010 est.)
country comparison to the world: 89

Crude oil—production: 0 bbl/day (2012 est.)
country comparison to the world: 197

Crude oil—exports: 0 bbl/day (2011 est.)
country comparison to the world: 156

Crude oil—imports: 0 bbl/day (2011 est.)
country comparison to the world: 95

Crude oil—proved reserves: 0 bbl (1 January 2013 es)
country comparison to the world: 166

Refined petroleum products—production: 0 bbl/day (2010 est.)
country comparison to the world: 176

Refined petroleum products—consumption: 19,520 bbl/day (2011 est.)
country comparison to the world: 129

Refined petroleum products—exports: 327 bbl/day (2010 est.)
country comparison to the world: 117

Refined petroleum products—imports: 47,050 bbl/day (2010 est.)
country comparison to the world: 71

Natural gas—production: 0 cu m (2011 est.)
country comparison to the world: 169

Natural gas—consumption: 0 cu m (2010 est.)
country comparison to the world: 174

Natural gas—exports: 0 cu m (2011 est.)
country comparison to the world: 151

Natural gas—imports: 0 cu m (2011 est.)
country comparison to the world: 99

Natural gas—proved reserves: 0 cu m (1 January 2013 es)
country comparison to the world: 172

Carbon dioxide emissions from consumption of energy: 6.83 million Mt (2011 est.)
country comparison to the world: 115

COMMUNICATIONS

Telephones—main lines in use: 229,700 (2012)
country comparison to the world: 125

Telephones—mobile cellular: 539,500 (2012)
country comparison to the world: 168

Telephone system: *general assessment:* automatic system featuring submarine cable and microwave radio relay between islands
domestic: combined fixed-line and mobile-cellular subscribership exceeds 180 per 100 persons
international: country code—356; submarine cable connects to Italy; satellite earth station—1 Intelsat (Atlantic Ocean) (2011)

Broadcast media: 2 publicly owned TV stations, Television Malta (TVM) broadcasting nationally plus an educational channel; several privately owned national television stations, two of which are owned by political parties; Italian and British broadcast programs are available; multi-channel cable and satellite TV services are available; publicly owned radio broadcaster operates 1 station; roughly 20 commercial radio stations (2011)

Internet country code: .mt

Internet hosts: 14,754 (2012)
country comparison to the world: 125

Internet users: 240,600 (2009)
country comparison to the world: 137

TRANSPORTATION

Airports: 1 (2013)
country comparison to the world: 226

Airports—with paved runways: *total:* 1
over 3,047 m: 1 (2013)

Heliports: 2 (2013)

Roadways: *total:* 3,096 km
country comparison to the world: 164
paved: 2,704 km
unpaved: 392 km (2008)

Merchant marine: *total:* 1,650
country comparison to the world: 4
by type: bulk carrier 544, cargo 351, carrier 1, chemical tanker 324, container 117, liquefied gas 36, passenger 50, passenger/cargo 18, petroleum tanker 160, refrigerated cargo 7, roll on/roll off 22, specialized tanker 2, vehicle carrier 18
foreign-owned: 1,437 (Angola 7, Azerbaijan 1, Belgium 7, Bermuda 15, Bulgaria 8, Canada 5, China 6, Croatia 6, Cyprus 32, Denmark 34, Egypt 1, Estonia 16, Finland 3, France 8, Germany 135, Greece 469, Hong Kong 4, India 3, Iran 48, Ireland 4, Israel 3, Italy 45, Japan 5, Kuwait 3, Latvia 8, Lebanon 6, Libya 5, Luxembourg 3, Malaysia 1, Monaco 3, Netherlands 3, Norway 96, Oman 5, Poland 21, Portugal 3, Romania 7, Russia 45, Saudi Arabia 2, Singapore 4, Slovenia 4, South Korea 2, Spain 8, Sweden 1, Switzerland 20, Syria 4, Turkey 233, UAE 1, UK 21, Ukraine 29, US 34)
registered in other countries: 2 (Panama 2) (2010)

Ports and terminals: *major seaport(s):* Marsaxlokk (Malta Freeport), Valletta
container port(s) (TEUs): Marsaxlokk (2,360,000)

MILITARY

Military branches: Armed Forces of Malta (AFM; includes land, maritime, and air elements) (2013)

Military service age and obligation: 17 years 6 months of age for voluntary military service; no conscription (2013)

Manpower available for military service:
males age 16-49: 95,499
females age 16-49: 90,919 (2010 est.)

Manpower fit for military service:
males age 16-49: 79,645
females age 16-49: 75,684 (2010 est.)

Manpower reaching militarily significant age annually: *male:* 2,554
female: 2,385 (2010 est.)

Military expenditures: 0.61% of GDP (2012)
country comparison to the world: 122
0.61% of GDP (2011)
0.61% of GDP (2010)

TRANSNATIONAL ISSUES

Disputes—international: none

Refugees and internally displaced persons:
refugees (country of origin): 5,041 Somalia (2012)

Illicit drugs: minor transshipment point for hashish from North Africa to Western Europe

MARSHALL ISLANDS

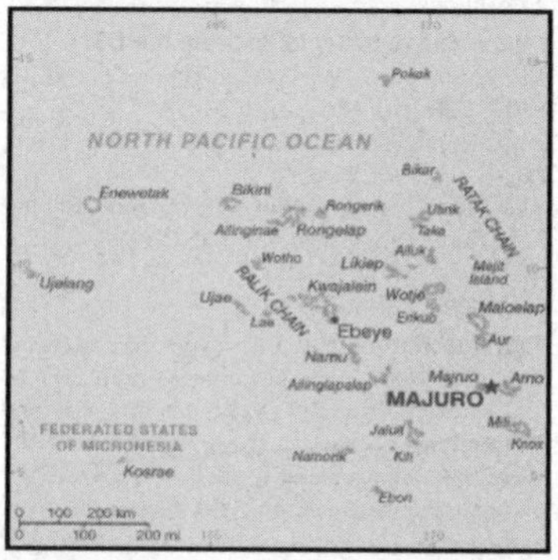

INTRODUCTION

Background: After almost four decades under US administration as the easternmost part of the UN Trust Territory of the Pacific Islands, the Marshall Islands attained independence in 1986 under a Compact of Free Association. Compensation claims continue as a result of US nuclear testing on some of the atolls between 1947 and 1962. The Marshall Islands hosts the US Army Kwajalein Atoll (USAKA) Reagan Missile Test Site, a key installation in the US missile defense network.

GEOGRAPHY

Location: Oceania, two archipelagic island chains of 29 atolls, each made up of many small islets, and five single islands in the North Pacific Ocean, about half way between Hawaii and Australia

Geographic coordinates: 9 00 N, 168 00 E

Map references: Oceania

Area: *total:* 181 sq km
country comparison to the world: 217
land: 181 sq km
water: 0 sq km
note: the archipelago includes 11,673 sq km of lagoon waters and encompasses the atolls of Bikini, Enewetak, Kwajalein, Majuro, Rongelap, and Utirik

Area—comparative: about the size of Washington, DC

Land boundaries: 0 km

Coastline: 370.4 km

Maritime claims: *territorial sea:* 12 nm
contiguous zone: 24 nm
exclusive economic zone: 200 nm

Climate: tropical; hot and humid; wet season May to November; islands border typhoon belt

Terrain: low coral limestone and sand islands

Elevation extremes: *lowest point:* Pacific Ocean 0 m
highest point: unnamed location on Likiep 10 m

Natural resources: coconut products, marine products, deep seabed minerals

Land use: *arable land:* 11.11%
permanent crops: 44.44%
other: 44.44% (2011)

Irrigated land: 0 sq km (2011)

Natural hazards: infrequent typhoons

Environment—current issues: inadequate supplies of potable water; pollution of Majuro lagoon from household waste and discharges from fishing vessels

Environment—international agreements:
party to: Biodiversity, Climate Change, Climate Change-Kyoto Protocol, Desertification, Hazardous Wastes, Law of the Sea, Ozone Layer Protection, Ship Pollution, Wetlands, Whaling
signed, but not ratified: none of the selected agreements

Geography—note: the islands of Bikini and Enewetak are former US nuclear test sites; Kwajalein atoll, famous as a World War II battleground, surrounds the world's largest lagoon and is used as a US missile test range; the island city of Ebeye is the second largest settlement in the Marshall Islands, after the capital of Majuro, and one of the most densely populated locations in the Pacific

PEOPLE AND SOCIETY

Nationality: *noun:* Marshallese (singular and plural)
adjective: Marshallese

Ethnic groups: Marshallese 92.1%, mixed Marshallese 5.9%, other 2% (2006)

Languages: Marshallese (official) 98.2%, other languages 1.8% (1999 census)
note: English (official), widely spoken as a second language

Religions: Protestant 54.8%, Assembly of God 25.8%, Roman Catholic 8.4%, Bukot nan Jesus 2.8%, Mormon 2.1%, other Christian 3.6%, other 1%, none 1.5% (1999 census)

Population: 70,983 (July 2014 est.)
country comparison to the world: 203

Age structure:
0-14 years: 36.6% (male 13,244/female 12,741)
15-24 years: 17.5% (male 6,305/female 6,087)
25-54 years: 36.9% (male 13,308/female 12,856)
55-64 years: 3.4% (male 2,078/female 1,938)
65 years and over: 3.3% (male 1,187/female 1,239) (2014 est.)

Median age: *total:* 22.5 years
male: 22.5 years
female: 22.6 years (2014 est.)

Population growth rate: 1.72% (2014 est.)
country comparison to the world: 72

Birth rate: 26.36 births/1,000 population (2014 est.)
country comparison to the world: 47

Death rate: 4.24 deaths/1,000 population (2014 est.)
country comparison to the world: 208

Net migration rate: -4.92 migrant(s)/1,000 population (2014 est.)
country comparison to the world: 194

Urbanization: *urban population:* 72% of total population (2010)
rate of urbanization: 2.3% annual rate of change (2010-15 est.)

Major urban areas—population: MAJURO (capital) 30,000 (2009)

Sex ratio: *at birth:* 1.05 male(s)/female
0-14 years: 1.04 male(s)/female
15-24 years: 1.04 male(s)/female
25-54 years: 1.04 male(s)/female
55-64 years: 1.04 male(s)/female
65 years and over: 0.95 male(s)/female
total population: 1.04 male(s)/female (2014 est.)

Infant mortality rate: *total:* 21.39 deaths/1,000 live births
country comparison to the world: 85
male: 24.09 deaths/1,000 live births
female: 18.55 deaths/1,000 live births (2014 est.)

Life expectancy at birth: *total population:* 72.58 years
country comparison to the world: 133
male: 70.42 years
female: 74.84 years (2014 est.)

Total fertility rate: 3.22 children born/woman (2014 est.)
country comparison to the world: 51

Contraceptive prevalence rate: 44.6% (2007)

Health expenditures: 16.5% of GDP (2011)
country comparison to the world: 5

Physicians density: 0.44 physicians/1,000 population (2010)

Hospital bed density: 2.7 beds/1,000 population (2010)

Drinking water source:
improved:
urban: 93.3% of population
rural: 97.4% of population
total: 94.4% of population
unimproved:
urban: 6.7% of population
rural: 2.6% of population
total: 5.6% of population (2011 est.)

Sanitation facility access:
improved:
urban: 83.9% of population
rural: 54.9% of population
total: 75.7% of population
unimproved:
urban: 16.1% of population
rural: 45.1% of population
total: 24.3% of population (2011 est.)

HIV/AIDS—adult prevalence rate: NA

HIV/AIDS—people living with HIV/AIDS: NA

HIV/AIDS—deaths: NA

Obesity—adult prevalence rate: 45.4% (2008)
country comparison to the world: 9

Education expenditures: 12.2% of GDP (2003)
country comparison to the world: 3

Literacy: *definition:* age 15 and over can read and write
total population: 93.7%
male: 93.6%
female: 93.7% (1999)

School life expectancy (primary to tertiary education): *total:* 12 years
male: 11 years
female: 12 years (2003)

GOVERNMENT

Country name: *conventional long form:* Republic of the Marshall Islands
conventional short form: Marshall Islands
local long form: Republic of the Marshall Islands
local short form: Marshall Islands
abbreviation: RMI
former: Trust Territory of the Pacific Islands, Marshall Islands District

Government type: constitutional government in free association with the US; the Compact of Free Association entered into force on 21 October 1986 and the Amended Compact entered into force in May 2004

Capital: *name:* Majuro

geographic coordinates: 7 06 N, 171 23 E
time difference: UTC+12 (17 hours ahead of Washington, DC during Standard Time)

Administrative divisions: 24 municipalities; Ailinglaplap, Ailuk, Arno, Aur, Bikini & Kili, Ebon, Enewetak & Ujelang, Jabat, Jaluit, Kwajalein, Lae, Lib, Likiep, Majuro, Maloelap, Mejit, Mili, Namdrik, Namu, Rongelap, Ujae, Utrik, Wotho, Wotje

Independence: 21 October 1986 (from the US-administered UN trusteeship)

National holiday: Constitution Day, 1 May (1979)

Constitution: effective 1 May 1979; amended several times, last in 1990 (2005)

Legal system: mixed legal system of US and English common law, customary law, and local statutes

International law organization participation: accepts compulsory ICJ jurisdiction with reservations; accepts ICCt jurisdiction

Suffrage: 18 years of age; universal

Executive branch: *chief of state:* President Christopher J. LOEAK (since 17 January 2012); note—the president is both the chief of state and head of government
head of government: President Christopher J. LOEAK (since 17 January 2012)
cabinet: Cabinet selected by the president from among the members of the legislature (For more information visit the World Leaders website)
elections: president elected by Nitijela (legislature) from among its members for a four-year term; election last held on 3 January 2012 (next to be held in 2016)
election results: Nitijela elected Christopher J. LOEAK president on 3 January 2012

Legislative branch: unicameral legislature or Nitijela (33 seats; members elected by popular vote to serve four-year terms)
elections: last held on 21 November 2011 (next to be held by November 2015)
election results: percent of vote by party—NA; seats by party—independents 33
note: the Council of Chiefs or Ironij is a 12-member body comprised of tribal chiefs that advises on matters affecting customary law and practice

Judicial branch: *highest court(s):* Supreme Court (consists of the chief justice and other judges as prescribed by law)
judge selection and term of office: judges appointed by the Cabinet on the recommendation of the Judicial Service Commission and upon the approval of the Nitijela; judges appointed until retirement, normally at age 72
subordinate courts: High Court; District Courts; Traditional Rights Court; Community Courts

Political parties and leaders: traditionally there have been no formally organized political parties; what has existed more closely resembles factions or interest groups because they do not have party headquarters, formal platforms, or party structures; the following two "groupings" have competed in legislative balloting in recent years—Aelon Kein Ad Party [Michael KABUA] and United Democratic Party or UDP [Litokwa TOMEING]

Political pressure groups and leaders: NA

International organization participation: ACP, ADB, AOSIS, FAO, G-77, IAEA, IBRD, ICAO, IDA, IFAD, IFC, ILO, IMF, IMO, IMSO, Interpol, IOC, ITU, OPCW, PIF, Sparteca, SPC, UN, UNCTAD, UNESCO, WHO

Diplomatic representation in the US:
chief of mission: Ambassador Charles R. PAUL (since 6 September 2011)
chancery: 2433 Massachusetts Avenue NW, Washington, DC 20008
telephone: [1] (202) 234-5414
FAX: [1] (202) 232-3236
consulate(s) general: Honolulu, Springdale (AR)

Diplomatic representation from the US:
chief of mission: Ambassador Thomas H. ARMBRUSTER (since 16 August 2012)
embassy: Oceanside, Mejen Weto, Long Island, Majuro
mailing address: P. O. Box 1379, Majuro, Republic of the Marshall Islands 96960-1379
telephone: [692] 247-4011
FAX: [692] 247-4012

Flag description: blue with two stripes radiating from the lower hoist-side corner—orange (top) and white; a white star with four large rays and 20 small rays appears on the hoist side above the two stripes; blue represents the Pacific Ocean, the orange stripe signifies the Ralik Chain or sunset and courage, while the white stripe signifies the Ratak Chain or sunrise and peace; the star symbolizes the cross of Christianity, each of the 24 rays designates one of the electoral districts in the country and the four larger rays highlight the principal cultural centers of Majuro, Jaluit, Wotje, and Ebeye; the rising diagonal band can also be interpreted as representing the equator, with the star showing the archipelago's position just to the north

National anthem: *name:* "Forever Marshall Islands"
lyrics/music: Amata KABUA
note: adopted 1981

ECONOMY

Economy—overview: US assistance and lease payments for the use of Kwajalein Atoll as a US military base are the mainstay of this small island country. The Marshall Islands received roughly $1 billion in aid from the US during 1986-2001 under the original Compact of Free Association (Compact). In 2002 and 2003, the US and the Marshall Islands renegotiated the Compact's financial package for a 20-year period, from 2004 to 2024. Under the amended Compact, the Marshall Islands will receive roughly $1.5 billion in direct US assistance. Agricultural production, primarily subsistence, is concentrated on small farms; the most important commercial crops are coconuts and breadfruit. Industry is limited to handicrafts, tuna processing, and copra. Tourism holds some potential. The islands and atolls have few natural resources, and imports exceed exports. Under the amended Compact, the US is also funding, jointly with the Marshall Islands, a Trust Fund for the people of the Marshall Islands that will provide an income stream beyond 2024 when direct Compact aid is to end.

GDP (purchasing power parity): $486 million (2013 est.)
country comparison to the world: 216
$475.4 million (2012 est.)
$467.2 million (2011 est.)

GDP (official exchange rate): $193 million (2013 est.)

GDP—real growth rate: 2.3% (2013 est.)
country comparison to the world: 134
1.9% (2012 est.)
0.8% (2011 est.)

GDP—per capita (PPP): $8,700 (2013 est.)
country comparison to the world: 127
$8,700 (2012 est.)
$8,800 (2011 est.)

GDP—composition, by sector of origin:
agriculture: 14.3%
industry: 13.9%
services: 71.8% (2011 est.)

Agriculture—products: coconuts, tomatoes, melons, taro, breadfruit, fruits; pigs, chickens

Industries: copra, tuna processing, tourism, craft items (from seashells, wood, and pearls)

Industrial production growth rate: NA%

Labor force: 10,480 (2011 est.)
country comparison to the world: 216

Labor force—by occupation:
agriculture: 11%
industry: 16.3%
services: 72.7% (2011 est.)

Unemployment rate: 36% (2006 est.)
country comparison to the world: 188
30.9% (2000 est.)

Population below poverty line: NA%

Household income or consumption by percentage share: *lowest 10%:* NA%
highest 10%: NA%

Budget: *revenues:* $105.4 million
expenditures: $104.7 million (FY09 est.)

Taxes and other revenues: 54.6% of GDP (FY09 est.)
country comparison to the world: 9

Budget surplus (+) or deficit (-):
0.4% of GDP (FY09 est.)
country comparison to the world: 35

Fiscal year: 1 October—30 September

Inflation rate (consumer prices): 12.9% (2008 est.)
country comparison to the world: 215
3% (2005 est.)

Exports: $50.14 million (2011 est.)
country comparison to the world: 196
$9.1 million (2000 est.)

Exports—commodities: copra cake, coconut oil, handicrafts, fish
Imports: $118.7 million (2011 est.)
country comparison to the world: 210
$54.7 million (2000 est.)

Imports—commodities: foodstuffs, machinery and equipment, fuels, beverages, tobacco

Debt—external: $87 million (2008 est.)
country comparison to the world: 191
$86.5 million (FY99/00 est.)

Exchange rates: the US dollar is used

COMMUNICATIONS

Telephones—main lines in use: 4,400 (2010)
country comparison to the world: 212

Telephones—mobile cellular: 3,800 (2010)
country comparison to the world: 215

Telephone system: *general assessment:* digital switching equipment; modern services include telex, cellular, Internet, international calling, caller ID, and leased data circuits
domestic: Majuro Atoll and Ebeye and Kwajalein islands have regular, seven-digit, direct-dial telephones; other islands interconnected by high frequency radiotelephone (used mostly for government purposes) and mini-satellite telephones
international: country code—692; satellite earth stations—2 Intelsat (Pacific Ocean); US Government satellite communications system on Kwajalein (2005)

Broadcast media: no TV broadcast station; a cable network is available on Majuro with programming via videotape replay and satellite relays; 4 radio broadcast stations; American Armed Forces Radio and Television Service (AFRTS) provides satellite radio and television service to Kwajalein Atoll (2009)

Internet country code: .mh

Internet hosts: 3 (2012)
country comparison to the world: 232

Internet users: 2,200 (2009)
country comparison to the world: 210

TRANSPORTATION

Airports: 15 (2013)
country comparison to the world: 146

Airports—with paved runways: *total:* 4
1,524 to 2,437 m: 3
914 to 1,523 m: 1 (2013)

Airports—with unpaved runways: *total:* 1 1
914 to 1,523 m: 10
under 914 m: 1 (2013)

Roadways: *total:* 2,028 km (includes 75 km of expressways) (2007)
country comparison to the world: 175

Merchant marine: *total:* 1,593

country comparison to the world: 7
by type: barge carrier 1, bulk carrier 524, cargo 65, carrier 1, chemical tanker 351, container 226, liquefied gas 88, passenger 7, passenger/cargo 1, petroleum tanker 297, refrigerated cargo 13, roll on/roll off 9, vehicle carrier 10
foreign-owned: 1,468 (Belgium 1, Bermuda 35, Brazil 1, Canada 8, China 14, Croatia 12, Cyprus 40, Denmark 7, Egypt 1, France 7, Germany 248, Greece 408, Hong Kong 3, India 10, Indonesia 1, Iraq 2, Ireland 6, Italy 1, Japan 59, Jersey 11, Kuwait 2, Latvia 19, Malaysia 11, Mexico 2, Monaco 30, Netherlands 21, Norway 75, Pakistan 1, Qatar 29, Romania 2, Russia 5, Singapore 30, Slovenia 6, South Korea 41, Sweden 1, Switzerland 12, Taiwan 8, Turkey 70, UAE 12, UK 12, Ukraine 1, US 200) (2010)

Ports and terminals: *major seaport(s):* Enitwetak Island, Kwajalein, Majuro

MILITARY

Military branches: no regular military forces; Marshall Islands Police (2012)

Manpower available for military service:
males age 16-49: 16,446 (2010 est.)

Manpower fit for military service:
males age 16-49: 13,568
females age 16-49: 13,606 (2010 est.)

Manpower reaching militarily significant age annually: *male:* 653
female: 631 (2010 est.)

Military—note: defense is the responsibility of the US

TRANSNATIONAL ISSUES

Disputes—international: claims US territory of Wake Island

Trafficking in persons: *current situation:* The Marshall Islands are a destination country for women from East Asia subjected to sex trafficking; foreign women are reportedly forced into prostitution in bars frequented by crew members of fishing vessels; some Chinese women are recruited to the Marshall Islands with promises of legitimate work and are subsequently forced into prostitution

tier rating: Tier 2 Watch List—The Marshall Islands do not fully comply with the minimum standards for the elimination of trafficking; however, it is making significant efforts to do so; the government has not identified any victims, investigated any trafficking cases, or prosecuted any offenders under the country's 2011 anti-trafficking law; the government also has no mechanism in place to ensure that trafficking victims receive access to legal, medical, or psychological services; no public awareness campaigns on the dangers of human trafficking have been undertaken (2013)

MAURITANIA

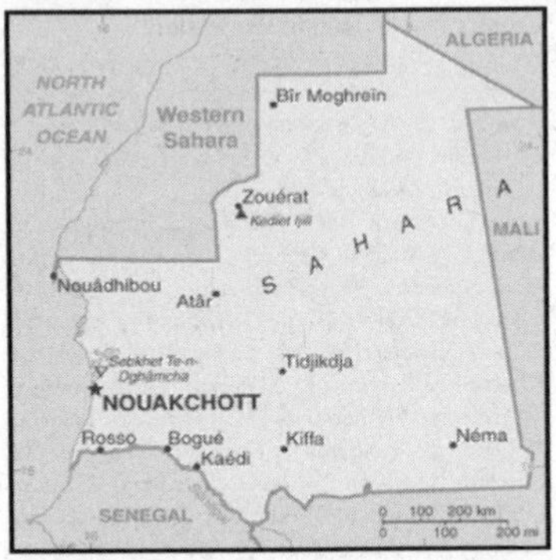

INTRODUCTION

Background: Independent from France in 1960, Mauritania annexed the southern third of the former Spanish Sahara (now Western Sahara) in 1976 but relinquished it after three years of raids by the Polisario guerrilla front seeking independence for the territory. Maaouya Ould Sid Ahmed TAYA seized power in a coup in 1984 and ruled Mauritania with a heavy hand for more than two decades. A series of presidential elections that he held were widely seen as flawed. A bloodless coup in August 2005 deposed President TAYA and ushered in a military council that oversaw a transition to democratic rule. Independent candidate Sidi Ould Cheikh ABDALLAHI was inaugurated in April 2007 as Mauritania's first freely and fairly elected president. His term ended prematurely in August 2008 when a military junta led by General Mohamed Ould Abdel AZIZ deposed him and installed a military council government. AZIZ was subsequently elected president in July 2009 and sworn in the following month. AZIZ sustained injuries from an accidental shooting by his own troops in October 2012 but has continued to maintain his authority. The country continues to experience ethnic tensions among its black population (Afro-Mauritanians) and white and black Moor (Arab-Berber) communities, and confronts a terrorism threat by al-Qa'ida in the Islamic Maghreb (AQIM).

GEOGRAPHY

Location: Western Africa, bordering the North Atlantic Ocean, between Senegal and Western Sahara

Geographic coordinates: 20 00 N, 12 00 W

Map references: Africa

Area: *total:* 1,030,700 sq km
country comparison to the world: 29
land: 1,030,700 sq km
water: 0 sq km

Area—comparative: slightly larger than three times the size of New Mexico

Land boundaries: *total:* 5,074 km
border countries: Algeria 463 km, Mali 2,237 km, Senegal 813 km, Western Sahara 1,561 km

Coastline: 754 km

Maritime claims: *territorial sea:* 12 nm
contiguous zone: 24 nm
exclusive economic zone: 200 nm
continental shelf: 200 nm or to the edge of the continental margin

Climate: desert; constantly hot, dry, dusty

Terrain: mostly barren, flat plains of the Sahara; some central hills

Elevation extremes: *lowest point:* Sebkhet Te-n-Dghamcha -5 m
highest point: Kediet Ijill 915 m

Natural resources: iron ore, gypsum, copper, phosphate, diamonds, gold, oil, fish

Land use: *arable land:* 0.44%
permanent crops: 0.01%
other: 99.55% (2011)

Irrigated land: 450.1 sq km (2004)

Total renewable water resources: 11.4 cu km (2011)

Freshwater withdrawal (domestic/industrial/agricultural): *total:* 1.35 cu km/yr (7%/2%/91%)
per capita: 420.2 cu m/yr (2005)

Natural hazards: hot, dry, dust/sand-laden sirocco wind blows primarily in March and April; periodic droughts

Environment—current issues: overgrazing, deforestation, and soil erosion aggravated by drought are contributing to desertification; limited natural freshwater resources away from the Senegal, which is the only perennial river; locust infestation

Environment—international agreements:
party to: Biodiversity, Climate Change, Climate Change-Kyoto Protocol, Desertification, Endangered Species, Hazardous Wastes, Law of the Sea, Ozone Layer Protection, Ship Pollution, Wetlands, Whaling
signed, but not ratified: none of the selected agreements

Geography—note: most of the population is concentrated in the cities of Nouakchott and Nouadhibou and along the Senegal River in the southern part of the country

PEOPLE AND SOCIETY

Nationality: *noun:* Mauritanian(s)
adjective: Mauritanian

Ethnic groups: black Moors (Haratines—Arab-speaking slaves, former slaves, and their descendants of African origin, enslaved by white Moors) 40%, white Moors (of Arab-Berber descent, known as Bidhan) 30%, black Africans (non-Arabic speaking, Halpulaar, Soninke, Wolof, and Bamara ethnic groups) 30%

Languages: Arabic (official and national), Pulaar, Soninke, Wolof (all national languages), French, Hassaniya (a variety of Arabic)

Religions: Muslim (official) 100%

Population: 3,516,806 (July 2014 est.)
country comparison to the world: 133

Age structure:
0-14 years: 39.5% (male 697,156/female 691,548)
15-24 years: 20% (male 343,214/female 358,533)
25-54 years: 32.5% (male 528,133/female 613,324)
55-64 years: 3.6% (male 71,265/female 87,086)
65 years and over: 3.5% (male 53,705/female 72,842) (2014 est.)

Dependency ratios:
total dependency ratio: 76.3 %
youth dependency ratio: 70.7 %
elderly dependency ratio: 5.6 %
potential support ratio: 17.9 (2013)

Median age: *total:* 19.9 years
male: 19 years
female: 20.9 years (2014 est.)

Population growth rate: 2.26% (2014 est.)
country comparison to the world: 40

Birth rate: 31.83 births/1,000 population (2014 est.)
country comparison to the world: 36

Death rate: 8.35 deaths/1,000 population (2014 est.)
country comparison to the world: 87

Net migration rate: -0.85 migrant(s)/1,000 population (2014 est.)
country comparison to the world: 146

Urbanization: *urban population:* 41.5% of total population (2011)
rate of urbanization: 2.91% annual rate of change (2010-15 est.)

Major urban areas—population: NOUAKCHOTT (capital) 709,000 (2009)

Sex ratio: *at birth:* 1.03 male(s)/female
0-14 years: 1.01 male(s)/female
15-24 years: 0.96 male(s)/female
25-54 years: 0.86 male(s)/female
55-64 years: 0.93 male(s)/female
65 years and over: 0.74 male(s)/female
total population: 0.93 male(s)/female (2014 est.)

Mother's mean age at first birth: 21.9 (2001 est.)

Maternal mortality rate: 510 deaths/100,000 live births (2010)
country comparison to the world: 19

Infant mortality rate: *total:* 56.06 deaths/1,000 live births
country comparison to the world: 28
male: 61.04 deaths/1,000 live births
female: 50.93 deaths/1,000 live births (2014 est.)

Life expectancy at birth: *total population:* 62.28 years
country comparison to the world: 188
male: 60 years
female: 64.63 years (2014 est.)

Total fertility rate: 4.07 children born/woman (2014 est.)
country comparison to the world: 39

Contraceptive prevalence rate: 9.3% (2007)

Health expenditures: 5.4% of GDP (2011)
country comparison to the world: 125

Physicians density: 0.13 physicians/1,000 population (2009)

Hospital bed density: 0.4 beds/1,000 population (2006)

Drinking water source:
improved:
urban: 52.3% of population
rural: 47.7% of population
total: 49.6% of population
unimproved:
urban: 47.7% of population
rural: 52.3% of population
total: 50.4% of population (2011 est.)

Sanitation facility access:
improved:
urban: 51.1% of population
rural: 9.2% of population
total: 26.6% of population
unimproved:
urban: 48.9% of population
rural: 90.8% of population
total: 73.4% of population (2011 est.)

HIV/AIDS—adult prevalence rate: 0.4% (2012 est.)
country comparison to the world: 83

HIV/AIDS—people living with HIV/AIDS: 10,500 (2012 est.)

country comparison to the world: 100

HIV/AIDS—deaths: 800 (2012 est.)
country comparison to the world: 81

Major infectious diseases: *degree of risk:* very high
food or waterborne diseases: bacterial and protozoal diarrhea, hepatitis A, and typhoid fever
vectorborne diseases: malaria and dengue fever
respiratory disease: meningococcal meningitis
animal contact disease: rabies (2013)

Obesity—adult prevalence rate: 12.7% (2008)
country comparison to the world: 127

Children under the age of 5 years underweight: 19.5% (2012)
country comparison to the world: 32

Education expenditures: 3.7% of GDP (2011)
country comparison to the world: 120

Literacy: *definition:* age 15 and over can read and write
total population: 58.6%
male: 65.3%
female: 52% (2011 est.)

School life expectancy (primary to tertiary education): *total:* 8 years
male: 8 years
female: 8 years (2012)

Child labor—children ages 5-14:
total number: 127,251
percentage: 16 % (2007 est.)

GOVERNMENT

Country name: *conventional long form:* Islamic Republic of Mauritania
conventional short form: Mauritania
local long form: Al Jumhuriyah al Islamiyah al Muritaniyah
local short form: Muritaniyah

Government type: military junta

Capital: *name:* Nouakchott

geographic coordinates: 18 04 N, 15 58 W
time difference: UTC 0 (5 hours ahead of Washington, DC during Standard Time)

Administrative divisions: 13 regions (wilayas, singular—wilaya); Adrar, Assaba, Brakna, Dakhlet Nouadhibou, Gorgol, Guidimaka, Hodh ech Chargui, Hodh el Gharbi, Inchiri, Nouakchott, Tagant, Tiris Zemmour, Trarza

Independence: 28 November 1960 (from France)

National holiday: Independence Day, 28 November (1960)

Constitution: previous 1964; latest adopted 12 July 1991; amended 2006, 2012 (2012)

Legal system: mixed legal system of Islamic and French civil law

International law organization participation: has not submitted an ICJ jurisdiction declaration; non-party state to the ICCt

Suffrage: 18 years of age; universal

Executive branch: *chief of state:* President Mohamed Ould Abdel AZIZ (since 5 August 2009); note—AZIZ, who deposed democratically elected President Sidi Ould Cheikh ABDELLAHI in a coup and installed himself as President of the High State Council on 6 August 2008, retired from the military and stepped down from the presidency in April 2009 to run for president; he was elected president in an election held on 18 July 2009
head of government: Prime Minister Moulaye Ould Mohamed LAGHDAF (since 14 August 2008)
cabinet: Council of Ministers (For more information visit the World Leaders website)
elections: president elected by popular vote for a five-year term; election last held on 18 July 2009 (next to be held by 2014)
election results: percent of vote—Mohamed Ould Abdel AZIZ 52.6%, Messaoud Ould BOULKHEIR 16.3%, Ahmed Ould DADDAH 13.7%, other 17.4%

Legislative branch: bicameral legislature consists of the Senate or Majlis al-Shuyukh (56 seats; 53 members elected by municipal leaders and 3 members elected for Mauritanians abroad to serve six-year terms; a portion of seats up for election every two years) and the National Assembly or Al Jamiya Al Wataniya (146 seats; 106 members elected in single- and multi-member constituencies to serve five-year terms and 40 are elected nationwide through a closed list proportional representation system to serve five-year terms; of the 40 seats elected at the nationwide level, 20 are reserved for women)
elections: Senate—last held in November 2009; National Assembly—first round last held on 23 November and second round on 21 December 2013
election results: Senate—percent of vote by party—NA; seats by party—CPM (Coalition of Majority Parties) 45, COD 7, RNRD-TAWASSOUL 4; National Assembly—percent of vote by party—NA; seats by party—UPR 75, RNRD-TAWASSOUL 16, El Wiam 10, APP 7, UDP 6, El Karam Party 6, AJD/MR 4, Surge of Youth for the Nation 4, El Vadila Party 3, PUD 3, Ravah Party 3, PRDR 3, others 6

Judicial branch: *highest court(s):* Supreme Court or Cour Supreme (subdivided into 1 criminal and 2 civil chambers, each with a president and 5 counselors); Constitutional Council (consists of 6 members)
judge selection and term of office: Supreme Court president appointed by the president of the republic to serve a 5-year renewable term; Constitutional Council members appointed—3 by the president of the republic, 2 by the president of the National Assembly, and 1 by the president of the Senate; members serve single, 9-year terms with one-third of membership renewed every 3 years
subordinate courts: High Court of Justice (cases involving treason and criminal acts of high government officials); courts of appeal; wilaya (regional) courts (located at the headquarters of each of the 13 regions); commercial and labor courts; criminal courts; moughataa (district) courts; informal/customary courts

Political parties and leaders: Alliance for Justice and Democracy/Movement for Renewal or AJD/MR [Ibrahima Moctar SARR]; Alternative or El-Badil [Mohamed Yahdhi Ould MOCTAR HACEN]; Coalition of Majority Parties or CPM (parties supporting the regime including PRDR, UPR, UDP, RD, HATEM-PMUC, UCD); Coalition for Pacific Alternation or CAP (coalition of opposition parties, including APP, El Wiam, and Sawab); Coordination of Democratic Opposition or COD [Ahmed Ould DADDAH] (coalition of 11 opposition political; parties including RNRD-TAWASSOUL, RFD, UFP, PNDD-ADIL, Alternative or El-Badil); Democratic Renewal or RD [Moustapha Ould ABDEIDARRAHMANE]; El Karama Party [Cheikhna Ould Mohamed Ould HAJBOU]; El Vadila Party [Ethmane Ould Ahmed ABOULMAALY]; El Wiam [Boidiel Ould HOUMEIT]; Mauritanian Party for Unity and Change or HATEM-PMUC [Saleh Ould HANENA]; National Pact for Democracy and Development or PNDD-ADIL [Yahya Ould Ahmed El WAGHEF]; (independents formerly supporting President Abdellahi); National Rally for Freedom, Democracy and Equality or RNLDE; National Rally for Reform and Development or RNRD-TAWASSOUL [Mohamed Jamil MANSOUR] (moderate; Islamists); Party of Unity and Development or PUD [Mohamed BARO]; Popular Progressive Alliance or APP [Messaoud Ould BOULKHEIR]; Popular Front or FP [Mohamed Lemine Ch'bih Ould CHEIKH MALAININE]; Rally of Democratic Forces or RFD [Ahmed Ould DADDAH]; Ravah Party; Republican Party for Democracy and Renewal or PRDR [Mintata Mint HIDEID]; Sawab [Abdel Salem Ould HORMA]; Socialist and Democratic Unity Party or PUDS [Mahfouz Weld AZIZ]; Surge of Youth for the Nation [Lalla CHERIVA]; Union for Democracy and Progress or UDP [Naha Mint MOUKNASS]; Union for the Republic or UPR [Mohamed Mahmoud Ould Mohamed LEMINE]; Union of Democratic Center or UCD [Cheikh Sid'Ahmed Ould BABA]; Union of the Forces for Progress or UFP [Mohamed Ould MAOULOUD]

Political pressure groups and leaders: General Confederation of Mauritanian Workers or CGTM [Abdallahi Ould MOHAMED, secretary general]; Independent Confederation of Mauritanian Workers or CLTM [Samory Ould BEYE]; Mauritanian Workers Union or UTM [Mohamed Ely Ould BRAHIM, secretary general]
other: Arab nationalists; Ba'thists; Islamists

International organization participation: ABEDA, ACP, AfDB, AFESD, AMF, AMU, AU, CAEU (candidate), EITI (compliant country), FAO, G-77, IAEA, IBRD, ICAO, ICRM, IDA, IDB, IFAD, IFC, IFRCS, IHO (pending member), ILO, IMF, IMO, Interpol, IOC, IOM, IPU, ISO (correspondent), ITSO, ITU, ITUC (NGOs), LAS, MIGA, MIUSMA, NAM, OIC, OIF, OPCW, UN, UNCTAD, UNESCO, UNIDO, UNWTO, UPU, WCO, WHO, WIPO, WMO, WTO

Diplomatic representation in the US:
chief of mission: Ambassador Mohamed Lemine El HAYCEN (since 28 July 2010)
chancery: 2129 Leroy Place NW, Washington, DC 20008
telephone: [1] (202) 232-5700 through 5701
FAX: [1] (202) 319-2623

Diplomatic representation from the US:
chief of mission: Ambassador (vacant); Charge d'Affaires David REIMER
embassy: 288 Rue Abdallaye, Rue 42-100 (between Presidency building and Spanish Embassy), Nouakchott
mailing address: BP 222, Nouakchott
telephone: [222] 4525-2660 through 2663
FAX: [222] 4525-1592

Flag description: green with a yellow five-pointed star above a yellow, horizontal crescent; the closed side of the crescent is down; the crescent, star, and color green are traditional symbols of Islam; the gold color stands for the sands of the Sahara

National symbol(s): star and crescent

National anthem: *name:* "Hymne National de la Republique Islamique de Mauritanie" (National Anthem of the Islamic Republic of Mauritania)
lyrics/music: Baba Ould CHEIKH/traditional, arranged by Tolia NIKIPROWETZKY
note: adopted 1960; the unique rhythm of the Mauritanian anthem makes it particularly challenging to sing

ECONOMY

Economy—overview: Mauritania's economy is dominated by natural resources and agriculture. Half the population still depends on agriculture and livestock for a livelihood, even though many of the nomads and subsistence farmers were forced into the cities by recurrent droughts in the 1970s and 1980s. Mauritania's extensive mineral resources include iron ore, gold, copper, gypsum, and phosphate rock and exploration is ongoing for uranium, crude oil, and natural gas. Extractive commodities make up 75% of Mauritania's total exports. The nation's coastal waters are among the richest fishing areas in the world, and fishing accounts for 20% of budget revenues, but overexploitation by foreigners threatens this key source of revenue. Risks to Mauritania's economy include its recurring exposure to droughts, dependence on foreign aid and investment, and insecurity in neighboring Mali, as well as significant shortages of infrastructure, institutional capacity, and human capital.

GDP (purchasing power parity): $8.204 billion (2013 est.)
country comparison to the world: 156
$7.708 billion (2012 est.)
$7.212 billion (2011 est.)
note: data are in 2013 US dollars

GDP (official exchange rate): $4.183 billion (2013 est.)

GDP—real growth rate: 6.4% (2013 est.)
country comparison to the world: 31
6.9% (2012 est.)
3.6% (2011 est.)

GDP—per capita (PPP): $2,200 (2013 est.)
country comparison to the world: 191
$2,100 (2012 est.)
$2,000 (2011 est.)
note: data are in 2013 US dollars

Gross national saving: 27.4% of GDP (2013 est.)
country comparison to the world: 38
26.2% of GDP (2012 est.)
39.3% of GDP (2011 est.)

GDP—composition, by end use:
household consumption: 52.4%
government consumption: 22.7%
investment in fixed capital: 61.9%
investment in inventories: -8.9%
exports of goods and services: 56.8%
imports of goods and services: -84.9% (2013 est.)

GDP—composition, by sector of origin:
agriculture: 16.9%
industry: 54.6%
services: 28.5% (2013 est.)

Agriculture—products: dates, millet, sorghum, rice, corn; cattle, sheep

Industries: fish processing, oil production, mining (iron ore, gold, and copper)
note: gypsum deposits have never been exploited

Industrial production growth rate: 8% (2013 est.)
country comparison to the world: 23

Labor force: 1.318 million (2007)
country comparison to the world: 135

Labor force—by occupation: *agriculture:* 50%
industry: 10%
services: 40% (2001 est.)

Unemployment rate: 30% (2008 est.)
country comparison to the world: 184
20% (2004 est.)

Population below poverty line: 40% (2004 est.)

Household income or consumption by percentage share: *lowest 10%:* 2.5%
highest 10%: 29.5% (2000)

Distribution of family income—Gini index: 39 (2000)
country comparison to the world: 67
37.3 (1995)

Budget: *revenues:* $1.677 billion
expenditures: $1.702 billion (2013 est.)

Taxes and other revenues: 40.1% of GDP (2013 est.)
country comparison to the world: 41

Budget surplus (+) or deficit (-): -0.6% of GDP (2013 est.)
country comparison to the world: 58

Fiscal year: calendar year

Inflation rate (consumer prices): 4.6% (2013 est.)
country comparison to the world: 149
4.9% (2012 est.)

Central bank discount rate: 9% (31 December 2009 est.)
country comparison to the world: 17
12% (31 December 2007)

Commercial bank prime lending rate: 18% (31 December 2013 est.)
country comparison to the world: 30
17% (31 December 2012 est.)

Stock of domestic credit: $1.739 billion (31 December 2013 est.)
country comparison to the world: 135
$1.514 billion (31 December 2012 est.)

Market value of publicly traded shares: $NA

Current account balance: -$1.24 billion (2013 est.)
country comparison to the world: 124
-$1.263 billion (2012 est.)

Exports: $2.728 billion (2013 est.)
country comparison to the world: 132
$2.642 billion (2012 est.)

Exports—commodities: iron ore, fish and fish products, gold, copper, petroleum

Exports—partners: China 50.5%, Italy 7.8%, Japan 7.3%, France 4.9%, Spain 4.2%, Cote dIvoire 4.1%, Netherlands 4% (2012)

Imports: $3.355 billion (2013 est.)
country comparison to the world: 142
$3.176 billion (2012 est.)

Imports—commodities: machinery and equipment, petroleum products, capital goods, foodstuffs, consumer goods

Imports—partners: China 12.9%, Netherlands 10.5%, US 7.8%, France 7.8%, Brazil 5.6%, Germany 5.5%, Spain 5.1%, Belgium 4.7% (2012)

Debt—external: $3.233 billion (31 December 2013 est.)
country comparison to the world: 135
$2.922 billion (31 December 2012 est.)

Exchange rates: ouguiyas (MRO) per US dollar—
298.1 (2013 est.)
296.6 (2012 est.)
275.89 (2010 est.)
262.4 (2009)
238.2 (2008)

ENERGY

Electricity—production: 701 million kWh (2010 est.)
country comparison to the world: 154

Electricity—consumption: 651.9 million kWh (2010 est.)
country comparison to the world: 161

Electricity—exports: 0 kWh (2012 est.)
country comparison to the world: 169

Electricity—imports: 0 kWh (2012 est.)
country comparison to the world: 171

Electricity—installed generating capacity: 263,000 kW (2010 est.)
country comparison to the world: 153

Electricity—from fossil fuels: 63.1% of total installed capacity (2010 est.)
country comparison to the world: 128

Electricity—from nuclear fuels: 0% of total installed capacity (2010 est.)
country comparison to the world: 141

Electricity—from hydroelectric plants: 36.9% of total installed capacity (2010 est.)
country comparison to the world: 63

Electricity—from other renewable sources: 0% of total installed capacity (2010 est.)
country comparison to the world: 203

Crude oil—production: 6,577 bbl/day (2012 est.)
country comparison to the world: 95

Crude oil—exports: 7,337 bbl/day (2010 est.)
country comparison to the world: 62

Crude oil—imports: 0 bbl/day (2010 est.)
country comparison to the world: 94

Crude oil—proved reserves: 20 million bbl (1 January 2013 es)
country comparison to the world: 84

Refined petroleum products—production: 0 bbl/day (2010 est.)
country comparison to the world: 175

Refined petroleum products—consumption: 18,120 bbl/day (2011 est.)
country comparison to the world: 133

Refined petroleum products—exports: 0 bbl/day (2010 est.)
country comparison to the world: 199

Refined petroleum products—imports: 12,810 bbl/day (2010 est.)
country comparison to the world: 126

Natural gas—production: 0 cu m (2011 est.)
country comparison to the world: 168

Natural gas—consumption: 0 cu m (2010 est.)
country comparison to the world: 173

Natural gas—exports: 0 cu m (2011 est.)
country comparison to the world: 150

Natural gas—imports: 0 cu m (2011 est.)
country comparison to the world: 98

Natural gas—proved reserves: 28.32 billion cu m (1 January 2013 es)
country comparison to the world: 71

Carbon dioxide emissions from consumption of energy: 1.774 million Mt (2011 est.)
country comparison to the world: 151

COMMUNICATIONS

Telephones—main lines in use: 65,100 (2012)
country comparison to the world: 158

Telephones—mobile cellular: 4.024 million (2012)
country comparison to the world: 121

Telephone system: *general assessment:* limited system of cable and open-wire lines, minor microwave radio relay links, and radiotelephone communications stations; mobile-cellular services expanding rapidly
domestic: Mauritel, the national telecommunications company, was privatized in 2001 but remains the monopoly provider of fixed-line services; fixed-line teledensity 2 per 100 persons; mobile-cellular network coverage extends mainly to urban areas with a teledensity of roughly 106 per 100 persons; mostly cable and open-wire lines; a domestic satellite telecommunications system links Nouakchott with regional capitals
international: country code—222; satellite earth stations—3 (1 Intelsat—Atlantic Ocean, 2 Arabsat); fiber-optic and Asymmetric Digital Subscriber Line (ADSL) cables for Internet access (2009)

Broadcast media: one state-run TV (Television de Mauritanie) and one state-run radio network (Radio de Mauritanie); Television de Mauritanie has three channels, Al Mahadra station (for Islamic content) and Channels 1 and 2, which cover news, sports, and other programming; Radio de Mauritanie runs 12 regional stations as well as a radio station for youth and the Holy Quran station; five private TV channels and five private radio stations also broadcast from Mauritania; six private international radio stations broadcast in Mauritania on the FM band; with satellite connections, Mauritanians also have access to hundreds of foreign TV channels (2013)

Internet country code: .mr

Internet hosts: 22 (2012)
country comparison to the world: 220

Internet users: 75,000 (2009)
country comparison to the world: 170

TRANSPORTATION

Airports: 30 (2013)
country comparison to the world: 116

Airports—with paved runways: *total:* 9
2,438 to 3,047 m: 5
1,524 to 2,437 m: 4 (2013)

Airports—with unpaved runways: *total:* 2 1
2,438 to 3,047 m: 1
1,524 to 2,437 m: 10
914 to 1,523 m: 8
under 914 m: 2 (2013)

Railways: 728 km
standard gauge: 728 km 1.435-m gauge (2008)

Roadways: *total:* 10,628 km

country comparison to the world: 133

paved: 3,158 km

unpaved: 7,470 km (2010)

Waterways: (some navigation is possible on the Senegal River) (2011)

Ports and terminals: *major seaport(s):* Nouadhibou, Nouakchott

MILITARY

Military branches: Mauritanian Armed Forces: Army, Mauritanian Navy (Marine Mauritanienne; includes naval infantry), Islamic Republic of Mauritania Air Group (Groupement Aerienne Islamique de Mauritanie, GAIM) (2013)

Military service age and obligation: 18 is the legal minimum age for voluntary military service; no conscription (2012)

Manpower available for military service:
males age 16-49: 718,713
females age 16-49: 804,622 (2010 est.)

Manpower fit for military service:
males age 16-49: 480,042
females age 16-49: 581,473 (2010 est.)

Manpower reaching militarily significant age annually: *male:* 36,116

female: 36,826 (2010 est.)

TRANSNATIONAL ISSUES

Disputes—international: Mauritanian claims to Western Sahara remain dormant

Refugees and internally displaced persons: *refugees (country of origin):* 26,000 (Western Saharan—Sahrawis) (2012); 57,406 (Mali) (2014)

Trafficking in persons: *current situation:* Mauritania is a source, transit, and destination country for men, women, and children subjected to conditions of forced labor and sex trafficking; adults and children from traditional slave castes are subjected to slavery-related practices rooted in ancestral master-slave relationships; Mauritanian boys called talibe are trafficked within the country by religious teachers for forced begging; Mauritanian girls, as well as girls from Mali, Senegal, The Gambia, and other West African countries are forced into domestic servitude; Mauritanian women and girls are forced into prostitution in the country or transported to countries in the Middle East for the same purpose

tier rating: Tier 3—Mauritania does not fully comply with the minimum standards for the elimination of trafficking and is not making significant efforts to do so; after the previous year's unprecedented progress in prosecuting and convicting trafficking offenders, the government has not convicted any traffickers; the government has not provided adequate protective services to victims or ensure their referral to NGOs, which provide the majority of care to trafficking victims and generally do not receive government financial support; the absence of measures in place to identify trafficking victims among vulnerable populations may have led to victims being punished for acts committed as a result of being trafficked; the effectiveness of the 2007 anti-slavery law remains impaired because the slaves, many of whom are illiterate, are first required to file a legal complaint, and the government provides no programs to assist victims in lodging slavery complaints (2013)

MAURITIUS

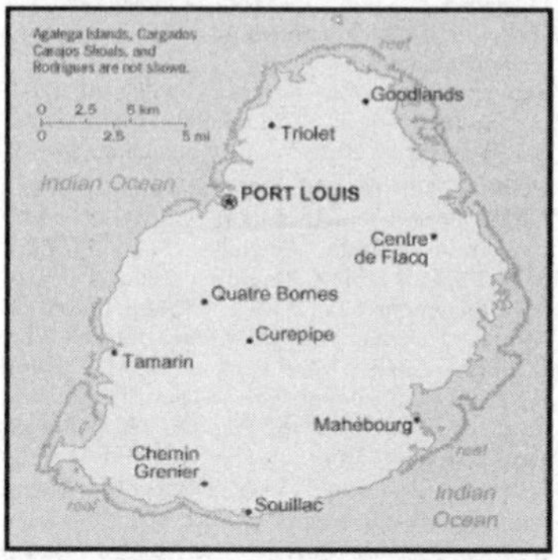

INTRODUCTION

Background: Although known to Arab and Malay sailors as early as the 10th century, Mauritius was first explored by the Portuguese in the 16th century and subsequently settled by the Dutch—who named it in honor of Prince Maurits van NASSAU—in the 17th century. The French assumed control in 1715, developing the island into an important naval base overseeing Indian Ocean trade, and establishing a plantation economy of sugar cane. The British captured the island in 1810, during the Napoleonic Wars. Mauritius remained a strategically important British naval base, and later an air station, playing an important role during World War II for anti-submarine and convoy operations, as well as the collection of signals intelligence. Independence from the UK was attained in 1968. A stable democracy with regular free elections and a positive human rights record, the country has attracted considerable foreign investment and has earned one of Africa's highest per capita incomes.

GEOGRAPHY

Location: Southern Africa, island in the Indian Ocean, east of Madagascar

Geographic coordinates: 20 17 S, 57 33 E

Map references: Africa

Area: *total:* 2,040 sq km
country comparison to the world: 181
land: 2,030 sq km
water: 10 sq km
note: includes Agalega Islands, Cargados Carajos Shoals (Saint Brandon), and Rodrigues

Area—comparative: almost 11 times the size of Washington, DC

Land boundaries: 0 km

Coastline: 177 km

Maritime claims: measured from claimed archipelagic straight baselines
territorial sea: 12 nm
exclusive economic zone: 200 nm
continental shelf: 200 nm or to the edge of the continental margin

Climate: tropical, modified by southeast trade winds; warm, dry winter (May to November); hot, wet, humid summer (November to May)

Terrain: small coastal plain rising to discontinuous mountains encircling central plateau

Elevation extremes: *lowest point:* Indian Ocean 0 m
highest point: Mont Piton 828 m

Natural resources: arable land, fish

Land use: *arable land:* 38.24%
permanent crops: 1.96%
other: 59.8% (2011)

Irrigated land: 212.2 sq km (2003)

Total renewable water resources: 2.75 cu km (2011)

Freshwater withdrawal (domestic/industrial/agricultural): *total:* 0.73 cu km/yr (30%/3%/68%)
per capita: 568.2 cu m/yr (2003)

Natural hazards: cyclones (November to April); almost completely surrounded by reefs that may pose maritime hazards

Environment—current issues: water pollution, degradation of coral reefs

Environment—international agreements: *party to:* Antarctic-Marine Living Resources, Biodiversity, Climate Change, Climate Change-Kyoto Protocol, Desertification, Endangered Species, Environmental Modification, Hazardous Wastes, Law of the Sea, Marine Life Conservation, Ozone Layer Protection, Ship Pollution, Wetlands
signed, but not ratified: none of the selected agreements

Geography—note: the main island, from which the country derives its name, is of volcanic origin and is almost entirely surrounded by coral reefs; former home of the dodo, a large flightless bird related to pigeons, driven to extinction by the end of the 17th century through a combination of hunting and the introduction of predatory species

PEOPLE AND SOCIETY

Nationality: *noun:* Mauritian(s)
adjective: Mauritian

Ethnic groups: Indo-Mauritian 68%, Creole 27%, Sino-Mauritian 3%, Franco-Mauritian 2%

Languages: Creole 86.5%, Bhojpuri 5.3%, French 4.1%, two languages 1.4%, other 2.6% (includes English, the official language, which is spoken by less than 1% of the population), unspecified 0.1% (2011 est.)

Religions: Hindu 48.5%, Roman Catholic 26.3%, Muslim 17.3%, other Christian 6.4%, other 0.6%, none 0.7%, unspecified 0.1% (2011 est.)

Population: 1,331,155 (July 2014 est.)
country comparison to the world: 156

Age structure:
0-14 years: 21% (male 143,064/female 137,021)
15-24 years: 15.5% (male 104,257/female 102,233)
25-54 years: 44.1% (male 293,607/female 294,029)
55-64 years: 8.4% (male 68,749/female 76,407)
65 years and over: 8% (male 45,145/female 66,643) (2014 est.)

Dependency ratios:
total dependency ratio: 39.8 %
youth dependency ratio: 27.6 %
elderly dependency ratio: 12.2 %
potential support ratio: 8.2 (2013)

Median age: *total:* 33.9 years
male: 33.1 years
female: 34.8 years (2014 est.)

Population growth rate: 0.66% (2014 est.)
country comparison to the world: 148

Birth rate: 13.46 births/1,000 population (2014 est.)
country comparison to the world: 149

Death rate: 6.85 deaths/1,000 population (2014 est.)
country comparison to the world: 139

Net migration rate: 0 migrant(s)/1,000 population (2014 est.)
country comparison to the world: 88

Urbanization: *urban population:* 41.8% of total population (2011)
rate of urbanization: 0.57% annual rate of change (2010-15 est.)

Major urban areas—population: PORT LOUIS (capital) 149,000 (2009)

Sex ratio: *at birth:* 1.05 male(s)/female
0-14 years: 1.04 male(s)/female
15-24 years: 1.02 male(s)/female
25-54 years: 1 male(s)/female
55-64 years: 0.97 male(s)/female
65 years and over: 0.67 male(s)/female
total population: 0.97 male(s)/female (2014 est.)

Maternal mortality rate: 60 deaths/100,000 live births (2010)
country comparison to the world: 99

Infant mortality rate: *total:* 10.59 deaths/1,000 live births
country comparison to the world: 136
male: 12.59 deaths/1,000 live births
female: 8.5 deaths/1,000 live births (2014 est.)

Life expectancy at birth: *total population:* 75.17 years
country comparison to the world: 98
male: 71.71 years
female: 78.81 years (2014 est.)

Total fertility rate: 1.77 children born/woman (2014 est.)
country comparison to the world: 160

Contraceptive prevalence rate: 75.8% (2002)

Health expenditures: 5.9% of GDP (2011)
country comparison to the world: 115

Physicians density: 1.06 physicians/1,000 population (2004)

Hospital bed density: 3.4 beds/1,000 population (2011)

Drinking water source:
improved:
urban: 99.9% of population
rural: 99.7% of population
total: 99.8% of population
unimproved:
urban: 0.1% of population
rural: 0.3% of population
total: 0.2% of population (2011 est.)

Sanitation facility access:
improved:
urban: 91.6% of population
rural: 89.9% of population
total: 90.6% of population
unimproved:
urban: 8.4% of population
rural: 10.1% of population
total: 9.4% of population (2011 est.)

HIV/AIDS—adult prevalence rate: 1.2% (2012 est.)
country comparison to the world: 40

HIV/AIDS—people living with HIV/AIDS: 10,500 (2012 est.)
country comparison to the world: 101

HIV/AIDS—deaths: 700 (2012 est.)
country comparison to the world: 84

Obesity—adult prevalence rate: 18.5% (2008)
country comparison to the world: 105

Education expenditures: 3.5% of GDP (2012)
country comparison to the world: 123

Literacy: *definition:* age 15 and over can read and write
total population: 88.8%
male: 91.1%
female: 86.7% (2011 est.)

School life expectancy (primary to tertiary education): *total:* 16 years
male: 15 years
female: 16 years (2012)

Unemployment, youth ages 15-24: *total:* 23.7%
country comparison to the world: 44
male: 20.4%
female: 28.4% (2012)

GOVERNMENT

Country name: *conventional long form:* Republic of Mauritius
conventional short form: Mauritius
local long form: Republic of Mauritius
local short form: Mauritius

Government type: parliamentary democracy

Capital: *name:* Port Louis

geographic coordinates: 20 09 S, 57 29 E
time difference: UTC+4 (9 hours ahead of Washington, DC during Standard Time)

Administrative divisions: 9 districts and 3 dependencies*; Agalega Islands*, Black River, Cargados Carajos Shoals*, Flacq, Grand Port, Moka, Pamplemousses, Plaines Wilhems, Port Louis, Riviere du Rempart, Rodrigues*, Savanne

Independence: 12 March 1968 (from the UK)

National holiday: Independence Day, 12 March (1968)

Constitution: several previous; latest adopted 12 March 1968; amended many times, last in 2012 (2012)

Legal system: civil legal system based on French civil law with some elements of English common law

International law organization participation: accepts compulsory ICJ jurisdiction with reservations; accepts ICCt jurisdiction

Suffrage: 18 years of age; universal

Executive branch: *chief of state:* President Rajkeswur Kailash PURRYAG (since 21 July 2012); note—former President Sir Anerood JUGNAUTH resigned on 31 March 2012
head of government: Prime Minister Navinchandra RAMGOOLAM (since 5 July 2005)
cabinet: Council of Ministers appointed by the president on the recommendation of the prime minister (For more information visit the World Leaders website)
elections: president and vice president elected by the National Assembly for five-year terms (eligible for a second term); elections last held on 21 July 2012 (next to be held in 2017); prime minister and deputy prime minister appointed by the president, responsible to the National Assembly; note—former President Sir Anerood JUGNAUTH resigned on 31 March 2012
election results: Rajkeswur Kailash PURRYAG elected president by unanimous vote; percent of vote by the National Assembly—NA

Legislative branch: unicameral National Assembly (70 seats; 62 members elected by popular vote, 8 appointed by the election commission to give representation to various ethnic minorities; members to serve five-year terms)
elections: last held on 5 May 2010 (next to be held in 2015)
election results: percent of vote by party—NA; seats by party—AF 41, MMM 18, MR 2, FSM 1; appointed seats—to be assigned 8; note—as of 4 March 2014 seats by party were AF 38, MMM 19, MSM 9, FSM 1, MMSD 1, OPR 1, other 1

Judicial branch: *highest court(s):* Supreme Court of Mauritius (consists of the chief justice, a senior puisne judge, and 17 puisne judges)
judge selection and term of office: chief justice appointed by the president after consultation with the prime minister; senior puisne judge appointed by the president with the advice of the chief justice; other puisne judges appointed by the president with the advice of the Judicial and Legal Commission, a 4-member body of judicial officials including the chief justice; all judges serve until retirement at age 62
subordinate courts: Court of Civil Appeal; Court of Criminal Appeal; Public Bodies Appeal Tribunal (formed by a 2008 constitutional amendment)

Political parties and leaders: Alliance of the Future or AF [Navinchandra RAMGOOLAM] (governing coalition—includes MLP, MMSM, MR, MSD, PMSD); Mauritian Labor Party or MLP [Navinchandra RAMGOOLAM]; Mauritian Militant Movement or MMM [Paul BERENGER]; Militant Socialist Movement or MSM [Pravind JUGNAUTH]; Maurition Social Democratic Party or PMSD [Xavier Luc DUVAL]; Mauritian Solidarity Front of FSM [Cehl FAKEERMEEAH]; Mauritian Social Democratic Movement or MMSD [Eric GUIMBEAU]; Mauritian Militant Socialist Movement or MSMM [Madan DULLOO]; Rodrigues Movement or MR [Joseph (Nicholas) Von MALLY]; Rodrigues Peoples Organization or OPR [Serge CLAIR]

Political pressure groups and leaders: LALIT Political Party; Blok 104. Rezistans ek Alternativ (Resistence and Alternative), Say No to Coal!
other: various labor unions

International organization participation: ACP, AfDB, AOSIS, AU, C, CD, COMESA, CPLP (associate), FAO, G-77, IAEA, IBRD, ICAO, ICC (NGOs), ICRM, IDA, IFAD, IFC, IFRCS, IHO, ILO, IMF, IMO, IMSO, InOC, Interpol, IOC, IOM, IPU, ISO, ITSO, ITU, ITUC (NGOs), MIGA, NAM, OIF, OPCW, PCA, SAARC (observer), SADC, UN, UNCTAD, UNESCO, UNIDO, UNWTO, UPU, WCO, WFTU (NGOs), WHO, WIPO, WMO, WTO

Diplomatic representation in the US:
chief of mission: Ambassador Somduth SOBORUN (since 28 January 2011)
chancery: 1709 N Street NW, Washington, DC 20036; administrative offices—3201 Connecticut Avenue NW, Suite 441, Washington, DC 20036
telephone: [1] (202) 244-1491 through 1492
FAX: [1] (202) 966-0983

Diplomatic representation from the US:
chief of mission: Ambassador Sharon VILLAROSA (since 10 September 2012; note—also accredited to
Seychelles
embassy: 4th Floor, Rogers House, John Kennedy Street, Port Louis
mailing address: international mail: P. O. Box 544, Port Louis; US mail: American Embassy, Port Louis, US Department of State, Washington, DC 20521-2450
telephone: [230] 202-4400
FAX: [230] 208-9534

Flag description: four equal horizontal bands of red (top), blue, yellow, and green; red represents self-determination and independence, blue the Indian Ocean surrounding the island, yellow has been interpreted as the new light of independence, golden sunshine, or the bright future, and green can symbolize either agriculture or the lush vegetation of the island

National anthem: *name:* "Motherland"
lyrics/music: Jean Georges PROSPER/Philippe GENTIL
note: adopted 1968

ECONOMY

Economy—overview: Since independence in 1968, Mauritius has developed from a low-income, agriculturally based economy to a middle-income diversified economy with growing industrial, financial, and tourist sectors. Mauritius has achieved steady and strong growth over the last several decades, resulting in more equitable income distribution, increased life expectancy, lowered infant mortality, and a much-improved infrastructure. The economy rests on sugar, tourism, textiles and apparel, and financial services, and is expanding into fish processing, information and communications technology, and hospitality and property development. Sugarcane is grown on about 90% of the cultivated land area and accounts for 15% of export earnings. The government's development strategy centers on creating vertical and horizontal clusters of development in these sectors. Mauritius has attracted more than 32,000 offshore entities, many aimed at commerce in India, South Africa, and China. Investment in the banking sector alone has reached over $1 billion. Mauritius, with its strong textile sector, has been well poised to take advantage of the Africa Growth and Opportunity Act (AGOA). Mauritius' sound economic policies and prudent banking practices helped to mitigate negative effects of the global financial crisis in 2008-09. GDP grew in the 3-4% per year range in 2010-13, and the country continues to expand its trade and investment outreach around the globe.

GDP (purchasing power parity): $20.95 billion (2013 est.)
country comparison to the world: 131
$20.26 billion (2012 est.)
$19.61 billion (2011 est.)
note: data are in 2013 US dollars

GDP (official exchange rate): $11.9 billion (2013 est.)

GDP—real growth rate: 3.4% (2013 est.)
country comparison to the world: 103
3.3% (2012 est.)
3.8% (2011 est.)

GDP—per capita (PPP): $16,100 (2013 est.)
country comparison to the world: 86
$15,600 (2012 est.)
$15,200 (2011 est.)
note: data are in 2013 US dollars

Gross national saving: 32% of GDP (2013 est.)
country comparison to the world: 20
32% of GDP (2012 est.)
31% of GDP (2011 est.)

GDP—composition, by end use:
household consumption: 74.1%
government consumption: 13.2%
investment in fixed capital: 22%
investment in inventories: 1.5%
exports of goods and services: 54.6%
imports of goods and services: -65.4% (2013 est.)

GDP—composition, by sector of origin:
agriculture: 4.5%
industry: 22%
services: 73.4% (2013 est.)

Agriculture—products: sugarcane, tea, corn, potatoes, bananas, pulses; cattle, goats; fish

Industries: food processing (largely sugar milling), textiles, clothing, mining, chemicals, metal products, transport equipment, nonelectrical machinery, tourism

Industrial production growth rate: 0.2% (2013 est.)
country comparison to the world: 164

Labor force: 637,600 (2013 est.)
country comparison to the world: 153

Labor force—by occupation:
agriculture and fishing: 9%
construction and industry: 30%
transportation and communication: 7%
trade, restaurants, hotels: 22%
finance: 6%
other services: 25% (2007)

Unemployment rate: 8.3% (2013 est.)
country comparison to the world: 94
8.1% (2012 est.)

Population below poverty line: 8% (2006 est.)

Household income or consumption by percentage share: *lowest 10%:* NA%
highest 10%: NA%

Distribution of family income—Gini index: 39 (2006 est.)
country comparison to the world: 66
37 (1987 est.)

Budget: *revenues:* $2.507 billion
expenditures: $2.736 billion (2013 est.)

Taxes and other revenues: 21.1% of GDP (2013 est.)
country comparison to the world: 156

Budget surplus (+) or deficit (-):
-1.9% of GDP (2013 est.)
country comparison to the world: 84

Public debt: 58% of GDP (2013 est.)
country comparison to the world: 52
57.7% of GDP (2012 est.)

Fiscal year: 1 July—30 June

Inflation rate (consumer prices): 3.5% (2013 est.)
country comparison to the world: 123
3.9% (2012 est.)

Central bank discount rate: 9% (31 December 2010 est.)

Commercial bank prime lending rate: 8.5% (31 December 2013 est.)
country comparison to the world: 110
8.67% (31 December 2012 est.)

Stock of narrow money: $2.475 billion (31 December 2013 est.)
country comparison to the world: 122
$2.378 billion (31 December 2012 est.)

Stock of broad money: $11.73 billion (31 December 2013 est.)
country comparison to the world: 99
$11.38 billion (31 December 2012 est.)

Stock of domestic credit: $13.03 billion (31 December 2013 est.)
country comparison to the world: 93
$12.87 billion (31 December 2012 est.)

Market value of publicly traded shares:
$7.093 billion (31 December 2012 est.)
country comparison to the world: 76
$7.667 billion (31 December 2011)
$7.442 billion (31 December 2010 est.)

Current account balance: -$1.099 billion (2013 est.)
country comparison to the world: 120
-$1.175 billion (2012 est.)

Exports: $2.788 billion (2013 est.)
country comparison to the world: 131
$2.673 billion (2012 est.)

Exports—commodities: clothing and textiles, sugar, cut flowers, molasses, fish, primates (for research)

Exports—partners: UK 19.3%, France 16.4%, US 9.9%, South Africa 9.8%, Spain 7.5%, Italy 6.9%, Madagascar 6.8% (2012)

Imports: $4.953 billion (2013 est.)
country comparison to the world: 128
$5.104 billion (2012 est.)

Imports—commodities: manufactured goods, capital equipment, foodstuffs, petroleum products, chemicals

Imports—partners: India 23.1%, China 16%, France 8.5%, South Africa 6.5% (2012)

Reserves of foreign exchange and gold: $3.286 billion (31 December 2013 est.)
country comparison to the world: 106
$3.046 billion (31 December 2012 est.)

Debt—external: $2.894 billion (31 December 2013 est.)
country comparison to the world: 138
$2.606 billion (31 December 2012 est.)

Stock of direct foreign investment—at home: NA

Stock of direct foreign investment—abroad: NA

Exchange rates: Mauritian rupees (MUR) per US dollar—
30.89 (2013 est.)
30.051 (2012 est.)
30.784 (2010 est.)
31.96 (2009)
27.973 (2008)

ENERGY

Electricity—production: 2.628 billion kWh (2011 est.)
country comparison to the world: 131

Electricity—consumption: 2.358 billion kWh (2010 est.)
country comparison to the world: 136

Electricity—exports: 0 kWh (2012 est.)
country comparison to the world: 168

Electricity—imports: 0 kWh (2012 est.)
country comparison to the world: 170

Electricity—installed generating capacity: 900,200 kW (2010 est.)
country comparison to the world: 124

Electricity—from fossil fuels: 75.7% of total installed capacity (2010 est.)
country comparison to the world: 98

Electricity—from nuclear fuels: 0% of total installed capacity (2010 est.)
country comparison to the world: 140

Electricity—from hydroelectric plants: 6.6% of total installed capacity (2010 est.)
country comparison to the world: 121

Electricity—from other renewable sources: 17.8% of total installed capacity (2010 est.)
country comparison to the world: 8

Crude oil—production: 0 bbl/day (2012 est.)
country comparison to the world: 196

Crude oil—exports: 0 bbl/day (2010 est.)
country comparison to the world: 155

Crude oil—imports: 0 bbl/day (2010 est.)
country comparison to the world: 93

Crude oil—proved reserves: 0 bbl (1 January 2013 es)
country comparison to the world: 165

Refined petroleum products—production: 0 bbl/day (2010 est.)
country comparison to the world: 174

Refined petroleum products—consumption: 24,710 bbl/day (2011 est.)
country comparison to the world: 122

Refined petroleum products—exports: 0 bbl/day (2010 est.)
country comparison to the world: 198

Refined petroleum products—imports: 20,620 bbl/day (2010 est.)
country comparison to the world: 105

Natural gas—production: 0 cu m (2011 est.)
country comparison to the world: 167

Natural gas—consumption: 0 cu m (2010 est.)
country comparison to the world: 172

Natural gas—exports: 0 cu m (2011 est.)
country comparison to the world: 149

Natural gas—imports: 0 cu m (2011 est.)
country comparison to the world: 97

Natural gas—proved reserves: 0 cu m (1 January 2013 es)
country comparison to the world: 171

Carbon dioxide emissions from consumption of energy: 5.06 million Mt (2011 est.)
country comparison to the world: 124

COMMUNICATIONS

Telephones—main lines in use: 349,100 (2012)
country comparison to the world: 109

Telephones—mobile cellular: 1.485 million (2012)
country comparison to the world: 152

Telephone system: *general assessment:* small system with good service
domestic: monopoly over fixed-line services terminated in 2005; fixed-line teledensity roughly 30 per 100 persons; mobile-cellular services launched in 1989 with current teledensity roughly 100 per 100 persons
international: country code—230; landing point for the SAFE submarine cable that provides links to Asia and South Africa where it connects to the SAT-3/WASC submarine cable that provides further links to parts of East Africa, and Europe; satellite earth station—1 Intelsat (Indian Ocean); new microwave link to Reunion; HF radiotelephone links to several countries (2011)

Broadcast media: the government maintains control over TV broadcasting through the Mauritius Broadcasting Corporation (MBC), which operates 3 analog and 10 digital TV stations; MBC is a shareholder in a local company that operates 2 pay-TV stations; the state retains the largest radio broadcast network with multiple stations; several private radio broadcasters have entered the market since 2001; transmissions of at least 2 international broadcasters are available (2007)

Internet country code: .mu

Internet hosts: 51,139 (2012)
country comparison to the world: 95

Internet users: 290,000 (2009)
country comparison to the world: 131

TRANSPORTATION

Airports: 5 (2013)
country comparison to the world: 180

Airports—with paved runways: *total:* 2
over 3,047 m: 1
914 to 1,523 m: 1 (2013)

Airports—with unpaved runways: *total:* 3
914 to 1,523 m: 2
under 914 m: 1 (2013)

Roadways: *total:* 2,149 km
country comparison to the world: 173
paved: 2,149 km (includes 75 km of expressways) (2012)

Merchant marine: *total:* 4
country comparison to the world: 129
by type: passenger/cargo 2, petroleum tanker 1, refrigerated cargo 1 (2010)

Ports and terminals: *major seaport(s):* Port Louis

MILITARY

Military branches: no regular military forces; Mauritius Police Force, Special Mobile Force, National Coast Guard (2011)

Manpower available for military service: *males age 16-49:* 343,628 (2010 est.)

Manpower fit for military service: *males age 16-49:* 280,596
females age 16-49: 283,317 (2010 est.)

Manpower reaching militarily significant age annually: *male:* 10,193
female: 10,104 (2010 est.)

Military expenditures: 0.19% of GDP (2012)
country comparison to the world: 130
0.16% of GDP (2011)
0.19% of GDP (2010)

TRANSNATIONAL ISSUES

Disputes—international: Mauritius and Seychelles claim the Chagos Islands; claims French-administered Tromelin Island

Illicit drugs: consumer and transshipment point for heroin from South Asia; small amounts of cannabis produced and consumed locally; significant offshore financial industry creates potential for money laundering, but corruption levels are relatively low and the government appears generally to be committed to regulating its banking industry

MEXICO

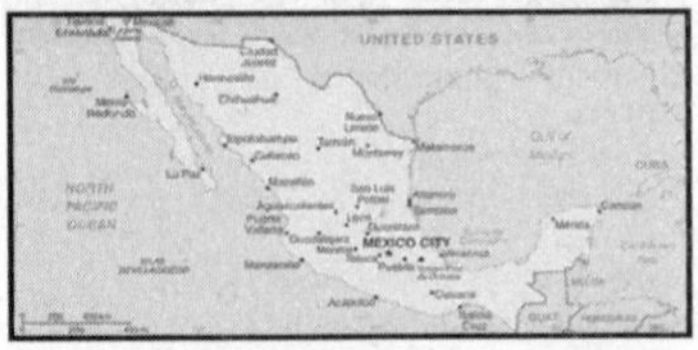

INTRODUCTION

Background: The site of several advanced Amerindian civilizations—including the Olmec, Toltec, Teotihuacan, Zapotec, Maya, and Aztec—Mexico was conquered and colonized by Spain in the early 16th century. Administered as the Viceroyalty of New Spain for three centuries, it achieved its independence early in the 19th century. The global financial crisis beginning in late 2008 caused a massive economic downturn the following year, although growth returned quickly in 2010. Ongoing economic and social concerns include low real wages, underemployment for a large segment of the population, inequitable income distribution, and few advancement opportunities for the largely indigenous population in the impoverished southern states. The elections held in 2000 marked the first time since the 1910 Mexican Revolution that an opposition candidate—Vicente FOX of the National Action Party (PAN)—defeated the party in government, the Institutional Revolutionary Party (PRI). He was succeeded in 2006 by another PAN candidate Felipe CALDERON, but the PRI regained the presidency in 2012. Since 2007, Mexico's powerful drug-trafficking organizations have engaged in bloody feuding, resulting in tens of thousands of drug-related homicides.

GEOGRAPHY

Location: North America, bordering the Caribbean Sea and the Gulf of Mexico, between Belize and the United States and bordering the North Pacific Ocean, between Guatemala and the United States

Geographic coordinates: 23 00 N, 102 00 W

Map references: North America

Area: *total:* 1,964,375 sq km
country comparison to the world: 14
land: 1,943,945 sq km
water: 20,430 sq km

Area—comparative: slightly less than three times the size of Texas

Land boundaries: *total:* 4,353 km
border countries: Belize 250 km, Guatemala 962 km, US 3,141 km

Coastline: 9,330 km

Maritime claims: *territorial sea:* 12 nm
contiguous zone: 24 nm
exclusive economic zone: 200 nm
continental shelf: 200 nm or to the edge of the continental margin

Climate: varies from tropical to desert

Terrain: high, rugged mountains; low coastal plains; high plateaus; desert

Elevation extremes: *lowest point:* Laguna Salada -10 m
highest point: Volcan Pico de Orizaba 5,700 m

Natural resources: petroleum, silver, copper, gold, lead, zinc, natural gas, timber

Land use: *arable land:* 12.98%
permanent crops: 1.36%
other: 85.66% (2011)

Irrigated land: 64,600 sq km (2009)

Total renewable water resources: 457.2 cu km (2011)

Freshwater withdrawal (domestic/industrial/agricultural): *total:* 80.4 cu km/yr (14%/9%/77%)
per capita: 700.4 cu m/yr (2009)

Natural hazards: tsunamis along the Pacific coast, volcanoes and destructive earthquakes in the center and south, and hurricanes on the Pacific, Gulf of Mexico, and Caribbean coasts
volcanism: volcanic activity in the central-southern part of the country; the volcanoes in Baja California are mostly dormant; Colima (elev. 3,850 m), which erupted in 2010, is Mexico's most active volcano and is responsible for causing periodic evacuations of nearby villagers; it has been deemed a Decade Volcano by the International Association of Volcanology and Chemistry of the Earth's Interior, worthy of study due to its explosive history and close proximity to human populations; Popocatepetl (elev. 5,426 m) poses a threat to Mexico City; other historically active volcanoes include Barcena, Ceboruco, El Chichon, Michoacan-Guanajuato, Pico de Orizaba, San Martin, Socorro, and Tacana

Environment—current issues: scarcity of hazardous waste disposal facilities; rural to urban migration; natural freshwater resources scarce and polluted in north, inaccessible and poor quality in center and extreme southeast; raw sewage and industrial effluents polluting rivers in urban areas; deforestation; widespread erosion; desertification; deteriorating agricultural lands; serious air and water pollution in the national capital and urban centers along US-Mexico border; land subsidence in Valley of Mexico caused by groundwater depletion
note: the government considers the lack of clean water and deforestation national security issues

Environment—international agreements:
party to: Biodiversity, Climate Change, Climate Change-Kyoto Protocol, Desertification, Endangered Species, Hazardous Wastes, Law of the Sea, Marine Dumping, Marine Life Conservation, Ozone Layer Protection, Ship Pollution, Wetlands, Whaling
signed, but not ratified: none of the selected agreements

Geography—note: strategic location on southern border of US; corn (maize), one of the world's major grain crops, is thought to have originated in Mexico

PEOPLE AND SOCIETY

Nationality: *noun:* Mexican(s)
adjective: Mexican

Ethnic groups: mestizo (Amerindian-Spanish) 60%, Amerindian or predominantly Amerindian 30%, white 9%, other 1%

Languages: Spanish only 92.7%, Spanish and indigenous languages 5.7%, indigenous only 0.8%, unspecified 0.8%
note: indigenous languages include various Mayan, Nahuatl, and other regional languages (2005)

Religions: Roman Catholic 82.7%, Pentecostal 1.6%, Jehovah's Witnesses 1.4%, other Evangelical Churches 5%, other 1.9%, none 4.7%, unspecified 2.7% (2010 est.)

Population: 120,286,655 (July 2014 est.)
country comparison to the world: 12

Age structure: *0-14 years:* 27.9% (male 17,188,577/female 16,423,421)
15-24 years: 18.1% (male 10,999,445/female 10,741,999)
25-54 years: 40.4% (male 23,385,321/female 25,200,511)
55-64 years: 6.6% (male 3,850,792/female 4,527,074)
65 years and over: 6.9% (male 3,594,675/female 4,374,840) (2014 est.)

Dependency ratios:
total dependency ratio: 53.6 %
youth dependency ratio: 43.7 %
elderly dependency ratio: 9.8 %
potential support ratio: 10.2 (2013)

Median age: *total:* 27.3 years
male: 26.3 years
female: 28.4 years (2014 est.)

Population growth rate: 1.21% (2014 est.)
country comparison to the world: 98

Birth rate: 19.02 births/1,000 population (2014 est.)
country comparison to the world: 91

Death rate: 5.24 deaths/1,000 population (2014 est.)
country comparison to the world: 183

Net migration rate: -1.64 migrant(s)/1,000 population (2014 est.)
country comparison to the world: 158

Urbanization: *urban population:* 78% of total population (2010)
rate of urbanization: 1.2% annual rate of change (2010-15 est.)
note: Mexico City is the second-largest urban agglomeration in the Western Hemisphere, after Sao Paulo (Brazil), but before New York-Newark (US)

Major urban areas—population: MEXICO CITY (capital) 19.319 million; Guadalajara 4.338 million; Monterrey 3.838 million; Puebla 2.278 million; Tijuana 1.629 million (2009)

Sex ratio: *at birth:* 1.05 male(s)/female
0-14 years: 1.05 male(s)/female
15-24 years: 1.02 male(s)/female
25-54 years: 0.93 male(s)/female
55-64 years: 0.96 male(s)/female
65 years and over: 0.81 male(s)/female
total population: 0.96 male(s)/female (2014 est.)

Mother's mean age at first birth: 21.3
note: median age at first birth among women 25-29 (2006 est.)

Maternal mortality rate: 50 deaths/100,000 live births (2010)
country comparison to the world: 108

Infant mortality rate: *total:* 12.58 deaths/1,000 live births
country comparison to the world: 123
male: 14 deaths/1,000 live births
female: 11.08 deaths/1,000 live births (2014 est.)

Life expectancy at birth: *total population:* 75.43 years
country comparison to the world: 94
male: 72.67 years
female: 78.32 years (2014 est.)

Total fertility rate: 2.29 children born/woman (2014 est.)
country comparison to the world: 95

Contraceptive prevalence rate: 70.9% (2006)

Health expenditures: 6.4% of GDP (2009)
country comparison to the world: 97

Physicians density: 1.96 physicians/1,000 population (2009)

Hospital bed density: 1.7 beds/1,000 population (2010)

Drinking water source:
improved:
urban: 95.9% of population
rural: 89.3% of population
total: 94.4% of population
unimproved:
urban: 4.1% of population
rural: 10.7% of population
total: 5.6% of population (2011 est.)

Sanitation facility access:
improved:
urban: 86.7% of population
rural: 77.4% of population
total: 84.7% of population
unimproved:
urban: 13.3% of population
rural: 22.6% of population
total: 15.3% of population (2011 est.)

HIV/AIDS—adult prevalence rate: 0.2% (2012 est.)
country comparison to the world: 115

HIV/AIDS—people living with HIV/AIDS: 174,300 (2012 est.)
country comparison to the world: 32

HIV/AIDS—deaths: NA

Major infectious diseases: *degree of risk:* intermediate
food or waterborne diseases: bacterial diarrhea and hepatitis A
vectorborne disease: dengue fever (2013)

Obesity—adult prevalence rate: 32.1% (2008)
country comparison to the world: 23

Children under the age of 5 years underweight: 2.8% (2012)
country comparison to the world: 115

Education expenditures: 5.1% of GDP (2009)
country comparison to the world: 72

Literacy: *definition:* age 15 and over can read and write
total population: 93.5%

male: 94.8%
female: 92.3% (2011 est.)

School life expectancy (primary to tertiary education): *total:* 13 years
male: 13 years
female: 13 years (2011)

Child labor—children ages 5-14: *total number:* 1,105,617
percentage: 5 % (2009 est.)

Unemployment, youth ages 15-24: *total:* 9.4%
country comparison to the world: 113
male: 9.1%
female: 9.9% (2012)

GOVERNMENT

Country name: *conventional long form:* United Mexican States
conventional short form: Mexico
local long form: Estados Unidos Mexicanos
local short form: Mexico

Government type: federal republic

Capital: *name:* Mexico City (Distrito Federal)

geographic coordinates: 19 26 N, 99 08 W
time difference: UTC-6 (1 hour behind Washington, DC during Standard Time)
daylight saving time: +1hr, begins first Sunday in April; ends last Sunday in October
note: Mexico is divided into three time zones

Administrative divisions: 31 states (estados, singular—estado) and 1 federal district* (distrito federal); Aguascalientes, Baja California, Baja California Sur, Campeche, Chiapas, Chihuahua, Coahuila de Zaragoza, Colima, Distrito Federal*, Durango, Guanajuato, Guerrero, Hidalgo, Jalisco, Mexico, Michoacan de Ocampo, Morelos, Nayarit, Nuevo Leon, Oaxaca, Puebla, Queretaro de Arteaga, Quintana Roo, San Luis Potosi, Sinaloa, Sonora, Tabasco, Tamaulipas, Tlaxcala, Veracruz de Ignacio de la Llave (Veracruz), Yucatan, Zacatecas

Independence: 16 September 1810 (declared); 27 September 1821 (recognized by Spain)

National holiday: Independence Day, 16 September (1810)

Constitution: several previous; latest approved 5 February 1917; amended many times, last in 2012 (2012)

Legal system: civil law system with US constitutional law theory influence; judicial review of legislative acts

International law organization participation: accepts compulsory ICJ jurisdiction with reservations; accepts ICCt jurisdiction

Suffrage: 18 years of age; universal and compulsory (but not enforced)

Executive branch: *chief of state:* President Enrique PENA NIETO (since 1 December 2012); note—the president is both the chief of state and head of government
head of government: President Enrique PENA NIETO (since 1 December 2012)
cabinet: Cabinet appointed by the president; note—appointment of attorney general, the head of the Bank of Mexico, and senior treasury officials require consent of the Senate (For more information visit the World Leaders website)
elections: president elected by popular vote for a single six-year term; election last held on 1 July 2012 (next to be held July 2018)
election results: Enrique PENA NIETO elected president; percent of vote—Enrique PENA NIETO (PRI) 38.21%, Andres Manuel LOPEZ OBRADOR (PRD) 31.59%, Josefina Eugenia VAZQUEZ Mota (PAN) 25.41%, other 4.79%

Legislative branch: bicameral National Congress or Congreso de la Union consists of the Senate or Camara de Senadores (128 seats; 96 members elected by popular vote to serve six-year terms, and 32 seats allocated on the basis of each party's popular vote) and the Chamber of Deputies or Camara de Diputados (500 seats; 300 members are elected by popular vote; remaining 200 members are allocated on the basis of each party's popular vote; members to serve three-year terms)
elections: Senate—last held on 1 July 2012 for all of the seats (next to be held on 1 July 2018); Chamber of Deputies—last held on 1 July 2012 (next to be held on 5 July 2015)
election results: Senate—percent of vote by party—NA; seats by party—PRI 52, PAN 38, PRD 22, PVEM 9, PT 4, Movimiento Ciudadano 2, PANAL 1; Chamber of Deputies—percent of vote by party—NA; seats by party—PRI 208, PAN 114, PRD 100, PVEM 33, PT 19, Movimiento Ciudadano 16, PANAL 10

Judicial branch: *highest court(s):* Supreme Court of Justice or Suprema Corte de Justicia de la Nacion (consists of 21 ministers or judges and 5 supernumerary judges)
judge selection and term of office: judges nominated by the president and approved by the Senate; judges serve for life
subordinate courts: federal level includes Electoral Tribunal, circuit, collegiate, and unitary courts; state level and district level courts

Political parties and leaders: Citizen's Movement (Movimiento Ciudadano) [Dante DELGADO Rannaoro]; Institutional Revolutionary Party (Partido Revolucionario Institucional) or PRI [Cesar CAMACHO Quiroz]; Labor Party (Partido del Trabajo) or PT [Alberto ANAYA Gutierrez]; Mexican Green Ecological Party (Partido Verde Ecologista de Mexico) or PVEM [vacant]; National Action Party (Partido Accion Nacional) or PAN [Gustavo MADERO Munoz]; New Alliance Party (Partido Nueva Alianza) or PNA/PANAL [Luis CASTRO Obregon]; Party of the Democratic Revolution (Partido de la Revolucion Democratica) or PRD [Jesus ZAMBRANO Grijalva]

Political pressure groups and leaders: Businessmen's Coordinating Council or CCE; Confederation of Employers of the Mexican Republic or COPARMEX; Confederation of Industrial Chambers or CONCAMIN; Confederation of Mexican Workers or CTM; Confederation of National Chambers of Commerce or CONCANACO; Coordinator for Foreign Trade Business Organizations or COECE; Federation of Unions Providing Goods and Services or FESEBES; National Chamber of Transformation Industries or CANACINTRA; National Confederation of Popular Organizations or CNOP; National Coordinator for Education Workers or CNTE; National Peasant Confederation or CNC; National Small Business Chamber or CANACOPE; National Syndicate of Education Workers or SNTE; National Union of Workers or UNT; Popular Assembly of the People of Oaxaca or APPO; Roman Catholic Church

International organization participation: APEC, BCIE, BIS, CAN (observer), Caricom (observer), CD, CDB, CE (observer), CELAC, CSN (observer), EBRD, FAO, FATF, G-20, G-3, G-15, G-24, IADB, IAEA, IBRD, ICAO, ICC (national committees), ICRM, IDA, IFAD, IFC, IFRCS, IHO, ILO, IMF, IMO, IMSO, Interpol, IOC, IOM, IPU, ISO, ITSO, ITU, ITUC (NGOs), LAES, LAIA, MIGA, NAFTA, NAM (observer), NEA, OAS, OECD, OPANAL, OPCW, Paris Club (associate), PCA, SICA (observer), UN, UNASUR (observer), UNCTAD, UNESCO, UNHCR, UNIDO, Union Latina (observer), UNWTO, UPU, WCO, WFTU (NGOs), WHO, WIPO, WMO, WTO

Diplomatic representation in the US:
chief of mission: Ambassador Eduardo MEDINA MORA Icaza (since 11 January 2013)
chancery: 1911 Pennsylvania Avenue NW, Washington, DC 20006
telephone: [1] (202) 728-1600
FAX: [1] (202) 728-1698
consulate(s) general: Anchorage, Atlanta, Austin, Boston, Chicago, Dallas, Denver, El Paso (TX), Houston, Laredo (TX), Los Angeles, Miami, New York, Nogales (AZ), Phoenix, Sacramento (CA), San Antonio, San Diego, San Francisco, San Jose (CA), San Juan (Puerto Rico), Saint Paul (MN)
consulate(s): Albuquerque, Anchorage (AK), Boise (ID), Brownsville (TX), Calexico (CA), Del Rio (TX), Detroit, Douglas (AZ), Eagle Pass (TX), Fresno (CA), Indianapolis (IN), Kansas City (MO), Las Vegas (NV), Little Rock (AR), McAllen (TX), Midland (TX), New Orleans, Omaha (NE), Orlando (FL), Oxnard (CA), Philadelphia, Portland (OR), Presidio (TX), Raleigh (NC), Salt Lake City, San Bernardino (CA), Santa Ana (CA), Seattle, Tucson (AZ), Yuma (AZ); note—Washington DC Consular Section located in a separate building from the Mexican Embassy and has jurisdiction over DC, parts of Virginia, Maryland, and West Virginia

Diplomatic representation from the US:
chief of mission: Ambassador Earl Anthony WAYNE (since 2 August 2011)
embassy: Paseo de la Reforma 305, Colonia Cuauhtemoc, 06500 Mexico, Distrito Federal
mailing address: P. O. Box 9000, Brownsville, TX 78520-9000
telephone: [52] (55) 5080-2000
FAX: [52] (55) 5080-2834
consulate(s) general: Ciudad Juarez, Guadalajara, Hermosillo, Matamoros, Merida, Monterrey, Nogales, Nuevo Laredo, Tijuana

Flag description: three equal vertical bands of green (hoist side), white, and red; Mexico's coat of arms (an eagle with a snake in its beak perched on a cactus) is centered in the white band; green signifies hope, joy, and love; white represents peace and honesty; red stands for hardiness, bravery, strength, and valor; the coat of arms is derived from a legend that the wandering Aztec people were to settle at a location where they would see an eagle on a cactus eating a snake; the city they founded, Tenochtitlan, is now Mexico City
note: similar to the flag of Italy, which is shorter, uses lighter shades of red and green, and does not have anything in its white band

National symbol(s): golden eagle

National anthem: *name:* "Himno Nacional Mexicano" (National Anthem of Mexico)
lyrics/music: Francisco Gonzalez BOCANEGRA/ Jaime Nuno ROCA
note: adopted 1943, in use since 1854; the anthem is also known as "Mexicanos, al grito de Guerra" (Mexicans, to the War Cry); according to tradition, Francisco Gonzalez BOCANEGRA, an accomplished poet, was uninterested in submitting lyrics to a national anthem contest; his fiancee locked him in a room and refused to release him until the lyrics were completed

ECONOMY

Economy—overview: Mexico has a free market economy in the trillion dollar class. It contains a mixture of modern and outmoded industry and agriculture, increasingly dominated by the private sector. Recent administrations have expanded competition in seaports, railroads, telecommunications, electricity generation, natural gas distribution, and airports. Per capita income is roughly one-third that of the US; income distribution remains highly unequal. Since the implementation of the North American Free Trade Agreement (NAFTA) in 1994, Mexico's share of US imports has increased from 7% to 12%, and its share of Canadian imports has doubled to 5.5%. Mexico has free trade agreements with over 50 countries including Guatemala, Honduras, El Salvador, the European Free Trade Area, and Japan - putting more than 90% of trade under free trade agreements. In 2012 Mexico formally joined the Trans-Pacific Partnership negotiations and in July it formed the Pacific Alliance with Peru, Colombia and Chile. In 2007, during its first year in office, the Felipe CALDERON administration was able to garner support from the opposition to successfully pass pension and fiscal reforms. The administration passed an energy reform measure in 2008 and another fiscal reform in 2009. Mexico's GDP plunged 6.2% in 2009 as world demand for exports dropped, asset prices tumbled, and remittances and investment declined. GDP recovered during 2010-13 with exports—particularly to the United States—leading the way. In November 2012, Mexico's legislature passed a comprehensive labor reform which was signed into law by former President Felipe CALDERON. Mexico's new PRI government, led by President Enrique PENA NIETO, has emphasized economic reforms during its first year in office, passing education, energy, financial, fiscal and telecommunications reform legislation. Nevertheless, administration estimates show GDP growth slowed in 2013 to just over 1%.

GDP (purchasing power parity): $1.845 trillion (2013 est.)
country comparison to the world: 11
$1.823 trillion (2012 est.)
$1.76 trillion (2011 est.)
note: data are in 2013 US dollars

GDP (official exchange rate): $1.327 trillion (2013 est.)

GDP—real growth rate: 1.2% (2013 est.)
country comparison to the world: 169
3.6% (2012 est.)
4% (2011 est.)

GDP—per capita (PPP): $15,600 (2013 est.)
country comparison to the world: 88
$15,600 (2012 est.)
$15,200 (2011 est.)
note: data are in 2013 US dollars

Gross national saving: 21% of GDP (2013 est.)
country comparison to the world: 76
21.3% of GDP (2012 est.)
21.2% of GDP (2011 est.)

GDP—composition, by end use:
household consumption: 69.1%
government consumption: 11.8%
investment in fixed capital: 22.7%
investment in inventories: -1%
exports of goods and services: 31.2%
imports of goods and services: -33.8% (2013 est.)

GDP—composition, by sector of origin:
agriculture: 3.6%
industry: 36.6%
services: 59.8% (2013 est.)

Agriculture—products: corn, wheat, soybeans, rice, beans, cotton, coffee, fruit, tomatoes; beef, poultry, dairy products; wood products

Industries: food and beverages, tobacco, chemicals, iron and steel, petroleum, mining, textiles, clothing, motor vehicles, consumer durables, tourism

Industrial production growth rate: 3.5% (2013 est.)
country comparison to the world: 85

Labor force: 51.48 million (2013 est.)
country comparison to the world: 13

Labor force—by occupation: *agriculture:* 13.4%
industry: 24.1%
services: 61.9% (2011)

Unemployment rate: 4.9% (2013 est.)
country comparison to the world: 44
5.3% (2012 est.)
note: underemployment may be as high as 25%

Population below poverty line: 52.3%
note: based on food-based definition of poverty; asset based poverty amounted to more than 47% (2012 est.)

Household income or consumption by percentage share: *lowest 10%:* 2%
highest 10%: 37.5% (2010)

Distribution of family income—Gini index: 48.3 (2008)
country comparison to the world: 25
53.1 (1998)

Budget: *revenues:* $291.2 billion
expenditures: $324.1 billion (2013 est.)

Taxes and other revenues: 21.9% of GDP (2013 est.)
country comparison to the world: 149

Budget surplus (+) or deficit (-):
-2.5% of GDP (2013 est.)
country comparison to the world: 105

Public debt: 37.7% of GDP (2013 est.)
country comparison to the world: 99
35.8% of GDP (2012 est.)

Fiscal year: calendar year

Inflation rate (consumer prices): 4% (2013 est.)
country comparison to the world: 134
3.6% (2012 est.)

Central bank discount rate: 4.5% (31 December 2012 est.)
country comparison to the world: 82
4.5% (31 December 2011 est.)

Commercial bank prime lending rate: 4.7% (31 December 2013 est.)
country comparison to the world: 160
4.73% (31 December 2012 est.)

Stock of narrow money: $174.2 billion (31 December 2012 est.)
country comparison to the world: 23
$170.5 billion (31 December 2011 est.)

Stock of broad money: $713 billion (31 December 2013 est.)
country comparison to the world: 20
$671.8 billion (31 December 2012 est.)

Stock of domestic credit: $444.6 billion (31 December 2013 est.)
country comparison to the world: 27
$404.4 billion (31 December 2012 est.)

Market value of publicly traded shares: $525.1 billion (31 December 2012 est.)
country comparison to the world: 22
$408.7 billion (31 December 2011)
$454.3 billion (31 December 2010 est.)

Current account balance: -$14.18 billion (2013 est.)
country comparison to the world: 182
-$11.84 billion (2012 est.)

Exports: $370.9 billion (2013 est.)
country comparison to the world: 17
$349.6 billion (2012 est.)

Exports—commodities: manufactured goods, oil and oil products, silver, fruits, vegetables, coffee, cotton

Exports—partners: US 78% (2012)

Imports: $370.7 billion (2013 est.)
country comparison to the world: 16
$350.9 billion (2012 est.)

Imports—commodities: metalworking machines, steel mill products, agricultural machinery, electrical equipment, car parts for assembly, repair parts for motor vehicles, aircraft, and aircraft parts

Imports—partners: US 49.9%, China 15.4%, Japan 4.8% (2012)

Reserves of foreign exchange and gold: $167.1 billion (31 December 2013 est.)
country comparison to the world: 18
$149.2 billion (31 December 2012 est.)

Debt—external: $354.9 billion (31 December 2013 est.)
country comparison to the world: 32
$286.4 billion (31 December 2012 est.)

Stock of direct foreign investment—at home: $435.3 billion (31 December 2013 est.)
country comparison to the world: 19
$400.9 billion (31 December 2012 est.)

Stock of direct foreign investment—abroad: $141.2 billion (31 December 2013 est.)
country comparison to the world: 26
$133 billion (31 December 2012 est.)

Exchange rates: Mexican pesos (MXN) per US dollar—
12.76 (2013 est.)
13.17 (2012 est.)
12.636 (2010 est.)
13.514 (2009)
11.016 (2008)

ENERGY

Electricity—production: 296 billion kWh (2012 est.)
country comparison to the world: 1 4

Electricity—consumption: 212.3 billion kWh (2010 est.)
country comparison to the world: 18

Electricity—exports: 1.286 billion kWh (2012 est.)
country comparison to the world: 54

Electricity—imports: 603 million kWh (2012 est.)
country comparison to the world: 74

Electricity—installed generating capacity: 62 million kW (2010 est.)
country comparison to the world: 16

Electricity—from fossil fuels: 76.2% of total installed capacity (2010 est.)
country comparison to the world: 96

Electricity—from nuclear fuels: 2.2% of total installed capacity (2010 est.)
country comparison to the world: 25

Electricity—from hydroelectric plants: 18.3% of total installed capacity (2010 est.)
country comparison to the world: 95

Electricity—from other renewable sources: 3.3% of total installed capacity (2010 est.)
country comparison to the world: 54

Crude oil—production: 2.936 million bbl/day (2012 est.)
country comparison to the world: 9

Crude oil—exports: 1.46 million bbl/day (2010 est.)
country comparison to the world: 10

Crude oil—imports: 0 bbl/day (2010 est.)
country comparison to the world: 98

Crude oil—proved reserves: 10.26 billion bbl (1 January 2013 es)
country comparison to the world: 18

Refined petroleum products—production: 1.364 million bbl/day (2010 est.)
country comparison to the world: 15

Refined petroleum products—consumption: 2.133 million bbl/day (2011 est.)
country comparison to the world: 12

Refined petroleum products—exports: 189,100 bbl/day (2010 est.)
country comparison to the world: 33

Refined petroleum products—imports: 607,400 bbl/day (2010 est.)
country comparison to the world: 11

Natural gas—production: 53.96 billion cu m (2012 est.)
country comparison to the world: 17

Natural gas—consumption: 59.15 billion cu m (2011 est.)
country comparison to the world: 14

Natural gas—exports: 11 million cu m (2012 est.)
country comparison to the world: 51

Natural gas—imports: 17.24 billion cu m (2012 est.)
country comparison to the world: 22

Natural gas—proved reserves: 487.7 billion cu m (1 January 2013 es)
country comparison to the world: 32

Carbon dioxide emissions from consumption of energy: 462.3 million Mt (2011 est.)
country comparison to the world: 14

COMMUNICATIONS

Telephones—main lines in use: 20.22 million (2012)
country comparison to the world: 14

Telephones—mobile cellular: 100.786 million (2012)
country comparison to the world: 13

Telephone system: *general assessment:* adequate telephone service for business and government; improving quality and increasing mobile cellular availability, with mobile subscribers far outnumbering fixed-line subscribers; domestic satellite system with 120 earth stations; extensive microwave radio relay network; considerable use of fiber-optic cable and coaxial cable
domestic: despite the opening to competition in January 1997, Telmex remains dominant; Fixed-line teledensity is less than 20 per 100 persons; mobile-cellular teledensity is about 80 per 100 persons
international: country code—52; Columbus-2 fiber-optic submarine cable with access to the US, Virgin Islands, Canary Islands, Spain, and Italy; the Americas Region Caribbean Ring System (ARCOS-1) and the MAYA-1 submarine cable system together provide access to Central America, parts of South America and the Caribbean, and the US; satellite earth stations—120 (32 Intelsat, 2 Solidaridad (giving Mexico improved access to South America, Central America, and much of the US as well as enhancing domestic communications), 1 Panamsat, numerous Inmarsat mobile earth stations); linked to Central American Microwave System of trunk connections (2011)

Broadcast media: many TV stations and more than 1,400 radio stations with most privately owned; the Televisa group once had a virtual monopoly in TV broadcasting, but new broadcasting groups and foreign satellite and cable operators are now available (2012)

Internet country code: .mx

Internet hosts: 16.233 million (2012)
country comparison to the world: 9

Internet users: 31.02 million (2009)
country comparison to the world: 12

TRANSPORTATION

Airports: 1,714 (2013)
country comparison to the world: 3

Airports—with paved runways: *total:* 243
over 3,047 m: 12
2,438 to 3,047 m: 32
1,524 to 2,437 m: 80
914 to 1,523 m: 86
under 914 m: 33 (2013)

Airports—with unpaved runways: *total:* 1,471
over 3,047 m: 1
2,438 to 3,047 m: 1
1,524 to 2,437 m: 42
914 to 1,523 m: 281
under 914 m: 1,146 (2013)

Heliports: 1 (2013)

Pipelines: gas 18,074 km; liquid petroleum 2,102 km; oil 8,775 km; oil/gas/water 369 km; refined products 7,565 km; water 123 km (2013)

Railways: *total:* 17,166 km
country comparison to the world: 16
standard gauge: 17,166 km 1.435-m gauge (22 km electrified) (2008)

Roadways: *total:* 377,660 km
country comparison to the world: 18
paved: 137,544 km (includes 7,176 km of expressways)
unpaved: 240,116 km (2012)

Waterways: 2,900 km (navigable rivers and coastal canals mostly connected with ports on the country's east coast) (2012)
country comparison to the world: 34

Merchant marine: *total:* 5 2
country comparison to the world: 70
by type: bulk carrier 5, cargo 3, chemical tanker 11, liquefied gas 3, passenger/cargo 10, petroleum tanker 17, roll on/roll off 3
foreign-owned: 5 (France 1, Greece 2, South Africa 1, UAE 1)
registered in other countries: 12 (Antigua and Barbuda 1, Marshall Islands 2, Panama 5, Portugal 1, Spain 1, Venezuela 1, unknown 1) (2010)

Ports and terminals: *major seaport(s):* Altamira, Coatzacoalcos, Lazaro Cardenas, Manzanillo, Salina Cruz, Veracruz
oil terminals: Cayo Arcas terminal, Dos Bocas terminal

MILITARY

Military branches: Secretariat of National Defense (Secretaria de Defensa Nacional, Sedena): Army (Ejercito), Mexican Air Force (Fuerza Aerea Mexicana, FAM); Secretariat of the Navy (Secretaria de Marina, Semar): Mexican Navy (Armada de Mexico (ARM); includes Naval Air Force (FAN), Mexican Naval Infantry Corps (Cuerpo de Infanteria de Marina, Mexmar or CIM)) (2013)

Military service age and obligation: 18 years of age for compulsory military service, conscript service obligation is 12 months; 16 years of age with consent for voluntary enlistment; conscripts serve only in the Army; Navy and Air Force service is all voluntary; women are eligible for voluntary military service; cadets enrolled in military schools from the age of 15 are considered members of the armed forces (2012)

Manpower available for military service:
males age 16-49: 28,815,506
females age 16-49: 30,363,558 (2010 est.)

Manpower fit for military service:
males age 16-49: 23,239,866
females age 16-49: 25,642,549 (2010 est.)

Manpower reaching militarily significant age annually: *male:* 1,105,371
female: 1,067,007 (2010 est.)

Military expenditures: 0.59% of GDP (2012)
country comparison to the world: 124
0.56% of GDP (2011)
0.59% of GDP (2010)

TRANSNATIONAL ISSUES

Disputes—international: abundant rainfall in recent years along much of the Mexico-US border region has ameliorated periodically strained water-sharing arrangements; the US has intensified security measures to monitor and control legal and illegal personnel, transport, and commodities across its border with Mexico; Mexico must deal with thousands of impoverished Guatemalans and other Central Americans who cross the porous border looking for work in Mexico and the United States; Belize and Mexico are working to solve minor border demarcation discrepancies arising from inaccuracies in the 1898 border treaty

Refugees and internally displaced persons:
IDPs: 160,000 (government's quashing of Zapatista uprising in 1994 in eastern Chiapas Region; drug cartel violence and government's military response since 2007; violence between and within indigenous groups) (2011)
stateless persons: 7 (2012)

Illicit drugs: major drug-producing and transit nation; world's second largest opium poppy cultivator; opium poppy cultivation in 2009 rose 31% over 2008 to 19,500 hectares yielding a potential production of 50 metric tons of pure heroin, or 125 metric tons of "black tar" heroin, the dominant form of Mexican heroin in the western United States; marijuana cultivation increased 45% to 17,500 hectares in 2009; government conducts the largest independent illicit-crop eradication program in the world; continues as the primary transshipment country for US-bound cocaine from South America, with an estimated 95% of annual cocaine movements toward the US stopping in Mexico; major drug syndicates control the majority of drug trafficking throughout the country; producer and distributor of ecstasy; significant money-laundering center; major supplier of heroin and largest foreign supplier of marijuana and methamphetamine to the US market (2007)

MICRONESIA, FEDERATED STATES OF

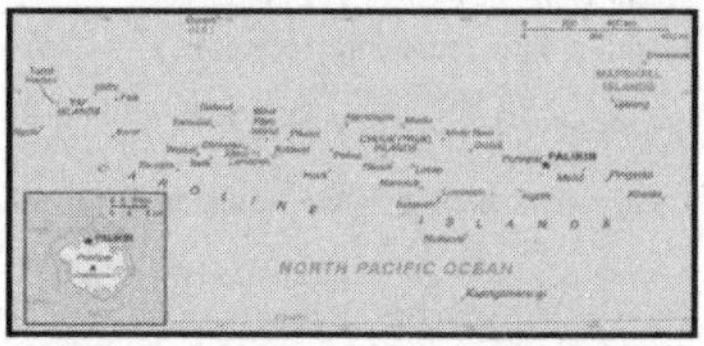

INTRODUCTION

Background: The Caroline Islands are a widely scattered archipelago in the western Pacific Ocean; they became part of a UN Trust Territory under US administration following World War II. The eastern four island groups adopted a constitution in 1979 and chose to become the Federated States of Micronesia. (The fifth, westernmost island group became Palau.) Independence came in 1986 under a Compact of Free Association with the US, which was amended and renewed in 2004. Present concerns include large-scale unemployment, overfishing, and overdependence on US aid.

GEOGRAPHY

Location: Oceania, island group in the North Pacific Ocean, about three-quarters of the way from Hawaii to Indonesia

Geographic coordinates: 6 55 N, 158 15 E

Map references: Oceania

Area: *total:* 702 sq km
country comparison to the world: 191
land: 702 sq km
water: 0 sq km (fresh water only)
note: includes Pohnpei (Ponape), Chuuk (Truk) Islands, Yap Islands, and Kosrae (Kosaie)

Area—comparative: four times the size of Washington, DC (land area only)

Land boundaries: 0 km

Coastline: 6,112 km

Maritime claims: *territorial sea:* 12 nm
exclusive economic zone: 200 nm

Climate: tropical; heavy year-round rainfall, especially in the eastern islands; located on southern edge of the typhoon belt with occasionally severe damage

Terrain: islands vary geologically from high mountainous islands to low, coral atolls; volcanic outcroppings on Pohnpei, Kosrae, and Chuuk

Elevation extremes: *lowest point:* Pacific Ocean 0 m
highest point: Dolohmwar (Totolom) 791 m

Natural resources: timber, marine products, deep-seabed minerals, phosphate

Land use: *arable land:* 2.86%
permanent crops: 24.29%
other: 72.86% (2011)

Irrigated land: NA

Natural hazards: typhoons (June to December)

Environment—current issues: overfishing, climate change, pollution

Environment—international agreements: party to: Biodiversity, Climate Change, Climate Change-Kyoto Protocol, Desertification, Hazardous Wastes, Law of the Sea, Ozone Layer Protection
signed, but not ratified: none of the selected agreements

Geography—note: four major island groups totaling 607 islands

PEOPLE AND SOCIETY

Nationality:
noun: Micronesian(s)
adjective: Micronesian; Chuukese, Kosraen(s), Pohnpeian(s), Yapese

Ethnic groups: Chuukese 48.8%, Pohnpeian 24.2%, Kosraean 6.2%, Yapese 5.2%, Yap outer islands 4.5%, Asian 1.8%, Polynesian 1.5%, other 6.4%, unknown 1.4% (2000 census)

Languages: English (official and common language), Chuukese, Kosrean, Pohnpeian, Yapese, Ulithian, Woleaian, Nukuoro, Kapingamarangi

Religions: Roman Catholic 54.7%, Protestant 41.1% (includes Congregational 38.5%, Baptist 1.1%, Seventh Day Adventist 0.8%, Assembly of God .7%), Mormon 1.5%, other 1.9%, none 0.7%, unspecified 0.1% (2010 est.)

Population: 105,681 (July 2014 est.)
country comparison to the world: 193

Age structure:
0-14 years: 31.9% (male 17,120/female 16,561)
15-24 years: 20.2% (male 10,755/female 10,609)
25-54 years: 38% (male 19,483/female 20,686)
55-64 years: 3.4% (male 3,440/female 3,477)
65 years and over: 3.2% (male 1,576/female 1,974) (2014 est.)

Dependency ratios:
total dependency ratio: 64.4 %
youth dependency ratio: 57.7 %
elderly dependency ratio: 6.7 %
potential support ratio: 14.9 (2013)

Median age: *total:* 23.8 years
male: 23.2 years
female: 24.4 years (2014 est.)

Population growth rate: -0.42% (2014 est.)
country comparison to the world: 220

Birth rate: 20.97 births/1,000 population (2014 est.)
country comparison to the world: 80

Death rate: 4.25 deaths/1,000 population (2014 est.)
country comparison to the world: 207

Net migration rate: -20.93 migrant(s)/1,000 population (2014 est.)
country comparison to the world: 220

Urbanization: *urban population:* 23% of total population (2010)
rate of urbanization: 1.3% annual rate of change (2010-15 est.)

Major urban areas—population: PALIKIR (capital) 7,000 (2009)

Sex ratio: *at birth:* 1.05 male(s)/female
0-14 years: 1.03 male(s)/female
15-24 years: 1.01 male(s)/female
25-54 years: 0.94 male(s)/female
55-64 years: 0.98 male(s)/female
65 years and over: 0.77 male(s)/female
total population: 0.99 male(s)/female (2014 est.)

Maternal mortality rate: 100 deaths/100,000 live births (2010)
country comparison to the world: 71

Infant mortality rate: *total:* 21.93 deaths/1,000 live births
country comparison to the world: 81
male: 24.28 deaths/1,000 live births
female: 19.47 deaths/1,000 live births (2014 est.)

Life expectancy at birth: *total population:* 72.35 years
country comparison to the world: 135
male: 70.34 years
female: 74.45 years (2014 est.)

Total fertility rate: 2.55 children born/woman (2014 est.)
country comparison to the world: 78

Health expenditures: 13.4% of GDP (2011)
country comparison to the world: 7

Physicians density: 0.18 physicians/1,000 population (2009)

Hospital bed density: 3.2 beds/1,000 population (2009)

Drinking water source:
improved:
urban: 94.7% of population
rural: 87.5% of population
total: 89.1% of population
unimproved:
urban: 5.3% of population
rural: 12.5% of population
total: 10.9% of population (2011 est.)

Sanitation facility access:
improved:
urban: 83.3% of population
rural: 47% of population
total: 55.2% of population
unimproved:
urban: 16.7% of population
rural: 53% of population
total: 44.8% of population (2011 est.)

HIV/AIDS—adult prevalence rate: NA

HIV/AIDS—people living with HIV/AIDS: NA

HIV/AIDS—deaths: NA

Obesity—adult prevalence rate: 40.6% (2008)
country comparison to the world: 12

Education expenditures: NA

Literacy: *definition:* age 15 and over can read and write
total population: 89%
male: 91%
female: 88% (1980 est.)

GOVERNMENT

Country name: *conventional long form:* Federated States of Micronesia
conventional short form: none
local long form: Federated States of Micronesia
local short form: none
former: Trust Territory of the Pacific Islands, Ponape, Truk, and Yap Districts
abbreviation: FSM

Government type: constitutional government in free association with the US; the Compact of Free Association entered into force on 3 November 1986 and the Amended Compact entered into force in May 2004

Capital: *name:* Palikir
geographic coordinates: 6 55 N, 158 09 E
time difference: UTC+11 (16 hours ahead of Washington, DC during Standard Time)

Administrative divisions: 4 states; Chuuk (Truk), Kosrae (Kosaie), Pohnpei (Ponape), Yap

Independence: 3 November 1986 (from the US-administered UN trusteeship)

National holiday: Constitution Day, 10 May (1979)

Constitution: drafted June 1975, ratified 1 October 1978, entered into force 10 May 1979; amended 1990 (2012)

Legal system: mixed legal system of common and customary law

International law organization participation:

has not submitted an ICJ jurisdiction declaration; non-party state to the ICCt

Suffrage: 18 years of age; universal

Executive branch: *chief of state:* President Emanuel MORI (since 11 May 2007); Vice President Alik L. ALIK (since 11 May 2007); note—the president is both the chief of state and head of government
head of government: President Emanuel MORI (since 11 May 2007); Vice President Alik L. ALIK (since 11 May 2007)
cabinet: Cabinet includes the vice president and the heads of the eight executive departments (For more information visit the World Leaders website)
elections: president and vice president elected by Congress from among the four senators at large for a four-year term (eligible for a second term); election last held on 11 May 2011 (next to be held in May 2015); note—a proposed constitutional amendment to establish popular elections for president and vice president failed
election results: Emanuel MORI reelected president by Congress unopposed; Alik L. ALIK reelected vice president

Legislative branch: unicameral Congress (14 seats; 4—one elected from each state to serve four-year terms and 10—elected from single-member districts delineated by population to serve two-year terms; members elected by popular vote)
elections: last held on 5 March 2013 (next to be held in March 2015)
election results: percent of vote—NA; seats—independents 14

Judicial branch: *highest court(s):* Federated States of Micronesia (FSM) Supreme Court (consists of the chief justice and not more than 5 associate justices and organized into appellate and criminal divisions)
judge selection and term of office: justices appointed by the president of the Federated States of Micronesia with the approval of two-thirds of Congress; justices appointed for life
subordinate courts: the highest state-level courts are: Chuuk Supreme Court; Korsae State Court; Pohnpei State Court; Yap State Court

Political parties and leaders: no formal parties

Political pressure groups and leaders: NA

International organization participation: ACP, ADB, AOSIS, FAO, G-77, IBRD, ICAO, ICRM, IDA, IFC, IFRCS, IMF, IOC, IOM, IPU, ITSO, ITU, MIGA, OPCW, PIF, Sparteca, SPC, UN, UNCTAD, UNESCO, WHO, WMO
Diplomatic representation in the US:
chief of mission: Ambassador Asterio R. TAKESY (since 13 January 2012)
chancery: 1725 N Street NW, Washington, DC 20036
telephone: [1] (202) 223-4383
FAX: [1] (202) 223-4391
consulate(s) general: Honolulu, Tamuning (Guam)

Diplomatic representation from the US:
chief of mission: Ambassador Dorothea-Maria (Doria) ROSEN (since 9 August 2012)
embassy: 101 Upper Pics Road, Kolonia
mailing address: P. O. Box 1286, Kolonia, Pohnpei, 96941; U.S. Embassy in Micronesia, 4120 Kolonia Place, Washington, D.C. 20521-4120
telephone: [691] 320-2187
FAX: [691] 320-2186

Flag description: light blue with four white five-pointed stars centered; the stars are arranged in a diamond pattern; blue symbolizes the Pacific Ocean, the stars represent the four island groups of Chuuk, Kosrae, Pohnpei, and Yap

National anthem: *name:* "Patriots of Micronesia"
lyrics/music: unknown
note: adopted 1991; the anthem is also known as "Across All Micronesia;" the music is based on the 1820 German patriotic song "Ich hab mich ergeben," which was the West German national anthem from 1949-1950; variants of this tune are used in Johannes Brahms' "Festival Overture" and Gustav Mahler's "Third Symphony"

ECONOMY

Economy—overview: Economic activity consists of subsistence farming and fishing and government which is funded largely by Compact of Free Association (Compact) assistance provided by the US. The islands have few known mineral deposits worth commercial exploration. The potential for tourism is also limited by isolation, lack of adequate facilities, and limited air and water connections hinder development. Under the terms of the original Compact, the US provided $1.3 billion in grants and aid in 1986-2001. The US and the Federated States of Micronesia (FSM) negotiated a second (amended) Compact agreement in 2002-2003 that took effect in 2004. The amended Compact runs for a 20-year period to 2024; during which the US will provide roughly $2.1 billion to the FSM. The amended Compact also includes a Trust Fund for the people of the FSM which is to provide an income stream beyond 2024 when Compact grants are to end. The country's medium-term economic outlook appears fragile because of reduced US assistance and lackluster performance of its small and stagnant private sector.

GDP (purchasing power parity): $754 million (2013 est.)
country comparison to the world: 210
$749.1 million (2012 est.)
$746.8 million (2011 est.)
note: GDP supplemented by grant aid, averaging perhaps $100 million annually

GDP (official exchange rate): $339 million (2013 est.)

GDP—real growth rate: 0.6% (2013 est.)
country comparison to the world: 181
0.4% (2012 est.)
2.1% (2011 est.)

GDP—per capita (PPP): $7,300 (2013 est.)
country comparison to the world: 140
$7,200 (2012 est.)
$7,200 (2011 est.)

GDP—composition, by sector of origin:
agriculture: 14%
industry: 12%
services: 74% (2011 est.)

Agriculture—products: black pepper, tropical fruits and vegetables, coconuts, bananas, cassava (tapioca), sakau (kava), Kosraen citrus, betel nuts, sweet potatoes; pigs, chickens; fish

Industries: tourism, construction; fish processing, specialized aquaculture; craft items (from shell, wood, and pearls)

Industrial production growth rate: NA%

Labor force: 15,920 (2011)
country comparison to the world: 213

Labor force—by occupation:
agriculture: 0.9%
industry: 20.6%
services: 78.5%
note: two-thirds of the labor force are government employees (2011 est.)

Unemployment rate: 22% (2000 est.)
country comparison to the world: 167

Population below poverty line: 26.7% (2000)

Household income or consumption by percentage share: *lowest 10%:* NA%
highest 10%: NA%

Budget: *revenues:* $107 million
expenditures: $102 million (FY10/11 est.)

Taxes and other revenues: 31.6% of GDP (FY10/11 est.)
country comparison to the world: 83

Budget surplus (+) or deficit (-):
1.5% of GDP (FY10/11 est.)
country comparison to the world: 22

Fiscal year: 1 October—30 September

Inflation rate (consumer prices): 3.4% (2011 est.)
country comparison to the world: 122
3.5% (2010 est.)

Commercial bank prime lending rate: 14.35% (31 December 2013 est.)
country comparison to the world: 47
14.35% (31 December 2012 est.)

Stock of narrow money: $27.22 million (31 December 2011 est.)
country comparison to the world: 188
$27.22 million

Stock of broad money: $118.4 million (31 December 2011 est.)
country comparison to the world: 189
$113.9 million (31 December 2010 est.)

Stock of domestic credit: $-56.77 million (31 December 2011 est.)
country comparison to the world: 183
$56.77 million

Current account balance: -$34.3 million (FY05 est.)
country comparison to the world: 65

Exports: $24.9 million (2009 est.)
country comparison to the world: 204
$14 million (2004 est.)

Exports—commodities: fish, garments, bananas, black pepper, sakau (kava), betel nuts

Imports: $132.7 million (2004)
country comparison to the world: 208

Imports—commodities: food, manufactured goods, machinery and equipment, beverages

Reserves of foreign exchange and gold: $75.06 million (31 December 2011 est.)
country comparison to the world: 167
$75.06 million

Debt—external: $60.8 million (FY05 est.)
country comparison to the world: 193

Exchange rates: the US dollar is used

ENERGY

Electricity—production: 192 million kWh (2002)
country comparison to the world: 184

Electricity—consumption: 178.6 million kWh (2002)
country comparison to the world: 187

Electricity—exports: 0 kWh (2002)
country comparison to the world: 136

Electricity—imports: 0 kWh (2002)
country comparison to the world: 143

COMMUNICATIONS

Telephones—main lines in use: 8,400 (2012)
country comparison to the world: 202

Telephones—mobile cellular: 27,600 (2012)
country comparison to the world: 208

Telephone system: *general assessment:* adequate system
domestic: islands interconnected by shortwave radiotelephone (used mostly for government purposes), satellite (Intelsat) ground stations, and some coaxial and fiber-optic cable; mobile-cellular service available on Kosrae, Pohnpei, and Yap
international: country code—691; satellite earth stations—5 Intelsat (Pacific Ocean) (2002)

Broadcast media: no TV broadcast stations; each state has a multi-channel cable service with TV transmissions carrying roughly 95% imported programming and 5% local programming; about a half dozen radio stations (2009)

Internet country code: .fm

Internet hosts: 4,668 (2012)
country comparison to the world: 147

Internet users: 17,000 (2009)
country comparison to the world: 196

TRANSPORTATION

Airports: 6 (2013)
country comparison to the world: 172

Airports—with paved runways: *total:* 6
1,524 to 2,437 m: 4
914 to 1,523 m: 2 (2013)

Roadways: *total:* 240 km
country comparison to the world: 207
paved: 42 km
unpaved: 198 km (2000)

Merchant marine: *total:* 3
country comparison to the world: 138
by type: cargo 1, passenger/cargo 2 (2010)

Ports and terminals: *major seaport(s):* Colonia (Tomil Harbor), Lele Harbor, Pohnepi Harbor

MILITARY

Military branches: no regular military forces (2012)

Manpower available for military service:
males age 16-49: 26,712 (2010 est.)

Manpower fit for military service:
males age 16-49: 22,008
females age 16-49: 23,501 (2010 est.)

Manpower reaching militarily significant age annually: *male:* 1,276

female: 1,253 (2010 est.)

Military—note: defense is the responsibility of the US

TRANSNATIONAL ISSUES

Disputes—international: none

Trafficking in persons: *current situation:* Micronesia is a source, and to a limited extent, destination country for women subjected to sex trafficking; Micronesian women are fraudulently recruited for jobs in the US and its territories only to be forced into prostitution or labor upon arrival; Micronesian and foreign women and children are also reportedly prostituted on fishing vessels in Micronesia or its territorial waters, as well as restaurants and clubs frequented by fishermen; complaints of nonpayment and inhuman treatment on fishing boats has led to investigations of labor trafficking

tier rating: Tier 2 Watch List—Micronesia does not fully comply with the minimum standards for the elimination of trafficking; however, it is making significant efforts to do so; despite passage of implementing regulations for Micronesia's 2012 trafficking law, the government has not reported any investigations, prosecutions, or convictions for sex or labor trafficking; the government also makes no efforts to identify trafficking victims and refer them to protective services; no NGOs provide services to victims; limited efforts are made to increase the public's awareness of human trafficking (2013)

Illicit drugs: major consumer of cannabis

MIDWAY ISLANDS

INTRODUCTION

Background: The US took formal possession of the islands in 1867. The laying of the trans-Pacific cable, which passed through the islands, brought the first residents in 1903. Between 1935 and 1947, Midway was used as a refueling stop for trans-Pacific flights. The US naval victory over a Japanese fleet off Midway in 1942 was one of the turning points of World War II. The islands continued to serve as a naval station until closed in 1993. Today the islands are a US National Wildlife Refuge. From 1996 to 2001 the refuge was open to the public; it is now temporarily closed.

GEOGRAPHY

Location: Oceania, atoll in the North Pacific Ocean, about one-third of the way from Honolulu to Tokyo

Geographic coordinates: 28 12 N, 177 22 W

Map references: Oceania

Area: *total:* 6.2 sq km
land: 6.2 sq km
water: 0 sq km
note: includes Eastern Island, Sand Island, and Spit Island

Area—comparative: about nine times the size of The Mall in Washington, DC

Land boundaries: 0 km

Coastline: 15 km

Maritime claims: *territorial sea:* 12 nm
exclusive economic zone: 200 nm

Climate: subtropical; moderated by prevailing easterly winds

Terrain: low, nearly level

Elevation extremes: *lowest point:* Pacific Ocean 0 m
highest point: unnamed location 13 m

Natural resources: wildlife, terrestrial and aquatic

Land use: *arable land:* 0%
permanent crops: 0%
other: 100% (2011)

Irrigated land: 0 sq km (2011)

Natural hazards: NA

Environment—current issues: NA

Geography—note: a coral atoll managed as a national wildlife refuge and open to the public for wildlife-related recreation in the form of wildlife observation and photography, sport fishing, snorkeling, and scuba diving; in 2000 the lands and waters of the Midway National Wildlife Refuge were also designated as the Battle of Midway National Monument; Henderson Airfield on Sand Island continues to serve as an emergency landing field for military and civilian aircraft transiting the Pacific Ocean (2012)

PEOPLE AND SOCIETY

Population: no indigenous inhabitants; approximately 40 people make up the staff of US Fish and Wildlife Service and their services contractor living at the atoll (July 2013 est.)

GOVERNMENT

Country name: *conventional long form:* none
conventional short form: Midway Islands

Dependency status: unincorporated territory of the US; formerly administered from Washington, DC, by the US Navy; on 31 October 1996, through a presidential executive order, the jurisdiction and control of the atoll was transferred to the Fish and Wildlife Service of the US Department of the Interior as part of the National Wildlife Refuge System

Legal system: the laws of the US, where applicable, apply

Flag description: the flag of the US is used

TRANSPORTATION

Airports—with paved runways: *total:* 2
1,524 to 2,437 m: 2 (2013)

Airports—with unpaved runways: *total:* 1
914 to 1,523 m: 1 (2013)

Ports and terminals: *major seaport(s):* Sand Island

Transportation—note: Henderson Field on Sand Island serves as an emergency landing site for aircraft crossing the Pacific Ocean

MILITARY

Military—note: defense is the responsibility of the US

TRANSNATIONAL ISSUES

Disputes—international: none

MOLDOVA

INTRODUCTION

Background: Part of Romania during the interwar period, Moldova was incorporated into the Soviet Union at the close of World War II. Although the country has been independent from the USSR since 1991, Russian forces have remained on Moldovan territory east of the Nistru River supporting the separatist region of Transnistria, composed of a Slavic majority population (mostly Ukrainians and Russians), but with a sizeable ethnic Moldovan minority. One of the poorest nations in Europe, Moldova became the first former Soviet state to elect a communist, Vladimir VORONIN, as its president in 2001. VORONIN served as Moldova's president until he resigned in September 2009, following the opposition's gain of a narrow majority in July parliamentary elections and the Communist Party's (PCRM) subsequent inability to attract the three-fifths of parliamentary votes required to elect a president and, by doing so, put into place a permanent government. Four Moldovan opposition parties formed a new coalition, the Alliance for European Integration (AEI), iterations of which have acted as Moldova's governing coalitions since. Moldova experienced significant political uncertainty between 2009 and early

2012, holding three general elections and numerous presidential ballots in parliament, all of which failed to secure a president. Following November 2010 parliamentary elections, a reconstituted AEI-coalition consisting of three of the four original AEI parties formed a government, and in March 2012 was finally able to elect an independent as president. As of late May 2013, the ruling coalition—comprised of two of the original AEI parties and a splinter group from a third—is called the Pro-European Coalition. In November 2013, the Moldovan Government initialed an Association Agreement with the European Union (EU), advancing the coalition's policy priority of EU integration.

GEOGRAPHY

Location: Eastern Europe, northeast of Romania

Geographic coordinates: 47 00 N, 29 00 E

Map references: Europe

Area: *total:* 33,851 sq km
country comparison to the world: 140
land: 32,891 sq km
water: 960 sq km

Area—comparative: slightly larger than Maryland

Land boundaries: *total:* 1,390 km
border countries: Romania 450 km, Ukraine 940 km

Coastline: 0 km (landlocked)

Maritime claims: none (landlocked)

Climate: moderate winters, warm summers

Terrain: rolling steppe, gradual slope south to Black Sea

Elevation extremes: *lowest point:* Dniester (Nistru) 2 m
highest point: Dealul Balanesti 430 m

Natural resources: lignite, phosphorites, gypsum, arable land, limestone

Land use: *arable land:* 53.47%
permanent crops: 8.77%
other: 37.75% (2011)

Irrigated land: 2,283 sq km (2011)

Total renewable water resources: 11.65 cu km (2011)

Freshwater withdrawal (domestic/industrial/agricultural): *total:* 1.07 cu km/yr (14%/83%/4%)
per capita: 290 cu m/yr (2010)

Natural hazards: landslides

Environment—current issues: heavy use of agricultural chemicals, including banned pesticides such as DDT, has contaminated soil and groundwater; extensive soil erosion from poor farming methods

Environment—international agreements: *party to:* Air Pollution, Air Pollution-Persistent Organic Pollutants, Biodiversity, Climate Change, Climate Change-Kyoto Protocol, Desertification, Endangered Species, Hazardous Wastes, Ozone Layer Protection, Ship Pollution, Wetlands
signed, but not ratified: none of the selected agreements

Geography—note: landlocked; well endowed with various sedimentary rocks and minerals including sand, gravel, gypsum, and limestone

PEOPLE AND SOCIETY

Nationality: *noun:* Moldovan(s)
adjective: Moldovan

Ethnic groups: Moldovan/Romanian 78.2%, Ukrainian 8.4%, Russian 5.8%, Gagauz 4.4%, Bulgarian 1.9%, other 1.3% (2004 census)
note: internal disputes with ethnic Slavs in the Transnistrian region

Languages: Moldovan (official, virtually the same as the Romanian language), Russian, Gagauz (a Turkish dialect)

Religions: Eastern Orthodox 98%, Jewish 1.5%, Baptist and other 0.5% (2000)

Population: 3,583,288 (July 2014 est.)
country comparison to the world: 132

Age structure: 0-14 years: 17.7% (male 326,968/female 306,948)
15-24 years: 14.2% (male 262,559/female 246,283)
25-54 years: 43.9% (male 785,392/female 786,421)
55-64 years: 11.1% (male 214,899/female 255,046)
65 years and over: 10.7% (male 151,629/female 247,143) (2014 est.)

Dependency ratios:
total dependency ratio: 38.8 %
youth dependency ratio: 23 %
elderly dependency ratio: 15.8 %
potential support ratio: 6.3 (2013)

Median age: *total:* 35.7 years
male: 33.9 years
female: 37.7 years (2014 est.)

Population growth rate: -1.02% (2014 est.)
country comparison to the world: 231

Birth rate: 12.21 births/1,000 population (2014 est.)
country comparison to the world: 161

Death rate: 12.6 deaths/1,000 population (2014 est.)
country comparison to the world: 24

Net migration rate: -9.8 migrant(s)/1,000 population (2014 est.)
country comparison to the world: 215

Urbanization: *urban population:* 47.7% of total population (2011)
rate of urbanization: 0.79% annual rate of change (2010-15 est.)

Major urban areas—population: CHISINAU (capital) 650,000 (2009)

Sex ratio: *at birth:* 1.06 male(s)/female
0-14 years: 1.07 male(s)/female
15-24 years: 1.07 male(s)/female
25-54 years: 1 male(s)/female
55-64 years: 0.95 male(s)/female
65 years and over: 0.6 male(s)/female
total population: 0.94 male(s)/female (2014 est.)

Mother's mean age at first birth: 23.5 (2010 est.)

Maternal mortality rate: 41 deaths/100,000 live births (2010)
country comparison to the world: 114

Infant mortality rate: *total:* 12.93 deaths/1,000 live births
country comparison to the world: 122
male: 14.82 deaths/1,000 live births
female: 10.93 deaths/1,000 live births (2014 est.)

Life expectancy at birth: *total population:* 70.12 years
country comparison to the world: 152
male: 66.25 years
female: 74.24 years (2014 est.)

Total fertility rate: 1.56 children born/woman (2014 est.)
country comparison to the world: 183

Contraceptive prevalence rate: 67.8% (2005)

Health expenditures: 11.4% of GDP (2011)
country comparison to the world: 11

Physicians density: 3.64 physicians/1,000 population (2011)

Hospital bed density: 6.2 beds/1,000 population (2011)

Drinking water source:
improved:
urban: 99.4% of population
rural: 93.3% of population
total: 96.2% of population
unimproved:
urban: 0.6% of population
rural: 6.7% of population
total: 3.8% of population (2011 est.)

Sanitation facility access:
improved:
urban: 89% of population
rural: 83.4% of population
total: 86.1% of population
unimproved:
urban: 11% of population
rural: 16.6% of population
total: 13.9% of population (2011 est.)

HIV/AIDS—adult prevalence rate: 0.7% (2012 est.)
country comparison to the world: 59

HIV/AIDS—people living with HIV/AIDS: 18,700 (2012 est.)
country comparison to the world: 83

HIV/AIDS—deaths: 1,300 (2012 est.)
country comparison to the world: 68

Obesity—adult prevalence rate: 21.2% (2008)
country comparison to the world: 91

Children under the age of 5 years underweight: 3.2% (2005)
country comparison to the world: 111

Education expenditures: 8.4% of GDP (2012)
country comparison to the world: 10

Literacy: *definition:* age 15 and over can read and write
total population: 99%
male: 99.5%
female: 98.5% (2011 est.)

School life expectancy (primary to tertiary education): *total:* 12 years
male: 12 years
female: 12 years (2012)

Child labor—children ages 5-14: *total number:* 72,364
percentage: 16 % (2009 est.)

Unemployment, youth ages 15-24: *total:* 13.1%
country comparison to the world: 95
male: 12.8%
female: 13.4% (2012)

GOVERNMENT

Country name: *conventional long form:* Republic of Moldova
conventional short form: Moldova
local long form: Republica Moldova
local short form: Moldova

former: Moldavian Soviet Socialist Republic, Moldovan Soviet Socialist Republic

Government type: republic

Capital: *name:* Chisinau in Romanian (Kishinev in Russian)
note: pronounced KEE-shee-now (KIH-shi-nyev)

geographic coordinates: 47 00 N, 28 51 E
time difference: UTC+2 (7 hours ahead of Washington, DC during Standard Time)
daylight saving time: +1hr, begins last Sunday in March; ends last Sunday in October

Administrative divisions: 32 raions (raioane, singular—raion), 3 municipalities (municipii, singular—municipiul), 1 autonomous territorial unit (unitatea teritoriala autonoma), and 1 territorial unit (unitatea teritoriala)
raions: Anenii Noi, Basarabeasca, Briceni, Cahul, Cantemir, Calarasi, Causeni, Cimislia, Criuleni, Donduseni, Drochia, Dubasari, Edinet, Falesti, Floresti, Glodeni, Hincesti, Ialoveni, Leova, Nisporeni, Ocnita, Orhei, Rezina, Riscani, Singerei, Soldanesti, Soroca, Stefan-Voda, Straseni, Taraclia, Telenesti, Ungheni
municipalities: Balti, Bender, Chisinau
autonomous territorial unit: Gagauzia
territorial unit: Stinga Nistrului (Transnistria)

Independence: 27 August 1991 (from the Soviet Union)

National holiday: Independence Day, 27 August (1991)

Constitution: previous 1978; latest adopted 29 July 1994, effective 27 August 1994; amended 2003 (2011)

Legal system: civil law system with Germanic law influences; Constitutional Court review of legislative acts

International law organization participation: has not submitted an ICJ jurisdiction declaration; accepts ICCt jurisdiction

Suffrage: 18 years of age; universal

Executive branch: *chief of state:* President Nicolae TIMOFTI (since 23 March 2012)
head of government: Prime Minister Iurie LEANCA (since 25 April 2013; acting until 30 May 2013, sworn in on 31 May 2013)
cabinet: Cabinet selected by president, subject to approval of Parliament (For more information visit the World Leaders website)
elections: president elected by Parliament for a four-year term (eligible for a second term); election last held 16 March 2012 (next to be held in March 2016); note—prime minister designated by the president upon consultation with Parliament; within 15 days from designation, the prime minister-designate must request a vote of confidence from the Parliament regarding his/her work program and entire cabinet; the prime minister and Cabinet received a vote of confidence 30 May 2013
election results: Nicolae TIMOFTI elected president; parliamentary votes—62 of 101 votes Iurie LEANCA designated prime minister; parliamentary votes of confidence—58 of 101

Legislative branch: unicameral Parliament or Parlamentul (101 seats; members elected on an at-large basis by popular vote to serve four-year terms)
elections: last held on 28 November 2010 (next to be held in November 2014); note—this was the third parliamentary election in less than two years; the earlier parliaments (elected 5 April 2009 and 29 July 2009) were dissolved after they could not elect a presidential candidate with the necessary three-fifths majority
election results: percent of vote by party—PCRM 39.3%, PLDM 29.4%, PD 12.7%, PL 10%, other 8.6%; seats by party—PCRM 42, PLDM 32, PD 15, PL 12; note—in November of 2011, 3 legislators defected from the Communist Party (PCRM) and voted with the PLDM, PD, and PL governing coalition—termed the Alliance for European Integration (AEI)—to reach a 62-seat majority sufficient to elect a new president; the 3 former PCRM legislators are now aligned with the Party of Socialists, and in 2012 an additional 5 legislators defected from the PCRM; 1 PLDM legislator also defected and is independent

Judicial branch: *highest court(s):* Supreme Court of Justice (consists of a chief judges, 3 deputy-chief judges, 45 judges, and 7 assistant judges); Constitutional Court (consists of the court president and 6 judges) note—the Constitutional Court is autonomous to the other branches of government; the Court interprets the Constitution and reviews the constitutionality of parliamentary laws and decisions, decrees of the president, and acts of the government.
judge selection and term of office: Supreme Court of Justice judges appointed by Parliament upon the recommendation of the Supreme Council of the Magistracy; all judges serve 4-year renewable terms; Constitutional Court judges appointed 2 each by Parliament, the Moldovan president, and the Higher Council of Magistracy; court president elected by other court judges for a 3-year term; other judges appointed for 6-year terms
subordinate courts: Courts of Appeal; Court of Business Audit; municipal courts

Political parties and leaders: represented in Parliament; Communist Party of the Republic of Moldova or PCRM [Vladimir VORONIN]; Democratic Party or PD [Marian LUPU]; Liberal Democratic Party or PLDM [Vladimir FILAT]; Liberal Party or PL [Mihai GHIMPU]; Liberal Reformers Party or PLR [Ion HADARCA]; Pro-European Coalition (coalition of the PD, PLDM, and PLR); not represented in Parliament; Christian Democratic People's Party or PPCD [Iurie ROSCA]; Conservative Party or PC [Natalia NIRCA]; Ecological Party of Moldova "Green Alliance" or PEMAVE [Vladimir BRAGA]; European Action Movement or MAE [Veaceslav UNTILA]; For Nation and Country Party or PpNT [Sergiu MOCANU]; Humanist Party of Moldova or PUM [Valeriu PASAT]; Labor Party or PM [Gheorghe SIMA]; National Liberal Party or PNL [Vitalia PAVLICENKO]; Party of Socialists or PSRM [Igor DODON]; Patriots of Moldova Party or PPM [Mihail GARBUZ]; Popular Republican Party or PPR [Nicolae ANDRONIC]; Republican Party of Moldova or PRM [Andrei STRATAN]; Roma Social Political Movement of the Republic of Moldova or MRRM [Ion BUCUR]; Social Democratic Party or PSD [Victor SELIN]; Social Political Movement "Equality" or MR [Valeriy KLIMENCO]; United Moldova Party or PMUEM [Vladimir TURCAN]

Political pressure groups and leaders: NA

International organization participation: BSEC, CD, CE, CEI, CIS, EAEC (observer), EAPC, EBRD, FAO, GCTU, GUAM, IAEA, IBRD, ICAO, ICC (NGOs), ICRM, IDA, IFAD, IFC, IFRCS, ILO, IMF, IMO, Interpol, IOC, IOM, IPU, ISO (correspondent), ITU, ITUC (NGOs), MIGA, OIF, OPCW, OSCE, PFP, SELEC, UN, UNCTAD, UNESCO, UNHCR, UNIDO, Union Latina, UNMIL, UNMISS, UNOCI, UNWTO, UPU, WCO, WHO, WIPO, WMO, WTO

Diplomatic representation in the US:
chief of mission: Ambassador Igor MUNTEANU (since 7 September 2010)
chancery: 2101 S Street NW, Washington, DC 20008
telephone: [1] (202) 667-1130
FAX: [1] (202) 667-2624

Diplomatic representation from the US:
chief of mission: Ambassador William H. MOSER (since 6 September 2011)
embassy: 103 Mateevici Street, Chisinau MD-2009
mailing address: use embassy street address
telephone: [373] (22) 40-8300
FAX: [373] (22) 23-3044

Flag description: three equal vertical bands of blue (hoist side), yellow, and red; emblem in center of flag is of a Roman eagle of gold outlined in black with a red beak and talons carrying a yellow cross in its beak and a green olive branch in its right talons and a yellow scepter in its left talons; on its breast is a shield divided horizontally red over blue with a stylized aurochs head, star, rose, and crescent all in black-outlined yellow; based on the color scheme of the flag of Romania—with which Moldova shares a history and culture—but Moldova's blue band is lighter; the reverse of the flag does not display any coat of arms
note: one of only three national flags that differ on their obverse and reverse sides—the others are Paraguay and Saudi Arabia

National symbol(s): aurochs (a type of wild cattle)

National anthem: *name:* "Limba noastra" (Our Language)
lyrics/music: Alexei MATEEVICI/Alexandru CRISTEA
note: adopted 1994

ECONOMY

Economy—overview: Despite recent progress, Moldova remains one of the poorest countries in Europe. With a moderate climate and good farmland, Moldova's economy relies heavily on its agriculture sector, featuring fruits, vegetables, wine, and tobacco. Moldova also depends on annual remittances of about $1.6 billion from the roughly one million Moldovans working in Europe, Russia, and other former Soviet Bloc countries. With few natural energy resources, Moldova imports almost all of its energy supplies from Russia and Ukraine. Moldova's dependence on Russian energy is underscored by a growing $5 billion debt to Russian natural gas supplier Gazprom, largely the result of unreimbursed natural gas consumption in the separatist Transnistria region. In August 2013, work began on a new pipeline between Moldova and Romania that may eventually break Russia's monopoly on Moldova's gas supplies. The government's goal of EU integration has resulted in some market-oriented progress. Moldova experienced better than expected economic growth in 2013 due to increased agriculture production, to economic policies adopted by the Moldovan government since 2009, and to the receipt of EU trade preferences. Moldova is poised to sign an Association Agreement and a Deep and Comprehensive Free Trade Agreement with the EU during fall 2014, connecting Moldovan products to the world's largest market. Still, growth has been hampered by high prices for Russian natural gas, a Russian import ban on Moldovan wine, increased foreign scrutiny of Moldovan agricultural products, and by Moldova's large external debt. Over the longer term, Moldova's economy remains vulnerable to political uncertainty, weak administrative capacity, vested bureaucratic interests, corruption, higher fuel prices, Russian pressure, and the illegal separatist regime in Moldova's Transnistria region.

GDP (purchasing power parity): $13.25 billion (2013 est.)
country comparison to the world: 149
$12.16 billion (2012 est.)
$12.26 billion (2011 est.)
note: data are in 2013 US dollars

GDP (official exchange rate): $7.932 billion (2013 est.)

GDP—real growth rate: 8.9% (2013 est.)
country comparison to the world: 8
-0.7% (2012 est.)
6.8% (2011 est.)

GDP—per capita (PPP): $3,800 (2013 est.)
country comparison to the world: 171
$3,500 (2012 est.)
$3,500 (2011 est.)
note: data are in 2013 US dollars

Gross national saving: 16.9% of GDP (2013 est.)
country comparison to the world: 99
16.1% of GDP (2012 est.)
11.8% of GDP (2011 est.)

GDP—composition, by end use:
household consumption: 92.9%
government consumption: 20.6%
investment in fixed capital: 22.6%
investment in inventories: 1.7%
exports of goods and services: 44.1%
imports of goods and services: -81.9% (2013 est.)

GDP—composition, by sector of origin:
agriculture: 13.8%
industry: 19.9%
services: 66.2% (2013 est.)

Agriculture—products: vegetables, fruits, grapes, grain, sugar beets, sunflower seed, tobacco; beef, milk; wine

Industries: sugar, vegetable oil, food processing, agricultural machinery; foundry equipment, refrigerators and freezers, washing machines; hosiery, shoes, textiles

Industrial production growth rate: 6.8% (2013 est.)
country comparison to the world: 37

Labor force: 1.206 million (2013 est.)
country comparison to the world: 139

Labor force—by occupation:
agriculture: 26.4%
industry: 13.2%
services: 60.4% (2012 est.)

Unemployment rate: 5.8% (2013 est.)
country comparison to the world: 56
5.6% (2012 est.)

Population below poverty line:
21.9% (2010 est.)

Household income or consumption by percentage share: *lowest 10%:* 3.3%
highest 10%: 26% (2010 est.)

Distribution of family income—Gini index:
33 (2010)
country comparison to the world: 100
33.2 (2003)

Budget: *revenues:* $2.931 billion
expenditures: $3.071 billion
note: National Public Budget (2013 est.)

Taxes and other revenues: 37% of GDP (2013 est.)
country comparison to the world: 56

Budget surplus (+) or deficit (-):
-1.8% of GDP (2013 est.)
country comparison to the world: 79

Public debt: 16.6% of GDP (2013 est.)
country comparison to the world: 140
17.8% of GDP (2012 est.)

Fiscal year: calendar year

Inflation rate (consumer prices): 4.6% (2013 est.)
country comparison to the world: 150
4.6% (2012 est.)

Central bank discount rate: 3.5% (31 December 2013)
country comparison to the world: 81
4.5% (31 December 2012)
note: this is the basic rate on short-term operations

Commercial bank prime lending rate: 12.26% (31 December 2013 est.)
country comparison to the world: 58
13.34% (31 December 2012 est.)

Stock of narrow money: $2.154 billion (31 December 2013 est.)
country comparison to the world: 126
$1.701 billion (31 December 2012 est.)

Stock of broad money: $4.974 billion (31 December 2013 est.)
country comparison to the world: 129
$4.088 billion (31 December 2012 est.)

Stock of domestic credit: $2.978 billion (31 December 2013 est.)
country comparison to the world: 126
$2.908 billion (31 December 2012 est.)

Market value of publicly traded shares: $65.28 million (31 December 2012 est.)
country comparison to the world: 119
$51.46 million (31 December 2012)
$20.71 million

Current account balance: -$507.7 million (2013 est.)
country comparison to the world: 101
-$495.3 million (2012 est.)

Exports: $2.399 billion (2013 est.)
country comparison to the world: 139
$2.162 billion (2012 est.)

Exports—commodities: foodstuffs, textiles, machinery

Exports—partners: Russia 26.3%, Romania 17.2%, Italy 7.7%, Ukraine 5.9%, Turkey 5.3%, Germany 4.7%, GB 4.4% (2012 est.)

Imports: $5.493 billion (2013 est.)
country comparison to the world: 124
$5.213 billion (2012 est.)

Imports—commodities: mineral products and fuel, machinery and equipment, chemicals, textiles

Imports—partners: Russia 14.3%, Romania 13.1%, Ukraine 12%, China 8.7%, Germany 7.2%, Turkey 6.9%, Italy 6.3% (2012 est.)

Reserves of foreign exchange and gold: $2.814 billion (31 December 2013 est.)
country comparison to the world: 111
$2.513 billion (31 December 2012 est.)

Debt—external: $6.218 billion (30 September, 2013 est.)
country comparison to the world: 115
$5.984 billion (31 December 2012 est.)

Stock of direct foreign investment—at home:
$3.448 billion (31 December 2012 est.)
country comparison to the world: 92
$3.262 billion (31 December 2011 est.)

Stock of direct foreign investment—abroad:
$108.2 million (31 December 2012)
country comparison to the world: 87
$88.42 million (31 December 2011)

Exchange rates: Moldovan lei (MDL) per US dollar—
12.592 (2013 est.)
12.112 (2012 est.)
12.369 (2010 est.)
11.11 (2009)
10.326 (2008)

ENERGY

Electricity—production: 932 million kWh (2012 est.)
country comparison to the world: 149

Electricity—consumption: 4.211 billion kWh (2012 est.)
country comparison to the world: 122

Electricity—exports: 0 kWh (2012 est.)
country comparison to the world: 163

Electricity—imports: 3.297 billion kWh (2012 est.)
country comparison to the world: 45

Electricity—installed generating capacity: 439,900 kW
country comparison to the world: 142
note: excludes Transnistria (2013 est.)

Electricity—from fossil fuels: 96.4% of total installed capacity (2013 est.)
country comparison to the world: 66

Electricity—from nuclear fuels: 0% of total installed capacity (2013 est.)
country comparison to the world: 132

Electricity—from hydroelectric plants: 3.6% of total installed capacity (2013 est.)
country comparison to the world: 127

Electricity—from other renewable sources:
0% of total installed capacity (2013 est.)
country comparison to the world: 198

Crude oil—production: 221 bbl/day (2012 est.)
country comparison to the world: 117

Crude oil—exports: 0 bbl/day (2012 est.)
country comparison to the world: 148

Crude oil—imports: 0 bbl/day (2012 est.)
country comparison to the world: 87

Crude oil—proved reserves: 7,330 bbl (1 January 2013 es)
country comparison to the world: 100

Refined petroleum products—production:
321 bbl/day (2012 est.)
country comparison to the world: 114

Refined petroleum products—consumption:
15,320 bbl/day (2012 est.)
country comparison to the world: 142

Refined petroleum products—exports: 552 bbl/day (2012 est.)
country comparison to the world: 112

Refined petroleum products—imports: 15,280 bbl/day (2012 est.)
country comparison to the world: 119

Natural gas—production: 0 cu m (2012 est.)
country comparison to the world: 160

Natural gas—consumption: 1.095 billion cu m (2012 est.)
country comparison to the world: 87

Natural gas—exports: 0 cu m (2012 est.)
country comparison to the world: 141

Natural gas—imports: 1.095 billion cu m
country comparison to the world: 57
note: excludes Transnistria (2012 est.)

Natural gas—proved reserves: 0 cu m (1 January 2013 es)
country comparison to the world: 164

Carbon dioxide emissions from consumption of energy: 6.467 million Mt (2011 est.)
country comparison to the world: 121

COMMUNICATIONS

Telephones—main lines in use: 1.206 million (2012)
country comparison to the world: 6 9

Telephones—mobile cellular: 4.08 million (2012)
country comparison to the world: 120

Telephone system: *general assessment:* poor service outside Chisinau; some modernization is under way
domestic: multiple private operators of GSM mobile-cellular telephone service are operating; GPRS system is being introduced; a CDMA mobile telephone network began operations in 2007; combined fixed-line and mobile-cellular teledensity 100 per 100 persons
international: country code—373; service through Romania and Russia via landline; satellite earth stations - at least 3 (Intelsat, Eutelsat, and Intersputnik) (2011)

Broadcast media: state-owned national radio-TV broadcaster operates 2 TV and 2 radio stations; a total of nearly 40 terrestrial TV channels and some 50 radio stations are in operation; Russian and Romanian channels also are available (2007)

Internet country code: .md

Internet hosts: 711,564 (2012)
country comparison to the world: 51

Internet users: 1.333 million (2009)
country comparison to the world: 89

TRANSPORTATION

Airports: 7 (2013)
country comparison to the world: 169

Airports—with paved runways: *total:* 5
over 3,047 m: 1
2,438 to 3,047 m: 2
1,524 to 2,437 m: 2 (2013)

Airports—with unpaved runways: *total:* 2
1,524 to 2,437 m: 1
under 914 m: 1 (2013)

Pipelines: gas 1,906 km (2013)

Railways: *total:* 1,190 km
country comparison to the world: 86
broad gauge: 1,176 km 1.520-m gauge
standard gauge: 14 km 1.435-m gauge (2008)

Roadways: *total:* 9,352 km
country comparison to the world: 136
paved: 8,835 km
unpaved: 517 km (2012)

Waterways: 558 km (in public use on Danube, Dniester and Prut rivers) (2011)
country comparison to the world: 83

Merchant marine: *total:* 121
country comparison to the world: 45
by type: bulk carrier 7, cargo 88, carrier 1, chemical tanker 3, passenger/cargo 7, petroleum tanker

2, refrigerated cargo 1, roll on/roll off 11, specialized tanker 1
foreign-owned: 63 (Bulgaria 1, Denmark 1, Egypt 5, Greece 1, Israel 2, Lebanon 1, Pakistan 1, Romania 2, Russia 5, Syria 5, Turkey 18, UK 3, Ukraine 14, Yemen 4) (2010)

MILITARY

Military branches: National Army: Land Forces Command, Air Forces Command (includes air defense unit), Logistics Command (2013)

Military service age and obligation: 18 years of age for compulsory or voluntary military service; male registration required at age 16; 1-year service obligation (2012)

Manpower available for military service:
males age 16-49: 1,143,440
females age 16-49: 1,156,958 (2010 est.)

Manpower fit for military service:
males age 16-49: 875,224
females age 16-49: 969,903 (2010 est.)

Manpower reaching militarily significant age annually: *male:* 28,213

female: 26,614 (2010 est.)

Military expenditures: 0.3% of GDP (2012)
country comparison to the world: 128
0.3% of GDP (2011)
0.3% of GDP (2010)

TRANSNATIONAL ISSUES

Disputes—international: Moldova and Ukraine operate joint customs posts to monitor the transit of people and commodities through Moldova's break-away Transnistria region, which remains under the auspices of an Organization for Security and Cooperation in Europe-mandated peacekeeping mission comprised of Moldovan, Transnistrian, Russian, and Ukrainian troops

Refugees and internally displaced persons: *stateless persons:* 1,998 (2012)

Illicit drugs: limited cultivation of opium poppy and cannabis, mostly for CIS consumption; transshipment point for illicit drugs from Southwest Asia via Central Asia to Russia, Western Europe, and possibly the US; widespread crime and underground economic activity

MONACO

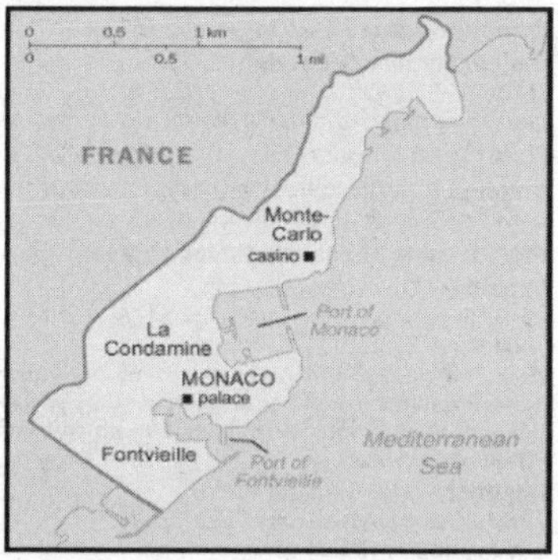

INTRODUCTION

Background: The Genoese built a fortress on the site of present day Monaco in 1215. The current ruling GRIMALDI family first seized temporary control in 1297, and again in 1331, but were not able to permanently secure their holding until 1419. Economic development was spurred in the late 19th century with a railroad linkup to France and the opening of a casino. Since then, the principality's mild climate, splendid scenery, and gambling facilities have made Monaco world famous as a tourist and recreation center.

GEOGRAPHY

Location: Western Europe, bordering the Mediterranean Sea on the southern coast of France, near the border with Italy

Geographic coordinates: 43 44 N, 7 24 E

Map references: Europe

Area: *total:* 2 sq km
country comparison to the world: 250
land: 2 sq km
water: 0 sq km

Area—comparative: about three times the size of The Mall in Washington, DC

Land boundaries: *total:* 4.4 km
border countries: France 4.4 km

Coastline: 4.1 km

Maritime claims: *territorial sea:* 12 nm
exclusive economic zone: 12 nm

Climate: Mediterranean with mild, wet winters and hot, dry summers

Terrain: hilly, rugged, rocky

Elevation extremes: *lowest point:* Mediterranean Sea 0 m
highest point: Mont Agel 140 m

Natural resources: none

Land use: *arable land:* 0%
permanent crops: 1%
other: 99% (urban area) (2011)

Irrigated land: NA

Natural hazards: NA

Environment—current issues: NA

Environment—international agreements: party to: Air Pollution, Air Pollution-Sulfur 94, Air Pollution-Volatile Organic Compounds, Biodiversity, Climate Change, Climate Change-Kyoto Protocol, Desertification, Endangered Species, Hazardous Wastes, Law of the Sea, Marine Dumping, Ozone Layer Protection, Ship Pollution, Wetlands, Whaling
signed, but not ratified: none of the selected agreements

Geography—note: second-smallest independent state in the world (after Holy See); almost entirely urban

PEOPLE AND SOCIETY

Nationality: *noun:* Monegasque(s) or Monacan(s)
adjective: Monegasque or Monacan

Ethnic groups: French 47%, Monegasque 16%, Italian 16%, other 21%

Languages: French (official), English, Italian, Monegasque

Religions: Roman Catholic 90% (official), other 10%

Population: 30,508 (July 2014 est.)
country comparison to the world: 218

Age structure:
0-14 years: 11.7% (male 1,828/female 1,742)
15-24 years: 9.2% (male 1,445/female 1,371)
25-54 years: 35.1% (male 5,332/female 5,363)
55-64 years: 29.5% (male 2,223/female 2,203)
65 years and over: 28.7% (male 4,020/female 4,981) (2014 est.)

Median age: *total:* 51.1 years
male: 50 years
female: 52.3 years (2014 est.)

Population growth rate: 0.06% (2014 est.)
country comparison to the world: 186

Birth rate: 6.72 births/1,000 population (2014 est.)
country comparison to the world: 224

Death rate: 9.01 deaths/1,000 population (2014 est.)
country comparison to the world: 68

Net migration rate: 2.85 migrant(s)/1,000 population (2014 est.)
country comparison to the world: 35

Urbanization: *urban population:* 100% of total population (2010)
rate of urbanization: 0.3% annual rate of change (2010-15 est.)

Sex ratio: *at birth:* 1.04 male(s)/female
0-14 years: 1.05 male(s)/female
15-24 years: 1.05 male(s)/female
25-54 years: 0.99 male(s)/female
55-64 years: 0.95 male(s)/female
65 years and over: 0.81 male(s)/female
total population: 0.95 male(s)/female (2014 est.)

Infant mortality rate: *total:* 1.81 deaths/1,000 live births
country comparison to the world: 224
male: 2.05 deaths/1,000 live births
female: 1.56 deaths/1,000 live births (2014 est.)

Life expectancy at birth: *total population:* 89.57 years
country comparison to the world: 1
male: 85.66 years
female: 93.64 years (2014 est.)

Total fertility rate: 1.52 children born/woman (2014 est.)
country comparison to the world: 190

Health expenditures: 4.3% of GDP (2011)
country comparison to the world: 157

Physicians density: 7.06 physicians/1,000 population (2011)

Hospital bed density: 16.5 beds/1,000 population (2011)

Drinking water source:
improved:
urban: 100% of population
total: 100% of population (2011 est.)

Sanitation facility access:
improved:
urban: 100% of population
total: 100% of population
unimproved:
urban: 0% of population
total: 0% of population (2011 est.)

HIV/AIDS—adult prevalence rate: NA

HIV/AIDS—people living with HIV/AIDS: NA

HIV/AIDS—deaths: NA

Education expenditures: 1.6% of GDP (2011)
country comparison to the world: 169

Literacy: *definition:* age 15 and over can read and write
total population: 99%
male: 99%

female: 99% (2003 est.)

Unemployment, youth ages 15-24: *total:* 6.9%
country comparison to the world: 130
male: 6.6%
female: 7.4% (2000)

GOVERNMENT

Country name: *conventional long form:* Principality of Monaco
conventional short form: Monaco
local long form: Principaute de Monaco
local short form: Monaco

Government type: constitutional monarchy

Capital: *name:* Monaco

geographic coordinates: 43 44 N, 7 25 E
time difference: UTC+1 (6 hours ahead of Washington, DC during Standard Time)
daylight saving time: +1hr, begins last Sunday in March; ends last Sunday in October

Administrative divisions: none; there are no first-order administrative divisions as defined by the US Government, but there are four quarters (quartiers, singular—quartier); Fontvieille, La Condamine, Monaco-Ville, Monte-Carlo; note—Moneghetti, a part of La Condamine, is sometimes called the 5th quarter of Monaco

Independence: 1419 (beginning of permanent rule by the House of GRIMALDI)

National holiday: National Day (Saint Rainier's Day), 19 November (1857)

Constitution: previous 1911 (suspended 1959); latest adopted 17 December 1962; amended 2002 (2013)

Legal system: civil law system influenced by French legal tradition

International law organization participation: has not submitted an ICJ jurisdiction declaration; non-party state to the ICCt

Suffrage: 18 years of age; universal

Executive branch: *chief of state:* Prince ALBERT II (since 6 April 2005)
head of government: Minister of State Michel ROGER (since 29 March 2010)
cabinet: Council of Government under the authority of the monarch (For more information visit the World Leaders website)
elections: the monarchy is hereditary; minister of state appointed by the monarch from a list of three French national candidates presented by the French Government

Legislative branch: unicameral National Council or Conseil National (24 seats; 16 members elected by list majority system, 8 by proportional representation to serve five-year terms)
elections: last held on 10 February 2013 (next to be held in February 2018)
election results: percent of vote by party—Horizon Monaco 50.3%, Union Monegasque 39%, Renaissance 10.7%; seats by party—Horizon Monaco 20, Union Monegasque 3, Renaissance 1

Judicial branch: *highest court(s):* Supreme Court (consists of 5 permanent members and 2 substitutes)
judge selection and term of office: Supreme Court members appointed by the monarch upon the proposals of the National Council, State Council, Crown Council, Court of Appeal, and Trial Court
subordinate courts: Court of Appeal; Civil Court of First Instance

Political parties and leaders: Horizon Monaco [Laurent NOUVION]; Renaissance [SBM (public corporation)]; Union Monegasque [Stephane VALERI]

Political pressure groups and leaders: NA

International organization participation: CD, CE, FAO, IAEA, ICAO, ICC (national committees), ICRM, IFRCS, IHO, IMO, IMSO, Interpol, IOC, IPU, ITSO, ITU, OAS (observer), OIF, OPCW, OSCE, Schengen Convention (de facto member), UN, UNCTAD, UNESCO, UNIDO, Union Latina, UNWTO, UPU, WHO, WIPO, WMO

Diplomatic representation in the US:
chief of mission: Ambassador Maguy MACCARIO-DOYLE (since 3 December 2013)
chancery: 3400 International Drive NW, Suite 2K-100, Washington, DC 20008
telephone: (202) 234-1530
FAX: (202) 244-7656
consulate(s) general: New York

Diplomatic representation from the US: the US does not have an embassy in Monaco; the US Ambassador to France is accredited to Monaco; the US Consul General in Marseille (France), under the authority of the US ambassador to France, handles diplomatic and consular matters concerning Monaco

Flag description: two equal horizontal bands of red (top) and white; the colors are those of the ruling House of Grimaldi and have been in use since 1339, making the flag one of the world's oldest national banners note: similar to the flag of Indonesia which is longer and the flag of Poland which is white (top) and red

National anthem: *name:* "A Marcia de Muneghu" (The March of Monaco)
lyrics/music: Louis NOTARI/Charles ALBRECHT
note: music adopted 1867, lyrics adopted 1931; although French is commonly spoken, only the Monegasque lyrics are official; the French version is known as "Hymne Monegasque" (Monegasque Anthem); the words are generally only sung on official occasions

ECONOMY

Economy—overview: Monaco, bordering France on the Mediterranean coast, is a popular resort, attracting tourists to its casino and pleasant climate. The principality also is a banking center and has successfully sought to diversify into services and small, high-value-added, nonpolluting industries. The state has no income tax and low business taxes and thrives as a tax haven both for individuals who have established residence and for foreign companies that have set up businesses and offices. Monaco, however, is not a tax-free shelter; it charges nearly 20% value-added tax, collects stamp duties, and companies face a 33% tax on profits unless they can show that three-quarters of profits are generated within the principality. Monaco's reliance on tourism and banking for its economic growth has left it vulnerable to a downturn in France and other European economies which are the principality's main trade partners. In 2009, Monaco's GDP fell by 11.5% as the euro-zone crisis precipitated a sharp drop in tourism and retail activity and home sales. A modest recovery ensued in 2010, but Monaco's economic prospects remain uncertain, and tied to future euro-zone growth. Weak economic growth also has deteriorated public finances as the principality recorded budget deficits in 2011-12. Monaco was formally removed from the OECD's "grey list" of uncooperative tax jurisdictions in late 2009, but continues to face international pressure to abandon its banking secrecy laws and help combat tax evasion. The state retains monopolies in a number of sectors, including tobacco, the telephone network, and the postal service. Living standards are high, roughly comparable to those in prosperous French metropolitan areas.

GDP (purchasing power parity): $5.748 billion (2011 est.)
country comparison to the world: 167
$5.47 billion (2010 est.)
$5.337 billion (2009 est.)
note: data are in 2011 US dollars

GDP (official exchange rate): $5.748 billion (2011 est.)

GDP—real growth rate: 5.1% (2011 est.)
country comparison to the world: 55
2.5% (2010 est.)
-11.5% (2009)

GDP—per capita (PPP): $65,500 (2011)
country comparison to the world: 6

GDP—composition, by sector of origin:
agriculture: 0%
industry: 10%
services: 90% (2011)

Agriculture—products: none

Industries: banking, insurance, tourism, construction, small-scale industrial and consumer products

Industrial production growth rate: NA%

Labor force: 50,580
country comparison to the world: 191
note: includes workers from all foreign countries (2011 est.)

Unemployment rate: 0% (2011)
country comparison to the world: 2

Population below poverty line: NA%

Household income or consumption by percentage share: *lowest 10%:* NA%
highest 10%: NA%

Budget: *revenues:* $1.044 billion
expenditures: $1.111 billion (2011 est.)

Taxes and other revenues: 19.6% of GDP (2011 est.)
country comparison to the world: 169

Budget surplus (+) or deficit (-):
-1.3% of GDP (2011 est.)
country comparison to the world: 66

Fiscal year: calendar year

Inflation rate (consumer prices): 1.5% (2010)
country comparison to the world: 40

Market value of publicly traded shares: $NA

Exports: $802.4 million (2011)
country comparison to the world: 166
$684.9 million (2010)
note: full customs integration with France, which collects and rebates Monegasque trade duties; also participates in EU market system through customs union with France

Imports: $786.9 million (2011)
country comparison to the world: 185
$850.2 million (2010)
note: full customs integration with France, which collects and rebates Monegasque trade duties; also participates in EU market system through customs union with France

Debt—external: $NA

Exchange rates: euros (EUR) per US dollar—
0.7634 (2013 est.)
0.7752 (2012 est.)
0.755 (2010 est.)
0.7198 (2009 est.)
0.6827 (2008 est.)

COMMUNICATIONS

Telephones—main lines in use: 44,500 (2012)
country comparison to the world: 166

Telephones—mobile cellular: 33,200 (2012)
country comparison to the world: 207

Telephone system: *general assessment:* modern automatic telephone system; the country's sole fixed line operator offers a full range of services to residential and business customers
domestic: combined fixed-line and mobile-cellular teledensity exceeds 200 per 100 persons
international: country code—377; no satellite earth stations; connected by cable into the French communications system (2011)

Broadcast media: TV Monte-Carlo (TMC) operates a TV network; cable TV available; Radio Monte-Carlo has extensive radio networks in France and Italy with French-language broadcasts to France beginning in the 1960s and Italian-language broadcasts to Italy beginning in the 1970s; other radio stations include Riviera Radio and Radio Monaco (2012)

Internet country code: .mc

Internet hosts: 26,009 (2012)

country comparison to the world: 111

Internet users: 23,000 (2009)
country comparison to the world: 191

TRANSPORTATION

Heliports: 1 (2012)

Roadways: *total:* 77 km
country comparison to the world: 217
paved: 77 km (2010)

Merchant marine:
registered in other countries: 64 (Bahamas 8, Bermuda 2, Liberia 8, Malta 3, Marshall Islands 30, Panama 11, Saint Vincent and the Grenadines 2) (2010)
country comparison to the world: 63

Ports and terminals: *major seaport(s):* Monaco

MILITARY

Military branches: no regular military forces; Directorate of Public Security (2012)

Manpower available for military service:
males age 16-49: 5,749 (2010 est.)

Manpower fit for military service:
males age 16-49: 4,629
females age 16-49: 4,597 (2010 est.)

Manpower reaching militarily significant age annually: *male:* 153
female: 141 (2010 est.)

Military—note: defense is the responsibility of France

TRANSNATIONAL ISSUES

Disputes—international: none

MONGOLIA

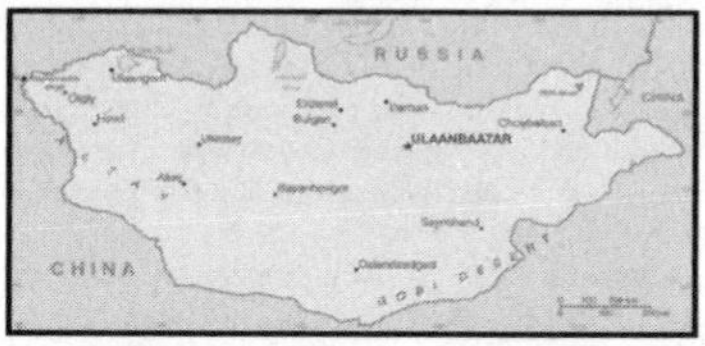

INTRODUCTION

Background: The Mongols gained fame in the 13th century when under Chinggis KHAAN they established a huge Eurasian empire through conquest. After his death the empire was divided into several powerful Mongol states, but these broke apart in the 14th century. The Mongols eventually retired to their original steppe homelands and in the late 17th century came under Chinese rule. Mongolia won its independence in 1921 with Soviet backing and a communist regime was installed in 1924. The modern country of Mongolia, however, represents only part of the Mongols' historical homeland; more ethnic Mongolians live in the Inner Mongolia Autonomous Region in the People's Republic of China than in Mongolia. Following a peaceful democratic revolution, the ex-communist Mongolian People's Revolutionary Party (MPRP) won elections in 1990 and 1992, but was defeated by the Democratic Union Coalition (DUC) in the 1996 parliamentary election. The MPRP won an overwhelming majority in the 2000 parliamentary election, but the party lost seats in the 2004 election and shared power with democratic coalition parties from 2004-08. The MPRP regained a solid majority in the 2008 parliamentary elections but nevertheless formed a coalition government with the Democratic Party that lasted until January 2012. In 2009, current President ELBEGDORJ of the Democratic Party was elected to office and was re-elected for his second term in June 2013. In 2010, the MPRP voted to retake the name of the Mongolian People's Party (MPP), a name it used in the early 1920s. Shortly thereafter, a new party was formed by former president ENKHBAYAR, which adopted the MPRP name. In the 2012 Parliamentary elections, a coalition of four political parties led by the Democratic Party, gained control of the Parliament.

GEOGRAPHY

Location: Northern Asia, between China and Russia

Geographic coordinates: 46 00 N, 105 00 E

Map references: Asia

Area: *total:* 1,564,116 sq km
country comparison to the world: 19
land: 1,553,556 sq km
water: 10,560 sq km

Area—comparative: slightly smaller than Alaska

Land boundaries: *total:* 8,220 km
border countries: China 4,677 km, Russia 3,543 km

Coastline: 0 km (landlocked)

Maritime claims: none (landlocked)

Climate: desert; continental (large daily and seasonal temperature ranges)

Terrain: vast semidesert and desert plains, grassy steppe, mountains in west and southwest; Gobi Desert in south-central

Elevation extremes: *lowest point:* Hoh Nuur 560 m
highest point: Nayramadlin Orgil (Huyten Orgil) 4,374 m

Natural resources: oil, coal, copper, molybdenum, tungsten, phosphates, tin, nickel, zinc, fluorspar, gold, silver, iron

Land use: *arable land:* 0.39%
permanent crops: 0%
other: 99.61% (2011)

Irrigated land: 843 sq km (2003)

Total renewable water resources: 34.8 cu km (2011)

Freshwater withdrawal (domestic/industrial/agricultural): *total:* 0.55 cu km/yr (13%/43%/44%)
per capita: 196.8 cu m/yr (2009)

Natural hazards: dust storms; grassland and forest fires; drought; "zud," which is harsh winter conditions

Environment—current issues: limited natural freshwater resources in some areas; the policies of former Communist regimes promoted rapid urbanization and industrial growth that had negative effects on the environment; the burning of soft coal in power plants and the lack of enforcement of environmental laws severely polluted the air in Ulaanbaatar; deforestation, overgrazing, and the converting of virgin land to agricultural production increased soil erosion from wind and rain; desertification and mining activities had a deleterious effect on the environment

Environment—international agreements:
party to: Biodiversity, Climate Change, Climate Change-Kyoto Protocol, Desertification, Endangered Species, Environmental Modification, Hazardous Wastes, Law of the Sea, Ozone Layer Protection, Ship Pollution, Wetlands, Whaling
signed, but not ratified: none of the selected agreements

Geography—note: landlocked; strategic location between China and Russia

PEOPLE AND SOCIETY

Nationality: *noun:* Mongolian(s)
adjective: Mongolian

Ethnic groups: Khalkh 81.9%, Kazak 3.8%, Dorvod 2.7%, Bayad 2.1%, Buryat-Bouriates 1.7%, Zakhchin 1.2%, Dariganga 1%, Uriankhai 1%, other 4.6% (2010 est.)

Languages: Khalkha Mongol 90% (official), Turkic, Russian (1999)

Religions: Buddhist 53%, Muslim 3%, Christian 2.2%, Shamanist 2.9%, other 0.4%, none 38.6% (2010 est.)

Population: 2,953,190 (July 2014 est.)
country comparison to the world: 139

Age structure:
0-14 years: 26.8% (male 404,051/female 388,546)
15-24 years: 18.7% (male 278,912/female 273,167)
25-54 years: 44.5% (male 636,799/female 677,236)
55-64 years: 4.1% (male 80,267/female 94,021)
65 years and over: 4% (male 49,314/female 70,877) (2014 est.)

Dependency ratios:
total dependency ratio: 45.1 %
youth dependency ratio: 39.6 %
elderly dependency ratio: 5.5 %
potential support ratio: 18.1 (2013)

Median age: *total:* 27.1 years
male: 26.3 years
female: 27.8 years (2014 est.)

Population growth rate: 1.37% (2014 est.)
country comparison to the world: 89

Birth rate: 20.88 births/1,000 population (2014 est.)
country comparison to the world: 81

Death rate: 6.38 deaths/1,000 population (2014 est.)
country comparison to the world: 156

Net migration rate: -0.85 migrant(s)/1,000 population (2014 est.)
country comparison to the world: 145

Urbanization: *urban population:* 68.5% of total population (2011)
rate of urbanization: 2.81% annual rate of change (2010-15 est.)

Major urban areas—population: ULAANBAATAR (capital) 949,000 (2009)

Sex ratio: *at birth:* 1.05 male(s)/female
0-14 years: 1.04 male(s)/female

15-24 years: 1.02 male(s)/female
25-54 years: 0.94 male(s)/female
55-64 years: 0.96 male(s)/female
65 years and over: 0.77 male(s)/female
total population: 1 male(s)/female (2014 est.)

Maternal mortality rate: 63 deaths/100,000 live births (2010)
country comparison to the world: 96

Infant mortality rate: *total:* 23.15 deaths/1,000 live births
country comparison to the world: 79
male: 26.4 deaths/1,000 live births
female: 19.75 deaths/1,000 live births (2014 est.)

Life expectancy at birth: *total population:* 68.98 years
country comparison to the world: 158
male: 64.72 years
female: 73.45 years (2014 est.)

Total fertility rate: 2.22 children born/woman (2014 est.)
country comparison to the world: 100

Contraceptive prevalence rate: 55% (2010)

Health expenditures: 5.3% of GDP (2011)
country comparison to the world: 129

Physicians density: 2.76 physicians/1,000 population (2008)

Hospital bed density: 6.8 beds/1,000 population (2011)

Drinking water source:
improved:
urban: 100% of population
rural: 53.1% of population
total: 85.3% of population
unimproved:
urban: 0% of population
rural: 46.9% of population
total: 14.7% of population (2011 est.)

Sanitation facility access:
improved:
urban: 64% of population
rural: 29.1% of population
total: 53% of population
unimproved:
urban: 36% of population
rural: 70.9% of population
total: 47% of population (2011 est.)

HIV/AIDS—adult prevalence rate: less than 0.1% (2009 est.)
country comparison to the world: 161

HIV/AIDS—people living with HIV/AIDS: fewer than 500 (2009 est.)
country comparison to the world: 160

HIV/AIDS—deaths: fewer than 100 (2009 est.)
country comparison to the world: 140

Obesity—adult prevalence rate: 14.4% (2008)
country comparison to the world: 122

Children under the age of 5 years underweight: 5.3% (2005)
country comparison to the world: 88

Education expenditures: 5.5% of GDP (2011)
country comparison to the world: 58

Literacy: *definition:* age 15 and over can read and write
total population: 97.4%
male: 96.8%
female: 97.9% (2011 est.)

School life expectancy (primary to tertiary education): *total:* 15 years
male: 14 years
female: 16 years (2012)

Child labor—children ages 5-14: *total number:* 106,203
percentage: 18 % (2005 est.)

Unemployment, youth ages 15-24: *total:* 11.9%
country comparison to the world: 100
male: 10.7%
female: 13.2% (2011)

GOVERNMENT

Country name: *conventional long form:* none
conventional short form: Mongolia
local long form: none
local short form: Mongol Uls
former: Outer Mongolia

Government type: parliamentary

Capital: *name:* Ulaanbaatar

geographic coordinates: 47 55 N, 106 55 E
time difference: UTC+8 (13 hours ahead of Washington, DC during Standard Time)

Administrative divisions: 21 provinces (aymguud, singular—aymag) and 1 municipality* (singular—hot); Arhangay, Bayanhongor, Bayan-Olgiy, Bulgan, Darhan-Uul, Dornod, Dornogovi, Dundgovi, Dzavhan (Zavkhan), Govi-Altay, Govisumber, Hentiy, Hovd, Hovsgol, Omnogovi, Orhon, Ovorhangay, Selenge, Suhbaatar, Tov, Ulaanbaatar*, Uvs

Independence: 11 July 1921 (from China)

National holiday: Independence Day/Revolution Day, 11 July (1921)

Constitution: several previous; latest adopted 13 January 1992, effective 12 February 1992; amended 1999, 2001 (2011)

Legal system: civil law system influenced by Soviet and Romano-Germanic legal systems; constitution ambiguous on judicial review of legislative acts

International law organization participation: has not submitted an ICJ jurisdiction declaration; accepts ICCt jurisdiction

Suffrage: 18 years of age; universal

Executive branch: *chief of state:* President Tsakhia ELBEGDORJ (since 18 June 2009)
head of government: Prime Minister Norov ALTANKHUYAG (since 9 August 2012); Deputy Prime Minister Dendev TERBISHDAGVA (since 20 August 2012)
cabinet: Cabinet nominated by the prime minister in consultation with the president and confirmed by the State Great Hural (parliament) (For more information visit the World Leaders website)
elections: presidential candidates nominated by political parties represented in State Great Hural and elected by popular vote for a four-year term (eligible for a second term); election last held on 26 June 2013 (next to be held in June 2017); following legislative elections, leaders of the majority party or a majority coalition usually elect the prime minister of the State Great Hural
election results: in elections in June 2013, Tsakhia ELBEGDORJ elected president; percent of vote—Tsakhia ELBEGDORJ 50.2%, Badmaanyambuu BAT-ERDENE 42%, Natsag UDVAL 6.5%, others 1.3%

Legislative branch: unicameral State Great Hural (76 seats; of which 48 members are directly elected from 26 electoral districts, while 28 members are proportionally elected based on a party's share of the total votes; all serve four-year terms)
elections: last held on 28 June 2012 (next to be held in June 2016)
election results: percent of vote by party—NA; seats by party—DP 33, MPP 25, Justice Coalition 11, others 5, vacant 2

Judicial branch: *highest court(s):* Supreme Court (consists of the Chief Justice and 16 judges organized into civil, criminal, and administrative chambers); Constitutional Court or Tsets (consists of a chairman and 8 members)
judge selection and term of office: Supreme Court chief justice and judges appointed by the president upon recommendation to the State Great Hural by the General Council of Courts; term of appointment is for life; chairman of the Constitutional Court elected from among its members; members appointed by the State Great Heral upon nominations—3 each by the president, the State Great Hural, and the Supreme Court; term of appointment is 6 years; chairmanship limited to a single renewable 3-year term
subordinate courts: aimag (provincial) and capital city appellate courts; soum, inter-soum, and district courts; Administrative Cases Courts (established in 2004)

Political parties and leaders: Civil Will-Green Party or CWGP [Sanjaasuren OYUN]; Democratic Party or DP [Norov ALTANHUYAG]; Justice Coalition (includes MPRP and MNDP); Mongolian National Democratic Party or MNDP [Mendsaikhan ENKHSAIKHAN]; Mongolian People's Party or MPP [Miyegombo ENKHBOLD]; Mongolian People's Revolutionary Party or MPRP [Nambar ENKHBAYAR]

Political pressure groups and leaders:
other: human rights groups; women's groups

International organization participation: ADB, ARF, CD, CICA, CP, EBRD, EITI (compliant country), FAO, G-77, IAEA, IBRD, ICAO, ICC (NGOs), ICRM, IDA, IFAD, IFC, IFRCS, ILO, IMF, IMO, IMSO, Interpol, IOC, IOM, IPU, ISO, ITSO, ITU, ITUC, MIGA, MINURSO, MONUSCO, NAM, OPCW, OSCE, SCO (observer), UN, UNAMID, UNCTAD, UNESCO, UNIDO, UNISFA, UNMISS, UNWTO, UPU, WCO, WHO, WIPO, WMO, WTO

Diplomatic representation in the US:
chief of mission: Ambassador Bulgaa ALTANGEREL (since 8 January 2013)
chancery: 2833 M Street NW, Washington, DC 20007
telephone: [1] (202) 333-7117
FAX: [1] (202) 298-9227
consulate(s) general: New York, San Francisco

Diplomatic representation from the US:
chief of mission: Ambassador Piper Anne Wind CAMPBELL (since 6 August 2012)
embassy: Denver Street #3, 11th Micro Region, Big Ring Road, Ulaanbaatar, 14190 Mongolia
mailing address: PSC 461, Box 300, FPO AP 96521-0002; P.O. Box 341, Ulaanbaatar-14192
telephone: [976] 7007-6001
FAX: [976] 7007-6016

Flag description: three equal, vertical bands of red (hoist side), blue, and red; centered on the hoist-side red band in yellow is the national emblem ("soyombo"—a columnar arrangement of abstract and geometric representation for fire, sun, moon, earth, water, and the yin-yang symbol);

blue represents the sky, red symbolizes progress and prosperity

National symbol(s): soyombo emblem

National anthem: *name:* "Mongol ulsyn toriin duulal" (National Anthem of Mongolia)
lyrics/music: Tsendiin DAMDINSUREN/Bilegiin DAMDINSUREN and Luvsanjamts MURJORJ
note: music adopted 1950, lyrics adopted 2006; the anthem's lyrics have been altered on numerous occasions

ECONOMY

Economy—overview: Mongolia's extensive mineral deposits and attendant growth in mining-sector activities have transformed Mongolia's economy, which traditionally has been dependent on herding and agriculture. Mongolia's copper, gold, coal, molybdenum, fluorspar, uranium, tin, and tungsten deposits, among others, have attracted foreign direct investment. Soviet assistance, at its height one-third of GDP, disappeared almost overnight in 1990 and 1991 at the time of the dismantlement of the USSR. The following decade saw Mongolia endure both deep recession, because of political inaction and natural disasters, as well as economic growth, because of reform-embracing, free-market economics and extensive privatization of the formerly state-run economy. The country opened a fledgling stock exchange in 1991. Mongolia joined the World Trade Organization in 1997 and seeks to expand its participation in regional economic and trade regimes. Growth averaged nearly 9% per year in 2004-08 largely because of high copper prices globally and new gold production. By late 2008, Mongolia was hit hard by the global financial crisis. Slower global economic growth hurt the country's exports, notably copper, and slashed government revenues. As a result, Mongolia's real economy contracted 1.3% in 2009. In early 2009, the International Monetary Fund reached a $236 million Stand-by Arrangement with Mongolia and the country has largely emerged from the crisis with better regulations and closer supervision. The banking sector strengthened but weaknesses remain. In October 2009, Mongolia passed long-awaited legislation on an investment agreement to develop the Oyu Tolgoi mine, considered to be among the world's largest untapped copper-gold deposits. Mongolia's ongoing dispute with a foreign investor over Oyu Tolgoi, however, has called into question the attractiveness of Mongolia as a destination for foreign direct investment. Negotiations to develop the massive Tavan Tolgoi coal field also have stalled. The economy has grown more than 10% per year since 2010, largely on the strength of commodity exports to nearby countries and high government spending domestically. Mongolia's economy, however, faces near-term economic risks from the government's loose fiscal and monetary policies, which are contributing to high inflation, and from uncertainties in foreign demand for Mongolian exports. Trade with China represents more than half of Mongolia's total external trade—China receives more than 90% of Mongolia's exports and is Mongolia's largest supplier. Mongolia has relied on Russia for energy supplies, leaving it vulnerable to price increases; in the first 11 months of 2013, Mongolia purchased 76% of its gasoline and diesel fuel and a substantial amount of electric power from Russia. A drop in foreign direct investment and a decrease in Chinese demand for Mongolia's mineral exports are putting pressure on Mongolia's balance of payments. Remittances from Mongolians working abroad, particularly in South Korea, are significant.

GDP (purchasing power parity): $17.03 billion (2013 est.)
country comparison to the world: 140
$15.23 billion (2012 est.)
$13.57 billion (2011 est.)
note: data are in 2013 US dollars

GDP (official exchange rate): $11.14 billion (2013 est.)

GDP—real growth rate: 11.8% (2013 est.)
country comparison to the world: 5
12.3% (2012 est.)
17.5% (2011 est.)

GDP—per capita (PPP): $5,900 (2013 est.)
country comparison to the world: 152
$5,400 (2012 est.)
$4,900 (2011 est.)
note: data are in 2013 US dollars

GDP—composition, by end use:
household consumption: 58.5%
government consumption: 14.9%
investment in fixed capital: 55.8%
investment in inventories: 0%
exports of goods and services: 50%
imports of goods and services: -79.2% (2013 est.)

GDP—composition, by sector of origin:
agriculture: 16.5%
industry: 32.6%
services: 50.9% (2013 est.)

Agriculture—products: wheat, barley, vegetables, forage crops; sheep, goats, cattle, camels, horses

Industries: construction and construction materials; mining (coal, copper, molybdenum, fluorspar, tin, tungsten, and gold); oil; food and beverages; processing of animal products, cashmere and natural fiber manufacturing

Industrial production growth rate: 11% (2013 est.)
country comparison to the world: 10

Labor force: 1.037 million (2011 est.)
country comparison to the world: 141

Labor force—by occupation:
agriculture: 33%
industry: 10.6%
services: 56.4% (2011)

Unemployment rate: 9% (2011 est.)
country comparison to the world: 99
13% (2010)

Population below poverty line: 29.8% (2011 est.)

Household income or consumption by percentage share: *lowest* 10%: 3%
highest 10%: 28.4% (2008)

Distribution of family income—Gini index: 36.5 (2008)
country comparison to the world: 84
32.8 (2002)

Budget: *revenues:* $3.462 billion
expenditures: $4.36 billion (2013 est.)

Taxes and other revenues: 31.1% of GDP (2013 est.)
country comparison to the world: 86

Budget surplus (+) or deficit (-): -8.1% of GDP (2013 est.)
country comparison to the world: 197

Fiscal year: calendar year

Inflation rate (consumer prices): 8.2% (2013 est.)
country comparison to the world: 195
15% (2012 est.)

Central bank discount rate: 13.25% (31 December 2012)
country comparison to the world: 15
12.25% (31 December 2011 est.)

Commercial bank prime lending rate: 17.5% (31 December 2013 est.)
country comparison to the world: 25
18.2% (31 December 2012 est.)

Stock of narrow money: $1.219 billion (31 December 2013 est.)
country comparison to the world: 144
$1.318 billion (31 December 2012 est.)

Stock of broad money: $6.329 billion (31 December 2013 est.)
country comparison to the world: 120
$5.472 billion (31 December 2012 est.)

Stock of domestic credit: $3.297 billion (31 December 2013 est.)
country comparison to the world: 124
$3.09 billion (31 December 2012 est.)

Market value of publicly traded shares: $1.293 billion (31 December 2012 est.)
country comparison to the world: 100
$1.579 billion (31 December 2011)
$1.093 billion (31 December 2010 est.)

Current account balance: -$3.639 billion (2013 est.)
country comparison to the world: 162
-$3.362 billion (2012 est.)

Exports: $4.294 billion (2013 est.)
country comparison to the world: 116
$4.382 billion (2012 est.)

Exports—commodities: copper, apparel, livestock, animal products, cashmere, wool, hides, fluorspar, other nonferrous metals, coal, crude oil

Exports—partners: China 89%, Canada 4.1% (2012)

Imports: $5.696 billion (2013 est.)
country comparison to the world: 121
$5.934 billion (2012 est.)

Imports—commodities: machinery and equipment, fuel, cars, food products, industrial consumer goods, chemicals, building materials, cigarettes and tobacco, appliances, soap and detergent

Imports—partners: China 37.5%, Russia 25.6%, US 9.4%, South Korea 6.1%, Japan 4.9% (2012)

Debt—external: $4.954 billion (31 December 2013 est.)
country comparison to the world: 122
$4.669 billion (31 December 2012 est.)

Stock of direct foreign investment—at home: $1.69 billion (31 December 2013 est.)
country comparison to the world: 99
$4.452 billion (31 December 2012 est.)

Stock of direct foreign investment—abroad: $NA (31 December 2013 est.)
$44 million (31 December 2012 est.)

Exchange rates: togrog/tugriks (MNT) per US dollar—
1,444.3 (2013 est.)
1,357.6 (2012 est.)
1,357.1 (2010 est.)

1,442.8 (2009)
1,170 (2007)

ENERGY

Electricity—production: 4.48 billion kWh (2010 est.)
country comparison to the world: 120

Electricity—consumption: 3.951 billion kWh (2010 est.)
country comparison to the world: 123

Electricity—exports: 22 million kWh (2010 est.)
country comparison to the world: 88

Electricity—imports: 263 million kWh (2010 est.)
country comparison to the world: 82

Electricity—installed generating capacity: 833,200 kW (2010 est.)
country comparison to the world: 127

Electricity—from fossil fuels: 99.9% of total installed capacity (2010 est.)
country comparison to the world: 44

Electricity—from nuclear fuels: 0% of total installed capacity (2010 est.)
country comparison to the world: 133

Electricity—from hydroelectric plants: 0% of total installed capacity (2010 est.)
country comparison to the world: 182

Electricity—from other renewable sources: 0.1% of total installed capacity (2010 est.)
country comparison to the world: 102

Crude oil—production: 9,935 bbl/day (2012 est.)
country comparison to the world: 91

Crude oil—exports: 5,680 bbl/day (2010 est.)
country comparison to the world: 64

Crude oil—imports: 0 bbl/day (2010 est.)
country comparison to the world: 88

Crude oil—proved reserves: NA bbl

Refined petroleum products—production: 0 bbl/day (2010 est.)
country comparison to the world: 169

Refined petroleum products—consumption: 21,610 bbl/day (2011 est.)
country comparison to the world: 125

Refined petroleum products—exports: 0 bbl/day (2010 est.)
country comparison to the world: 194

Refined petroleum products—imports: 17,360 bbl/day (2010 est.)
country comparison to the world: 109

Natural gas—production: 0 cu m (2011 est.)
country comparison to the world: 161

Natural gas—consumption: 0 cu m (2010 est.)
country comparison to the world: 167

Natural gas—exports: 0 cu m (2011 est.)
country comparison to the world: 142

Natural gas—imports: 0 cu m (2011 est.)
country comparison to the world: 92

Natural gas—proved reserves: 0 cu m (1 January 2013 es)
country comparison to the world: 165

Carbon dioxide emissions from consumption of energy: 10.21 million Mt (2011 est.)
country comparison to the world: 100

COMMUNICATIONS

Telephones—main lines in use: 176,700 (2012)
country comparison to the world: 129

Telephones—mobile cellular: 3.375 million (2012)
country comparison to the world: 126

Telephone system: *general assessment:* network is improving with international direct dialing available in many areas; a fiber-optic network has been installed that is improving broadband and communication services between major urban centers with multiple companies providing inter-city fiber-optic cable services
domestic: very low fixed-line teledensity; there are multiple mobile-cellular providers and subscribership is increasing
international: country code—976; satellite earth stations—7 (2011)

Broadcast media: following a law passed in 2005, Mongolia's state-run radio and TV provider converted to a public service provider; also available are private radio and TV broadcasters, as well as multi-channel satellite and cable TV providers; more than 100 radio stations, including some 20 via repeaters for the public broadcaster; transmissions of multiple international broadcasters are available (2008)

Internet country code: .mn

Internet hosts: 20,084 (2012)
country comparison to the world: 118

Internet users: 330,000 (2008)
country comparison to the world: 125

TRANSPORTATION

Airports: 44 (2013)
country comparison to the world: 9 8

Airports—with paved runways: *total:* 1 5
over 3,047 m: 2
2,438 to 3,047 m: 10
1,524 to 2,437 m: 3 (2013)

Airports—with unpaved runways: *total:* 2 9
over 3,047 m: 2
2,438 to 3,047 m: 2
1,524 to 2,437 m: 24
under 914 m: 1 (2013)

Heliports: 1 (2013)

Railways: *total:* 1,908 km
country comparison to the world: 73
broad gauge: 1,908 km 1.520-m gauge
note: the railway is 50 percent owned by the Russian State Railway (2010)

Roadways: *total:* 49,249 km
country comparison to the world: 78
paved: 4,800 km
unpaved: 44,449 km (2013)

Waterways: 580 km (the only waterway in operation is Lake Hovsgol) (135 km); Selenge River (270 km) and Orhon River (175 km) are navigable but carry little traffic; lakes and rivers freeze in winter, they are open from May to September) (2010)
country comparison to the world: 82

Merchant marine: *total:* 5 7
country comparison to the world: 68
by type: bulk carrier 21, cargo 25, chemical tanker 1, container 2, liquefied gas 2, passenger/cargo 2, roll on/roll off 3, vehicle carrier 1
foreign-owned: 44 (Indonesia 2, Japan 2, North Korea 1, Russia 2, Singapore 3, Ukraine 1, Vietnam 33) (2010)

MILITARY

Military branches: Mongolian Armed Forces (Mongol ulsyn zevsegt huchin): Mongolian Army (includes Mongolian Air and Air Defense, which is to become a separate service in 2015); there is no navy (2013)

Military service age and obligation: 18-25 years of age for compulsory and voluntary military service; conscript service obligation is 12 months in land or air defense forces or police; a small portion of Mongolian land forces (2.5 percent) is comprised of contract soldiers; women cannot be deployed overseas for military operations (2012)

Manpower available for military service:
males age 16-49: 898,546
females age 16-49: 891,192 (2010 est.)

Manpower fit for military service:
males age 16-49: 726,199
females age 16-49: 756,628 (2010 est.)

Manpower reaching militarily significant age annually: *male:* 30,829
female: 29,648 (2010 est.)

Military expenditures:
1.12% of GDP (2012)
country comparison to the world: 92
0.99% of GDP (2011)
1.12% of GDP (2010)

TRANSNATIONAL ISSUES

Disputes—international: none

Refugees and internally displaced persons: *stateless persons:* 220 (2012)

MONTENEGRO

INTRODUCTION

Background: The use of the name Crna Gora or Black Mountain (Montenegro) began in the 13th century in reference to a highland region in the Serbian province of Zeta. The later medieval state of Zeta maintained its existence until 1496 when Montenegro finally fell under Ottoman rule. Over subsequent centuries Montenegro managed to maintain a level of autonomy within the Ottoman Empire. From the 16th to 19th centuries, Montenegro was a theocracy ruled by a series of bishop princes; in 1852, it transformed into a secular principality. Montenegro was recognized as an independent sovereign principality at the Congress of Berlin in 1878. After World War I, during which Montenegro fought on the side of the Allies, Montenegro was absorbed by the Kingdom of Serbs, Croats, and Slovenes, which became the Kingdom of Yugoslavia in 1929; at the conclusion of World War II, it became a constituent republic of the Socialist Federal Republic of Yugoslavia. When the latter dissolved in 1992, Montenegro federated with Serbia, creating the Federal Republic of Yugoslavia and, after 2003, shifting to a looser State Union of Serbia and Montenegro. In May 2006, Montenegro invoked its right under the Constitutional Charter of Serbia and Montenegro to hold a referendum on independence from the state union. The vote for severing ties with Serbia barely exceeded 55%—the threshold set by the EU—allowing Montenegro to formally restore its independence on 3 June 2006.

GEOGRAPHY

Location: Southeastern Europe, between the Adriatic Sea and Serbia

Geographic coordinates: 42 30 N, 19 18 E

Map references: Europe

Area: *total:* 13,812 sq km
country comparison to the world: 162
land: 13,452 sq km
water: 360 sq km

Area—comparative: slightly smaller than Connecticut

Land boundaries: *total:* 625 km
border countries: Albania 172 km, Bosnia and Herzegovina 225 km, Croatia 25 km, Kosovo 79 km, Serbia 124 km

Coastline: 293.5 km

Maritime claims: *territorial sea:* 12 nm
continental shelf: defined by treaty

Climate: Mediterranean climate, hot dry summers and autumns and relatively cold winters with heavy snowfalls inland

Terrain: highly indented coastline with narrow coastal plain backed by rugged high limestone mountains and plateaus

Elevation extremes: *lowest point:* Adriatic Sea 0 m
highest point: Bobotov Kuk 2,522 m

Natural resources: bauxite, hydroelectricity

Land use: *arable land:* 12.45%
permanent crops: 1.16%
other: 86.39% (2011)

Irrigated land: 24.12 sq km (2010)

Natural hazards: destructive earthquakes

Environment—current issues: pollution of coastal waters from sewage outlets, especially in tourist-related areas such as Kotor

Environment—international agreements:
party to: Air Pollution, Biodiversity, Climate Change, Climate Change-Kyoto Protocol, Desertification, Hazardous Wastes, Law of the Sea, Marine Dumping, Marine Life Conservation, Ozone Layer Protection, Ship Pollution
signed, but not ratified: none of the selected agreements

Geography—note: strategic location along the Adriatic coast

PEOPLE AND SOCIETY

Nationality: *noun:* Montenegrin(s)
adjective: Montenegrin

Ethnic groups: Montenegrin 45%, Serbian 28.7%, Bosniak 8.7%, Albanian 4.9%, Muslim 3.3%, Roma 1%, Croat 1%, other 2.6%, unspecified 4.9% (2011 est.)

Languages: Serbian 42.9%, Montenegrin (official) 37%, Bosnian 5.3%, Albanian 5.3%, Serbo-Croat 2%, other 3.5%, unspecified 4% (2011 est.)

Religions: Orthodox 72.1%, Muslim 19.1%, Catholic 3.4%, atheist 1.2%, other 1.5%, unspecified 2.6% (2011 est.)

Population: 650,036 (July 2014 est.)
country comparison to the world: 168

Age structure:
0-14 years: 15.2% (male 48,231/female 50,659)
15-24 years: 10.8% (male 33,085/female 37,029)
25-54 years: 47.1% (male 164,644/female 141,380)
55-64 years: 14% (male 41,765/female 42,075)
65 years and over: 13.8% (male 36,081/female 55,087) (2014 est.)

Dependency ratios:
total dependency ratio: 46.7 %
youth dependency ratio: 27.5 %
elderly dependency ratio: 19.2 %
potential support ratio: 5.2 (2013)

Median age: *total:* 39.2 years
male: 38.2 years
female: 40.5 years (2014 est.)

Population growth rate: -0.49% (2014 est.)
country comparison to the world: 223

Birth rate: 10.59 births/1,000 population (2014 est.)
country comparison to the world: 182

Death rate: 9.3 deaths/1,000 population (2014 est.)
country comparison to the world: 61

Urbanization: *urban population:* 61% of total population (2010)
rate of urbanization: 0.1% annual rate of change (2010-15 est.)

Major urban areas—population: PODGORICA (capital) 144,000 (2009)

Sex ratio: *at birth:* 1.07 male(s)/female
0-14 years: 0.95 male(s)/female
15-24 years: 0.89 male(s)/female
25-54 years: 1.17 male(s)/female
55-64 years: 0.99 male(s)/female
65 years and over: 0.66 male(s)/female
total population: 0.99 male(s)/female (2014 est.)

Mother's mean age at first birth: 26.3 (2009 est.)

Maternal mortality rate: 8 deaths/100,000 live births (2010)
country comparison to the world: 160

Contraceptive prevalence rate: 39.4% (2005/06)

Health expenditures: 9.3% of GDP (2011)
country comparison to the world: 39

Physicians density: 2.03 physicians/1,000 population (2010)

Hospital bed density: 4 beds/1,000 population (2010)

Drinking water source:
improved:
urban: 99.6% of population
rural: 95.3% of population
total: 98% of population
unimproved:
urban: 0.4% of population
rural: 4.7% of population
total: 2% of population (2011 est.)

Sanitation facility access:
improved:
urban: 91.9% of population
rural: 86.8% of population
total: 90% of population
unimproved:
urban: 8.1% of population
rural: 13.2% of population
total: 10% of population (2011 est.)

Major infectious diseases: *degree of risk:* intermediate
food or waterborne diseases: bacterial diarrhea
vectorborne disease: Crimean-Congo hemorrhagic fever (2013)

Obesity—adult prevalence rate: 22.5% (2008)
country comparison to the world: 79

Children under the age of 5 years underweight: 2.2% (2006)
country comparison to the world: 121

Education expenditures: NA

Literacy: *definition:* age 15 and over can read and write
total population: 98.5%
male: 99.4%
female: 97.6% (2011 est.)

School life expectancy (primary to tertiary education): *total:* 15 years
male: 15 years
female: 16 years (2010)

Child labor—children ages 5-14: *total number:* 8,520
percentage: 10 % (2005 est.)

Unemployment, youth ages 15-24: *total:* 41.1%
country comparison to the world: 11
male: 42.3%
female: 39.7% (2012)

GOVERNMENT

Country name: *conventional long form:* none
conventional short form: Montenegro

local long form: none
local short form: Crna Gora
former: People's Republic of Montenegro, Socialist Republic of Montenegro, Republic of Montenegro

Government type: republic

Capital: *name:* Podgorica; note—the Old Royal Capital is Cetinje mentioned in the constitution

geographic coordinates: 42 26 N, 19 16 E
time difference: UTC+1 (6 hours ahead of Washington, DC during Standard Time)
daylight saving time: +1 hr, begins last Sunday in March; ends last Sunday in October

Administrative divisions: 23 municipalities (opstine, singular—opstina); Andrijevica, Bar, Berane, Bijelo Polje, Budva, Cetinje, Danilovgrad, Gusinje, Herceg Novi, Kolasin, Kotor, Mojkovac, Niksic, Petnijica, Plav, Pljevlja, Pluzine, Podgorica, Rozaje, Savnik, Tivat, Ulcinj, Zabljak

Independence: 3 June 2006 (from the State Union of Serbia and Montenegro)

National holiday: National Day, 13 July (1878)

Constitution: several previous; latest adopted 22 October 2007; note—in early 2013, Montenegro's parliamentary constitutional committee began debate on proposed amendments (2013)

Legal system: civil law

International law organization participation: has not submitted an ICJ jurisdiction declaration; accepts ICC jurisdiction

Suffrage: 18 years of age; universal

Executive branch: *chief of state:* President Filip VUJANOVIC (since 6 April 2008)
head of government: Prime Minister Milo DJUKANOVIC (since 4 December 2012)
cabinet: Ministers act as cabinet (For more information visit the World Leaders website)
elections: president elected by direct vote for five-year term (eligible for a second term); election last held on 7 April 2013 (next to be held in 2018); prime minister proposed by president, accepted by Assembly
election results: Filip VUJANOVIC reelected president; Filip VUJANOVIC 51.2%, Miodrag LEKIC 48.8%%

Legislative branch: unicameral Assembly (81 seats; members elected by direct vote to serve four-year terms)
elections: last held on 14 October 2012 (next to be held by 2016)
election results: percent of vote by party/coalition—Coalition for European Montenegro 45.6%, Democratic Front 22.8%, SNP 11.1%, Positive Montenegro 8.2%, Bosniak Party, 4.2%, other (including Albanian and Croatian minority parties) 8.1%; seats by party—Coalition for European Montenegro 39, Democratic Front 20, SNP 9, Positive Montenegro 7, Bosniak Party 3, Albanian and Croatian minority parties 3

Judicial branch: *highest court(s):* Supreme Court or Vrhovni Sud (consists of the court president and 6 judges); Constitutional Court or Ustavni Sud (consists of the court president and 6 judges)
judge selection and term of office: president of Supreme Court proposed jointly by the president of Montenegro, the speaker of the Assembly, and the prime minister; other judges elected by the Judicial Council; court president term is 5 years; term of other judges is 9 years; Constitutional Court judges proposed by the president of Montenegro and elected by the Assembly; court president elected among its members; term of judges is 9 years; court president term is 3 years
subordinate courts: Administrative Court; Court of Appeal; regional and first instance courts

Political parties and leaders: Albanian Coalition (includes Democratic League in Montenegro or DSCG [Mehmed BARDHI], Democratic Party [Fatmir; DJEKA], and Albanian Alternative or AA [Djerdj DAMAJ]); Bosniak Party or BS [Rafet HUSOVIC]; Coalition for European Montenegro (bloc) [Milo DJUKANOVIC] (includes Democratic Party of Socialists or DPS [Milo; DJUKANOVIC], Liberal Party of Montenegro or LP [Andrija POPOCVIC], and the Social Democratic Party or SDP [Ranko; KRIVOKAPIC]); Coalition FORCA for Unity (includes FORCA [Nazif CUNGU] and Civic Initiative [Vaselj Sinistaj]); Croatian Civic Initiative or HGI [Marija VUCINOVIC]; Democratic Center or DC [Goran BATRICEVIC]; Democratic Front (bloc) [Miodrag LEKIC] (includes New Serb Democracy or NOVA [Andrija MANDIC] and Movement for; Change or PZP [Nebojsa MEDOJEVIC], a splinter faction of the Socialist People's Party or SNP); Democratic Union of Albanians or DUA [Mehmet ZENKA]; Just Montenegro [Rade BOJOVIC]; Positive Montenegro [Darko PAJOVIC]; Serbian National Alliance (bloc) (includes Party of Serb Radicals or SSR, Democratic Serb Party or DSS [Ranko KADIC], and the Serbian National Council); Serbian Unity (bloc) (includes Serbian People's Party or NS [Predrag POPOVIC], the Serb List or SL, the Serbian Homeland; Party, the Serbian Radical Party, and the Democratic Centre of Boka or DCB [Dejan COROVIC]); Socialist People's Party or SNP [Srdan MILIC]; Together (bloc) (includes Pensioners' Party [Vojo VULETIC], Disabled and Social Justice, and the Yugoslav Communist; Party of Montenegro or JKPCG)

Political pressure groups and leaders: NA

International organization participation: CE, CEI, EAPC, EBRD, FAO, IAEA, IBRD, ICAO, ICC (NGOs), ICRM, IDA, IFC, IFRCS, IHO (pending member), ILO, IMF, IMO, IMSO, Interpol, IOC, IOM, IPU, ISO (correspondent), ITSO, ITU, ITUC (NGOs), MIGA, NAM (observer), OIF (observer), OPCW, OSCE, PCA, PFP, SELEC, UN, UNCTAD, UNESCO, UNHCR, UNIDO, UNMIL, UNWTO, UPU, WCO, WHO, WIPO, WMO, WTO

Diplomatic representation in the US:
chief of mission: Ambassador Srdjan DARMANOVIC (since 30 November 2010)
chancery: 1610 New Hampshire Avenue NW, Washington, DC, 20009
telephone: [1] (202) 234-6108
FAX: [1] (202) 234-6109
consulate(s) general: New York

Diplomatic representation from the US:
chief of mission: Ambassador Sue K. BROWN (since 27 April 2011)
embassy: Dzona Dzeksona 2, 81000 Podgorica, Montenegro
mailing address: use embassy street address
telephone: [382] (0) 20 410 500
FAX: [382] (0) 20 241 358

Flag description: a red field bordered by a narrow golden-yellow stripe with the Montenegrin coat of arms centered; the arms consist of a double-headed golden eagle—symbolizing the unity of church and state—surmounted by a crown; the eagle holds a golden scepter in its right claw and a blue orb in its left; the breast shield over the eagle shows a golden lion passant on a green field in front of a blue sky; the lion is symbol of episcopal authority and harkens back to the three and a half centuries that Montenegro was ruled as a theocracy

National symbol(s): double-headed eagle

National anthem: *name:* "Oj, svijetla majska zoro" (Oh, Bright Dawn of May)
lyrics/music: Sekula DRLJEVIC/unknown, arranged by Zarko MIKOVIC
note: adopted 2004; the anthem's music is based on a Montenegrin folk song

ECONOMY

Economy—overview: Montenegro's economy is slowly transitioning to a market system, but the state sector remains large and additional institutional changes are needed. The economy relies heavily on foreign tourism and the export of refined metals. Unprofitable state-owned enterprises, especially the Podgorica Aluminum Kombine, the country's largest exporter, weigh heavily on public finances. During the MILOSEVIC era, Montenegro severed its economy from Serbia, maintained its own central bank, adopted the Deutsche Mark, then shifted to the euro—rather than the Yugoslav dinar—as official currency, collected customs tariffs, and managed its own budget. The 2006 dissolution of the loose political union between Serbia and Montenegro led to separate memberships in several international financial institutions, such as the European Bank for Reconstruction and Development. In January 2007, Montenegro joined the World Bank and IMF. Montenegro became the 156th member of World Trade Organization in December 2011. The European Council (EC) granted candidate country status to Montenegro at the December 2010 session. Montenegro began negotiations to join the EC in June, 2012, having met the conditions set down by the European Council, which called on Montenegro to take steps to fight corruption and organized crime. Unemployment and disparities in regional development, especially in the north, remain key political and economic problems. The global financial crisis had a significant negative impact on the economy, due to a credit crunch, a decline in the real estate sector, and a fall in aluminum exports. The Government of Montenegro increased value added tax (VAT) from 17% in 2012 to 19% in 2013 and raised income tax rates from 9% to 15% for those earning over 480 a month. In 2013, the government also retrenched by freezing pensions and limiting salary increases for public enterprises and members of the parliament.

GDP (purchasing power parity): $7.429 billion (2013 est.)
country comparison to the world: 159
$7.318 billion (2012 est.)
$7.358 billion (2011 est.)
note: data are in 2013 US dollars

GDP (official exchange rate): $4.518 billion (2013 est.)

GDP—real growth rate: 1.5% (2013 est.)
country comparison to the world: 160
-0.5% (2012 est.)
3.2% (2011 est.)

GDP—per capita (PPP): $11,900 (2013 est.)
country comparison to the world: 107
$11,800 (2012 est.)
$11,900 (2011 est.)
note: data are in 2013 US dollars

GDP—composition, by end use:
household consumption: 84.4%
government consumption: 22.1%
investment in fixed capital: 18.4%
investment in inventories: 1.1%
exports of goods and services: 40.2%
imports of goods and services: -66.2% (2011 est.)

GDP—composition, by sector of origin:
agriculture: 0.8%
industry: 11.3%
services: 87.9% (2011)

Agriculture—products: tobacco, potatoes, citrus fruits, olives, grapes; sheep

Industries: steelmaking, aluminum, agricultural processing, consumer goods, tourism

Labor force: 251,300 (2011 est.)
country comparison to the world: 166

Labor force—by occupation:

agriculture: 6.3%
industry: 20.9%
services: 72.8% (2011 est.)

Unemployment rate: 19.1% (2012 est.)
country comparison to the world: 159
11.5% (2011 est.)

Population below poverty line: 6.6% (2010 est.)

Distribution of family income—Gini index: 24.3 (2010)
country comparison to the world: 137
30 (2003)

Budget: *revenues:* $1.68 billion
expenditures: $1.58 billion (2012 est.)

Taxes and other revenues: 37.2% of GDP (2012 est.)
country comparison to the world: 54

Budget surplus (+) or deficit (-): 2.2% of GDP (2012 est.)
country comparison to the world: 15

Public debt: 52.1% of GDP (2012 est.)
country comparison to the world: 62
45% of GDP (2011 est.)
note: data cover general government debt, and includes debt instruments issued (or owned) by government entities other than the treasury; the data include treasury debt held by foreign entities; the data include debt issued by subnational entities, as well as intra-governmental debt; intra-governmental debt consists of treasury borrowings from surpluses in the social funds, such as for retirement, medical care, and unemployment; debt instruments for the social funds are not sold at public auctions

Fiscal year: calendar year

Inflation rate (consumer prices): 4% (2012)
country comparison to the world: 135
3% (2011)

Commercial bank prime lending rate: 9.69% (31 December 2011 est.)
country comparison to the world: 93
9.53% (31 December 2010 est.)

Stock of narrow money: $749 million (31 December 2011 est.)
country comparison to the world: 155
$783.3 million (31 December 2010 est.)

Stock of broad money: $1.982 billion (31 December 2011 est.)
country comparison to the world: 150
$2.01 billion (31 December 2010 est.)

Stock of domestic credit: $3.29 billion (31 December 2009)
country comparison to the world: 125
$3.771 billion (31 December 2008)

Market value of publicly traded shares: $3.827 billion (31 December 2012 est.)
country comparison to the world: 92
$3.322 billion (31 December 2011)
$3.604 billion (31 December 2010 est.)

Current account balance: -$1.938 billion (2012 est.)
country comparison to the world: 141
-$1.927 billion (2011 est.)

Exports: $489.2 million (2012 est.)
country comparison to the world: 176
$640 million (2011 est.)

Exports—partners: Croatia 22.7%, Serbia 22.7%, Slovenia 7.8% (2012 est.)

Imports: $2.4 billion (2012 est.)
country comparison to the world: 158
$2.5 billion (2011 est.)

Imports—partners: Serbia 29.3%, Greece 8.7%, China 7.1% (2012 est.)

Reserves of foreign exchange and gold: $400 million (31 December 2011)
country comparison to the world: 150

Debt—external: $1.7 billion (2012 est.)
country comparison to the world: 147
$1.2 billion (2011 est.)

Exchange rates: euros (EUR) per US dollar—
0.7634 (2013 est.)
0.7752 (2012 est.)
0.755 (2010 est.)
0.7198 (2009 est.)
0.6827 (2008 est.)

ENERGY

Electricity—production: 3.945 billion kWh (2010 est.)
country comparison to the world: 124

Electricity—consumption: 3.279 billion kWh (2010 est.)
country comparison to the world: 128

Electricity—exports: 730 million kWh (2010 est.)
country comparison to the world: 61

Electricity—imports: 732 million kWh (2010 est.)
country comparison to the world: 68

Electricity—installed generating capacity: 868,000 kW (2010 est.)
country comparison to the world: 125

Electricity—from fossil fuels: 24.2% of total installed capacity (2010 est.)
country comparison to the world: 187

Electricity—from nuclear fuels: 0% of total installed capacity (2010 est.)
country comparison to the world: 136

Electricity—from hydroelectric plants: 75.8% of total installed capacity (2010 est.)
country comparison to the world: 18

Electricity—from other renewable sources: 0% of total installed capacity (2010 est.)
country comparison to the world: 201

Crude oil—production: 0 bbl/day (2012 est.)
country comparison to the world: 193

Crude oil—exports: 0 bbl/day (2010 est.)
country comparison to the world: 151

Crude oil—imports: 0 bbl/day (2010 est.)
country comparison to the world: 91

Crude oil—proved reserves: 0 bbl (1 January 2012 es)
country comparison to the world: 162

Refined petroleum products—production: 0 bbl/day (2010 est.)
country comparison to the world: 172

Refined petroleum products—consumption: 4,446 bbl/day (2011 est.)
country comparison to the world: 173

Refined petroleum products—exports: 369.3 bbl/day (2010 est.)
country comparison to the world: 115

Refined petroleum products—imports: 3,300 bbl/day (2010 est.)
country comparison to the world: 168

Natural gas—production: 0 cu m (2011 est.)
country comparison to the world: 164

Natural gas—consumption: 0 cu m (2010 est.)
country comparison to the world: 170

Natural gas—exports: 0 cu m (2011 est.)
country comparison to the world: 145

Natural gas—imports: 0 cu m (2011 est.)
country comparison to the world: 95

Natural gas—proved reserves: 0 cu m (1 January 2013 es)
country comparison to the world: 168

Carbon dioxide emissions from consumption of energy: 2.166 million Mt (2011 est.)
country comparison to the world: 146

COMMUNICATIONS

Telephones—main lines in use: 163,000 (2012)
country comparison to the world: 131

Telephones—mobile cellular: 1.126 million (2012)
country comparison to the world: 154

Telephone system: general assessment: modern telecommunications system with access to European satellites
domestic: GSM mobile-cellular service, available through multiple providers with national coverage, is growing
international: country code—382; 2 international switches connect the national system (2011)

Broadcast media: state-funded national radio-TV broadcaster operates 2 terrestrial TV networks, 1 satellite TV channel, and 2 radio networks; 4 public TV stations and some 20 private TV stations; 14 local public radio stations and more than 40 private radio stations (2007)

Internet country code: .me

Internet hosts: 10,088 (2012)
country comparison to the world: 135

Internet users: 280,000 (2009)
country comparison to the world: 133

TRANSPORTATION

Airports: 5 (2013)
country comparison to the world: 181

Airports—with paved runways: *total:* 5
2,438 to 3,047 m: 2
1,524 to 2,437 m: 1
914 to 1,523 m: 1
under 914 m: 1 (2013)

Heliports: 1 (2012)

Railways: *total:* 250 km
country comparison to the world: 124
standard gauge: 250 km 1.435-m gauge (169 km electrified) (2010)

Roadways: *total:* 7,763 km
country comparison to the world: 142
paved: 5,365 km
unpaved: 2,398 km (2010)

Merchant marine: *total:* 2
country comparison to the world: 141
by type: cargo 1, passenger/cargo 1
registered in other countries: 4 (Bahamas 2, Honduras 1, Slovakia 1) (2010)

Ports and terminals: *major seaport(s):* Bar

MILITARY

Military branches: Armed Forces of the Republic of Montenegro: Army of Montenegro (includes Montenegrin Navy (Mornarica Crne Gore, MCG)), Air Force (2011)

Military service age and obligation: 18 is the legal minimum age for voluntary military service; no conscription (2012)

Manpower fit for military service:
males age 16-49: 149,159
females age 16-49: 131,823 (2010 est.)

Manpower reaching militarily significant age annually: *male:* 3,120
female: 3,677 (2010 est.)

Military expenditures: 1.87% of GDP (2012)
country comparison to the world: 46
1.95% of GDP (2011)
1.87% of GDP (2010)

TRANSNATIONAL ISSUES

Disputes—international: none

Refugees and internally displaced persons:
refugees (country of origin): 8,504 (Kosovo) (2012)
stateless persons: 3,383 (2012)

MONTSERRAT

INTRODUCTION

Background: English and Irish colonists from St. Kitts first settled on Montserrat in 1632; the first African slaves arrived three decades later. The British and French fought for possession of the island for most of the 18th century, but it finally was confirmed as a British possession in 1783. The island's sugar plantation economy was converted to small farm landholdings in the mid 19th century. Much of this island was devastated and two-thirds of the population fled abroad because of the eruption of the Soufriere Hills Volcano that began on 18 July 1995. Montserrat has endured volcanic activity since, with the last eruption occurring in July 2003.

GEOGRAPHY

Location: Caribbean, island in the Caribbean Sea, southeast of Puerto Rico

Geographic coordinates: 16 45 N, 62 12 W

Map references: Central America and the Caribbean

Area: *total:* 102 sq km
country comparison to the world: 226
land: 102 sq km
water: 0 sq km

Area—comparative: about 0.6 times the size of Washington, DC

Land boundaries: 0 km

Coastline: 40 km

Maritime claims: *territorial sea:* 3 nm
exclusive fishing zone: 200 nm

Climate: tropical; little daily or seasonal temperature variation

Terrain: volcanic island, mostly mountainous, with small coastal lowland

Elevation extremes: *lowest point:* Caribbean Sea 0 m
highest point: lava dome in English's Crater (in the Soufriere Hills volcanic complex) estimated at over 930 m (2006)

Natural resources: NEGL

Land use: *arable land:* 20%
permanent crops: 0%
other: 80% (2011)

Irrigated land: NA

Natural hazards: volcanic eruptions; severe hurricanes (June to November)
volcanism: Soufriere Hills volcano (elev. 915 m), has erupted continuously since 1995; a massive eruption in 1997 destroyed most of the capital, Plymouth, and resulted in approximately half of the island becoming uninhabitable

Environment—current issues: land erosion occurs on slopes that have been cleared for cultivation

Geography—note: the island is entirely volcanic in origin and comprised of three major volcanic centers of differing ages

PEOPLE AND SOCIETY

Nationality: *noun:* Montserratian(s)
adjective: Montserratian

Ethnic groups: African/black 88.4%, mixed 3.7%, hispanic/Spanish 3%, caucasian/white 2.7%, East Indian/Indian 1.5%, other 0.7% (2011 est.)

Languages: English

Religions: Protestant 67.1% (includes Anglican 21.8%, Methodist 17%, Pentecostal 14.1%, Seventh Day Adventist 10.5%, and Church of God 3.7%), Roman Catholic 11.6%, Rastafarian 1.4%, other 6.5%, none 2.6%, unspecified 10.8% (2001 est.)

Population: 5,215 (July 2014 est.)
country comparison to the world: 231
note: an estimated 8,000 refugees left the island following the resumption of volcanic activity in July 1995; some have returned

Age structure: *0-14 years:* 17.6% (male 472/female 445)
15-24 years: 21.5% (male 588/female 531)
25-54 years: 47.9% (male 1,190/female 1,309)
55-64 years: 6.1% (male 160/female 200)
65 years and over: 6.2% (male 196/female 124) (2014 est.)

Median age: *total:* 31.4 years
male: 30.9 years
female: 31.9 years (2014 est.)

Population growth rate: 0.48% (2014 est.)
country comparison to the world: 157

Birth rate: 11.31 births/1,000 population (2014 est.)
country comparison to the world: 174

Death rate: 6.52 deaths/1,000 population (2014 est.)
country comparison to the world: 151

Net migration rate: 0 migrant(s)/1,000 population (2014 est.)
country comparison to the world: 89

Urbanization: *urban population:* 14% of total population (2010)
rate of urbanization: 2.4% annual rate of change (2010-15 est.)

Sex ratio: *at birth:* 1.04 male(s)/female
0-14 years: 1.06 male(s)/female
15-24 years: 1.11 male(s)/female
25-54 years: 0.91 male(s)/female
55-64 years: 1 male(s)/female
65 years and over: 1.55 male(s)/female
total population: 1 male(s)/female (2014 est.)

Infant mortality rate: *total:* 13.66 deaths/1,000 live births
country comparison to the world: 116
male: 10.54 deaths/1,000 live births
female: 16.92 deaths/1,000 live births (2014 est.)

Life expectancy at birth:
total population: 73.9 years
country comparison to the world: 119
male: 75.48 years
female: 72.24 years (2014 est.)

Total fertility rate: 1.29 children born/woman (2014 est.)
country comparison to the world: 216

Drinking water source:
improved:
urban: 98.9% of population
rural: 99% of population
total: 99% of population
unimproved:
urban: 1.1% of population
rural: 1% of population
total: 1% of population (2011 est.)

Sanitation facility access:
improved:
urban: 82.9% of population
rural: 82.9% of population
total: 82.9% of population
unimproved:
urban: 17.1% of population
rural: 17.1% of population
total: 17.1% of population (2007 est.)

HIV/AIDS—adult prevalence rate: NA

HIV/AIDS—people living with HIV/AIDS: NA

HIV/AIDS—deaths: NA

Literacy: *definition:* age 15 and over has ever attended school
total population: 97%
male: 97%
female: 97% (1970 est.)

School life expectancy (primary to tertiary education): *total:* 15 years
male: 14 years
female: 17 years (2007)

GOVERNMENT

Country name: *conventional long form:* none
conventional short form: Montserrat

Dependency status: overseas territory of the UK

Government type: NA

Capital: *name:* Plymouth

geographic coordinates: 16 42 N, 62 13 W
time difference: UTC-4 (1 hour ahead of Washington, DC during Standard Time)
note: Plymouth was abandoned in 1997 because of volcanic activity; interim government buildings have been built at Brades Estate in the Carr's Bay/Little Bay vicinity at the northwest end of Montserrat

Administrative divisions: 3 parishes; Saint Anthony, Saint Georges, Saint Peter

Independence: none (overseas territory of the UK)

National holiday: Birthday of Queen ELIZABETH II, second Saturday in June (1926)

Constitution: previous 1960; latest effective 1 September 2010; amended 2011 (2012)

Legal system: English common law

Suffrage: 18 years of age; universal

Executive branch: *chief of state:* Queen ELIZABETH II (since 6 February 1952); represented by Governor Adrian DAVIS (since 8 April 2011)
head of government: Premier Rueben T. MEADE (since 27 September 2011); note—the office of premier came into effect with the new Constitution Order; he replaces the Chief Minister
cabinet: Executive Council consists of the governor, the premier, 3 other ministers, the attorney general, and the finance secretary (For more information visit the World Leaders website)
elections: the monarchy is hereditary; governor appointed by the monarch; following legislative elections, the leader of the majority party usually becomes premier

Legislative branch: unicameral Legislative Council (11 seats; 9 members popularly elected to serve five-year terms; the attorney general and financial secretary sit as ex-officio members)
elections: last held on 8 September 2009 (next to be held by 2014)
election results: percent of vote by party—NA; seats by party—MCAP 6, independents 3
Judicial branch: highest court(s): the Eastern Caribbean Supreme Court (ECSC) is the itinerant superior court of record for the 9-member Organization of Eastern Caribbean States to include Montserrat; the ECSC—with its headquarters on St. Lucia—is headed by the chief justice and is comprised of the Court of Appeal with 3 justices and the High Court with 16 judges; sittings of the Court of Appeal and High Court rotate among the 9 member states; 1 judge of the Supreme Court is a resident of Montserrat and presides over the High Court note—Montserrat is also a member of the Caribbean Court of Justice

judge selection and term of office: Eastern Caribbean Supreme Court chief justice appointed by Her Majesty, Queen ELIZABETH II; other justices and judges appointed by the Judicial and Legal Services Commission; Court of Appeal justices appointed for life with mandatory retirement at age 65; High Court judges appointed for life with mandatory retirement at age 62
subordinate courts: magistrate's court

Political parties and leaders: Montserrat Democratic Party or MDP [Lowell LEWIS]; Movement for Change and Prosperity or MCAP [Roselyn CASSELL-SEALY]; New People's Liberation Movement or NPLM [John A. OSBORNE]

Political pressure groups and leaders: NA

International organization participation: Caricom, CDB, Interpol (subbureau), OECS, UPU

Diplomatic representation in the US: none (overseas territory of the UK)

Diplomatic representation from the US: none (overseas territory of the UK)

Flag description: blue, with the flag of the UK in the upper hoist-side quadrant and the Montserratian coat of arms centered in the outer half of the flag; the arms feature a woman in green dress, Erin, the female personification of Ireland, standing beside a yellow harp and embracing a large dark cross with her right arm; Erin and the harp are symbols of Ireland reflecting the territory's Irish ancestry; blue represents awareness, trustworthiness, determination, and righteousness

National anthem: note: as a territory of the United Kingdom, "God Save the Queen" is official (see United Kingdom)

ECONOMY

Economy—overview: Severe volcanic activity, which began in July 1995, has put a damper on this small, open economy. A catastrophic eruption in June 1997 closed the airport and seaports, causing further economic and social dislocation. Two-thirds of the 12,000 inhabitants fled the island. Some began to return in 1998 but lack of housing limited the number. The agriculture sector continued to be affected by the lack of suitable land for farming and the destruction of crops. Prospects for the economy depend largely on developments in relation to the volcanic activity and on public sector construction activity. Half of the island remains uninhabitable. In January 2013, the EU announced the disbursement of a $55.2 million aid package to Montserrat in order to boost the country's economic recovery, with a specific focus on public finance management, public sector reform, and prudent economic management.

GDP (purchasing power parity): $43.78 million (2006 est.)
country comparison to the world: 225

GDP (official exchange rate): $NA

GDP—real growth rate: 3.5% (2008 est.)
country comparison to the world: 100

GDP—per capita (PPP): $8,500 (2006 est.)
country comparison to the world: 128

GDP—composition, by end use:
household consumption: 84.8%
government consumption: 47.1%
investment in fixed capital: 26%
investment in inventories: 0%
exports of goods and services: 23%
imports of goods and services: -80.9% (2013 est.)

GDP—composition, by sector of origin:
agriculture: 1.6%
industry: 23.2%
services: 75.1% (2013 est.)

Agriculture—products: cabbages, carrots, cucumbers, tomatoes, onions, peppers; livestock products

Industries: tourism, rum, textiles, electronic appliances

Industrial production growth rate: 2%
country comparison to the world: 128

Labor force: 4,521 (2012)
country comparison to the world: 223

Unemployment rate: 6% (1998 est.)
country comparison to the world: 61

Population below poverty line: NA%

Household income or consumption by percentage share: *lowest* 10%: NA%
highest 10%: NA%

Budget: *revenues:* $31.4 million
expenditures: $37.04 million (2011 est.)

Fiscal year: 1 April—31 March

Inflation rate (consumer prices): 4.5% (2013 est.)
country comparison to the world: 145
4.8% (2012 est.)

Central bank discount rate: 10.99% (31 December 2010 est.)
country comparison to the world: 53
6.5% (31 December 2009 est.)

Commercial bank prime lending rate: 8.3% (31 December 2013 est.)
country comparison to the world: 115
8.16% (31 December 2012 est.)

Stock of narrow money: $19.5 million (31 December 2013 est.)
country comparison to the world: 189
$17.54 million (31 December 2012 est.)

Stock of broad money: $89.96 million (31 December 2013 est.)
country comparison to the world: 191
$81.79 million (31 December 2012 est.)

Stock of domestic credit: $4.074 million (31 December 2012 est.)
country comparison to the world: 180
$5.185 million (31 December 2011 est.)

Exports: $3.6 million (2013 est.)
country comparison to the world: 218
$2.3 million (2012 est.)

Exports—commodities: electronic components, plastic bags, apparel; hot peppers, limes, live plants; cattle

Imports: $30 million (2013 est.)
country comparison to the world: 218
$32.5 million (2012 est.)

Imports—commodities: machinery and transportation equipment, foodstuffs, manufactured goods, fuels, lubricants, and related materials

Reserves of foreign exchange and gold: $32.08 million (31 December 2012 est.)
country comparison to the world: 169
$24.81 million (31 December 2011 est.)

Debt—external: $8.9 million (1997)
country comparison to the world: 198

Exchange rates: East Caribbean dollars (XCD) per US dollar—
2.7 (2013 est.)
2.7 (2012 est.)
2.7 (2010 est.)
2.7 (2009)

ENERGY

Electricity—production: 24 million kWh (2010 est.)
country comparison to the world: 213

Electricity—consumption: 22.32 million kWh (2010 est.)
country comparison to the world: 213

Electricity—exports: 0 kWh (2012 est.)
country comparison to the world: 164

Electricity—imports: 0 kWh (2012 est.)
country comparison to the world: 167

Electricity—installed generating capacity: 10,000 kW (2010 est.)
country comparison to the world: 205

Electricity—from fossil fuels: 100% of total installed capacity (2010 est.)
country comparison to the world: 23

Electricity—from nuclear fuels: 0% of total installed capacity (2010 est.)
country comparison to the world: 134

Electricity—from hydroelectric plants: 0% of total installed capacity (2010 est.)
country comparison to the world: 183

Electricity—from other renewable sources: 0% of total installed capacity (2010 est.)
country comparison to the world: 199

Crude oil—production: 0 bbl/day (2012 est.)
country comparison to the world: 192

Crude oil—exports: 0 bbl/day (2010 est.)
country comparison to the world: 149

Crude oil—imports: 0 bbl/day (2010 est.)
country comparison to the world: 89

Crude oil—proved reserves: 0 bbl (1 January 2013 es)
country comparison to the world: 160

Refined petroleum products—production: 0 bbl/day (2010 est.)
country comparison to the world: 170

Refined petroleum products—consumption: 1,000 bbl/day (2011 est.)
country comparison to the world: 201

Refined petroleum products—exports: 0 bbl/day (2010 est.)
country comparison to the world: 195

Refined petroleum products—imports: 568.5 bbl/day (2010 est.)
country comparison to the world: 203

Natural gas—production: 0 cu m (2011 est.)
country comparison to the world: 162

Natural gas—consumption: 0 cu m (2010 est.)
country comparison to the world: 168

Natural gas—exports: 0 cu m (2011 est.)
country comparison to the world: 143

Natural gas—imports: 0 cu m (2011 est.)
country comparison to the world: 93

Natural gas—proved reserves: 0 cu m (1 January 2013 es)
country comparison to the world: 166

Carbon dioxide emissions from consumption of energy: 87,860 Mt (2011 est.)
country comparison to the world: 206

COMMUNICATIONS

Telephones—main lines in use: 3,000 (2012)
country comparison to the world: 214

Telephones—mobile cellular: 4,000 (2012)
country comparison to the world: 214

Telephone system: general assessment: modern and fully digitalized
domestic: combined fixed-line and mobile-cellular teledensity exceeds 100 per 100 persons
international: country code—1-664; landing point for the East Caribbean Fiber System (ECFS) optic submarine cable with links to 13 other islands in the eastern Caribbean extending from the British Virgin Islands to Trinidad (2011)

Broadcast media: Radio Montserrat, a public radio broadcaster, transmits on 1 station and has a repeater transmission to a second station; repeater transmissions from the GEM Radio Network of Trinidad and Tobago provide another 2 radio stations; cable and satellite TV available (2007)

Internet country code: .ms

Internet hosts: 2,431 (2012)
country comparison to the world: 160

Internet users: 1,200 (2009)
country comparison to the world: 213

TRANSPORTATION

Airports: 1 (2013)
country comparison to the world: 225

Airports—with paved runways: *total:* 1
under 914 m: 1 (2013)

Roadways: *note:* volcanic eruptions that began in 1995 destroyed most of the 227 km road system; a new road infrastructure has been built on the north end of the island (2008)

Ports and terminals: *major seaport(s):* Little Bay, Plymouth

MILITARY

Military branches: no regular military forces; Royal Montserrat Police Force (2011)

Manpower available for military service:
males age 16-49: 1,353 (2010 est.)

Manpower fit for military service:
males age 16-49: 1,135
females age 16-49: 1,223 (2010 est.)

Manpower reaching militarily significant age annually: *male:* 3 5
female: 34 (2010 est.)

Military—note: defense is the responsibility of the UK

TRANSNATIONAL ISSUES

Disputes—international: none

Illicit drugs: transshipment point for South American narcotics destined for the US and Europe

MOROCCO

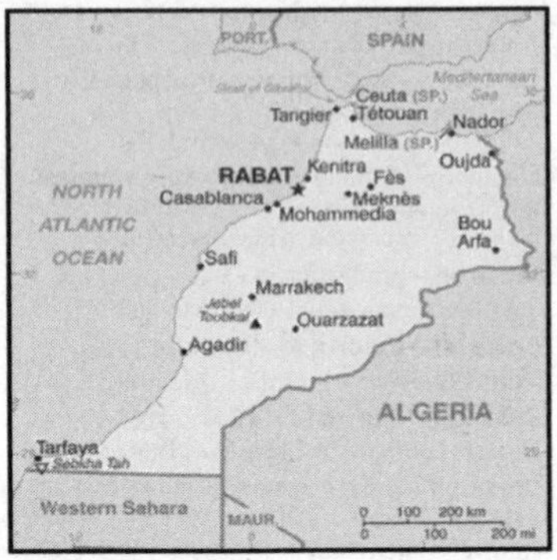

INTRODUCTION

Background: In 788, about a century after the Arab conquest of North Africa, a series of Moroccan Muslim dynasties began to rule in Morocco. In the 16th century, the Sa'adi monarchy, particularly under Ahmad al-MANSUR (1578-1603), repelled foreign invaders and inaugurated a golden age. The Alaouite Dynasty, to which the current Moroccan royal family belongs, dates from the 17th century. In 1860, Spain occupied northern Morocco and ushered in a half century of trade rivalry among European powers that saw Morocco's sovereignty steadily erode; in 1912, the French imposed a protectorate over the country. A protracted independence struggle with France ended successfully in 1956. The internationalized city of Tangier and most Spanish possessions were turned over to the new country that same year. Sultan MOHAMMED V, the current monarch's grandfather, organized the new state as a constitutional monarchy and in 1957 assumed the title of king. Although Morocco is not the UN-recognized Administering Power for the Western Sahara, it exercises de facto administrative control over 80% of the territory. The UN since 1991 has monitored a ceasefire between Morocco and the Polisario Front and leads ongoing negotiations over the status of the territory. King MOHAMMED VI in early 2011 responded to the spread of pro-democracy protests in the region by implementing a reform program that included a new constitution, passed by popular referendum in July 2011, under which some new powers were extended to parliament and the prime minister but ultimate authority remains in the hands of the monarch. In November 2012, the Justice and Development Party—a moderate Islamist party—won the largest number of seats in parliamentary elections, becoming the first Islamist party to lead the Moroccan Government.

GEOGRAPHY

Location: Northern Africa, bordering the North Atlantic Ocean and the Mediterranean Sea, between Algeria and Western Sahara

Geographic coordinates: 32 00 N, 5 00 W

Map references: Africa

Area: *total:* 446,550 sq km
country comparison to the world: 58
land: 446,300 sq km
water: 250 sq km

Area—comparative: slightly larger than California

Land boundaries: *total:* 2,017.9 km
border countries: Algeria 1,559 km, Western Sahara 443 km, Spain (Ceuta) 6.3 km, Spain (Melilla) 9.6 km

Coastline: 1,835 km

Maritime claims: *territorial sea:* 12 nm
contiguous zone: 24 nm
exclusive economic zone: 200 nm
continental shelf: 200 m depth or to the depth of exploitation

Climate: Mediterranean, becoming more extreme in the interior

Terrain: northern coast and interior are mountainous with large areas of bordering plateaus, intermontane valleys, and rich coastal plains

Elevation extremes: *lowest point:* Sebkha Tah -55 m
highest point: Jebel Toubkal 4,165 m

Natural resources: phosphates, iron ore, manganese, lead, zinc, fish, salt

Land use: *arable land:* 17.79%
permanent crops: 2.6%
other: 79.61% (2011)

Irrigated land: 14,850 sq km (2004)

Total renewable water resources: 29 cu km (2011)

Freshwater withdrawal (domestic/industrial/agricultural): *total:* 12.61 cu km/yr (12%/4%/84%)
per capita: 428.1 cu m/yr (2005)

Natural hazards: northern mountains geologically unstable and subject to earthquakes; periodic droughts

Environment—current issues: land degradation/desertification (soil erosion resulting from farming of marginal areas, overgrazing, destruction of vegetation); water supplies contaminated by raw sewage; siltation of reservoirs; oil pollution of coastal waters

Environment—international agreements:
party to: Biodiversity, Climate Change, Climate Change-Kyoto Protocol, Desertification, Endangered Species, Hazardous Wastes, Law of the Sea, Marine Dumping, Ozone Layer Protection, Ship Pollution, Wetlands, Whaling
signed, but not ratified: Environmental Modification

Geography—note: strategic location along Strait of Gibraltar

PEOPLE AND SOCIETY

Nationality: *noun:* Moroccan(s)
adjective: Moroccan

Ethnic groups: Arab-Berber 99%, other 1%

Languages: Arabic (official), Berber languages (Tamazight (official), Tachelhit, Tarifit), French (often the language of business, government, and diplomacy)

Religions: Muslim 99% (official; virtually all Sunni,

Population: 32,987,206 (July 2014 est.)

country comparison to the world: 39

Age structure:
0-14 years: 26.7% (male 4,479,676/female 4,342,605)
15-24 years: 17.7% (male 2,899,041/female 2,931,856)
25-54 years: 42% (male 6,693,877/female 7,146,696)
55-64 years: 6.3% (male 1,200,733/female 1,203,447)
65 years and over: 6.3% (male 940,291/female 1,148,984) (2014 est.)

Dependency ratios:
total dependency ratio: 48.9 %
youth dependency ratio: 41.5 %
elderly dependency ratio: 7.4 %
potential support ratio: 13.5 (2013)

Median age: *total:* 28.1 years
male: 27.5 years
female: 28.7 years (2014 est.)

Population growth rate: 1.02% (2014 est.)
country comparison to the world: 117

Birth rate: 18.47 births/1,000 population (2014 est.)
country comparison to the world: 100

Death rate: 4.79 deaths/1,000 population (2014 est.)
country comparison to the world: 196

Net migration rate: -3.46 migrant(s)/1,000 population (2014 est.)
country comparison to the world: 186

Urbanization: *urban population:* 57% of total population (2011)
rate of urbanization: 1.62% annual rate of change (2010-15 est.)

Major urban areas—population: Casablanca 3.245 million; RABAT (capital) 1.77 million; Fes 1.044 million; Marrakech 909,000; Tangier 768,000 (2009)

Sex ratio: *at birth:* 1.05 male(s)/female
0-14 years: 1.03 male(s)/female
15-24 years: 0.99 male(s)/female
25-54 years: 0.94 male(s)/female
55-64 years: 0.97 male(s)/female
65 years and over: 0.82 male(s)/female
total population: 0.97 male(s)/female (2014 est.)

Mother's mean age at first birth: 25.4 (2004 est.)

Maternal mortality rate: 100 deaths/100,000 live births (2010)
country comparison to the world: 70

Infant mortality rate: *total:* 24.52 deaths/1,000 live births
country comparison to the world: 74
male: 28.96 deaths/1,000 live births
female: 19.87 deaths/1,000 live births (2014 est.)

Life expectancy at birth: *total population:* 76.51 years
country comparison to the world: 78
male: 73.44 years
female: 79.74 years (2014 est.)

Total fertility rate: 2.15 children born/woman (2014 est.)
country comparison to the world: 105

Contraceptive prevalence rate: 67.4% (2011)

Health expenditures: 6% of GDP (2011)
country comparison to the world: 109

Physicians density: 0.62 physicians/1,000 population (2009)

Hospital bed density: 1.1 beds/1,000 population (2009)

Drinking water source:
improved:
urban: 98.2% of population
rural: 60.8% of population
total: 82.1% of population
unimproved:
urban: 1.8% of population
rural: 39.2% of population
total: 17.9% of population (2011 est.)

Sanitation facility access:
improved:
urban: 83.1% of population
rural: 52% of population
total: 69.8% of population
unimproved:
urban: 16.9% of population
rural: 48% of population
total: 30.2% of population (2011 est.)

HIV/AIDS—adult prevalence rate: 0.1% (2012 est.)
country comparison to the world: 162

HIV/AIDS—people living with HIV/AIDS: 30,000 (2012 est.)
country comparison to the world: 71

HIV/AIDS—deaths: 1,200 (2012 est.)
country comparison to the world: 70

Obesity—adult prevalence rate: 16.4% (2008)
country comparison to the world: 114

Children under the age of 5 years underweight: 3.1% (2011)
country comparison to the world: 113

Education expenditures: 5.4% of GDP (2009)
country comparison to the world: 59

Literacy: *definition:* age 15 and over can read and write
total population: 67.1%
male: 76.1%
female: 57.6% (2011 est.)

School life expectancy (primary to tertiary education): *total:* 11 years
male: 12 years
female: 11 years (2010)

Child labor—children ages 5-14: *total number:* 500,960
percentage: 8 % (2007 est.)

Unemployment, youth ages 15-24: *total:* 18.6%
country comparison to the world: 65
male: 18.4%
female: 19.2% (2012)

GOVERNMENT

Country name: *conventional long form:* Kingdom of Morocco
conventional short form: Morocco
local long form: Al Mamlakah al Maghribiyah
local short form: Al Maghrib

Government type: constitutional monarchy

Capital: *name:* Rabat

geographic coordinates: 34 01 N, 6 49 W
time difference: UTC 0 (5 hours ahead of Washington, DC during Standard Time)
daylight saving time: +1 hr, begins last Sunday in April; ends last Sunday in September

Administrative divisions: 15 regions; Grand Casablanca, Chaouia-Ouardigha, Doukkala-Abda, Fes-Boulemane, Gharb-Chrarda-Beni Hssen, Guelmim-Es Smara, Laayoune-Boujdour-Sakia El Hamra, Marrakech-Tensift-Al Haouz, Meknes-Tafilalet, Oriental, Rabat-Sale-Zemmour-Zaer, Souss-Massa-Draa, Tadla-Azilal, Tanger-Tetouan, Taza-Al Hoceima-Taounate
note: Morocco claims the territory of Western Sahara, the political status of which is considered undetermined by the US Government; portions of the regions Guelmim-Es Smara and Laayoune-Boujdour-Sakia El Hamra as claimed by Morocco lie within Western Sahara; Morocco also claims Oued Eddahab-Lagouira, another region that falls entirely within Western Sahara

Independence: 2 March 1956 (from France)

National holiday: Throne Day (accession of King MOHAMMED VI to the throne), 30 July (1999)

Constitution: several previous; latest drafted 17 June 2011, approved by referendum 1 July 2011; note—sources disagree on whether the 2011 referendum was for a new constitution or for reforms to the previous constitution (2011)

Legal system: mixed legal system of civil law based on French law and Islamic law; judicial review of legislative acts by Supreme Court

International law organization participation: has not submitted an ICJ jurisdiction declaration; non-party state to the ICCt

Suffrage: 18 years of age; universal

Executive branch: *chief of state:* King MOHAMMED VI (since 30 July 1999)
head of government: Prime Minister Abdelillah BENKIRANE (since 29 November 2011)
cabinet: Council of Ministers appointed by the prime minister as well as Minister Delegates to each ministry appoined by the Palace (For more information visit the World Leaders website)
elections: the monarchy is hereditary; prime minister appointed by the monarch from the winning party following legislative elections

Legislative branch: bicameral Parliament consists of the Chamber of Counselors or Majlis al-Mustacharin (270 seats—to be reduced to a maximum of 120; members elected indirectly by local councils, professional organizations, and labor syndicates to serve six-year terms; one-third of the members are elected every three years) and Chamber of Representatives or Majlis al-Nuwab (395 seats; members elected by popular vote to serve five-year terms)
elections: Chamber of Counselors—last held on 3 October 2009 (next pending legislation by the 2011 constitution); Chamber of Representatives—last held on 25 November 2011 (next to be held in 2016)
election results: Chamber of Counselors—percent of vote by party—NA; seats by party—NA; Chamber of Representatives—percent of vote by party—NA; seats by party—PJD 107, PI 60, RNI 52, PAM 47, USFP 39, MP 32, UC 23, PPS 18, other 17

Judicial branch: *highest court(s):* Supreme Court or Court of Cassation (consists of 5-judge panels organized into civil, family matters, commercial, administrative, social, and criminal sections)
judge selection and term of office: Supreme Court judges appointed by the monarch upon the recommendation of the Supreme Council of the Judiciary
subordinate courts: courts of appeal; regional and sadad courts (for religious, civil and administrative, and penal adjudication)

Political parties and leaders: Action Party or PA [Mohammed EL IDRISSI]; Al Ahd (The Covenant) Party [Najib EL OUAZZANI]; Alliance des Libert'es (Alliance of Liberties) or ADL [Ali BELHAJ]; An-Nahj Ad-Dimocrati or An-Nahj [Abdellah EL HARIF]; Authenticity and Modernity Party or PAM [Mustapha BAKKOURY, secretary general]; Choura et Istiqlal (Consultation and Independence) Party or PCI [Abdelwahed MAACH]; Citizens' Forces or FC [Abderrahman LAHJOUJI]; Citizenship and Development Initiative or ICD [Mohamed BENHAMOU]; Constitutional Union Party or UC [Mohammed ABIED]; Constitutional Union Party or UC [Mohammed ABIED]; Democratic and Social Movement or MDS [Mahmoud ARCHANE]; Democratic Forces Front or FFD [Touhami EL KHIARI]; Democratic Socialist Vanguard Party or PADS [Ahmed BENJELLOUN]; Democratic Society Party or PSD [Zhor CHEKKAFI]; Democratic Union or UD

[Bouazza IKKEN]; Environment and Development Party or PED [Ahmed EL ALAMI]; Istiqlal (Independence) Party or PI [Hamid CHABAT]; Labor Party or LP [Abdelkrim BENATIK]; Moroccan Liberal Party or PML [Mohamed ZIANE]; National Democratic Party or PND [Abdallah KADIRI]; National Ittihadi Congress Party or CNI [Abdelmajid BOUZOUBAA]; National Popular Movement or MNP [Mahjoubi AHERDANE]; National Rally of Independents or RNI [Salaheddine MEZOUAR]; National Union of Popular Forces or UNFP [Abdellah IBRAHIM]; Party of Justice and Development or PJD [Abdelillah BENKIRANE]; Popular Movement or MP [Mohamed LAENSER]; Progress and Socialism Party or PPS [Nabil BENABDELLAH]; Reform and Development Party or PRD [Abderrahmane EL KOUHEN]; Renaissance and Virtue Party or PRV [Mohamed KHALIDI]; Renewal and Equity Party or PRE [Chakir ACHABAR]; Social Center Party or PSC [Lahcen MADIH]; Socialist Democratic Party or PSD [Aissa OUARDIGHI]; Socialist Union of Popular Forces or USFP [Driss LACHGAR]; Unified Socialist Left Party or PGSU [Mohamed Ben Said AIT IDDER]

Political pressure groups and leaders: Democratic Confederation of Labor or CDT [Noubir AMAOUI]; General Union of Moroccan Workers or UGTM [Abderrazzak AFILAL]; Justice and Charity Organization or JCO; Moroccan Employers Association or CGEM [Hassan CHAMI]; National Labor Union of Morocco or UNMT [Abdelslam MAATI]; Union of Moroccan Workers or UMT [Mahjoub BENSEDDIK]

International organization participation: ABEDA, AfDB, AFESD, AMF, AMU, CAEU, CD, EBRD, FAO, G-11, G-77, IAEA, IBRD, ICAO, ICC (national committees), ICRM, IDA, IDB, IFAD, IFC, IFRCS, IHO, ILO, IMF, IMO, IMSO, Interpol, IOC, IOM, IPU, ISO, ITSO, ITU, ITUC (NGOs), LAS, MIGA, MONUSCO, NAM, OAS (observer), OIC, OIF, OPCW, OSCE (partner), Paris Club (associate), PCA, UN, UN Security Council (temporary), UNCTAD, UNESCO, UNHCR, UNIDO, UNOCI, UNSC (temporary), UNWTO, UPU, WCO, WHO, WIPO, WMO, WTO

Diplomatic representation in the US:
chief of mission: Ambassador Mohammed Rachad BOUHLAL (since 22 December 2011)
chancery: 1601 21st Street NW, Washington, DC 20009
telephone: [1] (202) 462-7979
FAX: [1] (202) 462-7643
consulate(s) general: New York

Diplomatic representation from the US:
chief of mission: Ambassador (vacant); Charge d'Affaires Matthew LUSSENHOP (since July 2013)
embassy: 2 Avenue de Mohamed El Fassi, Rabat
mailing address: Unit 9400, Box 021, DPO AE 09718
telephone: [212] (537) 76 22 65
FAX: [212] (537) 76 56 61
consulate(s) general: Casablanca

Flag description: red with a green pentacle (five-pointed, linear star) known as Sulayman's (Solomon's) seal in the center of the flag; red and green are traditional colors in Arab flags, although the use of red is more commonly associated with the Arab states of the Persian gulf; the pentacle represents the five pillars of Islam and signifies the association between God and the nation; design dates to 1912

National symbol(s): pentacle symbol; lion

National anthem: *name:* "Hymne Cherifien" (Hymn of the Sharif)
lyrics/music: Ali Squalli HOUSSAINI/Leo MORGAN
note: music adopted 1956, lyrics adopted 1970

ECONOMY

Economy—overview: Morocco has capitalized on its proximity to Europe and relatively low labor costs to build a diverse, open, market-oriented economy. In the 1980s Morocco was a heavily indebted country before pursuing austerity measures and pro-market reforms, overseen by the IMF. Since taking the throne in 1999, King MOHAMMED VI has presided over a stable economy marked by steady growth, low inflation, and gradually falling unemployment, although a poor harvest and economic difficulties in Europe contributed to an economic slowdown in 2012. Industrial development strategies and infrastructure improvements—most visibly illustrated by a new port and free trade zone near Tangier—are improving Morocco's competitiveness. Morocco also seeks to expand its renewable energy capacity with a goal of making renewable 40% of electricity output by 2020. Key sectors of the economy include agriculture, tourism, phosphates, textiles, apparel, and subcomponents. To boost exports, Morocco entered into a bilateral Free Trade Agreement with the United States in 2006 and an Advanced Status agreement with the European Union in 2008. Despite Morocco's economic progress, the country suffers from high unemployment, poverty, and illiteracy, particularly in rural areas. In 2011 and 2012, high prices on fuel—which is subsidized and almost entirely imported—strained the government's budget and widened the country's current account deficit. In the fall of 2013, Morocco capped some of its fuel subsidies in an effort to gradually reduce the country's large budgetary deficit. Key economic challenges for Morocco include fighting corruption and reforming the education system, the judiciary, and the government's costly subsidy program.

GDP (purchasing power parity): $180 billion (2013 est.)
country comparison to the world: 60
$171.2 billion (2012 est.)
$166.7 billion (2011 est.)
note: data are in 2013 US dollars

GDP (official exchange rate): $104.8 billion (2013 est.)

GDP—real growth rate: 5.1% (2013 est.)
country comparison to the world: 53
2.7% (2012 est.)
5% (2011 est.)

GDP—per capita (PPP): $5,500 (2013 est.)
country comparison to the world: 155
$5,300 (2012 est.)
$5,200 (2011 est.)
note: data are in 2013 US dollars

Gross national saving: 25.4% of GDP (2013 est.)
country comparison to the world: 48
25.1% of GDP (2012 est.)
27.6% of GDP (2011 est.)

GDP—composition, by end use:
household consumption: 59.5%
government consumption: 19.1%
investment in fixed capital: 30.8%
investment in inventories: 3.7%
exports of goods and services: 35.4%
imports of goods and services: -48.5% (2013 est.)

GDP—composition, by sector of origin:
agriculture: 15.1%
industry: 31.7%
services: 53.2% (2012 est.)

Agriculture—products: barley, wheat, citrus fruits, grapes, vegetables, olives; livestock; wine

Industries: phosphate rock mining and processing, food processing, leather goods, textiles, construction, energy, tourism

Industrial production growth rate: 1.2% (2013 est.)
country comparison to the world: 142

Labor force: 11.73 million (2013 est.)
country comparison to the world: 46

Labor force—by occupation: *agriculture:* 44.6%
industry: 19.8%
services: 35.5% (2006 est.)

Unemployment rate: 9.5% (2013 est.)
country comparison to the world: 103
9% (2012 est.)

Population below poverty line: 15% (2007 est.)

Household income or consumption by percentage share: *lowest 10%:* 2.7%
highest 10%: 33.2% (2007)

Distribution of family income—Gini index: 40.9 (2007 est.)
country comparison to the world: 54
39.5 (1999 est.)

Budget: *revenues:* $26.07 billion
expenditures: $34.51 billion (2013 est.)

Taxes and other revenues: 24.9% of GDP (2013 est.)
country comparison to the world: 131

Budget surplus (+) or deficit (-):
-8% of GDP (2013 est.)
country comparison to the world: 196

Public debt: 76.9% of GDP (2013 est.)
country comparison to the world: 31
71.2% of GDP (2012 est.)

Fiscal year: calendar year

Inflation rate (consumer prices): 2.5% (2013 est.)
country comparison to the world: 93
1.2% (2012 est.)

Central bank discount rate: 6.5% (31 December 2010 est.)
country comparison to the world: 100
3.31% (31 December 2009 est.)

Commercial bank prime lending rate: 6.3% (31 December 2013 est.)
country comparison to the world: 134
6.3% (31 December 2012 est.)

Stock of narrow money: $75.71 billion (31 December 2013 est.)
country comparison to the world: 42
$71.51 billion (31 December 2012 est.)

Stock of broad money: $90.76 billion (31 December 2013 est.)
country comparison to the world: 57
$84.52 billion (31 December 2012 est.)

Stock of domestic credit: $121 billion (31 December 2013 est.)
country comparison to the world: 50
$111.6 billion (31 December 2012 est.)

Market value of publicly traded shares: $52.63 billion (31 December 2012 est.)
country comparison to the world: 48
$60.09 billion (31 December 2011)
$69.15 billion (31 December 2010 est.)

Current account balance: -$9.595 billion (2013 est.)
country comparison to the world: 176
-$9.843 billion (2012 est.)

Exports: $16.78 billion (2013 est.)
country comparison to the world: 76
$16.99 billion (2012 est.)

Exports—commodities: clothing and textiles, electric components, inorganic chemicals, transistors, crude minerals, fertilizers (including phosphates), petroleum products, citrus fruits, vegetables, fish

Exports—partners: France 21%, Spain 17.3%, Brazil 5.4%, India 4.9%, US 4.6% (2012)

Imports: $38.66 billion (2013 est.)
country comparison to the world: 62
$38.88 billion (2012 est.)

Imports—commodities: crude petroleum, textile fabric, telecommunications equipment, wheat, gas and electricity, transistors, plastics

Imports—partners: Spain 13.1%, France 12.1%, China 6.9%, US 6.8%, Saudi Arabia 6.2%, Italy 5.1%, Russia 5%, Germany 4.9% (2012)

Reserves of foreign exchange and gold: $19.16 billion (31 December 2013 est.)
country comparison to the world: 61
$17.54 billion (31 December 2012 est.)

Debt—external: $36.51 billion (31 December 2013 est.)
country comparison to the world: 68
$32.15 billion (31 December 2012 est.)

Stock of direct foreign investment—at home: $51.82 billion (31 December 2013 est.)
country comparison to the world: 54
$48.18 billion (31 December 2012 est.)

Stock of direct foreign investment—abroad: $1.972 billion (31 December 2013 est.)
country comparison to the world: 73
$2.423 billion (31 December 2012 est.)

Exchange rates: Moroccan dirhams (MAD) per US dollar—
8.439 (2013 est.)
8.6026 (2012 est.)
8.4172 (2010 est.)
8.0571 (2009)
7.526 (2008)

ENERGY

Electricity—production: 21.13 billion kWh (2010 est.)
country comparison to the world: 7 1

Electricity—consumption: 23.61 billion kWh (2010 est.)
country comparison to the world: 67

Electricity—exports: 0 kWh (2012 est.)
country comparison to the world: 167

Electricity—imports: 3.94 billion kWh (2010 est.)
country comparison to the world: 41

Electricity—installed generating capacity: 6.62 million kW (2010 est.)
country comparison to the world: 69

Electricity—from fossil fuels: 69.3% of total installed capacity (2010 est.)
country comparison to the world: 109

Electricity—from nuclear fuels: 0% of total installed capacity (2010 est.)
country comparison to the world: 139

Electricity—from hydroelectric plants: 19.4% of total installed capacity (2010 est.)
country comparison to the world: 93

Electricity—from other renewable sources: 4.3% of total installed capacity (2010 est.)
country comparison to the world: 47

Crude oil—production: 5,057 bbl/day (2012 est.)
country comparison to the world: 99

Crude oil—exports: 0 bbl/day (2010 est.)
country comparison to the world: 154

Crude oil—imports: 122,900 bbl/day (2010 est.)
country comparison to the world: 45

Crude oil—proved reserves: 680,000 bbl (1 January 2013 es)
country comparison to the world: 98

Refined petroleum products—production: 131,500 bbl/day (2010 est.)
country comparison to the world: 67

Refined petroleum products—consumption: 203,600 bbl/day (2011 est.)
country comparison to the world: 58

Refined petroleum products—exports: 20,830 bbl/day (2010 est.)
country comparison to the world: 72

Refined petroleum products—imports: 143,000 bbl/day (2010 est.)
country comparison to the world: 40

Natural gas—production: 60 million cu m (2011 est.)
country comparison to the world: 86

Natural gas—consumption: 560 million cu m (2010 est.)
country comparison to the world: 97

Natural gas—exports: 0 cu m (2011 est.)
country comparison to the world: 148

Natural gas—imports: 150 million cu m (2011 est.)
country comparison to the world: 73

Natural gas—proved reserves: 1.444 billion cu m (1 January 2013 es)
country comparison to the world: 101

Carbon dioxide emissions from consumption of energy: 43.71 million Mt (2011 est.)
country comparison to the world: 68

COMMUNICATIONS

Telephones—main lines in use: 3.28 million (2012)
country comparison to the world: 4 7

Telephones—mobile cellular: 39.016 million (2012)
country comparison to the world: 31

Telephone system: *general assessment:* good system composed of open-wire lines, cables, and microwave radio relay links; principal switching centers are Casablanca and Rabat; national network nearly 100% digital using fiber-optic links; improved rural service employs microwave radio relay; Internet available but expensive
domestic: fixed-line teledensity is roughly 10 per 100 persons; mobile-cellular subscribership exceeds 100 per 100 persons
international: country code—212; landing point for the Atlas Offshore, Estepona-Tetouan, Euroafrica, Spain-Morocco, and SEA-ME-WE-3 fiber-optic telecommunications undersea cables that provide connectivity to Asia, the Middle East, and Europe; satellite earth stations—2 Intelsat (Atlantic Ocean) and 1 Arabsat; microwave radio relay to Gibraltar, Spain, and Western Sahara; coaxial cable and microwave radio relay to Algeria; participant in Medarabtel; fiber-optic cable link from Agadir to Algeria and Tunisia (2011)

Broadcast media: 2 TV broadcast networks with state-run Radio-Television Marocaine (RTM) operating one network and the state partially owning the other; foreign TV broadcasts are available via satellite dish; 3 radio broadcast networks with RTM operating one; the government-owned network includes 10 regional radio channels in addition to its national service (2007)

Internet country code: .ma

Internet hosts: 277,338 (2012)
country comparison to the world: 66

Internet users: 13.213 million (2009)
country comparison to the world: 29

TRANSPORTATION

Airports: 55 (2013)
country comparison to the world: 8 6

Airports—with paved runways: *total:* 3 1
over 3,047 m: 11
2,438 to 3,047 m: 9
1,524 to 2,437 m: 7
914 to 1,523 m: 4 (2013)

Airports—with unpaved runways: *total:* 2 4
2,438 to 3,047 m: 1
1,524 to 2,437 m: 7
914 to 1,523 m: 11
under 914 m: 5 (2013)

Heliports: 1 (2013)

Pipelines: gas 944 km; oil 270 km; refined products 175 km (2013)

Railways: *total:* 2,067 km
country comparison to the world: 70
standard gauge: 2,067 km 1.435-m gauge (1,022 km electrified) (2008)

Roadways: *total:* 58,395 km
country comparison to the world: 74
paved: 41,116 km (includes 1,080 km of expressways)
unpaved: 17,279 km (2010)

Merchant marine: *total:* 2 6
country comparison to the world: 88
by type: cargo 1, chemical tanker 3, container 6, passenger/cargo 14, roll on/roll off 2
foreign-owned: 14 (France 3, Germany 1, Italy 1, Spain 9)
registered in other countries: 4 (Gibraltar 4) (2010)

Ports and terminals: *major seaport(s):* Casablanca, Jorf Lasfar, Mohammedia, Safi, Tangier
container port(s) (TEUs): Tangier (2,093,408)

MILITARY

Military branches: Royal Armed Forces (Forces Armees Royales, FAR): Royal Moroccan Army (includes Air Defense), Royal Moroccan Navy (includes Coast Guard, Marines), Royal Moroccan Air Force (Al Quwwat al Jawyiya al Malakiya Marakishiya; Force Aerienne Royale Marocaine) (2010)

Military service age and obligation: 20 years of age for voluntary military service; no conscription; service obligation—18 months (2012)

Manpower available for military service:
males age 16-49: 8,252,682
females age 16-49: 8,691,419 (2010 est.)

Manpower fit for military service:
males age 16-49: 7,026,016
females age 16-49: 7,377,045 (2010 est.)

Manpower reaching militarily significant age annually: *male:* 300,327
female: 298,366 (2010 est.)

Military expenditures: 3.55% of GDP (2012)
country comparison to the world: 14
3.37% of GDP (2011)
3.55% of GDP (2010)

TRANSNATIONAL ISSUES

Disputes—international: claims and administers Western Sahara whose sovereignty remains unresolved; Morocco protests Spain's control over the coastal enclaves of Ceuta, Melilla, and Penon de Velez de la Gomera, the islands of Penon de Alhucemas and Islas Chafarinas, and surrounding waters; both countries claim Isla Perejil (Leila Island); discussions have not progressed on a comprehensive maritime delimitation, setting limits on resource exploration and refugee interdiction, since Morocco's 2002 rejection of Spain's unilateral designation of a median line from the Canary Islands; Morocco serves as one of the primary launching areas of illegal migration into Spain from North Africa; Algeria's border with

Morocco remains an irritant to bilateral relations, each nation accusing the other of harboring militants and arms smuggling; the National Liberation Front's assertions of a claim to Chirac Pastures in southeastern Morocco is a dormant dispute

Trafficking in persons: *current situation:* Morocco is a source, destination, and transit country for men, women, and children who are subjected to forced labor and sex trafficking; Moroccan adults and children are exploited for forced labor and forced prostitution in the Middle East and Europe; some Moroccan girls recruited to work as maids experience conditions of forced labor, while some Moroccan boys are forced to work as apprentices in the artisan and construction industries and in mechanic shops; women and children from sub-Saharan Africa and South Asia who voluntarily enter Morocco are subsequently coerced into prostitution or, less frequently, domestic service; women and children from Cote d'Ivoire, the Democratic Republic of the Congo, and Nigeria are also vulnerable to sex trafficking and, to a lesser extent, forced labor in Morocco
tier rating: Tier 2 Watch List—Morocco does not comply with the minimum standards for the elimination of trafficking; however, it is making significant efforts to do so; the government does not demonstrate progress in investigating, prosecuting, convicting, and adequately punishing trafficking offenders and has failed to provide law enforcement data; it has not developed or employed systematic procedures to proactively identify trafficking victims among vulnerable groups, particularly the sub-Saharan migrant community, but has made some efforts to offer protective services to Moroccan women and child trafficking victims; Morocco continues to lack a single comprehensive anti-trafficking law (2013)

Illicit drugs: one of the world's largest producers of illicit hashish; shipments of hashish mostly directed to Western Europe; transit point for cocaine from South America destined for Western Europe; significant consumer of cannabis

MOZAMBIQUE

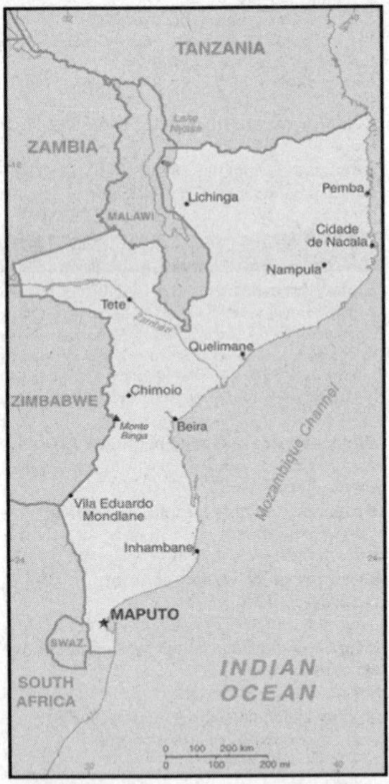

INTRODUCTION

Background: Almost five centuries as a Portuguese colony came to a close with independence in 1975. Large-scale emigration, economic dependence on South Africa, a severe drought, and a prolonged civil war hindered the country's development until the mid 1990s. The ruling Front for the Liberation of Mozambique (Frelimo) party formally abandoned Marxism in 1989, and a new constitution the following year provided for multiparty elections and a free market economy. A UN-negotiated peace agreement between Frelimo and rebel Mozambique National Resistance (Renamo) forces ended the fighting in 1992. In December 2004, Mozambique underwent a delicate transition as Joaquim CHISSANO stepped down after 18 years in office. His elected successor, Armando Emilio GUEBUZA, promised to continue the sound economic policies that have encouraged foreign investment. President GUEBUZA was reelected to a second term in October 2009. However, the elections were flawed by voter fraud, questionable disqualification of candidates, and Frelimo use of government resources during the campaign. As a result, Freedom House removed Mozambique from its list of electoral democracies.

GEOGRAPHY

Location: Southeastern Africa, bordering the Mozambique Channel, between South Africa and Tanzania

Geographic coordinates: 18 15 S, 35 00 E

Map references: Africa

Area: *total:* 799,380 sq km
country comparison to the world: 35
land: 786,380 sq km
water: 13,000 sq km

Area—comparative: slightly less than twice the size of California

Land boundaries: *total:* 4,571 km
border countries: Malawi 1,569 km, South Africa 491 km, Swaziland 105 km, Tanzania 756 km, Zambia 419 km, Zimbabwe 1,231 km

Coastline: 2,470 km

Maritime claims: *territorial sea:* 12 nm
exclusive economic zone: 200 nm

Climate: tropical to subtropical

Terrain: mostly coastal lowlands, uplands in center, high plateaus in northwest, mountains in west

Elevation extremes: *lowest point:* Indian Ocean 0 m
highest point: Monte Binga 2,436 m

Natural resources: coal, titanium, natural gas, hydropower, tantalum, graphite

Land use: *arable land:* 6.51%
permanent crops: 0.25%
other: 93.24% (2011)

Irrigated land: 1,181 sq km (2003)

Total renewable water resources: 217.1 cu km (2011)

Freshwater withdrawal (domestic/industrial/agricultural): *total:* 0.88 cu km/yr (26%/4%/70%)
per capita: 46.05 cu m/yr (2005)

Natural hazards: severe droughts; devastating cyclones and floods in central and southern provinces

Environment—current issues: a long civil war and recurrent drought in the hinterlands have resulted in increased migration of the population to urban and coastal areas with adverse environmental consequences; desertification; pollution of surface and coastal waters; elephant poaching for ivory is a problem

Environment—international agreements:
party to: Biodiversity, Climate Change, Climate Change-Kyoto Protocol, Desertification, Endangered Species, Hazardous Wastes, Law of the Sea, Ozone Layer Protection, Ship Pollution, Wetlands
signed, but not ratified: none of the selected agreements

Geography—note: the Zambezi flows through the north-central and most fertile part of the country

PEOPLE AND SOCIETY

Nationality: *noun:* Mozambican(s)
adjective: Mozambican

Ethnic groups: African 99.66% (Makhuwa, Tsonga, Lomwe, Sena, and others), Europeans 0.06%, Euro-Africans 0.2%, Indians 0.08%

Languages: Emakhuwa 25.3%, Portuguese (official) 10.7%, Xichangana 10.3%, Cisena 7.5%, Elomwe 7%, Echuwabo 5.1%, other Mozambican languages 30.1%, other 4% (1997 census)

Religions: Roman Catholic 28.4%, Muslim 17.9%, Zionist Christian 15.5%, Protestant 12.2% (includes Pentecostal 10.9% and Anglican 1.3%), other 6.7%, none 18.7%, unspecified 0.7% (2007 est.)

Population: 24,692,144 (July 2014 est.)
country comparison to the world: 51
note: estimates for this country explicitly take into account the effects of excess mortality due to AIDS; this can result in lower life expectancy, higher infant mortality, higher death rates, lower population growth rates, and changes in the distribution of population by age and sex than would otherwise be expected

Age structure: *0-14 years:* 45.3% (male 5,627,116/female 5,566,260)
15-24 years: 21.3% (male 2,566,298/female 2,689,695)

25-54 years: 27% (male 3,113,095/female 3,553,266)
55-64 years: 2.9% (male 404,988/female 448,814)
65 years and over: 2.9% (male 332,013/female 390,599) (2014 est.)
Dependency ratios:
total dependency ratio: 94.8 %
youth dependency ratio: 88.4 %
elderly dependency ratio: 6.4 %
potential support ratio: 15.6 (2013)

Median age: *total:* 16.9 years
male: 16.3 years
female: 17.5 years (2014 est.)

Population growth rate: 2.45% (2014 est.)
country comparison to the world: 34

Birth rate: 38.83 births/1,000 population (2014 est.)
country comparison to the world: 11

Death rate: 12.34 deaths/1,000 population (2014 est.)
country comparison to the world: 25

Net migration rate: -2.02 migrant(s)/1,000 population (2014 est.)
country comparison to the world: 167

Urbanization: *urban population:* 31.2% of total population (2011)
rate of urbanization: 3.05% annual rate of change (2010-15 est.)

Major urban areas—population: MAPUTO (capital) 1.589 million; Matola 761,000 (2009)

Sex ratio: *at birth:* 1.02 male(s)/female
0-14 years: 1.01 male(s)/female
15-24 years: 0.95 male(s)/female
25-54 years: 0.88 male(s)/female
55-64 years: 0.95 male(s)/female
65 years and over: 0.85 male(s)/female
total population: 0.95 male(s)/female (2014 est.)

Mother's mean age at first birth: 18.8 (2003 est.)

Maternal mortality rate: 490 deaths/100,000 live births (2010)
country comparison to the world: 20

Infant mortality rate: *total:* 72.42 deaths/1,000 live births
country comparison to the world: 13
male: 74.53 deaths/1,000 live births
female: 70.26 deaths/1,000 live births (2014 est.)

Life expectancy at birth: *total population:* 52.6 years
country comparison to the world: 213
male: 51.85 years
female: 53.37 years (2014 est.)

Total fertility rate: 5.27 children born/woman (2014 est.)
country comparison to the world: 12

Contraceptive prevalence rate: 11.6% (2011)

Health expenditures: 6.6% of GDP (2011)
country comparison to the world: 95

Physicians density: 0.03 physicians/1,000 population (2008)

Hospital bed density: 0.7 beds/1,000 population (2011)

Drinking water source:
improved:
urban: 78% of population
rural: 33.2% of population
total: 47.2% of population
unimproved:
urban: 22% of population
rural: 66.8% of population
total: 52.8% of population (2011 est.)

Sanitation facility access:
improved:
urban: 40.9% of population
rural: 9.2% of population
total: 19.1% of population
unimproved:
urban: 59.1% of population
rural: 90.8% of population
total: 80.9% of population (2011 est.)

HIV/AIDS—adult prevalence rate: 11.1% (2012 est.)
country comparison to the world: 8

HIV/AIDS—people living with HIV/AIDS: 1,554,700 (2012 est.)
country comparison to the world: 5

HIV/AIDS—deaths: 76,800 (2012 est.)
country comparison to the world: 5

Major infectious diseases: *degree of risk:* very high
food or waterborne diseases: bacterial and protozoal diarrhea, hepatitis A, and typhoid fever
vectorborne diseases: malaria and dengue fever
water contact disease: schistosomiasis
animal contact disease: rabies (2013)

Obesity—adult prevalence rate: 4.9% (2008)
country comparison to the world: 158

Children under the age of 5 years underweight: 15.6% (2011)
country comparison to the world: 46

Education expenditures: 5% of GDP (2006)
country comparison to the world: 78

Literacy: *definition:* age 15 and over can read and write
total population: 56.1%
male: 70.8%
female: 42.8% (2010 est.)

School life expectancy (primary to tertiary education): *total:* 10 years
male: 10 years
female: 9 years (2011)

Child labor—children ages 5-14: *total number:* 1,369,080
percentage: 22 % (2008 est.)

GOVERNMENT

Country name: *conventional long form:* Republic of Mozambique
conventional short form: Mozambique
local long form: Republica de Mocambique
local short form: Mocambique
former: Portuguese East Africa

Government type: republic

Capital: *name:* Maputo

geographic coordinates: 25 57 S, 32 35 E
time difference: UTC+2 (7 hours ahead of Washington, DC during Standard Time)

Administrative divisions: 10 provinces (provincias, singular—provincia), 1 city (cidade)*; Cabo Delgado, Gaza, Inhambane, Manica, Maputo, Cidade de Maputo*, Nampula, Niassa, Sofala, Tete, Zambezia

Independence: 25 June 1975 (from Portugal)

National holiday: Independence Day, 25 June (1975)

Constitution: previous 1975, 1990; latest adopted 16 November 2004, effective 21 December 2004; note—draft amendments planned for parliamentary review in late 2013 (2013)

Legal system: mixed legal system of Portuguese civil law, Islamic law, and customary law

International law organization participation: has not submitted an ICJ jurisdiction declaration; non-party state to the ICCt

Suffrage: 18 years of age; universal

Executive branch: *chief of state:* President Armando Emilio GUEBUZA (since 2 February 2005)
head of government: Prime Minister Alberto Clementino Antonio VAQUINA (since 8 October 2012)
cabinet: Cabinet (For more information visit the World Leaders website)
elections: president elected by popular vote for a five-year term (eligible for three terms); election last held on 28 October 2009 (next to be held in 2014); prime minister appointed by the president
election results: Armando GUEBUZA reelected president; percent of vote—Armando GUEBUZA 76.3%, Afonso DHLAKAMA 14.9%, Daviz SIMANGO 8.8%

Legislative branch: unicameral Assembly of the Republic or Assembleia da Republica (250 seats; members directly elected by popular vote to serve five-year terms)
elections: last held on 28 October 2009 (next to be held in 2014)
election results: percent of vote by party—FRELIMO 74.7%, RENAMO 17.7%, MDM 3.9%, other 3.7%; seats by party—FRELIMO 191, RENAMO 51, MDM 8

Judicial branch: *highest court(s):* Supreme Court (consists of the court president, vice president, and 5 judges); Constitutional Council (consists of 7 judges) note—the Higher Council of the Judiciary is responsible for judiciary management and discipline
judge selection and term of office: Supreme Court president and vice president appointed by Mozambique president in consultation with the Higher Council of the Judiciary (CSMJ) and with ratification by the legislature; other judges elected by the legislature; judges serve 5-year renewable terms; Constitutional Council judges appointed—1 by the president, 5 by the legislature, and 1 by the CSMJ; judges serve 5-year nonrenewable terms
subordinate courts: Administrative Court (capital city only); provincial courts or Tribunais Judicias de Provincia; District Courts or Tribunais Judicias de Districto; customs courts; maritime courts; courts marshal; labor courts; community courts

Political parties and leaders: Democratic Movement of Mozambique (Movimento Democratico de Mocambique) or MDM [Daviz SIMANGO]; Front for the Liberation of Mozambique (Frente de Libertacao de Mocambique) or FRELIMO [Armando Emilio; GUEBUZA]; Mozambique National Resistance (Resistencia Nacional Mocambicana) or RENAMO [Afonso DHLAKAMA]

Political pressure groups and leaders: Mozambican League of Human Rights (Liga Mocambicana dos Direitos Humanos) or LDH [Alice MABOTE, president]

International organization participation: ACP, AfDB, AU, C, CD, CPLP, EITI (compliant country), FAO, G-77, IAEA, IBRD, ICAO, ICC (NGOs), ICRM, IDA, IDB, IFAD, IFC, IFRCS, IHO, ILO, IMF, IMO, IMSO, Interpol, IOC, IOM, IPU, ISO (correspondent), ITSO, ITU, ITUC

(NGOs), MIGA, NAM, OIC, OIF (observer), OPCW, SADC, UN, UNCTAD, UNESCO, UNHCR, UNIDO, Union Latina, UNISFA, UNWTO, UPU, WCO, WFTU (NGOs), WHO, WIPO, WMO, WTO

Diplomatic representation in the US:
chief of mission: Ambassador Amelia Narciso Matos SUMBANA (since 2 November 2009)
chancery: 1525 New Hampshire Avenue NW, Washington, DC 20036
telephone: [1] (202) 293-7146
FAX: [1] (202) 835-0245

Diplomatic representation from the US:
chief of mission: Ambassador Douglas M. GRIFFITHS (since 6 July 2012)
embassy: Avenida Kenneth Kuanda 193, Maputo
mailing address: P. O. Box 783, Maputo
telephone: [258] (21) 492797
FAX: [258] (21) 490114

Flag description: three equal horizontal bands of green (top), black, and yellow with a red isosceles triangle based on the hoist side; the black band is edged in white; centered in the triangle is a yellow five-pointed star bearing a crossed rifle and hoe in black superimposed on an open white book; green represents the riches of the land, white peace, black the African continent, yellow the country's minerals, and red the struggle for independence; the rifle symbolizes defense and vigilance, the hoe refers to the country's agriculture, the open book stresses the importance of education, and the star represents Marxism and internationalism

National anthem: *name:* "Patria Amada" (Lovely Fatherland)
lyrics/music: Salomao J. MANHICA/unknown
note: adopted 2002

ECONOMY

Economy—overview: At independence in 1975, Mozambique was one of the world's poorest countries. Socialist mismanagement and a brutal civil war from 1977-92 exacerbated the situation. In 1987, the government embarked on a series of macroeconomic reforms designed to stabilize the economy. These steps, combined with donor assistance and with political stability since the multi-party elections in 1994, have led to dramatic improvements in the country's growth rate. Fiscal reforms, including the introduction of a value-added tax and reform of the customs service, have improved the government's revenue collection abilities. In spite of these gains, Mozambique remained dependent upon foreign assistance for 40% of its 2012 annual budget and over half the population remained below the poverty line. Subsistence agriculture continues to employ the vast majority of the country's work force and smallholder agricultural productivity and productivity growth is weak. A substantial trade imbalance persists although aluminum production from the Mozal smelter has significantly boosted export earnings in recent years. In 2012, The Mozambican government took over Portugal's last remaining share in the Cahora Bassa Hydroelectricity Company (HCB), a significant contributor to the Southern African Power Pool. The government has plans to expand the Cahora Bassa Dam and build additional dams to increase its electricity exports and fulfill the needs of its burgeoning domestic industries. Mozambique's once substantial foreign debt has been reduced through forgiveness and rescheduling under the IMF's Heavily Indebted Poor Countries (HIPC) and Enhanced HIPC initiatives, and is now at a manageable level. In July 2007, the US government's Millennium Challenge Corporation (MCC) signed a $506.9 million Compact with Mozambique. Compact projects will end in September 2013 and are focusing on improving sanitation, roads, agriculture, and the business regulation environment in an effort to spur economic growth in the four northern provinces of the country. Citizens rioted in September 2010, after fuel, water, electricity, and bread price increases were announced. In an attempt to lessen the negative impact on people, the government implemented subsidies, decreased taxes and tariffs, and instituted other fiscal measures. Mozambique grew at an average annual rate of 6%-8% in the decade up to 2013, one of Africa's strongest performances. Mozambique's ability to attract large investment projects in natural resources is expected to fuel continued high growth in coming years. Revenues from these vast resources, including natural gas, coal, titanium and hydroelectric capacity, could overtake donor assistance within five years.

GDP (purchasing power parity): $28.15 billion (2013 est.)
country comparison to the world: 116
$26.31 billion (2012 est.)
$24.49 billion (2011 est.)
note: data are in 2013 US dollars

GDP (official exchange rate): $14.67 billion (2013 est.)

GDP—real growth rate: 7% (2013 est.)
country comparison to the world: 19
7.4% (2012 est.)
7.3% (2011 est.)

GDP—per capita (PPP): $1,200 (2013 est.)
country comparison to the world: 214
$1,200 (2012 est.)
$1,100 (2011 est.)
note: data are in 2013 US dollars

Gross national saving: -5.6% of GDP (2013 est.)
country comparison to the world: 156
-4.6% of GDP (2012 est.)
0.8% of GDP (2011 est.)

GDP—composition, by end use:
household consumption: 71.4%
government consumption: 16.9%
investment in fixed capital: 33.8%
investment in inventories: -1.6%
exports of goods and services: 30%
imports of goods and services: -50.5% (2013 est.)

GDP—composition, by sector of origin:
agriculture: 28.7%
industry: 24.9%
services: 46.4% (2013 est.)

Agriculture—products: cotton, cashew nuts, sugarcane, tea, cassava (tapioca), corn, coconuts, sisal, citrus and tropical fruits, potatoes, sunflowers; beef, poultry

Industries: aluminum, petroleum products, chemicals (fertilizer, soap, paints), textiles, cement, glass, asbestos, tobacco, food, beverages

Industrial production growth rate: 8% (2013 est.)
country comparison to the world: 27

Labor force: 10.55 million (2013 est.)
country comparison to the world: 49

Labor force—by occupation: *agriculture:* 81%
industry: 6%
services: 13% (1997 est.)

Unemployment rate: 17% (2007 est.)
country comparison to the world: 150
21% (1997 est.)

Population below poverty line: 52% (2009 est.)

Household income or consumption by percentage share: *lowest 10%:* 1.9%
highest 10%: 36.7% (2008)

Distribution of family income—Gini index: 45.6 (2008)
country comparison to the world: 37
47.3 (2002)

Budget: *revenues:* $4.808 billion
expenditures: $6.101 billion (2013 est.)

Taxes and other revenues: 32.8% of GDP (2013 est.)
country comparison to the world: 74

Budget surplus (+) or deficit (-):
-8.8% of GDP (2013 est.)
country comparison to the world: 201

Public debt: 46.7% of GDP (2013 est.)
country comparison to the world: 77
42.2% of GDP (2012 est.)

Fiscal year: calendar year

Inflation rate (consumer prices): 4.4% (2013 est.)
country comparison to the world: 143
2.1% (2012 est.)

Central bank discount rate: 9.5% (17 January 2013 est.)
country comparison to the world: 101
3.25% (31 December 2010 est.)

Commercial bank prime lending rate: 15.6% (31 December 2013 est.)
country comparison to the world: 32
16.81% (31 December 2012 est.)

Stock of narrow money: $4.665 billion (31 December 2013 est.)
country comparison to the world: 103
$4.335 billion (31 December 2012 est.)

Stock of broad money: $6.856 billion (31 December 2013 est.)
country comparison to the world: 116
$6.242 billion (31 December 2012 est.)

Stock of domestic credit: $4.438 billion (31 December 2013 est.)
country comparison to the world: 118
$3.951 billion (31 December 2012 est.)

Market value of publicly traded shares: $NA

Current account balance: -$5.884 billion (2013 est.)
country comparison to the world: 171
-$5.168 billion (2012 est.)

Exports: $3.92 billion (2013 est.)
country comparison to the world: 123
$3.47 billion (2012 est.)

Exports—commodities: aluminum, prawns, cashews, cotton, sugar, citrus, timber; bulk electricity

Exports—partners: South Africa 31.3%, Belgium 12.8%, China 9%, Italy 7.9%, Spain 6.2%, India 5.8% (2012)

Imports: $7.068 billion (2013 est.)
country comparison to the world: 113
$6.168 billion (2012 est.)

Imports—commodities: machinery and equipment, vehicles, fuel, chemicals, metal products, foodstuffs, textiles

Imports—partners: South Africa 30.5%, China 12.3%, India 11.6%, US 5.1%, Portugal 4.8%, Australia 4.5% (2012)

Reserves of foreign exchange and gold: $2.99 billion (31 December 2013 est.)
country comparison to the world: 107
$2.77 billion (31 December 2012 est.)

Debt—external: $6.276 billion (31 December 2013 est.)
country comparison to the world: 114
$4.7 billion (31 December 2012 est.)

Exchange rates: meticais (MZM) per US dollar—
30 (2013 est.)
28.383 (2012 est.)
33.96 (2010 est.)
26.28 (2009)
24.125 (2008)

ENERGY

Electricity—production: 14.83 billion kWh (2012 est.)
country comparison to the world: 83

Electricity—consumption: 10.19 billion kWh (2012 est.)
country comparison to the world: 89

Electricity—exports: 9.462 billion kWh (2012 est.)
country comparison to the world: 21

Electricity—imports: 8.537 billion kWh (2012 est.)
country comparison to the world: 26

Electricity—installed generating capacity: 2.428 million kW (2010 est.)
country comparison to the world: 96

Electricity—from fossil fuels: 0.1% of total installed capacity (2012 est.)
country comparison to the world: 209

Electricity—from nuclear fuels: 0% of total installed capacity (2012 est.)
country comparison to the world: 146

Electricity—from hydroelectric plants: 99.9% of total installed capacity (2012 est.)
country comparison to the world: 2

Electricity—from other renewable sources: 0% of total installed capacity (2012 est.)
country comparison to the world: 206

Crude oil—production: 20 bbl/day (2012 est.)
country comparison to the world: 128

Crude oil—exports: 0 bbl/day (2010 est.)
country comparison to the world: 158

Crude oil—imports: 0 bbl/day (2010 est.)
country comparison to the world: 99

Crude oil—proved reserves: 0 bbl (1 January 2013 es)
country comparison to the world: 168

Refined petroleum products—production: 991.6 bbl/day (2010 est.)
country comparison to the world: 111

Refined petroleum products—consumption: 19,580 bbl/day (2011 est.)
country comparison to the world: 128

Refined petroleum products—exports: 953.4 bbl/day (2010 est.)
country comparison to the world: 107

Refined petroleum products—imports: 16,140 bbl/day (2010 est.)
country comparison to the world: 116

Natural gas—production: 3.82 billion cu m (2011 est.)
country comparison to the world: 55

Natural gas—consumption: 80 million cu m (2010 est.)
country comparison to the world: 107

Natural gas—exports: 3.3 billion cu m (2011 est.)
country comparison to the world: 38

Natural gas—imports: 0 cu m (2011 est.)
country comparison to the world: 101

Natural gas—proved reserves: 127.4 billion cu m (1 January 2013 es)
country comparison to the world: 51

Carbon dioxide emissions from consumption of energy: 3.426 million Mt (2011 est.)
country comparison to the world: 135

COMMUNICATIONS

Telephones—main lines in use: 88,100 (2012)
country comparison to the world: 148

Telephones—mobile cellular: 8.108 million (2012)
country comparison to the world: 91

Telephone system: *general assessment:* a fair telecommunications system that is shackled with a heavy state presence, lack of competition, and high operating costs and charges
domestic: stagnation in the fixed-line network contrasts with rapid growth in the mobile-cellular network; mobile-cellular coverage now includes all the main cities and key roads, including those from Maputo to the South African and Swaziland borders, the national highway through Gaza and Inhambane provinces, the Beira corridor, and from Nampula to Nacala; extremely low fixed-line teledensity; despite significant growth in mobile-cellular services, teledensity remains low at about 35 per 100 persons
international: country code—258; landing point for the EASSy and SEACOM fiber-optic submarine cable systems; satellite earth stations—5 Intelsat (2 Atlantic Ocean and 3 Indian Ocean) (2011)

Broadcast media: 1 state-run TV station supplemented by private TV station; Portuguese state TV's African service, RTP Africa, and Brazilian-owned TV Miramar are available; state-run radio provides nearly 100% territorial coverage and broadcasts in multiple languages; a number of privately owned and community-operated stations; transmissions of multiple international broadcasters are available (2007)

Internet country code: .mz

Internet hosts: 89,737 (2012)
country comparison to the world: 82

Internet users: 613,600 (2009)
country comparison to the world: 113

TRANSPORTATION

Airports: 98 (2013)
country comparison to the world: 57

Airports—with paved runways: *total:* 21
over 3,047 m: 1
2,438 to 3,047 m: 2
1,524 to 2,437 m: 9
914 to 1,523 m: 5
under 914 m: 4 (2013)

Airports—with unpaved runways: *total:* 77
2,438 to 3,047 m: 1
1,524 to 2,437 m: 9
914 to 1,523 m: 29
under 914 m: 38 (2013)

Pipelines: gas 972 km; refined products 278 km (2013)

Railways: *total:* 4,787 km
country comparison to the world: 38
narrow gauge: 4,787 km 1.067-m gauge (2008)

Roadways: *total:* 30,331 km
country comparison to the world: 96
paved: 6,303 km
unpaved: 24,028 km (2009)

Waterways: 460 km (Zambezi River navigable to Tete and along Cahora Bassa Lake) (2010)
country comparison to the world: 86

Merchant marine: *total:* 2
country comparison to the world: 143
by type: cargo 2
foreign-owned: 2 (Belgium 2) (2010)

Ports and terminals: *major seaport(s):* Beira, Maputo, Nacala

MILITARY

Military branches: Mozambique Armed Defense Forces (Forcas Armadas de Defesa de Mocambique, FADM): Mozambique Army, Mozambique Navy (Marinha de Guerra de Mocambique, MGM), Mozambique Air Force (Forca Aerea de Mocambique, FAM) (2012)

Military service age and obligation: registration for military service is mandatory for all males and females at 18 years of age; 18-35 years of age for selective compulsory military service; 18 years of age for voluntary service; 2-year service obligation; women may serve as officers or enlisted (2012)

Manpower available for military service:
males age 16-49: 4,613,367 (2010 est.)

Manpower fit for military service:
males age 16-49: 2,677,473

females age 16-49: 2,941,073 (2010 est.)

Manpower reaching militarily significant age annually: *male:* 274,602
female: 280,008 (2010 est.)

TRANSNATIONAL ISSUES

Disputes—international: South Africa has placed military units to assist police operations along the border of Lesotho, Zimbabwe, and Mozambique to control smuggling, poaching, and illegal migration

Illicit drugs: southern African transit point for South Asian hashish and heroin, and South American cocaine probably destined for the European and South African markets; producer of cannabis (for local consumption) and methaqualone (for export to South Africa); corruption and poor regulatory capability make the banking system vulnerable to money laundering, but the lack of a well-developed financial infrastructure limits the country's utility as a money-laundering center

N

NAMIBIA

INTRODUCTION

Background: South Africa occupied the German colony of South-West Africa during World War I and administered it as a mandate until after World War II, when it annexed the territory. In 1966 the Marxist South-West Africa People's Organization (SWAPO) guerrilla group launched a war of independence for the area that became Namibia, but it was not until 1988 that South Africa agreed to end its administration in accordance with a UN peace plan for the entire region. Namibia has been governed by SWAPO since the country won independence in 1990. Hifikepunye POHAMBA was elected president in November 2004 in a landslide victory replacing Sam NUJOMA who led the country during its first 14 years of self rule. POHAMBA was reelected in November 2009.

GEOGRAPHY

Location: Southern Africa, bordering the South Atlantic Ocean, between Angola and South Africa

Geographic coordinates: 22 00 S, 17 00 E

Map references: Africa

Area: *total:* 824,292 sq km
country comparison to the world: 34
land: 823,290 sq km
water: 1,002 sq km

Area—comparative: slightly more than half the size of Alaska

Land boundaries: *total:* 3,936 km
border countries: Angola 1,376 km, Botswana 1,360 km, South Africa 967 km, Zambia 233 km

Coastline: 1,572 km

Maritime claims: *territorial sea:* 12 nm
contiguous zone: 24 nm
exclusive economic zone: 200 nm

Climate: desert; hot, dry; rainfall sparse and erratic

Terrain: mostly high plateau; Namib Desert along coast; Kalahari Desert in east

Elevation extremes: *lowest point:* Atlantic Ocean 0 m
highest point: Konigstein 2,606 m

Natural resources: diamonds, copper, uranium, gold, silver, lead, tin, lithium, cadmium, tungsten, zinc, salt, hydropower, fish
note: suspected deposits of oil, coal, and iron ore

Land use: *arable land:* 0.97%
permanent crops: 0.01%
other: 99.02% (2011)

Irrigated land: 75.73 sq km (2003)

Total renewable water resources: 17.72 cu km (2011)

Freshwater withdrawal (domestic/industrial/agricultural): *total:* 0.29 cu km/yr (25%/5%/70%)
per capita: 146 cu m/yr (2002)

Natural hazards: prolonged periods of drought

Environment—current issues: limited natural freshwater resources; desertification; wildlife poaching; land degradation has led to few conservation areas

Environment—international agreements:
party to: Antarctic-Marine Living Resources, Biodiversity, Climate Change, Climate Change-Kyoto Protocol, Desertification, Endangered Species, Hazardous Wastes, Law of the Sea, Ozone Layer Protection, Wetlands
signed, but not ratified: none of the selected agreements

Geography—note: first country in the world to incorporate the protection of the environment into its constitution; some 14% of the land is protected, including virtually the entire Namib Desert coastal strip

PEOPLE AND SOCIETY

Nationality: *noun:* Namibian(s)
adjective: Namibian

Ethnic groups: black 87.5%, white 6%, mixed 6.5%
note: about 50% of the population belong to the Ovambo tribe and 9% to the Kavangos tribe; other ethnic groups include Herero 7%, Damara 7%, Nama 5%, Caprivian 4%, Bushmen 3%, Baster 2%, Tswana 0.5%

Languages: English (official) 7%, Afrikaans (common language of most of the population and about 60% of the white population), German 32%, indigenous languages (includes Oshivambo, Herero, Nama) 1%

Religions: Christian 80% to 90% (at least 50% Lutheran), indigenous beliefs 10% to 20%

Population: 2,198,406 (July 2013 est.)
country comparison to the world: 143
note: estimates for this country explicitly take into account the effects of excess mortality due to AIDS; this can result in lower life expectancy, higher infant mortality, higher death rates, lower population growth rates, and changes in the distribution of population by age and sex than would otherwise be expected (July 2014 est.)

Age structure: *0-14 years:* 31.7% (male 352,368/female 345,593)
15-24 years: 23.1% (male 256,965/female 251,276)
25-54 years: 35.9% (male 410,736/female 378,678)
55-64 years: 4.4% (male 47,832/female 58,602)
65 years and over: 4.3% (male 41,697/female 54,659) (2014 est.)

Dependency ratios:
total dependency ratio: 65.5 %
youth dependency ratio: 59.6 %
elderly dependency ratio: 5.9 %
potential support ratio: 17 (2013)

Median age: *total:* 22.8 years
male: 22.8 years
female: 22.8 years (2014 est.)

Population growth rate: 0.67% (2014 est.)
country comparison to the world: 147

Birth rate: 20.28 births/1,000 population (2014 est.)
country comparison to the world: 83

Death rate: 13.6 deaths/1,000 population (2014 est.)
country comparison to the world: 15

Net migration rate: 0.05 migrant(s)/1,000 population (2014 est.)
country comparison to the world: 76

Urbanization: *urban population:* 38.4% of total population (2011)
rate of urbanization: 3.14% annual rate of change (2010-15 est.)

Major urban areas—population: WINDHOEK (capital) 342,000 (2009)

Sex ratio: *at birth:* 1.03 male(s)/female
0-14 years: 1.02 male(s)/female
15-24 years: 1.02 male(s)/female
25-54 years: 1.09 male(s)/female
55-64 years: 1.02 male(s)/female
65 years and over: 0.78 male(s)/female
total population: 1.02 male(s)/female (2014 est.)

Mother's mean age at first birth: 21.4 (2007 est.)

Maternal mortality rate: 200 deaths/100,000 live births (2010)
country comparison to the world: 53

Infant mortality rate: *total:* 45.64 deaths/1,000 live births
country comparison to the world: 46
male: 48.6 deaths/1,000 live births
female: 42.59 deaths/1,000 live births (2014 est.)

Life expectancy at birth: *total population:* 51.85 years
country comparison to the world: 215
male: 52.22 years
female: 51.46 years (2014 est.)

Total fertility rate: 2.25 children born/woman (2014 est.)
country comparison to the world: 98

Contraceptive prevalence rate: 55.1% (2006/07)

Health expenditures: 5.3% of GDP (2011)
country comparison to the world: 132

Physicians density: 0.37 physicians/1,000 population (2007)

Hospital bed density: 2.7 beds/1,000 population (2009)

Drinking water source:
improved:
urban: 98.5% of population
rural: 90.3% of population
total: 93.4% of population
unimproved:
urban: 1.5% of population
rural: 9.7% of population
total: 6.6% of population (2011 est.)

Sanitation facility access:
improved:
urban: 57.1% of population
rural: 16.9% of population
total: 32.3% of population
unimproved:
urban: 42.9% of population
rural: 83.1% of population
total: 67.7% of population (2011 est.)

HIV/AIDS—adult prevalence rate: 13.3% (2012 est.)
country comparison to the world: 6

HIV/AIDS—people living with HIV/AIDS: 220,100 (2012 est.)
country comparison to the world: 27

HIV/AIDS—deaths: 5,000 (2012 est.)
country comparison to the world: 40

Major infectious diseases: *degree of risk:* high
food or waterborne diseases: bacterial diarrhea, hepatitis A, and typhoid fever
vectorborne disease: malaria
water contact disease: schistosomiasis (2013)

Obesity—adult prevalence rate: 9.5% (2008)

country comparison to the world: 133

Children under the age of 5 years underweight: 17.5% (2007)
country comparison to the world: 39

Education expenditures: 8.4% of GDP (2010)
country comparison to the world: 9

Literacy: *definition:* age 15 and over can read and write
total population: 88.8%
male: 89%
female: 88.5% (2010 est.)

School life expectancy (primary to tertiary education): *total:* 11 years
male: 11 years
female: 11 years (2006)

Unemployment, youth ages 15-24: *total:* 40.1%
country comparison to the world: 13
male: 29.4%
female: 34.3% (2012)

GOVERNMENT

Country name: *conventional long form:* Republic of Namibia
conventional short form: Namibia
local long form: Republic of Namibia
local short form: Namibia
former: German South-West Africa (Sued-West Afrika), South-West Africa

Government type: republic

Capital: *name:* Windhoek

geographic coordinates: 22 34 S, 17 05 E
time difference: UTC+1 (6 hours ahead of Washington, DC during Standard Time)
daylight saving time: +1hr, begins first Sunday in September; ends first Sunday in April

Administrative divisions: 14 regions; Erongo, Hardap, //Karas, Kavango East, Kavango West, Khomas, Kunene, Ohangwena, Omaheke, Omusati, Oshana, Oshikoto, Otjozondjupa, Zambezi; note—the Karas Region was renamed //Karas in September 2013 to include the alveolar lateral click of the Khoekhoegowab language

Independence: 21 March 1990 (from South African mandate)

National holiday: Independence Day, 21 March (1990)

Constitution: drafted 9 February 1990, signed 16 March 1990, entered into force 21 March 1990; amended 1998, 2010 (2010)

Legal system: mixed legal system of uncodified civil law based on Roman-Dutch law and customary law

International law organization participation: has not submitted an ICJ jurisdiction declaration; accepts ICCt jurisdiction

Suffrage: 18 years of age; universal

Executive branch: *chief of state:* President Hifikepunye POHAMBA (since 21 March 2005); note—the president is both the chief of state and head of government
head of government: President Hifikepunye POHAMBA (since 21 March 2005); Prime Minister Hage GEINGOB (since 4 December 2012)
cabinet: Cabinet appointed by the president from among the members of the National Assembly (For more information visit the World Leaders website)
elections: president elected by popular vote for a five-year term (eligible for a second term); if no single candidate receives a majority of the vote in the first round of voting, a run-off election is scheduled between the two candidates with the greatest vote count; election last held on 27-28 November 2009 (next to be held in 2014)
election results: Hifikepunye POHAMBA reelected president; percent of vote—Hifikepunye POHAMBA 76.4%, Hidipo HAMUTENYA 11.0%, Katuutire KAURA 3.0%, Kuaima RIRUAKO 2.9%, Justus GAROEB 2.4%, Ignatius SHIXWAMENI 1.3%, Hendrick MUDGE 1.2%, other 1.8%

Legislative branch: bicameral legislature consists of the National Council, primarily an advisory body (26 seats; two members chosen from each regional council to serve six-year terms), and the National Assembly (72 seats; members elected by popular vote to serve five-year terms, an additional six nonvoting members are appointed by the president)
elections: National Council—elections for regional councils to determine members of the National Council held on 26-27 November 2010 (next to be held in 2016); National Assembly—last held on 26-27 November 2009 (next to be held in November 2014)
election results: National Council—percent of vote by party—NA; seats by party—SWAPO 24, UDF 1, DTA 1; National Assembly—percent of vote by party—SWAPO 75.3%, RDP 11.3%, DTA 3.1%, NUDO 3.0%, UDF 2.4%, APP 1.4%, RP 0.8%, COD 0.7%, SWANU 0.6%, other 1.3%; seats by party—SWAPO 54, RDP 8, DTA 2, NUDO 2, UDF 2, APP 1, COD 1, RP 1, SWANU 1

Judicial branch: highest court(s): Supreme Court (consists of the chief justice and at least 3 judges in quorum sessions)
judge selection and term of office: judges appointed by the president of Namibia upon the recommendation of the Judicial Service Commission; judges serve until age 65 but can be extended by the president until age 70
subordinate courts: High Court; Labor Court; regional and district magistrates' courts; community courts

Political parties and leaders: All People's Party or APP [Ignatius SHIXWAMENI]; Congress of Democrats or COD [Benjamin ULENGA]; Democratic Turnhalle Alliance of Namibia or DTA [Katuutire KAURA]; Monitor Action Group or MAG [Jurie VILJOEN]; National Democratic Movement for Change or NamDMC; National Unity Democratic Organization or NUDO [Kuaima RIRUAKO]; Rally for Democracy and Progress or RDP [Hidipo HAMUTENYA]; Republican Party or RP [Hendrick MUDGE]; South West Africa National Union or SWANU [Usutuaije MAAMBERUA]; South West Africa People's Organization or SWAPO [Hifikepunye POHAMBA]; United Democratic Front or UDF [Justus GAROEB]

Political pressure groups and leaders: National Society for Human Rights or NSHR (NAMRIGHTS as of 2010); various labor unions

International organization participation: ACP, AfDB, AU, C, CD, FAO, G-77, IAEA, IBRD, ICAO, ICRM, IDA, IFAD, IFC, IFRCS, ILO, IMF, IMO, Interpol, IOC, IOM, IPU, ISO, ITSO, ITU, ITUC (NGOs), MIGA, NAM, OPCW, SACU, SADC, UN, UNAMID, UNCTAD, UNESCO, UNHCR, UNIDO, UNISFA, UNMIL, UNMISS, UNOCI, UNWTO, UPU, WCO, WHO, WIPO, WMO, WTO

Diplomatic representation in the US:
chief of mission: Ambassador Martin ANDJABA (since 3 September 2010)
chancery: 1605 New Hampshire Avenue NW, Washington, DC 20009
telephone: [1] (202) 986-0540
FAX: [1] (202) 986-0443

Diplomatic representation from the US:
chief of mission: Ambassador Wanda L. NESBITT (since 20 July 2010)
embassy: 14 Lossen Street, Windhoek
mailing address: Private Bag 12029 Ausspannplatz, Windhoek
telephone: [264] (61) 295-8500
FAX: [264] (61) 295-8603

Flag description: a wide red stripe edged by narrow white stripes divides the flag diagonally from lower hoist corner to upper fly corner; the upper hoist-side triangle is blue and charged with a yellow, 12-rayed sunburst; the lower fly-side triangle is green; red signifies the heroism of the people and their determination to build a future of equal opportunity for all; white stands for peace, unity, tranquility, and harmony; blue represents the Namibian sky and the Atlantic Ocean, the country's precious water resources and rain; the yellow sun denotes power and existence; green symbolizes vegetation and agricultural resources

National anthem: *name:* "Namibia, Land of the Brave"
lyrics/music: Axali DOESEB
note: adopted 1991

ECONOMY

Economy—overview: The economy is heavily dependent on the extraction and processing of minerals for export. Mining accounts for 11.5% of GDP, but provides more than 50% of foreign exchange earnings. Rich alluvial diamond deposits make Namibia a primary source for gem-quality diamonds. Marine diamond mining is becoming increasingly important as the terrestrial diamond supply has dwindled. Namibia is the world's fourth-largest producer of uranium. It also produces large quantities of zinc and is a small producer of gold and other minerals. The mining and quarrying sectors employs only about 1.8% of the population. Namibia normally imports about 50% of its cereal requirements; in drought years food shortages are a major problem in rural areas. A high per capita GDP, relative to the region, hides one of the world's most unequal income distributions, as shown by Namibia's 59.7 GINI coefficient. The Namibian economy is closely linked to South Africa with the Namibian dollar pegged one-to-one to the South African rand. Namibia receives 30%-40% of its revenues from the Southern African Customs Union (SACU). Volatility in the size of Namibia's annual SACU allotment complicates budget planning. Namibia's economy remains vulnerable to volatility in the price of uranium and other commodities. The rising cost of mining diamonds, increasingly from the sea, has reduced profit margins. Namibian authorities recognize these issues and have emphasized the need to increase higher value raw materials, manufacturing, and services, especially in the logistics and transportation sectors.

GDP (purchasing power parity): $17.79 billion (2013 est.)
country comparison to the world: 139
$17.05 billion (2012 est.)
$16.23 billion (2011 est.)
note: data are in 2013 US dollars

GDP (official exchange rate): $12.3 billion (2013 est.)

GDP—real growth rate: 4.4% (2013 est.)
country comparison to the world: 71
5% (2012 est.)
5.7% (2011 est.)

GDP—per capita (PPP): $8,200 (2013 est.)
country comparison to the world: 132
$7,900 (2012 est.)
$7,600 (2011 est.)
note: data are in 2013 US dollars

Gross national saving: 18.5% of GDP (2013 est.)
country comparison to the world: 86
18.1% of GDP (2012 est.)
15.3% of GDP (2011 est.)

GDP—composition, by end use:
household consumption: 59.9%
government consumption: 26.2%
investment in fixed capital: 22.8%
investment in inventories: 0.5%
exports of goods and services: 41.4%
imports of goods and services: -50.9% (2013 est.)

GDP—composition, by sector of origin:
agriculture: 7.7%
industry: 29.6%
services: 62.6% (2013 est.)

Agriculture—products: millet, sorghum, peanuts, grapes; livestock; fish

Industries: meatpacking, fish processing, dairy products, pasta and beverages; mining (diamonds, lead, zinc, tin, silver, tungsten, uranium, copper)

Industrial production growth rate: 5.6% (2013 est.)
country comparison to the world: 47

Labor force: 928,200 (2013 est.)
country comparison to the world: 146

Labor force—by occupation:
agriculture: 16.3%
industry: 22.4%
services: 61.3%
note: about half of Namibia's people are unemployed while about two-thirds live in rural areas; roughly two-thirds of rural dwellers rely on subsistence agriculture (2008 est.)

Unemployment rate: 51.2% (2008 est.)
country comparison to the world: 195
36.7% (2004 est.)

Population below poverty line: 55.8%
note: the UNDP's 2005 Human Development Report indicated that 34.9% of the population live on $1 per day and 55.8% live on $2 per day (2005 est.)

Household income or consumption by percentage share: *lowest 10%:* 2.4%
highest 10%: 42% (2010)

Distribution of family income—Gini index:
59.7 (2010)
country comparison to the world: 6
70.7 (2003)

Budget: *revenues:* $4.325 billion
expenditures: $5.126 billion (2013 est.)

Taxes and other revenues: 35.2% of GDP (2013 est.)
country comparison to the world: 64

Budget surplus (+) or deficit (-):
-6.5% of GDP (2013 est.)
country comparison to the world: 185

Public debt: 27.2% of GDP (2013 est.)
country comparison to the world: 127

25.8% of GDP (2012 est.)

Fiscal year: 1 April—31 March

Inflation rate (consumer prices): 5.5% (2013 est.)
country comparison to the world: 162
6.5% (2012 est.)

Central bank discount rate: 12% (31 December 2010 est.)
country comparison to the world: 40
7% (31 December 2009 est.)

Commercial bank prime lending rate: 8.2% (31 December 2013 est.)
country comparison to the world: 108
8.7% (31 December 2012 est.)

Stock of narrow money: $2.723 billion (31 December 2013 est.)
country comparison to the world: 119
$2.941 billion (31 December 2012 est.)

Stock of broad money: $7.22 billion (31 December 2013 est.)
country comparison to the world: 114
$7.228 billion (31 December 2012 est.)

Stock of domestic credit: $5.942 billion (31 December 2013 est.)
country comparison to the world: 111
$6.266 billion (31 December 2012 est.)

Market value of publicly traded shares: $1.305 billion (31 December 2012 est.)
country comparison to the world: 105
$1.152 billion (31 December 2011)
$1.176 billion (31 December 2010 est.)

Current account balance: -$658.4 million (2013 est.)
country comparison to the world: 109
-$414 million (2012 est.)

Exports: $5.124 billion (2013 est.)
country comparison to the world: 114
$4.883 billion (2012 est.)

Exports—commodities: diamonds, copper, gold, zinc, lead, uranium; cattle, white fish and mollusks

Imports: $7.084 billion (2013 est.)
country comparison to the world: 112
$6.44 billion (2012 est.)

Imports—commodities: foodstuffs; petroleum products and fuel, machinery and equipment, chemicals

Reserves of foreign exchange and gold: $2.267 billion (31 December 2013 est.)
country comparison to the world: 118
$1.738 billion (31 December 2012 est.)

Debt—external: $4.312 billion (31 December 2013 est.)
country comparison to the world: 127
$4.292 billion (31 December 2012 est.)

Stock of direct foreign investment—at home: $NA

Stock of direct foreign investment—abroad: $NA

Exchange rates: Namibian dollars (NAD) per US dollar—
9.282 (2013 est.)
8.2031 (2012 est.)
7.3212 (2010 est.)
8.42 (2009)
7.75 (2008)

ENERGY

Electricity—production: 1.643 billion kWh (2012 est.)
country comparison to the world: 140

Electricity—consumption: 3.635 billion kWh (2012 est.)
country comparison to the world: 125

Electricity—exports: 91 million kWh (2012 est.)
country comparison to the world: 77

Electricity—imports: 2.519 billion kWh (2012 est.)
country comparison to the world: 52

Electricity—installed generating capacity: 508,000 kW (2012 est.)
country comparison to the world: 137

Electricity—from fossil fuels: 33.3% of total installed capacity (2012 est.)
country comparison to the world: 174

Electricity—from nuclear fuels: 0% of total installed capacity (2012 est.)
country comparison to the world: 203

Electricity—from hydroelectric plants: 66.7% of total installed capacity (2012 est.)
country comparison to the world: 24

Electricity—from other renewable sources: 0% of total installed capacity (2012 est.)
country comparison to the world: 139

Crude oil—production: 0 bbl/day (2012 est.)
country comparison to the world: 143

Crude oil—exports: 0 bbl/day (2010 est.)
country comparison to the world: 204

Crude oil—imports: 0 bbl/day (2010 est.)
country comparison to the world: 140

Crude oil—proved reserves: 0 bbl (1 January 2013 es)
country comparison to the world: 205

Refined petroleum products—production: 0 bbl/day (2012 est.)
country comparison to the world: 207

Refined petroleum products—consumption: 22,990 bbl/day (2011 est.)
country comparison to the world: 124

Refined petroleum products—exports: 0 bbl/day (2010 est.)
country comparison to the world: 143

Refined petroleum products—imports: 20,810 bbl/day (2012 est.)
country comparison to the world: 104

Natural gas—production: 0 cu m (2012 est.)
country comparison to the world: 207

Natural gas—consumption: 0 cu m (2012 est.)
country comparison to the world: 207

Natural gas—exports: 0 cu m (2012 est.)
country comparison to the world: 206

Natural gas—imports: 0 cu m (2012 est.)
country comparison to the world: 148

Natural gas—proved reserves: 62.29 billion cu m (1 January 2013 es)
country comparison to the world: 63

Carbon dioxide emissions from consumption of energy: 3.217 million Mt (2011 est.)
country comparison to the world: 138

COMMUNICATIONS

Telephones—main lines in use: 171,000 (2012)
country comparison to the world: 130

Telephones—mobile cellular: 2.435 million (2012)
country comparison to the world: 137

Telephone system: *general assessment:* good system; core fiber-optic network links most centers and connections are now digital
domestic: multiple mobile-cellular providers with a combined subscribership of more than 100 telephones per 100 persons
international: country code—264; fiber-optic cable to South Africa, microwave radio relay link to Botswana, direct links to other neighboring countries; connected to the South African Far East (SAFE) submarine cable through South Africa; satellite earth stations—4 Intelsat (2010)

Broadcast media: 1 private and 1 state-run TV station; satellite and cable TV service is available; state-run radio service broadcasts in multiple languages; about a dozen private radio stations; transmissions of multiple international broadcasters are available (2007)

Internet country code: .na

Internet hosts: 78,280 (2012)
country comparison to the world: 84

Internet users: 127,500 (2009)
country comparison to the world: 151

TRANSPORTATION

Airports: 112 (2013)
country comparison to the world: 5 2

Airports—with paved runways: *total:* 1 9
over 3,047 m: 4

2,438 to 3,047 m: 2
1,524 to 2,437 m: 12
914 to 1,523 m: 1 (2013)

Airports—with unpaved runways: *total:* 93
1,524 to 2,437 m: 25
914 to 1,523 m: 52
under 914 m: 16 (2013)

Railways: *total:* 2,626 km
country comparison to the world: 64
narrow gauge: 2,626 km 1.067-m gauge (2008)

Roadways: *total:* 44,138 km
country comparison to the world: 82
paved: 6,387 km
unpaved: 37,751 km (2010)

Merchant marine: *total:* 1
country comparison to the world: 152
by type: cargo 1 (2010)

Ports and terminals: *major seaport(s):* Luderitz, Walvis Bay

MILITARY

Military branches: Namibian Defense Force (NDF): Army, Navy, Air Force (2013)

Military service age and obligation: 18 years of age for voluntary military service; no conscription (2012)

Manpower available for military service:
males age 16-49: 568,231 (2010 est.)

Manpower fit for military service:
males age 16-49: 351,431
females age 16-49: 311,513 (2010 est.)

Manpower reaching militarily significant age annually: *male:* 26,413
female: 26,038 (2010 est.)

Military expenditures: 3.11% of GDP (2012)
country comparison to the world: 19
3.38% of GDP (2011)
3.11% of GDP (2010)

TRANSNATIONAL ISSUES

Disputes—international: concerns from international experts and local populations over the Okavango Delta ecology in Botswana and human displacement scuttled Namibian plans to construct a hydroelectric dam on Popa Falls along the Angola-Namibia border; the governments of South Africa and Namibia have not signed or ratified the text of the 1994 Surveyor's General agreement placing the boundary in the middle of the Orange River; Namibia has supported, and in 2004 Zimbabwe dropped objections to, plans between Botswana and Zambia to build a bridge over the Zambezi River, thereby de facto recognizing a short, but not clearly delimited, Botswana-Zambia boundary in the river

Trafficking in persons: *current situation:* Namibia is predominantly a country of origin and destination for children and, to a lesser extent, women subjected to forced labor and sex trafficking; victims lured by promises of legitimate jobs are forced to work in hazardous condition in urban centers and on commercial farms; traffickers exploit Namibian children, as well as children from Angola, Zambia, and Zimbabwe, for forced labor in agriculture, cattle herding, domestic service, and criminal activities; children are also forced into prostitution, often catering to tourists from southern Africa and Europe; girls of the San tribe are particularly vulnerable

tier rating: Tier 2 Watch List—Namibia does not fully comply with the minimum standards for the elimination of trafficking; however, it is making significant efforts to do so; in 2012, the government launched a National Plan of Action on Gender-Based Violence, which included addressing human trafficking but did not complete its draft comprehensive anti-trafficking legislation or obtain parliamentary passage of the Child Care and Protection Bill, which would criminalize child trafficking; a process has been developed for referring trafficking victims for assistance but a system for screening potential victims and providing official designation of trafficking victim status is lacking (2013)

NAURU

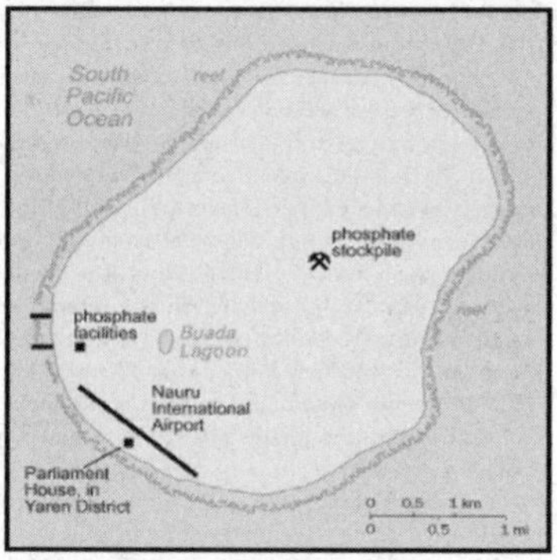

INTRODUCTION

Background: The exact origins of the Nauruans are unclear since their language does not resemble any other in the Pacific region. Germany annexed the island in 1888. A German-British consortium began mining the island's phosphate deposits early in the 20th century. Australian forces occupied Nauru in World War I; it subsequently became a League of Nations mandate. After the Second World War—and a brutal occupation by Japan—Nauru became a UN trust territory. It achieved independence in 1968 and joined the UN in 1999 as the world's smallest independent republic.

GEOGRAPHY

Location: Oceania, island in the South Pacific Ocean, south of the Marshall Islands

Geographic coordinates: 0 32 S, 166 55 E

Map references: Oceania

Area: *total:* 21 sq km
country comparison to the world: 240
land: 21 sq km
water: 0 sq km

Area—comparative: about 0.1 times the size of Washington, DC

Land boundaries: 0 km

Coastline: 30 km

Maritime claims: *territorial sea:* 12 nm
contiguous zone: 24 nm
exclusive economic zone: 200 nm

Climate: tropical with a monsoonal pattern; rainy season (November to February)

Terrain: sandy beach rises to fertile ring around raised coral reefs with phosphate plateau in center

Elevation extremes: *lowest point:* Pacific Ocean 0 m
highest point: unnamed elevation along plateau rim 61 m

Natural resources: phosphates, fish

Land use: *arable land:* 0%
permanent crops: 20%
other: 80% (2011)

Irrigated land: NA

Natural hazards: periodic droughts

Environment—current issues: limited natural freshwater resources, roof storage tanks collect rainwater but mostly dependent on a single, aging desalination plant; intensive phosphate mining during the past 90 years—mainly by a UK, Australia, and NZ consortium—has left the central 90% of Nauru a wasteland and threatens limited remaining land resources

Environment—international agreements:
party to: Biodiversity, Climate Change, Climate Change-Kyoto Protocol, Desertification, Hazardous Wastes, Law of the Sea, Marine Dumping, Ozone Layer Protection, Whaling
signed, but not ratified: none of the selected agreements

Geography—note: Nauru is one of the three great phosphate rock islands in the Pacific Ocean—the others are Banaba (Ocean Island) in Kiribati and Makatea in French Polynesia; only 53 km south of Equator

PEOPLE AND SOCIETY

Nationality: *noun:* Nauruan(s)
adjective: Nauruan

Ethnic groups: Nauruan 58%, other Pacific Islander 26%, Chinese 8%, European 8%

Languages: Nauruan 93% (official, a distinct Pacific Island language), English 2% (widely understood, spoken, and used for most government and commercial purposes), other 5% (includes I-Kiribati 2% and Chinese 2%)
note: percentages represent main language spoken at home; Nauruan is spoken by 95% of the population, English by 66%, and other languages by 12% (2011 est.)

Religions: Protestant 60.4% (includes Nauru Congregational 33.7%, Assembly of God 13%, Nauru Independent Church 9.5%, Baptist 1.5%, and Seventh Day Adventist .7%), Roman Catholic 33%, other 2.8%, none 1.8%, unspecified 1.1% (2011 est.)

Population: 9,488 (July 2014 est.)
country comparison to the world: 227

Age structure:
0-14 years: 32.5% (male 1,359/female 1,720)
15-24 years: 16.9% (male 828/female 773)
25-54 years: 42.7% (male 2,013/female 2,040)
55-64 years: 1.9% (male 228/female 343)

65 years and over: 1.8% (male 73/female 111) (2014 est.)

Median age: *total:* 25.3 years
male: 25.6 years
female: 25 years (2014 est.)

Population growth rate: 0.56% (2014 est.)
country comparison to the world: 151

Birth rate: 25.61 births/1,000 population (2014 est.)
country comparison to the world: 51

Death rate: 5.9 deaths/1,000 population (2014 est.)
country comparison to the world: 172

Net migration rate: -14.12 migrant(s)/1,000 population (2014 est.)
country comparison to the world: 218

Urbanization: *urban population:* 100% of total population (2010)
rate of urbanization: 0.6% annual rate of change (2010-15 est.)

Sex ratio: *at birth:* 0.84 male(s)/female
0-14 years: 0.79 male(s)/female
15-24 years: 1.07 male(s)/female
25-54 years: 0.99 male(s)/female
55-64 years: 0.9 male(s)/female
65 years and over: 0.78 male(s)/female
total population: 0.91 male(s)/female (2014 est.)

Infant mortality rate: *total:* 8.21 deaths/1,000 live births
country comparison to the world: 153
male: 10.54 deaths/1,000 live births
female: 6.27 deaths/1,000 live births (2014 est.)

Life expectancy at birth: *total population:* 66.4 years
country comparison to the world: 169
male: 62.3 years
female: 69.83 years (2014 est.)

Total fertility rate: 2.93 children born/woman (2014 est.)
country comparison to the world: 59

Contraceptive prevalence rate: 35.6% (2007)

Health expenditures: 9.8% of GDP (2011)
country comparison to the world: 28

Physicians density: 0.71 physicians/1,000 population (2010)

Drinking water source:
improved:
urban: 96% of population
total: 96% of population
unimproved:
urban: 4% of population
total: 4% of population (2011 est.)

Sanitation facility access:
improved:
urban: 65.6% of population
total: 65.6% of population
unimproved:
urban: 34.4% of population
total: 34.4% of population (2011 est.)

HIV/AIDS—adult prevalence rate: NA

HIV/AIDS—people living with HIV/AIDS: NA

HIV/AIDS—deaths: NA

Obesity—adult prevalence rate: 71.1% (2008)
country comparison to the world: 2

Children under the age of 5 years underweight: 4.8% (2007)
country comparison to the world: 91

Education expenditures: NA

Literacy: NA

School life expectancy (primary to tertiary education): *total:* 9 years
male: 9 years
female: 10 years (2008)

GOVERNMENT

Country name: *conventional long form:* Republic of Nauru
conventional short form: Nauru
local long form: Republic of Nauru
local short form: Nauru
former: Pleasant Island

Government type: republic

Capital: no official capital; government offices in Yaren District
time difference: UTC+12 (17 hours ahead of Washington, DC during Standard Time)

Administrative divisions: 14 districts; Aiwo, Anabar, Anetan, Anibare, Baiti, Boe, Buada, Denigomodu, Ewa, Ijuw, Meneng, Nibok, Uaboe, Yaren

Independence: 31 January 1968 (from the Australia-, NZ-, and UK-administered UN trusteeship)

National holiday: Independence Day, 31 January (1968)

Constitution: effective 29 January 1968; amended 1968, 2009; note—in early 2013, further amendments were introduced (2013)

Legal system: mixed legal system of common law based on the English model and customary law

International law organization participation: has not submitted an ICJ jurisdiction declaration; accepts ICCt jurisdiction

Suffrage: 20 years of age; universal and compulsory

Executive branch: *chief of state:* President Baron WAQA (since 11 June 2013); note—the president is both chief of state and head of government
head of government: President Baron WAQA (since 11 June 2013)
cabinet: Cabinet appointed by the president from among the members of parliament (For more information visit the World Leaders website)
elections: president elected by parliament for a three-year term; election last held on 11 June 2013 (next to be held in 2016)
election results: Baron WAQA elected in a parliamentary vote of 13 to 5

Legislative branch: unicameral parliament (19 seats; members elected by popular vote to serve three-year terms)
elections: last held on 8 June 2013 (next to be held in 2016)
election results: percent of vote—NA; seats—independents 19

Judicial branch: *highest court(s):* Supreme Court (consists of a chief justice and 1 judge)
judge selection and term of office: judges appointed by the president to serve until age 65
subordinate courts: District Court, Family Court

Political parties and leaders: Democratic Party [Kennan ADEANG]; Nauru First (Naoero Amo) Party; Nauru Party (informal)
note: loose multiparty system

Political pressure groups and leaders: Woman Information and News Agency (women's issues)

International organization participation: ACP, ADB, AOSIS, C, FAO, G-77, ICAO, Interpol, IOC, IOM, ITU, OPCW, PIF, Sparteca, SPC, UN, UNCTAD, UNESCO, UPU, WHO

Diplomatic representation in the US:
chief of mission: Ambassador Marlene Inemwin MOSES (since 10 February 2006)
chancery: 800 2nd Avenue, Suite 400 D, New York, NY 10017
telephone: [1] (212) 937-0074
FAX: [1] (212) 937-0079
consulate(s): Agana (Guam)

Diplomatic representation from the US: the US does not have an embassy in Nauru; the US Ambassador to Fiji, currently Ambassador Frankie A. REED, is accredited to Nauru

Flag description: blue with a narrow, horizontal, yellow stripe across the center and a large white 12-pointed star below the stripe on the hoist side; blue stands for the Pacific Ocean, the star indicates the country's location in relation to the Equator (the yellow stripe) and the 12 points symbolize the 12 original tribes of Nauru

National anthem: *name:* "Nauru Bwiema" (Song of Nauru)
lyrics/music: Margaret HENDRIE/Laurence Henry HICKS
note: adopted 1968

ECONOMY

Economy—overview: Revenues of this tiny island traditionally have come from exports of phosphates. Few other resources exist, with most necessities being imported, mainly from Australia, its former occupier and later major source of support. In 2005 an Australian company entered into an agreement to exploit remaining supplies. Primary reserves of phosphates were exhausted and mining ceased in 2006, but mining of a deeper layer of "secondary phosphate" in the interior of the island began the following year. The secondary phosphate deposits may last another 30 years. The rehabilitation of mined land and the replacement of income from phosphates are serious long-term problems. In anticipation of the exhaustion of Nauru's phosphate deposits, substantial amounts of phosphate income were invested in trust funds to help cushion the transition and provide for Nauru's economic future. As a result of heavy spending from the trust funds, the government faced virtual bankruptcy. To cut costs the government has frozen wages and reduced overstaffed public service departments. Nauru lost further revenue in 2008 with the closure of Australia's refugee processing center, making it almost totally dependent on food imports and foreign aid. Housing, hospitals, and other capital plant are deteriorating. The cost to Australia of keeping the government and economy afloat continues to climb. Few comprehensive statistics on the Nauru economy exist with estimates of Nauru's GDP varying widely.

GDP (purchasing power parity): $60 million (2005 est.)
country comparison to the world: 224

GDP (official exchange rate): $NA

GDP—real growth rate: NA%

GDP—per capita (PPP): $5,000 (2005 est.)
country comparison to the world: 160

GDP—composition, by sector of origin: *agriculture:* 6.1%

industry: 33%
services: 60.8% (2009 est.)

Agriculture—products: coconuts

Industries: phosphate mining, offshore banking, coconut products

Industrial production growth rate: NA%

Labor force—by occupation: *note:* employed in mining phosphates, public administration, education, and transportation

Unemployment rate: 90% (2004 est.)
country comparison to the world: 202

Population below poverty line: NA%

Household income or consumption by percentage share: *lowest* 10%: NA%
highest 10%: NA%

Budget: *revenues:* $13.5 million
expenditures: $13.5 million (2005)

Fiscal year: 1 July—30 June

Inflation rate (consumer prices): NA% (2011 est.)

Exports: $64,000 (2005 est.)
country comparison to the world: 221

Exports—commodities: phosphates

Imports: $20 million (2004 est.)
country comparison to the world: 220

Imports—commodities: food, fuel, manufactures, building materials, machinery

Debt—external: $33.3 million (2004 est.)
country comparison to the world: 196

Exchange rates: Australian dollars (AUD) per US dollar—
1.031 (2013)
0.9658 (2011 est.)
1.0902 (2010)
1.2822 (2009)
1.2059 (2008)

ENERGY

Electricity—production: 35 million kWh (2010 est.)
country comparison to the world: 209

Electricity—consumption: 32.55 million kWh (2010 est.)
country comparison to the world: 209

Electricity—exports: 0 kWh (2012 est.)
country comparison to the world: 178

Electricity—imports: 0 kWh (2012 est.)
country comparison to the world: 179

Electricity—installed generating capacity: 1,000 kW (2010 est.)
country comparison to the world: 210

Electricity—from fossil fuels: 100% of total installed capacity (2010 est.)
country comparison to the world: 27

Electricity—from nuclear fuels: 0% of total installed capacity (2010 est.)
country comparison to the world: 154

Electricity—from hydroelectric plants: 0% of total installed capacity (2010 est.)
country comparison to the world: 190

Electricity—from other renewable sources: 0% of total installed capacity (2010 est.)
country comparison to the world: 108

Crude oil—production: 0 bbl/day (2012 est.)
country comparison to the world: 203

Crude oil—exports: 0 bbl/day (2010 est.)
country comparison to the world: 164

Crude oil—imports: 0 bbl/day (2010 est.)
country comparison to the world: 106

Crude oil—proved reserves: 0 bbl (1 January 2013 es)
country comparison to the world: 173

Refined petroleum products—production: 0 bbl/day (2010 est.)
country comparison to the world: 183

Refined petroleum products—consumption: 1,000 bbl/day (2011 est.)
country comparison to the world: 200

Refined petroleum products—exports: 0 bbl/day (2010 est.)
country comparison to the world: 205

Refined petroleum products—imports: 1,075 bbl/day (2010 est.)
country comparison to the world: 193

Natural gas—production: 0 cu m (2011 est.)
country comparison to the world: 176

Natural gas—consumption: 0 cu m (2010 est.)
country comparison to the world: 181

Natural gas—exports: 0 cu m (2011 est.)
country comparison to the world: 158

Natural gas—imports: 0 cu m (2011 est.)
country comparison to the world: 109

Natural gas—proved reserves: 0 cu m (1 January 2013 es)
country comparison to the world: 179

Carbon dioxide emissions from consumption of energy: 168,800 Mt (2011 est.)
country comparison to the world: 196

COMMUNICATIONS

Telephones—main lines in use: 1,900 (2009)
country comparison to the world: 219

Telephones—mobile cellular: 6,800 (2012)
country comparison to the world: 213

Telephone system: *general assessment:* adequate local and international radiotelephone communication provided via Australian facilities
international: country code—674; satellite earth station—1 Intelsat (Pacific Ocean)

Broadcast media: 1 government-owned TV station broadcasting programs from New Zealand sent via satellite or on videotape; 1 government-owned radio station, broadcasting on AM and FM, utilizes Australian and British programs (2009)

Internet country code: . n r

Internet hosts: 8,162 (2012)
country comparison to the world: 138

TRANSPORTATION

Airports: 1 (2013)
country comparison to the world: 229

Airports—with paved runways: *total:* 1
1,524 to 2,437 m: 1 (2013)

Roadways: *total:* 30 km
country comparison to the world: 219
paved: 24 km
unpaved: 6 km (2002)

Ports and terminals: *major seaport(s):* Nauru

MILITARY

Military branches: no regular military forces (2012)

Manpower available for military service:
males age 16-49: 2,542 (2010 est.)

Manpower fit for military service:
males age 16-49: 1,823
females age 16-49: 2,034 (2010 est.)

Manpower reaching militarily significant age annually:
male: 7 4
female: 78 (2010 est.)

Military—note: Nauru maintains no defense forces; under an informal agreement, defense is the responsibility of Australia

TRANSNATIONAL ISSUES

Disputes—international: none

NAVASSA ISLAND

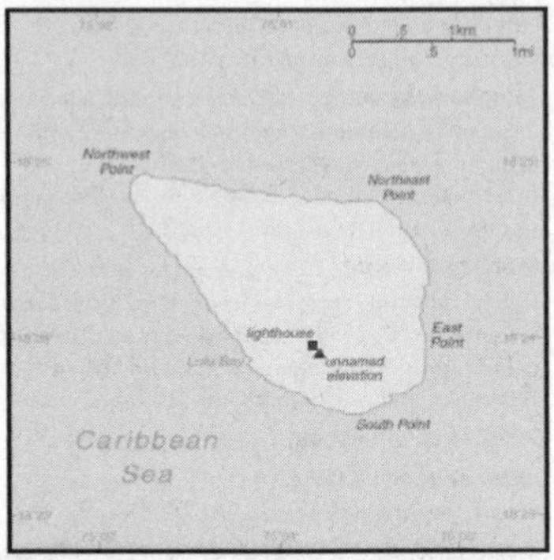

INTRODUCTION

Background: This uninhabited island was claimed by the US in 1857 for its guano. Mining took place between 1865 and 1898. The lighthouse, built in 1917, was shut down in 1996 and administration of Navassa Island transferred from the US Coast Guard to the Department of the Interior. A 1998 scientific expedition to the island described it as a unique preserve of Caribbean biodiversity; the following year it became a National Wildlife Refuge and annual scientific expeditions have continued.

GEOGRAPHY

Location: Caribbean, island in the Caribbean Sea, 35 miles west of Tiburon Peninsula of Haiti

Geographic coordinates: 18 25 N, 75 02 W

Map references: Central America and the Caribbean

Area: *total:* 5.4 sq km
country comparison to the world: 246
land: 5.4 sq km
water: 0 sq km

Area—comparative: about nine times the size of The Mall in Washington, DC

Land boundaries: 0 km

Coastline: 8 km

Maritime claims: *territorial sea:* 12 nm
exclusive economic zone: 200 nm

Climate: marine, tropical

Terrain: raised coral and limestone plateau, flat to undulating; ringed by vertical white cliffs (9 to 15 m high)

Elevation extremes: *lowest point:* Caribbean Sea 0 m
highest point: unnamed elevation on southwest side 77 m

Natural resources: guano

Land use: *arable land:* 0%
permanent crops: 0%
other: 100% (2011)

Natural hazards: hurricanes

Environment—current issues: NA

Geography—note: strategic location 160 km south of the US Naval Base at Guantanamo Bay, Cuba; mostly exposed rock with numerous solution holes (limestone sinkholes) but with enough grassland to support goat herds; dense stands of fig trees, scattered cactus

PEOPLE AND SOCIETY

Population: uninhabited
note: transient Haitian fishermen and others camp on the island

GOVERNMENT

Country name: *conventional long form:* none
conventional short form: Navassa Island

Dependency status: unorganized, unincorporated territory of the US; administered by the Fish and Wildlife Service, US Department of the Interior from the Caribbean Islands National Wildlife Refuge in Boqueron, Puerto Rico; in September 1996, the Coast Guard ceased operations and maintenance of Navassa Island Light, a 46-meter-tall lighthouse on the southern side of the island; there has also been a private claim advanced against the island

Legal system: the laws of the US, where applicable, apply

Diplomatic representation from the US: none (territory of the US)

Flag description: the flag of the US is used

ECONOMY

Economy—overview: Subsistence fishing and commercial trawling occur within refuge waters.

TRANSPORTATION

Ports and terminals: none; offshore anchorage only

MILITARY

Military—note: defense is the responsibility of the US

TRANSNATIONAL ISSUES

Disputes—international: claimed by Haiti, source of subsistence fishing

NEPAL

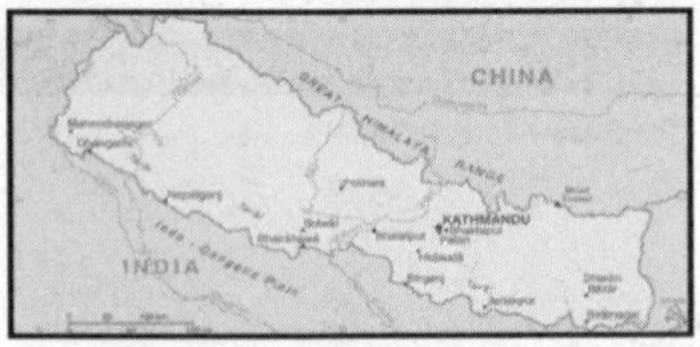

INTRODUCTION

Background: In 1951, the Nepali monarch ended the century-old system of rule by hereditary premiers and instituted a cabinet system of government. Reforms in 1990 established a multiparty democracy within the framework of a constitutional monarchy. An insurgency led by Maoists broke out in 1996. The ensuing 10-year civil war between Maoist and government forces witnessed the dissolution of the cabinet and parliament and assumption of absolute power by the king in 2002. Several weeks of mass protests in April 2006 were followed by several months of peace negotiations between the Maoists and government officials, and culminated in a late 2006 peace accord and the promulgation of an interim constitution. Following a nationwide election in April 2008, the newly formed Constituent Assembly (CA) declared Nepal a federal democratic republic and abolished the monarchy at its first meeting the following month. The CA elected the country's first president in July. Between 2008 and 2011 there were four different coalition governments, led twice by the United Communist Party of Nepal-Maoist, which received a plurality of votes in the 2008 CA election, and twice by the Communist Party of Nepal-United Marxist-Leninist (UML). After the CA failed to draft a constitution by the May 2012 deadline set by the Supreme Court, then Prime Minister Baburam BHATTARAI dissolved the CA. Months of negotiations ensued until March 2013 when the major political parties agreed to create an interim government headed by then Chief Justice Khil Raj REGMI with a mandate to hold elections for a new CA. Elections were held in November 2013, in which and the Nepali Congress won the largest share of the seats in the CA and in February 2014 formed a coalition government with the second place UML and with Nepali Congress President Sushil KOIRALA as prime minister

GEOGRAPHY

Location: Southern Asia, between China and India

Geographic coordinates: 28 00 N, 84 00 E

Map references: Asia

Area: *total:* 147,181 sq km
country comparison to the world: 94
land: 143,351 sq km
water: 3,830 sq km

Area—comparative: slightly larger than Arkansas

Land boundaries: *total:* 2,926 km

border countries: China 1,236 km, India 1,690 km

Coastline: 0 km (landlocked)

Maritime claims: none (landlocked)

Climate: varies from cool summers and severe winters in north to subtropical summers and mild winters in south

Terrain: Tarai or flat river plain of the Ganges in south, central hill region, rugged Himalayas in north

Elevation extremes: *lowest point:* Kanchan Kalan 70 m
highest point: Mount Everest 8,850 m (highest point in Asia)

Natural resources: quartz, water, timber, hydropower, scenic beauty, small deposits of lignite, copper, cobalt, iron ore

Land use: *arable land:* 16%
permanent crops: 0.8%
other: 83.2% (2011)

Irrigated land: 11,680 sq km (2003)

Total renewable water resources: 210.2 cu km (2011)

Freshwater withdrawal (domestic/industrial/agricultural): *total:* 9.5 cu km/yr (2%/0%/98%)
per capita: 334.7 cu m/yr (2006)

Natural hazards: severe thunderstorms; flooding; landslides; drought and famine depending on the timing, intensity, and duration of the summer monsoons

Environment—current issues: deforestation (overuse of wood for fuel and lack of alternatives); contaminated water (with human and animal wastes, agricultural runoff, and industrial effluents); wildlife conservation; vehicular emissions

Environment—international agreements: *party to:* Biodiversity, Climate Change, Climate Change-Kyoto Protocol, Desertification, Endangered Species, Hazardous Wastes, Law of the Sea, Ozone Layer Protection, Tropical Timber 83, Tropical Timber 94, Wetlands
signed, but not ratified: Marine Life Conservation

Geography—note: landlocked; strategic location between China and India; contains eight of world's 10 highest peaks, including Mount Everest and Kanchenjunga—the world's tallest and third tallest—on the borders with China and India respectively

PEOPLE AND SOCIETY

Nationality: *noun:* Nepali (singular and plural)
adjective: Nepali

Ethnic groups: Chhettri 16.6%, Brahman-Hill 12.2%, Magar 7.1%, Tharu 6.6%, Tamang 5.8%, Newar 5%, Kami 4.8%, Muslim 4.4%, Yadav 4%, Rai 2.3%, Gurung 2%, Damai/Dholii 1.8%, Thakuri 1.6%, Limbu 1.5%, Sarki 1.4%, Teli 1.4%, Chamar/Harijan/Ram 1.3%, Koiri/Kushwaha 1.2%, other 23%
note: 125 caste/ethnic groups were reported in the 2011 national census (2011 est.)

Languages: Nepali (official) 44.6%, Maithali 11.7%, Bhojpuri 6%, Tharu 5.8%, Tamang 5.1%, Newar 3.2%, Magar 3%, Bajjika 3%, Urdu 2.6%, Avadhi 1.9%, Limbu 1.3%, Gurung 1.2%, other 10.4%, unspecified 0.2% note: 123 languages reported as mother tongue in 2011 national census; many in government and business also speak English (2011 est.)

Religions: Hindu 81.3%, Buddhist 9%, Muslim 4.4%, Kirant 3%, Christian 1.4%, other 0.5%, unspecifed 0.2% (2011 est.)

Population: 30,986,975 (July 2014 est.)
country comparison to the world: 42

Age structure:
0-14 years: 31.6% (male 4,989,268/female 4,805,381)
15-24 years: 22.6% (male 3,521,421/female 3,484,203)
25-54 years: 35.7% (male 5,273,079/female 5,775,404)
55-64 years: 4.5% (male 847,431/female 886,760)
65 years and over: 4.5% (male 648,917/female 755,111) (2014 est.)

Dependency ratios:
total dependency ratio: 66.1 %
youth dependency ratio: 57.6 %
elderly dependency ratio: 8.5 %
potential support ratio: 11.7 (2013)

Median age: *total:* 22.9 years
male: 22.2 years
female: 23.6 years (2014 est.)

Population growth rate: 1.82% (2014 est.)
country comparison to the world: 66

Birth rate: 21.07 births/1,000 population (2014 est.)
country comparison to the world: 79

Death rate: 6.62 deaths/1,000 population (2014 est.)
country comparison to the world: 145

Net migration rate: 3.71 migrant(s)/1,000 population (2014 est.)
country comparison to the world: 32

Urbanization: *urban population:* 17% of total population (2011)
rate of urbanization: 3.62% annual rate of change (2010-15 est.)

Major urban areas—population: KATHMANDU (capital) 990,000 (2009)

Sex ratio: *at birth:* 1.04 male(s)/female
0-14 years: 1.04 male(s)/female
15-24 years: 1.01 male(s)/female
25-54 years: 0.91 male(s)/female
55-64 years: 0.97 male(s)/female
65 years and over: 0.87 male(s)/female
total population: 0.96 male(s)/female (2014 est.)

Mother's mean age at first birth: 20.1
note: median age at first birth among women 25-29 (2011 est.)

Maternal mortality rate: 170 deaths/100,000 live births (2010)
country comparison to the world: 60

Infant mortality rate: *total:* 40.43 deaths/1,000 live births
country comparison to the world: 53
male: 40.5 deaths/1,000 live births
female: 40.35 deaths/1,000 live births (2014 est.)

Life expectancy at birth: *total population:* 67.19 years
country comparison to the world: 165
male: 65.88 years
female: 68.56 years (2014 est.)

Total fertility rate: 2.3 children born/woman (2014 est.)
country comparison to the world: 93

Contraceptive prevalence rate: 49.7% (2011)

Health expenditures: 5.4% of GDP (2011)
country comparison to the world: 126

Physicians density: 0.21 physicians/1,000 population (2004)

Hospital bed density: 4.7 beds/1,000 population (2009)

Drinking water source:
improved:
urban: 91.2% of population
rural: 86.8% of population
total: 87.6% of population
unimproved:
urban: 8.8% of population
rural: 13.2% of population
total: 12.4% of population (2011 est.)

Sanitation facility access:
improved:
urban: 50.1% of population
rural: 32.4% of population
total: 35.4% of population
unimproved:
urban: 49.9% of population
rural: 67.6% of population
total: 64.6% of population (2011 est.)

HIV/AIDS—adult prevalence rate: 0.3% (2012 est.)
country comparison to the world: 99

HIV/AIDS—people living with HIV/AIDS: 48,700 (2012 est.)
country comparison to the world: 61

HIV/AIDS—deaths: 4,100 (2012 est.)
country comparison to the world: 44

Major infectious diseases: *degree of risk:* high
food or waterborne diseases: bacterial diarrhea, hepatitis A and E, and typhoid fever
vectorborne disease: Japanese encephalitis, malaria, and dengue fever (2013)

Obesity—adult prevalence rate: 1.4% (2008)
country comparison to the world: 189

Children under the age of 5 years underweight: 29.1% (2011)
country comparison to the world: 18

Education expenditures: 4.7% of GDP (2010)
country comparison to the world: 87

Literacy: *definition:* age 15 and over can read and write
total population: 57.4%
male: 71.1%
female: 46.7% (2011 est.)

School life expectancy (primary to tertiary education): *total:* 12 years
male: 12 years
female: 13 years (2011)

Child labor—children ages 5-14:
total number: 2,467,549
percentage: 34 % (2008 est.)

GOVERNMENT

Country name: *conventional long form:* Federal Democratic Republic of Nepal
conventional short form: Nepal
local long form: Sanghiya Loktantrik Ganatantra Nepal
local short form: Nepal

Government type: federal democratic republic

Capital: *name:* Kathmandu

geographic coordinates: 27 43 N, 85 19 E
time difference: UTC+5.75 (10.75 hours ahead of Washington, DC during Standard Time)

Administrative divisions: 14 zones (anchal, singular and plural); Bagmati, Bheri, Dhawalagiri, Gandaki, Janakpur, Karnali, Kosi, Lumbini, Mahakali, Mechi, Narayani, Rapti, Sagarmatha, Seti

Independence: 1768 (unified by Prithvi Narayan SHAH)

National holiday: Republic Day, 29 May

Constitution: several previous; latest entered into force 15 January 2007 (interim); note -a Constituent Assembly (CA) elected in 2008 to draft and promulgate a new constitution was unsuccessful and was disolved in mid-2012; a new CA was elected in late 2013 and the parties have committed to promulgating a new constitution within one year of the CAs first sitting of January 2014 (2013)

Legal system: English common law and Hindu legal concepts

International law organization participation: has not submitted an ICJ jurisdiction declaration; non-party state to the ICCt

Suffrage: 18 years of age; universal

Executive branch: *chief of state:* President Ram Baran YADAV (since 23 July 2008); Vice President Paramananda JHA (since 23 July 2008)
head of government: Prime Minister Sushil KOIRALA (since 11 February 2014)
cabinet: Prime Minister Koirala on 25 February 2014 appointed the cabinet ministers; the cabinet is dominated by the Nepali Congress and the Communist Party of Nepal-United Marxist-Leninist (For more information visit the World Leaders website)
elections: president elected by Parliament; term extends until the new constitution is promulgated; president elected on 21 July 2008; date of next election NA
election results: Ram Baran YADAV elected president by the Constituent Assembly in a second round of voting on 21 July 2008; Ram Baran YADAV 308, Ram Jaja Prasad SINGH 282

Legislative branch: unicameral Constituent Assembly (601 seats; 240 members elected by direct popular vote, 335 by proportional representation, and 26 appointed by the Cabinet (Council of Ministers); note—interim government Chairman REGMI convened Nepal's second Constituency Assembly on 22 January 2014
elections: last held on 19 November 2013 (next to be held NA)
election results: percent of vote by party—NC 26%, CPN-UML 24%, Unified Communist Party of Nepal (Maoist) 15%, Rastriya Prajatantra Party Nepal 7%; other 26%; seats by party—NC 196, CPN-UML 175, UCPN(M) 80, Rastriya

Prajantantra Party Nepal 24, other smaller parties 100; note—26 seats filled by the new Cabinet have not yet been appointed

Judicial branch: *highest court(s):* Supreme Court (consists of the chief justice and up to 14 judges note—Nepal's judiciary was restructured under its 2007 Interim Constitution
judge selection and term of office: the Supreme Court chief justice appointed by the prime minister on the recommendation of the Constitutional Council; other judges are appointed by the prime minister on the recommendation of the Judicial Council; judges serve until age 65
subordinate courts: appellate and district courts

Political parties and leaders:
note: 120 political parties participated in the 19 November 2013 election and the 30 parties listed below were elected to serve in the Constituent Assembly
Akhanda Nepal Party [Kumar KHADKA]; Communist Party of Nepal-Marxist Leninist [C.P. MAINALI]; Communist Party of Nepal-Unified Marxist-Leninist or UML [Jhalanath KHANAL]; Communist Party of Nepal (United) [Chandra Dev JOSHI]; Dalit Janajati Party [Bishwendra PASHWAN]; Federal Socialist Party [Ashok RAI]; Jana Jagaran Party Nepal [Lok Mani DHAKAL]; Khambuwan Rastriya Morcha-Nepal [Ram Kumar RAI]; Madhesi People's Rights Forum-Democratic [Bijay Kumar GACHCHADAR]; Madhesi People's Rights Forum-Nepal [Upendra YADAV]; Madhesi People's Rights Forum-Republican [Raj Kishore YADAV]; Madhes Samata Party Nepal [Meghraj SAHANI]; National Madhes Socialist Party [Sharat Singh BHANDARI]; Nepal Pariwar Dal [Ek Nath DHAKAL]; Nepal Workers and Peasants Party [Narayan Man BIJUKCHHE]; Nepali Congress [Sushil KOIRALA]; Nepali Janata Dal [Hari Charan SAH]; Nepa Rastriya Party [Keshav Man SHAKYA]; Rastriya Janamorcha Nepal [Chitra Bahadur K.C.]; Rastriya Janamukti Party [Malwar Singh THAPA]; Rastriya Prajatantra Party [Surya Bahadur THAPA]; Rastriya Prajatantra Party-Nepal [Kamal THAPA]; Sadbhavana Party [Rajendra MAHATO]; Samajbadi Janata Party Nepal [Prem Bahadur SINGH]; Sanghiya Sadbhavana Party [Anil JHA]; Sanghiye Lokatantrik Rastriya Manch [Rukmini CHAUDARY]; Terai Madhes Democratic Party [Mahantha THAKUR]; Terai Madhes Sadbhavana Party-Nepal [Mahendra YADAV]; Tharuhat Terai Party Nepal [Bhanuram CHAUDARY]; Unified Communist Party of Nepal (Maoist) or UCPN(M) [Pushpa Kamal DAHAL, also known as PRACHANDA]

Political pressure groups and leaders: The Communist Party of Nepal—Maoist (CPN-M); note—this party split from the UCPN(M) in June 2012,opposed the November 2013 elections, and is not represented in the current Constituent Assembly
other: a variety of groups advocating regional autonomy such as the Federal State Limbuwan Council in far eastern Nepal

International organization participation: ADB, BIMSTEC, CD, CP, FAO, G-77, IAEA, IBRD, ICAO, ICC, ICRM, IDA, IFAD, IFC, IFRCS, ILO, IMF, IMO, Interpol, IOC, IOM, IPU, ISO (correspondent), ITSO, ITU, ITUC (NGOs), MIGA, MINURSO, MINUSMA, MINUSTAH, MONUSCO, NAM, OPCW, SAARC, SACEP, UN, UNAMID, UNCTAD, UNESCO, UNIDO, UNIFIL, UNISFA, UNMIL, UNMISS, UNMIT, UNOCI, UNTSO, UNWTO, UPU, WCO, WFTU (NGOs), WHO, WIPO, WMO, WTO

Diplomatic representation in the US:
chief of mission: ambassador (vacant); Chargé d'Affaires Rishi Ram GHIMIRE (since 22 January 2014)
chancery: 2131 Leroy Place NW, Washington, DC 20008
telephone: [1] (202) 667-4550
FAX: [1] (202) 667-5534
consulate(s) general: New York

Diplomatic representation from the US:
chief of mission: Ambassador Peter W. BODDE (since 21 September 2012)
embassy: Maharajgunj, Kathmandu
mailing address: use embassy street address
telephone: [977] (1) 423-4000
FAX: [977] (1) 400-7272

Flag description: red with a blue border around the unique shape of two overlapping right triangles; the smaller, upper triangle bears a white stylized moon and the larger, lower triangle displays a white 12-pointed sun; the color red represents the rhododendron (Nepal's national flower) and is a sign of victory and bravery, the blue border signifies peace and harmony; the two right triangles are a combination of two single pennons (pennants) that originally symbolized the Himalaya Mountains while their charges represented the families of the king (upper) and the prime minister, but today they are understood to denote Hinduism and Buddhism, the country's two main religions; the moon represents the serenity of the Nepalese people and the shade and cool weather in the Himalayas, while the sun depicts the heat and higher temperatures of the lower parts of Nepal; the moon and the sun are also said to express the hope that the nation will endure as long as these heavenly bodies
note: Nepal is the only country in the world whose flag is not rectangular or square

National symbol(s): rhododendron blossom

National anthem: *name:* "Sayaun Thunga Phool Ka" (Hundreds of Flowers)
lyrics/music: Pradeep Kumar RAI/Ambar GURUNG
note: adopted 2007; after the abolition of the monarchy in 2006, a new anthem was required because of the previous anthem's praise for the king

ECONOMY

Economy—overview: Nepal is among the poorest and least developed countries in the world, with about one-quarter of its population living below the poverty line. Nepal is heavily dependent on remittances, which amount to as much as 22-25% of GDP. Agriculture is the mainstay of the economy, providing a livelihood for more than 70% of the population and accounting for a little over one-third of GDP. Industrial activity mainly involves the processing of agricultural products, including pulses, jute, sugarcane, tobacco, and grain. Nepal has considerable scope for exploiting its potential in hydropower, with an estimated 42,000 MW of commercially feasible capacity, but political uncertainty and a difficult business climate have hampered foreign investment. Additional challenges to Nepal's growth include its landlocked geographic location, persistent power shortages, underdeveloped transportation infrastructure, civil strife and labor unrest, and its susceptibility to natural disaster. The lack of political consensus in the past several years has delayed national budgets and prevented much-needed economic reform, although the government passed a full budget in 2013.

GDP (purchasing power parity): $42.06 billion (2013 est.)
country comparison to the world: 104
$40.57 billion (2012 est.)
$38.7 billion (2011 est.)
note: data are in 2013 US dollars

GDP (official exchange rate): $19.34 billion (2013 est.)

GDP—real growth rate: 3.6% (2013 est.)
country comparison to the world: 89
4.9% (2012 est.)
3.4% (2011 est.)

GDP—per capita (PPP): $1,500 (2013 est.)
country comparison to the world: 205
$1,500 (2012 est.)
$1,400 (2011 est.)
note: data are in 2013 US dollars

GDP—composition, by end use:
household consumption: 81.2%
government consumption: 10%
investment in fixed capital: 21.6%
investment in inventories: 14.6%
exports of goods and services: 10.3%
imports of goods and services: -37.7% (2013 est.)

GDP—composition, by sector of origin:
agriculture: 36.8%
industry: 14.5%
services: 48.7% (2013 est.)

Agriculture—products: pulses, rice, corn, wheat, sugarcane, jute, root crops; milk, water buffalo meat

Industries: tourism, carpets, textiles; small rice, jute, sugar, and oilseed mills; cigarettes, cement and brick production

Industrial production growth rate: 1.5% (2013 est.)
country comparison to the world: 137

Labor force: 16 million
country comparison to the world: 39
note: severe lack of skilled labor (2011 est.)

Labor force—by occupation: *agriculture:* 75%
industry: 7%
services: 18% (2010 est.)

Unemployment rate: 46% (2008 est.)
country comparison to the world: 193
42% (2004 est.)

Population below poverty line: 25.2% (2011 est.)

Household income or consumption by percentage share: *lowest 10%:* 3.2%
highest 10%: 29.5% (2011)

Distribution of family income—Gini index: 32.8 (2010)
country comparison to the world: 102
47.2 (2008 est.)

Budget: *revenues:* $3.3 billion
expenditures: $3.9 billion (FY12/13)

Taxes and other revenues: 17.1% of GDP (FY12/13)
country comparison to the world: 182

Budget surplus (+) or deficit (-):
-3.1% of GDP (FY12/13)
country comparison to the world: 126

Public debt: 28% of GDP
country comparison to the world: 126

Fiscal year: 16 July—15 July

Inflation rate (consumer prices): 9.6% (2013 est.)
country comparison to the world: 207
9.5% (2012 est.)

Central bank discount rate: 6% (31 December 2010 est.)
country comparison to the world: 49
6.5% (31 December 2009 est.)

Commercial bank prime lending rate: 9% (31 December 2013 est.)
country comparison to the world: 117
8% (31 December 2012 est.)

Stock of narrow money: $3.553 billion (31 December 2013 est.)
country comparison to the world: 114
$3.104 billion (31 December 2012 est.)

Stock of broad money: $11.49 billion (31 December 2013 est.)
country comparison to the world: 100
$11.71 billion (31 December 2012 est.)

Stock of domestic credit: $13.46 billion (31 December 2013 est.)
country comparison to the world: 90
$11.88 billion (31 December 2012 est.)

Market value of publicly traded shares: $4.16 billion (31 December 2012 est.)
country comparison to the world: 90
$3.849 billion (31 December 2011)
$5.235 billion (31 December 2010 est.)

Current account balance: $648 million (2013 est.)
country comparison to the world: 50
$283.9 million (2012 est.)

Exports: $1.06 billion (2013 est.)
country comparison to the world: 156
$1.004 billion (2012 est.)

Exports—commodities: clothing, pulses, carpets, textiles, juice, pashima, jute goods

Exports—partners: India 93.9%, Bangladesh 4%, Italy 0.4% (2013 est.)

Imports: $6.329 billion (2013 est.)
country comparison to the world: 119
$5.951 billion (2012 est.)

Imports—commodities: petroleum products, machinery and equipment, gold, electrical goods, medicine

Imports—partners: UAE 6.2%, South Korea 3.1%, China 2.5% (2013 est.)

Reserves of foreign exchange and gold: $6.574 billion (15 January 2014 est.)
country comparison to the world: 85
$5.833 billion (15 July 2013 est.)

Debt—external: $3.956 billion (31 December 2011 est.)
country comparison to the world: 128
$3.673 billion (31 December 2010 est.)

Stock of direct foreign investment—at home: $103 million
country comparison to the world: 105

Stock of direct foreign investment—abroad: $NA

Exchange rates: Nepalese rupees (NPR) per US dollar—
87.96 (2013 est.)
85.2 (2012 est.)
73.16 (2010 est.)
77.44 (2009)
65.21 (2008)

ENERGY

Electricity—production: 3.431 billion kWh (2012 est.)
country comparison to the world: 128

Electricity—consumption: 2.745 billion kWh (2010 est.)
country comparison to the world: 133

Electricity—exports: 30 million kWh (2010 est.)
country comparison to the world: 86

Electricity—imports: 694 million kWh (2010 est.)
country comparison to the world: 71

Electricity—installed generating capacity: 721,000 kW (2010 est.)
country comparison to the world: 129

Electricity—from fossil fuels: 7.9% of total installed capacity (2010 est.)
country comparison to the world: 198

Electricity—from nuclear fuels: 0% of total installed capacity (2010 est.)
country comparison to the world: 153

Electricity—from hydroelectric plants: 92.1% of total installed capacity (2010 est.)
country comparison to the world: 10

Electricity—from other renewable sources: 0% of total installed capacity (2010 est.)
country comparison to the world: 107

Crude oil—production: 0 bbl/day (2012 est.)
country comparison to the world: 202

Crude oil—exports: 0 bbl/day (2010 est.)
country comparison to the world: 163

Crude oil—imports: 0 bbl/day (2010 est.)
country comparison to the world: 105

Crude oil—proved reserves: 0 bbl (1 January 2013 es)
country comparison to the world: 172

Refined petroleum products—production: 0 bbl/day (2010 est.)
country comparison to the world: 182

Refined petroleum products—consumption: 18,430 bbl/day (2011 est.)
country comparison to the world: 132

Refined petroleum products—exports: 0 bbl/day (2010 est.)
country comparison to the world: 204

Refined petroleum products—imports: 21,960 bbl/day (2010 est.)
country comparison to the world: 102

Natural gas—production: 0 cu m (2011 est.)
country comparison to the world: 175

Natural gas—consumption: 0 cu m (2010 est.)
country comparison to the world: 180

Natural gas—exports: 0 cu m (2011 est.)
country comparison to the world: 157

Natural gas—imports: 0 cu m (2011 est.)
country comparison to the world: 108

Natural gas—proved reserves: 0 cu m (1 January 2013 es)
country comparison to the world: 178

Carbon dioxide emissions from consumption of energy: 3.173 million Mt (2011 est.)
country comparison to the world: 139

COMMUNICATIONS

Telephones—main lines in use: 834,000 (2013)
country comparison to the world: 8 3

Telephones—mobile cellular: 18.138 million (2013)
country comparison to the world: 54

Telephone system: *general assessment:* poor telephone and telegraph service; fair radiotelephone communication service and mobile-cellular telephone network
domestic: mobile-cellular telephone subscribership base is increasing with roughly 90% of the population living in areas covered by mobile carriers
international: country code—977; radiotelephone communications; microwave and fiber landlines to India; satellite earth station—1 Intelsat (Indian Ocean) (2011)

Broadcast media: state operates 2 TV stations as well as national and regional radio stations; roughly 30 independent TV channels are registered with only about half in regular operation; nearly 400 FM radio stations are licensed with roughly 300 operational (2007)

Internet country code: . n p

Internet hosts: 41,256 (2012)
country comparison to the world: 100

Internet users: 577,800 (2009)
country comparison to the world: 116

TRANSPORTATION

Airports: 47 (2013)
country comparison to the world: 9 4

Airports—with paved runways: *total:* 1 1
over 3,047 m: 1
1,524 to 2,437 m: 3
914 to 1,523 m: 6
under 914 m: 1 (2013)

Airports—with unpaved runways: *total:* 3 6
1,524 to 2,437 m: 1
914 to 1,523 m: 6
under 914 m: 29 (2013)

Railways: *total:* 59 km
country comparison to the world: 129
narrow gauge: 59 km 0.762-m gauge (2008)

Roadways: *total:* 10,844 km
country comparison to the world: 132
paved: 4,952 km
unpaved: 5,892 km (2010)

MILITARY

Military branches: Nepal Army (2012)

Military service age and obligation: 18 years of age for voluntary military service; no conscription (2014)

Manpower available for military service:
males age 16-49: 6,941,152
females age 16-49: 7,618,397 (2010 est.)

Manpower fit for military service:
males age 16-49: 5,260,878
females age 16-49: 5,947,512 (2010 est.)

Manpower reaching militarily significant age annually: *male*: 380,172
female: 367,103 (2010 est.)

Military expenditures: NA% (2012)
1.41% of GDP (2011)
NA% (2010)

TRANSNATIONAL ISSUES

Disputes—international: joint border commission continues to work on contested sections of boundary with India, including the 400 square kilometer dispute over the source of the Kalapani River; India has instituted a stricter border regime to restrict transit of Maoist insurgents and illegal cross-border activities Refugees and internally displaced persons:

refugees (country of origin): 15,0000-20,000 (Tibet/China) (2012); 29,813 (Bhutan) (2014)
IDPs: 50,000 (remaining from ten-year Maoist insurgency that officially ended in 2006; figure does not include people displaced since 2007 by inter-communal violence and insecurity in the Terai region) (2012)
stateless persons: 800,000 (2011); note—in 2007-2008 the government distributed 2.6 million citizenship certificates to the 3.4 million people without one; the remaining 800,000 without citizenship certificates are not necessarily stateless, and the UNHCR is working with the Nepali Government to clarify their situation; lesser numbers of Bhutanese Hindu refugees of Nepali origin (the Lhotsampa) who were stripped of Bhutanese nationality and forced to flee their country in the late 1980s and early 1990s—and undocumented Tibetan refugees who arrived in Nepal prior to the 1990s—are considered stateless

Illicit drugs: illicit producer of cannabis and hashish for the domestic and international drug markets; transit point for opiates from Southeast Asia to the West

NETHERLANDS

INTRODUCTION

Background: The Dutch United Provinces declared their independence from Spain in 1579; during the 17th century, they became a leading seafaring and commercial power, with settlements and colonies around the world. After a 20-year French occupation, a Kingdom of the Netherlands was formed in 1815. In 1830 Belgium seceded and formed a separate kingdom. The Netherlands remained neutral in World War I, but suffered invasion and occupation by Germany in World War II. A modern, industrialized nation, the Netherlands is also a large exporter of agricultural products. The country was a founding member of NATO and the EEC (now the EU) and participated in the introduction of the euro in 1999. In October 2010, the former Netherlands Antilles was dissolved and the three smallest islands—Bonaire, Sint Eustatius, and Saba—became special municipalities in the Netherlands administrative structure. The larger islands of Sint Maarten and Curacao joined the Netherlands and Aruba as constituent countries forming the Kingdom of the Netherlands.

GEOGRAPHY

Location: Western Europe, bordering the North Sea, between Belgium and Germany

Geographic coordinates: 52 30 N, 5 45 E

Map references: Europe

Area: *total*: 41,543 sq km
country comparison to the world: 135
land: 33,893 sq km
water: 7,650 sq km

Area—comparative: slightly less than twice the size of New Jersey

Land boundaries: *total*: 1,027 km
border countries: Belgium 450 km, Germany 577 km

Coastline: 451 km

Maritime claims: *territorial sea*: 12 nm
contiguous zone: 24 nm
exclusive fishing zone: 200 nm

Climate: temperate; marine; cool summers and mild winters

Terrain: mostly coastal lowland and reclaimed land (polders); some hills in southeast

Elevation extremes: *lowest point*: Zuidplaspolder -7 m
highest point: Mount Scenery 862 m (on the island of Saba in the Caribbean, now considered an integral part of the Netherlands following the dissolution of the Netherlands Antilles)
note: the highest point on continental Netherlands is Vaalserberg at 322 m

Natural resources: natural gas, petroleum, peat, limestone, salt, sand and gravel, arable land

Land use: *arable land*: 25.08%
permanent crops: 0.88%
other: 74.04% (2011)

Irrigated land: 4,572 sq km (2007)

Total renewable water resources: 91 cu km (2011)

Freshwater withdrawal (domestic/industrial/agricultural): *total*: 10.61 cu km/yr (12%/88%/1%)
per capita: 636.7 cu m/yr (2008)

Natural hazards: flooding

Environment—current issues: water pollution in the form of heavy metals, organic compounds, and nutrients such as nitrates and phosphates; air pollution from vehicles and refining activities; acid rain

Environment—international agreements: party to: Air Pollution, Air Pollution-Nitrogen Oxides, Air Pollution-Persistent Organic Pollutants, Air Pollution-Sulfur 85, Air Pollution-Sulfur 94, Air Pollution-Volatile Organic Compounds, Antarctic-Environmental Protocol, Antarctic-Marine Living Resources, Antarctic Treaty, Biodiversity, Climate Change, Climate Change-Kyoto Protocol, Desertification, Endangered Species, Environmental Modification, Hazardous Wastes, Law of the Sea, Marine Dumping, Marine Life Conservation, Ozone Layer Protection, Ship Pollution, Tropical Timber 83, Tropical Timber 94, Wetlands, Whaling
signed, but not ratified: none of the selected agreements

Geography—note: located at mouths of three major European rivers (Rhine, Maas or Meuse, and Schelde)

PEOPLE AND SOCIETY

Nationality: *noun*: Dutchman(men), Dutchwoman (women)
adjective: Dutch

Ethnic groups: Dutch 80.7%, EU 5%, Indonesian 2.4%, Turkish 2.2%, Surinamese 2%, Moroccan 2%, Caribbean 0.8%, other 4.8% (2008 est.)

Languages: Dutch (official), Frisian (official)

Religions: Roman Catholic 30%, Protestant 20% (Dutch Reformed 11%, Calvinist 6%, other Protestant 3%), Muslim 5.8%, other 2.2%, none 42% (2006)

Population: 16,877,351 (July 2014 est.)
country comparison to the world: 66

Age structure:
0-14 years: 16.9% (male 1,460,234/female 1,393,766)
15-24 years: 12.2% (male 1,046,323/female 1,006,114)
25-54 years: 40.4% (male 3,423,777/female 3,399,378)
55-64 years: 17.6% (male 1,088,860/female 1,094,574)
65 years and over: 17.1% (male 1,331,258/female 1,633,067) (2014 est.)

Dependency ratios:
total dependency ratio: 51.7 %
youth dependency ratio: 25.9 %
elderly dependency ratio: 25.8 %
potential support ratio: 3.9 (2013)

Median age: *total*: 42.1 years
male: 41.2 years
female: 42.9 years (2014 est.)

Population growth rate: 0.42% (2014 est.)
country comparison to the world: 161

Birth rate: 10.83 births/1,000 population (2014 est.)

country comparison to the world: 181

Death rate: 8.57 deaths/1,000 population (2014 est.)
country comparison to the world: 76

Net migration rate: 1.97 migrant(s)/1,000 population (2014 est.)
country comparison to the world: 48

Urbanization: *urban population:* 83% of total population (2010)
rate of urbanization: 0.8% annual rate of change (2010-15 est.)

Major urban areas—population: AMSTERDAM (capital) 1.044 million; Rotterdam 1.008 million; The Hague (seat of government) 629,000 (2009)

Sex ratio: *at birth:* 1.05 male(s)/female
0-14 years: 1.05 male(s)/female
15-24 years: 1.04 male(s)/female
25-54 years: 1.01 male(s)/female
55-64 years: 0.98 male(s)/female
65 years and over: 0.8 male(s)/female
total population: 0.98 male(s)/female (2014 est.)

Mother's mean age at first birth: 28.9 (2005 est.)

Maternal mortality rate: 6 deaths/100,000 live births (2010)
country comparison to the world: 171

Infant mortality rate: *total:* 3.66 deaths/1,000 live births
country comparison to the world: 205
male: 3.95 deaths/1,000 live births
female: 3.35 deaths/1,000 live births (2014 est.)

Life expectancy at birth: *total population:* 81.12 years
country comparison to the world: 22
male: 79.02 years
female: 83.34 years (2014 est.)

Total fertility rate: 1.78 children born/woman (2014 est.)
country comparison to the world: 157

Contraceptive prevalence rate: 69%
note: percent of women aged 18-45 (2008)

Health expenditures: 12% of GDP (2011)
country comparison to the world: 9

Physicians density: 3.92 physicians/1,000 population (2007)

Hospital bed density: 4.7 beds/1,000 population (2009)

Drinking water source:
improved:
urban: 100% of population
rural: 100% of population
total: 100% of population
unimproved:
urban: 0% of population
rural: 0% of population
total: 0% of population (2011 est.)

Sanitation facility access:
improved:
urban: 100% of population
rural: 100% of population
total: 100% of population
unimproved:
urban: 0% of population
rural: 0% of population
total: 0% of population (2011 est.)

HIV/AIDS—adult prevalence rate: 0.2% (2009 est.)
country comparison to the world: 103

HIV/AIDS—people living with HIV/AIDS: 22,000 (2009 est.)
country comparison to the world: 79

HIV/AIDS—deaths: fewer than 100 (2009 est.)
country comparison to the world: 139

Obesity—adult prevalence rate: 18.8% (2008)
country comparison to the world: 103

Education expenditures: 5.9% of GDP (2011)
country comparison to the world: 45

Literacy: *definition:* age 15 and over can read and write
total population: 99%
male: 99%
female: 99% (2003 est.)

School life expectancy (primary to tertiary education): *total:* 18 years
male: 18 years
female: 18 years (2011)

Unemployment, youth ages 15-24: *total:* 9.5%
country comparison to the world: 110
male: 8.9%
female: 10% (2012)

GOVERNMENT

Country name: *conventional long form:* Kingdom of the Netherlands
conventional short form: Netherlands
local long form: Koninkrijk der Nederlanden
local short form: Nederland

Government type: constitutional monarchy

Capital: *name:* Amsterdam

geographic coordinates: 52 21 N, 4 55 E
time difference: UTC+1 (6 hours ahead of Washington, DC during Standard Time)
daylight saving time: +1hr, begins last Sunday in March; ends last Sunday in October
note: The Hague is the seat of government; time descriptions apply to the continental Netherlands only, not to the Caribbean components

Administrative divisions: 12 provinces (provincies, singular—provincie); Drenthe, Flevoland, Fryslan (Friesland), Gelderland, Groningen, Limburg, Noord-Brabant (North Brabant), Noord-Holland (North Holland), Overijssel, Utrecht, Zeeland (Zealand), Zuid-Holland (South Holland)

Dependent areas: Aruba, Curacao, Sint Maarten

Independence: 23 January 1579 (the northern provinces of the Low Countries conclude the Union of Utrecht breaking with Spain; on 26 July 1581 they formally declared their independence with an Act of Abjuration; however, it was not until 30 January 1648 and the Peace of Westphalia that Spain recognized this independence)

National holiday: King's Day (for 2014, the holiday will be on 26 April; thereafter it will fall on the King's Birthday of 27 April (1967))

Constitution: previous 1597, 1798; latest adopted 24 August 1815 (substantially revised in 1848); amended many times, last in 2010 (2013)

Legal system: civil law system based on the French system; constitution does not permit judicial review of acts of the States General

International law organization participation: accepts compulsory ICJ jurisdiction with reservations; accepts ICCt jurisdiction

Suffrage: 18 years of age; universal

Executive branch: *chief of state:* King WILLEM-ALEXANDER (since 30 April 2013)
head of government: Prime Minister Mark RUTTE (since 14 October 2010); Deputy Prime Minister Lodewijk ASSCHER (since 5 November 2012); note—Mark RUTTE tendered his resignation 23 April 2012; new elections were held on 12 September 2012 in which his party won the most seats; during the interim period he remained in office in a care-taking position; he was sworn in again to be prime minister on 5 November 2012
cabinet: Council of Ministers appointed by the monarch (For more information visit the World Leaders website)
elections: the monarchy is hereditary; following Second Chamber elections, the leader of the majority party or leader of a majority coalition usually appointed prime minister by the monarch; deputy prime ministers appointed by the monarch
note: there is also a Council of State composed of the monarch, heir apparent, and councilors that provides consultations to the cabinet on legislative and administrative policy

Legislative branch: bicameral States General or Staten Generaal consists of the First Chamber or Eerste Kamer (75 seats; members indirectly elected by the country's 12 provincial councils to serve four-year terms) and the Second Chamber or Tweede Kamer (150 seats; members elected by popular vote to serve at most four-year terms)
elections: First Chamber—last held on May 2011 (next to be held in May 2015); Second Chamber—last held on 12 September 2012 (next to be held by September 2016)
election results: First Chamber—percent of vote by party—NA; seats by party—VVD 16, PvdA 14, CDA 11, PVV 10, SP 8, D66 5, GL 5, other 6; Second Chamber—percent of vote by party—VVD 26.6%, PvdA 24.8%, PVV, 10.1%, SP 9.7%, CDA 8.5%, D66 8.0%, CU 3.1%, GL 6.7%, other 2.5%; seats by party—VVD 41, PvdA 38, PVV 15, SP 15, CDA 13, D66 12, CU 5, GL 4, other 7

Judicial branch: *highest court(s):* Supreme Court or Hoge Raad (consists of 41 judges: the president, 6 vice-presidents, 31 justices or raadsheren, and 3 justices in exceptional service, referred to as buitengewone dienst); the court is divided into criminal, civil, tax, and ombuds chambers
judge selection and term of office: justices appointed by the monarch from a list provided by the Second Chamber of the States General; justices appointed for life or until mandatory retirement at age 70
subordinate courts: courts of appeal; district courts, each with up to 5 subdistrict courts

Political parties and leaders: Christian Democratic Appeal or CDA [Sybrand VAN HAERSMA BUMA]; Christian Union or CU [Arie SLOB]; Democrats 66 or D66 [Alexander PECHTOLD]; Green Left or GL [Bram VAN OJIK]; Labor Party or PvdA [Diederik SAMSOM]; Party for Freedom or PVV [Geert WILDERS]; Party for the Animals or PvdD [Marianne THIEME]; People's Party for Freedom and Democracy or VVD [Halbe ZIJLSTRA]; Reformed Political Party or SGP [Kees VAN DER STAAIJ]; Socialist Party or SP [Emile ROEMER]; plus a few minor parties

Political pressure groups and leaders: Christian Trade Union Federation or CNV [Jaap SMIT]; Confederation of Netherlands Industry and Employers or VNO-NCW [Bernard WIENTJES]; Federation for Small and Medium-sized businesses or MKB [Hans BIESHEUVEL]; Netherlands Trade Union Federation or FNV [Ton HEERTS]; Social Economic Council or SER [Wiebe DRAIJER]; Trade Union Federation of Middle and High Personnel or MHP [Reginald VISSER]

International organization participation: ADB (nonregional member), AfDB (nonregional member), Arctic Council (observer), Australia Group, Benelux, BIS, CBSS (observer), CD, CE, CERN, EAPC, EBRD, ECB, EIB, EITI (implementing country), EMU, ESA, EU, FAO, FATF, G-10,

IADB, IAEA, IBRD, ICAO, ICC (national committees), ICRM, IDA, IEA, IFAD, IFC, IFRCS, IGAD (partners), IHO, ILO, IMF, IMO, IMSO, Interpol, IOC, IOM, IPU, ISO, ITSO, ITU, ITUC (NGOs), MIGA, MINUSMA, NATO, NEA, NSG, OAS (observer), OECD, OPCW, OSCE, Paris Club, PCA, Schengen Convention, SELEC (observer), UN, UNAMID, UNCTAD, UNESCO, UNHCR, UNIDO, UNMISS, UNRWA, UNTSO, UNWTO, UPU, WCO, WHO, WIPO, WMO, WTO, ZC

Diplomatic representation in the US:
chief of mission: Ambassador Rudolf Simon BEKINK (since 20 July 2012)
chancery: 4200 Linnean Avenue NW, Washington, DC 20008
telephone: [1] (202) 244-5300, [1] 877-388-2443
FAX: [1] (202) 362-3430
consulate(s) general: Chicago, Miami, New York, San Francisco
consulate(s): Boston

Diplomatic representation from the US:
chief of mission: ambassador (vacant); Charge d'Affaires Adam STERLING (since July 2013)
embassy: Lange Voorhout 102, 2514 EJ, The Hague
mailing address: PSC 71, Box 1000, APO AE 09715
telephone: [31] (70) 310-2209
FAX: [31] (70) 310-2207
consulate(s) general: Amsterdam

Flag description: three equal horizontal bands of red (top), white, and blue; similar to the flag of Luxembourg, which uses a lighter blue and is longer; the colors were those of WILLIAM I, Prince of Orange, who led the Dutch Revolt against Spanish sovereignty in the latter half of the 16th century; originally the upper band was orange, but because it tended to fade to red over time, the red shade was eventually made the permanent color; the banner is perhaps the oldest tricolor in continuous use

National symbol(s): lion

National anthem: *name:* "Het Wilhelmus" (The William)
lyrics/music: Philips VAN MARNIX van Sint Aldegonde (presumed)/unknown
note: adopted 1932, in use since the 17th century, making it the oldest national anthem in the world; also known as "Wilhelmus van Nassouwe" (William of Nassau), it is in the form of an acrostic, where the first letter of each stanza spells the name of the leader of the Dutch Revolt

ECONOMY

Economy—overview: The Dutch economy is the sixth-largest economy in the euro-zone and is noted for its stable industrial relations, moderate unemployment and inflation, a sizable trade surplus, and an important role as a European transportation hub. Industrial activity is predominantly in food processing, chemicals, petroleum refining, and electrical machinery. A highly mechanized agricultural sector employs only 2% of the labor force but provides large surpluses for the food-processing industry and for exports. The Netherlands, along with 11 of its EU partners, began circulating the euro currency on 1 January 2002. After 26 years of uninterrupted economic growth, the Dutch economy—highly dependent on an international financial sector and international trade—contracted by 3.5% in 2009 as a result of the global financial crisis. The Dutch financial sector suffered, due in part to the high exposure of some Dutch banks to U.S. mortgage-backed securities. In 2008, the government nationalized two banks and injected billions of dollars of capital into other financial institutions, to prevent further deterioration of a crucial sector. The government also sought to boost the domestic economy by accelerating infrastructure programs, offering corporate tax breaks for employers to retain workers, and expanding export credit facilities. The stimulus programs and bank bailouts, however, resulted in a government budget deficit of 5.3% of GDP in 2010 that contrasted sharply with a surplus of 0.7% in 2008. The government of Prime Minister Mark RUTTE began implementing fiscal consolidation measures in early 2011, mainly reductions in expenditures, which resulted in an improved budget deficit in 2011. In 2012-13 tax revenues dropped, GDP contracted, and the budget deficit deteriorated. Although jobless claims continued to grow, the unemployment rate remained relatively low at 6.8 percent.

GDP (purchasing power parity): $696.3 billion (2013 est.)
country comparison to the world: 24
$705.3 billion (2012 est.)
$714.2 billion (2011 est.)
note: data are in 2013 US dollars

GDP (official exchange rate): $800.5 billion (2013 est.)

GDP—real growth rate: -1.3% (2013 est.)
country comparison to the world: 205
-1.2% (2012 est.)
0.9% (2011 est.)

GDP—per capita (PPP): $41,400 (2013 est.)
country comparison to the world: 24
$42,100 (2012 est.)
$42,800 (2011 est.)
note: data are in 2013 US dollars

Gross national saving: 26.2% of GDP (2013 est.)
country comparison to the world: 42
27.5% of GDP (2012 est.)
28.3% of GDP (2011 est.)

GDP—composition, by end use:
household consumption: 45.3%
government consumption: 27.7%
investment in fixed capital: 15.7%
investment in inventories: 0.4%
exports of goods and services: 86%
imports of goods and services: -75.2% (2013 est.)

GDP—composition, by sector of origin:
agriculture: 2.6%
industry: 25.4%
services: 72.1% (2013 est.)

Agriculture—products: grains, potatoes, sugar beets, fruits, vegetables; livestock

Industries: agroindustries, metal and engineering products, electrical machinery and equipment, chemicals, petroleum, construction, microelectronics, fishing

Industrial production growth rate: 1% (2013 est.)
country comparison to the world: 146

Labor force: 7.879 million (2013 est.)
country comparison to the world: 61

Labor force—by occupation:
agriculture: 2%
industry: 18%
services: 80% (2005 est.)

Unemployment rate: 6.8% (2013 est.)
country comparison to the world: 71
5.3% (2012 est.)

Population below poverty line: 10.5% (2005)

Household income or consumption by percentage share: *lowest 10%:* 2.5%
highest 10%: 22.9% (1999)

Distribution of family income—Gini index: 30.9 (2007)
country comparison to the world: 114
32.6 (1994)

Budget: *revenues:* $370.4 billion
expenditures: $400.6 billion (2013 est.)

Taxes and other revenues: 46.3% of GDP (2013 est.)
country comparison to the world: 19

Budget surplus (+) or deficit (-):
-3.8% of GDP (2013 est.)
country comparison to the world: 142

Public debt: 73.3% of GDP (2013 est.)
country comparison to the world: 35
71.1% of GDP (2012 est.)
note: data cover general government debt, and includes debt instruments issued (or owned) by government entities other than the treasury; the data include treasury debt held by foreign entities; the data include debt issued by subnational entities, as well as intra-governmental debt; intra-governmental debt consists of treasury borrowings from surpluses in the social funds, such as for retirement, medical care, and unemployment, debt instruments for the social funds are not sold at public auctions

Fiscal year: calendar year

Inflation rate (consumer prices): 2.8% (2013 est.)
country comparison to the world: 102
2.8% (2012 est.)

Central bank discount rate: 0.75% (31 December 2013)
country comparison to the world: 130
1.5% (31 December 2010)
note: this is the European Central Bank's rate on the marginal lending facility, which offers overnight credit to banks in the euro area

Commercial bank prime lending rate: 2.3% (31 December 2013 est.)
country comparison to the world: 178
2.65% (31 December 2012 est.)

Stock of narrow money: $401.1 billion (31 December 2013 est.)
country comparison to the world: 15
$389.9 billion (31 December 2012 est.)
note: see entry for the European Union for money supply in the euro area; the European Central Bank (ECB) controls monetary policy for the 17 members of the Economic and Monetary Union (EMU); individual members of the EMU do not control the quantity of money circulating within their own borders

Stock of broad money: $1.169 trillion (31 December 2013 est.)
country comparison to the world: 17
$1.136 trillion (31 December 2012 est.)

Stock of domestic credit: $1.736 trillion (31 December 2013 est.)
country comparison to the world: 13
$1.7 trillion (31 December 2012 est.)

Market value of publicly traded shares: $651 billion (31 December 2012 est.)
country comparison to the world: 19
$594.7 billion (31 December 2011)
$661.2 billion (31 December 2010 est.)

Current account balance: $82.9 billion (2013 est.)
country comparison to the world: 4
$77.02 billion (2012 est.)

Exports: $551 billion (2013 est.)
country comparison to the world: 8
$540.3 billion (2012 est.)

Exports—commodities: machinery and equipment, chemicals, fuels; foodstuffs

Exports—partners: Germany 26.5%, Belgium 13.7%, France 8.8%, UK 8%, Italy 4.5% (2012)

Imports: $477.8 billion (2013 est.)
country comparison to the world: 10
$476.5 billion (2012 est.)

Imports—commodities: machinery and transport equipment, chemicals, fuels, foodstuffs, clothing

Imports—partners: Germany 13.8%, China 12%, Belgium 8.4%, UK 6.7%, Russia 6.4%, US 6.1% (2012)

Reserves of foreign exchange and gold: $54.82 billion (31 December 2012 est.)
country comparison to the world: 35
$51.27 billion (31 December 2011 est.)

Debt—external: $2.504 trillion (31 December 2012 est.)
country comparison to the world: 9
$2.482 trillion (31 December 2011)

Stock of direct foreign investment—at home: $567.8 billion (31 December 2013 est.)
country comparison to the world: 15
$560.2 billion (31 December 2012 est.)

Stock of direct foreign investment—abroad: $967 billion (31 December 2013 est.)
country comparison to the world: 10
$953.8 billion (31 December 2012 est.)

Exchange rates: euros (EUR) per US dollar—
0.7634 (2013 est.)
0.7752 (2012 est.)
0.755 (2010 est.)
0.7198 (2009 est.)
0.6827 (2008 est.)

ENERGY

Electricity—production: 106.7 billion kWh (2011 est.)
country comparison to the world: 3 3

Electricity—consumption: 110 billion kWh (2010 est.)
country comparison to the world: 31

Electricity—exports: 15.05 billion kWh (2012 est.)
country comparison to the world: 13

Electricity—imports: 32.16 billion kWh (2012 est.)
country comparison to the world: 6

Electricity—installed generating capacity: 26.62 million kW (2010 est.)
country comparison to the world: 31

Electricity—from fossil fuels: 83.6% of total installed capacity (2010 est.)
country comparison to the world: 90

Electricity—from nuclear fuels: 1.9% of total installed capacity (2010 est.)
country comparison to the world: 28

Electricity—from hydroelectric plants: 0.1% of total installed capacity (2010 est.)
country comparison to the world: 149

Electricity—from other renewable sources: 14.3% of total installed capacity (2010 est.)
country comparison to the world: 15

Crude oil—production: 71,720 bbl/day (2012 est.)
country comparison to the world: 56

Crude oil—exports: 10,220 bbl/day (2010 est.)
country comparison to the world: 58

Crude oil—imports: 1.027 million bbl/day (2010 est.)
country comparison to the world: 12

Crude oil—proved reserves: 243.9 million bbl (1 January 2013 es)
country comparison to the world: 57

Refined petroleum products—production: 1.248 million bbl/day (2010 est.)
country comparison to the world: 17

Refined petroleum products—consumption: 1.01 million bbl/day (2011 est.)
country comparison to the world: 21

Refined petroleum products—exports: 2.138 million bbl/day (2010 est.)
country comparison to the world: 4

Refined petroleum products—imports: 2.079 million bbl/day (2010 est.)
country comparison to the world: 3

Natural gas—production: 80.78 billion cu m (2012 est.)
country comparison to the world: 11

Natural gas—consumption: 54.85 billion cu m (2010 est.)
country comparison to the world: 16

Natural gas—exports: 74.06 billion cu m (2012 est.)
country comparison to the world: 6

Natural gas—imports: 35.74 billion cu m (2012 est.)
country comparison to the world: 17

Natural gas—proved reserves: 1.23 trillion cu m (1 January 2013 es)
country comparison to the world: 24

Carbon dioxide emissions from consumption of energy: 253 million Mt (2011 est.)
country comparison to the world: 26

COMMUNICATIONS

Telephones—main lines in use: 7.086 million (2012)
country comparison to the world: 2 5

Telephones—mobile cellular: 19.643 million (2012)
country comparison to the world: 50

Telephone system: *general assessment:* highly developed and well maintained
domestic: extensive fixed-line fiber-optic network; large cellular telephone system with 5 major operators utilizing the third generation of the Global System for Mobile Communications (GSM) technology; one in five households now use Voice over the Internet Protocol (VoIP) services
international: country code—31; submarine cables provide links to the US and Europe; satellite earth stations—5 (3 Intelsat—1 Indian Ocean and 2 Atlantic Ocean, 1 Eutelsat, and 1 Inmarsat (2011)

Broadcast media: more than 90% of households are connected to cable or satellite TV systems that provide a wide range of domestic and foreign channels; public service broadcast system includes multiple broadcasters, 3 with a national reach and the remainder operating in regional and local markets; 2 major nationwide commercial television companies, each with 3 or more stations, and many commercial TV stations in regional and local markets; nearly 600 radio stations with a mix of public and private stations providing national or regional coverage (2008)

Internet country code: .nl

Internet hosts: 13.699 million (2012)
country comparison to the world: 11

Internet users: 14.872 million (2009)
country comparison to the world: 27

TRANSPORTATION

Airports: 29 (2013)
country comparison to the world: 120

Airports—with paved runways: *total:* 2 3
over 3,047 m: 3
2,438 to 3,047 m: 11
1,524 to 2,437 m: 1
914 to 1,523 m: 6
under 914 m: 2 (2013)

Airports—with unpaved runways: *total:* 6
914 to 1,523 m: 4
under 914 m: 2 (2013)

Heliports: 1 (2013)

Pipelines: condensate 81 km; gas 8,531 km; oil 578 km; refined products 716 km (2013)

Railways: *total:* 3,013 km
country comparison to the world: 56

standard gauge: 3,013 km 1.435-m gauge (2,195 km electrified) (2012)

Roadways: *total:* 139,295 km (includes 2,758 km of expressways) (2012)
country comparison to the world: 36

Waterways: 6,237 km (navigable for ships of 50 tons) (2012)
country comparison to the world: 22

Merchant marine: *total:* 744
country comparison to the world: 15
by type: bulk carrier 4, cargo 514, carrier 15, chemical tanker 56, container 67, liquefied gas 21, passenger 17, passenger/cargo 14, petroleum tanker 4, refrigerated cargo 10, roll on/roll off 19, specialized tanker 3
foreign-owned: 196 (Australia 1, Bermuda 1, Denmark 27, Finland 13, France 2, Germany 86, Ireland 8, Italy 6, Japan 1, Norway 19, Sweden 12, UAE 4, US 16)
registered in other countries: 233 (Antigua and Barbuda 17, Bahamas 23, Belize 1, Canada 1, Curacao 43, Cyprus 23, Germany 1, Gibraltar 34, Italy 2, Liberia 31, Luxembourg 3, Malta 3, Marshall Islands 21, Panama 6, Paraguay 1, Philippines 17, Russia 2, Saint Vincent and the Grenadines 1, Singapore 1, UK 1, unknown 1) (2010)

Ports and terminals: *major seaport(s):* IJmuiden, Vlissingen
river port(s): Amsterdam (Nordsee Kanaal); Moerdijk (Hollands Diep River); Rotterdam (Rhine River); Terneuzen (Western Scheldt River)
container port(s) (TEUs): Rotterdam (11,876,920)

MILITARY

Military branches: Royal Netherlands Army, Royal Netherlands Navy (includes Naval Air Service and Marine Corps), Royal Netherlands Air Force (Koninklijke Luchtmacht, KLu), Royal Military Police (2012)

Military service age and obligation: 17 years of age for an all-volunteer force (2012)

Manpower available for military service:
males age 16-49: 3,911,098
females age 16-49: 3,817,031 (2010 est.)

Manpower fit for military service:
males age 16-49: 3,201,328
females age 16-49: 3,122,889 (2010 est.)

Manpower reaching militarily significant age annually: *male:* 103,462 *female:* 98,383 (2010 est.)

Military expenditures: 1.27% of GDP (2012)
country comparison to the world: 82
1.35% of GDP (2011)
1.27% of GDP (2010)

TRANSNATIONAL ISSUES

Disputes—international: none

Refugees and internally displaced persons: *refugees (country of origin):* 18,255 (Iraq); 15,715 (Somalia); 5,697 (Afghanistan) (2012)
stateless persons: 2,005 (2012)

Illicit drugs: major European producer of synthetic drugs, including ecstasy, and cannabis cultivator; important gateway for cocaine, heroin, and hashish entering Europe; major source of US-bound ecstasy; large financial sector vulnerable to money laundering; significant consumer of ecstasy

NEW CALEDONIA

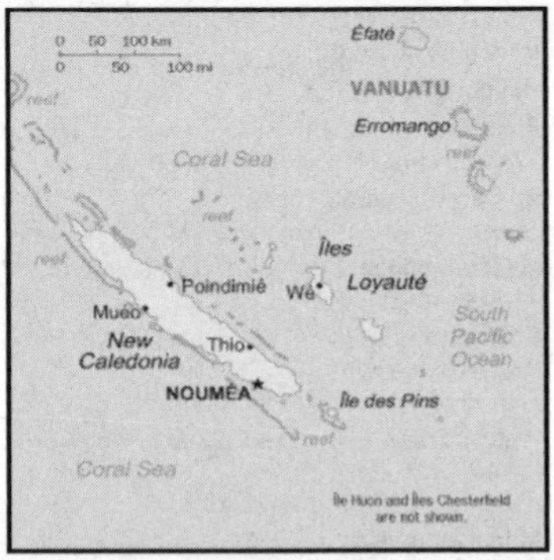

INTRODUCTION

Background: Settled by both Britain and France during the first half of the 19th century, the island became a French possession in 1853. It served as a penal colony for four decades after 1864. Agitation for independence during the 1980s and early 1990s ended in the 1998 Noumea Accord, which over a period of 15 to 20 years will transfer an increasing amount of governing responsibility from France to New Caledonia. The agreement also commits France to conduct a referendum between 2014 and 2018 to decide whether New Caledonia should assume full sovereignty and independence.

GEOGRAPHY

Location: Oceania, islands in the South Pacific Ocean, east of Australia

Geographic coordinates: 21 30 S, 165 30 E

Map references: Oceania

Area: *total:* 18,575 sq km
country comparison to the world: 156
land: 18,275 sq km
water: 300 sq km

Area—comparative: slightly smaller than New Jersey

Land boundaries: 0 km

Coastline: 2,254 km

Maritime claims: *territorial sea:* 12 nm
exclusive economic zone: 200 nm

Climate: tropical; modified by southeast trade winds; hot, humid

Terrain: coastal plains with interior mountains

Elevation extremes: *lowest point:* Pacific Ocean 0 m
highest point: Mont Panie 1,628 m

Natural resources: nickel, chrome, iron, cobalt, manganese, silver, gold, lead, copper

Land use: *arable land:* 0.38%
permanent crops: 0.27%
other: 99.34% (2011)

Irrigated land: 100 sq km (2003)

Natural hazards: cyclones, most frequent from November to March
volcanism: Matthew and Hunter Islands are historically active

Environment—current issues: erosion caused by mining exploitation and forest fires

Geography—note: consists of the main island of New Caledonia (one of the largest in the Pacific Ocean), the archipelago of Iles Loyaute, and numerous small, sparsely populated islands and atolls

PEOPLE AND SOCIETY

Nationality: *noun:* New Caledonian(s)
adjective: New Caledonian

Ethnic groups: Kanak 40.3%, European 29.2%, Wallisian, Futunian 8.7%, Tahitian 2%, Indonesian 1.6%, Vietnamese 1%, Ni-Vanuatu 0.9%, other 16.2% (2009 est.)

Languages: French (official), 33 Melanesian-Polynesian dialects

Religions: Roman Catholic 60%, Protestant 30%, other 10%

Population: 267,840 (July 2014 est.)
country comparison to the world: 183

Age structure:
0-14 years: 23.6% (male 32,311/female 30,926)
15-24 years: 17% (male 23,218/female 22,260)
25-54 years: 42.8% (male 57,646/female 56,939)
55-64 years: 8.5% (male 10,698/female 11,128)
65 years and over: 8.2% (male 10,135/female 12,579) (2014 est.)

Dependency ratios:
total dependency ratio: 48.3 %
youth dependency ratio: 33.6 %
elderly dependency ratio: 14.7 %
potential support ratio: 6.8 (2013)

Median age: *total:* 31.1 years
male: 30.4 years
female: 31.7 years (2014 est.)

Population growth rate: 1.42% (2014 est.)
country comparison to the world: 85

Birth rate: 15.57 births/1,000 population (2014 est.)
country comparison to the world: 128

Death rate: 5.45 deaths/1,000 population (2014 est.)
country comparison to the world: 177

Net migration rate: 4.06 migrant(s)/1,000 population
country comparison to the world: 31
note: there has been steady emigration from Wallis and Futuna to New Caledonia (2014 est.)

Urbanization: *urban population:* 57% of total population (2010)
rate of urbanization: 1.4% annual rate of change (2010-15 est.)

Major urban areas—population: NOUMEA (capital) 144,000 (2009)

Sex ratio: *at birth:* 1.05 male(s)/female
0-14 years: 1.05 male(s)/female
15-24 years: 1.04 male(s)/female
25-54 years: 1.01 male(s)/female
55-64 years: 1 male(s)/female
65 years and over: 0.81 male(s)/female
total population: 1 male(s)/female (2014 est.)

Infant mortality rate: *total:* 5.46 deaths/1,000 live births
country comparison to the world: 177
male: 6.43 deaths/1,000 live births
female: 4.43 deaths/1,000 live births (2014 est.)

Life expectancy at birth: *total population:* 77.31 years
country comparison to the world: 68
male: 73.29 years
female: 81.54 years (2014 est.)

Total fertility rate: 1.99 children born/woman (2014 est.)

country comparison to the world: 127

Drinking water source:
improved:
urban: 98.5% of population
rural: 98.5% of population
total: 98.5% of population
unimproved:
urban: 1.5% of population
rural: 1.5% of population
total: 1.5% of population (2011 est.)

Sanitation facility access:
improved:
urban: 100% of population
rural: 100% of population
total: 100% of population
unimproved:
urban: 0% of population
rural: 0% of population
total: 0% of population (2011 est.)

HIV/AIDS—adult prevalence rate: NA

HIV/AIDS—people living with HIV/AIDS: NA

HIV/AIDS—deaths: NA

Literacy: *definition:* age 15 and over can read and write
total population: 96.2%
male: 96.8%
female: 95.5% (1996 census)

GOVERNMENT

Country name: *conventional long form:* Territory of New Caledonia and Dependencies
conventional short form: New Caledonia
local long form: Territoire des Nouvelle-Caledonie et Dependances
local short form: Nouvelle-Caledonie

Dependency status: territorial collectivity (or a sui generis collectivity) of France since 1998

Government type: parliamentary representative democracy

Capital: *name:* Noumea

geographic coordinates: 22 16 S, 166 27 E
time difference: UTC+11 (16 hours ahead of Washington, DC during Standard Time)

Administrative divisions: none (overseas territory of France); there are no first-order administrative divisions as defined by the US Government, but there are three provinces named Province des Iles, Province Nord, and Province Sud

Independence: none (overseas territory of France); note—a referendum on independence was held in 1998 but did not pass; a new referendum is scheduled to take place between 2014 and 2018

National holiday: Fete de la Federation, 14 July (1789); note—the local holiday is New Caledonia Day, 24 September (1853)

Constitution: 4 October 1958 (French Constitution with changes as reflected in Noumea Accord of 5 May 1998) (2013)

Legal system: civil law system based on French law; the 1988 Matignon Accords (signed in the Matignon Hotel) set up a ten-year period of development during which the Kanak community received substantial autonomy but agreed not to raise the independece issue

Suffrage: 18 years of age; universal

Executive branch: *chief of state:* President Francois HOLLANDE (since 15 May 2012); represented by High Commissioner Jean-Jacques BROT (since 2 February 2013)
head of government: President of the Government Harold MARTIN (since 3 March 2011); note—since 3 March 2011, three different governments of Harold MARTIN have collapsed over the choice of a flag that will be used while it is being decolonized; President Harold MARTIN is head of a caretaker government
cabinet: Cabinet consisting of 11 members elected from and by the Territorial Congress (For more information visit the World Leaders website)
elections: French president elected by popular vote for a five-year term; high commissioner appointed by the French president on the advice of the French Ministry of Interior; president of the government elected by the members of the Territorial Congress for a five-year term (no term limits); note—last election held on 10 June 2011 (next to be held in June 2016)

Legislative branch: unicameral Territorial Congress or Congres du territoire (54 seats; members belong to the three Provincial Assemblies, or Assemblees Provinciales, elected by popular vote to serve five-year terms)
elections: last held on 9 May 2009 (next to be held on 10 May 2014)
election results: percent of vote by party—NA; seats by party—UMP 13, Caledonia Together 10, UC 8, UNI 8, AE 6, FLNKS 3, Labor Party 3, other 3
note: the Customary Senate is the assembly of the various traditional councils of the Kanaks, the indigenous population, which rules on laws affecting the indigenous population; New Caledonia holds two seats in the French Senate; elections last held on 21 September 2008 (next to be held not later than September 2014); results—percent of vote by party—NA; seats by party—UMP 2; New Caledonia also elects two seats to the French National Assembly; elections last held on 17 June 2012 (next to be held by June 2017); results—percent of vote by party—NA; seats by party—UMP 2

Judicial branch: *highest court(s):* Court of Appeal in Noumea or Cour d'Appel (the highest local judicial court; organized into civil, commercial, social, and pre-trial investigation chambers; number of judges NA); Conseil d'Etat (the highest local administrative court; number of judges NA) note—final appeals are heard before the Court of Cassation or Cour de Cassation, in Paris
judge selection and term of office: NA
subordinate courts: Courts of First Instance include: civil, juvenile, commercial, labor, police, criminal, Assizes, and also a pre-trial investigation chamber; Joint Commerce Tribunal; administrative courts

Political parties and leaders: Caledonia Together [Philippe GOMES]; Caledonian Union or UC [Daniel GOA]; Front National or FN [Marine LE PEN]; Kanak Socialist Front for National Liberation or FLNKS (includes PALIKA, UNI, UC, and UPM); Labor Party (Labor Party) [Louis Kotra UREGEI]; National Union for Independence (Union Nationale pour l'Independance) or UNI; Parti de Liberation Kanak or PALIKA [Paul NEAOUTYINE]; Progressive Melanesian Union (Union Progressiste Mellanesienne) or UPM; Socialist Group [Jean Pierre BEL]; Socialist Kanak Liberation or LKS [Nidoish NAISSELINE]; The Future Together or AE [Harold MARTIN]; The Rally or UMP [Pierre GROGIER]; Union of Pro-Independence Co-operation Committees [Francois BURCK]

Political pressure groups and leaders: NA

International organization participation: PIF (associate member), SPC, UPU, WFTU (NGOs)

Diplomatic representation in the US: none (overseas territory of France)

Diplomatic representation from the US: none (overseas territory of France)

Flag description: the flag of France is used

National symbol(s): kagu bird

National anthem: *name:* "Soyons unis, devenons freres" (Let Us Be United, Let Us Become Brothers)
lyrics/music: Chorale Melodia (a local choir)
note: adopted 2008; the anthem contains a mixture of lyrics in both French and Nengone (an indigenous language); as a self-governing territory of France, in addition to the local anthem, "La Marseillaise" is official (see France)

ECONOMY

Economy—overview: New Caledonia has about 25% of the world's known nickel reserves. Only a small amount of the land is suitable for cultivation, and food accounts for about 20% of imports. In addition to nickel, substantial financial support from France—equal to more than 15% of GDP—and tourism are keys to the health of the economy; during 2009-10, France sent more development assistance to New Caledonia than to any of its other overseas territories. Substantial new investment in the nickel industry, combined with the recovery of global nickel prices, brightens the economic outlook for the next several years.

GDP (purchasing power parity): $9.28 billion (2008 est.)
country comparison to the world: 154
$3.158 billion (2003 est.)

GDP (official exchange rate): $9.28 billion (2008 est.)

GDP—real growth rate: 0.6% (2008 est.)
country comparison to the world: 180

GDP—per capita (PPP): $37,700 (2008 est.)
country comparison to the world: 33
$15,000 (2003 est.)

GDP—composition, by end use:
household consumption: 63.5%
government consumption: 27.6%
investment in fixed capital: 29.2%
investment in inventories: 0%
exports of goods and services: 25.1%
imports of goods and services: -45.4% (2013 est.)

GDP—composition, by sector of origin:
agriculture: 2.1%
industry: 30%
services: 67.9% (2013 est.)

Agriculture—products: vegetables; beef, deer, other livestock products; fish

Industries: nickel mining and smelting

Industrial production growth rate: 8% (2013 est.)
country comparison to the world: 25

Labor force: 106,400 (2010)
country comparison to the world: 183

Labor force—by occupation: *agriculture:* 20%
industry: 20%
services: 60% (2002)

Unemployment rate: 17.1% (2004)
country comparison to the world: 151

Population below poverty line: NA%

Household income or consumption by percentage share: *lowest 10%:* NA%
highest 10%: NA%

Budget: *revenues:* $996 million
expenditures: $1.072 billion (2001 est.)

Budget surplus (+) or deficit (-):
NA% of GDP

Fiscal year: calendar year

Inflation rate (consumer prices): 1.7% (2013 est.)
country comparison to the world: 48
1.7% (2012 est.)

Market value of publicly traded shares: $NA

Exports: $1.321 billion (2012 est.)
country comparison to the world: 151
$1.661 billion (2011 est.)

Exports—commodities: ferronickels, nickel ore, fish

Exports—partners: Japan 17.2%, France 16.3%, South Korea 12.3%, China 9.6%, Australia 8.4%, Belgium 4.9% (2012)

Imports: $3.245 billion (2012 est.)
country comparison to the world: 143
$3.698 billion (2011 est.)

Imports—commodities: machinery and equipment, fuels, chemicals, foodstuffs

Imports—partners: France 33.5%, Singapore 22.5%, Australia 11.7%, NZ 5.1% (2012)

Debt—external: $79 million (1998 est.)
country comparison to the world: 192

Exchange rates: Comptoirs Francais du Pacifique francs (XPF) per US dollar—
85.74 (2011 est.)
90.01 (2010 est.)

ENERGY

Electricity—production: 1.978 billion kWh (2010 est.)
country comparison to the world: 135

Electricity—consumption: 1.84 billion kWh (2010 est.)
country comparison to the world: 140

Electricity—exports: 0 kWh (2012 est.)
country comparison to the world: 173

Electricity—imports: 0 kWh (2012 est.)
country comparison to the world: 175

Electricity—installed generating capacity: **499,000 kW (2010 est.)**
country comparison to the world: 138

Electricity—from fossil fuels: 76.8% of total installed capacity (2010 est.)
country comparison to the world: 95

Electricity—from nuclear fuels: 0% of total installed capacity (2010 est.)
country comparison to the world: 147

Electricity—from hydroelectric plants: 15.6% of total installed capacity (2010 est.)
country comparison to the world: 99

Electricity—from other renewable sources: 7.6% of total installed capacity (2010 est.)
country comparison to the world: 31

Crude oil—production: 0 bbl/day (2012 est.)
country comparison to the world: 199

Crude oil—exports: 0 bbl/day (2010 est.)
country comparison to the world: 159

Crude oil—imports: 0 bbl/day (2010 est.)
country comparison to the world: 100

Crude oil—proved reserves: 0 bbl (1 January 2013 es)
country comparison to the world: 169

Refined petroleum products—production: 0 bbl/day (2010 est.)
country comparison to the world: 178

Refined petroleum products—consumption: 13,640 bbl/day (2011 est.)
country comparison to the world: 148

Refined petroleum products—exports: 116.9 bbl/day (2010 est.)
country comparison to the world: 120

Refined petroleum products—imports: 14,670 bbl/day (2010 est.)
country comparison to the world: 121

Natural gas—production: 0 cu m (2011 est.)
country comparison to the world: 171

Natural gas—consumption: 0 cu m (2010 est.)
country comparison to the world: 176

Natural gas—exports: 0 cu m (2011 est.)
country comparison to the world: 153

Natural gas—imports: 0 cu m (2011 est.)
country comparison to the world: 102

Natural gas—proved reserves: 0 cu m (1 January 2013 es)
country comparison to the world: 174

Carbon dioxide emissions from consumption of energy: 3.026 million Mt (2011 est.)
country comparison to the world: 140

COMMUNICATIONS

Telephones—main lines in use: 80,000 (2012)
country comparison to the world: 151

Telephones—mobile cellular: 231,000 (2012)
country comparison to the world: 178

Telephone system: *general assessment:* a submarine cable network connection between New Caledonia and Australia, completed in 2007, increased

network capacity and improved high-speed connectivity and access to international networks
domestic: combined fixed-line and mobile-cellular telephone subscribership exceeds 100 per 100 persons
international: country code—687; satellite earth station—1 Intelsat (Pacific Ocean) (2010)

Broadcast media: the publicly owned French Overseas Network (RFO), which operates in France's overseas departments and territories, broadcasts over the RFO Nouvelle Caledonie TV and radio stations; a small number of privately owned radio stations also broadcast (2008)

Internet country code: .nc

Internet hosts: 34,231 (2012)
country comparison to the world: 104

Internet users: 85,000 (2009)
country comparison to the world: 165

TRANSPORTATION

Airports: 25 (2013)
country comparison to the world: 128

Airports—with paved runways: *total:* 1 2
over 3,047 m: 1
914 to 1,523 m: 10
under 914 m: 1 (2013)

Airports—with unpaved runways: *total:* 1 3
914 to 1,523 m: 5
under 914 m: 8 (2013)

Heliports: 8 (2013)

Roadways: *total:* 5,622 km (2006)
country comparison to the world: 151

Merchant marine: registered in other countries: 3 (France 3) (2010)
country comparison to the world: 135

Ports and terminals: *major seaport(s):* Noumea

MILITARY

Military branches: no regular military forces; French military, police, and gendarmerie (2012)

Manpower available for military service:
males age 16-49: 68,219 (2010 est.)

Manpower fit for military service:
males age 16-49: 56,233
females age 16-49: 55,983 (2010 est.)

Manpower reaching militarily significant age annually:
male: 2,272
female: 2,167 (2010 est.)

Military—note: defense is the responsibility of France

TRANSNATIONAL ISSUES

Disputes—international: Matthew and Hunter Islands east of New Caledonia claimed by France and Vanuatu

NEW ZEALAND

INTRODUCTION

Background: The Polynesian Maori reached New Zealand in about A.D. 800. In 1840, their chieftains entered into a compact with Britain, the Treaty of Waitangi, in which they ceded sovereignty to Queen Victoria while retaining territorial rights. That same year, the British began the first organized colonial settlement. A series of land wars between 1843 and 1872 ended with the defeat of the native peoples. The British colony of New Zealand became an independent dominion in 1907 and supported the UK militarily in both world wars. New Zealand's full participation in a number of defense alliances lapsed by the 1980s. In recent years, the government has sought to address longstanding Maori grievances.

GEOGRAPHY

Location: Oceania, islands in the South Pacific Ocean, southeast of Australia

Geographic coordinates: 41 00 S, 174 00 E

Map references: Oceania

Area: *total:* 267,710 sq km
country comparison to the world: 76
land: 267,710 sq km
water: NA
note: includes Antipodes Islands, Auckland Islands, Bounty Islands, Campbell Island, Chatham Islands, and Kermadec Islands

Area—comparative: almost twice the size of North Carolina; about the size of Colorado

Land boundaries: 0 km

Coastline: 15,134 km Maritime claims: *territorial sea:* 12 nm
contiguous zone: 24 nm
exclusive economic zone: 200 nm
continental shelf: 200 nm or to the edge of the continental margin

Climate: temperate with sharp regional contrasts

Terrain: predominately mountainous with some large coastal plains

Elevation extremes: *lowest point:* Pacific Ocean 0 m
highest point: Aoraki-Mount Cook 3,754 m

Natural resources: natural gas, iron ore, sand, coal, timber, hydropower, gold, limestone

Land use: *arable land:* 1.76%
permanent crops: 0.27%
other: 97.98% (2011)

Irrigated land: 6,193 sq km (2007)

Total renewable water resources: 327 cu km (2011)

Freshwater withdrawal (domestic/industrial/agricultural): *total:* 4.75 cu km/yr (23%/5%/72%)
per capita: 1,200 cu m/yr (2010)

Natural hazards: earthquakes are common, though usually not severe; volcanic activity
volcanism: significant volcanism on North Island; Ruapehu (elev. 2,797 m), which last erupted in 2007, has a history of large eruptions in the past century; Taranaki has the potential to produce dangerous avalanches and lahars; other historically active volcanoes include Okataina, Raoul Island, Tongariro, and White Island

Environment—current issues: deforestation; soil erosion; native flora and fauna hard-hit by invasive species

Environment—international agreements:
party to: Antarctic-Environmental Protocol, Antarctic-Marine Living Resources, Antarctic Treaty, Biodiversity, Climate Change, Climate Change-Kyoto Protocol, Desertification, Endangered Species, Environmental Modification, Hazardous Wastes, Law of the Sea, Marine Dumping, Ozone Layer Protection, Ship Pollution, Tropical Timber 83, Tropical Timber 94, Wetlands, Whaling
signed, but not ratified: Antarctic Seals, Marine Life Conservation

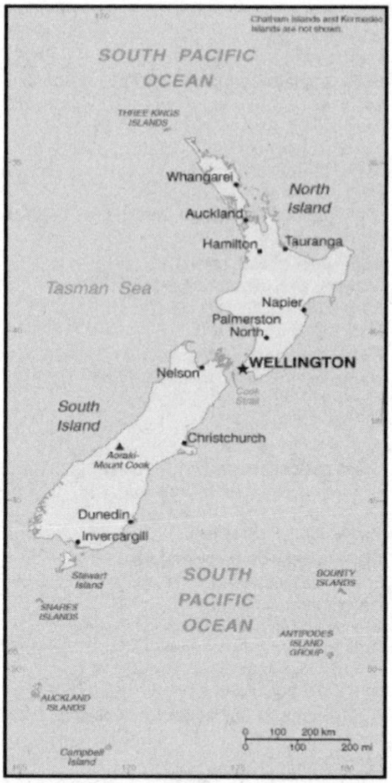

Geography—note: almost 90% of the population lives in cities; Wellington is the southernmost national capital in the world

PEOPLE AND SOCIETY

Nationality: *noun:* New Zealander(s)
adjective: New Zealand

Ethnic groups: European 71.2%, Maori 14.1%, Asian 11.3%, Pacific peoples 7.6%, Middle Eastern, Latin American, African 1.1%, other 1.6%, not stated or unidentified 5.4%
note: based on the 2013 census of the usually resident population; percentages add up to more than 100% because people were able to identify more than one ethnic group (2013 est.)

Languages: English (de facto official) 89.8%, Maori (de jure official) 3.5%, Samoan 2%, Hindi 1.6%, French 1.2%, Northern Chinese 1.2%, Yue 1%, Other or not stated 20.5%, New Zealand Sign Language (de jure official)
note: shares sum to 120.8% due to multiple responses on census (2013 est.)

Religions: Christian 44.3% (Catholic 11.6%, Anglican 10.8%, Presbyterian and Congregational 7.8%, Methodist, 2.4%, Pentecostal 1.8%, other 9.9%), Hindu 2.1%, Buddhist 1.4%, Maori Christian 1.3%, Islam 1.1%, other religion 1.4% (includes Judaism, Spiritualism and New Age religions, Baha'i, Asian religions other than Buddhism), no religion 38.5%, not stated or unidentified 8.2%, objected to answering 4.1%
note: based on the 2013 census of the usually resident population; percentages add up to more than 100% because people were able to identify more than one religion (2013 est.)

Population: 4,401,916 (July 2014 est.)
country comparison to the world: 127

Age structure:
0-14 years: 20% (male 450,985/female 429,184)
15-24 years: 13.9% (male 313,711/female 298,427)
25-54 years: 40.4% (male 890,678/female 888,565)
55-64 years: 14.3% (male 245,084/female 255,879)
65 years and over: 14% (male 290,429/female 338,974) (2014 est.)

Dependency ratios:
total dependency ratio: 51.9 %
youth dependency ratio: 30.7 %
elderly dependency ratio: 21.2 %
potential support ratio: 4.7 (2013)

Median age: *total:* 37.6 years
male: 36.7 years
female: 38.4 years (2014 est.)

Population growth rate: 0.83% (2014 est.)
country comparison to the world: 132

Birth rate: 13.4 births/1,000 population (2014 est.)
country comparison to the world: 151

Death rate: 7.3 deaths/1,000 population (2014 est.)
country comparison to the world: 124

Net migration rate: 2.23 migrant(s)/1,000 population (2014 est.)
country comparison to the world: 45

Urbanization: *urban population:* 86% of total population (2010)
rate of urbanization: 0.9% annual rate of change (2010-15 est.)

Major urban areas—population: Auckland 1.36 million; WELLINGTON (capital) 391,000 (2009)

Sex ratio: *at birth:* 1.05 male(s)/female
0-14 years: 1.05 male(s)/female
15-24 years: 1.05 male(s)/female
25-54 years: 1 male(s)/female
55-64 years: 0.99 male(s)/female
65 years and over: 0.85 male(s)/female
total population: 0.99 male(s)/female (2014 est.)

Mother's mean age at first birth: 27.7 (2008 est.)

Maternal mortality rate: 15 deaths/100,000 live births (2010)
country comparison to the world: 144

Infant mortality rate: *total:* 4.59 deaths/1,000 live births
country comparison to the world: 184
male: 5.14 deaths/1,000 live births
female: 4.01 deaths/1,000 live births (2014 est.)

Life expectancy at birth: *total population:* 80.93 years
country comparison to the world: 26
male: 78.88 years
female: 83.08 years (2014 est.)

Total fertility rate: 2.05 children born/woman (2014 est.)
country comparison to the world: 119

Contraceptive prevalence rate: 75%
note: percent of women aged 20-49 (1995)

Health expenditures: 10.1% of GDP (2011)
country comparison to the world: 24

Physicians density: 2.74 physicians/1,000 population (2010)

Hospital bed density: 2.3 beds/1,000 population (2011)

Drinking water source:
improved:
urban: 100% of population
rural: 100% of population
total: 100% of population
unimproved:
urban: 0% of population
rural: 0% of population
total: 0% of population (2011 est.)

HIV/AIDS—adult prevalence rate: 0.1% (2009 est.)
country comparison to the world: 163

HIV/AIDS—people living with HIV/AIDS: 2,500 (2009 est.)
country comparison to the world: 137

HIV/AIDS—deaths: fewer than 100 (2009 est.)
country comparison to the world: 138

Obesity—adult prevalence rate: 28.3% (2008)
country comparison to the world: 34

Education expenditures: 7.4% of GDP (2012)
country comparison to the world: 16

Literacy: *definition:* age 15 and over can read and write
total population: 99%
male: 99%
female: 99% (2003 est.)

School life expectancy (primary to tertiary education): *total:* 19 years
male: 19 years
female: 20 years (2011)

Unemployment, youth ages 15-24: *total:* 17.7%
country comparison to the world: 69
male: 17.3%
female: 18.1% (2012)

GOVERNMENT

Country name: *conventional long form:* none
conventional short form: New Zealand
abbreviation: NZ

Government type: parliamentary democracy and a Commonwealth realm

Capital: *name:* Wellington
geographic coordinates: 41 18 S, 174 47 E
time difference: UTC+12 (17 hours ahead of Washington, DC during Standard Time)
daylight saving time: +1hr, begins last Sunday in September; ends first Sunday in April
note: New Zealand is divided into two time zones—New Zealand standard time (12 hours in advance of UTC), and Chatham Islands time (45 minutes in advance of New Zealand standard time)

Administrative divisions: 16 regions and 1 territory*; Auckland, Bay of Plenty, Canterbury, Chatham Islands*, Gisborne, Hawke's Bay, Manawatu-Wanganui, Marlborough, Nelson, Northland, Otago, Southland, Taranaki, Tasman, Waikato, Wellington, West Coast

Dependent areas: Cook Islands, Niue, Tokelau

Independence: 26 September 1907 (from the UK)

National holiday: Waitangi Day (Treaty of Waitangi established British sovereignty over New Zealand), 6 February (1840); ANZAC Day (commemorated as the anniversary of the landing of troops of the Australian and New Zealand Army Corps during World War I at Gallipoli, Turkey), 25 April (1915)

Constitution: Constitution Act 1986 (the principal formal charter) adopted and effective 1 January 1987; amended 1999, 2005 (2013)

Legal system: common law system, based on English model, with special legislation and land courts for the Maori

International law organization participation: accepts compulsory ICJ jurisdiction with reservations; accepts ICCt jurisdiction

Suffrage: 18 years of age; universal

Executive branch: *chief of state:* Queen ELIZABETH II (since 6 February 1952); represented by Governor General Lt Gen Sir Jerry MATEPARAE (since 31 August 2011)
head of government: Prime Minister John KEY (since 19 November 2008); Deputy Prime Minister Simon William ENGLISH (since 19 November 2008)
cabinet: Executive Council appointed by the governor general on the recommendation of the prime minister (For more information visit the World Leaders website)
elections: the monarchy is hereditary; governor general appointed by the monarch; following legislative elections, the leader of the majority party or the leader of a majority coalition usually appointed prime minister by the governor general; deputy prime minister appointed by the governor general

Legislative branch: unicameral House of Representatives—commonly called Parliament (usually 120 seats; 70 members elected by popular vote in single-member constituencies including 7 Maori constituencies, 50 proportional seats chosen from party lists; serve three-year terms)
elections: last held on 26 November 2011 (next to be held not later than November 2014)
election results: percent of vote by party—National Party 48%, Labor Party 27.1%, Green Party 10.6%, NZ First 6.8%, Maori 1.4%, ACT Party 1.1%, Mana 1%, United Future 0.6%, other 3.43%; seats by party—National Party 60, Labor Party 34, Green Party 13, NZ First 8, Maori 3, ACT Party 1, Mana 1, United Future 1
note: results of 2011 election saw the total number of seats decline to 121

Judicial branch: *highest court(s):* Supreme Court (consists of 5 justices including the chief justice) note—the Supreme Court in 2004 replaced the Judicial Committee of the Privy Council, in London, as the final appeals court
judge selection and term of office: justices appointed by the governor-general on the recommendation of the attorney-general; justices appointed for life
subordinate courts: Court of Appeal; High Court; tribunals and authorities; district courts; specialized courts for issues related to employment, environment, Maori lands, and military

Political parties and leaders: ACT New Zealand [Rodney HIDE]; Green Party [Russel NORMAN and Metiria TUREI]; Mana Party [Hone HARAWIRA]; Maori Party [Tariana TURIA and Dr. Pita SHARPLES]; New Zealand National Party [John KEY]; New Zealand First Party or NZ First [Winston PETERS]; New Zealand Labor Party [Phil GOFF]; Jim Anderton's Progressive Party [James (Jim) ANDERTON]; United Future New Zealand [Peter DUNNE]

Political pressure groups and leaders: Women's Electoral Lobby or WEL
other: apartheid groups; civil rights groups; farmers groups; Maori; nuclear weapons groups; women's rights groups

International organization participation: ADB, ANZUS (US suspended security obligations to NZ on 11 August 1986), APEC, ARF, ASEAN (dialogue partner), Australia Group, BIS, C, CD, CP, EAS, EBRD, FAO, FATF, IAEA, IBRD, ICAO, ICC (national committees), ICRM, IDA, IEA, IFAD, IFC, IFRCS, IHO, ILO, IMF, IMO, IMSO, Interpol, IOC, IOM, IPU, ISO, ITSO, ITU, ITUC (NGOs), MIGA, NSG, OECD, OPCW, Paris Club (associate), PCA, PIF, Sparteca, SPC, UN, UNCTAD, UNESCO, UNHCR, UNIDO, UNMISS, UNMIT, UNTSO, UPU, WCO, WFTU (NGOs), WHO, WIPO, WMO, WTO

Diplomatic representation in the US:
chief of mission: Ambassador Michael Kenneth MOORE (since 5 August 2010)
chancery: 37 Observatory Circle NW, Washington, DC 20008
telephone: [1] (202) 328-4800
FAX: [1] (202) 667-5227
consulate(s) general: New York, Pago Pago (American Samoa), Santa Monica (CA)

Diplomatic representation from the US:
chief of mission: Ambassador (vacant); Charge d' Affaires Marie C. DAMOUR note—also accredited to Samoa
embassy: 29 Fitzherbert Terrace, Thorndon, Wellington
mailing address: P. O. Box 1190, Wellington; PSC 467, Box 1, APO AP 96531-1034
telephone: [64] (4) 462-6000
FAX: [64] (4) 499-0490
consulate(s) general: Auckland

Flag description: blue with the flag of the UK in the upper hoist-side quadrant with four red five-pointed stars edged in white centered in the outer half of the flag; the stars represent the Southern Cross constellation

National symbol(s): Southern Cross constellation (four, five-pointed stars); kiwi (bird), silver fern

National anthem: *name:* "God Defend New Zealand"
lyrics/music: Thomas BRACKEN [English], Thomas Henry SMITH [Maori]/John Joseph WOODS
note: adopted 1940 as national song, adopted 1977 as co-national anthem; New Zealand has two national anthems with equal status; as a commonwealth realm, in addition to "God Defend New Zealand," "God Save the Queen" serves as a national anthem (see United Kingdom); "God Save the Queen" normally is played only when a member of the royal family or the governor-general is present; in all other cases, "God Defend New Zealand" is played

Government—note:

ECONOMY

Economy—overview: Over the past 20 years the government has transformed New Zealand from an agrarian economy dependent on concessionary British market access to a more industrialized, free market economy that can compete globally. This dynamic growth has boosted real incomes—but left behind some at the bottom of the ladder—and broadened and deepened the technological capabilities of the industrial sector. Per capita income rose for ten consecutive years until 2007 in purchasing power parity terms, but fell in 2008-09. Debt-driven consumer spending drove robust growth in the first half of the decade, helping fuel a large balance of payments deficit that posed a challenge for economic managers. Inflationary pressures caused the central bank to raise its key rate steadily from January 2004 until it was among the highest in the OECD in 2007-08; international capital inflows attracted to the high rates further strengthened the currency and housing market, however, aggravating the current account deficit. The economy fell into recession before the start of the global financial crisis and contracted for five consecutive quarters in 2008-09. In line with global peers, the central bank cut interest rates aggressively and the government developed fiscal stimulus measures. The economy pulled out of recession late in 2009, and achieved 2-3% per year growth in 2010-13. Nevertheless, key trade sectors remain vulnerable to weak external demand. The government plans to raise productivity growth and develop infrastructure, while reining in government spending.

GDP (purchasing power parity): $136 billion (2013 est.)
country comparison to the world: 64
$132.7 billion (2012 est.)
$129.2 billion (2011 est.)
note: data are in 2013 US dollars

GDP (official exchange rate): $181.1 billion (2013 est.)

GDP—real growth rate: 2.5% (2013 est.)
country comparison to the world: 127
2.7% (2012 est.)
1.4% (2011 est.)

GDP—per capita (PPP): $30,400 (2013 est.)
country comparison to the world: 46
$29,900 (2012 est.)
$29,300 (2011 est.)
note: data are in 2013 US dollars

Gross national saving: 15.9% of GDP (2013 est.)
country comparison to the world: 106
14.5% of GDP (2012 est.)
14.5% of GDP (2011 est.)

GDP—composition, by end use:
household consumption: 58.1%
government consumption: 19.9%
investment in fixed capital: 20.2%
investment in inventories: 0.5%
exports of goods and services: 30%
imports of goods and services: -28.7% (2013 est.)

GDP—composition, by sector of origin:
agriculture: 5%
industry: 25.5%
services: 69.5% (2013 est.)

Agriculture—products: dairy products, lamb and mutton; wheat, barley, potatoes, pulses, fruits, vegetables; wool, beef; fish

Industries: food processing, wood and paper products, textiles, machinery, transportation equipment, banking and insurance, tourism, mining

Industrial production growth rate: 1.9% (2013 est.)
country comparison to the world: 129

Labor force: 2.413 million (2013 est.)
country comparison to the world: 113

Labor force—by occupation: *agriculture:* 7%
industry: 19%
services: 74% (2006 est.)

Unemployment rate: 6.4% (2013 est.)
country comparison to the world: 65
6.9% (2012 est.)

Population below poverty line: NA%

Household income or consumption by percentage share: *lowest 10%:* NA%
highest 10%: NA%

Distribution of family income—Gini index: 36.2 (1997)
country comparison to the world: 86

Budget: *revenues:* $69.17 billion
expenditures: $72.65 billion (2013 est.)

Taxes and other revenues: 38.2% of GDP (2013 est.)
country comparison to the world: 51

Budget surplus (+) or deficit (-):
-1.9% of GDP (2013 est.)
country comparison to the world: 83

Public debt: 38.4% of GDP (2013 est.)
country comparison to the world: 97
38.1% of GDP (2012 est.)

Fiscal year: 1 April—31 March
note: this is the fiscal year for tax purposes

Inflation rate (consumer prices): 1.3% (2013 est.)
country comparison to the world: 35
1.1% (2012 est.)

Central bank discount rate: 2.5% (31 December 2009)
country comparison to the world: 73
5% (31 December 2008)

Commercial bank prime lending rate: 5.7% (31 December 2013 est.)
country comparison to the world: 140
5.82% (31 December 2012 est.)

Stock of narrow money: $30.03 billion (31 December 2013 est.)
country comparison to the world: 60
$29.87 billion (31 December 2012 est.)

Stock of broad money: $91.28 billion (31 December 2013 est.)
country comparison to the world: 56
$84.55 billion (31 December 2012 est.)

Stock of domestic credit: $256.3 billion (31 December 2013 est.)
country comparison to the world: 37
$265.6 billion (31 December 2012 est.)

Market value of publicly traded shares: $79.8 billion (31 December 2012 est.)
country comparison to the world: 44
$71.66 billion (31 December 2011)
$71.83 billion (31 December 2010 est.)

Current account balance: -$8.358 billion (2013 est.)
country comparison to the world: 173
-$8.508 billion (2012 est.)

Exports: $37.84 billion (2013 est.)
country comparison to the world: 62
$37.87 billion (2012 est.)

Exports—commodities: dairy products, meat, wood and wood products, fish, machinery

Exports—partners: Australia 21.1%, China 15%, US 9.2%, Japan 7% (2012)

Imports: $37.35 billion (2013 est.)
country comparison to the world: 63
$37.04 billion (2012 est.)

Imports—commodities: machinery and equipment, vehicles, aircraft, petroleum, electronics, textiles, plastics

Imports—partners: China 16.4%, Australia 15.2%, US 9.3%, Japan 6.5%, Singapore 4.8%, Germany 4.4% (2012)

Reserves of foreign exchange and gold: $20.01 billion (31 December 2013 est.)
country comparison to the world: 60
$17.58 billion (31 December 2012 est.)

Debt—external: $81.36 billion (31 December 2013 est.)
country comparison to the world: 52
$85.18 billion (31 December 2012 est.)

Stock of direct foreign investment—at home: $84.2 billion (31 December 2013 est.)
country comparison to the world: 46
$81.36 billion (31 December 2012 est.)

Stock of direct foreign investment—abroad: $59.08 billion (31 December 2009)
country comparison to the world: 37

Exchange rates: New Zealand dollars (NZD) per US dollar—
1.247 (2013 est.)
1.2334 (2012 est.)
1.3874 (2010 est.)
1.6002 (2009)
1.4151 (2008)

ENERGY

Electricity—production: 43.54 billion kWh (2011 est.)
country comparison to the world: 5 6

Electricity—consumption: 40.76 billion kWh (2010 est.)
country comparison to the world: 52

Electricity—exports: 0 kWh (2012 est.)
country comparison to the world: 180

Electricity—imports: 0 kWh (2012 est.)
country comparison to the world: 181

Electricity—installed generating capacity: 9.679 million kW (2010 est.)
country comparison to the world: 58

Electricity—from fossil fuels: 31.7% of total installed capacity (2010 est.)
country comparison to the world: 178

Electricity—from nuclear fuels: 0% of total installed capacity (2010 est.)
country comparison to the world: 157

Electricity—from hydroelectric plants: 54.2% of total installed capacity (2010 est.)
country comparison to the world: 38

Electricity—from other renewable sources: 14% of total installed capacity (2010 est.)
country comparison to the world: 16

Crude oil—production: 48,190 bbl/day (2012 est.)
country comparison to the world: 64

Crude oil—exports: 47,290 bbl/day (2010 est.)
country comparison to the world: 46

Crude oil—imports: 99,810 bbl/day (2010 est.)
country comparison to the world: 50

Crude oil—proved reserves: 81.4 million bbl (1 January 2013 es)
country comparison to the world: 74

Refined petroleum products—production: 109,700 bbl/day (2010 est.)
country comparison to the world: 72

Refined petroleum products—consumption: 148,900 bbl/day (2011 est.)
country comparison to the world: 67

Refined petroleum products—exports: 2,471 bbl/day (2010 est.)
country comparison to the world: 98

Refined petroleum products—imports: 41,170 bbl/day (2010 est.)
country comparison to the world: 80

Natural gas—production: 4.59 billion cu m (2012 est.)
country comparison to the world: 53

Natural gas—consumption: 4.537 billion cu m (2010 est.)
country comparison to the world: 65

Natural gas—exports: 0 cu m (2012 est.)
country comparison to the world: 161

Natural gas—imports: 0 cu m (2012 est.)
country comparison to the world: 112

Natural gas—proved reserves: 29.42 billion cu m (1 January 2013 es)
country comparison to the world: 69

Carbon dioxide emissions from consumption of energy: 37.17 million Mt (2011 est.)
country comparison to the world: 71

COMMUNICATIONS

Telephones—main lines in use: 1.88 million (2012)
country comparison to the world: 6 1

Telephones—mobile cellular: 4.922 million (2012)
country comparison to the world: 113

Telephone system: *general assessment:* excellent domestic and international systems
domestic: combined fixed-line and mobile-cellular telephone subscribership exceeds 150 per 100 persons
international: country code—64; the Southern Cross submarine cable system provides links to Australia, Fiji, and the US; satellite earth stations—8 (1 Inmarsat—Pacific Ocean, 7 other) (2011)

Broadcast media: state-owned Television New Zealand operates multiple TV networks and state-owned Radio New Zealand operates 3 radio networks and an external shortwave radio service to the South Pacific region; a small number of national commercial TV and radio stations and many regional commercial television and radio stations are available; cable and satellite TV systems are available (2008)

Internet country code: . n z

Internet hosts: 3.026 million (2012)
country comparison to the world: 34

Internet users: 3.4 million (2009)
country comparison to the world: 62

TRANSPORTATION

Airports: 123 (2013)
country comparison to the world: 4 8

Airports—with paved runways: *total:* 3 9
over 3,047 m: 2
2,438 to 3,047 m: 1
1,524 to 2,437 m: 12
914 to 1,523 m: 23
under 914 m: 1 (2013)

Airports—with unpaved runways: *total:* 8 4
1,524 to 2,437 m: 3
914 to 1,523 m: 33
under 914 m: 48 (2013)

Pipelines: condensate 331 km; gas 1,936 km; liquid petroleum gas 172 km; oil 288 km; refined products 198 km (2013)

Railways: *total:* 4,128 km
country comparison to the world: 42
narrow gauge: 4,128 km 1.067-m gauge (506 km electrified) (2008)

Roadways: *total:* 94,160 km
country comparison to the world: 50
paved: 62,759 km (includes 199 km of expressways)
unpaved: 32,143 km (2012)

Merchant marine: *total:* 1 5
country comparison to the world: 101
by type: bulk carrier 3, cargo 3, chemical tanker 1, container 1, passenger/cargo 5, petroleum tanker 2
foreign-owned: 7 (Germany 2, Hong Kong 1, South Africa 1, Switzerland 2, UK 1)
registered in other countries: 5 (Antigua and Barbuda 2, Cook Islands 2, Samoa 1) (2010)

Ports and terminals: *major seaport(s):* Auckland, Lyttelton, Manukau Harbor, Marsden Point, Tauranga, Wellington

MILITARY

Military branches: New Zealand Defense Force (NZDF): New Zealand Army; Royal New Zealand Navy; Royal New Zealand Air Force (Te Hokowhitu o Kahurangi, RNZAF) (2013)

Military service age and obligation: 17 years of age for voluntary military service; soldiers cannot be deployed until the age of 18; no conscription; 3

years of secondary education required; must be a citizen of NZ, the UK, Australia, Canada, or the US, and resident of NZ for the previous 5 years (2013)

Manpower available for military service:
males age 16-49: 1,019,798
females age 16-49: 1,003,429 (2010 est.)

Manpower fit for military service:
males age 16-49: 843,526
females age 16-49: 828,779 (2010 est.)

Manpower reaching militarily significant age annually: *male:* 30,846
female: 28,825 (2010 est.)

Military expenditures: 1.13% of GDP (2012)
country comparison to the world: 89
1.12% of GDP (2011)
1.13% of GDP (2010)

TRANSNATIONAL ISSUES

Disputes—international: asserts a territorial claim in Antarctica (Ross Dependency)

Illicit drugs: significant consumer of amphetamines

NICARAGUA

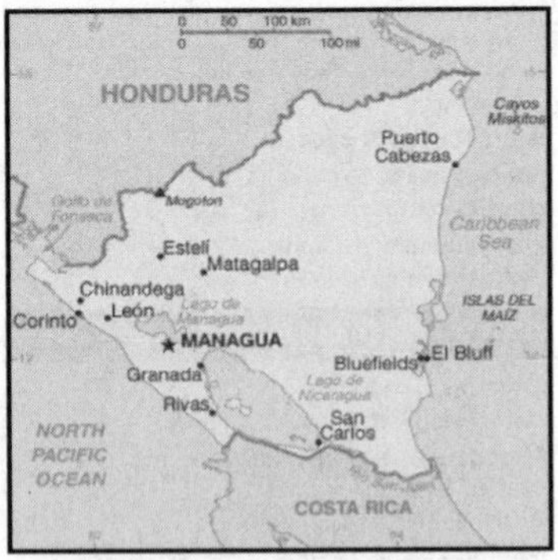

INTRODUCTION

Background: The Pacific coast of Nicaragua was settled as a Spanish colony from Panama in the early 16th century. Independence from Spain was declared in 1821 and the country became an independent republic in 1838. Britain occupied the Caribbean Coast in the first half of the 19th century, but gradually ceded control of the region in subsequent decades. Violent opposition to governmental manipulation and corruption spread to all classes by 1978 and resulted in a short-lived civil war that brought the Marxist Sandinista guerrillas to power in 1979. Nicaraguan aid to leftist rebels in El Salvador caused the US to sponsor anti-Sandinista contra guerrillas through much of the 1980s. After losing free and fair elections in 1990, 1996, and 2001, former Sandinista President Daniel ORTEGA Saavedra was elected president in 2006 and reelected in 2011. The 2008 municipal elections, 2010 regional elections, November 2011 presidential elections, and 2012 municipal elections were marred by widespread irregularities. Nicaragua's infrastructure and economy—hard hit by the earlier civil war and by Hurricane Mitch in 1998—are slowly being rebuilt, but democratic institutions have been weakened under the ORTEGA administration.

GEOGRAPHY

Location: Central America, bordering both the Caribbean Sea and the North Pacific Ocean, between Costa Rica and Honduras

Geographic coordinates: 13 00 N, 85 00 W

Map references: Central America and the Caribbean

Area: *total:* 130,370 sq km
country comparison to the world: 98
land: 119,990 sq km
water: 10,380 sq km

Area—comparative: slightly larger than Pennsylvania; slightly smaller than New York state

Land boundaries: *total:* 1,231 km
border countries: Costa Rica 309 km, Honduras 922 km

Coastline: 910 km

Maritime claims: *territorial sea:* 12 nm
contiguous zone: 24 nm
continental shelf: natural prolongation

Climate: tropical in lowlands, cooler in highlands

Terrain: extensive Atlantic coastal plains rising to central interior mountains; narrow Pacific coastal plain interrupted by volcanoes

Elevation extremes: *lowest point:* Pacific Ocean 0 m
highest point: Mogoton 2,438 m

Natural resources: gold, silver, copper, tungsten, lead, zinc, timber, fish

Land use: *arable land:* 14.57%
permanent crops: 1.76%
other: 83.66% (2011)

Irrigated land: 942.4 sq km (2003)

Total renewable water resources: 196.6 cu km (2011)

Freshwater withdrawal (domestic/industrial/agricultural): *total:* 1.39 cu km/yr (23%/4%/73%)
per capita: 265.9 cu m/yr (2008)

Natural hazards: destructive earthquakes; volcanoes; landslides; extremely susceptible to hurricanes
volcanism: significant volcanic activity; Cerro Negro (elev. 728 m), which last erupted in 1999, is one of Nicaragua's most active volcanoes; its lava flows and ash have been known to cause significant damage to farmland and buildings; other historically active volcanoes include Concepcion, Cosiguina, Las Pilas, Masaya, Momotombo, San Cristobal, and Telica

Environment—current issues: deforestation; soil erosion; water pollution

Environment—international agreements:
party to: Biodiversity, Climate Change, Climate Change-Kyoto Protocol, Desertification, Endangered Species, Environmental Modification, Hazardous Wastes, Law of the Sea, Ozone Layer Protection, Ship Pollution, Wetlands, Whaling
signed, but not ratified: none of the selected agreements

Geography—note: largest country in Central America; contains the largest freshwater body in Central America, Lago de Nicaragua

PEOPLE AND SOCIETY

Nationality: *noun:* Nicaraguan(s)
adjective: Nicaraguan

Ethnic groups: mestizo (mixed Amerindian and white) 69%, white 17%, black 9%, Amerindian 5%

Languages: Spanish (official) 95.3%, Miskito 2.2%, Mestizo of the Caribbean coast 2%, other 0.5%
note: English and indigenous languages found on the Caribbean coast (2005 est.)

Religions: Roman Catholic 58.5%, Protestant 23.2% (Evangelical 21.6%, Moravian 1.6%), Jehovah's Witnesses 0.9%, other 1.6%, none 15.7% (2005 est.)

Demographic profile: Despite being one of the poorest countries in Latin America, Nicaragua has improved its access to potable water and sanitation and has ameliorated its life expectancy, infant and child mortality, and immunization rates. However, income distribution is very uneven, and the poor, agriculturalists, and indigenous people continue to have less access to healthcare services. Nicaragua's total fertility rate has fallen from around 6 children per woman in 1980 to just above replacement level today, but the high birth rate among adolescents perpetuates a cycle of poverty and low educational attainment. Nicaraguans emigrate primarily to Costa Rica and to a lesser extent the United States. Nicaraguan men have been migrating seasonally to Costa Rica to harvest bananas and coffee since the early 20th century. Political turmoil, civil war, and natural disasters from the 1970s through the 1990s dramatically increased the flow of refugees and permanent migrants seeking jobs, higher wages, and better social and healthcare benefits. Since 2000, Nicaraguan emigration to Costa Rica has slowed and stabilized. Today roughly 300,000 Nicaraguans are permanent residents of Costa Rica—about 75% of the foreign population—and thousands more migrate seasonally for work, many illegally.

Population: 5,848,641 (July 2014 est.)
country comparison to the world: 111

Age structure:
0-14 years: 29.3% (male 873,545/female 839,853)
15-24 years: 22.4% (male 657,076/female 652,856)
25-54 years: 38% (male 1,051,656/female 1,173,084)
55-64 years: 4.8% (male 147,405/female 169,618)
65 years and over: 4.7% (male 127,699/female 155,849) (2014 est.)

Dependency ratios:
total dependency ratio: 59.9 %
youth dependency ratio: 52.5 %
elderly dependency ratio: 7.4 %

potential support ratio: 13.5 (2013)

Median age: *total:* 24.2 years
male: 23.3 years
female: 25.1 years (2014 est.)

Population growth rate: 1.02% (2014 est.)
country comparison to the world: 118

Birth rate: 18.41 births/1,000 population (2014 est.)
country comparison to the world: 103

Death rate: 5.07 deaths/1,000 population (2014 est.)
country comparison to the world: 185

Net migration rate: -3.13 migrant(s)/1,000 population (2014 est.)
country comparison to the world: 179

Urbanization: *urban population:* 57% of total population (2010)
rate of urbanization: 2% annual rate of change (2010-15 est.)

Major urban areas—population: MANAGUA (capital) 934,000 (2009)

Sex ratio: *at birth:* 1.05 male(s)/female
0-14 years: 1.04 male(s)/female
15-24 years: 1.01 male(s)/female
25-54 years: 0.9 male(s)/female
55-64 years: 0.96 male(s)/female
65 years and over: 0.83 male(s)/female
total population: 0.96 male(s)/female (2014 est.)

Mother's mean age at first birth: 19.7
note: median age at first birth among women 25-29 (2007 est.)

Maternal mortality rate: 95 deaths/100,000 live births (2010)
country comparison to the world: 76

Infant mortality rate: *total:* 20.36 deaths/1,000 live births
country comparison to the world: 88
male: 23.36 deaths/1,000 live births
female: 17.2 deaths/1,000 live births (2014 est.)

Life expectancy at birth: *total population:* 72.72 years
country comparison to the world: 130
male: 70.57 years
female: 74.98 years (2014 est.)

Total fertility rate: 1.99 children born/woman (2014 est.)
country comparison to the world: 128

Contraceptive prevalence rate: 72.4% (2006/07)

Health expenditures: 10.1% of GDP (2009)
country comparison to the world: 26

Physicians density: 0.37 physicians/1,000 population (2003)

Hospital bed density: 1.1 beds/1,000 population (2011)

Drinking water source:
improved:
urban: 97.6% of population
rural: 67.8% of population
total: 85% of population
unimproved:
urban: 2.4% of population
rural: 32.2% of population
total: 15% of population (2011 est.)

Sanitation facility access:
improved:
urban: 63.2% of population
rural: 37% of population
total: 52.1% of population
unimproved:
urban: 36.8% of population
rural: 63% of population
total: 47.9% of population (2011 est.)

HIV/AIDS—adult prevalence rate: 0.3% (2012 est.)
country comparison to the world: 100

HIV/AIDS—people living with HIV/AIDS: 9,600 (2012 est.)
country comparison to the world: 106

HIV/AIDS—deaths: 100 (2012 est.)
country comparison to the world: 137

Major infectious diseases: *degree of risk:* high
food or waterborne diseases: bacterial diarrhea, hepatitis A, and typhoid fever
vectorborne disease: dengue fever and malaria (2013)

Obesity—adult prevalence rate: 22.2% (2008)
country comparison to the world: 81

Children under the age of 5 years underweight: 5.7% (2007)
country comparison to the world: 85

Education expenditures: 4.6% of GDP (2010)
country comparison to the world: 88

Literacy: *definition:* age 15 and over can read and write
total population: 78%
male: 78.1%
female: 77.9% (2005 est.)

School life expectancy (primary to tertiary education): *total:* 11 years
male: 10 years
female: 11 years (2002)

Child labor—children ages 5-14:
total number: 223,992
percentage: 14 %
note: data represents children ages 5-17 (2005 est.)

Unemployment, youth ages 15-24: *total:* 8.6%
country comparison to the world: 118
male: 8.1%
female: 9.7% (2006)

GOVERNMENT

Country name: *conventional long form:* Republic of Nicaragua
conventional short form: Nicaragua
local long form: Republica de Nicaragua
local short form: Nicaragua

Government type: republic

Capital: *name:* Managua

geographic coordinates: 12 08 N, 86 15 W
time difference: UTC-6 (1 hour behind Washington, DC during Standard Time)

Administrative divisions: 15 departments (departamentos, singular—departamento) and 2 autonomous regions* (regiones autonomistas, singular—region autonoma); Atlantico Norte*, Atlantico Sur*, Boaco, Carazo, Chinandega, Chontales, Esteli, Granada, Jinotega, Leon, Madriz, Managua, Masaya, Matagalpa, Nueva Segovia, Rio San Juan, Rivas

Independence: 15 September 1821 (from Spain)

National holiday: Independence Day, 15 September (1821)

Constitution: several previous; latest adopted 19 November 1986, effective 9 January 1987; amended several times, last in 2007 (2007)

Legal system: civil law system; Supreme Court may review administrative acts

International law organization participation: accepts compulsory ICJ jurisdiction with reservations; non-party state to the ICCt

Suffrage: 16 years of age; universal

Executive branch: *chief of state:* President Jose Daniel ORTEGA Saavedra (since 10 January 2007); Vice President Moises Omar HALLESLEVENS Acevedo (since 10 January 2012); note—the president is both chief of state and head of government
head of government: President Jose Daniel ORTEGA Saavedra (since 10 January 2007); Vice President Moises Omar HALLESLEVENS Acevedo (since 10 January 2012)
cabinet: Council of Ministers appointed by the president (For more information visit the World Leaders website)
elections: president and vice president elected on the same ticket by popular vote for a five-year term; election last held on 6 November 2011 (next to be held by November 2016)
election results: Jose Daniel ORTEGA Saavedra reelected president; percent of vote—Jose Daniel ORTEGA Saavedra 62.5%, Fabio GADEA 31%, Arnoldo ALEMAN 5.9%, other 0.6%

Legislative branch: unicameral National Assembly or Asamblea Nacional (92 seats; 90 members elected by proportional representation and party lists to serve five-year terms; 1 seat for the previous president, 1 seat for the runner-up in previous presidential election)
elections: last held on 6 November 2011 (next to be held by November 2016)
election results: percent of vote by party—NA; seats by party—FSLN 62, PLI/MRS 26, PLC 2

Judicial branch: *highest court(s):* Supreme Court or Corte Suprema de Justicia (consists of 16 judges organized into administrative, civil, criminal, and constitutional chambers)
judge selection and term of office: Supreme Court judges elected by the National Assembly to serve 5-year staggered terms
subordinate courts: Appeals Court; first instance civil, criminal, and military courts

Political parties and leaders: Alliance for the Republic or APRE [Carlos CANALES]; Conservative Party or PC [Alejandro BOLANOS Davis]; Independent Liberal Party or PLI [Indalecio RODRIGUEZ]; Liberal Constitutionalist Party or PLC [Maria Haydee OSUNA]; Nicaraguan Liberal Alliance or ALN [Alejandro MEJIA Ferreti]; Sandinista National Liberation Front or FSLN [Jose Daniel ORTEGA Saavedra]; Sandinista Renovation Movement or MRS [Ana Margarita VIJIL]; Political pressure groups and leaders; National Workers Front or FNT (a Sandinista umbrella group of eight labor unions including: Farm Workers Association or ATC, Health; Workers Federation or FETASALUD, Heroes and Martyrs Confederation of Professional Associations or CONAPRO, National Association; of Educators of Nicaragua or ANDEN, National Union of Employees or UNE, National Union of Farmers and Ranchers or UNAG, Sandinista Workers Central or CST, and Union of Journalists of Nicaragua or UPN); Permanent Congress of Workers or CPT (an umbrella group of four non-Sandinista labor unions including: Autonomous Nicaraguan; Workers Central or CTN-A, Confederation of Labor Unification or CUS, Independent General Confederation of Labor or CGT-I, and Labor

Action and Unity Central or CAUS); Nicaraguan Workers' Central or CTN (an independent labor union); Superior Council of Private Enterprise or COSEP (a confederation of business groups)

International organization participation: BCIE, CACM, CD, CELAC, FAO, G-77, IADB, IAEA, IBRD, ICAO, ICRM, IDA, IFAD, IFC, IFRCS, ILO, IMF, IMO, Interpol, IOC, IOM, IPU, ISO (correspondent), ITSO, ITU, ITUC (NGOs), LAES, LAIA, LAIA (observer), MIGA, NAM, OAS, OPANAL, OPCW, PCA, Petrocaribe, SICA, UN, UNCTAD, UNESCO, UNHCR, UNIDO, Union Latina, UNWTO, UPU, WCO, WHO, WIPO, WMO, WTO

Diplomatic representation in the US:
chief of mission: Ambassador Francisco Obadiah CAMPBELL Hooker (since 23 June 2010)
chancery: 1627 New Hampshire Avenue NW, Washington, DC 20009
telephone: [1] (202) 939-6570, 6573
FAX: [1] (202) 939-6545
consulate(s) general: Houston, Los Angeles, Miami, New Orleans, New York, San Francisco

Diplomatic representation from the US:
chief of mission: Ambassador Phyllis M. POWERS (since 24 April 2012)
embassy: Kilometer 5.5 Carretera Sur, Managua
mailing address: American Embassy Managua, APO AA 34021
telephone: [505] 2252-7100, 2252-7888; 2252-7634 (after hours)
FAX: [505] 2252-7250

Flag description: three equal horizontal bands of blue (top), white, and blue with the national coat of arms centered in the white band; the coat of arms features a triangle encircled by the words REPUBLICA DE NICARAGUA on the top and AMERICA CENTRAL on the bottom; the banner is based on the former blue-white-blue flag of the Federal Republic of Central America; the blue bands symbolize the Pacific Ocean and the Caribbean Sea, while the white band represents the land between the two bodies of water
note: similar to the flag of El Salvador, which features a round emblem encircled by the words REPUBLICA DE EL SALVADOR EN LA AMERICA CENTRAL centered in the white band; also similar to the flag of Honduras, which has five blue stars arranged in an X pattern centered in the white band

National symbol(s): turquoise-browed motmot (bird)

National anthem: *name:* "Salve a ti, Nicaragua" (Hail to Thee, Nicaragua)
lyrics/music: Salomon Ibarra MAYORGA/traditional, arranged by Luis Abraham DELGADILLO
note: although only officially adopted in 1971, the music was approved in 1918 and the lyrics in 1939; the tune, originally from Spain, was used as an anthem for Nicaragua from the 1830's until 1876

ECONOMY

Economy—overview: Nicaragua, the poorest country in Central America and the second poorest in the Western Hemisphere, has widespread underemployment and poverty. The Dominican Republic-Central America-United States Free Trade Agreement (CAFTA-DR) has been in effect since April 2006 and has expanded export opportunities for many agricultural and manufactured goods. Textiles and agriculture combined account for nearly 50% of Nicaragua's exports. The ORTEGA administration's promotion of mixed business initiatives, owned by the Nicaraguan and Venezuelan state oil firms, together with the weak rule of law, could undermine the investment climate for domestic and international private firms in the near-term. Nicaragua relied on an IMF external credit facility to meet internal- and external-debt financing obligations. The most recent IMF program ended in 2011 and Nicaragua is currently in negotiations for a new program. Nicaragua depends heavily on foreign development assistance, however, donors have curtailed this funding in response to November 2008 and subsequent electoral fraud. Nicaragua still struggles with a relatively high public debt burden.

GDP (purchasing power parity): $27.86 billion (2013 est.)
country comparison to the world: 118
$26.74 billion (2012 est.)
$25.42 billion (2011 est.)
note: data are in 2013 US dollars

GDP (official exchange rate): $11.28 billion (2013 est.)

GDP—real growth rate: 4.2% (2013 est.)
country comparison to the world: 72
5.2% (2012 est.)
5.4% (2011 est.)

GDP—per capita (PPP): $4,500 (2013 est.)
country comparison to the world: 166
$4,400 (2012 est.)
$4,200 (2011 est.)
note: data are in 2013 US dollars

GDP—composition, by end use:
household consumption: 86.1%
government consumption: 10.3%
investment in fixed capital: 34.4%
exports of goods and services: 38.6%
imports of goods and services: -69.5% (2013 est.)

GDP—composition, by sector of origin:
agriculture: 17.1%
industry: 25.5%
services: 57.5% (2013 est.)

Agriculture—products: coffee, bananas, sugarcane, rice, corn, tobacco, sesame, soya, beans; beef, veal, pork, poultry, dairy products; shrimp, lobsters, cotton

Industries: food processing, chemicals, machinery and metal products, knit and woven apparel, petroleum refining and distribution, beverages, footwear, wood, electric wire harness manufacturing, mining

Industrial production growth rate: 3% (2013 est.)
country comparison to the world: 101

Labor force: 3.039 million (2013 est.)
country comparison to the world: 103

Labor force—by occupation: *agriculture:* 28%
industry: 19%
services: 53% (2010 est.)

Unemployment rate: 7.2% (2013 est.)
country comparison to the world: 78
7.4% (2012 est.)
note: underemployment was 46.5% in 2008

Population below poverty line: 42.5% (2009)

Household income or consumption by percentage share: *lowest 10%:* 1.4%
highest 10%: 41.8% (2005)

Distribution of family income—Gini index: 40.5 (2010)
country comparison to the world: 56
60.3 (1998)

Budget: *revenues:* $2.885 billion
expenditures: $2.918 billion (2013 est.)

Taxes and other revenues: 25.6% of GDP (2013 est.)
country comparison to the world: 120

Budget surplus (+) or deficit (-): -0.3% of GDP (2013 est.)
country comparison to the world: 49

Public debt: 57.4% of GDP (2013 est.)
country comparison to the world: 53
58.6% of GDP (2012 est.)
note: official data; data cover general Government Debt, and includes debt instruments issued (or owned) by Government entities other than the treasury; the data include treasury debt held by foreign entities, as well as intra-governmental debt; intra-governmental debt consists of treasury borrowings from surpluses in the social funds, such as retirement, medical care, and unemployment, debt instruments for the social funds are not sold at public auctions; Nicaragua rebased its GDP figures in 2012, which reduced the figures for debt as a percentage of GDP

Fiscal year: calendar year

Inflation rate (consumer prices): 7.4% (2013 est.)
country comparison to the world: 189
7.2% (2012 est.)

Central bank discount rate: 3% (31 December 2010 est.)

Commercial bank prime lending rate: 12% (31 December 2013 est.)
country comparison to the world: 70
11.99% (31 December 2012 est.)

Stock of narrow money: $923.6 million (31 December 2013 est.)
country comparison to the world: 152
$788.4 million (31 December 2012 est.)

Stock of broad money: $3.136 billion (31 December 2011 est.)
country comparison to the world: 143
$2.924 billion (31 December 2010 est.)

Stock of domestic credit: $4.268 billion (31 December 2013 est.)
country comparison to the world: 120
$4.567 billion (31 December 2012 est.)

Market value of publicly traded shares: $NA

Current account balance: -$1.578 billion (2013 est.)
country comparison to the world: 134
-$1.35 billion (2012 est.)

Exports: $4.278 billion (2013 est.)
country comparison to the world: 117
$4.157 billion (2012 est.)

Exports—commodities: coffee, beef, gold, sugar, peanuts, shrimp and lobster, tobacco, cigars, automobile wiring harnesses, textiles, apparel, cotton

Exports—partners: US 55.6%, Canada 8.6%, Venezuela 7.3%, El Salvador 4.2% (2012)

Imports: $6.608 billion (2013 est.)
country comparison to the world: 116
$6.45 billion (2012 est.)

Imports—commodities: consumer goods, machinery and equipment, raw materials, petroleum products

Imports—partners: US 19%, Venezuela 14.8%, Mexico 12.2%, Costa Rica 8.5%, Guatemala 8%, China 7.9%, El Salvador 4.7% (2012)

Reserves of foreign exchange and gold: $1.89 billion (31 December 2013 est.)
country comparison to the world: 124
$1.887 billion (31 December 2012 est.)

Debt—external: $8.16 billion (31 December 2013 est.)
country comparison to the world: 105
$7.79 billion (31 December 2012 est.)

Exchange rates: cordobas (NIO) per US dollar—
24.77 (2013 est.)
23.547 (2012 est.)
21.356 (2010 est.)
20.34 (2009)
19.374 (2008)

ENERGY

Electricity—production: 3.824 billion kWh (2011 est.)
country comparison to the world: 125

Electricity—consumption: 2.941 billion kWh (2011 est.)
country comparison to the world: 132

Electricity—exports: 43 million kWh (2010 est.)
country comparison to the world: 83

Electricity—imports: 10 million kWh (2010 est.)
country comparison to the world: 106

Electricity—installed generating capacity: 1.108 million kW (2011 est.)
country comparison to the world: 123

Electricity—from fossil fuels: 66% of total installed capacity (2011 est.)
country comparison to the world: 119

Electricity—from nuclear fuels: 0% of total installed capacity (2011 est.)
country comparison to the world: 156

Electricity—from hydroelectric plants: 9.5% of total installed capacity (2011 est.)
country comparison to the world: 116

Electricity—from other renewable sources: 24.5% of total installed capacity (2011 est.)
country comparison to the world: 5

Crude oil—production: 0 bbl/day (2011 est.)
country comparison to the world: 204

Crude oil—exports: 0 bbl/day (2011 est.)
country comparison to the world: 165

Crude oil—imports: 16,020 bbl/day (2011 est.)
country comparison to the world: 71

Crude oil—proved reserves: 0 bbl (1 January 2013 es)
country comparison to the world: 174

Refined petroleum products—production: 15,870 bbl/day (2010 est.)
country comparison to the world: 98

Refined petroleum products—consumption: 30,690 bbl/day (2011 est.)
country comparison to the world: 113

Refined petroleum products—exports: 999.6 bbl/day (2011 est.)
country comparison to the world: 106

Refined petroleum products—imports: 15,830 bbl/day (2011 est.)
country comparison to the world: 118

Natural gas—production: 0 cu m (2012 est.)
country comparison to the world: 178

Natural gas—consumption: 0 cu m (2012 est.)
country comparison to the world: 183

Natural gas—exports: 0 cu m (2012 est.)
country comparison to the world: 160

Natural gas—imports: 0 cu m (2012 est.)
country comparison to the world: 111

Natural gas—proved reserves: 0 cu m (1 January 2013 es)
country comparison to the world: 181

Carbon dioxide emissions from consumption of energy: 5.035 million Mt (2011 est.)
country comparison to the world: 125

COMMUNICATIONS

Telephones—main lines in use: 320,000 (2012)
country comparison to the world: 112

Telephones—mobile cellular: 5.346 million (2012)
country comparison to the world: 108

Telephone system: *general assessment:* system being upgraded by foreign investment; nearly all installed telecommunications capacity now uses digital technology, owing to investments since privatization of the formerly state-owned telecommunications company
domestic: since privatization, access to fixed-line and mobile-cellular services has improved; fixed-line teledensity roughly 5 per 100 persons; mobile-cellular telephone subscribership has increased to roughly 85 per 100 persons
international: country code—505; the Americas Region Caribbean Ring System (ARCOS-1) fiber optic submarine cable provides connectivity to South and Central America, parts of the Caribbean, and the US; satellite earth stations—1 Intersputnik (Atlantic Ocean region) and 1 Intelsat (Atlantic Ocean) (2011)

Broadcast media: multiple privately owned terrestrial TV networks, supplemented by cable TV in most urban areas; of more than 100 radio stations, nearly all are privately owned; Radio Nicaragua is government-owned and Radio Sandino is controlled by the Sandinista National Liberation Front (FSLN) (2007)

Internet country code: .ni

Internet hosts: 296,068 (2012)
country comparison to the world: 63

Internet users: 199,800 (2009)
country comparison to the world: 141

TRANSPORTATION

Airports: 147 (2013)
country comparison to the world: 40

Airports—with paved runways: *total:* 12
2,438 to 3,047 m: 3
1,524 to 2,437 m: 2
914 to 1,523 m: 3
under 914 m: 4 (2013)

Airports—with unpaved runways: *total:* 135
1,524 to 2,437 m: 1
914 to 1,523 m: 15
under 914 m: 119 (2013)

Pipelines: oil 54 km (2013)

Roadways: *total:* 22,111 km
country comparison to the world: 104
paved: 2,850 km
unpaved: 19,261 km (2010)

Waterways: 2,220 km (navigable waterways as well as the use of the large Lake Managua and Lake Nicaragua; rivers serve only the sparsely populated eastern part of the country) (2011)
country comparison to the world: 40

Ports and terminals: *major seaport(s):* Bluefields, Corinto

MILITARY

Military branches: National Army of Nicaragua (Ejercito Nacional de Nicaragua, ENN; includes Navy, Air Force) (2013)

Military service age and obligation: 18-30 years of age for voluntary military service; no conscription; tour of duty 18-36 months; requires Nicaraguan nationality and 6th-grade education (2012)

Manpower available for military service:
males age 16-49: 1,452,107
females age 16-49: 1,552,698 (2010 est.)

Manpower fit for military service:
males age 16-49: 1,227,757
females age 16-49: 1,335,653 (2010 est.)

Manpower reaching militarily significant age annually: *male:* 69,093
female: 67,522 (2010 est.)

Military expenditures: 0.63% of GDP (2012)
country comparison to the world: 120
0.53% of GDP (2011)
0.63% of GDP (2010)

TRANSNATIONAL ISSUES

Disputes—international: the 1992 ICJ ruling for El Salvador and Honduras advised a tripartite resolution to establish a maritime boundary in the Gulf of Fonseca, which considers Honduran access to the Pacific; legal dispute over navigational rights of San Juan River on border with Costa Rica

Illicit drugs: transshipment point for cocaine destined for the US and transshipment point for arms-for-drugs dealing

NIGER

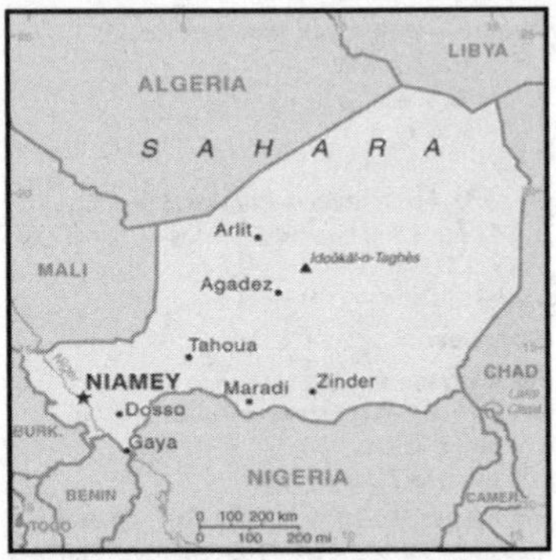

INTRODUCTION

Background: Niger became independent from France in 1960 and experienced single-party and military rule until 1991, when Gen. Ali SAIBOU was forced by public pressure to allow multiparty elections, which resulted in a democratic government in 1993. Political infighting brought the government to a standstill and in 1996 led to a coup by Col. Ibrahim BARE. In 1999, BARE was killed in a counter coup by military officers who restored democratic rule and held elections that brought Mamadou TANDJA to power in December of that year. TANDJA was reelected in 2004 and in 2009 spearheaded a constitutional amendment that would allow him to extend his term as president. In February 2010, a military coup deposed TANDJA, immediately suspended the constitution, and dissolved the Cabinet. ISSOUFOU Mahamadou emerged victorious from a crowded field in the election following the coup and was inaugurated in April 2011. Niger is one of the poorest countries in the world with minimal government services and insufficient funds to develop its resource base. The largely agrarian and subsistence-based economy is frequently disrupted by extended droughts common to the Sahel region of Africa. The Nigerien Movement for Justice, a predominantly ethnic Tuareg rebel group, emerged in February 2007, and attacked several military targets in Niger's northern region throughout 2007 and 2008. Successful government offensives in 2009 ended the rebellion. Niger is facing increased security concerns on its borders from various external threats including insecurity in Libya, spillover from the conflict in Mali, and violent extremism in northeastern Nigeria.

GEOGRAPHY

Location: Western Africa, southeast of Algeria

Geographic coordinates: 16 00 N, 8 00 E

Map references: Africa

Area: *total:* 1.267 million sq km
country comparison to the world: 22
land: 1,266,700 sq km
water: 300 sq km

Area—comparative: slightly less than twice the size of Texas

Land boundaries: *total:* 5,697 km
border countries: Algeria 956 km, Benin 266 km, Burkina Faso 628 km, Chad 1,175 km, Libya 354 km, Mali 821 km, Nigeria 1,497 km

Coastline: 0 km (landlocked)

Maritime claims: none (landlocked)

Climate: desert; mostly hot, dry, dusty; tropical in extreme south

Terrain: predominately desert plains and sand dunes; flat to rolling plains in south; hills in north

Elevation extremes: *lowest point:* Niger River 200 m
highest point: Idoukal-n-Taghes 2,022 m

Natural resources: uranium, coal, iron ore, tin, phosphates, gold, molybdenum, gypsum, salt, petroleum

Land use: *arable land:* 11.79%
permanent crops: 0.05%
other: 88.16% (2011)

Irrigated land: 736.6 sq km (2005)

Total renewable water resources: 33.65 cu km (2011)

Freshwater withdrawal (domestic/industrial/agricultural): *total:* 0.98 cu km/yr (30%/3%/67%)
per capita: 70.53 cu m/yr (2005)

Natural hazards: recurring droughts

Environment—current issues: overgrazing; soil erosion; deforestation; desertification; wildlife populations (such as elephant, hippopotamus, giraffe, and lion) threatened because of poaching and habitat destruction

Environment—international agreements: *party to:* Biodiversity, Climate Change, Climate Change-Kyoto Protocol, Desertification, Endangered Species, Environmental Modification, Hazardous Wastes, Ozone Layer Protection, Wetlands
signed, but not ratified: Law of the Sea

Geography—note: landlocked; one of the hottest countries in the world; northern four-fifths is desert, southern one-fifth is savanna, suitable for livestock and limited agriculture

PEOPLE AND SOCIETY

Nationality: *noun:* Nigerien(s)
adjective: Nigerien

Ethnic groups: Haoussa 55.4%, Djerma Sonrai 21%, Tuareg 9.3%, Peuhl 8.5%, Kanouri Manga 4.7%, other 1.2% (2001 census)

Languages: French (official), Hausa, Djerma

Religions: Muslim 80%, other (includes indigenous beliefs and Christian) 20%

Population: 17,466,172 (July 2014 est.)
country comparison to the world: 63

Age structure:
0-14 years: 49.8% (male 4,387,785/female 4,308,312)
15-24 years: 18.4% (male 1,586,720/female 1,626,457)
25-54 years: 25.9% (male 2,261,287/female 2,266,576)
55-64 years: 2.6% (male 294,446/female 274,268)
65 years and over: 2.6% (male 234,079/female 226,242) (2014 est.)

Dependency ratios:
total dependency ratio: 111.5 %
youth dependency ratio: 105.9 %
elderly dependency ratio: 5.5 %
potential support ratio: 18.1 (2013)

Median age: *total:* 15.1 years
male: 15 years
female: 15.2 years (2014 est.)

Population growth rate: 3.28% (2014 est.)
country comparison to the world: 7

Birth rate: 46.12 births/1,000 population (2014 est.)
country comparison to the world: 1

Death rate: 12.73 deaths/1,000 population (2014 est.)
country comparison to the world: 22

Net migration rate: -0.58 migrant(s)/1,000 population (2014 est.)
country comparison to the world: 137

Urbanization: *urban population:* 17.8% of total population (2011)
rate of urbanization: 4.91% annual rate of change (2010-15 est.)

Major urban areas—population: NIAMEY (capital) 1.004 million (2009)

Sex ratio: *at birth:* 1.03 male(s)/female
0-14 years: 1.02 male(s)/female
15-24 years: 0.98 male(s)/female
25-54 years: 1 male(s)/female
55-64 years: 1.01 male(s)/female
65 years and over: 1.03 male(s)/female
total population: 1.01 male(s)/female (2014 est.)

Mother's mean age at first birth: 18 (2006 est.)

Maternal mortality rate: 590 deaths/100,000 live births (2010)
country comparison to the world: 14
Infant mortality rate: *total:* 86.27 deaths/1,000 live births
country comparison to the world: 7
male: 90.86 deaths/1,000 live births
female: 81.53 deaths/1,000 live births (2014 est.)

Life expectancy at birth: *total population:* 54.74 years
country comparison to the world: 208
male: 53.54 years
female: 55.97 years (2014 est.)

Total fertility rate: 6.89 children born/woman (2014 est.)
country comparison to the world: 1

Contraceptive prevalence rate: 13.9% (2012)

Health expenditures: 5.3% of GDP (2011)
country comparison to the world: 128

Physicians density: 0.02 physicians/1,000 population (2008)

Hospital bed density: 0.31 beds/1,000 population (2005)

Drinking water source:
improved:
urban: 100% of population
rural: 39.5% of population
total: 50.3% of population
unimproved:
urban: 0% of population
rural: 60.5% of population
total: 49.7% of population (2011 est.)

Sanitation facility access:
improved:
urban: 34% of population
rural: 4.3% of population

total: 9.6% of population
unimproved:
urban: 66% of population
rural: 95.7% of population
total: 90.4% of population (2011 est.)

HIV/AIDS—adult prevalence rate: 0.5% (2012 est.)
country comparison to the world: 71

HIV/AIDS—people living with HIV/AIDS: 46,300 (2012 est.)
country comparison to the world: 62

HIV/AIDS—deaths: 3,400 (2012 est.)
country comparison to the world: 49

Major infectious diseases: *degree of risk:* very high
food or waterborne diseases: bacterial and protozoal diarrhea, hepatitis A, and typhoid fever
vectorborne diseases: malaria and dengue fever
water contact disease: schistosomiasis
respiratory disease: meningococcal meningitis
animal contact disease: rabies
note: highly pathogenic H5N1 avian influenza has been identified in this country; it poses a negligible risk with extremely rare cases possible among US citizens who have close contact with birds (2013)

Obesity—adult prevalence rate: 2.4% (2008)
country comparison to the world: 180

Children under the age of 5 years underweight: 39.9% (2006)
country comparison to the world: 4

Education expenditures: 4.2% of GDP (2011)
country comparison to the world: 101

Literacy: *definition:* age 15 and over can read and write
total population: 28.7%
male: 42.9%
female: 15.1% (2005 est.)

School life expectancy (primary to tertiary education): *total:* 5 years
male: 6 years
female: 5 years (2012)

Child labor—children ages 5-14:
total number: 1,557,913
percentage: 43 % (2006 est.)

Unemployment, youth ages 15-24: *total:* 3.2%
country comparison to the world: 142
male: 4%
female: 1.7% (2001)

GOVERNMENT

Country name: *conventional long form:* Republic of Niger
conventional short form: Niger
local long form: Republique du Niger
local short form: Niger

Government type: republic

Capital: *name:* Niamey

geographic coordinates: 13 31 N, 2 07 E
time difference: UTC+1 (6 hours ahead of Washington, DC during Standard Time)

Administrative divisions: 8 regions (regions, singular—region) includes 1 capital district* (communite urbaine); Agadez, Diffa, Dosso, Maradi, Niamey*, Tahoua, Tillaberi, Zinder

Independence: 3 August 1960 (from France)

National holiday: Republic Day, 18 December (1958); note—commemorates the founding of the Republic of Niger which predated independence from France in 1960

Constitution: several previous; passed by referendum 31 October 2010, entered into force 25 November 2010 (2014) (2010)

Legal system: mixed legal system of civil law (based on French civil law), Islamic law, and customary law

International law organization participation: has not submitted an ICJ jurisdiction declaration; accepts ICCt jurisdiction

Suffrage: 18 years of age; universal

Executive branch: *chief of state:* President ISSOUFOU Mahamadou (since 7 April 2011)
head of government: Prime Minister Brigi RAFINI (since 7 April 2011); appointed by the president and shares some executive responsibilities with the president
cabinet: 37-member Cabinet appointed by the president; note—in August 2013, the president authorized a cabinet reshuffle and increased its membership to 37 from 26 in order to create a government of national unity (For more information visit the World Leaders website)
elections: president elected by popular vote for a five-year term (eligible for a second term); candidate must receive a majority of the votes to be elected president; a presidential election to restore civilian rule was held 31 January 2011 with a runoff election between ISSOUFOU Mahamadou (PNDS-Tarayya) and Seini OUMAROU (MNSD-Nassara) held on 12 March 2011
election results: ISSOUFOU Mahamadou elected president in a runoff election; percent of vote—ISSOUFOU Mahamadou 58%, Seini OUMAROU 42%

Legislative branch: unicameral National Assembly (113 seats; members elected by popular vote to serve five-year terms)
elections: last held on 31 January 2011
election results: percent of vote by party—PNDS-Tarrayya 33%, MNSD-Nassara 21%, MODEN/FA-Lumana 20%, ANDP-Zaman Lahiya 7.5%, RDP-Jama'a 6.5%, UDR-Tabbat 5.4%, CDS-Rahama 3.3%, UNI 1%; seats by party—PNDS-Tarrayya 37, MNSD-Nassara 26, MODEN/FA-Lumana 25, ANDP-Zaman Lahiya 8, RDP-Jama'a **7, UDR-Tabbat 6, CDS-Rahama 3, UNI 1**

Judicial branch: *highest court(s):* Constitutional Court (consists of 7 judges); High Court of Justice (consists of 7 members)
judge selection and term of office: Constitutional Court judges nominated/elected—1 by the president of the Republic, 1 by the president of the National Assembly, 2 by peer judges, 2 by peer lawyers, 1 law professor by peers, and 1 from within Nigerien society; all appointed by the president; judges serve 6-year nonrenewable terms with one-third of membership renewed every 2 years; High Judicial Court members selected from among the legislature and judiciary; members serve 5-year terms
subordinate courts: Court of Cassation; Council of State; Court of Finances; various specialized tribunals and customary courts

Political parties and leaders: Democratic and Social Convention-Rahama or CDS-Rahama [Mahamane OUSMANE]; National Movement for a Society of Development-Nassara or MNSD-Nassara [Seini OUMAROU]; National Union of Independents or UNI [Amadou DJIBO ALI]; Nigerien Alliance for Democracy and Progress-Zaman Lahiya or ANDP-Zaman Lahiya [Moussa Moumouni; DJERMAKOYE]; Nigerien Democratic Movement for an African Federation or MODEN/FA Lumana [Hama AMADOU]; Nigerien Party for Democracy and Socialism or PNDS-Tarrayya [Mohamed BAZOUM]; Rally for Democracy and Progress-Jama'a or RDP-Jama'a [Hamid ALGABID]; Social and Democratic Rally or RSD-Gaskiyya [Cheiffou AMADOU]; Union for Democracy and the Republic-Tabbat or UDR-Tabbat [Amadou Boubacar CISSE]
note: the SPLM and SPLM-DC are banned political parties

International organization participation: ACP, AfDB, AU, CD, ECOWAS, EITI (compliant country), Entente, FAO, FZ, G-77, IAEA, IBRD, ICAO, ICRM, IDA, IDB, IFAD, IFC, IFRCS, ILO, IMF, Interpol, IOC, IOM, IPU, ISO (correspondent), ITSO, ITU, ITUC (NGOs), MIGA, MINUSMA, MONUSCO, NAM, OIC, OIF, OPCW, UN, UNCTAD, UNESCO, UNIDO, UNMIL, UNOCI, UNWTO, UPU, WADB (regional), WAEMU, WCO, WFTU (NGOs), WHO, WIPO, WMO, WTO

Diplomatic representation in the US:
chief of mission: Ambassador Maman Sambo SIDIKOU (since 2 December 2011)
chancery: 2204 R Street NW, Washington, DC 20008
telephone: [1] (202) 483-4224 through 4227
FAX: [1] (202)483-3169

Diplomatic representation from the US:
chief of mission: Ambassador (vacant); Charge d'Affaires Richard BELL (since September 2012)
embassy: BP 11201, Rue Des Ambassades, Niamey
mailing address: 2420 Niamey Pl, Washington DC 20521-2420
telephone: [227] 20-73-31-69 or [227] 20-72-39-41
FAX: [227] 20-73-55-60

Flag description: three equal horizontal bands of orange (top), white, and green with a small orange disk centered in the white band; the orange band denotes the drier northern regions of the Sahara; white stands for purity and innocence; green symbolizes hope and the fertile and productive southern and western areas, as well as the Niger River; the orange disc represents the sun and the sacrifices made by the people
note: similar to the flag of India, which has a blue spoked wheel centered in the white band

National anthem: *name:* "La Nigerienne" (The Nigerien)
lyrics/music: Maurice Albert THIRIET/Robert JACQUET and Nicolas Abel Francois FRIONNET
note: adopted 1961

ECONOMY

Economy—overview: Niger is a landlocked, Sub-Saharan nation, whose economy centers on subsistence crops, livestock, and some of the world's largest uranium deposits. Agriculture contributes about one-third of GDP and provides livelihood for about nine-tenths of the population. Drought, desertification, and strong population growth have undercut the economy. Niger shares a common currency, the CFA franc, and a common central bank, the Central Bank of West African

States (BCEAO), with seven other members of the West African Monetary Union. Debt relief has significantly reduced Niger's annual debt service obligations, freeing funds for expenditures on basic health care, primary education, HIV/AIDS prevention, rural infrastructure, and other programs geared at poverty reduction. Nearly half of the government's budget is derived from foreign donor resources. The economy in recent years has been hurt by terrorist activity and kidnappings near its uranium mines and instability in Mali. Future growth may be sustained by exploitation of oil, gold, coal, and other mineral resources. Niger has sizable reserves of oil and oil production, which began in 2012, along with refining, and exports are expected to grow through 2016. However, oil revenues have fallen well short of predictions, mainly because of logistical challenges. Food insecurity and drought remain perennial problems for Niger. The mining sector may be affected by the government's attempt to renegotiate extraction rights contracts.

GDP (purchasing power parity): $13.98 billion (2013 est.)
country comparison to the world: 147
$13.17 billion (2012 est.)
$11.84 billion (2011 est.)
note: data are in 2013 US dollars

GDP (official exchange rate): $7.304 billion (2013 est.)

GDP—real growth rate: 6.2% (2013 est.)
country comparison to the world: 34
11.2% (2012 est.)
2.2% (2011 est.)

GDP—per capita (PPP): $800 (2013 est.)
country comparison to the world: 222
$800 (2012 est.)
$800 (2011 est.)
note: data are in 2013 US dollars

Gross national saving: 23.7% of GDP (2013 est.)
country comparison to the world: 59
22% of GDP (2012 est.)
25.3% of GDP (2011 est.)

GDP—composition, by end use:
household consumption: 61%
government consumption: 25.1%
investment in fixed capital: 44.7%
investment in inventories: 0%
exports of goods and services: 26.3%
imports of goods and services: -57.1% (2013 est.)

GDP—composition, by sector of origin:
agriculture: 35.2%
industry: 14.2%
services: 50.6% (2013 est.)

Agriculture—products: cowpeas, cotton, peanuts, millet, sorghum, cassava (manioc), rice; cattle, sheep, goats, camels, donkeys, horses, poultry

Industries: uranium mining, petroleum, cement, brick, soap, textiles, food processing, chemicals, slaughterhouses

Industrial production growth rate: 5.7% (2013 est.)
country comparison to the world: 44

Labor force: 4.688 million (2007)
country comparison to the world: 83

Labor force—by occupation:
agriculture: 90%
industry: 6%
services: 4% (1995)

Unemployment rate: NA%

Population below poverty line: 63% (1993 est.)

Household income or consumption by percentage share: *lowest 10%:* 3.7%
highest 10%: 28.5% (2007)

Distribution of family income—Gini index: 34 (2007)
country comparison to the world: 95
50.5 (1995)

Budget: *revenues:* $1.911 billion (2013 est.)
expenditures: $2.086 billion (2013 est.)

Taxes and other revenues: 26.2% of GDP (2013 est.)
country comparison to the world: 114

Budget surplus (+) or deficit (-):
-2.4% of GDP (2013 est.)
country comparison to the world: 96

Fiscal year: calendar year

Inflation rate (consumer prices): 1.9% (2013 est.)
country comparison to the world: 63
0.5% (2012 est.)

Central bank discount rate: 4.25% (31 December 2009)
country comparison to the world: 79
4.75% (31 December 2008)

Commercial bank prime lending rate: 4% (31 December 2013 est.)
country comparison to the world: 164
4% (31 December 2012 est.)

Stock of narrow money: $1.388 billion (31 December 2013 est.)
country comparison to the world: 143
$1.284 billion (31 December 2012 est.)

Stock of broad money: $1.74 billion (31 December 2013 est.)
country comparison to the world: 156
$1.61 billion (31 December 2012 est.)

Stock of domestic credit: $992.7 million (31 December 2013 est.)
country comparison to the world: 155
$915 million (31 December 2012 est.)

Market value of publicly traded shares: $NA

Current account balance: -$1.45 billion (2013 est.)
country comparison to the world: 132
-$1.453 billion (2012 est.)

Exports: $1.539 billion (2013 est.)
country comparison to the world: 147
$1.458 billion (2012 est.)

Exports—commodities: uranium ore, livestock, cowpeas, onions

Exports—partners: Nigeria 40.3%, US 17.2%, India 14.3%, Italy 8.6%, China 7.8%, Ghana 5.3% (2012)

Imports: $2.314 billion (2013 est.)
country comparison to the world: 160
$2.273 billion (2012 est.)

Imports—commodities: foodstuffs, machinery, vehicles and parts, petroleum, cereals

Imports—partners: France 14.4%, China 11.3%, Nigeria 10.1%, French Polynesia 9.2%, Togo 5.1%, Cote dIvoire 4.5% (2012)

Debt—external: $1.556 billion (31 December 2013 est.)
country comparison to the world: 150
$1.551 billion (31 December 2012 est.)

Exchange rates: Communaute Financiere Africaine francs (XOF) per US dollar—
500.7 (2013 est.)
510.53 (2012 est.)
495.28 (2010)
472.19 (2009)
447.81 (2008)

ENERGY

Electricity—production: 250 million kWh (2010 est.)
country comparison to the world: 179

Electricity—consumption: 832.5 million kWh (2010 est.)
country comparison to the world: 155

Electricity—exports: 0 kWh (2012 est.)
country comparison to the world: 175

Electricity—imports: 600 million kWh (2010 est.)
country comparison to the world: 75

Electricity—installed generating capacity: 134,000 kW (2010 est.)
country comparison to the world: 167

Electricity—from fossil fuels: 100% of total installed capacity (2010 est.)
country comparison to the world: 26

Electricity—from nuclear fuels: 0% of total installed capacity (2010 est.)
country comparison to the world: 149

Electricity—from hydroelectric plants: 0% of total installed capacity (2010 est.)
country comparison to the world: 188

Electricity—from other renewable sources: 0% of total installed capacity (2010 est.)
country comparison to the world: 208

Crude oil—production: 20,000 bbl/day (2012 est.)
country comparison to the world: 79

Crude oil—exports: 0 bbl/day (2010 est.)
country comparison to the world: 161

Crude oil—imports: 0 bbl/day (2010 est.)
country comparison to the world: 102

Crude oil—proved reserves: NA bbl (1 January 2013 es)

Refined petroleum products—production: 0 bbl/day (2010 est.)
country comparison to the world: 180

Refined petroleum products—consumption: 5,629 bbl/day (2011 est.)
country comparison to the world: 165

Refined petroleum products—exports: 0 bbl/day (2010 est.)
country comparison to the world: 202

Refined petroleum products—imports: 5,136 bbl/day (2010 est.)
country comparison to the world: 150

Natural gas—production: 0 cu m (2011 est.)
country comparison to the world: 173

Natural gas—consumption: 0 cu m (2010 est.)
country comparison to the world: 178

Natural gas—exports: 0 cu m (2011 est.)
country comparison to the world: 155

Natural gas—imports: 0 cu m (2011 est.)
country comparison to the world: 104

Natural gas—proved reserves: 0 cu m (1 January 2013 es)
country comparison to the world: 176

Carbon dioxide emissions from consumption of energy: 1.272 million Mt (2011 est.)
country comparison to the world: 160

COMMUNICATIONS

Telephones—main lines in use: 100,500 (2012)
country comparison to the world: 145

Telephones—mobile cellular: 5.4 million (2012)
country comparison to the world: 107

Telephone system: *general assessment:* inadequate; small system of wire, radio telephone communications, and microwave radio relay links concentrated in the southwestern area of Niger
domestic: combined fixed-line and mobile-cellular teledensity remains only about 30 per 100 persons despite a rapidly increasing cellular subscribership base; domestic satellite system with 3 earth stations and 1 planned
international: country code—227; satellite earth stations—2 Intelsat (1 Atlantic Ocean and 1 Indian Ocean) (2010)

Broadcast media: state-run TV station; 3 private TV stations provide a mix of local and foreign programming; state-run radio has only radio station with a national reach; about 30 private radio stations operate locally; as many as 100 community radio stations broadcast; transmissions of multiple international broadcasters are available (2007)

Internet country code: .ne

Internet hosts: 454 (2012)
country comparison to the world: 185

Internet users: 115,900 (2009)
country comparison to the world: 155

TRANSPORTATION

Airports: 30 (2013)
country comparison to the world: 115

Airports—with paved runways: *total:* 1 0
2,438 to 3,047 m: 3
1,524 to 2,437 m: 6
914 to 1,523 m: 1 (2013)

Airports—with unpaved runways: *total:* 2 0
1,524 to 2,437 m: 3
914 to 1,523 m: 15
under 914 m: 2 (2013)

Heliports: 1 (2013)

Roadways: *total:* 18,949 km
country comparison to the world: 114
paved: 3,912 km
unpaved: 15,037 km (2010)

Waterways: 300 km (the Niger, the only major river, is navigable to Gaya between September and March) (2012)
country comparison to the world: 94

MILITARY

Military branches: Nigerien Armed Forces (Forces Armees Nigeriennes, FAN): Army, Nigerien Air Force (Force Aerienne du Niger) (2012)

Military service age and obligation: 18 is the presumed legal minimum age for compulsory or voluntary military service; enlistees must be Nigerien citizens and unmarried; 2-year service term; women may serve in health care (2012)

Manpower available for military service:
males age 16-49: 3,329,184
females age 16-49: 3,267,669 (2010 est.)

Manpower fit for military service:
males age 16-49: 2,194,570
females age 16-49: 2,219,416 (2010 est.)

Manpower reaching militarily significant age annually: *male:* 186,348
female: 180,779 (2010 est.)

Military expenditures: 1.06% of GDP (2012)
country comparison to the world: 96
NA% (2011)
1.06% of GDP (2010)

TRANSNATIONAL ISSUES

Disputes—international: Libya claims about 25,000 sq km in a currently dormant dispute in the Tommo region; location of Benin-Niger-Nigeria tripoint is unresolved; only Nigeria and Cameroon have heeded the Lake Chad Commission's admonition to ratify the delimitation treaty that also includes the Chad-Niger and Niger-Nigeria boundaries; the dispute with Burkina Faso was referred to the ICJ in 2010

Refugees and internally displaced persons: *refugees (country of origin):* 49,770 (Mali) (2013); 10,044 (Nigeria) (2014)
IDPs: undetermined (unknown how many of the 11,000 people displaced by clashes between government forces and the Tuareg militant group, Niger Movement for Justice, in 2007 are still displaced; inter-communal violence) (2012)

NIGERIA

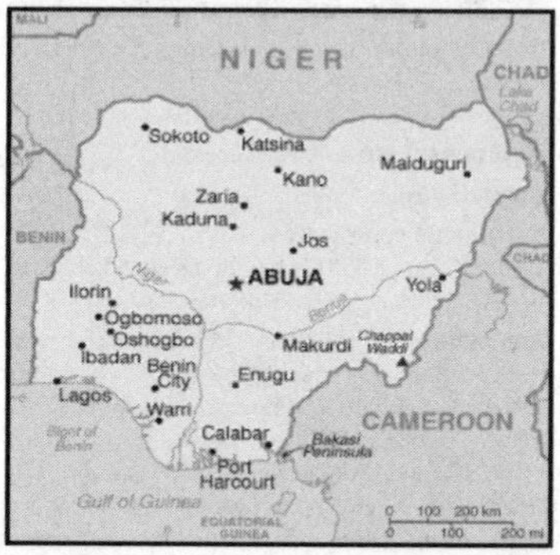

INTRODUCTION

Background: British influence and control over what would become Nigeria and Africa's most populous country grew through the 19th century. A series of constitutions after World War II granted Nigeria greater autonomy; independence came in 1960. Following nearly 16 years of military rule, a new constitution was adopted in 1999, and a peaceful transition to civilian government was completed. The government continues to face the daunting task of reforming a petroleum-based economy, whose revenues have been squandered through corruption and mismanagement, and institutionalizing democracy. In addition, Nigeria continues to experience longstanding ethnic and religious tensions. Although both the 2003 and 2007 presidential elections were marred by significant irregularities and violence, Nigeria is currently experiencing its longest period of civilian rule since independence. The general elections of April 2007 marked the first civilian-to-civilian transfer of power in the country's history and the elections of 2011 were generally regarded as credible. In January 2014, Nigeria assumed a nonpermanent seat on the UN Security Council for the 2014-15 term.

GEOGRAPHY

Location: Western Africa, bordering the Gulf of Guinea, between Benin and Cameroon

Geographic coordinates: 10 00 N, 8 00 E

Map references: Africa

Area: *total:* 923,768 sq km
country comparison to the world: 32
land: 910,768 sq km
water: 13,000 sq km

Area—comparative: slightly more than twice the size of California

Land boundaries: *total:* 4,047 km
border countries: Benin 773 km, Cameroon 1,690 km, Chad 87 km, Niger 1,497 km

Coastline: 853 km

Maritime claims: *territorial sea:* 12 nm
exclusive economic zone: 200 nm
continental shelf: 200 m depth or to the depth of exploitation

Climate: varies; equatorial in south, tropical in center, arid in north

Terrain: southern lowlands merge into central hills and plateaus; mountains in southeast, plains in north

Elevation extremes: *lowest point:* Atlantic Ocean 0 m
highest point: Chappal Waddi 2,419 m

Natural resources: natural gas, petroleum, tin, iron ore, coal, limestone, niobium, lead, zinc, arable land

Land use: *arable land:* 38.97%

permanent crops: 3.46%
other: 57.57% (2011)

Irrigated land: 2,932 sq km (2004)

Total renewable water resources: 286.2 cu km (2011)

Freshwater withdrawal (domestic/industrial/agricultural): *total:* 13.11 cu km/yr (31%/15%/54%)
per capita: 89.21 cu m/yr (2005)

Natural hazards: periodic droughts; flooding

Environment—current issues: soil degradation; rapid deforestation; urban air and water pollution; desertification; oil pollution—water, air, and soil; has suffered serious damage from oil spills; loss of arable land; rapid urbanization

Environment—international agreements:
party to: Biodiversity, Climate Change, Climate Change-Kyoto Protocol, Desertification, Endangered Species, Hazardous Wastes, Law of the Sea, Marine Dumping, Marine Life Conservation, Ozone Layer Protection, Ship Pollution, Wetlands
signed, but not ratified: none of the selected agreements

Geography—note: the Niger enters the country in the northwest and flows southward through tropical rain forests and swamps to its delta in the Gulf of Guinea

PEOPLE AND SOCIETY

Nationality: *noun:* Nigerian(s)
adjective: Nigerian

Ethnic groups: Nigeria, Africa's most populous country, is composed of more than 250 ethnic groups; the following are the most populous and politically influential: Hausa and Fulani 29%, Yoruba 21%, Igbo (Ibo) 18%, Ijaw 10%, Kanuri 4%, Ibibio 3.5%, Tiv 2.5%

Languages: English (official), Hausa, Yoruba, Igbo (Ibo), Fulani, over 500 additional indigenous languages

Religions: Muslim 50%, Christian 40%, indigenous beliefs 10%

Population: 177,155,754 (July 2014 est.)
country comparison to the world: 8
note: estimates for this country explicitly take into account the effects of excess mortality due to AIDS; this can result in lower life expectancy, higher infant mortality, higher death rates, lower population growth rates, and changes in the distribution of population by age and sex than would otherwise be expected

Age structure:
0-14 years: 43.2% (male 39,151,304/female 37,353,737)
15-24 years: 19.3% (male 17,486,117/female 16,732,533)
25-54 years: 30.5% (male 27,697,644/female 26,285,816)
55-64 years: 3.1% (male 3,393,631/female 3,571,301)
65 years and over: 3% (male 2,621,845/female 2,861,826) (2014 est.)

Dependency ratios:
total dependency ratio: 89 %
youth dependency ratio: 83.8 %
elderly dependency ratio: 5.2 %
potential support ratio: 19.3 (2013)

Median age: *total:* 18.2 years
male: 18.1 years
female: 18.3 years (2014 est.)

Population growth rate: 2.47% (2014 est.)
country comparison to the world: 33

Birth rate: 38.03 births/1,000 population (2014 est.)
country comparison to the world: 12

Death rate: 13.16 deaths/1,000 population (2014 est.)
country comparison to the world: 19

Net migration rate: -0.22 migrant(s)/1,000 population (2014 est.)
country comparison to the world: 120

Urbanization: *urban population:* 49.6% of total population (2011)
rate of urbanization: 3.75% annual rate of change (2010-15 est.)

Major urban areas—population: Lagos 10.203 million; Kano 3.304 million; Ibadan 2.762 million; ABUJA (capital) 1.857 million; Kaduna 1.519 million (2009)

Sex ratio: *at birth:* 1.06 male(s)/female
0-14 years: 1.05 male(s)/female
15-24 years: 1.05 male(s)/female
25-54 years: 1.05 male(s)/female
55-64 years: 1.04 male(s)/female
65 years and over: 0.85 male(s)/female
total population: 1.01 male(s)/female (2014 est.)

Mother's mean age at first birth: 20.9 (2008 est.)

Maternal mortality rate: 630 deaths/100,000 live births (2010)
country comparison to the world: 11

Infant mortality rate: *total:* 74.09 deaths/1,000 live births
country comparison to the world: 10
male: 79.02 deaths/1,000 live births
female: 68.87 deaths/1,000 live births (2014 est.)

Life expectancy at birth: *total population:* 52.62 years
country comparison to the world: 212
male: 51.63 years
female: 53.66 years (2014 est.)

Total fertility rate: 5.25 children born/woman (2014 est.)
country comparison to the world: 13

Contraceptive prevalence rate: 14.1% (2011)

Health expenditures: 5.3% of GDP (2011)
country comparison to the world: 127

Physicians density: 0.4 physicians/1,000 population (2008)

Hospital bed density: 0.53 beds/1,000 population (2004)

Drinking water source:
improved:
urban: 75.1% of population
rural: 47.3% of population
total: 61.1% of population
unimproved:
urban: 24.9% of population
rural: 52.7% of population
total: 38.9% of population (2011 est.)

Sanitation facility access:
improved:
urban: 33.2% of population
rural: 28.1% of population
total: 30.6% of population
unimproved:
urban: 66.8% of population
rural: 71.9% of population
total: 69.4% of population (2011 est.)

HIV/AIDS—adult prevalence rate: 3.1% (2012 est.)
country comparison to the world: 20

HIV/AIDS—people living with HIV/AIDS: 3,426,600 (2012 est.)
country comparison to the world: 2

HIV/AIDS—deaths: 239,700 (2012 est.)
country comparison to the world: 1

Major infectious diseases: *degree of risk:* very high
food or waterborne diseases: bacterial and protozoal diarrhea, hepatitis A and E, and typhoid fever
vectorborne diseases: malaria, dengue fever, and yellow fever
water contact diseases: leptospirosis and schistosomiasis
respiratory disease: meningococcal meningitis
aerosolized dust or soil contact disease: one of the most highly endemic areas for Lassa fever
animal contact disease: rabies
note: highly pathogenic H5N1 avian influenza has been identified in this country; it poses a negligible risk with extremely rare cases possible among US citizens who have close contact with birds (2013)

Obesity—adult prevalence rate: 6.5% (2008)
country comparison to the world: 146

Children under the age of 5 years underweight: 24.4% (2011)
country comparison to the world: 26

Education expenditures: NA

Literacy: *definition:* age 15 and over can read and write
total population: 61.3%
male: 72.1%
female: 50.4% (2010 est.)

School life expectancy (primary to tertiary education): *total:* 9 years
male: 10 years
female: 8 years (2005)

Child labor—children ages 5-14: *total number:* 11,396,823
percentage: 29 % (2007 est.)

GOVERNMENT

Country name: *conventional long form:* Federal Republic of Nigeria
conventional short form: Nigeria

Government type: federal republic

Capital: *name:* Abuja
geographic coordinates: 9 05 N, 7 32 E
time difference: UTC+1 (6 hours ahead of Washington, DC during Standard Time)

Administrative divisions: 36 states and 1 territory*; Abia, Adamawa, Akwa Ibom, Anambra, Bauchi, Bayelsa, Benue, Borno, Cross River, Delta, Ebonyi, Edo, Ekiti, Enugu, Federal Capital Territory*, Gombe, Imo, Jigawa, Kaduna, Kano, Katsina, Kebbi, Kogi, Kwara, Lagos, Nasarawa, Niger, Ogun, Ondo, Osun, Oyo, Plateau, Rivers, Sokoto, Taraba, Yobe, Zamfara

Independence: 1 October 1960 (from the UK)

National holiday: Independence Day (National Day), 1 October (1960)

Constitution: several previous; latest adopted 5 May 1999, effective 29 May 1999; amended 2010 (2010)

Legal system: mixed legal system of English common law, Islamic law (in 12 northern states), and traditional law

International law organization participation: accepts compulsory ICJ jurisdiction with reservations; accepts ICCt jurisdiction

Suffrage: 18 years of age; universal

Executive branch: *chief of state:* President Goodluck JONATHAN (since 5 May 2010, acting since 9 February 2010); Vice President Mohammed Namadi SAMBO (since 19 May 2010); note—the president is both the chief of state and head of government; JONATHAN assumed the presidency on 5 May 2010 following the death of President YAR'ADUA; JONATHAN was elected president on 16 April 2011
head of government: President Goodluck JONATHAN (since 5 May 2010, acting since 9 February 2010); Vice President Mohammed Namadi SAMBO (since 19 May 2010)
cabinet: Federal Executive Council (For more information visit the World Leaders website)
elections: president elected by popular vote for a four-year term (eligible for a second term); election last held on 16 April 2011 (next to be held in February 2015)
election results: Goodluck JONATHAN elected president; percent of vote—Goodluck JONATHAN 58.9%, Muhammadu BUHARI 32.0%, Nuhu RIBADU 5.4%, Ibrahim SHEKARAU 2.4%, other 1.3%

Legislative branch: bicameral National Assembly consists of the Senate (109 seats, 3 from each state plus 1 from Abuja; members elected by popular vote to serve four-year terms) and House of Representatives (360 seats; members elected by popular vote to serve four-year terms)
elections: Senate—last held on 9 and 26 April 2011 (next to be held in February 2015); House of Representatives—last held on 9 and 26 April 2011 (next to be held in February 2015)
election results: Senate—percent of vote by party—NA; seats by party—PDP 73, ACN 17, ANPP 7, CPC 6, LP 4, other 2; House of Representatives—percent of vote by party—NA; seats by party—PDP 205, ACN 69, CPC 36, ANPP 28, LP 9, APGA 6, ACC 5, other 2; note—due to logistical problems elections in a number of constituencies were held on 26 April 2011

Judicial branch: *highest court(s):* Supreme Court (consists of the chief justice and 15 justices)
judge selection and term of office: judges appointed by the president on the recommendation of the National Judicial Council, a 23-member independent body of federal and state judicial officials; judge appointments confirmed by the Senate; judges serve until age 65
subordinate courts: Court of Appeal; Federal High Court; High Court of the Federal Capital Territory; Sharia Court of Appeal of the Federal Capital Territory; Customary Court of Appeal of the Federal Capital Territory; state court system similar in structure to federal system

Political parties and leaders: Accord Party or ACC [Mohammad Lawal MALADO]; Action Congress of Nigeria or ACN [Adebisi Bamidele AKANDE]; All Nigeria Peoples Party or ANPP [Ogbonnaya C. ONU]; All Progressives Congress [Adebisi Bamidele AKANDE, acting]; All Progressives Grand Alliance or APGA [Victor C. UMEH]; Congress for Progressive Change or CPC [Tony MOMOH]; Democratic Peoples Party or DPP [Jeremiah USENI]; Labor Party [Chief Dan NWANYANWU]; Peoples Democratic Party or PDP [Adamu MU'AZU]

Political pressure groups and leaders: Academic Staff Union for Universities or ASUU; Campaign for Democracy or CD; Civil Liberties Organization or CLO; Committee for the Defense of Human Rights or CDHR; Constitutional Right Project or CRP; Human Right Africa; National Association of Democratic Lawyers or NADL; National Association of Nigerian Students or NANS; Nigerian Bar Association or NBA; Nigerian Labor Congress or NLC; Nigerian Medical Association or NMA; the press; Universal Defenders of Democracy or UDD

International organization participation: ACP, AfDB, AU, C, CD, D-8, ECOWAS, EITI (compliant country), FAO, G-15, G-24, G-77, IAEA, IBRD, ICAO, ICC (national committees), ICRM, IDA, IDB, IFAD, IFC, IFRCS, IHO, ILO, IMF, IMO, IMSO, Interpol, IOC, IOM, IPU, ISO, ITSO, ITU, ITUC (NGOs), MIGA, MINURSO, MINUSMA, MONUSCO, NAM, OAS (observer), OIC, OPCW, OPEC, PCA, UN, UN Security Council (temporary), UNAMID, UNCTAD, UNESCO, UNHCR, UNIDO, UNIFIL, UNISFA, UNITAR, UNMIL, UNMISS, UNOCI, UNWTO, UPU, WCO, WFTU (NGOs), WHO, WIPO, WMO, WTO

Diplomatic representation in the US:
chief of mission: Ambassador Adebowale Ibidapo ADEFUYE (since 26 March 2010)
chancery: 3519 International Court NW, Washington, DC 20008
telephone: [1] (202) 986-8400
FAX: [1] (202) 362-6541
consulate(s) general: Atlanta, New York

Diplomatic representation from the US:
chief of mission: Ambassador James F. ENTWISTLE (since 28 October 2013)
embassy: Plot 1075 Diplomatic Drive, Central District Area, Abuja
mailing address: P. O. Box 5760, Garki, Abuja
telephone: [234] (9) 461-4000
FAX: [234] (9) 461-4171

Flag description: three equal vertical bands of green (hoist side), white, and green; the color green represents the forests and abundant natural wealth of the country, white stands for peace and unity

National symbol(s): eagle

National anthem: *name:* "Arise Oh Compatriots, Nigeria's Call Obey"
lyrics/music: John A. ILECHUKWU, Eme Etim AKPAN, B. A. OGUNNAIKE, Sotu OMOIGUI and P. O. ADERIBIGBE/Benedict Elide ODIASE
note: adopted 1978; the lyrics are a mixture of five of the top entries in a national contest

ECONOMY

Economy—overview: Following an April 2014 statistical "rebasing" exercise, Nigeria has emerged as Africa's largest economy, with 2013 GDP estimated at US$ 502 billion. Oil has been a dominant source of government revenues since the 1970s. Regulatory constraints and security risks have limited new investment in oil and natural gas, and Nigeria's oil production contracted in 2012 and 2013. Nevertheless, the Nigerian economy has continued to grow at a rapid 6-8% per annum (pre-rebasing), driven by growth in agriculture, telecommunications, and services, and the medium-term outlook for Nigeria is good, assuming oil output stabilizes and oil prices remain strong. Fiscal authorities pursued countercyclical policies in 2011-2013, significantly reducing the budget deficit. Monetary policy has also been responsive and effective. Following the 2008-9 global financial crises, the banking sector was effectively recapitalized and regulation enhanced. Despite its strong fundamentals, oil-rich Nigeria has been hobbled by inadequate power supply, lack of infrastructure, delays in the passage of legislative reforms, an inefficient property registration system, restrictive trade policies, an inconsistent regulatory environment, a slow and ineffective judicial system, unreliable dispute resolution mechanisms, insecurity, and pervasive corruption. Economic diversification and strong growth have not translated into a significant decline in poverty levels—over 62% of Nigeria's 170 million people live in extreme poverty. President JONATHAN has established an economic team that includes experienced and reputable members and has announced plans to increase transparency, continue to diversify production, and further improve fiscal management. The government is working to develop stronger public-private partnerships for roads, agriculture, and power.

GDP (purchasing power parity): $478.5 billion (2013 est.)
country comparison to the world: 31
$450.4 billion (2012 est.)
$422.6 billion (2011 est.)
note: data are in 2013 US dollars

GDP (official exchange rate): $292 billion (2013 est.)

GDP—real growth rate: 6.2% (2013 est.)
country comparison to the world: 35
6.6% (2012 est.)
7.4% (2011 est.)

GDP—per capita (PPP): $2,800 (2013 est.)
country comparison to the world: 180
$2,700 (2012 est.)
$2,600 (2011 est.)
note: data are in 2013 US dollars

Gross national saving: 15.5% of GDP (2013 est.)
country comparison to the world: 108
15.9% of GDP (2012 est.)
15.4% of GDP (2011 est.)

GDP—composition, by end use:
household consumption: 50.3%
government consumption: 12.8%
investment in fixed capital: 9.8%
investment in inventories: 0%
exports of goods and services: 49.9%
imports of goods and services: -22.8% (2013 est.)

GDP—composition, by sector of origin:
agriculture: 30.9%
industry: 43%
services: 26% (2012 est.)

Agriculture—products: cocoa, peanuts, cotton, palm oil, corn, rice, sorghum, millet, cassava (tapioca), yams, rubber; cattle, sheep, goats, pigs; timber; fish

Industries: crude oil, coal, tin, columbite; rubber products, wood; hides and skins, textiles, cement and other construction materials, food products, footwear, chemicals, fertilizer, printing, ceramics, steel

Industrial production growth rate: 0.9% (2013 est.)
country comparison to the world: 155

Labor force: 51.53 million (2011 est.)
country comparison to the world: 12

Labor force—by occupation:
agriculture: 70%
industry: 10%
services: 20% (1999 est.)

Unemployment rate: 23.9% (2011 est.)
country comparison to the world: 172
4.9% (2011 est.)

Population below poverty line: 70% (2010 est.)

Household income or consumption by percentage share: *lowest 10%:* 1.8%
highest 10%: 38.2% (2010 est.)

Distribution of family income—Gini index: 43.7 (2003)
country comparison to the world: 47
50.6 (1997)

Budget: *revenues:* $23.85 billion
expenditures: $31.51 billion (2013 est.)

Taxes and other revenues: 8.2% of GDP (2013 est.)
country comparison to the world: 211

Budget surplus (+) or deficit (-):
-2.6% of GDP (2013 est.)
country comparison to the world: 109

Public debt: 19.3% of GDP (2013 est.)
country comparison to the world: 135
17.9% of GDP (2012 est.)

Fiscal year: calendar year

Inflation rate (consumer prices): 8.7% (2013 est.)
country comparison to the world: 200
12.2% (2012 est.)

Central bank discount rate: 4.25% (31 December 2010 est.)
country comparison to the world: 59
6% (31 December 2009 est.)

Commercial bank prime lending rate: 15.5% (31 December 2013 est.)
country comparison to the world: 33
16.79% (31 December 2012 est.)

Stock of narrow money: $46.48 billion (31 December 2013 est.)
country comparison to the world: 49
$44.41 billion (31 December 2012 est.)

Stock of broad money: $98.75 billion (31 December 2013 est.)
country comparison to the world: 53
$96.34 billion (31 December 2012 est.)

Stock of domestic credit: $93.46 billion (31 December 2013 est.)
country comparison to the world: 53
$93.5 billion (31 December 2012 est.)

Market value of publicly traded shares: $56.39 billion (31 December 2012 est.)
country comparison to the world: 54
$39.27 billion (31 December 2011)
$50.88 billion (31 December 2010 est.)

Current account balance: $16.16 billion (2013 est.)
country comparison to the world: 19
$20.35 billion (2012 est.)

Exports: $93.55 billion (2013 est.)
country comparison to the world: 38
$95.68 billion (2012 est.)

Exports—commodities: petroleum and petroleum products 95%, cocoa, rubber

Exports—partners: US 16.8%, India 11.5%, Netherlands 8.6%, Spain 7.8%, Brazil 7.6%, UK 5.1%, Germany 4.9%, Japan 4.1%, France 4.1% (2012)

Imports: $55.98 billion (2013 est.)
country comparison to the world: 52
$53.36 billion (2012 est.)

Imports—commodities: machinery, chemicals, transport equipment, manufactured goods, food and live animals

Imports—partners: China 18.3%, US 10.1%, India 5.5% (2012)

Reserves of foreign exchange and gold: $47.7 billion (31 December 2013 est.)
country comparison to the world: 43
$46.41 billion (31 December 2012 est.)

Debt—external: $15.73 billion (31 December 2013 est.)
country comparison to the world: 86
$13.4 billion (31 December 2012 est.)

Stock of direct foreign investment—at home: $84.56 billion (31 December 2013 est.)
country comparison to the world: 45
$76.75 billion (31 December 2012 est.)

Stock of direct foreign investment—abroad: $9.212 billion (31 December 2013 est.)
country comparison to the world: 56
$7.444 billion (31 December 2012 est.)

Exchange rates: nairas (NGN) per US dollar—
156.8 (2013 est.)
156.81 (2012 est.)
150.3 (2010 est.)
148.9 (2009)
117.8 (2008)

ENERGY

Electricity—production: 24.87 billion kWh (2010 est.)
country comparison to the world: 6 8

Electricity—consumption: 20.38 billion kWh (2010 est.)
country comparison to the world: 69

Electricity—exports: 0 kWh (2012 est.)
country comparison to the world: 177

Electricity—imports: 0 kWh (2012 est.)
country comparison to the world: 178

Electricity—installed generating capacity: 5.9 million kW (2010 est.)
country comparison to the world: 72

Electricity—from fossil fuels: 67.1% of total installed capacity (2010 est.)
country comparison to the world: 114

Electricity—from nuclear fuels: 0% of total installed capacity (2010 est.)
country comparison to the world: 151

Electricity—from hydroelectric plants: 32.8% of total installed capacity (2010 est.)
country comparison to the world: 70

Electricity—from other renewable sources: 0% of total installed capacity (2010 est.)
country comparison to the world: 209

Crude oil—production: 2.524 million bbl/day (2012 est.)
country comparison to the world: 12

Crude oil—exports: 2.341 million bbl/day (2010 est.)
country comparison to the world: 5

Crude oil—imports: 0 bbl/day (2010 est.)
country comparison to the world: 104

Crude oil—proved reserves: 37.2 billion bbl (1 January 2013 es)
country comparison to the world: 10

Refined petroleum products—production: 101,300 bbl/day (2010 est.)
country comparison to the world: 73

Refined petroleum products—consumption: 271,600 bbl/day (2011 est.)
country comparison to the world: 46

Refined petroleum products—exports: 18,750 bbl/day (2010 est.)
country comparison to the world: 73

Refined petroleum products—imports: 151,700 bbl/day (2010 est.)
country comparison to the world: 38

Natural gas—production: 31.36 billion cu m (2011 est.)
country comparison to the world: 29

Natural gas—consumption: 5.03 billion cu m (2010 est.)
country comparison to the world: 62

Natural gas—exports: 25.96 billion cu m (2011 est.)
country comparison to the world: 16

Natural gas—imports: 0 cu m (2011 est.)
country comparison to the world: 106

Natural gas—proved reserves: 5.153 trillion cu m (1 January 2013 es)
country comparison to the world: 9

Carbon dioxide emissions from consumption of energy: 75.96 million Mt (2011 est.)
country comparison to the world: 47

COMMUNICATIONS

Telephones—main lines in use: 418,200 (2012)
country comparison to the world: 102

Telephones—mobile cellular: 112.78 million (2012)
country comparison to the world: 10

Telephone system: *general assessment:* further expansion and modernization of the fixed-line telephone network is needed; network quality remains a problem
domestic: the addition of a second fixed-line provider in 2002 resulted in faster growth but subscribership remains only about 1 per 100 persons; mobile-cellular services growing rapidly, in part responding to the shortcomings of the fixed-line network; multiple cellular providers operate nationally with subscribership base approaching 60 per 100 persons
international: country code—234; landing point for the SAT-3/WASC fiber-optic submarine cable that provides connectivity to Europe and Asia; satellite earth stations—3 Intelsat (2 Atlantic Ocean and 1 Indian Ocean) (2010)

Broadcast media: nearly 70 federal government-controlled national and regional TV stations; all 36 states operate TV stations; several private TV stations operational; cable and satellite TV subscription services are available; network of federal government-controlled national, regional, and state radio stations; roughly 40 state government-owned radio stations typically carry their own programs except for news broadcasts; about 20 private radio stations; transmissions of international broadcasters are available (2007)

Internet country code: .ng

Internet hosts: 1,234 (2012)
country comparison to the world: 169

Internet users: 43.989 million (2009)
country comparison to the world: 9

TRANSPORTATION

Airports: 54 (2013)
country comparison to the world: 8 7

Airports—with paved runways: *total:* 4 0

over 3,047 m: 10
2,438 to 3,047 m: 12
1,524 to 2,437 m: 9
914 to 1,523 m: 6
under 914 m: 3 (2013)

Airports—with unpaved runways: *total:* 1 4
1,524 to 2,437 m: 2
914 to 1,523 m: 9
under 914 m: 3 (2013)

Heliports: 5 (2013)

Pipelines: condensate 124 km; gas 4,045 km; liquid petroleum gas 164 km; oil 4,441 km; refined products 3,940 km (2013)

Railways: *total:* 3,505 km
country comparison to the world: 50
narrow gauge: 3,505 km 1.067-m gauge (2008)

Roadways: *total:* 193,200 km
country comparison to the world: 27
paved: 28,980 km
unpaved: 164,220 km (2004)

Waterways: 8,600 km (Niger and Benue rivers and smaller rivers and creeks) (2011)
country comparison to the world: 15

Merchant marine: *total:* 8 9
country comparison to the world: 54
by type: cargo 2, chemical tanker 28, liquefied gas 1, passenger/cargo 1, petroleum tanker 56, specialized tanker 1
foreign-owned: 3 (India 1, UK 2)
registered in other countries: 33 (Bahamas 2, Bermuda 11, Comoros 1, Italy 1, Liberia 4, North Korea 1, Panama 6, Seychelles 1, unknown 6) (2010)

Ports and terminals: *major seaport(s):* Bonny Inshore Terminal, Calabar, Lagos

Transportation—note: the International Maritime Bureau reports the territorial and offshore waters in the Niger Delta and Gulf of Guinea as high risk for piracy and armed robbery against ships; in 2012, 27 commercial vessels were boarded or attacked compared with 10 attacks in 2011; crews were robbed and stores or cargoes stolen; Nigerian pirates have extended the range of their attacks to as far away as Cote d'Ivoire

MILITARY

Military branches: Nigerian Armed Forces: Army, Navy, Air Force (2013)

Military service age and obligation: 18 years of age for voluntary military service; no conscription (2012)

Manpower available for military service:
males age 16-49: 37,087,711
females age 16-49: 35,232,127 (2010 est.)

Manpower fit for military service:
males age 16-49: 20,839,976
females age 16-49: 19,867,683 (2010 est.)
Manpower reaching militarily significant age annually: *male:* 1,767,428
female: 1,687,719 (2010 est.)

Military expenditures: 0.89% of GDP (2012)
country comparison to the world: 109
0.98% of GDP (2011)
0.89% of GDP (2010)

TRANSNATIONAL ISSUES

Disputes—international: Joint Border Commission with Cameroon reviewed 2002 ICJ ruling on the entire boundary and bilaterally resolved differences, including June 2006 Greentree Agreement that immediately cedes sovereignty of the Bakassi Peninsula to Cameroon with a phase-out of Nigerian control within two years while resolving patriation issues; the ICJ ruled on an equidistance settlement of Cameroon-Equatorial Guinea-Nigeria maritime boundary in the Gulf of Guinea, but imprecisely defined coordinates in the ICJ decision and a sovereignty dispute between Equatorial Guinea and Cameroon over an island at the mouth of the Ntem River all contribute to the delay in implementation; only Nigeria and Cameroon have heeded the Lake Chad Commission's admonition to ratify the delimitation treaty which also includes the Chad-Niger and Niger-Nigeria boundaries; location of Benin-Niger-Nigeria tripoint is unresolved

Refugees and internally displaced persons: *refugees (country of origin):* 5,299 (Liberia) (2011)
IDPs: undetermined (communal violence between Christians and Muslims, political violence; flooding; forced evictions; competition for resources; displacement is mostly short-term) (2012)

Illicit drugs: a transit point for heroin and cocaine intended for European, East Asian, and North American markets; consumer of amphetamines; safe haven for Nigerian narcotraffickers operating worldwide; major money-laundering center; massive corruption and criminal activity; Nigeria has improved some anti-money-laundering controls, resulting in its removal from the Financial Action Task Force's (FATF's) Noncooperative Countries and Territories List in June 2006; Nigeria's anti-money-laundering regime continues to be monitored by FATF

NIUE

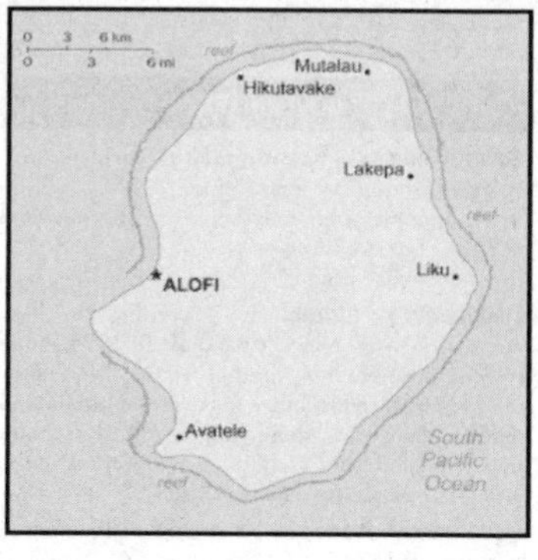

INTRODUCTION

Background: Niue's remoteness, as well as cultural and linguistic differences between its Polynesian inhabitants and those of the adjacent Cook Islands, has caused it to be separately administered by New Zealand. The population of the island continues to drop (from a peak of 5,200 in 1966 to an estimated 1,229 in 2013) with substantial emigration to New Zealand 2,400 km to the southwest.

GEOGRAPHY

Location: Oceania, island in the South Pacific Ocean, east of Tonga

Geographic coordinates: 19 02 S, 169 52 W

Map references: Oceania

Area: *total:* 260 sq km
country comparison to the world: 213
land: 260 sq km
water: 0 sq km

Area—comparative: 1.5 times the size of Washington, DC

Land boundaries: 0 km

Coastline: 64 km

Maritime claims: *territorial sea:* 12 nm
exclusive economic zone: 200 nm

Climate: tropical; modified by southeast trade winds

Terrain: steep limestone cliffs along coast, central plateau

Elevation extremes: *lowest point:* Pacific Ocean 0 m
highest point: unnamed elevation near Mutalau settlement 68 m

Natural resources: fish, arable land

Land use: *arable land:* 3.85%
permanent crops: 11.54%
other: 84.62% (2011)

Irrigated land: NA

Natural hazards: typhoons

Environment—current issues: increasing attention to conservationist practices to counter loss of soil fertility from traditional slash and burn agriculture

Environment—international agreements: *party to:* Biodiversity, Climate Change, Climate Change-Kyoto Protocol, Desertification, Law of the Sea, Ozone Layer Protection

Geography—note: one of world's largest coral islands

PEOPLE AND SOCIETY

Nationality: *noun:* Niuean(s)
adjective: Niuean

Ethnic groups: Niuen 66.5%, part-Niuen 13.4%, non-Niuen 20.1% (includes 12% European and Asian and 8% Pacific Islanders) (2011 est.)

Languages: Niuean (official) 46% (a Polynesian language closely related to Tongan and Samoan), Niuean and English 32%, English (official) 11%, Niuean and others 5%, other 6% (2011 est.)

Religions: Ekalesia Niue (Congregational Christian Church of Niue—a Protestant church founded by missionaries from the London Missionary Society) 67%, other Protestant 3% (includes Seventh Day Adventist 1%, Presbyterian 1%, and Methodist 1%), Mormon 10%, Roman Catholic 10%, Jehovah's Witnesses 2%, other 6%, none 2% (2011 est.)

Population: 1,190 (July 2014 est.)
country comparison to the world: 237

Population growth rate: -0.03% (2014 est.)
country comparison to the world: 201

Urbanization: *urban population:* 38% of total population (2010)
rate of urbanization: -1.3% annual rate of change (2010-15 est.)

Sex ratio: NA

Infant mortality rate: total: NA
male: NA
female: NA

Life expectancy at birth: *total population:* NA
male: NA
female: NA

Total fertility rate: NA (2014 est.)

Health expenditures: 14.6% of GDP (2011)
country comparison to the world: 6

Physicians density: 6 physicians/1,000 population (2008)

Drinking water source:
improved:
urban: 98.5% of population
rural: 98.5% of population
total: 98.6% of population
unimproved:
urban: 1.5% of population
rural: 1.5% of population
total: 1.4% of population (2011 est.)

Sanitation facility access:
improved:
urban: 100% of population
rural: 100% of population
total: 100% of population
unimproved:
urban: 0% of population
rural: 0% of population
total: 0% of population (2011 est.)

HIV/AIDS—adult prevalence rate: NA

HIV/AIDS—people living with HIV/AIDS: NA

HIV/AIDS—deaths: NA

Education expenditures: NA

Literacy: *definition:* NA
total population: 95%
male: NA
female: NA

School life expectancy (primary to tertiary education): *total:* 13 years
male: 12 years
female: 15 years (2005)

GOVERNMENT

Country name: *conventional long form:* none
conventional short form: Niue
note: pronunciation falls between nyu-way and new-way, but not like new-wee
former: Savage Island

Dependency status: self-governing in free association with New Zealand since 1974; Niue fully responsible for internal affairs; New Zealand retains responsibility for external affairs and defense; however, these responsibilities confer no rights of control and are only exercised at the request of the Government of Niue

Government type: self-governing parliamentary democracy

Capital: *name:* Alofi

geographic coordinates: 19 01 S, 169 55 W
time difference: UTC-11 (6 hours behind Washington, DC during Standard Time)

Administrative divisions: none; note—there are no first-order administrative divisions as defined by the US Government, but there are 14 villages at the second order

Independence: 19 October 1974 (Niue became a self-governing parliamentary government in free association with New Zealand)

National holiday: Waitangi Day (Treaty of Waitangi established British sovereignty over New Zealand), 6 February (1840)

Constitution: several previous (New Zealand colonial statutes); latest 19 October 1974 (Niue Constitution Act 1974); amended 1992, 2007 (2007)

Legal system: English common law

Suffrage: 18 years of age; universal

Executive branch: *chief of state:* Queen ELIZABETH II (since 6 February 1952); represented by Governor General of New Zealand Anand SATYANAND (since 23 August 2006); the UK and New Zealand are represented by New Zealand High Commissioner Mark BLUMSKY (since September 2011)
head of government: Premier Toke TALAGI (since 18 June 2008)
cabinet: Cabinet consists of the premier and 3 ministers (For more information visit the World Leaders website)
elections: the monarchy is hereditary; premier elected by the Legislative Assembly for a three-year term; election last held on 16 May 2011 (next to be held in 2014)
election results: Toke TALAGI reelected premier in Legislative Assembly vote; Toke TALAGI—11, Togia SIONEHOLO—8

Legislative branch: unicameral Legislative Assembly (20 seats; members elected by popular vote to serve three-year terms; six elected from a common roll and 14 are village representatives)
elections: last held on 12 April 2014 (next to be held in 2017)
election results: percent of vote by party—NA; seats by party—20 independents

Judicial branch: *highest court(s):* Court of Appeal (consists of the chief justice and up to 3 judges); note—the Judicial Committee of the Privy Council (in London) is the final appeal court beyond the Niue Court of Appeal note—Niue is a participant in the Pacific Judicial Development Program; the program is designed to build governance and the rule of law in 15 Pacific island countries
judge selection and term of office: Niue chief justice appointed by the governor-general on the advice of the Cabinet and tendered by the premier; other judges appointed by the governor-general on the advice of the Cabinet and tendered by the chief justice and the minister of justice; judges serve until age 68
subordinate courts: High Court

Political parties and leaders: Alliance of Independents or AI; Niue People's Action Party or NPP [Young VIVIAN]

Political pressure groups and leaders: NA

International organization participation: ACP, AOSIS, FAO, IFAD, OPCW, PIF, Sparteca, SPC, UNESCO, UPU, WHO, WMO

Diplomatic representation in the US: none (self-governing territory in free association with New Zealand)

Diplomatic representation from the US: none (self-governing territory in free association with New Zealand)

Flag description: yellow with the flag of the UK in the upper hoist-side quadrant; the flag of the UK bears five yellow five-pointed stars—a large star on a blue disk in the center and a smaller star on each arm of the bold red cross; the larger star stands for Niue, the smaller stars recall the Southern Cross constellation on the New Zealand flag and symbolize links with that country; yellow represents the bright sunshine of Niue and the warmth and friendship between Niue and New Zealand

National anthem: *name:* "Ko e Iki he Lagi" (The Lord in Heaven)
lyrics/music: unknown/unknown, prepared by Sioeli FUSIKATA
note: adopted 1974

ECONOMY

Economy—overview: The economy suffers from the typical Pacific island problems of geographic isolation, few resources, and a small population. Government expenditures regularly exceed revenues, and the shortfall is made up by critically needed grants from New Zealand that are used to pay wages to public employees. Niue has cut government expenditures by reducing the public service by almost half. The agricultural sector consists mainly of subsistence gardening, although some cash crops are grown for export. Industry consists primarily of small factories to process passion fruit, lime oil, honey, and coconut cream. The sale of postage stamps to foreign collectors is an important source of revenue. The island in recent years has suffered a serious loss of population because of emigration to New Zealand. Efforts to increase GDP include the promotion of tourism and financial services, although the International Banking Repeal Act of 2002 resulted in the termination of all offshore banking licenses. Economic aid from New Zealand in FY08/09 was US$5.7 million. While in the process of rebuilding, Niue has been dependent on foreign aid.

GDP (purchasing power parity): $10.01 million (2003 est.)
country comparison to the world: 228

GDP (official exchange rate): $10.01 million (2003)

GDP—real growth rate: 6.2% (2003 est.)
country comparison to the world: 33

GDP—per capita (PPP): $5,800 (2003 est.)
country comparison to the world: 153

GDP—composition, by sector of origin:
agriculture: 23.5%
industry: 26.9%
services: 49.5% (2003)

Agriculture—products: coconuts, passion fruit, honey, limes, taro, yams, cassava (tapioca), sweet potatoes; pigs, poultry, beef cattle

Industries: handicrafts, food processing

Industrial production growth rate: NA%

Labor force: 663 (2001)
country comparison to the world: 231

Labor force—by occupation:
note: most work on family plantations; paid work exists only in government service, small industry, and the Niue Development Board

Unemployment rate: 12% (2001)
country comparison to the world: 122

Population below poverty line: NA%

Household income or consumption by percentage share: *lowest* 10%: NA%
highest 10%: NA%

Budget: *revenues:* $15.07 million
expenditures: $16.33 million (FY04/05)

Budget surplus (+) or deficit (-):
-12.6% of GDP (FY04/05)
country comparison to the world: 211

Fiscal year: 1 April—31 March

Inflation rate (consumer prices): 4% (2005)
country comparison to the world: 136

Exports: $201,400 (2004)
country comparison to the world: 220

Exports—commodities: canned coconut cream, copra, honey, vanilla, passion fruit products, pawpaws, root crops, limes, footballs, stamps, handicrafts

Imports: $9.038 million (2004)
country comparison to the world: 222

Imports—commodities: food, live animals, manufactured goods, machinery, fuels, lubricants, chemicals, drugs

Debt—external: $418,000 (2002 est.)
country comparison to the world: 201

Exchange rates: New Zealand dollars (NZD) per US dollar—
1.247 (2013)
1.2334 (2012)
1.3874 (2010)
1.6002 (2009)
1.4151 (2008)

ENERGY

Electricity—production: 3 million kWh (2010 est.)
country comparison to the world: 216

Electricity—consumption: 2.79 million kWh (2010 est.)
country comparison to the world: 216

Electricity—exports: 0 kWh (2012 est.)
country comparison to the world: 174

Electricity—imports: 0 kWh (2012 est.)
country comparison to the world: 176

Electricity—installed generating capacity: 1,000 kW (2010 est.)
country comparison to the world: 211

Electricity—from fossil fuels: 100% of total installed capacity (2010 est.)
country comparison to the world: 25

Electricity—from nuclear fuels: 0% of total installed capacity (2010 est.)
country comparison to the world: 148

Electricity—from hydroelectric plants: 0% of total installed capacity (2010 est.)
country comparison to the world: 187

Electricity—from other renewable sources: 0% of total installed capacity (2010 est.)
country comparison to the world: 207

Crude oil—production: 0 bbl/day (2012 est.)
country comparison to the world: 200

Crude oil—exports: 0 bbl/day (2010 est.)
country comparison to the world: 160

Crude oil—imports: 0 bbl/day (2010 est.)
country comparison to the world: 101

Crude oil—proved reserves: 0 bbl (1 January 2013 es)
country comparison to the world: 170

Refined petroleum products—production: 0 bbl/day (2010 est.)
country comparison to the world: 179

Refined petroleum products—consumption: NA bbl/day (2011 est.)

Refined petroleum products—exports: 0 bbl/day (2010 est.)
country comparison to the world: 201

Refined petroleum products—imports: 22.57 bbl/day (2010 est.)
country comparison to the world: 209

Natural gas—production: 0 cu m (2011 est.)
country comparison to the world: 172

Natural gas—consumption: 0 cu m (2010 est.)
country comparison to the world: 177

Natural gas—exports: 0 cu m (2011 est.)
country comparison to the world: 154

Natural gas—imports: 0 cu m (2011 est.)
country comparison to the world: 103

Natural gas—proved reserves: 0 cu m (1 January 2013 es)
country comparison to the world: 175

Carbon dioxide emissions from consumption of energy: 3,050 Mt (2011 est.)
country comparison to the world: 211

COMMUNICATIONS

Telephone system:
domestic: single-line telephone system connects all villages on island
international: country code—683 (2001)

Broadcast media: 1 government-owned TV station with many of the programs supplied by Television New Zealand; 1 government-owned radio station broadcasting in AM and FM (2009)

Internet country code: . n u

Internet hosts: 79,508 (2012)
country comparison to the world: 83

Internet users: 1,100 (2009)
country comparison to the world: 214

TRANSPORTATION

Airports: 1 (2013)
country comparison to the world: 227

Airports—with paved runways: *total:* 1
1,524 to 2,437 m: 1 (2012)

Airports—with unpaved runways: *total:* 1
1,524 to 2,437 m: 1 (2013)

Roadways: *total:* 120 km
country comparison to the world: 213
paved: 120 km (2011)

Ports and terminals: *major seaport(s):* Alofi

MILITARY

Military branches: no regular indigenous military forces; Police Force

Military—note: defense is the responsibility of New Zealand

TRANSNATIONAL ISSUES

Disputes—international: none

NORFOLK ISLAND

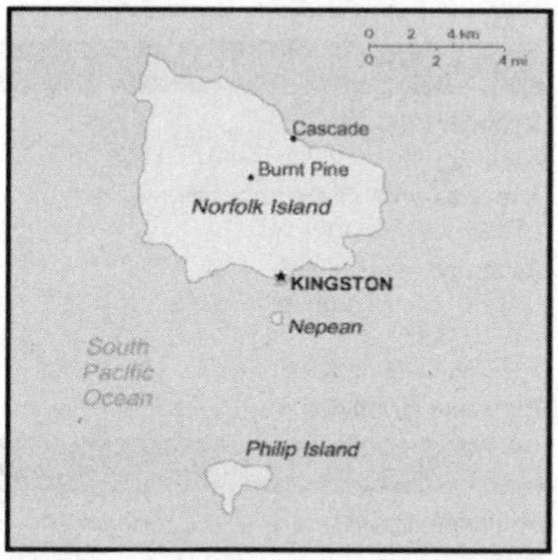

INTRODUCTION

Background: Two British attempts at establishing the island as a penal colony (1788-1814 and 1825-55) were ultimately abandoned. In 1856, the island was resettled by Pitcairn Islanders, descendants of the Bounty mutineers and their Tahitian companions.

GEOGRAPHY

Location: Oceania, island in the South Pacific Ocean, east of Australia

Geographic coordinates: 29 02 S, 167 57 E

Map references: Oceania

Area: *total:* 36 sq km
country comparison to the world: 235
land: 36 sq km
water: 0 sq km

Area—comparative: about 0.2 times the size of Washington, DC

Land boundaries: 0 km

Coastline: 32 km

Maritime claims: *territorial sea:* 12 nm
exclusive fishing zone: 200 nm

Climate: subtropical; mild, little seasonal temperature variation

Terrain: volcanic formation with mostly rolling plains

Elevation extremes: *lowest point:* Pacific Ocean 0 m
highest point: Mount Bates 319 m

Natural resources: fish

Land use: *arable land:* 0%
permanent crops: 0%
other: 100% (2011)

Irrigated land: NA

Natural hazards: typhoons (especially May to July)

Environment—current issues: NA

Geography—note: most of the 32 km coastline consists of almost inaccessible cliffs, but the land slopes down to the sea in one small southern area on Sydney Bay, where the capital of Kingston is situated

PEOPLE AND SOCIETY

Nationality: *noun:* Norfolk Islander(s)
adjective: Norfolk Islander(s)

Ethnic groups: Australian 79.5%, New Zealander 13.3%, Filipino 1.1%, English 1%, other 1.8%, unspecified 0.8% (2011 est.)

Languages: English (official) 67.6%, other 32.4% (includes Norfolk Island 23.7%, which is a mixture of 18th century English and ancient Tahitian) (2011 est.)

Religions: Protestant 49.6% (Anglican 31.8%, Uniting Church in Australia 10.6%, Seventh-Day Adventist 3.2%), Roman Catholic 11.7%, other 8.6%, none 23.5%, unspecified 6.6% (2011 est.)

Population: 2,210 (July 2014 est.)
country comparison to the world: 233

Age structure: *0-14 years:* 20.2%
15-64 years: 63.9%
65 years and over: 15.9% (2013 est.)

Population growth rate: 0.01% (2014 est.)
country comparison to the world: 194

Sex ratio: NA

Infant mortality rate: *total:* NA
male: NA
female: NA

Life expectancy at birth: *total population:* NA
male: NA
female: NA

Total fertility rate: NA (2014 est.)

HIV/AIDS—adult prevalence rate: NA

HIV/AIDS—people living with HIV/AIDS: NA

HIV/AIDS—deaths: NA

Literacy: NA

GOVERNMENT

Country name: *conventional long form:* Territory of Norfolk Island
conventional short form: Norfolk Island

Dependency status: self-governing territory of Australia; administered from Canberra by the Department of Regional Australia, Local Government, Arts and Sport

Government type: NA

Capital: *name:* Kingston

geographic coordinates: 29 03 S, 167 58 E
time difference: UTC+11.5 (16.5 hours ahead of Washington, DC during Standard Time)

Administrative divisions: none (territory of Australia)

Independence: none (territory of Australia)

National holiday: Bounty Day (commemorates the arrival of Pitcairn Islanders), 8 June (1856)

Constitution: previous 1913, 1957; latest effective 7 August 1979; amended many times, last in 2010 (2011)

Legal system: English common law and the laws of Australia

Suffrage: 18 years of age; universal

Executive branch: *chief of state:* Queen ELIZABETH II (since 6 February 1952); represented by the Australian governor general
head of government: Administrator Neil POPE (since 1 April 2012)

cabinet: Executive Council made up of 4 of the 9 members of the Legislative Assembly; the council devises government policy and acts as an advisor to the administrator (For more information visit the World Leaders website)
elections: the monarchy is hereditary; governor general appointed by the monarch; administrator appointed by the governor general of Australia for a two year term and represents the monarch and Australia

Legislative branch: unicameral Legislative Assembly (9 seats; members elected by electors who have nine equal votes each but only four votes can be given to any one candidate; members to serve three-year terms)
elections: last held on 13 March 2013 (next to be held in 2016)
election results: seats—independents 8; Norfolk Liberals 1

Judicial branch: *highest court(s):* Supreme Court of Norfolk Island (consists of the chief justice and NA justices) note—appeals beyond the Supreme Court of Norfolk Island are heard by the Federal Court of Australia
judge selection and term of office: justices appointed by the governor general of Australia from among justices of the Federal Court of Australia; justices serve until mandatory retirement at age 70
subordinate courts: Petty Court of Sessions; specialized courts including a Coroner's Court and the Employment Tribunal

Political parties and leaders: Norfolk Island Labor Party [Mike KELLY]; Norfolk Liberals [John BROWN]

Political pressure groups and leaders: none

International organization participation: UPU

Diplomatic representation in the US: none (territory of Australia)

Diplomatic representation from the US: none (territory of Australia)

Flag description: three vertical bands of green (hoist side), white, and green with a large green Norfolk Island pine tree centered in the slightly wider white band; green stands for the rich vegetation on the island, and the pine tree—endemic to the island—is a symbol of Norfolk Island
note: somewhat reminiscent of the flag of Canada with its use of only two colors and depiction of a prominent local floral symbol in the central white band

National symbol(s): Norfolk Island pine

National anthem: *name:* "Come Ye Blessed"
lyrics/music: New Testament/John Prindle SCOTT
note: the local anthem, whose lyrics consist of the words from Matthew 25:34-36, 40, is also known as "The Pitcairn Anthem;" as a territory of Australia, "God Save the Queen" is official (see Australia), however, the island does not recognize "Advance Australia Fair"

ECONOMY

Economy—overview: Norfolk Island is suffering from a severe economic downturn. Tourism, the primary economic activity, is the main driver of economic growth. The agricultural sector has become self sufficient in the production of beef, poultry, and eggs.

GDP (purchasing power parity): $NA

Agriculture—products: Norfolk Island pine seed, Kentia palm seed, cereals, vegetables, fruit; cattle, poultry

Industries: tourism, light industry, ready mixed concrete

Labor force: 978 (2006)
country comparison to the world: 230

Labor force—by occupation: *agriculture:* 6%
industry: 14%
services: 80% (2006 est.)

Budget: *revenues:* $4.6 million
expenditures: $4.8 million (FY99/00)

Fiscal year: 1 July—30 June

Exports: $NA

Exports—commodities: postage stamps, seeds of the Norfolk Island pine and Kentia palm, small quantities of avocados

Imports: $NA

Imports—commodities: NA

Debt—external: $NA

Exchange rates: Australian dollars (AUD) per US dollar—
1.031 (2013)
0.9658 (2012)
1.0902 (2010)
1.2822 (2009)
1.2059 (2008)

COMMUNICATIONS

Telephone system: *general assessment:* adequate
domestic: free local calls
international: country code—672; submarine cable links with Australia and New Zealand; satellite earth station—1

Broadcast media: 1 local radio station; broadcasts of several Australian radio and TV stations available via satellite (2009)

Internet country code: .nf

Internet hosts: 128 (2012)
country comparison to the world: 204

TRANSPORTATION

Airports: 1 (2013)
country comparison to the world: 228

Airports—with paved runways: *total:* 1
1,524 to 2,437 m: 1 (2013)

Roadways: *total:* 80 km
country comparison to the world: 216
paved: 53 km
unpaved: 27 km (2008)

Ports and terminals: *major seaport(s):* Kingston

MILITARY

Military—note: defense is the responsibility of Australia

TRANSNATIONAL ISSUES

Disputes—international: none

NORTHERN MARIANA ISLANDS

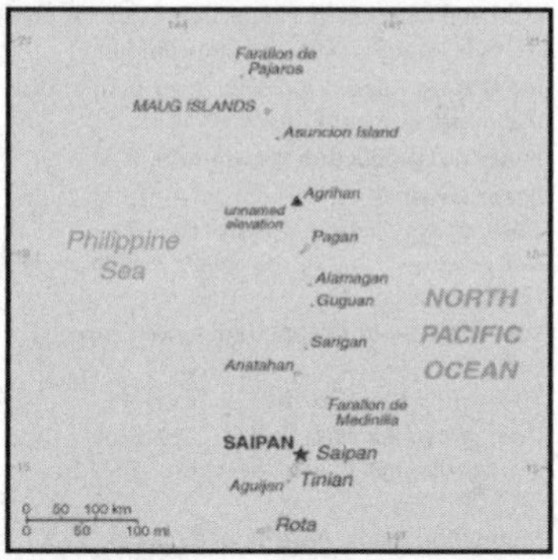

INTRODUCTION

Background: Under US administration as part of the UN Trust Territory of the Pacific, the people of the Northern Mariana Islands decided in the 1970s not to seek independence but instead to forge closer links with the US. Negotiations for territorial status began in 1972. A covenant to establish a commonwealth in political union with the US was approved in 1975, and came into force on 24 March 1976. A new government and constitution went into effect in 1978.

GEOGRAPHY

Location: Oceania, islands in the North Pacific Ocean, about three-quarters of the way from Hawaii to the Philippines

Geographic coordinates: 15 12 N, 145 45 E

Map references: Oceania

Area: *total:* 464 sq km
country comparison to the world: 197
land: 464 sq km
water: 0 sq km
note: consists of 14 islands including Saipan, Rota, and Tinian

Area—comparative: 2.5 times the size of Washington, DC

Land boundaries: 0 km

Coastline: 1,482 km

Maritime claims: *territorial sea:* 12 nm
exclusive economic zone: 200 nm

Climate: tropical marine; moderated by northeast trade winds, little seasonal temperature variation; dry season December to June, rainy season July to October

Terrain: southern islands are limestone with level terraces and fringing coral reefs; northern islands are volcanic

Elevation extremes: *lowest point:* Pacific Ocean 0 m
highest point: unnamed elevation on Agrihan 965 m

Natural resources: arable land, fish

Land use: *arable land:* 2.17%
permanent crops: 2.17%
other: 95.65% (2011)

Irrigated land: 1 sq km (2011)

Natural hazards: active volcanoes on Pagan and Agrihan; typhoons (especially August to November)

Environment—current issues: contamination of groundwater on Saipan may contribute to disease; clean-up of landfill; protection of endangered species conflicts with development

Geography—note: strategic location in the North Pacific Ocean

PEOPLE AND SOCIETY

Nationality: *noun:* NA (US citizens)
adjective: NA

Ethnic groups: Asian 50% (includes Filipino 35.3%, Chinese 6.8%, Korean 4.2%, and other Asian 3.7%), Native Hawaiian or other Pacific Islander 34.9% (includes Chamorro 23.9%, Carolinian 4.6%, and other Native Hawaiian or Pacific Islander 6.4%), other 2.5%, two or more ethnicities or races 12.7% (2010 est.)

Languages: Philippine languages 32.8%, Chamorro (official) 24.1%, English (official) 17%, other Pacific island languages 10.1%, Chinese 6.8%, other Asian languages 7.3%, other 1.9% (2010 est.)

Religions: Christian (Roman Catholic majority, although traditional beliefs and taboos may still be found)

Population: 51,483 (July 2014 est.)
country comparison to the world: 210

Age structure:
0-14 years: 25.9% (male 6,944/female 6,393)
15-24 years: 14.5% (male 4,133/female 3,348)
25-54 years: 44.9% (male 9,793/female 13,340)
55-64 years: 4.6% (male 2,798/female 2,372)
65 years and over: 4.3% (male 1,122/female 1,240) (2014 est.)

Median age: *total:* 31.6 years
male: 29.4 years
female: 32.2 years (2014 est.)

Population growth rate: 1.13% (2014 est.)
country comparison to the world: 107

Birth rate: 18.94 births/1,000 population (2014 est.)
country comparison to the world: 94

Death rate: 3.61 deaths/1,000 population (2014 est.)
country comparison to the world: 214

Net migration rate: -4.02 migrant(s)/1,000 population (2014 est.)
country comparison to the world: 190

Urbanization: *urban population:* 91% of total population (2010)
rate of urbanization: 1.7% annual rate of change (2010-15 est.)

Major urban areas—population: SAIPAN (capital) NA (2009)

Sex ratio: *at birth:* 1.06 male(s)/female
0-14 years: 1.09 male(s)/female
15-24 years: 1.23 male(s)/female
25-54 years: 0.73 male(s)/female
55-64 years: 0.93 male(s)/female
65 years and over: 0.91 male(s)/female
total population: 0.93 male(s)/female (2014 est.)

Infant mortality rate: *total:* 5.5 deaths/1,000 live births
country comparison to the world: 176
male: 5.88 deaths/1,000 live births
female: 5.09 deaths/1,000 live births (2014 est.)

Life expectancy at birth: *total population:* 77.64 years
country comparison to the world: 63
male: 74.98 years
female: 80.46 years (2014 est.)

Total fertility rate: 2.01 children born/woman (2014 est.)
country comparison to the world: 122

Drinking water source:
improved:
urban: 96.5% of population
rural: 96.5% of population
total: 96.5% of population
unimproved:
urban: 3.5% of population
rural: 3.5% of population
total: 3.5% of population (2011 est.)

Sanitation facility access:
improved:
urban: 97.9% of population
rural: 97.9% of population
total: 97.9% of population
unimproved:
urban: 2.1% of population
rural: 2.1% of population
total: 2.1% of population (2011 est.)

HIV/AIDS—adult prevalence rate: NA

HIV/AIDS—people living with HIV/AIDS: NA

HIV/AIDS—deaths: NA

Literacy: *definition:* age 15 and over can read and write
total population: 97%
male: 97%
female: 96% (1980 est.)

Unemployment, youth ages 15-24: *total:* 5.9%
country comparison to the world: 133
male: 11.2%
female: 4.4% (2003)

GOVERNMENT

Country name: *conventional long form:* Commonwealth of the Northern Mariana Islands
conventional short form: Northern Mariana Islands
abbreviation: CNMI
former: Trust Territory of the Pacific Islands, Mariana Islands District

Dependency status: commonwealth in political union with the US; federal funds to the Commonwealth administered by the US Department of the Interior, Office of Insular Affairs

Government type: commonwealth; self-governing with locally elected governor, lieutenant governor, and legislature

Capital: *name:* Saipan

geographic coordinates: 15 12 N, 145 45 E
time difference: UTC+10 (15 hours ahead of Washington, DC during Standard Time)

Administrative divisions: none (commonwealth in political union with the US); there are no first-order administrative divisions as defined by the US

Government, but there are four municipalities at the second order: Northern Islands, Rota, Saipan, Tinian

Independence: none (commonwealth in political union with the US)

National holiday: Commonwealth Day, 8 January (1978)

Constitution: partially effective 1 January 1978 (Constitution of the Commonwealth of the Northern Mariana Islands); fully effective 4 November 1986 (Covenant Agreement); amended several times, last in 2012 (2012)

Legal system: US system applies, except for customs, wages, immigration laws, and taxation

Suffrage: 18 years of age; universal; note—indigenous inhabitants are US citizens but do not vote in US presidential elections

Executive branch: *chief of state:* President Barack H. OBAMA (since 20 January 2009); Vice President Joseph R. BIDEN (since 20 January 2009)
head of government: Governor Eloy S. INOS (since 20 February 2013); Lieutenant Governor Jude U. HOFSCHNEIDER (since 20 February 2013)
cabinet: the cabinet consists of the heads of the 10 principal departments under the executive branch who are appointed by the governor with the advice and consent of the Senate; other members include special assistants to the governor and office heads appointed by and reporting directly to the governor (For more information visit the World Leaders website)
elections: under the US Constitution, residents of unincorporated territories, such as the Commonwealth of the Northern Mariana Islands, do not vote in elections for US president and vice president; however, they may vote in the Democratic and Republican party presidential primary elections; governor and lieutenant governor elected on the same ticket by popular vote for four-year terms (eligible for a second term); election last held on 7 November 2009 with a run-off election held on 23 November 2009 (next to be held in 2014)
election results: Benigno R. FITIAL reelected governor in a run-off election held 23 November 2009; percent of vote—Benigno R. FITIAL 51.4%, Heinz HOFSCHNEIDER 48.6%
note: Benigno R. FITIAL was impeached by House of Representatives on 11-12 February 2013 and resigns on 20 February 2013; Eloy INOS was sworn in as governor the same day

Legislative branch: bicameral legislature consists of the Senate (9 seats; members elected by popular vote to serve four-year staggered terms) and the House of Representatives (20 seats; members elected by popular vote to serve two-year terms)
elections: Senate—last held on 6 November 2012 (next to be held in November 2014); House of Representatives—last held on 6 November 2012 (next to be held in November 2014)
election results: Senate—percent of vote by party—NA; seats by party—Covenant Party 3, Republican Party 3, Democratic Party 1, independents 2; House of Representatives—percent of vote by party—NA; seats by party—Republican Party 4, Covenant Party 3, independents 13
note: the Northern Mariana Islands elects one nonvoting delegate to the US House of Representatives; election last held on 6 November 2012 (next to be held in November 2014); seats by party—independent 1

Judicial branch: *highest court(s):* Supreme Court of the Commonwealth of the Northern Marianna Islands or CNMI (consists of the chief justice and 2 associate justices); US Federal District Court (consists of 1 judge); note—US Federal District Court jurisdiction limited to US federal laws note—appeals beyond the Northern Mariannas Islands Supreme Court are referred to the US Supreme Court
judge selection and term of office: judges of the Supreme Court of the CNMI appointed by the governor and confirmed by the CNMI Senate; judges appointed for 8-year terms and can serve another term if approved through voter election; US Federal District Court judges appointed by the US president and confirmed by the US Senate; judges appointed for renewable 10-year terms
subordinate courts: Superior Court

Political parties and leaders: Covenant Party [Benigno R. FITIAL]; Democratic Party [Dr. Carlos S. CAMACHO]; Republican Party [Juan S. REYES]

Political pressure groups and leaders: NA

International organization participation: SPC, UPU

Flag description: blue, with a white, five-pointed star superimposed on a gray latte stone (the traditional foundation stone used in building) in the center, surrounded by a wreath; blue symbolizes the Pacific Ocean, the star represents the Commonwealth; the latte stone and the floral head wreath display elements of the native Chamorro culture

National symbol(s): latte stone

National anthem: *name:* "Gi Talo Gi Halom Tasi" (In the Middle of the Sea)
lyrics/music: Jose S. PANGELINAN [Chamoru], David PETER [Carolinian]/Wilhelm GANZHORN
note: adopted 1996; the Carolinian version of the song is known as "Satil Matawal Pacifico;" as a commonwealth of the United States, in addition to the local anthem, "The Star-Spangled Banner" is official (see United States)

ECONOMY

Economy—overview: The Northern Mariana Islands' economy benefits substantially from financial assistance from the US. The tourist industry employs approximately a quarter of the work force and accounts for roughly one-fourth of GDP. As a share of total arrivals, the number of Japanese tourists has dropped recently to less than half, while Korean visitors account for roughly one-third. Annual tourist arrivals have remained below 400,000 since 2007. Other services such as trade are also important to the local economy. The small agriculture sector is made up of cattle ranches and small farms producing coconuts, breadfruit, tomatoes, and melons.

GDP (purchasing power parity): $733 million (2010 est.)
country comparison to the world: 211
note: GDP estimate includes US subsidy

GDP (official exchange rate): $733 million (2010 est.)

GDP—per capita (PPP): $13,600 (2010 est.)
country comparison to the world: 98

GDP—composition, by sector of origin:
agriculture: 1.7%
industry: 3.3%
services: 95% (2010)

Agriculture—products: vegetables and melons, fruits and nuts; ornamental plants; livestock, poultry and eggs; fish and aquaculture products

Industries: tourism, banking, construction, fishing, handicrafts, other services

Industrial production growth rate: NA%

Labor force: 38,450
country comparison to the world: 199
note: nearly 29,000 of these were foreign workers (2005 est.)

Labor force—by occupation: *agriculture:* 1.9%
industry: 10%
services: 88.1% (2010 est.)

Unemployment rate: 11.2% (2010 est.)
country comparison to the world: 118
8% (2005 est.)

Population below poverty line: NA%

Household income or consumption by percentage share: *lowest 10%:* NA%
highest 10%: NA%

Budget: *revenues:* $260 million
expenditures: $318.2 million (FY10/11)

Taxes and other revenues: 35.5% of GDP (FY10/11 est.)
country comparison to the world: 62

Budget surplus (+) or deficit (-):
-7.9% of GDP (FY10/11 est.)
country comparison to the world: 194

Fiscal year: 1 October—30 September

Inflation rate (consumer prices): -2.7% (2012 est.)
country comparison to the world: 1

Exports: $98.2 million (2008)
country comparison to the world: 191

Exports—commodities: garments

Imports: $214.4 million (2001)
country comparison to the world: 204

Imports—commodities: food, construction equipment and materials, petroleum products

Debt—external: $NA

Exchange rates: the US dollar is used

ENERGY

Electricity—production: 60,600 kWh (January 2009)
country comparison to the world: 217

Electricity—consumption: 48,300 kWh (January 2009)
country comparison to the world: 218

Electricity—exports: 0 kWh (January 2009 est.)
country comparison to the world: 122

Electricity—imports: 0 kWh (January 2009 est.)
country comparison to the world: 129

COMMUNICATIONS

Telephone system: *international:* country code—1-670; satellite earth stations—2 Intelsat (Pacific Ocean)

Broadcast media: 1 TV broadcast station on Saipan; multi-channel cable TV services are available on Saipan; 9 licensed radio broadcast stations (2009)

Internet country code: .mp

Internet hosts: 17 (2012)
country comparison to the world: 222

TRANSPORTATION

Airports: 5 (2013)
country comparison to the world: 179

Airports—with paved runways: *total:* 3
2,438 to 3,047 m: 2
1,524 to 2,437 m: 1 (2013)

Airports—with unpaved runways: *total:* 2
2,438 to 3,047 m: 1
under 914 m: 1 (2013)

Heliports: 1 (2013)

Roadways: *total:* 536 km (2008)
country comparison to the world: 193

Ports and terminals: *major seaport(s):* Saipan, Tinian, Rota

MILITARY

Manpower fit for military service:
males age 16-49: 8,793
females age 16-49: 11,569 (2010 est.)

Manpower reaching militarily significant age annually: *male:* 410
female: 306 (2010 est.)

Military—note: defense is the responsibility of the US

TRANSNATIONAL ISSUES

Disputes—international: none

NORWAY

INTRODUCTION

Background: Two centuries of Viking raids into Europe tapered off following the adoption of Christianity by King Olav TRYGGVASON in 994. Conversion of the Norwegian kingdom occurred over the next several decades. In 1397, Norway was absorbed into a union with Denmark that lasted more than four centuries. In 1814, Norwegians resisted the cession of their country to Sweden and adopted a new constitution. Sweden then invaded Norway but agreed to let Norway keep its constitution in return for accepting the union under a Swedish king. Rising nationalism throughout the 19th century led to a 1905 referendum granting Norway independence. Although Norway remained neutral in World War I, it suffered heavy losses to its shipping. Norway proclaimed its neutrality at the outset of World War II, but was nonetheless occupied for five years by Nazi Germany (1940-45). In 1949, neutrality was abandoned and Norway became a member of NATO. Discovery of oil and gas in adjacent waters in the late 1960s boosted Norway's economic fortunes. In referenda held in 1972 and 1994, Norway rejected joining the EU. Key domestic issues include immigration and integration of ethnic minorities, maintaining the country's extensive social safety net with an aging population, and preserving economic competitiveness.

GEOGRAPHY

Location: Northern Europe, bordering the North Sea and the North Atlantic Ocean, west of Sweden

Geographic coordinates: 62 00 N, 10 00 E

Map references: Europe

Area: *total:* 323,802 sq km
country comparison to the world: 68
land: 304,282 sq km
water: 19,520 sq km

Area—comparative: slightly larger than New Mexico

Land boundaries: *total:* 2,542 km
border countries: Finland 727 km, Sweden 1,619 km, Russia 196 km

Coastline: 25,148 km (includes mainland 2,650 km, as well as long fjords, numerous small islands, and minor indentations 22,498 km; length of island coastlines 58,133 km)

Maritime claims: *territorial sea:* 12 nm
contiguous zone: 10 nm
exclusive economic zone: 200 nm
continental shelf: 200 nm

Climate: temperate along coast, modified by North Atlantic Current; colder interior with increased precipitation and colder summers; rainy year-round on west coast

Terrain: glaciated; mostly high plateaus and rugged mountains broken by fertile valleys; small, scattered plains; coastline deeply indented by fjords; arctic tundra in north

Elevation extremes: *lowest point:* Norwegian Sea 0 m
highest point: Galdhopiggen 2,469 m

Natural resources: petroleum, natural gas, iron ore, copper, lead, zinc, titanium, pyrites, nickel, fish, timber, hydropower

Land use: *arable land:* 2.52%
permanent crops: 0.01%
other: 97.46% (2011)

Irrigated land: 1,149 sq km (2007)

Total renewable water resources: 382 cu km (2011)

Freshwater withdrawal (domestic/industrial/agricultural): *total:* 2.94 cu km/yr (28%/43%/29%)
per capita: 622.4 cu m/yr (2006)

Natural hazards: rockslides, avalanches
volcanism: Beerenberg (elev. 2,227 m) on Jan Mayen Island in the Norwegian Sea is the country's only active volcano

Environment—current issues: water pollution; acid rain damaging forests and adversely affecting lakes, threatening fish stocks; air pollution from vehicle emissions

Environment—international agreements:
party to: Air Pollution, Air Pollution-Nitrogen Oxides, Air Pollution-Persistent Organic Pollutants, Air Pollution-Sulfur 85, Air Pollution-Sulfur 94, Air Pollution-Volatile Organic Compounds, Antarctic-Environmental Protocol, Antarctic-Marine Living Resources, Antarctic Seals, Antarctic Treaty, Biodiversity, Climate Change, Climate Change-Kyoto Protocol, Desertification, Endangered Species, Environmental Modification, Hazardous Wastes, Law of the Sea, Marine Dumping, Ozone Layer Protection, Ship Pollution, Tropical Timber 83, Tropical Timber 94, Wetlands, Whaling
signed, but not ratified: none of the selected agreements

Geography—note: about two-thirds mountains; some 50,000 islands off its much-indented coastline; strategic location adjacent to sea lanes and air routes in North Atlantic; one of the most rugged and longest coastlines in the world

PEOPLE AND SOCIETY

Nationality: *noun:* Norwegian(s)
adjective: Norwegian

Ethnic groups: Norwegian 94.4% (includes Sami, about 60,000), other European 3.6%, other 2% (2007 estimate)

Languages: Bokmal Norwegian (official), Nynorsk Norwegian (official), small Sami- and Finnish-speaking minorities
note: Sami is an official language in nine municipalities

Religions: Church of Norway (Evangelical Lutheran—official) 82.1%, other Christian 3.9%, Muslim 2.3%, Roman Catholic 1.8%, other 2.4%, unspecified 7.5% (2011 est.)

Population: 5,147,792 (July 2014 est.)
country comparison to the world: 121

Age structure: *0-14 years:* 18.2% (male 480,176/female 456,128)
15-24 years: 13.1% (male 347,873/female 329,021)
25-54 years: 40.8% (male 1,080,339/female 1,021,370)
55-64 years: 16.1% (male 305,094/female 298,134)
65 years and over: 16.8% (male 375,909/female 453,748) (2014 est.)

Dependency ratios:
total dependency ratio: 52.6 %
youth dependency ratio: 28.5 %
elderly dependency ratio: 24.1 %
potential support ratio: 4.1 (2013)

Median age: *total:* 39.1 years
male: 38.2 years
female: 39.9 years (2014 est.)

Population growth rate: 1.19% (2014 est.)
country comparison to the world: 101

Birth rate: 12.09 births/1,000 population (2014 est.)
country comparison to the world: 165

Death rate: 8.19 deaths/1,000 population (2014 est.)
country comparison to the world: 94

Net migration rate: 7.96 migrant(s)/1,000 population (2014 est.)
country comparison to the world: 18

Urbanization: *urban population:* 79% of total population (2010)
rate of urbanization: 1.2% annual rate of change (2010-15 est.)

Major urban areas—population: OSLO (capital) 875,000 (2009)

Sex ratio: *at birth:* 1.06 male(s)/female
0-14 years: 1.05 male(s)/female
15-24 years: 1.06 male(s)/female
25-54 years: 1.06 male(s)/female
55-64 years: 1.01 male(s)/female
65 years and over: 0.78 male(s)/female
total population: 0.98 male(s)/female (2014 est.)

Mother's mean age at first birth: 28.4 (2011 est.)

Maternal mortality rate: 7 deaths/100,000 live births (2010)
country comparison to the world: 167

Infant mortality rate: *total:* 2.48 deaths/1,000 live births
country comparison to the world: 221
male: 2.79 deaths/1,000 live births
female: 2.15 deaths/1,000 live births (2014 est.)

Life expectancy at birth: *total population:* 81.6 years
country comparison to the world: 17
male: 79.63 years
female: 83.69 years (2014 est.)

Total fertility rate: 1.86 children born/woman (2014 est.)
country comparison to the world: 145

Contraceptive prevalence rate: 88.4%
note: percent of women aged 20-44 (2005)

Health expenditures: 9.1% of GDP (2011)
country comparison to the world: 42

Physicians density: 3.7 physicians/1,000 population (2011)

Hospital bed density: 3.3 beds/1,000 population (2010)

Drinking water source:
improved:
urban: 100% of population
rural: 100% of population
total: 100% of population
unimproved:
urban: 0% of population
rural: 0% of population
total: 0% of population (2011 est.)

Sanitation facility access:
improved:
urban: 100% of population
rural: 100% of population
total: 100% of population
unimproved:
urban: 0% of population
rural: 0% of population
total: 0% of population (2011 est.)

HIV/AIDS—adult prevalence rate: 0.1% (2009 est.)
country comparison to the world: 164

HIV/AIDS—people living with HIV/AIDS: 4,000 (2009 est.)
country comparison to the world: 127

HIV/AIDS—deaths: fewer than 100 (2009 est.)
country comparison to the world: 136

Obesity—adult prevalence rate: 21.5% (2008)
country comparison to the world: 84

Education expenditures: 6.9% of GDP (2010)
country comparison to the world: 21

Literacy: *definition:* age 15 and over can read and write
total population: 100%
male: 100%
female: 100%

School life expectancy (primary to tertiary education): *total:* 18 years
male: 17 years
female: 18 years (2011)

Unemployment, youth ages 15-24: *total:* 8.6%
country comparison to the world: 117
male: 10%
female: 7.2% (2012)

GOVERNMENT

Country name: *conventional long form:* Kingdom of Norway
conventional short form: Norway
local long form: Kongeriket Norge
local short form: Norge

Government type: constitutional monarchy

Capital: *name:* Oslo
geographic coordinates: 59 55 N, 10 45 E
time difference: UTC+1 (6 hours ahead of Washington, DC during Standard Time)
daylight saving time: +1hr, begins last Sunday in March; ends last Sunday in October

Administrative divisions: 19 counties (fylker, singular—fylke); Akershus, Aust-Agder, Buskerud, Finnmark, Hedmark, Hordaland, More og Romsdal, Nordland, Nord-Trondelag, Oppland, Oslo, Ostfold, Rogaland, Sogn og Fjordane, Sor-Trondelag, Telemark, Troms, Vest-Agder, Vestfold

Dependent areas: Bouvet Island, Jan Mayen, Svalbard

Independence: 7 June 1905 (Norway declared the union with Sweden dissolved); 26 October 1905 (Sweden agreed to the repeal of the union)

National holiday: Constitution Day, 17 May (1814)

Constitution: drafted spring 1814, adopted 16 May 1814, signed by Constituent Assembly 17 May 1814; amended many times, last in 2012 (2012)

Legal system: mixed legal system of civil, common, and customary law; Supreme Court can advise on legislative acts

International law organization participation: accepts compulsory ICJ jurisdiction with reservations; accepts ICCt jurisdiction

Suffrage: 18 years of age; universal

Executive branch: *chief of state:* King HARALD V (since 17 January 1991); Heir Apparent Crown Prince HAAKON MAGNUS, son of the monarch (born 20 July 1973)
head of government: Prime Minister Erna SOLBERG (since 16 October 2013)
cabinet: State Council appointed by the monarch with the approval of parliament (For more information visit the World Leaders website)
elections: the monarchy is hereditary; following parliamentary elections, the leader of the majority party or the leader of the majority coalition usually appointed prime minister by the monarch with the approval of the parliament

Legislative branch: modified unicameral Parliament or Storting (169 seats; members elected by popular vote by proportional representation to serve four-year terms)
elections: last held on 9 September 2013 (next to be held in September 2017)
election results: percent of vote by party—Ap 30.8%, H 26.3%, FrP 16.3%, KrF 5.6%, Sp 5.5%, V 5.2%, SV 4.1%, MDG 2.8, other 2.7%; seats by party—Ap 55, H 48, FrP 29, Sp 10, KrF 10, V 9, SV 7, MDG 1

Judicial branch: *highest court(s):* Supreme Court or Hoyesterett (consists of the chief justice and 18 associate justices) note—in addition to professionally trained judges, there are elected lay judges that sit on the bench with professional judges in the Courts of Appeal and district courts
judge selection and term of office: justices appointed by the monarch (King in Council) upon the recommendation of the Judicial Appointments Board; justice retirement mandatory at age 70
subordinate courts: Courts of Appeal or Lagmensrett; regional and district courts; Conciliation Boards; ordinary and special courts

Political parties and leaders: Center Party or Sp [Liv Signe NAVARSETE]; Christian Democratic Party or KrF [Knut Arild HAREIDE]; Conservative Party or H [Erna SOLBERG]; Labor Party or Ap [Jens STOLTENBERG]; Liberal Party or V [Trine SKEI-GRANDE]; Progress Party or FrP [Siv JENSEN]; Socialist Left Party or SV [Audun LYSBAKKEN]

Political pressure groups and leaders: Confederation of Norwegian Enterprise (Naeringslivets Hovedorganisasjon) or NHO [President Tore; ULSTEIN; CEO Kristin SKOGEN LUND]; Norwegian Confederation of Trade Unions (Landsorganisasjonen i Norge) or LO [Gerd KRISTIANSEN]
other: environmental groups; media; digital privacy movements

International organization participation: ADB (nonregional member), AfDB (nonregional member), Arctic Council, Australia Group, BIS, CBSS, CD, CE, CERN, EAPC, EBRD, EFTA, EITI (implementing country), ESA, FAO, FATF,

IADB, IAEA, IBRD, ICAO, ICC (national committees), ICRM, IDA, IEA, IFAD, IFC, IFRCS, IGAD (partners), IHO, ILO, IMF, IMO, IMSO, Interpol, IOC, IOM, IPU, ISO, ITSO, ITU, ITUC (NGOs), MIGA, MINUSMA, MONUSCO, NATO, NC, NEA, NIB, NSG, OAS (observer), OECD, OPCW, OSCE, Paris Club, PCA, Schengen Convention, UN, UNCTAD, UNESCO, UNHCR, UNIDO, UNITAR, UNMISS, UNRWA, UNTSO, UNWTO, UPU, WCO, WHO, WIPO, WMO, WTO, ZC

Diplomatic representation in the US:
chief of mission: Ambassador Kare Reidar AAS (since 22 August 2013)
chancery: 2720 34th Street NW, Washington, DC 20008
telephone: [1] (202) 333-6000
FAX: [1] (202) 469-3990
consulate(s) general: Houston, New York, San Francisco

Diplomatic representation from the US:
chief of mission: Ambassador (vacant); Charge d'Affaires Julie Furuta-Toy (since 27 September 2013)
embassy: Henrik Ibsens gate 48, 0244 Oslo; note—the embassy will move to Huseby in the near future
mailing address: PSC 69, Box 1000, APO AE 09707
telephone: [47] 21-30-85-40
FAX: [47] 22-44-33-63, 22-56-27-51

Flag description: red with a blue cross outlined in white that extends to the edges of the flag; the vertical part of the cross is shifted to the hoist side in the style of the Dannebrog (Danish flag); the colors recall Norway's past political unions with Denmark (red and white) and Sweden (blue)

National symbol(s): lion

National anthem: *name:* "Ja, vi elsker dette landet" (Yes, We Love This Country)
lyrics/music: lyrics/music: Bjornstjerne BJORNSON/Rikard NORDRAAK
note: adopted 1864; in addition to the national anthem, "Kongesangen" (Song of the King), which uses the tune of "God Save the Queen," serves as the royal anthem

ECONOMY

Economy—overview: The Norwegian economy is a prosperous mixed economy, with a vibrant private sector, a large state sector, and an extensive social safety net. The government controls key areas, such as the vital petroleum sector, through extensive regulation and large-scale state-majority-owned enterprises. The country is richly endowed with natural resources—petroleum, hydropower, fish, forests, and minerals—and is highly dependent on the petroleum sector, which accounts for the largest portion of export revenue and about 30% of government revenue. Norway is the world's third-largest natural gas exporter; and seventh largest oil exporter, making one of its largest offshore oil finds in 2011. Norway opted to stay out of the EU during a referendum in November 1994; nonetheless, as a member of the European Economic Area, it contributes sizably to the EU budget. In anticipation of eventual declines in oil and gas production, Norway saves state revenue from the petroleum sector in the world's largest sovereign wealth fund, valued at over $830 billion in January 2014 and uses the fund's return to help finance public expenses. After solid GDP growth in 2004-07, the economy slowed in 2008, and contracted in 2009, before returning to positive growth in 2010-13. Nevertheless, the government budget remains in surplus.

GDP (purchasing power parity): $282.2 billion (2013 est.)
country comparison to the world: 47
$277.8 billion (2012 est.)
$269.7 billion (2011 est.)
note: data are in 2013 US dollars

GDP (official exchange rate): $515.8 billion (2013 est.)

GDP—real growth rate: 1.6% (2013 est.)
country comparison to the world: 151
3% (2012 est.)
1.3% (2011 est.)

GDP—per capita (PPP): $55,400 (2013 est.)
country comparison to the world: 10
$55,100 (2012 est.)
$54,200 (2011 est.)
note: data are in 2013 US dollars

Gross national saving: 38.2% of GDP (2013 est.)
country comparison to the world: 13
39.4% of GDP (2012 est.)
37% of GDP (2011 est.)

GDP—composition, by end use:
household consumption: 40.5%
government consumption: 21.6%
investment in fixed capital: 21.7%
investment in inventories: 3.4%
exports of goods and services: 39.9%
imports of goods and services: -27.1% (2013 est.)

GDP—composition, by sector of origin:
agriculture: 1.2%
industry: 42.3%
services: 56.5% (2013 est.)

Agriculture—products: barley, wheat, potatoes; pork, beef, veal, milk; fish

Industries: petroleum and gas, food processing, shipbuilding, pulp and paper products, metals, chemicals, timber, mining, textiles, fishing

Industrial production growth rate: -3% (2013 est.)
country comparison to the world: 185

Labor force: 2.707 million (2014 est.)
country comparison to the world: 109

Labor force—by occupation:
agriculture: 2.2%
industry: 20.2%
services: 77.6% (2012)

Unemployment rate: 3.6% (2013 est.)
country comparison to the world: 29
3.2% (2012 est.)

Population below poverty line: NA%

Household income or consumption by percentage share: *lowest 10%:* 3.9%
highest 10%: 21% (2008)

Distribution of family income—Gini index:
25 (2008)
country comparison to the world: 133
25.8 (1995)

Budget: *revenues:* $292.8 billion
expenditures: $225 billion (2013 est.)

Taxes and other revenues: 56.8% of GDP (2013 est.)
country comparison to the world: 6

Budget surplus (+) or deficit (-):
13.1% of GDP (2013 est.)
country comparison to the world: 4

Public debt: 30.1% of GDP (2013 est.)
country comparison to the world: 123
29.1% of GDP (2012 est.)
note: data cover general government debt, and includes debt instruments issued (or owned) by government entities other than the treasury; the data exclude treasury debt held by foreign entities; the data exclude debt issued by subnational entities, as well as intra-governmental debt; intra-governmental debt consists of treasury borrowings from surpluses in the social funds, such as for retirement, medical care, and unemployment; debt instruments for the social funds are not sold at public auctions

Fiscal year: calendar year

Inflation rate (consumer prices): 1.9% (2013 est.)
country comparison to the world: 64
0.7% (2012 est.)

Central bank discount rate: 6.25% (31 December 2010 est.)
country comparison to the world: 116
1.75% (31 December 2009 est.)

Commercial bank prime lending rate: 3.4% (31 December 2013 est.)
country comparison to the world: 166
3.7% (31 December 2012 est.)

Stock of narrow money: $146.3 billion (31 December 2013 est.)
country comparison to the world: 27
$152.1 billion (31 December 2012 est.)

Stock of broad money: $312.9 billion (31 December 2013 est.)
country comparison to the world: 30
$318.5 billion (31 December 2012 est.)

Stock of domestic credit: $706.4 billion (31 December 2013 est.)
country comparison to the world: 21
$705.4 billion (31 December 2012 est.)

Market value of publicly traded shares: $252.9 billion (31 December 2012 est.)
country comparison to the world: 30
$219.2 billion (31 December 2011)
$250.9 billion (31 December 2010 est.)

Current account balance: $67.4 billion (2013 est.)
country comparison to the world: 7
$71.87 billion (2012 est.)

Exports: $154.2 billion (2013 est.)
country comparison to the world: 33
$166 billion (2012 est.)

Exports—commodities: petroleum and petroleum products, machinery and equipment, metals, chemicals, ships, fish

Exports—partners: UK 25.6%, Germany 12.6%, Netherlands 12%, France 6.7%, Sweden 6.3%, US 5% (2012)

Imports: $90.14 billion (2013 est.)
country comparison to the world: 36
$89.05 billion (2012 est.)

Imports—commodities: machinery and equipment, chemicals, metals, foodstuffs

Imports—partners: Sweden 13.6%, Germany 12.4%, China 9.3%, Denmark 6.3%, UK 6.1%, US 5.4% (2012)

Reserves of foreign exchange and gold: $51.86 billion (31 December 2012 est.)
country comparison to the world: 39
$49.4 billion (31 December 2011 est.)

Debt—external: $720.6 billion (31 December 2012 est.)
country comparison to the world: 21
$595.7 billion (31 December 2011)
note: Norway is a net external creditor

Stock of direct foreign investment—at home:
$274.5 billion (31 December 2013 est.)
country comparison to the world: 21

$256.8 billion (31 December 2012 est.)

Stock of direct foreign investment—abroad: $264.3 billion (31 December 2013 est.)
country comparison to the world: 20
$241.3 billion (31 December 2012 est.)

Exchange rates: Norwegian kroner (NOK) per US dollar—
5.802 (2013 est.)
5.8162 (2012 est.)
6.0442 (2010 est.)
6.288 (2009)
5.6361 (2008)

ENERGY

Electricity—production: 125.2 billion kWh (2011 est.)
country comparison to the world: 2 9

Electricity—consumption: 120.9 billion kWh (2010 est.)
country comparison to the world: 28

Electricity—exports: 22.17 billion kWh (2012 est.)
country comparison to the world: 8

Electricity—imports: 4.168 billion kWh (2012 est.)
country comparison to the world: 39

Electricity—installed generating capacity: 30.18 million kW (2010 est.)
country comparison to the world: 28

Electricity—from fossil fuels: 2% of total installed capacity (2010 est.)
country comparison to the world: 202

Electricity—from nuclear fuels: 0% of total installed capacity (2010 est.)
country comparison to the world: 152

Electricity—from hydroelectric plants: 91.7% of total installed capacity (2010 est.)
country comparison to the world: 11

Electricity—from other renewable sources: 1.9% of total installed capacity (2010 est.)
country comparison to the world: 70

Crude oil—production: 1.902 million bbl/day (2012 est.)
country comparison to the world: 14

Crude oil—exports: 1.602 million bbl/day (2010 est.)
country comparison to the world: 9

Crude oil—imports: 11,320 bbl/day (2010 est.)
country comparison to the world: 76

Crude oil—proved reserves: 5.366 billion bbl (1 January 2010 es)
country comparison to the world: 24

Refined petroleum products—production: 307,700 bbl/day (2010 est.)
country comparison to the world: 42

Refined petroleum products—consumption: 255,200 bbl/day (2011 est.)
country comparison to the world: 51

Refined petroleum products—exports: 349,600 bbl/day (2010 est.)
country comparison to the world: 21

Refined petroleum products—imports: 100,000 bbl/day (2010 est.)
country comparison to the world: 51

Natural gas—production: 114.7 billion cu m (2012 est.)
country comparison to the world: 7

Natural gas—consumption: 5.506 billion cu m (2010 est.)
country comparison to the world: 57

Natural gas—exports: 107.3 billion cu m (2012 est.)
country comparison to the world: 3

Natural gas—imports: 0 cu m (2011 est.)
country comparison to the world: 107

Natural gas—proved reserves: 2.07 trillion cu m (1 January 2013 es)
country comparison to the world: 17

Carbon dioxide emissions from consumption of energy: 45.87 million Mt (2011 est.)
country comparison to the world: 67

COMMUNICATIONS

Telephones—main lines in use: 1.465 million (2012)
country comparison to the world: 6 6

Telephones—mobile cellular: 5.732 million (2012)
country comparison to the world: 103

Telephone system: *general assessment:* modern in all respects; one of the most advanced telecommunications networks in Europe
domestic: Norway has a domestic satellite system; the prevalence of rural areas encourages the wide use of mobile-cellular systems
international: country code—47; 2 buried coaxial cable systems; submarine cables provide links to other Nordic countries and Europe; satellite earth stations—NA Eutelsat, NA Intelsat (Atlantic Ocean), and 1 Inmarsat (Atlantic and Indian Ocean regions); note—Norway shares the Inmarsat earth station with the other Nordic countries (Denmark, Finland, Iceland, and Sweden) (2011)

Broadcast media: state-owned public radio-TV broadcaster operates 3 nationwide TV stations, 3 nationwide radio stations, and 16 regional radio stations; roughly a dozen privately owned television stations broadcast nationally and roughly another 25 local TV stations broadcasting; nearly 75% of households have access to multi-channel cable or satellite TV; 2 privately owned radio stations broadcast nationwide and another 240 stations operate locally (2008)

Internet country code: .no

Internet hosts: 3.588 million (2012)
country comparison to the world: 29

Internet users: 4.431 million (2009)
country comparison to the world: 53

TRANSPORTATION

Airports: 95 (2013)
country comparison to the world: 6 1

Airports—with paved runways: *total:* 6 7
2,438 to 3,047 m: 14
1,524 to 2,437 m: 10
914 to 1,523 m: 22
under 914 m: 21 (2013)

Airports—with unpaved runways: *total:* 2 8
914 to 1,523 m: 6
under 914 m: 22 (2013)

Heliports: 1 (2013)

Pipelines: condensate 578 km; condensate/gas 220 km; gas 8,044 km; oil 3,794 km; oil/gas/water 457 km; water 96 km (2013)

Railways: *total:* 4,237 km
country comparison to the world: 39
standard gauge: 4,237 km 1.435-m gauge (2,784 km electrified) (2012)

Roadways: *total:* 93,870 km (includes 393 km of expressways)
country comparison to the world: 51
paved: 75,754 km
unpaved: 18,116 km (2013)

Waterways: 1,577 km (2010)
country comparison to the world: 52

Merchant marine: *total:* 585
country comparison to the world: 19
by type: bulk carrier 55, cargo 105, carrier 5, chemical tanker 121, combination ore/oil 12, liquefied gas 47, passenger 3, passenger/cargo 121, petroleum tanker 54, refrigerated cargo 9, roll on/roll off 4, vehicle carrier 49
foreign-owned: 81 (Bermuda 24, Canada 1, Cyprus 1, Denmark 7, France 5, Iceland 2, Lithuania 1, Saudi Arabia 3, Sweden 27, US 10)
registered in other countries: 974 (Antigua and Barbuda 9, Bahamas 186, Barbados 38, Belize 2, Bermuda 5, Brazil 3, Canada 4, Chile 1, Comoros 1, Cook Islands 8, Croatia 2, Curacao 2, Cyprus 14, Denmark 2, Dominica 1, Equatorial Guinea 1, Estonia 2, Faroe Islands 13, Gibraltar 46, Hong Kong 48, Indonesia 3, Isle of Man 30, Italy 6, Liberia 38, Libya 1, Malta 96, Marshall Islands 75, Netherlands 19, Panama 81, Portugal 2, Saint Kitts and Nevis 3, Saint Vincent and the Grenadines 13, Singapore 153, Spain 10, Sweden 3, UK 32, US 17, Vanuatu 1, unknown 3) (2010)

Ports and terminals: *major seaport(s):* Bergen, Haugesund, Maaloy, Mongstad, Narvik, Sture

MILITARY

Military branches: Norwegian Army (Haeren), Royal Norwegian Navy (Kongelige Norske Sjoeforsvaret, RNoN; includes Coastal Rangers and Coast Guard (Kystvakt)), Royal Norwegian Air Force (Kongelige Norske Luftforsvaret, RNoAF), Home Guard (Heimevernet, HV) (2013)

Military service age and obligation: 19-35 years of age for male compulsory military service; 16 years of age in wartime; 17 years of age for male volunteers; 18 years of age for women; 1-year service obligation followed by 4-5 refresher training periods through ages 35-60, totalling 18 months (2012)

Manpower available for military service:
males age 16-49: 1,079,043
females age 16-49: 1,051,210 (2010 est.)

Manpower fit for military service:
males age 16-49: 888,761
females age 16-49: 865,697 (2010 est.)

Manpower reaching militarily significant age annually: *male:* 32,290
female: 30,777 (2010 est.)

Military expenditures: 1.4% of GDP (2012)
country comparison to the world: 72
1.47% of GDP (2011)
1.4% of GDP (2010)

TRANSNATIONAL ISSUES

Disputes—international: Norway asserts a territorial claim in Antarctica (Queen Maud Land and its continental shelf); Denmark (Greenland) and Norway have made submissions to the Commission on the Limits of the Continental shelf (CLCS) and Russia is collecting additional data to augment its 2001 CLCS submission; Norway and Russia signed a comprehensive maritime boundary agreement in 2010

Refugees and internally displaced persons: *refugees (country of origin):* 8,870 (Somalia); 5,727 (Iraq); 7,129 (Eritrea); 5,984 (Afghanistan) (2012)
stateless persons: 2,313 (2012)

OMAN

INTRODUCTION

Background: The inhabitants of the area of Oman have long prospered on Indian Ocean trade. In the late 18th century, a newly established sultanate in Muscat signed the first in a series of friendship treaties with Britain. Over time, Oman's dependence on British political and military advisors increased, but it never became a British colony. In 1970, QABOOS bin Said Al-Said overthrew his father, and he has since ruled as sultan. His extensive modernization program has opened the country to the outside world while preserving the longstanding close ties with the UK. Oman's moderate, independent foreign policy has sought to maintain good relations with all Middle Eastern countries. Inspired by the popular uprisings that swept the Middle East and North Africa beginning in January 2011, some Omanis began staging marches, demonstrations, and sit-ins calling mostly for more jobs and economic benefits and an end to corruption. In response to those protester demands, QABOOS in 2011 pledged to implement economic and political reforms, such as granting legislative and regulatory powers to the Majlis al-Shura and introducing unemployment benefits. Additionally, in August 2012, the Sultan announced a royal directive mandating the speedy implementation of a national job creation plan for thousands of public and private sector jobs. As part of the government's efforts to decentralize authority and allow greater citizen participation in local governance, Oman successfully conducted its first municipal council elections in December 2012. Announced by the Sultan in 2011, the municipal councils will have the power to advise the Royal Court on the needs of local districts across Oman's 11 governorates.

GEOGRAPHY

Location: Middle East, bordering the Arabian Sea, Gulf of Oman, and Persian Gulf, between Yemen and UAE

Geographic coordinates: 21 00 N, 57 00 E

Map references: Middle East

Area: *total:* 309,500 sq km
country comparison to the world: 71
land: 309,500 sq km
water: 0 sq km

Area—comparative: slightly smaller than Kansas

Land boundaries: *total:* 1,374 km
border countries: Saudi Arabia 676 km, UAE 410 km, Yemen 288 km

Coastline: 2,092 km

Maritime claims: *territorial sea:* 12 nm
contiguous zone: 24 nm
exclusive economic zone: 200 nm

Climate: dry desert; hot, humid along coast; hot, dry interior; strong southwest summer monsoon (May to September) in far south

Terrain: central desert plain, rugged mountains in north and south

Elevation extremes: *lowest point:* Arabian Sea 0 m
highest point: Jabal Shams 2,980 m

Natural resources: petroleum, copper, asbestos, some marble, limestone, chromium, gypsum, natural gas

Land use: *arable land:* 0.1%
permanent crops: 0.12%
other: 99.77% (2011)

Irrigated land: 588.5 sq km (2004)

Total renewable water resources: 1.4 cu km (2011)

Freshwater withdrawal (domestic/industrial/agricultural): *total:* 1.32 cu km/yr (10%/1%/88%)
per capita: 515.8 cu m/yr (2003)

Natural hazards: summer winds often raise large sandstorms and dust storms in interior; periodic droughts

Environment—current issues: rising soil salinity; beach pollution from oil spills; limited natural freshwater resources

Environment—international agreements:
party to: Biodiversity, Climate Change, Climate Change-Kyoto Protocol, Desertification, Hazardous Wastes, Law of the Sea, Marine Dumping, Ozone Layer Protection, Ship Pollution, Whaling
signed, but not ratified: none of the selected agreements

Geography—note: strategic location on Musandam Peninsula adjacent to Strait of Hormuz, a vital transit point for world crude oil

PEOPLE AND SOCIETY

Nationality: *noun:* Omani(s)
adjective: Omani

Ethnic groups: Arab, Baluchi, South Asian (Indian, Pakistani, Sri Lankan, Bangladeshi), African

Languages: Arabic (official), English, Baluchi, Urdu, Indian dialects

Religions: Muslim (official; majority are Ibadhi, lesser numbers of Sunni and Shia)) 85.9%, Christian 6.5%, Hindu 5.5%, Buddhist 0.8%, Jewish
note: approximately 75% of Omani citizens, who compose almost 70% of the country's total population, are Ibadhi Muslims; the Omani government does not keep statistics on religious affiliation (2013) (2010 est.)

Population: 3,219,775 (July 2014 est.)
country comparison to the world: 136
note: immigrants make up just over 30% of the total population, according to UN data (2013)

Age structure: *0-14 years:* 30.4% (male 501,352/female 476,333)
15-24 years: 19.9% (male 335,404/female 304,261)
25-54 years: 42.6% (male 801,539/female 569,187)
55-64 years: 3.3% (male 67,085/female 58,254)
65 years and over: 3.2% (male 53,320/female 53,040) (2014 est.)

Dependency ratios:
total dependency ratio: 35.7 %
youth dependency ratio: 31.9 %
elderly dependency ratio: 3.8 %
potential support ratio: 26.2 (2013)

Median age: *total:* 24.9 years
male: 26.1 years
female: 23.4 years (2014 est.)

Population growth rate: 2.06% (2014 est.)
country comparison to the world: 49

Birth rate: 24.47 births/1,000 population (2014 est.)
country comparison to the world: 59

Death rate: 3.38 deaths/1,000 population (2014 est.)
country comparison to the world: 219

Net migration rate: -0.45 migrant(s)/1,000 population (2014 est.)
country comparison to the world: 133

Urbanization: *urban population:* 73.4% of total population (2011)
rate of urbanization: 2.23% annual rate of change (2010-15 est.)

Major urban areas—population: MUSCAT (capital) 634,000 (2009)

Sex ratio: *at birth:* 1.05 male(s)/female
0-14 years: 1.05 male(s)/female
15-24 years: 1.1 male(s)/female
25-54 years: 1.41 male(s)/female
55-64 years: 1.2 male(s)/female
65 years and over: 1.03 male(s)/female
total population: 1.22 male(s)/female (2014 est.)

Maternal mortality rate: 32 deaths/100,000 live births (2010)
country comparison to the world: 122

Infant mortality rate: *total:* 14 deaths/1,000 live births
country comparison to the world: 112
male: 14.29 deaths/1,000 live births
female: 13.69 deaths/1,000 live births (2014 est.)

Life expectancy at birth: *total population:* 74.97 years
country comparison to the world: 103
male: 73.07 years
female: 76.97 years (2014 est.)

Total fertility rate: 2.86 children born/woman (2014 est.)
country comparison to the world: 64

Contraceptive prevalence rate: 31.7% (2000)

Health expenditures: 2.3% of GDP (2011)
country comparison to the world: 188

Physicians density: 2.05 physicians/1,000 population (2010)

Hospital bed density: 1.8 beds/1,000 population (2009)

Drinking water source:
improved:
urban: 94.8% of population
rural: 85.2% of population
total: 92.3% of population
unimproved:
urban: 5.2% of population
rural: 14.8% of population
total: 7.7% of population (2011 est.)

Sanitation facility access:
improved:
urban: 97.3% of population
rural: 94.7% of population
total: 96.6% of population
unimproved:
urban: 2.7% of population
rural: 5.3% of population
total: 3.4% of population (2011 est.)

HIV/AIDS—adult prevalence rate: 0.1% (2009 est.)
country comparison to the world: 165

HIV/AIDS—people living with HIV/AIDS: 1,100 (2009 est.)
country comparison to the world: 144

HIV/AIDS—deaths: fewer than 100 (2009 est.)
country comparison to the world: 135

Obesity—adult prevalence rate: 20.9% (2008)
country comparison to the world: 94

Children under the age of 5 years underweight: 8.6% (2009)
country comparison to the world: 72

Education expenditures: 4.3% of GDP (2009)
country comparison to the world: 100

Literacy: *definition:* age 15 and over can read and write
total population: 86.9%
male: 90.2%
female: 81.8% (2010 est.)

School life expectancy (primary to tertiary education): *total:* 14 years
male: 13 years
female: 14 years (2011)

GOVERNMENT

Country name: *conventional long form:* Sultanate of Oman
conventional short form: Oman
local long form: Saltanat Uman
local short form: Uman
former: Muscat and Oman

Government type: monarchy

Capital: *name:* Muscat

geographic coordinates: 23 37 N, 58 35 E
time difference: UTC+4 (9 hours ahead of Washington, DC during Standard Time)

Administrative divisions: 11 governorates (muhafazat, singular—muhafazat); Ad Dakhiliyah, Al Buraymi, Al Wusta, Az Zahirah, Janub al Batinah (Al Batinah South), Janub ash Sharqiyah (Ash Sharqiyah South), Masqat (Muscat), Musandam, Shamal al Batinah (Al Batinah North), Shamal ash Sharqiyah (Ash Sharqiyah North), Zufar (Dhofar)

Independence: 1650 (expulsion of the Portuguese)

National holiday: Birthday of Sultan QABOOS, 18 November (1940)

Constitution: previous 1996 (The Basic Law of the Sultanate of Oman serves as the constitution); latest amended by royal decree in 2011 (2011)

Legal system: mixed legal system of Anglo-Saxon law and Islamic law

International law organization participation: has not submitted an ICJ jurisdiction declaration; non-party state to the ICCt

Suffrage: 21 years of age; universal; note—members of the military and security forces by law are not allowed to vote

Executive branch: *chief of state:* Sultan and Prime Minister QABOOS bin Said Al-Said (sultan since 23 July 1970 and prime minister since 23 July 1972); note—the monarch is both the chief of state and head of government
head of government: Sultan and Prime Minister QABOOS bin Said Al-Said (sultan since 23 July 1970 and prime minister since 23 July 1972)
cabinet: Cabinet appointed by the monarch (For more information visit the World Leaders website)
elections: the Ruling Family Council determines a successor from the Sultan's extended family; if the Council cannot form a consensus within three days of the Sultan's death or incapacitation, the Defense Council will relay a predetermined heir as chosen by the Sultan

Legislative branch: bicameral—consists of Majlis al-Dawla or upper chamber (71 seats; members appointed by the sultan; has only advisory powers) and Majlis al-Shura or lower chamber (84 seats; members elected by popular vote to serve four-year terms; body has authority to draft legislation but is subordinate to the Sultan)
elections: (Majlis al-Shura) last held on 15 October 2011 (next to be held in October 2015)
election results: percent of vote by party—NA; seats by party—NA; note—three prominent figures from the Arab Spring 2011 protests won seats; one woman also won a seat

Judicial branch: *highest court(s):* Supreme Court (consists of 5 judges)
judge selection and term of office: judges nominated by the 9-member Supreme Judicial Council (chaired by the monarch) and appointed by the monarch; judge tenure NA
subordinate courts: Courts of Appeal; Courts of First Instance; sharia courts; magistrates' courts

Political parties and leaders: political parties are illegal

Political pressure groups and leaders: none

International organization participation: ABEDA, AFESD, AMF, CAEU, FAO, G-77, GCC, IAEA, IBRD, ICAO, ICC (NGOs), IDA, IDB, IFAD, IFC, IHO, ILO, IMF, IMO, IMSO, Interpol, IOC, IPU, ISO, ITSO, ITU, LAS, MIGA, NAM, OIC, OPCW, UN, UNCTAD, UNESCO, UNIDO, UNWTO, UPU, WCO, WFTU (NGOs), WHO, WIPO, WMO, WTO

Diplomatic representation in the US:
chief of mission: Ambassador Hunaina bint Sultan bin Ahmad al-MUGHAIRI (since 9 November 2005)
chancery: 2535 Belmont Road, NW, Washington, DC 20008
telephone: [1] (202) 387-1980
FAX: [1] (202) 745-4933

Diplomatic representation from the US:
chief of mission: Ambassador Greta C. HOLTZ (since 27 September 2012)
embassy: Jamait Ad Duwal Al Arabiyya Street, Al Khuwair area, Muscat
mailing address: P. O. Box 202, P.C. 115, Madinat Al Sultan Qaboos, Muscat
telephone: [968] 24-643-400
FAX: [968] 24-64-37-40

Flag description: three horizontal bands of white, red, and green of equal width with a broad, vertical, red band on the hoist side; the national emblem (a khanjar dagger in its sheath superimposed on two crossed swords in scabbards) in white is centered near the top of the vertical band; white represents peace and prosperity, red recalls battles against foreign invaders, and green symbolizes the Jebel Akhdar (Green Mountains) and fertility

National symbol(s): Khanjar dagger superimposed on two crossed swords

National anthem: *name:* "Nashid as-Salaam as-Sultani" (The Sultan's Anthem)
lyrics/music: Rashid bin Uzayyiz al KHUSAIDI/ James Frederick MILLS, arranged by Bernard EBBINGHAUS
note: adopted 1932; new words were written after QABOOS bin Said al Said gained power in 1970; the anthem was first performed by the band of a British ship as a salute to the Sultan during a 1932 visit to Muscat; the bandmaster of the HMS Hawkins was asked to write a salutation to the Sultan on the occasion of his visiting the ship

ECONOMY

Economy—overview: Oman is a middle-income economy that is heavily dependent on dwindling oil resources. Because of declining reserves and a rapidly growing labor force, Muscat has actively pursued a development plan that focuses on diversification, industrialization, and privatization, with the objective of reducing the oil sector's contribution to GDP to 9% by 2020 and creating more jobs to employ the rising numbers of Omanis entering the workforce. Tourism and gas-based industries are key components of the government's diversification strategy. However, increases in social welfare benefits, particularly since the Arab Spring, will challenge the government's ability to effectively balance its budget if oil revenues decline. By using enhanced oil recovery techniques, Oman succeeded in increasing oil production, giving the country more time to diversify, and the increase in global oil prices through 2011 provided the government greater financial resources to invest in non-oil sectors. In 2012, continued surpluses resulting from sustained high oil prices and increased enhanced oil recovery allowed the government to maintain growth in social subsidies and public sector job creation. However, the Sultan made widely reported statements indicating this would not be sustainable, and called for expanded efforts to support SME development and entrepreneurship. Government agencies and large oligarchic group companies heeded his call, announcing new initiatives to spin off non-essential functions to entrepreneurs, incubate new businesses, train and mentor up and coming business people, and provide financing for start-ups. In response to fast growth in household indebtedness, the Central Bank reduced the ceiling on personal interest loans from 8 to 7%, lowered mortgage rates, capped the percentage of consumer loans at 50% of borrower's salaries for personal loans and 60% for housing loans, and limited maximum repayment terms to 10 and 25 years respectively.

GDP (purchasing power parity): $94.86 billion (2013 est.)
country comparison to the world: 77
$90.28 billion (2012 est.)
$85.99 billion (2011 est.)
note: data are in 2013 US dollars

GDP (official exchange rate): $81.95 billion (2013 est.)

GDP—real growth rate: 5.1% (2013 est.)
country comparison to the world: 52
5% (2012 est.)

4.5% (2011 est.)

GDP—per capita (PPP): $29,800 (2013 est.)
country comparison to the world: 50
$29,200 (2012 est.)
$28,700 (2011 est.)
note: data are in 2013 US dollars

Gross national saving: 36.2% of GDP (2013 est.)
country comparison to the world: 15
37.4% of GDP (2012 est.)
41% of GDP (2011 est.)

GDP—composition, by end use:
household consumption: 30.5%
government consumption: 17.8%
investment in fixed capital: 27.3%
investment in inventories: -0.5%
exports of goods and services: 63.8%
imports of goods and services: -39.4% (2013 est.)

GDP—composition, by sector of origin:
agriculture: 1%
industry: 64.4%
services: 34.6% (2013 est.)

Agriculture—products: dates, limes, bananas, alfalfa, vegetables; camels, cattle; fish

Industries: crude oil production and refining, natural and liquefied natural gas (LNG) production; construction, cement, copper, steel, chemicals, optic fiber

Industrial production growth rate: 3.5% (2013 est.)
country comparison to the world: 86

Labor force: 968,800
country comparison to the world: 144
note: about 60% of the labor force is non-national (2007)

Labor force—by occupation:
agriculture: NA%
industry: NA%
services: NA%

Unemployment rate: 15% (2004 est.)
country comparison to the world: 142

Population below poverty line: NA%

Household income or consumption by percentage share: *lowest* 10%: NA%
highest 10%: NA%

Budget: *revenues:* $34.42 billion
expenditures: $35.48 billion (2013 est.)

Taxes and other revenues: 42% of GDP (2013 est.)
country comparison to the world: 30

Budget surplus (+) or deficit (-):
-1.3% of GDP (2013 est.)
country comparison to the world: 68

Public debt: 4.4% of GDP (2013 est.)
country comparison to the world: 159
4.3% of GDP (2012 est.)

Fiscal year: calendar year

Inflation rate (consumer prices): 1.6% (2013 est.)
country comparison to the world: 42
2.9% (2012 est.)

Central bank discount rate: 2% (31 December 2010 est.)
country comparison to the world: 143
0.05% (31 December 2009 est.)

Commercial bank prime lending rate: 5.8% (31 December 2013 est.)
country comparison to the world: 144
5.65% (31 December 2012 est.)

Stock of narrow money: $9.537 billion (31 December 2013 est.)
country comparison to the world: 80
$9.083 billion (31 December 2012 est.)

Stock of broad money: $71.42 billion (31 December 2010 est.)
country comparison to the world: 61
$63.16 billion (31 December 2009 est.)

Stock of domestic credit: $29.97 billion (31 December 2013 est.)
country comparison to the world: 71
$27.62 billion (31 December 2012 est.)

Market value of publicly traded shares: $20.11 billion (31 December 2012 est.)
country comparison to the world: 63
$19.72 billion (31 December 2011)
$20.27 billion (31 December 2010 est.)

Current account balance: $7.249 billion (2013 est.)
country comparison to the world: 28
$8.312 billion (2012 est.)

Exports: $56.22 billion (2013 est.)
country comparison to the world: 57
$52.14 billion (2012 est.)

Exports—commodities: petroleum, reexports, fish, metals, textiles

Exports—partners: China 31.8%, Japan 12.9%, UAE 10.4%, South Korea 10%, Thailand 4.4%, Singapore 4.4% (2012)

Imports: $30.75 billion (2013 est.)
country comparison to the world: 67
$25.63 billion (2012 est.)

Imports—commodities: machinery and transport equipment, manufactured goods, food, livestock, lubricants

Imports—partners: UAE 24.1%, Japan 12.5%, India 8.5%, China 6.3%, US 6.1% (2012)

Reserves of foreign exchange and gold: $17.7 billion (31 December 2013 est.)
country comparison to the world: 62
$14.4 billion (31 December 2012 est.)

Debt—external: $10.84 billion (31 December 2013 est.)
country comparison to the world: 99
$9.99 billion (31 December 2012 est.)

Stock of direct foreign investment—at home: $NA

Stock of direct foreign investment—abroad: $NA

Exchange rates: Omani rials (OMR) per US dollar—
0.3845 (2013 est.)
0.3845 (2012 est.)
0.3845 (2010 est.)
0.3845 (2009)
0.3845 (2008)

ENERGY

Electricity—production: 18.63 billion kWh (2010 est.)
country comparison to the world: 7 6

Electricity—consumption: 15.32 billion kWh (2010 est.)
country comparison to the world: 76

Electricity—exports: 0 kWh (2012 est.)
country comparison to the world: 171

Electricity—imports: 0 kWh (2012 est.)
country comparison to the world: 173

Electricity—installed generating capacity: 4.265 million kW (2010 est.)
country comparison to the world: 78

Electricity—from fossil fuels: 100% of total installed capacity (2010 est.)
country comparison to the world: 24

Electricity—from nuclear fuels: 0% of total installed capacity (2010 est.)
country comparison to the world: 143

Electricity—from hydroelectric plants: 0% of total installed capacity (2010 est.)
country comparison to the world: 185

Electricity—from other renewable sources: 0% of total installed capacity (2010 est.)
country comparison to the world: 204

Crude oil—production: 923,800 bbl/day (2012 est.)
country comparison to the world: 26

Crude oil—exports: 705,100 bbl/day (2010 est.)
country comparison to the world: 20

Crude oil—imports: 0 bbl/day (2010 est.)
country comparison to the world: 96

Crude oil—proved reserves: 5.5 billion bbl (1 January 2013 es)
country comparison to the world: 22

Refined petroleum products—production: 164,600 bbl/day (2010 est.)
country comparison to the world: 60

Refined petroleum products—consumption: 98,000 bbl/day (2011 est.)
country comparison to the world: 79

Refined petroleum products—exports: 47,710 bbl/day (2010 est.)
country comparison to the world: 61

Refined petroleum products—imports: 2,390 bbl/day (2010 est.)
country comparison to the world: 177

Natural gas—production: 35.94 billion cu m (2012 est.)
country comparison to the world: 27

Natural gas—consumption: 17.53 billion cu m (2011 est.)
country comparison to the world: 37

Natural gas—exports: 10.93 billion cu m (2011 est.)
country comparison to the world: 23

Natural gas—imports: 1.95 billion cu m (2011 est.)
country comparison to the world: 51

Natural gas—proved reserves: 849.5 billion cu m (1 January 2013 es)
country comparison to the world: 29

Carbon dioxide emissions from consumption of energy: 52.67 million Mt (2011 est.)
country comparison to the world: 60

COMMUNICATIONS

Telephones—main lines in use: 305,000 (2012)
country comparison to the world: 115

Telephones—mobile cellular: 5.278 million (2012)
country comparison to the world: 109

Telephone system: *general assessment:* modern system consisting of open-wire, microwave, and radiotelephone communication stations; limited coaxial cable; domestic satellite system with 8 earth stations

domestic: fixed-line and mobile-cellular subscribership both increasing with fixed-line phone service gradually being introduced to remote villages using wireless local loop systems
international: country code—968; the Fiber-Optic Link Around the Globe (FLAG) and the SEA-ME-WE-3 submarine cable provide connectivity to Asia, the Middle East, and Europe; satellite earth stations—2 Intelsat (Indian Ocean), 1 Arabsat (2008)

Broadcast media: 1 state-run TV broadcaster; TV stations transmitting from Saudi Arabia, the UAE, and Yemen available via satellite TV; state-run radio operates multiple stations; first private radio station began operating in 2007 and 2 additional stations now operating (2007)

Internet country code: .om

Internet hosts: 14,531 (2012)
country comparison to the world: 127

Internet users: 1.465 million (2009)
country comparison to the world: 83

TRANSPORTATION

Airports: 132 (2013)
country comparison to the world: 4 4

Airports—with paved runways: *total:* 1 3
over 3,047 m: 7
2,438 to 3,047 m: 5
914 to 1,523 m: 1 (2013)

Airports—with unpaved runways: *total:* 119
over 3,047 m: 2
2,438 to 3,047 m: 7
1,524 to 2,437 m: 51
914 to 1,523 m: 33
under 914 m: 26 (2013)

Heliports: 3 (2013)

Pipelines: condensate 106 km; gas 4,224 km; oil 3,558 km; oil/gas/water 33 km; refined products 264 km (2013)

Roadways: *total:* 60,240 km
country comparison to the world: 70
paved: 29,685 km (includes 1,943 km of expressways)
unpaved: 30,545 km (2012)

Merchant marine: *total:* 5
country comparison to the world: 125
by type: chemical tanker 1, passenger 1, passenger/cargo 3
registered in other countries: 15 (Malta 5, Panama 10) (2010)

Ports and terminals: *major seaport(s):* Mina' Qabus, Salalah, Suhar
container port(s) (TEUs): Salalah (3,200,000)

MILITARY

Military branches: Sultan's Armed Forces (SAF): Royal Army of Oman, Royal Navy of Oman, Royal Air Force of Oman (al-Quwwat al-Jawwiya al-Sultanat Oman) (2013)

Military service age and obligation: 18-30 years of age for voluntary military service; no conscription (2012)

Manpower available for military service:
males age 16-49: 985,957
females age 16-49: 737,812 (2010 est.)

Manpower fit for military service:
males age 16-49: 837,886
females age 16-49: 642,427 (2010 est.)

Manpower reaching militarily significant age annually: *male:* 31,959
female: 30,264 (2010 est.)

Military expenditures: 8.61% of GDP (2012)
country comparison to the world: 2
6.13% of GDP (2011)
8.61% of GDP (2010)

TRANSNATIONAL ISSUES

Disputes—international: boundary agreement reportedly signed and ratified with UAE in 2003 for entire border, including Oman's Musandam Peninsula and Al Madhah exclave, but details of the alignment have not been made public

PACIFIC OCEAN

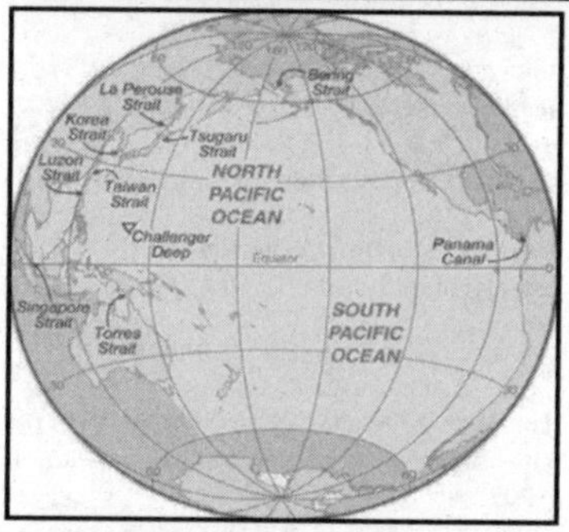

INTRODUCTION

Background: The Pacific Ocean is the largest of the world's five oceans (followed by the Atlantic Ocean, Indian Ocean, Southern Ocean, and Arctic Ocean). Strategically important access waterways include the La Perouse, Tsugaru, Tsushima, Taiwan, Singapore, and Torres Straits. The decision by the International Hydrographic Organization in the spring of 2000 to delimit a fifth ocean, the Southern Ocean, removed the portion of the Pacific Ocean south of 60 degrees south.

GEOGRAPHY

Location: body of water between the Southern Ocean, Asia, Australia, and the Western Hemisphere

Geographic coordinates: 0 00 N, 160 00 W

Map references: Political Map of the World

Area: *total*: 155.557 million sq km
note: includes Bali Sea, Bering Sea, Bering Strait, Coral Sea, East China Sea, Gulf of Alaska, Gulf of Tonkin, Philippine Sea, Sea of Japan, Sea of Okhotsk, South China Sea, Tasman Sea, and other tributary water bodies

Area—comparative: about 15 times the size of the US; covers about 28% of the global surface; almost equal to the total land area of the world

Coastline: 135,663 km

Climate: planetary air pressure systems and resultant wind patterns exhibit remarkable uniformity in the south and east; trade winds and westerly winds are well-developed patterns, modified by seasonal fluctuations; tropical cyclones (hurricanes) may form south of Mexico from June to October and affect Mexico and Central America; continental influences cause climatic uniformity to be much less pronounced in the eastern and western regions at the same latitude in the North Pacific Ocean; the western Pacific is monsoonal—a rainy season occurs during the summer months, when moisture-laden winds blow from the ocean over the land, and a dry season during the winter months, when dry winds blow from the Asian landmass back to the ocean; tropical cyclones (typhoons) may strike southeast and east Asia from May to December

Terrain: surface currents in the northern Pacific are dominated by a clockwise, warm-water gyre (broad circular system of currents) and in the southern Pacific by a counterclockwise, cool-water gyre; in the northern Pacific, sea ice forms in the Bering Sea and Sea of Okhotsk in winter; in the southern Pacific, sea ice from Antarctica reaches its northernmost extent in October; the ocean floor in the eastern Pacific is dominated by the East Pacific Rise, while the western Pacific is dissected by deep trenches, including the Mariana Trench, which is the world's deepest

Elevation extremes: *lowest point:* Challenger Deep in the Mariana Trench -10,924 m
highest point: sea level 0 m

Natural resources: oil and gas fields, polymetallic nodules, sand and gravel aggregates, placer deposits, fish

Natural hazards: surrounded by a zone of violent volcanic and earthquake activity sometimes referred to as the "Pacific Ring of Fire"; subject to tropical cyclones (typhoons) in southeast and east Asia from May to December (most frequent from July to October); tropical cyclones (hurricanes) may form south of Mexico and strike Central America and Mexico from June to October (most common in August and September); cyclical El Nino/La Nina phenomenon occurs in the equatorial Pacific, influencing weather in the Western Hemisphere and the western Pacific; ships subject to superstructure icing in extreme north from October to May; persistent fog in the northern Pacific can be a maritime hazard from June to December

Environment—current issues: endangered marine species include the dugong, sea lion, sea otter, seals, turtles, and whales; oil pollution in Philippine Sea and South China Sea Geography—note: the major chokepoints are the Bering Strait, Panama Canal, Luzon Strait, and the Singapore Strait; the Equator divides the Pacific Ocean into the North Pacific Ocean and the South Pacific Ocean; dotted with low coral islands and rugged volcanic islands in the southwestern Pacific Ocean

ECONOMY

Economy—overview: The Pacific Ocean is a major contributor to the world economy and particularly to those nations its waters directly touch. It provides low-cost sea transportation between East and West, extensive fishing grounds, offshore oil and gas fields, minerals, and sand and gravel for the construction industry. In 1996, over 60% of the world's fish catch came from the Pacific Ocean. Exploitation of offshore oil and gas reserves is playing an ever-increasing role in the energy supplies of the US, Australia, NZ, China, and Peru. The high cost of recovering offshore oil and gas, combined with the wide swings in world prices for oil since 1985, has led to fluctuations in new drillings.

TRANSPORTATION

Ports and terminals: *major seaport(s)*: Bangkok (Thailand), Hong Kong (China), Kao-hsiung (Taiwan), Los Angeles (US), Manila (Philippines), Pusan (South Korea), San Francisco (US), Seattle (US), Shanghai (China), Singapore, Sydney (Australia), Vladivostok (Russia), Wellington (NZ), Yokohama (Japan)

Transportation—note: the Inside Passage offers protected waters from southeast Alaska to Puget Sound (Washington state); the International Maritime Bureau reports the territorial waters of littoral states and offshore waters in the South China Sea as high risk for piracy and armed robbery against ships; numerous commercial vessels have been attacked and hijacked both at anchor and while underway; hijacked vessels are often disguised and cargoes stolen; crew and passengers are often held for ransom, murdered, or cast adrift

TRANSNATIONAL ISSUES PACIFIC OCEAN

Disputes—international: some maritime disputes (see littoral states)

PAKISTAN

INTRODUCTION

Background: The Indus Valley civilization, one of the oldest in the world and dating back at least 5,000 years, spread over much of what is presently Pakistan. During the second millennium B.C., remnants of this culture fused with the migrating Indo-Aryan peoples. The area underwent successive invasions in subsequent centuries from the Persians, Greeks, Scythians, Arabs (who brought Islam), Afghans, and Turks. The Mughal Empire flourished in the 16th and 17th centuries; the British came to dominate the region in the 18th century. The separation in 1947 of British India into the Muslim state of Pakistan (with West and East sections) and largely Hindu India was never satisfactorily resolved, and India and Pakistan fought two wars—in 1947-48 and 1965—over the disputed Kashmir territory. A third war between these countries in 1971—in which India capitalized on Islamabad's marginalization of Bengalis in Pakistani politics—resulted in East Pakistan becoming the separate nation of Bangladesh. In response to Indian nuclear weapons testing, Pakistan conducted its own tests in 1998. India-Pakistan relations have been rocky since the November 2008 Mumbai attacks, but both countries are taking small steps to put relations back on track. In February 2008, Pakistan held parliamentary elections and in September 2008, after the resignation of former President MUSHARRAF, elected Asif Ali ZARDARI to the presidency. Pakistani government and military leaders are struggling to control domestic insurgents, many of whom are located in the tribal areas adjacent to the border with Afghanistan.

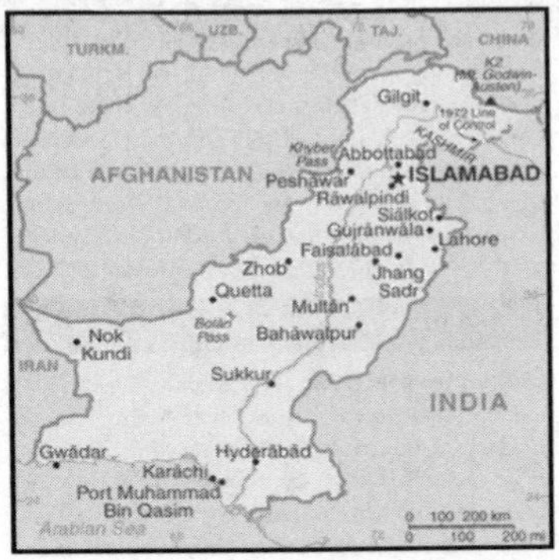

GEOGRAPHY

Location: Southern Asia, bordering the Arabian Sea, between India on the east and Iran and Afghanistan on the west and China in the north

Geographic coordinates: 30 00 N, 70 00 E

Map references: Asia

Area: *total:* 796,095 sq km
country comparison to the world: 36
land: 770,875 sq km
water: 25,220 sq km

Area—comparative: slightly more than five times the size of Georgia; slightly less than twice the size of California

Land boundaries: *total:* 6,774 km
border countries: Afghanistan 2,430 km, China 523 km, India 2,912 km, Iran 909 km

Coastline: 1,046 km

Maritime claims: *territorial sea:* 12 nm
contiguous zone: 24 nm
exclusive economic zone: 200 nm
continental shelf: 200 nm or to the edge of the continental margin

Climate: mostly hot, dry desert; temperate in northwest; arctic in north

Terrain: flat Indus plain in east; mountains in north and northwest; Balochistan plateau in west

Elevation extremes: *lowest point:* Indian Ocean 0 m
highest point: K2 (Mt. Godwin-Austen) 8,611 m

Natural resources: land, extensive natural gas reserves, limited petroleum, poor quality coal, iron ore, copper, salt, limestone

Land use: *arable land:* 26.02%
permanent crops: 1.05%
other: 72.93% (2011)

Irrigated land: 199,900 sq km (2008)

Total renewable water resources: 246.8 cu km (2011)

Freshwater withdrawal (domestic/industrial/agricultural): *total:* 183.5 cu km/yr (5%/1%/94%)
per capita: 1,038 cu m/yr (2008)

Natural hazards: frequent earthquakes, occasionally severe especially in north and west; flooding along the Indus after heavy rains (July and August)

Environment—current issues: water pollution from raw sewage, industrial wastes, and agricultural runoff; limited natural freshwater resources; most of the population does not have access to potable water; deforestation; soil erosion; desertification

Environment—international agreements: *party to:* Biodiversity, Climate Change, Climate Change-Kyoto Protocol, Desertification, Endangered Species, Environmental Modification, Hazardous Wastes, Law of the Sea, Marine Dumping, Ozone Layer Protection, Ship Pollution, Wetlands
signed, but not ratified: Marine Life Conservation

Geography—note: controls Khyber Pass and Bolan Pass, traditional invasion routes between Central Asia and the Indian Subcontinent

PEOPLE AND SOCIETY

Nationality: *noun:* Pakistani(s)
adjective: Pakistani

Ethnic groups: Punjabi 44.68%, Pashtun (Pathan) 15.42%, Sindhi 14.1%, Sariaki 8.38%, Muhajirs 7.57%, Balochi 3.57%, other 6.28%

Languages: Punjabi 48%, Sindhi 12%, Saraiki (a Punjabi variant) 10%, Pashto (alternate name, Pashtu) 8%, Urdu (official) 8%, Balochi 3%, Hindko 2%, Brahui 1%, English (official; lingua franca of Pakistani elite and most government ministries), Burushaski, and other 8%

Religions: Muslim (official) 96.4% (Sunni 85-90%, Shia 10-15%), other (includes Christian and Hindu) 3.6% (2010 est.)

Population: 196,174,380 (July 2014 est.)
country comparison to the world: 7

Age structure:
0-14 years: 33.3% (male 33,595,949/female 31,797,766)
15-24 years: 21.5% (male 21,803,617/female 20,463,184)
25-54 years: 35.7% (male 36,390,119/female 33,632,395)
55-64 years: 4.3% (male 5,008,681/female 5,041,434)
65 years and over: 4.3% (male 3,951,190/female 4,490,045) (2014 est.)

Dependency ratios:
total dependency ratio: 61.8 %
youth dependency ratio: 54.7 %
elderly dependency ratio: 7.1 %
potential support ratio: 14.1 (2013)

Median age: *total:* 22.6 years
male: 22.6 years
female: 22.6 years (2014 est.)

Population growth rate: 1.49% (2014 est.)
country comparison to the world: 80

Birth rate: 23.19 births/1,000 population (2014 est.)
country comparison to the world: 71

Death rate: 6.58 deaths/1,000 population (2014 est.)
country comparison to the world: 147

Net migration rate: -1.69 migrant(s)/1,000 population (2014 est.)
country comparison to the world: 160

Urbanization: *urban population:* 36.2% of total population (2011)
rate of urbanization: 2.68% annual rate of change (2010-15 est.)

Major urban areas—population: Karachi 13.125 million; Lahore 7.132 million; Faisalabad 2.849 million; Rawalpindi 2.026 million; ISLAMABAD (capital) 832,000 (2009)

Sex ratio: *at birth:* 1.05 male(s)/female
0-14 years: 1.06 male(s)/female
15-24 years: 1.07 male(s)/female
25-54 years: 1.08 male(s)/female
55-64 years: 1.06 male(s)/female
65 years and over: 0.89 male(s)/female
total population: 1.06 male(s)/female (2014 est.)

Mother's mean age at first birth: 22.7 (2007 est.)

Maternal mortality rate: 260 deaths/100,000 live births (2010)
country comparison to the world: 44

Infant mortality rate: *total:* 57.48 deaths/1,000 live births
country comparison to the world: 25
male: 60.67 deaths/1,000 live births
female: 54.13 deaths/1,000 live births (2014 est.)

Life expectancy at birth: *total population:* 67.05 years
country comparison to the world: 167
male: 65.16 years
female: 69.03 years (2014 est.)

Total fertility rate: 2.86 children born/woman (2014 est.)
country comparison to the world: 63

Contraceptive prevalence rate: 27% (2007/08)

Health expenditures: 2.5% of GDP (2011)
country comparison to the world: 185

Physicians density: 0.81 physicians/1,000 population (2009)

Hospital bed density: 0.6 beds/1,000 population (2010)

Drinking water source:
improved:
urban: 95.7% of population
rural: 89% of population
total: 91.4% of population
unimproved:
urban: 4.3% of population
rural: 11% of population
total: 8.6% of population (2011 est.)

Sanitation facility access:
improved:
urban: 71.8% of population
rural: 33.6% of population
total: 47.4% of population
unimproved:
urban: 28.2% of population
rural: 66.4% of population
total: 52.6% of population (2011 est.)

HIV/AIDS—adult prevalence rate: 0.1% (2012 est.)
country comparison to the world: 166

HIV/AIDS—people living with HIV/AIDS: 86,700 (2012 est.)
country comparison to the world: 47

HIV/AIDS—deaths: 3,500 (2012 est.)
country comparison to the world: 48

Major infectious diseases: *degree of risk:* high
food or waterborne diseases: bacterial diarrhea, hepatitis A and E, and typhoid fever
vectorborne diseases: dengue fever and malaria
animal contact disease: rabies
note: highly pathogenic H5N1 avian influenza has been identified in this country; it poses a negligible risk with extremely rare cases possible among US citizens who have close contact with birds (2013)

Obesity—adult prevalence rate: 5.5% (2008)
country comparison to the world: 153

Children under the age of 5 years underweight: 30.9% (2011)

country comparison to the world: 14

Education expenditures: 2.1% of GDP (2012)
country comparison to the world: 164

Literacy: *definition:* age 15 and over can read and write
total population: 54.9%
male: 68.6%
female: 40.3% (2009 est.)

School life expectancy (primary to tertiary education): *total:* 8 years
male: 8 years
female: 7 years (2012)

Unemployment, youth ages 15-24: *total:* 7.7%
country comparison to the world: 124
male: 7%
female: 10.5% (2008)

GOVERNMENT

Country name: *conventional long form:* Islamic Republic of Pakistan
conventional short form: Pakistan
local long form: Jamhuryat Islami Pakistan
local short form: Pakistan
former: West Pakistan

Government type: federal republic

Capital: *name:* Islamabad

geographic coordinates: 33 41 N, 73 03 E
time difference: UTC+5 (10 hours ahead of Washington, DC during Standard Time)

Administrative divisions: 4 provinces, 1 territory*, and 1 capital territory**; Balochistan, Federally Administered Tribal Areas*, Islamabad Capital Territory**, Khyber Pakhtunkhwa (formerly North-West Frontier Province), Punjab, Sindh
note: the Pakistani-administered portion of the disputed Jammu and Kashmir region consists of *two administrative entities:* Azad Kashmir and Gilgit-Baltistan

Independence: 14 August 1947 (from British India)

National holiday: Pakistan Day (also referred to as Pakistan Resolution Day or Republic Day), 23 March (1940); note—commemorates both the adoption of the Lahore Resolution by the All-India Muslim League during its 22-24 March 1940 session, which called for the creation of independent Muslim states, and the adoption of the first constitution of Pakistan during the transition to the Islamic Republic of Pakistan on 23 March 1956

Constitution: several previous; latest endorsed 12 April 1973, passed 19 April 1973, entered into force 14 August 1973 (suspended and restored several times); amended many times, last in 2012 (2012)

Legal system: common law system with Islamic law influence

International law organization participation: accepts compulsory ICJ jurisdiction with reservations; non-party state to the ICCt

Suffrage: 18 years of age; universal; note—there are joint electorates and reserved parliamentary seats for women and non-Muslims

Executive branch: *chief of state:* President Mamnoon HUSSAIN (since 9 September 2013)
head of government: Prime Minister Mohammad Nawaz SHARIF (since 5 June 2013)
cabinet: Cabinet appointed by the president upon the advice of the prime minister (For more information visit the World Leaders website)
elections: president elected by secret ballot through an Electoral College comprising the members of the Senate, National Assembly, and provincial assemblies for a five-year term; election last held on 9 September 2013 (next to be held in 2018); prime minister selected by the National Assembly
election results: Mamnoon HUSSAIN elected president; Mamnoon HUSSAIN 432 votes, Wajihuddin AHMED 77 votes

Legislative branch: bicameral parliament or Majlis-e-Shoora consists of the Senate (104 seats; members indirectly elected by provincial assemblies and the territories' representatives in the National Assembly to serve six-year terms; one half are elected every three years) and the National Assembly (342 seats; 272 members elected by popular vote; 60 seats reserved for women; 10 seats reserved for non-Muslims; members serve five-year terms)
elections: Senate—last held on 2 March 2012 (next to be held in March 2015); National Assembly—last held on 11 May 2013 (next to be held in 2018)
election results: Senate—percent of vote by party—NA; seats by party—PPPP 41, PML-N 14, ANP 12, JUI-F 7, MQM 7, PML-Q 5, BNP-A 4, NPP 1, PML-F 1, independents 12; National Assembly—percent of votes by party—NA; seats by party as of June 2013)—PML-N 126, PPPP 31, PTI 28, MQM 18, JUI-F 10, PML-F 5, other 22, independents 25, unfilled seats 7; 60 seats reserved for women, 10 seats reserved for non-Muslims

Judicial branch: *highest court(s):* Supreme Court of Pakistan (consists of the chief justice and 16 judges)
judge selection and term of office: justices nominated by an 8-member Majlis-e-Shoora (parliamentary) Committee upon the recommendation of the Judicial Commission (a 9-member body of several judges and other judicial professionals), and appointed by the president of Pakistan; justices can serve until age 65
subordinate courts: High Courts; Federal Shariat Court; provincial and district civil and criminal courts; specialized courts for issues such as taxation, banking, customs, etc.

Political parties and leaders: Awami National Party or ANP [Asfandyar Wali KHAN]; Balochistan National Party-Awami or BNP-A; Balochistan National Party-Hayee Group or BNP-H [Dr. Hayee BALOCH]; Balochistan National Party-Mengal or BNP-M; Jamaat-i Islami or JI [Syed Munawar HASAN]; Jamhoori Watan Party or JWP; Jamiat Ahle Hadith or JAH [Sajid MIR]; Jamiat-i Ulema-i Islam Fazl-ur Rehman or JUI-F [Fazl-ur REHMAN]; Jamiat-i Ulema-i Islam Sami-ul HAQ or JUI-S [Sami ul-HAQ]; Jamiat-i Ulema-i Pakistan or JUP [Abul Khair ZUBAIR]; Millat-e-Jafferia [Allama Sajid NAQVI]; Muttahida Qaumi Movement or MQM [Altaf HUSSAIN]; National Peoples Party or NPP; Pakhtun-khwa Milli Awami Party or PKMAP [Mahmood Khan ACHAKZAI]; Pakistan Awami Tehrik or PAT [Tahir ul QADRI]; Pakistan Muslim League-Quaid-i Azam or PML-Q [Chaudhry Shujaat HUSSAIN]; Pakistan Muslim League-Functional or PML-F [Pir PAGARO]; Pakistan Muslim League-Nawaz or PML-N [Nawaz SHARIF]; Pakistan Peoples Party Parliamentarians or PPPP [Bilawal Bhutto ZARDARI, chairman; Asif Ali; ZARDARI, co-chairman]; Pakistan Peoples Party-S [Aftab Ahmad SHERPAO]; Quami Watan Party or QWP [Aftab Ahmed Khan SHERPAO]; Pakistan Tehrik-e Insaaf or PTI [Imran KHAN]
note: political alliances in Pakistan can shift frequently

Political pressure groups and leaders:
other: military (most important political force); ulema (clergy); landowners; industrialists; small merchants

International organization participation: ADB, ARF, ASEAN (dialogue partner), C, CICA, CP, D-8, ECO, FAO, G-11, G-24, G-77, IAEA, IBRD, ICAO, ICC (national committees), ICRM, IDA, IDB, IFAD, IFC, IFRCS, IHO, ILO, IMF, IMO, IMSO, Interpol, IOC, IOM, IPU, ISO, ITSO, ITU, ITUC (NGOs), LAIA (observer), MIGA, MINURSO, MONUSCO, NAM, OAS (observer), OIC, OPCW, PCA, SAARC, SACEP, SCO (observer), UN, UNAMID, UNCTAD, UNESCO, UNHCR, UNIDO, UNISFA, UNMIL, UNMIT, UNOCI, UNWTO, UPU, WCO, WFTU (NGOs), WHO, WIPO, WMO, WTO

Diplomatic representation in the US:
chief of mission: Ambassador Jalil Abbas JILANI (since 10 March 2014)
chancery: 3517 International Court, Washington, DC 20008
telephone: [1] (202) 243-6500
FAX: [1] (202) 686-1534
consulate(s) general: Chicago, Houston, Los Angeles, New York, Sunnyvale (CA)
consulate(s): Chicago, Houston

Diplomatic representation from the US:
chief of mission: Ambassador Richard OLSON (since 24 September 2012)
embassy: Diplomatic Enclave, Ramna 5, Islamabad
mailing address: 8100 Islamabad Pl., Washington, DC 20521-8100
telephone: [92] (51) 208-0000
FAX: [92] (51) 227-6427
consulate(s) general: Karachi
consulate(s): Lahore, Peshawar

Flag description: green with a vertical white band (symbolizing the role of religious minorities) on the hoist side; a large white crescent and star are centered in the green field; the crescent, star, and color green are traditional symbols of Islam

National symbol(s): star and crescent

National anthem: *name:* "Qaumi Tarana" (National Anthem)
lyrics/music: Abu-Al-Asar Hafeez JULLANDHURI/Ahmed Ghulamali CHAGLA
note: adopted 1954; the anthem is also known as "Pak sarzamin shad bad" (Blessed Be the Sacred **Land)**

ECONOMY

Economy—overview: Decades of internal political disputes and low levels of foreign investment have led to slow growth and underdevelopment in Pakistan. Agriculture accounts for more than one-fifth of output and two-fifths of employment. Textiles account for most of Pakistan's export earnings, and Pakistan's failure to expand a viable export base for other manufactures has left the country vulnerable to shifts in world demand. Official unemployment was 6.6% in 2013, but this fails to capture the true picture, because much of the economy is informal and underemployment remains high. Over the past few years, low growth and high inflation, led by a spurt in food prices, have increased the amount of poverty. As a result of political and economic instability, the Pakistani rupee has depreciated more than 40% since 2007. The government agreed to an International

Monetary Fund Standby Arrangement in November 2008 in response to a balance of payments crisis. Although the economy has stabilized since the crisis, it has failed to recover. Foreign investment has not returned, due to investor concerns related to governance, energy, security, and a slow-down in the global economy. Remittances from overseas workers, averaging about $1 billion a month since March 2011, remain a bright spot for Pakistan. However, after a small current account surplus in fiscal year 2011 (July 2010/June 2011), Pakistan's current account turned to deficit in the following two years, spurred by higher prices for imported oil and lower prices for exported cotton. Pakistan remains stuck in a low-income, low-growth trap, with growth averaging about 3.5% per year from 2008 to 2013. Pakistan must address long standing issues related to government revenues and energy production in order to spur the amount of economic growth that will be necessary to employ its growing and rapidly urbanizing population, more than half of which is under 22. Other long term challenges include expanding investment in education and healthcare, adapting to the effects of climate change and natural disasters, and reducing dependence on foreign donors.

GDP (purchasing power parity): $574.1 billion (2013 est.)
country comparison to the world: 27
$554.2 billion (2012 est.)
$531 billion (2011 est.)
note: data are in 2013 US dollars

GDP (official exchange rate): $236.5 billion (2013 est.)

GDP—real growth rate: 3.6% (2013 est.)
country comparison to the world: 90
4.4% (2012 est.)
3.7% (2011 est.)

GDP—per capita (PPP): $3,100 (2013 est.)
country comparison to the world: 176
$3,100 (2012 est.)
$3,000 (2011 est.)
note: data are in 2013 US dollars

Gross national saving: 12.7% of GDP (2013 est.)
country comparison to the world: 121
13.3% of GDP (2012 est.)
12.9% of GDP (2011 est.)

GDP—composition, by end use:
household consumption: 81%
government consumption: 10.8%
investment in fixed capital: 12.6%
investment in inventories: 1.6%
exports of goods and services: 12.7%
imports of goods and services: -18.8% (2013 est.)

GDP—composition, by sector of origin:
agriculture: 25.3%
industry: 21.6%
services: 53.1% (2013 est.)

Agriculture—products: cotton, wheat, rice, sugarcane, fruits, vegetables; milk, beef, mutton, eggs

Industries: textiles and apparel, food processing, pharmaceuticals, construction materials, paper products, fertilizer, shrimp

Industrial production growth rate: 3.5% (2013 est.)
country comparison to the world: 87

Labor force: 59.21 million
country comparison to the world: 10
note: extensive export of labor, mostly to the Middle East, and use of child labor (2012 est.)

Labor force—by occupation:
agriculture: 45.1%
industry: 20.7%
services: 34.2% (2010 est.)

Unemployment rate: 6.6% (2013 est.)
country comparison to the world: 68
6% (2012 est.)
note: substantial underemployment exists

Population below poverty line: 22.3% (FY05/06 est.)

Household income or consumption by percentage share: *lowest 10%:* 3.9%
highest 10%: 39.3% (FY05/06)

Distribution of family income—Gini index: 30.6 (FY07/08)
country comparison to the world: 117
41 (FY98/99)

Budget: *revenues:* $29.71 billion
expenditures: $47.97 billion (2013 est.)

Taxes and other revenues: 12.6% of GDP (2013 est.)
country comparison to the world: 201

Budget surplus (+) or deficit (-):
-7.7% of GDP (2013 est.)
country comparison to the world: 193

Public debt: 54.6% of GDP (2013 est.)
country comparison to the world: 58
52.1% of GDP (2012 est.)

Fiscal year: 1 July—30 June

Inflation rate (consumer prices): 7.7% (2013 est.)
country comparison to the world: 192
9.7% (2012 est.)

Central bank discount rate: 12% (31 January 2012 est.)
country comparison to the world: 13
14% (31 December 2010 est.)

Commercial bank prime lending rate: 11.5% (31 December 2013 est.)
country comparison to the world: 63
12.41% (31 December 2012 est.)

Stock of narrow money: $71.96 billion (31 December 2013 est.)
country comparison to the world: 43
$62.29 billion (31 December 2012 est.)

Stock of broad money: $93.11 billion (31 December 2013 est.)
country comparison to the world: 55
$82.63 billion (31 December 2012 est.)

Stock of domestic credit: $106.8 billion (31 December 2013 est.)
country comparison to the world: 51
$94.65 billion (31 December 2012 est.)

Market value of publicly traded shares: $43.68 billion (31 December 2012 est.)
country comparison to the world: 56
$32.76 billion (31 December 2011)
$38.17 billion (31 December 2010 est.)

Current account balance: -$2.36 billion (2013 est.)
country comparison to the world: 148
-$2.072 billion (2012 est.)

Exports: $25.05 billion (2013 est.)
country comparison to the world: 70
$24.71 billion (2012 est.)

Exports—commodities: textiles (garments, bed linen, cotton cloth, yarn), rice, leather goods, sports goods, chemicals, manufactures, carpets and rugs

Exports—partners: US 13.6%, China 11.1%, UAE 8.5%, Afghanistan 7.8% (2012)

Imports: $39.27 billion (2013 est.)
country comparison to the world: 61
$40.07 billion (2012 est.)

Imports—commodities: petroleum, petroleum products, machinery, plastics, transportation equipment, edible oils, paper and paperboard, iron and steel, tea

Imports—partners: China 19.7%, Saudi Arabia 12.3%, UAE 12.1%, Kuwait 6.3% (2012)

Reserves of foreign exchange and gold: $11.18 billion (31 December 2013 est.)
country comparison to the world: 73
$13.8 billion (31 December 2012 est.)

Debt—external: $52.43 billion (31 December 2013 est.)
country comparison to the world: 61
$54.5 billion (31 December 2012 est.)

Stock of direct foreign investment—at home: $24.33 billion (31 December 2013 est.)
country comparison to the world: 68
$22.73 billion (31 December 2012 est.)

Stock of direct foreign investment—abroad: $1.569 billion (31 December 2013 est.)
country comparison to the world: 76
$1.519 billion (31 December 2012 est.)

Exchange rates: Pakistani rupees (PKR) per US dollar—
100.4 (2013 est.)
93.3952 (2012 est.)
85.194 (2010 est.)
81.71 (2009)
70.64 (2008)

ENERGY

Electricity—production: 94.65 billion kWh (2011 est.)
country comparison to the world: 3 5

Electricity—consumption: 70.1 billion kWh (2011 est.)
country comparison to the world: 39

Electricity—exports: 0 kWh (2012 est.)
country comparison to the world: 182

Electricity—imports: 0 kWh (2012 est.)
country comparison to the world: 185

Electricity—installed generating capacity: 22.27 million kW (2010 est.)
country comparison to the world: 36

Electricity—from fossil fuels: 68.3% of total installed capacity (2010 est.)
country comparison to the world: 112

Electricity—from nuclear fuels: 2.1% of total installed capacity (2010 est.)
country comparison to the world: 27

Electricity—from hydroelectric plants: 29.6% of total installed capacity (2010 est.)
country comparison to the world: 80

Electricity—from other renewable sources: 0% of total installed capacity (2010 est.)
country comparison to the world: 112

Crude oil—production: 61,660 bbl/day (2012 est.)
country comparison to the world: 59

Crude oil—exports: 0 bbl/day (2010 est.)
country comparison to the world: 167

Crude oil—imports: 151,200 bbl/day (2010 est.)
country comparison to the world: 42

Crude oil—proved reserves: 247.5 million bbl (1 January 2013 es)
country comparison to the world: 56

Refined petroleum products—production: 210,100 bbl/day (2010 est.)
country comparison to the world: 53

Refined petroleum products—consumption: 426,700 bbl/day (2011 est.)
country comparison to the world: 34

Refined petroleum products—exports: 34,660 bbl/day (2010 est.)
country comparison to the world: 68

Refined petroleum products—imports: 227,100 bbl/day (2010 est.)
country comparison to the world: 25

Natural gas—production: 39.15 billion cu m (2011 est.)
country comparison to the world: 24

Natural gas—consumption: 42.9 billion cu m (2011 est.)
country comparison to the world: 23

Natural gas—exports: 0 cu m (2011 est.)
country comparison to the world: 164

Natural gas—imports: 0 cu m (2011 est.)
country comparison to the world: 116

Natural gas—proved reserves: 679.6 billion cu m (1 January 2013 es)
country comparison to the world: 31

Carbon dioxide emissions from consumption of energy: 139.7 million Mt (2011 est.)
country comparison to the world: 34

COMMUNICATIONS

Telephones—main lines in use: 5.803 million (2012)
country comparison to the world: 2 9

Telephones—mobile cellular: 125 million (2013)
country comparison to the world: 9

Telephone system: *general assessment:* the telecommunications infrastructure is improving dramatically with foreign and domestic investments in fixed-line and mobile-cellular networks; system consists of microwave radio relay, coaxial cable, fiber-optic cable, cellular, and satellite networks;
domestic: mobile-cellular subscribership has skyrocketed, exceeding 110 million by the end of 2011, up from only about 300,000 in 2000; more than 90 percent of Pakistanis live within areas that have cell phone coverage and more than half of all Pakistanis have access to a cell phone; fiber systems are being constructed throughout the country to aid in network growth; fixed line availability has risen only marginally over the same period and there are still difficulties getting fixed-line service to rural areas

International: country code—92; landing point for the SEA-ME-WE-3 and SEA-ME-WE-4 submarine cable systems that provide links to Asia, the Middle East, and Europe; satellite earth stations—3 Intelsat (1 Atlantic Ocean and 2 Indian Ocean); 3 operational international gateway exchanges (1 at Karachi and 2 at Islamabad); microwave radio relay to neighboring countries (2011)

Broadcast media: media is government regulated; 1 dominant state-owned TV broadcaster, Pakistan Television Corporation (PTV), operates a network consisting of 5 channels; private TV broadcasters are permitted; to date 69 foreign satellite channels are operational; the state-owned radio network operates more than 40 stations; nearly 100 commercially licensed privately owned radio stations provide programming mostly limited to music and talk shows (2007)

Internet country code: .pk

Internet hosts: 365,813 (2012)
country comparison to the world: 57

Internet users: 20.431 million (2009)
country comparison to the world: 20

TRANSPORTATION

Airports: 151 (2013)
country comparison to the world: 3 7

Airports—with paved runways: *total:* 108
over 3,047 m: 15
2,438 to 3,047 m: 20
1,524 to 2,437 m: 43
914 to 1,523 m: 20
under 914 m: 10 (2013)

Airports—with unpaved runways: *total:* 4 3
2,438 to 3,047 m: 1
1,524 to 2,437 m: 9
914 to 1,523 m: 9
under 914 m: 24 (2013)

Heliports: 23 (2013)

Pipelines: gas 12,646 km; oil 2,576 km; refined products 1,087 km (2013)

Railways: *total:* 7,791 km
country comparison to the world: 27
broad gauge: 7,479 km 1.676-m gauge (293 km electrified)
narrow gauge: 312 km 1.000-m gauge (2007)

Roadways: *total:* 262,256 km
country comparison to the world: 20
paved: 189,218 km (includes 708 km of expressways)
unpaved: 73,038 km (2010)

Merchant marine: *total:* 1 1
country comparison to the world: 110
by type: bulk carrier 5, cargo 3, petroleum tanker 3
registered in other countries: 11 (Comoros 5, Marshall Islands 1, Moldova 1, Panama 3, Saint Kitts and Nevis 1) (2010)

Ports and terminals: *major seaport(s):* Karachi, Port Muhammad Bin Qasim
container port(s) (TEUs): Karachi (1,545,434)

MILITARY

Military branches: Pakistan Army (includes National Guard), Pakistan Navy (includes Marines and Maritime Security Agency), Pakistan Air Force (Pakistan Fiza'ya) (2013)

Military service age and obligation: 16-23 years of age for voluntary military service; soldiers cannot be deployed for combat until age 18; the Pakistani Air Force and Pakistani Navy have inducted their first female pilots and sailors; the Pakistan Air Force recruits aviation technicians at age 15; service obligation (Navy) 10-18 years; retirement required after 18-30 years service or age 40-52 (2012)

Manpower available for military service:
males age 16-49: 48,453,305
females age 16-49: 44,898,096 (2010 est.)

Manpower fit for military service:
males age 16-49: 37,945,440
females age 16-49: 37,381,549 (2010 est.)

Manpower reaching militarily significant age annually: *male:* 2,237,723
female: 2,104,906 (2010 est.)

Military expenditures: 3.04% of GDP (2012)
country comparison to the world: 20
3.13% of GDP (2011)
3.04% of GDP (2010)

TRANSNATIONAL ISSUES

Disputes—international: various talks and confidence-building measures cautiously have begun to defuse tensions over Kashmir, particularly since the October 2005 earthquake in the region; Kashmir nevertheless remains the site of the world's largest and most militarized territorial dispute with portions under the de facto administration of China (Aksai Chin), India (Jammu and Kashmir), and Pakistan (Azad Kashmir and Northern Areas); UN Military Observer Group in India and Pakistan has maintained a small group of peacekeepers since 1949; India does not recognize Pakistan's ceding historic Kashmir lands to China in 1964; India and Pakistan have maintained their 2004 cease-fire in Kashmir and initiated discussions on defusing the armed standoff in the Siachen glacier region; Pakistan protests India's fencing the highly militarized Line of Control and construction of the Baglihar Dam on the Chenab River in Jammu and Kashmir, which is part of the larger dispute on water sharing of the Indus River and its tributaries; to defuse tensions and prepare for discussions on a maritime boundary, India and Pakistan seek technical resolution of the disputed boundary in Sir Creek estuary at the mouth of the Rann of Kutch in the Arabian Sea; Pakistani maps continue to show the Junagadh claim in India's Gujarat State; by 2005, Pakistan, with UN assistance, repatriated 2.3 million Afghan refugees leaving slightly more than a million, many of whom remain at their own choosing; Pakistan has sent troops across and built fences along some remote tribal areas of its treaty-defined Durand Line border with Afghanistan, which serve as bases for foreign terrorists and other illegal activities; Afghan, Coalition, and Pakistan military meet periodically to clarify the alignment of the boundary on the ground and on maps

Refugees and internally displaced persons:
refugees (country of origin): 2.6 million (1.6 million registered, 1 million undocumented) (Afghanistan) (2014)
IDPs: more than 1 million (primarily includes IDPs who remain displaced by counter-terrorism and counter-insurgency operations and violent conflict between armed non-state groups in the Federally Administered Tribal Areas (FATA) and Khyber-Paktunkwa Province; individuals also have been displaced by repeated monsoon floods) (2014)

Illicit drugs: significant transit area for Afghan drugs, including heroin, opium, morphine, and hashish, bound for Iran, Western markets, the Gulf States, Africa, and Asia; financial crimes related to drug trafficking, terrorism, corruption, and smuggling remain problems; opium poppy cultivation estimated to be 2,300 hectares in 2007 with 600 of those hectares eradicated; federal and provincial authorities continue to conduct anti-poppy campaigns that utilizes forced eradication, fines, and arrests

PALAU

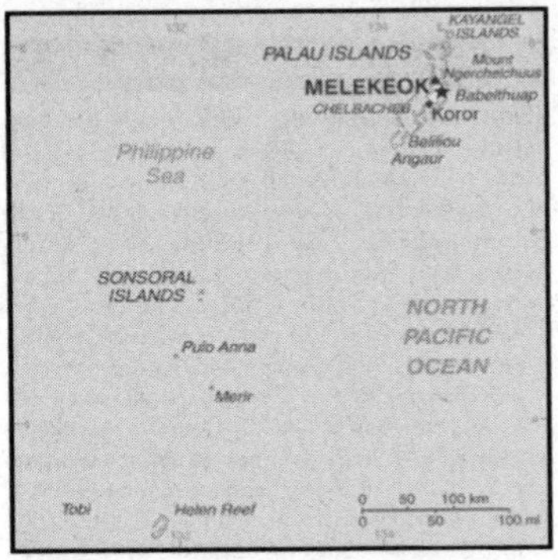

INTRODUCTION

Background: After three decades as part of the UN Trust Territory of the Pacific under US administration, this westernmost cluster of the Caroline Islands opted for independence in 1978 rather than join the Federated States of Micronesia. A Compact of Free Association with the US was approved in 1986 but not ratified until 1993. It entered into force the following year when the islands gained independence.

GEOGRAPHY

Location: Oceania, group of islands in the North Pacific Ocean, southeast of the Philippines

Geographic coordinates: 7 30 N, 134 30 E

Map references: Oceania

Area: *total:* 459 sq km
country comparison to the world: 198
land: 459 sq km
water: 0 sq km

Area—comparative: slightly more than 2.5 times the size of Washington, DC

Land boundaries: 0 km

Coastline: 1,519 km

Maritime claims: *territorial sea:* 3 nm
exclusive fishing zone: 200 nm

Climate: tropical; hot and humid; wet season May to November

Terrain: varying geologically from the high, mountainous main island of Babelthuap to low, coral islands usually fringed by large barrier reefs

Elevation extremes: *lowest point:* Pacific Ocean 0 m
highest point: Mount Ngerchelchuus 242 m

Natural resources: forests, minerals (especially gold), marine products, deep-seabed minerals

Land use: *arable land:* 2.17%
permanent crops: 4.35%
other: 93.48% (2011)

Irrigated land: NA

Natural hazards: typhoons (June to December)

Environment—current issues: inadequate facilities for disposal of solid waste; threats to the marine ecosystem from sand and coral dredging, illegal fishing practices, and overfishing

Environment—international agreements: *party to:* Biodiversity, Climate Change, Climate Change-Kyoto Protocol, Desertification, Law of the Sea, Ozone Layer Protection, Wetlands, Whaling
signed, but not ratified: none of the selected agreements

Geography—note: westernmost archipelago in the Caroline chain, consists of six island groups totaling more than 300 islands; includes World War II battleground of Beliliou (Peleliu) and world-famous rock islands

PEOPLE AND SOCIETY

Nationality: *noun:* Palauan(s)
adjective: Palauan

Ethnic groups: Palauan (Micronesian with Malayan and Melanesian admixtures) 72.5%, Carolinian 1%, other Micronesian 2.4%, Filipino 16.3%, Chinese 1.6%, Vietnamese 1.6%, other Asian 3.4%, white 0.9%, other 0.3% (2005 est.)

Languages: Palauan (official on most islands) 66.6%, Carolinian 0.7%, other Micronesian 0.7%, English (official) 15.5%, Filipino 10.8%, Chinese 1.8%, other Asian 2.6%, other 1.3%
note: Sonsoral (Sonsoralese and English are official), Tobi (Tobi and English are official), and Angaur (Angaur, Japanese, and English are official) (2005 est.)

Religions: Roman Catholic 49.4%, Protestant 30.9% (includes Protestant (general) 23.1%, Seventh Day Adventist 5.3%, and other Protestant 2.5%), Modekngei 8.7% (indigenous to Palau), Jehovah's Witnesses 1.1%, other 8.8%, none or unspecified 1.1% (2005 est.)

Population: 21,186 (July 2014 est.)
country comparison to the world: 220

Age structure:
0-14 years: 20.5% (male 2,239/female 2,101)
15-24 years: 17.4% (male 1,835/female 1,855)
25-54 years: 46.4% (male 5,985/female 3,842)
55-64 years: 7.1% (male 642/female 1,188)
65 years and over: 6.8% (male 410/female 1,089) (2014 est.)

Median age: *total:* 33 years
male: 32.5 years
female: 34.2 years (2014 est.)

Population growth rate: 0.37% (2014 est.)
country comparison to the world: 163

Birth rate: 10.95 births/1,000 population (2014 est.)
country comparison to the world: 177

Death rate: 7.93 deaths/1,000 population (2014 est.)
country comparison to the world: 103

Net migration rate: 0.66 migrant(s)/1,000 population (2014 est.)
country comparison to the world: 66

Urbanization: *urban population:* 83% of total population (2010)
rate of urbanization: 1.4% annual rate of change (2010-15 est.)

Sex ratio: *at birth:* 1.05 male(s)/female
0-14 years: 1.07 male(s)/female
15-24 years: 0.99 male(s)/female
25-54 years: 1.56 male(s)/female
55-64 years: 1.1 male(s)/female
65 years and over: 0.4 male(s)/female
total population: 1.12 male(s)/female (2014 est.)

Infant mortality rate: *total:* 11.46 deaths/1,000 live births
country comparison to the world: 130
male: 13.01 deaths/1,000 live births
female: 9.81 deaths/1,000 live births (2014 est.)

Life expectancy at birth: *total population:* 72.6 years
country comparison to the world: 132
male: 69.43 years
female: 75.96 years (2014 est.)

Total fertility rate: 1.71 children born/woman (2014 est.)
country comparison to the world: 170

Contraceptive prevalence rate: 32.8%
note: percent of women aged 15-44 (2003)

Health expenditures: 10.6% of GDP (2011)
country comparison to the world: 18

Physicians density: 1.38 physicians/1,000 population (2010)

Hospital bed density: 4.8 beds/1,000 population (2010)

Drinking water source:
improved:
urban: 97% of population
rural: 86% of population
total: 95.3% of population
unimproved:
urban: 3% of population
rural: 14% of population
total: 4.7% of population (2011 est.)

Sanitation facility access:
improved:
urban: 100% of population
rural: 100% of population
total: 100% of population
unimproved:
urban: 0% of population
rural: 0% of population
total: 0% of population (2011 est.)

HIV/AIDS—adult prevalence rate: NA

HIV/AIDS—people living with HIV/AIDS: NA

HIV/AIDS—deaths: NA

Obesity—adult prevalence rate: 48.9% (2008)
country comparison to the world: 7

Education expenditures: 7.3% of GDP (2002)
country comparison to the world: 17

Literacy: *definition:* age 15 and over can read and write
total population: 92%
male: 93%
female: 90% (1980 est.)

School life expectancy (primary to tertiary education): *total:* 14 years
male: 13 years
female: 15 years (2000)

GOVERNMENT

Country name: *conventional long form:* Republic of Palau

conventional short form: Palau
local long form: Beluu er a Belau
local short form: Belau
former: Trust Territory of the Pacific Islands, Palau District

Government type: constitutional government in free association with the US; the Compact of Free Association entered into force on 1 October 1994

Capital: *name:* Melekeok

geographic coordinates: 7 29 N, 134 38 E
time difference: UTC+9 (14 hours ahead of Washington, DC during Standard Time)

Administrative divisions: 16 states; Aimeliik, Airai, Angaur, Hatohobei, Kayangel, Koror, Melekeok, Ngaraard, Ngarchelong, Ngardmau, Ngatpang, Ngchesar, Ngeremlengui, Ngiwal, Peleliu, Sonsorol

Independence: 1 October 1994 (from the US-administered UN trusteeship)

National holiday: Constitution Day, 9 July (1979)

Constitution: ratified 9 July 1980, effective 1 January 1981; amended 1992, 2004 (2011)

Legal system: mixed legal system of civil, common, and customary law

International law organization participation: has not submitted an ICJ jurisdiction declaration; non-party state to the ICCt

Suffrage: 18 years of age; universal

Executive branch: *chief of state:* President Tommy REMENGESAU (since 17 January 2013); Vice President Antonio BELLS (since 17 January 2013); note—the president is both the chief of state and head of government
head of government: President Tommy REMENGESAU (since 17 January 2013); Vice President Antonio BELLS (since 17 January 2013)
cabinet: NA (For more information visit the World Leaders website)
elections: president and vice president elected on separate tickets by popular vote for four-year terms (eligible for a second term); election last held on 6 November 2012 (next to be held in November 2016)
election results: percent of vote—Tommy REMENGESAU 58%, Johnson TORIBIONG 42%

Legislative branch: bicameral National Congress or Olbiil Era Kelulau (OEK) consists of the Senate (9 seats; members elected by popular vote on a population basis to serve four-year terms) and the House of Delegates (16 seats; members elected by popular vote to serve four-year terms)
elections: Senate—last held on 6 November 2012 (next to be held in November 2016); House of Delegates—last held on 6 November 2012 (next to be held in November 2016)
election results: Senate—percent of vote—NA; seats—independents 9; House of Delegates—percent of vote—NA; seats—independents 16

Judicial branch: *highest court(s):* Supreme Court (consists of the chief justice and 3 associate justices organized into appellate trial divisions; also within the Supreme Court organization are the Common Pleas and Land Courts)
judge selection and term of office: justices nominated by a 7-member independent body consisting of judges, presidential appointees, and lawyers, and appointed by the president; judges appointed until mandatory retirement at age 65
subordinate courts: National Court and other 'inferior' courts

Political parties and leaders: none

Political pressure groups and leaders: NA

International organization participation: ACP, ADB, AOSIS, FAO, IAEA, IBRD, ICAO, ICRM, IDA, IFC, IFRCS, ILO, IMF, IMO, IMSO, IOC, IPU, MIGA, OPCW, PIF, Sparteca, SPC, UN, UNAMID, UNCTAD, UNESCO, WHO

Diplomatic representation in the US:
chief of mission: Ambassador Hersey KYOTA (since 12 November 1997)
chancery: 1701 Pennsylvania Avenue NW, Suite 300, Washington, DC 20006
telephone: [1] (202) 452-6814
FAX: [1] (202) 452-6281
consulate(s): Tamuning (Guam)

Diplomatic representation from the US:
chief of mission: Ambassador Helen P. REED-ROWE (since 27 September 2013)
embassy: Koror (no street address)
mailing address: P. O. Box 6028, Koror, Republic of Palau 96940
telephone: [680] 587-2920
FAX: [680] 587-2911

Flag description: light blue with a large yellow disk shifted slightly to the hoist side; the blue color represents the ocean, the disk represents the moon; Palauans consider the full moon to be the optimum time for human activity; it is also considered a symbol of peace, love, and tranquility

National anthem: *name:* "Belau rekid" (Our Palau)
lyrics/music: multiple/Ymesei O. EZEKIEL
note: adopted 1980

ECONOMY

Economy—overview: The economy consists of tourism and other services such as trade, subsistence agriculture, and fishing. Government is a major employer of the work force relying on financial assistance from the US under the Compact of Free Association (Compact) with the US. The Compact took effect, after the end of the UN trusteeship on 1 October 1994. The US provided Palau with roughly $700 million in aid for the first 15 years following commencement of the Compact in 1994 in return for unrestricted access to its land and waterways for strategic purposes. Business and leisure tourist arrivals numbered over 109,000 in 2011, for a 27% increase over 2010. The population enjoys a per capita income roughly double that of the Philippines and much of Micronesia. Long-run prospects for tourism have been bolstered by the expansion of air travel in the Pacific, the rising prosperity of industrial East Asia, and the willingness of foreigners to finance infrastructure development. Proximity to Guam, the region's major destination for tourists from East Asia, and a regionally competitive tourist infrastructure enhance Palau's advantage as a destination.

GDP (purchasing power parity): $245.5 million (2013 est.)
country comparison to the world: 218
$237.2 million (2012 est.)
$223.2 million (2011 est.)
note: GDP estimate includes US subsidy

GDP (official exchange rate): $221 million (2011 est.)

GDP—real growth rate: 3.5% (2013 est.)
country comparison to the world: 97
6.3% (2012 est.)
6.9% (2011 est.)

GDP—per capita (PPP): $10,500 (2011 est.)
country comparison to the world: 116
$7,600 (2005 est.)

GDP—composition, by sector of origin:
agriculture: 3.2%
industry: 20%
services: 76.8% (2012 est.)

Agriculture—products: coconuts, copra, cassava (tapioca), sweet potatoes; fish

Industries: tourism, craft items (from shell, wood, pearls), construction, garment making

Industrial production growth rate: NA%

Labor force: 9,777 (2005)
country comparison to the world: 217

Labor force—by occupation: *agriculture:* 20%
industry: NA%
services: NA% (1990)

Unemployment rate: 4.2% (2005 est.)
country comparison to the world: 36

Population below poverty line: NA%

Household income or consumption by percentage share: *lowest 10%:* NA%
highest 10%: NA%

Budget: *revenues:* $89 million
expenditures: $94.3 million (2010 est.)

Taxes and other revenues: 40.3% of GDP (2010 est.)
country comparison to the world: 40

Budget surplus (+) or deficit (-):
-2.4% of GDP (2010 est.)
country comparison to the world: 99

Fiscal year: 1 October—30 September

Inflation rate (consumer prices): 2.7% (2011 est.)
country comparison to the world: 100
1.6% (2010 est.)

Market value of publicly traded shares: $NA

Current account balance: -$20.8 million (2010 est.)
country comparison to the world: 63
$15.09 million (FY03/04)

Exports: $12.3 million (2010 est.)
country comparison to the world: 210
$5.882 million (2004 est.)

Exports—commodities: shellfish, tuna, copra, garments

Imports: $113.4 million (2010 est.)
country comparison to the world: 211
$107.3 million (2004 est.)

Imports—commodities: machinery and equipment, fuels, metals; foodstuffs

Debt—external: $0 (FY99/00)
country comparison to the world: 204

Exchange rates: the US dollar is used

COMMUNICATIONS

Telephones—main lines in use: 7,300 (2012)
country comparison to the world: 205

Telephones—mobile cellular: 17,150 (2012)
country comparison to the world: 210

Telephone system: domestic: fixed-line and mobile-cellular services available with a combined subscribership of roughly 100 per 100 persons
international: country code—680; satellite earth station—1 Intelsat (Pacific Ocean) (2009)

Broadcast media: no TV stations; a cable TV network covers the major islands and provides access to rebroadcasts, on a delayed basis, of a number of US stations as well as access to a number of real-time satellite TV channels; about a half dozen radio stations with 1 government-owned **(2009)**

Internet country code: .pw

Internet hosts: 4 (2012)
country comparison to the world: 231

TRANSPORTATION

Airports: 3 (2013)
country comparison to the world: 194

Airports—with paved runways: *total:* 1
1,524 to 2,437 m: 1 (2013)

Airports—with unpaved runways: *total:* 2
1,524 to 2,437 m: 2 (2013)

Ports and terminals: *major seaport(s):* Koror

MILITARY

Military branches: no regular military forces; Palau National Police (2009)

Manpower available for military service:
males age 16-49: 6,987 (2010 est.)

Manpower fit for military service:
males age 16-49: 5,272
females age 16-49: 3,969 (2010 est.)

Manpower reaching militarily significant age annually: *male:* 216
female: 222 (2010 est.)

Military—note: defense is the responsibility of the US; under a Compact of Free Association between Palau and the US, the US military is granted access to the islands for 50 years, but it has not stationed any military forces there (2008)

TRANSNATIONAL ISSUES

Disputes—international: maritime delineation negotiations continue with Philippines, Indonesia

PALMYRA ATOLL

INTRODUCTION

Background: The Kingdom of Hawaii claimed the atoll in 1862, and the US included it among the Hawaiian Islands when it annexed the archipelago in 1898. The Hawaii Statehood Act of 1959 did not include Palmyra Atoll, which is now part privately owned by the Nature Conservancy and part US Government-owned and administered as a nature preserve. The lagoons and surrounding waters within the 12-nautical-mile US territorial seas were transferred to the US Fish and Wildlife Service and were designated a National Wildlife Refuge in January 2001.

GEOGRAPHY

Location: Oceania, atoll in the North Pacific Ocean, about half way between Hawaii and American Samoa

Geographic coordinates: 5 52 N, 162 04 W

Map references: Oceania

Area: *total:* 11.9 sq km
land: 11.9 sq km
water: 0 sq km

Area—comparative: about 20 times the size of The Mall in Washington, DC

Land boundaries: 0 km

Coastline: 14.5 km

Maritime claims: *territorial sea:* 12 nm
exclusive economic zone: 200 nm

Climate: equatorial, hot, and very rainy

Terrain: very low

Elevation extremes: *lowest point:* Pacific Ocean 0 m
highest point: unnamed location 2 m

Natural resources: terrestrial and aquatic wildlife

Land use: *arable land:* 0%
permanent crops: 0%
other: 100% (forests and woodlands) (2011)

Natural hazards: NA

Environment—current issues: NA

Geography—note: about 50 islets covered with dense vegetation, coconut trees, and balsa-like trees up to 30 meters tall

PEOPLE AND SOCIETY

Population: no indigenous inhabitants
note: 4 to 20 Nature Conservancy staff, US Fish and
Wildlife staff (July 2008 est.)

GOVERNMENT

Country name: *conventional long form:* none
conventional short form: Palmyra Atoll

Dependency status: incorporated territory of the US; privately owned, but administered from Washington, DC, by the Fish and Wildlife Service of the US Department of the Interior; the Office of Insular Affairs of the US Department of the Interior continues to administer nine excluded areas comprising certain tidal and submerged lands within the 12 nm territorial sea or within the lagoon Legal system: the laws of the US, where applicable, apply

Flag description: the flag of the US is used

TRANSPORTATION

Airports—with unpaved runways: total: 1
1,524 to 2,437 m: 1 (2013)

Ports and terminals: West Lagoon

MILITARY

Military—note: defense is the responsibility of the US

TRANSNATIONAL ISSUES

Disputes—international: none

PANAMA

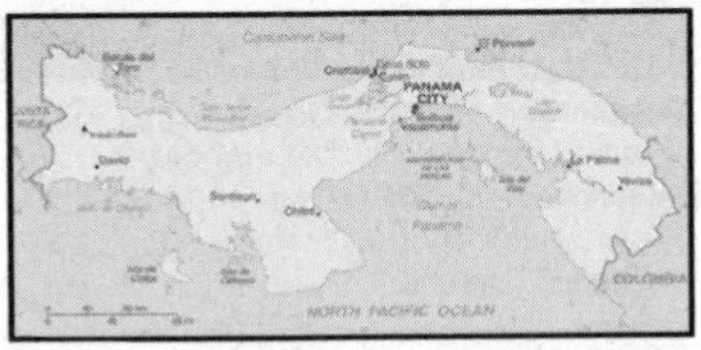

INTRODUCTION

Background: Explored and settled by the Spanish in the 16th century, Panama broke with Spain in 1821 and joined a union of Colombia, Ecuador, and Venezuela - named the Republic of Gran Colombia. When the latter dissolved in 1830, Panama remained part of Colombia. With US backing, Panama seceded from Colombia in 1903 and promptly signed a treaty with the US allowing for the construction of a canal and US sovereignty over a strip of land on either side of the structure (the Panama Canal Zone). The Panama Canal was built by the US Army Corps of Engineers between 1904 and 1914. In 1977, an agreement was signed for the complete transfer of the Canal from the US to Panama by the end of the century. Certain portions of the Zone and increasing responsibility over the Canal were turned over in the subsequent decades. With US help, dictator Manuel NORIEGA was deposed in 1989. The entire Panama Canal, the area supporting the Canal, and remaining US military bases were transferred to Panama by the end of 1999. In October 2006, Panamanians approved an ambitious plan (estimated to cost $5.3 billion) to expand the Canal. The project, which began in 2007 and could double the Canal's capacity, is expected to be completed in 2015.

GEOGRAPHY

Location: Central America, bordering both the Caribbean Sea and the North Pacific Ocean, between Colombia and Costa Rica

Geographic coordinates: 9 00 N, 80 00 W

Map references: Central America and the Caribbean

Area: *total:* 75,420 sq km
country comparison to the world: 118
land: 74,340 sq km
water: 1,080 sq km

Area—comparative: slightly smaller than South Carolina

Land boundaries: *total:* 555 km
border countries: Colombia 225 km, Costa Rica 330 km

Coastline: 2,490 km

Maritime claims: *territorial sea:* 12 nm
contiguous zone: 24 nm
exclusive economic zone: 200 nm or edge of continental margin

Climate: tropical maritime; hot, humid, cloudy; prolonged rainy season (May to January), short dry season (January to May)

Terrain: interior mostly steep, rugged mountains and dissected, upland plains; coastal areas largely plains and rolling hills

Elevation extremes: *lowest point:* Pacific Ocean 0 m
highest point: Volcan Baru 3,475 m

Natural resources: copper, mahogany forests, shrimp, hydropower

Land use: *arable land:* 7.16%
permanent crops: 2.51%
other: 90.33% (2011)

Irrigated land: 346.2 sq km (2003)

Total renewable water resources: 148 cu km (2011)

Freshwater withdrawal (domestic/industrial/agricultural): *total:* 0.91 cu km/yr (27%/2%/71%)
per capita: 296.1 cu m/yr (2005)

Natural hazards: occasional severe storms and forest fires in the Darien area

Environment—current issues: water pollution from agricultural runoff threatens fishery resources;

deforestation of tropical rain forest; land degradation and soil erosion threatens siltation of Panama Canal; air pollution in urban areas; mining threatens natural resources

Environment—international agreements: *party to:* Biodiversity, Climate Change, Climate Change-Kyoto Protocol, Desertification, Endangered Species, Environmental Modification, Hazardous Wastes, Law of the Sea, Marine Dumping, Ozone Layer Protection, Ship Pollution, Tropical Timber 83, Tropical Timber 94, Wetlands, Whaling
signed, but not ratified: Marine Life Conservation

Geography—note: strategic location on eastern end of isthmus forming land bridge connecting North and South America; controls Panama Canal that links North Atlantic Ocean via Caribbean Sea with North Pacific Ocean

PEOPLE AND SOCIETY

Nationality: *noun:* Panamanian(s)
adjective: Panamanian

Ethnic groups: mestizo (mixed Amerindian and white) 70%, Amerindian and mixed (West Indian) 14%, white 10%, Amerindian 6%

Languages: Spanish (official), English 14%
note: many Panamanians are bilingual

Religions: Roman Catholic 85%, Protestant 15%

Demographic profile: Panama is a country of demographic and economic contrasts. It is in the midst of a demographic transition, characterized by steadily declining rates of fertility, mortality, and population growth, but disparities persist based on wealth, geography, and ethnicity. Panama has one of the fastest growing economies in Latin America and dedicates substantial funding to social programs, yet poverty and inequality remain prevalent. The indigenous population accounts for a growing share of Panama's poor and extreme poor, while the non-indigenous rural poor have been more successful at rising out of poverty through rural-to-urban labor migration. The government's large expenditures on untargeted, indirect subsidies for water, electricity, and fuel have been ineffective, but its conditional cash transfer program has shown some promise in helping to decrease extreme poverty among the indigenous population. Panama has expanded access to education and clean water, but the availability of sanitation and, to a lesser extent, electricity remains poor. The increase in secondary schooling—led by female enrollment—is spreading to rural and indigenous areas, which probably will help to alleviate poverty if educational quality and the availability of skilled jobs improve. Inadequate access to sanitation contributes to a high incidence of diarrhea in Panama's children, which is one of the main causes of Panama's elevated chronic malnutrition rate, especially among indigenous communities.

Population: 3,608,431 (July 2014 est.)
country comparison to the world: 131

Age structure:
0-14 years: 27.4% (male 504,710/female 484,166)
15-24 years: 17.3% (male 317,875/female 306,378)
25-54 years: 40.1% (male 733,588/female 714,859)
55-64 years: 7.8% (male 131,899/female 135,015)
65 years and over: 7.6% (male 129,091/female 150,850) (2014 est.)

Dependency ratios:
total dependency ratio: 55.1 %
youth dependency ratio: 43.9 %
elderly dependency ratio: 11.2 %
potential support ratio: 8.9 (2013)

Median age: *total:* 28.3 years
male: 27.9 years
female: 28.7 years (2014 est.)

Population growth rate: 1.35% (2014 est.)
country comparison to the world: 91

Birth rate: 18.61 births/1,000 population (2014 est.)
country comparison to the world: 98

Death rate: 4.77 deaths/1,000 population (2014 est.)
country comparison to the world: 198

Net migration rate: -0.32 migrant(s)/1,000 population (2014 est.)
country comparison to the world: 126

Urbanization: *urban population:* 75% of total population (2010)
rate of urbanization: 2.3% annual rate of change (2010-15 est.)

Major urban areas—population: PANAMA CITY (capital) 1.346 million (2009)

Sex ratio: *at birth:* 1.05 male(s)/female
0-14 years: 1.04 male(s)/female
15-24 years: 1.04 male(s)/female
25-54 years: 1.03 male(s)/female
55-64 years: 1.01 male(s)/female
65 years and over: 0.86 male(s)/female
total population: 1.02 male(s)/female (2014 est.)

Mother's mean age at first birth: 21.1 (1976 est.)

Maternal mortality rate: 92 deaths/100,000 live births (2010)
country comparison to the world: 78

Infant mortality rate: *total:* 10.7 deaths/1,000 live births
country comparison to the world: 135
male: 11.46 deaths/1,000 live births
female: 9.92 deaths/1,000 live births (2014 est.)

Life expectancy at birth: *total population:* 78.3 years
country comparison to the world: 56
male: 75.51 years
female: 81.22 years (2014 est.)

Total fertility rate: 2.38 children born/woman (2014 est.)
country comparison to the world: 85

Contraceptive prevalence rate: 52.2% (2009)

Health expenditures: 8.2% of GDP (2011)
country comparison to the world: 59

Physicians density: 1.5 physicians/1,000 population (2000)

Hospital bed density: 2.4 beds/1,000 population (2010)

Drinking water source:
improved:
urban: 97% of population
rural: 85.8% of population
total: 94.2% of population
unimproved:
urban: 3% of population
rural: 14.2% of population
total: 5.8% of population (2011 est.)

Sanitation facility access:
improved:
urban: 76.9% of population
rural: 54.1% of population
total: 71.2% of population
unimproved:
urban: 23.1% of population
rural: 45.9% of population
total: 28.8% of population (2011 est.)

HIV/AIDS—adult prevalence rate: 0.7% (2012 est.)
country comparison to the world: 57

HIV/AIDS—people living with HIV/AIDS: 16,700 (2012 est.)
country comparison to the world: 87

HIV/AIDS—deaths: 600 (2012 est.)
country comparison to the world: 86

Major infectious diseases: *degree of risk:* intermediate
food or waterborne diseases: bacterial diarrhea
vectorborne disease: dengue fever (2013)

Obesity—adult prevalence rate: 25.4% (2008)
country comparison to the world: 55

Children under the age of 5 years underweight: 3.9% (2008)
country comparison to the world: 99

Education expenditures: 3.5% of GDP (2011)
country comparison to the world: 122

Literacy: *definition:* age 15 and over can read and write
total population: 94.1%
male: 94.7%
female: 93.5% (2010 est.)

School life expectancy (primary to tertiary education): *total:* 12 years
male: 12 years
female: 13 years (2011)

Child labor—children ages 5-14:
total number: 59,294
percentage: 7 %
note: data represents children ages 5-17 (2010 est.)

Unemployment, youth ages 15-24: *total:* 14.6%
country comparison to the world: 87
male: 8.7%
female: 10.3% (2012)

GOVERNMENT

Country name: *conventional long form:* Republic of Panama
conventional short form: Panama
local long form: Republica de Panama
local short form: Panama

Government type: constitutional democracy

Capital: *name:* Panama City

geographic coordinates: 8 58 N, 79 32 W
time difference: UTC-5 (same time as Washington, DC during Standard Time)

Administrative divisions: 9 provinces (provincias, singular—provincia) and 3 indigenous territories* (comarcas); Bocas del Toro, Chiriqui, Cocle, Colon, Darien, Embera-Wounaan*, Herrera, Kuna Yala*, Los Santos, Ngobe-Bugle*, Panama, Veraguas

Independence: 3 November 1903 (from Colombia; became independent from Spain on 28 November 1821)

National holiday: Independence Day, 3 November (1903)

Constitution: several previous; latest effective 11 October 1972; amended several times, last in 2004 (2010)

Legal system: civil law system; judicial review of legislative acts in the Supreme Court of Justice

International law organization participation: accepts compulsory ICJ jurisdiction with reservations; accepts ICCt jurisdiction

Suffrage: 18 years of age; universal and compulsory

Executive branch: chief of state: President Ricardo MARTINELLI Berrocal (since 1 July 2009); Vice President Juan Carlos VARELA Rodriguez (since 1 July 2009); note—the president is both the chief of state and head of government
head of government: President Ricardo MARTINELLI Berrocal (since 1 July 2009); Vice President Juan Carlos VARELA Rodriguez (since 1 July 2009)
cabinet: Cabinet appointed by the president (For more information visit the World Leaders website)
elections: president and vice president elected on the same ticket by popular vote for five-year terms (president not eligible for immediate reelection and must sit out two additional terms (10 years) before becoming eligible for reelection); election last held on 3 May 2009 (next to be held in May 2014)
election results: Ricardo MARTINELLI Berrocal elected president; percent of vote—Ricardo MARTINELLI Berrocal 60%, Balbina HERRERA 38%, Guillermo ENDARA Galimany 2%
note: the ruling government coalition—formerly comprised of CD (Democratic Change), Panamenista Party, MOLIRENA (Nationalist Republican Liberal Movement), and UP (Patriotic Union Party)—split in August 2011 when President

MARTINELLI relieved Vice President VARELA from his position as Foreign Minister prompting the Panamenistas to pull out of the coalition; UP has now merged with CD, and CD and the Panamenista Party will now run separate candidates for the presidency in 2014

Legislative branch: unicameral National Assembly or Asamblea Nacional (71 seats; members elected by popular vote to serve five-year terms)
elections: last held on 3 May 2009 (next to be held in May 2014)
election results: percent of vote by party—NA; seats by party—PRD 26, Panamenista 22, CD 14, UP 4, MOLIRENA 2, PP 1, independents 2; note—changes in political affiliation now reflect the following seat distribution: as of 13 February 2013—seats by party—CD 36, PRD 17, Panamenista 13, MOLIRENA 4, PP 1
note: legislators from outlying rural districts are chosen on a plurality basis while districts located in more populous towns and cities elect multiple legislators by means of a proportion-based formula

Judicial branch: *highest court(s):* Supreme Court of Justice or Corte Suprema de Justicia (consists of 9 magistrates and 9 alternates and divided into civil, criminal, administrative, and general business chambers)
judge selection and term of office: magistrates appointed by the president for staggered 10-year terms
subordinate courts: appellate courts or Tribunal Superior; Labor Supreme Courts; Court of Audit; circuit courts or Tribunal Circuital (2 each in 9 provinces); municipal courts; electoral, family, maritime, and adolescent courts

Political parties and leaders: Democratic Change or CD [Ricardo MARTINELLI Berrocal]; Democratic Revolutionary Party or PRD [Juan Carlos NAVARRO Quelquejeu]; Nationalist Republican Liberal Movement or MOLIRENA [Sergio GONZALEZ-Ruiz]; Panamenista Party [Juan Carlos VARELA Rodriguez] (formerly the Arnulfista Party); Popular Party or PP [Milton HENRIQUEZ] (formerly Christian Democratic Party or PDC)

Political pressure groups and leaders: Chamber of Commerce; Concertacion Nacional (mechanism for government of Panama to formally dialogue with representatives of civil society); National Council of Organized Workers or CONATO; National Council of Private Enterprise or CONEP; National Union of Construction and Similar Workers (SUNTRACS); Panamanian Association of Business Executives or APEDE; Panamanian Industrialists Society or SIP; Workers Confederation of the Republic of Panama or CTRP

International organization participation: BCIE, CAN (observer), CD, CELAC, CSN (observer), FAO, G-77, IADB, IAEA, IBRD, ICAO, ICC (national committees), ICRM, IDA, IFAD, IFC, IFRCS, ILO, IMF, IMO, IMSO, Interpol, IOC, IOM, IPU, ISO, ITSO, ITU, ITUC (NGOs), LAES, LAIA, MIGA, NAM, OAS, OPANAL, OPCW, PCA, SICA, UN, UNASUR (observer), UNCTAD, UNESCO, UNIDO, Union Latina, UNWTO, UPU, WCO, WFTU (NGOs), WHO, WIPO, WMO, WTO

Diplomatic representation in the US:
chief of mission: Ambassador Mario Ernesto JARAMILLO Castillo (since 17 February 2011)
chancery: 2862 McGill Terrace NW, Washington, DC 20008
telephone: [1] (202) 483-1407
FAX: [1] (202) 483-8413
consulate(s) general: Honolulu, Houston, Miami, New Orleans, New York, Philadelphia, San Diego, Tampa, Washington DC

Diplomatic representation from the US:
chief of mission: Ambassador Jonathan D. FARRAR (since 15 May 2012)
embassy: Edificio 783, Avenida Demetrio Basilio Lakas Panama, Apartado Postal 0816-02561, Zona 5, Panama City
mailing address: American Embassy Panama, Unit 0945, APO AA 34002; American Embassy Panama, 9100 Panama City PL, Washington, DC 20521-9100
telephone: [507] 317-5000
FAX: [507] 317-5568

Flag description: divided into four, equal rectangles; the top quadrants are white (hoist side) with a blue five-pointed star in the center and plain red; the bottom quadrants are plain blue (hoist side) and white with a red five-pointed star in the center; the blue and red colors are those of the main political parties (Conservatives and Liberals respectively) and the white denotes peace between them; the blue star stands for the civic virtues of purity and honesty, the red star signifies authority and law

National symbol(s): harpy eagle

National anthem: *name:* "Himno Istmeno" (Isthmus Hymn)
lyrics/music: Jeronimo DE LA OSSA/Santos A. JORGE
note: adopted 1925

ECONOMY

Economy—overview: Panama's dollar-based economy rests primarily on a well-developed services sector that accounts for more than three-quarters of GDP. Services include operating the Panama Canal, logistics, banking, the Colon Free Zone, insurance, container ports, flagship registry, and tourism. Economic growth will be bolstered by the Panama Canal expansion project that began in 2007 and is estimated to be completed by 2015 at a cost of $5.3 billion—about 10-15% of current GDP. The expansion project will more than double the Canal's capacity, enabling it to accommodate ships that are too large to traverse the existing canal. The United States and China are the top users of the Canal. Panama is also constructing a metro system in Panama City, valued at $1.2 billion and scheduled to be completed by 2014. Panama's booming transportation and logistics services sectors, along with aggressive infrastructure development projects, have lead the economy to continued high growth in 2012. Foreign investment, at around 10% of GDP in both 2011 and 2012, has continued to be a source of growth. Strong economic performance has not translated into broadly shared prosperity, as Panama has the second worst income distribution in Latin America. About one-fourth of the population lives in poverty; however, from 2006 to 2012 poverty was reduced by 10 percentage points, while unemployment dropped from 12% to 4.5% of the labor force in 2013. The US-Panama Trade Promotion Agreement was approved by Congress and signed into law in October 2011, and entered into force in October 2012. Panama also achieved removal from the Organization of Economic Development's gray-list of tax havens by signing various double taxation treaties with other nations.

GDP (purchasing power parity): $61.54 billion (2013 est.)
country comparison to the world: 90
$57.24 billion (2012 est.)
$51.72 billion (2011 est.)
note: data are in 2013 US dollars

GDP (official exchange rate): $40.62 billion (2013 est.)

GDP—real growth rate: 7.5% (2013 est.)
country comparison to the world: 16
10.7% (2012 est.)
10.8% (2011 est.)

GDP—per capita (PPP): $16,500 (2013 est.)
country comparison to the world: 81
$15,700 (2012 est.)
$14,400 (2011 est.)
note: data are in 2013 US dollars

GDP—composition, by end use:
household consumption: 57.6%
government consumption: 13.1%
investment in fixed capital: 30.3%
investment in inventories: 0.9%
exports of goods and services: 81%
imports of goods and services: -82.9% (2013 est.)

GDP—composition, by sector of origin:
agriculture: 3.7%
industry: 17.9%
services: 78.4% (2013 est.)

Agriculture—products: bananas, rice, corn, coffee, sugarcane, vegetables; livestock; shrimp

Industries: construction, brewing, cement and other construction materials, sugar milling

Industrial production growth rate: 9.2% (2013 est.)
country comparison to the world: 18

Labor force: 1.54 million
country comparison to the world: 128
note: shortage of skilled labor, but an oversupply of unskilled labor (2013 est.)

Labor force—by occupation: *agriculture:* 17%
industry: 18.6%
services: 64.4% (2009 est.)

Unemployment rate: 4.5% (2013 est.)
country comparison to the world: 39
4.4% (2012 est.)

Population below poverty line: 26% (2012 est.)

Household income or consumption by percentage share: *lowest 10%:* 1.1%
highest 10%: 40.1% (2010 est.)

Distribution of family income—Gini index: 51.9 (2010 est.)
country comparison to the world: 16
56.1 (2003)

Budget: *revenues:* $10.33 billion
expenditures: $11.38 billion (2013 est.)

Taxes and other revenues: 25.4% of GDP (2013 est.)
country comparison to the world: 121

Budget surplus (+) or deficit (-): -2.6% of GDP (2013 est.)
country comparison to the world: 107

Public debt: 39.8% of GDP (2013 est.)
country comparison to the world: 90
39.6% of GDP (2012 est.)

Fiscal year: calendar year

Inflation rate (consumer prices): 4.1% (2013 est.)
country comparison to the world: 138
5.7% (2012 est.)

Commercial bank prime lending rate: 6.3% (31 December 2013 est.)
country comparison to the world: 127
6.91% (31 December 2012 est.)

Stock of narrow money: $8.976 billion (31 December 2013 est.)
country comparison to the world: 83
$7.659 billion (31 December 2012 est.)

Stock of broad money: $29.72 billion (31 December 2012 est.)
country comparison to the world: 75
$25.73 billion (31 December 2011 est.)

Stock of domestic credit: $35.57 billion (31 December 2013 est.)
country comparison to the world: 69
$32.27 billion (31 December 2012 est.)

Market value of publicly traded shares: $12.54 billion (31 December 2012 est.)
country comparison to the world: 69
$10.68 billion (31 December 2011)
$8.348 billion (31 December 2010 est.)

Current account balance: -$5.064 billion (2013 est.)
country comparison to the world: 168
-$3.267 billion (2012 est.)

Exports: $18.87 billion (2013 est.)
country comparison to the world: 73
$18.88 billion (2012 est.)
note: includes the Colon Free Zone

Exports—commodities: gold, bananas, shrimp, sugar, iron and steel waste, pineapples, watermelons

Exports—partners: US 20.2%, Canada 14.6%, Costa Rica 6.6%, Netherlands 5.9%, Sweden 4.8%, China 4.1%, Italy 4% (2012)

Imports: $26.61 billion (2013 est.)
country comparison to the world: 70
$24.61 billion (2012 est.)
note: includes the Colon Free Zone

Imports—commodities: fuel products, medicines, vehicles, iron and steel rods, cellular phones

Imports—partners: US 23.6%, China 6.4%, Costa Rica 4.6%, Mexico 4.4% (2012)

Reserves of foreign exchange and gold: $2.666 billion (31 December 2013 est.)
country comparison to the world: 113
$2.466 billion (31 December 2012 est.)

Debt—external: $15.22 billion (31 December 2013 est.)
country comparison to the world: 88
$13.56 billion (31 December 2012 est.)

Stock of direct foreign investment—at home: $32.89 billion (31 December 2013 est.)
country comparison to the world: 62
$29.27 billion (31 December 2012 est.)

Stock of direct foreign investment—abroad: $3.233 billion (31 December 2013 est.)
country comparison to the world: 67
$3.11 billion (31 December 2012 est.)

Exchange rates: balboas (PAB) per US dollar—
1 (2013 est.)
1 (2012 est.)
1 (2010 est.)
1 (2009)
1 (2008)

ENERGY

Electricity—production: 7.257 billion kWh (2010 est.)
country comparison to the world: 107

Electricity—consumption: 6.209 billion kWh (2010 est.)
country comparison to the world: 104

Electricity—exports: 39 million kWh (2010 est.)
country comparison to the world: 84

Electricity—imports: 72 million kWh (2011 est.)
country comparison to the world: 96

Electricity—installed generating capacity: 1.976 million kW (2010 est.)
country comparison to the world: 103

Electricity—from fossil fuels: 52.6% of total installed capacity (2010 est.)
country comparison to the world: 148

Electricity—from nuclear fuels: 0% of total installed capacity (2010 est.)
country comparison to the world: 162

Electricity—from hydroelectric plants: 47.4% of total installed capacity (2010 est.)
country comparison to the world: 45

Electricity—from other renewable sources: 0% of total installed capacity (2010 est.)
country comparison to the world: 113

Crude oil—production: 0 bbl/day (2012 est.)
country comparison to the world: 205

Crude oil—exports: 0 bbl/day (2010 est.)
country comparison to the world: 168

Crude oil—imports: 0 bbl/day (2010 est.)
country comparison to the world: 109

Crude oil—proved reserves: 0 bbl (1 January 2010 es)
country comparison to the world: 176

Refined petroleum products—production: 0 bbl/day (2010 est.)
country comparison to the world: 185

Refined petroleum products—consumption: 98,890 bbl/day (2011 est.)
country comparison to the world: 78

Refined petroleum products—exports: 0 bbl/day (2010 est.)
country comparison to the world: 207

Refined petroleum products—imports: 111,100 bbl/day (2010 est.)
country comparison to the world: 48

Natural gas—production: 0 cu m (2011 est.)
country comparison to the world: 181

Natural gas—consumption: 0 cu m (2010 est.)
country comparison to the world: 186

Natural gas—exports: 0 cu m (2011 est.)
country comparison to the world: 165

Natural gas—imports: 0 cu m (2011 est.)
country comparison to the world: 117

Natural gas—proved reserves: 0 cu m (1 January 2013 es)
country comparison to the world: 183

Carbon dioxide emissions from consumption of energy: 15.9 million Mt (2011 est.)
country comparison to the world: 91

COMMUNICATIONS

Telephones—main lines in use: 640,000 (2012)
country comparison to the world: 9 0

Telephones—mobile cellular: 6.77 million (2012)
country comparison to the world: 96

Telephone system: *general assessment:* domestic and international facilities well-developed
domestic: mobile-cellular telephone subscribership has increased rapidly
international: country code—507; landing point for the Americas Region Caribbean Ring System (ARCOS-1), the MAYA-1, and PAN-AM submarine cable systems that together provide links to the US and parts of the Caribbean, Central America, and South America; satellite earth stations—2 Intelsat (Atlantic Ocean); connected to the Central American Microwave System (2011)

Broadcast media: multiple privately owned TV networks and a government-owned educational TV station; multi-channel cable and satellite TV subscription services are available; more than 100 commercial radio stations (2007)

Internet country code: .pa

Internet hosts: 11,022 (2012)
country comparison to the world: 132

Internet users: 959,800 (2009)
country comparison to the world: 104

TRANSPORTATION

Airports: 117 (2013)
country comparison to the world: 4 9

Airports—with paved runways: *total:* 5 7
over 3,047 m: 1
2,438 to 3,047 m: 3
1,524 to 2,437 m: 3
914 to 1,523 m: 20
under 914 m: 30 (2013)

Airports—with unpaved runways: *total:* 6 0
1,524 to 2,437 m: 1
914 to 1,523 m: 8
under 914 m: 51 (2013)

Heliports: 3 (2013)

Pipelines: oil 128 km (2013)

Railways: *total:* 76 km
country comparison to the world: 127
standard gauge: 76 km 1.435-m gauge (2008)

Roadways: *total:* 15,137 km
country comparison to the world: 122
paved: 6,351 km
unpaved: 8,786 km (2010)

Waterways: 800 km (includes the 82-km Panama Canal that is being widened) (2011)
country comparison to the world: 73

Merchant marine: *total:* 6,413

country comparison to the world: 1
by type: barge carrier 1, bulk carrier 2,525, cargo 1,115, carrier 27, chemical tanker 588, combination ore/oil 1, container 742, liquefied gas 205, passenger 42, passenger/cargo 51, petroleum tanker 545, refrigerated cargo 191, roll on/roll off 87, specialized tanker 3, vehicle carrier 290
foreign-owned: 5,162 (Albania 4, Argentina 5, Australia 4, Bahamas 6, Bangladesh 5, Belgium 1, Bermuda 27, Brazil 3, Bulgaria 6, Burma 3, Canada 6, Chile 14, China 534, Colombia 2, Croatia 2, Cuba 2, Cyprus 5, Denmark 41, Ecuador 3, Egypt 11, Finland 2, France 7, Gabon 1, Germany 24, Gibraltar 1, Greece 379, Hong Kong 144, India 24, Indonesia 10, Iran 5, Ireland 1, Israel 1, Italy 25, Japan 2372, Jordan 11, Kuwait 12, Lebanon 2, Lithuania 3, Luxembourg 1, Malaysia 12, Maldives 2, Malta 2, Mexico 5, Monaco 11, Netherlands 6, Nigeria 6, Norway 81, Oman 10, Pakistan 3, Peru 9, Philippines 5, Portugal 10, Qatar 1, Romania 3, Russia 49, Saudi Arabia 11, Singapore 92, South Korea 373, Spain 30, Sweden 2, Switzerland 15, Syria 34, Taiwan 328, Tanzania 2, Thailand 6, Turkey 62, UAE 83, UK 37, Ukraine 8, US 90, Venezuela 13, Vietnam 43, Yemen 4)
registered in other countries: 1 (Honduras 1) (2010)

Ports and terminals: *major seaport(s):* Balboa, Colon, Cristobal
container port(s) (TEUs): Balboa (3,232,265), Colon (2,390,976), Manzanillo (2,391,066)

MILITARY

Military branches: no regular military forces; Panamanian Public Security Forces (subordinate to the Ministry of Public Security), comprising the National Police (PNP), National Air-Naval Service (SENAN), National Border Service (SENAFRONT) (2013)

Manpower available for military service:
males age 16-49: 890,006 (2010 est.)

Manpower fit for military service:
males age 16-49: 731,254
females age 16-49: 728,329 (2010 est.)

Manpower reaching militarily significant age annually: *male:* 32,142

female: 30,879 (2010 est.)

Military—note: on 10 February 1990, the government of then President ENDARA abolished Panama's military and reformed the security apparatus by creating the Panamanian Public Forces; in October 1994, Panama's Legislative Assembly approved a constitutional amendment prohibiting the creation of a standing military force but allowing the temporary establishment of special police units to counter acts of "external aggression"

TRANSNATIONAL ISSUES

Disputes—international: organized illegal narcotics operations in Colombia operate within the remote border region with Panama
Refugees and internally displaced persons:
refugees (country of origin): 15,723 (Colombia) (2012)

Illicit drugs: major cocaine transshipment point and primary money-laundering center for narcotics revenue; money-laundering activity is especially heavy in the Colon Free Zone; offshore financial center; negligible signs of coca cultivation; monitoring of financial transactions is improving; official corruption remains a major problem

PAPUA NEW GUINEA

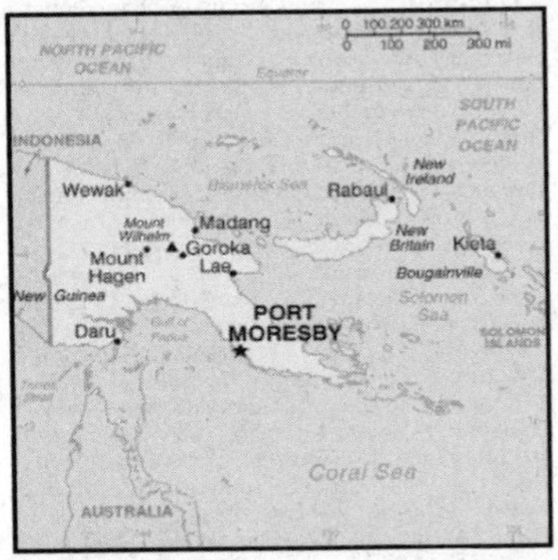

INTRODUCTION

Background: The eastern half of the island of New Guinea—second largest in the world—was divided between Germany (north) and the UK (south) in 1885. The latter area was transferred to Australia in 1902, which occupied the northern portion during World War I and continued to administer the combined areas until independence in 1975. A nine-year secessionist revolt on the island of Bougainville ended in 1997 after claiming some 20,000 lives.

GEOGRAPHY

Location: Oceania, group of islands including the eastern half of the island of New Guinea between the Coral Sea and the South Pacific Ocean, east of Indonesia

Geographic coordinates: 6 00 S, 147 00 E

Map references: Oceania

Area: *total:* 462,840 sq km
country comparison to the world: 55
land: 452,860 sq km
water: 9,980 sq km

Area—comparative: slightly larger than California

Land boundaries: *total:* 820 km
border countries: Indonesia 820 km

Coastline: 5,152 km

Maritime claims: measured from claimed archipelagic baselines
territorial sea: 12 nm
continental shelf: 200 m depth or to the depth of exploitation
exclusive fishing zone: 200 nm

Climate: tropical; northwest monsoon (December to March), southeast monsoon (May to October); slight seasonal temperature variation

Terrain: mostly mountains with coastal lowlands and rolling foothills

Elevation extremes: *lowest point:* Pacific Ocean 0 m
highest point: Mount Wilhelm 4,509 m

Natural resources: gold, copper, silver, natural gas, timber, oil, fisheries

Land use: *arable land:* 0.65%
permanent crops: 1.51%
other: 97.84% (2011)

Irrigated land: 0 sq km (2003)

Total renewable water resources: 801 cu km (2011)

Freshwater withdrawal (domestic/industrial/agricultural): *total:* 0.39 cu km/yr (57%/43%/0%)
per capita: 61.3 cu m/yr (2005)

Natural hazards: active volcanism; situated along the Pacific "Ring of Fire"; the country is subject to frequent and sometimes severe earthquakes; mud slides; tsunamis
volcanism: severe volcanic activity; Ulawun (elev. 2,334 m), one of Papua New Guinea's potentially most dangerous volcanoes, has been deemed a Decade Volcano by the International Association of Volcanology and Chemistry of the Earth's Interior, worthy of study due to its explosive history and close proximity to human populations; Rabaul (elev. 688 m) destroyed the city of Rabaul in 1937 and 1994; Lamington erupted in 1951 killing 3,000 people; Manam's 2004 eruption forced the island's abandonment; other historically active volcanoes include Bam, Bagana, Garbuna, Karkar, Langila, Lolobau, Long Island, Pago, St. Andrew Strait, Victory, and Waiowa

Environment—current issues: rain forest subject to deforestation as a result of growing commercial demand for tropical timber; pollution from mining projects; severe drought

Environment—international agreements:
party to: Antarctic Treaty, Biodiversity, Climate Change, Climate Change-Kyoto Protocol, Desertification, Endangered Species, Environmental Modification, Hazardous Wastes, Law of the Sea, Marine Dumping, Ozone Layer Protection, Ship Pollution, Tropical Timber 83, Tropical Timber 94, Wetlands
signed, but not ratified: none of the selected agreements

Geography—note: shares island of New Guinea with Indonesia; one of world's largest swamps along southwest coast

PEOPLE AND SOCIETY

Nationality: *noun:* Papua New Guinean(s)
adjective: Papua New Guinean

Ethnic groups: Melanesian, Papuan, Negrito, Micronesian, Polynesian

Languages: Tok Pisin (official), English (official), Hiri Motu (official), some 836 indigenous languages spoken (about 12% of the world's total); most languages have fewer than 1,000 speakers
note: Tok Pisin, a creole language, is widely used and understood; English is spoken by 1%-2%; Hiri Motu is spoken by less than 2%

Religions: Roman Catholic 27%, Protestant 69.4% (Evangelical Lutheran 19.5%, United Church 11.5%, Seventh-Day Adventist 10%, Pentecostal 8.6%, Evangelical Alliance 5.2%, Anglican 3.2%, Baptist 2.5%, other Protestant 8.9%), Baha'i 0.3%, indigenous beliefs and other 3.3% (2000 census)

Population: 6,552,730 (July 2014 est.)
country comparison to the world: 106

Age structure: *0-14 years:* 35% (male 1,165,911/female 1,125,104)
15-24 years: 19.7% (male 652,548/female 635,411)
25-54 years: 36.2% (male 1,226,213/female 1,146,951)
55-64 years: 3.9% (male 173,019/female 169,329)
65 years and over: 3.8% (male 134,396/female 123,848) (2014 est.)

Dependency ratios:
total dependency ratio: 69.3 %
youth dependency ratio: 64.3 %
elderly dependency ratio: 4.9 %
potential support ratio: 20.3 (2013)

Median age: *total:* 22.4 years
male: 22.6 years
female: 22.2 years (2014 est.)

Population growth rate: 1.84% (2014 est.)
country comparison to the world: 65

Birth rate: 24.89 births/1,000 population (2014 est.)
country comparison to the world: 57

Death rate: 6.53 deaths/1,000 population (2014 est.)
country comparison to the world: 150

Net migration rate: 0 migrant(s)/1,000 population (2014 est.)
country comparison to the world: 90

Urbanization: *urban population:* 13% of total population (2010)
rate of urbanization: 2.9% annual rate of change (2010-15 est.)

Major urban areas—population: PORT MORESBY (capital) 314,000 (2009)

Sex ratio: *at birth:* 1.05 male(s)/female
0-14 years: 1.04 male(s)/female
15-24 years: 1.03 male(s)/female
25-54 years: 1.07 male(s)/female
55-64 years: 1.05 male(s)/female
65 years and over: 1.14 male(s)/female
total population: 1.05 male(s)/female (2014 est.)

Maternal mortality rate: 230 deaths/100,000 live births (2010)
country comparison to the world: 51

Infant mortality rate: *total:* 39.67 deaths/1,000 live births
country comparison to the world: 54
male: 43.29 deaths/1,000 live births
female: 35.87 deaths/1,000 live births (2014 est.)

Life expectancy at birth: *total population:* 66.85 years
country comparison to the world: 168
male: 64.63 years
female: 69.19 years (2014 est.)

Total fertility rate: 3.24 children born/woman (2014 est.)
country comparison to the world: 50

Contraceptive prevalence rate: 32.4% (2007)

Health expenditures: 4.3% of GDP (2011)
country comparison to the world: 155

Physicians density: 0.05 physicians/1,000 population (2008)

Drinking water source:
improved:
urban: 89.2% of population
rural: 33.3% of population

total: 40.2% of population
unimproved:
urban: 10.8% of population
rural: 66.7% of population
total: 59.8% of population (2011 est.)

Sanitation facility access:
improved:
urban: 56.7% of population
rural: 13.3% of population
total: 18.7% of population
unimproved:
urban: 43.3% of population
rural: 86.7% of population
total: 81.3% of population (2011 est.)

HIV/AIDS—adult prevalence rate: 0.5% (2012 est.)
country comparison to the world: 72

HIV/AIDS—people living with HIV/AIDS: 24,900 (2012 est.)
country comparison to the world: 76

HIV/AIDS—deaths: 1,000 (2012 est.)
country comparison to the world: 78

Major infectious diseases: *degree of risk:* very high
food or waterborne diseases: bacterial diarrhea, hepatitis A, and typhoid fever
vectorborne diseases: dengue fever and malaria (2013)

Obesity—adult prevalence rate: 16.2% (2008)
country comparison to the world: 115

Children under the age of 5 years underweight: 18.1% (2005)
country comparison to the world: 37

Education expenditures: NA

Literacy: *definition:* age 15 and over can read and write
total population: 62.4%
male: 65.4%
female: 59.4% (2011 est.)

People—note: the indigenous population of Papua New Guinea is one of the most heterogeneous in the world; PNG has several thousand separate communities, most with only a few hundred people; divided by language, customs, and tradition, some of these communities have engaged in low-scale tribal conflict with their neighbors for millennia; the advent of modern weapons and modern migrants into urban areas has greatly magnified the impact of this lawlessness

GOVERNMENT

Country name: *conventional long form:* Independent State of Papua New Guinea
conventional short form: Papua New Guinea
local short form: Papuaniugini
former: Territory of Papua and New Guinea
abbreviation: PNG

Government type: constitutional parliamentary democracy and a Commonwealth realm

Capital: *name:* Port Moresby

geographic coordinates: 9 27 S, 147 11 E

time difference: UTC+10 (15 hours ahead of Washington, DC during Standard Time)

Administrative divisions: 20 provinces, 1 autonomous region*, and 1 district**; Bougainville*, Central, Chimbu, Eastern Highlands, East New Britain, East Sepik, Enga, Gulf, Hela, Jiwaka, Madang, Manus, Milne Bay, Morobe, National Capital**, New Ireland, Northern, Southern Highlands, Western, Western Highlands, West New Britain, West Sepik

Independence: 16 September 1975 (from the Australian-administered UN trusteeship)

National holiday: Independence Day, 16 September (1975)

Constitution: adopted 15 August 1975, effective at independence 16 September 1975; amended many times, last in 2003 (2013)

Legal system: mixed legal system of English common law and customary law

International law organization participation: has not submitted an ICJ jurisdiction declaration; non-party state to the ICCt

Suffrage: 18 years of age; universal

Executive branch: *chief of state:* Queen ELIZABETH II (since 6 February 1952); represented by Governor Michael OGIO (since 25 February 2011)
head of government: Prime Minister Peter Paire O'NEILL (since 2 August 2011); Deputy Prime Minister Leo DION (since 9 August 2012)
cabinet: National Executive Council appointed by the governor general on the recommendation of the prime minister (For more information visit the World Leaders website)
elections: the monarchy is hereditary; the governor general nominated by parliament and appointed by the chief of state; following legislative elections, the leader of the majority party or leader of the majority coalition usually appointed prime minister by the governor general acting in accordance with a decision of the parliament; Peter Paire O'NEILL elected prime minister by parliament on 3 August 2012 by a vote of 94 to 12

Legislative branch: unicameral National Parliament (111 seats, 89 filled from open electorates and 20 from provinces and national capital district; members elected by popular vote to serve five-year terms); constitution allows up to 126 seats
elections: last held from 23 June 2012 to 27 July 2012 (next to be held in June 2017)
election results: percent of vote by party—NA; seats by party—People's National Congress Party 27, Triumph Heritage Empowerment Party 12, PNG Party 8, National Alliance Party 7, United Resources Party 7, People's Party 6, People's Progess Party 6, other parties 22, independents 16
note: 14 other parties won 3 or fewer seats; association with political parties is fluid

Judicial branch: *highest court(s):* Supreme Court (consists of the chief justice, deputy chief justice, and 28 other judges); National Courts (10 courts located in the province capitals, with a total of 16 resident judges)
judge selection and term of office: chief justice appointed by the governor-general upon advice of the National Executive Council (cabinet) after consultation with the National Justice Administration Minister; deputy chief justice and other justices appointed by the Judicial and Legal Services Commission, a 5-member body to include the Supreme Court chief and deputy chief justices, the chief ombudsman, and a member of the National Parliament; citizen judges appointed for 10-year renewable terms; non-citizen judges appointed for 3-year renewable terms; appointment and tenure of National Court resident judges NA
subordinate courts: district, village, and juvenile courts

Political parties and leaders: National Alliance Party or NA [Patrick PRUAITCHI]; Papua New Guinea Party or PNGP [Beldan NEMAH]; People's National Congress Party or PNC [Peter Paire O'NEILL]; People's Party or PP; People's Progress Party or PPP; Triumph Heritage Empowerment Party or THE [Don POYLE]; United Resources Party or URP [William DUMA]
note: as of 13 March 2012, 41 political parties were registered

Political pressure groups and leaders: Centre for Environment Law and Community Rights or Celcor; [Damien ASE]; Community Coalition Against Corruption; National Council of Women; Transparency International PNG

International organization participation: ACP, ADB, AOSIS, APEC, ARF, ASEAN (observer), C, CD, CP, FAO, G-77, IAEA, IBRD, ICAO, ICRM, IDA, IFAD, IFC, IFRCS, IHO, ILO, IMF, IMO, Interpol, IOC, IOM, IOM (observer), IPU, ISO (correspondent), ITSO, ITU, MIGA, NAM, OPCW, PIF, Sparteca, SPC, UN, UNCTAD, UNESCO, UNIDO, UNMISS, UNWTO, UPU, WCO, WFTU (NGOs), WHO, WIPO, WMO, WTO

Diplomatic representation in the US:
chief of mission: Ambassador (vacant); Charge d'Affaires Elias Rahuromo WOHENGU
chancery: 1779 Massachusetts Avenue NW, Suite 805, Washington, DC 20036
telephone: [1] (202) 745-3680
FAX: [1] (202) 745-3679

Diplomatic representation from the US:
chief of mission: Ambassador Walter E. NORTH (since 7 November 2012); note—also accredited to the Solomon Islands and Vanuatu
embassy: Douglas Street, Port Moresby, N.C.D.
mailing address: 4240 Port Moresby Place, US Department of State, Washington DC 20521-4240
telephone: [675] 321-1455
FAX: [675] 321-3423

Flag description: divided diagonally from upper hoist-side corner; the upper triangle is red with a soaring yellow bird of paradise centered; the lower triangle is black with five, white, five-pointed stars of the Southern Cross constellation centered; red, black, and yellow are traditional colors of Papua New Guinea; the bird of paradise—endemic to the island of New Guinea—is an emblem of regional tribal culture and represents the emergence of Papua New Guinea as a nation; the Southern Cross, visible in the night sky, symbolizes Papua New Guinea's connection with Australia and several other countries in the South Pacific

National symbol(s): bird of paradise

National anthem: *name:* "O Arise All You Sons"
lyrics/music: Thomas SHACKLADY
note: adopted 1975

ECONOMY

Economy—overview: Papua New Guinea (PNG) is richly endowed with natural resources, but exploitation has been hampered by rugged terrain, land tenure issues, and the high cost of developing infrastructure. The economy has a small formal sector, focused mainly on the export of those natural resources, and an informal sector, employing the majority of the population. Agriculture provides a subsistence livelihood for 85% of the people. Mineral deposits, including copper, gold, and oil, account for nearly two-thirds of export earnings. Natural gas reserves amount to an estimated 155 billion cubic meters. A consortium led by a major American oil company is constructing a liquefied natural gas (LNG) production facility that could begin exporting in 2014. As the largest investment project in the country's history, it has the potential to double GDP in the near-term and triple Papua New Guinea's export revenue. An American-owned firm also opened PNG's first oil refinery in 2004 and is building a second LNG production facility. The government faces the challenge of ensuring transparency and accountability for revenues flowing from this and other large LNG projects. In 2011 and 2012, the National Parliament passed legislation that created an offshore Sovereign Wealth Fund (SWF) to manage government surpluses from mineral, oil, and natural gas projects. In recent years, the government has opened up markets in telecommunications and air transport, making both more affordable to the people. Numerous challenges still face the government of Peter O'NEILL, including providing physical security for foreign investors, regaining investor confidence, restoring integrity to state institutions, promoting economic efficiency by privatizing moribund state institutions, and maintaining good relations with Australia, its former colonial ruler. Other socio-cultural challenges could upend the economy including chronic law and order and land tenure issues. The global financial crisis had little impact because of continued foreign demand for PNG's commodities.

GDP (purchasing power parity): $19.96 billion (2013 est.)
country comparison to the world: 135
$18.93 billion (2012 est.)
$17.51 billion (2011 est.)
note: data are in 2013 US dollars

GDP (official exchange rate): $16.1 billion (2013 est.)

GDP—real growth rate: 5.4% (2013 est.)
country comparison to the world: 47
8.1% (2012 est.)
10.7% (2011 est.)

GDP—per capita (PPP): $2,900 (2013 est.)
country comparison to the world: 178
$2,800 (2012 est.)
$2,600 (2011 est.)
note: data are in 2013 US dollars

Gross national saving: -1.9% of GDP (2013 est.)
country comparison to the world: 152
-3.9% of GDP (2012 est.)
13.9% of GDP (2011 est.)

GDP—composition, by end use:
household consumption: 55.7%
government consumption: 8.9%
investment in fixed capital: 13.3%
investment in inventories: 18.4%
exports of goods and services: 53.6%
imports of goods and services: -49.9% (2013 est.)

GDP—composition, by sector of origin:
agriculture: 27.6%
industry: 39.1%
services: 33.3% (2013 est.)

Agriculture—products: coffee, cocoa, copra, palm kernels, tea, sugar, rubber, sweet potatoes, fruit, vegetables, vanilla; poultry, pork; shellfish

Industries: copra crushing, palm oil processing, plywood production, wood chip production; mining (gold, silver, and copper); crude oil production, petroleum refining; construction, tourism

Industrial production growth rate: 5.5% (2013 est.)
country comparison to the world: 50

Labor force: 4.077 million (2013 est.)
country comparison to the world: 90

Labor force—by occupation: *agriculture:* 85%
industry: NA%
services: NA% (2005 est.)

Unemployment rate: 1.9% (2008 est.)
country comparison to the world: 11
1.7% (2004)

Population below poverty line: 37% (2002 est.)

Household income or consumption by percentage share: *lowest 10%:* 1.7%
highest 10%: 40.5% (1996)

Distribution of family income—Gini index: 50.9 (1996)
country comparison to the world: 18

Budget: *revenues:* $4.359 billion
expenditures: $5.105 billion (2013 est.)

Taxes and other revenues: 27.1% of GDP (2013 est.)
country comparison to the world: 108

Budget surplus (+) or deficit (-): -4.6% of GDP (2013 est.)
country comparison to the world: 161

Public debt: 28.1% of GDP (2013 est.)
country comparison to the world: 125
25.5% of GDP (2012 est.)

Fiscal year: calendar year

Inflation rate (consumer prices): 3.8% (2013 est.)
country comparison to the world: 127
2.3% (2012 est.)

Central bank discount rate: 14% (31 December 2010 est.)
country comparison to the world: 45
6.92% (31 December 2009 est.)

Commercial bank prime lending rate: 10.6% (31 December 2013 est.)
country comparison to the world: 81
10.82% (31 December 2012 est.)

Stock of narrow money: $4.825 billion (31 December 2013 est.)
country comparison to the world: 101
$5.301 billion (31 December 2012 est.)

Stock of broad money: $7.366 billion (31 December 2013 est.)
country comparison to the world: 113
$8.068 billion (31 December 2012 est.)

Stock of domestic credit: $4.098 billion (31 December 2013 est.)
country comparison to the world: 121
$4.342 billion (31 December 2012 est.)

Market value of publicly traded shares: $10.71 billion (31 December 2012 est.)
country comparison to the world: 73
$8.999 billion (31 December 2011)
$9.742 billion (31 December 2010 est.)

Current account balance: -$2.396 billion (2013 est.)
country comparison to the world: 150
-$3.03 billion (2012 est.)

Exports: $5.392 billion (2013 est.)
country comparison to the world: 112
$5.602 billion (2012 est.)

Exports—commodities: oil, gold, copper ore, logs, palm oil, coffee, cocoa, crayfish, prawns

Exports—partners: Australia 30.1%, Japan 9.9%, China 5%, Germany 4.1% (2012)

Imports: $4.587 billion (2013 est.)
country comparison to the world: 133
$4.767 billion (2012 est.)

Imports—commodities: machinery and transport equipment, manufactured goods, food, fuels, chemicals

Imports—partners: Australia 36.3%, Singapore 13.8%, Malaysia 8.4%, China 7.9%, Japan 5.8%, US 4.8% (2012)

Reserves of foreign exchange and gold: $2.926 billion (31 December 2013 est.)
country comparison to the world: 108
$4.001 billion (31 December 2012 est.)

Debt—external: $13.61 billion (31 December 2013 est.)
country comparison to the world: 94
$12.96 billion (31 December 2012 est.)

Stock of direct foreign investment—at home: $NA

Stock of direct foreign investment—abroad: $NA

Exchange rates: kina (PGK) per US dollar—
2.278 (2013 est.)
2.0837 (2012 est.)
2.7193 (2010 est.)
2.7551 (2009)
2.6956 (2008)

ENERGY

Electricity—production: 3.35 billion kWh (2010 est.)
country comparison to the world: 129

Electricity—consumption: 3.116 billion kWh (2010 est.)
country comparison to the world: 130

Electricity—exports: 0 kWh (2012 est.)
country comparison to the world: 183

Electricity—imports: 0 kWh (2012 est.)
country comparison to the world: 186

Electricity—installed generating capacity: 700,000 kW (2010 est.)
country comparison to the world: 130

Electricity—from fossil fuels: 61.1% of total installed capacity (2010 est.)
country comparison to the world: 133

Electricity—from nuclear fuels: 0% of total installed capacity (2010 est.)
country comparison to the world: 164

Electricity—from hydroelectric plants: 30.9% of total installed capacity (2010 est.)
country comparison to the world: 79

Electricity—from other renewable sources: 8% of total installed capacity (2010 est.)
country comparison to the world: 29

Crude oil—production: 27,490 bbl/day (2012 est.)
country comparison to the world: 72

Crude oil—exports: 28,400 bbl/day (2010 est.)
country comparison to the world: 50

Crude oil—imports: 14,880 bbl/day (2010 est.)
country comparison to the world: 74

Crude oil—proved reserves: 154.3 million bbl (1 January 2013 es)
country comparison to the world: 64

Refined petroleum products—production: 17,330 bbl/day (2010 est.)
country comparison to the world: 95

Refined petroleum products—consumption: 36,320 bbl/day (2011 est.)
country comparison to the world: 110

Refined petroleum products—exports: 3,536 bbl/day (2010 est.)
country comparison to the world: 95

Refined petroleum products—imports: 5,937 bbl/day (2010 est.)
country comparison to the world: 145

Natural gas—production: 100 million cu m (2011 est.)
country comparison to the world: 83

Natural gas—consumption: 110 million cu m (2010 est.)
country comparison to the world: 106

Natural gas—exports: 0 cu m (2011 est.)
country comparison to the world: 167

Natural gas—imports: 0 cu m (2011 est.)
country comparison to the world: 118

Natural gas—proved reserves: 155.3 billion cu m (1 January 2013 es)
country comparison to the world: 49

Carbon dioxide emissions from consumption of energy: 3.279 million Mt (2011 est.)
country comparison to the world: 136

COMMUNICATIONS

Telephones—main lines in use: 139,000 (2012)
country comparison to the world: 140

Telephones—mobile cellular: 2.709 million (2012)
country comparison to the world: 134

Telephone system: *general assessment:* services are minimal; facilities provide radiotelephone and telegraph, coastal radio, aeronautical radio, and international radio communication services
domestic: access to telephone services is not widely available although combined fixed-line and mobile-cellular teledensity has increased to roughly 40 per 100 persons
international: country code—675; submarine cables to Australia and Guam; satellite earth station—1 Intelsat (Pacific Ocean); international radio communication service (2009)

Broadcast media: 2 TV stations, 1 commercial station operating since the late 1980s and 1 state-run station launched in 2008; satellite and cable TV services are available; state-run National Broadcasting Corporation operates 3 radio networks with multiple repeaters and about 20 provincial stations; several commercial radio stations with multiple transmission points as well as several community stations; transmissions of several international broadcasters are accessible (2009)

Internet country code: .pg

Internet hosts: 5,006 (2012)
country comparison to the world: 145

Internet users: 125,000 (2009)
country comparison to the world: 152

TRANSPORTATION

Airports: 561 (2013)
country comparison to the world: 1 2

Airports—with paved runways: *total:* 2 1
over 3,047 m: 1
2,438 to 3,047 m: 2
1,524 to 2,437 m: 12
914 to 1,523 m: 5
under 914 m: 1 (2013)

Airports—with unpaved runways: *total:* 540
1,524 to 2,437 m: 11
914 to 1,523 m: 53
under 914 m: 476 (2013)

Heliports: 2 (2013)

Pipelines: oil 264 km (2013)

Roadways: *total:* 9,349 km
country comparison to the world: 137
paved: 3,000 km
unpaved: 6,349 km (2011)

Waterways: 11,000 km (2011)
country comparison to the world: 12

Merchant marine: *total:* 3 1
country comparison to the world: 84
by type: bulk carrier 7, cargo 22, petroleum tanker 2
foreign-owned: 8 (Germany 1, Malaysia 1, UAE 6) (2010)

Ports and terminals: *major seaport(s):* Kimbe, Lae, Madang, Rabaul, Wewak

MILITARY

Military branches: Papua New Guinea Defense Force (PNGDF; includes Maritime Operations Element, Air Operations Element) (2013)

Military service age and obligation: 16 years of age for voluntary military service (with parental consent); no conscription; graduation from grade 12 required (2013)

Manpower available for military service:
males age 16-49: 1,568,210
females age 16-49: 1,478,965 (2010 est.)

Manpower fit for military service:
males age 16-49: 1,130,951
females age 16-49: 1,137,753 (2010 est.)

Manpower reaching militarily significant age annually: *male:* 67,781
female: 65,820 (2010 est.)

Military expenditures: 0.54% of GDP (2012)
country comparison to the world: 126
0.6% of GDP (2011)
0.54% of GDP (2010)

TRANSNATIONAL ISSUES

Disputes—international: relies on assistance from Australia to keep out illegal cross-border activities from primarily Indonesia, including goods smuggling, illegal narcotics trafficking, and squatters and secessionists

Refugees and internally displaced persons: *refugees (country of origin):* 9,368 (Indonesia) (2012)

Trafficking in persons: *current situation:* Papua New Guinea is a source, destination, and transit country for men, women, and children subjected to sex trafficking and forced labor; women and children are subjected to sex trafficking and domestic servitude; families may sell girls into forced marriages to settle debts, leaving them vulnerable to forced domestic service; local and Chinese men are forced to labor in logging and mining camps; migrant women from Malaysia, Thailand, China, and the Philippines are subjected to sex trafficking and domestic servitude at logging and mining camps, fisheries, and entertainment sites tier rating: Tier 3—Papua New Guinea does not fully comply with the minimum standards for the elimination of trafficking and is not making significant efforts to do so; despite acknowledging trafficking as a problem, the government has not enacted legislation to criminalize all forms of trafficking, investigated any suspected trafficking offenses, prosecuted or convicted any trafficking offenders under existing laws, addressed allegations of officials being complicit in human trafficking crimes, or identified or assisted any trafficking victims; Papua New Guinea is not a party to the 2000 UN TIP Protocol

Illicit drugs: major consumer of cannabis

PARACEL ISLANDS

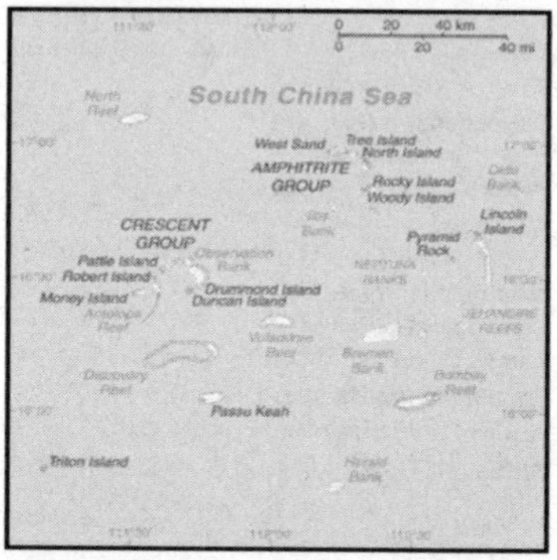

INTRODUCTION

Background: The Paracel Islands are surrounded by productive fishing grounds and by potential oil and gas reserves. In 1932, French Indochina annexed the islands and set up a weather station on Pattle Island; maintenance was continued by its successor, Vietnam. China has occupied all the Paracel Islands since 1974, when its troops seized a South Vietnamese garrison occupying the western islands. China built a military installation on Woody Island with an airfield and artificial harbor. The islands also are claimed by Taiwan and Vietnam.

GEOGRAPHY

Location: Southeastern Asia, group of small islands and reefs in the South China Sea, about one-third of the way from central Vietnam to the northern Philippines

Geographic coordinates: 16 30 N, 112 00 E

Map references: Southeast Asia

Area: *total:* ca. 7.75 sq km
land: ca. 7.75 sq km
water: 0 sq km

Area—comparative: NA

Land boundaries: 0 km

Coastline: 518 km

Maritime claims: NA

Climate: tropical

Terrain: mostly low and flat

Elevation extremes: *lowest point:* South China Sea 0 m
highest point: unnamed location on Rocky Island 14 m

Natural resources: none

Land use: *arable land:* 0%
permanent crops: 0%
other: 100% (2011)

Irrigated land: 0 sq km (2011)

Natural hazards: typhoons

Environment—current issues: NA

Geography—note: composed of 130 small coral islands and reefs divided into the northeast Amphitrite Group and the western Crescent Group

PEOPLE AND SOCIETY

Population: no indigenous inhabitants
note: there are scattered Chinese garrisons

GOVERNMENT

Country name: *conventional long form:* none
conventional short form: Paracel Islands

ECONOMY

Economy—overview: The islands have the potential for oil and gas development. Waters around the islands support commercial fishing, but the islands themselves are not populated on a permanent basis.

TRANSPORTATION

Airports: 1 (2013)
country comparison to the world: 230

Airports—with paved runways: total: 1
1,524 to 2,437 m: 1 (2013)

Ports and terminals: small Chinese port facilities on Woody Island and Duncan Island

MILITARY

Military—note: occupied by China

TRANSNATIONAL ISSUES

Disputes—international: occupied by China, also claimed by Taiwan and Vietnam

PARAGUAY

INTRODUCTION

Background: Paraguay achieved its independence from Spain in 1811. In the disastrous War of the Triple Alliance (1865-70)—between Paraguay and Argentina, Brazil, and Uruguay—Paraguay lost two-thirds of its adult males and much of its territory. The country stagnated economically for the next half century. Following the Chaco War of 1932-35 with Bolivia, Paraguay gained a large part of the Chaco lowland region. The 35-year military dictatorship of Alfredo STROESSNER ended in 1989, and, despite a marked increase in political infighting in recent years, Paraguay has held relatively free and regular presidential elections since the country's return to democracy.

GEOGRAPHY

Location: Central South America, northeast of Argentina, southwest of Brazil

Geographic coordinates: 23 00 S, 58 00 W

Map references: South America

Area: *total:* 406,752 sq km
country comparison to the world: 60
land: 397,302 sq km
water: 9,450 sq km

Area—comparative: slightly smaller than California

Land boundaries: *total:* 3,995 km
border countries: Argentina 1,880 km, Bolivia 750 km, Brazil 1,365 km

Coastline: 0 km (landlocked)

Maritime claims: none (landlocked)

Climate: subtropical to temperate; substantial rainfall in the eastern portions, becoming semiarid in the far west

Terrain: grassy plains and wooded hills east of Rio Paraguay; Gran Chaco region west of Rio Paraguay mostly low, marshy plain near the river, and dry forest and thorny scrub elsewhere

Elevation extremes: *lowest point:* junction of Rio Paraguay and Rio Parana 46 m
highest point: Cerro Pero 842 m

Natural resources: hydropower, timber, iron ore, manganese, limestone

Land use: *arable land:* 9.59%
permanent crops: 0.22%
other: 90.19% (2011)

Irrigated land: 670 sq km (2003)

Total renewable water resources: 336 cu km (2011)

Freshwater withdrawal (domestic/industrial/agricultural): *total:* 0.49 cu km/yr (20%/8%/71%)
per capita: 88.05 cu m/yr (2000)

Natural hazards: local flooding in southeast (early September to June); poorly drained plains may become boggy (early October to June)

Environment—current issues: deforestation; water pollution; inadequate means for waste disposal pose health risks for many urban residents; loss of wetlands

Environment—international agreements:
party to: Biodiversity, Climate Change, Climate Change-Kyoto Protocol, Desertification, Endangered Species, Hazardous Wastes, Law of the Sea, Ozone Layer Protection, Wetlands
signed, but not ratified: none of the selected agreements

Geography—note: landlocked; lies between Argentina, Bolivia, and Brazil; population concentrated in southern part of country

PEOPLE AND SOCIETY

Nationality: *noun:* Paraguayan(s)
adjective: Paraguayan

Ethnic groups: mestizo (mixed Spanish and Amerindian) 95%, other 5%

Languages: Spanish (official), Guarani (official)

Religions: Roman Catholic 89.6%, Protestant 6.2%, other Christian 1.1%, other or unspecified 1.9%, none 1.1% (2002 census)

Demographic profile: Paraguay falls below the Latin American average in several socioeconomic categories, including immunization rates, potable water, sanitation, and secondary school enrollment, and has greater rates of income inequality and child and maternal mortality. Paraguay's poverty rate has declined in recent years but remains high, especially in rural areas, with more than a third of the population below the poverty line. However, the well-being of the poor in many regions has improved in terms of housing quality and access to clean water, telephone service, and electricity. The fertility rate continues to drop, declining sharply from an average 4.3 births per woman in the late 1990s to about 2 in 2013, as a result of the greater educational attainment of women, increased use of contraception, and a desire for smaller families among young women. Paraguay is a country of emigration; it has not attracted large numbers of immigrants because of political instability, civil wars, years of dictatorship, and the greater appeal of neighboring countries. Paraguay first tried to encourage immigration in 1870 in order to rebound from the heavy death toll it suffered during the tried to encourage immigration in 1870 in order to rebound from the heavy death toll it suffered during the War of the Triple Alliance, but it received few European and Middle Eastern immigrants. In the 20th century, limited numbers of immigrants arrived from Lebanon, Japan, South Korea, and China, as well as Mennonites from Canada, Russia, and Mexico. Large flows of Brazilian immigrants have been arriving since the 1960s, mainly to work in agriculture. Paraguayans continue to emigrate to Argentina, Brazil, Uruguay, the United States, Italy, Spain, and France.

Population: 6,703,860 (July 2014 est.)
country comparison to the world: 105

Age structure:
0-14 years: 26.2% (male 892,315/female 861,915)
15-24 years: 20.5% (male 691,365/female 683,653)
25-54 years: 39.5% (male 1,326,281/female 1,323,194)
55-64 years: 6.6% (male 246,869/female 236,564)
65 years and over: 6.4% (male 206,089/female 235,615) (2014 est.)

Dependency ratios:
total dependency ratio: 61 %
youth dependency ratio: 52.2 %
elderly dependency ratio: 8.8 %
potential support ratio: 11.4 (2013)

Median age: *total:* 26.8 years
male: 26.6 years
female: 27 years (2014 est.)

Population growth rate: 1.19% (2014 est.)
country comparison to the world: 100

Birth rate: 16.66 births/1,000 population (2014 est.)
country comparison to the world: 118

Death rate: 4.64 deaths/1,000 population (2014 est.)
country comparison to the world: 200

Net migration rate: -0.08 migrant(s)/1,000 population (2014 est.)
country comparison to the world: 114

Urbanization: *urban population:* 61% of total population (2010)
rate of urbanization: 2.5% annual rate of change (2010-15 est.)

Major urban areas—population: ASUNCION (capital) 1.977 million (2009)

Sex ratio: *at birth:* 1.05 male(s)/female
0-14 years: 1.04 male(s)/female
15-24 years: 1.01 male(s)/female
25-54 years: 1 male(s)/female
55-64 years: 1.01 male(s)/female
65 years and over: 0.87 male(s)/female
total population: 1.01 male(s)/female (2014 est.)

Mother's mean age at first birth: 22.9
note: median age at first birth among women 25-29 (2008 est.)

Maternal mortality rate: 99 deaths/100,000 live births (2010)
country comparison to the world: 73

Infant mortality rate: *total:* 20.75 deaths/1,000 live births
country comparison to the world: 86
male: 24.39 deaths/1,000 live births
female: 16.93 deaths/1,000 live births (2014 est.)

Life expectancy at birth: *total population:* 76.8 years
country comparison to the world: 72
male: 74.16 years
female: 79.56 years (2014 est.)

Total fertility rate: 1.96 children born/woman (2014 est.)
country comparison to the world: 131

Contraceptive prevalence rate: 79.4%
note: percent of women aged 15-44 (2008)

Health expenditures: 9.7% of GDP (2011)
country comparison to the world: 29

Physicians density: 1.11 physicians/1,000 population (2002)

Hospital bed density: 1.3 beds/1,000 population (2011)

Drinking water source:
improved:
urban: 99.4% of population
rural: 66% of population
total: 86.5% of population
unimproved:
urban: 0.6% of population
rural: 34% of population
total: 13.5% of population (2010 est.)

Sanitation facility access:
improved:
urban: 89.9% of population
rural: 40.5% of population
total: 70.8% of population
unimproved:
urban: 10.1% of population
rural: 59.5% of population
total: 29.2% of population (2010 est.)

HIV/AIDS—adult prevalence rate: 0.3% (2012 est.)
country comparison to the world: 86

HIV/AIDS—people living with HIV/AIDS: 13,100 (2012 est.)
country comparison to the world: 96

HIV/AIDS—deaths: 300 (2012 est.)
country comparison to the world: 104

Major infectious diseases: *degree of risk:* intermediate
food or waterborne diseases: bacterial diarrhea, hepatitis A, and typhoid fever
vectorborne disease: dengue fever (2013)

Obesity—adult prevalence rate: 17.9% (2008)
country comparison to the world: 110

Children under the age of 5 years underweight: 3.4% (2005)
country comparison to the world: 104

Education expenditures: 4.8% of GDP (2011)
country comparison to the world: 84

Literacy: *definition:* age 15 and over can read and write
total population: 93.9%
male: 94.8%
female: 92.9% (2010 est.)

School life expectancy (primary to tertiary education): *total:* 13 years
male: 12 years
female: 13 years (2011)

Child labor—children ages 5-14:
total number: 205,297
percentage: 15 % (2004 est.)

Unemployment, youth ages 15-24: *total:* 11.2%
country comparison to the world: 104
male: 9%
female: 14.6% (2012)

GOVERNMENT

Country name: *conventional long form:* Republic of Paraguay
conventional short form: Paraguay
local long form: Republica del Paraguay
local short form: Paraguay

Government type: constitutional republic

Capital: *name:* Asuncion

geographic coordinates: 25 16 S, 57 40 W
time difference: UTC-4 (1 hour ahead of Washington, DC during Standard Time)
daylight saving time: +1hr, begins first Sunday in October; ends fourth Sunday in March

Administrative divisions: 17 departments (departamentos, singular—departamento) and 1 capital city*; Alto Paraguay, Alto Parana, Amambay, Asuncion*, Boqueron, Caaguazu, Caazapa, Canindeyu, Central, Concepcion, Cordillera, Guaira, Itapua, Misiones, Neembucu, Paraguari, Presidente Hayes, San Pedro

Independence: 14 May 1811 (from Spain)

National holiday: Independence Day, 14 May 1811 (observed 15 May)

Constitution: several previous; latest approved and promulgated 20 June 1992; amended 2011 (2011)

Legal system: civil law system with influences from Argentine, Spanish, Roman, and French civil law models; judicial review of legislative acts in Supreme Court of Justice

International law organization participation: accepts compulsory ICJ jurisdiction; accepts ICCt jurisdiction

Suffrage: 18 years of age; universal and compulsory until the age of 75

Executive branch: *chief of state:* President Horacio CARTES (since 15 August 2013); Vice President Juan AFARA Maciel (since 15 August 2013); note—the president is both the chief of state and head of government
head of government: President Horacio CARTES (since 15 August 2013); Vice President Juan AFARA Maciel (since 15 August 2013)
cabinet: Council of Ministers appointed by the president (For more information visit the World Leaders website)
elections: president and vice president elected on the same ticket by popular vote for a single five-year term; election last held on 21 April 2013 (next to be held in April 2018)
election results: Horacio CARTES elected president; percent of vote—Horacio CARTES 45.8%, Efrain ALEGRE 36.94%, Mario FERREIRO 5.88%, Anibal CARRILLO 3.32%, other 8.06%

Legislative branch: bicameral National Congress or Congreso Nacional consists of the Chamber of Senators or Camara de Senadores (45 seats; members elected by popular vote to serve five-year terms) and the Chamber of Deputies or Camara de Diputados (80 seats; members elected by popular vote to serve five-year terms)
elections: Chamber of Senators—last held on 21 April 2013 (next to be held in April 2018); Chamber of Deputies—last held on 21 April 2013 (next to be held in April 2018)
election results: Chamber of Senators—percent of vote by party—NA; seats by party—ANR 19, PLRA 12, FG 5, PDP 3, Avanza Pais 2, UNACE 2, PEN 1, PPQ 1; Chamber of Deputies—percent of vote by party—NA; seats by party—ANR 44, PLRA 27, Avanza Pais 2, PEN 2, UNACE 2, FG 1, PPQ 1, other 1

Judicial branch: *highest court(s):* Supreme Court of Justice or Corte Suprema de Justicia (consists of 9 justices divided 3 each into the Constitutional Court, Civil and Commercial Chamber, and Criminal Division
judge selection and term of office: justices proposed by the Council of Magistrates or Consejo de la Magistratura, a 6-member independent body, and appointed by the Chamber of Senators with presidential concurrence; judges appointed until mandatory retirement at age 75
subordinate courts: appellate courts; first instance courts; minor courts, including justices of the peace

Political parties and leaders: Asociacion Nacional Republicana—Colorado Party or ANR [Lilian SAMANIEGO]; Avanza Pais coalition [Adolfo FERREIRO]; Broad Front coalition (Frente Guasu) or FG [Fernando Armindo LUGO Mendez]; Movimiento Union Nacional de Ciudadanos Eticos or UNACE [Jorge OVIEDO MATTO]; Patria Querida (Beloved Fatherland Party) or PPQ [Sebastian ACHA]; Partido del Movimiento al Socialismo or P-MAS [Camilo Ernesto SOARES Machado]; Partido Democratica Progresista or PDP [Desiree MASI]; Partido Encuentro Nacional or PEN [Fernando CAMACHO Paredes]; Partido Liberal Radical Autentico or PLRA [Miguel ABDON SAGUIER]; Partido Pais Solidario or PPS [Carlos Alberto FILIZZOLA Pallares]; Partido Popular Tekojoja [Sixto PEREIRA]

Political pressure groups and leaders: Ahorristas Estafados or AE; National Coordinating Board of Campesino Organizations or MCNOC [Luis AGUAYO]; National Federation of Campesinos or FNC [Odilon ESPINOLA]; National Workers Central or CNT [Secretary General Juan TORRALES]; Paraguayan Workers Confederation or CPT; Roman Catholic Church; Unitary Workers Central or CUT [Jorge Guzman ALVARENGA Malgarejo];

International organization participation: CAN (associate), CD, CELAC, FAO, G-11, G-77, IADB, IAEA, IBRD, ICAO, ICRM, IDA, IFAD, IFC, IFRCS, ILO, IMF, IMO, Interpol, IOC, IOM, IPU, ISO (correspondent), ITSO, ITU, ITUC (NGOs), LAES, LAIA, Mercosur, MIGA, MINURSO, MINUSTAH, MONUSCO, NAM (observer), OAS, OPANAL, OPCW, PCA, UN, UNASUR, UNCTAD, UNESCO, UNFICYP, UNIDO, Union Latina, UNISFA, UNMIL, UNMISS, UNOCI, UNWTO, UPU, WCO, WHO, WIPO, WMO, WTO

Diplomatic representation in the US:

chief of mission: Ambassador Fernando Antonio PFANNL Caballero (since 9 January 2013)
chancery: 2400 Massachusetts Avenue NW, Washington, DC 20008
telephone: [1] (202) 483-6960 through 6962
FAX: [1] (202) 234-4508
consulate(s) general: Los Angeles, Miami, New York

Diplomatic representation from the US: Ambassador James H. THESSIN (since 8 September 2011)
embassy: 1776 Avenida Mariscal Lopez, Casilla Postal 402, Asuncion
mailing address: Unit 4711, DPO AA 34036-0001
telephone: [595] (21) 213-715
FAX: [595] (21) 213-728

Flag description: three equal, horizontal bands of red (top), white, and blue with an emblem centered in the white band; unusual flag in that the emblem is different on each side; the obverse (hoist side at the left) bears the national coat of arms (a yellow five-pointed star within a green wreath capped by the words REPUBLICA DEL PARAGUAY, all within two circles); the reverse (hoist side at the right) bears a circular seal of the treasury (a yellow lion below a red Cap of Liberty and the words PAZ Y JUSTICIA (Peace and Justice)); red symbolizes bravery and patriotism, white represents integrity and peace, and blue denotes liberty and generosity
note: the three color bands resemble those on the flag of the Netherlands; one of only three national flags that differ on their obverse and reverse sides—the others are Moldova and Saudi Arabia

National symbol(s): lion

National anthem: *name:* "Paraguayos, Republica o muerte!" (Paraguayans, The Republic or Death!)
lyrics/music: Francisco Esteban ACUNA de Figueroa/disputed
note: adopted 1934, in use since 1846; the anthem was officially adopted following its re-arrangement in 1934

ECONOMY

Economy—overview: Landlocked Paraguay has a market economy distinguished by a large informal sector, featuring re-export of imported consumer goods to neighboring countries, as well as the activities of thousands of microenterprises and urban street vendors. A large percentage of the population, especially in rural areas, derives its living from agricultural activity, often on a subsistence basis. Because of the importance of the informal sector, accurate economic measures are difficult to obtain. On a per capita basis, real income has stagnated at 1980 levels. The economy grew rapidly between 2003 and 2008 as growing world demand for commodities combined with high prices and favorable weather to support Paraguay's commodity-based export expansion. Paraguay is the sixth largest soy producer in the world. Drought hit in 2008, reducing agricultural exports and slowing the economy even before the onset of the global recession. The economy fell 3.8% in 2009, as lower world demand and commodity prices caused exports to contract. The government reacted by introducing fiscal and monetary stimulus packages. Growth resumed at a 13% level in 2010, the highest in South America, but slowed in 2011-12 as the stimulus subsided and severe drought and outbreaks of foot-and-mouth disease led to a drop in beef and other agricultural exports. The economy took another leap in 2013, largely due to strong export growth. Political uncertainty, corruption, limited progress on structural reform, and deficient infrastructure are the main obstacles to long-term growth.

GDP (purchasing power parity): $45.9 billion (2013 est.)
country comparison to the world: 100
$40.98 billion (2012 est.)
$41.49 billion (2011 est.)
note: data are in 2013 US dollars

GDP (official exchange rate): $30.56 billion (2013 est.)

GDP—real growth rate: 12% (2013 est.)
country comparison to the world: 4
-1.2% (2012 est.)
4.3% (2011 est.)

GDP—per capita (PPP): $6,800 (2013 est.)
country comparison to the world: 143
$6,100 (2012 est.)
$6,300 (2011 est.)
note: data are in 2013 US dollars

GDP—composition, by end use:
household consumption: 67.1%
government consumption: 12.8%
investment in fixed capital: 16.9%
investment in inventories: 0.4%
exports of goods and services: 52.1%
imports of goods and services: -49.4% (2013 est.)

GDP—composition, by sector of origin:
agriculture: 20.4%
industry: 17.7%
services: 61.9% (2013 est.)

Agriculture—products: cotton, sugarcane, soybeans, corn, wheat, tobacco, cassava (tapioca), fruits, vegetables; beef, pork, eggs, milk; timber

Industries: sugar, cement, textiles, beverages, wood products, steel, metallurgic, electric power

Industrial production growth rate: 5.6% (2013 est.)
country comparison to the world: 46

Labor force: 3.19 million (2013 est.)
country comparison to the world: 102

Labor force—by occupation: *agriculture:* 26.5%
industry: 18.5%
services: 55% (2008)

Unemployment rate: 6.6% (2013 est.)
country comparison to the world: 70
6.9% (2012 est.)

Population below poverty line: 34.7% (2010 est.)

Household income or consumption by percentage share: *lowest 10%:* 1%
highest 10%: 41.1% (2010 est.)

Distribution of family income—Gini index: 53.2 (2009)
country comparison to the world: 13
57.7 (1998)

Budget: *revenues:* $5.788 billion
expenditures: $6.287 billion (2013 est.)

Taxes and other revenues: 18.9% of GDP (2013 est.)
country comparison to the world: 174

Budget surplus (+) or deficit (-):
-1.6% of GDP (2013 est.)
country comparison to the world: 72

Public debt: 15.7% of GDP (2013 est.)
country comparison to the world: 141
14.7% of GDP (2012 est.)

Fiscal year: calendar year

Inflation rate (consumer prices): 2.3% (2013 est.)
country comparison to the world: 85
3.7% (2012 est.)

Central bank discount rate: 5.5% (31 December 2012 est.)
country comparison to the world: 58
6% (31 December 2011 est.)

Commercial bank prime lending rate: 28.9% (31 December 2013 est.)
country comparison to the world: 5
29.1% (31 December 2012 est.)

Stock of narrow money: $4.364 billion (31 December 2013 est.)
country comparison to the world: 108
$4.135 billion (31 December 2012 est.)

Stock of broad money: $8.215 billion (31 December 2013 est.)
country comparison to the world: 111
$7.637 billion (31 December 2012 est.)

Stock of domestic credit: $11 billion (31 December 2013 est.)
country comparison to the world: 97
$9.747 billion (31 December 2012 est.)

Market value of publicly traded shares: $962.3 million (31 December 2012 est.)
country comparison to the world: 107
$958.1 million (31 December 2011)
$42 million (31 December 2010 est.)

Current account balance: $1.376 billion (2013 est.)
country comparison to the world: 47
$115.6 million (2012 est.)

Exports: $14.7 billion (2013 est.)
country comparison to the world: 81
$11.9 billion (2012 est.)

Exports—commodities: soybeans, feed, cotton, meat, edible oils, wood, leather

Exports—partners: Uruguay 17.7%, Brazil 16.4%, Argentina 15.6%, Russia 12% (2012)

Imports: $12.37 billion (2013 est.)
country comparison to the world: 93
$11.06 billion (2012 est.)

Imports—commodities: road vehicles, consumer goods, tobacco, petroleum products, electrical machinery, tractors, chemicals, vehicle parts

Imports—partners: Brazil 24.2%, China 19.5%, Argentina 18.3%, US 11.5% (2012)

Reserves of foreign exchange and gold: $6.336 billion (31 December 2013 est.)
country comparison to the world: 86
$4.994 billion (31 December 2012 est.)

Debt—external: $7.013 billion (31 December 2013 est.)
country comparison to the world: 110
$5.985 billion (31 December 2012 est.)

Stock of direct foreign investment—at home: $4.526 billion (31 December 2013 est.)
country comparison to the world: 90
$4.145 billion (31 December 2012 est.)

Stock of direct foreign investment—abroad: $213.6 million (31 December 2013 est.)
country comparison to the world: 84
$213.6 million (31 December 2012 est.)

Exchange rates: guarani (PYG) per US dollar—
4,315.1 (2013 est.)
4,424.9 (2012 est.)
4,735.5 (2010 est.)
4,965.4 (2009)
4,337.7 (2008)

ENERGY

Electricity—production: 53.53 billion kWh (2010 est.)
country comparison to the world: 4 9

Electricity—consumption: 6.778 billion kWh (2010 est.)
country comparison to the world: 101

Electricity—exports: 46.12 billion kWh (2011 est.)
country comparison to the world: 4

Electricity—imports: 0 kWh (2012 est.)
country comparison to the world: 183

Electricity—installed generating capacity: 8.816 million kW (2010 est.)
country comparison to the world: 60

Electricity—from fossil fuels: 0.1% of total installed capacity (2010 est.)
country comparison to the world: 208

Electricity—from nuclear fuels: 0% of total installed capacity (2010 est.)
country comparison to the world: 159

Electricity—from hydroelectric plants: 99.9% of total installed capacity (2010 est.)
country comparison to the world: 3

Electricity—from other renewable sources: 0% of total installed capacity (2010 est.)
country comparison to the world: 110

Crude oil—production: 2,000 bbl/day (2012 est.)
country comparison to the world: 105

Crude oil—exports: 0 bbl/day (2010 est.)
country comparison to the world: 166

Crude oil—imports: 0 bbl/day (2010 est.)
country comparison to the world: 108

Crude oil—proved reserves: 0 bbl (1 January 2013 es)
country comparison to the world: 175

Refined petroleum products—production: 0 bbl/day (2010 est.)
country comparison to the world: 184

Refined petroleum products—consumption: 26,820 bbl/day (2011 est.)
country comparison to the world: 119

Refined petroleum products—exports: 0 bbl/day (2010 est.)
country comparison to the world: 206

Refined petroleum products—imports: 31,290 bbl/day (2010 est.)
country comparison to the world: 89

Natural gas—production: 0 cu m (2011 est.)
country comparison to the world: 180

Natural gas—consumption: 0 cu m (2010 est.)
country comparison to the world: 185

Natural gas—exports: 0 cu m (2011 est.)
country comparison to the world: 163

Natural gas—imports: 0 cu m (2011 est.)
country comparison to the world: 114

Natural gas—proved reserves: 0 cu m (1 January 2013 es)
country comparison to the world: 182

Carbon dioxide emissions from consumption of energy: 3.987 million Mt (2011 est.)
country comparison to the world: 132

COMMUNICATIONS

Telephones—main lines in use: 376,000 (2012)
country comparison to the world: 107

Telephones—mobile cellular: 6.79 million (2012)
country comparison to the world: 95

Telephone system: *general assessment:* the fixed-line market is a state monopoly and fixed-line telephone service is meager; principal switching center is in Asuncion
domestic: deficiencies in provision of fixed-line service have resulted in a rapid expansion of mobile-cellular services fostered by competition among multiple providers
international: country code—595; satellite earth station—1 Intelsat (Atlantic Ocean) (2010)

Broadcast media: 6 privately owned TV stations; about 75 commercial and community radio stations; 1 state-owned radio network (2010)

Internet country code: .py

Internet hosts: 280,658 (2012)
country comparison to the world: 65

Internet users: 1.105 million (2009)
country comparison to the world: 94

TRANSPORTATION

Airports: 799 (2013)
country comparison to the world: 9

Airports—with paved runways: *total:* 1 5
over 3,047 m: 3
1,524 to 2,437 m: 7
914 to 1,523 m: 5 (2013)

Airports—with unpaved runways: *total:* 784
1,524 to 2,437 m: 23
914 to 1,523 m: 290
under 914 m: 471 (2013)

Railways: *total:* 36 km
country comparison to the world: 132
standard gauge: 36 km 1.435-m gauge (2008)

Roadways: *total:* 32,059 km
country comparison to the world: 95
paved: 4,860 km
unpaved: 27,199 km (2010)

Waterways: 3,100 km (primarily on the Paraguay and Paraná river systems) (2012)
country comparison to the world: 33

Merchant marine: *total:* 1 9
country comparison to the world: 96
by type: cargo 13, container 3, passenger 1, petroleum tanker 1, roll on/roll off 1
foreign-owned: 6 (Argentina 5, Netherlands 1) (2010)

Ports and terminals: *river port(s):* Asuncion, Villeta, San Antonio, Encarnacion (Parana)

MILITARY

Military branches: Armed Forces Command (Commando de las Fuerzas Militares): Army, National Navy (Armada Nacional, includes Marine Corps, Naval Aviation, and Coast Guard), Paraguayan Air Force (Fuerza Aerea Paraguay, FAP), Logistics Command, War Materiel Directorate (2012)

Military service age and obligation: 18 years of age for compulsory and voluntary military service; conscript service obligation is 12 months for Army, 24 months for Navy; volunteers for the Air Force must be younger than 22 years of age with a secondary school diploma (2012)

Manpower available for military service:
males age 16-49: 1,678,335
females age 16-49: 1,675,352 (2010 est.)

Manpower fit for military service:
males age 16-49: 1,409,859
females age 16-49: 1,433,037 (2010 est.)

Manpower reaching militarily significant age annually: *male:* 73,367
female: 71,801 (2010 est.)

Military expenditures: 1.66% of GDP (2012)
country comparison to the world: 54
1.16% of GDP (2011)
1.66% of GDP (2010)

TRANSNATIONAL ISSUES

Disputes—international: unruly region at convergence of Argentina-Brazil-Paraguay borders is locus of money laundering, smuggling, arms and illegal narcotics trafficking, and fundraising for extremist organizations

Illicit drugs: major illicit producer of cannabis, most or all of which is consumed in Brazil, Argentina, and Chile; transshipment country for Andean cocaine headed for Brazil, other Southern Cone markets, and Europe; weak border controls, extensive corruption and money-laundering activity, especially in the Tri-Border Area; weak anti-money-laundering laws and enforcement

PERU

INTRODUCTION

Background: Ancient Peru was the seat of several prominent Andean civilizations, most notably that of the Incas whose empire was captured by Spanish conquistadors in 1533. Peruvian independence was declared in 1821, and remaining Spanish forces were defeated in 1824. After a dozen years of military rule, Peru returned to democratic leadership in 1980, but experienced economic problems and the growth of a violent insurgency. President Alberto FUJIMORI's election in 1990 ushered in a decade that saw a dramatic turnaround in the economy and significant progress in curtailing guerrilla activity. Nevertheless, the president's increasing reliance on authoritarian measures and an economic slump in the late 1990s generated mounting dissatisfaction with his regime, which led to his resignation in 2000. A caretaker government oversaw new elections in the spring of 2001, which installed Alejandro TOLEDO Manrique as the new head of government—Peru's first democratically elected president of indigenous ethnicity. The presidential election of 2006 saw the return of Alan GARCIA Perez who, after a disappointing presidential term from 1985 to 1990, oversaw a robust economic rebound. In June 2011, former army officer Ollanta HUMALA Tasso was elected president, defeating Keiko FUJIMORI Higuchi, the daughter of Alberto FUJIMORI. Since his election, HUMALA has carried on the sound, market-oriented economic policies of the three preceding administrations.

GEOGRAPHY

Location: Western South America, bordering the South Pacific Ocean, between Chile and Ecuador

Geographic coordinates: 10 00 S, 76 00 W

Map references: South America

Area: *total:* 1,285,216 sq km
country comparison to the world: 20
land: 1,279,996 sq km
water: 5,220 sq km

Area—comparative: slightly smaller than Alaska

Land boundaries: *total:* 7,461 km
border countries: Bolivia 1,075 km, Brazil 2,995 km, Chile 171 km, Colombia 1,800 km, Ecuador 1,420 km

Coastline: 2,414 km

Maritime claims: *territorial sea:* 200 nm
continental shelf: 200 nm

Climate: varies from tropical in east to dry desert in west; temperate to frigid in Andes

Terrain: western coastal plain (costa), high and rugged Andes in center (sierra), eastern lowland jungle of Amazon Basin (selva)

Elevation extremes: *lowest point:* Pacific Ocean 0 m
highest point: Nevado Huascaran 6,768 m

Natural resources: copper, silver, gold, petroleum, timber, fish, iron ore, coal, phosphate, potash, hydropower, natural gas

Land use: *arable land:* 2.84%
permanent crops: 0.66%
other: 96.5% (2011)

Irrigated land: 11,960 sq km (2003)

Total renewable water resources: 1,913 cu km (2011)

Freshwater withdrawal (domestic/industrial/agricultural): *total:* 19.34 cu km/yr (8%/10%/82%)
per capita: 727.6 cu m/yr (2005)

Natural hazards: earthquakes, tsunamis, flooding, landslides, mild volcanic activity
volcanism: volcanic activity in the Andes Mountains; Ubinas (elev. 5,672 m), which last erupted in 2009, is the country's most active volcano; other historically active volcanoes include El Misti, Huaynaputina, Sabancaya, and Yucamane

Environment—current issues: deforestation (some the result of illegal logging); overgrazing of the slopes of the costa and sierra leading to soil erosion; desertification; air pollution in Lima; pollution of rivers and coastal waters from municipal and mining wastes

Environment—international agreements:
party to: Antarctic-Environmental Protocol, Antarctic-Marine Living Resources, Antarctic Treaty, Biodiversity, Climate Change, Climate Change-Kyoto Protocol, Desertification, Endangered Species, Hazardous Wastes, Marine Dumping, Ozone Layer Protection, Ship Pollution, Tropical Timber 83, Tropical Timber 94, Wetlands, Whaling
signed, but not ratified: none of the selected agreements

Geography—note: shares control of Lago Titicaca, world's highest navigable lake, with Bolivia; a remote slope of Nevado Mismi, a 5,316 m peak, is the ultimate source of the Amazon River

PEOPLE AND SOCIETY

Nationality: *noun:* Peruvian(s)
adjective: Peruvian

Ethnic groups: Amerindian 45%, mestizo (mixed Amerindian and white) 37%, white 15%, black, Japanese, Chinese, and other 3%

Languages: Spanish (official) 84.1%, Quechua (official) 13%, Aymara (official) 1.7%, Ashaninka 0.3%, other native languages (includes a large number of minor Amazonian languages) 0.7%, other 0.2% (2007 Census)

Religions: Roman Catholic 81.3%, Evangelical 12.5%, other 3.3%, unspecified or none 2.9% (2007 Census)

Demographic profile: Peru's urban and coastal communities have benefited much more from recent economic growth than rural, Afro-Peruvian, indigenous, and poor populations of the Amazon and mountain regions. The poverty rate has dropped substantially during the last decade but remains stubbornly high at about 30% (more than 55% in rural areas). After remaining almost static for about a decade, Peru's malnutrition rate began falling in 2005, when the government introduced a coordinated strategy focusing on hygiene, sanitation, and clean water. School enrollment has improved, but achievement scores reflect ongoing problems with educational quality. Many poor children temporarily or permanently drop out of school to help support their families. About a quarter to a third of Peruvian children aged 6 to 14 work, often putting in long hours at hazardous mining or construction sites. Peru was a country of immigration in the 19th and early 20th centuries, but has become a country of emigration in the last few decades. Beginning in the 19th century, Peru brought in Asian contract laborers mainly to work on coastal plantations. Populations of Chinese and Japanese descent—among the largest in Latin America—are economically and culturally influential in Peru today. Peruvian emigration began rising in the 1980s due to an economic crisis and a violent internal conflict, but outflows have stabilized in the last few years as economic conditions have improved. Nonetheless, more than 2 million Peruvians have emigrated in the last decade, principally to the US, Spain, and Argentina.

Population: 30,147,935 (July 2014 est.)
country comparison to the world: 43

Age structure:
0-14 years: 27.3% (male 4,184,330/female 4,040,096)
15-24 years: 19.2% (male 2,894,168/female 2,889,409)
25-54 years: 39.4% (male 5,715,542/female 6,161,540)
55-64 years: 6.9% (male 1,071,688/female 1,125,100)
65 years and over: 6.7% (male 979,854/female 1,086,208) (2014 est.)

Dependency ratios:
total dependency ratio: 54.2 %
youth dependency ratio: 44.4 %
elderly dependency ratio: 9.9 %
potential support ratio: 10.1 (2013)

Median age: *total:* 27 years
male: 26.3 years
female: 27.7 years (2014 est.)

Population growth rate: 0.99% (2014 est.)
country comparison to the world: 120

Birth rate: 18.57 births/1,000 population (2014 est.)
country comparison to the world: 99

Death rate: 5.99 deaths/1,000 population (2014 est.)
country comparison to the world: 166

Net migration rate: -2.69 migrant(s)/1,000 population (2014 est.)
country comparison to the world: 175

Urbanization: *urban population:* 77% of total population (2010)
rate of urbanization: 1.6% annual rate of change (2010-15 est.)

Major urban areas—population: LIMA (capital) 8.769 million; Arequipa 778,000 (2009)

Sex ratio: *at birth:* 1.05 male(s)/female
0-14 years: 1.04 male(s)/female
15-24 years: 1 male(s)/female
25-54 years: 0.93 male(s)/female
55-64 years: 0.97 male(s)/female
65 years and over: 0.9 male(s)/female
total population: 0.97 male(s)/female (2014 est.)

Mother's mean age at first birth: 22.3
note: median age at first birth among women 25-29 (2012 est.)

Maternal mortality rate: 67 deaths/100,000 live births (2010)
country comparison to the world: 90

Infant mortality rate: *total:* 20.21 deaths/1,000 live births
country comparison to the world: 90
male: 22.44 deaths/1,000 live births
female: 17.88 deaths/1,000 live births (2014 est.)

Life expectancy at birth: *total population:* 73.23 years
country comparison to the world: 127
male: 71.23 years
female: 75.33 years (2014 est.)

Total fertility rate: 2.22 children born/woman (2014 est.)
country comparison to the world: 101

Contraceptive prevalence rate: 68.9% (2011)

Health expenditures: 4.8% of GDP (2011)
country comparison to the world: 145

Physicians density: 0.92 physicians/1,000 population (2009)

Hospital bed density: 1.5 beds/1,000 population (2011)

Drinking water source:
improved:
urban: 90.9% of population
rural: 66.1% of population
total: 85.3% of population
unimproved:
urban: 9.1% of population
rural: 33.9% of population
total: 14.7% of population (2011 est.)

Sanitation facility access:
improved:
urban: 81.3% of population
rural: 38.4% of population
total: 71.6% of population

unimproved:
urban: 18.7% of population
rural: 61.6% of population
total: 28.4% of population (2011 est.)

HIV/AIDS—adult prevalence rate: 0.4% (2012 est.)
country comparison to the world: 79

HIV/AIDS—people living with HIV/AIDS: 75,500 (2012 est.)
country comparison to the world: 51

HIV/AIDS—deaths: 4,100 (2012 est.)
country comparison to the world: 45

Major infectious diseases: *degree of risk:* very high
food or waterborne diseases: bacterial diarrhea, hepatitis A, and typhoid fever
vectorborne disease: dengue fever, malaria, and Bartonellosis (Oroya fever) (2013)

Obesity—adult prevalence rate: 15.7% (2008)
country comparison to the world: 117

Children under the age of 5 years underweight: 4.5% (2008)
country comparison to the world: 93

Education expenditures: 2.8% of GDP (2012)
country comparison to the world: 145

Literacy: *definition:* age 15 and over can read and write
total population: 89.6%
male: 94.9%
female: 84.6% (2007 est.)

School life expectancy (primary to tertiary education): *total:* 13 years
male: 13 years
female: 13 years (2010)

Child labor—children ages 5-14:
total number: 2,545,855
percentage: 34 %
note: data represents children ages 5-17 (2007 est.)

Unemployment, youth ages 15-24: *total:* 9.5%
country comparison to the world: 111
male: 9.4%
female: 9.7% (2011)

GOVERNMENT

Country name: *conventional long form:* Republic of Peru
conventional short form: Peru
local long form: Republica del Peru
local short form: Peru

Government type: constitutional republic

Capital: *name:* Lima

geographic coordinates: 12 03 S, 77 03 W
time difference: UTC-5 (same time as Washington, DC during Standard Time)

Administrative divisions: 25 regions (regiones, singular—region) and 1 province* (provincia); Amazonas, Ancash, Apurimac, Arequipa, Ayacucho, Cajamarca, Callao, Cusco, Huancavelica, Huanuco, Ica, Junin, La Libertad, Lambayeque, Lima, Lima*, Loreto, Madre de Dios, Moquegua, Pasco, Piura, Puno, San Martin, Tacna, Tumbes, Ucayali
note: Callao, the largest port in Peru, is also referred to as a constitutional province, the only province of the the Callao region

Independence: 28 July 1821 (from Spain)

National holiday: Independence Day, 28 July (1821)

Constitution: several previous; latest promulgated 29 December 1993, enacted 31 December 1993; amended several times, last in 2009 (2009)

Legal system: civil law system

International law organization participation: accepts compulsory ICJ jurisdiction with reservations; accepts ICCt jurisdiction

Suffrage: 18 years of age; universal and compulsory until the age of 70

Executive branch: *chief of state:* President Ollanta HUMALA Tasso (since 28 July 2011); First Vice President Marisol ESPINOZA Cruz (since 28 July 2011); Second Vice President (vacant); note—the president is both the chief of state and head of government
head of government: President Ollanta HUMALA Tasso (since 28 July 2011); First Vice President Marisol ESPINOZA Cruz (since 28 July 2011); Second Vice President (vacant)
note: Prime Minister Juan Federico JIMENEZ Mayor (since 23 July 2012) does not exercise executive power; this power rests with the president
cabinet: Council of Ministers appointed by the president (For more information visit the World Leaders website)
elections: president elected by popular vote for a five-year term (eligible for nonconsecutive reelection); presidential and congressional elections last held on 10 April 2011 with runoff election held on 6 June 2011 (next to be held in April 2016)
election results: Ollanta HUMALA Tasso elected president in runoff election; percent of vote—Ollanta HUMALA Tasso 51.5%, Keiko FUJIMORI Higuchi 48.5%

Legislative branch: unicameral Congress of the Republic of Peru or Congreso de la Republica del Peru (130 seats; members are elected by popular vote to serve five-year terms)
elections: last held on 10 April 2011 (next to be held in April 2016)
election results: percent of vote by party—Gana Peru 25.3%, Fuerza 2011 23%, PP 14.8%, Alliance for Great Change 14.4%, National Solidarity 10.2%, Peruvian Aprista Party 6.4%, other 5.9%; seats by party—Gana Peru 47, Fuerza 2011 37, PP 21, Alliance for Great Change 12, National Solidarity 9, Peruvian Aprista Party 4; note—defections by members of National Assembly are commonplace, resulting in frequent changes in the numbers of seats held by the various parties

Judicial branch: *highest court(s):* Supreme Court (consists of 16 judges and divided into civil, criminal, and constitutional-social sectors)
judge selection and term of office: justices proposed by the National Council of the Judiciary or National Judicial Council (a 7-member independent body), nominated by the president, and confirmed by the Congress (all appointments reviewed by the Council every 7 years; justices appointed for life or until age 70
subordinate courts: Court of Constitutional Guarantees; Superior Courts or Cortes Superiores; specialized civil, criminal, and mixed courts; two types of peace courts in which professional judges and selected members of the local communities preside

Political parties and leaders: Alliance for Great Change (Alianza por el Gran Cambio) (a coalition of the Alliance for Progress, Humanist; Party, National Restoration Party, and Popular Christian Party) [Pedro Pablo KUCZYNSKI]; Fuerza 2011 [Keiko FUJIMORI Higuchi]; Gana Peru (a coalition of Lima Para Todos, Peruvian Communist Party, Peruvian Nationalist Party, and; Peruvian Socialist Party) [Ollanta HUMALA Tasso]; National Solidarity (Solidaridad Nacional) or SN (a coalition of Cambio 90, Siempre Unidos, Todos por el; Peru, and Union for Peru or UPP) [Luis CASTANEDA Lossio]; Peru Posible or PP (a coalition of Accion Popular and Somos Peru) [Alejandro TOLEDO Manrique]; Peruvian Aprista Party (Partido Aprista Peruano) or PAP [Alan GARCIA Perez] (also referred to by its; original name Alianza Popular Revolucionaria Americana or APRA)

Political pressure groups and leaders: General Workers Confederation of Peru (Confederacion General de Trabajadores del Peru) or CGTP [Mario; HUAMAN]; Shining Path (Sendero Luminoso) or SL [Abimael GUZMAN Reynoso (imprisoned), Victor QUISPE Palomino; (top leader at-large)] (leftist guerrilla group)

International organization participation: APEC, BIS, CAN, CD, CELAC, EITI (compliant country), FAO, G-24, G-77, IADB, IAEA, IBRD, ICAO, ICC (NGOs), ICRM, IDA, IFAD, IFC, IFRCS, IHO, ILO, IMF, IMO, IMSO, Interpol, IOC, IOM, IPU, ISO, ITSO, ITU, ITUC (NGOs), LAES, LAIA, Mercosur (associate), MIGA, MINURSO, MINUSTAH, MONUSCO, NAM, OAS, OPANAL, OPCW, PCA, SICA (observer), UN, UNASUR, UNCTAD, UNESCO, UNIDO, Union Latina, UNISFA, UNMIL, UNMISS, UNOCI, UNWTO, UPU, WCO, WFTU (NGOs), WHO, WIPO, WMO, WTO

Diplomatic representation in the US:
chief of mission: Ambassador Harold Winston FORSYTH Mejia (since 29 August 2011)
chancery: 1700 Massachusetts Avenue NW, Washington, DC 20036
telephone: [1] (202) 833-9860 through 9869
FAX: [1] (202) 659-8124
consulate(s) general: Atlanta, Boston, Chicago, Dallas, Denver, Hartford (CT), Houston, Los Angeles, Miami, New York, Paterson (NJ), San Francisco

Diplomatic representation from the US:
chief of mission: Ambassador (vacant); Charge d'Affaires Michael J. Fitzpatrick (since 20 September 2013)
embassy: Avenida La Encalada, Cuadra 17 s/n, Surco, Lima 33
mailing address: P. O. Box 1995, Lima 1; American Embassy (Lima), APO AA 34031-5000
telephone: [51] (1) 618-2000
FAX: [51] (1) 618-2397

Flag description: three equal, vertical bands of red (hoist side), white, and red with the coat of arms centered in the white band; the coat of arms features a shield bearing a vicuna (representing fauna), a cinchona tree (the source of quinine, signifying flora), and a yellow cornucopia spilling out coins (denoting mineral wealth); red recalls blood shed for independence, white symbolizes peace

National symbol(s): vicuna (a camelid related to the llama)

National anthem: *name:* "Himno Nacional del Peru" (National Anthem of Peru)
lyrics/music: Jose DE LA TORRE Ugarte/Jose Bernardo ALZEDO
note: adopted 1822; the song won a national contest for an anthem

ECONOMY

Economy—overview: Peru's economy reflects its varied geography—an arid lowland coastal region, the central high sierra of the Andes, the dense forest of the Amazon, with tropical lands bordering Colombia and Brazil. A wide range of important mineral resources are found in the mountainous and coastal areas, and Peru's coastal waters provide excellent fishing grounds. The Peruvian economy has been growing by an average of 6.4% per year since 2002 with a stable/slightly appreciating exchange rate and low inflation, which in 2013 is expected to be below the upper limit of the Central Bank target range of 1 to 3%. Growth has been in the 6-9% range for the last three years, due partly to a leap in private investment, especially in the extractive sector, which accounts for more than 60% of Peru's total exports. Despite Peru's strong macroeconomic performance, dependence on minerals and metals exports and imported foodstuffs subjects the economy to fluctuations in world prices. Poor infrastructure hinders the spread of growth to Peru's non-coastal areas. Peru's rapid expansion coupled with cash transfers and other programs have helped to reduce the national poverty rate by 23 percentage points since 2002, but inequality persists and continues to pose a challenge for the new Ollanta HUMALA administration, which has championed a policy of social inclusion and a more equitable distribution of income. Peru's free trade policy has continued under the HUMALA administration; since 2006, Peru has signed trade deals with the US, Canada, Singapore, China, Korea, Mexico, Japan, the European Free Trade Association, Chile, and four other countries; concluded negotiations with Venezuela, Costa Rica, and Guatemala; and begun trade talks with two other Central American countries and the Trans-Pacific Partnership. Peru also has signed a trade pact with Chile, Colombia, and Mexico called the Pacific Alliance that rivals Mercosur in combined population, GDP, and trade. The US-Peru Trade Promotion Agreement entered into force 1 February 2009, opening the way to greater trade and investment between the two economies. Although Peru has continued to attract foreign investment, political activism and protests are hampering development of some projects related to natural resource extraction.

GDP (purchasing power parity): $344 billion (2013 est.)
country comparison to the world: 40
$327.3 billion (2012 est.)
$308 billion (2011 est.)
note: data are in 2013 US dollars

GDP (official exchange rate): $210.3 billion (2013 est.)

GDP—real growth rate: 5.1% (2013 est.)
country comparison to the world: 54
6.3% (2012 est.)
6.9% (2011 est.)

GDP—per capita (PPP): $11,100 (2013 est.)
country comparison to the world: 110
$10,700 (2012 est.)
$10,300 (2011 est.)
note: data are in 2013 US dollars

Gross national saving: 22.2% of GDP (2013 est.)
country comparison to the world: 67
23.3% of GDP (2012 est.)
23.4% of GDP (2011 est.)

GDP—composition, by end use:
household consumption: 62.4%
government consumption: 10.8%
investment in fixed capital: 27%
investment in inventories: 0.1%
exports of goods and services: 24.4%
imports of goods and services: -24.7% (2013 est.)

GDP—composition, by sector of origin:
agriculture: 6.2%
industry: 37.5%
services: 56.3% (2013 est.)

Agriculture—products: asparagus, coffee, cocoa, cotton, sugarcane, rice, potatoes, corn, plantains, grapes, oranges, pineapples, guavas, bananas, apples, lemons, pears, coca, tomatoes, mangoes, barley, medicinal plants, palm oil, marigold, onion, wheat, dry beans; poultry, beef, pork, dairy products; guinea pigs; fish

Industries: mining and refining of minerals; steel, metal fabrication; petroleum extraction and refining, natural gas and natural gas liquefaction; fishing and fish processing, cement, glass, textiles, clothing, food processing, beer, soft drinks, rubber, machinery, electrical machinery, chemicals, furniture

Industrial production growth rate: 5% (2013 est.)
country comparison to the world: 57

Labor force: 16.16 million
country comparison to the world: 38
note: individuals older than 14 years of age (2012 est.)

Labor force—by occupation: *agriculture:* 25.8%
industry: 17.4%
services: 56.8% (2011)

Unemployment rate: 3.6% (2012 est.)
country comparison to the world: 28
3.9% (2011 est.)
note: data are for metropolitan Lima; widespread underemployment

Population below poverty line: 25.8% (2012 est.)

Household income or consumption by percentage share: *lowest* 10%: 1.4%
highest 10%: 36.1% (2010 est.)

Distribution of family income—Gini index: 48.1 (2010)
country comparison to the world: 26
51 (2005)

Budget: *revenues:* $60.95 billion
expenditures: $58.91 billion (2013 est.)

Taxes and other revenues: 29% of GDP (2013 est.)
country comparison to the world: 97

Budget surplus (+) or deficit (-): 1% of GDP (2013 est.)
country comparison to the world: 26

Public debt: 14.9% of GDP (2013 est.)
country comparison to the world: 143
16.6% of GDP (2012 est.)
note: data cover general government debt, and includes debt instruments issued by government entities other than the treasury; the data exclude treasury debt held by foreign entities; the data include debt issued by subnational entities

Fiscal year: calendar year

Inflation rate (consumer prices): 2.9% (2013 est.)
country comparison to the world: 112
3.4% (2011 est.)
note: data are for metropolitan Lima, annual average

Central bank discount rate: 5.05% (31 December 2012)
country comparison to the world: 69
5.05% (31 December 2011)

Commercial bank prime lending rate: 20.3% (31 December 2013 est.)
country comparison to the world: 19
19.23% (31 December 2012 est.)
note: domestic currency lending rate, 90 day maturity

Stock of narrow money: $32.2 billion (31 December 2013 est.)
country comparison to the world: 58
$32.61 billion (31 December 2012 est.)

Stock of broad money: $80.91 billion (31 December 2013 est.)
country comparison to the world: 59
$77.62 billion (31 December 2012 est.)

Stock of domestic credit: $37.96 billion (31 December 2013 est.)
country comparison to the world: 66
$36.76 billion (31 December 2012 est.)

Market value of publicly traded shares: $153.4 billion (31 December 2012)
country comparison to the world: 40
$121.6 billion (31 December 2011)
$160.9 billion (31 December 2010)

Current account balance: -$10.31 billion (2013 est.)
country comparison to the world: 177
-$7.137 billion (2012 est.)

Exports: $41.48 billion (2013 est.)
country comparison to the world: 60
$45.64 billion (2012 est.)

Exports—commodities: copper, gold, lead, zinc, tin, iron ore, molybdenum, silver; crude petroleum and petroleum products, natural gas; coffee, asparagus and other vegetables, fruit, apparel and textiles, fishmeal, fish, chemicals, fabricated metal products and machinery, alloys

Exports—partners: China 19.9%, US 15.7%, Canada 9.5%, Japan 6.6%, Spain 5.2%, Chile 4.9% (2012)

Imports: $42.13 billion (2013 est.)
country comparison to the world: 59
$41.11 billion (2012 est.)

Imports—commodities: petroleum and petroleum products, chemicals, plastics, machinery, vehicles, color TV sets, power shovels, front-end loaders, telephones and telecommunication equipment, iron and steel, wheat, corn, soybean products, paper, cotton, vaccines and medicines

Imports—partners: US 24.6%, China 14%, Brazil 6.4%, Argentina 5%, Chile 4.8%, Colombia 4.2%, Ecuador 4.1%, Mexico 4% (2012)

Reserves of foreign exchange and gold: $65.15 billion (31 December 2013 est.)
country comparison to the world: 32
$64.17 billion (31 December 2012 est.)

Debt—external: $50.15 billion (31 December 2013 est.)
country comparison to the world: 62
$50.47 billion (31 December 2012 est.)
note: public debt component of total: $20.6 billion (31 December 2009)

Stock of direct foreign investment—at home: $76.57 billion (31 December 2013 est.)
country comparison to the world: 49
$63.51 billion (31 December 2012 est.)

Stock of direct foreign investment—abroad: $3.165 billion (31 December 2013 est.)
country comparison to the world: 68
$3.041 billion (31 December 2012 est.)

Exchange rates: nuevo sol (PEN) per US dollar—
2.699 (2013 est.)
2.6376 (2012 est.)
2.8251 (2010 est.)
3.0115 (2009)
2.91 (2008)

ENERGY

Electricity—production: 38.4 billion kWh (2012 est.)
country comparison to the world: 6 0

Electricity—consumption: 34.25 billion kWh (2011 est.)
country comparison to the world: 58

Electricity—exports: 112 million kWh (2010 est.)
country comparison to the world: 75

Electricity—imports: 0 kWh (2012 est.)
country comparison to the world: 184

Electricity—installed generating capacity: 8.613 million kW (2010 est.)
country comparison to the world: 61

Electricity—from fossil fuels: 60.1% of total installed capacity (2010 est.)
country comparison to the world: 134

Electricity—from nuclear fuels: 0% of total installed capacity (2010 est.)
country comparison to the world: 160

Electricity—from hydroelectric plants: 39.9% of total installed capacity (2010 est.)
country comparison to the world: 60

Electricity—from other renewable sources: 0% of total installed capacity (2010 est.)
country comparison to the world: 111

Crude oil—production: 160,400 bbl/day (2012 est.)
country comparison to the world: 42

Crude oil—exports: 15,610 bbl/day (2012 est.)
country comparison to the world: 55

Crude oil—imports: 99,590 bbl/day (2012 est.)
country comparison to the world: 51

Crude oil—proved reserves: 579.2 million bbl (1 January 2013 es)
country comparison to the world: 49

Refined petroleum products—production: 159,500 bbl/day (2012 est.)
country comparison to the world: 61

Refined petroleum products—consumption: 206,900 bbl/day (2012 est.)
country comparison to the world: 56

Refined petroleum products—exports: 82,080 bbl/day (2012 est.)
country comparison to the world: 49

Refined petroleum products—imports: 43,480 bbl/day (2012 est.)
country comparison to the world: 76

Natural gas—production: 32.4 billion cu m (2012)
country comparison to the world: 28

Natural gas—consumption: 5.49 billion cu m (2010 est.)
country comparison to the world: 59

Natural gas—exports: 8.73 billion cu m (2012 est.)
country comparison to the world: 29

Natural gas—imports: 0 cu m (2012)
country comparison to the world: 115

Natural gas—proved reserves: 359.6 billion cu m (1 January 2013 es)
country comparison to the world: 38

Carbon dioxide emissions from consumption of energy: 37.71 million Mt (2011 est.)
country comparison to the world: 70

COMMUNICATIONS

Telephones—main lines in use: 3.42 million (2012)
country comparison to the world: 4 5

Telephones—mobile cellular: 29.4 million (2012)
country comparison to the world: 36

Telephone system: *general assessment:* adequate for most requirements; nationwide microwave radio relay system and a domestic satellite system with 12 earth stations
domestic: fixed-line teledensity is only about 12 per 100 persons; mobile-cellular teledensity, spurred by competition among multiple providers, exceeds 100 telephones per 100 persons
international: country code—51; the South America-1 (SAM-1) and Pan American (PAN-AM) submarine cable systems provide links to parts of Central and South America, the Caribbean, and US; satellite earth stations—2 Intelsat (Atlantic Ocean) (2010)

Broadcast media: 10 major TV networks of which only one, Television Nacional de Peru, is state-owned; multi-channel cable TV services are available; in excess of 2,000 radio stations including a substantial number of indigenous language stations (2010)

Internet country code: .pe

Internet hosts: 234,102 (2012)
country comparison to the world: 70

Internet users: 9.158 million (2009)
country comparison to the world: 31

TRANSPORTATION

Airports: 191 (2013)
country comparison to the world: 3 0

Airports—with paved runways: *total:* 5 9
over 3,047 m: 5
2,438 to 3,047 m: 21
1,524 to 2,437 m: 16
914 to 1,523 m: 12
under 914 m: 5 (2013)

Airports—with unpaved runways: *total:* 132
2,438 to 3,047 m: 1
1,524 to 2,437 m: 19
914 to 1,523 m: 30
under 914 m: 82 (2013)

Heliports: 5 (2013)

Pipelines: extra heavy crude 786 km; gas 1,526 km; liquid petroleum gas 679 km; oil 1,033 km; refined products 15 km (2013)

Railways: *total:* 1,907 km
country comparison to the world: 74
standard gauge: 1,772 km 1.435-m gauge
narrow gauge: 135 km 0.914-m gauge (2012)

Roadways: *total:* 140,672 km (of which 18,698 km are paved)
country comparison to the world: 35
note: includes 24,593 km of national roads (of which 14,748 km are paved), 24,235 km of departmental roads (2,340 km paved), and 91,844 km of local roads (1,611 km paved) (2012)

Waterways: 8,808 km (there are 8,600 km of navigable tributaries on the Amazon system and 208 km on Lago Titicaca) (2011)
country comparison to the world: 14

Merchant marine: *total:* 2 2
country comparison to the world: 92
by type: cargo 2, chemical tanker 5, liquefied gas 2, petroleum tanker 13
foreign-owned: 8 (Chile 6, Ecuador 1, Spain 1)
registered in other countries: 9 (Panama 9) (2010)

Ports and terminals: *major seaport(s):* Callao, Matarani, Paita
river port(s): Iquitos, Pucallpa, Yurimaguas (Amazon)
oil terminals: Conchan oil terminal, La Pampilla oil terminal
container port(s) (TEUs): Callao (1,616,365)

MILITARY

Military branches: Peruvian Army (Ejercito Peruano), Peruvian Navy (Marina de Guerra del Peru, MGP; includes naval air, naval infantry, and Coast Guard), Air Force of Peru (Fuerza Aerea del Peru, FAP) (2013)

Military service age and obligation: 18-50 years of age for male and 18-45 years of age for female voluntary military service; no conscription (2012)

Manpower available for military service:
males age 16-49: 7,385,588
females age 16-49: 7,727,623 (2010 est.)

Manpower fit for military service:
males age 16-49: 5,788,629
females age 16-49: 6,565,097 (2010 est.)

Manpower reaching militarily significant age annually: *male:* 304,094
female: 298,447 (2010 est.)

Military expenditures: 1.28% of GDP (2012)
country comparison to the world: 81
1.15% of GDP (2011)
1.28% of GDP (2010)

TRANSNATIONAL ISSUES

Disputes—international: Chile and Ecuador rejected Peru's November 2005 unilateral legislation to shift the axis of their joint treaty-defined maritime boundaries along the parallels of latitude to equidistance lines which favor Peru; organized illegal narcotics operations in Colombia have penetrated Peru's shared border; Peru rejects Bolivia's claim to restore maritime access through a sovereign corridor through Chile along the Peruvian border

Refugees and internally displaced persons: *IDPs:* 150,000 (civil war from 1980-2000; most IDPs are indigenous peasants in Andean and Amazonian regions; as of 2011, no new information on the situation of these IDPs) (2011)

Illicit drugs: until 1996 the world's largest coca leaf producer, Peru is now the world's second largest producer of coca leaf, though it lags far behind Colombia; cultivation of coca in Peru was estimated at 40,000 hectares in 2009, a slight decrease over 2008; second largest producer of cocaine, estimated at 225 metric tons of potential pure cocaine in 2009; finished cocaine is shipped out from Pacific ports to the international drug market; increasing amounts of base and finished cocaine, however, are being moved to Brazil, Chile, Argentina, and Bolivia for use in the Southern Cone or transshipment to Europe and Africa; increasing domestic drug consumption

PHILIPPINES

INTRODUCTION

Background: The Philippine Islands became a Spanish colony during the 16th century; they were ceded to the US in 1898 following the Spanish-American War. In 1935 the Philippines became a self-governing commonwealth. Manuel QUEZON was elected president and was tasked with preparing the country for independence after a 10-year transition. In 1942 the islands fell under Japanese occupation during World War II, and US forces and Filipinos fought together during 1944-45 to regain control. On 4 July 1946 the Republic of the Philippines attained its independence. A 20-year rule by Ferdinand MARCOS ended in 1986, when a "people power" movement in Manila ("EDSA 1") forced him into exile and installed Corazon AQUINO as president. Her presidency was hampered by several coup attempts that prevented a return to full political stability and economic development. Fidel RAMOS was elected president in 1992. His administration was marked by increased stability and by progress on economic reforms. In 1992, the US closed its last military bases on the islands. Joseph ESTRADA was elected president in 1998. He was succeeded by his vice-president, Gloria MACAPAGAL-ARROYO, in January 2001 after ESTRADA's stormy impeachment trial on corruption charges broke down and another "people power" movement ("EDSA 2") demanded his resignation. MACAPAGAL-ARROYO was elected to a six-year term as president in May 2004. Her presidency was marred by several corruption allegations but the Philippine economy was one of the few to avoid contraction following the 2008 global financial crisis, expanding each year of her administration. Benigno AQUINO III was elected to a six-year term as president in May 2010. The Philippine Government faces threats from several groups, some of which are on the US Government's Foreign Terrorist Organization list. Manila has waged a decades-long struggle against ethnic Moro insurgencies in the southern Philippines, which has led to a peace accord with the Moro National Liberation Front and ongoing peace talks with the Moro Islamic Liberation Front. The decades-long Maoist-inspired New People's Army insurgency also operates through much of the country. The Philippines faces increased tension with China over disputed territorial and maritime claims in the South China Sea.

GEOGRAPHY

Location: Southeastern Asia, archipelago between the Philippine Sea and the South China Sea, east of Vietnam

Geographic coordinates: 13 00 N, 122 00 E

Map references: Southeast Asia

Area: *total:* 300,000 sq km

country comparison to the world: 73

land: 298,170 sq km

water: 1,830 sq km

Area—comparative: slightly less than twice the size of Georgia; slightly larger than Arizona

Land boundaries: 0 km

Coastline: 36,289 km

Maritime claims: *territorial sea:* irregular polygon extending up to 100 nm from coastline as defined by 1898 treaty; since late 1970s has also claimed polygonal-shaped area in South China Sea up to 285 nm in breadth
exclusive economic zone: 200 nm
continental shelf: to depth of exploitation

Climate: tropical marine; northeast monsoon (November to April); southwest monsoon (May to October)

Terrain: mostly mountains with narrow to extensive coastal lowlands

Elevation extremes: *lowest point:* Philippine Sea 0 m
highest point: Mount Apo 2,954 m

Natural resources: timber, petroleum, nickel, cobalt, silver, gold, salt, copper

Land use: *arable land:* 18%
permanent crops: 17.33%
other: 64.67% (2011)

Irrigated land: 18,790 sq km (2006)

Total renewable water resources: 479 cu km (2011)

Freshwater withdrawal (domestic/industrial/agricultural): *total:* 81.56 cu km/yr (8%/10%/82%)
per capita: 859.9 cu m/yr (2009)

Natural hazards: astride typhoon belt, usually affected by 15 and struck by five to six cyclonic storms each year; landslides; active volcanoes; destructive earthquakes; tsunamis
volcanism: significant volcanic activity; Taal (elev. 311 m), which has shown recent unrest and may erupt in the near future, has been deemed a Decade Volcano by the International Association of Volcanology and Chemistry of the Earth's Interior, worthy of study due to its explosive history and close proximity to human populations; Mayon (elev. 2,462 m), the country's most active volcano, erupted in 2009 forcing over 33,000 to be evacuated; other historically active volcanoes include Biliran, Babuyan Claro, Bulusan, Camiguin, Camiguin de Babuyanes, Didicas, Iraya, Jolo, Kanlaon, Makaturing, Musuan, Parker, Pinatubo and Ragang

Environment—current issues: uncontrolled deforestation especially in watershed areas; soil erosion; air and water pollution in major urban centers; coral reef degradation; increasing pollution of coastal mangrove swamps that are important fish breeding grounds

Environment—international agreements:
party to: Biodiversity, Climate Change, Climate Change-Kyoto Protocol, Desertification, Endangered Species, Hazardous Wastes, Law of the Sea, Marine Dumping, Ozone Layer Protection, Ship Pollution, Tropical Timber 83, Tropical Timber 94, Wetlands, Whaling
signed, but not ratified: Air Pollution-Persistent Organic Pollutants

Geography—note: the Philippine archipelago is made up of 7,107 islands; favorably located in relation to many of Southeast Asia's main
water bodies: the South China Sea, Philippine Sea, Sulu Sea, Celebes Sea, and Luzon Strait

PEOPLE AND SOCIETY

Nationality: *noun:* Filipino(s)
adjective: Philippine

Ethnic groups: Tagalog 28.1%, Cebuano 13.1%, Ilocano 9%, Bisaya/Binisaya 7.6%, Hiligaynon Ilonggo 7.5%, Bikol 6%, Waray 3.4%, other 25.3% (2000 census)

Languages: Filipino (official; based on Tagalog) and English (official); eight major dialects—Tagalog, Cebuano, Ilocano, Hiligaynon or Ilonggo, Bicol, Waray, Pampango, and Pangasinan

Religions: Catholic 82.9% (Roman Catholic 80.9%, Aglipayan 2%), Muslim 5%, Evangelical 2.8%, Iglesia ni Kristo 2.3%, other Christian 4.5%, other 1.8%, unspecified 0.6%, none 0.1% (2000 census)

Population: 107,668,231 (July 2014 est.)
country comparison to the world: 13

Age structure:
0-14 years: 33.7% (male 18,493,668/female 17,753,359)
15-24 years: 19% (male 10,416,358/female 10,044,724)
25-54 years: 37% (male 20,031,638/female 19,796,545)
55-64 years: 4.5% (male 2,882,719/female 3,372,485)
65 years and over: 4.4% (male 2,103,596/female 2,773,139) (2014 est.)

Dependency ratios:
total dependency ratio: 61.4 %
youth dependency ratio: 55.1 %

elderly dependency ratio: 6.3 %
potential support ratio: 15.9 (2013)

Median age: *total:* 23.5 years
male: 23 years
female: 24 years (2014 est.)

Population growth rate: 1.81% (2014 est.)
country comparison to the world: 67

Birth rate: 24.24 births/1,000 population (2014 est.)
country comparison to the world: 61

Death rate: 4.92 deaths/1,000 population (2014 est.)
country comparison to the world: 193

Net migration rate: -1.23 migrant(s)/1,000 population (2014 est.)
country comparison to the world: 155

Urbanization: *urban population:* 48.8% of total population (2011)
rate of urbanization: 2.16% annual rate of change (2010-15 est.)

Major urban areas—population: MANILA (capital) 11.449 million; Davao 1.48 million; Cebu City 845,000; Zamboanga 827,000 (2009)

Sex ratio: *at birth:* 1.05 male(s)/female
0-14 years: 1.04 male(s)/female
15-24 years: 1.04 male(s)/female
25-54 years: 1.01 male(s)/female
55-64 years: 1 male(s)/female
65 years and over: 0.76 male(s)/female
total population: 1 male(s)/female (2014 est.)

Mother's mean age at first birth: 23.1 (2008 est.)

Maternal mortality rate: 99 deaths/100,000 live births (2010)
country comparison to the world: 74

Infant mortality rate: *total:* 17.64 deaths/1,000 live births
country comparison to the world: 99
male: 19.99 deaths/1,000 live births
female: 15.17 deaths/1,000 live births (2014 est.)

Life expectancy at birth: *total population:* 72.48 years
country comparison to the world: 134
male: 69.52 years
female: 75.59 years (2014 est.)

Total fertility rate: 3.06 children born/woman (2014 est.)
country comparison to the world: 53

Contraceptive prevalence rate: 48.9% (2011)

Health expenditures: 4.1% of GDP (2011)
country comparison to the world: 159

Physicians density: 1.15 physicians/1,000 population (2004)

Hospital bed density: 1 beds/1,000 population (2011)

Drinking water source:
improved:
urban: 92.7% of population
rural: 92.1% of population
total: 92.4% of population
unimproved:
urban: 7.3% of population
rural: 7.9% of population
total: 7.6% of population (2011 est.)

Sanitation facility access:
improved:
urban: 79.2% of population
rural: 69.3% of population
total: 74.2% of population
unimproved:
urban: 20.8% of population
rural: 30.7% of population
total: 25.8% of population (2011 est.)

HIV/AIDS—adult prevalence rate: 0.1% (2012 est.)
country comparison to the world: 167

HIV/AIDS—people living with HIV/AIDS: 14,800 (2012 est.)
country comparison to the world: 91

HIV/AIDS—deaths: 300 (2012 est.)
country comparison to the world: 106

Major infectious diseases: *degree of risk:* high
food or waterborne diseases: bacterial diarrhea, hepatitis A, and typhoid fever
vectorborne diseases: dengue fever and malaria
water contact disease: leptospirosis (2013)

Obesity—adult prevalence rate: 6.3% (2008)
country comparison to the world: 148

Children under the age of 5 years underweight: 20.2% (2011)
country comparison to the world: 31

Education expenditures: 2.7% of GDP (2009)
country comparison to the world: 149

Literacy: *definition:* age 15 and over can read and write
total population: 95.4%
male: 95%
female: 95.8% (2008 est.)

School life expectancy (primary to tertiary education): *total:* 11 years
male: 11 years
female: 12 years (2009)

Unemployment, youth ages 15-24: *total:* 16.3%
country comparison to the world: 79
male: 15.2%
female: 18.3% (2011)

GOVERNMENT

Country name: *conventional long form:* Republic of the Philippines
conventional short form: Philippines
local long form: Republika ng Pilipinas
local short form: Pilipinas

Government type: republic

Capital: *name:* Manila

geographic coordinates: 14 36 N, 120 58 E
time difference: UTC+8 (13 hours ahead of Washington, DC during Standard Time)

Administrative divisions: 80 provinces and 39 chartered cities
provinces: Abra, Agusan del Norte, Agusan del Sur, Aklan, Albay, Antique, Apayao, Aurora, Basilan, Bataan, Batanes, Batangas, Biliran, Benguet, Bohol, Bukidnon, Bulacan, Cagayan, Camarines Norte, Camarines Sur, Camiguin, Capiz, Catanduanes, Cavite, Cebu, Compostela, Davao del Norte, Davao del Sur, Davao Oriental, Dinagat Islands, Eastern Samar, Guimaras, Ifugao, Ilocos Norte, Ilocos Sur, Iloilo, Isabela, Kalinga, Laguna, Lanao del Norte, Lanao del Sur, La Union, Leyte, Maguindanao, Marinduque, Masbate, Mindoro Occidental, Mindoro Oriental, Misamis Occidental, Misamis Oriental, Mountain Province, Negros Occidental, Negros Oriental, North Cotabato, Northern Samar, Nueva Ecija, Nueva Vizcaya, Palawan, Pampanga, Pangasinan, Quezon, Quirino, Rizal, Romblon, Samar, Sarangani, Siquijor, Sorsogon, South Cotabato, Southern Leyte, Sultan Kudarat, Sulu, Surigao del Norte, Surigao del Sur, Tarlac, Tawi-Tawi, Zambales, Zamboanga del Norte, Zamboanga del Sur, Zamboanga Sibugay
chartered cities: Angeles, Antipolo, Bacolod, Baguio, Butuan, Cagayan de Oro, Caloocan, Cebu, Cotabato, Dagupan, Davao, General Santos, Iligan, Iloilo, Lapu-Lapu, Las Pinas, Lucena, Makati, Malabon, Mandaluyong, Mandaue, Manila, Marikina, Muntinlupa, Naga, Navotas, Olongapo, Ormoc, Paranaque, Pasay, Pasig, Puerto Princesa, Quezon, San Juan, Santiago, Tacloban, Taguig, Valenzuela, Zamboanga (2012)

Independence: 12 June 1898 (independence proclaimed from Spain); 4 July 1946 (from the US)

National holiday: Independence Day, 12 June (1898); note—12 June 1898 was date of declaration of independence from Spain; 4 July 1946 was date of independence from US

Constitution: several previous; latest ratified 2 February 1987, effective 11 February 1987 (2013)

Legal system: mixed legal system of civil, common, Islamic, and customary law

International law organization participation: accepts compulsory ICJ jurisdiction with reservations; accepts ICCt jurisdiction

Suffrage: 18 years of age; universal

Executive branch: *chief of state:* President Benigno AQUINO (since 30 June 2010); Vice President Jejomar BINAY (since 30 June 2010); note—president is both chief of state and head of government
head of government: President Benigno AQUINO (since 30 June 2010)
cabinet: Cabinet appointed by the president with consent of Commission of Appointments (For more information visit the World Leaders website)
elections: president and vice president elected on separate tickets by popular vote for a single six-year term; election held on 10 May 2010 (next election to be held in May 2016)
election results: Benigno AQUINO elected president; percent of vote—Benigno AQUINO 42.1%, Joseph ESTRADA 26.3%, seven others 31.6%; Jejomar BINAY elected vice president; percent of vote Jejomar BINAY 41.6%, Manuel ROXAS 39.6%, six others 18.8%

Legislative branch: bicameral Congress or Kongreso consists of the Senate or Senado (24 seats—one-half elected every three years; members elected at large by popular vote to serve six-year terms) and the House of Representatives or Kapulungan Ng Nga Kinatawan (287 seats—230 members in one tier representing districts and 57 sectoral party-list members in a second tier representing special minorities elected on the basis of one seat for every 2% of the total vote but with each party limited to three seats); a party represented in one tier may not hold seats in the other tier; all House members are elected by popular vote to serve three-year terms
note: the constitution limits the House of Representatives to 250 members; the number of members allowed was increased, however, through legislation when in April 2009 the Philippine Supreme Court ruled that additional party members could sit in the House of Representatives if they received the required number of votes
elections: Senate—elections last held on 13 May 2013 (next to be held in May 2016); House of Representatives—elections last held on 13 May 2013 (next to be held in May 2016)

election results: Senate—percent of vote by party for 2013 election—UNA 26.94%, NP 15.3%, LP 11.32%, NPC 10.15%, LDP 5.38%, PDP-Laban 4.95%, others 9.72%, independents 16.24%; seats by party after 2013 election—UNA 5, NP 5, LP 4, Lakas 2, NPC 2, LDP 1, PDP-Laban 1, PRP 1, independents 3; House of Representatives—percent of vote by party—LP 38.3%, NPC 17.4%, UNA 11.4%, NUP 8.7%, NP 8.5%, Lakas 5.3%, independents 6.0%, others 4.4%; seats by party—LP 110, NPC 43, NUP 24, NP 17, Lakas 14, UNA 8, independents 6, others 12; party-list 57

Judicial branch: *highest court(s):* Supreme Court (consists of a chief justice and 14 associate justices)
judge selection and term of office: justices are appointed by the president on the recommendation of the Judicial and Bar Council, a constitutionally-created, 6-member body that recommends Supreme Court nominees; justices serve until age 70
subordinate courts: Court of Appeals; Sandiganbayan (special court for corruption cases of government officials); Court of Tax Appeals; regional, metropolitan, and municipal trial courts; sharia courts

Political parties and leaders: Laban ng Demokratikong Pilipino (Struggle of Filipino Democrats) or LDP [Edgardo ANGARA]; Lakas ng EDSA-Christian Muslim Democrats or Lakas-CMD [Manuel "Mar" ROXAS]; Liberal Party or LP [Manuel ROXAS]; Nacionalista Party or NP [Manuel "Manny" VILLAR]; Nationalist People's Coalition or NPC [Frisco SAN JUAN]; PDP-Laban [Aquilino PIMENTEL]; People's Reform Party [Miriam Defensor SANTIAGO]; Puwersa ng Masang Pilipino (Force of the Philippine Masses) or PMP [Joseph ESTRADA]
note: United Nationalist Alliance or [UNA]—PDP-Laban and PMP coalition for the 2013 election

Political pressure groups and leaders: Black and White Movement [Vicente ROMANO]; Kilosbayan [Jovito SALONGA]

International organization participation: ADB, APEC, APT, ARF, ASEAN, BIS, CD, CICA (observer), CP, EAS, FAO, G-24, G-77, IAEA, IBRD, ICAO, ICC (national committees), ICRM, IDA, IFAD, IFC, IFRCS, IHO, ILO, IMF, IMO, IMSO, Interpol, IOC, IOM, IPU, ISO, ITSO, ITU, ITUC (NGOs), MIGA, MINUSTAH, NAM, OAS (observer), OPCW, PCA, PIF (partner), UN, UNCTAD, UNDOF, UNESCO, UNHCR, UNIDO, Union Latina, UNISFA, UNMIL, UNMISS, UNMIT, UNMOGIP, UNOCI, UNWTO, UPU, WCO, WFTU (NGOs), WHO, WIPO, WMO, WTO

Diplomatic representation in the US:
chief of mission: Ambassador Jose L. CUISIA Jr. (since 7 April 2011)
chancery: 1600 Massachusetts Avenue NW, Washington, DC 20036
telephone: [1] (202) 467-9300
FAX: [1] (202) 467-9417
consulate(s) general: Chicago, Honolulu, Los Angeles, New York, San Francisco, Tamuning (Guam)

Diplomatic representation from the US:
chief of mission: Ambassador Philip S. GOLDBERG (since 21 November 2013)
embassy: 1201 Roxas Boulevard, Manila 1000
mailing address: PSC 500, FPO AP 96515-1000
telephone: [63] (2) 301-2000
FAX: [63] (2) 301-2017

Flag description: two equal horizontal bands of blue (top) and red; a white equilateral triangle is based on the hoist side; the center of the triangle displays a yellow sun with eight primary rays; each corner of the triangle contains a small, yellow, five-pointed star; blue stands for peace and justice, red symbolizes courage, the white equal-sided triangle represents equality; the rays recall the first eight provinces that sought independence from Spain, while the stars represent the three major geographical divisions of the country: Luzon, Visayas, and Mindanao; the design of the flag dates to 1897
note: in wartime the flag is flown upside down with the red band at the top

National symbol(s): Philippine eagle

National anthem: *name:* "Lupang Hinirang" (Chosen Land)
lyrics/music: Jose PALMA (revised by Felipe PADILLA de Leon)/Julian FELIPE
note: music adopted 1898, original Spanish lyrics adopted 1899, Filipino (Tagalog) lyrics adopted 1956; although the original lyrics were written in Spanish, later English and Filipino versions were created; today, only the Filipino version is used

ECONOMY

Economy—overview: The economy has weathered global economic and financial downturns better than its regional peers due to minimal exposure to troubled international securities, lower dependence on exports, relatively resilient domestic consumption, large remittances from four- to five-million overseas Filipino workers, and a rapidly expanding business process outsourcing industry. The current account balance had recorded consecutive surpluses since 2003; international reserves are at record highs; the banking system is stable; and the stock market was Asia's second best-performer in 2012. Efforts to improve tax administration and expenditure management have helped ease the Philippines' tight fiscal situation and reduce high debt levels. The Philippines has received several credit rating upgrades on its sovereign debt, and has had little difficulty tapping domestic and international markets to finance its deficits. Economic growth in the Philippines averaged 4.5% during the MACAPAGAL-ARROYO administration, but poverty worsened during her term. Growth has accelerated under the AQUINO government, but with limited progress thus far in bringing down unemployment, which hovers around 7%, and improving the quality of jobs. Underemployment is nearly 20% and more than 40% of the employed are estimated to be working in the informal sector. The AQUINO administration has been working to boost the budgets for education, health, cash transfers to the poor, and other social spending programs, and is relying on the private sector to help fund major infrastructure projects under its Public-Private Partnership program. Long term challenges include reforming governance and the judicial system, building infrastructure, improving regulatory predictability, and the ease of doing business, attracting higher levels of local and foreign investments. The Philippine Constitution and the other laws continue to restrict foreign ownership in important activities/sectors (such as land ownership and public utilities).

GDP (purchasing power parity): $454.3 billion (2013 est.)
country comparison to the world: 32
$425.3 billion (2012 est.)
$398.2 billion (2011 est.)
note: data are in 2013 US dollars

GDP (official exchange rate): $272.2 billion (2013 est.)

GDP—real growth rate: 6.8% (2013 est.)
country comparison to the world: 25
6.8% (2012 est.)
3.6% (2011 est.)

GDP—per capita (PPP): $4,700 (2013 est.)
country comparison to the world: 165
$4,400 (2012 est.)
$4,200 (2011 est.)
note: data are in 2013 US dollars

Gross national saving: 22.9% of GDP (2013 est.)
country comparison to the world: 63
21.3% of GDP (2012 est.)
23.6% of GDP (2011 est.)

GDP—composition, by end use:
household consumption: 72.6%
government consumption: 11.5%
investment in fixed capital: 20.2%
investment in inventories: -0.2%
exports of goods and services: 28.3%
imports of goods and services: -32.4% (2013 est.)

GDP—composition, by sector of origin:
agriculture: 11.2%
industry: 31.6%
services: 57.2% (2013 est.)

Agriculture—products: sugarcane, coconuts, rice, corn, bananas, cassavas, pineapples, mangoes; pork, eggs, beef; fish

Industries: electronics assembly, garments, footwear, pharmaceuticals, chemicals, wood products, food processing, petroleum refining, fishing

Industrial production growth rate: 9% (2013 est.)
country comparison to the world: 19

Labor force: 41.33 million (2013 est.)
country comparison to the world: 16

Labor force—by occupation: *agriculture:* 32%
industry: 15%
services: 53% (2012 est.)

Unemployment rate: 7.4% (2013 est.)
country comparison to the world: 80
7% (2012 est.)

Population below poverty line: 26.5% (2009 est.)

Household income or consumption by percentage share: *lowest 10%:* 2.6%
highest 10%: 33.6% (2009 est.)

Distribution of family income—Gini index:
44.8 (2009)
country comparison to the world: 42
46.6 (2003)

Budget: *revenues:* $38.88 billion

expenditures: $43.89 billion (2013 est.)

Taxes and other revenues: 14.3% of GDP (2013 est.)
country comparison to the world: 195

Budget surplus (+) or deficit (-):
-1.8% of GDP (2013 est.)
country comparison to the world: 78

Public debt: 50.2% of GDP (2013 est.)
country comparison to the world: 68
51.5% of GDP (2012 est.)
note: data cover debt issued by the national government, and excludes debt instruments issued by government entities other than the treasury; the data include treasury debt held by foreign entities; the data exclude debt issued by social security institutions, government-owned and controlled corporations, the Central Bank, and local government units

Fiscal year: calendar year

Inflation rate (consumer prices): 2.8% (2013 est.)
country comparison to the world: 107
3.2% (2012 est.)

Central bank discount rate: 5.3% (31 December 2012 est.)
country comparison to the world: 64
5.6% (31 December 2011 est.)

Commercial bank prime lending rate: 5.8% (31 December 2013 est.)
country comparison to the world: 143
5.68% (31 December 2012 est.)

Stock of narrow money: $43.67 billion (31 December 2013 est.)
country comparison to the world: 51
$39.01 billion (31 December 2012 est.)

Stock of broad money: $137.7 billion (31 December 2013 est.)
country comparison to the world: 49
$121.6 billion (31 December 2012 est.)

Stock of domestic credit: $150.3 billion (31 December 2013 est.)
country comparison to the world: 47
$129.4 billion (31 December 2012 est.)

Market value of publicly traded shares: $266.3 billion (31 December 2012)
country comparison to the world: 33
$198.4 billion (31 December 2011)
$202.2 billion (31 December 2010)

Current account balance: $7.512 billion (2013 est.)
country comparison to the world: 26
$7.126 billion (2012 est.)

Exports: $47.45 billion (2013 est.)
country comparison to the world: 58
$46.28 billion (2012 est.)

Exports—commodities: semiconductors and electronic products, transport equipment, garments, copper products, petroleum products, coconut oil, fruits

Exports—partners: Japan 19%, US 14.2%, China 11.8%, Singapore 9.3%, Hong Kong 9.2%, South Korea 5.5%, Thailand 4.7% (2012)

Imports: $63.91 billion (2013 est.)
country comparison to the world: 47
$61.49 billion (2012 est.)

Imports—commodities: electronic products, mineral fuels, machinery and transport equipment, iron and steel, textile fabrics, grains, chemicals, plastic

Imports—partners: US 11.5%, China 10.8%, Japan 10.4%, South Korea 7.3%, Singapore 7.1%, Thailand 5.6%, Saudi Arabia 5.6%, Indonesia 4.4%, Malaysia 4% (2012)

Reserves of foreign exchange and gold: $85.04 billion (31 December 2013 est.)
country comparison to the world: 26
$83.83 billion (31 December 2012 est.)

Debt—external: $72.81 billion (31 December 2013 est.)
country comparison to the world: 54
$74.88 billion (31 December 2012 est.)

Stock of direct foreign investment—at home: $33.28 billion (31 December 2013 est.)
country comparison to the world: 61
$30.38 billion (31 December 2012 est.)

Stock of direct foreign investment—abroad: $9.435 billion (31 December 2013 est.)
country comparison to the world: 54
$8.435 billion (31 December 2012 est.)

Exchange rates: Philippine pesos (PHP) per US dollar—
42.69 (2013 est.)
42.229 (2012 est.)
45.11 (2010 est.)
47.68 (2009)
44.439 (2008)

ENERGY

Electricity—production: 67.45 billion kWh (2011 est.)
country comparison to the world: 4 1

Electricity—consumption: 56.84 billion kWh (2010 est.)
country comparison to the world: 42

Electricity—exports: 0 kWh (2012 est.)
country comparison to the world: 186

Electricity—imports: 0 kWh (2012 est.)
country comparison to the world: 189

Electricity—installed generating capacity: 16.36 million kW (2010 est.)
country comparison to the world: 43

Electricity—from fossil fuels: 66.9% of total installed capacity (2010 est.)
country comparison to the world: 115

Electricity—from nuclear fuels: 0% of total installed capacity (2010 est.)
country comparison to the world: 168

Electricity—from hydroelectric plants: 20.8% of total installed capacity (2010 est.)
country comparison to the world: 90

Electricity—from other renewable sources: 12.3% of total installed capacity (2010 est.)
country comparison to the world: 21

Crude oil—production: 25,240 bbl/day (2012 est.)
country comparison to the world: 73

Crude oil—exports: 20,090 bbl/day (2010 est.)
country comparison to the world: 53

Crude oil—imports: 182,000 bbl/day (2010 est.)
country comparison to the world: 35

Crude oil—proved reserves: 138.5 million bbl (1 January 2013 es)
country comparison to the world: 67

Refined petroleum products—production: 181,300 bbl/day (2010 est.)
country comparison to the world: 57

Refined petroleum products—consumption: 315,600 bbl/day (2011 est.)
country comparison to the world: 42

Refined petroleum products—exports: 17,810 bbl/day (2010 est.)
country comparison to the world: 74

Refined petroleum products—imports: 147,900 bbl/day (2010 est.)
country comparison to the world: 39

Natural gas—production: 3.91 billion cu m (2012 est.)
country comparison to the world: 54

Natural gas—consumption: 2.86 billion cu m (2010 est.)
country comparison to the world: 73

Natural gas—exports: 0 cu m (2011 est.)
country comparison to the world: 171

Natural gas—imports: 0 cu m (2011 est.)
country comparison to the world: 121

Natural gas—proved reserves: 98.54 billion cu m (1 January 2013 es)
country comparison to the world: 54

Carbon dioxide emissions from consumption of energy: 81.15 million Mt (2011 est.)
country comparison to the world: 45

COMMUNICATIONS

Telephones—main lines in use: 3.939 million (2012)
country comparison to the world: 4 3

Telephones—mobile cellular: 103 million (2012)
country comparison to the world: 12

Telephone system: *general assessment:* good international radiotelephone and submarine cable services; domestic and interisland service adequate
domestic: telecommunications infrastructure includes the following platforms: fixed-line, mobile cellular, cable TV, over-the-air TV, radio and Very Small Aperture Terminal (VSAT), fiber-optic cable, and satellite; mobile-cellular communications now dominate the industry
international: country code—63; a series of submarine cables together provide connectivity to Asia, US, the Middle East, and Europe; multiple international gateways (2011)

Broadcast media: multiple national private TV and radio networks; multi-channel satellite and cable TV systems available; more than 350 TV stations—4 major TV networks operating nationwide with 1 being government-owned; some 1100 cable TV providers and some 1,200 radio stations broadcasting; the Philippines is scheduled to complete the switch from analog to digital broadcasting by the end of 2015 (2012)

Internet country code: . p h

Internet hosts: 425,812 (2012)
country comparison to the world: 52

Internet users: 8.278 million (2009)
country comparison to the world: 34

TRANSPORTATION

Airports: 247 (2013)
country comparison to the world: 2 4

Airports—with paved runways: *total:* 8 9
over 3,047 m: 4
2,438 to 3,047 m: 8
1,524 to 2,437 m: 33
914 to 1,523 m: 34
under 914 m: 10 (2013)

Airports—with unpaved runways: *total:* 158
1,524 to 2,437 m: 3
914 to 1,523 m: 56
under 914 m: 99 (2013)

Heliports: 2 (2013)

Pipelines: gas 567 km; oil 138 km; refined products 185 km (2013)

Railways: *total:* 995 km
country comparison to the world: 88
narrow gauge: 995 km 1.067-m gauge (484 km are in operation) (2010)

Roadways: *total:* 213,151 km
country comparison to the world: 23
paved: 54,481 km
unpaved: 158,670 km (2009)

Waterways: 3,219 km (limited to vessels with draft less than 1.5 m) (2011)
country comparison to the world: 31

Merchant marine: *total:* 446
country comparison to the world: 23
by type: bulk carrier 76, cargo 152, carrier 12, chemical tanker 27, container 17, liquefied gas 5, passenger 7, passenger/cargo 65, petroleum tanker 44, refrigerated cargo 20, roll on/roll off 11, vehicle carrier 10
foreign-owned: 159 (Bermuda 47, China 4, Denmark 2, Germany 2, Greece 5, Japan 77, Malaysia 1, Netherlands 17, Singapore 1, South Korea 1, Taiwan 1, UAE 1)
registered in other countries: 7 (Cyprus 1, Panama 5, unknown 1) (2010)

Ports and terminals: *major seaport(s):* Batangas, Cagayan de Oro, Cebu, Davao, Liman, Manila
container port(s) (TEUs): Manila (3,342,200)

Transportation—note: the International Maritime Bureau reports the territorial and offshore waters in the South China Sea as high risk for piracy and armed robbery against ships; numerous commercial vessels have been attacked and hijacked both at anchor and while underway; hijacked vessels are often disguised and cargo diverted to ports in East Asia; crews have been murdered or cast adrift

MILITARY

Military branches: Armed Forces of the Philippines (AFP): Army, Navy (includes Marine Corps), Air Force (2013)

Military service age and obligation: 17-23 years of age (officers 20-24) for voluntary military service; no conscription; applicants must be single male or female Philippine citizens with either 72 college credit hours (enlisted) or a baccalaureate degree (officers) (2013)

Manpower available for military service:
males age 16-49: 25,614,135
females age 16-49: 25,035,061 (2010 est.)

Manpower fit for military service:
males age 16-49: 20,142,940
females age 16-49: 21,427,792 (2010 est.)

Manpower reaching militarily significant age annually: *male:* 1,060,319
female: 1,021,069 (2010 est.)

Military expenditures: 1.19% of GDP (2012)
country comparison to the world: 86
1.21% of GDP (2011)
1.19% of GDP (2010)

TRANSNATIONAL ISSUES

Disputes—international: Philippines claims sovereignty over Scarborough Reef (also claimed by China together with Taiwan) and over certain of the Spratly Islands, known locally as the Kalayaan (Freedom) Islands, also claimed by China, Malaysia, Taiwan, and Vietnam; the 2002 "Declaration on the Conduct of Parties in the South China Sea," has eased tensions in the Spratly Islands but falls short of a legally binding "code of conduct" desired by several of the disputants; in March 2005, the national oil companies of China, the Philippines, and Vietnam signed a joint accord to conduct marine seismic activities in the Spratly Islands; Philippines retains a dormant claim to Malaysia's Sabah State in northern Borneo based on the Sultanate of Sulu's granting the Philippines Government power of attorney to pursue a sovereignty claim on his behalf; maritime delimitation negotiations continue with Palau

Refugees and internally displaced persons:
IDPs: about 4.5 million (government troops fighting the Moro Islamic Liberation Front, the Abu Sayyaf Group, and the New People's Army; clan feuds; natural disasters including typhoon Bopha (December 2012), the Bohol earthquake (October 2013), and typhoon Haiyan (November 2013)) (2013)
stateless persons: at least 115,772 (2014)

Illicit drugs: domestic methamphetamine production has been a growing problem in recent years despite government crackdowns; major consumer of amphetamines; longstanding marijuana producer mainly in rural areas where Manila's control is limited

PITCAIRN ISLANDS

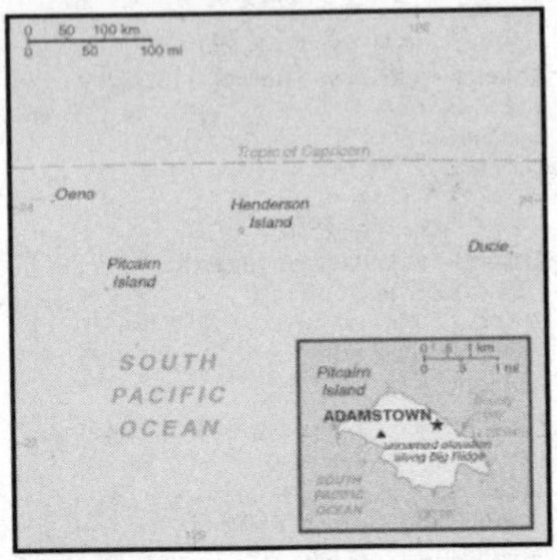

INTRODUCTION

Background: Pitcairn Island was discovered in 1767 by the British and settled in 1790 by the Bounty mutineers and their Tahitian companions. Pitcairn was the first Pacific island to become a British colony (in 1838) and today remains the last vestige of that empire in the South Pacific. Outmigration, primarily to New Zealand, has thinned the population from a peak of 233 in 1937 to less than 50 today.

GEOGRAPHY

Location: Oceania, islands in the South Pacific Ocean, about midway between Peru and New Zealand

Geographic coordinates: 25 04 S, 130 06 W

Map references: Oceania

Area: *total:* 47 sq km
country comparison to the world: 234
land: 47 sq km
water: 0 sq km

Area—comparative: about three tenths the size of Washington, DC

Land boundaries: 0 km

Coastline: 51 km

Maritime claims: *territorial sea:* 3 nm
exclusive economic zone: 200 nm

Climate: tropical; hot and humid; modified by southeast trade winds; rainy season (November to March)

Terrain: rugged volcanic formation; rocky coastline with cliffs

Elevation extremes: *lowest point:* Pacific Ocean 0 m
highest point: Big Ridge 347 m

Natural resources: miro trees (used for handicrafts), fish
note: manganese, iron, copper, gold, silver, and zinc have been discovered offshore

Land use: *arable land:* 0%
permanent crops: 0%
other: 100% (2011)

Irrigated land: NA

Natural hazards: typhoons (especially November to March)

Environment—current issues: deforestation (only a small portion of the original forest remains because of burning and clearing for settlement)

Geography—note: Britain's most isolated dependency; only the larger island of Pitcairn is inhabited but it has no port or natural harbor; supplies must be transported by rowed longboat from larger ships stationed offshore

PEOPLE AND SOCIETY

Nationality: *noun:* Pitcairn Islander(s)
adjective: Pitcairn Islander

Ethnic groups: descendants of the Bounty mutineers and their Tahitian wives

Languages: English (official), Pitkern (mixture of an 18th century English dialect and a Tahitian dialect)

Religions: Seventh-Day Adventist 100%

Population: 48 (July 2014 est.)
country comparison to the world: 240

Population growth rate: 0% (2014 est.)
country comparison to the world: 197

Urbanization: *urban population:* 0% of total population (2010)
rate of urbanization: 0% annual rate of change (2010-15 est.)

Sex ratio: NA

Infant mortality rate: total: NA
male: NA
female: NA

Life expectancy at birth: *total population:* NA
male: NA
female: NA

Total fertility rate: NA (2014 est.)

HIV/AIDS—adult prevalence rate: NA

HIV/AIDS—people living with HIV/AIDS: NA

HIV/AIDS—deaths: NA

Literacy: NA

GOVERNMENT

Country name: *conventional long form:* Pitcairn, Henderson, Ducie, and Oeno Islands
conventional short form: Pitcairn Islands

Dependency status: overseas territory of the UK

Government type: NA

Capital: *name:* Adamstown
geographic coordinates: 25 04 S, 130 05 W
time difference: UTC-9 (4 hours behind Washington, DC during Standard Time)

Administrative divisions: none (overseas territory of the UK)

Independence: none (overseas territory of the UK)

National holiday: Birthday of Queen ELIZABETH II, second Saturday in June (1926); Discovery Day, 2 July (1767)

Constitution: several previous; latest made 10 February 2010, presented 17 February 2010, effective 4 March 2010 (2010)

Legal system: local island by-laws

Suffrage: 18 years of age; universal with three years residency

Executive branch: *chief of state:* Queen ELIZABETH II (since 6 February 1952); represented by UK High Commissioner to New Zealand and Governor (nonresident) of the Pitcairn Islands Victoria M. TREADELL (since May 2010); Commissioner (nonresident) Leslie JAQUES (since September 2003) serves as liaison between the governor and the Island Council
head of government: Mayor and Chairman of the Island Council Shawn CHRISTIAN (since 13 November 2013)
cabinet: NA (For more information visit the World Leaders website)
elections: the monarchy is hereditary; governor and commissioner appointed by the monarch; island mayor elected by popular vote for a three-year term; election last held in November 2013 (next to be held not later than December 2016)
election results: Shawn CHRISTIAN elected mayor and chairman of the Island Council

Legislative branch: unicameral Island Council (10 seats; mayor, deputy mayor, 5 members elected by popular vote, 3 ex officio members including governor, deputy governor, and commissioner; deputy mayor and elected members serve two-year terms)
elections: last held on 13 November 2013 (next to be held not later than December 2015)
election results: percent of vote—NA; seats—5 independents

Judicial branch: *highest court(s):* Pitcairn Court of Appeal (consists of the court president, 2 judges, and the Supreme Court chief justice (ex-officio member); Pitcairn Supreme Court (consists of the chief justice and 2 judges) note—appeals beyond the Pitcairn Court of Appeal are heard by the Judicial Committee of the Privy Council (in London); note 2: the Court of Appeal was established in 2000 by an Order in Council
judge selection and term of office: all judges of both courts appointed by the governor of the Pitcairn Islands on the instructions of the Queen of England through the Secretary of State; all judges appointed until retirement, normally at age 75
subordinate courts: Magistrate's Court

Political parties and leaders: none

Political pressure groups and leaders: none

International organization participation: SPC, UPU

Diplomatic representation in the US: none (overseas territory of the UK)

Diplomatic representation from the US: none (overseas territory of the UK)

Flag description: blue with the flag of the UK in the upper hoist-side quadrant and the Pitcairn Islander coat of arms centered on the outer half of the flag; the green, yellow, and blue of the shield represents the island rising from the ocean; the green field features a yellow anchor surmounted by a bible (both the anchor and the bible were items found on the HMS Bounty); sitting on the crest is a Pitcairn Island wheelbarrow from which springs a slip of miro (a local plant)

National anthem: *name:* "We From Pitcairn Island"
lyrics/music: unknown/Frederick M. LEHMAN
note: serves as a local anthem; as a territory of the United Kingdom, "God Save the Queen" is official (see United Kingdom)

ECONOMY

Economy—overview: The inhabitants of this tiny isolated economy exist on fishing, subsistence farming, handicrafts, and postage stamps. The fertile soil of the valleys produces a wide variety of fruits and vegetables, including citrus, sugarcane, watermelons, bananas, yams, and beans. Bartering is an important part of the economy. The major sources of revenue are the sale of postage stamps to collectors and the sale of handicrafts to passing ships.

GDP (purchasing power parity): $NA

Agriculture—products: honey; wide variety of fruits and vegetables; goats, chickens; fish

Industries: postage stamps, handicrafts, beekeeping, honey

Labor force: 15 (2004)
country comparison to the world: 233

Labor force—by occupation: note: no business community in the usual sense; some public works; subsistence farming and fishing

Budget: *revenues:* $746,000
expenditures: $1.028 million (FY04/05)

Fiscal year: 1 April—31 March

Exports: $NA

Exports—commodities: fruits, vegetables, curios, stamps

Imports: $NA

Imports—commodities: fuel oil, machinery, building materials, flour, sugar, other foodstuffs

Exchange rates: New Zealand dollars (NZD) per US dollar—
1.247 (2013)
1.2334 (2012)
1.3874 (2010)
1.6002 (2009)
1.4151 (2008)

COMMUNICATIONS

Telephone system: *general assessment:* satellite-based phone services
domestic: local phone service with international connections via Internet
international: country code—872; satellite earth station—1 (Inmarsat)

Broadcast media: satellite TV from Fiji-based Sky Pacific offering a wide range of international channels

Internet country code: .pn

Internet hosts: 26 (2012)
country comparison to the world: 217

Communications—note: satellite-based local phone service and broadband Internet connections available in all homes

TRANSPORTATION

Ports and terminals: *major seaport(s):* Adamstown (on Bounty Bay)

MILITARY

Military—note: defense is the responsibility of the UK

TRANSNATIONAL ISSUES

Disputes—international: none

POLAND

INTRODUCTION

Background: Poland's history as a state begins near the middle of the 10th century. By the mid-16th century, the Polish-Lithuanian Commonwealth ruled a vast tract of land in central and eastern Europe. During the 18th century, internal disorders weakened the nation, and in a series of agreements between 1772 and 1795, Russia, Prussia, and Austria partitioned Poland among themselves. Poland regained its independence in 1918 only to be overrun by Germany and the Soviet Union in World War II. It became a Soviet satellite state following the war, but its government was comparatively tolerant and progressive. Labor turmoil in 1980 led to the formation of the independent trade union "Solidarity" that over time became a political force with over ten million members. Free elections in 1989 and 1990 won Solidarity control of the parliament and the presidency, bringing the communist era to a close. A "shock therapy" program during the early 1990s enabled the country to transform its economy into one of the most robust in Central Europe. Poland joined NATO in 1999 and the European Union in 2004. With its transformation to a democratic, market-oriented country largely completed and with large investments in defense, energy, and other infrastructure, Poland is an increasingly active member of Euro-Atlantic organizations.

GEOGRAPHY

Location: Central Europe, east of Germany

Geographic coordinates: 52 00 N, 20 00 E

Map references: Europe

Area: *total:* 312,685 sq km
country comparison to the world: 70
land: 304,255 sq km

water: 8,430 sq km

Area—comparative: slightly smaller than New Mexico

Land boundaries: *total:* 3,071 km
border countries: Belarus 418 km, Czech Republic 796 km, Germany 467 km, Lithuania 104 km, Russia (Kaliningrad Oblast) 210 km, Slovakia 541 km, Ukraine 535 km

Coastline: 440 km

Maritime claims: *territorial sea:* 12 nm
exclusive economic zone: defined by international treaties

Climate: temperate with cold, cloudy, moderately severe winters with frequent precipitation; mild summers with frequent showers and thundershowers

Terrain: mostly flat plain; mountains along southern border

Elevation extremes: *lowest point:* near Raczki Elblaskie -2 m
highest point: Rysy 2,499 m

Natural resources: coal, sulfur, copper, natural gas, silver, lead, salt, amber, arable land

Land use: *arable land:* 35.49%
permanent crops: 1.25%
other: 63.26% (2011)

Irrigated land: 1,157 sq km (2007)

Total renewable water resources: 61.6 cu km (2011)

Freshwater withdrawal (domestic/industrial/agricultural): *total:* 11.96 cu km/yr (31%/60%/10%)
per capita: 312.3 cu m/yr (2009)

Natural hazards: flooding

Environment—current issues: situation has improved since 1989 due to decline in heavy industry and increased environmental concern by post-Communist governments; air pollution nonetheless remains serious because of sulfur dioxide emissions from coal-fired power plants, and the resulting acid rain has caused forest damage; water pollution from industrial and municipal sources is also a problem, as is disposal of hazardous wastes; pollution levels should continue to decrease as industrial establishments bring their facilities up to EU code, but at substantial cost to business and the government

Environment—international agreements:
party to: Air Pollution, Antarctic-Environmental Protocol, Antarctic-Marine Living Resources, Antarctic Seals, Antarctic Treaty, Biodiversity, Climate Change, Climate Change-Kyoto Protocol, Desertification, Endangered Species, Environmental Modification, Hazardous Wastes, Law of the Sea, Marine Dumping, Ozone Layer Protection, Ship Pollution, Wetlands
signed, but not ratified: Air Pollution-Nitrogen Oxides, Air Pollution-Persistent Organic Pollutants, Air Pollution-Sulfur 94

Geography—note: historically, an area of conflict because of flat terrain and the lack of natural barriers on the North European Plain

PEOPLE AND SOCIETY

Nationality: *noun:* Pole(s)
adjective: Polish

Ethnic groups: Polish 96.9%, Silesian 1.1%, German 0.2%, Ukrainian 0.1%, other and unspecified 1.7%
note: represents ethnicity declared first (2011 est.)

Languages: Polish (official) 96.2%, Polish and non-Polish 2%, non-Polish 0.5%, unspecified 1.3% (2011 est.)

Religions: Catholic 87.2% (includes Roman Catholic 86.9% and Greek Catholic, Armenian Catholic, and Byzantine-Slavic Catholic .3%), Orthodox 1.3% (almost all are Polish Autocephalous Orthodox), Protestant 0.4% (mainly Augsburg Evangelical and Pentacostal), other 0.4% (includes Jehovah's Witness, Buddhist, Hare Krishna, Gaudiya Vaishnavism, Muslim, Jewish, Mormon), unspecified 10.8% (2012 est.)

Population: 38,346,279 (July 2014 est.)
country comparison to the world: 35

Age structure:
0-14 years: 14.6% (male 2,876,264/female 2,716,569)
15-24 years: 11.9% (male 2,333,627/female 2,235,228)
25-54 years: 43.8% (male 8,459,153/female 8,355,491)
55-64 years: 15% (male 2,658,106/female 2,973,933)
65 years and over: 14.5% (male 2,224,569/female 3,513,339) (2014 est.)

Dependency ratios:
total dependency ratio: 41.6 %
youth dependency ratio: 21.2 %
elderly dependency ratio: 20.4 %
potential support ratio: 4.9 (2013)

Median age: *total:* 39.5 years
male: 37.9 years
female: 41.3 years (2014 est.)

Population growth rate: -0.11% (2014 est.)
country comparison to the world: 203

Birth rate: 9.77 births/1,000 population (2014 est.)
country comparison to the world: 200

Death rate: 10.37 deaths/1,000 population (2014 est.)
country comparison to the world: 43

Net migration rate: -0.47 migrant(s)/1,000 population (2014 est.)
country comparison to the world: 134

Urbanization: *urban population:* 60.9% of total population (2011)
rate of urbanization: -0.04% annual rate of change (2010-15 est.)

Major urban areas—population: WARSAW (capital) 1.71 million; Krakow 756,000 (2009)

Sex ratio: *at birth:* 1.06 male(s)/female
0-14 years: 1.06 male(s)/female
15-24 years: 1.04 male(s)/female
25-54 years: 1.01 male(s)/female
55-64 years: 0.94 male(s)/female
65 years and over: 0.62 male(s)/female
total population: 0.94 male(s)/female (2014 est.)

Mother's mean age at first birth: 26.6 (2010 est.)

Maternal mortality rate: 5 deaths/100,000 live births (2010)
country comparison to the world: 175

Infant mortality rate: *total:* 6.19 deaths/1,000 live births
country comparison to the world: 168
male: 6.88 deaths/1,000 live births
female: 5.45 deaths/1,000 live births (2014 est.)

Life expectancy at birth:
total population: 76.65 years
country comparison to the world: 76
male: 72.74 years
female: 80.8 years (2014 est.)

Total fertility rate: 1.33 children born/woman (2014 est.)
country comparison to the world: 212

Contraceptive prevalence rate: 72.7%
note: 20-49 (1991)

Health expenditures: 6.7% of GDP (2011)
country comparison to the world: 91

Physicians density: 2.07 physicians/1,000 population (2010)

Hospital bed density: 6.6 beds/1,000 population (2010)

Drinking water source:
improved:
urban: 100% of population
unimproved:
urban: 0% of population (2011 est.)

Sanitation facility access:
improved:
urban: 95.5% of population
rural: 79.6% of population
total: 89.3% of population
unimproved:
urban: 4.5% of population
rural: 20.4% of population
total: 10.7% of population (2008 est.)

HIV/AIDS—adult prevalence rate: 0.1%; note—no country specific models provided (2009 est.)
country comparison to the world: 168

HIV/AIDS—people living with HIV/AIDS: 27,000 (2009 est.)
country comparison to the world: 74

HIV/AIDS—deaths: fewer than 200 (2009 est.)
country comparison to the world: 108

Major infectious diseases: *degree of risk:* intermediate
vectorborne disease: tickborne encephalitis
note: highly pathogenic H5N1 avian influenza has been identified in this country; it poses a negligible risk with extremely rare cases possible among US citizens who have close contact with birds (2013)

Obesity—adult prevalence rate: 25.3% (2008)
country comparison to the world: 56

Education expenditures: 5.2% of GDP (2010)
country comparison to the world: 65

Literacy: *definition:* age 15 and over can read and write
total population: 99.7%
male: 99.9%
female: 99.6% (2011 est.)

School life expectancy (primary to tertiary education): *total:* 16 years
male: 15 years
female: 16 years (2012)

Unemployment, youth ages 15-24: total: 26.5%
country comparison to the world: 36
male: 24.1%
female: 30% (2012)

GOVERNMENT

Country name: *conventional long form:* Republic of Poland
conventional short form: Poland
local long form: Rzeczpospolita Polska
local short form: Polska

Government type: republic

Capital: *name:* Warsaw
geographic coordinates: 52 15 N, 21 00 E
time difference: UTC+1 (6 hours ahead of Washington, DC during Standard Time)
daylight saving time: +1hr, begins last Sunday in March; ends last Sunday in October

Administrative divisions: 16 provinces (wojewodztwa, singular—wojewodztwo); Dolnoslaskie (Lower Silesia), Kujawsko-Pomorskie (Kuyavia-Pomerania), Lodzkie (Lodz), Lubelskie (Lublin), Lubuskie (Lubusz), Malopolskie (Lesser Poland), Mazowieckie (Masovia), Opolskie (Opole), Podkarpackie (Subcarpathia), Podlaskie, Pomorskie (Pomerania), Slaskie (Silesia), Swietokrzyskie (Holy Cross), Warminsko-Mazurskie

(Warmia-Masuria), Wielkopolskie (Greater Poland), Zachodniopomorskie (West Pomerania)

Independence: 11 November 1918 (republic proclaimed); notable earlier dates: 966 (adoption of Christianity, traditional founding date), 1 July 1569 (Polish-Lithuanian Commonwealth created)

National holiday: Constitution Day, 3 May (1791)

Constitution: several previous; latest adopted 2 April 1997, approved by referendum 25 May 1997, effective 17 October 1997; amended 2006, 2009 (2013)

Legal system: civil law system; changes gradually being introduced as part of broader democratization process; limited judicial review of legislative acts, but rulings of the Constitutional Tribunal are final

International law organization participation: accepts compulsory ICJ jurisdiction with reservations; accepts ICCt jurisdiction

Suffrage: 18 years of age; universal

Executive branch: *chief of state:* President Bronislaw KOMOROWSKI (since 6 August 2010)
head of government: Prime Minister Donald TUSK (since 16 November 2007); Deputy Prime Ministers Janusz PIECHOCINSKI (since 6 December 2012) and Elzbieta BIENKOWSKA (since 27 November 2013)
cabinet: Council of Ministers responsible to the prime minister and the Sejm; the prime minister proposes, the president appoints, and the Sejm approves the Council of Ministers (For more information visit the World Leaders website)
elections: president elected by popular vote for a five-year term (eligible for a second term); election last held on 20 June and 4 July 2010 (next to be held in 2015); prime minister and deputy prime ministers appointed by the president and confirmed by the Sejm
election results: Bronislaw KOMOROWSKI elected president; percent of popular vote—Bronislaw KOMOROWSKI 53%, Jaroslaw KACZYNSKI 47%

Legislative branch: bicameral legislature consists of an upper house, the Senate or Senat (100 seats; members elected by a majority vote on a provincial basis to serve four-year terms), and a lower house, the Sejm (460 seats; members elected under a complex system of proportional representation to serve four-year terms); the designation of National Assembly or Zgromadzenie Narodowe is only used on those rare occasions when the two houses meet jointly
elections: Senate—last held on 9 October 2011 (next to be held by October 2015); Sejm—last held on 9 October 2011 (next to be held by October 2015)
election results and current seat distribution: Senate—percent of vote by party—NA; seats by party—PO 63, PiS 29, PSL 2, SP 2, independents 4; as of 25 January 2014—PO 62, PiS 30, PSL 2, SP 2, independents 4; Sejm—percent of vote by party—PO 39.2%, PiS 29.9%, RP 10%, PSL 8.4%, SLD 8.2%, other 4.3%; seats by party - PO 206, PiS 137, RP 43, PSL 28, SLD 25, SP 19, independent 1, German minority 1; as of 25 January 2014 - PO 203, PiS 136, TR 36, PSL 33, SLD 26, SP 17, independent 8, German Minority 1
note: the German minority is exempt from the 5% threshold requirement for seats to the Sejm

Judicial branch: *highest court(s):* Supreme Court or Sad Najwyzszy (consists of the president of the Supreme Court and 116 judges organized in criminal, civil, labor and social insurance, and military chambers)
judge selection and term of office: president of the Supreme Court nominated by the General Assembly of the Supreme Court and selected by the president of Poland; other judges nominated by the 25-member National Judiciary Council, and appointed by the president of Poland; judges appointed until retirement, normally at age 65, but tenure can be extended
subordinate courts: Constitutional Tribunal; regional and appellate courts subdivided into military, civil, criminal, labor, and family courts

Political parties and leaders:; Civic Platform or PO [Donald TUSK, chairman; Rafal GRUPINSKI, parliamentary caucus leader]; Democratic Left Alliance or SLD [Leszek MILLER, chairman, parliamentary caucus leader]; Democratic Party or PD [Andrzej CELINSKI, chairman]; Democratic Party or SD [Pawel PISKORSKI, chairman]; German Minority of Lower Silesia or MNSO [Ryszard GALLA, representative]; Law and Justice or PiS [Jaroslaw KACZYNSKI, chairman; Mariusz BLASZCZAK, parliamentary caucus leader]; League of Polish Families or LPR [Witold BALAZAK, chairman]; Poland Comes First or PJN [Pawel KOWAL, chairperson]; Poland Together or PR [Jaroslaw GOWIN, chairman]; Polish People's Party or PSL [Janusz PIECHOCINSKI, chairman; Jan BURY, parliamentary caucus leader]; Social Democratic Party of Poland or SDPL [Wojciech FILEMONOWICZ, chairman]; Union of Labor or UP [Waldemar WITKOWSKI, chairman]; United Poland or SP [Zbigniew ZIOBRO, chairperson; Arkadiusz MULARCZYK, parliamentary caucus leader]; Your Movement or TR [Janusz PALIKOT, chairman, parliamentary caucus leader] (formerly Palikot's Your Movement)

Political pressure groups and leaders: All Poland Trade Union Alliance or OPZZ (trade union) [Jan GUZ]; Roman Catholic Church [Cardinal Stanislaw DZIWISZ, Archbishop Jozef MICHALIK]; Independent and Self-Governing Trade Union "Solidarity" [Piotr DUDA]

International organization participation: Arctic Council (observer), Australia Group, BIS, BSEC (observer), CBSS, CD, CE, CEI, CERN, EAPC, EBRD, EIB, ESA, EU, FAO, IAEA, IBRD, ICAO, ICC (national committees), ICRM, IDA, IEA, IFC, IFRCS, IHO, ILO, IMF, IMO, IMSO, Interpol, IOC, IOM, IPU, ISO, ITSO, ITU, ITUC (NGOs), MIGA, MONUSCO, NATO, NEA, NSG, OAS (observer), OECD, OIF (observer), OPCW, OSCE, PCA, Schengen Convention, UN, UNCTAD, UNESCO, UNHCR, UNIDO, UNMIL, UNMISS, UNOCI, UNWTO, UPU, WCO, WFTU (NGOs), WHO, WIPO, WMO, WTO, ZC

Diplomatic representation in the US:
chief of mission: Ambassador Ryszard SCHNEPF (since 28 September 2012)
chancery: 2640 16th Street NW, Washington, DC 20009
telephone: [1] (202) 234-3800 through 3802
FAX: [1] (202) 328-6271
consulate(s) general: Chicago, Los Angeles, New York

Diplomatic representation from the US:
chief of mission: Ambassador Stephen MULL (since 24 October 2012)
embassy: Aleje Ujazdowskie 29/31 00-540 Warsaw
mailing address: American Embassy Warsaw, US Department of State, Washington, DC 20521-5010 (pouch)
telephone: [48] (22) 504-2000
FAX: [48] (22) 504-2688
consulate(s) general: Krakow

Flag description: two equal horizontal bands of white (top) and red; colors derive from the Polish emblem—a white eagle on a red field
note: similar to the flags of Indonesia and Monaco which are red (top) and white

National symbol(s): white eagle

National anthem: *name:* "Mazurek Dabrowskiego" (Dabrowski's Mazurka)
lyrics/music: Jozef WYBICKI/traditional
note: adopted 1927; the anthem, commonly known as "Jeszcze Polska nie zginela" (Poland Has Not Yet Perished), was written in 1797; the lyrics resonate strongly with Poles because they reflect the numerous occasions in which the nation's lands have been occupied

ECONOMY

Economy—overview: Poland has pursued a policy of economic liberalization since 1990 and Poland's economy was the only one in the EU to avoid a recession through the 2008-09 economic downturn. Although EU membership and access to EU structural funds have provided a major boost to the economy since 2004, GDP per capita remains significantly below the EU average while unemployment continues to exceed the EU average. The government of Prime Minister Donald TUSK steered the Polish economy through the economic downturn by skillfully managing public finances and adopting controversial pension and tax reforms to further shore up public finances. While the Polish economy has performed well over the past five years, growth slowed in 2012 and 2013, in part due to the ongoing economic difficulties in the euro zone. Short-term, the key policy challenge will be to consolidate debt and spending without stifling economic growth. Over the longer term, Poland's economic performance could improve if the country addresses some of the remaining deficiencies in its road and rail infrastructure, business environment, rigid labor code, commercial court system, government red tape, and burdensome tax system.

GDP (purchasing power parity): $814 billion (2013 est.)
country comparison to the world: 22
$803.3 billion (2012 est.)
$788.6 billion (2011 est.)
note: data are in 2013 US dollars

GDP (official exchange rate): $513.9 billion (2013 est.)

GDP—real growth rate: 1.3% (2013 est.)
country comparison to the world: 165
1.9% (2012 est.)
4.5% (2011 est.)

GDP—per capita (PPP): $21,100 (2013 est.)
country comparison to the world: 69
$20,800 (2012 est.)
$20,500 (2011 est.)
note: data are in 2013 US dollars

Gross national saving: 16.8% of GDP (2013 est.)
country comparison to the world: 100
17.2% of GDP (2012 est.)
16.7% of GDP (2011 est.)

GDP—composition, by end use:
household consumption: 61.5%
government consumption: 17.6%
investment in fixed capital: 18.3%
investment in inventories: 0.6%
exports of goods and services: 46.7%
imports of goods and services: -44.7% (2013 est.)

GDP—composition, by sector of origin:
agriculture: 4%
industry: 33.3%

services: 62.7% (2013 est.)

Agriculture—products: potatoes, fruits, vegetables, wheat; poultry, eggs, pork, dairy

Industries: machine building, iron and steel, coal mining, chemicals, shipbuilding, food processing, glass, beverages, textiles

Industrial production growth rate: 5.2% (2013 est.)
country comparison to the world: 52

Labor force: 18.22 million (2013 est.)
country comparison to the world: 34

Labor force—by occupation: *agriculture:* 12.9%
industry: 30.2%
services: 57% (2010)

Unemployment rate: 13.5% (2013 est.)
country comparison to the world: 133
12.8% (2012 est.)

Population below poverty line: 10.6% (2008 est.)

Household income or consumption by percentage share: *lowest 10%:* 3.3%
highest 10%: 27.1% (2009 est.)

Distribution of family income—Gini index: 34.1 (2009)
country comparison to the world: 94
31.6 (1998)

Budget: *revenues:* $92.5 billion
expenditures: $92.47 billion (2013 est.)

Taxes and other revenues: 18% of GDP (2013 est.)
country comparison to the world: 176

Budget surplus (+) or deficit (-):
0% of GDP (2013 est.)
country comparison to the world: 42

Public debt: 48.2% of GDP (2013 est.)
country comparison to the world: 71
48.3% of GDP (2012 est.)
note: data cover general government debt, and includes debt instruments issued (or owned) by government entities other than the treasury; the data include treasury debt held by foreign entities, the data include subnational entities, as well as intra-governmental debt; intra-governmental debt consists of treasury borrowings from surpluses in the social funds, such as for retirement, medical care, and unemployment; debt instruments for the social funds are not sold at public auctions

Fiscal year: calendar year

Inflation rate (consumer prices): 1% (2013 est.)
country comparison to the world: 23
3.7% (2012 est.)

Central bank discount rate: 4.25% (31 December 2012 est.)
country comparison to the world: 96
4% (31 December 2010 est.)

Commercial bank prime lending rate: 6.9% (31 December 2013 est.)
country comparison to the world: 106
8.73% (31 December 2012 est.)

Stock of narrow money: $162 billion (31 December 2013 est.)
country comparison to the world: 24
$156.4 billion (31 December 2012 est.)

Stock of broad money: $291.1 billion (31 December 2013 est.)
country comparison to the world: 31
$290.5 billion (31 December 2012 est.)

Stock of domestic credit: $344.7 billion (31 December 2013 est.)
country comparison to the world: 31
$328.4 billion (31 December 2012 est.)

Market value of publicly traded shares: $177.7 billion (31 December 2012 est.)
country comparison to the world: 38
$138.2 billion (31 December 2011)
$190.2 billion (31 December 2010 est.)

Current account balance: -$11.06 billion (2013 est.)
country comparison to the world: 180
-$18.14 billion (2012 est.)

Exports: $202.3 billion (2013 est.)
country comparison to the world: 27
$191 billion (2012 est.)

Exports—commodities: machinery and transport equipment 37.8%, intermediate manufactured goods 23.7%, miscellaneous manufactured goods 17.1%, food and live animals 7.6%

Exports—partners: Germany 26%, UK 7%, Czech Republic 6.5%, France 6%, Russia 5.2%, Italy 5%, Netherlands 4.6% (2012)

Imports: $207.4 billion (2013 est.)
country comparison to the world: 26
$197.7 billion (2012 est.)

Imports—commodities: machinery and transport equipment 38%, intermediate manufactured goods 21%, chemicals 15%, minerals, fuels, lubricants, and related materials 9% (2011 est.)

Imports—partners: Germany 27.3%, Russia 12.2%, Netherlands 5.9%, China 5.4%, Italy 5.2%, Czech Republic 4.3%, France 4.2% (2012)

Reserves of foreign exchange and gold: $107.8 billion (31 December 2013 est.)
country comparison to the world: 23
$108.9 billion (31 December 2012 est.)

Debt—external: $365.2 billion (31 December 2013 est.)
country comparison to the world: 30
$364.2 billion (31 December 2012 est.)

Stock of direct foreign investment—at home: $248.2 billion (31 December 2013 est.)
country comparison to the world: 23
$246.5 billion (31 December 2012 est.)

Stock of direct foreign investment—abroad: $69.78 billion (31 December 2013 est.)
country comparison to the world: 33
$70.28 billion (31 December 2012 est.)

Exchange rates: zlotych (PLN) per US dollar—
3.175 (2013 est.)
3.2565 (2012 est.)
3.0153 (2010 est.)
3.1214 (2009)
2.3 (2008)

ENERGY

Electricity—production: 153.4 billion kWh (2011 est.)
country comparison to the world: 25

Electricity—consumption: 155 billion kWh (2010 est.)
country comparison to the world: 25

Electricity—exports: 12.64 billion kWh (2012)
country comparison to the world: 16

Electricity—imports: 9.803 billion kWh (2012 est.)
country comparison to the world: 24

Electricity—installed generating capacity: 33.36 million kW (2010 est.)
country comparison to the world: 25

Electricity—from fossil fuels: 89.2% of total installed capacity (2010 est.)
country comparison to the world: 77

Electricity—from nuclear fuels: 0% of total installed capacity (2010 est.)
country comparison to the world: 161

Electricity—from hydroelectric plants: 2.8% of total installed capacity (2010 est.)
country comparison to the world: 131

Electricity—from other renewable sources: 3.7% of total installed capacity (2010 est.)
country comparison to the world: 51

Crude oil—production: 27,680 bbl/day (2012 est.)
country comparison to the world: 71

Crude oil—exports: 3,615 bbl/day (2011 est.)
country comparison to the world: 66

Crude oil—imports: 547,900 bbl/day (2011 est.)
country comparison to the world: 18

Crude oil—proved reserves: 156.5 million bbl (1 January 2010 es)
country comparison to the world: 63

Refined petroleum products—production: 636,000 bbl/day (2012 est.)
country comparison to the world: 26

Refined petroleum products—consumption: 576,600 bbl/day (2011 est.)
country comparison to the world: 30

Refined petroleum products—exports: 68,970 bbl/day (2010 est.)
country comparison to the world: 56

Refined petroleum products—imports: 137,700 bbl/day (2010 est.)
country comparison to the world: 41

Natural gas—production: 6.193 billion cu m (2012 est.)
country comparison to the world: 51

Natural gas—consumption: 14.38 billion cu m (2011 est.)
country comparison to the world: 39

Natural gas—exports: 25.01 billion cu m (2012 est.)
country comparison to the world: 17

Natural gas—imports: 37.38 billion cu m (2012 est.)
country comparison to the world: 15

Natural gas—proved reserves: 92 billion cu m (1 January 2013 es)
country comparison to the world: 57

Carbon dioxide emissions from consumption of energy: 307.9 million Mt (2011 est.)
country comparison to the world: 21

COMMUNICATIONS

Telephones—main lines in use: 6.125 million (2012)
country comparison to the world: 28

Telephones—mobile cellular: 50.84 million (2012)
country comparison to the world: 27

Telephone system: *general assessment:* modernization of the telecommunications network has accelerated with market-based competition; fixed-line service, dominated by the former state-owned company, is dwarfed by the growth in mobile-cellular services
domestic: mobile-cellular service available since 1993 and provided by three nation-wide networks with a fourth provider beginning operations in late 2006; coverage is generally good with some gaps in the east; fixed-line service lags in rural areas
international: country code—48; international direct dialing with automated exchanges; satellite earth station—1 with access to Intelsat, Eutelsat, Inmarsat, and Intersputnik (2011)

Broadcast media: state-run public TV operates 2 national channels supplemented by 16 regional channels and several niche channels; privately owned entities operate several national TV networks and a number of special interest channels; many privately owned channels broadcasting locally; roughly half of all households are linked to either satellite or cable TV systems providing access to foreign television networks; state-run public radio operates 5 national networks and 17 regional radio stations; 2 privately owned national radio networks, several commercial stations broadcasting to multiple cities, and many privately owned local radio stations (2007)

Internet country code: .pl

Internet hosts: 13.265 million (2012)
country comparison to the world: 12

Internet users: 22.452 million (2009)
country comparison to the world: 19

TRANSPORTATION

Airports: 126 (2013)
country comparison to the world: 4 7

Airports—with paved runways: *total:* 8 7
over 3,047 m: 5
2,438 to 3,047 m: 30
1,524 to 2,437 m: 36
914 to 1,523 m: 10
under 914 m: 6 (2013)

Airports—with unpaved runways: *total:* 3 9
1,524 to 2,437 m: 1
914 to 1,523 m: 17
under 914 m: 21 (2013)

Heliports: 6 (2013)

Pipelines: gas 14,198 km; oil 1,374 km; refined products 777 km (2013)

Railways: *total:* 19,428 km
country comparison to the world: 15
broad gauge: 399 km 1.524-m gauge
standard gauge: 19,029 km 1.435-m gauge (11,805 km electrified) (2007)

Roadways: *total:* 412,035 km
country comparison to the world: 15
paved: 280,719 km (includes 2,418 km of expressways)
unpaved: 131,316 km (2012)

Waterways: 3,997 km (navigable rivers and canals) (2009)
country comparison to the world: 28

Merchant marine: *total:* 9
country comparison to the world: 117
by type: cargo 7, chemical tanker 1, passenger/cargo 1
registered in other countries: 106 (Antigua and Barbuda 2, Bahamas 34, Cyprus 24, Liberia 13, Malta 21, Saint Vincent and the Grenadines 3, Vanuatu 9) (2010)

Ports and terminals: *major seaport(s):* Gdansk, Gdynia, Swinoujscie
river port(s): Szczecin (River Oder)

MILITARY

Military branches: Polish Armed Forces: Land Forces, Navy, Air and Air Defense Aviation Forces, Special Forces (2013)

Military service age and obligation: 18-28 years of age for male and female voluntary military service; conscription phased out in 2009-12; service obligation shortened from 12 to 9 months in 2005; women only allowed to serve as officers and non-commissioned officers (2013)

Manpower available for military service:
males age 16-49: 9,531,855
females age 16-49: 9,298,593 (2010 est.)

Manpower fit for military service:
males age 16-49: 7,817,556
females age 16-49: 7,766,361 (2010 est.)

Manpower reaching militarily significant age annually: *male:* 221,889
female: 211,172 (2010 est.)

Military expenditures: 1.91% of GDP (2012)
country comparison to the world: 45
1.83% of GDP (2011)
1.91% of GDP (2010)

TRANSNATIONAL ISSUES

Disputes—international: as a member state that forms part of the EU's external border, Poland has implemented the strict Schengen border rules to restrict illegal immigration and trade along its eastern borders with Belarus and Ukraine

Refugees and internally displaced persons: *refugees (country of origin):* 14,938 (Russia) (2012)
stateless persons: 10,825 (2012)

Illicit drugs: despite diligent counternarcotics measures and international information sharing on cross-border crimes, a major illicit producer of synthetic drugs for the international market; minor transshipment point for Southwest Asian heroin and Latin American cocaine to Western Europe

PORTUGAL

INTRODUCTION

Background: Following its heyday as a global maritime power during the 15th and 16th centuries, Portugal lost much of its wealth and status with the destruction of Lisbon in a 1755 earthquake, occupation during the Napoleonic Wars, and the independence of Brazil, its wealthiest colony, in 1822. A 1910 revolution deposed the monarchy; for most of the next six decades, repressive governments ran the country. In 1974, a left-wing military coup installed broad democratic reforms. The following year, Portugal granted independence to all of its African colonies. Portugal is a founding member of NATO and entered the EC (now the EU) in 1986.

GEOGRAPHY

Location: Southwestern Europe, bordering the North Atlantic Ocean, west of Spain

Geographic coordinates: 39 30 N, 8 00 W

Map references: Europe

Area: *total:* 92,090 sq km
country comparison to the world: 111
land: 91,470 sq km
water: 620 sq km
note: includes Azores and Madeira Islands

Area—comparative: slightly smaller than Indiana

Land boundaries: *total:* 1,214 km
border countries: Spain 1,214 km

Coastline: 1,793 km

Maritime claims: *territorial sea:* 12 nm
contiguous zone: 24 nm
exclusive economic zone: 200 nm
continental shelf: 200 m depth or to the depth of exploitation

Climate: maritime temperate; cool and rainy in north, warmer and drier in south

Terrain: mountainous north of the Tagus River, rolling plains in south

Elevation extremes: *lowest point:* Atlantic Ocean 0 m
highest point: Ponta do Pico (Pico or Pico Alto) on Ilha do Pico in the Azores 2,351 m

Natural resources: fish, forests (cork), iron ore, copper, zinc, tin, tungsten, silver, gold, uranium, marble, clay, gypsum, salt, arable land, hydropower

Land use: *arable land:* 11.88%
permanent crops: 7.71%
other: 80.41% (2011)

Irrigated land: 5,837 sq km (2007)

Total renewable water resources: 68.7 cu km (2011)

Freshwater withdrawal (domestic/industrial/agricultural): *total:* 8.46 cu km/yr (12%/18%/69%)
per capita: 812 cu m/yr (2005)

Natural hazards: Azores subject to severe earthquakes
volcanism: limited volcanic activity in the Azores Islands; Fayal or Faial (elev. 1,043 m) last erupted in 1958; most volcanoes have not erupted in centuries; historically active volcanoes include Agua de Pau, Furnas, Pico, Picos Volcanic System, San Jorge, Sete Cidades, and Terceira

Environment—current issues: soil erosion; air pollution caused by industrial and vehicle emissions; water pollution, especially in coastal areas

Environment—international agreements:
party to: Air Pollution, Biodiversity, Climate Change, Climate Change-Kyoto Protocol, Desertification, Endangered Species, Hazardous Wastes, Law of the Sea, Marine Dumping, Marine Life Conservation, Ozone Layer Protection, Ship Pollution, Tropical Timber 83, Tropical Timber 94, Wetlands, Whaling
signed, but not ratified: Air Pollution-Persistent Organic Pollutants, Air Pollution-Volatile Organic Compounds, Environmental Modification

Geography—note: Azores and Madeira Islands occupy strategic locations along western sea approaches to Strait of Gibraltar

PEOPLE AND SOCIETY

Nationality: *noun:* Portuguese (singular and plural)
adjective: Portuguese

Ethnic groups: homogeneous Mediterranean stock; citizens of black African descent who immigrated to mainland during decolonization number less than 100,000; since 1990 East Europeans have entered Portugal

Languages: Portuguese (official), Mirandese (official, but locally used)

Religions: Roman Catholic 81%, other Christian 3.3%, other 0.6%, none 6.8%, unspecified 8.3% (2011 est.)

Population: 10,813,834 (July 2014 est.)
country comparison to the world: 80

Age structure:
0-14 years: 15.9% (male 893,902/female 821,062)
15-24 years: 11.4% (male 654,102/female 579,440)
25-54 years: 42.2% (male 2,304,503/female 2,260,556)
55-64 years: 18.6% (male 599,380/female 685,279)
65 years and over: 18.4% (male 824,062/female 1,191,548) (2014 est.)

Dependency ratios:
total dependency ratio: 50.5 %
youth dependency ratio: 22.2 %
elderly dependency ratio: 28.2 %
potential support ratio: 3.5 (2013)

Median age: *total:* 41.1 years
male: 39 years
female: 43.3 years (2014 est.)

Population growth rate: 0.12% (2014 est.)
country comparison to the world: 184

Birth rate: 9.42 births/1,000 population (2014 est.)
country comparison to the world: 202

Death rate: 10.97 deaths/1,000 population (2014 est.)
country comparison to the world: 36

Net migration rate: 2.74 migrant(s)/1,000 population (2014 est.)
country comparison to the world: 36

Urbanization: *urban population:* 61% of total population (2010)
rate of urbanization: 1% annual rate of change (2010-15 est.)

Major urban areas—population: LISBON (capital) 2.808 million; Porto 1.344 million (2009)

Sex ratio: *at birth:* 1.07 male(s)/female
0-14 years: 1.09 male(s)/female
15-24 years: 1.13 male(s)/female
25-54 years: 1.02 male(s)/female
55-64 years: 0.95 male(s)/female
65 years and over: 0.69 male(s)/female
total population: 0.95 male(s)/female (2014 est.)

Mother's mean age at first birth: 27.4 (2005 est.)

Maternal mortality rate: 8 deaths/100,000 live births (2010)
country comparison to the world: 162

Infant mortality rate: *total:* 4.48 deaths/1,000 live births
country comparison to the world: 188
male: 4.92 deaths/1,000 live births
female: 4.02 deaths/1,000 live births (2014 est.)

Life expectancy at birth: *total population:* 79.01 years
country comparison to the world: 49
male: 75.76 years
female: 82.47 years (2014 est.)

Total fertility rate: 1.52 children born/woman (2014 est.)
country comparison to the world: 189

Contraceptive prevalence rate: 86.8% (2005/06)

Health expenditures: 10.4% of GDP (2011)
country comparison to the world: 21

Physicians density: 3.76 physicians/1,000 population (2009)

Hospital bed density: 3.4 beds/1,000 population (2010)

Drinking water source:
improved:
urban: 99.7% of population
rural: 99.7% of population
total: 99.7% of population
unimproved:
urban: 0.3% of population
rural: 0.3% of population
total: 0.3% of population (2011 est.)

Sanitation facility access:
improved:
urban: 100% of population
rural: 100% of population
total: 100% of population
unimproved:
urban: 0% of population
rural: 0% of population
total: 0% of population (2011 est.)

HIV/AIDS—adult prevalence rate: 0.6% (2009 est.)
country comparison to the world: 63

HIV/AIDS—people living with HIV/AIDS: 42,000 (2009 est.)
country comparison to the world: 65

HIV/AIDS—deaths: fewer than 500 (2009 est.)
country comparison to the world: 93

Obesity—adult prevalence rate: 24% (2008)
country comparison to the world: 69

Education expenditures: 5.6% of GDP (2010)
country comparison to the world: 55

Literacy: *definition:* age 15 and over can read and write
total population: 95.4%
male: 97%
female: 94% (2011 est.)

School life expectancy (primary to tertiary education): *total:* 16 years
male: 16 years
female: 17 years (2010)
Child labor—children ages 5-14:
total number: 36,569
percentage: 3 %
note: data represents children ages 6-14 (2001 est.)

Unemployment, youth ages 15-24: *total:* 37.6%
country comparison to the world: 17 *male:* 36.4%
female: 39.1% (2012)

GOVERNMENT

Country name: *conventional long form:* Portuguese Republic
conventional short form: Portugal
local long form: Republica Portuguesa
local short form: Portugal

Government type: republic; parliamentary democracy

Capital: *name:* Lisbon

geographic coordinates: 38 43 N, 9 08 W
time difference: UTC 0 (5 hours ahead of Washington, DC during Standard Time)
daylight saving time: +1hr, begins last Sunday in March; ends last Sunday in October

Administrative divisions: 18 districts (distritos, singular—distrito) and 2 autonomous regions* (regioes autonomas, singular—regiao autonoma); Aveiro, Acores (Azores)*, Beja, Braga, Braganca, Castelo Branco, Coimbra, Evora, Faro, Guarda, Leiria, Lisboa (Lisbon), Madeira*, Portalegre, Porto, Santarem, Setubal, Viana do Castelo, Vila Real, Viseu

Independence: 1143 (Kingdom of Portugal recognized); 5 October 1910 (republic proclaimed)

National holiday: Portugal Day (Dia de Portugal), 10 June (1580); note—also called Camoes Day, the day that revered national poet Luis de Camoes (1524-80) died

Constitution: several previous; latest adopted 2 April 1976, effective 25 April 1976; amended several times, last in 2005 (2013)

Legal system: civil law system; Constitutional Court review of legislative acts

International law organization participation: accepts compulsory ICJ jurisdiction with reservations; accepts ICCt jurisdiction

Suffrage: 18 years of age; universal

Executive branch: *chief of state:* President Anibal CAVACO SILVA (since 9 March 2006)
head of government: Prime Minister Pedro Manuel PASSOS COELHO Mamede (since 21 June 2011)
cabinet: Council of Ministers appointed by the president on the recommendation of the prime minister (For more information visit the World Leaders website)
note: there is also a Council of State that acts as a consultative body to the president elections:

president elected by popular vote for a five-year term (eligible for a second term); election last held on 23 January 2011 (next to be held in January 2016); following legislative elections which must be held by October 2015, the leader of the majority party or leader of a majority coalition usually appointed prime minister by the president
election results: Anibal CAVACO SILVA reelected president; percent of vote—Anibal CAVACO SILVA 53%, Manuel ALEGRE 19.8%, Fernando NOBRE 14.1%, Francisco LOPES 7.1%, Manuel COELHO 4.5%, Defensor MOURA 1.6%

Legislative branch: unicameral Assembly of the Republic or Assembleia da Republica (230 seats; members elected by popular vote to serve four-year terms)
elections: last held on 5 June 2011 (next to be held by October 2015)
election results: percent of vote by party—PPD/PSD 38%, PS 28%, CDS/PP 11%, PCP/PEV (see CDU) 7%, BE 5%, other 11%; seats by party—PPD/PSD 108, PS 74, CDS/PP 24, PCP/PEV (see CDU) 16, BE 8

Judicial branch: *highest court(s):* Supreme Court or Supremo Tribunal de Justica (consists of 12 justices); Constitutional Court or Tribunal Constitucional (consists of 13 judges)
judge selection and term of office: Supreme Court justices nominated by the president and appointed by the Assembly of the Republic; judges appointed for life; Constitutional Court judges—10 elected by the Assembly and 3 elected by the other Constitutional Court judges; judges elected for 6-year non-renewable terms
subordinate courts: Supreme Administrative Court (Supremo Tribunal Administrativo); Audit Court (Tribunal de Contas); appellate, district, and municipal courts

Political parties and leaders: Democratic and Social Center/Popular Party or CDS/PP [Paulo PORTAS]; Social Democratic Party or PPD/PSD [Pedro PASSOS COELHO]; Socialist Party or PS [Antonio Jose SEGURO]; The Left Bloc or BE [Joao Pedro Furtado da Cunha SEMEDO and Catarina Soares MARTINS; Unitarian Democratic Coalition or CDU [Jeronimo DE SOUSA] (includes Portuguese Communist Party or PCP; and Ecologist Party ("The Greens") or PEV)

Political pressure groups and leaders: Armed Forces Officers' Association (AOFA) [Colonel Pereira CRACEL]; the Desperate Generation (youth movement protesting against low wages, precarious labor conditions, and unemployment); the General Workers Union or General Confederation of Portuguese Workers (UGT) [Carlos SILVA]; Portuguese National Workers' Conference (CGTP) [Armenio CARLOS]; TugaLeaks (a website that has become a mouthpiece for publicizing diverse protest action)
other: the media; labor unions

International organization participation: ADB (nonregional member), AfDB (nonregional member), Australia Group, BIS, CD, CE, CERN, CPLP, EAPC, EBRD, ECB, EIB, EMU, ESA, EU, FAO, FATF, IADB, IAEA, IBRD, ICAO, ICC (national committees), ICRM, IDA, IEA, IFAD, IFC, IFRCS, IHO, ILO, IMF, IMO, IMSO, Interpol, IOC, IOM, IPU, ISO, ITSO, ITU, ITUC (NGOs), LAIA (observer), MIGA, NATO, NEA, NSG, OAS (observer), OECD, OPCW, OSCE, Paris Club (associate), PCA, Schengen Convention, SELEC (observer), UN, UNCTAD, UNESCO, UNHCR, UNIDO, Union Latina, UNMIT, UNSC (temporary), UNWTO, UPU, WCO, WFTU (NGOs), WHO, WIPO, WMO, WTO, ZC

Diplomatic representation in the US:
chief of mission: Ambassador Nuno Filipe Alves Salvador e BRITO (since 10 February 2011)
chancery: 2012 Massachusetts Avenue NW, Washington, DC 20036
telephone: [1] (202) 350-5400
FAX: [1] (202) 462-3726
consulate(s) general: Boston, New York, Newark (NJ), San Francisco
consulate(s): New Bedford (MA), Providence (RI)

Diplomatic representation from the US:
chief of mission: Ambassador Robert A. SHERMAN (since 12 February 2014)
embassy: Avenida das Forcas Armadas, 1600-081 Lisbon
mailing address: Apartado 43033, 1601-301 Lisboa; PSC 83, APO AE 09726
telephone: [351] (21) 727-3300
FAX: [351] (21) 726-9109
consulate(s): Ponta Delgada (Azores)

Flag description: two vertical bands of green (hoist side, two-fifths) and red (three-fifths) with the national coat of arms (armillary sphere and Portuguese shield) centered on the dividing line; explanations for the color meanings are ambiguous, but a popular interpretation has green symbolizing hope and red the blood of those defending the nation

National symbol(s): armillary sphere (a spherical astrolabe modeling objects in the sky and representing the Republic)

National anthem: *name:* "A Portugesa" (The Song of the Portuguese)
lyrics/music: Henrique LOPES DE MENDOCA/Alfredo KEIL
note: adopted 1910; "A Portuguesa" was originally written to protest the Portuguese monarchy's acquiescence to the 1890 British ultimatum forcing Portugal to give up areas of Africa; the lyrics refer to the "insult" that resulted from the event

ECONOMY

Economy—overview: Portugal has become a diversified and increasingly service-based economy since joining the European Community—the EU's predecessor—in 1986. Over the following two decades, successive governments privatized many state-controlled firms and liberalized key areas of the economy, including the financial and telecommunications sectors. The country qualified for the Economic and Monetary Union (EMU) in 1998 and began circulating the euro on 1 January 2002 along with 11 other EU members. The economy grew by more than the EU average for much of the 1990s, but the rate of growth slowed in 2001-08. The economy contracted in 2009, and fell again from 2011 to 2013, as the government implemented spending cuts and tax increases to comply with conditions of an EU-IMF financial rescue package, signed in May 2011. Austerity measures also have contributed to record unemployment and a wave of emigration not seen since the 1960s. Booming exports will contribute to growth and employment in 2014, but the need to continue to reduce private- and public-sector debt could weigh on consumption and investment. The government of Pedro PASSOS COELHO has stated its intention to reduce labor market rigidity, and, this, along with steps to trim the budget deficit, could make Portugal more attractive to foreign investors. The government reduced the budget deficit from 10.1% of GDP in 2009 to 5.1% in 2013, lower than the EU-IMF fiscal target of 5.5%. Despite these efforts, public debt has continued to grow and, in 2013, stands among the highest in the EU. As a result, the government may have difficulty regaining full bond market financing when the EU-IMF financing program expires in May 2014.

GDP (purchasing power parity): $243.3 billion (2013 est.)
country comparison to the world: 54
$247.7 billion (2012 est.)
$256 billion (2011 est.)
note: data are in 2013 US dollars

GDP (official exchange rate): $219.3 billion (2013 est.)

GDP—real growth rate: -1.8% (2013 est.)
country comparison to the world: 211
-3.2% (2012 est.)
-1.3% (2011 est.)

GDP—per capita (PPP): $22,900 (2013 est.)
country comparison to the world: 64
$23,400 (2012 est.)
$24,000 (2011 est.)
note: data are in 2013 US dollars

Gross national saving: 15.4% of GDP (2013 est.)
country comparison to the world: 110
15% of GDP (2012 est.)
11.3% of GDP (2011 est.)

GDP—composition, by end use:
household consumption: 64.8%
government consumption: 18.1%
investment in fixed capital: 15.5%
investment in inventories: -0.4%
exports of goods and services: 42%
imports of goods and services: -40% (2013 est.)

GDP—composition, by sector of origin:
agriculture: 2.6%
industry: 22.2%
services: 75.2% (2013 est.)

Agriculture—products: grain, potatoes, tomatoes, olives, grapes; sheep, cattle, goats, pigs, poultry, dairy products; fish

Industries: textiles, clothing, footwear, wood and cork, paper, chemicals, auto-parts manufacturing, base metals, porcelain and ceramics, glassware, technology, telecommunications; dairy products, wine and other foods; ship construction and refurbishment; tourism

Industrial production growth rate: -1% (2013 est.)
country comparison to the world: 178

Labor force: 5.395 million (2013 est.)
country comparison to the world: 70

Labor force—by occupation: *agriculture:* 11.7%
industry: 28.5%
services: 59.8% (2009 est.)

Unemployment rate: 16.8% (2013 est.)
country comparison to the world: 149
15.7% (2012 est.)

Population below poverty line: 18% (2006)

Household income or consumption by percentage share: *lowest 10%:* 3.1%
highest 10%: 28.4% (1995 est.)

Distribution of family income—Gini index: 38.5 (2007)
country comparison to the world: 71
35.6 (1995)

Budget: *revenues:* $95.49 billion
expenditures: $106.8 billion (2013 est.)

Taxes and other revenues: 43.5% of GDP (2013 est.)
country comparison to the world: 24

Budget surplus (+) or deficit (-):
-5.1% of GDP (2013 est.)
country comparison to the world: 171

Public debt: 127.8% of GDP (2013 est.)
country comparison to the world: 6
123.6% of GDP (2012 est.)
note: data cover general government debt, and includes debt instruments issued (or owned) by government entities other than the treasury; the data include treasury debt held by foreign entities; the data include debt issued by subnational entities, as well as intra-governmental debt; intra-governmental debt consists of treasury borrowings from surpluses in the social funds, such as for retirement, medical care, and unemployment; debt instruments for the social funds are not sold at public auctions

Fiscal year: calendar year

Inflation rate (consumer prices): 0.4% (2013 est.)
country comparison to the world: 14
2.8% (2012 est.)

Central bank discount rate: 0.75% (31 December 2013)
country comparison to the world: 129
1.5% (31 December 2010)
note: this is the European Central Bank's rate on the marginal lending facility, which offers overnight credit to banks in the euro area

Commercial bank prime lending rate: 6% (31 December 2013 est.)
country comparison to the world: 133
6.37% (31 December 2012 est.)

Stock of narrow money: $86.57 billion (31 December 2013 est.)
country comparison to the world: 38
$88.92 billion (31 December 2012 est.)
note: see entry for the European Union for money supply in the euro area; the European Central Bank (ECB) controls monetary policy for the 17 members of the Economic and Monetary Union (EMU); individual members of the EMU do not control the quantity of money circulating within their own borders

Stock of broad money: $283.9 billion (31 December 2013 est.)
country comparison to the world: 32
$301.5 billion (31 December 2012 est.)

Stock of domestic credit: $408.3 billion (31 December 2013 est.)
country comparison to the world: 30
$433.6 billion (31 December 2012 est.)

Market value of publicly traded shares: $65.53 billion (31 December 2012 est.)
country comparison to the world: 47
$61.69 billion (31 December 2011)
$82 billion (31 December 2010 est.)

Current account balance: $1 billion (2013 est.)
country comparison to the world: 49
-$3.365 billion (2012 est.)

Exports: $61 billion (2013 est.)
country comparison to the world: 54
$58.29 billion (2012 est.)

Exports—commodities: agricultural products, food products, wine, oil products, chemical products, plastics and rubber, hides, leather, wood and cork, wood pulp and paper, textile materials, clothing, footwear, machinery and tools, base metals

Exports—partners: Spain 22.7%, Germany 12.4%, France 11.9%, Angola 6.5%, UK 5.3%, Netherlands 4.2% (2012)

Imports: $59 billion (2013 est.)
country comparison to the world: 51
$72.35 billion (2012 est.)

Imports—commodities: agricultural products, chemical products, vehicles and other transport material, optical and precision instruments, computer accessories and parts, semi-conductors and related devices, oil products, base metals, food products, textile materials

Imports—partners: Spain 32%, Germany 11.5%, France 6.7%, Italy 5.3%, Netherlands 4.9% (2012)

Reserves of foreign exchange and gold: $22.66 billion (31 December 2012 est.)
country comparison to the world: 55
$21.34 billion (31 December 2011 est.)

Debt—external: $508.3 billion (31 December 2012 est.)
country comparison to the world: 26
$482.2 billion (31 December 2011)

Stock of direct foreign investment—at home: $121.6 billion (31 December 2013 est.)
country comparison to the world: 38
$117.2 billion (31 December 2012 est.)

Stock of direct foreign investment—abroad: $71.26 billion (31 December 2013 est.)
country comparison to the world: 32
$71.26 billion (31 December 2012 est.)

Exchange rates: euros (EUR) per US dollar—
0.7634 (2013 est.)
0.7752 (2012 est.)
0.755 (2010 est.)
0.7198 (2009 est.)
0.6827 (2008 est.)

ENERGY

Electricity—production: 49.92 billion kWh (2011 est.)
country comparison to the world: 5 1

Electricity—consumption: 50.26 billion kWh (2010 est.)
country comparison to the world: 46

Electricity—exports: 2.873 billion kWh (2012 est.)
country comparison to the world: 35

Electricity—imports: 10.76 billion kWh (2012 est.)
country comparison to the world: 21

Electricity—installed generating capacity: 18.92 million kW (2010 est.)
country comparison to the world: 38

Electricity—from fossil fuels: 49% of total installed capacity (2010 est.)
country comparison to the world: 157

Electricity—from nuclear fuels: 0% of total installed capacity (2010 est.)
country comparison to the world: 163

Electricity—from hydroelectric plants: 21.5% of total installed capacity (2010 est.)
country comparison to the world: 88

Electricity—from other renewable sources: 24.1% of total installed capacity (2010 est.)
country comparison to the world: 6

Crude oil—production: 5,250 bbl/day (2012 est.)
country comparison to the world: 98

Crude oil—exports: 0 bbl/day (2010 est.)
country comparison to the world: 169

Crude oil—imports: 222,300 bbl/day (2010 est.)
country comparison to the world: 32

Crude oil—proved reserves: 0 bbl (1 January 2013 es)
country comparison to the world: 177

Refined petroleum products—production: 252,200 bbl/day (2010 est.)
country comparison to the world: 50

Refined petroleum products—consumption: 259,700 bbl/day (2011 est.)
country comparison to the world: 48

Refined petroleum products—exports: 61,010 bbl/day (2010 est.)
country comparison to the world: 58

Refined petroleum products—imports: 84,080 bbl/day (2010 est.)
country comparison to the world: 55

Natural gas—production: 4.904 billion cu m (2012 est.)
country comparison to the world: 52

Natural gas—consumption: 5.143 billion cu m (2010 est.)
country comparison to the world: 61

Natural gas—exports: 0 cu m (2011 est.)
country comparison to the world: 166

Natural gas—imports: 5.185 billion cu m (2011 est.)
country comparison to the world: 35

Natural gas—proved reserves: 0 cu m (1 January 2013 es)
country comparison to the world: 184

Carbon dioxide emissions from consumption of energy: 54.17 million Mt (2011 est.)
country comparison to the world: 57

COMMUNICATIONS

Telephones—main lines in use: 4.558 million (2012)
country comparison to the world: 35

Telephones—mobile cellular: 12.312 million (2012)
country comparison to the world: 70

Telephone system: *general assessment:* Portugal's telephone system has a state-of-the-art network with broadband, high-speed capabilities
domestic: integrated network of coaxial cables, open-wire, microwave radio relay, and domestic satellite earth stations
international: country code—351; a combination of submarine cables provide connectivity to Europe, North and East Africa, South Africa, the Middle East, Asia, and the US; satellite earth stations—3 Intelsat (2 Atlantic Ocean and 1 Indian Ocean), NA Eutelsat; tropospheric scatter to Azores (2010)

Broadcast media: Radio e Televisao de Portugal (RTP),the publicly-owned TV broadcaster, operates 2 domestic channels and external service channels to Africa; overall, roughly 40 domestic TV stations; viewers have widespread access to international broadcasters with more than half of all households connected to multi-channel cable or satellite TV systems; publicly owned radio operates 3 national networks and provides regional and external services; several privately owned national radio stations and some 300 regional and local commercial radio stations (2008)

Internet country code: . p t

Internet hosts: 3.748 million (2012)
country comparison to the world: 28

Internet users: 5.168 million (2009)
country comparison to the world: 45

TRANSPORTATION

Airports: 64 (2013)
country comparison to the world: 7 6

Airports—with paved runways: *total:* 4 3
over 3,047 m: 5
2,438 to 3,047 m: 7
1,524 to 2,437 m: 8
914 to 1,523 m: 15
under 914 m: 8 (2013)

Airports—with unpaved runways: *total:* 2 1
914 to 1,523 m: 1

under 914 m: 20 (2013)

Pipelines: gas 1,344 km; oil 11 km; refined products 188 km (2013)

Railways: *total:* 3,319 km
country comparison to the world: 53
broad gauge: 2,700 km 1.668-m gauge (1,436 km electrified)
narrow gauge: 192 km 1.000-m gauge; 427 km 0.760-m gauge (2008)

Roadways: *total:* 82,900 km
country comparison to the world: 57
paved: 71,294 km (includes 2,613 km of expressways)
unpaved: 11,606 km (2008)

Waterways: 210 km (on Douro River from Porto) (2011)
country comparison to the world: 96

Merchant marine: *total:* 109
country comparison to the world: 50
by type: bulk carrier 8, cargo 35, carrier 1, chemical tanker 21, container 7, liquefied gas 6, passenger 13, passenger/cargo 5, petroleum tanker 3, roll on/roll off 1, vehicle carrier 9
foreign-owned: 81 (Belgium 8, Colombia 1, Denmark 4, Germany 14, Greece 2, Italy 12, Japan 9, Mexico 1, Norway 2, Spain 18, Sweden 3, Switzerland 3, US 4)
registered in other countries: 15 (Cyprus 2, Malta 3, Panama 10) (2010)

Ports and terminals: *major seaport(s):* Leixoes, Lisbon, Setubal, Sines

MILITARY

Military branches: Portuguese Army (Exercito Portuguesa), Portuguese Navy (Marinha Portuguesa; includes Marine Corps), Portuguese Air Force (Forca Aerea Portuguesa, FAP) (2013)

Military service age and obligation: 18-30 years of age for voluntary military service; no compulsory military service, but conscription possible if insufficient volunteers available; women serve in the armed forces, on naval ships since 1993, but are prohibited from serving in some combatant specialties; reserve obligation to age 35 (2012)

Manpower available for military service:
males age 16-49: 2,566,264
females age 16-49: 2,458,297 (2010 est.)

Manpower fit for military service:
males age 16-49: 2,103,080
females age 16-49: 2,018,004 (2010 est.)

Manpower reaching militarily significant age annually: *male:* 62,208
female: 54,786 (2010 est.)

Military expenditures: 1.29% of GDP (2014)
country comparison to the world: 80
1.2% of GDP (2013)
1.78% of GDP (2012)

TRANSNATIONAL ISSUES

Disputes—international: Portugal does not recognize Spanish sovereignty over the territory of Olivenza based on a difference of interpretation of the 1815 Congress of Vienna and the 1801 Treaty of Badajoz

Refugees and internally displaced persons: *stateless persons:* 553 (2012)

Illicit drugs: seizing record amounts of Latin American cocaine destined for Europe; a European gateway for Southwest Asian heroin; transshipment point for hashish from North Africa to Europe; consumer of Southwest Asian heroin

PUERTO RICO

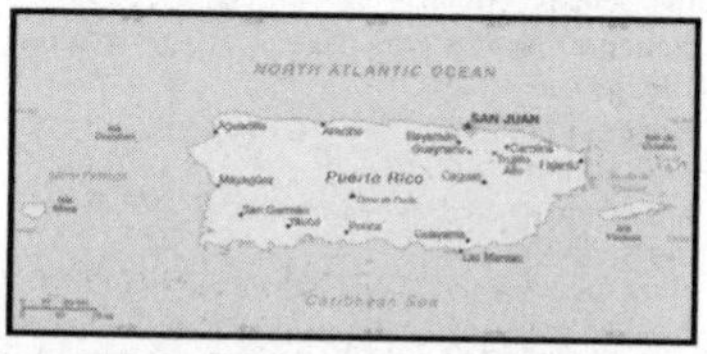

INTRODUCTION

Background: Populated for centuries by aboriginal peoples, the island was claimed by the Spanish Crown in 1493 following Christopher COLUMBUS' second voyage to the Americas. In 1898, after 400 years of colonial rule that saw the indigenous population nearly exterminated and African slave labor introduced, Puerto Rico was ceded to the US as a result of the Spanish-American War. Puerto Ricans were granted US citizenship in 1917. Popularly-elected governors have served since 1948. In 1952, a constitution was enacted providing for internal self government. In plebiscites held in 1967, 1993, and 1998, voters chose not to alter the existing political status with the US, but the results of a 2012 vote left open the possibility of American statehood.

GEOGRAPHY

Location: Caribbean, island between the Caribbean Sea and the North Atlantic Ocean, east of the Dominican Republic

Geographic coordinates: 18 15 N, 66 30 W

Map references: Central America and the Caribbean

Area: *total:* 13,790 sq km
country comparison to the world: 163
land: 8,870 sq km
water: 4,921 sq km

Area—comparative: slightly less than three times the size of Rhode Island

Land boundaries: 0 km

Coastline: 501 km

Maritime claims: *territorial sea:* 12 nm
exclusive economic zone: 200 nm

Climate: tropical marine, mild; little seasonal temperature variation

Terrain: mostly mountains with coastal plain belt in north; mountains precipitous to sea on west coast; sandy beaches along most coastal areas

Elevation extremes: *lowest point:* Caribbean Sea 0 m

highest point: Cerro de Punta 1,338 m

Natural resources: some copper and nickel; potential for onshore and offshore oil

Land use: *arable land:* 6.76%
permanent crops: 4.51%
other: 88.73% (2011)

Irrigated land: 220.4 sq km (2005)

Natural hazards: periodic droughts; hurricanes

Environment—current issues: erosion; occasional drought causing water shortages

Geography—note: important location along the Mona Passage—a key shipping lane to the Panama Canal; San Juan is one of the biggest and best natural harbors in the Caribbean; many small rivers and high central mountains ensure land is well watered; south coast relatively dry; fertile coastal plain belt in north

PEOPLE AND SOCIETY

Nationality: *noun:* Puerto Rican(s) (US citizens)
adjective: Puerto Rican

Ethnic groups: white 75.8%, black/African American 12.4%, other 8.5% (includes American Indian, Alaskan Native, Native Hawaiian, other Pacific Islander, and others), mixed 3.3%
note: 99% of the population is Latino (2010 est.)

Languages: Spanish, English

Religions: Roman Catholic 85%, Protestant and other 15%

Population: 3,620,897 (July 2014 est.)
country comparison to the world: 130

Age structure:
0-14 years: 18.1% (male 335,142/female 319,765)
15-24 years: 14.5% (male 267,596/female 256,487)
25-54 years: 38.5% (male 665,092/female 727,412)
55-64 years: 17% (male 197,256/female 238,139)
65 years and over: 16.4% (male 265,674/female 348,334) (2014 est.)

Dependency ratios:
total dependency ratio: 50.1 %
youth dependency ratio: 29.3 %
elderly dependency ratio: 20.9 %
potential support ratio: 4.8 (2013)

Median age: *total:* 38.7 years
male: 36.8 years
female: 40.5 years (2014 est.)

Population growth rate: -0.65% (2014 est.)
country comparison to the world: 227

Birth rate: 10.9 births/1,000 population (2014 est.)
country comparison to the world: 178

Death rate: 8.51 deaths/1,000 population (2014 est.)
country comparison to the world: 79

Net migration rate: -8.93 migrant(s)/1,000 population (2014 est.)
country comparison to the world: 211

Urbanization: *urban population:* 99% of total population (2010)
rate of urbanization: 0.5% annual rate of change (2010-15 est.)

Major urban areas—population: SAN JUAN (capital) 2.73 million (2009)

Sex ratio: *at birth:* 1.02 male(s)/female
0-14 years: 1.05 male(s)/female
15-24 years: 1.04 male(s)/female
25-54 years: 0.91 male(s)/female
55-64 years: 0.92 male(s)/female
65 years and over: 0.77 male(s)/female
total population: 0.92 male(s)/female (2014 est.)

Maternal mortality rate: 20 deaths/100,000 live births (2010)
country comparison to the world: 140

Infant mortality rate: *total:* 7.73 deaths/1,000 live births
country comparison to the world: 158
male: 8.53 deaths/1,000 live births
female: 6.91 deaths/1,000 live births (2014 est.)

Life expectancy at birth: *total population:* 79.09 years
country comparison to the world: 47
male: 75.46 years
female: 82.8 years (2014 est.)

Total fertility rate: 1.64 children born/woman (2014 est.)
country comparison to the world: 178

Contraceptive prevalence rate: 84.1%
note: percent of women aged 18-44 (2002)

Sanitation facility access:
improved:
urban: 99.3% of population
rural: 99.3% of population
total: 99.3% of population
unimproved:
urban: 0.7% of population
rural: 0.7% of population
total: 0.7% of population (2011 est.)

HIV/AIDS—adult prevalence rate: NA

HIV/AIDS—people living with HIV/AIDS: NA

HIV/AIDS—deaths: NA

Education expenditures: NA

Literacy: *definition:* age 15 and over can read and write
total population: 90.3%
male: 89.7%
female: 90.9% (2011 est.)

School life expectancy (primary to tertiary education): *total:* 16 years
male: 14 years
female: 17 years (2011)

Unemployment, youth ages 15-24: *total:* 26.6%
country comparison to the world: 35
male: 28.9%
female: 23.1% (2012)

GOVERNMENT

Country name: *conventional long form:* Commonwealth of Puerto Rico
conventional short form: Puerto Rico

Dependency status: unincorporated, organized territory of the US with commonwealth status; policy relations between Puerto Rico and the US conducted under the jurisdiction of the Office of the President

Government type: commonwealth

Capital: *name:* San Juan
geographic coordinates: 18 28 N, 66 07 W
time difference: UTC-4 (1 hour ahead of Washington, DC during Standard Time)

Administrative divisions: none (territory of the US with commonwealth status); there are no first-order administrative divisions as defined by the US Government, but there are 78 municipalities (municipios, singular—municipio) at the second order; Adjuntas, Aguada, Aguadilla, Aguas Buenas, Aibonito, Anasco, Arecibo, Arroyo, Barceloneta, Barranquitas, Bayamon, Cabo Rojo, Caguas, Camuy, Canovanas, Carolina, Catano, Cayey, Ceiba, Ciales, Cidra, Coamo, Comerio, Corozal, Culebra, Dorado, Fajardo, Florida, Guanica, Guayama, Guayanilla, Guaynabo, Gurabo, Hatillo, Hormigueros, Humacao, Isabela, Jayuya, Juana Diaz, Juncos, Lajas, Lares, Las Marias, Las Piedras, Loiza, Luquillo, Manati, Maricao, Maunabo, Mayaguez, Moca, Morovis, Naguabo, Naranjito, Orocovis, Patillas, Penuelas, Ponce, Quebradillas, Rincon, Rio Grande, Sabana Grande, Salinas, San German, San Juan, San Lorenzo, San Sebastian, Santa Isabel, Toa Alta, Toa Baja, Trujillo Alto, Utuado, Vega Alta, Vega Baja, Vieques, Villalba, Yabucoa, Yauco

Independence: none (territory of the US with commonwealth status)

National holiday: US Independence Day, 4 July (1776); Puerto Rico Constitution Day, 25 July (1952)

Constitution: previous 1900 (Organic Act, or Foraker Act); latest ratified 3 March 1952, approved 3 July 1952, effective 25 July 1952; note—constitutional amendments introduced in 2012 were rejected in a referendum (2013)

Legal system: civil law system based on the Spanish civil code and within the framework of the US federal system

Suffrage: 18 years of age; universal; note—island residents are US citizens but do not vote in US presidential elections

Executive branch: *chief of state:* President Barack H. OBAMA (since 20 January 2009); Vice President Joseph R. BIDEN (since 20 January 2009)
head of government: Governor Alejandro GARCIA Padilla (since 2 January 2013)
cabinet: Cabinet appointed by the governor with the consent of the legislature (For more information visit the World Leaders website)
elections: under the US Constitution, residents of unincorporated territories, such as Puerto Rico, do not vote in elections for US president and vice president; however, they may vote in Democratic and Republican party presidential primary elections; governor elected by popular vote for a four-year term (no term limits); election last held on 6 November 2012 (next to be held in November 2016)
election results: Alejandro GARCIA Padilla elected governor with 48.2% of the vote

Legislative branch: bicameral Legislative Assembly consists of the Senate (at least 27 seats; members directly elected by popular vote to serve four-year terms) and the House of Representatives (51 seats; members elected by popular vote to serve four-year terms)
elections: Senate—last held on 6 November 2012 (next to be held in November 2016); House of Representatives—last held on 6 November 2012 (next to be held in November 2016)
election results: Senate—percent of vote by party—NA; seats by party—PPD 18, PNP 8, PIP 1; House of Representatives—percent of vote by party—NA; seats by party—PPD 28, PNP 23
note: Puerto Rico elects, by popular vote, a resident commissioner to serve a four-year term as a nonvoting representative in the US House of Representatives; aside from not voting on the House floor, he enjoys all the rights of a member of Congress; elections last held 6 November 2012 (next to be held in November 2016); results—percent of vote by party—NA; seats by party—PNP 1

Judicial branch: *highest court(s):* Supreme Court (consists of the chief justice and 6 associate judges) note—the Commonwealth of Puerto Rico Judiciary Act of 2003 reformed the judicial system
judge selection and term of office: justices appointed by the governor with the advice and consent of the Senate; judges serve until compulsory retirement at age 75
subordinate courts: Court of Appeals; First Instance Court comprised of superior and municipal courts

Political parties and leaders: National Democratic Party [Roberto PRATS]; National Republican Party of Puerto Rico [Dr. Tiody FERRE]; New Progressive Party or PNP [Pedro ROSSELLO] (pro-US statehood); Popular Democratic Party or PPD [Anibal ACEVEDO-VILA] (pro-commonwealth); Puerto Rican Independence Party or PIP [Ruben BERRIOS Martinez] (pro-independence)

Political pressure groups and leaders: Boricua Popular Army or EPB (a revolutionary group also known as Los Macheteros)
note: the following radical groups are considered dormant by Federal law enforcement: Armed Forces for National Liberation or FALN, Armed Forces of Popular Resistance, Volunteers of the Puerto Rican Revolution

International organization participation: Caricom (observer), Interpol (subbureau), IOC, UNWTO (associate), UPU

Diplomatic representation in the US: none (territory of the US)

Diplomatic representation from the US: none (territory of the US with commonwealth status)

Flag description: five equal horizontal bands of red (top and bottom) alternating with white; a blue isosceles triangle based on the hoist side bears a large, white, five-pointed star in the center; the white star symbolizes Puerto Rico; the three sides of the triangle signify the executive, legislative and judicial parts of the government; blue stands for the sky and the coastal waters; red symbolizes the blood shed by warriors, while white represents liberty, victory, and peace
note: design initially influenced by the US flag, but similar to the Cuban flag, with the colors of the bands and triangle reversed

National symbol(s): Puerto Rican spindalis (bird); coqui (frog)

National anthem: *name:* "La Borinquena" (The Puerto Rican)
lyrics/music: Manuel Fernandez JUNCOS/Felix Astol ARTES
note: music adopted 1952, lyrics adopted 1977; the local anthem's name is a reference to the indigenous name of the island, Borinquen; the music was originally composed as a dance in 1867 and gained popularity in the early 20th century; there is some evidence that the music was written by Francisco RAMIREZ; as a commonwealth of the United States, "The Star-Spangled Banner" is official (see United States)

ECONOMY

Economy—overview: Puerto Rico has one of the most dynamic economies in the Caribbean region, however, growth has been negative for the past four years, and unemployment rose to nearly 16% in 2011. The industrial sector has surpassed agriculture as the primary locus of economic activity and income. Mainland US firms have invested heavily in Puerto Rico since the 1950s. US minimum wage laws apply. Sugar production has lost out to dairy production and other livestock products as the main source of income in the agricultural sector. Tourism has traditionally been an important source of income with estimated arrivals of more than 3.6 million tourists in 2008. Closing the budget deficit while restoring economic growth and employment remain the central concerns of the government.

GDP (purchasing power parity): $64.84 billion (2010 est.)
country comparison to the world: 87
$68.84 billion (2009 est.)
$71.51 billion (2008 est.)
note: data are in 2010 US dollars

GDP (official exchange rate): $93.52 billion (2010 est.)

GDP—real growth rate: -5.8% (2010 est.)
country comparison to the world: 217
-3.7% (2009 est.)
-2.8% (2008 est.)

GDP—per capita (PPP): $16,300 (2010 est.)
country comparison to the world: 84
$17,400 (2009 est.)
$18,100 (2008 est.)
note: data are in 2010 US dollars

GDP—composition, by end use:
household consumption: 88.2%
government consumption: 14.6%
investment in fixed capital: 14%
investment in inventories: 0.1%
exports of goods and services: 106.9%
imports of goods and services: -123.8% (2013 est.)

GDP—composition, by sector of origin:
agriculture: 0.7%
industry: 48.8%
services: 50.5% (2013 est.)

Agriculture—products: sugarcane, coffee, pineapples, plantains, bananas; livestock products, chickens

Industries: pharmaceuticals, electronics, apparel, food products, tourism

Industrial production growth rate: 0.5%
country comparison to the world: 158

Labor force: 1.286 million (March 2012)
country comparison to the world: 137

Labor force—by occupation: *agriculture:* 2.1%
industry: 19%
services: 79% (2005)

Unemployment rate: 16% (2011 est.)
country comparison to the world: 147
12% (2002 est.)

Population below poverty line: NA%

Household income or consumption by percentage share: *lowest 10%:* NA%
highest 10%: NA%

Budget: *revenues:* $6.7 billion
expenditures: $9.6 billion (FY99/00)

Taxes and other revenues: 7.2% of GDP (FY99/00)
country comparison to the world: 212

Budget surplus (+) or deficit (-):
-3.1% of GDP (FY99/00)
country comparison to the world: 125

Public debt: 96.5% of GDP (2013 est.)
country comparison to the world: 16
93.2% of GDP (2012 est.)

Fiscal year: 1 July—30 June
Inflation rate (consumer prices): 0.9% (2013 est.)
country comparison to the world: 20
2.6% (2012 est.)

Market value of publicly traded shares: $NA

Exports: $69.75 billion (2013 est.)
country comparison to the world: 50
$67.3 billion (2012 est.)

Exports—commodities: chemicals, electronics, apparel, canned tuna, rum, beverage concentrates, medical equipment

Imports: $47.32 billion (2013 est.)
country comparison to the world: 57
$49 billion (2012 est.)

Imports—commodities: chemicals, machinery and equipment, clothing, food, fish, petroleum products

Debt—external: $56.82 billion (31 December 2010 est.)
country comparison to the world: 59
$52.98 billion (31 December 2009 est.)

Exchange rates: the US dollar is used

ENERGY

Electricity—production: 20.02 billion kWh (2011 est.)
country comparison to the world: 7 3

Electricity—consumption: 19.43 billion kWh (2010 est.)
country comparison to the world: 70

Electricity—exports: 0 kWh (2012 est.)
country comparison to the world: 187

Electricity—imports: 0 kWh (2012 est.)
country comparison to the world: 190

Electricity—installed generating capacity: 5.571 million kW (2010 est.)

country comparison to the world: 74 Electricity—from fossil fuels:
97.2% of total installed capacity (2010 est.)
country comparison to the world: 63

Electricity—from nuclear fuels: 0% of total installed capacity (2010 est.)
country comparison to the world: 169

Electricity—from hydroelectric plants: 2.8% of total installed capacity (2010 est.)
country comparison to the world: 130

Electricity—from other renewable sources: 0% of total installed capacity (2010 est.)
country comparison to the world: 116

Crude oil—production: 673.7 bbl/day (2012 est.)
country comparison to the world: 113

Crude oil—exports: 0 bbl/day (2010 est.)
country comparison to the world: 172

Crude oil—imports: 0 bbl/day (2010 est.)
country comparison to the world: 112

Crude oil—proved reserves: 0 bbl (1 January 2013 es)
country comparison to the world: 179

Refined petroleum products—production: 0 bbl/day (2010 est.)
country comparison to the world: 187

Refined petroleum products—consumption: 151,600 bbl/day (2011 est.)
country comparison to the world: 65

Refined petroleum products—exports: 0 bbl/day (2010 est.)
country comparison to the world: 209

Refined petroleum products—imports: 176,000 bbl/day (2010 est.)
country comparison to the world: 30

Natural gas—production: 0 cu m (2011 est.)
country comparison to the world: 183

Natural gas—consumption: 770 million cu m (2010 est.)
country comparison to the world: 94

Natural gas—exports: 0 cu m (2011 est.)
country comparison to the world: 172

Natural gas—imports: 750 million cu m (2011 est.)
country comparison to the world: 62

Natural gas—proved reserves: 0 cu m (1 January 2013 es)
country comparison to the world: 186

Carbon dioxide emissions from consumption of energy: 28.53 million Mt (2011 est.)
country comparison to the world: 77

COMMUNICATIONS

Telephones—main lines in use: 780,200 (2012)
country comparison to the world: 87

Telephones—mobile cellular: 3.06 million (2012)
country comparison to the world: 130

Telephone system: *general assessment:* modern system integrated with that of the US by high-capacity submarine cable and Intelsat with high-speed data capability
domestic: digital telephone system; mobile-cellular services
international: country code—1-787, 939; submarine cables provide connectivity to the US, Caribbean, Central and South America; satellite earth station—1 Intelsat (2011)

Broadcast media: more than 30 TV stations operating; cable TV subscription services are available; roughly 125 radio stations (2007)

Internet country code: . p r

Internet hosts: 469 (2012)
country comparison to the world: 184

Internet users: 1 million (2009)
country comparison to the world: 100

TRANSPORTATION

Airports: 29 (2013)
country comparison to the world: 119

Airports—with paved runways: *total:* 1 7
over 3,047 m: 2
2,438 to 3,047 m: 1
1,524 to 2,437 m: 2
914 to 1,523 m: 7
under 914 m: 5 (2013)

Airports—with unpaved runways: *total:* 1 2
1,524 to 2,437 m: 1
914 to 1,523 m: 1
under 914 m: 10 (2013)

Roadways: *total:* 26,862 km (includes 454 km of expressways) (2012)
country comparison to the world: 99

Ports and terminals: *major seaport(s):* Ensenada Honda, Mayaguez, Playa de Guayanilla, Playa de Ponce, San Juan
container port(s) (TEUs): San Juan (1,484,595)

MILITARY

Military branches: no regular indigenous military forces; paramilitary National Guard, Police Force

Manpower fit for military service:
males age 16-49: 700,443
females age 16-49: 786,035 (2010 est.)

Manpower reaching militarily significant age annually: *male:* 30,517
female: 29,010 (2010 est.)

Military—note: defense is the responsibility of the US

TRANSNATIONAL ISSUES

Disputes—international: increasing numbers of illegal migrants from the Dominican Republic cross the Mona Passage to Puerto Rico each year looking for work

Q

QATAR

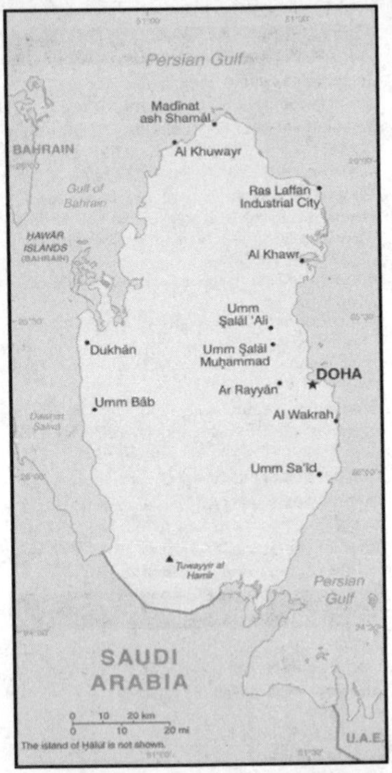

INTRODUCTION

Background: Ruled by the Al Thani family since the mid-1800s, Qatar transformed itself from a poor British protectorate noted mainly for pearling into an independent state with significant oil and natural gas revenues. During the late 1980s and early 1990s, the Qatari economy was crippled by a continuous siphoning off of petroleum revenues by the Amir, who had ruled the country since 1972. His son, the current Amir HAMAD bin Khalifa Al Thani, overthrew the father in a bloodless coup in 1995. In short order, HAMAD oversaw the creation of the pan-Arab satellite news network Al-Jazeera and Qatar's pursuit of a leadership role in mediating regional conflicts. In the 2000s, Qatar resolved its longstanding border disputes with both Bahrain and Saudi Arabia. As of 2007, oil and natural gas revenues had enabled Qatar to attain the highest per capita income in the world. Qatar has not experienced domestic unrest or violence like that seen in other Near Eastern and North African countries in 2010-11, due in part to its immense wealth. Since the outbreak of regional unrest, however, Doha has prided itself on its support for many of these popular revolutions, particularly in Libya and Syria. In mid-2013, HAMAD transferred power to his 33 year-old son, TAMIM bin Hamad—a peaceful abdication rare in the history of Arab Gulf states. TAMIM has prioritized improving the domestic welfare of Qataris, including establishing advanced healthcare and education systems and expanding the country's infrastructure in anticipation of Doha's hosting of the 2022 World Cup.

GEOGRAPHY

Location: Middle East, peninsula bordering the Persian Gulf and Saudi Arabia

Geographic coordinates: 25 30 N, 51 15 E

Map references: Middle East

Area: *total:* 11,586 sq km
country comparison to the world: 166
land: 11,586 sq km
water: 0 sq km

Area—comparative: slightly smaller than Connecticut

Land boundaries: *total:* 60 km
border countries: Saudi Arabia 60 km

Coastline: 563 km

Maritime claims: *territorial sea:* 12 nm
contiguous zone: 24 nm
exclusive economic zone: as determined by bilateral agreements or the median line

Climate: arid; mild, pleasant winters; very hot, humid summers

Terrain: mostly flat and barren desert covered with loose sand and gravel

Elevation extremes: *lowest point:* Persian Gulf 0 m
highest point: Tuwayyir al Hamir 103 m

Natural resources: petroleum, natural gas, fish

Land use: *arable land:* 1.21%
permanent crops: 0.17%
other: 98.62% (2011)

Irrigated land: 129.4 sq km (2003)

Total renewable water resources: 0.06 cu km (2011)

Freshwater withdrawal (domestic/industrial/agricultural): *total:* 0.44 cu km/yr (39%/2%/59%)
per capita: 376.9 cu m/yr (2005)

Natural hazards: haze, dust storms, sandstorms common

Environment—current issues: limited natural freshwater resources are increasing dependence on large-scale desalination facilities

Environment—international agreements:
party to: Biodiversity, Climate Change, Climate Change-Kyoto Protocol, Desertification, Endangered Species, Hazardous Wastes, Law of the Sea, Ozone Layer Protection, Ship Pollution
signed, but not ratified: none of the selected agreements

Geography—note: strategic location in central Persian Gulf near major petroleum deposits

PEOPLE AND SOCIETY

Nationality: *noun:* Qatari(s)
adjective: Qatari

Ethnic groups: Arab 40%, Indian 18%, Pakistani 18%, Iranian 10%, other 14%

Languages: Arabic (official), English commonly used as a second language

Religions: Muslim 77.5%, Christian 8.5%, other (includes mainly Hindu and other Indian religions) 14% (2004 est.)

Population: 2,123,160 (July 2014 est.)
country comparison to the world: 146

Age structure:
0-14 years: 12.5% (male 134,477/female 130,640)
15-24 years: 13.4% (male 208,278/female 75,889)
25-54 years: 69.9% (male 1,228,151/female 256,099)
55-64 years: 0.9% (male 55,386/female 16,156)
65 years and over: 0.8% (male 11,226/female 6,858) (2014 est.)

Dependency ratios:
total dependency ratio: 17.2 %
youth dependency ratio: 16 %
elderly dependency ratio: 1.2 %
potential support ratio: 83.9 (2013)

Median age: *total:* 32.6 years
male: 33.6 years
female: 28 years (2014 est.)

Population growth rate: 3.58% (2014 est.)
country comparison to the world: 5

Birth rate: 9.95 births/1,000 population (2014 est.)
country comparison to the world: 194

Death rate: 1.53 deaths/1,000 population (2014 est.)
country comparison to the world: 226

Net migration rate: 27.35 migrant(s)/1,000 population (2014 est.)
country comparison to the world: 2

Urbanization: *urban population:* 98.8% of total population (2011)
rate of urbanization: 3.01% annual rate of change (2010-15 est.)

Major urban areas—population: DOHA (capital) 427,000 (2009)

Sex ratio: *at birth:* 1.02 male(s)/female
0-14 years: 1.03 male(s)/female
15-24 years: 2.75 male(s)/female
25-54 years: 4.8 male(s)/female
55-64 years: 3.37 male(s)/female
65 years and over: 1.5 male(s)/female
total population: 3.29 male(s)/female (2014 est.)

Maternal mortality rate: 7 deaths/100,000 live births (2010)
country comparison to the world: 166

Infant mortality rate: *total:* 6.42 deaths/1,000 live births
country comparison to the world: 165
male: 6.67 deaths/1,000 live births
female: 6.16 deaths/1,000 live births (2014 est.)

Life expectancy at birth:
total population: 78.38 years
country comparison to the world: 53
male: 76.4 years
female: 80.4 years (2014 est.)

Total fertility rate: 1.92 children born/woman (2014 est.)
country comparison to the world: 136

Contraceptive prevalence rate: 43.2% (1998)

Health expenditures: 1.9% of GDP (2011)
country comparison to the world: 190

Physicians density: 2.76 physicians/1,000 population (2006)

Hospital bed density: 1.2 beds/1,000 population (2009)

Drinking water source:
improved:
urban: 100% of population
rural: 100% of population
total: 100% of population

unimproved:
urban: 0% of population
rural: 0% of population
0% of population (2011 est.)

Sanitation facility access:
improved:
urban: 100% of population
rural: 100% of population
total: 100% of population
unimproved:
urban: 0% of population
rural: 0% of population
total: 0% of population (2011 est.)

HIV/AIDS—adult prevalence rate: less than 0.1% (2009 est.)
country comparison to the world: 121

HIV/AIDS—people living with HIV/AIDS: fewer than 200 (2009 est.)
country comparison to the world: 162

HIV/AIDS—deaths: fewer than 100 (2009 est.)
country comparison to the world: 122

Obesity—adult prevalence rate: 33.2% (2008)
country comparison to the world: 16

Education expenditures: 2.5% of GDP (2008)
country comparison to the world: 154

Literacy: *definition:* age 15 and over can read and write
total population: 96.3%
male: 96.5%
female: 95.4% (2010 est.)

School life expectancy (primary to tertiary education): *total:* 14 years
male: 14 years
female: 14 years (2005)

Unemployment, youth ages 15-24: *total:* 1.3%
country comparison to the world: 146
male: 0.4%
female: 8.9% (2011)

GOVERNMENT

Country name: *conventional long form:* State of Qatar
conventional short form: Qatar
local long form: Dawlat Qatar
local short form: Qatar
note: closest approximation of the native pronunciation is cutter

Government type: emirate

Capital: *name:* Doha

geographic coordinates: 25 17 N, 51 32 E
time difference: UTC+3 (8 hours ahead of Washington, DC during Standard Time)

Administrative divisions: 7 municipalities (baladiyat, singular—baladiyah); Ad Dawhah, Al Khawr wa adh Dhakhirah, Al Wakrah, Ar Rayyan, Ash Shamal, Az Za'ayin, Umm Salal

Independence: 3 September 1971 (from the UK)

National holiday: National Day, 18 December (1878), anniversary of Al Thani family accession to the throne; Independence Day, 3 September (1971)

Constitution: previous 1972 (provisional); latest drafted 2 July 2002, approved by referendum 29 April 2003, endorsed 8 June 2004, effective 9 June 2005 (2013)

Legal system: mixed legal system of civil law and Islamic law (in family and personal matters)

International law organization participation: has not submitted an ICJ jurisdiction declaration; non-party state to the ICCt

Suffrage: 18 years of age; universal

Executive branch: *chief of state:* Amir TAMIM bin Hamad Al Thani (since 25 June 2013)
head of government: Prime Minister ABDALLAH bin Nasir bin Khalifa Al Thani (since 26 June 2013); Deputy Prime Minister Ahmad bin Abdallah al-MAHMUD (since 20 September 2011)
cabinet: Council of Ministers appointed by the amir (For more information visit the World Leaders website)
elections: the position of amir is hereditary

Legislative branch: unicameral Advisory Council or Majlis al-Shura (45 seats; 15 members appointed; 30 members to be elected by popular vote beginning mid- or late 2013, per the 2003 constitutional referendum)
note: the Advisory Council has limited legislative authority to draft and approve laws, but the Amir has final say on all matters; Qatar's first legislative elections were expected to be held in 2013, but HAMAD postponed them in a final legislative act prior to handing over power to TAMIN; there is currently no date set for Advisory Council elections; in principle the public would elect 30 members and the Amir would appoint 15; the Advisory Council would have authority to approve the national budget, hold ministers accountable through no-confidence votes, and propose legislation; Qatar in May 2011 held nationwide elections for the 29-member Central Municipal Council (CMC)—first elected in 1999—which has limited consultative authority aimed at improving municipal services

Judicial branch: *highest court(s):* Court of Cassation (consists of the court president and several judges); Supreme Constitutional Court (consists of the chief justice and 6 members) note—the Supreme Constitutional Court and the Judicial Supreme Council were established in 1999
judge selection and term of office: Cassation Court judges nominated by the Judicial Supreme Council, a 9-member independent body consisting of judiciary heads appointed by the monarch; judges appointed for 3-year renewable terms; Supreme Constitutional Court members nominated by the Judicial Supreme Council and appointed by the monarch; term of appointment NA
subordinate courts: Courts of Appeal; Courts of First Instance; Sharia Courts; Courts of Justice

Political parties and leaders: none

Political pressure groups and leaders: none

International organization participation: ABEDA, AFESD, AMF, CAEU, CD, CICA (observer), EITI (implementing country), FAO, G-77, GCC, IAEA, IBRD, ICAO, ICC (national committees), ICRM, IDA, IDB, IFAD, IFC, IFRCS, IHO, ILO, IMF, IMO, IMSO, Interpol, IOC, IOM (observer), IPU, ISO, ITSO, ITU, LAS, MIGA, NAM, OAPEC, OAS (observer), OIC, OPCW, OPEC, PCA, UN, UNCTAD, UNESCO, UNIDO, UNIFIL, UNWTO, UPU, WCO, WHO, WIPO, WMO, WTO

Diplomatic representation in the US:
chief of mission: Ambassador Jaham KUWARI (since 10 March 2014)
chancery: 2555 M Street NW, Washington, DC 20037
telephone: [1] (202) 274-1600 and 274-1603
FAX: [1] (202) 237-0061
consulates: Houston, Los Angeles, New York

Diplomatic representation from the US:
chief of mission: Ambassador Susan L. ZIADEH (since 11 September 2011)
embassy: Al-Luqta District, 22 February Road, Doha
mailing address: P. O. Box 2399, Doha
telephone: [974] 4496-6000
FAX: [974] 4488 4298

Flag description: maroon with a broad white serrated band (nine white points) on the hoist side; maroon represents the blood shed in Qatari wars, white stands for peace; the nine-pointed serrated edge signifies Qatar as the ninth member of the "reconciled emirates" in the wake of the Qatari-British treaty of 1916
note: the other eight emirates are the seven that compose the UAE and Bahrain; according to some sources, the dominant color was formerly red, but this darkened to maroon upon exposure to the sun and the new shade was eventually adopted

National anthem: *name:* "Al-Salam Al-Amiri" (The Peace for the Anthem)
lyrics/music: Sheikh MUBARAK bin Saif al-Thani/Abdul Aziz Nasser OBAIDAN
note: adopted 1996; the anthem was first performed that year at a meeting of the Gulf Cooperative Council hosted by Qatar

ECONOMY

Economy—overview: Qatar has prospered in the last several years with continued high real GDP growth. Throughout the financial crisis Qatari authorities sought to protect the local banking sector, with direct investments into domestic banks. GDP is driven largely by changes in oil prices and by investment in the energy sector. Economic policy is focused on developing Qatar's nonassociated natural gas reserves and increasing private and foreign investment in non-energy sectors, but oil and gas still account for more than 50% of GDP, roughly 85% of export earnings, and 50% of government revenues. Oil and gas have made Qatar the world's highest per-capita income country and the country with the lowest unemployment. Proved oil reserves in excess of 25 billion barrels should enable continued output at current levels for about 57 years. Qatar's proved reserves of natural gas exceed 25 trillion cubic meters, about 13% of the world total and third largest in the world. Qatar's successful 2022 World Cup bid is accelerating large-scale infrastructure projects such as Qatar's metro system, light rail system, the construction of a new port, roads, stadiums and related sporting infrastructure. The new Hamad International Airport is expected to open in mid-2014 with an annual passenger capacity of 24 million on initial opening and 50 million when complete.

GDP (purchasing power parity): $198.7 billion (2013 est.)
country comparison to the world: 56
$185.3 billion (2012 est.)
$171.4 billion (2011 est.)
note: data are in 2013 US dollars

GDP (official exchange rate): $213.1 billion (2013 est.)

GDP—real growth rate: 5.5% (2013 est.)
country comparison to the world: 46

8.1% (2012 est.)
13% (2011 est.)

GDP—per capita (PPP): $102,100 (2013 est.)
country comparison to the world: 1
$100,900 (2012 est.)
$100,400 (2011 est.)
note: data are in 2013 US dollars

Gross national saving: 54.1% of GDP (2013 est.)
country comparison to the world: 3
62.1% of GDP (2012 est.)
59.8% of GDP (2011 est.)

GDP—composition, by end use:
household consumption: 13.5%
government consumption: 13.8%
investment in fixed capital: 29.3%
investment in inventories: 2.5%
exports of goods and services: 71.7%
imports of goods and services: -30.8% (2013 est.)

GDP—composition, by sector of origin:
agriculture: 0.1%
industry: 72.2%
services: 27.7% (2013 est.)

Agriculture—products: fruits, vegetables; poultry, dairy products, beef; fish

Industries: liquefied natural gas, crude oil production and refining, ammonia, fertilizers, petrochemicals, steel reinforcing bars, cement, commercial ship repair

Industrial production growth rate: 2.9% (2013 est.)
country comparison to the world: 108

Labor force: 1.424 million (2013 est.)
country comparison to the world: 132

Unemployment rate: 0.3% (2013 est.)
country comparison to the world: 3
0.5% (2012 est.)

Population below poverty line: NA%

Household income or consumption by percentage share: *lowest 10%:* 1.3%
highest 10%: 35.9% (2007)

Budget: *revenues:* $77.54 billion
expenditures: $57.25 billion (2013 est.)

Taxes and other revenues: 38.8% of GDP (2013 est.)
country comparison to the world: 48

Budget surplus (+) or deficit (-):
9.1% of GDP (2013 est.)
country comparison to the world: 6

Public debt: 30.6% of GDP (2013 est.)
country comparison to the world: 120
32.8% of GDP (2012 est.)

Fiscal year: 1 April—31 March

Inflation rate (consumer prices): 3.1% (2013 est.)
country comparison to the world: 116
1.9% (2012 est.)

Central bank discount rate: 4.5% (31 December 2012 est.)
country comparison to the world: 74
4.93% (31 December 2011 est.)

Commercial bank prime lending rate: 5.3% (31 December 2013 est.)
country comparison to the world: 152
5.38% (31 December 2012 est.)

Stock of narrow money: $29.98 billion (31 December 2013 est.)
country comparison to the world: 61
$24.98 billion (31 December 2012 est.)

Stock of broad money: $136 billion (31 December 2013 est.)
country comparison to the world: 50
$104.7 billion (31 December 2012 est.)

Stock of domestic credit: $170.1 billion (31 December 2013 est.)
country comparison to the world: 44
$149.1 billion (31 December 2012 est.)

Market value of publicly traded shares: $126.4 billion (31 December 2012 est.)
country comparison to the world: 39
$125.4 billion (31 December 2011)
$123.6 billion (31 December 2010 est.)

Current account balance: $47.56 billion (2013 est.)
country comparison to the world: 14
$61.59 billion (2012 est.)

Exports: $12.7 billion (2013 est.)
country comparison to the world: 87
$133 billion (2012 est.)

Exports—commodities: liquefied natural gas (LNG), petroleum products, fertilizers, steel

Exports—partners: Japan 26.7%, South Korea 19%, India 12.1%, Singapore 5.7%, China 5.4% (2013 est.)

Imports: $39.58 billion (2013 est.)
country comparison to the world: 60
$27.73 billion (2012 est.)

Imports—commodities: machinery and transport equipment, food, chemicals

Imports—partners: US 14.2%, UAE 11.1%, Saudi Arabia 8.6%, UK 6.4%, Japan 6%, China 4.8%, Germany 4.7%, Italy 4.4%, France 4.4% (2013 est.)

Reserves of foreign exchange and gold: $40.09 billion (31 December 2013 est.)
country comparison to the world: 45
$33.19 billion (31 December 2012 est.)

Debt—external: $149.4 billion (31 December 2013 est.)
country comparison to the world: 37
$139.2 billion (31 December 2012 est.)

Stock of direct foreign investment—at home: $33.48 billion (31 December 2013 est.)
country comparison to the world: 60
$32.17 billion (31 December 2012 est.)

Stock of direct foreign investment—abroad: $28.86 billion (31 December 2013 est.)
country comparison to the world: 43
$26.86 billion (31 December 2012 est.)

Exchange rates: Qatari rials (QAR) per US dollar—
3.64 (2013 est.)
3.64 (2012 est.)
3.64 (2010 est.)
3.64 (2009)
3.64 (2008)

ENERGY

Electricity—production: 32.34 billion kWh (2011 est.)
country comparison to the world: 6 5

Electricity—consumption: 20.51 billion kWh (2010 est.)
country comparison to the world: 68

Electricity—exports: 0 kWh (2012 est.)
country comparison to the world: 185

Electricity—imports: 0 kWh (2012 est.)
country comparison to the world: 188

Electricity—installed generating capacity: 7.83 million kW (2011 est.)
country comparison to the world: 66

Electricity—from fossil fuels: 100% of total installed capacity (2010 est.)
country comparison to the world: 29

Electricity—from nuclear fuels: 0% of total installed capacity (2010 est.)
country comparison to the world: 166

Electricity—from hydroelectric plants: 0% of total installed capacity (2010 est.)
country comparison to the world: 192

Electricity—from other renewable sources: 0% of total installed capacity (2010 est.)
country comparison to the world: 115

Crude oil—production: 1.579 million bbl/day (2012 est.)
country comparison to the world: 19

Crude oil—exports: 1.389 million bbl/day (2012 est.)
country comparison to the world: 14

Crude oil—imports: 0 bbl/day (2010 est.)
country comparison to the world: 111

Crude oil—proved reserves: 25.38 billion bbl (1 January 2013 es)
country comparison to the world: 12

Refined petroleum products—production: 287,500 bbl/day (2010 est.)
country comparison to the world: 44

Refined petroleum products—consumption: 189,700 bbl/day (2012 est.)
country comparison to the world: 60

Refined petroleum products—exports: 210,000 bbl/day (2010 est.)
country comparison to the world: 31

Refined petroleum products—imports: 0 bbl/day (2010 est.)
country comparison to the world: 211

Natural gas—production: 133.2 billion cu m (2011 est.)
country comparison to the world: 6

Natural gas—consumption: 19.53 billion cu m (2012 est.)
country comparison to the world: 36

Natural gas—exports: 113.7 billion cu m (2011 est.)
country comparison to the world: 2

Natural gas—imports: 0 cu m (2011 est.)
country comparison to the world: 120

Natural gas—proved reserves: 25.2 trillion cu m (1 January 2013 es)
country comparison to the world: 3

Carbon dioxide emissions from consumption of energy: 64.46 million Mt (2011 est.)
country comparison to the world: 53

COMMUNICATIONS

Telephones—main lines in use: 327,000 (2012)
country comparison to the world: 111

Telephones—mobile cellular: 2.6 million (2012)
country comparison to the world: 136

Telephone system: *general assessment:* modern system centered in Doha
domestic: combined fixed and mobile-cellular telephone subscribership exceeds 130 telephones per 100 persons

international: country code—974; landing point for the Fiber-Optic Link Around the Globe (FLAG) submarine cable network that provides links to Asia, Middle East, Europe, and the US; tropospheric scatter to Bahrain; microwave radio relay to Saudi Arabia and the UAE; satellite earth stations—2 Intelsat (1 Atlantic Ocean and 1 Indian Ocean) and 1 Arabsat (2011)

Broadcast media: TV and radio broadcast licensing and access to local media markets are state controlled; home of the satellite TV channel Al-Jazeera, which was originally owned and financed by the Qatari government, but has evolved to independent corporate status; Al-Jazeera claims editorial independence in broadcasting; local radio transmissions include state, private, and international broadcasters on FM frequencies in Doha; in August 2013, Qatar's satellite company Es'hailSat launched its first communications satellite Es'hail 1 (manufactured in the US), which entered commercial service in December 2013 to provide improved television broadcasting capability and expand availability of voice and internet; Es'hailSat released a request for proposals in March 2014 for its second satellite to launch in 2016 (2014)

Internet country code: .qa

Internet hosts: 897 (2012)
country comparison to the world: 173

Internet users: 563,800 (2009)
country comparison to the world: 117

TRANSPORTATION

Airports: 6 (2013)
country comparison to the world: 178

Airports—with paved runways: *total:* 4
over 3,047 m: 3
1,524 to 2,437 m: 1 (2013)

Airports—with unpaved runways: *total:* 2
914 to 1,523 m: 1
under 914 m: 1 (2013)

Heliports: 1 (2013)

Pipelines: condensate 288 km; condensate/gas 221 km; gas 2,383 km; liquid petroleum gas 90 km; oil 745 km; refined products 103 km (2013)

Roadways: *total:* 9,830 km (2010)
country comparison to the world: 135

Merchant marine: *total:* 2 8
country comparison to the world: 87
by type: bulk carrier 3, chemical tanker 2, container 13, liquefied gas 6, petroleum tanker 4
foreign-owned: 6 (Kuwait 6)
registered in other countries: 35 (Liberia 5, Marshall Islands 29, Panama 1) (2010)

Ports and terminals: *major seaport(s):* Doha, Mesaieed (Umaieed), Ra's Laffan

MILITARY

Military branches: Qatari Emiri Land Force (QELF), Qatari Emiri Navy (QEN), Qatari Emiri Air Force (QEAF) (2013)

Military service age and obligation: conscription for males aged 18-35 (2014)

Manpower available for military service:
males age 16-49: 389,487
females age 16-49: 165,572 (2010 est.)

Manpower fit for military service:
males age 16-49: 321,974
females age 16-49: 140,176 (2010 est.)

Manpower reaching militarily significant age annually: *male:* 6,429
female: 5,162 (2010 est.)

TRANSNATIONAL ISSUES

Disputes—international: none

Refugees and internally displaced persons:
stateless persons: 1,200 (2012)

ROMANIA

INTRODUCTION

Background: The principalities of Wallachia and Moldavia—for centuries under the suzerainty of the Turkish Ottoman Empire—secured their autonomy in 1856; they were de facto linked in 1859 and formally united in 1862 under the new name of Romania. The country gained recognition of its independence in 1878. It joined the Allied Powers in World War I and acquired new territories—most notably Transylvania—following the conflict. In 1940, Romania allied with the Axis powers and participated in the 1941 German invasion of the USSR. Three years later, overrun by the Soviets, Romania signed an armistice. The post-war Soviet occupation led to the formation of a communist "people's republic" in 1947 and the abdication of the king. The decades-long rule of dictator Nicolae CEAUSESCU, who took power in 1965, and his Securitate police state became increasingly oppressive and draconian through the 1980s. CEAUSESCU was overthrown and executed in late 1989. Former communists dominated the government until 1996 when they were swept from power. Romania joined NATO in 2004 and the EU in 2007.

GEOGRAPHY

Location: Southeastern Europe, bordering the Black Sea, between Bulgaria and Ukraine

Geographic coordinates: 46 00 N, 25 00 E

Map references: Europe

Area: *total:* 238,391 sq km
country comparison to the world: 83
land: 229,891 sq km
water: 8,500 sq km

Area—comparative: slightly smaller than Oregon

Land boundaries: *total:* 2,508 km
border countries: Bulgaria 608 km, Hungary 443 km, Moldova 450 km, Serbia 476 km, Ukraine (north) 362 km, Ukraine (east) 169 km

Coastline: 225 km

Maritime claims: *territorial sea:* 12 nm
contiguous zone: 24 nm
exclusive economic zone: 200 nm
continental shelf: 200 m depth or to the depth of exploitation

Climate: temperate; cold, cloudy winters with frequent snow and fog; sunny summers with frequent showers and thunderstorms

Terrain: central Transylvanian Basin is separated from the Moldavian Plateau on the east by the Eastern Carpathian Mountains and separated from the Walachian Plain on the south by the Transylvanian Alps

Elevation extremes: *lowest point:* Black Sea 0 m
highest point: Moldoveanu 2,544 m

Natural resources: petroleum (reserves declining), timber, natural gas, coal, iron ore, salt, arable land, hydropower

Land use: *arable land:* 37.73%
permanent crops: 1.86%
other: 60.41% (2011)

Irrigated land: 6,153 sq km (2007)

Total renewable water resources: 211.9 cu km (2011)

Freshwater withdrawal (domestic/industrial/agricultural): *total:* 6.88 cu km/yr (22%/61%/17%)
per capita: 320.8 cu m/yr (2009)

Natural hazards: earthquakes, most severe in south and southwest; geologic structure and climate promote landslides

Environment—current issues: soil erosion and degradation; water pollution; air pollution in south from industrial effluents; contamination of Danube delta wetlands

Environment—international agreements:
party to: Air Pollution, Air Pollution-Persistent Organic Pollutants, Antarctic-Environmental Protocol, Antarctic Treaty, Biodiversity, Climate Change, Climate Change-Kyoto Protocol, Desertification, Endangered Species, Environmental Modification, Hazardous Wastes, Law of the Sea, Ozone Layer Protection, Ship Pollution, Wetlands
signed, but not ratified: none of the selected agreements

Geography—note: controls most easily traversable land route between the Balkans, Moldova, and Ukraine

PEOPLE AND SOCIETY

Nationality: *noun:* Romanian(s)
adjective: Romanian

Ethnic groups: Romanian 83.4%, Hungarian 6.1%, Roma 3.1%, Ukrainian 0.3%, German 0.2%, other 0.7%, unspecified 6.1% (2011 est.)

Languages: Romanian (official) 85.4%, Hungarian 6.3%, Romany (Gypsy) 1.2%, other 1%, unspecified 6.1% (2011 est.)

Religions: Eastern Orthodox (including all sub-denominations) 81.9%, Protestant (various denominations including Reformed and Pentecostal) 6.4%, Roman Catholic 4.3%, other (includes Muslim) 0.9%, none or atheist 0.2%, unspecified 6.3% (2011 est.)

Population: 21,729,871 (July 2014 est.)
country comparison to the world: 58

Age structure:
0-14 years: 14.6% (male 1,628,220/female 1,541,914)
15-24 years: 11.3% (male 1,258,746/female 1,197,681)
25-54 years: 45.7% (male 5,021,370/female 4,916,576)
55-64 years: 15.4% (male 1,320,781/female 1,508,878)
65 years and over: 15.1% (male 1,346,864/female 1,988,841) (2014 est.)

Dependency ratios:
total dependency ratio: 43.3 %
youth dependency ratio: 21.6 %
elderly dependency ratio: 21.7 %
potential support ratio: 4.6 (2013)

Median age: *total:* 39.8 years
male: 38.4 years
female: 41.4 years (2014 est.)

Population growth rate: -0.29% (2014 est.)
country comparison to the world: 216

Birth rate: 9.27 births/1,000 population (2014 est.)
country comparison to the world: 206

Death rate: 11.88 deaths/1,000 population (2014 est.)
country comparison to the world: 28

Net migration rate: -0.24 migrant(s)/1,000 population (2014 est.)
country comparison to the world: 123

Urbanization: *urban population:* 52.8% of total population (2011)
rate of urbanization: -0.18% annual rate of change (2010-15 est.)

Major urban areas—population: BUCHAREST (capital) 1.933 million (2009)

Sex ratio: *at birth:* 1.06 male(s)/female
0-14 years: 1.06 male(s)/female
15-24 years: 1.05 male(s)/female
25-54 years: 1.02 male(s)/female
55-64 years: 0.95 male(s)/female
65 years and over: 0.68 male(s)/female
total population: 0.95 male(s)/female (2014 est.)

Mother's mean age at first birth: 26 (2010 est.)

Maternal mortality rate: 27 deaths/100,000 live births (2010)
country comparison to the world: 127

Infant mortality rate: *total:* 10.16 deaths/1,000 live births
country comparison to the world: 140
male: 11.52 deaths/1,000 live births
female: 8.72 deaths/1,000 live births (2014 est.)

Life expectancy at birth:
total population: 74.69 years
country comparison to the world: 108
male: 71.23 years
female: 78.36 years (2014 est.)

Total fertility rate: 1.32 children born/woman (2014 est.)
country comparison to the world: 214

Contraceptive prevalence rate: 69.8%
note: percent of women aged 15-49 (2005)

Health expenditures: 5.9% of GDP (2010)
country comparison to the world: 116

Physicians density: 2.39 physicians/1,000 population (2010)

Hospital bed density: 6.3 beds/1,000 population (2010)

Drinking water source:
improved:
urban: 98.5% of population
rural: 75.6% of population
total: 87.7% of population
unimproved:
urban: 1.5% of population
rural: 24.4% of population
total: 12.3% of population (2008 est.)

Sanitation facility access:
improved:
urban: 87.9% of population
rural: 54.4% of population
total: 72.1% of population
unimproved:
urban: 12.1% of population
rural: 45.6% of population
total: 27.9% of population (2008 est.)

HIV/AIDS—adult prevalence rate: 0.1% (2009 est.)
country comparison to the world: 122

HIV/AIDS—people living with HIV/AIDS: 16,000 (2009 est.)
country comparison to the world: 88

HIV/AIDS—deaths: fewer than 1,000 (2009 est.)

country comparison to the world: 76

Obesity—adult prevalence rate: 19.1% (2008)
country comparison to the world: 101

Children under the age of 5 years underweight: 3.5% (2002)
country comparison to the world: 103

Education expenditures: 4.2% of GDP (2009)
country comparison to the world: 104

Literacy: *definition:* age 15 and over can read and write
total population: 97.7%
male: 98.3%
female: 97.1% (2011 est.)

School life expectancy (primary to tertiary education): *total:* 14 years
male: 14 years
female: 15 years (2011)

Child labor—children ages 5-14:
total number: 26,658
percentage: 1 % (2000 est.)

Unemployment, youth ages 15-24: *total:* 22.7%
country comparison to the world: 49
male: 22.3%
female: 23.2% (2012)

GOVERNMENT

Country name: *conventional long form:* none
conventional short form: Romania
local long form: none
local short form: Romania

Government type: republic

Capital: *name:* Bucharest

geographic coordinates: 44 26 N, 26 06 E
time difference: UTC+2 (7 hours ahead of Washington, DC during Standard Time)
daylight saving time: +1hr, begins last Sunday in March; ends last Sunday in October

Administrative divisions: 41 counties (judete, singular—judet) and 1 municipality* (municipiu); Alba, Arad, Arges, Bacau, Bihor, Bistrita-Nasaud, Botosani, Braila, Brasov, Bucuresti (Bucharest)*, Buzau, Calarasi, Caras-Severin, Cluj, Constanta, Covasna, Dambovita, Dolj, Galati, Gorj, Giurgiu, Harghita, Hunedoara, Ialomita, Iasi, Ilfov, Maramures, Mehedinti, Mures, Neamt, Olt, Prahova, Salaj, Satu Mare, Sibiu, Suceava, Teleorman, Timis, Tulcea, Vaslui, Valcea, Vrancea

Independence: 9 May 1877 (independence proclaimed from the Ottoman Empire; independence recognized on 13 July 1878 by the Treaty of Berlin); 26 March 1881 (kingdom proclaimed); 30 December 1947 (republic proclaimed)

National holiday: Unification Day (of Romania and Transylvania), 1 December (1918)

Constitution: several previous; latest adopted 21 November 1991, approved by referendum and effective 8 December 1991; amended 2003 (2014)

Legal system: civil law system

International law organization participation: has not submitted an ICJ jurisdiction declaration; accepts ICCt jurisdiction

Suffrage: 18 years of age; universal

Executive branch: *chief of state:* President Traian BASESCU (since 20 December 2004); note—President BASESCU has twice been temporarily suspended since assuming his post: first from 20 April-23 May 2007, second from 6 July-27 August 2012; he survived a national recall referendum on both occasions
head of government: Prime Minister Victor-Viorel PONTA (since 7 May 2012); Deputy Prime Ministers Daniel CONSTANTIN, Hunor KELEMAN, Gabriel OPREA (since 5 March 2014)
cabinet: Council of Ministers appointed by the prime minister (For more information visit the World Leaders website)
elections: president elected by popular vote for a five-year term (eligible for a second term); election last held on 22 November 2009 with runoff on 6 December 2009 (next to be held in November-December 2014); prime minister appointed by the president with the consent of the Parliament
election results: Traian BASESCU reelected president; percent of vote—Traian BASESCU 50.3%, Mircea GEOANA 49.7%

Legislative branch: bicameral Parliament or Parlament consists of the Senate or Senat (176 seats; members elected by popular vote in a mixed electoral system to serve four-year terms) and the Chamber of Deputies or Camera Deputatilor (412 seats; members elected by popular vote in a mixed electoral system to serve four-year terms)
elections: Senate—last held on 9 December 2012 (next by December 2016); Chamber of Deputies—last held on 9 December 2012 (next by December 2016)
election results: Senate—percent of vote by alliance/party—USL 60.1%, ARD 16.7%, PP-DD 14.6%, UDMR 5.3%, other 3.3%; seats by alliance/party—USL 122, ARD 24, PP-DD 21, UDMR 9; Chamber of Deputies - percent of vote by alliance/party—USL 58.6%, ARD 16.5%, PP-DD 14%, UDMR 5.2%, ethnic minorities 2.6%, other 3.1%; seats by alliance/party—USL 273, ARD 56, PP-DD 47, UDMR 18, ethnic minorities 18

Judicial branch: *highest court(s):* High Court of Cassation and Justice (consists of 111 judges and organized into civil, penal, commercial, contentious administrative and fiscal business, and joint sections); Supreme Constitutional Court (consists of 9 members)

judge selection and term of office: High Court of Cassation and Justice judges appointed by the president upon nomination by the Superior Council of Magistracy, a 19-member body mostly of judges, prosecutors, and law specialists; judges appointed for 6-year renewable terms; Constitutional Court members—6 elected by Parliament and 3 appointed by the president; members serve 9-year, non-renewable terms
subordinate courts: Courts of Appeal; regional tribunals; first instance courts; military and arbitration courts

Political parties and leaders: Christian-Democratic National Peasants' Party or PNT-CD [Aurelian PAVELESCU]; Civic Force or FC [Mihai-Razvan UNGUREANU]; Conservative Party or PC [Daniel CONSTANTIN] (formerly Humanist Party or PUR); Democratic Liberal Party or PDL [Vasile BLAGA] (formerly Democratic Party); Democratic Union of Hungarians in Romania or UDMR [Hunor KELEMEN]; National Liberal Party or PNL [Crin ANTONESCU]; National Union for Romania's Progress or UNPR [Gabriel OPREA]; New Republic Party or NR [Mihai NEAMTU]; People's Party—Dan Diaconescu or PP-DD [Dan DIACONESCU]; Popular Movement Party or PMP [Eugene TOMAC]; Social Democratic Party or PSD [Victor-Viorel PONTA] (formerly Party of Social Democracy in Romania or PDSR)

Political pressure groups and leaders:
other: various human rights and professional associations

International organization participation: Australia Group, BIS, BSEC, CBSS (observer), CD, CE, CEI, EAPC, EBRD, EIB, ESA, EU, FAO, G-9, IAEA, IBRD, ICAO, ICC (national committees), ICRM, IDA, IFAD, IFC, IFRCS, IHO, ILO, IMF, IMO, IMSO, Interpol, IOC, IOM, IPU, ISO, ITSO, ITU, ITUC (NGOs), LAIA (observer), MIGA, MONUSCO, NATO, NSG, OAS (observer), OIF, OPCW, OSCE, PCA, SELEC, UN, UNCTAD, UNESCO, UNHCR, UNIDO, Union Latina, UNMIL, UNMISS, UNOCI, UNWTO, UPU, WCO, WFTU (NGOs), WHO, WIPO, WMO, WTO, ZC

Diplomatic representation in the US:
chief of mission: Iulian BUGA (since 3 December 2013)
chancery: 1607 23rd Street NW, Washington, DC 20008
telephone: [1] (202) 332-4846, 4848, 4851, 4852
FAX: [1] (202) 232-4748
consulate(s) general: Chicago, Los Angeles, New York

Diplomatic representation from the US:
chief of mission: Ambassador (vacant); Charge d'Affaires Duane BUTCHER (since 14 December 2012)
embassy: Bulevardul Dr. Liviu Librescu 4-6, District 1, Bucharest, 015118
mailing address: American Embassy Bucharest, US Department of State, 5260 Bucharest Place, Washington, DC 20521-5260 (pouch)
telephone: [40] (21) 200-3300
FAX: [40] (21) 200-3442

Flag description: three equal vertical bands of blue (hoist side), yellow, and red; modeled after the flag of France, the colors are those of the principalities of Walachia (red and yellow) and Moldavia (red and blue), which united in 1862 to form Romania; the national coat of arms that used to be centered in the yellow band has been removed
note: now similar to the flag of Chad, whose blue band is darker; also resembles the flags of Andorra and Moldova

National symbol(s): golden eagle

National anthem: *name:* "Desteapta-te romane!" (Wake up, Romanian!)
lyrics/music: Andrei MURESIANU/Anton PANN
note: adopted 1990; the anthem was written during the 1848 Revolution

ECONOMY

Economy—overview: Romania, which joined the EU on 1 January 2007, began the transition from Communism in 1989 with a largely obsolete industrial base and a pattern of output unsuited to the country's needs. The country emerged in 2000 from a punishing three-year recession due to strong demand in EU export markets. Domestic consumption and investment fueled strong GDP growth, but led to large current account imbalances. Romania's macroeconomic gains have only recently started to spur creation of a middle class and to address Romania's widespread poverty. Corruption and red tape continue to permeate the business environment. As a result of the global financial crisis, Romania signed on to a $26 billion emergency assistance package from the IMF, the EU, and other international lenders. GDP contracted from 2009 to 2011. In March 2011, Romania and the IMF/EU/World Bank signed a 24-month precautionary stand-by agreement, worth $6.6 billion, to promote fiscal discipline, encourage progress on structural reforms, and strengthen financial sector stability. In September 2013, the Romanian authorities and the IMF/EU agreed to a follow-on stand-by agreement, worth $5.4 billion, to continue with reforms, although Bucharest announced that it does not intend to draw funds under the agreement. Economic growth accelerated in 2013, driven by strong industrial exports and an excellent agricultural harvest; in

December 2013 inflation dropped to a historical low annual rate of 1.6%; and the current account deficit was reduced substantially. Yet, progress on structural reforms is uneven and the economy still is vulnerable to shocks.

GDP (purchasing power parity): $280.7 billion (2013 est.)
country comparison to the world: 48
$275.2 billion (2012 est.)
$273.3 billion (2011 est.)
note: data are in 2013 US dollars

GDP (official exchange rate): $183.8 billion (2013 est.)

GDP—real growth rate: 2% (2013 est.)
country comparison to the world: 141
0.7% (2012 est.)
2.2% (2011 est.)

GDP—per capita (PPP): $13,200 (2013 est.)
country comparison to the world: 99
$12,900 (2012 est.)
$12,800 (2011 est.)
note: data are in 2013 US dollars

Gross national saving: 24.8% of GDP (2013 est.)
country comparison to the world: 50
23.3% of GDP (2012 est.)
22.4% of GDP (2011 est.)

GDP—composition, by end use:
household consumption: 72.7%
government consumption: 6.7%
investment in fixed capital: 25.9%
investment in inventories: 0.2%
exports of goods and services: 41.2%
imports of goods and services: -46.6% (2013 est.)

GDP—composition, by sector of origin:
agriculture: 10.8%
industry: 37.4%
services: 51.8% (2013 est.)

Agriculture—products: wheat, corn, barley, sugar beets, sunflower seed, potatoes, grapes; eggs, sheep

Industries: electric machinery and equipment, textiles and footwear, light machinery and auto assembly, mining, timber, construction materials, metallurgy, chemicals, food processing, petroleum refining

Industrial production growth rate: 2.6% (2013 est.)
country comparison to the world: 115

Labor force: 9.246 million (2013 est.)
country comparison to the world: 51

Labor force—by occupation: *agriculture:* 31.6%
industry: 21.1%
services: 47.3% (2010)

Unemployment rate: 4.8% (2013 est.)
country comparison to the world: 42
5.6% (2012 est.)

Population below poverty line: 22.2% (2011 est.)

Household income or consumption by percentage share: *lowest 10%:* 1.7%
highest 10%: 19.8% (2011 est.)

Distribution of family income—Gini index: 33.2 (2011)
country comparison to the world: 99
30 (2003)

Budget: *revenues:* $58.77 billion
expenditures: $62.99 billion (2013 est.)

Taxes and other revenues: 32% of GDP (2013 est.)
country comparison to the world: 82

Budget surplus (+) or deficit (-): -2.3% of GDP (2013 est.)
country comparison to the world: 91

Public debt: 36.7% of GDP (2013 est.)
country comparison to the world: 101
37.2% of GDP (2012 est.)
note: defined by the EU's Maastricht Treaty as consolidated general government gross debt at nominal value, outstanding at the end of the year in the following categories of government liabilities: currency and deposits, securities other than shares excluding financial derivatives, and loans; general government sector
comprises the subsectors: central government, state government, local government, and social security funds

Fiscal year: calendar year

Inflation rate (consumer prices): 4.1% (2013 est.)
country comparison to the world: 139
3.3% (2012 est.)

Central bank discount rate: 5.25% (31 December 2012)
country comparison to the world: 62
5.75% (31 December 2011)

Commercial bank prime lending rate: 9% (31 December 2013 est.)
country comparison to the world: 74
11.33% (31 December 2012 est.)

Stock of narrow money: $19.55 billion (31 December 2013 est.)
country comparison to the world: 65
$26.51 billion (31 December 2012 est.)

Stock of broad money: $67.67 billion (31 December 2013 est.)
country comparison to the world: 63
$66.07 billion (31 December 2012 est.)

Stock of domestic credit: $84.71 billion (31 December 2013 est.)
country comparison to the world: 57
$82.69 billion (31 December 2012 est.)

Market value of publicly traded shares: $15.93 billion (31 December 2012 est.)
country comparison to the world: 62
$21.2 billion (31 December 2011)
$32.38 billion (31 December 2010 est.)

Current account balance: -$2.26 billion (2013 est.)
country comparison to the world: 146
-$6.346 billion (2012 est.)

Exports: $61.24 billion (2013 est.)
country comparison to the world: 52
$51.29 billion (2012 est.)

Exports—commodities: machinery and equipment, metals and metal products, textiles and footwear, chemicals, agricultural products, minerals and fuels

Exports—partners: Germany 18.9%, Italy 12.3%, France 7.1%, Turkey 5.5%, Hungary 5.5% (2012)

Imports: $69.18 billion (2013 est.)
country comparison to the world: 43
$62.75 billion (2012 est.)

Imports—commodities: machinery and equipment, chemicals, fuels and minerals, metals, textile and products, agricultural products

Imports—partners: Germany 17.5%, Italy 11%, Hungary 9.1%, France 5.7%, Russia 4.4%, Poland 4.3%, Austria 4.2%, Kazakhstan 4.1% (2012)

Reserves of foreign exchange and gold: $53.41 billion (31 December 2013 est.)
country comparison to the world: 36
$46.71 billion (31 December 2012 est.)

Debt—external: $130.4 billion (31 December 2013 est.)
country comparison to the world: 42
$129.3 billion (31 December 2012 est.)

Stock of direct foreign investment—at home: $78.96 billion (31 December 2013 est.)
country comparison to the world: 47
$75.46 billion (31 December 2012 est.)

Stock of direct foreign investment—abroad: $2.677 billion (31 December 2013 est.)
country comparison to the world: 70
$2.727 billion (31 December 2012 est.)

Exchange rates: lei (RON) per US dollar—
3.41 (2013 est.)
3.4682 (2012 est.)
3.1779 (2010 est.)
3.0493 (2009)
2.5 (2008)

ENERGY

Electricity—production: 60.39 billion kWh (2011 est.)
country comparison to the world: 4 4

Electricity—consumption: 53.74 billion kWh (2011 est.)
country comparison to the world: 45

Electricity—exports: 2.457 billion kWh (2011 est.)
country comparison to the world: 40

Electricity—imports: 1.04 billion kWh (2011 est.)
country comparison to the world: 63

Electricity—installed generating capacity: 24.98 million kW (2011 est.)
country comparison to the world: 34

Electricity—from fossil fuels: 61.7% of total installed capacity (2011 est.)
country comparison to the world: 131

Electricity—from nuclear fuels: 9.4% of total installed capacity (2011 est.)
country comparison to the world: 19

Electricity—from hydroelectric plants: 27% of total installed capacity (2011 est.)
country comparison to the world: 83

Electricity—from other renewable sources: 1.9% of total installed capacity (2011 est.)
country comparison to the world: 72

Crude oil—production: 101,600 bbl/day (2012 est.)
country comparison to the world: 50

Crude oil—exports: 1,604 bbl/day (2010 est.)
country comparison to the world: 69

Crude oil—imports: 122,000 bbl/day (2010 est.)
country comparison to the world: 46

Crude oil—proved reserves: 600 million bbl (1 January 2013 es)
country comparison to the world: 47

Refined petroleum products—production: 218,700 bbl/day (2010 est.)
country comparison to the world: 52

Refined petroleum products—consumption: 218,200 bbl/day (2011 est.)
country comparison to the world: 54

Refined petroleum products—exports: 75,480 bbl/day (2010 est.)
country comparison to the world: 52

Refined petroleum products—imports: 44,070 bbl/day (2010 est.)
country comparison to the world: 75

Natural gas—production: 10.61 billion cu m (2011 est.)
country comparison to the world: 41

Natural gas—consumption: 14.2 billion cu m (2011 est.)
country comparison to the world: 41

Natural gas—exports: 0 cu m (2011 est.)
country comparison to the world: 170

Natural gas—imports: 3.16 billion cu m (2011 est.)
country comparison to the world: 42

Natural gas—proved reserves:
105.5 billion cu m (1 January 2013 es)
country comparison to the world: 53

Carbon dioxide emissions from consumption of energy: 86.19 million Mt (2011 est.)
country comparison to the world: 42

COMMUNICATIONS

Telephones—main lines in use: 4.68 million (2012)
country comparison to the world: 32

Telephones—mobile cellular: 22.7 million (2012)
country comparison to the world: 45

Telephone system: *general assessment:* the telecommunications sector is being expanded and modernized; domestic and international service improving rapidly, especially mobile-cellular services
domestic: more than 90 percent of telephone network is automatic; fixed-line teledensity exceeds 20 telephones per 100 persons; mobile-cellular teledensity roughly 110 telephones per 100 persons
international: country code—40; the Black Sea Fiber Optic System provides connectivity to Bulgaria and Turkey; satellite earth stations—10; digital, international, direct-dial exchanges operate in Bucharest (2011)

Broadcast media: a mixture of public and private TV stations; the public broadcaster operates multiple stations; roughly 100 private national, regional, and local stations; more than 75% of households are connected to multi-channel cable or satellite TV systems that provide access to Romanian, European, and international stations; state-owned public radio broadcaster operates 4 national networks and regional and local stations; more than 100 private radio stations (2008)

Internet country code: .ro

Internet hosts: 2.667 million (2012)
country comparison to the world: 35

Internet users: 7.787 million (2009)
country comparison to the world: 37

TRANSPORTATION

Airports: 45 (2013)
country comparison to the world: 9 7

Airports—with paved runways: *total:* 2 6
over 3,047 m: 4
2,438 to 3,047 m: 10
1,524 to 2,437 m: 11
under 914 m: 1 (2013)

Airports—with unpaved runways: *total:* 1 9
914 to 1,523 m: 5
under 914 m: 14 (2013)

Heliports: 2 (2013)

Pipelines: gas 3,726 km; oil 2,451 km (2013)

Railways: *total:* 10,777 km
country comparison to the world: 22
broad gauge: 134 km 1.524-m gauge
standard gauge: 10,639 km 1.435-m gauge (4,020 km electrified)
narrow gauge: 4 km 1.000-m gauge (2012)

Roadways: *total:* 84,185 km
country comparison to the world: 55
paved: 49,873 km (includes 337 km of expressways)
unpaved: 34,312 km (2012)

Waterways: 1,731 km (includes 1,075 km on the Danube River, 524 km on secondary branches, and 132 km on canals) (2010)
country comparison to the world: 46

Merchant marine: *total:* 5
country comparison to the world: 127
by type: cargo 1, passenger/cargo 2, petroleum tanker 1, roll on/roll off 1
foreign-owned: 1 (Russia 1)
registered in other countries: 31 (Georgia 7, Liberia 3, Malta 7, Marshall Islands 2, Moldova 2, Panama 3, Russia 1, Saint Vincent and the Grenadines 1, Sierra Leone 2, Tanzania 1, Togo 1, unknown 1) (2010)

Ports and terminals: *major seaport(s):* Constanta, Midia
river port(s): Braila, Galati (Galatz), Mancanului (Giurgiu), Tulcea (Danube River)

MILITARY

Military branches: Land Forces, Naval Forces (Fortele Naval, FN), Romanian Air Force (Fortele Aeriene Romane, FAR) (2013)

Military service age and obligation: 20-35 years of age for compulsory male military service; conscription ended 2006, but military service remains mandatory; 18 years of age for male and female voluntary service; all military inductees (including women) contract for an initial 5-year term of service, with subsequent successive 3-year terms until age 36 (2012)

Manpower available for military service:
males age 16-49: 5,601,234
females age 16-49: 5,428,939 (2010 est.)

Manpower fit for military service:
males age 16-49: 4,550,409
females age 16-49: 4,507,880 (2010 est.)

Manpower reaching militarily significant age annually: *male:* 117,798
female: 111,607 (2010 est.)

Military expenditures: 1.29% of GDP (2012)
country comparison to the world: 79
1.3% of GDP (2011)
1.29% of GDP (2010)

TRANSNATIONAL ISSUES

Disputes—international: the ICJ ruled largely in favor of Romania in its dispute submitted in 2004 over Ukrainian-administered Zmiyinyy/Serpilor (Snake) Island and Black Sea maritime boundary delimitation; Romania opposes Ukraine's reopening of a navigation canal from the Danube border through Ukraine to the Black Sea

Refugees and internally displaced persons:
stateless persons: 248 (2012)

Illicit drugs: major transshipment point for Southwest Asian heroin transiting the Balkan route and small amounts of Latin American cocaine bound for Western Europe; although not a significant financial center, role as a narcotics conduit leaves it vulnerable to laundering, which occurs via the banking system, currency exchange houses, and casinos

RUSSIA

INTRODUCTION

Background: Founded in the 12th century, the Principality of Muscovy, was able to emerge from over 200 years of Mongol domination (13th-15th centuries) and to gradually conquer and absorb surrounding principalities. In the early 17th century, a new Romanov Dynasty continued this policy of expansion across Siberia to the Pacific. Under PETER I (ruled 1682-1725), hegemony was extended to the Baltic Sea and the country was renamed the Russian Empire. During the 19th century, more territorial acquisitions were made in Europe and Asia. Defeat in the Russo-Japanese War of 1904-05 contributed to the Revolution of 1905, which resulted in the formation of a parliament and other reforms. Repeated devastating defeats of the Russian army in World War I led to widespread rioting in the major cities of the Russian Empire and to the overthrow in 1917 of the imperial household. The communists under Vladimir LENIN seized power soon after and formed the USSR. The brutal rule of Iosif STALIN (1928-53) strengthened communist rule and Russian dominance of the Soviet Union at a cost of tens of millions of lives. The Soviet economy and society stagnated in the following decades until General Secretary Mikhail GORBACHEV (1985-91) introduced glasnost (openness) and perestroika (restructuring) in an attempt to modernize communism, but his initiatives inadvertently released forces that by December 1991 splintered the USSR into Russia and 14 other independent republics. Since then, Russia has shifted its post-Soviet democratic ambitions in favor of a centralized semi-authoritarian state in which the leadership seeks to legitimize its rule through managed national elections, populist appeals by President PUTIN, and continued economic growth. Russia has severely disabled a Chechen rebel movement, although violence still occurs throughout the North Caucasus.

GEOGRAPHY

Location: North Asia bordering the Arctic Ocean, extending from Europe (the portion west of the Urals) to the North Pacific Ocean

Geographic coordinates: 60 00 N, 100 00 E

Map references: Asia

Area: *total:* 17,098,242 sq km
country comparison to the world: 1
land: 16,377,742 sq km
water: 720,500 sq km

Area—comparative: approximately 1.8 times the size of the US

Land boundaries: *total:* 20,241.5 km
border countries: Azerbaijan 284 km, Belarus 959 km, China (southeast) 3,605 km, China (south) 40 km, Estonia 290 km, Finland 1,313 km, Georgia 723 km, Kazakhstan 6,846 km, North Korea 17.5 km, Latvia 292 km, Lithuania (Kaliningrad Oblast) 227 km, Mongolia 3,441 km, Norway 196 km, Poland (Kaliningrad Oblast) 432 km, Ukraine 1,576 km

Coastline: 37,653 km

Maritime claims: *territorial sea:* 12 nm
contiguous zone: 24 nm
exclusive economic zone: 200 nm
continental shelf: 200 m depth or to the depth of exploitation

Climate: ranges from steppes in the south through humid continental in much of European Russia; subarctic in Siberia to tundra climate in the polar north; winters vary from cool along Black Sea coast to frigid in Siberia; summers vary from warm in the steppes to cool along Arctic coast

Terrain: broad plain with low hills west of Urals; vast coniferous forest and tundra in Siberia; uplands and mountains along southern border regions

Elevation extremes: *lowest point:* Caspian Sea -28 m
highest point: Gora El'brus 5,633 m (highest point in Europe)

Natural resources: wide natural resource base including major deposits of oil, natural gas, coal, and many strategic minerals, reserves of rare earth elements, timber
note: formidable obstacles of climate, terrain, and distance hinder exploitation of natural resources

Land use: *arable land:* 7.11%
permanent crops: 0.1%
other: 92.79% (2011)

Irrigated land: 43,460 sq km (2008)

Total renewable water resources: 4,508 cu km (2011)

Freshwater withdrawal (domestic/industrial/agricultural): *total:* 66.2 cu km/yr (20%/60%/20%)
per capita: 454.9 cu m/yr (2001)

Natural hazards: permafrost over much of Siberia is a major impediment to development; volcanic activity in the Kuril Islands; volcanoes and earthquakes on the Kamchatka Peninsula; spring floods and summer/autumn forest fires throughout Siberia and parts of European Russia
volcanism: significant volcanic activity on the Kamchatka Peninsula and Kuril Islands; the peninsula alone is home to some 29 historically active volcanoes, with dozens more in the Kuril Islands; Kliuchevskoi (elev. 4,835 m), which erupted in 2007 and 2010, is Kamchatka's most active volcano; Avachinsky and Koryaksky volcanoes, which pose a threat to the city of Petropavlovsk-Kamchatskiy, have been deemed Decade Volcanoes by the International Association of Volcanology and Chemistry of the Earth's Interior, worthy of study due to their explosive history and close proximity to human populations; other notable historically active volcanoes include Bezymianny, Chikurachki, Ebeko, Gorely, Grozny, Karymsky, Ketoi, Kronotsky, Ksudach, Medvezhia, Mutnovsky, Sarychev Peak, Shiveluch, Tiatia, Tolbachik, and Zheltovsky

Environment—current issues: air pollution from heavy industry, emissions of coal-fired electric plants, and transportation in major cities; industrial, municipal, and agricultural pollution of inland waterways and seacoasts; deforestation; soil erosion; soil contamination from improper application of agricultural chemicals; scattered areas of sometimes intense radioactive contamination; groundwater contamination from toxic waste; urban solid waste management; abandoned stocks of obsolete pesticides

Environment—international agreements:
party to: Air Pollution, Air Pollution-Nitrogen Oxides, Air Pollution-Sulfur 85, Antarctic-Environmental Protocol, Antarctic-Marine Living Resources, Antarctic Seals, Antarctic Treaty, Biodiversity, Climate Change, Climate Change-Kyoto Protocol, Desertification, Endangered Species, Environmental Modification, Hazardous Wastes, Law of the Sea, Marine Dumping, Ozone Layer Protection, Ship Pollution, Tropical Timber 83, Wetlands, Whaling
signed, but not ratified: Air Pollution-Sulfur 94

Geography—note: largest country in the world in terms of area but unfavorably located in relation to major sea lanes of the world; despite its size, much of the country lacks proper soils and climates (either too cold or too dry) for agriculture; Mount El'brus is Europe's tallest peak; Lake Baikal, the deepest lake in the world, is estimated to hold one fifth of the world's fresh water

PEOPLE AND SOCIETY

Nationality: *noun:* Russian(s)
adjective: Russian

Ethnic groups: Russian 77.7%, Tatar 3.7%, Ukrainian 1.4%, Bashkir 1.1%, Chuvash 1%, Chechen 1%, other 10.2%, unspecified 3.9% (2010 est.)

Languages: Russian (official) 96.3%, Dolgang 5.3%, German 1.5%, Chechen 1%, Tatar 3%, other 10.3%
note: shares sum to more than 100% because some respondents gave more than one answer on the census (2010 est.)

Religions: Russian Orthodox 15-20%, Muslim 10-15%, other Christian 2% (2006 est.)
note: estimates are of practicing worshipers; Russia has large populations of non-practicing believers and non-believers, a legacy of over seven decades of Soviet rule

Population: 142,470,272 (July 2014 est.)
country comparison to the world: 10

Age structure: *0-14 years:* 16.4% (male 11,980,138/female 11,344,818)
15-24 years: 10.7% (male 7,828,947/female 7,482,143)
25-54 years: 45.8% (male 31,928,886/female 33,319,671)
55-64 years: 13.3% (male 8,408,637/female 11,287,153)
65 years and over: 13.1% (male 5,783,983/female 13,105,896) (2014 est.)

Dependency ratios:
total dependency ratio: 40.5 %
youth dependency ratio: 22.2 %
elderly dependency ratio: 18.3 %
potential support ratio: 5.5 (2013)

Median age: *total:* 38.9 years
male: 36 years
female: 41.9 years (2014 est.)

Population growth rate: -0.03% (2014 est.)
country comparison to the world: 200

Birth rate: 11.87 births/1,000 population (2014 est.)
country comparison to the world: 168

Death rate: 13.83 deaths/1,000 population (2014 est.)
country comparison to the world: 10

Net migration rate: 1.69 migrant(s)/1,000 population (2014 est.)
country comparison to the world: 52

Urbanization: *urban population:* 73.8% of total population (2011)
rate of urbanization: 0.13% annual rate of change (2010-15 est.)

Major urban areas—population: MOSCOW (capital) 10.523 million; Saint Petersburg 4.575 million; Novosibirsk 1.397 million; Yekaterinburg 1.344 million; Nizhniy Novgorod 1.267 million (2009)

Sex ratio: *at birth:* 1.06 male(s)/female
0-14 years: 1.06 male(s)/female
15-24 years: 1.05 male(s)/female
25-54 years: 0.96 male(s)/female
55-64 years: 0.86 male(s)/female
65 years and over: 0.44 male(s)/female
total population: 0.86 male(s)/female (2014 est.)

Maternal mortality rate: 34 deaths/100,000 live births (2010)
country comparison to the world: 119

Infant mortality rate: *total:* 7.08 deaths/1,000 live births
country comparison to the world: 160
male: 7.93 deaths/1,000 live births
female: 6.18 deaths/1,000 live births (2014 est.)

Life expectancy at birth:
total population: 70.16 years
country comparison to the world: 151
male: 64.37 years
female: 76.3 years (2014 est.)

Total fertility rate: 1.61 children born/woman (2014 est.)
country comparison to the world: 179

Contraceptive prevalence rate: 79.5%
note: percent of women under age 50 (2007)

Health expenditures: 6.2% of GDP (2011)
country comparison to the world: 103

Physicians density: 4.31 physicians/1,000 population (2006)

Hospital bed density: 9.7 beds/1,000 population (2006)

Drinking water source:

improved:
urban: 98.7% of population
rural: 92.2% of population
total: 97% of population
unimproved:
urban: 1.3% of population
rural: 7.8% of population
total: 3% of population (2011 est.)

Sanitation facility access:
improved:
urban: 74.4% of population
rural: 59.3% of population
total: 70.4% of population
unimproved:
urban: 25.6% of population
rural: 40.7% of population
total: 29.6% of population (2011 est.)

HIV/AIDS—adult prevalence rate: 1% (2009 est.)
country comparison to the world: 47

HIV/AIDS—people living with HIV/AIDS: 980,000 (2009 est.)
country comparison to the world: 12

HIV/AIDS—deaths: NA

Major infectious diseases: *degree of risk:* intermediate
food or waterborne diseases: bacterial diarrhea
vectorborne disease: tickborne encephalitis
note: highly pathogenic H5N1 avian influenza has been identified in this country; it poses a negligible risk with extremely rare cases possible among US citizens who have close contact with birds (2013)

Obesity—adult prevalence rate: 26.5% (2008)
country comparison to the world: 46

Education expenditures: 4.1% of GDP (2008)
country comparison to the world: 110

Literacy: *definition:* age 15 and over can read and write
total population: 99.7%
male: 99.7%
female: 99.6% (2010 est.)

School life expectancy (primary to tertiary education): *total:* 14 years
male: 14 years
female: 15 years (2009)

Unemployment, youth ages 15-24: *total:* 14.8%
country comparison to the world: 84
male: 14.5%
female: 15.1% (2012)

GOVERNMENT

Country name: *conventional long form:* Russian Federation
conventional short form: Russia
local long form: Rossiyskaya Federatsiya
local short form: Rossiya
former: Russian Empire, Russian Soviet Federative Socialist Republic

Government type: federation

Capital: *name:* Moscow

geographic coordinates: 55 45 N, 37 36 E
time difference: UTC+4 (9 hours ahead of Washington, DC during Standard Time)
daylight saving time: +1hr; note—Russia has announced that it will remain on daylight saving time permanently, which began on 27 March 2011
note: Russia is divided into 9 time zones

Administrative divisions: 46 provinces (oblastey, singular—oblast), 21 republics (respublik, singular—respublika), 4 autonomous okrugs (avtonomnykh okrugov, singular—avtonomnyy okrug), 9 krays (krayev, singular—kray), 2 federal cities (goroda, singular—gorod), and 1 autonomous oblast (avtonomnaya oblast')
oblasts: Amur (Blagoveshchensk), Arkhangel'sk, Astrakhan', Belgorod, Bryansk, Chelyabinsk, Irkutsk, Ivanovo, Kaliningrad, Kaluga, Kemerovo, Kirov, Kostroma, Kurgan, Kursk, Leningrad, Lipetsk, Magadan, Moscow, Murmansk, Nizhniy Novgorod, Novgorod, Novosibirsk, Omsk, Orenburg, Orel, Penza, Pskov, Rostov, Ryazan', Sakhalin (Yuzhno-Sakhalinsk), Samara, Saratov, Smolensk, Sverdlovsk (Yekaterinburg), Tambov, Tomsk, Tula, Tver', Tyumen', Ul'yanovsk, Vladimir, Volgograd, Vologda, Voronezh, Yaroslavl'
republics: Adygeya (Maykop), Altay (Gorno-Altaysk), Bashkortostan (Ufa), Buryatiya (Ulan-Ude), Chechnya (Groznyy), Chuvashiya (Cheboksary), Dagestan (Makhachkala), Ingushetiya (Magas), Kabardino-Balkariya (Nal'chik), Kalmykiya (Elista), Karachayevo-Cherkesiya (Cherkessk), Kareliya (Petrozavodsk), Khakasiya (Abakan), Komi (Syktyvkar), Mariy-El (Yoshkar-Ola), Mordoviya (Saransk), North Ossetia (Vladikavkaz), Sakha [Yakutiya] (Yakutsk), Tatarstan (Kazan'), Tyva (Kyzyl), Udmurtiya (Izhevsk)
autonomous okrugs: Chukotka (Anadyr'), Khanty-Mansi (Khanty-Mansiysk), Nenets (Nar'yan-Mar), Yamalo-Nenets (Salekhard)
krays: Altay (Barnaul), Kamchatka (Petropavlovsk-Kamchatskiy), Khabarovsk, Krasnodar, Krasnoyarsk, Perm', Primorskiy [Maritime] (Vladivostok), Stavropol', Zabaykal'sk (Chita)
federal cities: Moscow [Moskva], Saint Petersburg [Sankt-Peterburg]
autonomous oblast: Yevrey [Jewish] (Birobidzhan)
note 1: administrative divisions have the same names as their administrative centers (exceptions have the administrative center name following in parentheses)
note 2: the United States does not recognize Russia's annexation of Ukraine's Autonomous Republic of Crimea and the municipality of Sevastopol, nor their redesignation as the Republic of Crimea and the Federal City of Sevastopol

Independence: 24 August 1991 (from the Soviet Union); notable earlier dates: 1157 (Principality of Vladimir-Suzdal created); 16 January 1547 (Tsardom of Muscovy established); 22 October 1721 (Russian Empire proclaimed); 30 December 1922 (Soviet Union established)

National holiday: Russia Day, 12 June (1990)

Constitution: several previous (during Russian Empire and Soviet eras); latest drafted 12 July 1993, adopted by referendum 12 December 1993, effective 25 December 1993; amended 2008 (2013)

Legal system: civil law system; judicial review of legislative acts

International law organization participation: has not submitted an ICJ jurisdiction declaration; non-party state to the ICCt

Suffrage: 18 years of age; universal

Executive branch: *chief of state:* President Vladimir Vladimirovich PUTIN (since 7 May 2012)
head of government: Premier Dmitriy Anatolyevich MEDVEDEV (since 8 May 2012); First Deputy Premier Igor Ivanovich SHUVALOV (since 12 May 2008); Deputy Premiers Arkadiy Vladimirovich DVORKOVICH (since 21 May 2012), Olga Yuryevna GOLODETS (since 21 May 2012), Aleksandr Gennadiyevich KHLOPONIN (since 19 January 2010), Dmitriy Nikolayevich KOZAK (since 14 October 2008), Dmitriy Olegovich ROGOZIN (since 23 December 2011), Sergey Eduardovich PRIKHODKO (since 22 May 2013), Yuriy Petrovich TRUTNEV (since 31 August 2013)
cabinet: the "Government" is composed of the premier, his deputies, and ministers; all are appointed by the president, and the premier is also confirmed by the Duma (For more information visit the World Leaders website)
note: there is also a Presidential Administration (PA) that provides staff and policy support to the president, drafts presidential decrees, and coordinates policy among government agencies; a Security Council also reports directly to the president
elections: president elected by popular vote for a six-year term (eligible for a second term); election last held 4 March 2012 (next to be held in March 2018); note—the term length was extended from four to six years in late 2008 and went into effect after the 2012 election; there is no vice president; if the president dies in office, cannot exercise his powers because of ill health, is impeached, or resigns, the premier serves as acting president until a new presidential election is held, which must be within three months; premier appointed by the president with the approval of the Duma
election results: Vladimir PUTIN elected president; percent of vote—Vladimir PUTIN 63.6%, Gennadiy ZYUGANOV 17.2%, Mikhail PROKHOROV 8%, Vladimir ZHIRINOVSKIY 6.2%, Sergey MIRONOV 3.9%, other 1.1%; Dmitriy MEDVEDEV approved as premier by Duma 299 to 144

Legislative branch: bicameral Federal Assembly or Federalnoye Sobraniye consists of an upper house, the Federation Council or Sovet Federatsii (166 seats; members appointed by the top executive and legislative officials in each of the 83 federal administrative units—oblasts, krays, republics, autonomous okrugs and oblasts, and the federal cities of Moscow and Saint Petersburg; members to serve four-year terms) and a lower house, the State Duma or Gosudarstvennaya Duma (450 seats; as of 2007, all members elected by proportional representation from party lists winning at least 7% of the vote; members elected by popular vote to serve four-year terms)
elections: State Duma—last held on 4 December 2011 (next to be held in December 2015)
election results: State Duma—United Russia 49.6%, CPRF 19.2%, Just Russia 13.2%, LDPR 11.7%, other 6.3%; total seats by party—United Russia 238, CPRF 92, Just Russia 64, LDPR 56

Judicial branch: *highest court(s):* Supreme Court of the Russian Federation (consists of 23 members); Constitutional Court (consists of 19 members); Superior Court of Arbitration (consists of a chairman and 4 deputy chairmen); note—as of January 2014 legislation was pending that would merge the Constitutional Court and Superior Court of Arbitration
judge selection and term of office: all members of Russia's three highest courts nominated by the president and appointed by the Federation Council (the upper house of the legislature); members of all three courts appointed for life
subordinate courts: Higher Arbitration Court; regional (kray) and provincial (oblast) courts; Moscow and St. Petersburg city courts; autonomous province and district courts; note—the 14 Russian Republics have court systems specified by their own constitutions

Political parties and leaders: seventy eight political parties are registered with Russia's Ministry of Justice (as of January 2014), but only

four parties maintain representation in Russia's national legislature:
A Just Russia [Sergey MIRONOV]; Communist Party of the Russian Federation or CPRF [Gennadiy ZYUGANOV]; Liberal Democratic Party of Russia or LDPR [Vladimir ZHIRINOVSKIY]; United Russia [Dmitriy MEDVEDEV]

Political pressure groups and leaders: Confederation of Labor of Russia (KTR); Federation of Independent Trade Unions of Russia; Golos Association in Defense of Voters' Rights; Memorial; Movement Against Illegal Migration; Russkiye; Solidarnost; The World Russian People's Congress; Union of the Committees of Soldiers' Mothers; Union of Russian Writers; other—business associations, environmental organizations, religious groups (especially those with Orthodox or Muslim affiliation), and veterans groups

International organization participation: APEC, Arctic Council, ARF, ASEAN (dialogue partner), BIS, BRICS, BSEC, CBSS, CD, CE, CERN (observer), CICA, CIS, CSTO, EAEC, EAPC, EAS, EBRD, FAO, FATF, G-20, GCTU, IAEA, IBRD, ICAO, ICC (national committees), ICRM, IDA, IFC, IFRCS, IHO, ILO, IMF, IMO, IMSO, Interpol, IOC, IOM (observer), IPU, ISO, ITSO, ITU, ITUC (NGOs), LAIA (observer), MIGA, MINURSO, MONUSCO, NSG, OAS (observer), OIC (observer), OPCW, OSCE, Paris Club, PCA, PFP, SCO, UN, UNCTAD, UNESCO, UNHCR, UNIDO, UNISFA, UNMIL, UNMISS, UNOCI, UNSC (permanent), UNTSO, UNWTO, UPU, WCO, WFTU (NGOs), WHO, WIPO, WMO, WTO, ZC

Diplomatic representation in the US:
chief of mission: Ambassador Sergey Ivanovich KISLYAK (since 16 September 2008)
chancery: 2650 Wisconsin Avenue NW, Washington, DC 20007
telephone: [1] (202) 298-5700, 5701, 5704, 5708
FAX: [1] (202) 298-5735
consulate(s) general: Houston, New York, San Francisco, Seattle

Diplomatic representation from the US:
chief of mission: Chargé d'Affaires Sheila GWALTNEY (since 27 February 2014)
embassy: Bolshoy Deviatinskiy Pereulok No. 8, 121099 Moscow
mailing address: PSC-77, APO AE 09721
telephone: [7] (495) 728-5000
FAX: [7] (495) 728-5090
consulate(s) general: Saint Petersburg, Vladivostok, Yekaterinburg

Flag description: three equal horizontal bands of white (top), blue, and red
note: the colors may have been based on those of the Dutch flag; despite many popular interpretations, there is no official meaning assigned to the colors of the Russian flag; this flag inspired other Slav countries to adopt horizontal tricolors of the same colors but in different arrangements, and so red, blue, and white became the Pan-Slav colors

National symbol(s): bear; double-headed eagle

National anthem: *name:* "Gimn Rossiyskoy Federatsii" (National Anthem of the Russian Federation)
lyrics/music: Sergey Vladimirovich MIKHALKOV/Aleksandr Vasilyevich ALEKSANDROV
note: in 2000, Russia adopted the tune of the anthem of the former Soviet Union (composed in 1939); the lyrics, also adopted in 2000, were written by the same person who authored the Soviet lyrics in 1943

ECONOMY

Economy—overview: Russia has undergone significant changes since the collapse of the Soviet Union, moving from a globally-isolated, centrally-planned economy towards a more market-based and globally-integrated economy, but stalling as a partially reformed, statist economy with a high concentration of wealth in officials' hands. Economic reforms in the 1990s privatized most industry, with notable exceptions in the energy and defense-related sectors. The protection of property rights is still weak and the private sector remains subject to heavy state interference. Russia is one of the world's leading producers of oil and natural gas and is also a top exporter of metals such as steel and primary aluminum. Russia's manufacturing sector is generally uncompetitive on world markets and is geared toward domestic consumption. Russia's reliance on commodity exports makes it vulnerable to boom and bust cycles that follow the volatile swings in global prices. The economy, which had averaged 7% growth during 1998-2008 as oil prices rose rapidly, was one of the hardest hit by the 2008-09 global economic crisis as oil prices plummeted and the foreign credits that Russian banks and firms relied on dried up. Slowly declining oil prices over the past few years and difficulty attracting foreign direct investment have contributed to a noticeable slowdown in GDP growth rates. In late 2013, the Russian Economic Development Ministry reduced its growth forecast through 2030 to an average of only 2.5% per year, down from its previous forecast of 4.0 to 4.2%. In 2014, following Russia's military intervention in Ukraine, prospects for economic growth declined further, with expectations that GDP growth could drop as low as zero.

GDP (purchasing power parity): $2.553 trillion (2013 est.)
country comparison to the world: 7
$2.52 trillion (2012 est.)
$2.437 trillion (2011 est.)
note: data are in 2013 US dollars

GDP (official exchange rate): $2.113 trillion (2013 est.)

GDP—real growth rate: 1.3% (2013 est.)
country comparison to the world: 166
3.4% (2012 est.)
4.3% (2011 est.)

GDP—per capita (PPP): $18,100 (2013 est.)
country comparison to the world: 77
$17,800 (2012 est.)
$17,100 (2011 est.)
note: data are in 2013 US dollars

Gross national saving: 28.3% of GDP (2013 est.)
country comparison to the world: 33
29.5% of GDP (2012 est.)
30.6% of GDP (2011 est.)

GDP—composition, by end use:
household consumption: 51.3%
government consumption: 18.8%
investment in fixed capital: 22%
investment in inventories: 1.4%
exports of goods and services: 29.6%
imports of goods and services: -23% (2013 est.)

GDP—composition, by sector of origin:
agriculture: 4.2%
industry: 37.5%
services: 58.3% (2013 est.)

Agriculture—products: grain, sugar beets, sunflower seed, vegetables, fruits; beef, milk

Industries: complete range of mining and extractive industries producing coal, oil, gas, chemicals, and metals; all forms of machine building from rolling mills to high-performance aircraft and space vehicles; defense industries including radar, missile production, and advanced electronic components, shipbuilding; road and rail transportation equipment; communications equipment; agricultural machinery, tractors, and construction equipment; electric power generating and transmitting equipment; medical and scientific instruments; consumer durables, textiles, foodstuffs, handicrafts

Industrial production growth rate: 0.1% (2013 est.)
country comparison to the world: 167

Labor force: 75.29 million (2013 est.)
country comparison to the world: 8

Labor force—by occupation: *agriculture:* 9.7%
industry: 27.8%
services: 62.5% (2012)

Unemployment rate: 5.8% (2013 est.)
country comparison to the world: 55
5.5% (2012 est.)

Population below poverty line: 11% (2013 est.)

Household income or consumption by percentage share: *lowest 10%:* 5.7%
highest 10%: 42.4% (2011 est.)

Distribution of family income—Gini index: 42 (2012)
country comparison to the world: 50
41.7 (2011)

Budget: *revenues:* $439 billion
expenditures: $450.3 billion (2013 est.)

Taxes and other revenues: 20.7% of GDP (2013 est.)
country comparison to the world: 159

Budget surplus (+) or deficit (-):
-0.5% of GDP (2013 est.)
country comparison to the world: 56

Public debt: 7.9% of GDP (2013 est.)
country comparison to the world: 150
8% of GDP (2012 est.)
note: data cover general government debt, and includes debt instruments issued (or owned) by government entities other than the treasury; the data include treasury debt held by foreign entities; the data include debt issued by subnational entities, as well as intra-governmental debt; intra-governmental debt consists of treasury borrowings from surpluses in the social funds, such as for retirement, medical care, and unemployment, debt instruments for the social funds are not sold at public auctions

Fiscal year: calendar year

Inflation rate (consumer prices): 6.8% (2013 est.)
country comparison to the world: 185
5.1% (2012 est.)

Central bank discount rate: 8.25% (31 December 2012 est.)
country comparison to the world: 32
8% (31 December 2011)
note: this is the so-called refinancing rate, but in Russia banks do not get refinancing at this rate; this is a reference rate used primarily for fiscal purposes

Commercial bank prime lending rate: 9.3% (31 December 2013 est.)
country comparison to the world: 99
9.1% (31 December 2012 est.)

Stock of narrow money: $452.8 billion (31 December 2012 est.)
country comparison to the world: 13
$399.3 billion (31 December 2011 est.)

Stock of broad money: $1.061 trillion (31 December 2012 est.)

country comparison to the world: 18
$893.1 billion (31 December 2011 est.)

Stock of domestic credit: $947 billion (31 December 2013 est.)
country comparison to the world: 17
$922.6 billion (31 December 2012 est.)

Market value of publicly traded shares: $874.7 billion (31 December 2012 est.)
country comparison to the world: 17
$796.4 billion (31 December 2011)
$1.005 trillion (31 December 2010 est.)

Current account balance: $74.8 billion (2012 est.)
country comparison to the world: 5
$71.43 billion (2012 est.)

Exports: $515 billion (2013 est.)
country comparison to the world: 9
$528 billion (2012 est.)

Exports—commodities: petroleum and petroleum products, natural gas, metals, wood and wood products, chemicals, and a wide variety of civilian and military manufactures

Exports—partners: Netherlands 14.6%, China 6.8%, Germany 6.8%, Italy 6.2%, Turkey 5.2%, Ukraine 5.2%, Belarus 4.7% (2012 est.)

Imports: $341 billion (2013 est.)
country comparison to the world: 17
$335.7 billion (2012 est.)

Imports—commodities: machinery, vehicles, pharmaceutical products, plastic, semi-finished metal products, meat, fruits and nuts, optical and medical instruments, iron, steel

Imports—partners: China 16.6%, Germany 12.2%, Ukraine 5.7%, Japan 5%, United States 4.9%, France 4.4%, Italy 4.3% (2012 est.)

Reserves of foreign exchange and gold: $515.6 billion (01 December 2013 est.)
country comparison to the world: 6
$537.6 billion (31 December 2012 est.)

Debt—external: $714.2 billion (30 September 2013 est.)
country comparison to the world: 22
$636.4 billion (31 December 2012 est.)

Stock of direct foreign investment—at home: $552.8 billion (31 December 2013 est.)
country comparison to the world: 16
$497.8 billion (31 December 2012 est.)

Stock of direct foreign investment—abroad: $439.2 billion (31 December 2013 est.)
country comparison to the world: 18
$387.2 billion (31 December 2012 est.)

Exchange rates: Russian rubles (RUB) per US dollar—
31.82 (2013 est.)
30.84 (2012 est.)
30.368 (2010 est.)
31.74 (2009)
24.853 (2008)

ENERGY

Electricity—production: 1.057 trillion kWh (2013 est.)
country comparison to the world: 4

Electricity—consumption: 1.038 trillion kWh (2012 est.)
country comparison to the world: 4

Electricity—exports: 19.14 billion kWh (2012 est.)
country comparison to the world: 11

Electricity—imports: 2.661 billion kWh (2012 est.)
country comparison to the world: 50

Electricity—installed generating capacity: 223.1 million kW (2012 est.)
country comparison to the world: 5

Electricity—from fossil fuels: 67.7% of total installed capacity (2012 est.)
country comparison to the world: 113

Electricity—from nuclear fuels: 17.8% of total installed capacity (2012 est.)
country comparison to the world: 12

Electricity—from hydroelectric plants: 15.1% of total installed capacity (2012 est.)
country comparison to the world: 101

Electricity—from other renewable sources: 0% of total installed capacity (2012 est.)
country comparison to the world: 117

Crude oil—production: 10.44 million bbl/day (2013 est.)
country comparison to the world: 3

Crude oil—exports: 4.72 million bbl/day (2013 est.)
country comparison to the world: 2

Crude oil—imports: 16,380 bbl/day (2012 est.)
country comparison to the world: 69

Crude oil—proved reserves: 80 billion bbl (1 January 2013 es)
country comparison to the world: 8

Refined petroleum products—production: 4.812 million bbl/day (2010 est.)
country comparison to the world: 4

Refined petroleum products—consumption: 3.196 million bbl/day (2012 est.)
country comparison to the world: 6

Refined petroleum products—exports: 2.92 million bbl/day (2012 est.)
country comparison to the world: 1

Refined petroleum products—imports: 24,300 bbl/day (2013 est.)
country comparison to the world: 97

Natural gas—production: 669.7 billion cu m (2013 est.)
country comparison to the world: 2

Natural gas—consumption: 457.2 billion cu m (2013 est.)
country comparison to the world: 2

Natural gas—exports: 196 billion cu m (2013 est.)
country comparison to the world: 1

Natural gas—imports: 32.5 billion cu m (2012 est.)
country comparison to the world: 18

Natural gas—proved reserves: 47.8 trillion cu m (1 January 2013 es)
country comparison to the world: 1

Carbon dioxide emissions from consumption of energy: 1.788 billion Mt (2011 est.)
country comparison to the world: 4

COMMUNICATIONS

Telephones—main lines in use: 42.9 million (2012)
country comparison to the world: 6

Telephones—mobile cellular: 261.9 million (2012)
country comparison to the world: 5

Telephone system: *general assessment:* the telephone system is experiencing significant changes; there are more than 1,000 companies licensed to offer communication services; access to digital lines has improved, particularly in urban centers; Internet and e-mail services are improving; Russia has made progress toward building the telecommunications infrastructure necessary for a market economy; the estimated number of mobile subscribers jumped from fewer than 1 million in 1998 to more than 235 million in 2011; fixed line service has improved but a large demand remains
domestic: cross-country digital trunk lines run from Saint Petersburg to Khabarovsk, and from Moscow to Novorossiysk; the telephone systems in 60 regional capitals have modern digital infrastructures; cellular services, both analog and digital, are available in many areas; in rural areas, the telephone services are still outdated, inadequate, and low density
international: country code—7; Russia is connected internationally by undersea fiber optic cables; satellite earth stations provide access to Intelsat, Intersputnik, Eutelsat, Inmarsat, and Orbita systems (2011)

Broadcast media: 6 national TV stations with the federal government owning 1 and holding a controlling interest in a second; state-owned Gazprom maintains a controlling interest in a third national channel; government-affiliated Bank Rossiya owns controlling interest in a fourth and fifth, while the sixth national channel is owned by the Moscow city administration; roughly 3,300 national, regional, and local TV stations with over two-thirds completely or partially controlled by the federal or local governments; satellite TV services are available; 2 state-run national radio networks with a third majority-owned by Gazprom; roughly 2,400 public and commercial radio stations (2007)

Internet country code: .ru; note—Russia also has responsibility for a legacy domain ".su" that was allocated to the Soviet Union and is being phased out

Internet hosts: 14.865 million (2012)
country comparison to the world: 10

Internet users: 40.853 million (2009)
country comparison to the world: 10

TRANSPORTATION

Airports: 1,218 (2013)
country comparison to the world: 5

Airports—with paved runways: *total:* 594
over 3,047 m: 54
2,438 to 3,047 m: 197
1,524 to 2,437 m: 123
914 to 1,523 m: 95
under 914 m: 125 (2013)

Airports—with unpaved runways: *total:* 624
over 3,047 m: 4
2,438 to 3,047 m: 13
1,524 to 2,437 m: 69
914 to 1,523 m: 81
under 914 m: 457 (2013)

Heliports: 49 (2013)

Pipelines: condensate 122 km; gas 163,872 km; liquid petroleum gas 1,378 km; oil 80,820 km; oil/gas/water 40 km; refined products 13,658 km; water 23 km (2013)

Railways: *total:* 87,157 km
country comparison to the world: 2
broad gauge: 86,200 km 1.520-m gauge (40,300 km electrified)
narrow gauge: 957 km 1.067-m gauge (on Sakhalin Island)
note: an additional 30,000 km of non-common carrier lines serve industries (2006)

Roadways: *total:* 1,283,387 km
country comparison to the world: 5
paved: 927,721 km (includes 39,143 km of expressways)
unpaved: 355,666 km (2012)

Waterways: 102,000 km (including 48,000 km with guaranteed depth; the 72,000 km system in

European Russia links Baltic Sea, White Sea, Caspian Sea, Sea of Azov, and Black Sea) (2009)
country comparison to the world: 2

Merchant marine: *total:* 1,143
country comparison to the world: 11
by type: bulk carrier 20, cargo 642, carrier 3, chemical tanker 57, combination ore/oil 42, container 13, passenger 15, passenger/cargo 7, petroleum tanker 244, refrigerated cargo 84, roll on/roll off 13, specialized tanker 3
foreign-owned: 155 (Belgium 4, Cyprus 13, Estonia 1, Ireland 1, Italy 14, Latvia 2, Netherlands 2, Romania 1, South Korea 1, Switzerland 3, Turkey 101, Ukraine 12)
registered in other countries: 439 (Antigua and Barbuda 3, Belgium 1, Belize 30, Bulgaria 2, Cambodia 50, Comoros 12, Cook Islands 1, Cyprus 46, Dominica 3, Georgia 6, Hong Kong 1, Kiribati 1, Liberia 109, Malaysia 2, Malta 45, Marshall Islands 5, Moldova 5, Mongolia 2, Panama 49, Romania 1, Saint Kitts and Nevis 13, Saint Vincent and the Grenadines 11, Sierra Leone 7, Singapore 2, Spain 6, Vanuatu 7, unknown 19) (2010)

Ports and terminals: *major seaport(s):* Kaliningrad, Nakhodka, Novorossiysk, Primorsk, Vostochnyy
river port(s): Saint Petersburg (Neva River)
oil terminal(s): Kavkaz oil terminal
container port(s) (TEUs): Saint Petersburg (2,365,174)

MILITARY

Military branches: Ground Troops (Sukhoputnyye Voyskia, SV), Navy (Voyenno-Morskoy Flot, VMF), Air Forces (Voyenno-Vozdushniye Sily, VVS); Airborne Troops (Vozdushno-Desantnyye Voyska, VDV), Missile Troops of Strategic Purpose (Raketnyye Voyska Strategicheskogo Naznacheniya, RVSN) referred to commonly as Strategic Rocket Forces, and Aerospace Defense Troops (Voyska Vozdushno-Kosmicheskoy Oborony or Voyska VKO) are independent "combat arms," not subordinate to any of the three branches; Russian Ground Troops include the *following combat arms:* motorized-rifle troops, tank troops, missile and artillery troops, air defense of the Ground Troops (2014)

Military service age and obligation: 18-27 years of age for compulsory or voluntary military service; males are registered for the draft at 17 years of age; service obligation is 1 year (conscripts can only be sent to combat zones after 6 months of training); reserve obligation for non-officers to age 50; enrollment in military schools from the age of 16, cadets classified as members of the armed forces
note: the chief of the General Staff Mobilization Directorate announced in May 2013 that for health reasons, only 65% of draftees called up during the spring 2013 draft campaign were fit for military service, and over 12% of these were sent for an additional medical examination (by way of comparison, 69.9% in 2012 and 57.7% in 2011 were deemed fit for military service); approximately 50% of draft-age Russian males receive some type of legal deferment each draft cycle (2014)

Manpower available for military service:
males age 16-49: 34,765,736
females age 16-49: 35,410,779 (2013 est.)

Manpower fit for military service:
males age 16-49: 22,597,728
females age 16-49: 23,017,006 (2013 est.)

Manpower reaching militarily significant age annually: *male:* 696,768
female: 664,847 (2013 est.)

Military expenditures: 4.47% of GDP (2012)
country comparison to the world: 8
4.13% of GDP (2011)
4.47% of GDP (2010)

TRANSNATIONAL ISSUES

Disputes—international: Russia remains concerned about the smuggling of poppy derivatives from Afghanistan through Central Asian countries; China and Russia have demarcated the once disputed islands at the Amur and Ussuri confluence and in the Argun River in accordance with the 2004 Agreement, ending their centuries-long border disputes; the sovereignty dispute over the islands of Etorofu, Kunashiri, Shikotan, and the Habomai group, known in Japan as the "Northern Territories" and in Russia as the "Southern Kurils," occupied by the Soviet Union in 1945, now administered by Russia, and claimed by Japan, remains the primary sticking point to signing a peace treaty formally ending World War II hostilities; Russia's military support and subsequent recognition of Abkhazia and South Ossetia independence in 2008 continue to sour relations with Georgia; Azerbaijan, Kazakhstan, and Russia ratified Caspian seabed delimitation treaties based on equidistance, while Iran continues to insist on a one-fifth slice of the sea; Norway and Russia signed a comprehensive maritime boundary agreement in 2010; various groups in Finland advocate restoration of Karelia (Kareliya) and other areas ceded to the Soviet Union following World War II but the Finnish Government asserts no territorial demands; Russia and Estonia signed a technical border agreement in May 2005, but Russia recalled its signature in June 2005 after the Estonian parliament added to its domestic ratification act a historical preamble referencing the Soviet occupation and Estonia's pre-war borders under the 1920 Treaty of Tartu; Russia contends that the preamble allows Estonia to make territorial claims on Russia in the future, while Estonian officials deny that the preamble has any legal impact on the treaty text; Russia demands better treatment of the Russian-speaking population in Estonia and Latvia; Lithuania and Russia committed to demarcating their boundary in 2006 in accordance with the land and maritime treaty ratified by Russia in May 2003 and by Lithuania in 1999; Lithuania operates a simplified transit regime for Russian nationals traveling from the Kaliningrad coastal exclave into Russia, while still conforming, as an EU member state with an EU external border, where strict Schengen border rules apply; preparations for the demarcation delimitation of land boundary with Ukraine have commenced; the dispute over the boundary between Russia and Ukraine through the Kerch Strait and Sea of Azov remains unresolved despite a December 2003 framework agreement and on-going expert-level discussions; Kazakhstan and Russia boundary delimitation was ratified on November 2005 and field demarcation should commence in 2007; Russian Duma has not yet ratified 1990 Bering Sea Maritime Boundary Agreement with the US; Denmark (Greenland) and Norway have made submissions to the Commission on the Limits of the Continental shelf (CLCS) and Russia is collecting additional data to augment its 2001 CLCS submission

Refugees and internally displaced persons:
IDPs: 8,500-28,450 (displacement from Chechnya and North Ossetia-Alania) (2011)
stateless persons: 178,000 (2012); note—Russia's stateless population consists of Roma, Meskhetian Turks, and ex-Soviet citizens from the former republics; between 2003 and 2010 more than 600,000 stateless people were naturalized; most Meskhetian Turks, followers of Islam with origins in Georgia, fled or were evacuated from Uzbekistan after a 1989 pogrom and have lived in Russia for more than the required five-year residency period; they continue to be denied registration for citizenship and basic rights by local Krasnodar Krai authorities on the grounds that they are temporary illegal migrants

Trafficking in persons: *current situation:* Russia is a source, transit, and destination country for men, women, and children who are subjected to forced labor and sex trafficking, although labor trafficking is the predominant problem; people from Russia and other countries in Europe, Central Asia, and Asia, including Vietnam and North Korea, are subjected to conditions of forced labor in Russia's construction, manufacturing, agriculture, repair shop, and domestic services industries, as well as forced begging and narcotics cultivation; North Koreans contracted under bilateral government arrangements to work in the timber industry in the Russian Far East reportedly are subjected to forced labor; Russian women and children were reported to be victims of sex trafficking in Russia, Northeast Asia, Europe, Central Asia, and the Middle East, while women from European, African, and Central Asian countries were reportedly forced into prostitution in Russia

tier rating: Tier 3—Russia does not fully comply with the minimum standards for the elimination of trafficking and because it is not deemed to be making significant efforts to do so was downgraded to Tier 3 after the maximum of two consecutive annual waivers; the number of prosecutions remains low compared to estimates of Russia's trafficking problem; the government did not develop or deploy a formal system for the identification of trafficking victims or their referral to protective services, although some victims were reportedly cared for through ad hoc efforts; the government has reported minimal efforts to identify or care for the large number of migrant workers vulnerable to labor exploitation and has not investigated allegations of slave-like conditions in North Korean-operated timber camps (2013)

Illicit drugs: limited cultivation of illicit cannabis and opium poppy and producer of methamphetamine, mostly for domestic consumption; government has active illicit crop eradication program; used as transshipment point for Asian opiates, cannabis, and Latin American cocaine bound for growing domestic markets, to a lesser extent Western and Central Europe, and occasionally to the US; major source of heroin precursor chemicals; corruption and organized crime are key concerns; major consumer of opiates

RWANDA

INTRODUCTION

Background: In 1959, three years before independence from Belgium, the majority ethnic group, the Hutus, overthrew the ruling Tutsi king. Over the next several years, thousands of Tutsis were killed, and some 150,000 driven into exile in neighboring countries. The children of these exiles later formed a rebel group, the Rwandan Patriotic Front (RPF), and began a civil war in 1990. The war, along with several political and economic upheavals, exacerbated ethnic tensions, culminating in April 1994 in a state-orchestrated genocide, in which Rwandans killed up to a million of their fellow citizens, including approximately three-quarters of the Tutsi population. The genocide ended later that same year when the predominantly Tutsi RPF, operating out of Uganda and northern Rwanda, defeated the national army and Hutu militias, and established an RPF-led government of national unity. Approximately 2 million Hutu refugees—many fearing Tutsi retribution—fled to neighboring Burundi, Tanzania, Uganda, and former Zaire. Since then, most of the refugees have returned to Rwanda, but several thousand remained in the neighboring Democratic Republic of the Congo (DRC, the former Zaire) and formed an extremist insurgency bent on retaking Rwanda, much as the RPF did in 1990. Rwanda held its first local elections in 1999 and its first post-genocide presidential and legislative elections in 2003. Rwanda in 2009 staged a joint military operation with the Congolese Army in DRC to rout out the Hutu extremist insurgency there, and Kigali and Kinshasa restored diplomatic relations. Rwanda also joined the Commonwealth in late 2009. In January 2013, Rwanda assumed a nonpermanent seat on the UN Security Council for the 2013-14 term.

GEOGRAPHY

Location: Central Africa, east of Democratic Republic of the Congo

Geographic coordinates: 2 00 S, 30 00 E

Map references: Africa

Area: *total:* 26,338 sq km
country comparison to the world: 149
land: 24,668 sq km
water: 1,670 sq km

Area—comparative: slightly smaller than Maryland

Land boundaries: *total:* 893 km
border countries: Burundi 290 km, Democratic Republic of the Congo 217 km, Tanzania 217 km, Uganda 169 km

Coastline: 0 km (landlocked)

Maritime claims: none (landlocked)

Climate: temperate; two rainy seasons (February to April, November to January); mild in mountains with frost and snow possible

Terrain: mostly grassy uplands and hills; relief is mountainous with altitude declining from west to east

Elevation extremes: *lowest point:* Rusizi River 950 m
highest point: Volcan Karisimbi 4,519 m

Natural resources: gold, cassiterite (tin ore), wolframite (tungsten ore), methane, hydropower, arable land

Land use: *arable land:* 46.32%
permanent crops: 9.49%
other: 44.19% (2011)

Irrigated land: 96.25 sq km (2007)

Total renewable water resources: 9.5 cu km (2011)

Freshwater withdrawal (domestic/industrial/agricultural): *total:* 0.15 cu km/yr (33%/11%/55%)
per capita: 17.25 cu m/yr (2005)

Natural hazards: periodic droughts; the volcanic Virunga mountains are in the northwest along the border with Democratic Republic of the Congo
volcanism: Visoke (elev. 3,711 m), located on the border with the Democratic Republic of the Congo, is the country's only historically active volcano

Environment—current issues: deforestation results from uncontrolled cutting of trees for fuel; overgrazing; soil exhaustion; soil erosion; widespread poaching

Environment—international agreements:
party to: Biodiversity, Climate Change, Climate Change-Kyoto Protocol, Desertification, Endangered Species, Hazardous Wastes, Ozone Layer Protection, Wetlands
signed, but not ratified: Law of the Sea

Geography—note: landlocked; most of the country is savanna grassland with the population predominantly rural

PEOPLE AND SOCIETY

Nationality: *noun:* Rwandan(s)
adjective: Rwandan

Ethnic groups: Hutu (Bantu) 84%, Tutsi (Hamitic) 15%, Twa (Pygmy) 1%

Languages: Kinyarwanda only (official, universal Bantu vernacular) 93.2%, Kinyarwanda and other language(s) 6.2%, French (official) and other language(s) 0.1%, English (official) and other language(s) 0.1%, Swahili (or Kiswahili, used in commercial centers) 0.02%, other 0.03%, unspecified 0.3% (2002 est.)

Religions: Roman Catholic 49.5%, Protestant 39.4% (includes Adventist 12.2% and other Protestant 27.2%), other Christian 4.5%, Muslim 1.8%, animist 0.1%, other 0.6%, none 3.6% (2001), unspecified 0.5% (2002 est.)

Population: 12,337,138 (July 2014 est.)
country comparison to the world: 74
note: estimates for this country explicitly take into account the effects of excess mortality due to AIDS; this can result in lower life expectancy, higher infant mortality, higher death rates, lower population growth rates, and changes in the distribution of population by age and sex than would otherwise be expected

Age structure:
0-14 years: 42.1% (male 2,617,472/female 2,575,429)
15-24 years: 18.9% (male 1,166,258/female 1,167,934)
25-54 years: 32.5% (male 2,010,034/female 1,994,582)
55-64 years: 2.5% (male 229,759/female 267,430)
65 years and over: 2.5% (male 125,862/female 182,378) (2014 est.)

Dependency ratios:
total dependency ratio: 82.8 %
youth dependency ratio: 78.5 %
elderly dependency ratio: 4.3 %
potential support ratio: 23 (2013)

Median age: *total:* 18.7 years
male: 18.4 years
female: 18.9 years (2014 est.)

Population growth rate: 2.63% (2014 est.)
country comparison to the world: 23

Birth rate: 34.61 births/1,000 population (2014 est.)
country comparison to the world: 28

Death rate: 9.18 deaths/1,000 population (2014 est.)
country comparison to the world: 64

Net migration rate: 0.9 migrant(s)/1,000 population (2014 est.)
country comparison to the world: 63

Urbanization: *urban population:* 19.1% of total population (2011)
rate of urbanization: 4.5% annual rate of change (2010-15 est.)

Major urban areas—population: KIGALI (capital) 909,000 (2009)

Sex ratio: *at birth:* 1.03 male(s)/female
0-14 years: 1.02 male(s)/female
15-24 years: 1 male(s)/female
25-54 years: 1.01 male(s)/female
55-64 years: 0.99 male(s)/female
65 years and over: 0.67 male(s)/female
total population: 0.99 male(s)/female (2014 est.)

Mother's mean age at first birth: 22.9
note: median age at first birth among women 25-29 (2010 est.)

Maternal mortality rate: 340 deaths/100,000 live births (2010)
country comparison to the world: 35

Infant mortality rate: *total:* 59.59 deaths/1,000 live births
country comparison to the world: 23
male: 63.11 deaths/1,000 live births
female: 55.96 deaths/1,000 live births (2014 est.)

Life expectancy at birth: *total population:* 59.26 years
country comparison to the world: 197
male: 57.73 years

female: 60.83 years (2014 est.)

Total fertility rate: 4.62 children born/woman (2014 est.)
country comparison to the world: 27

Contraceptive prevalence rate: 51.6% (2010/11)

Health expenditures: 10.8% of GDP (2011)
country comparison to the world: 17

Physicians density: 0.06 physicians/1,000 population (2010)

Hospital bed density: 1.6 beds/1,000 population (2007)

Drinking water source:
improved:
urban: 79.6% of population
rural: 66.4% of population
total: 68.9% of population
unimproved:
urban: 20.4% of population
rural: 33.6% of population
total: 31.1% of population (2011 est.)

Sanitation facility access:
improved:
urban: 61.3% of population
rural: 61.3% of population
total: 61.3% of population
unimproved:
urban: 38.7% of population
rural: 38.7% of population
total: 38.7% of population (2011 est.)

HIV/AIDS—adult prevalence rate: 2.9% (2012 est.)
country comparison to the world: 22

HIV/AIDS—people living with HIV/AIDS: 206,900 (2012 est.)
country comparison to the world: 30

HIV/AIDS—deaths: 5,600 (2012 est.)
country comparison to the world: 34

Major infectious diseases: *degree of risk:* very high
food or waterborne diseases: bacterial diarrhea, hepatitis A, and typhoid fever
vectorborne diseases: malaria and dengue fever
animal contact disease: rabies (2013)

Obesity—adult prevalence rate: 4.3% (2008)
country comparison to the world: 170

Children under the age of 5 years underweight: 11.7% (2011)
country comparison to the world: 63

Education expenditures: 5.1% of GDP (2013)
country comparison to the world: 73

Literacy: *definition:* age 15 and over can read and write
total population: 71.1%
male: 74.8%
female: 67.5% (2010 est.)

School life expectancy (primary to tertiary education): *total:* 10 years
male: 10 years
female: 10 years (2012)

Child labor—children ages 5-14:
total number: 783,113
percentage: 35 % (2000 est.)

People—note: Rwanda is the most densely populated country in Africa

GOVERNMENT

Country name: *conventional long form:* Republic of Rwanda
conventional short form: Rwanda
local long form: Republika y'u Rwanda
local short form: Rwanda
former: Ruanda, German East Africa

Government type: republic; presidential, multiparty system

Capital: *name:* Kigali
geographic coordinates: 1 57 S, 30 03 E
time difference: UTC+2 (7 hours ahead of Washington, DC during Standard Time)

Administrative divisions: 4 provinces (in French—provinces, singular—province; in Kinyarwanda—intara for singular and plural) and 1 city* (in French—ville; in Kinyarwanda—umujyi); Est (Eastern), Kigali*, Nord (Northern), Ouest (Western), Sud (Southern)

Independence: 1 July 1962 (from Belgium-administered UN trusteeship)

National holiday: Independence Day, 1 July (1962)

Constitution: several previous; latest adopted by referendum 26 May 2003, effective 4 June 2003; amended several times, last in 2010 (2013)

Legal system: mixed legal system of civil law, based on German and Belgian models, and customary law; judicial review of legislative acts in the Supreme Court

International law organization participation: has not submitted an ICJ jurisdiction declaration; non-party state to the ICCt

Suffrage: 18 years of age; universal

Executive branch: *chief of state:* President Paul KAGAME (since 22 April 2000)
head of government: Prime Minister Pierre Damien HABUMUREMYI (since 7 October 2011)
cabinet: Council of Ministers appointed by the president (For more information visit the World Leaders website)
elections: president elected by popular vote for a seven-year term (eligible for a second term); elections last held on 9 August 2010 (next to be held in 2017)
election results: Paul KAGAME elected to a second term as president; Paul KAGAME 93.1%, Jean NTAWUKURIRYAYO 5.1%, Prosper HIGIRO 1.4%, Alvera MUKABARAMBA 0.4%

Legislative branch: bicameral Parliament consists of Senate (26 seats; 12 members elected by local councils, 8 appointed by the president, 4 appointed by the Political Organizations Forum, 2 represent institutions of higher learning; members to serve eight-year terms) and Chamber of Deputies (80 seats; 53 members elected by popular vote, 24 women elected by local bodies, 3 selected by youth and disability organizations; members to serve five-year terms)
elections: Senate—NA; Chamber of Deputies—last held on 15 September 2008 (next to be held on 16-18 September 2013)
election results: percent of vote by party—RPF 78.8%, PSD 13.1%, PL 7.5%; seats by party—RPF 42, PSD 7, PL 4, additional 27 members indirectly elected

Judicial branch: *highest court(s):* Supreme Court (consists of the court president, vice president, and 12 judges; normally organized into 3-judge benches) note—the Gacaca Court was established in 2001 by the National Unity Government to try cases of genocide against the Tutsis
judge selection and term of office: judges nominated by the president of the republic, after consultation with the Cabinet and the Superior Council of the Judiciary (a 14-member body of judges, other judicial officials, and legal professionals), and approved by the Senate; court president and vice president appointed for 8-year nonrenewable terms; tenure of other judges NA
subordinate courts: High Court of the Republic; commercial courts including the High Commercial Court; intermediate courts; primary courts; Gacaca and military specialized courts

Political parties and leaders: Centrist Democratic Party or PDC [Agnes MUKABARANGA]; Democratic Popular Union of Rwanda or UDPR [Gonzague RWIGEMA]; Democratic Republican Movement or MDR [Celestin KABANDA] (officially banned); Islamic Democratic Party or PDI [Musa Fazil HARERIMANA]; Liberal Party or PL [Protais MITALI]; Party for Democratic Renewal (officially banned); Party for Progress and Concord or PPC [Alvera MUKABARAMBA]; Rwandan Patriotic Front or RPF [Paul KAGAME]; Rwandan Socialist Party or PSR [Jean Baptist RUCIBIGANGO]; Social Democratic Party or PSD [Vincent BIRUTA]; Socialist Party-Imberakuri or PS-Imberakuri [Christine MUKABUNANI]; Solidarity and Prosperity Party or PSP [Pheobe KANYANGE]

Political pressure groups and leaders: IBUKA (association of genocide survivors)

International organization participation: ACP, AfDB, AU, C, CEPGL, COMESA, EAC, EADB, FAO, G-77, IAEA, IBRD, ICAO, ICRM, IDA, IFAD, IFC, IFRCS, ILO, IMF, Interpol, IOC, IOM, IPU, ISO (correspondent), ITSO, ITU, ITUC (NGOs), MIGA, MINUSMA, NAM, OIF, OPCW, PCA, UN, UN Security Council (temporary), UNAMID, UNCTAD, UNESCO, UNHCR, UNIDO, UNISFA, UNMISS, UNWTO, UPU, WCO, WHO, WIPO, WMO, WTO

Diplomatic representation in the US:
chief of mission: Ambassador Mathilde MUKANTABANA (since 5 July 2013)
chancery: 1714 New Hampshire Avenue NW, Washington, DC 20009
telephone: [1] (202) 232-2882
FAX: [1] (202) 232-4544

Diplomatic representation from the US:
chief of mission: Ambassador Donald W. KORAN (since 8 August 2011)
embassy: 2657 Avenue de la Gendarmerie, Kigali
mailing address: B. P. 28, Kigali
telephone: [250] 596-400
FAX: [250] 596-591

Flag description: three horizontal bands of sky blue (top, double width), yellow, and green, with a golden sun with 24 rays near the fly end of the blue band; blue represents happiness and peace, yellow economic development and mineral wealth, green hope of prosperity and natural resources; the sun symbolizes unity, as well as enlightenment and transparency from ignorance

National anthem: *name:* "Rwanda nziza" (Rwanda, Our Beautiful Country)
lyrics/music: Faustin MURIGO/Jean-Bosco HASHAKAIMANA
note: adopted 2001

ECONOMY

Economy—overview: Rwanda is a poor rural country with about 90% of the population engaged in (mainly subsistence) agriculture and some mineral and agro-processing. Tourism, minerals, coffee and tea are Rwanda's main sources of foreign exchange. The 1994 genocide decimated Rwanda's fragile economic base, severely impoverished the population, particularly women, and temporarily stalled the country's ability to attract private and external investment. However, Rwanda has made substantial progress in stabilizing and rehabilitating its economy to pre-1994 levels. GDP has rebounded with an average annual growth of 7%-8% since 2003 and inflation has been reduced to single digits. Nonetheless, a significant percent of the population still live below the official poverty line. Despite Rwanda's fertile ecosystem, food production often does not keep pace with demand, requiring food imports. Rwanda continues to receive substantial aid money and obtained IMF-World Bank Heavily Indebted Poor Country (HIPC) initiative debt relief in 2005-06. In recognition of Rwanda's successful management of its macro economy, in 2010, the IMF graduated Rwanda to a Policy Support Instrument (PSI). Rwanda also received a Millennium Challenge Threshold Program in 2008. Africa's most densely populated country is trying to overcome the limitations of its small, landlocked economy by leveraging regional trade. Rwanda joined the East African Community and is aligning its budget, trade, and immigration policies with its regional partners. The government has embraced an expansionary fiscal policy to reduce poverty by improving education, infrastructure, and foreign and domestic investment and pursuing market-oriented reforms. Energy shortages, instability in neighboring states, and lack of adequate transportation linkages to other countries continue to handicap private sector growth. The Rwandan Government is seeking to become regional leader in information and communication technologies. In 2010, Rwanda neared completion of the first modern Special Economic Zone (SEZ) in Kigali. The SEZ seeks to attract investment in all sectors, but specifically in agribusiness, information and communications technologies, trade and logistics, mining, and construction. The global downturn hurt export demand and tourism, but economic growth has recovered, driven in large part by the services sector, but inflation has grown. On the back of this growth, government is gradually ending its fiscal stimulus policy while protecting aid to the poor.

GDP (purchasing power parity): $16.37 billion (2013 est.)
country comparison to the world: 142
$15.23 billion (2012 est.)
$14.1 billion (2011 est.)
note: data are in 2013 US dollars

GDP (official exchange rate): $7.7 billion (2013 est.)

GDP—real growth rate: 7.5% (2013 est.)
country comparison to the world: 15
8% (2012 est.)
8.2% (2011 est.)

GDP—per capita (PPP): $1,500 (2013 est.)
country comparison to the world: 204
$1,500 (2012 est.)
$1,400 (2011 est.)
note: data are in 2013 US dollars

Gross national saving: 12.6% of GDP (2013 est.)
country comparison to the world: 124
14.8% of GDP (2012 est.)
14.1% of GDP (2011 est.)

GDP—composition, by end use:
household consumption: 88.2%
government consumption: 9%
investment in fixed capital: 21.2%
investment in inventories: 0%
exports of goods and services: 11.3%
imports of goods and services: -29.7% (2013 est.)

GDP—composition, by sector of origin:
agriculture: 31.9%
industry: 14.8%
services: 53.3% (2013 est.)

Agriculture—products: coffee, tea, pyrethrum (insecticide made from chrysanthemums), bananas, beans, sorghum, potatoes; livestock

Industries: cement, agricultural products, small-scale beverages, soap, furniture, shoes, plastic goods, textiles, cigarettes

Industrial production growth rate: 6% (2013 est.)
country comparison to the world: 42

Labor force: 4.446 million (2007)
country comparison to the world: 86

Labor force—by occupation:
agriculture: 90%
industry and services: 10% (2000)

Unemployment rate: NA%

Population below poverty line: 44.9% (2011 est.)

Household income or consumption by percentage share: *lowest 10%:* 2.1%
highest 10%: 43.2% (2011 est.)

Distribution of family income—Gini index: 46.8 (2000)
country comparison to the world: 33
28.9 (1985)

Budget: *revenues:* $1.814 billion
expenditures: $2.146 billion (2013 est.)

Taxes and other revenues: 23.6% of GDP (2013 est.)
country comparison to the world: 140

Budget surplus (+) or deficit (-): -4.3% of GDP (2013 est.)
country comparison to the world: 154

Public debt: 23.5% of GDP (2013 est.)
country comparison to the world: 130
21.7% of GDP (2012 est.)

Fiscal year: calendar year

Inflation rate (consumer prices): 5.9% (2013 est.)
country comparison to the world: 169
6.3% (2012 est.)

Central bank discount rate: 7.75% (31 December 2010 est.)
country comparison to the world: 21
11.25% (31 December 2008)

Commercial bank prime lending rate: 16.3% (31 December 2013 est.)
country comparison to the world: 27
17.5% (31 December 2012 est.)

Stock of narrow money: $791.6 million (31 December 2013 est.)
country comparison to the world: 154
$671.2 million (31 December 2012 est.)

Stock of broad money: $1.445 billion (31 December 2013 est.)
country comparison to the world: 160
$1.137 billion (31 December 2012 est.)

Stock of domestic credit: $717.3 million (31 December 2013 est.)
country comparison to the world: 162
$557 million (31 December 2012 est.)

Market value of publicly traded shares: $NA

Current account balance: -$667.9 million (2013 est.)
country comparison to the world: 110
-$569.2 million (2012 est.)

Exports: $538.3 million (2013 est.)
country comparison to the world: 171
$512 million (2012 est.)

Exports—commodities: coffee, tea, hides, tin ore

Exports—partners: Kenya 30.5%, Democratic Republic of the Congo 12.2%, China 12.1%, Malaysia 10.7%, US 5.8%, Swaziland 4.9% (2012)

Imports: $1.937 billion (2013 est.)
country comparison to the world: 166
$1.871 billion (2012 est.)

Imports—commodities: foodstuffs, machinery and equipment, steel, petroleum products, cement and construction material

Imports—partners: Kenya 17.3%, Uganda 15.6%, UAE 8.9%, China 7.2%, India 5.6%, Tanzania 5%, Belgium 4.5%, Canada 4.1% (2012)

Reserves of foreign exchange and gold: $1.354 billion (31 December 2013 est.)
country comparison to the world: 128
$847.8 million (31 December 2012 est.)

Debt—external: $1.656 billion (31 December 2013 est.)
country comparison to the world: 148
$1.153 billion (31 December 2012 est.)

Stock of direct foreign investment—at home: $900.1 million (31 December 2013 est.)
country comparison to the world: 101
$743.3 million (31 December 2012 est.)

Stock of direct foreign investment—abroad: $12.9 million (31 December 2013 est.)
country comparison to the world: 92
$12.9 million (31 December 2012 est.)

Exchange rates: Rwandan francs (RWF) per US dollar—
633.6 (2013 est.)
616.6 (2012 est.)
583.13 (2010 est.)
568.18 (2009)
550 (2008)

ENERGY

Electricity—production: 280.2 million kWh (2010 est.)
country comparison to the world: 176

Electricity—consumption: 319.6 million kWh (2010 est.)
country comparison to the world: 172

Electricity—exports: 3 million kWh (2010 est.)
country comparison to the world: 91

Electricity—imports: 62 million kWh (2010 est.)
country comparison to the world: 97

Electricity—installed generating capacity: 57,250 kW (2010 est.)
country comparison to the world: 185

Electricity—from fossil fuels: 52.4% of total installed capacity (2010 est.)
country comparison to the world: 150

Electricity—from nuclear fuels: 0% of total installed capacity (2010 est.)

country comparison to the world: 170

Electricity—from hydroelectric plants: 47.2% of total installed capacity (2010 est.)
country comparison to the world: 46

Electricity—from other renewable sources: 0.4% of total installed capacity (2010 est.)
country comparison to the world: 86

Crude oil—production: 10 bbl/day (2012 est.)
country comparison to the world: 129

Crude oil—exports: 0 bbl/day (2010 est.)
country comparison to the world: 173

Crude oil—imports: 0 bbl/day (2010 est.)
country comparison to the world: 113

Crude oil—proved reserves: 0 bbl (1 January 2013 es)
country comparison to the world: 180

Refined petroleum products—production: 0 bbl/day (2010 est.)
country comparison to the world: 188

Refined petroleum products—consumption: 5,245 bbl/day (2011 est.)
country comparison to the world: 166

Refined petroleum products—exports: 0 bbl/day (2010 est.)
country comparison to the world: 210

Refined petroleum products—imports: 5,302 bbl/day (2010 est.)
country comparison to the world: 148

Natural gas—production: 0 cu m (2011 est.)
country comparison to the world: 184

Natural gas—consumption: 0 cu m (2010 est.)
country comparison to the world: 188

Natural gas—exports: 0 cu m (2011 est.)
country comparison to the world: 173

Natural gas—imports: 0 cu m (2011 est.)
country comparison to the world: 122

Natural gas—proved reserves: 56.63 billion cu m (1 January 2013 es)
country comparison to the world: 64

Carbon dioxide emissions from consumption of energy: 865,100 Mt (2011 est.)
country comparison to the world: 169

COMMUNICATIONS

Telephones—main lines in use: 44,400 (2012)
country comparison to the world: 167

Telephones—mobile cellular: 5.69 million (2012)
country comparison to the world: 104

Telephone system: *general assessment:* small, inadequate telephone system primarily serves business, education, and government
domestic: the capital, Kigali, is connected to the centers of the provinces by microwave radio relay and, recently, by cellular telephone service; much of the network depends on wire and HF radiotelephone; combined fixed-line and mobile-cellular telephone density has increased and now exceeds 40 telephones per 100 persons
international: country code—250; international connections employ microwave radio relay to neighboring countries and satellite communications to more distant countries; satellite earth stations—1 Intelsat (Indian Ocean) in Kigali (includes telex and telefax service) (2010)

Broadcast media: government owns and operates the only TV station; government-owned and operated Radio Rwanda has a national reach; 9 private radio stations; transmissions of multiple international broadcasters are available (2007)

Internet country code: .rw

Internet hosts: 1,447 (2012)
country comparison to the world: 168

Internet users: 450,000 (2009)
country comparison to the world: 118

TRANSPORTATION

Airports: 7 (2013)
country comparison to the world: 167

Airports—with paved runways: *total:* 4
over 3,047 m: 1
914 to 1,523 m: 2
under 914 m: 1 (2013)

Airports—with unpaved runways: *total:* 3
914 to 1,523 m: 2
under 914 m: 1 (2013)

Roadways: *total:* 4,700 km
country comparison to the world: 152
paved: 1,207 km
unpaved: 3,493 km (2012)

Waterways: (Lac Kivu navigable by shallow-draft barges and native craft) (2011)

Ports and terminals: *lake port(s):* Cyangugu, Gisenyi, Kibuye (Lake Kivu)

MILITARY

Military branches:
Rwanda Defense Force (RDF): Rwanda Army (Rwanda Land Force), Rwanda Air Force (Force Aerienne Rwandaise, FAR) (2013)

Military service age and obligation: 18 years of age for voluntary military service; no conscription; Rwandan citizenship is required, as is a 9th grade education for enlisted recruits and an A-level certificate for officer candidates; enlistment is either as contract (5-years, renewable twice) or career; retirement (for officers and senior NCOs) after 20 years of service or at 40-60 years of age (2012)

Manpower available for military service:
males age 16-49: 2,625,917
females age 16-49: 2,608,110 (2010 est.)

Manpower fit for military service:
males age 16-49: 1,685,066
females age 16-49: 1,749,580 (2010 est.)

Manpower reaching militarily significant age annually: *male:* 110,736
female: 110,328 (2010 est.)

Military expenditures: 1.12% of GDP (2012)
country comparison to the world: 93
1.19% of GDP (2011)
1.12% of GDP (2010)

TRANSNATIONAL ISSUES

Disputes—international: Burundi and Rwanda dispute two sq km (0.8 sq mi) of Sabanerwa, a farmed area in the Rukurazi Valley where the Akanyaru/Kanyaru River shifted its course southward after heavy rains in 1965; fighting among ethnic groups—loosely associated political rebels, armed gangs, and various government forces in Great Lakes region transcending the boundaries of Burundi, Democratic Republic of the Congo (DROC), Rwanda, and Uganda—abated substantially from a decade ago due largely to UN peacekeeping, international mediation, and efforts by local governments to create civil societies; nonetheless, 57,000 Rwandan refugees still reside in 21 African states, including Zambia, Gabon, and 20,000 who fled to Burundi in 2005 and 2006 to escape drought and recriminations from traditional courts investigating the 1994 massacres; the 2005 DROC and Rwanda border verification mechanism to stem rebel actions on both sides of the border remains in place

Refugees and internally displaced persons:
refugees (country of origin): 57,857 (Democratic Republic of the Congo) (2012)
IDPs: undetermined (fighting between government and insurgency in 1998-99; returning refugees) (2012)

Trafficking in persons: *current situation:* Rwanda is a source and, to a lesser extent, transit and destination country for women and children subjected to forced labor and sex trafficking; Rwandan girls and, to a lesser extent, boys are exploited in domestic servitude within the country; Rwandan girls are also forced into prostitution by older girls, women, and loosely organized prostitution networks; Rwandan women and children are subjected to forced agricultural and industrial labor, domestic servitude, and prostitution in Kenya, Uganda, Democratic Republic of the Congo, Tanzania, Burundi, Zambia, South Africa, France, the Netherlands, Malaysia, China, and the US; children in Rwanda-based refugee camps are brought to Kigali, Uganda, Kenya, Sudan, and South Sudan for use in the sex trade; a limited number of foreign nationals are moved through Rwanda to be exploited in third countries

tier rating: Tier 2 Watch List—Rwanda does not fully comply with the minimum standards for the elimination of trafficking; however, it is making significant efforts to do so; the government maintains strong efforts to investigate and prosecute some trafficking crimes but fails to stop M23 (an armed group in the eastern Democratic Republic of the Congo) from recruiting within Rwanda, which is at times reportedly supported by government officials, amounting to complicity in human trafficking; although the revised penal code covers almost all forms of human trafficking, its narrow definition may result in the confusion of trafficking with other crimes; other obstacles include a lack of awareness of human trafficking among officials and an inadequate number of investigators (2013)

SAINT BARTHELEMY

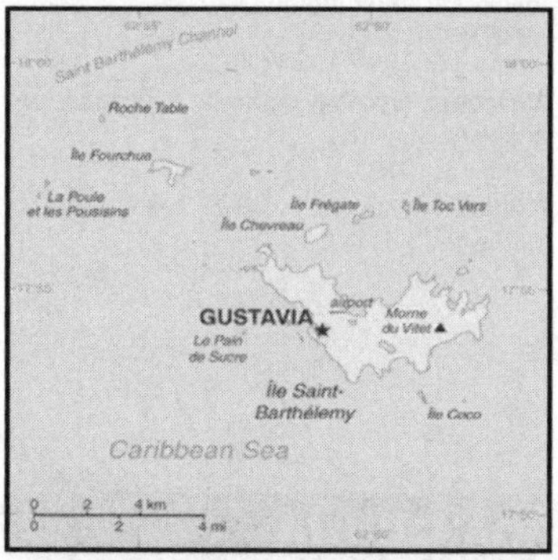

INTRODUCTION

Background: Discovered in 1493 by Christopher COLUMBUS who named it for his brother Bartolomeo, Saint Barthelemy was first settled by the French in 1648. In 1784, the French sold the island to Sweden, who renamed the largest town Gustavia, after the Swedish King GUSTAV III, and made it a free port; the island prospered as a trade and supply center during the colonial wars of the 18th century. France repurchased the island in 1877 and took control the following year. It was placed under the administration of Guadeloupe. Saint Barthelemy retained its free port status along with various Swedish appellations such as Swedish street and town names, and the three-crown symbol on the coat of arms. In 2003 the populace of the island voted to secede from Guadeloupe, and in 2007 the island became a French overseas collectivity.

GEOGRAPHY

Location: Caribbean, island between the Caribbean Sea and the North Atlantic Ocean; located in the Leeward Islands (northern) group; Saint Barthelemy lies east of the US Virgin Islands

Geographic coordinates: 17 90 N, 62 85 W

Map references: Central America and the Caribbean

Area: 21 sq km

Area—comparative: less than an eighth of the size of Washington, DC

Land boundaries: 0 km

Climate: tropical, with practically no variation in temperature; has two seasons (dry and humid)

Terrain: hilly, almost completely surrounded by shallow-water reefs, with plentiful beaches

Elevation extremes: *lowest point:* Caribbean Ocean 0 m
highest point: Morne du Vitet 286 m

Natural resources: has few natural resources, its beaches being the most important

Environment—current issues: with no natural rivers or streams, fresh water is in short supply, especially in summer, and provided by desalinization of sea water, collection of rain water, or imported via water tanker

PEOPLE AND SOCIETY

Ethnic groups: white, Creole (mulatto), black, Guadeloupe Mestizo (French-East Asia)

Languages: French (primary), English

Religions: Roman Catholic, Protestant, Jehovah's Witnesses

Population: 7,267 (July 2014 est.)
country comparison to the world: 229

Age structure:
0-14 years: 17.8% (male 664/female 631)
15-24 years: 6.9% (male 262/female 237)
25-54 years: 46.1% (male 1,829/female 1,524)
55-64 years: 14.2% (male 590/female 501)
65 years and over: 13.3% (male 514/female 515) (2014 est.)

Median age: *total:* 42.4 years
male: 42.4 years
female: 42.3 years (2014 est.)

Sex ratio: *at birth:* 1.03 male(s)/female
0-14 years: 1.05 male(s)/female
15-24 years: 1.11 male(s)/female
25-54 years: 1.2 male(s)/female
55-64 years: 1.13 male(s)/female
65 years and over: 1 male(s)/female
total population: 1.14 male(s)/female (2014 est.)

GOVERNMENT

Country name: *conventional long form:* Overseas Collectivity of Saint Barthelemy
conventional short form: Saint Barthelemy
local long form: Collectivite d'outre mer de Saint-Barthelemy
local short form: Saint-Barthelemy
abbreviation: Saint-Barth (French); St. Barts or St. Barths (English)

Dependency status: overseas collectivity of France

Capital: *name:* Gustavia

geographic coordinates: 17 53 N, 62 51 W
time difference: UTC-4 (1 hour ahead of Washington, DC, during Standard Time)

Independence: none (overseas collectivity of France)

National holiday: Fete de la Federation, 14 July (1789); note—local holiday is St. Barthelemy Day, 24 August (1572)

Constitution: 4 October 1958 (French Constitution) (2013)

Legal system: French civil law

Suffrage: 18 years of age, universal

Executive branch: *chief of state:* President Francois HOLLANDE (since 15 May 2012), represented by Prefect Philippe CHOPIN (since 16 November 2011)
head of government: President of the Territorial Council Bruno MAGRAS (since 16 July 2007)
cabinet: Executive Council; note—there is also an advisory, economic, social, and cultural council (For more information visit the World Leaders website)
elections: French president elected by popular vote for a five-year term; prefect appointed by the French president on the advice of the French Ministry of Interior; president of the Territorial Council elected by the members of the Council for a five-year term
election results: Bruno MAGRAS unanimously elected president by the Territorial Council on 16 July 2007 (next to be held in 2012)

Legislative branch: unicameral Territorial Council (19 seats; members elected by popular vote to serve five-year terms)
elections: last held on 18 March 2012 (next to be held in July 2017)
election results: percent of vote by party—SBA 73.8%, Ensemble pour Saint-Barthelemy 15.9%, Tous Unis pour Saint-Barthelemy 10.3%; seats by party—SBA 16, Ensemble pour Saint-Barthelemy 2, Tous Unis pour Saint-Barthelemy 1
note: Saint Barthelemy elects one seat to the French Senate; election last held on 21 September 2008 (next to be held in September 2014); results—percent of vote by party—NA; seats by party—UMP 1; one seat (shared with Saint Martin) was elected to the French National Assembly on 17 June 1012 (next to be held by June 2017); results—percent of vote by party—NA; seats by party—UMP 1

Political parties and leaders: Action-Equilibre-Transparence [Maxime DESOUCHES]; Ensemble pour Saint-Barthelemy [Benoit CHAUVIN]; Saint-Barth d'Abord! or SBA [Bruno MAGRAS]; Tous Unis pour Saint-Barthelemy [Karine MIOT-RICHARD]

Political pressure groups and leaders: The Marine Reserve (protection of fish); Rotary Club

International organization participation: UPU

Diplomatic representation in the US: none (overseas collectivity of France)

Diplomatic representation from the US: none (overseas collectivity of France)

Flag description: the flag of France is used

National anthem: *name:* "L'Hymne a St. Barthelemy" (Hymn to St. Barthelemy)
lyrics/music: Isabelle Massart DERAVIN/Michael VALENTI
note: local anthem in use since 1999; as a collectivity of France, "La Marseillaise" is official (see France)

ECONOMY

Economy—overview: The economy of Saint Barthelemy is based upon high-end tourism and duty-free luxury commerce, serving visitors primarily from North America. The luxury hotels and villas host 70,000 visitors each year with another 130,000 arriving by boat. The relative isolation and high cost of living inhibits mass tourism. The construction and public sectors also enjoy significant investment in support of tourism. With limited fresh water resources, all food must be imported, as must all energy resources and most manufactured goods. Employment is strong and attracts labor from Brazil and Portugal.

Exchange rates: euros (EUR) per US dollar—
0.7838 (2012 est.)
0.7185 (2011 est.)
0.755 (2010 est.)
0.7198 (2009 est.)
0.6827 (2008 est.)

COMMUNICATIONS

Telephone system: *general assessment:* fully integrated access
domestic: direct dial capability with both fixed and wireless systems
international: country code—590; undersea fiber-optic cable provides voice and data connectivity to Puerto Rico and Guadeloupe (2008)

Broadcast media: no local TV broadcasters; 3 FM radio channels (2 via repeater)

Internet country code: .bl; note—.gp, the Internet country code for Guadeloupe, and .fr, the Internet country code for France, might also be encountered

TRANSPORTATION

Airports: 1 (2013)
country comparison to the world: 234

Airports—with paved runways: *total:* 1
under 914 m: 1 (2013)

Ports and terminals: *major seaport(s):* Gustavia

Transportation—note: nearest airport for international flights is Princess Juliana International Airport (SXM) located on Sint Maarten

MILITARY

Manpower fit for military service:
males age 16-49: 1,495
females age 16-49: 1,263 (2010 est.)

Manpower reaching militarily significant age annually: *male:* 2 3
female: 21 (2010 est.)

Military—note: defense is the responsibility of France

SAINT HELENA, ASCENSION, AND TRISTAN DA CUNHA

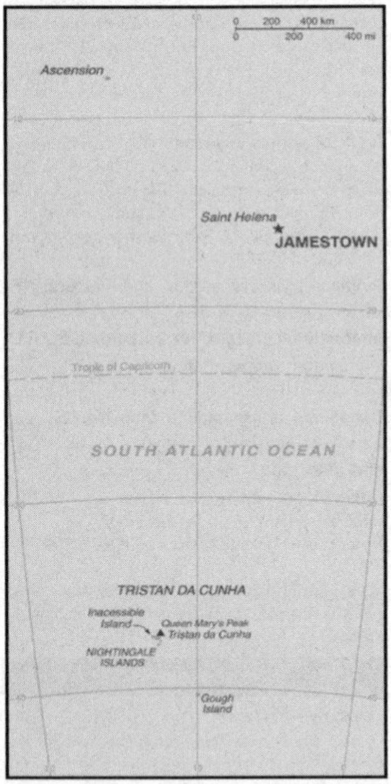

INTRODUCTION

Background: Saint Helena is a British Overseas Territory consisting of Saint Helena and Ascension Islands, and the island group of Tristan da Cunha. Saint Helena: Uninhabited when first discovered by the Portuguese in 1502, Saint Helena was garrisoned by the British during the 17th century. It acquired fame as the place of Napoleon BONAPARTE's exile from 1815 until his death in 1821, but its importance as a port of call declined after the opening of the Suez Canal in 1869. During the Anglo-Boer War in South Africa, several thousand Boer prisoners were confined on the island between 1900 and 1903.
Ascension Island: This barren and uninhabited island was discovered and named by the Portuguese in 1503. The British garrisoned the island in 1815 to prevent a rescue of Napoleon from Saint Helena. It served as a provisioning station for the Royal Navy's West Africa Squadron on anti-slavery patrol. The island remained under Admiralty control until 1922, when it became a dependency of Saint Helena. During World War II, the UK permitted the US to construct an airfield on Ascension in support of transatlantic flights to Africa and anti-submarine operations in the South Atlantic. In the 1960s the island became an important space tracking station for the US. In 1982, Ascension was an essential staging area for British forces during the Falklands War. It remains a critical refueling point in the air-bridge from the UK to the South Atlantic. the air-bridge from the UK to the South Atlantic.

Tristan da Cunha: The island group consists of the islands of Tristan da Cunha, Nightingale, Inaccessible, and Gough. Tristan da Cunha is named after its Portuguese discoverer (1506); it was garrisoned by the British in 1816 to prevent any attempt to rescue Napoleon from Saint Helena. Gough and Inaccessible Islands have been designated World Heritage Sites. South Africa leases a site for a meteorological station on Gough Island.

GEOGRAPHY

Location: islands in the South Atlantic Ocean, about midway between South America and Africa; Ascension Island lies 700 nm northwest of Saint Helena; Tristan da Cunha lies 2,300 nm southwest of Saint Helena

Geographic coordinates: *Saint Helena:* 15 57 S, 5 42 W
Ascension Island: 7 57 S, 14 22 W
Tristan da Cunha island group: 37 15 S, 12 30 W

Map references: Africa

Area: *total:* 308 sq km
country comparison to the world: 209
land: Saint Helena Island 122 sq km; Ascension Island 88 sq km; Tristan da Cunha island group 98 sq km
water: 0 sq km

Area—comparative: slightly more than twice the size of Washington, DC

Land boundaries: 0 km

Coastline: Saint Helena: 60 km
Ascension Island: NA
Tristan da Cunha: 40 km

Maritime claims: *territorial sea:* 12 nm
exclusive fishing zone: 200 nm

Climate:
Saint Helena: tropical marine; mild, tempered by trade winds
Ascension Island: tropical marine; mild, semi-arid
Tristan da Cunha: temperate marine; mild, tempered by trade winds (tends to be cooler than Saint Helena)

Terrain: the islands of this group result from volcanic activity associated with the Atlantic Mid-Ocean Ridge
Saint Helena: rugged, volcanic; small scattered plateaus and plains
Ascension: surface covered by lava flows and cinder cones of 44 dormant volcanoes; ground rises to the east
Tristan da Cunha: sheer cliffs line the coastline of the nearly circular island; the flanks of the central volcanic peak are deeply dissected; narrow coastal plain lies between The Peak and the coastal cliffs

Elevation extremes: *lowest point:* Atlantic Ocean 0 m
highest point: Queen Mary's Peak on Tristan da Cunha 2,060 m; Green Mountain on Ascension Island 859 m; Mount Actaeon on Saint Helena Island 818 m

Natural resources: fish, lobster

Land use: *arable land:* 10.26%
permanent crops: 0%
other: 89.74% (2011)

Irrigated land: NA

Natural hazards: active volcanism on Tristan da Cunha
volcanism: the island volcanoes of Tristan da Cunha (elev. 2,060 m) and Nightingale Island (elev. 365 m) experience volcanic activity; Tristan da Cunha erupted in 1962 and Nightingale in 2004

Environment—current issues: NA

Geography—note: Saint Helena harbors at least 40 species of plants unknown elsewhere in the world; Ascension is a breeding ground for sea turtles and sooty terns; Queen Mary's Peak on Tristan da Cunha is the highest island mountain in the South Atlantic and a prominent landmark on the sea lanes around southern Africa

PEOPLE AND SOCIETY

Nationality: *noun:* Saint Helenian(s)
adjective: Saint Helenian
note: referred to locally as "Saints"

Ethnic groups: African descent 50%, white 25%, Chinese 25%

Languages: English

Religions: Protestant (Anglican (majority), Baptist, Seventh-Day Adventist), Roman Catholic

Population: 7,776 (July 2014 est.)
country comparison to the world: 228
note: only Saint Helena, Ascension, and Tristan da Cunha islands are inhabited

Age structure:
0-14 years: 16.9% (male 669/female 643)
15-24 years: 11.9% (male 471/female 455)
25-54 years: 45.1% (male 1,737/female 1,773)
55-64 years: 13.7% (male 508/female 455)
65 years and over: 13.2% (male 543/female 522) (2014 est.)

Median age: *total:* 40.5 years
male: 40.5 years
female: 40.4 years (2014 est.)

Population growth rate: 0.27% (2014 est.)
country comparison to the world: 173

Birth rate: 10.03 births/1,000 population (2014 est.)
country comparison to the world: 191

Death rate: 7.33 deaths/1,000 population (2014 est.)
country comparison to the world: 121

Net migration rate: 0 migrant(s)/1,000 population (2014 est.)
country comparison to the world: 78

Urbanization: *urban population:* 39.5% of total population (2011)
rate of urbanization: -0.87% annual rate of change (2010-15 est.)

Major urban areas—population: JAMESTOWN (capital) 1,000 (2009)

Sex ratio: *at birth:* 1.05 male(s)/female
0-14 years: 1.04 male(s)/female
15-24 years: 1.04 male(s)/female
25-54 years: 0.98 male(s)/female
55-64 years: 1.02 male(s)/female
65 years and over: 1.01 male(s)/female
total population: 1.02 male(s)/female (2014 est.)

Infant mortality rate: *total:* 14.71 deaths/1,000 live births
country comparison to the world: 109
male: 17.35 deaths/1,000 live births
female: 11.93 deaths/1,000 live births (2014 est.)

Life expectancy at birth: *total population:* 79.21 years
country comparison to the world: 45
male: 76.27 years
female: 82.29 years (2014 est.)

Total fertility rate: 1.58 children born/woman (2014 est.)
country comparison to the world: 182

HIV/AIDS—adult prevalence rate: NA

HIV/AIDS—people living with HIV/AIDS: NA

HIV/AIDS—deaths: NA

Literacy: *definition:* age 20 and over can read and write
total population: 97%
male: 97%
female: 98% (1987 est.)

GOVERNMENT

Country name: *conventional long form:* Saint Helena, Ascension, and Tristan da Cunha
conventional short form: none

Dependency status: overseas territory of the UK

Government type: NA

Capital: *name:* Jamestown
geographic coordinates: 15 56 S, 5 43 W
time difference: UTC 0 (5 hours ahead of Washington, DC during Standard Time)

Administrative divisions: 3 administrative areas; Ascension, Saint Helena, Tristan da Cunha

Independence: none (overseas territory of the UK)

National holiday: Birthday of Queen ELIZABETH II, second Saturday in June (1926)

Constitution: several previous; latest effective 1 September 2009 (The St. Helena, Ascension and Tristan da Cunha Constitution Order 2009) (2013)

Legal system: English common law and local statutes

Suffrage: 18 years of age

Executive branch: *chief of state:* Queen ELIZABETH II (since 6 February 1952)
head of government: Governor Mark CAPES (since 29 October 2011)
note: the constitution order provides for an administrator for Ascension and Tristan da Cunha appointed by the governor
Administrator Ascension Island: Colin WELLS (since 27 October 2011)
Administrator Tristan da Cunha: Alex MITHAM (since 23 September 2013)
cabinet: Executive Council consists of the governor, 3 ex-officio officers, and 5 elected members of the Legislative Council (For more information visit the World Leaders website)
elections: none; the monarchy is hereditary; governor appointed by the monarch

Legislative branch: unicameral Legislative Council (17 seats, including a speaker and deputy speaker, 12 elected, and three ex-officio members; members elected by popular vote to serve four-year terms)
note: the Constitution Order provides for separate Island Councils for both Ascension and Tristan da Cunha
elections: last held on 4 November 2009 (next to be held in November 2013)
election results: percent of vote—NA; seats—independents 12

Judicial branch: *highest court(s):* Court of Appeal (consists of the court president and 2 justices); Supreme Court (consists of the chief justice—a non-resident—and NA judges) note—appeals beyond the Court of Appeal are heard by the Judicial Committee of the Privy Council (in London)
judge selection and term of office: court judges' appointments and tenures NA
subordinate courts: Magistrate's Court; Small Claims Court; Juvenile Court

Political parties and leaders: none

Political pressure groups and leaders:
other: private sector; unions

International organization participation: UPU

Diplomatic representation in the US: none (overseas territory of the UK)

Diplomatic representation from the US: none (overseas territory of the UK)

Flag description: blue with the flag of the UK in the upper hoist-side quadrant and the Saint Helenian shield centered on the outer half of the flag; the upper third of the shield depicts a white plover (wire bird) on a yellow field; the remainder of the shield depicts a rocky coastline on the left, offshore is a three-masted sailing ship with sails furled but flying an English flag

National symbol(s): Saint Helena plover (bird)

National anthem: *note:* as a territory of the UK, "God Save the Queen" is official (see United Kingdom)

ECONOMY

Economy—overview: The economy depends largely on financial assistance from the UK, which amounted to about $27 million in FY06/07 or more than twice the level of annual budgetary revenues. The local population earns income from fishing, raising livestock, and sales of handicrafts. Because there are few jobs, 25% of the work force has left to seek employment on Ascension Island, on the Falklands, and in the UK.

GDP (purchasing power parity): $31.1 million (FY09/10 est.)
country comparison to the world: 227

GDP (official exchange rate): $NA

GDP—real growth rate: NA%

GDP—per capita (PPP): $7,800 (FY09/10 est.)
country comparison to the world: 135

GDP—composition, by sector of origin:
agriculture: NA%
industry: NA%
services: NA%

Agriculture—products: coffee, corn, potatoes, vegetables; fish, lobster; livestock; timber

Industries: construction, crafts (furniture, lacework, fancy woodwork), fishing, philatelic sales

Industrial production growth rate: NA%

Labor force: 2,486 (1998 est.)
country comparison to the world: 228

Labor force—by occupation:
agriculture: 6%
industry: 48%
services: 46% (1987 est.)

Unemployment rate: 14% (1998 est.)
country comparison to the world: 136

Population below poverty line: NA%

Household income or consumption by percentage share: *lowest 10%:* NA%
highest 10%: NA%

Budget: *revenues:* $10.23 million
expenditures: $25.13 million

note: revenue data reflect locally raised revenues only; the budget deficit is resolved by grant aid from the UK (FY06/07 est.)

Fiscal year: 1 April—31 March

Inflation rate (consumer prices): 4% (2012 est.)
country comparison to the world: 132

Exports: $19 million (2004 est.)
country comparison to the world: 207

Exports—commodities: fish (frozen, canned, and salt-dried skipjack, tuna), coffee, handicrafts

Imports: $20.53 million (2010 est.)
country comparison to the world: 219

Imports—commodities: food, beverages, tobacco, fuel oils, animal feed, building materials, motor vehicles and parts, machinery and parts

Debt—external: $NA

Exchange rates: Saint Helenian pounds (SHP) per US dollar—
0.6391 (2013)
0.6307 (2012)
0.6472 (2010)
0.6175 (2009)
0.5302 (2008)

ENERGY

Electricity—production: 8 million kWh (2010 est.)
country comparison to the world: 215

Electricity—consumption: 7.44 million kWh (2010 est.)
country comparison to the world: 215

Electricity—exports: 0 kWh (2012 est.)
country comparison to the world: 193

Electricity—imports: 0 kWh (2012 est.)
country comparison to the world: 196

Electricity—installed generating capacity: 5,000 kW (2010 est.)
country comparison to the world: 208

Electricity—from fossil fuels: 100% of total installed capacity (2010 est.)
country comparison to the world: 33

Electricity—from nuclear fuels: 0% of total installed capacity (2010 est.)
country comparison to the world: 176

Electricity—from hydroelectric plants: 0% of total installed capacity (2010 est.)
country comparison to the world: 198

Electricity—from other renewable sources: 0% of total installed capacity (2010 est.)
country comparison to the world: 121

Crude oil—production: 0 bbl/day (2012 est.)
country comparison to the world: 211

Crude oil—exports: 0 bbl/day (2010 est.)
country comparison to the world: 179

Crude oil—imports: 0 bbl/day (2010 est.)
country comparison to the world: 118

Crude oil—proved reserves: 0 bbl (1 January 2013 es)
country comparison to the world: 185

Refined petroleum products—production: 0 bbl/day (2010 est.)
country comparison to the world: 192

Refined petroleum products—consumption: 100 bbl/day (2011 est.)
country comparison to the world: 210

Refined petroleum products—exports: 0 bbl/day (2010 est.)
country comparison to the world: 129

Refined petroleum products—imports: 63.12 bbl/day (2010 est.)
country comparison to the world: 208

Natural gas—production: 0 cu m (2011 est.)
country comparison to the world: 188

Natural gas—consumption: 0 cu m (2010 est.)
country comparison to the world: 192

Natural gas—exports: 0 cu m (2011 est.)
country comparison to the world: 180

Natural gas—imports: 0 cu m (2011 est.)
country comparison to the world: 128

Natural gas—proved reserves: 0 cu m (1 January 2013 es)
country comparison to the world: 191

Carbon dioxide emissions from consumption of energy: 9,100 Mt (2011 est.)
country comparison to the world: 210

COMMUNICATIONS

Telephones—main lines in use: 3,000 (2012)
country comparison to the world: 216

Telephone system: *general assessment:* can communicate worldwide
domestic: automatic digital network
international: country code (Saint Helena)—290, (Ascension Island)—247; international direct dialing; satellite voice and data communications; satellite earth stations—5 (Ascension Island—4, Saint Helena—1) (2010)

Broadcast media: St. Helena has no local TV station; 2 local radio stations, one of which is relayed to Ascension Island; satellite TV stations rebroadcast terrestrially; Ascension Island has no local TV station but has 1 local radio station and receives relays of broadcasts from 1 radio station on St. Helena; broadcasts from the British Forces Broadcasting Service (BFBS) are available, as well as TV services for the US military; Tristan da Cunha has 1 local radio station and receives BFBS TV and radio broadcasts (2007)

Internet country code: .sh; note—Ascension Island assigned .ac

Internet hosts: 6,729 (2012)
country comparison to the world: 141

Internet users: 900 (2009)
country comparison to the world: 215

Communications—note: South Africa maintains a meteorological station on Gough Island

TRANSPORTATION

Airports: 1 (2013)
country comparison to the world: 232

Airports—with paved runways: *total:* 1
over 3,047 m: 1 (2013)

Roadways: *total:* 198 km (Saint Helena 138 km, Ascension 40 km, Tristan da Cunha 20 km)
country comparison to the world: 209
paved: 168 km (Saint Helena 118 km, Ascension 40 km, Tristan da Cunha 10 km)
unpaved: 30 km (Saint Helena 20 km, Tristan da Cunha 10 km) (2002)

Ports and terminals: *major seaport(s):*
Saint Helena: Jamestown
Ascension Island: Georgetown
Tristan da Cunha: Calshot Harbor (Edinburgh)

Transportation—note: there is no air connection to Saint Helena or Tristan da Cunha; construction on the new international airport for Saint Helena began in 2012 with an estimated completion date of late 2015 or early 2016; the new airport will have a runway of 1,550 m capable of handling B737/A319 size aircraft

MILITARY

Manpower fit for military service:
males age 16-49: 1,565
females age 16-49: 1,579 (2010 est.)

Manpower reaching militarily significant age annually: *male:* 4 9
female: 48 (2010 est.)

Military—note: defense is the responsibility of the UK

TRANSNATIONAL ISSUES

Disputes—international: none

SAINT KITTS AND NEVIS

INTRODUCTION

Background: Carib Indians occupied the islands of the West Indies for hundreds of years before the British began settlement in 1623. In 1967, the island territory of Saint Christopher-Nevis-Anguilla became an associated state of the UK with full internal autonomy. The island of Anguilla rebelled and was allowed to secede in 1971. The remaining islands achieved independence in 1983 as Saint Kitts and Nevis. In 1998, a vote in Nevis on a referendum to separate from Saint Kitts fell short of the two-thirds majority needed. Nevis continues in its efforts to separate from Saint Kitts.

GEOGRAPHY

Location: Caribbean, islands in the Caribbean Sea, about one-third of the way from Puerto Rico to Trinidad and Tobago

Geographic coordinates: 17 20 N, 62 45 W

Map references: Central America and the Caribbean

Area: *total:* 261 sq km (Saint Kitts 168 sq km; Nevis 93 sq km)
country comparison to the world: 212
land: 261 sq km
water: 0 sq km

Area—comparative: one and a half times the size of Washington, DC

Land boundaries: 0 km

Coastline: 135 km

Maritime claims: *territorial sea:* 12 nm
contiguous zone: 24 nm

exclusive economic zone: 200 nm
continental shelf: 200 nm or to the edge of the continental margin

Climate: tropical, tempered by constant sea breezes; little seasonal temperature variation; rainy season (May to November)

Terrain: volcanic with mountainous interiors

Elevation extremes: *lowest point:* Caribbean Sea 0 m
highest point: Mount Liamuiga 1,156 m

Natural resources: arable land

Land use: *arable land:* 19.23%
permanent crops: 0.38%
other: 80.38% (2011)

Irrigated land: 0.18 sq km (2003)

Total renewable water resources: 0.02 cu km (2011)

Natural hazards: hurricanes (July to October)

Environment—current issues: NA

Environment—international agreements:
party to: Biodiversity, Climate Change, Climate Change-Kyoto Protocol, Desertification, Endangered Species, Hazardous Wastes, Law of the Sea, Marine Dumping, Ozone Layer Protection, Ship Pollution, Whaling
signed, but not ratified: none of the selected agreements

Geography—note: with coastlines in the shape of a baseball bat and ball, the two volcanic islands are separated by a 3-km-wide channel called The Narrows; on the southern tip of long, baseball bat-shaped Saint Kitts lies the Great Salt Pond; Nevis Peak sits in the center of its almost circular namesake island and its ball shape complements that of its sister island

PEOPLE AND SOCIETY

Nationality: *noun:* Kittitian(s), Nevisian(s)
adjective: Kittitian, Nevisian

Ethnic groups: predominantly black; some British, Portuguese, and Lebanese

Languages: English (official)

Religions: Anglican, other Protestant, Roman Catholic

Population: 51,538 (July 2014 est.)
country comparison to the world: 209

Age structure:
0-14 years: 21.4% (male 5,520/female 5,518)
15-24 years: 15.4% (male 3,904/female 4,028)
25-54 years: 45.1% (male 11,869/female 11,384)
55-64 years: 7.9% (male 2,637/female 2,610)
65 years and over: 7.8% (male 1,834/female 2,234) (2014 est.)

Median age: *total:* 33.5 years
male: 33.6 years
female: 33.4 years (2014 est.)

Population growth rate: 0.78% (2014 est.)
country comparison to the world: 142

Birth rate: 13.64 births/1,000 population (2014 est.)
country comparison to the world: 146

Death rate: 7.08 deaths/1,000 population (2014 est.)
country comparison to the world: 130

Net migration rate: 1.22 migrant(s)/1,000 population (2014 est.)
country comparison to the world: 58

Urbanization: *urban population:* 32% of total population (2010)
rate of urbanization: 1.8% annual rate of change (2010-15 est.)

Major urban areas—population: BASSETERRE (capital) 13,000 (2009)

Sex ratio: *at birth:* 1.02 male(s)/female
0-14 years: 1 male(s)/female
15-24 years: 0.97 male(s)/female
25-54 years: 1.04 male(s)/female
55-64 years: 1 male(s)/female
65 years and over: 0.8 male(s)/female
total population: 1 male(s)/female (2014 est.)

Infant mortality rate: *total:* 8.98 deaths/1,000 live births
country comparison to the world: 148
male: 6.11 deaths/1,000 live births
female: 11.91 deaths/1,000 live births (2014 est.)

Life expectancy at birth: *total population:* 75.29 years
country comparison to the world: 96
male: 72.88 years
female: 77.75 years (2014 est.)

Total fertility rate: 1.78 children born/woman (2014 est.)
country comparison to the world: 156

Health expenditures: 4.4% of GDP (2011)
country comparison to the world: 152

Physicians density: 1.17 physicians/1,000 population (2001)

Hospital bed density: 4.8 beds/1,000 population (2011)

Drinking water source:
improved:
urban: 98.3% of population
rural: 98.3% of population
total: 98.3% of population
unimproved:
urban: 1.7% of population
rural: 1.7% of population
total: 1.7% of population (2011 est.)

Sanitation facility access:
improved:
urban: 87.3% of population
rural: 87.3% of population
total: 87.3% of population
unimproved:
urban: 12.7% of population
rural: 12.7% of population
total: 12.7% of population (2007 est.)

HIV/AIDS—adult prevalence rate: NA

HIV/AIDS—people living with HIV/AIDS: NA

HIV/AIDS—deaths: NA

Obesity—adult prevalence rate: 40.7% (2008)
country comparison to the world: 11

Education expenditures: 4.2% of GDP (2007)
country comparison to the world: 105

Literacy: *definition:* age 15 and over has ever attended school
total population: 97.8%
male: NA
female: NA (2003 est.)

School life expectancy (primary to tertiary education): *total:* 13 years
male: 12 years
female: 13 years (2008)

GOVERNMENT

Country name: *conventional long form:* Federation of Saint Kitts and Nevis
conventional short form: Saint Kitts and Nevis
former: Federation of Saint Christopher and Nevis

Government type: parliamentary democracy and a Commonwealth realm

Capital: *name:* Basseterre

geographic coordinates: 17 18 N, 62 43 W
time difference: UTC-4 (1 hour ahead of Washington, DC during Standard Time)

Administrative divisions: 14 parishes; Christ Church Nichola Town, Saint Anne Sandy Point, Saint George Basseterre, Saint George Gingerland, Saint James Windward, Saint John Capesterre, Saint John Figtree, Saint Mary Cayon, Saint Paul Capesterre, Saint Paul Charlestown, Saint Peter Basseterre, Saint Thomas Lowland, Saint Thomas Middle Island, Trinity Palmetto Point

Independence: 19 September 1983 (from the UK)

National holiday: Independence Day, 19 September (1983)

Constitution: several previous; latest presented 22 June 1983, effective 23 June 1983 (2011)

Legal system: English common law

International law organization participation: has not submitted an ICJ jurisdiction declaration; accepts ICCt jurisdiction

Suffrage: 18 years of age; universal

Executive branch: *chief of state:* Queen ELIZABETH II (since 6 February 1952); represented by Governor General Sir Edmund LAWRENCE (since 2 January 2013)
head of government: Prime Minister Dr. Denzil DOUGLAS (since 6 July 1995); Deputy Prime Minister Sam CONDOR (since 6 July 1995)
cabinet: Cabinet appointed by the governor general in consultation with the prime minister (For more information visit the World Leaders website)
elections: the monarchy is hereditary; the governor general appointed by the monarch; following legislative elections, the leader of the majority party or leader of a majority coalition usually appointed prime minister by the governor general; deputy prime minister appointed by the governor general

Legislative branch: unicameral National Assembly (14 seats, 3 appointed and 11 popularly elected from single-member constituencies; members serve five-year terms)

elections: last held on 25 January 2010 (next to be held by 2015)
election results: percent of vote by party—NA; seats by party—SKNLP 6, CCM 2, PAM 2, NRP 1

Judicial branch: *highest court(s):* the Eastern Caribbean Supreme Court (ECSC) is the itinerant superior court of record for the 9-member Organization of Eastern Caribbean States which includes Saint Kitts and Nevis; the ECSC—with its headquarters on St. Lucia—is headed by the chief justice and comprised of the Court of Appeal with 3 justices and the High Court with 16 judges; sittings of the Court of Appeal and High Court rotate among the member states; 2 High Court judges reside on Saint Kitts and Nevis note—the Eastern Caribbean Supreme Court in 2003 replaced the Judicial Committee of the Privy Council (in London) as the final court of appeal on Saint Kitts and Nevis; Saint Kitts and Nevis is also a member of the Caribbean Court of Justice
judge selection and term of office: Eastern Caribbean Supreme Court chief justice appointed by Her Majesty, Queen ELIZABETH II; other justices and judges appointed by the Judicial and Legal Services Commission; Court of Appeal justices appointed for life with mandatory retirement at age 65; High Court judges appointed for life with mandatory retirement at age 62
subordinate courts: magistrates' courts

Political parties and leaders: Concerned Citizens Movement or CCM [Vance AMORY]; Nevis Reformation Party or NRP [Joseph PARRY]; People's Action Movement or PAM [Shawn RICHARDS]; Saint Kitts and Nevis Labor Party or SKNLP [Dr. Denzil DOUGLAS]

Political pressure groups and leaders: NA

International organization participation: ACP, AOSIS, C, Caricom, CDB, CELAC, FAO, G-77, IBRD, ICAO, ICRM, IDA, IFAD, IFC, IFRCS, ILO, IMF, IMO, Interpol, IOC, ITU, MIGA, NAM, OAS, OECS, OPANAL, OPCW, Petrocaribe, UN, UNCTAD, UNESCO, UNIDO, UPU, WHO, WIPO, WTO

Diplomatic representation in the US:
chief of mission: Ambassador Jacinth Lorna HENRY-MARTIN (since 14 February 2011)
chancery: 3216 New Mexico Avenue NW, Washington, DC 20016
telephone: [1] (202) 686-2636
FAX: [1] (202) 686-5740
consulate(s) general: Los Angeles, New York

Diplomatic representation from the US: the US does not have an embassy in Saint Kitts and Nevis; the US Ambassador to Barbados is accredited to Saint Kitts and Nevis

Flag description: divided diagonally from the lower hoist side by a broad black band bearing two white, five-pointed stars; the black band is edged in yellow; the upper triangle is green, the lower triangle is red; green signifies the island's fertility, red symbolizes the struggles of the people from slavery, yellow denotes year-round sunshine, and black represents the African heritage of the people; the white stars stand for the islands of Saint Kitts and Nevis, but can also express hope and liberty, or independence and optimism

National symbol(s): brown pelican

National anthem: *name:* "Oh Land of Beauty!"
lyrics/music: Kenrick Anderson GEORGES
note: adopted 1983

ECONOMY

Economy—overview: The economy of Saint Kitts and Nevis depends on tourism; since the 1970s tourism has replaced sugar as the traditional mainstay of the economy. Following the 2005 harvest, the government closed the sugar industry, after several decades of losses. To compensate for lost jobs, the government has embarked on a program to diversify the agricultural sector and to stimulate other sectors of the economy, such as export-oriented manufacturing and offshore banking. Roughly 200,000 tourists visited the islands in 2009, but reduced tourism arrivals and foreign investment led to an economic contraction in 2009-2012, and the economy returned to growth only in 2013. Like other tourist destinations in the Caribbean, St. Kitts and Nevis is vulnerable to damage from natural disasters and shifts in tourism demand. The government has made notable progress on reducing its public debt—from 154% of GDP in 2011 to 83% in 2013—although it still faces one of the highest levels in the world, largely attributable to public enterprise losses.

GDP (purchasing power parity): $952 million (2013 est.)
country comparison to the world: 205
$933.6 million (2012 est.)
$941.7 million (2011 est.)
note: data are in 2013 US dollars

GDP (official exchange rate): $767 million (2013 est.)

GDP—real growth rate: 1.9% (2013 est.)
country comparison to the world: 144
-0.9% (2012 est.)
-1.9% (2011 est.)

GDP—per capita (PPP): $16,300 (2013 est.)
country comparison to the world: 83
$16,300 (2012 est.)
$16,800 (2011 est.)
note: data are in 2013 US dollars

Gross national saving: 32.1% of GDP (2013 est.)
country comparison to the world: 19
34.5% of GDP (2012 est.)
32.4% of GDP (2011 est.)

GDP—composition, by end use:
household consumption: 72.1%
government consumption: 10.6%
investment in fixed capital: 28.4%
investment in inventories: 0%
exports of goods and services: 30.8%
imports of goods and services: -41.9% (2013 est.)

GDP—composition, by sector of origin:
agriculture: 1.8%
industry: 23.1%
services: 75.1% (2013 est.)

Agriculture—products: sugarcane, rice, yams, vegetables, bananas; fish

Industries: tourism, cotton, salt, copra, clothing, footwear, beverages

Industrial production growth rate: 0.5%
country comparison to the world: 160

Labor force: 18,170 (June 1995)
country comparison to the world: 210

Unemployment rate: 4.5% (1997)
country comparison to the world: 38

Population below poverty line: NA%

Household income or consumption by percentage share: *lowest 10%:* NA%
highest 10%: NA%

Budget: *revenues:* $222.2 million
expenditures: $185.2 million (2013 est.)

Taxes and other revenues: 29% of GDP (2013 est.)
country comparison to the world: 96

Budget surplus (+) or deficit (-):
4.8% of GDP (2013 est.)
country comparison to the world: 9

Public debt: 83% of GDP (2013 est.)
country comparison to the world: 25
144% of GDP (2012 est.)

Fiscal year: calendar year

Inflation rate (consumer prices): 2.2% (2013 est.)
country comparison to the world: 73
1.4% (2012 est.)

Central bank discount rate: 6.5% (31 December 2009)
country comparison to the world: 56
6.5% (31 December 2008)

Commercial bank prime lending rate: 8.9% (31 December 2013 est.)
country comparison to the world: 107
8.73% (31 December 2012 est.)

Stock of narrow money: $218.5 million (31 December 2013 est.)
country comparison to the world: 176
$200.4 million (31 December 2012 est.)

Stock of broad money: $867 million (31 December 2013 est.)
country comparison to the world: 171
$869.1 million (31 December 2012 est.)

Stock of domestic credit: $814.8 million (31 December 2013 est.)
country comparison to the world: 159
$809.6 million (31 December 2012 est.)

Market value of publicly traded shares: $598.4 million (31 December 2011)
country comparison to the world: 110
$598.4 million (31 December 2011)
$623.9 million (31 December 2010)

Current account balance: -$133.1 million (2013 est.)
country comparison to the world: 78
-$70.8 million (2012 est.)

Exports: $57.3 million (2013 est.)
country comparison to the world: 194
$68.6 million (2012 est.)

Exports—commodities: machinery, food, electronics, beverages, tobacco

Exports—partners: US 56%, Canada 9.8%, Bangladesh 6.2% (2012)

Imports: $355.4 million (2013 est.)
country comparison to the world: 194
$225.6 million (2012 est.)

Imports—commodities: machinery, manufactures, food, fuels

Imports—partners: US 31.7%, Trinidad and Tobago 19.9%, Italy 7%, Germany 6%, Barbados 4.7% (2012)

Debt—external: $158.9 million (31 December 2013 est.)
country comparison to the world: 188
$189.3 million (31 December 2012 est.)

Exchange rates: East Caribbean dollars (XCD) per US dollar—
2.7 (2013 est.)
2.7 (2012 est.)
2.7 (2010 est.)
2.7 (2009)

ENERGY

Electricity—production: 135 million kWh (2010 est.)
country comparison to the world: 192

Electricity—consumption: 125.6 million kWh (2010 est.)
country comparison to the world: 194

Electricity—exports: 0 kWh (2012 est.)

country comparison to the world: 190
Electricity—imports: 0 kWh (2012 est.)
country comparison to the world: 193
Electricity—installed generating capacity: 55,000 kW (2010 est.)
country comparison to the world: 186
Electricity—from fossil fuels: 100% of total installed capacity (2010 est.)
country comparison to the world: 31
Electricity—from nuclear fuels: 0% of total installed capacity (2010 est.)
country comparison to the world: 173
Electricity—from hydroelectric plants: 0% of total installed capacity (2010 est.)
country comparison to the world: 195
Electricity—from other renewable sources: 0% of total installed capacity (2010 est.)
country comparison to the world: 119
Crude oil—production: 0 bbl/day (2012 est.)
country comparison to the world: 208
Crude oil—exports: 0 bbl/day (2010 est.)
country comparison to the world: 175
Crude oil—imports: 0 bbl/day (2010 est.)
country comparison to the world: 116
Crude oil—proved reserves: 0 bbl (1 January 2013 es)
country comparison to the world: 182
Refined petroleum products—production: 0 bbl/day (2010 est.)
country comparison to the world: 190
Refined petroleum products—consumption: 1,496 bbl/day (2011 est.)
country comparison to the world: 195
Refined petroleum products—exports: 0 bbl/day (2010 est.)
country comparison to the world: 127
Refined petroleum products—imports: 1,784 bbl/day (2010 est.)
country comparison to the world: 182
Natural gas—production: 0 cu m (2011 est.)
country comparison to the world: 186
Natural gas—consumption: 0 cu m (2010 est.)
country comparison to the world: 190
Natural gas—exports: 0 cu m (2011 est.)
country comparison to the world: 176
Natural gas—imports: 0 cu m (2011 est.)
country comparison to the world: 125
Natural gas—proved reserves: 0 cu m (1 January 2013 es)
country comparison to the world: 188
Carbon dioxide emissions from consumption of energy: 302,700 Mt (2011 est.)
country comparison to the world: 188

COMMUNICATIONS

Telephones—main lines in use: 20,000 (2012)
country comparison to the world: 186
Telephones—mobile cellular: 84,000 (2012)
country comparison to the world: 196
Telephone system: *general assessment:* good interisland and international connections
domestic: interisland links via Eastern Caribbean Fiber Optic cable; construction of enhanced wireless infrastructure launched in November 2004; fixed-line teledensity about 40 per 100 persons; mobile-cellular teledensity is roughly 170 per 100 persons
international: country code—1-869; connected internationally by the East Caribbean Fiber Optic System (ECFS) and Southern Caribbean fiber optic system (SCF) submarine cables (2010)
Broadcast media: the government operates a national TV network that broadcasts on 2 channels; cable subscription services provide access to local and international channels; the government operates a national radio network; a mix of government-owned and privately owned broadcasters operate roughly 15 radio stations (2007)
Internet country code: .kn
Internet hosts: 54 (2012)
country comparison to the world: 213
Internet users: 17,000 (2009)
country comparison to the world: 197

TRANSPORTATION

Airports: 2 (2013)
country comparison to the world: 204
Airports—with paved runways: *total:* 2
1,524 to 2,437 m: 1
914 to 1,523 m: 1 (2013)
Railways: *total:* 50 km
country comparison to the world: 130
narrow gauge: 50 km 0.762-m gauge on Saint Kitts for tourists (2008)
Roadways: *total:* 383 km
country comparison to the world: 200
paved: 163 km
unpaved: 220 km (2002)
Merchant marine: *total:* 152
country comparison to the world: 38
by type: bulk carrier 16, cargo 81, chemical tanker 4, combination ore/oil 1, container 2, liquefied gas 3, passenger 2, passenger/cargo 7, petroleum tanker 27, refrigerated cargo 4, roll on/roll off 4, specialized tanker 1
foreign-owned: 73 (Belgium 1, China 1, Egypt 1, Greece 2, India 2, Japan 2, Malaysia 1, Norway 3, Pakistan 1, Russia 13, Singapore 10, Turkey 18, UAE 8, UK 1, Ukraine 8, US 1) (2010)
Ports and terminals: *major seaport(s):* Basseterre, Charlestown

MILITARY

Military branches: Ministry of Foreign Affairs, National Security, Labour, Immigration, and Social Security: Royal Saint Kitts and Nevis Defense Force (includes Coast Guard), Royal Saint Kitts and Nevis Police Force (2013)
Military service age and obligation: 18 years of age for voluntary military service; no conscription (2012)
Manpower available for military service:
males age 16-49: 13,506
females age 16-49: 13,089 (2010 est.)
Manpower fit for military service:
males age 16-49: 10,742
females age 16-49: 10,923 (2010 est.)
Manpower reaching militarily significant age annually: *male:* 380
female: 422 (2010 est.)

TRANSNATIONAL ISSUES

Disputes—international: joins other Caribbean states to counter Venezuela's claim that Aves Island sustains human habitation, a criterion under United Nations Convention on the Law of the Sea, which permits Venezuela to extend its Economic Exclusion Zone/continental shelf over a large portion of the eastern Caribbean Sea
Illicit drugs: transshipment point for South American drugs destined for the US and Europe; some money-laundering activity

SAINT LUCIA

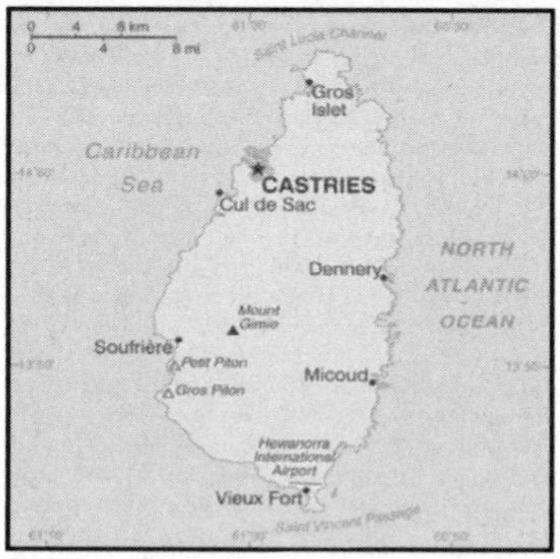

INTRODUCTION

Background: The island, with its fine natural harbor at Castries, was contested between England and France throughout the 17th and early 18th centuries (changing possession 14 times); it was finally ceded to the UK in 1814. Even after the abolition of slavery on its plantations in 1834, Saint Lucia remained an agricultural island, dedicated to producing tropical commodity crops. Self-government was granted in 1967 and independence in 1979.

GEOGRAPHY

Location: Caribbean, island between the Caribbean Sea and North Atlantic Ocean, north of Trinidad and Tobago
Geographic coordinates: 13 53 N, 60 58 W
Map references: Central America and the Caribbean
Area: *total:* 616 sq km
country comparison to the world: 193
land: 606 sq km
water: 10 sq km
Area—comparative: three and a half times the size of Washington, DC
Land boundaries: 0 km
Coastline: 158 km
Maritime claims: *territorial sea:* 12 nm
contiguous zone: 24 nm
exclusive economic zone: 200 nm
continental shelf: 200 nm or to the edge of the continental margin
Climate: tropical, moderated by northeast trade winds; dry season January to April, rainy season May to August

Terrain: volcanic and mountainous with some broad, fertile valleys

Elevation extremes:
lowest point: Caribbean Sea 0 m
highest point: Mount Gimie 950 m

Natural resources: forests, sandy beaches, minerals (pumice), mineral springs, geothermal potential

Land use: *arable land:* 4.84%
permanent crops: 11.29%
other: 83.87% (2011)

Irrigated land: 30 sq km (2007)

Freshwater withdrawal (domestic/industrial/agricultural): *total:* 0.02 cu km/yr (NA)
per capita: 98.22 cu m/yr (2005)

Natural hazards: hurricanes; volcanic activity

Environment—current issues: deforestation; soil erosion, particularly in the northern region

Environment—international agreements:
party to: Biodiversity, Climate Change, Climate Change-Kyoto Protocol, Desertification, Endangered Species, Environmental Modification, Hazardous Wastes, Law of the Sea, Marine Dumping, Ozone Layer Protection, Ship Pollution, Wetlands, Whaling
signed, but not ratified: none of the selected agreements

Geography—note: the twin Pitons (Gros Piton and Petit Piton), striking cone-shaped peaks south of Soufriere, are one of the scenic natural highlights of the Caribbean

PEOPLE AND SOCIETY

Nationality: *noun:* Saint Lucian(s)
adjective: Saint Lucian

Ethnic groups: black/African descent 85.3%, mixed 10.9%, East Indian 2.2%, other 1.6%, unspecified 0.1% (2010 est.)

Languages: English (official), French patois

Religions: Roman Catholic 61.5%, Protestant 25.5% (includes Seventh Day Adventist 10.4%, Pentecostal 8.9%, Baptist 2.2%, Anglican 1.6%, Church of God 1.5%, other Protestant .9%), other Christian 3.4% (includes Evangelical 2.3% and Jehovah's Witness 1.1%), Rastafarian 1.9%, other 0.4%, none 5.9%, unspecified 1.4% (2010 est.)

Population: 163,362 (July 2014 est.)
country comparison to the world: 187

Age structure:
0-14 years: 21.2% (male 17,814/female 16,809)
15-24 years: 16.6% (male 13,701/female 13,368)
25-54 years: 42.9% (male 33,695/female 36,445)
55-64 years: 10.5% (male 6,657/female 7,717)
65 years and over: 10.2% (male 7,760/female 9,396) (2014 est.)

Dependency ratios:
total dependency ratio: 48.6 %
youth dependency ratio: 35.6 %
elderly dependency ratio: 13 %
potential support ratio: 7.7 (2013)

Median age: *total:* 32.9 years
male: 31.7 years
female: 34 years (2014 est.)

Population growth rate: 0.35% (2014 est.)
country comparison to the world: 166

Birth rate: 13.94 births/1,000 population (2014 est.)
country comparison to the world: 141

Death rate: 7.32 deaths/1,000 population (2014 est.)
country comparison to the world: 122

Net migration rate: -3.13 migrant(s)/1,000 population (2014 est.)
country comparison to the world: 180

Urbanization: *urban population:* 28% of total population (2010)
rate of urbanization: 1.6% annual rate of change (2010-15 est.)

Major urban areas—population: CASTRIES (capital) 15,000 (2009)

Sex ratio: *at birth:* 1.06 male(s)/female
0-14 years: 1.06 male(s)/female
15-24 years: 1.03 male(s)/female
25-54 years: 0.93 male(s)/female
55-64 years: 0.95 male(s)/female
65 years and over: 0.83 male(s)/female
total population: 0.95 male(s)/female (2014 est.)

Maternal mortality rate: 35 deaths/100,000 live births (2010)
country comparison to the world: 117

Infant mortality rate: *total:* 11.75 deaths/1,000 live births
country comparison to the world: 127
male: 11.15 deaths/1,000 live births
female: 12.4 deaths/1,000 live births (2014 est.)

Life expectancy at birth:
total population: 77.41 years
country comparison to the world: 67
male: 74.69 years
female: 80.28 years (2014 est.)

Total fertility rate: 1.77 children born/woman (2014 est.)
country comparison to the world: 161

Health expenditures: 7.2% of GDP (2011)
country comparison to the world: 81

Physicians density: 0.47 physicians/1,000 population (2002)

Hospital bed density: 1.6 beds/1,000 population (2011)

Drinking water source:
improved:
urban: 98.4% of population
rural: 92.8% of population
total: 93.8% of population
unimproved:
urban: 1.6% of population
rural: 7.2% of population
total: 6.2% of population (2011 est.)

Sanitation facility access:
improved:
urban: 70.4% of population
rural: 64.1% of population
total: 65.2% of population
unimproved:
urban: 29.6% of population
rural: 35.9% of population
total: 34.8% of population (2011 est.)

HIV/AIDS—adult prevalence rate: NA

HIV/AIDS—people living with HIV/AIDS: NA

HIV/AIDS—deaths: NA

Obesity—adult prevalence rate: 21.4% (2008)
country comparison to the world: 87

Education expenditures: 4.1% of GDP (2012)
country comparison to the world: 107

Literacy: *definition:* age 15 and over has ever attended school
total population: 90.1%
male: 89.5%
female: 90.6% (2001 est.)

School life expectancy (primary to tertiary education): *total:* 12 years
male: 12 years
female: 13 years (2012)

Unemployment, youth ages 15-24: *total:* 40.8%
country comparison to the world: 12
male: 37.1%
female: 45.5% (2004)

GOVERNMENT

Country name: *conventional long form:* none
conventional short form: Saint Lucia

Government type: parliamentary democracy and a Commonwealth realm

Capital: *name:* Castries

geographic coordinates: 14 00 N, 61 00 W
time difference: UTC-4 (1 hour ahead of Washington, DC during Standard Time)

Administrative divisions: 10 districts; Anse-la-Raye, Canaries, Castries, Choiseul, Dennery, Gros-Islet, Laborie, Micoud, Soufriere, Vieux-Fort

Independence: 22 February 1979 (from the UK)

National holiday: Independence Day, 22 February (1979)

Constitution: previous 1958, 1960 (preindependence); latest presented 20 December 1978, effective 22 February 1979; note—a constitutional reform report was submitted to the St. Lucian Parliament in April 2013 (2013)

Legal system: English common law

International law organization participation: has not submitted an ICJ jurisdiction declaration; accepts ICCt jurisdiction

Suffrage: 18 years of age; universal

Executive branch: *chief of state:* Queen ELIZABETH II (since 6 February 1952); represented by Governor General Dame Pearlette LOUISY (since September 1997)
head of government: Prime Minister Kenny Davis ANTHONY (since 30 November 2011)
cabinet: Cabinet appointed by the governor general on the advice of the prime minister (For more information visit the World Leaders website)
elections: the monarchy is hereditary; the governor general appointed by the monarch; following legislative elections, the leader of the majority party or the leader of a majority coalition usually appointed prime minister by the governor general; deputy prime minister appointed by the governor general

Legislative branch: bicameral Parliament consists of the Senate (11 seats; six members appointed on the advice of the prime minister, three on the advice of the leader of the opposition, and two after consultation with religious, economic, and social groups) and the House of Assembly (17 seats; members elected by popular vote to serve five-year terms)
elections: House of Assembly—last held on 28 November 2011 (next to be held in 2016)
election results: House of Assembly—percent of vote by party—SLP 49.68%, UWP 45.83%; seats by party—SLP 11, UWP 6

Judicial branch: *highest court(s):* the Eastern Caribbean Supreme Court (ECSC) is the itinerant superior court of record for the 9-member Organization of Eastern Caribbean States; the ECSC—with its headquarters on St. Lucia—is headed by the chief justice and is comprised of the Court of Appeal with 3 justices and the High Court with 16 judges; sittings of the Court of Appeal and High Court rotate among the member states; 3 High Court judges reside on Saint Lucia note—Saint Lucia is a member of the Caribbean Court of Justice
judge selection and term of office: Eastern Caribbean Supreme Court chief justice appointed by Her Majesty, Queen ELIZABETH II; other justices and judges appointed by the Judicial and Legal Services Commission; Court of Appeal justices appointed for life with mandatory retirement at age 65; High Court judges appointed for life with mandatory retirement at age 62
subordinate courts: magistrate's court

Political parties and leaders: Lucian People's Movement or LPM [Therold PRUDENT]; Saint Lucia Labor Party or SLP [Kenny ANTHONY]; United Workers Party or UWP [Stephenson KING]

Political pressure groups and leaders: NA

International organization participation: ACP, AOSIS, C, Caricom, CD, CDB, CELAC, FAO, G-77, IBRD, ICAO, ICRM, IDA, IFAD, IFC, IFRCS, ILO, IMF, IMO, Interpol, IOC, ISO, ITU, ITUC (NGOs), MIGA, NAM, OAS, OECS, OIF, OPANAL, OPCW, Petrocaribe, UN, UNCTAD, UNESCO, UNIDO, UPU, WCO, WFTU (NGOs), WHO, WIPO, WMO, WTO

Diplomatic representation in the US:
chief of mission: Ambassador Sonia Merlyn JOHNNY (since 12 September 2012)
chancery: 3216 New Mexico Avenue NW, Washington, DC 20016
telephone: [1] (202) 364-6792 through 6795
FAX: [1] (202) 364-6723
consulate(s) general: Coral Gables (FL), New York

Diplomatic representation from the US: the US does not have an embassy in Saint Lucia; the US Ambassador to Barbados is accredited to Saint Lucia

Flag description: blue, with a gold isosceles triangle below a black arrowhead; the upper edges of the arrowhead have a white border; the blue color represents the sky and sea, gold stands for sunshine and prosperity, and white and black the racial composition of the island (with the latter being dominant); the two major triangles invoke the twin Pitons (Gros Piton and Petit Piton), cone-shaped volcanic plugs that are a symbol of the island

National symbol(s): twin pitons (volcanic peaks); Saint Lucia parrot

National anthem: *name:* "Sons and Daughters of St. Lucia"
lyrics/music: Charles JESSE/Leton Felix THOMAS
note: adopted 1967

ECONOMY

Economy—overview: The island nation has been able to attract foreign business and investment, especially in its offshore banking and tourism industries. Tourism is Saint Lucia's main source of jobs and income—accounting for 65% of GDP—and the island's main source of foreign exchange earnings. The manufacturing sector is the most diverse in the Eastern Caribbean area. Crops such as bananas, mangos, and avocados continue to be grown for export, but St. Lucia's once solid banana industry has been devastated by strong competition. Saint Lucia is vulnerable to a variety of external shocks, including volatile tourism receipts, natural disasters, and dependence on foreign oil. Furthermore, high public debt—77% of GDP in 2012—and high debt servicing obligations constrain the ANTHONY administration's ability to respond to adverse external shocks. St. Lucia has experienced anemic growth since the onset of the global financial crisis in 2008, largely because of a slowdown in tourism—airlines cut back on their routes to St. Lucia in 2012. Also, St. Lucia introduced a value added tax in 2012 of 15%, becoming the last country in the Eastern Caribbean to do so. In 2013, the government introduced a National Competitiveness and Productivity Council to address St. Lucia's high public wages and lack of productivity.

GDP (purchasing power parity): $2.216 billion (2013 est.)
country comparison to the world: 191
$2.211 billion (2012 est.)
$2.23 billion (2011 est.)
note: data are in 2013 US dollars

GDP (official exchange rate): $1.377 billion (2013 est.)

GDP—real growth rate: 0.2% (2013 est.)
country comparison to the world: 190
-0.9% (2012 est.)
1.8% (2011 est.)

GDP—per capita (PPP): $13,100 (2013 est.)
country comparison to the world: 100
$13,200 (2012 est.)
$13,400 (2011 est.)
note: data are in 2013 US dollars

Gross national saving: 17.4% of GDP (2013 est.)
country comparison to the world: 95
18.6% of GDP (2013 est.)
15.3% of GDP (2013 est.)

GDP—composition, by end use:
household consumption: 60.6%
government consumption: 19%
investment in fixed capital: 31.5%
investment in inventories: 0%
exports of goods and services: 50.3%
imports of goods and services: -61.3% (2013 est.)

GDP—composition, by sector of origin:
agriculture: 3.1%
industry: 17.4%
services: 79.5% (2013 est.)

Agriculture—products: bananas, coconuts, vegetables, citrus, root crops, cocoa

Industries: tourism; clothing, assembly of electronic components, beverages, corrugated cardboard boxes, lime processing, coconut processing

Industrial production growth rate: 2.6%
country comparison to the world: 114

Labor force: 79,700 (2012)
country comparison to the world: 184

Labor force—by occupation: *agriculture:* 21.7%
industry: 24.7%
services: 53.6% (2002 est.)

Unemployment rate: 20% (2003 est.)
country comparison to the world: 161

Population below poverty line: NA%

Household income or consumption by percentage share: *lowest 10%:* NA%
highest 10%: NA%

Budget: *revenues:* $185.2 million
expenditures: $222.2 million (2011 est.)

Taxes and other revenues: 13.4% of GDP (2011 est.)
country comparison to the world: 198

Budget surplus (+) or deficit (-):
-2.7% of GDP (2011 est.)
country comparison to the world: 114

Public debt: 77% of GDP (2012 est.)
country comparison to the world: 30
77% of GDP (2010 est.)

Fiscal year: 1 April—31 March

Inflation rate (consumer prices): 5.3% (2013 est.)
country comparison to the world: 159
4.2% (2012 est.)

Central bank discount rate: 6.5% (31 December 2010 est.)
country comparison to the world: 55
6.5% (31 December 2009 est.)

Commercial bank prime lending rate: 9.3% (31 December 2013 est.)
country comparison to the world: 94
9.5% (31 December 2012 est.)

Stock of narrow money: $270.3 million (31 December 2013 est.)
country comparison to the world: 172
$259.6 million (31 December 2012 est.)

Stock of broad money: $1.073 billion (31 December 2013 est.)
country comparison to the world: 167
$1.036 billion (31 December 2012 est.)

Stock of domestic credit: $1.699 billion (31 December 2013 est.)
country comparison to the world: 138
$1.598 billion (31 December 2012 est.)

Current account balance: -$210.2 million (2013 est.)
country comparison to the world: 87
-$184.4 million (2012 est.)

Exports: $206.8 million (2013 est.)
country comparison to the world: 183
$190.1 million (2012 est.)

Exports—commodities: bananas 41%, clothing, cocoa, avacados, mangoes, coconut oil

Exports—partners: US 13.9%, UK 10.3%, Peru 9.7%, Antigua and Barbuda 9.3%, Dominica 9.1%, France 9%, Barbados 8.1%, Trinidad and Tobago 7.6%, Grenada 6.2% (2012)

Imports: $592.7 million (2013 est.)
country comparison to the world: 190
$579.3 million (2012 est.)

Imports—commodities: food 23%, manufactured goods 21%, machinery and transportation equipment 19%, chemicals, fuels

Imports—partners: Brazil 57.4%, US 19%, Trinidad and Tobago 9% (2012)

Debt—external: $446.4 million (31 December 2013 est.)
country comparison to the world: 177
$438.7 million (31 December 2012 est.)

Exchange rates: East Caribbean dollars (XCD) per US dollar—
2.7 (2013 est.)
2.7 (2012 est.)
2.7 (2010 est.)
2.7 (2009)

ENERGY

Electricity—production: 362 million kWh (2011 est.)
country comparison to the world: 167

Electricity—consumption: 332.9 million kWh (2010 est.)
country comparison to the world: 171

Electricity—exports: 0 kWh (2012 est.)
country comparison to the world: 197

Electricity—imports: 0 kWh (2012 est.)
country comparison to the world: 200

Electricity—installed generating capacity: 76,000 kW (2010 est.)
country comparison to the world: 178

Electricity—from fossil fuels: 100% of total installed capacity (2010 est.)
country comparison to the world: 35

Electricity—from nuclear fuels: 0% of total installed capacity (2010 est.)
country comparison to the world: 180

Electricity—from hydroelectric plants: 0% of total installed capacity (2010 est.)
country comparison to the world: 201

Electricity—from other renewable sources: 0% of total installed capacity (2010 est.)
country comparison to the world: 124

Crude oil—production: 0 bbl/day (2012 est.)
country comparison to the world: 134

Crude oil—exports: 0 bbl/day (2010 est.)
country comparison to the world: 185

Crude oil—imports: 0 bbl/day (2010 est.)
country comparison to the world: 122

Crude oil—proved reserves: 0 bbl (1 January 2013 es)
country comparison to the world: 190
Refined petroleum products—production: 0 bbl/day (2010 est.)
country comparison to the world: 196
Refined petroleum products—consumption: 2,922 bbl/day (2011 est.)
country comparison to the world: 182
Refined petroleum products—exports: 0 bbl/day (2010 est.)
country comparison to the world: 132
Refined petroleum products—imports: 2,914 bbl/day (2010 est.)
country comparison to the world: 172
Natural gas—production: 0 cu m (2011 est.)
country comparison to the world: 192
Natural gas—consumption:—0 cu m (2010 est.)
country comparison to the world: 195
Natural gas—exports: 0 cu m (2011 est.)
country comparison to the world: 184
Natural gas—imports: 0 cu m (2011 est.)
country comparison to the world: 131
Natural gas—proved reserves: 0 cu m (1 January 2013 es)
country comparison to the world: 194
Carbon dioxide emissions from consumption of energy: 424,900 Mt (2011 est.)
country comparison to the world: 185

COMMUNICATIONS

Telephones—main lines in use: 36,800 (2012)
country comparison to the world: 172
Telephones—mobile cellular: 227,000 (2012)
country comparison to the world: 179
Telephone system: *general assessment:* an adequate system that is automatically switched
domestic: fixed-line teledensity is 25 per 100 persons and mobile-cellular teledensity is roughly 130 per 100 persons
international: country code—1-758; the East Caribbean Fiber Optic System (ECFS) and Southern Caribbean fiber optic system (SCF) submarine cables, along with Intelsat from Martinique, carry calls internationally; direct microwave radio relay link with Martinique and Saint Vincent and the Grenadines; tropospheric scatter to Barbados (2010)
Broadcast media: 3 privately owned TV stations; 1 public TV station operating on a cable network; multi-channel cable TV service available; a mix of state-owned and privately owned broadcasters operate nearly 25 radio stations including repeater transmission stations (2007)
Internet country code: .lc
Internet hosts: 100 (2012)
country comparison to the world: 209
Internet users: 142,900 (2009)
country comparison to the world: 149

TRANSPORTATION

Airports: 2 (2013)
country comparison to the world: 205
Airports—with paved runways: *total:* 2
2,438 to 3,047 m: 1
1,524 to 2,437 m: 1 (2013)
Roadways: *total:* 1,210 km
country comparison to the world: 181
paved: 847 km
unpaved: 363 km (2011)
Ports and terminals: *major seaport(s):* Castries, Cul-de-Sac, Vieux-Fort

MILITARY

Military branches: no regular military forces; Royal Saint Lucia Police Force (includes Special Service Unit, Marine Unit) (2012)
Military service age and obligation: 18 years of age for voluntary security service; no national army (2012)
Manpower available for military service:
males age 16-49: 41,414 (2010 est.)
Manpower fit for military service:
males age 16-49: 32,688
females age 16-49: 36,289 (2010 est.)
Manpower reaching militarily significant age annually: *male:* 1,574
female: 1,502 (2010 est.)

TRANSNATIONAL ISSUES

Disputes—international: joins other Caribbean states to counter Venezuela's claim that Aves Island sustains human habitation, a criterion under United Nations Convention on the Law of the Sea, which permits Venezuela to extend its Economic Exclusion Zone/continental shelf over a large portion of the eastern Caribbean Sea
Trafficking in persons: *current situation:* St. Lucia is a destination country for persons subjected to forced prostitution and forced labor; legal and illegal immigrants from Haiti, Jamaica, the Dominican Republic, Guyana, and South Asia, especially those working in domestic service, are vulnerable to human trafficking; some children under 18 are coerced to work in St. Lucia's commercial sex industry
tier rating: Tier 2 Watch List—St. Lucia does not fully comply with the minimum standards for the elimination of trafficking; however, it is making significant efforts to do so; the government did not report any investigations, prosecutions, or convictions of trafficking offenders or public officials complicit in human trafficking in 2012 or 2011, although a counter-trafficking act was passed in 2010; the government helps protect trafficking victims by funding an NGO and running a system of informal shelters but lacks formal procedures for identifying victims and referring them to available protection and assistance services; St. Lucia is not a party to the 2000 UN TIP Protocol (2013)
Illicit drugs: transit point for South American drugs destined for the US and Europe

SAINT MARTIN

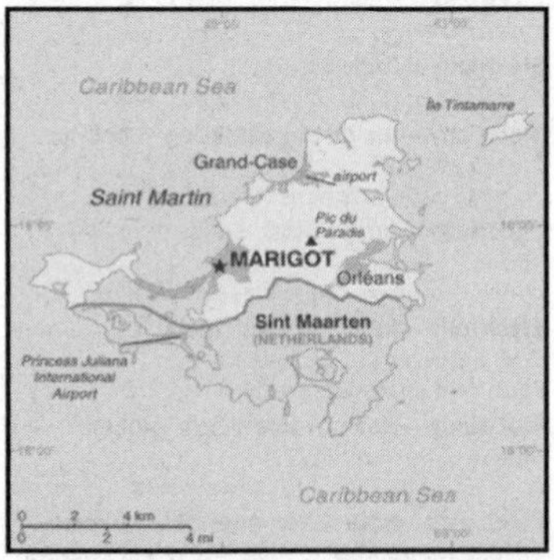

INTRODUCTION

Background: Although sighted by Christopher COLUMBUS in 1493 and claimed for Spain, it was the Dutch who occupied the island in 1631 and set about exploiting its salt deposits. The Spanish retook the island in 1633, but continued to be harassed by the Dutch. The Spanish finally relinquished Saint Martin to the French and Dutch, who divided it between themselves in 1648. Friction between the two sides caused the border to frequently fluctuate over the next two centuries, with the French eventually holding the greater portion of the island (about 57%). The cultivation of sugar cane introduced African slavery to the island in the late 18th century; the practice was not abolished until 1848. The island became a free port in 1939; the tourism industry was dramatically expanded during the 1970s and 1980s. In 2003, the populace of Saint Martin voted to secede from Guadeloupe and in 2007, the northern portion of the island became a French overseas collectivity. In 2010, the southern Dutch portion of the island became the independent nation of Sint Maarten within the Kingdom of the Netherlands.

GEOGRAPHY

Location: Caribbean, located in the Leeward Islands (northern) group; French part of the island of Saint Martin in the Caribbean Sea; Saint Martin lies east of the US Virgin Islands
Geographic coordinates: 18 05 N, 63 57 W
Map references: Central America and the Caribbean
Area: *total:* 54.4 sq km
country comparison to the world: 231
land: 54.4 sq km
water: NEGL
Area—comparative: more than one-third the size of Washington, DC
Land boundaries: *total:* 15 km
border countries: Sint Maarten 15 km
Coastline: 58.9 km (for entire island)
Climate: temperature averages 80-85 degrees all year long; low humidity, gentle trade winds, brief, intense rain showers; hurricane season stretches from July to November
Elevation extremes: *lowest point:* Caribbean Ocean 0 m
highest point: Pic du Paradis 424 m
Natural resources: salt

Natural hazards: subject to hurricanes from July to November

Environment—current issues: freshwater supply is dependent on desalinization of sea water

Geography—note: the island of Saint Martin is the smallest landmass in the world shared by two independent states, the French territory of Saint Martin and the Dutch territory of Sint Maarten

PEOPLE AND SOCIETY

Ethnic groups: Creole (mulatto), black, Guadeloupe Mestizo (French-East Asia), white, East Indian

Languages: French (official), English, Dutch, French Patois, Spanish, Papiamento (dialect of Netherlands Antilles)

Religions: Roman Catholic, Jehovah's Witnesses, Protestant, Hindu

Population: 31,530 (July 2014 est.)
country comparison to the world: 217

Age structure:
0-14 years: 26.6% (male 4,179/female 4,216)
15-24 years: 10.8% (male 1,721/female 1,678)
25-54 years: 47.2% (male 7,046/female 7,836)
55-64 years: 6.9% (male 1,246/female 1,420)
65 years and over: 6.6% (male 978/female 1,210) (2014 est.)

Median age: *total:* 31.8 years
male: 30.7 years
female: 32.7 years (2014 est.)

Sex ratio: *at birth:* 1.04 male(s)/female
0-14 years: 0.99 male(s)/female
15-24 years: 1.03 male(s)/female
25-54 years: 0.9 male(s)/female
55-64 years: 0.93 male(s)/female
65 years and over: 0.81 male(s)/female
total population: 0.93 male(s)/female (2014 est.)

GOVERNMENT

Country name: *conventional long form:* Overseas Collectivity of Saint Martin
conventional short form: Saint Martin
local long form: Collectivite d'outre mer de Saint-Martin
local short form: Saint-Martin

Dependency status: overseas collectivity of France

Capital: *name:* Marigot

geographical coordinates: 18 04 N, 63 05 W
time difference: UTC-4 (1 hour ahead of Washington, DC during Standard Time)

Independence: none (overseas collectivity of France)

National holiday: Fete de la Federation, 14 July (1789); note—local holiday is Schoalcher Day (Slavery Abolition Day) 12 July (1848)

Constitution: 4 October 1958 (French Constitution) (2013)

Legal system: French civil law

Suffrage: 18 years of age, universal

Executive branch: *chief of state:* President Francois HOLLANDE (since 15 May 2012), represented by Deputy Prefect Philippe CHOPIN (since 16 November 2011)
head of government: President of the Territorial Council Aline HANSON (since 17 April 2013)
cabinet: Executive Council; note—there is also an advisory economic, social, and cultural council (For more information visit the World Leaders website)
election: French president elected by popular vote to a five-year term; prefect appointed by the French president on the advice of the French Ministry of Interior; president of the Territorial Council elected by the members of the Council for a five-year term
election results: Aline HANSON elected president by the Territorial Council on 17 April 2013 (next to be held in 2018); note—Alaine RICHARDSON was removed from the post

Legislative branch: unicameral Territorial Council (23 seats; members are elected by popular vote to serve five-year terms)
elections: last held on 18 and 25 March 2012 (next to be held in July 2017)
election results: percent of seats by party—RRR 34.1%, Team Daniel Gibbs 2012 32%, UPP 13.3%, Saint-Martin pour tous 9.4%, other 11.2%; seats by party—NA; second round, percent of seats by party—RRR 56.9%, Team Daniel Gibbs 43.1%; seats by party—RRR 17, Team Daniel Gibbs 6
note: Saint Martin elects one member to the French Senate; election last held on 21 September 2008 (next to be held in September 2014); results—percent of vote by party—NA; seats by party—UMP 1; one seat (shared with Saint Barthelemy) was elected to the French National Assembly on 17 June 2012 (next to be held by June 2017); results—percent of vote by party—NA; seats by party—UMP 1

Political parties and leaders: Union Pour le Progres or UPP [Louis-Constant FLEMING]; Rassemblement Responsabilite Reussite or RRR [Alain RICHARDSON]; Reussir Saint-Martin [Jean-Luc HAMLET]; Saint-Martin pour tous; Team Daniel Gibbs

Political pressure groups and leaders: NA

International organization participation: UPU

Diplomatic representation in the US: none (overseas collectivity of France)

Diplomatic representation from the US: none (overseas collectivity of France)

Flag description: the flag of France is used

National symbol(s): brown pelican

National anthem: *name:* "O Sweet Saint Martin's Land"
lyrics/music: Gerard KEMPS
note: the song, written in 1958, is used as an unofficial anthem for the entire island (both French and Dutch sides); as a collectivity of France, in addition to the local anthem, "La Marseillaise" remains official on the French side (see France); as a constituent part of the Kingdom of the Netherlands, in addition to the local anthem, "Het Wilhelmus" remains official on the Dutch side (see Netherlands)

ECONOMY

Economy—overview: The economy of Saint Martin centers around tourism with 85% of the labor force engaged in this sector. Over one million visitors come to the island each year with most arriving through the Princess Juliana International Airport in Sint Maarten. No significant agriculture and limited local fishing means that almost all food must be imported. Energy resources and manufactured goods are also imported, primarily from Mexico and the United States. Saint Martin is reported to have the highest per capita income in the Caribbean.

GDP (purchasing power parity): $561.5 million (2005 est.)

GDP (official exchange rate): $561.5 million (2005 est.)

GDP—per capita (PPP): $19,300 (2005 est.)

GDP—composition, by sector of origin:
agriculture: 1%
industry: 15%
services: 84% (2000)

Industries: tourism, light industry and manufacturing, heavy industry

Labor force: 17,300 (2008 est.)
country comparison to the world: 212

Labor force—by occupation: 85% directly or indirectly employed in tourist industry

Imports—commodities: crude petroleum, food, manufactured items

Exchange rates: euros (EUR) per US dollar
0.7107 (2011 est.)
0.755 (2010 est.)
0.7198 (2009 est.)
0.6827 (2008 est.)

COMMUNICATIONS

Telephone system: *general assessment:* fully integrated access
domestic: direct dial capability with both fixed and wireless systems
international: country code—590; undersea fiber-optic cable provides voice and data connectivity to Puerto Rico and Guadeloupe (2009)

Broadcast media: 1 local TV station; access to about 20 radio stations, including RFO Guadeloupe radio broadcasts via repeater (2008)

Internet country code: .mf; note—.gp, the Internet country code for Guadeloupe, and .fr, the Internet country code for France, might also be encountered

TRANSPORTATION

Airports: 1 (2013)
country comparison to the world: 231

Airports—with paved runways: *total:* 1
914 to 1,523 m: 1 (2013)

Transportation—note: nearest airport for international flights is Princess Juliana International Airport (SXM) located on Sint Maarten

MILITARY

Manpower fit for military service:
males age 16-49: 6,435
females age 16-49: 6,967 (2010 est.)

Manpower reaching militarily significant age annually: *male:* 168
female: 168 (2010 est.)

Military—note: defense is the responsibility of France

SAINT PIERRE AND MIQUELON

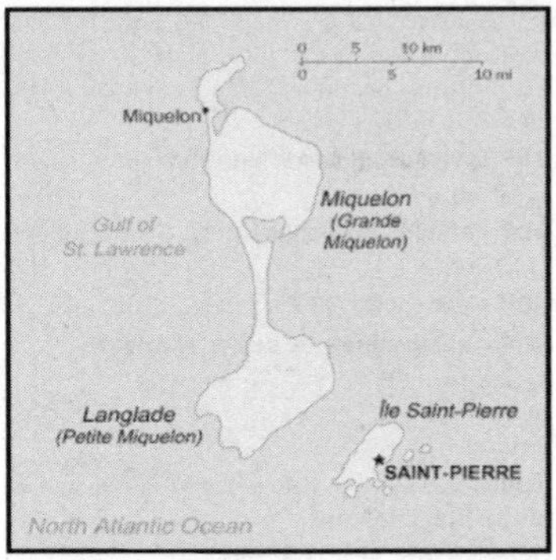

INTRODUCTION

Background: First settled by the French in the early 17th century, the islands represent the sole remaining vestige of France's once vast North American possessions.

GEOGRAPHY

Location: Northern North America, islands in the North Atlantic Ocean, south of Newfoundland (Canada)

Geographic coordinates: 46 50 N, 56 20 W

Map references: North America

Area: *total:* 242 sq km
country comparison to the world: 214
land: 242 sq km
water: 0 sq km
note: includes eight small islands in the Saint Pierre and the Miquelon groups

Area—comparative: one and half times the size of Washington, DC

Land boundaries: 0 km

Coastline: 120 km

Maritime claims: *territorial sea:* 12 nm
exclusive economic zone: 200 nm

Climate: cold and wet, with considerable mist and fog; spring and autumn are often windy

Terrain: mostly barren rock

Elevation extremes: *lowest point:* Atlantic Ocean 0 m
highest point: Morne de la Grande Montagne 240 m

Natural resources: fish, deepwater ports

Land use: *arable land:* 8.7%
permanent crops: 0%
other: 91.3% (2011)

Irrigated land: NA

Natural hazards: persistent fog throughout the year can be a maritime hazard

Environment—current issues: recent test drilling for oil in waters around Saint Pierre and Miquelon may bring future development that would impact the environment

Geography—note: vegetation scanty

PEOPLE AND SOCIETY

Nationality: *noun:* Frenchman(men), Frenchwoman (women)
adjective: French

Ethnic groups: Basques and Bretons (French fishermen)

Languages: French (official)

Religions: Roman Catholic 99%, other 1%

Population: 5,716 (July 2014 est.)
country comparison to the world: 230

Age structure:
0-14 years: 16.3% (male 481/female 450)
15-24 years: 8.5% (male 249/female 235)
25-54 years: 43.5% (male 1,234/female 1,252)
55-64 years: 17.9% (male 416/female 378)
65 years and over: 17.1% (male 421/female 600) (2014 est.)

Median age: *total:* 44.6 years
male: 44.2 years
female: 45 years (2014 est.)

Population growth rate: -1.02% (2014 est.)
country comparison to the world: 230

Birth rate: 7.7 births/1,000 population (2014 est.)
country comparison to the world: 223

Death rate: 9.27 deaths/1,000 population (2014 est.)
country comparison to the world: 63

Net migration rate: -8.57 migrant(s)/1,000 population (2014 est.)
country comparison to the world: 209

Urbanization: *urban population:* 91% of total population (2010)
rate of urbanization: 0.1% annual rate of change (2010-15 est.)

Major urban areas—population: SAINT-PIERRE (capital) 5,000 (2009)

Sex ratio: *at birth:* 1.1 male(s)/female
0-14 years: 1.07 male(s)/female
15-24 years: 1.06 male(s)/female
25-54 years: 0.99 male(s)/female
55-64 years: 0.96 male(s)/female
65 years and over: 0.69 male(s)/female
total population: 0.97 male(s)/female (2014 est.)

Infant mortality rate: *total:* 6.95 deaths/1,000 live births
country comparison to the world: 162
male: 8.07 deaths/1,000 live births
female: 5.76 deaths/1,000 live births (2014 est.)

Life expectancy at birth: *total population:* 80.26 years
country comparison to the world: 31
male: 77.95 years
female: 82.7 years (2014 est.)

Total fertility rate: 1.56 children born/woman (2014 est.)
country comparison to the world: 184

HIV/AIDS—adult prevalence rate: NA

HIV/AIDS—people living with HIV/AIDS: NA

HIV/AIDS—deaths: NA

Literacy: *definition:* age 15 and over can read and write
total population: 99%
male: 99%
female: 99% (1982 est.)

GOVERNMENT

Country name: *conventional long form:* Territorial Collectivity of Saint Pierre and Miquelon
conventional short form: Saint Pierre and Miquelon
local long form: Departement de Saint-Pierre et Miquelon
local short form: Saint-Pierre et Miquelon

Dependency status: self-governing territorial overseas collectivity of France

Government type: parliamentary representative democracy

Capital: *name:* Saint-Pierre
geographic coordinates: 46 46 N, 56 11 W
time difference: UTC-3 (2 hours ahead of Washington, DC during Standard Time)
daylight saving time: +1hr, begins second Sunday in March; ends first Sunday in November

Administrative divisions: none (territorial overseas collectivity of France); note—there are no first-order administrative divisions as defined by the US Government, but there are two communes—Saint Pierre, Miquelon at the second order

Independence: none (territorial collectivity of France; has been under French control since 1763)

National holiday: Fete de la Federation, 14 July (1789)

Constitution: 4 October 1958 (French Constitution) (2013)

Legal system: French civil law

Suffrage: 18 years of age; universal

Executive branch: *chief of state:* President Francois HOLLANDE (since 15 May 2012); represented by Prefect Patrice LATRON (since 16 November 2011)
head of government: President of the Territorial Council Stephane ARTANO (since 21 February 2007)
cabinet: NA (For more information visit the World Leaders website)
elections: French president elected by popular vote for a five-year term; election last held on 6 May 2012 (next to be held in 2017); prefect appointed by the French president on the advice of the French Ministry of Interior; president of the Territorial Council elected by the members of the council

Legislative branch: unicameral Territorial Council or Conseil Territorial (19 seats, 15 from Saint Pierre and 4 from Miquelon; members elected by popular vote to serve six-year terms)
elections: elections last held on 18 March 2012 (next to be held in March 2018)
election results: percent of vote by party—NA; seats by party—NA
note: Saint Pierre and Miquelon elect one member to the French Senate; elections last held on 21 September 2008 (next to be held in September 2014); results—percent of vote by party—NA; seats by party—UMP 1; Saint Pierre and Miquelon also elects one member to the French National Assembly; elections last held on 17 June 2012

(next to be held by June 2017); results—percent of vote by party—NA; seats by party—PRG 1

Judicial branch: *highest court(s)*: Superior Tribunal of Appeals or Tribunal Superieur d'Appel (composition NA)
judge selection and term of office: judge selection and tenure NA
subordinate courts: NA

Political parties and leaders: Archipelago Tomorrow or AD (affiliated with UDF/RPR list); Cap sur l'Avenir (affiliated with PRG); Left Radical Party or PRG; Rassemblement pour la Republique or RPR (now UMP); Saint Pierre and Miquelon 2000/Avenir Miquelon or SPM 2000/AM; Socialist Party or PS; Union pour la Democratie Francaise or UDF

Political pressure groups and leaders: NA

International organization participation: UPU, WFTU (NGOs)

Diplomatic representation in the US: none (territorial overseas collectivity of France)

Diplomatic representation from the US: none (territorial overseas collectivity of France)

Flag description: a yellow three-masted sailing ship facing the hoist side rides on a blue background with scattered, white, wavy lines under the ship; a continuous black-over-white wavy line divides the ship from the white wavy lines; on the hoist side, a vertical band is divided into three parts: the top part (called ikkurina) is red with a green diagonal cross extending to the corners overlaid by a white cross dividing the rectangle into four sections; the middle part has a white background with an ermine pattern; the third part has a red background with two stylized yellow lions outlined in black, one above the other; these three heraldic arms represent settlement by colonists from the Basque Country (top), Brittany, and Normandy; the blue on the main portion of the flag symbolizes the Atlantic Ocean and the stylized ship represents the Grande Hermine in which Jacques Cartier "discovered" the islands in 1536
note: the flag of France used for official occasions

National symbol(s): 16th-century sailing ship

National anthem: *note:* as a collectivity of France, "La Marseillaise" is official (see France)

ECONOMY

Economy—overview: The inhabitants have traditionally earned their livelihood by fishing and by servicing fishing fleets operating off the coast of Newfoundland. The economy has been declining, however, because of disputes with Canada over fishing quotas and a steady decline in the number of ships stopping at Saint Pierre. In 1992, an arbitration panel awarded the islands an exclusive economic zone of 12,348 sq km to settle a long-standing territorial dispute with Canada, although it represents only 25% of what France had sought. France heavily subsidizes the islands to the great betterment of living standards. The government hopes an expansion of tourism will boost economic prospects. Fish farming, crab fishing, and agriculture are being developed to diversify the local economy. Recent test drilling for oil may pave the way for development of the energy sector.

GDP (purchasing power parity): $215.3 million (2006 est.)
country comparison to the world: 219
note: supplemented by annual payments from France of about $60 million

GDP (official exchange rate): $215.3 million (2006 est.)

GDP—real growth rate: NA%

GDP—per capita (PPP): $34,900 (2006 est.)
country comparison to the world: 39

GDP—composition, by sector of origin:
agriculture: 2%
industry: 15%
services: 83% (2006 est.)

Agriculture—products: vegetables; poultry, cattle, sheep, pigs; fish

Industries: fish processing and supply base for fishing fleets; tourism

Industrial production growth rate: NA%

Labor force: 3,194 (2006)
country comparison to the world: 225

Labor force—by occupation: *agriculture:* 18%
industry: 41%
services: 41% (1996)

Unemployment rate: 9.9% (2008 est.)
country comparison to the world: 107

Population below poverty line: NA%

Household income or consumption by percentage share: *lowest 10%:* NA%
highest 10%: NA%

Budget: *revenues:* $70 million
expenditures: $60 million (1996)

Taxes and other revenues: 32.5% of GDP
country comparison to the world: 76

Budget surplus (+) or deficit (-):
4.6% of GDP
country comparison to the world: 10

Fiscal year: calendar year

Inflation rate (consumer prices): 4.5% (2010)
country comparison to the world: 148
8.1% (2005)

Exports: $6.641 million (2010 est.)
country comparison to the world: 216
$5.5 million (2005 est.)

Exports—commodities: fish and fish products, soybeans, animal feed, mollusks and crustaceans, fox and mink pelts

Imports: $95.35 million (2010 est.)
country comparison to the world: 213
$68.2 million (2005 est.)

Imports—commodities: meat, clothing, fuel, electrical equipment, machinery, building materials

Debt—external: $NA

Exchange rates: euros (EUR) per US dollar—
0.7634 (2013 est.)
0.7752 (2012 est.)
0.755 (2010 est.)
0.7198 (2009 est.)
0.6827 (2008 est.)

ENERGY

Electricity—production: 53 million kWh (2010 est.)
country comparison to the world: 205

Electricity—consumption: 49.29 million kWh (2010 est.)
country comparison to the world: 205

Electricity—exports: 0 kWh (2012 est.)
country comparison to the world: 189

Electricity—imports: 0 kWh (2012 est.)
country comparison to the world: 192

Electricity—installed generating capacity: 26,600 kW (2010 est.)
country comparison to the world: 200

Electricity—from fossil fuels: 97.7% of total installed capacity (2010 est.)
country comparison to the world: 59

Electricity—from nuclear fuels: 0% of total installed capacity (2010 est.)
country comparison to the world: 172

Electricity—from hydroelectric plants: 0% of total installed capacity (2010 est.)
country comparison to the world: 194

Electricity—from other renewable sources: 2.3% of total installed capacity (2010 est.)
country comparison to the world: 65

Crude oil—production: 0 bbl/day (2012 est.)
country comparison to the world: 207

Crude oil—exports: 0 bbl/day (2010 est.)
country comparison to the world: 174

Crude oil—imports: 0 bbl/day (2010 est.)
country comparison to the world: 115

Crude oil—proved reserves: 0 bbl (1 January 2013 es)
country comparison to the world: 181

Refined petroleum products—production: 0 bbl/day (2010 est.)
country comparison to the world: 189

Refined petroleum products—consumption: 974.1 bbl/day (2011 est.)
country comparison to the world: 205

Refined petroleum products—exports: 0 bbl/day (2010 est.)
country comparison to the world: 211

Refined petroleum products—imports: 584 bbl/day (2010 est.)
country comparison to the world: 201

Natural gas—production: 0 cu m (2011 est.)
country comparison to the world: 185

Natural gas—consumption: 0 cu m (2010 est.)
country comparison to the world: 189

Natural gas—exports: 0 cu m (2011 est.)
country comparison to the world: 175

Natural gas—imports: 0 cu m (2011 est.)
country comparison to the world: 124

Natural gas—proved reserves: 0 cu m (1 January 2013 es)
country comparison to the world: 187

Carbon dioxide emissions from consumption of energy: 91,430 Mt (2011 est.)
country comparison to the world: 205

COMMUNICATIONS

Telephones—main lines in use: 4,800 (2010)
country comparison to the world: 211

Telephone system: *general assessment:* adequate
international: country code—508; radiotelephone communication with most countries in the world; satellite earth station—1 in French domestic satellite system

Broadcast media: 2 TV stations with a third repeater station, all part of the French Overseas Network; radio stations on St. Pierre and on Miquelon are part of the French Overseas Network (2007)

Internet country code: .pm

Internet hosts: 15 (2012)
country comparison to the world: 224

TRANSPORTATION

Airports: 2 (2013)
country comparison to the world: 209

Airports—with paved runways: *total:* 2
1,524 to 2,437 m: 1
914 to 1,523 m: 1 (2013)

Roadways: *total:* 117 km
country comparison to the world: 214
paved: 80 km
unpaved: 37 km (2009)

Ports and terminals:
major seaport(s): Saint-Pierre

MILITARY

Manpower fit for military service:
males age 16-49: 1,064
females age 16-49: 1,069 (2010 est.)

Manpower reaching militarily significant age annually: *male:* 3 4
female: 32 (2010 est.)

Military—note: defense is the responsibility of France

TRANSNATIONAL ISSUES

Disputes—international: none

SAINT VINCENT AND THE GRENADINES

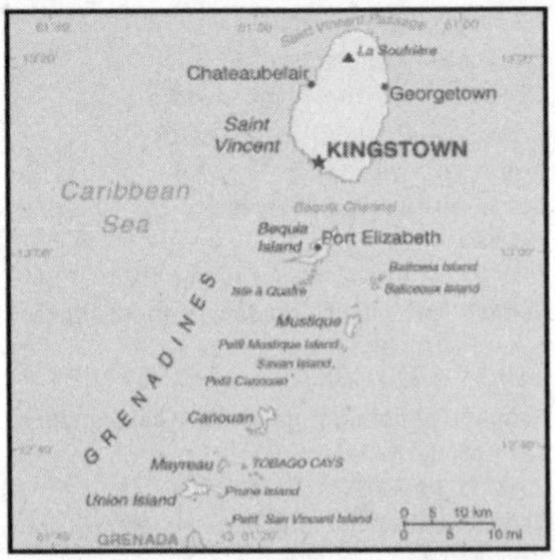

INTRODUCTION

Background: Resistance by native Caribs prevented colonization on Saint Vincent until 1719. Disputed between France and the United Kingdom for most of the 18th century, the island was ceded to the latter in 1783. Between 1960 and 1962, Saint Vincent and the Grenadines was a separate administrative unit of the Federation of the West Indies. Autonomy was granted in 1969 and independence in 1979.

GEOGRAPHY

Location: Caribbean, islands between the Caribbean Sea and North Atlantic Ocean, north of Trinidad and Tobago

Geographic coordinates: 13 15 N, 61 12 W

Map references: Central America and the Caribbean

Area: *total:* 389 sq km (Saint Vincent 344 sq km)
country comparison to the world: 204
land: 389 sq km
water: 0 sq km

Area—comparative: twice the size of Washington, DC

Land boundaries: 0 km

Coastline: 84 km

Maritime claims: *territorial sea:* 12 nm
contiguous zone: 24 nm
exclusive economic zone: 200 nm
continental shelf: 200 nm

Climate: tropical; little seasonal temperature variation; rainy season (May to November)

Terrain: volcanic, mountainous

Elevation extremes: *lowest point:* Caribbean Sea 0 m
highest point: La Soufriere 1,234 m

Natural resources: hydropower, cropland

Land use: *arable land:* 12.82%
permanent crops: 7.69%
other: 79.49% (2011)

Irrigated land: 10 sq km (2003)

Freshwater withdrawal (domestic/industrial/agricultural): *total:* 0.01 cu km/yr (NA)
per capita: 92.59 cu m/yr (1995)

Natural hazards: hurricanes; Soufriere volcano on the island of Saint Vincent is a constant threat

Environment—current issues: pollution of coastal waters and shorelines from discharges by pleasure yachts and other effluents; in some areas, pollution is severe enough to make swimming prohibitive

Environment—international agreements:
party to: Biodiversity, Climate Change, Climate Change-Kyoto Protocol, Desertification, Endangered Species, Environmental Modification, Hazardous Wastes, Law of the Sea, Marine Dumping, Ozone Layer Protection, Ship Pollution, Whaling
signed, but not ratified: none of the selected agreements

Geography—note: the administration of the islands of the Grenadines group is divided between Saint Vincent and the Grenadines and Grenada; Saint Vincent and the Grenadines is comprised of 32 islands and cays

PEOPLE AND SOCIETY

Nationality: *noun:* Saint Vincentian(s) or Vincentian(s)
adjective: Saint Vincentian or Vincentian

Ethnic groups: black 66%, mixed 19%, East Indian 6%, European 4%, Carib Amerindian 2%, other 3%

Languages: English, French patois

Religions: Protestant 75% (Anglican 47%, Methodist 28%), Roman Catholic 13%, other (includes Hindu, Seventh-Day Adventist, other Protestant) 12%

Population: 102,918 (July 2014 est.)
country comparison to the world: 196

Age structure:
0-14 years: 22.9% (male 11,858/female 11,661)
15-24 years: 16.7% (male 8,687/female 8,528)
25-54 years: 42.6% (male 22,781/female 21,065)
55-64 years: 8.6% (male 4,873/female 4,634)
65 years and over: 8.4% (male 4,083/female 4,748) (2014 est.)

Dependency ratios:
total dependency ratio: 47.6 %
youth dependency ratio: 37.3 %
elderly dependency ratio: 10.3 %
potential support ratio: 9.7 (2013)

Median age: *total:* 31.9 years
male: 32 years
female: 31.7 years (2014 est.)

Population growth rate: -0.29% (2014 est.)
country comparison to the world: 217

Birth rate: 13.85 births/1,000 population (2014 est.)
country comparison to the world: 144

Death rate: 7.12 deaths/1,000 population (2014 est.)
country comparison to the world: 128

Net migration rate: -9.6 migrant(s)/1,000 population (2014 est.)
country comparison to the world: 213

Urbanization: *urban population:* 49% of total population (2010)
rate of urbanization: 1% annual rate of change (2010-15 est.)

Major urban areas—population: KINGSTOWN (capital) 28,000 (2009)

Sex ratio: *at birth:* 1.03 male(s)/female
0-14 years: 1.02 male(s)/female
15-24 years: 1.02 male(s)/female
25-54 years: 1.08 male(s)/female
55-64 years: 1.03 male(s)/female
65 years and over: 0.84 male(s)/female
total population: 1.03 male(s)/female (2014 est.)

Maternal mortality rate: 48 deaths/100,000 live births (2010)
country comparison to the world: 109

Infant mortality rate:
total: 13.07 deaths/1,000 live births
country comparison to the world: 121
male: 14.24 deaths/1,000 live births
female: 11.87 deaths/1,000 live births (2014 est.)

Life expectancy at birth:
total population: 74.86 years
country comparison to the world: 106
male: 72.9 years
female: 76.88 years (2014 est.)

Total fertility rate: 1.84 children born/woman (2014 est.)
country comparison to the world: 151

Health expenditures: 4.9% of GDP (2011)
country comparison to the world: 142

Physicians density: 0.53 physicians/1,000 population (2001)

Hospital bed density: 2.7 beds/1,000 population (2011)

Drinking water source:

improved:
urban: 95.1% of population
rural: 95.1% of population
total: 95.1% of population
unimproved:
urban: 4.9% of population
rural: 4.9% of population
total: 4.9% of population (2011 est.)

Sanitation facility access:
improved:
rural: 95.1% of population
unimproved:
rural: 4.9% of population (2011 est.)

HIV/AIDS—adult prevalence rate: NA

HIV/AIDS—people living with HIV/AIDS: NA

HIV/AIDS—deaths: NA

Obesity—adult prevalence rate: 23.4% (2008)
country comparison to the world: 75

Education expenditures: 5.1% of GDP (2010)
country comparison to the world: 69

Literacy: *definition:* age 15 and over has ever attended school
total population: 96%
male: 96%
female: 96% (1970 est.)

School life expectancy (primary to tertiary education): *total:* 13 years
male: 13 years
female: 13 years (2004)

GOVERNMENT

Country name: *conventional long form:* none
conventional short form: Saint Vincent and the Grenadines

Government type: parliamentary democracy and a Commonwealth realm

Capital: *name:* Kingstown

geographic coordinates: 13 08 N, 61 13 W
time difference: UTC-4 (1 hour ahead of Washington, DC during Standard Time)

Administrative divisions: 6 parishes; Charlotte, Grenadines, Saint Andrew, Saint David, Saint George, Saint Patrick

Independence: 27 October 1979 (from the UK)

National holiday: Independence Day, 27 October (1979)

Constitution: several previous; latest presented 26 July 1979, effective 27 October 1979 (2009)

Legal system: English common law

International law organization participation: has not submitted an ICJ jurisdiction declaration; accepts ICCt jurisdiction

Suffrage: 18 years of age; universal

Executive branch: *chief of state:* Queen ELIZABETH II (since 6 February 1952); represented by Governor General Sir Fredrick Nathaniel BALLANTYNE (since 2 September 2002)
head of government: Prime Minister Ralph E. GONSALVES (since 29 March 2001)
cabinet: Cabinet appointed by the governor general on the advice of the prime minister (For more information visit the World Leaders website)
elections: the monarchy is hereditary; the governor general appointed by the monarch; following legislative elections, the leader of the majority party usually appointed prime minister by the governor general; deputy prime minister appointed by the governor general on the advice of the prime minister

Legislative branch: unicameral House of Assembly (21 seats, 15 elected representatives and 6 appointed senators; representatives elected by popular vote to serve five-year terms)
elections: last held on 13 December 2010 (next to be held in 2015)
election results: percent of vote by party—ULP 51.6%, NDP 47.8%, other 0.6%; seats by party—ULP 8, NDP 7

Judicial branch: *highest court(s):* the Eastern Caribbean Supreme Court (ECSC) is the itinerant superior court of record for the 9-member Organization of Eastern Caribbean States to include Saint Vincent and the Grenadines; the ECSC—with its headquarters on Saint Lucia—is headed by the chief justice and is comprised of the Court of Appeal with 3 justices and the High Court with 16 judges; sittings of the Court of Appeal and High Court rotate among the member states; 2 High Court judges reside on Saint Vincent and the Grenadines note—Saint Vincent and the Grenadines is a member of the Caribbean Court of Justice
judge selection and term of office: Eastern Caribbean Supreme Court chief justice appointed by Her Majesty, Queen ELIZABETH II; other justices and judges appointed by the Judicial and Legal Services Commission; Court of Appeal justices appointed for life with mandatory retirement at age 65; High Court judges appointed for life with mandatory retirement at age 62
subordinate courts: magistrates' courts

Political parties and leaders: New Democratic Party or NDP [Arnhim EUSTACE]; Unity Labor Party or ULP [Ralph GONSALVES] (formed by the coalition of Saint Vincent Labor Party or SVLP and the Movement for; National Unity or MNU)

Political pressure groups and leaders: NA

International organization participation: ACP, AOSIS, C, Caricom, CDB, CELAC, FAO, G-77, IBRD, ICAO, ICRM, IDA, IFAD, IFRCS, ILO, IMF, IMO, Interpol, IOC, IOM, ISO (subscriber), ITU, MIGA, NAM, OAS, OECS, OPANAL, OPCW, Petrocaribe, UN, UNCTAD, UNESCO, UNIDO, UPU, WFTU (NGOs), WHO, WIPO, WTO

Diplomatic representation in the US:
chief of mission: Ambassador La Celia A. PRINCE (since 30 May 2008)
chancery: 3216 New Mexico Avenue NW, Washington, DC 20016
telephone: [1] (202) 364-6730
FAX: [1] (202) 364-6736
consulate(s) general: New York

Diplomatic representation from the US: the US does not have an embassy in Saint Vincent and the Grenadines; the US Ambassador to Barbados is accredited to Saint Vincent and the Grenadines

Flag description: three vertical bands of blue (hoist side), gold (double width), and green; the gold band bears three green diamonds arranged in a V pattern, which stands for Vincent; the diamonds recall the islands as the "Gems of the Antilles"; blue conveys the colors of a tropical sky and crystal waters, yellow signifies the golden Grenadine sands, and green represents lush vegetation

National anthem: *name:* "St. Vincent! Land So Beautiful!"
lyrics/music: Phyllis Joyce MCCLEAN PUNNETT/Joel Bertram MIGUEL
note: adopted 1967

ECONOMY

Economy—overview: Success of the economy hinges upon seasonal variations in agriculture, tourism, and construction activity as well as remittance inflows. Much of the workforce is employed in banana production and tourism, but persistent high unemployment has prompted many to leave the islands. This lower-middle-income country is vulnerable to natural disasters—tropical storms wiped out substantial portions of crops in 1994, 1995, and 2002. In 2008, the islands had more than 200,000 tourist arrivals, mostly to the Grenadines, a drop of nearly 20% from 2007. Saint Vincent is home to a small offshore banking sector and has moved to adopt international regulatory standards. The government's ability to invest in social programs and respond to external shocks is constrained by its high public debt burden, which was 68% of GDP at the end of 2011. Weak recovery in the tourism and construction sectors will limit growth prospects in 2014.

GDP (purchasing power parity): $1.325 billion (2013 est.)
country comparison to the world: 199
$1.309 billion (2012 est.)
$1.288 billion (2011 est.)
note: data are in 2013 US dollars

GDP (official exchange rate): $742 million (2013 est.)

GDP—real growth rate: 1.3% (2013 est.)
country comparison to the world: 168
1.5% (2012 est.)
0.4% (2011 est.)

GDP—per capita (PPP): $12,100 (2013 est.)
country comparison to the world: 106
$11,900 (2012 est.)
$11,800 (2011 est.)
note: data are in 2013 US dollars

Gross national saving: -4.7% of GDP (2013 est.)
country comparison to the world: 155
-6.7% of GDP (2012 est.)
-4.2% of GDP (2011 est.)
GDP—composition, by end use:
household consumption: 92.3%
government consumption: 16.6%
investment in fixed capital: 23.7%
investment in inventories: 0%
exports of goods and services: 21.8%
imports of goods and services: -54.4% (2013 est.)

GDP—composition, by sector of origin:
agriculture: 5.4%
industry: 20.3%
services: 74.4% (2013 est.)

Agriculture—products: bananas, coconuts, sweet potatoes, spices; small numbers of cattle, sheep, pigs, goats; fish

Industries: tourism; food processing, cement, furniture, clothing, starch

Industrial production growth rate: 3% (2013 est.)
country comparison to the world: 97

Labor force: 57,520 (2007 est.)
country comparison to the world: 187

Labor force—by occupation: *agriculture:* 26%
industry: 17%
services: 57% (1980 est.)

Unemployment rate: 15% (2001 est.)
country comparison to the world: 143

Population below poverty line: NA%

Household income or consumption by percentage share: *lowest 10%:* NA%
highest 10%: NA%

Budget: *revenues:* $185.2 million
expenditures: $185.2 million (2013 est.)

Taxes and other revenues: 25% of GDP (2013 est.)
country comparison to the world: 129

Budget surplus (+) or deficit (-):
0% of GDP (2013 est.)
country comparison to the world: 45

Public debt: 68% of GDP (2011 est.)
country comparison to the world: 38

Fiscal year: calendar year

Inflation rate (consumer prices): 2.8% (2013 est.)
country comparison to the world: 109
2.6% (2012 est.)

Central bank discount rate: 6.5% (31 December 2010 est.)
country comparison to the world: 47
6.5% (31 December 2009 est.)

Commercial bank prime lending rate: 9.4% (31 December 2013 est.)
country comparison to the world: 96
9.43% (31 December 2012 est.)

Stock of narrow money: $142.2 million (31 December 2013 est.)
country comparison to the world: 181
$133.7 million (31 December 2012 est.)

Stock of broad money: $460.4 million (31 December 2013 est.)
country comparison to the world: 178
$438.5 million (31 December 2012 est.)

Stock of domestic credit: $423.2 million (31 December 2013 est.)
country comparison to the world: 171
$404.8 million (31 December 2012 est.)

Current account balance: -$207.7 million (2013 est.)
country comparison to the world: 85
-$215.9 million (2012 est.)

Exports: $45.7 million (2013 est.)
country comparison to the world: 197
$48.7 million (2012 est.)

Exports—commodities: bananas, eddoes and dasheen (taro), arrowroot starch; tennis racquets

Exports—partners: Trinidad and Tobago 14.5%, St. Lucia 12.9%, Turkey 12.7%, Barbados 10.7%, Dominica 8.5%, Grenada 8.1%, Antigua and Barbuda 7.3% (2012)

Imports: $301.5 million (2013 est.)
country comparison to the world: 200
$314.6 million (2012 est.)

Imports—commodities: foodstuffs, machinery and equipment, chemicals and fertilizers, minerals and fuels

Imports—partners: Singapore 28%, Trinidad and Tobago 22.6%, US 19%, China 5.6%, Barbados 5% (2012)

Reserves of foreign exchange and gold: $115 million (31 December 2013 est.)
country comparison to the world: 165
$111 million (31 December 2012 est.)

Debt—external: $255.3 million (31 December 2013 est.)
country comparison to the world: 186
$265 million (31 December 2012 est.)

Exchange rates: East Caribbean dollars (XCD) per US dollar—
2.7 (2013 est.)
2.7 (2012 est.)
2.7 (2010 est.)
2.7 (2009)

ENERGY

Electricity—production: 136 million kWh (2010 est.)
country comparison to the world: 191

Electricity—consumption: 126.5 million kWh (2010 est.)
country comparison to the world: 193

Electricity—exports: 0 kWh (2012 est.)
country comparison to the world: 209

Electricity—imports: 0 kWh (2012 est.)
country comparison to the world: 210

Electricity—installed generating capacity: 47,000 kW (2010 est.)
country comparison to the world: 190

Electricity—from fossil fuels: 85.1% of total installed capacity (2010 est.)
country comparison to the world: 87

Electricity—from nuclear fuels: 0% of total installed capacity (2010 est.)
country comparison to the world: 198

Electricity—from hydroelectric plants: 14.9% of total installed capacity (2010 est.)
country comparison to the world: 102

Electricity—from other renewable sources: 0% of total installed capacity (2010 est.)
country comparison to the world: 135

Crude oil—production: 0 bbl/day (2012 est.)
country comparison to the world: 141

Crude oil—exports: 0 bbl/day (2010 est.)
country comparison to the world: 201

Crude oil—imports: 0 bbl/day (2010 est.)
country comparison to the world: 136

Crude oil—proved reserves: 0 bbl (1 January 2013 es)
country comparison to the world: 202

Refined petroleum products—production: 0 bbl/day (2010 est.)
country comparison to the world: 205

Refined petroleum products—consumption: 1,948 bbl/day (2011 est.)
country comparison to the world: 189

Refined petroleum products—exports: 0 bbl/day (2010 est.)
country comparison to the world: 141

Refined petroleum products—imports: 1,474 bbl/day (2010 est.)
country comparison to the world: 186

Natural gas—production: 0 cu m (2011 est.)
country comparison to the world: 204

Natural gas—consumption: 0 cu m (2010 est.)
country comparison to the world: 204

Natural gas—exports: 0 cu m (2011 est.)
country comparison to the world: 201

Natural gas—imports: 0 cu m (2011 est.)
country comparison to the world: 145

Natural gas—proved reserves: 0 cu m (1 January 2013 es)
country comparison to the world: 203

Carbon dioxide emissions from consumption of energy: 198,900 Mt (2011 est.)
country comparison to the world: 195

COMMUNICATIONS

Telephones—main lines in use: 19,400 (2012)
country comparison to the world: 187

Telephones—mobile cellular: 135,500 (2012)
country comparison to the world: 187

Telephone system: *general assessment:* adequate islandwide, fully automatic telephone system
domestic: fixed-line teledensity exceeds 20 per 100 persons and mobile-cellular teledensity exceeds 125 per 100 persons
international: country code—1-784; the East Caribbean Fiber Optic System (ECFS) and Southern Caribbean fiber optic system (SCF) submarine cables carry international calls; connectivity also provided by VHF/UHF radiotelephone from Saint Vincent to Barbados; SHF radiotelephone to Grenada and Saint Lucia; access to Intelsat earth station in Martinique through Saint Lucia (2011)

Broadcast media: St. Vincent and the Grenadines Broadcasting Corporation operates 1 TV station and 5 repeater stations that provide near total coverage to the multi-island state; multichannel cable TV service available; a partially government-funded national radio service broadcasts on 1 station and has 2 repeater stations; about a dozen privately owned radio stations and repeater stations (2007)

Internet country code: .vc

Internet hosts: 305 (2012)
country comparison to the world: 190

Internet users: 76,000 (2009)
country comparison to the world: 169

TRANSPORTATION

Airports: 6 (2013)
country comparison to the world: 177

Airports—with paved runways: *total:* 5
1,524 to 2,437 m: 1
914 to 1,523 m: 3
under 914 m: 1 (2013)

Airports—with unpaved runways: *total:* 1
under 914 m: 1 (2013)

Roadways: *total:* 829 km
country comparison to the world: 187
paved: 580 km
unpaved: 249 km (2003)

Merchant marine: *total:* 412
country comparison to the world: 25
by type: bulk carrier 64, cargo 263, carrier 14, chemical tanker 4, container 18, liquefied gas 3, passenger 2, passenger/cargo 7, petroleum tanker 9, refrigerated cargo 12, roll on/roll off 15, specialized tanker 1
foreign-owned: 325 (Austria 1, Azerbaijan 1, Bangladesh 1, Belgium 7, Bermuda 1, Bulgaria 9, China 65, Croatia 8, Cyprus 3, Czech Republic 1, Denmark 9, Dominica 1, Egypt 2, Estonia 8, France 2, Germany 3, Greece 42, Guyana 2, Hong Kong 5, Israel 3, Italy 4, Japan 3, Kenya 2, Latvia 15, Lebanon 2, Lithuania 9, Monaco 2, Netherlands 1, Norway 13, Poland 3, Romania 1, Russia 11, Singapore 5, Slovenia 1, Sweden 10, Switzerland 7, Syria 9, Turkey 13, UAE 3, UK 6, Ukraine 12, US 18, Venezuela 1) (2010)

Ports and terminals: *major seaport(s):* Kingstown

MILITARY

Military branches: no regular military forces; Royal Saint Vincent and the Grenadines Police Force (RSVPF) (2013)

Manpower available for military service:
males age 16-49: 27,809 (2010 est.)

Manpower fit for military service:
males age 16-49: 22,875
females age 16-49: 22,015 (2010 est.)

Manpower reaching militarily significant age annually: *male:* 964
female: 953 (2010 est.)

TRANSNATIONAL ISSUES

Disputes—international: joins other Caribbean states to counter Venezuela's claim that Aves Island sustains human habitation, a criterion under United Nations Convention on the Law of the Sea, which permits Venezuela to extend its Economic Exclusion Zone/continental shelf over a large portion of the eastern Caribbean Sea

Illicit drugs: transshipment point for South American drugs destined for the US and Europe; small-scale cannabis cultivation

SAMOA

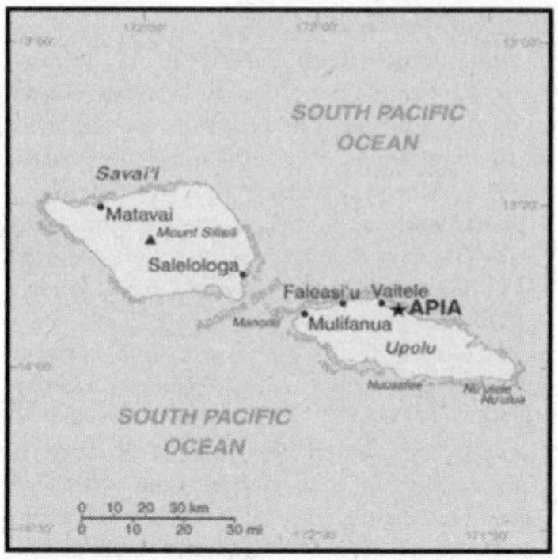

INTRODUCTION

Background: New Zealand occupied the German protectorate of Western Samoa at the outbreak of World War I in 1914. It continued to administer the islands as a mandate and then as a trust territory until 1962, when the islands became the first Polynesian nation to reestablish independence in the 20th century. The country dropped the "Western" from its name in 1997.

GEOGRAPHY

Location: Oceania, group of islands in the South Pacific Ocean, about half way between Hawaii and New Zealand

Geographic coordinates: 13 35 S, 172 20 W

Map references: Oceania

Area: *total:* 2,831 sq km

country comparison to the world: 178
land: 2,821 sq km
water: 10 sq km

Area—comparative: slightly smaller than Rhode Island

Land boundaries: 0 km

Coastline: 403 km

Maritime claims: *territorial sea:* 12 nm
contiguous zone: 24 nm
exclusive economic zone: 200 nm

Climate: tropical; rainy season (November to April), dry season (May to October)

Terrain: two main islands (Savaii, Upolu) and several smaller islands and uninhabited islets; narrow coastal plain with volcanic, rocky, rugged mountains in interior

Elevation extremes: *lowest point:* Pacific Ocean 0 m
highest point: Mount Silisili 1,857 m

Natural resources: hardwood forests, fish, hydropower

Land use: *arable land:* 2.82%
permanent crops: 7.75%
other: 89.44% (2011)

Irrigated land: NA

Natural hazards: occasional typhoons; active volcanism
volcanism: Savai'I Island (elev. 1,858 m), which last erupted in 1911, is historically active

Environment—current issues: soil erosion, deforestation, invasive species, overfishing

Environment—international agreements: *party to:* Biodiversity, Climate Change, Climate Change-Kyoto Protocol, Desertification, Hazardous Wastes, Law of the Sea, Ozone Layer Protection, Ship Pollution, Wetlands
signed, but not ratified: none of the selected agreements

Geography—note: occupies an almost central position within Polynesia

PEOPLE AND SOCIETY

Nationality: *noun:* Samoan(s)
adjective: Samoan

Ethnic groups: Samoan 92.6%, Euronesians (persons of European and Polynesian blood) 7%, Europeans 0.4% (2001 census)

Languages: Samoan (Polynesian) (official), English

Religions: Protestant 57.4% (Congregationalist 31.8%, Methodist 13.7%, Assembly of God 8%, Seventh-Day Adventist 3.9%), Roman Catholic 19.4%, Mormon 15.2%, Worship Centre 1.7%, other Christian 5.5%, other 0.7%, none 0.1%, unspecified 0.1% (2011 est.)

Population: 196,628 (July 2014 est.)
country comparison to the world: 185
note: prior estimates used official net migration data by sex, but a highly unusual pattern for 1993 lead to a significant imbalance in the sex ratios (more men and fewer women) and a seeming reduction in the female population; the revised total was calculated using a 1993 number that was an average of the 1992 and 1994 migration figures

Age structure:
0-14 years: 33.4% (male 33,842/female 31,749)
15-24 years: 20.1% (male 20,227/female 19,200)
25-54 years: 35.2% (male 35,872/female 33,355)
55-64 years: 5.4% (male 5,955/female 5,770)
65 years and over: 5.4% (male 4,647/female 6,011) (2014 est.)

Dependency ratios:
total dependency ratio: 75.1 %
youth dependency ratio: 66.1 %
elderly dependency ratio: 9 %
potential support ratio: 11.1 (2013)

Median age: *total:* 23.1 years
male: 22.9 years
female: 23.4 years (2014 est.)

Population growth rate: 0.59% (2014 est.)
country comparison to the world: 150

Birth rate: 21.29 births/1,000 population (2014 est.)
country comparison to the world: 78

Death rate: 5.32 deaths/1,000 population (2014 est.)
country comparison to the world: 180

Net migration rate: -10.12 migrant(s)/1,000 population (2014 est.)
country comparison to the world: 216

Urbanization: *urban population:* 20% of total population (2010)
rate of urbanization: 0% annual rate of change (2010-15 est.)

Major urban areas—population: APIA (capital) 36,000 (2009)

Sex ratio: *at birth:* 1.05 male(s)/female
0-14 years: 1.07 male(s)/female
15-24 years: 1.05 male(s)/female
25-54 years: 1.08 male(s)/female
55-64 years: 1.05 male(s)/female
65 years and over: 0.78 male(s)/female
total population: 1.05 male(s)/female (2014 est.)

Mother's mean age at first birth: 23.6
note: median age at first birth among women 25-29 (2009 est.)

Maternal mortality rate: 100 deaths/100,000 live births (2010)
country comparison to the world: 72

Infant mortality rate: *total:* 20.5 deaths/1,000 live births
country comparison to the world: 87
male: 24.18 deaths/1,000 live births
female: 16.63 deaths/1,000 live births (2014 est.)

Life expectancy at birth: *total population:* 73.21 years
country comparison to the world: 128
male: 70.32 years
female: 76.24 years (2014 est.)

Total fertility rate: 2.94 children born/woman (2014 est.)
country comparison to the world: 58

Contraceptive prevalence rate: 28.7% (2009)

Health expenditures: 7% of GDP (2011)
country comparison to the world: 84

Physicians density: 0.48 physicians/1,000 population (2008)

Hospital bed density: 1 beds/1,000 population (2005)

Drinking water source:
improved:
urban: 97.4% of population
rural: 98.3% of population
total: 98.1% of population
unimproved:
urban: 2.6% of population
rural: 1.7% of population
total: 1.9% of population (2011 est.)

Sanitation facility access:
improved:
urban: 93.4% of population
rural: 91.2% of population
total: 91.6% of population
unimproved:
urban: 6.6% of population
rural: 8.8% of population
total: 8.4% of population (2011 est.)

HIV/AIDS—adult prevalence rate: NA

HIV/AIDS—people living with HIV/AIDS: NA

HIV/AIDS—deaths: NA

Obesity—adult prevalence rate: 54.1% (2008)
country comparison to the world: 6

Education expenditures: 5.8% of GDP (2008)
country comparison to the world: 48

Literacy: *definition:* age 15 and over can read and write

total population: 98.8%
male: 99%
female: 98.6% (2003 est.)

School life expectancy (primary to tertiary education): *total:* 12 years
male: 12 years
female: 12 years (2000)

Unemployment, youth ages 15-24: *total:* 16.1%
country comparison to the world: 81
male: 13.8%
female: 22.2% (2011)

GOVERNMENT

Country name: *conventional long form:* Independent State of Samoa
conventional short form: Samoa
local long form: Malo Sa'oloto Tuto'atasi o Samoa
local short form: Samoa
former: Western Samoa

Government type: parliamentary democracy

Capital: *name:* Apia

geographic coordinates: 13 49 S, 171 46 W
time difference: UTC+13 (18 hours ahead of Washington, DC during Standard Time) +1hr, begins last Sunday in September; ends first Sunday in April

Administrative divisions: 11 districts; A'ana, Aiga-i-le-Tai, Atua, Fa'asaleleaga, Gaga'emauga, Gagaifomauga, Palauli, Satupa'itea, Tuamasaga, Va'a-o-Fonoti, Vaisigano

Independence: 1 January 1962 (from New Zealand-administered UN trusteeship)

National holiday: Independence Day Celebration, 1 June (1962); note—1 January 1962 is the date of independence from the New Zealand-administered UN trusteeship; it is observed in June

Constitution: several previous (preindependence); latest 1 January 1962; amended several times, last in 2013 (2013)

Legal system: mixed legal system of English common law and customary law; judicial review of legislative acts with respect to fundamental rights of the citizen

International law organization participation: has not submitted an ICJ jurisdiction declaration; accepts ICCt jurisdiction

Suffrage: 21 years of age; universal

Executive branch: *chief of state:* TUI ATUA Tupua Tamasese Efi (since 20 June 2007)
head of government: Prime Minister TUILA'EPA Lupesoliai Sailele Malielegaoi (since 1998); Deputy Prime Minister FONOTOE Pierre Lauofo (since 2011)
cabinet: Cabinet consists of 12 members appointed by the chief of state on the prime minister's advice (For more information visit the World Leaders website) elections: chief of state elected by the Legislative Assembly to serve a five-year term (no term limits); election last held on 20 July 2012 (next to be held in 2017); following legislative elections, the leader of the majority party usually appointed prime minister by the chief of state with the approval of the Legislative Assembly
election results: TUI ATUA Tupua Tamasese Efi unanimously elected by the Legislative Assembly

Legislative branch: unicameral Legislative Assembly or Fono (49 seats, 47 members elected by voters affiliated with traditional village-based electoral districts, 2 elected by independent, mostly non-Samoan or part-Samoan, voters who cannot (or choose not to) establish a village affiliation; only chiefs (matai) may stand for election to the Fono from the 47 village-based electorates; members serve five-year terms)
elections: election last held on 4 March 2011 (next election to be held not later than March 2016)
election results: percent of vote by party—NA; seats by party—HRPP 29, Tautua Samoa 13, independents 7

Judicial branch: *highest court(s):* Court of Appeal (consists of the chief justice and 2 Supreme Court judges and meets once or twice a year); Supreme Court (consists of the chief justice and several judges)
judge selection and term of office: chief justice appointed by the head of state upon the advice of the prime minister; other Supreme Court judges appointed by the Judicial Service Commission, a 3-member body chaired by the chief justice and includes the attorney general and an appointee of the Minister of Justice; judges normally appointed until retirement at age 68
subordinate courts: District Court; Magistrates' Courts; Land and Titles Courts; village fono or village chief councils

Political parties and leaders: Human Rights Protection Party or HRPP [Sailele Malielegaoi TUILA'EPA]; Samoa Christian Party or TCP [Tuala Tiresa MALIETOA]; Samoa Progressive Political Party or SPPP; Tautua Samoa [Palusalue FA'APO II]

Political pressure groups and leaders: NA

International organization participation: ACP, ADB, AOSIS, C, FAO, G-77, IBRD, ICAO, ICRM, IDA, IFAD, IFC, IFRCS, ILO, IMF, IMO, Interpol, IOC, IPU, ITU, ITUC (NGOs), MIGA, OPCW, PIF, Sparteca, SPC, UN, UNCTAD, UNESCO, UNIDO, UPU, WCO, WHO, WIPO, WMO, WTO

Diplomatic representation in the US:
chief of mission: Ambassador Aliioaiga Feturi ELISAIA (since 4 December 2003)
chancery: 800 Second Avenue, Suite 400J, New York, NY 10017
telephone: [1] (212) 599-6196 through 6197
FAX: [1] (212) 599-0797
consulate(s) general: Pago Pago (American Samoa)

Diplomatic representation from the US:
chief of mission: the US does not have an embassy in Samoa; the US Ambassador to New Zealand, currently Ambassador David HUEBNER, is accredited to Samoa
embassy: Accident Corporation Building, 5th Floor, Matafele, Apia
mailing address: P. O. Box 3430, Matafele, Apia
telephone: [685] 21436/21631/21452/22696
FAX: [685] 22030

Flag description: red with a blue rectangle in the upper hoist-side quadrant bearing five white five-pointed stars representing the Southern Cross constellation; red stands for courage, blue represents freedom, and white signifies purity

National symbol(s): Southern Cross constellation (five, five-pointed stars)

National anthem: *name:* "O le Fu'a o le Sa'olotoga o Samoa" (The Banner of Freedom)
lyrics/music: Sauni Liga KURESA
note: adopted 1962; the anthem is also known as "Samoa Tula'i" (Samoa Arise)

ECONOMY

Economy—overview: The economy of Samoa has traditionally been dependent on development aid, family remittances from overseas, agriculture, and fishing. The country is vulnerable to devastating storms. Agriculture employs roughly two-thirds of the labor force and furnishes 90% of exports, featuring coconut cream, coconut oil, and copra. The manufacturing sector mainly processes agricultural products. One factory in the Foreign Trade Zone employs 3,000 people to make automobile electrical harnesses for an assembly plant in Australia. Tourism is an expanding sector accounting for 25% of GDP; 122,000 tourists visited the islands in 2007. In late September 2009, an earthquake and the resulting tsunami severely damaged Samoa, and nearby American Samoa, disrupting transportation and power generation, and resulting in about 200 deaths. In December 2012, extensive flooding and wind damage from Tropical Cyclone Evan killed four people, displaced over 6,000, and damaged or destroyed an estimated 1,500 homes in Samoa's Upolu island. The Samoan Government has called for deregulation of the financial sector, encouragement of investment, and continued fiscal discipline, while at the same time protecting the environment. Observers point to the flexibility of the labor market as a basic strength for future economic advances. Foreign reserves are in a relatively healthy state, the external debt is stable, and inflation is low.

GDP (purchasing power parity): $1.145 billion (2013 est.)
country comparison to the world: 203
$1.144 billion (2012 est.)
$1.11 billion (2011 est.)
note: data are in 2013 US dollars

GDP (official exchange rate): $705 million (2013 est.)

GDP—real growth rate: 0.1% (2013 est.)
country comparison to the world: 195
3.1% (2012 est.)
1.3% (2011 est.)

GDP—per capita (PPP): $6,200 (2013 est.)
country comparison to the world: 149
$6,200 (2012 est.)
$6,100 (2011 est.)
note: data are in 2013 US dollars

GDP—composition, by sector of origin:
agriculture: 10.2%
industry: 25.9%
services: 64% (2013 est.)

Agriculture—products: coconuts, bananas, taro, yams, coffee, cocoa

Industries: food processing, building materials, auto parts

Industrial production growth rate: -4.8% (2013 est.)
country comparison to the world: 189

Labor force: 47,930 (2011 est.)
country comparison to the world: 193

Labor force—by occupation:
agriculture: 65%
industry: NA%
services: NA%

Unemployment rate: NA%

Population below poverty line: NA%

Household income or consumption by percentage share: *lowest 10%:* NA%
highest 10%: NA%

Budget: *revenues:* $215.6 million
expenditures: $258.7 million (2013 est.)

Taxes and other revenues: 30.6% of GDP (2013 est.)
country comparison to the world: 90

Budget surplus (+) or deficit (-):
-6.1% of GDP (2013 est.)
country comparison to the world: 181

Fiscal year: June 1—May 31

Inflation rate (consumer prices): 2.7% (2013 est.)
country comparison to the world: 99
2.1% (2012 est.)

Commercial bank prime lending rate: 10.2% (31 December 2013 est.)
country comparison to the world: 90
9.86% (31 December 2012 est.)

Stock of narrow money: $97.8 million (31 December 2013 est.)
country comparison to the world: 183
$97.71 million (31 December 2012 est.)

Stock of broad money: $305.8 million (31 December 2013 est.)
country comparison to the world: 185
$307.8 million (31 December 2012 est.)

Stock of domestic credit: $301.9 million (31 December 2013 est.)
country comparison to the world: 174
$312.1 million (31 December 2012 est.)

Market value of publicly traded shares: $NA

Current account balance: -$76.11 million (2011 est.)
country comparison to the world: 72
-$58.66 million (2010 est.)

Exports: $11.4 million (2011 est.)
country comparison to the world: 213

Exports—commodities: fish, coconut oil and cream, copra, taro, automotive parts, garments, beer

Exports—partners: American Samoa 48.4%, Australia 24% (2012)

Imports: $318.7 million (2011 est.)
country comparison to the world: 197

$280 million (2010 est.)

Imports—commodities: machinery and equipment, industrial supplies, foodstuffs

Imports—partners: NZ 19.2%, Singapore 18.6%, Fiji 17.6%, China 15.8%, Australia 5.9%, US 5.4% (2012)

Reserves of foreign exchange and gold: $168.7 million (31 December 2012 est.)
country comparison to the world: 163
$168.7 million (31 December 2012 est.)

Debt—external: $368.3 million (31 December 2011 est.)
country comparison to the world: 182
$368.3 million (31 December 2011 est.)

Exchange rates: tala (SAT) per US dollar—
2.319 (2013 est.)
2.2923 (2012 est.)
2.4847 (2010 est.)

ENERGY

Electricity—production: 120.2 million kWh (2010 est.)
country comparison to the world: 195

Electricity—consumption: 111.8 million kWh (2010 est.)
country comparison to the world: 195

Electricity—exports: 0 kWh (2012 est.)
country comparison to the world: 214

Electricity—imports: 0 kWh (2012 est.)
country comparison to the world: 215

Electricity—installed generating capacity:
41,100 kW (2010 est.)
country comparison to the world: 194

Electricity—from fossil fuels: 70.6% of total installed capacity (2010 est.)
country comparison to the world: 106

Electricity—from nuclear fuels: 0% of total installed capacity (2010 est.)
country comparison to the world: 206

Electricity—from hydroelectric plants: 29.2% of total installed capacity (2010 est.)
country comparison to the world: 81

Electricity—from other renewable sources:
0.2% of total installed capacity (2010 est.)
country comparison to the world: 98

Crude oil—production: 0 bbl/day (2012 est.)
country comparison to the world: 146

Crude oil—exports: 0 bbl/day (2010 est.)
country comparison to the world: 207

Crude oil—imports: 0 bbl/day (2010 est.)
country comparison to the world: 143

Crude oil—proved reserves: 0 bbl (1 January 2013 es)
country comparison to the world: 208

Refined petroleum products—production: 0 bbl/day (2010 est.)
country comparison to the world: 210

Refined petroleum products—consumption:
1,070 bbl/day (2011 est.)
country comparison to the world: 198

Refined petroleum products—exports: 0 bbl/day (2010 est.)
country comparison to the world: 145

Refined petroleum products—imports: 1,149 bbl/day (2010 est.)
country comparison to the world: 192

Natural gas—production: 0 cu m (2011 est.)
country comparison to the world: 210

Natural gas—consumption: 0 cu m (2010 est.)
country comparison to the world: 210

Natural gas—exports: 0 cu m (2011 est.)
country comparison to the world: 209

Natural gas—imports: 0 cu m (2011 est.)
country comparison to the world: 80

Natural gas—proved reserves: 0 cu m (1 January 2013 es)
country comparison to the world: 208

Carbon dioxide emissions from consumption of energy: 146,600 Mt (2011 est.)
country comparison to the world: 203

COMMUNICATIONS

Telephones—main lines in use: 35,300 (2010)
country comparison to the world: 173

Telephones—mobile cellular: 167,400 (2010)
country comparison to the world: 183

Telephone system: *general assessment:* adequate
domestic: combined fixed-line and mobile-cellular teledensity roughly 100 telephones per 100 persons
international: country code—685; satellite earth station—1 Intelsat (Pacific Ocean) (2007)

Broadcast media: state-owned TV station privatized in 2008; 4 privately-owned television broadcast stations; about a half dozen privately owned radio stations and one state-owned radio station; TV and radio broadcasts of several stations from American Samoa are available (2009)

Internet country code: .ws

Internet hosts: 18,013 (2012)
country comparison to the world: 120

Internet users: 9,000 (2009)
country comparison to the world: 202

TRANSPORTATION

Airports: 4 (2013)
country comparison to the world: 187

Airports—with paved runways: *total:* 1
2,438 to 3,047 m: 1 (2013)

Airports—with unpaved runways: *total:* 3
under 914 m:
3 (2013)

Roadways: *total:* 2,337 km
country comparison to the world: 172
paved: 332 km
unpaved: 2,005 km (2001)

Merchant marine: *total:* 2
country comparison to the world: 146
by type: cargo 1, passenger/cargo 1
foreign-owned: 1 (NZ 1) (2010)

Ports and terminals: *major seaport(s):* Apia

MILITARY

Military branches: no regular military forces; Samoa Police Force (2008)

Manpower available for military service:
males age 16-49: 47,906 (2010 est.)

Manpower fit for military service:
males age 16-49: 38,260
females age 16-49: 38,032 (2010 est.)

Manpower reaching militarily significant age annually: *male:* 2,221
female: 2,062 (2010 est.)

Military—note: Samoa has no formal defense structure or regular armed forces; informal defense ties exist with NZ, which is required to consider any Samoan request for assistance under the 1962 Treaty of Friendship

TRANSNATIONAL ISSUES

Disputes—international: none

SAN MARINO

INTRODUCTION

Background: Geographically the third smallest state in Europe (after the Holy See and Monaco), San Marino also claims to be the world's oldest republic. According to tradition, it was founded by a Christian stonemason named Marinus in A.D. 301. San Marino's foreign policy is aligned with that of the European Union, although it is not a member; social and political trends in the republic track closely with those of its larger neighbor, Italy.

GEOGRAPHY

Location: Southern Europe, an enclave in central Italy

Geographic coordinates: 43 46 N, 12 25 E

Map references: Europe

Area: total: 61 sq km
country comparison to the world: 229
land: 61 sq km
water: 0 sq km

Area—comparative: about one third times the size of Washington, DC

Land boundaries: *total:* 39 km
border countries: Italy 39 km

Coastline: 0 km (landlocked)

Maritime claims: none (landlocked)

Climate: Mediterranean; mild to cool winters; warm, sunny summers

Terrain: rugged mountains

Elevation extremes: *lowest point:* Torrente Ausa 55 m
highest point: Monte Titano 755 m

Natural resources: building stone

Land use: *arable land:* 16.67%
permanent crops: 0%
other: 83.33% (2011)

Irrigated land: NA

Natural hazards: NA

Environment—current issues: air pollution; urbanization decreasing rural farmlands

Environment—international agreements: *party to:* Biodiversity, Climate Change, Desertification, Whaling
signed, but not ratified: Air Pollution

Geography—note: landlocked; smallest independent state in Europe after the Holy See and Monaco; dominated by the Apennines

People and Society

Nationality: *noun:* Sammarinese (singular and plural)
adjective: Sammarinese

Ethnic groups: Sammarinese, Italian

Languages: Italian

Religions: Roman Catholic

Population: 32,742 (July 2014 est.)
country comparison to the world: 215

Age structure:
0-14 years: 16% (male 2,779/female 2,445)
15-24 years: 10.9% (male 1,822/female 1,733)
25-54 years: 42.4% (male 6,552/female 7,328)
55-64 years: 18.8% (male 1,957/female 1,957)
65 years and over: 18.5% (male 2,756/female 3,413) (2014 est.)

Median age: *total:* 43.6 years
male: 42.6 years
female: 44.4 years (2014 est.)

Population growth rate: 0.87% (2014 est.)
country comparison to the world: 127

Birth rate: 8.7 births/1,000 population (2014 est.)
country comparison to the world: 215

Death rate: 8.31 deaths/1,000 population (2014 est.)
country comparison to the world: 91

Net migration rate: 8.31 migrant(s)/1,000 population (2014 est.)
country comparison to the world: 16

Urbanization: *urban population:* 94% of total population (2010)
rate of urbanization: 0.6% annual rate of change (2010-15 est.)

Sex ratio: *at birth:* 1.1 male(s)/female
0-14 years: 1.14 male(s)/female
15-24 years: 1.05 male(s)/female
25-54 years: 0.89 male(s)/female
55-64 years: 0.94 male(s)/female
65 years and over: 0.8 male(s)/female
total population: 0.94 male(s)/female (2014 est.)

Infant mortality rate: *total:* 4.52 deaths/1,000 live births
country comparison to the world: 185
male: 4.71 deaths/1,000 live births
female: 4.31 deaths/1,000 live births (2014 est.)

Life expectancy at birth: *total population:* 83.18 years
country comparison to the world: 5
male: 80.64 years
female: 85.94 years (2014 est.)

Total fertility rate: 1.49 children born/woman (2014 est.)
country comparison to the world: 193

Health expenditures: 7.2% of GDP (2010)
country comparison to the world: 80

Physicians density: 4.88 physicians/1,000 population (2011)

Hospital bed density: 3.9 beds/1,000 population (2011)

HIV/AIDS—adult prevalence rate: NA

HIV/AIDS—people living with HIV/AIDS: NA

HIV/AIDS—deaths: NA

Education expenditures: NA

Literacy: *definition:* age 10 and over can read and write
total population: 96%
male: 97%
female: 95%

School life expectancy (primary to tertiary education): *total:* 15 years
male: 15 years
female: 16 years (2011)

GOVERNMENT

Country name: *conventional long form:* Republic of San Marino
conventional short form: San Marino
local long form: Repubblica di San Marino
local short form: San Marino

Government type: republic

Capital: *name:* San Marino

geographic coordinates: 43 56 N, 12 25 E
time difference: UTC+1 (6 hours ahead of Washington, DC during Standard Time)
daylight saving time: +1hr, begins last Sunday in March; ends last Sunday in October

Administrative divisions: 9 municipalities (castelli, singular—castello); Acquaviva, Borgo Maggiore, Chiesanuova, Domagnano, Faetano, Fiorentino, Montegiardino, San Marino Citta, Serravalle

Independence: 3 September 301

National holiday: Founding of the Republic, 3 September (A.D. 301)

Constitution: consists of several legislative instruments, chief among them the Statutes (Leges Statuti) of 1600 and the Declaration of Citizen Rights of 1974; latter document amended 2000, 2002 (2013)

Legal system: civil law system with Italian civil law influences

International law organization participation: has not submitted an ICJ jurisdiction declaration; accepts ICCt jurisdiction

Suffrage: 18 years of age; universal

Executive branch: *chief of state:* Co-chiefs of State Captain Regent Valeria CIAVATTA and Captain Regent Luca BSECCARI (for the period 1 April-1 October 2014)
head of government: Secretary of State for Foreign and Political Affairs Pasquale VALENTINI (since 5 December 2012)
cabinet: Congress of State elected by the Great and General Council for a five-year term (For more information visit the World Leaders website)
elections: co-chiefs of state (captains regent) elected by the Grand and General Council for a six-month term; election last held on 17 September 2013 (next to be held in March 2014); secretary of state for foreign and political affairs elected by the Grand and General Council for a five-year term; election last held on 11 November 2012 (next to be held by November 2017)
election results: Anna Maria MUCCIOLI and Gian Carlo CAPICCHIONI elected captains regent; percent of legislative vote—NA; Pasquale VALENTINI elected secretary of state for foreign and political affairs; percent of legislative vote—NA
note: the popularly elected parliament (Grand and General Council) selects two of its members to serve as the captains regent (co-chiefs of state) for a six-month period; they preside over meetings of the Grand and General Council and its cabinet (Congress of State), which has nine other members, all are selected by the Grand and General Council; assisting the captains regent are

nine secretaries of state; the secretary of state for Foreign Affairs has assumed some prime ministerial roles

Legislative branch: unicameral Grand and General Council or Consiglio Grande e Generale (60 seats; members elected by popular vote to serve five-year terms)
elections: last held on 11 November 2012 (next to be held by November 2017)
election results: percent of vote by party—San Marino Common Good coalition (San Marino Bene Comune) 50.7% (PDCS 29.5%, PSD 14.3%, AP 6.7%), Entente for the Country coalition (Intesa per Il Paese) 22.3% (PS 12.1%, UPR 8.4%, USDM 1.7%), Active Citizenry coalition (Cittadinanza Attiva) 16.1% (SU 9.1%, Civic 10 6.7%), Civic Movement R.E.T.E. 6.3%, For San Marino 2.8%, San Marino 3.0 1.8%; seats by party—San Marino Common Good coalition 35 (PDCS 21, PSD 10, AP 4), Entente for the Country coalition 12 (PS 7, UPR 5), Active Citizenry 9 (SU 5, Civic 10 4), Civic Movement R.E.T.E. 4

Judicial branch: *highest court(s):* Council of Twelve or Consiglio dei XII (consists of 12 members) note—the College of Guarantors for the Constitutionality and General Norms functions as San Marino's constitutional court
judge selection and term of office: judges elected by the Grand and General Council from among its own to serve 5-year terms
subordinate courts: first instance and first appeal criminal, administrative, and civil courts; justices of the peace or conciliatory judges

Political parties and leaders:
San Marino Common Good: Christian Democrats or PDCS [Marco GATTI]; Party of Socialists and Democrats or PSD [Gerardo GIOVAGNOLI]; Popular Alliance or AP [Stefano PALMIERI]
Entente for the Country: Socialist Party or PS [Augusto CASALI]; Union for the Republic or UPR [Giovanni LONFERNINI]; Sammarinese Union of Moderates or USDM [Romeo MORRI and Glauco SANSOVINI]
Active Citizenship: United Left or SU [Alessandro ROSSI]; Civic 10 [Mateo CIACCI]

other: Civic Movement R.E.T.E. (Network) [Gloria ARCANGELONI]; For San Marino [Emilio DELLA BALDA]; San Marino 3.0 [Simone DELLA VALLE]

Political pressure groups and leaders: NA

International organization participation: CE, FAO, IAEA, IBRD, ICAO, ICC (NGOs), ICRM, IDA, IFRCS, ILO, IMF, IMO, Interpol, IOC, IOM (observer), IPU, ITU, ITUC (NGOs), LAIA (observer), OPCW, OSCE, Schengen Convention (de facto member), UN, UNCTAD, UNESCO, Union Latina, UNWTO, UPU, WHO, WIPO

Diplomatic representation in the US: chief of mission: Ambassador Paolo RONDELLI (since 16 July 2007)
chancery: 1711 N Street NW, 2nd floor, Washington, DC 20036
telephone: 202-223-2418
FAX: 202-223-2748

Diplomatic representation from the US: the US does not have an embassy in San Marino; the ambassador to Italy is accredited to San Marino

Flag description: two equal horizontal bands of white (top) and light blue with the national coat of arms superimposed in the center; the main colors derive from the shield of the coat of arms, which features three white towers on three peaks on a blue field; the towers represent three castles built on San Marino's highest feature, Mount *Titano:* Guaita, Cesta, and Montale; the coat of arms is flanked by a wreath, below a crown and above a scroll bearing the word LIBERTAS (Liberty); the white and blue colors are also said to stand for peace and liberty respectively

National symbol(s): three peaks each displaying a tower

National anthem: *name:* "Inno Nazionale della Repubblica" (National Anthem of the Republic)
lyrics/music: none/Federico CONSOLO
note: adopted 1894; the music for the lyric-less anthem is based on a 10th century chorale piece

ECONOMY

Economy—overview: San Marino's economy relies heavily on tourism, the banking industry and the manufacture and export of ceramics, clothing, fabrics, furniture, paints, spirits, tiles, and wine. The manufacturing and financial sectors account for more than half of San Marino's GDP. The per capita level of output and standard of living are comparable to those of the most prosperous regions of Italy. The economy benefits from foreign investment due to its relatively low corporate taxes and low taxes on interest earnings. The income tax rate is also very low, about one-third the average EU level. San Marino does not issue public debt securities; when necessary, it finances deficits by drawing down central bank deposits. San Marino's economy has been contracting since 2008, largely due to weakened demand from Italy—which accounts for nearly 90% of its export market—and financial sector consolidation. Difficulties in the banking sector, the recent global economic downturn, and the sizeable decline in tax revenues have contributed to negative real GDP growth. The government has adopted measures to counter the economic downturn, including subsidized credit to businesses and is seeking to shift its growth model away from a reliance on bank and tax secrecy. San Marino continues to work towards harmonizing its fiscal laws with EU and international standards. In September 2009, the OECD removed San Marino from its list of tax havens that have yet to fully adopt global tax standards, and in 2010 San Marino signed Tax Information Exchange Agreements with most major countries. In 2013 San Marino's Government signed a Double Taxation Agreement with Italy, but a referendum on EU membership failed to reach the quorum needed to bring it to a vote.

GDP (purchasing power parity): $1.306 billion (2013 est.)
country comparison to the world: 200
$1.353 billion (2012 est.)
$1.409 billion (2011 est.)
note: data are in 2013 US dollars

GDP (official exchange rate): $1.866 billion (2013 est.)

GDP—real growth rate: -3.5% (2013 est.)
country comparison to the world: 214
-4% (2012 est.)
-2.5% (2011 est.)

GDP—per capita (PPP): $0 (2013 est.)
country comparison to the world: 229
$55,000 (2012 est.)
$60,800 (2011 est.)

GDP—composition, by end use:
exports of goods and services: 176.6%
imports of goods and services: -153.3%

GDP—composition, by sector of origin:
agriculture: 0.1%
industry: 39.2%
services: 60.7% (2009)

Agriculture—products: wheat, grapes, corn, olives; cattle, pigs, horses, beef, cheese, hides

Industries: tourism, banking, textiles, electronics, ceramics, cement, wine

Industrial production growth rate: -1.1% (2012 est.)
country comparison to the world: 180

Labor force: 21,960 (September 2013)
country comparison to the world: 209

Labor force—by occupation:
agriculture: 0.2%
industry: 33.5%
services: 66.3% (September 2013 es)

Unemployment rate: 7% (2012)
country comparison to the world: 75
5.5% (2011)

Population below poverty line: NA%

Household income or consumption by percentage share: *lowest* 10%: NA%
highest 10%: NA%

Budget: *revenues:* $667.7 million
expenditures: $721.8 million (2011)

Taxes and other revenues: 35.8% of GDP (2011)
country comparison to the world: 61

Budget surplus (+) or deficit (-):
-2.9% of GDP (2012 est.)
country comparison to the world: 120

Public debt: 25.8% of GDP (2013 est.)
country comparison to the world: 128
20.3% of GDP (2012 est.)

Fiscal year: calendar year

Inflation rate (consumer prices): 2.8% (2012 est.)
country comparison to the world: 108
2% (2011)

Commercial bank prime lending rate: 5.92% (31 December 2011 est.)
country comparison to the world: 150
5.38% (31 December 2010 est.)

Stock of narrow money: $1.326 billion (31 December 2007)

Stock of broad money: $4.584 billion (31 December 2007)
country comparison to the world: 131
$4.584 billion

Stock of domestic credit: $8.822 billion (30 September 2010)
country comparison to the world: 102
$8.008 billion (31 December 2009)

Market value of publicly traded shares: $NA

Exports: $3.827 billion (2011 est.)
country comparison to the world: 125
$2.576 billion (2010 est.)

Exports—commodities: building stone, lime, wood, chestnuts, wheat, wine, baked goods, hides, ceramics

Exports—partners: Italy 82.3% (2012 est.)

Imports: $2.551 billion (2011 est.)
country comparison to the world: 154
$2.132 billion (2010 est.)

Imports—commodities: wide variety of consumer manufactures, food, energy

Imports—partners: Italy 81.8% (2012 est.)

Reserves of foreign exchange and gold: $308.6 million (2012 est.)
country comparison to the world: 156
$341.9 million (2011)

Debt—external: $NA

Exchange rates: euros (EUR) per US dollar—
0.7634 (2012 est.)
0.7752 (2011 est.)

0.755 (2010 est.)
0.7198 (2009 est.)
0.6827 (2008 est.)

COMMUNICATIONS

Telephones—main lines in use: 18,700 (2012)
country comparison to the world: 189

Telephones—mobile cellular: 36,000 (2011)
country comparison to the world: 205

Telephone system: *general assessment:* automatic telephone system completely integrated into Italian system
domestic: combined fixed-line and mobile-cellular teledensity 170 telephones per 100 persons
international: country code—378; connected to Italian international network (2011)

Broadcast media: state-owned public broadcaster operates 1 TV station and 3 radio stations; receives radio and TV broadcasts from Italy (2012)

Internet country code: .sm

Internet hosts: 11,015 (2012)
country comparison to the world: 133

Internet users: 17,000 (2009)
country comparison to the world: 195

TRANSPORTATION

Roadways: *total:* 292 km
country comparison to the world: 205
paved: 292 km (2006)

MILITARY

Military branches: no regular military forces; voluntary Military Corps (Corpi Militari) performs ceremonial duties and limited police support functions (2010)

Military service age and obligation: 18 is the legal minimum age for voluntary military service; no conscription; government has the authority to call up all San Marino citizens from 16-60 years of age to service in the military (2012)

Manpower available for military service:
males age 16-49: 6,892 (2010 est.)

Manpower fit for military service:
males age 16-49: 5,565
females age 16-49: 6,067 (2010 est.)

Manpower reaching militarily significant age annually: *male:* 186
female: 166 (2010 est.)

Military—note: defense is the responsibility of Italy

TRANSNATIONAL ISSUES

Disputes—international: none

SAO TOME AND PRINCIPE

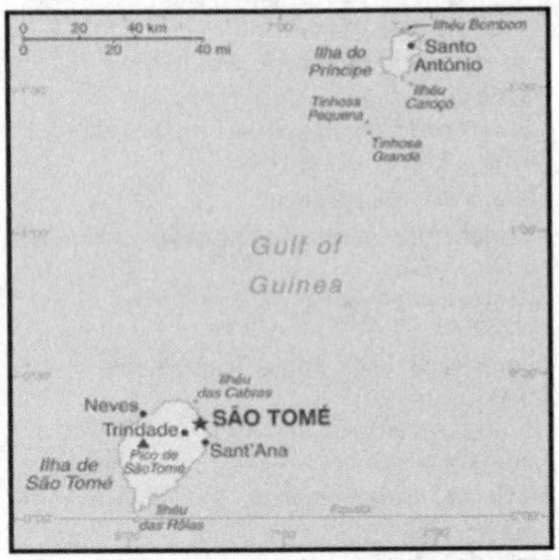

INTRODUCTION

Background: Discovered and claimed by Portugal in the late 15th century, the islands' sugar-based economy gave way to coffee and cocoa in the 19th century—all grown with African plantation slave labor, a form of which lingered into the 20th century. While independence was achieved in 1975, democratic reforms were not instituted until the late 1980s. The country held its first free elections in 1991, but frequent internal wrangling between the various political parties precipitated repeated changes in leadership and two failed coup attempts in 1995 and 2003. In 2012, three opposition parties combined in a no confidence vote to bring down the majority government of former Prime Minister Patrice TROVOADA. The new government of Prime Minister Gabriel Arcanjo Ferreira DA COSTA is entirely composed of opposition party members with limited experience in governance. New oil discoveries in the Gulf of Guinea may attract increased attention to the small island nation.

GEOGRAPHY

Location: Central Africa, islands in the Gulf of Guinea, just north of the Equator, west of Gabon

Geographic coordinates: 1 00 N, 7 00 E

Map references: Africa

Area: *total:* 964 sq km
country comparison to the world: 185
land: 964 sq km
water: 0 sq km

Area—comparative: more than five times the size of Washington, DC

Land boundaries: 0 km

Coastline: 209 km

Maritime claims: measured from claimed archipelagic baselines
territorial sea: 12 nm
exclusive economic zone: 200 nm

Climate: tropical; hot, humid; one rainy season (October to May)

Terrain: volcanic, mountainous

Elevation extremes: *lowest point:* Atlantic Ocean 0 m
highest point: Pico de Sao Tome 2,024 m

Natural resources: fish, hydropower

Land use: *arable land:* 9.06%
permanent crops: 40.62%
other: 50.31% (2011)

Irrigated land: 97 sq km (2003)

Natural hazards: NA

Environment—current issues: deforestation; soil erosion and exhaustion

Environment—international agreements:
party to: Biodiversity, Climate Change, Climate Change-Kyoto Protocol, Desertification, Endangered Species, Environmental Modification, Law of the Sea, Ozone Layer Protection, Ship Pollution, Wetlands
signed, but not ratified: none of the selected agreements

Geography—note: the smallest country in Africa; the two main islands form part of a chain of extinct volcanoes and both are mountainous

PEOPLE AND SOCIETY

Nationality: *noun:* Sao Tomean(s)
adjective: Sao Tomean

Ethnic groups: mestico, angolares (descendants of Angolan slaves), forros (descendants of freed slaves), servicais (contract laborers from Angola, Mozambique, and Cabo Verde), tongas (children of servicais born on the islands), Europeans (primarily Portuguese), Asians (mostly Chinese)

Languages: Portuguese 98.4% (official), Forro 36.2%, Cabo Verdian 8.5%, French 6.8%, Angolar 6.6%, English 4.9%, Lunguie 1%, other (including sign language) 2.4%
note: shares sum to more than 100% because some respondents gave more than one answer on the census (2012 est.)

Religions: Catholic 55.7%, Adventist 4.1%, Assembly of God 3.4%, New Apostolic 2.9%, Mana 2.3%, Universal Kingdom of God 2%, Jehovah's Witness 1.2%, other 6.2%, none 21.2%, unspecified 1% (2012 est.)

Population: 190,428 (July 2014 est.)
country comparison to the world: 186

Age structure:
0-14 years: 43.5% (male 42,170/female 40,750)
15-24 years: 19.8% (male 19,085/female 18,573)
25-54 years: 30.3% (male 28,232/female 29,410)
55-64 years: 2.9% (male 3,010/female 3,612)
65 years and over: 3% (male 2,523/female 3,063) (2014 est.)

Dependency ratios:
total dependency ratio: 81.8 %
youth dependency ratio: 75.6 %
elderly dependency ratio: 6.1 %
potential support ratio: 16.3 (2013)

Median age: *total:* 17.8 years
male: 17.3 years
female: 18.2 years (2014 est.)

Population growth rate: 1.89% (2014 est.)
country comparison to the world: 60

Birth rate: 35.12 births/1,000 population (2014 est.)
country comparison to the world: 24

Death rate: 7.45 deaths/1,000 population (2014 est.)
country comparison to the world: 115

Net migration rate: -8.79 migrant(s)/1,000 population (2014 est.)
country comparison to the world: 210

Urbanization: *urban population:* 62.7% of total population (2011)
rate of urbanization: 3.01% annual rate of change (2010-15 est.)

Major urban areas—population: SAO TOME (capital) 60,000 (2009)

Sex ratio: *at birth:* 1.03 male(s)/female
0-14 years: 1.04 male(s)/female
15-24 years: 1.03 male(s)/female
25-54 years: 0.96 male(s)/female
55-64 years: 1 male(s)/female
65 years and over: 0.84 male(s)/female
total population: 1 male(s)/female (2014 est.)

Mother's mean age at first birth: 19.4
note: median age at first birth among women 25-29 (2009 est.)

Maternal mortality rate: 70 deaths/100,000 live births (2010)
country comparison to the world: 88

Infant mortality rate: *total:* 49.16 deaths/1,000 live births
country comparison to the world: 41
male: 51.16 deaths/1,000 live births
female: 47.1 deaths/1,000 live births (2014 est.)

Life expectancy at birth:
total population: 64.22 years
country comparison to the world: 177
male: 62.94 years
female: 65.53 years (2014 est.)

Total fertility rate: 4.67 children born/woman (2014 est.)
country comparison to the world: 25

Contraceptive prevalence rate: 38.4% (2008/09)

Health expenditures: 7.7% of GDP (2011)
country comparison to the world: 69

Physicians density: 0.49 physicians/1,000 population (2004)

Hospital bed density: 2.9 beds/1,000 population (2011)

Drinking water source:
improved:
urban: 98.9% of population
rural: 93.6% of population
total: 97% of population
unimproved:
urban: 1.1% of population
rural: 6.4% of population
total: 3% of population (2011 est.)

Sanitation facility access:
improved:
urban: 40.8% of population
rural: 23.3% of population
total: 34.3% of population
unimproved:
urban: 59.2% of population
rural: 76.7% of population
total: 65.7% of population (2011 est.)

HIV/AIDS—adult prevalence rate: 1% (2012 est.)
country comparison to the world: 46

HIV/AIDS—people living with HIV/AIDS: 1,400 (2012 est.)
country comparison to the world: 141

HIV/AIDS—deaths: 100 (2012 est.)
country comparison to the world: 154

Major infectious diseases: *degree of risk:* high
food or waterborne diseases: bacterial diarrhea, hepatitis A, and typhoid fever
vectorborne diseases: malaria and dengue fever
water contact disease: schistosomiasis (2013)

Obesity—adult prevalence rate: 9.5% (2008)
country comparison to the world: 132

Children under the age of 5 years underweight: 14.4% (2009)
country comparison to the world: 52

Education expenditures: 9.5% of GDP (2010)
country comparison to the world: 6

Literacy: *definition:* age 15 and over can read and write
total population: 69.5%
male: 80.3%
female: 60.1% (2008 est.)

School life expectancy (primary to tertiary education): *total:* 11 years
male: 11 years
female: 11 years (2012)

Child labor—children ages 5-14:
total number: 3,235
percentage: 8 % (2006 est.)

GOVERNMENT

Country name: *conventional long form:* Democratic Republic of Sao Tome and Principe
conventional short form: Sao Tome and Principe
local long form: Republica Democratica de Sao Tome e Principe
local short form: Sao Tome e Principe

Government type: republic

Capital: *name:* Sao Tome

geographic coordinates: 0 20 N, 6 44 E
time difference: UTC 0 (5 hours ahead of Washington, DC during Standard Time)

Administrative divisions: 2 provinces; Principe, Sao Tome
note: Principe has had self government since 29 April 1995

Independence: 12 July 1975 (from Portugal)

National holiday: Independence Day, 12 July (1975)

Constitution: approved 5 November 1975; revised several times, last in 2003 (2012)

Legal system: mixed legal system of civil law base on the Portuguese model and customary law

International law organization participation: has not submitted an ICJ jurisdiction declaration; non-party state to the ICCt

Suffrage: 18 years of age; universal

Executive branch: *chief of state:* President Manuel Pinto DA COSTA (since 3 September 2011)
head of government: Prime Minister Gabriel Arcanjo Ferreira DA COSTA (since 12 December 2012)
cabinet: Council of Ministers appointed by the president on the proposal of the prime minister (For more information visit the World Leaders website)
elections: president elected by popular vote for a five-year term (eligible for a second term); election last held on 17 July and 7 August 2011 (next to be held in 2016); prime minister chosen by the National Assembly and approved by the president
election results: Manuel Pinto DA COSTA elected president in a run-off election; percent of vote—Manuel Pinto DA COSTA 52.9%, Evaristo CARVALHO 47.1%

Legislative branch: unicameral National Assembly or Assembleia Nacional (55 seats; members elected by popular vote to serve four-year terms)
elections: last held on 1 August 2010 (next to be held in 2014)
election results: percent of vote by party—NA; seats by party—ADI 26, MLSTP-PSD 21, PCD 7, MDFM 1

Judicial branch: *highest court(s):* Supreme Court (consists of 5 judges); Constitutional Court (consists of 5 judges, 3 of which are from the Supreme Court)
judge selection and term of office: Supreme Court judges appointed by the National Assembly; judge tenure NA; Constitutional Court judges nominated by the president of the republic and elected by the National Assembly for 5-year terms
subordinate courts: Court of First Instance; Audit Court

Political parties and leaders: Force for Change Democratic Movement or MDFM [Fradigue Bandeira Melo DE MENEZES]; Independent Democratic Action or ADI [Patrice TROVOADA]; Movement for the Liberation of Sao Tome and Principe-Social Democratic Party or MLSTP-PSD [Aurelio MARTINS]; Party for Democratic Convergence or PCD [Leonel Mario D'ALVA]; other small parties

Political pressure groups and leaders: Association of Sao Tome and Principe NGOs or FONG
other: the media

International organization participation: ACP, AfDB, AOSIS, AU, CD, CPLP, EITI (candidate country), FAO, G-77, IBRD, ICAO, ICRM, IDA, IFAD, IFC, IFRCS, ILO, IMF, IMO, Interpol, IOC, IOM (observer), IPU, ITU, ITUC (NGOs), NAM, OIF, OPCW, UN, UNCTAD, UNESCO, UNIDO, Union Latina, UNWTO, UPU, WCO, WHO, WIPO, WMO, WTO (observer)

Diplomatic representation in the US:
chief of mission: Ambassador Carlos Filomeno Azevedo AGOSTINHO das Neves (since 3 December 2013)
chancery: 1211 Connecticut Avenue NW, Suite 300, Washington, DC 20036
telephone: [1] (202) 775-2075, 2076
FAX: [1] (202) 775-2077

Diplomatic representation from the US: the US does not have an embassy in Sao Tome and Principe; the Ambassador to Gabon is accredited to Sao Tome and Principe on a nonresident basis and makes periodic visits to the islands

Flag description: three horizontal bands of green (top), yellow (double width), and green with two black five-pointed stars placed side by side in the center of the yellow band and a red isosceles triangle based on the hoist side; green stands for the country's rich vegetation, red recalls the struggle for independence, and yellow represents cocoa, one of the country's main agricultural products; the two stars symbolize the two main islands
note: uses the popular Pan-African colors of Ethiopia

National anthem: *name:* "Independencia total" (Total Independence)
lyrics/music: Alda Neves DA GRACA do Espirito Santo/Manuel dos Santos Barreto de Sousa e ALMEIDA
note: adopted 1975

ECONOMY

Economy—overview: This small, poor island economy has become increasingly dependent on cocoa since independence in 1975. Cocoa production has substantially declined in recent years because of drought and mismanagement. Sao Tome and Principe has to import fuels, most manufactured goods, consumer goods, and a substantial amount of food, making it vulnerable to fluctuations in global commodity prices. Over the years, it has had difficulty servicing its external debt and has relied heavily on concessional aid and debt rescheduling. Sao Tome and Principe benefited from $200 million in debt relief in December 2000 under the Highly Indebted Poor Countries (HIPC) program, which helped bring down the country's $300 million debt burden. In August 2005, the government signed on to a new 3-year IMF Poverty Reduction and Growth Facility (PRGF) program worth $4.3 million. In April 2011 the country completed a Threshold Country Program with The Millennium Challenge Corporation to help increase tax revenues, reform customs, and improve the business environment. Considerable potential exists for development of a tourist industry, and the government has taken steps to expand facilities in recent years. The government also has attempted to reduce price controls and subsidies. Potential exists for the development of petroleum resources in Sao Tome and Principe's territorial waters in the oil-rich Gulf of Guinea, which are being jointly developed in a 60-40 split with Nigeria, but any actual production is at least several years off. The first production licenses were sold in 2004, though a dispute over licensing with Nigeria delayed the country's receipt of more than $20 million in signing bonuses for almost a year. Maintaining control of inflation, fiscal discipline, and increasing flows of foreign direct investment into the oil sector are the major economic problems facing the country.

GDP (purchasing power parity): $421 million (2013 est.)
country comparison to the world: 217
$402.4 million (2012 est.)
$387.8 million (2011 est.)
note: data are in 2013 US dollars

GDP (official exchange rate): $311 million (2013 est.)

GDP—real growth rate: 4.5% (2013 est.)
country comparison to the world: 67
4% (2012 est.)
4.9% (2011 est.)

GDP—per capita (PPP): $2,200 (2013 est.)
country comparison to the world: 190
$2,200 (2012 est.)
$2,300 (2011 est.)
note: data are in 2013 US dollars

Gross national saving: 32.7% of GDP (2013 est.)
country comparison to the world: 17
27.4% of GDP (2012 est.)
16.8% of GDP (2011 est.)

GDP—composition, by end use:
household consumption: 137.6%
government consumption: 12%
investment in fixed capital: 53.1%
investment in inventories: -1.4%
exports of goods and services: 13.2%
imports of goods and services: -114.5% (2013 est.)

GDP—composition, by sector of origin:
agriculture: 13.7%
industry: 19.5%
services: 66.8% (2013 est.)

Agriculture—products: cocoa, coconuts, palm kernels, copra, cinnamon, pepper, coffee, bananas, papayas, beans; poultry; fish

Industries: light construction, textiles, soap, beer, fish processing, timber

Industrial production growth rate: 4% (2013 est.)
country comparison to the world: 71

Labor force: 52,490 (2007)
country comparison to the world: 189

Labor force—by occupation:
note: population mainly engaged in subsistence agriculture and fishing; shortages of skilled workers

Unemployment rate: NA%

Population below poverty line: 66.2% (2009 est.)

Household income or consumption by percentage share: *lowest 10%:* NA%
highest 10%: NA%

Budget: *revenues:* $100.9 million
expenditures: $133.3 million (2013 est.)

Taxes and other revenues: 32.5% of GDP (2013 est.)
country comparison to the world: 77

Budget surplus (+) or deficit (-):
-10.4% of GDP (2013 est.)
country comparison to the world: 207

Public debt: 65.5% of GDP (2013 est.)
country comparison to the world: 42
75.5% of GDP (2012 est.)

Fiscal year: calendar year

Inflation rate (consumer prices): 8.7% (2013 est.)
country comparison to the world: 199
10.6% (2012 est.)

Central bank discount rate: 16% (31 December 2009)
country comparison to the world: 4
28% (31 December 2008)

Commercial bank prime lending rate: 26% (31 December 2013 est.)
country comparison to the world: 11
26% (31 December 2012 est.)

Stock of narrow money: $47.43 million (31 December 2013 est.)
country comparison to the world: 186
$38.63 million (31 December 2012 est.)

Stock of broad money: $109.9 million (31 December 2013 est.)
country comparison to the world: 190
$99.74 million (31 December 2012 est.)

Stock of domestic credit: $97.37 million (31 December 2013 est.)
country comparison to the world: 178
$94.99 million (31 December 2012 est.)

Market value of publicly traded shares: $NA

Current account balance: -$59 million (2013 est.)
country comparison to the world: 71
-$58.7 million (2012 est.)

Exports: $12.1 million (2013 est.)
country comparison to the world: 212
$12.2 million (2012 est.)

Exports—commodities: cocoa 80%, copra, coffee, palm oil

Exports—partners: Netherlands 33.3%, Belgium 21.8%, Spain 11%, Nigeria 5.6%, US 5.1% (2012)

Imports: $112.8 million (2013 est.)
country comparison to the world: 212
$115.1 million (2012 est.)

Imports—commodities: machinery and electrical equipment, food products, petroleum products

Imports—partners: Portugal 63.1%, Gabon 5.4% (2012)

Reserves of foreign exchange and gold: $46.6 million (31 December 2013 est.)
country comparison to the world: 168
$51.59 million (31 December 2012 est.)

Debt—external: $406.8 million (31 December 2013 est.)
country comparison to the world: 181
$313.3 million (31 December 2012 est.)

Exchange rates: dobras (STD) per US dollar—
18,702 (2013 est.)
19,068 (2012 est.)
18,499 (2010 est.)
16,209 (2009)
14,900 (2008)

ENERGY

Electricity—production: 30 million kWh (2010 est.)
country comparison to the world: 211

Electricity—consumption: 27.9 million kWh (2010 est.)
country comparison to the world: 211

Electricity—exports: 0 kWh (2012)
country comparison to the world: 203

Electricity—imports: 0 kWh (2012 est.)
country comparison to the world: 206

Electricity—installed generating capacity:
14,000 kW (2010 est.)
country comparison to the world: 202

Electricity—from fossil fuels: 57.1% of total installed capacity (2010 est.)
country comparison to the world: 139

Electricity—from nuclear fuels: 0% of total installed capacity (2010 est.)
country comparison to the world: 189

Electricity—from hydroelectric plants: 42.9% of total installed capacity (2010 est.)
country comparison to the world: 56

Electricity—from other renewable sources:
0% of total installed capacity (2010 est.)
country comparison to the world: 130

Crude oil—production: 0 bbl/day (2012 est.)
country comparison to the world: 138

Crude oil—exports: 0 bbl/day (2010 est.)
country comparison to the world: 192

Crude oil—imports: 0 bbl/day (2010 est.)
country comparison to the world: 129

Crude oil—proved reserves: 0 bbl (1 January 2010 es)
country comparison to the world: 197

Refined petroleum products—production: 0 bbl/day (2010 est.)
country comparison to the world: 200

Refined petroleum products—consumption:
903.5 bbl/day (2011 est.)
country comparison to the world: 207

Refined petroleum products—exports: 0 bbl/day (2010 est.)
country comparison to the world: 136

Refined petroleum products—imports: 889 bbl/day (2010 est.)
country comparison to the world: 196

Natural gas—production: 0 cu m (2011 est.)
country comparison to the world: 199

Natural gas—consumption: 0 cu m (2010 est.)
country comparison to the world: 200

Natural gas—exports: 0 cu m (2011 est.)
country comparison to the world: 193

Natural gas—imports: 0 cu m (2011 est.)
country comparison to the world: 138

Natural gas—proved reserves: 0 cu m (1 January 2013 es)

country comparison to the world: 200

Carbon dioxide emissions from consumption of energy: 151,600 Mt (2011 est.)
country comparison to the world: 199

COMMUNICATIONS

Telephones—main lines in use: 8,000 (2012)
country comparison to the world: 204

Telephones—mobile cellular: 122,000 (2012)
country comparison to the world: 190

Telephone system: *general assessment:* local telephone network of adequate quality with most lines connected to digital switches
domestic: combined fixed-line and mobile-cellular teledensity roughly 65 telephones per 100 persons
international: country code—239; satellite earth station—1 Intelsat (Atlantic Ocean) (2010)

Broadcast media: 1 government-owned TV station; 1 government-owned radio station; 3 independent local radio stations authorized in 2005 with 2 operating at the end of 2006; transmissions of multiple international broadcasters are available (2007)

Internet country code: .st

Internet hosts: 1,678 (2012)
country comparison to the world: 165

Internet users: 26,700 (2009)
country comparison to the world: 184

TRANSPORTATION

Airports: 2 (2013)
country comparison to the world: 206

Airports—with paved runways: *total:* 2
1,524 to 2,437 m: 1
914 to 1,523 m: 1 (2013)

Roadways: *total:* 320 km
country comparison to the world: 202
paved: 218 km
unpaved: 102 km (2000)

Merchant marine: *total:* 3
country comparison to the world: 139
by type: bulk carrier 1, cargo 2
foreign-owned: 2 (China 1, Greece 1) (2010)

Ports and terminals: *major seaport(s):* Sao Tome

MILITARY

Military branches: Armed Forces of Sao Tome and Principe (Forcas Armadas de Sao Tome e Principe, FASTP): Army, Coast Guard of Sao Tome e Principe (Guarda Costeira de Sao Tome e Principe, GCSTP); also called "Navy"), Presidential Guard (2013)

Military service age and obligation: 18 is the legal minimum age for compulsory military service; 17 is the legal minimum age for voluntary service (2012)

Manpower available for military service:
males age 16-49: 39,182
females age 16-49: 39,845 (2010 est.)

Manpower fit for military service:
males age 16-49: 27,310
females age 16-49: 29,279 (2010 est.)

Manpower reaching militarily significant age annually: *male:* 2,076
female: 2,003 (2010 est.)

Military—note: Sao Tome and Principe's army is a tiny force with almost no resources at its disposal and would be wholly ineffective operating unilaterally; infantry equipment is considered simple to operate and maintain but may require refurbishment or replacement after 25 years in tropical climates; poor pay, working conditions, and alleged nepotism in the promotion of officers have been problems in the past, as reflected in the 1995 and 2003 coups; these issues are being addressed with foreign assistance aimed at improving the army and its focus on realistic security concerns; command is exercised from the president, through the Minister of Defense, to the Chief of the Armed Forces staff (2005)

TRANSNATIONAL ISSUES

Disputes—international: none

SAUDI ARABIA

INTRODUCTION

Background: Saudi Arabia is the birthplace of Islam and home to Islam's two holiest shrines in Mecca and Medina. The king's official title is the Custodian of the Two Holy Mosques. The modern Saudi state was founded in 1932 by ABD AL-AZIZ bin Abd al-Rahman Al SAUD (Ibn Saud) after a 30-year campaign to unify most of the Arabian Peninsula. One of his male descendants rules the country today, as required by the country's 1992 Basic Law. King ABDALLAH bin Abd al-Aziz ascended to the throne in 2005. Following Iraq's invasion of Kuwait in 1990, Saudi Arabia accepted the Kuwaiti royal family and 400,000 refugees while allowing Western and Arab troops to deploy on its soil for the liberation of Kuwait the following year. The continuing presence of foreign troops on Saudi soil after the liberation of Kuwait became a source of tension between the royal family and the public until all operational US troops left the country in 2003. Major terrorist attacks in May and November 2003 spurred a strong on-going campaign against domestic terrorism and extremism. King ABDALLAH since 2005 has worked to incrementally modernize the Kingdom—driven by personal ideology and political pragmatism—through a series of social and economic initiatives, including expanding employment and social opportunities for women, attracting foreign investment, increasing the role of the private sector in the economy, and discouraging businesses from hiring foreign workers. The Arab Spring inspired protests - increasing in number since 2011 but usually small in size—over primarily domestic issues among Saudi Arabia's majority Sunni population. Riyadh has taken a cautious but firm approach by arresting some protesters but releasing most of them quickly, and by using its state-sponsored clerics to counter political and Islamist activism. In addition, Saudi Arabia has seen protests among the Shia populace in the Eastern Province, who have protested primarily against the detention of political prisoners, endemic discrimination, and Bahraini and Saudi Government actions in Bahrain. Protests are met by a strong police presence, with some arrests, but not the level of bloodshed seen in protests elsewhere in the region. In response to the unrest, King ABDALLAH in February and March 2011 announced a series of benefits to Saudi citizens including funds to build affordable housing, salary increases for government workers, and unemployment entitlements. To promote increased political participation, the government held elections nationwide in September 2011 for half the members of 285 municipal councils—a body that holds little influence in the Saudi Government. Also in September, the king announced that women will be allowed to run for and vote in future municipal elections—first held in 2005—and serve as full members of the advisory Consultative Council. The country remains a leading producer of oil and natural gas and holds about 17% of the world's proven oil reserves. The government continues to pursue economic reform and diversification, particularly since Saudi Arabia's accession to the WTO in 2005, and promotes foreign investment in the kingdom. A burgeoning population, aquifer depletion, and an economy largely dependent on petroleum output and prices are ongoing governmental concerns.

GEOGRAPHY

Location: Middle East, bordering the Persian Gulf and the Red Sea, north of Yemen

Geographic coordinates: 25 00 N, 45 00 E

Map references: Middle East

Area: *total:* 2,149,690 sq km
country comparison to the world: 13
land: 2,149,690 sq km
water: 0 sq km

Area—comparative: slightly more than one-fifth the size of the US

Land boundaries: *total:* 4,431 km
border countries: Iraq 814 km, Jordan 744 km, Kuwait 222 km, Oman 676 km, Qatar 60 km, UAE 457 km, Yemen 1,458 km

Coastline: 2,640 km

Maritime claims: *territorial sea:* 12 nm
contiguous zone: 18 nm
continental shelf: not specified

Climate: harsh, dry desert with great temperature extremes

Terrain: mostly uninhabited, sandy desert

Elevation extremes: *lowest point:* Persian Gulf 0 m
highest point: Jabal Sawda' 3,133 m

Natural resources: petroleum, natural gas, iron ore, gold, copper

Land use: *arable land:* 1.45%
permanent crops: 0.11%
other: 98.44% (2011)

Irrigated land: 16,200 sq km (2004)

Total renewable water resources: 2.4 cu km (2011)

Freshwater withdrawal (domestic/industrial/agricultural): *total:* 23.67 cu km/yr (9%/3%/88%)
per capita: 928.1 cu m/yr (2006)

Natural hazards: frequent sand and dust storms
volcanism: despite many volcanic formations, there has been little activity in the past few centuries; volcanoes include Harrat Rahat, Harrat Khaybar, Harrat Lunayyir, and Jabal Yar

Environment—current issues: desertification; depletion of underground water resources; the lack of perennial rivers or permanent water bodies has prompted the development of extensive seawater desalination facilities; coastal pollution from oil spills

Environment—international agreements:
party to: Biodiversity, Climate Change, Climate Change-Kyoto Protocol, Desertification, Endangered Species, Hazardous Wastes, Law of the Sea, Marine Dumping, Ozone Layer Protection, Ship Pollution
signed, but not ratified: none of the selected agreements

Geography—note: Saudi Arabia is the largest country in the world without a river; extensive coastlines on the Persian Gulf and Red Sea provide great leverage on shipping (especially crude oil) through the Persian Gulf and Suez Canal

PEOPLE AND SOCIETY

Nationality: *noun:* Saudi(s)
adjective: Saudi or Saudi Arabian

Ethnic groups: Arab 90%, Afro-Asian 10%

Languages: Arabic (official)

Religions: Muslim (official; citizens are 85-90% Sunni and 10-15% Shia), other (includes Eastern Orthodox, Protestant, Roman Catholic, Jewish, Hindu, Buddhist, and Sikh) (2012 est.)
note: despite having a large expatriate community of various faiths (more than 30% of the population), most forms of public religious expression inconsistent with the government-sanctioned interpretation of Sunni Islam are restricted; non-Muslims are not allowed to have Saudi citizenship and non-Muslim places of worship are not permitted (2013) (2012 est.)

Population: 27,345,986 (July 2014 est.)
country comparison to the world: 47
note: immigrants make up more than 30% of the total population, according to UN data (2013)

Age structure:
0-14 years: 27.6% (male 3,869,961/female 3,681,616)
15-24 years: 19.3% (male 2,832,538/female 2,458,339)
25-54 years: 45.4% (male 7,086,004/female 5,323,373)
55-64 years: 3.2% (male 674,571/female 555,136)
65 years and over: 3.1% (male 444,302/female 420,146) (2014 est.)

Dependency ratios:
total dependency ratio: 46.9 %
youth dependency ratio: 42.6 %
elderly dependency ratio: 4.2 %
potential support ratio: 23.6 (2013)

Median age: *total:* 26.4 years
male: 27.3 years
female: 25.3 years (2014 est.)

Population growth rate: 1.49% (2014 est.)
country comparison to the world: 81

Birth rate: 18.78 births/1,000 population (2014 est.)
country comparison to the world: 96

Death rate: 3.32 deaths/1,000 population (2014 est.)
country comparison to the world: 220

Net migration rate: -0.59 migrant(s)/1,000 population (2014 est.)
country comparison to the world: 138

Urbanization: *urban population:* 82.3% of total population (2011)
rate of urbanization: 2.38% annual rate of change (2010-15 est.)

Major urban areas—population: RIYADH (capital) 4.725 million; Jeddah 3.234 million; Mecca 1.484 million; Medina 1.104 million; Ad Dammam 902,000 (2009)

Sex ratio: *at birth:* 1.05 male(s)/female
0-14 years: 1.05 male(s)/female
15-24 years: 1.15 male(s)/female
25-54 years: 1.33 male(s)/female
55-64 years: 1.2 male(s)/female
65 years and over: 1.08 male(s)/female
total population: 1.21 male(s)/female (2014 est.)

Maternal mortality rate: 24 deaths/100,000 live births (2010)
country comparison to the world: 133

Infant mortality rate: *total:* 14.58 deaths/1,000 live births
country comparison to the world: 110
male: 16.73 deaths/1,000 live births
female: 12.32 deaths/1,000 live births (2014 est.)

Life expectancy at birth: *total population:* 74.82 years
country comparison to the world: 107
male: 72.79 years
female: 76.94 years (2014 est.)

Total fertility rate: 2.17 children born/woman (2014 est.)
country comparison to the world: 104

Contraceptive prevalence rate: 23.8% (2007)

Health expenditures: 3.7% of GDP (2011)
country comparison to the world: 173

Physicians density: 0.94 physicians/1,000 population (2008)

Hospital bed density: 2.2 beds/1,000 population (2009)

Drinking water source:
improved:
urban: 97% of population
rural: 97% of population
total: 97% of population
unimproved:
urban: 3% of population
rural: 3% of population
total: 3% of population (2011 est.)

Sanitation facility access:
improved:
urban: 100% of population
rural: 100% of population
total: 100% of population
unimproved:
urban: 0% of population
rural: 0% of population
total: 0% of population (2011 est.)

HIV/AIDS—adult prevalence rate: 0.01% (2001 est.)
country comparison to the world: 169

HIV/AIDS—people living with HIV/AIDS: NA

HIV/AIDS—deaths: NA

Obesity—adult prevalence rate: 33% (2008)
country comparison to the world: 19

Children under the age of 5 years underweight: 5.3% (2005)
country comparison to the world: 87

Education expenditures: 5.1% of GDP (2008)
country comparison to the world: 68

Literacy: *definition:* age 15 and over can read and write
total population: 87.2%
male: 90.8%
female: 82.2% (2011 est.)

School life expectancy (primary to tertiary education): *total:* 16 years
male: 15 years
female: 16 years (2012)

Unemployment, youth ages 15-24: *total:* 28.3%
country comparison to the world: 31
male: 20.8%
female: 54.4% (2012)

GOVERNMENT

Country name: *conventional long form:* Kingdom of Saudi Arabia
conventional short form: Saudi Arabia
local long form: Al Mamlakah al Arabiyah as Suudiyah
local short form: Al Arabiyah as Suudiyah

Government type: monarchy

Capital: *name:* Riyadh

geographic coordinates: 24 39 N, 46 42 E
time difference: UTC+3 (8 hours ahead of Washington, DC during Standard Time)

Administrative divisions: 13 provinces (mintaqat, singular—mintaqah); Al Bahah, Al Hudud ash Shamaliyah (Northern Border), Al Jawf, Al Madinah (Medina), Al Qasim, Ar Riyad (Riyadh), Ash Sharqiyah (Eastern), 'Asir, Ha'il, Jazan, Makkah (Mecca), Najran, Tabuk

Independence: 23 September 1932 (unification of the kingdom)

National holiday: Unification of the Kingdom, 23 September (1932)

Constitution: 1 March 1992—Basic Law of Government, issued by royal decree, serves as the constitutional framework and is based on the Qur'an and the life and tradition of the Prophet Muhammad (2013)

Legal system: Islamic (sharia) legal system with some elements of Egyptian, French, and customary law; note—several secular codes have been introduced; commercial disputes handled by special committees

International law organization participation: has not submitted an ICJ jurisdiction declaration; non-party state to the ICCt

Suffrage: 21 years of age; male

Executive branch: *chief of state:* King and Prime Minister ABDALLAH bin Abd al-Aziz Al Saud (since 1 August 2005); Heir Apparent Crown Prince SALMAN bin Abd al-Aziz Al Saud, born 31 December 1935); Deputy Crown Prince MUQRIN bin Abd al-Aziz Al Saud (born 15 September 1945); note—the monarch is both chief of state and head of government
head of government: King and Prime Minister ABDALLAH bin Abd al-Aziz Al Saud (since 1 August 2005); Deputy Prime Minister SALMAN bin Abd al-Aziz Al Saud (since 19 June 2012); Second Deputy Prime Minister MUQRIN bin Abd al-Aziz Al Saud (since February 2013)
cabinet: Council of Ministers appointed by the monarch every four years and includes many royal family members (For more information visit the World Leaders website)
elections: none; the monarchy is hereditary; note—an Allegiance Commission created by royal decree in October 2006 established a committee of Saudi princes that will play a role in selecting future Saudi kings, but the system will not take effect until after King ABDALLAH's successor inherits the throne

Legislative branch: Consultative Council or Majlis al-Shura (150 members and a chairman appointed by the monarch to serve four-year terms); note—though the Council of Ministers announced in October 2003 its intent to introduce elections for a third of the Majlis al-Shura incrementally over a period of four to five years, to date no such elections have been held or announced

Judicial branch: *highest court(s):* High Court (consists of the court chief and organized into circuits with 3-judge panels except the criminal circuit which has a 5-judge panel for cases involving major punishments) note—in 2005, King Abdullah issued decrees approving an overhaul of the judicial system and which were incorporated in the Judiciary Law of 2007; one change was the replacement of the Supreme Council of Justice with the High Court
judge selection and term of office: the High Court chief and chiefs of the High Court Circuits appointed by royal decree following the recommendation of the Supreme Judiciary Council, a 10-member body of high level judges and other judicial heads; new judges and assistant judges serve 1- and 2- year probations, respectively, before permanent assignment
subordinate courts: Court of Appeals; first-degree courts composed of general, criminal, personal status, and commercial courts, and the Labor Court; hierarchy of administrative courts

Political parties and leaders: none

Political pressure groups and leaders: Ansar Al Marah (supports women's rights); Freedom and Justice Coalition (supports Shia rights)
other: gas companies; religious groups

International organization participation: ABEDA, AfDB (nonregional member), AFESD, AMF, BIS, CAEU, CP, FAO, G-20, G-77, GCC, IAEA, IBRD, ICAO, ICC (national committees), ICRM, IDA, IDB, IFAD, IFC, IFRCS, IHO, ILO, IMF, IMO, IMSO, Interpol, IOC, IOM (observer), IPU, ISO, ITSO, ITU, LAS, MIGA, NAM, OAPEC, OAS (observer), OIC, OPCW, OPEC, PCA, UN, UNCTAD, UNESCO, UNIDO, UNRWA, UNWTO, UPU, WCO, WFTU (NGOs), WHO, WIPO, WMO, WTO

Diplomatic representation in the US:
chief of mission: Ambassador Adil al-Ahmad al-JUBAYR (since 21 February 2007)
chancery: 601 New Hampshire Avenue NW, Washington, DC 20037
telephone: [1] (202) 342-3800
FAX: [1] (202) 944-3113
consulate(s) general: Houston, Los Angeles, New York

Diplomatic representation from the US:
chief of mission: Ambassador Joseph WESTPHAL (since 26 March 2014)
embassy: Collector Road M, Diplomatic Quarter, Riyadh
mailing address: American Embassy, Unit 61307, APO AE 09803-1307; International Mail: P. O. Box 94309, Riyadh 11693
telephone: [966] (1) 488-3800
FAX: [966] (1) 488-7360
consulate(s) general: Dhahran, Jiddah (Jeddah)

Flag description: green, a traditional color in Islamic flags, with the Shahada or Muslim creed in large white Arabic script (translated as "There is no god but God; Muhammad is the Messenger of God") above a white horizontal saber (the tip points to the hoist side); design dates to the early twentieth century and is closely associated with the Al Saud family which established the kingdom in 1932; the flag is manufactured with differing obverse and reverse sides so that the Shahada reads—and the sword points—correctly from right to left on both sides
note: one of only three national flags that differ on their obverse and reverse sides—the others are Moldova and Paraguay

National symbol(s): palm tree surmounting two crossed swords

National anthem: *name:* "Aash Al Maleek" (Long Live Our Beloved King)
lyrics/music: Ibrahim KHAFAJI/Abdul Rahman al-KHATEEB
note: music adopted 1947, lyrics adopted 1984

ECONOMY

Economy—overview: Saudi Arabia has an oil-based economy with strong government controls over major economic activities. It possesses about 16% of the world's proven petroleum reserves, ranks as the largest exporter of petroleum, and plays a leading role in OPEC. The petroleum sector accounts for roughly 80% of budget revenues, 45% of GDP, and 90% of export earnings. Saudi Arabia is encouraging the growth of the private sector in order to diversify its economy and to employ more Saudi nationals. Diversification efforts are focusing on power generation, telecommunications, natural gas exploration, and petrochemical sectors. Over 6 million foreign workers play an important role in the Saudi economy, particularly in the oil and service sectors, while Riyadh is struggling to reduce unemployment among its own nationals. Saudi officials are particularly focused on employing its large youth population, which generally lacks the education and technical skills the private sector needs. Riyadh has substantially boosted spending on job training and education, most recently with the opening of the King Abdallah University of Science and Technology—Saudi Arabia's first co-educational university. As part of its effort to attract foreign investment, Saudi Arabia acceded to the WTO in 2005. The government has begun establishing six "economic cities" in different regions of the country to promote foreign investment and plans to spend $373 billion between 2010 and 2014 on social development and infrastructure projects to advance Saudi Arabia's economic development.

GDP (purchasing power parity): $927.8 billion (2013 est.)
country comparison to the world: 20
$895.8 billion (2012 est.)
$852.1 billion (2011 est.)
note: data are in 2013 US dollars

GDP (official exchange rate): $718.5 billion (2013 est.)

GDP—real growth rate: 3.6% (2013 est.)
country comparison to the world: 88
5.1% (2012 est.)
8.6% (2011 est.)

GDP—per capita (PPP): $31,300 (2013 est.)
country comparison to the world: 44
$30,900 (2012 est.)
$30,000 (2011 est.)
note: data are in 2013 US dollars

Gross national saving: 45% of GDP (2013 est.)
country comparison to the world: 8
48.8% of GDP (2012 est.)
50.5% of GDP (2011 est.)

GDP—composition, by end use:
household consumption: 29.7%
government consumption: 21.7%
investment in fixed capital: 23.5%
investment in inventories: 3.5%
exports of goods and services: 52.9%
imports of goods and services: -31.4% (2013 est.)

GDP—composition, by sector of origin:
agriculture: 2%
industry: 62.5%
services: 35.5% (2013 est.)

Agriculture—products: wheat, barley, tomatoes, melons, dates, citrus; mutton, chickens, eggs, milk

Industries: crude oil production, petroleum refining, basic petrochemicals, ammonia, industrial gases, sodium hydroxide (caustic soda), cement, fertilizer, plastics, metals, commercial ship repair, commercial aircraft repair, construction

Industrial production growth rate: 2.7% (2013 est.)
country comparison to the world: 112

Labor force: 8.412 million
country comparison to the world: 57
note: about 80% of the labor force is non-national (2013 est.)

Labor force—by occupation: *agriculture:* 6.7%
industry: 21.4%
services: 71.9% (2005 est.)

Unemployment rate: 10.5% (2013 est.)
country comparison to the world: 110
10.6% (2012 est.)
note: data are for Saudi males only (local bank estimates; some estimates range as high as 25%)

Population below poverty line: NA%

Household income or consumption by percentage share: *lowest 10%:* NA%
highest 10%: NA%

Budget: *revenues:* $302.6 billion
expenditures: $258.4 billion (2013 est.)

Taxes and other revenues: 42.1% of GDP (2013 est.)
country comparison to the world: 29

Budget surplus (+) or deficit (-): 6.2% of GDP (2013 est.)
country comparison to the world: 7

Public debt: 12.2% of GDP (2013 est.)
country comparison to the world: 147
11.8% of GDP (2012 est.)

Fiscal year: calendar year

Inflation rate (consumer prices): 3.7% (2013 est.)
country comparison to the world: 126
2.9% (2012 est.)

Central bank discount rate: 2.5% (31 December 2008)

Commercial bank prime lending rate: 6.7% (31 December 2013 est.)
country comparison to the world: 129
6.8% (31 December 2012 est.)

Stock of narrow money: $263.8 billion (31 December 2013 est.)
country comparison to the world: 17
$236.6 billion (31 December 2012 est.)

Stock of broad money: $416.3 billion (31 December 2013 est.)
country comparison to the world: 25
$371.7 billion (31 December 2012 est.)

Stock of domestic credit: $-52.29 billion (31 December 2013 est.)
country comparison to the world: 190
$-74.71 billion (31 December 2012 est.)

Market value of publicly traded shares: $373.4 billion (31 December 2012 est.)
country comparison to the world: 25
$338.9 billion (31 December 2011)
$353.4 billion (31 December 2010 est.)

Current account balance: $132.2 billion (2013 est.)
country comparison to the world: 3
$164.8 billion (2012 est.)

Exports: $376.3 billion (2013 est.)
country comparison to the world: 16
$388.4 billion (2012 est.)

Exports—commodities: petroleum and petroleum products 90%

Exports—partners: US 14.2%, China 13.6%, Japan 13.6%, South Korea 9.9%, India 8.2%, Singapore 4.3% (2012)

Imports: $147 billion (2013 est.)
country comparison to the world: 31
$141.8 billion (2012 est.)

Imports—commodities: machinery and equipment, foodstuffs, chemicals, motor vehicles, textiles

Imports—partners: China 13.5%, US 13.2%, South Korea 6.6%, Germany 6.5%, India 6.3%, Japan 6% (2012)

Reserves of foreign exchange and gold: $739.5 billion (31 December 2013 est.)
country comparison to the world: 4
$656.9 billion (31 December 2012 est.)

Debt—external: $149.4 billion (31 December 2013 est.)
country comparison to the world: 36
$136.3 billion (31 December 2012 est.)

Stock of direct foreign investment—at home: $240.6 billion (31 December 2013 est.)
country comparison to the world: 24
$223.2 billion (31 December 2012 est.)

Stock of direct foreign investment—abroad: $26.08 billion (31 December 2013 est.)
country comparison to the world: 45
$22.12 billion (31 December 2012 est.)

Exchange rates: Saudi riyals (SAR) per US dollar—
3.75 (2013 est.)
3.75 (2012 est.)
3.75 (2010 est.)
3.75 (2009)
3.75 (2008)

ENERGY

Electricity—production: 239.2 billion kWh (2011 est.)
country comparison to the world: 1 9

Electricity—consumption: 190.9 billion kWh (2010 est.)
country comparison to the world: 20

Electricity—exports: 0 kWh (2012 est.)
country comparison to the world: 188

Electricity—imports: 0 kWh (2012 est.)
country comparison to the world: 191

Electricity—installed generating capacity: 49.05 million kW (2010 est.)
country comparison to the world: 20

Electricity—from fossil fuels: 100% of total installed capacity (2010 est.)
country comparison to the world: 30

Electricity—from nuclear fuels: 0% of total installed capacity (2010 est.)
country comparison to the world: 171

Electricity—from hydroelectric plants: 0% of total installed capacity (2010 est.)
country comparison to the world: 193

Electricity—from other renewable sources: 0% of total installed capacity (2010 est.)
country comparison to the world: 118

Crude oil—production: 11.73 million bbl/day (2012 est.)
country comparison to the world: 1

Crude oil—exports: 6.88 million bbl/day (2011 est.)
country comparison to the world: 1

Crude oil—imports: 0 bbl/day (2011 est.)
country comparison to the world: 114

Crude oil—proved reserves: 267.9 billion bbl (1 January 2013 es)
country comparison to the world: 2

Refined petroleum products—production: 1.935 million bbl/day (2010 est.)
country comparison to the world: 11

Refined petroleum products—consumption: 2.817 million bbl/day (2011 est.)
country comparison to the world: 7

Refined petroleum products—exports: 1.471 million bbl/day (2010 est.)
country comparison to the world: 5

Refined petroleum products—imports: 196,700 bbl/day (2010 est.)
country comparison to the world: 26

Natural gas—production: 103.2 billion cu m (2012 est.)
country comparison to the world: 9

Natural gas—consumption: 99.23 billion cu m (2011 est.)
country comparison to the world: 7

Natural gas—exports: 0 cu m (2011 est.)
country comparison to the world: 174

Natural gas—imports: 0 cu m (2011 est.)
country comparison to the world: 123

Natural gas—proved reserves: 8.15 trillion cu m (1 January 2013 es)
country comparison to the world: 6

Carbon dioxide emissions from consumption of energy: 513.5 million Mt (2011 est.)
country comparison to the world: 11

COMMUNICATIONS

Telephones—main lines in use: 4.8 million (2012)
country comparison to the world: 31

Telephones—mobile cellular: 53 million (2012)
country comparison to the world: 26

Telephone system: *general assessment:* modern system including a combination of extensive microwave radio relays, coaxial cables, and fiber-optic cables
domestic: mobile-cellular subscribership has been increasing rapidly
international: country code—966; landing point for the international submarine cable Fiber-Optic Link Around the Globe (FLAG) and for both the SEA-ME-WE-3 and SEA-ME-WE-4 submarine cable networks providing connectivity to Asia, Middle East, Europe, and US; microwave radio relay to Bahrain, Jordan, Kuwait, Qatar, UAE, Yemen, and Sudan; coaxial cable to Kuwait and Jordan; satellite earth stations—5 Intelsat (3 Atlantic Ocean and 2 Indian Ocean), 1 Arabsat, and 1 Inmarsat (Indian Ocean region) (2011)

Broadcast media: broadcast media are state-controlled; state-run TV operates 4 networks; Saudi Arabia is a major market for pan-Arab satellite TV broadcasters; state-run radio operates several networks; multiple international broadcasters are available (2007)

Internet country code: .sa

Internet hosts: 145,941 (2012)
country comparison to the world: 79

Internet users: 9.774 million (2009)
country comparison to the world: 30

TRANSPORTATION

Airports: 214 (2013)
country comparison to the world: 2 6

Airports—with paved runways: *total:* 8 2
over 3,047 m: 33
2,438 to 3,047 m: 16
1,524 to 2,437 m: 27
914 to 1,523 m: 2
under 914 m: 4 (2013)

Airports—with unpaved runways: *total:* 132
2,438 to 3,047 m: 7
1,524 to 2,437 m: 72
914 to 1,523 m: 37
under 914 m: 16 (2013)

Heliports: 10 (2013)

Pipelines: condensate 209 km; gas 2,940 km; liquid petroleum gas 1,183 km; oil 5,117 km; refined products 1,151 km (2013)

Railways: *total:* 1,378 km
country comparison to the world: 81
standard gauge: 1,378 km 1.435-m gauge (with branch lines and sidings) (2008)

Roadways: *total:* 221,372 km
country comparison to the world: 22
paved: 47,529 km (includes 3,891 km of expressways)
unpaved: 173,843 km (2006)

Merchant marine: *total:* 72
country comparison to the world: 61
by type: cargo 1, chemical tanker 25, container 4, liquefied gas 2, passenger/cargo 10, petroleum tanker 20, refrigerated cargo 3, roll on/roll off 7
foreign-owned: 15 (Egypt 1, Greece 4, Kuwait 4, UAE 6)
registered in other countries: 55 (Bahamas 16, Dominica 2, Liberia 20, Malta 2, Norway 3, Panama 11, Tanzania 1) (2010)

Ports and terminals: *major seaport(s):* Ad Dammam, Al Jubayl, Jeddah, Yanbu al Bahr
container port(s) (TEUs): Ad Dammam (1,492,315), Jeddah (4,010,448)

MILITARY

Military branches: Ministry of Defense and Aviation Forces: Royal Saudi Land Forces, Royal Saudi Naval Forces (includes Marine Forces and Special Forces), Royal Saudi Air Force (Al-Quwwat al-Jawwiya al-Malakiya as-Sa'udiya), Royal Saudi Air Defense Forces, Royal Saudi Strategic Rocket Forces, Saudi Arabian National Guard (SANG)

Military service age and obligation: 17 is the legal minimum age for voluntary military service; no conscription (2012)

Manpower available for military service:
males age 16-49: 8,644,522
females age 16-49: 6,601,985 (2010 est.)

Manpower fit for military service:
males age 16-49: 7,365,624
females age 16-49: 5,677,819 (2010 est.)

Manpower reaching militarily significant age annually: *male:* 261,105
female: 244,763 (2010 est.)

Military expenditures: 7.98% of GDP (2012)
country comparison to the world: 3
7.25% of GDP (2011)
7.98% of GDP (2010)

TRANSNATIONAL ISSUES

Disputes—international: Saudi Arabia has reinforced its concrete-filled security barrier along sections of the now fully demarcated border with Yemen to stem illegal cross-border activities; Kuwait and Saudi Arabia continue discussions on a maritime boundary with Iran; Saudi Arabia claims Egyptian-administered islands of Tiran and Sanafir

Refugees and internally displaced persons: *refugees (country of origin):* 291,000 (Palestinian Territories) (2009)
stateless persons: 70,000 (2012); note—thousands of biduns (stateless Arabs) are descendants of nomadic tribes who were not officially registered when national borders were established, while others migrated to Saudi Arabia in search of jobs; some have temporary identification cards that must be renewed every five years, but their rights remain restricted; most Palestinians have only legal resident status; some naturalized Yemenis were made stateless after being stripped of their passports when Yemen backed Iraq in its

invasion of Kuwait in 1990; Saudi women cannot pass their citizenship on to their children, so if they marry a non-national, their children risk statelessness

Trafficking in persons: *current situation:* Saudi Arabia is a destination country for men and women subjected to forced labor and, to a lesser extent, forced prostitution; men and women from Bangladesh, India, Sri Lanka, Nepal, Pakistan, the Philippines, Indonesia, Sudan, Ethiopia, Kenya, and many other countries voluntarily travel to Saudi Arabia as domestic servants or other low-skilled laborers, but some subsequently face conditions indicative of involuntary servitude (many are forced to work months or years beyond their contract term because employers withhold passports and required exit visas); women, primarily from Asian and African countries, are believed to be forced into prostitution in Saudi Arabia; others were reportedly kidnapped and forced into prostitution after running away from abusive employers; Yemeni, Nigerian, Pakistani, Afghan, Chadian, and Sudanese children were subjected to forced labor as beggars and street vendors in Saudi Arabia, facilitated by criminal gangs
tier rating: Tier 3—Saudi Arabia does not fully comply with the minimum standards for the elimination of trafficking and is not making significant efforts to do so; fewer victims were identified and referred to protection services than in the previous reporting period; the sponsorship system, including the exit visa requirement, continues to restrict the freedom of movement of migrant workers and hamper the ability of victims to pursue legal cases against their employers; however, the government has implemented regulations mandating the formation of unified recruitment companies to replace the sponsorship model; no specialized shelter was available to victims of sex trafficking or male victims of trafficking (2013)

Illicit drugs: death penalty for traffickers; improving anti-money-laundering legislation and enforcement

SENEGAL

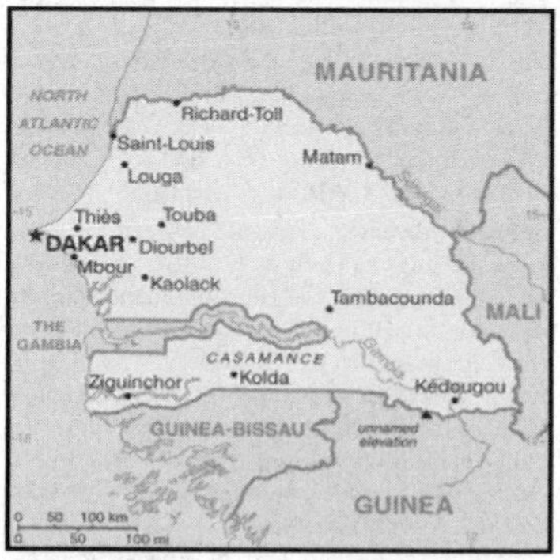

INTRODUCTION

Background: The French colonies of Senegal and the French Sudan were merged in 1959 and granted their independence as the Mali Federation in 1960. The union broke up after only a few months. Senegal joined with The Gambia to form the nominal confederation of Senegambia in 1982. The envisaged integration of the two countries was never carried out, and the union was dissolved in 1989. The Movement of Democratic Forces in the Casamance (MFDC) has led a low-level separatist insurgency in southern Senegal since the 1980s, and several peace deals have failed to resolve the conflict. Nevertheless, Senegal remains one of the most stable democracies in Africa and has a long history of participating in international peacekeeping and regional mediation. Senegal was ruled by a Socialist Party for 40 years until Abdoulaye WADE was elected president in 2000. He was reelected in 2007 and during his two terms amended Senegal's constitution over a dozen times to increase executive power and to weaken the opposition. His decision to run for a third presidential term sparked a large public backlash that led to his defeat in a March 2012 runoff election with Macky SALL.

GEOGRAPHY

Location: Western Africa, bordering the North Atlantic Ocean, between Guinea-Bissau and Mauritania

Geographic coordinates: 14 00 N, 14 00 W

Map references: Africa

Area: *total:* 196,722 sq km
country comparison to the world: 88
land: 192,530 sq km
water: 4,192 sq km

Area—comparative: slightly smaller than South Dakota

Land boundaries: *total:* 2,640 km
border countries: The Gambia 740 km, Guinea 330 km, Guinea-Bissau 338 km, Mali 419 km, Mauritania 813 km

Coastline: 531 km

Maritime claims: *territorial sea:* 12 nm
contiguous zone: 24 nm
exclusive economic zone: 200 nm
continental shelf: 200 nm or to the edge of the continental margin

Climate: tropical; hot, humid; rainy season (May to November) has strong southeast winds; dry season (December to April) dominated by hot, dry, harmattan wind

Terrain: generally low, rolling, plains rising to foothills in southeast

Elevation extremes: *lowest point:* Atlantic Ocean 0 m
highest point: unnamed elevation southwest of Kedougou 581 m

Natural resources: fish, phosphates, iron ore

Land use: *arable land:* 19.57%
permanent crops: 0.28%
other: 80.15% (2011)

Irrigated land: 1,197 sq km (2003)

Total renewable water resources: 38.8 cu km (2011)

Freshwater withdrawal (domestic/industrial/agricultural): *total:* 2.22 cu km/yr (4%/3%/93%)
per capita: 221.6 cu m/yr (2002)

Natural hazards: lowlands seasonally flooded; periodic droughts

Environment—current issues: wildlife populations threatened by poaching; deforestation; overgrazing; soil erosion; desertification; overfishing
Environment—international agreements:
party to: Biodiversity, Climate Change, Climate Change-Kyoto Protocol, Desertification, Endangered Species, Hazardous Wastes, Law of the Sea, Marine Life Conservation, Ozone Layer Protection, Ship Pollution, Wetlands, Whaling
signed, but not ratified: none of the selected agreements

Geography—note: westernmost country on the African continent; The Gambia is almost an enclave within Senegal

PEOPLE AND SOCIETY

Nationality: *noun:* Senegalese (singular and plural)
adjective: Senegalese

Ethnic groups: Wolof 43.3%, Pular 23.8%, Serer 14.7%, Jola 3.7%, Mandinka 3%, Soninke 1.1%, European and Lebanese 1%, other 9.4%

Languages: French (official), Wolof, Pulaar, Jola, Mandinka

Religions: Muslim 94% (most adhere to one of the four main Sufi brotherhoods), Christian 5% (mostly Roman Catholic), indigenous beliefs 1%

Population: 13,635,927 (July 2014 est.)
country comparison to the world: 73

Age structure:
0-14 years: 42.5% (male 2,908,431/female 2,880,258)
15-24 years: 20.5% (male 1,388,530/female 1,401,109)
25-54 years: 30.4% (male 1,892,403/female 2,253,576)
55-64 years: 2.9% (male 225,942/female 289,920)
65 years and over: 2.9% (male 179,444/female 216,314) (2014 est.)

Dependency ratios:
total dependency ratio: 86.9 %
youth dependency ratio: 81.3 %
elderly dependency ratio: 5.6 %
potential support ratio: 17.9 (2013)

Median age: *total:* 18.4 years
male: 17.5 years
female: 19.3 years (2014 est.)

Population growth rate: 2.48% (2014 est.)
country comparison to the world: 32

Birth rate: 35.09 births/1,000 population (2014 est.)
country comparison to the world: 25

Death rate: 8.65 deaths/1,000 population (2014 est.)
country comparison to the world: 75

Net migration rate: -1.66 migrant(s)/1,000 population (2014 est.)
country comparison to the world: 159

Urbanization: *urban population:* 42.5% of total population (2011)
rate of urbanization: 3.32% annual rate of change (2010-15 est.)

Major urban areas—population: DAKAR (capital) 2.777 million (2009)

Sex ratio: *at birth:* 1.03 male(s)/female
0-14 years: 1.01 male(s)/female
15-24 years: 0.99 male(s)/female
25-54 years: 0.84 male(s)/female
55-64 years: 0.94 male(s)/female
65 years and over: 0.85 male(s)/female
total population: 0.94 male(s)/female (2014 est.)

Mother's mean age at first birth: 21.4
note: median age at first birth among women 25-29 (2011 est.)

Maternal mortality rate: 370 deaths/100,000 live births (2010)
country comparison to the world: 28

Infant mortality rate: *total:* 52.72 deaths/1,000 live births
country comparison to the world: 35
male: 58.91 deaths/1,000 live births
female: 46.35 deaths/1,000 live births (2014 est.)

Life expectancy at birth: *total population:* 60.95 years
country comparison to the world: 192
male: 58.94 years
female: 63.02 years (2014 est.)

Total fertility rate: 4.52 children born/woman (2014 est.)
country comparison to the world: 29

Contraceptive prevalence rate: 13.1% (2010/11)

Health expenditures: 6% of GDP (2011)
country comparison to the world: 107

Physicians density: 0.06 physicians/1,000 population (2008)

Hospital bed density: 0.3 beds/1,000 population (2008)

Drinking water source:
improved:
urban: 93.2% of population
rural: 58.7% of population
total: 73.4% of population
unimproved:
urban: 6.8% of population
rural: 41.3% of population
total: 26.6% of population (2011 est.)

Sanitation facility access:
improved:
urban: 67.9% of population
rural: 39.1% of population
total: 51.4% of population
unimproved:
urban: 32.1% of population
rural: 60.9% of population
total: 48.6% of population (2011 est.)

HIV/AIDS—adult prevalence rate: 0.5% (2012 est.)
country comparison to the world: 68

HIV/AIDS—people living with HIV/AIDS: 42,800 (2012 est.)
country comparison to the world: 64

HIV/AIDS—deaths: 1,900 (2012 est.)
country comparison to the world: 60

Major infectious diseases: *degree of risk:* very high
food or waterborne diseases: bacterial and protozoal diarrhea, hepatitis A, and typhoid fever
vectorborne diseases: dengue fever, malaria, and yellow fever
water contact disease: schistosomiasis
respiratory disease: meningococcal meningitis
animal contact disease: rabies (2013)

Obesity—adult prevalence rate: 6.8% (2008)
country comparison to the world: 145

Children under the age of 5 years underweight: 14.4% (2012)
country comparison to the world: 51

Education expenditures: 5.6% of GDP (2010)
country comparison to the world: 53

Literacy: *definition:* age 15 and over can read and write
total population: 49.7%
male: 61.8%
female: 38.7% (2009 est.)

School life expectancy (primary to tertiary education): *total:* 8 years
male: 8 years
female: 8 years (2010)

Child labor—children ages 5-14:
total number: 657,216
percentage: 22 % (2005 est.)

Unemployment, youth ages 15-24: *total:* 14.8%
country comparison to the world: 83
male: 11.9%
female: 20.1% (2006)

GOVERNMENT

Country name: *conventional long form:* Republic of Senegal
conventional short form: Senegal
local long form: Republique du Senegal
local short form: Senegal
former: Senegambia (along with The Gambia), Mali Federation

Government type: republic

Capital: *name:* Dakar

geographic coordinates: 14 44 N, 17 38 W
time difference: UTC 0 (5 hours ahead of Washington, DC during Standard Time)

Administrative divisions: 14 regions (regions, singular—region); Dakar, Diourbel, Fatick, Kaffrine, Kaolack, Kedougou, Kolda, Louga, Matam, Saint-Louis, Sedhiou, Tambacounda, Thies, Ziguinchor

Independence: 4 April 1960 (from France); note—complete independence achieved upon dissolution of federation with Mali on 20 August 1960

National holiday: Independence Day, 4 April (1960)

Constitution: previous 1959 (preindependence), 1963; latest adopted by referendum 7 January 2001, promulgated 22 January 2001; amended many times, last in 2008 (2011)

Legal system: civil law system based on French law; judicial review of legislative acts in Constitutional Court

International law organization participation: accepts compulsory ICJ jurisdiction with reservations; accepts ICCt jurisdiction

Suffrage: 18 years of age; universal

Executive branch: *chief of state:* President Macky SALL (since 2 April 2012)
head of government: Prime Minister Aminata TOURE (since 3 September 2013)
cabinet: Council of Ministers appointed by the prime minister in consultation with the president (For more information visit the World Leaders website)
elections: president elected by popular vote for a seven-year term (eligible for a second term); election last held on 26 February 2012 with a second round runoff on 25 March 2012 (next to be held 2019); prime minister appointed by the president
election results: Macky SALL elected president; percent of votes in a runoff—Macky SALL 65.8%, Abdoulaye WADE 34.2%

Legislative branch: unicameral National Assembly or Assemblee Nationale (150 seats; 90 members elected by direct popular vote and 60 elected by proportional representation from party lists to serve five-year terms)
elections: National Assembly—last held on 1 July 2012 (next to be held in 2017)
election results: National Assembly results—percent of vote by party—NA; seats by party—Benno Bokk Yakaar coalition 119, PDS 12, Bokk Giss Giss coalition 4, MCRN-Bes Du Nakk 4, PVD 2, MRDS 2, URD 1, AJ/PADS 1, other 5

Judicial branch: *highest court(s):* Highest Appeals Court or Cour de Cassation (consists of 13 judges including the court president); Constitutional Council (consists of 5 members including the court president, vice-president, and 3 judges)
judge selection and term of office: Highest Appeals Court judges' tenure NA; Constitutional Council members appointed by the president of the republic to serve 6-year terms with renewal of 3 members every two years
subordinate courts: Court of Appeals; regional and first instance courts

Political parties and leaders: African Party of Independence [Majhemout DIOP]; Alliance for the Republic-Yakaar [Macky SALL]; Alliance of Forces of Progress or AFP [Moustapha NIASSE]; And-Jef/African Party for Democracy and Socialism or AJ/PADS [Landing SAVANE]; Benno Bokk Yakaar coaltion [Macky SALL]; Benno Siggil Senegal (a coalition of opposition parties); Bokk Giss Giss coalition [Pape DIOP]; Citizen Movement for National Reform or MCRN-Bes Du Nakk; Democratic League-Labor Party Movement or LD-MPT [Dr. Abdoulaye BATHILY]; Front for Socialism and Democracy/Benno Jubel or FSD/BJ [Cheikh Abdoulaye Bamba DIEYE]; Gainde Centrist Bloc or BGC [Jean-Paul DIAS]; Independence and Labor Party or PIT [Amath DANSOKHO]; Jef-Jel [Talla SYLLA]; National Democratic Rally or RND [Madior DIOUF]; Party for Truth and Development or PVD [Ahmadou Kara MBACKE]; People's Labor Party or PTP [El Hadji DIOUF]; Reform Party or PR [Abdourahim AGNE]; Republican Movement for Socialism and Democracy or MRDS; Rewmi Party [Idrissa SECK]; Senegalese Democratic Party or PDS [Abdoulaye WADE]; Socialist Party or PS [Ousmane Tanor DIENG]; SOPI Coalition [Abdoulaye WADE] (a coalition led by the PDS); Synergy for Ethics and Transparency [Aminata TALL]; Union for Democratic Renewal or URD [Djibo Leyti KA]

Political pressure groups and leaders:
other: labor; students; Sufi brotherhoods, including the Mourides and Tidjanes; teachers

International organization participation: ACP, AfDB, AU, CD, CPLP (associate), ECOWAS, FAO, FZ, G-15, G-77, IAEA, IBRD, ICAO, ICC (national committees), ICRM, IDA, IDB, IFAD, IFC, IFRCS, ILO, IMF, IMO, IMSO, Interpol, IOC, IOM, IPU, ISO, ITSO, ITU, ITUC (NGOs), MIGA, MINUSMA, MONUSCO, NAM, OIC, OIF, OPCW, PCA, UN, UNAMID, UNCTAD, UNESCO, UNIDO, Union Latina, UNMIL, UNMISS, UNOCI, UNWTO, UPU, WADB (regional), WAEMU, WCO, WFTU (NGOs), WHO, WIPO, WMO, WTO

Diplomatic representation in the US:
chief of mission: Ambassador Cheikh NIANG (since 13 July 2012)
embassy: 2215 M Street, NW, Washington, DC 20037
telephone: [1] (202) 234-0540
FAX: [1] (202) 332-6315
consulate(s) general: Houston, New York

Diplomatic representation from the US:
chief of mission: Ambassador Lewis LUKENS (since 11 July 2011) note—also accredited to Guinea-Bissau
embassy: Route des Almadies, Dakar
mailing address: B. P. 49, Dakar
telephone: [221] 33-879-4000
FAX: [221] 33-822-2991

Flag description: three equal vertical bands of green (hoist side), yellow, and red with a small green five-pointed star centered in the yellow band; green represents Islam, progress, and hope; yellow signifies natural wealth and progress; red symbolizes sacrifice and determination; the star denotes unity and hope
note: uses the popular Pan-African colors of Ethiopia; the colors from left to right are the same as those of neighboring Mali and the reverse of those on the flag of neighboring Guinea

National symbol(s): lion

National anthem: *name:* "Pincez Tous vos Koras, Frappez les Balafons" (Pluck Your Koras, Strike the Balafons)
lyrics/music: *Leopold Sedar SENGHOR/Herbert PEPPER*
note: adopted 1960; the lyrics were written by Leopold Sedar SENGHOR, Senegal's first president; the anthem is sometimes played incorporating the Koras (harp-like stringed instruments) and Balafons (types of xylophones) mentioned in the title

ECONOMY

Economy—overview: Senegal's economy is driven by agriculture and that sector is the primary source of employment for the rural areas. The country's key export industries are phosphate mining, fertilizer production, and commercial fishing. The country is also working on iron ore and oil exploration projects. senegal relies heavily on donor assistance and foreign direct investment. President Macky SALL, who was elected in March 2012 under a reformist policy agenda, inherited an economy with a weak infrastructure, challenging business environment, and a culture of overspending that still plagued the country in 2013. The IMF completed a non-dispersing, Policy Support Initiative program in December 2010 and approved a new three-year policy support instrument to assist with economic reforms. The economy continues to suffer from unreliable power supplies and rising costs of living, which has led to public protests and high unemployment and has prompted migrants to flee Senegal in search of better job opportunities in Europe.

GDP (purchasing power parity): $27.72 billion (2013 est.)
country comparison to the world: 119
$26.65 billion (2012 est.)
$25.74 billion (2011 est.)
note: data are in 2013 US dollars

GDP (official exchange rate): $15.36 billion (2013 est.)

GDP—real growth rate: 4% (2013 est.)
country comparison to the world: 78
3.5% (2012 est.)
2.6% (2011 est.)

GDP—per capita (PPP): $2,100 (2013 est.)
country comparison to the world: 193
$2,000 (2012 est.)
$2,000 (2011 est.)
note: data are in 2013 US dollars

Gross national saving: 22.4% of GDP (2013 est.)
country comparison to the world: 65
19.3% of GDP (2012 est.)
20.2% of GDP (2011 est.)

GDP—composition, by end use:
household consumption: 81.8%
government consumption: 9%
investment in fixed capital: 31%
investment in inventories: 0%
exports of goods and services: 25.6%
imports of goods and services: -47.4% (2013 est.)

GDP—composition, by sector of origin:
agriculture: 14.9%
industry: 22.7%
services: 62.4% (2013 est.)

Agriculture—products: peanuts, millet, corn, sorghum, rice, cotton, tomatoes, green vegetables; cattle, poultry, pigs; fish

Industries: agricultural and fish processing, phosphate mining, fertilizer production, petroleum refining; iron ore, zircon, and gold mining, construction materials, ship construction and repair

Industrial production growth rate: 3% (2013 est.)
country comparison to the world: 100

Labor force: 6.096 million (2013 est.)
country comparison to the world: 67

Labor force—by occupation:
agriculture: 77.5%
industry and services: 22.5% (2007 est.)

Unemployment rate: 48% (2007 est.)
country comparison to the world: 194

Population below poverty line: 54% (2001 est.)

Household income or consumption by percentage share: *lowest 10%:* 2.5%
highest 10%: 30.1% (2005)

Distribution of family income—Gini index: 41.3 (2001)
country comparison to the world: 52
41.3 (1995)

Budget: *revenues:* $3.555 billion
expenditures: $4.366 billion (2013 est.)

Taxes and other revenues: 23.2% of GDP (2013 est.)
country comparison to the world: 144

Budget surplus (+) or deficit (-):
-5.3% of GDP (2013 est.)
country comparison to the world: 173

Public debt: 38.4% of GDP (2013 est.)
country comparison to the world: 96
38.8% of GDP (2012 est.)

Fiscal year: calendar year

Inflation rate (consumer prices): 0.8% (2013 est.)
country comparison to the world: 17
1.4% (2012 est.)

Central bank discount rate: 0.25% (31 December 2010 est.)
country comparison to the world: 85
4.25% (31 December 2009 est.)

Commercial bank prime lending rate: 13.8% (31 December 2013 est.)
country comparison to the world: 49
14.3% (31 December 2012 est.)

Stock of narrow money: $3.809 billion (31 December 2013 est.)
country comparison to the world: 111
$3.577 billion (31 December 2012 est.)

Stock of broad money: $6.193 billion (31 December 2013 est.)
country comparison to the world: 123
$5.826 billion (31 December 2012 est.)

Stock of domestic credit: $4.574 billion (31 December 2013 est.)
country comparison to the world: 117
$4.509 billion (31 December 2012 est.)

Market value of publicly traded shares: $NA

Current account balance: -$1.291 billion (2013 est.)
country comparison to the world: 128
-$1.618 billion (2012 est.)

Exports: $2.691 billion (2013 est.)
country comparison to the world: 133
$2.382 billion (2012 est.)

Exports—commodities: fish, groundnuts (peanuts), petroleum products, phosphates, cotton

Exports—partners: Mali 14.4%, Switzerland 14.1%, India 11.9%, France 4.7%, Guinea 4.2% (2012)

Imports: $5.61 billion (2013 est.)
country comparison to the world: 122
$5.733 billion (2012 est.)

Imports—commodities: food and beverages, capital goods, fuels

Imports—partners: France 16.2%, Nigeria 12.9%, India 6.3%, China 6.3%, UK 4.6% (2012)

Reserves of foreign exchange and gold: $2.15 billion (31 December 2013 est.)
country comparison to the world: 121
$2.082 billion (31 December 2012 est.)

Debt—external: $4.375 billion (31 December 2013 est.)
country comparison to the world: 126
$4.221 billion (31 December 2012 est.)

Exchange rates: Communaute Financiere Africaine francs (XOF) per US dollar—
500.7 (2013 est.)
510.53 (2012 est.)
495.28 (2010)
472.19 (2009)
447.81 (2008)

ENERGY

Electricity—production: 2.769 billion kWh (2010 est.)
country comparison to the world: 130

Electricity—consumption: 2.22 billion kWh (2010 est.)
country comparison to the world: 138

Electricity—exports: 0 kWh (2012 est.)
country comparison to the world: 192

Electricity—imports: 0 kWh (2012 est.)
country comparison to the world: 195

Electricity—installed generating capacity: 638,000 kW (2010 est.)
country comparison to the world: 131

Electricity—from fossil fuels: 99.7% of total installed capacity (2010 est.)
country comparison to the world: 49

Electricity—from nuclear fuels: 0% of total installed capacity (2010 est.)
country comparison to the world: 175

Electricity—from hydroelectric plants: 0% of total installed capacity (2010 est.)
country comparison to the world: 197

Electricity—from other renewable sources: 0.3% of total installed capacity (2010 est.)
country comparison to the world: 91

Crude oil—production: 0 bbl/day (2011 est.)
country comparison to the world: 210

Crude oil—exports: 0 bbl/day (2010 est.)
country comparison to the world: 178

Crude oil—imports: 15,500 bbl/day (2010 est.)
country comparison to the world: 73

Crude oil—proved reserves: 0 bbl (1 January 2013 es)
country comparison to the world: 184

Refined petroleum products—production: 15,100 bbl/day (2010 est.)
country comparison to the world: 99

Refined petroleum products—consumption: 40,600 bbl/day (2011 est.)
country comparison to the world: 107

Refined petroleum products—exports: 561.8 bbl/day (2010 est.)
country comparison to the world: 111

Refined petroleum products—imports: 23,760 bbl/day (2010 est.)
country comparison to the world: 98

Natural gas—production: 20 million cu m (2011 est.)
country comparison to the world: 88

Natural gas—consumption: 20 million cu m (2010 est.)
country comparison to the world: 110

Natural gas—exports: 0 cu m (2011 est.)
country comparison to the world: 179

Natural gas—imports: 0 cu m (2011 est.)
country comparison to the world: 127

Natural gas—proved reserves: 0 cu m
country comparison to the world: 190

Carbon dioxide emissions from consumption of energy: 7.088 million Mt (2011 est.)
country comparison to the world: 112

COMMUNICATIONS

Telephones—main lines in use: 338,200 (2012)
country comparison to the world: 110

Telephones—mobile cellular: 11.47 million (2012)
country comparison to the world: 73

Telephone system: *general assessment:* good system with microwave radio relay, coaxial cable and fiber-optic cable in trunk system
domestic: above-average urban system with a fiber-optic network; nearly two-thirds of all fixed-line connections are in Dakar where a call-center industry is emerging; expansion of fixed-line services in rural areas needed; mobile-cellular service is expanding rapidly
international: country code—221; the SAT-3/WASC fiber-optic cable provides connectivity to Europe and Asia while Atlantis-2 provides connectivity to South America; satellite earth station—1 Intelsat (Atlantic Ocean) (2010)

Broadcast media: state-run Radiodiffusion Television Senegalaise (RTS) operates 2 TV stations; a few private TV subscription channels rebroadcast foreign channels without providing any local news or programs; RTS operates a national radio network and a number of regional FM stations; many community and private-broadcast radio stations are available; transmissions of at least 2 international broadcasters are accessible on FM in Dakar (2007)

Internet country code: .sn

Internet hosts: 237 (2012)
country comparison to the world: 197

Internet users: 1.818 million (2009)
country comparison to the world: 76

TRANSPORTATION

Airports: 20 (2013)
country comparison to the world: 136

Airports—with paved runways: *total:* 9
over 3,047 m: 2
1,524 to 2,437 m: 6
914 to 1,523 m: 1 (2013)

Airports—with unpaved runways: *total:* 1 1
1,524 to 2,437 m: 7
914 to 1,523 m: 3
under 914 m: 1 (2013)

Pipelines: gas 43 km; refined products 8 km (2013)

Railways: *total:* 906 km
country comparison to the world: 92
narrow gauge: 906 km 1.000-m gauge (2008)

Roadways: *total:* 14,008 km
country comparison to the world: 125
paved: 4,099 km (includes 7 km of expressways)
unpaved: 9,909 km (2003)

Waterways: 1,000 km (primarily on the Senegal, Saloum, and Casamance rivers) (2012)
country comparison to the world: 64

Merchant marine: *total:* 1
country comparison to the world: 150
by type: passenger/cargo 1 (2010)

Ports and terminals: *major seaport(s):* Dakar

MILITARY

Military branches: Senegalese Armed Forces: Army, Senegalese National Navy (Marine Senegalaise, MNS), Senegalese Air Force (Armee de l'Air du Senegal) (2013)

Military service age and obligation: 18 years of age for voluntary military service; 20 years of age for selective conscript service; service obligation is 2 years; women have been accepted into military service since 2008 (2013)

Manpower available for military service:
males age 16-49: 2,699,196
females age 16-49: 3,018,565 (2010 est.)

Manpower fit for military service:
males age 16-49: 1,788,493
females age 16-49: 2,133,370 (2010 est.)

Manpower reaching militarily significant age annually: *male:* 145,509
female: 145,064 (2010 est.)

TRANSNATIONAL ISSUES

Disputes—international: The Gambia and Guinea-Bissau attempt to stem separatist violence, cross border raids, and arms smuggling into their countries from Senegal's Casamance region, and in 2006, respectively accepted 6,000 and 10,000 Casamance residents fleeing the conflict; 2,500 Guinea-Bissau residents fled into Senegal in 2006 to escape armed confrontations along the border

Refugees and internally displaced persons:
refugees (country of origin): 13,702 (Mauritania) (2012)
IDPs: 10,000-40,000 (clashes between government troops and separatists in Casamance region) (2012)

Illicit drugs: transshipment point for Southwest and Southeast Asian heroin and South American cocaine moving to Europe and North America; illicit cultivator of cannabis

SERBIA

INTRODUCTION

Background: The Kingdom of Serbs, Croats, and Slovenes was formed in 1918; its name was changed to Yugoslavia in 1929. Communist Partisans resisted the Axis occupation and division of Yugoslavia from 1941 to 1945 and fought nationalist opponents and collaborators as well. The military and political movement headed by Josip Broz "TITO" (Partisans) took full control of Yugoslavia when their domestic rivals and the occupiers were defeated in 1945. Although communists, TITO and his successors (Tito died in 1980) managed to steer their own path between the Warsaw Pact nations and the West for the next four and a half decades. In 1989, Slobodan MILOSEVIC became president of the Republic of Serbia and his ultranationalist calls for Serbian domination led to the violent breakup of Yugoslavia along ethnic lines. In 1991, Croatia, Slovenia, and Macedonia declared independence, followed by Bosnia in 1992. The remaining republics of Serbia and Montenegro declared a new Federal Republic of Yugoslavia (FRY) in April 1992 and under MILOSEVIC's leadership, Serbia led various military campaigns to unite ethnic Serbs in neighboring republics into a "Greater Serbia." These actions were ultimately unsuccessful and, after international intervention, led to the signing of the Dayton Peace Accords in 1995. MILOSEVIC retained control over Serbia and eventually became president of the FRY in 1997. In 1998, an ethnic Albanian insurgency in the formerly autonomous Serbian province of Kosovo provoked a Serbian counterinsurgency campaign that resulted in massacres and massive expulsions of ethnic Albanians living in Kosovo. The MILOSEVIC government's rejection of a proposed international settlement led to NATO's bombing of Serbia in the spring of 1999. Serbian military and police forces withdrew from Kosovo in June 1999, and the UN Security Council authorized an interim UN administration and a NATO-led security force in Kosovo. FRY elections in late 2000 led to the ouster of MILOSEVIC and the installation of democratic government. In 2003, the FRY became the State Union of Serbia and Montenegro, a loose federation of the two republics. Widespread violence predominantly targeting ethnic Serbs in Kosovo in March 2004 let to more intense calls to address Kosovo's status, and the UN began facilitating status talks in 2006. In June 2006, Montenegro seceded from the federation and declared itself an independent nation. Serbia subsequently gave notice that it was the successor state to the union of Serbia and Montenegro. In February 2008, after nearly two years of inconclusive negotiations, Kosovo declared itself independent of Serbia—an action Serbia refuses to recognize. At Serbia's request, the UN General Assembly (UNGA) in October 2008 sought an advisory opinion from the International Court of Justice (ICJ) on whether Kosovo's unilateral declaration of independence was in accordance with international law. In a ruling considered unfavorable to Serbia, the ICJ issued an advisory opinion in July 2010 stating that international law did not prohibit declarations of independence. In late 2010, Serbia agreed to an EU-drafted UNGA Resolution acknowledging the ICJ's decision and calling for a new round of talks between Serbia and Kosovo, this time on practical issues rather than Kosovo's status. The EU-moderated Belgrade-Pristina dialogue began in March 2011 and was raised to the level of prime ministers in October 2012. Serbia and Kosovo signed the first agreement of principles governing the normalization of relations between the two countries in April 2013 and are in the process of implementing its provisions.

GEOGRAPHY

Location: Southeastern Europe, between Macedonia and Hungary

Geographic coordinates: 44 00 N, 21 00 E

Map references: Europe

Area: *total:* 77,474 sq km
country comparison to the world: 117
land: 77,474 sq km
water: 0 sq km

Area—comparative: slightly smaller than South Carolina

Land boundaries: *total:* 2,026 km
border countries: Bosnia and Herzegovina 302 km, Bulgaria 318 km, Croatia 241 km, Hungary 151 km, Kosovo 352 km, Macedonia 62 km, Montenegro 124 km, Romania 476 km

Coastline: 0 km (landlocked)

Maritime claims: none (landlocked)

Climate: in the north, continental climate (cold winters and hot, humid summers with well-distributed rainfall); in other parts, continental and Mediterranean climate (relatively cold winters with heavy snowfall and hot, dry summers and autumns)

Terrain: extremely varied; to the north, rich fertile plains; to the east, limestone ranges and basins; to the southeast, ancient mountains and hills

Elevation extremes: *lowest point:* Danube and Timok Rivers 35 m
highest point: Midzor 2,169 m

Natural resources: oil, gas, coal, iron ore, copper, zinc, antimony, chromite, gold, silver, magnesium, pyrite, limestone, marble, salt, arable land

Land use: *arable land:* 37.28%
permanent crops: 3.41%
other: 59.31% (2011)

Irrigated land: 919.6 sq km (2011)

Total renewable water resources: 162.2 cu km (note—includes Kosovo) (2011)

Natural hazards: destructive earthquakes

Environment—current issues: air pollution around Belgrade and other industrial cities; water pollution from industrial wastes dumped into the Sava which flows into the Danube

Environment—international agreements:
party to: Air Pollution, Biodiversity, Climate Change, Climate Change-Kyoto Protocol, Desertification, Endangered Species, Hazardous Wastes, Law of the Sea, Marine Dumping, Marine Life Conservation, Ozone Layer Protection, Ship Pollution, Wetlands
signed, but not ratified: none of the selected agreements

Geography—note: controls one of the major land routes from Western Europe to Turkey and the Near East

PEOPLE AND SOCIETY

Nationality: *noun:* Serb(s)
adjective: Serbian

Ethnic groups: Serb 83.3%, Hungarian 3.5%, Romany 2.1%, Bosniak 2%, other 5.7%, undeclared or unknown 3.4% (2011 est.)

Languages: Serbian (official) 88.1%, Hungarian 3.4%, Bosnian 1.9%, Romany 1.4%, other 3.4%, undeclared or unknown 1.8%
note: Serbian, Hungarian, Slovak, Romanian, Croatian, and Rusyn all official in Vojvodina (2011 est.)

Religions: Serbian Orthodox 84.6%, Catholic 5%, Muslim 3.1%, Protestant 1%, atheist 1.1%, other 0.8%, undeclared or unknown 4.5% (2011 est.)

Population: 7,209,764 (July 2014 est.)
country comparison to the world: 101
note: does not include the population of Kosovo

Age structure:
0-14 years: 14.8% (male 549,469/female 515,988)
15-24 years: 11.6% (male 432,471/female 407,367)
25-54 years: 41.6% (male 1,512,888/female 1,488,099)
55-64 years: 17.2% (male 511,516/female 551,117)
65 years and over: 16.9% (male 508,751/female 732,098) (2014 est.)

Dependency ratios:
total dependency ratio: 44 %
youth dependency ratio: 23.4 %
elderly dependency ratio: 20.7 %
potential support ratio: 4.8 (2013)

Median age: *total:* 41.9 years
male: 40.2 years
female: 43.6 years (2014 est.)

Population growth rate: -0.46% (2014 est.)
country comparison to the world: 221

Birth rate: 9.13 births/1,000 population (2014 est.)
country comparison to the world: 208

Death rate: 13.71 deaths/1,000 population (2014 est.)
country comparison to the world: 12

Net migration rate: 0 migrant(s)/1,000 population (2014 est.)

country comparison to the world: 79

Urbanization: *urban population:* 56% of total population (2010)
rate of urbanization: 0.6% annual rate of change (2010-15 est.)

Major urban areas—population: BELGRADE (capital) 1.115 million (2009)

Sex ratio: *at birth:* 1.07 male(s)/female
0-14 years: 1.07 male(s)/female
15-24 years: 1.06 male(s)/female
25-54 years: 1.02 male(s)/female
55-64 years: 0.95 male(s)/female
65 years and over: 0.69 male(s)/female
total population: 0.95 male(s)/female (2014 est.)

Mother's mean age at first birth: 27.2 (2010 est.)

Maternal mortality rate: 12 deaths/100,000 live births (2010)
country comparison to the world: 149

Infant mortality rate: *total:* 6.16 deaths/1,000 live births
country comparison to the world: 170
male: 7.1 deaths/1,000 live births
female: 5.16 deaths/1,000 live births (2014 est.)

Life expectancy at birth: *total population:* 75.02 years
country comparison to the world: 101
male: 72.17 years
female: 78.07 years (2014 est.)

Total fertility rate: 1.42 children born/woman (2014 est.)
country comparison to the world: 204

Contraceptive prevalence rate: 60.8% (2010)

Health expenditures: 10.4% of GDP (2011)
country comparison to the world: 22

Physicians density: 2.11 physicians/1,000 population (2009)

Hospital bed density: 5.4 beds/1,000 population (2009)

Drinking water source:
improved:
urban: 99.5% of population
rural: 98.9% of population
total: 99.2% of population
unimproved:
urban: 0.5% of population
rural: 1.1% of population
total: 0.8% of population (2011 est.)

Sanitation facility access:
improved:
urban: 98.5% of population
rural: 95.6% of population
total: 97.2% of population
unimproved:
urban: 1.5% of population
rural: 4.4% of population
total: 2.8% of population (2011 est.)

HIV/AIDS—adult prevalence rate: 0.1% (2009 est.)
country comparison to the world: 140

HIV/AIDS—people living with HIV/AIDS: 6,400 (2009 est.)
country comparison to the world: 121

HIV/AIDS—deaths: fewer than 100 (2009 est.)
country comparison to the world: 155

Major infectious diseases: *degree of risk:* intermediate
food or waterborne diseases: bacterial diarrhea
note: highly pathogenic H5N1 avian influenza has been identified in this country; it poses a negligible risk with extremely rare cases possible among US citizens who have close contact with birds (2013)

Obesity—adult prevalence rate: 24.8% (2008)
country comparison to the world: 63

Children under the age of 5 years underweight: 1.6% (2010)
country comparison to the world: 126

Education expenditures: 4.8% of GDP (2011)
country comparison to the world: 82

Literacy: *definition:* age 15 and over can read and write
total population: 98%
male: 99.2%
female: 96.9% (2011 est.)

School life expectancy (primary to tertiary education): *total:* 14 years
male: 13 years
female: 14 years (2012)

Child labor—children ages 5-14:
total number: 36,141
percentage: 4 % (2005 est.)

Unemployment, youth ages 15-24:
total: 51.1% (2012)
country comparison to the world: 7

GOVERNMENT

Country name: *conventional long form:* Republic of Serbia
conventional short form: Serbia
local long form: Republika Srbija
local short form: Srbija
former: People's Republic of Serbia, Socialist Republic of Serbia

Government type: republic

Capital: *name:* Belgrade (Beograd)

geographic coordinates: 44 50 N, 20 30 E
time difference: UTC+1 (6 hours ahead of Washington, DC during Standard Time)
daylight saving time: +1hr, begins last Sunday in March; ends last Sunday in October

Administrative divisions: 122 municipalities (opstine, singular—opstina) and 23 cities (gradovi, singular—grad)
municipalities: Ada, Aleksandrovac, Aleksinac, Alibunar, Apatin, Arandelovac, Arilje, Babusnica, Bac, Backa Palanka, Backa Topola, Backi Petrovac, Bajina Basta, Batocina, Becej, Bela Crkva, Bela Palanka, Beocin, Blace, Bogatic, Bojnik, Boljevac, Bor, Bosilegrad, Brus, Bujanovac, Cajetina, Cicevac, Coka, Crna Trava, Cuprija, Despotovac, Dimitrov, Doljevac, Gadzin Han, Golubac, Gornji Milanovac, Indija, Irig, Ivanjica, Kanjiza, Kikinda, Kladovo, Knic, Knjazevac, Koceljeva, Kosjeric, Kovacica, Kovin, Krupanj, Kucevo, Kula, Kursumlija, Lajkovac, Lapovo, Lebane, Ljig, Ljubovija, Lucani, Majdanpek, Mali Idos, Mali Zvornik, Malo Crnice, Medveda, Merosina, Mionica, Negotin, Nova Crnja, Nova Varos, Novi Becej, Novi Knezevac, Odzaci, Opovo, Osecina, Paracin, Pecinci, Petrovac na Mlavi, Pirot, Plandiste, Pozega, Presevo, Priboj, Prijepolje, Prokuplje, Raca, Raska, Razanj, Rekovac, Ruma, Secanj, Senta, Sid, Sjenica, Smederevska Palanka, Sokobanja, Srbobran, Sremski Karlovci, Stara Pazova, Surdulica, Svilajnac, Svrljig, Temerin, Titel, Topola, Trgoviste, Trstenik, Tutin, Ub, Varvarin, Velika Plana, Veliko Gradiste, Vladicin Han, Vladimirci, Vlasotince, Vrbas, Vrnjacka Banja, Vrsac, Zabalj, Zabari, Zagubica, Zitiste, Zitorada
cities: Beograd, Cacak, Jagodina, Kragujevac, Kraljevo, Krusevac, Leskovac, Loznica, Nis, Novi Pazar, Novi Sad, Pancevo, Pozarevac, Sabac, Smederevo, Sombor, Sremska Mitrovica, Subotica, Uzice, Vajevo, Vranje, Zajecar, Zrenjanin

Independence: 5 June 2006 (from Serbia and Montenegro)

National holiday: National Day, 15 February

Constitution: many previous; latest approved by referendum 28-29 October 2006, adopted 30 September 2006, effective 8 November 2006 (2011)

Legal system: civil law system

International law organization participation: has not submitted an ICJ jurisdiction declaration; accepts ICCt jurisdiction

Suffrage: 18 years of age, 16 if employed; universal

Executive branch: *chief of state:* President Tomislav NIKOLIC (since 31 May 2012)
head of government: Prime Minister Aleksandar VUCIC (since 22 April 2014)
cabinet: Republican Ministries act as cabinet (For more information visit the World Leaders website)
elections: president elected by direct vote for a five-year term (eligible for a second term); election last held on 20 May 2012 (next to be held in 2017); prime minister elected by the National Assembly
election results: Tomislav NIKOLIC elected president in runoff election; NIKOLIC 51.2% of the vote, Boris TADIC 48.8% of the vote

Legislative branch: unicameral National Assembly (250 seats; deputies elected according to party lists to serve four-year terms)
elections: last held on 16 March 2016 (next to be held by March 2020)
election results: percent of vote by party/coalition—SNS-led Coalition 48.4%, SPS/PUPS/JS 13.5%, DS 6.0%, Boris Tadic Coalition 5.7%, DSS 4.2%, Dveri 3.6%, LDP-led Coalition 3.4%, URS 3.0%, SVM 2.1%, Enough of that 4.3%, SRS 2.0%, SDA 1.0%, PDD .7%, other and invalid 1.2%; seats by party/coalition—SNS-led Coalition 158, SPS/PUPS/JS 44, DS 19, Boris Tadic Coalition 18, SVM 6, SDA 3, PDD 2

Judicial branch: *highest court(s):* Supreme Court of Cassation (consists of more than 60 judges organized into 3- and 5-member panels for criminal, civil, and administrative cases); Constitutional Court (consists of 15 judges) note—in 2003, specialized panels on war crimes were established within the Serbian court system; the panels have jurisdiction over alleged violations of the Basic Criminal Code and crimes against humanity, international law, and criminal acts as defined by the Statute of the International Criminal Tribunal for the former Yugoslavia
judge selection and term of office: Supreme Court justices proposed by the High Judicial Council (HJC), an 11-member body of which 7 are judges, and elected by the National Assembly; Constitutional Court judges appointed—5 each by the National Assembly, the president, and the Supreme Court of Cassation; judges of both courts appointed to permanent tenure by the HJC
subordinate courts: appellate courts, higher courts, and municipal and district courts; courts of special jurisdiction include the Administrative

Court, Appellate Commercial Court, and two levels of misdemeanor courts

Political parties and leaders: Alliance of Vojvodina Hungarians or SVM [Istvan PASZTOR]; Boris Tadic Coalition [Boris TADIC] (includes New Democratic Party-Greens or NDS-Z [Boris TADIC], League; of Social Democrats of Vojvodina or LSV [Nenad CANAK], Together for Serbia or ZSS [Dusan PETROVIC], Democratic Alliance of Vojvodina Hungarians or VMDK [Aron CSONKA], Together for Vojvodina [Olena; PAPUGA], Democratic Left of Roma or DLR [Jovan DAMJANOVIC]); Democratic Party of Serbia or DSS [Aleksandar Popovic]; Enough of That [Sasa RADULOVIC]; Party for Democratic Action or PDD [Riza HALIMI]; Party of Democratic Action of the Sandzak or SDA [Sulejman UGLJANIN]; Serbian Radical Party or SRS [Vojislav SESELJ]; SNS-led Coalition/A Future We Believe In [Aleksandar VUCIC] (includes Serbian Progressive Party or SNS; [Aleksandar VUCIC], Social Democratic Party of Serbia or SDPS [Rasim LJAJIC], New Serbia or NS [Velimir; ILIC], Movement of Socialists or PS [Aleksandar VULIN], and Serbian Renewal Movement or SPO [Vuk; DRASKOVIC]); United Regions of Serbia [Mladan DINKIC]; With Democratic Party for Democratic Serbia/Democratic Party or DS [Dragan DJILAS]; SPS/PUPS/JS [Ivica DACIC] (includes Socialist Party of Serbia or SPS [Ivica DACIC], Party of United; Pensioners of Serbia or PUPS [Jovan KRKOBABIC], United Serbia or JS [Dragan "Palma" MARKOVIC]); LDP-led Coalition [Cedomir JOVANOVIC] (includes Liberal Democratic Party of LDP [Cedomir JOVANOVIC], Bosniak Democratic Union of Sandzak or BDZS [Esad DZUDZEVIC], Social Democratic Union of SDU [Zarko; KORAC])

Political pressure groups and leaders: 1389 (Serbian nationalist movement); Dveri—Movement for the Life of Serbia [Bosko OBRADOVIC]; Obraz (Orthodox clero-fascist organization); SNP NASI (Serbian National Movement NASI)

International organization participation: BIS, BSEC, CD, CE, CEI, EAPC, EBRD, EU (candidate country), FAO, G-9, IAEA, IBRD, ICAO, ICC (national committees), ICRM, IDA, IFC, IFRCS, IHO, ILO, IMF, IMO, IMSO, Interpol, IOC, IOM, IPU, ISO, ITSO, ITU, ITUC (NGOs), MIGA, MONUSCO, NAM (observer), OAS (observer), OIF (observer), OPCW, OSCE, PCA, PFP, SELEC, UN, UNCTAD, UNESCO, UNFICYP, UNHCR, UNIDO, UNIFIL, UNMIL, UNOCI, UNWTO, UPU, WCO, WHO, WIPO, WMO, WTO (observer)

Diplomatic representation in the US:
chief of mission: Ambassador (vacant); Charge d'Affaires Vladimir JOVICIC (since 3 December 2013)
chancery: 2134 Kalorama Road NW, Washington, DC 20008
telephone: [1] (202) 332-0333
FAX: [1] (202) 332-3933
consulate(s) general: Chicago, New York

Diplomatic representation from the US:
chief of mission: Ambassador Michael KIRBY (since 11 September 2012)
embassy: 92 Bulevar kneza Aleksandra Karadjordjevica, 11040 Belgrade, Serbia
mailing address: 5070 Belgrade Place, Washington, DC 20521-5070
telephone: [381] (11) 706-4000
FAX: [381] (11) 706-4005

Flag description: three equal horizontal stripes of red (top), blue, and white—the Pan-Slav colors representing freedom and revolutionary ideals; charged with the coat of arms of Serbia shifted slightly to the hoist side; the principal field of the coat of arms represents the Serbian state and displays a white two-headed eagle on a red shield; a smaller red shield on the eagle represents the Serbian nation, and is divided into four quarters by a white cross; interpretations vary as to the meaning and origin of the white, curved symbols resembling firesteels or Cyrillic "C's" in each quarter; a royal crown surmounts the coat of arms
note: the Pan-Slav colors were inspired by the 19th-century flag of Russia

National symbol(s): double-headed eagle

National anthem: *name:* "Boze pravde" (God of Justice)
lyrics/music: Jovan DORDEVIC/Davorin JENKO
note: adopted 1904; the song was originally written as part of a play in 1872 and has been used as an anthem by the Serbian people throughout the 20th and 21st centuries

ECONOMY

Economy—overview: Serbia has a transitional economy largely dominated by market forces, but the state sector remains significant in certain areas and many institutional reforms are needed. The economy relies on manufacturing and exports, driven largely by foreign investment. MILOSEVIC-era mismanagement of the economy, an extended period of international economic sanctions, civil war, and the damage to Yugoslavia's infrastructure and industry during the NATO airstrikes in 1999 left the economy only half the size it was in 1990. After the ousting of former Federal Yugoslav President MILOSEVIC in September 2000, the Democratic Opposition of Serbia (DOS) coalition government implemented stabilization measures and embarked on a market reform program. After renewing its membership in the IMF in December 2000, Serbia continued to reintegrate into the international community by rejoining the World Bank (IBRD) and the European Bank for Reconstruction and Development (EBRD). Serbia has made progress in trade liberalization and enterprise restructuring and privatization, but many large enterprises—including the power utilities, telecommunications company, natural gas company, and others—remain in state hands. Serbia has made some progress towards EU membership, signing a Stabilization and Association Agreement with Brussels in May 2008, and with full implementation of the Interim Trade Agreement with the EU in February 2010, gained candidate status in March 2012. In January 2014, Serbia's EU accession talks officially opened. Serbia's negotiations with the World Trade Organization are advanced, with the country's complete ban on the trade and cultivation of agricultural biotechnology products representing the primary remaining obstacle to accession. Serbia's program with the IMF was frozen in early 2012 because the 2012 budget approved by parliament deviated from the program parameters; the arrangement is now void. However, an IMF mission visited Serbia in February 2014 to initiate discussions with Serbian authorities on a possible new IMF arrangement and these talks will continue following the formation of the new government. High unemployment and stagnant household incomes are ongoing political and economic problems. Structural economic reforms needed to ensure the country's long-term prosperity have largely stalled since the onset of the global financial crisis. Growing budget deficits constrain the use of stimulus efforts to revive the economy and contribute to growing concern of a public debt crisis, given that Serbia's total public debt as a share of GDP doubled between 2008 and 2013. Serbia's concerns about inflation and exchange-rate stability may preclude the use of expansionary monetary policy. During the recent election campaign, the victorious SNS party promised comprehensive economic reform during the first half of 2014 to address issues with the fiscal deficit, state-owned enterprises, the labor market, construction permits, bankruptcy and privatization, and other areas. Major challenges ahead include: high unemployment rates and the need for job creation; high government expenditures for salaries, pensions, healthcare, and unemployment benefits; a growing need for new government borrowing; rising public and private foreign debt; attracting new foreign direct investment; and getting the IMF program back on track. Other serious longer-term challenges include an inefficient judicial system, high levels of corruption, and an aging population. Factors favorable to Serbia's economic growth include its strategic location, a relatively inexpensive and skilled labor force, and free trade agreements with the EU, Russia, Turkey, and countries that are members of the Central European Free Trade Agreement (CEFTA).

GDP (purchasing power parity): $80.47 billion (2013 est.)
country comparison to the world: 81
$78.89 billion (2012 est.)
$80.3 billion (2011 est.)
note: data are in 2013 US dollars

GDP (official exchange rate): $43.68 billion (2013 est.)

GDP—real growth rate: 2% (2013 est.)
country comparison to the world: 142
-1.7% (2012 est.)
1.6% (2011 est.)

GDP—per capita (PPP): $11,100 (2013 est.)
country comparison to the world: 111
$10,900 (2012 est.)
$11,100 (2011 est.)
note: data are in 2013 US dollars

Gross national saving: 26.7% of GDP
country comparison to the world: 40
28.3% of GDP
22.6% of GDP

GDP—composition, by end use:
household consumption: 75.8%
government consumption: 19.2%
investment in fixed capital: 16.3%
investment in inventories: 5.4%
exports of goods and services: 42.7%
imports of goods and services: -59.4% (2013 est.)

GDP—composition, by sector of origin:
agriculture: 7.9%
industry: 31.8%
services: 60.3% (2013 est.)

Agriculture—products: wheat, maize, sunflower, sugar beets, fruits (raspberries, apples, sour cherry), vegetables (tomatoes, peppers, potatoes), beef/

pork meat and meat products, milk and dairy products, grapes/wine

Industries: automobiles, base metals, furniture, food processing, machinery, chemicals, sugar, tires, clothes, pharmaceuticals

Industrial production growth rate: 5.5% (2013 est.)
country comparison to the world: 48

Labor force: 1.703 million (2013 est.)
country comparison to the world: 125

Labor force—by occupation:
agriculture: 23.9%
industry: 16.5%
services: 59.6% (2013 est.)

Unemployment rate: 20.1% (2013 est.)
country comparison to the world: 163
22.4% (2012 est.)

Population below poverty line: 9.1% (2013 est.)

Distribution of family income—Gini index: 38 (2013 est.)
country comparison to the world: 72
28.2 (2008 est.)

Budget: *revenues:* $17.47 billion
expenditures: $19.6 billion
note: this is the consolidated budget, including both central government and local goverment budgets (2013 est.)

Taxes and other revenues: 40% of GDP (2013 est.)
country comparison to the world: 43

Budget surplus (+) or deficit (-):
-4.9% of GDP (2013 est.)
country comparison to the world: 164

Public debt: 61.2% of GDP (2013 est.)
country comparison to the world: 46
59.3% of GDP (2012 est.)
note: data cover general government debt, and includes debt instruments issued or owned by government entities other than the treasury (for which the GOS issued guarantees); the data include treasury debt held by foreign entities; the data include debt issued by subnational entities (for which the GOS issued guarantees), as well as intra-governmental debt; intra-governmental debt consists of treasury borrowings from surpluses in the social funds, such as for retirement, medical care, and unemployment, debt instruments for the social funds are not sold at public auctions

Inflation rate (consumer prices): 2.2% (2013 est.)
country comparison to the world: 81
12.2% (2012 est.)

Central bank discount rate: 9.5% (18 March 2014)
country comparison to the world: 20
11.75% (6 February 2013)

Commercial bank prime lending rate: 13.85% (31 December 2013 est.)
country comparison to the world: 43
14.99% (31 December 2012 est.)

Stock of narrow money: $4.626 billion (31 December 2013 est.)
country comparison to the world: 105
$3.595 billion (31 December 2012 est.)

Stock of broad money: $20.47 billion (31 December 2013 est.)
country comparison to the world: 85
$19.12 billion (31 December 2012 est.)

Stock of domestic credit: $25.48 billion (31 December 2013 est.)
country comparison to the world: 73
$26.26 billion (31 December 2012 est.)

Market value of publicly traded shares: $9.199 billion (31 December 2013 est.)
country comparison to the world: 77
$7.451 billion (31 December 2012)
$8.365 billion (31 December 2011 est.)

Current account balance: -$1.807 billion (2013 est.)
country comparison to the world: 138
-$4.012 billion (2012 est.)

Exports: $14.61 billion (2013 est.)
country comparison to the world: 82
$11.35 billion (2012 est.)

Exports—commodities: iron and steel, rubber, clothes, wheat, fruit and vegetables, nonferrous metals, electric appliances, metal products, weapons and ammunition, automobiles

Imports: $20.54 billion (2013 est.)
country comparison to the world: 78
$19.01 billion (2012 est.)

Reserves of foreign exchange and gold: $15.87 billion (31 December 2013 est.)
country comparison to the world: 67
$14.4 billion (31 December 2012 est.)

Debt—external: $33.6 billion (31 December 2013 est.)
country comparison to the world: 71
$33.42 billion (31 December 2012 est.)

Stock of direct foreign investment—at home:
$26.41 billion (31 December 2009 est.)
country comparison to the world: 66
$11.95 billion (2006 est.)

Stock of direct foreign investment—abroad:
$NA

Exchange rates: Serbian dinars (RSD) per US dollar—
85.67 (2013 est.)
87.992 (2012 est.)
77.729 (2010 est.)
67.634 (2009)
62.9 (2008)

ENERGY

Electricity—production: 37.65 billion kWh (2013 est.)
country comparison to the world: 61

Electricity—consumption: 28.04 billion kWh (2013 est.)
country comparison to the world: 63

Electricity—exports: 5.707 billion kWh (2013 est.)
country comparison to the world: 26

Electricity—imports: 5.835 billion kWh (2013 est.)
country comparison to the world: 34

Electricity—installed generating capacity:
7.379 million kW (2013 est.)
country comparison to the world: 67

Electricity—from fossil fuels: 57.5% of total installed capacity (2013 est.)
country comparison to the world: 138

Electricity—from nuclear fuels: 0% of total installed capacity (2013 est.)
country comparison to the world: 167

Electricity—from hydroelectric plants: 39% of total installed capacity (2013 est.)
country comparison to the world: 62

Electricity—from other renewable sources:
3.5% of total installed capacity (2013 est.)
country comparison to the world: 53

Crude oil—production: 24,500 bbl/day (2013 est.)
country comparison to the world: 74

Crude oil—exports: 0 bbl/day (2013 est.)
country comparison to the world: 171

Crude oil—imports: 33,330 bbl/day (2013 est.)
country comparison to the world: 62

Crude oil—proved reserves: 77.5 million bbl (1 January 2013 es)
country comparison to the world: 75

Refined petroleum products—production:
65,720 bbl/day (2013 est.)
country comparison to the world: 79

Refined petroleum products—consumption:
72,770 bbl/day (2013 est.)
country comparison to the world: 89

Refined petroleum products—exports: 16,060 bbl/day (2013 est.)
country comparison to the world: 77

Refined petroleum products—imports: 31,120 bbl/day (2013 est.)
country comparison to the world: 90

Natural gas—production: 484.7 million cu m (2013 est.)
country comparison to the world: 71

Natural gas—consumption: 2.827 billion cu m (2013 est.)
country comparison to the world: 74

Natural gas—exports: 0 cu m (2013 est.)
country comparison to the world: 169

Natural gas—imports: 2.45 billion cu m (2013 est.)
country comparison to the world: 45

Natural gas—proved reserves: 48.14 billion cu m (1 January 2013 es)
country comparison to the world: 66

Carbon dioxide emissions from consumption of energy: 62 million Mt (2013 est.)
country comparison to the world: 55

COMMUNICATIONS

Telephones—main lines in use: 2.977 million (2012)
country comparison to the world: 5 0

Telephones—mobile cellular: 9.138 million (2012)
country comparison to the world: 85

Telephone system: *general assessment:* replacements of, and upgrades to, telecommunications equipment damaged during the 1999 war has resulted in a modern digitalized telecommunications system
domestic: wireless service, available through multiple providers with national coverage, is growing very rapidly; best telecommunications services are centered in urban centers; 3G mobile network launched in 2007
international: country code—381 (2011)

Internet country code: . r s

Internet hosts: 1.102 million (2012)
country comparison to the world: 44

Internet users: 4.107 million (2009)
country comparison to the world: 57

TRANSPORTATION

Airports: 26 (2013)
country comparison to the world: 127

Airports—with paved runways: *total:* 1 0
over 3,047 m: 2
2,438 to 3,047 m: 3
1,524 to 2,437 m: 3
914 to 1,523 m: 2 (2013)

Airports—with unpaved runways: *total:* 1 6
1,524 to 2,437 m: 1
914 to 1,523 m: 10
under 914 m: 5 (2013)

Heliports: 2 (2012)

Railways: *total:* 3,809 km
country comparison to the world: 46

standard gauge: 3,809 km 1.435-m gauge (1,279 km electrified) (2010)

Roadways: *total:* 44,248 km
country comparison to the world: 81
paved: 28,000 km
unpaved: 16,248 km (2010)

Waterways: 587 km (primarily on the Danube and Sava rivers) (2009)
country comparison to the world: 81

MILITARY

Military branches: Serbian Armed Forces (Vojska Srbije, VS): Land Forces Command (includes Riverine Component, consisting of a river flotilla on the Danube), Air and Air Defense Forces Command (2012)

Military service age and obligation: 18 years of age for voluntary military service; conscription abolished December 2010; reserve obligation to age 60 for men and age 50 for women (2013)

Manpower fit for military service:
males age 16-49: 1,395,426
females age 16-49: 1,356,415 (2010 est.)

Manpower reaching militarily significant age annually: *male:* 43,945
female: 41,080 (2010 est.)

Military expenditures: 2.21% of GDP (2012)
country comparison to the world: 37
2.28% of GDP (2011)
2.21% of GDP (2010)

TRANSNATIONAL ISSUES

Disputes—international: Serbia with several other states protest the US and other states' recognition of Kosovo's declaration of its status as a sovereign and independent state in February 2008; ethnic Serbian municipalities along Kosovo's northern border challenge final status of Kosovo-Serbia boundary; several thousand NATO-led Kosovo Force peacekeepers under United Nations Interim Administration Mission in Kosovo authority continue to keep the peace within Kosovo between the ethnic Albanian majority and the Serb minority in Kosovo; Serbia delimited about half of the boundary with Bosnia and Herzegovina, but sections along the Drina River remain in dispute

Refugees and internally displaced persons:
refugees (country of origin): 49,931 (Croatia); 16,418 (Bosnia and Herzegovina) (2012)
IDPs: 228,215 (most are Kosovar Serbs some are Roma, Ashkalis, and Egyptian (RAE); some RAE IDPs are unregistered) (2011)
stateless persons: 8,500 (includes stateless persons in Kosovo) (2012)

Illicit drugs: transshipment point for Southwest Asian heroin moving to Western Europe on the Balkan route; economy vulnerable to money laundering

SEYCHELLES

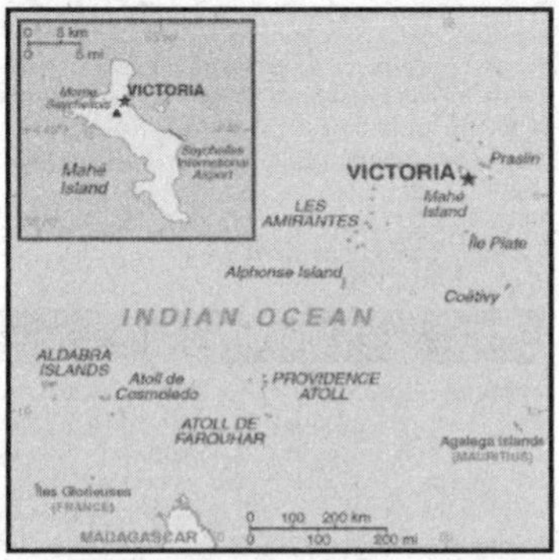

INTRODUCTION

Background: A lengthy struggle between France and Great Britain for the islands ended in 1814, when they were ceded to the latter. Independence came in 1976. Socialist rule was brought to a close with a new constitution and free elections in 1993. President France-Albert RENE, who had served since 1977, was re-elected in 2001, but stepped down in 2004. Vice President James Alix MICHEL took over the presidency and in July 2006 was elected to a new five-year term; he was reelected in May 2011.

GEOGRAPHY

Location: archipelago in the Indian Ocean, northeast of Madagascar

Geographic coordinates: 4 35 S, 55 40 E

Map references: Africa

Area: *total:* 455 sq km
country comparison to the world: 199
land: 455 sq km
water: 0 sq km

Area—comparative: 2.5 times the size of Washington, DC

Land boundaries: 0 km

Coastline: 491 km

Maritime claims: *territorial sea:* 12 nm
contiguous zone: 24 nm
exclusive economic zone: 200 nm
continental shelf: 200 nm or to the edge of the continental margin

Climate: tropical marine; humid; cooler season during southeast monsoon (late May to September); warmer season during northwest monsoon (March to May)

Terrain: Mahe Group is granitic, narrow coastal strip, rocky, hilly; others are coral, flat, elevated reefs

Elevation extremes: *lowest point:* Indian Ocean 0 m
highest point: Morne Seychellois 905 m

Natural resources: fish, copra, cinnamon trees

Land use: *arable land:* 2.17%
permanent crops: 4.35%
other: 93.48% (2011)

Irrigated land: 2.6 sq km (2003)

Natural hazards: lies outside the cyclone belt, so severe storms are rare; occasional short droughts

Environment—current issues: water supply depends on catchments to collect rainwater

Environment—international agreements:
party to: Biodiversity, Climate Change, Climate Change-Kyoto Protocol, Desertification, Endangered Species, Hazardous Wastes, Law of the Sea, Marine Dumping, Ozone Layer Protection, Ship Pollution, Wetlands
signed, but not ratified: none of the selected agreements

Geography—note: the constitution of the Republic of Seychelles lists 155 islands: 42 granitic and 113 coralline; by far the largest island is Mahe, which is home to about 90% of the population and the site of the capital city of Victoria

PEOPLE AND SOCIETY

Nationality: *noun:* Seychellois (singular and plural)
adjective: Seychellois

Ethnic groups: mixed French, African, Indian, Chinese, and Arab

Languages: Seychellois Creole (official) 89.1%, English (official) 5.1%, French (official) 0.7%, other 3.8%, unspecified 1.4% (2010 est.)

Religions: Roman Catholic 76.2%, Protestant 10.6% (Anglican 6.1%, Pentecoastal Assembly 1.5%, Seventh-Day Adventist 1.2%, other Protestant 1.6), other Christian 2.4%, Hindu 2.4%, Muslim 1.6%, other non-Christian 1.1%, unspecified 4.8%, none 0.9% (2010 est.)

Population: 91,650 (July 2014 est.)
country comparison to the world: 198

Age structure:
0-14 years: 20.9% (male 9,808/female 9,320)
15-24 years: 14.2% (male 6,827/female 6,190)
25-54 years: 49.4% (male 23,787/female 21,456)
55-64 years: 7.3% (male 3,915/female 3,632)
65 years and over: 7.3% (male 2,592/female 4,123) (2014 est.)

Dependency ratios:
total dependency ratio: 42.6 %
youth dependency ratio: 31.6 %
elderly dependency ratio: 11 %
potential support ratio: 9.1 (2013)

Median age: *total:* 33.9 years
male: 33.4 years
female: 34.5 years (2014 est.)

Population growth rate: 0.87% (2014 est.)
country comparison to the world: 129

Birth rate: 14.54 births/1,000 population (2014 est.)
country comparison to the world: 136

Death rate: 6.9 deaths/1,000 population (2014 est.)
country comparison to the world: 138

Net migration rate: 1 migrant(s)/1,000 population (2014 est.)
country comparison to the world: 61

Urbanization: *urban population:* 53.6% of total population (2011)
rate of urbanization: 1.05% annual rate of change (2010-15 est.)

Major urban areas—population: VICTORIA (capital) 26,000 (2009)

Sex ratio: *at birth:* 1.03 male(s)/female
0-14 years: 1.05 male(s)/female
15-24 years: 1.1 male(s)/female
25-54 years: 1.11 male(s)/female
55-64 years: 1.05 male(s)/female
65 years and over: 0.61 male(s)/female
total population: 1.04 male(s)/female (2014 est.)

Infant mortality rate: *total:* 10.77 deaths/1,000 live births

country comparison to the world: 134
male: 13.48 deaths/1,000 live births
female: 7.98 deaths/1,000 live births (2014 est.)

Life expectancy at birth:
total population: 74.25 years
country comparison to the world: 113
male: 69.66 years
female: 78.98 years (2014 est.)

Total fertility rate: 1.88 children born/woman (2014 est.)
country comparison to the world: 141

Health expenditures: 3.8% of GDP (2011)
country comparison to the world: 170

Physicians density: 1.51 physicians/1,000 population (2004)

Hospital bed density: 3.6 beds/1,000 population (2011)

Drinking water source:
improved:
urban: 96.3% of population
rural: 96.3% of population
total: 96.3% of population
unimproved:
urban: 3.7% of population
rural: 3.7% of population
total: 3.7% of population (2011 est.)

Sanitation facility access:
improved:
urban: 97.1% of population
rural: 97.1% of population
total: 97.1% of population
unimproved:
urban: 2.9% of population
rural: 2.9% of population
total: 2.9% of population (2011 est.)

HIV/AIDS—adult prevalence rate: NA

HIV/AIDS—people living with HIV/AIDS: NA

HIV/AIDS—deaths: NA

Obesity—adult prevalence rate: 23.9% (2008)
country comparison to the world: 70

Education expenditures: 3.6% of GDP (2011)
country comparison to the world: 121

Literacy: *definition:* age 15 and over can read and write
total population: 91.8%
male: 91.4%
female: 92.3% (2011 est.)

School life expectancy (primary to tertiary education): *total:* 12 years
male: 11 years
female: 12 years (2011)

Unemployment, youth ages 15-24: *total:* 20.3% (2002)
country comparison to the world: 58

GOVERNMENT

Country name: *conventional long form:* Republic of Seychelles
conventional short form: Seychelles
local long form: Republic of Seychelles
local short form: Seychelles

Government type: republic

Capital: *name:* Victoria

geographic coordinates: 4 37 S, 55 27 E
time difference: UTC+4 (9 hours ahead of Washington, DC during Standard Time)

Administrative divisions: 25 administrative districts; Anse aux Pins, Anse Boileau, Anse Etoile, Anse Royale, Au Cap, Baie Lazare, Baie Sainte Anne, Beau Vallon, Bel Air, Bel Ombre, Cascade, Glacis, Grand Anse Mahe, Grand Anse Praslin, Inner Islands, La Riviere Anglaise, Les Mamalles, Mont Buxton, Mont Fleuri, Plaisance, Pointe Larue, Port Glaud, Roche Caiman, Saint Louis, Takamaka

Independence: 29 June 1976 (from the UK)

National holiday: Constitution Day (National Day), 18 June (1993)

Constitution: previous 1970, 1979; latest drafted May 1993, approved by referendum 18 June 1993, effective 23 June 1993; amended many times, last in 2011 (2011)

Legal system: mixed legal system of English common law, French civil law, and customary law

International law organization participation: has not submitted an ICJ jurisdiction declaration; accepts ICCt jurisdiction

Suffrage: 18 years of age; universal

Executive branch: *chief of state:* President James Alix MICHEL (since 14 April 2004); Vice President Danny FAURE (since 1 July 2010); note—the president is both the chief of state and head of government
head of government: President James Alix MICHEL (since 14 April 2004); Vice President Danny FAURE (since 1 July 2010)
cabinet: Council of Ministers appointed by the president (For more information visit the World Leaders website)
elections: president elected by popular vote for a five-year term (eligible for two more terms); election last held on 19-21 May 2011 (next to be held in 2016)
election results: President James MICHEL elected president; percent of vote—James MICHEL 55.5%, Wavel RAMKALAWAN 41.4%, Philippe BOULLE 1.7%, Ralph VOLCERE 1.5%; note—this was the second election in which President James MICHEL participated; he was originally sworn in as president after former president France Albert RENE stepped down in April 2004

Legislative branch: unicameral National Assembly or Assemblee Nationale (34 seats; 25 members elected by popular vote, 9 allocated on a proportional basis to parties winning at least 10% of the vote; members to serve five-year terms)
elections: last held on 29 September—1 October 2011 (next to be held in 2016); note—the National Assembly was dissolved in July 2011 resulting in early elections

election results: percent of vote by party—PL 88.6%, PDM 10.9%, independents 0.6%; seats by party—PL 31, PDM 1, vacant 2; note—the ruling SPPF changed its name to People's Party (Party Lepep) in June 2009; the SNP and NDP boycotted the 2011 elections

Judicial branch: *highest court(s):* Seychelles Court of Appeal (consists of the court president and 4 justices; Supreme Court of Seychelles (consists of the chief justice and 5 pusine judges); Constitutional Court (consists of 3 Supreme Court judges)

judge selection and term of office: all judges appointed by the president of the republic upon the recommendation of the Constitutional Appointments Committee, a 3-member body, with 1 member appointed by the president of the republic, 1 by the opposition leader in the National Assembly, and 1 by the other 2 appointees; judges appointed until retirement at age 70
subordinate courts: Magistrates' Courts of Seychelles; Family Tribunal for issues such as domestic violence, and child custody and maintenance

Political parties and leaders: Democratic Party or DP [Paul CHOW]; People's Party (Parti Lepep) or PL [James Alix MICHEL]; Popular Democratic Movement or PDM [David PIERRE]; Seychelles National Party or SNP [Wavel RAMKALAWAN] (formerly the United Opposition or UO); Seychelles United Party or SUP [Ralph VOLCERE]

Political pressure groups and leaders: Roman Catholic Church
other: trade unions

International organization participation: ACP, AfDB, AOSIS, AU, C, CD, COMESA, FAO, G-77, IAEA, IBRD, ICAO, ICRM, IDA, IFAD, IFC, IFRCS, ILO, IMF, IMO, InOC, Interpol, IOC, IOM, IPU, ISO (correspondent), ITU, MIGA, NAM, OIF, OPCW, SADC, UN, UNCTAD, UNESCO, UNIDO, UNWTO, UPU, WCO, WHO, WIPO, WMO, WTO (observer)

Diplomatic representation in the US:
chief of mission: Ambassador Marie-Louise Cecile POTTER (since 6 September 2012)
chancery: 800 Second Avenue, Suite 400C, New York, NY 10017
telephone: [1] (212) 972-1785
FAX: [1] (212) 972-1786

Diplomatic representation from the US: the US does not have an embassy in Seychelles; the US Ambassador to Mauritius is accredited to Seychelles

Flag description: five oblique bands of blue (hoist side), yellow, red, white, and green (bottom) radiating from the bottom of the hoist side; the oblique bands are meant to symbolize a dynamic new country moving into the future; blue represents sky and sea, yellow the sun giving light and life, red the peoples' determination to work for the future in unity and love, white social justice and harmony, green the land and natural environment

National anthem: *name:* "Koste Seselwa" (Seychellois Unite)
lyrics/music: David Francois Marc ANDRE and George Charles Robert PAYET
note: adopted 1996

ECONOMY

Economy—overview: Since independence in 1976, per capita output in this Indian Ocean archipelago has expanded to roughly seven times the pre-independence, near-subsistence level, moving the island into the upper-middle-income group of countries. Growth has been led by the tourist sector, which employs about 30% of the labor force and provides more than 70% of hard currency earnings, and by tuna fishing. In recent years, the government has encouraged foreign investment to upgrade hotels and other services. At the same time, the government has moved to reduce the dependence on tourism by promoting the development of farming, fishing, and small-scale manufacturing. In 2008, having depleted its foreign exchange reserves, Seychelles defaulted on interest payments due on a $230 million Eurobond, requested assistance from the International Monetary Fund (IMF), and immediately enacted a number of significant structural reforms, including liberalization of the exchange rate, reform of the public sector to include layoffs, and the selling of some state assets. In December 2013, the IMF declared that Seychelles had successfully transitioned to a market-based economy with full employment and a fiscal surplus.

GDP (purchasing power parity): $2.404 billion (2013 est.)
country comparison to the world: 188
$2.326 billion (2012 est.)
$2.261 billion (2011 est.)
note: data are in 2013 US dollars

GDP (official exchange rate): $1.271 billion (2013 est.)

GDP—real growth rate: 3.3% (2013 est.)
country comparison to the world: 107

2.9% (2012 est.)
5% (2011 est.)

GDP—per capita (PPP): $25,900 (2013 est.)
country comparison to the world: 57
$25,300 (2012 est.)
$24,900 (2011 est.)
note: data are in 2013 US dollars

Gross national saving: 18.7% of GDP (2013 est.)
country comparison to the world: 85
10.6% of GDP (2012 est.)
6.3% of GDP (2011 est.)

GDP—composition, by end use:
household consumption: 92.3%
government consumption: 11.9%
investment in fixed capital: 28.2%
investment in inventories: 15.2%
exports of goods and services: 35.1%
imports of goods and services: -82.7% (2013 est.)

GDP—composition, by sector of origin:
agriculture: 2%
industry: 18.7%
services: 79.4% (2013 est.)

Agriculture—products: coconuts, cinnamon, vanilla, sweet potatoes, cassava (tapioca), copra, bananas; poultry; tuna

Industries: fishing, tourism, processing of coconuts and vanilla, coir (coconut fiber) rope, boat building, printing, furniture; beverages

Industrial production growth rate: 3.7% (2013 est.)
country comparison to the world: 81

Labor force: 39,560 (2006)
country comparison to the world: 197

Labor force—by occupation:
agriculture: 3%
industry: 23%
services: 74% (2006)

Unemployment rate: 2% (2006 est.)
country comparison to the world: 14

Population below poverty line: NA%

Household income or consumption by percentage share: *lowest 10%:* 4.7%
highest 10%: 15.4% (2007)

Budget: *revenues:* $516.7 million
expenditures: $491.7 million (2013 est.)

Taxes and other revenues: 40.7% of GDP (2013 est.)
country comparison to the world: 35

Budget surplus (+) or deficit (-):
2% of GDP (2013 est.)
country comparison to the world: 18

Public debt: 51.8% of GDP (2013 est.)
country comparison to the world: 64
68.4% of GDP (2012 est.)

Fiscal year: calendar year

Inflation rate (consumer prices): 4.3% (2013 est.)
country comparison to the world: 141
7.1% (2012 est.)

Central bank discount rate: 11.17% (31 December 2010 est.)

Commercial bank prime lending rate: 12.4% (31 December 2013 est.)
country comparison to the world: 66
12.19% (31 December 2012 est.)

Stock of narrow money: $380.7 million (31 December 2013 est.)
country comparison to the world: 165
$301.5 million (31 December 2012 est.)

Stock of broad money: $584.4 million (31 December 2013 est.)
country comparison to the world: 175
$383.1 million (31 December 2012 est.)

Stock of domestic credit: $617.6 million (31 December 2013 est.)
country comparison to the world: 164
$408.1 million (31 December 2012 est.)

Market value of publicly traded shares: $NA

Current account balance: -$140 million (2013 est.)
country comparison to the world: 80
-$208.9 million (2012 est.)

Exports: $516.7 million (2013 est.)
country comparison to the world: 172
$493.3 million (2012 est.)

Exports—commodities: canned tuna, frozen fish, cinnamon bark, copra, petroleum products (reexports)

Exports—partners: France 27.7%, UK 17.6%, Japan 15.2%, Italy 10.6% (2012)

Imports: $846.4 million (2013 est.)
country comparison to the world: 182
$889.6 million (2012 est.)

Imports—commodities: machinery and equipment, foodstuffs, petroleum products, chemicals, other manufactured goods

Imports—partners: Saudi Arabia 24%, Spain 12.1%, France 5.9% (2012)

Reserves of foreign exchange and gold: $362.4 million (31 December 2013 est.)
country comparison to the world: 153
$318.7 million (31 December 2012 est.)

Debt—external: $1.719 billion (31 December 2013 est.)
country comparison to the world: 146
$1.733 billion (31 December 2012 est.)

Exchange rates: Seychelles rupees (SCR) per US dollar—
12 (2013 est.)
13.704 (2012 est.)
12.068 (2010 est.)
13.61 (2009)
8 (2008)

ENERGY

Electricity—production: 283 million kWh (2010 est.)
country comparison to the world: 175

Electricity—consumption: 263.2 million kWh (2010 est.)
country comparison to the world: 180

Electricity—exports: 0 kWh (2012 est.)
country comparison to the world: 191

Electricity—imports: 0 kWh (2012 est.)
country comparison to the world: 194

Electricity—installed generating capacity: 89,000 kW (2010 est.)
country comparison to the world: 175

Electricity—from fossil fuels: 100% of total installed capacity (2010 est.)
country comparison to the world: 32

Electricity—from nuclear fuels: 0% of total installed capacity (2010 est.)
country comparison to the world: 174

Electricity—from hydroelectric plants: 0% of total installed capacity (2010 est.)
country comparison to the world: 196

Electricity—from other renewable sources: 0% of total installed capacity (2010 est.)
country comparison to the world: 120

Crude oil—production: 0 bbl/day (2012 est.)
country comparison to the world: 209

Crude oil—exports: 0 bbl/day (2010 est.)
country comparison to the world: 176

Crude oil—imports: 0 bbl/day (2010 est.)
country comparison to the world: 117

Crude oil—proved reserves: 0 bbl (1 January 2010 es)
country comparison to the world: 183

Refined petroleum products—production: 0 bbl/day (2010 est.)
country comparison to the world: 191

Refined petroleum products—consumption: 7,793 bbl/day (2011 est.)
country comparison to the world: 159

Refined petroleum products—exports: 0 bbl/day (2010 est.)
country comparison to the world: 128

Refined petroleum products—imports: 6,316 bbl/day (2010 est.)
country comparison to the world: 140

Natural gas—production: 0 cu m (2011 est.)
country comparison to the world: 187

Natural gas—consumption: 0 cu m (2010 est.)
country comparison to the world: 191

Natural gas—exports: 0 cu m (2011 est.)
country comparison to the world: 177

Natural gas—imports: 0 cu m (2011 est.)
country comparison to the world: 126

Natural gas—proved reserves: 0 cu m (1 January 2013 es)
country comparison to the world: 189

Carbon dioxide emissions from consumption of energy: 1.088 million Mt (2011 est.)
country comparison to the world: 165

COMMUNICATIONS

Telephones—main lines in use: 28,900 (2012)
country comparison to the world: 177

Telephones—mobile cellular: 138,300 (2012)
country comparison to the world: 185

Telephone system: *general assessment:* effective system
domestic: combined fixed-line and mobile-cellular teledensity exceeds 170 telephones per 100 persons; radiotelephone communications between islands in the archipelago
international: country code—248; direct radiotelephone communications with adjacent island countries and African coastal countries; satellite earth station—1 Intelsat (Indian Ocean) (2011)

Broadcast media: the government operates the only terrestrial TV station, which provides local programming and airs broadcasts from international services; multi-channel cable and satellite TV are available; the government operates 1 AM and 1 FM radio station; transmissions of 2 international broadcasters are accessible in Victoria (2007)

Internet country code: .sc

Internet hosts: 247 (2012)
country comparison to the world: 195

Internet users: 32,000 (2008)
country comparison to the world: 180

TRANSPORTATION

Airports: 14 (2013)
country comparison to the world: 150

Airports—with paved runways: *total:* 7
2,438 to 3,047 m: 1
914 to 1,523 m: 5
under 914 m: 1 (2013)

Airports—with unpaved runways: *total:* 7
914 to 1,523 m: 2
under 914 m: 5 (2013)

Heliports: 1 (2013)

Roadways: *total:* 508 km
country comparison to the world: 194
paved: 490 km

unpaved: 18 km (2010)

Merchant marine: *total:* 9
country comparison to the world: 118
by type: cargo 1, carrier 1, chemical tanker 6, petroleum tanker 1
foreign-owned: 3 (Hong Kong 1, Nigeria 1, South Africa 1) (2010)

Ports and terminals: *major seaport(s):* Victoria

MILITARY

Military branches: Seychelles Defense Force: Army, Coast Guard (includes Naval Wing, Air Wing), National Guard (2005)

Military service age and obligation: 18 years of age for voluntary military service (younger with parental consent); no conscription (2012)

Manpower available for military service:
males age 16-49: 26,257
females age 16-49: 23,996 (2010 est.)

Manpower fit for military service:
males age 16-49: 20,231
females age 16-49: 19,891 (2010 est.)

Manpower reaching militarily significant age annually: *male:* 686
female: 650 (2010 est.)

Military expenditures: 0.89% of GDP (2012)
country comparison to the world: 110
0.82% of GDP (2011)
0.89% of GDP (2010)

TRANSNATIONAL ISSUES

Disputes—international: Mauritius and Seychelles claim the Chagos Islands (UK-administered British Indian Ocean Territory)

Trafficking in persons: *current situation:* Seychelles is a source and destination country for Seychellois children and foreign women subjected to sex trafficking; Seychellois girls and, to a lesser extent, boys are forced into prostitution in nightclubs, bars, guest houses, hotels, brothels, private homes, and on the streets by peers, family members, and pimps; foreign tourists, sailors, and migrant workers contribute to the demand for commercial sex acts in Seychelles; some of the large population of foreign migrant workers reportedly experience the underpayment of wages and substandard housing

tier rating: Tier 2 Watch List—Seychelles does not fully comply with the minimum standards for the elimination of trafficking; however, it is making significant efforts to do so; the government has failed to report any investigations, prosecutions, or convictions of trafficking offenses; the government also has not identified or provided protective services to any trafficking victims and punished victims for crimes committed as a result of being trafficked, although it has acknowledged the need for specialized training of officials in recognizing, investigating, and prosecuting trafficking offenses, it did not provide any such training during the reporting period (2013)

SIERRA LEONE

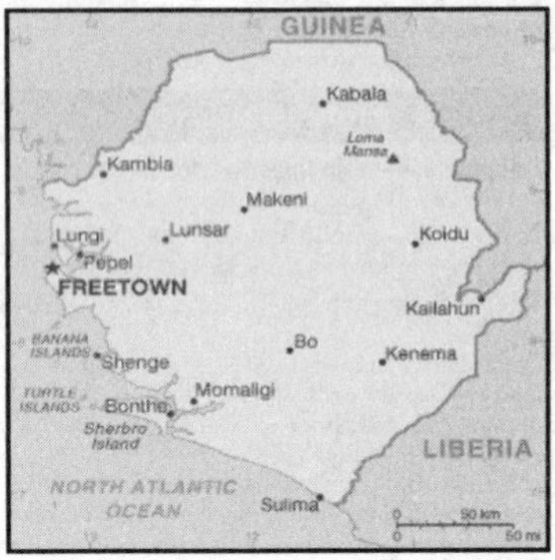

INTRODUCTION

Background: Democracy is slowly being reestablished after the civil war from 1991 to 2002 that resulted in tens of thousands of deaths and the displacement of more than 2 million people (about a third of the population). The military, which took over full responsibility for security following the departure of UN peacekeepers at the end of 2005, is increasingly developing as a guarantor of the country's stability. The armed forces remained on the sideline during the 2007 and 2012 national elections, and over the past year have deployed over 850 peacekeepers in the African Union Mission in Somalia (AMISOM). As of January 2014, Sierra Leone also fielded 122 staff for five UN peacekeeping missions. In March 2014, the closure of the UN Integrated Peacebuilding Office in Sierra Leone (UNIPSIL) marked the end of more than 15 years of peacekeeping and political operations in Sierra Leone. The government's priorities include furthering development, creating jobs, and stamping out endemic corruption.

GEOGRAPHY

Location: Western Africa, bordering the North Atlantic Ocean, between Guinea and Liberia

Geographic coordinates: 8 30 N, 11 30 W

Map references: Africa

Area: *total:* 71,740 sq km
country comparison to the world: 119
land: 71,620 sq km
water: 120 sq km

Area—comparative: slightly smaller than South Carolina

Land boundaries: *total:* 958 km
border countries: Guinea 652 km, Liberia 306 km

Coastline: 402 km

Maritime claims: *territorial sea:* 12 nm
contiguous zone: 24 nm
exclusive economic zone: 200 nm
continental shelf: 200 nm

Climate: tropical; hot, humid; summer rainy season (May to December); winter dry season (December to April)

Terrain: coastal belt of mangrove swamps, wooded hill country, upland plateau, mountains in east

Elevation extremes: *lowest point:* Atlantic Ocean 0 m
highest point: Loma Mansa (Bintimani) 1,948 m

Natural resources: diamonds, titanium ore, bauxite, iron ore, gold, chromite

Land use: *arable land:* 15.33%
permanent crops: 1.88%
other: 82.79% (2011)

Irrigated land: 293.6 sq km (2003)

Total renewable water resources: 160 cu km (2011)

Freshwater withdrawal (domestic/industrial/agricultural): *total:* 0.21 cu km/yr (52%/26%/22%)
per capita: 38.74 cu m/yr (2005)

Natural hazards: dry, sand-laden harmattan winds blow from the Sahara (December to February); sandstorms, dust storms

Environment—current issues: rapid population growth pressuring the environment; overharvesting of timber, expansion of cattle grazing, and slash-and-burn agriculture have resulted in deforestation and soil exhaustion; civil war depleted natural resources; overfishing

Environment—international agreements:
party to: Biodiversity, Climate Change, Climate Change-Kyoto Protocol, Desertification, Endangered Species, Law of the Sea, Marine Life Conservation, Ozone Layer Protection, Ship Pollution, Wetlands
signed, but not ratified: Environmental Modification

Geography—note: rainfall along the coast can reach 495 cm (195 inches) a year, making it one of the wettest places along coastal, western Africa

PEOPLE AND SOCIETY

Nationality: *noun:* Sierra Leonean(s)
adjective: Sierra Leonean

Ethnic groups: Temne 35%, Mende 31%, Limba 8%, Kono 5%, Kriole 2% (descendants of freed Jamaican slaves who were settled in the Freetown area in the late-18th century; also known as Krio), Mandingo 2%, Loko 2%, other 15% (includes refugees from Liberia's recent civil war, and small numbers of Europeans, Lebanese, Pakistanis, and Indians) (2008 census)

Languages: English (official, regular use limited to literate minority), Mende (principal vernacular in the south), Temne (principal vernacular in the north), Krio (English-based Creole, spoken by the descendants of freed Jamaican slaves who were settled in the Freetown area, a lingua franca and a first language for 10% of the population but understood by 95%)

Religions: Muslim 60%, Christian 10%, indigenous beliefs 30%

Population: 5,743,725 (July 2014 est.)
country comparison to the world: 112

Age structure:
0-14 years: 41.9% (male 1,198,553/female 1,208,775)
15-24 years: 18.8% (male 524,819/female 557,142)
25-54 years: 31.6% (male 872,284/female 943,626)
55-64 years: 3.7% (male 101,856/female 123,164)
65 years and over: 3.7% (male 91,198/female 122,308) (2014 est.)

Dependency ratios:
total dependency ratio: 79.3 %
youth dependency ratio: 74.5 %
elderly dependency ratio: 4.8 %
potential support ratio: 20.9 (2013)

Median age: *total:* 19 years

male: 18.5 years
female: 19.6 years (2014 est.)

Population growth rate: 2.33% (2014 est.)
country comparison to the world: 37

Birth rate: 37.4 births/1,000 population (2014 est.)
country comparison to the world: 15

Death rate: 11.03 deaths/1,000 population (2014 est.)
country comparison to the world: 33

Net migration rate: -3.12 migrant(s)/1,000 population
country comparison to the world: 178
note: refugees currently in surrounding countries are slowly returning (2014 est.)

Urbanization: *urban population:* 39.2% of total population (2011)
rate of urbanization: 3.04% annual rate of change (2010-15 est.)

Major urban areas—population: FREETOWN (capital) 875,000 (2009)

Sex ratio: *at birth:* 1.03 male(s)/female
0-14 years: 0.99 male(s)/female
15-24 years: 0.94 male(s)/female
25-54 years: 0.92 male(s)/female
55-64 years: 0.94 male(s)/female
65 years and over: 0.78 male(s)/female
total population: 0.94 male(s)/female (2014 est.)

Mother's mean age at first birth: 19 (2008 est.)

Maternal mortality rate: 890 deaths/100,000 live births (2010)
country comparison to the world: 5

Infant mortality rate: *total:* 73.29 deaths/1,000 live births
country comparison to the world: 11
male: 81.84 deaths/1,000 live births
female: 64.49 deaths/1,000 live births (2014 est.)

Life expectancy at birth: *total population:* 57.39 years
country comparison to the world: 201
male: 54.85 years
female: 60 years (2014 est.)

Total fertility rate: 4.83 children born/woman (2014 est.)
country comparison to the world: 19

Contraceptive prevalence rate: 11% (2010)

Health expenditures: 18.8% of GDP (2011)
country comparison to the world: 2

Physicians density: 0.02 physicians/1,000 population (2010)

Hospital bed density: 0.4 beds/1,000 population (2006)

Drinking water source:
improved:
urban: 84.1% of population
rural: 40.3% of population
total: 57.5% of population
unimproved:
urban: 15.9% of population
rural: 59.7% of population
total: 42.5% of population (2011 est.)

Sanitation facility access:
improved:
urban: 22.5% of population
rural: 6.7% of population
total: 12.9% of population
unimproved:
urban: 77.5% of population
rural: 93.3% of population
total: 87.1% of population (2011 est.)

HIV/AIDS—adult prevalence rate: 1.5% (2012 est.)
country comparison to the world: 31

HIV/AIDS—people living with HIV/AIDS: 57,700 (2012 est.)
country comparison to the world: 59

HIV/AIDS—deaths: 3,300 (2012 est.)
country comparison to the world: 51

Major infectious diseases:
degree of risk: very high
food or waterborne diseases: bacterial and protozoal diarrhea, hepatitis A, and typhoid fever
vectorborne diseases: malaria, dengue fever, and yellow fever
water contact disease: schistosomiasis
animal contact disease: rabies
aerosolized dust or soil contact disease: Lassa fever (2013)

Obesity—adult prevalence rate: 6.8% (2008)
country comparison to the world: 144

Children under the age of 5 years underweight: 18.6% (2010)
country comparison to the world: 35

Education expenditures: 2.9% of GDP (2012)
country comparison to the world: 141

Literacy: *definition:* age 15 and over can read and write English, Mende, Temne, or Arabic
total population: 43.3%
male: 54.7%
female: 32.6% (2011 est.)

School life expectancy (primary to tertiary education): *total:* 7 years
male: 8 years
female: 6 years (2001)

Child labor—children ages 5-14:
total number: 573,287
percentage: 48 % (2005 est.)

GOVERNMENT

Country name: *conventional long form:* Republic of Sierra Leone
conventional short form: Sierra Leone
local long form: Republic of Sierra Leone
local short form: Sierra Leone

Government type: constitutional democracy

Capital: *name:* Freetown

geographic coordinates: 8 29 N, 13 14 W
time difference: UTC 0 (5 hours ahead of Washington, DC during Standard Time)

Administrative divisions: 3 provinces and 1 area*; Eastern, Northern, Southern, Western*

Independence: 27 April 1961 (from the UK)

National holiday: Independence Day, 27 April (1961)

Constitution: several previous; latest in effect 1 October 1991; amended several times, last in 2010; note—in mid-2013 a committee was formed to review the constitution (2013)

Legal system: mixed legal system of English common law and customary law

International law organization participation: has not submitted an ICJ jurisdiction declaration; accepts ICCt jurisdiction

Suffrage: 18 years of age; universal

Executive branch: *chief of state:* President Ernest Bai KOROMA (since 17 September 2007); note—the president is both the chief of state and head of government
head of government: President Ernest Bai KOROMA (since 17 September 2007)
cabinet: Ministers of State appointed by the president with the approval of the House of Representatives; the cabinet is responsible to the president (For more information visit the World Leaders website)
elections: president elected by popular vote for a five-year term (eligible for a second term); election last held on 17 November 2012 (next to be held in 2017)
election results: Ernest Bai KOROMA elected to a second term; percent of vote—Ernest Bai KOROMA 58.7%, Julius Maada BIO 37.4%, other 3.9%

Legislative branch: unicameral Parliament (124 seats; 112 members elected by popular vote, 12 filled by paramount chiefs elected in separate elections; members to serve five-year terms)
elections: last held on 17 November 2012 (next to be held in 2017)
election results: percent of vote by party—NA; seats by party—APC 69, SLPP 43

Judicial branch: *highest court(s):* Superior Court of Judicature (consists of the Supreme Court—at the apex—with the chief justice and 4 other judges, the Court of Appeal with the chief justice and 7 other judges, and the High Court of Justice with the chief justice and 9 other judges; note – the Judicature has jurisdiction in all civil, criminal, and constitutional matters
judge selection and term of office: Supreme Court chief justice and other judges of the Judicature appointed by the president on the advice of the Judicial and Legal Service Commission (a 7-member independent body of judges, presidential appointees, and the Commission chairman) and subject to the approval of Parliament; all Judicature judges appointed until retirement at age 65
subordinate courts: magistrates' courts; District Appeals Court; local courts

Political parties and leaders: All People's Congress or APC [Ernest Bai KOROMA]; Peace and Liberation Party or PLP [Kandeh Baba CONTEH]; People's Movement for Democratic Change or PMDC [Charles MARGAI]; Sierra Leone People's Party or SLPP [Sumanu KAPEN]; United Democratic Movement or UDM [Mohamed BANGURA]; numerous others

Political pressure groups and leaders: other: student unions; trade unions

International organization participation: ACP, AfDB, AU, C, ECOWAS, EITI (candidate country), FAO, G-77, IAEA, IBRD, ICAO, ICRM, IDA, IDB, IFAD, IFC, IFRCS, IHO (pending member), ILO, IMF, IMO, Interpol, IOC, IOM, IPU, ISO (correspondent), ITU, ITUC (NGOs), MIGA, MINUSMA, NAM, OIC, OPCW, UN, UNAMID, UNCTAD, UNESCO, UNIDO, UNIFIL, UNISFA, UNMIT, UNWTO, UPU, WCO, WFTU (NGOs), WHO, WIPO, WMO, WTO

Diplomatic representation in the US:
chief of mission: Ambassador Bockari Kortu STEVENS (since 28 March 2008)
chancery: 1701 19th Street NW, Washington, DC 20009
telephone: [1] (202) 939-9261 through 9263
FAX: [1] (202) 483-1793

Diplomatic representation from the US:
chief of mission: Ambassador (vacant); Charge d'Affaires Kathleen FITZGIBBON (since 2 October 2013)
embassy: Southridge-Hill Station, Freetown
mailing address: use embassy street address
telephone: [232] (76) 515 000 or (76) 515 000
FAX: [232] (76) 515 355

Flag description: three equal horizontal bands of green (top), white, and blue; green symbolizes agriculture, mountains, and natural resources, white represents unity and justice, and blue the sea and the natural harbor in Freetown

National symbol(s): lion

National anthem: *name:* "High We Exalt Thee, Realm of the Free"
lyrics/music: Clifford Nelson FYLE/John Joseph AKA
note: adopted 1961

ECONOMY

Economy—overview: Sierra Leone is extremely poor. Nearly half of the working-age population engages in subsistence agriculture. The country possesses substantial mineral, agricultural, and fishery resources, but it is still recovering from a civil war that ended in the early 2000s that destroyed most institutions. In recent years economic growth has been driven by mining—particularly of iron ore and oil exploration. The country exports rutile, diamonds, and bauxite, and is vulnerable to fluctuations in international commodity prices. The country relies on external assistance to meet its budgetary needs; overseas grants make up one-fourth of total revenue. Corruption is a hindrance to foreign investment, although from 2011 to 2012 the country's Anti-Corruption Commission increased convictions of high-level officials from nine to 22 and recovered millions of dollars. In December 2013, the US Millennium Challenge Corporation (MCC) did not hold a vote on the reselection of Sierra Leone because the country did not pass MCC's Scorecard Corruption indicator; however, MCC continues compact development through a more limited engagement.

GDP (purchasing power parity): $9.156 billion (2013 est.)
country comparison to the world: 155
$8.079 billion (2012 est.)
$7.016 billion (2011 est.)
note: data are in 2013 US dollars

GDP (official exchange rate): $4.607 billion (2013 est.)

GDP—real growth rate: 13.3% (2013 est.)
country comparison to the world: 2
15.2% (2012 est.)
6% (2011 est.)

GDP—per capita (PPP): $1,400 (2013 est.)
country comparison to the world: 208
$1,300 (2012 est.)
$1,200 (2011 est.)
note: data are in 2013 US dollars

Gross national saving: 27.8% of GDP (2013 est.)
country comparison to the world: 35
17.2% of GDP (2012 est.)
-1% of GDP (2011 est.)

GDP—composition, by end use:
household consumption: 77.8%
government consumption: 6.8%
investment in fixed capital: 36.7%
investment in inventories: 0.8%
exports of goods and services: 9.7%
imports of goods and services: -31.8% (2013 est.)

GDP—composition, by sector of origin:
agriculture: 47.9%
industry: 18.6%
services: 33.5% (2013 est.)

Agriculture—products: rice, coffee, cocoa, palm kernels, palm oil, peanuts; poultry, cattle, sheep, pigs; fish

Industries: diamond mining; iron ore, rutile and bauxite mining; small-scale manufacturing (beverages, textiles, cigarettes, footwear); petroleum refining, small commercial ship repair

Industrial production growth rate: 42%
country comparison to the world: 1

Labor force: 2.207 million (2007 est.)
country comparison to the world: 119

Labor force—by occupation: *agriculture:* NA%
industry: NA%
services: NA%

Unemployment rate: NA%

Population below poverty line: 70.2% (2004)

Household income or consumption by percentage share: *lowest 10%:* 2.6%
highest 10%: 33.6% (2003)

Distribution of family income—Gini index: 62.9 (1989)
country comparison to the world: 4

Budget: *revenues:* $614.8 million
expenditures: $754.4 million (2013 est.)

Taxes and other revenues: 13.3% of GDP (2013 est.)
country comparison to the world: 199

Budget surplus (+) or deficit (-):
-3% of GDP (2013 est.)
country comparison to the world: 121

Public debt: 31.1% of GDP (2013 est.)
country comparison to the world: 116
36.5% of GDP (2012 est.)

Fiscal year: calendar year

Inflation rate (consumer prices): 11.1% (2013 est.)
country comparison to the world: 212
12.9% (2012 est.)

Central bank discount rate: NA%

Commercial bank prime lending rate: 20.5% (31 December 2013 est.)
country comparison to the world: 16
21% (31 December 2012 est.)

Stock of narrow money: $355.7 million (31 December 2013 est.)
country comparison to the world: 166
$324.7 million (31 December 2012 est.)

Stock of broad money: $1.001 billion (31 December 2013 est.)
country comparison to the world: 169
$772.6 million (31 December 2012 est.)

Stock of domestic credit: $567.7 million (31 December 2013 est.)
country comparison to the world: 166
$429.1 million (31 December 2012 est.)

Market value of publicly traded shares: $NA

Current account balance: -$463.3 million (2013 est.)
country comparison to the world: 97
-$862.5 million (2012 est.)

Exports: $1.563 billion (2013 est.)
country comparison to the world: 146
$953.4 million (2012 est.)

Exports—commodities: diamonds, rutile, cocoa, coffee, fish

Exports—partners: China 51.1%, Belgium 18.2%, Japan 7.7%, Turkey 4.8% (2012)

Imports: $1.637 billion (2013 est.)
country comparison to the world: 171
$1.597 billion (2012 est.)

Imports—commodities: foodstuffs, machinery and equipment, fuels and lubricants, chemicals

Imports—partners: China 16.5%, India 10.2%, South Africa 7.6%, US 6.7%, UK 6.7%, Belgium 4.6% (2012)

Debt—external: $1.331 billion (31 December 2013 est.)
country comparison to the world: 152
$1.172 billion (31 December 2012 est.)

Stock of direct foreign investment—at home: $2.394 billion (31 December 2013 est.)
country comparison to the world: 96
$1.719 billion (31 December 2012 est.)

Exchange rates: leones (SLL) per US dollar—
4,320.8 (2013 est.)
4,344 (2012 est.)
3,978.1 (2010 est.)

ENERGY

Electricity—production: 145 million kWh (2010 est.)
country comparison to the world: 189

Electricity—consumption: 134.9 million kWh (2010 est.)
country comparison to the world: 192

Electricity—exports: 0 kWh (2012 est.)
country comparison to the world: 194

Electricity—imports: 0 kWh (2012 est.)
country comparison to the world: 197

Electricity—installed generating capacity: 102,000 kW (2010 est.)
country comparison to the world: 171

Electricity—from fossil fuels: 47.1% of total installed capacity (2010 est.)
country comparison to the world: 161

Electricity—from nuclear fuels: 0% of total installed capacity (2010 est.)
country comparison to the world: 177

Electricity—from hydroelectric plants: 52.9% of total installed capacity (2010 est.)
country comparison to the world: 40

Electricity—from other renewable sources: 0% of total installed capacity (2010 est.)
country comparison to the world: 122

Crude oil—production: 25.39 bbl/day (2012 est.)
country comparison to the world: 126

Crude oil—exports: 0 bbl/day (2010 est.)
country comparison to the world: 181

Crude oil—imports: 0 bbl/day (2010 est.)
country comparison to the world: 120

Crude oil—proved reserves: 0 bbl (1 January 2013 es)
country comparison to the world: 187

Refined petroleum products—production: 0 bbl/day (2010 est.)
country comparison to the world: 194

Refined petroleum products—consumption: 8,768 bbl/day (2011 est.)
country comparison to the world: 155

Refined petroleum products—exports: 0 bbl/day (2010 est.)
country comparison to the world: 130

Refined petroleum products—imports: 9,373 bbl/day (2010 est.)
country comparison to the world: 132

Natural gas—production: 0 cu m (2011 est.)
country comparison to the world: 189

Natural gas—consumption: 0 cu m (2010 est.)
country comparison to the world: 193

Natural gas—exports: 0 cu m (2011 est.)
country comparison to the world: 181

Natural gas—imports: 0 cu m (2011 est.)
country comparison to the world: 129

Natural gas—proved reserves: 0 cu m (1 January 2013 es)
country comparison to the world: 192

Carbon dioxide emissions from consumption of energy: 1.492 million Mt (2011 est.)
country comparison to the world: 153

COMMUNICATIONS

Telephones—main lines in use: 18,000 (2012)
country comparison to the world: 190

Telephones—mobile cellular: 2.21 million (2012)
country comparison to the world: 143

Telephone system: *general assessment:* marginal telephone service with poor infrastructure

domestic: the national microwave radio relay trunk system connects Freetown to Bo and Kenema; while mobile-cellular service is growing rapidly from a small base, service area coverage remains limited
international: country code—232; satellite earth station—1 Intelsat (Atlantic Ocean) (2009)

Broadcast media: 1 government-owned TV station; 1 private TV station began operating in 2005; a pay-TV service began operations in late 2007; 1 government-owned national radio station; about two dozen private radio stations primarily clustered in major cities; transmissions of several international broadcasters are available (2007)

Internet country code: .sl

Internet hosts: 282 (2012)
country comparison to the world: 191

Internet users: 14,900 (2009)
country comparison to the world: 199

TRANSPORTATION

Airports: 8 (2013)
country comparison to the world: 164

Airports—with paved runways: *total:* 1
over 3,047 m: 1 (2013)

Airports—with unpaved runways: *total:* 7
914 to 1,523 m: 7 (2013)

Heliports: 2 (2013)

Roadways: *total:* 11,300 km
country comparison to the world: 131
paved: 904 km
unpaved: 10,396 km (2002)

Waterways: 800 km (600 km navigable year round) (2011)
country comparison to the world: 72

Merchant marine: *total:* 215
country comparison to the world: 34
by type: bulk carrier 22, cargo 120, carrier 2, chemical tanker 19, container 6, liquefied gas 3, passenger/cargo 2, petroleum tanker 28, refrigerated cargo 7, roll on/roll off 4, specialized tanker 1, vehicle carrier 1
foreign-owned: 98 (Bangladesh 1, China 19, Cyprus 2, Egypt 3, Estonia 2, Hong Kong 7, Japan 4, Lebanon 2, North Korea 2, Romania 2, Russia 7, Singapore 9, Syria 13, Taiwan 7, Turkey 9, UAE 1, UK 1, Ukraine 5, Yemen 2) (2010)

Ports and terminals: *major seaport(s):* Freetown, Pepel, Sherbro Islands

MILITARY

Military branches: Republic of Sierra Leone Armed Forces (RSLAF): Army (includes Maritime Wing and Air Wing) (2013)

Military service age and obligation: 18 is the legal minimum age for voluntary military service (younger with parental consent); women are eligible to serve; no conscription; candidates must be HIV negative (2012)

Manpower available for military service:
males age 16-49: 1,183,093 (2010 est.)

Manpower fit for military service:
males age 16-49: 731,898
females age 16-49: 838,032 (2010 est.)

Manpower reaching militarily significant age annually: *male:* 54,212
female: 57,154 (2010 est.)

Military expenditures: 0.72% of GDP (2012)
country comparison to the world: 118
0.8% of GDP (2011)
0.72% of GDP (2010)

TRANSNATIONAL ISSUES

Disputes—international: as domestic fighting among disparate ethnic groups, rebel groups, warlords, and youth gangs in Cote d'Ivoire, Guinea, Liberia, and Sierra Leone gradually abates, the number of refugees in border areas has begun to slowly dwindle; Sierra Leone considers excessive Guinea's definition of the flood plain limits to define the left bank boundary of the Makona and Moa rivers and protests Guinea's continued occupation of these lands including the hamlet of Yenga occupied since 1998

SINGAPORE

INTRODUCTION

Background: Singapore was founded as a British trading colony in 1819. It joined the Malaysian Federation in 1963 but separated two years later and became independent. Singapore subsequently became one of the world's most prosperous countries with strong international trading links (its port is one of the world's busiest in terms of tonnage handled) and with per capita GDP equal to that of the leading nations of Western Europe.

GEOGRAPHY

Location: Southeastern Asia, islands between Malaysia and Indonesia

Geographic coordinates: 1 22 N, 103 48 E

Map references: Southeast Asia

Area: *total:* 697 sq km
country comparison to the world: 192
land: 687 sq km
water: 10 sq km

Area—comparative: slightly more than 3.5 times the size of Washington, DC

Land boundaries: 0 km

Coastline: 193 km

Maritime claims: *territorial sea:* 3 nm
exclusive fishing zone: within and beyond territorial sea, as defined in treaties and practice

Climate: tropical; hot, humid, rainy; two distinct monsoon seasons—Northeastern monsoon (December to March) and Southwestern monsoon (June to September); inter-monsoon—frequent afternoon and early evening thunderstorms

Terrain: lowland; gently undulating central plateau contains water catchment area and nature preserve

Elevation extremes: *lowest point:* Singapore Strait 0 m
highest point: Bukit Timah 166 m

Natural resources: fish, deepwater ports

Land use: *arable land:* 0.89%
permanent crops: 0.14%
other: 98.97% (2011)

Irrigated land: NA

Total renewable water resources: 0.6 cu km (2011)

Freshwater withdrawal (domestic/industrial/agricultural): *total:* 0.19 cu km/yr (47%/53%/0%)
per capita: 81.97 cu m/yr (2005)

Natural hazards: NA

Environment—current issues: industrial pollution; limited natural freshwater resources; limited land availability presents waste disposal problems; seasonal smoke/haze resulting from forest fires in Indonesia

Environment—international agreements:
party to: Biodiversity, Climate Change, Climate Change-Kyoto Protocol, Desertification, Endangered Species, Hazardous Wastes, Law of the Sea, Ozone Layer Protection, Ship Pollution
signed, but not ratified: none of the selected agreements

Geography—note: focal point for Southeast Asian sea routes

PEOPLE AND SOCIETY

Nationality: *noun:* Singaporean(s)
adjective: Singapore

Ethnic groups: Chinese 74.2%, Malay 13.3%, Indian 9.2%, other 3.3% (2012 est.)

Languages: Mandarin (official) 36.3%, English (official) 29.8%, Hokkien 8.1%, Tamil (official) 4.4%, Cantonese 4.1%, Teochew 3.2%, Malay (official) 1.2%, other Chinese dialects 1.1%, other 1.7% (2010 est.)

Religions: Buddhist 33.9%, Muslim 14.3%, Taoist 11.3%, Catholic 7.1%, Hindu 5.2%, other Christian 11%, other 0.7%, none 16.4% (2010 est.)

Population: 5,567,301 (July 2014 est.)
country comparison to the world: 116

Age structure:
0-14 years: 13.4% (male 381,452/female 364,050)
15-24 years: 17.8% (male 487,593/female 502,637)
25-54 years: 50.3% (male 1,365,872/female 1,434,495)
55-64 years: 8.5% (male 279,243/female 278,852)
65 years and over: 8.1% (male 214,665/female 258,442) (2014 est.)

Dependency ratios:
total dependency ratio: 35.6 %
youth dependency ratio: 21.8 %
elderly dependency ratio: 13.8 %
potential support ratio: 7.2 (2013)

Median age: *total:* 33.8 years
male: 33.7 years
female: 33.9 years (2014 est.)

Population growth rate: 1.92% (2014 est.)
country comparison to the world: 57

Birth rate: 8.1 births/1,000 population (2014 est.)
country comparison to the world: 221

Death rate: 3.42 deaths/1,000 population (2014 est.)
country comparison to the world: 218

Net migration rate: 14.55 migrant(s)/1,000 population (2014 est.)
country comparison to the world: 8

Urbanization: *urban population:* 100% of total population (2011)
rate of urbanization: 1.1% annual rate of change (2010-15 est.)

Sex ratio: *at birth:* 1.07 male(s)/female
0-14 years: 1.05 male(s)/female
15-24 years: 0.97 male(s)/female
25-54 years: 0.95 male(s)/female
55-64 years: 0.96 male(s)/female
65 years and over: 0.82 male(s)/female
total population: 0.96 male(s)/female (2014 est.)

Mother's mean age at first birth: 29.4 (2008 est.)

Maternal mortality rate: 3 deaths/100,000 live births (2010)
country comparison to the world: 182

Infant mortality rate: *total:* 2.53 deaths/1,000 live births
country comparison to the world: 220
male: 2.69 deaths/1,000 live births
female: 2.36 deaths/1,000 live births (2014 est.)

Life expectancy at birth: *total population:* 84.38 years
country comparison to the world: 4
male: 81.86 years
female: 87.07 years (2014 est.)

Total fertility rate: 0.8 children born/woman (2014 est.)
country comparison to the world: 224

Contraceptive prevalence rate: 62%

note: percent of women aged 15-44 (1997)

Health expenditures: 4.6% of GDP (2011)
country comparison to the world: 150

Physicians density: 1.92 physicians/1,000 population (2010)

Hospital bed density: 2.7 beds/1,000 population (2011)

Drinking water source:
improved:
urban: 100% of population
total: 100% of population
unimproved:
urban: 0% of population
total: 0% of population (2011 est.)

Sanitation facility access:
improved:
urban: 100% of population
total: 100% of population
unimproved:
urban: 0% of population
total: 0% of population (2011 est.)

HIV/AIDS—adult prevalence rate: 0.1% (2009 est.)
country comparison to the world: 141

HIV/AIDS—people living with HIV/AIDS: 3,400 (2009 est.)
country comparison to the world: 131

HIV/AIDS—deaths: fewer than 100 (2009 est.)
country comparison to the world: 153

Obesity—adult prevalence rate: 7.1% (2008)
country comparison to the world: 142

Children under the age of 5 years underweight: 3.3% (2000)
country comparison to the world: 109

Education expenditures: 3% of GDP (2013)
country comparison to the world: 140

Literacy: *definition:* age 15 and over can read and write
total population: 95.9%
male: 98%
female: 93.8% (2010 est.)

Unemployment, youth ages 15-24: *total:* 6.7% (2012)
country comparison to the world: 131

GOVERNMENT

Country name: *conventional long form:* Republic of Singapore
conventional short form: Singapore
local long form: Republic of Singapore
local short form: Singapore

Government type: parliamentary republic

Capital: *name:* Singapore

geographic coordinates: 1 17 N, 103 51 E
time difference: UTC+8 (13 hours ahead of Washington, DC during Standard Time)

Administrative divisions: none

Independence: 9 August 1965 (from Malaysian Federation)

National holiday: National Day, 9 August (1965)

Constitution: several previous; latest adopted 22 December 1965; amended several times, last in 2010 (2013)

Legal system: English common law

International law organization participation: has not submitted an ICJ jurisdiction declaration; non-party state to the ICCt

Suffrage: 21 years of age; universal and compulsory

Executive branch: *chief of state:* President Tony TAN Keng Yam (since 1 September 2011)
head of government: Prime Minister LEE Hsien Loong (since 12 August 2004); Deputy Prime Minister TEO Chee Hean (since 1 April 2009) and Deputy Prime Minister Tharman SHANMUGARATNAM (since 21 May 2011)
cabinet: appointed by president, responsible to parliament (For more information visit the World Leaders website)
elections: president elected by popular vote for six-year term; election last held on 27 August 2011 (next to be held by August 2017); following legislative elections, leader of majority party or leader of majority coalition usually appointed prime minister by president; deputy prime ministers appointed by president
election results: Tony TAN Keng Yam elected president from a field of four candidates with 35.2% of the votes cast

Legislative branch: unicameral Parliament (87 seats; members elected by popular vote to serve five-year terms); note—in addition, there are up to nine nominated members (NMP) and up to nine Non-Constituency Members of Parliament (NCMP); traditionally, members of parties that came closest to winning seats may be appointed as NCMPs; NMPs are appointed by the president to ensure that a wide range of community views are present in Parliament; NMPs are independent and non-partisan members
elections: last held on 7 May 2011 (next to be held by 2017)
election results: percent of vote by party—PAP 60.1%, WP 12.8%, NSP 12.1%, others 15%; seats by party—PAP 81, WP 6; (seats as of February 2013 PAP 80, WP 7)

Judicial branch: *highest court(s):* Supreme Court (consists of the president or chief justice and 16 justices and organized into an upper tier Appeal Court and a lower tier High Court)
judge selection and term of office: all judges appointed by the president from candidates recommended by the prime minister after consultation with the chief justice; justices appointed for life
subordinate courts: district, magistrates', juvenile, family, community, and coroners' courts; small claims tribunals

Political parties and leaders: National Solidarity Party or NSP [Jeannette CHONG-ARULDROSS]; People's Action Party or PAP [LEE Hsien Loong]; Reform Party [Kenneth JEYARETNAM]; Singapore Democratic Alliance or SDA [Desmond LIM] (includes Singapore Justice Party or SJP [Desmond; LIM] and Singapore National Malay Organization/Pertubuhan Kebangsaan Melayu Singapura or PKMS [Abu; Bin MOHAMED]); Singapore Democratic Party or SDP [CHEE Soon Juan]; Singapore People's Party or SPP [CHIAM See Tong]; Workers' Party or WP [LOW Thia Khiang]

Political pressure groups and leaders: none

International organization participation: ADB, AOSIS, APEC, ARF, ASEAN, BIS, C, CP, EAS, FATF, G-77, IAEA, IBRD, ICAO, ICC (national committees), ICRM, IDA, IFC, IFRCS, IHO, ILO, IMF, IMO, IMSO, Interpol, IOC, IPU, ISO, ITSO, ITU, ITUC (NGOs), MIGA, NAM, OPCW, PCA, UN, UNCTAD, UNESCO, UNMIT, UPU, WCO, WHO, WIPO, WMO, WTO

Diplomatic representation in the US:
chief of mission: Ambassador Ashok Kumar MIRPURI (since 24 July 2012)
chancery: 3501 International Place NW, Washington, DC 20008
telephone: [1] (202) 537-3100
FAX: [1] (202) 537-0876
consulate(s) general: New York, San Francisco
Diplomatic representation from the US:

chief of mission: Ambassador Kirk WAGER (since 4 September 2013)
embassy: 27 Napier Road, Singapore 258508
mailing address: FPO AP 96507-0001
telephone: [65] 6476-9100
FAX: [65] 6476-9340

Flag description: two equal horizontal bands of red (top) and white; near the hoist side of the red band, there is a vertical, white crescent (closed portion is toward the hoist side) partially enclosing five white five-pointed stars arranged in a circle; red denotes brotherhood and equality; white signifies purity and virtue; the waxing crescent moon symbolizes a young nation on the ascendancy; the five stars represent the nation's ideals of democracy, peace, progress, justice, and equality

National symbol(s): lion, merlion (mythical half lion-half fish creature), orchid

National anthem: *name:* "Majulah Singapura" (Onward Singapore)
lyrics/music: ZUBIR Said
note: adopted 1965; the anthem, which was first performed in 1958 at the Victoria Theatre, is sung only in Malay

ECONOMY

Economy—overview: Singapore has a highly developed and successful free-market economy. It enjoys a remarkably open and corruption-free environment, stable prices, and a per capita GDP higher than that of most developed countries. The economy depends heavily on exports, particularly in consumer electronics, information technology products, pharmaceuticals, and on a growing financial services sector. The economy contracted 0.6% in 2009 as a result of the global financial crisis, but rebounded 15.1% in 2010, on the strength of renewed exports, before slowing to in 2011-13, largely a result of soft demand for exports during the second European recession. Over the longer term, the government hopes to establish a new growth path that focuses on raising productivity. Singapore has attracted major investments in pharmaceuticals and medical technology production and will continue efforts to establish Singapore as Southeast Asia's financial and high-tech hub.

GDP (purchasing power parity): $339 billion (2013 est.)
country comparison to the world: 41
$327.4 billion (2012 est.)
$323.2 billion (2011 est.)
note: data are in 2013 US dollars

GDP (official exchange rate): $287.4 billion (2013 est.)

GDP—real growth rate: 3.5% (2013 est.)
country comparison to the world: 91
1.3% (2012 est.)
5.2% (2011 est.)

GDP—per capita (PPP): $62,400 (2013 est.)
country comparison to the world: 7
$61,600 (2012 est.)
$62,300 (2011 est.)
note: data are in 2013 US dollars

Gross national saving: 48.3% of GDP (2013 est.)
country comparison to the world: 5
45.6% of GDP (2012 est.)
46.8% of GDP (2011 est.)

GDP—composition, by end use:
household consumption: 41%
government consumption: 9.7%
investment in fixed capital: 25.6%
investment in inventories: 4.5%
exports of goods and services: 195.8%
imports of goods and services: -176.7% (2013 est.)

GDP—composition, by sector of origin:
agriculture: 0%
industry: 27.3%
services: 72.7% (2013 est.)

Agriculture—products: orchids, vegetables; poultry, eggs; fish, ornamental fish

Industries: electronics, chemicals, financial services, oil drilling equipment, petroleum refining, rubber processing and rubber products, processed food and beverages, ship repair, offshore platform construction, life sciences, entrepot trade

Industrial production growth rate: 3.5% (2013 est.)
country comparison to the world: 83

Labor force: 3.428 million
country comparison to the world: 99
note: excludes non-residents (2013 est.)

Labor force—by occupation: *agriculture:* 0.1%
industry: 19.6%
services: 80.3%
note: excludes non-residents (2011)

Unemployment rate: 2.1% (2013 est.)
country comparison to the world: 15
1.9% (2012 est.)

Population below poverty line: NA%

Household income or consumption by percentage share: *lowest 10%:* 4.4%
highest 10%: 23.2% (2008)

Distribution of family income—Gini index: 47.8 (2012)
country comparison to the world: 27
48.1 (2008)

Budget: *revenues:* $44.48 billion
expenditures: $42.47 billion
note: expenditures include both operational and development expenditures (2013 est.)

Taxes and other revenues: 15.5% of GDP (2013 est.)
country comparison to the world: 190

Budget surplus (+) or deficit (-): 0.7% of GDP (2013 est.)
country comparison to the world: 31

Public debt: 113.6% of GDP (2013 est.)
country comparison to the world: 10
111.4% of GDP (2012 est.)
note: for Singapore, public debt consists largely of Singapore Government Securities (SGS) issued to assist the Central Provident Fund (CPF), which administers Singapore's defined contribution pension fund; special issues of SGS are held by the CPF, and are non-tradable; the government has not borrowed to finance deficit expenditures since the 1980s; Singapore has no external public debt

Fiscal year: 1 April—31 March

Inflation rate (consumer prices): 2.4% (2013 est.)
country comparison to the world: 88
4.6% (2012 est.)

Commercial bank prime lending rate: 5.4% (31 December 2013 est.)
country comparison to the world: 151
5.38% (31 December 2012 est.)

Stock of narrow money: $124.8 billion (31 December 2013 est.)
country comparison to the world: 29
$115 billion (31 December 2012 est.)

Stock of broad money: $400.9 billion (31 December 2013 est.)
country comparison to the world: 26
$388.6 billion (31 December 2012 est.)

Stock of domestic credit: $302.7 billion (31 December 2013 est.)
country comparison to the world: 35
$281.1 billion (31 December 2012 est.)

Market value of publicly traded shares: $414.1 billion (31 December 2012 est.)
country comparison to the world: 26
$308.3 billion (31 December 2011)
$370.1 billion (31 December 2010 est.)

Current account balance: $52.19 billion (2013 est.)
country comparison to the world: 13
$51.44 billion (2012 est.)

Exports: $442.9 billion (2013 est.)
country comparison to the world: 15
$435.8 billion (2012 est.)

Exports—commodities: machinery and equipment (including electronics and telecommunications), pharmaceuticals and other chemicals, refined petroleum products, food and beverages

Exports—partners: Malaysia 12.3%, Hong Kong 10.9%, China 10.8%, Indonesia 10.6%, US 5.5%, Japan 4.6%, Australia 4.2%, South Korea 4% (2012)

Imports: $380.3 billion (2013 est.)
country comparison to the world: 15
$374.9 billion (2012 est.)

Imports—commodities: machinery and equipment, mineral fuels, chemicals, foodstuffs, consumer goods

Imports—partners: Malaysia 10.6%, China 10.3%, US 10.2%, South Korea 6.8%, Japan 6.2%, Indonesia 5.3%, Saudi Arabia 4.5%, UAE 4.1% (2012)

Reserves of foreign exchange and gold: $270.5 billion (31 December 2013 est.)
country comparison to the world: 12
$259.1 billion (31 December 2012 est.)

Debt—external: $1.174 trillion (31 December 2012 est.)
country comparison to the world: 16
$1.088 trillion (31 December 2011 est.)

Stock of direct foreign investment—at home: $800 billion (31 December 2013 est.)
country comparison to the world: 10
$741 billion (31 December 2012 est.)

Stock of direct foreign investment—abroad: $445.1 billion (31 December 2013 est.)
country comparison to the world: 16
$416.9 billion (31 December 2012 est.)

Exchange rates: Singapore dollars (SGD) per US dollar—
1.25 (2013 est.)
1.2497 (2012 est.)
1.3635 (2010 est.)
1.4545 (2009)
1.415 (2008)

ENERGY

Electricity—production: 44.41 billion kWh (2011 est.)
country comparison to the world: 5 4

Electricity—consumption: 40.62 billion kWh (2010 est.)
country comparison to the world: 53

Electricity—exports: 0 kWh (2012 est.)
country comparison to the world: 195

Electricity—imports: 0 kWh (2012 est.)
country comparison to the world: 198

Electricity—installed generating capacity: 10.25 million kW (2010 est.)
country comparison to the world: 54

Electricity—from fossil fuels: 99.8% of total installed capacity (2010 est.)
country comparison to the world: 46

Electricity—from nuclear fuels: 0% of total installed capacity (2010 est.)
country comparison to the world: 178

Electricity—from hydroelectric plants: 0% of total installed capacity (2010 est.)
country comparison to the world: 199

Electricity—from other renewable sources: 0.2% of total installed capacity (2010 est.)
country comparison to the world: 93

Crude oil—production: 20,170 bbl/day (2012 est.)
country comparison to the world: 77

Crude oil—exports: 0 bbl/day (2011 est.)
country comparison to the world: 182

Crude oil—imports: 1.137 million bbl/day (2010 est.)
country comparison to the world: 10

Crude oil—proved reserves: 0 bbl (1 January 2013 es)
country comparison to the world: 188

Refined petroleum products—production: 1.357 million bbl/day (2011 est.)
country comparison to the world: 16

Refined petroleum products—consumption: 1.25 million bbl/day (2011 est.)
country comparison to the world: 19

Refined petroleum products—exports: 1.14 million bbl/day (2010 est.)
country comparison to the world: 7

Refined petroleum products—imports: 1.348 million bbl/day (2010 est.)
country comparison to the world: 5

Natural gas—production: 0 cu m (2011 est.)
country comparison to the world: 190

Natural gas—consumption: 8.778 billion cu m (2011 est.)
country comparison to the world: 51

Natural gas—exports: 0 cu m (2011 est.)
country comparison to the world: 182

Natural gas—imports: 8.78 billion cu m (2011 est.)
country comparison to the world: 32

Natural gas—proved reserves: 0 cu m (1 January 2013 es)
country comparison to the world: 193

Carbon dioxide emissions from consumption of energy: 212.4 million Mt (2011 est.)
country comparison to the world: 28

COMMUNICATIONS

Telephones—main lines in use: 1.99 million (2012)
country comparison to the world: 5 8

Telephones—mobile cellular: 8.063 million (2012)
country comparison to the world: 92

Telephone system: *general assessment:* excellent service
domestic: excellent domestic facilities; launched 3G wireless service in February 2005; combined fixed-line and mobile-cellular teledensity more than 180 telephones per 100 persons; multiple providers of high-speed Internet connectivity and the government is close to completing an island-wide roll out of a high-speed fiber-optic broadband network
international: country code—65; numerous submarine cables provide links throughout Asia, Australia, the Middle East, Europe, and US; satellite earth stations—4; supplemented by VSAT coverage (2011)

Broadcast media: state controls broadcast media; 8 domestic TV stations operated by MediaCorp which is wholly owned by a state investment company; broadcasts from Malaysian and Indonesian stations available; satellite dishes banned; multi-channel cable TV service available; a total of 18 domestic radio stations broadcasting with MediaCorp operating more than a dozen and another 4 stations are closely linked to the ruling party or controlled by the Singapore Armed Forces Reservists Association; many Malaysian and Indonesian radio stations are available

Internet country code: .sg

Internet hosts: 1.96 million (2012)
country comparison to the world: 39

Internet users: 3.235 million (2009)
country comparison to the world: 65

TRANSPORTATION

Airports: 9 (2013)
country comparison to the world: 158

Airports—with paved runways: *total:* 9
over 3,047 m: 2
2,438 to 3,047 m: 2
1,524 to 2,437 m: 3
914 to 1,523 m: 1
under 914 m: 1 (2013)

Pipelines: gas 122 km; refined products 8 km (2013)

Roadways: *total:* 3,425 km
country comparison to the world: 163
paved: 3,425 km (includes 161 km of expressways) (2012)

Merchant marine: *total:* 1,599
country comparison to the world: 6
by type: bulk carrier 247, cargo 109, carrier 6, chemical tanker 256, container 339, liquefied gas 131, petroleum tanker 436, refrigerated cargo 13, roll on/roll off 5, vehicle carrier 57
foreign-owned: 966 (Australia 12, Bangladesh 1, Belgium 1, Bermuda 25, Brazil 9, Chile 6, China 29, Cyprus 6, Denmark 149, France 3, Germany 32, Greece 22, Hong Kong 46, India 21, Indonesia 60, Italy 5, Japan 164, Malaysia 27, Netherlands 1, Norway 153, Russia 2, South Africa 13, South Korea 3, Sweden 11, Switzerland 3, Taiwan 77, Thailand 33, UAE 10, UK 6, US 36)
registered in other countries: 344 (Australia 2, Bahamas 7, Bangladesh 7, Belize 4, Cambodia 3, Cyprus 1, France 3, Honduras 11, Hong Kong 13, Indonesia 46, Italy 1, Kiribati 9, Liberia 22, Malaysia 13, Maldives 4, Malta 4, Marshall Islands 30, Mongolia 3, North Korea 1, Panama 92, Philippines 1, Saint Kitts and Nevis 10, Saint Vincent and the Grenadines 5, Sierra Leone 9, Thailand 1, Tuvalu 19, US 16, Vanuatu 2, unknown 5) (2010)

Ports and terminals: *major seaport(s):* Singapore
major container port(s) (TEUs): Singapore

Transportation—note: the International Maritime Bureau reports the territorial and offshore waters in the South China Sea as high risk for piracy and armed robbery against ships; numerous commercial vessels have been attacked and hijacked both at anchor and while underway; hijacked vessels are often disguised and cargo diverted to ports in East Asia; crews have been murdered or cast adrift

MILITARY

Military branches: Singapore Armed Forces: Army, Navy, Air Force (includes Air Defense) (2013)

Military service age and obligation: 18-21 years of age for male compulsory military service; 16 1/2 years of age for volunteers; 2-year conscript service obligation, with a reserve obligation to age 40 (enlisted) or age 50 (officers) (2012)

Manpower available for military service:
males age 16-49: 1,255,902 (2010 est.)

Manpower fit for military service:
males age 16-49: 1,018,839
females age 16-49: 1,087,134 (2010 est.)

Manpower reaching militarily significant age annually: *male:* 27,098
female: 25,368 (2010 est.)

Military expenditures: 3.52% of GDP (2012)
country comparison to the world: 15
3.47% of GDP (2011)
3.52% of GDP (2010)

TRANSNATIONAL ISSUES

Disputes—international: disputes persist with Malaysia over deliveries of fresh water to Singapore, Singapore's extensive land reclamation works, bridge construction, and maritime boundaries in the Johor and Singapore Straits; in 2008, ICJ awarded sovereignty of Pedra Branca (Pulau Batu Puteh/Horsburgh Island) to Singapore, and Middle Rocks to Malaysia, but did not rule on maritime regimes, boundaries, or disposition of South Ledge; Indonesia and Singapore continue to work on finalization of their 1973 maritime boundary agreement by defining unresolved areas north of Indonesia's Batam Island; piracy remains a problem in the Malacca Strait

Illicit drugs: drug abuse limited because of aggressive law enforcement efforts; as a transportation and financial services hub, Singapore is vulnerable, despite strict laws and enforcement, as a venue for money laundering

SINT MAARTEN

INTRODUCTION

Background: Although sighted by Christopher COLUMBUS in 1493 and claimed for Spain, it was the Dutch who occupied the island in 1631 and set about exploiting its salt deposits. The Spanish retook the island in 1633, but continued to be harassed by the Dutch. The Spanish finally relinquished the island of Saint Martin to the French and Dutch, who divided it amongst themselves in 1648. The establishment of cotton, tobacco, and sugar plantations dramatically expanded African slavery on the island in the 18th and 19th centuries; the practice was not abolished in the Dutch half until 1863. The island's economy declined until 1939 when it became a free port; the tourism industry was dramatically expanded beginning in the 1950s. In 1954, Sint Maarten and several other Dutch Caribbean possessions became part of the Kingdom of the Netherlands as the Netherlands Antilles. In a 2000 referendum, the citizens of Sint Maarten voted to become a self-governing country within the Kingdom of the Netherlands. The change in status became effective in October of 2010 with the dissolution of the Netherlands Antilles.

GEOGRAPHY

Location: Caribbean, located in the Leeward Islands (northern) group; Dutch part of the island of Saint Martin in the Caribbean Sea; Sint Maarten lies east of the US Virgin Islands

Geographic coordinates: 18 4 N, 63 4 W

Map references: Central America and the Caribbean

Area: *total:* 34 sq km
country comparison to the world: 236
land: 34 sq km
water: 0 sq km
note: Dutch part of the island of Saint Martin

Area—comparative: one-fifth the size of Washington, DC

Land boundaries: *total:* 15 km
border countries: Saint Martin (France) 15 km

Coastline: 364 km

Maritime claims: *territorial sea:* 12 nm
exclusive fishing zone: 12 nm

Climate: tropical marine climate, ameliorated by northeast trade winds, results in moderate temperatures; average rainfall of 1500 mm/year; hurricane season stretches from July to November

Terrain: low, hilly terrain, volcanic origin

Elevation extremes: *lowest point:* Caribbean Sea 0 m
highest point: Mount Flagstaff 386 m

Natural resources: fish, salt

Land use: *arable land:* 10%
permanent crops: 0%
other: 90% (2011)

Irrigated land: NA

Natural hazards: subject to hurricanes from July to November

Environment—current issues: NA

Geography—note: the northern border is shared with the French overseas collectivity of Saint Martin; together, these two entities make up the smallest landmass in the world shared by two self-governing states

PEOPLE AND SOCIETY

Languages: English (official) 67.5%, Spanish 12.9%, Creole 8.2%, Dutch (official) 4.2%, Papiamento (a Spanish-Portuguese-Dutch-English dialect) 2.2%, French 1.5%, other 3.5% (2001 census)

Religions: Roman Catholic 39%, Protestant 44.8% (Pentecostal 11.6%, Seventh-Day Adventist 6.2%, other Protestant 27%), none 6.7%, other 5.4%, Jewish 3.4%, not reported 0.7% (2001 census)

Population: 39,689 (July 2013 est.)
country comparison to the world: 213

Age structure: *0-14 years:* 19.7% (male 3,986/female 3,704)
15-24 years: 16.3% (male 3,130/female 3,253)
25-54 years: 45.3% (male 8,626/female 9,077)
55-64 years: 12.9% (male 2,448/female 2,596)
65 years and over: 5.8% (male 1,087/female 1,181) (2013 est.)

Median age: *total:* 39.7 years
male: 38.9 years
female: 40.4 years (2013 est.)

Population growth rate: 1.51% (2013 est.)
country comparison to the world: 79

Birth rate: 13 births/1,000 population (2013 est.)
country comparison to the world: 154

Death rate: 4.51 deaths/1,000 population (2013 est.)
country comparison to the world: 203

Net migration rate: 6.63 migrant(s)/1,000 population (2013 est.)
country comparison to the world: 21

Sex ratio: *at birth:* 1.05 male(s)/female
0-14 years: 1.08 male(s)/female
15-24 years: 0.96 male(s)/female
25-54 years: 0.95 male(s)/female
55-64 years: 0.94 male(s)/female
65 years and over: 0.92 male(s)/female

total population: 0.97 male(s)/female (2013 est.)

Infant mortality rate: *total:* 9.05 deaths/1,000 live births
country comparison to the world: 146
male: 9.84 deaths/1,000 live births
female: 8.22 deaths/1,000 live births (2013 est.)

Life expectancy at birth: *total population:* 77.61 years
country comparison to the world: 65
male: 75.34 years
female: 79.99 years (2013 est.)

Total fertility rate: 2.09 children born/woman (2013 est.)
country comparison to the world: 110

HIV/AIDS—adult prevalence rate: NA

HIV/AIDS—people living with HIV/AIDS: NA

HIV/AIDS—deaths: NA

GOVERNMENT

Country name: *Dutch long form:* Land Sint Maarten
Dutch short form: Sint Maarten
English long form: Country of Sint Maarten
English short form: Sint Maarten
former: Netherlands Antilles; Curacao and Dependencies

Dependency status: constituent country within the Kingdom of the Netherlands; full autonomy in internal affairs granted in 2010; Dutch Government responsible for defense and foreign affairs

Government type: parliamentary

Capital: *name:* Philipsburg

geographic coordinates: 18 1 N, 63 2 W

time difference: UTC-4 (1 hour ahead of Washington, DC during Standard Time)

Administrative divisions: none (part of the Kingdom of the Netherlands)

Independence: none (part of the Kingdom of the Netherlands)

National holiday: Queen's Day (Birthday of Queen-Mother JULIANA and accession to the throne of her oldest daughter BEATRIX), 30 April (1909 and 1980)

Constitution: Staatsregeling, 10 October 2010; revised Kingdom Charter pending previous 1947, 1955; latest adopted 21 July 2010, entered into force 10 October 2010 (regulates governance of Sint Maarten but is subordinate to the Charter for the Kingdom of the Netherlands); note—in October 2010, with the dissolution of the Netherlands Antilles, Sint Maarten became a constituent country within the Kingdom of the Netherlands (2013)

Legal system: based on Dutch civil law system with some English common law influence

Suffrage: 18 years of age; universal

Executive branch: *chief of state:* Queen BEATRIX of the Netherlands (since 30 April 1980); represented by Governor General Eugene HOLIDAY (since 10 October 2010)

head of government: Sarah WESCOTT-WILLIAMS (since 10 October 2010)

cabinet: Cabinet (For more information visit the World Leaders website)

elections: the monarch is hereditary; governor general appointed by the monarch for a six-year term; following legislative elections, the leader of the majority party is usually elected prime minister by the legislature

Legislative branch: unicameral parliament or Staten (15 seats; members elected by popular vote for four-year term)

elections: last held 17 September 2010 (next to be held in 2014)

election results: percent of vote by party—National Alliance 45.9%, UPP 36.1%, Democratic Party 17.1%, other .9%; seats by party - National Alliance 7, UPP 6, Democratic Party 2

Judicial branch: *highest court(s):* Joint Court of Justice of Aruba, Curacao, Sint Maarten, and of Bonaire, Sint Eustatitus, and Saba or "Joint Court of Justice" (consists of the presiding judge, other members, and their substitutes); final appeals heard by the Supreme Court, in The Hague, Netherlands
note—prior to 2010, the Joint Court of Justice was the Common Court of Justice of the Netherlands Antilles and Aruba

judge selection and term of office: Joint Court judges appointed by the monarch for life

subordinate courts: Courts in First Instance

Political parties and leaders: Democratic Party or DP [Sarah WESCOTT-WILLIAMS]; National Alliance or NA [William MARLIN]; United People's Party or UPP [Theodore HEYLIGER]; Concordia Political Alliance or CPA [Jeffery RICHARDSON]

Diplomatic representation in the US: none (represented by the Kingdom of the Netherlands)

Diplomatic representation from the US: the US does not have an embassy in Sint Maarten; the Consul General to Curacao, currently Consul General James R. Moore, is accredited to Sint Maarten

Flag description: two equal horizontal bands of red (top) and blue with a white isosceles triangle based on the hoist side; the center of the triangle displays the Sint Maarten coat of arms; the arms consist of an orange-bordered blue shield prominently displaying the white court house in Philipsburg, as well as a bouquet of yellow sage (the national flower) in the upper left, and the silhouette of a Dutch-French friendship monument in the upper right; the shield is surmounted by a yellow rising sun in front of which is a Brown Pelican in flight; a yellow scroll below the shield bears the motto: SEMPER PROGREDIENS (Always Progressing); the three main colors are identical to those on the Dutch flag *note:* the flag somewhat resembles that of the Philippines, but with the main red and blue bands reversed; the banner more closely evokes the wartime Philippine flag

National anthem: *name:* "O Sweet Saint Martin's Land"

lyrics/music: Gerard KEMPS
note: the song, written in 1958, is used as an unofficial anthem for the entire island (both French and Dutch sides); as a collectivity of France, in addition to the local anthem, "La Marseillaise" is official on the French side (see France); as a constituent part of the Kingdom of the Netherlands, in addition to the local anthem, "Het Wilhelmus" is official on the Dutch side (see Netherlands)

ECONOMY

Economy—overview: The economy of Sint Maarten centers around tourism with nearly four-fifths of the labor force engaged in this sector. Nearly two million visitors come to the island each year by cruise ship and roughly 500,000 visitors arrived through Princess Juliana International Airport in 2012. Cruise ships and yachts also call on Sint Maarten's numerous ports and harbors. No significant agriculture and limited local fishing means that almost all food must be imported. Energy resources and manufactured goods are also imported. Sint Maarten had the highest per capita income among the five islands that formerly comprised the Netherlands Antilles.

GDP (purchasing power parity): $798.3 million (2010 est.)
country comparison to the world: 209
$794.7 million (2008 est.)
$748.9 million (2007 est.)

GDP (official exchange rate): $794.7 million (2008)

GDP—real growth rate: 4% (2012 est.)
country comparison to the world: 75
1.6% (2008 est.)
4.5% (2007 est.)

GDP—per capita (PPP): $15,400 (2008 est.)
country comparison to the world: 89

GDP—composition, by sector of origin:
agriculture: 0.4%
industry: 18.3%
services: 81.3% (2008 est.)

Agriculture—products: sugar

Industries: tourism, light industry, and manufacturing

Labor force: 23,200 (2008 est.)
country comparison to the world: 208

Labor force—by occupation: *agriculture:* 1.1%
industry: 15.2%
services: 83.7% (2008 est.)

Unemployment rate: 12% (2012 est.)
country comparison to the world: 123
10.6% (2008 est.)

Inflation rate (consumer prices): 4% (2012 est.)
country comparison to the world: 133
0.7% (2009 est.)

Exports—commodities: sugar

Exchange rates: Netherlands Antillean guilders (ANG) per US dollar - 1.79 (2012)
1.79 (2011); 1.79 (2009)
1.79 (2008); 1.79 (2007)
note: The Netherland Antillean guilder was replaced by the newly created Caribbean guilder in 2013

ENERGY

Electricity—production: 304.3 million kWh (2008 est.)
country comparison to the world: 171

COMMUNICATIONS

Telephone system: *general assessment:* generally adequate facilities
domestic: extensive interisland microwave radio relay links
international: country code—1-721; the Americas Region Caribbean Ring System (ARCOS-1) and the Americas-2 submarine cable systems provide connectivity to Central America, parts of South America and the Caribbean, and the US; satellite earth stations—2 Intelsat (Atlantic Ocean) (2010)

Internet country code: .sx; note—IANA has designated .sx for Sint Maarten, but has not yet assigned it to a sponsoring organization

Internet hosts: NA

Internet users: NA

TRANSPORTATION

Airports: 1 (2013)
country comparison to the world: 233

Airports—with paved runways: *total:* 1
1,524 to 2,437 m: 1 (2012)

Roadways: *total:* 53 km
country comparison to the world: 218

Ports and terminals:
major seaport(s): Philipsburg
oil terminals: Coles Bay oil terminal

MILITARY

Military branches: no regular military forces (2012)

Military—note: defense is the responsibility of the Kingdom of the Netherlands

SLOVAKIA

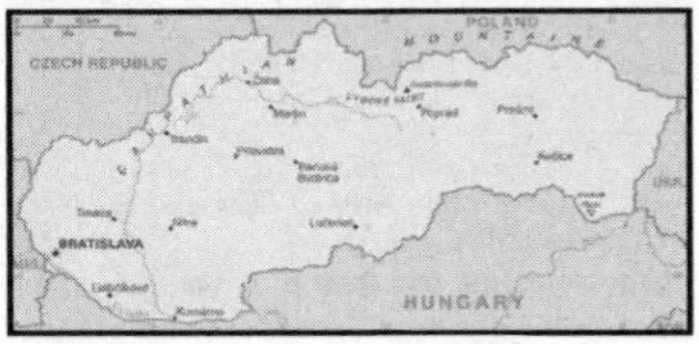

INTRODUCTION

Background: Slovakia's roots can be traced to the 9th century state of Great Moravia. Subsequently, the Slovaks became part of the Hungarian Kingdom, where they remained for the next 1,000 years. Following the formation of the dual Austro-Hungarian monarchy in 1867, language and education policies favoring the use of Hungarian (Magyarization) resulted in a strengthening of Slovak nationalism and a cultivation of cultural ties with the closely related Czechs, who were under Austrian rule. After the dissolution of the Austro-Hungarian Empire at the close of World War I, the Slovaks joined the Czechs to form Czechoslovakia. During the interwar period, Slovak nationalist leaders pushed for autonomy within Czechoslovakia, and in 1939 Slovakia became an independent state allied with Nazi Germany. Following World War II, Czechoslovakia was reconstituted and came under communist rule within Soviet-dominated Eastern Europe. In 1968, an invasion by Warsaw Pact troops ended the efforts of the country's leaders to liberalize communist rule and create "socialism with a human face," ushering in a period of repression known as "normalization." The peaceful "Velvet Revolution" swept the Communist Party from power at the end of 1989 and inaugurated a return to democratic rule and a market economy. On 1 January 1993, the country underwent a nonviolent "velvet divorce" into its two national components, Slovakia and the Czech Republic. Slovakia joined both NATO and the EU in the spring of 2004 and the euro zone on 1 January 2009.

GEOGRAPHY

Location: Central Europe, south of Poland

Geographic coordinates: 48 40 N, 19 30 E

Map references: Europe

Area: *total:* 49,035 sq km
country comparison to the world: 131
land: 48,105 sq km
water: 930 sq km

Area—comparative: about twice the size of New Hampshire

Land boundaries: *total:* 1,474 km
border countries: Austria 91 km, Czech Republic 197 km, Hungary 676 km, Poland 420 km, Ukraine 90 km

Coastline: 0 km (landlocked)

Maritime claims: none (landlocked)

Climate: temperate; cool summers; cold, cloudy, humid winters

Terrain: rugged mountains in the central and northern part and lowlands in the south

Elevation extremes: *lowest point:* Bodrok River 94 m
highest point: Gerlachovsky Stit 2,655 m

Natural resources: brown coal and lignite; small amounts of iron ore, copper and manganese ore; salt; arable land

Land use: *arable land:* 28.36%
permanent crops: 0.41%
other: 71.22% (2011)

Irrigated land: 1,720 sq km (2007)

Total renewable water resources: 50.1 cu km (2011)

Freshwater withdrawal (domestic/industrial/agricultural): *total:* 0.69 cu km/yr (47%/51%/3%)
per capita: 126.7 cu m/yr (2010)

Natural hazards: NA

Environment—current issues: air pollution from metallurgical plants presents human health risks; acid rain damaging forests

Environment—international agreements: *party to:* Air Pollution, Air Pollution-Nitrogen Oxides, Air Pollution-Persistent Organic Pollutants, Air Pollution-Sulfur 85, Air Pollution-Sulfur 94, Air Pollution-Volatile Organic Compounds, Antarctic Treaty, Biodiversity, Climate Change, Climate Change-Kyoto Protocol, Desertification, Endangered Species, Environmental Modification, Hazardous Wastes, Law of the Sea, Ozone Layer Protection, Ship Pollution, Wetlands, Whaling
signed, but not ratified: none of the selected agreements

Geography—note: landlocked; most of the country is rugged and mountainous; the Tatra Mountains in the north are interspersed with many scenic lakes and valleys

PEOPLE AND SOCIETY

Nationality: *noun:* Slovak(s)
adjective: Slovak

Ethnic groups: Slovak 80.7%, Hungarian 8.5%, Roma 2%, other and unspecified 8.8% (2011 est.)

Languages: Slovak (official) 78.6%, Hungarian 9.4%, Roma 2.3%, Ruthenian 1%, other or unspecified 8.8% (2011 est.)

Religions: Roman Catholic 62%, Protestant 8.2%, Greek Catholic 3.8%, other or unspecified 12.5%, none 13.4% (2011 est.)

Population: 5,443,583 (July 2014 est.)
country comparison to the world: 117

Age structure:
0-14 years: 15.2% (male 422,636/female 403,626)
15-24 years: 12.2% (male 341,500/female 322,287)
25-54 years: 45.2% (male 1,241,930/female 1,218,706)
55-64 years: 13.9% (male 347,438/female 388,461)
65 years and over: 13.4% (male 288,010/female 468,989) (2014 est.)

Dependency ratios:
total dependency ratio: 38.9 %
youth dependency ratio: 20.9 %
elderly dependency ratio: 18 %
potential support ratio: 5.6 (2013)

Median age: *total:* 39.2 years
male: 37.5 years
female: 41 years (2014 est.)

Population growth rate: 0.03% (2014 est.)
country comparison to the world: 189

Birth rate: 10.01 births/1,000 population (2014 est.)
country comparison to the world: 192

Death rate: 9.7 deaths/1,000 population (2014 est.)
country comparison to the world: 52

Net migration rate: 0.01 migrant(s)/1,000 population (2014 est.)
country comparison to the world: 77

Urbanization: *urban population:* 54.7% of total population (2011)
rate of urbanization: 0.06% annual rate of change (2010-15 est.)

Major urban areas—population: BRATISLAVA (capital) 428,000 (2009)

Sex ratio: *at birth:* 1.07 male(s)/female
0-14 years: 1.05 male(s)/female
15-24 years: 1.06 male(s)/female
25-54 years: 1.02 male(s)/female
55-64 years: 0.94 male(s)/female
65 years and over: 0.6 male(s)/female
total population: 0.94 male(s)/female (2014 est.)

Mother's mean age at first birth: 27.3 (2010 est.)

Maternal mortality rate: 6 deaths/100,000 live births (2010)
country comparison to the world: 172

Infant mortality rate: *total:* 5.35 deaths/1,000 live births
country comparison to the world: 178
male: 6 deaths/1,000 live births
female: 4.66 deaths/1,000 live births (2014 est.)

Life expectancy at birth:
total population: 76.69 years
country comparison to the world: 75
male: 73.09 years
female: 80.52 years (2014 est.)

Total fertility rate: 1.39 children born/woman (2014 est.)
country comparison to the world: 209

Contraceptive prevalence rate: 79.8%
note: percent of women aged 15-44 (1997)

Health expenditures: 9% of GDP (2010)
country comparison to the world: 44

Physicians density: 3 physicians/1,000 population (2007)

Hospital bed density: 6.4 beds/1,000 population (2010)

Drinking water source:
improved:
urban: 100% of population
rural: 100% of population
total: 100% of population
unimproved:
urban: 0% of population
rural: 0% of population
total: 0% of population (2011 est.)

Sanitation facility access:
improved:
urban: 99.9% of population
rural: 99.6% of population
total: 99.7% of population
unimproved:
urban: 0.1% of population
rural: 0.4% of population
total: 0.3% of population (2011 est.)

HIV/AIDS—adult prevalence rate: less than 0.1% (2009 est.)
country comparison to the world: 142

HIV/AIDS—people living with HIV/AIDS: fewer than 500 (2009 est.)
country comparison to the world: 156

HIV/AIDS—deaths: fewer than 100 (2009 est.)
country comparison to the world: 152

Obesity—adult prevalence rate: 25.4% (2008)
country comparison to the world: 54

Education expenditures: 4.2% of GDP (2010)
country comparison to the world: 103

Literacy: *definition:* age 15 and over can read and write
total population: 99.6%
male: 99.7%
female: 99.6% (2004)

School life expectancy (primary to tertiary education): *total:* 12 years
male: 12 years
female: 12 years (2012)

Unemployment, youth ages 15-24: *total:* 34%
country comparison to the world: 21
male: 35%
female: 32.5% (2012)

GOVERNMENT

Country name: *conventional long form:* Slovak Republic
conventional short form: Slovakia
local long form: Slovenska republika
local short form: Slovensko

Government type: parliamentary democracy

Capital: *name:* Bratislava

geographic coordinates: 48 09 N, 17 07 E
time difference: UTC+1 (6 hours ahead of Washington, DC during Standard Time)
daylight saving time: +1hr, begins last Sunday in March; ends last Sunday in October

Administrative divisions: 8 regions (kraje, singular—kraj); Banskobystricky, Bratislavsky, Kosicky, Nitriansky, Presovsky, Trenciansky, Trnavsky, Zilinsky

Independence: 1 January 1993 (Czechoslovakia split into the Czech Republic and Slovakia)

National holiday: Constitution Day, 1 September (1992)

Constitution: several previous (preindependence); latest passed by legislature 1 September 1992, signed 3 September 1992, effective 1 October 1992; amended several times, last in 2011 (2011)

Legal system: civil law system based on Austro-Hungarian codes; note—legal code modified to comply with the obligations of Organization on Security and Cooperation in Europe and to expunge Marxist-Leninist legal system International law organization participation: accepts compulsory ICJ jurisdiction with reservations; accepts ICCt jurisdiction

Suffrage: 18 years of age; universal

Executive branch: *chief of state:* President Ivan GASPAROVIC (since 15 June 2004)
head of government: Prime Minister Robert FICO (since 4 April 2012); Deputy Prime Ministers Robert KALINAK, Peter KAZIMIR, Miroslav LAJCAK (since 4 April 2012), Lubomir VAZNY (since 26 November 2012)
cabinet: Cabinet appointed by the president on the recommendation of the prime minister (For more information visit the World Leaders website)
elections: president elected by popular vote for a five-year term (eligible for a second term); election last held on 15 and 29 March 2014 (next to be held in March 2019); following National Council elections, the leader of the majority party or the leader of a majority coalition usually appointed prime minister by the president

election results: Andrej KISKA elected president in runoff; percent of vote—Andrej KISKA 59.4%, Robert FICO 40.6%; note—KISKA is to be sworn in on 15 June 2014

Legislative branch: unicameral National Council of the Slovak Republic or Narodna Rada Slovenskej Republiky (150 seats; members elected on the basis of proportional representation to serve four-year terms)
elections: last held on 10 March 2012 (next to be held in 2016)
election results: percent of vote by party—Smer-SD 44.4%, KDH 8.8%, OLaNO 8.6%, Most-Hid 6.9%, SDKU-DS 6.1%, SaS 5.9%, other 19.3%; seats by party—Smer-SD 83, KDH 16, OLaNO 16, Most-Hid 13, SDKU-DS 11, SaS 11

Judicial branch: *highest court(s):* Supreme Court of the Slovak Republic (consists of 78 judges—as of 2003—organized into criminal, civil, commercial, and administrative divisions with 3- and 5-judge panels; Constitutional Court (consists of 13 judges)
judge selection and term of office: Supreme Court judge candidates proposed by the Judicial Council of the Slovak Republic, a 17-member independent body to include the Supreme Court chief justice and presidential and governmental appointees; judges appointed by the president for life with mandatory retirement at age 65; Constitutional Court judges nominated by the National Council of the Republic and appointed by the president; judges appointed for 12-year terms
subordinate courts: regional and district civil courts; Higher Military Court; military district courts; Court of Audit

Political parties and leaders:
parties in the Parliament: Christian Democratic Movement or KDH [Jan FIGEL]; Direction-Social Democracy or Smer-SD [Robert FICO]; Freedom and Solidarity or SaS [Richard SULIK]; Most-Hid or Bridge [Bela BUGAR]; Ordinary People and Independent Personalities or OLaNO [Igor MATOVIC]; Slovak Democratic and Christian Union-Democratic Party or SDKU-DS [Pavol FRESO]
selected parties outside the Parliament: Civic Conservative Party or OKS [Ondrej DOSTAL]; Nation and Justice—Our Party or NAS [Anna BELOUSOVOVA]; Party of the Democratic Left or SDL [Jozef DURICA]; Party of the Hungarian Coalition or SMK [Jozsef BERENYI]; People's Party—Our Slovakia or LSNS [Marian KOTLEBA]; Slovak National Party or SNS [Andrej DANKO]

Political pressure groups and leaders: Association of Towns and Villages or ZMOS; Confederation of Trade Unions or KOZ; Entrepreneurs Association of Slovakia or ZPS; Federation of Employers' Associations of the Slovak Republic; Medical Trade Association or LOZ; National Union of Employers or RUZ; Slovak Chamber of Commerce and Industry or SOPK; The Business Alliance of Slovakia or PAS

International organization participation: Australia Group, BIS, BSEC (observer), CBSS (observer), CD, CE, CEI, CERN, EAPC, EBRD, ECB, EIB, EMU, EU, FAO, IAEA, IBRD, ICAO, ICC (national committees), ICRM, IDA, IEA, IFC, IFRCS, ILO, IMF, IMO, IMSO, Interpol, IOC, IOM, IPU, ISO, ITU, ITUC (NGOs), MIGA, NATO, NEA, NSG, OAS (observer), OECD, OIF (observer), OPCW, OSCE, PCA, Schengen Convention, SELEC (observer), UN, UNCTAD, UNESCO, UNFICYP, UNIDO, UNTSO, UNWTO, UPU, WCO, WFTU (NGOs), WHO, WIPO, WMO, WTO, ZC

Diplomatic representation in the US:
chief of mission: Ambassador Peter KMEC (since 17 September 2012)
chancery: 3523 International Court NW, Washington, DC 20008
telephone: [1] (202) 237-1054
FAX: [1] (202) 237-6438
consulate(s) general: New York

Diplomatic representation from the US:
chief of mission: Ambassador Theodore SEDGWICK (since 4 July 2010)
embassy: Hviezdoslavovo Namestie 4, 81102 Bratislava
mailing address: P.O. Box 309, 814 99 Bratislava
telephone: [421] (2) 5443-3338
FAX: [421] (2) 5441-8861

Flag description: three equal horizontal bands of white (top), blue, and red derive from the Pan-Slav colors; the Slovakian coat of arms (consisting of a red shield bordered in white and bearing a white double-barred cross of St. Cyril and St. Methodius surmounting three blue hills) is centered over the bands but offset slightly to the hoist side
note: the Pan-Slav colors were inspired by the 19th-century flag of Russia

National symbol(s): double-barred cross (Cross of St. Cyril and St. Methodius) surmounting three peaks

National anthem: *name:* "Nad Tatrou sa blyska" (Lightning Over the Tatras)
lyrics/music: Janko MATUSKA/traditional
note: adopted 1993, in use since 1844; the anthem's music is based on the Slovak folk song "Kopala studienku"

ECONOMY

Economy—overview: Slovakia has made significant economic reforms since its separation from the Czech Republic in 1993. After a period of relative stagnation in the early and mid 1990s, reforms to the taxation, healthcare, pension, and social welfare systems helped Slovakia consolidate its budget, get on track to join the EU in 2004, and adopt the euro in January 2009. Major privatizations are nearly complete, the banking sector is almost entirely in foreign hands, and the government has facilitated a foreign investment boom with business friendly policies. Foreign direct investment (FDI), especially in the automotive and electronic sectors, fueled much of the growth until 2008. Cheap, skilled labor, low taxes, no dividend taxes, a relatively liberal labor code, and a favorable geographical location are Slovakia's main advantages to foreign investors. Growth returned, following a contraction in 2009, but has remained sluggish in large part due to continued weakness in external demand. In 2012 the government of Prime Minister Robert FICO rolled back some of Slovakia's pro-growth reforms to help shore up public finances. Corruption and slow dispute resolution remain key factors constraining economic growth.

GDP (purchasing power parity): $133.4 billion (2013 est.)
country comparison to the world: 66
$132.3 billion (2012 est.)
$129.6 billion (2011 est.)
note: data are in 2013 US dollars

GDP (official exchange rate): $96.96 billion (2013 est.)

GDP—real growth rate: 0.8% (2013 est.)
country comparison to the world: 177
2% (2012 est.)
3.2% (2011 est.)

GDP—per capita (PPP): $24,700 (2013 est.)
country comparison to the world: 61
$24,500 (2012 est.)
$24,000 (2011 est.)
note: data are in 2013 US dollars

Gross national saving: 21.1% of GDP (2013 est.)
country comparison to the world: 75
23% of GDP (2012 est.)
21.8% of GDP (2011 est.)

GDP—composition, by end use:
household consumption: 58%
government consumption: 16.9%
investment in fixed capital: 19.9%
investment in inventories: -2.2%
exports of goods and services: 97.5%
imports of goods and services: -90.2% (2013 est.)

GDP—composition, by sector of origin:
agriculture: 3.1%
industry: 30.8%
services: 47% (2013 est.)

Agriculture—products: grains, potatoes, sugar beets, hops, fruit; pigs, cattle, poultry; forest products

Industries: metal and metal products; food and beverages; electricity, gas, coke, oil, nuclear fuel; chemicals and manmade fibers; machinery; paper and printing; earthenware and ceramics; transport vehicles; textiles; electrical and optical apparatus; rubber products

Industrial production growth rate: 6.5% (2013 est.)
country comparison to the world: 39

Labor force: 2.727 million (2013 est.)
country comparison to the world: 108

Labor force—by occupation: *agriculture:* 3.5%
industry: 27%
services: 69.4% (December 2009)

Unemployment rate: 14.4% (2013 est.)
country comparison to the world: 138
13.6% (2012 est.)

Population below poverty line: 21% (2002)

Household income or consumption by percentage share: *lowest 10%:* 4.4%
highest 10%: 22.4% (2009 est.)

Distribution of family income—Gini index: 26 (2005)
country comparison to the world: 132
26.3 (1996)

Budget: *revenues:* $32.41 billion

expenditures: $35.72 billion (2013 est.)

Taxes and other revenues: 33.4% of GDP (2013 est.)
country comparison to the world: 72

Budget surplus (+) or deficit (-): -3.4% of GDP (2013 est.)
country comparison to the world: 136

Public debt: 55.5% of GDP (2013 est.)
country comparison to the world: 56
52.1% of GDP (2012 est.)
note: data cover general Government Gross Debt, and includes debt instruments issued (or owned) by Government entities, including sub-sectors of central government, state government, local government, and social security funds.

Fiscal year: calendar year

Inflation rate (consumer prices): 1.7% (2013 est.)
country comparison to the world: 45
3.6% (2012 est.)

Central bank discount rate: 1.75% (31 December 2011 est.)
country comparison to the world: 117
1.75% (31 December 2010 est.)
note: this is the European Central Bank's rate on the marginal lending facility, which offers overnight credit to banks from the euro area; Slovakia became a member of the Economic and Monetary Union (EMU) on 1 January 2009

Commercial bank prime lending rate: 3.3% (31 December 2013 est.)
country comparison to the world: 171
3.47% (31 December 2012 est.)

Stock of narrow money: $38.48 billion (31 December 2013 est.)
country comparison to the world: 55
$37.14 billion (31 December 2012 est.)
note: see entry for the European Union for money supply in the euro area; the European Central Bank (ECB) controls monetary policy for the 17 members of the Economic and Monetary Union (EMU); individual members of the EMU do not control the quantity of money circulating within their own borders

Stock of broad money: $59.89 billion (31 December 2013 est.)
country comparison to the world: 66
$56.57 billion (31 December 2012 est.)

Stock of domestic credit: $72.6 billion (31 December 2013 est.)
country comparison to the world: 60
$68.47 billion (31 December 2012 est.)

Market value of publicly traded shares: $4.611 billion (31 December 2012 est.)
country comparison to the world: 85
$4.736 billion (31 December 2011)
$4.15 billion (31 December 2010 est.)

Current account balance: $3.315 billion (2013 est.)
country comparison to the world: 33
$2.096 billion (2012 est.)

Exports: $82.7 billion (2013 est.)
country comparison to the world: 45
$80.67 billion (2012 est.)

Exports—commodities: machinery and electrical equipment 35.9%, vehicles 21%, base metals 11.3%, chemicals and minerals 8.1%, plastics 4.9% (2009 est.)

Exports—partners: Germany 22.3%, Czech Republic 14.9%, Poland 8.8%, Hungary 7.8%, Austria 7%, France 5.6%, Italy 4.9%, UK 4.1% (2012)

Imports: $77.96 billion (2013 est.)
country comparison to the world: 39
$75.99 billion (2012 est.)

Imports—commodities: machinery and transport equipment 31%, mineral products 13%, vehicles 12%, base metals 9%, chemicals 8%, plastics 6% (2009 est.)

Imports—partners: Germany 18.6%, Czech Republic 18%, Russia 9.9%, Austria 8%, Hungary 6.8%, Poland 6%, South Korea 4.1% (2012)

Reserves of foreign exchange and gold: $2.258 billion (31 December 2013 est.)
country comparison to the world: 119
$2.519 billion (31 December 2012 est.)

Debt—external: $68.44 billion (31 December 2012 est.)
country comparison to the world: 55
$68.61 billion (31 December 2011 est.)

Stock of direct foreign investment—at home: $63.99 billion (31 December 2013 est.)
country comparison to the world: 50
$62.49 billion (31 December 2012 est.)

Stock of direct foreign investment—abroad: $11.15 billion (31 December 2013 est.)
country comparison to the world: 52
$11.09 billion (31 December 2012 est.)

Exchange rates: euros (EUR) per US dollar—
0.7634 (2013 est.)
0.7752 (2012 est.)
0.755 (2010 est.)
0.7198 (2009 est.)
0.6827 (2008 est.)

ENERGY

Electricity—production: 24.39 billion kWh (2011 est.)
country comparison to the world: 69

Electricity—consumption: 26.27 billion kWh (2010 est.)
country comparison to the world: 64

Electricity—exports: 13.08 billion kWh (2012 est.)
country comparison to the world: 15

Electricity—imports: 13.88 billion kWh (2012 est.)
country comparison to the world: 12

Electricity—installed generating capacity: 7.855 million kW (2010 est.)
country comparison to the world: 65

Electricity—from fossil fuels: 42.2% of total installed capacity (2010 est.)
country comparison to the world: 167

Electricity—from nuclear fuels: 23.2% of total installed capacity (2010 est.)
country comparison to the world: 5

Electricity—from hydroelectric plants: 20.4% of total installed capacity (2010 est.)
country comparison to the world: 91

Electricity—from other renewable sources: 2.6% of total installed capacity (2010 est.)
country comparison to the world: 64

Crude oil—production: 9,277 bbl/day (2012 est.)
country comparison to the world: 92

Crude oil—exports: 262.5 bbl/day (2010 est.)
country comparison to the world: 73

Crude oil—imports: 108,400 bbl/day (2010 est.)
country comparison to the world: 49

Crude oil—proved reserves: 9 million bbl (1 January 2013 es)
country comparison to the world: 92

Refined petroleum products—production: 129,600 bbl/day (2010 est.)
country comparison to the world: 68

Refined petroleum products—consumption: 83,910 bbl/day (2011 est.)
country comparison to the world: 83

Refined petroleum products—exports: 70,520 bbl/day (2010 est.)
country comparison to the world: 55

Refined petroleum products—imports: 28,380 bbl/day (2010 est.)
country comparison to the world: 94

Natural gas—production: 105 million cu m (2012 est.)
country comparison to the world: 82

Natural gas—consumption: 6.468 billion cu m (2011 est.)
country comparison to the world: 56

Natural gas—exports: 45.43 billion cu m (2012 est.)
country comparison to the world: 9

Natural gas—imports: 50.18 billion cu m (2012 est.)
country comparison to the world: 6

Natural gas—proved reserves: 14.16 billion cu m (1 January 2013 es)
country comparison to the world: 80

Carbon dioxide emissions from consumption of energy: 34.88 million Mt (2011 est.)
country comparison to the world: 74

COMMUNICATIONS

Telephones—main lines in use: 975,000 (2012)
country comparison to the world: 77

Telephones—mobile cellular: 6.095 million (2012)
country comparison to the world: 101

Telephone system: *general assessment:* Slovakia has a modern telecommunications system that has expanded dramatically in recent years with the growth in cellular services
domestic: analog system is now receiving digital equipment and is being enlarged with fiber-optic cable, especially in the larger cities; 3 companies provide nationwide cellular services
international: country code—421; 3 international exchanges (1 in Bratislava and 2 in Banska Bystrica) are available; Slovakia is participating in several international telecommunications projects that will increase the availability of external services (2011)

Broadcast media: state-owned public broadcaster, Radio and Television of Slovakia (RTVS), operates 3 national TV stations and multiple national and regional radio networks; roughly 35 privately owned TV stations operating nationally, regionally, and locally; about 40% of households are connected to multi-channel cable or satellite TV; more than 20 privately owned radio stations (2008)

Internet country code: .sk

Internet hosts: 1.384 million (2012)
country comparison to the world: 41

Internet users: 4.063 million (2009)
country comparison to the world: 58

TRANSPORTATION

Airports: 35 (2013)
country comparison to the world: 111

Airports—with paved runways: *total:* 21
over 3,047 m: 2
2,438 to 3,047 m: 2
1,524 to 2,437 m: 3
914 to 1,523 m: 3
under 914 m: 11 (2013)

Airports—with unpaved runways: *total:* 14
914 to 1,523 m: 9
under 914 m: 5 (2013)

Heliports: 1 (2013)

Pipelines: gas 6,774 km; oil 419 km (2013)

Railways: *total:* 3,622 km
country comparison to the world: 49
broad gauge: 99 km 1.520-m gauge
standard gauge: 3,473 km 1.435-m gauge (1,615 km electrified)
narrow gauge: 50 km 1.000-m or 0.750-m gauge (2008)

Roadways: *total:* 43,916 km
country comparison to the world: 83
paved: 38,238 km (includes 417 km of expressways)
unpaved: 5,678 km (2010)

Waterways: 172 km (on Danube River) (2012)
country comparison to the world: 100

Merchant marine: *total:* 11
country comparison to the world: 109
by type: cargo 9, refrigerated cargo 2
foreign-owned: 11 (Germany 3, Ireland 1, Italy 2, Montenegro 1, Slovenia 1, Turkey 1, Ukraine 2) (2010)

Ports and terminals: *river port(s):* Bratislava, Komarno (Danube)

MILITARY

Military branches: Armed Forces of the Slovak Republic (Ozbrojene Sily Slovenskej Republiky): Land Forces (Pozemne Sily), Air Forces (Vzdusne Sily) (2010)

Military service age and obligation: 18-30 years of age for voluntary military service; conscription in peacetime suspended in 2006; women are eligible to serve (2012)

Manpower available for military service:
males age 16-49: 1,405,310
females age 16-49: 1,369,897 (2010 est.)

Manpower fit for military service:
males age 16-49: 1,156,113
females age 16-49: 1,139,380 (2010 est.)

Manpower reaching militarily significant age annually: *male:* 31,646
female: 30,219 (2010 est.)

Military expenditures: 1.12% of GDP (2012)
country comparison to the world: 91
1.1% of GDP (2011)
1.12% of GDP (2010)

TRANSNATIONAL ISSUES

Disputes—international: bilateral government, legal, technical and economic working group negotiations continued in 2006 between Slovakia and Hungary over Hungary's completion of its portion of the Gabcikovo-Nagymaros hydroelectric dam project along the Danube; as a member state that forms part of the EU's external border, Slovakia has implemented the strict Schengen border rules

Refugees and internally displaced persons: *stateless persons:* 1,523 (2013)

Illicit drugs: transshipment point for Southwest Asian heroin bound for Western Europe; producer of synthetic drugs for regional market; consumer of ecstasy

SLOVENIA

INTRODUCTION

Background: The Slovene lands were part of the Austro-Hungarian Empire until the latter's dissolution at the end of World War I. In 1918, the Slovenes joined the Serbs and Croats in forming a new multinational state, which was named Yugoslavia in 1929. After World War II, Slovenia became a republic of the renewed Yugoslavia, which though communist, distanced itself from Moscow's rule. Dissatisfied with the exercise of power by the majority Serbs, the Slovenes succeeded in establishing their independence in 1991 after a short 10-day war. Historical ties to Western Europe, a strong economy, and a stable democracy have assisted in Slovenia's transformation to a modern state. Slovenia acceded to both NATO and the EU in the spring of 2004; it joined the eurozone in 2007.

GEOGRAPHY

Location: south Central Europe, Julian Alps between Austria and Croatia

Geographic coordinates: 46 07 N, 14 49 E

Map references: Europe

Area: *total:* 20,273 sq km
country comparison to the world: 155
land: 20,151 sq km
water: 122 sq km

Area—comparative: slightly smaller than New Jersey

Land boundaries: *total:* 1,086 km
border countries: Austria 330 km, Croatia 455 km, Hungary 102 km, Italy 199 km

Coastline: 46.6 km

Maritime claims: *territorial sea:* 12 nm

Climate: Mediterranean climate on the coast, continental climate with mild to hot summers and cold winters in the plateaus and valleys to the east

Terrain: a short coastal strip on the Adriatic, an alpine mountain region adjacent to Italy and Austria, mixed mountains and valleys with numerous rivers to the east

Elevation extremes: *lowest point:* Adriatic Sea 0 m
highest point: Triglav 2,864 m

Natural resources: lignite coal, lead, zinc, building stone, hydropower, forests

Land use: *arable land:* 8.31%
permanent crops: 1.33%
other: 90.36% (2011)

Irrigated land: 76.04 sq km (2010)

Total renewable water resources: 31.87 cu km (2011)

Freshwater withdrawal (domestic/industrial/agricultural): *total:* 0.94 cu km/yr (18%/82%/0%)
per capita: 462.9 cu m/yr (2009)

Natural hazards: flooding; earthquakes

Environment—current issues: Sava River polluted with domestic and industrial waste; pollution of coastal waters with heavy metals and toxic chemicals; forest damage near Koper from air pollution (originating at metallurgical and chemical plants) and resulting acid rain

Environment—international agreements:
party to: Air Pollution, Air Pollution-Nitrogen Oxides, Air Pollution-Persistent Organic Pollutants, Air Pollution-Sulfur 94, Biodiversity, Climate Change, Climate Change-Kyoto Protocol, Desertification, Endangered Species, Environmental Modification, Hazardous Wastes, Law of the Sea, Marine Dumping, Ozone Layer Protection, Ship Pollution, Wetlands, Whaling
signed, but not ratified: none of the selected agreements

Geography—note: despite its small size, this eastern Alpine country controls some of Europe's major transit routes

PEOPLE AND SOCIETY

Nationality: *noun:* Slovene(s)
adjective: Slovenian

Ethnic groups: Slovene 83.1%, Serb 2%, Croat 1.8%, Bosniak 1.1%, other or unspecified 12% (2002 census)

Languages: Slovenian (official) 91.1%, Serbo-Croatian 4.5%, other or unspecified 4.4%, Italian (official, only in municipalities where Italian national communities reside), Hungarian (official, only in municipalities where Hungarian national communities reside) (2002 census)

Religions: Catholic 57.8%, Muslim 2.4%, Orthodox 2.3%, other Christian 0.9%, unaffiliated 3.5%, other or unspecified 23%, none 10.1% (2002 census)

Population: 1,988,292 (July 2014 est.)
country comparison to the world: 148

Age structure:
0-14 years: 13.4% (male 137,407/female 129,111)
15-24 years: 10% (male 101,754/female 96,973)
25-54 years: 43.9% (male 441,079/female 432,476)
55-64 years: 17.9% (male 145,013/female 148,704)
65 years and over: 17.5% (male 142,954/female 212,821) (2014 est.)

Dependency ratios:
total dependency ratio: 46 %
youth dependency ratio: 20.9 %
elderly dependency ratio: 25.2 %
potential support ratio: 4 (2013)

Median age: *total:* 43.5 years
male: 41.7 years
female: 45.2 years (2014 est.)

Population growth rate: -0.23% (2014 est.)
country comparison to the world: 215

Birth rate: 8.54 births/1,000 population (2014 est.)
country comparison to the world: 217

Death rate: 11.25 deaths/1,000 population (2014 est.)
country comparison to the world: 32

Net migration rate: 0.37 migrant(s)/1,000 population (2014 est.)
country comparison to the world: 73

Urbanization: *urban population:* 50% of total population (2010)
rate of urbanization: 0.2% annual rate of change (2010-15 est.)

Major urban areas—population: LJUBLJANA (capital) 260,000 (2009)

Sex ratio: *at birth:* 1.07 male(s)/female
0-14 years: 1.06 male(s)/female
15-24 years: 1.05 male(s)/female
25-54 years: 1.02 male(s)/female
55-64 years: 0.95 male(s)/female
65 years and over: 0.66 male(s)/female
total population: 0.95 male(s)/female (2014 est.)

Mother's mean age at first birth: 28.7 (2010 est.)

Maternal mortality rate: 12 deaths/100,000 live births (2010)
country comparison to the world: 150

Infant mortality rate: *total:* 4.04 deaths/1,000 live births
country comparison to the world: 198
male: 4.56 deaths/1,000 live births
female: 3.49 deaths/1,000 live births (2014 est.)

Life expectancy at birth: *total population:* 77.83 years
country comparison to the world: 61
male: 74.21 years
female: 81.69 years (2014 est.)

Total fertility rate: 1.33 children born/woman (2014 est.)
country comparison to the world: 213

Contraceptive prevalence rate: 78.9%
note: percent of women aged 15-44 (1994/95)

Health expenditures: 9% of GDP (2010)
country comparison to the world: 43

Physicians density: 2.54 physicians/1,000 population (2010)

Hospital bed density: 4.6 beds/1,000 population (2010)

Drinking water source:
improved:
urban: 99.8% of population
rural: 99.4% of population
total: 99.6% of population
unimproved:
urban: 0.2% of population
rural: 0.6% of population
total: 0.4% of population (2011 est.)

Sanitation facility access:
improved:
urban: 100% of population
rural: 100% of population
total: 100% of population
unimproved:
urban: 0% of population
rural: 0% of population
total: 0% of population (2011 est.)

HIV/AIDS—adult prevalence rate: less than 0.1% (2009 est.)
country comparison to the world: 143

HIV/AIDS—people living with HIV/AIDS: fewer than 1,000 (2009 est.)
country comparison to the world: 145

HIV/AIDS—deaths: fewer than 100 (2009 est.)
country comparison to the world: 151

Obesity—adult prevalence rate: 28.6% (2008)
country comparison to the world: 33

Education expenditures: 5.7% of GDP (2010)
country comparison to the world: 51

Literacy: *definition:* NA
total population: 99.7%
male: 99.7%
female: 99.7% (2011 est.)

School life expectancy (primary to tertiary education): *total:* 17 years
male: 16 years
female: 18 years (2012)

Unemployment, youth ages 15-24: *total:* 20.6%
country comparison to the world: 57
male: 20.3%
female: 21% (2012)

GOVERNMENT

Country name: *conventional long form:* Republic of Slovenia
conventional short form: Slovenia
local long form: Republika Slovenija
local short form: Slovenija
former: People's Republic of Slovenia, Socialist Republic of Slovenia

Government type: parliamentary republic

Capital: *name:* Ljubljana

geographic coordinates: 46 03 N, 14 31 E
time difference: UTC+1 (6 hours ahead of Washington, DC during Standard Time)
daylight saving time: +1hr, begins last Sunday in March; ends last Sunday in October

Administrative divisions: 200 municipalities (obcine, singular—obcina) and 11 urban municipalities (mestne obcine, singular—mestna obcina)
municipalities: Ajdovscina, Apace, Beltinci, Benedikt, Bistrica ob Sotli, Bled, Bloke, Bohinj, Borovnica, Bovec, Braslovce, Brda, Brezice, Brezovica, Cankova, Cerklje na Gorenjskem, Cerknica, Cerkno, Cerkvenjak, Cirkulane, Crensovci, Crna na Koroskem, Crnomelj, Destrnik, Divaca, Dobje, Dobrepolje, Dobrna, Dobrova-Polhov Gradec, Dobrovnik/Dobronak, Dolenjske Toplice, Dol pri Ljubljani, Domzale, Dornava, Dravograd, Duplek, Gorenja Vas-Poljane, Gorisnica, Gorje, Gornja Radgona, Gornji Grad, Gornji Petrovci, Grad, Grosuplje, Hajdina, Hoce-Slivnica, Hodos, Horjul, Hrastnik, Hrpelje-Kozina, Idrija, Ig, Ilirska Bistrica, Ivancna Gorica, Izola/Isola, Jesenice, Jezersko, Jursinci, Kamnik, Kanal, Kidricevo, Kobarid, Kobilje, Kocevje, Komen, Komenda, Kosanjevica na Krki, Kostel, Kozje, Kranjska Gora, Krizevci, Krsko, Kungota, Kuzma, Lasko, Lenart, Lendava/Lendva, Litija, Ljubno, Ljutomer, Log-Dragomer, Logatec, Loska Dolina, Loski Potok, Lovrenc na Pohorju, Luce, Lukovica, Majsperk, Makole, Markovci, Medvode, Menges, Metlika, Mezica, Miklavz na Dravskem Polju, Miren-Kostanjevica, Mirna, Mirna Pec, Mislinja, Mokronog-Trebelno, Moravce, Moravske Toplice, Mozirje, Muta, Naklo, Nazarje, Odranci, Oplotnica, Ormoz, Osilnica, Pesnica, Piran/Pirano, Pivka, Podcetrtek, Podlehnik, Podvelka, Poljcane, Polzela, Postojna, Prebold, Preddvor, Prevalje, Puconci, Race-Fram, Radece, Radenci, Radlje ob Dravi, Radovljica, Ravne na Koroskem, Razkrizje, Recica ob Savinji, Rence-Vogrsko, Ribnica, Ribnica na Pohorju, Rogaska Slatina, Rogasovci, Rogatec, Ruse, Selnica ob Dravi, Semic, Sevnica, Sezana, Slovenska Bistrica, Slovenske Konjice, Sodrazica, Solcava, Sredisce ob Dravi, Starse, Straza, Sveta Ana, Sveta Trojica v Slovenskih Goricah, Sveti Andraz v Slovenskih Goricah, Sveti Jurij ob Scavnici, Sveti Jurij v Slovenskih Goricah, Sveti Tomaz, Salovci, Sempeter-Vrtojba, Sencur, Sentilj, Sentjernej, Sentjur, Sentrupert, Skocjan, Skofja Loka, Skofljica, Smarje pri Jelsah, Smarjeske Toplice, Smartno ob Paki, Smartno pr
urban municipalities: Celje, Koper-Capodistria, Kranj, Ljubljana, Maribor, Murska Sobota, Nova Gorica, Novo Mesto, Ptuj, Slovenj Gradec, Velenje

Independence: 25 June 1991 (from Yugoslavia)

National holiday: Independence Day/Statehood Day, 25 June (1991)

Constitution: previous 1974 (preindependence); latest passed by legislature 23 December 1991; amended several times, last in 2013 (2013)

Legal system: civil law system

International law organization participation: has not submitted an ICJ jurisdiction declaration; accepts ICCt jurisdiction

Suffrage: 18 years of age, 16 if employed; universal

Executive branch: *chief of state:* President Borut PAHOR (since 22 December 2012)
head of government: Prime Minister Alenka BRATUSEK (since 20 March 2013)
cabinet: Council of Ministers nominated by the prime minister and elected by the National Assembly (For more information visit the World Leaders website)
elections: president elected by popular vote for a five-year term (eligible for a second term); election last held on 11 November and a runoff on 2 December 2012 (next presidential election to be held in 2017); following National Assembly elections, the leader of the majority party or the leader of a majority coalition usually nominated to become prime minister by the president and elected by the National Assembly
election results: Borut PAHOR elected president; percent of vote—Borut PAHOR 67.4%, Danilo TURK 32.6%; on February 27, 2013 a no-confidence vote in Parliament resulted in Alenka BRATUSEK becoming prime minister designate; BRATUSEK became prime minister (Slovenia's

first female prime minister) on 20 March 2013 after her cabinet was approved

Legislative branch: bicameral Parliament consists of a National Council or Drzavni Svet (40 seats; members indirectly elected by an electoral college to serve five-year terms; note—this is primarily an advisory body with limited legislative powers; it may propose laws, ask to review any National Assembly decision, and call national referenda) and the National Assembly or Drzavni Zbor (90 seats; 88 members are elected on a proportional basis and 2 are elected by the Italian and Hungarian minorities through a majoritarian, preferential system; members elected by popular vote to serve four-year terms)
elections: National Assembly—last held on 4 December 2011 (next to be held in 2015)
election results: percent of vote by party—PS 28.6%, SDS 26.2%, SD 10.5%, LGV 8.4%, DeSUS 7%, SLS 6.9%, NSi 4.8%, other 7.6%; seats by party—PS 28, SDS 26, SD 10, LGV 8, DeSUS 6, SLS 6, NSi 4, Hungarian minority 1, Italian minority 1

Judicial branch: *highest court(s):* Supreme Court (consists of the court president and 37 judges organized into 7 departments—civil, criminal, commercial, labor and social security, administrative, registry, and international cooperation); Constitutional Court (consists of the court president, vice president, and 7 judges)

judge selection and term of office: Supreme Court president and vice president appointed by the National Assembly upon the proposal of the Minister of Justice based on the opinions of the Judicial Council, an 11-member independent body elected by the National Assembly from proposals submitted by the president, attorneys, law universities, and sitting judges; other Supreme Court judges elected by the National Assembly from candidates proposed by the Judicial Council; Supreme Court judge term NA; Constitutional Court judges appointed by the National Assembly from nominations by the president of the republic; Constitutional Court president selected from among their own for a 3-year term; other judges elected for single 9-year terms
subordinate courts: county, district, regional, and high courts; specialized labor-related and social courts; Court of Audit; Administrative Court

Political parties and leaders: Civic List or DL [Gregor VIRANT] (formerly LGV); Democratic Party of Pensioners of Slovenia or DeSUS [Karl ERJAVEC]; New Slovenia or NSi [Ljudmila NOVAK]; Positive Slovenia or PS [Alenka BRATUSEK (interim)]; Slovene People's Party or SLS [Radovan ZERJAV]; Slovenian Democratic Party or SDS [Janez JANSA]; Social Democrats or SD [Igor LUKSIC] (formerly ZLSD)

Political pressure groups and leaders: Slovenian Roma Association [Jozek Horvat MUC]; various trade and public sector employee unions
other: Catholic Church

International organization participation: Australia Group, BIS, CD, CE, CEI, EAPC, EBRD, ECB, EIB, EMU, ESA (cooperating state), EU, FAO, IADB, IAEA, IBRD, ICAO, ICC (national committees), ICRM, IDA, IFC, IFRCS, IHO, ILO, IMF, IMO, Interpol, IOC, IOM, IPU, ISO, ITU, MIGA, NATO, NEA, NSG, OAS (observer), OECD, OIF (observer), OPCW, OSCE, PCA, Schengen Convention, SELEC, UN, UNCTAD, UNESCO, UNHCR, UNIDO, UNIFIL, UNTSO, UNWTO, UPU, WCO, WHO, WIPO, WMO, WTO, ZC

Diplomatic representation in the US:
chief of mission: Ambassador Bozo CERAR (since 6 September 2013)
chancery: 2410 California Street N.W., Washington, DC 20008
telephone: [1] (202) 386-6601
FAX: [1] (202) 386-6633
consulate(s) general: Cleveland, New York

Diplomatic representation from the US:
chief of mission: Ambassador Joseph A. MUSSOMELI (since 29 October 2010)
embassy: Presernova 31, 1000 Ljubljana
mailing address: American Embassy Ljubljana, US Department of State, 7140 Ljubljana Place, Washington, DC 20521-7140
telephone: [386] (1) 200-5500
FAX: [386] (1) 200-5555

Flag description: three equal horizontal bands of white (top), blue, and red, derive from the medieval coat of arms of the Duchy of Carniola; the Slovenian seal (a shield with the image of Triglav, Slovenia's highest peak, in white against a blue background at the center; beneath it are two wavy blue lines depicting seas and rivers, and above it are three six-pointed stars arranged in an inverted triangle, which are taken from the coat of arms of the Counts of Celje, the great Slovene dynastic house of the late 14th and early 15th centuries) appears in the upper hoist side of the flag centered on the white and blue bands

National symbol(s): Mount Triglav

National anthem: *name:* "Zdravljica" (A Toast)
lyrics/music: France PRESEREN/Stanko PREMRL
note: adopted 1989; the anthem was originally written in 1848; the full poem, whose seventh verse is used as the anthem, speaks of pan-Slavic nationalism

ECONOMY

Economy—overview: With excellent infrastructure, a well-educated work force, and a strategic location between the Balkans and Western Europe, Slovenia has one of the highest per capita GDPs in Central Europe. Slovenia became the first 2004 European Union entrant to adopt the euro (on 1 January 2007) and has experienced one of the most stable political transitions in Central and Southeastern Europe. In March 2004, Slovenia became the first transition country to graduate from borrower status to donor partner at the World Bank. In 2007, Slovenia was invited to begin the process for joining the OECD; it became a member in 2012. However, long-delayed privatizations, particularly within Slovenia's largely state-owned and increasingly indebted banking sector, have fueled investor concerns since 2012 that the country would need EU-IMF financial assistance. In 2013, the European Commission granted Slovenia permission to begin recapitalizing ailing lenders and transferring their nonperforming assets into a "bad bank" established to restore bank balance sheets. Yield-seeking bond investors' strong demand for Slovenian debt helped the government in 2013 to continue to finance itself independently on international markets. The government has embarked on a program of state asset sales intended to bolster investor confidence in the economy, which in 2014 is poised to contract 1%, its third-year of recession.

GDP (purchasing power parity): $56.5 billion (2013 est.)
country comparison to the world: 93
$58 billion (2012 est.)
$59.52 billion (2011 est.)
note: data are in 2013 US dollars

GDP (official exchange rate): $46.82 billion (2013 est.)

GDP—real growth rate: -2.6% (2013 est.)
country comparison to the world: 212
-2.5% (2012 est.)
0.7% (2011 est.)

GDP—per capita (PPP): $27,400 (2013 est.)
country comparison to the world: 55
$28,200 (2012 est.)
$29,000 (2011 est.)
note: data are in 2013 US dollars

Gross national saving: 18.1% of GDP (2013 est.)
country comparison to the world: 88
19.8% of GDP (2012 est.)
20.1% of GDP (2011 est.)

GDP—composition, by end use:
household consumption: 58.4%
government consumption: 21.2%
investment in fixed capital: 17.7%
investment in inventories: -5.2%
exports of goods and services: 81.1%
imports of goods and services: -73.2% (2013 est.)

GDP—composition, by sector of origin:
agriculture: 2.8%
industry: 28.9%
services: 68.3% (2013 est.)

Agriculture—products: potatoes, hops, wheat, sugar beets, corn, grapes; cattle, sheep, poultry

Industries: ferrous metallurgy and aluminum products, lead and zinc smelting; electronics (including military electronics), trucks, automobiles, electric power equipment, wood products, textiles, chemicals, machine tools

Industrial production growth rate: 1.5% (2013 est.)
country comparison to the world: 136

Labor force: 923,200 (2013 est.)
country comparison to the world: 147

Labor force—by occupation: *agriculture:* 2.2%
industry: 35%
services: 62.8% (2009)

Unemployment rate: 12.4% (2013 est.)
country comparison to the world: 127
12% (2012 est.)

Population below poverty line: 13.6% (2011)

Household income or consumption by percentage share: *lowest 10%:* 3.9%
highest 10%: 19.8% (2011)

Distribution of family income—Gini index: 23.8 (2011)
country comparison to the world: 138
23.8 (2004)

Budget: *revenues:* $19.1 billion
expenditures: $21.44 billion (2013 est.)

Taxes and other revenues: 40.8% of GDP (2013 est.)
country comparison to the world: 34

Budget surplus (+) or deficit (-):
-5% of GDP (2013 est.)
country comparison to the world: 169

Public debt: 58.8% of GDP (2013 est.)
country comparison to the world: 51
47.6% of GDP (2012 est.)
note: defined by the EU's Maastricht Treaty as consolidated general government gross debt at

nominal value, outstanding at the end of the year in the following categories of government liabilities: currency and deposits, securities other than shares excluding financial derivatives, and loans; general government sector
comprises the subsectors: central government, state government, local government, and social security funds

Fiscal year: calendar year

Inflation rate (consumer prices): 2.1% (2013 est.)
country comparison to the world: 72
2.6% (2012 est.)

Central bank discount rate: 0.75% (31 December 2013)
country comparison to the world: 128
1.5% (31 December 2012)

note: this is the European Central Bank's rate on the marginal lending facility, which offers overnight credit to banks in the euro area

Commercial bank prime lending rate: 5.7% (31 December 2013 est.)
country comparison to the world: 142
5.73% (31 December 2012 est.)

Stock of narrow money: $11.83 billion (31 December 2013 est.)
country comparison to the world: 74
$16.12 billion (31 December 2010 est.)
note: see entry for the European Union for money supply in the euro area; the European Central Bank (ECB) controls monetary policy for the 17 members of the Economic and Monetary Union (EMU); individual members of the EMU do not control the quantity of money circulating within their own borders

Stock of broad money: $25.4 billion (31 December 2013 est.)
country comparison to the world: 77
$25.37 billion (31 December 2012 est.)

Stock of domestic credit: $42.41 billion (31 December 2013 est.)
country comparison to the world: 63
$46.2 billion (31 December 2012 est.)

Market value of publicly traded shares: $6.475 billion (31 December 2012 est.)
country comparison to the world: 79
$6.326 billion (31 December 2011)
$9.428 billion (31 December 2010 est.)

Current account balance: $1.977 billion (2013 est.)
country comparison to the world: 41
$1.491 billion (2012 est.)

Exports: $28.29 billion (2013 est.)
country comparison to the world: 66
$27.81 billion (2012 est.)

Exports—commodities: manufactured goods, machinery and transport equipment, chemicals, food

Exports—partners: Germany 20%, Italy 12%, Austria 7.9%, Croatia 6.2%, France 4.8%, Russia 4.6% (2012)

Imports: $28.02 billion (2013 est.)
country comparison to the world: 68
$27.95 billion (2012 est.)

Imports—commodities: machinery and transport equipment, manufactured goods, chemicals, fuels and lubricants, food

Imports—partners: Italy 16.5%, Germany 16.3%, Austria 10.4%, Croatia 4.8%, Hungary 4% (2012)

Reserves of foreign exchange and gold: $993.7 million (31 December 2013 est.)
country comparison to the world: 135
$951.9 million (31 December 2012 est.)

Debt—external: $53.9 billion (31 December 2012 est.)
country comparison to the world: 60
$52.07 billion (31 December 2011)

Stock of direct foreign investment—at home: $17.96 billion (31 December 2013 est.)
country comparison to the world: 73
$16.96 billion (31 December 2012 est.)

Stock of direct foreign investment—abroad: $9.378 billion (31 December 2013 est.)
country comparison to the world: 55
$8.878 billion (31 December 2012 est.)

Exchange rates: euros (EUR) per US dollar—
0.7634 (2013 est.)
0.7752 (2012 est.)
0.755 (2010 est.)
0.7198 (2009 est.)
0.6827 (2008 est.)

ENERGY

Electricity—production: 15.17 billion kWh (2011 est.)
country comparison to the world: 80

Electricity—consumption: 12.6 billion kWh (2010 est.)
country comparison to the world: 86

Electricity—exports: 5.915 billion kWh (2012 est.)
country comparison to the world: 25

Electricity—imports: 5.002 billion kWh (2012 est.)
country comparison to the world: 37

Electricity—installed generating capacity: 3.193 million kW (2010 est.)
country comparison to the world: 85

Electricity—from fossil fuels: 38% of total installed capacity (2010 est.)
country comparison to the world: 171

Electricity—from nuclear fuels: 20.9% of total installed capacity (2010 est.)
country comparison to the world: 7

Electricity—from hydroelectric plants: 33.6% of total installed capacity (2010 est.)
country comparison to the world: 66

Electricity—from other renewable sources: 1.9% of total installed capacity (2010 est.)
country comparison to the world: 71

Crude oil—production: 305 bbl/day (2012 est.)
country comparison to the world: 115

Crude oil—exports: 0 bbl/day (2010 est.)
country comparison to the world: 180

Crude oil—imports: 0 bbl/day (2010 est.)
country comparison to the world: 119

Crude oil—proved reserves: 0 bbl (1 January 2013 es)
country comparison to the world: 186

Refined petroleum products—production: 0 bbl/day (2010 est.)
country comparison to the world: 193

Refined petroleum products—consumption: 52,930 bbl/day (2011 est.)
country comparison to the world: 96

Refined petroleum products—exports: 14,210 bbl/day (2010 est.)
country comparison to the world: 80

Refined petroleum products—imports: 68,320 bbl/day (2010 est.)
country comparison to the world: 60

Natural gas—production: 2 million cu m (2011 est.)
country comparison to the world: 95

Natural gas—consumption: 1.06 billion cu m (2010 est.)
country comparison to the world: 88

Natural gas—exports: 1.181 billion cu m (2012 est.)
country comparison to the world: 44

Natural gas—imports: 2.07 billion cu m (2012 est.)
country comparison to the world: 48

Natural gas—proved reserves: NA cu m (1 January 2013 es)

Carbon dioxide emissions from consumption of energy: 15.83 million Mt (2011 est.)
country comparison to the world: 92

COMMUNICATIONS

Telephones—main lines in use: 825,000 (8012)
country comparison to the world: 84

Telephones—mobile cellular: 2.246 million (2012)
country comparison to the world: 141

Telephone system: *general assessment:* well-developed telecommunications infrastructure
domestic: combined fixed-line and mobile-cellular teledensity roughly 150 telephones per 100 persons
international: country code—386 (2011)

Broadcast media: public TV broadcaster, Radiotelevizija Slovenija (RTV), operates a system of national and regional TV stations; 35 domestic commercial TV stations operating nationally, regionally, and locally; about 60% of households are connected to multi-channel cable TV; public radio broadcaster operates 3 national and 4 regional stations; more than 75 regional and local commercial and non-commercial radio stations (2007)

Internet country code: .si

Internet hosts: 415,581 (2012)
country comparison to the world: 54

Internet users: 1.298 million (2009)
country comparison to the world: 92

TRANSPORTATION

Airports: 16 (2013)
country comparison to the world: 143

Airports—with paved runways: *total:* 7
over 3,047 m: 1
2,438 to 3,047 m: 1
1,524 to 2,437 m: 1
914 to 1,523 m: 3
under 914 m: 1 (2013)

Airports—with unpaved runways: *total:* 9
1,524 to 2,437 m: 1
914 to 1,523 m: 3
under 914 m: 5 (2013)

Pipelines: gas 844 km; oil 5 km (2013)

Railways: *total:* 1,228 km
country comparison to the world: 84
standard gauge: 1,228 km 1.435-m gauge (503 km electrified) (2007)

Roadways: *total:* 38,985 km
country comparison to the world: 91

paved: 38,985 km (includes 769 km of expressways) (2012)

Waterways: (there is some transport on the Drava River) (2012)

Merchant marine: *registered in other countries:* 24 (Cyprus 5, Liberia 7, Malta 4, Marshall Islands 6, Saint Vincent and the Grenadines 1, Slovakia 1) (2010)
country comparison to the world: 90

Ports and terminals: *major seaport(s):* Koper

MILITARY

Military branches: Slovenian Armed Forces (Slovenska Vojska, SV): Forces Command (with ground units, naval element, air and air defense brigade); Administration for Civil Protection and Disaster Relief (ACPDR) (2013)

Military service age and obligation: 18-25 years of age for voluntary military service; conscription abolished in 2003 (2012)

Manpower available for military service:
males age 16-49: 477,592
females age 16-49: 464,301 (2010 est.)

Manpower fit for military service:
males age 16-49: 392,075
females age 16-49: 380,077 (2010 est.)

Manpower reaching militarily significant age annually: *male:* 9,818
female: 9,395 (2010 est.)

Military expenditures: 1.18% of GDP (2012)
country comparison to the world: 88
1.32% of GDP (2011)
1.18% of GDP (2010)

TRANSNATIONAL ISSUES

Disputes—international: since the breakup of Yugoslavia in the early 1990s, Croatia and Slovenia have each claimed sovereignty over Pirin Bay and four villages, and Slovenia has objected to Croatia's claim of an exclusive economic zone in the Adriatic Sea; in 2009, however Croatia and Slovenia signed a binding international arbitration agreement to define their disputed land and maritime borders, which led to Slovenia lifting its objections to Croatia joining the EU; Slovenia continues to impose a hard border Schengen regime with Croatia, which joined the EU in 2013 but has not yet fulfilled Schengen requirements; as a member state that forms part of the EU's external border, Slovenia has implemented the strict Schengen border rules to curb illegal migration and commerce through southeastern Europe while encouraging close cross-border ties with Croatia

Illicit drugs: minor transit point for cocaine and Southwest Asian heroin bound for Western Europe, and for precursor chemicals

SOLOMON ISLANDS

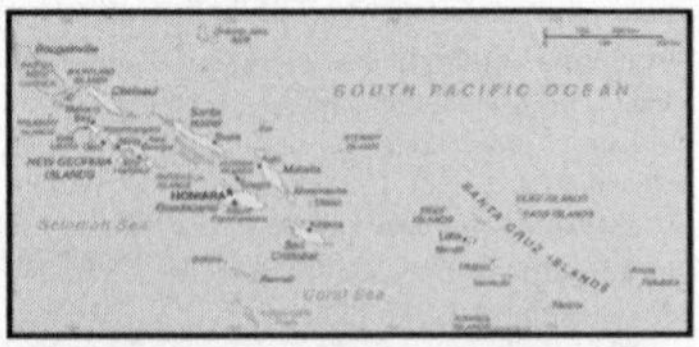

INTRODUCTION

Background: The UK established a protectorate over the Solomon Islands in the 1890s. Some of the most bitter fighting of World War II occurred on this archipelago. Self-government was achieved in 1976 and independence two years later. Ethnic violence, government malfeasance, and endemic crime have undermined stability and civil society. In June 2003, then Prime Minister Sir Allan KEMAKEZA sought the assistance of Australia in reestablishing law and order; the following month, an Australian-led multinational force arrived to restore peace and disarm ethnic militias. The Regional Assistance Mission to the Solomon Islands (RAMSI) has generally been effective in restoring law and order and rebuilding government institutions.

GEOGRAPHY

Location: Oceania, group of islands in the South Pacific Ocean, east of Papua New Guinea

Geographic coordinates: 8 00 S, 159 00 E

Map references: Oceania

Area: *total:* 28,896 sq km
country comparison to the world: **144**
land: 27,986 sq km
water: 910 sq km

Area—comparative: slightly smaller than Maryland

Land boundaries: 0 km

Coastline: 5,313 km

Maritime claims: measured from claimed archipelagic baselines
territorial sea: 12 nm
exclusive economic zone: 200 nm
continental shelf: 200 nm

Climate: tropical monsoon; few extremes of temperature and weather

Terrain: mostly rugged mountains with some low coral atolls

Elevation extremes: *lowest point:* Pacific Ocean 0 m
highest point: Mount Popomanaseu 2,310 m

Natural resources: fish, forests, gold, bauxite, phosphates, lead, zinc, nickel

Land use: *arable land:* 0.62%
permanent crops: 2.25%
other: 97.13% (2011)

Irrigated land: NA

Total renewable water resources: 44.7 cu km (2011)

Natural hazards: typhoons, but rarely destructive; geologically active region with frequent earthquakes, tremors, and volcanic activity; tsunamis
volcanism: Tinakula (elev. 851 m) has frequent eruption activity, while an eruption of Savo (elev. 485 m) could affect the capital Honiara on nearby Guadalcanal

Environment—current issues: deforestation; soil erosion; many of the surrounding coral reefs are dead or dying

Environment—international agreements: party to: Biodiversity, Climate Change, Climate Change-Kyoto Protocol, Desertification, Environmental Modification, Law of the Sea, Marine Dumping, Marine Life Conservation, Ozone Layer Protection, Whaling
signed, but not ratified: none of the selected agreements

Geography—note: strategic location on sea routes between the South Pacific Ocean, the Solomon Sea, and the Coral Sea; on 2 April 2007 an undersea earthquake measuring 8.1 on the Richter scale occurred 345 km WNW of the capital Honiara; the resulting tsunami devastated coastal areas of Western and Choiseul provinces with dozens of deaths and thousands dislocated; the provincial capital of Gizo was especially hard hit

PEOPLE AND SOCIETY

Nationality: *noun:* Solomon Islander(s)
adjective: Solomon Islander

Ethnic groups: Melanesian 95.3%, Polynesian 3.1%, Micronesian 1.2%, other 0.3% (2009 est.)

Languages: Melanesian pidgin (in much of the country is lingua franca), English (official but spoken by only 1%-2% of the population), 120 indigenous languages

Religions: Protestant 73.4% (Church of Melanesia 31.9%, South Sea Evangelical 17.1%, Seventh Day Adventist 11.7%, United Church 10.1%, Christian Fellowship Church 2.5%), Roman Catholic 19.6%, other Christian 2.9%, other 1.3%, unspecified 0.1%, none 0.03% (2009 est.)

Population: 609,883 (July 2014 est.)
country comparison to the world: 169

Age structure:
0-14 years: 36.2% (male 113,744/female 107,193)
15-24 years: 20% (male 62,656/female 59,280)
25-54 years: 35.4% (male 109,891/female 105,760)
55-64 years: 4.1% (male 13,197/female 13,359)
65 years and over: 4% (male 11,952/female 12,851) (2014 est.)

Dependency ratios:
total dependency ratio: 77.1 %
youth dependency ratio: 71.2 %
elderly dependency ratio: 6 %
potential support ratio: 16.8 (2013)

Median age: *total:* 21.6 years
male: 21.4 years
female: 21.8 years (2014 est.)

Population growth rate: 2.07% (2014 est.)
country comparison to the world: 48

Birth rate: 26.33 births/1,000 population (2014 est.)
country comparison to the world: 48

Death rate: 3.86 deaths/1,000 population (2014 est.)
country comparison to the world: 211

Net migration rate: -1.78 migrant(s)/1,000 population (2014 est.)
country comparison to the world: 162
Urbanization: urban population: 19% of total population (2010)
rate of urbanization: 4.2% annual rate of change (2010-15 est.)

Major urban areas—population: HONIARA (capital) 72,000 (2009)
Sex ratio: *at birth:* 1.05 male(s)/female
0-14 years: 1.06 male(s)/female
15-24 years: 1.06 male(s)/female
25-54 years: 1.04 male(s)/female
55-64 years: 1.04 male(s)/female
65 years and over: 0.95 male(s)/female
total population: 1.04 male(s)/female (2014 est.)
Maternal mortality rate: 93 deaths/100,000 live births (2010)
country comparison to the world: 77
Infant mortality rate: *total:* 16.17 deaths/1,000 live births
country comparison to the world: 102
male: 18.43 deaths/1,000 live births
female: 13.8 deaths/1,000 live births (2014 est.)
Life expectancy at birth: *total population:* 74.89 years
country comparison to the world: 105
male: 72.27 years
female: 77.64 years (2014 est.)
Total fertility rate: 3.36 children born/woman (2014 est.)
country comparison to the world: 47
Contraceptive prevalence rate: 34.6% (2006/07)
Health expenditures: 8.8% of GDP (2011)
country comparison to the world: 49
Physicians density: 0.22 physicians/1,000 population (2009)
Hospital bed density: 1.4 beds/1,000 population (2005)
Drinking water source:
improved:
urban: 93% of population
rural: 75.7% of population
total: 79.3% of population
unimproved:
urban: 7% of population
rural: 24.3% of population
total: 20.7% of population (2011 est.)
Sanitation facility access:
improved:
urban: 81.4% of population
rural: 15% of population
total: 28.5% of population
unimproved:
urban: 18.6% of population
rural: 85% of population
total: 71.5% of population (2011 est.)
HIV/AIDS—adult prevalence rate: NA
HIV/AIDS—people living with HIV/AIDS: NA
HIV/AIDS—deaths: NA
Obesity—adult prevalence rate: 30% (2008)
country comparison to the world: 27
Children under the age of 5 years underweight: 11.5% (2007)
country comparison to the world: 64
Education expenditures: 7.3% of GDP (2010)
country comparison to the world: 18
Literacy: *definition:* age 15 and over can read and write
total population: 84.1%
male: 88.9%
female: 79.2%
School life expectancy (primary to tertiary education): *total:* 9 years
male: 10 years
female: 9 years (2007)

GOVERNMENT

Country name: *conventional long form:* none
conventional short form: Solomon Islands
local long form: none
local short form: Solomon Islands
former: British Solomon Islands
Government type: parliamentary democracy and a Commonwealth realm
Capital: *name:* Honiara
geographic coordinates: 9 26 S, 159 57 E
time difference: UTC+11 (16 hours ahead of Washington, DC during Standard Time)
Administrative divisions: 9 provinces and 1 capital territory*; Central, Choiseul, Guadalcanal, Honiara*, Isabel, Makira, Malaita, Rennell and Bellona, Temotu, Western
Independence: 7 July 1978 (from the UK)
National holiday: Independence Day, 7 July (1978)
Constitution: adopted 31 May 1978, effective 7 July 1978; amended several times, last in 2010 (2012)
Legal system: mixed legal system of English common law and customary law
International law organization participation: has not submitted an ICJ jurisdiction declaration; non-party state to the ICCt
Suffrage: 21 years of age; universal
Executive branch: *chief of state:* Queen ELIZABETH II (since 6 February 1952); represented by Governor General Frank KABUI (since 7 July 2009)
head of government: Prime Minister Gordon Darcy LILO (since 16 November 2011)
cabinet: Cabinet consists of 20 members appointed by the governor general on the advice of the prime minister from among the members of parliament (For more information visit the World Leaders website)
elections: the monarchy is hereditary; governor general appointed by the monarch on the advice of parliament for up to five years (eligible for a second term); following legislative elections, the leader of the majority party or the leader of a majority coalition usually elected prime minister by parliament; deputy prime minister appointed by the governor general on the advice of the prime minister from among the members of parliament; Gordon Darcy LILO elected on 16 November 2011
Legislative branch: unicameral National Parliament (50 seats; members elected from single-member constituencies by popular vote to serve four-year terms) elections: last held on 4 August 2010 (next to be held in 2014)
election results: percent of vote by party—NA; seats by party—SIDP 14, OUR 4, SIPRA 3, RDP 3, IDP 2, DDP 2, PCP 1, PFP 1, RUPP 1, SILP 1, SINP 1, independents 17
Judicial branch: *highest court(s):* Court of Appeal (consists of the court president, and ex officio members to include the High Court chief justice and its puisne judges); High Court (consists of the chief justice and puisne judges as prescribed by the National Parliament)
judge selection and term of office: Court of Appeal and High Court president, chief justices, and puisne judges appointed by the governor-general upon recommendation of the Judicial and Legal Service Commission, chaired by the chief justice to include 5 members, mostly judicial officials and legal professionals; all judges appointed until retirement at age 60
subordinate courts: Magistrates' Courts; local courts; Customary Land Appeal Court
Political parties and leaders: Direct Development Party or DDP [Dick HA'AMORI]; Independent Democratic Party or IDP [Snyder RINI]; People's Alliance Party or PAP [James MEKAB]; People's Congress Party or PCP [Fred FONO]; People's Federation Party or PFP [Rudolf DORA]; Ownership, Unity, and Responsibility Party or OUR [Manasseh SOGAVARE]; Reform Democratic Party or RDP [Danny PHILIP]; Rural and Urban Political Party or RUPP [Samuel MANETOALI]; Solomon Islands Democratic Party or SIDP [Steve ABANA]; Solomon Islands Liberal Party or SILP [Derek SIKUA]; Solomon Islands National Party or SINP [Francis HILLY]; Solomon Islands Party for Rural Advancement or SIPRA [Job D. TAUSINGA]; United Party [Sir Peter KENILOREA]
note: in general, Solomon Islands politics is characterized by fluid coalitions
Political pressure groups and leaders: Isatabu Freedom Movement (IFM); Malaita Eagle Force (MEF)
note: these rival armed ethnic factions crippled the Solomon Islands in a wave of violence from 1999 to 2003
International organization participation: ACP, ADB, AOSIS, C, EITI (candidate country), ESCAP, FAO, G-77, IBRD, ICAO, ICRM, IDA, IFAD, IFC, IFRCS, ILO, IMF, IMO, IOC, ITU, MIGA, OPCW, PIF, Sparteca, SPC, UN, UNCTAD, UNESCO, UPU, WFTU, WHO, WMO, WTO
Diplomatic representation in the US:
chief of mission: Ambassador Collin David BECK (since 31 March 2004)
chancery: 800 Second Avenue, Suite 400L, New York, NY 10017
telephone: [1] (212) 599-6192, 6193
FAX: [1] (212) 661-8925
Diplomatic representation from the US: the US does not have an embassy in the Solomon Islands; the US ambassador to Papua New Guinea, currently Ambassador Walter E. North, is accredited to the Solomon Islands
Flag description: divided diagonally by a thin yellow stripe from the lower hoist-side corner; the upper triangle (hoist side) is blue with five white five-pointed stars arranged in an X pattern; the lower triangle is green; blue represents the ocean; green the land; and yellow sunshine; the five stars stand for the five main island groups of the Solomon Islands
National anthem: *name:* "God Save Our Solomon Islands"
lyrics/music: Panapasa BALEKANA and Matila BALEKANA/Panapasa BALEKANA
note: adopted 1978

ECONOMY

Economy—overview: The bulk of the population depends on agriculture, fishing, and forestry for at least part of its livelihood. Most manufactured goods and petroleum products must be imported. The islands are rich in undeveloped mineral resources such as lead, zinc, nickel, and gold. Prior to the arrival of The Regional Assistance Mission to the Solomon Islands (RAMSI), severe ethnic violence, the closing of key businesses, and an empty government treasury culminated in economic collapse. RAMSI's efforts to restore law and order and economic stability have led to modest growth as the economy rebuilds.
GDP (purchasing power parity): $1.958 billion (2013 est.)
country comparison to the world: 194
$1.883 billion (2012 est.)
$1.798 billion (2011 est.)
note: data are in 2013 US dollars
GDP (official exchange rate): $1.099 billion (2013 est.)

GDP—real growth rate: 4% (2013 est.)
country comparison to the world: 80
4.8% (2012 est.)
10.7% (2011 est.)

GDP—per capita (PPP): $3,400 (2013 est.)
country comparison to the world: 175
$3,300 (2012 est.)
$3,300 (2011 est.)
note: data are in 2013 US dollars

GDP—composition, by sector of origin:
agriculture: 50%
industry: 10.6%
services: 39.4% (2013 est.)

Agriculture—products: cocoa, coconuts, palm kernels, rice, potatoes, vegetables, fruit; cattle, pigs; fish; timber

Industries: fish (tuna), mining, timber

Industrial production growth rate: 14%
country comparison to the world: 3

Labor force: 202,500 (2007)
country comparison to the world: **170**

Labor force—by occupation: *agriculture:* 75%
industry: 5%
services: 20% (2000 est.)

Unemployment rate: NA%

Population below poverty line: NA%

Household income or consumption by percentage share: *lowest 10%:* NA%
highest 10%: NA%

Budget: *revenues:* $437.3 million
expenditures: $409.9 million (2013 est.)

Taxes and other revenues: 39.8% of GDP (2013 est.)
country comparison to the world: 44

Budget surplus (+) or deficit (-):
2.5% of GDP (2013 est.)
country comparison to the world: 14

Fiscal year: calendar year

Inflation rate (consumer prices): 2.6% (2012 est.)
country comparison to the world: 98
2.6% (2012 est.)

Commercial bank prime lending rate: 11.2% (31 December 2013 est.)
country comparison to the world: 75
11.28% (31 December 2012 est.)

Stock of narrow money: $335.3 million (31 December 2013 est.)
country comparison to the world: 168
$326.3 million (31 December 2012 est.)

Stock of broad money: $417.9 million (31 December 2013 est.)
country comparison to the world: 181
$417.4 million (31 December 2012 est.)

Stock of domestic credit: $41.38 million (31 December 2013 est.)
country comparison to the world: 179
$37.73 million (31 December 2012 est.)

Current account balance: -$1.2 million (2012 est.)
country comparison to the world: 60
-$60.6 million (2011 est.)

Exports: $493.1 million
country comparison to the world: 175
$415.2 million (2011 est.)

Exports—commodities: timber, fish, copra, palm oil, cocoa

Exports—partners: China 50.8%, Australia 17.5% (2012)

Imports: $446 million (2012 est.)
country comparison to the world: 192
$446 million (2012 est.)

Imports—commodities: food, plant and equipment, manufactured goods, fuels, chemicals

Imports—partners: Singapore 27.2%, Australia 25.7%, China 7.1%, NZ 4.9%, Malaysia 4.8% (2012)

Debt—external: $255.5 million (31 December 2011 est.)
country comparison to the world: 185
$166 million (2004)

Exchange rates: Solomon Islands dollars (SBD) per US dollar—
7.318 (2013 est.)
7.3552 (2012 est.)
8.0645 (2010 est.)

ENERGY

Electricity—production: 82 million kWh (2010 est.)
country comparison to the world: 202

Electricity—consumption: 76.26 million kWh (2010 est.)
country comparison to the world: 201

Electricity—exports: 0 kWh (2012 est.)
country comparison to the world: 110

Electricity—imports: 0 kWh (2012 est.)
country comparison to the world: 121

Electricity—installed generating capacity: 36,000 kW (2010 est.)
country comparison to the world: 196

Electricity—from fossil fuels: 100% of total installed capacity (2010 est.)
country comparison to the world: 8

Electricity—from nuclear fuels: 0% of total installed capacity (2010 est.)
country comparison to the world: 55

Electricity—from hydroelectric plants: 0% of total installed capacity (2010 est.)
country comparison to the world: 160

Electricity—from other renewable sources: 0% of total installed capacity (2010 est.)
country comparison to the world: 160

Crude oil—production: 0 bbl/day (2012 est.)
country comparison to the world: 156

Crude oil—exports: 0 bbl/day (2010 est.)
country comparison to the world: 90

Crude oil—imports: 0 bbl/day (2010 est.)
country comparison to the world: 164

Crude oil—proved reserves: 0 bbl (1 January 2013 es)
country comparison to the world: 110

Refined petroleum products—production: 0 bbl/day (2010 est.)
country comparison to the world: 125

Refined petroleum products—consumption: 1,728 bbl/day (2011 est.)
country comparison to the world: 192

Refined petroleum products—exports: 0 bbl/day (2010 est.)
country comparison to the world: 156

Refined petroleum products—imports: 1,463 bbl/day (2010 est.)
country comparison to the world: 187

Natural gas—production: 0 cu m (2011 est.)
country comparison to the world: 107

Natural gas—consumption: 0 cu m (2010 est.)
country comparison to the world: 123

Natural gas—exports: 0 cu m (2011 est.)
country comparison to the world: 70

Natural gas—imports: 0 cu m (2011 est.)
country comparison to the world: 165

Natural gas—proved reserves: 0 cu m (1 January 2013 es)
country comparison to the world: 117

Carbon dioxide emissions from consumption of energy: 203,200 Mt (2011 est.)
country comparison to the world: 194

COMMUNICATIONS

Telephones—main lines in use: 8,060 (2012)
country comparison to the world: 203

Telephones—mobile cellular: 302,100 (2012)
country comparison to the world: 175

Telephone system: *domestic:* mobile-cellular telephone density is about 50 per 100 persons
international: country code—677; satellite earth station—1 Intelsat (Pacific Ocean) (2011)

Broadcast media: Solomon Islands Broadcasting Corporation (SIBC) is the sole TV broadcaster with 1 station; multi-channel pay-TV is available; SIBC operates 2 national radio stations and 2 provincial stations; 2 local commercial radio stations; Radio Australia is available via satellite feed (2009)

Internet country code: .sb

Internet hosts: 4,370 (2012)
country comparison to the world: 148

Internet users: 10,000 (2009)
country comparison to the world: 201

TRANSPORTATION

Airports: 36 (2013)
country comparison to the world: 110

Airports—with paved runways: *total:* 1
1,524 to 2,437 m: 1 (2013)

Airports—with unpaved runways: *total:* 3 5
1,524 to 2,437 m: 1
914 to 1,523 m: 10
under 914 m: 24 (2013)

Heliports: 3 (2013)

Roadways: *total:* 1,390 km
country comparison to the world: 178
paved: 34 km
unpaved: 1,356 km
note: includes 920 km of private plantation roads (2011)

Ports and terminals: *major seaport(s):* Honiara, Malloco Bay, Viru Harbor, Tulaghi

MILITARY

Military branches: no regular military forces; Royal Solomon Islands Police Force (2013)

Manpower available for military service:
males age 16-49: 142,913 (2010 est.)

Manpower fit for military service:
males age 16-49: 118,921
females age 16-49: 118,164 (2010 est.)

Manpower reaching militarily significant age annually: male: 6,483
female: 6,098 (2010 est.)

TRANSNATIONAL ISSUES

Disputes—international: since 2003, the Regional Assistance Mission to Solomon Islands, consisting of police, military, and civilian advisors drawn from 15 countries, has assisted in reestablishing and maintaining civil and political order while reinforcing regional stability and security

Trafficking in persons: current situation: The Solomon Islands is a source and destination country for local and Southeast Asian men and women subjected to forced labor and forced prostitution; women from China, Indonesia, Malaysia, and the Philippines are recruited for legitimate work and upon arrival are forced into prostitution; men from Indonesia and Malaysia recruited to work in the Solomon Islands' mining and logging industries may be subjected to forced labor; local children are forced into prostitution near foreign logging camps, on fishing vessels, and at hotel and other entertainment venues; some local children are also sold by their parents for marriage to foreign workers or put up for "informal adoption" and then find themselves forced into domestic servitude or forced prostitution

tier rating: Tier 2 Watch List—The Solomon Islands does not fully comply with the minimum standards for the elimination of trafficking; however, it is making significant efforts to do so; the government has formed an ad hoc Solomon Islands Trafficking-in-Persons Advisory Committee and established an informal victim assistance referral procedure for law enforcement; the government did not pass the necessary implementing regulations for anti-trafficking legislation enacted in 2012, preventing authorities from using the new law to prosecute alleged traffickers; the government continues to rely on civil society or religious organizations to provide limited services to victims; the Solomon Islands is not a party to the 2000 UN TIP Protocol (2013)

SOMALIA

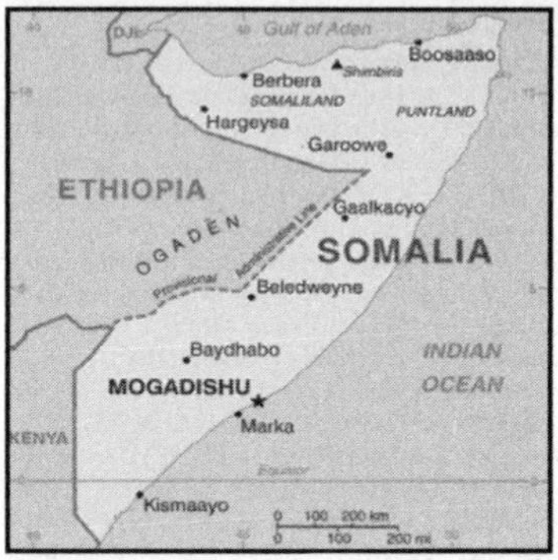

INTRODUCTION

Background: Britain withdrew from British Somaliland in 1960 to allow its protectorate to join with Italian Somaliland and form the new nation of Somalia. In 1969, a coup headed by Mohamed SIAD Barre ushered in an authoritarian socialist rule characterized by the persecution, jailing, and torture of political opponents and dissidents. After the regime's collapse early in 1991, Somalia descended into turmoil, factional fighting, and anarchy. In May 1991, northern clans declared an independent Republic of Somaliland that now includes the administrative regions of Awdal, Woqooyi Galbeed, Togdheer, Sanaag, and Sool. Although not recognized by any government, this entity has maintained a stable existence and continues efforts to establish a constitutional democracy, including holding municipal, parliamentary, and presidential elections. The regions of Bari, Nugaal, and northern Mudug comprise a neighboring semi-autonomous state of Puntland, which has been self-governing since 1998 but does not aim at independence; it has also made strides toward reconstructing a legitimate, representative government but has suffered some civil strife. Puntland disputes its border with Somaliland as it also claims portions of eastern Sool and Sanaag. Beginning in 1993, a two-year UN humanitarian effort (primarily in the south) was able to alleviate famine conditions, but when the UN withdrew in 1995, having suffered significant casualties, order still had not been restored. In 2000, the Somalia National Peace Conference (SNPC) held in Djibouti resulted in the formation of an interim government, known as the Transitional National Government (TNG). When the TNG failed to establish adequate security or governing institutions, the Government of Kenya, under the auspices of the Intergovernmental Authority on Development (IGAD), led a subsequent peace process that concluded in October 2004 with the election of Abdullahi YUSUF Ahmed as President of a second interim government, known as the Transitional Federal Government (TFG) of the Somali Republic. The TFG included a 275-member parliamentary body, known as the Transitional Federal Parliament (TFP). President YUSUF resigned late in 2008 while United Nations-sponsored talks between the TFG and the opposition Alliance for the Re-Liberation of Somalia (ARS) were underway in Djibouti. In January 2009, following the creation of a TFG-ARS unity government, Ethiopian military forces, which had entered Somalia in December 2006 to support the TFG in the face of advances by the opposition Islamic Courts Union (ICU), withdrew from the country. The TFP was doubled in size to 550 seats with the addition of 200 ARS and 75 civil society members of parliament. The expanded parliament elected Sheikh SHARIF Sheikh Ahmed, the former ICU and ARS chairman as president in January 2009. The creation of the TFG was based on the Transitional Federal Charter (TFC), which outlined a five-year mandate leading to the establishment of a new Somali constitution and a transition to a representative government following national elections. In 2009, the TFP amended the TFC to extend TFG's mandate until 2011 and in 2011 Somali principals agreed to institute political transition by August 2012. The transition process ended in September 2012 when clan elders replaced the TFP by appointing 275 members to a new parliament who subsequently elected a new president.

GEOGRAPHY

Location: Eastern Africa, bordering the Gulf of Aden and the Indian Ocean, east of Ethiopia

Geographic coordinates: 10 00 N, 49 00 E

Map references: Africa

Area: *total:* 637,657 sq km
country comparison to the world: 44
land: 627,337 sq km
water: 10,320 sq km

Area—comparative: almost five times the size of Alabama; slightly smaller than Texas

Land boundaries: *total:* 2,340 km
border countries: Djibouti 58 km, Ethiopia 1,600 km, Kenya 682 km

Coastline: 3,025 km

Maritime claims: *territorial sea:* 200 nm

Climate: principally desert; northeast monsoon (December to February), moderate temperatures in north and hot in south; southwest monsoon (May to October), torrid in the north and hot in the south, irregular rainfall, hot and humid periods (tangambili) between monsoons

Terrain: mostly flat to undulating plateau rising to hills in north

Elevation extremes: *lowest point:* Indian Ocean 0 m
highest point: Shimbiris 2,416 m

Natural resources: uranium and largely unexploited reserves of iron ore, tin, gypsum, bauxite, copper, salt, natural gas, likely oil reserves

Land use: *arable land:* 1.73%
permanent crops: 0.05%
other: 98.23% (2011)

Irrigated land: 2,000 sq km (2003)

Total renewable water resources: 14.7 cu km (2011)

Freshwater withdrawal (domestic/industrial/agricultural): *total:* 3.3 cu km/yr (0%/0%/99%)
per capita: 377.6 cu m/yr (2003)

Natural hazards: recurring droughts; frequent dust storms over eastern plains in summer; floods during rainy season

Environment—current issues: famine; use of contaminated water contributes to human health problems; deforestation; overgrazing; soil erosion; desertification

Environment—international agreements:
party to: Biodiversity, Desertification, Endangered Species, Law of the Sea, Ozone Layer Protection
signed, but not ratified: none of the selected agreements

Geography—note: strategic location on Horn of Africa along southern approaches to Bab el Mandeb and route through Red Sea and Suez Canal

PEOPLE AND SOCIETY

Nationality: *noun:* Somali(s)
adjective: Somali

Ethnic groups: Somali 85%, Bantu and other non-Somali 15% (including 30,000 Arabs)

Languages: Somali (official), Arabic (official, according to the Transitional Federal Charter), Italian, English

Religions: Sunni Muslim (Islam) (official, according to the Transitional Federal Charter)

Population: 10,428,043 (July 2014 est.)
country comparison to the world: 85
note: this estimate was derived from an official census taken in 1975 by the Somali Government; population counting in Somalia is complicated by the large number of nomads and by refugee movements in response to famine and clan warfare

Age structure: *0-14 years:* 44% (male 2,293,746/ female 2,298,442)

15-24 years: 18.9% (male 995,102/female 970,630)
25-54 years: 31.2% (male 1,681,705/female 1,571,586)
55-64 years: 2.3% (male 180,622/female 199,059)
65 years and over: 2.3% (male 92,707/female 144,444) (2014 est.)

Dependency ratios:
total dependency ratio: 100.1 %
youth dependency ratio: 94.4 %
elderly dependency ratio: 5.7 %
potential support ratio: 17.7 (2013)

Median age: *total:* 17.7 years
male: 17.9 years
female: 17.6 years (2014 est.)

Population growth rate: 1.75% (2014 est.)
country comparison to the world: 70

Birth rate: 40.87 births/1,000 population (2014 est.)
country comparison to the world: 8

Death rate: 13.91 deaths/1,000 population (2014 est.)
country comparison to the world: 9

Net migration rate: -9.51 migrant(s)/1,000 population (2014 est.)
country comparison to the world: 212

Urbanization: *urban population:* 37.7% of total population (2011)
rate of urbanization: 3.79% annual rate of change (2010-15 est.)

Major urban areas—population: MOGADISHU (capital) 1.353 million (2009)

Sex ratio: *at birth:* 1.03 male(s)/female
0-14 years: 1 male(s)/female
15-24 years: 1.03 male(s)/female
25-54 years: 1.07 male(s)/female
55-64 years: 1.01 male(s)/female
65 years and over: 0.66 male(s)/female
total population: 1.01 male(s)/female (2014 est.)

Maternal mortality rate: 1,000 deaths/100,000 live births (2010)
country comparison to the world: 3

Infant mortality rate: *total:* 100.14 deaths/1,000 live births
country comparison to the world: 3
male: 108.89 deaths/1,000 live births
female: 91.12 deaths/1,000 live births (2014 est.)

Life expectancy at birth: *total population:* 51.58 years
country comparison to the world: 217
male: 49.58 years
female: 53.65 years (2014 est.)

Total fertility rate: 6.08 children born/woman (2014 est.)
country comparison to the world: 4

Contraceptive prevalence rate: 14.6% (2006)

Physicians density: 0.04 physicians/1,000 population (2006)

Drinking water source:
improved:
urban: 66.4% of population
rural: 7.2% of population
total: 29.5% of population
unimproved:
urban: 33.6% of population
rural: 92.8% of population
total: 70.5% of population (2011 est.)

Sanitation facility access:
improved:
urban: 52% of population
rural: 6.3% of population
total: 23.6% of population
unimproved:
urban: 48% of population
rural: 93.7% of population
total: 76.4% of population (2011 est.)

HIV/AIDS—adult prevalence rate: 0.5% (2012 est.)
country comparison to the world: 69

HIV/AIDS—people living with HIV/AIDS: 31,200 (2012 est.)
country comparison to the world: 70

HIV/AIDS—deaths: 2,500 (2012 est.)
country comparison to the world: 55

Major infectious diseases: *degree of risk:* very high
food or waterborne diseases: bacterial and protozoal diarrhea, hepatitis A and E, and typhoid fever
vectorborne diseases: dengue fever, malaria, and Rift Valley fever
water contact disease: schistosomiasis
animal contact disease: rabies (2013)

Obesity—adult prevalence rate: 4.8% (2008)
country comparison to the world: 162

Children under the age of 5 years underweight: 32.8% (2006)
country comparison to the world: 10

Education expenditures: NA

Literacy: *definition:* age 15 and over can read and write
total population: 37.8%
male: 49.7%
female: 25.8% (2001 est.)

Child labor—children ages 5-14:
total number: 1,148,265
percentage: 49 % (2006 est.)

GOVERNMENT

Country name: *conventional long form:* Federal Republic of Somalia
conventional short form: Somalia
local long form: Jamhuuriyadda Federaalkaa Soomaaliya
local short form: Soomaaliya
former: Somali Republic, Somali Democratic Republic

Government type: in the process of building a federal parliamentary republic

Capital: *name:* Mogadishu

geographic coordinates: 2 04 N, 45 20 E
time difference: UTC+3 (8 hours ahead of Washington, DC during Standard Time)

Administrative divisions: 18 regions (plural—NA, singular—gobolka); Awdal, Bakool, Banaadir, Bari, Bay, Galguduud, Gedo, Hiiraan, Jubbada Dhexe (Middle Jubba), Jubbada Hoose (Lower Jubba), Mudug, Nugaal, Sanaag, Shabeellaha Dhexe (Middle Shabeelle), Shabeellaha Hoose (Lower Shabeelle), Sool, Togdheer, Woqooyi Galbeed

Independence: 1 July 1960 (from a merger of British Somaliland that became independent from the UK on 26 June 1960 and Italian Somaliland that became independent from the Italian-administered UN trusteeship on 1 July 1960 to form the Somali Republic)

National holiday: Foundation of the Somali Republic, 1 July (1960); note—26 June (1960) in Somaliland

Constitution: previous 1961, 1979; latest drafted 12 June 2012, approved 1 August 2012 (provisional) (2012)

Legal system: mixed legal system of civil law, Islamic law, and customary law (referred to as Xeer)

International law organization participation: accepts compulsory ICJ jurisdiction with reservations; non-party state to the ICCt

Suffrage: 18 years of age; universal

Executive branch: *chief of state:* President HASSAN SHEIKH Mahamud (since 10 September 2012)
head of government: Prime Minister ABDIWELLI Sheikh Ahmed (since 21 December 2013); Deputy Prime Minister Ridwan HIRSI Mohamed (since 17 January 2014)
cabinet: Cabinet appointed by the prime minister, approved by the National Parliament; note—new cabinet sworn in 22 January 2014 (For more information visit the World Leaders website)
elections: president elected by the National Parliament; election last held 10 September 2012
election results: HASSAN SHEIKH Mahamud elected president; National Parliament vote—HASSAN SHEIKH Mahamud 190, Sheikh SHARIF Sheikh Ahmed 79; the prime minister is chosen by the president and confirmed by the National Parliament

Legislative branch: bicameral National Parliament consisting of the House of the People of the Federal Parliament (275 seats, elected by Somali citizens) and the Upper House of the Federal Parliament (54 seats, elected by people of the federal member states)
note: the inaugural House of the People in September 2012 was appointed by clan elders; as of December 2013, the Upper House has not been formed

Judicial branch: *highest court(s):* the provisional constitution stipulates the establishment of the Constitutional Court (consists of 5 judges including the chief judge and deputy chief judge) note—under the terms of the 2004 Transitional National Charter (TNC), a Supreme Court based in Mogadishu and an Appeal Court were established; yet most regions have reverted to local forms of conflict resolution, either secular, traditional Somali customary law, or sharia Islamic law
judge selection and term of office: judges appointed by the president upon proposal of the Judicial Service Commission, a 9-member judicial and administrative body; judge tenure NA
subordinate courts: federal- and federal member state-level courts; military courts; sharia (Islamic) courts

Political parties and leaders: none

Political pressure groups and leaders:
other: numerous clan and sub-clan factions exist both in support and in opposition to the transitional government

International organization participation: ACP, AfDB, AFESD, AMF, AU, CAEU (candidate), FAO, G-77, IBRD, ICAO, ICRM, IDA, IDB, IFAD, IFC, IFRCS, IGAD, ILO, IMF, IMO, Interpol, IOC, IOM, ITSO, ITU, LAS, NAM, OIC, UN, UNCTAD, UNESCO, UNHCR, UNIDO, UPU, WFTU (NGOs), WHO, WIPO, WMO

Diplomatic representation in the US: Somalia does not have an embassy in the US (ceased operations on 8 May 1991); note—the Somali Government is represented in the US through its Permanent Mission to the UN

Diplomatic representation from the US: the US does not have an embassy in Somalia; US interests are represented by the US Special Representative for Somalia, Ambassador James P. MCANULTY, operating out of the US Embassy in Nairobi, Kenya at United Nations Avenue,
Nairobi; mailing address: Unit 64100, Nairobi; APO AE 09831; telephone: [254] (20) 363-6000; FAX [254] (20) 363-6157

Flag description: light blue with a large white five-pointed star in the center; the blue field was originally influenced by the flag of the UN, but today is said to denote the sky and the neighboring Indian Ocean; the five points of the star represent the five regions in the horn of Africa that are inhabited by Somali people: the former British Somaliland and Italian Somaliland (which together make up Somalia), Djibouti, Ogaden (Ethiopia), and the North East Province (Kenya)

National symbol(s): leopard

National anthem: *name:* "Qolobaa Calankeed" (Every Nation Has its own Flag)
lyrics/music: lyrics/music: Abdullahi QARSHE
note: adopted 2012; written in 1959

Government—note: regional and local governing bodies continue to exist and control various areas of the country, including the self-declared Republic of Somaliland in northwestern Somalia and the semi-autonomous state of Puntland in northeastern Somalia

ECONOMY

Economy—overview: Despite the lack of effective national governance, Somalia maintains an informal economy largely based on livestock, remittance/money transfer companies, and telecommunications. Agriculture is the most important sector with livestock normally accounting for about 40% of GDP and more than 50% of export earnings. Nomads and semi-pastoralists, who are dependent upon livestock for their livelihood, make up a large portion of the population. Livestock, hides, fish, charcoal, and bananas are Somalia's principal exports, while sugar, sorghum, corn, qat, and machined goods are the principal imports. Somalia's small industrial sector, based on the processing of agricultural products, has largely been looted and the machinery sold as scrap metal. Telecommunication firms provide wireless services in most major cities and offer the lowest international call rates on the continent. Mogadishu's main market offers a variety of goods from food to electronic gadgets. Hotels continue to operate and are supported with private-security militias. Somalia's government lacks the ability to collect domestic revenue, and arrears to the IMF have continued to grow. Somalia's capital city—Mogadishu—has witnessed the development of the city's first gas stations, supermarkets, and flights between Europe (Istanbul-Mogadishu) since the collapse of central authority in 1991. This economic growth has yet to expand outside of Mogadishu, and within the city, security concerns dominate business. In the absence of a formal banking sector, money transfer/remittance services have sprouted throughout the country, handling up to $1.6 billion in remittances annually, although international concerns over the money transfers into Somalia currently threatens these services.

GDP (purchasing power parity): $5.896 billion (2010 est.)
country comparison to the world: 165
$5.75 billion (2009 est.)
$5.607 billion (2008 est.)
note: data are in 2010 US dollars

GDP (official exchange rate): $2.372 billion (2010 est.)

GDP—real growth rate: 2.6% (2010 est.)
country comparison to the world: 125
2.6% (2012 est.)
2.6% (2008 est.)

GDP—per capita (PPP): $600 (2010 est.)
country comparison to the world: 227
$600 (2009 est.)
$600 (2008 est.)
note: data are in 2013 US dollars

GDP—composition, by end use:
household consumption: 72.6%
government consumption: 8.7%
investment in fixed capital: 20%
investment in inventories: 0.1% 0.3%
imports of goods and services: -1.7%

GDP—composition, by sector of origin:
agriculture: 59.3%
industry: 7.2%
services: 33.5% (2012 est.)

Agriculture—products: bananas, sorghum, corn, coconuts, rice, sugarcane, mangoes, sesame seeds, beans; cattle, sheep, goats; fish

Industries: a few light industries, including sugar refining, textiles, wireless communication

Industrial production growth rate: NA%

Labor force: 3.447 million (2007)
country comparison to the world: 98

Labor force—by occupation: *agriculture:* 71%
industry and services: 29% (1975)

Unemployment rate: NA%

Population below poverty line: NA%

Household income or consumption by percentage share: *lowest* 10%: NA%
highest 10%: NA%

Budget: *revenues:* $NA
expenditures: $NA

Fiscal year: NA

Inflation rate (consumer prices): NA%
note: businesses print their own money, so inflation rates cannot be easily determined

Central bank discount rate: NA%

Commercial bank prime lending rate: NA%

Exports: $515.8 million (2012 est.)
country comparison to the world: 173
$594.3 million (2011 est.)

Exports—commodities: livestock, bananas, hides, fish, charcoal, scrap metal

Exports—partners: UAE 51.7%, Yemen 18.1%, Oman 13% (2012)

Imports: $1.263 billion (2010 est.)
country comparison to the world: 176
$798 million (2006 est.)

Imports—commodities: manufactures, petroleum products, foodstuffs, construction materials, qat

Imports—partners: Djibouti 27.3%, India 13.2%, Kenya 7.1%, China 6.7%, Pakistan 6.4%, Oman 5.1%, UAE 5%, Yemen 4.4% (2012)

Debt—external: $3.05 billion (31 December 2011 est.)
country comparison to the world: 136
$2.942 billion (31 December 2010 est.)

Exchange rates: Somali shillings (SOS) per US dollar—
1,600 (2012 est.)
31,900 (2011 est.)

ENERGY

Electricity—production: 310 million kWh (2010 est.)
country comparison to the world: 170

Electricity—consumption: 288.3 million kWh (2010 est.)
country comparison to the world: 176

Electricity—exports: 0 kWh (2012 est.)
country comparison to the world: 196

Electricity—imports: 0 kWh (2012 est.)
country comparison to the world: 199

Electricity—installed generating capacity: 80,000 kW (2010 est.)
country comparison to the world: 177

Electricity—from fossil fuels: 100% of total installed capacity (2010 est.)
country comparison to the world: 34

Electricity—from nuclear fuels: 0% of total installed capacity (2010 est.)
country comparison to the world: 179

Electricity—from hydroelectric plants: 0% of total installed capacity (2010 est.)
country comparison to the world: 200

Electricity—from other renewable sources: 0% of total installed capacity (2010 est.)
country comparison to the world: 123

Crude oil—production: 0 bbl/day (2012 est.)
country comparison to the world: 133

Crude oil—exports: 0 bbl/day (2010 est.)
country comparison to the world: 183

Crude oil—imports: 0 bbl/day (2010 est.)
country comparison to the world: 121

Crude oil—proved reserves: 0 bbl (1 January 2013 es)
country comparison to the world: 189

Refined petroleum products—production: 0 bbl/day (2010 est.)
country comparison to the world: 195

Refined petroleum products—consumption: 5,659 bbl/day (2011 est.)
country comparison to the world: 164

Refined petroleum products—exports: 0 bbl/day (2010 est.)
country comparison to the world: 131

Refined petroleum products—imports: 5,399 bbl/day (2010 est.)
country comparison to the world: 147

Natural gas—production: 0 cu m (2011 est.)
country comparison to the world: 191

Natural gas—consumption: 0 cu m (2010 est.)
country comparison to the world: 194

Natural gas—exports: 0 cu m (2011 est.)
country comparison to the world: 183

Natural gas—imports: 0 cu m (2011 est.)
country comparison to the world: 130

Natural gas—proved reserves: 5.663 billion cu m (1 January 2013 es)
country comparison to the world: 91

Carbon dioxide emissions from consumption of energy: 753,400 Mt (2011 est.)
country comparison to the world: 172

COMMUNICATIONS

Telephones—main lines in use: 100,000 (2012)
country comparison to the world: 146

Telephones—mobile cellular: 658,000 (2012)
country comparison to the world: 162

Telephone system: *general assessment*: the public telecommunications system was almost completely destroyed or dismantled during the civil war; private companies offer limited local fixed-line service and private wireless companies offer service in most major cities while charging the lowest international rates on the continent
domestic: local cellular telephone systems have been established in Mogadishu and in several other population centers with one company beginning to provide 3G services in late 2012
international: country code—252; Mogadishu is a landing point for the EASSy fiber-optic submarine cable system linking East Africa with Europe and North America (2010)

Broadcast media: 2 private TV stations rebroadcast Al-Jazeera and CNN; Somaliland has 1 government-operated TV station and Puntland has 1 private TV station; the transitional government operates Radio Mogadishu; 1 SW and roughly 10 private FM radio stations broadcast in Mogadishu; several radio stations operate in central and southern regions; Somaliland has 1 government-operated radio station; Puntland has roughly a half dozen private radio stations; transmissions of at least 2 international broadcasters are available (2007)

Internet country code: .so

Internet hosts: 186 (2012)
country comparison to the world: 202

Internet users: 106,000 (2009)
country comparison to the world: 159

TRANSPORTATION

Airports: 61 (2013)
country comparison to the world: 8 0

Airports—with paved runways: *total*: 6
over 3,047 m: 4
2,438 to 3,047 m: 1
1,524 to 2,437 m: 1 (2013)

Airports—with unpaved runways: *total*: 5 5
over 3,047 m: 1
2,438 to 3,047 m: 5
1,524 to 2,437 m: 20
914 to 1,523 m: 23
under 914 m: 6 (2013)

Roadways: *total*: 22,100 km
country comparison to the world: 105
paved: 2,608 km
unpaved: 19,492 km (2000)

Merchant marine: *total*: 1
country comparison to the world: 148
by type: cargo 1 (2008)

Ports and terminals: *major seaport(s)*: Berbera, Kismaayo

Transportation—note: despite a dramatic drop in the number of attacks in 2012, the International Maritime Bureau continues to report the territorial and offshore waters in the Gulf of Aden and Indian Ocean as a region of significant risk for piracy and armed robbery against ships accounting for 25% of all attacks in 2012; 75 vessels, including commercial shipping and pleasure craft, were attacked or hijacked both at anchor and while underway compared with 237 in 2011; the number of hijackings off the coast of Somalia was reduced to 14 in 2012, down from 28 in 2011; as of April 2013, 77 vessels and 7 hostages were being held for ransom by Somali pirates; the presence of several naval task forces in the Gulf of Aden and additional anti-piracy measures on the part of ship operators, including the use of on-board armed security teams, have reduced piracy incidents in that body of water; in response Somali-based pirates, using hijacked fishing trawlers as "mother ships" to extend their range, shifted operations as far south as the Mozambique Channel, eastward to the vicinity of the Maldives, and northeastward to the Strait of Hormuz

MILITARY

Military branches: National Security Force (NSF): Somali Army (2011)

Military service age and obligation: 18 is the legal minimum age for compulsory and voluntary military service (2012)

Manpower available for military service:
males age 16-49: 2,260,175
females age 16-49: 2,159,293 (2010 est.)

Manpower fit for military service:
males age 16-49: 1,331,894
females age 16-49: 1,357,051 (2010 est.)

Manpower reaching militarily significant age annually: *male*: 101,634
female: 101,072 (2010 est.)

TRANSNATIONAL ISSUES

Disputes—international: Ethiopian forces invaded southern Somalia and routed Islamist Courts from Mogadishu in January 2007; "Somaliland" secessionists provide port facilities in Berbera to landlocked Ethiopia and have established commercial ties with other regional states; "Puntland" and "Somaliland" "governments" seek international support in their secessionist aspirations and overlapping border claims; the undemarcated former British administrative line has little meaning as a political separation to rival clans within Ethiopia's Ogaden and southern Somalia's Oromo region; Kenya works hard to prevent the clan and militia fighting in Somalia from spreading south across the border, which has long been open to nomadic pastoralists

Refugees and internally displaced persons: *IDPs*: 1.1 million (civil war since 1988, clan-based competition for resources; 2011 famine; insecurity because of fighting between al-Shabaab and TFG allied forces) (2012)

SOUTH AFRICA

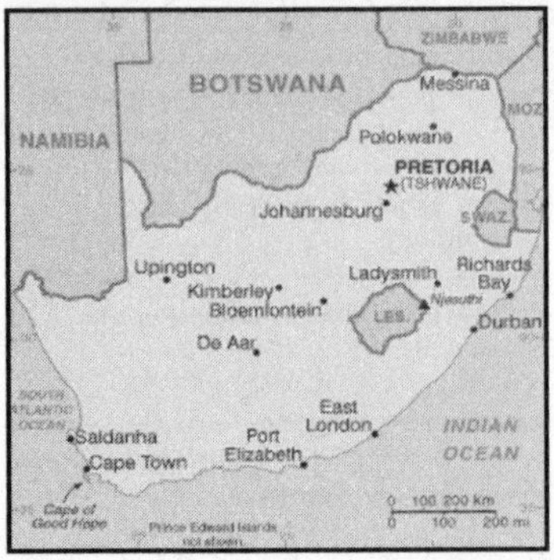

INTRODUCTION

Background: Dutch traders landed at the southern tip of modern day South Africa in 1652 and established a stopover point on the spice route between the Netherlands and the Far East, founding the city of Cape Town. After the British seized the Cape of Good Hope area in 1806, many of the Dutch settlers (the Boers) trekked north to found their own republics. The discovery of diamonds (1867) and gold (1886) spurred wealth and immigration and intensified the subjugation of the native inhabitants. The Boers resisted British encroachments but were defeated in the Second Anglo Boer War (1899-1902); however, the British and the Afrikaners, as the Boers became known, ruled together beginning in 1910 under the Union of South Africa, which became a republic in 1961 after a whites-only referendum. In 1948, the National Party was voted into power and instituted a policy of apartheid—the separate development of the races - which favored the white minority at the expense of the black majority. The African National Congress (ANC) led the opposition to apartheid and many top ANC leaders, such as Nelson MANDELA, spent decades in South Africa's prisons. Internal protests and insurgency, as well as boycotts by some Western nations and institutions, led to the regime's eventual willingness to negotiate a peaceful transition to majority rule. The first multi-racial elections in 1994 brought an end to apartheid and ushered in majority rule under an ANC-led government. South Africa since then has struggled to address apartheid-era imbalances in decent housing, education, and health care. ANC infighting, which has grown in recent years, came to a head in September 2008 when President Thabo MBEKI resigned, and Kgalema MOTLANTHE, the party's General-Secretary, succeeded him as interim president. Jacob ZUMA became president after the ANC won general elections in April 2009. National presidential and parliamentary elections are scheduled for May 2014.

GEOGRAPHY

Location: Southern Africa, at the southern tip of the continent of Africa

Geographic coordinates: 29 00 S, 24 00 E

Map references: Africa

Area: *total:* 1,219,090 sq km
country comparison to the world: 25
land: 1,214,470 sq km
water: 4,620 sq km
note: includes Prince Edward Islands (Marion Island and Prince Edward Island)

Area—comparative: slightly less than twice the size of Texas

Land boundaries: *total:* 4,862 km
border countries: Botswana 1,840 km, Lesotho 909 km, Mozambique 491 km, Namibia 967 km, Swaziland 430 km, Zimbabwe 225 km

Coastline: 2,798 km

Maritime claims: *territorial sea:* 12 nm
contiguous zone: 24 nm
exclusive economic zone: 200 nm
continental shelf: 200 nm or to edge of the continental margin

Climate: mostly semiarid; subtropical along east coast; sunny days, cool nights

Terrain: vast interior plateau rimmed by rugged hills and narrow coastal plain

Elevation extremes: *lowest point:* Atlantic Ocean 0 m
highest point: Njesuthi 3,408 m

Natural resources: gold, chromium, antimony, coal, iron ore, manganese, nickel, phosphates, tin, rare earth elements, uranium, gem diamonds, platinum, copper, vanadium, salt, natural gas

Land use: *arable land:* 9.87%
permanent crops: 0.34%
other: 89.79% (2011)

Irrigated land: 16,700 sq km (2012)

Total renewable water resources: 51.4 cu km (2011)

Freshwater withdrawal (domestic/industrial/agricultural): *total:* 12.5 cu km/yr (36%/7%/57%)
per capita: 271.7 cu m/yr (2005)

Natural hazards: prolonged droughts
volcanism: the volcano forming Marion Island in the Prince Edward Islands, which last erupted in 2004, is South Africa's only active volcano

Environment—current issues: lack of important arterial rivers or lakes requires extensive water conservation and control measures; growth in water usage outpacing supply; pollution of rivers from agricultural runoff and urban discharge; air pollution resulting in acid rain; soil erosion; desertification

Environment—international agreements:
party to: Antarctic-Environmental Protocol, Antarctic-Marine Living Resources, Antarctic Seals, Antarctic Treaty, Biodiversity, Climate Change, Climate Change-Kyoto Protocol, Desertification, Endangered Species, Hazardous Wastes, Law of the Sea, Marine Dumping, Marine Life Conservation, Ozone Layer Protection, Ship Pollution, Wetlands, Whaling
signed, but not ratified: none of the selected agreements

Geography—note: South Africa completely surrounds Lesotho and almost completely surrounds Swaziland

PEOPLE AND SOCIETY

Nationality: *noun:* South African(s)
adjective: South African

Ethnic groups: black African 79.2%, white 8.9%, colored 8.9%, Indian/Asian 2.5%, other 0.5% (2011 est.)

Languages: IsiZulu (official) 22.7%, IsiXhosa (official) 16%, Afrikaans (official) 13.5%, English (official) 9.6%, Sepedi (offcial) 9.1%, Setswana (official) 8%, Sesotho (official) 7.6%, Xitsonga (official) 4.5%, siSwati (official) 2.5%, Tshivenda (official) 2.4%, isiNdebele (official) 2.1%, sign language 0.5%, other 1.6% (2011 est.)

Religions: Protestant 36.6% (Zionist Christian 11.1%, Pentecostal/Charismatic 8.2%, Methodist 6.8%, Dutch Reformed 6.7%, Anglican 3.8%), Catholic 7.1%, Muslim 1.5%, other Christian 36%, other 2.3%, unspecified 1.4%, none 15.1% (2001 census)

Population: 48,375,645 (July 2014 est.)
country comparison to the world: 28
note: Statistics South Africa (the national statistical agency of South Africa) estimates the country's mid-year 2013 total population to be 52,981,991, which takes into account the findings of South Africa's 2011 census; estimates for this country explicitly take into account the effects of excess mortality due to AIDS; this can result in lower life expectancy, higher infant mortality, higher death rates, lower population growth rates, and changes in the distribution of population by age and sex than would otherwise be expected

Age structure: *0-14 years:* 28.3% (male 6,859,518/female 6,815,185)
15-24 years: 20.2% (male 4,914,394/female 4,866,121)
25-54 years: 38.2% (male 9,543,746/female 8,923,605)
55-64 years: 6.3% (male 1,470,282/female 1,950,499)
65 years and over: 6.1% (male 1,205,657/female 1,826,638) (2014 est.)

Dependency ratios:
total dependency ratio: 53.9 %
youth dependency ratio: 45.4 %
elderly dependency ratio: 8.5 %
potential support ratio: 11.7 (2013)

Median age: *total:* 25.7 years
male: 25.4 years
female: 26 years (2014 est.)

Population growth rate: -0.48% (2014 est.)
country comparison to the world: 222

Birth rate: 18.94 births/1,000 population (2014 est.)
country comparison to the world: 93

Death rate: 17.49 deaths/1,000 population (2014 est.)
country comparison to the world: 1

Net migration rate: -6.27 migrant(s)/1,000 population
country comparison to the world: 200
note: there is an increasing flow of Zimbabweans into South Africa and Botswana in search of better economic opportunities (2014 est.)

Urbanization: *urban population:* 62% of total population (2011)
rate of urbanization: 1.21% annual rate of change (2010-15 est.)

Major urban areas—population: Johannesburg 3.607 million; Cape Town 3.353 million; Ekurhuleni (East Rand) 3.144 million; Durban 2.837 million; PRETORIA (capital) 1.404 million (2009)

Sex ratio: *at birth:* 1.02 male(s)/female
0-14 years: 1.01 male(s)/female
15-24 years: 1.01 male(s)/female
25-54 years: 1.07 male(s)/female
55-64 years: 0.98 male(s)/female
65 years and over: 0.67 male(s)/female
total population: 0.99 male(s)/female (2014 est.)

Mother's mean age at first birth: 22.5 (2003 est.)

Maternal mortality rate: 300 deaths/100,000 live births (2010)
country comparison to the world: 38

Infant mortality rate: *total:* 41.61 deaths/1,000 live births
country comparison to the world: 51
male: 45.25 deaths/1,000 live births
female: 37.9 deaths/1,000 live births (2014 est.)

Life expectancy at birth: total population: 49.56 years
country comparison to the world: 222
male: 50.52 years
female: 48.58 years (2014 est.)

Total fertility rate: 2.23 children born/woman (2014 est.)
country comparison to the world: 99

Contraceptive prevalence rate: 59.9% (2003/04)

Health expenditures: 8.5% of GDP (2011)
country comparison to the world: 54

Physicians density: 0.76 physicians/1,000 population (2011)

Hospital bed density: 2.8 beds/1,000 population (2005)

Drinking water source:
improved:
urban: 99% of population
rural: 79.3% of population
total: 91.5% of population
unimproved:
urban: 1% of population
rural: 20.7% of population
total: 8.5% of population (2011 est.)

Sanitation facility access:
improved:
urban: 84.3% of population
rural: 57.1% of population
total: 74% of population
unimproved:
urban: 15.7% of population
rural: 42.9% of population
total: 26% of population (2011 est.)

HIV/AIDS—adult prevalence rate: 17.9% (2012 est.)
country comparison to the world: 4

HIV/AIDS—people living with HIV/AIDS: 6,070,800 (2012 est.)
country comparison to the world: 1

HIV/AIDS—deaths: 235,100 (2012 est.)

country comparison to the world: 2

Major infectious diseases: *degree of risk:* intermediate
food or waterborne diseases: bacterial diarrhea, hepatitis A, and typhoid fever
water contact disease: schistosomiasis (2013)

Obesity—adult prevalence rate: 31.3% (2008)
country comparison to the world: 24

Children under the age of 5 years underweight: 8.7% (2008)
country comparison to the world: 71

Education expenditures: 6% of GDP (2010)
country comparison to the world: 42

Literacy: *definition:* age 15 and over can read and write
total population: 93%
male: 93.9%
female: 92.2% (2011 est.)

Unemployment, youth ages 15-24: *total:* 51.5%
country comparison to the world: 6
male: 47.1%
female: 56.9% (2012)

GOVERNMENT

Country name: *conventional long form:* Republic of South Africa
conventional short form: South Africa
former: Union of South Africa
abbreviation: RSA

Government type: republic

Capital: *name:* Pretoria (administrative capital)

geographic coordinates: 25 42 S, 28 13 E
time difference: UTC+2 (7 hours ahead of Washington, DC during Standard Time)
note: Cape Town (legislative capital); Bloemfontein (judicial capital)

Administrative divisions: 9 provinces; Eastern Cape, Free State, Gauteng, KwaZulu-Natal, Limpopo, Mpumalanga, Northern Cape, North West, Western Cape

Independence: 31 May 1910 (Union of South Africa formed from four British colonies: Cape Colony, Natal, Transvaal, and Orange Free State); 31 May 1961 (republic declared); 27 April 1994 (majority rule)

National holiday: Freedom Day, 27 April (1994)

Constitution: several previous; latest drafted 8 May 1996, approved 4 December 1997, effective 4 February 1997; amended many times, last in 2013 (2013)

Legal system: mixed legal system of Roman-Dutch civil law, English common law, and customary law

International law organization participation: has not submitted an ICJ jurisdiction declaration; accepts ICCt jurisdiction

Suffrage: 18 years of age; universal

Executive branch: *chief of state:* President Jacob ZUMA (since 9 May 2009); Deputy President Kgalema MOTLANTHE (since 11 May 2009); note—the president is both the chief of state and head of government
head of government: President Jacob ZUMA (since 9 May 2009); Deputy President Kgalema MOTLANTHE (since 11 May 2009)
cabinet: Cabinet appointed by the president (For more information visit the World Leaders website)
elections: president elected by the National Assembly for a five-year term (eligible for a second term); election last held on 6 May 2009 (next to be held on 7 May 2014)
election results: Jacob ZUMA elected president; National Assembly vote—Jacob ZUMA (ANC) 277, Mvume DANDALA (COPE) 47, other 76

Legislative branch: bicameral Parliament consisting of the National Council of Provinces (90 seats; 10 members elected by each of the nine provincial legislatures for five-year terms; has special powers to protect regional interests, including the safeguarding of cultural and linguistic traditions among ethnic minorities) and the National Assembly (400 seats; members elected by popular vote under a system of proportional representation to serve five-year terms)
elections: National Assembly and National Council of Provinces—last held on 22 April 2009 (next to be held on 7 May 2014)
election results: National Council of Provinces—percent of vote by party—NA; seats by party—NA; National Assembly—percent of vote by party—ANC 65.9%, DA 16.7%, COPE 7.4%, IFP 4.6%, other 5.4%; seats by party—ANC 264, DA 67, COPE 30, IFP 18, other 21

Judicial branch: *highest court(s):* Supreme Court of Appeals (consists of the court president, deputy president, and 21 judges); Constitutional Court (consists of the chief and deputy chief justices and 9 judges)
judge selection and term of office: Supreme Court of Appeals president and vice-president appointed by the national president after consultation with the Joint Services Commission (JSC), a 22-member body of judicial and other government officials, and a law academics; other Supreme Court judges appointed by the national president on the advice of the JSC and hold office until discharged from active service in terms of an Act of Parliament; Constitutional Court chief and deputy chief justices appointed by the national president after consultation with the JSC and with heads of the National Assembly; other Constitutional Court judges appointed by the national president after consultation with the chief justice and leaders of the National Assembly; Constitutional Court judges appointed for 12-year non-renewable terms or until age 70
subordinate courts: High Courts; Magistrates' Courts; labor courts; land claims courts;

Political parties and leaders: African Christian Democratic Party or ACDP [Kenneth MESHOE]; African National Congress or ANC [Jacob ZUMA]; Congress of the People or COPE [Mosiuoa LEKOTA]; Democratic Alliance or DA [Helen ZILLE]; Economic Freedom Fighters or EFF [Julius MALEMA]; Freedom Front Plus or FF+ [Pieter MULDER]; Inkatha Freedom Party or IFP [Mangosuthu BUTHELEZI]; Pan-Africanist Congress or PAC [Alton MPHETHI]; United Christian Democratic Party or UCDP [Lucas MANGOPE]; United Democratic Movement or UDM [Bantu HOLOMISA]

Political pressure groups and leaders: Congress of South African Trade Unions or COSATU [Zwelinzima VAVI, general secretary]; South African Communist Party or SACP [Blade NZIMANDE, general secretary]; South African National Civics Organization or SANCO [Richard MDAKANE, national president]
note: COSATU and SACP are in a formal alliance with the ANC

International organization participation: ACP, AfDB, AU, BIS, BRICS, C, CD, FAO, FATF, G-20, G-24, G-77, IAEA, IBRD, ICAO, ICC (national committees), ICRM, IDA, IFAD, IFC, IFRCS, IHO, ILO, IMF, IMO, IMSO, Interpol, IOC, IOM, IPU, ISO, ITSO, ITU, ITUC (NGOs), MIGA, MONUSCO, NAM, NSG, OECD (Enhanced Engagement, OPCW, Paris Club (associate), PCA, SACU, SADC, UN, UNAMID, UNCTAD, UNESCO, UNHCR, UNIDO, UNITAR, UNSC (temporary), UNWTO, UPU, WCO, WFTU (NGOs), WHO, WIPO, WMO, WTO, ZC

Diplomatic representation in the US:
chief of mission: Ambassador Ebrahim RASOOL (since 4 August 2010)
chancery: 3051 Massachusetts Avenue NW, Washington, DC 20008
telephone: [1] (202) 232-4400
FAX: [1] (202) 265-1607
consulate(s) general: Chicago, Los Angeles, New York

Diplomatic representation from the US:
chief of mission: Ambassador Patrick GASPARD (since 1 August 2013)
embassy: 877 Pretorius Street, Arcadia, Pretoria
mailing address: P. O. Box 9536, Pretoria 0001
telephone: [27] (12) 431-4000
FAX: [27] (12) 342-2299
consulate(s) general: Cape Town, Durban, Johannesburg

Flag description: two equal width horizontal bands of red (top) and blue separated by a central green band that splits into a horizontal Y, the arms of which end at the corners of the hoist side; the Y embraces a black isosceles triangle from which the arms are separated by narrow yellow bands; the red and blue bands are separated from the green band and its arms by narrow white stripes; the flag colors do not have any official symbolism, but the Y stands for the "convergence of diverse elements within South African society, taking the road ahead in unity"; black, yellow, and green are found on the flag of the African National Congress, while red, white, and blue are the colors in the flags of the Netherlands and the UK, whose settlers ruled South Africa during the colonial era
note: the South African flag is one of only two national flags to display six colors as part of its primary design, the other is South Sudan's

National symbol(s): springbok antelope

National anthem: *name:* "National Anthem of South Africa"
lyrics/music: Enoch SONTONGA and Cornelius Jacob LANGENHOVEN/Enoch SONTONGA and Marthinus LOURENS de Villiers
note: adopted 1994; the anthem is a combination of "N'kosi Sikelel' iAfrica" (God Bless Africa) and "Die Stem van Suid Afrika" (The Call of South Africa), which were respectively the anthems of the non-white and white communities under apartheid; the official lyrics contain a mixture of Xhosa, Zulu, Sesotho, Afrikaans, and English; the music incorporates the melody used in the Tanzanian and Zambian anthems

ECONOMY

Economy—overview: South Africa is a middle-income, emerging market with an abundant supply of natural resources; well-developed financial, legal, communications, energy, and transport sectors and a stock exchange that is the 16th largest in the world. Even though the country's modern infrastructure supports a relatively efficient distribution of goods to major urban centers throughout the region, unstable electricity supplies retard growth. The global financial crisis reduced commodity prices and world demand. GDP fell nearly 2% in 2009 but has recovered since then, albeit slowly with 2014 growth projected at about 2%. Unemployment, poverty, and inequality—among the highest in the world—remain a challenge. Official unemployment is at nearly 25% of the work force, and runs significantly higher among black youth. Eskom, the state-run power company, has built two new power stations and installed new power demand management programs to improve power grid reliability. Construction delays at two additional plants, however, mean South Africa is operating on a razor thin margin; economists judge that growth cannot exceed 3% until those plants come on line. South Africa's economic policy has focused on controlling inflation, however, the country has had significant budget deficits that restrict its ability to deal with pressing economic problems. The current government faces growing pressure from special interest groups to use state-owned enterprises to deliver basic services to low-income areas and to increase job growth.

GDP (purchasing power parity): $595.7 billion (2013 est.)
country comparison to the world: 26
$584 billion (2012 est.)
$569.5 billion (2011 est.)
note: data are in 2013 US dollars

GDP (official exchange rate): $353.9 billion (2013 est.)

GDP—real growth rate: 2% (2013 est.)
country comparison to the world: 139
2.5% (2012 est.)
3.5% (2011 est.)

GDP—per capita (PPP): $11,500 (2013 est.)
country comparison to the world: 108
$11,400 (2012 est.)
$11,300 (2011 est.)
note: data are in 2013 US dollars

Gross national saving: 15.1% of GDP (2013 est.)
country comparison to the world: 111
13.2% of GDP (2012 est.)
16.1% of GDP (2011 est.)

GDP—composition, by end use:
household consumption: 63.8%
government consumption: 24%
investment in fixed capital: 22%
investment in inventories: -0.8%
exports of goods and services: 30.6%
imports of goods and services: -39.6% (2013 est.)

GDP—composition, by sector of origin:
agriculture: 2.6%
industry: 29%
services: 68.4% (2013 est.)

Agriculture—products: corn, wheat, sugarcane, fruits, vegetables; beef, poultry, mutton, wool, dairy products

Industries: mining (world's largest producer of platinum, gold, chromium), automobile assembly, metalworking, machinery, textiles, iron and steel, chemicals, fertilizer, foodstuffs, commercial ship repair

Industrial production growth rate: 0.9% (2013 est.)
country comparison to the world: 154

Labor force: 18.54 million (2013 est.)
country comparison to the world: 33

Labor force—by occupation: *agriculture:* 9%
industry: 26%
services: 65% (2007 est.)

Unemployment rate: 24.9% (2013 est.)
country comparison to the world: 173
25.1% (2012 est.)

Population below poverty line: 31.3% (2009 est.)

Household income or consumption by percentage share: *lowest 10%:* 1.2%
highest 10%: 51.7% (2009 est.)

Distribution of family income—Gini index: 63.1 (2005)
country comparison to the world: 2
59.3 (1994)

Budget: *revenues:* $88.53 billion
expenditures: $105.5 billion (2013 est.)

Taxes and other revenues: 25% of GDP (2013 est.)
country comparison to the world: 130

Budget surplus (+) or deficit (-): -4.8% of GDP (2013 est.)
country comparison to the world: 162

Public debt: 45.4% of GDP (2013 est.)
country comparison to the world: 81
42.3% of GDP (2012 est.)

Fiscal year: 1 April—31 March

Inflation rate (consumer prices): 5.8% (2013 est.)
country comparison to the world: 166
5.7% (2012 est.)

Central bank discount rate: 5% (31 December 2012)
country comparison to the world: 42
7% (31 December 2009)

Commercial bank prime lending rate: 8.5% (31 December 2013 est.)
country comparison to the world: 104
8.75% (31 December 2012 est.)

Stock of narrow money: $110.2 billion (31 December 2013 est.)
country comparison to the world: 33
$122 billion (31 December 2012 est.)

Stock of broad money: $198 billion (31 December 2013 est.)
country comparison to the world: 37
$220.1 billion (31 December 2012 est.)

Stock of domestic credit: $252.6 billion (31 December 2013 est.)
country comparison to the world: 38
$298.8 billion (31 December 2012 est.)

Market value of publicly traded shares: $1.038 trillion (31 December 2012)
country comparison to the world: 16
$855.7 billion (31 December 2011)
$1.013 trillion (31 December 2010)

Current account balance: -$23.78 billion (2013 est.)
country comparison to the world: 183
-$24.07 billion (2012 est.)

Exports: $91.05 billion (2013 est.)
country comparison to the world: 42
$93.48 billion (2012 est.)

Exports—commodities: gold, diamonds, platinum, other metals and minerals, machinery and equipment

Exports—partners: China 11.8%, US 8.3%, Japan 6%, Germany 5.7%, India 4.2% (2012)

Imports: $99.55 billion (2013 est.)
country comparison to the world: 34
$102.6 billion (2012 est.)

Imports—commodities: machinery and equipment, chemicals, petroleum products, scientific instruments, foodstuffs

Imports—partners: China 14.4%, Germany 10.1%, Saudi Arabia 7.7%, US 7.4%, Japan 4.6%, India 4.5% (2012)

Reserves of foreign exchange and gold: $48.46 billion (31 December 2013 est.)
country comparison to the world: 42
$50.7 billion (31 December 2012 est.)

Debt—external: $139 billion (31 December 2013 est.)
country comparison to the world: 39
$130.4 billion (31 December 2012 est.)

Stock of direct foreign investment—at home: $143.3 billion (31 December 2013 est.)
country comparison to the world: 34
$139 billion (31 December 2012 est.)

Stock of direct foreign investment—abroad: $87.67 billion (31 December 2013 est.)
country comparison to the world: 30
$82.82 billion (31 December 2012 est.)

Exchange rates: rand (ZAR) per US dollar—
9.576 (2013 est.)
8.2031 (2012 est.)
7.3212 (2010 est.)
8.42 (2009)
7.9576 (2008)

ENERGY

Electricity—production: 257.9 billion kWh (2012 est.)
country comparison to the world: 16

Electricity—consumption: 234.2 billion kWh (2012 est.)
country comparison to the world: 16

Electricity—exports: 15.04 billion kWh (2012 est.)
country comparison to the world: 14

Electricity—imports: 11.89 billion kWh (2011 est.)
country comparison to the world: 17

Electricity—installed generating capacity: 44.26 million kW (2010 est.)
country comparison to the world: 22

Electricity—from fossil fuels: 90.8% of total installed capacity (2010 est.)
country comparison to the world: 73

Electricity—from nuclear fuels: 4.1% of total installed capacity (2010 est.)
country comparison to the world: 23

Electricity—from hydroelectric plants: 1.5% of total installed capacity (2010 est.)
country comparison to the world: 141

Electricity—from other renewable sources: 0.5% of total installed capacity (2010 est.)
country comparison to the world: 84

Crude oil—production: 181,000 bbl/day (2012 est.)
country comparison to the world: 40

Crude oil—exports: 0 bbl/day (2010 est.)
country comparison to the world: 177

Crude oil—imports: 385,100 bbl/day (2010 est.)
country comparison to the world: 24

Crude oil—proved reserves: 15 million bbl (1 January 2013 es)
country comparison to the world: 86

Refined petroleum products—production: 437,600 bbl/day (2010 est.)
country comparison to the world: 33

Refined petroleum products—consumption: 590,900 bbl/day (2011 est.)
country comparison to the world: 29

Refined petroleum products—exports: 80,460 bbl/day (2010 est.)
country comparison to the world: 51

Refined petroleum products—imports: 79,010 bbl/day (2010 est.)
country comparison to the world: 57

Natural gas—production: 1.28 billion cu m (2011 est.)
country comparison to the world: 62

Natural gas—consumption: 4.01 billion cu m (2010 est.)
country comparison to the world: 67

Natural gas—exports: 0 cu m (2011 est.)
country comparison to the world: 178

Natural gas—imports: 3.3 billion cu m (2011 est.)
country comparison to the world: 41

Natural gas—proved reserves: 16 billion cu m (1 January 2012 es)
country comparison to the world: 78

Carbon dioxide emissions from consumption of energy: 461.6 million Mt (2011 est.)
country comparison to the world: 15

COMMUNICATIONS

Telephones—main lines in use: 4.03 million (2012)
country comparison to the world: 4 2

Telephones—mobile cellular: 68.4 million (2012)
country comparison to the world: 19

Telephone system: *general assessment:* the system is the best developed and most modern in Africa
domestic: combined fixed-line and mobile-cellular teledensity is roughly 140 telephones per 100 persons; consists of carrier-equipped open-wire lines, coaxial cables, microwave radio relay links, fiber-optic cable, radiotelephone communication stations, and wireless local loops; key centers are Bloemfontein, Cape Town, Durban, Johannesburg, Port Elizabeth, and Pretoria
international: country code—27; the SAT-3/WASC and SAFE fiber-optic submarine cable systems connect South Africa to Europe and Asia; the EASSy fiber-optic cable system connects with Europe and North America; satellite earth stations—3 Intelsat (1 Indian Ocean and 2 Atlantic Ocean) (2011)

Broadcast media: the South African Broadcasting Corporation (SABC) operates 4 TV stations, 3 are free-to-air and 1 is pay TV; e.tv, a private station, is accessible to more than half the population; multiple subscription TV services provide a mix of local and international channels; well developed mix of public and private radio stations at the national, regional, and local levels; the SABC radio network, state-owned and controlled but nominally independent, operates 18 stations, one for each of the 11 official languages, 4 community stations, and 3 commercial stations; more than 100 community-based stations extend coverage to rural areas (2007)

Internet country code: . z a

Internet hosts: 4.761 million (2012)
country comparison to the world: 23

Internet users: 4.42 million (2009)
country comparison to the world: 54

TRANSPORTATION

Airports: 566 (2013)
country comparison to the world: 11

Airports—with paved runways: *total:* 144
over 3,047 m: 11
2,438 to 3,047 m: 7
1,524 to 2,437 m: 52
914 to 1,523 m: 65
under 914 m: 9 (2013)

Airports—with unpaved runways: *total:* 422
2,438 to 3,047 m: 1
1,524 to 2,437 m: 31
914 to 1,523 m: 258
under 914 m: 132 (2013)

Heliports: 1 (2013)

Pipelines: condensate 94 km; gas 1,293 km; oil 992 km; refined products 1,460 km (2013)

Railways: *total:* 20,192 km
country comparison to the world: 14
narrow gauge: 19,756 km 1.065-m gauge (8,271 km electrified); 122 km 0.750-m gauge; 314 km 0.610-m gauge (2008)

Roadways: *total:* 364,131 km
country comparison to the world: 19
paved: 62,995 km (includes 254 km of expressways)
unpaved: 301,136 km (2002)

Merchant marine: *total:* 3
country comparison to the world: 134
by type: petroleum tanker 3
registered in other countries: 19 (Australia 1, Isle of Man 2, Mexico 1, NZ 1, Seychelles 1, Singapore 13) (2010)

Ports and terminals: *major seaport(s):* Cape Town, Durban, Port Elizabeth, Richards Bay, Saldanha Bay
container port(s) (TEUs): Durban (2,712,975)

MILITARY

Military branches: South African National Defense Force (SANDF): South African Army, South African Navy (SAN), South African Air Force (SAAF), South African Military Health Services (2013)

Military service age and obligation: 18 years of age for voluntary military service; women are eligible to serve in noncombat roles; 2-year service obligation (2012)

Manpower available for military service:
males age 16-49: 13,439,781
females age 16-49: 12,473,641 (2010 est.)

Manpower fit for military service:
males age 16-49: 7,617,063
females age 16-49: 6,476,264 (2010 est.)

Manpower reaching militarily significant age annually: *male:* 482,122
female: 485,017 (2010 est.)

Military expenditures: 1% of GDP (2013)
country comparison to the world: 101
1.16% of GDP (2012)
1.14% of GDP (2011)
1.16% of GDP (2010)

Military—note: with the end of apartheid and the establishment of majority rule, former military, black homelands forces, and ex-opposition forces were integrated into the South African National Defense Force (SANDF); as of 2003 the integration process was considered complete

TRANSNATIONAL ISSUES

Disputes—international: South Africa has placed military units to assist police operations along the border of Lesotho, Zimbabwe, and Mozambique to control smuggling, poaching, and illegal migration; the governments of South Africa and Namibia have not signed or ratified the text of the 1994 Surveyor's General agreement placing the boundary in the middle of the Orange River

Refugees and internally displaced persons: *refugees (country of origin):* 17,864 (Somalia); 13,386 (Democratic Republic of Congo); 5,805 (Angola); 5,538 (Ethiopia) (2012)

Illicit drugs: transshipment center for heroin, hashish, and cocaine, as well as a major cultivator of marijuana in its own right; cocaine and heroin consumption on the rise; world's largest market for illicit methaqualone, usually imported illegally from India through various east African countries, but increasingly producing its own synthetic drugs for domestic consumption; attractive venue for money launderers given the increasing level of organized criminal and narcotics activity in the region and the size of the South African economy

SOUTH GEORGIA AND SOUTH SANDWICH ISLANDS

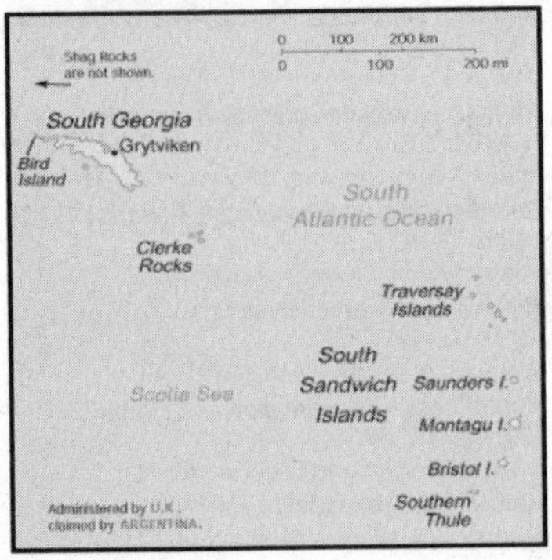

INTRODUCTION

Background: The islands, with large bird and seal populations, lie approximately 1,000 km east of the Falkland Islands and have been under British administration since 1908 - except for a brief period in 1982 when Argentina occupied them. Grytviken, on South Georgia, was a 19th and early 20th century whaling station. Famed explorer Ernest SHACKLETON stopped there in 1914 en route to his ill-fated attempt to cross Antarctica on foot. He returned some 20 months later with a few companions in a small boat and arranged a successful rescue for the rest of his crew, stranded off the Antarctic Peninsula. He died in 1922 on a subsequent expedition and is buried in Grytviken. Today, the station houses scientists from the British Antarctic Survey. Recognizing the importance of preserving the marine stocks in adjacent waters, the UK, in 1993, extended the exclusive fishing zone from 12 nm to 200 nm around each island.

GEOGRAPHY

Location: Southern South America, islands in the South Atlantic Ocean, east of the tip of South America

Geographic coordinates: 54 30 S, 37 00 W

Map references: South America

Area: *total:* 3,903 sq km
country comparison to the world: 177

land: 3,903 sq km
water: 0 sq km
note: includes Shag Rocks, Black Rock, Clerke Rocks, South Georgia Island, Bird Island, and the South Sandwich Islands, which consist of 11 islands Island, and the South Sandwich Islands, which consist of 11 islands

Area—comparative: slightly larger than Rhode Island

Land boundaries: 0 km

Coastline: NA

Maritime claims: *territorial sea:* 12 nm
exclusive fishing zone: 200 nm

Climate: variable, with mostly westerly winds throughout the year interspersed with periods of calm; nearly all precipitation falls as snow

Terrain: most of the islands, rising steeply from the sea, are rugged and mountainous; South Georgia is largely barren and has steep, glacier-covered mountains; the South Sandwich Islands are of volcanic origin with some active volcanoes

Elevation extremes: *lowest point:* Atlantic Ocean 0 m
highest point: Mount Paget (South Georgia) 2,934 m

Natural resources: fish

Land use: *arable land:* 0%
permanent crops: 0%
other: 100% (largely covered by permanent ice and snow with some sparse vegetation consisting of grass, moss, and lichen) (2011)

Irrigated land: 0 sq km (2011)

Natural hazards: the South Sandwich Islands have prevailing weather conditions that generally make them difficult to approach by ship; they are also subject to active volcanism

Environment—current issues: NA

Geography—note: the north coast of South Georgia has several large bays, which provide good anchorage; reindeer, introduced early in the 20th century, live on South Georgia

PEOPLE AND SOCIETY

Population: no indigenous inhabitants
note: the small military garrison on South Georgia withdrew in March 2001 replaced by a permanent group of scientists of the British Antarctic Survey, which also has a biological station on Bird Island; the South Sandwich Islands are uninhabited

GOVERNMENT

Country name: *conventional long form:* South Georgia and the South Sandwich Islands
conventional short form: South Georgia and South Sandwich Islands
abbreviation: SGSSI

Dependency status: overseas territory of the UK, also claimed by Argentina; administered from the Falkland Islands by a commissioner, who is concurrently governor of the Falkland Islands, representing Queen ELIZABETH II

Legal system: the laws of the UK where applicable apply; the senior magistrate from the Falkland Islands presides over the Magistrates Court

Diplomatic representation in the US: none (overseas territory of the UK, also claimed by Argentina)

Diplomatic representation from the US: none (overseas territory of the UK, also claimed by Argentina)

Flag description: blue, with the flag of the UK in the upper hoist-side quadrant and the South Georgia and South Sandwich Islands coat of arms centered on the outer half of the flag; the coat of arms features a shield with a golden lion rampant, holding a torch; the shield is supported by a fur seal on the left and a Macaroni penguin on the right; a reindeer appears above the crest, and below the shield on a scroll is the motto LEO TERRAM PROPRIAM PROTEGAT (Let the Lion Protect its Own Land)); the lion with the torch represents the UK and discovery; the background of the shield, blue and white estoiles, are found in the coat of arms of James Cook, discoverer of the islands; all the outer supporting animals represented are native to the islands

ECONOMY

Economy—overview: Some fishing takes place in adjacent waters. There is a potential source of income from harvesting finfish and krill. The islands receive income from postage stamps produced in the UK, sale of fishing licenses, and harbor and landing fees from tourist vessels. Tourism from specialized cruise ships is increasing rapidly.

TRANSPORTATION

Ports and terminals: *major seaport(s):* Grytviken

MILITARY

Military—note: defense is the responsibility of the UK

TRANSNATIONAL ISSUES

Disputes—international: Argentina, which claims the islands in its constitution and briefly occupied them by force in 1982, agreed in 1995 to no longer seek settlement by force

SOUTHERN OCEAN

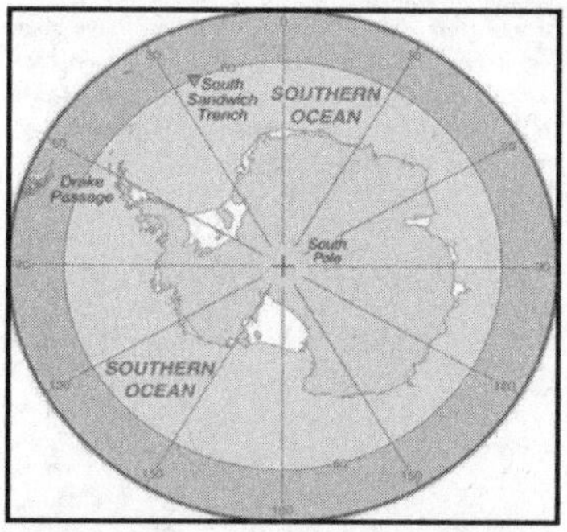

INTRODUCTION

Background: A large body of recent oceanographic research has shown that the Antarctic Circumpolar Current (ACC), an ocean current that flows from west to east around Antarctica, plays a crucial role in global ocean circulation. The region where the cold waters of the ACC meet and mingle with the warmer waters of the north defines a distinct border - the Antarctic Convergence—which fluctuates with the seasons, but which encompasses a discrete body of water and a unique ecologic region. The Convergence concentrates nutrients, which promotes marine plant life, and which, in turn, allows for a greater abundance of animal life. In 2000, the International Hydrographic Organization delimited the waters within the Convergence as a fifth world ocean—the Southern Ocean—by combining the southern portions of the Atlantic Ocean, Indian Ocean, and Pacific Ocean. The Southern Ocean extends from the coast of Antarctica north to 60 degrees south latitude, which coincides with the Antarctic Treaty Limit and which approximates the extent of the Antarctic Convergence. As such, the Southern Ocean is now the fourth largest of the world's five oceans (after the Pacific Ocean, Atlantic Ocean, and Indian Ocean, but larger than the Arctic Ocean). It should be noted that inclusion of the Southern Ocean does not imply recognition of this feature as one of the world's primary oceans by the US Government.

GEOGRAPHY

Location: body of water between 60 degrees south latitude and Antarctica

Geographic coordinates: 60 00 S, 90 00 E (nominally), but the Southern Ocean has the unique distinction of being a large circumpolar body of water totally encircling the continent of Antarctica; this ring of water lies between 60 degrees south latitude and the coast of Antarctica and encompasses 360 degrees of longitude

Map references: Antarctic Region

Area: *total:* 20.327 million sq km

note: includes Amundsen Sea, Bellingshausen Sea, part of the Drake Passage, Ross Sea, a small part of the Scotia Sea, Weddell Sea, and other tributary water bodies

Area—comparative: slightly more than twice the size of the US

Coastline: 17,968 km

Climate: sea temperatures vary from about 10 degrees Celsius to -2 degrees Celsius; cyclonic storms travel eastward around the continent and frequently are intense because of the temperature contrast between ice and open ocean; the ocean area from about latitude 40 south to the Antarctic Circle has the strongest average winds found anywhere on Earth; in winter the ocean freezes outward to 65 degrees south latitude in the Pacific sector and 55 degrees south latitude in the Atlantic sector, lowering surface temperatures well below 0 degrees Celsius; at some coastal points intense persistent drainage winds from the interior keep the shoreline ice-free throughout the winter

Terrain: the Southern Ocean is deep, 4,000 to 5,000 m over most of its extent with only limited areas of shallow water; the Antarctic continental shelf is generally narrow and unusually deep, its edge lying at depths of 400 to 800 m (the global mean is 133 m); the Antarctic icepack grows from an average minimum of 2.6 million sq km in March to about 18.8 million sq km in September, better than a sixfold increase in area; the Antarctic Circumpolar Current (21,000 km in length) moves perpetually eastward; it is the world's largest ocean current, transporting 130 million cubic meters of water per second—100 times the flow of all the world's rivers

Elevation extremes: *lowest point:* -7,235 m at the southern end of the South Sandwich Trench
highest point: sea level 0 m

Natural resources: probable large and possible giant oil and gas fields on the continental margin; manganese nodules, possible placer deposits, sand and gravel, fresh water as icebergs; squid, whales, and seals—none exploited; krill, fish

Natural hazards: huge icebergs with drafts up to several hundred meters; smaller bergs and iceberg fragments; sea ice (generally 0.5 to 1 m thick) with sometimes dynamic short-term variations and with large annual and interannual variations; deep continental shelf floored by glacial deposits varying widely over short distances; high winds and large waves much of the year; ship icing, especially May-October; most of region is remote from sources of search and rescue

Environment—current issues: increased solar ultraviolet radiation resulting from the Antarctic ozone hole in recent years, reducing marine primary productivity (phytoplankton) by as much as 15% and damaging the DNA of some fish; illegal, unreported, and unregulated fishing in recent years, especially the landing of an estimated five to six times more Patagonian toothfish than the regulated fishery, which is likely to affect the sustainability of the stock; large amount of incidental mortality of seabirds resulting from long-line fishing for toothfish
note: the now-protected fur seal population is making a strong comeback after severe overexploitation in the 18th and 19th centuries

Environment—international agreements: the Southern Ocean is subject to all international agreements regarding the world's oceans; in addition, it is subject to these agreements specific to the Antarctic
region: International Whaling Commission (prohibits commercial whaling south of 40 degrees south [south of 60 degrees south between 50 degrees and 130 degrees west]); Convention on the Conservation of Antarctic Seals (limits sealing); Convention on the Conservation of Antarctic Marine Living Resources (regulates fishing)
note: many nations (including the US) prohibit mineral resource exploration and exploitation south of the fluctuating Polar Front (Antarctic Convergence), which is in the middle of the Antarctic Circumpolar Current and serves as the dividing line between the cold polar surface waters to the south and the warmer waters to the north

Geography—note: the major chokepoint is the Drake Passage between South America and Antarctica; the Polar Front (Antarctic Convergence) is the best natural definition of the northern extent of the Southern Ocean; it is a distinct region at the middle of the Antarctic Circumpolar Current that separates the cold polar surface waters to the south from the warmer waters to the north; the Front and the Current extend entirely around Antarctica, reaching south of 60 degrees south near New Zealand and near 48 degrees south in the far South Atlantic coinciding with the path of the maximum westerly winds

ECONOMY

Economy—overview: Fisheries in 2006-07 landed 126,976 metric tons, of which 82% (104,586 tons) was krill (Euphausia superba) and 9.5% (12,027 tons) Patagonian toothfish (Dissostichus eleginoides—also known as Chilean sea bass), compared to 127,910 tons in 2005-06 of which 83% (106,591 tons) was krill and 9.7% (12,396 tons) Patagonian toothfish (estimated fishing from the area covered by the Convention of the Conservation of Antarctic Marine Living Resources (CCAMLR), which extends slightly beyond the Southern Ocean area). International agreements were adopted in late 1999 to reduce illegal, unreported, and unregulated fishing, which in the 2000-01 season landed, by one estimate, 8,376 metric tons of Patagonian and Antarctic toothfish. In the 2007-08 Antarctic summer, 45,213 tourists visited the Southern Ocean, compared to 35,552 in 2006-07, and 29,799 in 2005-06 (estimates provided to the Antarctic Treaty by the International Association of Antarctica Tour Operators (IAATO), and does not include passengers on overflights and those flying directly in and out of Antarctica). flying directly in and out of Antarctica).

TRANSPORTATION

Ports and terminals: *major seaport(s):* McMurdo, Palmer, and offshore anchorages in Antarctica
note: few ports or harbors exist on the southern side of the Southern Ocean; ice conditions limit use of most to short periods in midsummer; even then some cannot be entered without icebreaker escort; most Antarctic ports are operated by government research stations and, except in an emergency, are not open to commercial or private vessels

Transportation—note: Drake Passage offers alternative to transit through the Panama Canal

TRANSNATIONAL ISSUES

Disputes—international: Antarctic Treaty defers claims (see Antarctica entry), but Argentina, Australia, Chile, France, NZ, Norway, and UK assert claims (some overlapping), including the continental shelf in the Southern Ocean; several states have expressed an interest in extending those continental shelf claims under the United Nations Convention on the Law of the Sea to include undersea ridges; the US and most other states do not recognize the land or maritime claims of other states and have made no claims themselves (the US and Russia have reserved the right to do so); no formal claims exist in the waters in the sector between 90 degrees west and 150 degrees west an interest in extending those continental shelf claims under the United Nations Convention on the Law of the Sea to include undersea ridges; the US and most other states do not recognize the land or maritime claims of other states and have made no claims themselves (the US and Russia have reserved the right to do so); no formal claims exist in the waters in the sector between 90 degrees west and 150 degrees west

SOUTH SUDAN

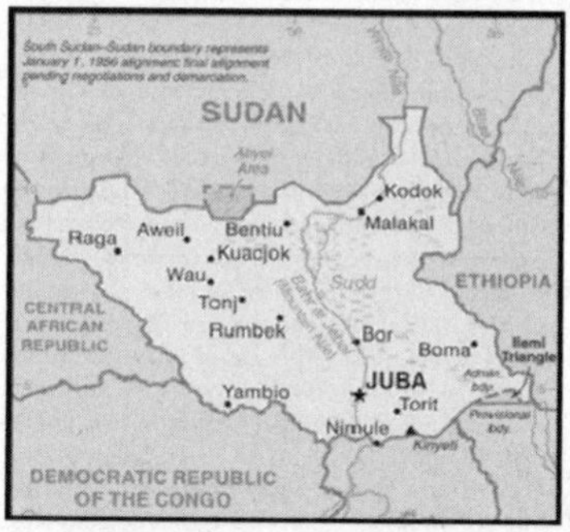

INTRODUCTION

Background: Egypt attempted to colonize the region of southern Sudan by establishing the province of Equatoria in the 1870s. Islamic Mahdist revolutionaries overran the region in 1885, but in 1898 a British force was able to overthrow the Mahdist regime. An Anglo-Egyptian Sudan was established the following year with Equatoria being the southernmost of its eight provinces. The isolated region was largely left to itself over the following decades, but Christian missionaries converted much of the population and facilitated the spread of English. When Sudan gained its independence in 1956, it was with the understanding that the southerners would be able to participate fully in the political system. When the Arab Khartoum government reneged on its promises, a mutiny began that led to two prolonged periods of conflict (1955-1972 and 1983-2005) in which perhaps 2.5 million people died—mostly civilians - due to starvation and drought. Ongoing peace talks finally resulted in a Comprehensive Peace Agreement, signed in January 2005. As part of this agreement the south was granted a six-year period of autonomy to be followed by a referendum on final status. The result of this referendum, held in January 2011, was a vote of 98% in favor of secession. Independence was attained on 9 July 2011. Since independence South Sudan has struggled with good governance and nation building and has attempted to control rebel militia groups operating in its territory. Economic conditions have deteriorated since January 2012 when the government decided to shut down oil production following bilateral disagreements with Sudan.

GEOGRAPHY

Location: East-Central Africa; south of Sudan, north of Uganda and Kenya, west of Ethiopia

Geographic coordinates: 8 00 N, 30 00 E

Map references: Africa

Area: *total:* 644,329 sq km
country comparison to the world: 42

Area—comparative: slightly smaller than Texas

Land boundaries: *total:* 5,413 km
border countries: Central African Republic 989 km, Democratic Republic of the Congo 639 km, Ethiopia 934 km, Kenya 232 km, Sudan 2,184 km, Uganda 435 km
note: South Sudan-Sudan boundary represents 1 January 1956 alignment; final alignment pending negotiations and demarcation; final sovereignty status of Abyei Area pending negotiations between South Sudan and Sudan

Coastline: 0 km (landlocked)

Maritime claims: none (landlocked)

Climate: hot with seasonal rainfall influenced by the annual shift of the Inter-Tropical Convergence Zone; rainfall is heaviest in the upland areas of the south and diminishes to the north

Terrain: the terrain gradually rises from plains in the north and center to southern highlands along the border with Uganda and Kenya; the White Nile, flowing north out of the uplands of Central Africa, is the major geographic feature of the country supporting agriculture and extensive wild animal populations; The Sudd (a name derived from floating vegetation that hinders navigation) is a large swampy area of more than 100,000 sq km fed by the waters of the White Nile that dominates the center of the country

Elevation extremes: *Lowest point:* NA
highest point: Kinyeti 3,187 m

Natural resources: hydropower, fertile agricultural land, gold, diamonds, petroleum, hardwoods, limestone, iron ore, copper, chromium ore, zinc, tungsten, mica, silver

Geography—note: The Sudd is a vast swamp in South Sudan, formed by the White Nile, comprising more than 15% of the total area; it is one of the world's largest wetlands

PEOPLE AND SOCIETY

Nationality: *noun:* South Sudanese (singular and plural)
adjective: South Sudanese

Ethnic groups: Dinka 35.8%, Nuer 15.6%, Shilluk, Azande, Bari, Kakwa, Kuku, Murle, Mandari, Didinga, Ndogo, Bviri, Lndi, Anuak, Bongo, Lango, Dungotona, Acholi (2011 est.)

Languages: English (official), Arabic (includes Juba and Sudanese variants), regional languages include Dinka, Nuer, Bari, Zande, Shilluk

Religions: animist, Christian

Population: 11,562,695 (July 2014 est.)
country comparison to the world: 75

Age structure:
0-14 years: 45.8% (male 2,699,556/female 2,593,241)
15-24 years: 19.9% (male 1,210,962/female 1,084,810)
25-54 years: 29.1% (male 1,622,776/female 1,742,842)
55-64 years: 2.1% (male 198,106/female 166,664)
65 years and over: 2.1% (male 136,932/female 106,806) (2014 est.)

Dependency ratios:
total dependency ratio: 83.8 %
youth dependency ratio: 77.4 %
elderly dependency ratio: 6.4 %
potential support ratio: 15.6 (2013)

Median age: *total:* 16.8 years
male: 16.6 years
female: 17 years (2014 est.)

Population growth rate: 4.12% (2014 est.)
country comparison to the world: 3

Birth rate: 37.68 births/1,000 population (2014 est.)
country comparison to the world: 13

Death rate: 8.42 deaths/1,000 population (2014 est.)
country comparison to the world: 82

Net migration rate: 11.94 migrant(s)/1,000 population (2014 est.)
country comparison to the world: 13

Urbanization: *urban population:* 18% of total population (2011)
rate of urbanization: 4.23% annual rate of change (2010-15 est.)

Major urban areas—population: JUBA (capital) 250,000 (2008 est.)

Maternal mortality rate: 2,054 deaths/100,000 live births (2006)
country comparison to the world: 1

Infant mortality rate: *total:* 68.16 deaths/1,000 live births (2014 est.)
country comparison to the world: 16

Total fertility rate: 5.43 children born/woman (2014 est.)
country comparison to the world: 11

Contraceptive prevalence rate: 3.5% (2006)

Drinking water source:
63.4% of population
55% of population
56.5% of population
36.6% of population
45% of population
43.5% of population (2011 est.)

Sanitation facility access:
improved:
urban: 15.8% of population
rural: 7.3% of population
total: 8.9% of population
unimproved:
urban: 84.2% of population
rural: 92.7% of population
total: 91.1% of population (2011 est.)

HIV/AIDS—adult prevalence rate: 2.7% (2012 est.)
country comparison to the world: 24

HIV/AIDS—people living with HIV/AIDS: 153,800 (2012 est.)
country comparison to the world: 33

HIV/AIDS—deaths: 12,900 (2012 est.)
country comparison to the world: 22

Major infectious diseases: *degree of risk:* very high
food or waterborne disease: bacterial and protozoal diarrhea, hepatitis A and E, and typhoid fever
vectorborne disease: malaria, dengue fever, trypanosomiasis-Gambiense (African sleeping sickness)
water contact disease: schistosomiasis
respiratory disease: meningococcal meningitis
animal contact disease: rabies (2013)

Children under the age of 5 years underweight: 32.5% (2006)
country comparison to the world: 11

Literacy: *definition:* age 15 and over can read and write
total population: 27%
male: 40%
female: 16% (2009)

GOVERNMENT

Country name: *conventional long form:* Republic of South Sudan
conventional short form: South Sudan

Government type: republic

Capital: *name:* Juba

geographic coordinates: 04 51 N 31 37 E
time difference: UTC+3 (8 hours ahead of Washington, DC during Standard Time)

Administrative divisions: 10 states; Central Equatoria, Eastern Equatoria, Jonglei, Lakes, Northern Bahr el Ghazal, Unity, Upper Nile, Warrap, Western Bahr el Ghazal, Western Equatoria

Independence: 9 July 2011 (from Sudan)

National holiday: Independence Day, 9 July (2011)

Constitution: previous 2005 (preindependence); latest signed 7 July 2011 (Transitional Constitution of the Republic of South Sudan, 2011); note—in January 2013, the mandate of the South Sudan National Constitutional Review Commission to address additional constitutional amendments was extended (2013)

Suffrage: 18 years of age; universal

Executive branch: *chief of state:* President Salva KIIR Mayardit (since 9 July 2011); Vice President James Wani IGGA (since 23 August 2013); note—the president is both chief of state and head of government
head of government: President Salva KIIR Mayardit (since 9 July 2011); Vice President James Wani IGGA (since 23 August 2013)
cabinet: National Council of Ministers; appointed by the president and approved by a resolution from the Legislative Assembly (For more information visit the World Leaders website)
elections: president elected by popular vote for a four-year term; election last held on 11-15 April 2010 (next to be held in 2015)
election results: Salva KIIR Mayardit elected president; percent of vote—Salva KIIR Mayardit 93%, Lam AKOL 7%

Legislative branch: bicameral National Legislature consists of the National Legislative Assembly (332 seats) and the Council of States (50 seats); members serve four-year terms
elections: National Legislative Assembly—last held 11-15 April 2010 (next to be held in 2015); Council of States—established and members appointed 1 August 2011
election results: National Legislative Assembly—percent of vote by party—NA; seats by party—SPLM 251, SPLM-DC 6, NCP 3, independent 6, unknown 66; Council of States—seats by party—SPLM 20, unknown 30
note: a presidential decree of 1 August 2011 reconstituted the National Legislative Assembly, as permitted under Article 94 of the Transitional Constitution, to include the 170 members elected 11-15 April 2010, 96 former members of the National Assembly of the Republic of Sudan, and 66 newly appointed members for a total of 332; a presidential decree also established a Council of States, initially with 50 members—the 20 former members of the Council of States of the Republic of Sudan plus an additional 30 appointed representatives

Judicial branch: *highest court(s):* Supreme Court of South Sudan (consists 7 justices including the court president and deputy president and organized into panels of 3 justices except when sitting as a Constitutional panel of all 7 justices)
judge selection and term of office: judges appointed by the president upon proposal of the Judicial Service Council, a 9-member judicial and administrative body; judge tenure NA

subordinate courts:
national level: Courts of Appeal; High Courts; County Courts; state level: High Courts; County Courts; customary courts; other specialized courts and tribunals

Political parties and leaders: Sudan People's Liberation Movement or SPLM [Salva KIIR Mayardit]; Sudan People's Liberation Movement for Democratic Change or SPLM-DC [Lam AKOL]

International organization participation: AU, IBRD, ICAO, IDA, IFAD, IFC, IFRCS, ILO, IMF, Interpol, IOM, ITU, MIGA, UN, UNCTAD, UNESCO, UPU

Diplomatic representation in the US:
chief of mission: Ambassador (vacant)
chancery: 1233 20th St. NW, Suite 602, Washington, DC 20036
telephone: [1] (202) 293-7940
FAX: [1] (202) 293-7941

Diplomatic representation from the US:
chief of mission: Ambassador Susan D. PAGE (since 18 October 2011)
embassy: located on Kololo Road adjacent to the EU's compound, Juba
telephone: [211] (0) 912-105-188

Flag description: three equal horizontal bands of black (top), red, and green; the red band is edged in white; a blue isosceles triangle based on the hoist side contains a gold, five-pointed star; black represents the people of South Sudan, red the blood shed in the struggle for freedom, green the verdant land, and blue the waters of the Nile; the gold star represents the unity of the states making up South Sudan
note: resembles the flag of Kenya; one of only two national flags to display six colors as part of its primary design, the other is South Africa's

National symbol(s): African fish eagle

National anthem: *name:* South Sudan Oyee! (Hooray!)
lyrics/music: collective of 49 poets/Juba University students and teachers
note: adopted 2011; the anthem was selected in a national contest

ECONOMY

Economy—overview: Following several decades of civil war with Sudan, industry and infrastructure in landlocked South Sudan are severely underdeveloped and poverty is widespread. Subsistence agriculture provides a living for the vast majority of the population. Property rights are insecure and price signals are weak, because markets are not well organized. South Sudan has little infrastructure—approximately 250 of paved roads. Electricity is produced mostly by costly diesel generators and indoor plumbing and potable water are scarce. South Sudan depends largely on imports of goods, services, and capital—mainly from Uganda, Kenya and Sudan. Nevertheless, South Sudan does have abundant natural resources. At independence in 2011, South Sudan produced nearly three-fourths of former Sudan's total oil output of nearly a half million barrels per day. The government of South Sudan derives nearly 98% of its budget revenues from oil. Oil is exported through two pipelines that run to refineries and shipping facilities at Port Sudan on the Red Sea. The economy of South Sudan will remain linked to Sudan for some time, given the long lead time and great expense required to build another pipeline, should the government decide to do so. In January 2012 South Sudan suspended production of oil because of its dispute with Sudan over transshipment fees. This suspension lasted fifteen months and had a devastating impact on GDP, which declined by 48% in 2012. With the resumption of oil flows the economy rebounded strongly during the second half of calendar year 2013. This occurred in spite of the fact that oil production, at an average level of 222,000 barrels per day, was 40% lower compared with 2011, prior to the shutdown. GDP is estimated to have grown by about 25% in 2013. However, the outbreak of conflict on December 15, 2013 combined with a further reduction of oil exports, means that GDP growth forecasts for 2014 are being revised downwards again, and poverty and food insecurity are rising. South Sudan holds one of the richest agricultural areas in Africa with fertile soils and abundant water supplies. Currently the region supports 10-20 million head of cattle. South Sudan is currently burdened by considerable debt, accrued largely in 2012, based on rapidly accumulating arrears, and increased military spending. South Sudan has received more than $4 billion in foreign aid since 2005, largely from the UK, the US, Norway, and the Netherlands. Following independence, South Sudan's central bank issued a new currency, the South Sudanese Pound, allowing a short grace period for turning in the old currency. Annual inflation peaked at 79.5% in May 2012 but declined rapidly thereafter, to an average of 1.7% in 2013. Following the December 2013 outbreak of violence, inflation is on the rise again. Long-term challenges include diversifying the formal economy, alleviating poverty, maintaining macroeconomic stability, improving tax collection and financial management and improving the business environment.

GDP (purchasing power parity): $14.71 billion (2013 est.)
country comparison to the world: 144
$11.79 billion (2012 est.)
$22.49 billion (2011 est.)
note: data are in 2013 US dollars

GDP (official exchange rate): $11.77 billion (2013 est.)

GDP—real growth rate: 24.7% (2013 est.)
country comparison to the world: 1
-47.6% (2012 est.)
NA% (2011 est.)

GDP—per capita (PPP): $1,400 (2013 est.)
country comparison to the world: 207
$1,100 (2012 est.)
$2,300 (2011 est.)

GDP—composition, by end use:
household consumption: 34.9%
government consumption: 17.1%
investment in fixed capital: 10.4%
exports of goods and services: 64.9%
imports of goods and services: -27.2% (2011 est.)

Agriculture—products: sorghum, maize, rice, millet, wheat, gum arabic, sugarcane, mangoes, papayas, bananas, sweet potatoes, sunflower, cotton, sesame, cassava (manioc), beans, peanuts; cattle, sheep

Population below poverty line: 50.6% (2009)

Inflation rate (consumer prices): 79% (May 2012 est.)
country comparison to the world: 224

Exchange rates: South Sudanese pounds (SSP) per US dollar—
0.7634 (2013 est.)
0.7752 (2012 est.)

ENERGY

Electricity—production: 881.3 million kWh (2010 est.)
country comparison to the world: 150

Electricity—consumption: 694.1 million kWh (2010 est.)
country comparison to the world: 159

Electricity—exports: 0 kWh (2012 est.)
country comparison to the world: 181

Electricity—imports: 0 kWh (2012 est.)
country comparison to the world: 182

Electricity—installed generating capacity: 255,200 kW (2010 est.)
country comparison to the world: 154

Electricity—from fossil fuels: 30.7% of total installed capacity (2010 est.)
country comparison to the world: 182

Electricity—from nuclear fuels: 0% of total installed capacity (2010 est.)
country comparison to the world: 158

Electricity—from hydroelectric plants: 66.3% of total installed capacity (2010 est.)
country comparison to the world: 26

Electricity—from other renewable sources:
3% of total installed capacity (2010 est.)
country comparison to the world: 59

Crude oil—production: 86,480 bbl/day (2012 est.)
country comparison to the world: 51

Crude oil—exports: 291,800 bbl/day (2010 est.)
country comparison to the world: 26

Crude oil—imports: 0 bbl/day (2010 est.)
country comparison to the world: 107

Crude oil—proved reserves: 3.75 billion bbl (1 January 2013 es)
country comparison to the world: 29

Refined petroleum products—imports: 13,050 bbl/day
country comparison to the world: 125

Natural gas—production: 0 cu m (2011 est.)
country comparison to the world: 179

Natural gas—consumption: 0 cu m (2010 est.)
country comparison to the world: 184

Natural gas—exports: 0 cu m (2011 est.)
country comparison to the world: 162

Natural gas—imports: 0 cu m (2011 est.)
country comparison to the world: 113

Natural gas—proved reserves: 63.71 billion cu m (1 January 2013 es)
country comparison to the world: 61

Carbon dioxide emissions from consumption of energy: 2.016 million Mt (2011 est.)
country comparison to the world: 148

COMMUNICATIONS

Telephones—main lines in use: 2,200 (2012)
country comparison to the world: 217

Telephones—mobile cellular: 2 million (2012)
country comparison to the world: 146

Telephone system: *international:* country code—211

Broadcast media: TV is controlled by the government; several private FM stations are operational in South Sudan; some foreign radio broadcasts are available

Internet country code: . ss

TRANSPORTATION

Airports: 85 (2013)
country comparison to the world: 6 4

Airports—with paved runways: *total:* 3
2,438 to 3,047 m: 1
1,524 to 2,437 m: 2 (2013)

Airports—with unpaved runways: *total:* 8 2
2,438 to 3,047 m: 1
1,524 to 2,437 m: 12
914 to 1,523 m: 35
under 914 m: 34 (2013)

Heliports: 1 (2013)

Railways: 248 km; note—a narrow guage, single-track railroad between Babonosa (Sudan) and Wau, the only existing rail system, was repaired in 2010 with $250 million in United Nations funds (2014)

Roadways: 7,000 km; note—little of the road network is paved and much of it is in disrepair; a 192 km paved road between the capital, Juba, and Nimule on the Ugandan border was constructed with USAID funds in 2012 (2012)

Waterways: see entry for Sudan

MILITARY

Military branches: Sudan People's Liberation Army (SPLA)

Military service age and obligation: 18 is the legal minimum age for compulsory and voluntary military service; the Government of South Sudan signed a revised action plan with the UN in March 2012 to demobilize all child soldiers within the SPLA; UNICEF reported 250 confirmed cases of the SPLA's association with children at the end of 2012 (2012)

Military expenditures: 10.32% of GDP (2012)
country comparison to the world: 1
5.8% of GDP (2011)
10.32% of GDP (2010)

TRANSNATIONAL ISSUES

Disputes—international: South Sudan-Sudan boundary represents 1 January 1956 alignment, final alignment pending negotiations and demarcation; final sovereignty status of Abyei Area pending negotiations between South Sudan and Sudan; periodic violent skirmishes with South Sudanese residents over water and grazing rights persist among related pastoral populations along the border with the Central African Republic; the boundary that separates Kenya and South Sudan's sovereignty is unclear in the "Ilemi Triangle," which Kenya has administered since colonial times

Refugees and internally displaced persons:
refugees (country of origin): 214,722 (Sudan); 14,208 (Democratic Republic of the Congo); 6,052 (Ethiopia) (2014)
IDPs: 916,900 (alleged coup attempt and ethnic conflict beginning in December 2013; information is lacking on those
displaced in earlier years by: fighting in Abyei between the Sudanese Armed Forces and the Sudan People's Liberation Army (SPLA) in May 2011; clashes between the SPLA and dissident militia groups in South Sudan; inter-ethnic conflicts over resources and cattle; attacks from the Lord's Resistance Army; floods and drought) (2014)

Trafficking in persons: *current situation:* South Sudan is a source and destination country for men, women, and children subjected to forced labor and sex trafficking; South Sudanese women and girls, particularly those who are internally displaced or from rural areas, are vulnerable to forced labor and sexual exploitation in urban centers; the rising number of street children and child laborers are also exploited for forced labor and prostitution; women and girls from Uganda, Kenya, Ethiopia, and Democratic Republic of the Congo are trafficked to South Sudan with promises of legitimate jobs and are forced into the sex trade; inter-ethnic abductions continue in some communities in South Sudan

tier rating: Tier 2 Watch List—South Sudan does not fully comply with the minimum standards for the elimination of trafficking; however, it is making significant efforts to do so; the government has made progress in implementing its UN-backed action plan to eliminate the use of child soldiers in its armed forces, but it has not demonstrated evidence of increasing efforts to address other forms of trafficking; the government has not taken steps to proactively identify trafficking victims among vulnerable populations and has not deployed a system to transfer victims to organizations to receive care; the government continues to indiscriminately arrest individuals in prostitution, including child sex trafficking victims, and sentence them to prison (2013)

SPAIN

INTRODUCTION

Background: Spain's powerful world empire of the 16th and 17th centuries ultimately yielded command of the seas to England. Subsequent failure to embrace the mercantile and industrial revolutions caused the country to fall behind Britain, France, and Germany in economic and political power. Spain remained neutral in World War I and II but suffered through a devastating civil war (1936-39). A peaceful transition to democracy following the death of dictator Francisco FRANCO in 1975, and rapid economic modernization (Spain joined the EU in 1986) gave Spain a dynamic and rapidly growing economy and made it a global champion of freedom and human rights. More recently the government has had to focus on measures to reverse a severe economic recession that began in mid-2008. Austerity measures implemented to reduce a large budget deficit and reassure foreign investors have led to one of the highest unemployment rates in Europe.

GEOGRAPHY

Location: Southwestern Europe, bordering the Mediterranean Sea, North Atlantic Ocean, Bay of Biscay, and Pyrenees Mountains; southwest of France

Geographic coordinates: 40 00 N, 4 00 W

Map references: Europe

Area: *total:* 505,370 sq km
country comparison to the world: 52
land: 498,980 sq km
water: 6,390 sq km
note: there are two autonomous cities—Ceuta and Melilla—and 17 autonomous communities including Balearic Islands and Canary Islands, and three small Spanish possessions off the coast of Morocco—Islas Chafarinas, Penon de Alhucemas, and Penon de Velez de la Gomera

Area—comparative: almost five times the size of Kentucky; slightly more than twice the size of Oregon

Land boundaries: *total:* 1,917.8 km
border countries: Andorra 63.7 km, France 623 km, Gibraltar 1.2 km, Portugal 1,214 km, Morocco (Ceuta) 6.3 km, Morocco (Melilla) 9.6 km

Coastline: 4,964 km

Maritime claims: *territorial sea:* 12 nm
contiguous zone: 24 nm
exclusive economic zone: 200 nm (applies only to the Atlantic Ocean)

Climate: temperate; clear, hot summers in interior, more moderate and cloudy along coast; cloudy, cold winters in interior, partly cloudy and cool along coast

Terrain: large, flat to dissected plateau surrounded by rugged hills; Pyrenees Mountains in north

Elevation extremes: *lowest point:* Atlantic Ocean 0 m
highest point: Pico de Teide (Tenerife) on Canary Islands 3,718 m

Natural resources: coal, lignite, iron ore, copper, lead, zinc, uranium, tungsten, mercury, pyrites, magnesite, fluorspar, gypsum, sepiolite, kaolin, potash, hydropower, arable land

Land use: *arable land:* 24.75%
permanent crops: 9.29%
other: 65.96% (2011)

Irrigated land: 34,700 sq km (2011)

Total renewable water resources: 111.5 cu km (2011)

Freshwater withdrawal (domestic/industrial/agricultural): *total:* 32.46 cu km/yr (18%/22%/61%)
per capita: 698.7 cu m/yr (2008)

Natural hazards: periodic droughts, occasional flooding
volcanism: volcanic activity in the Canary Islands, located off Africa's northwest coast; Teide (elev. 3,715 m) has been deemed a Decade Volcano by the International Association of Volcanology and Chemistry of the Earth's Interior, worthy of study due to its explosive history and close proximity to human populations; La Palma (elev. 2,426 m), which last erupted in 1971, is the most active of the Canary Islands volcanoes; Lanzarote is the only other historically active volcano

Environment—current issues: pollution of the Mediterranean Sea from raw sewage and effluents from the offshore production of oil and gas; water quality and quantity nationwide; air pollution; deforestation; desertification

Environment—international agreements:
party to: Air Pollution, Air Pollution-Nitrogen Oxides, Air Pollution-Sulfur 94, Air Pollution-Volatile Organic Compounds, Antarctic-Environmental Protocol, Antarctic-Marine Living Resources, Antarctic Treaty, Biodiversity, Climate Change, Climate Change-Kyoto Protocol, Desertification, Endangered Species, Environmental Modification, Hazardous Wastes, Law of the Sea, Marine Dumping, Marine Life Conservation, Ozone Layer Protection, Ship Pollution, Tropical Timber 83, Tropical Timber 94, Wetlands, Whaling
signed, but not ratified: Air Pollution-Persistent Organic Pollutants

Geography—note: strategic location along approaches to Strait of Gibraltar; Spain controls a number of territories in northern Morocco including the enclaves of Ceuta and Melilla, and the islands of Penon de Velez de la Gomera, Penon de Alhucemas, and Islas Chafarinas

PEOPLE AND SOCIETY

Nationality: *noun:* Spaniard(s)
adjective: Spanish

Ethnic groups: composite of Mediterranean and Nordic types

Languages: Castilian Spanish (official) 74%, Catalan 17%, Galician 7%, and Basque 2%
note: Catalan is official in Catalonia, the Balearic Islands, and the Valencian Community (where it is known as Valencian); in the northwest corner of Catalonia (Vall d'Aran), Aranese is official along with Catalan; Galician is official in Galicia; Basque is official in the Basque Country and in the Basque-speaking area of Navarre

Religions: Roman Catholic 94%, other 6%

Population: 47,737,941 (July 2014 est.)
country comparison to the world: 29

Age structure:
0-14 years: 15.4% (male 3,791,781/female 3,575,157)
15-24 years: 9.6% (male 2,370,289/female 2,212,511)
25-54 years: 45.9% (male 11,158,451/female 10,752,197)
55-64 years: 17.6% (male 2,662,055/female 2,799,379)
65 years and over: 17.5% (male 3,582,643/female 4,833,478) (2014 est.)

Dependency ratios:
total dependency ratio: 49.5 %
youth dependency ratio: 23 %
elderly dependency ratio: 26.6 %
potential support ratio: 3.8 (2013)

Median age: *total:* 41.6 years
male: 40.4 years
female: 42.9 years (2014 est.)

Population growth rate: 0.81% (2014 est.)
country comparison to the world: 135

Birth rate: 9.88 births/1,000 population (2014 est.)
country comparison to the world: 197

Death rate: 9 deaths/1,000 population (2014 est.)
country comparison to the world: 69

Net migration rate: 7.24 migrant(s)/1,000 population (2014 est.)
country comparison to the world: 19

Urbanization: *urban population:* 77% of total population (2010)
rate of urbanization: 1% annual rate of change (2010-15 est.)

Major urban areas—population: MADRID (capital) 5.762 million; Barcelona 5.029 million; Valencia 812,000 (2009)

Sex ratio: *at birth:* 1.07 male(s)/female
0-14 years: 1.06 male(s)/female
15-24 years: 1.07 male(s)/female
25-54 years: 1.04 male(s)/female
55-64 years: 0.98 male(s)/female
65 years and over: 0.74 male(s)/female
total population: 0.97 male(s)/female (2014 est.)

Mother's mean age at first birth: 29.3 (2006 est.)

Maternal mortality rate: 6 deaths/100,000 live births (2010)
country comparison to the world: 170

Infant mortality rate: *total:* 3.33 deaths/1,000 live births
country comparison to the world: 212
male: 3.66 deaths/1,000 live births
female: 2.97 deaths/1,000 live births (2014 est.)
Life expectancy at birth:
total population: 81.47 years
country comparison to the world: 18
male: 78.47 years
female: 84.67 years (2014 est.)

Total fertility rate: 1.48 children born/woman (2014 est.)
country comparison to the world: 194

Contraceptive prevalence rate: 65.7% (2006)

Health expenditures: 9.6% of GDP (2010)
country comparison to the world: 31

Physicians density: 3.96 physicians/1,000 population (2011)

Hospital bed density: 3.2 beds/1,000 population (2010)

Drinking water source:
improved:
urban: 99.9% of population
rural: 100% of population
total: 100% of population
unimproved:
urban: 0.1% of population
rural: 0% of population
total: 0% of population (2011 est.)

Sanitation facility access:
improved:
urban: 100% of population
rural: 100% of population
total: 100% of population
unimproved:
urban: 0% of population
rural: 0% of population
total: 0% of population (2011 est.)

HIV/AIDS—adult prevalence rate: 0.4% (2009 est.)
country comparison to the world: 84

HIV/AIDS—people living with HIV/AIDS: 130,000 (2009 est.)
country comparison to the world: 38

HIV/AIDS—deaths: 1,600 (2009 est.)
country comparison to the world: 64

Obesity—adult prevalence rate: 26.6% (2008)
country comparison to the world: 45

Education expenditures: 5% of GDP (2010)
country comparison to the world: 80

Literacy: *definition:* age 15 and over can read and write
total population: 97.7%
male: 98.5%
female: 97% (2010 est.)

School life expectancy (primary to tertiary education): *total:* 17 years
male: 17 years
female: 18 years (2011)

Unemployment, youth ages 15-24: *total:* 53.2%
country comparison to the world: 5
male: 54.4%
female: 51.8% (2012)

GOVERNMENT

Country name: *conventional long form:* Kingdom of Spain
conventional short form: Spain
local long form: Reino de Espana
local short form: Espana

Government type: parliamentary monarchy

Capital: *name:* Madrid

geographic coordinates: 40 24 N, 3 41 W
time difference: UTC+1 (6 hours ahead of Washington, DC during Standard Time)
daylight saving time: +1hr, begins last Sunday in March; ends last Sunday in October
note: Spain is divided into two time zones including the Canary Islands

Administrative divisions: 17 autonomous communities (comunidades autonomas, singular—comunidad autonoma) and 2 autonomous cities* (ciudades autonomas, singular—ciudad autonoma); Andalucia; Aragon; Asturias; Canarias (Canary Islands); Cantabria; Castilla-La Mancha; Castilla y Leon; Cataluna (Castilian), Catalunya (Catalan), Catalonha (Aranese) [Catalonia]; Ceuta*; Comunidad Valenciana (Castilian), Comunitat Valenciana (Valencian) [Valencian Community]; Extremadura; Galicia; Illes Baleares (Balearic Islands); La Rioja; Madrid; Melilla*; Murcia; Navarra (Castilian), Nafarroa (Basque) [Navarre]; Pais Vasco (Castilian), Euskadi (Basque) [Basque Country]
note: the autonomous cities of Ceuta and Melilla plus three small islands of Islas Chafarinas, Penon de Alhucemas, and Penon de Velez de la Gomera, administered directly by the Spanish central government, are all along the coast of Morocco and are collectively referred to as Places of Sovereignty (Plazas de Soberania)

Independence: 1492; the Iberian peninsula was characterized by a variety of independent kingdoms prior to the Muslim occupation that began in the early 8th century A.D. and lasted nearly seven centuries; the small Christian redoubts of the north began the reconquest almost immediately, culminating in the seizure of Granada in 1492; this event completed the unification of several kingdoms and is traditionally considered the forging of present-day Spain

National holiday: National Day, 12 October (1492); year when Columbus first set foot in the Americas

Constitution: previous 1812; latest approved by legislature 31 October 1978, passed by referendum 6 December 1978, signed by the king 27 December 1978, effective 29 December 1978; amended 1992, 2011 (2013)

Legal system: civil law system with regional variations

International law organization participation: accepts compulsory ICJ jurisdiction with reservations; accepts ICCt jurisdiction

Suffrage: 18 years of age; universal

Executive branch: *chief of state:* King JUAN CARLOS I (since 22 November 1975); Heir Apparent Prince FELIPE, son of the monarch, born 30 January 1968
head of government: President of the Government (Prime Minister equivalent) Mariano RAJOY (since 20 December 2011); Vice President (and Minister of the President's Office) Soraya SAENZ DE SANTAMARIA (since 22 December 2011)
cabinet: Council of Ministers designated by the president (For more information visit the World Leaders website)
note: there is also a Council of State that is the supreme consultative organ of the government, but its recommendations are non-binding
elections: the monarchy is hereditary; following legislative elections, the leader of the majority party or the leader of the majority coalition usually proposed president by the monarch and elected by the National Assembly; election last held on 20 November 2011 (next to be held in November 2015); vice president and Council of Ministers are appointed by the president
election results: Mariano RAJOY elected President of the Government; percent of vote—44.62%

Legislative branch: bicameral; General Courts or Las Cortes Generales (National Assembly) consists of the Senate or Senado (257 seats as of 2013; 208 members directly elected by popular vote and the other 49—as of 2013 - appointed by the regional legislatures and 265 seats as of 2014; 208 members directly elected by popular vote and the other 57—as of 2014—appointed by the regional legislatures; members to serve four-year terms) and the Congress of Deputies or Congreso de los Diputados (350 seats; each of the 50 electoral provinces fills a minimum of two seats and the North African enclaves of Ceuta and Melilla fill one seat each with members serving a four-year term; the other 248 members are determined by proportional representation based on popular vote on block lists who serve four-year terms)
elections: Senate—last held on 20 November 2011 (next to be held by November 2015); Congress of Deputies—last held on 20 November 2011 (next to be held by November 2015)
election results: Senate—percent of vote by party—NA; seats by party—PP 136, PSOE 48, CiU 9, Entesa (PSC-PSOE) 7, EAJ/PNV 4, other 4, members appointed by regional legislatures 49; Congress of Deputies - percent of vote by party—PP 44.6%, PSOE 28.8%, CiU 4.2%, IU 6.9%, Amaiur 1.4%, UPyD 4.7%, EAJ/PNV 1.3%, other 8.1%; seats by party—PP 186, PSOE 110, CiU 16, IU 11, Amaiur 7, UPyD 5, EAJ/PNV 5, other 10

Judicial branch: *highest court(s):* Supreme Court or Tribunal Supremo (consists of the court president and organized into the Civil Room with a president and 9 magistrates, the Penal Room with a president and 14 magistrates, the Administrative Room with a president and 32 magistrates, the Social Room with a president and 12 magistrates, and the Military Room with a president and 7 magistrates); Constitutional Court or Tribunal Constitucional de Espana (consists of 12 judges)
judge selection and term of office: Supreme Court judges appointed by the monarch from candidates proposed by the General Council of the Judicial Power, a 20-member body chaired by the monarch and includes presidential appointees, and lawyers and jurists elected by the National Assembly; judge tenure NA; Constitutional Court judges appointed by the monarch for 9-year terms
subordinate courts: National Court; High Courts of Justice (in each of the autonomous communities); provincial courts; courts of first instance

Political parties and leaders: Amaiur [collective leadership] (a separatist political coalition that advocates Basque independence from Spain) Basque Nationalist Party or PNV or EAJ [Inigo URKULLU Renteria]; Canarian Coalition or CC [Claudina MORALES Rodriquez] (a coalition of five parties); Ciutadans [Albert Rivera] (an anti-separatist Catalan party); Convergence and Union or CiU [Artur MAS i Gavarro] (a coalition of the Democratic Convergence of Catalonia or CDC [Artur MAS i Gavarro] and the Democratic Union of Catalonia or UDC [Josep Antoni DURAN i LLEIDA]); Entesa Catalonia de Progress (a Senate coalition grouping four Catalan parties—PSC, ERC, ICV, EUA) Galician Nationalist Bloc or BNG [Guillerme VAZQUEZ Vazquez]; Initiative for Catalonia Greens or ICV [Joan HERRERA i Torres]; Yes to the Future or Geroa Bai [collective leadership] (a coalition of four Navarran parties) Popular Party or PP [Mariano RAJOY Brey]; Republican Left of Catalonia or ERC [Oriol JUNQUERAS i Vies]; Spanish Socialist Workers Party or PSOE [Alfredo Perez RUBALCABA]; Union of People of Navarra or UPN [Yolanda BARCINA Angulo]; Union, Progress and Democracy or UPyD [Rosa DIEZ Gonzalez]; United Left or IU [Cayo LARA Moya] (a coalition of parties including the Communist Party of Spain or PCE and other small parties)

Political pressure groups and leaders: Association for Victims of Terrorism or AVT (grassroots organization devoted primarily to supporting victims of the Basque Fatherland and Liberty (ETA) terrorist organization) 15-M or 15 May protest movement, which is also known as the Indignados, Spanish for the "indignant ones" (a loose association of grassroots organizations that advocate for greater accountability and transparency in Spanish

politics, increased social justice and job creation) Socialist General Union of Workers or UGT and the smaller independent Workers Syndical Union or USO Trade Union Confederation of Workers' Commissions or CC.OO. Spanish Confederation of Employers' Organizations or CEOE
other: business and landowning interests; Catholic Church; free labor unions (authorized in April 1977); university students

International organization participation: ADB (nonregional member), AfDB (nonregional member), Arctic Council (observer), Australia Group, BCIE, BIS, CAN (observer), CBSS (observer), CD, CE, CERN, EAPC, EBRD, ECB, EIB, EITI (implementing country), EMU, ESA, EU, FAO, FATF, IADB, IAEA, IBRD, ICAO, ICRM, IDA, IEA, IFAD, IFC, IFRCS, IHO, ILO, IMF, IMO, IMSO, Interpol, IOC, IOM, IPU, ISO, ITSO, ITU, ITUC (NGOs), LAIA (observer), MIGA, NATO, NEA, NSG, OAS (observer), OECD, OPCW, OSCE, Paris Club, PCA, Schengen Convention, SELEC (observer), SICA (observer), UN, UNCTAD, UNESCO, UNHCR, UNIDO, UNIFIL, Union Latina, UNRWA, UNWTO, UPU, WCO, WHO, WIPO, WMO, WTO, ZC

Diplomatic representation in the US:
chief of mission: Ambassador Ramon GIL-CASARES Satrustegui (since 5 June 2012)
chancery: 2375 Pennsylvania Avenue NW, Washington, DC 20037
telephone: [1] (202) 452-0100, 728-2340
FAX: [1] (202) 833-5670
consulate(s) general: Boston, Chicago, Houston, Los Angeles, Miami, New York, San Francisco, San Juan (Puerto Rico)

Diplomatic representation from the US:
chief of mission: Ambassador James COSTOS (since 22 August 2013); note—also accredited to Andorra
embassy: Serrano 75, 28006 Madrid
mailing address: PSC 61, APO AE 09642
telephone: [34] (91) 587-2200
FAX: [34] (91) 587-2303
consulate(s) general: Barcelona

Flag description: three horizontal bands of red (top), yellow (double width), and red with the national coat of arms on the hoist side of the yellow band; the coat of arms is quartered to display the emblems of the traditional kingdoms of Spain (clockwise from upper left, Castile, Leon, Navarre, and Aragon) while Granada is represented by the stylized pomegranate at the bottom of the shield; the arms are framed by two columns representing the Pillars of Hercules, which are the two promontories (Gibraltar and Ceuta) on either side of the eastern end of the Strait of Gibraltar; the red scroll across the two columns bears the imperial motto of "Plus Ultra" (further beyond) referring to Spanish lands beyond Europe; the triband arrangement with the center stripe twice the width of the outer dates to the 18th century
note: the red and yellow colors are related to those of the oldest Spanish kingdoms: Aragon, Castile, Leon, and Navarre

National symbol(s): Pillars of Hercules

National anthem: *name:* "Himno Nacional Espanol" (National Anthem of Spain)
lyrics/music: none/unknown
note: officially in use between 1770 and 1931, restored in 1939; the Spanish anthem has no lyrics; in the years prior to 1931 it became known as "Marcha Real" (The Royal March); it first appeared in a 1761 military bugle call book and was replaced by "Himno de Riego" in the years between 1931 and 1939; the long version of the anthem is used for the king, while the short version is used for the prince, prime minister, and occasions such as sporting events

ECONOMY

Economy—overview: Spain experienced a prolonged recession in the wake of the global financial crisis. GDP contracted by 3.7% in 2009, ending a 16-year growth trend, and continued contracting through most of 2013. Economic growth resumed in late 2013, albeit only modestly, as credit contraction in the private sector, fiscal austerity, and high unemployment continued to weigh on domestic consumption and investment. Exports, however, have been resilient throughout the economic downturn, partially offsetting declines in domestic consumption and helped to bring Spain's current account into surplus in 2013 for the first time since 1986. The unemployment rate rose from a low of about 8% in 2007 to more than 26% in 2013, straining Spain's public finances as spending on social benefits increased while tax revenues fell. Spain's budget deficit peaked at 11.4% of GDP in 2009. Spain gradually reduced the deficit to just under 7% of GDP in 2013, slightly above the 6.5% target negotiated between Spain and the EU. Public debt has increased substantially – from 60.1% of GDP in 2010 to 93.4% in 2013. Rising labor productivity, moderating labor costs, and lower inflation have helped to improve foreign investor interest in the economy and to reduce government borrowing costs. The government's ongoing efforts to implement reforms—labor, pension, health, tax, and education—are aimed at supporting investor sentiment. The government also has shored up struggling banks exposed to Spain's depressed domestic construction and real estate sectors by successfully completing an EU-funded restructuring and recapitalization program in December 2013.

GDP (purchasing power parity): $1.389 trillion (2013 est.)
country comparison to the world: 15
$1.407 trillion (2012 est.)
$1.43 trillion (2011 est.)
note: data are in 2013 US dollars

GDP (official exchange rate): $1.356 trillion (2013 est.)

GDP—real growth rate: -1.3% (2013 est.)
country comparison to the world: 206
-1.6% (2012 est.)
0.1% (2011 est.)

GDP—per capita (PPP): $30,100 (2013 est.)
country comparison to the world: 47
$30,500 (2012 est.)
$31,000 (2011 est.)
note: data are in 2013 US dollars

Gross national saving: 18.9% of GDP (2013 est.)
country comparison to the world: 83
18.6% of GDP (2012 est.)
17.5% of GDP (2011 est.)

GDP—composition, by end use:
household consumption: 59%
government consumption: 19.9%
investment in fixed capital: 18.4%
investment in inventories: 0.4%
exports of goods and services: 32.8%
imports of goods and services: -30.4% (2013 est.)

GDP—composition, by sector of origin:
agriculture: 3.1%
industry: 26%
services: 70.8% (2013 est.)

Agriculture—products: grain, vegetables, olives, wine grapes, sugar beets, citrus; beef, pork, poultry, dairy products; fish

Industries: textiles and apparel (including footwear), food and beverages, metals and metal manufactures, chemicals, shipbuilding, automobiles, machine tools, tourism, clay and refractory products, footwear, pharmaceuticals, medical equipment

Industrial production growth rate: -1.2% (2013 est.)
country comparison to the world: 181

Labor force: 23.2 million (2013 est.)
country comparison to the world: 29

Labor force—by occupation: *agriculture:* 4.2%
industry: 24%
services: 71.7% (2009 est.)

Unemployment rate: 26.3% (2013 est.)
country comparison to the world: 176
25.1% (2012 est.)

Population below poverty line: 21.1% (2012)

Household income or consumption by percentage share: *lowest 10%:* 2.6%
highest 10%: 26.6% (2000)

Distribution of family income—Gini index: 32 (2005)
country comparison to the world: 107
32.5 (1990)

Budget: *revenues:* $505.1 billion
expenditures: $597.3 billion (2013 est.)

Taxes and other revenues: 37.1% of GDP (2013 est.)
country comparison to the world: 55

Budget surplus (+) or deficit (-):
-6.8% of GDP (2013 est.)
country comparison to the world: 186

Public debt: 93.7% of GDP (2013 est.)
country comparison to the world: 18
85.9% of GDP (2012 est.)

Fiscal year: calendar year

Inflation rate (consumer prices): 1.8% (2013 est.)
country comparison to the world: 55
2.4% (2012 est.)

Central bank discount rate: 0.75% (31 December 2013)
country comparison to the world: 127
1.5% (31 December 2010)
note: this is the European Central Bank's rate on the marginal lending facility, which offers overnight credit to banks in the euro area

Commercial bank prime lending rate: 8% (31 December 2013 est.)
country comparison to the world: 113
8.3% (31 December 2012 est.)

Stock of narrow money: $777.3 billion (31 December 2013 est.)
country comparison to the world: 8
$785.2 billion (31 December 2012 est.)
note: see entry for the European Union for money supply in the euro area; the European Central Bank (ECB) controls monetary policy for the 17 members of the Economic and Monetary Union (EMU); individual members of the EMU do not control the quantity of money circulating within their own borders

Stock of broad money: $2.003 trillion (31 December 2013 est.)
country comparison to the world: 9
$2.096 trillion (31 December 2012 est.)

Stock of domestic credit: $2.936 trillion (31 December 2013 est.)
country comparison to the world: 10
$3.045 trillion (31 December 2012 est.)

Market value of publicly traded shares: $995.1 billion (31 December 2012 est.)
country comparison to the world: 12
$1.031 trillion (31 December 2011)
$1.172 trillion (31 December 2010 est.)

Current account balance: $2.1 billion (2013 est.)
country comparison to the world: 39

-$15.14 billion (2012 est.)

Exports: $458 billion (2013 est.)
country comparison to the world: 14
$432 billion (2012 est.)

Exports—commodities: machinery, motor vehicles; foodstuffs, pharmaceuticals, medicines, other consumer goods

Exports—partners: France 16.8%, Germany 10.8%, Italy 7.7%, Portugal 7.1%, UK 6.5% (2012)

Imports: $431 billion (2013 est.)
country comparison to the world: 14
$422 billion (2012 est.)

Imports—commodities: machinery and equipment, fuels, chemicals, semifinished goods, foodstuffs, consumer goods, measuring and medical control instruments

Imports—partners: Germany 11.8%, France 11.5%, Italy 6.7%, China 5.6%, Netherlands 5.4%, UK 4.1% (2012)

Reserves of foreign exchange and gold: $50.59 billion (31 December 2012 est.)
country comparison to the world: 40
$47.1 billion (31 December 2011 est.)

Debt—external: $2.278 trillion (31 December 2012 est.)
country comparison to the world: 10
$2.269 trillion (31 December 2011)

Stock of direct foreign investment—at home: $779.5 billion (31 December 2013 est.)
country comparison to the world: 11
$725.3 billion (31 December 2012 est.)

Stock of direct foreign investment—abroad: $714.4 billion (31 December 2013 est.)
country comparison to the world: 12
$710.2 billion (31 December 2012 est.)

Exchange rates: euros (EUR) per US dollar—
0.7634 (2013 est.)
0.7752 (2012 est.)
0.755 (2010 est.)
0.7198 (2009 est.)
0.6827 (2008 est.)

ENERGY

Electricity—production: 276.8 billion kWh (2011 est.)
country comparison to the world: 15

Electricity—consumption: 249.7 billion kWh (2011 est.)
country comparison to the world: 14

Electricity—exports: 19.59 billion kWh (2012 est.)
country comparison to the world: 10

Electricity—imports: 8.209 billion kWh (2012 est.)
country comparison to the world: 28

Electricity—installed generating capacity: 101.7 million kW (2010 est.)
country comparison to the world: 12

Electricity—from fossil fuels: 48.7% of total installed capacity (2010 est.)
country comparison to the world: 158

Electricity—from nuclear fuels: 7.3% of total installed capacity (2010 est.)
country comparison to the world: 21

Electricity—from hydroelectric plants: 13% of total installed capacity (2010 est.)
country comparison to the world: 107

Electricity—from other renewable sources: 25.8% of total installed capacity (2010 est.)
country comparison to the world: 4

Crude oil—production: 29,290 bbl/day (2012 est.)
country comparison to the world: 68

Crude oil—exports: 0 bbl/day (2010 est.)
country comparison to the world: 184

Crude oil—imports: 1.061 million bbl/day (2010 est.)
country comparison to the world: 11

Crude oil—proved reserves: 150 million bbl (1 January 2013 es)
country comparison to the world: 65

Refined petroleum products—production: 1.189 million bbl/day (2010 est.)
country comparison to the world: 18

Refined petroleum productsvconsumption: 1.384 million bbl/day (2011 est.)
country comparison to the world: 17

Refined petroleum products—exports: 249,500 bbl/day (2010 est.)
country comparison to the world: 26

Refined petroleum products—imports: 566,200 bbl/day (2010 est.)
country comparison to the world: 12

Natural gas—production: 61 million cu m (2012 est.)
country comparison to the world: 85

Natural gas—consumption: 35.82 billion cu m (2010 est.)
country comparison to the world: 26

Natural gas—exports: 4.414 billion cu m (2012 est.)
country comparison to the world: 36

Natural gas—imports: 36.75 billion cu m (2012 est.)
country comparison to the world: 16

Natural gas—proved reserves: 2.548 billion cu m (1 January 2013 es)
country comparison to the world: 98

Carbon dioxide emissions from consumption of energy: 318.6 million Mt (2011 est.)
country comparison to the world: 20

COMMUNICATIONS

Telephones—main lines in use: 19.22 million (2012)
country comparison to the world: 15

Telephones—mobile cellular: 50.663 million (2012)
country comparison to the world: 28

Telephone system: *general assessment:* well-developed, modern facilities; fixed-line teledensity exceeds 40 per 100 persons
domestic: combined fixed-line and mobile-cellular teledensity exceeds 150 telephones per 100 persons
international: country code—34; submarine cables provide connectivity to Europe, Middle East, Asia, and US; satellite earth stations—2 Intelsat (1 Atlantic Ocean and 1 Indian Ocean), NA Eutelsat; tropospheric scatter to adjacent countries (2011)

Broadcast media: a mixture of both publicly operated and privately owned TV and radio stations; overall, hundreds of TV channels are available including national, regional, local, public, and international channels; satellite and cable TV systems available; multiple national radio networks, a large number of regional radio networks, and a larger number of local radio stations; overall, hundreds of radio stations (2008)

Internet country code: .es

Internet hosts: 4.228 million (2012)
country comparison to the world: 26

Internet users: 28.119 million (2009)
country comparison to the world: 14

TRANSPORTATION

Airports: 150 (2013)
country comparison to the world: 3 8

Airports—with paved runways: *total:* 9 9
over 3,047 m: 18
2,438 to 3,047 m: 14
1,524 to 2,437 m: 19
914 to 1,523 m: 24
under 914 m: 24 (2013)

Airports—with unpaved runways: *total:* 5 1
1,524 to 2,437 m: 2
914 to 1,523 m: 13
under 914 m: 36 (2013)

Heliports: 10 (2013)

Pipelines: gas 10,481 km; oil 616 km; refined products 3,461 km (2013)

Railways: *total:* 15,293 km
country comparison to the world: 19
broad gauge: 11,919 km 1.668-m gauge (6,950 km electrified)
standard gauge: 1,392 km 1.435-m gauge (1,054 km electrified)
narrow gauge: 1,954 km 1.000-m gauge (815 km electrified); 28 km 0.914-m gauge (2008)

Roadways: *total:* 683,175 km
country comparison to the world: 10
paved: 683,175 km (includes 16,205 km of expressways) (2011)

Waterways: 1,000 km (2012)
country comparison to the world: 65

Merchant marine: *total:* 132
country comparison to the world: 44
by type: bulk carrier 7, cargo 19, chemical tanker 8, container 5, liquefied gas 12, passenger/cargo 43, petroleum tanker 18, refrigerated cargo 4, roll on/roll off 9, vehicle carrier 7
foreign-owned: 27 (Canada 4, Germany 4, Italy 1, Mexico 1, Norway 10, Russia 6, Switzerland 1)
registered in other countries: 103 (Angola 1, Argentina 3, Bahamas 6, Brazil 12, Cabo Verde 1, Cyprus 6, Ireland 1, Malta 8, Morocco 9, Panama 30, Peru 1, Portugal 18, Uruguay 5, Venezuela 1, unknown 1) (2010)

Ports and terminals: *major seaport(s):* Algeciras, Barcelona, Bilbao, Cartagena, Huelva, Tarragona, Valencia (Spain); Las Palmas, Santa Cruz de Tenerife (Canary Islands)
container port(s) (TEUs): Algeciras (3,608,301), Barcelona (2,033,747), Valencia (4,327,371); Las Palmas (1,287,389)

MILITARY

Military branches: Spanish Armed Forces: Army (Ejercito de Tierra), Spanish Navy (Armada Espanola, AE; includes Marine Corps), Spanish Air Force (Ejercito del Aire Espanola, EdA) (2013)

Military service age and obligation: 18-26 years of age for voluntary military service by a Spanish citizen or legal immigrant, 2-3 year obligation; women allowed to serve in all SAF branches, including combat units; no conscription, but Spanish Government retains right to mobilize citizens 19-25 years of age in a national emergency; mandatory retirement of non-NCO enlisted personnel at age 45 or 58, depending on service length (2013)

Manpower available for military service: *males age 16-49:* 11,759,557
females age 16-49: 11,204,688 (2010 est.)

Manpower fit for military service: *males age 16-49:* 9,603,939
females age 16-49: 9,116,928 (2010 est.)

Manpower reaching militarily significant age annually: *male:* 217,244
female: 205,278 (2010 est.)

Military expenditures: 0.86% of GDP (2012)
country comparison to the world: 111
0.95% of GDP (2011)
0.86% of GDP (2010)

TRANSNATIONAL ISSUES

Disputes—international: in 2002, Gibraltar residents voted overwhelmingly by referendum to reject any "shared sovereignty" arrangement; the Government of Gibraltar insists on equal participation in talks between the UK and Spain; Spain disapproves of UK plans to grant Gibraltar greater autonomy; Morocco protests Spain's control over the coastal enclaves of Ceuta, Melilla, and the islands of Penon de Velez de la Gomera, Penon de Alhucemas, and Islas Chafarinas, and surrounding waters; both countries claim Isla Perejil (Leila Island); Morocco serves as the primary launching site of illegal migration into Spain from North Africa; Portugal does not recognize Spanish sovereignty over the territory of Olivenza based on a difference of interpretation of the 1815 Congress of Vienna and the 1801 Treaty of Badajoz

Refugees and internally displaced persons: *stateless persons:* 36 (2012)

Illicit drugs: despite rigorous law enforcement efforts, North African, Latin American, Galician, and other European traffickers take advantage of Spain's long coastline to land large shipments of cocaine and hashish for distribution to the European market; consumer for Latin American cocaine and North African hashish; destination and minor transshipment point for Southwest Asian heroin; money-laundering site for Colombian narcotics trafficking organizations and organized crime

SPRATLY ISLANDS

INTRODUCTION

Background: The Spratly Islands consist of more than 100 small islands or reefs. They are surrounded by rich fishing grounds and potentially by gas and oil deposits. They are claimed in their entirety by China, Taiwan, and Vietnam, while portions are claimed by Malaysia and the Philippines. About 45 islands are occupied by relatively small numbers of military forces from China, Malaysia, the Philippines, Taiwan, and Vietnam. Since 1985 Brunei has claimed a continental shelf that overlaps a southern reef but has not made any formal claim to the reef. Brunei claims an exclusive economic zone over this area.

GEOGRAPHY

Location: Southeastern Asia, group of reefs and islands in the South China Sea, about two-thirds of the way from southern Vietnam to the southern Philippines

Geographic coordinates: 8 38 N, 111 55 E

Map references: Southeast Asia

Area: *total:* less than 5 sq km
country comparison to the world: 248
land: less than 5 sq km
water: 0 sq km
note: includes 100 or so islets, coral reefs, and sea mounts scattered over an area of nearly 410,000 sq km of the central South China Sea

Area—comparative: NA

Land boundaries: 0 km

Coastline: 926 km

Maritime claims: NA

Climate: tropical

Terrain: flat

Elevation extremes: *lowest point:* South China Sea 0 m
highest point: unnamed location on Southwest Cay 4 m

Natural resources: fish, guano, undetermined oil and natural gas potential

Land use: *arable land:* 0%
permanent crops: 0%
other: 100% (2011)

Irrigated land: 5,700 sq km (2006)

Natural hazards: typhoons; numerous reefs and shoals pose a serious maritime hazard

Environment—current issues: NA

Geography—note: strategically located near several primary shipping lanes in the central South China Sea; includes numerous small islands, atolls, shoals, and coral reefs

PEOPLE AND SOCIETY

Population: no indigenous inhabitants
note: there are scattered garrisons occupied by military personnel of several claimant states

GOVERNMENT

Country name: *conventional long form:* none
conventional short form: Spratly Islands

ECONOMY

Economy—overview: Economic activity is limited to commercial fishing. The proximity to nearby oil—and gas-producing sedimentary basins suggests the potential for oil and gas deposits, but the region is largely unexplored. There are no reliable estimates of potential reserves. Commercial exploitation has yet to be developed.

TRANSPORTATION

Airports: 4 (2013)
country comparison to the world: 191

Airports—with paved runways: *total:* 3
914 to 1,523 m: 2
under 914 m: 1 (2013)

Airports—with unpaved runways: *total:* 1
914 to 1,523 m: 1 (2013)

Heliports: 3 (2013)

Ports and terminals: none; offshore anchorage only

MILITARY

Military—note: Spratly Islands consist of more than 100 small islands or reefs of which about 45 are claimed and occupied by China, Malaysia, the Philippines, Taiwan, and Vietnam

TRANSNATIONAL ISSUES

Disputes—international: all of the Spratly Islands are claimed by China (including Taiwan) and Vietnam; parts of them are claimed by Brunei, Malaysia and the Philippines; despite no public territorial claim to Louisa Reef, Brunei implicitly lays claim by including it within the natural prolongation of its continental shelf and basis for a seabed median with Vietnam; claimants in November 2002 signed the "Declaration on the Conduct of Parties in the South China Sea," which has eased tensions but falls short of a legally binding "code of conduct"; in March 2005, the national oil companies of China, the Philippines, and Vietnam signed a joint accord to conduct marine seismic activities in the Spratly Islands

SRI LANKA

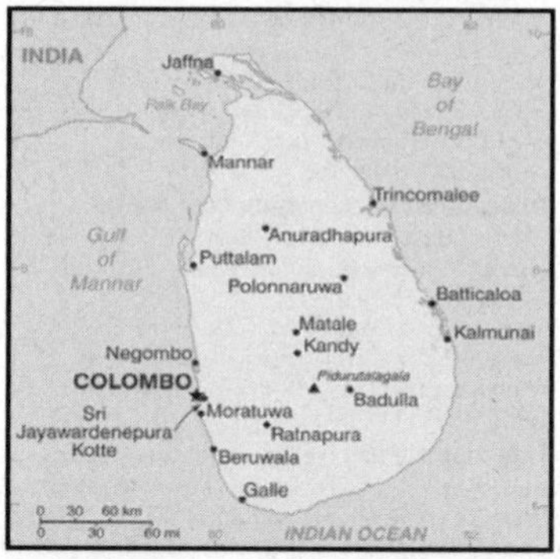

INTRODUCTION

Background: The first Sinhalese arrived in Sri Lanka late in the 6th century B.C., probably from northern India. Buddhism was introduced in about the mid-third century B.C., and a great civilization developed at the cities of Anuradhapura (kingdom from circa 200 B.C. to circa A.D. 1000) and Polonnaruwa (from about 1070 to 1200). In the 14th century, a south Indian dynasty established a Tamil kingdom in northern Sri Lanka. The coastal areas of the island were controlled by the Portuguese in the 16th century and by the Dutch in the 17th century. The island was ceded to the British in 1796, became a crown colony in 1802, and was formally united under British rule by 1815. As Ceylon, it became independent in 1948; its name was changed to Sri Lanka in 1972. Tensions between the Sinhalese majority and Tamil separatists erupted into war in 1983. After two decades of fighting, the government and Liberation Tigers of Tamil Eelam (LTTE) formalized a cease-fire in February 2002 with Norway brokering peace negotiations. Violence between the LTTE and government forces intensified in 2006, but the government regained control of the Eastern Province in 2007. By May 2009, the government announced that its military had defeated the remnants of the LTTE. Since the end of the conflict, the government has enacted an ambitious program of economic development projects, many of which are financed by loans from the Government of China. In addition to efforts to reconstruct its economy, the government has resettled more than 95% of those civilians who were displaced during the final phase of the conflict and released the vast majority of former LTTE combatants captured by Government Security Forces. At the same time, there has been little progress on more contentious and politically difficult issues such as reaching a political settlement with Tamil elected representatives and holding accountable those alleged to have been involved in human rights violations and other abuses during the conflict.

GEOGRAPHY

Location: Southern Asia, island in the Indian Ocean, south of India

Geographic coordinates: 7 00 N, 81 00 E

Map references: Asia

Area: *total:* 65,610 sq km
country comparison to the world: 122
land: 64,630 sq km
water: 980 sq km

Area—comparative: slightly larger than West Virginia

Land boundaries: 0 km

Coastline: 1,340 km

Maritime claims: *territorial sea:* 12 nm
contiguous zone: 24 nm
exclusive economic zone: 200 nm
continental shelf: 200 nm or to the edge of the continental margin

Climate: tropical monsoon; northeast monsoon (December to March); southwest monsoon (June to October)

Terrain: mostly low, flat to rolling plain; mountains in south-central interior

Elevation extremes: *lowest point:* Indian Ocean 0 m
highest point: Pidurutalagala 2,524 m

Natural resources: limestone, graphite, mineral sands, gems, phosphates, clay, hydropower

Land use: *arable land:* 18.29%
permanent crops: 14.94%
other: 66.77% (2011)

Irrigated land: 5,700 sq km (2003)

Total renewable water resources: 52.8 cu km (2011)

Freshwater withdrawal (domestic/industrial/agricultural): *total:* 12.95 cu km/yr (6%/6%/87%)
per capita: 638.8 cu m/yr (2005)

Natural hazards: occasional cyclones and tornadoes

Environment—current issues: deforestation; soil erosion; wildlife populations threatened by poaching and urbanization; coastal degradation from mining activities and increased pollution; freshwater resources being polluted by industrial wastes and sewage runoff; waste disposal; air pollution in Colombo

Environment—international agreements:
party to: Biodiversity, Climate Change, Climate Change-Kyoto Protocol, Desertification, Endangered Species, Environmental Modification, Hazardous Wastes, Law of the Sea, Ozone Layer Protection, Ship Pollution, Wetlands
signed, but not ratified: Marine Life Conservation

Geography—note: strategic location near major Indian Ocean sea lanes

PEOPLE AND SOCIETY

Nationality: *noun:* Sri Lankan(s)
adjective: Sri Lankan

Ethnic groups: Sinhalese 73.8%, Sri Lankan Moors 7.2%, Indian Tamil 4.6%, Sri Lankan Tamil 3.9%, other 0.5%, unspecified 10% (2001 census provisional data)

Languages: Sinhala (official and national language) 74%, Tamil (national language) 18%, other 8%
note: English, spoken competently by about 10% of the population, is commonly used in government and is referred to as the link language in the constitution

Religions: Buddhist (official) 69.1%, Muslim 7.6%, Hindu 7.1%, Christian 6.2%, unspecified 10% (2001 census provisional data)

Population: 21,866,445 (July 2014 est.)
country comparison to the world: 57

Age structure: *0-14 years:* 24.7% (male 2,758,360/female 2,648,073)
15-24 years: 14.9% (male 1,651,901/female 1,606,465)
25-54 years: 42.1% (male 4,504,395/female 4,708,288)
55-64 years: 8.7% (male 966,295/female 1,117,310)
65 years and over: 8.4% (male 812,669/female 1,092,689) (2014 est.)

Dependency ratios:
total dependency ratio: 50.7 %
youth dependency ratio: 37.9 %
elderly dependency ratio: 12.8 %
potential support ratio: 7.8 (2013)

Median age: *total:* 31.8 years
male: 30.6 years
female: 32.9 years (2014 est.)

Population growth rate: 0.86% (2014 est.)
country comparison to the world: 130

Birth rate: 16.24 births/1,000 population (2014 est.)
country comparison to the world: 122

Death rate: 6.06 deaths/1,000 population (2014 est.)
country comparison to the world: 164

Net migration rate: -1.54 migrant(s)/1,000 population (2014 est.)
country comparison to the world: 157

Urbanization: *urban population:* 15.1% of total population (2011)
rate of urbanization: 1.36% annual rate of change (2010-15 est.)

Major urban areas—population: COLOMBO (capital) 681,000 (2009)

Sex ratio: *at birth:* 1.04 male(s)/female
0-14 years: 1.04 male(s)/female
15-24 years: 1.03 male(s)/female
25-54 years: 0.96 male(s)/female
55-64 years: 0.96 male(s)/female
65 years and over: 0.75 male(s)/female
total population: 0.96 male(s)/female (2014 est.)

Mother's mean age at first birth: 22.6
note: median age at first birth among women 25-29 (2000 est.)

Maternal mortality rate: 35 deaths/100,000 live births (2010)
country comparison to the world: 118

Infant mortality rate: *total:* 9.02 deaths/1,000 live births
country comparison to the world: 147
male: 9.98 deaths/1,000 live births
female: 8.02 deaths/1,000 live births (2014 est.)

Life expectancy at birth: *total population:* 76.35 years
country comparison to the world: 83
male: 72.85 years
female: 79.99 years (2014 est.)

Total fertility rate: 2.13 children born/woman (2014 est.)
country comparison to the world: 107

Contraceptive prevalence rate: 68% (2006/07)

Health expenditures: 3.4% of GDP (2011)
country comparison to the world: 177

Physicians density: 0.49 physicians/1,000 population (2006)

Hospital bed density: 3.1 beds/1,000 population (2004)

Drinking water source: improved:
urban: 98.8% of population
rural: 91.5% of population
total: 92.6% of population
unimproved:

urban: 1.2% of population
rural: 8.5% of population
total: 7.4% of population (2011 est.)

Sanitation facility access: improved:
urban: 82.7% of population
rural: 92.6% of population
total: 91.1% of population
unimproved:
urban: 17.36% of population
rural: 7.4% of population
total: 8.9% of population (2011 est.)

HIV/AIDS—adult prevalence rate: 0.1% (2012 est.)
country comparison to the world: 144

HIV/AIDS—people living with HIV/AIDS: 3,000 (2012 est.)
country comparison to the world: 134

HIV/AIDS—deaths: 200 (2012 est.)
country comparison to the world: 113

Major infectious diseases:
degree of risk: high
food or waterborne diseases: bacterial diarrhea and hepatitis A
vectorborne disease: dengue fever
water contact disease: leptospirosis
animal contact disease: rabies (2013)

Obesity—adult prevalence rate: 5.1% (2008)
country comparison to the world: 155

Children under the age of 5 years underweight: 21.6% (2009)
country comparison to the world: 28

Education expenditures: 1.7% of GDP (2012)
country comparison to the world: 168

Literacy: *definition:* age 15 and over can read and write
total population: 91.2%
male: 92.6%
female: 90% (2010 census)

School life expectancy (primary to tertiary education): *total:* 14 years
male: 13 years
female: 14 years (2012)

Unemployment, youth ages 15-24: *total:* 17.3%
country comparison to the world: 74
male: 14%
female: 23.5% (2012)

GOVERNMENT

Country name: *conventional long form:* Democratic Socialist Republic of Sri Lanka
conventional short form: Sri Lanka
local long form: Shri Lanka Prajatantrika Samajavadi Janarajaya/Ilankai Jananayaka Choshalichak Kutiyarachu
local short form: Shri Lanka/Ilankai
former: Serendib, Ceylon

Government type: republic

Capital: *name:* Colombo
geographic coordinates: 6 55 N, 79 50 E
time difference: UTC+5.5 (10.5 hours ahead of Washington, DC during Standard Time)
note: Sri Jayewardenepura Kotte (legislative capital)

Administrative divisions: 9 provinces; Central, Eastern, North Central, Northern, North Western, Sabaragamuwa, Southern, Uva, Western

Independence: 4 February 1948 (from the UK)

National holiday: Independence Day, 4 February (1948)

Constitution: several previous; latest adopted 16 August 1978, certified 31 August 1978; amended many times, last in 2010 (2010)

Legal system: mixed legal system of Roman-Dutch civil law, English common law, and Jaffna Tamil customary law

International law organization participation: has not submitted an ICJ jurisdiction declaration; non-party state to the ICCt

Suffrage: 18 years of age; universal

Executive branch: *chief of state:* President Mahinda Percy RAJAPAKSA (since 19 November 2005); note—the president is both the chief of state and head of government; Dissanayake Mudiyanselage JAYARATNE holds the largely ceremonial title of prime minister (since 21 April 2010)
head of government: President Mahinda Percy RAJAPAKSA (since 19 November 2005)
cabinet: Cabinet appointed by the president in consultation with the prime minister (For more information visit the World Leaders website)
elections: president elected by popular vote for a six-year term, eligible for a second term; election last held on 26 January 2010 (next to be held in 2016)
election results: Mahinda Percy RAJAPAKSA reelected president for second term; percent of vote—Mahinda Percy RAJAPAKSA 57.88%, Sarath FONSEKA 40.15%, other 1.97%

Legislative branch: unicameral Parliament (225 seats; members elected by popular vote on the basis of an open-list, proportional representation system by electoral district to serve six-year terms)
elections: last held on 8 April 2010 with a repoll in two electorates held on 20 April 2010 (next to be held by April 2016)
election results: percent of vote by alliance or party—United People's Freedom Alliance 60.93%, United National Party 29.34%, Democratic National Alliance 5.49%, Tamil National Alliance 2.9%, other 1.34%; seats by alliance or party—United People's Freedom Alliance 144, United National Party 60, Tamil National Alliance 14, Democratic National Alliance 7

Judicial branch: *highest court(s):* Supreme Court of the Republic (consists of the chief justice and 10 justices); note—the court has exclusive jurisdiction to review legislation
judge selection and term of office: the chief justice appointed by the president; the other justices appointed by the president with the advice of the chief justice; all justices hold office until age 65
subordinate courts: Court of Appeals; High Courts; Magistrate's Courts; municipal and primary courts

Political parties and leaders:
Coalitions and leaders: Democratic National Alliance, led by General (Retired) Sarath FONSEKA
Janatha Vimukthi Peramuna or JVP [Somawansa AMARASINGHE]; Tamil National Alliance led by Illandai Tamil Arasu Kachchi [R. SAMPANTHAN]; United National Front led by United National Party [Ranil WICKREMESINGHE]; United People's Freedom Alliance led by Sri Lanka Freedom Party [Mahinda RAJAPAKSA]

Political pressure groups and leaders: Buddhist clergy; labor unions; hard-line nationalist Sinhalese groups such as the National Movement Against Terrorism; Sinhalese Buddhist lay groups

International organization participation: ABEDA, ADB, ARF, BIMSTEC, C, CD, CP, FAO, G-11, G-15, G-24, G-77, IAEA, IBRD, ICAO, ICC (national committees), ICRM, IDA, IFAD, IFC, IFRCS, IHO, ILO, IMF, IMO, IMSO, Interpol, IOC, IOM, IPU, ISO, ITSO, ITU, ITUC (NGOs), MIGA, MINURSO, MINUSTAH, MONUSCO, NAM, OAS (observer), OPCW, PCA, SAARC, SACEP, SCO (dialogue member), UN, UNCTAD, UNESCO, UNIDO, UNIFIL, UNISFA, UNMISS, UNWTO, UPU, WCO, WFTU (NGOs), WHO, WIPO, WMO, WTO

Diplomatic representation in the US:
chief of mission: Ambassador Designate Prasad KARIYAWASAM (since 2014)
chancery: 2148 Wyoming Avenue NW, Washington, DC 20008
telephone: [1] (202) 483-4025 through 4028
FAX: [1] (202) 232-7181
consulate(s) general: Los Angeles
consulate(s): New York

Diplomatic representation from the US:
chief of mission: Ambassador Michele J. SISON (since 29 September 2012); note—also accredited to Maldives
embassy: 210 Galle Road, Colombo 3
mailing address: P. O. Box 106, Colombo
telephone: [94] (11) 249-8500
FAX: [94] (11) 243-7345

Flag description: yellow with two panels; the smaller hoist-side panel has two equal vertical bands of green (hoist side) and orange; the other larger panel depicts a yellow lion holding a sword on a dark red rectangular field that also displays a yellow bo leaf in each corner; the yellow field appears as a border around the entire flag and extends between the two panels; the lion represents Sinhalese ethnicity, the strength of the nation, and bravery; the sword demonstrates the sovereignty of the nation; the four bo leaves—symbolizing Buddhism and its influence on the country—stand for the four virtues of kindness, friendliness, happiness, and equanimity; orange signifies Sri Lankan Tamils, green the Sri Lankan Moors; dark red represents the European Burghers, but also refers to the rich colonial background of the country; yellow denotes other ethnic groups; also referred to as the Lion Flag

National symbol(s):
lion

National anthem: *name:* "Sri Lanka Matha" (Mother Sri Lanka)
lyrics/music: Ananda SAMARKONE
note: adopted 1951

ECONOMY

Economy—overview: Sri Lanka continues to experience strong economic growth following the end of the 26-year conflict with the Liberation Tigers of Tamil Eelam. The government has been pursuing large-scale reconstruction and development projects in its efforts to spur growth in war-torn and disadvantaged areas, develop small and medium enterprises and increase agricultural productivity. The government's high debt payments and bloated civil service have contributed to historically high budget deficits, but fiscal consolidation efforts and strong GDP growth in recent years have helped bring down the government's fiscal deficit. However, low tax revenues are a major concern. The 2008-09 global financial crisis and recession exposed Sri Lanka's economic vulnerabilities and nearly caused a balance of payments crisis. Agriculture slowed due to a drought and weak global demand affected exports and trade. In early 2012, Sri Lanka floated the rupee, resulting in a sharp depreciation, and took steps to curb imports. A large trade deficit remains a concern, but strong remittances from Sri Lankan workers abroad help offset the trade deficit. Government debt of about 80% of GDP remains among the highest in emerging markets.

GDP (purchasing power parity): $134.5 billion (2013 est.)
country comparison to the world: 65
$126.6 billion (2012 est.)

$119 billion (2011 est.)
note: data are in 2013 US dollars

GDP (official exchange rate): $65.12 billion (2013 est.)

GDP—real growth rate: 6.3% (2013 est.)
country comparison to the world: 32
6.4% (2012 est.)
8.2% (2011 est.)

GDP—per capita (PPP): $6,500 (2013 est.)
country comparison to the world: 145
$6,100 (2012 est.)
$5,800 (2011 est.)
note: data are in 2013 US dollars

Gross national saving: 27% of GDP (2013 est.)
country comparison to the world: 39
24% of GDP (2012 est.)
22.1% of GDP (2011 est.)

GDP—composition, by end use:
household consumption: 69.7%
government consumption: 13.2%
investment in fixed capital: 29%
investment in inventories: 1.7%
exports of goods and services: 20.1%
imports of goods and services: -33.7% (2013 est.)

GDP—composition, by sector of origin:
agriculture: 10.6%
industry: 32.4%
services: 57% (2013 est.)

Agriculture—products: rice, sugarcane, grains, pulses, oilseed, spices, vegetables, fruit, tea, rubber, coconuts; milk, eggs, hides, beef; fish

Industries: processing of rubber, tea, coconuts, tobacco and other agricultural commodities; telecommunications, insurance, banking; tourism, shipping; clothing, textiles; cement, petroleum refining, information technology services, construction

Industrial production growth rate: 10% (2013 est.)
country comparison to the world: 15

Labor force: 8.528 million (2013 est.)
country comparison to the world: 55

Labor force—by occupation: *agriculture:* 31.8%
industry: 25.8%
services: 42.4% (June 2012)

Unemployment rate: 5.1% (2013 est.)
country comparison to the world: 49
4% (2012 est.)

Population below poverty line: 8.9% (2010 est.)

Household income or consumption by percentage share: *lowest 10%:* 1.6%
highest 10%: 39.5% (2009)

Distribution of family income—Gini index: 49 (2010)
country comparison to the world: 24
46 (1995)

Budget: *revenues:* $8.43 billion
expenditures: $12.57 billion (2013 est.)

Taxes and other revenues: 12.9% of GDP (2013 est.)
country comparison to the world: 200

Budget surplus (+) or deficit (-):
-6.4% of GDP (2013 est.)
country comparison to the world: 184

Public debt: 78.4% of GDP (2013 est.)
country comparison to the world: 29
79.1% of GDP (2012 est.)
note: covers central government debt, and excludes debt instruments directly owned by government entities other than the treasury (e.g. commercial bank borrowings of a government corporation); the data includes treasury debt held by foreign entities as well as intra-governmental debt; intra-governmental debt consists of treasury borrowings from surpluses in the social funds, such as for retirement; sub-national entities are usually not permitted to sell debt instruments

Fiscal year: calendar year

Inflation rate (consumer prices): 4.7% (2013 est.)
country comparison to the world: 151
9.2% (2012 est.)

Central bank discount rate: 6.5% (31 December 2013 est.)
country comparison to the world: 34
7.5% (19 December 2012 est.)

Commercial bank prime lending rate: 9.88% (31 December 2013 est.)
country comparison to the world: 46
14.4% (31 December 2012 est.)

Stock of narrow money: $3.629 billion (31 December 2013 est.)
country comparison to the world: 113
$3.539 billion (31 December 2012 est.)

Stock of broad money: $23.55 billion (31 December 2013 est.)
country comparison to the world: 81
$20.39 billion (31 December 2012 est.)

Stock of domestic credit: $32.98 billion (31 December 2013 est.)
country comparison to the world: 70
$28.86 billion (31 December 2012 est.)

Market value of publicly traded shares: $18.48 billion (31 November 2013 est.)
country comparison to the world: 66
$17.05 billion (31 December 2012)
$19.44 billion (31 December 2011 est.)

Current account balance: -$2.452 billion (2013 est.)
country comparison to the world: 152
-$3.931 billion (2012 est.)

Exports: $10.39 billion (2013 est.)
country comparison to the world: 93
$9.774 billion (2012 est.)

Exports—commodities: textiles and apparel, tea and spices; rubber manufactures; precious stones; coconut products, fish

Exports—partners: US 20.4%, UK 9.9%, India 5.8%, Italy 4.7%, Belgium 4.3%, Germany 4.3% (2012)

Imports: $18 billion (2013 est.)
country comparison to the world: 81
$19.19 billion (2012 est.)

Imports—commodities: petroleum, textiles, machinery and transportation equipment, building materials, mineral products, foodstuffs

Imports—partners: India 22.7%, Singapore 8.8%, UAE 7.7%, China 7%, Iran 6.1%, Malaysia 4.5% (2012)

Reserves of foreign exchange and gold: $7.2 billion (31 December 2013 est.)
country comparison to the world: 83
$6.9 billion (31 December 2012 est.)

Debt—external: $33.67 billion (31 December 2013 est.)
country comparison to the world: 70
$29.39 billion (31 December 2012 est.)

Stock of direct foreign investment—at home: $NA

Stock of direct foreign investment—abroad: $NA

Exchange rates: Sri Lankan rupees (LKR) per US dollar—
129.6 (2013 est.)
127.6 (2012 est.)
113.06 (2010 est.)
114.95 (2009)
108.33 (2008)

ENERGY

Electricity—production: 11.8 billion kWh (2012 est.)
country comparison to the world: 92

Electricity—consumption: 8.927 billion kWh (2011 est.)
country comparison to the world: 91

Electricity—exports: 0 kWh (2012 est.)
country comparison to the world: 116

Electricity—imports: 0 kWh (2012 est.)
country comparison to the world: 125

Electricity—installed generating capacity: 2.685 million kW (2010 est.)
country comparison to the world: 92

Electricity—from fossil fuels: 53.8% of total installed capacity (2011 est.)
country comparison to the world: 146

Electricity—from nuclear fuels: 0% of total installed capacity (2011 est.)
country comparison to the world: 61

Electricity—from hydroelectric plants: 44.6% of total installed capacity (2011 est.)
country comparison to the world: 54

Electricity—from other renewable sources: 1.6% of total installed capacity (2011 est.)
country comparison to the world: 77

Crude oil—production: 0 bbl/day (2012 est.)
country comparison to the world: 159

Crude oil—exports: 0 bbl/day (2010 est.)
country comparison to the world: 95

Crude oil—imports: 36,380 bbl/day (2010 est.)
country comparison to the world: 60

Crude oil—proved reserves: 0 bbl (1 January 2013 es)
country comparison to the world: 115

Refined petroleum products—production: 35,440 bbl/day (2010 est.)
country comparison to the world: 86

Refined petroleum products—consumption: 89,620 bbl/day (2011 est.)
country comparison to the world: 81

Refined petroleum products—exports: 0 bbl/day (2010 est.)
country comparison to the world: 162

Refined petroleum products—imports: 44,270 bbl/day (2010 est.)
country comparison to the world: 74

Natural gas—production: 0 cu m (2012 est.)
country comparison to the world: 113

Natural gas—consumption: 0 cu m (2012 est.)
country comparison to the world: 129

Natural gas—exports: 0 cu m (2012 est.)
country comparison to the world: 77

Natural gas—imports: 0 cu m (2012 est.)
country comparison to the world: 172

Natural gas—proved reserves: 0 cu m (1 January 2013 es)
country comparison to the world: 122

Carbon dioxide emissions from consumption of energy: 13.1 million Mt (2011 est.)
country comparison to the world: 95

COMMUNICATIONS

Telephones—main lines in use: 2.796 million (2013)
country comparison to the world: 52

Telephones—mobile cellular: 19.533 million (2013)
country comparison to the world: 51

Telephone system: *general assessment:* telephone services have improved significantly and are available in most parts of the country

domestic: national trunk network consists mostly of digital microwave radio relay; fiber-optic links now in use in Colombo area and fixed wireless local loops have been installed; competition is strong in mobile cellular systems and mobile cellular subscribership is increasing
international: country code—94; the SEA-ME-WE-3 and SEA-ME-WE-4 submarine cables provide connectivity to Asia, Australia, Middle East, Europe, US; satellite earth stations—2 Intelsat (Indian Ocean) (2011)

Broadcast media: government operates 8 TV channels and a radio network; multi-channel satellite and cable TV subscription services available; 35 private TV stations and about 50 radio stations (2012)

Internet country code: .lk

Internet hosts: 9,552 (2012)
country comparison to the world: 136

Internet users: 1.777 million (2009)
country comparison to the world: 77

TRANSPORTATION

Airports: 19 (2013)
country comparison to the world: 138

Airports—with paved runways: *total:* 1 5
over 3,047 m: 2
1,524 to 2,437 m: 6
914 to 1,523 m: 7 (2013)

Airports—with unpaved runways: *total:* 4
914 to 1,523 m: 1
under 914 m: 3 (2013)

Heliports: 1 (2013)

Railways: *total:* 1,449 km
country comparison to the world: 80
broad gauge: 1,449 km 1.676-m gauge (2007)

Roadways: *total:* 114,093 km
country comparison to the world: 41
paved: 16,977 km
unpaved: 97,116 km (2010)

Waterways: 160 km (primarily on rivers in southwest) (2012)
country comparison to the world: 101
Merchant marine: total: 2 1
country comparison to the world: 94
by type: bulk carrier 4, cargo 13, chemical tanker 1, container 1, petroleum tanker 2
foreign-owned: 8 (Germany 8) (2010)

Ports and terminals: *major seaport(s):* Colombo
container port(s) (TEUs): Colombo (3,651,963)

MILITARY

Military branches: Sri Lanka Army, Sri Lanka Navy, Sri Lanka Air Force (2013)

Military service age and obligation: 18-22 years of age for voluntary military service; no conscription; 5-year service obligation (Air Force) (2012)

Manpower available for military service:
males age 16-49: 5,342,147
females age 16-49: 5,466,409 (2010 est.)

Manpower fit for military service:
males age 16-49: 4,177,432
females age 16-49: 4,574,833 (2010 est.)

Manpower reaching militarily significant age annually: *male:* 167,026
female: 162,587 (2010 est.)

Military expenditures: 2.43% of GDP (2012)
country comparison to the world: 31
2.89% of GDP (2011)
2.43% of GDP (2010)

TRANSNATIONAL ISSUES

Disputes—international: none

Refugees and internally displaced persons:
IDPs: as many as 90,000 (civil war; more than half displaced prior to 2008; many of the more than 480,000 IDPs registered as returnees have not reached durable solutions) (2014)

Trafficking in persons: *current situation:* Sri Lanka is primarily a source and, to a much lesser extent, a destination country for men, women, and children subjected to forced labor and sex trafficking; some Sri Lankan adults and children who migrate willingly to Saudi Arabia, Kuwait, Qatar, the United Arab Emirates, Jordan, Bahrain, Lebanon, Iraq, Afghanistan, Malaysia, and Singapore to work as domestic servants, construction workers, or garment factory workers face conditions indicative of forced labor; some Sri Lankan women are forced into prostitution in Jordan, Singapore, Maldives, and other countries; within Sri Lanka, women and children are subjected to sex trafficking in brothels, while other children are forced to work in the agriculture, fireworks, and fish-drying industries

tier rating: Tier 2 Watch List—Sri Lanka does not fully comply with the minimum standards for the elimination of trafficking; however, it is making significant efforts to do so; law enforcement efforts and victim protection, particularly identification, are very weak, with no reported prosecutions or convictions under the country's penal code article prohibiting human trafficking; government employees' complicity in trafficking offenses remains a problem; the government has not approved its draft standard operating procedures for identifying trafficking victims and referring them to protective services, consequently, victims may have been punished for crimes committed as a direct result of being trafficked; the government adopted an anti-trafficking action plan in 2012 (2013)

SUDAN

INTRODUCTION

Background: Military regimes favoring Islamic-oriented governments have dominated national politics since independence from Anglo-Egyptian co rule in 1956. Sudan was embroiled in two prolonged civil wars during most of the remainder of the 20th century. These conflicts were rooted in northern economic, political, and social domination of largely non-Muslim, non-Arab southern Sudanese. The first civil war ended in 1972 but another broke out in 1983. Peace talks gained momentum in 2002-04 with the signing of several accords. The final North/South Comprehensive Peace Agreement (CPA), signed in January 2005, granted the southern rebels autonomy for six years followed by a referendum on independence for Southern Sudan. The referendum was held in January 2011 and indicated overwhelming support for independence. South Sudan became independent on 9 July 2011. Sudan and South Sudan have yet to fully implement security and economic agreements signed on September 27, 2012 relating to the normalization of relations between the two countries. The final disposition of the contested Abyei region has also to be decided. Since South Sudan's independence, conflict has broken out between the government and the Sudan People's Liberation Movement-North (SPLM-N) in Southern Kordofan and Blue Nile states, which has resulted in 1.2 million internally displaced persons or severely affected persons in need of humanitarian assistance. A separate conflict, which broke out in the western region of Darfur in 2003, has displaced nearly two million people and caused an estimated 200,000 to 400,000 deaths. Violence in Darfur in 2013 resulted in an additional estimated 6,000 civilians killed and 500,000 displaced. The UN and the African Union have jointly commanded a Darfur peacekeeping operation known as the African Union-United Nations Hybrid Mission in Darfur (UNAMID) since 2007. Peacekeeping troops have struggled to stabilize the situation and have increasingly become targets for attacks by armed groups. In 2013, 16 peacekeepers were killed, UNAMID's deadliest year so far. Sudan also has faced refugee influxes from neighboring countries, primarily Ethiopia, Eritrea, Chad, Central African Republic, and South Sudan. Armed conflict, poor transport infrastructure, and government denial of access have impeded the provision of humanitarian assistance to affected populations. Geography :: Sudan Location: north-eastern Africa, bordering the Red Sea, between Egypt and Eritrea

Geographic coordinates: 15 00 N, 30 00 E

Map references: Africa

Area: *total:* 1,861,484 sq km
country comparison to the world: 16
land: NA
water: NA

Area—comparative: slightly less than one-fifth the size of the US

Land boundaries: *total:* 6,751 km
border countries: Central African Republic 175 km, Chad 1,360 km, Egypt 1,275 km, Eritrea 605 km, Ethiopia 769 km, Libya 383 km, South Sudan 2,184 km
note: Sudan-South Sudan boundary represents 1 January 1956 alignment; final alignment pending negotiations and demarcation; final sovereignty

status of Abyei region pending negotiations between Sudan and South Sudan

Coastline: 853 km

Maritime claims: *territorial sea:* 12 nm
contiguous zone: 18 nm
continental shelf: 200 m depth or to the depth of exploitation

Climate: hot and dry; arid desert; rainy season varies by region (April to November)

Terrain: generally flat, featureless plain; desert dominates the north

Elevation extremes: *lowest point:* Red Sea 0 m
highest point: Jabal Marrah 3,071 m

Natural resources: petroleum; small reserves of iron ore, copper, chromium ore, zinc, tungsten, mica, silver, gold; hydropower

Land use: *arable land:* 6.76%
permanent crops: 0.07%
other: 93.17% (2011)

Irrigated land: 18,900 sq km (2010)

Total renewable water resources: 64.5 cu km (2011)

Freshwater withdrawal (domestic/industrial/agricultural): *total:* 27.59 cu km/yr (4%/1%/95%)
per capita: 683.4 cu m/yr (2005)

Natural hazards: dust storms and periodic persistent droughts

Environment—current issues: inadequate supplies of potable water; wildlife populations threatened by excessive hunting; soil erosion; desertification; periodic drought

Environment—international agreements:
party to: Biodiversity, Climate Change, Climate Change-Kyoto Protocol, Desertification, Endangered Species, Hazardous Wastes, Law of the Sea, Ozone Layer Protection, Wetlands
signed, but not ratified: none of the selected agreements

Geography—note: dominated by the Nile and its tributaries

PEOPLE AND SOCIETY

Nationality: *noun:* Sudanese (singular and plural)
adjective: Sudanese

Ethnic groups: Sudanese Arab (approximately 70%), Fur, Beja, Nuba, Fallata

Languages: Arabic (official), English (official), Nubian, Ta Bedawie, Fur
note: program of "Arabization" in process

Religions: Sunni Muslim, small Christian minority

Population: 35,482,233 (July 2014 est.)
country comparison to the world: 37

Age structure:
0-14 years: 40.8% (male 7,356,059/female 7,131,497)
15-24 years: 20.2% (male 3,704,700/female 3,476,847)
25-54 years: 31.8% (male 5,465,816/female 5,800,619)
55-64 years: 3.3% (male 737,831/female 652,428)
65 years and over: 3.3% (male 633,083/female 523,353) (2014 est.)

Dependency ratios:
total dependency ratio: 79.9 %
youth dependency ratio: 74.1 %
elderly dependency ratio: 5.8 %
potential support ratio: 17.1 (2013)

Median age: *total:* 19.1 years
male: 18.9 years
female: 19.4 years (2014 est.)

Population growth rate: 1.78% (2014 est.)
country comparison to the world: 68

Birth rate: 30.01 births/1,000 population (2014 est.)
country comparison to the world: 42

Death rate: 7.87 deaths/1,000 population (2014 est.)
country comparison to the world: 105

Net migration rate: -4.36 migrant(s)/1,000 population (2014 est.)
country comparison to the world: 192

Urbanization: *urban population:* 33.2% of total population (2011)
rate of urbanization: 2.6% annual rate of change (2010-15 est.)

Major urban areas—population: KHARTOUM (capital) 5.021 million (2009)

Sex ratio: *at birth:* 1.05 male(s)/female
0-14 years: 1.03 male(s)/female
15-24 years: 1.07 male(s)/female
25-54 years: 0.94 male(s)/female
55-64 years: 1.02 male(s)/female
65 years and over: 1.24 male(s)/female
total population: 1.02 male(s)/female (2014 est.)

Maternal mortality rate: 730 deaths/100,000 live births (2010)
country comparison to the world: 9

Infant mortality rate: *total:* 52.86 deaths/1,000 live births
country comparison to the world: 34
male: 58.29 deaths/1,000 live births
female: 47.15 deaths/1,000 live births (2014 est.)

Life expectancy at birth: total population: 63.32 years
country comparison to the world: 185
male: 61.27 years
female: 65.46 years (2014 est.)

Total fertility rate: 3.92 children born/woman (2014 est.)
country comparison to the world: 40

Contraceptive prevalence rate: 9% (2010)

Health expenditures: 8.4% of GDP (2011)
country comparison to the world: 57

Physicians density: 0.28 physicians/1,000 population (2008)

Hospital bed density: 0.7 beds/1,000 population (2009)

Drinking water source: improved:
urban: 66% of population
rural: 50.2% of population
total: 55.4% of population
unimproved:
urban: 34% of population
rural: 49.8% of population
total: 44.6% of population (2011 est.)

Sanitation facility access: improved:
urban: 43.9% of population
rural: 13.4% of population
total: 23.5% of population
unimproved:
urban: 56.1% of population
rural: 86.6% of population
total: 76.5% of population (2011 est.)

HIV/AIDS—adult prevalence rate: 1.1% (2009 est.)
country comparison to the world: 41

HIV/AIDS—people living with HIV/AIDS: 260,000 (2009 est.)
country comparison to the world: 22

HIV/AIDS—deaths: 12,000 (2009 est.)
country comparison to the world: 24

Major infectious diseases: *degree of risk:* very high
food or waterborne diseases: bacterial and protozoal diarrhea, hepatitis A and E, and typhoid fever
vectorborne diseases: malaria, dengue fever, and Rift Valley fever
water contact disease: schistosomiasis
respiratory disease: meningococcal meningitis
animal contact disease: rabies
note: highly pathogenic H5N1 avian influenza has been identified in this country; it poses a negligible risk with extremely rare cases possible among US citizens who have close contact with birds (2013)

Obesity—adult prevalence rate: 6% (2008)
country comparison to the world: 150

Children under the age of 5 years underweight: 31.7% (2006)
country comparison to the world: 12

Literacy: *definition:* age 15 and over can read and write
total population: 71.9%
male: 80.7%
female: 63.2%
note: pre-secession of South Sudan (2011 est.)

School life expectancy (primary to tertiary education): *total:* 4 years (2000)

GOVERNMENT

Country name: *conventional long form:* Republic of the Sudan
conventional short form: Sudan
local long form: Jumhuriyat as-Sudan
local short form: As-Sudan
former: Anglo-Egyptian Sudan

Government type: Federal republic ruled by the National Congress Party the (NCP), which came to power by military coup in 1989; the CPA-mandated Government of National Unity, which between 2005 and 2011 provided a percentage of leadership posts to the southern Sudan-based Sudan People's Liberation Movement (SPLM), was disbanded following the secession of South Sudan.

Capital: *name:* Khartoum

geographic coordinates: 15 36 N, 32 32 E
time difference: UTC+3 (8 hours ahead of Washington, DC during Standard Time)

Administrative divisions: 17 states (wilayat, singular—wilayah); Al Bahr al Ahmar (Red Sea), Al Jazira (Gezira), Al Khartoum (Khartoum), Al Qadarif (Gedaref), An Nil al Abyad (White Nile), An Nil al Azraq (Blue Nile), Ash Shamaliyya (Northern), Gharb Darfur (Western Darfur), Janub Darfur (Southern Darfur), Janub Kurdufan (Southern Kordofan), Kassala, Nahr an Nil (River Nile), Sharq Darfur (Eastern Darfur), Shimal Darfur (Northern Darfur), Shimal Kurdufan (Northern Kordofan), Sinnar, Wasat Darfur (Central Darfur)

Independence: 1 January 1956 (from Egypt and the UK)

National holiday: Independence Day, 1 January (1956)

Constitution: previous 1998; latest (interim) adopted 6 July 2005, effective 9 July 2005; note—in 2011, the Government of Sudan initiated a process for drafting a new constitution (2013)

Legal system: mixed legal system of Islamic law and English common law

International law organization participation: accepts compulsory ICJ jurisdiction with reservations; withdrew acceptance of ICCt jurisdiction in 2008

Suffrage: 17 years of age; universal

Executive branch: *chief of state:* President Umar Hassan Ahmad al-BASHIR (since 16 October 1993); First Vice President BAKRI Hassan Salih, Second Vice President Hasabu Mohamed ABDEL RAHMIN (both since 3 December 2013) note—the president is both the chief of state and head of government
head of government: President Umar Hassan Ahmad al-BASHIR (since 16 October 1993); First Vice President BAKRI Hassan Salih, Second Vice President Hasabu Mohamed ABDEL RAHMAN (both since 9 December 2013)
cabinet: Council of Ministers appointed by the president; note—the NCP (formerly the National Islamic Front or NIF) dominates al-BASHIR's cabinet (For more information visit the World Leaders website)
elections: election on 11-15 April 2010 (next to be held in 2015)
election results: Umar Hassan Ahmad al-BASHIR reelected president; percent of vote—Umar Hassan Ahmad al-BASHIR 68.2%, Yasir ARMAN 21.7%, Abdullah Deng NHIAL 3.9%, others 6.2%
note: al-BASHIR assumed power as chairman of Sudan's Revolutionary Command Council for National Salvation (RCC) in June 1989 and served concurrently as chief of state, chairman of the RCC, prime minister, and minister of defense until mid-October 1993 when he was appointed president by the RCC; he was elected president by popular vote for the first time in March 1996

Legislative branch: bicameral National Legislature consists of a Council of States (50 seats; members indirectly elected by state legislatures to serve six-year terms) and a National Assembly (450 seats; 60% from geographic constituencies, 25% from a women's list, and 15% from party lists; members to serve six-year terms)
elections: last held on 11-15 April 2010 (next to be held in 2015)
election results: National Assembly—percent of vote by party—NA; seats by party—NCP 323, SPLM 99, PCP 4, DUP 4, UFP 3, URDP 2, DUPO 2, SPLM-DC 2, other 7, vacant 4; composition of National Assembly following South Sudan's independence—seats by party—NCP 317, SPLM 8, PCP 4, DUP 4, UFP 3, URDP 2, DUPO 1, UP 1, UNP 1, UCLP 1, MB 1, independent 3, vacant 8
note: the mandate of the members from the south was terminated upon independence by the Republic of South Sudan effective 9 July 2011 and membership in Sudan's National Assembly was reduced to 354; it is unclear whether this total will be retained for the next election or whether the previous total of 450 will be reconstituted

Judicial branch: *highest court(s):* National Supreme Court (consists of 70 judges organized into panels of 3 judges; court includes 4 circuits that operate outside the capital); Constitutional Court (consists of 9 justices including the court president); note—the Constitutional Court resides outside the national judiciary
judge selection and term of office: National Supreme Court and Constitutional Court judges appointed by the president of the republic upon the recommendation of the National Judicial Service Commission, an independent body chaired by the chief justice of the republic and members including other judges and judicial and legal officials; Supreme Court judge tenure NA; Constitutional Court judges appointed for 7 years
subordinate courts: National Court of Appeals; other national courts (not specified in the 2005 Interim National Constitution as to national or local authority); township and rural (peoples') courts

Political parties and leaders: Democratic Unionist Party or DUP [Muhammad Uthman al-MIRGHANI]; Muslim Brotherhood or MB; National Congress Party or NCP [Umar Hassan al-BASHIR]; National Umma Party or UP [Siddiq al-MAHDI]; Popular Congress Party or PCP [Hassan al-TURABI]; Reform Now Party or RNP [Dr. Ghazi Salah ADDEEN]; Sudanese Communist Party (SCP) [Mohammed Moktar Al-KHATEEB]; Sudanese Congress Party [Ibrahim Al Shiek ABDULRAHMAN]; Unionist Movement Party or UMP [Nagla AL-AZHARI]

Political pressure groups and leaders: Sudan People's Liberation Movement-North (SPLM-N) [Malik AGAR]; Sudan Revolutionary Front (SRF) [Malik AGAR] National Consensus Front (NCF) [Farouq ABU ISSA] Darfur rebel groups including the Justice and Equality Movement or JEM [Gibril Fidail IBRAHIM], the Sudan Liberation Movement or SLM-AW [Abdel Wahid NUR] [various factional leaders], Sudan Liberation or SLM-MM /[Minni Arkou MINAWI]

International organization participation: ABEDA, ACP, AfDB, AFESD, AMF, AU, CAEU, COMESA, FAO, G-77, IAEA, IBRD, ICAO, ICC (NGOs), ICRM, IDA, IDB, IFAD, IFC, IFRCS, IGAD, ILO, IMF, IMO, Interpol, IOC, IOM, IPU, ISO, ITSO, ITU, LAS, MIGA, NAM, OIC, OPCW, PCA, UN, UNCTAD, UNESCO, UNHCR, UNIDO, UNWTO, UPU, WCO, WFTU (NGOs), WHO, WIPO, WMO, WTO (observer)

Diplomatic representation in the US:
chief of mission: Ambassador (vacant); Charge d'Affaires Elhafiz Eisa Abdulla ADAM
chancery: 2210 Massachusetts Avenue NW, Washington, DC 20008
telephone: [1] (202) 338-8565
FAX: [1] (202) 667-2406

Diplomatic representation from the US:
chief of mission: Ambassador (vacant); Deputy Chief of Mission Christopher ROWAN (since December 2012)
embassy: Sharia Ali Abdul Latif Street, Khartoum
mailing address: P.O. Box 699, Kilo 10, Soba, Khartoum; APO AE 09829
telephone: [249] (187)-0-(22000)
FAX: [249] (183) 774-137

Flag description: three equal horizontal bands of red (top), white, and black with a green isosceles triangle based on the hoist side; colors and design based on the Arab Revolt flag of World War I, but the meanings of the colors are expressed as follows: red signifies the struggle for freedom, white is the color of peace, light, and love, black represents Sudan itself (in Arabic 'Sudan' means black), green is the color of Islam, agriculture, and prosperity

National symbol(s): secretary bird

National anthem: *name:* "Nahnu Djundulla Djundulwatan" (We Are the Army of God and of Our Land)
lyrics/music: Sayed Ahmad Muhammad SALIH/ Ahmad MURJAN
note: adopted 1956; the song originally served as the anthem of the Sudanese military

ECONOMY

Economy—overview: Sudan is an extremely poor country that has experienced protracted social conflict, civil war, and, in July 2011, the loss of three-quarters of its oil production due to the secession of South Sudan. The oil sector had driven much of Sudan's GDP growth since 1999. For nearly a decade, the economy boomed on the back of rising oil production, high oil prices, and significant inflows of foreign direct investment. Since the economic shock of South Sudan's secession, Sudan has struggled to stabilize its economy and make up for the loss of foreign exchange earnings. The interruption of oil production in South Sudan in 2012 for over a year and the consequent loss of oil transit fees further exacerbated the fragile state of Sudan's economy. Sudan is also subject to comprehensive US sanctions. Sudan is attempting to develop non-oil sources of revenues, such as gold mining, while carrying out an austerity program to reduce expenditures. The world's largest exporter of gum Arabic, Sudan produces 75-80% of the world's total output. Agriculture continues to employ 80% of the work force. Sudan introduced a new currency, still called the Sudanese pound, following South Sudan's secession, but the value of the currency has fallen since its introduction. Khartoum formally devalued the currency in June 2012, when it passed austerity measures that included gradually repealing fuel subsidies. Sudan also faces rising inflation, which reached 47% on an annual basis in November 2012, but subsided to 25% in 2013. Ongoing conflicts in Southern Kordofan, Darfur, and the Blue Nile states, lack of basic infrastructure in large areas, and reliance by much of the population on subsistence agriculture keep close to half of the population at or below the poverty line.

GDP (purchasing power parity): $89.97 billion (2013 est.)
country comparison to the world: 79
$86.59 billion (2012 est.)
$89.51 billion (2011 est.)
note: data are in 2013 US dollars

GDP (official exchange rate):
$52.5 billion (2013 est.)

GDP—real growth rate: 3.9% (2013 est.)
country comparison to the world: 81
-3.3% (2012 est.)
-1.8% (2011 est.)

GDP—per capita (PPP): $2,600 (2013 est.)
country comparison to the world: 182
$2,600 (2012 est.)
$2,700 (2011 est.)
note: data are in 2013 US dollars

Gross national saving: 26.6% of GDP (2013 est.)
country comparison to the world: 41
18.1% of GDP (2012 est.)
26.8% of GDP (2011 est.)

GDP—composition, by end use:
household consumption: 64.1%
government consumption: 11.3%
investment in fixed capital: 23.2%
investment in inventories: 3.4%
exports of goods and services: 17.9%
imports of goods and services: -19.9% (2013 est.)

GDP—composition, by sector of origin:
agriculture: 27.4%
industry: 33.6%
services: 39% (2013 est.)

Agriculture—products: cotton, groundnuts (peanuts), sorghum, millet, wheat, gum arabic, sugarcane, cassava (tapioca), mangoes, papaya, bananas, sweet potatoes, sesame; sheep and other livestock

Industries: oil, cotton ginning, textiles, cement, edible oils, sugar, soap distilling, shoes, petroleum refining, pharmaceuticals, armaments, automobile/light truck assembly

Industrial production growth rate: 11% (2013 est.)
country comparison to the world: 11

Labor force: 11.92 million (2007 est.)
country comparison to the world: 45

Labor force—by occupation: *agriculture:* 80%
industry: 7%
services: 13% (1998 est.)

Unemployment rate: 20% (2012 est.)
country comparison to the world: 162
18.7% (2002 est.)

Population below poverty line: 46.5% (2009 est.)

Household income or consumption by percentage share: *lowest 10%:* 2.7%
highest 10%: 26.7% (2009 est.)

Budget: *revenues:* $4.513 billion
expenditures: $6.842 billion (2013 est.)

Taxes and other revenues: 8.6% of GDP (2013 est.)
country comparison to the world: 210

Budget surplus (+) or deficit (-):
-4.4% of GDP (2013 est.)
country comparison to the world: 156

Public debt: 111% of GDP (2013 est.)
country comparison to the world: 12
101.7% of GDP (2012 est.)

Fiscal year: calendar year

Inflation rate (consumer prices): 25% (2013 est.)
country comparison to the world: 219
37.4% (2012 est.)

Stock of narrow money: $8.035 billion (31 December 2013 est.)
country comparison to the world: 88
$7.927 billion (31 December 2012 est.)

Stock of broad money: $12.82 billion (31 December 2013 est.)
country comparison to the world: 94
$13.23 billion (31 December 2012 est.)

Stock of domestic credit: $9.785 billion (31 December 2013 est.)
country comparison to the world: 100
$11.64 billion (31 December 2012 est.)

Market value of publicly traded shares: $NA

Current account balance: -$1.98 billion (2013 est.)
country comparison to the world: 143
-$5.282 billion (2012 est.)

Exports: $4.145 billion (2013 est.)
country comparison to the world: 120
$3.368 billion (2012 est.)

Exports—commodities: gold; oil and petroleum products; cotton, sesame, livestock, groundnuts, gum arabic, sugar

Exports—partners: UAE 63.2%, Saudi Arabia 9.2%, Ethiopia 5.3% (2012)

Imports: $5.941 billion (2013 est.)
country comparison to the world: 120
$8.123 billion (2012 est.)

Imports—commodities: foodstuffs, manufactured goods, refinery and transport equipment, medicines and chemicals, textiles, wheat

Imports—partners: Macau 18.1%, India 8.8%, Saudi Arabia 7.9%, Egypt 6.7%, UAE 5.2% (2012)

Reserves of foreign exchange and gold: $202.2 million (31 December 2013 est.)
country comparison to the world: 159
$192.6 million (31 December 2012 est.)

Debt—external: $40.92 billion (31 December 2013 est.)
country comparison to the world: 65
$39.54 billion (31 December 2012 est.)

Exchange rates: Sudanese pounds (SDG) per US dollar—
5.83 (2013 est.)
3.57 (2012 est.)
2.31 (2010 est.)
2.3 (2009)
2.1 (2008)

ENERGY

Electricity—production: 7.193 billion kWh (2010 est.)
country comparison to the world: 109

Electricity—consumption: 5.665 billion kWh (2010 est.)
country comparison to the world: 110

Electricity—exports: 0 kWh (2012 est.)
country comparison to the world: 198

Electricity—imports: 0 kWh (2012 est.)
country comparison to the world: 201

Electricity—installed generating capacity:
2.083 million kW (2010 est.)
country comparison to the world: 99

Electricity—from fossil fuels: 30.7% of total installed capacity (2010 est.)
country comparison to the world: 181

Electricity—from nuclear fuels: 0% of total installed capacity (2010 est.)
country comparison to the world: 181

Electricity—from hydroelectric plants: 66.3% of total installed capacity (2010 est.)
country comparison to the world: 27

Electricity—from other renewable sources:
3% of total installed capacity (2010 est.)
country comparison to the world: 61

Crude oil—production: 28,830 bbl/day (2012 est.)
country comparison to the world: 69

Crude oil—exports: 97,270 bbl/day (2010 est.)
country comparison to the world: 37

Crude oil—imports: 0 bbl/day (2010 est.)
country comparison to the world: 123

Crude oil—proved reserves: 1.25 billion bbl (1 January 2013 es)
country comparison to the world: 40

Refined petroleum products—production:
124,900 bbl/day (2010 est.)
country comparison to the world: 70

Refined petroleum products—consumption:
95,450 bbl/day (2011 est.)
country comparison to the world: 80

Refined petroleum products—exports: 14,950 bbl/day (2010 est.)
country comparison to the world: 78

Refined petroleum products—imports: 4,349 bbl/day (2008 est.)
country comparison to the world: 160

Natural gas—production: 0 cu m (2011 est.)
country comparison to the world: 193

Natural gas—consumption: 0 cu m (2010 est.)
country comparison to the world: 196

Natural gas—exports: 0 cu m (2011 est.)
country comparison to the world: 185

Natural gas—imports: 0 cu m (2011 est.)
country comparison to the world: 132

Natural gas—proved reserves: 21.24 billion cu m (1 January 2013 es)
country comparison to the world: 76

Carbon dioxide emissions from consumption of energy: 16.45 million Mt (2011 est.)
country comparison to the world: 89

COMMUNICATIONS

Telephones—main lines in use: 425,000 (2012)
country comparison to the world: 101

Telephones—mobile cellular: 27.659 million (2012)
country comparison to the world: 38

Telephone system: *general assessment:* well-equipped system by regional standards and being upgraded; cellular communications started in 1996 and have expanded substantially with wide coverage of most major cities
domestic: consists of microwave radio relay, cable, fiber optic, radiotelephone communications, tropospheric scatter, and a domestic satellite system with 14 earth stations
international: country code—249; linked to the EASSy and FLAG fiber-optic submarine cable systems; satellite earth stations—1 Intelsat (Atlantic Ocean), 1 Arabsat (2010)

Broadcast media: the Sudanese Government directly controls TV and radio, requiring that both media reflect government policies; TV has a permanent military censor; a private radio station is in operation (2007)

Internet country code: . s d

Internet hosts: 99 (2012)
country comparison to the world: 210

Internet users: 4.2 million (2008)
country comparison to the world: 56

TRANSPORTATION

Airports: 74 (2013)
country comparison to the world: 7 0

Airports—with paved runways: *total:* 1 6
over 3,047 m: 2
2,438 to 3,047 m: 10
1,524 to 2,437 m: 2
under 914 m: 2 (2013)

Airports—with unpaved runways: *total:* 5 8
2,438 to 3,047 m: 1
1,524 to 2,437 m: 17
914 to 1,523 m: 28
under 914 m: 12 (2013)

Heliports: 6 (2013)

Pipelines: gas 156 km; oil 4,070 km; refined products 1,613 km (2013)

Railways: *total:* 5,978 km
country comparison to the world: 30
narrow gauge: 4,578 km 1.067-m gauge; 1,400 km 0.600-m gauge for cotton plantations (2008)

Roadways: *total:* 11,900 km

country comparison to the world: 128
paved: 4,320 km
unpaved: 7,580 km (2000)

Waterways: 4,068 km (1,723 km open year round on White and Blue Nile rivers) (2011)
country comparison to the world: 25

Merchant marine: *total:* 2
country comparison to the world: 140
by type: cargo 2 (2010)

Ports and terminals: *major seaport(s):* Port Sudan

MILITARY

Military branches: Sudanese Armed Forces (SAF): Land Forces, Navy (includes Marines), Sudanese Air Force (Sikakh al-Jawwiya as-Sudaniya), Popular Defense Forces (2011)

Military service age and obligation: 18-33 years of age for male and female compulsory or voluntary military service; 1-2 year service obligation; a requirement that completion of national service was mandatory before entering public or private sector employment has been cancelled (2012)

Manpower available for military service:
males age 16-49: 10,433,973
females age 16-49: 10,411,443 (2010 est.)

Manpower fit for military service:
males age 16-49: 6,475,530
females age 16-49: 6,840,885 (2010 est.)

Manpower reaching militarily significant age annually: *male:* 532,030
female: 512,476 (2010 est.)

TRANSNATIONAL ISSUES

Disputes—international: the effects of Sudan's almost constant ethnic and rebel militia fighting since the mid-20th century have penetrated all of the neighboring states; Chad wishes to be a helpful mediator in resolving the Darfur conflict, and in 2010 established a joint border monitoring force with Sudan, which has helped to reduce cross-border banditry and violence; as of 2006, Chad, Ethiopia, Kenya, Central African Republic, Democratic Republic of the Congo, and Uganda provided shelter for over a half million Sudanese refugees, which include 240,000 Darfur residents driven from their homes by Janjawid armed militia and Sudanese military forces; as of January 2011, Sudan, in turn, hosted about 138,700 Eritreans, 43,000 Chadians, and smaller numbers of Ethiopians; Sudan accuses Eritrea of supporting Sudanese rebel groups; efforts to demarcate the porous boundary with Ethiopia proceed slowly due to civil and ethnic fighting in eastern Sudan; Sudan claims but Egypt de facto administers security and economic development of Halaib region north of the 22nd parallel boundary; periodic violent skirmishes with Sudanese residents over water and grazing rights persist among related pastoral populations along the border with the Central African Republic; South Sudan-Sudan boundary represents 1 January 1956 alignment, final alignment pending negotiations and demarcation; final sovereignty status of Abyei Area pending negotiations between South Sudan and Sudan

Refugees and internally displaced persons: *refugees (country of origin):* 112,283 (Eritrea); 32,220 (Chad) (2012); 60,568 (South Sudan) (2014)
IDPs: 2.641 million (civil war 1983-2005; ongoing conflict in Darfur region; government and rebel fighting along South Sudan border; inter-tribal clashes) (2013)

Trafficking in persons: *current situation:* Sudan is a source, transit, and destination country for men, women, and children who are subjected to forced labor and sex trafficking; Sudanese women and girls, particularly those from rural areas or who are internally displaced, are vulnerable to forced labor as domestic workers in homes throughout the country; some of these women and girls are subsequently sexually abused by male occupants of the household or forced to engage in commercial sex acts; Sudanese women and girls are subjected to domestic servitude in Middle Eastern countries and to forced sex trafficking in European countries; some Sudanese men who voluntarily migrate to the Middle East as low-skilled laborers face conditions indicative of forced labor; Sudanese children in Saudi Arabia are used in forced begging and street vending; Sudan is a transit and destination country for Ethiopian and Eritrean women subjected to domestic servitude in Sudan and Middle Eastern countries; Sudan is a destination for Ethiopian, Somali, and possibly Thai women subjected to forced prostitution; Sudanese children in Darfur are forcibly conscripted, at times through abduction, and used by armed groups and government security forces

tier rating: Tier 3—Sudan does not fully comply with the minimum standards for the elimination of trafficking and is not making significant efforts to do so; while the government has taken some initial steps to draft anti-trafficking legislation, prosecute suspected traffickers, demobilize and reintegrate child soldiers, and has convened its first workshop to discuss human trafficking, its efforts to combat human trafficking through law enforcement, protection, or prevention measures are undertaken in an ad hoc fashion, rather than as the result of strategic planning; the government has not employed a system for proactively identifying trafficking victims among vulnerable populations or a referral process for transferring victims to organizations providing care; its proxy militias reportedly unlawfully recruited and used child soldiers during the reporting period; the government has not taken action to conclude a proposed action plan with the UN to address the problem (2013)

SURINAME

INTRODUCTION

Background: First explored by the Spaniards in the 16th century and then settled by the English in the mid-17th century, Suriname became a Dutch colony in 1667. With the abolition of African slavery in 1863, workers were brought in from India and Java. Independence from the Netherlands was granted in 1975. Five years later the civilian government was replaced by a military regime that soon declared a socialist republic. It continued to exert control through a succession of nominally civilian administrations until 1987, when international pressure finally forced a democratic election. In 1990, the military overthrew the civilian leadership, but a democratically elected government—a four-party coalition—returned to power in 1991. The coalition expanded to eight parties in 2005 and ruled until August 2010, when voters returned former military leader Desire BOUTERSE and his opposition coalition to power.

GEOGRAPHY

Location: Northern South America, bordering the North Atlantic Ocean, between French Guiana and Guyana

Geographic coordinates: 4 00 N, 56 00 W

Map references: South America

Area: *total:* 163,820 sq km
country comparison to the world: 92
land: 156,000 sq km
water: 7,820 sq km

Area—comparative: slightly larger than Georgia

Land boundaries: *total:* 1,703 km
border countries: Brazil 593 km, French Guiana 510 km, Guyana 600 km

Coastline: 386 km

Maritime claims: *territorial sea:* 12 nm
exclusive economic zone: 200 nm

Climate: tropical; moderated by trade winds

Terrain: mostly rolling hills; narrow coastal plain with swamps

Elevation extremes: *lowest point:* unnamed location in the coastal plain -2 m
highest point: Juliana Top 1,230 m

Natural resources: timber, hydropower, fish, kaolin, shrimp, bauxite, gold, and small amounts of nickel, copper, platinum, iron ore

Land use: *arable land:* 0.36%
permanent crops: 0.04%
other: 99.6% (2011)

Irrigated land: 511.8 sq km (2003)

Total renewable water resources: 122 cu km (2011)

Freshwater withdrawal (domestic/industrial/agricultural): *total:* 0.67 cu km/yr (6%/4%/90%)
per capita: 1,396 cu m/yr (2006)

Natural hazards: NA

Environment—current issues: deforestation as timber is cut for export; pollution of inland waterways by small-scale mining activities

Environment—international agreements: party to: Biodiversity, Climate Change, Climate Change-Kyoto Protocol, Desertification, Endangered Species, Law of the Sea, Marine Dumping,

Ozone Layer Protection, Ship Pollution, Tropical Timber 94, Wetlands, Whaling
signed, but not ratified: none of the selected agreements

Geography—note: smallest independent country on South American continent; mostly tropical rain forest; great diversity of flora and fauna that, for the most part, is increasingly threatened by new development; relatively small population, mostly along the coast

PEOPLE AND SOCIETY

Nationality: *noun:* Surinamer(s)
adjective: Surinamese

Ethnic groups: Hindustani (also known locally as "East Indians"; their ancestors emigrated from northern India in the latter part of the 19th century) 37%, Creole (mixed white and black) 31%, Javanese 15%, "Maroons" (their African ancestors were brought to the country in the 17th and 18th centuries as slaves and escaped to the interior) 10%, Amerindian 2%, Chinese 2%, white 1%, other 2%

Languages: Dutch (official), English (widely spoken), Sranang Tongo (Surinamese, sometimes called Taki-Taki, is native language of Creoles and much of the younger population and is lingua franca among others), Caribbean Hindustani (a dialect of Hindi), Javanese

Religions: Hindu 27.4%, Protestant 25.2% (predominantly Moravian), Roman Catholic 22.8%, Muslim 19.6%, indigenous beliefs 5%

Demographic profile: Suriname is a pluralistic society consisting primarily of Creoles (persons of mixed African and European heritage), the descendants of escaped African slaves known as Maroons, and the descendants of Indian and Javanese contract workers. The country overall is in full, post-industrial demographic transition, with a low fertility rate, a moderate mortality rate, and a rising life expectancy. However, the Maroon population of the rural interior lags behind because of lower educational attainment and contraceptive use, higher malnutrition, and significantly less access to electricity, potable water, sanitation, infrastructure, and health care. Some 350,000 people of Surinamese descent live in the Netherlands, Suriname's former colonial ruler. In the 19th century, better-educated, largely Dutch-speaking Surinamese began emigrating to the Netherlands. World War II interrupted the outflow, but it resumed after the war when Dutch labor demands grew—emigrants included all segments of the Creole population. Suriname still is strongly influenced by the Netherlands because most Surinamese have relatives living there and it is the largest supplier of development aid. Other emigration destinations include French Guiana and the United States. Suriname's immigration rules are flexible, and the country is easy to enter illegally because rainforests obscure its borders. Since the mid-1980s, Brazilians have settled in Suriname's capital, Paramaribo, or eastern Suriname, where they mine gold. This immigration is likely to slowly re-orient Suriname toward its Latin American roots.

Population: 573,311 (July 2014 est.)
country comparison to the world: 171

Age structure: *0-14 years:* 26.2% (male 76,565/female 73,676)
15-24 years: 17.6% (male 51,322/female 49,313)
25-54 years: 44.1% (male 128,620/female 124,034)
55-64 years: 5.7% (male 18,140/female 19,158)
65 years and over: 5.6% (male 14,041/female 18,442) (2014 est.)

Dependency ratios:
total dependency ratio: 51.6 %
youth dependency ratio: 41.5 %
elderly dependency ratio: 10.1 %
potential support ratio: 9.9 (2013)

Median age: *total:* 28.6 years
male: 28.3 years
female: 29 years (2014 est.)

Population growth rate: 1.12% (2014 est.)
country comparison to the world: 110

Birth rate: 16.73 births/1,000 population (2014 est.)
country comparison to the world: 116

Death rate: 6.13 deaths/1,000 population (2014 est.)
country comparison to the world: 162

Net migration rate: 0.57 migrant(s)/1,000 population (2014 est.)
country comparison to the world: 68

Urbanization: *urban population:* 69% of total population (2010)
rate of urbanization: 1.5% annual rate of change (2010-15 est.)

Major urban areas—population: PARAMARIBO (capital) 259,000 (2009)

Sex ratio: *at birth:* 1.05 male(s)/female
0-14 years: 1.04 male(s)/female
15-24 years: 1.04 male(s)/female
25-54 years: 1.04 male(s)/female
55-64 years: 1.01 male(s)/female
65 years and over: 0.77 male(s)/female
total population: 1.01 male(s)/female (2014 est.)

Maternal mortality rate: 130 deaths/100,000 live births (2010)
country comparison to the world: 63

Infant mortality rate: *total:* 27.07 deaths/1,000 live births
country comparison to the world: 68
male: 31.5 deaths/1,000 live births
female: 22.41 deaths/1,000 live births (2014 est.)

Life expectancy at birth: *total population:* 71.69 years
country comparison to the world: 144
male: 69.31 years
female: 74.18 years (2014 est.)

Total fertility rate: 2.01 children born/woman (2014 est.)
country comparison to the world: 124

Contraceptive prevalence rate: 45.6% (2006)

Health expenditures:

5.3% of GDP (2011)

country comparison to the world: 134

Physicians density: 0.91 physicians/1,000 population (2004)

Hospital bed density: 3.1 beds/1,000 population (2010)

Drinking water source: improved:
urban: 96.6% of population
rural: 81.1% of population
total: 91.9% of population
unimproved:
urban: 3.4% of population
rural: 18.9% of population
total: 8.1% of population (2011 est.)

Sanitation facility access:
improved:
urban: 90.3% of population
rural: 66.2% of population
total: 83% of population
unimproved:
urban: 9.7% of population
rural: 33.8% of population
total: 17% of population (2011 est.)

HIV/AIDS—adult prevalence rate: 1.1% (2012 est.)
country comparison to the world: 42

HIV/AIDS—people living with HIV/AIDS: 4,000 (2012 est.)
country comparison to the world: 126

HIV/AIDS—deaths: 100 (2012 est.)
country comparison to the world: 150

Major infectious diseases:
degree of risk: very high
food or waterborne diseases: bacterial and protozoal diarrhea, hepatitis A, and typhoid fever
vectorborne disease: dengue fever and malaria (2013)

Obesity—adult prevalence rate: 25.1% (2008)
country comparison to the world: 60

Children under the age of 5 years underweight: 5.8% (2010)
country comparison to the world: 83

Education expenditures: NA

Literacy: *definition:* age 15 and over can read and write
total population: 94.7%
male: 95.4%
female: 94% (2010 est.)

School life expectancy (primary to tertiary education): *total:* 12 years
male: 11 years
female: 13 years (2002)

Child labor—children ages 5-14: total number: 6,094
percentage: 6 % (2006 est.)

Unemployment, youth ages 15-24: *total:* 21.5% (2004)
country comparison to the world: 54

GOVERNMENT

Country name: *conventional long form:* Republic of Suriname
conventional short form: Suriname
local long form: Republiek Suriname
local short form: Suriname
former: Netherlands Guiana, Dutch Guiana

Government type: constitutional democracy

Capital: *name:* Paramaribo

geographic coordinates: 5 50 N, 55 10 W
time difference: UTC-3 (2 hours ahead of Washington, DC during Standard Time)

Administrative divisions: 10 districts (distrikten, singular—distrikt); Brokopondo, Commewijne, Coronie, Marowijne, Nickerie, Para, Paramaribo, Saramacca, Sipaliwini, Wanica

Independence: 25 November 1975 (from the Netherlands)

National holiday: Independence Day, 25 November (1975)

Constitution: previous 1975; latest ratified 30 September 1987, effective 30 October 1987; amended 1992; note—in 2012, the president appointed a commission to revise the constitution (2012)

Legal system: civil law system influenced by Dutch civil law; note—the Commissie Nieuw Surinaamse Burgerlijk Wetboek completed drafting a new civil code in February 2009 International law organization participation: accepts compulsory ICJ jurisdiction with reservations; accepts ICCt jurisdiction

Suffrage: 18 years of age; universal

Executive branch: *chief of state:* President Desire Delano BOUTERSE (since 12 August 2010); Vice President Robert AMEERALI (since 12 August 2010); note—the president is both the chief of state and head of government
head of government: President Desire Delano BOUTERSE (since 12 August 2010); Vice President Robert AMEERALI (since 12 August 2010)
cabinet: Cabinet of Ministers appointed by the president (For more information visit the World Leaders website)
elections: president and vice president elected by the National Assembly or, if no presidential or vice presidential candidate receives a two-thirds constitutional majority in the National Assembly after two votes, by a simple majority in the larger United People's Assembly (893 representatives from the national, local, and regional councils), for five-year terms (no term limits); election last held on 19 July 2010 (next to be held in 2015)
election results: Desire Delano BOUTERSE elected president; percent of vote—Desire Delano BOUTERSE 70.6%, Chandrikapersad SATOKHI 25.5%, other 3.9%

Legislative branch: unicameral National Assembly or Nationale Assemblee (51 seats; members elected by popular vote to serve five-year terms)
elections: last held on 25 May 2010 (next to be held in May 2015)
election results: percent of vote by party—Mega Combination 45.1%, New Front 27.5%, A-Com 13.7%, People's Alliance 11.8%, DOE 1.9%; seats by party—Mega Combination 23, New Front 14, A-Com 7, People's Alliance 6, DOE 1

Judicial branch: *highest court(s):* High Court of Justice of Suriname (consists of the court president, vice president, and 4 judges) note—Suriname can appeal beyond its High Court to the Caribbean Court of Justice, with final appeal to the Judicial Committee of the Privy Council (in London)
judge selection and term of office: court judges appointed by the national president after consultation with the High Court; judges appointed for life
subordinate courts: cantonal courts

Political parties and leaders: A-Combination (a coalition that includes the General Liberation and Development Party ABOP; [Ronnie BRUNSWIJK], and SEEKA [Paul ABENA]); Basic Party for Renewal and Democracy or BVD [Dilip SARDJOE]; Basic Party for Renewal and Democracy or PVF [Soedeschand JAIRAM]; Democratic Union Suriname or DUS [Japhet DIEKO]; Mega Combination Coalition (a coalition that joined with A-Combination and the PL to form a majority in Parliament in 2010—includes the National Democratic Party or NDP [Desire Delano BOUTERSE] (largest party in the coalition), Progressive Worker and Farmer's Union or PALU [Jim HOK], Party for National Unity and Solidarity of the Highest Order or KTPI [Willy SOEMITA], DNP-2000 [Jules WIJDENBOSCH], Union of Brotherhood and Unity in Politics BEP [Caprino ALENDY], and New Suriname or NS [Nanan PANDAY]); National Union or NU [P. VAN LEEUWAARDE]; New Front for Democracy and Development or NF (a coalition made up of the National Party of Suriname or NPS [Runaldo VENETIAAN], United Reform Party or VHP [Ramdien SARDJOE], Democratic Alternative 1991 or DA-91—an independent, business-oriented party [Winston JESSURUN], Surinamese Labor Party or SPA [Siegfried GILDS]); Party for Democracy and Development in Unity or DOE [Carl BREEVELD]; Party for the Permanent Prosperity Republic Suriname or PVRS People's Alliance, Pertjaja Luhur's or PL [Paul SOMOHARDJO](includes D-21 [Soewarta MOESTADJA] and Pendawa Lima [Raymond SAPEON], which merged with PL in 2010)
note: BVD and PVF participated in the elections as a coalition (BVD/PVF) in the most recent elections, but separated after the election

Political pressure groups and leaders: Association of Indigenous Village Chiefs [Ricardo PANE]; Association of Saramaccan Authorities or Maroon [Head Captain WASE]; Women's Parliament Forum or PVF [Iris GILLIAD]

International organization participation: ACP, AOSIS, Caricom, CD, CELAC, FAO, G-77, IADB, IBRD, ICAO, ICRM, IDA, IDB, IFAD, IFRCS, IHO, ILO, IMF, IMO, Interpol, IOC, IPU, ISO (correspondent), ITU, ITUC (NGOs), LAES, MIGA, NAM, OAS, OIC, OPANAL, OPCW, PCA, Petrocaribe, UN, UNASUR, UNCTAD, UNESCO, UNIDO, UPU, WHO, WIPO, WMO, WTO

Diplomatic representation in the US:
chief of mission: Ambassador Subhas-Chandra MUNGRA (since 28 January 2011)
chancery: Suite 460, 4301 Connecticut Avenue NW, Washington, DC 20008
telephone: [1] (202) 244-7488
FAX: [1] (202) 244-5878
consulate(s) general: Miami

Diplomatic representation from the US:
chief of mission: Ambassador Jay N. ANANIA (since 1 October 2012)
embassy: Dr. Sophie Redmondstraat 129, Paramaribo
mailing address: US Department of State, PO Box 1821, Paramaribo
telephone: [597] 472-900
FAX: [597] 410-972

Flag description: five horizontal bands of green (top, double width), white, red (quadruple width), white, and green (double width); a large, yellow, five-pointed star is centered in the red band; red stands for progress and love; green symbolizes hope and fertility; white signifies peace, justice, and freedom; the star represents the unity of all ethnic groups; from its yellow light the nation draws strength to bear sacrifices patiently while working toward a golden future

National anthem: *name:* "God zij met ons Suriname!" (God Be With Our Suriname)
lyrics/music: Cornelis Atses HOEKSTRA and Henry DE ZIEL/Johannes Corstianus DE PUY
note: adopted 1959; the anthem, originally adapted from a Sunday school song written in 1893, contains lyrics in both Dutch and Sranang Tongo

ECONOMY

Economy—overview: The economy is dominated by the mining industry, with exports of alumina, gold, and oil accounting for about 85% of exports and 25% of government revenues, making the economy highly vulnerable to mineral price volatility. Economic growth has remained at about 4-5% per year in 2010-13, but the government's budget was strained by high inflation in 2010. In January 2011, the government devalued the currency by 20% and raised taxes to reduce the budget deficit. As a result of these measures, inflation has receded to about 4% in 2013. Suriname's economic prospects for the medium term will depend on continued commitment to responsible monetary and fiscal policies and to the introduction of structural reforms to liberalize markets and promote competition. The government's reliance on revenue from extractive industries will temper Suriname's economic outlook, especially if gold prices continue their downward trend.

GDP (purchasing power parity): $7.12 billion (2013 est.)
country comparison to the world: 161
$6.801 billion (2012 est.)
$6.492 billion (2011 est.)
note: data are in 2013 US dollars

GDP (official exchange rate): $5.009 billion (2013 est.)

GDP—real growth rate: 4.7% (2013 est.)
country comparison to the world: 62
4.8% (2012 est.)
4.7% (2011 est.)

GDP—per capita (PPP): $12,900 (2013 est.)
country comparison to the world: 101
$12,500 (2012 est.)
$12,100 (2011 est.)
note: data are in 2013 US dollars

GDP—composition, by end use:
household consumption: 73.8%
government consumption: 9.9%
investment in fixed capital: 5%
investment in inventories: 19.7%
exports of goods and services: 43.2%
imports of goods and services: -51.6% (2013 est.)

GDP—composition, by sector of origin:
agriculture: 8.9%
industry: 36.6%
services: 54.5% (2013 est.)

Agriculture—products: rice, bananas, palm kernels, coconuts, plantains, peanuts; beef, chickens; shrimp; forest products

Industries: bauxite and gold mining, alumina production; oil, lumbering, food processing, fishing

Industrial production growth rate: 4% (2013 est.)
country comparison to the world: 73

Labor force: 165,600 (2007)
country comparison to the world: 176

Labor force—by occupation: *agriculture:* 8%
industry: 14%
services: 78% (2004)

Unemployment rate: 9% (2008)
country comparison to the world: 100
12.1% (2006)

Population below poverty line: 70% (2002 est.)

Household income or consumption by percentage share: *lowest 10%:* NA%
highest 10%: NA%

Budget: *revenues:* $826.6 million
expenditures: $939.7 million (2010 est.)

Taxes and other revenues: 16.5% of GDP (2010 est.)
country comparison to the world: 185

Budget surplus (+) or deficit (-):
-2.3% of GDP (2010 est.)
country comparison to the world: 90

Fiscal year: calendar year

Inflation rate (consumer prices): 4.2% (2013 est.)
country comparison to the world: 140
5% (2012 est.)

Commercial bank prime lending rate: 12% (31 December 2013 est.)
country comparison to the world: 72
11.73% (31 December 2012 est.)

Stock of narrow money: $1.132 billion (31 December 2012 est.)
country comparison to the world: 148
$1.075 billion (31 December 2011 est.)

Stock of broad money: $3.005 million (31 December 2013 est.)
country comparison to the world: 192
$2.463 million (31 December 2012 est.)

Stock of domestic credit: $939.4 million (31 December 2013 est.)
country comparison to the world: 156
$1.275 billion (31 December 2012 est.)

Market value of publicly traded shares: $NA

Current account balance: $102.5 million (2013 est.)
country comparison to the world: 58
$241.4 million (2012 est.)

Exports: $2.512 billion (2013 est.)
country comparison to the world: 137
$2.564 billion (2012 est.)

Exports—commodities: alumina, gold, crude oil, lumber, shrimp and fish, rice, bananas

Exports—partners: US 25.7%, Belgium 17.4%, UAE 11.5%, Canada 10.3%, Guyana 5.8%, France 5.5%, Barbados 4.2% (2012)

Imports: $1.778 billion (2013 est.)
country comparison to the world: 168
$1.761 billion (2012 est.)

Imports—commodities: capital equipment, petroleum, foodstuffs, cotton, consumer goods

Imports—partners: US 26%, Netherlands 16%, China 9.9%, UAE 8.1%, Antigua and Barbuda 6.7%, Netherlands Antilles 4.9%, Japan 4.3% (2012)

Reserves of foreign exchange and gold: $1.008 billion (31 December 2012 est.)
country comparison to the world: 134
$816.9 million (31 December 2011 est.)

Debt—external: $860 million (31 December 2013 est.)
country comparison to the world: 165
$810.8 million (31 December 2012 est.)

Exchange rates: Surinamese dollars (SRD) per US dollar—
3.3 (2012 est.)
3.3 (2012 est.)
2.7454 (2010 est.)
2.745 (2009)
2.745 (2008)

ENERGY

Electricity—production: 1.57 billion kWh (2010 est.)
country comparison to the world: 141

Electricity—consumption: 1.423 billion kWh (2010 est.)
country comparison to the world: 147

Electricity—exports: 0 kWh (2012 est.)
country comparison to the world: 179

Electricity—imports: 0 kWh (2012 est.)
country comparison to the world: 180

Electricity—installed generating capacity: 410,000 kW (2010 est.)
country comparison to the world: 145

Electricity—from fossil fuels: 53.9% of total installed capacity (2010 est.)
country comparison to the world: 145

Electricity—from nuclear fuels: 0% of total installed capacity (2010 est.)
country comparison to the world: 155

Electricity—from hydroelectric plants: 46.1% of total installed capacity (2010 est.)
country comparison to the world: 48

Electricity—from other renewable sources: 0% of total installed capacity (2010 est.)
country comparison to the world: 109

Crude oil—production: 15,270 bbl/day (2012 est.)
country comparison to the world: 82

Crude oil—exports: 7,621 bbl/day (2010 est.)
country comparison to the world: 61

Crude oil—imports: 0.66 bbl/day (2010 est.)
country comparison to the world: 82

Crude oil—proved reserves: 76.8 million bbl (1 January 2013 es)
country comparison to the world: 76

Refined petroleum products—production: 7,462 bbl/day (2010 est.)
country comparison to the world: 105

Refined petroleum products—consumption: 14,100 bbl/day (2011 est.)
country comparison to the world: 146

Refined petroleum products—exports: 1,015 bbl/day (2010 est.)
country comparison to the world: 105

Refined petroleum products—imports: 6,454 bbl/day (2010 est.)
country comparison to the world: 139

Natural gas—production: 0 cu m (2011 est.)
country comparison to the world: 177

Natural gas—consumption: 0 cu m (2010 est.)
country comparison to the world: 182

Natural gas—exports: 0 cu m (2011 est.)
country comparison to the world: 159

Natural gas—imports: 0 cu m (2011 est.)
country comparison to the world: 110

Natural gas—proved reserves: 0 cu m (1 January 2011 es)
country comparison to the world: 180

Carbon dioxide emissions from consumption of energy: 2.335 million Mt (2011 est.)
country comparison to the world: 145

COMMUNICATIONS

Telephones—main lines in use: 83,000 (2012)
country comparison to the world: 149

Telephones—mobile cellular: 977,000 (2012)
country comparison to the world: 158

Telephone system: *general assessment:* international facilities are good
domestic: combined fixed-line and mobile-cellular teledensity 185 telephones per 100 persons; microwave radio relay network
international: country code—597; satellite earth stations—2 Intelsat (Atlantic Ocean) (2010)

Broadcast media: 2 state-owned TV stations; 1 state-owned radio station; multiple private radio and TV stations (2007)

Internet country code: . sr

Internet hosts: 188 (2012)
country comparison to the world: 201

Internet users: 163,000 (2009)
country comparison to the world: 146

TRANSPORTATION

Airports: 55 (2013)
country comparison to the world: 8 5

Airports—with paved runways: *total:* 6
over 3,047 m: 1
under 914 m: 5 (2013)

Airports—with unpaved runways: *total:* 4 9
914 to 1,523 m: 4
under 914 m: 45 (2013)

Pipelines: oil 50 km (2013)

Roadways: *total:* 4,304 km
country comparison to the world: 154
paved: 1,130 km
unpaved: 3,174 km (2003)

Waterways: 1,200 km (most navigable by ships with drafts up to 7 m) (2011)
country comparison to the world: 61

Ports and terminals: *major seaport(s):* Paramaribo, Wageningen

MILITARY

Military branches: *Suriname Armed Forces:* Ground Forces, Naval Forces, Air Forces (2010)

Military service age and obligation: 18 is the legal minimum age for voluntary military service; no conscription; personnel drawn almost exclusively from the Creole community (2012)

Manpower available for military service: *males age 16-49:* 134,218
females age 16-49: 134,439 (2010 est.)

Manpower fit for military service: *males age 16-49:* 109,445
females age 16-49: 112,538 (2010 est.)

Manpower reaching militarily significant age annually: *male:* 4,119
female: 4,106 (2010 est.)

TRANSNATIONAL ISSUES

Disputes—international: area claimed by French Guiana between Riviere Litani and Riviere Marouini (both headwaters of the Lawa); Suriname claims a triangle of land between the New and Kutari/Koetari rivers in a historic dispute over the headwaters of the Courantyne; Guyana seeks United Nations Convention on the Law of the Sea arbitration to resolve the longstanding dispute with Suriname over the axis of the territorial sea boundary in potentially oil-rich waters

Trafficking in persons: *current situation:* Suriname is a source, destination, and transit country for women, men, and children who are subjected to sex trafficking and forced labor; women and girls from Suriname, Guyana, Brazil, and the Dominican Republic are subjected to sex trafficking in the country, sometimes around mining camps; debt bondage and sex trafficking are reported to occur within the Chinese migrant community; migrant workers in agriculture and on fishing boats and children working in informal urban sectors and gold mines are vulnerable to forced labor

tier rating: Tier 2 Watch List—Suriname does not fully comply with the minimum standards for the elimination of trafficking; however, it is making significant efforts to do so; the government has prosecuted an increased number of sex trafficking cases and identified an increased number of child sex trafficking victims; accountability for trafficking offenses continues to be a problem as no offenders have been convicted and the complicity of local officials remains a concern; authorities do not have a formal system for referring victims to NGOs that provide services but reported doing so on an ad hoc basis; the government's interagency anti-trafficking working group drafted an anti-trafficking policy in 2012 (2013)

Illicit drugs: growing transshipment point for South American drugs destined for Europe via the Netherlands and Brazil; transshipment point for arms-for-drugs dealing

SVALBARD

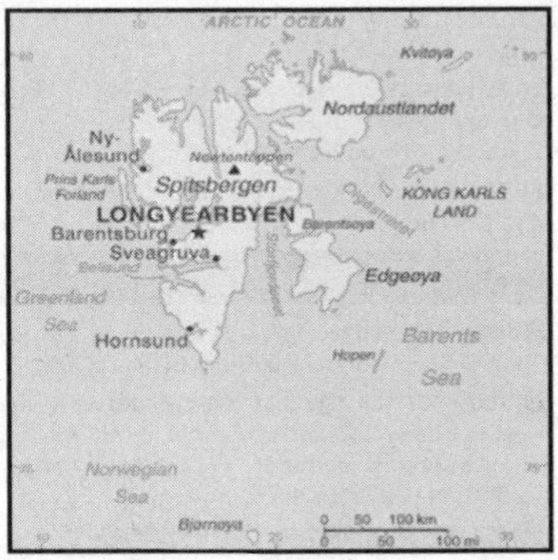

INTRODUCTION

Background: First discovered by the Norwegians in the 12th century, the islands served as an international whaling base during the 17th and 18th centuries. Norway's sovereignty was recognized in 1920; five years later it officially took over the territory.

GEOGRAPHY

Location: Northern Europe, islands between the Arctic Ocean, Barents Sea, Greenland Sea, and Norwegian Sea, north of Norway

Geographic coordinates: 78 00 N, 20 00 E

Map references: Europe

Area: *total:* 62,045 sq km
country comparison to the world: 125
land: 62,045 sq km
water: 0 sq km
note: includes Spitsbergen and Bjornoya (Bear Island)

Area—comparative: slightly smaller than West Virginia

Land boundaries: 0 km

Coastline: 3,587 km

Maritime claims: *territorial sea:* 4 nm
exclusive fishing zone: 200 nm unilaterally claimed by Norway but not recognized by Russia

Climate: arctic, tempered by warm North Atlantic Current; cool summers, cold winters; North Atlantic Current flows along west and north coasts of Spitsbergen, keeping water open and navigable most of the year

Terrain: wild, rugged mountains; much of high land ice covered; west coast clear of ice about one-half of the year; fjords along west and north coasts

Elevation extremes: *lowest point:* Arctic Ocean 0 m
highest point: Newtontoppen 1,717 m

Natural resources: coal, iron ore, copper, zinc, phosphate, wildlife, fish

Land use: *arable land:* 0%
permanent crops: 0%
other: 100% (no trees; the only bushes are crowberry and cloudberry) (2011)

Irrigated land: NA

Natural hazards: ice floes often block the entrance to Bellsund (a transit point for coal export) on the west coast and occasionally make parts of the northeastern coast inaccessible to maritime traffic

Environment—current issues: NA

Geography—note: northernmost part of the Kingdom of Norway; consists of nine main islands; glaciers and snowfields cover 60% of the total area; Spitsbergen Island is the site of the Svalbard Global Seed Vault, a seed repository established by the Global Crop Diversity Trust and the Norwegian Government

PEOPLE AND SOCIETY

Ethnic groups: Norwegian 55.4%, Russian and Ukrainian 44.3%, other 0.3% (1998)

Languages: Norwegian, Russian

Population: 1,872 (July 2014 est.)
country comparison to the world: 234

Population growth rate: -0.03% (2014 est.)
country comparison to the world: 199

Sex ratio: NA

Infant mortality rate: *total:* NA
male: NA
female: NA

Life expectancy at birth:
total population: NA
male: NA
female: NA

Total fertility rate: NA (2014 est.)

HIV/AIDS—adult prevalence rate: 0% (2001 est.)
country comparison to the world: 170

HIV/AIDS—deaths: 0 (2001 est.)
country comparison to the world: 158

Literacy: NA

GOVERNMENT

Country name: *conventional long form:* none
conventional short form: Svalbard (sometimes referred to as Spitsbergen)

Dependency status: territory of Norway; administered by the Polar Department of the Ministry of Justice, through a governor (sysselmann) residing in Longyearbyen, Spitsbergen; by treaty (9 February 1920) sovereignty was awarded to Norway

Government type: NA

Capital: *name:* Longyearbyen

geographic coordinates: 78 13 N, 15 38 E
time difference: UTC+1 (6 hours ahead of Washington, DC during Standard Time)
daylight saving time: +1hr, begins last Sunday in March; ends last Sunday in October

Independence: none (territory of Norway)

Legal system: the laws of Norway where applicable apply

Executive branch: *chief of state:* King HARALD V of Norway (since 17 January 1991)
head of government: Governor Odd Olsen INGERO (since September 2009); Assistant Governor Lars Erik ALHEIM
elections: none; the monarchy is hereditary; governor and assistant governor responsible to the Polar Department of the Ministry of Justice

Political pressure groups and leaders: NA

International organization participation: none

Flag description: the flag of Norway is used

National anthem: *note:* as a territory of Norway, "Ja, vi elsker dette landet" is official (see Norway)

ECONOMY

Economy—overview: Coal mining, tourism, and international research are the major revenue sources on Svalbard. Coal mining is the dominant economic activity and a treaty of 9 February 1920 gave the 41 signatories equal rights to exploit mineral deposits, subject to Norwegian regulation. Although US, UK, Dutch, and Swedish coal companies have mined in the past, the only companies still engaging in this are Norwegian and Russian. The settlements on Svalbard are essentially company towns. The Norwegian state-owned coal company employs nearly 60% of the Norwegian population on the island, runs many of the local services, and provides most of the local infrastructure. There is also some hunting of seal, reindeer, and fox. Goods such as alcohol, tobacco, and vehicles, normally highly taxed on mainland Norway, are considerably cheaper in Svalbard in an effort by the Norwegian government to entice more people to live on the Arctic archipelago. By law, the Norwegians collect only enough taxes to pay for the needs of the local government; none of tax proceeds go to Norway.

GDP (purchasing power parity): $6.313 billion

GDP—real growth rate: NA%

Labor force: 1,234 (2003)
country comparison to the world: 229

Budget: *revenues:* $NA
expenditures: $NA

Taxes and other revenues: NA% of GDP

Budget surplus (+) or deficit (-):
NA% of GDP

Exports: $NA

Imports: $NA

Exchange rates: Norwegian kroner (NOK) per US dollar—
5.802 (2013)
5.8162 (2012)
6.0442 (2010)
6.288 (2009)
5.6361 (2008)

COMMUNICATIONS

Telephone system: *general assessment:* adequate
domestic: local telephone service
international: country code—47-790; satellite earth station—1 of unknown type (for communication with Norwegian mainland only) (2005)

Broadcast media: the Norwegian Broadcasting Corporation (NRK) began direct TV transmission to Svalbard via satellite in 1984; Longyearbyen households have access to 3 NRK radio and 2 TV stations (2008)

Internet country code: .sj

TRANSPORTATION

Airports: 4 (2013)
country comparison to the world: 188

Airports—with paved runways: *total:* 1
2,438 to 3,047 m: 1 (2013)

Airports—with unpaved runways: *total:* 3
under 914 m: 3 (2013)

Heliports: 1 (2013)

Ports and terminals: *major seaport(s):* Barentsburg, Longyearbyen, Ny-Alesund, Pyramiden

MILITARY

Military branches: no regular military forces

Military—note: Svalbard is a territory of Norway, demilitarized by treaty on 9 February 1920; Norwegian military activity is limited to fisheries surveillance by the Norwegian Coast Guard

TRANSNATIONAL ISSUES

Disputes—international: despite recent discussions, Russia and Norway dispute their maritime limits in the Barents Sea and Russia's fishing rights beyond Svalbard's territorial limits within the Svalbard Treaty zone

SWAZILAND

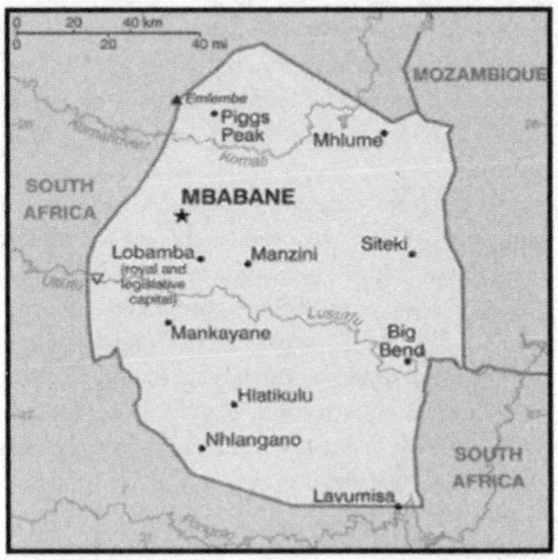

INTRODUCTION

Background: Autonomy for the Swazis of southern Africa was guaranteed by the British in the late 19th century; independence was granted in 1968. Student and labor unrest during the 1990s pressured King MSWATI III, Africa's last absolute monarch, to grudgingly allow political reform and greater democracy, although he has backslid on these promises in recent years. A constitution came into effect in 2006, but the legal status of political parties remains unclear. The African United Democratic Party tried unsuccessfully to register as an official political party in mid 2006. Talks over the constitution broke down between the government and progressive groups in 2007. Swaziland recently surpassed Botswana as the country with the world's highest known HIV/AIDS prevalence rate.

GEOGRAPHY

Location: Southern Africa, between Mozambique and South Africa

Geographic coordinates: 26 30 S, 31 30 E

Map references: Africa

Area: *total:* 17,364 sq km
country comparison to the world: 159
land: 17,204 sq km
water: 160 sq km

Area—comparative: slightly smaller than New Jersey

Land boundaries: *total:* 535 km
border countries: Mozambique 105 km, South Africa 430 km

Coastline: 0 km (landlocked)

Maritime claims: none (landlocked)

Climate: varies from tropical to near temperate

Terrain: mostly mountains and hills; some moderately sloping plains

Elevation extremes: *lowest point:* Great Usutu River 21 m
highest point: Emlembe 1,862 m

Natural resources: asbestos, coal, clay, cassiterite, hydropower, forests, small gold and diamond deposits, quarry stone, and talc

Land use: *arable land:* 10.08%
permanent crops: 0.86%
other: 89.06% (2011)

Irrigated land: 498.5 sq km (2003)

Total renewable water resources: 4.51 cu km (2011)

Freshwater withdrawal (domestic/industrial/agricultural): *total:* 1.04 cu km/yr (4%/2%/94%)
per capita: 962.1 cu m/yr (2005)

Natural hazards: drought

Environment—current issues: limited supplies of potable water; wildlife populations being depleted because of excessive hunting; overgrazing; soil degradation; soil erosion

Environment—international agreements:
party to: Biodiversity, Climate Change, Climate Change-Kyoto Protocol, Desertification, Endangered Species, Hazardous Wastes, Ozone Layer Protection
signed, but not ratified: Law of the Sea

Geography—note: landlocked; almost completely surrounded by South Africa

PEOPLE AND SOCIETY

Nationality: *noun:* Swazi(s)
adjective: Swazi

Ethnic groups: African 97%, European 3%

Languages: English (official, used for government business), siSwati (official)

Religions: Zionist 40% (a blend of Christianity and indigenous ancestral worship), Roman Catholic 20%, Muslim 10%, other (includes Anglican, Baha'i, Methodist, Mormon, Jewish) 30%

Population: 1,419,623 (July 2014 est.)
country comparison to the world: 155
note: estimates for this country explicitly take into account the effects of excess mortality due to AIDS; this can result in lower life expectancy, higher infant mortality, higher death rates, lower population growth rates, and changes in the distribution of population by age and sex than would otherwise be expected

Age structure: *0-14 years:* 36.5% (male 261,715/female 255,949)
15-24 years: 22.3% (male 160,283/female 156,685)
25-54 years: 33.2% (male 241,958/female 229,140)
55-64 years: 3.8% (male 23,739/female 36,469)
65 years and over: 3.7% (male 21,321/female 32,364) (2014 est.)

Dependency ratios:
total dependency ratio: 70.4 %
youth dependency ratio: 64.4 %
elderly dependency ratio: 5.9 %
potential support ratio: 16.8 (2013)

Median age: *total:* 21 years
male: 20.7 years
female: 21.3 years (2014 est.)

Population growth rate: 1.14% (2014 est.)
country comparison to the world: 105

Birth rate: 25.18 births/1,000 population (2014 est.)
country comparison to the world: 54

Death rate: 13.75 deaths/1,000 population (2014 est.)
country comparison to the world: 11

Net migration rate: 0 migrant(s)/1,000 population (2014 est.)
country comparison to the world: 80

Urbanization: *urban population:* 21.2% of total population (2011)
rate of urbanization: 1.19% annual rate of change (2010-15 est.)

Major urban areas—population: MBABANE (capital) 74,000 (2009)

Sex ratio: *at birth:* 1.03 male(s)/female
0-14 years: 1.02 male(s)/female
15-24 years: 1.02 male(s)/female
25-54 years: 1.06 male(s)/female

55-64 years: 1 male(s)/female
65 years and over: 0.69 male(s)/female
total population: 0.99 male(s)/female (2014 est.)

Mother's mean age at first birth: 19.5 (2007 est.)

Maternal mortality rate: 320 deaths/100,000 live births (2010)
country comparison to the world: 36

Infant mortality rate: *total:* 54.82 deaths/1,000 live births
country comparison to the world: 32
male: 58.8 deaths/1,000 live births
female: 50.72 deaths/1,000 live births (2014 est.)

Life expectancy at birth: *total population:* 50.54 years
country comparison to the world: 219
male: 51.04 years
female: 50.04 years (2014 est.)

Total fertility rate: 2.88 children born/woman (2014 est.)
country comparison to the world: 61

Contraceptive prevalence rate: 65.2% (2010)

Health expenditures: 8% of GDP (2011)
country comparison to the world: 63

Physicians density: 0.17 physicians/1,000 population (2009)

Hospital bed density: 2.1 beds/1,000 population (2011)

Drinking water source:
improved:
urban: 93.2% of population
rural: 66.5% of population
total: 72.2% of population
unimproved:
urban: 6.8% of population
rural: 33.5% of population
total: 27.8% of population (2011 est.)

Sanitation facility access:
improved:
urban: 63% of population
rural: 55.3% of population
total: 57% of population
unimproved:
urban: 37% of population
rural: 44.7% of population
total: 43% of population (2011 est.)

HIV/AIDS—adult prevalence rate: 26.5% (2012 est.)
country comparison to the world: 1

HIV/AIDS—people living with HIV/AIDS: 212,900 (2012 est.)
country comparison to the world: 29

HIV/AIDS—deaths: 5,500 (2012 est.)
country comparison to the world: 35

Major infectious diseases:
degree of risk: intermediate
food or waterborne diseases: bacterial diarrhea, hepatitis A, and typhoid fever
vectorborne disease: malaria
water contact disease: schistosomiasis (2013)

Obesity—adult prevalence rate: 19.7% (2008)
country comparison to the world: 98

Children under the age of 5 years underweight: 5.8% (2010)
country comparison to the world: 84

Education expenditures: 8.3% of GDP (2011)
country comparison to the world: 12

Literacy: *definition:* age 15 and over can read and write
total population: 87.8%
male: 88.4%
female: 87.3% (2011 est.)

School life expectancy (primary to tertiary education): *total:* 11 years
male: 12 years
female: 11 years (2011)

Child labor—children ages 5-14:
total number: 28,043
percentage: 9 % (2000 est.)

GOVERNMENT

Country name: *conventional long form:* Kingdom of Swaziland
conventional short form: Swaziland
local long form: Umbuso weSwatini
local short form: eSwatini

Government type: monarchy

Capital: *name:* Mbabane

geographic coordinates: 26 19 S, 31 08 E
time difference: UTC+2 (7 hours ahead of Washington, DC during Standard Time)
note: Lobamba (royal and legislative capital)

Administrative divisions: 4 districts; Hhohho, Lubombo, Manzini, Shiselweni

Independence: 6 September 1968 (from the UK)

National holiday: Independence Day, 6 September (1968)

Constitution: previous 1968, 1978; latest signed by the king 26 July 2005, effective 8 February 2006 (2013)

Legal system: mixed legal system of civil, common, and customary law

International law organization participation: accepts compulsory ICJ jurisdiction with reservations; non-party state to the ICCt

Suffrage: 18 years of age

Executive branch: *chief of state:* King MSWATI III (since 25 April 1986)
head of government: Prime Minister Barnabas Sibusiso DLAMINI (since 23 October 2008); Deputy Prime Minister Themba Nhlanganiso MASUKU (since 2008)
cabinet: Cabinet recommended by the prime minister and confirmed by the monarch (For more information visit the World Leaders website)
elections: none; the monarchy is hereditary; prime minister appointed by the monarch from among the elected members of the House of Assembly

Legislative branch: bicameral Parliament or Libandla consists of the Senate (30 seats; 10 members elected by the House of Assembly and 20 appointed by the monarch; members to serve five-year terms) and the House of Assembly (65 seats; 10 members appointed by the monarch and 55 elected by popular vote; members to serve five-year terms)
elections: House of Assembly—last held on 20 September 2013 (next scheduled for September 2018)
election results: House of Assembly—balloting is done on a nonparty basis; candidates for election nominated by the local council of each constituency and for each constituency the three candidates with the most votes in the first round of voting are narrowed to a single winner by a second round

Judicial branch: *highest court(s):* the Supreme Court of the Judicature comprising the Supreme Court (consists of the chief justice and at least 5 justices) and the High Court (consists of the chief justice—ex officio—and at least 4 justices); note—the Supreme Court has jurisdiction in all constitutional matters note—the national constitution as amended in 2006 shifted judicial power from the monarch and vested it exclusively in the judiciary
judge selection and term of office: justices of the Supreme Court of the Judicature are appointed by the monarch on the advice of the Judicial Service Commission or JCS, a judicial advisory body consisting of the Supreme Court Chief Justice, 4 members appointed by the monarch, and the JCS head; justices of both courts eligible for retirement at age 65 with mandatory retirement at age 75 for Supreme Court justices and at age 70 for High Court justices
subordinate courts: magistrates' courts; National Swazi Courts for administering customary/traditional law (jurisdiction restricted to customary law for Swazi citizens)

Political parties and leaders: the status of political parties, previously banned, is unclear under the 2006 Constitution and currently being debated; the following are considered political associations; African United Democratic Party or AUDP [Stanley MAUNDZISA, president]; Imbokodvo National Movement or INM; Ngwane National Liberatory Congress or NNLC [Obed DLAMINI, president]; People's United Democratic Movement or PUDEMO [Mario MASUKU, president]

Political pressure groups and leaders: Swaziland Democracy Campaign; Swaziland Federation of Trade Unions; Swaziland Solidarity Network or SSN

International organization participation: ACP, AfDB, AU, C, COMESA, FAO, G-77, IAEA, IBRD, ICAO, ICRM, IDA, IFAD, IFC, IFRCS, ILO, IMF, IMO, Interpol, IOC, IOM, ISO (correspondent), ITSO, ITU, ITUC (NGOs), MIGA, NAM, OPCW, PCA, SACU, SADC, UN, UNCTAD, UNESCO, UNIDO, UNWTO, UPU, WCO, WHO, WIPO, WMO, WTO

Diplomatic representation in the US:
chief of mission: Ambassador Abednigo Mandla NTSHANGASE (since 19 July 2010)
chancery: 1712 New Hampshire Avenue, NW, Washington, DC 20009
telephone: [1] (202) 234-5002
FAX: [1] (202) 234-8254

Diplomatic representation from the US:
chief of mission: Ambassador Makila JAMES (since 27 August 2012)
embassy: 7th Floor, Central Bank Building, Mahlokohla St., Mbabane
mailing address: P. O. Box 199, Mbabane
telephone: [268] 404-6441
FAX: [268] 404-5959

Flag description: three horizontal bands of blue (top), red (triple width), and blue; the red band is edged in yellow; centered in the red band is a large black and white shield covering two spears and a staff decorated with feather tassels, all placed horizontally; blue stands for peace and stability, red represents past struggles, and yellow the mineral resources of the country; the shield, spears, and staff symbolize protection from the country's enemies, while the black and white of the shield are meant to portray black and white people living in peaceful coexistence

National symbol(s): lion; elephant

National anthem: *name:* "Nkulunkulu Mnikati wetibusiso temaSwati" (Oh God, Bestower of the Blessings of the Swazi)
lyrics/music: Andrease Enoke Fanyana SIMELANE/David Kenneth RYCROFT
note: adopted 1968; the anthem uses elements of both ethnic Swazi and Western music styles

ECONOMY

Economy—overview: Surrounded by South Africa, except for a short border with Mozambique, Swaziland depends heavily on South Africa from which it receives more than 90% of its imports and to which it sends 60% of its exports. Swaziland's currency is pegged to the South African rand, effectively subsuming Swaziland's monetary policy to South Africa. The government is heavily dependent on customs duties from the Southern African Customs Union (SACU), and worker remittances from South Africa supplement domestically earned income. Subsistence agriculture employs approximately 70% of the population. The manufacturing sector has diversified since the mid-1980s. Sugar and wood pulp were major foreign exchange earners; however, the wood pulp producer closed in January 2010, and sugar is now the main export earner. Mining has declined in importance in recent years with only coal and quarry stone mines remaining active. Customs revenues plummeted due to the global economic crisis and a drop in South African imports. The resulting decline in revenue has pushed the country into a fiscal crisis. Swaziland is looking to other countries, including South Africa, for assistance, but continues to struggle to meet its monthly payroll and fund government programs. With an estimated 40% unemployment rate, Swaziland's need to increase the number and size of small and medium enterprises and attract foreign direct investment is acute. Overgrazing, soil depletion, drought, and floods persist as problems for the future. More than one-fourth of the population needed emergency food aid in 2006-07 because of drought, and more than one-quarter of the adult population has been infected by HIV/AIDS, as of 2013.

GDP (purchasing power parity): $6.259 billion (2013 est.)
country comparison to the world: 164
$6.259 billion (2012 est.)
$6.354 billion (2011 est.)
note: data are in 2013 US dollars

GDP (official exchange rate): $3.807 billion (2013 est.)

GDP—real growth rate: 0% (2013 est.)
country comparison to the world: 197
-1.5% (2012 est.)
0.3% (2011 est.)

GDP—per capita (PPP): $5,700 (2013 est.)
country comparison to the world: 154
$5,800 (2012 est.)
$6,000 (2011 est.)
note: data are in 2013 US dollars

Gross national saving: 10.1% of GDP (2013 est.)
country comparison to the world: 134
13.4% of GDP (2012 est.)
4.5% of GDP (2011 est.)

GDP—composition, by end use:
household consumption: 86.2%
government consumption: 21.5%
investment in fixed capital: 10.1%
investment in inventories: 0%
exports of goods and services: 57.4%
imports of goods and services: -75.3% (2013 est.)

GDP—composition, by sector of origin:
agriculture: 7.6%
industry: 47.8%
services: 44.6% (2013 est.)

Agriculture—products: sugarcane, cotton, corn, tobacco, rice, citrus, pineapples, sorghum, peanuts; cattle, goats, sheep

Industries: coal, wood pulp, sugar, soft drink concentrates, textiles and apparel

Industrial production growth rate: 0.4% (2013 est.)
country comparison to the world: 162

Labor force: 424,100 (2011 est.)
country comparison to the world: 158

Labor force—by occupation: *agriculture:* 70%
industry: NA%
services: NA%

Unemployment rate: 40% (2006 est.)
country comparison to the world: 190

Population below poverty line: 69% (2006)

Household income or consumption by percentage share: *lowest 10%:* 1.7%
highest 10%: 40.1% (2010 est.)

Distribution of family income—Gini index: 50.4 (2001)
country comparison to the world: 20

Budget: *revenues:* $1.274 billion
expenditures: $1.316 billion (2013 est.)

Taxes and other revenues: 33.5% of GDP (2013 est.)
country comparison to the world: 71

Budget surplus (+) or deficit (-): -1.1% of GDP (2013 est.)
country comparison to the world: 64

Fiscal year: 1 April—31 March

Inflation rate (consumer prices): 6.1% (2013 est.)
country comparison to the world: 174
8.9% (2012 est.)

Central bank discount rate: 6.5% (31 December 2010 est.)
country comparison to the world: 52
6.5% (31 December 2009 est.)

Commercial bank prime lending rate: 8.5% (31 December 2013 est.)
country comparison to the world: 105
8.75% (31 December 2012 est.)

Stock of narrow money: $421.6 million (31 December 2013 est.)
country comparison to the world: 163
$403.3 million (31 December 2012 est.)

Stock of broad money: $1.142 billion (31 December 2013 est.)
country comparison to the world: 165
$1.138 billion (31 December 2012 est.)

Stock of domestic credit: $763.3 million (31 December 2013 est.)
country comparison to the world: 160
$762.9 million (31 December 2012 est.)

Market value of publicly traded shares: $203.1 million (31 December 2007)
country comparison to the world: 114
$203.1 million (31 December 2007)
$199.9 million

Current account balance: -$1.5 million (2013 est.)
country comparison to the world: 61
$53 million (2012 est.)

Exports: $1.603 billion (2013 est.)
country comparison to the world: 145
$1.681 billion (2012 est.)

Exports—commodities: soft drink concentrates, sugar, wood pulp, cotton yarn, refrigerators, citrus and canned fruit

Imports: $1.545 billion (2013 est.)
country comparison to the world: 172
$1.578 billion (2012 est.)

Imports—commodities: motor vehicles, machinery, transport equipment, foodstuffs, petroleum products, chemicals

Reserves of foreign exchange and gold: $801.4 million (31 December 2013 est.)
country comparison to the world: 143
$741 million (31 December 2012 est.)

Debt—external: $609.5 million (31 December 2013 est.)
country comparison to the world: 172
$604.8 million (31 December 2012 est.)

Stock of direct foreign investment—at home: $NA

Stock of direct foreign investment—abroad: $NA

Exchange rates: emalangeni per US dollar—
9.575 (2013 est.)
8.2031 (2012 est.)

7.3212 (2010 est.)
8.42 (2009)
7.75 (2008)

ENERGY

Electricity—production: 496 million kWh (2010 est.)
country comparison to the world: 164

Electricity—consumption: 1.058 billion kWh (2010 est.)
country comparison to the world: 149

Electricity—exports: 0 kWh (2012)
country comparison to the world: 215

Electricity—imports: 564 million kWh (2011 est.)
country comparison to the world: 76

Electricity—installed generating capacity: 149,000 kW (2010 est.)
country comparison to the world: 163

Electricity—from fossil fuels: 59.7% of total installed capacity (2010 est.)
country comparison to the world: 135

Electricity—from nuclear fuels: 0% of total installed capacity (2010 est.)
country comparison to the world: 207

Electricity—from hydroelectric plants: 40.3% of total installed capacity (2010 est.)
country comparison to the world: 59

Electricity—from other renewable sources: 0% of total installed capacity (2010 est.)
country comparison to the world: 142

Crude oil—production: 0 bbl/day (2012 est.)
country comparison to the world: 147

Crude oil—exports: 0 bbl/day (2010 est.)
country comparison to the world: 208

Crude oil—imports: 0 bbl/day (2010 est.)
country comparison to the world: 144

Crude oil—proved reserves: 0 bbl (1 January 2010 es)
country comparison to the world: 209

Refined petroleum products—production: 0 bbl/day (2010 est.)
country comparison to the world: 211

Refined petroleum products—consumption: 4,567 bbl/day (2011 est.)
country comparison to the world: 171

Refined petroleum products—exports: 0 bbl/day (2010 est.)
country comparison to the world: 146

Refined petroleum products—imports: 4,761 bbl/day (2010 est.)
country comparison to the world: 155

Natural gas—production: 0 cu m (2011 est.)
country comparison to the world: 211

Natural gas—consumption: 0 cu m (2010 est.)
country comparison to the world: 211

Natural gas—exports: 0 cu m (2011 est.)
country comparison to the world: 210

Natural gas—imports: 0 cu m (2011 est.)
country comparison to the world: 81

Natural gas—proved reserves: 0 cu m (1 January 2013 es)
country comparison to the world: 209

Carbon dioxide emissions from consumption of energy: 1.024 million Mt (2011 est.)
country comparison to the world: 167

COMMUNICATIONS

Telephones—main lines in use: 48,600 (2012)
country comparison to the world: 164

Telephones—mobile cellular: 805,000 (2012)
country comparison to the world: 160

Telephone system: *general assessment:* a somewhat modern but not an advanced system
domestic: single source for mobile-cellular service with a geographic coverage of about 90% and a rising subscribership base; combined fixed-line and mobile cellular teledensity roughly 60 telephones per 100 persons in 2011; telephone system consists of carrier-equipped, open-wire lines and low-capacity, microwave radio relay
international: country code—268; satellite earth station—1 Intelsat (Atlantic Ocean) (2009)

Broadcast media: state-owned TV station; satellite dishes are able to access South African providers; state-owned radio network with 3 channels; 1 private radio station (2007)

Internet country code: .sz

Internet hosts: 2,744 (2012)
country comparison to the world: 158

Internet users: 90,100 (2009)
country comparison to the world: 162

TRANSPORTATION

Airports: 14 (2013)
country comparison to the world: 149

Airports—with paved runways: *total:* 2
over 3,047 m: 1
2,438 to 3,047 m: 1 (2013)

Airports—with unpaved runways: *total:* 1 2
914 to 1,523 m: 5
under 914 m: 7 (2013)

Railways: *total:* 301 km
country comparison to the world: 120
narrow gauge: 301 km 1.067-m gauge (2008)

Roadways: *total:* 3,594 km
country comparison to the world: 160
paved: 1,078 km
unpaved: 2,516 km (2002)

MILITARY

Military branches: Umbutfo Swaziland Defense Force (USDF): Ground Force (includes Air Wing (no operational aircraft)) (2013)

Military service age and obligation: 18-30 years of age for male and female voluntary military service; no conscription; compulsory HIV testing required, only HIV-negative applicants accepted (2012)

Manpower available for military service:
males age 16-49: 344,038 (2010 est.)

Manpower fit for military service:
males age 16-49: 201,853
females age 16-49: 175,477 (2010 est.)

Manpower reaching militarily significant age annually: *male:* 16,168
female: 15,763 (2010 est.)

Military expenditures:
3.17% of GDP (2012)
country comparison to the world: 17
3.11% of GDP (2011)
3.17% of GDP (2010)

TRANSNATIONAL ISSUES

Disputes—international: in 2006, Swazi king advocated resorting to ICJ to claim parts of Mpumalanga and KwaZulu-Natal from South Africa

SWEDEN

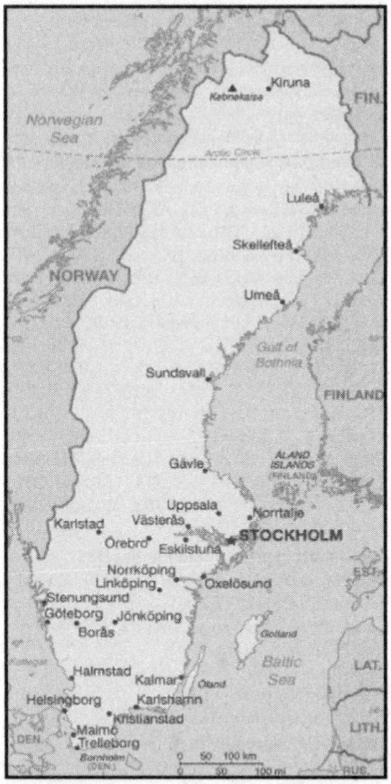

INTRODUCTION

Background: A military power during the 17th century, Sweden has not participated in any war for almost two centuries. An armed neutrality was preserved in both world wars. Sweden's long-successful economic formula of a capitalist system intermixed with substantial welfare elements was challenged in the 1990s by high unemployment and in 2000-02 and 2009 by the global economic downturns, but fiscal discipline over the past several years has allowed the country to weather economic vagaries. Sweden joined the EU in 1995, but the public rejected the introduction of the euro in a 2003 referendum.

GEOGRAPHY

Location: Northern Europe, bordering the Baltic Sea, Gulf of Bothnia, Kattegat, and Skagerrak, between Finland and Norway

Geographic coordinates: 62 00 N, 15 00 E

Map references: Europe

Area: *total:* 450,295 sq km
country comparison to the world: 56
land: 410,335 sq km
water: 39,960 sq km

Area—comparative: slightly larger than California

Land boundaries: *total:* 2,233 km
border countries: Finland 614 km, Norway 1,619 km

Coastline: 3,218 km

Maritime claims: *territorial sea:* 12 nm (adjustments made to return a portion of straits to high seas)
exclusive economic zone: agreed boundaries or midlines
continental shelf: 200 m depth or to the depth of exploitation

Climate: temperate in south with cold, cloudy winters and cool, partly cloudy summers; subarctic in north

Terrain: mostly flat or gently rolling lowlands; mountains in west

Elevation extremes: *lowest point:* reclaimed bay of Lake Hammarsjon, near Kristianstad -2.4 m
highest point: Kebnekaise 2,111 m

Natural resources: iron ore, copper, lead, zinc, gold, silver, tungsten, uranium, arsenic, feldspar, timber, hydropower

Land use: *arable land:* 5.8%
permanent crops: 0.02%
other: 94.18% (2011)

Irrigated land: 1,597 sq km (2007)

Total renewable water resources: 174 cu km (2011)

Freshwater withdrawal (domestic/industrial/agricultural): *total:* 2.62 cu km/yr (37%/59%/4%)
per capita: 285.6 cu m/yr (2007)

Natural hazards: ice floes in the surrounding waters, especially in the Gulf of Bothnia, can interfere with maritime traffic

Environment—current issues: acid rain damage to soils and lakes; pollution of the North Sea and the Baltic Sea

Environment—international agreements:
party to: Air Pollution, Air Pollution-Nitrogen Oxides, Air Pollution-Persistent Organic Pollutants, Air Pollution-Sulfur 85, Air Pollution-Sulfur 94, Air Pollution-Volatile Organic Compounds, Antarctic-Environmental Protocol, Antarctic-Marine Living Resources, Antarctic Treaty, Biodiversity, Climate Change, Climate Change-Kyoto Protocol, Desertification, Endangered Species, Environmental Modification, Hazardous Wastes, Law of the Sea, Marine Dumping, Ozone Layer Protection, Ship Pollution, Tropical Timber 83, Tropical Timber 94, Wetlands, Whaling
signed, but not ratified: none of the selected agreements

Geography—note: strategic location along Danish Straits linking Baltic and North Seas

PEOPLE AND SOCIETY

Nationality: *noun:* Swede(s)
adjective: Swedish

Ethnic groups: *indigenous population:* Swedes with Finnish and Sami minorities; foreign-born or first-generation
immigrants: Finns, Yugoslavs, Danes, Norwegians, Greeks, Turks

Languages: Swedish (official), small Sami- and Finnish-speaking minorities

Religions: Lutheran 87%, other (includes Roman Catholic, Orthodox, Baptist, Muslim, Jewish, and Buddhist) 13%

Population: 9,723,809 (July 2014 est.)
country comparison to the world: 91

Age structure:
0-14 years: 16.9% (male 847,611/female 800,213)
15-24 years: 12.3% (male 617,054/female 582,755)
25-54 years: 39.2% (male 1,937,091/female 1,872,070)
55-64 years: 19.8% (male 571,079/female 568,093)
65 years and over: 20.5% (male 882,653/female 1,045,190) (2014 est.)

Dependency ratios:
total dependency ratio: 56.8 %
youth dependency ratio: 26.5 %
elderly dependency ratio: 30.3 %
potential support ratio: 3.3 (2013)

Median age: *total:* 41.2 years
male: 40.2 years
female: 42.2 years (2014 est.)

Population growth rate: 0.79% (2014 est.)
country comparison to the world: 140

Birth rate: 11.92 births/1,000 population (2014 est.)
country comparison to the world: 167

Death rate: 9.45 deaths/1,000 population (2014 est.)
country comparison to the world: 58

Net migration rate: 5.46 migrant(s)/1,000 population (2014 est.)
country comparison to the world: 25

Urbanization: *urban population:* 85% of total population (2010)
rate of urbanization: 0.6% annual rate of change (2010-15 est.)

Major urban areas—population: STOCKHOLM (capital) 1.279 million (2009)

Sex ratio: *at birth:* 1.06 male(s)/female
0-14 years: 1.06 male(s)/female
15-24 years: 1.06 male(s)/female
25-54 years: 1.04 male(s)/female
55-64 years: 1 male(s)/female
65 years and over: 0.81 male(s)/female
total population: 0.98 male(s)/female (2014 est.)

Mother's mean age at first birth: 28.6 (2005 est.)

Maternal mortality rate: 4 deaths/100,000 live births (2010)
country comparison to the world: 179

Infant mortality rate: *total:* 2.6 deaths/1,000 live births
country comparison to the world: 219
male: 2.88 deaths/1,000 live births
female: 2.3 deaths/1,000 live births (2014 est.)

Life expectancy at birth:
total population: 81.89 years
country comparison to the world: 12
male: 80.03 years
female: 83.87 years (2014 est.)

Total fertility rate: 1.88 children born/woman (2014 est.)
country comparison to the world: 142

Contraceptive prevalence rate: 75.2%
note: percent of women aged 18-44 (1996)

Health expenditures: 9.4% of GDP (2011)

country comparison to the world: 36

Physicians density: 3.8 physicians/1,000 population (2010)

Hospital bed density: 2.7 beds/1,000 population (2010)

Drinking water source:
improved:
urban: 100% of population
rural: 100% of population
total: 100% of population
unimproved:
urban: 0% of population
rural: 0% of population
total: 0% of population (2011 est.)

Sanitation facility access:
improved:
urban: 100% of population
rural: 100% of population
total: 100% of population
unimproved:
urban: 0% of population
rural: 0% of population
total: 0% of population (2011 est.)

HIV/AIDS—adult prevalence rate: 0.1% (2009 est.)
country comparison to the world: 145

HIV/AIDS—people living with HIV/AIDS: 8,100 (2009 est.)
country comparison to the world: 111

HIV/AIDS—deaths: fewer than 100 (2009 est.)
country comparison to the world: 149

Obesity—adult prevalence rate: 18.6% (2008)
country comparison to the world: 104

Education expenditures: 7% of GDP (2010)
country comparison to the world: 20

Literacy: *definition:* age 15 and over can read and write
total population: 99%
male: 99%
female: 99% (2003 est.)

School life expectancy (primary to tertiary education): *total:* 16 years
male: 15 years
female: 17 years (2011)

Unemployment, youth ages 15-24: total: 23.7%
country comparison to the world: 45
male: 25%
female: 22.3% (2012)

GOVERNMENT

Country name: *conventional long form:* Kingdom of Sweden
conventional short form: Sweden
local long form: Konungariket Sverige
local short form: Sverige

Government type: constitutional monarchy

Capital: *name:* Stockholm

geographic coordinates: 59 20 N, 18 03 E
time difference: UTC+1 (6 hours ahead of Washington, DC during Standard Time)
daylight saving time: +1hr, begins last Sunday in March; ends last Sunday in October

Administrative divisions: 21 counties (lan, singular and plural); Blekinge, Dalarna, Gavleborg, Gotland, Halland, Jamtland, Jonkoping, Kalmar, Kronoberg, Norrbotten, Orebro, Ostergotland, Skane, Sodermanland, Stockholm, Uppsala, Varmland, Vasterbotten, Vasternorrland, Vastmanland, Vastra Gotaland

Independence: 6 June 1523 (Gustav VASA elected king)

National holiday: National Day, 6 June (1983); note—from 1916 to 1982 this date was celebrated as Swedish Flag Day

Constitution: several previous; latest adopted 1 January 1975; amended several times, last in 2011 (2011)

Legal system: civil law system influenced by Roman-Germanic law and customary law

International law organization participation: accepts compulsory ICJ jurisdiction with reservations; accepts ICCt jurisdiction

Suffrage: 18 years of age; universal

Executive branch: *chief of state:* King CARL XVI GUSTAF (since 19 September 1973); Heir Apparent Princess VICTORIA Ingrid Alice Desiree, daughter of the monarch (born 14 July 1977)
head of government: Prime Minister Fredrik REINFELDT (since 5 October 2006); Deputy Prime Minister Jan BJORKLUND (since 5 October 2010)
cabinet: Cabinet appointed by the prime minister (For more information visit the World Leaders website)
elections: the monarchy is hereditary; following legislative elections, the leader of the majority party or the leader of the majority coalition usually becomes the prime minister

Legislative branch: unicameral Parliament or Riksdag (349 seats; members are elected by popular vote on a proportional representation basis to serve four-year terms)
elections: last held on 19 September 2010 (next to be held in September 2014)
election results: percent of vote by party—SAP 30.7%, Moderate Party 30.1%, Green Party 7.3%, FP 7.1%, C 6.6%, SD 5.7%, KD 5.6%, V 5.6%, others 1.3%; seats by party—SAP 112, Moderate Party 107, Green Party 25, FP 24, C 23, SD 20, KD 19, V 19

Judicial branch: *highest court(s):* Supreme Court of Sweden (consists of 16 justices including the court chairman; Supreme Administrative Court (consists of 18 justices including the court president)
judge selection and term of office: Supreme Court and Supreme Administrative Court justices nominated by the Board of Judges, a 9-member nominating body consisting of high-level judges, prosecutors, and members of Parliament; justices appointed by the Government; following a probationary period, justices' appointments are permanent
subordinate courts: first instance and appellate general and administrative courts; specialized courts that handle cases such as land and environment, immigration, labor, markets, and patents

Political parties and leaders: Center Party (Centerpartiet) or C [Annie LOOF]; Christian Democrats (Kristdemokraterna) or KD [Goran HAGGLUND]; Green Party (Miljopartiet de Grona); [spokespersons Asa ROMSON and Gustav FRIDOLIN]; Left Party (Vansterpartiet) (formerly Communist Party) or V [Jonas SJOSTEDT]; Liberal People's Party (Folkpartiet) or FP [Jan BJORKLUND]; Moderate Party (Moderaterna) or M [Fredrik REINFELDT]; Social Democratic Party (Socialdemokraterna) or SDP [Stefan LOFVEN]; Sweden Democrats (Sverigedemokraterna) or SD [Jimmie AKESSON]

Political pressure groups and leaders: Children's Rights in Society; Swedish Confederation of Professional Employees or TCO; Swedish Trade Union Confederation (Landsorganisationen) or LO [Wanja LUNDBY-WEDIN]
other: environmental groups; media

International organization participation: ADB (nonregional member), AfDB (nonregional member), Arctic Council, Australia Group, BIS, CBSS, CD, CE, CERN, EAPC, EBRD, EIB, EITI (implementing country), ESA, EU, FAO, FATF, G-9, G-10, IADB, IAEA, IBRD, ICAO, ICC (national committees), ICRM, IDA, IEA, IFAD, IFC, IFRCS, IGAD (partners), IHO, ILO, IMF, IMO, IMSO, Interpol, IOC, IOM, IPU, ISO, ITSO, ITU, ITUC (NGOs), MIGA, MINUSMA, MONUSCO, NC, NEA, NIB, NSG, OAS (observer), OECD, OPCW, OSCE, Paris Club, PCA, PFP, Schengen Convention, UN, UNCTAD, UNESCO, UNHCR, UNIDO, UNISFA, UNMISS, UNMOGIP, UNRWA, UNTSO, UPU, WCO, WFTU (NGOs), WHO, WIPO, WMO, WTO, ZC

Diplomatic representation in the US:
chief of mission: Ambassador Bjorn O. LYRVALL (since 12 September 2013)
chancery: The House of Sweden, 2900 K Street NW, Washington, DC 20007
telephone: [1] (202) 467-2600
FAX: [1] (202) 467-2699
consulate(s) general: New York

Diplomatic representation from the US:
chief of mission: Ambassador Mark Francis BRZEZINSKI (since 14 November 2011)
embassy: Dag Hammarskjolds Vag 31, SE-11589 Stockholm
mailing address: American Embassy Stockholm, US Department of State, 5750 Stockholm Place, Washington, DC 20521-5750
telephone: [46] (08) 783 53 00
FAX: [46] (08) 661 19 64

Flag description: blue with a golden yellow cross extending to the edges of the flag; the vertical part of the cross is shifted to the hoist side in the style of the Dannebrog (Danish flag); the colors reflect those of the Swedish coat of arms—three gold crowns on a blue field

National symbol(s): three crowns; lion

National anthem: *name:* "Du Gamla, Du Fria" (Thou Ancient, Thou Free)
lyrics/music: Richard DYBECK/traditional
note: in use since 1844; the anthem, also known as "Sang till Norden" (Song of the North), is based on a Swedish folk tune; it has never been officially adopted by the government; "Kungssangen" (The King's Song) serves as the royal anthem and is played in the presence of the royal family and during certain state ceremonies

ECONOMY

Economy—overview: Aided by peace and neutrality for the whole of the 20th century, Sweden has achieved an enviable standard of living under a mixed system of high-tech capitalism and extensive welfare benefits. It has a modern distribution system, excellent internal and external communications, and a highly skilled labor force. In September 2003, Swedish voters turned down entry into the euro system concerned about the impact on the economy and sovereignty. Timber, hydropower, and iron ore constitute the resource base of an economy heavily oriented toward foreign trade. Privately owned firms account for vast majority of industrial output, of which the engineering sector accounts for about 50% of output and exports. Agriculture accounts for little more than 1% of GDP and of employment. Until 2008, Sweden was in the midst of a sustained economic upswing, boosted by increased domestic demand and strong exports. This, and robust finances, offered the center-right government considerable scope to implement its reform program aimed at increasing employment, reducing welfare dependence, and streamlining the state's role in the economy. Despite strong finances and underlying fundamentals, the Swedish economy slid into recession in the third quarter of 2008 and the contraction continued in 2009 as deteriorating global conditions reduced export demand and consumption. Strong exports of commodities and a return to profitability by Sweden's banking sector drove a rebound in 2010, but growth slipped in 2013, as a result of continued economic weakness in the EU—Sweden's main export market.

GDP (purchasing power parity): $393.8 billion (2013 est.)
country comparison to the world: 35
$390.4 billion (2012 est.)
$386.7 billion (2011 est.)
note: data are in 2013 US dollars

GDP (official exchange rate): $552 billion (2013 est.)

GDP—real growth rate: 0.9% (2013 est.)
country comparison to the world: 176
1% (2012 est.)
2.9% (2011 est.)

GDP—per capita (PPP): $40,900 (2013 est.)
country comparison to the world: 26
$40,900 (2012 est.)
$40,800 (2011 est.)
note: data are in 2013 US dollars

Gross national saving: 25.8% of GDP (2013 est.)
country comparison to the world: 45
25.8% of GDP (2012 est.)
26.9% of GDP (2011 est.)

GDP—composition, by end use:
household consumption: 48.6%
government consumption: 26.8%
investment in fixed capital: 18.3%
investment in inventories: 0.4%
exports of goods and services: 45.8%
imports of goods and services: -39.9% (2013 est.)

GDP—composition, by sector of origin:
agriculture: 2%
industry: 31.3%
services: 66.8% (2013 est.)

Agriculture—products: barley, wheat, sugar beets; meat, milk

Industries: iron and steel, precision equipment (bearings, radio and telephone parts, armaments), wood pulp and paper products, processed foods, motor vehicles

Industrial production growth rate: -1% (2013 est.)
country comparison to the world: 177

Labor force: 5.107 million (2013 est.)
country comparison to the world: 74

Labor force—by occupation: *agriculture:* 1.1%
industry: 28.2%
services: 70.7% (2008 est.)

Unemployment rate: 8.1% (2013 est.)
country comparison to the world: 92
8% (2012 est.)

Population below poverty line: NA%

Household income or consumption by percentage share: *lowest 10%:* 3.6%
highest 10%: 22.2% (2000)

Distribution of family income—Gini index: 23 (2005)
country comparison to the world: 139
25 (1992)

Budget: *revenues:* $283.5 billion
expenditures: $294.7 billion (2013 est.)

Taxes and other revenues: 51.4% of GDP (2013 est.)
country comparison to the world: 12

Budget surplus (+) or deficit (-):
-2% of GDP (2013 est.)
country comparison to the world: 85

Public debt: 41.5% of GDP (2013 est.)
country comparison to the world: 85
38.2% of GDP (2012 est.)
note: data cover general government debt, and includes debt instruments issued (or owned) by government entities other than the treasury; the data include treasury debt held by foreign entities; the data include debt issued by subnational entities, as well as intra-governmental debt; intra-governmental debt consists of treasury borrowings from surpluses in the social funds, such as for retirement, medical care, and unemployment; debt instruments for the social funds are not sold at public auctions

Fiscal year: calendar year

Inflation rate (consumer prices): 0% (2013 est.)
country comparison to the world: 6
0.9% (2012 est.)

Central bank discount rate: 5.5% (31 December 2010 est.)
country comparison to the world: 139
0.5% (31 December 2009 est.)

Commercial bank prime lending rate: 3.3% (31 December 2013 est.)
country comparison to the world: 169
3.57% (31 December 2012 est.)

Stock of narrow money: $254.3 billion (31 December 2013 est.)
country comparison to the world: 18
$260.1 billion (31 December 2012 est.)

Stock of broad money: $349.4 billion (31 December 2013 est.)
country comparison to the world: 28
$347 billion (31 December 2012 est.)

Stock of domestic credit: $798 billion (31 December 2013 est.)
country comparison to the world: 18
$792.5 billion (31 December 2012 est.)

Market value of publicly traded shares: $560.5 billion (31 December 2012 est.)
country comparison to the world: 20
$470.1 billion (31 December 2011)
$581.2 billion (31 December 2010 est.)

Current account balance: $39 billion (2013 est.)
country comparison to the world: 15
$36.31 billion (2012 est.)

Exports: $181.5 billion (2013 est.)
country comparison to the world: 28
$184.8 billion (2012 est.)

Exports—commodities: machinery 35%, motor vehicles, paper products, pulp and wood, iron and steel products, chemicals

Exports—partners: Norway 10.4%, Germany 10.3%, UK 8.1%, Finland 6.8%, Denmark 6.7%, Netherlands 5.5%, US 5.5%, Belgium 5%, France 4.8% (2012)

Imports: $158 billion (2013 est.)
country comparison to the world: 30
$163.3 billion (2012 est.)

Imports—commodities: machinery, petroleum and petroleum products, chemicals, motor vehicles, iron and steel; foodstuffs, clothing

Imports—partners: Germany 17.4%, Denmark 8.5%, Norway 8.4%, UK 6.5%, Netherlands 6.4%, Russia 5.6%, Finland 5.1%, China 4.9%, France 4.2% (2012)

Reserves of foreign exchange and gold: $52.23 billion (31 December 2012 est.)
country comparison to the world: 37
$50.35 billion (31 December 2011 est.)

Debt—external: $1.039 trillion (31 December 2012 est.)
country comparison to the world: 18
$992.5 billion (31 December 2011)

Stock of direct foreign investment—at home: $519.3 billion (31 December 2013 est.)
country comparison to the world: 17
$500.8 billion (31 December 2012 est.)

Stock of direct foreign investment—abroad: $558.8 billion (31 December 2013 est.)
country comparison to the world: 15
$527.8 billion (31 December 2012 est.)

Exchange rates: Swedish kronor (SEK) per US dollar—
6.58 (2013 est.)
6.77 (2012 est.)
7.2075 (2010 est.)
7.6529 (2009)
6.4074 (2008)

ENERGY

Electricity—production: 148.7 billion kWh (2011 est.)
country comparison to the world: 26

Electricity—consumption: 136 billion kWh (2010 est.)
country comparison to the world: 26

Electricity—exports: 31.28 billion kWh (2012 est.)
country comparison to the world: 6

Electricity—imports: 11.68 billion kWh (2012 est.)
country comparison to the world: 18

Electricity—installed generating capacity: 36.51 million kW (2010 est.)
country comparison to the world: 24

Electricity—from fossil fuels: 13% of total installed capacity (2010 est.)
country comparison to the world: 194

Electricity—from nuclear fuels: 24.6% of total installed capacity (2010 est.)
country comparison to the world: 4

Electricity—from hydroelectric plants: 45.5% of total installed capacity (2010 est.)
country comparison to the world: 49

Electricity—from other renewable sources: 16.6% of total installed capacity (2010 est.)
country comparison to the world: 11

Crude oil—production: 11,270 bbl/day (2012 est.)
country comparison to the world: 87

Crude oil—exports: 0 bbl/day (2010 est.)
country comparison to the world: 186

Crude oil—imports: 398,100 bbl/day (2010 est.)
country comparison to the world: 22

Crude oil—proved reserves: 0 bbl (1 January 2013 es)
country comparison to the world: 191

Refined petroleum products—production: 419,400 bbl/day (2010 est.)
country comparison to the world: 35

Refined petroleum products—consumption: 316,000 bbl/day (2011 est.)
country comparison to the world: 41

Refined petroleum products—exports: 261,700 bbl/day (2010 est.)
country comparison to the world: 24

Refined petroleum products—imports: 187,300 bbl/day (2010 est.)
country comparison to the world: 27

Natural gas—production: 0 cu m (2011 est.)
country comparison to the world: 194

Natural gas—consumption: 1.53 billion cu m (2010 est.)
country comparison to the world: 81

Natural gas—exports: 0 cu m (2011 est.)
country comparison to the world: 186

Natural gas—imports: 1.129 billion cu m (2012 est.)
country comparison to the world: 56

Natural gas—proved reserves: 0 cu m (1 January 2013 es)
country comparison to the world: 195

Carbon dioxide emissions from consumption of energy: 53.15 million Mt (2011 est.)
country comparison to the world: 59

COMMUNICATIONS

Telephones—main lines in use: 4.321 million (2012)
country comparison to the world: 41

Telephones—mobile cellular: 11.643 million (2012)
country comparison to the world: 71

Telephone system: *general assessment:* highly developed telecommunications infrastructure; ranked among leading countries for fixed-line, mobile-cellular, Internet and broadband penetration
domestic: coaxial and multiconductor cables carry most of the voice traffic; parallel microwave radio relay systems carry some additional telephone channels
international: country code—46; submarine cables provide links to other Nordic countries and Europe; satellite earth stations—1 Intelsat (Atlantic Ocean), 1 Eutelsat, and 1 Inmarsat (Atlantic and Indian Ocean regions); note—Sweden shares the Inmarsat earth station with the other Nordic countries (Denmark, Finland, Iceland, and Norway) (2011)

Broadcast media: publicly owned TV broadcaster operates 2 terrestrial networks plus regional stations; multiple privately owned TV broadcasters operating nationally, regionally, and locally; about 50 local TV stations; widespread access to pan-Nordic and international broadcasters through multi-channel cable and satellite TV; publicly owned radio broadcaster operates 3 national stations and a network of 25 regional channels; roughly 100 privately owned local radio stations with some consolidating into near national networks; an estimated 900 community and neighborhood radio stations broadcast intermittently (2008)

Internet country code: .se

Internet hosts: 5.978 million (2010)
country comparison to the world: 19

Internet users: 8.398 million (2009)
country comparison to the world: 33

TRANSPORTATION

Airports: 231 (2013)
country comparison to the world: 2 5

Airports—with paved runways: *total:* 149
over 3,047 m: 3
2,438 to 3,047 m: 12
1,524 to 2,437 m: 75
914 to 1,523 m: 22
under 914 m: 37 (2013)

Airports—with unpaved runways: *total:* 8 2
914 to 1,523 m: 5
under 914 m: 77 (2013)

Heliports: 2 (2013)

Pipelines: gas 1,626 km (2013)

Railways: *total:* 11,633 km
country comparison to the world: 21
standard gauge: 11,568 km 1.435-m gauge (7,567 km electrified)
narrow gauge: 65 km 1.000-m gauge (65 km electrified) (2008)

Roadways: *total:* 579,564 km (includes 1,913 km of expressways)
country comparison to the world: 12
paved: 135,444 km
unpaved: 444,412 km
note: includes 104,705 km of state roads, 433,034 km of private roads, and 41,825 km of municipal roads (2010)

Waterways: 2,052 km (2010)
country comparison to the world: 41

Merchant marine: *total:* 135
country comparison to the world: 42
by type: bulk carrier 4, cargo 16, carrier 1, chemical tanker 15, passenger 5, passenger/cargo 36, petroleum tanker 11, roll on/roll off 30, vehicle carrier 17
foreign-owned: 35 (Denmark 4, Estonia 3, Finland 16, Germany 3, Ireland 1, Italy 5, Norway 3)
registered in other countries: 189 (Bahamas 11, Barbados 4, Bermuda 14, Canada 2, Cook Islands 3, Cyprus 5, Denmark 15, Faroe Islands 11, Finland 1, France 4, Gibraltar 11, Italy 1, Liberia 12, Malta 1, Marshall Islands 1, Netherlands 12, Norway 27, Panama 2, Portugal 3, Saint Vincent and the Grenadines 10, Singapore 11, UK 28) (2010)

Ports and terminals: *major seaport(s):* Brofjorden, Goteborg, Helsingborg, Karlshamn, Lulea, Malmo, Stockholm, Trelleborg, Visby

MILITARY

Military branches: Swedish Armed Forces (Forsvarsmakten): Army (Armen), Royal Swedish Navy (Marinen), Swedish Air Force (Svenska Flygvapnet) (2010)

Military service age and obligation: 18-47 years of age for male and female voluntary military service; Swedish citizenship required; service
obligation: 7.5 months (Army), 7-15 months (Navy), 8-12 months (Air Force); the Swedish Parliament has abolished compulsory military service, with exclusively voluntary recruitment as of July 2010; conscription remains an option in emergencies; after completing initial service, soldiers have a reserve commitment until age 47 (2013)

Manpower available for military service:
males age 16-49: 2,065,691
females age 16-49: 1,996,764 (2010 est.)

Manpower fit for military service:
males age 16-49: 1,709,055
females age 16-49: 1,650,432 (2010 est.)

Manpower reaching militarily significant age annually: *male:* 54,960
female: 52,275 (2010 est.)

Military expenditures: 1.18% of GDP (2012)
country comparison to the world: 87
1.17% of GDP (2011)
1.18% of GDP (2010)

TRANSNATIONAL ISSUES

Disputes—international: none

Refugees and internally displaced persons:
refugees (country of origin): 24,741 (Iraq); 19,416 (Somalia); 8,454 (Afghanistan); 6,414 (Eritrea); 6,051 (Syria) (2012)
stateless persons: 9,596 (2012); note—the majority of stateless people come from the Middle East and Somalia

SWITZERLAND

INTRODUCTION

Background: The Swiss Confederation was founded in 1291 as a defensive alliance among three cantons. In succeeding years, other localities joined the original three. The Swiss Confederation secured its independence from the Holy Roman Empire in 1499. A constitution of 1848, subsequently modified in 1874, replaced the confederation with a centralized federal government. Switzerland's sovereignty and neutrality have long been honored by the major European powers, and the country was not involved in either of the two world wars. The political and economic integration of Europe over the past half century, as well as Switzerland's role in many UN and international organizations, has strengthened Switzerland's ties with its neighbors. However, the country did not officially become a UN member until 2002. Switzerland remains active in many UN and international organizations but retains a strong commitment to neutrality.

GEOGRAPHY

Location: Central Europe, east of France, north of Italy

Geographic coordinates: 47 00 N, 8 00 E

Map references: Europe

Area: *total:* 41,277 sq km
country comparison to the world: 136
land: 39,997 sq km
water: 1,280 sq km

Area—comparative: slightly less than twice the size of New Jersey

Land boundaries: *total:* 1,852 km
border countries: Austria 164 km, France 573 km, Italy 740 km, Liechtenstein 41 km, Germany 334 km

Coastline: 0 km (landlocked)

Maritime claims: none (landlocked)

Climate: temperate, but varies with altitude; cold, cloudy, rainy/snowy winters; cool to warm, cloudy, humid summers with occasional showers

Terrain: mostly mountains (Alps in south, Jura in northwest) with a central plateau of rolling hills, plains, and large lakes

Elevation extremes: *lowest point:* Lake Maggiore 195 m
highest point: Dufourspitze 4,634 m

Natural resources: hydropower potential, timber, salt

Land use: *arable land:* 9.8%
permanent crops: 0.57%
other: 89.63% (2011)

Irrigated land: 550 sq km (2007)

Total renewable water resources: 53.5 cu km (2011)

Freshwater withdrawal (domestic/industrial/agricultural): *total:* 2.61 cu km/yr (39%/58%/3%)
per capita: 360.3 cu m/yr (2010)

Natural hazards: avalanches, landslides; flash floods

Environment—current issues: air pollution from vehicle emissions and open-air burning; acid rain; water pollution from increased use of agricultural fertilizers; loss of biodiversity

Environment—international agreements:
party to: Air Pollution, Air Pollution-Nitrogen Oxides, Air Pollution-Persistent Organic Pollutants, Air Pollution-Sulfur 85, Air Pollution-Sulfur 94, Air Pollution-Volatile Organic Compounds, Antarctic Treaty, Biodiversity, Climate Change, Climate Change-Kyoto Protocol, Desertification, Endangered Species, Environmental Modification, Hazardous Wastes, Marine Dumping, Marine Life Conservation, Ozone Layer Protection, Ship Pollution, Tropical Timber 83, Tropical Timber 94, Wetlands, Whaling
signed, but not ratified: Law of the Sea

Geography—note: landlocked; crossroads of northern and southern Europe; along with southeastern France, northern Italy, and southwestern Austria, has the highest elevations in the Alps

PEOPLE AND SOCIETY

Nationality: *noun:* Swiss (singular and plural)
adjective: Swiss

Ethnic groups: German 65%, French 18%, Italian 10%, Romansch 1%, other 6%

Languages: German (official) 64.9%, French (official) 22.6%, Italian (official) 8.3%, Serbo-Croatian 2.5%, Albanian 2.6%, Portuguese 3.4%, Spanish 2.2%, English 4.6%, Romansch (official) 0.5%, other 5.1%
note: German, French, Italian, and Romansch are all national and official languages; totals more than 100% because some respondents indicated more than one main principal language (2012 est.)

Religions: Roman Catholic 38.2%, Protestant 26.9%, Muslim 4.9%, other Christian 5.7%, other 1.6%, none 21.4%, unspecified 1.3% (2012 est.)

Population: 8,061,516 (July 2014 est.)
country comparison to the world: 96

Age structure:
0-14 years: 15.1% (male 627,952/female 591,528)
15-24 years: 11.4% (male 469,536/female 451,547)
25-54 years: 43.9% (male 1,775,571/female 1,760,456)
55-64 years: 17.5% (male 484,278/female 486,220)
65 years and over: 17.3% (male 616,009/female 798,419) (2014 est.)

Dependency ratios:
total dependency ratio: 48.1 %
youth dependency ratio: 21.9 %
elderly dependency ratio: 26.2 %
potential support ratio: 3.8 (2013)

Median age: *total:* 42 years
male: 41 years
female: 42.9 years (2014 est.)

Population growth rate: 0.78% (2014 est.)
country comparison to the world: 141

Birth rate: 10.48 births/1,000 population (2014 est.)
country comparison to the world: 185

Death rate: 8.1 deaths/1,000 population (2014 est.)
country comparison to the world: 96

Net migration rate: 5.43 migrant(s)/1,000 population (2014 est.)
country comparison to the world: 26

Urbanization: *urban population:* 74% of total population (2010)
rate of urbanization: 0.5% annual rate of change (2010-15 est.)

Major urban areas—population: Zurich 1.143 million; BERN (capital) 346,000 (2009)

Sex ratio: *at birth:* 1.06 male(s)/female
0-14 years: 1.06 male(s)/female
15-24 years: 1.04 male(s)/female
25-54 years: 1.01 male(s)/female
55-64 years: 0.97 male(s)/female
65 years and over: 0.76 male(s)/female
total population: 0.97 male(s)/female (2014 est.)

Mother's mean age at first birth: 30.2 (2010 est.)

Maternal mortality rate: 8 deaths/100,000 live births (2010)
country comparison to the world: 159

Infant mortality rate: *total:* 3.73 deaths/1,000 live births
country comparison to the world: 203
male: 4.12 deaths/1,000 live births
female: 3.32 deaths/1,000 live births (2014 est.)

Life expectancy at birth: *total population:* 82.39 years
country comparison to the world: 8
male: 80.1 years
female: 84.81 years (2014 est.)

Total fertility rate: 1.54 children born/woman (2014 est.)
country comparison to the world: 188

Contraceptive prevalence rate: 82%
note: percent of women aged 20-49 (1994/95)

Health expenditures: 10.9% of GDP (2011)
country comparison to the world: 15

Physicians density: 4.08 physicians/1,000 population (2010)

Hospital bed density: 5 beds/1,000 population (2010)

Drinking water source:
improved:
urban: 100% of population
rural: 100% of population
total: 100% of population
unimproved:
urban: 0% of population
rural: 0% of population
total: 0% of population (2011 est.)

Sanitation facility access:
improved:
urban: 100% of population
rural: 100% of population
total: 100% of population

unimproved:
urban: 0% of population
rural: 0% of population
total: 0% of population (2011 est.)

HIV/AIDS—adult prevalence rate: 0.4% (2009 est.)
country comparison to the world: 80

HIV/AIDS—people living with HIV/AIDS: 18,000 (2009 est.)
country comparison to the world: 85

HIV/AIDS—deaths: fewer than 100 (2009 est.)
country comparison to the world: 148

Obesity—adult prevalence rate: 17.5% (2008)
country comparison to the world: 111

Education expenditures: 5.2% of GDP (2010)
country comparison to the world: 66

Literacy: *definition:* age 15 and over can read and write
total population: 99%
male: 99%
female: 99% (2003 est.)

School life expectancy (primary to tertiary education): *total:* 16 years
male: 16 years
female: 16 years (2011)

Unemployment, youth ages 15-24: *total:* 8.4%
country comparison to the world: 119
male: 8.8%
female: 8.1% (2012)

GOVERNMENT

Country name: *conventional long form:* Swiss Confederation
conventional short form: Switzerland
local long form: Schweizerische Eidgenossenschaft (German); Confederation Suisse (French); Confederazione Svizzera (Italian); Confederaziun Svizra (Romansh)
local short form: Schweiz (German); Suisse (French); Svizzera (Italian); Svizra (Romansh)

Government type: formally a confederation but similar in structure to a federal republic

Capital: *name:* Bern
geographic coordinates: 46 55 N, 7 28 E
time difference: UTC+1 (6 hours ahead of Washington, DC during Standard Time)
daylight saving time: +1hr, begins last Sunday in March; ends last Sunday in October

Administrative divisions: 26 cantons (cantons, singular—canton in French; cantoni, singular—cantone in Italian; Kantone, singular—Kanton in German); Aargau, Appenzell Ausserrhoden, Appenzell Innerrhoden, Basel-Landschaft, Basel-Stadt, Bern/Berne, Fribourg/Freiburg, Geneve, Glarus, Graubuenden/Grischun/Grigioni, Jura, Luzern, Neuchatel, Nidwalden, Obwalden, Sankt Gallen, Schaffhausen, Schwyz, Solothurn, Thurgau, Ticino, Uri, Valais/Wallis, Vaud, Zug, Zuerich
note: 6 of the cantons—Appenzell Ausserrhoden, Appenzell Innerrhoden, Basel-Landschaft, Basel-Stadt, Nidwalden, Obwalden—are referred to as half cantons because they elect only one member to the Council of States and, in popular referendums where a majority of popular votes and a majority of cantonal votes are required, these six cantons only have a half vote

Independence: 1 August 1291 (founding of the Swiss Confederation)

National holiday: Founding of the Swiss Confederation, 1 August (1291)

Constitution: previous 1848, 1874 (extensive revision of 1848 version); latest adopted by referendum 18 April 1999, effective 1 January 2000; amended several times, last in 2012 (2012)

Legal system: civil law system; judicial review of legislative acts, except for federal decrees of a general obligatory character

International law organization participation: accepts compulsory ICJ jurisdiction with reservations; accepts ICCt jurisdiction

Suffrage: 18 years of age; universal

Executive branch: *chief of state:* President of the Swiss Confederation Didier BURKHALTER (since 1 January 2014); Vice President Simonetta SOMMARUGA (since 1 January 2014; note—the Federal Council, which is comprised of seven federal councillors, constitutes the federal government of Switzerland; council members rotate in one-year terms as federal president (chief of state and head of government)
head of government: President of the Swiss Confederation Didier BURKHALTER (since 1 January 2014); Vice President Simonetta SOMMARUGA (since 1 January 2014)
cabinet: Federal Council or Bundesrat (in German), Conseil Federal (in French), Consiglio Federale (in Italian) is elected by the Federal Assembly usually from among its members for a four-year term (For more information visit the World Leaders website)
elections: president and vice president elected by the Federal Assembly from among the members of the Federal Council for a one-year term (they may not serve consecutive terms); election last held on 5 December 2012 (next to be held in early December 2013)
election results: Didier BURKHALTER elected president; number of Federal Assembly votes—183 of 202; Simonetta SOMMARUGA elected vice president

Legislative branch: bicameral Federal Assembly or Bundesversammlung (in German), Assemblee Federale (in French), Assemblea Federale (in Italian) consists of the Council of States or Staenderat (in German), Conseil des Etats (in French), Consiglio degli Stati (in Italian) (46 seats; membership consists of 2 representatives from each canton and 1 from each half canton; members serve four-year terms) and the National Council or Nationalrat (in German), Conseil National (in French), Consiglio Nazionale (in Italian) (200 seats; members elected by popular vote on the basis of proportional representation serve four-year terms)
elections: Council of States—last held in most cantons on 23 October 2011 (each canton determines when the next election will be held); National Council—last held on 23 October 2011 (next to be held in October 2015)
election results: Council of States—percent of vote by party—NA; seats by party—CVP 13, FDP 11, SVP 5, SPS 11, other 6; National Council—percent of vote by party—SVP 26.6%, SPS 18.7%, FDP 15.1%, CVP 12.3%, Green Party 8.4%, GLP 5.4%, BDP 5.4%, other 8.1%; seats by party—SVP 54, SPS 46, FDP 30, CVP 28, Green Party 15, GLP 12, BDP 9, other small parties 6

Judicial branch: *highest court(s):* Federal Supreme Court (consists of 38 judges and 31 substitutes and organized into 5 sections)
judge selection and term of office: judges elected by the Federal Assembly for 6-year terms; note—judges are affiliated with political parties and are elected according to linguistic and regional criteria in approximate proportion to the level of party representation in the Federal Assembly
subordinate courts: Federal Criminal Court (began in 2004); Federal Administrative Court (began in 2007); note—each of Switzerland's 26 cantons has its own courts

Political parties and leaders: Christian Democratic People's Party (Christlichdemokratische Volkspartei der Schweiz or CVP, Parti Democrate-Chretien Suisse or PDC, Partito Popolare Democratico Svizzero or PPD, Partida Cristiandemocratica dalla Svizra or PCD) [Christophe DARBELLAY]; Conservative Democratic Party (Buergerlich-Demokratische Partei Schweiz or BDP, Parti Bourgeois Democratique Suisse or PBD, Partito Borghese Democratico Svizzero or PBD, Partido burgais democratica Svizera or PBD) [Martin LANDOLT]; Free Democratic Party or FDP.The Liberals (FDP.Die Liberalen, PLR.Les Liberaux-Radicaux, PLR.I Liberali, Ils Liberals) [Philipp MUELLER]; Green Liberal Party (Grunliberale or GLP, Parti vert liberale or PVL, Partito Verde-Liberale or PVL, Partida Verde Liberale or PVL) [Martin BAEUMLE]; Green Party (Gruene Partei der Schweiz or Gruene, Parti Ecologiste Suisse or Les Verts, Partito Ecologista Svizzero or I Verdi, Partida Ecologica Svizra or La Verda) [Adele THORENS]; Social Democratic Party (Sozialdemokratische Partei der Schweiz or SPS, Parti Socialiste Suisse or PSS, Partito Socialista; Svizzero or PSS, Partida Socialdemocratica de la Svizra or PSS) [Christian LEVRAT] Swiss People's Party (Schweizerische Volkspartei or SVP, Union Democratique du Centre or UDC, Unione Democratica di Centro or UDC, Uniun Democratica dal Center or UDC) [Toni BRUNNER]; and other minor parties

Political pressure groups and leaders: NA

International organization participation: ADB (nonregional member), AfDB (nonregional member), Australia Group, BIS, CD, CE, CERN, EAPC, EBRD, EFTA, EITI (implementing country), ESA, FAO, FATF, G-10, IADB, IAEA, IBRD, ICAO, ICC (national committees), ICRM, IDA, IEA, IFAD, IFC, IFRCS, IGAD (partners), ILO, IMF, IMO, IMSO, Interpol, IOC, IOM, IPU, ISO, ITSO, ITU, ITUC (NGOs), LAIA (observer), MIGA, MINUSMA, MONUSCO, NEA, NSG, OAS (observer), OECD, OIF, OPCW, OSCE, Paris Club, PCA, PFP, Schengen Convention, UN, UNCTAD, UNESCO, UNHCR, UNIDO, UNITAR, UNMISS, UNRWA, UNTSO, UNWTO, UPU, WCO, WHO, WIPO, WMO, WTO, ZC

Diplomatic representation in the US:
chief of mission: Ambassador Manuel SAGER (since 1 November 2010)
chancery: 2900 Cathedral Avenue NW, Washington, DC 20008
telephone: [1] (202) 745-7900
FAX: [1] (202) 387-2564
consulate(s) general: Atlanta, Chicago, Los Angeles, New York, San Francisco
consulate(s): Boston

Diplomatic representation from the US:
chief of mission: Ambassador (vacant); Charge d'Affaires Jeffrey R. CELLARS (since 22 July 2013); note—also accredited to Liechtenstein
embassy: Sulgeneckstrasse 19, CH-3007 Bern
mailing address: use Embassy street address
telephone: [41] (031) 357-70-11
FAX: [41] (031) 357-73-44

Flag description: red square with a bold, equilateral white cross in the center that does not extend to the edges of the flag; various medieval legends purport to describe the origin of the flag; a white cross used as identification for troops of the Swiss Confederation is first attested at the Battle of Laupen (1339)

National symbol(s): Swiss cross (white cross on red field; arms equal length)

National anthem: *name:* "Schweizerpsalm" [German] "Cantique Suisse" [French] "Salmo svizzero," [Italian] "Psalm svizzer" [Romansch] (Swiss Psalm)
lyrics/music: Leonhard WIDMER [German], Charles CHATELANAT [French], Camillo VALSANGIACOMO [Italian], and Flurin CAMATHIAS [Romansch]/Alberik ZWYSSIG
note: unofficially adopted 1961, official adoption 1981; the anthem has been popular in a number of Swiss cantons since its composition (in German) in 1841; translated into the other three official languages of the country (French, Italian, and Romansch), it is official in each of those languages

ECONOMY

Economy—overview: Switzerland is a peaceful, prosperous, and modern market economy with low unemployment, a highly skilled labor force, and a per capita GDP among the highest in the world. Switzerland's economy benefits from a highly developed service sector, led by financial services, and a manufacturing industry that specializes in high-technology, knowledge-based production. Its economic and political stability, transparent legal system, exceptional infrastructure, efficient capital markets, and low corporate tax rates also make Switzerland one of the world's most competitive economies. The Swiss have brought their economic practices largely into conformity with the EU's to enhance their international competitiveness, but some trade protectionism remains, particularly for its small agricultural sector. The fate of the Swiss economy is tightly linked to that of its neighbors in the euro zone, which purchases half of all Swiss exports. The global financial crisis of 2008 and resulting economic downturn in 2009 stalled export demand and put Switzerland in a recession. The Swiss National Bank (SNB) during this period effectively implemented a zero-interest rate policy to boost the economy as well as prevent appreciation of the franc, and Switzerland's economy began to recover in 2010. The sovereign debt crises currently unfolding in neighboring euro-zone countries pose a significant risk to Switzerland's financial stability and are driving up demand for the Swiss franc by investors seeking a safe-haven currency. The independent SNB has upheld its zero-interest rate policy and conducted major market interventions to prevent further appreciation of the Swiss franc, but parliamentarians have urged it to do more to weaken the currency. The franc's strength has made Swiss exports less competitive and weakened the country's growth outlook; GDP growth fell below 2% per year during 2011-13. Switzerland has also come under increasing pressure from individual neighboring countries, the EU, the US, and international institutions to reform its banking secrecy laws. Consequently, the government agreed to conform to OECD regulations on administrative assistance in tax matters, including tax evasion. The government has renegotiated its double taxation agreements with numerous countries, including the US, to incorporate the OECD standard, and is considering the possibility of imposing taxes on bank deposits held by foreigners. These steps will have a lasting impact on Switzerland's long history of bank secrecy.

GDP (purchasing power parity): $370.3 billion (2013 est.)
country comparison to the world: 37
$363.9 billion (2012 est.)
$360.1 billion (2011 est.)
note: data are in 2013 US dollars

GDP (official exchange rate): $646.2 billion (2013 est.)

GDP—real growth rate: 1.7% (2013 est.)
country comparison to the world: 149
1% (2012 est.)
1.8% (2011 est.)

GDP—per capita (PPP): $46,000 (2013 est.)
country comparison to the world: 15
$45,500 (2012 est.)
$45,300 (2011 est.)
note: data are in 2013 US dollars

Gross national saving: 31.5% of GDP (2013 est.)
country comparison to the world: 23
31.5% of GDP (2012 est.)
27.3% of GDP (2011 est.)

GDP—composition, by end use:
household consumption: 57.4%
government consumption: 11.5%
investment in fixed capital: 20.3%
investment in inventories: 0.7%
exports of goods and services: 50.4%
imports of goods and services: -40.2% (2013 est.)

GDP—composition, by sector of origin:
agriculture: 0.7%
industry: 26.8%
services: 72.5% (2013 est.)

Agriculture—products: grains, fruits, vegetables; meat, eggs

Industries: machinery, chemicals, watches, textiles, precision instruments, tourism, banking, and insurance

Industrial production growth rate: 2.2% (2013 est.)
country comparison to the world: 122

Labor force: 4.976 million (2013 est.)
country comparison to the world: 77

Labor force—by occupation: *agriculture:* 3.4%
industry: 23.4%
services: 73.2% (2010)

Unemployment rate: 2.9% (2013 est.)
country comparison to the world: 22
2.9% (2012 est.)

Population below poverty line: 7.9% (2010)

Household income or consumption by percentage share: *lowest 10%:* 7.5%
highest 10%: 19% (2007)

Distribution of family income—Gini index: 29.6 (2010)
country comparison to the world: 121
33.1 (1992)

Budget: *revenues:* $210 billion
expenditures: $208.5 billion
note: includes federal, cantonal, and municipal accounts (2013 est.)

Taxes and other revenues: 32.5% of GDP (2013 est.)
country comparison to the world: 78

Budget surplus (+) or deficit (-):
0.2% of GDP (2013 est.)
country comparison to the world: 40

Public debt: 34.3% of GDP (2013 est.)
country comparison to the world: 108
54.5% of GDP (2010)
note: general government gross debt; gross debt consists of all liabilities that require payment or payments of interest and/or principal by the debtor to the creditor at a date or dates in the future; includes debt liabilities in the form of SDRs, currency and deposits, debt securities, loans, insurance, pensions and standardized guarantee schemes, and other accounts payable; all liabilities in the GFSM 2001 system are debt, except for equity and investment fund shares and financial derivatives and employee stock options

Fiscal year: calendar year

Inflation rate (consumer prices): -0.4% (2013 est.)
country comparison to the world: 5
-0.7% (2012 est.)

Central bank discount rate: 0.5% (31 December 2010 est.)
country comparison to the world: 133
0.75% (31 December 2009 est.)

Commercial bank prime lending rate: 2.7% (31 December 2013 est.)
country comparison to the world: 177
2.69% (31 December 2012 est.)

Stock of narrow money: $525.9 billion (31 December 2013 est.)
country comparison to the world: 11
$534.4 billion (31 December 2012 est.)

Stock of broad money: $1.36 trillion (31 December 2013 est.)
country comparison to the world: 14
$1.215 trillion (31 December 2012 est.)

Stock of domestic credit: $1.395 trillion (31 December 2013 est.)
country comparison to the world: 14
$1.247 trillion (31 December 2012 est.)

Market value of publicly traded shares: $1.079 trillion (31 December 2012 est.)
country comparison to the world: 14
$932.2 billion (31 December 2011)
$1.229 trillion (31 December 2010 est.)

Current account balance: $65.6 billion (2013 est.)
country comparison to the world: 8
$63.82 billion (2012 est.)

Exports: $312.3 billion (2013 est.)
country comparison to the world: 20
$332.1 billion (2012 est.)
note: trade data exclude trade with Switzerland

Exports—commodities: machinery, chemicals, metals, watches, agricultural products

Exports—partners: Germany 18.5%, United States 11.61%, Italy 7.61%, France 6.96%, United Kingdom 5.67% (2013 est.)

Imports: $275.7 billion (2013 est.)
country comparison to the world: 19
$296.2 billion (2012 est.)

Imports—commodities: machinery, chemicals, vehicles, metals; agricultural products, textiles

Imports—partners: Germany 28.19%, Italy 10.46%, France 8.49%, United States 6.08%, China 5.75%, Austria 4.4% (2013 est.)

Reserves of foreign exchange and gold: $531.1 billion (31 December 2012 est.)

country comparison to the world: 5
$331.9 billion (31 December 2011 est.)

Debt—external: $1.544 trillion (31 December 2012 est.)
country comparison to the world: 12
$1.424 trillion (31 December 2011)

Stock of direct foreign investment—at home: $968.9 billion (31 December 2013 est.)
country comparison to the world: 9
$955.1 billion (31 December 2012 est.)

Stock of direct foreign investment—abroad: $1.432 trillion (31 December 2013 est.)
country comparison to the world: 5
$1.381 trillion (31 December 2012 est.)

Exchange rates: Swiss francs (CHF) per US dollar—
0.9542 (2013 est.)
0.9374 (2012 est.)
1.0429 (2010 est.)
1.0881 (2009)
1.0774 (2008)

ENERGY

Electricity—production: 60.18 billion kWh (2011 est.)
country comparison to the world: 45

Electricity—consumption: 60.42 billion kWh (2011 est.)
country comparison to the world: 41

Electricity—exports: 34.57 billion kWh (2012 est.)
country comparison to the world: 5

Electricity—imports: 32.25 billion kWh (2012 est.)
country comparison to the world: 5

Electricity—installed generating capacity: *18.07 million kW (2010 est.)*
country comparison to the world: 41

Electricity—from fossil fuels: 3.1% of total installed capacity (2010 est.)
country comparison to the world: 200

Electricity—from nuclear fuels: 18% of total installed capacity (2010 est.)
country comparison to the world: 11

Electricity—from hydroelectric plants: 65.9% of total installed capacity (2010 est.)
country comparison to the world: 28

Electricity—from other renewable sources: 3% of total installed capacity (2010 est.)
country comparison to the world: 60

Crude oil—production: 3,613 bbl/day (2012 est.)
country comparison to the world: 100

Crude oil—exports: 0 bbl/day (2011 est.)
country comparison to the world: 187

Crude oil—imports: 258,200 bbl/day (2011 est.)
country comparison to the world: 29

Crude oil—proved reserves: 0 bbl (1 January 2013 es)
country comparison to the world: 192

Refined petroleum products—production: 96,710 bbl/day (2010 est.)
country comparison to the world: 75

Refined petroleum products—consumption: 258,200 bbl/day (2011 est.)
country comparison to the world: 50

Refined petroleum products—exports: 7,585 bbl/day (2010 est.)
country comparison to the world: 87

Refined petroleum products—imports: 157,600 bbl/day (2010 est.)
country comparison to the world: 36

Natural gas—production: 0 cu m (2011 est.)
country comparison to the world: 195

Natural gas—consumption: 3.2 billion cu m (2012 est.)
country comparison to the world: 71

Natural gas—exports: 8.494 billion cu m (2012 est.)
country comparison to the world: 31

Natural gas—imports: 11.77 billion cu m (2012 est.)
country comparison to the world: 26

Natural gas—proved reserves: 0 cu m (1 January 2011 es)
country comparison to the world: 196

Carbon dioxide emissions from consumption of energy: 43.36 million Mt (2011 est.)
country comparison to the world: 69

COMMUNICATIONS

Telephones—main lines in use: 4.382 million (2012)
country comparison to the world: 38

Telephones—mobile cellular: 10.46 million (2012)
country comparison to the world: 77

Telephone system: *general assessment:* highly developed telecommunications infrastructure with excellent domestic and international services
domestic: ranked among leading countries for fixed-line teledensity and infrastructure; mobile-cellular subscribership roughly 125 per 100 persons; extensive cable and microwave radio relay networks
international: country code—41; satellite earth stations—2 Intelsat (Atlantic Ocean and Indian Ocean) (2011)

Broadcast media: the publicly owned radio and TV broadcaster, Swiss Broadcasting Corporation (SRG/SSR), operates 7 national TV networks, 3 broadcasting in German, 2 in Italian, and 2 in French; private commercial TV stations broadcast regionally and locally; TV broadcasts from stations in Germany, Italy, and France are widely available via multi-channel cable and satellite TV services; SRG/SSR operates 18 radio stations that, along with private broadcasters, provide national to local coverage (2009)

Internet country code: .ch

Internet hosts: 5.301 million (2012)
country comparison to the world: 20

Internet users: 6.152 million (2009)
country comparison to the world: 42

TRANSPORTATION

Airports: 63 (2013)
country comparison to the world: 7 8

Airports—with paved runways: *total:* 4 0
over 3,047 m: 3
2,438 to 3,047 m: 2
1,524 to 2,437 m: 12
914 to 1,523 m: 6
under 914 m: 17 (2013)

Airports—with unpaved runways: *total:* 2 3
under 914 m: 23 (2013)

Heliports: 2 (2013)

Pipelines: gas 1,800 km; oil 94 km; refined products 7 km (2013)

Railways: *total:* 4,876 km
country comparison to the world: 37
standard gauge: 3,846 km 1.435-m gauge (3,591 km electrified)
narrow gauge: 1,020 km 1.000-m gauge (1,013 km electrified); 10 km 0.800-m gauge (10 km electrified) (2008)

Roadways: *total:* 71,464 km
country comparison to the world: 65
paved: 71,464 km (includes 1,415 of expressways) (2011)

Waterways: 1,292 km (there are 1,227 km of waterways on lakes and rivers for public transport and another 65 km on the Rhine River between Basel-Rheinfelden and Schaffhausen-Bodensee used for the transport of commercial goods) (2010)
country comparison to the world: 58

Merchant marine: *total:* 3 8
country comparison to the world: 78
by type: bulk carrier 19, cargo 9, chemical tanker 5, container 4, petroleum tanker 1
registered in other countries: 127 (Antigua and Barbuda 7, Bahamas 1, Belize 1, Cayman Islands 1, France 5, Germany 2, Hong Kong 5, Italy 13, Liberia 25, Luxembourg 1, Malta 20, Marshall Islands 12, NZ 2, Panama 15, Portugal 3, Russia 3, Saint Vincent and the Grenadines 7, Singapore 3, Spain 1) (2010)

Ports and terminals: *river port(s):* Basel (Rhine)

MILITARY

Military branches: Swiss Armed Forces: Land Forces, Swiss Air Force (Schweizer Luftwaffe) (2013)

Military service age and obligation: 19-26 years of age for male compulsory military service; 18 years of age for voluntary male and female military service; every Swiss male has to serve at least 260 days in the armed forces; conscripts receive 18 weeks of mandatory training, followed by seven 3-week intermittent recalls for training during the next 10 years (2012)

Manpower available for military service:
males age 16-49: 1,828,043
females age 16-49: 1,786,552 (2010 est.)

Manpower fit for military service:
males age 16-49: 1,493,509
females age 16-49: 1,459,450 (2010 est.)

Manpower reaching militarily significant age annually: *male:* 46,562
female: 42,585 (2010 est.)

Military expenditures: 0.76% of GDP (2012)
country comparison to the world: 117
0.75% of GDP (2011)
0.76% of GDP (2010)

TRANSNATIONAL ISSUES

Disputes—international: none

Refugees and internally displaced persons:
refugees (country of origin): 10,981 (Eritrea) (2012)
stateless persons: 69 (2012)

Illicit drugs: a major international financial center vulnerable to the layering and integration stages of money laundering; despite significant legislation and reporting requirements, secrecy rules persist and nonresidents are permitted to conduct business through offshore entities and various intermediaries; transit country for and consumer of South American cocaine, Southwest Asian heroin, and Western European synthetics; domestic cannabis cultivation and limited ecstasy production

SYRIA

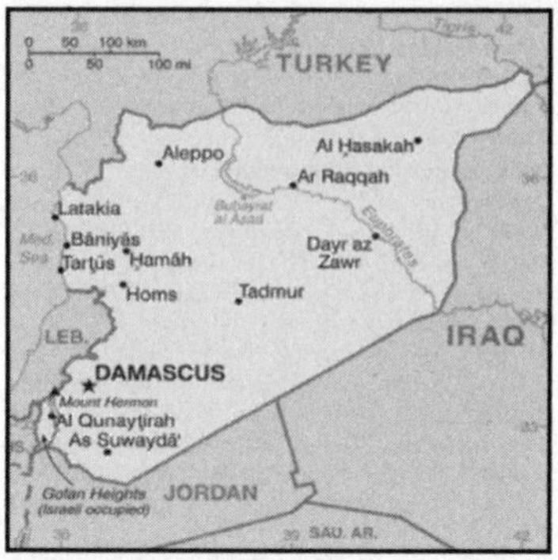

INTRODUCTION

Background: Following World War I, France acquired a mandate over the northern portion of the former Ottoman Empire province of Syria. The French administered the area as Syria until granting it independence in 1946. The new country lacked political stability, however, and experienced a series of military coups during its first decades. Syria united with Egypt in February 1958 to form the United Arab Republic. In September 1961, the two entities separated, and the Syrian Arab Republic was reestablished. In November 1970, Hafiz al-ASAD, a member of the socialist Ba'th Party and the minority Alawi sect, seized power in a bloodless coup and brought political stability to the country. In the 1967 Arab-Israeli War, Syria lost the Golan Heights to Israel. During the 1990s, Syria and Israel held occasional peace talks over its return. Following the death of President al-ASAD, his son, Bashar al-ASAD, was approved as president by popular referendum in July 2000. Syrian troops—stationed in Lebanon since 1976 in an ostensible peacekeeping role - were withdrawn in April 2005. During the July-August 2006 conflict between Israel and Hizballah, Syria placed its military forces on alert but did not intervene directly on behalf of its ally Hizballah. In May 2007 Bashar al-ASAD's second term as president was approved by popular referendum. Influenced by major uprisings that began elsewhere in the region, antigovernment protests broke out in the southern province of Dar'a in March 2011 with protesters calling for the repeal of the restrictive Emergency Law allowing arrests without charge, the legalization of political parties, and the removal of corrupt local officials. Since then demonstrations and unrest have spread to nearly every city in Syria, but the size and intensity of protests have fluctuated over time. The government responded to unrest with a mix of concessions—including the repeal of the Emergency Law and approving new laws permitting new political parties and liberalizing local and national elections—and force. However, the government's response has failed to meet opposition demands for ASAD to step down, and the government's ongoing security operations to quell unrest and widespread armed opposition activity have led to extended violent clashes between government forces and oppositionists. International pressure on the ASAD regime has intensified since late 2011, as the Arab League, EU, Turkey, and the United States have expanded economic sanctions against the regime. Lakhdar BRAHIMI, current Joint Special Representative of the United Nations and the League of Arab States on the Syrian crisis, in October 2012 began meeting with regional heads of state to assist in brokering a cease-fire. In December 2012, the National Coalition of Syrian Revolution and Opposition Forces was recognized by more than 130 countries as the sole legitimate representative of the Syrian people. Unrest persisted in 2013, and the death toll among Syrian Government forces, opposition forces, and civilians has topped 100,000. In January 2014, the Syrian Opposition Coalition and Syrian regime began peace talks at the UN sponsored Geneva II conference.

GEOGRAPHY

Location: Middle East, bordering the Mediterranean Sea, between Lebanon and Turkey

Geographic coordinates: 35 00 N, 38 00 E

Map references: Middle East

Area: *total:* 185,180 sq km
country comparison to the world: 89
land: 183,630 sq km
water: 1,550 sq km
note: includes 1,295 sq km of Israeli-occupied territory

Area—comparative: slightly more than 1.5 times the size of Pennsylvania

Land boundaries: *total:* 2,253 km
border countries: Iraq 605 km, Israel 76 km, Jordan 375 km, Lebanon 375 km, Turkey 822 km

Coastline: 193 km

Maritime claims: *territorial sea:* 12 nm
contiguous zone: 24 nm

Climate: mostly desert; hot, dry, sunny summers (June to August) and mild, rainy winters (December to February) along coast; cold weather with snow or sleet periodically in Damascus

Terrain: primarily semiarid and desert plateau; narrow coastal plain; mountains in west

Elevation extremes: *lowest point:* unnamed location near Lake Tiberias -200 m
highest point: Mount Hermon 2,814 m

Natural resources: petroleum, phosphates, chrome and manganese ores, asphalt, iron ore, rock salt, marble, gypsum, hydropower

Land use: *arable land:* 24.9%
permanent crops: 5.69%
other: 69.41% (2011)

Irrigated land: 13,410 sq km (2010)

Total renewable water resources: 16.8 cu km (2011)

Freshwater withdrawal (domestic/industrial/agricultural): *total:* 16.76 cu km/yr (9%/4%/88%)
per capita: 867.4 cu m/yr (2005)

Natural hazards: dust storms, sandstorms
volcanism: Syria's two historically active volcanoes, Es Safa and an unnamed volcano near the Turkish border have not erupted in centuries

Environment—current issues: deforestation; overgrazing; soil erosion; desertification; water pollution from raw sewage and petroleum refining wastes; inadequate potable water

Environment—international agreements: *party to:* Biodiversity, Climate Change, Climate Change-Kyoto Protocol, Desertification, Endangered Species, Hazardous Wastes, Ozone Layer Protection, Ship Pollution, Wetlands
signed, but not ratified: Environmental Modification

Geography—note: the capital of Damascus—located at an oasis fed by the Barada River—is thought to be one of the world's oldest continuously inhabited cities; there are 41 Israeli settlements and civilian land use sites in the Israeli-occupied Golan Heights (2010 est.)

PEOPLE AND SOCIETY

Nationality: *noun:* Syrian(s)
adjective: Syrian

Ethnic groups: Arab 90.3%, Kurds, Armenians, and other 9.7%

Languages: Arabic (official), Kurdish, Armenian, Aramaic, Circassian (widely understood); French, English (somewhat understood)

Religions: Muslim 87% (official; includes Sunni 74% and Alawi, Ismaili, and Shia 13%), Christian (includes Orthodox, Uniate, and Nestorian) 10% (includes Orthodox, Uniate, and Nestorian), Druze 3%, Jewish (few remaining in Damascus and Aleppo)

Population: 17,951,639 (July 2014 est.)
country comparison to the world: 61
note: approximately 18,900 Israeli settlers live in the Golan Heights (2012)

Age structure:
0-14 years: 33.1% (male 3,046,922/female 2,898,060)
15-24 years: 20.2% (male 1,833,802/female 1,789,854)
25-54 years: 37.9% (male 3,406,744/female 3,396,756)
55-64 years: 3.9% (male 429,644/female 440,980)
65 years and over: 3.9% (male 320,946/female 387,931) (2014 est.)

Dependency ratios:
total dependency ratio: 64.3 %
youth dependency ratio: 57.7 %
elderly dependency ratio: 6.7 %
potential support ratio: 15 (2013)

Median age: *total:* 23.3 years
male: 22.9 years
female: 23.7 years (2014 est.)

Population growth rate: -9.73% (2014 est.)
country comparison to the world: 233

Birth rate: 22.76 births/1,000 population (2014 est.)
country comparison to the world: 74

Death rate: 6.51 deaths/1,000 population (2014 est.)
country comparison to the world: 152

Net migration rate: -113.51 migrant(s)/1,000 population (2014 est.)
country comparison to the world: 222

Urbanization: *urban population:* 56.1% of total population (2011)
rate of urbanization: 2.36% annual rate of change (2010-15 est.)

Major urban areas—population: Aleppo 2.985 million; DAMASCUS (capital) 2.527 million; Hims 1.276 million; Hamah 854,000 (2009)

Sex ratio: *at birth:* 1.06 male(s)/female
0-14 years: 1.05 male(s)/female
15-24 years: 1.03 male(s)/female
25-54 years: 1 male(s)/female
55-64 years: 1.01 male(s)/female
65 years and over: 0.85 male(s)/female
total population: 1.03 male(s)/female (2014 est.)

Maternal mortality rate: 70 deaths/100,000 live births (2010)
country comparison to the world: 87

Infant mortality rate: *total:* 15.79 deaths/1,000 live births
country comparison to the world: 103
male: 18.14 deaths/1,000 live births
female: 13.31 deaths/1,000 live births (2014 est.)

Life expectancy at birth: *total population:* 68.41 years
country comparison to the world: 161
male: 61.4 years
female: 75.84 years (2014 est.)

Total fertility rate: 2.68 children born/woman (2014 est.)
country comparison to the world: 73

Contraceptive prevalence rate: 58.3% (2006)

Health expenditures: 3.7% of GDP (2011)
country comparison to the world: 172

Physicians density: 1.5 physicians/1,000 population (2008)

Hospital bed density: 1.5 beds/1,000 population (2010)

Drinking water source:
improved:
urban: 92.6% of population
rural: 86.5% of population
total: 89.9% of population
unimproved:
urban: 7.4% of population
rural: 13.5% of population
total: 10.1% of population (2011 est.)

Sanitation facility access:
improved:
urban: 96.1% of population
rural: 94% of population
total: 95.2% of population
unimproved:
urban: 3.9% of population
rural: 6% of population
total: 4.8% of population (2011 est.)

HIV/AIDS—adult prevalence rate: less than 0.1% (2001 est.)
country comparison to the world: 146

HIV/AIDS—people living with HIV/AIDS: fewer than 500 (2003 est.)
country comparison to the world: 158

HIV/AIDS—deaths: fewer than 200 (2003 est.)
country comparison to the world: 110

Obesity—adult prevalence rate: 27.1% (2008)
country comparison to the world: 41

Children under the age of 5 years underweight: 10.1% (2009)
country comparison to the world: 70

Education expenditures: 5.1% of GDP (2009)
country comparison to the world: 70

Literacy: *definition:* age 15 and over can read and write
total population: 84.1%
male: 90.3%
female: 77.7% (2011 est.)

School life expectancy (primary to tertiary education): *total:* 12 years
male: 12 years
female: 12 years (2011)

Child labor—children ages 5-14:
total number: 192,915
percentage: 4 % (2006 est.)

Unemployment, youth ages 15-24: *total:* 19.2%
country comparison to the world: 63
male: 15.3%
female: 40.2% (2010)

GOVERNMENT

Country name: *conventional long form:* Syrian Arab Republic
conventional short form: Syria
local long form: Al Jumhuriyah al Arabiyah as Suriyah
local short form: Suriyah
former: United Arab Republic (with Egypt)

Government type: republic under an authoritarian regime

Capital: *name:* Damascus
geographic coordinates: 33 30 N, 36 18 E
time difference: UTC+2 (7 hours ahead of Washington, DC during Standard Time)
daylight saving time: +1hr, begins midnight on the last Friday in March; ends at midnight on the first Friday in November

Administrative divisions: 14 provinces (muhafazat, singular—muhafazah); Al Hasakah, Al Ladhiqiyah (Latakia), Al Qunaytirah, Ar Raqqah, As Suwayda', Dar'a, Dayr az Zawr, Dimashq (Damascus), Halab, Hamah, Hims (Homs), Idlib, Rif Dimashq (Damascus Countryside), Tartus

Independence: 17 April 1946 (from League of Nations mandate under French administration)

National holiday: Independence Day, 17 April (1946)

Constitution: several previous; latest issued 15 February 2012, passed by referendum 26 February 2012 (2013)

Legal system: mixed legal system of civil and Islamic law (for family courts)

International law organization participation: has not submitted an ICJ jurisdiction declaration; non-party state to the ICCt

Suffrage: 18 years of age; universal

Executive branch: *chief of state:* President Bashar al-ASAD (since 17 July 2000); Vice President Farouk al-SHARA (since 21 February 2006); Vice President Najah al-ATTAR (since 23 March 2006)
head of government: Prime Minister Wael al-HALQI (since 9 August 2012); Deputy Prime Ministers Fahd Jasim al-FURAYJ, Lt. Gen., Walid al-MUALEM
cabinet: Council of Ministers appointed by the president; note—new Council appointed on 14 April 2011 (For more information visit the World Leaders website)
elections: president approved by popular referendum for a second 7-year term (the 2012 constitution allows for two successive 7-year terms); referendum last held on 27 May 2007 (next to be held on June 2014); the president appoints the vice presidents, prime minister, and deputy prime ministers
election results: Bashar al-ASAD approved as president; percent of vote—Bashar al-ASAD 97.6%, other 2.4%

Legislative branch: unicameral People's Assembly or Majlis al-Shaab (250 seats; members elected by popular vote to serve four-year terms)
elections: last held on 7 May 2012 (next to be held in 2016)
election results: percent of vote by party—NA; seats by party—NA

Judicial branch: *highest court(s):* Court of Cassation (organized into civil, criminal, religious, and military divisions, each with 3 judges); Supreme Constitutional Court (consists of 4 members)
judge selection and term of office: Court of Cassation judges appointed by the Supreme Judicial Council or SJC, a judicial management body headed by the minister of justice with 7 members including the national president; judge tenure NA; Supreme Constitutional Court judges nominated by the president and appointed by the SJC; judges appointed for 4-year renewable terms
subordinate courts: courts of first instance; magistrates' courts; religious and military courts; Economic Security Court

Political parties and leaders:
legal parties:
National Progressive Front or NPF [President Bashar al-ASAD, Dr. Suleiman QADDAH] (includes; Arab Socialist Renaissance (Ba'th) Party [President Bashar al-ASAD]; Socialist Unionist Democratic Party [Fadlallah Nasr al-DIN]; Syrian Arab Socialist Union or ASU [Safwan al-QUDSI]; Syrian Communist Party (two branches) [Wissal Farha BAKDASH, Yusuf Rashid FAYSAL]; Syrian Social Nationalist Party [As'ad HARDAN]; Unionist Socialist Party [Fayez ISMAIL])
Kurdish parties (considered illegal): Kurdish Azadi Party; Kurdish Democratic Accord Party (al Wifaq); Kurdish Democratic Party (al Parti-Ibrahim wing); Kurdish Democratic Party (al Parti-Mustafa wing); Kurdish Democratic Party in Syria or KDP-S; Kurdish Democratic Patriotic/National Party; Kurdish Democratic Progressive Party or KDPP-Darwish; Kurdish Democratic Progressive Party or KDPP-Muhammad; Kurdish Democratic Union Party or PYD [Salih Muslim MOHAMMAD]; Kurdish Democratic Unity Party; Kurdish Democratic Yekiti Party; Kurdish Future Party or KFP; Kurdish Future Party [Rezan HASSAN]; Kurdish Left Party; Kurdish Yekiti (Union) Party; Syrian Kurdish Democratic Party
other parties: Syrian Democratic Party [Mustafa QALAAJI]

Political pressure groups and leaders: Free Syrian Army; Syrian Muslim Brotherhood or SMB [Muhammad Riyad al-SHAQFAH] (operates in exile in London); Syrian Opposition Coalition or National Coalition of Syrian Revolutionary and Opposition Forces; [al-Asi- al-JARBAL]
note: there are also hundreds of local groups that organize protests and stage armed attacks

International organization participation: ABEDA, AFESD, AMF, CAEU, FAO, G-24, G-77, IAEA, IBRD, ICAO, ICC (national committees), ICRM, IDA, IDB, IFAD, IFC, IFRCS, IHO, ILO, IMF, IMO, Interpol, IOC, IPU, ISO, ITSO, ITU, MIGA, NAM, OAPEC, OIC, UN, UNCTAD, UNESCO, UNIDO, UNRWA, UNWTO, UPU, WCO, WFTU (NGOs), WHO, WIPO, WMO, WTO (observer)

Diplomatic representation in the US:
note: embassy ceased operation since 18 March 2014
chief of mission: Ambassador (vacant); Charge d'Affaires Mounir KOUDMANI
chancery: 2215 Wyoming Avenue NW, Washington, DC 20008
telephone: [1] (202) 232-6313
FAX: [1] (202) 265-4585

Diplomatic representation from the US:
chief of mission: Ambassador Robert Stephen FORD (since 7 January 2011); note—on 6 February 2012, the US closed its embassy in Damascus
embassy: Abou Roumaneh, Al-Mansour Street, No. 2, Damascus
mailing address: P. O. Box 29, Damascus
telephone: [963] (11) 3391-4444
FAX: [963] (11) 3391-3999

Flag description: three equal horizontal bands of red (top), white, and black; two small, green,

five-pointed stars in a horizontal line centered in the white band; the band colors derive from the Arab Liberation flag and represent oppression (black), overcome through bloody struggle (red), to be replaced by a bright future (white); identical to the former flag of the United Arab Republic (1958-1961) where the two stars represented the constituent states of Syria and Egypt; the current design dates to 1980
note: similar to the flag of Yemen, which has a plain white band, Iraq, which has an Arabic inscription centered in the white band, and that of Egypt, which has a gold Eagle of Saladin centered in the white band

National symbol(s): hawk

National anthem: *name:* "Humat ad-Diyar" (Guardians of the Homeland)
lyrics/music: Khalil Mardam BEY/Mohammad Salim FLAYFEL and Ahmad Salim FLAYFEL
note: adopted 1936, restored 1961; between 1958 and 1961, while Syria was a member of the United Arab Republic with Egypt, the country had a different anthem

ECONOMY

Economy—overview: Despite modest economic growth and reform prior to the outbreak of unrest, Syria's economy continues to deteriorate amid the ongoing conflict that began in 2011. The economy further contracted in 2013 because of international sanctions, widespread infrastructure damage, reduced domestic consumption and production, and sharply rising inflation. The government has struggled to address the effects of economic decline, which include dwindling foreign exchange reserves, rising budget and trade deficits, and the decreasing value of the Syrian pound. The ongoing conflict and economic decline have created a humanitarian crisis, prompting widespread need for international aid. Prior to the unrest, Damascus began liberalizing economic policies, including cutting lending interest rates, opening private banks, consolidating multiple exchange rates, raising prices on some subsidized items, and establishing the Damascus Stock Exchange. The economy remains highly regulated by the government. Long-run economic constraints include foreign trade barriers, declining oil production, high unemployment, rising budget deficits, increasing pressure on water supplies caused by heavy use in agriculture, rapid population growth, industrial expansion, and water pollution.

GDP (purchasing power parity): $107.6 billion (2011 est.)
country comparison to the world: 73
$110.1 billion (2010 est.)
$106.5 billion (2009 est.)
note: data are in 2011 US dollars the war driven deterioration of the economy resulted in a disappearance of quality national level statistics in 2012-13

GDP (official exchange rate): $64.7 billion (2011 est.)

GDP—real growth rate: NA% (2012 est.)
-2.3% (2011 est.)
3.4% (2010 est.)

GDP—per capita (PPP): $5,100 (2011 est.)
country comparison to the world: 159
$5,100 (2010 est.)
$5,200 (2010 est.)
note: data are in 2011 US dollars

Gross national saving: 5.4% of GDP (2013 est.)
country comparison to the world: 147
12.8% of GDP (2012 est.)
15% of GDP (2011 est.)

GDP—composition, by end use:
household consumption: 68.3%
government consumption: 19.7%
investment in fixed capital: 20.1%
investment in inventories: 9.3%
exports of goods and services: 11.3%
imports of goods and services: -28.6% (2013 est.)

GDP—composition, by sector of origin:
agriculture: 17.6%
industry: 22.2%
services: 60.2% (2013 est.)

Agriculture—products: wheat, barley, cotton, lentils, chickpeas, olives, sugar beets; beef, mutton, eggs, poultry, milk

Industries: petroleum, textiles, food processing, beverages, tobacco, phosphate rock mining, cement, oil seeds crushing, car assembly

Industrial production growth rate: -20.6% (2013 est.)
country comparison to the world: 193

Labor force: 5.014 million (2013 est.)
country comparison to the world: 75

Labor force—by occupation: *agriculture:* 17%
industry: 16%
services: 67% (2008 est.)

Unemployment rate: 17.8% (2013 est.)
country comparison to the world: 156
18% (2012 est.)

Population below poverty line: 11.9% (2006 est.)

Household income or consumption by percentage share: *lowest 10%:* NA%
highest 10%: NA%

Budget: *revenues:* $2.38 billion
expenditures: $7.56 billion (2013 est.)

Taxes and other revenues: 3.7% of GDP (2013 est.)
country comparison to the world: 214

Budget surplus (+) or deficit (-):
-8% of GDP (2013 est.)
country comparison to the world: 195

Public debt: 58.9% of GDP (2013 est.)
country comparison to the world: 50
52.4% of GDP (2012 est.)

Fiscal year: calendar year

Inflation rate (consumer prices): 59.1% (2013 est.)
country comparison to the world: 223
36.9% (2012 est.)

Central bank discount rate: 0.75% (31 December 2013 est.)
country comparison to the world: 71
5% (31 December 2012 est.)

Commercial bank prime lending rate: 10.5% (31 December 2013 est.)
country comparison to the world: 73
11.7% (31 December 2012 est.)

Stock of narrow money: $8.097 billion (31 December 2013 est.)
country comparison to the world: 87
$16.78 billion (31 December 2012 est.)

Stock of broad money: $12.77 billion (31 December 2013 est.)
country comparison to the world: 95
$27.11 billion (31 December 2012 est.)

Stock of domestic credit: $7.777 billion (31 December 2013 est.)
country comparison to the world: 105
$17.41 billion (31 December 2012 est.)

Market value of publicly traded shares: $NA

Current account balance: -$5.879 billion (2013 est.)
country comparison to the world: 170
-$6.706 billion (2012 est.)

Exports: $2.675 billion (2013 est.)
country comparison to the world: 134
$3.876 billion (2012 est.)

Exports—commodities: crude oil, minerals, petroleum products, fruits and vegetables, cotton fiber, textiles, clothing, meat and live animals, wheat

Exports—partners: Iraq 58.4%, Saudi Arabia 9.7%, Kuwait 6.4%, UAE 5.5%, Libya 4.1% (2012)

Imports: $8.917 billion (2013 est.)
country comparison to the world: 105
$10.78 billion (2012 est.)

Imports—commodities: machinery and transport equipment, electric power machinery, food and livestock, metal and metal products, chemicals and chemical products, plastics, yarn, paper

Imports—partners: Saudi Arabia 22.8%, UAE 11.2%, Iran 8.3%, China 7.3%, Iraq 6.8% (2012)

Reserves of foreign exchange and gold: $1.895 billion (31 December 2013 est.)
country comparison to the world: 123
$4.793 billion (31 December 2012 est.)

Debt—external: $9.796 billion (31 December 2013 est.)
country comparison to the world: 100
$8.394 billion (31 December 2012 est.)

Exchange rates: Syrian pounds (SYP) per US dollar—
105.3 (2013 est.)
64.392 (2012 est.)
11.225 (2010 est.)
46.708 (2009)
46.5281 (2008)

ENERGY

Electricity—production: 43.76 billion kWh (2010 est.)
country comparison to the world: 55

Electricity—consumption: 35.61 billion kWh (2010 est.)
country comparison to the world: 56

Electricity—exports: 1.043 billion kWh (2010 est.)
country comparison to the world: 55

Electricity—imports: 0 kWh (2012 est.)
country comparison to the world: 202

Electricity—installed generating capacity: 8.323 million kW (2010 est.)
country comparison to the world: 62

Electricity—from fossil fuels: 89.2% of total installed capacity (2010 est.)
country comparison to the world: 78

Electricity—from nuclear fuels: 0% of total installed capacity (2010 est.)
country comparison to the world: 182

Electricity—from hydroelectric plants: 10.8% of total installed capacity (2010 est.)
country comparison to the world: 112

Electricity—from other renewable sources: 0% of total installed capacity (2010 est.)
country comparison to the world: 125

Crude oil—production: 182,500 bbl/day (2012 est.)
country comparison to the world: 39

Crude oil—exports: 152,400 bbl/day (2010 est.)
country comparison to the world: 34

Crude oil—imports: 0 bbl/day (2010 est.)
country comparison to the world: 124

Crude oil—proved reserves: 2.5 billion bbl (1 January 2013 es)
country comparison to the world: 33

Refined petroleum products—production: 253,600 bbl/day (2010 est.)
country comparison to the world: 49

Refined petroleum products—consumption: 258,800 bbl/day (2011 est.)
country comparison to the world: 49

Refined petroleum products—exports: 36,210 bbl/day (2010 est.)
country comparison to the world: 66

Refined petroleum products—imports: 104,800 bbl/day (2010 est.)
country comparison to the world: 50

Natural gas—production: 7.87 billion cu m (2011 est.)
country comparison to the world: 45

Natural gas—consumption: 9.63 billion cu m (2010 est.)
country comparison to the world: 48

Natural gas—exports: 0 cu m (2011 est.)
country comparison to the world: 187

Natural gas—imports: 250 million cu m (2011 est.)
country comparison to the world: 69

Natural gas—proved reserves: 240.7 billion cu m (1 January 2013 es)
country comparison to the world: 45

Carbon dioxide emissions from consumption of energy: 63.14 million Mt (2011 est.)
country comparison to the world: 54

COMMUNICATIONS

Telephones—main lines in use: 4.425 million (2012)
country comparison to the world: 36

Telephones—mobile cellular: 12.928 million (2012)
country comparison to the world: 66

Telephone system: *general assessment:* fair system currently undergoing significant improvement and digital upgrades, including fiber-optic technology and expansion of the network to rural areas; the armed insurgency that began in 2011 has led to major disruptions to the network and has caused telephone and Internet outages throughout the country
domestic: the number of fixed-line connections has increased markedly since 2000; mobile-cellular service growing with telephone subscribership nearly 60 per 100 persons in 2011
international: country code—963; submarine cable connection to Egypt, Lebanon, and Cyprus; satellite earth stations—1 Intelsat (Indian Ocean) and 1 Intersputnik (Atlantic Ocean region); coaxial cable and microwave radio relay to Iraq, Jordan, Lebanon, and Turkey; participant in Medarabtel (2011)

Broadcast media: state-run TV and radio broadcast networks; state operates 2 TV networks and a satellite channel; roughly two-thirds of Syrian homes have a satellite dish providing access to foreign TV broadcasts; 3 state-run radio channels; first private radio station launched in 2005; private radio broadcasters prohibited from transmitting news or political content (2007)

Internet country code: .sy

Internet hosts: 416 (2012)
country comparison to the world: 187

Internet users: 4.469 million (2009)
country comparison to the world: 52

TRANSPORTATION

Airports: 90 (2013)
country comparison to the world: 6 2

Airports—with paved runways: *total:* 2 9
over 3,047 m: 5
2,438 to 3,047 m: 16
914 to 1,523 m: 3
under 914 m: 5 (2013)

Airports—with unpaved runways: *total:* 6 1
1,524 to 2,437 m: 1
914 to 1,523 m: 12
under 914 m: 48 (2013)

Heliports: 6 (2013)

Pipelines: gas 3,170 km; oil 2,029 km (2013)

Railways: *total:* 2,052 km
country comparison to the world: 72
standard gauge: 1,801 km 1.435-m gauge
narrow gauge: 251 km 1.050-m gauge (2008)

Roadways: *total:* 69,873 km
country comparison to the world: 67
paved: 63,060 km
unpaved: 6,813 km (2010)

Waterways: 900 km (navigable but not economically significant) (2011)
country comparison to the world: 69

Merchant marine: *total:* 1 9
country comparison to the world: 95
by type: bulk carrier 4, cargo 14, carrier 1
registered in other countries: 166 (Barbados 1, Belize 4, Bolivia 4, Cambodia 22, Comoros 5, Dominica 4, Georgia 24, Lebanon 2, Liberia 1, Malta 4, Moldova 5, North Korea 4, Panama 34, Saint Vincent and the Grenadines 9, Sierra Leone 13, Tanzania 23, Togo 6, unknown 1) (2010)

Ports and terminals: *major seaport(s):* Baniyas, Latakia, Tartus

MILITARY

Military branches: Syrian Armed Forces: Land Forces, Naval Forces, Air Forces (includes Air Defense Forces) (2013)

Military service age and obligation: 18 years of age for compulsory and voluntary military service; conscript service obligation is 18 months; women are not conscripted but may volunteer to serve; re-enlistment obligation 5 years, with retirement after 15 years or age 40 (enlisted) or 20 years or age 45 (NCOs) (2012)

Manpower available for military service:
males age 16-49: 5,889,837
females age 16-49: 5,660,751 (2010 est.)

Manpower fit for military service:
males age 16-49: 5,055,510
females age 16-49: 4,884,151 (2010 est.)

Manpower reaching militarily significant age annually: *male:* 256,698
female: 244,712 (2010 est.)

TRANSNATIONAL ISSUES

Disputes—international: Golan Heights is Israeli-occupied with the almost 1,000-strong UN Disengagement Observer Force patrolling a buffer zone since 1964; lacking a treaty or other documentation describing the boundary, portions of the Lebanon-Syria boundary are unclear with several sections in dispute; since 2000, Lebanon has claimed Shab'a Farms in the Golan Heights; 2004 Agreement and pending demarcation settles border dispute with Jordan

Refugees and internally displaced persons: *refugees (country of origin):* 87,741 (Iraq) (2012); 507,904 (Palestinian Refugees (UNRWA)) (2013)
note: the ongoing civil war had created more than 2.7 million Syrian refugees—dispersed in Egypt, Iraq, Jordan, Lebanon, and Turkey—as of February 2014
IDPs: 6.5 million (ongoing civil war since 2011) (2014)
stateless persons: 221,000 (2012); note—Syria's stateless population is composed of Kurds and Palestinians; stateless persons are prevented from voting, owning land, holding certain jobs, receiving food subsidies or public healthcare, enrolling in public schools, or being legally married to Syrian citizens; in 1962, some 120,000 Syrian Kurds were stripped of their Syrian citizenship, rendering them and their descendants stateless; in 2011, the Syrian Government granted citizenship to thousands of Syrian Kurds as a means of appeasement; however, resolving the question of statelessness is not a priority given Syria's ongoing civil war

Trafficking in persons: *current situation:* due to Syria's political uprising and violent unrest, hundreds of thousands of Syrians, foreign migrant workers, and refugees have fled the country and are vulnerable to human trafficking; the lack of security and inaccessibility of the majority of the country makes it impossible to conduct a thorough analysis of the ongoing conflict and the scope and magnitude of Syria's human trafficking situation; prior to the uprising, Syria was principally a destination country for women and children subjected to forced labor or sex trafficking; thousands of women—the majority from Indonesia, the Philippines, Somalia, and Ethiopia—were recruited to work as domestic servants but were subsequently subjected to forced labor; Filipina domestic workers continue to be sent to Syria and are vulnerable to forced labor; the Syrian armed forces and opposition forces are using Syrian children in combat and support roles and as human shields; Iraqi women and girls continue to be sexually exploited, and Syrian children still face conditions of

forced labor tier rating: Tier 3—the government does not fully comply with the minimum standards for the elimination of trafficking and is not making significant efforts to do so; the government does not demonstrate evidence of increasing efforts to investigate and punish trafficking offenses, provide protective services to victims, inform the public about human trafficking, or provide much-needed anti-trafficking training to law enforcement and social welfare officials; the government does not refer any victims to NGO-operated shelters and has failed to institute procedures for the identification, interview, and referral of trafficking victims; the status of the national plan of action against trafficking is unknown (2013)

Illicit drugs: a transit point for opiates, hashish, and cocaine bound for regional and Western markets; weak anti-money-laundering controls and bank privatization may leave it vulnerable to money laundering

TAIWAN

INTRODUCTION

Background: In 1895, military defeat forced China's Qing Dynasty to cede Taiwan to Japan. Taiwan came under Chinese Nationalist control after World War II. Following the communist victory on the mainland in 1949, 2 million Nationalists fled to Taiwan and established a government using the 1947 constitution drawn up for all of China. Beginning in the 1950s, the ruling authorities gradually democratized and incorporated the local population within the governing structure. This process expanded rapidly in the 1980s. In 2000, Taiwan underwent its first peaceful transfer of power from the Nationalist (Kuomintang or KMT) to the Democratic Progressive Party. Throughout this period, the island prospered and became one of East Asia's economic "Tigers." The dominant political issues continue to be management of sensitive relations between Taiwan and China—specifically the question of Taiwan's eventual status—as well as domestic priorities for economic reform and growth.

GEOGRAPHY

Location: Eastern Asia, islands bordering the East China Sea, Philippine Sea, South China Sea, and Taiwan Strait, north of the Philippines, off the southeastern coast of China

Geographic coordinates: 23 30 N, 121 00 E

Map references: Southeast Asia

Area: *total:* 35,980 sq km
country comparison to the world: 139
land: 32,260 sq km
water: 3,720 sq km
note: includes the Pescadores, Matsu, and Quemoy islands

Area—comparative: slightly smaller than Maryland and Delaware combined

Land boundaries: 0 km

Coastline: 1,566.3 km

Maritime claims: *territorial sea:* 12 nm
exclusive economic zone: 200 nm

Climate: tropical; marine; rainy season during southwest monsoon (June to August); cloudiness is persistent and extensive all year

Terrain: eastern two-thirds mostly rugged mountains; flat to gently rolling plains in west

Elevation extremes: *lowest point:* South China Sea 0 m
highest point: Yu Shan 3,952 m

Natural resources: small deposits of coal, natural gas, limestone, marble, and asbestos

Land use: *arable land:* 24%
permanent crops: 1%
other: 75% (2011)

Irrigated land: NA

Total renewable water resources: 67 cu km (2011)

Natural hazards: earthquakes; typhoons
volcanism: Kueishantao Island (elev. 401 m), east of Taiwan, is its only historically active volcano, although it has not erupted in centuries

Environment—current issues: air pollution; water pollution from industrial emissions, raw sewage; contamination of drinking water supplies; trade in endangered species; low-level radioactive waste disposal

Environment—international agreements:
party to: none of the selected agreements because of Taiwan's international status

Geography—note: strategic location adjacent to both the Taiwan Strait and the Luzon Strait

PEOPLE AND SOCIETY

Nationality: *noun:* Taiwan (singular and plural)
note: example—he or she is from Taiwan; they are from Taiwan
adjective: Taiwan (or Taiwanese)

Ethnic groups: Taiwanese (including Hakka) 84%, mainland Chinese 14%, indigenous 2%

Languages: Mandarin Chinese (official), Taiwanese (Min), Hakka dialects

Religions: mixture of Buddhist and Taoist 93%, Christian 4.5%, other 2.5%

Population: 23,359,928 (July 2014 est.)
country comparison to the world: 52

Age structure:
0-14 years: 14% (male 1,683,381/female 1,575,789)
15-24 years: 13.4% (male 1,613,197/female 1,526,344)
25-54 years: 47.4% (male 5,539,606/female 5,539,654)
55-64 years: 12% (male 1,506,657/female 1,571,208)
65 years and over: 11.6% (male 1,301,420/female 1,502,672) (2014 est.)

Median age: *total:* 39.2 years
male: 38.5 years
female: 39.9 years (2014 est.)

Population growth rate: 0.25% (2014 est.)
country comparison to the world: 177

Birth rate: 8.55 births/1,000 population (2014 est.)
country comparison to the world: 216

Death rate: 6.97 deaths/1,000 population (2014 est.)
country comparison to the world: 135

Net migration rate: 0.9 migrant(s)/1,000 population (2014 est.)
country comparison to the world: 62

Sex ratio: *at birth:* 1.07 male(s)/female
0-14 years: 1.07 male(s)/female
15-24 years: 1.06 male(s)/female
25-54 years: 1 male(s)/female
55-64 years: 0.99 male(s)/female
65 years and over: 0.89 male(s)/female
total population: 1 male(s)/female (2014 est.)

Infant mortality rate: *total:* 4.49 deaths/1,000 live births
country comparison to the world: 186
male: 4.9 deaths/1,000 live births
female: 4.06 deaths/1,000 live births (2014 est.)

Life expectancy at birth:
total population: 79.84 years
country comparison to the world: 38
male: 76.72 years
female: 83.2 years (2014 est.)

Total fertility rate: 1.11 children born/woman (2014 est.)
country comparison to the world: 222

HIV/AIDS—adult prevalence rate: NA

HIV/AIDS—people living with HIV/AIDS: NA

HIV/AIDS—deaths: NA

Literacy: *definition:* age 15 and over can read and write
total population: 96.1%
male: NA
female: NA (2003)

GOVERNMENT

Country name: *conventional long form:* none
conventional short form: Taiwan
local long form: none
local short form: Taiwan
former: Formosa

Government type: multiparty democracy

Capital: *name:* Taipei

geographic coordinates: 25 02 N, 121 31 E
time difference: UTC+8 (13 hours ahead of Washington, DC during Standard Time)

Administrative divisions: includes main island of Taiwan plus smaller islands nearby and off coast of China's Fujian Province; Taiwan is divided into 14 counties (hsien, singular and plural), 3 municipalities (shih, singular and plural), and 5 special municipalities (chih-hsia-shih, singular and plural)
note: Taiwan uses a variety of romanization systems; while a modified Wade-Giles system still dominates, the city of Taipei has adopted a Pinyin romanization for street and place names within its boundaries; other local authorities use different romanization systems; names for administrative divisions that follow are taken from the Taiwan Yearbook 2007 published by the Government Information Office in Taipei.
counties: Changhua, Chiayi (county), Hsinchu (county), Hualien, Kinmen, Lienchiang, Miaoli, Nantou, Penghu, Pingtung, Taitung, Taoyuan, Yilan, Yunlin
municipalities: Chiayi (city), Hsinchu (city), Keelung (city)
municipalities: Chiayi (city), Hsinchu (city), Keelung (city)
special municipalities: Kaohsiung (city), New Taipei (city), Taichung (city), Tainan (city), Taipei (city)

National holiday: Republic Day (Anniversary of the Chinese Revolution), 10 October (1911)

Constitution: previous 1912, 1931; latest adopted 25 December 1946, promulgated 1 January 1947, effective 25 December 1947; revised several times, last in 2005 (2013)

Legal system: civil law system

International law organization participation: has not submitted an ICJ jurisdiction declaration; non-party state to the ICCt

Suffrage: 20 years of age; universal

Executive branch: *chief of state*: President MA Ying-jeou (since 20 May 2008); Vice President WU Den-yih (since 20 May 2012)
head of government: Premier JIANG Yi-huah (President of the Executive Yuan) (since 18 February 2013); Vice Premier MAO Chi-kuo (Vice President of the Executive Yuan) (since 18 February 2013)
cabinet: Executive Yuan—ministers appointed by president on recommendation of premier (For more information visit the World Leaders website)
elections: president and vice president elected on the same ticket by popular vote for four-year terms (eligible for a second term); election last held on 14 January 2012 (next to be held in January 2016); premier appointed by the president; vice premiers appointed by the president on the recommendation of the premier
election results: MA Ying-jeou elected president; percent of vote—MA Ying-jeou 51.6%, TSAI Ing-wen 45.6%, James SOONG Chu-ye 2.8%

Legislative branch: unicameral Legislative Yuan (113 seats—73 district members elected by popular vote, 34 at-large members elected on basis of proportion of islandwide votes received by participating political parties, 6 elected by popular vote among aboriginal populations; members to serve four-year terms); parties must receive 5% of vote to qualify for at-large seats
elections: Legislative Yuan—last held on 14 January 2012 (next to be held in January 2016)
election results: Legislative Yuan—percent of vote by party—KMT 44.6%, DPP 34.6%, TSU 9.0%, PFP 5.5%, others 6.3%; seats by party—KMT 64, DPP 40, PFP 3, TSU 3, NPSU 2, independent 1

Judicial branch: *highest court(s)*: Supreme Court (consists of the court president, vice president, and approximately 100 judges organized into 8 civil and 12 criminal divisions, each with a division chief justice and 4 associate justices); Constitutional Court (consists of the court president, vice president, and 13 justices)
judge selection and term of office: both Supreme Court and Constitutional Court justices appointed by the president of the republic with the approval of the Legislative Yuan; Supreme Court justices appointed for life; Constitutional Court president, vice-president, and 8 grand justices serve 4-year terms and remaining justices serve 8-year terms
subordinate courts: high courts; district courts; hierarchy of administrative courts

Political parties and leaders: Democratic Progressive Party or DPP [SU Tseng-chang]; Kuomintang or KMT (Nationalist Party) [MA Ying-jeou]; New Party [YOK Mu-ming]; Non-Partisan Solidarity Union or NPSU [LIN Pin-kuan]; People First Party or PFP [James SOONG Chu-ye]; Taiwan Solidarity Union or TSU [HUANG Kun-huei]

Political pressure groups and leaders: environmental groups; independence movement; various business groups
note: debate on Taiwan independence has become acceptable within the mainstream of domestic politics on Taiwan; public opinion polls consistently show a substantial majority of Taiwan people supports maintaining Taiwan's status quo for the foreseeable future; advocates of Taiwan independence oppose the stand that the island will eventually unify with mainland China; advocates of eventual unification predicate their goal on the democratic transformation of the mainland

International organization participation: ADB, APEC, BCIE, ICC (national committees), IOC, ITUC (NGOs), WTO

Diplomatic representation in the US: none; commercial and cultural relations with the people in the United States are maintained through an unofficial instrumentality, the Taipei Economic and Cultural Representative Office in the United States (TECRO), a private nonprofit corporation that performs citizen and consular services similar to those at diplomatic posts
representative: KING Pu-tsung
office: 4201 Wisconsin Avenue NW, Washington, DC 20016
telephone: [1] 202 895-1800
Taipei Economic and Cultural Offices (branch offices): Atlanta, Boston, Chicago, Guam, Houston, Honolulu, Kansas City, Los Angeles, Miami, New York, San Francisco, Seattle

Diplomatic representation from the US: none; commercial and cultural relations with the people on Taiwan are maintained through an unofficial instrumentality, the American Institute in Taiwan (AIT), a private nonprofit corporation that performs citizen and consular services similar to those at diplomatic posts
director: Christopher J. MARUT
office: #7 Lane 134, Hsin Yi Road, Section 3, Taipei 106, Taiwan
telephone: [1] [886] (02) 2162-2000
FAX: [1] [886] (02) 2162-2251
other offices: Kaohsiung

Flag description: red field with a dark blue rectangle in the upper hoist-side corner bearing a white sun with 12 triangular rays; the blue and white design of the canton (symbolizing the sun of progress) dates to 1895; it was later adopted as the flag of the Kuomintang Party; blue signifies liberty, justice, and democracy; red stands for fraternity, sacrifice, and nationalism, white represents equality, frankness, and the people's livelihood; the 12 rays of the sun are those of the months and the twelve traditional Chinese hours (each ray equals two hours)

National symbol(s): white, 12-rayed sun on blue field

National anthem: *name*: "Zhonghua Minguo guoge" (National Anthem of the Republic of China)
lyrics/music: HU Han-min, TAI Chi-t'ao, and LIAO Chung-k'ai/CHENG Mao-Yun
note: adopted 1930; the anthem is also the song of the Kuomintang Party; it is informally known as "San Min Chu I" or "San Min Zhu Yi" (Three Principles of the People); because of political pressure from China, "Guo Qi Ge" (National Banner Song) is used at international events rather than the official anthem of Taiwan; the "National Banner Song" has gained popularity in Taiwan and is commonly used during flag raisings

ECONOMY

Economy—overview: Taiwan has a dynamic capitalist economy with gradually decreasing government guidance of investment and foreign trade. Exports, led by electronics, machinery, and petrochemicals have provided the primary impetus for economic development. This heavy dependence on exports exposes the economy to fluctuations in world demand. Taiwan's diplomatic isolation, low birth rate, and rapidly aging population are other major long-term challenges. Free trade agreements have proliferated in East Asia over the past several years, and following the landmark Economic Cooperation Framework Agreement (ECFA) signed with China in June 2010, Taiwan in July 2013 signed a free trade deal with New Zealand—Taipei's first-ever with a country with which it does not maintain diplomatic relations—and in November inked a trade pact with Singapore. Negotiations continue on follow-on components of ECFA regarding trade in goods and a dispute resolution mechanism; a trade in services agreement is under review in the legislature. Taiwan's Total Fertility rate of just over one child per woman is among the lowest in the world, raising the prospect of future labor shortages, falling domestic demand, and declining tax revenues. Taiwan's population is aging quickly, with the number of people over 65 accounting for 11.2% of the island's total population as of 2012. The island runs a large overall trade surplus largely because of its surplus with China, and its foreign reserves are the world's sixth largest, behind China, Japan, Saudi Arabia, Russia, and Switzerland. In 2006 China overtook the US to become Taiwan's second-largest source of imports after Japan. China is also the island's number one destination for foreign direct investment. Taiwan since 2009 has gradually loosened rules governing Chinese investment on the island, and has also secured greater market access for its investors in the mainland. In August 2012, Taiwan Central Bank signed a memorandum of understanding on cross-Strait currency settlement with its Chinese counterpart. The MOU allows for the direct settlement of Chinese RMB and the New Taiwan dollar across the Strait, which could help develop Taiwan into a local RMB hub. Closer economic links with the mainland bring greater opportunities for the Taiwan economy, but also poses new challenges as the island becomes more economically dependent on China while political differences remain unresolved.

GDP (purchasing power parity): $926.4 billion (2013 est.)
country comparison to the world: 21
$906.6 billion (2012 est.)
$894.7 billion (2011 est.)
note: data are in 2013 US dollars

GDP (official exchange rate): $484.7 billion (2013 est.)

GDP—real growth rate: 2.2% (2013 est.)
country comparison to the world: 136
1.3% (2012 est.)
4.1% (2011 est.)

GDP—per capita (PPP): $39,600 (2013 est.)
country comparison to the world: 28
$38,900 (2012 est.)
$38,500 (2011 est.)
note: data are in 2013 US dollars

Gross national saving: 31.3% of GDP (2013 est.)

country comparison to the world: 24
30.3% of GDP (2012 est.)
29.6% of GDP (2011 est.)

GDP—composition, by end use:
household consumption: 59.5%
government consumption: 12.2%
investment in fixed capital: 19.4%
investment in inventories: 0.3%
exports of goods and services: 73.1%
imports of goods and services: -64.5% (2013 est.)

GDP—composition, by sector of origin:
agriculture: 2%
industry: 29.4%
services: 68.6% (2013 est.)

Agriculture—products: rice, vegetables, fruit, tea, flowers; pigs, poultry; fish

Industries: electronics, communications and information technology products, petroleum refining, chemicals, textiles, iron and steel, machinery, cement, food processing, vehicles, consumer products, pharmaceuticals

Industrial production growth rate: 1.8% (2013 est.)
country comparison to the world: 132

Labor force: 11.55 million (2013 est.)
country comparison to the world: 47

Labor force—by occupation: *agriculture:* 5%
industry: 36.2%
services: 58.8% (2012 est.)

Unemployment rate: 4.1% (2013 est.)
country comparison to the world: 35
4.2% (2012 est.)

Population below poverty line: 1.5% (2012 est.)

Household income or consumption by percentage share: *lowest 10%:* 6.4%
highest 10%: 40.3% (2010)

Distribution of family income—Gini index: 34.2 (2011)
country comparison to the world: 93
32.6 (2000)

Budget: *revenues:* $78.24 billion
expenditures: $90.38 billion (2013 est.)

Taxes and other revenues: 16.1% of GDP (2013 est.)
country comparison to the world: 187

Budget surplus (+) or deficit (-):
-2.5% of GDP (2013 est.)
country comparison to the world: 100

Public debt: 38.9% of GDP (2013 est.)
country comparison to the world: 94
35.8% of GDP (2012 est.)
note: data for central government

Fiscal year: calendar year

Inflation rate (consumer prices): 1.1% (2013 est.)
country comparison to the world: 26
1.9% (2012 est.)

Central bank discount rate: 1.88% (31 December 2012)
country comparison to the world: 114
1.88% (31 December 2011)

Commercial bank prime lending rate: 2.9% (31 December 2013 est.)
country comparison to the world: 176
2.88% (31 December 2012 est.)

Stock of narrow money: $450.1 billion (31 December 2013 est.)
country comparison to the world: 14
$426.2 billion (31 December 2012 est.)

Stock of broad money: $1.189 trillion (31 December 2013 est.)
country comparison to the world: 16
$1.152 trillion (31 December 2012 est.)

Stock of domestic credit: $753.5 billion (31 December 2013 est.)
country comparison to the world: 19
$743.1 billion (31 December 2012 est.)

Market value of publicly traded shares: $831.9 billion (31 December 2012)
country comparison to the world: 18
$784.1 billion (31 December 2011)
$738.3 billion (31 December 2010)

Current account balance: $56.66 billion (2013 est.)
country comparison to the world: 9
$49.92 billion (2012 est.)

Exports: $305.8 billion (2013 est.)
country comparison to the world: 21
$299.8 billion (2012 est.)

Exports—commodities: electronics, flat panels, machinery; metals; textiles, plastics, chemicals; optical, photographic, measuring, and medical instruments

Exports—partners: China 27.1%, Hong Kong 13.2%, US 10.3%, Japan 6.4%, Singapore 4.4% (2012 est.)

Imports: $268.5 billion (2013 est.)
country comparison to the world: 20
$268.8 billion (2012 est.)

Imports—commodities: electronics, machinery, crude petroleum, precision instruments, organic chemicals, metals

Imports—partners: Japan 17.6%, China 16.1%, US 9.5% (2012 est.)

Reserves of foreign exchange and gold: $414.5 billion (31 December 2013 est.)
country comparison to the world: 7
$408.5 billion (31 December 2012 est.)

Debt—external: $146.8 billion (31 December 2013 est.)
country comparison to the world: 38
$130.8 billion (31 December 2012 est.)

Stock of direct foreign investment—at home: $62.94 billion (31 December 2013 est.)
country comparison to the world: 51
$59.36 billion (31 December 2012 est.)

Stock of direct foreign investment—abroad: $240.3 billion (31 December 2013 est.)
country comparison to the world: 22
$226.1 billion (31 December 2012 est.)

Exchange rates: New Taiwan dollars (TWD) per US dollar—
29.77 (2013 est.)
29.616 (2012 est.)
31.648 (2010 est.)
33.061 (2009)
31.53 (2008)

ENERGY

Electricity—production: 252.2 billion kWh (2011 est.)
country comparison to the world: 17

Electricity—consumption: 242.2 billion kWh (2011 est.)
country comparison to the world: 15

Electricity—exports: 0 kWh (2011 est.)
country comparison to the world: 206

Electricity—imports: 0 kWh (2011 est.)
country comparison to the world: 208

Electricity—installed generating capacity: 48.75 million kW (2011 est.)
country comparison to the world: 21

Electricity—from fossil fuels: 77.2% of total installed capacity (2011 est.)
country comparison to the world: 94

Electricity—from nuclear fuels: 10.6% of total installed capacity (2011 est.)
country comparison to the world: 17

Electricity—from hydroelectric plants: 5.3% of total installed capacity (2011 est.)
country comparison to the world: 124

Electricity—from other renewable sources: 6.9% of total installed capacity (2011 est.)
country comparison to the world: 35

Crude oil—production: 21,680 bbl/day (2012 est.)
country comparison to the world: 75

Crude oil—exports: 0 bbl/day (2011 est.)
country comparison to the world: 194

Crude oil—imports: 885,900 bbl/day (2010 est.)
country comparison to the world: 14

Crude oil—proved reserves: 2.38 million bbl (1 January 2013 es)
country comparison to the world: 95

Refined petroleum products—production: 920,200 bbl/day (2011 est.)
country comparison to the world: 21

Refined petroleum products—consumption: 786,100 bbl/day (2011 est.)
country comparison to the world: 24

Refined petroleum products—exports: 255,000 bbl/day (2011 est.)
country comparison to the world: 25

Refined petroleum products—imports: 304,700 bbl/day (2011 est.)
country comparison to the world: 20

Natural gas—production: 330.2 million cu m (2011 est.)
country comparison to the world: 75

Natural gas—consumption: 16.37 billion cu m (2011 est.)
country comparison to the world: 38

Natural gas—exports: 0 cu m (2011 est.)
country comparison to the world: 196

Natural gas—imports: 15.9 billion cu m (2011 est.)
country comparison to the world: 24

Natural gas—proved reserves: 6.229 billion cu m (1 January 2013 es)
country comparison to the world: 88

Carbon dioxide emissions from consumption of energy: 293.3 million Mt (2011 est.)
country comparison to the world: 24

COMMUNICATIONS

Telephones—main lines in use: 15.998 million (2012)
country comparison to the world: 17

Telephones—mobile cellular: 29.455 million (2012)
country comparison to the world: 35

Telephone system: *general assessment:* provides telecommunications service for every business and private need

domestic: thoroughly modern; completely digitalized
international: country code—886; roughly 15 submarine fiber cables provide links throughout Asia, Australia, the Middle East, Europe, and the US; satellite earth stations—2 (2011)

Broadcast media: 5 nationwide television networks operating roughly 75 TV stations; about 85% of households utilize multi-channel cable TV; national and regional radio networks with about 170 radio stations (2008)

Internet country code: .tw

Internet hosts: 6.272 million (2012)
country comparison to the world: 18

Internet users: 16.147 million (2009)
country comparison to the world: 24

TRANSPORTATION

Airports: 37 (2013)
country comparison to the world: 107

Airports—with paved runways: *total:* 3 5
over 3,047 m: 8
2,438 to 3,047 m: 7
1,524 to 2,437 m: 10
914 to 1,523 m: 8
under 914 m: 2 (2013)

Airports—with unpaved runways: *total:* 2
1,524 to 2,437 m: 1
under 914 m: 1 (2013)

Heliports: 31 (2013)

Pipelines: condensate 25 km; gas 802 km; oil 241 km (2013)

Railways: *total:* 1,580 km
country comparison to the world: 79
standard gauge: 345 km 1.435-m gauge (345 km electrified)
narrow gauge: 1,085 km 1.067-m gauge (685 km electrified); 150 km 0.762-m gauge
note: the 0.762 gauge track belongs to three entities, the Forestry Bureau, Taiwan Cement, and TaiPower (2009)

Roadways: *total:* 41,475 km
country comparison to the world: 86
paved: 41,033 km (includes 720 km of expressways)
unpaved: 442 km (2009)

Merchant marine: *total:* 112
country comparison to the world: 47
by type: bulk carrier 35, cargo 20, chemical tanker 1, container 31, passenger/cargo 4, petroleum tanker 12, refrigerated cargo 7, roll on/roll off 2
foreign-owned: 3 (France 2, Vietnam 1)
registered in other countries: 579 (Argentina 2, Cambodia 1, Honduras 1, Hong Kong 25, Indonesia 1, Italy 10, Kiribati 2, Liberia 94, Marshall Islands 8, Panama 328, Philippines 1, Sierra Leone 7, Singapore 77, South Korea 1, Thailand 1, UK 11, Vanuatu 1, unknown 8) (2010)

Ports and terminals: *major seaport(s):* Chilung (Keelung), Kaohsiung, Hualian, Taichung
container port(s) (TEUs): Chilung (Keelung) (1,749,388), Kaohsiung (9,363,289), Taichung (1,383,578)

MILITARY

Military branches: Army, Navy (includes Marine Corps), Air Force, Coast Guard Administration, Armed Forces Reserve Command, Combined Service Forces Command, Armed Forces Police Command

Military service age and obligation: 18-35 years of age for compulsory and voluntary military service; service obligation is 2 years; women may enlist; women in Air Force service are restricted to noncombat roles; reserve obligation to age 30 (Army); the Ministry of Defense is in the process of implementing a voluntary enlistment system over the period 2010-2015, although nonvolunteers will still be required to perform alternative service or go through 4 months of military training (2012)

Manpower available for military service:
males age 16-49: 6,183,567
females age 16-49: 6,006,676 (2010 est.)

Manpower fit for military service:
males age 16-49: 5,074,173
females age 16-49: 4,951,088 (2010 est.)

Manpower reaching militarily significant age annually: *male:* 166,190
female: 155,306 (2010 est.)

TRANSNATIONAL ISSUES

Disputes—international: involved in complex dispute with Brunei, China, Malaysia, the Philippines, and Vietnam over the Spratly Islands, and with China and the Philippines over Scarborough Reef; the 2002 "Declaration on the Conduct of Parties in the South China Sea" has eased tensions but falls short of a legally binding "code of conduct" desired by several of the disputants; Paracel Islands are occupied by China, but claimed by Taiwan and Vietnam; in 2003, China and Taiwan became more vocal in rejecting both Japan's claims to the uninhabited islands of the Senkaku-shoto (Diaoyu Tai) and Japan's unilaterally declared exclusive economic zone in the East China Sea where all parties engage in hydrocarbon prospecting

Illicit drugs: regional transit point for heroin, methamphetamine, and precursor chemicals; transshipment point for drugs to Japan; major problem with domestic consumption of methamphetamine and heroin; rising problems with use of ketamine and club drugs

TAJIKISTAN

INTRODUCTION

Background: The Tajik people came under Russian rule in the 1860s and 1870s, but Russia's hold on Central Asia weakened following the Revolution of 1917. Bands of indigenous guerrillas (called "basmachi") fiercely contested Bolshevik control of the area, which was not fully reestablished until 1925. Tajikistan was first created as an autonomous republic within Uzbekistan in 1924, but the USSR designated Tajikistan a separate republic in 1929 and transferred to it much of present-day Sughd province. Ethnic Uzbeks form a substantial minority in Tajikistan. Tajikistan became independent in 1991 following the breakup of the Soviet Union, and experienced a civil war between regional factions from 1992 to 1997. Tajikistan endured several domestic security incidents during 2010-12, including armed conflict between government forces and local strongmen in the Rasht Valley and between government forces and criminal groups in Gorno-Badakhshan Autonomous Oblast. The country remains the poorest in the former Soviet sphere. Tajikistan became a member of the World Trade Organization in March 2013. However, its economy continues to face major challenges, including dependence on remittances from Tajikistanis working in Russia, pervasive corruption, and the major role narcotrafficking plays in the country's informal economy.

GEOGRAPHY

Location: Central Asia, west of China, south of Kyrgyzstan

Geographic coordinates: 39 00 N, 71 00 E

Map references: Asia

Area: *total:* 143,100 sq km
country comparison to the world: 96
land: 141,510 sq km
water: 2,590 sq km

Area—comparative: slightly smaller than Wisconsin

Land boundaries: *total:* 3,651 km
border countries: Afghanistan 1,206 km, China 414 km, Kyrgyzstan 870 km, Uzbekistan 1,161 km

Coastline: 0 km (landlocked)

Maritime claims: none (landlocked)

Climate: midlatitude continental, hot summers, mild winters; semiarid to polar in Pamir Mountains

Terrain: Pamir and Alay Mountains dominate landscape; western Fergana Valley in north, Kofarnihon and Vakhsh Valleys in southwest

Elevation extremes: *lowest point:* Syr Darya (Sirdaryo) 300 m
highest point: Qullai Ismoili Somoni 7,495 m

Natural resources: hydropower, some petroleum, uranium, mercury, brown coal, lead, zinc, antimony, tungsten, silver, gold

Land use: *arable land:* 5.96%
permanent crops: 0.91%
other: 93.13% (2011)

Irrigated land: 7,421 sq km (2009)

Total renewable water resources: 21.91 cu km (2011)

Freshwater withdrawal (domestic/industrial/agricultural): *total:* 11.49 cu km/yr (6%/4%/91%)
per capita: 1,740 cu m/yr (2006)

Natural hazards: earthquakes; floods

Environment—current issues: inadequate sanitation facilities; increasing levels of soil salinity; industrial pollution; excessive pesticides

Environment—international agreements: *party to:* Biodiversity, Climate Change, Climate Change-Kyoto Protocol, Desertification, Environmental Modification, Ozone Layer Protection, Wetlands
signed, but not ratified: none of the selected agreements

Geography—note: landlocked; mountainous region dominated by the Trans-Alay Range in the north and the Pamirs in the southeast; highest point, Qullai Ismoili Somoni (formerly Communism Peak), was the tallest mountain in the former USSR

PEOPLE AND SOCIETY

Nationality: *noun:* Tajikistani(s)
adjective: Tajikistani

Ethnic groups: Tajik 79.9%, Uzbek 15.3%, Russian 1.1%, Kyrgyz 1.1%, other 2.6% (2000 census)
note: estimates of Uzbek proportion can range as high as 25% depending on how mixed Tajik-Uzbek families (largely in border areas) are counted

Languages: Tajik (official), Russian widely used in government and business

Religions: Sunni Muslim 85%, Shia Muslim 5%, other 10% (2003 est.)

Population: 8,051,512 (July 2014 est.)
country comparison to the world: 97

Age structure:
0-14 years: 33% (male 1,352,150/female 1,304,615)
15-24 years: 20.1% (male 819,936/female 796,211)
25-54 years: 38.9% (male 1,547,863/female 1,586,218)
55-64 years: 3.2% (male 178,161/female 210,616)
65 years and over: 3.2% (male 107,137/female 148,605) (2014 est.)

Dependency ratios:
total dependency ratio: 64.1 %
youth dependency ratio: 58.9 %
elderly dependency ratio: 5.2 %
potential support ratio: 19.1 (2013)

Median age: *total:* 23.5 years
male: 23 years
female: 24 years (2014 est.)

Population growth rate: 1.75% (2014 est.)
country comparison to the world: 69

Birth rate: 24.99 births/1,000 population (2014 est.)
country comparison to the world: 56

Death rate: 6.28 deaths/1,000 population (2014 est.)
country comparison to the world: 158

Net migration rate: -1.17 migrant(s)/1,000 population (2014 est.)
country comparison to the world: 152

Urbanization: *urban population:* 26.5% of total population (2011)
rate of urbanization: 1.66% annual rate of change (2010-15 est.)

Major urban areas—population: DUSHANBE (capital) 704,000 (2009)

Sex ratio: *at birth:* 1.05 male(s)/female
0-14 years: 1.04 male(s)/female
15-24 years: 1.03 male(s)/female
25-54 years: 0.98 male(s)/female
55-64 years: 0.99 male(s)/female
65 years and over: 0.73 male(s)/female
total population: 0.99 male(s)/female (2014 est.)

Mother's mean age at first birth: 22.8
note: median age at first birth among women 25-29 (2012 est.)

Maternal mortality rate: 65 deaths/100,000 live births (2010)
country comparison to the world: 93

Infant mortality rate: *total:* 35.03 deaths/1,000 live births
country comparison to the world: 64
male: 39.42 deaths/1,000 live births
female: 30.42 deaths/1,000 live births (2014 est.)

Life expectancy at birth:
total population: 67.06 years
country comparison to the world: 166
male: 63.96 years
female: 70.32 years (2014 est.)

Total fertility rate: 2.76 children born/woman (2014 est.)
country comparison to the world: 71

Contraceptive prevalence rate: 27.9% (2012)

Health expenditures: 5.8% of GDP (2011)
country comparison to the world: 117

Physicians density: 1.9 physicians/1,000 population (2011)

Hospital bed density: 5.5 beds/1,000 population (2011)

Drinking water source:
improved:
urban: 91.8% of population
rural: 56.5% of population
total: 65.9% of population
unimproved:
urban: 8.2% of population
rural: 43.5% of population
total: 34.1% of population (2011 est.)

Sanitation facility access:
improved:
urban: 95.4% of population
rural: 94.4% of population
total: 94.7% of population
unimproved:
urban: 4.6% of population
rural: 5.6% of population
total: 5.3% of population (2011 est.)

HIV/AIDS—adult prevalence rate: 0.3% (2012 est.)
country comparison to the world: 94

HIV/AIDS—people living with HIV/AIDS: 11,900 (2012 est.)

country comparison to the world: 98

HIV/AIDS—deaths: 500 (2012 est.)
country comparison to the world: 87

Major infectious diseases:
degree of risk: high
food or waterborne diseases: bacterial diarrhea, hepatitis A, and typhoid fever
vectorborne disease: malaria (2013)

Obesity—adult prevalence rate: 8.6% (2008)
country comparison to the world: 136

Children under the age of 5 years underweight: 15% (2007)
country comparison to the world: 49

Education expenditures: 3.9% of GDP (2011)
country comparison to the world: 114

Literacy: *definition:* age 15 and over can read and write
total population: 99.7%
male: 99.8%
female: 99.6% (2011 est.)

School life expectancy (primary to tertiary education): *total:* 11 years
male: 12 years
female: 10 years (2011)

Child labor—children ages 5-14:
total number: 164,432
percentage: 10 % (2005 est.)

Unemployment, youth ages 15-24: *total:* 16.7%
country comparison to the world: 77
male: 19.2%
female: 13.7% (2009)

GOVERNMENT

Country name: *conventional long form:* Republic of Tajikistan
conventional short form: Tajikistan
local long form: Jumhurii Tojikiston
local short form: Tojikiston
former: Tajik Soviet Socialist Republic

Government type: republic

Capital: *name:* Dushanbe

geographic coordinates: 38 33 N, 68 46 E
time difference: UTC+5 (10 hours ahead of Washington, DC during Standard Time)

Administrative divisions: 2 provinces (viloyatho, singular—viloyat), 1 autonomous province* (viloyati mukhtor), 1 capital region** (viloyati poytakht), and 1 area referred to as Districts Under Republic Administration***; Dushanbe**, Khatlon (Qurghonteppa), Kuhistoni Badakhshon [Gorno-Badakhshan]* (Khorugh), Nohiyahoi Tobei Jumhuri***, Sughd (Khujand)
note: the administrative center name follows in parentheses

Independence: 9 September 1991 (from the Soviet Union)

National holiday: Independence Day (or National Day), 9 September (1991)

Constitution: several previous; latest adopted 6 November 1994; amended 1999, 2003 (2009)

Legal system: civil law system

International law organization participation: has not submitted an ICJ jurisdiction declaration; accepts ICCt jurisdiction

Suffrage: 18 years of age; universal

Executive branch: *chief of state:* President Emomali RAHMON (since 6 November 1994; head of state and Supreme Assembly chairman since 19 November 1992)
head of government: Prime Minister Qohir RASULZODA (since 23 November 2013); First Deputy Prime Minister Davlatali SAIDOV (since 19 November 2013)
cabinet: Council of Ministers appointed by the president, approved by the Supreme Assembly (For more information visit the World Leaders website)
elections: president elected by popular vote for a seven-year term (technically eligible for two terms); election last held on 6 November 2013 (next to be held in November 2020); prime minister appointed by the president
election results: Emomali RAHMON reelected president; percent of vote—Emomali RAHMON 83.9%, Ismoil TALBAKOV 5%, other 11.1%

Legislative branch: bicameral Supreme Assembly or Majlisi Oli consists of the National Assembly (upper chamber) or Majlisi Milli (34 seats; 25 members selected by local deputies, 8 appointed by the president; 1 seat reserved for the former president; members serve five-year terms) and the Assembly of Representatives (lower chamber) or Majlisi Namoyandagon (63 seats; 41 members elected through constituencies, 22 members elected through party selection; members serve five-year terms)
elections: National Assembly—last held on 28 February 2010 (next to be held in February 2015); Assembly of Representatives—last held on 28 February 2010 (next to be held in February 2015)
election results: National Assembly—percent of vote by party—NA; seats by party—NA;

Assembly of Representatives—percent of vote by party—PDPT 71%, IRPT 8.2%, CPT 7%, APT 5.1%, PERT 5.1%, other 3.6%; seats by party—PDPT 55, IRPT 2, CPT 2, APT 2, PERT 2

Judicial branch: *highest court(s):* Supreme Court (consists of the chairman, deputy chairmen, and 34 judges organized into civil, criminal, and military chambers); Constitutional Court (consists of the court chairman, vice-president, and 5 judges); High Economic Court (consists 16 judicial positions)
judge selection and term of office: Supreme Court, Constitutional Court, and High Economic Court judges nominated by the president of the republic and approved by the National Assembly; judges of all three courts appointed for 10-year renewable terms with no limit on terms, but last appointment must occur before the age of 65
subordinate courts: regional and district courts; Dushanbe City Court; viloyat (province level) courts; Court of Gorno-Badakhshan Autonomous Region

Political parties and leaders: Agrarian Party of Tajikistan or APT [Amir QARAQULOV]; Communist Party of Tajikistan or CPT [Shodi SHABDOLOV]; Democratic Party of Tajikistan [Saidjafar ISMONOV]; Islamic Revival Party of Tajikistan or IRPT [Muhiddin KABIRI]; Party of Economic Reform of Tajikistan or PERT [Olimjon BOBOEV]; People's Democratic Party of Tajikistan or PDPT [Emomali RAHMON]; Social Democratic Party of Tajikistan or SDPT [Rahmatullo ZOYIROV]; Socialist Party of Tajikistan or SPT [Abduhalim GHAFOROV]

Political pressure groups and leaders: influential religious leader Akbar TURAJONZODA; unregistered Youth Party of Tajikistan [Izzat AMON]; unregistered opposition group Guruhi-24 (Group-24) [Umarali QUVVATOV]; Vatandor (Patriot) Movement [Dodojon ATOVULLOEV]; unregistered presidential candidate of Union of Reformist Forces of Tajikistan Oynihol BOBONAZAROVA; unregistered New Tajikistan party [Zayd SAIDOV]

International organization participation: ADB, CICA, CIS, CSTO, EAEC, EAPC, EBRD, ECO, FAO, G-77, GCTU, IAEA, IBRD, ICAO, ICC (NGOs), ICRM, IDA, IDB, IFAD, IFC, IFRCS, ILO, IMF, Interpol, IOC, IOM, IPU, ISO (correspondent), ITSO, ITU, MIGA, MINUSMA, NAM (observer), OIC, OPCW, OSCE, PFP, SCO, UN, UNCTAD, UNESCO, UNIDO, UNWTO, UPU, WCO, WFTU (NGOs), WHO, WIPO, WMO, WTO

Diplomatic representation in the US:
chief of mission: Ambassador Nuriddin SHAMSOV (since 30 July 2012)
chancery: 1005 New Hampshire Avenue NW, Washington, DC 20037
telephone: [1] (202) 223-6090
FAX: [1] (202) 223-6091

Diplomatic representation from the US:
chief of mission: Ambassador Susan M. ELLIOTT (since 25 July 2012)
embassy: 109-A Ismoili Somoni Avenue, Dushanbe 734019
mailing address: 7090 Dushanbe Place, Dulles, VA 20189
telephone: [992] (37) 229-20-00
FAX: [992] (37) 229-20-50

Flag description: three horizontal stripes of red (top), a wider stripe of white, and green; a gold crown surmounted by seven gold, five-pointed stars is located in the center of the white stripe; red represents the sun, victory, and the unity of the nation, white stands for purity, cotton, and mountain snows, while green is the color of Islam and the bounty of nature; the crown symbolizes the Tajik people; the seven stars signify the Tajik magic number "seven"—a symbol of perfection and the embodiment of happiness

National symbol(s): crown surmounted by seven, five-pointed stars

National anthem: *name:* "Surudi milli" (National Anthem)
lyrics/music: Gulnazar KELDI/Suleiman YUDAKOV
note: adopted 1991; after the fall of the Soviet Union, Tajikistan kept the music of the anthem from its time as a Soviet republic but adopted new lyrics

ECONOMY

Economy—overview: Tajikistan has one of the lowest per capita GDPs among the 15 former Soviet republics. The 1992-1997 civil war severely damaged an already weak economic infrastructure and caused a sharp decline in industrial and agricultural production. Because of a lack of employment opportunities in Tajikistan, more than one million Tajik citizens work abroad—roughly 90% in Russia—supporting families in Tajikistan through remittances. Less than 7% of the land area is arable and cotton is the most important crop. Until 2008, cotton production was closely monitored and controlled by the government. In the wake of the National Bank of Tajikistan's admission in December 2007 that it had directed the AgroInvestBank to improperly lend money to politically connected investors in the cotton sector, the IMF canceled its stand-by assistance program in Tajikistan. As part of the Tajik government's subsequent reforms, over a half billion dollars in farmer debt has been forgiven. In 2008 Tajikistan passed new law authorizing farmers to decide for themselves what crops to grow, and this has resulted in a gradual decrease in cotton output. Tajikistan imports approximately 60% of its food, most of which comes by rail. Uzbekistan closed one of the rail lines into Tajikistan in late 2011, hampering the transit of goods to and from the southern part of the country. As a result, food and fuel prices increased to the highest levels since 2002. Mineral resources include silver, gold, uranium, and tungsten. Industry consists mainly of small obsolete factories in food processing and light industry, substantial hydropower facilities, and a large aluminum plant—currently operating below 25% of capacity. Electricity output expanded with the completion of the Sangtuda-1 hydropower dam—finished in 2009 with Russian investment. The smaller Sangtuda-2 hydropower dam, built with Iranian investment, began operating in 2012 at a limited capacity. The Tajik government is tens of millions of dollars in arrears for both Sangtuda dams, and Sangtuda-2 has been closed for "maintenance" since January 2014. The government is pinning its drive for energy independence on completion of the Roghun dam, which is scheduled for mid-2014. In 2010, the government began a coerced sale of shares in the Roghun enterprise to its population, ultimately raising over $180 million before stopping under intense criticism from international donors, but the dam is likely to cost billions of dollars. The World Bank funded two feasibility studies (technical-economic, and social-environmental) for the dam. If built according to plan, Roghun will be the tallest dam in the world, will operate year around, and will significantly expand Tajikistan's electricity output. In 2013, the Tajik government finalized an agreement to import one million tons of fuel and oil products from Russia each year, at reduced prices. Tajikistan's economic situation remains fragile due to uneven implementation of structural reforms, corruption, weak governance, seasonal power shortages, and its large external debt burden.

GDP (purchasing power parity): $19.2 billion (2013 est.)
country comparison to the world: 137
$17.88 billion (2012 est.)
$16.63 billion (2011 est.)
note: data are in 2013 US dollars

GDP (official exchange rate): $8.513 billion (2013 est.)

GDP—real growth rate: 7.4% (2013 est.)
country comparison to the world: 18
7.5% (2012 est.)
7.4% (2011 est.)

GDP—per capita (PPP): $2,300 (2013 est.)
country comparison to the world: 189
$2,200 (2012 est.)
$2,100 (211 est.)
note: data are in 2013 US dollars

Gross national saving: 12.4% of GDP (2013 est.)
country comparison to the world: 125
17.8% of GDP (2012 est.)
10% of GDP (2011 est.)

GDP—composition, by end use:
household consumption: 97%
government consumption: 12%
investment in fixed capital: 14%
investment in inventories: 6.7%
exports of goods and services: 13.7%
imports of goods and services: -48.5% (2013 est.)

GDP—composition, by sector of origin:
agriculture: 21.1%
industry: 23.2%
services: 55.7% (2013 est.)

Agriculture—products: cotton, grain, fruits, grapes, vegetables; cattle, sheep, goats

Industries: aluminum, cement, vegetable oil

Industrial production growth rate: 3.9% (2013 est.)
country comparison to the world: 76

Labor force: 2.209 million (2013 est.)
country comparison to the world: 118

Labor force—by occupation: *agriculture:* 46.5%
industry: 10.7%
services: 42.8% (2013 est.)

Unemployment rate: 2.5% (2013 est.)
country comparison to the world: 20
2.5% (2012 est.)
note: official rates; actual unemployment is much higher

Population below poverty line: 35.6% (2013 est.)

Household income or consumption by percentage share: *lowest 10%:* NA%
highest 10%: NA% (2009 est.)

Distribution of family income—Gini index: 32.6 (2006)
country comparison to the world: 104
34.7 (1998)

Budget: *revenues:* $2.425 billion
expenditures: $2.423 billion (2013 est.)

Taxes and other revenues: 28.5% of GDP (2013 est.)
country comparison to the world: 102

Budget surplus (+) or deficit (-):
0% of GDP (2013 est.)
country comparison to the world: 43

Public debt: 6.5% of GDP
country comparison to the world: 154
NA%

Fiscal year: calendar year

Inflation rate (consumer prices): 3.7% (2013 est.)
country comparison to the world: 124
5.8% (2012 est.)

Central bank discount rate: 4.8% (31 December 2013 est.)
country comparison to the world: 54
6.5% (31 December 2012 est.)

Commercial bank prime lending rate: 22% (31 December 2013 est.)
country comparison to the world: 29
17.13% (31 December 2012 est.)

Stock of narrow money: $1.044 billion (31 December 2013 est.)
country comparison to the world: 150
$1.191 billion (31 December 2012 est.)

Stock of broad money: $2.033 billion (31 December 2013 est.)
country comparison to the world: 149
$1.555 billion (31 December 2012 est.)

Stock of domestic credit: $1.611 billion (31 December 2013 est.)
country comparison to the world: 140
$1.196 billion (31 December 2012 est.)

Market value of publicly traded shares: $NA
$NA
$NA

Current account balance: -$330 million (2013 est.)
country comparison to the world: 92
-$246.2 million (2012 est.)

Exports: $1.163 billion (2013 est.)
country comparison to the world: 154
$826.6 million (2012 est.)

Exports—commodities: aluminum, electricity, cotton, fruits, vegetable oil, textiles

Exports—partners: Turkey 40.7%, Russia 10.6%, Iran 9.9%, Afghanistan 8.7%, China 7.4%, Kazakhstan 7.4%, Switzerland 6.6% (2012 est.)

Imports: $4.121 billion (2013 est.)
country comparison to the world: 137
$3.778 billion (2012 est.)

Imports—commodities: petroleum products, aluminum oxide, machinery and equipment, foodstuffs

Imports—partners: Russia 22%, Kazakhstan 15.2%, China 14.5%, Lithuania 4.7%, Kyrgyzstan 4.4%, Turkey 4.4%, Iran 4.3% (2012 est.)

Reserves of foreign exchange and gold: $1.072 billion (31 December 2013 est.)
country comparison to the world: 133
$972 million (31 December 2012 est.)

Debt—external: $2.162 billion (31 December 2013 est.)
country comparison to the world: 142
$3.439 billion (31 December 2012 est.)

Stock of direct foreign investment—at home: $2.272 billion (31 December 2013 est.)
country comparison to the world: 97

Stock of direct foreign investment—abroad: $NA (31 December 2010 est.)
$16.3 billion (31 December 2009 est.)

Exchange rates: Tajikistani somoni (TJS) per US dollar—
4.76 (2013 est.)
4.76 (2012 est.)
4.379 (2010 est.)
4.1428 (2009)
3.4563 (2008)

ENERGY

Electricity—production: 17.09 billion kWh (2013 est.)
country comparison to the world: 78

Electricity—consumption: 16.09 billion kWh (2013 est.)
country comparison to the world: 75

Electricity—exports: 1 billion kWh (2013 est.)
country comparison to the world: 57

Electricity—imports: 300.5 million kWh (2012 est.)
country comparison to the world: 81

Electricity—installed generating capacity: 4.476 million kW (2013 est.)
country comparison to the world: 77

Electricity—from fossil fuels: 9% of total installed capacity (2013 est.)
country comparison to the world: 197

Electricity—from nuclear fuels: 0% of total installed capacity (2013 est.)
country comparison to the world: 185

Electricity—from hydroelectric plants: 91% of total installed capacity (2013 est.)
country comparison to the world: 12

Electricity—from other renewable sources: 0% of total installed capacity (2013 est.)
country comparison to the world: 126

Crude oil—production: 553 bbl/day (2013 est.)
country comparison to the world: 114

Crude oil—exports: 0 bbl/day (2013 est.)
country comparison to the world: 188

Crude oil—imports: 0 bbl/day (2013 est.)
country comparison to the world: 125

Crude oil—proved reserves: 12 million bbl (1 January 2013 es)
country comparison to the world: 88

Refined petroleum products—production: 400 bbl/day
country comparison to the world: 113

Refined petroleum products—consumption: 20,090 bbl/day (2013 est.)
country comparison to the world: 127

Refined petroleum products—exports: 500 bbl/day (2013 est.)
country comparison to the world: 114

Refined petroleum products—imports: 20,090 bbl/day (2013 est.)
country comparison to the world: 106

Natural gas—production: 3.928 million cu m (2013 est.)
country comparison to the world: 94

Natural gas—consumption: 3.928 million cu m (2013 est.)
country comparison to the world: 113

Natural gas—exports: 0 cu m (2013 est.)
country comparison to the world: 189

Natural gas—imports: 0 cu m (2013 est.)
country comparison to the world: 134

Natural gas—proved reserves: 5.663 billion cu m (1 January 2013 es)
country comparison to the world: 92

Carbon dioxide emissions from consumption of energy: 2.618 million Mt (2013 est.)
country comparison to the world: 142

COMMUNICATIONS

Telephones—main lines in use: 393,000 (2012)
country comparison to the world: 106

Telephones—mobile cellular: 6.528 million (2012)
country comparison to the world: 98

Telephone system: *general assessment:* foreign investment in the telephone system has resulted in major improvements; conversion of the existing fixed network from analogue to digital was completed in 2012
domestic: fixed line availability has not changed significantly since 1998 while mobile cellular subscribership, aided by competition among multiple operators, has expanded rapidly; coverage now extends to all major cities and towns
international: country code—992; linked by cable and microwave radio relay to other CIS republics and by leased connections to the Moscow international gateway switch; Dushanbe linked by Intelsat to international gateway switch in Ankara (Turkey); satellite earth stations—3 (2 Intelsat and 1 Orbita) (2011)

Broadcast media: state-run TV broadcaster transmits nationally on 4 stations and regionally on 4 stations; 11 independent TV stations broadcast locally and regionally; some households are able to receive Russian and other foreign stations via cable and satellite; state-run radio broadcaster operates Radio Tajikistan, Voice of Dushanbe, and several regional stations; a small number of independent radio stations (2010)

Internet country code: .tj

Internet hosts: 6,258 (2012)
country comparison to the world: 142

Internet users: 700,000 (2009)
country comparison to the world: 110

TRANSPORTATION

Airports: 24 (2013)
country comparison to the world: 131

Airports—with paved runways: *total:* 17
over 3,047 m: 2
2,438 to 3,047 m: 4
1,524 to 2,437 m: 5
914 to 1,523 m: 3
under 914 m: 3 (2013)

Airports—with unpaved runways: *total:* 7
1,524 to 2,437 m: 1
914 to 1,523 m: 1
under 914 m: 5 (2013)

Pipelines: gas 549 km; oil 38 km (2013)

Railways: *total:* 680 km
country comparison to the world: 103

broad gauge: 680 km 1.520-m gauge (2008)

Roadways: *total:* 27,767 km (2000)
country comparison to the world: 98

Waterways: 200 km (along Vakhsh River) (2011)
country comparison to the world: 99

MILITARY

Military branches: Ground Forces, Air and Air Defense Forces, Mobile Forces (2013)

Military service age and obligation: 18-27 years of age for compulsory or voluntary military service; 2-year conscript service obligation; males required to undergo compulsory military training between ages 16 and 55; males can enroll in military schools from at least age 15 (2012)

Manpower available for military service:
males age 16-49: 2,012,790
females age 16-49: 2,020,618 (2010 est.)

Manpower fit for military service:
males age 16-49: 1,490,267
females age 16-49: 1,675,083 (2010 est.)

Manpower reaching militarily significant age annually: *male:* 76,430
female: 74,038 (2010 est.)

TRANSNATIONAL ISSUES

Disputes—international: in 2006, China and Tajikistan pledged to commence demarcation of the revised boundary agreed to in the delimitation of 2002; talks continue with Uzbekistan to delimit border and remove minefields; disputes in Isfara Valley delay delimitation with Kyrgyzstan

Refugees and internally displaced persons: *stateless persons:* 2,300 (2012)

Illicit drugs: major transit country for Afghan narcotics bound for Russian and, to a lesser extent, Western European markets; limited illicit cultivation of opium poppy for domestic consumption; Tajikistan seizes roughly 80% of all drugs captured in Central Asia and stands third worldwide in seizures of opiates (heroin and raw opium); significant consumer of opiates

TANZANIA

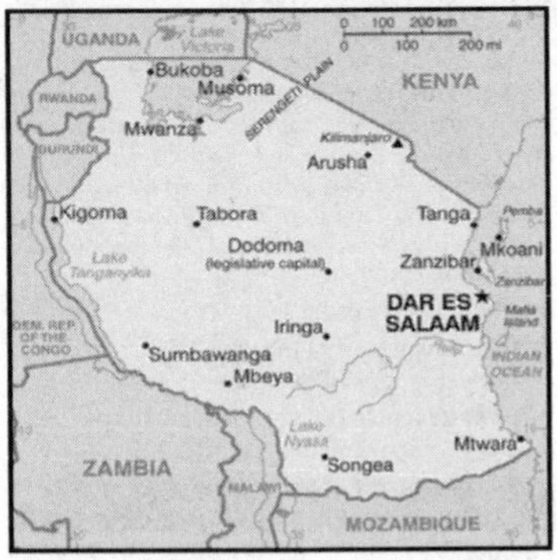

INTRODUCTION

Background: Shortly after achieving independence from Britain in the early 1960s, Tanganyika and Zanzibar merged to form the nation of Tanzania in 1964. One-party rule ended in 1995 with the first democratic elections held in the country since the 1970s. Zanzibar's semi-autonomous status and popular opposition led to two contentious elections since 1995, which the ruling party won despite international observers' claims of voting irregularities. The formation of a government of national unity between Zanzibar's two leading parties succeeded in minimizing electoral tension in 2010.

GEOGRAPHY

Location: Eastern Africa, bordering the Indian Ocean, between Kenya and Mozambique

Geographic coordinates: 6 00 S, 35 00 E

Map references: Africa

Area: *total:* 947,300 sq km
country comparison to the world: 31
land: 885,800 sq km
water: 61,500 sq km
note: includes the islands of Mafia, Pemba, and Zanzibar

Area—comparative: slightly larger than twice the size of California

Land boundaries: *total:* 3,861 km
border countries: Burundi 451 km, Democratic Republic of the Congo 459 km, Kenya 769 km, Malawi 475 km, Mozambique 756 km, Rwanda 217 km, Uganda 396 km, Zambia 338 km

Coastline: 1,424 km

Maritime claims: *territorial sea:* 12 nm
exclusive economic zone: 200 nm

Climate: varies from tropical along coast to temperate in highlands

Terrain: plains along coast; central plateau; highlands in north, south

Elevation extremes: *lowest point:* Indian Ocean 0 m
highest point: Kilimanjaro 5,895 m (highest point in Africa)

Natural resources: hydropower, tin, phosphates, iron ore, coal, diamonds, gemstones, gold, natural gas, nickel

Land use: *arable land:* 12.25%
permanent crops: 1.79%
other: 85.96% (2011)

Irrigated land: 1,843 sq km (2003)

Total renewable water resources: 96.27 cu km (2011)

Freshwater withdrawal (domestic/industrial/agricultural): *total:* 5.18 cu km/yr (10%/0%/89%)
per capita: 144.7 cu m/yr (2002)

Natural hazards: flooding on the central plateau during the rainy season; drought
volcanism: limited volcanic activity; Ol Doinyo Lengai (elev. 2,962 m) has emitted lava in recent years; other historically active volcanoes include Kieyo and Meru

Environment—current issues: soil degradation; deforestation; desertification; destruction of coral reefs threatens marine habitats; recent droughts affected marginal agriculture; wildlife threatened by illegal hunting and trade, especially for ivory

Environment—international agreements: *party to:* Biodiversity, Climate Change, Climate Change-Kyoto Protocol, Desertification, Endangered Species, Hazardous Wastes, Law of the Sea, Ozone Layer Protection, Wetlands
signed, but not ratified: none of the selected agreements

Geography—note: Kilimanjaro is the highest point in Africa and one of only two mountains on the continent that has glaciers (the other is Mount Kenya); bordered by three of the largest lakes on the continent: Lake Victoria (the world's second-largest freshwater lake) in the north, Lake Tanganyika (the world's second deepest) in the west, and Lake Nyasa (Lake Malawi) in the southwest

PEOPLE AND SOCIETY

Nationality: *noun:* Tanzanian(s)
adjective: Tanzanian

Ethnic groups: mainland—African 99% (of which 95% are Bantu consisting of more than 130 tribes), other 1% (consisting of Asian, European, and Arab); Zanzibar—Arab, African, mixed Arab and African

Languages: Kiswahili or Swahili (official), Kiunguja (name for Swahili in Zanzibar), English (official, primary language of commerce, administration, and higher education), Arabic (widely spoken in Zanzibar), many local languages
note: Kiswahili (Swahili) is the mother tongue of the Bantu people living in Zanzibar and nearby coastal Tanzania; although Kiswahili is Bantu in structure and origin, its vocabulary draws on a variety of sources including Arabic and English; it has become the lingua franca of central and eastern Africa; the first language of most people is one of the local languages

Religions: mainland—Christian 30%, Muslim 35%, indigenous beliefs 35%; Zanzibar—more than 99% Muslim

Population: 49,639,138 (July 2014 est.)
country comparison to the world: 26
note: estimates for this country explicitly take into account the effects of excess mortality due to AIDS; this can result in lower life expectancy, higher infant mortality, higher death rates, lower population growth rates, and changes in the distribution of population by age and sex than would otherwise be expected

Age structure:
0-14 years: 44.6% (male 11,173,655/female 10,962,186)
15-24 years: 19.5% (male 4,838,216/female 4,841,338)
25-54 years: 29.5% (male 7,340,129/female 7,289,483)
55-64 years: 2.9% (male 745,214/female 985,524)
65 years and over: 2.9% (male 629,483/female 833,910) (2014 est.)

Dependency ratios:
total dependency ratio: 92.5 %
youth dependency ratio: 86.3 %
elderly dependency ratio: 6.2 %
potential support ratio: 16.2 (2013)

Median age: *total:* 17.4 years
male: 17.1 years
female: 17.7 years (2014 est.)

Population growth rate: 2.8% (2014 est.)
country comparison to the world: 18

Birth rate: 36.82 births/1,000 population (2014 est.)
country comparison to the world: 17

Death rate: 8.2 deaths/1,000 population (2014 est.)
country comparison to the world: 93

Net migration rate: -0.57 migrant(s)/1,000 population (2014 est.)
country comparison to the world: 136

Urbanization: *urban population:* 26.7% of total population (2011)
rate of urbanization: 4.77% annual rate of change (2010-15 est.)

Major urban areas—population: DAR ES SALAAM (capital) 3.207 million (2009)

Sex ratio: *at birth:* 1.03 male(s)/female
0-14 years: 1.02 male(s)/female
15-24 years: 1 male(s)/female
25-54 years: 1.01 male(s)/female
55-64 years: 0.99 male(s)/female
65 years and over: 0.76 male(s)/female
total population: 0.99 male(s)/female (2014 est.)

Mother's mean age at first birth: 19.6
note: median age at first birth among women 25-29 (2010 est.)

Maternal mortality rate: 460 deaths/100,000 live births (2010)

country comparison to the world: 23

Infant mortality rate: *total:* 43.74 deaths/1,000 live births
country comparison to the world: 49
male: 45.78 deaths/1,000 live births
female: 41.64 deaths/1,000 live births (2014 est.)

Life expectancy at birth:
total population: 61.24 years
country comparison to the world: 190
male: 59.91 years
female: 62.62 years (2014 est.)

Total fertility rate: 4.95 children born/woman (2014 est.)
country comparison to the world: 17

Contraceptive prevalence rate:
34.4% (2009/10)

Health expenditures: 7.3% of GDP (2011)
country comparison to the world: 78

Physicians density: 0.01 physicians/1,000 population (2006)

Hospital bed density: 0.7 beds/1,000 population (2010)

Drinking water source:
improved:
urban: 78.7% of population
rural: 44.1% of population
total: 53.3% of population
unimproved:
urban: 21.3% of population
rural: 55.9% of population
total: 46.7% of population (2011 est.)
Sanitation facility access:
improved:
urban: 24.2% of population
rural: 7.4% of population
total: 11.9% of population
unimproved:
urban: 75.8% of population
rural: 92.6% of population
total: 88.1% of population (2011 est.)

HIV/AIDS—adult prevalence rate: 5.1% (2012 est.)
country comparison to the world: 13

HIV/AIDS—people living with HIV/AIDS: 1,472,400 (2012 est.)
country comparison to the world: 7

HIV/AIDS—deaths: 80,000 (2012 est.)
country comparison to the world: 4

Major infectious diseases:
degree of risk: very high
food or waterborne diseases: bacterial diarrhea, hepatitis A, and typhoid fever
vectorborne diseases: malaria, dengue fever, and Rift Valley fever
water contact diseases: schistosomiasis and leptospirosis
animal contact disease: rabies (2013)

Obesity—adult prevalence rate: 5% (2008)
country comparison to the world: 156

Children under the age of 5 years underweight: 16.2% (2010)
country comparison to the world: 44

Education expenditures: 6.2% of GDP (2010)
country comparison to the world: 37

Literacy: *definition:* age 15 and over can read and write Kiswahili (Swahili), English, or Arabic
total population: 67.8%
male: 75.5%
female: 60.8% (2010 est.)

School life expectancy (primary to tertiary education): *total:* 9 years
male: 9 years
female: 9 years (2012)

Child labor—children ages 5-14:
total number: 2,815,085
percentage: 21 %
note: data represents children ages 5-17 and does not in (2006 est.)

Unemployment, youth ages 15-24: *total:* 7.1% (2011)
country comparison to the world: 129

GOVERNMENT

Country name: *conventional long form:* United Republic of Tanzania
conventional short form: Tanzania
local long form: Jamhuri ya Muungano wa Tanzania
local short form: Tanzania
former: United Republic of Tanganyika and Zanzibar

Government type: republic

Capital: *name:* Dar es Salaam

geographic coordinates: 6 48 S, 39 17 E
time difference: UTC+3 (8 hours ahead of Washington, DC during Standard Time)
note: legislative offices have been transferred to Dodoma, which is planned as the new national capital, and the National Assembly now meets there on a regular basis; the Executive Branch with all ministries and diplomatic representation remains located in Dar es Salaam

Administrative divisions: 30 regions; Arusha, Dar es Salaam, Dodoma, Geita, Iringa, Kagera, Kaskazini Pemba (Pemba North), Kaskazini Unguja (Zanzibar North), Katavi, Kigoma, Kilimanjaro, Kusini Pemba (Pemba South), Kusini Unguja (Zanzibar Central/South), Lindi, Manyara, Mara, Mbeya, Mjini Magharibi (Zanzibar Urban/West), Morogoro, Mtwara, Mwanza, Njombe, Pwani (Coast), Rukwa, Ruvuma, Shinyanga, Simiyu, Singida, Tabora, Tanga

Independence: 26 April 1964; Tanganyika became independent on 9 December 1961 (from UK-administered UN trusteeship); Zanzibar became independent on 10 December 1963 (from UK); Tanganyika united with Zanzibar on 26 April 1964 to form the United Republic of Tanganyika and Zanzibar; renamed United Republic of Tanzania on 29 October 1964

National holiday: Union Day (Tanganyika and Zanzibar), 26 April (1964)

Constitution: several previous; latest adopted 25 April 1977; amended many times, last in 2012; note—in 2012, the Tanzania Constitutional Review Commission was formed, and in June 2013, completed the first draft of a new constitution (2013)

Legal system: English common law; judicial review of legislative acts limited to matters of interpretation International law organization participation: has not submitted an ICJ jurisdiction declaration; accepts ICCt jurisdiction

Suffrage: 18 years of age; universal

Executive branch: *chief of state:* President Jakaya KIKWETE (since 21 December 2005); Vice President Mohammed Gharib BILAL (since 6 November 2010); note—the president is both chief of state and head of government
head of government: President Jakaya KIKWETE (since 21 December 2005); Vice President Mohammed Gharib BILAL (since 6 November 2010)
note: Zanzibar elects a president who is head of government for matters internal to Zanzibar; Ali Mohamed SHEIN elected to that office on 31 October 2010, sworn in 3 November 2010
cabinet: Cabinet appointed by the president from among the members of the National Assembly (For more information visit the World Leaders website)
elections: president and vice president elected on the same ballot by popular vote for five-year terms (eligible for a second term); election last held on 31 October 2010 (next to be held in 2015); prime minister appointed by the president
election results: Jakaya KIKWETE elected president; percent of vote—Jakaya KIKWETE 61.2%, Willibrod SLAA 26.3%, Ibrahim LIPUMBA 8.1%, other 4.4%

Legislative branch: unicameral National Assembly or Bunge (357 seats; 239 members elected by popular vote, 102 allocated to women nominated by the president, 5 to members of the Zanzibar House of Representatives; members serve five-year terms, up to 10 additional members appointed by the president, 1 seat reserved for the Attorney General); note—in addition to enacting laws that apply to the entire United Republic of Tanzania, the Assembly enacts laws that apply only to the mainland; Zanzibar has its own House of Representatives with jurisdiction exclusive to Zanzibar (the Zanzibar House of Representatives has 50 seats; members elected by universal suffrage to serve five-year terms)
elections: last held on 31 October 2010 (next to be held in 2015)
election results: National Assembly—percent of vote by party—NA; seats by party—CCM 259, CHADEMA 48, CUF 34, NCCR-M 4, other 7, Zanzibar representatives 5; Zanzibar House of Representatives—percent of vote by party—NA; seats by party—CCM 28, CUF 22

Judicial branch: *highest court(s):* Court of Appeal of the United Republic of Tanzania (consists of the chief justice and 14 justices); High Court of the United Republic for Mainland Tanzania (consists of the principal judge and 30 judges organized into commercial, land, and labor courts); High Court of Zanzibar (consists of the chief justice and NA judges)
judge selection and term of office: Court of Appeal and High Court justices appointed by the national president after consultation with the Judicial Service Commission for Tanzania, a judicial body of high level judges and 2 members appointed by the national president; Court of Appeal and High Court judges appointed until mandatory retirement at age 60 but can extended; High Court of Zanzibar judges appointed by the national president after consultation with the Judicial Commission of Zanzibar; judge tenure NA
subordinate courts: Resident Magistrates Courts; Kadhi courts (for Islamic family matters); district and primary courts

Political parties and leaders: Chama Cha Demokrasia na Maendeleo (Party of Democracy and Development) or CHADEMA [Willibrod SLAA]; Chama Cha Mapinduzi or CCM (Revolutionary Party) [Jakaya Mrisho KIKWETE]; Civic United Front or CUF [Ibrahim LIPUMBA]; Democratic Party or DP [Christopher MTIKLA] (unregistered) National Convention for Construction and Reform—Mageuzi or NCCR-M [Hashim RUNGWE]; Tanzania Labor Party or TLP [Mutamwega MUGAHWYA]; United Democratic Party or UDP [Fahma DOVUTWA]

Political pressure groups and leaders: Economic and Social Research Foundation or ESRF; Free Zanzibar; Tanzania Media Women's Association or TAMWA

International organization participation: ACP, AfDB, AU, C, CD, EAC, EADB, EITI (candidate country), FAO, G-77, IAEA, IBRD,

ICAO, ICC (NGOs), ICRM, IDA, IFAD, IFC, IFRCS, ILO, IMF, IMO, IMSO, Interpol, IOC, IOM, IPU, ISO, ITSO, ITU, ITUC (NGOs), MIGA, MONUSCO, NAM, OPCW, SADC, UN, UNAMID, UNCTAD, UNESCO, UNHCR, UNIDO, UNIFIL, UNISFA, UNMISS, UNOCI, UNWTO, UPU, WCO, WFTU (NGOs), WHO, WIPO, WMO, WTO

Diplomatic representation in the US:
chief of mission: Ambassador Liberata Rutageruka MULAMULA (since 17 July 2013)
chancery: 1232 22nd Street NW, Washington, DC 20037
telephone: [1] (202) 939-6125
FAX: [1] (202) 797-7408

Diplomatic representation from the US:
chief of mission: Ambassador Mark Bradley CHILDRESS (since 7 April 2014)
embassy: 686 Old Bagamoyo Road, Msasani, Dar es Salaam
mailing address: P. O. Box 9123, Dar es Salaam
telephone: [255] (22) 229-4000
FAX: [255] (22) 229-4970 or 4971

Flag description: divided diagonally by a yellow-edged black band from the lower hoist-side corner; the upper triangle (hoist side) is green and the lower triangle is blue; the banner combines colors found on the flags of Tanganyika and Zanzibar; green represents the natural vegetation of the country, gold its rich mineral deposits, black the native Swahili people, and blue the country's many lakes and rivers, as well as the Indian Ocean

National symbol(s): Uhuru (Freedom) torch

National anthem: *name:* "Mungu ibariki Afrika" (God Bless Africa)
lyrics/music: collective/Enoch Mankayi SONTONGA
note: adopted 1961; the anthem, which is also a popular song in Africa, shares the same melody with that of Zambia, but has different lyrics; the melody is also incorporated into South Africa's anthem

ECONOMY

Economy—overview: Tanzania is one of the world's poorest economies in terms of per capita income, however, it has achieved high overall growth rates based on gold production and tourism. Tanzania has largely completed its transition to a liberalized market economy, though the government retains a presence in sectors such as telecommunications, banking, energy, and mining. The economy depends on agriculture, which accounts for more than one-quarter of GDP, provides 85% of exports, and employs about 80% of the work force. The World Bank, the IMF, and bilateral donors have provided funds to rehabilitate Tanzania's aging economic infrastructure, including rail and port infrastructure that are important trade links for inland countries. Recent banking reforms have helped increase private-sector growth and investment, and the government has increased spending on agriculture to 7% of its budget. The financial sector in Tanzania has expanded in recent years and foreign-owned banks account for about 48% of the banking industry's total assets. Competition among foreign commercial banks has resulted in significant improvements in the efficiency and quality of financial services, though interest rates are still relatively high, reflecting high fraud risk. All land in Tanzania is owned by the government, which can lease land for up to 99 years. Proposed reforms to allow for land ownership, particularly foreign land ownership, remain unpopular. Continued donor assistance and solid macroeconomic policies supported a positive growth rate, despite the world recession. In 2008, Tanzania received the world's largest Millennium Challenge Compact grant, worth $698 million, and in December 2012 the Millennium Challenge Corporation selected Tanzania for a second Compact. Dar es Salaam used fiscal stimulus and loosened monetary policy to ease the impact of the global recession. GDP growth in 2009-13 was a respectable 6-7% per year due to high gold prices and increased production.

GDP (purchasing power parity): $79.29 billion (2013 est.)
country comparison to the world: 83
$74.12 billion (2012 est.)
$69.31 billion (2011 est.)
note: data are in 2013 US dollars

GDP (official exchange rate): $31.94 billion (2013 est.)

GDP—real growth rate: 7% (2013 est.)
country comparison to the world: 22
6.9% (2012 est.)
6.4% (2011 est.)

GDP—per capita (PPP): $1,700 (2013 est.)
country comparison to the world: 200
$1,600 (2012 est.)
$1,600 (2011 est.)
note: data are in 2013 US dollars

Gross national saving: 25.7% of GDP (2013 est.)
country comparison to the world: 47
25.2% of GDP (2012 est.)
17.4% of GDP (2011 est.)

GDP—composition, by end use:
household consumption: 60.3%
government consumption: 17.2%
investment in fixed capital: 40.2%
investment in inventories: 0.6%
exports of goods and services: 30.1%
imports of goods and services: -48.5% (2013 est.)

GDP—composition, by sector of origin:
agriculture: 27.6%
industry: 25%
services: 47.4% (2013 est.)

Agriculture—products: coffee, sisal, tea, cotton, pyrethrum (insecticide made from chrysanthemums), cashew nuts, tobacco, cloves, corn, wheat, cassava (tapioca), bananas, fruits, vegetables; cattle, sheep, goats

Industries: agricultural processing (sugar, beer, cigarettes, sisal twine); mining (diamonds, gold, and iron), salt, soda ash; cement, oil refining, shoes, apparel, wood products, fertilizer

Industrial production growth rate: 7.4% (2013 est.)
country comparison to the world: 29

Labor force: 25.59 million (2013 est.)
country comparison to the world: 27

Labor force—by occupation: *agriculture:* 80%
industry and services: 20% (2002 est.)

Unemployment rate: NA%

Population below poverty line: 36% (2002 est.)

Household income or consumption by percentage share: *lowest 10%:* 2.8%
highest 10%: 29.6% (2007)

Distribution of family income—Gini index: 37.6 (2007)
country comparison to the world: 77
34.6 (2000)

Budget: *revenues:* $7.117 billion
expenditures: $8.917 billion (2013 est.)

Taxes and other revenues: 22.3% of GDP (2013 est.)
country comparison to the world: 148

Budget surplus (+) or deficit (-): -5.6% of GDP (2013 est.)
country comparison to the world: 175

Public debt: 42.7% of GDP (2013 est.)
country comparison to the world: 83
41.7% of GDP (2012 est.)

Fiscal year: 1 July—30 June

Inflation rate (consumer prices): 7.8% (2013 est.)
country comparison to the world: 194
16% (2012 est.)

Central bank discount rate: 8.25% (31 December 2010 est.)
country comparison to the world: 98
3.7% (31 December 2009 est.)

Commercial bank prime lending rate: 13.6% (31 December 2013 est.)
country comparison to the world: 37
15.46% (31 December 2012 est.)

Stock of narrow money: $4.594 billion (31 December 2013 est.)
country comparison to the world: 106
$4.16 billion (31 December 2012 est.)

Stock of broad money: $7.702 billion (31 December 2013 est.)
country comparison to the world: 112
$6.824 billion (31 December 2012 est.)

Stock of domestic credit: $7.326 billion (31 December 2013 est.)
country comparison to the world: 107
$7.061 billion (31 December 2012 est.)

Market value of publicly traded shares: $1.803 billion (31 December 2012 est.)
country comparison to the world: 101
$1.539 billion (31 December 2011)
$1.264 billion (31 December 2010 est.)

Current account balance: -$4.857 billion (2013 est.)
country comparison to the world: 167
-$4.195 billion (2012 est.)

Exports: $5.92 billion (2013 est.)
country comparison to the world: 109
$5.912 billion (2012 est.)

Exports—commodities: gold, coffee, cashew nuts, manufactures, cotton

Exports—partners: India 15.2%, China 11.1%, Japan 6.2%, Germany 5.1%, UAE 4.8% (2012)

Imports: $11.16 billion (2013 est.)
country comparison to the world: 96
$10.32 billion (2012 est.)

Imports—commodities: consumer goods, machinery and transportation equipment, industrial raw materials, crude oil

Imports—partners: China 21.3%, India 16.3%, South Africa 6.4%, Kenya 6%, UAE 5% (2012)

Reserves of foreign exchange and gold: $4.343 billion (31 December 2013 est.)
country comparison to the world: 99
$4.053 billion (31 December 2012 est.)
note: excludes gold

Debt—external: $13.82 billion (31 December 2013 est.)
country comparison to the world: 92
$11.82 billion (31 December 2012 est.)

Stock of direct foreign investment—at home: $NA

Stock of direct foreign investment—abroad: $NA

Exchange rates: Tanzanian shillings (TZS) per US dollar—
1,609.2 (2013 est.)
1,583 (2012 est.)
1,409.3 (2010 est.)
1,320.3 (2009)

1,178.1 (2008)

ENERGY

Electricity—production: 4.302 billion kWh (2010 est.)
country comparison to the world: 122

Electricity—consumption: 3.403 billion kWh (2010 est.)
country comparison to the world: 126

Electricity—exports: 0 kWh (2012 est.)
country comparison to the world: 207

Electricity—imports: 50 million kWh (2010 est.)
country comparison to the world: 98

Electricity—installed generating capacity: 841,000 kW (2010 est.)
country comparison to the world: 126

Electricity—from fossil fuels: 33.2% of total installed capacity (2010 est.)
country comparison to the world: 175

Electricity—from nuclear fuels: 0% of total installed capacity (2010 est.)
country comparison to the world: 193

Electricity—from hydroelectric plants: 66.8% of total installed capacity (2010 est.)
country comparison to the world: 23

Electricity—from other renewable sources: 0% of total installed capacity (2010 est.)
country comparison to the world: 132

Crude oil—production: 10 bbl/day (2012 est.)
country comparison to the world: 130

Crude oil—exports: 0 bbl/day (2010 est.)
country comparison to the world: 195

Crude oil—imports: 0 bbl/day (2010 est.)
country comparison to the world: 132

Crude oil—proved reserves: 0 bbl (1 January 2013 es)
country comparison to the world: 199

Refined petroleum products—production: 0 bbl/day (2010 est.)
country comparison to the world: 202

Refined petroleum products—consumption: 43,310 bbl/day (2011 est.)
country comparison to the world: 104

Refined petroleum products—exports: 0 bbl/day (2010 est.)
country comparison to the world: 138

Refined petroleum products—imports: 30,750 bbl/day (2010 est.)
country comparison to the world: 91

Natural gas—production: 860 million cu m (2011 est.)
country comparison to the world: 67

Natural gas—consumption: 780 million cu m (2010 est.)
country comparison to the world: 93

Natural gas—exports: 0 cu m (2011 est.)
country comparison to the world: 197

Natural gas—imports: 0 cu m (2011 est.)
country comparison to the world: 141

Natural gas—proved reserves: 6.513 billion cu m (1 January 2013 es)
country comparison to the world: 87

Carbon dioxide emissions from consumption of energy: 7.228 million Mt (2011 est.)
country comparison to the world: 111

COMMUNICATIONS

Telephones—main lines in use: 161,100 (2011)
country comparison to the world: 133

Telephones—mobile cellular: 27.22 million (2012)
country comparison to the world: 39

Telephone system: *general assessment:* telecommunications services are marginal; system operating below capacity and being modernized for better service; small aperture terminal (VSAT) system under construction
domestic: fixed-line telephone network inadequate with less than 1 connection per 100 persons; mobile-cellular service, aided by multiple providers, is increasing rapidly and in 2011 exceeded a subscriber base of 50 telephones per 100 persons; trunk service provided by open-wire, microwave radio relay, tropospheric scatter, and fiber-optic cable; some links being made digital
international: country code—255; landing point for the EASSy fiber-optic submarine cable system linking East Africa with Europe and North America; satellite earth stations—2 Intelsat (1 Indian Ocean, 1 Atlantic Ocean) (2010)

Broadcast media: a state-owned TV station and multiple privately owned TV stations; state-owned national radio station supplemented by more than 40 privately owned radio stations; transmissions of several international broadcasters are available (2007)

Internet country code: . t z

Internet hosts: 26,074 (2012)
country comparison to the world: 110

Internet users: 678,000 (2009)
country comparison to the world: 111

TRANSPORTATION

Airports: 166 (2013)
country comparison to the world: 3 4

Airports—with paved runways: *total:* 1 0
over 3,047 m: 2
2,438 to 3,047 m: 2
1,524 to 2,437 m: 4
914 to 1,523 m: 2 (2013)

Airports—with unpaved runways: *total:* 156
over 3,047 m: 1
1,524 to 2,437 m: 24
914 to 1,523 m: 98
under 914 m: 33 (2013)

Pipelines: gas 311 km; oil 891 km; refined products 8 km (2013)

Railways: *total:* 3,689 km
country comparison to the world: 47
narrow gauge: 969 km 1.067-m gauge; 2,720 km 1.000-m gauge (2008)

Roadways: *total:* 86,472 km
country comparison to the world: 53
paved: 7,092 km
unpaved: 79,380 km (2010)

Waterways: (Lake Tanganyika, Lake Victoria, and Lake Nyasa (Lake Malawi) are the principal avenues of commerce with neighboring countries; the rivers are not navigable) (2011)

Merchant marine: *total:* 9 4
country comparison to the world: 52
by type: bulk carrier 6, cargo 66, carrier 4, chemical tanker 1, container 1, passenger/cargo 2, petroleum tanker 10, refrigerated cargo 1, roll on/roll off 3
foreign-owned: 42 (Japan 1, Romania 1, Saudi Arabia 1, Syria 23, Turkey 13, UAE 3)
registered in other countries: 3 (Panama 2, UK 1) (2010)

Ports and terminals: *major seaport(s):* Dar es Salaam, Zanzibar

Transportation—note: the International Maritime Bureau reports that shipping in territorial and offshore waters in the Indian Ocean remain at risk for piracy and armed robbery against ships, especially as Somali-based pirates extend their activities south; numerous commercial vessels have been attacked and hijacked both at anchor and while underway; crews have been robbed and stores or cargoes stolen

MILITARY

Military branches: Tanzania People's Defense Force (Jeshi la Wananchi la Tanzania, JWTZ): Army, Naval Wing (includes Coast Guard), Air Defense Command (includes Air Wing), National Service (2007)

Military service age and obligation: 18 years of age for voluntary military service; no conscription (2012)

Manpower available for military service:
males age 16-49: 9,985,445 (2010 est.)

Manpower fit for military service:
males age 16-49: 5,860,339
females age 16-49: 5,882,279 (2010 est.)

Manpower reaching militarily significant age annually: *male:* 512,294
female: 514,164 (2010 est.)

Military expenditures: 1.13% of GDP (2012)
country comparison to the world: 90
1.12% of GDP (2011)
1.13% of GDP (2010)

TRANSNATIONAL ISSUES

Disputes—international: Tanzania still hosts more than a half million refugees, more than any other African country, mainly from Burundi and the Democratic Republic of the Congo, despite the international community's efforts at repatriation; disputes with Malawi over the boundary in Lake Nyasa (Lake Malawi) and the meandering

Songwe River remain dormant Refugees and internally displaced persons:
refugees (country of origin): 63,330 (Democratic Republic of the Congo); 35,343 (Burundi) (2012)

Trafficking in persons: *current situation:* Tanzania is a source, transit, and destination country for men, women, and children subjected to forced labor and sex trafficking; the exploitation of young girls in domestic servitude continues to be Tanzania's largest human trafficking problem; Tanzanian boys are subject to forced labor mainly on farms but also in mines, in the commercial service sector, in the sex trade, and possibly on small fishing boats; internal trafficking is more prevalent than transnational trafficking and is usually facilitated by friends, family members, or intermediaries offering education or legitimate job opportunities; trafficking victims from Burundi, Kenya, Bangladesh, Nepal, Yemen, and India are to work in Tanzania's agricultural, mining, and domestic service sectors or may be sex trafficked

tier rating: Tier 2 Watch List—Tanzania does not fully comply with the minimum standards for the elimination of trafficking; however, it is making significant efforts to do so; law enforcement made modest anti-trafficking efforts but imposed punishments on offenders that were inadequate for the seriousness of the crimes committed; key victim protection provisions of the 2008 anti-trafficking act remain unimplemented; the government continues to refer child trafficking victims to NGOs for care but has no procedure for the referral of adult victims; the national anti-trafficking action plan has not been implemented; no public awareness campaigns about the dangers of trafficking are conducted (2013)

Illicit drugs: targeted by traffickers moving hashish, Afghan heroin, and South American cocaine transported down the East African coastline, through airports, or overland through Central Africa; Zanzibar likely used by traffickers for drug smuggling; traffickers in the past have recruited Tanzanian couriers to move drugs through Iran into East Asia

THAILAND

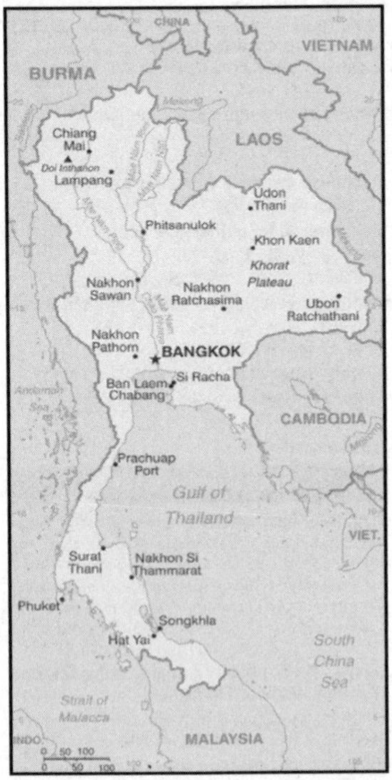

INTRODUCTION

Background: A unified Thai kingdom was established in the mid-14th century. Known as Siam until 1939, Thailand is the only Southeast Asian country never to have been taken over by a European power. A bloodless revolution in 1932 led to a constitutional monarchy. In alliance with Japan during World War II, Thailand became a US treaty ally in 1954 after sending troops to Korea and later fighting alongside the United States in Vietnam. Thailand since 2005 has experienced several rounds of political turmoil including a military coup in 2006 that ousted then Prime Minister THAKSIN Chinnawat, followed by large-scale street protests by competing political factions in 2008, 2009, and 2010. Demonstrations in 2010 culminated with clashes between security forces and pro-THAKSIN protesters, elements of which were armed, and resulted in at least 92 deaths and an estimated $1.5 billion in arson-related property losses. THAKSIN's youngest sister, YINGLAK Chinnawat, in 2011 led the Puea Thai Party to an electoral win and assumed control of the government. YINGLAK's leadership was almost immediately challenged by historic flooding in late 2011 that had large swathes of the country underwater and threatened to inundate Bangkok itself. A blanket amnesty bill for individuals involved in street protests, altered at the last minute to include all political crimes—including all convictions against THAKSIN—triggered large protests in Bangkok. In late 2013 demonstrations led by former opposition deputy leader SUTHEP Thaugsuban called for the establishment of an unelected "people's council" to replace YINGLUCK's government and reform the Thai political system. YINGLUCK dissolved parliament in December 2013 and proposed a new election for February 2014. Thailand's Constitutional Court invalidated the election in March 2014 on grounds that it was not completed within one day throughout the nation. Thailand has also experienced violence associated with the ethno-nationalist insurgency in Thailand's southern Malay-Muslim majority provinces. Since January 2004, thousands have been killed and wounded in the insurgency.

GEOGRAPHY

Location: Southeastern Asia, bordering the Andaman Sea and the Gulf of Thailand, southeast of Burma

Geographic coordinates: 15 00 N, 100 00 E

Map references: Southeast Asia

Area: *total*: 513,120 sq km
country comparison to the world: 51
land: 510,890 sq km
water: 2,230 sq km

Area—comparative: slightly more than twice the size of Wyoming

Land boundaries: *total*: 4,863 km
border countries: Burma 1,800 km, Cambodia 803 km, Laos 1,754 km, Malaysia 506 km

Coastline: 3,219 km

Maritime claims: *territorial sea*: 12 nm
exclusive economic zone: 200 nm
continental shelf: 200 m depth or to the depth of exploitation

Climate: tropical; rainy, warm, cloudy southwest monsoon (mid-May to September); dry, cool northeast monsoon (November to mid-March); southern isthmus always hot and humid

Terrain: central plain; Khorat Plateau in the east; mountains elsewhere

Elevation extremes: *lowest point*: Gulf of Thailand 0 m
highest point: Doi Inthanon 2,576 m

Natural resources: tin, rubber, natural gas, tungsten, tantalum, timber, lead, fish, gypsum, lignite, fluorite, arable land

Land use: *arable land*: 30.71%
permanent crops: 8.77%
other: 60.52% (2011)

Irrigated land: 64,150 sq km (2007)

Total renewable water resources: 438.6 cu km (2011)

Freshwater withdrawal (domestic/industrial/agricultural): *total*: 57.31 cu km/yr (5%/5%/90%)
per capita: 845.3 cu m/yr (2007)

Natural hazards: land subsidence in Bangkok area resulting from the depletion of the water table; droughts

Environment—current issues: air pollution from vehicle emissions; water pollution from organic and factory wastes; deforestation; soil erosion; wildlife populations threatened by illegal hunting

Environment—international agreements:
party to: Biodiversity, Climate Change, Climate Change-Kyoto Protocol, Desertification, Endangered Species, Hazardous Wastes, Marine Life Conservation, Ozone Layer Protection, Tropical Timber 83, Tropical Timber 94, Wetlands
signed, but not ratified: Law of the Sea

Geography—note: controls only land route from Asia to Malaysia and Singapore

PEOPLE AND SOCIETY

Nationality: *noun*: Thai (singular and plural)
adjective: Thai

Ethnic groups: Thai 95.9%, Burmese 2%, other 1.3% (2010 est.)

Languages: Thai (official) 90.7%, Burmese 1.3%, other 8%
note: English is a secondary language of the elite (2010 est.)

Religions: Buddhist (official) 93.6%, Muslim 4.9%, Christian 1.2%, other 0.2%, none 0.1% (2010 est.)

Population: 67,741,401 (July 2014 est.)
country comparison to the world: 21
note: estimates for this country explicitly take into account the effects of excess mortality due to AIDS; this can result in lower life expectancy, higher infant mortality, higher death rates, lower population growth rates, and changes in the distribution of population by age and sex than would otherwise be expected

Age structure:
0-14 years: 17.6% (male 6,117,993/female 5,827,981)
15-24 years: 15% (male 5,194,332/female 4,999,669)
25-54 years: 46.9% (male 15,685,882/female 16,097,245)
55-64 years: 9.5% (male 3,468,620/female 3,893,925)
65 years and over: 9.8% (male 2,830,418/female 3,625,336) (2014 est.)

Dependency ratios:
total dependency ratio: 38.6 %
youth dependency ratio: 25.2 %
elderly dependency ratio: 13.5 %
potential support ratio: 7.4 (2013)

Median age: *total*: 36.2 years
male: 35.3 years
female: 37.2 years (2014 est.)

Population growth rate: 0.35% (2014 est.)
country comparison to the world: 165

Birth rate: 11.26 births/1,000 population (2014 est.)
country comparison to the world: 175

Death rate: 7.72 deaths/1,000 population (2014 est.)
country comparison to the world: 111

Net migration rate: 0 migrant(s)/1,000 population (2014 est.)
country comparison to the world: 81

Urbanization: *urban population*: 34.1% of total population (2011)
rate of urbanization: 1.6% annual rate of change (2010-15 est.)

Major urban areas—population: BANGKOK (capital) 6.902 million (2009)

Sex ratio: *at birth*: 1.05 male(s)/female
0-14 years: 1.05 male(s)/female
15-24 years: 1.04 male(s)/female
25-54 years: 0.97 male(s)/female
55-64 years: 0.97 male(s)/female
65 years and over: 0.82 male(s)/female
total population: 0.98 male(s)/female (2014 est.)

Mother's mean age at first birth: 2 3
note: median age at first birth among women 25-29 (1987 est.)

Maternal mortality rate: 48 deaths/100,000 live births (2010)
country comparison to the world: 110

Infant mortality rate: *total*: 9.86 deaths/1,000 live births

country comparison to the world: 142
male: 10.82 deaths/1,000 live births
female: 8.85 deaths/1,000 live births (2014 est.)

Life expectancy at birth:
total population: 74.18 years
country comparison to the world: 115
male: 71 years
female: 77.54 years (2014 est.)

Total fertility rate: 1.5 children born/woman (2014 est.)
country comparison to the world: 192

Contraceptive prevalence rate: 79.6% (2009)

Health expenditures: 4.1% of GDP (2011)
country comparison to the world: 163

Physicians density: 0.3 physicians/1,000 population (2004)

Hospital bed density: 2.1 beds/1,000 population (2010)

Drinking water source:
improved:
urban: 96.7% of population
rural: 95.3% of population
total: 95.8% of population
unimproved:
urban: 3.3% of population
rural: 4.7% of population
total: 4.2% of population (2011 est.)
Sanitation facility access:
improved:
urban: 88.7% of population
rural: 95.9% of population
total: 93.4% of population
unimproved:
urban: 11.3% of population
rural: 4.1% of population
total: 6.6% of population (2011 est.)

HIV/AIDS—adult prevalence rate: 1.1% (2012 est.)
country comparison to the world: 43

HIV/AIDS—people living with HIV/AIDS: 443,100 (2012 est.)
country comparison to the world: 19

HIV/AIDS—deaths: 20,800 (2012 est.)
country comparison to the world: 17

Major infectious diseases:
degree of risk: very high
food or waterborne diseases: bacterial diarrhea
vectorborne diseases: dengue fever, Japanese encephalitis, and malaria
note: highly pathogenic H5N1 avian influenza has been identified in this country; it poses a negligible risk with extremely rare cases possible among US citizens who have close contact with birds (2013)

Obesity—adult prevalence rate: 8.8% (2008)
country comparison to the world: 135

Children under the age of 5 years underweight: 7% (2006)
country comparison to the world: 76

Education expenditures: 5.8% of GDP (2011)
country comparison to the world: 47

Literacy: *definition:* age 15 and over can read and write
total population: 93.5%
male: 95.6%
female: 91.5% (2005 est.)

School life expectancy (primary to tertiary education): *total:* 13 years
male: 13 years
female: 13 years (2009)

Child labor—children ages 5-14:
total number: 818,399
percentage: 8 % (2006 est.)

Unemployment, youth ages 15-24: *total:* 2.8%
country comparison to the world: 144
male: 2.5%
female: 3.1% (2012)

GOVERNMENT

Country name: *conventional long form:* Kingdom of Thailand
conventional short form: Thailand
local long form: Ratcha Anachak Thai
local short form: Prathet Thai
former: Siam

Government type: constitutional monarchy

Capital: *name:* Bangkok

geographic coordinates: 13 45 N, 100 31 E
time difference: UTC+7 (12 hours ahead of Washington, DC during Standard Time)

Administrative divisions: 77 provinces (changwat, singular and plural); Amnat Charoen, Ang Thong, Bueng Kan, Buriram, Chachoengsao, Chai Nat, Chaiyaphum, Chanthaburi, Chiang Mai, Chiang Rai, Chon Buri, Chumphon, Kalasin, Kamphaeng Phet, Kanchanaburi, Khon Kaen, Krabi, Krung Thep Mahanakhon (Bangkok), Lampang, Lamphun, Loei, Lop Buri, Mae Hong Son, Maha Sarakham, Mukdahan, Nakhon Nayok, Nakhon Pathom, Nakhon Phanom, Nakhon Ratchasima, Nakhon Sawan, Nakhon Si Thammarat, Nan, Narathiwat, Nong Bua Lamphu, Nong Khai, Nonthaburi, Pathum Thani, Pattani, Phangnga, Phatthalung, Phayao, Phetchabun, Phetchaburi, Phichit, Phitsanulok, Phra Nakhon Si Ayutthaya, Phrae, Phuket, Prachin Buri, Prachuap Khiri Khan, Ranong, Ratchaburi, Rayong, Roi Et, Sa Kaeo, Sakon Nakhon, Samut Prakan, Samut Sakhon, Samut Songkhram, Sara Buri, Satun, Sing Buri, Sisaket, Songkhla, Sukhothai, Suphan Buri, Surat Thani, Surin, Tak, Trang, Trat, Ubon Ratchathani, Udon Thani, Uthai Thani, Uttaradit, Yala, Yasothon

Independence: 1238 (traditional founding date; never colonized)

National holiday: Birthday of King PHUMIPHON (BHUMIBOL), 5 December (1927)

Constitution: many previous; latest approved by referendum 19 August 2007, effective 24 August 2007 (2013)

Legal system: civil law system with common law influences

International law organization participation: has not submitted an ICJ jurisdiction declaration; non-party state to the ICCt

Suffrage: 18 years of age; universal and compulsory

Executive branch: *chief of state:* King PHUMIPHON Adunyadet, also spelled BHUMIBOL Adulyadej (since 9 June 1946)
head of government: Prime Minister YINGLAK Chinnawat also spelled YINGLUCK Shinawatra (since 8 August 2011); Deputy Prime Minister KITTIRAT Na Ranong (since 28 October 2012); Deputy Prime Minister PHONGTHEP Thepkanchana also spelled PHONGTHEP Therkanchana (since 28 October 2012); Deputy Prime Minister PLODPRASOP Suraswadi (since 28 October 2012); Deputy Prime Minister PRACHA Promnok (since 24 March 2013); Deputy Prime Minister SURAPHONG Towijakchaikun also spelled SURAPONG Tovichakchaikul (since 28 October 2012); Deputy Prime Minister YUKHON Limlaemthong (since 25 March 2013)
cabinet: Council of Ministers (For more information visit the World Leaders website)
note: there is also a Privy Council advising the king
elections: the monarchy is hereditary; according to the 2007 constitution, the prime minister is elected from among members of the House of Representatives; following national elections for the House of Representatives, the leader of the party positioned to organize a majority coalition usually becomes prime minister by appointment by the king; the prime minister is limited to two four-year terms

Legislative branch: bicameral National Assembly or Rathasapha consisted of the Senate or Wuthisapha (150 seats; 76 members elected by popular vote representing 75 provinces and 1 metropolitan district (Bangkok), 74 appointed by the Senate Selection Committee; members serve six-year terms) and the House of Representatives or Sapha Phuthaen Ratsadon (500 seats; 375 members elected from 375 single-seat constituencies and 125 elected on proportional party-list basis; members serve four-year terms)
elections: Senate—last held on 30 March 2014; House of Representatives—last held on 2 February 2014, but later declared invalid by the Constitutional Court(the date of the new election has not been announced)
election results: Senate—percent of vote by party—NA; seats by party—NA; House of Representatives—percent of vote by party—NA; seats by party—NA
note: 74 senators were appointed on 19 February 2008 by a seven-member committee headed by the chief of the Constitutional Court; 76 senators were elected on 30 March 2014; elections to the Senate are non-partisan; registered political party members are disqualified from being senators

Judicial branch: *highest court(s):* Supreme Court of Justice (consists of the court president, 6 vice-presidents, and NA judges and organized into civil and criminal divisions); Constitutional Court (consists of the court president and 8 judges); Supreme Administrative Court (the number of judges determined by the Judicial Commission of the Administrative Courts)
judge selection and term of office: Supreme Court judges selected by the Judicial Commission of the Courts of Justice and approved by the monarch; judges' terms NA; Constitutional Court justices—3 judges drawn from the Supreme Court, 2 judges drawn from the Administrative Court, and 4 judge candidates selected by the Selective Committee for Judges of the Constitutional Court and confirmed by the Senate; judges appointed by the monarch to serve single 9-year terms; Supreme Administrative Court judges selected by the Judicial Commission of the Administrative Courts and appointed by the monarch; judge tenure NA
subordinate courts: courts of first instance and appeals courts within both the judicial and administrative systems; military courts

Political parties and leaders: Chat Pattana Party or CPN (Nation Development Party) [WANNARAT Channukul]; Chat Thai Phattana Party or CTP (Thai Nation Development Party) [THEERA Wongsamut]; Mahachon Party or Mass Party [APHIRAT Sirinawin]; Matubhum Party (Motherland Party) [Gen. SONTHI Bunyaratkalin]; Phalang Chon Party (People Chonburi Power Party) [SONTHAYA Khunpluem]; Phumjai (Bhumjai) Thai Party or PJT (Thai Pride) [ANUTIN Charnvirakul]; Prachathipat Party or DP (Democrat Party) [ABHISIT Wechachiwa, also spelled ABHISIT Vejjajiva]; Prachathipathai Mai Party (New Democracy Party) [SURATIN Phijarn]; Puea Thai Party (For Thais Party) or PTP [CHARUPHONG Rueangsuwan also spelled JARUPONG Ruangsuwan]; Rak Prathet Thai Party (Love Thailand Party) [CHUWIT Kamonwisit]; Rak Santi Party (Peace Conservation Party) [Pol. Lt. Gen. THAWIL Surachetphong]

Political pressure groups and leaders: Multicolor Group; People's Alliance for Democracy or PAD; People's Democratic Reform Committee or PDRC; Student and People Network for Thailand's Reform or STR; United Front for Democracy Against Dictatorship or UDD

International organization participation: ADB, APEC, ARF, ASEAN, BIMSTEC, BIS, CD, CICA, CP, EAS, FAO, G-77, IAEA, IBRD, ICAO, ICC (national committees), ICRM, IDA, IFAD, IFC, IFRCS, IHO, ILO, IMF, IMO, IMSO,

Interpol, IOC, IOM, IPU, ISO, ITSO, ITU, ITUC (NGOs), MIGA, NAM, OAS (observer), OIC (observer), OIF (observer), OPCW, OSCE (partner), PCA, PIF (partner), UN, UNAMID, UNCTAD, UNESCO, UNHCR, UNIDO, UNMOGIP, UNWTO, UPU, WCO, WFTU (NGOs), WHO, WIPO, WMO, WTO

Diplomatic representation in the US:
chief of mission: Ambassador WICHAWAT Isarabhakdi (since 3 December 2013)
chancery: 1024 Wisconsin Avenue NW, Suite 401, Washington, DC 20007
telephone: [1] (202) 944-3600
FAX: [1] (202) 944-3611
consulate(s) general: Chicago, Los Angeles, New York

Diplomatic representation from the US:
chief of mission: Ambassador Kristie A. KENNEY (since 10 January 2011)
embassy: 120-122 Wireless Road, Bangkok 10330
mailing address: APO AP 96546
telephone: [66] (2) 205-4000
FAX: [66] (2) 254-2990, 205-4131
consulate(s) general: Chiang Mai

Flag description: five horizontal bands of red (top), white, blue (double width), white, and red; the red color symbolizes the nation and the blood of life; white represents religion and the purity of Buddhism; blue stands for the monarchy
note: similar to the flag of Costa Rica but with the blue and red colors reversed

National symbol(s): garuda (mythical half-man, half-bird figure); elephant

National anthem: *name:* "Phleng Chat Thai" (National Anthem of Thailand)
lyrics/music: Luang SARANUPRAPAN/Phra JENDURIYANG
note: music adopted 1932, lyrics adopted 1939; by law, people are required to stand for the national anthem at 0800 and 1800 every day; the anthem is played in schools, offices, theaters, and on television and radio during this time; "Phleng Sansasoen Phra Barami" (A Salute to the Monarch) serves as the royal anthem and is played in the presence of the royal family and during certain state ceremonies

ECONOMY

Economy—overview: With a well-developed infrastructure, a free-enterprise economy, generally pro-investment policies, and strong export industries, Thailand achieved steady growth due largely to industrial and agriculture exports - mostly electronics, agricultural commodities, automobiles and parts, and processed foods. Unemployment, at less than 1% of the labor force, stands as one of the lowest levels in the world, which puts upward pressure on wages in some industries. Thailand also attracts nearly 2.5 million migrant workers from neighboring countries. The Thai government in 2013 implemented a nation-wide 300 baht ($10) per day minimum wage policy and deployed new tax reforms designed to lower rates on middle-income earners. The Thai economy has weathered internal and external economic shocks in recent years. The global economic recession severely cut Thailand's exports, with most sectors experiencing double-digit drops. In late 2011 Thailand's recovery was interrupted by historic flooding in the industrial areas in Bangkok and its five surrounding provinces, crippling the manufacturing sector. The government approved flood mitigation projects worth $11.7 billion, which were started in 2012, to prevent similar economic damage, and an additional $75 billion for infrastructure over the following seven years. This was expected to lead to an economic upsurge but growth has remained slow, in part due to ongoing political unrest and resulting uncertainties. Spending on infrastructure will require re-approval once a new government is seated.

GDP (purchasing power parity): $674.3 billion (2013 est.)
country comparison to the world: 25
$654 billion (2012 est.)
$614.2 billion (2011 est.)
note: data are in 2013 US dollars

GDP (official exchange rate): $400.9 billion (2013 est.)

GDP—real growth rate: 3.1% (2013 est.)
country comparison to the world: 111
6.5% (2012 est.)
0.1% (2011 est.)

GDP—per capita (PPP): $9,900 (2013 est.)
country comparison to the world: 118
$9,600 (2012 est.)
$9,100 (2011 est.)
note: data are in 2013 US dollars

Gross national saving: 28.7% of GDP (2013 est.)
country comparison to the world: 31
30.5% of GDP (2012 est.)
28.3% of GDP (2011 est.)

GDP—composition, by end use:
household consumption: 53.5%
government consumption: 13.3%
investment in fixed capital: 28.2%
investment in inventories: 0.9%
exports of goods and services: 70.6%
imports of goods and services: -66.6% (2013 est.)

GDP—composition, by sector of origin:
agriculture: 12.1%
industry: 43.6%
services: 44.2% (2013 est.)

Agriculture—products: rice, cassava (manioc), rubber, corn, sugarcane, coconuts, soybeans

Industries: tourism, textiles and garments, agricultural processing, beverages, tobacco, cement, light manufacturing such as jewelry and electric appliances, computers and parts, integrated circuits, furniture, plastics, automobiles and automotive parts; world's second-largest tungsten producer and third-largest tin producer

Industrial production growth rate: 4% (2013 est.)
country comparison to the world: 74

Labor force: 39.64 million (2013 est.)
country comparison to the world: 17

Labor force—by occupation: *agriculture:* 38.2%
industry: 13.6%
services: 48.2% (2011 est.)

Unemployment rate: 0.8% (2013 est.)
country comparison to the world: 4
0.7% (2012 est.)

Population below poverty line:
7.8% (2010 est.)

Household income or consumption by percentage share: *lowest 10%:* 2.8%
highest 10%: 31.5% (2009 est.)

Distribution of family income—Gini index:
53.6 (2009)
country comparison to the world: 12
42 (2002)

Budget: *revenues:* $80.91 billion
expenditures: $92.9 billion (2013 est.)

Taxes and other revenues: 20.2% of GDP (2013 est.)
country comparison to the world: 164

Budget surplus (+) or deficit (-):
-3% of GDP (2013 est.)
country comparison to the world: 123

Public debt: 47.5% of GDP (2013 est.)
country comparison to the world: 73
45.7% of GDP (2012 est.)
note: data cover general government debt, and includes debt instruments issued (or owned) by government entities other than the treasury; the data include treasury debt held by foreign entities; the data include debt issued by subnational entities, as well as intra-governmental debt; intra-governmental debt consists of treasury borrowings from surpluses in the social funds, such as for retirement, medical care, and unemployment; debt instruments for the social funds are sold at public auctions

Fiscal year: 1 October—30 September

Inflation rate (consumer prices): 2.2% (2013 est.)
country comparison to the world: 78
3% (2012 est.)

Central bank discount rate: 2.75% (31 December 2012 est.)
country comparison to the world: 102
3.25% (31 December 2011 est.)

Commercial bank prime lending rate: 7% (31 December 2013 est.)
country comparison to the world: 122
7.1% (31 December 2012 est.)

Stock of narrow money: $50.18 billion (31 December 2013 est.)
country comparison to the world: 46
$52.18 billion (31 December 2012 est.)

Stock of broad money: $516.4 billion (31 December 2013 est.)
country comparison to the world: 22
$488.6 billion (31 December 2012 est.)

Stock of domestic credit: $511.2 billion (31 December 2013 est.)
country comparison to the world: 26
$480.5 billion (31 December 2012 est.)

Market value of publicly traded shares: $383 billion (31 December 2012 est.)
country comparison to the world: 28
$268.5 billion (31 December 2011)
$277.7 billion (31 December 2010 est.)

Current account balance: -$1.117 billion (2013 est.)
country comparison to the world: 121
$2.759 billion (2012 est.)

Exports: $229.1 billion (2013 est.)
country comparison to the world: 26
$226.1 billion (2012 est.)

Exports—commodities: electronics, computer parts, automobiles and parts, electrical appliances, machinery and equipment, textiles and footwear, fishery products, rice, rubber

Exports—partners: China 11.7%, Japan 10.2%, US 9.9%, Hong Kong 5.7%, Malaysia 5.4%, Indonesia 4.9%, Singapore 4.7%, Australia 4.3% (2012)

Imports: $223 billion (2013 est.)
country comparison to the world: 25
$217.8 billion (2012 est.)

Imports—commodities: capital goods, intermediate goods and raw materials, consumer goods, fuels

Imports—partners: Japan 20%, China 14.9%, UAE 6.3%, Malaysia 5.3%, US 5.3% (2012)

Reserves of foreign exchange and gold: $167.6 billion (31 December 2013 est.)
country comparison to the world: 17
$181.6 billion (31 December 2012 est.)

Debt—external: $86.1 billion (31 December 2013 est.)
country comparison to the world: 50
$133.7 billion (31 December 2012 est.)

Stock of direct foreign investment—at home:
$193.7 billion (31 December 2013 est.)
country comparison to the world: 29
$185.7 billion (31 December 2012 est.)

Stock of direct foreign investment—abroad:
$65.14 billion (31 December 2013 est.)
country comparison to the world: 34
$56.14 billion (31 December 2012 est.)

Exchange rates: baht per US dollar—
30.59 (2013 est.)
31.083 (2012 est.)
31.686 (2010 est.)
34.286 (2009)
33.37 (2008)

ENERGY

Electricity—production: 173.3 billion kWh (2012 est.)
country comparison to the world: 24

Electricity—consumption: 169.4 billion kWh (2012 est.)
country comparison to the world: 23

Electricity—exports: 1.535 billion kWh (2012 est.)
country comparison to the world: 49

Electricity—imports: 9.575 billion kWh (2012 est.)
country comparison to the world: 25

Electricity—installed generating capacity: 32.6 million kW (2012 est.)
country comparison to the world: 27

Electricity—from fossil fuels: 89% of total installed capacity (2012 est.)
country comparison to the world: 79

Electricity—from nuclear fuels: 0% of total installed capacity (2012 est.)
country comparison to the world: 184

Electricity—from hydroelectric plants: 10.9% of total installed capacity (2012 est.)
country comparison to the world: 111

Electricity—from other renewable sources: 0.2% of total installed capacity (2012 est.)
country comparison to the world: 94

Crude oil—production: 433,300 bbl/day (2012 est.)
country comparison to the world: 32

Crude oil—exports: 32,200 bbl/day (2011 est.)
country comparison to the world: 48

Crude oil—imports: 793,900 bbl/day (2011 est.)
country comparison to the world: 15

Crude oil—proved reserves: 453.3 million bbl (1 January 2013 es)
country comparison to the world: 51

Refined petroleum products—production: 913,600 bbl/day (2011 est.)
country comparison to the world: 23

Refined petroleum products—consumption: 721,100 bbl/day (2011 est.)
country comparison to the world: 25

Refined petroleum products—exports: 192,400 bbl/day (2011 est.)
country comparison to the world: 32

Refined petroleum products—imports: 41,700 bbl/day (2011 est.)
country comparison to the world: 79

Natural gas—production: 36.99 billion cu m (2011 est.)
country comparison to the world: 26

Natural gas—consumption: 45.08 billion cu m (2010 est.)
country comparison to the world: 21

Natural gas—exports: country comparison to the world: 188

Natural gas—imports: 9.58 billion cu m (2011 est.)
country comparison to the world: 31

Natural gas—proved reserves: 284.9 billion cu m (1 January 2013 es)
country comparison to the world: 40

Carbon dioxide emissions from consumption of energy: 269.6 million Mt (2011 est.)
country comparison to the world: 25

COMMUNICATIONS

Telephones—main lines in use: 6.391 million (2012)
country comparison to the world: 26

Telephones—mobile cellular: 84.075 million (2012)
country comparison to the world: 17

Telephone system: *general assessment:* high quality system, especially in urban areas like Bangkok
domestic: fixed line system provided by both a government-owned and commercial provider; wireless service expanding rapidly
international: country code—66; connected to major submarine cable systems providing links throughout Asia, Australia, Middle East, Europe, and US; satellite earth stations—2 Intelsat (1 Indian Ocean, 1 Pacific Ocean) (2011)

Broadcast media: 6 terrestrial TV stations in Bangkok broadcast nationally via relay stations—2 of the networks are owned by the military, the other 4 are government-owned or controlled, leased to private enterprise, and all are required to broadcast government-produced news programs twice a day; multi-channel satellite and cable TV subscription services are available; radio frequencies have been allotted for more than 500 government and commercial radio stations; many small community radio stations operate with low-power transmitters (2008)

Internet country code: .th

Internet hosts: 3.399 million (2012)
country comparison to the world: 31

Internet users: 17.483 million (2009)
country comparison to the world: 23

TRANSPORTATION

Airports: 101 (2013)
country comparison to the world: 56

Airports—with paved runways: *total:* 63
over 3,047 m: 8
2,438 to 3,047 m: 12
1,524 to 2,437 m: 23
914 to 1,523 m: 14
under 914 m: 6 (2013)

Airports—with unpaved runways: *total:* 38
2,438 to 3,047 m: 1
1,524 to 2,437 m: 1
914 to 1,523 m: 10
under 914 m: 26 (2013)

Heliports: 7 (2013)

Pipelines: condensate 2 km; gas 5,900 km; liquid petroleum gas 85 km; oil 1 km; refined products 1,097 km (2013)

Railways: *total:* 4,071 km
country comparison to the world: 43
standard gauge: 29 km 1.435-m gauge (29 km electrified)
narrow gauge: 4,042 km 1.000-m gauge (2008)

Roadways: *total:* 180,053 km (includes 450 km of expressways) (2006)
country comparison to the world: 28

Waterways: 4,000 km (3,701 km navigable by boats with drafts up to 0.9 m) (2011)
country comparison to the world: 26

Merchant marine: *total:* 363
country comparison to the world: 28
by type: bulk carrier 31, cargo 99, chemical tanker 28, container 18, liquefied gas 36, passenger 1, passenger/cargo 10, petroleum tanker 114, refrigerated cargo 24, roll on/roll off 1, vehicle carrier 1
foreign-owned: 13 (China 1, Hong Kong 1, Malaysia 3, Singapore 1, Taiwan 1, UK 6)
registered in other countries: 46 (Bahamas 4, Belize 1, Honduras 2, Panama 6, Singapore 33) (2010)

Ports and terminals: *major seaport(s):* Bangkok, Laem Chabang, Map Ta Phut, Prachuap Port, Si Racha
container port(s) TEUs): Bangkok (1,305,229), Laem Chabang (5,731,063)

MILITARY

Military branches: Royal Thai Army (Kongthap Bok Thai, RTA), Royal Thai Navy (Kongthap Ruea Thai, RTN, includes Royal Thai Marine Corps), Royal Thai Air Force (Kongthap Agard Thai, RTAF) (2013)

Military service age and obligation: 21 years of age for compulsory military service; 18 years of age for voluntary military service; males register at 18 years of age; 2-year conscript service obligation (2012)

Manpower available for military service:
males age 16-49: 17,689,921
females age 16-49: 17,754,795 (2010 est.)

Manpower fit for military service:
males age 16-49: 13,308,372
females age 16-49: 14,182,567 (2010 est.)

Manpower reaching militarily significant age annually: *male:* 533,424
female: 509,780 (2010 est.)

Military expenditures: 1.47% of GDP (2012)
country comparison to the world: 61
1.6% of GDP (2011)
1.47% of GDP (2010)

TRANSNATIONAL ISSUES

Disputes—international: separatist violence in Thailand's predominantly Malay-Muslim southern provinces prompt border closures and controls with Malaysia to stem insurgent activities; Southeast Asian states have enhanced border surveillance to check the spread of avian flu; talks continue on completion of demarcation with Laos but disputes remain over several islands in the Mekong River; despite continuing border committee talks, Thailand must deal with Karen and other ethnic rebels, refugees, and illegal cross-border activities; Cambodia and Thailand dispute sections of boundary; in 2011 Thailand and Cambodia resorted to arms in the dispute over the location of the boundary on the precipice surmounted by Preah Vihear temple ruins, awarded to Cambodia by ICJ decision in 1962 and part of a planned UN World Heritage site; Thailand is studying the feasibility of jointly constructing the Hatgyi Dam on the Salween river near the border with Burma; in 2004, international environmentalist pressure prompted China to halt construction of 13 dams on the Salween River that flows through China, Burma, and Thailand; 140,000 mostly Karen refugees fleeing civil strife, political upheaval and economic stagnation in Burma live in remote camps in Thailand near the border

Refugees and internally displaced persons:
refugees (country of origin): 83,317 (Burma) (2012)
IDPs: undetermined (resurgence in ethno-nationalist violence in south of country since 2004) (2011)
stateless persons: 506,197 (2012); note—about half of Thailand's northern hill tribe people do not have citizenship and make up the bulk of Thailand's stateless population; most lack documentation showing they or one of their parents were born in Thailand; children born to Burmese refugees are not eligible for Burmese or Thai citizenship and are stateless; most Chao Lay, maritime nomadic peoples, who travel from island to island in the Andaman Sea west of Thailand are also stateless; stateless Rohingya refugees from Burma are considered illegal migrants by Thai authorities

and are detained in inhumane conditions or expelled; stateless persons are denied access to voting, property, education, employment, healthcare, and driving

Trafficking in persons: *current situation:* Thailand is a source, transit, and destination country for men, women, and children subjected to forced labor and sex trafficking; victims, who are most often from neighboring countries, especially Burma, and also China, Vietnam, Russia, Uzbekistan, and Fiji, migrate to Thailand in search of economic opportunities but are forced, coerced, or defrauded into labor or commercial sexual exploitation; forced laborers are exploited in fishing, low-end garment production, domestic service, and some are forced to beg; some men forced to work on fishing boats have reportedly been kept at sea for years; sex trafficking of Thai and migrant children and sex tourism remain significant problems; Thailand is a transit country for victims from North Korea, China, Vietnam, Pakistan, and Burma destined for exploitation in third countries, including Malaysia, Indonesia, Singapore, Russia, the Republic of Korea, the US, and Western European countries tier rating: Tier 2 Watch List—Thailand does not fully comply with the minimum standards for the elimination of trafficking; the government investigated more trafficking-related cases but prosecuted and convicted fewer trafficking offender in 2012 than it did in the previous year; widespread corruption among law enforcement personnel creates an enabling environment for human trafficking; local authorities lack an awareness of the elements of trafficking and are deficient at identifying and protecting victims; weak law enforcement, inadequate human and financial resources, and fragmented coordination among regulatory agencies in the fishing industry contributes to overall impunity for exploitive labor practices in this sector; no labor recruitment companies have been punished for forced labor or trafficking allegations (2013)

Illicit drugs: a minor producer of opium, heroin, and marijuana; transit point for illicit heroin en route to the international drug market from Burma and Laos; eradication efforts have reduced the area of cannabis cultivation and shifted some production to neighboring countries; opium poppy cultivation has been reduced by eradication efforts; also a drug money-laundering center; minor role in methamphetamine production for regional consumption; major consumer of methamphetamine since the 1990s despite a series of government crackdowns

TIMOR-LESTE

INTRODUCTION

Background: The Portuguese began to trade with the island of Timor in the early 16th century and colonized it in mid-century. Skirmishing with the Dutch in the region eventually resulted in an 1859 treaty in which Portugal ceded the western portion of the island. Imperial Japan occupied Portuguese Timor from 1942 to 1945, but Portugal resumed colonial authority after the Japanese defeat in World War II. East Timor declared itself independent from Portugal on 28 November 1975 and was invaded and occupied by Indonesian forces nine days later. It was incorporated into Indonesia in July 1976 as the province of Timor Timur (East Timor). An unsuccessful campaign of pacification followed over the next two decades, during which an estimated 100,000 to 250,000 individuals lost their lives. On 30 August 1999, in a UN-supervised popular referendum, an overwhelming majority of the people of Timor-Leste voted for independence from Indonesia. However, in the next three weeks, anti-independence Timorese militias—organized and supported by the Indonesian military—commenced a large-scale, scorched-earth campaign of retribution. The militias killed approximately 1,400 Timorese and forcibly pushed 300,000 people into western Timor as refugees. Most of the country's infrastructure, including homes, irrigation systems, water supply systems, and schools, and nearly 100% of the country's electrical grid were destroyed. On 20 September 1999, Australian-led peacekeeping troops deployed to the country and brought the violence to an end. On 20 May 2002, Timor-Leste was internationally recognized as an independent state. In 2006, internal tensions threatened the new nation's security when a military strike led to violence and a breakdown of law and order. At Dili's request, an Australian-led International Stabilization Force (ISF) deployed to Timor-Leste, and the UN Security Council established the UN Integrated Mission in Timor-Leste (UNMIT), which included an authorized police presence of over 1,600 personnel. The ISF and UNMIT restored stability, allowing for presidential and parliamentary elections in 2007 in a largely peaceful atmosphere. In February 2008, a rebel group staged an unsuccessful attack against the president and prime minister. The ringleader was killed in the attack, and most of the rebels surrendered in April 2008. Since the attack, the government has enjoyed one of its longest periods of post-independence stability, including successful 2012 elections for both the parliament and president. In late 2012, the UN Security Council voted to end its peacekeeping mission in Timor-Leste and both the ISF and UNMIT departed the country by the end of the year.

GEOGRAPHY

Location: Southeastern Asia, northwest of Australia in the Lesser Sunda Islands at the eastern end of the Indonesian archipelago; note—Timor-Leste includes the eastern half of the island of Timor, the Oecussi (Ambeno) region on the northwest portion of the island of Timor, and the islands of Pulau Atauro and Pulau Jaco

Geographic coordinates: 8 50 S, 125 55 E

Map references: Southeast Asia

Area: *total:* 14,874 sq km
country comparison to the world: 160
land: 14,874 sq km
water: 0 sq km

Area—comparative: slightly larger than Connecticut

Land boundaries: *total:* 228 km
border countries: Indonesia 228 km

Coastline: 706 km

Maritime claims: *territorial sea:* 12 nm
contiguous zone: 24 nm
exclusive fishing zone: 200 nm

Climate: tropical; hot, humid; distinct rainy and dry seasons

Terrain: mountainous

Elevation extremes: *lowest point:* Timor Sea, Savu Sea, and Banda Sea 0 m
highest point: Foho Tatamailau 2,963 m

Natural resources: gold, petroleum, natural gas, manganese, marble

Land use: *arable land:* 10.09%
permanent crops: 4.03%
other: 85.88% (2011)

Irrigated land: 346.5 sq km (2003)

Natural hazards: floods and landslides are common; earthquakes; tsunamis; tropical cyclones

Environment—current issues: widespread use of slash and burn agriculture has led to deforestation and soil erosion

Environment—international agreements:
party to: Biodiversity, Climate Change, Climate Change-Kyoto Protocol, Desertification
signed, but not ratified: none of the selected agreements

Geography—note: Timor comes from the Malay word for "East"; the island of Timor is part of the Malay Archipelago and is the largest and easternmost of the Lesser Sunda Islands

PEOPLE AND SOCIETY

Nationality: *noun:* Timorese
adjective: Timorese

Ethnic groups: Austronesian (Malayo-Polynesian), Papuan, small Chinese minority

Languages: Tetum (official), Portuguese (official), Indonesian, English
note: there are about 16 indigenous languages; Tetum, Galole, Mambae, and Kemak are spoken by a significant portion of the population

Religions: Roman Catholic 96.9%, Protestant / Evangelical 2.2%, Muslim 0.3%, other 0.6% (2005)

Population: 1,201,542 (July 2014 est.)
country comparison to the world: 160
note: other estimates range as low as 800,000

Age structure:
0-14 years: 42.4% (male 261,794/female 247,486)
15-24 years: 19.8% (male 120,256/female 117,268)
25-54 years: 29.3% (male 170,179/female 182,278)

55-64 years: 3.7% (male 29,867/female 28,156)
65 years and over: 3.6% (male 21,214/female 23,044) (2014 est.)

Dependency ratios:
total dependency ratio: 96.3 %
youth dependency ratio: 89.9 %
elderly dependency ratio: 6.4 %
potential support ratio: 15.5 (2013)

Median age: *total:* 18.5 years
male: 17.9 years
female: 19.1 years (2014 est.)

Population growth rate: 2.44% (2014 est.)
country comparison to the world: 35

Birth rate: 34.48 births/1,000 population (2014 est.)
country comparison to the world: 30

Death rate: 6.18 deaths/1,000 population (2014 est.)
country comparison to the world: 159

Net migration rate: -3.87 migrant(s)/1,000 population (2014 est.)
country comparison to the world: 189

Urbanization: *urban population:* 28.3% of total population (2011)
rate of urbanization: 4.25% annual rate of change (2010-15 est.)

Major urban areas—population: DILI (capital) 166,000 (2009)

Sex ratio: *at birth:* 1.07 male(s)/female
0-14 years: 1.06 male(s)/female
15-24 years: 1.03 male(s)/female
25-54 years: 0.93 male(s)/female
55-64 years: 1.01 male(s)/female
65 years and over: 0.96 male(s)/female
total population: 1.01 male(s)/female (2014 est.)

Mother's mean age at first birth: 22.1
note: median age at first birth among women 25-29 (2010 est.)

Maternal mortality rate: 300 deaths/100,000 live births (2010)
country comparison to the world: 41

Infant mortality rate: *total:* 38.79 deaths/1,000 live births
country comparison to the world: 56
male: 41.84 deaths/1,000 live births
female: 35.54 deaths/1,000 live births (2014 est.)

Life expectancy at birth:
total population: 67.39 years
country comparison to the world: 164
male: 65.87 years
female: 69.01 years (2014 est.)

Total fertility rate: 5.11 children born/woman (2014 est.)
country comparison to the world: 15

Contraceptive prevalence rate: 22.3% (2009/10)

Health expenditures: 5.1% of GDP (2011)
country comparison to the world: 140

Physicians density: 0.1 physicians/1,000 population (2004)

Hospital bed density: 5.9 beds/1,000 population (2010)

Drinking water source:
improved:
urban: 93% of population
rural: 59.6% of population
total: 69.1% of population
unimproved:
urban: 7% of population
rural: 40.4% of population
total: 30.9% of population (2011 est.)

Sanitation facility access:
improved:
urban: 67.6% of population
rural: 27.3% of population
total: 38.7% of population
unimproved:
urban: 32.4% of population
rural: 72.7% of population
total: 61.3% of population (2011 est.)

HIV/AIDS—adult prevalence rate: NA

HIV/AIDS—people living with HIV/AIDS: NA

HIV/AIDS—deaths: NA

Major infectious diseases:
degree of risk: very high
food or waterborne diseases: bacterial diarrhea, hepatitis A, and typhoid fever
vectorborne diseases: dengue fever and malaria (2013)

Obesity—adult prevalence rate: 2.7% (2008)
country comparison to the world: 178

Children under the age of 5 years underweight: 45.3% (2010)
country comparison to the world: 1

Education expenditures: 9.4% of GDP (2011)
country comparison to the world: 7

Literacy: *definition:* age 15 and over can read and write
total population: 58.3%
male: 63.6%
female: 53% (2010 est.)

School life expectancy (primary to tertiary education): *total:* 12 years
male: 12 years
female: 11 years (2010)

Child labor—children ages 5-14:
total number: 10,510
percentage: 4 % (2002 est.)

Unemployment, youth ages 15-24: *total:* 14.8%
country comparison to the world: 85
male: 10.4%
female: 22.7% (2010)

GOVERNMENT

Country name: *conventional long form:* Democratic Republic of Timor-Leste (pronounced TEE-mor LESS-tay)
conventional short form: Timor-Leste
local long form: Republika Demokratika Timor Lorosa'e [Tetum]; Republica Democratica de Timor-Leste [Portuguese]
local short form: Timor Lorosa'e [Tetum]; Timor-Leste [Portuguese]
former: East Timor, Portuguese Timor

Government type: republic

Capital: 1: Dili

geographic coordinates: 8 35 S, 125 36 E
time difference: UTC+9 (14 hours ahead of Washington, DC during Standard Time)

Administrative divisions: 13 administrative districts; Aileu, Ainaro, Baucau, Bobonaro (Maliana), Cova-Lima (Suai), Dili, Ermera (Gleno), Lautem (Los Palos), Liquica, Manatuto, Manufahi (Same), Oecussi (Ambeno), Viqueque
note: administrative divisions have the same names as their administrative centers (exceptions have the administrative center name following in parentheses)

Independence: 28 November 1975 (independence proclaimed from Portugal); note—20 May 2002 is the official date of international recognition of Timor-Leste's independence

National holiday: Proclamation of Independence Day, 28 November (1975)

Constitution: drafted 2001, approved 22 March 2002, entered into force 20 May 2002 (2013)

Legal system: civil law system based on the Portuguese model; note—penal and civil law codes to replace the Indonesian codes were passed by Parliament and promulgated in 2009 and 2011, respectively

International law organization participation: has not submitted an ICJ jurisdiction declaration; accepts ICCt jurisdiction

Suffrage: 17 years of age; universal

Executive branch: *chief of state:* President Taur Matan RUAK (Jose Maria de VASCONCELOS) (since 20 May 2012); note—the president plays a largely symbolic role but is the commander in chief of the military and is able to veto legislation, dissolve parliament, and call national elections
head of government: Prime Minister Kay Rala Xanana GUSMAO (since 8 August 2007); note—he formerly used the name Jose Alexandre GUSMAO; Vice Prime Minister Fernando "Lasama" de ARAUJO (since 8 August 2012)
cabinet: Council of Ministers (For more information visit the World Leaders website)
elections: the president is elected by popular vote for a five-year term (eligible for a second term); an election was held on 17 March 2012 with a run-off on 16 April 2012; following parliamentary elections, the president appoints the leader of the majority party or majority coalition as the prime minister
election results: Taur Matan RUAK elected president in 2012; percent of second-round vote—Taur Matan RUAK 61.2%, Francisco GUTTERES 38.8%

Legislative branch: unicameral National Parliament (the number of seats can vary from 52 to 65; members are elected by popular vote to serve five-year terms in a modified proportional representation system)
elections: elections were held on 7 July 2012 (next to be held in July 2017)
election results: percent of vote by party—CNRT 36%, FRETILIN 30%, PD 10%, Frenti-Mudanca 3%, others 21%; seats by party—CNRT 30, FRETILIN 25, PD 8, Frenti-Mudanca 2

Judicial branch: *highest court(s):* Supreme Court of Justice (consists of the court president and NA judges) note—the UN Justice System Programme, launched in 2003 and in 2008, is helping strengthen the country's justice system
judge selection and term of office: Supreme Court president appointed by the president of the republic from among the other court judges to serve a 4-year term; other Supreme Court judges appointed—1 by the Parliament, and the others by the Supreme Council for the Judiciary, a body presided by the Supreme Court president and includes mostly presidential and parliamentary appointees; other Supreme Court judge tenure NA
subordinate courts: Court of Appeal; district courts; magistrates' courts

Political parties and leaders: Democratic Party or PD [Fernando "Lasama" de ARAUJO]; Frenti-Mudanca [Jose Luis GUTERRES]; National Congress for Timorese Reconstruction or CNRT [Kay Rala Xanana GUSMAO]; Revolutionary Front of Independent Timor-Leste or FRETILIN [Mari ALKATIRI]; (only parties in Parliament are listed)

Political pressure groups and leaders: NA

International organization participation: ACP, ADB, AOSIS, ARF, ASEAN (observer), CPLP, EITI (compliant country), FAO, G-77, IBRD, ICAO, ICRM, IDA, IFAD, IFC, IFRCS, ILO, IMF, IMO, Interpol, IOC, IOM, IPU, ITU, MIGA, NAM, OPCW, PIF (observer), UN, UNCTAD, UNESCO, UNIDO, Union Latina, UNMISS, UNWTO, UPU, WCO, WHO, WMO

Diplomatic representation in the US:
chief of mission: Ambassador (vacant); Charge d'Affaires Julio da Costa FREITAS (since 16 July 2013)
chancery: 4201 Connecticut Avenue NW, Suite 504,Washington, DC 20008
telephone: [1] (202) 966-3202
FAX: [1] (202) 966-3205

Diplomatic representation from the US:
chief of mission: Ambassador (vacant); Charge d'Affaires Scott TICKNOR
embassy: Avenida de Portugal, Praia dos Coqueiros, Dili
mailing address: US Department of State, 8250 Dili Place, Washington, DC 20521-8250
telephone: (670) 332-4684
FAX: (670) 331-3206

Flag description: red, with a black isosceles triangle (based on the hoist side) superimposed on a slightly longer yellow arrowhead that extends to the center of the flag; a white star—pointing to the upper hoist-side corner of the flag—is in the center of the black triangle; yellow denotes the colonialism in Timor-Leste's past; black represents the obscurantism that needs to be overcome; red stands for the national liberation struggle; the white star symbolizes peace and serves as a guiding light

National anthem: *name:* "Patria" (Fatherland)
lyrics/music: Fransisco Borja DA COSTA/Afonso DE ARAUJO
note: adopted 2002; the song was first used as an anthem when Timor-Leste declared its independence from Portugal in 1975; the lyricist, Fransisco Borja DA COSTA, was killed in the Indonesian invasion just days after independence was declared

ECONOMY

Economy—overview: Since its 1999 independence, Timor-Leste has faced great challenges in rebuilding its infrastructure, strengthening the civil administration, and generating jobs for young people entering the work force. The development of oil and gas resources in offshore waters has greatly supplemented government revenues. This technology-intensive industry, however, has done little to create jobs for the unemployed in part because there are no production facilities in Timor-Leste. Gas is piped to Australia. In June 2005, the National Parliament unanimously approved the creation of a Petroleum Fund to serve as a repository for all petroleum revenues and to preserve the value of Timor-Leste's petroleum wealth for future generations. The Fund held assets of US$9.3 billion as of December 2011. The economy continues to recover from the mid-2006 outbreak of violence and civil unrest, which disrupted both private and public sector economic activity. Government spending increased markedly from 2009 through 2012, primarily on basic infrastructure, including electricity and roads. Limited experience in procurement and infrastructure building has hampered these projects. The underlying economic policy challenge the country faces remains how best to use oil-and-gas wealth to lift the non-oil economy onto a higher growth path and to reduce poverty. On the strength of its oil-wealth, the economy has achieved real growth between 8-12% per year for the last several years, among the highest sustained growth rates in the world.

GDP (purchasing power parity): $25.41 billion (2013 est.)
country comparison to the world: 125
$23.51 billion (2012 est.)
$21.72 billion (2011 est.)
note: data are in 2013 US dollars

GDP (official exchange rate): $6.129 billion
note: non-oil GDP (2013 est.)

GDP—real growth rate: 8.1% (2013 est.)
country comparison to the world: 10
8.3% (2012 est.)
12% (2011 est.)

GDP—per capita (PPP): $21,400 (2013 est.)
country comparison to the world: 68
$20,400 (2012 est.)
$19,400 (2011 est.)
note: data are in 2013 US dollars

GDP—composition, by end use:
household consumption: 16.7%
government consumption: 22.3%
investment in fixed capital: 16.5%
investment in inventories: 0%
exports of goods and services: 74%
imports of goods and services: -29.5% (2013 est.)

GDP—composition, by sector of origin:
agriculture: 2.6%
industry: 81.6%
services: 15.8% (2013 est.)

Agriculture—products: coffee, rice, corn, cassava (manioc), sweet potatoes, soybeans, cabbage, mangoes, bananas, vanilla

Industries: printing, soap manufacturing, handicrafts, woven cloth

Industrial production growth rate: 6.2% (2013 est.)
country comparison to the world: 41

Labor force: 418,200 (2009)
country comparison to the world: 159

Labor force—by occupation: *agriculture:* 64%
industry: 10%
services: 26% (2010)

Unemployment rate: 18.4% (2010 est.)
country comparison to the world: 158
20% (2006 est.)

Population below poverty line: 41% (2009 est.)

Household income or consumption by percentage share: *lowest 10%:* 4%
highest 10%: 27% (2007)

Distribution of family income—Gini index: 31.9 (2007 est.)
country comparison to the world: 109
38 (2002 est.)

Budget: *revenues:* $1.6 billion
expenditures: $1.7 billion (2013 est.)

Taxes and other revenues: 26.1% of GDP (2013 est.)
country comparison to the world: 115

Budget surplus (+) or deficit (-):
-1.6% of GDP (2013 est.)
country comparison to the world: 74

Fiscal year: calendar year

Inflation rate (consumer prices): 4.5% (2013 est.)
country comparison to the world: 146
11.8% (2012 est.)

Commercial bank prime lending rate: 12.3% (31 December 2013 est.)
country comparison to the world: 65
12.21% (31 December 2012 est.)

Stock of narrow money: $203.2 million (31 December 2013 est.)
country comparison to the world: 179
$205.8 million (31 December 2012 est.)

Stock of broad money: $433.4 million (31 December 2013 est.)
country comparison to the world: 180
$407 million (31 December 2012 est.)

Stock of domestic credit: $-300 million (31 December 2013 est.)
country comparison to the world: 184
$-681 million (31 December 2012 est.)

Market value of publicly traded shares: $NA

Current account balance: $2.375 billion (2011 est.)
country comparison to the world: 37
$1.161 billion (2007 est.)

Exports: $34.1 million (2011 est.)
country comparison to the world: 202
$17.8 million (2010 est.)
note: excludes oil

Exports—commodities: oil, coffee, sandalwood, marble
note: potential for vanilla exports

Imports: $689 million (2011 est.)
country comparison to the world: 188
$378 million (2010 est.)

Imports—commodities: food, gasoline, kerosene, machinery

Exchange rates: the US dollar is used

ENERGY

Electricity—production: 131.7 million kWh (2011 est.)
country comparison to the world: 193

Electricity—consumption: 67.59 million kWh (2011 est.)
country comparison to the world: 202

Electricity—exports: 0 kWh (2011 est.)
country comparison to the world: 205

Electricity—imports: 0 kWh (2011 est.)
country comparison to the world: 207

Crude oil—production: 79,490 bbl/day (2012 est.)
country comparison to the world: 54

Crude oil—exports: 87,000 bbl/day (2010 est.)
country comparison to the world: 39

Crude oil—imports: 0 bbl/day (2010 est.)
country comparison to the world: 130

Crude oil—proved reserves: 0 bbl (1 January 2013 es)
country comparison to the world: 198

Refined petroleum products—production: 0 bbl/day (2010 est.)
country comparison to the world: 201

Refined petroleum products—consumption: 2,755 bbl/day (2011 est.)
country comparison to the world: 184

Refined petroleum products—exports: 0 bbl/day (2010 est.)
country comparison to the world: 137

Refined petroleum products—imports: 1,264 bbl/day (2010 est.)
country comparison to the world: 190

Natural gas—production: 0 cu m (2011 est.)
country comparison to the world: 200

Natural gas—consumption: 0 cu m (2010 est.)
country comparison to the world: 201

Natural gas—exports: 0 cu m (2011 est.)
country comparison to the world: 195

Natural gas—imports: 0 cu m (2011 est.)
country comparison to the world: 139

Natural gas—proved reserves: 200 billion cu m (1 January 2006 es)
country comparison to the world: 46

Carbon dioxide emissions from consumption of energy: 211,100 Mt (2011 est.)
country comparison to the world: 192

COMMUNICATIONS

Telephones—main lines in use: 3,000 (2012)
country comparison to the world: 215

Telephones—mobile cellular: 621,000 (2012)
country comparison to the world: 163

Telephone system: *general assessment:* rudimentary service in urban and some rural areas, which is expanding with the entrance of new competitors
domestic: system suffered significant damage during the violence associated with independence; limited fixed-line services; mobile-cellular services have been expanding and are now available in urban and most rural areas
international: country code—670; international service is available (2012)

Broadcast media: 1 public TV broadcast station broadcasting nationally and 1 public radio broadcaster with stations in each of the 13 administrative districts; 1 commercial TV broadcast station, 3 commercial radio stations, and roughly 20 community radio stations (2012)

Internet country code: .tl

Internet hosts: 252 (2012)
country comparison to the world: 194

Internet users: 2,100 (2009)
country comparison to the world: 211

TRANSPORTATION

Airports: 6 (2013)
country comparison to the world: 176

Airports—with paved runways: *total:* 2
2,438 to 3,047 m: 1
1,524 to 2,437 m: 1 (2013)

Airports—with unpaved runways: *total:* 4
914 to 1,523 m: 2
under 914 m: 2 (2013)

Heliports: 8 (2013)

Roadways: *total:* 6,040 km
country comparison to the world: 149
paved: 2,600 km
unpaved: 3,440 km (2005)

Merchant marine: *total:* 1
country comparison to the world: 153
by type: passenger/cargo 1 (2010)

Ports and terminals: *major seaport(s):* Dili

MILITARY

Military branches: Timor-Leste Defense Force (Falintil-Forcas de Defesa de Timor-L'este, Falintil (F-FDTL)): Army, Navy (Armada) (2013)

Military service age and obligation: 18 years of age for voluntary military service; 18-month service obligation; no conscription but, as of May 2013, introduction of conscription was under discussion (2013)

Manpower available for military service:
males age 16-49: 305,643
females age 16-49: 293,052 (2010 est.)

Manpower fit for military service:
males age 16-49: 243,120
females age 16-49: 251,061 (2010 est.)

Manpower reaching militarily significant age annually: *male:* 12,737
female: 12,389 (2010 est.)

Military expenditures: 2.92% of GDP (2012)
country comparison to the world: 22
2.6% of GDP (2011)
2.92% of GDP (2010)

TRANSNATIONAL ISSUES

Disputes—international: three stretches of land borders with Timor-Leste have yet to be delimited, two of which are in the Oecussi exclave area, and no maritime or Economic Exclusion Zone boundaries have been established between the countries; maritime boundaries with Indonesia remain unresolved; many refugees who left Timor-Leste in 2003 still reside in Indonesia and refuse repatriation; in 2007, Australia and Timor-Leste signed a 50-year development zone and revenue sharing agreement in lieu of a maritime boundary

Illicit drugs: NA

TOGO

INTRODUCTION

Background: French Togoland became Togo in 1960. Gen. Gnassingbe EYADEMA, installed as military ruler in 1967, ruled Togo with a heavy hand for almost four decades. Despite the facade of multi-party elections instituted in the early 1990s, the government was largely dominated by President EYADEMA, whose Rally of the Togolese People (RPT) party has maintained power almost continually since 1967 and maintains a majority of seats in today's legislature. Upon EYADEMA's death in February 2005, the military installed the president's son, Faure GNASSINGBE, and then engineered his formal election two months later. Democratic gains since then allowed Togo to hold its first relatively free and fair legislative elections in October 2007. After years of political unrest and condemnation from international organizations for human rights abuses, Togo is finally being re-welcomed into the international community.

GEOGRAPHY

Location: Western Africa, bordering the Bight of Benin, between Benin and Ghana

Geographic coordinates: 8 00 N, 1 10 E

Map references: Africa

Area: *total:* 56,785 sq km
country comparison to the world: 126
land: 54,385 sq km
water: 2,400 sq km

Area—comparative: slightly smaller than West Virginia

Land boundaries: *total:* 1,647 km
border countries: Benin 644 km, Burkina Faso 126 km, Ghana 877 km

Coastline: 56 km

Maritime claims: *territorial sea:* 30 nm
exclusive economic zone: 200 nm

Climate: tropical; hot, humid in south; semiarid in north

Terrain: gently rolling savanna in north; central hills; southern plateau; low coastal plain with extensive lagoons and marshes

Elevation extremes: *lowest point:* Atlantic Ocean 0 m
highest point: Mont Agou 986 m

Natural resources: phosphates, limestone, marble, arable land

Land use: *arable land:* 44.2%
permanent crops: 3.7%
other: 52.1% (2011)

Irrigated land: 73 sq km (2003)

Total renewable water resources: 14.7 cu km (2011)

Freshwater withdrawal (domestic/industrial/agricultural): *total:* 0.17 cu km/yr (63%/3%/34%)
per capita: 33.46 cu m/yr (2005)

Natural hazards: hot, dry harmattan wind can reduce visibility in north during winter; periodic droughts

Environment—current issues: deforestation attributable to slash-and-burn agriculture and the use of wood for fuel; water pollution presents health hazards and hinders the fishing industry; air pollution increasing in urban areas

Environment—international agreements:
party to: Biodiversity, Climate Change, Climate Change-Kyoto Protocol, Desertification, Endangered Species, Law of the Sea, Ozone Layer Protection, Ship Pollution, Tropical Timber 83, Tropical Timber 94, Wetlands, Whaling
signed, but not ratified: none of the selected agreements

Geography—note: the country's length allows it to stretch through six distinct geographic regions; climate varies from tropical to savanna

PEOPLE AND SOCIETY

Nationality: *noun:* Togolese (singular and plural)
adjective: Togolese

Ethnic groups: African (37 tribes; largest and most important are Ewe, Mina, and Kabre) 99%, European and Syrian-Lebanese less than 1%

Languages: French (official, the language of commerce), Ewe and Mina (the two major African languages in the south), Kabye (sometimes spelled Kabiye) and Dagomba (the two major African languages in the north)

Religions: Christian 29%, Muslim 20%, indigenous beliefs 51%

Population: 7,351,374 (July 2014 est.)
country comparison to the world: 100
note: estimates for this country explicitly take into account the effects of excess mortality due to AIDS; this can result in lower life expectancy, higher infant mortality, higher death rates, lower population growth rates, and changes in the distribution of population by age and sex than would otherwise be expected

Age structure:
0-14 years: 40.7% (male 1,499,011/female 1,490,513)
15-24 years: 19.7% (male 723,237/female 726,350)
25-54 years: 32.1% (male 1,173,492/female 1,188,961)
55-64 years: 3.3% (male 145,743/female 163,384)
65 years and over: 3.2% (male 104,277/female 136,406) (2014 est.)

Dependency ratios:
total dependency ratio: 80.5 %
youth dependency ratio: 75.5 %
elderly dependency ratio: 5 %
potential support ratio: 20.1 (2013)

Median age: *total:* 19.6 years
male: 19.3 years
female: 19.8 years (2014 est.)

Population growth rate: 2.71% (2014 est.)
country comparison to the world: 22

Birth rate: 34.52 births/1,000 population (2014 est.)
country comparison to the world: 29

Death rate: 7.43 deaths/1,000 population (2014 est.)
country comparison to the world: 117

Net migration rate: 0 migrant(s)/1,000 population (2014 est.)
country comparison to the world: 82

Urbanization: *urban population:* 38% of total population (2011)
rate of urbanization: 3.3% annual rate of change (2010-15 est.)

Major urban areas—population: LOME (capital) 1.593 million (2009)

Sex ratio: *at birth:* 1.03 male(s)/female
0-14 years: 1.01 male(s)/female
15-24 years: 1 male(s)/female
25-54 years: 0.99 male(s)/female
55-64 years: 0.98 male(s)/female
65 years and over: 0.77 male(s)/female
total population: 0.98 male(s)/female (2014 est.)

Mother's mean age at first birth: 20 (1998 est.)

Maternal mortality rate: 300 deaths/100,000 live births (2010)
country comparison to the world: 40

Infant mortality rate: *total:* 46.73 deaths/1,000 live births
country comparison to the world: 44
male: 53.38 deaths/1,000 live births
female: 39.88 deaths/1,000 live births (2014 est.)

Life expectancy at birth:
total population: 64.06 years
country comparison to the world: 178
male: 61.49 years
female: 66.71 years (2014 est.)

Total fertility rate: 4.53 children born/woman (2014 est.)
country comparison to the world: 28

Contraceptive prevalence rate: 15.2% (2010)

Health expenditures: 8% of GDP (2011)
country comparison to the world: 62

Physicians density: 0.05 physicians/1,000 population (2008)

Hospital bed density: 0.7 beds/1,000 population (2011)

Drinking water source:
improved:
urban: 89.7% of population
rural: 40.1% of population
total: 59% of population
unimproved:
urban: 10.3% of population
rural: 59.9% of population
total: 41% of population (2011 est.)

Sanitation facility access:
improved:
urban: 25.5% of population
rural: 2.7% of population
total: 11.4% of population
unimproved:
urban: 74.5% of population
rural: 97.3% of population
total: 88.6% of population (2011 est.)

HIV/AIDS—adult prevalence rate: 2.9% (2012 est.)
country comparison to the world: 21

HIV/AIDS—people living with HIV/AIDS: 128,100 (2012 est.)
country comparison to the world: 40

HIV/AIDS—deaths: 7,200 (2012 est.)
country comparison to the world: 30

Major infectious diseases:
degree of risk: very high
food or waterborne diseases: bacterial and protozoal diarrhea, hepatitis A, and typhoid fever
vectorborne diseases: malaria, dengue fever, and yellow fever
respiratory disease: meningococcal meningitis
water contact disease: schistosomiasis
animal contact disease: rabies
note: highly pathogenic H5N1 avian influenza has been identified in this country; it poses a negligible risk with extremely rare cases possible among US citizens who have close contact with birds (2013)

Obesity—adult prevalence rate: 4.3% (2008)
country comparison to the world: 169

Children under the age of 5 years underweight: 16.5% (2010)
country comparison to the world: 41

Education expenditures: 4.5% of GDP (2011)
country comparison to the world: 91

Literacy: *definition:* age 15 and over can read and write
total population: 60.4%
male: 74.1%
female: 48% (2011 est.)

School life expectancy (primary to tertiary education): *total:* 12 years (2011)

Child labor—children ages 5-14:
total number: 774,801
percentage: 47 % (2010 est.)

GOVERNMENT

Country name: *conventional long form:* Togolese Republic
conventional short form: Togo
local long form: Republique Togolaise
local short form: none
former: French Togoland

Government type: republic under transition to multiparty democratic rule

Capital: *name:* Lome

geographic coordinates: 6 07 N, 1 13 E
time difference: UTC 0 (5 hours ahead of Washington, DC during Standard Time)

Administrative divisions: 5 regions (regions, singular—region); Centrale, Kara, Maritime, Plateaux, Savanes

Independence: 27 April 1960 (from French-administered UN trusteeship)

National holiday: Independence Day, 27 April (1960)

Constitution: several previous; latest adopted 27 September 1992, effective 14 October 1992; amended 2002, last in 2005 (2005)

Legal system: customary law system

International law organization participation: accepts compulsory ICJ jurisdiction with reservations; non-party state to the ICCt

Suffrage: 18 years of age; universal

Executive branch: *chief of state:* President Faure GNASSINGBE (since 4 May 2005);
head of government: Prime Minister Kwesi Seleagodji AHOOMEY-ZUNU (since 23 July 2012)
cabinet: Council of Ministers appointed by the president on the advice of the prime minister (For more information visit the World Leaders website)
elections: president elected by popular vote for a five-year term (no term limits); election last held on 4 March 2010 (next to be held in 2015); prime minister appointed by the president
election results: Faure GNASSINGBE reelected president; percent of vote—Faure GNASSINGBE 60.9%, Jean-Pierre FABRE 33.9%, Yawovi AGBOYIBO 3%, other 2.2%

Legislative branch: unicameral National Assembly (91 seats; members elected by popular vote to serve five-year terms)
elections: last held on 25 July 2013 (next to be held in 2018)
election results: percent of vote by party—NA; seats by party—UNIR 62, CST 19, Rainbow Alliance 6, UFC 3, independents 1

Judicial branch: *highest court(s):* Supreme Court or Cour Supreme (organized into the Criminal

Chamber and the Administrative Chamber, each with a chamber president and advisors); Constitutional Court (consists of 9 judges including the court president)
judge selection and term of office: Supreme Court president appointed by decree of the president of the republic upon the proposal of the Supreme Council of the Magistracy, a 9-member judicial, advisory, and disciplinary body; other judge appointments and judge tenure NA; Constitutional Court judges appointed by the National Assembly; judge tenure NA
subordinate courts: Court of Assizes (sessions court); appeals courts; tribunals of first instance (divided into civil, commercial, and correctional chambers; Court of State Security; military tribunal

Political parties and leaders:; Action Committee for Renewal or CAR [Yawovi AGBOYIBO]; Democratic Convention of African Peoples or CDPA; Movement of the Believers of Peace and Equality or MOCEP; National Alliance for Change or ANC [Jean-Pierre FABRE]; Pan-African Patriotic Convergence or CPP [Edem KODJO]; Rainbow Alliance (a colalition including: CAR and CDPA) [Brigitte Adjamagbo JOHNSON]; Rally for the Support for Development and Democracy or RSDD [Harry OLYMPIO]; Save Togo Collective or CST (a coalition including: ANC and PSR) [Ata Messan Zeus AJAVON; Socialist Pact for Renewal or PSR; Union for Democracy and Social Progress or UDPS [Gagou KOKOU]; Union for the Republic or UNIR [Faure GNASSINGBE]; Union of Forces for Change or UFC [Gilchrist OLYMPIO]

Political pressure groups and leaders: NA

International organization participation: ACP, AfDB, AU, ECOWAS, EITI (candidate country), Entente, FAO, FZ, G-77, IAEA, IBRD, ICAO, ICC (national committees), ICRM, IDA, IDB, IFAD, IFC, IFRCS, ILO, IMF, IMO, Interpol, IOC, IOM, IPU, ISO (correspondent), ITSO, ITU, ITUC (NGOs), MIGA, MINUSMA, NAM, OIC, OIF, OPCW, PCA, UN, UNAMID, UNCTAD, UNESCO, UNHCR, UNIDO, UNMIL, UNOCI, UNWTO, UPU, WADB (regional), WAEMU, WCO, WFTU (NGOs), WHO, WIPO, WMO, WTO

Diplomatic representation in the US:
chief of mission: Ambassador Limbiye Edawa Kadangha BARIKI (since 14 July 2009)
chancery: 2208 Massachusetts Avenue NW, Washington, DC 20008
telephone: [1] (202) 234-4212
FAX: [1] (202) 232-3190

Diplomatic representation from the US:
chief of mission: Ambassador Robert E. WHITEHEAD (since 3 May 2012)
embassy: 4332 Blvd. Gnassingbe Eyadema, Cite OUA, Lome
mailing address: B. P. 852, Lome; 2300 Lome Place, Washington, DC 20521-2300
telephone: [228] 2261-5470
FAX: [228] 2261-5501

Flag description: five equal horizontal bands of green (top and bottom) alternating with yellow; a white five-pointed star on a red square is in the upper hoist-side corner; the five horizontal stripes stand for the five different regions of the country; the red square is meant to express the loyalty and patriotism of the people; green symbolizes hope, fertility, and agriculture; yellow represents mineral wealth and faith that hard work and strength will bring prosperity; the star symbolizes life, purity, peace, dignity, and Togo's independence
note: uses the popular Pan-African colors of Ethiopia

National anthem: *name:* "Salut a toi, pays de nos aieux" (Hail to Thee, Land of Our Forefathers)
lyrics/music: Alex CASIMIR-DOSSEH
note: adopted 1960, restored 1992; this anthem was replaced by another during one-party rule between 1979 and 1992

ECONOMY

Economy—overview: This small, sub-Saharan economy depends heavily on both commercial and subsistence agriculture, which provides employment for a significant share of the labor force. Some basic foodstuffs must still be imported. Cocoa, coffee, and cotton generate about 40% of export earnings with cotton being the most important cash crop. Togo is among the world's largest producers of phosphate and Togo seeks to develop its carbonate phosphate reserves. The government's decade-long effort, supported by the World Bank and the IMF, to implement economic reform measures, encourage foreign investment, and bring revenues in line with expenditures has moved slowly. Progress depends on follow through on privatization, increased openness in government financial operations, progress toward legislative elections, and continued support from foreign donors. Foreign direct investment inflows have slowed over recent years. Togo completed its IMF Extended Credit Facility in 2011 and reached a HIPC debt relief completion point in 2010 at which 95% of the country's debt was forgiven. Togo continues to work with the IMF on structural reforms.

GDP (purchasing power parity): $7.348 billion (2013 est.)
country comparison to the world: 160
$6.964 billion (2012 est.)
$6.594 billion (2011 est.)
note: data are in 2013 US dollars

GDP (official exchange rate): $4.299 billion (2013 est.)

GDP—real growth rate: 5.5% (2013 est.)
country comparison to the world: 45
5.6% (2012 est.)
4.8% (2011 est.)

GDP—per capita (PPP): $1,100 (2013 est.)
country comparison to the world: 218
$1,100 (2012 est.)
$1,100 (2011 est.)
note: data are in 2013 US dollars

Gross national saving: 9.8% of GDP (2013 est.)
country comparison to the world: 137
8.7% of GDP (2012 est.)
10.7% of GDP (2011 est.)

GDP—composition, by end use:
household consumption: 87.5%
government consumption: 9.7%
investment in fixed capital: 18.7%
investment in inventories: 1.2%
exports of goods and services: 36.9%
imports of goods and services: -54% (2013 est.)

GDP—composition, by sector of origin:
agriculture: 27.6%
industry: 33.7%
services: 38.7% (2013 est.)

Agriculture—products: coffee, cocoa, cotton, yams, cassava (manioc), corn, beans, rice, millet, sorghum; livestock; fish

Industries: phosphate mining, agricultural processing, cement, handicrafts, textiles, beverages

Industrial production growth rate: 5.1% (2013 est.)
country comparison to the world: 53

Labor force: 2.595 million (2007)
country comparison to the world: 111

Labor force—by occupation: *agriculture:* 65%
industry: 5%
services: 30% (1998 est.)

Unemployment rate: NA%

Population below poverty line: 32% (1989 est.)

Household income or consumption by percentage share: *lowest 10%:* 3.3%
highest 10%: 27.1% (2006)

Budget: *revenues:* $825.8 million
expenditures: $983 million (2013 est.)

Taxes and other revenues: 19.2% of GDP (2013 est.)
country comparison to the world: 171

Budget surplus (+) or deficit (-):
-3.7% of GDP (2013 est.)
country comparison to the world: 138

Fiscal year: calendar year

Inflation rate (consumer prices): 2.2% (2013 est.)
country comparison to the world: 80
2.6% (2012 est.)

Central bank discount rate: 2.5% (31 December 2010 est.)
country comparison to the world: 86
4.25% (31 December 2009 est.)

Commercial bank prime lending rate: NA%

Stock of narrow money: $1.138 billion (31 December 2013 est.)
country comparison to the world: 147
$1.057 billion (31 December 2012 est.)

Stock of broad money: $1.971 billion (31 December 2013 est.)
country comparison to the world: 151
$1.819 billion (31 December 2012 est.)

Stock of domestic credit: $1.594 billion (31 December 2013 est.)
country comparison to the world: 141
$1.471 billion (31 December 2012 est.)

Market value of publicly traded shares: $NA

Current account balance: -$355.1 million (2013 est.)
country comparison to the world: 94
-$372.2 million (2012 est.)

Exports: $982.2 million (2013 est.)
country comparison to the world: 160
$960.5 million (2012 est.)

Exports—commodities: reexports, cotton, phosphates, coffee, cocoa

Exports—partners: India 14.2%, Lebanon 10.6%, Burkina Faso 7.6%, Benin 7.5%, China 6.1%, Niger 5.8%, Netherlands 5.2%, Ghana 4.4% (2012)

Imports: $1.677 billion (2013 est.)
country comparison to the world: 169
$1.604 billion (2012 est.)

Imports—commodities: machinery and equipment, foodstuffs, petroleum products

Imports—partners: China 40.4%, Netherlands 7.9%, France 5.4%, UK 5.3% (2012)

Reserves of foreign exchange and gold: $531.4 million (31 December 2013 est.)
country comparison to the world: 147
$441.6 million (31 December 2012 est.)

Debt—external: $719 million (31 December 2013 est.)
country comparison to the world: 169
$658.1 million (31 December 2012 est.)

Exchange rates: Communaute Financiere Africaine francs (XOF) per US dollar—
500.7 (2013 est.)
510.53 (2012 est.)
495.28 (2010 est.)
472.19 (2009)
447.81 (2008)

ENERGY

Electricity—production: 127.1 million kWh (2010 est.)
country comparison to the world: 194

Electricity—consumption: 676.1 million kWh (2010 est.)
country comparison to the world: 160

Electricity—exports: 0 kWh (2012 est.)
country comparison to the world: 202

Electricity—imports: 710 million kWh (2010 est.)
country comparison to the world: 70

Electricity—installed generating capacity: 85,000 kW (2010 est.)
country comparison to the world: 176

Electricity—from fossil fuels: 21.2% of total installed capacity (2010 est.)
country comparison to the world: 190

Electricity—from nuclear fuels: 0% of total installed capacity (2010 est.)
country comparison to the world: 188

Electricity—from hydroelectric plants: 78.8% of total installed capacity (2010 est.)
country comparison to the world: 16

Electricity—from other renewable sources: 0% of total installed capacity (2010 est.)
country comparison to the world: 129

Crude oil—production: 0 bbl/day (2012 est.)
country comparison to the world: 137

Crude oil—exports: 0 bbl/day (2010 est.)
country comparison to the world: 191

Crude oil—imports: 0 bbl/day (2010 est.)
country comparison to the world: 128

Crude oil—proved reserves: 0 bbl (1 January 2013 es)
country comparison to the world: 196

Refined petroleum products—production: 0 bbl/day (2010 est.)
country comparison to the world: 199

Refined petroleum products—consumption: 28,670 bbl/day (2011 est.)
country comparison to the world: 117

Refined petroleum products—exports: 0 bbl/day (2010 est.)
country comparison to the world: 135

Refined petroleum products—imports: 9,773 bbl/day (2010 est.)
country comparison to the world: 131

Natural gas—production: 0 cu m (2011 est.)
country comparison to the world: 198

Natural gas—consumption: 0 cu m (2010 est.)
country comparison to the world: 199

Natural gas—exports: 0 cu m (2011 est.)
country comparison to the world: 192

Natural gas—imports: 0 cu m (2011 est.)
country comparison to the world: 137

Natural gas—proved reserves: 0 cu m (1 January 2013 es)
country comparison to the world: 199

Carbon dioxide emissions from consumption of energy: 1.445 million Mt (2011 est.)
country comparison to the world: 156

COMMUNICATIONS

Telephones—main lines in use: 225,000 (2012)
country comparison to the world: 127

Telephones—mobile cellular: 3.518 million (2012)
country comparison to the world: 124

Telephone system: *general assessment:* fair system based on a network of microwave radio relay routes supplemented by open-wire lines and a mobile-cellular system
domestic: microwave radio relay and open-wire lines for conventional system; combined fixed-line and mobile-cellular teledensity roughly 50 telephones per 100 persons with mobile-cellular use predominating
international: country code—228; satellite earth stations—1 Intelsat (Atlantic Ocean), 1 Symphonie (2010)

Broadcast media: 2 state-owned TV stations with multiple transmission sites; 5 private TV stations broadcast locally; cable TV service is available; state-owned radio network with multiple stations; several dozen private radio stations and a few community radio stations; transmissions of multiple international broadcasters available (2007)

Internet country code: .tg

Internet hosts: 1,168 (2012)
country comparison to the world: 170

Internet users: 356,300 (2009)
country comparison to the world: 123

TRANSPORTATION

Airports: 8 (2013)
country comparison to the world: 162

Airports—with paved runways: *total:* 2
2,438 to 3,047 m: 2 (2013)

Airports—with unpaved runways: *total:* 6
914 to 1,523 m: 4
under 914 m: 2 (2013)

Railways: *total:* 568 km
country comparison to the world: 110
narrow gauge: 568 km 1.000-m gauge (2008)

Roadways: *total:* 11,652 km
country comparison to the world: 129
paved: 2,447 km
unpaved: 9,205 km (2007)

Waterways: 50 km (seasonally navigable by small craft on the Mono River depending on rainfall) (2011)
country comparison to the world: 103

Merchant marine: *total:* 6 1

country comparison to the world: 66
by type: bulk carrier 6, cargo 38, carrier 3, chemical tanker 5, container 3, passenger/cargo 1, petroleum tanker 3, refrigerated cargo 1, roll on/roll off 1 foreign-owned: 21 (China 1, Lebanon 6, Romania 1, Syria 6, Turkey 4, UAE 1, US 1, Yemen 1) (2010)

Ports and terminals: *major seaport(s):* Kpeme, Lome

MILITARY

Military branches: Togolese Armed Forces (Forces Armees Togolaise, FAT): Togolese Army (l'Armee de Terre), Togolese Navy (Forces Naval Togolaises), Togolese Air Force (Force Aerienne Togolaise, TAF), National Gendarmerie (2013)

Military service age and obligation: 18 years of age for compulsory and voluntary military service; 2-year service obligation (2012)

Manpower available for military service:
males age 16-49: 1,577,572
females age 16-49: 1,589,715 (2010 est.)

Manpower fit for military service:
males age 16-49: 1,104,536
females age 16-49: 1,158,061 (2010 est.)

Manpower reaching militarily significant age annually: *male:* 74,036
female: 73,515 (2010 est.)

Military expenditures: NA% (2012)
1.6% of GDP (2011)
NA% (2010)

TRANSNATIONAL ISSUES

Disputes—international: in 2001, Benin claimed Togo moved boundary monuments—joint commission continues to resurvey the boundary; in 2006, 14,000 Togolese refugees remain in Benin and Ghana out of the 40,000 who fled there in 2005; talks continue between Benin and Togo on funding the Adjrala hydroelectric dam on the Mona River

Refugees and internally displaced persons: *refugees (country of origin):* 17,371 (Ghana); 5,593 (Cote d'Ivoire) (2012)
IDPs: undetermined (2012)

Illicit drugs: transit hub for Nigerian heroin and cocaine traffickers; money laundering not a significant problem

TOKELAU

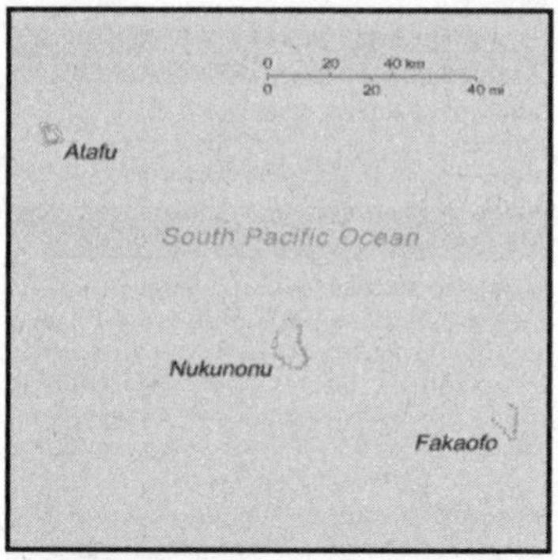

INTRODUCTION

Background: Originally settled by Polynesian emigrants from surrounding island groups, the Tokelau Islands were made a British protectorate in 1889. They were transferred to New Zealand administration in 1925. Referenda held in 2006 and 2007 to change the status of the islands from that of a New Zealand territory to one of free association with New Zealand did not meet the needed threshold for approval.

GEOGRAPHY

Location: Oceania, group of three atolls in the South Pacific Ocean, about one-half of the way from Hawaii to New Zealand

Geographic coordinates: 9 00 S, 172 00 W

Map references: Oceania

Area: *total:* 12 sq km
country comparison to the world: 242
land: 12 sq km
water: 0 sq km

Area—comparative: about 17 times the size of The Mall in Washington, DC

Land boundaries: 0 km

Coastline: 101 km

Maritime claims: *territorial sea:* 12 nm
exclusive economic zone: 200 nm

Climate: tropical; moderated by trade winds (April to November)

Terrain: low-lying coral atolls enclosing large lagoons

Elevation extremes: *lowest point:* Pacific Ocean 0 m
highest point: unnamed location 5 m

Natural resources: NEGL

Land use: *arable land:* 0% (soil is thin and infertile)
permanent crops: 60%
other: 40% (2011)

Irrigated land: NA

Natural hazards: lies in Pacific typhoon belt

Environment—current issues: limited natural resources and overcrowding are contributing to emigration to New Zealand

Geography—note: consists of three atolls (Atafu, Fakaofo, Nukunonu), each with a lagoon surrounded by a number of reef-bound islets of varying length and rising to over 3 m above sea level

PEOPLE AND SOCIETY4

Nationality: *noun:* Tokelauan(s)
adjective: Tokelauan

Ethnic groups: Tokelauan 65.3%, part Tokelauan/Samoan 8.7%, part Tokelauan/Tuvaluan 6.9%, part Tokelauan/other Pacific islander 1.9%, part Tokelauan/European 1%, Samoan 6.7%, Tuvaluan 2.8%, other Pacific islander 1.1%, other 5.1%, unspecified 0.4% (2011 est.)

Languages: Tokelauan 93.5% (a Polynesian language), English 58.9%, Samoan 45.5%, Tuvaluan 11.6%, Kiribati 2.7%, other 2.5%, none 4.1%, unspecified 0.6%
note: shares sum to more than 100% because some respondents gave more than one answer on the census (2011 ests.)

Religions: Congregational Christian Church 58.2%, Roman Catholic 36.6%, Presbyterian 1.8%, other Christian 2.8%, Spiritualism and New Age 0.1%, unspecified 0.5% (2011 est.)

Population: 1,337 (July 2014 est.)
country comparison to the world: 236

Age structure: *0-14 years:* 42%
15-64 years: 53%
65 years and over: 5% (2013 est.)

Population growth rate: -0.01% (2014 est.)
country comparison to the world: 198

Urbanization: *urban population:* 0% of total population (2010)
rate of urbanization: 0% annual rate of change (2010-15 est.)

Sex ratio: NA

Infant mortality rate: *total:* NA
male: NA
female: NA

Life expectancy at birth: *total population:* NA
male: NA
female: NA

Total fertility rate: NA (2014 est.)

Drinking water source:
improved:
rural: 97.4% of population
total: 97.4% of population
unimproved:
rural: 2.6% of population
total: 2.6% of population (2011 est.)

Sanitation facility access:
improved:
rural: 92.9% of population
total: 92.9% of population
unimproved:
rural: 7.1% of population
total: 7.1% of population (2011 est.)

HIV/AIDS—adult prevalence rate: NA

HIV/AIDS—people living with HIV/AIDS: NA

HIV/AIDS—deaths: NA

Obesity—adult prevalence rate: 63.4% (2007)
country comparison to the world: 4

Education expenditures: NA

Literacy: NA

School life expectancy (primary to tertiary education): *total:* 12 years
male: 12 years
female: 13 years (2003)

GOVERNMENT

Country name: *conventional long form:* none
conventional short form: Tokelau

Dependency status: self-administering territory of New Zealand; note—Tokelau and New Zealand have agreed to a draft constitution as Tokelau moves toward free association with New Zealand; a UN-sponsored referendum on self governance in October 2007 did not produce the two-thirds majority vote necessary for changing the political status

Government type: NA

Capital: none; each atoll has its own administrative center
time difference: UTC+13 (18 hours ahead of Washington, DC during Standard Time)

Administrative divisions: none (territory of New Zealand)

Independence: none (territory of New Zealand)

National holiday: Waitangi Day (Treaty of Waitangi established British sovereignty over New Zealand), 6 February (1840)

Constitution: many previous; latest effective 1 January 1949 (Tokelau Islands Act 1948); amended many times, last in 2007 (2012)

Legal system: common law system of New Zealand

Suffrage: 21 years of age; universal

Executive branch: *chief of state:* Queen ELIZABETH II (since 6 February 1952); represented by Governor General of New Zealand Anand SATYANAND (since 23 August 2006); New Zealand is represented by Administrator Jonathan KINGS (since February 2011)
head of government: Kuresa NASAU (since February 2014); note—position rotates annually among the 3 Faipule (village leaders)
cabinet: the Council for the Ongoing Government of Tokelau, consisting of 3 Faipule (village leaders) and 3 Pulenuku (village mayors), functions as a cabinet (For more information visit the World Leaders website)
elections: the monarchy is hereditary; governor general appointed by the monarch; administrator appointed by the Minister of Foreign Affairs and Trade in New Zealand; the head of government chosen from the Council of Faipule and serves a one-year term

Legislative branch: unicameral General Fono (20 seats; members elected by popular vote to serve three-year terms based upon proportional representation from the three islands—Atafu has 7 seats, Fakaofo has 7 seats, Nukunonu has 6 seats); note—the Tokelau Amendment Act of 1996 confers limited legislative power to the General Fono
elections: last held on 23 January 2014 (next to be held in 2017)
election results: independents 20

Judicial branch: *highest court(s):* Court of Appeal in New Zealand (consists of the court president and 8 judges sitting in 3- or 5-judge panels depending on the case)
judge selection and term of office: judges nominated by the Judicial Selection Committee and

approved by three-quarters majority of the Parliament; judge tenure NA
subordinate courts: High Court, in New Zealand; Council of Elders or Taupulega

Political parties and leaders: none

Political pressure groups and leaders: none

International organization participation: PIF (observer), SPC, UNESCO (associate), UPU

Diplomatic representation in the US: none (territory of New Zealand)

Diplomatic representation from the US: none (territory of New Zealand)

Flag description: a yellow stylized Tokelauan canoe on a dark blue field sails toward the manu—the Southern Cross constellation of four, white, five-pointed stars at the hoist side; the Southern Cross represents the role of Christianity in Tokelauan culture and, in conjunction with the canoe, symbolizes the country navigating into the future; the color yellow indicates happiness and peace, and the blue field represents the ocean on which the community relies

National symbol(s): tuluma (fishing tackle box)

National anthem: *name:* "Te Atua" (For the Almighty)
lyrics/music: unknown/Falani KALOLO
note: adopted 2008; in preparation for eventual self governance, Tokelau held a national contest to choose an anthem; as a territory of New Zealand, "God Defend New Zealand" and "God Save the Queen" are official (see New Zealand)

ECONOMY

Economy—overview: Tokelau's small size (three villages), isolation, and lack of resources greatly restrain economic development and confine agriculture to the subsistence level. The people rely heavily on aid from New Zealand—about $10 million annually in 2008 and 2009—to maintain public services. New Zealand's support amounts to 80% of Tokelau's recurrent government budget. An international trust fund, currently worth nearly US$32 million, was established in 2004 to provide Tokelau an independent source of revenue. The principal sources of revenue come from sales of copra, postage stamps, souvenir coins, and handicrafts. Money is also remitted to families from relatives in New Zealand.

GDP (purchasing power parity): $1.5 million (1993 est.)
country comparison to the world: 229

GDP (official exchange rate): $NA

GDP—real growth rate: NA%

GDP—per capita (PPP): $1,000 (1993 est.)
country comparison to the world: 220

GDP—composition, by sector of origin:
agriculture: NA%
industry: NA%
services: NA%

Agriculture—products: coconuts, copra, breadfruit, papayas, bananas; pigs, poultry, goats; fish

Industries: small-scale enterprises for copra production, woodworking, plaited craft goods; stamps, coins; fishing

Labor force: 440 (2001)
country comparison to the world: 232

Unemployment rate: NA%

Population below poverty line: NA%

Budget: *revenues:* $430,800
expenditures: $2.8 million (1987 est.)

Fiscal year: 1 April—31 March

Inflation rate (consumer prices): NA%

Exports: $0 (2002)
country comparison to the world: 223

Exports—commodities: stamps, copra, handicrafts

Imports: $969,200 (2002)
country comparison to the world: 223

Imports—commodities: foodstuffs, building materials, fuel

Exchange rates: New Zealand dollars (NZD) per US dollar—
1.247 (2013)
1.2334 (2012)
1.3874 (2010)
1.6002 (2009)
1.4151 (2008)

ENERGY

Crude oil—proved reserves: 0 bbl (1 January 2013 es)
country comparison to the world: 194

COMMUNICATIONS

Telephone system: *general assessment:* modern satellite-based communications system
domestic: radiotelephone service between islands
international: country code—690; radiotelephone service to Samoa; government-regulated telephone service (TeleTok); satellite earth stations—3 (2009)

Broadcast media: no TV stations; each atoll operates a radio service that provides shipping news and weather reports (2009)

Internet country code: .tk

Internet hosts: 2,069 (2012)
country comparison to the world: 162

Internet users: 800 (2008)
country comparison to the world: 216

TRANSPORTATION

Ports and terminals: none; offshore anchorage only

MILITARY

Military—note: defense is the responsibility of New Zealand

TRANSNATIONAL ISSUES

Disputes—international: Tokelau included American Samoa's Swains Island (Olosega) in its 2006 draft independence constitution

TONGA

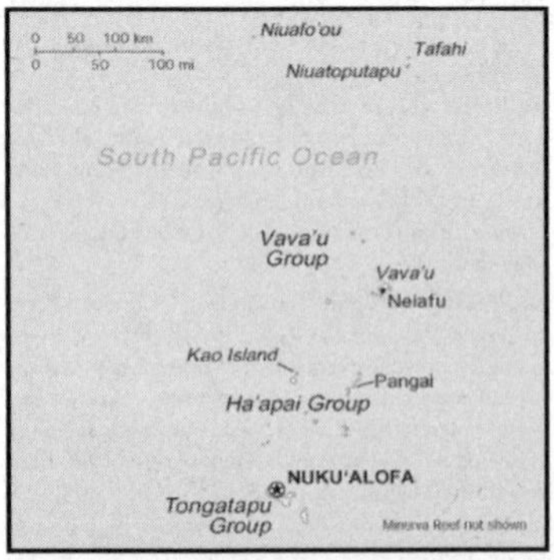

INTRODUCTION

Background: Tonga—unique among Pacific nations—never completely lost its indigenous governance. The archipelagos of "The Friendly Islands" were united into a Polynesian kingdom in 1845. Tonga became a constitutional monarchy in 1875 and a British protectorate in 1900; it withdrew from the protectorate and joined the Commonwealth of Nations in 1970. Tonga remains the only monarchy in the Pacific.

GEOGRAPHY

Location: Oceania, archipelago in the South Pacific Ocean, about two-thirds of the way from Hawaii to New Zealand

Geographic coordinates: 20 00 S, 175 00 W

Map references: Oceania

Area: *total:* 747 sq km
country comparison to the world: 190
land: 717 sq km
water: 30 sq km

Area—comparative: four times the size of Washington, DC

Land boundaries: 0 km

Coastline: 419 km

Maritime claims: *territorial sea:* 12 nm
exclusive economic zone: 200 nm
continental shelf: 200 m depth or to the depth of exploitation

Climate: tropical; modified by trade winds; warm season (December to May), cool season (May to December)

Terrain: most islands have limestone base formed from uplifted coral formation; others have limestone overlying volcanic base

Elevation extremes: *lowest point:* Pacific Ocean 0 m
highest point: unnamed elevation on Kao Island 1,033 m

Natural resources: fish, fertile soil

Land use: *arable land:* 21.33%
permanent crops: 14.67%
other: 64% (2011)

Irrigated land: NA

Natural hazards: cyclones (October to April); earthquakes and volcanic activity on Fonuafo'ou
volcanism: moderate volcanic activity; Fonualei (elev. 180 m) has shown frequent activity in recent years, while Niuafo'ou (elev. 260 m), which last erupted in 1985, has forced evacuations; other historically active volcanoes include Late and Tofua

Environment—current issues: deforestation results as more and more land is being cleared for agriculture and settlement; some damage to coral reefs from starfish and indiscriminate coral and shell collectors; overhunting threatens native sea turtle populations

Environment—international agreements: *party to:* Biodiversity, Climate Change, Climate Change-Kyoto Protocol, Desertification, Law of the Sea, Marine Dumping, Marine Life Conservation, Ozone Layer Protection, Ship Pollution
signed, but not ratified: none of the selected agreements

Geography—note: archipelago of 169 islands (36 inhabited)

PEOPLE AND SOCIETY

Nationality: *noun:* Tongan(s)
adjective: Tongan

Ethnic groups: Tongan 96.6%, part-Tongan 1.7%, other 1.7%, unspecified 0.03% (2006 est.)

Languages: English and Tongan 87%, Tongan (official) 10.7%, English (official) 1.2%, other 1.1%, uspecified 0.03% (2006 est.)

Religions: Protestant 64.9% (includes Free Wesleyan Church 37.3%, Free Church of Tonga 11.4%, Church of Tonga 7.2%, Tokaikolo Christian Church 2.6%, Assembly of God 2.3% Seventh Day Adventist 2.2%, Constitutional Church of Tonga .9%, Anglican .8% and Full Gospel Church .2%), Mormon 16.8%, Roman Catholic 15.6%, other 1.1%, none 0.03%, unspecified 1.7% (2006 est.)

Population: 106,440 (July 2014 est.)
country comparison to the world: 192

Age structure:
0-14 years: 35.6% (male 19,272/female 18,661)
15-24 years: 19.3% (male 10,514/female 10,016)
25-54 years: 33.3% (male 17,717/female 17,732)
55-64 years: 6.3% (male 2,852/female 3,013)
65 years and over: 6.2% (male 3,044/female 3,619) (2014 est.)

Dependency ratios:
total dependency ratio: 75.7 %
youth dependency ratio: 65.4 %
elderly dependency ratio: 10.3 %
potential support ratio: 9.7 (2013)

Median age: *total:* 22 years
male: 21.6 years
female: 22.5 years (2014 est.)

Population growth rate: 0.09% (2014 est.)
country comparison to the world: 185

Birth rate: 23.55 births/1,000 population (2014 est.)
country comparison to the world: 66

Death rate: 4.86 deaths/1,000 population (2014 est.)
country comparison to the world: 194

Net migration rate: -17.85 migrant(s)/1,000 population (2014 est.)
country comparison to the world: 219

Urbanization: *urban population:* 23% of total population (2010)
rate of urbanization: 0.8% annual rate of change (2010-15 est.)

Sex ratio: *at birth:* 1.03 male(s)/female
0-14 years: 1.03 male(s)/female
15-24 years: 1.05 male(s)/female
25-54 years: 1 male(s)/female
55-64 years: 1.01 male(s)/female
65 years and over: 0.86 male(s)/female
total population: 1.01 male(s)/female (2014 est.)

Maternal mortality rate: 110 deaths/100,000 live births (2010)
country comparison to the world: 66

Infant mortality rate: *total:* 12.36 deaths/1,000 live births
country comparison to the world: 125
male: 12.78 deaths/1,000 live births
female: 11.93 deaths/1,000 live births (2014 est.)

Life expectancy at birth:
total population: 75.82 years
country comparison to the world: 88
male: 74.35 years
female: 77.34 years (2014 est.)

Total fertility rate: 3.36 children born/woman (2014 est.)
country comparison to the world: 48

Health expenditures: 5.3% of GDP (2011)
country comparison to the world: 133

Physicians density: 0.56 physicians/1,000 population (2010)

Hospital bed density: 2.6 beds/1,000 population (2010)

Drinking water source:
improved:
urban: 98.8% of population
rural: 99.4% of population
total: 99.2% of population
unimproved:
urban: 1.2% of population
rural: 0.6% of population
total: 0.8% of population (2011 est.)

Sanitation facility access:
improved:
urban: 99.3% of population
rural: 89.1% of population
total: 91.5% of population
unimproved:
urban: 0.7% of population
rural: 10.9% of population
total: 8.5% of population (2011 est.)

HIV/AIDS—adult prevalence rate: NA

HIV/AIDS—people living with HIV/AIDS: NA

HIV/AIDS—deaths: NA

Obesity—adult prevalence rate: 57.6% (2008)
country comparison to the world: 5

Education expenditures: 3.9% of GDP (2004)
country comparison to the world: 113

Literacy: *definition:* can read and write Tongan and/or English
total population: 99%
male: 99%
female: 99.1% (2006 est.)

School life expectancy (primary to tertiary education): *total:* 14 years
male: 13 years
female: 14 years (2002)

Unemployment, youth ages 15-24: *total:* 11.9%
country comparison to the world: 101
male: 9.9%
female: 15.1% (2003)

GOVERNMENT

Country name: *conventional long form:* Kingdom of Tonga
conventional short form: Tonga
local long form: Pule'anga Tonga
local short form: Tonga
former: Friendly Islands

Government type: constitutional monarchy

Capital: *name:* Nuku'alofa

geographic coordinates: 21 08 S, 175 12 W
time difference: UTC+13 (18 hours ahead of Washington, DC during Standard Time)

Administrative divisions: 5 island divisions; 'Eua, Ha'apai, Ongo Niua, Tongatapu, Vava'u

Independence: 4 June 1970 (from UK protectorate)

National holiday: National Day, 4 November (1875)

Constitution: adopted 4 November 1875; amended many times, last in 2013 (2013)

Legal system: English common law

International law organization participation: has not submitted an ICJ jurisdiction declaration; non-party state to the ICCt

Suffrage: 21 years of age; universal

Executive branch: *chief of state:* King TUPOU VI (since 18 March 2012); note—King George TUPOU V died on 18 March 2012 in Hong Kong; he was succeeded by his brother Crown Prince TUPOUTO'A Lavaka, who took the throne name TUPOU VI
head of government: Prime Minister Lord Siale'ataonga TU'IVAKANO (since 22 December 2010)
cabinet: Cabinet is nominated by the prime minister and appointed by the monarch (For more information visit the World Leaders website)
note: there is also a Privy Council that advises the monarch
elections: the monarchy is hereditary; prime minister and deputy prime minister elected by and from the members of parliament and appointed by the monarch
election results: Lord Siale'ataonga TU'IVAKANO elected by parliament on 21 December 2010 with 14 of 26 votes

Legislative branch: unicameral Legislative Assembly or Fale Alea (26 seats—9 for nobles elected from among the country's 29 nobles, 17 members elected by popular vote to serve four-year terms)
elections: last held on 25 November 2010 (next to be held in 2014)
election results: Peoples Representatives: percent of vote—independents 67.3%, Democratic Party 28.5%, other 4.2%; seats—Democratic Party 12, independents 5

Judicial branch: *highest court(s):* Court of Appeal (consists of the court president and a number of judges determined by the monarch); note—appeals beyond the Court of Appeal are brought before the King in Privy Council, the monarch's advisory organ that has both judicial and legislative powers
judge selection and term of office: judge appointments and tenures made by the King in Privy Council, judge appointments subject to consent of the Legislative Assembly
subordinate courts: Supreme Court; Magistrate's Courts; Land Courts

Political parties and leaders: Democratic Party of the Friendly Islands [Samuela 'Akilisi POHIVA] People's Democratic Party or PDP [Tesina FUKO] Sustainable Nation-Building Party [Sione FONUA] Tonga Democratic Labor Party [NA] Tonga Human Rights and Democracy Movement or THRDM [NA]

Political pressure groups and leaders: Human Rights and Democracy Movement Tonga or HRDMT [Rev. Simote VEA, chairman] Public Servant's Association [Finau TUTONE]

International organization participation: ACP, ADB, AOSIS, C, FAO, G-77, IAEA, IBRD, ICAO, ICRM, IDA, IFAD, IFC, IFRCS, IHO, IMF, IMO, IMSO, Interpol, IOC, ITU, ITUC (NGOs), OPCW, PIF, Sparteca, SPC, UN, UNCTAD, UNESCO, UNIDO, UPU, WCO, WHO, WIPO, WMO, WTO

Diplomatic representation in the US:
chief of mission: Ambassador Mahe'uli'uli Sandhurst TUPOUNIUA (since 10 September 2013)
chancery: 800 Second Avenue, Suite 400B, New York, NY 10017
telephone: [1] (800) 345-6541
consulate(s) general: San Francisco

Diplomatic representation from the US: the US does not have an embassy in Tonga; the US ambassador to Fiji, currently Ambassador Frankie A. REED, is accredited to Tonga

Flag description: red with a bold red cross on a white rectangle in the upper hoist-side corner; the cross reflects the deep-rooted Christianity in Tonga; red represents the blood of Christ and his sacrifice; white signifies purity

National symbol(s): red cross on white field; arms equal length

National anthem: *name:* "Ko e fasi `o e tu"i `o e `Otu Tonga" (Song of the King of the Tonga Islands)
lyrics/music: Uelingatoni Ngu TUPOUMALOHI/Karl Gustavus SCHMITT
note: in use since 1875; the anthem is more commonly known as "Fasi Fakafonua" (National Song)

ECONOMY

Economy—overview: Tonga has a small, open, South Pacific island economy. It has a narrow export base in agricultural goods. Squash, vanilla beans, and yams are the main crops. Agricultural exports, including fish, make up two-thirds of total exports. The country must import a high proportion of its food, mainly from New Zealand. The country remains dependent on external aid and remittances from Tongan communities overseas to offset its trade deficit. Tourism is the second-largest source of hard currency earnings following remittances. Tonga had 39,000 visitors in 2006. The government is emphasizing the development of the private sector, especially the encouragement of investment, and is committing increased funds for health and education. Tonga has a reasonably sound basic infrastructure and well developed social services. High unemployment among the young, moderate inflation, pressures for democratic reform, and rising civil service expenditures are major issues facing the government.

GDP (purchasing power parity): $846 million (2013 est.)
country comparison to the world: 208
$837.3 million (2012 est.)
$831.3 million (2011 est.)
note: data are in 2013 US dollars

GDP (official exchange rate): $477 million (2013 est.)

GDP—real growth rate: 1% (2013 est.)
country comparison to the world: 175
0.7% (2012 est.)
1.9% (2011 est.)

GDP—per capita (PPP): $8,200 (2013 est.)
country comparison to the world: 133
$8,100 (2012 est.)
$8,100 (2011 est.)
note: data are in 2013 US dollars

GDP—composition, by end use:
household consumption: 95.9%
government consumption: 17.2%
investment in fixed capital: 29.9%
investment in inventories: 0%
exports of goods and services: 18.8%
imports of goods and services: -61.8% (2013 est.)

GDP—composition, by sector of origin:
agriculture: 20.9%
industry: 21.9%
services: 57.2% (2013 est.)

Agriculture—products: squash, coconuts, copra, bananas, vanilla beans, cocoa, coffee, ginger, black pepper; fish

Industries: tourism, construction, fishing

Industrial production growth rate: 1% (2013 est.)
country comparison to the world: 150

Labor force: 39,960 (2007)
country comparison to the world: 196

Labor force—by occupation: *agriculture:* 31.8%
industry: 30.6%
services: 2,003% (2003 est.)

Unemployment rate: 13% (FY03/04 est.)
country comparison to the world: 129

Population below poverty line: 24% (FY03/04)

Household income or consumption by percentage share: *lowest* 10%: NA%
highest 10%: NA%

Budget: *revenues:* $112.4 million
expenditures: $112.4 million (2013 est.)

Taxes and other revenues: 23.6% of GDP (2012 est.)
country comparison to the world: 139

Budget surplus (+) or deficit (-):
0% of GDP (2012 est.)
country comparison to the world: 46

Fiscal year: 1 July—30 June

Inflation rate (consumer prices): 2% (2013 est.)
country comparison to the world: 66
1.2% (2012 est.)

Commercial bank prime lending rate: 10.9% (31 December 2013 est.)
country comparison to the world: 84
10.36% (31 December 2012 est.)

Stock of narrow money: $85.97 million (31 December 2013 est.)
country comparison to the world: 185
$81.03 million (31 December 2012 est.)

Stock of broad money: $178.8 million (31 December 2013 est.)
country comparison to the world: 187
$186.6 million (31 December 2012 est.)

Stock of domestic credit: $110 million (31 December 2013 est.)
country comparison to the world: 177
$125.5 million (31 December 2012 est.)

Market value of publicly traded shares: $NA

Current account balance: -$43.3 million (2013 est.)
country comparison to the world: 67
-$48.5 million (2012 est.)

Exports: $9.1 million (2013 est.)
country comparison to the world: 214
$8.4 million (2012 est.)

Exports—commodities: squash, fish, vanilla beans, root crops

Exports—partners: South Korea 18.5%, US 17%, NZ 15.6%, Fiji 10.2%, Japan 9.5%, Samoa 8.6%, American Samoa 5.4%, Australia 5.1% (2012)

Imports: $122.5 million (2013 est.)
country comparison to the world: 209
$121.9 million (2012 est.)

Imports—commodities: foodstuffs, machinery and transport equipment, fuels, chemicals

Imports—partners: Fiji 35.7%, NZ 24.4%, US 10.5%, China 10.2% (2012)

Reserves of foreign exchange and gold: $147.1 million (31 December 2013 est.)
country comparison to the world: 164
$152.4 million (31 December 2012 est.)

Debt—external: $215.8 million (31 December 2013 est.)
country comparison to the world: 187
$198.6 million (31 December 2012 est.)

Stock of direct foreign investment—at home:
$61.39 million (31 December 2013 est.)
country comparison to the world: 107
$61.43 million (31 December 2012 est.)

Exchange rates: pa'anga (TOP) per US dollar—
1.78 (2013 est.)
1.72 (2012 est.)
1.906 (2010 est.)

ENERGY

Electricity—production: 41 million kWh (2010 est.)
country comparison to the world: 207

Electricity—consumption: 38.13 million kWh (2010 est.)
country comparison to the world: 207

Electricity—exports: 0 kWh (2012)
country comparison to the world: 201

Electricity—imports: 0 kWh (2012 est.)
country comparison to the world: 205

Electricity—installed generating capacity:
12,000 kW (2010 est.)
country comparison to the world: 203

Electricity—from fossil fuels: 100% of total installed capacity (2010 est.)
country comparison to the world: 37

Electricity—from nuclear fuels: 0% of total installed capacity (2010 est.)
country comparison to the world: 187

Electricity—from hydroelectric plants: 0% of total installed capacity (2010 est.)
country comparison to the world: 204

Electricity—from other renewable sources:
0% of total installed capacity (2010 est.)
country comparison to the world: 128

Crude oil—production: 0 bbl/day (2012 est.)
country comparison to the world: 136

Crude oil—exports: 0 bbl/day (2010 est.)
country comparison to the world: 190

Crude oil—imports: 0 bbl/day (2010 est.)
country comparison to the world: 127

Crude oil—proved reserves: 0 bbl (1 January 2010 es)
country comparison to the world: 195

Refined petroleum products—production: 0 bbl/day (2010 est.)
country comparison to the world: 198

Refined petroleum products—consumption:
1,221 bbl/day (2011 est.)
country comparison to the world: 196

Refined petroleum products—exports: 0 bbl/day (2010 est.)
country comparison to the world: 134

Refined petroleum products—imports: 1,202 bbl/day (2010 est.)
country comparison to the world: 191

Natural gas—production: 0 cu m (2011 est.)
country comparison to the world: 197

Natural gas—consumption: 0 cu m (2010 est.)
country comparison to the world: 198

Natural gas—exports: 0 cu m (2011 est.)
country comparison to the world: 191

Natural gas—imports: 0 cu m (2011 est.)
country comparison to the world: 136

Natural gas—proved reserves: 0 cu m (1 January 2013 es)
country comparison to the world: 198

Carbon dioxide emissions from consumption of energy: 154,600 Mt (2011 est.)
country comparison to the world: 198

COMMUNICATIONS

Telephones—main lines in use: 30,000 (2012)
country comparison to the world: 175

Telephones—mobile cellular: 56,000 (2012)
country comparison to the world: 201

Telephone system: *general assessment:* competition between Tonga Telecommunications Corporation (TCC) and Shoreline Communications Tonga (SCT) is accelerating expansion of telecommunications; SCT granted approval to introduce high-speed digital service for telephone, Internet, and television while TCC has exclusive rights to operate the mobile-phone network; international telecom services are provided by government-owned Tonga Telecommunications International
domestic: combined fixed-line and mobile-cellular teledensity about 80 telephones per 100 persons; fully automatic switched network
international: country code—676; satellite earth station—1 Intelsat (Pacific Ocean) (2011)

Broadcast media: 2 state-owned TV stations and 2 privately owned TV stations; satellite and cable TV services are available; 2 state-owned and 3 privately owned radio stations; Radio Australia broadcasts available via satellite (2009)

Internet country code: .to

Internet hosts: 5,367 (2012)
country comparison to the world: 144

Internet users: 8,400 (2009)
country comparison to the world: 203

TRANSPORTATION

Airports: 6 (2013)
country comparison to the world: 175

Airports—with paved runways: *total:* 1
2,438 to 3,047 m: 1 (2013)

Airports—with unpaved runways: *total:* 5
1,524 to 2,437 m: 1
914 to 1,523 m: 3
under 914 m: 1 (2013)

Roadways: *total:* 680 km
country comparison to the world: 189
paved: 184 km
unpaved: 496 km (2011)

Merchant marine: *total:* 7
country comparison to the world: 122
by type: cargo 4, carrier 1, passenger/cargo 2
foreign-owned: 2 (Australia 1, UK 1) (2010)

Ports and terminals: *major seaport(s):* Nuku'alofa, Neiafu, Pangai

MILITARY

Military branches: Tonga Defense Services (TDS): Land Force (Royal Guard), Maritime Force (includes Royal Marines, Air Wing) (2013)

Military service age and obligation: 16 years of age for voluntary enlistment (with parental consent); no conscription; the king retains the right to call up "all those capable of bearing arms" in wartime (2012)

Manpower available for military service:
males age 16-49: 24,460
females age 16-49: 24,041 (2010 est.)

Manpower fit for military service:
males age 16-49: 20,956
females age 16-49: 20,577 (2010 est.)

Manpower reaching militarily significant age annually: *male:* 1,196
female: 1,134 (2010 est.)

TRANSNATIONAL ISSUES

Disputes—international: none

TRINIDAD AND TOBAGO

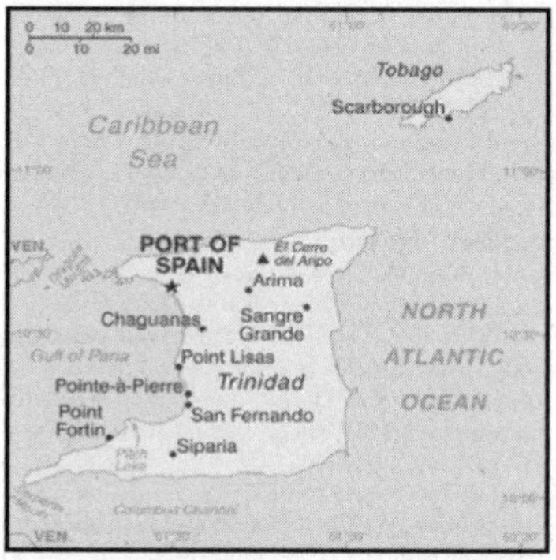

INTRODUCTION

Background: First colonized by the Spanish, the islands came under British control in the early 19th century. The islands' sugar industry was hurt by the emancipation of the slaves in 1834. Manpower was replaced with the importation of contract laborers from India between 1845 and 1917, which boosted sugar production as well as the cocoa industry. The discovery of oil on Trinidad in 1910 added another important export. Independence was attained in 1962. The country is one of the most prosperous in the Caribbean thanks largely to petroleum and natural gas production and processing. Tourism, mostly in Tobago, is targeted for expansion and is growing. The government is coping with a rise in violent crime.

GEOGRAPHY

Location: Caribbean, islands between the Caribbean Sea and the North Atlantic Ocean, northeast of Venezuela

Geographic coordinates: 11 00 N, 61 00 W

Map references: Central America and the Caribbean

Area: *total:* 5,128 sq km
country comparison to the world: 174
land: 5,128 sq km
water: 0 sq km

Area—comparative: slightly smaller than Delaware

Land boundaries: 0 km

Coastline: 362 km

Maritime claims: measured from claimed archipelagic baselines
territorial sea: 12 nm
contiguous zone: 24 nm
exclusive economic zone: 200 nm
continental shelf: 200 nm or to the outer edge of the continental margin

Climate: tropical; rainy season (June to December)

Terrain: mostly plains with some hills and low mountains

Elevation extremes: *lowest point:* Caribbean Sea 0 m
highest point: El Cerro del Aripo 940 m

Natural resources: petroleum, natural gas, asphalt

Land use: *arable land:* 4.87%
permanent crops: 4.29%
other: 90.84% (2011)

Irrigated land: 36 sq km (2003)

Total renewable water resources: 3.84 cu km (2011)

Freshwater withdrawal (domestic/industrial/agricultural): *total:* 0.23 cu km/yr (67%/25%/8%)
per capita: 177.9 cu m/yr (2005)

Natural hazards: outside usual path of hurricanes and other tropical storms

Environment—current issues: water pollution from agricultural chemicals, industrial wastes, and raw sewage; oil pollution of beaches; deforestation; soil erosion

Environment—international agreements: *party to:* Biodiversity, Climate Change, Climate Change-Kyoto Protocol, Desertification, Endangered Species, Hazardous Wastes, Law of the Sea, Marine Dumping, Marine Life Conservation, Ozone Layer Protection, Ship Pollution, Tropical Timber 83, Tropical Timber 94, Wetlands
signed, but not ratified: none of the selected agreements

Geography—note: Pitch Lake, on Trinidad's southwestern coast, is the world's largest natural reservoir of asphalt

PEOPLE AND SOCIETY

Nationality: *noun:* Trinidadian(s), Tobagonian(s)
adjective: Trinidadian, Tobagonian

Ethnic groups: East Indian 35.4%, African 34.2%, mixed—other 15.3%, mixed African/East Indian 7.7%, other 1.3%, unspecified 6.2% (2011 est.)

Languages: English (official), Caribbean Hindustani (a dialect of Hindi), French, Spanish, Chinese

Religions: Protestant 32.1% (Pentecostal/Evangelical/Full Gospel 12%, Baptist 6.9%, Anglican

5.7%, Seventh-Day Adventist 4.1%, Presbyterian/ Congretational 2.5, other Protestant .9), Roman Catholic 21.6%, Hindu 18.2%, Muslim 5%, Jehovah's Witness 1.5%, other 8.4%, none 2.2%, unspecified 11.1% (2011 est.)

Population: 1,223,916 (July 2014 est.)
country comparison to the world: 159

Age structure:
0-14 years: 19.4% (male 121,386/female 116,661)
15-24 years: 13% (male 82,779/female 76,785)
25-54 years: 46.9% (male 298,156/female 276,205)
55-64 years: 9.5% (male 67,738/female 68,535)
65 years and over: 9.1% (male 50,107/female 65,564) (2014 est.)

Dependency ratios:
total dependency ratio: 42.5 %
youth dependency ratio: 29.6 %
elderly dependency ratio: 12.9 %
potential support ratio: 7.8 (2013)

Median age: *total:* 34.4 years
male: 34 years
female: 34.9 years (2014 est.)

Population growth rate: -0.11% (2014 est.)
country comparison to the world: 205

Birth rate: 13.8 births/1,000 population (2014 est.)
country comparison to the world: 145

Death rate: 8.48 deaths/1,000 population (2014 est.)
country comparison to the world: 81

Net migration rate: -6.42 migrant(s)/1,000 population (2014 est.)
country comparison to the world: 201

Urbanization: *urban population:* 14% of total population (2010)
rate of urbanization: 3% annual rate of change (2010-15 est.)

Major urban areas—population: PORT-OF-SPAIN (capital) 57,000 (2009)

Sex ratio: *at birth:* 1.03 male(s)/female
0-14 years: 1.04 male(s)/female
15-24 years: 1.08 male(s)/female
25-54 years: 1.08 male(s)/female
55-64 years: 1.03 male(s)/female
65 years and over: 0.76 male(s)/female
total population: 1.03 male(s)/female (2014 est.)

Maternal mortality rate: 46 deaths/100,000 live births (2010)
country comparison to the world: 112

Infant mortality rate: *total:* 24.82 deaths/1,000 live births
country comparison to the world: 72
male: 26.05 deaths/1,000 live births
female: 23.57 deaths/1,000 live births (2014 est.)

Life expectancy at birth:
total population: 72.29 years
country comparison to the world: 136
male: 69.42 years
female: 75.24 years (2014 est.)

Total fertility rate: 1.71 children born/woman (2014 est.)
country comparison to the world: 171

Contraceptive prevalence rate: 42.5% (2006)

Health expenditures: 5.7% of GDP (2011)
country comparison to the world: 119

Physicians density: 1.18 physicians/1,000 population (2007)

Hospital bed density: 2.1 beds/1,000 population (2.1)

Drinking water source:
improved:
urban: 97.6% of population
rural: 93.3% of population
total: 93.9% of population
unimproved:
urban: 2.4% of population
rural: 6.7% of population
total: 6.1% of population (2011 est.)

Sanitation facility access:
improved:
urban: 92.1% of population
rural: 92.1% of population
total: 92.1% of population
unimproved:
urban: 7.9% of population
rural: 7.9% of population
total: 7.9% of population (2011 est.)

HIV/AIDS—adult prevalence rate: 1.6% (2012 est.)
country comparison to the world: 30

HIV/AIDS—people living with HIV/AIDS: 14,300 (2012 est.)
country comparison to the world: 93

HIV/AIDS—deaths: 500 (2012 est.)
country comparison to the world: 88

Obesity—adult prevalence rate: 29.3% (2008)
country comparison to the world: 31

Children under the age of 5 years underweight: 4.4% (2000)
country comparison to the world: 96

Education expenditures: 3.2% of GDP (2003)
country comparison to the world: 135

Literacy: *definition:* age 15 and over can read and write
total population: 98.8%
male: 99.2%
female: 98.5% (2011 est.)

School life expectancy (primary to tertiary education): *total:* 12 years
male: 12 years
female: 13 years (2004)

Child labor—children ages 5-14:
total number: 1,201
percentage: 1 % (2006 est.)

Unemployment, youth ages 15-24: *total:* 10.5%
country comparison to the world: 108
male: 8.8%
female: 12.9% (2008)

GOVERNMENT

Country name: *conventional long form:* Republic of Trinidad and Tobago
conventional short form: Trinidad and Tobago

Government type: parliamentary democracy

Capital: *name:* Port of Spain

geographic coordinates: 10 39 N, 61 31 W
time difference: UTC-4 (1 hour ahead of Washington, DC during Standard Time)

Administrative divisions: 9 regions, 3 boroughs, 2 cities, 1 ward

regions: Couva/Tabaquite/Talparo, Diego Martin, Mayaro/Rio Claro, Penal/Debe, Princes Town, Sangre Grande, San Juan/Laventille, Siparia, Tunapuna/Piarco
borough: Arima, Chaguanas, Point Fortin
cities: Port of Spain, San Fernando
ward: Tobago

Independence: 31 August 1962 (from the UK)

National holiday: Independence Day, 31 August (1962)

Constitution: previous 1962; latest 1976; amended many times, last in 2007 (2012)

Legal system: English common law; judicial review of legislative acts in the Supreme Court

International law organization participation: has not submitted an ICJ jurisdiction declaration; accepts ICCt jurisdiction

Suffrage: 18 years of age; universal

Executive branch: *chief of state:* President Anthony CARMONA (since 18 March 2013)
head of government: Prime Minister Kamla PERSAD-BISSESSAR (since 26 May 2010)
cabinet: Cabinet appointed from among the members of Parliament (For more information visit the World Leaders website)
elections: president elected by an electoral college, which consists of the members of the Senate and House of Representatives, for a five-year term (eligible for a second term); election last held on 15 February 2013 (next to be held by February 2018); the president usually appoints as prime minister the leader of the majority party in the House of Representatives
election results: as the only candidate nominated, Anthony CARMONA elected president; sworn in on 18 March 2013; percent of electoral college vote—100%

Legislative branch: bicameral Parliament consists of the Senate (31 seats; 16 members appointed by the ruling party, 9 by the president, 6 by the opposition party to serve a maximum term of five years) and the House of Representatives (41 seats; members are elected by popular vote to serve five-year terms)
elections: House of Representatives—last held on 24 May 2010 (next to be held in 2015)
election results: House of Representatives—percent of vote—NA; seats by party—UNC 21, PNM 12, COP 6, TOP 2
note: Tobago has a unicameral House of Assembly with 12 members serving four-year terms; last election held in January 2013; seats by party—PNM 12

Judicial branch: *highest court(s):* Supreme Court of the Judicature (consists of a chief justice for both the Court of Appeal with 12 judges and the High Court with 24 judges) note—Trinidad and Tobago can file appeals beyond its Supreme Court to the Caribbean Court of Justice, with final appeal to the Judicial Committee of the Privy Council (in London)
judge selection and term of office: Supreme Court chief justice appointed by the president after consultation with the prime minister and the parliamentary leader of the opposition; other judges appointed by the Judicial Legal Services Commission, headed by the chief justice and 5 members with judicial experience; all judges appointed for life with mandatory retirement normally at age 65
subordinate courts: Courts of Summary Criminal Jurisdiction; Petty Civil Courts; Family Court

Political parties and leaders: Congress of the People or COP [Prakash RAMADHAR]; Democratic Action Congress or DAC [Hochoy CHARLES] (only active in Tobago); Democratic National Alliance or DNA [Charles CARSON] (coalition of NAR, DDPT, MND); Movement for National Development or MND [Garvin NICHOLAS]; National Alliance for Reconstruction or NAR [Lennox SANKERSINGH]; People's National Movement or PNM [Keith ROWLEY]; Tobago Organization of the People or TOP [Ashworth JACK]; United National Congress or UNC

[Kamla PERSAD-BISSESSAR]; United National Congress or UNC [Kamla PERSAD-BISSESSAR]

Political pressure groups and leaders: Jamaat-al Muslimeen [Yasin ABU BAKR]

International organization participation: ACP, AOSIS, C, Caricom, CDB, CELAC, EITI (candidate country), FAO, G-24, G-77, IADB, IAEA, IBRD, ICAO, ICC (NGOs), ICRM, IDA, IFAD, IFC, IFRCS, IHO, ILO, IMF, IMO, Interpol, IOC, IOM, IPU, ISO, ITSO, ITU, ITUC; (NGOs), LAES, MIGA, NAM, OAS, OPANAL, OPCW, Paris Club; (associate), UN, UNCTAD, UNESCO, UNIDO, UPU, WCO, WFTU (NGOs), WHO, WIPO, WMO, WTO

Diplomatic representation in the US:
chief of mission: Ambassador Neil N. PARSAN (since 14 February 2011)
chancery: 1708 Massachusetts Avenue NW, Washington, DC 20036
telephone: [1] (202) 467-6490
FAX: [1] (202) 785-3130
consulate(s) general: Miami, New York

Diplomatic representation from the US:
chief of mission: Ambassador (vacant); Charge d'Affaires Margaret B. DIOP
embassy: 15 Queen's Park West, Port of Spain
mailing address: P. O. Box 752, Port of Spain
telephone: [1] (868) 622-6371 through 6376
FAX: [1] (868) 822-5905

Flag description: red with a white-edged black diagonal band from the upper hoist side; to the lower fly side; the colors represent the elements of earth, water, and fire; black stands for the wealth of the land and the dedication of; the people; white symbolizes the sea surrounding the islands, the; purity of the country's aspirations, and equality; red symbolizes the; warmth and energy of the sun, the vitality of the land, and the; courage and friendliness of its people

National symbol(s): scarlet ibis (bird of Trinidad); cocrico (bird of Tobago)

National anthem: *name:* "Forged From the Love of Liberty"
lyrics/music: Patrick Stanislaus CASTAGNE
note: adopted 1962; the song was originally created to serve as an anthem for the West Indies Federation; it was adopted by Trinidad and Tobago following the Federation's dissolution in 1962

ECONOMY

Economy—overview: Trinidad and Tobago has earned a reputation as an excellent; investment site for international businesses and has one of the; highest per capita incomes in Latin America. Economic growth; between 2000 and 2007 averaged slightly over 8%, significantly above; the regional average of about 3.7% for that same period; however, GDP; has slowed down since then and contracted during 2009-2011 due to; depressed natural gas prices and changing markets. Growth had been; fueled by investments in liquefied natural gas, petrochemicals, and; steel with additional upstream and downstream investment planned.; Trinidad and Tobago is the leading Caribbean producer of oil and gas, and its economy is heavily dependent upon these resources but it also; supplies manufactured goods, notably food products and beverages, as well as cement to the Caribbean region. Oil and gas account for; about 40% of GDP and 80% of exports, but only 5% of employment. Oil; production has declined over the last decade as the country focused; the majority of its efforts on natural gas. However, declining reserves, lack of government investment in the sector, and the changing global; gas market raises concern for the long-term growth of the country's; energy sector. Although Trinidad and Tobago enjoys cheap electricity; from natural gas, the renewable energy sector has recently garnered; increased interest. The country is also a regional financial center with; a well-regulated and stable financial system. Other sectors the; Government of Trinidad and Tobago targeted for increased; investment and projected growth include tourism, agriculture, information and communications technology, and shipping. The; economy benefits from a growing trade surplus with the US. The US is; Trinidad and Tobago's leading trade partner. The previous MANNING; administration benefited from fiscal surpluses fueled by the dynamic; export sector; however, declines in oil and gas prices have reduced; government revenues, challenging the current government's; commitment to maintaining high levels of public investment. Crime; and bureaucratic hurdles continue to be the biggest deterrents for; attracting more foreign direct investment and business. The; government's 2013 budget aims to boost revenue through increased; taxation and competitiveness.

GDP (purchasing power parity): $27.14 billion (2013 est.)
country comparison to the world: 121
$26.71 billion (2012 est.)
$26.66 billion (2011 est.)
note: data are in 2013 US dollars

GDP (official exchange rate): $27.13 billion (2013 est.)

GDP—real growth rate: 1.6% (2013 est.)
country comparison to the world: 153
0.2% (2012 est.)
-2.6% (2011 est.)

GDP—per capita (PPP): $20,300 (2013 est.)
country comparison to the world: 70
$20,100 (2012 est.)
$20,100 (2011 est.)
note: data are in 2013 US dollars

Gross national saving: 18.2% of GDP (2013 est.)
country comparison to the world: 87
20% of GDP (2012 est.)
28.1% of GDP (2011 est.)

GDP—composition, by end use:
household consumption: 56.1%
government consumption: 16.9%
investment in fixed capital: 15.4%
investment in inventories: -20.2%
exports of goods and services: 94.3%
imports of goods and services: -62.5% (2013 est.)

GDP—composition, by sector of origin:
agriculture: 0.3%
industry: 57.7%
services: 42% (2013 est.)

Agriculture—products: cocoa, rice, citrus, coffee, vegetables; poultry; sugar

Industries: petroleum and petroleum products, liquefied natural gas (LNG), methanol, ammonia, urea, steel products, beverages, food processing, cement, cotton textiles

Industrial production growth rate: 1.2% (2013 est.)
country comparison to the world: 141

Labor force: 621,000 (2013 est.)
country comparison to the world: 156

Labor force—by occupation: *agriculture:* 3.8%
manufacturing, mining, and quarrying: 12.8%
construction and utilities: 20.4%
services: 62.9% (2007 est.)

Unemployment rate: 5.9% (2013 est.)
country comparison to the world: 57
5.6% (2012 est.)

Population below poverty line: 17% (2007 est.)

Household income or consumption by percentage share: *lowest 10%:* NA%
highest 10%: NA%

Budget: *revenues:* $7.847 billion
expenditures: $8.323 billion (2013 est.)

Taxes and other revenues: 28.9% of GDP (2013 est.)
country comparison to the world: 98

Budget surplus (+) or deficit (-):
-1.8% of GDP (2013 est.)
country comparison to the world: 77

Public debt: 37.1% of GDP (2013 est.)
country comparison to the world: 100
37.9% of GDP (2012 est.)

Fiscal year: 1 October—30 September

Inflation rate (consumer prices): 5.4% (2013 est.)
country comparison to the world: 160
9.2% (2012 est.)

Central bank discount rate: 4.25% (31 December 2010 est.)
country comparison to the world: 38
7.25% (31 December 2009 est.)

Commercial bank prime lending rate: 7.5% (31 December 2013 est.)
country comparison to the world: 118
7.7% (31 December 2012 est.)

Stock of narrow money: $7.044 billion (31 December 2013 est.)
country comparison to the world: 92
$6.221 billion (31 December 2012 est.)

Stock of broad money: $20.12 billion (31 December 2013 est.)
country comparison to the world: 86
$17.82 billion (31 December 2012 est.)

Stock of domestic credit: $6.403 billion (31 December 2013 est.)
country comparison to the world: 109
$6.059 billion (31 December 2012 est.)

Market value of publicly traded shares: $15.17 billion (31 December 2012 est.)
country comparison to the world: 67
$14.73 billion (31 December 2011)
$12.16 billion (31 December 2010 est.)

Current account balance: $414.1 million (2013 est.)
country comparison to the world: 52
$959 million (2012 est.)

Exports: $12.86 billion (2013 est.)
country comparison to the world: 85
$12.98 billion (2012 est.)

Exports—commodities: petroleum and petroleum products, liquefied natural gas, methanol, ammonia, urea, steel products, beverages, cereal and cereal products, sugar, cocoa, coffee, citrus fruit, vegetables, flowers

Exports—partners: US 42.1%, Chile 7.1%, Argentina 6.5%, Spain 4.5% (2012)

Imports: $9.638 billion (2013 est.)
country comparison to the world: 103
$9.065 billion (2012 est.)

Imports—commodities: mineral fuels, lubricants, machinery, transportation equipment, manufactured goods, food, chemicals, live animals

Imports—partners: US 33.1%, Brazil 8.1%, Colombia 7.7%, Gabon 5.5%, Canada 4.4%, China 4.2% (2012)

Reserves of foreign exchange and gold: $10.07 billion (31 December 2013 est.)
country comparison to the world: 76
$9.897 billion (31 December 2012 est.)

Debt—external: $4.823 billion (31 December 2013 est.)
country comparison to the world: 124
$4.722 billion (31 December 2012 est.)

Stock of direct foreign investment—at home: $102 billion (31 December 2008 est.)
country comparison to the world: 42
$12.44 billion (2007)

Stock of direct foreign investment—abroad: $3.829 billion (2007)
country comparison to the world: 65

Exchange rates: Trinidad and Tobago dollars (TTD) per US dollar—
6.411 (2013 est.)
6.3907 (2012 est.)
6.3755 (2010 est.)
6.3099 (2009)
6.2896 (2008)

ENERGY

Electricity—production: 7.998 billion kWh (2010 est.)
country comparison to the world: 99

Electricity—consumption: 7.586 billion kWh (2010 est.)
country comparison to the world: 97

Electricity—exports: 0 kWh (2012 est.)
country comparison to the world: 199

Electricity—imports: 0 kWh (2012 est.)
country comparison to the world: 203

Electricity—installed generating capacity: 1.605 million kW (2010 est.)
country comparison to the world: 113

Electricity—from fossil fuels: 99.7% of total installed capacity (2010 est.)
country comparison to the world: 47

Electricity—from nuclear fuels: 0% of total installed capacity (2010 est.)
country comparison to the world: 183

Electricity—from hydroelectric plants: 0% of total installed capacity (2010 est.)
country comparison to the world: 202

Electricity—from other renewable sources: 0.3% of total installed capacity (2010 est.)
country comparison to the world: 90

Crude oil—production: 119,300 bbl/day (2012 est.)
country comparison to the world: 46

Crude oil—exports: 75,340 bbl/day (2010 est.)
country comparison to the world: 43

Crude oil—imports: 70,260 bbl/day (2010 est.)
country comparison to the world: 52

Crude oil—proved reserves: 728.3 million bbl (1 January 2013 es)
country comparison to the world: 44

Refined petroleum products—production: 132,300 bbl/day (2010 est.)
country comparison to the world: 66

Refined petroleum products—consumption: 41,000 bbl/day (2011 est.)
country comparison to the world: 105

Refined petroleum products—exports: 106,500 bbl/day (2010 est.)
country comparison to the world: 43

Refined petroleum products—imports: 1,598 bbl/day (2010 est.)
country comparison to the world: 185

Natural gas—production: 40.6 billion cu m (2011 est.)
country comparison to the world: 22

Natural gas—consumption: 23.32 billion cu m (2010 est.)
country comparison to the world: 32

Natural gas—exports: 17.64 billion cu m (2011 est.)
country comparison to the world: 20

Natural gas—imports: 0 cu m (2011 est.)
country comparison to the world: 133

Natural gas—proved reserves: 375.4 billion cu m (1 January 2013 es)
country comparison to the world: 36

Carbon dioxide emissions from consumption of energy: 52.07 million Mt (2011 est.)
country comparison to the world: 62

COMMUNICATIONS

Telephones—main lines in use: 287,000 (2012)
country comparison to the world: 119

Telephones—mobile cellular: 1.884 million (2012)
country comparison to the world: 147

Telephone system: *general assessment:* excellent international service; good local service
domestic: combined fixed-line and mobile-cellular teledensity roughly 170 telephones per 100 persons
international: country code—1-868; submarine cable systems provide connectivity to US and parts of the Caribbean and South America; satellite earth station—1 Intelsat (Atlantic Ocean); tropospheric scatter to Barbados and Guyana (2011)

Broadcast media: 5 TV networks, one of which is state-owned, broadcast on multiple stations; multiple cable TV subscription service providers; multiple radio networks, one state-owned, broadcast over about 35 stations (2007)

Internet country code: .tt

Internet hosts: 241,690 (2012)
country comparison to the world: 69

Internet users: 593,000 (2009)
country comparison to the world: 115

TRANSPORTATION

Airports: 4 (2013)
country comparison to the world: 189

Airports—with paved runways: *total:* 2
over 3,047 m: 1
2,438 to 3,047 m: 1 (2013)

Airports—with unpaved runways: *total:* 2
914 to 1,523 m: 1
under 914 m: 1 (2013)

Pipelines: condensate 257 km; condensate/gas 11 km; gas 1,567 km; oil 587 km (2013)

Roadways: *total:* 8,320 km
country comparison to the world: 139
paved: 4,252 km
unpaved: 4,068 km (2001)

Merchant marine: *total:* 4
country comparison to the world: 130
by type: passenger 1, passenger/cargo 2, petroleum tanker 1
registered in other countries: 2 (unknown 2) (2010)

Ports and terminals: *major seaport(s):* Point Fortin, Point Lisas, Port of Spain, Scarborough
oil terminals: Galeota Point terminal

MILITARY

Military branches: Trinidad and Tobago Defense Force (TTDF): Trinidad and Tobago; Army, Coast Guard, Air Guard, Defense Force Reserves (2010)

Military service age and obligation: 18-25 years of age for voluntary military service (16 years of age with parental consent); no conscription; Trinidad and Tobago citizenship; and completion of secondary school required (2012)

Manpower available for military service:
males age 16-49: 341,764
females age 16-49: 317,899 (2010 est.)

Manpower fit for military service:
males age 16-49: 269,824
females age 16-49: 261,735 (2010 est.)

Manpower reaching militarily significant age annually: *male:* 8,164
female: 7,503 (2010 est.)

TRANSNATIONAL ISSUES

Disputes—international: Barbados and Trinidad and Tobago abide by the April 2006 Permanent Court of Arbitration decision delimiting a maritime boundary and limiting catches of flying fish in Trinidad and Tobago's exclusive economic zone; in 2005, Barbados and Trinidad and Tobago agreed to compulsory international arbitration under United Nations Convention on the Law of the Sea challenging whether the northern limit of Trinidad and Tobago's and Venezuela's maritime boundary extends into Barbadian waters; Guyana has also expressed its intention to include itself in the arbitration as the Trinidad and Tobago-Venezuela maritime boundary may extend into its waters as well

Trafficking in persons: *current situation:* Trinidad and Tobago is a destination and transit country for adults and children subjected to sex trafficking and adults subjected to forced labor; local victims have been trafficked to the US and the UK for sexual exploitation, while women and girls from South America and the Dominican Republic have been subjected to sex trafficking in Trinidad and Tobago's brothels and clubs; some economic migrants from the Caribbean region and Asia have had their passports held and experienced forced labor conditions; children are vulnerable to forced labor, including scavenging trash; the country is a potential transit point for human trafficking to Caribbean and South American destinations

tier rating: Tier 2 Watch List—Trinidad and Tobago does not fully comply with the minimum standards for the elimination of trafficking; however, it is making significant efforts to do so; in 2013, the government proclaimed its anti-trafficking law and established a counter-trafficking unit, but authorities did not use the law to its full effect; despite victim protections in the new law, the government has failed to properly screen and protect hundreds of potential trafficking victims; the reported complicity of public officials in trafficking offenses is also an obstacle (2013)

Illicit drugs: transshipment point for South American drugs destined for the US and Europe; producer of cannabis

TUNISIA

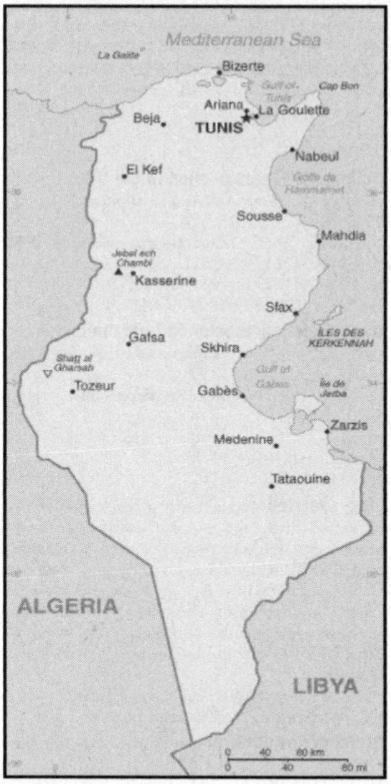

INTRODUCTION

Background: Rivalry between French and Italian interests in Tunisia culminated in a French invasion in 1881 and the creation of a protectorate. Agitation for independence in the decades following World War I was finally successful in getting the French to recognize Tunisia as an independent state in 1956. The country's first president, Habib BOURGUIBA, established a strict one-party state. He dominated the country for 31 years, repressing Islamic fundamentalism and establishing rights for women unmatched by any other Arab nation. In November 1987, BOURGUIBA was removed from office and replaced by Zine el Abidine BEN ALI in a bloodless coup. Street protests that began in Tunis in December 2010 over high unemployment, corruption, widespread poverty, and high food prices escalated in January 2011, culminating in rioting that led to hundreds of deaths. On 14 January 2011, the same day BEN ALI dismissed the government, he fled the country, and by late January 2011, a "national unity government" was formed. Elections for the new Constituent Assembly were held in late October 2011, and in December, it elected human rights activist Moncef MARZOUKI as interim president. The Assembly began drafting a new constitution in February 2012 and, after several iterations and a months-long political crisis that stalled the transition, ratified the document in January 2014. Presidential and parliamentary elections for a permanent government could be held by the end of 2014.

GEOGRAPHY

Location: Northern Africa, bordering the Mediterranean Sea, between Algeria and Libya

Geographic coordinates: 34 00 N, 9 00 E

Map references: Africa

Area: *total:* 163,610 sq km
country comparison to the world: 93
land: 155,360 sq km
water: 8,250 sq km

Area—comparative: slightly larger than Georgia

Land boundaries: *total:* 1,424 km
border countries: Algeria 965 km, Libya 459 km

Coastline: 1,148 km

Maritime claims: *territorial sea:* 12 nm
contiguous zone: 24 nm
exclusive economic zone: 12 nm

Climate: temperate in north with mild, rainy winters and hot, dry summers; desert in south

Terrain: mountains in north; hot, dry central plain; semiarid south merges into the Sahara

Elevation extremes:
lowest point: Shatt al Gharsah -17 m
highest point: Jebel ech Chambi 1,544 m

Natural resources: petroleum, phosphates, iron ore, lead, zinc, salt

Land use: *arable land:* 17.35%
permanent crops: 14.63%
other: 68.02% (2011)

Irrigated land: 3,970 sq km (2003)

Total renewable water resources: 4.6 cu km (2011)

Freshwater withdrawal (domestic/industrial/agricultural): *total:* 2.85 cu km/yr (14%/4%/82%)
per capita: 295.8 cu m/yr (2001)

Natural hazards: NA

Environment—current issues: toxic and hazardous waste disposal is ineffective and poses health risks; water pollution from raw sewage; limited natural freshwater resources; deforestation; overgrazing; soil erosion; desertification

Environment—international agreements:
party to: Biodiversity, Climate Change, Climate Change-Kyoto Protocol, Desertification, Endangered Species, Environmental Modification, Hazardous Wastes, Law of the Sea, Marine Dumping, Ozone Layer Protection, Ship Pollution, Wetlands
signed, but not ratified: Marine Life Conservation

Geography—note: strategic location in central Mediterranean; Malta and Tunisia are discussing the commercial exploitation of the continental shelf between their countries, particularly for oil exploration

PEOPLE AND SOCIETY

Nationality: *noun:* Tunisian(s)
adjective: Tunisian

Ethnic groups: Arab 98%, European 1%, Jewish and other 1%

Languages: Arabic (official, one of the languages of commerce), French (commerce), Berber (Tamazight)

Religions: Muslim (official; Sunni) 99.1%, other (includes Christian, Jewish, Shia Muslim, and Baha'i) 1%

Population: 10,937,521 (July 2014 est.)
country comparison to the world: 79

Age structure:
0-14 years: 23% (male 1,298,262/female 1,219,086)
15-24 years: 16% (male 879,755/female 871,954)
25-54 years: 44.6% (male 2,373,765/female 2,509,750)
55-64 years: 7.9% (male 468,278/female 454,170)
65 years and over: 7.7% (male 423,350/female 439,151) (2014 est.)

Dependency ratios:
total dependency ratio: 43.6 %
youth dependency ratio: 33.3 %
elderly dependency ratio: 10.3 %
potential support ratio: 9.7 (2013)

Median age: *total:* 31.4 years
male: 31 years
female: 31.8 years (2014 est.)

Population growth rate: 0.92% (2014 est.)
country comparison to the world: 126

Birth rate: 16.9 births/1,000 population (2014 est.)
country comparison to the world: 112

Death rate: 5.94 deaths/1,000 population (2014 est.)
country comparison to the world: 168

Net migration rate: -1.74 migrant(s)/1,000 population (2014 est.)
country comparison to the world: 161

Urbanization: *urban population:* 66.3% of total population (2011)
rate of urbanization: 1.34% annual rate of change (2010-15 est.)

Major urban areas—population: TUNIS (capital) 759,000 (2009)

Sex ratio: *at birth:* 1.07 male(s)/female
0-14 years: 1.07 male(s)/female
15-24 years: 1.01 male(s)/female
25-54 years: 0.95 male(s)/female
55-64 years: 0.99 male(s)/female
65 years and over: 0.96 male(s)/female
total population: 0.99 male(s)/female (2014 est.)

Maternal mortality rate: 56 deaths/100,000 live births (2010)
country comparison to the world: 104

Infant mortality rate: *total:* 23.19 deaths/1,000 live births
country comparison to the world: 78
male: 26.63 deaths/1,000 live births
female: 19.51 deaths/1,000 live births (2014 est.)

Life expectancy at birth:
total population: 75.68 years
country comparison to the world: 92
male: 73.6 years
female: 77.9 years (2014 est.)

Total fertility rate: 2 children born/woman (2014 est.)
country comparison to the world: 126

Contraceptive prevalence rate: 63% (2012)

Health expenditures: 6.2% of GDP (2011)
country comparison to the world: 104

Physicians density: 1.22 physicians/1,000 population (2010)

Hospital bed density: 2.1 beds/1,000 population (2010)

Drinking water source:
improved:
urban: 100% of population
rural: 89.2% of population
total: 96.4% of population
unimproved:
urban: 0% of population

rural: 10.8% of population
total: 3.6% of population (2011 est.)

Sanitation facility access:
improved:
urban: 97.3% of population
rural: 75% of population
total: 89.8% of population
unimproved:
urban: 2.7% of population
rural: 25% of population
total: 10.2% of population (2011 est.)

HIV/AIDS—adult prevalence rate: 0.1% (2012 est.)
country comparison to the world: 147

HIV/AIDS—people living with HIV/AIDS: 2,300 (2012 est.)
country comparison to the world: 138

HIV/AIDS—deaths: 100 (2012 est.)
country comparison to the world: 147

Obesity—adult prevalence rate: 22.3% (2008)
country comparison to the world: 80

Children under the age of 5 years underweight: 3.3% (2006)
country comparison to the world: 110

Education expenditures: 6.2% of GDP (2012)
country comparison to the world: 38

Literacy: *definition:* age 15 and over can read and write
total population: 79.1%
male: 87.4%
female: 71.1% (2010 est.)

School life expectancy (primary to tertiary education): *total:* 15 years
male: 14 years
female: 15 years (2010)

Unemployment, youth ages 15-24: *total:* 42.3% (2011)
country comparison to the world: 10

GOVERNMENT

Country name: *conventional long form:* Tunisian Republic
conventional short form: Tunisia
local long form: Al Jumhuriyah at Tunisiyah
local short form: Tunis

Government type: republic

Capital: *name:* Tunis

geographic coordinates: 36 48 N, 10 11 E
time difference: UTC+1 (6 hours ahead of Washington, DC during Standard Time)

Administrative divisions: 24 governorates (wilayat, singular—wilayah); Beja (Bajah), Ben Arous (Bin 'Arus), Bizerte (Banzart), Gabes (Qabis), Gafsa (Qafsah), Jendouba (Jundubah), Kairouan (Al Qayrawan), Kasserine (Al Qasrayn), Kebili (Qibili), Kef (Al Kaf), L'Ariana (Aryanah), Mahdia (Al Mahdiyah), Manouba (Manubah), Medenine (Madanin), Monastir (Al Munastir), Nabeul (Nabul), Sfax (Safaqis), Sidi Bouzid (Sidi Bu Zayd), Siliana (Silyanah), Sousse (Susah), Tataouine (Tatawin), Tozeur (Tawzar), Tunis, Zaghouan (Zaghwan)

Independence: 20 March 1956 (from France)

National holiday: Independence Day, 20 March (1956); Revolution and Youth Day, 14 January (2011)

Constitution: several previous; latest approved by Constituent Assembly 26 January 2014 (2014)

Legal system: mixed legal system of civil law, based on the French civil code, and Islamic law; some judicial review of legislative acts in the Supreme Court in joint session

International law organization participation: has not submitted an ICJ jurisdiction declaration; non-party state to the ICCt

Suffrage: 18 years of age; universal except for active government security forces (including the police and the military), people with mental disabilities, people who have served more than three months in prison (criminal cases only), and people given a suspended sentence of more than six months

Executive branch: *note:* the interim government will remain in power pending a general election slated for late 2014
chief of state: President Moncef MARZOUKI (since 12 December 2011)
head of government: Prime Minister Mehdi JOMAA (since 29 January 2014)
cabinet: selected by the prime minister and approved by the Constituent Assembly (For more information visit the World Leaders website)
elections: president elected by Constituent Assembly; election last held on 12 December 2011 (next to be held NA); prime minister appointed by the president
election results: President MARZOUKI elected by Constituent Assembly with 153 of 156 votes

Legislative branch: unicameral Constituent Assembly (217 seats); note—the legislative role of the Constituent Assembly remains unclear
elections: initial election of 217 Constituent Assembly members held on 23 October 2011 (next to be held NA)
election results: percent of vote by party—NA; seats by party—al-Nahda 89, CPR 29, Popular Petition 26, FDTL 20, PDP 16, PDM 5, The Initiative 5, Afek Tounes 4, PCOT 3, other minor parties each with fewer than three seats 20

Judicial branch: *highest court(s):* Court of Cassation or Cour de Cassation (organized into civil and criminal chambers and consists of NA judges)
judge selection and term of office: judges nominated by the Higher Magistracy Council (also called the Superior Council of the Judiciary), a 7-member body of judges and prosecutors; judges appointed by presidential decree; judge tenure NA
subordinate courts: Administrative Court; Courts of Appeal; Housing Court; courts of first instance; lower district courts; military courts

Political parties and leaders: Afek Tounes [Emna MINF]; Alliance for Tunisia (a coalition of Tunisia's Call [Beji Caid ESSEBSI], Republican Party [Maya JRIBI and Najib CHBBI],Democratic Path [Ahmed BRAHIM]); al-Nahda (The Renaissance) [Rachid GHANNOUCHI]; Congress Party for the Republic or CPR [Moncef MARZOUKI]; Democratic Forum for Labor and Liberties or FDTL (Ettakatol) [Mustapha Ben JAAFAR]; Democratic Modernist Pole or PDM (a coalition); Democratic Socialist Movement or MDS; Et-Tajdid Movement [Ahmed IBRAHIM]; Et-Tajdid Movement [Ahmed IBRAHIM]; Green Party for Progress or PVP [Mongi KHAMASSI]; Liberal Social Party or PSL [Mondher THABET]; Movement of Socialist Democrats or MDS [Ismail BOULAHYA]; Popular Petition (Aridha Chaabia) [Hachemi HAMDI]; Popular Unity Party or PUP [Mohamed BOUCHIHA]; Progressive Democratic Party or PDP [Maya JERIBI]; The Initiative [Kamel MORJANE] (formerly the Constitutional Democratic Rally or RCD); Tunisian Workers' Communist Party or PCOT [Hamma HAMMAMI]; Unionist Democratic Union or UDU [Ahmed INOUBLI]

Political pressure groups and leaders: 18 October Group [collective leadership]; Tunisian League for Human Rights or LTDH [Mokhtar TRIFI]; Tunisian General Labor Union or UGTT [Hassine ABASSI]

International organization participation: ABEDA, AfDB, AFESD, AMF, AMU, AU, BSEC (observer), CD, EBRD, FAO, G-11, G-77, IAEA, IBRD, ICAO, ICC (national committees), ICRM, IDA, IDB, IFAD, IFC, IFRCS, IHO, ILO, IMF, IMO, IMSO, Interpol, IOC, IOM, IPU, ISO, ITSO, ITU, ITUC (NGOs), LAS, MIGA, MONUSCO, NAM, OAPEC, OAS (observer), OIC, OIF, OPCW, OSCE (partner), UN, UNCTAD, UNESCO, UNHCR, UNIDO, UNOCI, UNWTO, UPU, WCO, WFTU (NGOs), WHO, WIPO, WMO, WTO

Diplomatic representation in the US:
chief of mission: Ambassador (vacant); Charge d'Affaires Kais DARRAGI
chancery: 1515 Massachusetts Avenue NW, Washington, DC 20005
telephone: [1] (202) 862-1850
FAX: [1] (202) 862-1858

Diplomatic representation from the US:
chief of mission: Ambassador Jake WALLES (since 24 July 2012)
embassy: Zone Nord-Est des Berges du Lac Nord de Tunis 1053
mailing address: use embassy street address
telephone: [216] 71 107-000
FAX: [216] 71 963-263

Flag description: red with a white disk in the center bearing a red crescent nearly encircling a red five-pointed star; resembles the Ottoman flag (red banner with white crescent and star) and recalls Tunisia's history as part of the Ottoman Empire; red represents the blood shed by martyrs in the struggle against oppression, white stands for peace; the crescent and star are traditional symbols of Islam
note: the flag is based on that of Turkey, itself a successor state to the Ottoman Empire

National symbol(s): encircled red star and crescent

National anthem: *name:* "Humat Al Hima" (Defenders of the Homeland)
lyrics/music: Mustafa Sadik AL-RAFII and Aboul-Qacem ECHEBBI/Mohamad Abdel WAHAB
note: adopted 1957, replaced 1958, restored 1987; Mohamad Abdel WAHAB also composed the music for the anthem of the United Arab Emirates

ECONOMY

Economy—overview: Tunisia's diverse, market-oriented economy has long been cited as a success story in Africa and the Middle East, but it faces an array of challenges during the country's ongoing political transition. Following an ill-fated experiment with socialist economic policies in the 1960s, Tunisia embarked on a successful strategy focused on bolstering exports, foreign investment, and tourism, all of which have become central to the country's economy. Key exports now include textiles and apparel, food products, petroleum products, chemicals, and phosphates, with about 80% of exports bound for Tunisia's main economic partner, the European Union. Tunisia's liberal strategy, coupled with investments in education and infrastructure, fueled decades of 4-5% annual GDP growth and improving living standards. Former President (1987-2011) Zine el Abidine BEN ALI continued these policies, but as his reign wore on cronyism and corruption stymied economic performance and unemployment rose among the country's growing ranks of university graduates. These grievances contributed to the January 2011 overthrow of BEN ALI, sending Tunisia's economy into a tailspin as tourism and investment declined sharply. During 2012 and 2013, the Tunisian Government's focus on the political transition led to a neglect of the economy that resulted in several downgrades of Tunisia's credit rating. As the economy recovers, Tunisia's government faces challenges reassuring businesses and investors, bringing budget and current account deficits under control, shoring up the country's financial system, bringing down high unemployment, and reducing economic disparities between the more developed coastal region and the impoverished interior.

GDP (purchasing power parity): $108.4 billion (2013 est.)
country comparison to the world: 72
$105.4 billion (2012 est.)
$101.8 billion (2011 est.)
note: data are in 2013 US dollars

GDP (official exchange rate): $48.38 billion (2013 est.)

GDP—real growth rate: 2.8% (2013 est.)
country comparison to the world: 124
3.6% (2012 est.)
-1.9% (2011 est.)

GDP—per capita (PPP): $9,900 (2013 est.)
country comparison to the world: 119
$9,800 (2012 est.)
$9,500 (2011 est.)
note: data are in 2013 US dollars

Gross national saving: 26.1% of GDP (2013 est.)
country comparison to the world: 43
25.4% of GDP (2012 est.)
24.1% of GDP (2011 est.)

GDP—composition, by end use:
household consumption: 66.5%
government consumption: 18.4%
investment in fixed capital: 22.6%
investment in inventories: 3.5%
exports of goods and services: 49.2%
imports of goods and services: -60.1% (2013 est.)

GDP—composition, by sector of origin:
agriculture: 8.6%
industry: 30.4%
services: 61% (2013 est.)

Agriculture—products: olives, olive oil, grain, tomatoes, citrus fruit, sugar beets, dates, almonds; beef, dairy products

Industries: petroleum, mining (particularly phosphate and iron ore), tourism, textiles, footwear, agribusiness, beverages

Industrial production growth rate: 3% (2013 est.)
country comparison to the world: 98

Labor force: 3.974 million (2013 est.)
country comparison to the world: 91

Labor force—by occupation: *agriculture:* 18.3%
industry: 31.9%
services: 49.8% (2009 est.)

Unemployment rate: 17.2% (2013 est.)
country comparison to the world: 152
17.4% (2012 est.)

Population below poverty line: 3.8% (2005 est.)

Household income or consumption by percentage share: *lowest* 10%: 2.3%
highest 10%: 31.5% (2000)

Distribution of family income—Gini index: 40 (2005 est.)
country comparison to the world: 59
41.7 (1995 est.)

Budget: *revenues:* $12.16 billion
expenditures: $15.8 billion (2013 est.)

Taxes and other revenues: 25.1% of GDP (2013 est.)
country comparison to the world: 128

Budget surplus (+) or deficit (-):
-7.5% of GDP (2013 est.)
country comparison to the world: 191

Public debt: 51.1% of GDP (2013 est.)
country comparison to the world: 65
46.1% of GDP (2012 est.)

Fiscal year: calendar year

Inflation rate (consumer prices): 6.1% (2013 est.)
country comparison to the world: 175
5.6% (2012 est.)

Central bank discount rate: 5.75% (31 December 2010 est.)

Commercial bank prime lending rate: 7.31% (31 December 2012 est.)
country comparison to the world: 131
6.76% (31 December 2011 est.)

Stock of narrow money: $13.08 billion (31 December 2013 est.)
country comparison to the world: 72
$13.44 billion (31 December 2012 est.)

Stock of broad money: $29.8 billion (31 December 2013 est.)
country comparison to the world: 74
$30.72 billion (31 December 2012 est.)

Stock of domestic credit: $35.59 billion (31 December 2013 est.)
country comparison to the world: 68
$36.09 billion (31 December 2012 est.)

Market value of publicly traded shares: $8.887 billion (31 December 2012 est.)
country comparison to the world: 72
$9.662 billion (31 December 2011)
$10.68 billion (31 December 2010 est.)

Current account balance: -$4.556 billion (2013 est.)
country comparison to the world: 165
-$3.773 billion (2012 est.)

Exports: $17.46 billion (2013 est.)
country comparison to the world: 74
$17.07 billion (2012 est.)

Exports—commodities: clothing, semi-finished goods and textiles, agricultural products, mechanical goods, phosphates and chemicals, hydrocarbons, electrical equipment

Exports—partners: France 26.2%, Italy 16%, Germany 9.4%, Libya 7.6%, US 4.3% (2012)

Imports: $24.95 billion (2013 est.)
country comparison to the world: 73
$23.1 billion (2012 est.)

Imports—commodities: textiles, machinery and equipment, hydrocarbons, chemicals, foodstuffs

Imports—partners: France 19.8%, Italy 16.7%, Germany 7.3%, China 6%, Spain 5.3%, Algeria 4.4% (2012)

Reserves of foreign exchange and gold: $8.113 billion (31 December 2013 est.)
country comparison to the world: 78
$8.36 billion (31 December 2012 est.)

Debt—external: $26.95 billion (31 December 2013 est.)
country comparison to the world: 75
$24.6 billion (31 December 2012 est.)

Stock of direct foreign investment—at home: $34.64 billion (31 December 2013 est.)
country comparison to the world: 59
$33.4 billion (31 December 2012 est.)

Stock of direct foreign investment—abroad: $295 million (31 December 2013 est.)
country comparison to the world: 83
$285 million (31 December 2012 est.)

Exchange rates: Tunisian dinars (TND) per US dollar—
1.638 (2013 est.)
1.5619 (2012 est.)
1.4314 (2010 est.)
1.3503 (2009)
1.211 (2008)

ENERGY

Electricity—production: 15.14 billion kWh (2010 est.)
country comparison to the world: 81

Electricity—consumption: 13.29 billion kWh (2010 est.)
country comparison to the world: 82

Electricity—exports: 0 kWh (2010 est.)
country comparison to the world: 204

Electricity—imports: 19 million kWh (2010 est.)
country comparison to the world: 105

Electricity—installed generating capacity: 3.652 million kW (2010 est.)
country comparison to the world: 82

Electricity—from fossil fuels: 96.8% of total installed capacity (2010 est.)
country comparison to the world: 65

Electricity—from nuclear fuels: 0% of total installed capacity (2010 est.)
country comparison to the world: 190

Electricity—from hydroelectric plants: 1.7% of total installed capacity (2010 est.)
country comparison to the world: 139

Electricity—from other renewable sources: 1.5% of total installed capacity (2010 est.)
country comparison to the world: 78

Crude oil—production: 68,310 bbl/day (2012 est.)
country comparison to the world: 57

Crude oil—exports: 77,980 bbl/day (2010 est.)
country comparison to the world: 42

Crude oil—imports: 3,680 bbl/day (2010 est.)
country comparison to the world: 80

Crude oil—proved reserves: 425 million bbl (1 January 2013 es)
country comparison to the world: 52

Refined petroleum products—production: 11,170 bbl/day (2010 est.)
country comparison to the world: 103

Refined petroleum products—consumption: 88,380 bbl/day (2011 est.)
country comparison to the world: 82

Refined petroleum products—exports: 3,391 bbl/day (2010 est.)

country comparison to the world: 96 Refined petroleum products—imports:
80,980 bbl/day (2010 est.)
country comparison to the world: 56

Natural gas—production: 1.93 billion cu m (2011 est.)
country comparison to the world: 58

Natural gas—consumption: 3.28 billion cu m (2010 est.)
country comparison to the world: 69

Natural gas—exports: 0 cu m (2011 est.)
country comparison to the world: 194

Natural gas—imports: 1.78 billion cu m (2011 est.)
country comparison to the world: 52

Natural gas—proved reserves: 65.13 billion cu m (1 January 2013 es)
country comparison to the world: 60

Carbon dioxide emissions from consumption of energy: 20.52 million Mt (2011 est.)
country comparison to the world: 84

COMMUNICATIONS

Telephones—main lines in use: 1.105 million (2012)
country comparison to the world: 71

Telephones—mobile cellular: 12.84 million (2012)
country comparison to the world: 68

Telephone system: *general assessment:* above the African average and continuing to be upgraded; key centers are Sfax, Sousse, Bizerte, and Tunis; telephone network is completely digitized; Internet access available throughout the country
domestic: in an effort to jumpstart expansion of the fixed-line network, the government has awarded a concession to build and operate a VSAT network with international connectivity; rural areas are served by wireless local loops; competition between the two mobile-cellular service providers has resulted in lower activation and usage charges and a strong surge in subscribership; a third mobile, fixed, and ISP operator was licensed in 2009 and began offering services in 2010; expansion of mobile-cellular services to include multimedia messaging and e-mail and Internet to mobile phone services also leading to a surge in subscribership; overall fixed-line and mobile-cellular teledensity has reached about 125 telephones per 100 persons
international: country code—216; a landing point for the SEA-ME-WE-4 submarine cable system that provides links to Europe, Middle East, and Asia; satellite earth stations—1 Intelsat (Atlantic Ocean) and 1 Arabsat; coaxial cable and microwave radio relay to Algeria and Libya; participant in Medarabtel; 2 international gateway digital switches (2011)

Broadcast media: broadcast media is mainly government-controlled; the state-run Tunisian Radio and Television Establishment (ERTT) operates 2 national TV networks, several national radio networks, and a number of regional radio stations; 1 TV and 3 radio stations are privately owned and report domestic news stories directly from the official Tunisian news agency; the state retains control of broadcast facilities and transmitters through L'Office National de la Telediffusion; Tunisians also have access to Egyptian, pan-Arab, and European satellite TV channels (2007)

Internet country code: .tn

Internet hosts: 576 (2012)
country comparison to the world: 180

Internet users: 3.5 million (2009)
country comparison to the world: 60

TRANSPORTATION

Airports: 29 (2013)
country comparison to the world: 118

Airports—with paved runways: *total:* 15
over 3,047 m: 4
2,438 to 3,047 m: 6
1,524 to 2,437 m: 2
914 to 1,523 m: 3 (2013)

Airports—with unpaved runways: *total:* 14
1,524 to 2,437 m: 1
914 to 1,523 m: 5
under 914 m: 8 (2013)

Pipelines: condensate 68 km; gas 3,111 km; oil 1,381 km; refined products 453 km (2013)

Railways: *total:* 2,165 km (1,991 in use)
country comparison to the world: 69
standard gauge: 471 km 1.435-m gauge
narrow gauge: 1,694 km 1.000-m gauge (65 km electrified) (2011)

Roadways: *total:* 19,418 km
country comparison to the world: 112
paved: 14,756 km (includes 357 km of expressways)
unpaved: 4,662 km (2010)
Merchant marine: total: 9
country comparison to the world: 116
by type: bulk carrier 1, cargo 2, passenger/cargo 4, roll on/roll off 2 (2010)

Ports and terminals: *major seaport(s):* Bizerte, Gabes, Rades, Sfax, Skhira

MILITARY

Military branches: Tunisian Armed Forces (Forces Armees Tunisiens, FAT): Tunisian Army (includes Tunisian Air Defense Force), Tunisian Navy, Republic of Tunisia Air Force (Al-Quwwat al-Jawwiya al-Jamahiriyah At'Tunisia) (2012)

Military service age and obligation: 20-23 years of age for compulsory service, one year service obligation; 18-23 years of age for voluntary service; Tunisian nationality required (2012)

Manpower available for military service:
males age 16-49: 2,846,572
females age 16-49: 2,952,180 (2010 est.)

Manpower fit for military service:
males age 16-49: 2,397,716
females age 16-49: 2,484,097 (2010 est.)

Manpower reaching militarily significant age annually: *male:* 90,436
female: 87,346 (2010 est.)

Military expenditures: 1.55% of GDP (2012)
country comparison to the world: 57
1.34% of GDP (2011)
1.55% of GDP (2010)

TRANSNATIONAL ISSUES

Disputes—international: none

Trafficking in persons: *current situation:* Tunisia is a source, destination, and possible transit country for men, women, and children subjected to forced labor and sex trafficking; Tunisia's increased number of street children, children working to support their families, and migrants who have fled unrest in neighboring countries are vulnerable to human trafficking; Tunisian women recruited into Lebanon's entertainment industry are forced into prostitution on arrival and other Tunisian women are forced into prostitution in Jordan; some Tunisian girls employed in domestic work are held in conditions of forced labor

tier rating: Tier 2 Watch List—Tunisia does not fully comply with the minimum standards for the elimination of trafficking; however, it is making significant efforts to do so; the government continues to maintain that human trafficking is not a widespread problem in Tunisia, which undermines awareness campaigns and does not differentiate human trafficking from migrant smuggling; prior commitments to enact draft anti-trafficking legislation were not fulfilled, and the government has not developed or implemented procedures to identify proactively trafficking victims; the government has assisted an unidentified number of trafficking victims in its shelters for vulnerable groups (2013)

TURKEY

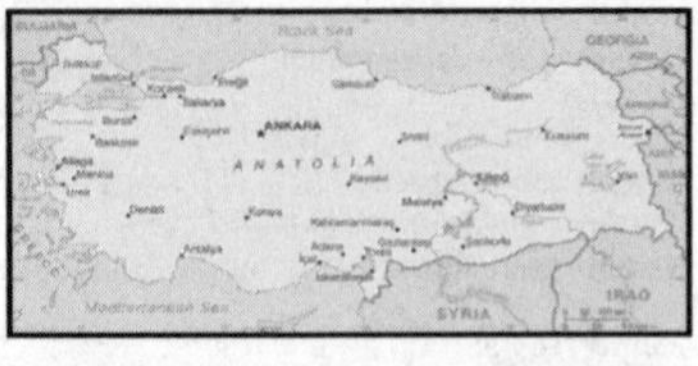

INTRODUCTION

Background: Modern Turkey was founded in 1923 from the Anatolian remnants of the defeated Ottoman Empire by national hero Mustafa KEMAL, who was later honored with the title Ataturk or "Father of the Turks." Under his leadership, the country adopted wide-ranging social, legal, and political reforms. After a period of one-party rule, an experiment with multi-party politics led to the 1950 election victory of the opposition Democratic Party and the peaceful transfer of power. Since then, Turkish political parties have multiplied, but democracy has been fractured by periods of instability and intermittent military coups (1960, 1971, 1980), which in each case eventually resulted in a return of political power to civilians. In 1997, the military again helped engineer the ouster—popularly dubbed a "post-modern coup"—of the then Islamic-oriented government. Turkey intervened militarily on Cyprus in 1974 to prevent a Greek takeover of the island and has since acted as patron state to the "Turkish Republic of Northern Cyprus," which only Turkey recognizes. A separatist insurgency begun in 1984 by the Kurdistan Workers' Party (PKK)—now known as the Kurdistan People's Congress or Kongra-Gel (KGK)—has dominated the Turkish military's attention and claimed more than 30,000 lives. After the capture of the group's leader in 1999, the insurgents largely withdrew from Turkey mainly to northern Iraq. In 2013, KGK and the Turkish Government agreed to a ceasefire that continues despite slow progress in ongoing peace talks. Turkey joined the UN in 1945 and in 1952 it became a member of NATO. In 1964, Turkey became an associate member of the European Community. Over the past decade, it has undertaken many reforms to strengthen its democracy and economy; it began accession membership talks with the European Union in 2005.

GEOGRAPHY

Location: Southeastern Europe and Southwestern Asia (that portion of Turkey west of the Bosporus is geographically part of Europe), bordering the Black Sea, between Bulgaria and Georgia, and bordering the Aegean Sea and the Mediterranean Sea, between Greece and Syria

Geographic coordinates: 39 00 N, 35 00 E

Map references: Middle East

Area: *total:* 783,562 sq km
country comparison to the world: 37
land: 769,632 sq km
water: 13,930 sq km

Area—comparative: slightly larger than Texas

Land boundaries: *total:* 2,648 km

border countries: Armenia 268 km, Azerbaijan 9 km, Bulgaria 240 km, Georgia 252 km, Greece 206 km, Iran 499 km, Iraq 352 km, Syria 822 km

Coastline: 7,200 km

Maritime claims: *territorial sea:* 6 nm in the Aegean Sea; 12 nm in Black Sea and in Mediterranean Sea
exclusive economic zone: in Black Sea only: to the maritime boundary agreed upon with the former USSR

Climate: temperate; hot, dry summers with mild, wet winters; harsher in interior

Terrain: high central plateau (Anatolia); narrow coastal plain; several mountain ranges

Elevation extremes: *lowest point:* Mediterranean Sea 0 m
highest point: Mount Ararat 5,166 m

Natural resources: coal, iron ore, copper, chromium, antimony, mercury, gold, barite, borate, celestite (strontium), emery, feldspar, limestone, magnesite, marble, perlite, pumice, pyrites (sulfur), clay, arable land, hydropower

Land use: *arable land:* 26.21%
permanent crops: 3.94%
other: 69.84% (2011)

Irrigated land: 53,400 sq km (2012)

Total renewable water resources: 211.6 cu km (2011)

Freshwater withdrawal (domestic/industrial/agricultural): *total:* 40.1 cu km/yr (14%/10%/76%)
per capita: 572.9 cu m/yr (2008)

Natural hazards: severe earthquakes, especially in northern Turkey, along an arc extending from the Sea of Marmara to Lake Van
volcanism: limited volcanic activity; its three historically active volcanoes; Ararat, Nemrut Dagi, and Tendurek Dagi have not erupted since the 19th century or earlier

Environment—current issues: water pollution from dumping of chemicals and detergents; air pollution, particularly in urban areas; deforestation; concern for oil spills from increasing Bosporus ship traffic

Environment—international agreements:
party to: Air Pollution, Antarctic Treaty, Biodiversity, Climate Change, Desertification, Endangered Species, Hazardous Wastes, Ozone Layer Protection, Ship Pollution, Wetlands
signed, but not ratified: Environmental Modification

Geography—note: strategic location controlling the Turkish Straits (Bosporus, Sea of Marmara, Dardanelles) that link Black and Aegean Seas; Mount Ararat, the legendary landing place of Noah's ark, is in the far eastern portion of the country

PEOPLE AND SOCIETY

Nationality: *noun:* Turk(s)
adjective: Turkish

Ethnic groups: Turkish 70-75%, Kurdish 18%, other minorities 7-12% (2008 est.)

Languages: Turkish (official), Kurdish, other minority languages

Religions: Muslim 99.8% (mostly Sunni), other 0.2% (mostly Christians and Jews)

Population: 81,619,392 (July 2014 est.)
country comparison to the world: 17

Age structure:
0-14 years: 25.5% (male 10,660,110/female 10,179,850)
15-24 years: 16.8% (male 6,989,099/female 6,709,480)
25-54 years: 42.9% (male 17,650,790/female 17,358,730)
55-64 years: 6.7% (male 3,289,605/female 3,291,199)
65 years and over: 6.6% (male 2,517,219/female 2,973,310) (2014 est.)

Dependency ratios:
total dependency ratio: 49.3 %
youth dependency ratio: 38.3 %
elderly dependency ratio: 11 %
potential support ratio: 9.1 (2013)

Median age: *total:* 29.6 years
male: 29.2 years
female: 30 years (2014 est.)

Population growth rate: 1.12% (2014 est.)
country comparison to the world: 108

Birth rate: 16.86 births/1,000 population (2014 est.)
country comparison to the world: 114

Death rate: 6.12 deaths/1,000 population (2014 est.)
country comparison to the world: 163

Net migration rate: 0.46 migrant(s)/1,000 population (2014 est.)
country comparison to the world: 71

Urbanization: *urban population:* 71.5% of total population (2011)
rate of urbanization: 2.4% annual rate of change (2010-15 est.)

Major urban areas—population: Istanbul 10.378 million; ANKARA (capital) 3.846 million; Izmir 2.679 million; Bursa 1.559 million; Adana 1.339 million (2009)

Sex ratio: *at birth:* 1.05 male(s)/female
0-14 years: 1.05 male(s)/female
15-24 years: 1.04 male(s)/female
25-54 years: 1.02 male(s)/female
55-64 years: 1.02 male(s)/female
65 years and over: 0.84 male(s)/female
total population: 1.02 male(s)/female (2014 est.)

Mother's mean age at first birth: 22.9 (2003 est.)

Maternal mortality rate: 20 deaths/100,000 live births (2010)
country comparison to the world: 139

Infant mortality rate: *total:* 21.43 deaths/1,000 live births
country comparison to the world: 84
male: 22.48 deaths/1,000 live births
female: 20.32 deaths/1,000 live births (2014 est.)

Life expectancy at birth:
total population: 73.29 years
country comparison to the world: 124
male: 71.33 years
female: 75.35 years (2014 est.)

Total fertility rate: 2.08 children born/woman (2014 est.)
country comparison to the world: 113

Contraceptive prevalence rate: 73% (2008)

Health expenditures: 6.7% of GDP (2011)
country comparison to the world: 90

Physicians density: 1.71 physicians/1,000 population (2011)

Hospital bed density: 2.5 beds/1,000 population (2010)

Drinking water source:
improved:
urban: 100% of population
rural: 99.1% of population
total: 99.7% of population
unimproved:
urban: 0% of population
rural: 0.9% of population
total: 0.3% of population (2011 est.)

Sanitation facility access:
improved:
urban: 97.2% of population
rural: 75.5% of population
total: 91% of population
unimproved:
urban: 2.8% of population
rural: 24.5% of population
total: 9% of population (2011 est.)

HIV/AIDS—adult prevalence rate: less than 0.1%; note—no country specific models provided (2009 est.)
country comparison to the world: 148

HIV/AIDS—people living with HIV/AIDS: 4,600 (2009 est.)
country comparison to the world: 124

HIV/AIDS—deaths: fewer than 200 (2009 est.)
country comparison to the world: 117

Obesity—adult prevalence rate: 27.8% (2008)
country comparison to the world: 36

Children under the age of 5 years underweight: 3.5% (2004)
country comparison to the world: 102

Education expenditures: 2.9% of GDP (2006)
country comparison to the world: 142

Literacy: *definition:* age 15 and over can read and write
total population: 94.1%
male: 97.9%
female: 90.3% (2011 est.)

School life expectancy (primary to tertiary education): *total:* 14 years
male: 15 years
female: 14 years (2011)

Child labor—children ages 5-14:
total number: 321,866
percentage: 3 %
note: data represents children ages 6-14 (2006 est.)

Unemployment, youth ages 15-24: *total:* 17.5%
country comparison to the world: 71
male: 16.3%
female: 19.9% (2012)

GOVERNMENT

Country name: *conventional long form:* Republic of Turkey
conventional short form: Turkey
local long form: Turkiye Cumhuriyeti
local short form: Turkiye

Government type: republican parliamentary democracy

Capital: *name:* Ankara

geographic coordinates: 39 56 N, 32 52 E
time difference: UTC+2 (7 hours ahead of Washington, DC during Standard Time)
daylight saving time: +1hr, begins last Sunday in March; ends last Sunday in October

Administrative divisions: 81 provinces (iller, singular—ili); Adana, Adiyaman, Afyonkarahisar, Agri, Aksaray, Amasya, Ankara, Antalya, Ardahan, Artvin, Aydin, Balikesir, Bartin, Batman, Bayburt, Bilecik, Bingol, Bitlis, Bolu, Burdur, Bursa, Canakkale, Cankiri, Corum, Denizli, Diyarbakir, Duzce, Edirne, Elazig, Erzincan, Erzurum, Eskisehir, Gaziantep, Giresun, Gumushane, Hakkari, Hatay, Igdir, Isparta, Istanbul, Izmir (Smyrna), Kahramanmaras, Karabuk, Karaman, Kars, Kastamonu, Kayseri, Kilis, Kirikkale, Kirklareli, Kirsehir, Kocaeli, Konya, Kutahya, Malatya, Manisa, Mardin, Mersin, Mugla, Mus,

Nevsehir, Nigde, Ordu, Osmaniye, Rize, Sakarya, Samsun, Sanliurfa, Siirt, Sinop, Sirnak, Sivas, Tekirdag, Tokat, Trabzon (Trebizond), Tunceli, Usak, Van, Yalova, Yozgat, Zonguldak

Independence: 29 October 1923 (successor state to the Ottoman Empire)

National holiday: Republic Day, 29 October (1923)

Constitution: several previous; latest ratified 9 November 1982; amended 2001, 2007, 2010 (2010)

Legal system: civil law system based on various European legal systems notably the Swiss civil code; note—member of the European Court of Human Rights (ECHR), although Turkey claims limited derogations on the ratified European Convention on Human Rights

International law organization participation: has not submitted an ICJ jurisdiction declaration; non-party state to the ICCt

Suffrage: 18 years of age; universal

Executive branch: *chief of state:* President Abdullah GUL (since 28 August 2007)
head of government: Prime Minister Recep Tayyip ERDOGAN (since 14 March 2003)
cabinet: Council of Ministers appointed by the president on the nomination of the prime minister (For more information visit the World Leaders website)
elections: president elected directly for a five-year term (eligible for a second term); prime minister appointed by the president from among members of parliament
election results: on 28 August 2007 the National Assembly elected Abdullah GUL president on the third ballot; National Assembly vote - 3 3 9
note: in October 2007 Turkish voters approved a referendum package of constitutional amendments including a provision for direct presidential elections

Legislative branch: unicameral Grand National Assembly of Turkey or Turkiye Buyuk Millet Meclisi (550 seats; members elected by popular vote to serve four-year terms)
elections: last held on 12 June 2011 (next likely to be held by June 2015)
election results: percent of vote by party—AKP 49.8%, CHP 25.9%, MHP 13%, independents 6.6%, other 4.7%; seats by party—AKP 326, CHP 135, MHP 53, independents 36; note—only parties surpassing the 10% threshold are entitled to parliamentary seats

Judicial branch: *highest court(s):* Constitutional Court (consists of 17 members); Supreme Court of Appeals organized into 15 divisions with 38 civil and criminal chambers and consisting of 250 high judges and 440 rapporteur judges)
judge selection and term of office: Constitutional Court judges appointed by the president from among candidates submitted by plenary assemblies of other courts, the Higher Education Council, senior government administrators, and lawyers; judges appointed for 12-year, non-renewable terms and with mandatory retirement at age 65; Supreme Court of Appeals judges appointed by the Supreme Council of Judges and Public Prosecutors; judge tenure NA
subordinate courts: Council of State (Danistay); Court of Accounts (Sayistay); Military High Court of Appeals; Military High Administrative Court

Political parties and leaders: Democratic Left Party or DSP [Masum TURKER]; Democratic Party or DP [Namik Kemal ZEYBEK]; Equality and Democracy Party or EDP [Ziva HALIS]; Felicity Party or SP [Mustafa KAMALAK] (sometimes translated as Contentment Party) Freedom and Solidarity Party or ODP [Alper TAS]; Grand Unity Party or BBP [Yalcin TOPCU]; Justice and Development Party or AKP [Recep Tayyip ERDOGAN]; Nationalist Movement Party or MHP [Devlet BAHCELI]; Peace and Democracy Party or BDP [Selahattin DEMIRTAS]; Republican People's Party or CHP [Kemal KILICDAROGLU]; Turkey Party or TP [Abdullatif SENER]
note: the parties listed above are some of the more significant of the 61 parties that Turkey had according to the Ministry of Interior statistics current as of May 2009

Political pressure groups and leaders: Confederation of Businessmen and Industrialists of Turkey or TUSKON [Rizanur MERAL]; Confederation of Public Sector Unions or KESK [Lami OZGEN]; Confederation of Revolutionary Workers Unions or DISK [Tayfun GORGUN]; Independent Industrialists' and Businessmen's Association or MUSIAD [Omer Cihad VARDAN]; Moral Rights Workers Union or Hak-Is [Mahmut ARSLAN]; Turkish Confederation of Employers' Unions or TISK [Tugrul KUDATGOBILIK]; Turkish Confederation of Labor or Turk-Is [Mustafa KUMLU]; Turkish Confederation of Tradesmen and Craftsmen or TESK [Bendevi PALANDOKEN]; Turkish Industrialists' and Businessmen's Association or TUSIAD [Umit BOYNER]; Turkish Union of Chambers of Commerce and Commodity Exchanges or TOBB [M. Rifat HISARCIKLIOGLU]

International organization participation: ADB (nonregional member), Australia Group, BIS, BSEC, CD, CE, CERN (observer), CICA, D-8, EAPC, EBRD, ECO, EU (candidate country), FAO, FATF, G-20, IAEA, IBRD, ICAO, ICC (national committees), ICRM, IDA, IDB, IEA, IFAD, IFC, IFRCS, IHO, ILO, IMF, IMO, IMSO, Interpol, IOC, IOM, IPU, ISO, ITSO, ITU, ITUC (NGOs), MIGA, NATO, NEA, NSG, OAS (observer), OECD, OIC, OPCW, OSCE, Paris Club (associate), PCA, SELEC, UN, UNCTAD, UNESCO, UNHCR, UNIDO, UNIFIL, UNRWA, UNWTO, UPU, WCO, WFTU (NGOs), WHO, WIPO, WMO, WTO, ZC

Diplomatic representation in the US:
chief of mission: Ambassador Sedar KILIC (since 16 April 1014)
chancery: 2525 Massachusetts Avenue NW, Washington, DC 20008
telephone: [1] (202) 612-6700
FAX: [1] (202) 612-6744
consulate(s) general: Chicago, Houston, New York, Newton (MA)

Diplomatic representation from the US:
chief of mission: Ambassador Francis J. RICCIARDONE, Jr. (since 3 January 2011)
embassy: 110 Ataturk Boulevard, Kavaklidere, 06100 Ankara
mailing address: PSC 93, Box 5000, APO AE 09823
telephone: [90] (312) 455-5555
FAX: [90] (312) 467-0019
consulate(s) general: Istanbul
consulate(s): Adana; note—there is a Consular Agent in Izmir

Flag description: red with a vertical white crescent moon (the closed portion is toward the hoist side) and white five-pointed star centered just outside the crescent opening; the flag colors and designs closely resemble those on the banner of the Ottoman Empire, which preceded modern-day Turkey; the crescent moon and star serve as insignia for the Turks, as well as being traditional symbols of Islam; according to legend, the flag represents the reflection of the moon and a star in a pool of blood of Turkish warriors

National symbol(s): star and crescent

National anthem: *name:* "Istiklal Marsi" (Independence March)
lyrics/music: Mehmet Akif ERSOY/Zeki UNGOR
note: lyrics adopted 1921, music adopted 1932; the anthem's original music was adopted in 1924; a new composition was agreed upon in 1932

ECONOMY

Economy—overview: Turkey's largely free-market economy is increasingly driven by its industry and service sectors, although its traditional agriculture sector still accounts for about 25% of employment. An aggressive privatization program has reduced state involvement in basic industry, banking, transport, and communication, and an emerging cadre of middle-class entrepreneurs is adding dynamism to the economy and expanding production beyond the traditional textiles and clothing sectors. The automotive, construction, and electronics industries, are rising in importance and have surpassed textiles within Turkey's export mix. Oil began to flow through the Baku-Tbilisi-Ceyhan pipeline in May 2006, marking a major milestone that will bring up to 1 million barrels per day from the Caspian to market. Several gas pipelines projects also are moving forward to help transport Central Asian gas to Europe through Turkey, which over the long term will help address Turkey's dependence on imported oil and gas to meet 97% of its energy needs. After Turkey experienced a severe financial crisis in 2001, Ankara adopted financial and fiscal reforms as part of an IMF program. The reforms strengthened the country's economic fundamentals and ushered in an era of strong growth—averaging more than 6% annually until 2008. Global economic conditions and tighter fiscal policy caused GDP to contract in 2009, but Turkey's well-regulated financial markets and banking system helped the country weather the global financial crisis and GDP rebounded strongly to around 9% in 2010-11, as exports returned to normal levels following the recession. Growth dropped to roughly 3% in 2012-13. Turkey's public sector debt to GDP ratio has fallen below 40%, and at least one rating agency upgraded Turkey's debt to investment grade in 2012. Turkey remains dependent on often volatile, short-term investment to finance its large trade deficit. The stock value of FDI reached nearly $195 billion at year-end 2013, reflecting Turkey's good growth even in the face of economic turmoil in Europe, the source of much of Turkey's FDI. Turkey's relatively high current account deficit, uncertainty related to monetary policy-making, and political turmoil within Turkey's neighborhood leave the economy vulnerable to destabilizing shifts in investor confidence.

GDP (purchasing power parity): $1.167 trillion (2013 est.)
country comparison to the world: 17
$1.124 trillion (2012 est.)
$1.101 trillion (2011 est.)
note: data are in 2013 US dollars

GDP (official exchange rate): $821.8 billion (2013 est.)

GDP—real growth rate: 3.8% (2013 est.)
country comparison to the world: 86
2.2% (2012 est.)
8.8% (2011 est.)

GDP—per capita (PPP): $15,300 (2013 est.)
country comparison to the world: 90
$15,000 (2012 est.)

$14,900 (2011 est.)
note: data are in 2013 US dollars

Gross national saving: 19.4% of GDP (2013 est.)
country comparison to the world: 79
20.2% of GDP (2012 est.)
23.6% of GDP (2011 est.)

GDP—composition, by end use:
household consumption: 71%
government consumption: 15.4%
investment in fixed capital: 19.4%
investment in inventories: 0%
exports of goods and services: 26.6%
imports of goods and services: -32.5% (2013 est.)

GDP—composition, by sector of origin:
agriculture: 8.9%
industry: 27.3%
services: 63.8% (2013 est.)

Agriculture—products: tobacco, cotton, grain, olives, sugar beets, hazelnuts, pulses, citrus; livestock

Industries: textiles, food processing, autos, electronics, mining (coal, chromate, copper, boron), steel, petroleum, construction, lumber, paper

Industrial production growth rate: 3.5% (2013 est.)
country comparison to the world: 84

Labor force: 27.91 million
country comparison to the world: 22
note: about 1.2 million Turks work abroad (2013 est.)

Labor force—by occupation: *agriculture:* 25.5%
industry: 26.2%
services: 48.4% (2010)

Unemployment rate: 9.3% (2013 est.)
country comparison to the world: 101
9.2% (2012 est.)
note: underemployment amounted to 4% in 2008

Population below poverty line: 16.9% (2010)

Household income or consumption by percentage share: *lowest 10%:* 2.1%
highest 10%: 30.3% (2008)

Distribution of family income—Gini index: 40.2 (2010)
country comparison to the world: 57
43.6 (2003)

Budget: *revenues:* $190.4 billion
expenditures: $207.9 billion (2013 est.)

Taxes and other revenues: 23.2% of GDP (2013 est.)
country comparison to the world: 145

Budget surplus (+) or deficit (-):
-2.1% of GDP (2013 est.)
country comparison to the world: 87

Public debt: 36.6% of GDP (2013 est.)
country comparison to the world: 102
37.6% of GDP (2012 est.)
note: data cover central government debt, and excludes debt instruments issued (or owned) by government entities other than the treasury; the data include treasury debt held by foreign entities; the data exclude debt issued by subnational entities, as well as intra-governmental debt; intra-governmental debt consists of treasury borrowings from surpluses in the social funds, such as for retirement, medical care, and unemployment; debt instruments for the social funds are sold at public auctions

Fiscal year: calendar year

Inflation rate (consumer prices): 7.6% (2013 est.)
country comparison to the world: 191
8.9% (2012 est.)

Central bank discount rate: 5.25% (31 December 2011)
country comparison to the world: 9
15% (22 December 2009)

Commercial bank prime lending rate: 18.5% (31 December 2013 est.)
country comparison to the world: 20
19% (31 December 2012 est.)

Stock of narrow money: $80.72 billion (31 December 2013 est.)
country comparison to the world: 41
$85.23 billion (31 December 2012 est.)

Stock of broad money: $383.5 billion (31 December 2013 est.)
country comparison to the world: 27
$405.6 billion (31 December 2012 est.)

Stock of domestic credit: $549.5 billion (31 December 2013 est.)
country comparison to the world: 24
$552.3 billion (31 December 2012 est.)

Market value of publicly traded shares: $308.8 billion (31 December 2012 est.)
country comparison to the world: 31
$201.8 billion (31 December 2011)
$306.7 billion (31 December 2010 est.)

Current account balance: -$58.35 billion (2013 est.)
country comparison to the world: 188
-$47.75 billion (2012 est.)

Exports: $167.6 billion (2013 est.)
country comparison to the world: 30
$163.3 billion (2012 est.)

Exports—commodities: apparel, foodstuffs, textiles, metal manufactures, transport equipment

Exports—partners: Germany 8.6%, Iraq 7.1%, Iran 6.5%, UK 5.7%, UAE 5.4%, Russia 4.4%, Italy 4.2%, France 4.1% (2012)

Imports: $242.9 billion (2013 est.)
country comparison to the world: 23
$228.6 billion (2012 est.)

Imports—commodities: machinery, chemicals, semi-finished goods, fuels, transport equipment

Imports—partners: Russia 11.3%, Germany 9%, China 9%, US 6%, Italy 5.6%, Iran 5.1% (2012)

Reserves of foreign exchange and gold: $117.6 billion (31 December 2013 est.)
country comparison to the world: 22
$119.2 billion (31 December 2012 est.)

Debt—external: $359.5 billion (31 December 2013 est.)
country comparison to the world: 31
$336.7 billion (31 December 2012 est.)

Stock of direct foreign investment—at home: $194.2 billion (31 December 2013 est.)
country comparison to the world: 28
$181.7 billion (31 December 2012 est.)

Stock of direct foreign investment—abroad: $33.44 billion (31 December 2013 est.)
country comparison to the world: 42
$30.94 billion (31 December 2012 est.)

Exchange rates: Turkish liras (TRY) per US dollar—
1.899 (2013 est.)
1.796 (2012 est.)
1.5028 (2010 est.)
1.55 (2009)
1.3179 (2008)

ENERGY

Electricity—production: 217.7 billion kWh (2011 est.)
country comparison to the world: 21

Electricity—consumption: 170.4 billion kWh (2010 est.)
country comparison to the world: 22

Electricity—exports: 1.49 billion kWh (2012 est.)
country comparison to the world: 51

Electricity—imports: 4.362 billion kWh (2012 est.)
country comparison to the world: 38

Electricity—installed generating capacity: 49.52 million kW (2010 est.)
country comparison to the world: 19

Electricity—from fossil fuels: 64.9% of total installed capacity (2010 est.)
country comparison to the world: 122

Electricity—from nuclear fuels: 0% of total installed capacity (2010 est.)
country comparison to the world: 191

Electricity—from hydroelectric plants: 32% of total installed capacity (2010 est.)
country comparison to the world: 72

Electricity—from other renewable sources: 3.1% of total installed capacity (2010 est.)
country comparison to the world: 58

Crude oil—production: 56,650 bbl/day (2012 est.)
country comparison to the world: 60

Crude oil—exports: 0 bbl/day (2010 est.)
country comparison to the world: 193

Crude oil—imports: 338,900 bbl/day (2010 est.)
country comparison to the world: 26

Crude oil—proved reserves: 270.4 million bbl (1 January 2013 es)
country comparison to the world: 54

Refined petroleum products—production: 418,200 bbl/day (2010 est.)
country comparison to the world: 36

Refined petroleum products—consumption: 706,100 bbl/day (2011 est.)
country comparison to the world: 26

Refined petroleum products—exports: 107,800 bbl/day (2010 est.)
country comparison to the world: 42

Refined petroleum products—imports: 301,300 bbl/day (2010 est.)
country comparison to the world: 22

Natural gas—production: 632 million cu m (2012 est.)
country comparison to the world: 69

Natural gas—consumption: 38.13 billion cu m (2010 est.)
country comparison to the world: 25

Natural gas—exports: 600 million cu m (2012 est.)
country comparison to the world: 45

Natural gas—imports: 45.92 billion cu m (2012 est.)
country comparison to the world: 10

Natural gas—proved reserves: 6.173 billion cu m (1 January 2013 es)
country comparison to the world: 89

Carbon dioxide emissions from consumption of energy: 296.3 million Mt (2011 est.)
country comparison to the world: 23

COMMUNICATIONS

Telephones—main lines in use: 13.86 million (2012)
country comparison to the world: 18

Telephones—mobile cellular: 67.68 million (2012)
country comparison to the world: 20

Telephone system: *general assessment:* comprehensive telecommunications network undergoing

rapid modernization and expansion, especially in mobile-cellular services
domestic: additional digital exchanges are permitting a rapid increase in subscribers; the construction of a network of technologically advanced intercity trunk lines, using both fiber-optic cable and digital microwave radio relay, is facilitating communication between urban centers; remote areas are reached by a domestic satellite system; combined fixed-line and mobile-cellular teledensity is roughly 100 telephones per 100 persons
international: country code—90; international service is provided by the SEA-ME-WE-3 submarine cable and by submarine fiber-optic cables in the Mediterranean and Black Seas that link Turkey with Italy, Greece, Israel, Bulgaria, Romania, and Russia; satellite earth stations—12 Intelsat; mobile satellite terminals—328 in the Inmarsat and Eutelsat systems (2010)

Broadcast media: Turkish Radio and Television Corporation (TRT) operates multiple TV and radio networks and stations; multiple privately owned national television stations and up to 300 private regional and local television stations; multi-channel cable TV subscriptions available; more than 1,000 private radio broadcast stations (2009)

Internet country code: . tr

Internet hosts: 7.093 million (2012)
country comparison to the world: 16

Internet users: 27.233 million (2009)
country comparison to the world: 15

TRANSPORTATION

Airports: 98 (2013)
country comparison to the world: 5 8

Airports—with paved runways: *total:* 9 1
over 3,047 m: 16
2,438 to 3,047 m: 38
1,524 to 2,437 m: 17
914 to 1,523 m: 16
under 914 m: 4 (2013)

Airports—with unpaved runways: *total:* 7
1,524 to 2,437 m: 1
914 to 1,523 m: 4
under 914 m: 2 (2013)

Heliports: 20 (2013)

Pipelines: gas 12,603 km; oil 3,038 km (2013)

Railways: *total:* 12,008 km
country comparison to the world: 20
standard gauge: 12,008 km 1.435-m gauge (3,216 km electrified) (2012)

Roadways: *total:* 385,748 km
country comparison to the world: 17
paved: 352,268 km (includes 2,127 km of expressways)
unpaved: 33,486 km (2012)

Waterways: 1,200 km (2010)
country comparison to the world: 60

Merchant marine: *total:* 629
country comparison to the world: 18
by type: bulk carrier 102, cargo 281, chemical tanker 80, container 42, liquefied gas 6, passenger 2, passenger/cargo 60, petroleum tanker 25, refrigerated cargo 1, roll on/roll off 29, specialized tanker 1
foreign-owned: 1 (Italy 1)
registered in other countries: 645 (Albania 1, Antigua and Barbuda 7, Azerbaijan 1, Bahamas 3, Barbados 1, Belize 16, Brazil 1, Cambodia 15, Comoros 8, Cook Islands 4, Curacao 5, Cyprus 1, Dominica 1, Georgia 14, Italy 4, Kazakhstan 1, Liberia 16, Malta 233, Marshall Islands 70, Moldova 18, Panama 62, Russia 101, Saint Kitts and Nevis 18, Saint Vincent and the Grenadines 13, Sierra Leone 9, Slovakia 1, Tanzania 13, Togo 4, Tuvalu 1, unknown 3) (2010)

Ports and terminals: *major seaport(s):* Aliaga, Ambarli, Diliskelesi, Eregli, Izmir, Kocaeli (Izmit), Mersin (Icel), Limani, Yarimca
container port(s) (TEUs): Ambarli (2,121,549), Mersin (Icel) (1,126,866)

MILITARY

Military branches: Turkish Armed Forces (TSK): Turkish Land Forces (Turk Kara Kuvvetleri), Turkish Naval Forces (Turk Deniz Kuvvetleri; includes naval air and naval infantry), Turkish Air Forces (Turk Hava Kuvvetleri) (2013)

Military service age and obligation: 21-41 years of age for male compulsory military service; 18 years of age for voluntary service; 15 months conscript obligation for non-university graduates, 6-12 months for university graduates; conscripts are called to register at age 20, for service at 21; women serve in the Turkish Armed Forces only as officers; reserve obligation to age 41; under a law passed in November 2011, men aged 30 and older, or who have worked 3 years in foreign countries, may pay $16,200 in lieu of mandatory military service (2013)

Manpower available for military service:
males age 16-49: 21,079,077
females age 16-49: 20,558,696 (2010 est.)

Manpower fit for military service:
males age 16-49: 17,664,510
females age 16-49: 17,340,816 (2010 est.)

Manpower reaching militarily significant age annually: *male:* 700,079
female: 670,328 (2010 est.)

Military expenditures: 2.31% of GDP (2012)
country comparison to the world: 35
2.28% of GDP (2011)
2.31% of GDP (2010)

Military—note: the ruling Justice and Development Party (AKP) has actively pursued the goal of asserting civilian control over the military since first taking power in 2002; the Turkish Armed Forces (TSK) role in internal security has been significantly reduced; the TSK leadership continues to be an influential institution within Turkey, but plays a much smaller role in politics; the Turkish military remains focused on the threats emanating from the Syrian civil war, Russia's actions in Ukraine, and the PKK insurgency; primary domestic threats are listed as fundamentalism (with the definition in some dispute with the civilian government), separatism (Kurdish discontent), and the extreme left wing; Ankara strongly opposed establishment of an autonomous Kurdish region in Iraq; an overhaul of the Turkish Land Forces Command (TLFC) taking place under the "Force 2014" program is to produce 20-30% smaller, more highly trained forces characterized by greater mobility and firepower and capable of joint and combined operations; the TLFC has taken on increasing international peacekeeping responsibilities including in Afghanistan; the Turkish Navy is a regional naval power that wants to develop the capability to project power beyond Turkey's coastal waters; the Navy is heavily involved in NATO, multinational, and UN operations; its roles include control of territorial waters and security for sea lines of communications; the Turkish Air Force adopted an "Aerospace and Missile Defense Concept" in 2002 and has initiated project work on an integrated missile defense system; Air Force priorities include attaining a modern deployable, survivable, and sustainable force structure, and establishing a sustainable command and control system; Turkey is a NATO ally and hosts NATO's Land Forces Command in Izmir, as well as the AN/TPY-2 radar as part of NATO Missile Defense (2008)

TRANSNATIONAL ISSUES

Disputes—international: complex maritime, air, and territorial disputes with Greece in the Aegean Sea; status of north Cyprus question remains; Syria and Iraq protest Turkish hydrological projects to control upper Euphrates waters; Turkey has expressed concern over the status of Kurds in Iraq; in 2009, Swiss mediators facilitated an accord reestablishing diplomatic ties between Armenia and Turkey, but neither side has ratified the agreement and the rapprochement effort has faltered; Turkish authorities have complained that blasting from quarries in Armenia might be damaging the medieval ruins of Ani, on the other side of the Arpacay valley;

Refugees and internally displaced persons:
refugees (country of origin): 11,322 (Iraq) (2012); 714,552 (Syria) (2014)
IDPs: at least 954,000-1.2 million (displaced from 1984-2005 because of fighting between Kurdish PKK and Turkish military; most IDPs are Kurds from eastern and southeastern provinces; no information available on persons displaced by development projects) (2012)
stateless persons: 780 (2012)

Illicit drugs: key transit route for Southwest Asian heroin to Western Europe and, to a lesser extent, the US—via air, land, and sea routes; major Turkish and other international trafficking organizations operate out of Istanbul; laboratories to convert imported morphine base into heroin exist in remote regions of Turkey and near Istanbul; government maintains strict controls over areas of legal opium poppy cultivation and over output of poppy straw concentrate; lax enforcement of money-laundering controls

TURKMENISTAN

INTRODUCTION

Background: Present-day Turkmenistan covers territory that has been at the crossroads of civilizations for centuries. The area was ruled in antiquity by various Persian empires, and was conquered by Alexander the Great, Muslim crusaders, the Mongols, Turkic warriors, and eventually the Russians. In medieval times Merv (today known as Mary) was one of the great cities of the Islamic world and an important stop on the Silk Road. Annexed by Russia in the late 1800s, Turkmenistan later figured prominently in the anti-Bolshevik movement in Central Asia. In 1924, Turkmenistan became a Soviet republic; it achieved independence upon the dissolution of the USSR in 1991. Extensive hydrocarbon/natural gas reserves, which have yet to be fully exploited, have begun to transform the country. Turkmenistan is moving to expand its extraction and delivery projects. The Government of Turkmenistan is actively working to diversify its gas export routes beyond the still important Russian pipeline network. In 2010, new gas export pipelines that carry Turkmen gas to China and to northern Iran began operating, effectively ending the Russian monopoly on Turkmen gas exports. President for Life Saparmurat NYYAZOW died in December 2006, and Turkmenistan held its first multi-candidate presidential election in February 2007. Gurbanguly BERDIMUHAMEDOW, a deputy cabinet chairman under NYYAZOW, emerged as the country's new president; he was chosen as president again in February 2012, in an election that the OSCE said lacked the freedoms necessary to create a competitive environment.

GEOGRAPHY

Location: Central Asia, bordering the Caspian Sea, between Iran and Kazakhstan

Geographic coordinates: 40 00 N, 60 00 E

Map references: Asia

Area: *total:* 488,100 sq km
country comparison to the world: 53
land: 469,930 sq km
water: 18,170 sq km

Area—comparative: slightly larger than California

Land boundaries: *total:* 3,736 km
border countries: Afghanistan 744 km, Iran 992 km, Kazakhstan 379 km, Uzbekistan 1,621 km

Coastline: 0 km; note—Turkmenistan borders the Caspian Sea (1,768 km)

Maritime claims: none (landlocked)

Climate: subtropical desert

Terrain: flat-to-rolling sandy desert with dunes rising to mountains in the south; low mountains along border with Iran; borders Caspian Sea in west

Elevation extremes: *lowest point:* Vpadina Akchanaya -81 m
note: Sarygamysh Koli is a lake in northern Turkmenistan with a water level that fluctuates above and below the elevation of Vpadina Akchanaya (the lake has dropped as low as -110 m)
highest point: Gora Ayribaba 3,139 m

Natural resources: petroleum, natural gas, sulfur, salt

Land use: *arable land:* 3.89%
permanent crops: 0.12%
other: 95.98% (2011)

Irrigated land: 19,910 sq km (2006)

Total renewable water resources: 24.77 cu km (2011)

Freshwater withdrawal (domestic/industrial/agricultural): *total:* 27.95 cu km/yr (3%/3%/94%)
per capita: 5,752 cu m/yr (2004)

Natural hazards: NA

Environment—current issues: contamination of soil and groundwater with agricultural chemicals, pesticides; salination, water logging of soil due to poor irrigation methods; Caspian Sea pollution; diversion of a large share of the flow of the Amu Darya into irrigation contributes to that river's inability to replenish the Aral Sea; desertification

Environment—international agreements:
party to: Biodiversity, Climate Change, Climate Change-Kyoto Protocol, Desertification, Hazardous Wastes, Ozone Layer Protection
signed, but not ratified: none of the selected agreements

Geography—note: landlocked; the western and central low-lying desolate portions of the country make up the great Garagum (Kara-Kum) desert, which occupies over 80% of the country; eastern part is plateau

PEOPLE AND SOCIETY

Nationality: *noun:* Turkmen(s)
adjective: Turkmen

Ethnic groups: Turkmen 85%, Uzbek 5%, Russian 4%, other 6% (2003)

Languages: Turkmen (official) 72%, Russian 12%, Uzbek 9%, other 7%

Religions: Muslim 89%, Eastern Orthodox 9%, unknown 2%

Population: 5,171,943 (July 2014 est.)
country comparison to the world: 120

Age structure:
0-14 years: 26.4% (male 691,076/female 673,310)
15-24 years: 20.2% (male 526,027/female 519,474)
25-54 years: 42.3% (male 1,082,821/female 1,102,716)
55-64 years: 4.2% (male 168,543/female 188,742)
65 years and over: 4.2% (male 95,391/female 123,843) (2014 est.)

Dependency ratios:
total dependency ratio: 48.3 %
youth dependency ratio: 42.2 %
elderly dependency ratio: 6.1 %
potential support ratio: 16.5 (2013)

Median age: *total:* 26.6 years
male: 26.2 years
female: 27.1 years (2014 est.)

Population growth rate: 1.14% (2014 est.)
country comparison to the world: 104

Birth rate: 19.46 births/1,000 population (2014 est.)
country comparison to the world: 89

Death rate: 6.16 deaths/1,000 population (2014 est.)
country comparison to the world: 161

Net migration rate: -1.86 migrant(s)/1,000 population (2014 est.)
country comparison to the world: 164

Urbanization: *urban population:* 48.7% of total population (2011)
rate of urbanization: 1.91% annual rate of change (2010-15 est.)

Major urban areas—population: ASHGABAT (capital) 637,000 (2009)

Sex ratio: *at birth:* 1.05 male(s)/female
0-14 years: 1.03 male(s)/female
15-24 years: 1.01 male(s)/female
25-54 years: 0.98 male(s)/female
55-64 years: 0.98 male(s)/female
65 years and over: 0.77 male(s)/female
total population: 0.98 male(s)/female (2014 est.)

Mother's mean age at first birth: 24.6 (2006 est.)

Maternal mortality rate: 67 deaths/100,000 live births (2010)
country comparison to the world: 89

Infant mortality rate:
total: 38.13 deaths/1,000 live births
country comparison to the world: 60
male: 45.63 deaths/1,000 live births
female: 30.26 deaths/1,000 live births (2014 est.)

Life expectancy at birth:
total population: 69.47 years
country comparison to the world: 155
male: 66.48 years
female: 72.61 years (2014 est.)

Total fertility rate: 2.1 children born/woman (2014 est.)
country comparison to the world: 108

Contraceptive prevalence rate: 61.8% (2000)

Health expenditures: 2.7% of GDP (2011)
country comparison to the world: 183

Physicians density: 2.44 physicians/1,000 population (2007)

Hospital bed density: 4.1 beds/1,000 population (2011)

Drinking water source:
improved:
urban: 89.1% of population
rural: 53.7% of population
total: 71% of population
unimproved:
urban: 10.9% of population
rural: 46.3% of population
total: 29% of population (2011 est.)

Sanitation facility access:
improved:
urban: 100% of population
rural: 98.2% of population
total: 99.1% of population

unimproved:
urban: 0% of population
rural: 1.8% of population
total: 0.9% of population (2011 est.)

HIV/AIDS—adult prevalence rate: less than 0.1% (2007 est.)
country comparison to the world: 149

HIV/AIDS—people living with HIV/AIDS: fewer than 200 (2007 est.)
country comparison to the world: 161

HIV/AIDS—deaths: fewer than 100 (2004 est.)
country comparison to the world: 146

Obesity—adult prevalence rate: 13.2% (2008)
country comparison to the world: 125

Children under the age of 5 years underweight: 10.5% (2000)
country comparison to the world: 68

Education expenditures: NA

Literacy: *definition:* age 15 and over can read and write
total population: 99.6%
male: 99.7%
female: 99.5% (2011 est.)

GOVERNMENT

Country name: *conventional long form:* none
conventional short form: Turkmenistan
local long form: none
local short form: Turkmenistan
former: Turkmen Soviet Socialist Republic

Government type: defines itself as a secular democracy and a presidential republic; in actuality displays authoritarian presidential rule, with power concentrated within the presidential administration

Capital: *name:* Ashgabat (Ashkhabad)

geographic coordinates: 37 57 N, 58 23 E
time difference: UTC+5 (10 hours ahead of Washington, DC during Standard Time)

Administrative divisions: 5 provinces (welayatlar, singular—welayat) and 1 independent city*: Ahal Welayaty (Anew), Ashgabat*, Balkan Welayaty (Balkanabat), Dashoguz Welayaty, Lebap Welayaty (Turkmenabat), Mary Welayaty
note: administrative divisions have the same names as their administrative centers (exceptions have the administrative center name following in parentheses)

Independence: 27 October 1991 (from the Soviet Union)

National holiday: Independence Day, 27 October (1991)

Constitution: adopted 18 May 1992; amended several times, last in 2008; note—sources disagree on whether the changes in 2008 are amendments or reflect a new constitution (2012)

Legal system: civil law system with Islamic law influences

International law organization participation: has not submitted an ICJ jurisdiction declaration; non-party state to the ICCt

Suffrage: 18 years of age; universal

Executive branch: *chief of state:* President Gurbanguly BERDIMUHAMEDOW (since 14 February 2007); note—the president is both the chief of state and head of government
head of government: President Gurbanguly BERDIMUHAMEDOW (since 14 February 2007)
cabinet: Cabinet of Ministers appointed by the president (For more information visit the World Leaders website)
elections: president elected by popular vote for a five-year term (eligible for a second term; election last held on 12 February 2012 (next to be held February 2017)
election results: Gurbanguly BERDIMUHAMEDOW reelected president; percent of vote—Gurbanguly BERDIMUHAMEDOW 97.1%, Annageldi YAZMYRADOW 1.1%, other candidates 1.8%

Legislative branch: unicameral parliament known as the National Assembly (Mejlis) (125 seats; members elected by popular vote to serve five-year terms)
elections: last held on 15 December 2013 (next to be held in December 2018)
election results: percent of vote by party—NA; seats by party—Democratic Party 47, Organization of Trade and Unions of Turkmenistan 33, Women's Union of Turkmenistan 16, Party of Industrialists and Entrepreneurs 14
note: in 26 September 2008, a new constitution of Turkmenistan abolished a second, 2,507-member legislative body known as the People's Council and expanded the number of deputies in the National Assembly from 65 to 125; the powers formerly held by the People's Council were divided up between the president and the National Assembly

Judicial branch: *highest court(s):* Supreme Court of Turkmenistan (consists of the court president and 21 associate judges)
judge selection and term of office: judges appointed by the president; judge tenure NA
subordinate courts: provincial, district, and city courts; High Commercial Court; military courts

Political parties and leaders: Democratic Party of Turkmenistan or DPT [Kasymguly BABAYEW]; Party of Industrialists and Entrepreneurs or PIE [Orazmammet MAMMEDOW] (party registered 21 August 2012)
note: a law authorizing the registration of political parties went into effect in January 2012; unofficial, small opposition movements exist abroad; the three most prominent opposition groups-in-exile are the National Democratic Movement of Turkmenistan (NDMT), the Republican Party of Turkmenistan, and the Watan (Fatherland) Party; the NDMT was led by former Foreign Minister Boris SHIKHMURADOV until his arrest and imprisonment in the wake of the 25 November 2002 attack on President NYYAZOW's motorcade

Political pressure groups and leaders: none

International organization participation: ADB, CIS (associate member, has not ratified the 1993 CIS charter although it participates in meetings and held the chairmanship of the CIS in 2012), EAPC, EBRD, ECO, FAO, G-77, IBRD, ICAO, ICRM, IDA, IDB, IFC, IFRCS, ILO, IMF, IMO, Interpol, IOC, IOM (observer), ISO (correspondent), ITU, MIGA, NAM, OIC, OPCW, OSCE, PFP, UN, UNCTAD, UNESCO, UNHCR, UNIDO, UNWTO, UPU, WCO, WFTU (NGOs), WHO, WIPO, WMO

Diplomatic representation in the US:
chief of mission: Ambassador Mered Bairamovich ORAZOW (since 14 February 2001)
chancery: 2207 Massachusetts Avenue NW, Washington, DC 20008
telephone: [1] (202) 588-1500
FAX: [1] (202) 280-1003

Diplomatic representation from the US:
chief of mission: Ambassador Robert E. PATTERSON (since 26 April 2011)
embassy: No. 9 1984 Street (formerly Pushkin Street), Ashgabat, Turkmenistan 744000
mailing address: 7070 Ashgabat Place, Washington, DC 20521-7070
telephone: [993] (12) 94-00-45
FAX: [993] (12) 94-26-14

Flag description: green field with a vertical red stripe near the hoist side, containing five tribal guls (designs used in producing carpets) stacked above two crossed olive branches; five white stars and a white crescent moon appear in the upper corner of the field just to the fly side of the red stripe; the green color and crescent moon represent Islam; the five stars symbolize the regions or welayats of Turkmenistan; the guls reflect the national identity of Turkmenistan where carpet-making has long been a part of traditional nomadic life
note: the flag of Turkmenistan is the most intricate of all national flags

National symbol(s): Akhal-Teke horse

National anthem: *name:* "Garassyz, Bitarap Turkmenistanyn" (Independent, Neutral, Turkmenistan State Anthem)
lyrics/music: collective/Veli MUKHATOV
note: adopted 1997, lyrics revised 2008; following the death of the President Saparmurat NYYAZOW, the lyrics were altered to eliminate references to the former president

ECONOMY

Economy—overview: Turkmenistan is largely a desert country with intensive agriculture in irrigated oases and sizeable gas and oil resources. The two largest crops are cotton, most of which is produced for export, and wheat, which is domestically consumed. Although agriculture accounts for roughly 7% of GDP, it continues to employ nearly half of the country's workforce. Turkmenistan's authoritarian regime has taken a cautious approach to economic reform, hoping to use gas and cotton export revenues to sustain its inefficient and highly corrupt economy. The government introduced a privatization plan in 2012, but the implementation of this initiative has been slow. Privatization goals remain limited. From 1998-2005, Turkmenistan suffered from the continued lack of adequate export routes for natural gas and from obligations on extensive short-term external debt. At the same time, however, total exports rose by an average of roughly 15% per year from 2003-08, largely because of higher international oil and gas prices. Additional pipelines to China, that began operation in early 2010, and increased pipeline capacity to Iran, have expanded Turkmenistan's export routes for its gas. Overall prospects in the near future are discouraging because of endemic corruption, a poor educational system, government misuse of oil and gas revenues, and Ashgabat's reluctance to adopt market-oriented reforms. The majority of Turkmenistan's economic statistics are state secrets. The present government established a State Agency for Statistics, but GDP numbers and other publicized figures are subject to wide margins of error. In particular, the rate of GDP growth is uncertain. Since his election, President BERDIMUHAMEDOW unified the country's dual currency exchange rate, ordered the redenomination of the manat, reduced state subsidies for gasoline, and initiated development of a special tourism zone on the Caspian Sea. Although foreign investment is encouraged, and some improvements in macroeconomic policy have been made, numerous bureaucratic obstacles impede international business activity.

GDP (purchasing power parity): $55.16 billion (2013 est.)
country comparison to the world: 95
$49.18 billion (2012 est.)
$44.27 billion (2011 est.)
note: data are in 2013 US dollars

GDP (official exchange rate): $40.56 billion (2013 est.)

GDP—real growth rate: 12.2% (2013 est.)
country comparison to the world: 3
11.1% (2012 est.)
14.7% (2011 est.)

GDP—per capita (PPP): $9,700 (2013 est.)
country comparison to the world: 122
$8,800 (2012 est.)
$8,000 (2011 est.)
note: data are in 2013 US dollars

Gross national saving: 12.6% of GDP (2013 est.)
country comparison to the world: 123
12.9% of GDP (2012 est.)
10.6% of GDP (2011 est.)

GDP—composition, by end use:
household consumption: 50%
government consumption: 12.8%
investment in fixed capital: 11.6%
investment in inventories: 0%
exports of goods and services: 56.4%
imports of goods and services: -30.8% (2013 est.)

GDP—composition, by sector of origin:
agriculture: 7.2%
industry: 24.4%
services: 68.4% (2013 est.)

Agriculture—products: cotton, grain, melons; livestock

Industries: natural gas, oil, petroleum products, textiles, food processing

Industrial production growth rate: 8% (2013 est.)
country comparison to the world: 26

Labor force: 2.3 million (2008 est.)
country comparison to the world: 116

Labor force—by occupation: *agriculture:* 48.2%
industry: 14%
services: 37.8% (2004 est.)

Unemployment rate: 60% (2004 est.)
country comparison to the world: 199

Population below poverty line: 30% (2004 est.)

Household income or consumption by percentage share: *lowest 10%:* 2.6%
highest 10%: 31.7% (1998)

Distribution of family income—Gini index: 40.8 (1998)
country comparison to the world: 55

Budget: *revenues:* $5.93 billion
expenditures: $5.474 billion (2013 est.)

Taxes and other revenues: 14.6% of GDP (2013 est.)
country comparison to the world: 194

Budget surplus (+) or deficit (-):
1.1% of GDP (2013 est.)
country comparison to the world: 24

Fiscal year: calendar year

Inflation rate (consumer prices): 9% (2013 est.)
country comparison to the world: 203
8.5% (2012 est.)

Stock of narrow money: $577.2 million (31 December 2013 est.)
country comparison to the world: 158
$526.3 million (31 December 2012 est.)

Stock of broad money: $1.199 billion (31 December 2013 est.)
country comparison to the world: 164
$1.058 billion (31 December 2012 est.)

Stock of domestic credit: $2.912 billion (31 December 2013 est.)
country comparison to the world: 127
$2.561 billion (31 December 2012 est.)

Market value of publicly traded shares: $NA

Current account balance: $285.9 million (2013 est.)
country comparison to the world: 56
$622.7 million (2012 est.)

Exports: $17.13 billion (2013 est.)
country comparison to the world: 75
$19.99 billion (2012 est.)

Exports—commodities: gas, crude oil, petrochemicals, textiles, cotton fiber

Exports—partners: China 69.6%, Italy 4.7% (2012)

Imports: $12.48 billion (2013 est.)
country comparison to the world: 92
$14.14 billion (2012 est.)

Imports—commodities: machinery and equipment, chemicals, foodstuffs

Imports—partners: China 19.5%, Turkey 17%, Russia 12.6%, UAE 6.8%, Ukraine 6%, Germany 4.7%, UK 4.2% (2012)

Reserves of foreign exchange and gold: $22.35 billion (31 December 2013 est.)
country comparison to the world: 56
$20.71 billion (31 December 2012 est.)

Debt—external: $428.9 million (31 December 2012 est.)
country comparison to the world: 180
$451.5 million (31 December 2011 est.)

Exchange rates: Turkmen manat (TMM) per US dollar—
2.85 (2013 est.)
2.85 (2012 est.)
2.85 (2010 est.)
2.85 (2009)
14,250 (2008)

ENERGY

Electricity—production: 19.97 billion kWh (2013 est.)
country comparison to the world: 7 4

Electricity—consumption: 17.08 billion kWh (2013 est.)
country comparison to the world: 72

Electricity—exports: 2.885 billion kWh (2013 est.)
country comparison to the world: 34

Electricity—imports: 0 kWh (2013 est.)
country comparison to the world: 209

Electricity—installed generating capacity: 2.852 million kW (2010 est.)
country comparison to the world: 88

Electricity—from fossil fuels: 100% of total installed capacity (2010 est.)
country comparison to the world: 38

Electricity—from nuclear fuels: 0% of total installed capacity (2010 est.)
country comparison to the world: 192

Electricity—from hydroelectric plants: 0% of total installed capacity (2010 est.)
country comparison to the world: 205

Electricity—from other renewable sources: 0% of total installed capacity (2010 est.)
country comparison to the world: 131

Crude oil—production: 244,100 bbl/day (2012 est.)
country comparison to the world: 36

Crude oil—exports: 67,000 bbl/day (2012 est.)
country comparison to the world: 44

Crude oil—imports: 0 bbl/day (2010 est.)
country comparison to the world: 131

Crude oil—proved reserves: 600 million bbl (1 January 2013 es)
country comparison to the world: 46

Refined petroleum products—production: 143,200 bbl/day (2010 est.)
country comparison to the world: 64

Refined petroleum products—consumption: 145,000 bbl/day (2011 est.)
country comparison to the world: 68

Refined petroleum products—exports: 64,360 bbl/day (2010 est.)
country comparison to the world: 57

Refined petroleum products—imports: 2,542 bbl/day (2010 est.)
country comparison to the world: 176

Natural gas—production: 64.4 billion cu m (2012 est.)
country comparison to the world: 13

Natural gas—consumption: 23.3 billion cu m (2012 est.)
country comparison to the world: 33

Natural gas—exports: 41.1 billion cu m (2012 est.)
country comparison to the world: 10

Natural gas—imports: 0 cu m (2013 est.)
country comparison to the world: 140

Natural gas—proved reserves: 17.5 trillion cu m (1 January 2013 es)
country comparison to the world: 4

Carbon dioxide emissions from consumption of energy: 51.85 million Mt (2011 est.)
country comparison to the world: 63

COMMUNICATIONS

Telephones—main lines in use: 575,000 (2012)
country comparison to the world: 94

Telephones—mobile cellular: 3.953 million (2012)
country comparison to the world: 123

Telephone system: *general assessment:* telecommunications network remains underdeveloped and progress toward improvement is slow; strict government control and censorship inhibits liberalization and modernization
domestic: Turkmentelekom, in cooperation with foreign partners, has installed high-speed fiber-optic lines and has upgraded most of the country's telephone exchanges and switching centers with new digital technology; combined fixed-line and mobile teledensity is about 80 per 100 persons; Russia's Mobile Telesystems, the only foreign mobile-cellular service provider in Turkmenistan, had its operating license suspended in December 2010 but was able to resume operations in September 2012; Turkmenistan's first telecommunication satellite is scheduled to be launched by the end of 2014; once in orbit, it is expected that the satellite will greatly improve connectivity in the country
international: country code—993; linked by fiber-optic cable and microwave radio relay to other CIS republics and to other countries by leased connections to the Moscow international gateway switch; an exchange in Ashgabat switches international traffic through Turkey via Intelsat; satellite earth stations—1 Orbita and 1 Intelsat (2012)

Broadcast media: broadcast media is government controlled and censored; 7 state-owned TV and 4 state-owned radio networks; satellite dishes and programming provide an alternative to the state-run media; officials sometimes limit access to satellite TV by removing satellite dishes (2007)

Internet country code: . t m

Internet hosts: 714 (2012)
country comparison to the world: 176

Internet users: 80,400 (2009)
country comparison to the world: 166

TRANSPORTATION

Airports: 26 (2013)

country comparison to the world: 126

Airports—with paved runways: *total:* 2 1
over 3,047 m: 1
2,438 to 3,047 m: 9
1,524 to 2,437 m: 9
914 to 1,523 m: 2 (2013)

Airports—with unpaved runways: *total:* 5
1,524 to 2,437 m: 1
under 914 m: 4 (2013)

Heliports: 1 (2013)

Pipelines: gas 7,500 km; oil 1,501 km (2013)

Railways: *total:* 2,980 km
country comparison to the world: 57
broad gauge: 2,980 km 1.520-m gauge (2008)

Roadways: *total:* 58,592 km
country comparison to the world: 72
paved: 47,577 km
unpaved: 11,015 km (2002)

Waterways: 1,300 km (Amu Darya and Kara Kum canal are important inland waterways) (2011)
country comparison to the world: 56

Merchant marine: *total:* 1 1
country comparison to the world: 112
by type: cargo 4, chemical tanker 1, petroleum tanker 5, refrigerated cargo 1 (2010)

Ports and terminals: *major seaport(s):* Turkmenbasy

MILITARY

Military branches: Turkmen Armed Forces: Ground Forces, Navy, Air and Air Defense Forces (2013)

Military service age and obligation: 18-27 years of age for compulsory male military service; 2-year conscript service obligation, or 1 year for university students; 20 years of age for voluntary service; males may enroll in military schools from age 15 (2013)

Manpower available for military service:
males age 16-49: 1,380,794
females age 16-49: 1,387,211 (2010 est.)

Manpower fit for military service:
males age 16-49: 1,066,649
females age 16-49: 1,185,538 (2010 est.)

Manpower reaching militarily significant age annually: *male:* 53,829
female: 52,988 (2010 est.)

TRANSNATIONAL ISSUES

Disputes—international: cotton monoculture in Uzbekistan and Turkmenistan creates water-sharing difficulties for Amu Darya river states; field demarcation of the boundaries with Kazakhstan commenced in 2005, but Caspian seabed delimitation remains stalled with Azerbaijan, Iran, and Kazakhstan due to Turkmenistan's indecision over how to allocate the sea's waters and seabed; bilateral talks continue with Azerbaijan on dividing the seabed and contested oilfields in the middle of the Caspian

Refugees and internally displaced persons: *stateless persons:* 8,947 (2012)

Trafficking in persons: *current situation:* Turkmenistan is a source, and to a much lesser degree, destination country for men, women, and children subjected to forced labor and sex trafficking; Turkmen in search of work in other countries are forced to work in textile sweatshops, construction, and domestic service; some Turkmen women and girls are sex trafficked abroad; Turkey is the primary trafficking destination, followed by Russia, the United Arab Emirates, and, to a lesser extent, the UK, Kazakhstan, and Cyprus; labor trafficking occurs within Turkmenistan, particularly in the construction industry, with victims identified from Uzbekistan, Ukraine, and Azerbaijan

tier rating: Tier 2 Watch List—Turkmenistan does not fully comply with the minimum standards for the elimination of trafficking; however, it is making significant efforts to do so; the government continues to convict trafficking offenders under its anti-trafficking statute; it employs no formal victim identification procedures and does not provide services or fund NGOs to provide services to victims; authorities punish some victims for crimes committed as a result of being trafficked; there continues to be no governmental coordinating body for anti-trafficking efforts or a national anti-trafficking action plan (2013)

Illicit drugs: transit country for Afghan narcotics bound for Russian and Western European markets; transit point for heroin precursor chemicals bound for Afghanistan

TURKS AND CAICOS ISLANDS

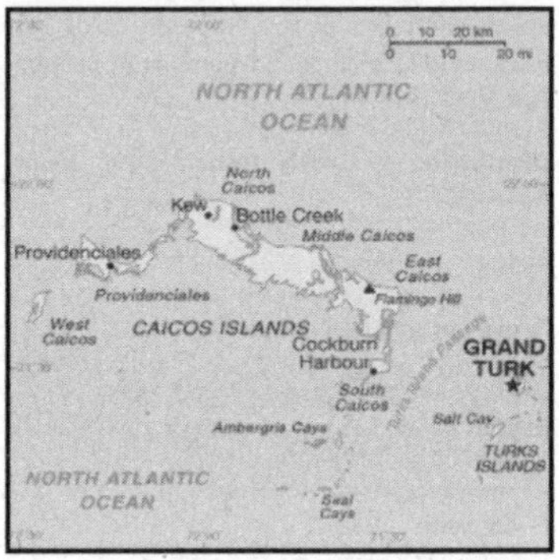

INTRODUCTION

Background: The islands were part of the UK's Jamaican colony until 1962, when they assumed the status of a separate crown colony upon Jamaica's independence. The governor of The Bahamas oversaw affairs from 1965 to 1973. With Bahamian independence, the islands received a separate governor in 1973. Although independence was agreed upon for 1982, the policy was reversed and the islands remain a British overseas territory.

GEOGRAPHY

Location: two island groups in the North Atlantic Ocean, southeast of The Bahamas, north of Haiti

Geographic coordinates: 21 45 N, 71 35 W

Map references: Central America and the Caribbean

Area: *total:* 948 sq km
country comparison to the world: 186
land: 948 sq km
water: 0 sq km

Area—comparative: 2.5 times the size of Washington, DC

Land boundaries: 0 km

Coastline: 389 km

Maritime claims: territorial sea: 12 nm
exclusive fishing zone: 200 nm

Climate: tropical; marine; moderated by trade winds; sunny and relatively dry

Terrain: low, flat limestone; extensive marshes and mangrove swamps

Elevation extremes:
lowest point: Caribbean Sea 0 m
highest point: Flamingo Hill 48 m

Natural resources: spiny lobster, conch

Land use: *arable land:* 1.05%
permanent crops: 0%
other: 98.95% (2011)

Irrigated land: NA

Natural hazards: frequent hurricanes

Environment—current issues: limited natural freshwater resources, private cisterns collect rainwater

Geography—note: about 40 islands (eight inhabited)

PEOPLE AND SOCIETY

Nationality: *noun:* none
adjective: none

Ethnic groups: black 87.6%, white 7.9%, mixed 2.5%, East Indian 1.3%, other 0.7% (2006)

Languages: English (official)

Religions: Protestant 72.8% (Baptist 35.8%, Church of God 11.7%, Anglican 10%, Methodist 9.3%, Seventh-Day Adventist 6%), Roman Catholic 11.4%, Jehovah's Witnesses 1.8%, other 14%

Population: 49,070 (July 2014 est.)
country comparison to the world: 212

Age structure:
0-14 years: 22.1% (male 5,536/female 5,332)
15-24 years: 14.8% (male 3,552/female 3,715)
25-54 years: 53.5% (male 13,333/female 12,931)
55-64 years: 4.2% (male 1,434/female 1,188)
65 years and over: 4.1% (male 910/female 1,139) (2014 est.)

Median age: *total:* 31.9 years
male: 32.2 years
female: 31.5 years (2014 est.)

Population growth rate: 2.58% (2014 est.)
country comparison to the world: 27

Birth rate: 16.61 births/1,000 population (2014 est.)
country comparison to the world: 119

Death rate: 3.08 deaths/1,000 population (2014 est.)
country comparison to the world: 222

Net migration rate: 12.23 migrant(s)/1,000 population (2014 est.)
country comparison to the world: 12

Urbanization: *urban population:* 93% of total population (2010)
rate of urbanization: 1.6% annual rate of change (2010-15 est.)

Major urban areas—population: GRAND TURK (capital) 6,000 (2009)

Sex ratio: *at birth:* 1.05 male(s)/female
0-14 years: 1.04 male(s)/female
15-24 years: 0.96 male(s)/female
25-54 years: 1.03 male(s)/female
55-64 years: 1.02 male(s)/female
65 years and over: 0.8 male(s)/female
total population: 1.02 male(s)/female (2014 est.)

Infant mortality rate: *total:* 10.97 deaths/1,000 live births
country comparison to the world: 131
male: 13.7 deaths/1,000 live births
female: 8.09 deaths/1,000 live births (2014 est.)

Life expectancy at birth:
total population: 79.55 years
country comparison to the world: 43
male: 76.8 years
female: 82.42 years (2014 est.)

Total fertility rate: 1.7 children born/woman (2014 est.)
country comparison to the world: 172

Drinking water source:
improved:
urban: 100% of population
rural: 100% of population
total: 100% of population (2010 est.)

Sanitation facility access:
improved:
urban: 81.4% of population
rural: 81.4% of population
total: 81.4% of population
unimproved:
urban: 18.6% of population
rural: 18.6% of population
total: 18.6% of population (2007 est.)

HIV/AIDS—adult prevalence rate: NA

HIV/AIDS—people living with HIV/AIDS: NA

HIV/AIDS—deaths: NA

Education expenditures: NA

Literacy: *definition:* age 15 and over has ever attended school
total population: 98%
male: 99%
female: 98% (1970 est.)

People—note: destination and transit point for illegal Haitian immigrants bound for the Turks and Caicos Islands, The Bahamas, and the US

GOVERNMENT

Country name: *conventional long form:* none
conventional short form: Turks and Caicos Islands
abbreviation: TCI

Dependency status: overseas territory of the UK

Government type: NA

Capital: *name:* Grand Turk (Cockburn Town)
geographic coordinates: 21 28 N, 71 08 W
time difference: UTC-5 (same time as Washington, DC during Standard Time)
daylight saving time: +1hr, begins second Sunday in March; ends first Sunday in November

Administrative divisions: none (overseas territory of the UK)

Independence: none (overseas territory of the UK)

National holiday: Constitution Day, 30 August (1976)

Constitution: several previous; latest signed 7 August 2012, effective 15 October 2012 (Turks and Caicos Constitution Order 2011) (2012)

Legal system: mixed legal system of English common law and civil law

Suffrage: 18 years of age; universal

Executive branch: *chief of state:* Queen ELIZABETH II (since 6 February 1952); represented by Governor Peter BECKINGHAM (since 9 October 2013)
head of government: Premier Rufus EWING (since 13 November 2012)
cabinet: consists of the governor, the premier, six ministers appointed by the governor from among the members of the House of Assembly, and the attorney general (For more information visit the World Leaders website)
elections: the monarch is hereditary; governor appointed by the monarch; following legislative elections, the leader of the majority party is appointed premier by the governor
note: the UK foreign minister has determined that sufficient progress has been made to reinstate local government under a new constitution that came into effect in October 2012

Legislative branch: unicameral House of Assembly consisting of 19 seats, 15 elected and 4 appointed by the governor; of elected members, five are elected at large and 10 from single member districts for four-year terms
elections: last held on 9 November 2012 (next to be held in 2016)
election results: percent of vote—NA; seats by party—PNP 8, PDM 7

Judicial branch: *highest court(s):* Supreme Court (consists of the chief justice and such number of other judges as determined by the governor); Court of Appeal (consists of the court president and 2 justices) note—appeals beyond the Supreme Court are heard by the Judicial Committee of the Privy Council, in London
judge selection and term of office: Supreme Court and Appeals Court judges appointed by the governor in accordance with the Judicial Service Commission, a 3-member body of high level judicial officials; Supreme Court judges appointed until mandatory retirement at age 65, but can be extended to age 70; Appeals Court judge tenure determined by individual terms of appointment
subordinate courts: magistrates' courts

Political parties and leaders: People's Democratic Movement or PDM [Oswald SKIPPINGS]; People's Progressive Party [NA]; Progressive National Party or PNP [Rufus EWING]

Political pressure groups and leaders: NA

International organization participation: Caricom (associate), CDB, Interpol (subbureau), UPU

Diplomatic representation in the US: none (overseas territory of the UK)

Diplomatic representation from the US: none (overseas territory of the UK)

Flag description: blue, with the flag of the UK in the upper hoist-side quadrant and the colonial shield centered on the outer half of the flag; the shield is yellow and displays a conch shell, a spiny lobster, and Turks Head cactus—three common elements of the islands' biota

National anthem: *name:* "This Land of Ours"
lyrics/music: Conrad HOWELL
note: serves as a local anthem; as a territory of the United Kingdom, "God Save the Queen" is the official anthem (see United Kingdom)

ECONOMY

Economy—overview: The Turks and Caicos economy is based on tourism, offshore financial services, and fishing. Most capital goods and food for domestic consumption are; imported. The US is the leading source of tourists, accounting for more than three-quarters of the 175,000 visitors that arrived in 2004. Major sources of government revenue also include fees from offshore financial activities and customs receipts.

GDP (purchasing power parity): $632 million (2007 est.)
country comparison to the world: 213
$568.3 million (2006 est.)

GDP (official exchange rate): $NA

GDP—real growth rate: 11.2% (2007 est.)
country comparison to the world: 6

GDP—per capita (PPP): $29,100 (2007 est.)
country comparison to the world: 52

GDP—composition, by end use:
household consumption: 29.6%
government consumption: 17.7%
investment in fixed capital: 52.9%
exports of goods and services: 76.2%
imports of goods and services: -76.3% (2013 est.)

GDP—composition, by sector of origin:
agriculture: 1%
industry: 22.5%
services: 76.5% (2013 est.)

Agriculture—products: corn, beans, cassava (tapioca), citrus fruits; fish

Industries: tourism, offshore financial services

Industrial production growth rate: 3%
country comparison to the world: 99

Labor force: 4,848 (1990 est.)
country comparison to the world: 222

Labor force—by occupation: *note:* about 33% in government and 20% in agriculture and fishing; significant numbers in tourism, financial, and other services

Unemployment rate: 10% (1997 est.)
country comparison to the world: 108

Population below poverty line: NA%

Household income or consumption by percentage share: *lowest 10%:* NA%
highest 10%: NA%

Budget: *revenues:* $434.1 million
expenditures: $437.6 million (2013 est.)

Fiscal year: calendar year

Inflation rate (consumer prices): 2.5% (2013 est.)
country comparison to the world: 94
2.5% (2012 est.)

Exports: $24.77 million (2008 est.)
country comparison to the world: 205

Exports—commodities: lobster, dried and fresh conch, conch shells

Imports: $591.3 million (2008 est.)
country comparison to the world: 191

Imports—commodities: food and beverages, tobacco, clothing, manufactures, construction materials

Debt—external: $NA

Exchange rates: the US dollar is used

ENERGY

Electricity—production: 200 million kWh (2010 est.)
country comparison to the world: 182

Electricity—consumption: 186 million kWh (2010 est.)
country comparison to the world: 186

Electricity—exports: 0 kWh (2012 est.)

country comparison to the world: 200
Electricity—imports: 0 kWh (2012 est.)
country comparison to the world: 204
Electricity—installed generating capacity: 50,000 kW (2010 est.)
country comparison to the world: 188
Electricity—from fossil fuels: 100% of total installed capacity (2010 est.)
country comparison to the world: 36
Electricity—from nuclear fuels: 0% of total installed capacity (2010 est.)
country comparison to the world: 186
Electricity—from hydroelectric plants: 0% of total installed capacity (2010 est.)
country comparison to the world: 203
Electricity—from other renewable sources: 0% of total installed capacity (2010 est.)
country comparison to the world: 127
Crude oil—production: 0 bbl/day (2012 est.)
country comparison to the world: 135
Crude oil—exports: 0 bbl/day (2010 est.)
country comparison to the world: 189
Crude oil—imports: 0 bbl/day (2010 est.)
country comparison to the world: 126
Crude oil—proved reserves: 0 bbl (1 January 2013 es)
country comparison to the world: 193
Refined petroleum products—production: 0 bbl/day (2010 est.)
country comparison to the world: 197
Refined petroleum products—consumption: 998.6 bbl/day (2011 est.)
country comparison to the world: 203
Refined petroleum products—exports: 0 bbl/day (2010 est.)
country comparison to the world: 133
Refined petroleum products—imports: 1,063 bbl/day (2010 est.)
country comparison to the world: 194
Natural gas—production: 0 cu m (2011 est.)
country comparison to the world: 196
Natural gas—consumption: 0 cu m (2010 est.)
country comparison to the world: 197
Natural gas—exports: 0 cu m (2011 est.)
country comparison to the world: 190
Natural gas—imports: 0 cu m (2011 est.)
country comparison to the world: 135
Natural gas—proved reserves: 0 cu m (1 January 2013 es)
country comparison to the world: 197
Carbon dioxide emissions from consumption of energy: 155,500 Mt (2011 est.)
country comparison to the world: 197

COMMUNICATIONS

Telephone system: *general assessment:* fully digital system with international direct dialing
domestic: full range of services available; GSM wireless service available
international: country code—1-649; the Americas Region Caribbean Ring System (ARCOS-1) fiber optic telecommunications submarine cable provides connectivity to South and Central America, parts of the Caribbean, and the US; satellite earth station—1 Intelsat (Atlantic Ocean) (2011)
Broadcast media: no local terrestrial TV stations, broadcasts from the Bahamas can be received and multi-channel cable and satellite TV services are available; government-run radio network operates alongside private broadcasters with a total of about 15 stations (2007)
Internet country code: .tc
Internet hosts: 73,217 (2012)
country comparison to the world: 86

TRANSPORTATION

Airports: 8 (2013)
country comparison to the world: 163
Airports—with paved runways: *total:* 6
2,438 to 3,047 m: 1
1,524 to 2,437 m: 3
914 to 1,523 m: 1
under 914 m: 1 (2013)
Airports—with unpaved runways: *total:* 2
under 914 m: 2 (2013)
Roadways: *total:* 121 km
country comparison to the world: 212
paved: 24 km
unpaved: 97 km (2003)
Ports and terminals: *major seaport(s):* Cockburn Harbour, Grand Turk, Providenciales

MILITARY

Manpower fit for military service:
males age 16-49: 11,842
females age 16-49: 11,755 (2010 est.)
Manpower reaching militarily significant age annually: *male:* 338
female: 342 (2010 est.)
Military—note: defense is the responsibility of the UK

TRANSNATIONAL ISSUES

Disputes—international: have received Haitians fleeing economic and civil disorder
Illicit drugs: transshipment point for South American narcotics destined for the US and Europe

TUVALU

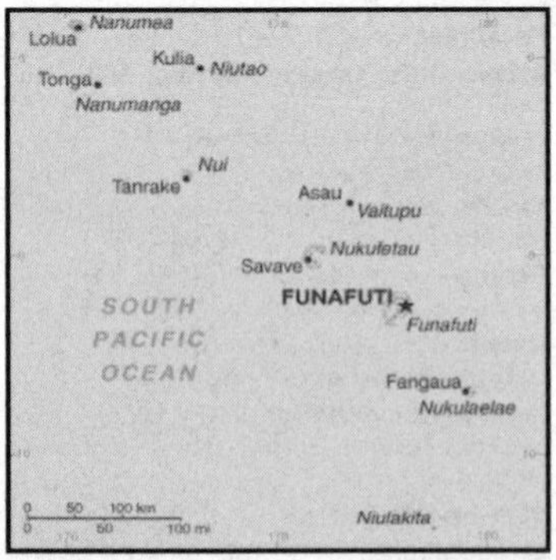

INTRODUCTION

Background: In 1974, ethnic differences within the British colony of the Gilbert and Ellice Islands caused the Polynesians of the Ellice Islands to vote for separation from the Micronesians of the Gilbert Islands. The following year, the Ellice Islands became the separate British colony of Tuvalu. Independence was granted in 1978. In 2000, Tuvalu negotiated a contract leasing its Internet domain name ".tv" for $50 million in royalties over a 12-year period.

GEOGRAPHY

Location: Oceania, island group consisting of nine coral atolls in the South Pacific Ocean, about one-half of the way from Hawaii to Australia
Geographic coordinates: 8 00 S, 178 00 E
Map references: Oceania
Area: *total:* 26 sq km
country comparison to the world: 238
land: 26 sq km
water: 0 sq km
Area—comparative: 0.1 times the size of Washington, DC
Land boundaries: 0 km
Coastline: 24 km
Maritime claims: *territorial sea:* 12 nm
contiguous zone: 24 nm
exclusive economic zone: 200 nm
Climate: tropical; moderated by easterly trade winds (March to November); westerly gales and heavy rain (November to March)
Terrain: low-lying and narrow coral atolls
Elevation extremes: *lowest point:* Pacific Ocean 0 m
highest point: unnamed location 5 m
Natural resources: fish
Land use: *arable land:* 0%
permanent crops: 60%
other: 40% (2011)
Irrigated land: NA
Natural hazards: severe tropical storms are usually rare, but in 1997 there were three cyclones; low levels of islands make them sensitive to changes in sea level
Environment—current issues: since there are no streams or rivers and groundwater is not potable, most water needs must be met by catchment systems with storage facilities (the Japanese Government has built one desalination plant and plans to build one other); beachhead erosion because of the use of sand for building materials; excessive clearance of forest undergrowth for use as fuel; damage to coral reefs from the spread of the Crown of Thorns starfish; Tuvalu is concerned about global increases in greenhouse gas emissions and their effect on rising sea levels, which threaten the country's underground water table; in 2000, the government appealed to Australia and New

Zealand to take in Tuvaluans if rising sea levels should make evacuation necessary

Environment—international agreements: *party to:* Biodiversity, Climate Change, Climate Change-Kyoto Protocol, Desertification, Law of the Sea, Ozone Layer Protection, Ship Pollution, Whaling
signed, but not ratified: none of the selected agreements

Geography—note: one of the smallest and most remote countries on Earth; six of the nine coral atolls—Nanumea, Nui, Vaitupu, Nukufetau, Funafuti, and Nukulaelae—have lagoons open to the ocean; Nanumaya and Niutao have landlocked lagoons; Niulakita does not have a lagoon

PEOPLE AND SOCIETY

Nationality: *noun:* Tuvaluan(s)
adjective: Tuvaluan

Ethnic groups: Polynesian 96%, Micronesian 4%

Languages: Tuvaluan (official), English (official), Samoan, Kiribati (on the island of Nui)

Religions: Protestant 98.4% (Church of Tuvalu (Congregationalist) 97%, Seventh-Day Adventist 1.4%), Baha'i 1%, other 0.6%

Population: 10,782 (July 2014 est.)
country comparison to the world: 225

Age structure:
0-14 years: 29.6% (male 1,636/female 1,553)
15-24 years: 20.6% (male 1,176/female 1,048)
25-54 years: 36.2% (male 1,901/female 1,999)
55-64 years: 5.4% (male 360/female 525)
65 years and over: 5.3% (male 242/female 342) (2014 est.)

Median age: *total:* 24.9 years
male: 23.7 years
female: 26.4 years (2014 est.)

Population growth rate: 0.8% (2014 est.)
country comparison to the world: 139

Birth rate: 23.74 births/1,000 population (2014 est.)
country comparison to the world: 64

Death rate: 8.9 deaths/1,000 population (2014 est.)
country comparison to the world: 71

Net migration rate: -6.86 migrant(s)/1,000 population (2014 est.)
country comparison to the world: 202

Urbanization: *urban population:* 50% of total population (2010)
rate of urbanization: 1.4% annual rate of change (2010-15 est.)

Sex ratio: *at birth:* 1.05 male(s)/female
0-14 years: 1.05 male(s)/female
15-24 years: 1.12 male(s)/female
25-54 years: 0.95 male(s)/female
55-64 years: 0.97 male(s)/female
65 years and over: 0.73 male(s)/female
total population: 0.97 male(s)/female (2014 est.)

Infant mortality rate: *total:* 31.69 deaths/1,000 live births
country comparison to the world: 66
male: 34.44 deaths/1,000 live births
female: 28.81 deaths/1,000 live births (2014 est.)

Life expectancy at birth:
total population: 65.81 years
country comparison to the world: 171
male: 63.69 years
female: 68.05 years (2014 est.)

Total fertility rate: 3.03 children born/woman (2014 est.)
country comparison to the world: 54

Contraceptive prevalence rate: 30.5% (2007)

Health expenditures: 17.3% of GDP (2011)
country comparison to the world: 4

Physicians density: 1.09 physicians/1,000 population (2009)

Hospital bed density: 5.6 beds/1,000 population (2001)

Drinking water source:
improved:
urban: 98.3% of population
rural: 97% of population
total: 97.7% of population
unimproved:
urban: 1.7% of population
rural: 3% of population
total: 2.3% of population (2011 est.)

Sanitation facility access:
improved:
urban: 86.3% of population
rural: 80.2% of population
total: 83.3% of population
unimproved:
urban: 13.7% of population
rural: 19.8% of population
total: 15.7% of population (2011 est.)

HIV/AIDS—adult prevalence rate: NA

HIV/AIDS—people living with HIV/AIDS: NA

HIV/AIDS—deaths: NA

Children under the age of 5 years underweight: 1.6% (2007)
country comparison to the world: 125

Education expenditures: NA

Literacy: NA

School life expectancy (primary to tertiary education): *total:* 11 years
male: 10 years
female: 11 years (2001)

GOVERNMENT

Country name: *conventional long form:* none
conventional short form: Tuvalu
local long form: none
local short form: Tuvalu
former: Ellice Islands
note: "Tuvalu" means "group of eight" referring to the country's eight traditionally inhabited islands

Government type: parliamentary democracy and a Commonwealth realm

Capital: *name:* Funafuti

geographic coordinates: 8 31 S, 179 13 E
time difference: UTC+12 (17 hours ahead of Washington, DC during Standard Time)
note: administrative offices are in Vaiaku Village on Fongafale Islet

Administrative divisions: 7 island councils and 1 town council*; Funafuti*, Nanumaga, Nanumea, Niutao, Nui, Nukufetau, Nukulaelae, Vaitupu

Independence: 1 October 1978 (from the UK)

National holiday: Independence Day, 1 October (1978)

Constitution: previous 1978 (at independence); latest effective 1 October 1986; amended 2007, 2010 (2010)

Legal system: mixed legal system of English common law and local customary law

International law organization participation: has not submitted an ICJ jurisdiction declaration; non-party state to the ICCt

Suffrage: 18 years of age; universal

Executive branch: *chief of state:* Queen ELIZABETH II (since 6 February 1952); represented by Governor General Iakoba TAEIA Italeli (since May 2010)
head of government: Prime Minister Enele SOPOAGA (since 5 August 2013)
cabinet: Cabinet appointed by the governor general on the recommendation of the prime minister (For more information visit the World Leaders website)
elections: the monarchy is hereditary; governor general appointed by the monarch on the recommendation of the prime minister; prime minister and deputy prime minister elected by and from the members of parliament following parliamentary elections
election results: Willie TELAVI removed as prime minister by the governor-general on 1 August 2013; Enele SOPOAGA elected 4 August 2013 in a 8 to 5 vote by the House of Assembly

Legislative branch: unicameral Parliament or Fale I Fono, also called House of Assembly (15 seats; members elected by popular vote to serve four-year terms)
elections: last held on 16 September 2010 (next to be held in 2014)
election results: percent of vote—NA; seats—independents 15; 10 members reelected

Judicial branch: *highest court(s):* Court of Appeal is the Fiji Court of Appeal on Fiji Island (consists of the chief justice who visits twice a year); High Court, located on Fiji, consists of the chief justice of Fiji who presides over its sessions
judge selection and term of office: chief justice appointed by the president of Fiji on the advice of the prime minister following consultation with the parliamentary leader of the opposition; justices of the Court of Appeal, and puisne judges of the High Court are appointed by the president of Fiji, upon the nomination of the Judicial Service Commission, after consulting with the Cabinet Minister and the committee of the House of Representatives responsible for the administration of justice; the chief justice and justices of Appeal generally required to retire at age 70; puisine judges appointed for not less than 4 years nor more than 7 years with mandatory retirement at age 65
subordinate courts: magistrates' courts; island courts; lands courts

Political parties and leaders: there are no political parties but members of parliament usually align themselves in informal groupings

Political pressure groups and leaders: none

International organization participation: ACP, ADB, AOSIS, C, FAO, IBRD, IDA, IFRCS (observer), ILO, IMF, IMO, IOC, ITU, OPCW, PIF, Sparteca, SPC, UN, UNCTAD, UNESCO, UNIDO, UPU, WHO

Diplomatic representation in the US:
chief of mission: Ambassador Aunese Makoi SIMATI (since 11 January 2013)
chancery: Note—Tuvalu does not have an embassy in Washington, D.C.; UN office located

at 800 2nd Avenue, Suite 400D, New York, NY 10017
telephone: [1] (212) 490-0534
FAX: [1] (212) 937-0692

Diplomatic representation from the US: the US does not have an embassy in Tuvalu; the US ambassador to Fiji, currently Ambassador Frankie A. REED, is accredited to Tuvalu

Flag description: light blue with the flag of the UK in the upper hoist-side quadrant; the outer half of the flag represents a map of the country with nine yellow, five-pointed stars on a blue field symbolizing the nine atolls in the ocean

National anthem: *name:* "Tuvalu mo te Atua" (Tuvalu for the Almighty)
lyrics/music: Afaese MANOA
note: adopted 1978; the anthem's name is also the nation's motto

ECONOMY

Economy—overview: Tuvalu consists of a densely populated, scattered group of nine coral atolls with poor soil. Only eight of the atolls are inhabited. The country has no known mineral resources and few exports and is almost entirely dependent upon imported food and fuel. Subsistence farming and fishing are the primary economic activities. Fewer than 1,000 tourists, on average, visit Tuvalu annually. Job opportunities are scarce and public sector workers make up most of those employed. About 15% of the adult male population work as seamen on merchant ships abroad, and remittances are a vital source of income contributing around $2 million in 2007. Substantial income is received annually from the Tuvalu Trust Fund (TTF) an international trust fund established in 1987 by Australia, NZ, and the UK and supported also by Japan and South Korea. Thanks to wise investments and conservative withdrawals, this fund grew from an initial $17 million to an estimated value of $77 million in 2006. The TTF contributed nearly $9 million towards the government budget in 2006 and is an important cushion for meeting shortfalls in the government's budget. The US Government is also a major revenue source for Tuvalu because of payments from a 1988 treaty on fisheries. In an effort to ensure financial stability and sustainability, the government is pursuing public sector reforms, including privatization of some government functions and personnel cuts. Tuvalu also derives royalties from the lease of its ".tv" Internet domain name with revenue of more than $2 million in 2006. A minor source of government revenue comes from the sale of stamps and coins. With merchandise exports only a fraction of merchandise imports, continued reliance must be placed on fishing and telecommunications license fees, remittances from overseas workers, official transfers, and income from overseas investments. Growing income disparities and the vulnerability of the country to climatic change are among leading concerns for the nation.

GDP (purchasing power parity): $40 million (2013 est.)
country comparison to the world: 226
$39.53 million (2012 est.)
$39.19 million (2011 est.)
note: data are in 2013 US dollars

GDP (official exchange rate): $38 million (2013 est.)

GDP—real growth rate: 1.1% (2013 est.)
country comparison to the world: 172
0.2% (2012 est.)
8.5% (2011 est.)

GDP—per capita (PPP): $3,500 (2013 est.)
country comparison to the world: 173
$3,500 (2012 est.)
$3,500 (2011 est.)

GDP—composition, by sector of origin:
agriculture: 16.6%
industry: 27.2%
services: 56.2% (2002)

Agriculture—products: coconuts; fish

Industries: fishing, tourism, copra

Industrial production growth rate: NA%

Labor force: 3,615 (2004 est.)
country comparison to the world: 224

Labor force—by occupation:
note: people make a living mainly through exploitation of the sea, reefs, and atolls and from wages sent home by those abroad (mostly workers in the phosphate industry and sailors)

Unemployment rate: NA%

Population below poverty line: NA%

Household income or consumption by percentage share: *lowest 10%:* NA%
highest 10%: NA%

Budget: *revenues:* $21.54 million
expenditures: $23.05 million (2006)

Taxes and other revenues: 56.7% of GDP (2006)
country comparison to the world: 7

Budget surplus (+) or deficit (-):
-4% of GDP (2006)
country comparison to the world: 144

Fiscal year: calendar year

Inflation rate (consumer prices): 3.8% (2006 est.)
country comparison to the world: 128

Current account balance: -$7.7 million (2010 est.)
country comparison to the world: 62
-$11.68 million (2003)

Exports: $600,000 (2010 est.)
country comparison to the world: 219
$1 million (2004 est.)

Exports—commodities: copra, fish

Imports: $16.5 million (2010 est.)
country comparison to the world: 221
$12.91 million (2005)

Imports—commodities: food, animals, mineral fuels, machinery, manufactured goods

Debt—external: $NA

Exchange rates: Tuvaluan dollars or Australian dollars (AUD) per US dollar—
1.031 (2011)
1.67 (2011 est.)
1.67 (2010)
1.2822 (2009)
1.2059 (2008)

COMMUNICATIONS

Telephones—main lines in use: 1,450 (2012)
country comparison to the world: 220

Telephones—mobile cellular: 2,800 (2012)
country comparison to the world: 217

Telephone system: *general assessment:* serves particular needs for internal communications
domestic: radiotelephone communications between islands
international: country code—688; international calls can be made by satellite (2007)

Broadcast media: no TV stations; many households use satellite dishes to watch foreign TV stations; 1 government-owned radio station, Radio Tuvalu, includes relays of programming from international broadcasters (2009)

Internet country code: .tv

Internet hosts: 145,158 (2012)
country comparison to the world: 80

Internet users: 4,200 (2008)
country comparison to the world: 206

TRANSPORTATION

Airports: 1 (2013)
country comparison to the world: 235

Airports—with unpaved runways: *total:* 1
1,524 to 2,437 m: 1 (2013)

Roadways: *total:* 8 km
country comparison to the world: 222
paved: 8 km (2011)

Merchant marine: *total:* 5 8
country comparison to the world: 67
by type: bulk carrier 4, cargo 24, chemical tanker 15, container 1, passenger 2, passenger/cargo 1, petroleum tanker 10, refrigerated cargo 1
foreign-owned: 33 (China 4, Indonesia 1, Maldives 1, Singapore 19, South Korea 1, Turkey 1, Vietnam 6) (2010)

Ports and terminals: *major seaport(s):* Funafuti

MILITARY

Military branches: no regular military forces; Tuvalu Police Force (2012)

Manpower fit for military service:
males age 16-49: 2,021
females age 16-49: 2,026 (2010 est.)

Manpower reaching militarily significant age annually: *male:* 119
female: 111 (2010 est.)

TRANSNATIONAL ISSUES

Disputes—international: none

UGANDA

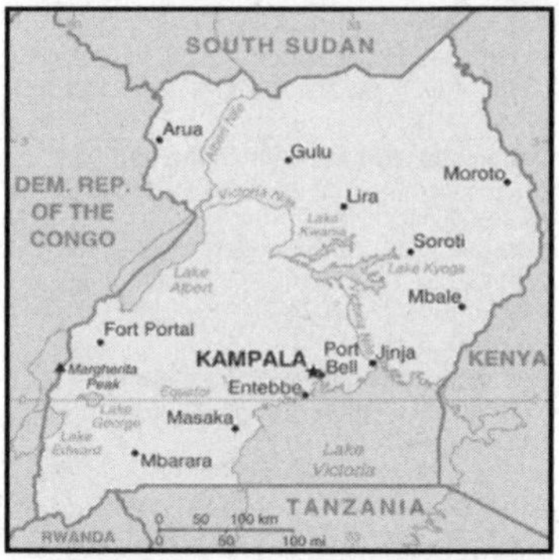

INTRODUCTION

Background: The colonial boundaries created by Britain to delimit Uganda grouped together a wide range of ethnic groups with different political systems and cultures. These differences prevented the establishment of a working political community after independence was achieved in 1962. The dictatorial regime of Idi AMIN (1971-79) was responsible for the deaths of some 300,000 opponents; guerrilla war and human rights abuses under Milton OBOTE (1980-85) claimed at least another 100,000 lives. The rule of Yoweri MUSEVENI since 1986 has brought relative stability and economic growth to Uganda. A constitutional referendum in 2005 cancelled a 19-year ban on multi-party politics.

GEOGRAPHY

Location: East-Central Africa, west of Kenya, east of the Democratic Republic of the Congo

Geographic coordinates: 1 00 N, 32 00 E

Map references: Africa

Area: *total:* 241,038 sq km
country comparison to the world: 81
land: 197,100 sq km
water: 43,938 sq km

Area—comparative: slightly smaller than Oregon

Land boundaries: *total:* 2,698 km
border countries: Democratic Republic of the Congo 765 km, Kenya 933 km, Rwanda 169 km, South Sudan 435 km, Tanzania 396 km

Coastline: 0 km (landlocked)

Maritime claims: none (landlocked)

Climate: tropical; generally rainy with two dry seasons (December to February, June to August); semiarid in northeast

Terrain: mostly plateau with rim of mountains

Elevation extremes: *lowest point:* Lake Albert 621 m
highest point: Margherita Peak on Mount Stanley 5,110 m

Natural resources: copper, cobalt, hydropower, limestone, salt, arable land, gold

Land use: *arable land:* 27.94%
permanent crops: 9.11%
other: 62.95% (2011)

Irrigated land: 144.2 sq km (2010)

Total renewable water resources: 66 cu km (2011)

Freshwater withdrawal (domestic/industrial/agricultural): *total:* 0.32 cu km/yr (41%/16%/43%)
per capita: 12.31 cu m/yr (2005)

Natural hazards: NA

Environment—current issues: draining of wetlands for agricultural use; deforestation; overgrazing; soil erosion; water hyacinth infestation in Lake Victoria; widespread poaching

Environment—international agreements:
party to: Biodiversity, Climate Change, Climate Change-Kyoto Protocol, Desertification, Endangered Species, Hazardous Wastes, Law of the Sea, Marine Life Conservation, Ozone Layer Protection, Wetlands
signed, but not ratified: Environmental Modification

Geography—note: landlocked; fertile, well-watered country with many lakes and rivers

PEOPLE AND SOCIETY

Nationality: noun: Ugandan(s)
adjective: Ugandan

Ethnic groups: Baganda 16.9%, Banyankole 9.5%, Basoga 8.4%, Bakiga 6.9%, Iteso 6.4%, Langi 6.1%, Acholi 4.7%, Bagisu 4.6%, Lugbara 4.2%, Bunyoro 2.7%, other 29.6% (2002 census)

Languages: English (official national language, taught in grade schools, used in courts of law and by most newspapers and some radio broadcasts), Ganda or Luganda (most widely used of the Niger-Congo languages, preferred for native language publications in the capital and may be taught in school), other Niger-Congo languages, Nilo-Saharan languages, Swahili, Arabic

Religions: Roman Catholic 41.9%, Protestant 42% (Anglican 35.9%, Pentecostal 4.6%, Seventh-Day Adventist 1.5%), Muslim 12.1%, other 3.1%, none 0.9% (2002 census)

Population: 35,918,915 (July 2014 est.)
country comparison to the world: 36
note: estimates for this country explicitly take into account the effects of excess mortality due to AIDS; this can result in lower life expectancy, higher infant mortality, higher death rates, lower population growth rates, and changes in the distribution of population by age and sex than would otherwise be expected

Age structure:
0-14 years: 48.7% (male 8,714,354/female 8,765,900)
15-24 years: 21.2% (male 3,775,679/female 3,833,574)
25-54 years: 25.7% (male 4,618,088/female 4,615,616)
55-64 years: 2.1% (male 405,740/female 447,118)
65 years and over: 2.1% (male 327,771/female 415,075) (2014 est.)

Dependency ratios:
total dependency ratio: 103.3 %
youth dependency ratio: 98.4 %
elderly dependency ratio: 4.9 %
potential support ratio: 20.3 (2013)

Median age: *total:* 15.5 years
male: 15.5 years
female: 15.6 years (2014 est.)

Population growth rate: 3.24% (2014 est.)
country comparison to the world: 9

Birth rate: 44.17 births/1,000 population (2014 est.)
country comparison to the world: 3

Death rate: 10.97 deaths/1,000 population (2014 est.)
country comparison to the world: 35

Net migration rate: -0.76 migrant(s)/1,000 population (2014 est.)
country comparison to the world: 144

Urbanization: *urban population:* 15.6% of total population (2011)
rate of urbanization: 5.74% annual rate of change (2010-15 est.)

Major urban areas—population: KAMPALA (capital) 1.535 million (2009)

Sex ratio: *at birth:* 1.03 male(s)/female
0-14 years: 0.99 male(s)/female
15-24 years: 0.99 male(s)/female
25-54 years: 1 male(s)/female
55-64 years: 0.99 male(s)/female
65 years and over: 0.8 male(s)/female
total population: 0.99 male(s)/female (2014 est.)

Mother's mean age at first birth: 18.9
note: median age at first birth among women 25-29 (2011 est.)

Maternal mortality rate: 310 deaths/100,000 live births (2010)
country comparison to the world: 37

Infant mortality rate: *total:* 60.82 deaths/1,000 live births
country comparison to the world: 21
male: 70.17 deaths/1,000 live births
female: 51.18 deaths/1,000 live births (2014 est.)

Life expectancy at birth:
total population: 54.46 years
country comparison to the world: 209
male: 53.1 years
female: 55.86 years (2014 est.)

Total fertility rate: 5.97 children born/woman (2014 est.)
country comparison to the world: 5

Contraceptive prevalence rate: 30% (2011)

Health expenditures: 9.5% of GDP (2011)
country comparison to the world: 32

Physicians density: 0.12 physicians/1,000 population (2005)

Hospital bed density: 0.5 beds/1,000 population (2010)

Drinking water source:
improved:
urban: 91.3% of population
rural: 71.7% of population
total: 74.8% of population
unimproved:
urban: 8.7% of population
rural: 28.3% of population
total: 25.2% of population (2011 est.)

Sanitation facility access:
improved:
urban: 33.9% of population
rural: 35.2% of population
total: 35% of population
unimproved:
urban: 66.1% of population
rural: 64.8% of population
total: 65% of population (2011 est.)

HIV/AIDS—adult prevalence rate: 7.2% (2012 est.)
country comparison to the world: 10

HIV/AIDS—people living with HIV/AIDS: 1,549,200 (2012 est.)
country comparison to the world: 6

HIV/AIDS—deaths: 63,300 (2012 est.)
country comparison to the world: 6

Major infectious diseases:
degree of risk: very high
food or waterborne diseases: bacterial diarrhea, hepatitis A and E, and typhoid fever

vectorborne diseases: malaria, dengue fever, and trypanosomiasis-Gambiense (African sleeping sickness)
water contact disease: schistosomiasis
animal contact disease: rabies (2013)

Obesity—adult prevalence rate: 4.3% (2008)
country comparison to the world: 167

Children under the age of 5 years underweight: 14.1% (2011)
country comparison to the world: 54

Education expenditures: 3.3% of GDP (2012)
country comparison to the world: 131

Literacy: *definition:* age 15 and over can read and write
total population: 73.2%
male: 82.6%
female: 64.6% (2010 est.)

School life expectancy (primary to tertiary education): *total:* 11 years
male: 11 years
female: 11 years (2009)

Child labor—children ages 5-14:
total number: 117,266
percentage: 25 %
note: data represents children ages 5-17 working in the (2010 est.)

Unemployment, youth ages 15-24: *total:* 5.4% (2009)
country comparison to the world: 136

GOVERNMENT

Country name: *conventional long form:* Republic of Uganda
conventional short form: Uganda

Government type: republic

Capital: *name:* Kampala

geographic coordinates: 0 19 N, 32 33 E
time difference: UTC+3 (8 hours ahead of Washington, DC during Standard Time)

Administrative divisions: 111 districts and 1 capital city*; Abim, Adjumani, Agago, Alebtong, Amolatar, Amudat, Amuria, Amuru, Apac, Arua, Budaka, Bududa, Bugiri, Buhweju, Buikwe, Bukedea, Bukomansimbi, Bukwa, Bulambuli, Buliisa, Bundibugyo, Bushenyi, Busia, Butaleja, Butambala, Buvuma, Buyende, Dokolo, Gomba, Gulu, Hoima, Ibanda, Iganga, Isingiro, Jinja, Kaabong, Kabale, Kabarole, Kaberamaido, Kalangala, Kaliro, Kalungu, Kampala*, Kamuli, Kamwenge, Kanungu, Kapchorwa, Kasese, Katakwi, Kayunga, Kibaale, Kiboga, Kibuku, Kiruhura, Kiryandongo, Kisoro, Kitgum, Koboko, Kole, Kotido, Kumi, Kween, Kyankwanzi, Kyegegwa, Kyenjojo, Lamwo, Lira, Luuka, Luwero, Lwengo, Lyantonde, Manafwa, Maracha, Masaka, Masindi, Mayuge, Mbale, Mbarara, Mitooma, Mityana, Moroto, Moyo, Mpigi, Mubende, Mukono, Nakapiripirit, Nakaseke, Nakasongola, Namayingo, Namutumba, Napak, Nebbi, Ngora, Ntoroko, Ntungamo, Nwoya, Otuke, Oyam, Pader, Pallisa, Rakai, Rubirizi, Rukungiri, Sembabule, Serere, Sheema, Sironko, Soroti, Tororo, Wakiso, Yumbe, Zombo

Independence: 9 October 1962 (from the UK)

National holiday: Independence Day, 9 October (1962)

Constitution: several previous; latest adopted 27 September 1995, promulgated 8 October 1995; amended many times, last in 2005 (2011)

Legal system: mixed legal system of English common law and customary law

International law organization participation: accepts compulsory ICJ jurisdiction with reservations; accepts ICCt jurisdiction

Suffrage: 18 years of age; universal

Executive branch: *chief of state:* President Lt. Gen. Yoweri Kaguta MUSEVENI (since seizing power on 26 January 1986); Vice President Edward SSEKANDI (since 24 May 2011) note—the president is both chief of state and head of government
head of government: President Lt. Gen. Yoweri Kaguta MUSEVENI (since seizing power on 26 January 1986); Prime Minister Amama MBABAZI (since 24 May 2011); note—the prime minister assists the president in the supervision of the cabinet
cabinet: Cabinet appointed by the president from among elected legislators (For more information visit the World Leaders website)
elections: president reelected by popular vote for a five-year term; election last held on 18 February 2011 (next to be held in 2016)
election results: Lt. Gen. Yoweri Kaguta MUSEVENI elected president; percent of vote—Lt. Gen. Yoweri Kaguta MUSEVENI 68.4%, Kizza BESIGYE 26.0%, other 5.6%

Legislative branch: unicameral National Assembly (375 seats; 238 members elected by popular vote, 112 women directly elected, 25 nominated by legally established special interest groups [army 10, disabled 5, youth 5, labor 5], additional ex-officio members may be nominated by the president; members serve five-year terms)
elections: last held on 18 February 2011 (next to be held in 2016)
election results: percent of vote by party—NA; seats by party—NRM 263, FDC 34, DP 12, UPC 10, UPDF 10, CP 1, JEEMA 1, independents 43, vacant 1; note—UPDF is the Uganda People's Defense Force

Judicial branch: *highest court(s):* Supreme Court of Uganda (consists of the chief justice and 5 justices)
judge selection and term of office: justices appointed by the president in consultation with the Judicial Service Commission (a 9-member independent advisory body) and with approval of the National Assembly; justices serve until mandatory retirement at age 70
subordinate courts: Court of Appeal (also sits as the Constitutional Court); High Court (includes 10 High Court Circuits and 7 High Court Divisions); Chief Magistrate Grade One and Grade Two Courts

Political parties and leaders: Conservative Party or CP [Ken LUKYAMUZI]; Democratic Party or DP [Norbert MAO]; Forum for Democratic Change or FDC [Muntu MUGISHA]; Inter-Party Co-operation or IPC (a coalition of opposition groups) Justice Forum or JEEMA [Asuman BASALIRWA]; National Resistance Movement or NRM [Yoweri MUSEVENI]; Peoples Progressive Party or PPP [Bidandi SSALI]; Ugandan People's Congress or UPC [Olara OTUNNU]
note: a national referendum in July 2005 opened the way for Uganda's transition to a multi-party political system

Political pressure groups and leaders: Lord's Resistance Army or LRA [Joseph KONY]; Parliamentary Advocacy Forum or PAFO; National Association of Women Organizations in Uganda or NAWOU [Florence NEKYON]; The Ugandan Coalition for Political Accountability to Women or COPAW

International organization participation: ACP, AfDB, AU, C, COMESA, EAC, EADB, FAO, G-77, IAEA, IBRD, ICAO, ICC (NGOs), ICRM, IDA, IDB, IFAD, IFC, IFRCS, IGAD, ILO, IMF, Interpol, IOC, IOM, IPU, ISO (correspondent), ITSO, ITU, ITUC (NGOs), MIGA, NAM, OIC, OPCW, PCA, UN, UNAMID, UNCTAD, UNESCO, UNHCR, UNIDO, UNOCI, UNWTO, UPU, WCO, WFTU (NGOs), WHO, WIPO, WMO, WTO

Diplomatic representation in the US:
chief of mission: Ambassador Oliver WONEKHA (since 6 June 2013)
chancery: 5911 16th Street NW, Washington, DC 20011
telephone: [1] (202) 726-7100 through 7102, 0416
FAX: [1] (202) 726-1727

Diplomatic representation from the US:
chief of mission: Ambassador Scott H. DELISI (since 18 July 2012)
embassy: 1577 Ggaba Road, Kampala
mailing address: P. O. Box 7007, Kampala
telephone: [256] (414) 259 791 through 93, 95
FAX: [256] (414) 259-794

Flag description: six equal horizontal bands of black (top), yellow, red, black, yellow, and red; a white disk is superimposed at the center and depicts a grey crowned crane (the national symbol) facing the hoist side; black symbolizes the African people, yellow sunshine and vitality, red African brotherhood; the crane was the military badge of Ugandan soldiers under the UK

National symbol(s): grey crowned crane

National anthem: *name:* "Oh Uganda, Land of Beauty!"
lyrics/music: George Wilberforce KAKOMOA
note: adopted 1962

ECONOMY

Economy—overview: Uganda has substantial natural resources, including fertile soils, regular rainfall, small deposits of copper, gold, and other minerals, and recently discovered oil. Uganda has never conducted a national minerals survey. Agriculture is the most important sector of the economy, employing over 80% of the work force. Coffee accounts for the bulk of export revenues. Since 1986, the government—with the support of foreign countries and international agencies—has acted to rehabilitate and stabilize the economy by undertaking currency reform, raising producer prices on export crops, increasing prices of petroleum products, and improving civil service wages. The policy changes are especially aimed at dampening inflation and boosting production and export earnings. Since 1990 economic reforms ushered in an era of solid economic growth based on continued investment in infrastructure, improved incentives for production and exports, lower inflation, better domestic security, and the return of exiled Indian-Ugandan entrepreneurs. The global economic downturn hurt Uganda's exports; however, Uganda's GDP growth has largely recovered due to past reforms and sound management of the downturn. Oil revenues and taxes will become a larger source of government funding as oil comes on line in the next few years. Instability in South Sudan is a risk for the Ugandan economy because Uganda's main export partner is Sudan, and Uganda is a key destination for Sudanese refugees. Unreliable power, high energy costs, inadequate transportation infrastructure, and corruption inhibit economic development and investor confidence.

GDP (purchasing power parity): $54.37 billion (2013 est.)
country comparison to the world: 96
$51.47 billion (2012 est.)
$50.08 billion (2011 est.)

note: data are in 2013 US dollars

GDP (official exchange rate): $22.6 billion (2013 est.)

GDP—real growth rate: 5.6% (2013 est.)
country comparison to the world: 44
2.8% (2012 est.)
6.2% (2011 est.)

GDP—per capita (PPP): $1,500 (2013 est.)
country comparison to the world: 206
$1,400 (2012 est.)
$1,500 (2011 est.)
note: data are in 2013 US dollars

Gross national saving: 17.4% of GDP (2013 est.)
country comparison to the world: 93
14.7% of GDP (2012 est.)
13.1% of GDP (2011 est.)

GDP—composition, by end use:
household consumption: 82.3%
government consumption: 7.6%
investment in fixed capital: 25.5%
investment in inventories: 0.2%
exports of goods and services: 22.8%
imports of goods and services: -38.3% (2013 est.)

GDP—composition, by sector of origin:
agriculture: 23.1%
industry: 26.9%
services: 50% (2013 est.)

Agriculture—products: coffee, tea, cotton, tobacco, cassava (tapioca), potatoes, corn, millet, pulses, cut flowers; beef, goat meat, milk, poultry

Industries: sugar, brewing, tobacco, cotton textiles; cement, steel production

Industrial production growth rate: 3.8% (2013 est.)
country comparison to the world: 78

Labor force: 17.4 million (2013 est.)
country comparison to the world: 35

Labor force—by occupation: *agriculture:* 82%
industry: 5%
services: 13% (1999 est.)

Unemployment rate: NA%

Population below poverty line: 24.5% (2009 est.)

Household income or consumption by percentage share: *lowest 10%:* 2.4%
highest 10%: 36.1% (2009 est.)

Distribution of family income—Gini index: 44.3 (2009)
country comparison to the world: 46
45.7 (2002)

Budget: *revenues:* $3.2 billion
expenditures: $3.803 billion (2013 est.)

Taxes and other revenues: 14.2% of GDP (2013 est.)
country comparison to the world: 197

Budget surplus (+) or deficit (-):
-2.7% of GDP (2013 est.)
country comparison to the world: 110

Public debt: 30.7% of GDP (2013 est.)
country comparison to the world: 119
26.3% of GDP (2012 est.)

Fiscal year: 1 July—30 June

Inflation rate (consumer prices): 6.2% (2013 est.)
country comparison to the world: 177
14% (2012 est.)

Central bank discount rate: 14% (31 December 2010 est.)
country comparison to the world: 28
9.65% (31 December 2009 est.)

Commercial bank prime lending rate: 23.7% (31 December 2013 est.)
country comparison to the world: 10
26.31% (31 December 2012 est.)

Stock of narrow money: $2.455 billion (31 December 2013 est.)
country comparison to the world: 123
$2.015 billion (31 December 2012 est.)

Stock of broad money: $4.049 billion (31 December 2013 est.)
country comparison to the world: 136
$3.293 billion (31 December 2012 est.)

Stock of domestic credit: $3.67 billion (31 December 2013 est.)
country comparison to the world: 122
$3.042 billion (31 December 2012 est.)

Market value of publicly traded shares: $7.294 billion (31 December 2012 est.)
country comparison to the world: 75
$7.727 billion (31 December 2011)
$1.788 billion (31 December 2011 est.)

Current account balance: -$1.908 billion (2013 est.)
country comparison to the world: 140
-$2.232 billion (2012 est.)

Exports: $3.156 billion (2013 est.)
country comparison to the world: 128
$2.811 billion (2012 est.)

Exports—commodities: coffee, fish and fish products, tea, cotton, flowers, horticultural products; gold

Exports—partners: Kenya 12.3%, Rwanda 10.3%, UAE 10.2%, Democratic Republic of the Congo 9.4%, Netherlands 6.1%, Germany 5.6%, Italy 4.4% (2012)

Imports: $4.858 billion (2013 est.)
country comparison to the world: 129
$5.187 billion (2012 est.)

Imports—commodities: capital equipment, vehicles, petroleum, medical supplies; cereals

Imports—partners: Kenya 15.6%, UAE 15.4%, China 12.8%, India 11.7%, South Africa 4.1%, Japan 4% (2012)

Reserves of foreign exchange and gold: $3.579 billion (31 December 2013 est.)
country comparison to the world: 102
$3.167 billion (31 December 2012 est.)
note: excludes gold

Debt—external: $5.223 billion (31 December 2013 est.)
country comparison to the world: 121
$4.461 billion (31 December 2012 est.)

Stock of direct foreign investment—at home: $NA

Stock of direct foreign investment—abroad: $NA

Exchange rates: Ugandan shillings (UGX) per US dollar—
2,604.6 (2013 est.)
2,505.6 (2012 est.)
2,177.6 (2010 est.)
2,030 (2009)
1,658.1 (2008)

ENERGY

Electricity—production: 2.406 billion kWh (2010 est.)
country comparison to the world: 132

Electricity—consumption: 2.192 billion kWh (2010 est.)
country comparison to the world: 139

Electricity—exports: 75 million kWh (2010)
country comparison to the world: 79

Electricity—imports: 29 million kWh (2011 est.)
country comparison to the world: 101

Electricity—installed generating capacity: 539,000 kW (2010 est.)
country comparison to the world: 135

Electricity—from fossil fuels: 31.5% of total installed capacity (2010 est.)
country comparison to the world: 180

Electricity—from nuclear fuels: 0% of total installed capacity (2010 est.)
country comparison to the world: 194

Electricity—from hydroelectric plants: 65.3% of total installed capacity (2010 est.)
country comparison to the world: 29

Electricity—from other renewable sources: 3.2% of total installed capacity (2010 est.)
country comparison to the world: 55

Crude oil—production: 0 bbl/day (2012 est.)
country comparison to the world: 139

Crude oil—exports: 0 bbl/day (2010 est.)
country comparison to the world: 196

Crude oil—imports: 0 bbl/day (2010 est.)
country comparison to the world: 133

Crude oil—proved reserves: 2.5 billion bbl (1 January 2010 es)
country comparison to the world: 34

Refined petroleum products—production: 0 bbl/day (2010 est.)
country comparison to the world: 203

Refined petroleum products—consumption: 16,930 bbl/day (2011 est.)
country comparison to the world: 138

Refined petroleum products—exports: 0 bbl/day (2010 est.)
country comparison to the world: 139

Refined petroleum products—imports: 22,990 bbl/day (2010 est.)
country comparison to the world: 99

Natural gas—production: 0 cu m (2011 est.)
country comparison to the world: 201

Natural gas—consumption: 0 cu m (2010 est.)
country comparison to the world: 202

Natural gas—exports: 0 cu m (2011 est.)
country comparison to the world: 198

Natural gas—imports: 0 cu m (2011 est.)
country comparison to the world: 142

Natural gas—proved reserves: 14.16 billion cu m (1 January 2013 es)
country comparison to the world: 79

Carbon dioxide emissions from consumption of energy: 3.244 million Mt (2011 est.)
country comparison to the world: 137

COMMUNICATIONS

Telephones—main lines in use: 315,000 (2012)
country comparison to the world: 113

Telephones—mobile cellular: 16.355 million (2012)
country comparison to the world: 58

Telephone system: *general assessment:* mobile cellular service is increasing rapidly, but the number of main lines is still deficient; work underway on a national backbone information and communications technology infrastructure; international phone networks and Internet connectivity provided through satellite and VSAT applications

domestic: intercity traffic by wire, microwave radio relay, and radiotelephone communication stations, fixed and mobile-cellular systems for short-range traffic; mobile-cellular teledensity about 50 per 100 persons in 2010
international: country code—256; satellite earth stations—1 Intelsat (Atlantic Ocean) and 1 Inmarsat; analog links to Kenya and Tanzania (2011)

Broadcast media: public broadcaster, Uganda Broadcasting Corporation (UBC), operates radio and TV networks; Uganda first began licensing privately owned stations in the 1990s; by 2007 there were nearly 150 radio and 35 TV stations, mostly based in and around Kampala; transmissions of multiple international broadcasters are available in Kampala (2007)

Internet country code: .ug

Internet hosts: 32,683 (2012)
country comparison to the world: 106

Internet users: 3.2 million (2009)
country comparison to the world: 66

TRANSPORTATION

Airports: 47 (2013)
country comparison to the world: 9 3

Airports—with paved runways: *total:* 5
over 3,047 m: 3
1,524 to 2,437 m: 1
914 to 1,523 m: 1 (2013)

Airports—with unpaved runways: *total:* 4 2
over 3,047 m: 1
1,524 to 2,437 m: 8
914 to 1,523 m: 26
under 914 m: 7 (2013)

Railways: *total:* 1,244 km
country comparison to the world: 83
narrow gauge: 1,244 km 1.000-m gauge (2008)

Roadways: *total:* 20,000 km (does not include local roads)
country comparison to the world: 109
paved: 3,264 km
unpaved: 16,736 km (2011)

Waterways: (there are no long navigable stretches of river in Uganda; parts of the Albert Nile that flow out of Lake Albert in the northwestern part of the country are navigable; several lakes including Lake Victoria and Lake Kyoga have substantial traffic; Lake Albert is navigable along a 200-km stretch from its northern tip to its southern shores) (2011)

Ports and terminals: *lake port(s):* Entebbe, Jinja, Port Bell (Lake Victoria)

MILITARY

Military branches: Uganda People's Defense Force (UPDF): Land Forces (includes Marine Unit), Uganda Air Force (2013)

Military service age and obligation: 18-26 years of age for voluntary military duty; 18-30 years of age for professionals; no conscription; 9-year service obligation; the government has stated that while recruitment under 18 years of age could occur with proper consent, "no person under the apparent age of 18 years shall be enrolled in the armed forces"; Ugandan citizenship and secondary education required (2012)

Manpower available for military service:
males age 16-49: 7,249,271
females age 16-49: 7,025,439 (2010 est.)

Manpower fit for military service:
males age 16-49: 4,313,068
females age 16-49: 4,200,901 (2010 est.)

Manpower reaching militarily significant age annually: *male:* 423,923
female: 420,236 (2010 est.)

Military expenditures: 1.45% of GDP (2012)
country comparison to the world: 68
3.73% of GDP (2011)
1.45% of GDP (2010)

TRANSNATIONAL ISSUES

Disputes—international: Uganda is subject to armed fighting among hostile ethnic groups, rebels, armed gangs, militias, and various government forces that extend across its borders; Ugandan refugees as well as members of the Lord's Resistance Army (LRA) seek shelter in southern Sudan and the Democratic Republic of the Congo's Garamba National Park; LRA forces have also attacked Kenyan villages across the border

Refugees and internally displaced persons:
refugees (country of origin): 127,021 (Democratic Republic of Congo); 14,684 (Rwanda); 10,728 (Burundi); 7,910 (Sudan) (2012); 119,787 (South Sudan); 18,534 (Somalia) (2014)
IDPs: 30,000 (displacement in northern Uganda because of fighting between government forces and the Lord's Resistance Army; as of 2011, most of the 1.8 million people displaced to IDP camps at the height of the conflict had returned home or resettled, but many had not found durable solutions) (2011)

UKRAINE

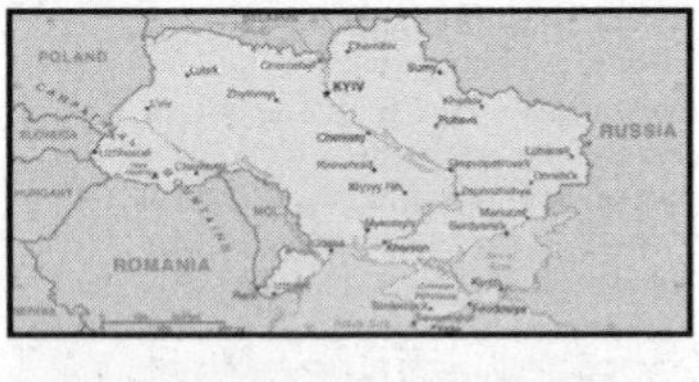

INTRODUCTION

Background: Ukraine was the center of the first eastern Slavic state, Kyivan Rus, which during the 10th and 11th centuries was the largest and most powerful state in Europe. Weakened by internecine quarrels and Mongol invasions, Kyivan Rus was incorporated into the Grand Duchy of Lithuania and eventually into the Polish-Lithuanian Commonwealth. The cultural and religious legacy of Kyivan Rus laid the foundation for Ukrainian nationalism through subsequent centuries. A new Ukrainian state, the Cossack Hetmanate, was established during the mid-17th century after an uprising against the Poles. Despite continuous Muscovite pressure, the Hetmanate managed to remain autonomous for well over 100 years. During the latter part of the 18th century, most Ukrainian ethnographic territory was absorbed by the Russian Empire. Following the collapse of czarist Russia in 1917, Ukraine was able to achieve a short-lived period of independence (1917-20), but was reconquered and forced to endure a brutal Soviet rule that engineered two forced famines (1921-22 and 1932-33) in which over 8 million died. In World War II, German and Soviet armies were responsible for some 7 to 8 million more deaths. Although final independence for Ukraine was achieved in 1991 with the dissolution of the USSR, democracy and prosperity remained elusive as the legacy of state control and endemic corruption stalled efforts at economic reform, privatization, and civil liberties. A peaceful mass protest "Orange Revolution" in the closing months of 2004 forced the authorities to overturn a rigged presidential election and to allow a new internationally monitored vote that swept into power a reformist slate under Viktor YUSHCHENKO. Subsequent internal squabbles in the YUSHCHENKO camp allowed his rival Viktor YANUKOVYCH to stage a comeback in parliamentary (Rada) elections and to become prime minister in August of 2006, and to be elected president in February 2010. In October 2012, Ukraine held Rada elections, widely criticized by Western observers as flawed due to use of government resources to favor ruling party candidates, interference with media access, and harassment of opposition candidates. President YANUKOVYCH's backtracking on a trade and cooperation agreement with the EU in November 2013—in favor of closer economic ties with Russia—led to a three-month protest occupation of Kyiv's central square. The government's eventual use of force to break up the protest camp in February 2014 led to all out pitched battles, scores of deaths, international condemnation, and the president's abrupt departure to Russia. An interim government under Acting President Oleksandr TURCHYNOV has scheduled new presidential elections for 25 May 2014. On 1 March 2014, one week after the overthrow in Kyiv, Russian President PUTIN ordered the invasion of Ukraine's Crimean Peninsula claiming the action was to protect ethnic Russians living there. On 16 March 2014, a "referendum" was held regarding the integration of Crimea into the Russian Federation. The "referendum" was condemned as illegitimate by the Ukrainian Government, the EU, the US, and the UN General Assembly. Russian forces now occupy Crimea and Russian authorities claim it as Russian territory. The Ukrainian Government asserts that Crimea remains part of Ukraine.

GEOGRAPHY

Location: Eastern Europe, bordering the Black Sea, between Poland, Romania, and Moldova in the west and Russia in the east

Geographic coordinates: 49 00 N, 32 00 E

Map references: Europe

Area: *total:* 603,550 sq km
country comparison to the world: 46
land: 579,330 sq km
water: 24,220 sq km

Area—comparative: almost four times the size of Georgia; slightly smaller than Texas

Land boundaries: *total:* 4,566 km
border countries: Belarus 891 km, Hungary 103 km, Moldova 940 km, Poland 428 km, Romania (south) 176 km, Romania (southwest) 362 km, Russia 1,576 km, Slovakia 90 km

Coastline: 2,782 km

Maritime claims: *territorial sea:* 12 nm
exclusive economic zone: 200 nm
continental shelf: 200 m or to the depth of exploitation

Climate: temperate continental; Mediterranean only on the southern Crimean coast; precipitation disproportionately distributed, highest in west and north, lesser in east and southeast; winters vary from cool along the Black Sea to cold farther inland; summers are warm across the greater part of the country, hot in the south

Terrain: most of Ukraine consists of fertile plains (steppes) and plateaus, mountains being found only in the west (the Carpathians), and in the Crimean Peninsula in the extreme south

Elevation extremes: *lowest point:* Black Sea 0 m
highest point: Hora Hoverla 2,061 m

Natural resources: iron ore, coal, manganese, natural gas, oil, salt, sulfur, graphite, titanium, magnesium, kaolin, nickel, mercury, timber, arable land

Land use: *arable land:* 53.85%
permanent crops: 1.48%
other: 44.67% (2011)

Irrigated land: 21,750 sq km (2010)

Total renewable water resources: 139.6 cu km (2011)

Freshwater withdrawal (domestic/industrial/agricultural): *total:* 19.24 cu km/yr (24%/69%/7%)
per capita: 415.7 cu m/yr (2010)

Natural hazards: NA

Environment—current issues: inadequate supplies of potable water; air and water pollution; deforestation; radiation contamination in the northeast from 1986 accident at Chornobyl' Nuclear Power Plant

Environment—international agreements:
party to: Air Pollution, Air Pollution-Nitrogen Oxides, Air Pollution-Sulfur 85, Antarctic-Environmental Protocol, Antarctic-Marine Living Resources, Antarctic Treaty, Biodiversity, Climate Change, Climate Change-Kyoto Protocol, Desertification, Endangered Species, Environmental Modification, Hazardous Wastes, Law of the Sea, Marine Dumping, Ozone Layer Protection, Ship Pollution, Wetlands
signed, but not ratified: Air Pollution-Persistent Organic Pollutants, Air Pollution-Sulfur 94, Air Pollution-Volatile Organic Compounds

Geography—note: strategic position at the crossroads between Europe and Asia; second-largest country in Europe

PEOPLE AND SOCIETY

Nationality: *noun:* Ukrainian(s)
adjective: Ukrainian

Ethnic groups: Ukrainian 77.8%, Russian 17.3%, Belarusian 0.6%, Moldovan 0.5%, Crimean Tatar 0.5%, Bulgarian 0.4%, Hungarian 0.3%, Romanian 0.3%, Polish 0.3%, Jewish 0.2%, other 1.8% (2001 est.)

Languages: Ukrainian (official) 67%, Russian (regional language) 24%, other (includes small Romanian-, Polish-, and Hungarian-speaking minorities) 9%
note: 2012 legislation enables a language spoken by at least 10% of an oblast's population to be given the status of "regional language," allowing for its use in courts, schools, and other government institutions; Ukrainian remains the country's only official nationwide language

Religions: Orthodox (includes Ukrainian Autocephalous Orthodox (UAOC), Ukrainian Orthodox—Kyiv Patriarchate (UOC-KP), Ukrainian Orthodox—Moscow Patriarchate (UOC-MP), Ukrainian Greek Catholic, Roman Catholic, Protestant, Muslim, Jewish
note: Ukraine's population is overwhelmingly Christian; the vast majority—up to two-thirds—identify themselves as Orthodox, but many do not specify a particular branch; the UOC-KP and the UOC-MP each represent less than a quarter of the country's adherents, the Ukrainian Greek Catholic Church accounts for 8-10%, and the UAOC accounts for 1-2%; Muslim and Jewish adherents each compose less than 1% of the total population (2013 est.)

Population: 44,291,413 (July 2014 est.)
country comparison to the world: 32

Age structure:
0-14 years: 14% (male 3,191,247/female 3,013,575)
15-24 years: 11.5% (male 2,610,172/female 2,501,795)
25-54 years: 45% (male 9,639,882/female 10,274,240)
55-64 years: 15.9% (male 2,581,380/female 3,433,568)
65 years and over: 15.6% (male 2,310,652/female 4,734,902) (2014 est.)

Dependency ratios:
total dependency ratio: 41.9 %
youth dependency ratio: 20.5 %
elderly dependency ratio: 21.4 %
potential support ratio: 4.7 (2013)

Median age: *total:* 40.6 years
male: 37.3 years
female: 43.7 years (2014 est.)

Population growth rate: -0.64% (2014 est.)
country comparison to the world: 226

Birth rate: 9.41 births/1,000 population (2014 est.)
country comparison to the world: 203

Death rate: 15.72 deaths/1,000 population (2014 est.)
country comparison to the world: 2

Net migration rate: -0.06 migrant(s)/1,000 population (2014 est.)
country comparison to the world: 113

Urbanization: *urban population:* 68.9% of total population (2011)
rate of urbanization: -0.26% annual rate of change (2010-15 est.)

Major urban areas—population: KYIV (capital) 2.779 million; Kharkiv 1.455 million; Dnipropetrovsk 1.013 million; Odesa 1.009 million; Donetsk 971,000 (2009)

Sex ratio: *at birth:* 1.07 male(s)/female
0-14 years: 1.06 male(s)/female
15-24 years: 1.04 male(s)/female
25-54 years: 0.94 male(s)/female
55-64 years: 0.85 male(s)/female
65 years and over: 0.49 male(s)/female
total population: 0.85 male(s)/female (2014 est.)

Mother's mean age at first birth: 23.1
note: median age at first birth among women 25-29 (2007 est.)

Maternal mortality rate: 32 deaths/100,000 live births (2010)
country comparison to the world: 121

Infant mortality rate: *total:* 8.1 deaths/1,000 live births
country comparison to the world: 154
male: 10.13 deaths/1,000 live births
female: 5.94 deaths/1,000 live births (2014 est.)

Life expectancy at birth:
total population: 69.14 years
country comparison to the world: 156
male: 63.78 years
female: 74.86 years (2014 est.)

Total fertility rate: 1.3 children born/woman (2014 est.)
country comparison to the world: 215

Contraceptive prevalence rate: 66.7% (2007)

Health expenditures: 7.3% of GDP (2011)
country comparison to the world: 77

Physicians density: 3.52 physicians/1,000 population (2011)

Hospital bed density: 8.7 beds/1,000 population (2009)

Drinking water source:
improved:
urban: 98.1% of population
rural: 97.7% of population
total: 98% of population
unimproved:
urban: 1.9% of population
rural: 2.3% of population
total: 2% of population (2011 est.)

Sanitation facility access:
improved:
urban: 96.5% of population
rural: 89.4% of population
total: 94.3% of population
unimproved:
urban: 3.5% of population
rural: 10.6% of population
total: 5.7% of population (2011 est.)

HIV/AIDS—adult prevalence rate: 0.9% (2012 est.)
country comparison to the world: 52

HIV/AIDS—people living with HIV/AIDS: 230,500 (2012 est.)
country comparison to the world: 26

HIV/AIDS—deaths: 18,100 (2012 est.)
country comparison to the world: 18

Obesity—adult prevalence rate: 21.3% (2008)
country comparison to the world: 89

Children under the age of 5 years underweight: 0.9% (2002)
country comparison to the world: 134

Education expenditures: 6.2% of GDP (2011)
country comparison to the world: 35

Literacy: *definition:* age 15 and over can read and write
total population: 99.7%
male: 99.8%
female: 99.7% (2011 est.)

School life expectancy (primary to tertiary education): *total:* 15 years
male: 15 years
female: 15 years (2012)

Child labor—children ages 5-14:
total number: 356,213
percentage: 7 % (2005 est.)

Unemployment, youth ages 15-24: *total:* 17.3%
country comparison to the world: 72
male: 18.1%
female: 16.1% (2012)

GOVERNMENT

Country name: *conventional long form:* none
conventional short form: Ukraine
local long form: none
local short form: Ukrayina

former: Ukrainian National Republic, Ukrainian State, Ukrainian Soviet Socialist Republic

Government type: republic

Capital: *name:* Kyiv (Kiev)
note: pronounced KAY-yiv

geographic coordinates: 50 26 N, 30 31 E
time difference: UTC+2 (7 hours ahead of Washington, DC during Standard Time)
daylight saving time: +1hr, begins last Sunday in March; ends last Sunday in October

Administrative divisions: 24 provinces (oblasti, singular—oblast'), 1 autonomous republic* (avtonomna respublika), and 2 municipalities (mista, singular—misto) with oblast status**; Cherkasy, Chernihiv, Chernivtsi, Crimea or Avtonomna Respublika Krym* (Simferopol'), Dnipropetrovs'k, Donets'k, Ivano-Frankivs'k, Kharkiv, Kherson, Khmel'nyts'kyy, Kirovohrad, Kyiv**, Kyiv, Luhans'k, L'viv, Mykolayiv, Odesa, Poltava, Rivne, Sevastopol'**, Sumy, Ternopil', Vinnytsya, Volyn' (Luts'k), Zakarpattya (Uzhhorod), Zaporizhzhya, Zhytomyr
note 1: administrative divisions have the same names as their administrative centers (exceptions have the administrative center name following in parentheses)
note 2: the United States does not recognize Russia's annexation of Ukraine's Autonomous Republic of Crimea and the municipality of Sevastopol, nor their redesignation as the Republic of Crimea and the Federal City of Sevastopol

Independence: 24 August 1991 (from the Soviet Union); notable earlier dates: ca. 982 (VOLODYMYR I consolidates Kyivan Rus), 1648 (establishment of Cossack Hetmanate)

National holiday: Independence Day, 24 August (1991); note—22 January 1918, the day Ukraine first declared its independence (from Soviet Russia) and the day the short-lived Western and Greater (Eastern) Ukrainian republics united (1919), is now celebrated as Unity Day

Constitution: several previous; latest adopted and ratified 28 June 1996; amended 2004, 2010; note—to revert to the 2004 version pending additional constitutional reforms (2014)

Legal system: civil law system; judicial review of legislative acts

International law organization participation: has not submitted an ICJ jurisdiction declaration; non-party state to the ICCt

Suffrage: 18 years of age; universal

Executive branch: *chief of state:* Acting President Oleksandr TURCHYNOV (since 23 February 2014)
head of government: Prime Minister Arseniy YATSENYUK (since 27 February 2014); First Deputy Prime Minister Vitaliy YAREMA, Deputy Prime Ministers Volodymyr HROYSMAN and Oleksandr SYCH (all since 27 February 2014)
cabinet: Cabinet of Ministers nominated by the president (For more information visit the World Leaders website)
note: there is also a National Security and Defense Council or NSDC originally created in 1992 as the National Security Council; the NSDC staff is tasked with developing national security policy on domestic and international matters and advising the president; a Presidential Administration helps draft presidential edicts and provides policy support to the president
elections: president elected by popular vote for a five-year term (eligible for a second term); election last held on 17 January 2010 with runoff on 7 February 2010 (next to be held in 25 May 2014); note—following the departure of President YANUKOVYCH in response to the EuroMaidan protests of February 2014, the presidential election was moved up to 25 May 2014
election results: Viktor YANUKOVYCH elected president; percent of vote—Viktor YANUKOVYCH 48.9%, Yuliya TYMOSHENKO 45.5%, other 5.6%

Legislative branch: unicameral Supreme Council or Verkhovna Rada (450 seats; 50% of seats allocated on a proportional basis to those parties that gain 5% or more of the national electoral vote and 50% to members elected in single mandate districts; members serve five-year terms)
elections: last held on 28 October 2012 (next to be held fall 2017)
election results: percent of vote by party—Party of Regions 30%, Batkivshchyna 25.5%, UDAR 14%, CPU 13.2%, Svoboda 10.4%, other parties 6.9%; seats by party—Party of Regions 185, Batkivshchyna 101, UDAR 40, Svoboda 37, CPU 32, United Center 3, People's Party 2, Radical 1, Union 1, independents 43, vacant 5; composition as of early April 2014—Party of Regions 120, Batkivshchyna 88, UDAR 42, "Economic Development" group 36, "Sovereign European Ukraine" group 36, Svoboda 35, CPU 32, independents 59, vacant 2

Judicial branch: *highest court(s):* Supreme Court of Ukraine (consists of 95 judges organized into civil, criminal, commercial, and administrative chambers, and a military panel); Constitutional Court (consists of 18 justices)
judge selection and term of office: Supreme Court judges proposed by the Supreme Council of Justice or SCJ (a 20-member independent body of judicial officials and other appointees) and appointed by presidential decree; judges initially appointed for 5 years and, if approved by the SCJ, serve until mandatory retirement at age 65; Constitutional Court justices appointed—6 each by the president, by the SCU, and by the Verkhovna Rada; justices appointed for 9-year non-renewable terms
subordinate courts: specialized high courts; Courts of Cassation; Courts of Appeal; regional, district, city, and town courts

Political parties and leaders: Batkivshchyna ("Fatherland") [Yuliya TYMOSHENKO]; Communist Party of Ukraine or CPU [Petro SYMONENKO]; Party of Regions [vacant]; People's Movement of Ukraine (Rukh) [Borys TARASYUK]; People's Party [Volodymyr LYTVYN]; Radical Party [Oleh LYASHKO]; Socialist Party of Ukraine or SPU [Oleksandr MOROZ]; Svoboda ("Freedom") [Oleh TYAHNYBOK]; Ukrainian Democratic Alliance for Reforms or UDAR [Vitaliy KLYCHKO]; Union [Lev MIRIMSKY]; United Center [Viktor BALOHA]

Political pressure groups and leaders: Committee of Voters of Ukraine [Oleksandr CHERNENKO]; OPORA [Olha AIVAZOVSKA]

International organization participation: Australia Group, BSEC, CBSS (observer), CD, CE, CEI, CICA (observer), CIS (participating member, has not signed the 1993 CIS charter although it participates in meetings), EAEC (observer), EAPC, EBRD, FAO, GCTU, GUAM, IAEA, IBRD, ICAO, ICC (national committees), ICRM, IDA, IFC, IFRCS, IHO, ILO, IMF, IMO, IMSO, Interpol, IOC, IOM, IPU, ISO, ITU, ITUC (NGOs), LAIA (observer), MIGA, MONUSCO, NAM (observer), NSG, OAS (observer), OIF (observer), OPCW, OSCE, PCA, PFP, SELEC (observer), UN, UNCTAD, UNESCO, UNIDO, UNMIL, UNMISS, UNWTO, UPU, WCO, WFTU (NGOs), WHO, WIPO, WMO, WTO, ZC

Diplomatic representation in the US:
chief of mission: Ambassador Oleksandr MOTSYK (since 24 June 2010)
chancery: 3350 M Street NW, Washington, DC 20007
telephone: [1] (202) 349-2920
FAX: [1] (202) 333-0817
consulate(s) general: Chicago, New York, San Francisco

Diplomatic representation from the US:
chief of mission: Ambassador Geoffrey R. PYATT (since 30 July 2013)
embassy: 4 Igor Sikorsky Street, 04112 Kyiv
mailing address: 5850 Kyiv Place, Washington, DC 20521-5850
telephone: [380] (44) 521-5000
FAX: [380] (44) 521-5155

Flag description: two equal horizontal bands of azure (top) and golden yellow represent grain fields under a blue sky

National symbol(s): trident (tryzub)

National anthem: *name:* "Shche ne vmerla Ukraina" (Ukraine Has Not Yet Perished)
lyrics/music: Paul CHUBYNSKYI/Mikhail VERBYTSKYI
note: music adopted 1991, lyrics adopted 2003; the song was first performed in 1864 at the Ukraine Theatre in Lviv; the lyrics, originally written in 1862, were revised in 2003

ECONOMY

Economy—overview: After Russia, the Ukrainian republic was the most important economic component of the former Soviet Union, producing about four times the output of the next-ranking republic. Its fertile black soil generated more than one-fourth of Soviet agricultural output, and its farms provided substantial quantities of meat, milk, grain, and vegetables to other republics. Likewise, its diversified heavy industry supplied the unique equipment (for example, large diameter pipes) and raw materials to industrial and mining sites (vertical drilling apparatus) in other regions of the former USSR. Shortly after independence in August 1991, the Ukrainian Government liberalized most prices and erected a legal framework for privatization, but widespread resistance to reform within the government and the legislature soon stalled reform efforts and led to some backtracking. Output by 1999 had fallen to less than 40% of the 1991 level. Ukraine's dependence on Russia for energy supplies and the lack of significant structural reform have made the Ukrainian economy vulnerable to external shocks. Ukraine depends on imports to meet about three-fourths of its annual oil and natural gas requirements and 100% of its nuclear fuel needs. After a two-week dispute that saw gas supplies cutoff to Europe, Ukraine agreed to 10-year gas supply and transit contracts with Russia in January 2009 that brought gas prices to "world" levels. The strict terms of the contracts have further hobbled Ukraine's cash-strapped state gas company, Naftohaz. Outside institutions—particularly the IMF—have encouraged Ukraine to quicken the pace and scope of reforms to foster economic growth. Ukrainian Government officials eliminated most tax and customs privileges in a March 2005 budget law, bringing more economic activity out of Ukraine's large shadow economy, but more improvements are needed, including fighting corruption, developing capital markets, and improving the legislative framework. Ukraine's economy was buoyant despite political turmoil between the prime minister and president until mid-2008. The economy contracted nearly 15% in 2009, among the worst economic performances in the world. In April 2010, Ukraine negotiated a price discount on Russian gas imports in exchange for extending Russia's lease on its naval base in Crimea. Movement toward an Association Agreement with the European Union, which would commit Ukraine to economic and financial reforms in exchange for preferential access to EU markets, was curtailed by the November 2013 decision of President YANUKOVYCH against signing this treaty. In response, on 17 December 2013 President YANUKOVYCH and President PUTIN concluded a financial assistance package containing $15 billion in loans and lower gas prices. However, the end of the YANUKOVYCH government in February 2014 caused Russia to halt further funding. With the formation of an interim government in late February 2014, the international community began efforts to stabilize the Ukrainian economy, including a 27 March 2014 IMF assistance package of $14-18 billion.

GDP (purchasing power parity): $337.4 billion (2013 est.)
country comparison to the world: 42
$336.1 billion (2012 est.)
$335.6 billion (2011 est.)
note: data are in 2013 US dollars

GDP (official exchange rate): $175.5 billion (2013 est.)

GDP—real growth rate: 0.4% (2013 est.)
country comparison to the world: 187
0.2% (2012 est.)
5.2% (2011 est.)

GDP—per capita (PPP): $7,400 (2013 est.)
country comparison to the world: 139
$7,400 (2012 est.)
$7,400 (2011 est.)
note: data are in 2013 US dollars

Gross national saving: 10.1% of GDP (2013 est.)
country comparison to the world: 135
10.1% of GDP (2012 est.)
14.5% of GDP (2011 est.)

GDP—composition, by end use:
household consumption: 72%
government consumption: 18.6%
investment in fixed capital: 17.8%
investment in inventories: -1.1%
exports of goods and services: 49.6%
imports of goods and services: -56.9% (2013 est.)

GDP—composition, by sector of origin:
agriculture: 9.9%
industry: 29.6%
services: 60.5%

(2013 est.)

Agriculture—products: grain, sugar beets, sunflower seeds, vegetables; beef, milk

Industries: coal, electric power, ferrous and nonferrous metals, machinery and transport equipment, chemicals, food processing

Industrial production growth rate: -5% (2013 est.)
country comparison to the world: 190

Labor force: 22.17 million (2013 est.)
country comparison to the world: 30

Labor force—by occupation: *agriculture:* 5.6%
industry: 26%
services: 68.4% (2012)

Unemployment rate: 8% (2013 est.)
country comparison to the world: 89
7.5% (2012 est.)
note: officially registered; large number of unregistered or underemployed workers

Population below poverty line: 24.1% (2010)

Household income or consumption by percentage share: *lowest 10%:* 3.8%
highest 10%: 22.5% (2011 est.)

Distribution of family income—Gini index: 28.2 (2009)

country comparison to the world: 123
29 (1999)

Budget: *revenues:* $57.4 billion
expenditures: $66.5 billion
note: this is the planned, consolidated budget (2013 est.)

Taxes and other revenues: 32.7% of GDP (2013 est.)
country comparison to the world: 75

Budget surplus (+) or deficit (-):
-5.2% of GDP (2013 est.)
country comparison to the world: 172

Public debt: 40.6% of GDP (2013 est.)
country comparison to the world: 88
36.6% of GDP (2012 est.)
note: the total public debt of $64.5 billion consists of: domestic public debt ($23.8 billion); external public debt ($26.1 billion); and sovereign guarantees ($14.6 billion)

Fiscal year: calendar year

Inflation rate (consumer prices): 0.7% (2013 est.)
country comparison to the world: 16
0.6% (2012 est.)

Central bank discount rate: 7.5% (31 January 2012 est.)
country comparison to the world: 19
11.97% (31 December 2010 est.)

Commercial bank prime lending rate: 16% (31 December 2013 est.)
country comparison to the world: 23
18.39% (31 December 2012 est.)

Stock of narrow money: $39.94 billion (31 December 2013 est.)
country comparison to the world: 54
$40.44 billion (31 December 2012 est.)

Stock of broad money: $100.3 billion (31 December 2013 est.)
country comparison to the world: 52
$96.48 billion (31 December 2012 est.)

Stock of domestic credit: $130.6 billion (31 December 2013 est.)
country comparison to the world: 49
$129.6 billion (31 December 2012 est.)

Market value of publicly traded shares: $20.71 billion (31 December 2012 est.)
country comparison to the world: 59
$25.56 billion (31 December 2011)
$39.46 billion (31 December 2010 est.)

Current account balance: -$11.92 billion (2013 est.)
country comparison to the world: 181
-$14.32 billion (2012 est.)

Exports: $71.14 billion (2013 est.)
country comparison to the world: 48
$70.24 billion (2012 est.)

Exports—commodities: ferrous and nonferrous metals, fuel and petroleum products, chemicals, machinery and transport equipment, food products

Exports—partners: Russia 25.6%, Turkey 5.4%, Egypt 4.2% (2012)

Imports: $87.21 billion (2013 est.)
country comparison to the world: 38
$89.71 billion (2012 est.)

Imports—commodities: energy, machinery and equipment, chemicals

Imports—partners: Russia 32.4%, China 9.3%, Germany 8%, Belarus 6%, Poland 4.2% (2012)

Reserves of foreign exchange and gold: $21.95 billion (31 December 2013 est.)
country comparison to the world: 57
$24.55 billion (31 December 2012 est.)

Debt—external: $138.3 billion (31 December 2013 est.)
country comparison to the world: 40
$136.5 billion (31 December 2012 est.)

Stock of direct foreign investment—at home: $61.46 billion (31 December 2013 est.)
country comparison to the world: 52
$54.46 billion (31 December 2012 est.)

Stock of direct foreign investment—abroad: $8.604 billion (31 December 2013 est.)
country comparison to the world: 58
$8.104 billion (31 December 2012 est.)

Exchange rates: hryvnia (UAH) per US dollar—
8.195 (2013 est.)
7.991 (2012 est.)
7.9356 (2010 est.)
7.7912 (2009)
4.9523 (2008)

ENERGY

Electricity—production: 198.1 billion kWh (2012 est.)
country comparison to the world: 22

Electricity—consumption: 175.3 billion kWh (2012 est.)
country comparison to the world: 21

Electricity—exports: 3.852 billion kWh (2012 est.)
country comparison to the world: 32

Electricity—imports: 1.909 billion kWh (2010 est.)
country comparison to the world: 54

Electricity—installed generating capacity: 54.88 million kW (2010 est.)
country comparison to the world: 18

Electricity—from fossil fuels: 64.1% of total installed capacity (2010 est.)
country comparison to the world: 124

Electricity—from nuclear fuels: 25.2% of total installed capacity (2010 est.)
country comparison to the world: 3

Electricity—from hydroelectric plants: 9.9% of total installed capacity (2010 est.)
country comparison to the world: 114

Electricity—from other renewable sources:
0.1% of total installed capacity (2010 est.)
country comparison to the world: 100

Crude oil—production: 80,400 bbl/day (2012 est.)
country comparison to the world: 52

Crude oil—exports: 0 bbl/day (2010 est.)
country comparison to the world: 197

Crude oil—imports: 155,300 bbl/day (2010 est.)
country comparison to the world: 39

Crude oil—proved reserves: 395 million bbl (1 January 2013 es)
country comparison to the world: 53

Refined petroleum products—production: 262,300 bbl/day (2010 est.)
country comparison to the world: 48

Refined petroleum products—consumption: 320,600 bbl/day (2011 est.)
country comparison to the world: 39

Refined petroleum products—exports: 80,980 bbl/day (2010 est.)
country comparison to the world: 50

Refined petroleum products—imports: 126,500 bbl/day (2010 est.)

country comparison to the world: 43

Natural gas—production: 19.8 billion cu m (2011 est.)
country comparison to the world: 33

Natural gas—consumption: 56.2 billion cu m (2010 est.)
country comparison to the world: 15

Natural gas—exports: 2.6 billion cu m (2010 est.)
country comparison to the world: 42

Natural gas—imports: 44.8 billion cu m (2011 est.)
country comparison to the world: 11

Natural gas—proved reserves: 1.104 trillion cu m (1 January 2013 es)
country comparison to the world: 26

Carbon dioxide emissions from consumption of energy: 304.4 million Mt (2011 est.)
country comparison to the world: 22

COMMUNICATIONS

Telephones—main lines in use: 12.182 million (2012)
country comparison to the world: 19

Telephones—mobile cellular: 59.344 million (2012)
country comparison to the world: 22

Telephone system: *general assessment:* Ukraine's telecommunication development plan emphasizes improving domestic trunk lines, international connections, and the mobile-cellular system
domestic: at independence in December 1991, Ukraine inherited a telephone system that was antiquated, inefficient, and in disrepair; more than 3.5 million applications for telephones could not be satisfied; telephone density is rising and the domestic trunk system is being improved; about one-third of Ukraine's networks are digital and a majority of regional centers now have digital switching stations; improvements in local networks and local exchanges continue to lag; the mobile-cellular telephone system's expansion has slowed, largely due to saturation of the market which has reached 125 mobile phones per 100 people
international: country code—380; 2 new domestic trunk lines are a part of the fiber-optic Trans-Asia-Europe (TAE) system and 3 Ukrainian links have been installed in the fiber-optic Trans-European Lines (TEL) project that connects 18 countries; additional international service is provided by the Italy-Turkey-Ukraine-Russia (ITUR) fiber-optic submarine cable and by an unknown number of earth stations in the Intelsat, Inmarsat, and Intersputnik satellite systems (2010)

Broadcast media: Ukraine's state-controlled nationwide TV broadcast channel (UT1) and a number of privately owned TV networks provide basic TV coverage; multi-channel cable and satellite TV services are available; Russian television broadcasts have a small audience nationwide, but larger audiences in the eastern and southern regions; Ukraine's radio broadcast market, a mix of independent and state-owned networks, is comprised of some 300 stations (2007)

Internet country code: .ua

Internet hosts: 2.173 million (2012)
country comparison to the world: 37

Internet users: 7.77 million (2009)
country comparison to the world: 38

TRANSPORTATION

Airports: 187 (2013)
country comparison to the world: 31

Airports—with paved runways: *total:* 108
over 3,047 m: 13
2,438 to 3,047 m: 42
1,524 to 2,437 m: 22
914 to 1,523 m: 3
under 914 m: 28 (2013)

Airports—with unpaved runways: *total:* 7 9
1,524 to 2,437 m: 5
914 to 1,523 m: 5
under 914 m: 69 (2013)

Heliports: 9 (2013)

Pipelines: gas 36,720 km; oil 4,514 km; refined products 4,363 km (2013)

Railways: *total:* 21,619 km
country comparison to the world: 12
broad gauge: 21,619 km 1.524-m gauge (10,242 km electrified) (2012)

Roadways: *total:* 169,694 km
country comparison to the world: 29
paved: 166,095 km (includes 17 km of expressways)
unpaved: 3,599 km (2012)

Waterways: 1,672 km (most on Dnieper River) (2012)
country comparison to the world: 47

Merchant marine: *total:* 134
country comparison to the world: 43
by type: bulk carrier 3, cargo 98, chemical tanker 1, passenger 6, passenger/cargo 5, petroleum tanker 8, refrigerated cargo 11, specialized tanker 2 registered in other countries: 172 (Belize 6, Cambodia 35, Comoros 10, Cyprus 3, Dominica 1, Georgia 10, Liberia 10, Malta 29, Marshall Islands 1, Moldova 14, Mongolia 1, Panama 8, Russia 12, Saint Kitts and Nevis 8, Saint Vincent and the Grenadines 12, Sierra Leone 5, Slovakia 2, unknown 5) (2010)

Ports and terminals: *major seaport(s):* Feodosiya (Theodosia), Illichivsk, Mariupol', Mykolayiv, Odesa, Yuzhnyy

MILITARY

Military branches: Ground Forces, Naval Forces, Air Forces (2013)

Military service age and obligation: 18-25 years of age for compulsory and voluntary military service; conscript service obligation is 12 months for Army and Air Force, 18 months for Navy (2012)

Manpower available for military service:
males age 16-49: 10,984,394
females age 16-49: 11.26 million (2010 est.)

Manpower fit for military service:
males age 16-49: 6,893,551
females age 16-49: 8,792,504 (2010 est.)

Manpower reaching militarily significant age annually: *male:* 246,397
female: 234,916 (2010 est.)

Military expenditures: 2.77% of GDP (2012)
country comparison to the world: 27
2.4% of GDP (2011)
2.77% of GDP (2010)

TRANSNATIONAL ISSUES

Disputes—international: 1997 boundary delimitation treaty with Belarus remains unratified due to unresolved financial claims, stalling demarcation and reducing border security; delimitation of land boundary with Russia is complete with preparations for demarcation underway; the dispute over the boundary between Russia and Ukraine through the Kerch Strait and Sea of Azov remains unresolved despite a December 2003 framework agreement and ongoing expert-level discussions; Moldova and Ukraine operate joint customs posts to monitor transit of people and commodities through Moldova's break-away Transnistria Region, which remains under the auspices of an Organization for Security and Cooperation in Europe-mandated peacekeeping mission comprised of Moldovan, Transnistrian, Russian, and Ukrainian troops; the ICJ ruled largely in favor of Romania in its dispute submitted in 2004 over Ukrainian-administered Zmiyinyy/Serpilor (Snake) Island and Black Sea maritime boundary delimitation; Romania opposes Ukraine's reopening of a navigation canal from the Danube border through Ukraine to the Black Sea

Refugees and internally displaced persons: *stateless persons:* 35,000 (2012); note—citizens of the former USSR who were permanently resident in Ukraine were granted citizenship upon Ukraine's independence in 1991, but some missed this window of opportunity; people arriving after 1991, Crimean Tatars, ethnic Koreans, people with expired Soviet passports, and people with no documents have difficulty acquiring Ukrainian citizenship; following the fall of the Soviet Union in 1989, thousands of Crimean Tatars and their descendants deported from Ukraine under the STALIN regime returned to their homeland, some being stateless and others holding the citizenship of Uzbekistan or other former Soviet republics; a 1998 bilateral agreement between Ukraine and Uzbekistan simplified the process of renouncing Uzbek citizenship and obtaining Ukrainian citizenship

Trafficking in persons: *current situation:* Ukraine is a source, transit, and, increasingly, destination country for men, women, and children subjected to forced labor and sex trafficking; Ukrainian victims are sex trafficked within Ukraine as well as in Russia, Poland, Iraq, Spain, Turkey, Cyprus, Seychelles, Portugal, the Czech Republic, Israel, Italy, the United Arab Emirates, Montenegro, UK, and Tunisia; foreigners from Moldova, Uzbekistan, Pakistan, Cameroon, and Azerbaijan are victims of labor trafficking in Ukraine; Ukrainian recruiters most often target Ukrainians from rural areas with limited job prospects by using fraud, coercion, and debt bondage
tier rating: Tier 2 Watch List—Ukraine does not fully comply with the minimum standards for the elimination of trafficking; however, it is making significant efforts to do so; the government reduced its anti-trafficking law enforcement efforts in 2012; as a result of the dismantling of the specialized anti-trafficking police unit in 2011, the number of trafficking investigations, prosecutions, and convictions have decreased; fewer victims are identified and the national referral mechanism does not function effectively in many regions, resulting in few victims being granted victim status by the government; the government did not fund any anti-trafficking protection activities in 2012 and continues to rely on international donors to assist victims (2013)

Illicit drugs: limited cultivation of cannabis and opium poppy, mostly for CIS consumption; some synthetic drug production for export to the West; limited government eradication program; used as transshipment point for opiates and other illicit drugs from Africa, Latin America, and Turkey to Europe and Russia; Ukraine has improved anti-money-laundering controls, resulting in its removal from the Financial Action Task Force's (FATF's) Noncooperative Countries and Territories List in February 2004; Ukraine's anti-money-laundering regime continues to be monitored by FATF

UNITED ARAB EMIRATES

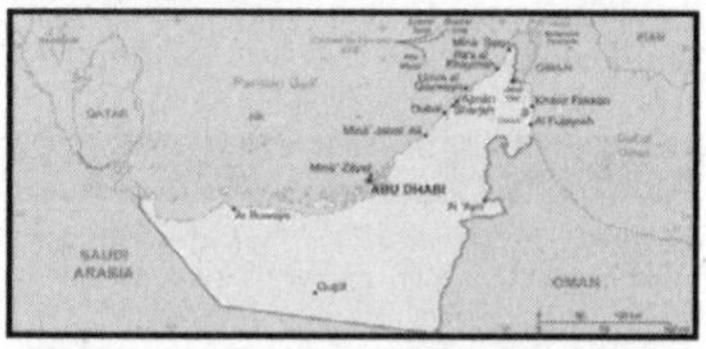

INTRODUCTION

Background: The Trucial States of the Persian Gulf coast granted the UK control of their defense and foreign affairs in 19th century treaties. In 1971, six of these states—Abu Dhabi, 'Ajman, Al Fujayrah, Ash Shariqah, Dubayy, and Umm al Qaywayn—merged to form the United Arab Emirates (UAE). They were joined in 1972 by Ra's al Khaymah. The UAE's per capita GDP is on par with those of leading West European nations. Its high oil revenues and its moderate foreign policy stance have allowed the UAE to play a vital role in the affairs of the region. For more than three decades, oil and global finance drove the UAE's economy. However, in 2008-09, the confluence of falling oil prices, collapsing real estate prices, and the international banking crisis hit the UAE especially hard. The UAE has essentially avoided the "Arab Spring" unrest seen elsewhere in the Middle East, though in March 2011, political activists and intellectuals signed a petition calling for greater public participation in governance that was widely circulated on the Internet. In an effort to stem potential further unrest, the government announced a multi-year, $1.6-billion infrastructure investment plan for the poorer northern emirates and aggressively pursued advocates of political reform.

GEOGRAPHY

Location: Middle East, bordering the Gulf of Oman and the Persian Gulf, between Oman and Saudi Arabia

Geographic coordinates: 24 00 N, 54 00 E

Map references: Middle East

Area: *total:* 83,600 sq km
country comparison to the world: 115
land: 83,600 sq km
water: 0 sq km

Area—comparative: slightly smaller than Maine

Land boundaries: *total:* 867 km
border countries: Oman 410 km, Saudi Arabia 457 km

Coastline: 1,318 km

Maritime claims: *territorial sea:* 12 nm
contiguous zone: 24 nm
exclusive economic zone: 200 nm
continental shelf: 200 nm or to the edge of the continental margin

Climate: desert; cooler in eastern mountains

Terrain: flat, barren coastal plain merging into rolling sand dunes of vast desert wasteland; mountains in east

Elevation extremes: *lowest point:* Persian Gulf 0 m
highest point: Jabal Yibir 1,527 m

Natural resources: petroleum, natural gas

Land use: *arable land:* 0.61%
permanent crops: 0.5%
other: 98.9% (2011)

Irrigated land: 920 sq km (2010)

Total renewable water resources: 0.15 cu km (2011)

Freshwater withdrawal (domestic/industrial/agricultural): *total:* 3.99 cu km/yr (15%/2%/83%)
per capita: 739.5 cu m/yr (2005)

Natural hazards: frequent sand and dust storms

Environment—current issues: lack of natural freshwater resources compensated by desalination plants; desertification; beach pollution from oil spills

Environment—international agreements: *party to:* Biodiversity, Climate Change, Climate Change-Kyoto Protocol, Desertification, Endangered Species, Hazardous Wastes, Marine Dumping, Ozone Layer Protection
signed, but not ratified: Law of the Sea

Geography—note: strategic location along southern approaches to Strait of Hormuz, a vital transit point for world crude oil

PEOPLE AND SOCIETY

Nationality: *noun:* Emirati(s)
adjective: Emirati

Ethnic groups: Emirati 19%, other Arab and Iranian 23%, South Asian 50%, other expatriates (includes Westerners and East Asians) 8% (1982)
note: less than 20% are UAE citizens (1982)

Languages: Arabic (official), Persian, English, Hindi, Urdu

Religions: Muslim (Islam; official) 76%, Christian 9%, other (primarily Hindu and Buddhist, less than 5% of the population consists of Parsi, Baha'i, Druze, Sikh, Ahmadi, Ismaili, Dawoodi Bohra Muslim, and Jewish) 15%
note: represents the total population; about 85% of the population consists of noncitizens (2005 est.)

Population: 5,628,805 (July 2014 est.)
country comparison to the world: 113
note: estimate is based on the results of the 2005 census that included a significantly higher estimate of net immigration of non-citizens than previous estimates; the United Arab Emirates' National Bureau of Statistics estimated the country's total population to have been 8,264,070 in 2010, based on census data

Age structure: *0-14 years:* 20.7% (male 597,476/female 570,275)
15-24 years: 13.7% (male 457,647/female 311,673)
25-54 years: 61.5% (male 2,639,018/female 820,915)
55-64 years: 1% (male 132,718/female 43,624)
65 years and over: 1% (male 35,071/female 20,388) (2014 est.)

Dependency ratios:
total dependency ratio: 18.6 %
youth dependency ratio: 18.1 %
elderly dependency ratio: 0.5 %
potential support ratio: 201.7 (2013)

Median age: *total:* 30.3 years
male: 32 years
female: 25 years (2014 est.)

Population growth rate: 2.71% (2014 est.)
country comparison to the world: 21

Birth rate: 15.54 births/1,000 population (2014 est.)
country comparison to the world: 129

Death rate: 1.99 deaths/1,000 population (2014 est.)
country comparison to the world: 225

Net migration rate: 13.58 migrant(s)/1,000 population (2014 est.)
country comparison to the world: 10

Urbanization: *urban population:* 84.4% of total population (2011)
rate of urbanization: 2.52% annual rate of change (2010-15 est.)

Major urban areas—population: ABU DHABI (capital) 666,000 (2009)

Sex ratio: *at birth:* 1.05 male(s)/female
0-14 years: 1.05 male(s)/female
15-24 years: 1.47 male(s)/female
25-54 years: 3.22 male(s)/female
55-64 years: 2.19 male(s)/female
65 years and over: 1.77 male(s)/female
total population: 2.19 male(s)/female (2014 est.)

Maternal mortality rate: 12 deaths/100,000 live births (2010)
country comparison to the world: 146

Infant mortality rate: *total:* 10.92 deaths/1,000 live births
country comparison to the world: 133
male: 12.73 deaths/1,000 live births
female: 9.01 deaths/1,000 live births (2014 est.)

Life expectancy at birth: total population: 77.09 years
country comparison to the world: 70
male: 74.49 years
female: 79.83 years (2014 est.)

Total fertility rate: 2.36 children born/woman (2014 est.)
country comparison to the world: 89

Contraceptive prevalence rate: 27.5% (1995)

Health expenditures: 3.3% of GDP (2011)
country comparison to the world: 178

Physicians density: 1.93 physicians/1,000 population (2007)

Hospital bed density: 1.9 beds/1,000 population (2008)

Drinking water source:
improved:
urban: 99.6% of population
rural: 100% of population
total: 99.6% of population
unimproved:
urban: 0.4% of population
rural: 0% of population
total: 0.4% of population (2011 est.)

Sanitation facility access:
improved:
urban: 98% of population
rural: 95.2% of population
total: 97.5% of population
unimproved:
urban: 2% of population
rural: 4.8% of population
total: 2.5% of population (2011 est.)

HIV/AIDS—adult prevalence rate: 0.2% (2001 est.)
country comparison to the world: 113

HIV/AIDS—people living with HIV/AIDS: NA

HIV/AIDS—deaths: NA

Obesity—adult prevalence rate: 32.7% (2008)
country comparison to the world: 22

Education expenditures: NA

Literacy: *definition:* age 15 and over can read and write
total population: 90%
male: 89.5%
female: 91.5% (2005 est.)

Unemployment, youth ages 15-24: *total:* 12.1%
country comparison to the world: 99
male: 7.9%
female: 21.8% (2008)

GOVERNMENT

Country name: *conventional long form:* United Arab Emirates
conventional short form: none
local long form: Al Imarat al Arabiyah al Muttahidah
local short form: none
former: Trucial Oman, Trucial States
abbreviation: UAE

Government type: federation with specified powers delegated to the UAE federal government and other powers reserved to member emirates

Capital: *name:* Abu Dhabi

geographic coordinates: 24 28 N, 54 22 E
time difference: UTC+4 (9 hours ahead of Washington, DC during Standard Time)

Administrative divisions: 7 emirates (imarat, singular—imarah); Abu Zaby (Abu Dhabi), 'Ajman, Al Fujayrah, Ash Shariqah (Sharjah), Dubayy (Dubai), Ra's al Khaymah, Umm al Qaywayn

Independence: 2 December 1971 (from the UK)

National holiday: Independence Day, 2 December (1971)

Constitution: previous 1971 (provisional); latest drafted in 1979, became permanent May 1996; amended 2009 (2012)

Legal system: mixed legal system of Islamic law and civil law

International law organization participation: has not submitted an ICJ jurisdiction declaration; non-party state to the ICCt

Suffrage: limited; note—rulers of the seven emirates each select a proportion of voters for the Federal National Council (FNC) that together account for about 12 percent of Emirati citizens

Executive branch: *chief of state:* President KHALIFA bin Zayid Al-Nuhayyan (since 3 November 2004), ruler of Abu Zaby (Abu Dhabi) (since 4 November 2004); Vice President and Prime Minister MUHAMMAD BIN RASHID Al-Maktum (since 5 January 2006)
head of government: Prime Minister Vice President MUHAMMAD BIN RASHID Al-Maktum (since 5 January 2006); Deputy Prime Ministers SAIF bin Zayid Al-Nuhayyan (since 11 May 2009) and MANSUR bin Zayid Al-Nuhayyan (since 11 May 2009)
cabinet: Council of Ministers appointed by the president (For more information visit the World Leaders website)
note: there is also a Federal Supreme Council (FSC) composed of the seven emirate rulers; the FSC is the highest constitutional authority in the UAE; establishes general policies and sanctions federal legislation; meets four times a year; Abu Zaby (Abu Dhabi) and Dubayy (Dubai) rulers have effective veto power
elections: president and vice president elected by the FSC for five-year terms (no term limits) from among the seven FSC members; election last held 3 November 2004 upon the death of the UAE's Founding Father and first President ZAYID bin Sultan Al Nuhayyan (next election NA); prime minister and deputy prime minister appointed by the president
election results: KHALIFA bin Zayid Al-Nuhayyan elected president by a unanimous vote of the FSC; MUHAMMAD bin Rashid Al-Maktum unanimously affirmed vice president after the 2006 death of his brother Sheikh MAKTUM bin Rashid Al-Maktum

Legislative branch: unicameral Federal National Council (FNC) or Majlis al-Ittihad al-Watani (40 seats; 20 members appointed by the rulers of the constituent states, 20 members elected to serve four-year terms)
elections: last held on 24 September 2011 (next to be held in 2015); note—the electoral college was expanded from 6,689 voters in the December 2006 election to 129,274 in the September 2011 election; elections for candidates rather than party lists; 469 candidates including 85 women ran for 20 contested FNC seats
election results: elected seats by emirate—Abu Dhabi 4, Dubai 4, Sharjah 3, Ras al-Khaimah 3, Ajman 2, Fujairah 2, Umm al-Quwain 2; note—number of appointed seats for each emirate are same as elected seats

Judicial branch: *highest court(s):* Federal Supreme Court (consists of the court president and 4 judges)
judge selection and term of office: judges appointed by the federal president following approval by the Federal Supreme Council, which includes the rulers of the 7 emirates; judge term NA
subordinate courts: Federal Court of Cassation (determines the constitutionality of laws promulgated at the federal and local (emirate) levels; federal level courts of first instance and appeals courts; each emirate has its own court system

Political parties and leaders: none; political parties are not allowed

Political pressure groups and leaders: NA

International organization participation: ABEDA, AfDB (nonregional member), AFESD, AMF, BIS, CAEU, CICA, FAO, G-77, GCC, IAEA, IBRD, ICAO, ICC (national committees), ICRM, IDA, IDB, IFAD, IFC, IFRCS, IHO, ILO, IMF, IMO, IMSO, Interpol, IOC, IPU, ISO, ITSO, ITU, LAS, MIGA, NAM, OAPEC, OIC, OIF (observer), OPCW, OPEC, PCA, UN, UNCTAD, UNESCO, UNIDO, UPU, WCO, WHO, WIPO, WMO, WTO

Diplomatic representation in the US:
chief of mission: Ambassador Yusif bin Mani bin Said al-UTAYBA (since 25 July 2008)
chancery: 3522 International Court NW, Suite 400, Washington, DC 20008
telephone: [1] (202) 243-2400
FAX: [1] (202) 243-2432

Diplomatic representation from the US:
chief of mission: Ambassador Michael H. CORBIN (since 25 July 2011)
embassy: Embassies District, Plot 38 Sector W59-02, Street No. 4, Abu Dhabi
mailing address: P. O. Box 4009, Abu Dhabi
telephone: [971] (2) 414-2200
FAX: [971] (2) 414-2603
consulate(s) general: Dubai

Flag description: three equal horizontal bands of green (top), white, and black with a wider vertical red band on the hoist side; the flag incorporates all four Pan-Arab colors, which in this case represent fertility (green), neutrality (white), petroleum resources (black), and unity (red); red was the traditional color incorporated into all flags of the emirates before their unification

National symbol(s): golden falcon

National anthem: *name:* "Nashid al-watani al-imarati" (National Anthem of the UAE)
lyrics/music: AREF Al Sheikh Abdullah Al Hassan/Mohamad Abdel WAHAB
note: music adopted 1971, lyrics adopted 1996; Mohamad Abdel WAHAB also composed the music for the anthem of Tunisia

ECONOMY

Economy—overview: The UAE has an open economy with a high per capita income and a sizable annual trade surplus. Successful efforts at economic diversification have reduced the portion of GDP based on oil and gas output to 25%. Since the discovery of oil in the UAE more than 30 years ago, the country has undergone a profound transformation from an impoverished region of small desert principalities to a modern state with a high standard of living. The government has increased spending on job creation and infrastructure expansion and is opening up utilities to greater private sector involvement. In April 2004, the UAE signed a Trade and Investment Framework Agreement with Washington and in November 2004 agreed to undertake negotiations toward a Free Trade Agreement with the US; however, those talks have not moved forward. The country's Free Trade Zones—offering 100% foreign ownership and zero taxes—are helping to attract foreign investors. The global financial crisis, tight international credit, and deflated asset prices constricted the economy in 2009. UAE authorities tried to blunt the crisis by increasing spending and boosting liquidity in the banking sector. The crisis hit Dubai hardest, as it was heavily exposed to depressed real estate prices. Dubai lacked sufficient cash to meet its debt obligations, prompting global concern about its solvency. The UAE Central Bank and Abu Dhabi-based banks bought the largest shares. In December 2009 Dubai received an additional $10 billion loan from the emirate of Abu Dhabi. Dependence on oil, a large expatriate workforce, and growing inflation pressures are significant long-term challenges. The UAE's strategic plan for the next few years focuses on diversification and creating more opportunities for nationals through improved education and increased private sector employment.

GDP (purchasing power parity): $269.8 billion (2013 est.)
country comparison to the world: 50
$259.3 billion (2012 est.)
$248.5 billion (2011 est.)
note: data are in 2013 US dollars

GDP (official exchange rate): $390 billion (2013 est.)

GDP—real growth rate: 4% (2013 est.)
country comparison to the world: 76
4.4% (2012 est.)
3.9% (2011 est.)

GDP—per capita (PPP): $29,900 (2013 est.)
country comparison to the world: 48
$29,600 (2012 est.)
$29,200 (2011 est.)
note: data are in 2013 US dollars

Gross national saving: 36.8% of GDP (2013 est.)
country comparison to the world: 14
40% of GDP (2012 est.)
37.6% of GDP (2011 est.)

GDP—composition, by end use:
household consumption: 51.9%
government consumption: 7%
investment in fixed capital: 23.1%
investment in inventories: 0.7%
exports of goods and services: 96%

imports of goods and services: -78.8% (2013 est.)

GDP—composition, by sector of origin:
agriculture: 0.6%
industry: 61.1%
services: 38.2% (2013 est.)

Agriculture—products: dates, vegetables, watermelons; poultry, eggs, dairy products; fish

Industries: petroleum and petrochemicals; fishing, aluminum, cement, fertilizers, commercial ship repair, construction materials, some boat building, handicrafts, textiles

Industrial production growth rate: 3.3% (2013 est.)
country comparison to the world: 90

Labor force: 4.588 million
country comparison to the world: 84
note: expatriates account for about 85% of the work force (2013 est.)

Labor force—by occupation: *agriculture:* 7%
industry: 15%
services: 78% (2000 est.)

Unemployment rate: 2.4% (2001)
country comparison to the world: 17

Population below poverty line: 19.5% (2003)

Household income or consumption by percentage share: *lowest 10%:* NA%
highest 10%: NA%

Budget: *revenues:* $138 billion
expenditures: $118.3 billion (2013 est.)

Taxes and other revenues: 35.4% of GDP (2013 est.)
country comparison to the world: 63

Budget surplus (+) or deficit (-):
5% of GDP (2013 est.)
country comparison to the world: 8

Public debt: 41.7% of GDP (2013 est.)
country comparison to the world: 84
42.6% of GDP (2012 est.)

Fiscal year: calendar year

Inflation rate (consumer prices): 1.3% (2013 est.)
country comparison to the world: 36
0.7% (2012 est.)

Central bank discount rate: NA%

Stock of narrow money: $96.11 billion (31 December 2013 est.)
country comparison to the world: 36
$81.46 billion (31 December 2012 est.)

Stock of broad money: $260.2 billion (31 December 2013 est.)
country comparison to the world: 33
$234.8 billion (31 December 2012 est.)

Stock of domestic credit: $308.1 billion (31 December 2013 est.)
country comparison to the world: 34
$293.4 billion (31 December 2012 est.)

Market value of publicly traded shares: $67.95 billion (31 December 2012 est.)
country comparison to the world: 45
$71.33 billion (31 December 2011)
$77.08 billion (31 December 2010 est.)

Current account balance: $52.67 billion (2013 est.)
country comparison to the world: 12
$66.56 billion (2012 est.)

Exports: $368.9 billion (2013 est.)
country comparison to the world: 18
$350.1 billion (2012 est.)

Exports—commodities: crude oil 45%, natural gas, reexports, dried fish, dates

Exports—partners: Japan 15.4%, India 13.4%, Iran 10.7%, Thailand 5.5%, Singapore 5.5%, South Korea 5.3% (2012)

Imports: $249.6 billion (2013 est.)
country comparison to the world: 21
$221.9 billion (2012 est.)

Imports—commodities: machinery and transport equipment, chemicals, food

Imports—partners: India 17%, China 13.7%, US 10.5%, Germany 5.1%, Japan 4.2% (2012)

Reserves of foreign exchange and gold: $58.04 billion (31 December 2013 est.)
country comparison to the world: 33
$47.04 billion (31 December 2012 est.)

Debt—external: $167.9 billion (31 December 2013 est.)
country comparison to the world: 35
$162.3 billion (31 December 2012 est.)

Stock of direct foreign investment—at home: $103 billion (31 December 2013 est.)
country comparison to the world: 41
$92.96 billion (31 December 2012 est.)

Stock of direct foreign investment—abroad: $61.96 billion (31 December 2013 est.)
country comparison to the world: 35
$58.46 billion (31 December 2012 est.)

Exchange rates: Emirati dirhams (AED) per US dollar—
3.673 (2013 est.)
3.6725 (2012 est.)
3.6725 (2010 est.)
3.673 (2009)
3.6725 (2008)

ENERGY

Electricity—production: 102.7 billion kWh (2011 est.)
country comparison to the world: 34

Electricity—consumption: 85.17 billion kWh (2010 est.)
country comparison to the world: 34

Electricity—exports: 0 kWh (2012 est.)
country comparison to the world: 94

Electricity—imports: 0 kWh (2012 est.)
country comparison to the world: 111

Electricity—installed generating capacity: 23.25 million kW (2010 est.)
country comparison to the world: 35

Electricity—from fossil fuels: 100% of total installed capacity (2010 est.)
country comparison to the world: 43

Electricity—from nuclear fuels: 0% of total installed capacity (2010 est.)
country comparison to the world: 33

Electricity—from hydroelectric plants: 0% of total installed capacity (2010 est.)
country comparison to the world: 153

Electricity—from other renewable sources: 0% of total installed capacity (2010 est.)
country comparison to the world: 147

Crude oil—production: 3.213 million bbl/day (2012 est.)
country comparison to the world: 7

Crude oil—exports: 2.142 million bbl/day (2010 est.)
country comparison to the world: 6

Crude oil—imports: 0 bbl/day (2010 est.)
country comparison to the world: 148

Crude oil—proved reserves: 97.8 billion bbl (1 January 2013 es)
country comparison to the world: 7

Refined petroleum products—production: 371,500 bbl/day (2010 est.)
country comparison to the world: 38

Refined petroleum products—consumption: 572,100 bbl/day (2011 est.)
country comparison to the world: 31

Refined petroleum products—exports: 382,300 bbl/day (2010 est.)
country comparison to the world: 18

Refined petroleum products—imports: 351,400 bbl/day (2010 est.)
country comparison to the world: 19

Natural gas—production: 52.31 billion cu m (2011 est.)
country comparison to the world: 18

Natural gas—consumption: 60.54 billion cu m (2010 est.)
country comparison to the world: 13

Natural gas—exports: 5.18 billion cu m (2011 est.)
country comparison to the world: 35

Natural gas—imports: 17.44 billion cu m (2011 est.)
country comparison to the world: 21

Natural gas—proved reserves: 6.089 trillion cu m (1 January 2013 es)
country comparison to the world: 7

Carbon dioxide emissions from consumption of energy: 245.4 million Mt (2011 est.)
country comparison to the world: 27

COMMUNICATIONS

Telephones—main lines in use: 1.967 million (2012)
country comparison to the world: 59

Telephones—mobile cellular: 13.775 million (2012)
country comparison to the world: 61

Telephone system: *general assessment:* modern fiber-optic integrated services; digital network with rapidly growing use of mobile-cellular telephones; key centers are Abu Dhabi and Dubai
domestic: microwave radio relay, fiber optic and coaxial cable
international: country code—971; linked to the international submarine cable FLAG (Fiber-Optic Link Around the Globe); landing point for both the SEA-ME-WE-3 and SEA-ME-WE-4 submarine cable networks; satellite earth stations—3 Intelsat (1 Atlantic Ocean and 2 Indian Ocean) and 1 Arabsat; tropospheric scatter to Bahrain; microwave radio relay to Saudi Arabia (2011)

Broadcast media: except for the many organizations now operating in Dubai's Media Free Zone, most TV and radio stations remain government-owned; widespread use of satellite dishes provides access to pan-Arab and other international broadcasts (2007)

Internet country code: .ae

Internet hosts: 337,804 (2012)
country comparison to the world: 61

Internet users: 3.449 million (2009)
country comparison to the world: 61

TRANSPORTATION

Airports: 43 (2013)
country comparison to the world: 100

Airports—with paved runways: *total:* 2 5
over 3,047 m: 12
2,438 to 3,047 m: 3
1,524 to 2,437 m: 5
914 to 1,523 m: 3

under 914 m: 2 (2013)

Airports—with unpaved runways: *total:* 1 8
over 3,047 m: 1
2,438 to 3,047 m: 1
1,524 to 2,437 m: 4
914 to 1,523 m: 6
under 914 m: 6 (2013)

Heliports: 5 (2013)

Pipelines: condensate 533 km; gas 3,277 km; liquid petroleum gas 300 km; oil 3,287 km; oil/gas/water 24 km; refined products 218 km; water 99 km (2013)

Roadways: *total:* 4,080 km
country comparison to the world: 157
paved: 4,080 km (includes 253 km of expressways) (2008)

Merchant marine: *total:* 6 1
country comparison to the world: 65
by type: bulk carrier 3, cargo 13, chemical tanker 8, container 7, liquefied gas 1, passenger/cargo 1, petroleum tanker 24, roll on/roll off 4
foreign-owned: 13 (Greece 3, Kuwait 10)
registered in other countries: 253 (Bahamas 23, Barbados 1, Belize 3, Cambodia 2, Comoros 8, Cyprus 3, Georgia 2, Gibraltar 5, Honduras 1, Hong Kong 1, India 4, Iran 2, Jordan 2, Liberia 37, Malta 1, Marshall Islands 12, Mexico 1, Netherlands 4, North Korea 2, Panama 83, Papua New Guinea 6, Philippines 1, Saint Kitts and Nevis 8, Saint Vincent and the Grenadines 3, Saudi Arabia 6, Sierra Leone 1, Singapore 10, Tanzania 3, Togo 1, UK 8, Vanuatu 1, unknown 8) (2010)

Ports and terminals: *major seaport(s):* Al Fujayrah, Mina' Jabal 'Ali (Dubai), Khor Fakkan (Khawr Fakkan), Mubarraz Island, Mina' Rashid (Dubai), Mina' Saqr (Ra's al Khaymah)
container port(s) (TEUs): Dubai Port (12,617,595), Khor Fakkan (Khawr Fakkan) (3,234,101)

MILITARY

Military branches: United Arab Emirates Armed Forces: Critical Infrastructure Coastal Patrol Agency (CNIA), Land Forces, Navy, Air Force and Air Defense, Border and Coast Guard Directorate (BCGD) (2012)

Military service age and obligation: 18 years of age for voluntary military service; 18 years of age for officers and women; no conscription; 16-22 years of age for candidates for the UAE Naval College (2012)

Manpower available for military service:
males age 16-49: 2,676,928 (includes non-nationals)
females age 16-49: 981,649 (2010 est.)

Manpower fit for military service:
males age 16-49: 2,229,366
females age 16-49: 842,759 (2010 est.)

Manpower reaching militarily significant age annually: *male:* 27,439
female: 24,419 (2010 est.)

Military expenditures: NA% (2012)
5.5% of GDP (2011)
NA% (2010)

TRANSNATIONAL ISSUES

Disputes—international: boundary agreement was signed and ratified with Oman in 2003 for entire border, including Oman's Musandam Peninsula and Al Madhah enclaves, but contents of the agreement and detailed maps showing the alignment have not been published; Iran and UAE dispute Tunb Islands and Abu Musa Island, which Iran occupies

Illicit drugs: the UAE is a drug transshipment point for traffickers given its proximity to Southwest Asian drug-producing countries; the UAE's position as a major financial center makes it vulnerable to money laundering; anti-money-laundering controls improving, but informal banking remains unregulated

UNITED KINGDOM

INTRODUCTION

Background: The United Kingdom has historically played a leading role in developing parliamentary democracy and in advancing literature and science. At its zenith in the 19th century, the British Empire stretched over one-fourth of the earth's surface. The first half of the 20th century saw the UK's strength seriously depleted in two world wars and the Irish Republic's withdrawal from the union. The second half witnessed the dismantling of the Empire and the UK rebuilding itself into a modern and prosperous European nation. As one of five permanent members of the UN Security Council and a founding member of NATO and the Commonwealth, the UK pursues a global approach to foreign policy. The UK is also an active member of the EU, although it chose to remain outside the Economic and Monetary Union. The Scottish Parliament, the National Assembly for Wales, and the Northern Ireland Assembly were established in 1999. The latter was suspended until May 2007 due to wrangling over the peace process, but devolution was fully completed in March 2010.

GEOGRAPHY

Location: Western Europe, islands—including the northern one-sixth of the island of Ireland—between the North Atlantic Ocean and the North Sea; northwest of France

Geographic coordinates: 54 00 N, 2 00 W

Map references: Europe

Area: *total:* 243,610 sq km
country comparison to the world: 80
land: 241,930 sq km
water: 1,680 sq km
note: includes Rockall and Shetland Islands

Area—comparative: twice the size of Pennsylvania; slightly smaller than Oregon

Land boundaries: *total:* 360 km
border countries: Ireland 360 km

Coastline: 12,429 km

Maritime claims: *territorial sea:* 12 nm
exclusive fishing zone: 200 nm
continental shelf: as defined in continental shelf orders or in accordance with agreed upon boundaries

Climate: temperate; moderated by prevailing southwest winds over the North Atlantic Current; more than one-half of the days are overcast

Terrain: mostly rugged hills and low mountains; level to rolling plains in east and southeast

Elevation extremes: *lowest point:* The Fens -4 m
highest point: Ben Nevis 1,343 m

Natural resources: coal, petroleum, natural gas, iron ore, lead, zinc, gold, tin, limestone, salt, clay, chalk, gypsum, potash, silica sand, slate, arable land

Land use: *arable land:* 24.88%
permanent crops: 0.18%
other: 74.93% (2011)

Irrigated land: 2,280 sq km (2005)

Total renewable water resources: 147 cu km (2011)

Freshwater withdrawal (domestic/industrial/agricultural): *total:* 13.03 cu km/yr (58%/33%/9%)
per capita: 213.2 cu m/yr (2008)

Natural hazards: winter windstorms; floods

Environment—current issues: continues to reduce greenhouse gas emissions (has met Kyoto Protocol target of a 12.5% reduction from 1990 levels and intends to meet the legally binding target and move toward a domestic goal of a 20% cut in emissions by 2010); by 2005 the government reduced the amount of industrial and commercial waste disposed of in landfill sites to 85% of 1998 levels and recycled or composted at least 25% of household waste, increasing to 33% by 2015

Environment—international agreements: *party to:* Air Pollution, Air Pollution-Nitrogen Oxides, Air Pollution-Persistent Organic Pollutants, Air Pollution-Sulfur 94, Air Pollution-Volatile Organic Compounds, Antarctic-Environmental Protocol, Antarctic-Marine Living Resources, Antarctic Seals, Antarctic Treaty, Biodiversity, Climate Change, Climate Change-Kyoto Protocol, Desertification, Endangered Species, Environmental Modification, Hazardous Wastes, Law of the Sea, Marine Dumping, Marine Life Conservation, Ozone Layer Protection, Ship Pollution, Tropical Timber 83, Tropical Timber 94, Wetlands, Whaling
signed, but not ratified: none of the selected agreements

Geography—note: lies near vital North Atlantic sea lanes; only 35 km from France and linked by tunnel under the English Channel; because of heavily indented coastline, no location is more than 125 km from tidal waters

PEOPLE AND SOCIETY

Nationality: *noun:* Briton(s), British (collective plural)
adjective: British

Ethnic groups: white 87.2%, black/African/Caribbean/black British 3%, Asian/Asian British: Indian 2.3%, Asian/Asian British: Pakistani 1.9%, mixed 2%, other 3.7% (2011 est.)

Languages: English
note: the following are recognized regional languages: Scots (about 30% of the population of Scotland), Scottish Gaelic (about 60,000 in Scotland), Welsh (about 20% of the population of Wales), Irish (about 10% of the population of

Northern Ireland), Cornish (some 2,000 to 3,000 in Cornwall) (2012)

Religions: Christian (includes Anglican, Roman Catholic, Presbyterian, Methodist) 59.5%, Muslim 4.4%, Hindu 1.3%, other 2%, none 25.7%, unspecified 7.2% (2011 est.)

Population: 63,742,977 (July 2014 est.)
country comparison to the world: 23

Age structure:
0-14 years: 17.3% (male 5,660,891/female 5,380,448)
15-24 years: 12.6% (male 4,116,859/female 3,945,146)
25-54 years: 41% (male 13,299,731/female 12,843,937)
55-64 years: 17.5% (male 3,621,110/female 3,702,717)
65 years and over: 17.3% (male 4,990,024/female 6,182,114) (2014 est.)

Dependency ratios:
total dependency ratio: 54 %
youth dependency ratio: 27.1 %
elderly dependency ratio: 26.9 %
potential support ratio: 3.7 (2013)

Median age: *total:* 40.4 years
male: 39.2 years
female: 41.6 years (2014 est.)

Population growth rate: 0.54% (2014 est.)
country comparison to the world: 152

Birth rate: 12.22 births/1,000 population (2014 est.)
country comparison to the world: 160

Death rate: 9.34 deaths/1,000 population (2014 est.)
country comparison to the world: 60

Net migration rate: 2.56 migrant(s)/1,000 population (2014 est.)
country comparison to the world: 38

Urbanization: *urban population:* 80% of total population (2010)
rate of urbanization: 0.7% annual rate of change (2010-15 est.)

Major urban areas—population: LONDON (capital) 8.615 million; Birmingham 2.296 million; Manchester 2.247 million; West Yorkshire 1.541 million; Glasgow 1.166 million (2009)

Sex ratio: *at birth:* 1.05 male(s)/female
0-14 years: 1.05 male(s)/female
15-24 years: 1.04 male(s)/female
25-54 years: 1.04 male(s)/female
55-64 years: 0.99 male(s)/female
65 years and over: 0.8 male(s)/female
total population: 0.99 male(s)/female (2014 est.)

Mother's mean age at first birth: 30 (2006 est.)

Maternal mortality rate: 12 deaths/100,000 live births (2010)
country comparison to the world: 148

Infant mortality rate: *total:* 4.44 deaths/1,000 live births
country comparison to the world: 189
male: 4.86 deaths/1,000 live births
female: 4 deaths/1,000 live births (2014 est.)

Life expectancy at birth:
total population: 80.42 years
country comparison to the world: 29
male: 78.26 years
female: 82.69 years (2014 est.)

Total fertility rate: 1.9 children born/woman (2014 est.)
country comparison to the world: 140

Contraceptive prevalence rate: 84%
note: percent of women aged 16-49 (2008/09)

Health expenditures: 9.3% of GDP (2011)
country comparison to the world: 37

Physicians density: 2.77 physicians/1,000 population (2011)

Hospital bed density: 3 beds/1,000 population (2010)

Drinking water source:
improved:
urban: 100% of population
rural: 100% of population
total: 100% of population
unimproved:
urban: 0% of population
rural: 0% of population
total: 0% of population (2011 est.)

Sanitation facility access:
improved:
urban: 100% of population
rural: 100% of population
total: 100% of population
unimproved:
urban: 0% of population
rural: 0% of population
total: 0% of population (2011 est.)

HIV/AIDS—adult prevalence rate: 0.2% (2009 est.)
country comparison to the world: 114

HIV/AIDS—people living with HIV/AIDS: 85,000 (2009 est.)
country comparison to the world: 48

HIV/AIDS—deaths: fewer than 1,000 (2009 est.)
country comparison to the world: 73

Obesity—adult prevalence rate: 26.9% (2008)
country comparison to the world: 43

Education expenditures: 6.2% of GDP (2010)
country comparison to the world: 36

Literacy: *definition:* age 15 and over has completed five or more years of schooling
total population: 99%
male: 99%
female: 99% (2003 est.)

School life expectancy (primary to tertiary education): *total:* 16 years
male: 16 years
female: 17 years (2011)

Unemployment, youth ages 15-24: *total:* 21%
country comparison to the world: 55
male: 23.8%
female: 17.9% (2012)

GOVERNMENT

Country name: *conventional long form:* United Kingdom of Great Britain and Northern Ireland; note—Great Britain includes England, Scotland, and Wales
conventional short form: United Kingdom
abbreviation: UK

Government type: constitutional monarchy and Commonwealth realm

Capital: *name:* London

geographic coordinates: 51 30 N, 0 05 W
time difference: UTC 0 (5 hours ahead of Washington, DC during Standard Time)
daylight saving time: +1hr, begins last Sunday in March; ends last Sunday in October
note: applies to the United Kingdom proper, not to its overseas dependencies or territories

Administrative divisions: England: 27 two-tier counties, 32 London boroughs and 1 City of London or Greater London, 36 metropolitan districts, 56 unitary authorities (including 4 single-tier counties*)
two-tier counties: Buckinghamshire, Cambridgeshire, Cumbria, Derbyshire, Devon, Dorset, East Sussex, Essex, Gloucestershire, Hampshire, Hertfordshire, Kent, Lancashire, Leicestershire, Lincolnshire, Norfolk, North Yorkshire, Northamptonshire, Nottinghamshire, Oxfordshire, Somerset, Staffordshire, Suffolk, Surrey, Warwickshire, West Sussex, Worcestershire
London boroughs and City of London or Greater London: Barking and Dagenham, Barnet, Bexley, Brent, Bromley, Camden, Croydon, Ealing, Enfield, Greenwich, Hackney, Hammersmith and Fulham, Haringey, Harrow, Havering, Hillingdon, Hounslow, Islington, Kensington and Chelsea, Kingston upon Thames, Lambeth, Lewisham, City of London, Merton, Newham, Redbridge, Richmond upon Thames, Southwark, Sutton, Tower Hamlets, Waltham Forest, Wandsworth, Westminster
metropolitan districts: Barnsley, Birmingham, Bolton, Bradford, Bury, Calderdale, Coventry, Doncaster, Dudley, Gateshead, Kirklees, Knowlsey, Leeds, Liverpool, Manchester, Newcastle upon Tyne, North Tyneside, Oldham, Rochdale, Rotherham, Salford, Sandwell, Sefton, Sheffield, Solihull, South Tyneside, St. Helens, Stockport, Sunderland, Tameside, Trafford, Wakefield, Walsall, Wigan, Wirral, Wolverhampton
unitary authorities: Bath and North East Somerset, Blackburn with Darwen, Bedford, Blackpool, Bournemouth, Bracknell Forest, Brighton and Hove, City of Bristol, Central Bedfordshire, Cheshire East, Cheshire West and Chester, Cornwall, Darlington, Derby, Durham County*, East Riding of Yorkshire, Halton, Hartlepool, Herefordshire*, Isle of Wight*, Isles of Scilly, City of Kingston upon Hull, Leicester, Luton, Medway, Middlesbrough, Milton Keynes, North East Lincolnshire, North Lincolnshire, North Somerset, Northumberland*, Nottingham, Peterborough, Plymouth, Poole, Portsmouth, Reading, Redcar and Cleveland, Rutland, Shropshire, Slough, South Gloucestershire, Southampton, Southend-on-Sea, Stockton-on-Tees, Stoke-on-Trent, Swindon, Telford and Wrekin, Thurrock, Torbay, Warrington, West Berkshire, Wiltshire, Windsor and Maidenhead, Wokingham, York

Northern Ireland: 13 borough councils, 11 district council areas, 1 city and district council, 1 city council
borough councils: Antrim, Ards, Ballymena, Ballymoney, Carrickfergus, Castlereagh, Coleraine, Craigavon, Dungannon and South Tyrone, Larne, Limavady, Newtownabbey, North Down
city and district councils: Armagh
city councils: Lisburn
district council areas: Belfast, Banbridge, Cookstown, Derry, Down, Fermanagh, Magherafelt, Moyle, Newry and Mourne, Omagh, Strabane
Scotland: 32 council areas
council areas: Aberdeen City, Aberdeenshire, Angus, Argyll and Bute, Clackmannanshire, Dumfries and Galloway, Dundee City, East Ayrshire, East Dunbartonshire, East Lothian, East Renfrewshire, City of Edinburgh, Eilean Siar (Western Isles), Falkirk, Fife, Glasgow City, Highland, Inverclyde, Midlothian, Moray, North Ayrshire, North Lanarkshire, Orkney Islands, Perth and Kinross, Renfrewshire, Shetland Islands, South Ayrshire, South Lanarkshire, Stirling, The Scottish Borders, West Dunbartonshire, West Lothian
Wales: 22 unitary authorities
unitary authorities: Blaenau Gwent; Bridgend; Caerphilly; Cardiff; Carmarthenshire; Ceredigion; Conwy; Denbighshire; Flintshire; Gwynedd; Isle of Anglesey; Merthyr Tydfil; Monmouthshire; Neath Port Talbot; Newport; Pembrokeshire; Powys; Rhondda Cynon Taff; Swansea; The Vale of Glamorgan; Torfaen; Wrexham

Dependent areas: Anguilla, Bermuda, British Indian Ocean Territory, British Virgin Islands, Cayman Islands, Falkland Islands, Gibraltar, Montserrat, Pitcairn Islands, Saint Helena, Ascension, and Tristan da Cunha, South Georgia and the South Sandwich Islands, Turks and Caicos Islands

Independence: 12 April 1927 (Royal and Parliamentary Titles Act establishes current name of the United Kingdom of Great Britain and *Northern Ireland); notable earlier dates:* 927 (minor English kingdoms united); 3 March 1284 (enactment of the Statute of Rhuddlan uniting England and Wales); 1536 (Act of Union formally incorporates England and Wales); 1 May 1707 (Acts of Union formally unite England and Scotland as Great Britain); 1 January 1801 (Acts of Union formally unite Great Britain and Ireland as the United Kingdom of Great Britain and Ireland); 6 December 1921 (Anglo-Irish Treaty formalizes partition of Ireland; six counties remain part of the United Kingdom and Northern Ireland)

National holiday: the UK does not celebrate one particular national holiday

Constitution: unwritten; partly statutes, partly common law and practice; note—recent additions include the Human Rights Act of 1998, the Constitutional Reform and Governance Act 2010, the Parliamentary Voting System and Constituencies Act 2011, and the Fixed-term Parliaments Act 2011 (2011)

Legal system: common law system; has nonbinding judicial review of Acts of Parliament under the Human Rights Act of 1998

International law organization participation: accepts compulsory ICJ jurisdiction with reservations; accepts ICCt jurisdiction

Suffrage: 18 years of age; universal

Executive branch: *chief of state:* Queen ELIZABETH II (since 6 February 1952); Heir Apparent Prince CHARLES (son of the queen, born 14 November 1948)
head of government: Prime Minister David CAMERON (since 11 May 2010)
cabinet: Cabinet of Ministers appointed by the prime minister (For more information visit the World Leaders website)
elections: the monarchy is hereditary; following legislative elections, the leader of the majority party or the leader of the majority coalition usually becomes the prime minister

Legislative branch: bicameral Parliament consists of House of Lords; note—membership is not fixed (780 seats; consisting of approximately 667 life peers, 88 hereditary peers, and 25 clergy—as of 13 January 2014) and House of Commons (650 seats since 2010 elections; members elected by popular vote to serve five-year terms unless the House is dissolved earlier)
elections: House of Lords—no elections (note—in 1999, as provided by the House of Lords Act, elections were held in the House of Lords to determine the 92 hereditary peers who would remain there; elections are held only as vacancies in the hereditary peerage arise); House of Commons—last held on 6 May 2010 (next to be held by June 2015)
election results: House of Commons—percent of vote by party—Conservative 36.1%, Labor 29%, Liberal Democrats 23%, other 11.9%; seats by party—Conservative 305, Labor 258, Liberal Democrat 57, other 30
note: in 1998 elections were held for a Northern Ireland Assembly (because of unresolved disputes among existing parties, the transfer of power from London to Northern Ireland came only at the end of 1999 and has been suspended four times, the latest occurring in October 2002 and lasting until 8 May 2007); in 1999, the UK held the first elections for a Scottish Parliament and a Welsh Assembly; the most recent elections for the Northern Ireland Assembly, the Scottish Parliament, and the Welsh Assembly took place in May 2011

Judicial branch: *highest court(s):* Supreme Court (consists of 12 justices including the court president and deputy president) note—the Supreme Court was established by the Constitutional Reform Act 2005 and implemented in October 2009, replacing the Appellate Committee of the House of Lords as the highest court in the United Kingdom
judge selection and term of office: judge candidates selected by an independent committee of several judicial commissions, followed by their recommendations to the prime minister, and appointed by Her Majesty The Queen; justices appointed during period of good behavior
subordinate courts: England and Wales—Court of Appeal (civil and criminal divisions); High Court; Crown Court; County Courts; Magistrates' Courts; Scotland—Court of Sessions; Sherrif Courts; High Court of Justiciary; tribunals; Northern Ireland—Court of Appeal in Northern Ireland; High Court; county courts; magistrates' courts; specialized tribunals

Political parties and leaders: Conservative [David CAMERON]; Alliance Party (Northerm Ireland) [David FORD]; Democratic Unionist Party or DUP (Northern Ireland) [Peter ROBINSON]; Labor Party [Ed MILIBAND]; Liberal Democrats (Lib Dems) [Nick CLEGG]; Party of Wales (Plaid Cymru) [Leanne WOOD]; Scottish National Party or SNP [Alex SALMOND]; Sinn Fein (Northern Ireland) [Gerry ADAMS]; Social Democratic and Labor Party or SDLP (Northern Ireland) [Alasdair MCDONNELL]; Ulster Unionist Party (Northern Ireland) [Mike NESBITT]; United Kingdom Independent Party or UKIP [Nigel FARAGE]

Political pressure groups and leaders: Campaign for Nuclear Disarmament; Confederation of British Industry; National Farmers' Union; Trades Union Congress

International organization participation: ADB (nonregional member), AfDB (nonregional member), Arctic Council (observer), Australia Group, BIS, C, CBSS (observer), CD, CDB, CE, CERN, EAPC, EBRD, EIB, EITI (implementing country), ESA, EU, FAO, FATF, G-20, G-5, G-7, G-8, G-10, IADB, IAEA, IBRD, ICAO, ICC (national committees), ICRM, IDA, IEA, IFAD, IFC, IFRCS, IGAD (partners), IHO, ILO, IMF, IMO, IMSO, Interpol, IOC, IOM, IPU, ISO, ITSO, ITU, ITUC (NGOs), MIGA, MINUSMA, MONUSCO, NATO, NEA, NSG, OAS (observer), OECD, OPCW, OSCE, Paris Club, PCA, PIF (partner), SELEC (observer), UN, UNCTAD, UNESCO, UNFICYP, UNHCR, UNIDO, UNISFA, UNMISS, UNRWA, UNSC (permanent), UPU, WCO, WHO, WIPO, WMO, WTO, ZC

Diplomatic representation in the US:
chief of mission: Ambassador Peter John WESTMACOTT (since 17 January 2012)
chancery: 3100 Massachusetts Avenue NW, Washington, DC 20008
telephone: [1] (202) 588-6500
FAX: [1] (202) 588-7850
consulate(s) general: Atlanta, Boston, Chicago, Denver, Houston, Los Angeles, Miami, New York, San Francisco
consulate(s): Dallas, Orlando (FL)

Diplomatic representation from the US:
chief of mission: Ambassador Matthew W. BARZUN (since 15 August 2013)
embassy: 24 Grosvenor Square, London, W1K 6AH note—a new embassy is scheduled to open by the end of 2017 in the Nine Elms area of Wandsworth
mailing address: PSC 801, Box 40, FPO AE 09498-4040
telephone: [44] (0) 20 7499-9000
FAX: [44] (0) 20 7629-9124
consulate(s) general: Belfast, Edinburgh

Flag description: blue field with the red cross of Saint George (patron saint of England) edged in white superimposed on the diagonal red cross of Saint Patrick (patron saint of Ireland), which is superimposed on the diagonal white cross of Saint Andrew (patron saint of Scotland); properly known as the Union Flag, but commonly called the Union Jack; the design and colors (especially the Blue Ensign) have been the basis for a number of other flags including other Commonwealth countries and their constituent states or provinces, and British overseas territories

National symbol(s): lion (Britain in general); lion, Tudor rose (England); lion, unicorn, thistle (Scotland); dragon, daffodil, leek (Wales); harp, flax (Northern Ireland)

National anthem: *name:* "God Save the Queen"
lyrics/music: unknown
note: in use since 1745; by tradition, the song serves as both the national and royal anthem of the United Kingdom; it is known as either "God Save the Queen" or "God Save the King," depending on the gender of the reigning monarch; it also serves as the royal anthem of many Commonwealth nations

ECONOMY

Economy—overview: The UK, a leading trading power and financial center, is the third largest economy in Europe after Germany and France. Over the past two decades, the government has greatly reduced public ownership. Agriculture is intensive, highly mechanized, and efficient by European standards, producing about 60% of food needs with less than 2% of the labor force. The UK has large coal, natural gas, and oil resources, but its oil and natural gas reserves are declining and the UK became a net importer of energy in 2005. Services, particularly banking, insurance, and business services, are key drivers of British GDP growth. Manufacturing, meanwhile, has declined in importance but still accounts for about 10% of economic output. After emerging from recession in 1992, Britain's economy enjoyed the longest period of expansion on record during which time growth outpaced most of Western Europe. In 2008, however, the global financial crisis hit the economy particularly hard, due to the importance of its financial sector. Falling home prices, high consumer debt, and the global economic slowdown compounded Britain's economic problems, pushing the economy into recession in the latter half of 2008 and prompting the then BROWN (Labour) government to implement a number of measures to stimulate the economy and stabilize the financial markets; these included nationalizing parts of the banking system, temporarily cutting taxes, suspending public sector borrowing rules, and moving forward public spending on capital projects. Facing burgeoning public deficits and debt levels, in 2010 the CAMERON-led coalition government (between Conservatives and Liberal Democrats) initiated a five-year austerity program, which aimed to lower London's budget deficit from about 11% of GDP in 2010 to nearly 1% by 2015. In November 2011, Chancellor of the Exchequer George OSBORNE announced additional austerity measures through 2017 largely due to the eurozone debt crisis. The CAMERON government raised the value added tax from 17.5% to 20% in 2011. It has pledged to reduce the corporation tax rate to 21% by 2014. The Bank of England (BoE) implemented an asset purchase program of £375 billion (approximately $605 billion) as of December 2013. During times of economic crisis, the BoE coordinates interest rate moves with the European Central Bank, but Britain remains outside the European Economic and Monetary Union (EMU). In 2012, weak consumer spending and subdued business investment weighed on the economy, however, in 2013 GDP grew 1.4%, accelerating unexpectedly in the second half of the year because of greater consumer spending and a recovering housing market. The budget deficit is falling but remains high at nearly 7% and public debt has continued to increase.

GDP (purchasing power parity): $2.378 trillion (2013 est.)
country comparison to the world: 9
$2.345 trillion (2012 est.)
$2.341 trillion (2011 est.)
note: data are in 2013 US dollars

GDP (official exchange rate): $2.49 trillion (2013 est.)

GDP—real growth rate: 1.4% (2013 est.)
country comparison to the world: 161
0.2% (2012 est.)
1.1% (2011 est.)

GDP—per capita (PPP): $37,300 (2013 est.)
country comparison to the world: 34
$37,100 (2012 est.)
$37,300 (2011 est.)
note: data are in 2013 US dollars

Gross national saving: 10.5% of GDP (2013 est.)
country comparison to the world: 133
11% of GDP (2012 est.)
13.7% of GDP (2011 est.)

GDP—composition, by end use:
household consumption: 66.5%
government consumption: 21.4%
investment in fixed capital: 13.8%
investment in inventories: 0.4%
exports of goods and services: 31.1%
imports of goods and services: -33.2% (2013 est.)

GDP—composition, by sector of origin:
agriculture: 0.7%
industry: 20.5%
services: 78.9% (2013 est.)

Agriculture—products: cereals, oilseed, potatoes, vegetables; cattle, sheep, poultry; fish

Industries: machine tools, electric power equipment, automation equipment, railroad equipment, shipbuilding, aircraft, motor vehicles and parts, electronics and communications equipment, metals, chemicals, coal, petroleum, paper and paper products, food processing, textiles, clothing, other consumer goods

Industrial production growth rate: -0.3% (2013 est.)
country comparison to the world: 171

Labor force: 32.32 million (2013 est.)
country comparison to the world: 20

Labor force—by occupation: *agriculture:* 1.4%
industry: 18.2%
services: 80.4% (2006 est.)

Unemployment rate: 7.7% (2013 est.)
country comparison to the world: 84
8% (2012 est.)

Population below poverty line: 14% (2006 est.)

Household income or consumption by percentage share: *lowest 10%:* 2.1%
highest 10%: 28.5% (1999)

Distribution of family income—Gini index: 40 (FY08/09)
country comparison to the world: 60
34 (2005)

Budget: *revenues:* $1.007 trillion
expenditures: $1.19 trillion (2013 est.)

Taxes and other revenues: 40.4% of GDP (2013 est.)
country comparison to the world: 38

Budget surplus (+) or deficit (-):
-7.4% of GDP (2013 est.)
country comparison to the world: 189

Public debt: 91.1% of GDP (2013 est.)
country comparison to the world: 20
88.7% of GDP (2012 est.)
note: data cover general government debt, and include debt instruments issued (or owned) by government entities other than the treasury; the data include treasury debt held by foreign entities; the data include debt issued by subnational entities, as well as intra-governmental debt; intra-governmental debt consists of treasury borrowings from surpluses in the social funds, such as for retirement, medical care, and unemployment; debt instruments for the social funds are not sold at public auctions

Fiscal year: 6 April—5 April
Inflation rate (consumer prices):
2.7% (2013 est.)
country comparison to the world: 101
2.8% (2012 est.)

Central bank discount rate: 0.5% (31 December 2012 est.)
country comparison to the world: 137
0.5% (31 December 2011 est.)

Commercial bank prime lending rate: 4.4% (31 December 2013 est.)
country comparison to the world: 163
4.22% (31 December 2012 est.)

Stock of narrow money: $103.8 billion (31 December 2013 est.)
country comparison to the world: 34
$101.8 billion (31 December 2012 est.)

Stock of broad money: $3.363 trillion (31 December 2013 est.)
country comparison to the world: 6
$3.401 trillion (31 December 2012 est.)

Stock of domestic credit: $3.636 trillion (31 December 2013 est.)
country comparison to the world: 7
$3.756 trillion (31 December 2012 est.)

Market value of publicly traded shares: $3.019 trillion
country comparison to the world: 5
$2.903 trillion (31 December 2011)
$3.107 trillion (31 December 2010 est.)

Current account balance: -$93.6 billion (2013 est.)
country comparison to the world: 192
-$93.6 billion (2012 est.)

Exports: $475.7 billion (2013 est.)
country comparison to the world: 11
$473 billion (2012 est.)

Exports—commodities: manufactured goods, fuels, chemicals; food, beverages, tobacco

Exports—partners: Germany 11.3%, US 10.5%, Netherlands 8.8%, France 7.4%, Ireland 6.2%, Belgium 5.1% (2012)

Imports: $646 billion (2013 est.)
country comparison to the world: 6
$643.5 billion (2012 est.)

Imports—commodities: manufactured goods, machinery, fuels; foodstuffs

Imports—partners: Germany 12.6%, China 8%, Netherlands 7.5%, US 6.7%, France 5.4%, Belgium 4.4%, Norway 4% (2012)

Reserves of foreign exchange and gold: $105.1 billion (31 December 2012 est.)
country comparison to the world: 24
$94.54 billion (31 December 2011 est.)

Debt—external: $9.457 trillion (31 December 2012 est.)
country comparison to the world: 3
$9.961 trillion (31 December 2011)

Stock of direct foreign investment—at home:
$1.407 trillion (31 December 2013 est.)
country comparison to the world: 3
$1.321 trillion (31 December 2012 est.)

Stock of direct foreign investment—abroad:
$1.884 trillion (31 December 2013 est.)
country comparison to the world: 2
$1.808 trillion (31 December 2012 est.)

Exchange rates: British pounds (GBP) per US dollar—
0.6391 (2013 est.)
0.6307 (2012 est.)
0.6472 (2010 est.)
0.6175 (2009)
0.5302 (2008)

ENERGY

Electricity—production: 342.1 billion kWh (2011 est.)
country comparison to the world: 12

Electricity—consumption: 329.3 billion kWh (2010 est.)
country comparison to the world: 12

Electricity—exports: 1.747 billion kWh (2012 est.)
country comparison to the world: 44

Electricity—imports: 13.79 billion kWh (2012 est.)
country comparison to the world: 13

Electricity—installed generating capacity:
93.45 million kW (2010 est.)
country comparison to the world: 13

Electricity—from fossil fuels: 75.4% of total installed capacity (2010 est.)
country comparison to the world: 99

Electricity—from nuclear fuels: 11.6% of total installed capacity (2010 est.)
country comparison to the world: 15

Electricity—from hydroelectric plants: 1.8% of total installed capacity (2010 est.)
country comparison to the world: 138

Electricity—from other renewable sources: 8.3% of total installed capacity (2010 est.)

country comparison to the world: 28 Crude oil—production:
1.009 million bbl/day (2012 est.)
country comparison to the world: 21

Crude oil—exports: 740,000 bbl/day (2010 est.)
country comparison to the world: 19

Crude oil—imports: 965,400 bbl/day (2010 est.)
country comparison to the world: 13

Crude oil—proved reserves: 3.122 billion bbl (1 January 2013 es)
country comparison to the world: 30

Refined petroleum products—production: 1.549 million bbl/day (2010 est.)
country comparison to the world: 14

Refined petroleum products—consumption: 1.608 million bbl/day (2011 est.)
country comparison to the world: 15

Refined petroleum products—exports: 679,700 bbl/day (2010 est.)
country comparison to the world: 10

Refined petroleum products—imports: 680,400 bbl/day (2010 est.)
country comparison to the world: 10

Natural gas—production: 40.99 billion cu m (2012 est.)
country comparison to the world: 21

Natural gas—consumption: 82.21 billion cu m (2011 est.)
country comparison to the world: 9

Natural gas—exports: 11.97 billion cu m (2012 est.)
country comparison to the world: 22

Natural gas—imports: 49.1 billion cu m (2012 est.)
country comparison to the world: 7

Natural gas—proved reserves: 246 billion cu m (1 January 2013 es)
country comparison to the world: 44

Carbon dioxide emissions from consumption of energy: 496.8 million Mt (2011 est.)
country comparison to the world: 12

COMMUNICATIONS

Telephones—main lines in use: 33.01 million (2012)
country comparison to the world: 9

Telephones—mobile cellular: 82.109 million (2012)
country comparison to the world: 18

Telephone system: *general assessment:* technologically advanced domestic and international system
domestic: equal mix of buried cables, microwave radio relay, and fiber-optic systems
international: country code—44; numerous submarine cables provide links throughout Europe, Asia, Australia, the Middle East, and US; satellite earth stations—10 Intelsat (7 Atlantic Ocean and 3 Indian Ocean), 1 Inmarsat (Atlantic Ocean region), and 1 Eutelsat; at least 8 large international switching centers (2011)

Broadcast media: public service broadcaster, British Broadcasting Corporation (BBC), is the largest broadcasting corporation in the world; BBC operates multiple TV networks with regional and local TV service; a mixed system of public and commercial TV broadcasters along with satellite and cable systems provide access to hundreds of TV stations throughout the world; BBC operates multiple national, regional, and local radio networks with multiple transmission sites; a large number of commercial radio stations as well as satellite radio services are available (2008)

Internet country code: .uk

Internet hosts: 8.107 million (2012)
country comparison to the world: 15

Internet users: 51.444 million (2009)
country comparison to the world: 7

TRANSPORTATION

Airports: 460 (2013)
country comparison to the world: 1 8

Airports—with paved runways: *total:* 271
over 3,047 m: 7
2,438 to 3,047 m: 29
1,524 to 2,437 m: 89
914 to 1,523 m: 80
under 914 m: 66 (2013)

Airports—with unpaved runways: *total:* 189
1,524 to 2,437 m: 3
914 to 1,523 m: 26
under 914 m: 160 (2013)

Heliports: 9 (2013)

Pipelines: condensate 502 km; condensate/gas 9 km; gas 28,603 km; liquid petroleum gas 59 km; oil 5,256 km; oil/gas/water 175 km; refined products 4,919 km; water 255 km (2013)

Railways: *total:* 16,454 km
country comparison to the world: 17
broad gauge: 303 km 1.600-m gauge (in Northern Ireland)
standard gauge: 16,151 km 1.435-m gauge (5,248 km electrified) (2008)

Roadways: *total:* 394,428 km
country comparison to the world: 16
paved: 394,428 km (includes 3,519 km of expressways) (2009)

Waterways: 3,200 km (620 km used for commerce) (2009)
country comparison to the world: 32

Merchant marine: *total:* 504
country comparison to the world: 22
by type: bulk carrier 33, cargo 76, carrier 4, chemical tanker 58, container 178, liquefied gas 6, passenger 7, passenger/cargo 66, petroleum tanker 18, refrigerated cargo 2, roll on/roll off 31, vehicle carrier 25
foreign-owned: 271 (Australia 1, Bermuda 6, China 7, Denmark 43, France 39, Germany 59, Hong Kong 12, Ireland 1, Italy 3, Japan 5, Netherlands 1, Norway 32, Sweden 28, Taiwan 11, Tanzania 1, UAE 8, US 14)
registered in other countries: 308 (Algeria 15, Antigua and Barbuda 1, Argentina 2, Australia 5, Bahamas 18, Barbados 6, Belgium 2, Belize 4, Bermuda 14, Bolivia 1, Brunei 2, Cabo Verde 1, Cambodia 1, Cayman Islands 2, Comoros 1, Cook Islands 2, Cyprus 7, Georgia 5, Gibraltar 6, Greece 6, Honduras 1, Hong Kong 33, Indonesia 2, Italy 2, Liberia 22, Liberia 32, Luxembourg 5, Malta 21, Marshall Islands 12, Marshall Islands 3, Moldova 3, Nigeria 2, NZ 1, Panama 37, Panama 5, Saint Kitts and Nevis 1, Saint Vincent and the Grenadines 6, Sierra Leone 1, Singapore 6, Thailand 6, Tonga 1, US 4, unknown 1) (2010)

Ports and terminals: *major seaport(s):* Dover, Felixstowe, Immingham, Liverpool, London, Southampton, Teesport (England); Forth Ports (Scotland); Milford Haven (Wales)
oil terminals: Fawley Marine terminal, Liverpool Bay terminal (England); Braefoot Bay terminal, Finnart oil terminal, Hound Point terminal (Scotland)
container port(s)(TEUs): Felixstowe (3,248,592), London (1,932,000), Southampton (1,324,581)

MILITARY

Military branches: Army, Royal Navy (includes Royal Marines), Royal Air Force (2013)

Military service age and obligation: 16-33 years of age (officers 17-28) for voluntary military service (with parental consent under 18); no conscription; women serve in military services, but are excluded from ground combat positions and some naval postings; as of October 2009, women comprised 12.1% of officers and 9% of enlisted personnel in the regular forces; must be citizen of the UK, Commonwealth, or Republic of Ireland; reservists serve a minimum of 3 years, to age 45 or 55; 17 years 6 months of age for voluntary military service by Nepalese citizens in the Brigade of Gurkhas; 16-34 years of age for voluntary military service by Papua New Guinean citizens (2012)

Manpower available for military service:
males age 16-49: 14,856,917
females age 16-49: 14,307,316 (2010 est.)

Manpower fit for military service:
males age 16-49: 12,255,452
females age 16-49: 11,779,679 (2010 est.)

Manpower reaching militarily significant age annually: *male:* 383,989
female: 365,491 (2010 est.)

Military expenditures: 2.49% of GDP (2012)
country comparison to the world: 28
2.48% of GDP (2011)
2.49% of GDP (2010)

TRANSNATIONAL ISSUES

Disputes—international: in 2002, Gibraltar residents voted overwhelmingly by referendum to reject any "shared sovereignty" arrangement between the UK and Spain; the Government of Gibraltar insisted on equal participation in talks between the two countries; Spain disapproved of UK plans to grant Gibraltar greater autonomy; Mauritius and Seychelles claim the Chagos Archipelago (British Indian Ocean Territory); in 2001, the former inhabitants of the archipelago, evicted 1967 - 1973, were granted U.K. citizenship and the right of return, followed by Orders in Council in 2004 that banned rehabitation, a High Court ruling reversed the ban, a Court of Appeal refusal to hear the case, and a Law Lords' decision in 2008 denied the right of return; in addition, the United Kingdom created the world's largest marine protection area around the Chagos islands prohibiting the extraction of any natural resources therein; UK rejects sovereignty talks requested by

Argentina, which still claims the Falkland Islands (Islas Malvinas) and South Georgia and the South Sandwich Islands; territorial claim in Antarctica (British Antarctic Territory) overlaps Argentine claim and partially overlaps Chilean claim; Iceland, the UK, and Ireland dispute Denmark's claim that the Faroe Islands' continental shelf extends beyond 200 nm

Refugees and internally displaced persons: *refugees (country of origin):* 15,132 (Somalia); 12,155 (Zimbabwe); 11,428 (Iran); 9,901 (Eritrea); 9,842 (Afghanistan);
5,752 (Iraq) (2012)
stateless persons: 205 (2012)

Illicit drugs: producer of limited amounts of synthetic drugs and synthetic precursor chemicals; major consumer of Southwest Asian heroin, Latin American cocaine, and synthetic drugs; money-laundering center

UNITED STATES

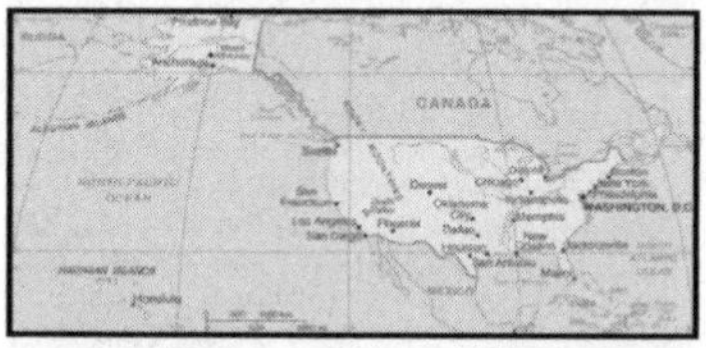

INTRODUCTION

Background: Britain's American colonies broke with the mother country in 1776 and were recognized as the new nation of the United States of America following the Treaty of Paris in 1783. During the 19th and 20th centuries, 37 new states were added to the original 13 as the nation expanded across the North American continent and acquired a number of overseas possessions. The two most traumatic experiences in the nation's history were the Civil War (1861-65), in which a northern Union of states defeated a secessionist Confederacy of 11 southern slave states, and the Great Depression of the 1930s, an economic downturn during which about a quarter of the labor force lost its jobs. Buoyed by victories in World Wars I and II and the end of the Cold War in 1991, the US remains the world's most powerful nation state. Since the end of World War II, the economy has achieved relatively steady growth, low unemployment and inflation, and rapid advances in technology.

GEOGRAPHY

Location: North America, bordering both the North Atlantic Ocean and the North Pacific Ocean, between Canada and Mexico

Geographic coordinates: 38 00 N, 97 00 W

Map references: North America

Area: *total:* 9,826,675 sq km
country comparison to the world: 3
land: 9,161,966 sq km
water: 664,709 sq km
note: includes only the 50 states and District of Columbia

Area—comparative: about half the size of Russia; about three-tenths the size of Africa; about half the size of South America (or slightly larger than Brazil); slightly larger than China; more than twice the size of the European Union

Land boundaries: *total:* 12,034 km
border countries: Canada 8,893 km (including 2,477 km with Alaska), Mexico 3,141 km
note: US Naval Base at Guantanamo Bay, Cuba is leased by the US and is part of Cuba; the base boundary is 28 km

Coastline: 19,924 km

Maritime claims: *territorial sea:* 12 nm
contiguous zone: 24 nm
exclusive economic zone: 200 nm
continental shelf: not specified

Climate: mostly temperate, but tropical in Hawaii and Florida, arctic in Alaska, semiarid in the great plains west of the Mississippi River, and arid in the Great Basin of the southwest; low winter temperatures in the northwest are ameliorated occasionally in January and February by warm chinook winds from the eastern slopes of the Rocky Mountains

Terrain: vast central plain, mountains in west, hills and low mountains in east; rugged mountains and broad river valleys in Alaska; rugged, volcanic topography in Hawaii

Elevation extremes: *lowest point:* Death Valley -86 m
highest point: Mount McKinley (Denali) 6,194 m (highest point in North America)
note: the peak of Mauna Kea (4,207 m above sea level) on the island of Hawaii rises about 10,200 m above the Pacific Ocean floor; by this measurement, it is the world's tallest mountain—higher than Mount Everest (8,850 m), which is recognized as the tallest mountain above sea level

Natural resources: coal, copper, lead, molybdenum, phosphates, rare earth elements, uranium, bauxite, gold, iron, mercury, nickel, potash, silver, tungsten, zinc, petroleum, natural gas, timber
note: the US has the world's largest coal reserves with 491 billion short tons accounting for 27% of the world's total

Land use: *arable land:* 16.29%
permanent crops: 0.26%
other: 83.44% (2011)

Irrigated land: 266,440 sq km (2007)

Total renewable water resources: 3,069 cu km (2011)

Freshwater withdrawal (domestic/industrial/agricultural): *total:* 478.4 cu km/yr (14%/46%/40%)
per capita: 1,583 cu m/yr (2005)

Natural hazards: tsunamis; volcanoes; earthquake activity around Pacific Basin; hurricanes along the Atlantic and Gulf of Mexico coasts; tornadoes in the Midwest and Southeast; mud slides in California; forest fires in the west; flooding; permafrost in northern Alaska, a major impediment to development
volcanism: volcanic activity in the Hawaiian Islands, Western Alaska, the Pacific Northwest, and in the Northern Mariana Islands; both Mauna Loa (elev. 4,170 m) in Hawaii and Mount Rainier (elev. 4,392 m) in Washington have been deemed Decade Volcanoes by the International Association of Volcanology and Chemistry of the Earth's Interior, worthy of study due to their explosive history and close proximity to human populations; Pavlof (elev. 2,519 m) is the most active volcano in Alaska's Aleutian Arc and poses a significant threat to air travel since the area constitutes a major flight path between North America and East Asia; St. Helens (elev. 2,549 m), famous for the devastating 1980 eruption, remains active today; numerous other historically active volcanoes exist, mostly concentrated in the
Aleutian arc and Hawaii; they include: in Alaska: Aniakchak, Augustine, Chiginagak, Fourpeaked, Iliamna, Katmai, Kupreanof, Martin, *Novarupta, Redoubt, Spurr, Wrangell; in Hawaii:* Trident, Ugashik-Peulik, Ukinrek Maars, Veniaminof; in the Northern Mariana Islands:
Anatahan; and in the Pacific Northwest: Mount Baker, Mount Hood

Environment—current issues: air pollution resulting in acid rain in both the US and Canada; large emitter of carbon dioxide from the burning of fossil fuels; water pollution from runoff of pesticides and fertilizers; limited natural freshwater resources in much of the western part of the country require careful management; desertification

Environment—international agreements: *party to:* Air Pollution, Air Pollution-Nitrogen Oxides, Antarctic-Environmental Protocol, Antarctic-Marine Living Resources, Antarctic Seals, Antarctic Treaty, Climate Change, Desertification, Endangered Species, Environmental Modification, Marine Dumping, Marine Life Conservation, Ozone Layer Protection, Ship Pollution, Tropical Timber 83, Tropical Timber 94, Wetlands, Whaling
signed, but not ratified: Air Pollution-Persistent Organic Pollutants, Air Pollution-Volatile Organic Compounds, Biodiversity, Climate Change-Kyoto Protocol, Hazardous Wastes

Geography—note: world's third-largest country by size (after Russia and Canada) and by population (after China and India); Mt. McKinley is highest point in North America and Death Valley the lowest point on the continent

PEOPLE AND SOCIETY

Nationality: *noun:* American(s)
adjective: American

Ethnic groups: white 79.96%, black 12.85%, Asian 4.43%, Amerindian and Alaska native 0.97%, native Hawaiian and other Pacific islander 0.18%, two or more races 1.61% (July 2007 estimate)
note: a separate listing for Hispanic is not included because the US Census Bureau considers Hispanic to mean persons of Spanish/Hispanic/Latino origin including those of Mexican, Cuban, Puerto Rican, Dominican Republic, Spanish, and Central or South American origin living in the US who may be of any race or ethnic group (white, black, Asian, etc.); about 15.1% of the total US population is Hispanic

Languages: English 82.1%, Spanish 10.7%, other Indo-European 3.8%, Asian and Pacific island 2.7%, other 0.7% (2000 census)
note: the US has no official national language, but English has acquired official status in 28 of the 50 states; Hawaiian is an official language in the state of Hawaii

Religions: Protestant 51.3%, Roman Catholic 23.9%, Mormon 1.7%, other Christian 1.6%, Jewish 1.7%, Buddhist 0.7%, Muslim 0.6%, other or unspecified 2.5%, unaffiliated 12.1%, none 4% (2007 est.)

Population: 318,892,103 (July 2014 est.)
country comparison to the world: 4

Age structure:
0-14 years: 19.4% (male 31,580,349/female 30,221,106)
15-24 years: 13.7% (male 22,436,057/female 21,321,861)
25-54 years: 39.9% (male 63,452,792/female 63,671,631)
55-64 years: 14.5% (male 19,309,019/female 20,720,284)
65 years and over: 13.9% (male 20,304,644/female 25,874,360) (2014 est.)

Dependency ratios:
total dependency ratio: 50.4 %
youth dependency ratio: 29.4 %
elderly dependency ratio: 21 %
potential support ratio: 4.8 (2013)

Median age: *total:* 37.6 years
male: 36.3 years
female: 39 years (2014 est.)

Population growth rate: 0.77% (2014 est.)
country comparison to the world: 143

Birth rate: 13.42 births/1,000 population (2014 est.)
country comparison to the world: 150

Death rate: 8.15 deaths/1,000 population (2014 est.)
country comparison to the world: 95

Net migration rate: 2.45 migrant(s)/1,000 population (2014 est.)
country comparison to the world: 40

Urbanization: *urban population:* 82% of total population (2010)
rate of urbanization: 1.2% annual rate of change (2010-15 est.)

Major urban areas—population: New York-Newark 19.3 million; Los Angeles-Long Beach-Santa Ana 12.675 million; Chicago 9.134 million; Miami 5.699 million; WASHINGTON, D.C. (capital) 4.421 million (2009)

Sex ratio: *at birth:* 1.05 male(s)/female
0-14 years: 1.05 male(s)/female
15-24 years: 1.05 male(s)/female
25-54 years: 1 male(s)/female
55-64 years: 0.97 male(s)/female
65 years and over: 0.77 male(s)/female
total population: 0.97 male(s)/female (2014 est.)

Mother's mean age at first birth: 25 (2006 est.)

Maternal mortality rate: 21 deaths/100,000 live births (2010)
country comparison to the world: 136

Infant mortality rate: total: 6.17 deaths/1,000 live births
country comparison to the world: 169
male: 6.75 deaths/1,000 live births
female: 5.56 deaths/1,000 live births (2014 est.)

Life expectancy at birth:
total population: 79.56 years
country comparison to the world: 42
male: 77.11 years
female: 81.94 years (2014 est.)

Total fertility rate: 2.01 children born/woman (2014 est.)
country comparison to the world: 123

Contraceptive prevalence rate: 76.4%
note: percent of women aged 15-44 (2010)

Health expenditures: 17.9% of GDP (2011)
country comparison to the world: 3

Physicians density: 2.42 physicians/1,000 population (2009)

Hospital bed density: 3 beds/1,000 population (2010)

Drinking water source:
improved:
urban: 99.8% of population
rural: 94% of population
total: 98.8% of population
unimproved:
urban: 0.2% of population
rural: 6% of population
total: 1.2% of population (2011 est.)

Sanitation facility access:
improved:
urban: 99.8% of population
rural: 98.6% of population
total: 99.6% of population
unimproved:
urban: 0.2% of population
rural: 1.4% of population
total: 0.4% of population (2011 est.)

HIV/AIDS—adult prevalence rate: 0.6% (2009 est.)
country comparison to the world: 64

HIV/AIDS—people living with HIV/AIDS: 1.2 million (2009 est.)
country comparison to the world: 9

HIV/AIDS—deaths: 17,000 (2012 est.)
country comparison to the world: 19

Obesity—adult prevalence rate: 33% (2008)
country comparison to the world: 18

Children under the age of 5 years underweight: 1.3% (2004)
country comparison to the world: 129

Education expenditures: 5.4% of GDP (2010)
country comparison to the world: 63

Literacy: *definition:* age 15 and over can read and write
total population: 99%
male: 99%
female: 99% (2003 est.)

School life expectancy (primary to tertiary education): *total:* 17 years
male: 16 years
female: 17 years (2011)

Unemployment, youth ages 15-24: *total:* 17.3%
country comparison to the world: 73
male: 18.7%
female: 15.7% (2011)

GOVERNMENT

Country name: *conventional long form:* United States of America
conventional short form: United States
abbreviation: US or USA

Government type: Constitution-based federal republic; strong democratic tradition

Capital: *name:* Washington, DC

geographic coordinates: 38 53 N, 77 02 W
time difference: UTC-5 (during Standard Time)
daylight saving time: +1hr, begins second Sunday in March; ends first Sunday in November
note: the 50 United States cover six time zones

Administrative divisions: 50 states and 1 district*; Alabama, Alaska, Arizona, Arkansas, California, Colorado, Connecticut, Delaware, District of Columbia*, Florida, Georgia, Hawaii, Idaho, Illinois, Indiana, Iowa, Kansas, Kentucky, Louisiana, Maine, Maryland, Massachusetts, Michigan, Minnesota, Mississippi, Missouri, Montana, Nebraska, Nevada, New Hampshire, New Jersey, New Mexico, New York, North Carolina, North Dakota, Ohio, Oklahoma, Oregon, Pennsylvania, Rhode Island, South Carolina, South Dakota, Tennessee, Texas, Utah, Vermont, Virginia, Washington, West Virginia, Wisconsin, Wyoming

Dependent areas: American Samoa, Baker Island, Guam, Howland Island, Jarvis Island, Johnston Atoll, Kingman Reef, Midway Islands, Navassa Island, Northern Mariana Islands, Palmyra Atoll, Puerto Rico, Virgin Islands, Wake Island
note: from 18 July 1947 until 1 October 1994, the US administered the Trust Territory of the Pacific Islands; it entered into a political
relationship with all four political entities: the Northern Mariana Islands is a commonwealth in political union with the US (effective 3 November 1986); the Republic of the Marshall Islands signed a Compact of Free Association with the US (effective 21 October 1986); the Federated States of Micronesia signed a Compact of Free Association with the US (effective 3 November 1986); Palau concluded a Compact of Free Association with the US (effective 1 October 1994)

Independence: 4 July 1776 (declared); 3 September 1783 (recognized by Great Britain)

National holiday: Independence Day, 4 July (1776)

Constitution: previous 1781 (Articles of Confederation and Perpetual Union); latest drafted July—September 1787, submitted to the Congress of the Confederation 20 September 1787, submitted for states' ratification 28 September 1787, ratification completed by nine states 21 June 1788, effective 4 March 1789; amended many times, last in 1992 (2013)

Legal system: common law system based on English common law at the federal level; state legal systems based on common law except Louisiana, which is based on Napoleonic civil code; judicial review of legislative acts

International law organization participation: withdrew acceptance of compulsory ICJ jurisdiction in 2005; withdrew acceptance of ICCt jurisdiction in 2002

Suffrage: 18 years of age; universal

Executive branch: *chief of state:* President Barack H. OBAMA (since 20 January 2009); Vice President Joseph R. BIDEN (since 20 January 2009); note—the president is both the chief of state and head of government
head of government: President Barack H. OBAMA (since 20 January 2009); Vice President Joseph R. BIDEN (since 20 January 2009)
cabinet: Cabinet appointed by the president with Senate approval (For more information visit the World Leaders website)
elections: president and vice president elected on the same ticket by a college of representatives who are elected directly from each state; president and vice president serve four-year terms (eligible for a second term); election last held 6 November 2012 (next to be held on 8 November 2016)
election results: Barack H. OBAMA reelected president; percent of popular vote—Barack H. OBAMA 50.6%, Mitt ROMNEY 47.9%, other 1.5%;

Legislative branch: bicameral Congress consists of the Senate (100 seats, 2 members elected from each state by popular vote to serve six-year terms; one-third elected every two years) and the House of Representatives (435 seats; members directly elected by popular vote to serve two-year terms)

elections: Senate—last held on 6 November 2012 (next to be held on 4 November 2014); House of Representatives—last held on 6 November 2012 (next to be held on 4 November 2014)
election results: Senate—percent of vote by party—NA; seats by party—Democratic Party 54, Republican Party 45, independent 1; House of Representatives—percent of vote by party—NA; seats by party—Democratic Party 201, Republican Party 234

Judicial branch: *highest court(s):* US Supreme Court (consists of 9 justices—the chief justice and 8 associate justices) note—The US court system consists of the federal court system and the state court systems; although each court system is responsible for hearing certain types of cases, neither is completely independent of the other, and the systems often interact
judge selection and term of office: president nominates, and with the advice and consent of the Senate, appoints Supreme Court justices; justices appointed for life
subordinate courts: Courts of Appeal (includes the US Court of Appeal for the Federal District and 12 regional appeals courts); 94 federal district courts in 50 states and territories

Political parties and leaders: Democratic Party [Debbie Wasserman SCHULTZ]; Green Party; Libertarian Party [Mark HINKLE]; Republican Party [Reince PRIEBUS]

Political pressure groups and leaders: environmentalists; business groups; labor unions; churches; ethnic groups; political action committees or PACs; health groups; education groups; civic groups; youth groups; transportation groups; agricultural groups; veterans groups; women's groups; reform lobbies

International organization participation: ADB (nonregional member), AfDB (nonregional member), ANZUS, APEC, Arctic Council, ARF, ASEAN (dialogue partner), Australia Group, BIS, BSEC (observer), CBSS (observer), CD, CE (observer), CERN (observer), CICA (observer), CP, EAPC, EAS, EBRD, EITI (implementing country), FAO, FATF, G-20, G-5, G-7, G-8, G-10, IADB, IAEA, IBRD, ICAO, ICC (national committees), ICRM, IDA, IEA, IFAD, IFC, IFRCS, IGAD (partners), IHO, ILO, IMF, IMO, IMSO, Interpol, IOC, IOM, ISO, ITSO, ITU, ITUC (NGOs), MIGA, MINUSTAH, MONUSCO, NAFTA, NATO, NEA, NSG, OAS, OECD, OPCW, OSCE, Paris Club, PCA, PIF (partner), SAARC (observer), SELEC (observer), SICA (observer), SPC, UN, UNCTAD, UNESCO, UNHCR, UNITAR, UNMIL, UNMISS, UNRWA, UNSC (permanent), UNTSO, UPU, WCO, WHO, WIPO, WMO, WTO, ZC

Flag description: 13 equal horizontal stripes of red (top and bottom) alternating with white; there is a blue rectangle in the upper hoist-side corner bearing 50 small, white, five-pointed stars arranged in nine offset horizontal rows of six stars (top and bottom) alternating with rows of five stars; the 50 stars represent the 50 states, the 13 stripes represent the 13 original colonies; the blue stands for loyalty, devotion, truth, justice, and friendship; red symbolizes courage, zeal, and fervency, while white denotes purity and rectitude of conduct; commonly referred to by its nickname of Old Glory
note: the design and colors have been the basis for a number of other flags, including Chile, Liberia, Malaysia, and Puerto Rico

National symbol(s): bald eagle

National anthem: *name:* "The Star-Spangled Banner"
lyrics/music: Francis Scott KEY/John Stafford SMITH
note: adopted 1931; during the War of 1812, after witnessing the successful American defense of Fort McHenry in Baltimore following British naval bombardment, Francis Scott KEY wrote the lyrics to what would become the national anthem; the lyrics were set to the tune of "The Anacreontic Song"; only the first verse is sung

ECONOMY

Economy—overview: The US has the largest and most technologically powerful economy in the world, with a per capita GDP of $49,800. In this market-oriented economy, private individuals and business firms make most of the decisions, and the federal and state governments buy needed goods and services predominantly in the private marketplace. US business firms enjoy greater flexibility than their counterparts in Western Europe and Japan in decisions to expand capital plant, to lay off surplus workers, and to develop new products. At the same time, they face higher barriers to enter their rivals' home markets than foreign firms face entering US markets. US firms are at or near the forefront in technological advances, especially in computers and in medical, aerospace, and military equipment; their advantage has narrowed since the end of World War II. The onrush of technology largely explains the gradual development of a "two-tier labor market" in which those at the bottom lack the education and the professional/technical skills of those at the top and, more and more, fail to get comparable pay raises, health insurance coverage, and other benefits. Since 1975, practically all the gains in household income have gone to the top 20% of households. Since 1996, dividends and capital gains have grown faster than wages or any other category of after-tax income. Imported oil accounts for nearly 55% of US consumption. Crude oil prices doubled between 2001 and 2006, the year home prices peaked; higher gasoline prices ate into consumers' budgets and many individuals fell behind in their mortgage payments. Oil prices climbed another 50% between 2006 and 2008, and bank foreclosures more than doubled in the same period. Besides dampening the housing market, soaring oil prices caused a drop in the value of the dollar and a deterioration in the US merchandise trade deficit, which peaked at $840 billion in 2008. The subprime mortgage crisis, falling home prices, investment bank failures, tight credit, and the global economic downturn pushed the United States into a recession by mid-2008. GDP contracted until the third quarter of 2009, making this the deepest and longest downturn since the Great Depression. To help stabilize financial markets, in October 2008 the US Congress established a $700 billion Troubled Asset Relief Program (TARP). The government used some of these funds to purchase equity in US banks and industrial corporations, much of which had been returned to the government by early 2011. In January 2009 the US Congress passed and President Barack OBAMA signed a bill providing an additional $787 billion fiscal stimulus to be used over 10 years—two-thirds on additional spending and one-third on tax cuts—to create jobs and to help the economy recover. In 2010 and 2011, the federal budget deficit reached nearly 9% of GDP. In 2012 the federal government reduced the growth of spending and the deficit shrank to 7.6% of GDP. Wars in Iraq and Afghanistan required major shifts in national resources from civilian to military purposes and contributed to the growth of the budget deficit and public debt. Through 2011, the direct costs of the wars totaled nearly $900 billion, according to US government figures. US revenues from taxes and other sources are lower, as a percentage of GDP, than those of most other countries. In March 2010, President OBAMA signed into law the Patient Protection and Affordable Care Act, a health insurance reform that was designed to extend coverage to an additional 32 million American citizens by 2016, through private health insurance for the general population and Medicaid for the impoverished. Total spending on health care—public plus private—rose from 9.0% of GDP in 1980 to 17.9% in 2010. In July 2010, the president signed the DODD-FRANK Wall Street Reform and Consumer Protection Act, a law designed to promote financial stability by protecting consumers from financial abuses, ending taxpayer bailouts of financial firms, dealing with troubled banks that are "too big to fail," and improving accountability and transparency in the financial system—in particular, by requiring certain financial derivatives to be traded in markets that are subject to government regulation and oversight. In December 2012, the Federal Reserve Board (Fed) announced plans to purchase $85 billion per month of mortgage-backed and Treasury securities in an effort to hold down long-term interest rates, and to keep short term rates near zero until unemployment drops below 6.5% or inflation rises above 2.5%. In late 2013, the Fed announced that it would begin scaling back long-term bond purchases to $75 billion per month in January 2014 and reduce them further as conditions warranted; the Fed, however, would keep short-term rates near zero so long as unemployment and inflation had not crossed the previously stated thresholds. Long-term problems include stagnation of wages for lower-income families, inadequate investment in deteriorating infrastructure, rapidly rising medical and pension costs of an aging population, energy shortages, and sizable current account and budget deficits.

GDP (purchasing power parity): $16.72 trillion (2013 est.)
country comparison to the world: 1
$16.47 trillion (2012 est.)
$16.02 trillion (2011 est.)
note: data are in 2013 US dollars

GDP (official exchange rate): $16.72 trillion (2013 est.)

GDP—real growth rate: 1.6% (2013 est.)
country comparison to the world: 156
2.8% (2012 est.)
1.8% (2011 est.)

GDP—per capita (PPP): $52,800 (2013 est.)
country comparison to the world: 13
$52,400 (2012 est.)
$51,400 (2011 est.)
note: data are in 2013 US dollars

Gross national saving: 13.5% of GDP (2013 est.)
country comparison to the world: 117
12.5% of GDP (2012 est.)
11.4% of GDP (2011 est.)

GDP—composition, by end use:
household consumption: 68.6%
government consumption: 18.6%
investment in fixed capital: 15.3%
investment in inventories: 0.4%
exports of goods and services: 13.4%
imports of goods and services: -16.3% (2013 est.)

GDP—composition, by sector of origin:
agriculture: 1.1%
industry: 19.5%
services: 79.4% (2013 est.)

Agriculture—products: wheat, corn, other grains, fruits, vegetables, cotton; beef, pork, poultry, dairy products; fish; forest products

Industries: highly diversified, world leading, high-technology innovator, second largest industrial output in world; petroleum, steel, motor vehicles, aerospace, telecommunications, chemicals, electronics, food processing, consumer goods, lumber, mining

Industrial production growth rate: 2.5% (2013 est.)
country comparison to the world: 116

Labor force: 155.4 million
country comparison to the world: 4
note: includes unemployed (2013 est.)

Labor force—by occupation: farming, forestry, and fishing: 0.7% manufacturing, extraction, transportation, and crafts: 20.3% managerial, professional, and technical: 37.3%
sales and office: 24.2%
other services: 17.6%
note: figures exclude the unemployed (2009)

Unemployment rate: 7.3% (2013 est.)
country comparison to the world: 79
8.1% (2012 est.)

Population below poverty line: 15.1% (2010 est.)

Household income or consumption by percentage share: *lowest* 10%: 2%
highest 10%: 30% (2007 est.)

Distribution of family income—Gini index: 45 (2007)
country comparison to the world: 41
40.8 (1997)

Budget: *revenues:* $2.849 trillion
expenditures: $3.517 trillion
note: for the US, revenues exclude social contributions of approximately $1.0 trillion; expenditures exclude social benefits of approximately $2.3 trillion (2013 est.)

Taxes and other revenues: 17% of GDP
country comparison to the world: 183
note: excludes contributions for social security and other programs; if social contributions were added, taxes and other revenues would amount to approximately 22% of GDP (2013 est.)

Budget surplus (+) or deficit (-):
-4% of GDP (2013 est.)
country comparison to the world: 148

Public debt: 71.8% of GDP (2013 est.)
country comparison to the world: 36
70% of GDP (2012 est.)
note: data cover only what the United States Treasury denotes as "Debt Held by the Public," which includes all debt instruments issued by the Treasury that are owned by non-US Government entities; the data include Treasury debt held by foreign entities; the data exclude debt issued by individual US states, as well as intra-governmental debt; intra-governmental debt consists of Treasury borrowings from surpluses in the trusts for Federal Social Security, Federal Employees, Hospital Insurance (Medicare and Medicaid), Disability and Unemployment, and several other smaller trusts; if data for intra-government debt were added, "Gross Debt" would increase by about one-third of GDP

Fiscal year: 1 October—30 September

Inflation rate (consumer prices): 1.5% (2013 est.)
country comparison to the world: 41
2.1% (2012 est.)

Central bank discount rate: 0.5% (31 December 2010)
country comparison to the world: 135
0.5% (31 December 2009)

Commercial bank prime lending rate: 3.3% (31 December 2013 est.)
country comparison to the world: 173
3.25% (31 December 2012 est.)

Stock of narrow money: $2.612 trillion (31 December 2013 est.)
country comparison to the world: 4
$2.311 trillion (31 December 2012 est.)

Stock of broad money: $12.99 trillion (31 December 2011 est.)
country comparison to the world: 3
$12.07 trillion (31 December 2010 est.)

Stock of domestic credit: $16.97 trillion (31 December 2013 est.)
country comparison to the world: 2
$16.17 trillion (31 December 2012 est.)

Market value of publicly traded shares: $18.67 trillion (31 December 2012 est.)
country comparison to the world: 1
$15.64 trillion (31 December 2011)
$17.14 trillion (31 December 2010 est.)

Current account balance: -$360.7 billion (2013 est.)
country comparison to the world: 193
-$440.4 billion (2012 est.)

Exports: $1.575 trillion (2013 est.)
country comparison to the world: 3
$1.561 trillion (2012 est.)

Exports—commodities: agricultural products (soybeans, fruit, corn) 9.2%, industrial supplies (organic chemicals) 26.8%, capital goods (transistors, aircraft, motor vehicle parts, computers, telecommunications equipment) 49.0%, consumer goods (automobiles, medicines) 15.0%

Exports—partners: Canada 18.9%, Mexico 14%, China 7.2%, Japan 4.5% (2012)

Imports: $2.273 trillion (2013 est.)
country comparison to the world: 2
$2.303 trillion (2012 est.)

Imports—commodities: agricultural products 4.9%, industrial supplies 32.9% (crude oil 8.2%), capital goods 30.4% (computers, telecommunications equipment, motor vehicle parts, office machines, electric power machinery), consumer goods 31.8% (automobiles, clothing, medicines, furniture, toys)

Imports—partners: China 19%, Canada 14.1%, Mexico 12%, Japan 6.4%, Germany 4.7% (2012)

Reserves of foreign exchange and gold: $150.2 billion (31 December 2012 est.)
country comparison to the world: 19
$148 billion (31 December 2011 est.)

Debt—external: $15.68 trillion (31 December 2012 est.)
country comparison to the world: 2
$15.51 trillion (31 December 2011)
note: approximately 4/5ths of US external debt is denominated in US dollars; foreign lenders have been willing to hold US dollar denominated debt instruments because they view the dollar as the world's reserve currency

Stock of direct foreign investment—at home: $2.815 trillion (31 December 2013 est.)
country comparison to the world: 1
$2.651 trillion (31 December 2012 est.)

Stock of direct foreign investment—abroad: $4.854 trillion (31 December 2013 est.)
country comparison to the world: 1
$4.453 trillion (31 December 2012 est.)

Exchange rates:
British pounds per US dollar: 0.6324 (2012 est.), 0.624 (2011 est.), 0.6472 (2010), 0.6175 (2009), 0.5302 (2008)
Canadian dollars per US dollar: (2013 est.), 1.001 (2012 est.), 0.9895 (2011 est), 1.0302 (2010 est.), 1.1431 (2009), 1.0364 (2008)
Chinese yuan per US dollar: (2012 est.), 6.311 (2012 est.), 6.4615 (20111 est.), 6.7703 (2010 est.), 6.8314 (2009), 6.9385 (2008)
euros per US dollar: 0.7838 (2012 est.), 0.7185 (2011 est.), 0.755 (2010 est.), 0.7198 (2009), 0.6827 (2008)
Japanese yen per US dollar: 79.42 (2012 est.), 79.81 (2011 est.), 87.78 (2010), 93.57 (2009), 103.58 (2008)

ENERGY

Electricity—production: 4.099 trillion kWh (2011 est.)
country comparison to the world: 2

Electricity—consumption: 3.886 trillion kWh (2010 est.)
country comparison to the world: 2

Electricity—exports: 12 billion kWh (2012 est.)
country comparison to the world: 19

Electricity—imports: 59.26 billion kWh (2012 est.)
country comparison to the world: 1

Electricity—installed generating capacity: 1.039 billion kW (2010 est.)
country comparison to the world: 2

Electricity—from fossil fuels: 75.3% of total installed capacity (2010 est.)
country comparison to the world: 100

Electricity—from nuclear fuels: 9.7% of total installed capacity (2010 est.)
country comparison to the world: 18

Electricity—from hydroelectric plants: 7.6% of total installed capacity (2010 est.)
country comparison to the world: 120

Electricity—from other renewable sources: 5.3% of total installed capacity (2010 est.)
country comparison to the world: 42

Crude oil—production: 11.11 million bbl/day (2012 est.)
country comparison to the world: 2

Crude oil—exports: 41,640 bbl/day (2010 est.)
country comparison to the world: 47

Crude oil—imports: 9.213 million bbl/day (2010 est.)
country comparison to the world: 2

Crude oil—proved reserves: 20.68 billion bbl (1 January 2013 es)
country comparison to the world: 13

Refined petroleum products—production: 18.45 million bbl/day (2010 est.)
country comparison to the world: 1

Refined petroleum products—consumption: 18.84 million bbl/day (2011 est.)
country comparison to the world: 1

Refined petroleum products—exports: 2.311 million bbl/day (2010 est.)
country comparison to the world: 2

Refined petroleum products—imports: 2.58 million bbl/day (2010 est.)
country comparison to the world: 2

Natural gas—production: 681.4 billion cu m (2012 est.)
country comparison to the world: 1

Natural gas—consumption: 689.9 billion cu m (2011 est.)
country comparison to the world: 1

Natural gas—exports: 45.84 billion cu m (2012 est.)
country comparison to the world: 8

Natural gas—imports: 88.77 billion cu m (2012 est.)
country comparison to the world: 3

Natural gas—proved reserves: 9.459 trillion cu m (1 January 2012 es)
country comparison to the world: 5

Carbon dioxide emissions from consumption of energy: 5.491 billion Mt (2011 est.)
country comparison to the world: 2

COMMUNICATIONS

Telephones—main lines in use: 139 million (2012)
country comparison to the world: 2

Telephones—mobile cellular: 310 million (2012)
country comparison to the world: 3

Telephone system: *general assessment:* a large, technologically advanced, multipurpose communications system
domestic: a large system of fiber-optic cable, microwave radio relay, coaxial cable, and domestic satellites carries every form of telephone traffic; a rapidly growing cellular system carries mobile telephone traffic throughout the country
international: country code—1; multiple ocean cable systems provide international connectivity; satellite earth stations—61 Intelsat (45 Atlantic Ocean and 16 Pacific Ocean), 5 Intersputnik (Atlantic Ocean region), and 4 Inmarsat (Pacific and Atlantic Ocean regions) (2011)

Broadcast media: 4 major terrestrial TV networks with affiliate stations throughout the country, plus cable and satellite networks, independent stations, and a limited public broadcasting sector that is largely supported by private grants; overall, thousands of TV stations broadcasting; multiple national radio networks with many affiliate stations; while most stations are commercial, National Public Radio (NPR) has a network of some 600 member stations; satellite radio available; overall, nearly 15,000 radio stations operating (2008)

Internet country code: .us

Internet hosts: 505 million (2012); note—the US Internet total host count includes the following top level domain host addresses: .us, .com, .edu, .gov, .mil, .net, and .org
country comparison to the world: 1

Internet users: 245 million (2009)
country comparison to the world: 2

TRANSPORTATION

Airports: 13,513 (2013)
country comparison to the world: 1

Airports—with paved runways: *total:* 5,054
over 3,047 m: 189
2,438 to 3,047 m: 235
1,524 to 2,437 m: 1,478
914 to 1,523 m: 2,249
under 914 m: 903 (2013)

Airports—with unpaved runways: *total:* 8,459
over 3,047 m: 1
2,438 to 3,047 m: 6
1,524 to 2,437 m: 140
914 to 1,523 m: 1,552
under 914 m: 6,760 (2013)

Heliports: 5,287 (2013)

Pipelines: natural gas 1,984,321 km; petroleum products 240,711 km (2013)

Railways: *total:* 224,792 km
country comparison to the world: 1
standard gauge: 224,792 km 1.435-m gauge (2007)

Roadways: *total:* 6,586,610 km
country comparison to the world: 1
paved: 4,304,715 km (includes 76,334 km of expressways)
unpaved: 2,281,895 km (2012)

Waterways: 41,009 km (19,312 km used for commerce; Saint Lawrence Seaway of 3,769 km, including the Saint Lawrence River of 3,058 km, is shared with Canada) (2012)
country comparison to the world: 5

Merchant marine: *total:* 393
country comparison to the world: 26
by type: barge carrier 6, bulk carrier 55, cargo 51, carrier 2, chemical tanker 30, container 84, passenger 18, passenger/cargo 56, petroleum tanker 35, refrigerated cargo 3, roll on/roll off 27, vehicle carrier 26
foreign-owned: 85 (Australia 1, Bermuda 5, Denmark 31, France 4, Germany 5, Malaysia 2, Norway 17, Singapore 16, UK 4)
registered in other countries: 794 (Antigua and Barbuda 7, Australia 2, Bahamas 109, Belgium 1, Bermuda 26, Canada 10, Cayman Islands 57, Comoros 2, Cyprus 5, Georgia 1, Greece 8, Honduras 1, Hong Kong 44, Indonesia 2, Ireland 2, Isle of Man 1, Italy 23, Liberia 53, Malta 34, Marshall Islands 200, Netherlands 16, Norway 10, Panama 90, Portugal 4, Saint Kitts and Nevis 1, Saint Vincent and the Grenadines 18, Singapore 36, South Korea 8, Togo 1, UK 14, Vanuatu 2, unknown 6) (2010)

Ports and terminals: *cargo ports (tonnage):* Baton Rouge, Corpus Christi, Hampton Roads, Houston, Long Beach, Los Angeles, New Orleans, New York, Plaquemines, Tampa, Texas City
container port(s) (TEUs): Hampton Roads (1,918,029), Houston (1,866,450), Long Beach (6,061,091), Los Angeles (7,940,511), New York/New Jersey (5,503,485), Oakland (2,342,504), Savannah (2,944,678), Seattle (2,033,535)(2011)
cruise departure ports (passengers): Miami (2,032,000), Port Everglades (1,277,000), Port Canaveral (1,189,000), Seattle (430,000), Long Beach (415,000) (2009)
oil terminals: LOOP terminal, Haymark terminal

MILITARY

Military branches: *United States Armed Forces:* US Army, US Navy (includes Marine Corps), US Air Force, US Coast Guard; note—Coast Guard administered in peacetime by the Department of Homeland Security, but in wartime reports to the Department of the Navy (2013)

Military service age and obligation: 18 years of age (17 years of age with parental consent) for male and female voluntary service; no conscription; maximum enlistment age 42 (Army), 27 (Air Force), 34 (Navy), 28 (Marines); service obligation 8 years, including 2-5 years active duty (Army), 2 years active (Navy), 4 years active (Air Force, Marines); DoD is eliminating prohibitions restricting women from assignments in units smaller than brigades or near combat units (2013)

Manpower available for military service:
males age 16-49: 73,270,043
females age 16-49: 71,941,969 (2010 est.)

Manpower fit for military service:
males age 16-49: 60,620,143
females age 16-49: 59,401,941 (2010 est.)

Manpower reaching militarily significant age annually: *male:* 2,161,727
female: 2,055,685 (2010 est.)

Military expenditures: 4.35% of GDP (2012)
country comparison to the world: 9
4.75% of GDP (2011)
4.35% of GDP (2010)

TRANSNATIONAL ISSUES

Disputes—international: the US has intensified domestic security measures and is collaborating closely with its neighbors, Canada and Mexico, to monitor and control legal and illegal personnel, transport, and commodities across the international borders; abundant rainfall in recent years along much of the Mexico-US border region has ameliorated periodically strained water-sharing arrangements; 1990 Maritime Boundary Agreement in the Bering Sea still awaits Russian Duma ratification; Canada and the United States dispute how to divide the Beaufort Sea and the status of the Northwest Passage but continue to work cooperatively to survey the Arctic continental shelf; The Bahamas and US have not been able to agree on a maritime boundary; US Naval Base at Guantanamo Bay is leased from Cuba and only mutual agreement or US abandonment of the area can terminate the lease; Haiti claims US-administered Navassa Island; US has made no territorial claim in Antarctica (but has reserved the right to do so) and does not recognize the claims of any other states; Marshall Islands claims Wake Island; Tokelau included American Samoa's Swains Island among the islands listed in its 2006 draft constitution

Refugees and internally displaced persons: *refugees (country of origin):* the US admitted 58,238 refugees during FY2012 including 15,070 (Bhutan); 14,160 (Burma); 12,163 (Iraq); 4,911 (Somalia); 1,948 (Cuba); 1,758 (Iran); 1,346 (Eritrea)

Illicit drugs: world's largest consumer of cocaine (shipped from Colombia through Mexico and the Caribbean), Colombian heroin, and Mexican heroin and marijuana; major consumer of ecstasy and Mexican methamphetamine; minor consumer of high-quality Southeast Asian heroin; illicit producer of cannabis, marijuana, depressants, stimulants, hallucinogens, and methamphetamine; money-laundering center

UNITED STATES PACIFIC ISLAND WILDLIFE REFUGES

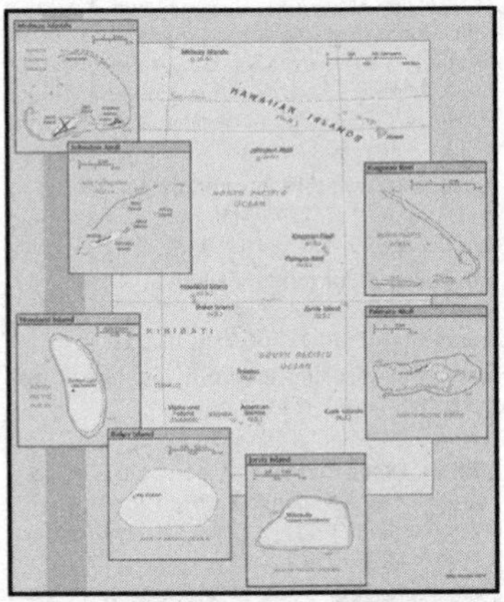

INTRODUCTION

Background: All of the following US Pacific island territories except Midway Atoll constitute the Pacific Remote Islands National Wildlife Refuge (NWR) Complex and as such are managed by the Fish and Wildlife Service of the US Department of the Interior. Midway Atoll NWR has been included in a Refuge Complex with the Hawaiian Islands NWR and also designated as part of Papahanaumokuakea Marine National Monument. These remote refuges are the most widespread collection of marineand terrestrial-life protected areas on the planet under a single country's jurisdiction. They sustain many endemic species including corals, fish, shellfish, marine mammals, seabirds, water birds, land birds, insects, and vegetation not found elsewhere.
Baker Island: The US took possession of the island in 1857. Its guano deposits were mined by US and British companies during the second half of the 19th century. In 1935, a short-lived attempt at colonization began on this island but was disrupted by World War II and thereafter abandoned. The island was established as a NWR in 1974.
Howland Island: Discovered by the US early in the 19th century, the uninhabited atoll was officially claimed by the US in 1857. Both US and British companies mined for guano deposits until about 1890. In 1935, a short-lived attempt at colonization began on this island, similar to the effort on nearby Baker Island, but was disrupted by World War II and thereafter abandoned. The famed American aviatrix Amelia EARHART disappeared while seeking out Howland Island as a refueling stop during her 1937 round-the-world flight; Earhart Light, a day beacon near the middle of the west coast, was named in her memory. The island was established as a NWR in 1974.
Jarvis Island: First discovered by the British in 1821, the uninhabited island was annexed by the US in 1858 but abandoned in 1879 after tons of guano had been removed. The UK annexed the island in 1889 but never carried out plans for further exploitation. The US occupied and reclaimed the island in 1935. It was abandoned in 1942 during World War II. The island was established as a NWR in 1974.
Johnston Atoll: Both the US and the Kingdom of Hawaii annexed Johnston Atoll in 1858, but it was the US that mined the guano deposits until the late 1880s. Johnston and Sand Islands were designated wildlife refuges in 1926. The US Navy took over the atoll in 1934. Subsequently, the US Air Force assumed control in 1948. The site was used for high-altitude nuclear tests in the 1950s and 1960s. Until late in 2000 the atoll was maintained as a storage and disposal site for chemical weapons. Munitions destruction, cleanup, and closure of the facility were completed by May 2005. The Fish and Wildlife Service and the US Air Force are currently discussing future management options; in the interim, Johnston Atoll and the three-mile Naval Defensive Sea around it remain under the jurisdiction and administrative control of the US Air Force.
Kingman Reef: The US annexed the reef in 1922. Its sheltered lagoon served as a way station for flying boats on Hawaii-to-American Samoa flights during the late 1930s. There are no terrestrial plants on the reef, which is frequently awash, but it does support abundant and diverse marine fauna and flora. In 2001, the waters surrounding the reef out to 12 nm were designated a US NWR.
Midway Islands: The US took formal possession of the islands in 1867. The laying of the trans-Pacific cable, which passed through the islands, brought the first residents in 1903. Between 1935 and 1947, Midway was used as a refueling stop for transpacific flights. The US naval victory over a Japanese fleet off Midway in 1942 was one of the turning points of World War II. The islands continued to serve as a naval station until closed in 1993. Today the islands are a NWR and are the site of the world's largest Laysan albatross colony.
Palmyra Atoll: The Kingdom of Hawaii claimed the atoll in 1862, and the US included it among the Hawaiian Islands when it annexed the archipelago in 1898. The Hawaii Statehood Act of 1959 did not include Palmyra Atoll, which is now partly privately owned by the Nature Conservancy with the rest owned by the Federal government and managed by the US Fish and Wildlife Service. These organizations are managing the atoll as a wildlife refuge. The lagoons and surrounding waters within the 12 nm US territorial seas were transferred to the US Fish and Wildlife Service and designated as a NWR in January 2001.

GEOGRAPHY

Location: Oceania
Baker Island: atoll in the North Pacific Ocean 1,830 nm (3,389 km) southwest of Honolulu, about half way between Hawaii and Australia
Howland Island: island in the North Pacific Ocean 1,815 nm (3,361 km) southwest of Honolulu, about half way between Hawaii and Australia
Jarvis Island: island in the South Pacific Ocean 1,305 nm (2,417 km) south of Honolulu, about half way between Hawaii and Cook Islands
Johnston Atoll: atoll in the North Pacific Ocean 717 nm (1,328 km) southwest of Honolulu, about one-third of the way from Hawaii to the Marshall Islands
Kingman Reef: reef in the North Pacific Ocean 930 nm (1,722 km) south of Honolulu, about half way between Hawaii and American Samoa
Midway Islands: atoll in the North Pacific Ocean 1,260 nm (2,334 km) northwest of Honolulu near the end of the Hawaiian Archipelago, about one-third of the way from Honolulu to Tokyo
Palmyra Atoll: atoll in the North Pacific Ocean 960 nm (1,778 km) south of Honolulu, about half way between Hawaii and American Samoa

Geographic coordinates: Baker Island: 0 13 N, 176 28 W
Howland Island: 0 48 N, 176 38 W
Jarvis Island: 0 23 S, 160 01 W
Johnston Atoll: 16 45 N, 169 31 W
Kingman Reef: 6 23 N, 162 25 W
Midway Islands: 28 12 N, 177 22 W
Palmyra Atoll: 5 53 N, 162 05 W

Map references: Oceania

Area: total—6,959.41 sq km; emergent land—22.41 sq km; submerged—6,937 sq km
country comparison to the world: 239
Baker Island: total—129.1 sq km; emergent land—2.1 sq km; submerged—127 sq km
Howland Island: total—138.6 sq km; emergent land—2.6 sq km; submerged—136 sq km
Jarvis Island: total—152 sq km; emergent land—5 sq km; submerged—147 sq km
Johnston Atoll: total—276.6 sq km; emergent land—2.6 sq km; submerged—274 sq km
Kingman Reef: total—1,958.01 sq km; emergent land—0.01 sq km; submerged—1,958 sq km
Midway Islands: total—2,355.2 sq km; emergent land—6.2 sq km; submerged—2,349 sq km
Palmyra Atoll: total—1,949.9 sq km; emergent land—3.9 sq km; submerged—1,946 sq km

Area—comparative: *Baker Island:* about two and a half times the size of The Mall in Washington, DC
Howland Island: about three times the size of The Mall in Washington, DC
Jarvis Island: about eight times the size of The Mall in Washington, DC
Johnston Atoll: about four and a half times the size of The Mall in Washington, DC
Kingman Reef: a little more than one and a half times the size of The Mall in Washington, DC
Midway Islands: about nine times the size of The Mall in Washington, DC
Palmyra Atoll: about 20 times the size of The Mall in Washington, DC

Land boundaries: none

Coastline: *Baker Island:* 4.8 km
Howland Island: 6.4 km
Jarvis Island: 8 km
Johnston Atoll: 34 km
Kingman Reef: 3 km
Midway Islands: 15 km
Palmyra Atoll: 14.5 km

Maritime claims: *territorial sea:* 12 nm
exclusive economic zone: 200 nm

Climate: Baker, Howland, and Jarvis Islands: equatorial; scant rainfall, constant wind, burning sun Johnston Atoll and Kingman Reef: tropical, but generally dry; consistent northeast trade winds with little seasonal temperature variation
Midway Islands: subtropical with cool, moist winters (December to February) and warm, dry summers (May to October); moderated by prevailing easterly winds; most of the 1,067 mm (42 in) of annual rainfall occurs during the winter
Palmyra Atoll: equatorial, hot; located within the low pressure area of the Intertropical Convergence Zone (ITCZ) where the northeast and southeast trade winds meet, it is extremely wet with between 4,000-5,000 mm (160-200 in) of rainfall each year

Terrain: low and nearly level sandy coral islands with narrow fringing reefs that have developed at the top of submerged volcanic mountains, which in most cases rise steeply from the ocean floor

Elevation extremes: *lowest point:* Pacific Ocean 0 m
highest point: Baker Island, unnamed location—8 m; Howland Island, unnamed location—3 m; Jarvis Island, unnamed location—7 m; Johnston Atoll, Sand Island—10 m; Kingman Reef, unnamed location—less than 2 m; Midway Islands, unnamed location—13 m; Palmyra Atoll, unnamed location—3 m

Natural resources: terrestrial and aquatic wildlife

Land use: *arable land:* 0%
permanent crops: 0%
other: 100% (2011)

Natural hazards: Baker, Howland, and Jarvis Islands: the narrow fringing reef surrounding the island poses a maritime hazard
Kingman Reef: wet or awash most of the time, maximum elevation of less than 2 m makes Kingman Reef a maritime hazard Midway Islands, Johnston, and Palmyra Atolls: NA

Environment—current issues: Baker, Howland, and Jarvis Islands, and Johnston Atoll: no natural freshwater resources
Kingman Reef: none
Midway Islands and Palmyra Atoll: NA

Geography—note: Baker, Howland, and Jarvis Islands: scattered vegetation consisting of grasses, prostrate vines, and low growing shrubs; primarily a nesting, roosting, and foraging habitat for seabirds, shorebirds, and marine wildlife; closed to the public
Johnston Atoll: Johnston Island and Sand Island are natural islands, which have been expanded by coral dredging; North Island (Akau) and East Island (Hikina) are manmade islands formed from coral dredging; the egg-shaped reef is 34 km in circumference; closed to the public
Kingman Reef: barren coral atoll with deep interior lagoon; closed to the public
Midway Islands: a coral atoll managed as a NWR and open to the public for wildlife-related recreation in the form of wildlife observation and photography
Palmyra Atoll: the high rainfall and resulting lush vegetation make the environment of this atoll unique among the US Pacific Island territories; supports a large undisturbed stand of Pisonia beach forest

PEOPLE AND SOCIETY

Population: no indigenous inhabitants
note: public entry is only by special-use permit from US Fish and Wildlife Service and generally restricted to scientists and educators; visited annually by US Fish and Wildlife Service
Johnston Atoll: in previous years, an average of 1,100 US military and civilian contractor personnel were present; as of May 2005, all US government personnel had left the island
Midway Islands: approximately 40 people make up the staff of US Fish and Wildlife Service and their services contractor living at the atoll
Palmyra Atoll: four to 20 Nature Conservancy, US Fish and Wildlife staff, and researchers

GOVERNMENT

Country name: *conventional long form:* none
conventional short form: Baker Island; Howland Island; Jarvis Island; Johnston Atoll; Kingman Reef; Midway Islands; Palmyra Atoll

Dependency status: unincorporated territories of the US; administered from Washington, DC by the Fish and Wildlife Service of the US Department of the Interior as part of the National Wildlife Refuge system
note on Palmyra Atoll: incorporated Territory of the US; partly privately owned and partly federally owned; administered from Washington, DC by the Fish and Wildlife Service of the US Department of the Interior; the Office of Insular Affairs of the US Department of the Interior continues to administer nine excluded areas comprising certain tidal and submerged lands within the 12 nm territorial sea or within the lagoon

Legal system: the laws of the US where applicable apply

Diplomatic representation from the US: none (territories of the US)

Flag description: the flag of the US is used

ECONOMY

Economy—overview: no economic activity

TRANSPORTATION

Airports: *Baker Island:* one abandoned World War II runway of 1,665 m covered with vegetation and unusable
Howland Island: airstrip constructed in 1937 for scheduled refueling stop on the round-the-world flight of Amelia EARHART and Fred NOONAN; the aviators left Lae, New Guinea, for Howland Island but were never seen again; the airstrip is no longer serviceable
Johnston Atoll: one closed and not maintained
Kingman Reef: lagoon was used as a halfway station between Hawaii and American Samoa by Pan American Airways for flying boats in 1937 and 1938
Midway Islands: 3—one operational (2,377 m paved); no fuel for sale except emergencies
Palmyra Atoll: 1—1,846 m unpaved runway; privately owned (2013)

Ports and terminals: *major seaport(s):* Baker, Howland, and Jarvis Islands, and Kingman Reef: none; offshore anchorage only
Johnston Atoll: Johnston Island
Midway Islands: Sand Island
Palmyra Atoll: West Lagoon

MILITARY

Military—note: defense is the responsibility of the US

TRANSNATIONAL ISSUES

Disputes—international: none

URUGUAY

INTRODUCTION

Background: Montevideo, founded by the Spanish in 1726 as a military stronghold, soon took advantage of its natural harbor to become an important commercial center. Claimed by Argentina but annexed by Brazil in 1821, Uruguay declared its independence four years later and secured its freedom in 1828 after a three-year struggle. The administrations of President Jose BATLLE in the early 20th century launched widespread political, social, and economic reforms that established a statist tradition. A violent Marxist urban guerrilla movement named the Tupamaros, launched in the late 1960s, led Uruguay's president to cede control of the government to the military in 1973. By yearend, the rebels had been crushed, but the military continued to expand its hold over the government. Civilian rule was not restored until 1985. In 2004, the left-of-center Frente Amplio Coalition won national elections that effectively ended 170 years of political control previously held by the Colorado and Blanco parties. Uruguay's political and labor conditions are among the freest on the continent.

GEOGRAPHY

Location: Southern South America, bordering the South Atlantic Ocean, between Argentina and Brazil

Geographic coordinates: 33 00 S, 56 00 W

Map references: South America

Area: *total:* 176,215 sq km
country comparison to the world: 91
land: 175,015 sq km
water: 1,200 sq km

Area—comparative: slightly smaller than the state of Washington

Land boundaries: *total:* 1,648 km
border countries: Argentina 580 km, Brazil 1,068 km

Coastline: 660 km

Maritime claims: *territorial sea:* 12 nm
contiguous zone: 24 nm
exclusive economic zone: 200 nm

continental shelf: 200 nm or edge of continental margin

Climate: warm temperate; freezing temperatures almost unknown

Terrain: mostly rolling plains and low hills; fertile coastal lowland

Elevation extremes: *lowest point:* Atlantic Ocean 0 m
highest point: Cerro Catedral 514 m

Natural resources: arable land, hydropower, minor minerals, fish

Land use: *arable land:* 10.25%
permanent crops: 0.22%
other: 89.52% (2011)

Irrigated land: 1,810 sq km (2003)

Total renewable water resources: 139 cu km (2011)

Freshwater withdrawal (domestic/industrial/agricultural): *total:* 3.66 cu km/yr (11%/2%/87%)
per capita: 1,101 cu m/yr (2000)

Natural hazards: seasonally high winds (the pampero is a chilly and occasional violent wind that blows north from the Argentine pampas), droughts, floods; because of the absence of mountains, which act as weather barriers, all locations are particularly vulnerable to rapid changes from weather fronts

Environment—current issues: water pollution from meat packing/tannery industry; inadequate solid/hazardous waste disposal

Environment—international agreements:
party to: Antarctic-Environmental Protocol, Antarctic-Marine Living Resources, Antarctic Treaty, Biodiversity, Climate Change, Climate Change-Kyoto Protocol, Desertification, Endangered Species, Environmental Modification, Hazardous Wastes, Law of the Sea, Ozone Layer Protection, Ship Pollution, Wetlands
signed, but not ratified: Marine Dumping, Marine Life Conservation

Geography—note: second-smallest South American country (after Suriname); most of the low-lying landscape (three-quarters of the country) is grassland, ideal for cattle and sheep raising

PEOPLE AND SOCIETY

Nationality: *noun:* Uruguayan(s)
adjective: Uruguayan

Ethnic groups: white 88%, mestizo 8%, black 4%, Amerindian (practically nonexistent)

Languages: Spanish (official), Portunol, Brazilero (Portuguese-Spanish mix on the Brazilian frontier)

Religions: Roman Catholic 47.1%, non-Catholic Christians 11.1%, nondenominational 23.2%, Jewish 0.3%, atheist or agnostic 17.2%, other 1.1% (2006)

Demographic profile: Uruguay rates high for most development indicators and is known for its secularism, liberal social laws, and well-developed social security, health, and educational systems. It is one of the few countries in Latin America and the Caribbean where the entire population has access to clean water. Uruguay's provision of free primary through university education has contributed to the country's high levels of literacy and educational attainment. However, the emigration of human capital has diminished the state's return on its investment in education. Remittances from the roughly 18% of Uruguayans abroad amount to less than 1 percent of national GDP. The emigration of young adults and a low birth rate are causing Uruguay's population to age rapidly. In the 1960s, Uruguayans for the first time emigrated en masse—primarily to Argentina and Brazil—because of economic decline and the onset of more than a decade of military dictatorship. Economic crises in the early 1980s and 2002 also triggered waves of emigration, but since 2002 more than 70% of Uruguayan emigrants have selected the US and Spain as destinations because of better job prospects. Uruguay had a tiny population upon its independence in 1828 and welcomed thousands of predominantly Italian and Spanish immigrants, but the country has not experienced large influxes of new arrivals since the aftermath of World War II. More recent immigrants include Peruvians and Arabs.

Population: 3,332,972 (July 2014 est.)
country comparison to the world: 135

Age structure:
0-14 years: 21% (male 356,851/female 344,576)
15-24 years: 16% (male 269,820/female 262,830)
25-54 years: 38.9% (male 639,766/female 658,257)
55-64 years: 13.9% (male 158,170/female 178,194)
65 years and over: 13.9% (male 185,132/female 279,376) (2014 est.)

Dependency ratios:
total dependency ratio: 56.2 %
youth dependency ratio: 34.1 %
elderly dependency ratio: 22 %
potential support ratio: 4.5 (2013)

Median age: *total:* 34.3 years
male: 32.6 years
female: 35.9 years (2014 est.)

Population growth rate: 0.26% (2014 est.)
country comparison to the world: 175

Birth rate: 13.18 births/1,000 population (2014 est.)
country comparison to the world: 152

Death rate: 9.48 deaths/1,000 population (2014 est.)
country comparison to the world: 57

Net migration rate: -1.08 migrant(s)/1,000 population (2014 est.)
country comparison to the world: 149

Urbanization: *urban population:* 92% of total population (2010)
rate of urbanization: 0.4% annual rate of change (2010-15 est.)

Major urban areas—population: MONTEVIDEO (capital) 1.633 million (2009)

Sex ratio: *at birth:* 1.04 male(s)/female
0-14 years: 1.04 male(s)/female
15-24 years: 1.03 male(s)/female
25-54 years: 0.97 male(s)/female
55-64 years: 0.93 male(s)/female
65 years and over: 0.66 male(s)/female
total population: 0.93 male(s)/female (2014 est.)

Maternal mortality rate: 29 deaths/100,000 live births (2010)
country comparison to the world: 124

Infant mortality rate: *total:* 8.97 deaths/1,000 live births
country comparison to the world: 149
male: 9.95 deaths/1,000 live births
female: 7.95 deaths/1,000 live births (2014 est.)

Life expectancy at birth:
total population: 76.81 years
country comparison to the world: 71
male: 73.67 years
female: 80.06 years (2014 est.)

Total fertility rate: 1.84 children born/woman (2014 est.)
country comparison to the world: 149

Contraceptive prevalence rate: 77%
note: percent of women aged 15-50 (2004)

Health expenditures: 8% of GDP (2011)
country comparison to the world: 61

Physicians density: 3.74 physicians/1,000 population (2008)

Hospital bed density: 3 beds/1,000 population (2011)

Drinking water source:
improved:
urban: 100% of population
rural: 97.6% of population
total: 99.8% of population
unimproved:
urban: 0% of population
rural: 2.4% of population
total: 0.2% of population (2011 est.)

Sanitation facility access:
improved:
urban: 99% of population
rural: 97.8% of population
total: 98.9% of population
unimproved:
urban: 1% of population
rural: 2.2% of population
total: 1.1% of population (2011 est.)

HIV/AIDS—adult prevalence rate: 0.7% (2012 est.)
country comparison to the world: 60

HIV/AIDS—people living with HIV/AIDS: 13,200 (2012 est.)
country comparison to the world: 95

HIV/AIDS—deaths: NA

Obesity—adult prevalence rate: 24.8% (2008)
country comparison to the world: 64

Children under the age of 5 years underweight: 4.5% (2011)
country comparison to the world: 94

Education expenditures: 4.5% of GDP (2011)
country comparison to the world: 92

Literacy: *definition:* age 15 and over can read and write
total population: 98.1%
male: 97.6%
female: 98.5% (2010 est.)

School life expectancy (primary to tertiary education): *total:* 16 years
male: 14 years
female: 17 years (2010)

Child labor—children ages 5-14:
total number: 51,879
percentage: 7 % (2006 est.)

Unemployment, youth ages 15-24: *total:* 18.5%
country comparison to the world: 66
male: 14.7%
female: 23.6% (2012)

GOVERNMENT

Country name: *conventional long form:* Oriental Republic of Uruguay
conventional short form: Uruguay
local long form: Republica Oriental del Uruguay
local short form: Uruguay
former: Banda Oriental, Cisplatine Province

Government type: constitutional republic

Capital: *name:* Montevideo

geographic coordinates: 34 51 S, 56 10 W
time difference: UTC-3 (2 hours ahead of Washington, DC during Standard Time)
daylight saving time: +1hr, begins first Sunday in October; ends second Sunday in March

Administrative divisions: 19 departments (departamentos, singular—departamento); Artigas, Canelones, Cerro Largo, Colonia, Durazno, Flores, Florida, Lavalleja, Maldonado, Montevideo, Paysandu, Rio Negro, Rivera, Rocha, Salto, San Jose, Soriano, Tacuarembo, Treinta y Tres

Independence: 25 August 1825 (from Brazil)

National holiday: Independence Day, 25 August (1825)

Constitution: several previous; latest approved by plebiscite 27 November 1966, effective 15 February 1967; amended several times, last in 2004 (2013)

Legal system: civil law system based on the Spanish civil code International law organization participation: accepts compulsory ICJ jurisdiction; accepts ICCt jurisdiction

Suffrage: 18 years of age; universal and compulsory

Executive branch: *chief of state:* President Jose "Pepe" MUJICA Cordano (since 1 March 2010); Vice President Danilo ASTORI Saragoza (since 1 March 2010); note—the president is both the chief of state and head of government
head of government: President Jose "Pepe" MUJICA Cordano (since 1 March 2010); Vice President Danilo ASTORI Saragoza (since 1 March 2010)
cabinet: Council of Ministers appointed by the president with parliamentary approval (For more information visit the World Leaders website)
elections: president and vice president elected on the same ticket by popular vote for five-year terms (may not serve consecutive terms); election last held on 29 November 2009 (next to be held in October 2014)
election results: Jose "Pepe" MUJICA Cordano elected president; percent of vote—Jose "Pepe" MUJICA Cordano 54.8%, Luis Alberto LACALLE 45.2%

Legislative branch: bicameral General Assembly or Asamblea General consists of Chamber of Senators or Camara de Senadores (30 seats; members elected by popular vote to serve five-year terms; vice president has one vote in the Senate) and Chamber of Representatives or Camara de Representantes (99 seats; members elected by popular vote to serve five-year terms)
elections: Chamber of Senators—last held on 25 October 2009 (next to be held in October 2014); Chamber of Representatives—last held on 25 October 2009 (next to be held in October 2014)
election results: Chamber of Senators—percent of vote by party—NA; seats by party—Frente Amplio 16, Blanco 9, Colorado Party 5; Chamber of Representatives—percent of vote by party—NA; seats by party—Frente Amplio 50, Blanco 30, Colorado Party 17, Independent Party 2

Judicial branch: *highest court(s):* Supreme Court of Justice (consists of 5 judges)
judge selection and term of office: judges nominated by the president and appointed in joint conference of the General Assembly; judges appointed for 10-year terms, with re-election after a lapse of 5 years following the previous term
subordinate courts: Courts of Appeal; District Courts (Juzgados Letrados); Peace Courts (Juzgados de Paz); Rural Courts (Juzgados Rurales)

Political parties and leaders: Broad Front (Frente Amplio)—formerly known as the Progressive Encounter/Broad Front Coalition or EP-FA [Monica XAVIER] (a broad governing coalition that includes Popular Participation Movement (MPP), New Space Party (Nuevo Espacio) [Rafael MICHELINI], Progressive Alliance (Alianza Progresista) [Rodolfo NIN NOVOA], Socialist Party [vacant], Communist Party [Eduardo LORIER], Uruguayan Assembly (Asamblea Uruguay) [Danilo ASTORI Saragoza], and Vertiente Artiguista [Enrique RUBIO]); Colorado Party (Vamos Uruguay) [Martha MONTANER]; Independent Party [Pablo MIERES]; National Party or Blanco [Luis Alberto HEBER]

Political pressure groups and leaders: Chamber of Commerce and Export of Agriproducts; Chamber of Industries (manufacturer's association); Exporters Union of Uruguay; National Chamber of Commerce and Services; PIT/CNT (powerful federation of Uruguayan Unions—umbrella labor organization); Rural Association of Uruguay (rancher's association); Uruguayan Network of Political Women
other: B'nai Brith; Catholic Church; students

International organization participation: CAN (associate), CD, CELAC, FAO, G-77, IADB, IAEA, IBRD, ICAO, ICC (national committees), ICRM, IDA, IFAD, IFC, IFRCS, IHO, ILO, IMF, IMO, Interpol, IOC, IOM, IPU, ISO, ITSO, ITU, LAES, LAIA, Mercosur, MIGA, MINURSO, MINUSTAH, MONUSCO, NAM (observer), OAS, OPANAL, OPCW, PCA, UN, UNASUR, UNCTAD, UNESCO, UNIDO, Union Latina, UNISFA, UNMOGIP, UNOCI, UNWTO, UPU, WCO, WHO, WIPO, WMO, WTO

Diplomatic representation in the US:
chief of mission: Ambassador Carlos Alberto GIANELLI Derois (since 11 September 2012)
chancery: 1913 I Street NW, Washington, DC 20006
telephone: [1] (202) 331-1313 through 1316
FAX: [1] (202) 331-8142
consulate(s) general: Chicago, Los Angeles, Miami, New York

Diplomatic representation from the US:
chief of mission: Ambassador Julissa REYNOSO (since 30 March 2012)
embassy: Lauro Muller 1776, Montevideo 11200
mailing address: APO AA 34035
telephone: [598] (2) 1770-2000
FAX: [598] (2) 1770-2128

Flag description: nine equal horizontal stripes of white (top and bottom) alternating with blue; a white square in the upper hoist-side corner with a yellow sun bearing a human face known as the Sun of May with 16 rays that alternate between triangular and wavy; the stripes represent the nine original departments of Uruguay; the sun symbol evokes the legend of the sun breaking through the clouds on 25 May 1810 as independence was first declared from Spain (Uruguay subsequently won its independence from Brazil)
note: the banner was inspired by the national colors of Argentina and by the design of the US flag

National symbol(s): Sun of May (a sun-with-face symbol)

National anthem: *name:* "Himno Nacional" (National Anthem of Uruguay)
lyrics/music: Francisco Esteban ACUNA de Figueroa/Francisco Jose DEBALI
note: adopted 1848; the anthem is also known as "Orientales, la Patria o la tumba!" ("Uruguayans, the Fatherland or Death!"); it is the world's longest national anthem in terms of music (105 bars; almost five minutes); generally only the first verse and chorus are sung

ECONOMY

Economy—overview: Uruguay has a free market economy characterized by an export-oriented agricultural sector, a well-educated work force, and high levels of social spending. Following financial difficulties in the late 1990s and early 2000s, economic growth for Uruguay averaged 8% annually during the period 2004-08. The 2008-09 global financial crisis put a brake on Uruguay's vigorous growth, which decelerated to 2.6% in 2009. Nevertheless, the country managed to avoid a recession and keep positive growth rates, mainly through higher public expenditure and investment, and GDP growth reached 8.9% in 2010 but slowed in 2012-13, the result of a renewed slowdown in the global economy and in Uruguay's main trade partners and Common Market of the South (Mercosur) counterparts, Argentina and Brazil. Uruguay has sought to expand trade within Mercosur and with non-Mercosur members. Uruguay's total merchandise trade with Mercosur since 2006 has increased by nearly 70% to more than $5 billion while its total trade with the world has almost doubled to roughly $23 billion in 2013.

GDP (purchasing power parity): $56.27 billion (2013 est.)
country comparison to the world: 94
$54.37 billion (2012 est.)
$52.31 billion (2011 est.)
note: data are in 2013 US dollars

GDP (official exchange rate): $57.11 billion (2013 est.)

GDP—real growth rate: 3.5% (2013 est.)
country comparison to the world: 99
3.9% (2012 est.)
6.5% (2011 est.)

GDP—per capita (PPP): $16,600 (2013 est.)
country comparison to the world: 80
$16,100 (2012 est.)
$15,500 (2011 est.)
note: data are in 2013 US dollars

Gross national saving: 17.3% of GDP (2013 est.)
country comparison to the world: 96
15.8% of GDP (2012 est.)
16.4% of GDP (2011 est.)

GDP—composition, by end use:
household consumption: 68.9%
government consumption: 13.6%
investment in fixed capital: 23.1%
investment in inventories: -0.8%
exports of goods and services: 25.8%
imports of goods and services: -30.5% (2013 est.)

GDP—composition, by sector of origin:
agriculture: 7.5%
industry: 21.5%
services: 71% (2013 est.)

Agriculture—products: soybeans, rice, wheat; beef, dairy products; fish; lumber, cellulose

Industries: food processing, electrical machinery, transportation equipment, petroleum products, textiles, chemicals, beverages

Industrial production growth rate: 6.6% (2013 est.)
country comparison to the world: 38

Labor force: 1.7 million (2013 est.)
country comparison to the world: 126

Labor force—by occupation: *agriculture:* 13%
industry: 14%
services: 73% (2010 est.)

Unemployment rate: 6.5% (2013 est.)
country comparison to the world: 67
6% (2012 est.)

Population below poverty line: 18.6% (2010 est.)

Household income or consumption by percentage share: *lowest 10%:* 1.9%
highest 10%: 34.4% (2010 est.)

Distribution of family income—Gini index: 45.3 (2010)
country comparison to the world: 40
44.8 (1999)

Budget: *revenues:* $17.14 billion
expenditures: $18.62 billion (2013 est.)

Taxes and other revenues: 30% of GDP (2013 est.)
country comparison to the world: 92

Budget surplus (+) or deficit (-):
-2.6% of GDP (2013 est.)
country comparison to the world: 108

Public debt: 62.8% of GDP (2013 est.)
country comparison to the world: 43
59.4% of GDP (2012 est.)
note: data cover general government debt, and include debt instruments issued (or owned) by government entities other than the treasury; the data include treasury debt held by foreign entities; the data include debt issued by subnational entities, as well as intra-governmental debt; intra-governmental debt consists of treasury borrowings from surpluses in the social funds, such as for retirement, medical care, and unemployment; debt instruments for the social funds are not sold at public auctions.

Fiscal year: calendar year

Inflation rate (consumer prices): 8.3% (2013 est.)
country comparison to the world: 196
8.1% (2012 est.)

Central bank discount rate: 9% (31 December 2012)
country comparison to the world: 29
8.75% (31 December 2011)
note: Uruguay's central bank uses the benchmark interest rate, rather than the discount rate, to conduct monetary policy; the rates shown here are the benchmark rates

Commercial bank prime lending rate: 11.3% (31 December 2013 est.)
country comparison to the world: 76
11.2% (31 December 2012 est.)

Stock of narrow money: $5.312 billion (31 December 2013 est.)
country comparison to the world: 98
$5.32 billion (31 December 2012 est.)

Stock of broad money: $8.689 billion (31 December 2013 est.)
country comparison to the world: 108
$8.648 billion (31 December 2012 est.)

Stock of domestic credit: $17.66 billion (31 December 2013 est.)
country comparison to the world: 85
$16.86 billion (31 December 2012 est.)

Market value of publicly traded shares: $175.4 million (31 December 2012 est.)
country comparison to the world: 116
$174.6 million (31 December 2011)
$156.9 million (31 December 2010 est.)

Current account balance: -$2.721 billion (2013 est.)
country comparison to the world: 156
-$2.69 billion (2012 est.)

Exports: $10.5 billion (2013 est.)
country comparison to the world: 92
$9.89 billion (2012 est.)

Exports—commodities: beef, soybeans, cellulose, rice, wheat, wood, dairy products; wool

Exports—partners: Brazil 18.6%, China 17.9%, Argentina 6.2%, Germany 4.3% (2012)

Imports: $12.5 billion (2013 est.)
country comparison to the world: 91
$12.26 billion (2012 est.)

Imports—commodities: refined oil, crude oil, passenger and other transportation vehicles, vehicle parts, cellular phones

Imports—partners: China 16.4%, Brazil 14.9%, Argentina 14.6%, US 9.1%, Paraguay 7.3% (2012)

Reserves of foreign exchange and gold: $16.32 billion (31 December 2013 est.)
country comparison to the world: 66
$13.6 billion (31 December 2012 est.)

Debt—external: $17.61 billion (31 December 2013 est.)
country comparison to the world: 84
$16.02 billion (31 December 2012 est.)

Stock of direct foreign investment—at home: $20.69 billion (31 December 2013 est.)
country comparison to the world: 72
$17.76 billion (31 December 2012 est.)

Stock of direct foreign investment—abroad: $422 million (31 December 2013 est.)
country comparison to the world: 81
$357 million (31 December 2012 est.)

Exchange rates: Uruguayan pesos (UYU) per US dollar—
20.58 (2013 est.)
20.311 (2012 est.)
20.059 (2010 est.)
22.568 (2009)
20.936 (2008)

ENERGY

Electricity—production: 9.5 billion kWh (2011 est.)
country comparison to the world: 95

Electricity—consumption: 7.96 billion kWh (2011 est.)
country comparison to the world: 94

Electricity—exports: 19 million kWh (2011 est.)
country comparison to the world: 89

Electricity—imports: 477 million kWh (2011 est.)
country comparison to the world: 80

Electricity—installed generating capacity: 2.588 million kW (2010 est.)
country comparison to the world: 93

Electricity—from fossil fuels: 39.8% of total installed capacity (2010 est.)
country comparison to the world: 170

Electricity—from nuclear fuels: 0% of total installed capacity (2010 est.)
country comparison to the world: 196

Electricity—from hydroelectric plants: 59.4% of total installed capacity (2010 est.)
country comparison to the world: 34

Electricity—from other renewable sources: 0.8% of total installed capacity (2010 est.)
country comparison to the world: 83

Crude oil—production: 1,183 bbl/day (2012 est.)
country comparison to the world: 107

Crude oil—exports: 0 bbl/day (2010 est.)
country comparison to the world: 199

Crude oil—imports: 38,680 bbl/day (2010 est.)
country comparison to the world: 59

Crude oil—proved reserves: 0 bbl (1 January 2009 es)
country comparison to the world: 201

Refined petroleum products—production: 43,440 bbl/day (2010 est.)
country comparison to the world: 84

Refined petroleum products—consumption: 51,100 bbl/day (2011 est.)
country comparison to the world: 98

Refined petroleum products—exports: 4,656 bbl/day (2010 est.)
country comparison to the world: 92

Refined petroleum products—imports: 16,420 bbl/day (2010 est.)
country comparison to the world: 112

Natural gas—production: 0 cu m (2011 est.)
country comparison to the world: 203

Natural gas—consumption: 80 million cu m (2010 est.)
country comparison to the world: 108

Natural gas—exports: 0 cu m (2011 est.)
country comparison to the world: 200

Natural gas—imports: 80 million cu m (2011 est.)
country comparison to the world: 74

Natural gas—proved reserves: 0 cu m (1 January 2013 es)
country comparison to the world: 202

Carbon dioxide emissions from consumption of energy: 8.326 million Mt (2011 est.)
country comparison to the world: 107

COMMUNICATIONS

Telephones—main lines in use: 1.01 million (2012)
country comparison to the world: 76

Telephones—mobile cellular: 5 million (2012)
country comparison to the world: 111

Telephone system:
general assessment: fully digitalized
domestic: most modern facilities concentrated in Montevideo; nationwide microwave radio relay network; overall fixed-line and mobile-cellular teledensity has reached 170 telephones per 100 persons
international: country code—598; the UNISOR submarine cable system provides direct connectivity to Brazil and Argentina; satellite earth stations—2 Intelsat (Atlantic Ocean) (2011)

Broadcast media: mixture of privately owned and state-run broadcast media; more than 100 commercial radio stations and about 20 TV channels; cable TV is available; many community radio and TV stations; adopted the hybrid Japanese/Brazilian HDTV standard (ISDB-T) in December 2010 (2010)

Internet country code: .uy

Internet hosts: 1.036 million (2012)
country comparison to the world: 45

Internet users: 1.405 million (2009)
country comparison to the world: 86

TRANSPORTATION

Airports: 133 (2013)

country comparison to the world: 4 3
Airports—with paved runways: *total:* 1 1
over 3,047 m: 1
1,524 to 2,437 m: 4
914 to 1,523 m: 4
under 914 m: 2 (2013)
Airports—with unpaved runways: *total:* 122
1,524 to 2,437 m: 3
914 to 1,523 m: 40
under 914 m: 79 (2013)
Pipelines: gas 257 km; oil 160 km (2013)
Railways: *total:* 1,641 km
country comparison to the world: 77
standard gauge: 1,641 km 1.435-m gauge (1,200 km operational) (2010)
Roadways: *total:* 77,732 km
country comparison to the world: 62
paved: 7,743 km
unpaved: 69,989 km (2010)
Waterways: 1,600 km (2011)
country comparison to the world: 50
Merchant marine: *total:* 1 6
country comparison to the world: 100
by type: bulk carrier 1, cargo 2, chemical tanker 3, passenger/cargo 6, petroleum tanker 3, roll on/roll off 1
foreign-owned: 8 (Argentina 1, Denmark 1, Greece 1, Spain 5)
registered in other countries: 1 (Liberia 1) (2010)
Ports and terminals: *major seaport(s):* Montevideo

MILITARY

Military branches: Uruguayan Armed Forces: Uruguayan National Army (Ejercito Nacional Uruguaya, ENU), Uruguayan National Navy (Armada Nacional del Uruguay; includes naval air arm, Naval Rifle Corps (Cuerpo de Fusileros Navales, Fusna), Maritime Prefecture in wartime), Uruguayan Air Force (Fuerza Aerea Uruguaya, FAU) (2012)
Military service age and obligation: 18-30 years of age (18-22 years of age for navy) for male or female voluntary military service; up to 40 years of age for specialists; enlistment is voluntary in peacetime, but the government has the authority to conscript in emergencies; minimum 6-year education (2013)
Manpower available for military service:
males age 16-49: 771,159
females age 16-49: 780,932 (2010 est.)
Manpower fit for military service:
males age 16-49: 649,025
females age 16-49: 654,903 (2010 est.)
Manpower reaching militarily significant age annually: *male:* 27,564
female: 26,811 (2010 est.)
Military expenditures: 1.95% of GDP (2012)
country comparison to the world: 43
1.94% of GDP (2011)
1.95% of GDP (2010)

TRANSNATIONAL ISSUES

Disputes—international: in 2010, the ICJ ruled in favor of Uruguay's operation of two paper mills on the Uruguay River, which forms the border with Argentina; the two countries formed a joint pollution monitoring regime; uncontested boundary dispute between Brazil and Uruguay over Braziliera/Brasiliera Island in the Quarai/Cuareim River leaves the tripoint with Argentina in question; smuggling of firearms and narcotics continues to be an issue along the Uruguay-Brazil border
Trafficking in persons: *current situation:* Uruguay is a source country for women and children subjected to sex trafficking and, to a lesser extent, a destination country for men, women, and children exploited in forced labor; most victims are women and girls exploited in sex trafficking; some Uruguayan women lured by fraudulent employment offers in Spain, Italy, and Argentina are forced into prostitution; foreign workers in domestic service and agriculture are vulnerable to forced labor in Uruguay; some human trafficking cases are reportedly linked to crime rings
tier rating: Tier 2 Watch List—Uruguay does not fully comply with the minimum standards for the elimination of trafficking; however, it is making significant efforts to do so; the government investigated and prosecuted several trafficking cases during 2012 but reported no convictions; authorities have increased funding and staffing for the national women's institute unit that is focused on sex trafficking and domestic violence, but specialized services remain inadequate and victim care services outside the capital are uneven; officials lack formal procedures for identifying trafficking victims (2013)
Illicit drugs: small-scale transit country for drugs mainly bound for Europe, often through sea-borne containers; law enforcement corruption; money laundering because of strict banking secrecy laws; weak border control along Brazilian frontier; increasing consumption of cocaine base and synthetic drugs

UZBEKISTAN

INTRODUCTION

Background: Russia conquered the territory of present-day Uzbekistan in the late 19th century. Stiff resistance to the Red Army after the Bolshevik Revolution was eventually suppressed and a socialist republic established in 1924. During the Soviet era, intensive production of "white gold" (cotton) and grain led to overuse of agrochemicals and the depletion of water supplies, which have left the land degraded and the Aral Sea and certain rivers half dry. Independent since 1991, the country has lessened its dependence on the cotton monoculture by diversifying agricultural production while developing its mineral and petroleum export capacity and increasing its manufacturing base. However, longserving septuagenarian President Islom KARIMOV, who rose through the ranks of the Soviet-era State Planning Committee (Gosplan), remains wedded to the concepts of a command economy, creating a challenging environment for foreign investment. Current concerns include post-KARIMOV succession, terrorism by Islamic militants, economic stagnation, and the curtailment of human rights and democratization.

GEOGRAPHY

Location: Central Asia, north of Turkmenistan, south of Kazakhstan
Geographic coordinates: 41 00 N, 64 00 E
Map references: Asia
Area: *total:* 447,400 sq km
country comparison to the world: 57
land: 425,400 sq km
water: 22,000 sq km
Area—comparative: slightly larger than California
Land boundaries: *total:* 6,221 km
border countries: Afghanistan 137 km, Kazakhstan 2,203 km, Kyrgyzstan 1,099 km, Tajikistan 1,161 km, Turkmenistan 1,621 km
Coastline: 0 km (doubly landlocked); note—Uzbekistan includes the southern portion of the Aral Sea with a 420 km shoreline
Maritime claims: none (doubly landlocked)
Climate: mostly midlatitude desert, long, hot summers, mild winters; semiarid grassland in east
Terrain: mostly flat-to-rolling sandy desert with dunes; broad, flat intensely irrigated river valleys along course of Amu Darya, Syr Darya (Sirdaryo), and Zarafshon; Fergana Valley in east surrounded by mountainous Tajikistan and Kyrgyzstan; shrinking Aral Sea in west
Elevation extremes:
lowest point: Sariqamish Kuli -12 m
highest point: Adelunga Toghi 4,301 m
Natural resources: natural gas, petroleum, coal, gold, uranium, silver, copper, lead and zinc, tungsten, molybdenum
Land use: *arable land:* 9.61%
permanent crops: 0.8%
other: 89.58% (2011)
Irrigated land: 41,980 sq km (2005)
Total renewable water resources: 48.87 cu km (2011)
Freshwater withdrawal (domestic/industrial/agricultural): *total:* 56 cu km/yr (7%/3%/90%)
per capita: 2,113 cu m/yr (2005)
Natural hazards: NA
Environment—current issues: shrinkage of the Aral Sea has resulted in growing concentrations of chemical pesticides and natural salts; these substances are then blown from the increasingly exposed lake bed and contribute to desertification and respiratory health problems; water pollution from industrial wastes and the heavy use of fertilizers and pesticides is the cause of many human health disorders; increasing soil salination; soil contamination from buried nuclear processing and

agricultural chemicals, including DDT Environment—international agreements:
party to: Biodiversity, Climate Change, Climate Change-Kyoto Protocol, Desertification, Endangered Species, Environmental Modification, Hazardous Wastes, Ozone Layer Protection, Wetlands
signed, but not ratified: none of the selected agreements

Geography—note: along with Liechtenstein, one of the only two doubly landlocked countries in the world

PEOPLE AND SOCIETY

Nationality: *noun:* Uzbekistani
adjective: Uzbekistani

Ethnic groups: Uzbek 80%, Russian 5.5%, Tajik 5%, Kazakh 3%, Karakalpak 2.5%, Tatar 1.5%, other 2.5% (1996 est.)

Languages: Uzbek (official) 74.3%, Russian 14.2%, Tajik 4.4%, other 7.1%

Religions: Muslim 88% (mostly Sunni), Eastern Orthodox 9%, other 3%

Population: 28,929,716 (July 2014 est.)
country comparison to the world: 45

Age structure:
0-14 years: 24.9% (male 3,693,838/female 3,514,734)
15-24 years: 20.5% (male 3,008,779/female 2,934,534)
25-54 years: 43% (male 6,178,921/female 6,255,715)
55-64 years: 4.8% (male 926,129/female 1,036,576)
65 years and over: 4.7% (male 588,881/female 791,609) (2014 est.)

Dependency ratios:
total dependency ratio: 49 %
youth dependency ratio: 42.6 %
elderly dependency ratio: 6.4 %
potential support ratio: 15.7 (2013)

Median age: *total:* 27.1 years
male: 26.6 years
female: 27.7 years (2014 est.)

Population growth rate: 0.93% (2014 est.)
country comparison to the world: 125

Birth rate: 17.02 births/1,000 population (2014 est.)
country comparison to the world: 109

Death rate: 5.29 deaths/1,000 population (2014 est.)
country comparison to the world: 181

Net migration rate: -2.46 migrant(s)/1,000 population (2014 est.)
country comparison to the world: 173

Urbanization: *urban population:* 36.2% of total population (2011)
rate of urbanization: 1.27% annual rate of change (2010-15 est.)

Major urban areas—population: TASHKENT (capital) 2.201 million (2009)

Sex ratio: *at birth:* 1.06 male(s)/female
0-14 years: 1.05 male(s)/female
15-24 years: 1.03 male(s)/female
25-54 years: 0.99 male(s)/female
55-64 years: 0.99 male(s)/female
65 years and over: 0.75 male(s)/female
total population: 0.99 male(s)/female (2014 est.)

Mother's mean age at first birth: 23.8 (2006 est.)

Maternal mortality rate: 28 deaths/100,000 live births (2010)
country comparison to the world: 126

Infant mortality rate: *total:* 19.84 deaths/1,000 live births
country comparison to the world: 91
male: 23.54 deaths/1,000 live births
female: 15.93 deaths/1,000 live births (2014 est.)

Life expectancy at birth:
total population: 73.29 years
country comparison to the world: 125
male: 70.25 years
female: 76.52 years (2014 est.)

Total fertility rate: 1.8 children born/woman (2014 est.)
country comparison to the world: 154

Contraceptive prevalence rate: 64.9% (2006)

Health expenditures: 5.4% of GDP (2011)
country comparison to the world: 123

Physicians density: 2.54 physicians/1,000 population (2010)

Hospital bed density: 4.5 beds/1,000 population (2010)

Drinking water source:
improved:
urban: 98.5% of population
rural: 80.9% of population
total: 87.3% of population
unimproved:
urban: 1.5% of population
rural: 19.1% of population
total: 12.7% of population (2011 est.)

Sanitation facility access:
improved:
urban: 100% of population
rural: 100% of population
total: 100% of population
unimproved:
urban: 0% of population
rural: 0% of population
total: 0% of population (2011 est.)

HIV/AIDS—adult prevalence rate: 0.1% (2012 est.)
country comparison to the world: 150

HIV/AIDS—people living with HIV/AIDS: 29,700 (2012 est.)
country comparison to the world: 72

HIV/AIDS—deaths: 2,400 (2012 est.)
country comparison to the world: 56

Obesity—adult prevalence rate: 15.1% (2008)
country comparison to the world: 119

Children under the age of 5 years underweight: 4.4% (2006)
country comparison to the world: 97

Education expenditures: NA

Literacy: *definition:* age 15 and over can read and write
total population: 99.4%
male: 99.6%
female: 99.2% (2011 est.)

School life expectancy (primary to tertiary education): *total:* 12 years
male: 12 years
female: 11 years (2011)

GOVERNMENT

Country name: *conventional long form:* Republic of Uzbekistan
conventional short form: Uzbekistan
local long form: O'zbekiston Respublikasi
local short form: O'zbekiston
former: Uzbek Soviet Socialist Republic

Government type: republic; authoritarian presidential rule, with little power outside the executive branch

Capital: *name:* Tashkent (Toshkent)
geographic coordinates: 41 19 N, 69 15 E
time difference: UTC+5 (10 hours ahead of Washington, DC during Standard Time)

Administrative divisions: 12 provinces (viloyatlar, singular—viloyat), 1 autonomous republic* (avtonom respublikasi), and 1 city** (shahar); Andijon Viloyati, Buxoro Viloyati, Farg'ona Viloyati, Jizzax Viloyati, Namangan Viloyati, Navoiy Viloyati, Qashqadaryo Viloyati (Qarshi), Qoraqalpog'iston Respublikasi [Karakalpakstan Republic]* (Nukus), Samarqand Viloyati, Sirdaryo Viloyati (Guliston), Surxondaryo Viloyati (Termiz), Toshkent Shahri [Tashkent City]**, Toshkent Viloyati [Tashkent province], Xorazm Viloyati (Urganch)
note: administrative divisions have the same names as their administrative centers (exceptions have the administrative center name following in parentheses)

Independence: 1 September 1991 (from the Soviet Union)

National holiday: Independence Day, 1 September (1991)

Constitution: several previous; latest adopted 8 December 1992; amended several times, last in 2012 (2012)

Legal system: civil law system

International law organization participation: has not submitted an ICJ jurisdiction declaration; non-party state to the ICCt

Suffrage: 18 years of age; universal

Executive branch: *chief of state:* President Islom KARIMOV (since 24 March 1990, when he was elected president by the then Supreme Soviet; first elected president of independent Uzbekistan in 1991)
head of government: Prime Minister Shavkat MIRZIYOYEV (since 11 December 2003); First Deputy Prime Minister Rustam AZIMOV (since 2 January 2008)
cabinet: Cabinet of Ministers appointed by the president with approval of both chambers of the Supreme Assembly (Oliy Majlis) (For more information visit the World Leaders website)
elections: president elected by popular vote for a five-year term (eligible for a second term; previously was a five-year term, extended by a 2002 constitutional amendment to seven years and changed back to five years in 2011); election last held on 23 December 2007 (next to be held first quarter 2015); prime minister, ministers, and deputy ministers appointed by the president; note—to present a facade of democracy, the president nominates a candidate for prime minister, who then must be approved by a majority vote in both chambers of parliament
election results: Islom KARIMOV reelected president; percent of vote—Islom KARIMOV 88.1%, Asliddin RUSTAMOV 3.2%, Dilorom TOSHMUHAMEDOVA 2.9%, Akmal SAIDOV 2.6%, other 3.2%

Legislative branch: bicameral Supreme Assembly or Oliy Majlis consists of an upper house or Senate (100 seats; 84 members elected by regional governing councils and 16 appointed by the president; members to serve five-year terms) and a lower house or Legislative Chamber (Qonunchilik Palatasi) (150 seats; 135 members elected by popular vote to serve five-year terms, while 15 spots reserved for the Ecological Movement of Uzbekistan)
elections: last held on 27 December 2009 and 10 January 2010 (next to be held in December 2014)
election results: Senate—percent of vote by party—NA; seats by party—NA; Legislative Chamber—percent of vote by party—NA; seats by party—LDPU 53, NDP 32, National Rebirth Party 31, Adolat 19
note: all parties in the Supreme Assembly support President Islom KARIMOV

Judicial branch: *highest court(s):* Supreme Court (consists of 34 judges organized in civil, criminal, and military sections); Constitutional Court (consists of 7 judges); Higher Economic Court (consists of 19 judges)
judge selection and term of office: judges of the 3 highest courts nominated by the president and confirmed by the Oliy Majlis; judges appointed for 5-year terms subject to reappointment
subordinate courts: regional, district, city, and town courts

Political parties and leaders: Ecological Movement of Uzbekistan (O'zbekiston Ekologik Harakati) [Boriy ALIXONOV]; Justice (Adolat) Social Democratic Party of Uzbekistan [Narimon UMAROV]; Liberal Democratic Party of Uzbekistan (O'zbekiston Liberal-Demokratik Partiyasi) or LDPU [Sodiqjon TURDIYEV]; National Rebirth Democratic Party of Uzbekistan (Milliy Tiklanish) [Sarvar OTAMURATOV]; People's Democratic Party of Uzbekistan (Xalq Demokratik Partiyas) or NDP [Hotamjon KETMONOV] (formerly Communist Party)

Political pressure groups and leaders: there are no significant opposition political parties or pressure groups operating in Uzbekistan

International organization participation: ADB, CICA, CIS, EAPC, EBRD, ECO, FAO, IAEA, IBRD, ICAO, ICC (NGOs), ICRM, IDA, IDB, IFAD, IFC, IFRCS, ILO, IMF, Interpol, IOC, ISO, ITSO, ITU, MIGA, NAM, OIC, OPCW, OSCE, PFP, SCO, UN, UNCTAD, UNESCO, UNIDO, UNWTO, UPU, WCO, WFTU (NGOs), WHO, WIPO, WMO, WTO (observer)

Diplomatic representation in the US:
chief of mission: Ambassador Baxtiyor GULOMOV (since 18 July 2013)
chancery: 1746 Massachusetts Avenue NW, Washington, DC 20036
telephone: [1] (202) 887-5300
FAX: [1] (202) 293-6804
consulate(s) general: New York

Diplomatic representation from the US:
chief of mission: Ambassador George KROL (since 10 June 2011)
embassy: 3 Moyqo'rq'on, 5th Block, Yunusobod District, Tashkent 100093
mailing address: use embassy street address
telephone: [998] (71) 120-5450
FAX: [998] (71) 120-6335

Flag description: three equal horizontal bands of blue (top), white, and green separated by red fimbriations with a white crescent moon (closed side to the hoist) and 12 white stars shifted to the hoist on the top band; blue is the color of the Turkic peoples and of the sky, white signifies peace and the striving for purity in thoughts and deeds, while green represents nature and is the color of Islam; the red stripes are the vital force of all living organisms that links good and pure ideas with the eternal sky and with deeds on earth; the crescent represents Islam and the 12 stars the months and constellations of the Uzbek calendar

National symbol(s): khumo (mythical bird)

National anthem: *name:* "O'zbekiston Respublikasining Davlat Madhiyasi" (National Anthem of the Republic of Uzbekistan)
lyrics/music: Abdulla ARIPOV/Mutal BURHANOV
note: adopted 1992; after the fall of the Soviet Union, Uzbekistan kept the music of the anthem from its time as a Soviet Republic but adopted new lyrics

ECONOMY

Economy—overview: Uzbekistan is a dry, landlocked country; 11% of the land is intensely cultivated, in irrigated river valleys. More than 60% of the population lives in densely populated rural communities. Export of hydrocarbons, primarily natural gas, provides a significant share of foreign exchange earnings. Other major export earners include gold and cotton. Despite ongoing efforts to diversify crops, Uzbekistani agriculture remains largely centered around cotton, although production has dropped by 35% since 1991. Uzbekistan is now the world's fifth largest cotton exporter and sixth largest producer. The country is addressing international criticism for the use of child labor in its cotton harvest. Following independence in September 1991, the government sought to prop up its Soviet-style command economy with subsidies and tight controls on production and prices. While aware of the need to improve the investment climate, the government still sponsors measures that often increase, not decrease, its control over business decisions. A sharp increase in the inequality of income distribution has hurt the lower ranks of society since independence. In 2003, the government accepted Article VIII obligations under the IMF, providing for full currency convertibility. However, strict currency controls and tightening of borders have lessened the effects of convertibility and have also led to some shortages that have further stifled economic activity. The Central Bank often delays or restricts convertibility, especially for consumer goods. Uzbekistan's growth has been driven primarily by state-led investments and a favorable export environment. In the past Uzbekistani authorities have accused US and other foreign companies operating in Uzbekistan of violating Uzbekistani laws and have frozen and even seized their assets. At the same time, the Uzbekistani Government has actively courted several major US and international corporations, offering financing and tax advantages. A major US automaker opened a powertrain manufacturing facility in Tashkent in November 2011, but there have been no sizable US investments since then. Diminishing foreign investment and difficulties transporting goods across borders further challenge the economy of Uzbekistan.

GDP (purchasing power parity): $112.6 billion (2013 est.)
country comparison to the world: 70
$105.2 billion (2012 est.)
$97.21 billion (2011 est.)
note: data are in 2013 US dollars

GDP (official exchange rate): $55.18 billion (2013 est.)

GDP—real growth rate: 7% (2013 est.)
country comparison to the world: 23
8.2% (2012 est.)
8.3% (2011 est.)

GDP—per capita (PPP): $3,800 (2013 est.)
country comparison to the world: 170
$3,600 (2012 est.)
$3,300 (2011 est.)
note: data are in 2013 US dollars

GDP—composition, by end use:
household consumption: 55.7%
government consumption: 16.6%
investment in fixed capital: 23.5%
investment in inventories: 4.9%
exports of goods and services: 28%
imports of goods and services: -31.3% (2011 est.)

GDP—composition, by sector of origin:
agriculture: 19.1%
industry: 32.2%
services: 48.7% (2013 est.)

Agriculture—products: cotton, vegetables, fruits, grain; livestock

Industries: textiles, food processing, machine building, metallurgy, mining, hydrocarbon extraction, chemicals

Industrial production growth rate: 7.1% (2013 est.)
country comparison to the world: 31

Labor force: 16.99 million (2013 est.)
country comparison to the world: 37

Labor force—by occupation: *agriculture:* 25.9%
industry: 13.2%
services: 60.9% (2012 est.)

Unemployment rate: 4.9% (2013 est.)
country comparison to the world: 47
4.9% (2012 est.)
note: officially measured by the Ministry of Labor, plus another 20% underemployed

Population below poverty line: 17% (2011 est.)

Household income or consumption by percentage share: *lowest 10%:* 2.8%
highest 10%: 29.6% (2003)

Distribution of family income—Gini index: 36.8 (2003)
country comparison to the world: 81
44.7 (1998)

Budget: *revenues:* $17.84 billion
expenditures: $18.05 billion (2013 est.)

Taxes and other revenues: 32.3% of GDP (2013 est.)
country comparison to the world: 80

Budget surplus (+) or deficit (-):
-0.4% of GDP (2013 est.)
country comparison to the world: 53

Public debt: 7.6% of GDP (2013 est.)
country comparison to the world: 151
6.2% of GDP (2012 est.)

Fiscal year: calendar year

Inflation rate (consumer prices): 10.1% (2013 est.)
country comparison to the world: 209
11.4% (2012 est.)

note: official data; based on independent analysis of consumer prices, inflation reached 22% in 2012

Stock of narrow money: $6.514 billion (31 December 2013 est.)
country comparison to the world: 93
$5.994 billion (31 December 2012 est.)

Stock of broad money: $10.88 billion (31 December 2013 est.)
country comparison to the world: 103
$9.463 billion (31 December 2012 est.)

Stock of domestic credit: $7.661 billion (31 December 2013 est.)
country comparison to the world: 106
$7.244 billion (31 December 2012 est.)

Market value of publicly traded shares: $NA (31 December 2012)
country comparison to the world: 109
$715.3 million (31 December 2006)

Current account balance: $1.801 billion (2013 est.)
country comparison to the world: 44
$1.807 billion (2012 est.)

Exports: $14.91 billion (2013 est.)
country comparison to the world: 80
$14.38 billion (2012 est.)

Exports—commodities: energy products, cotton, gold, mineral fertilizers, ferrous and nonferrous metals, textiles, food products, machinery, automobiles

Exports—partners: China 21.2%, Kazakhstan 15.9%, Turkey 15.8%, Russia 14.7%, Bangladesh 9.5%, Kyrgyzstan 4% (2012)

Imports: $12.64 billion (2013 est.)
country comparison to the world: 90
$12.06 billion (2012 est.)

Imports—commodities: machinery and equipment, foodstuffs, chemicals, ferrous and nonferrous metals

Imports—partners: Russia 20.7%, China 16.6%, South Korea 16.4%, Kazakhstan 12.5%, Germany 4.6%, Turkey 4.2%, Ukraine 4% (2012)

Reserves of foreign exchange and gold: $17 billion (31 December 2013 est.)
country comparison to the world: 64
$16 billion (31 December 2012 est.)

Debt—external: $8.773 billion (31 December 2013 est.)
country comparison to the world: 103
$7.342 billion (31 December 2012 est.)

Stock of direct foreign investment—at home: $NA

Stock of direct foreign investment—abroad: $NA

Exchange rates: Uzbekistani soum (UZS) per US dollar—
2,082.3 (2013 est.)
1,890.1 (2012 est.)
1,587.2 (2010 est.)
1,466.7 (2009)
1,317 (2008)

ENERGY

Electricity—production: 52.53 billion kWh (2012 est.)
country comparison to the world: 50

Electricity—consumption: 44.51 billion kWh (2010 est.)
country comparison to the world: 51

Electricity—exports: 12.09 billion kWh (2010 est.)
country comparison to the world: 18

Electricity—imports: 12 billion kWh (2010 est.)
country comparison to the world: 16

Electricity—installed generating capacity: 11.6 million kW (2010 est.)
country comparison to the world: 50

Electricity—from fossil fuels: 85.1% of total installed capacity (2010 est.)
country comparison to the world: 88

Electricity—from nuclear fuels: 0% of total installed capacity (2010 est.)
country comparison to the world: 197

Electricity—from hydroelectric plants: 14.9% of total installed capacity (2010 est.)
country comparison to the world: 103

Electricity—from other renewable sources: 0% of total installed capacity (2010 est.)
country comparison to the world: 134

Crude oil—production: 102,600 bbl/day (2012 est.)
country comparison to the world: 49

Crude oil—exports: 0 bbl/day (2010 est.)
country comparison to the world: 200

Crude oil—imports: 0 bbl/day (2010 est.)
country comparison to the world: 135

Crude oil—proved reserves: 594 million bbl (1 January 2013 es)
country comparison to the world: 48

Refined petroleum products—production: 92,300 bbl/day (2010 est.)
country comparison to the world: 76

Refined petroleum products—consumption: 137,100 bbl/day (2011 est.)
country comparison to the world: 71

Refined petroleum products—exports: 4,968 bbl/day (2010 est.)
country comparison to the world: 90

Refined petroleum products—imports: 655.9 bbl/day (2010 est.)
country comparison to the world: 200

Natural gas—production: 62.9 billion cu m (2012 est.)
country comparison to the world: 14

Natural gas—consumption: 46.8 billion cu m (2012 est.)
country comparison to the world: 19

Natural gas—exports: 13.4 billion cu m (2012 est.)
country comparison to the world: 21

Natural gas—imports: 0 cu m (2012 est.)
country comparison to the world: 144

Natural gas—proved reserves: 1.841 trillion cu m (1 January 2013 es)
country comparison to the world: 20

Carbon dioxide emissions from consumption of energy: 115.9 million Mt (2011 est.)
country comparison to the world: 38

COMMUNICATIONS

Telephones—main lines in use: 1.963 million (2012)
country comparison to the world: 60

Telephones—mobile cellular: 20.274 million (2012)
country comparison to the world: 48

Telephone system:
general assessment: digital exchanges in large cities and in rural areas
domestic: the state-owned telecommunications company, Uzbektelecom, owner of the fixed line telecommunications system, has used loans from the Japanese government and the China Development Bank to upgrade fixed-line services including conversion to digital exchanges; mobile-cellular services are provided by 3 private and 1 state-owned operator with a total subscriber base of 19 million as of January 2014
international: country code—998; linked by fiber-optic cable or microwave radio relay with CIS member states and to other countries by leased connection via the Moscow international gateway switch; the country also has a link to the Trans-Asia-Europe (TAE) fiber-optic cable; Uzbekistan has supported the national fiber optic backbone project of Afghanistan since 2008 (2009)

Broadcast media: government controls media; 14 state-owned broadcasters—10 TV and 4 radio—provide service to virtually the entire country; about 20 privately owned TV stations, overseen by local officials, broadcast to local markets; privately owned TV stations are required to lease transmitters from the government-owned Republic TV and Radio Industry Corporation; in 2013, the government closed TV and radio broadcasters affiliated with the National Association of Electronic Mass Media of Uzbekistan, a government-sponsored NGO for private broadcast media

Internet country code: .uz

Internet hosts: 56,075 (2012)
country comparison to the world: 94

Internet users: 4.689 million (2009)
country comparison to the world: 50

TRANSPORTATION

Airports: 53 (2013)
country comparison to the world: 89

Airports—with paved runways: *total:* 33
over 3,047 m: 6
2,438 to 3,047 m: 13
1,524 to 2,437 m: 6
914 to 1,523 m: 4
under 914 m: 4 (2013)

Airports—with unpaved runways: *total:* 20
2,438 to 3,047 m: 2
under 914 m: 18 (2013)

Pipelines: gas 10,401 km; oil 944 km (2013)

Railways: *total:* 4,230 km
country comparison to the world: 40
broad gauge: 4,200 km 1.520-m gauge (930 km electrified) (2012)

Roadways: *total:* 86,496 km
country comparison to the world: 52
paved: 75,511 km
unpaved: 10,985 km (2000)

Waterways: 1,100 km (2012)
country comparison to the world: 63

Ports and terminals: *river port(s):* Termiz (Amu Darya)

MILITARY

Military branches: Uzbek Armed Forces: Army, Air and Air Defense Forces (2013)

Military service age and obligation: 18 years of age for compulsory military service; 1-month or

1-year conscript service obligation for males; moving toward a professional military, but conscription in some form will continue; the military cannot accommodate everyone who wishes to enlist, and competition for entrance into the military is similar to the competition for admission to universities (2013)

Manpower available for military service:
males age 16-49: 7,887,292
females age 16-49: 7,886,459 (2010 est.)

Manpower fit for military service:
males age 16-49: 6,566,118
females age 16-49: 6,745,818 (2010 est.)

Manpower reaching militarily significant age annually: *male:* 306,404
female: 295,456 (2010 est.)

TRANSNATIONAL ISSUES

Disputes—international: prolonged drought and cotton monoculture in Uzbekistan and Turkmenistan created water-sharing difficulties for Amu Darya river states; field demarcation of the boundaries with Kazakhstan commenced in 2004; border delimitation of 130 km of border with Kyrgyzstan is hampered by serious disputes around enclaves and other areas

Refugees and internally displaced persons:
IDPs: undetermined (government forcibly relocated an estimated 3,400 people from villages near the Tajikistan border in 2000-2001; no new data is available) (2012)

Trafficking in persons: *current situation:* Uzbekistan is a source country for men, women, and children subjected to forced labor and women and children subjected to sex trafficking; adults and children are victims of government-organized forced labor during Uzbekistan's annual cotton harvest; some Uzbekistani adults are subjected to forced labor in Kazakhstan, Russia, and, to a much lesser extent, Ukraine in domestic service, agriculture, and the construction and oil industries; Uzbekistani women and children, lured with fraudulent job offers, are sex trafficked to countries in Central Asia, the Middle East, Europe, and Asia; small numbers of Tajikistani and Kyrgyzstani victims have been identified in Uzbekistan

tier rating: Tier 3—Uzbekistan does not fully comply with the minimum standards for the elimination of trafficking and because it is not deemed to be making significant efforts to do so, it was downgraded to Tier 3 after the maximum of two consecutive annual waivers; the government has identified an increased number of sex and transnational labor trafficking victims; for the first time a decree was implemented banning the forced labor of children under the age of 15 in the annual cotton harvest, but government-organized forced labor of adults and older children contines in the cotton and reportedly other sectors; Uzbekistan does not have a systematic process to proactively identify trafficking victims and refer them to protective services (2013)

Illicit drugs: transit country for Afghan narcotics bound for Russian and, to a lesser extent, Western European markets; limited illicit cultivation of cannabis and small amounts of opium poppy for domestic consumption; poppy cultivation almost wiped out by government crop eradication program; transit point for heroin precursor chemicals bound for Afghanistan

V

VANUATU

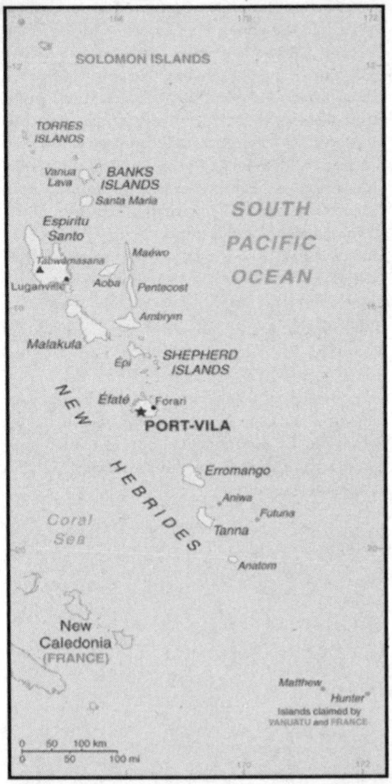

INTRODUCTION

Background: Multiple waves of colonizers, each speaking a distinct language, migrated to the New Hebrides in the millennia preceding European exploration in the 18th century. This settlement pattern accounts for the complex linguistic diversity found on the archipelago to this day. The British and French, who settled the New Hebrides in the 19th century, agreed in 1906 to an Anglo-French Condominium, which administered the islands until independence in 1980, when the new name of Vanuatu was adopted.

GEOGRAPHY

Location: Oceania, group of islands in the South Pacific Ocean, about three-quarters of the way from Hawaii to Australia

Geographic coordinates: 16 00 S, 167 00 E

Map references: Oceania

Area: *total:* 12,189 sq km
country comparison to the world: 164
land: 12,189 sq km
water: 0 sq km
note: includes more than 80 islands, about 65 of which are inhabited

Area—comparative: slightly larger than Connecticut

Land boundaries: 0 km

Coastline: 2,528 km

Maritime claims: measured from claimed archipelagic baselines *territorial sea:* 12 nm
contiguous zone: 24 nm
exclusive economic zone: 200 nm
continental shelf: 200 nm or to the edge of the continental margin

Climate: tropical; moderated by southeast trade winds from May to October; moderate rainfall from November to April; may be affected by cyclones from December to April

Terrain: mostly mountainous islands of volcanic origin; narrow coastal plains

Elevation extremes: *lowest point:* Pacific Ocean 0 m
highest point: Tabwemasana 1,877 m

Natural resources: manganese, hardwood forests, fish

Land use: *arable land:* 1.64%
permanent crops: 10.25%
other: 88.11% (2011)

Irrigated land: NA

Natural hazards: tropical cyclones or typhoons (January to April); volcanic eruption on Aoba (Ambae) island began on 27 November 2005, volcanism also causes minor earthquakes; tsunamis
volcanism: significant volcanic activity with multiple eruptions in recent years; Yasur (elev. 361 m), one of the world's most active volcanoes, has experienced continuous activity in recent centuries; other historically active volcanoes include, Aoba, Ambrym, Epi, Gaua, Kuwae, Lopevi, Suretamatai, and Traitor's Head

Environment—current issues: most of the population does not have access to a reliable supply of potable water; deforestation

Environment—international agreements:
party to: Antarctic-Marine Living Resources, Biodiversity, Climate Change, Climate Change-Kyoto Protocol, Desertification, Endangered Species, Law of the Sea, Marine Dumping, Ozone Layer Protection, Ship Pollution, Tropical Timber 94
signed, but not ratified: none of the selected agreements

Geography—note: a Y-shaped chain of four main islands and 80 smaller islands; several of the islands have active volcanoes and there are several underwater volcanoes as well

PEOPLE AND SOCIETY

Nationality: *noun:* Ni-Vanuatu (singular and plural)
adjective: Ni-Vanuatu

Ethnic groups: Ni-Vanuatu 97.6%, part Ni-Vanuatu 1.1%, other 1.3% (2009 est.)

Languages: local languages (more than 100) 63.2%, Bislama (official; creole) 33.7%, English (official) 2%, French (official) 0.6%, other 0.5% (2009 est.)

Religions: Protestant 70% (includes Presbyterian 27.9%, Anglican 15.1%, Seventh Day Adventist 12.5%, Assemblies of God 4.7%, Church of Christ 4.5%, Neil Thomas Ministry 3.1%, and Apostolic 2.2%), Roman Catholic 12.4%, customary beliefs 3.7% (including Jon Frum cargo cult), other 12.6%, none 1.1%, unspecified 0.2% (2009 est.)

Population: 266,937 (July 2014 est.)
country comparison to the world: 184

Age structure:
0-14 years: 37.3% (male 50,810/female 48,753)
15-24 years: 19.8% (male 26,341/female 26,620)
25-54 years: 34.2% (male 44,732/female 46,545)
55-64 years: 3.7% (male 6,751/female 6,599)
65 years and over: 3.6% (male 5,020/female 4,766) (2014 est.)

Dependency ratios:
total dependency ratio: 69.5 %
youth dependency ratio: 62.8 %
elderly dependency ratio: 6.7 %
potential support ratio: 15 (2013)

Median age: *total:* 21.1 years
male: 20.7 years
female: 21.4 years (2014 est.)

Population growth rate: 2.01% (2014 est.)
country comparison to the world: 51

Birth rate: 25.69 births/1,000 population (2014 est.)
country comparison to the world: 50

Death rate: 4.14 deaths/1,000 population (2014 est.)
country comparison to the world: 209

Net migration rate: -1.5 migrant(s)/1,000 population (2014 est.)
country comparison to the world: 156

Urbanization: *urban population:* 26% of total population (2010)
rate of urbanization: 4.2% annual rate of change (2010-15 est.)

Sex ratio: *at birth:* 1.05 male(s)/female
0-14 years: 1.04 male(s)/female
15-24 years: 0.99 male(s)/female
25-54 years: 0.96 male(s)/female
55-64 years: 1 male(s)/female
65 years and over: 1.07 male(s)/female
total population: 1.01 male(s)/female (2014 est.)

Maternal mortality rate: 110 deaths/100,000 live births (2010)
country comparison to the world: 68

Infant mortality rate: *total:* 16.41 deaths/1,000 live births
country comparison to the world: 101
male: 17.53 deaths/1,000 live births
female: 15.23 deaths/1,000 live births (2014 est.)

Life expectancy at birth:
total population: 72.72 years
country comparison to the world: 131
male: 71.16 years
female: 74.36 years (2014 est.)

Total fertility rate: 3.36 children born/woman (2014 est.)
country comparison to the world: 49

Contraceptive prevalence rate: 38.4% (2007)

Health expenditures: 4.1% of GDP (2011)
country comparison to the world: 160

Physicians density: 0.12 physicians/1,000 population (2008)

Hospital bed density: 1.7 beds/1,000 population (2008)

Drinking water source:
improved:
urban: 97.8% of population
rural: 88.3% of population
total: 90.6% of population
unimproved:
urban: 2.2% of population
rural: 11.7% of population
total: 9.4% of population (2011 est.)

Sanitation facility access:
improved:
urban: 65.1% of population
rural: 55.4% of population
total: 57.8% of population
unimproved:
urban: 34.9% of population
rural: 44.6% of population

total: 42.2% of population (2011 est.)

HIV/AIDS—adult prevalence rate: NA

HIV/AIDS—people living with HIV/AIDS: NA

HIV/AIDS—deaths: NA

Obesity—adult prevalence rate: 27.5% (2008)
country comparison to the world: 39

Children under the age of 5 years underweight: 11.7% (2007)
country comparison to the world: 62

Education expenditures: 5% of GDP (2009)
country comparison to the world: 79

Literacy: *definition:* age 15 and over can read and write
total population: 83.2%
male: NA 84.9%
female: NA 81.6% (2011 est.)

School life expectancy (primary to tertiary education): *total:* 11 years
male: 11 years
female: 10 years (2004)

GOVERNMENT

Country name: *conventional long form:* Republic of Vanuatu
conventional short form: Vanuatu
local long form: Ripablik blong Vanuatu
local short form: Vanuatu
former: New Hebrides

Government type: parliamentary republic

Capital: *name:* Port-Vila (on Efate)

geographic coordinates: 17 44 S, 168 19 E
time difference: UTC+11 (16 hours ahead of Washington, DC during Standard Time)

Administrative divisions: 6 provinces; Malampa, Penama, Sanma, Shefa, Tafea, Torba

Independence: 30 July 1980 (from France and the UK)

National holiday: Independence Day, 30 July (1980)

Constitution: effective 30 July 1980; amended 1981, 1983, 1988 (2006)

Legal system: mixed legal system of English common law, French law, and customary law

International law organization participation: has not submitted an ICJ jurisdiction declaration; accepts ICCt jurisdiction

Suffrage: 18 years of age; universal

Executive branch:
chief of state: President Iolu Johnson ABBIL (since 3 September 2009)
head of government: Prime Minister Moana CARCASSES Kalosil (since 23 March 2013)
cabinet: Council of Ministers appointed by the prime minister, responsible to parliament (For more information visit the World Leaders website)
elections: president elected for a five-year term by an electoral college consisting of parliament and the presidents of the regional councils; election for president last held on 2 September 2009 (next to be held in 2014); following legislative elections, the leader of the majority party or majority coalition usually elected prime minister by parliament from among its members; election for prime minister last held on 23 March 2013 (next to be held following general elections in 2016)
election results: Iolu Johnson ABBIL elected president, with 41 votes out of 58, on the third ballot on 2 September 2009; Moana CARCASSES Kalosil was elected prime minister following the resignation of Sato KILMAN on 21 March 2013

Legislative branch: unicameral Parliament (52 seats; members elected by popular vote to serve four-year terms)
elections: last held on 30 October 2012 (next to be held in 2016)
election results: percent of vote by party—NA; seats by party—VP 8, PPP 6, UMP 5, GJP 4, NUP 4, IG 3, GC 3, NAG 3, RMC 3, MPP 2, NIPDP 2, PSP 1, VLDP 1, VNP 1, VPDP 1, VRP 1, and independent 4; note—political party associations are fluid
note: the National Council of Chiefs advises on matters of culture and language

Judicial branch: *highest court(s):* Supreme Court (consists of a chief justice and 3 judges); note—appeals from the Supreme Court are considered by the Court of Appeal, constituted by 2 or more judges of the Supreme Court sitting together
judge selection and term of office: Supreme Court chief justice appointed by the president after consultation with the prime minister and the leader of the opposition; other judges are appointed by the president on the advice of the Judicial Service Commission, a 4-member advisory body; judges appointed until age of retirement
subordinate courts: magistrates' courts; island courts

Political parties and leaders: Greens Confederation or GC [Moana CARCASSES Kalosil]; Iauko Group or IG [NA]; Land and Justice Party (Graon mo Jastis Pati) or GJP [Ralph REGENVANU]; Melanesian Progressive Party or MPP [Barak SOPE]; Nagriamel movement or NAG [NA]; Natatok Indigenous People's Democratic Party or (NATATOK) or NIPDP [Alfred Roland CARLOT]; National United Party or NUP [Ham LINI]; People's Progressive Party or PPP [Sato KILMAN]; People's Service Party or PSP [Don KEN]; Reunification of Movement for Change or RMC [Charlot SALWAI]; Union of Moderate Parties or UMP [Serge VOHOR]; Vanua'aku Pati (Our Land Party) or VP [Edward NATAPEI]; Vanuatu Democratic Party [Maxime Carlot KORMAN]; Vanuatu Liberal Democratic Party or VLDP [Tapangararua WILLIE]; Vanuatu National Party or VNP [Issac HAMARILIU]; Vanuatu Progressive Development Party or VPDP [Robert Bohn SIKOL]; Vanuatu Republican Party or VRP [Marcellino PIPITE]

Political pressure groups and leaders: NA

International organization participation: ACP, ADB, AOSIS, C, FAO, G-77, IBRD, ICAO, ICRM, IDA, IFC, IFRCS, ILO, IMF, IMO, IMSO, IOC, IOM, ITU, ITUC (NGOs), MIGA, NAM, OAS (observer), OIF, OPCW, PIF, Sparteca, SPC, UN, UNCTAD, UNESCO, UNIDO, UNWTO, UPU, WCO, WFTU (NGOs), WHO, WIPO, WMO, WTO

Diplomatic representation in the US: Vanuatu does not have an embassy in the US; it does, however, have a Permanent Mission to the UN

Diplomatic representation from the US: the US does not have an embassy in Vanuatu; the US ambassador to Papua New Guinea, currently Ambassador Walter E. North, is accredited to Vanuatu

Flag description: two equal horizontal bands of red (top) and green with a black isosceles triangle (based on the hoist side) all separated by a black-edged yellow stripe in the shape of a horizontal Y (the two points of the Y face the hoist side and enclose the triangle); centered in the triangle is a boar's tusk encircling two crossed namele fern fronds, all in yellow; red represents the blood of boars and men, green the richness of the islands, and black the ni-Vanuatu people; the yellow Y-shape—which reflects the pattern of the islands in the Pacific Ocean—symbolizes the light of the Gospel spreading through the islands; the boar's tusk is a symbol of prosperity frequently worn as a pendant on the islands; the fern fronds represent peace

National symbol(s): boar's tusk

National anthem: *name:* "Yumi, Yumi, Yumi" (We, We, We)
lyrics/music: Francois Vincent AYSSAV
note: adopted 1980, the anthem is written in Bislama, a Creole language that mixes Pidgin English and French

ECONOMY

Economy—overview: This South Pacific island economy is based primarily on small-scale agriculture, which provides a living for about two-thirds of the population. Fishing, offshore financial services, and tourism, with nearly 197,000 visitors in 2008, are other mainstays of the economy. Mineral deposits are negligible; the country has no known petroleum deposits. A small light industry sector caters to the local market. Tax revenues come mainly from import duties. Economic development is hindered by dependence on relatively few commodity exports, vulnerability to natural disasters, and long distances from main markets and between constituent islands. In response to foreign concerns, the government has promised to tighten regulation of its offshore financial center. In mid-2002, the government stepped up efforts to boost tourism through improved air connections, resort development, and cruise ship facilities. Agriculture, especially livestock farming, is a second target for growth. Australia and New Zealand are the main suppliers of tourists and foreign aid.

GDP (purchasing power parity): $1.27 billion (2013 est.)
country comparison to the world: 202
$1.23 billion (2012 est.)
$1.203 billion (2011 est.)
note: data are in 2013 US dollars

GDP (official exchange rate): $828 million (2013 est.)

GDP—real growth rate: 3.3% (2013 est.)
country comparison to the world: 104
2.3% (2012 est.)
1.4% (2011 est.)

GDP—per capita (PPP): $4,800 (2013 est.)
country comparison to the world: 164
$4,900 (2012 est.)
$4,900 (2011 est.)
note: data are in 2013 US dollars

GDP—composition, by end use:
household consumption: 60.8%
government consumption: 17.8%
investment in fixed capital: 27.3%
investment in inventories: 0%
exports of goods and services: 41.5%
imports of goods and services: -47.3% (2013 est.)

GDP—composition, by sector of origin:
agriculture: 22.4%
industry: 9.7%
services: 67.9% (2013 est.)

Agriculture—products: copra, coconuts, cocoa, coffee, taro, yams, fruits, vegetables; beef; fish

Industries: food and fish freezing, wood processing, meat canning

Industrial production growth rate: 4.8% (2013 est.)
country comparison to the world: 58

Labor force: 115,900 (2007)
country comparison to the world: 182

Labor force—by occupation: *agriculture:* 65%

industry: 5%
services: 30% (2000 est.)

Unemployment rate: 1.7% (1999)
country comparison to the world: 9

Population below poverty line: NA%

Household income or consumption by percentage share: *lowest 10%:* NA%
highest 10%: NA%

Budget: *revenues:* $203.5 million
expenditures: $201.3 million (2013 est.)

Taxes and other revenues: 24.6% of GDP (2013 est.)
country comparison to the world: 134

Budget surplus (+) or deficit (-):
0.3% of GDP (2013 est.)
country comparison to the world: 38

Fiscal year: calendar year

Inflation rate (consumer prices): 1.9% (2013 est.)
country comparison to the world: 62
1.4% (2012 est.)

Central bank discount rate: 20% (31 December 2010 est.)
country comparison to the world: 61
6% (31 December 2009 est.)

Commercial bank prime lending rate: 6.7% (31 December 2013 est.)
country comparison to the world: 136
6% (31 December 2012 est.)

Stock of narrow money: $270.7 million (31 December 2013 est.)
country comparison to the world: 171
$264.1 million (31 December 2012 est.)

Stock of broad money: $644 million (31 December 2013 est.)
country comparison to the world: 174
$643.3 million (31 December 2012 est.)

Stock of domestic credit: $560.8 million (31 December 2013 est.)
country comparison to the world: 167
$549.4 million (31 December 2012 est.)

Market value of publicly traded shares: $NA

Current account balance: -$118 million (2013 est.)
country comparison to the world: 77
-$128.6 million (2012 est.)

Exports: $43.1 million (2013 est.)
country comparison to the world: 199
$57.5 million (2012 est.)

Exports—commodities: copra, beef, cocoa, timber, kava, coffee

Exports—partners: Thailand 41.9%, Cote dIvoire 30.5%, Japan 14.7% (2012)

Imports: $319.4 million (2013 est.)
country comparison to the world: 196
$322.6 million (2012 est.)

Imports—commodities: machinery and equipment, foodstuffs, fuels

Imports—partners: China 20.2%, Singapore 18.8%, US 15%, Japan 11.6%, Australia 10.4%, Fiji 5.2%, NZ 4.8% (2012)

Reserves of foreign exchange and gold: $174.2 million (31 December 2013 est.)
country comparison to the world: 162
$187.3 million (31 December 2012 est.)

Debt—external: $307.7 million (31 December 2011 est.)
country comparison to the world: 183
$258.9 million (31 December 2010 est.)

Stock of direct foreign investment—at home: $620.1 million (31 December 2013 est.)
country comparison to the world: 104
$565.1 million (31 December 2012 est.)

Stock of direct foreign investment—abroad: $21.3 million (31 December 2013 est.)
country comparison to the world: 91
$22.3 million (31 December 2012 est.)

Exchange rates: vatu (VUV) per US dollar—
92.38 (2013 est.)
92.64 (2012 est.)
96.91 (2010 est.)

ENERGY

Electricity—production: 55 million kWh (2010 est.)
country comparison to the world: 204

Electricity—consumption: 51.15 million kWh (2010 est.)
country comparison to the world: 204

Electricity—exports: 0 kWh (2012 est.)
country comparison to the world: 176

Electricity—imports: 0 kWh (2012 est.)
country comparison to the world: 177

Electricity—installed generating capacity: 28,000 kW (2010 est.)
country comparison to the world: 198

Electricity—from fossil fuels: 89.3% of total installed capacity (2010 est.)
country comparison to the world: 76

Electricity—from nuclear fuels: 0% of total installed capacity (2010 est.)
country comparison to the world: 150

Electricity—from hydroelectric plants: 0% of total installed capacity (2010 est.)
country comparison to the world: 189

Electricity—from other renewable sources: 10.7% of total installed capacity (2010 est.)
country comparison to the world: 25

Crude oil—production: 0 bbl/day (2012 est.)
country comparison to the world: 201

Crude oil—exports: 0 bbl/day (2010 est.)
country comparison to the world: 162

Crude oil—imports: 0 bbl/day (2010 est.)
country comparison to the world: 103

Crude oil—proved reserves: 0 bbl (1 January 2013 es)
country comparison to the world: 171

Refined petroleum products—production: 0 bbl/day (2010 est.)
country comparison to the world: 181

Refined petroleum products—consumption: 1,170 bbl/day (2011 est.)
country comparison to the world: 197

Refined petroleum products—exports: 0 bbl/day (2010 est.)
country comparison to the world: 203

Refined petroleum products—imports: 837.7 bbl/day (2010 est.)
country comparison to the world: 198

Natural gas—production: 0 cu m (2011 est.)
country comparison to the world: 174

Natural gas—consumption: 0 cu m (2010 est.)
country comparison to the world: 179

Natural gas—exports: 0 cu m (2011 est.)
country comparison to the world: 156

Natural gas—imports: 0 cu m (2011 est.)
country comparison to the world: 105

Natural gas—proved reserves: 0 cu m (1 January 2013 es)
country comparison to the world: 177

Carbon dioxide emissions from consumption of energy: 149,000 Mt (2011 est.)
country comparison to the world: 200

COMMUNICATIONS

Telephones—main lines in use: 5,800 (2012)
country comparison to the world: 208

Telephones—mobile cellular: 137,000 (2012)
country comparison to the world: 186

Telephone system:
international: country code—678; satellite earth station—1 Intelsat (Pacific Ocean)

Broadcast media: 1 state-owned TV station; multi-channel pay TV is available; state-owned Radio Vanuatu operates 2 radio stations; 2 privately owned radio broadcasters; programming from multiple international broadcasters is available (2008)

Internet country code: .vu

Internet hosts: 5,655 (2012)
country comparison to the world: 143

Internet users: 17,000 (2009)
country comparison to the world: 198

TRANSPORTATION

Airports: 31 (2013)
country comparison to the world: 114

Airports—with paved runways: *total:* 3
2,438 to 3,047 m: 1
1,524 to 2,437 m: 1
914 to 1,523 m: 1 (2013)

Airports—with unpaved runways: *total:* 2 8
914 to 1,523 m: 7
under 914 m: 21 (2013)

Roadways: *total:* 1,070 km
country comparison to the world: 184
paved: 256 km
unpaved: 814 km (2000)

Merchant marine: *total:* 7 7
country comparison to the world: 57
by type: bulk carrier 38, cargo 8, chemical tanker 2, container 1, liquefied gas 2, passenger 1, refrigerated cargo 24, vehicle carrier 1
foreign-owned: 72 (Belgium 1, Canada 5, China 1, Greece 3, Japan 39, Norway 1, Poland 9, Russia 7, Singapore 2, Taiwan 1, UAE 1, US 2) (2010)

Ports and terminals: *major seaport(s):* Forari Bay, Luganville (Santo, Espiritu Santo), Port-Vila

MILITARY

Military branches: no regular military forces; Vanuatu Police Force (VPF), Vanuatu Mobile Force (VMF; includes Police Maritime Wing (PMW)) (2013)

Manpower available for military service:
males age 16-49: 62,216 (2010 est.)

Manpower fit for military service:
males age 16-49: 43,331
females age 16-49: 44,927 (2010 est.)

Manpower reaching militarily significant age annually: *male:* 2,323
female: 2,230 (2010 est.)

TRANSNATIONAL ISSUES

Disputes—international: Matthew and Hunter Islands east of New Caledonia claimed by Vanuatu and France

VENEZUELA

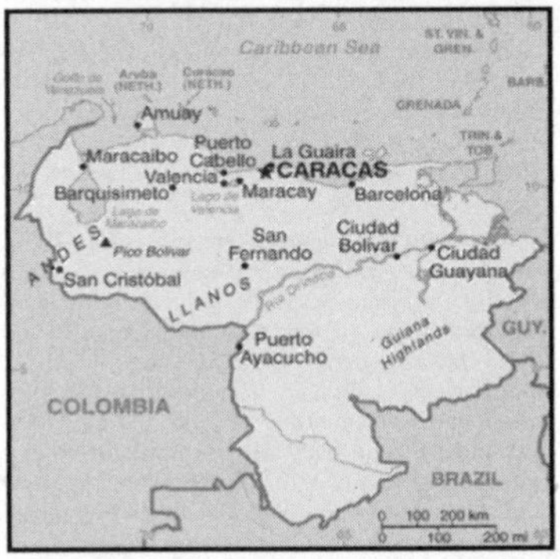

INTRODUCTION

Background: Venezuela was one of three countries that emerged from the collapse of Gran Colombia in 1830 (the others being Ecuador and New Granada, which became Colombia). For most of the first half of the 20th century, Venezuela was ruled by generally benevolent military strongmen, who promoted the oil industry and allowed for some social reforms. Democratically elected governments have held sway since 1959. Hugo CHAVEZ, president from 1999 to 2013, sought to implement his "21st Century Socialism," which purported to alleviate social ills while at the same time attacking capitalist globalization and existing democratic institutions. His hand-picked successor, President Nicolas MADURO, is continuing CHAVEZ's socialist program. Current
concerns include: a weakening of democratic institutions, political polarization, a politicized military, rampant violent crime, overdependence on the petroleum industry with its price fluctuations, and irresponsible mining operations that are endangering the rain forest and indigenous peoples.

GEOGRAPHY

Location: Northern South America, bordering the Caribbean Sea and the North Atlantic Ocean, between

Colombia and Guyana Geographic coordinates: 8 00 N, 66 00 W Map references:
South America Area: total: 912,050 sq km
country comparison to the world: 33
land: 882,050 sq km
water: 30,000 sq km

Area—comparative: almost six times the size of Georgia; slightly more than twice the size of California

Land boundaries: *total:* 4,993 km
border countries: Brazil 2,200 km, Colombia 2,050 km, Guyana 743 km

Coastline: 2,800 km

Maritime claims: *territorial sea:* 12 nm
contiguous zone: 15 nm
exclusive economic zone: 200 nm
continental shelf: 200 m depth or to the depth of exploitation

Climate: tropical; hot, humid; more moderate in highlands

Terrain: Andes Mountains and Maracaibo Lowlands in northwest; central plains (llanos); Guiana Highlands in southeast

Elevation extremes: *lowest point:* Caribbean Sea 0 m
highest point: Pico Bolivar 5,007 m

Natural resources: petroleum, natural gas, iron ore, gold, bauxite, other minerals, hydropower, diamonds

Land use: *arable land:* 2.85%
permanent crops: 0.71%
other: 96.44% (2011)

Irrigated land: 10,550 sq km (2008)

Total renewable water resources: 1,233 cu km (2011)

Freshwater withdrawal (domestic/industrial/agricultural): *total:* 9.06 cu km/yr (23%/4%/74%)
per capita: 358.6 cu m/yr (2008)

Natural hazards: subject to floods, rockslides, mudslides; periodic droughts

Environment—current issues: sewage pollution of Lago de Valencia; oil and urban pollution of Lago de Maracaibo; deforestation; soil degradation; urban and industrial pollution, especially along the Caribbean coast; threat to the rainforest ecosystem from irresponsible mining operations

Environment—international agreements:
party to: Antarctic Treaty, Biodiversity, Climate Change, Climate Change-Kyoto Protocol, Desertification, Endangered Species, Hazardous Wastes, Marine Life Conservation, Ozone Layer Protection, Ship Pollution, Tropical Timber 83, Tropical Timber 94, Wetlands
signed but not ratified:: none of the selected agreements

Geography—note: on major sea and air routes linking North and South America; Angel Falls in the Guiana Highlands is the world's highest waterfall

PEOPLE AND SOCIETY

Nationality: *noun:* Venezuelan(s)
adjective: Venezuelan

Ethnic groups: Spanish, Italian, Portuguese, Arab, German, African, indigenous people

Languages: Spanish (official), numerous indigenous dialects

Religions: nominally Roman Catholic 96%, Protestant 2%, other 2%

Demographic profile: Although poverty in Venezuela has declined during the CHAVEZ administration, dropping from nearly 50% in 1999 to about 27% in 2011, it remains high and some experts question how much of a role social expenditures have played in this poverty reduction. Progress in lowering poverty, income inequality, and unemployment may in fact be more closely linked to the rise and fall of prices for oil, Venezuela's dominant export. In the long-run, education and healthcare spending may increase economic growth and reduce income inequality, but rising costs and the staffing of new healthcare jobs with foreigners are slowing development. In the meantime, social investment has led to better living standards, including increased school enrollment, a substantial reduction in infant and child mortality, and greater access to potable water and sanitation. Since CHAVEZ came to power in 1999, more than a million predominantly middle- and upper-class Venezuelans are estimated to have emigrated. The brain drain is attributed to a repressive political system, lack of economic opportunities, steep inflation, a high crime rate, and corruption. Thousands of oil engineers emigrated to Canada, Colombia, and the United States following CHAVEZ's firing of over 20,000 employees of the state-owned petroleum company during a 2002-2003 oil strike. Additionally, thousands of Venezuelans of European descent have taken up residence in their ancestral homelands. Nevertheless, Venezuela continues to attract immigrants from South America and southern Europe because of its lenient migration policy and the availability of education and healthcare. Venezuela also has been a fairly accommodating host to more than 200,000 Colombian refugees.

Population: 28,868,486 (July 2014 est.)
country comparison to the world: 46

Age structure:
0-14 years: 28.2% (male 4,143,840/female 3,985,489)
15-24 years: 18.8% (male 2,723,856/female 2,697,672)
25-54 years: 39.6% (male 5,614,922/female 5,818,903)
55-64 years: 5.9% (male 1,030,898/female 1,137,894)
65 years and over: 5.8% (male 755,183/female 959,829) (2014 est.)

Dependency ratios:
total dependency ratio: 53.2 %
youth dependency ratio: 43.7 %
elderly dependency ratio: 9.5 %
potential support ratio: 10.6 (2013)

Median age: *total:* 26.9 years
male: 26.1 years
female: 27.6 years (2014 est.)

Population growth rate: 1.42% (2014 est.)
country comparison to the world: 86

Birth rate: 19.42 births/1,000 population (2014 est.)
country comparison to the world: 90

Death rate: 5.27 deaths/1,000 population (2014 est.)
country comparison to the world: 182

Net migration rate: 0 migrant(s)/1,000 population (2014 est.)
country comparison to the world: 83

Urbanization: *urban population:* 93% of total population (2010)
rate of urbanization: 1.7% annual rate of change (2010-15 est.)

Major urban areas—population: CARACAS (capital) 3.051 million; Maracaibo 2.153 million; Valencia 1.738 million; Barquisimeto 1.159 million; Maracay 1.04 million (2009)

Sex ratio: *at birth:* 1.05 male(s)/female
0-14 years: 1.04 male(s)/female
15-24 years: 1.01 male(s)/female
25-54 years: 0.97 male(s)/female
55-64 years: 0.98 male(s)/female
65 years and over: 0.79 male(s)/female
total population: 0.98 male(s)/female (2014 est.)

Maternal mortality rate: 92 deaths/100,000 live births (2010)
country comparison to the world: 79

Infant mortality rate: *total:* 19.33 deaths/1,000 live births
country comparison to the world: 93
male: 22.73 deaths/1,000 live births
female: 15.75 deaths/1,000 live births (2014 est.)

Life expectancy at birth:
total population: 74.39 years
country comparison to the world: 111
male: 71.26 years
female: 77.67 years (2014 est.)

Total fertility rate: 2.35 children born/woman (2014 est.)
country comparison to the world: 90

Contraceptive prevalence rate: 70.3% (1998)

Health expenditures: 5.2% of GDP (2011)
country comparison to the world: 138

Physicians density: 1.94 physicians/1,000 population (2001)

Hospital bed density: 0.9 beds/1,000 population (2011)

Drinking water source:
improved:
urban: 94.3% of population
rural: 75.3% of population
total: 92.9% of population
unimproved:
urban: 5.7% of population
rural: 24.7% of population
total: 7.1% of population (2007 est.)

Sanitation facility access:
improved:
urban: 93.6% of population
rural: 56.9% of population
total: 90.9% of population
unimproved:
urban: 6.4% of population
rural: 43.1% of population
total: 9.1% of population (2007 est.)

HIV/AIDS—adult prevalence rate: 0.6% (2012 est.)
country comparison to the world: 65

HIV/AIDS—people living with HIV/AIDS: 107,900 (2012 est.)
country comparison to the world: 43

HIV/AIDS—deaths: 3,800 (2012 est.)
country comparison to the world: 46

Major infectious diseases:
degree of risk: high
food or waterborne diseases: bacterial diarrhea and hepatitis A
vectorborne diseases: dengue fever and malaria (2013)

Obesity—adult prevalence rate: 30.3% (2008)
country comparison to the world: 26

Children under the age of 5 years underweight: 2.9% (2009)
country comparison to the world: 114

Education expenditures: 6.9% of GDP (2009)
country comparison to the world: 22

Literacy: *definition:* age 15 and over can read and write
total population: 95.5%
male: 95.7%
female: 95.4% (2009 est.)

School life expectancy (primary to tertiary education): *total:* 14 years
13 years
15 years (2008)

Child labor—children ages 5-14:
total number: 404,092
percentage: 8 % (2000 est.)

Unemployment, youth ages 15-24: *total:* 17.1%
country comparison to the world: 75
male: 14.3%
female: 22.6% (2012)

GOVERNMENT

Country name: *conventional long form:* Bolivarian Republic of Venezuela
conventional short form: Venezuela
local long form: Republica Bolivariana de Venezuela
local short form: Venezuela

Government type: federal republic

Capital: *name:* Caracas

geographic coordinates: 10 29 N, 66 52 W
time difference: UTC-4.5 (half an hour ahead of Washington, DC during Standard Time)

Administrative divisions: 23 states (estados, singular—estado), 1 capital district* (distrito capital), and 1 federal dependency** (dependencia federal); Amazonas, Anzoategui, Apure, Aragua, Barinas, Bolivar, Carabobo, Cojedes, Delta Amacuro, Dependencias Federales (Federal Dependencies)**, Distrito Capital (Capital District)*, Falcon, Guarico, Lara, Merida, Miranda, Monagas, Nueva Esparta, Portuguesa, Sucre, Tachira, Trujillo, Vargas, Yaracuy, Zulia
note: the federal dependency consists of 11 federally controlled island groups with a total of 72 individual islands

Independence: 5 July 1811 (from Spain)

National holiday: Independence Day, 5 July (1811)

Constitution: many previous; latest adopted 15 December 1999, effective 30 December 1999; amended 2009 (2013)

Legal system: civil law system based on the Spanish civil code

International law organization participation: has not submitted an ICJ jurisdiction declaration; state party to the ICCT

Suffrage: 18 years of age; universal

Executive branch: *chief of state:* President Nicolas MADURO Moros (since 8 March 2013); Executive Vice President Jorge Alberto ARREAZA Montserrat (since 8 March 2013); note—the president is both chief of state and head of government; former Executive Vice President Nicolas MADURO Moros assumed presidential responsibilities after the death of President Hugo CHAVEZ Frias on 5 March 2013, and was officially sworn in on 8 March 2013
head of government: President Nicolas MADURO Moros (since 8 March 2013); Executive Vice President Jorge Alberto ARREAZA Montserrat (since 8 March 2013)
cabinet: Council of Ministers appointed by the president (For more information visit the World Leaders website)
elections: president elected by popular vote for a six-year term (eligible for unlimited reelection); election last held on 14 April 2013; note—this was a special election held following the death of President Hugo CHAVEZ Frias on 5 March 2013; the next scheduled election after this is expected to be held in late 2018 pending official convocation by the country's electoral body)
note: in 1999, a National Constituent Assembly drafted a new constitution that increased the presidential term to six years; an election was subsequently held on 30 July 2000 under the terms of this constitution; in 2009, a national referendum approved the elimination of term limits on all elected officials, including the presidency
election results: Nicolas MADURO Moros elected president; percent of vote—Nicolas MADURO Moros 50.61%, Henrique CAPRILES Radonski 49.12%, other 0.24%

Legislative branch: unicameral National Assembly or Asamblea Nacional (165 seats; members elected by popular vote on a proportional basis to serve five-year terms; three seats reserved for the indigenous peoples of Venezuela)
elections: last held on 26 September 2010 (next to be held in 2015)
election results: percent of vote by party—pro-government 48.9%, opposition coalition 47.9%, other 3.2%; seats by party—pro-government 98, opposition 65, other 2

Judicial branch: *highest court(s):* Supreme Tribunal of Justice (consists of 32 judges organized into six divisions—constitutional, political administrative, electoral, civil appeals, criminal appeals, and social (mainly agrarian and labor issues)
judge selection and term of office: judges proposed by the Committee of Judicial Postulation (an independent body of organizations dealing with legal issues and of the organs of citizen power) and appointed by the National Assembly; judges serve non-renewable 12-year terms
subordinate courts: Superior or Appeals Courts (Tribunales Superiores); District Tribunals (Tribunales de Distrito); Courts of First Instance (Tribunales de Primera Instancia); Parish Courts (Tribunales de Parroquia); Justices of the Peace (Justicia de Paz) Network

Political parties and leaders: A New Time or UNT [Omar BARBOZA]; Brave People's Alliance or ABP [Antonio LEDEZMA]; Christian Democrats or COPEI [Roberto ENRIQUEZ]; Communist Party of Venezuela or PCV [Oscar FIGUERA]; Democratic Action or AD [Henry RAMOS ALLUP]; Fatherland for All or PPT [Rafael UZCATEGUI]; For Social Democracy or PODEMOS [Ismael GARCIA]; Justice First [Julio BORGES]; Movement Toward Socialism or MAS [Nicolas SOSA]; Popular Will or VP [Leopoldo LOPEZ]; Progressive Wave or AP [Henri FALCON]; The Democratic Unity Table or MUD [Ramon Guillermo AVELEDO]; The Radical Cause [Daniel SANTOLO]; United Socialist Party of Venezuela or PSUV [vacant]; Venezuelan Progressive Movement or MPV [Simon CALZADILLA]; Venezuela Project or PV [Henrique SALAS ROMER]

Political pressure groups and leaders: Bolivarian and Socialist Workers' Union (a ruling party labor union); Confederacion Venezolana de Industriales or Coindustria (a conservative business group); Consejos Comunales (pro-Chavez local cooperatives); FEDECAMARAS (a conservative business group); Union of Oil Workers of Venezuela or FUTPV; Venezuelan Confederation of Workers or CTV (opposition-oriented labor organization); various civil society groups and human rights organizations

International organization participation: Caricom (observer), CD, CDB, CELAC, FAO, G-15, G-24, G-77, IADB, IAEA, IBRD, ICAO, ICC (NGOs), ICCt, ICRM, IDA, IFAD, IFC, IFRCS, IHO, ILO, IMF, IMO, IMSO, Interpol, IOC, IOM, IPU, ITSO, ITU, ITUC (NGOs), LAES, LAIA, LAS (observer), Mercosur, MIGA, NAM, OAS, OPANAL, OPCW, OPEC, PCA, Petrocaribe, UN, UNASUR, UNCTAD, UNESCO, UNHCR, UNIDO, Union Latina, UNWTO, UPU, WCO, WFTU (NGOs), WHO, WIPO, WMO, WTO

Diplomatic representation in the US:
chief of mission: Ambassador (vacant)
chancery: 1099 30th Street NW, Washington, DC 20007
telephone: [1] (202) 342-2214
FAX: [1] (202) 342-6820

consulate(s) general: Boston, Chicago, Houston, Miami, New Orleans, New York, San Francisco, San Juan (Puerto Rico)

Diplomatic representation from the US:
chief of mission: Ambassador (vacant)
embassy: Calle F con Calle Suapure, Urbanizacion Colinas de Valle Arriba, Caracas 1080
mailing address: P. O. Box 62291, Caracas 1060-A; APO AA 34037
telephone: [58] (212) 975-6411, 907-8400 (after hours)
FAX: [58] (212) 907-8199

Flag description: three equal horizontal bands of yellow (top), blue, and red with the coat of arms on the hoist side of the yellow band and an arc of eight white five-pointed stars centered in the blue band; the flag retains the three equal horizontal bands and three main colors of the banner of Gran Colombia, the South American republic that broke up in 1830; yellow is interpreted as standing for the riches of the land, blue for the courage of its people, and red for the blood shed in attaining independence; the seven stars on the original flag represented the seven provinces in Venezuela that united in the war of independence; in 2006, then President Hugo CHAVEZ ordered an eighth star added to the star arc—a decision that sparked much controversy—to conform with the flag proclaimed by Simon Bolivar in 1827 and to represent the province of Guayana

National symbol(s): troupial (bird)

National anthem: *name:* "Gloria al bravo pueblo" (Glory to the Brave People)
lyrics/music: Vicente SALIAS/Juan Jose LANDAETA
note: adopted 1881; the lyrics were written in 1810, the music some years later; both SALIAS and LANDAETA were executed in 1814 during Venezuela's struggle for independence

ECONOMY

Economy—overview: Venezuela remains highly dependent on oil revenues, which account for roughly 95% of export earnings, about 45% of federal budget revenues, and around 12% of GDP. Fueled by high oil prices, record government spending helped to boost GDP growth in 2011, after a sharp drop in oil prices caused an economic contraction in 2009-10. Government spending, minimum wage hikes, and improved access to domestic credit created an increase in consumption which combined with supply problems to cause higher inflation—roughly 26% in 2011 and rising to more than 56% in 2013. Former President Hugo CHAVEZ's efforts to increase the government's control of the economy by nationalizing firms in the agribusiness, financial, construction, oil, and steel sectors hurt the private investment environment, reduced productive capacity, and slowed non-petroleum exports. In 2013, Venezuela continued to wrestle with a housing crisis, an electricity crisis, and rolling food and goods shortages—all of which were fallout from the government's unorthodox economic policies. The budget deficit for the entire government reached 17% of GDP in 2012. The deficit was trimmed to under 10% of GDP in 2013.

GDP (purchasing power parity): $407.4 billion (2013 est.)
country comparison to the world: 34
$403.3 billion (2012 est.)
$381.9 billion (2011 est.)
note: data are in 2013 US dollars

GDP (official exchange rate): $367.5 billion (2013 est.)

GDP—real growth rate: 1.6% (2013 est.)
country comparison to the world: 154
5.6% (2012 est.)
4.2% (2011 est.)

GDP—per capita (PPP): $13,600 (2013 est.)
country comparison to the world: 97
$13,700 (2012 est.)
$13,100 (2011 est.)
note: data are in 2013 US dollars

Gross national saving: 23.8% of GDP (2013 est.)
country comparison to the world: 58
28.9% of GDP (2012 est.)
30.8% of GDP (2011 est.)

GDP—composition, by end use:
household consumption: 62.3%
government consumption: 13.2%
investment in fixed capital: 17.3%
investment in inventories: 5.7%
exports of goods and services: 25%
imports of goods and services: -23.5% (2013 est.)

GDP—composition, by sector of origin:
agriculture: 3.7%
industry: 35.5%
services: 60.8% (2013 est.)

Agriculture—products: corn, sorghum, sugarcane, rice, bananas, vegetables, coffee; beef, pork, milk, eggs; fish

Industries: agricultural products, livestock, raw materials, machinery and equipment, transport equipment, construction materials, medical equipment, pharmaceuticals, chemicals, iron and steel products, and fuel

Industrial production growth rate: 1% (2013 est.)
country comparison to the world: 152

Labor force: 14.01 million (2013 est.)
country comparison to the world: 40

Labor force—by occupation: *agriculture:* 7.3%
industry: 21.8%
services: 70.9% (4th quarter, 2011)

Unemployment rate: 7.9% (2013 est.)
country comparison to the world: 86
7.8% (2012 est.)

Population below poverty line: 31.6% (2011 est.)

Household income or consumption by percentage share: *lowest 10%:* 1.7%
highest 10%: 32.7% (2006)

Distribution of family income—Gini index: 39 (2011)
country comparison to the world: 69
49.5 (1998)

Budget: *revenues:* $103.4 billion
expenditures: $139.4 billion (2013 est.)

Taxes and other revenues: 28.1% of GDP (2013 est.)
country comparison to the world: 105

Budget surplus (+) or deficit (-):
-9.8% of GDP (2013 est.)
country comparison to the world: 204

Public debt: 34.2% of GDP (2013 est.)
country comparison to the world: 109
26.8% of GDP (2012 est.)
note: data cover central government debt, as well as the debt of state-owned oil company PDVSA; the data include treasury debt held by foreign entities; the data include some debt issued by subnational entities, as well as intra-governmental debt; intra-governmental debt consists of treasury borrowings from surpluses in the social funds, such as for retirement, medical care, and unemployment; some debt instruments for the social funds are sold at public auctions

Fiscal year: calendar year

Inflation rate (consumer prices): 56.2% (2013 est.)
country comparison to the world: 222
21.1% (2012 est.)

Central bank discount rate: 29.5% (31 December 2010)
country comparison to the world: 3
29.5% (31 December 2009)

Commercial bank prime lending rate: 18% (31 December 2013 est.)
country comparison to the world: 34
16.38% (31 December 2012 est.)

Stock of narrow money: $181.4 billion (31 December 2013 est.)
country comparison to the world: 22
$162.7 billion (31 December 2012 est.)

Stock of broad money: $185.6 billion (31 December 2013 est.)
country comparison to the world: 39
$166.7 billion (31 December 2012 est.)

Stock of domestic credit: $176.7 billion (31 December 2013 est.)
country comparison to the world: 42
$160.1 billion (31 December 2012 est.)

Market value of publicly traded shares: $25.3 billion (31 December 2012 est.)
country comparison to the world: 84
$5.143 billion (31 December 2011)
$3.991 billion (31 December 2011 est.)

Current account balance: $3.195 billion (2013 est.)
country comparison to the world: 34
$11.02 billion (2012 est.)

Exports: $91.78 billion (2013 est.)
country comparison to the world: 41
$97.34 billion (2012 est.)

Exports—commodities: petroleum, bauxite and aluminum, minerals, chemicals, agricultural products, basic manufactures

Exports—partners: US 39.1%, China 14.3%, India 12%, Netherlands Antilles 7.8%, Cuba 4.6% (2012)

Imports: $59.32 billion (2013 est.)
country comparison to the world: 49
$59.31 billion (2012 est.)

Imports—commodities: agricultural products, livestock, raw materials, machinery and equipment, transport equipment, construction materials, medical equipment, pharmaceuticals, chemicals, iron and steel products

Imports—partners: US 31.7%, China 16.8%, Brazil 9.1%, Colombia 4.8% (2012)

Reserves of foreign exchange and gold: $21.15 billion (31 December 2013 est.)
country comparison to the world: 58
$29.89 billion (31 December 2012 est.)

Debt—external: $74.87 billion (31 December 2013 est.)
country comparison to the world: 53
$75.75 billion (31 December 2012 est.)

Stock of direct foreign investment—at home: $49.9 billion (31 December 2013 est.)
country comparison to the world: 55
$47.4 billion (31 December 2012 est.)

Stock of direct foreign investment—abroad: $21.94 billion (31 December 2013 est.)
country comparison to the world: 46
$21.25 billion (31 December 2012 est.)

Exchange rates: bolivars (VEB) per US dollar—
6.048 (2013 est.)
4.289 (2012 est.)
2.5821 (2010 est.)
2.147 (2009)
2.147 (2008)

ENERGY

Electricity—production: 127.6 billion kWh (2012 est.)
country comparison to the world: 28

Electricity—consumption: 85.05 billion kWh (2011 est.)
country comparison to the world: 35

Electricity—exports: 626 million kWh (2010 est.)
country comparison to the world: 62

Electricity—imports: 0 kWh (2010 est.)
country comparison to the world: 211

Electricity—installed generating capacity: 27.5 million kW (2012 est.)
country comparison to the world: 29

Electricity—from fossil fuels: 35.7% of total installed capacity (2012 est.)
country comparison to the world: 173

Electricity—from nuclear fuels: 0% of total installed capacity (2012 est.)
country comparison to the world: 199

Electricity—from hydroelectric plants: 64.3% of total installed capacity (2012 est.)
country comparison to the world: 30

Electricity—from other renewable sources: 0% of total installed capacity (2012 est.)
country comparison to the world: 136

Crude oil—production: 2.489 million bbl/day (2012 est.)
country comparison to the world: 13

Crude oil—exports: 1.645 million bbl/day (2010 est.)
country comparison to the world: 8

Crude oil—imports: 0 bbl/day (2010 est.)
country comparison to the world: 137

Crude oil—proved reserves: 297.6 billion bbl (1 January 2013 es)
country comparison to the world: 1

Refined petroleum products—production: 1.11 million bbl/day (2010 est.)
country comparison to the world: 19

Refined petroleum products—consumption: 571,000 bbl/day (2011 est.)
country comparison to the world: 32

Refined petroleum products—exports: 638,000 bbl/day (2010 est.)
country comparison to the world: 12

Refined petroleum products—imports: 16,660 bbl/day (2011 est.)
country comparison to the world: 111

Natural gas—production: 25.28 billion cu m (2012 est.)
country comparison to the world: 30

Natural gas—consumption: 27.11 billion cu m (2010 est.)
country comparison to the world: 30

Natural gas—exports: 0 cu m (2011 est.)
country comparison to the world: 202

Natural gas—imports: 2.11 billion cu m (2011 est.)
country comparison to the world: 46

Natural gas—proved reserves: 5.524 trillion cu m (1 January 2013 es)
country comparison to the world: 8

Carbon dioxide emissions from consumption of energy: 182.7 million Mt (2011 est.)
country comparison to the world: 33

COMMUNICATIONS

Telephones—main lines in use: 7.65 million (2012)
country comparison to the world: 24

Telephones—mobile cellular: 30.52 million (2012)
country comparison to the world: 34

Telephone system:
general assessment: modern and expanding
domestic: domestic satellite system with 3 earth stations; recent substantial improvement in telephone service in rural areas; substantial increase in digitalization of exchanges and trunk lines; installation of a national interurban fiber-optic network capable of digital multimedia services; combined fixed and mobile-cellular telephone subscribership 130 per 100 persons
international: country code—58; submarine cable systems provide connectivity to the Caribbean, Central and South America, and US; satellite earth stations—1 Intelsat (Atlantic Ocean) and 1 PanAmSat; participating with Colombia, Ecuador, Peru, and Bolivia in the construction of an international fiber-optic network; constructing submarine cable to provide connectivity to Cuba with an estimated date of completion in late 2011 (2010)

Broadcast media: government supervises a mixture of state-run and private broadcast media; 1 state-run TV network, 4 privately owned TV networks, a privately owned news channel with limited national coverage, and a government-backed pan-American channel; state-run radio network includes 65 news stations and roughly another 30 stations targeted at specific audiences; state-sponsored community broadcasters include 244 radio stations and 36 TV stations; the number of private broadcast radio stations has been declining, but many still remain in operation (2010)

Internet country code: .ve

Internet hosts: 1.016 million (2012)
country comparison to the world: 46

Internet users: 8.918 million (2009)
country comparison to the world: 32

TRANSPORTATION

Airports: 444 (2013)
country comparison to the world: 19

Airports—with paved runways: *total:* 127
over 3,047 m: 6
2,438 to 3,047 m: 9
1,524 to 2,437 m: 33
914 to 1,523 m: 62
under 914 m: 17 (2013)

Airports—with unpaved runways: *total:* 317
2,438 to 3,047 m: 3
1,524 to 2,437 m: 57
914 to 1,523 m: 127
under 914 m: 130 (2013)

Heliports: 3 (2013)

Pipelines: extra heavy crude 981 km; gas 5,941 km; oil 7,588 km; refined products 1,778 km (2013)

Railways: *total:* 806 km
country comparison to the world: 98
standard gauge: 806 km 1.435-m gauge (41 km electrified) (2008)

Roadways: *total:* 96,155 km
country comparison to the world: 48
paved: 32,308 km
unpaved: 63,847 km (2002)

Waterways: 7,100 km (the Orinoco River (400 km) and Lake de Maracaibo are navigable by oceangoing vessels) (2011)
country comparison to the world: 21

Merchant marine: *total:* 5 3
country comparison to the world: 69
by type: bulk carrier 4, cargo 12, chemical tanker 1, liquefied gas 5, passenger 1, passenger/cargo 14, petroleum tanker 16
foreign-owned: 9 (Denmark 1, Estonia 1, Germany 1, Greece 4, Mexico 1, Spain 1)
registered in other countries: 14 (Panama 13, Saint Vincent and the Grenadines 1) (2010)

Ports and terminals: *major seaport(s):* La Guaira, Maracaibo, Puerto Cabello, Punta Cardon
oil terminals: Jose terminal

Transportation—note: the International Maritime Bureau reports the territorial and offshore waters in the Caribbean Sea as a significant risk for piracy and armed robbery against ships; numerous vessels, including commercial shipping and pleasure craft, have been attacked and hijacked both at anchor and while underway; crews have been robbed and stores or cargoes stolen

MILITARY

Military branches: Bolivarian National Armed Forces (Fuerza Armada Nacional Bolivariana, FANB): Bolivarian Army (Ejercito Bolivariano, EB), Bolivarian Navy (Armada Bolivariana, AB; includes Naval Infantry, Coast Guard, Naval Aviation), Bolivarian Military Aviation (Aviacion Militar Bolivariana, AMB; includes Air National Guard), Bolivarian National Guard (Guardia Nacional Bolivaria, GNB) (2013) Military service age and obligation: 18-30 years of age for compulsory and voluntary military service; 30-month conscript service obligation; Navy requires 6th-grade education for enlisted personnel; all citizens of military service age (18-60 years old) are obligated to register for military service (2012)

Manpower available for military service:
males age 16-49: 7,013,854
females age 16-49: 7,165,661 (2010 est.)

Manpower fit for military service:
males age 16-49: 5,614,743
females age 16-49: 6,074,834 (2010 est.)

Manpower reaching militarily significant age annually: *male:* 277,210
female: 273,353 (2010 est.)

Military expenditures: 1.05% of GDP (2012)
country comparison to the world: 98
0.75% of GDP (2011)
1.05% of GDP (2010)

TRANSNATIONAL ISSUES

Disputes—international: claims all of the area west of the Essequibo River in Guyana, preventing any discussion of a maritime boundary; Guyana has expressed its intention to join Barbados in asserting claims before the United Nations Convention on the Law of the Sea that Trinidad and Tobago's maritime boundary with Venezuela extends into their waters; dispute with Colombia over maritime boundary and Venezuelan administered Los

Monjes islands near the Gulf of Venezuela; Colombian organized illegal narcotics and paramilitary activities penetrate Venezuela's shared border region; in 2006, an estimated 139,000 Colombians sought protection in 150 communities along the border in Venezuela; US, France, and the Netherlands recognize Venezuela's granting full effect to Aves Island, thereby claiming a Venezuelan Economic Exclusion Zone/continental shelf extending over a large portion of the eastern Caribbean Sea; Dominica, Saint Kitts and Nevis, Saint Lucia, and Saint Vincent and the Grenadines protest Venezuela's full effect claim

Refugees and internally displaced persons: *refugees (country of origin):* 203,563 (Colombia) (2012)

Trafficking in persons: *current situation:* Venezuela is a source, transit, and destination country for men, women, and children subjected to sex trafficking and forced labor; Venezuelan women and girls are trafficked within the country for sexual exploitation, lured from the nation's interior to urban and tourist areas; women from Colombia, Peru, Haiti, China, and South Africa are also reported to have been sexually exploited in Venezuela; some Venezuelan women are transported to Caribbean islands, particularly Aruba, Curacao, and Trinidad & Tobago, where they are subjected to forced prostitution; some Venezuelan children are forced to beg on the streets or work as domestic servants, while Ecuadorian children, who are often from indigenous communities, are subjected to forced labor

tier rating: Tier 2 Watch List—Venezuela does not fully comply with the minimum standards for the elimination of trafficking; however, it is making significant efforts to do so; the government has increased the investigation of forced labor crimes but has not publicly document progress on prosecutions and convictions of trafficking offenders or on victim identification or assistance; the government also does not report on the existence of formal procedures for identifying trafficking victims and referring them to victim services; authorities provide limited funding to some NGOs providing victim services; public service announcements and an awareness campaign on human trafficking have continued (2013)

Illicit drugs: small-scale illicit producer of opium and coca for the processing of opiates and coca derivatives; however, large quantities of cocaine, heroin, and marijuana transit the country from Colombia bound for US and Europe; significant narcotics-related money-laundering activity, especially along the border with Colombia and on Margarita Island; active eradication program primarily targeting opium; increasing signs of drug-related activities by Colombian insurgents on border

VIETNAM

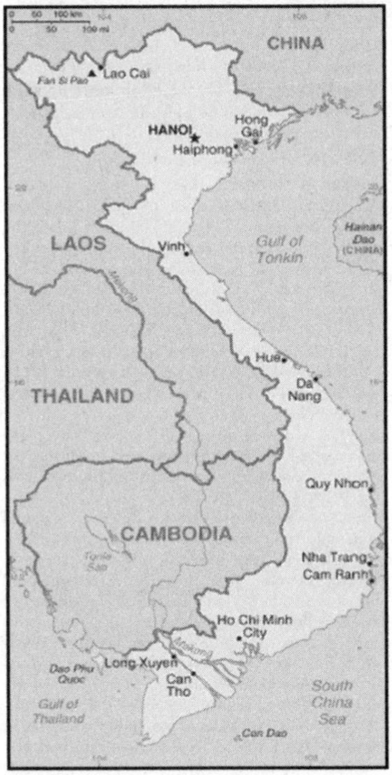

INTRODUCTION

Background: The conquest of Vietnam by France began in 1858 and was completed by 1884. It became part of French Indochina in 1887. Vietnam declared independence after World War II, but France continued to rule until its 1954 defeat by communist forces under Ho Chi MINH. Under the Geneva Accords of 1954, Vietnam was divided into the communist North and anti-communist South. US economic and military aid to South Vietnam grew through the 1960s in an attempt to bolster the government, but US armed forces were withdrawn following a cease-fire agreement in 1973. Two years later, North Vietnamese forces overran the South reuniting the country under communist rule. Despite the return of peace, for over a decade the country experienced little economic growth because of conservative leadership policies, the persecution and mass exodus of individuals—many of them successful South Vietnamese merchants—and growing international isolation. However, since the enactment of Vietnam's "doi moi" (renovation) policy in 1986, Vietnamese authorities have committed to increased economic liberalization and enacted structural reforms needed to modernize the economy and to produce more competitive, export-driven industries. The communist leaders, however, maintain control on political expression and have resisted outside calls to improve human rights. The country continues to experience small-scale protests from various groups - the vast majority connected to land-use issues, calls for increased political space, and the lack of equitable mechanisms for resolving disputes. Various ethnic minorities, such as the Montagnards of the Central Highlands and the Khmer Krom in the southern delta region, have also held protests.

GEOGRAPHY

Location: Southeastern Asia, bordering the Gulf of Thailand, Gulf of Tonkin, and South China Sea, as well as China, Laos, and Cambodia

Geographic coordinates: 16 10 N, 107 50 E

Map references: Southeast Asia

Area: *total:* 331,210 sq km
country comparison to the world: 66
land: 310,070 sq km
water: 21,140 sq km

Area—comparative: slightly larger than New Mexico

Land boundaries: *total:* 4,639 km
border countries: Cambodia 1,228 km, China 1,281 km, Laos 2,130 km

Coastline: 3,444 km (excludes islands)

Maritime claims: *territorial sea:* 12 nm
contiguous zone: 24 nm
exclusive economic zone: 200 nm
continental shelf: 200 nm or to the edge of the continental margin

Climate: tropical in south; monsoonal in north with hot, rainy season (May to September) and warm, dry season (October to March)

Terrain: low, flat delta in south and north; central highlands; hilly, mountainous in far north and northwest

Elevation extremes:
lowest point: South China Sea 0 m
highest point: Fan Si Pan 3,144 m

Natural resources: phosphates, coal, manganese, rare earth elements, bauxite, chromate, offshore oil and gas deposits, timber, hydropower

Land use: *arable land:* 19.64%
permanent crops: 11.18%
other: 69.18% (2011)

Irrigated land: 45,850 sq km (2005)

Total renewable water resources: 884.1 cu km (2011)

Freshwater withdrawal (domestic/industrial/agricultural): *total:* 82.03 cu km/yr (1%/4%/95%)
per capita: 965 cu m/yr (2005)

Natural hazards: occasional typhoons (May to January) with extensive flooding, especially in the Mekong River delta

Environment—current issues: logging and slash-and-burn agricultural practices contribute to deforestation and soil degradation; water pollution and overfishing threaten marine life populations; groundwater contamination limits potable water supply; growing urban industrialization and population migration are rapidly degrading environment in Hanoi and Ho Chi Minh City

Environment—international agreements:
party to: Biodiversity, Climate Change, Climate Change-Kyoto Protocol, Desertification, Endangered Species, Environmental Modification, Hazardous Wastes, Law of the Sea, Ozone Layer Protection, Ship Pollution, Wetlands
signed, but not ratified: none of the selected agreements

Geography—note: extending 1,650 km north to south, the country is only 50 km across at its narrowest point

PEOPLE AND SOCIETY

Nationality: *noun:* Vietnamese (singular and plural)
adjective: Vietnamese

Ethnic groups: Kinh (Viet) 85.7%, Tay 1.9%, Thai 1.8%, Muong 1.5%, Khmer 1.5%, Mong 1.2%, Nung 1.1%, others 5.3% (1999 census)

Languages: Vietnamese (official), English (increasingly favored as a second language), some French, Chinese, and Khmer, mountain area languages (Mon-Khmer and Malayo-Polynesian)

Religions: Buddhist 9.3%, Catholic 6.7%, Hoa Hao 1.5%, Cao Dai 1.1%, Protestant 0.5%, Muslim 0.1%, none 80.8% (1999 census)

Population: 93,421,835 (July 2014 est.)
country comparison to the world: 15

Age structure:
0-14 years: 24.3% (male 11,946,656/female 10,800,602)
15-24 years: 17.8% (male 8,598,360/female 8,023,377)
25-54 years: 44.8% (male 20,983,638/female 20,861,243)
55-64 years: 5.7% (male 3,149,494/female 3,763,309)
65 years and over: 5.6% (male 2,034,721/female 3,260,435) (2014 est.)

Dependency ratios:
total dependency ratio: 41.4 %
youth dependency ratio: 32.1 %
elderly dependency ratio: 9.3 %
potential support ratio: 10.7 (2013)

Median age: *total:* 29.2 years
male: 28.1 years
female: 30.2 years (2014 est.)

Population growth rate: 1% (2014 est.)
country comparison to the world: 119

Birth rate: 16.26 births/1,000 population (2014 est.)
country comparison to the world: 121

Death rate: 5.93 deaths/1,000 population (2014 est.)
country comparison to the world: 171

Net migration rate: -0.32 migrant(s)/1,000 population (2014 est.)
country comparison to the world: 129

Urbanization: *urban population:* 31% of total population (2011)
rate of urbanization: 3.03% annual rate of change (2010-15 est.)

Major urban areas—population: Ho Chi Minh City 5.976 million; HANOI (capital) 2.668 million; Haiphong 1.941 million; Da Nang 807,000 (2009)

Sex ratio: *at birth:* 1.12 male(s)/female
0-14 years: 1.11 male(s)/female
15-24 years: 1.07 male(s)/female
25-54 years: 1.01 male(s)/female
55-64 years: 1 male(s)/female
65 years and over: 0.62 male(s)/female
total population: 1 male(s)/female (2014 est.)

Mother's mean age at first birth: 22.6 (2002 est.)

Maternal mortality rate: 59 deaths/100,000 live births (2010)
country comparison to the world: 101

Infant mortality rate: *total:* 18.99 deaths/1,000 live births
country comparison to the world: 95
male: 19.35 deaths/1,000 live births
female: 18.58 deaths/1,000 live births (2014 est.)

Life expectancy at birth:
total population: 72.91 years
country comparison to the world: 129
male: 70.44 years
female: 75.65 years (2014 est.)

Total fertility rate: 1.85 children born/woman (2014 est.)
country comparison to the world: 147

Contraceptive prevalence rate: 77.8% (2010/11)

Health expenditures: 6.8% of GDP (2011)
country comparison to the world: 86

Physicians density: 1.22 physicians/1,000 population (2008)

Hospital bed density: 2.2 beds/1,000 population (2010)

Drinking water source:
improved:
urban: 99.5% of population
rural: 93.8% of population
total: 95.6% of population
unimproved:
urban: 0.5% of population
rural: 6.2% of population
total: 4.4% of population (2011 est.)

Sanitation facility access:
improved:
urban: 92.7% of population
rural: 66.7% of population
total: 74.8% of population
unimproved:
urban: 7.3% of population
rural: 33.3% of population
total: 25.2% of population (2011 est.)

HIV/AIDS—adult prevalence rate: 0.4% (2012 est.)
country comparison to the world: 81

HIV/AIDS—people living with HIV/AIDS: 259,200 (2012 est.)
country comparison to the world: 23

HIV/AIDS—deaths: 11,700 (2012 est.)
country comparison to the world: 25

Major infectious diseases:
degree of risk: very high
food or waterborne diseases: bacterial diarrhea, hepatitis A, and typhoid fever
vectorborne diseases: dengue fever, malaria, and Japanese encephalitis
note: highly pathogenic H5N1 avian influenza has been identified in this country; it poses a negligible risk with extremely rare cases possible among US citizens who have close contact with birds (2013)

Obesity—adult prevalence rate: 1.7% (2008)
country comparison to the world: 186

Children under the age of 5 years underweight: 12% (2011)
country comparison to the world: 60

Education expenditures: 6.3% of GDP (2010)
country comparison to the world: 33

Literacy: *definition:* age 15 and over can read and write
total population: 93.4%
male: 95.4%
female: 91.4% (2011 est.)

Child labor—children ages 5-14:
total number: 2,545,616
percentage: 16 % (2006 est.)

Unemployment, youth ages 15-24: *total:* 5.5%
country comparison to the world: 135
male: 4.6%
female: 6.5% (2012)

GOVERNMENT

Country name: *conventional long form:* Socialist Republic of Vietnam
conventional short form: Vietnam
local long form: Cong Hoa Xa Hoi Chu Nghia Viet Nam
local short form: Viet Nam
abbreviation: SRV

Government type: Communist state

Capital: *name:* Hanoi (Ha Noi)

geographic coordinates: 21 02 N, 105 51 E
time difference: UTC+7 (12 hours ahead of Washington, DC during Standard Time)

Administrative divisions: 58 provinces (tinh, singular and plural) and 5 municipalities (thanh pho, singular and plural)
provinces: An Giang, Bac Giang, Bac Kan, Bac Lieu, Bac Ninh, Ba Ria-Vung Tau, Ben Tre, Binh Dinh, Binh Duong, Binh Phuoc, Binh Thuan, Ca Mau, Cao Bang, Dak Lak, Dak Nong, Dien Bien, Dong Nai, Dong Thap, Gia Lai, Ha Giang, Ha Nam, Ha Tinh, Hai Duong, Hau Giang, Hoa Binh, Hung Yen, Khanh Hoa, Kien Giang, Kon Tum, Lai Chau, Lam Dong, Lang Son, Lao Cai, Long An, Nam Dinh, Nghe An, Ninh Binh, Ninh Thuan, Phu Tho, Phu Yen, Quang Binh, Quang Nam, Quang Ngai, Quang Ninh, Quang Tri, Soc Trang, Son La, Tay Ninh, Thai Binh, Thai Nguyen, Thanh Hoa, Thua Thien-Hue, Tien Giang, Tra Vinh, Tuyen Quang, Vinh Long, Vinh Phuc, Yen Bai
municipalities: Can Tho, Da Nang, Ha Noi, Hai Phong, Ho Chi Minh City (Saigon)

Independence: 2 September 1945 (from France)

National holiday: Independence Day, 2 September (1945)

Constitution: several previous; latest adopted 15 April 1992, effective 1 January 1995; amended 2001; note—in early 2013, the Vietnamese Government asked for public comment on its constitution (2013)

Legal system: civil law system; note—the civil code of 2005 reflects a European-style civil law

International law organization participation: has not submitted an ICJ jurisdiction declaration; non-party state to the ICCt

Suffrage: 18 years of age; universal

Executive branch: *chief of state:* President Truong Tan SANG (since 25 July 2011); Vice President Nguyen Thi DOAN (since 25 July 2007)
head of government: Prime Minister Nguyen Tan DUNG (since 27 June 2006); Deputy Prime Minister Vu Duc DAM (since 13 November 2013), Deputy Prime Minister Hoang Trung HAI (since 2 August 2007), Deputy Prime Minister Pham Binh MINH (since 13 November 2013), Deputy Prime Minister Vu Van NINH (since 3 August 2011), and Deputy Prime Minister Nguyen Xuan PHUC (since 3 August 2011)
cabinet: Cabinet appointed by president based on proposal of prime minister and confirmed by National Assembly (For more information visit the World Leaders website)
elections: president elected by the National Assembly from among its members for five-year term; last election held 25 July 2011 (next to be held in July 2016); prime minister appointed by the president from among the members of the National Assembly; deputy prime ministers appointed by the prime minister; appointment of prime minister and deputy prime ministers confirmed by National Assembly
election results: Truong Tan SANG elected president, percent of National Assembly vote—97%; Nguyen Tan DUNG elected prime minister, percent of National Assembly vote—94%

Legislative branch: unicameral National Assembly or Quoc Hoi (500 seats; members elected by popular vote to serve five-year terms)
elections: last held on 22 May 2011 (next to be held in May 2016)
election results: percent of vote by party—NA; seats by party—CPV 458, non-party CPV-approved 38, self-nominated 4; note—500 candidates were elected; the 496 CPV and non-party CPV-approved delegates were members of the Vietnamese Fatherland Front and were vetted prior to the election

Judicial branch: *highest court(s):* Supreme People's Court (consists of the chief justice and 13 judges)
judge selection and term of office: chief justice elected by the National Assembly on the recommendation of the president for a 5-year, renewable term; other judges appointed by the president for 5-year terms
subordinate courts: Court of Appeals; administrative, civil, criminal, economic, and labor courts; Central Military Court; People's Special Courts; note—the National Assembly can establish special tribunals

Political parties and leaders: Communist Party of Vietnam or CPV [Nguyen Phu TRONG]
note: other parties proscribed

Political pressure groups and leaders: 8406 Bloc; Democratic Party of Vietnam or DPV; People's Democratic Party Vietnam or PDP-VN; Alliance for Democracy
note: these groups advocate democracy but are not recognized by the government

International organization participation: ADB, APEC, ARF, ASEAN, CICA, CP, EAS, FAO, G-77, IAEA, IBRD, ICAO, ICC (NGOs), ICRM, IDA, IFAD, IFC, IFRCS, ILO, IMF, IMO, IMSO, Interpol, IOC, IOM, IPU, ISO, ITSO, ITU, MIGA, NAM, OIF, OPCW, PCA, UN, UNCTAD, UNESCO, UNIDO, UNWTO, UPU, WCO, WFTU (NGOs), WHO, WIPO, WMO, WTO

Diplomatic representation in the US:
chief of mission: Ambassador Nguyen Quoc CUONG (since 2 May 2011)
chancery: 1233 20th Street NW, Suite 400, Washington, DC 20036
telephone: [1] (202) 861-0737
FAX: [1] (202) 861-0917
consulate(s) general: Houston, New York, San Francisco
consulate: New York

Diplomatic representation from the US:
chief of mission: Ambassador David B. SHEAR (since 4 August 2011)
embassy: Rose Garden Building, 170 Ngoc Khanh St., Hanoi
mailing address: 7 Lang Ha Street, Ba Dinh District, Hanoi; 4550 Hanoi Place, Washington, DC 20521-4550
telephone: [84] (4) 3850-5000
FAX: [84] (4) 3850-5010
consulate(s) general: Ho Chi Minh City

Flag description: red field with a large yellow five-pointed star in the center; red symbolizes revolution and blood, the five-pointed star represents the five elements of the populace—peasants, workers, intellectuals, traders, and soldiers—that unite to build socialism

National symbol(s): yellow, five-pointed star on red field; lotus blossom

National anthem: *name:* "Tien quan ca" (The Song of the Marching Troops)
lyrics/music: Nguyen Van CAO
note: adopted as the national anthem of the Democratic Republic of Vietnam in 1945; it became the national anthem of the unified Socialist Republic of Vietnam in 1976; although it consists of two verses, only the first is used as the official anthem

ECONOMY

Economy—overview: Vietnam is a densely-populated developing country that has been transitioning from the rigidities of a centrally-planned economy since 1986. Vietnamese authorities have reaffirmed their commitment to economic modernization in recent years. Vietnam joined the World Trade Organization in January 2007, which has promoted more competitive, export-driven industries. Vietnam became an official negotiating partner in the Trans-Pacific Partnership trade agreement in 2010. Agriculture's share of economic output has continued to shrink from about 25% in 2000 to less than 20% in 2013, while industry's share increased from 36% to more than 42% in the same period. State-owned enterprises account for about 40% of GDP. Poverty has declined significantly, and Vietnam is working to create jobs to meet the challenge of a labor force that is growing by more than one million people every year. The global recession hurt Vietnam's export-oriented economy, with GDP in 2013 growing at 5%, the slowest rate of growth since 1999. In 2013, however, exports increased by more than 12%, year-on-year; several administrative actions brought the trade deficit back into balance. Between 2008 and 2011, Vietnam's managed currency, the dong, was devalued in excess of 20%, but its value remained relatively stable in 2013. Hanoi has oscillated between promoting growth and emphasizing macroeconomic stability in recent years. In February 2011, the government shifted from policies aimed at achieving a high rate of economic growth, which had stoked inflation, to those aimed at stabilizing the economy, through tighter monetary and fiscal control. Although Vietnam unveiled a broad, "three pillar" economic reform program in early 2012, proposing the restructuring of public investment, state-owned enterprises, and the banking sector, little perceptible progress has been made. Vietnam's economy continues to face challenges from an undercapitalized banking sector. Non-performing loans weigh heavily on banks and businesses.

GDP (purchasing power parity): $358.9 billion (2013 est.)
country comparison to the world: 39
$340.8 billion (2012 est.)
$323.8 billion (2011 est.)
note: data are in 2013 US dollars

GDP (official exchange rate): $170 billion (2013 est.)

GDP—real growth rate: 5.3% (2013 est.)
country comparison to the world: 50
5.2% (2012 est.)
6.2% (2011 est.)

GDP—per capita (PPP): $4,000 (2013 est.)
country comparison to the world: 169
$3,800 (2012 est.)
$3,700 (2011 est.)
note: data are in 2013 US dollars

Gross national saving: 38.4% of GDP (2013 est.)
country comparison to the world: 12
39% of GDP (2012 est.)
32.8% of GDP (2011 est.)

GDP—composition, by end use:
household consumption: 68.9%
government consumption: 6.8%
investment in fixed capital: 30.4%
investment in inventories: 3.1%
exports of goods and services: 84.7%
imports of goods and services: -93.9% (2013 est.)

GDP—composition, by sector of origin:
agriculture: 19.3%
industry: 38.5%
services: 42.2% (2013 est.)

Agriculture—products: paddy rice, coffee, rubber, tea, pepper, soybeans, cashews, sugar cane, peanuts, bananas; poultry; fish, seafood

Industries: food processing, garments, shoes, machine-building; mining, coal, steel; cement, chemical fertilizer, glass, tires, oil, mobile phones

Industrial production growth rate: 5% (2013 est.)
country comparison to the world: 55

Labor force: 52.93 million (2013 est.)
country comparison to the world: 11

Labor force—by occupation: *agriculture:* 48%
industry: 21%
services: 31% (2012)

Unemployment rate: 1.3% (2013 est.)
country comparison to the world: 7
3.2% (2012 est.)

Population below poverty line: 11.3% (2012 est.)

Household income or consumption by percentage share: *lowest 10%:* 3.2%
highest 10%: 30.2% (2008)

Distribution of family income—Gini index: 37.6 (2008)
country comparison to the world: 78
36.1 (1998)

Budget: *revenues:* $42.82 billion
expenditures: $50 billion (2013 est.)

Taxes and other revenues: 25.2% of GDP (2013 est.)
country comparison to the world: 125

Budget surplus (+) or deficit (-): -4.2% of GDP (2013 est.)
country comparison to the world: 152

Public debt: 48.2% of GDP (2013 est.)
country comparison to the world: 70
48.1% of GDP (2012 est.)
note: official data; data cover general government debt, and includes debt instruments issued (or owned) by government entities other than the treasury; the data include treasury debt held by foreign entities; the data include debt issued by subnational entities, as well as intra-governmental debt; intra-governmental debt consists of treasury borrowings from surpluses in the social funds, such as for retirement, medical care, and unemployment; debt instruments for the social funds are not sold at public auctions

Fiscal year: calendar year

Inflation rate (consumer prices): 6.8% (2013 est.)
country comparison to the world: 184
9.1% (2012 est.)

Central bank discount rate: 9% (31 December 2012)
country comparison to the world: 11
15% (31 December 2011)

Commercial bank prime lending rate: 10.5% (31 December 2013 est.)
country comparison to the world: 57
13.47% (31 December 2012 est.)

Stock of narrow money: $43.99 billion (31 December 2013 est.)
country comparison to the world: 50
$40.34 billion (31 December 2012 est.)

Stock of broad money: $184.9 billion (31 December 2013 est.)
country comparison to the world: 40
$165.9 billion (31 December 2012 est.)

Stock of domestic credit: $173.8 billion (31 December 2013 est.)
country comparison to the world: 43
$163.5 billion (31 December 2012 est.)

Market value of publicly traded shares: $38.2 billion (31 December 2011 est.)
country comparison to the world: 58
$26 billion (31 December 2011)
$37 billion (31 December 2010 est.)

Current account balance: $8.162 billion (2013 est.)
country comparison to the world: 25
$9.062 billion (2012 est.)

Exports: $128.9 billion (2013 est.)
country comparison to the world: 34
$114.6 billion (2012 est.)

Exports—commodities: clothes, shoes, electronics, seafood, crude oil, rice, coffee, wooden products, machinery

Exports—partners: US 17.8%, Japan 11.8%, China 11.2%, South Korea 5%, Malaysia 4.1% (2012)

Imports: $121.4 billion (2013 est.)
country comparison to the world: 33
$104.7 billion (2012 est.)

Imports—commodities: machinery and equipment, petroleum products, steel products, raw materials for the clothing and shoe industries, electronics, plastics, automobiles

Imports—partners: China 25.8%, South Korea 13.9%, Japan 10.4%, Singapore 6%, Thailand 5.2%, US 4.3% (2012)

Reserves of foreign exchange and gold: $32.49 billion (31 December 2013 est.)
country comparison to the world: 51
$26.11 billion (31 December 2012 est.)

Debt—external: $68.38 billion (31 December 2013 est.)
country comparison to the world: 56
$63.95 billion (31 December 2012 est.)

Stock of direct foreign investment—at home: $84.61 billion (31 December 2013 est.)
country comparison to the world: 44
$73.71 billion (31 December 2012 est.)

Stock of direct foreign investment—abroad: $7.7 billion (31 December 2009 est.)
country comparison to the world: 59
$5.3 billion (31 December 2008)

Exchange rates: dong (VND) per US dollar—
21,118 (2013 est.)
20,859 (2012 est.)
18,612.92 (2010 est.)
17,799.6 (2009)
16,548.3 (2008)

ENERGY

Electricity—production: 117 billion kWh (2012 est.)
country comparison to the world: 32

Electricity—consumption: 104 billion kWh (2012 est.)
country comparison to the world: 32

Electricity—exports: 964 million kWh (2010 est.)
country comparison to the world: 58

Electricity—imports: 2.7 billion kWh (2012 est.)
country comparison to the world: 49

Electricity—installed generating capacity: 26.3 million kW (2012 est.)
country comparison to the world: 32

Electricity—from fossil fuels: 55% of total installed capacity (2012 est.)
country comparison to the world: 144

Electricity—from nuclear fuels: 0% of total installed capacity (2012 est.)
country comparison to the world: 201

Electricity—from hydroelectric plants: 45% of total installed capacity (2012 est.)
country comparison to the world: 51

Electricity—from other renewable sources: 0.1% of total installed capacity (2012 est.)
country comparison to the world: 99

Crude oil—production: 363,500 bbl/day (2012 est.)
country comparison to the world: 33

Crude oil—exports: 188,000 bbl/day (2012 est.)
country comparison to the world: 30

Crude oil—imports: 0 bbl/day (2012 est.)
country comparison to the world: 139

Crude oil—proved reserves: 4.4 billion bbl (1 January 2013 es)
country comparison to the world: 26

Refined petroleum products—production: 112,000 bbl/day (2012 est.)
country comparison to the world: 71

Refined petroleum products—consumption: 259,900 bbl/day (2012 est.)
country comparison to the world: 47

Refined petroleum products—exports: 37,050 bbl/day (2012 est.)
country comparison to the world: 65

Refined petroleum products—imports: 184,900 bbl/day (2012 est.)
country comparison to the world: 28

Natural gas—production: 9.3 billion cu m (2012 est.)
country comparison to the world: 43

Natural gas—consumption: 10.2 billion cu m (2012 est.)
country comparison to the world: 46

Natural gas—exports: 0 cu m (2012 est.)
country comparison to the world: 204

Natural gas—imports: 890 million cu m (2012 est.)
country comparison to the world: 59

Natural gas—proved reserves: 699.4 billion cu m (1 January 2013 es)
country comparison to the world: 30

Carbon dioxide emissions from consumption of energy: 112.7 million Mt (2011 est.)
country comparison to the world: 39

COMMUNICATIONS

Telephones—main lines in use: 10.191 million (2012)
country comparison to the world: 21

Telephones—mobile cellular: 134.066 million (2012)
country comparison to the world: 8

Telephone system:
general assessment: Vietnam is putting considerable effort into modernization and expansion of its telecommunication system
domestic: all provincial exchanges are digitalized and connected to Hanoi, Da Nang, and Ho Chi Minh City by fiber-optic cable or microwave radio relay networks; main lines have been increased, and the use of mobile telephones is growing rapidly
international: country code—84; a landing point for the SEA-ME-WE-3, the C2C, and Thailand-Vietnam-Hong Kong submarine cable systems; the Asia-America Gateway submarine cable system, completed in 2009, provided new access links to Asia and the US; satellite earth stations—2 Intersputnik (Indian Ocean region) (2011)

Broadcast media: government controls all broadcast media exercising oversight through the Ministry of Information and Communication (MIC); government-controlled national TV provider, Vietnam Television (VTV), operates a network of 9 channels with several regional broadcasting centers; programming is relayed nationwide via a network of provincial and municipal TV stations; law limits access to satellite TV but many households are able to access foreign programming via home satellite equipment; government-controlled Voice of Vietnam, the national radio broadcaster, broadcasts on 6 channels and is repeated on AM, FM, and shortwave stations throughout Vietnam (2008)

Internet country code: .vn

Internet hosts: 189,553 (2012)
country comparison to the world: 74

Internet users: 23.382 million (2009)
country comparison to the world: 17

TRANSPORTATION

Airports: 45 (2013)
country comparison to the world: 9 6

Airports—with paved runways: *total:* 3 8
over 3,047 m: 10
2,438 to 3,047 m: 6
1,524 to 2,437 m: 13
914 to 1,523 m: 9 (2013)

Airports—with unpaved runways: *total:* 7
1,524 to 2,437 m: 1
914 to 1,523 m: 3
under 914 m: 3 (2013)

Heliports: 1 (2013)

Pipelines: condensate 72 km; condensate/gas 398 km; gas 955 km; oil 128 km; oil/gas/water 33 km; refined products 206 km; water 13 km (2013)

Railways: *total:* 2,632 km
country comparison to the world: 63
standard gauge: 527 km 1.435-m gauge
narrow gauge: 2,105 km 1.000-m gauge (2008)

Roadways: *total:* 206,633 km
country comparison to the world: 24
paved: 148,338 km
unpaved: 47,130 km (2013)

Waterways: 47,130 km (30,831 km weight under 50 tons) (2011)
country comparison to the world: 4

Merchant marine: *total:* 579
country comparison to the world: 20
by type: barge carrier 1, bulk carrier 142, cargo 335, chemical tanker 23, container 19, liquefied gas 7, passenger/cargo 1, petroleum tanker 48, refrigerated cargo 1, roll on/roll off 1, specialized tanker 1
registered in other countries: 86 (Cambodia 1, Kiribati 2, Mongolia 33, Panama 43, Taiwan 1, Tuvalu 6) (2010)

Ports and terminals:
major seaport(s): Cam Pha Port, Da Nang, Haiphong, Phu My, Quy Nhon
river port(s): Ho Chi Minh (Mekong)
container port(s) (TEUs): Haiphong (1,018,794), Saigon New Port (3,071,777)

Transportation—note: the International Maritime Bureau reports the territorial and offshore waters in the South China Sea as high risk for piracy and armed robbery against ships; numerous commercial vessels have been attacked and hijacked both at anchor and while underway; hijacked vessels are often disguised and cargo diverted to ports in East Asia; crews have been murdered or cast adrift

MILITARY

Military branches: People's Armed Forces: People's Army of Vietnam (PAVN; includes Vietnam People's Navy (with Naval Infantry), Vietnam People's Air and Air Defense Force, Border Defense Command, Coast Guard) (2013)

Military service age and obligation: 18-25 years of age for male compulsory and voluntary military service; females may volunteer for active duty military service; conscription typically takes place twice annually and service obligation is 18 months

(Army, Air Defense), 2 years (Navy and Air Force); 18-45 years of age (male) or 18-40 years of age (female) for Militia Force or Self Defense Force service; males may enroll in military schools at age 17 (2013)

Manpower available for military service:
males age 16-49: 25,649,738
females age 16-49: 24,995,692 (2010 est.)

Manpower fit for military service:
males age 16-49: 20,405,847
females age 16-49: 21,098,102 (2010 est.)

Manpower reaching militarily significant age annually: *male:* 847,743
female: 787,341 (2010 est.)

Military expenditures: 2.37% of GDP (2012)
country comparison to the world: 33
2.17% of GDP (2011)
2.37% of GDP (2010)

TRANSNATIONAL ISSUES

Disputes—international: southeast Asian states have enhanced border surveillance to check the spread of avian flu; Cambodia and Laos protest Vietnamese squatters and armed encroachments along border; Cambodia accuses Vietnam of a wide variety of illicit cross-border activities; progress on a joint development area with Cambodia is hampered by an unresolved dispute over sovereignty of offshore islands; an estimated 300,000 Vietnamese refugees reside in China; establishment of a maritime boundary with Cambodia is hampered by unresolved dispute over the sovereignty of offshore islands; the decade-long demarcation of the China-Vietnam land boundary was completed in 2009; China occupies the Paracel Islands also claimed by Vietnam and Taiwan; Brunei claims a maritime boundary extending beyond as far as a median with Vietnam, thus asserting an implicit claim to Lousia Reef; the 2002 "Declaration on the Conduct of Parties in the South China Sea" has eased tensions but falls short of a legally binding "code of conduct" desired by several of the disputants; Vietnam continues to expand construction of facilities in the Spratly Islands; in March 2005, the national oil companies of China, the Philippines, and Vietnam signed a joint accord to conduct marine seismic activities in the Spratly Islands; Economic Exclusion Zone negotiations with Indonesia are ongoing, and the two countries in Fall 2011 agreed to work together to reduce illegal fishing along their maritime boundary

Refugees and internally displaced persons: *stateless persons:* 11,500 (2012); note—Vietnam's stateless ethnic Chinese Cambodian population dates to the 1970s when thousands of Cambodians fled to Vietnam to escape the Khmer Rouge and were no longer recognized as Cambodian citizens; Vietnamese women who gave up their citizenship to marry foreign men have found themselves stateless after divorcing and returning home to Vietnam; the government addressed this problem in 2009, and Vietnamese women are beginning to reclaim their citizenship

Illicit drugs: minor producer of opium poppy; probable minor transit point for Southeast Asian heroin; government continues to face domestic opium/heroin/methamphetamine addiction problems despite longstanding crackdowns

VIRGIN ISLANDS

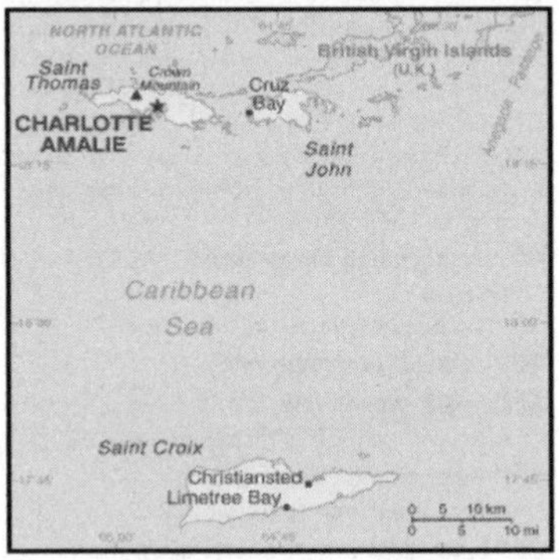

INTRODUCTION

Background: During the 17th century, the archipelago was divided into English and Dutch territorial units. Sugarcane, produced by African slave labor, drove the islands' economy during the 18th and early 19th centuries. In 1917, the US purchased the Danish portion, which had been in economic decline since the abolition of slavery in 1848.

GEOGRAPHY

Location: Caribbean, islands between the Caribbean Sea and the North Atlantic Ocean, east of Puerto Rico

Geographic coordinates: 18 20 N, 64 50 W

Map references: Central America and the Caribbean

Area: *total:* 1,910 sq km
country comparison to the world: 182
land: 346 sq km
water: 1,564 sq km

Area—comparative: twice the size of Washington, DC

Land boundaries: 0 km

Coastline: 188 km

Maritime claims: *territorial sea:* 12 nm
exclusive economic zone: 200 nm

Climate: subtropical, tempered by easterly trade winds, relatively low humidity, little seasonal temperature variation; rainy season September to November

Terrain: mostly hilly to rugged and mountainous with little level land

Elevation extremes: *lowest point:* Caribbean Sea 0 m
highest point: Crown Mountain 474 m

Natural resources: sun, sand, sea, surf

Land use: *arable land:* 2.86%
permanent crops: 2.86%
other: 94.29% (2011)

Irrigated land: 1 sq km (2011)

Natural hazards: several hurricanes in recent years; frequent and severe droughts and floods; occasional earthquakes

Environment—current issues: lack of natural freshwater resources

Geography—note: important location along the Anegada Passage—a key shipping lane for the Panama Canal; Saint Thomas has one of the best natural deepwater harbors in the Caribbean

PEOPLE AND SOCIETY

Nationality: *noun:* Virgin Islander(s) (US citizens)
adjective: Virgin Islander

Ethnic groups: black 76.2%, white 13.1%, Asian 1.1%, other 6.1%, mixed 3.5% (2000 census)

Languages: English 74.7%, Spanish or Spanish Creole 16.8%, French or French Creole 6.6%, other 1.9% (2000 census)

Religions: Protestant 59% (Baptist 42%, Episcopalian 17%), Roman Catholic 34%, other 7%

Population: 104,170 (July 2014 est.)
country comparison to the world: 195

Age structure:
0-14 years: 17.8% (male 9,386/female 9,207)
15-24 years: 10.3% (male 4,931/female 5,801)
25-54 years: 39% (male 18,350/female 22,231)
55-64 years: 18.6% (male 7,123/female 7,796)
65 years and over: 17.8% (male 8,758/female 10,587) (2014 est.)

Dependency ratios:
total dependency ratio: 58.1 %
youth dependency ratio: 32.7 %
elderly dependency ratio: 25.3 %
potential support ratio: 3.9 (2013)

Median age: *total:* 44.2 years
male: 44.5 years
female: 44 years (2014 est.)

Population growth rate: -0.56% (2014 est.)
country comparison to the world: 224

Birth rate: 10.49 births/1,000 population (2014 est.)
country comparison to the world: 184

Death rate: 8.24 deaths/1,000 population (2014 est.)
country comparison to the world: 92

Net migration rate: -7.84 migrant(s)/1,000 population (2014 est.)
country comparison to the world: 207

Urbanization: *urban population:* 95% of total population (2010)
rate of urbanization: -0.1% annual rate of change (2010-15 est.)

Major urban areas—population: CHARLOTTE AMALIE (capital) 54,000 (2009)

Sex ratio: *at birth:* 1.06 male(s)/female
0-14 years: 1.02 male(s)/female
15-24 years: 0.85 male(s)/female
25-54 years: 0.83 male(s)/female
55-64 years: 0.87 male(s)/female
65 years and over: 0.83 male(s)/female
total population: 0.88 male(s)/female (2014 est.)

Infant mortality rate: *total:* 6.79 deaths/1,000 live births
country comparison to the world: 163
male: 7.5 deaths/1,000 live births
female: 6.03 deaths/1,000 live births (2014 est.)

Life expectancy at birth:
total population: 79.75 years
country comparison to the world: 40
male: 76.7 years
female: 82.97 years (2014 est.)

Total fertility rate: 1.75 children born/woman (2014 est.)
country comparison to the world: 165

Contraceptive prevalence rate: 78.4%
note: percent of women aged 18-44 (2002)

Drinking water source:
improved:
urban: 100% of population
rural: 100% of population
total: 100% of population
unimproved:
urban: 0% of population
rural: 0% of population
total: 0% of population (2011 est.)

Sanitation facility access:
improved:
urban: 96.4% of population
rural: 96.4% of population
total: 96.4% of population
unimproved:
urban: 3.6% of population
rural: 3.6% of population
total: 3.6% of population (2011 est.)

HIV/AIDS—adult prevalence rate: NA

HIV/AIDS—people living with HIV/AIDS: NA

HIV/AIDS—deaths: NA

Literacy: *definition:* age 15 and over can read and write
total population: 90-95% est.
male: NA
female: NA (2005 est.)

GOVERNMENT

Country name: *conventional long form:* United States Virgin Islands
conventional short form: Virgin Islands
former: Danish West Indies
abbreviation: USVI

Dependency status: organized, unincorporated territory of the US with policy relations between the Virgin Islands and the US under the jurisdiction of the Office of Insular Affairs, US Department of the Interior

Government type: NA

Capital: *name:* Charlotte Amalie
geographic coordinates: 18 21 N, 64 56 W
time difference: UTC-4 (1 hour ahead of Washington, DC during Standard Time)

Administrative divisions: none (territory of the US); there are no first-order administrative divisions as defined by the US Government, but there are three islands at the second order; Saint Croix, Saint John, Saint Thomas

Independence: none (territory of the US)

National holiday: Transfer Day (from Denmark to the US), 31 March (1917)

Constitution: 22 July 1954—the Revised Organic Act of the Virgin Islands functions as a constitution for this territory of the US (2013)

Legal system: US common law

Suffrage: 18 years of age; universal; note—island residents are US citizens but do not vote in US presidential elections

Executive branch: *chief of state:* President Barack H. OBAMA (since 20 January 2009); Vice President Joseph R. BIDEN (since 20 January 2009)
head of government: Governor John DeJONGH (since 1 January 2007)
cabinet: NA (For more information visit the World Leaders website)
elections: under the US Constitution, residents of unincorporated territories, such as the Virgin Islands, do not vote in elections for US president and vice president; however, they may vote in the Democratic and Republican presidential primary elections; governor and lieutenant governor elected on the same ticket by popular vote for four-year terms (eligible for a second term); election last held on 2 November 2010 (next to be held in November 2014)
election results: John DeJONGH reelected governor; percent of vote—John DeJONGH 56.3%, Kenneth MAPP 43.6%

Legislative branch: unicameral Senate (15 seats; members are elected by popular vote to serve two-year terms)
elections: last held on 6 November 2012 (next to be held in November 2014)
election results: percent of vote by party—NA; seats by party—Democratic Party 10, ICM 2, independent 3
note: the Virgin Islands elects one non-voting representative to the US House of Representatives; election last held 6 November 2012 (next to be held on November 2014)

Judicial branch: *highest court(s):* Supreme Court of the Virgin Islands (consists of the chief justice and 2 associate justices); note—court established by US Congress in 2004 and assumed appellate jurisdiction in 2007
judge selection and term of office: justices appointed by the governor and confirmed by the Virgin Islands Senate; justices initially serve renewable 10-year terms; chief justice elected to position by peers for a 3-year term
subordinate courts: Superior Court (renamed in 2004 vice the Territorial Court); US Court of Appeals for the Third Circuit (has appellate jurisdiction over the District Court of the Virgin Islands; it is a territorial court and is not associated with a US federal judicial district); District Court of the Virgin Islands

Political parties and leaders: Democratic Party [Arturo WATLINGTON]; Independent Citizens' Movement or ICM [Usie RICHARDS]; Republican Party [Gary SPRAUVE]

Political pressure groups and leaders: NA

International organization participation: IOC, UPU, WFTU (NGOs)

Diplomatic representation in the US: none (territory of the US)

Diplomatic representation from the US: none (territory of the US)

Flag description: white field with a modified US coat of arms in the center; between the large blue initials V and I; the coat of arms shows; a yellow eagle holding an olive branch in its right talon and; three arrows in the left with a superimposed shield of seven; red and six white vertical stripes below a blue panel; white is; a symbol of purity, the letters stand for the Virgin Islands

National anthem: *name:* "Virgin Islands March"
lyrics/music: multiple/Alton Augustus ADAMS, Sr.
note: adopted 1963; serves as a local anthem; as a territory of the United States, "The Star-Spangled Banner" is official (see United States)

ECONOMY

Economy—overview: Tourism, trade, and other services are the primary economic; activities, accounting for roughly 57% of GDP and about half; of total civilian employment in 2010. The islands hosted; nearly 2.74 million visitors—2.2 million cruise ship and; 536,000 air passengers—in 2011. Industry and government; each account for about one-fifth of GDP. The manufacturing; sector consists of rum distilling, electronics, pharmaceuticals, and watch assembly. The agriculture sector is small, with; most food being imported. The islands are vulnerable to; damage from storms. The government is working to improve; fiscal discipline, to support construction projects in the; private sector, to expand tourist facilities, to reduce crime, and to protect the environment.

GDP (purchasing power parity): $1.577 billion (2004 est.)
country comparison to the world: 196

GDP (official exchange rate): $NA

GDP—real growth rate: 2% (2002 est.)
country comparison to the world: 143

GDP—per capita (PPP): $14,500 (2004 est.)
country comparison to the world: 92

GDP—composition, by sector of origin:
agriculture: 1%
industry: 19%
services: 80% (2003 est.)

Agriculture—products: fruit, vegetables, sorghum; Senepol cattle

Industries: tourism, watch assembly, rum distilling, construction, pharmaceuticals, electronics

Industrial production growth rate: NA%

Labor force: 49,820 (2007 est.)
country comparison to the world: 192

Labor force—by occupation: *agriculture:* 1%
industry: 19%
services: 80% (2003 est.)

Unemployment rate: 6.2% (2004)
country comparison to the world: 62

Population below poverty line: 28.9% (2002)

Household income or consumption by percentage share: *lowest 10%:* NA%
highest 10%: NA%

Budget: *revenues:* $837 million
expenditures: $837 million (FY08/09)

Fiscal year: 1 October—30 September

Inflation rate (consumer prices): 2.2% (2003)
country comparison to the world: 74

Exports: $4.234 billion (2001)
country comparison to the world: 119

Exports—commodities: refined petroleum products

Imports: $4.609 billion (2001)
country comparison to the world: 132

Imports—commodities: crude oil, foodstuffs, consumer goods, building materials

Debt—external: $NA

Exchange rates: the US dollar is used

ENERGY

Electricity—production: 794 million kWh (2011 est.)
country comparison to the world: 152

Electricity—consumption: 767.3 million kWh (2010 est.)
country comparison to the world: 158

Electricity—exports: 0 kWh (2012 est.)
country comparison to the world: 211

Electricity—imports: 0 kWh (2012 est.)
country comparison to the world: 213

Electricity—installed generating capacity: 323,000 kW (2010 est.)
country comparison to the world: 149

Electricity—from fossil fuels: 100% of total installed capacity (2010 est.)
country comparison to the world: 40

Electricity—from nuclear fuels: 0% of total installed capacity (2010 est.)
country comparison to the world: 202

Electricity—from hydroelectric plants: 0% of total installed capacity (2010 est.)
country comparison to the world: 207

Electricity—from other renewable sources: 0% of total installed capacity (2010 est.)
country comparison to the world: 138

Crude oil—production: 14,880 bbl/day (2012 est.)
country comparison to the world: 83

Crude oil—exports: 0 bbl/day (2010 est.)
country comparison to the world: 203

Crude oil—imports: 402,000 bbl/day (2010 est.)
country comparison to the world: 21

Crude oil—proved reserves: 0 bbl (1 January 2013 es)
country comparison to the world: 204

Refined petroleum products—production: 423,900 bbl/day (2010 est.)
country comparison to the world: 34

Refined petroleum products—consumption: 106,100 bbl/day (2011 est.)
country comparison to the world: 77

Refined petroleum products—exports: 316,100 bbl/day (2010 est.)
country comparison to the world: 23

Refined petroleum products—imports: 5,732 bbl/day (2010 est.)
country comparison to the world: 146

Natural gas—production: 0 cu m (2011 est.)
country comparison to the world: 206

Natural gas—consumption: 0 cu m (2010 est.)
country comparison to the world: 206

Natural gas—exports: 0 cu m (2011 est.)
country comparison to the world: 205

Natural gas—imports: 0 cu m (2011 est.)
country comparison to the world: 147

Natural gas—proved reserves: 0 cu m (1 January 2013 es)
country comparison to the world: 205

Carbon dioxide emissions from consumption of energy: 18.59 million Mt (2011 est.)
country comparison to the world: 87

COMMUNICATIONS

Telephones—main lines in use: 75,800 (2010)
country comparison to the world: 152

Telephones—mobile cellular: 80,300 (2005)
country comparison to the world: 197

Telephone system:
general assessment: modern system with total digital switching, uses fiber-optic cable and microwave radio relay
domestic: full range of services available
international: country code—1-340; submarine cable connections to US, the Caribbean, Central and South America; satellite earth stations—NA (2010)

Broadcast media: about a dozen TV broadcast stations including 1 public TV station; multichannel cable and satellite TV services are available; 24 radio stations (2009)

Internet country code: .vi

Internet hosts: 4,790 (2012)
country comparison to the world: 146

Internet users: 30,000 (2009)
country comparison to the world: 181

TRANSPORTATION

Airports: 2 (2013)
country comparison to the world: 207

Airports—with paved runways: *total:* 2
over 3,047 m: 1
1,524 to 2,437 m: 1 (2013)

Roadways: *total:* 1,260 km (2008)
country comparison to the world: 180

Ports and terminals:
major seaport(s): Charlotte Amalie, Christiansted, Cruz Bay, Frederiksted, Limetree Bay

MILITARY

Manpower fit for military service:
males age 16-49: 17,542
females age 16-49: 20,946 (2010 est.)

Manpower reaching militarily significant age annually: *male:* 744
female: 788 (2010 est.)

Military—note: defense is the responsibility of the US

TRANSNATIONAL ISSUES

Disputes—international: none

WAKE ISLAND

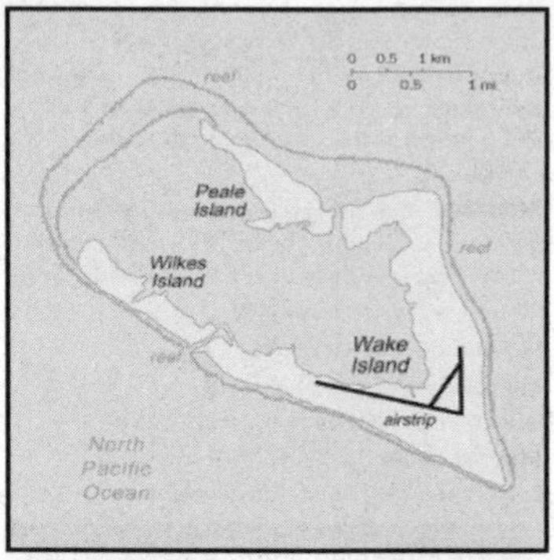

INTRODUCTION

Background: The US annexed Wake Island in 1899 for a cable station. An important air and naval base was constructed in 1940-41. In December 1941, the island was captured by the Japanese and held until the end of World War II. In subsequent years, Wake became a stopover and refueling site for military and commercial aircraft transiting the Pacific. Since 1974, the island's airstrip has been used by the US military, as well as for emergency landings. Operations on the island were suspended and all personnel evacuated in 2006 with the approach of super typhoon IOKE (category 5), but resultant damage was comparatively minor. A US Air Force repair team restored full capability to the airfield and facilities, and the island remains a vital strategic link in the Pacific region.

GEOGRAPHY

Location: Oceania, atoll in the North Pacific Ocean, about two-thirds of the way from Hawaii to the Northern Mariana Islands

Geographic coordinates: 19 17 N, 166 39 E

Map references: Oceania

Area: *total:* 6.5 sq km
country comparison to the world: 244
land: 6.5 sq km
water: 0 sq km

Area—comparative: about 11 times the size of The Mall in Washington, DC

Land boundaries: 0 km

Coastline: 19.3 km

Maritime claims: *territorial sea:* 12 nm
exclusive economic zone: 200 nm

Climate: tropical

Terrain: atoll of three low coral islands, Peale, Wake, and Wilkes, built up on an underwater volcano; central lagoon is former crater, islands are part of the rim

Elevation extremes: *lowest point:* Pacific Ocean 0 m
highest point: unnamed location 6 m

Natural resources: none

Land use: *arable land:* 0%
permanent crops: 0%
other: 100% (2011)

Irrigated land: 0 sq km (2011)

Natural hazards: occasional typhoons

Environment—current issues: NA

Geography—note: strategic location in the North Pacific Ocean; emergency landing location for transpacific flights

PEOPLE AND SOCIETY

Population: no indigenous inhabitants
note: approximately 150 military personnel and civilian contractors maintain and operate the airfield and communications facilities (2009)

GOVERNMENT

Country name:
conventional long form: none
conventional short form: Wake Island

Dependency status: unorganized, unincorporated territory of the US; administered from Washington, DC by the Department of the Interior; activities in the atoll are currently conducted by the US Air Force

Legal system: US common law

Flag description: the flag of the US is used

ECONOMY

Economy—overview: Economic activity is limited to providing services to military personnel and contractors located on the island. All food and manufactured goods must be imported.

COMMUNICATIONS

Telephone system: *general assessment:* satellite communications; 2 Defense Switched Network circuits off the Overseas Telephone System (OTS); located in the Hawaii area code—808

Broadcast media: American Armed Forces Radio and Television Service (AFRTS) provides satellite radio/TV broadcasts (2009)

TRANSPORTATION

Airports: 1 (2013)
country comparison to the world: 211

Airports—with paved runways: *total:* 1
2,438 to 3,047 m: 1 (2013)

Ports and terminals: none; two offshore anchorages for large ships

Transportation—note: there are no commercial or civilian flights to and from Wake Island, except in direct support of island missions; emergency landing is available

MILITARY

Military—note: defense is the responsibility of the US; the US Air Force is responsible for overall administration and operation of the island facilities; the launch support facility is administered by the US Missile Defense Agency (MDA)

TRANSNATIONAL ISSUES

Disputes—international: claimed by Marshall Islands

WALLIS AND FUTUNA

INTRODUCTION

Background: The Futuna island group was discovered by the Dutch in 1616 and Wallis by the British in 1767, but it was the French who declared a protectorate over the islands in 1842, and took official control of them between 1886 and 1888. Notably, Wallis and Futuna was the only French colony to side with the Vichy regime during World War II, a phase that ended in May of 1942 with the arrival of 2,000 American troops. In 1959, the inhabitants of the islands voted to become a French overseas territory and officially assumed this status in July 1961.

GEOGRAPHY

Location: Oceania, islands in the South Pacific Ocean, about two-thirds of the way from Hawaii to New Zealand

Geographic coordinates: 13 18 S, 176 12 W

Map references: Oceania

Area: *total:* 142 sq km
country comparison to the world: 221
land: 142 sq km
water: 0 sq km
note: includes Ile Uvea (Wallis Island), Ile Futuna (Futuna Island), Ile Alofi, and 20 islets

Area—comparative: 1.5 times the size of Washington, DC

Land boundaries: 0 km

Coastline: 129 km

Maritime claims: *territorial sea:* 12 nm
exclusive economic zone: 200 nm

Climate: tropical; hot, rainy season (November to April); cool, dry season (May to October); rains 2,500-3,000 mm per year (80% humidity); average temperature 26.6 degrees C

Terrain: volcanic origin; low hills

Elevation extremes: *lowest point:* Pacific Ocean 0 m
highest point: Mont Singavi (on Futuna) 765 m

Natural resources: NEGL

Land use: *arable land:* 7.14%
permanent crops: 35.71%
other: 57.15% (2011)

Irrigated land: NA

Natural hazards: NA

Environment—current issues: deforestation (only small portions of the original forests remain) largely as a result of the continued use of wood as the main fuel source; as a consequence of cutting down the forests, the mountainous terrain of Futuna is particularly prone to erosion; there are no permanent settlements on Alofi because of the lack of natural freshwater resources

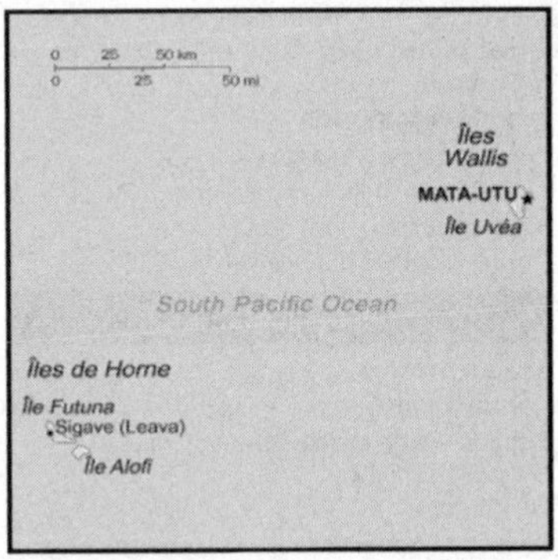

Geography—note: both island groups have fringing reefs

PEOPLE AND SOCIETY

Nationality: *noun:* Wallisian(s), Futunan(s), or Wallis and Futuna Islanders
adjective: Wallisian, Futunan, or Wallis and Futuna Islander

Ethnic groups: Polynesian

Languages: Wallisian (indigenous Polynesian language) 58.9%, Futunian 30.1%, French (official) 10.8%, other 0.2% (2003 census)

Religions: Roman Catholic 99%, other 1%

Population: 15,561 (July 2014 est.)
country comparison to the world: 224

Age structure:
0-14 years: 23.4% (male 1,902/female 1,741)
15-24 years: 17.8% (male 1,449/female 1,320)
25-54 years: 40.7% (male 3,147/female 3,183)
55-64 years: 8.9% (male 719/female 709)
65 years and over: 8.6% (male 663/female 728) (2014 est.)

Median age: *total:* 30.3 years
male: 29.3 years
female: 31.5 years (2014 est.)

Population growth rate: 0.33% (2014 est.)
country comparison to the world: 168

Birth rate: 13.56 births/1,000 population (2014 est.)
country comparison to the world: 148

Death rate: 4.95 deaths/1,000 population (2014 est.)
country comparison to the world: 189

Net migration rate: -5.27 migrant(s)/1,000 population
country comparison to the world: 195
note: there has been steady emigration from Wallis and Futuna to New Caledonia (2014 est.)

Urbanization: *urban population:* 0% of total population (2008)
rate of urbanization: 0% annual rate of change (2005-10 est.)

Sex ratio: *at birth:* 1.05 male(s)/female
0-14 years: 1.09 male(s)/female
15-24 years: 1.1 male(s)/female
25-54 years: 0.99 male(s)/female
55-64 years: 1.03 male(s)/female
65 years and over: 0.89 male(s)/female
total population: 1.02 male(s)/female (2014 est.)

Infant mortality rate: *total:* 4.49 deaths/1,000 live births
country comparison to the world: 187
male: 4.72 deaths/1,000 live births
female: 4.24 deaths/1,000 live births (2014 est.)

Life expectancy at birth:
total population: 79.42 years
country comparison to the world: 44
male: 76.43 years
female: 82.55 years (2014 est.)

Total fertility rate: 1.76 children born/woman (2014 est.)
country comparison to the world: 163

Drinking water source:
improved:
rural: 100% of population
total: 100% of population (2008 est.)

Sanitation facility access:
improved:
rural: 96% of population
total: 96% of population
unimproved:
rural: 4% of population
total: 4% of population (2008 est.)

HIV/AIDS—adult prevalence rate: NA

HIV/AIDS—people living with HIV/AIDS: NA

HIV/AIDS—deaths: NA

Literacy: *definition:* age 15 and over can read and write
total population: 50%
male: 50%
female: 50% (1969 est.)

GOVERNMENT

Country name: *conventional long form:* Territory of the Wallis and Futuna Islands
conventional short form: Wallis and Futuna
local long form: Territoire des Iles Wallis et Futuna
local short form: Wallis et Futuna

Dependency status: overseas territory of France

Government type: parliamentary representive democratic French overseas collectivity

Capital: *name:* Mata-Utu (on Ile Uvea)

geographic coordinates: 13 57 S, 171 56 W
time difference: UTC+12 (17 hours ahead of Washington, DC during Standard Time)

Administrative divisions: none (overseas territory of France); there are no first-order administrative divisions as defined by the US Government, but there are three kingdoms at the second order named Alo, Sigave, Wallis

Independence: none (overseas territory of France)

National holiday: Bastille Day, 14 July (1789)

Constitution: 4 October 1958 (French Constitution) (2013)

Legal system: French civil law

Suffrage: 18 years of age; universal

Executive branch: *chief of state:* President Francois HOLLANDE (since 15 May 2012); represented by High Administrator Michel JEANJEAN (since 10 June 2010)
head of government: President of the Territorial Assembly Vetelino NAU (since 4 April 2012)
cabinet: Council of the Territory consists of 3 kings and 3 members appointed by the high administrator on the advice of the Territorial Assembly (For more information visit the World Leaders website)
note: there are 3 traditional kings with limited powers
elections: French president elected by popular vote for a five-year term; high administrator appointed by the French president on the advice of the French Ministry of the Interior; the presidents of the Territorial Government and the Territorial Assembly elected by the members of the assembly

Legislative branch: unicameral Territorial Assembly or Assemblee Territoriale (20 seats; members elected by popular vote to serve five-year terms)
elections: last held on 22 March 2012 (next to be held in March 2017)
election results: percent of vote by party—NA; seats by party—PS 4, UMP 4, centrists, 3, other 9
note: Wallis and Futuna elects one senator to the French Senate and one deputy to the French National Assembly; French Senate—elections last held on 21 September 2008 (next to be held by September 2014); results—percent of vote by party—NA; seats—UMP 1; French National Assembly—elections last held on 17 June 2012 (next to be held by 2017); results—percent of vote by party—NA; seats—UMP 1

Judicial branch: *highest court(s):* Court of Appeal or Cour d'Appel, located in Noumea, New Caledonia
judge selection and term of office: NA
subordinate courts: note: justice generally administered under French law by the high administrator, but the three traditional kings administer customary law and there is a magistrate in Mata-Utu

Political parties and leaders: Lua Kae Tahi (Giscardians); Mouvement des Radicaux de Gauche or MRG; Rally for the Republic or RPR (UMP); Socialist Party or PS; Taumu'a Lelei; Union Populaire Locale or UPL; Union Pour la Democratie Francaise or UDF

Political pressure groups and leaders: NA

International organization participation: PIF (observer), SPC, UPU

Diplomatic representation in the US: none (overseas territory of France)

Diplomatic representation from the US: none (overseas territory of France)

Flag description: unofficial, local flag has a red field with four white isosceles triangles in the middle, representing the three native kings of the islands and the French administrator; the apexes of the triangles are oriented inward and at right angles to each other; the flag of France, outlined in white on two sides, is in the upper hoist quadrant
note: the design is derived from an original red banner with a white cross pattee that was introduced in the 19th century by French missionaries; the flag of France is used for official occasions

National symbol(s): red saltire (Saint Andrew's Cross) on a white square on a red field

National anthem: *note:* as a territory of France, "La Marseillaise" is official (see France)

ECONOMY

Economy—overview: The economy is limited to traditional subsistence agriculture, with 80% of labor force earnings from agriculture (coconuts and vegetables), livestock (mostly pigs), and fishing. About 4% of the population is employed in government. Revenues come from French Government subsidies, licensing of fishing rights to

Japan and South Korea, import taxes, and remittances from expatriate workers in New Caledonia.

GDP (purchasing power parity): $60 million (2004 est.)
country comparison to the world: 223

GDP (official exchange rate): $NA

GDP—real growth rate: NA%

GDP—per capita (PPP): $3,800 (2004 est.)
country comparison to the world: 172

GDP—composition, by sector of origin:
agriculture: NA%
industry: NA%
services: NA%

Agriculture—products: coconuts, breadfruit, yams, taro, bananas; pigs, goats; fish

Industries: copra, handicrafts, fishing, lumber

Industrial production growth rate: NA%

Labor force: 3,104 (2003)
country comparison to the world: 226

Labor force—by occupation: *agriculture:* 80%
industry: 4%
services: 16% (2001 est.)

Unemployment rate: 12.2% (2008)
country comparison to the world: 124

Population below poverty line: NA%

Household income or consumption by percentage share: *lowest 10%:* NA%
highest 10%: NA%

Budget: *revenues:* $29,730
expenditures: $31,330 (2004)

Public debt: 5.6% of GDP (2004 est.)
country comparison to the world: 157
note: offical data; data cover general government debt, and includes debt instruments issued (or owned) by government entities other than the treasury; the data include treasury debt held by foreign entities; the data include debt issued by subnational entities, as well as intra-governmental debt; intra-governmental debt consists of treasury borrowings from surpluses in the social funds, such as for retirement, medical care, and unemployment; debt instruments for the social funds are not sold at public auctions

Fiscal year: calendar year

Inflation rate (consumer prices): 2.8% (2005)
country comparison to the world: 105

Exports: $47,450 (2004)
country comparison to the world: 222

Exports—commodities: copra, chemicals, construction materials

Imports: $61.17 million (2004)
country comparison to the world: 217

Imports—commodities: chemicals, machinery, consumer goods

Debt—external: $3.67 million (2004)
country comparison to the world: 200

Exchange rates: Comptoirs Francais du Pacifique francs (XPF) per US dollar—
90.01 (February 2012)
87.59 (2007)

COMMUNICATIONS

Telephone system:
international: country code—681

Broadcast media: the publicly owned French Overseas Network (RFO), which broadcasts to France's overseas departments and territories, is carried on the RFO Wallis and Fortuna TV and radio stations (2008)

Internet country code: .wf

Internet hosts: 2,760 (2012)
country comparison to the world: 157

Internet users: 1,300 (2009)
country comparison to the world: 212

TRANSPORTATION

Airports: 2 (2013)
country comparison to the world: 203

Airports—with paved runways: *total:* 2
1,524 to 2,437 m: 1
914 to 1,523 m: 1 (2013)

Ports and terminals: *major seaport(s):* Leava, Mata-Utu

MILITARY

Manpower fit for military service:
males age 16-49: 3,376
females age 16-49: 3,314 (2010 est.)

Manpower reaching militarily significant age annually: *male:* 168
female: 139 (2010 est.)

Military—note: defense is the responsibility of France

TRANSNATIONAL ISSUES

Disputes—international: none

WEST BANK

INTRODUCTION

Background: From the early 16th century through 1917, the area now known as the West Bank fell under Ottoman rule. Following World War I, the Allied powers (France, UK, Russia) allocated the area to the British Mandate of Palestine. After World War II, the UN passed a resolution to establish two states within the Mandate, and designated a territory including what is now known as the West Bank as part of the proposed Arab state. Following the 1948 Arab-Israeli War the area was captured by Transjordan (later renamed Jordan). Jordan annexed the West Bank in 1950. In June 1967, Israel captured the West Bank and East Jerusalem during the 1967 Six-Day War. With the exception of East Jerusalem and the former Israeli-Jordanian border zone, the West Bank has remained under Israeli military control. Under a series of agreements signed between 1994 and 1999, Israel transferred to the Palestinian Authority (PA) security and civilian responsibility for many Palestinian-populated areas of the West Bank as well as the Gaza Strip. Negotiations to determine the permanent status of the West Bank and Gaza Strip stalled after the outbreak of an intifada in mid- 2000. In early 2003, the "Quartet" of the US, EU, UN, and Russia, presented a roadmap to a final peace settlement by 2005, calling for two states—Israel and a democratic Palestine. Following Palestinian leader Yasir ARAFAT's death in late 2004 and the subsequent election of Mahmud ABBAS (head of the Fatah political party) as the PLO Executive Committee Chairman and PA president, Israel and the PA agreed to move the peace process forward. Israel in late 2005 unilaterally withdrew all of its settlers and soldiers and dismantled its military facilities in the Gaza Strip and redeployed its military from several West Bank settlements but continues to control maritime, airspace, and other access. In early 2006, the Islamic Resistance Movement, HAMAS, won the Palestinian Legislative Council election and took control of the PA government. Attempts to form a unity government failed, and violent clashes between Fatah and HAMAS supporters ensued, culminating in HAMAS's violent seizure of all military and governmental institutions in the Gaza Strip. Fatah and HAMAS in early 2011 agreed to reunify the Gaza Strip and West Bank, but the factions have struggled to implement details on governance and security. The status quo remains with HAMAS in control of the Gaza Strip and the PA governing the West Bank. In late 2010, direct peace talks between the Israelis and Palestinians collapsed. In November 2012, the UN General Assembly upgraded the Palestinian status at the UN to that of an observer "state." The Israeli government and ABBAS returned to formal peace negotiations in July 2013.

GEOGRAPHY

Location: Middle East, west of Jordan, east of Israel

Geographic coordinates: 32 00 N, 35 15 E

Map references: Middle East

Area: *total:* 5,860 sq km
country comparison to the world: 172
land: 5,640 sq km
water: 220 sq km
note: includes West Bank, Latrun Salient, and the northwest quarter of the Dead Sea, but excludes Mt. Scopus; East Jerusalem and Jerusalem No Man's Land are also included only as a means of depicting the entire area occupied by Israel in 1967

Area—comparative: slightly smaller than Delaware

Land boundaries: *total:* 404 km
border countries: Israel 307 km, Jordan 97 km

Coastline: 0 km (landlocked)

Maritime claims: none (landlocked)

Climate: temperate; temperature and precipitation vary with altitude, warm to hot summers, cool to mild winters

Terrain: mostly rugged dissected upland, some vegetation in west, but barren in east

Elevation extremes: *lowest point:* Dead Sea -408 m
highest point: Tall Asur 1,022 m

Natural resources: arable land

Land use: *arable land:* 7.39%
permanent crops: 10.96%
other: 81.64% (2011)

Irrigated land: 240 sq km; note—includes Gaza Strip (2003)

Natural hazards: droughts

Environment—current issues: adequacy of freshwater supply; sewage treatment

Geography—note: landlocked; highlands are main recharge area for Israel's coastal aquifers; there are about 355 Israeli civilian sites including about 145 small outpost communities in the West Bank and 32 sites in East Jerusalem (2010 est.)

PEOPLE AND SOCIETY

Nationality: *noun:* NA
adjective: NA

Ethnic groups: Palestinian Arab and other 83%, Jewish 17%

Languages: Arabic, Hebrew (spoken by Israeli settlers and many Palestinians), English (widely understood)

Religions: Muslim (predominantly Sunni), Jewish, Christian and other

Population: 2,731,052 (July 2014 est.)
country comparison to the world: 142
note: approximately 341,400 Israeli settlers live in the West Bank (2012); approximately 196,400 Israeli settlers live in East Jerusalem (2011)

Age structure:
0-14 years: 33.7% (male 472,480/female 448,078)
15-24 years: 21.7% (male 303,578/female 289,119)
25-54 years: 36.4% (male 511,443/female 483,276)
55-64 years: 3.8% (male 59,762/female 59,372)
65 years and over: 3.8% (male 43,629/female 60,315) (2014 est.)

Dependency ratios:
total dependency ratio: 75.6 %
youth dependency ratio: 70.4 %
elderly dependency ratio: 5.2 %
potential support ratio: 19.2
note: data represents the Palestinian Territories (2013)

Median age: *total:* 22.4 years
male: 22.2 years
female: 22.5 years (2014 est.)

Population growth rate: 1.99% (2014 est.)
country comparison to the world: 52

Birth rate: 23.41 births/1,000 population (2014 est.)
country comparison to the world: 67

Death rate: 3.51 deaths/1,000 population (2014 est.)
country comparison to the world: 216

Net migration rate: 0 migrant(s)/1,000 population (2014 est.)
country comparison to the world: 84

Urbanization: *urban population:* 74.3% of total population (2011)
rate of urbanization: 3.1% annual rate of change (2005-10 est.)

Sex ratio: *at birth:* 1.06 male(s)/female
0-14 years: 1.05 male(s)/female
15-24 years: 1.05 male(s)/female
25-54 years: 1.06 male(s)/female
55-64 years: 1.04 male(s)/female
65 years and over: 0.71 male(s)/female
total population: 1.04 male(s)/female (2014 est.)

Maternal mortality rate: 64 deaths/100,000 live births (2010)
country comparison to the world: 95

Infant mortality rate: *total:* 13.49 deaths/1,000 live births
country comparison to the world: 117
male: 15.13 deaths/1,000 live births
female: 11.75 deaths/1,000 live births (2014 est.)

Life expectancy at birth:
total population: 75.69 years
country comparison to the world: 91
male: 73.58 years
female: 77.92 years (2014 est.)

Total fertility rate: 2.83 children born/woman (2014 est.)
country comparison to the world: 66

HIV/AIDS—adult prevalence rate: NA

HIV/AIDS—people living with HIV/AIDS: NA

HIV/AIDS—deaths: NA

Children under the age of 5 years underweight: 2.2% (2007)
country comparison to the world: 118

Literacy: *definition:* age 15 and over can read and write
total population: 95.3%
male: 97.9%
female: 92.6%
notes: estimates are for the Palestinian Territories (2011 est.)

Unemployment, youth ages 15-24: *total:* 38.8%
country comparison to the world: 15
male: 34.5%
female: 62.2%
note: includes Gaza (2012)

GOVERNMENT

Country name: *conventional long form:* none
conventional short form: West Bank

ECONOMY

Economy—overview: The West Bank—the larger of the two areas comprising the Palestinian territories—has sustained a moderate rate of economic growth since 2008. Inflows of donor aid and government spending have driven most of the gains, however. Private sector development has been weak. After a multiyear downturn following the start of the second intifada in 2000, overall standard-of-living measures have recovered and now exceed levels seen in the late 1990s. Despite the Palestinian Authority's (PA) successful implementation of economic and security reforms and the easing of some movement and access restrictions by the Israeli Government, Israeli closure policies continue to disrupt labor and trade flows, industrial capacity, and basic commerce, eroding the productive capacity of the West Bank economy. The biggest impediments to economic improvements in the West Bank remain Palestinians' inability to access land and resources in Israeli-controlled areas, import and export restrictions, and a high-cost capital structure. The PA for the foreseeable future will continue to rely heavily on donor aid for its budgetary needs, and West Bank economic activity will depend largely on the PA's ability to attract such aid.

GDP (purchasing power parity): $8.022 billion (2011 est.)
country comparison to the world: 157
$7.589 billion (2010 est.)
$7.106 billion (2009 est.)
note: includes Gaza Strip

GDP (official exchange rate): $6.641 billion
note: includes Gaza Strip (2008 est.)

GDP—real growth rate: 5.7% (2011 est.)
country comparison to the world: 42
6.8% (2010 est.)
7% (2009 est.)
note: includes Gaza Strip

GDP—per capita (PPP): $2,900 (2008 est.)
country comparison to the world: 179
note: includes Gaza Strip

GDP—composition, by end use:
household consumption: 99.5%
government consumption: 29.5%
investment in fixed capital: 18%
investment in inventories: 0%
exports of goods and services: 14.9%
imports of goods and services: -62% (2013 est.)

GDP—composition, by sector of origin:
agriculture: 4.2%
industry: 17.9%
services: 77.9%
note: includes Gaza Strip (2012 est.)

Agriculture—products: olives, citrus fruit, vegetables; beef, dairy products

Industries: small-scale manufacturing, quarrying, textiles, soap, olive-wood carvings, and mother-of-pearl souvenirs

Industrial production growth rate: 3%
country comparison to the world: 95

Labor force: 1.025 million (2013 est.)
country comparison to the world: 142

Labor force—by occupation: *agriculture:* 16.1%
industry: 28.4%
services: 55.5%
note: includes Gaza Strip (2010 est.)

Unemployment rate: 22.5% (2013 est.)
country comparison to the world: 169
23% (2012 est.)

Population below poverty line: 18.3% (2010 est.)

Household income or consumption by percentage share: *lowest 10%:* 3.2%
highest 10%: 28.2% (2009 est.)

Budget: *revenues:* $2.1 billion
expenditures: $3.2 billion
note: includes Palestinian Authority expenditures in the Gaza
Strip (2011 est.)

Taxes and other revenues: 31.6% of GDP (2011 est.)
country comparison to the world: 84

Budget surplus (+) or deficit (-):
-16.6% of GDP (2011 est.)
country comparison to the world: 214

Fiscal year: calendar year

Inflation rate (consumer prices): 1.7% (2013 est.)
country comparison to the world: 47
2.8% (2012 est.)
note: includes Gaza Strip

Commercial bank prime lending rate: 6.8% (31 December 2013 est.)
country comparison to the world: 126
6.97% (31 December 2012 est.)

Stock of narrow money: $232.2 million (31 December 2013 est.)
country comparison to the world: 174
$180.2 million (31 December 2012 est.)

Stock of broad money: $9.301 billion (31 December 2013 est.)
country comparison to the world: 106
$8.143 billion (31 December 2012 est.)

Stock of domestic credit: $1.248 billion (31 December 2013 est.)
country comparison to the world: 149
$1.042 billion (31 December 2012 est.)

Market value of publicly traded shares: $2.634 billion (31 December 2012 est.)
country comparison to the world: 96
$2.532 billion (31 December 2011)
$2.45 billion (31 December 2010 est.)

Current account balance: -$2.1 billion (2011 est.)
country comparison to the world: 145
-$690.7 million (2010 est.)

Exports: $666.1 million (2010 est.)
country comparison to the world: 168
$846.1 million (2011 est.)
note: includes Gaza Strip

Exports—commodities: stone, olives, fruit, vegetables, limestone

Imports: $5.474 billion (2011 est.)
country comparison to the world: 125
$4.319 billion (2010 est.)
note: data include the Gaza Strip

Imports—commodities: food, consumer goods, construction materials, petroleum, chemicals

Debt—external: $1.04 billion (2010 est.)
country comparison to the world: 162
$1.3 billion (2007 est.)
note: data include the Gaza Strip

Exchange rates: new Israeli shekels (ILS) per US dollar—
3.621 (2013 est.)
3.856 (2012 est.)
3.73 (2010)
3.932 (2009)
3.588 (2008)

ENERGY

Electricity—production: 445 million kWh (2010 est.)
country comparison to the world: 165

Electricity—consumption: 4.573 billion kWh (2010 est.)
country comparison to the world: 118

Electricity—exports: 0 kWh (2012)
country comparison to the world: 212

Electricity—imports: 550 million kWh (2011 est.)
country comparison to the world: 77

Electricity—installed generating capacity:
140,000 kW
country comparison to the world: 165
note: includes Gaza Strip (2010 est.)

Electricity—from fossil fuels: 100% of total installed capacity (2010 est.)
country comparison to the world: 41

Electricity—from nuclear fuels: 0% of total installed capacity (2010 est.)
country comparison to the world: 204

Electricity—from hydroelectric plants: 0% of total installed capacity (2010 est.)
country comparison to the world: 208

Electricity—from other renewable sources:
0% of total installed capacity (2010 est.)
country comparison to the world: 140

Crude oil—production: 0 bbl/day (2012 est.)
country comparison to the world: 144

Crude oil—exports: 0 bbl/day (2010 est.)
country comparison to the world: 205

Crude oil—imports: 0 bbl/day (2010 est.)
country comparison to the world: 141

Crude oil—proved reserves: 0 bbl (1 January 2009 es)
country comparison to the world: 206

Refined petroleum products—production: 0 bbl/day (2010 est.)
country comparison to the world: 208

Refined petroleum products—consumption:
29,310 bbl/day (2011 est.)
country comparison to the world: 115

Refined petroleum products—exports: 514.8 bbl/day (2010 est.)
country comparison to the world: 113

Refined petroleum products—imports: 16,330 bbl/day (2010 est.)
country comparison to the world: 114

Natural gas—production: 0 cu m (2011 est.)
country comparison to the world: 208

Natural gas—consumption: 0 cu m (2010 est.)
country comparison to the world: 208

Natural gas—exports: 0 cu m (2011 est.)
country comparison to the world: 207

Natural gas—imports: 0 cu m (2011 est.)
country comparison to the world: 78

Natural gas—proved reserves: 0 cu m (1 January 2013 es)
country comparison to the world: 206

Carbon dioxide emissions from consumption of energy: 2.502 million Mt (2011 est.)
country comparison to the world: 143

COMMUNICATIONS

Telephones—main lines in use: 406,000 (includes Gaza Strip) (2012)
country comparison to the world: 104

Telephones—mobile cellular: 3.041 million (includes Gaza Strip) (2012)
country comparison to the world: 132

Telephone system:
general assessment: continuing political and economic instability has impeded significant liberalization of the telecommunications industry
domestic: Israeli company BEZEK and the Palestinian company PALTEL are responsible for fixed line services; PALTEL plans to establish a fiber-optic connection to Jordan to route domestic mobile calls; the Palestinian JAWWAL company and WATANIYA PALESTINE provide cellular services
international: country code—970; 1 international switch in Ramallah (2009)

Broadcast media: the Palestinian Authority operates 1 TV and 1 radio station; about 30 independent TV and 25 radio stations; both Jordanian TV and satellite TV are accessible (2008)

Internet country code: .ps; note—same as Gaza Strip

Internet users: 1.379 million (includes Gaza Strip) (2009)
country comparison to the world: 88

TRANSPORTATION

Airports: 2 (2013)
country comparison to the world: 208

Airports—with paved runways: *total:* 2
1,524 to 2,437 m: 1
under 914 m: 1 (2013)

Heliports: 1 (2013)

Roadways: *total:* 4,686 km
country comparison to the world: 153
paved: 4,686 km
note: includes Gaza Strip (2010)

MILITARY

Manpower fit for military service:
males age 16-49: 579,248
females age 16-49: 547,782 (2010 est.)

Manpower reaching militarily significant age annually: *male:* 30,925
female: 29,440 (2010 est.)

TRANSNATIONAL ISSUES

Disputes—international: the current status of the West Bank is subject to the Israeli-Palestinian Interim Agreement—permanent status to be determined through further negotiation; Israel continues construction of a "seam line" separation barrier along parts of the Green Line and within the West Bank; Israel withdrew from four settlements in the northern West Bank in August 2005; since 1948, about 350 peacekeepers from the UN Truce Supervision Organization (UNTSO), headquartered in Jerusalem, monitor ceasefires, supervise armistice agreements, prevent isolated incidents from escalating, and assist other UN personnel in the region

Refugees and internally displaced persons:
refugees (country of origin): 748,899 (Palestinian refugees (UNRWA)) (2013)
IDPs: 160,000 (persons displaced within both the Gaza strip and the West Bank since 1967; as estimated by unofficial sources) (2011)

WESTERN SAHARA

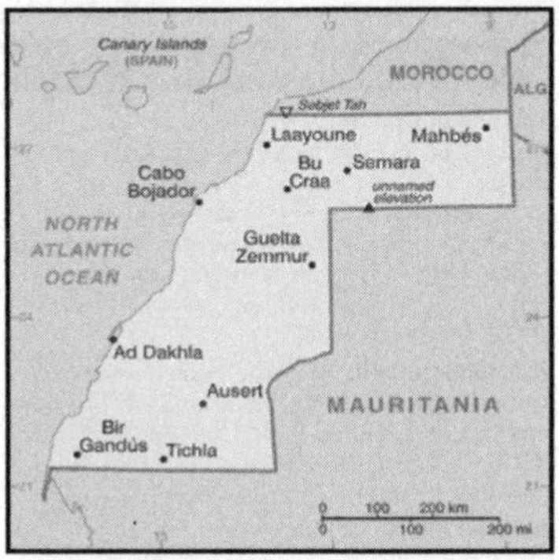

INTRODUCTION

Background: Western Sahara is a disputed territory on the northwest coast of Africa bordered by Morocco, Mauritania, and Algeria. After Spain withdrew from its former colony of Spanish Sahara in 1976, Morocco annexed the northern two-thirds of Western Sahara and claimed the rest of the territory in 1979, following Mauritania's withdrawal. A guerrilla war with the Polisario Front contesting Morocco's sovereignty ended in a 1991 cease-fire and the establishment of a UN peacekeeping operation. As part of this effort, the UN sought to offer a choice to the peoples of the Western Sahara between independence (favored by the Polisario Front) or integration into Morocco. A proposed referendum never took place due to lack of agreement on voter eligibility. The 2,700 km- (1,700 mi-) long defensive sand berm, built by the Moroccans from 1980 to 1987 and running the length of the territory, continues to separate the opposing forces with Morocco controlling the roughly 80 percent of the territory west of the berm. Local demonstrations criticizing the Moroccan authorities occur regularly, and there are periodic ethnic tensions between the native Sahrawi population and Moroccan immigrants. Morocco maintains a heavy security presence in the territory.

GEOGRAPHY

Location: Northern Africa, bordering the North Atlantic Ocean, between Mauritania and Morocco

Geographic coordinates: 24 30 N, 13 00 W

Map references: Africa

Area: *total:* 266,000 sq km
country comparison to the world: 78
land: 266,000 sq km
water: 0 sq km

Area—comparative: about the size of Colorado

Land boundaries: *total:* 2,046 km
border countries: Algeria 42 km, Mauritania 1,561 km, Morocco 443 km

Coastline: 1,110 km

Maritime claims: contingent upon resolution of sovereignty issue

Climate: hot, dry desert; rain is rare; cold offshore air currents produce fog and heavy dew

Terrain: mostly low, flat desert with large areas of rocky or sandy surfaces rising to small mountains in south and northeast

Elevation extremes: *lowest point:* Sebjet Tah -55 m
highest point: unnamed elevation 805 m

Natural resources: phosphates, iron ore

Land use: *arable land:* 0.02%
permanent crops: 0%
other: 99.98% (2011)

Irrigated land: NA

Natural hazards: hot, dry, dust/sand-laden sirocco wind can occur during winter and spring; widespread harmattan haze exists 60% of time, often severely restricting visibility

Environment—current issues: sparse water and lack of arable land

Environment—international agreements:
party to: none of the selected agreements

Geography—note: the waters off the coast are particularly rich fishing areas

PEOPLE AND SOCIETY

Nationality: *noun:* Sahrawi(s), Sahraoui(s)
adjective: Sahrawi, Sahrawian, Sahraouian

Ethnic groups: Arab, Berber

Languages: Standard Arabic (national), Hassaniya Arabic, Moroccan Arabic

Religions: Muslim

Population: 554,795 (July 2013 est.)
country comparison to the world: 172
note: estimate is based on projections by age, sex, fertility, mortality, and migration; fertility and mortality are based on data from neighboring countries (July 2014 est.)

Age structure:
0-14 years: 38.1% (male 106,868/female 104,574)
15-24 years: 19.7% (male 54,970/female 54,217)
25-54 years: 33.7% (male 91,986/female 95,114)
55-64 years: 3.7% (male 12,408/female 14,159)
65 years and over: 3.6% (male 9,002/female 11,497) (2014 est.)

Dependency ratios:
total dependency ratio: 41.2 %
youth dependency ratio: 37.5 %
elderly dependency ratio: 3.7 %
potential support ratio: 27 (2013)

Median age: *total:* 20.8 years
male: 20.3 years
female: 21.3 years (2014 est.)

Population growth rate: 2.89% (2014 est.)
country comparison to the world: 15

Birth rate: 30.71 births/1,000 population (2014 est.)
country comparison to the world: 40

Death rate: 8.49 deaths/1,000 population (2014 est.)
country comparison to the world: 80

Urbanization: *urban population:* 82% of total population (2011)
rate of urbanization: 3.49% annual rate of change (2010-15 est.)

Major urban areas—population: Laayoune 237,000 (2011)

Sex ratio: *at birth:* 1.04 male(s)/female
0-14 years: 1.02 male(s)/female
15-24 years: 1.01 male(s)/female
25-54 years: 0.97 male(s)/female
55-64 years: 0.99 male(s)/female
65 years and over: 0.78 male(s)/female
total population: 0.98 male(s)/female (2014 est.)

Infant mortality rate: *total:* 56.09 deaths/1,000 live births
country comparison to the world: 27
male: 61.04 deaths/1,000 live births
female: 50.93 deaths/1,000 live births (2014 est.)

Life expectancy at birth:
total population: 62.27 years
country comparison to the world: 189
male: 60 years
female: 64.63 years (2014 est.)

Total fertility rate: 4.07 children born/woman (2014 est.)
country comparison to the world: 38

HIV/AIDS—adult prevalence rate: NA

HIV/AIDS—people living with HIV/AIDS:
NA HIV/AIDS—deaths: NA

Literacy: NA

GOVERNMENT

Country name: *conventional long form:* none
conventional short form: Western Sahara
former: Rio de Oro, Saguia el Hamra, Spanish Sahara

Government type: legal status of territory and issue of sovereignty unresolved; territory contested by Morocco and Polisario Front (Popular Front for the Liberation of the Saguia el Hamra and Rio de Oro), which in February 1976 formally proclaimed a government-in-exile, the Sahrawi Arab Democratic Republic (SADR), based out of refugee camps near Tindouf, Algeria, led by President Mohamed ABDELAZIZ

Capital: Laayoune (administrative center)
time difference: UTC 0 (5 hours ahead of Washington, DC during Standard Time)
daylight saving time: +1hr, begins last Sunday in April; ends last Sunday in September

Administrative divisions: none (territory west of the berm under de facto Moroccan control)

Suffrage: none; (residents of Moroccan-controlled Western Sahara participate in Moroccan elections)

Executive branch: none

Political pressure groups and leaders: none

International organization participation: AU, CAN (observer), WFTU (NGOs)

Diplomatic representation in the US: none

Diplomatic representation from the US: none

ECONOMY

Economy—overview: Western Sahara has a small market-based economy whose main industries are fishing, phosphate mining, and pastoral nomadism. The territory's arid desert climate makes sedentary agriculture difficult, and Western Sahara imports much of its food. The Moroccan Government administers Western Sahara's economy and is a key source of employment, infrastructure development, and social spending in the territory. Western Sahara's unresolved legal status makes the exploitation of its natural resources a contentious issue between Morocco and the Polisario. Morocco and the EU in December 2013 finalized a four-year agreement allowing European vessels to fish off the coast of Morocco, including disputed waters off the coast of Western Sahara. Oil has never been found in Western Sahara in commercially significant quantities, but Morocco and the Polisario have quarreled over who has the right to authorize and benefit from oil exploration in the territory. Western Sahara's main long-term economic challenge is the development of a more diverse set of industries capable of providing greater employment and income to the territory.

GDP (purchasing power parity): $906.5 million (2007 est.)
country comparison to the world: 207

GDP (official exchange rate): $NA

GDP—real growth rate: NA%

GDP—per capita (PPP): $2,500 (2007 est.)
country comparison to the world: 187

GDP—composition, by sector of origin:
agriculture: NA%
industry: NA%
services: 40% (2007 est.)

Agriculture—products: fruits and vegetables (grown in the few oases); camels, sheep, goats (kept by nomads); fish

Industries: phosphate mining, handicrafts

Industrial production growth rate: NA%

Labor force: 144,000 (2010 est.)
country comparison to the world: 178

Labor force—by occupation: *agriculture:* 50%
industry and services: 50% (2005 est.)

Unemployment rate: NA%

Population below poverty line: NA%

Household income or consumption by percentage share: *lowest 10%:* NA%
highest 10%: NA%

Budget: *revenues:* $NA
expenditures: $NA

Fiscal year: calendar year

Inflation rate (consumer prices): NA%

Exports: $NA

Exports—commodities: phosphates 62%

Imports: $NA

Imports—commodities: fuel for fishing fleet, foodstuffs

Debt—external: $NA

Exchange rates: Moroccan dirhams (MAD) per US dollar—
8.439 (2013)
8.6026 (2012)
8.4172 (2010)
8.0571 (2009)
7.526 (2008)

ENERGY

Electricity—production: 90 million kWh (2010 est.)
country comparison to the world: 201

Electricity—consumption: 83.7 million kWh (2010 est.)
country comparison to the world: 200

Electricity—exports: 0 kWh (2012 est.)
country comparison to the world: 213

Electricity—imports: 0 kWh (2012 est.)
country comparison to the world: 214

Electricity—installed generating capacity: 58,000 kW (2010 est.)
country comparison to the world: 184

Electricity—from fossil fuels: 100% of total installed capacity (2010 est.)
country comparison to the world: 42

Electricity—from nuclear fuels: 0% of total installed capacity (2010 est.)
country comparison to the world: 205

Electricity—from hydroelectric plants: 0% of total installed capacity (2010 est.)
country comparison to the world: 209

Electricity—from other renewable sources: 0% of total installed capacity (2010 est.)
country comparison to the world: 141

Crude oil—production: 0 bbl/day (2012 est.)
country comparison to the world: 145

Crude oil—exports: 0 bbl/day (2010 est.)
country comparison to the world: 206

Crude oil—imports: 0 bbl/day (2010 est.)
country comparison to the world: 142

Crude oil—proved reserves: 0 bbl (1 January 2013 es)
country comparison to the world: 207

Refined petroleum products—production: 0 bbl/day (2010 est.)
country comparison to the world: 209

Refined petroleum products—consumption: 1,948 bbl/day (2011 est.)
country comparison to the world: 188

Refined petroleum products—exports: 0 bbl/day (2010 est.)
country comparison to the world: 144

Refined petroleum products—imports: 1,702 bbl/day (2010 est.)
country comparison to the world: 184

Natural gas—production: 0 cu m (2011 est.)
country comparison to the world: 209

Natural gas—consumption: 0 cu m (2010 est.)
country comparison to the world: 209

Natural gas—exports: 0 cu m (2011 est.)
country comparison to the world: 208

Natural gas—imports: 0 cu m (2011 est.)
country comparison to the world: 79

Natural gas—proved reserves: 0 cu m (1 January 2013 es)
country comparison to the world: 207

Carbon dioxide emissions from consumption of energy: 316,700 Mt (2011 est.)
country comparison to the world: 187

COMMUNICATIONS

Telephone system:
general assessment: sparse and limited system
domestic: NA
international: country code—212; tied into Morocco's system by microwave radio relay, tropospheric scatter, and satellite; satellite earth stations—2 Intelsat (Atlantic Ocean) linked to Rabat, Morocco (2008)

Broadcast media: Morocco's state-owned broadcaster, Radio-Television Marocaine (RTM), operates a radio service from Laayoune and relays TV service; a Polisario-backed radio station also broadcasts (2008)

Internet country code: .eh

TRANSPORTATION

Airports: 6 (2013)
country comparison to the world: 174

Airports—with paved runways: *total:* 3
2,438 to 3,047 m: 3 (2013)

Airports—with unpaved runways: *total:* 3
1,524 to 2,437 m: 1
914 to 1,523 m: 1
under 914 m: 1 (2013)

Ports and terminals:
major seaport(s): Ad Dakhla, Laayoune (El Aaiun)

MILITARY

Manpower fit for military service:
males age 16-49: 79,489
females age 16-49: 87,362 (2010 est.)

Manpower reaching militarily significant age annually: *male:* 5,523
female: 5,429 (2010 est.)

TRANSNATIONAL ISSUES

Disputes—international: many neighboring states reject Moroccan administration of Western Sahara; several states have extended diplomatic relations to the "Sahrawi Arab Democratic Republic" represented by the Polisario Front in exile in Algeria, while others recognize Moroccan sovereignty over Western Sahara; most of the approximately 90,000 Sahrawi refugees have been sheltered in camps in Tindouf, Algeria since the 1980s

WORLD

INTRODUCTION

Background: Globally, the 20th century was marked by: (a) two devastating world wars; (b) the Great Depression of the 1930s; (c) the end of vast colonial empires; (d) rapid advances in science and technology, from the first airplane flight at Kitty Hawk, North Carolina (US) to the landing on the moon; (e) the Cold War between the Western alliance and the Warsaw Pact nations; (f) a sharp rise in living standards in North America, Europe, and Japan; (g) increased concerns about environmental degradation including deforestation, energy and water shortages, declining biological diversity, and air pollution; (h) the onset of the AIDS epidemic; and (i) the ultimate emergence of the US as the only world superpower. The planet's population continues to explode: from 1 billion in 1820 to 2 billion in 1930, 3 billion in 1960, 4 billion in 1974, 5 billion in 1987, 6 billion in 1999, and 7 billion in 2012. For the 21st century, the continued exponential growth in science and technology raises both hopes (e.g., advances in medicine and agriculture) and fears (e.g., development of even more lethal weapons of war).

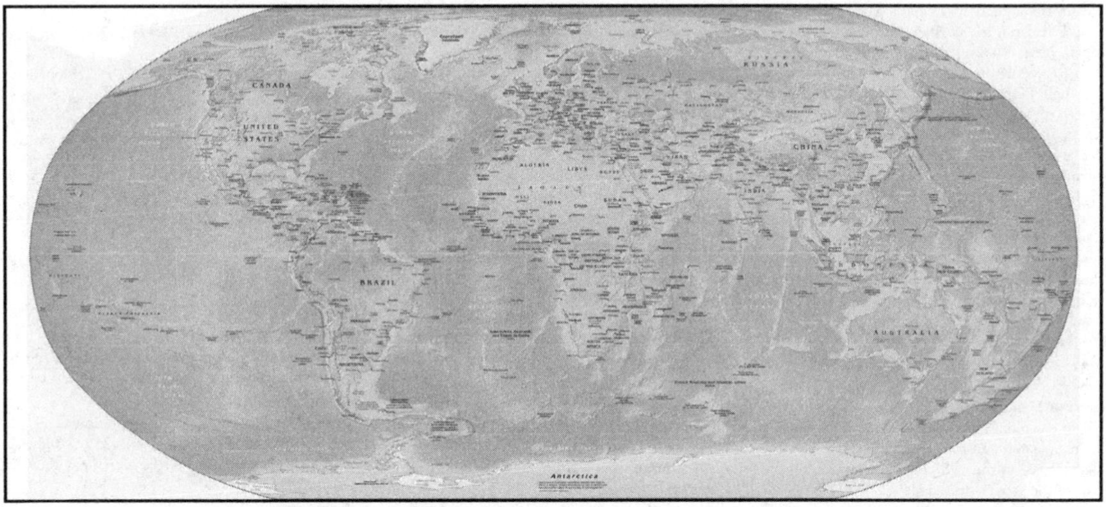

GEOGRAPHY

Geographic overview: The surface of the earth is approximately 70.9% water and 29.1% land. The former portion is divided into large water bodies termed oceans. The World Factbook recognizes and describes five oceans, which are in decreasing order of size: the Pacific Ocean, Atlantic Ocean, Indian Ocean, Southern Ocean, and Arctic Ocean.

The land portion is generally divided into several, large, discrete landmasses termed continents. Depending on the convention used, the number of continents can vary from five to seven. The most common classification recognizes seven, which are (from largest to smallest): Asia, Africa, North America, South America, Antarctica, Europe, and Australia. Asia and Europe are sometimes lumped together into a Eurasian continent resulting in six continents. Alternatively, North and South America are sometimes grouped as simply the Americas, resulting in a continent total of six (or five, if the Eurasia designation is used).

North America is commonly understood to include the island of Greenland, the isles of the Caribbean, and to extend south all the way to the Isthmus of Panama. The easternmost extent of Europe is generally defined as being the Ural Mountains and the Ural River; on the southeast the Caspian Sea; and on the south the Caucasus Mountains, the Black Sea, and the Mediterranean. Portions of Azerbaijan, Georgia, Kazakhstan, Russia, and Turkey fall within both Europe and Asia, but in every instance the larger section is in Asia. These countries are considered part of both continents. Armenia and Cyprus, which lie completely in Western Asia, are geopolitically European countries.

Asia usually incorporates all the islands of the Philippines, Malaysia, and Indonesia. The islands of the Pacific are often lumped with Australia into a "land mass" termed Oceania or Australasia. Africa's northeast termed Oceania or Australasia. Africa's northeast extremity is frequently delimited at the Isthmus of Suez, but for geopolitical purposes, the Egyptian Sinai Peninsula is often included as part of Africa.

Although the above groupings are the most common, different continental dispositions are recognized or taught in certain parts of the world, with some arrangements more heavily based on cultural spheres rather than physical geographic considerations.

Map references: Political Map of the World , Physical Map of the World , Standard Time Zones of the World , World Oceans

Area: *total:* 510.072 million sq km
land: 148.94 million sq km
water: 361.132 million sq km
note: 70.9% of the world's surface is water, 29.1% is land

Area—comparative: land area about 16 times the size of the US
top fifteen World Factbook entities ranked by size: Pacific Ocean 155.557 million sq km; Atlantic Ocean 76.762 million sq km; Indian Ocean 68.556 million sq km; Southern Ocean 20.327 million sq km; Russia 17,098,242 sq km; Arctic Ocean 14.056 million sq km; Antarctica 14 million sq km; Canada 9,984,670 sq km; United States 9,826,675 sq km; China 9,596,961 sq km; Brazil 8,514,877 sq km; Australia 7,741,220 sq km; European Union 4,324,782 sq km; India 3,287,263 sq km; Argentina 2,780,400 sq km
top ten largest water bodies: Pacific Ocean 155.557 million sq km; Atlantic Ocean 76.762 million sq km; Indian Ocean 68.556 million sq km; Southern Ocean 20.327 million sq km; Arctic Ocean 14.056 million sq km; Coral Sea 4,184,100 sq km; South China Sea 3,595,900 sq km; Caribbean Sea 2.834 million sq km; Bering Sea 2.52 million sq km; Mediterranean Sea 2.469 million sq km
top ten largest landmasses: Asia 44,568,500 sq km; Africa 30.065 million sq km; North America 24.473 million sq km; South America 17.819 million sq km; Antarctica 14 million sq km; Europe 9.948 million sq km; Australia 7,741,220 sq km; Greenland 2,166,086 sq km; New Guinea 785,753 sq km; Borneo 751,929 sq km
top ten largest islands: Greenland 2,166,086 sq km; New Guinea (Indonesia, Papua New Guinea) 785,753 sq km; Borneo (Brunei, Indonesia, Malaysia) 751,929 sq km; Madagascar 587,713 sq km; Baffin Island (Canada) 507,451 sq km; Sumatra (Indonesia) 472,784 sq km; Honshu (Japan) 227,963 sq km; Victoria Island (Canada) 217,291 sq km; Great Britain (United Kingdom) 209,331 sq km; Ellesmere Island (Canada) 196,236 sq km

Land boundaries: the land boundaries in the world total 251,060 km (not counting shared boundaries twice); two nations, China and Russia, each border 14 other countries
note: 46 nations and other areas are landlocked, these
include: Afghanistan, Andorra, Armenia, Austria, Azerbaijan, Belarus, Bhutan, Bolivia, Botswana, Burkina Faso, Burundi, Central African Republic, Chad, Czech Republic, Ethiopia, Holy See (Vatican City), Hungary, Kazakhstan, Kosovo, Kyrgyzstan, Laos, Lesotho, Liechtenstein, Luxembourg, Macedonia, Malawi, Mali, Moldova, Mongolia, Nepal, Niger, Paraguay, Rwanda, San Marino, Serbia, Slovakia, South Sudan, Swaziland, Switzerland, Tajikistan, Turkmenistan, Uganda, Uzbekistan, West Bank, Zambia, Zimbabwe; two of these, Liechtenstein and Uzbekistan, are doubly landlocked

Coastline: 356,000 km
note: 95 nations and other entities are islands that border no other countries, they include: American Samoa, Anguilla, Antigua and Barbuda, Aruba, Ashmore and Cartier Islands, The Bahamas, Bahrain, Baker Island, Barbados, Bermuda, Bouvet Island, British Indian Ocean Territory, British Virgin Islands, Cabo Verde, Cayman Islands, Christmas Island, Clipperton Island, Cocos (Keeling) Islands, Comoros, Cook Islands, Coral Sea Islands, Cuba, Curacao, Cyprus, Dominica, Falkland Islands (Islas Malvinas), Faroe Islands, Fiji, French Polynesia, French Southern and Antarctic Lands, Greenland, Grenada, Guam, Guernsey,

Heard Island and McDonald Islands, Howland Island, Iceland, Isle of Man, Jamaica, Jan Mayen, Japan, Jarvis Island, Jersey, Johnston Atoll, Kingman Reef, Kiribati, Madagascar, Maldives, Malta, Marshall Islands, Mauritius, Mayotte, Federated States of Micronesia, Midway Islands, Montserrat, Nauru, Navassa Island, New Caledonia, New Zealand, Niue, Norfolk Island, Northern Mariana Islands, Palau, Palmyra Atoll, Paracel Islands, Philippines, Pitcairn Islands, Puerto Rico, Saint Barthelemy, Saint Helena, Saint Kitts and Nevis, Saint Lucia, Saint Pierre and Miquelon, Saint Vincent and the Grenadines, Samoa, Sao Tome and Principe, Seychelles, Singapore, Sint Maarten, Solomon Islands, South Georgia and the South Sandwich Islands, Spratly Islands, Sri Lanka, Svalbard, Tokelau, Tonga, Trinidad and Tobago, Turks and Caicos Islands, Tuvalu, Vanuatu, Virgin Islands, Wake Island, Wallis and Futuna, Taiwan

Maritime claims: a variety of situations exist, but in general, most countries make the following claims measured from the mean low-tide baseline as described in the 1982 UN Convention on the Law of the Sea: territorial sea—12 nm, contiguous zone—24 nm, and exclusive economic zone—200 nm; additional zones provide for exploitation of continental shelf resources and an exclusive fishing zone; boundary situations with neighboring states prevent many countries from extending their fishing or economic zones to a full 200 nm

Climate: a wide equatorial band of hot and humid tropical climates—bordered north and south by subtropical temperate zones—that separate two large areas of cold and dry polar climates

Terrain: the greatest ocean depth is the Mariana Trench at 10,924 m in the Pacific Ocean

Elevation extremes: *lowest point:* Bentley Subglacial Trench (Antarctica) -2,555 m
note: in the oceanic realm, Challenger Deep in the Mariana Trench is the lowest point, lying -10,924 m below the surface of the Pacific Ocean
highest point: Mount Everest 8,850 m
top ten highest mountains (measured from sea level): Mount Everest (China-Nepal) 8,850 m; K2 (Pakistan) 8,611 m; Kanchenjunga (India-Nepal) 8,598 m; Lhotse (Nepal) 8,516 m; Makalu (China-Nepal) 8,463 m; Cho Oyu (China-Nepal) 8,201 m; Dhaulagiri (Nepal) 8,167 m; Manaslu (Nepal) 8,163 m; Nanga Parbat (Pakistan) 8,125 m; Anapurna (Nepal) 8,091 m

Natural resources: the rapid depletion of nonrenewable mineral resources, the depletion of forest areas and wetlands, the extinction of animal and plant species, and the deterioration in air and water quality (especially in some countries of Eastern Europe, the former USSR, and China) pose serious long-term problems that governments and peoples are only beginning to address

Land use: *arable land:* 10.43%
permanent crops: 1.15%
other: 88.42% (2011)

Irrigated land: 3,096,621.45 sq km (2011 est.)

Total renewable water resources: 53,789.29 cu km (2011)

Natural hazards: large areas subject to severe weather (tropical cyclones); natural disasters (earthquakes, landslides, tsunamis, volcanic eruptions)
volcanism: volcanism is a fundamental driver and consequence of plate tectonics, the physical process reshaping the Earth's lithosphere; the world is home to more than 1,500 potentially active volcanoes, with over 500 of these having erupted in historical times; an estimated 500 million people live near these volcanoes; associated dangers include lava flows, lahars (mudflows), pyroclastic flows, ash clouds, ash fall, ballistic projectiles, gas emissions, landslides, earthquakes, and tsunamis; in the 1990s, the International Association of Volcanology and Chemistry of the Earth's Interior, created a list of 16 Decade Volcanoes worthy of special study because of their great potential for destruction: Avachinsky-Koryaksky (Russia), Colima (Mexico), Etna (Italy), Galeras (Colombia), Mauna Loa (United States), Merapi (Indonesia), Nyiragongo (Democratic Republic of the Congo), Rainier (United States), Sakurajima (Japan), Santa Maria (Guatemala), Santorini (Greece), Taal (Philippines), Teide (Spain), Ulawun (Papua New Guinea), Unzen (Japan), Vesuvius (Italy)

Environment—current issues: large areas subject to overpopulation, industrial disasters, pollution (air, water, acid rain, toxic substances), loss of vegetation (overgrazing, deforestation, desertification), loss of wildlife, soil degradation, soil depletion, erosion; global warming becoming a greater concern Geography—note: the world is now thought to be about 4.55 billion years old, just about one-third of the 13.8-billion-year age estimated for the universe

PEOPLE AND SOCIETY

Languages: Mandarin Chinese 12.44%, Spanish 4.85%, English 4.83%, Arabic 3.25%, Hindi 2.68%, Bengali 2.66%, Portuguese 2.62%, Russian 2.12%, Japanese 1.8%, Standard German 1.33%, Javanese 1.25% (2009 est.)
note 1: percents are for "first language" speakers only; the six UN languages—Arabic, Chinese (Mandarin), English, French, Russian, and Spanish (Castilian)—are the mother tongue or second language of about half of the world's population, and are the official languages in more than half the states in the world; some 150 to 200 languages have more than a million speakers
note 2: all told, there are an estimated 7,100 languages spoken in the world; aproximately 80% of these languages are spoken by less than 100,000 people; about 50 languages are spoken by only 1 person; communities that are isolated from each other in mountainous regions often develop multiple languages; Papua New Guinea, for example, boasts about 836 separate languages
note 3: approximately 2,300 languages are spoken in Asia, 2,150, in Africa, 1,311 in the Pacific, 1,060 in the Americas, and 280 in Europe

Religions: Christian 33.39% (of which Roman Catholic 16.85%, Protestant 6.15%, Orthodox 3.96%, Anglican 1.26%), Muslim 22.74%, Hindu 13.8%, Buddhist 6.77%, Sikh 0.35%, Jewish 0.22%, Baha'i 0.11%, other religions 10.95%, non-religious 9.66%, atheists 2.01% (2010 est.)

Population: 7,095,217,980 (July 2013 est.)
top ten most populous countries (in millions): China 1,349.59; India 1,220.80; United States 316.67; Indonesia 251.16; Brazil 201.01; Pakistan 193.24; Nigeria 174.51; Bangladesh 163.65; Russia 142.50; Japan 127.25

Age structure:
0-14 years: 26% (male 956,360,171/female 893,629,520)
15-24 years: 16.8% (male 613,806,639/female 577,904,561)
25-54 years: 40.6% (male 1,478,739,525/female 1,447,244,791)
55-64 years: 8.4% (male 298,092,946/female 312,206,795)
65 years and over: 8.2% (male 265,453,689/female 331,172,947) (2013 est.)

Dependency ratios:
total dependency ratio: 52 %
youth dependency ratio: 39.9 %
elderly dependency ratio: 12.1 %
potential support ratio: 8.3 (2013)

Median age: *total:* 29.4 years
male: 28.7 years
female: 30.2 years (2013 est.)

Population growth rate: 1.1%
note: this rate results in about 148 net additions to the worldwide population every minute or 2.5 every second (2013 est.)

Birth rate: 18.9 births/1,000 population
note: this rate results in about 255 worldwide births per minute or 4.3 births every second (2013 est.)

Death rate: 7.9 deaths/1,000 population
note: this rate results in about 107 worldwide deaths per minute or 1.8 deaths every second (2013 est.)

Urbanization: *urban population:* 50.5% of total population (2010)
rate of urbanization: 1.85% annual rate of change (2010-15 est.)
ten largest urban agglomerations: Tokyo (Japan)—36,669,000; Delhi (India)—22,157,000; Sao Paulo (Brazil)—20,262,000; Mumbai (India)—20,041,000; Mexico City (Mexico)—19,460,000; New York-Newark (US)V—19,425,000; Shanghai (China)—16,575,000; Kolkata (India)—15,552,000; Dhaka (Bangladesh)—14,648,000; Karachi (Pakistan)—13,125,000 (2009)

Sex ratio: *at birth:* 1.07 male(s)/female
0-14 years: 1.07 male(s)/female
15-24 years: 1.06 male(s)/female
25-54 years: 1.02 male(s)/female
55-64 years: 0.96 male(s)/female
65 years and over: 0.8 male(s)/female
total population: 1.01 male(s)/female (2013 est.)

Infant mortality rate: *total:* 37.61 deaths/1,000 live births
male: 39.39 deaths/1,000 live births
female: 35.69 deaths/1,000 live births (2013 est.)

Life expectancy at birth:
total population: 68.09 years
male: 66.09 years
female: 70.24 years (2013 est.)

Total fertility rate: 2.45 children born/woman (2013 est.)

Hospital bed density: 2.9 beds/1,000 population (2005)

Drinking water source:
improved:
urban: 96.3% of population
rural: 80.9% of population
total: 88.9% of population
unimproved:
urban: 3.7% of population
rural: 19.1% of population
total: 11.1% of population (2011 est.)

Sanitation facility access:
improved:

urban: 79.9% of population
rural: 47% of population
total: 64.1% of population
unimproved:
urban: 20.1% of population
rural: 53% of population
total: 35.9% of population (2011 est.)

HIV/AIDS—adult prevalence rate: 0.8% (2009 est.)

HIV/AIDS—people living with HIV/AIDS: 35.3 million (2009 est.)

HIV/AIDS—deaths: 1.6 million (2009 est.)

Literacy: *definition:* age 15 and over can read and write
total population: 84.1%
male: 88.6%
female: 79.7%
note: almost three-quarters of the world's 775 million illiterate adults are found in only ten countries (in descending order: India, China, Pakistan, Bangladesh, Nigeria, Ethiopia, Egypt, Brazil, Indonesia, and the Democratic Republic of the Congo); of all the illiterate adults in the world, two-thirds are women; extremely low literacy rates are concentrated in South and West Asia and Sub-Saharan Africa (2010 est.)

School life expectancy (primary to tertiary education): *total:* 12 years
male: 12 years
female: 12 years (2011)

GOVERNMENT

Administrative divisions: 195 countries, 72 dependent areas and other entities

Legal system: the legal systems of nearly all countries are generally modeled upon elements of five main types: civil law (including French law, the Napoleonic Code, Roman law, Roman-Dutch law, and Spanish law); common law (including United States law); customary law; mixed or pluralistic law; and religious law (including Islamic law); an additional type of legal system—international law—governs the conduct of independent nations in their relationships with one another International law organization participation: all members of the UN are parties to the statute that established the International Court of Justice (ICJ) or World Court; 54 countries have accepted jurisdiction of the ICJ as compulsory with reservations and 14 countries have accepted ICJ jurisdiction as compulsory without reservations; states parties to the Rome Statute of the International Criminal Court (ICCt) are those countries that have ratified or acceded to the Rome Statute, the treaty that established the Court; a total of 121 (effective 1 July 2012) countries have accepted jurisdiction of the ICCt (see Appendix B for a clarification on the differing mandates of the ICJ and ICCt)

ECONOMY

Economy—overview: The international financial crisis of 2008-09 led to the first downturn in global output since 1946 and presented the world with a major new challenge: determining what mix of fiscal and monetary policies to follow to restore growth and jobs, while keeping inflation and debt under control. Financial stabilization and stimulus programs that started in 2009-11, combined with lower tax revenues in 2009-10, required most countries to run large budget deficits. Treasuries issued new public debt—totaling $7.6 trillion since 2008—to pay for the additional expenditures. To keep interest rates low, most central banks monetized that debt, injecting large sums of money into their economies—between December 2008 and December 2012 the global money supply increased by more than 31%. Governments now are faced with the difficult task of spurring current growth and employment without saddling their economies with so much debt that they sacrifice long-term growth and financial stability. And when economic activity picks up, central banks will confront the difficult task of containing inflation without raising interest rates so high they snuff out further growth.

Fiscal and monetary data for 2012 are currently available for 180 countries, which together account for 98.5% of World GDP. Of the 180 countries, 85 pursued unequivocally expansionary policies, boosting government spending while also expanding their money supply spending while also expanding their money supply relatively rapidly—faster than the world average of 4.1%; 37 followed restrictive fiscal and monetary policies, reducing government spending and holding money growth to less than the 4.1% average; and the remaining 58 followed a mix of counterbalancing fiscal and monetary policies, either reducing government spending while accelerating money growth, or boosting spending while curtailing money growth.

(For more information, see attached spreadsheet, Fiscal and Monetary Data, 2008-2012.)

In 2012, fiscal policy shifted towards greater austerity for a majority of the countries. In an attempt to attack their deficit and debt problems head-on, nearly 5 out of 6 countries slowed the rate of growth of government spending, and 1 in 3 countries actually lowered the level of their expenditures. The global growth rate for government expenditures dropped from 5.9% in 2010 and 10.1% in 2011, to just 1.4% in 2012. Roughly 1 out of 3 central banks tightened monetary policy, decelerating the rate of growth of their money supply, and about 1 out of 7 actually withdrew money from circulation. Growth of the global money supply, as measured by the narrowly defined M1, slowed from 8.7% in 2009 and 10.4% in 2010 to 5.2% in 2011 and 4.1% in 2012.

These policy choices significantly affected economic performance. The global budget deficit narrowed to roughly $2.7 trillion in 2012, or 3.8% of World GDP. But growth of the world economy slipped from 5.1% in 2010 and 3.7% in 2011, to just 3.1% in 2012. And world unemployment increased to 9.2%.

Countries with expansionary fiscal and monetary policies achieved significantly higher rates of growth, lower unemployment, higher growth of tax revenues, and greater success reducing the public debt burden than those countries that chose contractionary policies. In 2012, the 85 countries that followed a pro-growth approach achieved a median GDP growth rate of 4.9%, compared to just 0.8% for the 37 countries with restrictive fiscal and monetary policies, a difference of more than 4 percentage points. Among the 85, China grew 7.8%, Indonesia 6.0%, Mexico 4.0%, Russia 3.4%, Turkey 3.0%, the United States 2.2%, and Canada 1.9%, while among the 37, Brazil grew 1.3%, Germany 0.7%, France 0.1%, Belgium -0.2%, Netherlands -0.5%, Spain -1.4%, and Italy -2.3%. The median unemployment rate for the 37 countries jumped to 11.5%, while the median for the pro-growth countries held steady at 7.3%.

Faster GDP growth and lower unemployment rates translated into increased tax revenues and a lower debt burden. Revenues for the 85 expansionary countries grew at a median rate of 10.8%, whereas tax revenues fell at a median rate of 6.2% for the 37 countries that chose austere economic policies. Budget balances improved for about half of the 37, but, for most, debt grew faster than GDP, and the median level of their public debt as a share of GDP increased 2.5 percentage points, to 57.8%. On the other hand, budget balances deteriorated for most of the 85 pro-growth countries, but GDP growth outpaced increases in debt, and the median level of public debt as a share of GDP actually declined slightly (-0.1 percentage points).

The world recession has suppressed inflation rates—world inflation declined 1.0 percentage point in 2012 to about 4.0%. At the same time, the median inflation rate for the 85 pro-growth countries, at 5.5%, was 2.5 percentage points higher than that for the countries that followed more austere fiscal and monetary policies. Overall, the latter countries also improved their current account balances by shedding imports; as a result, current account balances deteriorated for most of the countries that pursued pro-growth policies. Slower growth of world income reduced import demand and crude oil prices fell. Consequently, the dollar value of world trade grew just 1% in 2012, compared with 18% in 2011.

Beyond the current global slowdown, the world faces several long-standing economic challenges. The addition of 80 million people each year to an already overcrowded globe is exacerbating the problems of pollution, waste-disposal, epidemics, water-shortages, famine, over-fishing of oceans, deforestation, desertification, and depletion of non-renewable resources. The nation-state, as a bedrock economic-political institution, is steadily losing control over international flows of people, goods, services, funds, and technology. The introduction of the euro as the common currency of much of Western Europe in January 1999, while paving the way for an integrated economic powerhouse, has created economic risks because the participating nations have varying income levels and growth rates, and hence, require a different mix of monetary and fiscal policies. Governments, especially in Western Europe, face the difficult political problem of channeling resources away from welfare programs in order to increase investment and strengthen incentives to seek employment. Because of their own internal problems and priorities, the industrialized countries are unable to devote sufficient resources to deal effectively with the poorer areas of the world, which, at least from an economic point of view, are becoming further marginalized. The terrorist attacks on the US on 11 September 2001 accentuated a growing risk to global prosperity—the diversion of resources away from capital investments to counter-terrorist programs.

Despite these vexing problems, the world economy also shows great promise. Technology has made possible further advances in a wide range of fields, from agriculture, to medicine, alternative energy, metallurgy, and transportation. Improved global communications have greatly reduced the costs of international trade, helping the world gain from the international division of labor, raise living standards, and reduce income disparities among nations. Much of the resilience of the world economy in the aftermath of the financial crisis resulted from government and central bank leaders resulted from government and central bank leaders around the globe working in concert to stem the financial onslaught, knowing well the lessons of past economic failures.

GDP (purchasing power parity): $87.18 trillion (2013 est.)
$84.78 trillion (2012 est.)
$82.24 trillion (2011 est.)
note: data are in 2013 US dollars

GDP (official exchange rate):

GWP (gross world product): $73.87 trillion (2013 est.)

GDP—real growth rate: 2.8% (2013 est.)
3.1% (2012 est.)
3.8% (2011 est.)

GDP—per capita (PPP): $13,100 (2013 est.)
$12,800 (2012 est.)
$12,600 (2011 est.)
note: data are in 2013 US dollars

GDP—composition, by end use:
household consumption: 62%
government consumption: 18.5%
investment in fixed capital: 19.4%
investment in inventories: 0.5%
exports of goods and services: 29.3%
imports of goods and services: -29.7% (2011 est.)

GDP—composition, by sector of origin:
agriculture: 5.9%
industry: 30.5%
services: 63.6% (2012 est.)

Industries: dominated by the onrush of technology, especially in computers, robotics, telecommunications, and medicines and medical equipment; most of these advances take place in OECD nations; only a small portion of non-OECD countries have succeeded in rapidly adjusting to these technological forces; the accelerated development of new technologies is complicating already grim environmental problems

Industrial production growth rate: 3.9% (2011 est.)

Labor force: 3.314 billion (2013 est.)

Labor force—by occupation: *agriculture:* 35.4%
industry: 22.8%
services: 41.8% (2008)

Unemployment rate: 9% (2013 est.)
8.2% (2012 est.)
note: 30% combined unemployment and underemployment in many non-industrialized countries; developed countries typically 4%-12% unemployment (2007 est.)

Household income or consumption by percentage share: *lowest* 10%: 2.8%
highest 10%: 28.2% (2008 est.)

Distribution of family income—Gini index: 39 (2007 est.)
37.2 (1998 est.)

Budget: *revenues:* $22.37 trillion
expenditures: $24.69 trillion (2013 est.)

Taxes and other revenues: 30.3% of GDP (2013 est.)

Budget surplus (+) or deficit (-):
-3.1% of GDP (2013 est.)

Public debt: 64.8% of GDP (2013 est.)
64.7% of GDP (2012 est.)

Inflation rate (consumer prices): world average 4% (2013 est.)
developed countries 1.6% (2013 est.)
developing countries 5.6% (2013 est.)
note: the above estimates are weighted averages; inflation in developed countries is 0% to 4% typically, in developing countries, 5% to 10% typically; national inflation rates vary widely in individual cases; inflation rates have declined for most countries for the last several years, held in check by increasing international competition from several low wage countries, and by soft demand as a result of the world financial crisis (2013 est.)

Stock of narrow money: $27.6 trillion (31 December 2013 est.)
$26.88 trillion (31 December 2012 est.)

Stock of broad money: $83.41 trillion (31 December 2013 est.)
$79.08 trillion (31 December 2012 est.)

Stock of domestic credit: $87.58 trillion (31 December 2013 est.)
$85.82 trillion (31 December 2012 est.)

Market value of publicly traded shares: $53.87 trillion (31 December 2012 est.)
$47.13 trillion (31 December 2011)
$54.61 trillion (31 December 2010 est.)

Exports: $18.48 trillion (2013 est.)
$18.19 trillion (2012 est.)

Exports—commodities: the whole range of industrial and agricultural goods and services top ten—share of world trade: electrical machinery, including computers 14.8%; mineral fuels, including oil, coal, gas, and refined products 14.4%; nuclear reactors, boilers, and parts 14.2%; cars, trucks, and buses 8.9%; scientific and precision instruments 3.5%; plastics 3.4%; iron and steel 2.7%; organic chemicals 2.6%; pharmaceutical products 2.6%; diamonds, pearls, and precious stones 1.9%

Imports: $18.09 trillion (2013 est.)
$17.93 trillion (2012 est.)

Imports—commodities: the whole range of industrial and agricultural goods and services top ten—share of world trade: see listing for exports

Debt—external: $72.82 trillion (31 December 2013 est.)
$70.43 trillion (31 December 2012 est.)
note: this figure is the sum total of all countries' external debt, both public and private

Stock of direct foreign investment—at home:
$24.6 trillion (31 December 2013 est.)
$23.14 trillion (31 December 2012 est.)

Stock of direct foreign investment—abroad:
$25.34 trillion (31 December 2013 est.)
$23.83 trillion (31 December 2012 est.)

ENERGY

Electricity—production: 21.11 trillion kWh (2010 est.)

Electricity—consumption: 19.46 trillion kWh (2010 est.)

Electricity—exports: 650 billion kWh (2012 est.)

Electricity—imports: 669.6 billion kWh (2012 est.)

Electricity—installed generating capacity:
5.281 billion kW (2010 est.)

Electricity—from fossil fuels: 66.2% of total installed capacity (2010 est.)

Electricity—from nuclear fuels: 7.5% of total installed capacity (2010 est.)

Electricity—from hydroelectric plants: 18.1% of total installed capacity (2010 est.)

Electricity—from other renewable sources: 5.8% of total installed capacity (2010 est.)

Crude oil—production: 89.04 million bbl/day (2012 est.)

Crude oil—exports: 43.93 million bbl/day (2010 est.)

Crude oil—imports: 44.89 million bbl/day (2010 est.)

Crude oil—proved reserves: 1.63 trillion bbl (1 January 2013 es)

Refined petroleum products—production: 82.72 million bbl/day (2010 est.)

Refined petroleum products—consumption: 87.6 million bbl/day (2011 est.)

Refined petroleum products—exports: 25.56 million bbl/day (2010 est.)

Refined petroleum products—imports: 24.64 million bbl/day (2010 est.)

Natural gas—production: 3.452 trillion cu m (2011 est.)

Natural gas—consumption: 3.272 trillion cu m (2010 est.)

Natural gas—exports: 1.332 trillion cu m (2011 est.)

Natural gas—imports: 1.652 trillion cu m (2011 est.)

Natural gas—proved reserves: 194.9 trillion cu m (1 January 2013 es)

Carbon dioxide emissions from consumption of energy: 32.62 billion Mt (2011 est.)

COMMUNICATIONS

Telephones—main lines in use: 1.2 billion (2011)

Telephones—mobile cellular: 6 billion (2011)

Internet users: 2.1 billion (2010)

TRANSPORTATION

Airports: total airports—41,821 (2013)
top ten by passengers: Atlanta (ATL)—95,672,104; Beijing (PEK)—81,908,740; London (LHR)—70,051,902; Tokyo (HND)—67,824,747; Chicago (ORD)—67,124,607; Los Angeles (LAX)—63,849,335; Paris (CDG)—61,478,475; Dallas/Fort Worth (DFW)—58,887,570; Dubai (DXB)—58,392,171; Jakarta (CGK)—57,839,056 (2013) top ten by cargo (metric tons): Hong Kong (HKG)—4,120,348; Memphis (MEM)—4,053,865; Shanghai (PVG)—2,969,554; Anchorage (ANC)—2,470,147; Incheon (ICN)—2,461,229; Dubai (DXB)—2,294,614; Louisville (SDF)—2,186,937; Frankfurt (FRA)—2,067,698; Tokyo (NRT)—2,014,500; Paris (CDG)—1,940,850 (2013) (2013) 2,014,500; Paris (CDG)—1,940,850 (2013) (2013)

Heliports: 6,524 (2013)

Railways: *total:* 657,382 km (2013)

Roadways: *total:* 64,285,009 km (2013)

Waterways: 2,293,412 km

top ten longest rivers: Nile (Africa) 6,693 km; Amazon (South America) 6,436 km; Mississippi-Missouri (North America) 6,238 km; Yenisey-Angara (Asia) 5,981 km; Ob-Irtysh (Asia) 5,569 km; Yangtze (Asia) 5,525 km; Yellow (Asia) 4,671 km; Amur (Asia) 4,352 km; Lena (Asia) 4,345 km; Congo (Africa) 4,344 km
note: rivers are not necessarily navigable along the entire length; if measured by volume, the Amazon is the largest river in the world
top ten largest natural lakes (by surface area): Caspian Sea (Azerbaijan, Iran, Kazakhstan, Russia, Turkmenistan) 372,960 sq km; Lake Superior (Canada, United States) 82,414 sq km; Lake Victoria (Kenya, Tanzania, Uganda) 69,490 sq km; Lake Huron (Canada, United States) 59,596 sq km; Lake Michigan (United States) 57,441 sq km; Lake Tanganyika (Burundi, Democratic Republic of the Congo, Tanzania, Zambia) 32,890 sq km; Great Bear Lake (Canada) 31,800 sq km; Lake Baikal (Russia) 31,494 sq km; Lake Nyasa (Malawi, Mozambique, Tanzania) 30,044 sq km; Great Slave Lake (Canada) 28,400 sq km
note: the areas of the lakes are subject to seasonal variation; only the Caspian Sea is saline, the rest are fresh water (2013)

Ports and terminals: top ten container ports as measured by Twenty-Foot Equivalent Units (TEUs) throughput: Shanghai (China)—31,739,000; Singapore (Singapore)—29,937,700; Hong Kong (China)—24,384,000; Shenzhen (China)—22,570,800; Busan (South Korea)—16,163,842; Ningbo (China)—14,719,200; Guangzhou (China)—14,260,400; Qingdao (China)—13,020,100; Dubai (UAE)—12,617,595;—Rotterdam (Netherlands)—11,876,920 (2011)

Transportation—note: the International Maritime Bureau (IMB) reports that 2011 saw a very slight (1%) decrease in global pirate activities with marginally fewer people taken hostage at sea; in 2011, pirates attacked a total of 439 ships world-wide including hijacking 45 ships, capturing 802 seafarers, and killing eight; while the Horn of Africa remains the most dangerous area for maritime shipping, accounting for more than 50% of all attacks in 2011, a number of attacks also occurred in the coastal waters of Indonesia, the South China Sea, Bangladesh, and West Africa; as of July 2012, there were 189 attacks worldwide with 20 hijackings; the Horn of Africa remains the most dangerous region in 2012 with 70 attacks, 13 hijackings, 212 hostages seized; as of July 2012, Somali pirates held 11 vessels and 174 hostages; the decrease in successful pirate attacks is due, in part, to more aggressive anti-piracy operations by international naval forces as well as the increased use of armed security teams aboard merchant ships

MILITARY

Military expenditures: 2.42% of GDP (2012)
2.51% of GDP (2011)
2.42% of GDP (2010)

WORLD

Disputes—international: stretching over 250,000 km, the world's 322 international land boundaries separate 195 independent states and 71 dependencies, areas of special sovereignty, and other miscellaneous entities; ethnicity, culture, race, religion, and language have divided states into separate political entities as much as history, physical terrain, political fiat, or conquest, resulting in sometimes arbitrary and imposed boundaries; most maritime states have claimed limits that include territorial seas and exclusive economic zones; overlapping limits due to adjacent or opposite coasts create the potential for 430 bilateral maritime boundaries of which 209 have agreements that include contiguous and non-contiguous segments; boundary, borderland/resource, and territorial disputes vary in intensity from managed or dormant to violent or militarized; undemarcated, indefinite, porous, and unmanaged boundaries tend to encourage illegal cross-border activities, uncontrolled migration, and confrontation; territorial disputes may evolve from historical and/or cultural claims, or they may be brought on by resource competition; ethnic and cultural clashes continue to be responsible for much of the territorial fragmentation and internal displacement of the estimated 6.6 million people and cross-border displacements of 8.6 million refugees around the world as of early 2006; just over one million refugees were repatriated in the same period; other sources of contention include access to water and mineral (especially hydrocarbon) resources, fisheries, and arable land; armed conflict prevails not so much between the uniformed armed forces of independent states as between stateless armed entities that detract from the sustenance and welfare of local populations, leaving the community of nations to cope with resultant refugees, hunger, disease, impoverishment, and environmental degradation

Refugees and internally displaced persons: the United Nations High Commissioner for Refugees (UNHCR) estimated that as of the end of 2012 there were 45.2 million people forcibly displaced worldwide; this includes 15.4 million refugees, 937,000 asylum seekers, and 28.8 million conflict IDPs (another 32.4 million IDPs were displaced by natural disasters); the UNHCR estimates there are currently 10-12 million stateless persons (2012)

Trafficking in persons: *current situation:* approximately 800,000 people, mostly women and children, are trafficked annually across national borders, not including the millions who are trafficked within their own countries; at least 80% of the victims are female and up to 50% are minors; 75% of all victims are trafficked into commercial sexual exploitation; almost two-thirds of the global victims are trafficked intra-regionally within East Asia and the Pacific (260,000 to 280,000 people) and Europe and Eurasia (170,000 to 210,000 people) (2012)

Tier 2 Watch List: (44 countries) Afghanistan, Albania, Angola, Bahrain, Barbados, Belarus, Burma, Burundi, Cambodia, Chad, Comoros, Djibouti, Federated States of Micronesia, The Gambia, Guinea, Guyana, Haiti, Honduras, Kenya, Lebanon, Lesotho, Liberia, Madagascar, Malaysia, Maldives, Mali, Marshall Islands, Morocco, Namibia, Rwanda, Saint Lucia, Seychelles, Solomon Islands, South Sudan, Sri Lanka, Suriname, Tanzania, Thailand, Trinidad and Tobago, Tunisia, Turkmenistan, Ukraine, Uruguay, Venezuela

Tier 3: (21 countries) Algeria, Central African Republic, China, Democratic Republic of Congo, Cuba, Equatorial Guinea, Eritrea, Guinea-Bissau, Iran, North Korea, Kuwait, Libya, Mauritania, Papua New Guinea, Russia, Saudi Arabia, Sudan, Syria, Uzbekistan, Yemen, Zimbabwe (2013)

Illicit drugs: *cocaine:* worldwide coca leaf cultivation in 2007 amounted to 232,500 hectares; Colombia produced slightly more than two-thirds of the worldwide crop, followed by Peru and Bolivia; potential pure cocaine production decreased 7% to 865 metric tons in 2007; Colombia conducts an aggressive coca eradication campaign, but both Peruvian and Bolivian Governments are hesitant to eradicate coca in key growing areas; 551 metric tons of export-quality cocaine (85% pure) is documented to have been seized or destroyed in 2005; US consumption of export quality cocaine is estimated to have been in excess of 380 metric tons
opiates: worldwide illicit opium poppy cultivation continued to increase in 2007, with a potential opium production of 8,400 metric tons, reaching the highest levels recorded since estimates began in mid-1980s; Afghanistan is world's primary opium producer, accounting for 95% of the global supply; Southeast Asia—responsible for 9% of global opium—saw marginal increases in production; Latin America produced 1% of global opium, but most was refined into heroin destined for the US market; if all potential opium was processed into pure heroin, the potential global production would be 1,000 metric tons of heroin in 2007

YEMEN

INTRODUCTION

Background: North Yemen became independent of the Ottoman Empire in 1918. The British, who had set up a protectorate area around the southern port of Aden in the 19th century, withdrew in 1967 from what became South Yemen. Three years later, the southern government adopted a Marxist orientation. The massive exodus of hundreds of thousands of Yemenis from the south to the north contributed to two decades of hostility between the states. The two countries were formally unified as the Republic of Yemen in 1990. A southern secessionist movement and brief civil war in 1994 was quickly subdued. In 2000, Saudi Arabia and Yemen agreed to a delimitation of their border. Fighting in the northwest between the government and the Huthis, a Zaydi Shia minority, began in 2004 and has since resulted in six rounds of fighting—the last ended in early 2010 with a cease-fire that continues to hold. The southern secessionist movement was revitalized in 2008 when a popular socioeconomic protest movement initiated the prior year took on political goals including secession. Public rallies in Sana'a against then President SALIH—inspired by similar demonstrations in Tunisia and Egypt—slowly built momentum starting in late January 2011 fueled by complaints over high unemployment, poor economic conditions, and corruption. By the following month, some protests had resulted in violence, and the demonstrations had spread to other major cities. By March the opposition had hardened its demands and was unifying behind calls for SALIH's immediate ouster, and prominent military and tribal leaders began defecting from SALIH's camp. The Gulf Cooperation Council (GCC) in late April 2011, in an attempt to mediate the crisis in Yemen, proposed an agreement in which the president would step down in exchange for immunity from prosecution. SALIH's refusal to sign an agreement led to heavy street fighting and his injury in an explosion in June 2011. The UN Security Council passed Resolution 2014 in October 2011 calling on both sides to end the violence and complete a power transfer deal. In late November 2011, SALIH signed the GCC-brokered agreement to step down and to transfer some of his powers to Vice President Abd Rabuh Mansur HADI. Following elections in February 2012, won by HADI, SALIH formally transferred his powers. In accordance with the GCC initiative, Yemen launched a National Dialogue in March 2013 to discuss key constitutional, political, and social issues. HADI concluded the National Dialogue in January 2014. Subsequent steps in the transition process include constitutional drafting, a constitutional referendum, and national elections.

GEOGRAPHY

Location: Middle East, bordering the Arabian Sea, Gulf of Aden, and Red Sea, between Oman and Saudi Arabia

Geographic coordinates: 15 00 N, 48 00 E

Map references: Middle East

Area: *total:* 527,968 sq km
country comparison to the world: 50
land: 527,968 sq km
water: 0 sq km
note: includes Perim, Socotra, the former Yemen Arab Republic (YAR or North Yemen), and the former People's Democratic Republic of Yemen (PDRY or South Yemen)

Area—comparative: almost four times the size of Alabama; slightly larger than twice the size of Wyoming

Land boundaries: *total:* 1,746 km
border countries: Oman 288 km, Saudi Arabia 1,458 km

Coastline: 1,906 km

Maritime claims: *territorial sea:* 12 nm
contiguous zone: 24 nm
exclusive economic zone: 200 nm
continental shelf: 200 nm or to the edge of the continental margin

Climate: mostly desert; hot and humid along west coast; temperate in western mountains affected by seasonal monsoon; extraordinarily hot, dry, harsh desert in east

Terrain: narrow coastal plain backed by flat-topped hills and rugged mountains; dissected upland desert plains in center slope into the desert interior of the Arabian Peninsula

Elevation extremes: *lowest point:* Arabian Sea 0 m
highest point: Jabal an Nabi Shu'ayb 3,760 m

Natural resources: petroleum, fish, rock salt, marble; small deposits of coal, gold, lead, nickel, and copper; fertile soil in west

Land use: *arable land:* 2.2%
permanent crops: 0.55%
other: 97.25% (2011)

Irrigated land: 6,801 sq km (2004)

Total renewable water resources: 2.1 cu km (2011)

Freshwater withdrawal (domestic/industrial/agricultural): *total:* 3.57 cu km/yr (7%/2%/91%)
per capita: 162.4 cu m/yr (2005)

Natural hazards: sandstorms and dust storms in summer volcanism: limited volcanic activity; Jebel at Tair (Jabal al-Tair, Jebel Teir, Jabal al-Tayr, Jazirat at-Tair) (elev. 244 m), which forms an island in the Red Sea, erupted in 2007 after awakening from dormancy; other historically active volcanoes include Harra of Arhab, Harras of Dhamar, Harra es-Sawad, and Jebel Zubair, although many of these have not erupted in over a century

Environment—current issues: limited natural freshwater resources; inadequate supplies of potable water; overgrazing; soil erosion; desertification

Environment—international agreements:
party to: Biodiversity, Climate Change, Climate Change-Kyoto Protocol, Desertification, Endangered Species, Environmental Modification, Hazardous Wastes, Law of the Sea, Ozone Layer Protection
signed, but not ratified: none of the selected agreements

Geography—note: strategic location on Bab el Mandeb, the strait linking the Red Sea and the Gulf of Aden, one of world's most active shipping lanes

PEOPLE AND SOCIETY

Nationality: *noun:* Yemeni(s)
adjective: Yemeni

Ethnic groups: predominantly Arab; but also Afro-Arab, South Asians, Europeans

Languages: Arabic (official)

Religions: Muslim 99.1% (official; virtually all are citizens, an estimated 65% are Sunni and 35% are Shia), other 0.9% (includes Jewish, Baha'i, Hindu, and Christian; many are refugees or temporary foreign residents) (2010 est.)

Population: 26,052,966 (July 2014 est.)
country comparison to the world: 48

Age structure:
0-14 years: 41.7% (male 5,523,744/female 5,336,795)
15-24 years: 21.1% (male 2,789,510/female 2,709,263)
25-54 years: 30.9% (male 4,106,917/female 3,933,852)
55-64 years: 2.6% (male 450,185/female 515,255)
65 years and over: 2.6% (male 320,426/female 367,019) (2014 est.)

Dependency ratios:
total dependency ratio: 75.6 %
youth dependency ratio: 70.6 %
elderly dependency ratio: 5.1 %
potential support ratio: 19.8 (2013)

Median age: *total:* 18.6 years
male: 18.5 years
female: 18.7 years (2014 est.)

Population growth rate: 2.72% (2014 est.)
country comparison to the world: 20

Birth rate: 31.02 births/1,000 population (2014 est.)
country comparison to the world: 39

Death rate: 6.45 deaths/1,000 population (2014 est.)
country comparison to the world: 154

Net migration rate: 2.61 migrant(s)/1,000 population (2014 est.)
country comparison to the world: 37

Urbanization: *urban population:* 32.3% of total population (2011)
rate of urbanization: 4.78% annual rate of change (2010-15 est.)

Major urban areas—population: SANAA (capital) 2.229 million (2009)

Sex ratio: *at birth:* 1.05 male(s)/female
0-14 years: 1.04 male(s)/female

15-24 years: 1.03 male(s)/female
25-54 years: 1.04 male(s)/female
55-64 years: 1.03 male(s)/female
65 years and over: 0.9 male(s)/female
total population: 1.03 male(s)/female (2014 est.)

Mother's mean age at first birth: 19.2
note: median age at first birth among women 25-29 (1997 est.)

Maternal mortality rate: 200 deaths/100,000 live births (2010)
country comparison to the world: 57

Infant mortality rate: *total:* 50.41 deaths/1,000 live births
country comparison to the world: 38
male: 54.71 deaths/1,000 live births
female: 45.88 deaths/1,000 live births (2014 est.)

Life expectancy at birth:
total population: 64.83 years
country comparison to the world: 175
male: 62.72 years
female: 67.04 years (2014 est.)

Total fertility rate: 4.09 children born/woman (2014 est.)
country comparison to the world: 36

Contraceptive prevalence rate: 27.7% (2006)

Health expenditures: 5.5% of GDP (2011)
country comparison to the world: 122

Physicians density: 0.2 physicians/1,000 population (2010)

Hospital bed density: 0.7 beds/1,000 population (2010)

Drinking water source:
improved:
urban: 72% of population
rural: 46.5% of population
total: 54.8% of population
unimproved:
urban: 28% of population
rural: 53.5% of population
total: 54.8% of population (2011 est.)

Sanitation facility access:
improved:
urban: 92.5% of population
rural: 34.1% of population
total: 53% of population
unimproved:
urban: 7.5% of population
rural: 65.9% of population
total: 47% of population (2011 est.)

HIV/AIDS—adult prevalence rate: 0.1% (2012 est.)
country comparison to the world: 151

HIV/AIDS—people living with HIV/AIDS: 18,800 (2012 est.)
country comparison to the world: 82

HIV/AIDS—deaths: 800 (2012 est.)
country comparison to the world: 82

Major infectious diseases:
degree of risk: high
food or waterborne diseases: bacterial diarrhea, hepatitis A, and typhoid fever
vectorborne diseases: dengue fever and malaria
water contact disease: schistosomiasis (2013)

Obesity—adult prevalence rate: 14.5% (2008)
country comparison to the world: 121

Children under the age of 5 years underweight: 43.1% (2003)
country comparison to the world: 3

Education expenditures: 5.2% of GDP (2008)
country comparison to the world: 67

Literacy: *definition:* age 15 and over can read and write
total population: 65.3%
male: 82.1%
female: 48.5% (2011 est.)

School life expectancy (primary to tertiary education): *total:* 9 years
male: 11 years
female: 8 years (2011)

Child labor—children ages 5-14:
total number: 1,334,288
percentage: 23 % (2006 est.)

Unemployment, youth ages 15-24: *total:* 33.7%
country comparison to the world: 22
male: 26%
female: 74% (2010)

GOVERNMENT

Country name:
conventional long form: Republic of Yemen
conventional short form: Yemen
local long form: Al Jumhuriyah al Yamaniyah
local short form: Al Yaman
former: Yemen Arab Republic [Yemen (Sanaa) or North Yemen] and People's Democratic Republic of Yemen [Yemen (Aden) or South Yemen]

Government type: republic

Capital: *name:* Sanaa

geographic coordinates: 15 21 N, 44 12 E
time difference: UTC+3 (8 hours ahead of Washington, DC during Standard Time)

Administrative divisions: 20 governorates (muhafazat, singular—muhafazah) and 1 municipality*; Abyan, 'Adan (Aden), Ad Dali', Al Bayda', Al Hudaydah, Al Jawf, Al Mahrah, Al Mahwit, Amanat al 'Asimah (Sanaa City)*, 'Amran, Dhamar, Hadramawt, Hajjah, Ibb, Lahij, Ma'rib, Raymah, Sa'dah, San'a' (Sanaa), Shabwah, Ta'izz Independence: 22 May 1990 (Republic of Yemen was established with the merger of the Yemen Arab Republic [Yemen (Sanaa) or North Yemen] and the Marxist-dominated People's Democratic Republic of Yemen [Yemen (Aden) or South Yemen]); note—previously North Yemen became independent in November 1918 (from the Ottoman Empire) and became a republic with the overthrow of the theocratic Imamate in 1962; South Yemen became independent on 30 November 1967 (from the UK)

National holiday: Unification Day, 22 May (1990)

Constitution: adopted by referendum 16 May 1991 (following unification); amended several times, last in 2009; note—in early 2013, the Yemeni Government launched a National Dialogue to seek reforms and recommendations for a new constitution (2013)

Legal system: mixed legal system of Islamic law, Napoleonic law, English common law, and customary law

International law organization participation: has not submitted an ICJ jurisdiction declaration; non-party state to the ICCt

Suffrage: 18 years of age; universal

Executive branch: *chief of state:* President Abd Rabuh Mansur HADI (Field Marshal) (since 25 February 2012)
head of government: Prime Minister Muhammad Salim BA SINDWAH (since 27 November 2011)
cabinet: on 27 November 2011, Vice President HADI requested Interim Prime Minister Muhammad Salim BA SINDWAH to form a new government following the resignation of President SALIH on 24 November 2011 (For more information visit the World Leaders website)
elections: president elected by popular vote for a seven-year term based on constitution; however a special election was held on 21 February 2012 to remove Ali Abdallah SALIH based on a GCC-mediated deal during the political crisis of 2011 (next election expected in 2014); vice president appointed by the president but position is vacant; prime minister appointed by the president
election results: Abd Rabuh Mansur HADI elected as a consensus president with about 50% popular participation; no other candidates

Legislative branch: bicameral legislature consisting of a Shura Council (111 seats; members appointed by the president) and House of Representatives (301 seats; members elected by popular vote in single-member constituencies to serve six-year terms)
elections: last held on 27 April 2003 (scheduled April 2009 election postponed)
election results: House of Representatives percent of vote by party—NA; seats by party—GPC 238, Islah 47, YSP 6, Nasserite Unionist Party 3, National Arab Socialist Ba'th Party 2, independents 5

Judicial branch: *highest court(s):* Supreme Court (consists of the president of the Court, 2 deputies, and nearly 50 judges; court organized into constitutional, civil, commercial, family, administrative, criminal, military, and appeals scrutiny divisions)
judge selection and term of office: judges appointed by the Supreme Judicial Council, chaired by the president of the republic and consisting of 10 high-ranking judicial officers; judges appointed for life with mandatory retirement at age 65
subordinate courts: appeal courts; district or first instance courts; commercial courts

Political parties and leaders: General People's Congress or GPC [Ali Abdallah SALIH, Abd Rabuh Mansur HADI]; Islamic Reform Grouping or Islah [Muhammed Abdallah al-YADUMI, Abdul Wahab al-ANSI]; Nasserite Unionist Party [Sultan al-ATWANI]; Yemeni Socialist Party or YSP [Yasin Said NU'MAN]
note: there are at least seven more active political parties

Political pressure groups and leaders: Muslim Brotherhood; Women National Committee
other: conservative tribal groups; Huthis, southern secessionist groups; al-Qa'ida in the Arabian Peninsula (AQAP)

International organization participation: AFESD, AMF, CAEU, CD, EITI (compliant country), FAO, G-77, IAEA, IBRD, ICAO, ICRM, IDA, IDB, IFAD, IFC, IFRCS, ILO, IMF, IMO, IMSO, Interpol, IOC, IOM, IPU, ISO, ITSO, ITU, ITUC (NGOs), LAS, MIGA, MINURSO, MINUSMA, MONUSCO, NAM, OAS (observer), OIC, OPCW, UN, UNAMID, UNCTAD, UNESCO, UNHCR, UNIDO, UNISFA, UNMIL, UNMIS, UNOCI, UNWTO, UPU, WCO, WFTU (NGOs), WHO, WIPO, WMO, WTO (observer)

Diplomatic representation in the US:
chief of mission: Ambassador (vacant); Charge d'Affaires Adel Ali Ahmed AL-SUNAINI
chancery: 2319 Wyoming Avenue NW, Washington, DC 20008
telephone: [1] (202) 965-4760
FAX: [1] (202) 337-2017

Diplomatic representation from the US:
chief of mission: Ambassador (vacant); Charge d'Affaires Karen H. SASAHARA (since July 2013)
embassy: Sa'awan Street, Sanaa
mailing address: P. O. Box 22347, Sanaa
telephone: [967] (1) 755-2000 ext. 2153 or 2266
FAX: [967] (1) 303-182

Flag description: three equal horizontal bands of red (top), white, and black; the band colors derive from the Arab Liberation flag and represent oppression (black), overcome through bloody struggle (red), to be replaced by a bright future (white)
note: similar to the flag of Syria, which has two green stars in the white band, and of Iraq, which has an Arabic inscription centered in the white band; also similar to the flag of Egypt, which has a heraldic eagle centered in the white band

National symbol(s): golden eagle

National anthem: *name:* "al-qumhuriyatu l-muttahida" (United Republic)
lyrics/music: Abdullah Abdulwahab NOA'MAN/ Ayyoab Tarish ABSI
note: adopted 1990; the music first served as the anthem for South Yemen before unification with North Yemen in 1990

ECONOMY

Economy—overview: Yemen is a low income country that is highly dependent on declining oil resources for revenue. Petroleum accounts for roughly 25% of GDP and 63% of government revenue. Yemen has tried to counter the effects of its declining oil resources and continuing attacks on its oil pipelines by diversifying its economy through an economic reform program initiated in 2006 that is designed to bolster non-oil sectors of the economy and foreign investment. In October 2009, Yemen exported its first liquefied natural gas as part of this diversification effort. In January 2010, the international community established the Friends of Yemen group that aims to support Yemen's efforts toward economic and political reform. In 2012, the Friends of Yemen pledged nearly $7 billion in assistance to Yemen. The Yemeni Government also endorsed a Mutual Accountability Framework to facilitate the efficient implementation of donor aid. The unrest that began in early 2011 caused GDP to plunge almost 11% in 2011. Availability of basic services, including electricity, water, and fuel, has improved since the transition, but progress toward achieving more sustainable economic stability has been slow and uneven. Yemen continues to face difficult long-term challenges, including declining water resources, high unemployment, severe food scarcity, and a high population growth rate.

GDP (purchasing power parity): $61.63 billion (2013 est.)
country comparison to the world: 89
$58.45 billion (2012 est.)
$57.36 billion (2011 est.)
note: data are in 2013 US dollars

GDP (official exchange rate): $43.89 billion (2013 est.)

GDP—real growth rate: 3.8% (2013 est.)
country comparison to the world: 85
0.1% (2012 est.)
-10.5% (2011 est.)

GDP—per capita (PPP): $2,500 (2013 est.)
country comparison to the world: 186
$2,500 (2012 est.)
$2,500 (2011 est.)
note: data are in 2013 US dollars

Gross national saving: 4.2% of GDP (2013 est.)
country comparison to the world: 148
9.6% of GDP (2012 est.)
6.3% of GDP (2011 est.)

GDP—composition, by end use:
household consumption: 80.3%
government consumption: 12.5%
investment in fixed capital: 18.4%
investment in inventories: -4%
exports of goods and services: 17.8%
imports of goods and services: -24.9% (2013 est.)

GDP—composition, by sector of origin:
agriculture: 7.7%
industry: 30.9%
services: 61.4% (2013 est.)

Agriculture—products: grain, fruits, vegetables, pulses, qat, coffee, cotton; dairy products, livestock (sheep, goats, cattle, camels), poultry; fish

Industries: crude oil production and petroleum refining; small-scale production of cotton textiles and leather goods; food processing; handicrafts; small aluminum products factory; cement; commercial ship repair; natural gas production

Industrial production growth rate: 4.8% (2013 est.)
country comparison to the world: 59

Labor force: 7.1 million (2013 est.)
country comparison to the world: 63

Labor force—by occupation: *note:* most people are employed in agriculture and herding; services, construction, industry, and commerce account for less than one-fourth of the labor force

Unemployment rate: 35% (2003 est.)
country comparison to the world: 187

Population below poverty line: 45.2% (2003)

Household income or consumption by percentage share: *lowest 10%:* 2.9%
highest 10%: 30.8% (2005)

Distribution of family income—Gini index: 37.7 (2005)
country comparison to the world: 74
33.4 (1998)

Budget: *revenues:* $7.769 billion
expenditures: $12.31 billion (2013 est.)

Taxes and other revenues: 17.7% of GDP (2013 est.)
country comparison to the world: 177

Budget surplus (+) or deficit (-): -10.3% of GDP (2013 est.)
country comparison to the world: 206

Public debt: 47.1% of GDP (2013 est.)
country comparison to the world: 74
45.4% of GDP (2012 est.)

Fiscal year: calendar year

Inflation rate (consumer prices): 11.8% (2013 est.)
country comparison to the world: 213
9.9% (2012 est.)

Central bank discount rate: NA%

Commercial bank prime lending rate: 22% (31 December 2013 est.)
country comparison to the world: 12
23% (31 December 2012 est.)

Stock of narrow money: $5.753 billion (31 December 2013 est.)
country comparison to the world: 96
$5.142 billion (31 December 2012 est.)

Stock of broad money: $14.2 billion (31 December 2013 est.)
country comparison to the world: 91
$12.35 billion (31 December 2012 est.)

Stock of domestic credit: $11.2 billion (31 December 2013 est.)
country comparison to the world: 94
$9.576 billion (31 December 2012 est.)

Market value of publicly traded shares: $NA

Current account balance: -$3.312 billion (2013 est.)
country comparison to the world: 161
-$985 million (2012 est.)

Exports: $6.694 billion (2013 est.)
country comparison to the world: 105
$7.57 billion (2012 est.)

Exports—commodities: crude oil, coffee, dried and salted fish, liquefied natural gas

Exports—partners: China 41%, Thailand 19.2%, India 11.4%, South Korea 4.4% (2013 est.)

Imports: $10.97 billion (2013 est.)
country comparison to the world: 97
$12.49 billion (2012 est.)

Imports—commodities: food and live animals, machinery and equipment, chemicals

Imports—partners: EU 48.8%, UAE 9.8%, Switzerland 8.8%, China 7.4%, India 5.8% (2013 est.)

Reserves of foreign exchange and gold: $5.538 billion (31 December 2013 est.)
country comparison to the world: 92
$6.158 billion (31 December 2012 est.)

Debt—external: $7.806 billion (31 December 2013 est.)
country comparison to the world: 107
$7.419 billion (31 December 2012 est.)

Stock of direct foreign investment—at home: $NA

Exchange rates: Yemeni rials (YER) per US dollar—
214.9 (2013 est.)
214.35 (2012 est.)
219.59 (2010 est.)
202.85 (2009)
199.76 (2008)

ENERGY

Electricity—production: 7.292 billion kWh (2010 est.)
country comparison to the world: 106

Electricity—consumption: 5.515 billion kWh (2010 est.)
country comparison to the world: 111

Electricity—exports: 0 kWh (2012 est.)
country comparison to the world: 216

Electricity—imports: 0 kWh (2012 est.)
country comparison to the world: 216

Electricity—installed generating capacity: 1.53 million kW (2011 est.)
country comparison to the world: 114

Electricity—from fossil fuels: 100% of total installed capacity (2010 est.)
country comparison to the world: 2

Electricity—from nuclear fuels: 0% of total installed capacity (2010 est.)
country comparison to the world: 208

Electricity—from hydroelectric plants: 0% of total installed capacity (2010 est.)
country comparison to the world: 210

Electricity—from other renewable sources: 0% of total installed capacity (2010 est.)
country comparison to the world: 143

Crude oil—production: 156,500 bbl/day (2012 est.)
country comparison to the world: 43

Crude oil—exports: 175,200 bbl/day (2010 est.)
country comparison to the world: 31

Crude oil—imports: 0 bbl/day (2010 est.)
country comparison to the world: 145

Crude oil—proved reserves: 3 billion bbl (1 January 2013 es)
country comparison to the world: 31

Refined petroleum products—production: 86,330 bbl/day (2010 est.)
country comparison to the world: 77

Refined petroleum products—consumption: 177,000 bbl/day (2011 est.)
country comparison to the world: 62

Refined petroleum products—exports: 14,330 bbl/day (2010 est.)
country comparison to the world: 79

Refined petroleum products—imports: 59,050 bbl/day (2010 est.)
country comparison to the world: 62

Natural gas—production: 9.62 billion cu m (2011 est.)
country comparison to the world: 42

Natural gas—consumption: 869.9 million cu m (2011 est.)
country comparison to the world: 91

Natural gas—exports: 8.75 billion cu m (2011 est.)
country comparison to the world: 28

Natural gas—imports: 0 cu m (2011 est.)
country comparison to the world: 82

Natural gas—proved reserves: 478.5 billion cu m (1 January 2013 es)
country comparison to the world: 33

Carbon dioxide emissions from consumption of energy: 23.75 million Mt (2011 est.)
country comparison to the world: 80

COMMUNICATIONS

Telephones—main lines in use: 1.1 million (2012)
country comparison to the world: 72

Telephones—mobile cellular: 13.9 million (2012)
country comparison to the world: 60

Telephone system: *general assessment:* since unification in 1990, efforts have been made to create a national telecommunications network
domestic: the national network consists of microwave radio relay, cable, tropospheric scatter, GSM and CDMA mobile-cellular telephone systems; fixed-line and mobile-cellular teledensity remains low by regional standards
international: country code—967; landing point for the international submarine cable Fiber-Optic Link Around the Globe (FLAG); satellite earth stations—3 Intelsat (2 Indian Ocean and 1 Atlantic Ocean), 1 Intersputnik (Atlantic Ocean region), and 2 Arabsat; microwave radio relay to Saudi Arabia and Djibouti (2006)

Broadcast media: state-run TV with 2 stations; state-run radio with 2 national radio stations and 5 local stations; stations from Oman and Saudi Arabia can be accessed (2007)

Internet country code: .ye

Internet hosts: 33,206 (2012)
country comparison to the world: 105

Internet users: 2.349 million (2009)
country comparison to the world: 71

TRANSPORTATION

Airports: 57 (2013)
country comparison to the world: 8 3

Airports—with paved runways: *total:* 17
over 3,047 m: 4
2,438 to 3,047 m: 9
1,524 to 2,437 m: 3
914 to 1,523 m: 1 (2013)

Airports—with unpaved runways: *total:* 4 0
over 3,047 m: 3
2,438 to 3,047 m: 5
1,524 to 2,437 m: 7
914 to 1,523 m: 16
under 914 m: 9 (2013)

Pipelines: gas 641 km; liquid petroleum gas 22 km; oil 1,370 km (2013)

Roadways: *total:* 71,300 km
country comparison to the world: 66
paved: 6,200 km
unpaved: 65,100 km (2005)

Merchant marine: *total:* 5
country comparison to the world: 126
by type: chemical tanker 2, petroleum tanker 2, roll on/roll off 1
registered in other countries: 14 (Moldova 4, Panama 4, Sierra Leone 2, Togo 1, unknown 3) (2010)

Ports and terminals: *major seaport(s):* Aden, Al Hudaydah, Al Mukalla

Transportation—note: the International Maritime Bureau reports offshore waters in the Gulf of Aden are high risk for piracy; numerous vessels, including commercial shipping and pleasure craft, have been attacked and hijacked both at anchor and while underway; crew, passengers, and cargo are held for ransom; the presence of several naval task forces in the Gulf of Aden and additional anti-piracy measures on the part of ship operators reduced the incidence of piracy in that body of water by more than half in 2010

MILITARY

Military branches: Land Forces, Naval and Coastal Defense Forces (includes Marines), Air and Air Defense Force (al-Quwwat al-Jawwiya al-Yemeniya), Border Guards, Stategic Reserve Forces (2013)

Military service age and obligation: 18 is the legal minimum age for voluntary military service; no conscription; 2-year service obligation (2012)

Manpower available for military service:
males age 16-49: 5,652,256
females age 16-49: 5,387,160 (2010 est.)

Manpower fit for military service:
males age 16-49: 4,056,944
females age 16-49: 4,116,895 (2010 est.)

Manpower reaching militarily significant age annually: *male:* 287,141
female: 277,612 (2010 est.)

Military expenditures: 4.02% of GDP (2012)
country comparison to the world: 11
3.48% of GDP (2011)
4.02% of GDP (2010)

Military—note: a Coast Guard was established in 2002

TRANSNATIONAL ISSUES

Disputes—international: Saudi Arabia has reinforced its concrete-filled security barrier along sections of the fully demarcated border with Yemen to stem illegal cross-border activities

Refugees and internally displaced persons: *refugees (country of origin):* 5,221 (Ethiopia) (2012); 230,878 (Somalia) (2014)
IDPs: 309,823 (conflict in Sa'ada governorate; clashes between AQAP and government forces) (2014)

Trafficking in persons: *current situation:* Yemen is a source and, to a much lesser extent, transit and destination country for men, women, and children subjected to forced labor and sex trafficking; some Yemeni children, mostly boys, migrate to Yemeni cities or across the border to Saudi Arabia and, less frequently Oman, where they end up as forced laborers in domestic service or small shops, beggars, or prostitutes; some of the large number of child workers in Yemen also face conditions of forced labor; other Yemeni children are conscripted into the government's armed forces or tribal or rebel militias; to a lesser degree, Yemen is a country of origin for girls trafficked within country or to Saudi Arabia to work as prostitutes in hotels and clubs; additionally, Yemen is a destination and transit country for women and children from the Horn of Africa who are looking for work or have received false job offers in the Gulf states but are subjected to sexual exploitation or forced labor upon arrival; reports indicate that adults and children are still sold or inherited as slaves in Yemen

tier rating: Tier 3—Yemen does not fully comply with the minimum standards for the elimination of trafficking and is not making significant efforts to do so; prolonged political, economic, and security crises impeded the government's modest anti-trafficking efforts; the government has not instituted formal procedures to identify and protect victims of trafficking or investigate or prosecute officials complicit in trafficking-related crimes; no known efforts have been made to investigate or punish the practice of chattel slavery; the government has taken some steps to prevent the recruitment of children in the armed forces, but it is unclear if efforts have been made to remove child soldiers from the military and provide them with protective or rehabilitative services; no progress has been made in implementing Yemen's 2008 national action plan on trafficking (2013)

Z

ZAMBIA

INTRODUCTION

Background: The territory of Northern Rhodesia was administered by the [British] South Africa Company from 1891 until it was taken over by the UK in 1923. During the 1920s and 1930s, advances in mining spurred development and immigration. The name was changed to Zambia upon independence in 1964. In the 1980s and 1990s, declining copper prices, economic mismanagement and a prolonged drought hurt the economy. Elections in 1991 brought an end to one-party rule, but the subsequent vote in 1996 saw blatant harassment of opposition parties. The election in 2001 was marked by administrative problems with three parties filing a legal petition challenging the election of ruling party candidate Levy MWANAWASA. MWANAWASA was reelected in 2006 in an election that was deemed free and fair. Upon his abrupt death in August 2008, he was succeeded by his vice president, Rupiah BANDA, who subsequently won a special presidential by-election in October 2008. Michael SATA was elected president in September 2011.

GEOGRAPHY

Location: Southern Africa, east of Angola, south of the Democratic Republic of the Congo

Geographic coordinates: 15 00 S, 30 00 E

Map references: Africa

Area: *total:* 752,618 sq km
country comparison to the world: 39
land: 743,398 sq km
water: 9,220 sq km

Area—comparative: slightly larger than Texas

Land boundaries: *total:* 5,664 km
border countries: Angola 1,110 km, Democratic Republic of the Congo 1,930 km, Malawi 837 km, Mozambique 419 km, Namibia 233 km, Tanzania 338 km, Zimbabwe 797 km

Coastline: 0 km (landlocked)

Maritime claims: none (landlocked)

Climate: tropical; modified by altitude; rainy season (October to April)

Terrain: mostly high plateau with some hills and mountains

Elevation extremes: *lowest point:* Zambezi river 329 m
highest point: unnamed elevation in Mafinga Hills 2,301 m

Natural resources: copper, cobalt, zinc, lead, coal, emeralds, gold, silver, uranium, hydropower

Land use: *arable land:* 4.52%
permanent crops: 0.05%
other: 95.44% (2011)

Irrigated land: 1,559 sq km (2003)

Total renewable water resources: 105.2 cu km (2011)

Freshwater withdrawal (domestic/industrial/agricultural): *total:* 1.57 cu km/yr (18%/8%/73%)
per capita: 147 cu m/yr (2002)

Natural hazards: periodic drought; tropical storms (November to April)

Environment—current issues: air pollution and resulting acid rain in the mineral extraction and refining region; chemical runoff into watersheds; poaching seriously threatens rhinoceros, elephant, antelope, and large cat populations; deforestation; soil erosion; desertification; lack of adequate water treatment presents human health risks

Environment—international agreements:
party to: Biodiversity, Climate Change, Climate Change-Kyoto Protocol, Desertification, Endangered Species, Hazardous Wastes, Law of the Sea, Ozone Layer Protection, Wetlands
signed, but not ratified: none of the selected agreements

Geography—note: landlocked; the Zambezi forms a natural riverine boundary with Zimbabwe; Lake Kariba on the Zambia-Zimbabwe border forms the world's largest reservoir by volume (180 cu km; 43 cu mi)

PEOPLE AND SOCIETY

Nationality: *noun:* Zambian(s)
adjective: Zambian

Ethnic groups: Bemba 21%, Tonga 13.6%, Chewa 7.4%, Lozi 5.7%, Nsenga 5.3%, Tumbuka 4.4%, Ngoni 4%, Lala 3.1%, Kaonde 2.9%, Namwanga 2.8%, Lunda (north Western) 2.6%, Mambwe 2.5%, Luvale 2.2%, Lamba 2.1%, Ushi 1.9%, Lenje 1.6%, Bisa 1.6%, Mbunda 1.2%, other 13.4%, unspecified 1% (2010 est.)

Languages: Bembe 33.4%, Nyanja 14.7%, Tonga 11.4%, Chewa 4.5%, Lozi 5.5%, Nsenga 2.9%, Tumbuka 2.5%, Lunda (North Western) 1.9%, Kaonde 1.8%, Lala 1.8%, Lamba 1.8%, English (official) 1.7%, Luvale 1.5%, Mambwe 1.3%, Namwanga 1.2%, Lenje 1.1%, Bisa 1%, other 9.4%, unspecified 0.4%
note: Zambia is said to have over 70 languages, although man of these may be considered dialects; all of Zambia's major languages are members of the Bantu family (2010 est.)

Religions: Protestant 75.3%, Roman Catholic 20.2%, other 2.7% (includes Muslim Buddhist, Hindu, and Baha'i), none 1.8% (2010 est.)

Population: 14,638,505 (July 2014 est.)
country comparison to the world: 71
note: estimates for this country explicitly take into account the effects of excess mortality due to AIDS; this can result in lower life expectancy, higher infant mortality, higher death rates, lower population growth rates, and changes in the distribution of population by age and sex than would otherwise be expected

Age structure:
0-14 years: 46.2% (male 3,393,388/female 3,362,850)
15-24 years: 20% (male 1,465,009/female 1,467,555)
25-54 years: 28.5% (male 2,105,768/female 2,072,314)
55-64 years: 2.4% (male 199,098/female 222,214)
65 years and over: 2.4% (male 151,471/female 198,838) (2014 est.)

Dependency ratios:
total dependency ratio: 97 %
youth dependency ratio: 91.8 %
elderly dependency ratio: 5.2 %
potential support ratio: 19.4 (2013)

Median age: *total:* 16.7 years
male: 16.6 years
female: 16.8 years (2014 est.)

Population growth rate: 2.88% (2014 est.)
country comparison to the world: 16

Birth rate: 42.46 births/1,000 population (2014 est.)
country comparison to the world: 4

Death rate: 12.92 deaths/1,000 population (2014 est.)
country comparison to the world: 21

Net migration rate: -0.72 migrant(s)/1,000 population (2014 est.)
country comparison to the world: 142

Urbanization: *urban population:* 39.2% of total population (2011)
rate of urbanization: 4.15% annual rate of change (2010-15 est.)

Major urban areas—population: LUSAKA (capital) 1.413 million (2009)

Sex ratio: *at birth:* 1.03 male(s)/female
0-14 years: 1.01 male(s)/female
15-24 years: 1 male(s)/female
25-54 years: 1.02 male(s)/female
55-64 years: 1 male(s)/female
65 years and over: 0.75 male(s)/female
total population: 1 male(s)/female (2014 est.)

Mother's mean age at first birth: 19.2 (2007 est.)

Maternal mortality rate: 440 deaths/100,000 live births (2010)
country comparison to the world: 26

Infant mortality rate: *total:* 66.62 deaths/1,000 live births
country comparison to the world: 17
male: 72.15 deaths/1,000 live births
female: 60.94 deaths/1,000 live births (2014 est.)

Life expectancy at birth:
total population: 51.83 years
country comparison to the world: 216
male: 50.24 years
female: 53.48 years (2014 est.)

Total fertility rate: 5.76 children born/woman (2014 est.)
country comparison to the world: 7

Contraceptive prevalence rate: 40.8% (2007)

Health expenditures: 6.1% of GDP (2011)
country comparison to the world: 105

Physicians density: 0.07 physicians/1,000 population (2010)

Hospital bed density: 2 beds/1,000 population (2010)

Drinking water source:
improved:
urban: 86% of population
rural: 50.1% of population
total: 64.1% of population
unimproved:
urban: 14% of population
rural: 49.9% of population
total: 35.9% of population (2011 est.)

Sanitation facility access:
improved:
urban: 55.8% of population
rural: 33.2% of population
total: 42.1% of population
unimproved:

urban: 44.2% of population
rural: 66.8% of population
total: 57.9% of population (2011 est.)

HIV/AIDS—adult prevalence rate: 12.7% (2012 est.)
country comparison to the world: 7

HIV/AIDS—people living with HIV/AIDS: 1,106,400 (2012 est.)
country comparison to the world: 11

HIV/AIDS—deaths: 30,300 (2012 est.)
country comparison to the world: 14

Major infectious diseases:
degree of risk: very high
food or waterborne diseases: bacterial and protozoal diarrhea, hepatitis A, and typhoid fever
vectorborne diseases: malaria and dengue fever
water contact disease: schistosomiasis
animal contact disease: rabies (2013)

Obesity—adult prevalence rate: 3.6% (2008)
country comparison to the world: 174

Children under the age of 5 years underweight: 14.9% (2007)
country comparison to the world: 50

Education expenditures: 1.3% of GDP (2008)
country comparison to the world: 170

Literacy: *definition:* age 15 and over can read and write English
total population: 61.4%
male: 71.9%
female: 51.8% (2007 est.)

School life expectancy (primary to tertiary education): *total:* 14 years
male: 14 years
female: 13 years (2012)

Child labor—children ages 5-14:
total number: 1,000,850
percentage: 41 %
note: data represents children ages 7-14 (2005 est.)

Unemployment, youth ages 15-24: *total:* 23.4% (2005)
country comparison to the world: 46

GOVERNMENT

Country name: *conventional long form:* Republic of Zambia
conventional short form: Zambia
former: Northern Rhodesia

Government type: republic

Capital: *name:* Lusaka

geographic coordinates: 15 25 S, 28 17 E
time difference: UTC+2 (7 hours ahead of Washington, DC during Standard Time)

Administrative divisions: 10 provinces; Central, Copperbelt, Eastern, Luapula, Lusaka, Muchinga, Northern, North-Western, Southern, Western

Independence: 24 October 1964 (from the UK)

National holiday: Independence Day, 24 October (1964)

Constitution: several previous; latest adopted 24 August 1991, promulgated 30 August 1991; amended 1996; note—in late 2013, a constitution committee submitted a draft constitution to the government, but the government has not yet publicly released the final copy or presented a plan to adopt the document (2013)

Legal system: mixed legal system of English common law and customary law; judicial review of legislative acts in an ad hoc constitutional council

International law organization participation: has not submitted an ICJ jurisdiction declaration; accepts ICCt jurisdiction

Suffrage: 18 years of age; universal

Executive branch: *chief of state:* President Michael Chilufya SATA (since 23 September 2011); Vice President Guy SCOTT (since 30 September 2011); the president is both the chief of state and head of government
head of government: President Michael Chilufya SATA (since 23 September 2011); Vice President Guy SCOTT (since 30 September 2011)
cabinet: Cabinet appointed by the president from among the members of the National Assembly, along with eight unelected members (For more information visit the World Leaders website)
elections: president elected by popular vote for a five-year term (eligible for a second term); election last held on 20 September 2011 (next to be held in 2016); vice president appointed by the president
election results: Michael Chilufya SATA elected president; percent of vote—Michael SATA 43.3%, Rupiah BANDA 36.2%, Hakainde HICHILEMA 18.5%, other 2.0%

Legislative branch: unicameral National Assembly (158 seats; 150 members are elected by popular vote, 8 members appointed by the president, to serve five-year terms)
elections: last held on 20 September 2011 (next to be held in 2016); note—over 25 by-elections, prompted by resignation, death, change of party or legal nullification have taken place since September 2011
election results: percent of vote by party—NA; seats by party—PF 60, MMD 55, UPND 28, ADD 1, FDD 1, independents 3; seats not determined 2; note—seats as of 4 March 2014—PF 69, MMD 41, UPND 31, ADD 1, FDD 1, independents 2, pending court decision 7, other 6

Judicial branch: *highest court(s):* Supreme Court (consists of 9 judges)
judge selection and term of office: Supreme Court judges appointed by the president and ratified by the National Assembly; judge tenure NA
subordinate courts: High Court; magistrate's courts and local courts

Political parties and leaders: Alliance for Democracy and Development or ADD [Charles MILUPI]; Alliance for a Better Zambia or ABZ [Frank BWALYA]; Christian Democratic Party or CDP [Daniel PULE]; Forum for Democracy and Development or FDD [Edith NAWAKWI]; Heritage Party or HP [Godfrey MIYANDA]; Movement for Multiparty Democracy or MMD [Nevers MUMBA]; National Restoration Party or NAREP [Elias CHIPIMO]; National Revolution Party or NRP [Cosmo MUMBA]; Party of Unity for Democracy and Development or PUDD [Dan PULE]; Party of Unity for Democracy and Development or PUDD [Dan PULE]; Patriotic Front or PF [Michael SATA]; Republican Progressive Party or RPP [James LUKUKU]; United National Independence Party or UNIP [Tilyenji KAUNDA]; United Party for National Development or UPND [Hakainde HICHILEMA]

Political pressure groups and leaders: NA

International organization participation: ACP, AfDB, AU, C, COMESA, EITI (compliant country), FAO, G-77, IAEA, IBRD, ICAO, ICRM, IDA, IFAD, IFC, IFRCS, ILO, IMF, Interpol, IOC, IOM, IPU, ISO (correspondent), ITSO, ITU, ITUC (NGOs), MIGA, MONUSCO, NAM, OPCW, PCA, SADC, UN, UNAMID, UNCTAD, UNESCO, UNHCR, UNIDO, UNISFA, UNMIL, UNMISS, UNWTO, UPU, WCO, WHO, WIPO, WMO, WTO

Diplomatic representation in the US:
chief of mission: Ambassador Palan MULONDA (since 8 January 2013)
chancery: 2419 Massachusetts Avenue NW, Washington, DC 20008
telephone: [1] (202) 265-9717 through 9719
FAX: [1] (202) 332-0826

Diplomatic representation from the US:
chief of mission: Ambassador (vacant); Charge d'Affaires David J. YOUNG
embassy: Ibex Hill, Lusaka
mailing address: P. O. Box 31617, Lusaka
telephone: [260] (211) 357-000
FAX: [260]) (211) 357-224

Flag description: green field with a panel of three vertical bands of red (hoist side), black, and orange below a soaring orange eagle, on the outer edge of the flag; green stands for the country's natural resources and vegetation, red symbolizes the struggle for freedom, black the people of Zambia, and orange the country's mineral wealth; the eagle represents the people's ability to rise above the nation's problems

National symbol(s): African fish eagle

National anthem: *name:* "Lumbanyeni Zambia" (Stand and Sing of Zambia, Proud and Free)
lyrics/music: multiple/Enoch Mankayi SONTONGA
note: adopted 1964; the melody, from the popular song "God Bless Africa," is the same as that of Tanzania but with different lyrics; the melody is also incorporated into South Africa's anthem

ECONOMY

Economy—overview: Zambia's economy has experienced strong growth in recent years, with real GDP growth in 2005-13 more than 6% per year. Privatization of government-owned copper mines in the 1990s relieved the government from covering mammoth losses generated by the industry and greatly increased copper mining output and profitability to spur economic growth. Copper output has increased steadily since 2004, due to higher copper prices and foreign investment. Zambia's dependency on copper makes it vulnerable to depressed commodity prices, but record high copper prices and a bumper maize crop in 2010 helped Zambia rebound quickly from the world economic slowdown that began in 2008. Zambia has made some strides to improve the ease of doing business. Regulatory changes by the current government in 2012-2013 included Statutory Instruments (SI) Number 33 (mandating use of the kwacha for domestic transactions) and SI Number 55 (monitoring foreign exchange transactions). Along with problems of fiscal management and weakening global copper prices, these SI's were perceived as undermining confidence in Zambia's economy and currency, leading to sharp depreciation of the kwacha in March 2014. In response, the Minister of Finance revoked SI 33 and 55 in late March 2014. Despite a strong economy, poverty remains a significant problem in Zambia, made worse by a high birth rate, relatively high HIV/AIDS burden, and by market distorting agricultural policies.

GDP (purchasing power parity): $25.47 billion (2013 est.)
country comparison to the world: 124
$24.01 billion (2012 est.)
$22.39 billion (2011 est.)
note: data are in 2013 US dollars

GDP (official exchange rate): $22.24 billion (2013 est.)

GDP—real growth rate: 6% (2013 est.)
country comparison to the world: 37
7.2% (2012 est.)
6.8% (2011 est.)

GDP—per capita (PPP): $1,800 (2013 est.)
country comparison to the world: 199
$1,700 (2012 est.)
$1,600 (2011 est.)

note: data are in 2013 US dollars

Gross national saving: 14.5% of GDP (2013 est.)
country comparison to the world: 113
19.4% of GDP (2012 est.)
23.7% of GDP (2011 est.)

GDP—composition, by end use:
household consumption: 60%
government consumption: 26.5%
investment in fixed capital: 19.1%
investment in inventories: 1%
exports of goods and services: 36.2%
imports of goods and services: -42.9% (2013 est.)

GDP—composition, by sector of origin:
agriculture: 19.8%
industry: 33.8%
services: 46.5% (2013 est.)

Agriculture—products: corn, sorghum, rice, peanuts, sunflower seed, vegetables, flowers, tobacco, cotton, sugarcane, cassava (tapioca), coffee; cattle, goats, pigs, poultry, milk, eggs, hides

Industries: copper mining and processing, emerald mining, construction, foodstuffs, beverages, chemicals, textiles, fertilizer, horticulture

Industrial production growth rate: 8% (2013 est.)
country comparison to the world: 24

Labor force: 6.275 million (2013 est.)
country comparison to the world: 65

Labor force—by occupation: *agriculture:* 85%
industry: 6%
services: 9% (2004)

Unemployment rate: 14% (2006 est.)
country comparison to the world: 137
50% (2000 est.)

Population below poverty line: 64% (2006)

Household income or consumption by percentage share: *lowest 10%:* 1.2%
highest 10%: 38.8% (2004)

Distribution of family income—Gini index: 50.8 (2004)
country comparison to the world: 19
52.6 (1998)

Budget: *revenues:* $4.814 billion
expenditures: $6.687 billion (2013 est.)

Taxes and other revenues: 21.6% of GDP (2013 est.)
country comparison to the world: 152

Budget surplus (+) or deficit (-):
-8.4% of GDP (2013 est.)
country comparison to the world: 199

Public debt: 31.8% of GDP (2013 est.)
country comparison to the world: 113
29.5% of GDP (2012 est.)

Fiscal year: calendar year

Inflation rate (consumer prices): 7.1% (2013 est.)
country comparison to the world: 188
6.6% (2012 est.)

Central bank discount rate: 8.39% (31 December 2009)
country comparison to the world: 12
14.49% (31 December 2008)

Commercial bank prime lending rate: 10.4% (31 December 2013 est.)
country comparison to the world: 67
12.15% (31 December 2012 est.)

Stock of narrow money: $2.299 billion (31 December 2013 est.)
country comparison to the world: 124
$2.185 billion (31 December 2012 est.)

Stock of broad money: $5.047 billion (31 December 2013 est.)
country comparison to the world: 128
$4.86 billion (31 December 2012 est.)

Stock of domestic credit: $5.458 billion (31 December 2013 est.)
country comparison to the world: 113
$3.833 billion (31 December 2012 est.)

Market value of publicly traded shares: $3.004 billion (31 December 2012 est.)
country comparison to the world: 89
$4.009 billion (31 December 2011)
$2.817 billion (31 December 2010 est.)

Current account balance: -$1.25 billion (2013 est.)
country comparison to the world: 125
-$189.9 million (2012 est.)

Exports: $8.547 billion (2013 est.)
country comparison to the world: 100
$9.414 billion (2012 est.)

Exports—commodities: copper/cobalt, cobalt, electricity; tobacco, flowers, cotton

Exports—partners: China 43.4%, South Africa 7.2%, Democratic Republic of the Congo 6.7%, South Korea 5.4%, India 4.7%, UAE 4.3%, Egypt 4.1% (2012)

Imports: $8.216 billion (2013 est.)
country comparison to the world: 109
$7.961 billion (2012 est.)

Imports—commodities: machinery, transportation equipment, petroleum products, electricity, fertilizer, foodstuffs, clothing

Imports—partners: South Africa 36.7%, Democratic Republic of the Congo 19.8%, China 10.4%, Kuwait 6% (2012)

Reserves of foreign exchange and gold: $2.833 billion (31 December 2013 est.)
country comparison to the world: 110
$3.042 billion (31 December 2012 est.)

Debt—external: $5.985 billion (31 December 2013 est.)
country comparison to the world: 118
$5.618 billion (31 December 2012 est.)

Stock of direct foreign investment—at home: $NA

Stock of direct foreign investment—abroad: $NA

Exchange rates: Zambian kwacha (ZMK) per US dollar—
5.3 (2013 est.)
5.1 (2012 est.)
4,797.1 (2010 est.)
5,046.1 (2009)
3,512.9 (2008)

ENERGY

Electricity—production: 11.19 billion kWh (2010 est.)
country comparison to the world: 93

Electricity—consumption: 7.96 billion kWh (2010 est.)
country comparison to the world: 95

Electricity—exports: 578 million kWh (2010)
country comparison to the world: 63

Electricity—imports: 23 million kWh (2011 est.)
country comparison to the world: 102

Electricity—installed generating capacity: 1.679 million kW (2010 est.)
country comparison to the world: 110

Electricity—from fossil fuels: 0.4% of total installed capacity (2010 est.)
country comparison to the world: 206

Electricity—from nuclear fuels: 0% of total installed capacity (2010 est.)
country comparison to the world: 209

Electricity—from hydroelectric plants: 99.6% of total installed capacity (2010 est.)
country comparison to the world: 5

Electricity—from other renewable sources: 0% of total installed capacity (2010 est.)
country comparison to the world: 144

Crude oil—production: 174.6 bbl/day (2012 est.)
country comparison to the world: 119

Crude oil—exports: 0 bbl/day (2010 est.)
country comparison to the world: 209

Crude oil—imports: 12,500 bbl/day (2010 est.)
country comparison to the world: 75

Crude oil—proved reserves: 0 bbl (1 January 2013 es)
country comparison to the world: 210

Refined petroleum products—production: 12,900 bbl/day (2010 est.)
country comparison to the world: 102

Refined petroleum products—consumption: 19,260 bbl/day (2011 est.)
country comparison to the world: 130

Refined petroleum products—exports: 254.1 bbl/day (2010 est.)
country comparison to the world: 118

Refined petroleum products—imports: 1,272 bbl/day (2010 est.)
country comparison to the world: 189

Natural gas—production: 0 cu m (2011 est.)
country comparison to the world: 212

Natural gas—consumption: 0 cu m (2010 est.)
country comparison to the world: 212

Natural gas—exports: 0 cu m (2011 est.)
country comparison to the world: 211

Natural gas—imports: 0 cu m (2011 est.)
country comparison to the world: 83

Natural gas—proved reserves: 0 cu m (1 January 2013 es)
country comparison to the world: 210

Carbon dioxide emissions from consumption of energy: 2.434 million Mt (2011 est.)
country comparison to the world: 144

COMMUNICATIONS

Telephones—main lines in use: 82,500 (2012)
country comparison to the world: 150

Telephones—mobile cellular: 10.525 million (2012)
country comparison to the world: 76

Telephone system:
general assessment: among the best in sub-Saharan Africa
domestic: high-capacity microwave radio relay connects most larger towns and cities; several cellular telephone services in operation and network coverage is improving; domestic satellite system being installed to improve telephone service in rural areas; Internet service is widely available; very small aperture terminal (VSAT) networks are operated by private firms
international: country code—260; satellite earth stations—2 Intelsat (1 Indian Ocean and 1 Atlantic Ocean), 3 owned by Zamtel (2010)

Broadcast media: state-owned Zambia National Broadcasting Corporation (ZNBC) operates 1 TV station and is the principal local-content provider; several private TV stations; multi-channel subscription TV services are available; ZNBC operates 3 radio networks; about 2 dozen private radio stations; relays of at least 2 international broadcasters are accessible in Lusaka and Kitwe (2007)

Internet country code: .zm

Internet hosts: 16,571 (2012)
country comparison to the world: 122

Internet users: 816,200 (2009)
country comparison to the world: 105

TRANSPORTATION

Airports: 88 (2013)
country comparison to the world: 63

Airports—with paved runways: *total:* 8
over 3,047 m: 1
2,438 to 3,047 m: 3
1,524 to 2,437 m: 3
914 to 1,523 m: 1 (2013)

Airports—with unpaved runways: *total:* 8 0
2,438 to 3,047 m: 1
1,524 to 2,437 m: 5
914 to 1,523 m: 53
under 914 m: 21 (2013)

Pipelines: oil 771 km (2013)

Railways: *total:* 2,922 km
country comparison to the world: 58
narrow gauge: 2,157 km 1.067-m gauge
note: includes 1,860 km of the Tanzania-Zambia Railway Authority (TAZARA) (2013)

Roadways: *total:* 67,671 km
country comparison to the world: 68

paved: 9,403 km

unpaved: 31,051 km

Waterways:
2,250 km (includes Lake Tanganyika and the Zambezi and Luapula rivers) (2010)
country comparison to the world: 39

Ports and terminals:

river port(s): Mpulungu (Zambezi)

MILITARY

Military branches: Zambian National Defense Force (ZNDF): Zambia Army, Zambia Air Force, National Service (paramilitary youth organization) (2012)

Military service age and obligation: national registration required at age 16; 18-25 years of age for male and female voluntary military service (16 years of age with parental consent); no conscription; Zambian citizenship required; grade 12 certification required; mandatory HIV testing on enlistment; mandatory retirement for officers at age 65 (Army, Air Force) (2012)

Manpower available for military service:
males age 16-49: 3,041,069
females age 16-49: 2,948,291 (2010 est.)

Manpower fit for military service:
males age 16-49: 1,745,656
females age 16-49: 1,688,670 (2010 est.)

Manpower reaching militarily significant age annually: *male:* 158,592
female: 158,805 (2010 est.)

Military expenditures: 1.55% of GDP (2012)
country comparison to the world: 58
1.59% of GDP (2011)
1.55% of GDP (2010)

TRANSNATIONAL ISSUES

Disputes—international: in 2004, Zimbabwe dropped objections to plans between Botswana and Zambia to build a bridge over the Zambezi River, thereby de facto recognizing a short, but not clearly delimited, Botswana-Zambia boundary in the river

Refugees and internally displaced persons:
refugees (country of origin): 14,871 (Democratic Republic of the Congo); 5,963 (Rwanda) (2012)

Illicit drugs: transshipment point for moderate amounts of methaqualone, small amounts of heroin, and cocaine bound for southern Africa and possibly Europe; a poorly developed financial infrastructure coupled with a government commitment to combating money laundering make it an unattractive venue for money launderers; major consumer of cannabis

ZIMBABWE

INTRODUCTION

Background: The UK annexed Southern Rhodesia from the [British] South Africa Company in 1923. A 1961 constitution was formulated that favored whites in power. In 1965 the government unilaterally declared its independence, but the UK did not recognize the act and demanded more complete voting rights for the black African majority in the country (then called Rhodesia). UN sanctions and a guerrilla uprising finally led to free elections in 1979 and independence (as Zimbabwe) in 1980. Robert MUGABE, the nation's first prime minister, has been the country's only ruler (as president since 1987) and has dominated the country's political system since independence. His chaotic land redistribution campaign, which began in 1997 and intensified after 2000, caused an exodus of white farmers, crippled the economy, and ushered in widespread shortages of basic commodities. Ignoring international condemnation, MUGABE rigged the 2002 presidential election to ensure his reelection. In April 2005, the capital city of Harare embarked on Operation Restore Order, ostensibly an urban rationalization program, which resulted in the destruction of the homes or businesses of 700,000 mostly poor supporters of the opposition. President MUGABE in June 2007 instituted price controls on all basic commodities causing panic buying and leaving store shelves empty for months; a period of increasing hyperinflation ensued. General elections held in March 2008 contained irregularities but still amounted to a censure of the ZANU-PF-led government with the opposition winning a majority of seats in parliament. MDC-T opposition leader Morgan TSVANGIRAI won the most votes in the presidential polls, but not enough to win outright. In the lead up to a run-off election in late June 2008, considerable violence enacted against opposition party members led to the withdrawal of TSVANGIRAI from the ballot. Extensive evidence of violence and intimidation resulted in international condemnation of the process. Difficult negotiations over a power-sharing "government of national unity," in which MUGABE remained president and TSVANGIRAI became prime minister, were finally settled in February 2009, although the leaders failed to agree upon many key outstanding governmental issues. MUGABE was reelected president in June 2013 in balloting that was severely flawed and internationally condemned. As a prerequisite to holding the elections, Zimbabwe enacted a new constitution by referendum, although many provisions in the new constitution have yet to be codified in law.

GEOGRAPHY

Location: Southern Africa, between South Africa and Zambia

Geographic coordinates: 20 00 S, 30 00 E

Map references: Africa

Area: *total:* 390,757 sq km
country comparison to the world: 61
land: 386,847 sq km
water: 3,910 sq km

Area—comparative: slightly larger than Montana

Land boundaries: *total:* 3,066 km
border countries: Botswana 813 km, Mozambique 1,231 km, South Africa 225 km, Zambia 797 km

Coastline: 0 km (landlocked)

Maritime claims: none (landlocked)

Climate: tropical; moderated by altitude; rainy season (November to March)

Terrain: mostly high plateau with higher central plateau (high veld); mountains in east

Elevation extremes: *lowest point:* junction of the Runde and Save Rivers 162 m
highest point: Inyangani 2,592 m

Natural resources: coal, chromium ore, asbestos, gold, nickel, copper, iron ore, vanadium, lithium, tin, platinum group metals

Land use: *arable land:* 10.49%
permanent crops: 0.31%
other: 89.2% (2011)

Irrigated land: 1,735 sq km (2003)

Total renewable water resources: 20 cu km (2011)

Freshwater withdrawal (domestic/industrial/agricultural): *total:* 4.21 cu km/yr (14%/7%/79%)
per capita: 333.5 cu m/yr (2002)

Natural hazards: recurring droughts; floods and severe storms are rare

Environment—current issues: deforestation; soil erosion; land degradation; air and water pollution; the black rhinoceros herd—once the largest concentration of the species in the world—has been significantly reduced by poaching; poor mining practices have led to toxic waste and heavy metal pollution

Environment—international agreements:
party to: Biodiversity, Climate Change, Desertification, Endangered Species, Law of the Sea, Ozone Layer Protection
signed, but not ratified: none of the selected agreements

Geography—note: landlocked; the Zambezi forms a natural riverine boundary with Zambia; in full flood (February-April) the massive Victoria Falls on the river forms the world's largest curtain of falling water; Lake Kariba on the Zambia-Zimbabwe border forms the world's largest reservoir by volume (180 cu km; 43 cu mi)

PEOPLE AND SOCIETY

Nationality: *noun:* Zimbabwean(s)
adjective: Zimbabwean

Ethnic groups: African 98% (Shona 82%, Ndebele 14%, other 2%), mixed and Asian 1%, white less than 1%

Languages: English (official), Shona, Sindebele (the language of the Ndebele, sometimes called Ndebele), numerous but minor tribal dialects

Religions: syncretic (part Christian, part indigenous beliefs) 50%, Christian 25%, indigenous beliefs 24%, Muslim and other 1%

Population: 13,771,721 (July 2014 est.)
country comparison to the world: 72
note: estimates for this country explicitly take into account the effects of excess mortality due to AIDS; this can result in lower life expectancy, higher infant mortality, higher death rates, lower population growth rates, and changes in the distribution of population by age and sex than would otherwise be expected

Age structure:
0-14 years: 38.4% (male 2,670,642/female 2,615,440)
15-24 years: 22.1% (male 1,527,964/female 1,520,255)
25-54 years: 32.3% (male 2,298,355/female 2,153,659)
55-64 years: 3.5% (male 180,554/female 318,410)
65 years and over: 3.6% (male 193,385/female 293,057) (2014 est.)

Dependency ratios:
total dependency ratio: 76.4 %
youth dependency ratio: 69.6 %
elderly dependency ratio: 6.8 %
potential support ratio: 14.7 (2013)

Median age: *total:* 20.2 years
male: 19.9 years
female: 20.4 years (2014 est.)

Population growth rate: 4.36% (2014 est.)
country comparison to the world: 2

Birth rate: 32.47 births/1,000 population (2014 est.)
country comparison to the world: 34

Death rate: 10.62 deaths/1,000 population (2014 est.)
country comparison to the world: 39

Net migration rate: 21.78 migrant(s)/1,000 population
country comparison to the world: 3
note: there is an increasing flow of Zimbabweans into South Africa and Botswana in search of better economic opportunities (2014 est.)

Urbanization: *urban population:* 38.6% of total population (2011)
rate of urbanization: 3.4% annual rate of change (2010-15 est.)

Major urban areas—population: HARARE (capital) 1.606 million (2009)

Sex ratio: *at birth:* 1.03 male(s)/female
0-14 years: 1.02 male(s)/female
15-24 years: 1.01 male(s)/female
25-54 years: 1.07 male(s)/female
55-64 years: 1 male(s)/female
65 years and over: 0.7 male(s)/female
total population: 0.95 male(s)/female (2014 est.)

Mother's mean age at first birth: 20.5
note: median age at first birth among women 25-29 (2011 est.)

Maternal mortality rate: 570 deaths/100,000 live births (2010)
country comparison to the world: 15

Infant mortality rate: *total:* 26.55 deaths/1,000 live births
country comparison to the world: 70
male: 28.88 deaths/1,000 live births
female: 24.15 deaths/1,000 live births (2014 est.)

Life expectancy at birth:
total population: 55.68 years
country comparison to the world: 204
male: 55.4 years
female: 55.97 years (2014 est.)

Total fertility rate: 3.56 children born/woman (2014 est.)
country comparison to the world: 44

Contraceptive prevalence rate: 58.5% (2010/11)

Physicians density: 0.06 physicians/1,000 population (2009)

Hospital bed density: 1.7 beds/1,000 population (2011)

Drinking water source:
improved:
urban: 97.1% of population
rural: 69.2% of population
total: 80% of population
unimproved:
urban: 2.9% of population
rural: 30.8% of population
total: 20% of population (2011 est.)

Sanitation facility access:
improved:
urban: 51.7% of population
rural: 33% of population
total: 40.2% of population
unimproved:
urban: 48.3% of population
rural: 67% of population
total: 59.8% of population (2011 est.)

HIV/AIDS—adult prevalence rate: 14.7% (2012 est.)
country comparison to the world: 5

HIV/AIDS—people living with HIV/AIDS: 1,368,100 (2012 est.)
country comparison to the world: 8

HIV/AIDS—deaths: 39,500 (2012 est.)
country comparison to the world: 10

Major infectious diseases:
degree of risk: very high
food or waterborne diseases: bacterial and protozoal diarrhea, hepatitis A, and typhoid fever
vectorborne diseases: malaria and dengue fever
water contact disease: schistosomiasis
animal contact disease: rabies (2013)

Obesity—adult prevalence rate: 7% (2008)
country comparison to the world: 143

Children under the age of 5 years underweight: 10.1% (2011)
country comparison to the world: 69

Education expenditures: 2.5% of GDP (2010)
country comparison to the world: 155

Literacy: *definition:* age 15 and over can read and write English
total population: 83.6%
male: 87.8%
female: 80.1% (2011 est.)

School life expectancy (primary to tertiary education): *total:* 9 years
male: 10 years
female: 9 years (2003)

Unemployment, youth ages 15-24: *total:* 7.6%
country comparison to the world: 125
male: 7.6%
female: 7.6% (2004)

GOVERNMENT

Country name:
conventional long form: Republic of Zimbabwe
conventional short form: Zimbabwe
former: Southern Rhodesia, Rhodesia

Government type: parliamentary democracy

Capital: *name:* Harare

geographic coordinates: 17 49 S, 31 02 E
time difference: UTC+2 (7 hours ahead of Washington, DC during Standard Time)

Administrative divisions: 8 provinces and 2 cities* with provincial status; Bulawayo*, Harare*, Manicaland, Mashonaland Central, Mashonaland East, Mashonaland West, Masvingo, Matabeleland North, Matabeleland South, Midlands

Independence: 18 April 1980 (from the UK)

National holiday: Independence Day, 18 April (1980)

Constitution: previous 1979; latest approved by referendum 16 March 2013, approved by Parliament 9 May 2013 (2013)

Legal system: mixed legal system of English common law, Roman-Dutch civil law, and customary law

International law organization participation: has not submitted an ICJ jurisdiction declaration; non-party state to the ICCt

Suffrage: 18 years of age; universal

Executive branch: *chief of state:* Executive President Robert Gabriel MUGABE (since 31 December 1987); Vice President Joice MUJURU (since 6 December 2004)

head of government: Executive President Robert Gabriel MUGABE (since 31 December 1987)
note—according to the new constitution, following the 31 July 2013 presidential elections the position of Prime Minister was abolished
cabinet: Cabinet appointed by the president; responsible to the House of Assembly (For more information visit the World Leaders website)
elections: presidential candidates nominated with a nomination paper signed by at least 10 registered voters (at least one from each province) and elected by popular vote for a five-year term (no term limits); elections last held on 31 July 2013 (next to be held in 2018); co-vice presidents drawn from party leadership
election results: Robert Gabriel MUGABE reelected president; percent of vote—Robert Gabriel MUGABE 61.1%, Morgan TSVANGIRAI 34.4%, Welshman NCUBE 2.7% other 1.8%; note—the election process was considered flawed and roundly criticised by election monitors and international bodies; both the AU and the SADC endoresed the results of the election with some concerns

Legislative branch: bicameral Parliament consists of a Senate (80 seats—60 members elected by popular vote for a five-year term, 18 traditional chiefs elected by the Council of Chiefs and 2 seats reserved for people with disabilities) and a House of Assembly (270 seats—members elected by popular vote for five-year terms and 60 seats reserved for women who are identified by their parties and nominated by proportional representation)
elections: last held on 31 July 2013 (next to be held in 2018)
election results: Senate—percent of vote by party—NA; seats by party—ZANU-PF 37 MD-T 21, MDC-N 2, chiefs 18, people with disabilities 2; House of Assembly—percent of vote by party—NA; seats by party—ZANU-PF 197, MDC-T 70, MDC-N 2, independent 1

Judicial branch:
highest court(s): Supreme Court (consists of the chief justice and 4 judges)
judge selection and term of office: Supreme Court judges appointed by the president upon recommendation of the Judicial Service Commission, an independent body consisting of the chief justice, Public Service Commission chairman, attorney general, and 2-3 members appointed by the president; judges normally serve until age 65, but can elect to serve until age 70
subordinate courts: High Court, regional magistrate courts, and special courts

Political parties and leaders: African National Party or ANP [Egypt DZINEMUNHENZVA]; Movement for Democratic Change—Tsvangirai or MDC-T [Morgan TSVANGIRAI]; Movement for Democratic Change—Ncube or MDC-N [Welshman NCUBE]; Peace Action is Freedom for All or PAFA; United Parties [Abel MUZOREWA]; United People's Party or UPP [Daniel SHUMBA]; Zimbabwe African National Union-Ndonga or ZANU-Ndonga [Wilson KUMBULA]; Zimbabwe African National Union-Patriotic Front or ZANU-PF [Robert Gabriel MUGABE]; Zimbabwe African Peoples Union or ZAPU [Dumiso DABENGWA]; Zimbabwe Youth in Alliance or ZIYA

Political pressure groups and leaders: Crisis in Zimbabwe Coalition; National Constitutional Assembly or NCA [Lovemore MADHUKU]; Women of Zimbabwe Arise or WOZA [Jenni WILLIAMS]; Zimbabwe Congress of Trade Unions or ZCTU [Wellington CHIBEBE]

International organization participation: ACP, AfDB, AU, COMESA, FAO, G-15, G-77, IAEA, IBRD, ICAO, ICRM, IDA, IFAD, IFC, IFRCS, ILO, IMF, IMO, Interpol, IOC, IOM, IPU, ISO, ITSO, ITU, ITUC (NGOs), MIGA, NAM, OPCW, PCA, SADC, UN, UNAMID, UNCTAD, UNESCO, UNIDO, UNISFA, UNMIL, UNMISS, UNOCI, UNWTO, UPU, WCO, WFTU (NGOs), WHO, WIPO, WMO, WTO

Diplomatic representation in the US:
chief of mission: Ambassador (vacant); Charge d'Affaires Richard CHIBUWE (since April 2014)
chancery: 1608 New Hampshire Avenue NW, Washington, DC 20009
telephone: [1] (202) 332-7100
FAX: [1] (202) 483-9326

Diplomatic representation from the US:
chief of mission: Ambassador David Bruce WHARTON (since 15 November 2012)
embassy: 172 Herbert Chitepo Avenue, Harare
mailing address: P. O. Box 3340, Harare
telephone: [263] (4) 250-593 through 250-594
FAX: [263] (4) 796-488, or 722-618

Flag description: seven equal horizontal bands of green, yellow, red, black, red, yellow, and green with a white isosceles triangle edged in black with its base on the hoist side; a yellow Zimbabwe bird representing the long history of the country is superimposed on a red five-pointed star in the center of the triangle, which symbolizes peace; green represents agriculture, yellow mineral wealth, red the blood shed to achieve independence, and black stands for the native people

National symbol(s): Zimbabwe bird symbol, African fish eagle, flame lily

National anthem: *name:* "Kalibusiswe Ilizwe leZimbabwe" [Northern Ndebele language] "Simudzai Mureza WeZimbabwe" [Shona] (Blessed Be the Land of Zimbabwe)
lyrics/music: Solomon MUTSWAIRO/Fred Lecture CHANGUNDEGA
note: adopted 1994

ECONOMY

Economy—overview: Zimbabwe's economy is growing despite continuing political uncertainty. Following a decade of contraction from 1998 to 2008, Zimbabwe's economy recorded real growth of roughly 10% per year in 2010-11, before slowing in 2012-13 due poor harvests and low diamond revenues. The government of Zimbabwe faces a number of difficult economic problems, including infrastructure and regulatory deficiencies, ongoing indigenization pressure, policy uncertainty, a large external debt burden, and insufficient formal employment. Until early 2009, the Reserve Bank of Zimbabwe routinely printed money to fund the budget deficit, causing hyperinflation. Dollarization in early 2009—which allowed currencies such as the Botswana pula, the South Africa rand, and the US dollar to be used locally—ended hyperinflation and reduced inflation below 10% per year, but exposed structural weaknesses that continue to inhibit broad-based growth.

GDP (purchasing power parity): $7.496 billion (2013 est.)
country comparison to the world: 158
$7.265 billion (2012 est.)
$6.957 billion (2011 est.)
note: data are in 2013 US dollars

GDP (official exchange rate): $10.48 billion
note: in 2009, the Zimbabwean dollar was taken out of circulation, making Zimbabwe's GDP at the official exchange rate a highly inaccurate statistic (2013 est.)

GDP—real growth rate: 3.2% (2013 est.)
country comparison to the world: 108
4.4% (2012 est.)
10.6% (2011 est.)

GDP—per capita (PPP): $600 (2013 est.)
country comparison to the world: 226
$600 (2012 est.)
$500 (2011 est.)
note: data are in 2013 US dollars

GDP—composition, by end use:
household consumption: 68.5%
government consumption: 30.4%
investment in fixed capital: 22.2%
exports of goods and services: 68.4%
imports of goods and services: -89.4% (2013 est.)

GDP—composition, by sector of origin:
agriculture: 20.1%
industry: 25.4%
services: 54.5% (2013 est.)

Agriculture—products: corn, cotton, tobacco, wheat, coffee, sugarcane, peanuts; sheep, goats, pigs

Industries: mining (coal, gold, platinum, copper, nickel, tin, diamonds, clay, numerous metallic and nonmetallic ores), steel; wood products, cement, chemicals, fertilizer, clothing and footwear, foodstuffs, beverages

Industrial production growth rate: 3.7% (2013 est.)
country comparison to the world: 82

Labor force: 3.939 million (2013 est.)
country comparison to the world: 92

Labor force—by occupation: *agriculture:* 66%
industry: 10%
services: 24% (1996)

Unemployment rate: 95% (2009 est.)
country comparison to the world: 203
80% (2005 est.)
note: figures reflect underemployment; true unemployment is unknown and, under current economic conditions, unknowable

Population below poverty line: 68% (2004)

Household income or consumption by percentage share: *lowest 10%:* 2%
highest 10%: 40.4% (1995)

Distribution of family income—Gini index: 50.1 (2006)
country comparison to the world: 23
50.1 (1995)

Budget: *revenues:* $1.05 trillion
expenditures: $1.187 trillion

Taxes and other revenues: NA% of GDP

Budget surplus (+) or deficit (-): NA% of GDP

Public debt: 202.4% of GDP (2013 est.)
country comparison to the world: 2
244.2% of GDP (2012 est.)

Fiscal year: calendar year

Inflation rate (consumer prices): 8.5% (2013 est.)

country comparison to the world: 198
8.2% (2012 est.)

Central bank discount rate: 7.17% (31 December 2010 est.)
country comparison to the world: 1
975% (31 December 2007)

Commercial bank prime lending rate: 28% (31 December 2013 est.)
country comparison to the world: 4
30% (31 December 2012 est.)

Stock of narrow money: $23.03 billion (31 December 2013 est.)
country comparison to the world: 64
$12.27 billion (31 December 2012 est.)
note: Zimbabwe's central bank no longer publishes data on monetary aggregates, except for bank deposits, which amounted to $2.1 billion in November 2010; the Zimbabwe dollar stopped circulating in early 2009; since then, the US dollar and South African rand have been the most frequently used currencies; there are no reliable estimates of the amount of foreign currency circulating in Zimbabwe

Stock of broad money: $22.7 billion (31 December 2012 est.)
country comparison to the world: 82
$47.61 billion (31 December 2013 est.)

Stock of domestic credit: $14.06 billion (31 December 2013 est.)
country comparison to the world: 89
$9.844 billion (31 December 2012 est.)

Market value of publicly traded shares: $11.82 billion (31 December 2012 est.)
country comparison to the world: 68
$10.9 billion (31 December 2011)
$11.48 billion (31 December 2010 est.)

Current account balance: -$576 million (2013 est.)
country comparison to the world: 105
-$416.5 million (2012 est.)

Exports: $3.144 billion (2013 est.)
country comparison to the world: 129
$3.314 billion (2012 est.)

Exports—commodities: platinum, cotton, tobacco, gold, ferroalloys, textiles/clothing

Exports—partners: China 21.1%, South Africa 15.1%, Democratic Republic of the Congo 12.1%, Botswana 10.8%, Italy 4.6% (2012)

Imports: $4.571 billion (2013 est.)
country comparison to the world: 134
$4.569 billion (2012 est.)

Imports—commodities: machinery and transport equipment, other manufactures, chemicals, fuels, food products

Imports—partners: South Africa 51.9%, China 10% (2012)

Reserves of foreign exchange and gold: $437 million (31 December 2013 est.)
country comparison to the world: 148
$575.6 million (31 December 2012 est.)

Debt—external: $8.445 billion (31 December 2013 est.)
country comparison to the world: 104
$8.765 billion (31 December 2012 est.)

Stock of direct foreign investment—at home: $NA

Stock of direct foreign investment—abroad: $NA

Exchange rates: Zimbabwean dollars (ZWD) per US dollar—
234.25 (2010)
234.25 (2009)
9,686.8 (2007)
note: the dollar was adopted as a legal currency in 2009; since then the Zimbabwean dollar has experienced hyperinflation and is essentially worthless

ENERGY

Electricity—production: 7.808 billion kWh (2010 est.)
country comparison to the world: 100

Electricity—consumption: 12.57 billion kWh (2010 est.)
country comparison to the world: 87

Electricity—exports: 56 million kWh (2010 est.)
country comparison to the world: 82

Electricity—imports: 5.338 billion kWh (2010 est.)
country comparison to the world: 36

Electricity—installed generating capacity: 2.035 million kW (2010 est.)
country comparison to the world: 101

Electricity—from fossil fuels: 66.6% of total installed capacity (2010 est.)
country comparison to the world: 116

Electricity—from nuclear fuels: 0% of total installed capacity (2010 est.)
country comparison to the world: 210

Electricity—from hydroelectric plants: 33.4% of total installed capacity (2010 est.)
country comparison to the world: 68

Electricity—from other renewable sources: 0% of total installed capacity (2010 est.)
country comparison to the world: 145

Crude oil—production: 120 bbl/day (2012 est.)
country comparison to the world: 121

Crude oil—exports: 0 bbl/day (2010 est.)
country comparison to the world: 210

Crude oil—imports: 0 bbl/day (2010 est.)
country comparison to the world: 146

Crude oil—proved reserves: 0 bbl (1 January 2013 es)
country comparison to the world: 211

Refined petroleum products—production: 0 bbl/day (2010 est.)
country comparison to the world: 212

Refined petroleum products—consumption: 19,030 bbl/day (2011 est.)
country comparison to the world: 131

Refined petroleum products—exports: 0 bbl/day (2010 est.)
country comparison to the world: 147

Refined petroleum products—imports: 13,290 bbl/day (2010 est.)
country comparison to the world: 124

Natural gas—production: 0 cu m (2011 est.)
country comparison to the world: 213

Natural gas—consumption: 0 cu m (2010 est.)
country comparison to the world: 213

Natural gas—exports: 0 cu m (2011 est.)
country comparison to the world: 212

Natural gas—imports: 0 cu m (2011 est.)
country comparison to the world: 84

Natural gas—proved reserves: 0 cu m (1 January 2013 es)
country comparison to the world: 211

Carbon dioxide emissions from consumption of energy: 8.875 million Mt (2011 est.)
country comparison to the world: 104

COMMUNICATIONS

Telephones—main lines in use: 301,600 (2012)
country comparison to the world: 117

Telephones—mobile cellular: 12.614 million (2012)
country comparison to the world: 69

Telephone system:
general assessment: system was once one of the best in Africa, but now suffers from poor maintenance
domestic: consists of microwave radio relay links, open-wire lines, radiotelephone communication stations, fixed wireless local loop installations, and a substantial mobile-cellular network; Internet connection is available in Harare and planned for all major towns and for some of the smaller ones
international: country code—263; satellite earth stations—2 Intelsat; 2 international digital gateway exchanges (in Harare and Gweru) (2010)

Broadcast media: government owns all local radio and TV stations; foreign shortwave broadcasts and satellite TV are available to those who can afford antennas and receivers; in rural areas, access to TV broadcasts is extremely limited (2007)

Internet country code: .zw

Internet hosts: 30,615 (2012)
country comparison to the world: 108

Internet users: 1.423 million (2009)
country comparison to the world: 84

TRANSPORTATION

Airports: 196 (2013)
country comparison to the world: 2 9

Airports—with paved runways: *total:* 1 7
over 3,047 m: 3
2,438 to 3,047 m: 2
1,524 to 2,437 m: 5
914 to 1,523 m: 7 (2013)

Airports—with unpaved runways: *total:* 179
1,524 to 2,437 m: 3
914 to 1,523 m: 104
under 914 m: 72 (2013)

Pipelines: refined products 270 km (2013)

Railways: *total:* 3,427 km
country comparison to the world: 51
narrow gauge: 3,427 km 1.067-m gauge (313 km electrified) (2008)

Roadways: *total:* 97,267 km
country comparison to the world: 47
paved: 18,481 km
unpaved: 78,786 km (2002)

Waterways: (some navigation possible on Lake Kariba) (2011)

Ports and terminals: *river port(s):* Binga, Kariba (Zambezi)

MILITARY

Military branches: Zimbabwe Defense Forces (ZDF): Zimbabwe National Army (ZNA), Air Force of Zimbabwe (AFZ) (2012)

Military service age and obligation: 18-24 years of age for voluntary military service; no conscription; women are eligible to serve (2012)

Manpower available for military service:
males age 16-49: 2,616,051
females age 16-49: 2,868,376 (2010 est.)

Manpower fit for military service:
males age 16-49: 1,528,166
females age 16-49: 1,646,041 (2010 est.)

Manpower reaching militarily significant age annually: *male:* 154,870
female: 152,550 (2010 est.)

Military expenditures: 2.94% of GDP (2012)
country comparison to the world: 21
2.05% of GDP (2011)
2.94% of GDP (2010)

TRANSNATIONAL ISSUES

Disputes—international: Namibia has supported, and in 2004 Zimbabwe dropped objections to, plans between Botswana and Zambia to build a bridge over the Zambezi River, thereby de facto recognizing a short, but not clearly delimited, Botswana-Zambia boundary in the river; South Africa has placed military units to assist police operations along the border of Lesotho, Zimbabwe, and Mozambique to control smuggling, poaching, and illegal migration

Refugees and internally displaced persons:
IDPs: undetermined (political violence, human rights violations, land reform, and economic collapse) (2012)

Trafficking in persons: *current situation:* Zimbabwe is a source, transit, and destination country for men, women, and children subjected to forced labor and sex trafficking; Zimbabwean women and girls from towns bordering South Africa, Mozambique, and Zambia are subjected to prostitution, sometimes being sold by their parents; Zimbabwean men, women, and children are subjected to forced labor in agriculture and domestic service in rural areas, as well as domestic servitude and sex trafficking in cities and towns; Zimbabwean women and men are lured into exploitative labor situations in Angola, Botswana, Mozambique, the United Arab Emirates, Malaysia, Nigeria, and South Africa with false job offers, while women and girls are lured to China, Egypt, the UK, and Canada and forced into prostitution; adults and children from Bangladesh, Somalia, India, Pakistan, the Democratic Republic of the Congo, Malawi, Mozambique, and Zambia are trafficked through Zimbabwe en route to South Africa

tier rating: Tier 3—Zimbabwe does not fully comply with the minimum standards for the elimination of trafficking and is not making significant efforts to do so; tangible efforts to investigate and prosecute trafficking offenses, including those allegedly involving government officials, and to protect victims remain minimal; the government continues to rely on an international organization to provide law enforcement training and on NGOs to identify and assist victims without government support for such work; a national trafficking awareness campaign was launched in November 2012 (2013)

Illicit drugs: transit point for cannabis and South Asian heroin, mandrax, and methamphetamines en route to South Africa

APPENDIX A

ABBREVIATIONS

ABEDA	Arab Bank for Economic Development in Africa
ACP Group	African, Caribbean, and Pacific Group of States
ADB	Asian Development Bank
AfDB	African Development Bank
AFESD	Arab Fund for Economic and Social Development
AG	Australia Group
Air Pollution	Convention on Long-Range Transboundary Air Pollution
Air Pollution-Nitrogen Oxides	Protocol to the 1979 Convention on Long-Range Transboundary Air Pollution Concerning the Control of Emissions of Nitrogen Oxides or Their Transboundary Fluxes
Air Pollution-Persistent Organic Pollutants	Protocol to the 1979 Convention on Long-Range Transboundary Air Pollution on Persistent Organic Pollutants
Air Pollution-Sulphur 85	Protocol to the 1979 Convention on Long-Range Transboundary Air Pollution on the Reduction of Sulphur Emissions or Their Transboundary Fluxes by at Least 30%
Air Pollution-Sulphur 94	Protocol to the 1979 Convention on Long-Range Transboundary Air Pollution on Further Reduction of Sulphur Emissions
Air Pollution-Volatile Organic Compounds	Protocol to the 1979 Convention on Long-Range Transboundary Air Pollution Concerning the Control of Emissions of Volatile Organic Compounds or Their Transboundary Fluxes
AMF	Arab Monetary Fund
AMU	Arab Maghreb Union
Antarctic Marine Living Resources	Convention on the Conservation of Antarctic Marine Living Resources
Antarctic Seals	Convention for the Conservation of Antarctic Seals
Antarctic-Environmental Protocol	Protocol on Environmental Protection to the Antarctic Treaty
ANZUS	Australia-New Zealand-United States Security Treaty
AOSIS	Alliance of Small Island States
APEC	Asia-Pacific Economic Cooperation
Arabsat	Arab Satellite Communications Organization
ARF	ASEAN Regional Forum
ASEAN	Association of Southeast Asian Nations
AU	African Union
Autodin	Automatic Digital Network
BA	Baltic Assembly
bbl/day	barrels per day
BCIE	Central American Bank for Economic Integration
BDEAC	Central African States Development Bank
Benelux	Benelux Union
BGN	United States Board on Geographic Names
BIMSTEC	Bay of Bengal Initiative for Multi-sectoral Technical and Economic Cooperation
Biodiversity	Convention on Biological Diversity
BIS	Bank for International Settlements
BRICS	(Brazil, Russia, India, China, and South Africa)
BSEC	Black Sea Economic Cooperation Zone
C	Commonwealth
CD	Community of Democracies
c.i.f.	cost, insurance, and freight
CACM	Central American Common Market
CAEU	Council of Arab Economic Unity
CAN	Andean Community
Caricom	Caribbean Community and Common Market
CB	citizen's band mobile radio communications
CBSS	Council of the Baltic Sea States
CCC	Customs Cooperation Council
CDB	Caribbean Development Bank
CE	Council of Europe
CEI	Central European Initiative
CELAC	Community of Latin America and Caribbean States
CEMA	Council for Mutual Economic Assistance
CEMAC	Economic and Monetary Community of Central Africa

CEPGL	Economic Community of the Great Lakes Countries
CERN	European Organization for Nuclear Research
CIA	Central Intelligence Agency
CICA	Conference of Interaction and Confidence-Building Measures in Asia
CIS	Commonwealth of Independent States
CITES	see Endangered Species
Climate Change	United Nations Framework Convention on Climate Change
Climate Change-Kyoto Protocol	Kyoto Protocol to the United Nations Framework Convention on Climate Change
COCOM	Coordinating Committee on Export Controls
COMESA	Common Market for Eastern and Southern Africa
Comsat	Communications Satellite Corporation
CP	Colombo Plan
CPLP	Comunidade dos Paises de Lingua Portuguesa
CSN	South American Community of Nations became UNASUL—Union of South American Nations
CSTO	Collective Security Treaty Organization
CTBTO	Preparatory Commission for the Nuclear-Test-Ban Treaty Organization
CY	calendar year
D-8	Developing Eight
DC	developed country
DDT	dichloro-diphenyl-trichloro-ethane
Desertification	United Nations Convention to Combat Desertification in Those Countries Experiencing Serious Drought and/or Desertification, Particularly in Africa
DIA	United States Defense Intelligence Agency
DSN	Defense Switched Network
DST	daylight savings time
DWT	deadweight ton
EAC	East African Community
EADB	East African Development Bank
EAEC	Eurasian Economic Community
EAPC	Euro-Atlantic Partnership Council
EAS	East Asia Summit
EBRD	European Bank for Reconstruction and Development
EC	European Community or European Commission
ECA	Economic Commission for Africa
ECB	European Central Bank
ECE	Economic Commission for Europe
ECLAC	Economic Commission for Latin America and the Caribbean
ECO	Economic Cooperation Organization
ECOSOC	Economic and Social Council
ECOWAS	Economic Community of West African States
ECSC	European Coal and Steel Community
EE	Eastern Europe
EEC	European Economic Community
EEZ	exclusive economic zone
EFTA	European Free Trade Association
EIB	European Investment Bank
EITI	Extractive Industry Trnsparency Iniative
EMU	European Monetary Union
Endangered Species	Convention on the International Trade in Endangered Species of Wild Flora and Fauna (CITES)
Entente	Council of the Entente
Environmental Modification	Convention on the Prohibition of Military or Any Other Hostile Use of Environmental Modification Techniques
ESA	European Space Agency
ESCAP	Economic and Social Commission for Asia and the Pacific
ESCWA	Economic and Social Commission for Western Asia
est.	estimate
EU	European Union
Euratom	European Atomic Energy Community
Eutelsat	European Telecommunications Satellite Organization
Ex-Im	Export-Import Bank of the United States

f.o.b.	free on board
FAO	Food and Agriculture Organization
FATF	Financial Action Task Force
FAX	facsimile
FLS	Front Line States
FOC	flags of convenience
FSU	former Soviet Union
FY	fiscal year
FZ	Franc Zone
G-3	Group of 3
G-5	Group of 5
G-6	Group of 6
G-7	Group of 7
G-8	Group of 8
G-9	Group of 9
G-10	Group of 10
G-15	Group of 15
G-11	Group of 11
G-20	Group of 20
G-24	Group of 24
G-77	Group of 77
GATT	General Agreement on Tariffs and Trade; now WTO
GCC	Gulf Cooperation Council
GCN	Global Caribbean Network
GCTU	General Confederation of Trade Unions
GDP	gross domestic product
GMT	Greenwich Mean Time
GNP	gross national product
GRT	gross register ton
GSM	global system for mobile cellular communications
GUAM	Organization for Democracy and Economic Development; acronym for member states—Georgia, Ukraine, Azerbaijan, Moldova
GWP	gross world product
Hazardous Wastes	Basel Convention on the Control of Transboundary Movements of Hazardous Wastes and Their Disposal
HF	high-frequency
HIV/AIDS	human immunodeficiency virus/acquired immune deficiency syndrome
IADB	Inter-American Development Bank
IAEA	International Atomic Energy Agency
IANA	Internet Assigned Numbers Authority
IBRD	International Bank for Reconstruction and Development (World Bank)
ICAO	International Civil Aviation Organization
ICC	International Chamber of Commerce
ICCt	International Criminal Court
ICJ	International Court of Justice (World Court)
ICRC	International Committee of the Red Cross
ICRM	International Red Cross and Red Crescent Movement
ICSID	International Center for Settlement of Investment Disputes
ICTR	International Criminal Tribunal for Rwanda
ICTY	International Criminal Tribunal for the former Yugoslavia
IDA	International Development Association
IDB	Islamic Development Bank
IDP	Internally Displaced Person
IEA	International Energy Agency
IFAD	International Fund for Agricultural Development
IFC	International Finance Corporation
IFRCS	International Federation of Red Cross and Red Crescent Societies
IGAD	Inter-Governmental Authority on Development
IHO	International Hydrographic Organization
ILO	International Labor Organization
IMF	International Monetary Fund
IMO	International Maritime Organization

IMSO	International Mobile Satellite Organization
inmarsat	International Maritime Satellite Organization
InOC	Indian Ocean Commission
Intelsat	International Telecommunications Satellite Organization
Interpol	International Criminal Police Organization
Intersputnik	International Organization of Space Communications
IOC	International Olympic Committee
IOM	International Organization for Migration
IPU	Inter-Parliamentary Union
ISO	International Organization for Standardization
ISP	Internet Service Provider
ITC	International Trade Center
ITSO	International Telecommunications Satellite Organization
ITU	International Telecommunication Union
ITUC	International Trade Union Confederation, the successor to ICFTU (International Confederation of Free Trade Unions) and the WCL (World Confederation of Labor)
kHz	kilohertz
km	kilometer
kW	kilowatt
kWh	kilowatt-hour
LAES	Latin American and Caribbean Economic System
LAIA	Latin American Integration Association
LAS	League of Arab States
Law of the Sea	United Nations Convention on the Law of the Sea (LOS)
LDC	less developed country
LLDC	least developed country
London Convention	see Marine Dumping
LOS	see Law of the Sea
m	meter
Marecs	Maritime European Communications Satellite
Marine Dumping	Convention on the Prevention of Marine Pollution by Dumping Wastes and Other Matter
Marine Life Conservation	Convention on Fishing and Conservation of Living Resources of the High Seas
MARPOL	see Ship Pollution
Medarabtel	Middle East Telecommunications Project of the International Telecommunications Union
Mercosur	Southern Cone Common Market
MHz	megahertz
MICAH	International Civilian Support Mission in Haiti
MIGA	Multilateral Investment Guarantee Agency
MINURCAT	United Nations Mission in the Central African Republic and Chad
MINURSO	United Nations Mission for the Referendum in Western Sahara
MINUSTAH	United Nations Stabilization Mission in Haiti
MONUSCO	United Nations Organization Stabilization Mission in the Democratic Republic of the Congo
NA	not available
NAFTA	North American Free Trade Agreement
NAM	Nonaligned Movement
NATO	North Atlantic Treaty Organization
NC	Nordic Council
NEA	Nuclear Energy Agency
NEGL	negligible
NGA	National Geospatial-Intelligence Agency
NGO	nongovernmental organization
NIB	Nordic Investment Bank
NIC	newly industrializing country
NIE	newly industrializing economy
NIS	new independent states
nm	nautical mile
NMT	Nordic Mobile Telephone
NSG	Nuclear Suppliers Group
Nuclear Test Ban	Treaty Banning Nuclear Weapons Tests in the Atmosphere, in Outer Space, and Under Water

NZ	New Zealand
OAPEC	Organization of Arab Petroleum Exporting Countries
OAS	Organization of American States
OAU	Organization of African Unity; see African Union
ODA	official development assistance
OECD	Organization for Economic Cooperation and Development
OECS	Organization of Eastern Caribbean States
OHCHR	Office of the United Nations High Commissioner for Human Rights
OIC	Organization of the Islamic Conference
OIF	International Organization of the French-speaking World
OOF	other official flows
OPANAL	Agency for the Prohibition of Nuclear Weapons in Latin America and the Caribbean
OPCW	Organization for the Prohibition of Chemical Weapons
OPEC	Organization of Petroleum Exporting Countries
OSCE	Organization for Security and Cooperation in Europe
Ozone Layer Protection	Montreal Protocol on Substances That Deplete the Ozone Layer
PCA	Permanent Court of Arbitration
PFP	Partnership for Peace
PIF	Pacific Islands Forum
PPP	purchasing power parity
Ramsar	see Wetlands
RG	Rio Group
SAARC	South Asian Association for Regional Cooperation
SACEP	South Asia Co-operative Environment Program
SACU	Southern African Customs Union
SADC	Southern African Development Community
SAFE	South African Far East Cable
SCO	Shanghai Cooperation Organization
SECI	Southeast European Cooperative Initiative
SELEC	Convention of the Southeast European Law Enforcement Centers (successor to SECI)
SHF	super-high-frequency
Ship Pollution	Protocol of 1978 Relating to the International Convention for the Prevention of Pollution From Ships, 1973 (MARPOL)
SICA	Central American Integration System
Sparteca	South Pacific Regional Trade and Economic Cooperation Agreement
SPC	Secretariat of the Pacific Communities
SPF	South Pacific Forum
sq km	square kilometer
sq mi	square mile
TAT	Trans-Atlantic Telephone
TEU	Twenty-Foot Equivalent Unit, a unit of measure for containerized cargo capacity
Tropical Timber 83	International Tropical Timber Agreement, 1983
Tropical Timber 94	International Tropical Timber Agreement, 1994
UAE	United Arab Emirates
UDEAC	Central African Customs and Economic Union
UHF	ultra-high-frequency
UK	United Kingdom
UN	United Nations
UN-AIDS	Joint United Nations Program on HIV/AIDS
UNAMA	United Nations Assistance Mission in Afghanistan
UNAMID	African Union/United Nations Hybrid Operation in Darfur
UNASUR	Union of South American Nations
UNCLOS	United Nations Convention on the Law of the Sea, also know as LOS
UNCTAD	United Nations Conference on Trade and Development
UNDCP	United Nations Drug Control Program
UNDEF	United Nations Democracy Fund
UNDOF	United Nations Disengagement Observer Force
UNDP	United Nations Development Program
UNEP	United Nations Environment Program
UNESCO	United Nations Educational, Scientific, and Cultural Organization
UNFICYP	United Nations Peace-keeping Force in Cyprus
UNFPA	United Nations Population Fund

UN-Habitat	United Nations Center for Human Settlements
UNHCR	United Nations High Commissioner for Refugees
UNICEF	United Nations Children's Fund
UNICRI	United Nations Interregional Crime and Justice Research Institute
UNIDIR	United Nations Institute for Disarmament Research
UNIDO	United Nations Industrial Development Organization
UNIFIL	United Nations Interim Force in Lebanon
UNISFA	United Nations Interim Force for Abyei
UNITAR	United Nations Institute for Training and Research
UNMIK	United Nations Interim Administration Mission in Kosovo
UNMIL	United Nations Mission in Liberia
UNMIS	United Nations Mission in the Sudan
UNMISS	United Nations Mission in South Sudan
UNMIT	United Nations Integrated Mission in Timor-Leste
UNMOGIP	United Nations Military Observer Group in India and Pakistan
UNOCI	United Nations Operation in Cote d'Ivoire
UNODC	United Nations Office of Drugs and Crime
UNOPS	United Nations Office of Project Services
UNRISD	United Nations Research Institute for Social Development
UNRWA	United Nations Relief and Works Agency for Palestine Refugees in the Near East
UNSC	United Nations Security Council
UNSSC	Untied Nations System Staff College
UNTSO	United Nations Truce Supervision Organization
UNU	United Nations University
UNWTO	World Tourism Organization
UPU	Universal Postal Union
US	United States
USSR	Union of Soviet Socialist Republics (Soviet Union); used for information dated before 25 December 1991
UTC	Coordinated Universal Time
UV	ultra violet
VHF	very-high-frequency
VSAT	very small aperture terminal
WADB	West African Development Bank
WAEMU	West African Economic and Monetary Union
WCL	World Confederation of Labor
WCO	World Customs Organization
Wetlands	Convention on Wetlands of International Importance Especially As Waterfowl Habitat
WEU	Western European Union
WFP	World Food Program
WFTU	World Federation of Trade Unions
Whaling	International Convention for the Regulation of Whaling
WHO	World Health Organization
WIPO	World Intellectual Property Organization
WMO	World Meteorological Organization
WP	Warsaw Pact
WTO	World Trade Organization
ZC	Zangger Committee

APPENDIX B

INTERNATIONAL ORGANIZATIONS AND GROUPS

advanced developing countries
another term for those less developed countries (LDCs) with particularly rapid industrial development; see newly industrializing economies (NIEs)

advanced economies
a term used by the International Monetary FUND (IMF) for the top group in its hierarchy of advanced economies, countries in transition, and developing countries; it includes the following 33 advanced economies: Australia, Austria, Belgium, Canada, Cyprus, Czech Republic, Denmark, Finland, France, Germany, Greece, Hong Kong, Iceland, Ireland, Israel, Italy, Japan, South Korea, Luxembourg, Malta, Netherlands, NZ, Norway, Portugal, Singapore, Slovak Republic, Slovenia, Spain, Sweden, Switzerland, Taiwan, UK, US; note—this group would presumably also cover the following nine smaller countries of Andorra, Bermuda, Faroe Islands, Guernsey, Holy See, Jersey, Liechtenstein, Monaco, and San Marino that are included in the more comprehensive group of "developed countries"

African Development Bank Group (AfDB)
note—regional multilateral development finance institution temporarily located in Tunis, Tunisia; the Bank Group consists of the African Development Bank, the African Development Fund, and the Nigerian Trust Fund
established—10 September 1964
aim—to promote economic development and social progress
regional members—(53) Algeria, Angola, Benin, Botswana, Burkina Faso, Burundi, Cameroon, cabo Verde, Central African Republic, Chad, Comoros, Democratic Republic of the Congo, Republic of the Congo, Cote d'Ivoire, Djibouti, Egypt, Equatorial Guinea, Eritrea, Ethiopia, Gabon, The Gambia, Ghana, Guinea, Guinea-Bissau, Kenya, Lesotho, Liberia, Libya, Madagascar, Malawi, Mali, Mauritania, Mauritius, Morocco, Mozambique, Namibia, Niger, Nigeria, Rwanda, Sao Tome and Principe, Senegal, Seychelles, Sierra Leone, Somalia, South Africa, Sudan, Swaziland, Tanzania, Togo, Tunisia, Uganda, Zambia, Zimbabwe
nonregional members—(25) Argentina, Austria, Belgium, Brazil, Canada, China, Denmark, Finland, France, Germany, India, Italy, Japan, South Korea, Kuwait, Netherlands, Norway, Portugal, Saudi Arabia, Spain, Sweden, Switzerland, UAE (ADF members only), UK, US

African Union (AU)
note—replaces Organization of African Unity (OAU)
established—8 July 2001
aim—to achieve greater unity among African States; to defend states' integrity and independence; to accelerate political, social, and economic integration; to encourage international cooperation; to promote democratic principles and institutions
members—(54) Algeria, Angola, Benin, Botswana, Burkina Faso, Burundi, Cabo Verde, Cameroon, Central African Republic, Chad, Comoros, Democratic Republic of the Congo, Republic of the Congo, Cote d'Ivoire, Djibouti, Egypt, Equatorial Guinea, Eritrea, Ethiopia, Gabon, The Gambia, Ghana, Guinea (suspended), Guinea-Bissau, Kenya, Lesotho, Liberia, Libya, Madagascar, Malawi, Mali, Mauritania, Mauritius, Mozambique, Namibia, Niger, Nigeria, Rwanda, Sahrawi Arab Democratic Republic (Western Sahara), Sao Tome and Principe, Senegal, Seychelles, Sierra Leone, Somalia, South Africa, South Sudan, Sudan, Swaziland, Tanzania, Togo, Tunisia, Uganda, Zambia, Zimbabwe, Uganda, Yemen, Zambia, Zimbabwe

African Union/United Nations Hybrid Operation in Darfur (UNAMID)
established—31 July 2007
aim—to contribute to the restoration of security conditions which will allow safe humanitarian assistance throughout Darfur, to contribute to the protection of civilian populations under imminent threat of physical attack, to monitor, observe compliance with, and verify the implementation of various ceasefire agreements
members—(47) Bangladesh, Benin, Bolivia, Burkina Faso, Burundi, Cambodia, Cameroon, China, Cote d'Ivoire, Djibouti, Ecuador, Egypt, Ethiopia, The Gambia, Germany, Ghana, Indonesia, Iran, Jordan, Kenya, South Korea,Kyrgyzstan, Lesotho, Malawi, Malaysia, Mali, Mongolia, Namibia, Nepal, Nigeria, Pakistan, Palau, Peru, Rwanda,Senegal, Sierra Leone, South Africa, Tajikistan, Tanzania, Thailand, Togo, Tunisia, Turkey

African, Caribbean, and Pacific Group of States (ACP Group)
established—6 June 1975
aim—to manage their preferential economic and aid relationship with the EU
members—(79) Angola, Antigua and Barbuda, The Bahamas, Barbados, Belize, Benin, Botswana, Burkina Faso, Burundi, cabo Verde, Cameroon, Central African Republic, Chad, Comoros, Democratic Republic of the Congo, Republic of the Congo, Cook Islands, Cote d'Ivoire, Cuba, Djibouti, Dominica, Dominican Republic, Equatorial Guinea, Eritrea, Ethiopia, Fiji, Gabon, The Gambia, Ghana, Grenada, Guinea, Guinea-Bissau, Guyana, Haiti, Jamaica, Kenya, Kiribati, Lesotho, Liberia, Madagascar, Malawi, Mali, Marshall Islands, Mauritania, Mauritius, Federated States of Micronesia, Mozambique, Namibia, Nauru, Niger, Nigeria, Niue, Palau, Papua New Guinea, Rwanda, Saint Kitts and Nevis, Saint Lucia, Saint Vincent and the Grenadines, Samoa, Sao Tome and Principe, Senegal, Seychelles, Sierra Leone, Solomon Islands, Somalia, South Africa, Sudan, Suriname, Swaziland, Tanzania, Timor-Leste, Togo, Tonga, Trinidad and Tobago, Tuvalu, Uganda, Vanuatu, Zambia, Zimbabwe

Agency for the Prohibition of Nuclear Weapons in Latin America and the Caribbean (OPANAL)
note—acronym from Organismo para la Proscripcion de las Armas Nucleares en la America Latina y el Caribe (OPANAL)
established—14 February 1967 under the Treaty of Tlatelolco; effective—25 April 1969 on the 11th ratification
aim—to encourage the peaceful uses of atomic energy and prohibit nuclear weapons
members—(33) Antigua and Barbuda, Argentina, The Bahamas, Barbados, Belize, Bolivia, Brazil, Chile, Colombia, Costa Rica, Cuba, Dominica, Dominican Republic, Ecuador, El Salvador, Grenada, Guatemala, Guyana, Haiti, Honduras, Jamaica, Mexico, Nicaragua, Panama, Paraguay, Peru, Saint Kitts and Nevis, Saint Lucia, Saint Vincent and the Grenadines, Suriname, Trinidad and Tobago, Uruguay, Venezuela

Alliance of Small Island States (AOSIS)
established—November 1990
aim—to call attention to threats of sea-level rise and coral bleaching to small islands and lowlying coastal developing states from global warming; to emphasize the importance of information and information technology in the process of achieving sustainable development
members—(39) Antigua and Barbuda, The Bahamas, Barbados, Belize, Cabo Verde, Comoros, Cook Islands, Cuba, Dominica, Dominican Republic, Fiji, Grenada, Guinea-Bissau, Guyana, Haiti, Jamaica, Kiribati, Maldives, Marshall Islands, Mauritius, Federated States of Micronesia, Nauru, Niue, Palau, Papua New Guinea, St. Kitts and Nevis, St. Lucia, St. Vincent and the Grenadines, Samoa, Sao Tome and Principe, Seychelles, Singapore, Solomon Islands, Suriname, Timor-Leste, Tonga, Trinidad and Tobago, Tuvalu, Vanuatu
observers—(5) American Samoa, Guam, Netherlands Antilles, Puerto Rico, U.S. Virgin Islands

Andean Community (CAN)
note—formerly known as the Andean Group (AG) and the Andean Common Market (Ancom)
established—26 May 1969; present name established 1 October 1992; effective—16 October 1969
aim—to promote harmonious development through economic integration
members—(4) Bolivia, Colombia, Ecuador, Peru
associate members—(5) Argentina, Brazil, Chile, Paraguay, Uruguay
observers—(1) Spain

Arab Bank for Economic Development in Africa (ABEDA)
note—also known as Banque Arabe de Developpement Economique en Afrique (BADEA)
established—18 February 1974; effective—16 September 1974
aim—to promote economic development
members—(17 plus the Palestine Liberation Organization) Algeria, Bahrain, Egypt, Iraq, Jordan, Kuwait, Lebanon, Libya, Mauritania, Morocco, Oman, Qatar, Saudi Arabia, Sudan, Syria, Tunisia, UAE, Palestine Liberation Organization; note—these are all the members of the Arab League excluding Comoros, Djibouti, Somalia, Yemen

Arab Fund for Economic and Social Development (AFESD)
established—16 May 1968
aim—to promote economic and social development
members—(20 plus the Palestine Liberation Organization) Algeria, Bahrain, Djibouti, Egypt, Iraq, Jordan, Kuwait, Lebanon, Libya, Mauritania, Morocco, Oman, Qatar, Saudi Arabia, Somalia (suspended 1993), Sudan, Syria, Tunisia, UAE, Yemen, Palestine Liberation Organization

Arab Maghreb Union (AMU)
established—17 February 1989
aim—to promote cooperation and integration among the Arab states of northern Africa
members—(5) Algeria, Libya, Mauritania, Morocco, Tunisia

Arab Monetary Fund (AMF)
established—27 April 1976; effective—2 February 1977
aim—to promote Arab cooperation, development, and integration in monetary and economic affairs
members—(21 plus the Palestine Liberation Organization) Algeria, Bahrain, Comoros, Djibouti, Egypt, Iraq, Jordan, Kuwait, Lebanon, Libya, Mauritania, Morocco, Oman, Qatar, Saudi Arabia, Somalia, Sudan, Syria, Tunisia, UAE, Yemen, Palestine Liberation Organization

Arctic Council
established—18 September 1996
aim—to address the common concerns and challenges faced by Arctic governments and the people of the Arctic; to protect the Arctic environment
members—(8) Canada, Denmark (Greenland, Faroe Islands), Finland, Iceland, Norway, Russia, Sweden, US
permanent participants—(6) Aleut International Association, Arctic Athabaskan Council, Gwich'in Council International, Inuit Circumpolar Conference, Russian Association of Indigenous People of the North, Saami Council
observers—(12) China, France, Germany, India, Italy, Japan, South Korea, Netherlands, Poland, Singapore, Spain, UK

ASEAN Regional Forum (ARF)
established—25 July 1994
aim—to foster constructive dialogue and consultation on political and security issues of common interest and concern
members—(27) Australia, Bangladesh, Brunei, Burma, Cambodia, Canada, China, EU, India, Indonesia, Japan, North Korea, South Korea, Laos, Malaysia, Mongolia, NZ, Pakistan, Papua New Guinea, Philippines, Russia, Singapore, Sri Lanka, Thailand, Timor-Leste, US, Vietnam

Asia-Pacific Economic Cooperation (APEC)
established—7 November 1989
aim—to promote trade and investment in the Pacific basin
members—(21) Australia, Brunei, Canada, Chile, China, Hong Kong, Indonesia, Japan, South Korea, Malaysia, Mexico, NZ, Papua New Guinea, Peru, Philippines, Russia, Singapore, Taiwan, Thailand, US, Vietnam
observers—(3) Association of Southeast Asian Nations, Pacific Economic Cooperation Council, Pacific Islands Forum Secretariat

Asian Development Bank (ADB)
established—19 December 1966
aim—to promote regional economic cooperation
members—(48) Afghanistan, Armenia, Australia, Azerbaijan, Bangladesh, Bhutan, Brunei, Burma, Cambodia, China, Cook Islands, Fiji, Georgia, Hong Kong, India, Indonesia, Japan, Kazakhstan, Kiribati, South Korea, Kyrgyzstan, Laos, Malaysia, Maldives, Marshall Islands, Federated States of Micronesia, Mongolia, Nauru, Nepal, NZ, Pakistan, Palau, Papua New Guinea, Philippines, Samoa, Singapore, Solomon Islands, Sri Lanka, Taiwan, Tajikistan, Thailand, Timor- Leste, Tonga, Turkmenistan, Tuvalu, Uzbekistan, Vanuatu, Vietnam

nonregional members—(19) Austria, Belgium, Canada, Denmark, Finland, France, Germany, Ireland, Italy, Luxembourg, Netherlands, Norway, Portugal, Spain, Sweden, Switzerland, Turkey, UK, US

Association of Southeast Asian Nations (ASEAN)
established—8 August 1967
aim—to encourage regional economic, social, and cultural cooperation among the non-Communist countries of Southeast Asia
members—(10) Brunei, Burma, Cambodia, Indonesia, Laos, Malaysia, Philippines, Singapore, Thailand, Vietnam
dialogue partners—(11) Australia, Canada, China, EU, India, Japan, South Korea, NZ, Russia, US
observers—(2) Papua New Guinea, Timor-Leste

Australia Group (AG)
established—June 1985
aim—to consult on and coordinate export controls related to chemical and biological weapons
members—(42) Argentina, Australia, Austria, Belgium, Bulgaria, Canada, Croatia, Cyprus, Czech Republic, Denmark, Estonia, European Commission, Finland, France, Germany, Greece, Hungary, Iceland, Ireland, Italy, Japan, South Korea, Latvia, Lithuania, Luxembourg, Malta, Mexico, Netherlands, NZ, Norway, Poland, Portugal, Romania, Slovakia, Slovenia, Spain, Sweden, Switzerland, Turkey, Ukraine, UK, US

Australia-New Zealand-United States Security Treaty (ANZUS)
established—1 September 1951; effective—29 April 1952
aim—to implement a trilateral mutual security agreement, although the US suspended security obligations to NZ on 11 August 1986; Australia and the US continue to hold annual meetings
members—(3) Australia, NZ, US

Baltic Assembly (BA)
established—12 May 1990
aim—to thoroughly discuss various cooperation issues between Baltic states
members—(3) Estonia, Latvia, Lithuania

Bank for International Settlements (BIS)
established—20 January 1930; effective—17 March 1930
aim—to promote cooperation among central banks in international financial settlements
members—(60) Algeria, Argentina, Australia, Austria, Belgium, Bosnia and Herzegovina, Brazil, Bulgaria, Canada, Chile, China, Colombia, Croatia, Czech Republic, Denmark, European Central Bank, Estonia, Finland, France, Germany, Greece, Hong Kong, Hungary, Iceland, India, Indonesia, Ireland, Israel, Italy, Japan, South Korea, Latvia, Lithuania, Luxembourg, Macedonia, Malaysia, Mexico, Netherlands, NZ, Norway, Peru, Philippines, Poland, Portugal, Romania, Russia, Saudi Arabia, Serbia, Singapore, Slovakia, Slovenia, South Africa, Spain, Sweden, Switzerland, Thailand, Turkey, UAE, UK, US; note—Montenegro has a separate central bank; its links with BIS are currently under review

Bay of Bengal Initiative for Multi-Sectoral Technical and Economic Cooperation (BIMSTEC)
established—June 1997
aim—to foster socio-economic cooperation among members
members—(7) Bangladesh, Bhutan, Burma, India, Nepal, Sri Lanka, Thailand

Benelux Union (Benelux)
note—acronym from Belgium, Netherlands, and Luxembourg; was formerly known as Benelux Economic Union
established—3 February 1958; effective—1 November 1960; changed names 17 June 2008
aim—to develop closer economic and legal cooperation and integration
members—(3) Belgium, Luxembourg, Netherlands

Big Seven
note—membership is the same as the Group of 7
established—1975
aim—to discuss and coordinate major economic policies
members—(7) Big Six (Canada, France, Germany, Italy, Japan, UK) plus the US

Black Sea Economic Cooperation Zone (BSEC)
established—25 June 1992
aim—to enhance regional stability through economic cooperation
members—(12) Albania, Armenia, Azerbaijan, Bulgaria, Georgia, Greece, Moldova, Romania, Russia, Serbia, Turkey, Ukraine; note—Macedonia is in the process of joining
observers—(17) Austria, Belarus, Black Sea Commission, EU, Croatia, Czech Republic, Egypt, Energy Charter Secretariat, France, Germany, International Black Sea Club, Israel, Italy, Poland, Slovakia, Tunisia, US; note—Bosnia and Herzegovina and Slovenia have applied for observer status

BRICS
note—note: the name of the organization stands for the first letter of each of the five members' names
established—BRIC established 16 June 2009; BRICS established 24 December 2011
aim—to seek common ground in political and economic venues; to achieve peace, security, development, and cooperation; to contribute significantly to the development of humanity and to establish a more equitable world
members—(5) Brazil, Russia, India, China, South Africa

Caribbean Community and Common Market (Caricom)
established—4 July 1973; effective—1 August 1973
aim—to promote economic integration and development, especially among the less developed countries
members—(15) Antigua and Barbuda, The Bahamas, Barbados, Belize, Dominica, Grenada, Guyana, Haiti, Jamaica, Montserrat, Saint Kitts and Nevis, Saint Lucia, Saint Vincent and the Grenadines, Suriname, Trinidad and Tobago

associate members—(5) Anguilla, Bermuda, British Virgin Islands, Cayman Islands, Turks and Caicos Islands
observers—(8) Aruba, Colombia, Curacao, Dominican Republic, Mexico, Puerto Rico, Sint Maarten, Venezuela

Caribbean Development Bank (CDB)
established—18 October 1969; effective—26 January 1970
aim—to promote economic development and cooperation
regional members—(21) Anguilla, Antigua and Barbuda, The Bahamas, Barbados, Belize, British Virgin Islands, Cayman Islands, Colombia, Dominica, Grenada, Guyana, Haiti, Jamaica, Mexico, Montserrat, Saint Kitts and Nevis, Saint Lucia, Saint Vincent and the Grenadines, Trinidad and Tobago, Turks and Caicos Islands, Venezuela
nonregional members—(5) Canada, China, Germany, Italy, UK

Central African Customs and Economic Union (UDEAC)
see *Economic and Monetary Community of Central Africa (CEMAC)*

Central African States Development Bank (BDEAC)
note—acronym from Banque de Developpement des Etats de I'Afrique Centrale
established—3 December 1975
aim—to provide loans for economic development
members—(11) African Development Bank (AfDB), Cameroon, Central African States Bank (BEAC), Central African Republic, Chad, Republic of the Congo, Equatorial Guinea, France, Gabon, Kuwait, Libya

Central American Bank for Economic Integration (BCIE)
note—acronym from Banco Centroamericano de Integracion Economico
established—13 December 1960 signature of Articles of Agreement; 31 May 1961 began operations
aim—to promote economic integration and development
members—(5) Costa Rica, El Salvador, Guatemala, Honduras, Nicaragua
nonregional members—(7) Argentina, Colombia, Dominican Republic, Mexico, Panama, Spain, Taiwan

Central American Common Market (CACM)
established—13 December 1960, collapsed in 1969, reinstated in 1991
aim—to promote establishment of a Central American Common Market
members—(5) Costa Rica, El Salvador, Guatemala, Honduras, Nicaragua

Central American Integration System (SICA)
established—13 December 1991; operational 1 February 1993
aim—to strengthen democracy; to set up a new model of regional security; to promote freedom; to achieve a regional system of welfare and economic and social justice; to attain economic unity and strengthen the area as an economic bloc; to act as a bloc in international matters
members—(7) Belize, Costa Rica, El Salvador, Guatemala, Honduras, Nicaragua, Panama
associated member—(1) Dominican Republic
observers—(15) Argentina, Australia, Brazil, Chile, China, France, Germany, Holy See, Italy, Japan, South Korea, Mexico, Peru, Spain, US

Central European Initiative (CEI)
note—evolved from the Quadrilateral Initiative and the Hexagonal Initiative
established—11 November 1989 as the Quadrilateral Initiative, 27 July 1991 became the Hexagonal Initiative, July 1992 its present name was adopted
aim—to form an economic and political cooperation group for the region between the Adriatic and the Baltic Seas
members—(18) Albania, Austria, Belarus, Bosnia and Herzegovina, Bulgaria, Croatia, Czech Republic, Hungary, Italy, Macedonia, Moldova, Montenegro, Poland, Romania, Serbia, Slovakia, Slovenia, Ukraine

centrally planned economies
a term applied mainly to the traditionally Communist states that looked to the former USSR for leadership; most are now evolving toward more democratic and market-oriented systems; also known formerly as the Second World or as the Communist countries; through the 1980s, this group included Albania, Bulgaria, Cambodia, China, Cuba, Czechoslovakia, German Democratic Republic, Hungary, North Korea, Laos, Mongolia, Poland, Romania, USSR, Vietnam, Yugoslavia, but now is limited to Cuba and North Korea, and less so to China

Collective Security Treaty Organization (CSTO)
established—7 October 2002
aim—to coordinate military and political cooperation, to develop multilateral structures and mechanisms of cooperation for ensuring national security of the member states
members—(7) Armenia, Belarus, Kazakhstan, Kyrgyzstan, Russia, Tajikistan, Uzbekistan

Colombo Plan (CP)
established—May 1950 proposal was adopted; 1 July 1951 commenced full operations
aim—to promote economic and social development in Asia and the Pacific
members—(27) Afghanistan, Australia, Bangladesh, Bhutan, Brunei, Burma, Fiji, India, Indonesia, Iran, Japan, South Korea, Laos, Malaysia, Maldives, Mongolia, Nepal, NZ, Pakistan, Papua New Guinea, Philippines, Saudi Arabia, Singapore, Sri Lanka, Thailand, US, Vietnam

Common Market for Eastern and Southern Africa (COMESA)
note—formerly known as Preferential Trade Area for Eastern and Southern Africa (PTA)
established—treaty signed 5 November 1993; treaty ratified 8 December 1994

aim—recognizing, promoting and protecting fundamental human rights, commitment to the principles of liberty and rule of law, maintaining peace and stability through the promotion and strengthening of good neighborliness, commitment to peaceful settlement of disputes among member states
members—(19) Burundi, Comoros, Democratic Republic of the Congo, Djibouti, Egypt, Eritrea, Ethiopia, Kenya, Libya, Madagascar, Malawi, Mauritius, Rwanda, Seychelles, Sudan, Swaziland, Uganda, Zambia, Zimbabwe

Commonwealth (C)
note—also known as Commonwealth of Nations
established—31 December 1931
aim—to foster multinational cooperation and assistance, as a voluntary association that evolved from the British Empire
members—(53) Antigua and Barbuda, Australia, The Bahamas, Bangladesh, Barbados, Belize, Botswana, Brunei, Cameroon, Canada, Cyprus, Dominica, Fiji (suspended), Ghana, Grenada, Guyana, India, Jamaica, Kenya, Kiribati, Lesotho, Malawi, Malaysia, Maldives, Malta, Mauritius, Mozambique, Namibia, Nauru, NZ, Nigeria, Pakistan (reinstated 2004), Papua New Guinea, Rwanda, Saint Kitts and Nevis, Saint Lucia, Saint Vincent and the Grenadines, Samoa, Seychelles, Sierra Leone, Singapore, Solomon Islands, South Africa, Sri Lanka, Swaziland, Tanzania, Tonga, Trinidad and Tobago, Tuvalu, Uganda, UK, Vanuatu, Zambia; note—on 7 December 2003 Zimbabwe withdrew its membership from the Commonwealth

Commonwealth of Independent States (CIS)
established—8 December 1991; effective—21 December 1991
aim—to coordinate intercommonwealth relations and to provide a mechanism for the orderly dissolution of the USSR
members—(11) Armenia, Azerbaijan, Belarus, Kazakhstan, Kyrgyzstan, Moldova, Russia, Tajikistan, Turkmenistan (unofficial), Ukraine (unofficial), Uzbekistan; note—neither Ukraine as a participating member nor Turkmenistan as an associate member have signed the 1993 CIS charter, although both participate in meetings; Georgia left the organization in August 2009

Communist countries
traditionally the Marxist-Leninist states with authoritarian governments and command economies based on the Soviet model; most of the original and the successor states are no longer Communist; see centrally planned economies

Community of Democracies (CD)
established—27 June 2000
aim—"to respect and uphold core democratic principles and practices" including free and fair elections, freedom of speech and expression, equal access to education, rule of law, and freedom of peaceful assembly
signatories of the Warsaw Declaration—(110) Albania, Algeria, Argentina, Armenia, Australia, Austria, Azerbaijan, Bangladesh, Belgium, Belize, Benin, Bolivia, Bosnia and Herzegovina, Botswana, Brazil, Bulgaria, Burkina Faso, Cabo Verde, Canada, Chile, Colombia, Costa Rica, Croatia, Cyprus, Czech Republic, Denmark, Dominica, Dominican Republic, Ecuador, Egypt, El Salvador, Estonia, Finland, Georgia, Germany, Greece, Guatemala, Guyana, Haiti, Honduras, Hungary, Iceland, India, Indonesia, Ireland, Israel, Italy, Japan, Jordan, Kenya, South Korea, Kuwait, Latvia, Lesotho, Liechtenstein, Lithuania, Luxembourg, Macedonia, Madagascar, Malawi, Mali, Malta, Mauritius, Mexico, Moldova, Monaco, Mongolia, Morocco, Mozambique, Namibia, Nepal, Netherlands, NZ, Nicaragua, Niger, Nigeria, Norway, Panama, Papua New Guinea, Paraguay, Peru, Philippines, Poland, Portugal, Qatar, Romania, Russia, Saint Lucia, Sao Tome and Principe, Senegal, Seychelles, Slovakia, Slovenia, South Africa, Spain, Sri Lanka, Suriname, Sweden, Switzerland, Tanzania, Thailand, Tunisia, Turkey, Ukraine, UK, US, Uruguay, Venezuela, Yemen, Yugoslavia

Community of Latin American and Caribbean States (CELAC)
note—successor to the Rio Group and the Latin America and Caribbean Summit on Integration and Development
established—created 23 February 2010; established July 2011
aim—to deepen the integration within Latin American and to reduce the influence of the US in the politics and economics of that part of the world
members—(33) Antigua and Barbuda, Argentina, The Bahamas, Barbados, Belize, Bolivia, Brazil, Chile, Colombia, Costa Rica, Cuba, Dominica, Dominican Republic, Ecuador, El Salvador, Grenada, Guatemala, Guyana, Haiti, Honduras, Jamaica, Mexico, Nicaragua, Panama, Paraguay, Peru, St. Kitts and Nevis, St. Lucia, St. Vincent and the Grenadines, Suriname, Trinidad and Tobago, Uruguay, Venezuela

Comuinidade dos Paises de Lingua Portuguesa (CPLP)
established—1996
aim—to establish a forum for friendship among Portuguese-speaking nations where Portuguese is an official language
members—(8) Angola, Brazil, cabo Verde, Guinea-Bissau, Mozambique, Portugal, Sao Tome and Principe, Timor-Leste
associate observers—(3) Equatorial Guinea, Mauritius, Senegal

Conference of Interaction and Confidence-Building Measures in Asia (CICA)
established—proposed 5 October 1992; established 14 September 1999
aim—promoting a multi-national forum for enhancing cooperation towards promoting peace, security, and stability in Asia
members—(23 and the Palestine Liberation Organization) Afghanistan, Azerbaijan, Bahrain, Cambodia, China, Egypt, India, Iraq, Iran, Israel, Jordan, Kazakhstan, Kyrgyzstan, Mongolia, Pakistan, South Korea, Russia, Tajikistan, Thailand, Turkey, UAE, Uzbekistan, Vietnam, and the Palestine Liberation Organization
observers—(13) Bangladesh, Indonesia, Japan, League of Arab States, Malaysia, OSCE, Parliamentary Assembly of the Turkic Speaking Countries, Philippines, Qatar, Sri Lanka, Ukraine, UN, US

Convention of the Southeast European Law Enforcement Center (SELEC)
note—successor to Southeast European Cooperative Initiative (SECI) formed in 1996 to help the Southeast European countries rebuild and stabilize through access to resources
established—7 October 2011
aim—to provide support for Member States and enhance coordination in preventing and combating crime in trans-border activity
members—(13) Albania, Bosnia and Herzegovina, Bulgaria, Croatia, Greece, Hungary, Macedonia, Moldova, Montenegro, Romania, Serbia, Slovenia, Turkey

observers—(15) Austria, Azerbaijan, Belgium, Canada, France, Georgia, Germany, Italy, Japan, The Netherlands, Portugal, Spain, Ukraine, UK, US

Coordinating Committee on Export Controls (COCOM)
established in 1949 to control the export of strategic products and technical data from member countries to proscribed destinations; members were: Australia, Belgium, Canada, Denmark, France, Germany, Greece, Italy, Japan, Luxembourg, Netherlands, Norway, Portugal, Spain, Turkey, UK, US; abolished 31 March 1994; COCOM members established a new organization, the Wassenaar Arrangement, with expanded membership on 12 July 1996 that focuses on nonproliferation export controls as opposed to East-West control of advanced technology

Council for Mutual Economic Assistance (CEMA)
note—also known as CMEA or Comecon
established 25 January 1949 to promote the development of socialist economies and abolished 1 January 1991; members included Afghanistan (observer), Albania (had not participated since 1961 break with USSR), Angola (observer), Bulgaria, Cuba, Czechoslovakia, Ethiopia (observer), GDR, Hungary, Laos (observer), Mongolia, Mozambique (observer), Nicaragua (observer), Poland, Romania, USSR, Vietnam, Yemen (observer), Yugoslavia (associate)

Council of Arab Economic Unity (CAEU)
established—3 June 1957; effective—30 May 1964
aim—to promote economic integration among Arab nations
members—(17 plus the Palestine Liberation Organization) Algeria, Bahrain, Egypt, Iraq, Jordan, Kuwait, Lebanon, Libya, Morocco, Oman, Qatar, Saudi Arabia, Sudan, Syria, Tunisia, UAE, Yemen, Palestine Liberation Organization
—(4) Comoros, Djibouti, Mauritania, Somalia

Council of Europe (CE)
established—5 May 1949; effective—3 August 1949
aim—to promote increased unity and quality of life in Europe
members—(47) Albania, Andorra, Armenia, Austria, Azerbaijan, Belgium, Bosnia and Herzegovina, Bulgaria, Croatia, Cyprus, Czech Republic, Denmark, Estonia, Finland, France, Georgia, Germany, Greece, Hungary, Iceland, Ireland, Italy, Latvia, Liechtenstein, Lithuania, Luxembourg, Macedonia, Malta, Moldova, Monaco, Montenegro, Netherlands, Norway, Poland, Portugal, Romania, Russia, San Marino, Serbia, Slovakia, Slovenia, Spain, Sweden, Switzerland, Turkey, Ukraine, UK
observers—(6) Canada, Holy See, Israel, Japan, Mexico, US

Council of the Baltic Sea States (CBSS)
established—6 March 1992
aim—to promote cooperation among the Baltic Sea states in the areas of aid to new democratic institutions, economic development, humanitarian aid, energy and the environment, cultural programs and education, and transportation and communication
members—(12) Denmark, Estonia, EC, Finland, Germany, Iceland, Latvia, Lithuania, Norway, Poland, Russia, Sweden
observers—(10) Belarus, France, Italy, Netherlands, Romania, Spain, Slovakia, Ukraine, UK, US

Council of the Entente (Entente)
established—29 May 1959
aim—to promote economic, social, and political coordination
members—(5) Benin, Burkina Faso, Cote d'Ivoire, Niger, Togo

countries in transition
a term used by the International Monetary Fund (IMF) for the middle group in its hierarchy of formerly centrally planned economies; IMF statistics include the following 28 countries in transition: Albania, Armenia, Azerbaijan, Belarus, Bosnia and Herzegovina, Bulgaria, Croatia, Czech Republic, Estonia, Georgia, Hungary, Kazakhstan, Kyrgyzstan, Latvia, Lithuania, Macedonia, Moldova, Mongolia, Montenegro, Poland, Romania, Russia, Serbia, Slovakia, Slovenia, Tajikistan, Turkmenistan, Ukraine, Uzbekistan; note—this group is identical to the group traditionally referred to as the "former USSR/Eastern Europe" except for the addition of Mongolia

Customs Cooperation Council (CCC)
note—see World Customs Organization (WCO)

developed countries (DCs)
the top group in the hierarchy of developed countries (DCs), former USSR/Eastern Europe (former USSR/EE), and less developed countries (LDCs); includes the market-oriented economies of the mainly democratic nations in the Organization for Economic Cooperation and Development (OECD), Bermuda, Israel, South Africa, and the European ministates; also known as the First World, high- income countries, the North, industrial countries; generally have a per capita GDP in excess of $15,000 although four OECD countries and South Africa have figures well under $15,000 and eight of the excluded OPEC countries have figures of more than $20,000; the DCs include: Andorra, Australia, Austria, Belgium, Bermuda, Canada, Denmark, Faroe Islands, Finland, France, Germany, Greece, Holy See, Iceland, Ireland, Israel, Italy, Japan, Liechtenstein, Luxembourg, Malta, Monaco, Netherlands, NZ, Norway, Portugal, San Marino, South Africa, Spain, Sweden, Switzerland, Turkey, UK, US; note—similar to the new International Monetary Fund (IMF) term "advanced economies" that adds Hong Kong, South Korea, Singapore, and Taiwan but drops Malta, Mexico, South Africa, and Turkey

developing countries
a term used by the International Monetary Fund (IMF) for the bottom group in its hierarchy of advanced economies, countries in transition, and developing countries; IMF statistics include the following 126 developing countries: Afghanistan, Algeria, Angola, Antigua and Barbuda, Argentina, Aruba, The Bahamas, Bahrain, Bangladesh, Barbados, Belize, Benin, Bhutan, Bolivia, Botswana, Brazil, Burkina Faso, Burma, Burundi, Cambodia, Cameroon, cabo Verde, Central African Republic, Chad, Chile, China, Colombia, Comoros, Democratic Republic of the Congo, Republic of the Congo, Costa Rica, Cote d'Ivoire, Cyprus, Djibouti, Dominica, Dominican Republic, Ecuador, Egypt, El Salvador, Equatorial Guinea, Ethiopia, Fiji, Gabon, The Gambia, Ghana, Grenada, Guatemala, Guinea, Guinea-Bissau, Guyana, Haiti, Honduras, India, Indonesia, Iran, Iraq, Jamaica, Jordan, Kenya, Kiribati, Kuwait, Laos, Lebanon, Lesotho, Liberia, Libya, Madagascar, Malawi, Malaysia, Maldives, Mali, Malta, Marshall Islands, Mauritania, Mauritius, Mexico, Federated States of Micronesia, Morocco, Mozambique, Namibia,

Nepal, Netherlands Antilles, Nicaragua, Niger, Nigeria, Oman, Pakistan, Panama, Papua New Guinea, Paraguay, Peru, Philippines, Qatar, Rwanda, Saint Kitts and Nevis, Saint Lucia, Saint Vincent and the Grenadines, Samoa, Sao Tome and Principe, Saudi Arabia, Senegal, Seychelles, Sierra Leone, Solomon Islands, Somalia, South Africa, Sri Lanka, Sudan, Suriname, Swaziland, Syria, Tanzania, Thailand, Togo, Trinidad and Tobago, Tunisia, Turkey, UAE, Uganda, Uruguay, Vanuatu, Venezuela, Vietnam, Yemen, Zambia, Zimbabwe; note—this category would presumably also cover the following 46 other countries that are traditionally included in the more comprehensive group of "less developed countries": American Samoa, Anguilla, British Virgin Islands, Brunei, Cayman Islands, Christmas Island, Cocos Islands, Cook Islands, Cuba, Eritrea, Falkland Islands, French Guiana, French Polynesia, Gaza Strip, Gibraltar, Greenland, Grenada, Guadeloupe, Guam, Guernsey, Isle of Man, Jersey, North Korea, Macau, Martinique, Mayotte, Montserrat, Nauru, New Caledonia, Niue, Norfolk Island, Northern Mariana Islands, Palau, Pitcairn Islands, Puerto Rico, Reunion, Saint Helena, Ascension, and Tristan da Cunha, Saint Pierre and Miquelon, Tokelau, Tonga, Turks and Caicos Islands, Tuvalu, Virgin Islands, Wallis and Futuna, West Bank, Western Sahara

Developing Eight (D-8)
established—15 June 1997
aim—to improve developing countries' positions in the world economy, diversify and create new opportunities in trade relations, enhance participation in decision-making at the international level, provide better standards of living
member—(8) Bangladesh, Egypt, Indonesia, Iran, Malaysia, Nigeria, Pakistan, Turkey

East African Community (EAC)
note—originally established in 1967, it was disbanded in 1977
established—January 2001
aim—to establish a political and economic union among the countries
members—(5) Burundi, Kenya, Rwanda, Tanzania, Uganda

East African Development Bank (EADB)
established—6 June 1967; effective—1 December 1967
aim—to promote economic development
members—(4) Kenya, Rwanda, Tanzania, Uganda

East Asia Summit (EAS)
established—14 December 2005
aim—to promote cooperation in political and security issues; to promote development, financial stability, energy security, economic integration and growth; to eradicate poverty and narrow the development gap in East Asia, and to promote deeper cultural understanding
members—(18) Australia, Brunei, Burma, Cambodia, China, India, Indonesia, Japan, South Korea, Laos, Malaysia, NZ, Philippines, Russia, Singapore, Thailand, US, Vietnam

Economic and Monetary Community of Central Africa (CEMAC)
note—was formerly the Central African Customs and Economic Union (UDEAC)
established—8 December 1964; effective—1 January 1966
aim—to promote the establishment of a Central African Common Market
members—(7) Cameroon, Central African Republic, Chad, Democratic Republic of the Congo, Equatorial Guinea, Gabon, The Gambia

Economic and Monetary Union (EMU)
note—an integral part of the European Union; also known as the European Economic and Monetary Union
established—1-2 December 1969 (proposed at summit conference of heads of government; 7 February 1992 (Maastricht Treaty signed)
aim—to promote a single market by creating a single currency, the euro; timetable—2 May 1998: European exchange rates fixed for 1 January 1999; 1 January 1999: all banks and stock exchanges begin using euros; 1 January 2002: the euro goes into circulation; 1 July 2002 local currencies no longer accepted
members—(18) Austria, Belgium, Cyprus, Estonia, Finland, France, Germany, Greece, Ireland, Italy, Latvia, Luxembourg, Malta, Netherlands, Portugal, Slovakia, Slovenia, Spain

Economic and Social Council (ECOSOC)
established—26 June 1945; effective—24 October 1945
aim—to coordinate the economic and social work of the UN; includes five regional commissions (Economic Commission for Africa, Economic Commission for Europe, Economic Commission for Latin America and the Caribbean, Economic and Social Commission for Asia and the Pacific, Economic and Social Commission for Western Asia) and nine functional commissions (Commission for Social Development, Commission on Human Rights, Commission on Narcotic Drugs, Commission on the Status of Women, Commission on Population and Development, Statistical Commission, Commission on Science and Technology for Development, Commission on Sustainable Development, and Commission on Crime Prevention and Criminal Justice)
members—(54) selected on a rotating basis from all regions

Economic Community of the Great Lakes Countries (CEPGL)
note—acronym from Communaute Economique des Pays des Grands Lacs
established—20 September 1976
aim—to promote regional economic cooperation and integration
members—(3) Burundi, Democratic Republic of the Congo, Rwanda; note—organization collapsed because of fighting in 1998; reactivated in 2006

Economic Community of West African States (ECOWAS)
established—28 May 1975
aim—to promote regional economic cooperation
members—(15) Benin, Burkina Faso, Cabo Verde, Cote d'Ivoire, The Gambia, Ghana, Guinea, Guinea-Bissau, Liberia, Mali, Niger, Nigeria, Senegal, Sierra Leone, Togo

Economic Cooperation Organization (ECO)
established—27-29 January 1985

aim—to promote regional cooperation in trade, transportation, communications, tourism, cultural affairs, and economic development
members—(10) Afghanistan, Azerbaijan, Iran, Kazakhstan, Kyrgyzstan, Pakistan, Tajikistan, Turkey, Turkmenistan, Uzbekistan

Eurasian Economic Community (EAEC or EurasEC)
note—merged with Central Asian Cooperation Organization (CACO) in 2005
established—May 2001
aim—to create a common economic and energy policy
members—(6) Belarus, Kazakhstan, Kyrgyzstan, Russia, Tajikistan, Uzbekistan
observers—(3) Armenia, Moldova, Ukraine

Euro-Atlantic Partnership Council (EAPC)
note—began as the North Atlantic Cooperation Council (NACC); an extension of NATO
established—8 November 1991; effective—20 December 1991
aim—to discuss cooperation on mutual political and security issues
members—(50) Albania, Armenia, Austria, Azerbaijan, Belarus, Belgium, Bosnia and Herzegovina, Bulgaria, Canada, Croatia, Czech Republic, Denmark, Estonia, Finland, France, Georgia, Germany, Greece, Hungary, Iceland, Ireland, Italy, Kazakhstan, Kyrgyzstan, Latvia, Lithuania, Luxembourg, Macedonia, Malta, Moldova, Montenegro, Netherlands, Norway, Poland, Portugal, Romania, Russia, Serbia, Slovakia, Slovenia, Spain, Sweden, Switzerland, Tajikistan, Turkey, Turkmenistan, Ukraine, UK, US, Uzbekistan

European Bank for Reconstruction and Development (EBRD)
established—8-9 January 1990 (proposals made); 15 April 1991 (bank inaugurated)
aim—to facilitate the transition of seven centrally planned economies in Europe (Bulgaria, former Czechoslovakia, Hungary, Poland, Romania, former USSR, and former Yugoslavia) to market economies by committing 60% of its loans to privatization
members—(66) Albania, Armenia, Australia, Austria, Azerbaijan, Belarus, Belgium, Bosnia and Herzegovina, Bulgaria, Canada, Croatia, Cyprus, Czech Republic, Denmark, Egypt, EU, European Investment Bank (EIB), Estonia, Finland, France, Georgia, Germany, Greece, Hungary, Iceland, Ireland, Israel, Italy, Japan, Jordan, Kazakhstan, South Korea, Kosovo, Kyrgyzstan, Latvia, Liechtenstein, Lithuania, Luxembourg, Macedonia, Malta, Mexico, Moldova, Mongolia, Montenegro, Morocco, Netherlands, NZ, Norway, Poland, Portugal, Romania, Russia, Serbia, Slovakia, Slovenia, Spain, Sweden, Switzerland, Tajikistan, Tunisia, Turkey, Turkmenistan, Ukraine, UK, US, Uzbekistan

European Central Bank (ECB)
established—1 June 1998
aim—to administer the monetary policy of the EU Eurozone member states
members—(18) Austria, Belgium, Cyprus, Estonia, Finland, France, Germany, Greece, Ireland, Italy, Latvia, Luxembourg, Malta, Netherlands, Portugal, Slovakia, Slovenia, Spain

European Community (or European Communities, EC)
established 8 April 1965 to integrate the European Atomic Energy Community (Euratom), the European Coal and Steel Community (ECSC), the European Economic Community (EEC or Common Market), and to establish a completely integrated common market and an eventual federation of Europe; merged into the European Union (EU) on 7 February 1992; member states at the time of merger were Belgium, Denmark, France, Germany, Greece, Ireland, Italy, Luxembourg, Netherlands, Portugal, Spain, UK

European Free Trade Association (EFTA)
established—4 January 1960; effective—3 May 1960
aim—to promote expansion of free trade
members—(4) Iceland, Liechtenstein, Norway, Switzerland

European Investment Bank (EIB)
established—25 March 1957; effective—1 January 1958
aim—to promote economic development of the EU and its predecessors, the EEC and the EC
members—(28) Austria, Belgium, Bulgaria, Croatia, Cyprus, Czech Republic, Denmark, Estonia, Finland, France, Germany, Greece, Hungary, Ireland, Italy, Latvia, Lithuania, Luxembourg, Malta, Netherlands, Poland, Portugal, Romania, Slovakia, Slovenia, Spain, Sweden, UK

European Organization for Nuclear Research (CERN)
note—acronym retained from the predecessor organization Conseil Europeenne pour la Recherche Nucleaire
established—1 July 1953; effective—29 September 1954
aim—to foster nuclear research for peaceful purposes only
members—(20) Austria, Belgium, Bulgaria, Czech Republic, Denmark, Finland, France, Germany, Greece, Hungary, Italy, Netherlands, Norway, Poland, Portugal, Slovakia, Spain, Sweden, Switzerland, UK
observers—(7) EC, India, Japan, Russia, Turkey, United Nations Educational, Scientific, and Cultural Organization (UNESCO), US

European Space Agency (ESA)
established—31 May 1975
aim—to promote peaceful cooperation in space research and technology
members—(20) Austria, Belgium, Czech Republic, Denmark, Finland, France, Germany, Greece, Ireland, Italy, Luxembourg, Netherlands, Norway, Poland, Portugal, Romania, Spain, Sweden, Switzerland, UK
cooperating states—(3) Estonia, Hungary, Slovenia

European Union (EU)
note—see European Union entry at the end of the "country" listings

Extractive Industry Transparency Initiative (EITI)
established—October 2002 Initiative announced; June 2003 first EITC Plenary Conference
aim—to set a global standard for transparency in the extractive industries in an effort to make natural resources benefit all

stake holders or implementing countries—(17) Australia, Belgium, Canada, Denmark, Finland, France, Germany, Italy, Japan, Netherlands, Norway, Qatar, Spain, Sweden, Switzerland, UK, US
compliant countries—(23) Albania, Azerbaijan, Burkina Faso, Cameroon, Congo, Cote d'Ivoire, Ghana, Iraq, Kazakhstan, Kyrgyzstan, Liberia, Mali, Mauritania, Mongolia, Mozambique, Niger, Nigeria, Peru, Tanzania, Timor-Leste, Togo, Yemen, Zambia; note - Central African Republic is suspended
candidate countries—(13) Afghanistan, Chad, Guatemala, Guinea, Honduras, Indonesia, Philippines, Sao Tome and Principe, Senegal, Solomon Islands, Tajikistan, Trinidad and Tobago, Ukraine; note - Democratic Republic of the Congo, Madagascar, and Sierra Leone are suspended

Financial Action Task Force (FATF)
established—by G-7 Summit in Paris in 1989
aim—to develop and promote policies to combat money laundering and terrorist financing
members—(36) Argentina, Australia, Austria, Belgium, Brazil, Canada, China, Denmark, EC, Finland, France, Germany, Greece, Gulf Cooperation Council, Hong Kong, Iceland, India, Ireland, Italy, Japan, South Korea, Luxembourg, Mexico, Netherlands (Aruba, Curacao, Sint Maarten), NZ, Norway, Portugal, Russia, Singapore, South Africa, Spain, Sweden, Switzerland, Turkey, UK, US

First World
another term for countries with advanced, industrialized economies; this term is fading from use; see developed countries (DCs)

Food and Agriculture Organization (FAO)
established—16 October 1945
aim—to raise living standards and increase availability of agricultural products; a UN specialized agency
members—(195) includes all UN member countries except Liechtenstein (192 total); plus Cook Islands, EU, and Niue
associate members—(2) Faroe Islands, Tokelau

former Soviet Union (FSU)
former term often used to identify as a group the successor nations to the Soviet Union or USSR; this group of 15 countries consists of: Armenia, Azerbaijan, Belarus, Estonia, Georgia, Kazakhstan, Kyrgyzstan, Latvia, Lithuania, Moldova, Russia, Tajikistan, Turkmenistan, Ukraine, Uzbekistan

former USSR/Eastern Europe (former USSR/EE)
the middle group in the hierarchy of developed countries (DCs), former USSR/Eastern Europe (former USSR/EE), and less developed countries (LDCs); these countries are in political and economic transition and may well be grouped differently in the near future; this group of 27 countries consists of: Albania, Armenia, Azerbaijan, Belarus, Bosnia and Herzegovina, Bulgaria, Croatia, Czech Republic, Estonia, Georgia, Hungary, Kazakhstan, Kyrgyzstan, Latvia, Lithuania, Macedonia, Moldova, Poland, Romania, Russia, Slovakia, Slovenia, Tajikistan, Turkmenistan, Ukraine, Uzbekistan, Yugoslavia; this group is identical to the IMF group "countries in transition" except for the IMF's inclusion of Mongolia

Four Dragons
the four small Asian less developed countries (LDCs) that have experienced unusually rapid economic growth; also known as the Four Tigers; this group consists of Hong Kong, South Korea, Singapore, Taiwan; these countries are included in the IMF's "advanced economies" group

Franc Zone (FZ)
note—also known as Conference des Ministres des Finances des Pays de la Zone Franc
established—1964
aim—to form a monetary union among countries whose currencies were linked to the French franc
members—(16) Benin, Burkina Faso, Cameroon, Central African Republic, Chad, Comoros, Republic of the Congo, Cote d'Ivoire, Equatorial Guinea, France, Gabon, Guinea-Bissau, Mali, Niger, Senegal, Togo

Front Line States (FLS)
established to achieve black majority rule in South Africa; has since gone out of existence; members included Angola, Botswana, Mozambique, Namibia, Tanzania, Zambia, Zimbabwe

General Agreement on Tariffs and Trade (GATT)
see the World Trade Organization (WTO)

General Confederation of Trade Unions (GCTU)
established—16 April 1992
aim—to consolidate trade union actions to protect citizens' social and labor rights and interests, to help secure trade unions' rights and guarantees, and to strengthen international trade union solidarity
members—(10) Armenia, Azerbaijan, Belarus, Georgia, Kazakhstan, Kyrgyzstan, Moldova, Russia, Tajikistan, Ukraine

Group of 10 (G-10)
note—also known as the Paris Club; includes the wealthiest members of the IMF who provide most of the money to be loaned and act as the informal steering committee; name persists despite increased membership
established—October 1962
aim—to coordinate credit policy
members—(11) Belgium, Canada, France, Germany, Italy, Japan, Netherlands, Sweden, Switzerland, UK, US
observers—(4) BIS, EC, IMF, OECD

Group of 11 (G-11)
established—2006
aim—to narrow the income gap with the world's richest nations
members—(11) Croatia, Ecuador, El Salvador, Georgia, Honduras, Indonesia, Jordan, Morocco, Pakistan, Paraguay, Sri Lanka

Group of 15 (G-15)
note—byproduct of the Nonaligned Movement; name persists despite increased membership
established—September 1989
aim—to promote economic cooperation among developing nations; to act as the main political organ for the Nonaligned Movement
members—(17) Algeria, Argentina, Brazil, Chile, Egypt, India, Indonesia, Iran, Jamaica, Kenya, Malaysia, Mexico, Nigeria, Senegal, Sri Lanka, Venezuela, Zimbabwe

Group of 20 (G-20)
established—created 1999; inaugurated 15-16 December 1999
aim—to promote open and constructive discussion between industrial and emerging-market countries on any issues related to global economic stability; helps to support growth and development across the globe
members—(20) Argentina, Australia, Brazil, Canada, China, EU, France, Germany, India, Indonesia, Italy, Japan, South Korea, Mexico, Russia, Saudi Arabia, South Africa, Turkey, UK, US

Group of 24 (G-24)
established—1 August 1989
aim—to promote the interests of developing countries in Africa, Asia, and Latin America within the IMF
members—(24) Algeria, Argentina, Brazil, Colombia, Democratic Republic of the Congo, Cote d'Ivoire, Egypt, Ethiopia, Gabon, Ghana, Guatemala, India, Iran, Lebanon, Mexico, Nigeria, Pakistan, Peru, Philippines, South Africa, Sri Lanka, Syria, Trinidad and Tobago, Venezuela
observers—(1) China

Group of 3 (G-3)
established—September 1990
aim—mechanism for policy coordination
members—(2) Colombia, Mexico; note—Panama shows interest in joining

Group of 5 (G-5)
note—with the addition of Italy, Canada, and Russia, it is now known as the Group of 8 or G-8; meanwhile the Group of 5 now refers to Brazil, China, India, Mexico, and South Africa
established—22 September 1985
aim—to coordinate the economic policies of five major noncommunist economic powers
members—(5) France, Germany, Japan, UK, US

Group of 6 (G-6)
also known as Groupe des Six Sur le Desarmement (not to be confused with the Big Six) was established in 22 May 1984 with the aim of achieving nuclear disarmament; its members were Argentina, Greece, India, Mexico, Sweden, Tanzania

Group of 7 (G-7)
note—membership is the same as the Big Seven
established—22 September 1985
aim—to facilitate economic cooperation among the seven major noncommunist economic powers
members—(7) Group of 5 (France, Germany, Japan, UK, US) plus Canada and Italy

Group of 77 (G-77)
established—15 June1964; October 1967 first ministerial meeting
aim—to promote economic cooperation among developing countries; name persists in spite of increased membership
members—(132 plus the Palestine Liberation Organization) Afghanistan, Algeria, Angola, Antigua and Barbuda, Argentina, The Bahamas, Bahrain, Bangladesh, Barbados, Belize, Benin, Bhutan, Bolivia, Bosnia and Herzegovina, Botswana, Brazil, Brunei, Burkina Faso, Burma, Burundi, Cambodia, Cabo Verde, Cameroon, Central African Republic, Chad, Chile, China, Colombia, Comoros, Democratic Republic of the Congo, Republic of the Congo, Costa Rica, Cote d'Ivoire, Cuba, Djibouti, Dominica, Dominican Republic, Ecuador, Egypt, El Salvador, Equatorial Guinea, Eritrea, Ethiopia, Fiji, Gabon, The Gambia, Ghana, Grenada, Guatemala, Guinea, Guinea-Bissau, Guyana, Haiti, Honduras, India, Indonesia, Iran, Iraq, Jamaica, Jordan, Kenya, Kiribati, North Korea, Kuwait, Laos, Lebanon, Lesotho, Liberia, Libya, Madagascar, Malawi, Malaysia, Maldives, Mali, Marshall Islands, Mauritania, Mauritius, Federated States of Micronesia, Mongolia, Morocco, Mozambique, Namibia, Nauru, Nepal, Nicaragua, Niger, Nigeria, Oman, Pakistan, Panama, Papua New Guinea, Paraguay, Peru, Philippines, Qatar, Rwanda, Saint Kitts and Nevis, Saint Lucia, Saint Vincent and the Grenadines, Samoa, Sao Tome and Principe, Saudi Arabia, Senegal, Seychelles, Sierra Leone, Singapore, Solomon Islands, Somalia, South Africa, Sri Lanka, Sudan, Suriname, Swaziland, Syria, Tajikistan, Tanzania, Thailand, Timor-Leste, Togo, Tonga, Trinidad and Tobago, Tunisia, Turkmenistan, Uganda, UAE, Uruguay, Vanuatu, Venezuela, Vietnam, Yemen, Zambia, Zimbabwe, Palestine Liberation Organization

Group of 8 (G-8)
established—October 1975
aim—to facilitate economic cooperation among the developed countries (DCs) that participated in the Conference on International Economic Cooperation (CIEC), held in several sessions between December 1975 and 3 June 1977
members—(8) Canada, EU, France, Germany, Italy, Japan, UK, US

Group of 9 (G-9)
established—NA
aim—to discuss matters of mutual interest on an informal basis
members—(9) Austria, Belgium, Bulgaria, Denmark, Finland, Hungary, Romania, Serbia, Sweden

Gulf Cooperation Council (GCC)
note—also known as the Cooperation Council for the Arab States of the Gulf

established—25 May 1981
aim—to promote regional cooperation in economic, social, political, and military affairs
members—(6) Bahrain, Kuwait, Oman, Qatar, Saudi Arabia, UAE

high income countries
another term for the industrialized countries with high per capita GDPs; see developed countries (DCs)

Indian Ocean Commission (InOC)
established—21 December 1982
aim—to organize and promote regional cooperation in all sectors, especially economic
members—(5) Comoros, France (for Reunion), Madagascar, Mauritius, Seychelles

industrial countries
another term for the developed countries; see developed countries (DCs)

Inter-American Development Bank (IADB)
note—also known as Banco Interamericano de Desarrollo (BID)
established—8 April 1959; effective—30 December 1959
aim—to promote economic and social development in Latin America
members—(48) Argentina, Austria, The Bahamas, Barbados, Belgium, Belize, Bolivia, Brazil, Canada, Chile, China, Colombia, Costa Rica, Croatia, Denmark, Dominican Republic, Ecuador, El Salvador, Finland, France, Germany, Guatemala, Guyana, Haiti, Honduras, Israel, Italy, Jamaica, Japan, South Korea, Mexico, Netherlands, Nicaragua, Norway, Panama, Paraguay, Peru, Portugal, Slovenia, Spain, Suriname, Sweden, Switzerland, Trinidad and Tobago, UK, US, Uruguay, Venezuela

Inter-Governmental Authority on Development (IGAD)
note—formerly known as Inter-Governmental Authority on Drought and Development (IGADD)
established—15-16 January 1986 as the Inter-Governmental Authority on Drought and Development; revitalized—21 March 1996 as the Inter-Governmental Authority on Development
aim—to promote a social, economic, and scientific community among its members
members—(6) Djibouti, Ethiopia, Kenya, Somalia, Sudan, Uganda; note—Eritrea declared its suspension in 2007
partners—(20) Austria, Belgium, Canada, Denmark, EC, France, Germany, Greece, International Organization for Migration, Ireland, Italy, Japan, Netherlands, Norway, Sweden, Switzerland, UK, UN Development Program, US, World Bank

Inter-Parliamentary Union (IPU)
established—1889
aim—fosters contacts among parliamentarians, considers and expresses views of international interest and concern with the purpose of bringing about action by parliaments and parliamentarians, contributes to the defense and promotion of human rights, contributes to better knowledge of representative institutions
members—(162 and the Palestine Liberation Organization) Afghanistan, Albania, Algeria, Andorra, Angola, Argentina, Armenia, Australia, Austria, Azerbaijan, Bahrain, Bangladesh, Belarus, Belgium, Benin, Bhutan, Bolivia, Bosnia and Herzegovina, Botswana, Brazil, Bulgaria, Burkina Faso, Burma, Burundi, Cambodia, Cabo Verde, Cameroon, Canada, Chad, Chile, China, Colombia, Democratic Republic of the Congo, Republic of the Congo, Costa Rica, Cote d'Ivoire, Croatia, Cuba, Cyprus, Czech Republic, Denmark, Djibouti, Dominican Republic, Ecuador, El Salvador, Equatorial Guinea, Estonia, Ethiopia, Finland, France, Gabon, The Gambia, Georgia, Germany, Ghana, Greece, Guatemala, Guinea-Bissau, Haiti, Honduras, Hungary, Iceland, India, Indonesia, Iran, Iraq, Ireland, Israel, Italy, Japan, Jordan, Kazakhstan, Kenya, North Korea, South Korea, Kuwait, Kyrgyzstan, Laos, Latvia, Lebanon, Lesotho, Libya, Liechtenstein, Lithuania, Luxembourg, Macedonia, Malawi, Malaysia, Maldives, Mali, Malta, Mauritania, Mauritius, Mexico, Federated States of Micronesia, Moldova, Monaco, Mongolia, Montenegro, Morocco, Mozambique, Namibia, Nepal, Netherlands, NZ, Nicaragua, Niger, Nigeria, Norway, Oman, Pakistan, Palau, Panama, Papua New Guinea, Paraguay, Peru, Philippines, Poland, Portugal, Qatar, Romania, Russia, Rwanda, Samoa, San Marino, Sao Tome and Principe, Saudi Arabia, Senegal, Serbia, Seychelles, Sierra Leone, Singapore, Slovakia, Slovenia, Somalia, South Africa, South Sudan, Spain, Sri Lanka, Sudan, Suriname, Sweden, Switzerland, Syria, Tanzania, Tajikistan, Thailand, Timor-Leste, Togo, Trinidad and Tobago, Tunisia, Turkey, Uganda, Ukraine, UAE, UK, Uruguay, Venezuela, Vietnam, Yemen, Zambia, Zimbabwe, Palestine Liberation Organization
associate members—(10) Andean Parliament, Central American Parliament, East African Legislative Assembly, European Parliament, Inter-Parliamentary Committee of the West African Economic and Monetary Union, Latin American Parliament, Parliament of the Economic Community of West African States, Parliament of the Economic and Monetary Community of Central Africa, Parliamentary Assembly of the Council of Europe, Transitional Arab Parliament

International Atomic Energy Agency (IAEA)
established—26 October 1956; effective—29 July 1957
aim—to promote peaceful uses of atomic energy
members—(162) Afghanistan, Albania, Algeria, Angola, Argentina, Armenia, Australia, Austria, Azerbaijan, The Bahamas, Bahrain, Bangladesh, Belarus, Belgium, Belize, Benin, Bolivia, Bosnia and Herzegovina, Botswana, Brazil, Brunei, Bulgaria, Burkina Faso, Burma, Burundi, Cabo Verde, Cambodia, Cameroon, Canada, Central African Republic, Chad, Chile, China, Colombia, Democratic Republic of the Congo, Republic of the Congo, Costa Rica, Cote d'Ivoire, Croatia, Cuba, Cyprus, Czech Republic, Denmark, Dominica, Dominican Republic, Ecuador, Egypt, El Salvador, Eritrea, Estonia, Ethiopia, Fiji, Finland, France, Gabon, Georgia, Germany, Ghana, Greece, Guatemala, Haiti, Holy See, Honduras, Hungary, Iceland, India, Indonesia, Iran, Iraq, Ireland, Israel, Italy, Jamaica, Japan, Jordan, Kazakhstan, Kenya, South Korea, Kuwait, Kyrgyzstan, Laos, Latvia, Lebanon, Lesotho, Liberia, Libya, Liechtenstein, Lithuania, Luxembourg, Macedonia, Madagascar, Malawi, Malaysia, Mali, Malta, Marshall Islands, Mauritania, Mauritius, Mexico, Moldova, Monaco, Mongolia, Montenegro, Morocco, Mozambique, Namibia, Nepal, Netherlands, NZ, Nicaragua, Niger, Nigeria, Norway, Oman, Pakistan, Palau, Panama, Papua New Guinea, Paraguay, Peru, Philippines, Poland, Portugal, Qatar, Romania, Russia, Rwanda, San Marino, Saudi Arabia, Senegal, Serbia, Seychelles, Sierra Leone, Singapore, Slovakia, Slovenia, South Africa, Spain, Sri Lanka, Sudan, Swaziland, Sweden, Switzerland, Syria, Tajikistan, Tanzania, Thailand, Togo, Tonga, Trinidad and Tobago, Tunisia, Turkey, Uganda, Ukraine, UAE, UK, US, Uruguay, Uzbekistan, Venezuela, Vietnam, Yemen, Zambia, Zimbabwe

International Bank for Reconstruction and Development (IBRD)
note—also known as the World Bank
established—22 July 1944; effective—27 December 1945
aim—to provide economic development loans; a UN specialized agency
members—(188) includes all UN member countries except Andorra, Cuba, North Korea, Liechtenstein, Monaco, Nauru; plus Kosovo

International Chamber of Commerce (ICC)
established—1919
aim—to promote free trade and private enterprise and to represent business interests at national and international levels
members—128 plus the Palestine Liberation Organization
countries with national committees—(93 and the Palestine Liberation Organization) Albania, Algeria, Argentina, Australia, Austria, Bahrain, Bangladesh, Belgium, Bolivia, Brazil, Bulgaria, Burkina Faso, Cameroon, Canada, Caribbean, Chile, China, Colombia, Costa Rica, Croatia, Cuba, Cyprus, Czech Republic, Denmark, Dominican Republic, Ecuador, Egypt, El Salvador, Estonia, Finland, France, Georgia, Germany, Ghana, Greece, Guatemala, Hong Kong, Hungary, Iceland, India, Indonesia, Iran, Ireland, Israel, Italy, Japan, Jordan, Kenya, South Korea, Kuwait, Lebanon, Lithuania, Luxembourg, Macao, Madagascar, Malaysia, Mexico, Monaco, Morocco, Netherlands, NZ, Nigeria, Norway, Pakistan, Panama, Philippines, Poland, Portugal, Qatar, Romania, Russia, Saudi Arabia, Senegal, Serbia, Singapore, Slovakia, Slovenia, South Africa, Spain, Sri Lanka, Sweden, Switzerland, Syria, Taiwan, Thailand, Togo, Tunisia, Turkey, Ukraine, UAE, UK, US, Uruguay, Palestine Liberation Organization; note—Peru is restructuring
countries with no national committees having direct members—(35) Afghanistan, Andorra, Armenia, Azerbaijan, Belarus, Bermuda, Bosnia and Herzegovina, Botswana, Democratic Republic of the Congo, Burma, Cote d'Ivoire, Eritrea, Ethiopia, Gibraltar, Haiti, Honduras, Iraq, North Korea, Latvia, Liberia, Macedonia, Malta, Mauritania, Mauritius, Moldova, Mongolia, Montenegro, Mozambique, Oman, Peru, Sudan, Tajikistan, Tanzania, Uganda, Vietnam

International Civil Aviation Organization (ICAO)
established—7 December 1944; effective—4 April 1947
aim—to promote international cooperation in civil aviation; a UN specialized agency
members—(191) includes all UN member countries except Dominica, Liechtenstein, and Tuvalu (190 total); plus Cook Islands

International Civilian Support Mission in Haiti (MICAH)
established 17 December 1999 to promote respect for human rights; members included Argentina, Benin, Canada, France, India, Mali, Niger, Senegal, Togo, Tunisia, US; closed 2001

International Committee of the Red Cross (ICRC)
established—17 February 1863
aim—to provide humanitarian aid in wartime
members—(15-25 individuals) all Swiss nationals

International Court of Justice (ICJ)
also known as the World Court; primary judicial organ of the UN
established—26 June 1945 with the signing of the UN Charter (inaugural sitting of the Court was on 18 April 1946); superseded Permanent Court of International Justice (attached to the League of Nations)
aim—to settle disputes submitted by member states and to provide advice to UN organs and other international agencies
members—(15 judges) elected by the UN General Assembly and Security Council to represent all principal legal systems; judges elected to nine-year terms (eligible for two additional terms); elections held every three years for one-third of the judges
jurisdiction—based on the principle of consent in contentious issues; consent to compulsory jurisdiction is outlined in Statute 36 of the ICJ; states provide declarations of consent to compulsory jurisdiction of the ICJ either with or without reservations (date in parens after each state is when the declaration was deposited with the UN Secretary-General); Haiti, Luxembourg, Nicaragua, and Uruguay deposited declarations with the Permanent Court of International Justice prior to 1945 and these were later transferred to the ICJ)
states accepting compulsory jurisdiction with reservations—(56) Australia (22 March 2002), Barbados (1 August 1980), Belgium (17 June 1958), Botswana (16 March 1970), Bulgaria (21 June 1992), Cambodia (19 September 1957), Canada (10 May 1994), Democratic Republic of the Congo (8 February 1989), Cote d'Ivoire (29 September 2001), Cyprus (3 September 2002), Denmark (10 December 1956), Djibouti (2 September 2005), Egypt (22 July 1957), Estonia (31 October 1991), Finland (25 June 1958), The Gambia (22 June 1966), Germany (30 April 2008), Greece (10 January 1994), Guinea (4 December 1998), Honduras (6 June 1986), Hungary (22 October 1992), India (18 September 1974), Japan (9 July 2007), Kenya (19 April 1965), Lesotho (6 September 2000), Liberia (20 March 1952), Liechtenstein (29 March 1950), Lithuania (26 September 2012), Madagascar (2 July 1992), Malawi (12 December 1966), Malta (2 September 1983), Marshall Islands (23 April 2013), Mauritius (23 September 1968), Mexico (28 October 1947), Netherlands (1 August 1956), New Zealand (23 September 1977), Nicaragua (24 September 1929), Nigeria (30 April 1998), Norway (25 June 1996), Pakistan (13 September 1960), Panama (25 October 1921), Peru (7 July 2003), Philippines (18 January 1972), Poland (25 March 1996), Portugal (25 February 2005), Senegal (2 December 1985), Slovakia (28 May 2004), Somalia (11 April 1963), Spain (20 October 1990), Sudan (2 January 1958), Suriname (31 August 1987), Swaziland (26 May 1969), Sweden (6 April 1957), Switzerland (28 July 1948), Togo (25 October 1979), Uganda (3 October 1963), United Kingdom (5 July 2004)
states accepting compulsory jurisdiction without reservations—(13) Austria (19 May 1971), Cameroon (3 March 1994), Costa Rica (20 February 1973), Dominica (31 March 2006), Dominican Republic (30 September 1924), Georgia (20 June 1995), Guinea-Bissau (7 August 1989), Haiti (4 October 1921), Ireland (15 December 2011), Luxembourg (15 September 1930), Paraguay (25 September 1996), Timor-Leste (21 September 2012), Uruguay (28 January 1921)

International Criminal Court (ICCt)
established—1 July 2002
aim—to hold all individuals and countries accountable to international laws of conduct; to specify international standards of conduct; to provide an important mechanism for implementing these standards; to ensure that perpetrators are brought to justice
members—21 judges (three judges form the Presidency) and six judges each in the Pre-trial, Trial, and Appeals Divisions; judges elected by secret ballot by the Assembly of States Parties to the Rome Statute for nine-year terms (not eligible for reelection) governed by the Statute

of the International Criminal Court treaty (or Rome Statute), adopted 17 July 1998 at the UN Conference of Plenipotentiaries in Rome and entered into force 1 July 2002
states accepting jurisdiction—(122) Afghanistan, Albania, Andorra, Antigua and Barbuda, Argentina, Australia, Austria, Bangladesh, Barbados, Belgium, Belize, Benin, Bolivia, Bosnia and Herzegovina, Botswana, Brazil, Bulgaria, Burkina Faso, Burundi, Cambodia, Canada, Cabo Verde, Central African Republic, Chad, Chile, Colombia, Comoros, Cook Islands, Democratic Republic of the Congo, Republic of the Congo, Costa Rica, Cote d'Ivoire, Croatia, Cyprus, Czech Republic, Denmark, Djibouti, Dominica, Dominican Republic, Ecuador, Estonia, Fiji, Finland, France, Gabon, The Gambia, Georgia, Germany, Ghana, Greece, Grenada, Guatemala, Guinea, Guyana, Honduras, Hungary, Iceland, Ireland, Italy, Japan, Jordan, Kenya, South Korea, Latvia, Lesotho, Liberia, Liechtenstein, Lithuania, Luxembourg, Macedonia, Madagascar, Malawi, Maldives, Mali, Malta, Marshall Islands, Mauritius, Mexico, Moldova, Mongolia, Montenegro, Namibia, Nauru, Netherlands, NZ, Niger, Nigeria, Norway, Panama, Paraguay, Peru, Philippines, Poland, Portugal, Romania, Saint Kitts and Nevis, Saint Lucia, Saint Vincent and the Grenadines, Samoa, San Marino, Senegal, Serbia, Seychelles, Sierra Leone, Slovakia, Slovenia, South Africa, Spain, Suriname, Sweden, Switzerland, Tajikistan, Tanzania, Timor-Leste, Trinidad and Tobago, Tunisia, Uganda, UK, Uruguay, Vanuatu, Venezuela, Zambia

International Criminal Police Organization (Interpol)
established—September 1923 set up as the International Criminal Police Commission; 13 June 1956 constitution modified and present name adopted
aim—to promote international cooperation among police authorities in fighting crime
members—(190) Afghanistan, Albania, Algeria, Andorra, Angola, Antigua and Barbuda, Argentina, Armenia, Aruba, Australia, Austria, Azerbaijan, The Bahamas, Bahrain, Bangladesh, Barbados, Belarus, Belgium, Belize, Benin, Bhutan, Bolivia, Bosnia and Herzegovina, Botswana, Brazil, Brunei, Bulgaria, Burkina Faso, Burma, Burundi, Cabo Verde, Cambodia, Cameroon, Canada, Central African Republic, Chad, Chile, China, Colombia, Comoros, Democratic Republic of the Congo, Republic of the Congo, Costa Rica, Cote d'Ivoire, Croatia, Cuba, Curacao, Cyprus, Czech Republic, Denmark, Djibouti, Dominica, Dominican Republic, Ecuador, Egypt, El Salvador, Equatorial Guinea, Eritrea, Estonia, Ethiopia, Fiji, Finland, France, Gabon, The Gambia, Georgia, Germany, Ghana, Greece, Grenada, Guatemala, Guinea, Guinea-Bissau, Guyana, Haiti, Holy See, Honduras, Hungary, Iceland, India, Indonesia, Iran, Iraq, Ireland, Israel, Italy, Jamaica, Japan, Jordan, Kazakhstan, Kenya, South Korea, Kuwait, Kyrgyzstan, Laos, Latvia, Lebanon, Lesotho, Liberia, Libya, Liechtenstein, Lithuania, Luxembourg, Macedonia, Madagascar, Malawi, Malaysia, Maldives, Mali, Malta, Marshall Islands, Mauritania, Mauritius, Mexico, Moldova, Monaco, Mongolia, Montenegro, Morocco, Mozambique, Namibia, Nauru, Nepal, Netherlands, NZ, Nicaragua, Niger, Nigeria, Norway, Oman, Pakistan, Panama, Papua New Guinea, Paraguay, Peru, Philippines, Poland, Portugal, Qatar, Romania, Russia, Rwanda, Saint Kitts and Nevis, Saint Lucia, Saint Vincent and the Grenadines, Samoa, San Marino, Sao Tome and Principe, Saudi Arabia, Senegal, Serbia, Seychelles, Sierra Leone, Singapore, Sint Maarten, Slovakia, Slovenia, Somalia, South Africa, South Sudan, Spain, Sri Lanka, Sudan, Suriname, Swaziland, Sweden, Switzerland, Syria, Tajikistan, Tanzania, Thailand, Timor-Leste, Togo, Tonga, Trinidad and Tobago, Tunisia, Turkey, Turkmenistan, Uganda, Ukraine, UAE, UK, US, Uruguay, Uzbekistan, Venezuela, Vietnam, Yemen, Zambia, Zimbabwe
subbureaus—(11) American Samoa, Anguilla, Bermuda, British Virgin Islands, Cayman Islands, Gibraltar, Hong Kong, Macau, Montserrat, Puerto Rico, Turks and Caicos Islands

International Development Association (IDA)
established—26 January 1960; effective—24 September 1960
aim—to provide economic loans for low-income countries; UN specialized agency and IBRD affiliate
members—(173) Afghanistan, Albania, Algeria, Angola, Argentina, Armenia, Australia, Austria, Azerbaijan, The Bahamas, Bangladesh, Barbados, Belgium, Belize, Benin, Bhutan, Bolivia, Bosnia and Herzegovina, Botswana, Brazil, Burkina Faso, Burma, Burundi, Cabo Verde, Cambodia, Cameroon, Canada, Central African Republic, Chad, Chile, China, Colombia, Comoros, Democratic Republic of the Congo, Republic of the Congo, Costa Rica, Cote d'Ivoire, Croatia, Cyprus, Czech Republic, Denmark, Djibouti, Dominica, Dominican Republic, Ecuador, Egypt, El Salvador, Equatorial Guinea, Eritrea, Estonia, Ethiopia, EU, Fiji, Finland, France, Gabon, The Gambia, Georgia, Germany, Ghana, Greece, Grenada, Guatemala, Guinea, Guinea-Bissau, Guyana, Haiti, Honduras, Hungary, Iceland, India, Indonesia, Iran, Iraq, Ireland, Israel, Italy, Japan, Jordan, Kazakhstan, Kenya, Kiribati, South Korea, Kosovo, Kuwait, Kyrgyzstan, Laos, Latvia, Lebanon, Lesotho, Liberia, Libya, Lithuania, Luxembourg, Macedonia, Madagascar, Malawi, Malaysia, Maldives, Mali, Marshall Islands, Mauritania, Mauritius, Mexico, Federated States of Micronesia, Moldova, Mongolia, Montenegro, Morocco, Mozambique, Nepal, Netherlands, NZ, Nicaragua, Niger, Nigeria, Norway, Oman, Pakistan, Palau, Panama, Papua New Guinea, Paraguay, Peru, Philippines, Poland, Portugal, Russia, Rwanda, Saint Kitts and Nevis, Saint Lucia, Saint Vincent and the Grenadines, Samoa, Sao Tome and Principe, Saudi Arabia, Senegal, Serbia, Sierra Leone, Singapore, Slovakia, Slovenia, Solomon Islands, Somalia, South Africa, South Sudan, Spain, Sri Lanka, Sudan, Swaziland, Sweden, Switzerland, Syria, Tajikistan, Tanzania, Thailand, Timor-Leste, Togo, Tonga, Trinidad and Tobago, Tunisia, Turkey, Tuvalu, Uganda, Ukraine, UAE, UK, US, Uzbekistan, Vanuatu, Vietnam, Yemen, Zambia, Zimbabwe

International Energy Agency (IEA)
established—15 November 1974
aim—to promote cooperation on energy matters, especially emergency oil sharing and relations between oil consumers and oil producers; established by the OECD
members—(29) Australia, Austria, Belgium, Canada, Czech Republic, Denmark, EC, Finland, France, Germany, Greece, Hungary, Ireland, Italy, Japan, South Korea, Luxembourg, Netherlands, NZ, Norway, Poland, Portugal, Slovakia, Spain, Sweden, Switzerland, Turkey, UK, US

International Federation of Red Cross and Red Crescent Societies (IFRCS)
note—formerly known as League of Red Cross and Red Crescent Societies (LORCS)
established—5 May 1919
aim—to organize, coordinate, and direct international relief actions; to promote humanitarian activities; to represent and encourage the development of National Societies; to bring help to victims of armed conflicts, refugees, and displaced people; to reduce the vulnerability of people through development programs
members—(187 plus the Palestine Liberation Organization) Afghanistan, Albania, Algeria, Andorra, Angola, Antigua and Barbuda, Argentina, Armenia, Australia, Austria, Azerbaijan, The Bahamas, Bahrain, Bangladesh, Barbados, Belarus, Belgium, Belize, Benin, Bolivia, Bosnia and Herzegovina, Botswana, Brazil, Brunei, Bulgaria, Burkina Faso, Burma, Burundi, Cabo Verde, Cambodia, Cameroon, Canada, Central African Republic, Chad, Chile, China, Colombia, Comoros, Democratic Republic of the Congo, Republic of the Congo, Cook Islands, Costa Rica, Cote d'Ivoire, Croatia, Cuba, Czech Republic, Denmark, Djibouti, Dominica, Dominican Republic, Ecuador, Egypt, El Salvador, Equatorial Guinea, Estonia, Ethiopia, Fiji, Finland, France, Gabon, The Gambia, Georgia, Germany, Ghana, Greece, Grenada,

Guatemala, Guinea, Guinea-Bissau, Guyana, Haiti, Honduras, Hungary, Iceland, India, Indonesia, Iran, Iraq, Ireland, Israel, Italy, Jamaica, Japan, Jordan, Kazakhstan, Kenya, Kiribati, North Korea, South Korea, Kuwait, Kyrgyzstan, Laos, Latvia, Lebanon, Lesotho, Liberia, Libya, Liechtenstein, Lithuania, Luxembourg, Macedonia, Madagascar, Malawi, Malaysia, Maldives, Mali, Malta, Mauritania, Mauritius, Mexico, Federated States of Micronesia, Moldova, Monaco, Mongolia, Montenegro, Morocco, Mozambique, Namibia, Nepal, Netherlands, NZ, Nicaragua, Niger, Nigeria, Norway, Pakistan, Palau, Panama, Papua New Guinea, Paraguay, Peru, Philippines, Poland, Portugal, Qatar, Romania, Russia, Rwanda, Saint Kitts and Nevis, Saint Lucia, Saint Vincent and the Grenadines, Samoa, San Marino, Sao Tome and Principe, Saudi Arabia, Senegal, Serbia, Seychelles, Sierra Leone, Singapore, Slovakia, Slovenia, Solomon Islands, Somalia, South Africa, South Sudan, Spain, Sri Lanka, Sudan, Suriname, Swaziland, Sweden, Switzerland, Syria, Tajikistan, Tanzania, Thailand, Timor-Leste, Togo, Tonga, Trinidad and Tobago, Tunisia, Turkey, Turkmenistan, Uganda, Ukraine, UAE, UK, US, Uruguay, Uzbekistan, Vanuatu, Venezuela, V
observers—(3) Cyprus, Eritrea, and Tuvalu

International Finance Corporation (IFC)
established—25 May 1955; effective—24 July 1956
aim—to support private enterprise in international economic development; a UN specialized agency and IBRD affiliate
members—(183) includes all UN member countries except Andorra, Brunei, Cuba, North Korea, Liechtenstein, Monaco, Nauru, Saint Vincent and the Grenadines, San Marino, Tuvalu; plus Kosovo

International Fund for Agricultural Development (IFAD)
established—November 1974
aim—to promote agricultural development; a UN specialized agency
members—(168)
List A—(23 industrialized aid contributors) Belgium, Canada, Denmark, Estonia, Finland, France, Germany, Greece, Hungary, Iceland, Ireland, Italy, Japan, Luxembourg, Netherlands, NZ, Norway, Portugal, Spain, Sweden, Switzerland, UK, US
List B—(12 petroleum-exporting aid contributors) Algeria, Gabon, Indonesia, Iran, Iraq, Kuwait, Libya, Nigeria, Qatar, Saudi Arabia, UAE, Venezuela
List C—(133 aid recipients) Afghanistan, Albania, Angola, Antigua and Barbuda, Argentina, Armenia, Azerbaijan, The Bahamas, Bangladesh, Barbados, Belize, Benin, Bhutan, Bolivia, Bosnia and Herzegovina, Botswana, Brazil, Burkina Faso, Burma, Burundi, Cabo Verde, Cambodia, Cameroon, Central African Republic, Chad, Chile, China, Colombia, Comoros, Democratic Republic of the Congo, Republic of the Congo, Cook Islands, Costa Rica, Cote d'Ivoire, Croatia, Cuba, Cyprus, Djibouti, Dominica, Dominican Republic, Ecuador, Egypt, El Salvador, Equatorial Guinea, Eritrea, Ethiopia, Fiji, The Gambia, Georgia, Ghana, Grenada, Guatemala, Guinea, Guinea-Bissau, Guyana, Haiti, Honduras, India, Israel, Jamaica, Jordan, Kazakhstan, Kenya, Kiribati, North Korea, South Korea, Kyrgyzstan, Laos, Lebanon, Lesotho, Liberia, Macedonia, Madagascar, Malawi, Malaysia, Maldives, Mali, Malta, Marshall Islands, Mauritania, Mauritius, Mexico, Moldova, Mongolia, Morocco, Mozambique, Namibia, Nauru, Nepal, Nicaragua, Niger, Niue, Oman, Pakistan, Panama, Papua New Guinea, Paraguay, Peru, Philippines, Romania, Rwanda, Saint Kitts and Nevis, Saint Lucia, Saint Vincent and the Grenadines, Samoa, Sao Tome and Principe, Senegal, Seychelles, Sierra Leone, Solomon Islands, Somalia, South Africa, South Sudan, Sri Lanka, Sudan, Suriname, Swaziland, Syria, Tajikistan, Tanzania, Thailand, Timor-Leste, Togo, Tonga, Trinidad and Tobago, Tunisia, Turkey, Tuvalu, Uganda, Uruguay, Uzbekistan, Vanuatu, Vietnam, Yemen, Zambia, Zimbabwe

International Hydrographic Organization (IHO)
note—name changed from International Hydrographic Bureau on 22 September 1970
established—June 1919; effective—June 1921
aim—to train hydrographic surveyors and nautical cartographers to achieve standardization in nautical charts and electronic chart displays; to provide advice on nautical cartography and hydrography; to develop the sciences in the field of hydrography and techniques used for descriptive oceanography
members—(81) Algeria, Argentina, Australia, Bahrain, Bangladesh, Belgium, Brazil, Burma, Cameroon, Canada, Chile, China (including Hong Kong and Macau), Colombia, Democratic Republic of the Congo, Croatia, Cuba, Cyprus, Denmark, Dominican Republic, Ecuador, Egypt, Estonia, Fiji, Finland, France, Germany, Greece, Guatemala, Iceland, India, Indonesia, Iran, Ireland, Italy, Jamaica, Japan, North Korea, South Korea, Kuwait, Latvia, Malaysia, Mauritius, Mexico, Monaco, Morocco, Mozambique, Netherlands, NZ, Nigeria, Norway, Oman, Pakistan, Papua New Guinea, Peru, Philippines, Poland, Portugal, Qatar, Romania, Russia, Saudi Arabia, Serbia, Singapore, Slovenia, South Africa, Spain, Sri Lanka, Suriname, Sweden, Syria, Thailand, Tonga, Trinidad and Tobago, Tunisia, Turkey, Ukraine, UAE, UK, US, Uruguay, Venezuela; note—members approved but waiting for Instrument of Accession: Bulgaria, Mauritania, Montenegro, Sierra Leone

International Labor Organization (ILO)
established—28 June 1919 set up as part of Treaty of Versailles; 11 April 1919 became operative; 14 December 1946 affiliated with the UN
aim—to deal with world labor issues; a UN specialized agency
members—(185) includes all UN member countries except Andorra, Bhutan, North Korea, Liechtenstein, Federated States of Micronesia, Monaco, Nauru, Tonga; note—includes the following dependencies: Netherlands (Aruba, Curacao, Sint Maarten)

International Maritime Organization (IMO)
note—name changed from Intergovernmental Maritime Consultative Organization (IMCO) on 22 May 1982
established—6 March 1948 set up as the Inter-Governmental Maritime Consultative Organization; effective—17 March 1958
aim—to deal with international maritime affairs; a UN specialized agency
members—(170) includes all UN member countries except Afghanistan, Andorra, Armenia, Belarus, Bhutan, Botswana, Burkina Faso, Burundi, Central African Republic, Chad, Kyrgyzstan, Laos, Lesotho, Liechtenstein, Mali, Federated States of Micronesia, Nauru, Niger, Rwanda, South Sudan, Swaziland, Tajikistan, Uzbekistan, Zambia; and Cook Islands
associate members—(3) Faroe Islands, Hong Kong, Macau

International Mobile Satellite Organization (IMSO)
established—15 April 1999
aim—acts as watchdog over Inmarsat (International Maritime Satellite Organization), a private company, to make sure it follows ICAO standards and recommended practices; plays an active role in the development of international telecommunications policies

members—(98) Algeria, Antigua and Barbuda, Argentina, Australia, The Bahamas, Bahrain, Bangladesh, Belarus, Belgium, Bosnia and Herzegovina, Brazil, Brunei, Bulgaria, Cameroon, Canada, Chile, China, Colombia, Comoros, Cook Islands, Costa Rica, Croatia, Cuba, Cyprus, Czech Republic, Denmark, Egypt, Finland, France, Gabon, Germany, Ghana, Greece, Hungary, Iceland, India, Indonesia, Iran, Iraq, Israel, Italy, Japan, Kenya, North Korea, South Korea, Kuwait, Latvia, Lebanon, Liberia, Libya, Malaysia, Malta, Marshall Islands, Mauritius, Mexico, Monaco, Mongolia, Montenegro, Morocco, Mozambique, Netherlands, NZ, Nigeria, Norway, Oman, Pakistan, Palau, Panama, Peru, Philippines, Poland, Portugal, Qatar, Romania, Russia, Saudi Arabia, Senegal, Serbia, Singapore, Slovakia, South Africa, Spain, Sri Lanka, Sweden, Switzerland, Tanzania, Thailand, Tonga, Tunisia, Turkey, Ukraine, UAE, UK, US, Vanuatu, Venezuela, Vietnam, Yemen

International Monetary Fund (IMF)
established—22 July 1944; effective—27 December 1945
aim—to promote world monetary stability and economic development; a UN specialized agency
members—(188) includes all UN member countries except Andorra, Cuba, North Korea, Liechtenstein, Monaco, Nauru; plus Kosovo; note—includes the following dependencies or areas of special interest: China (Hong Kong and Macau), Netherlands (Aruba, Curacao, Sint Maarten)

International Olympic Committee (IOC)
established—23 June 1894
aim—to promote the Olympic ideals and administer the Olympic games: 2012 Summer Olympics in London, UK; 2014 Winter Olympics in Sochi, Russia
National Olympic Committees—(204 and the Palestine Liberation Organization) Afghanistan, Albania, Algeria, American Samoa, Andorra, Angola, Antigua and Barbuda, Argentina, Armenia, Aruba, Australia, Austria, Azerbaijan, The Bahamas, Bahrain, Bangladesh, Barbados, Belarus, Belgium, Belize, Benin, Bermuda, Bhutan, Bolivia, Bosnia and Herzegovina, Botswana, Brazil, British Virgin Islands, Brunei, Bulgaria, Burkina Faso, Burma, Burundi, Cabo Verde, Cambodia, Cameroon, Canada, Cayman Islands, Central African Republic, Chad, Chile, China, Colombia, Comoros, Democratic Republic of the Congo, Republic of the Congo, Cook Islands, Costa Rica, Cote d'Ivoire, Croatia, Cuba, Cyprus, Czech Republic, Denmark, Djibouti, Dominica, Dominican Republic, Ecuador, Egypt, El Salvador, Equatorial Guinea, Eritrea, Estonia, Ethiopia, Fiji, Finland, France, Gabon, The Gambia, Georgia, Germany, Ghana, Greece, Grenada, Guam, Guatemala, Guinea, Guinea-Bissau, Guyana, Haiti, Honduras, Hong Kong, Hungary, Iceland, India, Indonesia, Iran, Iraq, Ireland, Israel, Italy, Jamaica, Japan, Jordan, Kazakhstan, Kenya, Kiribati, North Korea, South Korea, Kuwait, Kyrgyzstan, Laos, Latvia, Lebanon, Lesotho, Liberia, Libya, Liechtenstein, Lithuania, Luxembourg, Macedonia, Madagascar, Malawi, Malaysia, Maldives, Mali, Malta, Marshall Islands, Mauritania, Mauritius, Mexico, Federated States of Micronesia, Moldova, Monaco, Mongolia, Montenegro, Morocco, Mozambique, Namibia, Nauru, Nepal, Netherlands, NZ, Nicaragua, Niger, Nigeria, Norway, Oman, Pakistan, Palau, Panama, Papua New Guinea, Paraguay, Peru, Philippines, Poland, Portugal, Puerto Rico, Qatar, Romania, Russia, Rwanda, Saint Kitts and Nevis, Saint Lucia, Saint Vincent and the Grenadines, Samoa, San Marino, Sao Tome and Principe, Saudi Arabia, Senegal, Serbia, Seychelles, Sierra Leone, Singapore, Slovakia, Slovenia, Solomon Islands, Somalia, South Africa, Spain, Sri Lanka, Sudan, Suriname, Swaziland, Sweden, Switzerland, Syria, Taiwan, Tajikistan, Tanzania, Thailand, Timor-Leste, Togo, Tonga, Trinidad and Tobago, Tunisia, Turkey, Turkmenistan, Tuvalu, Uganda, Ukraine, UAE, UK, US, Uruguay, Uzbekistan, Vanuatu, Venezuela, Vietnam, Virgin Islands, Yemen, Zambia, Zimbabwe, Palestine Liberation Organization

International Organization for Migration (IOM)
note—established as Provisional Intergovernmental Committee for the Movement of Migrants from Europe; renamed Intergovernmental Committee for European Migration (ICEM) on 15 November 1952; renamed Intergovernmental Committee for Migration (ICM) in November 1980; current name adopted 14 November 1989
established—5 December 1951
aim—to facilitate orderly international emigration and immigration
members—(151) Afghanistan, Albania, Algeria, Angola, Antigua and Barbuda, Argentina, Armenia, Australia, Austria, Azerbaijan, The Bahamas, Bangladesh, Belarus, Belgium, Belize, Benin, Bolivia, Bosnia and Herzegovina, Botswana, Brazil, Bulgaria, Burkina Faso, Burma, Burundi, Cabo Verde, Cambodia, Cameroon, Canada, Central African Republic, Chad, Chile, Colombia, Comoros, Democratic Republic of the Congo, Republic of the Congo, Costa Rica, Cote d'Ivoire, Croatia, Cyprus, Czech Republic, Denmark, Djibouti, Dominican Republic, Ecuador, Egypt, El Salvador, Estonia, Ethiopia, Finland, France, Gabon, The Gambia, Georgia, Germany, Ghana, Greece, Guatemala, Guinea, Guinea-Bissau, Guyana, Haiti, Holy See, Honduras, Hungary, India, Iran, Ireland, Israel, Italy, Jamaica, Japan, Jordan, Kazakhstan, Kenya, South Korea, Kyrgyzstan, Latvia, Lesotho, Liberia, Libya, Lithuania, Luxembourg, Madagascar, Malawi, Maldives, Mali, Malta, Mauritania, Mauritius, Mexico, Federation of Micronesia, Moldova, Mongolia, Montenegro, Morocco, Mozambique, Namibia, Nauru, Nepal, Netherlands, NZ, Nicaragua, Niger, Nigeria, Norway, Pakistan, Panama, Papua New Guinea, Paraguay, Peru, Philippines, Poland, Portugal, Romania, Rwanda, Saint Vincent and the Grenadines, Senegal, Serbia, Seychelles, Sierra Leone, Slovakia, Slovenia, Somalia, South Africa, South Sudan, Spain, Sri Lanka, Sudan, Suriname, Swaziland, Sweden, Switzerland, Tajikistan, Tanzania, Thailand, Timor-Leste, Togo, Trinidad and Tobago, Tunisia, Turkey, Uganda, Ukraine, UK, US, Uruguay, Vanuatu, Venezuela, Vietnam, Yemen, Zambia, Zimbabwe
observers—(12) Bahrain, Bhutan, China, Cuba, Indonesia, Macedonia, Qatar, Russia, San Marino, Sao Tome and Principe, Saudi Arabia, Turkmenistan

International Organization for Standardization (ISO)
established—February 1947
aim—to promote the development of international standards with a view to facilitating international exchange of goods and services and to developing cooperation in the sphere of intellectual, scientific, technological and economic activity
members—(114 national standards organizations) Algeria, Argentina, Armenia, Australia, Austria, Azerbaijan, Bahrain, Bangladesh, Barbados, Belarus, Belgium, Bosnia and Herzegovina, Botswana, Brazil, Bulgaria, Cameroon, Canada, Chile, China, Colombia, Democratic Republic of the Congo, Costa Rica, Cote d'Ivoire, Croatia, Cuba, Cyprus, Czech Republic, Denmark, Ecuador, Egypt, El Salvador, Estonia, Ethiopia, Fiji, Finland, France, Gabon, Germany, Ghana, Greece, Hungary, Iceland, India, Indonesia, Iran, Iraq, Ireland, Israel, Italy, Jamaica, Japan, Jordan, Kazakhstan, Kenya, North Korea, South Korea, Kuwait, Lebanon, Libya, Lithuania, Luxembourg, Macedonia, Malaysia, Mali, Malta, Mauritius, Mexico, Mongolia, Morocco, Namibia, Netherlands, NZ, Nigeria, Norway, Oman, Pakistan, Panama, Peru, Philippines, Poland, Portugal, Qatar, Romania, Russia, Rwanda, Saint Lucia, Saudi Arabia, Senegal, Serbia, Singapore, Slovakia, Slovenia, South Africa, Spain, Sri Lanka, Sudan, Sweden, Switzerland, Syria, Tanzania, Thailand, Trinidad and Tobago, Tunisia, Turkey, Uganda, Ukraine, UAE, UK, US, Uruguay, Uzbekistan, Vietnam, Yemen, Zimbabwe

correspondent members—(45 plus the Palestine Liberation Organization) Afghanistan, Albania, Angola, Benin, Bhutan, Bolivia, Brunei, Burkina Faso, Burma, Burundi, Cambodia, Republic of the Congo, Dominica, Dominican Republic, Eritrea, Gabon, The Gambia, Georgia, Guatemala, Guinea, Guyana, Hong Kong, Kyrgyzstan, Latvia, Lesotho, Liberia, Macau, Madagascar, Malawi, Mauritania, Moldova, Montenegro, Mozambique, Nepal, Nicaragua, Niger, Papua New Guinea, Paraguay, Seychelles, Sierra Leone, Suriname, Swaziland, Tajikistan, Togo, Turkmenistan, Zambia, Palestine Liberation Organization
subscriber members—(4) Antigua and Barbuda, Honduras, Laos, Saint Vincent and the Grenadines

International Organization of the French-speaking World (OIF)
note—name changed from Agency of Cultural and Technical Cooperation (ACCT) in 1997; also known as Organisation Internationale de la Francophonie
established—20 March 1970
aim—founded around a common language to promote and spread the cultures of its members and to reinforce cultural and technical cooperation between them
members—(57) Albania, Andorra, Armenia, Belgium, Benin, Bulgaria, Burkina Faso, Burundi, Cabo Verde, Cambodia, Cameroon, Canada, Canada - New Brunswick, Canada - Quebec, Central African Republic, Chad, Comoros, Democratic Republic of Congo, Republic of Congo, Cote d'Ivoire, Cyprus, Djibouti, Dominica, Egypt, Equatorial Guinea, France, French Community of Belgium, Gabon, Ghana, Greece, Guinea, Guinea-Bissau, Haiti, Laos, Lebanon, Luxembourg, Macedonia, Madagascar, Mali, Mauritania, Mauritius, Moldova, Monaco, Morocco, Niger, Qatar, Romania, Rwanda, Saint Lucia, Sao Tome and Principe, Senegal, Seychelles, Switzerland, Togo, Tunisia, Vanuatu, Vietnam
observers—(20) Austria, Bosnia and Herzegovina, Croatia, Czech Republic, Dominican Republic, Estonia, Georgia, Hungary, Latvia, Lithuania, Montenegro, Mozambique, Poland, Serbia, Slovakia, Slovenia, Thailand, Ukraine, UAE, Uruguay

International Red Cross and Red Crescent Movement (ICRM)
established—1928
aim—to promote worldwide humanitarian aid through the International Committee of the Red Cross (ICRC) in wartime, and International Federation of Red Cross and Red Crescent Societies (IFRCS; formerly League of Red Cross and Red Crescent Societies or LORCS) in peacetime
National Societies—(187 countries and the Palestine Liberation Organization); note—same as membership for International Federation of Red Cross and Red Crescent Societies (IFRCS)

International Telecommunication Satellite Organization (ITSO)
established—August 1964
aim—to act as a watchdog over Intelsat, Ltd., a private company, to make sure it provides on a global and non-discriminatory basis public telecommunication services
members—(150) Afghanistan, Algeria, Angola, Argentina, Armenia, Australia, Austria, Azerbaijan, The Bahamas, Bahrain, Bangladesh, Barbados, Belgium, Benin, Bhutan, Bolivia, Bosnia and Herzegovina, Botswana, Brazil, Brunei, Bulgaria, Burkina Faso, Cabo Verde, Cameroon, Canada, Central African Republic, Chad, Chile, China, Colombia, Comoros, Democratic Republic of the Congo, Republic of the Congo, Costa Rica, Cote d'Ivoire, Croatia, Cuba, Cyprus, Czech Republic, Denmark, Dominican Republic, Ecuador, Egypt, El Salvador, Equatorial Guinea, Estonia, Ethiopia, Fiji, Finland, France, Gabon, The Gambia, Georgia, Germany, Ghana, Greece, Guatemala, Guinea, Guinea-Bissau, Haiti, Holy See, Honduras, Hungary, Iceland, India, Indonesia, Iran, Iraq, Ireland, Israel, Italy, Jamaica, Japan, Jordan, Kazakhstan, Kenya, North Korea, South Korea, Kuwait, Kyrgyzstan, Lebanon, Libya, Liechtenstein, Luxembourg, Madagascar, Malawi, Malaysia, Mali, Malta, Mauritania, Mauritius, Mexico, the Federated States of Micronesia, Monaco, Mongolia, Montenegro, Morocco, Mozambique, Namibia, Nepal, Netherlands, NZ, Nicaragua, Niger, Nigeria, Norway, Oman, Pakistan, Panama, Papua New Guinea, Paraguay, Peru, Philippines, Poland, Portugal, Qatar, Romania, Russia, Rwanda, Saudi Arabia, Senegal, Serbia, Singapore, Somalia, South Africa, Spain, Sri Lanka, Sudan, Swaziland, Sweden, Switzerland, Syria, Tajikistan, Tanzania, Thailand, Togo, Trinidad and Tobago, Tunisia, Turkey, Uganda, UAE, UK, US, Uruguay, Uzbekistan, Venezuela, Vietnam, Yemen, Zambia, Zimbabwe

International Telecommunication Union (ITU)
established—17 May 1865 set up as the International Telegraph Union; 9 December 1932 adopted present name; effective—1 January 1934; affiliated with the UN—15 November 1947
aim—to deal with world telecommunications issues; a UN specialized agency
members—(193) includes all UN member countries except Palau (192 total); plus Holy See

International Trade Union Confederation (ITUC)
note—its predecessors were the International Confederation of Free Trade Unions (ICFTU) and the World Confederation of Labor (WCL)
established—3 November 2006
aim—to promote the trade union movement
members—(325 affiliated organizations in 156 countries or territories and the Palestine Liberation Organization as of 2013) Albania, Algeria, Angola, Antigua and Barbuda, Aruba, Argentina, Australia, Austria, Azerbaijan, Bahrain, Bangladesh, Barbados, Belarus, Belgium, Belize, Benin, Bermuda, Bonaire, Bosnia and Herzegovina, Botswana, Brazil, Bulgaria, Burkina Faso, Burma, Burundi, Cabo Verde, Cambodia, Cameroon, Canada, Central African Republic, Chad, Chile, Colombia, Comoros, Democratic Republic of the Congo, Republic of the Congo, Cook Islands, Costa Rica, Cote d'Ivoire, Croatia, Curacao, Cyprus, Czech Republic, Denmark, Djibouti, Dominica, Dominican Republic, Ecuador, El Salvador, Eritrea, Estonia, Ethiopia, Fiji, Finland, France, French Polynesia, Gabon, The Gambia, Georgia, Germany, Ghana, Greece, Grenada, Guatemala, Guinea, Guinea-Bissau, Haiti, Holy See, Honduras, Hong Kong, Hungary, Iceland, India, Indonesia, Ireland, Israel, Italy, Japan, Jordan, Kenya, Kiribati, South Korea, Kosovo, Kuwait, Latvia, Liberia, Liechtenstein, Lithuania, Luxembourg, Macedonia, Madagascar, Malawi, Malaysia, Mali, Malta, Mauritania, Mauritius, Mexico, Moldova, Mongolia, Montenegro, Morocco, Mozambique, Namibia, Nepal, Netherlands, New Caledonia, NZ, Nicaragua, Niger, Nigeria, Norway, Pakistan, Panama, Paraguay, Peru, Philippines, Poland, Portugal, Romania, Russia, Rwanda, Saint Lucia, Samoa, San Marino, Sao Tome and Principe, Senegal, Serbia, Sierra Leone, Singapore, Slovakia, South Africa, Spain, Sri Lanka, Suriname, Swaziland, Sweden, Switzerland, Taiwan, Tanzania, Thailand, Togo, Tonga, Trinidad and Tobago, Tunisia, Turkey, Uganda, Ukraine, UK, US, Vanuatu, Venezuela, Yemen, Zambia, Zimbabwe, and the Palestine Liberation Organization

Islamic Development Bank (IDB)
established—15 December 1973 by declaration of intent; effective—12 August 1974
aim—to promote Islamic economic aid and social development
members—(55 plus the Palestine Liberation Organization) Afghanistan, Albania, Algeria, Azerbaijan, Bahrain, Bangladesh, Benin, Brunei, Burkina Faso, Cameroon, Chad, Comoros, Cote d'Ivoire, Djibouti, Egypt, Gabon, The Gambia, Guinea, Guinea-Bissau, Indonesia, Iran, Iraq, Jordan, Kazakhstan, Kuwait, Kyrgyzstan, Lebanon, Libya, Malaysia, Maldives, Mali, Mauritania, Morocco, Mozambique, Niger, Nigeria, Oman, Pakistan, Qatar, Saudi Arabia, Senegal, Sierra Leone, Somalia, Sudan, Suriname, Syria, Tajikistan, Togo, Tunisia, Turkey, Turkmenistan, Uganda, UAE, Uzbekistan, Yemen, Palestine Liberation Organization

Latin American and Caribbean Economic System (LAES)
note—also known as Sistema Economico Latinoamericana (SELA)
established—17 October 1975
aim—to promote economic and social development through regional cooperation
members—(28) Argentina, the Bahamas, Barbados, Belize, Bolivia, Brazil, Chile, Colombia, Costa Rica, Cuba, Dominican Republic, Ecuador, El Salvador, Grenada, Guatemala, Guyana, Haiti, Honduras, Jamaica, Mexico, Nicaragua, Panama, Paraguay, Peru, Suriname, Trinidad and Tobago, Uruguay, Venezuela

Latin American Integration Association (LAIA)
note—also known as Asociacion Latinoamericana de Integracion (ALADI)
established—12 August 1980; effective—18 March 1981
aim—to promote freer regional trade
members—(14) Argentina, Bolivia, Brazil, Chile, Colombia, Cuba, Ecuador, Mexico, Nicaragua, Panama, Paraguay, Peru, Uruguay, Venezuela
observers—(29) China, Corporacion Andina de Fomento, Costa Rica, Dominican Republic, EC, El Salvador, Guatemala, Honduras, Inter-American Development Bank, Inter-American Institute for Cooperation on Agriculture, Italy, Japan, South Korea, Latin America Economic System, Nicaragua, Organizacion Panamericana de la Salud, Organizacion Mundial de la Salud, Organization of American States, Pakistan, Portugal, Romania, Russia, San Marino, Secretaria General Iberoamericana, Spain, Switzerland, Ukraine, United Nations Development Program, United Nations Economic Commission for Latin America and the Caribbean

League of Arab States (LAS)
note—also known as Arab League (AL)
established—22 March 1945
aim—to promote economic, social, political, and military cooperation
members—(20 plus the Palestine Liberation Organization) Algeria, Bahrain, Comoros, Djibouti, Egypt, Iraq, Jordan, Kuwait, Lebanon, Libya, Mauritania, Morocco, Oman, Qatar, Saudi Arabia, Somalia, Sudan, Tunisia, UAE, Yemen, Palestine Liberation Organization
observers—(4) Brazil, Eritrea, India, Venezuela

least developed countries (LLDCs)
that subgroup of the less developed countries (LDCs) initially identified by the UN General Assembly in 1971 as having no significant economic growth, per capita GDPs normally less than $1,000, and low literacy rates; also known as the undeveloped countries; the 44 LLDCs are: Afghanistan, Bangladesh, Benin, Bhutan, Burkina Faso, Burma, Burundi, Cambodia, Cameroon, Central African Republic, Chad, Comoros, Democratic Republic of the Congo, Cote d'Ivoire, Equatorial Guinea, Eritrea, Ethiopia, The Gambia, Ghana, Guinea, Guinea-Bissau, Haiti, Kenya, Lesotho, Liberia, Malawi, Mali, Moldova, Mozambique, Nepal, Niger, Rwanda, Sao Tome and Principe, Senegal, Sierra Leone, Somalia, Sudan, Tajikistan, Tanzania, Togo, Tokelau, Tuvalu, Uganda, Zambia

less developed countries (LDCs)
the bottom group in the hierarchy of developed countries (DCs), former USSR/Eastern Europe (former USSR/EE), and less developed countries (LDCs); mainly countries and dependent areas with low levels of output, living standards, and technology; per capita GDPs are generally below $5,000 and often less than $1,500; however, the group also includes a number of countries with high per capita incomes, areas of advanced technology, and rapid rates of growth; includes the advanced developing countries, developing countries, Four Dragons (Four Tigers), least developed countries (LLDCs), low-income countries, middle-income countries, newly industrializing economies (NIEs), the South, Third World, underdeveloped countries, undeveloped countries; the 172 LDCs are: Afghanistan, Algeria, American Samoa, Angola, Anguilla, Antigua and Barbuda, Argentina, Aruba, The Bahamas, Bahrain, Bangladesh, Barbados, Belize, Benin, Bhutan, Bolivia, Botswana, Brazil, British Virgin Islands, Brunei, Burkina Faso, Burma, Burundi, Cabo Verde, Cambodia, Cameroon, Cayman Islands, Central African Republic, Chad, Chile, China, Christmas Island, Cocos Islands, Colombia, Comoros, Democratic Republic of the Congo, Republic of the Congo, Cook Islands, Costa Rica, Cote d'Ivoire, Cuba, Cyprus, Djibouti, Dominica, Dominican Republic, Ecuador, Egypt, El Salvador, Equatorial Guinea, Eritrea, Ethiopia, Falkland Islands, Fiji, French Guiana, French Polynesia, Gabon, The Gambia, Gaza Strip, Ghana, Gibraltar, Greenland, Grenada, Guadeloupe, Guam, Guatemala, Guernsey, Guinea, Guinea-Bissau, Guyana, Haiti, Honduras, Hong Kong, India, Indonesia, Iran, Iraq, Isle of Man, Jamaica, Jersey, Jordan, Kenya, Kiribati, North Korea, South Korea, Kuwait, Laos, Lebanon, Lesotho, Liberia, Libya, Macau, Madagascar, Malawi, Malaysia, Maldives, Mali, Marshall Islands, Martinique, Mauritania, Mauritius, Mayotte, Federated States of Micronesia, Mongolia, Montserrat, Morocco, Mozambique, Namibia, Nauru, Nepal, Netherlands Antilles, New Caledonia, Nicaragua, Niger, Nigeria, Niue, Norfolk Island, Northern Mariana Islands, Oman, Palau, Pakistan, Panama, Papua New Guinea, Paraguay, Peru, Philippines, Pitcairn Islands, Puerto Rico, Qatar, Reunion, Rwanda, Saint Helena, Ascension, and Tristan da Cunha, Saint Kitts and Nevis, Saint Lucia, Saint Pierre and Miquelon, Saint Vincent and the Grenadines, Samoa, Sao Tome and Principe, Saudi Arabia, Senegal, Seychelles, Sierra Leone, Singapore, Solomon Islands, Somalia, Sri Lanka, Sudan, Suriname, Swaziland, Syria, Taiwan, Tanzania, Thailand, Togo, Tokelau, Tonga, Trinidad and Tobago, Tunisia, Turks and Caicos Islands, Tuvalu, UAE, Uganda, Uruguay, Vanuatu, Venezuela, Vietnam, Virgin Islands, Wallis and Futuna, West Bank, Western Sahara, Yemen, Zambia, Zimbabwe; note—similar to the new International Monetary Fund (IMF) term "developing countries" which adds Malta, Mexico, South Africa, and Turkey but omits in its recently published statistics American Samoa, Anguilla, British Virgin Islands, Brunei, Cayman Islands, Christmas Island, Cocos Islands, Cook Islands, Cuba, Eritrea, Falkland Islands, French Guiana, French Polynesia, Gaza Strip, Gibraltar, Greenland, Grenada, Guadeloupe, Guam, Guernsey, Isle of Man, Jersey, North Korea, Macau, Martinique, Mayotte, Montserrat, Nauru, New Caledonia, Niue, Norfolk Island, Northern Mariana Islands, Palau, Pitcairn Islands, Puerto Rico, Reunion, Saint Helena, Ascension, and Tristan

da Cunha, Saint Pierre and Miquelon, Tokelau, Tonga, Turks and Caicos Islands, Tuvalu, Virgin Islands, Wallis and Futuna, West Bank, Western Sahara

low-income countries
another term for those less developed countries with below-average per capita GDPs; see less developed countries (LDCs)

middle-income countries
another term for those less developed countries with above-average per capita GDPs; see less developed countries (LDCs)

Multilateral Investment Guarantee Agency (MIGA)
established—12 April 1988
aim—encourages flow of foreign direct investment among member countries by offering investment insurance, consultation, and negotiation on conditions for foreign investment and technical assistance; a UN specialized agency
members—(179) includes all UN member countries except Andorra, Bhutan, Brunei, Burma, Cuba, Kiribati, North Korea, Liechtenstein, Marshall Islands, Monaco, Nauru, San Marino, Somalia, Tonga, Tuvalu; plus Kosovo

Near Abroad
Russian term for the 14 non-Russian successor states of the USSR, in which 25 million ethnic Russians live and in which Moscow has expressed a strong national security interest; the 14 countries are Armenia, Azerbaijan, Belarus, Estonia, Georgia, Kazakhstan, Kyrgyzstan, Latvia, Lithuania, Moldova, Tajikistan, Turkmenistan, Ukraine, Uzbekistan

new independent states (NIS)
a term referring to all the countries of the FSU except the Baltic countries (Estonia, Latvia, Lithuania)

newly industrializing countries (NICs)
former term for the newly industrializing economies; see newly industrializing economies (NIEs)

newly industrializing economies (NIEs)
that subgroup of the less developed countries (LDCs) that has experienced particularly rapid industrialization of their economies; formerly known as the newly industrializing countries (NICs); also known as advanced developing countries; usually includes the Four Dragons (Hong Kong, South Korea, Singapore, Taiwan), and Brazil

Nonaligned Movement (NAM)
established—1-6 September 1961
aim—to establish political and military cooperation apart from the traditional East or West blocs
members—(119 plus the Palestine Liberation Organization) Afghanistan, Algeria, Angola, Antigua and Barbuda, Azerbaijan, The Bahamas, Bahrain, Bangladesh, Barbados, Belarus, Belize, Benin, Bhutan, Bolivia, Botswana, Brunei, Burkina Faso, Burma, Burundi, Cabo Verde, Cambodia, Cameroon, Central African Republic, Chad, Chile, Colombia, Comoros, Democratic Republic of the Congo, Republic of the Congo, Cote d'Ivoire, Cuba, Djibouti, Dominica, Dominican Republic, Ecuador, Egypt, Equatorial Guinea, Eritrea, Ethiopia, Fiji, Gabon, The Gambia, Ghana, Grenada, Guatemala, Guinea, Guinea-Bissau, Guyana, Haiti, Honduras, India, Indonesia, Iran, Iraq, Jamaica, Jordan, Kenya, North Korea, Kuwait, Laos, Lebanon, Lesotho, Liberia, Libya, Madagascar, Malawi, Malaysia, Maldives, Mali, Mauritania, Mauritius, Mongolia, Morocco, Mozambique, Namibia, Nepal, Nicaragua, Niger, Nigeria, Oman, Pakistan, Panama, Papua New Guinea, Peru, Philippines, Qatar, Rwanda, Saint Kitts and Nevis, Saint Lucia, Saint Vincent and the Grenadines, Sao Tome and Principe, Saudi Arabia, Senegal, Seychelles, Sierra Leone, Singapore, Somalia, South Africa, Sri Lanka, Sudan, Suriname, Swaziland, Syria, Tanzania, Thailand, Timor-Leste, Togo, Trinidad and Tobago, Tunisia, Turkmenistan, Uganda, UAE, Uzbekistan, Vanuatu, Venezuela, Vietnam, Yemen, Zambia, Zimbabwe, Palestine Liberation Organization
observers—(17) Argentina, Armenia, Bosnia and Herzegovina, Brazil, China, Costa Rica, Croatia, El Salvador, Kazakhstan, Kyrgyzstan, Mexico, Montenegro, Paraguay, Serbia, Tajikistan, Ukraine, Uruguay

Nordic Council (NC)
established—16 March 1952; effective—12 February 1953
aim—to promote regional economic, cultural, and environmental cooperation
members—(5) Denmark (including Faroe Islands and Greenland), Finland (including Aland Islands), Iceland, Norway, Sweden
observers—(6) Estonia, Latvia, Lithuania, and the Sami (Lapp) local parliaments of Finland, Norway, and Sweden

Nordic Investment Bank (NIB)
established—4 December 1975; effective—1 June 1976
aim—to promote economic cooperation and development
members—(8) Denmark (including Faroe Islands and Greenland), Estonia, Finland (including Aland Islands), Iceland, Latvia, Lithuania, Norway, Sweden

North
a popular term for the rich industrialized countries generally located in the northern portion of the Northern Hemisphere; the counterpart of the South; see developed countries (DCs)

North American Free Trade Agreement (NAFTA)
established—17 December 1992
aim—to eliminate trade barriers, promote fair competition, increase investment opportunities, provide protection of intellectual property rights, and create procedures to settle disputes
members—(3) Canada, Mexico, US

North Atlantic Treaty Organization (NATO)
established—4 April 1949
aim—to promote mutual defense and cooperation

members—(28) Albania, Belgium, Bulgaria, Canada, Croatia, Czech Republic, Denmark, Estonia, France, Germany, Greece, Hungary, Iceland, Italy, Latvia, Lithuania, Luxembourg, Netherlands, Norway, Poland, Portugal, Romania, Slovakia, Slovenia, Spain, Turkey, UK, US

Nuclear Energy Agency (NEA)
note—also known as OECD Nuclear Energy Agency
established—1 February 1958
aim—to promote the peaceful uses of nuclear energy; associated with OECD
members—(31) Australia, Austria, Belgium, Canada, Czech Republic, Denmark, Finland, France, Germany, Greece, Hungary, Iceland, Ireland, Italy, Japan, South Korea, Luxembourg, Mexico, Netherlands, Norway, Poland, Portugal, Russia, Slovakia, Slovenia, Spain, Sweden, Switzerland, Turkey, UK, US

Nuclear Suppliers Group (NSG)
note—also known as the London Suppliers Group or the London Group
established—1974; effective—1975
aim—to establish guidelines for exports of nuclear materials, processing equipment for uranium enrichment, and technical information to countries of proliferation concern and regions of conflict and instability
members—(48) Argentina, Australia, Austria, Belarus, Belgium, Brazil, Bulgaria, Canada, China, Croatia, Cyprus, Czech Republic, Denmark, Estonia, Finland, France, Germany, Greece, Hungary, Iceland, Ireland, Italy, Japan, Kazakhstan, South Korea, Latvia, Lithuania, Luxembourg, Malta, Mexico, Netherlands, NZ, Norway, Poland, Portugal, Romania, Russia, Serbia, Slovakia, Slovenia, South Africa, Spain, Sweden, Switzerland, Turkey, Ukraine, UK, US
observer—(2) Chairman of the Zangger Committee, European Commission (a policy-planning body for the EU)

Organization for Democracy and Economic Development (GUAM)
note—acronym standing for the member countries, Georgia, Ukraine, Azerbaijan, Moldova; formerly known as GUUAM before Uzbekistan withdrew in 5 May 2005
established—7 June 2001
aim—commits the countries to cooperation and assistance in social and economic development, the strengthening and broadening of trade and economic relations, and the development and effective use of transport and communications, highways, and related infrastructure crossing the boundaries of the member states
members—(4) Azerbaijan, Georgia, Moldova, Ukraine

Organization for Economic Cooperation and Development (OECD)
established—14 December 1960; effective—30 September 1961
aim—to promote economic cooperation and development
members—(34) Australia, Austria, Belgium, Canada, Chile, Czech Republic, Denmark, Estonia, Finland, France, Germany, Greece, Hungary, Iceland, Ireland, Israel, Italy, Japan, South Korea, Luxembourg, Mexico, Netherlands, NZ, Norway, Poland, Portugal, Slovakia, Slovenia, Spain, Sweden, Switzerland, Turkey, UK, US
special member—(1) EC

Organization for Security and Cooperation in Europe (OSCE)
note—formerly the Conference on Security and Cooperation in Europe (CSCE) established 3 July 1975
established—1 January 1995
aim—to foster the implementation of human rights, fundamental freedoms, democracy, and the rule of law; to act as an instrument of early warning, conflict prevention, and crisis management; and to serve as a framework for conventional arms control and confidence building measures
members—(57) Albania, Andorra, Armenia, Austria, Azerbaijan, Belarus, Belgium, Bosnia and Herzegovina, Bulgaria, Canada, Croatia, Cyprus, Czech Republic, Denmark, Estonia, Finland, France, Georgia, Germany, Greece, Holy See, Hungary, Iceland, Ireland, Italy, Kazakhstan, Kyrgyzstan, Latvia, Liechtenstein, Lithuania, Luxembourg, Macedonia, Malta, Moldova, Monaco, Mongolia, Montenegro, Netherlands, Norway, Poland, Portugal, Romania, Russia, San Marino, Serbia, Slovakia, Slovenia, Spain, Sweden, Switzerland, Tajikistan, Turkey, Turkmenistan, Ukraine, UK, US, Uzbekistan
partners for cooperation—(11) Afghanistan, Algeria, Australia, Egypt, Israel, Japan, Jordan, South Korea, Morocco, Thailand, Tunisia

Organization for the Prohibition of Chemical Weapons (OPCW)
established—29 April 1997
aim—to enforce the Convention on the Prohibition of the Development, Production, Stockpiling, and Use of Chemical Weapons and on Their Destruction; to provide a forum for consultation and cooperation among the signatories of the Convention
members (countries that have ratified the Convention)—(190) Afghanistan, Albania, Algeria, Andorra, Antigua and Barbuda, Argentina, Armenia, Australia, Austria, Azerbaijan, The Bahamas, Bahrain, Bangladesh, Barbados, Belarus, Belgium, Belize, Benin, Bhutan, Bolivia, Bosnia and Herzegovina, Botswana, Brazil, Brunei, Bulgaria, Burkina Faso, Burundi, Cabo Verde, Cambodia, Cameroon, Canada, Central African Republic, Chad, Chile, China, Colombia, Comoros, Democratic Republic of the Congo, Republic of the Congo, Cook Islands, Costa Rica, Cote d'Ivoire, Croatia, Cuba, Cyprus, Czech Republic, Denmark, Dominica, Dominican Republic, Djibouti, Ecuador, El Salvador, Equatorial Guinea, Eritrea, Estonia, Ethiopia, Fiji, Finland, France, Gabon, The Gambia, Georgia, Germany, Ghana, Greece, Grenada, Guatemala, Guinea, Guinea-Bissau, Guyana, Haiti, Holy See, Honduras, Hungary, Iceland, India, Indonesia, Iran, Iraq, Ireland, Italy, Jamaica, Japan, Jordan, Kazakhstan, Kenya, Kiribati, South Korea, Kuwait, Kyrgyzstan, Laos, Latvia, Lebanon, Lesotho, Liberia, Libya, Liechtenstein, Lithuania, Luxembourg, Macedonia, Madagascar, Malawi, Malaysia, Maldives, Mali, Malta, Marshall Islands, Mauritania, Mauritius, Mexico, Federated States of Micronesia, Moldova, Monaco, Mongolia, Montenegro, Morocco, Mozambique, Namibia, Nauru, Nepal, Netherlands, NZ, Nicaragua, Niger, Nigeria, Niue, Norway, Oman, Pakistan, Palau, Panama, Papua New Guinea, Paraguay, Peru, Philippines, Poland, Portugal, Qatar, Romania, Russia, Rwanda, Saint Kitts and Nevis, Saint Lucia, Saint Vincent and the Grenadines, Samoa, San Marino, Sao Tome and Principe, Saudi Arabia, Senegal, Serbia, Seychelles, Sierra Leone, Singapore, Slovakia, Slovenia, Solomon Islands, Somalia, South Africa, Spain, Sri Lanka, Sudan,

Suriname, Swaziland, Sweden, Switzerland, Syria, Tajikistan, Tanzania, Thailand, Timor-Leste, Togo, Tonga, Trinidad and Tobago, Tunisia, Turkey, Turkmenistan, Tuvalu, Uganda, Ukraine, UAE, UK, US, Uruguay, Uzbekis
signatory states (countries that have signed, but not ratified, the Convention)—(2) Burma, Israel

Organization of African Unity (OAU)
see African Union

Organization of American States (OAS)
established—14 April 1890 as the International Union of American Republics; 30 April 1948 adopted present charter; effective—13 December 1951
aim—to promote regional peace and security as well as economic and social development
members—(35) Antigua and Barbuda, Argentina, The Bahamas, Barbados, Belize, Bolivia, Brazil, Canada, Chile, Colombia, Costa Rica, Cuba (suspended), Dominica, Dominican Republic, Ecuador, El Salvador, Grenada, Guatemala, Guyana, Haiti, Honduras, Jamaica, Mexico, Nicaragua, Panama, Paraguay, Peru, Saint Kitts and Nevis, Saint Lucia, Saint Vincent and the Grenadines, Suriname, Trinidad and Tobago, US, Uruguay, Venezuela
observers—(68) Albania, Algeria, Angola, Armenia, Austria, Azerbaijan, Belgium, Benin, Bosnia and Herzegovina, Bulgaria, China, Croatia, Cyprus, Czech Republic, Denmark, Egypt, Equatorial Guinea, Estonia, EU, Finland, France, Georgia, Germany, Ghana, Greece, Holy See, Hungary, Iceland, India, Ireland, Israel, Italy, Japan, Kazakhstan, South Korea, Latvia, Lebanon, Lithuania, Luxembourg, Macedonia, Malta, Monaco, Morocco, Netherlands, Nigeria, Norway, Pakistan, Philippines, Poland, Portugal, Qatar, Romania, Russia, Saudi Arabia, Serbia, Slovakia, Slovenia, Spain, Sri Lanka, Sweden, Switzerland, Thailand, Tunisia, Turkey, Ukraine, UK, Vanuatu, Yemen

Organization of Arab Petroleum Exporting Countries (OAPEC)
established—9 January 1968
aim—to promote cooperation in the petroleum industry
members—(11) Algeria, Bahrain, Egypt, Iraq, Kuwait, Libya, Qatar, Saudi Arabia, Syria, Tunisia (suspended), UAE

Organization of Eastern Caribbean States (OECS)
established—18 June 1981; effective—4 July 1981
aim—to promote political, economic, and defense cooperation
members—(9) Anguilla, Antigua and Barbuda, British Virgin Islands, Dominica, Grenada, Montserrat, Saint Kitts and Nevis, Saint Lucia, Saint Vincent and the Grenadines

Organization of Islamic Cooperation (OIC)
note—formerly the Organization of the Islamic Conference
established—22-25 September 1969
aim—to promote Islamic solidarity in economic, social, cultural, and political affairs
members—(56 plus the Palestine Liberation Organization) Afghanistan, Albania, Algeria, Azerbaijan, Bahrain, Bangladesh, Benin, Brunei, Burkina Faso, Cameroon, Chad, Comoros, Cote d'Ivoire, Djibouti, Egypt, Gabon, The Gambia, Guinea, Guinea-Bissau, Guyana, Indonesia, Iran, Iraq, Jordan, Kazakhstan, Kuwait, Kyrgyzstan, Lebanon, Libya, Malaysia, Maldives, Mali, Mauritania, Morocco, Mozambique, Niger, Nigeria, Oman, Pakistan, Qatar, Saudi Arabia, Senegal, Sierra Leone, Somalia, Sudan, Suriname, Syria, Tajikistan, Togo, Tunisia, Turkey, Turkmenistan, Uganda, UAE, Uzbekistan, Yemen, Palestine Liberation Organization
observers—(12) AU, Bosnia and Herzegovina, Central African Republic, ECO, LAS, Moro National Liberation Front, NAM, Parliamentary Union of the OIC Member States, Russia, Thailand, Turkish Muslim Community of Kibris, UN

Organization of Petroleum Exporting Countries (OPEC)
established—14 September 1960
aim—to coordinate petroleum policies
members—(12) Algeria, Angola, Ecuador, Iran, Iraq, Kuwait, Libya, Nigeria, Qatar, Saudi Arabia, UAE, Venezuela; note—Indonesia left OPEC in 2008

Pacific Alliance
established—28 April 2011
aim—to reduce trade barriers between member countries, to install visa-free travel, to install a common stock exchange, and to set up joint embassies in some countries
members—(5) Chile, Columbia, Costa Rica, Mexico, Peru
observers—(29) Australia, Canada, China, Dominican Republic, Ecuador, El Salvador , Finland, France, Germany, Guatemala, Honduras, India, Israel, Italy, Japan, Morocco, Netherlands, New Zealand, Panama, Paraguay, Portugal, Singapore, South Korea, Spain, Switzerland, Turkey, United Kingdom, United States, Uruguay

Pacific Community (SPC)
local name of the Secretariat of the Pacific Community

Pacific Islands Forum (PIF)
note—formerly known as South Pacific Forum (SPF)
established—5 August 1971
aim—to promote regional cooperation in political matters
members—(16) Australia, Cook Islands, Fiji, Kiribati, Marshall Islands, Federated States of Micronesia, Nauru, NZ, Niue, Palau, Papua New Guinea, Samoa, Solomon Islands, Tonga, Tuvalu, Vanuatu
associate members—(2) French Polynesia, New Caledonia
partners—(14) Canada, China, EU, France, India, Indonesia, Italy, Japan, South Korea, Malaysia, Philippines, Thailand, UK, US
observers—(12) ACP Group, American Samoa, Asia Development Bank, The Commonwealth, Commonwealth of the Northern Marianas, Guam, Timor-Leste (special observer), Tokelau, UN, Wallis and Futuna, Western and Central Pacific Fisheries Commission, the World Bank

Paris Club
established—1956
aim—to provide a forum for debtor countries to negotiate rescheduling of debt service payments or loans extended by governments or official agencies of participating countries; to help restore normal trade and project finance to debtor countries
members—(19) Australia, Austria, Belgium, Canada, Denmark, Finland, France, Germany, Ireland, Italy, Japan, Netherlands, Norway, Russia, Spain, Sweden, Switzerland, UK, US
associate members—(13) Abu Dhabi, Argentina, Brazil, Israel, South Korea, Kuwait, Mexico, Morocco, NZ, Portugal, South Africa, Trinidad and Tobago, Turkey

Partnership for Peace (PFP)
established—10-11 January 1994
aim—to expand and intensify political and military cooperation throughout Europe, increase stability, diminish threats to peace, and build relationships by promoting the spirit of practical cooperation and commitment to democratic principles that underpin NATO; program under the auspices of NATO
members—(22) Armenia, Austria, Azerbaijan, Belarus, Bosnia and Herzegovina, Finland, Georgia, Ireland, Kazakhstan, Kyrgyzstan, Macedonia, Malta, Moldova, Montenegro, Russia, Serbia, Sweden, Switzerland, Tajikistan, Turkmenistan, Ukraine, Uzbekistan; note—a nation that becomes a member of NATO is no longer a member of PFP

Permanent Court of Arbitration (PCA)
established—29 July 1899
aim—to facilitate the settlement of international disputes
members—(115) Albania, Argentina, Australia, Austria, Bahrain, Bangladesh, Belarus, Belgium, Belize, Benin, Bolivia, Brazil, Bulgaria, Burkina Faso, Cambodia, Cameroon, Canada, Chile, China, Colombia, Democratic Republic of the Congo, Costa Rica, Croatia, Cuba, Cyprus, Czech Republic, Denmark, Dominican Republic, Ecuador, Egypt, El Salvador, Eritrea, Estonia, Ethiopia, Fiji, Finland, France, Germany, Greece, Guatemala, Guyana, Haiti, Honduras, Hungary, Iceland, India, Iran, Iraq, Ireland, Israel, Italy, Japan, Jordan, Kenya, South Korea, Kuwait, Kyrgyzstan, Laos, Latvia, Lebanon, Libya, Liechtenstein, Lithuania, Luxembourg, Macedonia, Madagascar, Malaysia, Malta, Mauritius, Mexico, Montenegro, Morocco, Netherlands, NZ, Nicaragua, Nigeria, Norway, Pakistan, Panama, Paraguay, Peru, Philippines, Poland, Portugal, Qatar, Romania, Russia, Rwanda, Saudi Arabia, Senegal, Serbia, Singapore, Slovakia, Slovenia, South Africa, Spain, Sri Lanka, Sudan, Suriname, Swaziland, Sweden, Switzerland, Thailand, Togo, Turkey, Uganda, Ukraine, UAE, UK, US, Uruguay, Venezuela, Vietnam, Zambia, Zimbabwe

Petrocaribe
established—29 June 2005
aim—to eliminate existing social inequities, to foster high standards of living, to promote effective people's participation in shaping their own destiny
members—(18) Antigua and Barbuda, The Bahamas, Belize, Cuba, Dominica, Dominican Republic, Grenada, Guatemala, Guyana, Haiti, Honduras, Jamaica, Nicaragua, St. Kitts and Nevis, St. Lucia, St. Vincent and the Grenadines, Suriname, Venezuela

Rio Group (RG)
note—formerly known as Grupo de los Ocho, established NA December 1986; composed of the Contadora Group and the Lima Group established in 1988 to consult on regional Latin American issues; its members were Argentina, Belize, Bolivia, Brazil, Chile, Colombia, Costa Rica, Cuba, Dominican Republic, Ecuador, El Salvador, Guatemala, Guyana, Haiti, Honduras, Jamaica (representing CARICOM), Mexico, Nicaragua, Panama, Paraguay, Peru, Uruguay, Venezuela; in 2010 joined with the Caribbean Summit on Integration and Development (CALC) to form the Community of Latin American and Caribbean States (CELAC)

Schengen Convention
established—signed June 1990; effective March 1995
aim—to allow free movement within an area without internal border controls
members—(26) Austria, Belgium, Czech Republic, Denmark, Estonia, Finland, France, Germany, Greece, Hungary, Iceland, Italy, Latvia, Liechtenstein, Lithuania, Luxembourg, Malta, Netherlands, Norway, Poland, Portugal, Slovakia, Slovenia, Spain, Sweden, Switzerland; note- UK and Ireland have not joined; Cyprus will probably join in the near future; Bulgaria and Romania are still not fully implemented
De Facto members (microstates within or between Schengen states)—(5) Andorra, Holy See, Liechtenstein, Monaco, San Marino

Second World
another term for the traditionally Marxist-Leninist states of the USSR and Eastern Europe, with authoritarian governments and command economies based on the Soviet model; the term is fading from use; see centrally planned economies

Secretariat of the Pacific Community (SPC)
established—6 February 1947; effective 29 July 1948
aim—to serve island development in 22 Pacific countries; to develop technical assistance and professional, scientific, and research support; to build planning and management capability
members—(26) America Samoa, Australia, Cook Islands, Fiji, France, French Polynesia, Guam, Kiribati, Marshall Islands, Federated States of Micronesia, Nauru, New Caledonia, Niue, Northern Mariana Islands, NZ, Palau, Papua New Guinea, Pitcairn Islands, Samoa, Solomon Islands, Tokelau, Tonga, Tuvalu, Vanuatu, US, Wallis and Futuna

Shanghai Cooperation Organization (SCO)
established—15 June 2001
aim—to combat terrorism, extremism, and separatism; to safeguard regional security through mutual trust, disarmament, and cooperative security; and to increase cooperation in political, trade, economic, scientific and technological, cultural, and educational fields
members—(6) China, Kazakhstan, Kyrgyzstan, Russia, Tajikistan, Uzbekistan
dialogue members—(3) Belarus, Sri Lanka Turkey

observers—(5) Afghanistan, India, Iran, Mongolia, Pakistan

socialist countries
in general, countries in which the government owns and plans the use of the major factors of production; note—the term is sometimes used incorrectly as a synonym for Communist countries

South
a popular term for the poorer, less industrialized countries generally located south of the developed countries; the counterpart of the North; see less developed countries (LDCs)

South American Community of Nations (CSN)
established on 9 December 2004; its aim was to coordinate common policies regarding multilateral organizations, to integrate physical infrastructure, and to consolidate the merger of CAN and Mercosur; the members were Argentina, Bolivia, Brazil, Chile, Colombia, Ecuador, Guyana, Paraguay, Peru, Surinam, Uruguay, Venezuela; in 2008 it became Union of South American Nations (UNASUR)

South Asia Co-operative Environment Program (SACEP)
established—January 1983
aim—to promote regional cooperation in South Asia in the field of environment, both natural and human, and on issues of economic and social development; to support conservation and management of natural resources of the region
members—(8) Afghanistan, Bangladesh, Bhutan, India, Maldives, Nepal, Pakistan, Sri Lanka

South Asian Association for Regional Cooperation (SAARC)
established—8 December 1985
aim—to promote economic, social, and cultural cooperation
members—(8) Afghanistan, Bangladesh, Bhutan, India, Maldives, Nepal, Pakistan, Sri Lanka
observers—(9) Australia, Burma, China, EU, Iran, Japan, South Korea, Mauritius, US

South Pacific Forum (SPF)
note—see Pacific Island Forum

South Pacific Regional Trade and Economic Cooperation Agreement (Sparteca)
established—1981
aim—to redress unequal trade relationships of Australia and New Zealand with small island economies in the Pacific region
members—(16) Australia, Cook Islands, Fiji (suspended), Kiribati, Marshall Islands, Federated States of Micronesia, Nauru, NZ, Niue, Palau, Papua New Guinea, Samoa, Solomon Islands, Tonga, Tuvalu, Vanuatu

Southern African Customs Union (SACU)
established—11 December 1969
aim—to promote free trade and cooperation in customs matters
members—(5) Botswana, Lesotho, Namibia, South Africa, Swaziland

Southern African Development Community (SADC)
note—evolved from the Southern African Development Coordination Conference (SADCC)
established—17 August 1992
aim—to promote regional economic development and integration
members—(15) Angola, Botswana, Democratic Republic of the Congo, Lesotho, Madagascar, Malawi, Mauritius, Mozambique, Namibia, Seychelles, South Africa, Swaziland, Tanzania, Zambia, Zimbabwe

Southern Cone Common Market (Mercosur) or Southern Common Market
note—also known as Mercado Comun del Cono Sur (Mercosur)
established—26 March 1991
aim—to increase regional economic cooperation
members—(6) Argentina, Bolivia, Brazil, Paraguay (suspended), Uruguay, Venezuela
associate members—(6) Chile, Colombia, Ecuador, Guyana, Peru, Surinam

Third World
another term for the less developed countries; the term is obsolescent; see less developed countries (LDCs)

underdeveloped countries
refers to those less developed countries with the potential for above-average economic growth; see less developed countries (LDCs)

undeveloped countries
refers to those extremely poor less developed countries (LDCs) with little prospect for economic growth; see least developed countries (LLDCs)

Union Latina
established—15 May 1954; became functional 1983
aim—to project, protect, and promote the common heritage and unifying identities of the Latin, and Latin-influenced, world
members—(36) Andorra, Angola, Bolivia, Brazil, Cabo Verde, Chile, Colombia, Cote d'Ivoire, Costa Rica, Cuba, Dominican Republic, Ecuador, El Salvador, France, Guatemala, Guinea-Bissau, Haiti, Honduras, Italy, Moldova, Monaco, Mozambique, Nicaragua, Panama, Paraguay, Peru, Philippines, Portugal, Romania, San Marino, Sao Tome and Principe, Senegal, Spain, Timor-Leste, Uruguay, Venezuela
observers—(4) Argentina, Holy See, Mexico, Order of Malta

Union of South American Nations (UNASUR—Spanish; UNASUL—Portuguese)
formerly South American Community of Nations (CSN) which terminated on 16 April 2007
established—23 May 2008
aim—to model a community after the European Union which will include a common currency, parliament, passport, and defense policy
members—(12) Argentina, Bolivia, Brazil, Chile, Colombia, Ecuador, Guyana, Paraguay, Peru, Suriname, Uruguay, Venezuela
observers—(2) Mexico, Panama

United Nations (UN)
established—26 June 1945; effective—24 October 1945
aim—to maintain international peace and security and to promote cooperation involving economic, social, cultural, and humanitarian problems
constituent organizations—the UN is composed of six principal organs and numerous subordinate agencies and bodies as follows:
1) *Secretariat*
2) *General Assembly*: International Computing Center (ICC), International Trade Center (ITC), Joint United Nations Program on HIV/AIDS (UN-AIDS), Office of the United Nations High Commissioner for Refugees (UNHCR), United Nations Center for Human Settlements (UN-Habitat), United Nations Children's Fund (UNICEF), United Nations Conference on Trade and Development (UNCTAD), United Nations Development Program (UNDP), United Nations Environment Program (UNEP), United Nations Institute for Disarmament Research (UNIDIR), United Nations Institute for Training and Research (UNITAR), United Nations Interregional Crime and Justice Research Institute (UNICRI), United Nations Office on Drugs and Crime (UNODC), United Nations Population Fund (UNFPA), United Nations Office of Project Services (UNOPS), United Nations Relief and Works Agency for Palestine Refugees in the Near East (UNRWA), United Nations Research Institute for Social Development (UNRISD), United Nations System Staff College (UNSSC), United Nations University (UNU), United Nations Women, World Food Program (WFP)
3) *Security Council*: International Criminal Tribunal for the Former Yugoslavia (ICTY), International Criminal Tribunal for Rwanda (ICTR), United Nations Compensation Commission, United Nations Disengagement Observer Force (UNDOF), African Union/United Nations Hybrid Operation in Darfur (UNAMID), United Nations Assistance Mission in Afghanistan (UNAMA), United Nations Interim Administration Mission in Kosovo (UNMIK), United Nations Interim Force for Abyei (UNIFSA), United Nations Interim Force in Lebanon (UNIFIL), United Nations Mission in Liberia (UNMIL), United Nations Military Observer Group in India and Pakistan (UNMOGIP), United Nations Multidimensional Integrated Stabilization Mission in Mali (MINUSMA), United Nations Operation in Cote d'Ivoire (UNOCI), United Nations Mission for the Referendum in Western Sahara (MINURSO), United Nations Mission in South Sudan (UNMISS), United Nations Organization Stabilization Mission in the Democratic Republic of the Congo (MONUSCO), United Nations Peace-Keeping Force in Cyprus (UNFICYP), United Nations Stabilization Mission in Haiti (MINUSTAH), and United Nations Truce Supervision Organization (UNTSO)
4) *Economic and Social Council (ECOSOC)*: Commission for Social Development, Commission on Crime Prevention and Criminal Justice, Commission on Narcotics Drugs, Commission on Population and Development, Commission on Science and Technology for Development, Commission on Sustainable Development, Commission on the Status of Women, Economic and Social Commission for Asia and the Pacific (ESCAP), Economic and Social Commission for Western Asia (ESCWA), Economic Commission for Africa (ECA), Economic Commission for Europe (ECE), Economic Commission for Latin America and the Caribbean (ECLAC), Statistical Commission, Food and Agriculture Organization of the United Nations (FAO), International Atomic Energy Agency (IAEA), Preparatory Commission for the Nuclear-Test-Ban Treaty Organization (CTBTO), International Bank for Reconstruction and Development (IBRD), International Center for Secretariat of Investment Disputes (ICSID), International Civil Aviation Organization (ICAO), International Development Association (IDA), International Finance Corporation (IFC), International Fund for Agricultural Development (IFAD), International Labor Organization (ILO), International Maritime Organization (IMO), International Monetary Fund (IMF), International Telecommunication Union (ITU), Multilateral Investment Guarantee Agency (MIGA), Statistical Commission, United Nations Educational, Scientific, and Cultural Organization (UNESCO), United Nations Forum on Forests, United Nations Industrial Development Organization (UNIDO), Universal Postal Union (UPU), World Health Organization (WHO), World Intellectual Property Organization (WIPO), World Meteorological Organization (WMO), World Tourism Organization (UNWTO), and World Trade Organization (WTO), Statistical Commission, UN Forum on Forests
5) *Trusteeship Council* (inactive; no trusteeships at this time)
6) *International Court of Justice (ICJ)*
UN members—(193) Afghanistan, Albania, Algeria, Andorra, Angola, Antigua and Barbuda, Argentina, Armenia, Australia, Austria, Azerbaijan, The Bahamas, Bahrain, Bangladesh, Barbados, Belarus, Belgium, Belize, Benin, Bhutan, Bolivia, Bosnia and Herzegovina, Botswana, Brazil, Brunei, Bulgaria, Burkina Faso, Burma, Burundi, Cabo Verde, Cambodia, Cameroon, Canada, Central African Republic, Chad, Chile, China, Colombia, Comoros, Democratic Republic of the Congo, Republic of the Congo, Costa Rica, Cote d'Ivoire, Croatia, Cuba, Cyprus, Czech Republic, Denmark, Djibouti, Dominica, Dominican Republic, Ecuador, Egypt, El Salvador, Equatorial Guinea, Eritrea, Estonia, Ethiopia, Fiji, Finland, France, Gabon, The Gambia, Georgia, Germany, Ghana, Greece, Grenada, Guatemala, Guinea, Guinea-Bissau, Guyana, Haiti, Honduras, Hungary, Iceland, India, Indonesia, Iran, Iraq, Ireland, Israel, Italy, Jamaica, Japan, Jordan, Kazakhstan, Kenya, Kiribati, North Korea, South Korea, Kuwait, Kyrgyzstan, Laos, Latvia, Lebanon, Lesotho, Liberia, Libya, Liechtenstein, Lithuania, Luxembourg, Macedonia, Madagascar, Malawi, Malaysia, Maldives, Mali, Malta, Marshall Islands, Mauritania, Mauritius, Mexico, Federated States of Micronesia, Moldova, Monaco, Mongolia, Montenegro, Morocco, Mozambique, Namibia, Nauru, Nepal, Netherlands, NZ, Nicaragua, Niger, Nigeria, Norway, Oman, Pakistan, Palau, Panama, Papua New Guinea, Paraguay, Peru, Philippines, Poland, Portugal, Qatar, Romania, Russia, Rwanda, Saint Kitts and Nevis, Saint Lucia, Saint Vincent and the Grenadines, Samoa, San Marino, Sao Tome and Principe, Saudi Arabia, Senegal, Serbia, Seychelles, Sierra Leone, Singapore, Slovakia, Slovenia, Solomon Islands, Somalia, South Africa, South Sudan, Spain, Sri Lanka, Sudan, Suriname, Swaziland, Sweden, Switzerland, Syria, Tajikistan, Tanzania, Thailand, Timor-Leste, Togo, Tonga, Trinidad and Tobago, Tunisia, Turkey, Turkmenistan, Tuvalu, Uganda, Ukraine, UAE, UK, US, Uruguay, Uzbekistan, Vanuatu, Venezuela, Vietnam, Yemen, Zambia, Zimbabwe; note—all UN members are represented in the General Assembly
observers—(1 plus the Palestine Liberation Organization) Holy See, Palestine Liberation Organization

United Nations Assistance Mission in Afghanistan (UNAMA)
established—January 2010
aim—to support the government of Afghanistan, in its attempt to improve security, governance, and economic development and regional cooperation; protect civilians and support efforts to support human rights
note—gives civilian support only

United Nations Children's Fund (UNICEF)
note—acronym retained from the predecessor organization, UN International Children's Emergency Fund
established—11 December 1946
aim—to help establish child health and welfare services
executive board members—(36) selected on a rotating basis from all regions

United Nations Conference on Trade and Development (UNCTAD)
established—30 December 1964
aim—to promote international
trade members—(194) all UN members plus Holy See

United Nations Development Program (UNDP)
established—22 November 1965
aim—to provide technical assistance to stimulate economic and social development
members (executive board)—(36) selected on a rotating basis from all regions

United Nations Disengagement Observer Force (UNDOF)
established—31 May 1974
aim—to observe the 1973 Arab-Israeli cease-fire; established by the UN Security Council
members—(6) Fiji, India, Ireland, Nepal, Netherlands, Philippines

United Nations Educational, Scientific, and Cultural Organization (UNESCO)
established—16 November 1945; effective—4 November 1946
aim—to promote cooperation in education, science, and culture
members—(194 plus the Palestine Liberation Organization) includes all UN member countries except Liechtenstein (192 total); plus Cook Islands, Niue, and the Palestine Liberation Organization
associate members—(9) Anguilla, Aruba, British Virgin Islands, Cayman Islands, Curacao, Faroe Islands, Macau, Sint Maarten, Tokelau

United Nations Environment Program (UNEP)
established—15 December 1972
aim—to promote international cooperation on all environmental matters
members—(58) selected on a rotating basis from all regions

United Nations General Assembly
established—26 June 1945
effective—24 October 1945
aim—to function as the primary deliberative organ of the UN
members—(193) all UN members are represented in the General Assembly

United Nations High Commissioner for Refugees (UNHCR)
established—3 December 1949; effective—1 January 1951
aim—to ensure the humanitarian treatment of refugees and find permanent solutions to refugee problems
members (executive committee)—(87) Algeria, Argentina, Australia, Austria, Azerbaijan, Bangladesh, Belgium, Benin, Brazil, Bulgaria, Cameroon, Canada, Chile, China, Colombia, Democratic Republic of the Congo, Republic of the Congo, Costa Rica, Cote d'Ivoire, Croatia, Cyprus, Denmark, Djibouti, Ecuador, Egypt, Estonia, Ethiopia, Finland, France, Germany, Ghana, Greece, Guinea, Holy See, Hungary, India, Iran, Ireland, Israel, Italy, Japan, Jordan, Kenya, South Korea, Lebanon, Lesotho, Luxembourg, Macedonia, Madagascar, Mexico, Moldova, Montenegro, Morocco, Mozambique, Namibia, Netherlands, NZ, Nicaragua, Nigeria, Norway, Pakistan, Philippines, Poland, Portugal, Romania, Russia, Rwanda, Serbia, Slovenia, Somalia, South Africa, Spain, Sudan, Sweden, Switzerland, Tanzania, Thailand, Togo, Tunisia, Turkey, Turkmenistan, Uganda, UK, US, Venezuela, Yemen, Zambia

United Nations Industrial Development Organization (UNIDO)
established—17 November 1966; effective—1 January 1967
aim—UN specialized agency that promotes industrial development especially among the members
members—(174) includes all UN member countries except Andorra, Antigua and Barbuda, Australia, Brunei, Canada, Estonia, Iceland, Kiribati, Latvia, Liechtenstein, Marshall Islands, Federated States of Micronesia, Nauru, Palau, San Marino, Singapore, Solomon Islands, South Sudan, US

United Nations Institute for Training and Research (UNITAR)
established—11 December 1963 adoption of the resolution establishing the Institute; effective—24 March 1965
aim—to help the UN become more effective through training and research
members (Board of Trustees)—(12) Algeria, Brazil, Republic of the Congo, Guatemala, India, Iran, Jamaica, Nigeria, Norway, Russia, South Africa, Switzerland; note - the UN Secretary General can appoint up to 30 members

United Nations Integrated Mission in Timor-Leste (UNMIT)
established—25 August 2006
aim—to support the Government, to support the electoral process, to ensure the restoration and maintenance of public security
members—(15) Australia, Bangladesh, Brazil, China, Fiji, Japan, India, Malaysia, Nepal, NZ, Pakistan, Philippines, Portugal, Sierra Leone, Singapore

United Nations Interim Administration Mission in Kosovo (UNMIK)
established—10 June 1999
aim—to promote the establishment of substantial autonomy and self-government in Kosovo; to perform basic civilian administrative functions; to support the reconstruction of key infrastructure and humanitarian and disaster relief
note—gives civilian support only; works closely with NATO Kosovo Force (KFOR)

United Nations Interim Force in Lebanon (UNIFIL)
established—19 March 1978
aim—to confirm the withdrawal of Israeli forces, and assist in reestablishing Lebanese authority in southern Lebanon; established by the UN Security Council
members—(37) Armenia, Austria, Bangladesh, Belarus, Belgium, Brazil, Brunei, Cambodia, China, Croatia, Cyprus, El Salvador, Finland, France, Germany, Ghana, Greece, Guatemala, Hungary, India, Indonesia, Ireland, Italy, Kenya, South Korea, Macedonia, Malaysia, Nepal, Nigeria, Qatar, Serbia, Sierra Leone, Slovenia, Spain, Sri Lanka, Tanzania, Turkey

United Nations Interim Security Force for Abyei (UNISFA)
established—27 June 2011
aim—to protect civilians and humanitarian workers in Abyei
members—(28) Benin, Bolivia, Brazil, Burundi, Cambodia, Ecuador, Ethiopia, Ghana, Guatemala, Guinea, India, Mongolia, Namibia, Nepal, Nigeria, Paraguay, Peru, Philippines, Russia, Rwanda, Sierra Leone, Sri Lanka, Tanzania, Ukraine, Uruguay, Yemen, Zambia, Zimbabwe

United Nations Military Observer Group in India and Pakistan (UNMOGIP)
established—24 January 1949
aim—to observe the 1949 India-Pakistan cease-fire; established by the UN Security Council
members—(9) Chile, Croatia, Finland, Italy, South Korea, Philippines, Sweden, Thailand, Uruguay

United Nations Mission for the Referendum in Western Sahara (MINURSO)
established—29 April 1991
aim—to supervise the cease-fire and conduct a referendum in Western Sahara; established by the UN Security Council
members—(30) Argentina, Austria, Bangladesh, Brazil, China, Croatia, Egypt, El Salvador, France, Ghana, Guinea, Honduras, Hungary, Ireland, Italy, South Korea, Malawi, Malaysia, Mongolia, Nepal, Nigeria, Pakistan, Paraguay, Peru, Poland, Russia, Sri Lanka, Togo, Uruguay, Yemen

United Nations Mission in Liberia (UNMIL)
established—19 September 2003
aim—to support the cease-fire agreement and peace process, protect UN facilities and people, support humanitarian activities, and assist in national security reform
members—(43) Bangladesh, Benin, Bolivia, Brazil, Bulgaria, China, Croatia, Denmark, Ecuador, Egypt, El Salvador, Ethiopia, Finland, France, The Gambia, Ghana, Indonesia, Jordan, Kenya, South Korea, Kyrgyzstan, Malaysia, Moldova, Montenegro, Namibia, Nepal, Niger, Nigeria, Pakistan, Paraguay, Peru, Philippines, Poland, Romania, Russia, Senegal, Serbia, Togo, Ukraine, US, Yemen, Zambia, Zimbabwe

United Nations Mission in the Central African Republic and Chad (MINURCAT)
established on 25 September 2007; to create the security and conditions which will to contribute to the protection of refugees, displaced persons, and citizens in danger, to facilitate the provision of humanitarian assistance in eastern Chad and the northeastern Central African Republic, to create favorable conditions for the reconstruction and economic and social development of these areas; members were Bangladesh, Benin, Burkina Faso, Democratic Republic of the Congo, Egypt, Ethiopia, Ghana, Ireland, Kenya, Mali, Mongolia, Namibia, Nepal, Nigeria, Norway, Pakistan, Poland, Russia, Rwanda, Senegal, Serbia, Sri Lanka, Togo, Tunisia, US; MINURCAT was dissolved in December 2010

United Nations Mission in the Republic of South Sudan (UNMISS)
established—8 July 2011
aim—to consolidate peace and security and to establish the conditions in South Sudan which will strengthen its ability to govern effectively and democratically and establish good relations with its neighbors
members—(54) Australia, Bangladesh, Belarus, Benin, Bolivia, Brazil, Cambodia, Canada, China, Denmark, Ecuador, Egypt, El Salvador, Fiji, Germany, Ghana, Guatemala, Guinea, India, Indonesia, Italy, Japan, Jordan, Kenya, South Korea, Kyrgyzstan, Moldova, Mongolia, Namibia, Nepal, Netherlands, NZ, Nigeria, Norway, Papua New Guinea, Paraguay, Peru, Poland, Romania, Russia, Rwanda, Senegal, Sri Lanka, Sweden, Switzerland, Tanzania, Timor-Leste, Togo, Uganda, Ukraine, UK, US, Yemen, Zambia

United Nations Mission in the Sudan (UNMIS)
established in March 2005 to support implementation of the comprehensive Peace Agreement by monitoring and verifying the implementation of the Cease Fire Agreement, by observing and monitoring movements of armed groups, and by helping disarm, demobilizing and reintegrating armed bands; members were Australia, Bangladesh, Belgium, Benin, Bolivia, Brazil, Burkina Faso, Cambodia, Canada, China, Croatia, Denmark, Ecuador, Egypt, El Salvador, Fiji, Finland, Germany, Greece, Guatemala, Guinea, India, Indonesia, Iran, Japan, Jordan, Kenya, Kyrgyzstan, Malaysia, Moldova, Mongolia, Morocco, Namibia, Nepal, Netherland, NZ, Niger, Norway, Pakistan, Paraguay, Peru, Philippines, Poland, Qatar, Romania, Russia, Rwanda, Sierra Leone, Spain, Sweden, Switzerland, Tanzania, Thailand, Turkey, Uganda, Ukraine, UK, Yemen, Zambia, Zimbabwe; UNMIS was dissolved on 9 July 2011

United Nations Multidimensional Integrated Stabilization Mission in Mali, MINUSMA
established—25 April 2013
aim—to support political processes and carry out a number of security-related tasks
members—(36) Bangladesh, Benin, Burkina Faso, Cambodia, Chad, China, Cote d'Ivoire, Denmark, Dominican Republic, Estonia, Finland, France, The Gambia, Germany, Ghana, Guinea, Guinea-Bissau, Italy, Jordan, Kenya, Liberia, Mauritania, Nepal, Netherlands, Niger, Nigeria, Norway, Rwanda, Senegal, Sierra Leone, Sweden, Switzerland, Togo, UK, US, Yemen

United Nations Operation in Cote d'Ivoire (UNOCI)
established—27 February 2004
aim—to facilitate the implementation by the Ivorian parties of the peace agreement signed by them in January 2003
members—(44) Bangladesh, Benin, Bolivia, Brazil, Chad, China, Ecuador, Egypt, El Salvador, Ethiopia, France, The Gambia, Ghana, Guatemala, Guinea, India, Ireland, Jordan, South Korea, Malawi, Moldova, Morocco, Namibia, Nepal, Niger, Nigeria, Pakistan, Paraguay, Peru, Philippines, Poland, Romania, Russia, Senegal, Serbia, Tanzania, Togo, Tunisia, Uganda, Ukraine, Uruguay, Yemen, Zambia, Zimbabwe

United Nations Organization Stabilization Mission in the Democratic Republic of the Congo (MONUSCO)
established—28 May 2010
aim—to protect the civilians; to assist the government in the areas of stabilization and peace consolidation
members—(49) Algeria, Bangladesh, Belgium, Benin, Bolivia, Bosnia and Herzegovina, Burkina Faso, Cameroon, Canada, China, Czech Republic, Egypt, France, Ghana, Guatemala, Guinea, India, Indonesia, Ireland, Jordan, Kenya, Malawi, Malaysia, Mali, Mongolia, Morocco, Nepal, Niger, Nigeria, Pakistan, Paraguay, Peru, Poland, Romania, Russia, Senegal, Serbia, South Africa, Sri Lanka, Sweden, Switzerland, Tanzania, Tunisia, Ukraine, UK, US, Uruguay, Yemen, Zambia

United Nations Peacekeeping Force in Cyprus (UNFICYP)
established—4 March 1964
aim—to serve as a peacekeeping force between Greek Cypriots and Turkish Cypriots in Cyprus; established by the UN Security Council
members—(13) Argentina, Austria, Brazil, Canada, Chile, China, Croatia, Hungary, Paraguay, Serbia, Slovakia, Ukraine, UK

United Nations Population Fund (UNFPA)
note—acronym retained from predecessor organization UN Fund for Population Activities
established—July 1967
aim—to assist both developed and developing countries to deal with their population problems
members (executive board)—(36) selected on a rotating basis from all regions

United Nations Relief and Works Agency for Palestine Refugees in the Near East (UNRWA)
established—8 December 1949
aim—to provide assistance to Palestinian refugees
members (advisory commission)—(25) Australia, Belgium, Canada, Denmark, Egypt, Finland, France, Germany, Ireland, Italy, Japan, Jordan, Kuwait, Lebanon, Luxembourg, Netherlands, Norway, Saudi Arabia, Spain, Sweden, Switzerland, Syria, Turkey, UK, US
observers—(3) EC, LAS, Palestine Liberation Organization

United Nations Research Institute for Social Development (UNRISD)
established—1963
aim—to conduct research into the problems of economic development during different phases of economic growth
members—no country members, but a Board of Directors consisting of a chairman appointed by the UN Secretary General and 10 members confirmed by ECOSOC and a representative of the Secretary General

United Nations Secretariat
established—26 June 1945; effective—24 October 1945
aim—to serve as the primary administrative organ of the UN; a Secretary General is appointed for a five-year term by the General Assembly on the recommendation of the Security Council
members—the UN Secretary General and staff

United Nations Security Council (UNSC)
established—26 June 1945; effective—24 October 1945
aim—to maintain international peace and security
permanent members—(5) China, France, Russia, UK, US
nonpermanent members— (10) elected for two-year terms by the UN General Assembly; Argentina (2013-14),Australia (2013-14), Chad (2014-15), Chile (2014-15), Jordan (2014-15), Lithuania (2014-15), Luxembourg(2013-14), South Korea (2013-14), Nigeria (2014-15), Rwanda (2013-14)

United Nations Truce Supervision Organization (UNTSO)
established—June 1948
aim—to supervise the 1948 Arab-Israeli cease-fire; currently supports timely deployment of reinforcements to other peacekeeping operations in the region as needed; initially established by the UN Security Council
members—(24) Argentina, Australia, Austria, Belgium, Canada, Chile, China, Denmark, Estonia, Finland, France, Ireland, Italy, Nepal, Netherlands, NZ, Norway, Russia, Serbia, Slovakia, Slovenia, Sweden, Switzerland, US

United Nations Trusteeship Council
established on 26 June 1945, effective on 24 October 1945, to supervise the administration of the 11 UN trust territories; members were China, France, Russia, UK, US; it formally suspended operations 1 November 1994 after the Trust Territory of the Pacific Islands (Palau) became the Republic of Palau, a constitutional government in free association with the US; the Trusteeship Council was not dissolved

United Nations University (UNU)
established—3 December 1973
aim—to conduct research in development, welfare, and human survival and to train scholars
members—(16 members of UNU Council and the Rector are appointed by the Secretary General of the United Nations and the Director General of UNESCO)

Universal Postal Union (UPU)
established—9 October 1874, affiliated with the UN 15 November 1947; effective—1 July 1948
aim—to promote international postal cooperation; a UN specialized agency
members—(192) includes all UN member countries except Andorra, Marshall Islands, Federated States of Micronesia, Palau (189 total); plus Aruba, Curacao, and Sint Maarten; and Holy See; and Overseas Territories of the UK; note - includes the following dependencies or areas of special interest: Australia (Norfolk Island), China (Hong Kong, Macau), Denmark (Faroe Islands, Greenland), France (French Guiana, French Polynesia including Clipperton Island, French Southern and Antarctic Lands, Guadeloupe, Martinique, Mayotte, New Caledonia, Reunion, Saint Barthelemy, Saint Martin, Saint Pierre and Miquelon, Scattered Islands [Bassas da India, Europe, Juan de Nova, Glorioso Islands, Tromelin], Wallis and Futuna), Netherlands (Aruba, Curacao, Sint Maarten), NZ (Cook Island, Niue, Tokelau), UK (Guernsey, Isle of Man, Jersey; Anguilla, Bermuda, British Indian Ocean Territory, British Virgin Islands, Cayman Islands, Falkland Islands,

Gibraltar, Montserrat, Pitcairn Islands, Saint Helena, Ascension, and Tristan da Cunha, South Georgia and South Sandwich Islands, Turks and Caicos), US (American Samoa, Guam, Northern Mariana Islands, Puerto Rico, Virgin Islands)

Warsaw Pact (WP)
established 14 May 1955 to promote mutual defense; members met 1 July 1991 to dissolve the alliance; member states at the time of dissolution were: Bulgaria, Czechoslovakia, Hungary, Poland, Romania, and the USSR; earlier members included German Democratic Republic (GDR) and Albania

West African Development Bank (WADB)
note—also known as Banque Ouest-Africaine de Developpement (BOAD); is a financial institution of WAEMU
established—14 November 1973
aim—to promote regional economic development and integration
regional members—(8) Benin, Burkina Faso, Cote d'Ivoire, Guinea-Bissau, Mali, Niger, Senegal, Togo

West African Economic and Monetary Union (WAEMU)
note—also known as Union Economique et Monetaire Ouest Africaine (UEMOA)
established—1 August 1994
aim—to increase competitiveness of members' economic markets; to create a common market
members—(8) Benin, Burkina Faso, Cote d'Ivoire, Guinea-Bissau, Mali, Niger, Senegal, Togo

Western European Union (WEU)
established 23 October 1954; effective—6 May 1955; aim to provide mutual defense and to move toward political unification; 10 members: Belgium, France, Germany, Greece, Italy, Luxembourg, Netherlands, Portugal, Spain, UK; 6 associate members: Czech Republic, Hungary, Iceland, Norway, Poland, Turkey; 7 associate partners: Bulgaria, Estonia, Latvia, Lithuania, Romania, Slovakia, Slovenia; 5 observers: Austria, Denmark, Finland, Ireland, Sweden; note—to cease existence completely by June 2011

World Bank Group
includes International Bank for Reconstruction and Development (IBRD), International Development Association (IDA), International Finance Corporation (IFC), and Multilateral Investment Guarantee Agency (MIGA)

World Confederation of Labor (WCL)
established 19 June 1920 as the International Federation of Christian Trade Unions (IFCTU), renamed 4 October 1968; aim was to promote the trade union movement; on 31 October 2006 it merged with the International Confederation of Free Trade Unions (ICFTU) to form the International Trade Union Confederation (ITUC); members were (105 national organizations) Antigua and Barbuda, Argentina, Aruba, Austria, Bangladesh, Belgium, Belize, Benin, Bolivia, Brazil, Bulgaria, Burkina Faso, Cameroon, Canada, Central African Republic, Chad, Chile, Colombia, Democratic Republic of the Congo, Republic of the Congo, Costa Rica, Cote d'Ivoire, Cuba, Cyprus, Czech Republic, Denmark, Dominica, Dominican Republic, Ecuador, El Salvador, France, French Guiana, Gabon, The Gambia, Ghana, Guadeloupe, Guatemala, Guinea, Guyana, Haiti, Honduras, Hong Kong, Hungary, India, Indonesia, Iran, Italy, Japan, Kazakhstan, South Korea, Liberia, Libya, Liechtenstein, Lithuania, Luxembourg, Macedonia, Madagascar, Malawi, Malaysia, Malta, Martinique, Mauritania, Mauritius, Mexico, Morocco, Namibia, Nepal, Netherlands, Nicaragua, Niger, Pakistan, Panama, Paraguay, Peru, Philippines, Poland, Portugal, Puerto Rico, Romania, Rwanda, Saint Lucia, Saint Vincent and the Grenadines, Sao Tome and Principe, Senegal, Serbia, Sierra Leone, Singapore, Slovakia, South Africa, Spain, Sri Lanka, Suriname, Switzerland, Taiwan, Thailand, Togo, Trinidad and Tobago, Ukraine, US, Uruguay, Venezuela, Vietnam, Zambia, Zimbabwe

World Customs Organization (WCO)
note—began as the Customs Cooperation Council (CCC)
established—15 December 1950
aim—to promote international cooperation in customs matters
members—(180) Afghanistan, Albania, Algeria, Andorra, Angola, Argentina, Armenia, Australia, Austria, Azerbaijan, The Bahamas, Bahrain, Bangladesh, Barbados, Belarus, Belgium, Belize, Benin, Bermuda, Bhutan, Bolivia, Bosnia and Herzegovina, Botswana, Brazil, Brunei, Bulgaria, Burkina Faso, Burma, Burundi, Cabo Verde, Cambodia, Cameroon, Canada, Central African Republic, Chad, Chile, China, Colombia, Comoros, Democratic Republic of the Congo, Republic of the Congo, Costa Rica, Cote d'Ivoire, Croatia, Cuba, Curacao, Cyprus, Czech Republic, Denmark, Djibouti, Dominican Republic, EU, Ecuador, Egypt, El Salvador, Eritrea, Estonia, Ethiopia, Fiji, Finland, France, Gabon, The Gambia, Georgia, Germany, Ghana, Greece, Guatemala, Guinea, Guinea-Bissau, Guyana, Haiti, Honduras, Hong Kong, Hungary, Iceland, India, Indonesia, Iran, Iraq, Ireland, Israel, Italy, Jamaica, Japan, Jordan, Kazakhstan, Kenya, South Korea, Kuwait, Kyrgyzstan, Laos, Latvia, Lebanon, Lesotho, Liberia, Libya, Lithuania, Luxembourg, Macau, Macedonia, Madagascar, Malawi, Malaysia, Maldives, Mali, Malta, Mauritania, Mauritius, Mexico, Moldova, Mongolia, Montenegro, Morocco, Mozambique, Namibia, Nepal, Netherlands, NZ, Nicaragua, Niger, Nigeria, Norway, Oman, Pakistan, Panama, Papua New Guinea, Paraguay, Peru, Philippines, Poland, Portugal, Qatar, Romania, Russia, Rwanda, Saint Lucia, Samoa, Sao Tome and Principe, Saudi Arabia, Senegal, Serbia, Seychelles, Sierra Leone, Singapore, Slovakia, Slovenia, Somalia, South Africa, South Sudan, Spain, Sri Lanka, Sudan, Swaziland, Sweden, Switzerland, Syria, Tajikistan, Tanzania, Thailand, Timor-Leste, Togo, Tonga, Trinidad and Tobago, Tunisia, Turkey, Turkmenistan, Uganda, Ukraine, UAE, UK, US, Uruguay, Uzbekistan, Vanuatu, Venezuela, Vietnam, Yemen, Zambia, Zimbabwe

World Federation of Trade Unions (WFTU)
established—3 October 1945
aim—to promote the trade union movement
members—(in 2013 there were 126 participating nations and territories and the Palestine Liberation Organization); (in 2009 there were 125 nations and the Palestine Liberation Organization) Afghanistan, Albania, Angola, Antigua and Barbuda, Argentina, Armenia, Australia, Austria, Azerbaijan, Bahrain, Bangladesh, Barbados, Belarus, Benin, Bolivia, Botswana, Brazil, Bulgaria, Burkina Faso, Cambodia, Cameroon, Canada, Chile, Colombia, Democratic Republic of the Congo, Republic of the Congo, Costa Rica, Cote d'Ivoire, Cuba, Cyprus, Czech Republic, Djibouti, Dominican Republic, Ecuador, Egypt, El Salvador, Eritrea, Ethiopia, Fiji, Finland, France, French Guiana, The Gambia, Ghana, Greece, Guadeloupe, Guatemala, Guinea, Guinea-Bissau, Guyana, Haiti, Honduras, Hungary, India, Indonesia, Iran, Iraq, Jamaica, Japan, Jordan, Kazakhstan, North Korea, Kuwait, Kyrgyzstan, Laos, Lebanon, Lesotho, Liberia, Libya, Madagascar, Malawi, Malaysia, Mali, Martinique, Mauritius, Mexico, Mozambique, Nepal, New Caledonia, NZ, Niger, Nigeria, Oman, Pakistan, Panama, Papua New Guinea, Peru, Philippines, Poland, Portugal, Puerto Rico, Reunion, Romania, Russia, Saint Lucia, Saint Pierre and Miquelon, Saint Vincent and the Grenadines, Saudi Arabia, Senegal, Sierra Leone, Slovakia, Solomon Islands, Somalia, South Africa, Sri Lanka, Sudan,

Sweden, Syria, Tajikistan, Tanzania, Thailand, Togo, Trinidad and Tobago, Tunisia, Turkey, Turkmenistan, Uganda, Ukraine, Uruguay, Uzbekistan, Vanuatu, Venezuela, Vietnam, Yemen, Zimbabwe, Palestine Liberation Organization

World Food Program (WFP)
established—24 November 1961
aim—to provide food aid in support of economic development or disaster relief; an ECOSOC organization
members (Executive Board)—(36) selected on a rotating basis from all regions

World Health Organization (WHO)
established—22 July 1946; effective—7 April 1948
aim—to deal with health matters worldwide; a UN specialized agency
members—(194) includes all UN member countries except Liechtenstein (192 total); plus Cook Islands and Niue

World Intellectual Property Organization (WIPO)
established—14 July 1967; effective—26 April 1970
aim—to furnish protection for literary, artistic, and scientific works; a UN specialized agency
members—(185) includes all UN member countries except Marshall Islands, Federated States of Micronesia, Nauru, Palau, Solomon Islands, South Sudan, Timor-Leste, Tuvalu (185 total); plus Holy See

World Meteorological Organization (WMO)
established—11 October 1947; effective—4 April 1951
aim—to sponsor meteorological cooperation; a UN specialized agency
members—(185) includes all UN member countries except Andorra, Equatorial Guinea, Grenada, Liechtenstein, Marshall Islands, Nauru, Palau, Saint Kitts and Nevis, Saint Vincent and the Grenadines, San Marino (183 total); plus Cook Islands and Niue

World Tourism Organization (UNWTO)
established—2 January 1975
aim—to promote tourism as a means of contributing to economic development, international understanding, and peace
members—(156) Afghanistan, Albania, Algeria, Andorra, Angola, Argentina, Armenia, Australia, Austria, Azerbaijan, The Bahamas, Bahrain, Bangladesh, Belarus, Benin, Bhutan, Bolivia, Bosnia and Herzegovina, Botswana, Brazil, Brunei, Bulgaria, Burkina Faso, Burma, Burundi, Cabo Verde, Cambodia, Cameroon, Central African Republic, Chad, Chile, China, Colombia, Democratic Republic of the Congo, Republic of the Congo, Costa Rica, Cote d'Ivoire, Croatia, Cuba, Cyprus, Czech Republic, Djibouti, Dominican Republic, Ecuador, Egypt, El Salvador, Equatorial Guinea, Eritrea, Ethiopia, Fiji, France, Gabon, The Gambia, Georgia, Germany, Ghana, Greece, Guatemala, Guinea, Guinea-Bissau, Haiti, Honduras, Hungary, India, Indonesia, Iran, Iraq, Israel, Italy, Jamaica, Japan, Jordan, Kazakhstan, Kenya, North Korea, South Korea, Kuwait, Kyrgyzstan, Laos, Lebanon, Lesotho, Liberia, Libya, Lithuania, Macedonia, Madagascar, Malawi, Malaysia, Maldives, Mali, Malta, Mauritania, Mauritius, Mexico, Moldova, Monaco, Mongolia, Montenegro, Morocco, Mozambique, Namibia, Nepal, Netherlands, Nicaragua, Niger, Nigeria, Norway, Oman, Pakistan, Panama, Papua New Guinea, Paraguay, Peru, Philippines, Poland, Portugal, Qatar, Romania, Russia, Rwanda, San Marino, Sao Tome and Principe, Saudi Arabia, Senegal, Serbia, Seychelles, Sierra Leone, Slovakia, Slovenia, South Africa, Spain, Sri Lanka, Sudan, Swaziland, Switzerland, Syria, Tajikistan, Tanzania, Thailand, Timor-Leste, Togo, Trinidad and Tobago, Tunisia, Turkey, Turkmenistan, Uganda, Ukraine, UAE, Uruguay, Uzbekistan, Vanuatu, Venezuela, Vietnam, Yemen, Zambia, Zimbabwe
associate members—(6) Aruba, Flemish Community of Belgium, Hong Kong, Macau, Madeira Islands, Puerto Rico
observers—(1 plus Palestine Liberation Organization) Holy See, Palestine Liberation Organization

World Trade Organization (WTO)
note—succeeded General Agreement on Tariff and Trade (GATT)
established—15 April 1994; effective—1 January 1995
aim—to provide a forum to resolve trade conflicts between members and to carry on negotiations with the goal of further lowering and/or eliminating tariffs and other trade barriers
members—(159) Albania, Angola, Antigua and Barbuda, Argentina, Armenia, Australia, Austria, Bahrain, Bangladesh, Barbados, Belgium, Belize, Benin, Bolivia, Botswana, Brazil, Brunei, Bulgaria, Burkina Faso, Burma, Burundi, Cabo Verde, Cambodia, Cameroon, Canada, Central African Republic, Chad, Chile, China, Colombia, Democratic Republic of the Congo, Republic of the Congo, Costa Rica, Cote d'Ivoire, Croatia, Cuba, Cyprus, Czech Republic, Denmark, Djibouti, Dominica, Dominican Republic, Ecuador, Egypt, El Salvador, Estonia, EU, Fiji, Finland, France, Gabon, The Gambia, Georgia, Germany, Ghana, Greece, Grenada, Guatemala, Guinea, Guinea-Bissau, Guyana, Haiti, Honduras, Hong Kong, Hungary, Iceland, India, Indonesia, Ireland, Israel, Italy, Jamaica, Japan, Jordan, Kenya, South Korea, Kuwait, Kyrgyzstan, Laos, Latvia, Lesotho, Liechtenstein, Lithuania, Luxembourg, Macau, Macedonia, Madagascar, Malawi, Malaysia, Maldives, Mali, Malta, Mauritania, Mauritius, Mexico, Moldova, Mongolia, Montenegro, Morocco, Mozambique, Namibia, Nepal, Netherlands, NZ, Nicaragua, Niger, Nigeria, Norway, Oman, Pakistan, Panama, Papua New Guinea, Paraguay, Peru, Philippines, Poland, Portugal, Qatar, Romania, Russia, Rwanda, Saint Kitts and Nevis, Saint Lucia, Saint Vincent and the Grenadines, Samoa, Saudi Arabia, Senegal, Sierra Leone, Singapore, Slovakia, Slovenia, Solomon Islands, South Africa, Spain, Sri Lanka, Suriname, Swaziland, Sweden, Switzerland, Taiwan, Tajikistan, Tanzania, Thailand, Togo, Tonga, Trinidad and Tobago, Tunisia, Turkey, Uganda, Ukraine, UAE, UK, US, Uruguay, Vanuatu, Venezuela, Vietnam, Zambia, Zimbabwe
observers—(25) Afghanistan, Algeria, Andorra, Azerbaijan, The Bahamas, Belarus, Bhutan, Bosnia and Herzegovina, Comoros, Equatorial Guinea, Ethiopia, Holy See, Iran, Iraq, Kazakhstan, Lebanon, Liberia, Libya, Sao Tome and Principe, Serbia, Seychelles, Sudan, Syria, Uzbekistan, Yemen; note - with the exception of the Holy See, an observer must start accession negotiations within five years of becoming observers

Zangger Committee (ZC)
established—early 1970s
aim—to establish guidelines for the export control provisions of the Nonproliferation of Nuclear Weapons Treaty (NPT)
members—(39) Argentina, Australia, Austria, Belarus, Belgium, Bulgaria, Canada, China, Croatia, Czech Republic, Denmark, Finland, France, Germany, Greece, Hungary, Ireland, Italy, Japan, Kazakhstan, South Korea, Luxembourg, Netherlands, NZ, Norway, Poland, Portugal, Romania, Russia, Slovakia, Slovenia, South Africa, Spain, Sweden, Switzerland, Turkey, Ukraine, UK, US
observers—(1) European Commission

APPENDIX C

SELECTED ENVIRONMENTAL AGREEMENTS

Air Pollution
see Convention on Long-Range Transboundary Air Pollution

Air Pollution-Nitrogen Oxides
see Protocol to the 1979 Convention on Long-Range Transboundary Air Pollution Concerning the Control of Emissions of Nitrogen Oxides or Their Transboundary Fluxes

Air Pollution-Persistent Organic Pollutants
see Protocol to the 1979 Convention on Long-Range Transboundary Air Pollution on Persistent Organic Pollutants

Air Pollution-Sulphur 85
see Protocol to the 1979 Convention on Long-Range Transboundary Air Pollution on the Reduction of Sulphur Emissions or Their Transboundary Fluxes by at least 30%

Air Pollution-Sulphur 94
see Protocol to the 1979 Convention on Long-Range Transboundary Air Pollution on Further Reduction of Sulphur Emissions

Air Pollution-Volatile Organic Compounds
see Protocol to the 1979 Convention on Long-Range Transboundary Air Pollution Concerning the Control of Emissions of Volatile Organic Compounds or Their Transboundary Fluxes

Antarctic—Environmental Protocol
see Protocol on Environmental Protection to the Antarctic Treaty

Antarctic Treaty
opened for signature—1 December 1959
entered into force—23 June 1961
objective—to ensure that Antarctica is used for peaceful purposes only (such as international cooperation in scientific research); to defer the question of territorial claims asserted by some nations and not recognized by others; to provide an international forum for management of the region; applies to land and ice shelves south of 60 degrees south latitude
parties—(50) Argentina, Australia, Austria, Belarus, Belgium, Brazil, Bulgaria, Canada, Chile, China, Colombia, Cuba, Czech Republic, Denmark, Ecuador, Estonia, Finland, France, Germany, Greece, Guatemala, Hungary, India, Italy, Japan, North Korea, South Korea, Malaysia, Monaco, Netherlands, NZ, Norway, Pakistan, Papua New Guinea, Peru, Poland, Portugal, Romania, Russia, Slovakia, South Africa, Spain, Sweden, Switzerland, Turkey, Ukraine, UK, US, Uruguay, Venezuela

Basel Convention on the Control of Transboundary Movements of Hazardous Wastes and Their Disposal
note—abbreviated as Hazardous Wastes
opened for signature—22 March 1989
entered into force—5 May 1992
objective—to reduce transboundary movements of wastes subject to the Convention to a minimum consistent with the environmentally sound and efficient management of such wastes; to minimize the amount and toxicity of wastes generated and ensure their environmentally sound management as closely as possible to the source of generation; and to assist LDCs in environmentally sound management of the hazardous and other wastes they generate
parties—(171) Albania, Algeria, Andorra, Antigua and Barbuda, Argentina, Armenia, Australia, Austria, Azerbaijan, The Bahamas, Bahrain, Bangladesh, Barbados, Belarus, Belgium, Belize, Benin, Bhutan, Bolivia, Bosnia and Herzegovina, Botswana, Brazil, Brunei, Bulgaria, Burkina Faso, Burundi, Cambodia, Cameroon, Canada, Cape Verde, Central African Republic, Chad, Chile, China, Colombia, Comoros, Democratic Republic of the Congo, Republic of the Congo, Cook Islands, Costa Rica, Cote d'Ivoire, Croatia, Cuba, Cyprus, Czech Republic, Denmark, Djibouti, Dominica, Dominican Republic, Ecuador, Egypt, El Salvador, Equatorial Guinea, Eritrea, Estonia, Ethiopia, EU, Finland, France, Gabon, The Gambia, Georgia, Germany, Ghana, Greece, Guatemala, Guinea, Guinea-Bissau, Guyana, Honduras, Hungary, Iceland, India, Indonesia, Iran, Ireland, Israel, Italy, Jamaica, Japan, Jordan, Kazakhstan, Kenya, Kiribati, North Korea, South Korea, Kuwait, Kyrgyzstan, Latvia, Lebanon, Lesotho, Liberia, Libya, Liechtenstein, Lithuania, Luxembourg, Macedonia, Madagascar, Malawi, Malaysia, Maldives, Mali, Malta, Marshall Islands, Mauritania, Mauritius, Mexico, Federated States of Micronesia, Moldova, Monaco, Mongolia, Montenegro, Morocco, Mozambique, Namibia, Nauru, Nepal, Netherlands, NZ, Nicaragua, Niger, Nigeria, Norway, Oman, Pakistan, Panama, Papua New Guinea, Paraguay, Peru, Philippines, Poland, Portugal, Qatar, Romania, Russia, Rwanda, Saint Kitts and Nevis, Saint Lucia, Saint Vincent and the Grenadines, Samoa, Saudi Arabia, Senegal, Serbia, Seychelles, Singapore, Slovakia, Slovenia, South Africa, Spain, Sri Lanka, Sudan, Swaziland, Sweden, Switzerland, Syria, Tanzania, Thailand, Trinidad and Tobago, Tunisia, Turkey, Turkmenistan, Uganda, Ukraine, UAE, UK, Uruguay, Uzbekistan, Venezuela, Vietnam, Yemen, Zambia
countries that have signed, but not yet ratified—(3) Afghanistan, Haiti, US

Biodiversity
see Convention on Biological Diversity

Climate Change
see United Nations Framework Convention on Climate Change

Climate Change-Kyoto Protocol
see Kyoto Protocol to the United Nations Framework Convention on Climate Change

Convention for the Conservation of Antarctic Seals
note—abbreviated as Antarctic Seals
opened for signature—1 June 1972
entered into force—11 March 1978
objective—to promote and achieve the protection, scientific study, and rational use of Antarctic seals, and to maintain a satisfactory balance within the ecological system of Antarctica
parties—(16) Argentina, Australia, Belgium, Brazil, Canada, Chile, France, Germany, Italy, Japan, Norway, Poland, Russia, South Africa, UK, US
countries that have signed, but not yet ratified—(1) NZ

Convention on Biological Diversity
note—abbreviated as Biodiversity
opened for signature—5 June 1992
entered into force—29 December 1993
objective—to develop national strategies for the conservation and sustainable use of biological diversity and to address the fair and equitable sharing of benefits arising out of the utilization of genetic resources
parties—(191) Afghanistan, Albania, Algeria, Andorra, Angola, Antigua and Barbuda, Argentina, Armenia, Australia, Austria, Azerbaijan, The Bahamas, Bahrain, Bangladesh, Barbados, Belarus, Belgium, Belize, Benin, Bhutan, Bolivia, Bosnia and Herzegovina, Botswana, Brazil, Brunei, Bulgaria, Burkina Faso, Burma, Burundi, Cambodia, Cameroon, Canada, Cape Verde, Central African Republic, Chad, Chile, China, Colombia, Comoros, Democratic Republic of the Congo, Republic of the Congo, Cook Islands, Costa Rica, Cote d'Ivoire, Croatia, Cuba, Cyprus, Czech Republic, Denmark, Djibouti, Dominica, Dominican Republic, Ecuador, Egypt, El Salvador, Equatorial Guinea, Eritrea, Estonia, Ethiopia, EU, Fiji, Finland, France, Gabon, The Gambia, Georgia, Germany, Ghana, Greece, Grenada, Guatemala, Guinea, Guinea-Bissau, Guyana, Haiti, Honduras, Hungary, Iceland, India, Indonesia, Iran, Iraq, Ireland, Israel, Italy, Jamaica, Japan, Jordan, Kazakhstan, Kenya, Kiribati, North Korea, South Korea, Kuwait, Kyrgyzstan, Laos, Latvia, Lebanon, Lesotho, Liberia, Libya, Liechtenstein, Lithuania, Luxembourg, Macedonia, Madagascar, Malawi, Malaysia, Maldives, Mali, Malta, Marshall Islands, Mauritania, Mauritius, Mexico, Federated States of Micronesia, Moldova, Monaco, Mongolia, Montenegro, Morocco, Mozambique, Namibia, Nauru, Nepal, Netherlands, NZ, Nicaragua, Niger, Nigeria, Niue, Norway, Oman, Pakistan, Palau, Panama, Papua New Guinea, Paraguay, Peru, Philippines, Poland, Portugal, Qatar, Romania, Russia, Rwanda, Saint Kitts and Nevis, Saint Lucia, Saint Vincent and the Grenadines, Samoa, San Marino, Sao Tome and Principe, Saudi Arabia, Senegal, Serbia, Seychelles, Sierra Leone, Singapore, Slovakia, Slovenia, Solomon Islands, Somalia, South Africa, Spain, Sri Lanka, Sudan, Suriname, Swaziland, Sweden, Switzerland, Syria, Tajikistan, Tanzania, Thailand, Timor-Leste, Togo, Tonga, Trinidad and Tobago, Tunisia, Turkey, Turkmenistan, Tuvalu, Uganda, Ukraine, UAE, UK, Uruguay, Uzbekistan, Vanuatu, Venezuela, Vietnam, Yemen, Zambia, Zimbabwe
countries that have signed, but not yet ratified—(1) US

Convention on Fishing and Conservation of Living Resources of the High Seas
note—abbreviated as Marine Life Conservation
opened for signature—29 April 1958
entered into force—20 March 1966
objective—to solve through international cooperation the problems involved in the conservation of living resources of the high seas, considering that because of the development of modern technology some of these resources are in danger of being overexploited
parties—(39) Australia, Belgium, Bosnia and Herzegovina, Burkina Faso, Cambodia, Colombia, Republic of the Congo, Denmark, Dominican Republic, Fiji, Finland, France, Haiti, Jamaica, Kenya, Lesotho, Madagascar, Malawi, Malaysia, Mauritius, Mexico, Montenegro, Netherlands, Nigeria, Portugal, Senegal, Serbia, Sierra Leone, Solomon Islands, South Africa, Spain, Switzerland, Thailand, Tonga, Trinidad and Tobago, Uganda, UK, US, Venezuela
countries that have signed, but not yet ratified—(21) Afghanistan, Argentina, Bolivia, Canada, Costa Rica, Cuba, Ghana, Iceland, Indonesia, Iran, Ireland, Israel, Lebanon, Liberia, Nepal, NZ, Pakistan, Panama, Sri Lanka, Tunisia, Uruguay

Convention on Long-Range Transboundary Air Pollution
note—abbreviated as Air Pollution
opened for signature—13 November 1979
entered into force—16 March 1983
objective—to protect the human environment against air pollution and, as far as possible, to gradually reduce and prevent air pollution, including long-range transboundary air pollution
parties—(51) Albania, Armenia, Austria, Azerbaijan, Belarus, Belgium, Bosnia and Herzegovina, Bulgaria, Canada, Croatia, Cyprus, Czech Republic, Denmark, Estonia, EU, Finland, France, Georgia, Germany, Greece, Hungary, Iceland, Ireland, Italy, Kazakhstan, Kyrgyzstan, Latvia, Liechtenstein, Lithuania, Luxembourg, Macedonia, Malta, Moldova, Monaco, Montenegro, Netherlands, Norway, Poland, Portugal, Romania, Russia, Serbia, Slovakia, Slovenia, Spain, Sweden, Switzerland, Turkey, Ukraine, UK, US
countries that have signed, but not yet ratified—(2) Holy See, San Marino

Convention on Wetlands of International Importance Especially as Waterfowl Habitat (Ramsar)
note—abbreviated as Wetlands
opened for signature—2 February 1971
entered into force—21 December 1975
objective—to stem the progressive encroachment on and loss of wetlands now and in the future
parties—(168) Albania, Algeria, Andorra, Antigua and Barbuda, Argentina, Armenia, Australia, Austria, Azerbaijan, The Bahamas, Bahrain, Bangladesh, Barbados, Belarus, Belgium, Belize, Benin, Bhutan, Bolivia, Bosnia and Herzegovina, Botswana, Brazil, Bulgaria, Burkina Faso, Burma, Burundi, Cambodia, Cameroon, Canada, Cape Verde, Central African Republic, Chad, Chile, China, Colombia, Comoros, Democratic Republic of the Congo, Republic of the Congo, Costa Rica, Cote d'Ivoire, Croatia, Cuba, Cyprus, Czech Republic, Denmark, Djibouti, Dominican Republic, Ecuador, Egypt, El Salvador, Equatorial Guinea, Estonia, Fiji, Finland, France, Gabon, The Gambia, Georgia, Germany, Ghana, Greece, Grenada, Guatemala, Guinea, Guinea-Bissau, Honduras, Hungary, Gambia, Georgia, Germany, Ghana, Greece, Grenada, Guatemala, Guinea, Guinea-Bissau, Honduras, Hungary, Iceland, India, Indonesia, Iran, Iraq, Ireland, Israel, Italy, Jamaica, Japan, Jordan, Kazakhstan, Kenya, Kiribati, South Korea, Kyrgyzstan, Laos, Latvia, Lebanon, Lesotho, Liberia, Libya, Liechtenstein, Lithuania, Luxembourg, Macedonia, Madagascar, Malawi, Malaysia, Mali, Malta, Marshall Islands, Mauritania, Mauritius, Mexico, Moldova, Monaco,

Mongolia, Montenegro, Morocco, Mozambique, Namibia, Nepal, Netherlands, NZ, Nicaragua, Niger, Nigeria, Norway, Oman, Pakistan, Palau, Panama, Papua New Guinea, Paraguay, Peru, Philippines, Poland, Portugal, Romania, Russia, Rwanda, Saint Lucia, Samoa, Sao Tome and Principe, Senegal, Serbia, Seychelles, Sierra Leone, Slovakia, Slovenia, South Africa, South Sudan, Spain, Sri Lanka, Sudan, Suriname, Swaziland, Sweden, Switzerland, Syria, Tanzania, Tajikistan, Thailand, Togo, Trinidad and Tobago, Tunisia, Turkey, Turkmenistan, Uganda, Ukraine, UAE, UK, US, Uruguay, Uzbekistan, Venezuela, Vietnam, Yemen, Zambia, Zimbabwe

Convention on the Conservation of Antarctic Marine Living Resources
note—abbreviated as Antarctic-Marine Living Resources
opened for signature—5 May 1980
entered into force—7 April 1982
objective—to safeguard the environment and protect the integrity of the ecosystem of the seas surrounding Antarctica, and to conserve Antarctic marine living resources
parties—(34) Argentina, Australia, Belgium, Brazil, Bulgaria, Canada, Chile, China, Cook Islands, EU, Finland, France, Germany, Greece, India, Italy, Japan, South Korea, Mauritius, Namibia, Netherlands, NZ, Norway, Peru, Poland, Russia, South Africa, Spain, Sweden, Ukraine, UK, US, Uruguay, Vanuatu

Convention on the International Trade in Endangered Species of Wild Flora and Fauna (CITES)
note—abbreviated as Endangered Species
opened for signature—3 March 1973
entered into force—1 July 1975
objective—to protect certain endangered species from overexploitation by means of a system of import/export permits
parties—(179) Afghanistan, Albania, Algeria, Angola, Antigua and Barbuda, Argentina, Armenia, Australia, Austria, Azerbaijan, The Bahamas, Bahrain, Bangladesh, Barbados, Belarus, Belgium, Belize, Benin, Bhutan, Bolivia, Bosnia and Herzegovina, Botswana, Brazil, Brunei, Bulgaria, Burkina Faso, Burma, Burundi, Cambodia, Cameroon, Canada, Cape Verde, Central African Republic, Chad, Chile, China, Colombia, Comoros, Democratic Republic of the Congo, Republic of the Congo, Costa Rica, Cote d'Ivoire, Croatia, Cuba, Cyprus, Czech Republic, Denmark, Djibouti, Dominica, Dominican Republic, Ecuador, Egypt, El Salvador, Equatorial Guinea, Eritrea, Estonia, Ethiopia, Fiji, Finland, France, Gabon, The Gambia, Georgia, Germany, Ghana, Greece, Grenada, Guatemala, Guinea, Guinea-Bissau, Guyana, Honduras, Hungary, Iceland, India, Indonesia, Iran, Ireland, Israel, Italy, Jamaica, Japan, Jordan, Kazakhstan, Kenya, South Korea, Kuwait, Kyrgyzstan, Laos, Latvia, Lebanon, Lesotho, Liberia, Libya, Liechtenstein, Lithuania, Luxembourg, Macedonia, Madagascar, Malawi, Malaysia, Maldives, Mali, Malta, Mauritania, Mauritius, Mexico, Moldova, Monaco, Mongolia, Montenegro, Morocco, Mozambique, Namibia, Nepal, Netherlands, NZ, Nicaragua, Niger, Nigeria, Norway, Oman, Palau, Pakistan, Panama, Papua New Guinea, Paraguay, Peru, Philippines, Poland, Portugal, Qatar, Romania, Russia, Rwanda, Saint Kitts and Nevis, Saint Lucia, Saint Vincent and the Grenadines, Samoa, San Marino, Sao Tome and Principe, Saudi Arabia, Senegal, Serbia, Seychelles, Sierra Leone, Singapore, Slovakia, Slovenia, Solomon Islands, Somalia, South Africa, Spain, Sri Lanka, Sudan, Suriname, Swaziland, Sweden, Switzerland, Syria, Tanzania, Thailand, Togo, Trinidad and Tobago, Tunisia, Turkey, Uganda, Ukraine, UAE, UK, US, Uruguay, Uzbekistan, Vanuatu, Venezuela, Vietnam, Yemen, Zambia, Zimbabwe

Convention on the Prevention of Marine Pollution by Dumping Wastes and Other Matter (London Convention)
note—abbreviated as Marine Dumping
opened for signature—29 December 1972
entered into force—30 August 1975
objective—to promote effective control of all sources of marine pollution and to take all practicable steps to prevent pollution of the sea by dumping and to encourage regional agreements supplementary to the Convention
parties—(87) Afghanistan, Antigua and Barbuda, Argentina, Australia, Azerbaijan, Barbados, Belarus, Belgium, Benin, Bolivia, Brazil, Bulgaria, Canada, Cape Verde, Chile, China, Democratic Republic of the Congo, Costa Rica, Cote d'Ivoire, Croatia, Cuba, Cyprus, Denmark, Dominican Republic, Egypt, Equatorial Guinea, Finland, France, Cote d'Ivoire, Croatia, Cuba, Cyprus, Denmark, Dominican Republic, Egypt, Equatorial Guinea, Finland, France, Gabon, Germany, Greece, Guatemala, Haiti, Honduras, Hong Kong (associate member), Hungary, Iceland, Iran, Ireland, Italy, Jamaica, Japan, Jordan, Kenya, Kiribati, South Korea, Libya, Luxembourg, Malta, Mexico, Monaco, Montenegro, Morocco, Nauru, Netherlands, NZ, Nigeria, Norway, Oman, Pakistan, Panama, Papua New Guinea, Peru, Philippines, Poland, Portugal, Russia, Saint Lucia, Saint Vincent and the Grenadines, Serbia, Seychelles, Sierra Leon, Slovenia, Solomon Islands, South Africa, Spain, Suriname, Sweden, Switzerland, Syria, Tanzania, Tonga, Tunisia, Ukraine, UAE, UK, US, Vanuatu
associate members to the London Convention—(2) Faroe Islands, Macau
countries that have signed, but not yet ratified—(3) Chad, Kuwait, Uruguay

Convention on the Prohibition of Military or Any Other Hostile Use of Environmental Modification Techniques
note—abbreviated as Environmental Modification
opened for signature—18 May 1977
entered into force—5 October 1978
objective—to prohibit the military or other hostile use of environmental modification techniques in order to further world peace and trust among nations
parties—(76) Afghanistan, Algeria, Antigua and Barbuda, Argentina, Armenia, Australia, Austria, Bangladesh, Belarus, Belgium, Benin, Brazil, Bulgaria, Canada, Cameroon, Cape Verde, Chile, China, Costa Rica, Cuba, Cyprus, Czech Republic, Denmark, Dominica, Egypt, Estonia, Finland, Germany, Ghana, Greece, Guatemala, Honduras, Hungary, India, Ireland, Italy, Japan, Kazakhstan, North Korea, South Korea, Kuwait, Laos, Lithuania, Malawi, Mauritius, Mongolia, Netherlands, NZ, Nicaragua, Niger, Norway, Pakistan, Panama, Papua New Guinea, Poland, Romania, Russia, Saint Lucia, Saint Vincent and the Grenadines, Sao Tome and Principe, Slovakia, Slovenia, Solomon Islands, Spain, Sri Lanka, Sweden, Switzerland, Tajikistan, Tunisia, Ukraine, UK, US, Uruguay, Uzbekistan, Vietnam, Yemen
countries that have signed, but not yet ratified—(16) Bolivia, Democratic Republic of the Congo, Ethiopia, Holy See, Iceland, Iran, Iraq, Lebanon, Liberia, Luxembourg, Morocco, Portugal, Sierra Leone, Syria, Turkey, Uganda

Desertification
see United Nations Convention to Combat Desertification in those Countries Experiencing Serious Drought and/or Desertification, Particularly in Africa

Endangered Species
see Convention on the International Trade in Endangered Species of Wild Flora and Fauna (CITES)

Environmental Modification
see Convention on the Prohibition of Military or Any Other Hostile Use of Environmental Modification Techniques

Hazardous Wastes
see Basel Convention on the Control of Transboundary Movements of Hazardous Wastes and Their Disposal

International Convention for the Regulation of Whaling
note—abbreviated as Whaling
opened for signature—2 December 1946
entered into force—10 November 1948
objective—to protect all species of whales from overhunting; to establish a system of international regulation for the whale fisheries to ensure proper conservation and development of whale stocks; and to safeguard for future generations the great natural resources represented by whale stocks
parties—(88) Antigua and Barbuda, Argentina, Australia, Austria, Belgium, Belize, Benin, Brazil, Bulgaria, Cambodia, Cameroon, Chile, China, Colombia, Republic of the Congo, Costa Rica, Cote D'Ivoire, Croatia, Cyprus, Czech Republic, Denmark, Dominica, Dominican Republic, Ecuador, Eritrea, Estonia, Finland, France, Gabon, The Gambia, Germany, Ghana, Greece, Grenada, Guatemala, Guinea, Guinea-Bissau, Hungary, Iceland, India, Ireland, Israel, Italy, Japan, Kenya, Kiribati, South Korea, Laos, Lithuania, Luxembourg, Mali, Marshall Islands, Mauritania, Mexico, Monaco, Mongolia, Morocco, Nauru, Netherlands, NZ, Nicaragua, Norway, Oman, Palau, Panama, Peru, Mexico, Monaco, Mongolia, Morocco, Nauru, Netherlands, NZ, Nicaragua, Norway, Oman, Palau, Panama, Peru, Poland, Portugal, Romania, Russia, Saint Kitts and Nevis, Saint Lucia, Saint Vincent and the Grenadines, San Marino, Senegal, Slovakia, Slovenia, Solomon Islands, South Africa, Spain, Suriname, Sweden, Switzerland, Tanzania, Togo, Tuvalu, UK, US, Uruguay

International Tropical Timber Agreement, 1983
note—abbreviated as Tropical Timber 83
opened for signature—18 November 1983
entered into force—1 April 1985; this agreement was superseded by the International Tropical Timber Agreement, 1994
objective—to provide an effective framework for cooperation between tropical timber producers and consumers and to encourage the development of national policies aimed at sustainable utilization and conservation of tropical forests and their genetic resources
parties—(59) Australia, Austria, Belgium, Bolivia, Brazil, Burma, Cambodia, Cameroon, Canada, Central African Republic, China, Colombia, Democratic Republic of the Congo, Republic of the Congo, Cote d'Ivoire, Denmark, Ecuador, Egypt, EU, Fiji, Finland, France, Gabon, Germany, Ghana, Greece, Guatemala, Guyana, Honduras, India, Indonesia, Ireland, Italy, Japan, South Korea, Liberia, Luxembourg, Malaysia, Mexico, Nepal, Netherlands, NZ, Nigeria, Norway, Panama, Papua New Guinea, Peru, Philippines, Portugal, Russia, Spain, Suriname, Sweden, Switzerland, Thailand, Togo, Trinidad and Tobago, UK, US, Vanuatu, Venezuela

International Tropical Timber Agreement, 1994
note—abbreviated as Tropical Timber 94
opened for signature—1 April 1994
entered into force—1 January 1997 (provisional application)
objective—to provide a framework for international cooperation on conservation and sustainable development of tropical timber and enhance the capacity of members to implement a strategy for achieving exports of tropical timber and timber products from sustainably managed sources by the year 2000; to establish a fund to assist tropical timper producers in obtaining the resources necessary to reach this objective
parties—(61) Australia, Austria, Belgium, Bolivia, Brazil, Burma, Cambodia, Cameroon, Canada, Central African Republic, China, Colombia, Democratic Republic of the Congo, Republic of the Congo, Cote d'Ivoire, Denmark, Ecuador, Egypt, EU, Fiji, Finland, France, Gabon, Germany, Ghana, Greece, Guatemala, Guyana, Honduras, India, Indonesia, Ireland, Italy, Japan, South Korea, Liberia, Luxembourg, Malaysia, Mexico, Nepal, Netherlands, NZ, Nigeria, Norway, Panama, Papua New Guinea, Peru, Philippines, Poland, Portugal, Spain, Suriname, Sweden, Switzerland, Thailand, Togo, Trinidad and Tobago, UK, US, Vanuatu, Venezuela

Kyoto Protocol to the United Nations Framework Convention on Climate Change
note—abbreviated as Climate Change-Kyoto Protocol
opened for signature—16 March 1998
entered into force—23 February 2005
objective—to further reduce greenhouse gas emissions by enhancing the national programs of developed countries aimed at this goal and by establishing percentage reduction targets for the developed countries
parties—(192) Albania, Algeria, Angola, Antigua and Barbuda, Argentina, Armenia, Australia, Austria, Azerbaijan, The Bahamas, Bahrain, Bangladesh, Barbados, Belarus, Belgium, Belize, Benin, Bhutan, Bolivia, Bosnia and Herzegovina, Botswana, Brazil, Brunei, Bulgaria, Burkina Faso, Burma, Burundi, Cambodia, Cameroon, Cape Verde, Central African Republic, Chad, Chile, China, Colombia, Comoros, Democratic Republic of the Congo, Republic of the Congo, Cook Island, Costa Rica, Cote d'Ivoire, Croatia, Cuba, Cyprus, Czech Republic, Denmark, Djibouti, Dominica, Dominican Republic, Ecuador, Egypt, El Salvador, Equatorial Guinea, Eritrea, Estonia, Ethiopia, EU, Fiji, Finland, France, Gabon, The Gambia, Georgia, Germany, Ghana, Greece, Grenada, Guatemala, Guinea, Guinea-Bissau, Guyana, Haiti, Honduras, Hungary, Iceland, India, Indonesia, Iran, Iraq, Ireland, Israel, Italy, Jamaica, Japan, Jordan, Kazakhstan, Kenya, Kiribati, North Korea, South Korea, Kuwait, Kyrgyzstan, Laos, Latvia, Lebanon, Lesotho, Liberia, Libya, Liechtenstein, Lithuania, Luxembourg, Macedonia, Madagascar, Malawi, Malaysia, Maldives, Mali, Malta, Marshall Islands, Mauritania, Mauritius, Mexico, Federated States of Micronesia, Moldova, Monaco, Mongolia, Montenegro, Morocco, Mozambique, Namibia, Nauru, Nepal, Netherlands, NZ, Nicaragua, Niger, Nigeria, Niue, Norway, Oman, Pakistan, Palau, Panama, Papua New Guinea, Paraguay, Peru, Philippines, Poland, Nigeria, Niue, Norway, Oman, Pakistan, Palau, Panama, Papua New Guinea, Paraguay, Peru, Philippines, Poland, Portugal, Qatar, Romania, Russia, Rwanda, Saint Kitts and Nevis, Saint Lucia, Saint Vincent and the Grenadines, Samoa, San Marino, Sao Tome and Principe, Saudi Arabia, Senegal, Serbia, Seychelles, Sierra Leone, Singapore, Slovakia, Slovenia, Solomon Islands, Somalia, South Africa, Spain, Sri Lanka, Sudan, Suriname, Swaziland, Sweden, Switzerland, Syria, Tajikistan, Tanzania, Thailand, Timor-Leste, Togo, Tonga, Trinidad

and Tobago, Tunisia, Turkey, Turkmenistan, Tuvalu, Uganda, Ukraine, UAE, UK, Uruguay, Uzbekistan, Vanuatu, Venezuela, Vietnam, Yemen, Zam ia, Zimbabwe
countries that have signed, but not yet ratified—(1) US

Law of the Sea
see United Nations Convention on the Law of the Sea (LOS)

Marine Dumping
see Convention on the Prevention of Marine Pollution by Dumping Wastes and Other Matter (London Convention)

Marine Life Conservation
see Convention on Fishing and Conservation of Living Resources of the High Seas

Montreal Protocol on Substances That Deplete the Ozone Layer
note—abbreviated as Ozone Layer Protection
opened for signature—16 September 1987
entered into force—1 January 1989
objective—to protect the ozone layer by controlling emissions of substances that deplete it
parties—(197) Afghanistan, Albania, Algeria, Andorra, Angola, Antigua and Barbuda, Argentina, Armenia, Australia, Austria, Azerbaijan, The Bahamas, Bahrain, Bangladesh, Barbados, Belarus, Belgium, Belize, Benin, Bhutan, Bolivia, Bosnia and Herzegovina, Botswana, Brazil, Brunei, Bulgaria, Burkina Faso, Burma, Burundi, Cambodia, Cameroon, Canada, Cape Verde, Central African Republic, Chad, Chile, China, Colombia, Comoros, Democratic Republic of the Congo, Republic of the Congo, Cook Islands, Costa Rica, Cote d'Ivoire, Croatia, Cuba, Cyprus, Czech Republic, Denmark, Djibouti, Dominica, Dominican Republic, Ecuador, Egypt, El Salvador, Equatorial Guinea, Eritrea, Estonia, Ethiopia, EU, Fiji, Finland, France, Gabon, The Gambia, Georgia, Germany, Ghana, Greece, Grenada, Guatemala, Guinea, Guinea-Bissau, Guyana, Haiti, Holy See, Honduras, Hungary, Iceland, India, Indonesia, Iran, Iraq, Ireland, Israel, Italy, Jamaica, Japan, Jordan, Kazakhstan, Kenya, Kiribati, North Korea, South Korea, Kuwait, Kyrgyzstan, Laos, Latvia, Lebanon, Lesotho, Liberia, Libya, Liechtenstein, Lithuania, Luxembourg, Macedonia, Madagascar, Malawi, Malaysia, Maldives, Mali, Malta, Marshall Islands, Mauritania, Mauritius, Mexico, Federated States of Micronesia, Moldova, Monaco, Mongolia, Montenegro, Morocco, Mozambique, Namibia, Nauru, Nepal, Netherlands, NZ, Nicaragua, Niger, Nigeria, Niue, Norway, Oman, Pakistan, Palau, Panama, Papua New Guinea, Paraguay, Peru, Philippines, Poland, Portugal, Qatar, Romania, Russia, Rwanda, Saint Kitts and Nevis, Saint Lucia, Saint Vincent and the Grenadines, Samoa, San Marino, Sao Tome and Principe, Saudi Arabia, Senegal, Serbia, Seychelles, Sierra Leone, Singapore, Slovakia, Slovenia, Solomon Islands, Somalia, South Africa, South Sudan, Spain, Sri Lanka, Sudan, Suriname, Swaziland, Sweden, Switzerland, Syria, Tajikistan, Tanzania, Thailand, Timor-Leste, Togo, Tonga, Trinidad and Tobago, Tunisia, Turkey, Turkmenistan, Tuvalu, Uganda, Ukraine, UAE, UK, US, Ur guay, Uzbekistan, Vanuatu, Venezuela, Vietnam, Yemen, Zambia, Zimbabwe

Nuclear Test Ban
see Treaty Banning Nuclear Weapons Tests in the Atmosphere, in Outer Space, and Under Water

Ozone Layer Protection
see Montreal Protocol on Substances That Deplete the Ozone Layer

Protocol of 1978 Relating to the International Convention for the Prevention of Pollution From Ships, 1973 (MARPOL)
note—abbreviated as Ship Pollution
opened for signature—1 June 1978
entered into force—2 October 1983
objective—to modify the International Convention for the Prevention of Pollution from Ships, 1973, including by extending the period of compliance under the Convention by three years
parties—(152) Albania, Algeria, Angola, Antigua and Barbuda, Argentina, Australia, Austria, Azerbaijan, The Bahamas, Bahrain, Bangladesh, Barbados, Belarus, Belgium, Belize, Benin, Bolivia, Brazil, Brunei, Bulgaria, Burma, Cambodia, Canada, Cape Verde, Chile, China, Colombia, Comoros, Republic of Congo, Cote d'Ivoire, Croatia, Cuba, Cyprus, Czech Republic, Denmark, Djibouti, Dominica, Dominican Republic, Ecuador, Egypt, El Salvador, Equatorial Guinea, Estonia, Faroe Islands, Finland, France, Gabon, The Gambia, Georgia, Germany, Ghana, Greece, Guatemala, Guinea, Guyana, Honduras, Hong Kong, Hungary, Iceland, India, Indonesia, Iran, Ireland, Israel, Italy, Jamaica, Japan, Jordan, Kazakhstan, Kenya, Kiribati, North Korea, South Korea, Kuwait, Latvia, Lebanon, Liberia, Lithuania, Luxembourg, Libya, Macau, Madagascar, Malawi, Malaysia, Maldives, Malta, Marshall Islands, Mauritania, Mauritius, Mexico, Moldova, Monaco, Mongolia, Montenegro, Morocco, Mozambique, Namibia, Netherlands, NZ, Nicaragua, Nigeria, Norway, Nuie, Oman, Pakistan, Palau, Panama, Papua New Guinea, Peru, Philippines, Poland, Portugal, Qatar Romania, Russia, Saint Kitts and Nevis, Saint Lucia, Saint Vincent and the Grenadines, Samoa, Sao Tome and Principe, Saudi Arabia, Senegal, Serbia, Seychelles, Sierra Leone, Singapore, Slovakia, Slovenia, Solomon Islands, South Africa, Spain, Sri Lanka, Suriname, Sweden, Switzerland, Syria, Tanzania, Togo, Tonga, Trinidad and Tobago, Tunisia, Turkey, Turkmenistan, Tuvalu, Ukraine, UAE, UK, US, Uruguay, Vanuatu, Venezuela, Vietnam

Protocol on Environmental Protection to the Antarctic Treaty
note—abbreviated as Antarctic-Environmental Protocol
opened for signature—4 October 1991
entered into force—14 January 1998
objective—to provide for comprehensive protection of the Antarctic environment and dependent and associated ecosystems; applies to the area covered by the Antarctic Treaty
consultative parties—(28) Argentina, Australia, Belgium, Brazil, Bulgaria, Chile, China, Ecuador, Finland, France, Germany, India, Italy, Japan, South Korea, Netherlands, NZ, Norway, Peru, Poland, Russia, South Africa, Spain, Sweden, Ukraine, UK, US, Uruguay
non consultative parties—(22) Austria, Belarus, Canada, Colombia, Cuba, Czech Republic, Denmark, Estonia, Greece, Guatemala, Hungary, North Korea, Malaysia, Monaco, Pakistan, Papua New Guinea, Romania, Slovakia, Switzerland, Turkey, Venezuela

Protocol to the 1979 Convention on Long-Range Transboundary Air Pollution Concerning the Control of Emissions of Nitrogen Oxides or Their Transboundary Fluxes
note—abbreviated as Air Pollution-Nitrogen Oxides
opened for signature—31 October 1988
entered into force—14 February 1991
objective—to provide for the control or reduction national of nitrogen oxide emissions and their transboundary fluxes
parties—(35) Albania, Austria, Belarus, Belgium, Bulgaria, Canada, Croatia, Cyprus, Czech Republic, Denmark, Estonia, EU, Finland, France, Germany, Greece, Hungary, Ireland, Italy, Liechtenstein, Lithuania, Luxembourg, Macedonia, Netherlands, Norway, Poland, Russia, Slovakia, Slovenia, Spain, Sweden, Switzerland, Ukraine, UK, US

Protocol to the 1979 Convention on Long-Range Transboundary Air Pollution Concerning the Control of Emissions of Volatile Organic Compounds or Their Transboundary Fluxes
note—abbreviated as Air Pollution-Volatile Organic Compounds
opened for signature—18 November 1991
entered into force—29 September 1997
objective—to provide for the control and reduction of national emissions of volatile organic compounds in order to reduce their transboundary fluxes
parties—(23) (24) Austria, Belgium, Bulgaria, Croatia, Czech Republic, Denmark, Estonia, Finland, France, Germany, Hungary, Italy, Liechtenstein, Lithuania, Luxembourg, Macedonia, Monaco, Netherlands, Norway, Slovakia, Spain, Sweden, Switzerland, UK Sweden, Switzerland, UK
countries that have signed, but not yet ratified—(6) Canada, EU, Greece, Portugal, Ukraine, US

Protocol to the 1979 Convention on Long-Range Transboundary Air Pollution on Further Reduction of Sulphur Emissions
note—abbreviated as Air Pollution-Sulphur 94
opened for signature—14 June 1994
entered into force—5 August 1998
objective—to provide for a further reduction in national sulfur emissions or transboundary fluxes on a regional basis within Europe
parties—(29) Austria, Belgium, Bulgaria, Canada, Croatia, Cyprus, Czech Republic, Denmark, EU, Finland, France, Germany, Greece, Hungary, Ireland, Italy, Liechtenstein, Lithuania, Luxembourg, Macedonia, Monaco, Netherlands, Norway, Slovakia, Slovenia, Spain, Sweden, Switzerland, UK
countries that have signed, but not yet ratified—(3) Poland, Russia, Ukraine

Protocol to the 1979 Convention on Long-Range Transboundary Air Pollution on Persistent Organic Pollutants
note—abbreviated as Air Pollution-Persistent Organic Pollutants
opened for signature—24 June 1998
entered into force—23 October 2003
objective—to provide for the control, reduction, or elimination of discharges, emissions of persistent organic pollutants
parties—(33) Austria, Belgium, Bulgaria, Canada, Croatia, Cyprus, Czech Republic, Denmark, Estonia, EU, Finland, France, Germany, Hungary, Iceland, Italy, Latvia, Liechtenstein, Lithuania, Luxembourg, Macedonia, Moldova, Montenegro, Netherlands, Norway, Romania, Serbia, Slovakia, Slovenia, Spain, Sweden, Switzerland, UK
countries that have signed, but not yet ratified—(8) Armenia, Greece, Ireland, Poland, Portugal, Spain, Ukraine, US

Protocol to the 1979 Convention on Long-Range Transboundary Air Pollution on the Reduction of Sulphur Emissions or Their Transboundary Fluxes by at Least 30%
note—abbreviated as Air Pollution-Sulphur 85
opened for signature—8 July 1985
entered into force—2 September 1987
objective—to provide for national reductions in sulfur emissions or transboundary fluxes by 30% of 1980 emission or transboundary flux levels by no later than 1993
parties—(23) Albania, Austria, Belarus, Belgium, Bulgaria, Canada, Czech Republic, Denmark, Estonia, Finland, France, Germany, Hungary, Italy, Liechtenstein, Lithuania, Luxembourg, Macedonia, Netherlands, Norway, Russia, Slovakia, Sweden, Switzerland, Ukraine

Ship Pollution
see Protocol of 1978 Relating to the International Convention for the Prevention of Pollution From Ships, 1973 (MARPOL)

Treaty Banning Nuclear Weapon Tests in the Atmosphere, in Outer Space, and Under Water
note—abbreviated as Nuclear Test Ban
opened for signature—5 August 1963
entered into force—10 October 1963
objective—to ban nuclear weapons testing in the atmosphere, outer space, or under water
parties—(124) Afghanistan, Antigua and Barbuda, Argentina, Armenia, Australia, Austria, The Bahamas, Bangladesh, Belarus, Belgium, Benin, Bhutan, Bolivia, Bosnia and Herzegovina, Botswana, Brazil, Bulgaria, Burma, Canada, Cape Verde, Central African Republic, Chad, Chile, China, Colombia, Costa Rica, Cote d'Ivoire, Croatia, Cyprus, Czech Republic, Democratic Republic of the Congo, Denmark, Dominican Republic, Ecuador, Egypt, El Salvador, Fiji, Finland, Gabon, The Gambia, Germany, Ghana, Greece, Guatemala, Honduras, Hungary, Iceland, India, Indonesia, Iran, Iraq, Ireland, Israel, Italy, Jamaica, Japan, Jordan, Kenya, South Korea, Kuwait, Laos, Lebanon, Liberia, Libya, Luxembourg, Madagascar, Malawi, Malaysia, Malta, Mauritania, Mauritius, Mexico, Mongolia, Montenegro, Morocco, Nepal, Netherlands, New Zealand, Nicaragua, Niger, Nigeria, Norway, Panama, Pakistan, Papua New Guinea, Peru, Philippines, Poland, Romania, Russia, Rwanda, Samoa, San Marino, Senegal, Serbia, Seychelles, Sierra Leone, Singapore, Slovakia, Slovenia, South Africa, Spain, Sri Lanka, Sudan, Suriname, Swaziland, Sweden, Switzerland, Syria, Tanzania, Thailand, Togo, Tonga, Trinidad and Tobago, Tunisia, Turkey, Uganda, Ukraine, UK, US, Uruguay, Venezuela, Yemen, Zambia
countries that have signed, but not yet ratified—(11) Algeria, Burkina Faso, Burundi, Cameroon, Ethiopia, Haiti, Mali, Paraguay, Portugal, Somalia, Vietnam

Tropical Timber 83
see International Tropical Timber Agreement, 1983

Tropical Timber 94
see International Tropical Timber Agreement, 1994

United Nations Convention on the Law of the Sea (LOS)
note—abbreviated as Law of the Sea
opened for signature—10 December 1982
entered into force—16 November 1994
objective—to provide a comprehensive legal regime for the sea and oceans
parties—(164) Albania, Algeria, Angola, Antigua and Barbuda, Argentina, Armenia, Australia, Austria, The Bahamas, Bahrain, Bangladesh, Barbados, Belarus, Belgium, Belize, Benin, Bolivia, Bosnia and Herzegovina, Botswana, Brazil, Brunei, Bulgaria, Burkina Faso, Burma, Cameroon, Canada, Cape Verde, Chad, Chile, China, Comoros, Democratic Republic of the Congo, Republic of the Congo, Cook Islands, Costa Rica, Cote d'Ivoire, Croatia, Cuba, Cyprus, Czech Republic, Denmark, Djibouti, Dominica, Dominican Republic, Egypt, Equatorial Guinea, Estonia, EU, Fiji, Finland, France, Gabon, The Gambia, Georgia, Germany, Ghana, Greece, Grenada, Guatemala, Guinea, Guinea-Bissau, Guyana, Haiti, Honduras, Hungary, Iceland, India, Indonesia, Iraq, Ireland, Italy, Jamaica, Japan, Jordan, Kenya, Kiribati, South Korea, Kuwait, Laos, Latvia, Lebanon, Lesotho, Liberia, Lithuania, Luxembourg, Macedonia, Madagascar, Malawi, Malaysia, Maldives, Mali, Malta, Marshall Islands, Mauritania, Mauritius, Mexico, Federated States of Micronesia, Moldova, Monaco, Mongolia, Montenegro, Morocco, Mozambique, Namibia, Nauru, Nepal, Netherlands, NZ, Nicaragua, Nigeria, Niue, Norway, Oman, Pakistan, Palau, Panama, Papua New Guinea, Paraguay, Philippines, Poland, Portugal, Qatar, Romania, Russia, Saint Kitts and Nevis, Saint Lucia, Saint Vincent and the Grenadines, Samoa, Sao Tome and Principe, Saudi Arabia, Senegal, Serbia, Seychelles, Sierra Leone, Singapore, Slovakia, Slovenia, Solomon Islands, Somalia, South Africa, Spain, Sri Lanka, Sudan, Suriname, Swaziland, Sweden, Switzerland, Tanzania, Thailand, Timor-Liste, Togo, Tonga, Trinidad and Tobago, Tunisia, Tuvalu, Uganda, Ukraine, UK, Uruguay, Vanuatu, Vietnam, Yemen, Zambia, Zimbabwe
countries that have signed, but not yet ratified—(15) Afghanistan, Bhutan, Burundi, Cambodia, Central African Republic, Colombia, El Salvador, Ethiopia, Iran, North Korea, Libya, Liechtenstein, Niger, Rwanda, UAE

United Nations Convention to Combat Desertification in Those Countries Experiencing Serious Drought and/or Desertification, Particularly in Africa
note—abbreviated as Desertification
opened for signature—14 October 1994
entered into force—26 December 1996
objective—to combat desertification and mitigate the effects of drought through an integrated framework that is consistent with Agenda 21, employing international cooperation and partnership arrangements, and effective action at all levels
parties—(195) Afghanistan, Albania, Algeria, Andorra, Angola, Antigua and Barbuda, Argentina, Armenia, Australia, Austria, Azerbaijan, The Bahamas, Bahrain, Bangladesh, Barbados, Belarus, Belgium, Belize, Benin, Bhutan, Bolivia, Bosnia and Herzegovina, Botswana, Brazil, Brunei, Bulgaria, Burkina Faso, Burma, Burundi, Cambodia, Cameroon, Canada, Cape Verde, Central African Republic, Chad, Chile, China, Colombia, Comoros, Democratic Republic of the Congo, Republic of the Congo, Cook Islands, Costa Rica, Cote d'Ivoire, Croatia, Cuba, Cyprus, Czech Republic, Denmark, Djibouti, Dominica, Dominican Republic, Ecuador, Egypt, El Salvador, Equatorial Guinea, Eritrea, Estonia, Ethiopia, EU, Fiji, Finland, France, Gabon, The Gambia, Georgia, Germany, Ghana, Greece, Grenada, Guatemala, Guinea, Guinea-Bissau, Guyana, Haiti, Honduras, Hungary, Iceland, India, Indonesia, Iran, Iraq, Ireland, Israel, Italy, Jamaica, Japan, Jordan, Kazakhstan, Kenya, Kiribati, North Korea, South Korea, Kuwait, Kyrgyzstan, Laos, Latvia, Lebanon, Lesotho, Liberia, Libya, Liechtenstein, Lithuania, Luxembourg, Macedonia, Madagascar, Malawi, Malaysia, Maldives, Mali, Malta, Marshall Islands, Mauritania, Mauritius, Mexico, Federated States of Micronesia, Moldova, Monaco, Mongolia, Montenegro, Morocco, Mozambique, Namibia, Nauru, Nepal, Netherlands, NZ, Nicaragua, Niger, Nigeria, Niue, Norway, Oman, Pakistan, Palau, Panama, Papua New Guinea, Paraguay, Peru, Philippines, Poland, Portugal, Qatar, Romania, Russia, Rwanda, Saint Kitts and Nevis, Saint Lucia, Saint Vincent and the Grenadines, Samoa, San Marino, Sao Tome and Principe, Saudi Arabia, Senegal, Serbia, Seychelles, Sierra Leone, Singapore, Slovakia, Slovenia, Solomon Islands, Somalia, South Africa, Spain, Sri Lanka, Sudan, Suriname, Swaziland, Sweden, Switzerland, Syria, Tajikistan, Thailand, Tanzania, Timor-Leste, Togo, Tonga, Trinidad and Tobago, Tunisia, Turkey, Turkmenistan, Tuvalu, Uganda, Ukraine, UAE, UK, US, Uruguay, Uzbekistan Vanu tu, Venezuela, Vietnam, Yemen, Zambia, Zimbabwe

United Nations Framework Convention on Climate Change
note—abbreviated as Climate Change
opened for signature—9 May 1992
entered into force—21 March 1994
objective—to achieve stabilization of greenhouse gas concentrations in the atmosphere at a low enough level to prevent dangerous anthropogenic interference with the climate system
parties—(195) Afghanistan, Albania, Algeria, Andorra, Angola, Antigua and Barbuda, Argentina, Armenia, Australia, Austria, Azerbaijan, The Bahamas, Bahrain, Bangladesh, Barbados, Belarus, Belgium, Belize, Benin, Bhutan, Bolivia, Bosnia and Herzegovina, Botswana, Brazil, Brunei, Bulgaria, Burkina Faso, Burma, Burundi, Cambodia, Cameroon, Canada, Cape Verde, Central African Republic, Chad, Chile, China, Colombia, Comoros, Democratic Republic of the Congo, Republic of the Congo, Cook Islands, Costa Rica, Cote d'Ivoire, Croatia, Cuba, Cyprus, Czech Republic, Denmark, Djibouti, Dominica, Dominican Republic, Ecuador, Egypt, El Salvador, Equatorial Guinea, Eritrea, Estonia, Ethiopia, EU, Fiji, Finland, France, Gabon, The Gambia, Georgia, Germany, Ghana, Greece, Grenada, Guatemala, Guinea, Guinea-Bissau, Guyana, Haiti, Honduras, Hungary, Iceland, India, Indonesia, Iran, Iraq, Ireland, Israel, Italy, Jamaica, Japan, Jordan, Kazakhstan, Kenya, Kiribati, North Korea, South Korea, Kuwait, Kyrgyzstan, Laos, Latvia, Lebanon, Lesotho, Liberia, Libya, Liechtenstein, Lithuania, Luxembourg, Macedonia, Madagascar, Malawi, Malaysia, Maldives, Mali, Malta, Marshall Islands, Mauritania, Mauritius, Mexico, Federated States of Micronesia, Moldova, Monaco, Mongolia, Montenegro, Morocco, Mozambique, Namibia, Nauru, Nepal, Netherlands, NZ, Nicaragua, Niger, Nigeria, Niue, Norway, Oman, Pakistan, Palau, Panama, Papua New Guinea, Paraguay, Peru, Philippines, Poland, Portugal, Qatar, Romania, Russia, Rwanda, Saint Kitts and Nevis, Saint Lucia, Saint Vincent and the Grenadines, Samoa, San Marino, Sao Tome and Principe, Saudi Arabia, Senegal, Serbia, Seychelles, Sierra Leone, Singapore, Slovakia, Slovenia, Solomon Islands, Somalia, South Africa, Spain, Sri Lanka, Sudan, Suriname, Swaziland, Sweden, Switzerland, Syria, Tajikistan, Tanzania, Thailand, Timor-Leste, Togo, Tonga, Trinidad and Tobago, Tunisia, Turkey, Turkmenistan, Tuvalu, Uganda, Ukraine, UAE, UK, US, Uruguay, Uzbekistan, Vanu tu, Venezuela, Vietnam, Yemen, Zambia, Zimbabwe

Wetlands
see Convention on Wetlands of International Importance Especially As Waterfowl Habitat (Ramsar)

Whaling
see International Convention for the Regulation of Whaling

APPENDIX D

CROSS-REFERENCE LIST OF COUNTRY DATA CODES

GEOPOLITICAL ENTITIES and CODES (formerly FIPS PUB 10-4): FIPS PUB 10-4 was withdrawn by the National Institute of Standards and Technology on September 2, 2008 based on Public Law 104-113 (codified OMB Circular A-119 and the National Technology Transfer and Advancement Act of 1995). The National Geospatial-Intelligence Agency (NGA), as the maintenance authority for FIPS PUB 10-4, has continued to maintain and provide regular updates to its content in a document known as Geopolitical Entities and Codes (GEC) (Formerly FIPS 1PUB 10-4).

ISO 3166: Codes for the Representation of Names of Countries (ISO 3166) is prepared by the International Organization for Standardization. ISO 3166 includes two- and three-character alphabetic codes and three-digit numeric codes that may be needed for activities involving exchange of data with international organizations that have adopted that standard. Except for the numeric codes, ISO 3166 codes have been adopted in the US as FIPS 104-1: American National Standard Codes for the Representation of Names of Countries, Dependencies, and Areas of Special Sovereignty for Information Interchange.

STANAG 1059: Letter Codes for Geographical Entities (8th edition, 2004) is a Standardization Agreement (STANAG) established and maintained by the North Atlantic Treaty Organization (NATO/OTAN) for the purpose of providing a common set of geo-spatial identifiers for countries, territories, and possessions. The 8th edition established trigraph codes for each country based upon the ISO 3166-1 alpha-3 character sets. These codes are used throughout NATO.

Internet: The Internet country code is the two-letter digraph maintained by the International Organization for Standardization (ISO) in the ISO 3166 Alpha-2 list and used by the Internet Assigned Numbers Authority (IANA) to establish country-coded top-level domains (ccTLDs).

Entity	GEC	ISO 3166			Stanag	Internet	Comment
Afghanistan	AF	AF	AFG	004	AFG	.af	
Akrotiri	AX	–	–	–	–	–	
Albania	AL	AL	ALB	008	ALB	.al	
Algeria	AG	DZ	DZA	012	DZA	.dz	
American Samoa	AQ	AS	ASM	016	ASM	.as	
Andorra	AN	AD	AND	020	AND	.ad	
Angola	AO	AO	AGO	024	AGO	.ao	
Anguilla	AV	AI	AIA	660	AIA	.ai	
Antarctica	AY	AQ	ATA	010	ATA	.aq	ISO defines as the territory south of 60 degrees south latitude
Antigua and Barbuda	AC	AG	ATG	028	ATG	.ag	
Argentina	AR	AR	ARG	032	ARG	.ar	
Armenia	AM	AM	ARM	051	ARM	.am	
Aruba	AA	AW	ABW	533	ABW	.aw	
Ashmore and Cartier Islands	AT	–	–	–	AUS	–	ISO includes with Australia
Australia	AS	AU	AUS	036	AUS	.au	ISO includes Ashmore and Cartier Islands, Coral Sea Islands
Austria	AU	AT	AUT	040	AUT	.at	
Azerbaijan	AJ	AZ	AZE	031	AZE	.az	
Bahamas, The	BF	BS	BHS	044	BHS	.bs	
Bahrain	BA	BH	BHR	048	BHR	.bh	
Baker Island	FQ	–	–	–	UMI	–	ISO includes with the US Minor Outlying Islands
Bangladesh	BG	BD	BGD	050	BGD	.bd	
Barbados	BB	BB	BRB	052	BRB	.bb	
Bassas da India	BS	–	–	–	–	–	administered as part of French Southern and Antarctic Lands; no ISO codes assigned
Belarus	BO	BY	BLR	112	BLR	.by	
Belgium	BE	BE	BEL	056	BEL	.be	
Belize	BH	BZ	BLZ	084	BLZ	.bz	
Benin	BN	BJ	BEN	204	BEN	.bj	
Bermuda	BD	BM	BMU	060	BMU	.bm	

Entity	GEC	ISO 3166			Stanag	Internet	Comment
Bhutan	BT	BT	BTN	064	BTN	.bt	
Bolivia	BL	BO	BOL	068	BOL	.bo	
Bosnia and Herzegovina	BK	BA	BIH	070	BIH	.ba	
Botswana	BC	BW	BWA	072	BWA	.bw	
Bouvet Island	BV	BV	BVT	074	BVT	.bv	
Brazil	BR	BR	BRA	076	BRA	.br	
British Indian Ocean Territory	IO	IO	IOT	086	IOT	.io	
British Virgin Islands	VI	VG	VGB	092	VGB	.vg	
Brunei	BX	BN	BRN	096	BRN	.bn	
Bulgaria	BU	BG	BGR	100	BGR	.bg	
Burkina Faso	UV	BF	BFA	854	BFA	.bf	
Burma	BM	MM	MMR	104	MMR	.mm	ISO uses the name Myanmar
Burundi	BY	BI	BDI	108	BDI	.bi	
Cabo Verde	CV	CV	CPV	132	CPV	.cv	
Cambodia	CB	KH	KHM	116	KHM	.kh	
Cameroon	CM	CM	CMR	120	CMR	.cm	
Canada	CA	CA	CAN	124	CAN	.ca	
Cayman Islands	CJ	KY	CYM	136	CYM	.ky	
Central African Republic	CT	CF	CAF	140	CAF	.cf	
Chad	CD	TD	TCD	148	TCD	.td	
Chile	CI	CL	CHL	152	CHL	.cl	
China	CH	CN	CHN	156	CHN	.cn	see also Taiwan
Christmas Island	KT	CX	CXR	162	CXR	.cx	
Clipperton Island	IP	–	–	–	FYP	–	ISO includes with France
Cocos (Keeling) Islands	CK	CC	CCK	166	AUS	.cc	
Colombia	CO	CO	COL	170	COL	.co	
Comoros	CN	KM	COM	174	COM	.km	
Congo, Democratic Republic of the	CG	CD	COD	180	COD	.cd	formerly Zaire
Congo, Republic of the	CF	CG	COG	178	COG	.cg	
Cook Islands	CW	CK	COK	184	COK	.ck	
Coral Sea Islands	CR	–	–	–	AUS	–	ISO includes with Australia
Costa Rica	CS	CR	CRI	188	CRI	.cr	
Cote d'Ivoire	IV	CI	CIV	384	CIV	.ci	
Croatia	HR	HR	HRV	191	HRV	.hr	
Cuba	CU	CU	CUB	192	CUB	.cu	
Curacao	UC	CW	CUW	531	–	.cw	
Cyprus	CY	CY	CYP	196	CYP	.cy	
Czech Republic	EZ	CZ	CZE	203	CZE	.cz	
Denmark	DA	DK	DNK	208	DNK	.dk	
Dhekelia	DX	–	–	–	–	–	
Djibouti	DJ	DJ	DJI	262	DJI	.dj	
Dominica	DO	DM	DMA	212	DMA	.dm	
Dominican Republic	DR	DO	DOM	214	DOM	.do	

Entity	GEC	ISO 3166			Stanag	Internet	Comment
Ecuador	EC	EC	ECU	218	ECU	.ec	
Egypt	EG	EG	EGY	818	EGY	.eg	
El Salvador	ES	SV	SLV	222	SLV	.sv	
Equatorial Guinea	EK	GQ	GNQ	226	GNQ	.gq	
Eritrea	ER	ER	ERI	232	ERI	.er	
Estonia	EN	EE	EST	233	EST	.ee	
Ethiopia	ET	ET	ETH	231	ETH	.et	
Europa Island	EU	–	–	–	–	–	administered as part of French Southern and Antarctic Lands; no ISO codes assigned
Falkland Islands (Islas Malvinas)	FK	FK	FLK	238	FLK	.fk	
Faroe Islands	FO	FO	FRO	234	FRO	.fo	
Fiji	FJ	FJ	FJI	242	FJI	.fj	
Finland	FI	FI	FIN	246	FIN	.fi	
France	FR	FR	FRA	250	FRA	.fr	ISO includes metropolitan France along with the dependencies of Clipperton Island, French Guiana, French Polynesia, French Southern and Antarctic Lands, Guadeloupe, Martinique, Mayotte, New Caledonia, Reunion, Saint Pierre and Miquelon, Wallis and Futuna
France, Metropolitan	–	FX	FXX	249	–	.fx	ISO limits to the European part of France
French Guiana	FG	GF	GUF	254	GUF	.gf	
French Polynesia	FP	PF	PYF	258	PYF	.pf	
French Southern and Antarctic Lands	FS	TF	ATF	260	ATF	.tf	FIPS 10-4 does not include the French-claimed portion of Antarctica (Terre Adelie)
Gabon	GB	GA	GAB	266	GAB	.ga	
Gambia, The	GA	GM	GMB	270	GMB	.gm	
Gaza Strip	GZ	PS	PSE	275	PSE	.ps	ISO identifies as Occupied Palestinian Territory
Georgia	GG	GE	GEO	268	GEO	.ge	
Germany	GM	DE	DEU	276	DEU	.de	
Ghana	GH	GH	GHA	288	GHA	.gh	
Gibraltar	GI	GI	GIB	292	GIB	.gi	
Glorioso Islands	GO	–	–	–	–	–	administered as part of French Southern and Antarctic Lands; no ISO codes assigned
Greece	GR	GR	GRC	300	GRC	.gr	For its internal communications, the European Union recommends the use of the code EL in lieu of the ISO 3166-2 code of GR
Greenland	GL	GL	GRL	304	GRL	.gl	
Grenada	GJ	GD	GRD	308	GRD	.gd	
Guadeloupe	GP	GP	GLP	312	GLP	.gp	
Guam	GQ	GU	GUM	316	GUM	.gu	
Guatemala	GT	GT	GTM	320	GTM	.gt	

Entity	GEC	ISO 3166			Stanag	Internet	Comment
Guernsey	GK	GG	GGY	831	UK	.gg	
Guinea	GV	GN	GIN	324	GIN	.gn	
Guinea-Bissau	PU	GW	GNB	624	GNB	.gw	
Guyana	GY	GY	GUY	328	GUY	.gy	
Haiti	HA	HT	HTI	332	HTI	.ht	
Heard Island and McDonald Islands	HM	HM	HMD	334	HMD	.hm	
Holy See (Vatican City)	VT	VA	VAT	336	VAT	.va	
Honduras	HO	HN	HND	340	HND	.hn	
Hong Kong	HK	HK	HKG	344	HKG	.hk	
Howland Island	HQ	–	–	–	UMI	–	ISO includes with the US Minor Outlying Islands
Hungary	HU	HU	HUN	348	HUN	.hu	
Iceland	IC	IS	ISL	352	ISL	.is	
India	IN	IN	IND	356	IND	.in	
Indonesia	ID	ID	IDN	360	IDN	.id	
Iran	IR	IR	IRN	364	IRN	.ir	
Iraq	IZ	IQ	IRQ	368	IRQ	.iq	
Ireland	EI	IE	IRL	372	IRL	.ie	
Isle of Man	IM	IM	IMN	833	UK	.im	
Israel	IS	IL	ISR	376	ISR	.il	
Italy	IT	IT	ITA	380	ITA	.it	
Jamaica	JM	JM	JAM	388	JAM	.jm	
Jan Mayen	JN	–	–	–	SJM	–	ISO includes with Svalbard
Japan	JA	JP	JPN	392	JPN	.jp	
Jarvis Island	DQ	–	–	–	UMI	–	ISO includes with the US Minor Outlying Islands
Jersey	JE	JE	JEY	832	UK	.je	
Johnston Atoll	JQ	–	–	–	UMI	–	ISO includes with the US Minor Outlying Islands
Jordan	JO	JO	JOR	400	JOR	.jo	
Juan de Nova Island	JU	–	–	–	–	–	administered as part of French Southern and Antarctic Lands; no ISO codes assigned
Kazakhstan	KZ	KZ	KAZ	398	KAZ	.kz	
Kenya	KE	KE	KEN	404	KEN	.ke	
Kingman Reef	KQ	–	–	–	UMI	–	ISO includes with the US Minor Outlying Islands
Kiribati	KR	KI	KIR	296	KIR	.ki	
Korea, North	KN	KP	PRK	408	PRK	.kp	
Korea, South	KS	KR	KOR	410	KOR	.kr	
Kosovo	KV	XK	XKS	–	–	–	XK and XKS are ISO 3166 user assigned codes; ISO 3166 Maintenace Authority has not assigned codes
Kuwait	KU	KW	KWT	414	KWT	.kw	
Kyrgyzstan	KG	KG	KGZ	417	KGZ	.kg	

Entity	GEC	ISO 3166			Stanag	Internet	Comment
Laos	LA	LA	LAO	418	LAO	.la	
Latvia	LG	LV	LVA	428	LVA	.lv	
Lebanon	LE	LB	LBN	422	LBN	.lb	
Lesotho	LT	LS	LSO	426	LSO	.ls	
Liberia	LI	LR	LBR	430	LBR	.lr	
Libya	LY	LY	LBY	434	LBY	.ly	
Liechtenstein	LS	LI	LIE	438	LIE	.li	
Lithuania	LH	LT	LTU	440	LTU	.lt	
Luxembourg	LU	LU	LUX	442	LUX	.lu	
Macau	MC	MO	MAC	446	MAC	.mo	
Macedonia	MK	MK	MKD	807	FYR	.mk	
Madagascar	MA	MG	MDG	450	MDG	.mg	
Malawi	MI	MW	MWI	454	MWI	.mw	
Malaysia	MY	MY	MYS	458	MYS	.my	
Maldives	MV	MV	MDV	462	MDV	.mv	
Mali	ML	ML	MLI	466	MLI	.ml	
Malta	MT	MT	MLT	470	MLT	.mt	
Marshall Islands	RM	MH	MHL	584	MHL	.mh	
Martinique	MB	MQ	MTQ	474	MTQ	.mq	
Mauritania	MR	MR	MRT	478	MRT	.mr	
Mauritius	MP	MU	MUS	480	MUS	.mu	
Mayotte	MF	YT	MYT	175	FRA	.yt	
Mexico	MX	MX	MEX	484	MEX	.mx	
Micronesia, Federated States of	FM	FM	FSM	583	FSM	.fm	
Midway Islands	MQ	–	–	–	UMI	–	ISO includes with the US Minor Outlying Islands
Moldova	MD	MD	MDA	498	MDA	.md	
Monaco	MN	MC	MCO	492	MCO	.mc	
Mongolia	MG	MN	MNG	496	MNG	.mn	
Montenegro	MJ	ME	MNE	499	MNE	.me	
Montserrat	MH	MS	MSR	500	MSR	.ms	
Morocco	MO	MA	MAR	504	MAR	.ma	
Mozambique	MZ	MZ	MOZ	508	MOZ	.mz	
Myanmar	–	–	–	–	–	–	see Burma
Namibia	WA	NA	NAM	516	NAM	.na	
Nauru	NR	NR	NRU	520	NRU	.nr	
Navassa Island	BQ	–	–	–	UMI	–	ISO includes with the US Minor Outlying Islands
Nepal	NP	NP	NPL	524	NPL	.np	
Netherlands	NL	NL	NLD	528	NLD	.nl	
Netherlands Antilles	NT				ANT	.an	disestablished in October 2010 this entity no longer exists; ISO deleted the codes in December 2010
New Caledonia	NC	NC	NCL	540	NCL	.nc	

Entity	GEC	ISO 3166			Stanag	Internet	Comment
New Zealand	NZ	NZ	NZL	554	NZL	.nz	
Nicaragua	NU	NI	NIC	558	NIC	.ni	
Niger	NG	NE	NER	562	NER	.ne	
Nigeria	NI	NG	NGA	566	NGA	.ng	
Niue	NE	NU	NIU	570	NIU	.nu	
Norfolk Island	NF	NF	NFK	574	NFK	.nf	
Northern Mariana Islands	CQ	MP	MNP	580	MNP	.mp	
Norway	NO	NO	NOR	578	NOR	.no	
Oman	MU	OM	OMN	512	OMN	.om	
Pakistan	PK	PK	PAK	586	PAK	.pk	
Palau	PS	PW	PLW	585	PLW	.pw	
Palmyra Atoll	LQ	–	–	–	UMI	–	ISO includes with the US Minor Outlying Islands
Panama	PM	PA	PAN	591	PAN	.pa	
Papua New Guinea	PP	PG	PNG	598	PNG	.pg	
Paracel Islands	PF	–	–	–	–	–	
Paraguay	PA	PY	PRY	600	PRY	.py	
Peru	PE	PE	PER	604	PER	.pe	
Philippines	RP	PH	PHL	608	PHL	.ph	
Pitcairn Islands	PC	PN	PCN	612	PCN	.pn	
Poland	PL	PL	POL	616	POL	.pl	
Portugal	PO	PT	PRT	620	PRT	.pt	
Puerto Rico	RQ	PR	PRI	630	PRI	.pr	
Qatar	QA	QA	QAT	634	QAT	.qa	
Reunion	RE	RE	REU	638	REU	.re	
Romania	RO	RO	ROU	642	ROU	.ro	
Russia	RS	RU	RUS	643	RUS	.ru	
Rwanda	RW	RW	RWA	646	RWA	.rw	
Saint Barthelemy	TB	BL	BLM	652	–	.bl	ccTLD .fr and .gp may also be used
Saint Helena, Ascension, and Tristan da Cunha	SH	SH	SHN	654	SHN	.sh	includes Saint Helena Island, Ascension Island, and the Tristan da Cunha archipelago
Saint Kitts and Nevis	SC	KN	KNA	659	KNA	.kn	
Saint Lucia	ST	LC	LCA	662	LCA	.lc	
Saint Martin	RN	MF	MAF	663	–	.mf	ccTLD .fr and .gp may also be used
Saint Pierre and Miquelon	SB	PM	SPM	666	SPM	.pm	
Saint Vincent and the Grenadines	VC	VC	VCT	670	VCT	.vc	
Samoa	WS	WS	WSM	882	WSM	.ws	
San Marino	SM	SM	SMR	674	SMR	.sm	
Sao Tome and Principe	TP	ST	STP	678	STP	.st	
Saudi Arabia	SA	SA	SAU	682	SAU	.sa	
Senegal	SG	SN	SEN	686	SEN	.sn	
Serbia	RI	RS	SRB	688	–	.rs	

Entity	GEC	ISO 3166			Stanag	Internet	Comment
Seychelles	SE	SC	SYC	690	SYC	.sc	
Sierra Leone	SL	SL	SLE	694	SLE	.sl	
Singapore	SN	SG	SGP	702	SGP	.sg	
Sint Maarten	NN	SX	SXM	534	–	.sx	
Slovakia	LO	SK	SVK	703	SVK	.sk	
Slovenia	SI	SI	SVN	705	SVN	.si	
Solomon Islands	BP	SB	SLB	090	SLB	.sb	
Somalia	SO	SO	SOM	706	SOM	.so	
South Africa	SF	ZA	ZAF	710	ZAF	.za	
South Georgia and the Islands	SX	GS	SGS	239	SGS	.gs	
South Sudan	OD	SS	SSD	728	–	–	IANA has designated .ss as the ccTLD for South Sudan, however it has not been activated in DNS root zone
Spain	SP	ES	ESP	724	ESP	.es	
Spratly Islands	PG	–	–	–	–	–	
Sri Lanka	CE	LK	LKA	144	LKA	.lk	
Sudan	SU	SD	SDN	729	SDN	.sd	
Suriname	NS	SR	SUR	740	SUR	.sr	
Svalbard	SV	SJ	SJM	744	SJM	.sj	ISO includes Jan Mayen
Swaziland	WZ	SZ	SWZ	748	SWZ	.sz	
Sweden	SW	SE	SWE	752	SWE	.se	
Switzerland	SZ	CH	CHE	756	CHE	.ch	
Syria	SY	SY	SYR	760	SYR	.sy	
Taiwan	TW	TW	TWN	158	TWN	.tw	
Tajikistan	TI	TJ	TJK	762	TJK	.tj	
Tanzania	TZ	TZ	TZA	834	TZA	.tz	
Thailand	TH	TH	THA	764	THA	.th	
Timor-Leste	TT	TL	TLS	626	TLS	.tl	
Togo	TO	TG	TGO	768	TGO	.tg	
Tokelau	TL	TK	TKL	772	TKL	.tk	
Tonga	TN	TO	TON	776	TON	.to	
Trinidad and Tobago	TD	TT	TTO	780	TTO	.tt	
Tromelin Island	TE	–	–	–	–	–	administered as part of French Southern and Antarctic Lands; no ISO codes assigned
Tunisia	TS	TN	TUN	788	TUN	.tn	
Turkey	TU	TR	TUR	792	TUR	.tr	
Turkmenistan	TX	TM	TKM	795	TKM	.tm	
Turks and Caicos Islands	TK	TC	TCA	796	TCA	.tc	
Tuvalu	TV	TV	TUV	798	TUV	.tv	
Uganda	UG	UG	UGA	800	UGA	.ug	
Ukraine	UP	UA	UKR	804	UKR	.ua	
United Arab Emirates	AE	AE	ARE	784	ARE	.ae	

Entity	GEC	ISO 3166			Stanag	Internet	Comment
United Kingdom	UK	GB	GBR	826	GBR	.uk	for its internal communications, the European Union recommends the use of the code UK in lieu of the ISO 3166-2 code of GB
United States	US	US	USA	840	USA	.us	
United States Minor Outlying Islands	–	UM	UMI	581	–	.um	ISO includes Baker Island, Howland Island, Jarvis Island, Johnston Atoll, Kingman Reef, Midway Islands, Navassa Island, Palmyra Atoll, Wake Island
Uruguay	UY	UY	URY	858	URY	.uy	
Uzbekistan	UZ	UZ	UZB	860	UZB	.uz	
Vanuatu	NH	VU	VUT	548	VUT	.vu	
Venezuela	VE	VE	VEN	862	VEN	.ve	
Vietnam	VM	VN	VNM	704	VNM	.vn	
Virgin Islands	VQ	VI	VIR	850	VIR	.vi	
Virgin Islands (UK)	–	–	–	–	–	.vg	see British Virgin Islands
Virgin Islands (US)	–	–	–	–	–	.vi	see Virgin Islands
Wake Island	WQ	–	–	–	UMI	–	ISO includes with the US Minor Outlying Islands
Wallis and Futuna	WF	WF	WLF	876	WLF	.wf	
West Bank	WE	PS	PSE	275	PSE	.ps	ISO identifies as Occupied Palestinian Territory
Western Sahara	WI	EH	ESH	732	ESH	.eh	
Western Samoa	–	–	–	–	–	.ws	see Samoa
World	–	–	–	–	–	–	the Factbook uses the W data code from DIAM 65-18 Geopolitical Data Elements and Related Features, Data Standard No. 3, December 1994, published by the Defense Intelligence Agency
Yemen	YM	YE	YEM	887	YEM	.ye	
Zaire	–	–	–	–	–	–	see Democratic Republic of the Congo
Zambia	ZA	ZM	ZMB	894	ZMB	.zm	
Zimbabwe	ZI	ZW	ZWE	716	ZWE	.zw	

APPENDIX E

CROSS-REFERENCE LIST OF HYDROGRAPHIC DATA CODES

IHO 23-4th: *Limits of Oceans and Seas,* Special Publication 23, Draft 4th Edition 1986, published by the International Hydrographic Bureau of the International Hydrographic Organization.

IHO 23-3rd: *Limits of Oceans and Seas,* Special Publication 23, 3rd Edition 1953, published by the International Hydrographic Organization.

ACIC M 49-1: *Chart of Limits of Seas and Oceans,* revised January 1958, published by the Aeronautical Chart and Information Center (ACIC), United States Air Force.

DIAM 65-18: *Geopolitical Data Elements and Related Features,* Data Standard No. 4, Defense Intelligence Agency Manual 65-18, December 1994, published by the Defense Intelligence Agency. The US Government has not yet adopted a standard for hydrographic codes similar to the Federal Information Processing Standards (FIPS) 10-4 country codes. The names and limits of the following oceans and seas are not always directly comparable because of differences in the customers, needs, and requirements of the individual organizations. Even the number of principal water bodies varies from organization to organization. *Fact book* users, for example, find the Atlantic Ocean and Pacific Ocean entries useful, but none of the following standards include those oceans in their entirety. Nor is there any provision for combining codes or overcodes to aggregate water bodies. The recently delimited Southern Ocean is not included.

Principal Oceans and Seas of the World With Hydrographic Codes by Institution

	IHO 23-4th	IHO 23-3rd*	ACIC M 49-1	DIAM 65-18
Arctic Ocean	9	17	A	5A
Atlantic Ocean	–	–	–	–
Baltic Sea	2	1	B26	7B
Eastern Mediterranean	3.1.2	28 B	–	8E
Indian Ocean	5	45	F	6A
Mediterranean Sea	3.1	28	B11	–
North Atlantic Ocean	1	23	B	1A
North Pacific Ocean	7	57	D	3A
Pacific Ocean	–	–	–	–
South Atlantic Ocean	4	32	C	2A
South China and Eastern Archipelagic Seas	6	49, 48	D18 plus others	3U plus others
South Pacific Ocean	8	61	E	4A
Western Mediterranean	3.1.1	28 A	–	8W

*The letters after the numbers are subdivisions, not footnotes.

APPENDIX F

CROSS-REFERENCE LIST OF GEOGRAPHIC NAMES

Name	Entry in *The World Factbook*	Latitude (deg min)	Longitude (deg min)
Abidjan (capital)	Cote d'Ivoire	5 19 N	4 02 W
Abkhazia (region)	Georgia	43 00 N	41 00 E
Abu Dhabi (capital)	United Arab Emirates	24 28 N	54 22 E
Abu Musa (island)	Iran	25 52 N	55 03 E
Abuja (capital)	Nigeria	9 12 N	7 11 E
Abyssinia (former name for Ethiopia)	Ethiopia	8 00 N	38 00 E
Acapulco (city)	Mexico	16 51 N	99 55 W
Accra (capital)	Ghana	5 33 N	0 13 W
Adamstown (capital)	Pitcairn Islands	25 04 S	130 05 W
Addis Ababa (capital)	Ethiopia	9 02 N	38 42 E
Adelie Land (claimed by France; also Terre Adelie)	Antarctica	66 30 S	139 00 E
Aden (city)	Yemen	12 46 N	45 01 E
Aden, Gulf of	Indian Ocean	12 30 N	48 00 E
Admiralty Island	United States (Alaska)	57 44 N	134 20 W
Admiralty Islands	Papua New Guinea	2 10 S	147 00 E
Adriatic Sea	Atlantic Ocean	42 30 N	16 00 E
Adygey (region)	Russia	44 30 N	40 10 E
Aegean Islands	Greece	38 00 N	25 00 E
Aegean Sea	Atlantic Ocean	38 30 N	25 00 E
Afars and Issas, French Territory of the (or FTAI; former name for Djibouti)	Djibouti	11 30 N	43 00 E
Afghanestan (local name for Afghanistan)	Afghanistan	33 00 N	65 00 E
Agalega Islands	Mauritius	10 25 S	56 40 E
Agana (city; former name for Hagatna)	Guam	13 28 N	144 45 E
Ajaccio (city)	France (Corsica)	41 55 N	8 44 E
Ajaria (region)	Georgia	41 45 N	42 10 E
Akmola (city; former name for Astana)	Kazakhstan	51 10 N	71 30 E
Aksai Chin (region)	China (de facto), India (claimed)	35 00 N	79 00 E
Al Arabiyah as Suudiyah (local name for Saudi Arabia)	Saudi Arabia	25 00 N	45 00 E
Al Bahrayn (local name for Bahrain)	Bahrain	26 00 N	50 33 E
Al Imarat al Arabiyah al Muttahidah (local name for the United Arab Emirates)	United Arab Emirates	24 00 N	54 00 E
Al Iraq (local name for Iraq)	Iraq	33 00 N	44 00 E
Al Jaza'ir (local name for Algeria)	Algeria	28 00 N	3 00 E
Al Kuwayt (local name for Kuwait)	Kuwait	29 30 N	45 45 E
Al Maghrib (local name for Morocco)	Morocco	32 00 N	5 00 W
Al Urdun (local name for Jordan)	Jordan	31 00 N	36 00 E
Al Yaman (local name for Yemen)	Yemen	15 00 N	48 00 E
Aland Islands	Finland	60 15 N	20 00 E
Alaska (state)	United States	65 00 N	153 00 W
Alaska, Gulf of	Pacific Ocean	58 00 N	145 00 W
Alboran Sea	Atlantic Ocean	36 00 N	2 30 W
Aldabra Islands (Groupe d'Aldabra)	Seychelles	9 25 S	46 22 E
Alderney (island)	Guernsey	49 43 N	2 12 W
Aleutian Islands	United States (Alaska)	52 00 N	176 00 W
Alexander Archipelago (island group)	United States (Alaska)	57 00 N	134 00 W

Name	Entry in *The World Factbook*	Latitude (deg min)	Longitude (deg min)
Alexander Island	Antarctica	71 00 S	70 00 W
Alexandretta (region; former name for Iskenderun)	Turkey	36 34 N	36 08 E
Alexandria (city)	Egypt	31 12 N	29 54 E
Algiers (capital)	Algeria	36 47 N	2 03 E
Alhucemas, Penon de (island group)	Spain	35 13 N	3 53 W
Alma-Ata (city; former name for Almaty)	Kazakhstan	43 15 N	76 57 E
Almaty (former capital)	Kazakhstan	43 15 N	76 57 E
Alofi (capital)	Niue	19 01 S	169 55 W
Alphonse Island	Seychelles	7 01 S	52 45 E
Alsace (region)	France	48 30 N	7 20 E
Amami Strait	Pacific Ocean	28 40 N	129 30 E
Amindivi Islands (former name for Laccadive Islands)	India	11 30 N	72 30 E
Amirante Isles (island group; also Les Amirantes)	Seychelles	6 00 S	53 10 E
Amman (capital)	Jordan	31 57 N	35 56 E
Amsterdam (capital)	Netherlands	52 23 N	4 54 E
Amsterdam Island (Ile Amsterdam)	French Southern and Antarctic Lands	37 52 S	77 32 E
Amundsen Sea	Southern Ocean	72 30 S	112 00 W
Amur River	China, Russia	52 56 N	141 10 E
Amurskiy Liman (strait)	Pacific Ocean	53 00 N	141 30 E
Anadyrskiy Zaliv (gulf)	Pacific Ocean	64 00 N	177 00 E
Anatolia (region)	Turkey	39 00 N	35 00 E
Andaman Islands	India	12 00 N	92 45 E
Andaman Sea	Indian Ocean	10 00 N	95 00 E
Andorra la Vella (capital)	Andorra	42 30 N	1 30 E
Andros (island)	Greece	37 45 N	24 42 E
Andros Island	The Bahamas	24 26 N	77 57 W
Anegada Passage	Atlantic Ocean	18 30 N	63 40 W
Angkor Wat (ruins)	Cambodia	13 26 N	103 50 E
Anglo-Egyptian Sudan (former name for Sudan)	Sudan	15 00 N	30 00 E
Anjouan (island)	Comoros	12 15 S	44 25 E
Ankara (capital)	Turkey	39 56 N	32 52 E
Annobon (island)	Equatorial Guinea	1 25 S	5 36 E
Antananarivo (capital)	Madagascar	18 52 S	47 30 E
Antigua (island)	Antigua and Barbuda	14 34 N	90 44 W
Antipodes Islands	New Zealand	49 41 S	178 43 E
Antwerp (city)	Belgium	51 13 N	4 25 E
Aomen (local Chinese short-form name for Macau)	Macau	22 10 N	113 33 E
Aozou Strip (region)	Chad	22 00 N	18 00 E
Apia (capital)	Samoa	13 50 S	171 44 W
Aqaba, Gulf of	Indian Ocean	29 00 N	34 30 E
Arab, Shatt al (river)	Iran, Iraq	29 57 N	48 34 E
Arabian Sea	Indian Ocean	15 00 N	65 00 E
Arafura Sea	Pacific Ocean	9 00 S	133 00 E
Aral Sea	Kazakhstan, Uzbekistan	45 00 N	60 00 E
Argun River	China, Russia	53 20 N	121 28 E
Aru Sea	Pacific Ocean	6 15 S	135 00 E
As-Sudan (local name for Sudan)	Sudan	15 00 N	30 00 E
Ascension Island	Saint Helena, Ascension, and Tristan da Cunha	7 57 S	14 22 W
Ashgabat, Ashkhabad (capital)	Turkmenistan	37 57 N	58 23 E

Name	Entry in *The World Factbook*	Latitude (deg min)	Longitude (deg min)
Asmara, Asmera (capital)	Eritrea	15 20 N	38 53 E
Assumption Island	Seychelles	9 46 S	46 34 E
Astana (capital; formerly Akmola)	Kazakhstan	51 10 N	71 30 E
Asuncion (capital)	Paraguay	25 16 S	57 40 W
Asuncion Island	Northern Mariana Islands	19 40 N	145 24 E
Atacama (desert)	Chile	23 00 S	70 10 W
Atacama (region)	Chile	24 30 S	69 15 W
Athens (capital)	Greece	37 59 N	23 44 E
Attu Island	United States	52 55 N	172 57 E
Auckland (city)	New Zealand	36 52 S	174 46 E
Auckland Islands	New Zealand	51 00 S	166 30 E
Australes, Iles (island group; also Iles Tubuai)	French Polynesia	23 20 S	151 00 W
Avarua (capital)	Cook Islands	21 12 S	159 46 W
Axel Heiberg Island	Canada	79 30 N	90 00 W
Azad Kashmir (region)	Pakistan	34 30 N	74 00 E
Azarbaycan, Azerbaidzhan (local name for Azerbaijan)	Azerbaijan	40 30 N	47 30 E
Azores (islands)	Portugal	38 30 N	28 00 W
Azov, Sea of	Atlantic Ocean	49 00 N	36 00 E
Bab el Mandeb (strait)	Indian Ocean	12 40 N	43 20 E
Babuyan Channel	Pacific Ocean	18 44 N	121 40 E
Babuyan Islands	Philippines	19 10 N	121 40 E
Baffin Bay	Arctic Ocean	73 00 N	66 00 W
Baffin Island	Canada	68 00 N	70 00 W
Baghdad (capital)	Iraq	33 21 N	44 25 E
Baku (capital; also Baki, Baky)	Azerbaijan	40 23 N	49 51 E
Balabac Strait	Pacific Ocean	7 35 N	117 00 E
Balearic Islands	Spain	39 30 N	3 00 E
Balearic Sea (Iberian Sea)	Atlantic Ocean (Mediterranean Sea)	40 30 N	2 00 E
Bali (island)	Indonesia	8 20 S	115 00 E
Bali Sea	Indian Ocean	7 45 S	115 30 E
Balintang Channel	Pacific Ocean	19 49 N	121 40 E
Balintang Islands	Philippines	19 55 N	122 10 E
Balkan Peninsula	Albania, Bosnia and Herzegovina, Bulgaria, Croatia, Greece, Kosovo, Macedonia, Montenegro, Romania, Serbia, Slovenia, Turkey (European part)	42 00 N	23 00 E
Balleny Islands	Antarctica	67 00 S	163 00 E
Balochistan (region)	Pakistan	28 00 N	63 00 E
Baltic Sea	Atlantic Ocean	57 00 N	19 00 E
Bamako (capital)	Mali	12 39 N	8 00 W
Banaba (Ocean Island)	Kiribati	0 52 S	169 35 E
Banat (region)	Hungary, Romania, Serbia	45 30 N	21 00 E
Banda Sea	Pacific Ocean	5 00 S	128 00 E
Bandar Seri Begawan (capital)	Brunei	4 53 N	114 56 E
Bangka (island)	Indonesia	2 30 S	106 00 E
Bangkok (capital)	Thailand	13 45 N	100 31 E
Bangui (capital)	Central African Republic	4 22 N	18 35 E
Banjul (capital)	The Gambia	13 28 N	16 39 W
Banks Island	Canada	75 15 N	121 30 W

Name	Entry in *The World Factbook*	Latitude (deg min)	Longitude (deg min)
Banks Island	Australia	10 12 S	142 16 E
Banks Islands (Iles Banks)	Vanuatu	14 00 S	167 30 E
Barbuda (island)	Antigua and Barbuda	17 38 N	61 48 W
Barcelona (city)	Spain	41 25 N	2 13 E
Barents Sea	Arctic Ocean	74 00 N	36 00 E
Barranquilla (city)	Colombia	10 59 N	74 48 W
Bashi Channel	Pacific Ocean	22 00 N	121 00 E
Basilan Strait	Pacific Ocean	6 49 N	122 05 E
Basque Provinces	Spain	43 00 N	2 30 W
Bass Strait	Pacific Ocean	39 20 S	145 30 E
Bassas da India	Indian Ocean	21 30 S	39 50 E
Basse-Terre (capital)	France (Guadeloupe)	16 00 N	61 44 W
Basseterre (capital)	Saint Kitts and Nevis	17 18 N	62 43 W
Bastia (city)	France (Corsica)	42 42 N	9 27 E
Basutoland (former name for Lesotho)	Lesotho	29 30 S	28 30 E
Batan Islands	Philippines	20 30 N	121 50 E
Bavaria (region; also Bayern)	Germany	48 30 N	11 30 E
Beagle Channel	Atlantic Ocean	54 53 S	68 10 W
Bear Island (see Bjornoya)	Svalbard	74 26 N	19 05 E
Beaufort Sea	Arctic Ocean	73 00 N	140 00 W
Bechuanaland (former name for Botswana)	Botswana	22 00 S	24 00 E
Beijing (capital)	China	39 56 N	116 24 E
Beirut (capital)	Lebanon	33 53 N	35 30 E
Bekaa Valley	Lebanon	34 00 N	36 05 E
Belau (Palau Islands)	Palau	7 30 N	134 30 E
Belep Islands (Iles Belep)	New Caledonia	19 45 S	163 40 E
Belfast (city)	United Kingdom	54 36 N	5 55 W
Belgian Congo (former name for Democratic Republic of the Congo)	Democratic Republic of the Congo	0 00 N	25 00 E
Belgie, Belgique (local name for Belgium)	Belgium	50 50 N	4 00 E
Belgrade (capital)	Serbia	44 50 N	20 30 E
Belize City	Belize	17 30 N	88 12 W
Belle Isle, Strait of	Atlantic Ocean	51 35 N	56 30 W
Bellingshausen Sea	Southern Ocean	71 00 S	85 00 W
Belmopan (capital)	Belize	17 15 N	88 46 W
Belorussia (former name for Belarus)	Belarus	53 00 N	28 00 E
Benadir (region; former name of Italian Somaliland)	Somalia	4 00 N	46 00 E
Bengal (region)	Bangladesh, India	24 30 N	88 15 E
Bengal, Bay of	Indian Ocean	15 00 N	90 00 E
Berau, Gulf of	Pacific Ocean	2 30 S	132 30 E
Bering Island	Russia	55 00 N	166 30 E
Bering Sea	Pacific Ocean	60 00 N	175 00 W
Bering Strait	Pacific Ocean	65 30 N	169 00 W
Berkner Island	Antarctica	79 30 S	49 30 W
Berlin (capital)	Germany	52 31 N	13 24 E
Berlin, East (former name for eastern sector of Berlin)	Germany	52 30 N	13 33 E
Berlin, West (former name for western sector of Berlin)	Germany	52 30 N	13 20 E
Bern (capital)	Switzerland	46 57 N	7 26 E
Bessarabia (region)	Moldova, Romania, Ukraine	47 00 N	28 30 E
Bharat (local name for India)	India	20 00 N	77 00 E
Bhopal (city)	India	23 16 N	77 24 E

Name	Entry in *The World Factbook*	Latitude (deg min)	Longitude (deg min)
Biafra (region)	Nigeria	5 30 N	7 30 E
Big Diomede Island	Russia	65 46 N	169 06 W
Bijagos, Arquipelago dos (island group)	Guinea-Bissau	11 25 N	16 20 W
Bikini Atoll	Marshall Islands	11 35 N	165 23 E
Bilbao (city)	Spain	43 15 N	2 58 W
Bioko (island)	Equatorial Guinea	3 30 N	8 42 E
Biscay, Bay of	Atlantic Ocean	44 00 N	4 00 W
Bishkek (capital)	Kyrgyzstan	42 54 N	74 36 E
Bishop Rock	United Kingdom	49 52 N	6 27 W
Bismarck Archipelago (island group)	Papua New Guinea	5 00 S	150 00 E
Bismarck Sea	Pacific Ocean	4 00 S	148 00 E
Bissau (capital)	Guinea-Bissau	11 51 N	15 35 W
Bjornoya (Bear Island)	Svalbard	74 26 N	19 05 E
Black Forest (region)	Germany	48 00 N	8 15 E
Black Rock (island)	South Georgia and the South Sandwich Islands	53 39 S	41 48 W
Black Sea	Atlantic Ocean	43 00 N	35 00 E
Bloemfontein (judicial capital)	South Africa	29 12 S	26 07 E
Bo Hai (gulf)	Pacific Ocean	38 00 N	120 00 E
Boa Vista (island)	Cabo Verde	16 05 N	22 50 W
Bogota (capital)	Colombia	4 36 N	74 05 W
Bohemia (region)	Czech Republic	50 00 N	14 30 E
Bombay (city; see Mumbai)	India	18 58 N	72 50 E
Bonaire (island)	Netherlands	12 10 N	68 15 W
Bonifacio, Strait of	Atlantic Ocean (Mediterranean Sea)	41 01 N	14 00 E
Bonin Islands	Japan	27 00 N	142 10 E
Bonn (former capital)	Germany	50 44 N	7 05 E
Bophuthatswana (region; enclave)	South Africa	26 30 S	25 30 E
Bora-Bora (island)	French Polynesia	16 30 S	151 45 W
Bordeaux (city)	France	44 50 N	0 34 W
Borneo (island)	Brunei, Indonesia, Malaysia	0 30 N	114 00 E
Bornholm (island)	Denmark	55 10 N	15 00 E
Bosna i Hercegovina (local name for Bosnia and Herzegovina)	Bosnia and Herzegovina	44 00 N	18 00 E
Bosnia (political region)	Bosnia and Herzegovina	44 00 N	18 00 E
Bosporus (strait)	Atlantic Ocean	41 00 N	29 00 E
Bothnia, Gulf of	Atlantic Ocean	63 00 N	20 00 E
Bougainville (island)	Papua New Guinea	6 00 S	155 00 E
Bougainville Strait	Pacific Ocean	6 40 S	156 10 E
Bounty Islands	New Zealand	47 43 S	174 00 E
Bourbon Island (former name of Reunion)	Reunion	21 06 S	55 36 E
Brasilia (capital)	Brazil	15 47 S	47 55 W
Bratislava (capital)	Slovakia	48 09 N	17 07 E
Brazzaville (capital)	Republic of the Congo	4 16 S	15 17 E
Bridgetown (capital)	Barbados	13 06 N	59 37 W
Brisbane (city)	Australia	27 28 S	153 02 E
Bristol Bay	Pacific Ocean	57 00 N	160 00 W
Bristol Channel	Atlantic Ocean	51 18 N	3 30 W
Britain (see Great Britain)	United Kingdom	54 00 N	2 00 W
British Bechuanaland (region; former name for northwest South Africa)	South Africa	27 30 S	23 30 E
British Central African Protectorate (former name of Nyasaland)	Malawi	13 30 S	34 00 E

Name	Entry in *The World Factbook*	Latitude (deg min)	Longitude (deg min)
British East Africa (former name for British possessions in eastern Africa)	Kenya, Tanzania, Uganda	1 00 N	38 00 E
British Guiana (former name for Guyana)	Guyana	5 00 N	59 00 W
British Honduras (former name for Belize)	Belize	17 15 N	88 45 W
British Solomon Islands (former name for Solomon Islands)	Solomon Islands	8 00 S	159 00 E
British Somaliland (former name for northern Somalia)	Somalia	10 00 N	49 00 E
Brussels (capital)	Belgium	50 50 N	4 20 E
Bubiyan (island)	Kuwait	29 47 N	48 10 E
Bucharest (capital)	Romania	44 26 N	26 06 E
Budapest (capital)	Hungary	47 30 N	19 05 E
Buenos Aires (capital)	Argentina	34 36 S	58 27 W
Bujumbura (capital)	Burundi	3 23 S	29 22 E
Bukovina (region)	Romania, Ukraine	48 00 N	26 00 E
Byelarus (local name for Belarus)	Belarus	53 00 N	28 00 E
Byelorussia (former name for Belarus)	Belarus	53 00 N	28 00 E
Cabinda (province)	Angola	5 33 S	12 12 E
Cabot Strait	Atlantic Ocean	47 20 N	59 30 W
Caicos Islands	Turks and Caicos Islands	21 56 N	71 58 W
Cairo (capital)	Egypt	30 03 N	31 15 E
Calcutta (city)	India	22 32 N	88 21 E
Calgary (city)	Canada	51 02 N	114 04 W
California, Gulf of	Pacific Ocean	28 00 N	112 00 W
Cameroun (local name for Cameroon)	Cameroon	6 00 N	12 00 E
Campbell Island	New Zealand	52 33 S	169 09 E
Campeche, Bay of	Atlantic Ocean (Gulf of Mexico)	20 00 N	94 00 W
Canal Zone (former name for US possessions in Panama)	Panama	9 00 N	79 45 W
Canarias Sea	Atlantic Ocean	28 00 N	16 00 W
Canary Islands	Spain	28 00 N	15 30 W
Canberra (capital)	Australia	35 17 S	149 08 E
Cancun (city)	Mexico	21 10 N	86 50 W
Canton (city; now Guangzhou)	China	23 06 N	113 16 E
Canton Island (Kanton Island)	Kiribati	2 49 S	171 40 W
Cape Juby (region; former name for Southern Morocco)	Morocco	27 53 N	12 58 W
Cape Province (region; former name for Northern, Western, and Eastern Cape Provinces of South Africa)	South Africa	31 30 S	22 30 E
Cape Town (legislative capital)	South Africa	33 57 S	18 25 E
Cape of Good Hope (cape; also alternate name for Cape Province of South Africa)	South Africa	34 15 S	18 20 E
Caracas (capital)	Venezuela	10 30 N	66 56 W
Cargados Carajos Shoals	Mauritius	16 25 S	59 38 E
Caribbean Sea	Atlantic Ocean	15 00 N	73 00 W
Caroline Islands	Federated States of Micronesia, Palau	7 30 N	148 00 E
Carpatho-Ukraine (region; former name for Zakarpattya oblast')	Ukraine	48 22 N	23 32 E
Carpentaria, Gulf of	Pacific Ocean	14 00 S	139 00 E
Casablanca (city)	Morocco	33 35 N	7 34 W
Castries (capital)	Saint Lucia	14 01 N	61 00 W
Catalonia (region)	Spain	42 00 N	2 00 E
Cato Island	Australia	23 15 S	155 32 E
Caucasus (region)	Russia	42 00 N	45 00 E
Cayenne (capital)	French Guiana	4 56 N	52 20 W

Name	Entry in *The World Factbook*	Latitude (deg min)	Longitude (deg min)
Celebes (island)	Indonesia	2 00 S	121 00 E
Celebes Sea	Pacific Ocean	3 00 N	122 00 E
Celtic Sea	Atlantic Ocean	51 00 N	6 30 W
Central African Empire (former name for Central African Republic)	Central African Republic	7 00 N	21 00 E
Ceram (Seram) Sea	Pacific Ocean	2 30 S	129 30 E
Ceska Republika (local name for Czech Republic)	Czech Republic	49 45 N	15 30 E
Ceskoslovensko (former local name for Czechoslovakia)	Czech Republic, Slovakia	49 00 N	17 30 E
Cetinje (capital city)	Montenegro	42 24 N	18 55 E
Ceuta (city)	Spain	35 53 N	5 19 W
Ceylon (former name for Sri Lanka)	Sri Lanka	7 00 N	81 00 E
Chafarinas, Islas (island)	Spain	35 12 N	2 26 W
Chagos Archipelago (Oil Islands)	British Indian Ocean Territory	6 00 S	71 30 E
Challenger Deep (Mariana Trench)	Pacific Ocean	11 22 N	142 36 E
Channel Islands	Guernsey, Jersey	49 20 N	2 20 W
Charlotte Amalie (capital)	Virgin Islands	18 21 N	64 56 W
Chatham Islands	New Zealand	44 00 S	176 30 W
Chechnya (region; also Chechnia)	Russia	43 15 N	45 40 E
Cheju Strait	Pacific Ocean	34 00 N	126 30 E
Cheju-do (island)	Korea, South	33 20 N	126 30 E
Chengdu (city)	China	30 43 N	104 04 E
Chennai (city; also Madras)	India	13 04 N	80 16 E
Chesterfield Islands (Iles Chesterfield)	New Caledonia	19 52 S	158 15 E
Chihli, Gulf of (see Bo Hai)	Pacific Ocean	38 30 N	120 00 E
Chiloe (island)	Chile	42 50 S	74 00 W
China, People's Republic of	China	35 00 N	105 00 E
China, Republic of	Taiwan	23 30 N	121 00 E
Chisinau (capital; also Kishinev)	Moldova	47 00 N	28 50 E
Choiseul (island)	Solomon Islands	7 05 S	121 00 E
Choson (local name for North Korea)	North Korea	40 00 N	127 00 E
Christmas Island (Indian Ocean)	Australia	10 25 S	105 39 E
Christmas Island (Pacific Ocean; also Kiritimati)	Kiribati	1 52 N	157 20 W
Chukchi Sea	Arctic Ocean	69 00 N	171 00 W
Chuuk Islands (Truk Islands)	Federated States of Micronesia	7 25 N	151 47 W
Cilicia (region)	Turkey	36 50 N	34 30 E
Ciskei (enclave)	South Africa	33 00 S	27 00 E
Citta del Vaticano (local name for Vatican City)	Holy See	41 54 N	12 27 E
Cochin China (region)	Vietnam	11 00 N	107 00 E
Coco, Isla del (island)	Costa Rica	5 32 N	87 04 W
Cocos Islands	Cocos (Keeling) Islands	12 30 S	96 50 E
Colombo (capital)	Sri Lanka	6 56 N	79 51 E
Colon, Archipielago de (Galapagos Islands)	Ecuador	0 00 N	90 30 W
Commander Islands (Komandorskiye Ostrova)	Russia	55 00 N	167 00 E
Comores (local name for Comoros)	Comoros	12 10 S	44 15 E
Con Son (islands)	Vietnam	8 43 N	106 36 E
Conakry (capital)	Guinea	9 31 N	13 43 W
Confederatio Helvetica (local name for Switzerland)	Switzerland	47 00 N	8 00 E
Congo (Brazzaville) (former name for Republic of the Congo)	Republic of the Congo	1 00 S	15 00 E
Congo (Leopoldville) (former name for the Democratic Republic of the Congo)	Democratic Republic of the Congo	0 00 N	25 00 E
Constantinople (city; former name for Istanbul)	Turkey	41 01 N	28 58 E

Name	Entry in *The World Factbook*	Latitude (deg min)	Longitude (deg min)
Cook Strait	Pacific Ocean	41 15 S	174 30 E
Copenhagen (capital)	Denmark	55 40 N	12 35 E
Coral Sea	Pacific Ocean	15 00 S	150 00 E
Corfu (island)	Greece	39 40 N	19 45 E
Corinth (region)	Greece	37 56 N	22 56 E
Corisco (island)	Equatorial Guinea	0 55 N	9 19 E
Corn Islands (Islas del Maiz)	Nicaragua	12 15 N	83 00 W
Corocoro Island	Guyana, Venezuela	3 38 N	66 50 W
Corsica (island; also Corse)	France	42 00 N	9 00 E
Cosmoledo Group (island group; also Atoll de Cosmoledo)	Seychelles	9 43 S	47 35 E
Cotonou (former capital)	Benin	6 21 N	2 26 E
Cotopaxi (volcano)	Ecuador	0 39 S	78 26 W
Courantyne River	Guyana, Suriname	5 57 N	57 06 W
Cozumel (island)	Mexico	20 30 N	86 55 W
Crete (island)	Greece	35 15 N	24 45 E
Crimea (region)	Ukraine	45 00 N	34 00 E
Crimean Peninsula	Ukraine	45 00 N	34 00 E
Crooked Island Passage	Atlantic Ocean	22 55 N	74 35 W
Crozet Islands (Iles Crozet)	French Southern and Antarctic Lands	46 30 S	51 00 E
Cyclades (island group)	Greece	37 00 N	25 10 E
Cyrenaica (region)	Libya	31 00 N	22 00 E
Czechoslovakia (former name for the entity that subsequently split into the Czech Republic and Slovakia)	Czech Republic, Slovakia	49 00 N	18 00 E
D'Entrecasteaux Islands	Papua New Guinea	9 30 S	150 40 E
Dagestan (region)	Russia	43 00 N	47 00 E
Dahomey (former name for Benin)	Benin	9 30 N	2 15 E
Daito Islands	Japan	43 00 N	17 00 E
Dakar (capital)	Senegal	14 40 N	17 26 W
Dalmatia (region)	Croatia	43 00 N	17 00 E
Daman (city; also Damao)	India	20 10 N	73 00 E
Damascus (capital)	Syria	33 30 N	36 18 E
Danger Islands (see Pukapuka Atoll)	Cook Islands	10 53 S	165 49 W
Danish Straits	Atlantic Ocean	58 00 N	11 00 E
Danish West Indies (former name for the Virgin Islands)	Virgin Islands	18 20 N	64 50 W
Danmark (local name)	Denmark	56 00 N	10 00 E
Danzig (city; former name for Gdansk)	Poland	54 23 N	18 40 E
Dao Bach Long Vi (island)	Vietnam	20 08 N	107 44 E
Dar es Salaam (capital)	Tanzania	6 48 S	39 17 E
Dardanelles (strait)	Atlantic Ocean	40 15 N	26 25 E
Davis Strait	Atlantic Ocean	67 00 N	57 00 W
Dead Sea	Israel, Jordan, West Bank	32 30 N	35 30 E
Deception Island	Antarctica	62 56 S	60 34 W
Denmark Strait	Atlantic Ocean	67 00 N	24 00 W
Desolation Islands (Isles Kerguelen)	French Southern and Antarctic Lands	49 30 S	69 30 E
Deutschland (local name for Germany)	Germany	51 00 N	9 00 E
Devils Island (Ile du Diable)	French Guiana	5 17 N	52 35 W
Devon Island	Canada	76 00 N	87 00 W
Dhaka (capital)	Bangladesh	23 43 N	90 25 E
Dhivehi Raajje (local name for Maldives)	Maldives	3 15 N	73 00 E
Dhofar (region)	Oman	17 00 N	54 10 E

Name	Entry in *The World Factbook*	Latitude (deg min)	Longitude (deg min)
Diego Garcia (island)	British Indian Ocean Territory	7 20 S	72 25 E
Diego Ramirez (islands)	Chile	56 30 S	68 43 W
Dili (capital)	Timor-Leste	8 35 S	125 36 E
Dilmun (former name for Bahrain)	Bahrain	7 00 N	81 00 E
Diomede Islands	Russia (Big Diomede), United States (Little Diomede)	65 47 N	169 00 W
Diu (region)	India	20 42 N	70 59 E
Djibouti (capital)	Djibouti	11 30 N	43 15 E
Dnieper (river)	Belarus, Russia, Ukraine (Dnyapro, Dnepr, Dnipro)	46 30 N	32 18 E
Dniester (river)	Moldova, Ukraine (Nistru, Dnister)	46 18 N	30 17 E
Dobruja (region)	Bulgaria, Romania	43 30 N	28 00 E
Dodecanese (island group)	Greece	36 00 N	27 05 E
Dodoma (city)	Tanzania	6 11 S	35 45 E
Doha (capital)	Qatar	25 17 N	51 32 E
Donets Basin	Russia, Ukraine	48 15 N	38 30 E
Douala (city)	Cameroon	4 03 N	9 42 E
Douglas (capital)	Man, Isle of	54 09 N	4 28 W
Dover, Strait of	Atlantic Ocean	51 00 N	1 30 E
Drake Passage	Atlantic Ocean, Southern Ocean	60 00 S	60 00 W
Druk Yul (local name for Bhutan)	Bhutan	27 30 N	90 30 E
Dubai, Dubayy (city)	United Arab Emirates	25 18 N	55 18 E
Dublin (capital)	Ireland	53 20 N	6 15 W
Duesseldorf (city)	Germany	51 13 N	6 47 E
Durban (city)	South Africa	29 51 S	31 02 E
Dushanbe (capital)	Tajikistan	38 35 N	68 48 E
Dutch Antilles (former name for the Netherlands Antilles)	Aruba, Curacao, Sint Maarten	12 10 N	68 30 W
Dutch East Indies (former name for Indonesia)	Indonesia	5 00 S	120 00 E
Dutch Guiana (former name for Suriname)	Suriname	4 00 N	56 00 W
Dutch West Indies (former name for the Netherlands Antilles)	Aruba, Curacao, Sint Maarten	12 10 N	68 30 W
Dzungarian Gate (valley)	China, Kazakhstan	45 25 N	82 25 E
East China Sea	Pacific Ocean	30 00 N	126 00 E
East Frisian Islands	Germany	53 44 N	7 25 E
East Germany (German Democratic Republic; former name for eastern portion of Germany)	Germany	52 00 N	13 00 E
East Korea Strait (Eastern Channel or Tsushima Strait)	Pacific Ocean	34 00 N	129 00 E
East Pakistan (former name for Bangladesh)	Bangladesh	24 00 N	90 00 E
East Siberian Sea	Arctic Ocean	74 00 N	166 00 E
Easter Island (Isla de Pascua)	Chile	27 07 S	109 22 W
Eastern Channel (East Korea Strait or Tsushima Strait)	Pacific Ocean	34 00 N	129 00 E
Eastern Samoa (former name for American Samoa)	American Samoa	14 20 S	170 00 W
Edinburgh (city)	United Kingdom	55 57 N	3 11 W
Eesti (local name for Estonia)	Estonia	59 00 N	26 00 E
Eire (local name for Ireland)	Ireland	53 00 N	8 00 W
Elba (island)	Italy	42 46 N	10 17 E
Elemi Triangle (region)	Ethiopia (claimed), Kenya (de facto), Sudan (claimed)	5 00 N	35 30 E
Ellada, Ellas (local name for Greece)	Greece	39 00 N	22 00 E
Ellef Ringnes Island	Canada	78 00 N	103 00 W
Ellesmere Island	Canada	81 00 N	80 00 W
Ellice Islands	Tuvalu	8 00 S	178 00 E

Name	Entry in *The World Factbook*	Latitude (deg min)	Longitude (deg min)
Ellsworth Land (region)	Antarctica	75 00 S	92 00 W
Elobey, Islas de (island group)	Equatorial Guinea	0 59 N	9 33 E
Enderbury Island	Kiribati	3 08 S	171 05 W
Enewetak Atoll (Eniwetok Atoll)	Marshall Islands	11 30 N	162 15 E
England (region)	United Kingdom	52 30 N	1 30 W
English Channel	Atlantic Ocean	50 20 N	1 00 W
Eniwetok Atoll (see Enewetak Atoll)	Marshall Islands	11 30 N	162 15 E
Eolie, Isole (island group)	Italy	38 30 N	15 00 E
Epirus, Northern (region)	Albania, Greece	40 00 N	20 30 E
Episkopi Cantonment (capital)	Akrotiri, Dhekelia	34 40 N	32 51 E
Ertra (local name for Eritrea)	Eritrea	15 00 N	39 00 E
Espana	Spain	40 00 N	4 00 W
Essequibo (region; claimed by Venezuela)	Guyana	6 59 N	58 23 W
Etorofu (island; also Iturup)	Russia (de facto)	44 55 N	147 40 E
Europa Island	Indian Ocean	22 20 S	40 22 E
Farquhar Group (island group; also Atoll de Farquhar)	Seychelles	10 10 S	51 10 E
Fashoda (town; also Kodok)	South Sudan	9 53 N	32 7 E
Fergana Valley	Kyrgyzstan, Tajikistan, Uzbekistan	41 00 N	72 00 E
Fernando Po (island; see Bioko)	Equatorial Guinea	3 30 N	8 42 E
Fernando de Noronha (island group)	Brazil	3 51 S	32 25 W
Filipinas (local name for the Philippines; also Pilipinas)	Philippines	13 00 N	122 00 E
Finland, Gulf of	Atlantic Ocean (Baltic Sea)	60 00 N	27 00 E
Fiume (city; former name for Rijeka)	Croatia	45 19 N	14 25 E
Florence (city)	Italy	43 46 N	11 16 E
Flores (island)	Indonesia	8 45 S	121 00 E
Flores Sea	Pacific Ocean	7 40 S	119 45 E
Florida, Straits of	Atlantic Ocean	25 00 N	79 45 W
Fongafale (largest island of Funafuti)	Tuvalu	8 30 S	179 12 E
Former Soviet Union (FSU)	Armenia, Azerbaijan, Belarus, Estonia, Georgia, Kazakhstan, Kyrgyzstan, Latvia, Lithuania, Moldova, Russia, Tajikistan, Turkmenistan, Ukraine, Uzbekistan		
Formosa (island)	Taiwan	23 30 N	121 00 E
Formosa Strait (see Taiwan Strait)	Pacific Ocean	24 00 N	119 00 E
Foroyar (local name for Faroe Islands)	Faroe Islands	62 00 N	7 00 W
Fort-de-France (capital)	Martinique	14 36 N	61 05 W
Frankfurt am Main (city)	Germany	50 07 N	8 41 E
Franz Josef Land (island group)	Russia	81 00 N	55 00 E
Freetown (capital)	Sierra Leone	8 30 N	13 15 W
French Cameroon (former name for Cameroon)	Cameroon	6 00 N	12 00 E
French Guinea (former name for Guinea)	Guinea	11 00 N	10 00 W
French Indochina (former name for French possessions in southeast Asia)	Cambodia, Laos, Vietnam	15 00 N	107 00 E
French Morocco (former name for Morocco)	Morocco	32 00 N	5 00 W
French Somaliland (former name for Djibouti)	Djibouti	11 30 N	43 00 E
French Sudan (former name for Mali)	Mali	17 00 N	4 00 W
French Territory of the Afars and Issas (or FTAI; former name for Djibouti)	Djibouti	11 30 N	43 00 E
French Togoland (former name for Togo)	Togo	8 00 N	1 10 E

Name	Entry in *The World Factbook*	Latitude (deg min)	Longitude (deg min)
French West Indies (former name for French possessions in the West Indies)	Guadeloupe, Martinique	16 30 N	62 00 W
Friendly Islands	Tonga	20 00 S	175 00 W
Frisian Islands	Denmark, Germany, Netherlands	53 35 N	6 40 E
Frunze (city; former name for Bishkek)	Kyrgyzstan	42 54 N	74 36 E
Funafuti (capital, atoll)	Tuvalu	8 30 S	179 12 E
Fundy, Bay of	Atlantic Ocean	45 00 N	66 00 W
Futuna Islands (Hoorn Islands/Iles de Horne)	Wallis and Futuna	14 19 S	178 05 W
Fyn (island)	Denmark	55 20 N	10 25 E
Gaborone (capital)	Botswana	24 45 S	25 55 E
Galapagos Islands (Archipielago de Colon)	Ecuador	0 00 N	90 30 W
Galicia (region)	Spain	42 45 N	8 10 E
Galicia (region)	Poland, Ukraine	49 30 N	23 00 E
Galilee (region)	Israel	32 54 N	35 20 E
Galleons Passage	Atlantic Ocean	11 00 N	60 55 W
Gambier Islands (Iles Gambier)	French Polynesia	23 09 S	134 58 W
Gaspar Strait	Pacific Ocean	3 00 S	107 00 E
Gdansk (city; formerly Danzig)	Poland	54 23 N	18 40 E
Geneva (city)	Switzerland	46 12 N	6 10 E
Genoa (city)	Italy	44 25 N	8 57 E
George Town (capital)	Cayman Islands	19 20 N	81 23 W
George Town (city)	Malaysia	5 26 N	100 16 E
George Town (city)	The Bahamas	23 30 N	75 46 W
Georgetown (capital)	Guyana	6 48 N	58 10 W
Georgetown (city)	The Gambia	13 30 N	14 47 W
German Democratic Republic (East Germany; former name for eastern portion of Germany)	Germany	52 00 N	13 00 E
German Southwest Africa (former name for Namibia)	Namibia	22 00 S	17 00 E
Germany, Federal Republic of	Germany	51 00 N	9 00 E
Gibraltar (city, peninsula)	Gibraltar	36 11 N	5 22 W
Gibraltar, Strait of	Atlantic Ocean	35 57 N	5 36 W
Gidi Pass	Egypt	30 13 N	33 09 E
Gilbert Islands	Kiribati	1 25 N	173 00 E
Glorioso Islands	Indian Ocean	11 30 S	47 20 E
Goa (state)	India	15 20 N	74 00 E
Gobi (desert)	China, Mongolia	42 30 N	107 00 E
Godthab (capital; also Nuuk)	Greenland	64 11 N	51 44 W
Golan Heights (region)	Syria	33 00 N	35 45 E
Gold Coast (former name for Ghana)	Ghana	8 00 N	2 00 W
Golfo San Jorge (gulf)	Atlantic Ocean	46 00 S	66 00 W
Golfo San Matias (gulf)	Atlantic Ocean	41 30 S	64 00 W
Good Hope, Cape of	South Africa	34 24 S	18 30 E
Goteborg (city)	Sweden	57 43 N	11 58 E
Gotland (island)	Sweden	57 30 N	18 33 E
Gough Island	Saint Helena, Ascension, and Tristan da Cunha	40 20 S	9 55 W
Graham Land (region)	Antarctica	65 00 S	64 00 W
Gran Chaco (region)	Argentina, Paraguay	24 00 S	60 00 W
Grand Bahama (island)	The Bahamas	26 40 N	78 35 W
Grand Banks (fishing ground)	Atlantic Ocean	47 06 N	55 48 W

Name	Entry in *The World Factbook*	Latitude (deg min)	Longitude (deg min)
Grand Cayman (island)	Cayman Islands	19 20 N	81 20 W
Grand Turk (capital; also Cockburn Town)	Turks and Caicos Islands	21 28 N	71 08 W
Great Australian Bight	Indian Ocean	35 00 S	130 00 E
Great Belt (strait; also Store Baelt)	Atlantic Ocean	55 30 N	11 00 E
Great Bitter Lake	Egypt	30 20 N	32 23 E
Great Britain (island)	United Kingdom	54 00 N	2 00 W
Great Channel	Indian Ocean	6 25 N	94 20 E
Great Inagua (island)	The Bahamas	21 00 N	73 20 W
Great Rift Valley	Ethiopia, Kenya	0 30 N	36 00 E
Greater Sunda Islands	Brunei, Indonesia, Malaysia	2 00 S	110 00 E
Green Islands	Papua New Guinea	4 30 S	154 10 E
Greenland Sea	Arctic Ocean	79 00 N	5 00 W
Grenadines, Northern (island group)	Saint Vincent and the Grenadines	13 15 N	61 12 W
Grenadines, Southern (island group)	Grenada	12 07 N	61 40 W
Grytviken (town; on South Georgia)	South Georgia and the South Sandwich Islands	54 15 S	36 45 W
Guadalahara (city)	Mexico	20 40 N	103 24 W
Guadalcanal (island)	Solomon Islands	9 32 S	160 12 E
Guadalupe, Isla de (island)	Mexico	29 11 N	118 17 W
Guangzhou (city; also Canton)	China	23 09 N	113 21 E
Guantanamo Bay (US Naval Base)	Cuba	20 00 N	75 08 W
Guatemala (capital)	Guatemala	14 38 N	90 31 W
Guine-Bissau (local name for Guinea-Bissau)	Guinea-Bissau	12 00 N	15 00 W
Guinea Ecuatorial (local name for Equatorial Guinea)	Equatorial Guinea	2 00 N	10 00 E
Guinea, Gulf of	Atlantic Ocean	3 00 N	2 30 E
Guinee (local name for Guinea)	Guinea	11 00 N	10 00 W
Gustavia (capital)	Saint Barthelemy	17 53 N	62 51 W
Guyane Francaise (local name for French Guiana)	French Guiana	4 00 N	53 00 W
Ha'apai Group (island group)	Tonga	19 42 S	174 29 W
Habomai Islands	Russia (de facto)	43 30 N	146 10 E
Hadhramaut (region)	Yemen	15 00 N	50 00 E
Hagatna (capital; formerly Agana)	Guam	13 28 N	144 45 E
Hague, The (seat of government)	Netherlands	52 05 N	4 18 E
Haifa (city)	Israel	32 50 N	35 00 E
Hainan Dao (island)	China	19 00 N	109 30 E
Haiphong (city)	Vietnam	20 52 N	106 41 E
Hala'ib Triangle (region)	Egypt (claimed), Sudan (de facto)	22 30 N	35 00 E
Halifax (city)	Canada	44 39 N	63 36 W
Halmahera (island)	Indonesia	1 00 N	128 00 E
Halmahera Sea	Pacific Ocean	0 30 S	129 00 E
Hamburg (city)	Germany	53 34 N	9 59 E
Hamilton (capital)	Bermuda	32 17 N	64 46 W
Han-guk (local name for South Korea	South Korea	37 00 N	127 30 E
Hanoi (capital)	Vietnam	21 02 N	105 51 E
Harare (capital)	Zimbabwe	17 50 S	31 03 E
Harvey Islands (former name for Cook Islands)	Cook Islands	21 14 S	159 46 W
Hatay (province)	Turkey	36 30 N	36 15 E
Havana (capital)	Cuba	23 08 N	82 22 W
Hawaii (island)	United States	19 45 N	155 45 W
Hawaiian Islands	United States	21 00 N	157 45 W

Name	Entry in *The World Factbook*	Latitude (deg min)	Longitude (deg min)
Hawar (island)	Bahrain	25 40 N	50 47 E
Hayastan (local name for Armenia)	Armenia	40 00 N	45 00 E
Heard Island	Heard Island and McDonald Islands	53 06 S	73 30 E
Hejaz (region)	Saudi Arabia	24 30 N	38 30 E
Helsinki (capital)	Finland	60 10 N	24 58 E
Herzegovina (political region)	Bosnia and Herzegovina	44 00 N	18 00 E
Hiiumaa (island)	Estonia	58 50 N	22 30 E
Hispaniola (island)	Dominican Republic, Haiti	18 45 N	71 00 W
Ho Chi Minh City (formerly Saigon)	Vietnam	10 45 N	106 40 E
Hokkaido (island)	Japan	44 00 N	143 00 E
Holland (region)	Netherlands	52 30 N	5 45 E
Hong Kong (special administrative region)	Hong Kong	22 15 N	114 10 E
Honiara (capital)	Solomon Islands	9 26 S	159 57 E
Honshu (island)	Japan	36 00 N	138 00 E
Hormuz, Strait of	Indian Ocean	26 34 N	56 15 E
Horn of Africa (region)	Djibouti, Eritrea, Ethiopia, Somalia	8 00 N	48 00 E
Horn, Cape (Cabo de Hornos)	Chile	55 59 S	67 16 W
Horne, Iles de (island group)	Wallis and Futuna	14 19 S	178 05 W
Hrvatska (local name for Croatia)	Croatia	45 10 N	15 30 E
Hudson Bay	Arctic Ocean	60 00 N	86 00 W
Hudson Strait	Arctic Ocean	62 00 N	71 00 W
Hunter Island	New Caledonia, Vanuatu	22 24 S	172 06 E
Iberian Peninsula	Portugal, Spain	40 00 N	5 00 W
Iceland Sea	Arctic Ocean	68 00 N	20 00 W
Ifni (region; former name of part of Spanish West Africa)	Morocco	29 22 N	10 09 W
Inaccessible Island	Saint Helena, Ascension, and Tristan da Cunha	37 17 S	12 40 W
Indochina (region)	Cambodia, Laos, Vietnam	15 00 N	107 00 E
Ingushetia (region)	Russia	43 15 N	45 00 E
Inhambane (region)	Mozambique	22 30 S	34 30 E
Inini (former name for French Guiana)	French Guiana	4 00 N	53 00 W
Inland Sea	Japan	34 20 N	133 30 E
Inner Hebrides (islands)	United Kingdom	56 30 N	6 20 W
Inner Mongolia (region; also Nei Mongol)	China	42 00 N	113 00 E
Ionian Islands	Greece	38 30 N	20 30 E
Ionian Sea	Atlantic Ocean	38 30 N	18 00 E
Irian Jaya (province)	Indonesia	5 00 S	138 00 E
Irish Sea	Atlantic Ocean	53 30 N	5 20 W
Iron Gate (river gorge)	Romania, Serbia	44 41 N	22 31 E
Iskenderun (region; formerly Alexandretta)	Turkey	36 34 N	36 08 E
Islamabad (capital)	Pakistan	33 42 N	73 10 E
Island (local name for Iceland)	Iceland	65 00 N	18 00 W
Islas Malvinas (island group)	Falkland Islands (Islas Malvinas)	51 45 S	59 00 W
Istanbul (city)	Turkey	41 01 N	28 58 E
Istrian Peninsula	Croatia, Slovenia	45 00 N	14 00 E
Italia (local name for Italy)	Italy	42 50 N	12 50 E
Italian East Africa (former name for Italian possessions in eastern Africa)	Eritrea, Ethiopia, Somalia	8 00 N	38 00 E
Italian Somaliland (former name for southern Somalia)	Somalia	10 00 N	49 00 E

Name	Entry in *The World Factbook*	Latitude (deg min)	Longitude (deg min)
Ittihad al-Imarat al-Arabiyah (local name for the United Arab Emirates)	United Arab Emirates	24 00 N	54 00 E
Iturup (island; see Etorofu)	Russia (de facto)	44 55 N	147 40 E
Ityop'iya (local name for Ethiopia)	Ethiopia	8 00 N	38 00 E
Ivory Coast (former name for Cote d'Ivoire)	Cote d'Ivoire	8 00 N	5 00 W
Iwo Jima (island)	Japan	24 47 N	141 20 E
Izmir (region)	Turkey	38 25 N	27 10 E
Jakarta (capital)	Indonesia	6 10 S	106 48 E
James Bay	Arctic Ocean	54 00 N	80 00 W
Jamestown (capital)	Saint Helena, Ascension, and Tristan da Cunha	15 56 S	5 44 W
Jammu (city)	India	32 42 N	74 52 E
Jammu and Kashmir (region)	India, Pakistan	34 00 N	76 00 E
Japan, Sea of	Pacific Ocean	40 00 N	135 00 E
Jars, Plain of	Laos	19 27 N	103 10 E
Java (island)	Indonesia	7 30 S	110 00 E
Java Sea	Pacific Ocean	5 00 S	110 00 E
Jerusalem (capital, proclaimed)	Israel, West Bank	31 47 N	35 14 E
Jiddah, Jeddah (city)	Saudi Arabia	21 30 N	39 12 E
Johannesburg (city)	South Africa	26 15 S	28 00 E
Joseph Bonaparte Gulf	Pacific Ocean	14 00 S	128 45 E
Juan Fernandez, Islas de (island group)	Chile	33 00 S	80 00 W
Juan de Fuca, Strait of	Pacific Ocean	48 18 N	124 00 W
Juan de Nova Island	Indian Ocean	17 03 S	42 45 E
Juba (capital)	South Sudan	04 51 N	31 37 E
Jubal, Strait of	Indian Ocean	27 40 N	33 55 E
Judaea (region)	Israel, West Bank	31 35 N	35 00 E
Jugoslavia, Jugoslavija (local names for Yugoslavia, a former Balkan federation)	Bosnia and Herzegovina, Croatia, Macedonia, Montenegro, Serbia, Slovenia	43 00 N	21 00 E
Jutland (region)	Denmark	56 00 N	9 15 E
Juventud, Isla de la (Isle of Youth)	Cuba	21 40 N	82 50 W
Kabardino-Balkaria (region)	Russia	43 30 N	43 30 E
Kabul (capital)	Afghanistan	34 31 N	69 12 E
Kaduna (city)	Nigeria	10 33 N	7 27 E
Kailas Range	China, India	30 00 N	82 00 E
Kalaallit Nunaat (local name for Greenland)	Greenland	72 00 N	40 00 W
Kalahari (desert)	Botswana, Namibia	24 30 S	21 00 E
Kalimantan (region)	Indonesia	0 00 N	115 00 E
Kaliningrad (region; formerly part of East Prussia)	Russia	54 30 N	21 00 E
Kamaran (island)	Yemen	15 21 N	42 34 E
Kamchatka Peninsula (Poluostrov Kamchatka)	Russia	56 00 N	160 00 E
Kampala (capital)	Uganda	0 19 N	32 25 E
Kampuchea (former name for Cambodia)	Cambodia	13 00 N	105 00 E
Kane Basin (portion of channel)	Arctic Ocean	79 30 N	68 00 W
Kanton Island	Kiribati	2 49 S	171 40 W
Kara Sea	Arctic Ocean	76 00 N	80 00 E
Karachevo-Cherkessia (region)	Russia	43 40 N	41 50 E
Karachi (city)	Pakistan	24 51 N	67 03 E
Karafuto (island; former name for southern Sakhalin Island)	Russia	50 00 N	143 00 E
Karakoram Pass	China, India	35 30 N	77 50 E
Karelia, Kareliya (region)	Finland, Russia	63 15 N	30 48 E

Name	Entry in *The World Factbook*	Latitude (deg min)	Longitude (deg min)
Karelian Isthmus	Russia	60 25 N	30 00 E
Karimata Strait	Pacific Ocean	2 05 S	108 40 E
Kashmir (region)	India, Pakistan	34 00 N	76 00 E
Katanga (region)	Democratic Republic of the Congo	10 00 S	26 00 E
Kathmandu (capital)	Nepal	27 43 N	85 19 E
Kattegat (strait)	Atlantic Ocean	57 00 N	11 00 E
Kauai Channel	Pacific Ocean	21 45 N	158 50 W
Kazakstan (former name for Kazakhstan)	Kazakhstan	48 00 N	68 00 E
Keeling Islands	Cocos (Keeling) Islands	12 30 S	96 50 E
Kerguelen, Iles (island group)	French Southern and Antarctic Lands	49 30 S	69 30 E
Kermadec Islands	New Zealand	29 50 S	178 15 W
Kerulen River	China, Mongolia	48 48 N	117 00 E
Khabarovsk (city)	Russia	48 27 N	135 06 E
Khanka, Lake	China, Russia	45 00 N	132 24 E
Khartoum (capital)	Sudan	15 36 N	32 32 E
Khios (island)	Greece	38 22 N	26 04 E
Khmer Republic (former name for Cambodia)	Cambodia	13 00 N	105 00 E
Khuriya Muriya Islands (Kuria Muria Islands)	Oman	17 30 N	56 00 E
Khyber Pass	Afghanistan, Pakistan	34 05 N	71 10 E
Kibris (Turkish local name for Cyprus)	Cyprus	35 00 N	33 00 E
Kiel Canal (Nord-Ostsee Kanal)	Atlantic Ocean	53 53 N	9 08 E
Kiev (city; former name for Kyiv)	Ukraine	50 26 N	30 31 E
Kigali (capital)	Rwanda	1 57 S	30 04 E
Kingston (capital)	Jamaica	18 00 N	76 48 W
Kingston (capital)	Norfolk Island	29 03 S	167 58 E
Kingstown (capital)	Saint Vincent and the Grenadines	13 09 N	61 14 W
Kinshasa (capital)	Democratic Republic of the Congo	4 18 S	15 18 E
Kipros (Greek local name for Cyprus)	Cyprus	35 00 N	33 00 E
Kirghiziya, Kirgizia (former name for Kyrgyzstan)	Kyrgyzstan	41 00 N	75 00 E
Kirguizstan (local name for Kyrgyzstan)	Kyrgyzstan	41 00 N	75 00 E
Kiritimati (Christmas Island)	Kiribati	1 52 N	157 20 W
Kishinev (see Chisinau)	Moldova	47 00 N	28 50 E
Kithira Strait	Atlantic Ocean	36 00 N	23 00 E
Kobe (city)	Japan	34 41 N	135 10 E
Kodiak Island	United States	57 49 N	152 23 W
Kodok (town; also Fashoda)	South Sudan	9 53 N	32 7 E
Kola Peninsula (Kol'skiy Poluostrov)	Russia	67 20 N	37 00 E
Kolonia (town; former capital; changed to Palikir)	Federated States of Micronesia	6 58 N	158 13 E
Korea Bay	Pacific Ocean	39 00 N	124 00 E
Korea Strait	Pacific Ocean	34 00 N	129 00 E
Korea, Democratic People's Republic of	North Korea	40 00 N	127 00 E
Korea, Republic of	South Korea	37 00 N	127 30 E
Koror (capital)	Palau	7 20 N	134 29 E
Kosovo (region)	Kosovo	42 30 N	21 00 E
Kosrae (island)	Federated States of Micronesia	5 20 N	163 00 E
Kowloon (city)	Hong Kong	22 18 N	114 10 E
Kra, Isthmus of	Burma, Thailand	10 20 N	99 00 E
Krakatoa (volcano)	Indonesia	6 07 S	105 24 E

Name	Entry in *The World Factbook*	Latitude (deg min)	Longitude (deg min)
Krakow (city)	Poland	50 03 N	19 56 E
Kuala Lumpur (capital)	Malaysia	3 10 N	101 42 E
Kunashiri (island; also Kunashir)	Russia (de facto)	44 20 N	146 00 E
Kunlun Mountains	China	36 00 N	84 00 E
Kuril Islands	Russia (de facto)	46 10 N	152 00 E
Kuwait (capital)	Kuwait	29 20 N	47 59 E
Kuznetsk Basin	Russia	54 00 N	86 00 E
Kwajalein Atoll	Marshall Islands	9 05 N	167 20 E
Kyiv (capital)	Ukraine	50 26 N	30 31 E
Kyushu (island)	Japan	33 00 N	131 00 E
La Paz (administrative capital)	Bolivia	16 30 S	68 09 W
La Perouse Strait	Pacific Ocean	45 45 N	142 00 E
Labrador (peninsula, region)	Canada	54 00 N	62 00 W
Labrador Sea	Atlantic Ocean	60 00 N	55 00 W
Laccadive Islands	India	10 00 N	73 00 E
Laccadive Sea	Indian Ocean	7 00 N	76 00 E
Lagos (former capital)	Nigeria	6 27 N	3 24 E
Lahore (city)	Pakistan	31 33 N	74 23 E
Lake Erie	Atlantic Ocean	42 30 N	81 00 W
Lake Huron	Atlantic Ocean	45 00 N	83 00 W
Lake Michigan	Atlantic Ocean	43 30 N	87 30 W
Lake Ontario	Atlantic Ocean	43 30 N	78 00 W
Lake Superior	Atlantic Ocean	48 00 N	88 00 W
Lakshadweep (Laccadive Islands)	India	10 00 N	73 00 E
Lantau Island	Hong Kong	22 15 N	113 55 E
Lao (local name for Laos)	Laos	18 00 N	105 00 E
Laptev Sea	Arctic Ocean	76 00 N	126 00 E
Las Palmas (city)	Spain (Canary Islands)	28 06 N	15 24 W
Latakia (region)	Syria	36 00 N	35 50 E
Latvija (local name for Latvia)	Latvia	57 00 N	25 00 E
Lau Group (island group)	Fiji	18 20 S	178 30 E
Lefkosa (see Nicosia)	Cyprus	35 10 N	33 22 E
Leipzig (city)	Germany	51 21 N	12 23 E
Lemnos (island)	Greece	39 54 N	25 21 E
Leningrad (city; former name for Saint Petersburg)	Russia	59 55 N	30 15 E
Lesser Sunda Islands	Indonesia	9 00 S	120 00 E
Lesvos (island)	Greece	39 15 N	26 15 E
Leyte (island)	Philippines	10 50 N	124 50 E
Liancourt Rocks (claimed by Japan)	South Korea	37 15 N	131 50 E
Liaodong Wan (gulf)	Pacific Ocean	40 30 N	121 20 E
Liban (local name for Lebanon)	Lebanon	33 50 N	36 50 E
Libreville (capital)	Gabon	0 23 N	9 27 E
Lietuva (local name for Lithuania)	Lithuania	56 00 N	24 00 E
Ligurian Sea	Atlantic Ocean	43 30 N	9 00 E
Lilongwe (capital)	Malawi	13 59 S	33 44 E
Lima (capital)	Peru	12 03 S	77 03 W
Lincoln Sea	Arctic Ocean	83 00 N	56 00 W
Line Islands	Jarvis Island, Kingman Reef, Kiribati, Palmyra Atoll	0 05 N	157 00 W
Lion, Gulf of	Atlantic Ocean	43 20 N	4 00 E
Lisbon (capital)	Portugal	38 43 N	9 08 W

Name	Entry in *The World Factbook*	Latitude (deg min)	Longitude (deg min)
Little Belt (strait; also Lille Baelt)	Atlantic Ocean	55 05 N	9 55 E
Ljubljana (capital)	Slovenia	46 03 N	14 31 E
Llanos (region)	Venezuela	8 00 N	68 00 W
Lobamba (city)	Swaziland	26 27 S	31 12 E
Lombok (island)	Indonesia	8 28 S	116 40 E
Lombok Strait	Indian Ocean	8 30 S	115 50 E
Lome (capital)	Togo	6 08 N	1 13 E
London (capital)	United Kingdom	51 30 N	0 10 W
Longyearbyen (capital)	Svalbard	78 13 N	15 33 E
Lord Howe Island	Australia	31 30 S	159 00 E
Lorraine (region)	France	48 42 N	6 11 E
Louisiade Archipelago	Papua New Guinea	11 00 S	153 00 E
Lourenco Marques (city; former name for Maputo)	Mozambique	25 56 S	32 34 E
Loyalty Islands (Iles Loyaute)	New Caledonia	21 00 S	167 00 E
Luanda (capital)	Angola	8 48 S	13 14 E
Lubnan (local name for Lebanon)	Lebanon	33 50 N	36 50 E
Lubumbashi (city)	Democratic Republic of the Congo	11 40 S	27 28 E
Lusaka (capital)	Zambia	15 25 S	28 17 E
Luxembourg (capital)	Luxembourg	49 45 N	6 10 E
Luzon (island)	Philippines	16 00 N	121 00 E
Luzon Strait	Pacific Ocean	20 30 N	121 00 E
Lyakhov Islands	Russia	73 45 N	138 00 E
Macao	Macau	22 10 N	113 33 E
Macau (special administrative region)	China	22 10 N	113 33 E
Macquarie Island	Australia	54 36 S	158 54 E
Madagasikara (local name for Madagascar)	Madagascar	20 00 S	47 00 E
Maddalena, Isola	Italy	41 13 N	09 24 E
Madeira Islands	Portugal	32 40 N	16 45 W
Madras (city; see Chennai)	India	13 04 N	80 16 E
Madrid (capital)	Spain	40 24 N	3 41 W
Magellan, Strait of	Atlantic Ocean	54 00 S	71 00 W
Maghreb (region)	Algeria, Libya, Mauritania, Morocco, Tunisia	34 00 N	3 00 E
Magreb (local name for Morocco)	Morocco	32 00 N	5 00 W
Magyarorszag (local name for Hungary)	Hungary	47 00 N	20 00 E
Mahe Island	Seychelles	4 41 S	55 30 E
Maiz, Islas del (Corn Islands)	Nicaragua	12 15 N	83 00 W
Majorca Island (Isla de Mallorca)	Spain	39 30 N	3 00 E
Majuro (capital)	Marshall Islands	7 05 N	171 08 E
Makassar Strait	Pacific Ocean	2 00 S	117 30 E
Makedonija (local name for Macedonia)	Macedonia	41 50 N	22 00 E
Malabo (capital)	Equatorial Guinea	3 45 N	8 47 E
Malacca, Strait of	Indian Ocean	2 30 N	101 20 E
Malagasy Republic	Madagascar	20 00 S	47 00 E
Malay Archipelago	Brunei, Indonesia, Malaysia, Papua New Guinea, Philippines	2 30 N	120 00 E
Malay Peninsula	Malaysia, Thailand	7 10 N	100 35 E
Male (capital)	Maldives	4 10 N	73 31 E
Mallorca, Isla de (island; also Majorca)	Spain	39 30 N	3 00 E
Malmady (region)	Belgium	50 26 N	6 02 E

Name	Entry in *The World Factbook*	Latitude (deg min)	Longitude (deg min)
Malpelo, Isla de (island)	Colombia	4 00 N	90 30 W
Malta Channel	Atlantic Ocean	56 44 N	26 53 E
Malvinas, Islas (island group)	Falkland Islands (Islas Malvinas)	51 45 S	59 00 W
Mamoutzou (capital)	Mayotte	12 47 S	45 14 E
Managua (capital)	Nicaragua	12 09 N	86 17 W
Manama (capital)	Bahrain	26 13 N	50 35 E
Manchukuo (former state)	China	44 00 N	124 00 E
Manchuria (region)	China	44 00 N	124 00 E
Manila (capital)	Philippines	14 35 N	121 00 E
Manipa Strait	Pacific Ocean	3 20 S	127 23 E
Mannar, Gulf of	Indian Ocean	8 30 N	79 00 E
Manua Islands	American Samoa	14 13 S	169 35 W
Maputo (capital)	Mozambique	25 58 S	32 35 E
Marcus Island (Minami-tori-shima)	Japan	24 16 N	154 00 E
Margarita, Isla (island)	Venezuela	10 00 N	64 00 W
Mariana Islands	Guam, Northern Mariana Islands	16 00 N	145 30 E
Marie Byrd Land (region)	Antarctica	77 00 S	130 00 W
Marigot (capital)	Saint Martin	18 04 N	63 05 W
Marion Island	South Africa	46 51 S	37 52 E
Marmara, Sea of	Atlantic Ocean	40 40 N	28 15 E
Marquesas Islands (Iles Marquises)	French Polynesia	9 00 S	139 30 W
Marseille (city)	France	43 18 N	5 23 E
Martin Vaz, Ilhas (island group)	Brazil	20 30 S	28 51 W
Mas a Tierra (Robinson Crusoe Island)	Chile	33 38 S	78 52 W
Mascarene Islands	Mauritius, Reunion	21 00 S	57 00 E
Maseru (capital)	Lesotho	29 28 S	27 30 E
Mata-Utu (capital)	Wallis and Futuna	13 57 S	171 56 W
Matsu (island)	Taiwan	26 13 N	119 56 E
Matthew Island	New Caledonia, Vanuatu	22 20 S	171 20 E
Mauritanie (local name for Mauritania)	Mauritania	20 00 N	12 00 W
Mazatlan (city)	Mexico	23 13 N	106 25 W
Mbabane (capital)	Swaziland	26 18 S	31 06 E
McDonald Islands	Heard Island and McDonald Islands	53 06 S	73 30 E
Mecca (city)	Saudi Arabia	21 27 N	39 49 E
Mediterranean Sea	Atlantic Ocean	36 00 N	15 00 E
Melbourne (city)	Australia	37 49 S	144 58 E
Melilla (exclave)	Spain	35 19 N	2 58 W
Memel (region)	Lithuania	55 43 N	21 30 E
Mesopotamia (region)	Iraq	33 00 N	44 00 E
Messina, Strait of	Atlantic Ocean	38 15 N	15 35 E
Mexico City (capital)	Mexico	19 24 N	99 09 W
Mexico, Gulf of	Atlantic Ocean	25 00 N	90 00 W
Middle Congo (former name for Republic of the Congo)	Republic of the Congo	1 00 S	15 00 E
Milan (city)	Italy	45 28 N	9 11 E
Milwaukee Deep (Puerto Rico Trench)	Atlantic Ocean	19 55 N	65 27 W
Minami-tori-shima (Marcus Island)	Japan	24 16 N	154 00 E
Mindanao (island)	Philippines	8 00 N	125 00 E
Mindanao Sea	Pacific Ocean	9 15 N	124 30 E
Mindoro (island)	Philippines	12 50 N	121 05 E

Name	Entry in *The World Factbook*	Latitude (deg min)	Longitude (deg min)
Mindoro Strait	Pacific Ocean	12 20 N	120 40 E
Mingrelia (region)	Georgia	42 30 N	41 52 E
Minicoy Island	India	8 17 N	73 02 E
Minorca Island (Isla de Menorca)	Spain	40 00 N	4 00 E
Minsk (capital)	Belarus	53 54 N	27 34 E
Misr (local name for Egypt)	Egypt	27 00 N	30 00 E
Mitla Pass	Egypt	30 02 N	32 54 E
Mocambique (local name for Mozambique)	Mozambique	18 15 S	35 00 E
Mogadishu (capital)	Somalia	2 04 N	45 22 E
Moldavia (region)	Moldova, Romania	47 00 N	29 00 E
Molucca Sea	Pacific Ocean	2 00 N	127 00 E
Moluccas (Spice Islands)	Indonesia	2 00 S	128 00 E
Mombasa (city)	Kenya	4 03 S	39 40 E
Mona Passage	Atlantic Ocean	18 30 N	67 45 W
Monaco (capital)	Monaco	43 44 N	7 25 E
Mongol Uls (local name for Mongolia)	Mongolia	46 00 N	105 00 E
Monrovia (capital)	Liberia	6 18 N	10 47 W
Monterrey (city)	Mexico	25 40 N	100 19 W
Montevideo (capital)	Uruguay	34 53 S	56 11 W
Montreal (city)	Canada	45 31 N	73 34 W
Moravia (region)	Czech Republic	49 30 N	17 00 E
Moravian Gate (pass)	Czech Republic	49 35 N	17 50 E
Moroni (capital)	Comoros	11 41 S	43 16 E
Mortlock Islands (Nomoi Islands)	Federated States of Micronesia	5 30 N	153 40 E
Moscow (capital)	Russia	55 45 N	37 35 E
Mount Pinatubo (volcano)	Philippines	15 08 N	120 21 E
Mozambique Channel	Indian Ocean	19 00 S	41 00 E
Mumbai (city; also Bombay)	India	18 58 N	72 50 E
Munich, Muenchen (city)	Germany	48 08 N	11 35 E
Muritaniyah (local name for Mauritania)	Mauritania	20 00 N	12 00 W
Musandam Peninsula	Oman, United Arab Emirates	26 18 N	56 24 E
Muscat (capital)	Oman	23 37 N	58 35 E
Muscat and Oman (former name for Oman)	Oman	21 00 N	57 00 E
Myanma, Myanmar	Burma	22 00 N	98 00 E
N'Djamena (capital)	Chad	12 07 N	15 03 E
Nagorno-Karabakh (region)	Azerbaijan	40 00 N	46 40 E
Nairobi (capital)	Kenya	1 17 S	36 49 E
Namib (desert)	Namibia	24 00 S	15 00 E
Nampo-shoto (island group)	Japan	30 00 N	140 00 E
Nan Madol (ruins)	Federated States of Micronesia	6 85 N	158 35 E
Naples (city)	Italy	40 51 N	14 15 E
Nassau (capital)	The Bahamas	25 05 N	77 21 W
Natal (region)	South Africa	29 00 S	30 25 E
Natuna Besar Islands	Indonesia	3 30 N	102 30 E
Natuna Sea	Pacific Ocean	3 30 N	108 00 E
Naxcivan (region)	Azerbaijan	39 20 N	45 20 E
Naxos (island)	Greece	37 05 N	25 30 E
Nederland (local name for the Netherlands)	Netherlands	52 30 N	5 45 E
Nederlandse Antillen (local name for the former Netherlands Antilles)	Curacao, Sint Maarten	12 15 N	68 45 W
Negev (region)	Israel	30 30 N	34 55 E

Name	Entry in *The World Factbook*	Latitude (deg min)	Longitude (deg min)
Negros (island)	Philippines	10 00 N	123 00 E
Nejd (region)	Saudi Arabia	24 05 N	45 15 E
Netherlands Antilles (former name of Dutch Caribbean dependencies)	Curacao, Sint Maarten	12 15 N	68 45 W
Netherlands East Indies (former name for Indonesia)	Indonesia	5 00 S	120 00 E
Netherlands Guiana (former name for Suriname)	Suriname	4 00 N	56 00 W
Nevis (island)	Saint Kitts and Nevis	17 09 N	62 35 W
New Britain (island)	Papua New Guinea	6 00 S	150 00 E
New Delhi (capital)	India	28 36 N	77 12 E
New Guinea (island)	Indonesia, Papua New Guinea	5 00 S	140 00 E
New Hebrides (island group)	Vanuatu	16 00 S	167 00 E
New Ireland (island)	Papua New Guinea	3 20 N	152 00 E
New Siberian Islands	Russia	75 00 N	142 00 E
New Territories (mainland region)	Hong Kong	22 24 N	114 10 E
Newfoundland (island, with mainland area, and a province)	Canada	52 00 N	56 00 W
Niamey (capital)	Niger	13 31 N	2 07 E
Nicobar Islands	India	8 00 N	93 30 E
Nicosia (capital; also Lefkosia)	Cyprus	35 10 N	33 22 E
Nightingale Island	Saint Helena, Ascension, and Tristan da Cunha	37 25 S	12 30 W
Nihon, Nippon (local name for Japan)	Japan	36 00 N	138 00 E
Nomoi Islands (Mortlock Islands)	Federated States of Micronesia	5 30 N	153 40 E
Norge (local name for Norway)	Norway	62 00 N	10 00 E
Norman Isles (Channel Islands)	Guernsey, Jersey	49 20 N	2 20 W
North Atlantic Ocean	Atlantic Ocean	30 00 N	45 00 W
North Channel	Atlantic Ocean	55 10 N	5 40 W
North Frisian Islands	Denmark, Germany	54 50 N	8 12 E
North Greenland Sea	Arctic Ocean	78 00 N	5 00 W
North Island	New Zealand	39 00 S	176 00 E
North Ossetia (region)	Russia	43 00 N	44 10 E
North Pacific Ocean	Pacific Ocean	30 00 N	165 00 W
North Sea	Atlantic Ocean	56 00 N	4 00 E
North Vietnam (former name for northern portion of Vietnam)	Vietnam	23 00 N	106 00 E
North Yemen (Yemen Arab Republic; now part of Yemen)	Yemen	15 00 N	44 00 E
Northeast Providence Channel	Atlantic Ocean	25 40 N	77 09 W
Northern Areas	Pakistan	36 0 N	75 0 E
Northern Cyprus (region)	Cyprus	35 15 N	33 44 E
Northern Epirus (region)	Albania, Greece	40 00 N	20 30 E
Northern Grenadines (political region)	Saint Vincent and the Grenadines	12 45 N	61 15 W
Northern Ireland	United Kingdom	54 40 N	6 45 W
Northern Rhodesia (former name for Zambia)	Zambia	15 00 S	30 00 E
Northwest Passages	Arctic Ocean	74 40 N	100 00 W
Norwegian Sea	Atlantic Ocean	66 00 N	6 00 E
Nouakchott (capital)	Mauritania	18 06 N	15 57 W
Noumea (capital)	New Caledonia	22 16 S	166 27 E
Nouvelle-Caledonie (local name for New Caledonia)	New Caledonia	21 30 S	165 30 E
Nouvelles Hebrides (former name for Vanuatu)	Vanuatu	16 00 S	167 00 E
Novaya Zemlya (islands)	Russia	74 00 N	57 00 E
Nubia (region)	Egypt, Sudan	20 30 N	33 00 E
Nuku'alofa (capital)	Tonga	21 08 S	175 12 W
Nunavut (region)	Canada	72 00 N	90 00 W

Name	Entry in *The World Factbook*	Latitude (deg min)	Longitude (deg min)
Nuuk (capital; also Godthab)	Greenland	64 11 N	51 44 W
Nyasaland (former name for Malawi)	Malawi	13 30 S	34 00 E
Nyassa (region)	Mozambique	13 30 S	37 00 E
Oahu (island)	United States (Hawaii)	21 30 N	158 00 W
Ocean Island (Banaba)	Kiribati	0 52 S	169 35 E
Ocean Island (Kure Island)	United States	28 25 N	178 20 W
Oesterreich (local name for Austria)	Austria	47 20 N	13 20 E
Ogaden (region)	Ethiopia, Somalia	7 00 N	46 00 E
Oil Islands (Chagos Archipelago)	British Indian Ocean Territory	6 00 S	71 30 E
Okhotsk, Sea of	Pacific Ocean	53 00 N	150 00 E
Okinawa (island group)	Japan	26 30 N	128 00 E
Oland (island)	Sweden	56 45 N	16 40 E
Oman, Gulf of	Indian Ocean	24 30 N	58 30 E
Ombai Strait	Pacific Ocean	8 30 S	125 00 E
Oran (city)	Algeria	35 43 N	0 43 W
Orange River Colony (region; former name of Free State Province of South Africa)	South Africa	28 20 S	26 40 E
Oranjestad (capital)	Aruba	12 33 N	70 06 W
Oresund (The Sound) (strait)	Atlantic Ocean	55 50 N	12 40 E
Orkney Islands	United Kingdom	59 00 N	3 00 W
Osaka (city)	Japan	34 42 N	135 30 E
Oslo (capital)	Norway	59 55 N	10 45 E
Osumi Strait (Van Diemen Strait)	Pacific Ocean	31 00 N	131 00 E
Otranto, Strait of	Atlantic Ocean	40 00 N	19 00 E
Ottawa (capital)	Canada	45 25 N	75 40 W
Ouagadougou (capital)	Burkina Faso	12 22 N	1 31 W
Outer Hebrides (islands)	United Kingdom	57 45 N	7 00 W
Outer Mongolia (region)	Mongolia	46 00 N	105 00 E
P'yongyang (capital)	North Korea	39 01 N	125 45 E
Pacific Islands, Trust Territory of the (former name of a large area of the western North Pacific Ocean)	Marshall Islands, Federated States of Micronesia, Northern Mariana Islands, Palau	10 00 N	155 00 E
Pagan (island)	Northern Mariana Islands	18 08 N	145 47 E
Pago Pago (capital)	American Samoa	14 16 S	170 42 W
Palawan (island)	Philippines	9 30 N	118 30 E
Palermo (city)	Italy	38 07 N	13 21 E
Palestine (region)	Israel, West Bank	32 00 N	35 15 E
Palikir (capital)	Federated States of Micronesia	6 55 N	158 08 E
Palk Strait	Indian Ocean	10 00 N	79 45 E
Pamirs (mountains)	China, Tajikistan	38 00 N	73 00 E
Pampas (region)	Argentina	35 00 S	63 00 W
Panama (capital)	Panama	8 58 N	79 32 W
Panama Canal	Panama	9 00 N	79 45 W
Panama, Gulf of	Pacific Ocean	8 00 N	79 30 W
Panay (island)	Philippines	11 15 N	122 30 E
Pantelleria, Isola di (island)	Italy	36 47 N	12 00 E
Papeete (capital)	French Polynesia	17 32 S	149 34 W
Paramaribo (capital)	Suriname	5 50 N	55 10 W
Parece Vela (island)	Japan	20 20 N	136 00 E
Paris (capital)	France	48 52 N	2 20 E
Pascua, Isla de (Easter Island)	Chile	27 07 S	109 22 W
Pashtunistan (region)	Afghanistan, Pakistan	32 00 N	69 00 E

Name	Entry in *The World Factbook*	Latitude (deg min)	Longitude (deg min)
Passion, Ile de la (island)	Clipperton Island	10 17 N	109 13 W
Patagonia (region)	Argentina	48 00 S	61 00 W
Peking (see Beijing)	China	39 56 N	116 24 E
Pelagian Islands (Isole Pelagie)	Italy	35 40 N	12 40 E
Peleliu (Beliliou) (island)	Palau	7 01 N	134 15 E
Peloponnese (peninsula)	Greece	37 30 N	22 25 E
Pemba Island	Tanzania	5 20 S	39 45 E
Penang Island	Malaysia	5 23 N	100 15 E
Pentland Firth (channel)	Atlantic Ocean	58 44 N	3 13 W
Perim (island)	Yemen	12 39 N	43 25 E
Perouse Strait, La	Pacific Ocean	44 45 N	142 00 E
Persia (former name for Iran)	Iran	32 00 N	53 00 E
Persian Gulf	Indian Ocean	27 00 N	51 00 E
Perth (city)	Australia	31 56 S	115 50 E
Pescadores (islands)	Taiwan	23 30 N	119 30 E
Peshawar (city)	Pakistan	34 01 N	71 40 E
Peter I Island	Antarctica	68 48 S	90 35 W
Petrograd (city; former name for Saint Petersburg)	Russia	59 55 N	30 15 E
Philip Island	Norfolk Island	29 08 S	167 57 E
Philippine Sea	Pacific Ocean	20 00 N	134 00 E
Philipsburg (capital)	Sint Maarten	18 1 N	63 2 W
Phnom Penh (capital)	Cambodia	11 33 N	104 55 E
Phoenix Islands	Kiribati	3 30 S	172 00 W
Pinatubo, Mount (volcano)	Philippines	15 08 N	120 21 E
Pines, Isle of (island; former name for Isla de la Juventud)	Cuba	21 40 N	82 50 W
Pleasant Island	Nauru	0 32 S	166 55 E
Plymouth (capital)	Montserrat	16 44 N	62 14 W
Podgorica (administrative capital)	Montenegro	42 26 N	19 16 E
Polska (local name)	Poland	52 00 N	20 00 E
Polynesie Francaise (local name for French Polynesia)	French Polynesia	15 00 S	140 00 W
Pomerania (region)	Germany, Poland	53 40 N	15 35 E
Ponape (Pohnpei) (island)	Federated States of Micronesia	6 55 N	158 15 E
Port Louis (capital)	Mauritius	20 10 S	57 30 E
Port Moresby (capital)	Papua New Guinea	9 30 S	147 10 E
Port-Vila (capital)	Vanuatu	17 44 S	168 19 E
Port-au-Prince (capital)	Haiti	18 32 N	72 20 W
Port-of-Spain (capital)	Trinidad and Tobago	10 39 N	61 31 W
Porto-Novo (capital)	Benin	6 29 N	2 37 E
Portuguese East Africa (former name for Mozambique)	Mozambique	18 15 S	35 00 E
Portuguese Guinea (former name for Guinea-Bissau)	Guinea-Bissau	12 00 N	15 00 W
Portuguese Timor (former name for Timor-Leste)	Timor-Leste	9 00 S	126 00 E
Poznan (city)	Poland	52 25 N	16 55 E
Prague (capital)	Czech Republic	50 05 N	14 28 E
Praia (capital)	Cabo Verde	14 55 N	23 31 W
Prathet Thai (local name for Thailand)	Thailand	15 00 N	100 00 E
Pretoria (administrative capital)	South Africa	25 42 S	28 13 E
Prevlaka peninsula	Croatia	42 24 N	18 31 E
Pribilof Islands	United States	57 00 N	170 00 W
Prince Edward Island	Canada	46 20 N	63 20 W
Prince Edward Islands	South Africa	46 35 S	38 00 E
Prince Patrick Island	Canada	76 30 N	119 00 W

Name	Entry in *The World Factbook*	Latitude (deg min)	Longitude (deg min)
Principe (island)	Sao Tome and Principe	1 38 N	7 25 E
Pristina, Prishtina, Prishtine (capital)	Kosovo	42 40 N	21 10 E
Prussia (region)	Germany, Poland, Russia	53 00 N	14 00 E
Pukapuka Atoll	Cook Islands	10 53 S	165 49 W
Punjab (region)	India, Pakistan	30 50 N	73 30 E
Puntland (region)	Somalia	8 21 N	49 08 E
Qazaqstan (local name for Kazakhstan)	Kazakhstan	48 00 N	68 00 E
Qita Ghazzah (local name Gaza Strip)	Gaza Strip	31 25 N	34 20 E
Quebec (city)	Canada	46 48 N	71 15 W
Queen Charlotte Islands	Canada	53 00 N	132 00 W
Queen Elizabeth Islands	Canada	78 00 N	95 00 W
Queen Maud Land (claimed by Norway)	Antarctica	73 30 S	12 00 E
Quemoy (island)	Taiwan	24 27 N	118 23 E
Quito (capital)	Ecuador	0 13 S	78 30 W
Rabat (capital)	Morocco	34 02 N	6 51 W
Ralik Chain (island group)	Marshall Islands	8 00 N	167 00 E
Rangoon (capital; also Yangon)	Burma	16 47 N	96 10 E
Rapa Nui (Easter Island)	Chile	27 07 S	109 22 W
Ratak Chain (island group)	Marshall Islands	9 00 N	171 00 E
Red Sea	Indian Ocean	20 00 N	38 00 E
Redonda (island)	Antigua and Barbuda	16 55 N	62 19 W
Republica Dominicana (local name for Dominican Republic)	Dominican Republic	19 00 N	70 40 W
Republique Centrafricain (local name for Central African Republic)	Central African Republic	7 00 N	21 00 E
Republique Francaise (local name for France)	France	46 00 N	2 00 E
Republique Gabonaise (local name for Gabon)	Gabon	1 00 S	11 45 E
Republique Rwandaise (local name for Rwanda)	Rwanda	2 00 S	30 00 E
Republique Togolaise (local name for Togo)	Togo	8 00 N	1 10 E
Revillagigedo Island	United States (Alaska)	55 35 N	131 06 W
Revillagigedo Islands	Mexico	19 00 N	112 45 W
Reykjavik (capital)	Iceland	64 09 N	21 57 W
Rhodes (island)	Greece	36 10 N	28 00 E
Rhodesia, Northern (former name for Zambia)	Zambia	15 00 S	30 00 E
Rhodesia, Southern (former name for Zimbabwe)	Zimbabwe	20 00 S	30 00 E
Riga (capital)	Latvia	56 57 N	24 06 E
Riga, Gulf of	Atlantic Ocean	57 30 N	23 30 E
Rio Muni (mainland region)	Equatorial Guinea	1 30 N	10 00 E
Rio de Janiero (city)	Brazil	22 55 S	43 17 W
Rio de Oro (region)	Western Sahara	23 45 N	15 45 W
Rio de la Plata (gulf)	Atlantic Ocean	35 00 S	59 00 W
Riyadh (capital)	Saudi Arabia	24 38 N	46 43 E
Road Town (capital)	British Virgin Islands	18 27 N	64 37 W
Robinson Crusoe Island (Mas a Tierra)	Chile	33 38 S	78 52 W
Rocas, Atol das (island)	Brazil	3 51 S	33 49 W
Rockall (island)	United Kingdom	57 35 N	13 48 W
Rodrigues (island)	Mauritius	19 42 S	63 25 E
Rome (capital)	Italy	41 54 N	12 29 E
Roncador Cay (island)	Colombia	13 32 N	80 03 W
Roosevelt Island	Antarctica	79 30 S	162 00 W
Roseau (capital)	Dominica	15 18 N	61 24 W
Ross Dependency (claimed by New Zealand)	Antarctica	80 00 S	180 00 E

Name	Entry in *The World Factbook*	Latitude (deg min)	Longitude (deg min)
Ross Island	Antarctica	81 30 S	175 00 W
Ross Sea	Antarctica, Southern Ocean	76 00 S	175 00 W
Rossiya (local name for Russia)	Russia	60 00 N	100 00 E
Rota (island)	Northern Mariana Islands	14 10 N	145 12 E
Rotuma (island)	Fiji	12 30 S	177 05 E
Ruanda (former name for Rwanda)	Rwanda	2 00 S	30 00 E
Rub al Khali (desert)	Saudi Arabia	19 30 N	49 00 E
Rumelia (region)	Albania, Bulgaria, Macedonia	42 00 N	22 30 E
Ruthenia (region; former name for Carpatho-Ukraine)	Ukraine	48 22 N	23 32 E
Ryukyu Islands	Japan	26 30 N	128 00 E
Saar (region)	Germany	49 25 N	7 00 E
Saaremaa (island)	Estonia	58 25 N	22 30 E
Saba (island)	Netherlands	17 38 N	63 10 W
Sabah (state)	Malaysia	5 20 N	117 10 E
Sable Island	Canada	43 55 N	59 50 W
Safety Islands (Iles du Salut)	French Guiana	5 20 N	52 37 W
Sahara Occidental (former name for Western Sahara)	Western Sahara	24 30 N	13 00 W
Sahel (region)	Burkina Faso, Chad, The Gambia, Guinea- Bissau, Mali, Mauritania, Niger, Senegal	15 00 N	8 00 W
Saigon (city; former name for Ho Chi Minh City)	Vietnam	10 45 N	106 40 E
Saint Brandon (Cargados Carajos Shoals)	Mauritius	16 25 S	59 38 E
Saint Christopher (island)	Saint Kitts and Nevis	17 20 N	62 45 W
Saint Christopher and Nevis	Saint Kitts and Nevis	17 20 N	62 45 W
Saint Eustatius (island)	Netherlands	17 30 N	63 00 W
Saint George's (capital)	Grenada	12 03 N	61 45 W
Saint George's Channel	Atlantic Ocean	52 00 N	6 00 W
Saint Helena Island	Saint Helena, Ascension, and Tristan da Cunha	15 57 S	5 42 W
Saint Helens, Mount (volcano)	United States	46 15 N	122 12 W
Saint Helier (capital)	Jersey	49 12 N	2 07 W
Saint John (city)	Canada (New Brunswick)	45 16 N	66 04 W
Saint John's (capital)	Antigua and Barbuda	17 06 N	61 51 W
Saint Lawrence Island	United States	49 30 N	67 00 W
Saint Lawrence Seaway	Atlantic Ocean	49 15 N	67 00 W
Saint Lawrence, Gulf of	Atlantic Ocean	48 00 N	62 00 W
Saint Paul Island	Canada	47 12 N	60 09 W
Saint Paul Island	United States	57 11 N	170 16 W
Saint Paul Island (Ile Saint-Paul)	French Southern and Antarctic Lands	38 43 S	77 29 E
Saint Peter Port (capital)	Guernsey	49 27 N	2 32 W
Saint Peter and Saint Paul Rocks (Penedos de Sao Pedro e Sao Paulo)	Brazil	0 23 N	29 23 W
Saint Petersburg (city; former capital)	Russia	59 55 N	30 15 E
Saint Thomas (island)	Virgin Islands	18 21 N	64 55 W
Saint Vincent Passage	Atlantic Ocean	13 30 N	61 00 W
Saint-Denis (capital)	Reunion	20 52 S	55 28 E
Saint-Pierre (capital)	Saint Pierre and Miquelon	46 46 N	56 11 W
Saipan (island)	Northern Mariana Islands	15 12 N	145 45 E
Sak'art'velo (local name for Georgia)	Georgia	42 00 N	43 30 E
Sakhalin Island (Ostrov Sakhalin)	Russia	51 00 N	143 00 E
Sakishima Islands	Japan	24 30 N	124 00 E

Name	Entry in *The World Factbook*	Latitude (deg min)	Longitude (deg min)
Sala y Gomez, Isla (island)	Chile	26 28 S	105 00 W
Salisbury (city; former name for Harare)	Zimbabwe	17 50 S	105 00 W
Salzburg (city)	Austria	47 48 N	13 02 E
Samar (island)	Philippines	12 00 N	125 00 E
Samaria (region)	West Bank	32 15 N	35 10 E
Samoa Islands	American Samoa, Samoa	14 00 S	171 00 W
Samos (island)	Greece	37 48 N	26 44 E
San Ambrosio, Isla (island)	Chile	26 21 S	79 52 W
San Andres y Providencia, Archipielago (island group)	Colombia	13 00 N	81 30 W
San Bernardino Strait	Pacific Ocean	12 32 N	124 10 E
San Felix, Isla (island)	Chile	26 17 S	80 05 W
San Jose (capital)	Costa Rica	9 56 N	84 05 W
San Juan (capital)	Puerto Rico	18 28 N	66 07 W
San Marino (capital)	San Marino	43 56 N	12 25 E
San Salvador (capital)	El Salvador	13 42 N	89 12 W
Sanaa (capital)	Yemen	15 21 N	44 12 E
Sandzak (region)	Montenegro, Serbia	43 05 N	19 45 E
Santa Cruz (city)	Bolivia	17 48 S	63 10 W
Santa Cruz Islands	Solomon Islands	11 00 S	166 15 E
Santa Sede (local name for the Holy See)	Holy See	41 54 N	12 27 E
Santiago (capital)	Chile	33 27 S	70 40 W
Santo Antao (island)	Cabo Verde	17 05 N	25 10 W
Santo Domingo (capital)	Dominican Republic	18 28 N	69 54 W
Sao Paulo (city)	Brazil	23 35 S	46 43 W
Sao Pedro e Sao Paulo, Penedos de (rocks)	Brazil	0 23 N	29 23 W
Sao Tiago (island)	Cabo Verde	15 05 N	23 40 W
Sao Tome (island)	Sao Tome and Principe	0 12 N	6 39 E
Sapporo (city)	Japan	43 04 N	141 20 E
Sapudi Strait	Pacific Ocean	7 05 S	114 10 E
Sarajevo (capital)	Bosnia and Herzegovina	43 52 N	18 25 E
Sarawak (state)	Malaysia	2 30 N	113 30 E
Sardinia (island)	Italy	40 00 N	9 00 E
Sargasso Sea (region)	Atlantic Ocean	30 00 N	55 00 W
Sark (island)	Guernsey	49 26 N	2 21 W
Savage Island (former name for Niue)	Niue	19 02 S	169 52 W
Savu Sea	Pacific Ocean	9 30 S	122 00 E
Saxony (region)	Germany	51 00 N	13 00 E
Schleswig-Holstein (region)	Germany	54 31 N	9 33 E
Schweiz (local German name for Switzerland)	Switzerland	47 00 N	8 00 E
Scopus, Mount	Israel, West Bank	31 48 N	35 14 E
Scotia Sea	Atlantic Ocean, Southern Ocean	56 00 S	40 00 W
Scotland (region)	United Kingdom	57 00 N	4 00 W
Scott Island	Antarctica	67 24 S	179 55 W
Senegambia (region; former name of confederation of Senegal and The Gambia)	The Gambia, Senegal	13 50 N	15 25 W
Senyavin Islands	Federated States of Micronesia	6 55 N	158 00 E
Seoul (capital)	South Korea	37 34 N	127 00 E
Serendib (former name for Sri Lanka)	Sri Lanka	7 00 N	81 00 E
Serrana Bank (shoal)	Colombia	14 25 N	80 16 W
Serranilla Bank (shoal)	Colombia	15 51 N	79 46 W

Name	Entry in *The World Factbook*	Latitude (deg min)	Longitude (deg min)
Settlement, The (capital)	Christmas Island	10 25 S	105 43 E
Severnaya Zemlya (island group; also Northland)	Russia	79 30 N	98 00 E
Shaba (region)	Democratic Republic of the Congo	8 00 S	27 00 E
Shag Island	Heard Island and McDonald Islands	53 00 S	72 30 E
Shag Rocks	South Georgia and the South Sandwich Islands	53 33 S	42 02 W
Shanghai (city)	China	31 14 N	121 30 E
Shenyang (city; also Mukden)	China	41 46 N	123 24 E
Shetland Islands	United Kingdom	60 30 N	1 30 W
Shikoku (island)	Japan	33 45 N	133 30 E
Shikotan (island)	Russia (de facto)	43 47 N	146 45 E
Shqiperia (local name for Albania)	Albania	41 00 N	20 00 E
Siam (former name for Thailand)	Thailand	15 00 N	100 00 E
Siberia (region)	Russia	60 00 N	100 00 E
Sibutu Passage	Pacific Ocean	4 50 N	119 35 E
Sicily (island)	Italy	37 30 N	14 00 E
Sicily, Strait of	Atlantic Ocean	37 20 N	11 20 E
Sidra, Gulf of	Atlantic Ocean	31 30 N	18 00 E
Sikkim (state)	India	27 50 N	88 30 E
Silesia (region)	Czech Republic, Germany, Poland	51 00 N	17 00 E
Sinai Peninsula	Egypt	29 30 N	34 00 E
Singapore (capital)	Singapore	1 17 N	103 51 E
Singapore Strait	Pacific Ocean	1 15 N	104 00 E
Sinkiang (autonomous region; also Xinjiang)	China	42 00 N	86 00 E
Sint Eustatius (island)	Netherlands	17 29 N	62 58 W
Sint Maarten (island; also Saint-Martin)	Sint Maarten, Saint Martin	18 04 N	63 04 W
Sjaelland (island)	Denmark	55 30 N	12 00 E
Skagerrak (strait)	Atlantic Ocean	57 45 N	9 00 E
Skopje (capital)	Macedonia	41 59 N	21 26 E
Slavonia (region)	Croatia	45 27 N	18 00 E
Slovenija (local name for Slovenia)	Slovenia	46 00 N	15 00 E
Slovensko (local name for Slovakia)	Slovakia	48 40 N	19 30 E
Smyrna (region; former name for Izmir)	Turkey	38 25 N	27 10 E
Society Islands (Iles de la Societe)	French Polynesia	17 00 S	150 00 W
Socotra (island)	Yemen	12 30 N	54 00 E
Sofia (capital)	Bulgaria	42 41 N	23 19 E
Solomon Islands, northern	Papua New Guinea	6 00 S	155 00 E
Solomon Islands, southern	Solomon Islands	8 00 S	159 00 E
Solomon Sea	Pacific Ocean	8 00 S	153 00 E
Somaliland (region)	Somalia	9 30 N	46 00 E
Somers Islands (former name for Bermuda)	Bermuda	32 20 N	64 45 W
Songkhla (city)	Thailand	7 12 N	100 36 E
Sound, The (strait; also Oresund)	Atlantic Ocean	55 50 N	12 40 E
South Atlantic Ocean	Atlantic Ocean	30 00 S	15 00 W
South China Sea	Pacific Ocean	10 00 N	113 00 E
South Georgia (island)	South Georgia and the South Sandwich Islands	54 15 S	36 45 W
South Island	New Zealand	43 00 S	171 00 E
South Korea	South Korea	37 00 N	127 30 E

Name	Entry in *The World Factbook*	Latitude (deg min)	Longitude (deg min)
South Orkney Islands	Antarctica	61 00 S	45 00 W
South Ossetia (region)	Georgia	42 20 N	44 00 E
South Pacific Ocean	Pacific Ocean	30 00 S	130 00 W
South Sandwich Islands	South Georgia and the South Sandwich Islands	57 45 S	26 30 W
South Shetland Islands	Antarctica	62 00 S	59 00 W
South Tyrol (region)	Italy	46 30 N	10 30 E
South Vietnam (former name for the southern portion of Vietnam)	Vietnam	12 00 N	108 00 E
South Yemen (People's Democratic Republic of Yemen; now part of Yemen)	Yemen	14 00 N	48 00 E
South-West Africa (former name for Namibia)	Namibia	22 00 S	17 00 E
Southern Grenadines (island group)	Grenada	12 20 N	61 30 W
Southern Rhodesia (former name for Zimbabwe)	Zimbabwe	20 00 S	30 00 E
Soviet Union (former name of a large Eurasian empire, roughly coequal with the former Russian Empire)	Armenia, Azerbaijan, Belarus, Estonia, Georgia, Kazakhstan, Kyrgyzstan, Latvia, Lithuania, Moldova, Russia, Tajikistan, Turkmenistan, Ukraine, Uzbekistan		
Spanish Guinea (former name for Equatorial Guinea)	Equatorial Guinea	2 00 N	10 00 E
Spanish Morocco (former name for northern Morocco)	Morocco	32 00 N	7 00 W
Spanish North Africa (exclaves)	Spain (Ceuta, Islas Chafarinas, Melilla, Penon de Alhucemas, Penon de Velez de la Gomera)	35 15 N	4 00 W
Spanish Sahara (former name)	Western Sahara	24 30 N	13 00 W
Spanish West Africa (former name for Ifni and Spanish Sahara)	Morocco, Western Sahara	25 00 N	13 00 W
Spice Islands (Moluccas)	Indonesia	2 00 S	28 00 E
Spitsbergen (island)	Svalbard	78 00 N	20 00 E
Srbija (local name for Serbia)	Serbia	44 00 N	21 00 E
St. John's (city)	Canada (Newfoundland)	47 34 N	52 43 W
Stanley (capital)	Falkland Islands (Islas Malvinas)	51 42 S	57 41 W
Stockholm (capital)	Sweden	59 20 N	18 03 E
Strasbourg (city)	France	48 35 N	7 44 E
Stuttgart (city)	Germany	48 46 N	9 11 E
Sucre (constitutional capital)	Bolivia	19 02 S	65 17 W
Suez Canal	Egypt	29 55 N	32 33 E
Suez, Gulf of	Indian Ocean	28 10 N	33 27 E
Suisse (local French name for Switzerland)	Switzerland	47 00 N	8 00 E
Sulawesi (island; Celebes)	Indonesia	2 00 S	121 00 E
Sulawesi Sea	Pacific Ocean	3 00 N	122 00 E
Sulu Archipelago (island group)	Philippines	6 00 N	121 00 E
Sulu Sea	Pacific Ocean	8 00 N	120 00 E
Sumatra (island)	Indonesia	0 00 N	102 00 E
Sumba (island)	Indonesia	10 00 S	120 00 E
Sumba Strait	Pacific Ocean	9 10 S	120 00 E
Sumbawa (island)	Indonesia	8 30 S	118 00 E
Sunda Islands (Soenda Isles)	Indonesia, Malaysia	2 00 S	110 00 E
Sunda Strait	Indian Ocean	6 00 S	105 45 E
Suomi (local name for Finland)	Finland	64 00 N	26 00 E
Surabaya (city)	Indonesia	7 13 S	112 45 E
Surigao Strait	Pacific Ocean	10 15 N	125 23 E

Name	Entry in *The World Factbook*	Latitude (deg min)	Longitude (deg min)
Surinam (former name for Suriname)	Suriname	4 00 N	56 00 W
Suriyah (local name for Syria)	Syria	35 00 N	38 00 E
Surtsey (volcanic island)	Iceland	63 17 N	20 40 W
Suva (capital)	Fiji	18 08 S	178 25 E
Sverdlovsk (city; also Yekaterinburg)	Russia	56 50 N	60 39 E
Sverige (local name for Sweden)	Sweden	62 00 N	15 00 E
Svizzera (local Italian name for Switzerland)	Switzerland	47 00 N	8 00 E
Swains Island	American Samoa	11 03 S	171 15 W
Swan Islands	Honduras	17 25 S	83 56 W
Sydney (city)	Australia	33 53 S	151 13 E
T'bilisi (capital)	Georgia	41 43 N	44 49 E
Tadzhikistan (former name for Tajikistan)	Tajikistan	39 00 N	71 00 E
Tahiti (island)	French Polynesia	17 37 S	149 27 W
Taipei (capital)	Taiwan	25 03 N	121 30 E
Taiwan Strait	Pacific Ocean	24 00 N	119 00 E
Tallinn (capital)	Estonia	59 25 N	24 45 E
Tanganyika (former name for the mainland portion of Tanzania)	Tanzania	6 00 S	35 00 E
Tangier (city)	Morocco	35 48 N	5 45 W
Tannu-Tuva (region)	Russia	51 25 N	94 45 E
Tarawa (island)	Kiribati	1 25 N	173 00 E
Tartary, Gulf of	Pacific Ocean	50 00 N	141 00 E
Tashkent (capital)	Uzbekistan	41 20 N	69 18 E
Tasman Sea	Pacific Ocean	4 30 S	168 00 E
Tasmania (island)	Australia	43 00 S	147 00 E
Tatar Strait	Pacific Ocean	50 00 N	141 00 E
Taymyr Peninsula (Poluostrov Taymyr)	Russia	76 00 N	104 00 E
Tchad (local name for Chad)	Chad	15 00 N	19 00 E
Tegucigalpa (capital)	Honduras	14 06 N	87 13 W
Tehran (capital)	Iran	35 40 N	51 26 E
Tel Aviv (capital, de facto)	Israel	32 05 N	34 48 E
Teluk Bone (gulf)	Pacific Ocean	4 00 S	120 45 E
Teluk Tomini (gulf)	Pacific Ocean	0 30 S	121 00 E
Terre Adelie (claimed by France; also Adelie Land)	Antarctica	66 30 S	139 00 E
Terres Australes et Antarctiques Francaises (local name for the French Southern and Antarctic Lands)	French Southern and Antarctic Lands	43 00 S	67 00 E
Thailand, Gulf of	Pacific Ocean	10 00 N	101 00 E
The Former Yugoslav Republic of Macedonia	Macedonia	41 50 N	22 00 E
Thessaloniki (city; also Salonika)	Greece	40 38 N	22 57 E
Thimphu (capital)	Bhutan	27 28 N	89 39 E
Thuringia (region)	Germany	51 00 N	11 00 E
Thurston Island	Antarctica	72 20 S	99 00 W
Tiberias, Lake	Israel	32 48 N	35 35 E
Tibet (autonomous region; also Xizang)	China	32 00 N	90 00 E
Tibilisi (see T'bilisi)	Georgia	41 43 N	44 49 E
Tien Shan (mountains)	China, Kyrgyzstan	42 00 N	80 00 E
Tierra del Fuego (island, island group)	Argentina, Chile	54 00 S	69 00 W
Timor (island)	Timor-Leste, Indonesia	9 00 S	125 00 E
Timor Lorosa'e (local name for Timor-Leste)	Timor-Leste	9 00 N	126 00 E
Timor Sea	Pacific Ocean	11 00 S	128 00 E
Tinian (island)	Northern Mariana Islands	15 00 N	145 38 E
Tiran, Strait of	Indian Ocean	28 00 N	34 27 E

Name	Entry in *The World Factbook*	Latitude (deg min)	Longitude (deg min)
Tirana, Tirane (capital)	Albania	41 20 N	19 50 E
Tirol, Tyrol (region)	Austria, Italy	47 00 N	11 00 E
Tobago (island)	Trinidad and Tobago	11 15 N	60 40 W
Tokyo (capital)	Japan	35 42 N	139 46 E
Tonkin, Gulf of	Pacific Ocean	20 00 N	108 00 E
Toronto (city)	Canada	43 40 N	79 23 W
Torres Strait	Pacific Ocean	10 25 S	142 10 E
Torshavn (capital)	Faroe Islands	62 01 N	6 46 W
Toshkent (see Tashkent)	Uzbekistan	41 20 N	69 18 E
Transcarpathia (region; alternate name for Carpatho-Ukraine)	Ukraine	48 22 N	23 32 E
Transjordan (former name for Jordan)	Jordan	31 00 N	36 00 E
Transkei (enclave)	South Africa	32 15 S	28 15 E
Transvaal (region; former name for northeastern South Africa)	South Africa	25 10 S	29 25 E
Transylvania (region)	Romania	46 30 N	24 00 E
Trindade, Ilha de (island)	Brazil	20 31 S	29 20 W
Trinidad (island)	Trinidad and Tobago	10 22 N	61 15 W
Tripoli (capital)	Libya	32 54 N	13 11 E
Tripoli (city)	Lebanon	34 26 N	35 51 E
Tripolitania (region)	Libya	31 00 N	14 00 E
Tristan da Cunha Group (island group)	Saint Helena, Ascension, and Tristan da Cunha	37 15 S	12 30 W
Trobriand Islands	Papua New Guinea	8 38 S	151 04 E
Tromelin Island	Indian Ocean	15 52 S	54 25 E
Trucial Coast (former name for the United Arab Emirates)	United Arab Emirates	24 00 N	54 00 E
Trucial Oman (former name for the United Arab Emirates)	United Arab Emirates	24 00 N	54 00 E
Trucial States (former name for the United Arab Emirates)	United Arab Emirates	24 00 N	54 00 E
Truk Islands (former name for the Chuuk Islands)	Federated States of Micronesia	7 25 N	151 47 E
Tsugaru Strait	Pacific Ocean	41 35 N	141 00 E
Tuamotu Islands (Iles Tuamotu)	French Polynesia	19 00 S	142 00 W
Tubuai Islands (Iles Tubuai)	French Polynesia	23 00 S	150 00 W
Tunb al Kubra (island)	Iran	26 14 N	55 19 E
Tunb as Sughra (island)	Iran	26 14 N	55 09 E
Tunis (capital)	Tunisia	36 48 N	10 11 E
Turin (city)	Italy	45 04 N	7 40 E
Turkish Straits (see Bosporus and Dardenelles)	Atlantic Ocean	40 40 N	28 00 E
Turkiye (local name for Turkey)	Turkey	39 00 N	35 00 E
Turkmenia, Turkmeniya (former name for Turkmenistan)	Turkmenistan	40 00 N	60 00 E
Turks Island Passage	Atlantic Ocean	21 40 N	71 00 W
Tuscany (region)	Italy	43 25 N	11 00 E
Tutuila (island)	American Samoa	14 18 S	170 42 W
Tyrrhenian Sea	Atlantic Ocean	40 00 N	12 00 E
Ubangi-Shari (former name for the Central African Republic	Central African Republic	6 38 N	20 33 E
Ukrayina (local name for Ukraine)	Ukraine	49 00 N	32 00 E
Ulaanbaatar (capital)	Mongolia	47 55 N	106 53 E
Ullung-do (island)	South Korea	37 29 N	130 52 E
Ulster (region)	Ireland, United Kingdom	54 35 N	7 00 W
Uman (local name for Oman)	Oman	21 00 N	57 00 E
Unimak Pass (strait)	Pacific Ocean	54 20 N	164 50 W

Name	Entry in *The World Factbook*	Latitude (deg min)	Longitude (deg min)
Union of Soviet Socialist Republics or USSR (former name of a large Eurasian empire, roughly coequal with the former Russian Empire)	Armenia, Azerbaijan, Belarus, Estonia, Georgia, Kazakhstan, Kyrgyzstan, Latvia, Lithuania, Moldova, Russia, Tajikistan, Turkmenistan, Ukraine, Uzbekistan		
United Arab Republic or UAR (former name for a federation between Egypt and Syria)	Egypt, Syria		
Upper Volta (former name for Burkina Faso)	Burkina Faso	13 00 N	2 00 W
Ural Mountains	Kazakhstan, Russia	60 00 N	60 00 E
Urdunn (local name for Jordan)	Jordan	31 00 N	36 00 E
Urundi (former name for Burundi)	Burundi	3 30 S	30 00 E
Ussuri River	China, Russia	48 28 N	135 02 E
Vaduz (capital)	Liechtenstein	47 09 N	9 31 E
Vakhan (Wakhan Corridor)	Afghanistan	37 00 N	73 00 E
Valletta (capital)	Malta	35 54 N	14 31 E
Valley, The (capital)	Anguilla	18 13 N	63 04 W
Van Diemen Strait (Osumi Strait)	Pacific Ocean	31 00 N	131 00 E
Vancouver (city)	Canada	49 16 N	123 08 W
Vancouver Island	Canada	49 45 N	126 00 W
Vatican City (capital)	Holy See	41 54 N	12 27 E
Velez de la Gomera, Penon de (island)	Spain	35 11 N	4 18 W
Venda (enclave)	South Africa	23 00 S	31 00 E
Verde Island Passage	Pacific Ocean	13 34 N	120 51 E
Victoria (capital)	Seychelles	4 38 S	55 27 E
Victoria (island)	Canada	71 00 N	110 00 W
Victoria Land (region)	Antarctica	72 00 S	155 00 E
Vienna (capital)	Austria	48 12 N	16 22 E
Vientiane (capital)	Laos	17 58 N	102 36 E
Vilnius (capital)	Lithuania	54 41 N	25 19 E
Viti Levu (island)	Fiji	18 00 S	178 00 E
Vladivostok (city)	Russia	43 10 N	131 56 E
Vojvodina (region)	Serbia	45 35 N	20 00 E
Volcano Islands	Japan	25 00 N	141 00 E
Vostok Island	Kiribati	10 06 S	152 23 W
Wake Atoll	Wake Island	19 17 N	166 39 E
Wakhan Corridor (see Vakhan)	Afghanistan	37 00 N	73 00 E
Walachia (region)	Romania	44 45 N	26 05 E
Wales (region)	United Kingdom	52 30 N	3 30 W
Wallis Islands	Wallis and Futuna	13 17 S	176 10 W
Walvis Bay (city; former exclave)	Namibia	22 59 S	14 31 E
Warsaw (capital)	Poland	52 15 N	21 00 E
Washington, DC (capital)	United States	38 53 N	77 02 W
Weddell Sea	Southern Ocean	72 00 S	45 00 W
Wellington (capital)	New Zealand	41 28 S	174 51 E
West Frisian Islands	Netherlands	53 26 N	5 30 E
West Germany (Federal Republic of Germany; former name for western portion of Germany)	Germany	53 22 N	5 20 E
West Island (capital)	Cocos (Keeling) Islands	12 10 S	96 55 E
West Korea Strait (Western Channel)	Pacific Ocean	34 40 N	129 00 E
West Pakistan (former name for present-day Pakistan)	Pakistan	30 00 N	70 00 E
West Siberian Plain	Russia	60 00 N	75 00 E
Western Channel (West Korea Strait)	Pacific Ocean	34 40 N	129 00 E

Name	Entry in *The World Factbook*	Latitude (deg min)	Longitude (deg min)
Western Samoa (former name for Samoa)	Samoa	13 35 S	172 20 W
Wetar Strait	Pacific Ocean	8 20 S	126 30 E
White Sea	Arctic Ocean	65 30 N	38 00 E
Wilkes Land (region)	Antarctica	71 00 S	120 00 E
Willemstad (capital)	Curacao	12 06 N	68 56 W
Windhoek (capital)	Namibia	22 34 S	17 06 E
Windward Passage	Atlantic Ocean	20 00 N	73 50 W
Winnipeg (city)	Canada	49 53 N	97 10 W
Wrangel Island (Ostrov Vrangelya)	Russia	71 14 N	179 36 W
Xianggang (local name for Hong Kong)	Hong Kong	22 15 N	114 10 E
Y'israel (local name for Israel)	Israel	31 30 N	34 45 E
Yaitopya (local name for Ethiopia)	Ethiopia	8 00 N	38 00 E
Yalu River	China, North Korea	39 55 N	124 20 E
Yamoussoukro (capital)	Cote d'Ivoire	6 49 N	5 17 W
Yangon (see Rangoon)	Burma	16 47 N	96 10 E
Yaounde (capital)	Cameroon	3 52 N	11 31 E
Yap Islands	Federated States of Micronesia	9 30 N	138 00 E
Yaren (governmental center)	Nauru	0 32 S	166 55 E
Yekaterinburg (city; formerly Sverdlovsk)	Russia	56 50 N	60 39 E
Yellow Sea	Pacific Ocean	36 00 N	123 00 E
Yemen Arab Republic (also Yemen (Sanaa); former name for northern portion of Yemen)	Yemen	15 00 N	44 00 E
Yemen, People's Democratic Republic of (also Yemen (Aden); former name for southern portion of Yemen)	Yemen	14 00 N	46 00 E
Yerevan (capital)	Armenia	40 11 N	44 30 E
Yokohama (city)	Japan	35 26 N	139 37 E
Youth, Isle of (Isla de la Juventud)	Cuba	21 40 N	82 50 W
Yucatan Channel	Atlantic Ocean	21 45 N	85 45 W
Yucatan Peninsula	Mexico	19 30 N	89 00 W
Yugoslavia (former name for a federation of Serbia and Montenegro)	Montenegro, Serbia	43 00 N	21 00 E
Yugoslavia, Kingdom of (former name for a Balkan federation)	Bosnia and Herzegovina, Croatia, Macedonia, Montenegro, Serbia, Slovenia	43 00 N	19 00 E
Yugoslavia, Socialist Federal Republic of (former name for a Balkan federation)	Bosnia and Herzegovina, Croatia, Macedonia, Montenegro, Serbia, Slovenia	43 00 N	19 00 E
Zagreb (capital)	Croatia	45 48 N	15 58 E
Zaire (former name for the Democratic Republic of the Congo)	Democratic Republic of the Congo	15 00 S	30 00 E
Zakhalinskiy Zaliv (bay)	Pacific Ocean	54 00 N	142 00 E
Zaliv Shelikhova (bay)	Pacific Ocean	60 00 N	157 30 E
Zambezia (region)	Mozambique	16 00 S	37 00 E
Zanzibar (island)	Tanzania	6 10 S	39 11 E
Zhong Guo, Zhonghua (local name for China)	China	35 00 N	105 00 E
Zion, Mount (locale in Jerusalem)	Israel, West Bank	31 46 N	35 14 E
Zurich (city)	Switzerland	47 23 N	8 32 E

APPENDIX G

WEIGHTS AND MEASURES

Note: At this time, only three countries—Burma, Liberia, and the US—have not adopted the International System of Units (SI, or metric system) as their official system of weights and measures. Although use of the metric system has been sanctioned by law in the US since 1866, it has been slow in displacing the American adaptation of the British Imperial System known as the US Customary System. The US is the only industrialized nation that does not mainly use the metric system in its commercial and standards activities, but there is increasing acceptance in science, medicine, government, and many sectors of industry.

Mathematical Notation

Mathematical Power	Name
10^{18} or 1,000,000,000,000,000,000	one quintillion
10^{15} or 1,000,000,000,000,000	one quadrillion
10^{12} or 1,000,000,000,000	one trillion
10^{9} or 1,000,000,000	one billion
10^{6} or 1,000,000	one million
10^{3} or 1,000	one thousand
10^{2} or 100	one hundred
10^{1} or 10	ten
10^{0} or 1	one
10^{-1} or 0.1	one-tenth
10^{-2} or 0.01	one-hundredth
10^{-3} or 0.001	one-thousandth
10^{-6} or 0.000 001	one-millionth
10^{-9} or 0.000 000 001	one-billionth
10^{-12} or 0.000 000 000 001	one-trillionth
10^{-15} or 0.000 000 000 000 001	one-quadrillionth
10^{-18} or 0.000 000 000 000 000 001	one-quintillionth

Metric Interrelationships

Prefix	Symbol	Length, weight, or capacity
yotta	Y	10^{24}
zetta	Z	10^{21}
exa	E	10^{18}
peta	P	10^{15}
tera	T	10^{12}
giga	G	10^{9}
mega	M	10^{6}
kilo	k	10^{3}
hecto	h	10^{2}
deka	da	10^{1}
basic unit	–	1 meter, 1 gram, 1 liter
deci	d	10^{-1}
centi	c	10^{-2}
milli	m	10^{-3}
micro	u	10^{-6}
nano	n	10^{-9}
pico	p	10^{-12}
femto	f	10^{-15}
atto	a	10^{-18}
zepto	z	10^{-21}
yocto	y	10^{-24}

Conversion Factors

To Convert From	To	Multiply By
acres	ares	40.468 564 224
acres	hectares	0.404 685 642 24
acres	square feet	43,560
acres	square kilometers	0.004 046 856 422 4
acres	square meters	4,046.856 422 4
acres	square miles (statute)	0.001 562 50
acres	square yards	4,840
ares	square meters	100
ares	square yards	119.599
barrels, US beer	gallons	31
barrels, US beer	liters	117.347 77
barrels, US petroleum	gallons (British)	34.97
barrels, US petroleum	gallons (US)	42
barrels, US petroleum	liters	158.987 29
barrels, US proof spirits	gallons	40
barrels, US proof spirits	liters	151.416 47
bushels (US)	bushels (British)	0.968 9
bushels (US)	cubic feet	1.244 456
bushels (US)	cubic inches	2,150.42
bushels (US)	cubic meters	0.035 239 07
bushels (US)	cubic yards	0.046 090 96
bushels (US)	dekaliters	3.523 907
bushels (US)	dry pints	64
bushels (US)	dry quarts	32
bushels (US)	liters	35.239 070 17
bushels (US)	pecks	4
cables	fathoms	120
cables	meters	219.456
cables	yards	240
carat	milligrams	200
centimeters	feet	0.032 808 40
centimeters	inches	0.393 700 8
centimeters	meters	0.01
centimeters	yards	0.010 936 13
centimeters, cubic	cubic inches	0.061 023 744
centimeters, square	square feet	0.001 076 39
centimeters, square	square inches	0.155 000 31
centimeters, square	square meters	0.000 1
centimeters, square	square yards	0.000 119 599
chains, square surveyor's	ares	4.046 86
chains, square surveyor's	square feet	4,356
chains, surveyor's	feet	66
chains, surveyor's	meters	20.116 8
chains, surveyor's	rods	4
cords of wood	cubic feet	128
cords of wood	cubic meters	3.624 556
cords of wood	cubic yards	4.740 7
cups	liquid ounces (US)	8
cups	liters	0.236 588 2
degrees Celsius	degrees Fahrenheit	multiply by 1.8 and add 32
degrees Fahrenheit	degrees Celsius	subtract 32 and divide by 1.8

Conversion Factors

To Convert From	To	Multiply By
dekaliters	bushels	0.283 775 9
dekaliters	cubic feet	0.353 146 7
dekaliters	cubic inches	610.237 4
dekaliters	dry pints	18.161 66
dekaliters	dry quarts	9.080 829 8
dekaliters	liters	10
dekaliters	pecks	1.135 104
drams, avoirdupois	avoirdupois ounces	0.062 55
drams, avoirdupois	grains	27.344
drams, avoirdupois	grams	1.771 845 2
drams, troy	grains	60
drams, troy	grams	3.887 934 6
drams, troy	scruples	3
drams, troy	troy ounces	0.125
drams, liquid (US)	cubic inches	0.226
drams, liquid (US)	liquid drams (British)	1.041
drams, liquid (US)	liquid ounces	0.125
drams, liquid (US)	milliliters	3.696 69
drams, liquid (US)	minims	60
fathoms	feet	6
fathoms	meters	1.828 8
feet	centimeters	30.48
feet	inches	12
feet	kilometers	0.000 304 8
feet	meters	0.304 8
feet	statute miles	0.000 189 39
feet	yards	0.333 333 3
feet, cubic	bushels	0.803 563 95
feet, cubic	cubic decimeters	28.316 847
feet, cubic	cubic inches	1,728
feet, cubic	cubic meters	0.028 316 846 592
feet, cubic	cubic yards	0.037 037 04
feet, cubic	dry pints	51.428 09
feet, cubic	dry quarts	25.714 05
feet, cubic	gallons	7.480 519
feet, cubic	gills	239.376 6
feet, cubic	liquid ounces	957.506 5
feet, cubic	liquid pints	59.844 16
feet, cubic	liquid quarts	29.922 08
feet, cubic	liters	28.316 846 592
feet, cubic	pecks	3.214 256
feet, square	acres	0.000 022 956 8
feet, square	square centimeters	929.030 4
feet, square	square decimeters	9.290 304
feet, square	square inches	144
feet, square	square meters	0.092 903 04
feet, square	square yards	0.111 111 1
furlongs	feet	660
furlongs	inches	7,920
furlongs	meters	201.168
furlongs	statute miles	0.125

Conversion Factors

To Convert From	To	Multiply By
furlongs	yards	220
gallons, liquid (US)	cubic feet	0.133 680 6
gallons, liquid (US)	cubic inches	231
gallons, liquid (US)	cubic meters	0.003 785 411 784
gallons, liquid (US)	cubic yards	0.004 951 13
gallons, liquid (US)	gills (US)	32
gallons, liquid (US)	liquid gallons (British)	0.832 67
gallons, liquid (US)	liquid ounces	128
gallons, liquid (US)	liquid pints	8
gallons, liquid (US)	liquid quarts	4
gallons, liquid (US)	liters	3.785 411 784
gallons, liquid (US)	milliliters	3,785.411 784
gallons, liquid (US)	minims	61,440
gills (US)	centiliters	11.829 4
gills (US)	cubic feet	0.004 177 517
gills (US)	cubic inches	7.218 75
gills (US)	gallons	0.031 25
gills (US)	gills (British)	0.832 67
gills (US)	liquid ounces	4
gills (US)	liquid pints	0.25
gills (US)	liquid quarts	0.125
gills (US)	liters	0.118 294 118 25
gills (US)	milliliters	118.294 118 25
gills (US)	minims	1,920
grains	avoirdupois drams	0.036 571 43
grains	avoirdupois ounces	0.002 285 71
grains	avoirdupois pounds	0.000 142 86
grains	grams	0.064 798 91
grains	kilograms	0.000 064 798 91
grains	milligrams	64.798 910
grains	pennyweights	0.042
grains	scruples	0.05
grains	troy drams	0.016 6
grains	troy ounces	0.002 083 33
grains	troy pounds	0.000 173 61
grams	avoirdupois drams	0.564 383 39
grams	avoirdupois ounces	0.035 273 961
grams	avoirdupois pounds	0.002 204 622 6
grams	grains	15.432 361
grams	kilograms	0.001
grams	milligrams	1,000
grams	troy ounces	0.032 150 746 6
grams	troy pounds	0.002 679 23
hands (height of horse)	centimeters	10.16
hands (height of horse)	inches	4
hectares	acres	2.471 053 8
hectares	square feet	107,639.1
hectares	square kilometers	0.01
hectares	square meters	10,000
hectares	square miles	0.003 861 02
hectares	square yards	11,959.90

Conversion Factors

To Convert From	To	Multiply By
hundredweights, long	avoirdupois pounds	112
hundredweights, long	kilograms	50.802 345
hundredweights, long	long tons	0.05
hundredweights, long	metric tons	0.050 802 345
hundredweights, long	short tons	0.056
hundredweights, short	avoirdupois pounds	100
hundredweights, short	kilograms	45.359 237
hundredweights, short	long tons	0.044 642 86
hundredweights, short	metric tons	0.045 359 237
hundredweights, short	short tons	0.05
inches	centimeters	2.54
inches	feet	0.083 333 33
inches	meters	0.025 4
inches	millimeters	25.4
inches	yards	0.027 777 78
inches, cubic	bushels	0.000 465 025
inches, cubic	cubic centimeters	16.387 064
inches, cubic	cubic feet	0.000 578 703 7
inches, cubic	cubic meters	0.000 016 387 064
inches, cubic	cubic yards	0.000 021 433 47
inches, cubic	dry pints	0.029 761 6
inches, cubic	dry quarts	0.014 880 8
inches, cubic	gallons	0.004 329 0
inches, cubic	gills	0.138 528 1
inches, cubic	liquid ounces	0.554 112 6
inches, cubic	liquid pints	0.034 632 03
inches, cubic	liquid quarts	0.017 316 02
inches, cubic	liters	0.016 387 064
inches, cubic	milliliters	16.387 064
inches, cubic	minims (US)	265.974 0
inches, cubic	pecks	0.001 860 10
inches, square	square centimeters	6.451 600
inches, square	square feet	0.006 944 44
inches, square	square meters	0.000 645 16
inches, square	square yards	0.000 771 605
kilograms	avoirdupois drams	564.383 4
kilograms	avoirdupois ounces	35.273 962
kilograms	avoirdupois pounds	2.204 622 622
kilograms	grains	15,432.36
kilograms	grams	1,000
kilograms	long tons	0.000 984 2
kilograms	metric tons	0.001
kilograms	short hundredweights	0.022 046 23
kilograms	short tons	0.001 102 31
kilograms	troy ounces	32.150 75
kilograms	troy pounds	2.679 229
kilometers	meters	1,000
kilometers	statute miles	0.621 371 192
kilometers, square	acres	247.105 38
kilometers, square	hectares	100
kilometers, square	square meters	1,000,000

Conversion Factors To Convert From	To	Multiply By
kilometers, square	statute miles	0.386 102 16
knots (nautical mi/hr)	kilometers/hour	1.852
knots (nautical mi/hr)	statute miles/hour	1.151
leagues, nautical	kilometers	5.556
leagues, nautical	nautical miles	3
leagues, statute	kilometers	4.828 032
leagues, statute	statute miles	3
links, square surveyor's	square centimeters	404.686
links, square surveyor's	square inches	62.726 4
links, surveyor's	centimeters	20.116 8
links, surveyor's	chains	0.01
links, surveyor's	inches	7.92
liters	bushels	0.028 377 59
liters	cubic feet	0.035 314 67
liters	cubic inches	61.023 74
liters	cubic meters	0.001
liters	cubic yards	0.001 307 95
liters	dekaliters	0.1
liters	dry pints	1.816 166
liters	dry quarts	0.908 082 98
liters	gallons	0.264 172 052
liters	gills (US)	8.453 506
liters	liquid ounces	33.814 02
liters	liquid pints	2.113 376
liters	liquid quarts	1.056 688 2
liters	milliliters	1,000
liters	pecks	0.113 510 4
meters	centimeters	100
meters	feet	3.280 839 895
meters	inches	39.370 079
meters	kilometers	0.001
meters	millimeters	1,000
meters	statute miles	0.000 621 371
meters	yards	1.093 613 298
meters, cubic	bushels	28.377 59
meters, cubic	cubic feet	35.314 666 7
meters, cubic	cubic inches	61,023.744
meters, cubic	cubic yards	1.307 950 619
meters, cubic	gallons	264.172 05
meters, cubic	liters	1,000
meters, cubic	pecks	113.510 4
meters, square	acres	0.000 247 105 38
meters, square	hectares	0.000 1
meters, square	square centimeters	10,000
meters, square	square feet	10.763 910 4
meters, square	square inches	1,550.003 1
meters, square	square yards	1.195 990 046
microns	meters	0.000 001
microns	inches	0.000 039 4
mils	inches	0.001
mils	millimeters	0.025 4

Conversion Factors

To Convert From	To	Multiply By
miles, nautical	kilometers	1.852 0
miles, nautical	statute miles	1.150 779 4
miles, statute	centimeters	160,934.4
miles, statute	feet	5,280
miles, statute	furlongs	8
miles, statute	inches	63,360
miles, statute	kilometers	1.609 344
miles, statute	meters	1,609.344
miles, statute	rods	320
miles, statute	yards	1,760
miles, square nautical	square kilometers	3.429 904
miles, square nautical	square statute miles	1.325
miles, square statute	acres	640
miles, square statute	hectares	258.998 811 033 6
miles, square statute	sections	1
miles, square statute	square kilometers	2.589 988 110 336
miles, square statute	square nautical miles	0.755 miles
miles, square statute	square rods	102,400
milligrams	grains	0.015 432 358 35
milliliters	cubic inches	0.061 023 744
milliliters	gallons	0.000 264 17
milliliters	gills (US)	0.008 453 5
milliliters	liquid ounces	0.033 814 02
milliliters	liquid pints	0.002 113 4
milliliters	liquid quarts	0.001 056 7
milliliters	liters	0.001
milliliters	minims	16.230 73
millimeters	inches	0.039 370 078 7
minims (US)	cubic inches	0.003 759 77
minims (US)	gills (US)	0.000 520 83
minims (US)	liquid ounces	0.002 083 33
minims (US)	milliliters	0.061 611 52
minims (US)	minims (British)	1.041
ounces, avoirdupois	avoirdupois drams	16
ounces, avoirdupois	avoirdupois pounds	0.062 5
ounces, avoirdupois	grains	437.5
ounces, avoirdupois	grams	28.349 523 125
ounces, avoirdupois	kilograms	0.028 349 523 125
ounces, avoirdupois	troy ounces	0.911 458 3
ounces, avoirdupois	troy pounds	0.075 954 86
ounces, liquid (US)	cubic feet	0.001 044 38
ounces, liquid (US)	centiliters	2.957 35
ounces, liquid (US)	cubic inches	1.804 687 5
ounces, liquid (US)	gallons	0.007 812 5
ounces, liquid (US)	gills (US)	0.25
ounces, liquid (US)	liquid drams	8
ounces, liquid (US)	liquid ounces (British)	1.041
ounces, liquid (US)	liquid pints	0.062 5
ounces, liquid (US)	liquid quarts	0.031 25
ounces, liquid (US)	liters	0.029 573 53
ounces, liquid (US)	milliliters	29.573 529 6

Conversion Factors

To Convert From	To	Multiply By
ounces, liquid (US)	minims	480
ounces, troy	avoirdupois drams	17.554 29
ounces, troy	avoirdupois ounces	1.097 143
ounces, troy	avoirdupois pounds	0.068 571 43
ounces, troy	grains	480
ounces, troy	grams	31.103 476 8
ounces, troy	pennyweights	20
ounces, troy	troy drams	8
ounces, troy	troy pounds	0.083 333 3
paces (US)	centimeters	76.2
paces (US)	inches	30
pecks (US)	bushels	0.25
pecks (US)	cubic feet	0.311 114
pecks (US)	cubic inches	537.605
pecks (US)	cubic meters	0.008 809 77
pecks (US)	cubic yards	0.011 522 74
pecks (US)	dekaliters	0.880 976 75
pecks (US)	dry pints	16
pecks (US)	dry quarts	8
pecks (US)	liters	8.809 767 5
pecks (US)	pecks (British)	0.968 9
pennyweights	grains	24
pennyweights	grams	1.555 173 84
pennyweights	troy ounces	0.05
pints, dry (US)	bushels	0.015 625
pints, dry (US)	cubic feet	0.019 444 63
pints, dry (US)	cubic inches	33.600 312 5
pints, dry (US)	dekaliters	0.055 061 05
pints, dry (US)	dry pints (British)	0.968 9
pints, dry (US)	dry quarts	0.5
pints, dry (US)	liters	0.550 610 47
pints, liquid (US)	cubic feet	0.016 710 07
pints, liquid (US)	cubic inches	28.875
pints, liquid (US)	deciliters	4.731 76
pints, liquid (US)	gallons	0.125
pints, liquid (US)	gills (US)	4
pints, liquid (US)	liquid ounces	16
pints, liquid (US)	liquid pints (British)	0.832 67
pints, liquid (US)	liquid quarts	0.5
pints, liquid (US)	liters	0.473 176 473
pints, liquid (US)	milliliters	473.176 473
pints, liquid (US)	minims	7,680
points (typographical)	inches	0.013 837
points (typographical)	millimeters	0.351 459 8
pounds, avoirdupois	avoirdupois drams	256
pounds, avoirdupois	avoirdupois ounces	16
pounds, avoirdupois	grains	7,000
pounds, avoirdupois	grams	453.592 37
pounds, avoirdupois	kilograms	0.453 592 37
pounds, avoirdupois	long tons	0.000 446 428 6
pounds, avoirdupois	metric tons	0.000 453 592 37

Conversion Factors

To Convert From	To	Multiply By
pounds, avoirdupois	quintals	0.004 535 92
pounds, avoirdupois	short tons	0.000 5
pounds, avoirdupois	troy ounces	14.583 33
pounds, avoirdupois	troy pounds	1.215 278
pounds, troy	avoirdupois drams	210.651 4
pounds, troy	avoirdupois ounces	13.165 71
pounds, troy	avoirdupois pounds	0.822 857 1
pounds, troy	grains	5,760
pounds, troy	grams	373.241 721 6
pounds, troy	kilograms	0.373 241 721 6
pounds, troy	pennyweights	240
pounds, troy	troy ounces	12
quarts, dry (US)	bushels	0.031 25
quarts, dry (US)	cubic feet	0.038 889 25
quarts, dry (US)	cubic inches	67.200 625
quarts, dry (US)	dekaliters	0.110 122 1
quarts, dry (US)	dry pints	2
quarts, dry (US)	dry quarts (British)	0.968 9
quarts, dry (US)	liters	1.101 221
quarts, dry (US)	pecks	0.125
quarts, dry (US)	pints, dry (US)	2
quarts, liquid (US)	cubic feet	0.033 420 14
quarts, liquid (US)	cubic inches	57.75
quarts, liquid (US)	deciliters	9.463 53
quarts, liquid (US)	gallons	0.25
quarts, liquid (US)	gills (US)	8
quarts, liquid (US)	liquid ounces	32
quarts, liquid (US)	liquid pints (US)	2
quarts, liquid (US)	liquid quarts (British)	0.832 67
quarts, liquid (US)	liters	0.946 352 946
quarts, liquid (US)	milliliters	946.352 946
quarts, liquid (US)	minims	15,360
quintals	avoirdupois pounds	220.462 26
quintals	kilograms	100
quintals	metric tons	0.1
rods	feet	16.5
rods	meters	5.029 2
rods	yards	5.5
rods, square	acres	0.006 25
rods, square	square meters	25.292 85
rods, square	square yards	30.25
scruples	grains	20
scruples	grams	1.295 978 2
scruples	troy drams	0.333
sections (US)	square kilometers	2.589 988 1
sections (US)	square statute miles	1
spans	centimeters	22.86
spans	inches	9
steres	cubic meters	1
steres	cubic yards	1.307 95
tablespoons	milliliters	14.786 76

Conversion Factors To Convert From	To	Multiply By
tablespoons	teaspoons	3
teaspoons	milliliters	4.928 922
teaspoons	tablespoons	0.333 333
ton-miles, long	metric ton-kilometers	1.635 169
ton-miles, short	metric ton-kilometers	1.459 972
tons, gross register	cubic feet of permanently enclosed space	100
tons, gross register	cubic meters of permanently enclosed space	2.831 684 7
tons, long (deadweight)	avoirdupois ounces	35,840
tons, long (deadweight)	avoirdupois pounds	2,240
tons, long (deadweight)	kilograms	1,016.046 909 8
tons, long (deadweight)	long hundredweights	20
tons, long (deadweight)	metric tons	1.016 046 908 8
tons, long (deadweight)	short hundredweights	22.4
tons, long (deadweight)	short tons	1.12
tons, metric	avoirdupois pounds	2,204.623
tons, metric	kilograms	1,000
tons, metric	long hundredweights	19.684 130 3
tons, metric	long tons	0.984 206 5
tons, metric	quintals	10
tons, metric	short hundredweights	22.046 23
tons, metric	short tons	1.102 311 3
tons, metric	troy ounces	32,150.75
tons, net register	cubic feet of permanently enclosed space for cargo and passengers	100
tons, net register	cubic meters of permanently enclosed space for cargo and passengers	2.831 684 7
tons, shipping	cubic feet of permanently enclosed cargo space	42
tons, shipping	cubic meters of permanently enclosed cargo space	1.189 307 574
tons, short	avoirdupois pounds	2,000
tons, short	kilograms	907.184 74
tons, short	long hundredweights	17.857 14
tons, short	long tons	0.892 857 1
tons, short	metric tons	0.907 184 74
tons, short	short hundredweights	20
townships (US)	sections	36
townships (US)	square kilometers	93.239 572
townships (US)	square statute miles	36
miles, square statute	acres	640
miles, square statute	hectares	258.998 811 033 6
miles, square statute	square feet	27,878,400
miles, square statute	square meters	2,589,988.110 336
miles, square statute	square yards	3,097,600
yards	centimeters	91.44
yards	feet	3
yards	inches	36
yards	meters	0.914 4
yards	miles	0.000 568 18
yards, cubic	bushels	21.696 227
yards, cubic	cubic feet	27
yards, cubic	cubic inches	46,656

Conversion Factors

To Convert From	To	Multiply By
yards, cubic	cubic meters	0.764 554 857 984
yards, cubic	gallons	201.974 0
yards, cubic	liters	764.554 857 984
yards, cubic	pecks	86.784 91
yards, square	acres	0.000 206 611 6
yards, square	hectares	0.000 083 612 736
yards, square	square centimeters	8,361.273 6
yards, square	square feet	9
yards, square	square inches	1,296
yards, square	square meters	0.836 127 36
yards, square	square miles	0.000 000 322 830 6

AFRICA

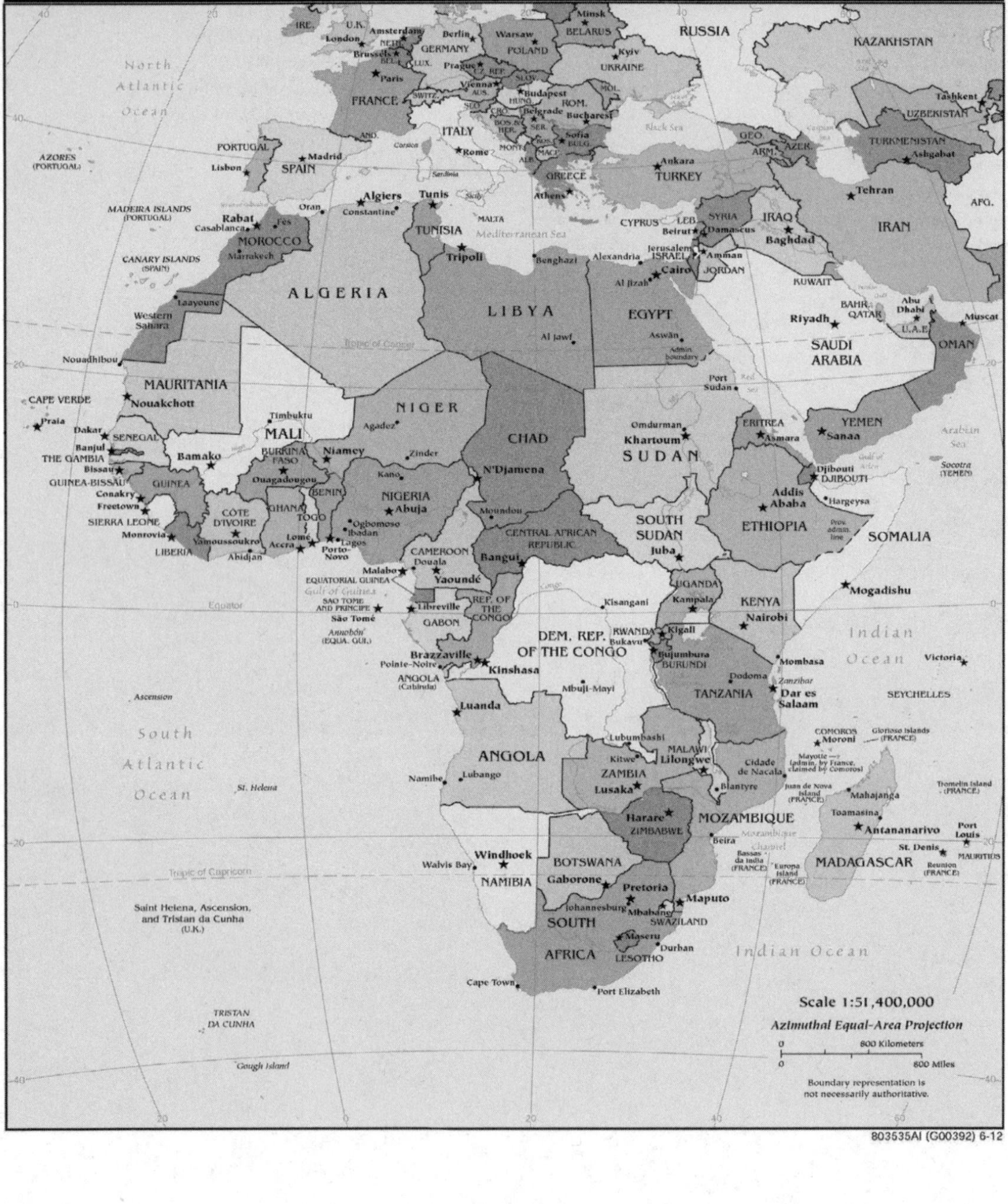

803535AI (G00392) 6-12

ANTARCTIC REGION

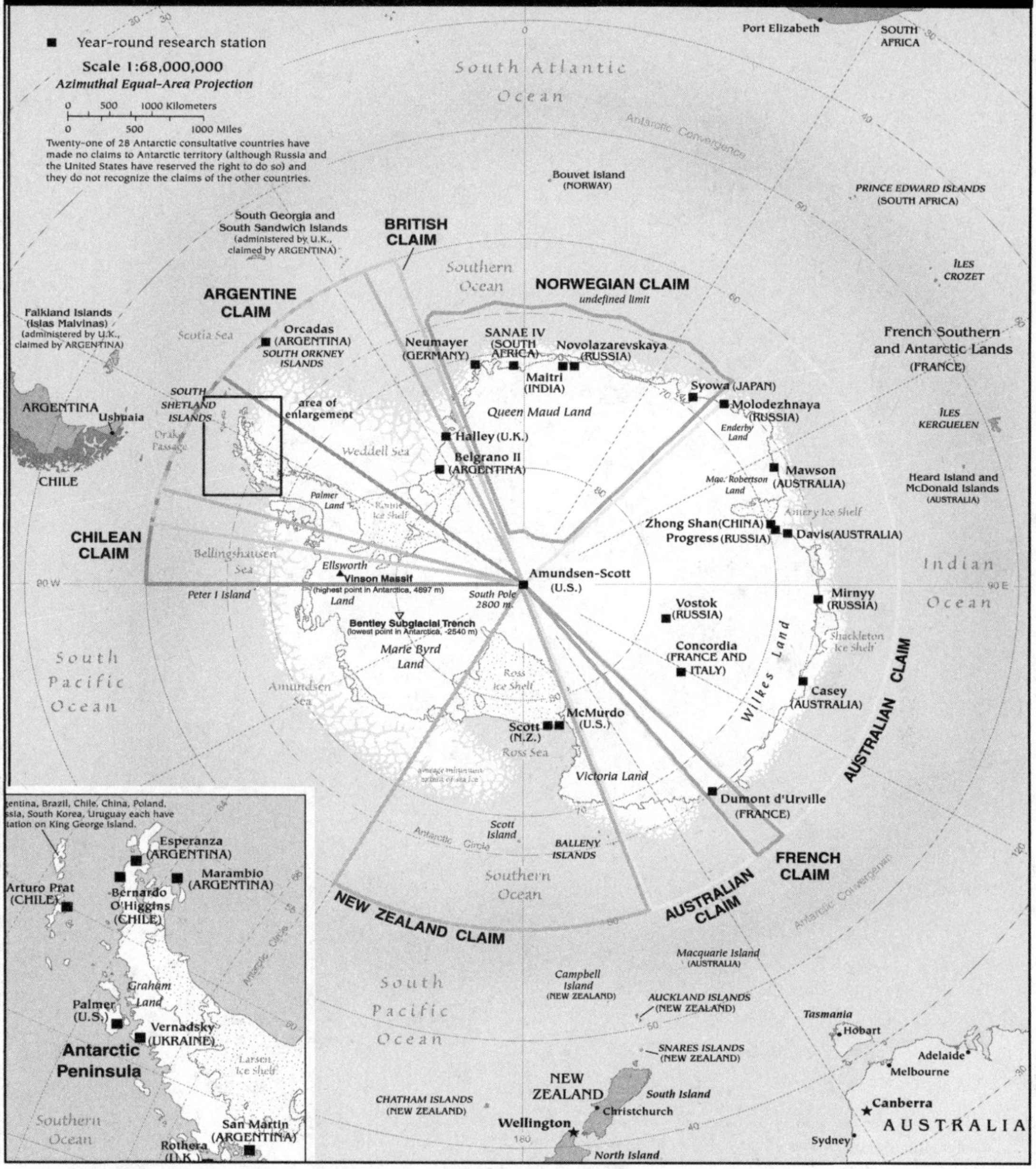
■ Year-round research station
Scale 1:68,000,000
Azimuthal Equal-Area Projection
0 500 1000 Kilometers
0 500 1000 Miles
Twenty-one of 28 Antarctic consultative countries have made no claims to Antarctic territory (although Russia and the United States have reserved the right to do so) and they do not recognize the claims of the other countries.
South Atlantic Ocean
Antarctic Convergence
Port Elizabeth
SOUTH AFRICA
Bouvet Island (NORWAY)
PRINCE EDWARD ISLANDS (SOUTH AFRICA)
ÎLES CROZET
French Southern and Antarctic Lands (FRANCE)
ÎLES KERGUELEN
Heard Island and McDonald Islands (AUSTRALIA)
South Georgia and South Sandwich Islands (administered by U.K., claimed by ARGENTINA)
BRITISH CLAIM
Southern Ocean
NORWEGIAN CLAIM
undefined limit
ARGENTINE CLAIM
Falkland Islands (Islas Malvinas) (administered by U.K., claimed by ARGENTINA)
Scotia Sea
Orcadas (ARGENTINA)
SOUTH ORKNEY ISLANDS
Neumayer (GERMANY)
SANAE IV (SOUTH AFRICA)
Novolazarevskaya (RUSSIA)
Maitri (INDIA)
Syowa (JAPAN)
Molodezhnaya (RUSSIA)
Enderby Land
Queen Maud Land
ARGENTINA
Ushuaia
SOUTH SHETLAND ISLANDS
Drake Passage
area of enlargement
Halley (U.K.)
Belgrano II (ARGENTINA)
Weddell Sea
CHILE
Mawson (AUSTRALIA)
Mac. Robertson Land
Amery Ice Shelf
Palmer Land
Ronne Ice Shelf
Zhong Shan (CHINA)
Progress (RUSSIA)
Davis (AUSTRALIA)
CHILEAN CLAIM
Bellingshausen Sea
Ellsworth Land
Vinson Massif (highest point in Antarctica, 4897 m)
Amundsen-Scott (U.S.)
South Pole 2800 m
Indian Ocean
90 W
90 E
Peter I Island
Mirnyy (RUSSIA)
Vostok (RUSSIA)
Bentley Subglacial Trench (lowest point in Antarctica, -2540 m)
Marie Byrd Land
Shackleton Ice Shelf
South Pacific Ocean
Concordia (FRANCE AND ITALY)
Wilkes Land
Ross Ice Shelf
Amundsen Sea
Casey (AUSTRALIA)
AUSTRALIAN CLAIM
McMurdo (U.S.)
Scott (N.Z.)
Ross Sea
Victoria Land
Dumont d'Urville (FRANCE)
Scott Island
BALLENY ISLANDS
Antarctic Circle
FRENCH CLAIM
Southern Ocean
NEW ZEALAND CLAIM
AUSTRALIAN CLAIM
Macquarie Island (AUSTRALIA)
Campbell Island (NEW ZEALAND)
AUCKLAND ISLANDS (NEW ZEALAND)
South Pacific Ocean
Tasmania
Hobart
SNARES ISLANDS (NEW ZEALAND)
Adelaide
Melbourne
NEW ZEALAND
South Island
Christchurch
CHATHAM ISLANDS (NEW ZEALAND)
Wellington
North Island
Canberra
AUSTRALIA
Sydney
…gentina, Brazil, Chile, China, Poland, …ssia, South Korea, Uruguay each have …tation on King George Island.
Esperanza (ARGENTINA)
Marambio (ARGENTINA)
Arturo Prat (CHILE)
Bernardo O'Higgins (CHILE)
Graham Land
Palmer (U.S.)
Vernadsky (UKRAINE)
Antarctic Peninsula
Larsen Ice Shelf
Southern Ocean
San Martín (ARGENTINA)
Rothera (U.K.)

ARCTIC REGION

ASIA

803537AI (G00543) 6-12

CENTRAL AMERICA AND THE CARIBBEAN

EUROPE

803539AI (G00772) 6-12

MIDDLE EAST

803540AI (G00412) 6-12

NORTH AMERICA

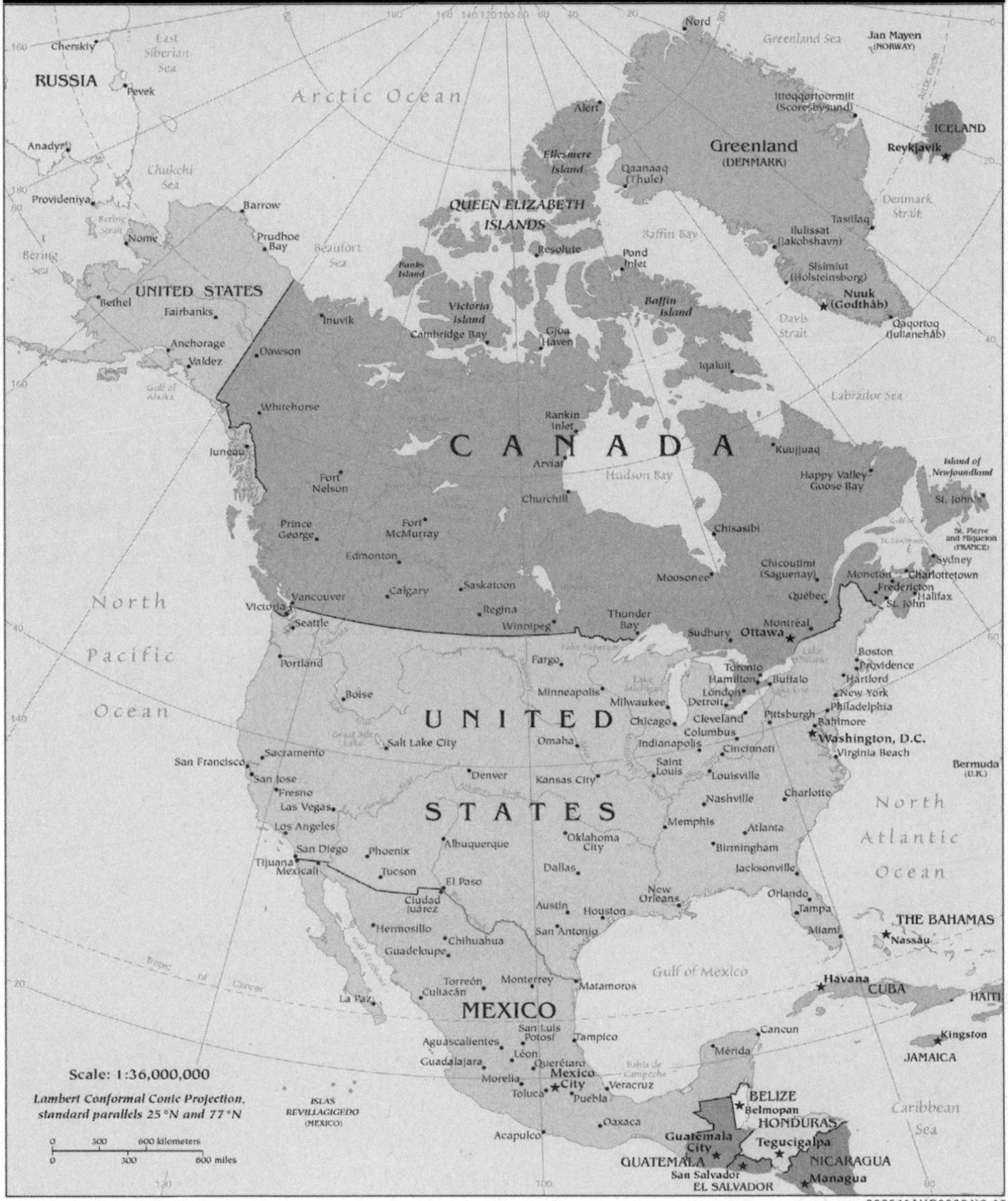

803541AI(G00694)6-12

OCEANIA

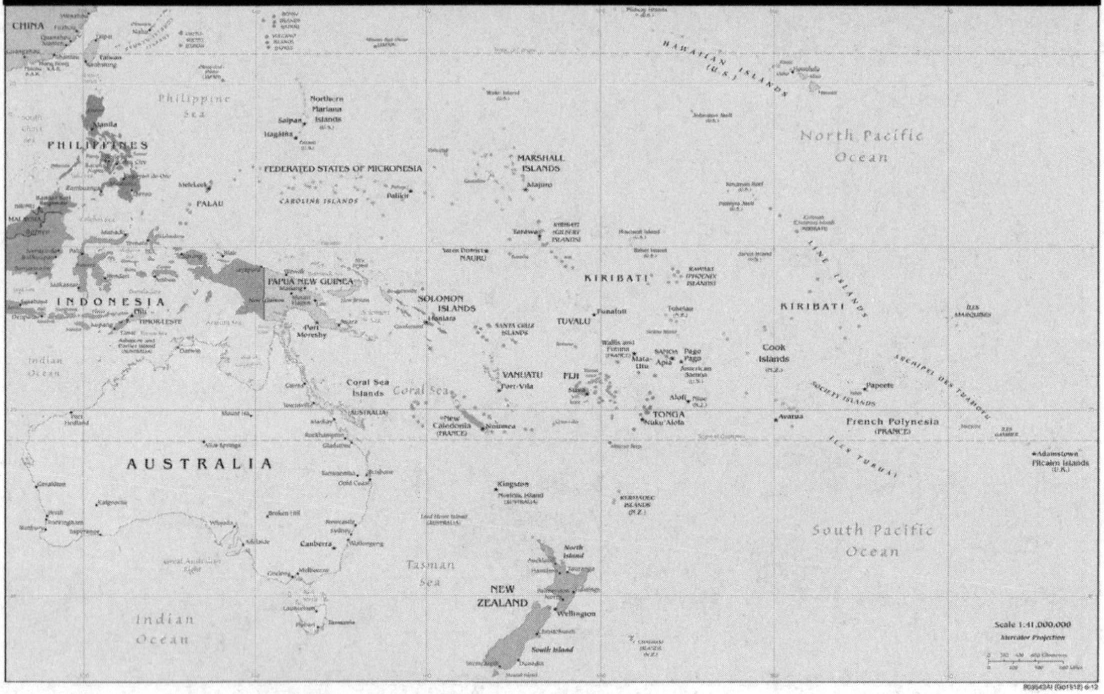
CHINA
Philippine Sea
Northern Mariana Islands (U.S.)
Saipan
Hagåtña
PHILIPPINES
Manila
FEDERATED STATES OF MICRONESIA
CAROLINE ISLANDS
Palikir
PALAU
MARSHALL ISLANDS
Majuro
HAWAIIAN ISLANDS (U.S.)
North Pacific Ocean
Tarawa
NAURU
KIRIBATI
LINE ISLANDS
INDONESIA
Dili
TIMOR-LESTE
PAPUA NEW GUINEA
Port Moresby
SOLOMON ISLANDS
Honiara
TUVALU
Funafuti
Wallis and Futuna (FRANCE)
Mata-Utu
SAMOA
Apia
Pago Pago
American Samoa (U.S.)
Cook Islands (N.Z.)
Indian Ocean
Coral Sea Islands (AUSTRALIA)
Coral Sea
VANUATU
Port-Vila
FIJI
Suva
Alofi
TONGA
Nuku'alofa
Avarua
Papeete
French Polynesia (FRANCE)
New Caledonia (FRANCE)
Noumea
AUSTRALIA
Adamstown
Pitcairn Islands (U.K.)
Kingston
Norfolk Island (AUSTRALIA)
South Pacific Ocean
Canberra
Tasman Sea
NEW ZEALAND
Wellington
North Island
South Island
Indian Ocean
Scale 1:41,000,000
Mercator Projection

PHYSICAL MAP OF THE WORLD

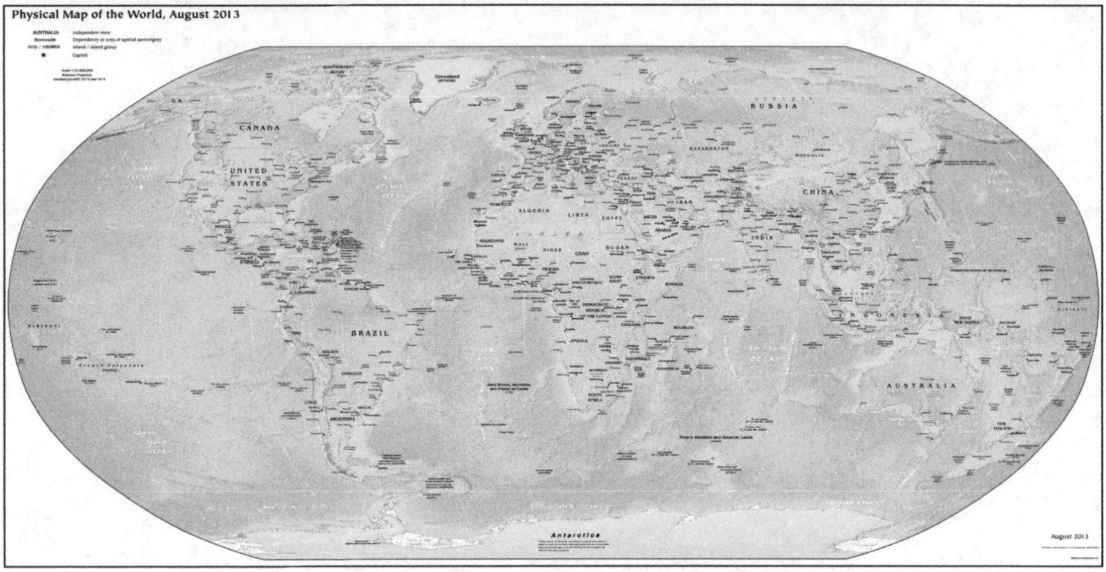

POLITICAL MAP OF THE WORLD

SOUTH AMERICA

803543AI (G00186) 6-12

PHYSICAL MAP OF SOUTHEAST ASIA

SOUTHEAST ASIA

803620AI (G00834) 8-13

STANDARD TIME ZONE OF THE WORLD

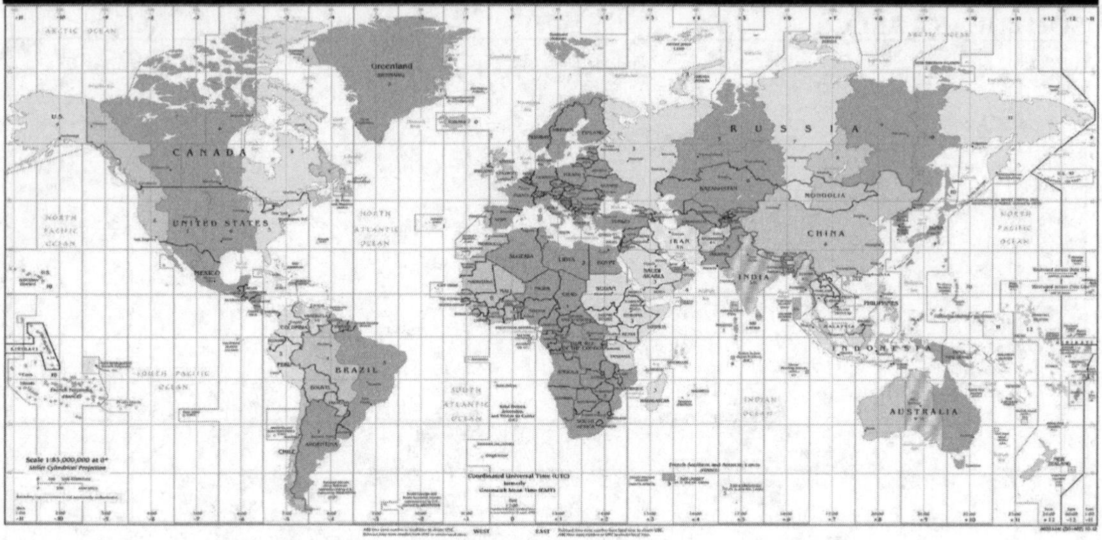

UNITED STATES

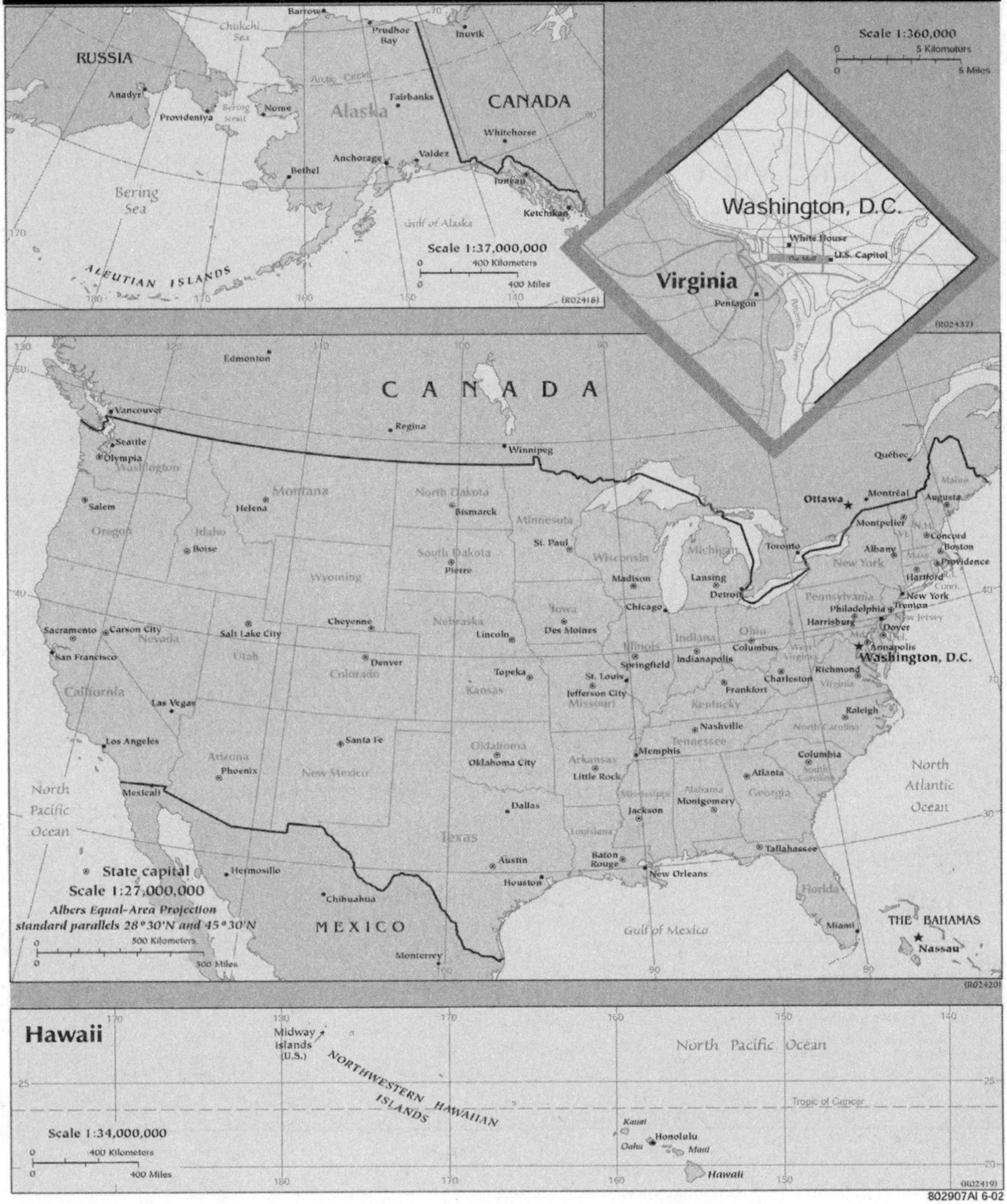

802907AI 6-02

CENTRAL BALKAN REGION

803403AI (G01093) 6-09